BURTON'S
LEGAL
THESAURUS

BURTON'S LEGAL THESAURUS

Fourth Edition

William C. Burton

McGraw-Hill

New York   Chicago   San Francisco   Lisbon   London
Madrid   Mexico City   Milan   New Delhi   San Juan
Seoul   Singapore   Sydney   Toronto

The McGraw·Hill Companies

Copyright © 2007, 1998, 1992, 1980 by William C. Burton. All rights reserved. Printed in the United States of America. Except as permitted under the United States Copyright Act of 1976, no part of this publication may be reproduced or distributed in any form or by any means, or stored in a data base or retrieval system, without the prior written permission of the publisher.

1 2 3 4 5 6 7 8 9 0   SDB/SDB   0 9 8 7 6

ISBN-13: 978-0-07-147262-3
ISBN-10:   0-07-147262-2

McGraw-Hill books are available at special quantity discounts to use as premiums and sales promotions, or for use in corporate training programs. For more information, please write to the Director of Special Sales, Professional Publishing, McGraw-Hill, Two Penn Plaza, New York, NY 10121-2298. Or contact your local bookstore.

Printed in China.

Library of Congress Cataloging-in-Publication Data

Burton, William C.
    Burton's legal thesaurus / William C. Burton.—4th ed.
        p.   cm.
    Includes index.
    ISBN 0-07-147262-2 (pbk. : alk. paper)
    1. Law—United States—Terminology.   2. English language—Synonyms and antonyms.
  I. Title.   II. Title: Legal thesaurus.

KF156.B856   2006
349.730′4—dc22   2006050566

EDITORIAL STAFF

Fourth Edition

by
William C. Burton
Author

Brian Burton
Editor

Executive Assistant
Jenise Hayes

Assistants
Vanita Vishnubhakat
Harold L. Harris

FIRST EDITION

Stephen C. DeCosta
Editor
Michal Hoschander Malen
Associate Editor

EDITORIAL BOARD

Legal Editorial Consultant
Joan Gudesblatt

Editorial Consultants
Barbara Wiberg Alverson   Arlene Rogat

Editorial Assistant
Yvonne Antokas Montesantos

Compilation Editors
Dorit King   Ethel Jane Osterman   Camille Capobianco Taranto

Assistants
Karen Dritto   Ronald M. Malen   Michele M. Mandelbaum

WILLIAM C. BURTON is a partner in the nationally recognized law firm of D'Amato & Lynch, New York, New York. He has served as a New York State Assistant Attorney General and as Assistant to the New York Special Prosecutor. He founded the Burton Awards for Legal Achievement, which is now run in association with the Library of Congress and the Law Library. The national program rewards excellent legal writers who are partners in the nation's 1,000 largest law firms and law school students in the over 220 law schools. He is the author of many articles in professional publications, and is admitted to the practice of law in New York and Florida.

CONTENTS

FOREWORD

In the legal community absolute understanding is the measure of perfection. Perfection in the reaim of the courts is the just resolution of issues of fact and questions of law. The primary tool for resolving conflicts among civilized people is through communication by written and oral language. The root of all language is the individual word.

In the English language, each word may have several meanings. Often, it is the use of a specific word or term upon which a case or controversy may hinge. Only by using precise language can the waters remain clear and unmuddied allowing justice to take its course unfettered by those who would mislead or misrepresent.

It is through the use of such a tool as the Legal Thesaurus that one may find the precise term to fit the nuances of a particular situation. It may be too much to expect such a tool to eradicate the confusion between " scienter" and "malice." The difference between "no law" and "no unreasonable law" may also be beyond its scope. But it should clearly demonstrate that "all deliberate speed" is not synonymous with "as slowly as feasible."

WILLIAM O. DOUGLAS
Justice, U.S. Supreme Court
1939–1975

OCTOBER 22, 1979

INTRODUCTION

For over a quarter of a century, before the publication of this book, lawyers could only use Roget's *Thesaurus* in legal writing. During that time, other general reference tools have been available, but members of the legal profession never had a thesaurus to assist them in their professional work. This book was compiled to meet that need. Through its use, hopefully, ambiguities and redundancies will be eliminated and replaced by clear and concise, plain language.

The fourth edition adds many new and contemporary words. It also includes many words and expressions that lawyers use frequently but were excluded from prior editions. By now including words commonly used but not technical we feel the book is greatly improved and fortified as a reference tool.

For the members of the judiciary, clear and precise language is not only important, it is indispensible. Every word that is written is subject to close scrutiny and interpretation. These words and their usage become precedents and shape the future development of the law.

To members of the bar, persuasive language is extremely important. Written arguments are regularly submitted to the Courts to sway the outcome of pending litigation. Plain language laws also require lawyers to simplify complex legalistic language and use clear and understandable wording.

To students of the law, precise and accurate expression is similarly critical whenever the nature and functions of jurisprudence are evaluated and these assessments are reduced to writings.

This reference book was compiled to assist judges, lawyers, and students of the law in their desire to convey their thoughts, arguments, and contentions effectively and persuasively.

The concept of a legal thesaurus was born out of necessity. It has its beginning in 1974 when the author was preparing a memorandum of law and found himself continuously repeating the same legal words. He looked for a legal thesaurus and learned that no such volume had ever been published.

He resolved to have such a book compiled. Five years later, under his direction, a staff of lawyers, librarians, and trained professionals had fulfilled the need that had been foreseen. Since the original publication, thousands of topical and frequently used entries have been incorporated into the book.

This book provides the broadest array of words that fit the thoughts to be conveyed. In addition to synonyms, the entries include relate words. All expressions and colloquialisms that are archaic and stilted have been omitted. The words provided are not always synonyms but are related in their meaning and provide a full panoply of possible words to be used by a writer.

Since a wide range of words is provided, some of which are not exact synonyms, the user should consult a legal dictionary to determine precise meanings, nuances, and variations in usage. Only when the true meaning of each word offered is understood can the user select the most appropriate synonym or related word to replace it.

At the outset, three criteria were used by the editors to select the main entries that are included in this book: First, those words that are strictly legal; second, those words that are not strictly legal but which are commonly used by members of the legal profession; and third, those words that are not legal and not widely used by lawyers but are sufficiently sophisticated to warrant their use by attorneys. A fourth category includes words that are regularly used by lawyers.

In selection of the main headings, words that have multiple parts of speech were evaluated. In each case, the noun, adjective, verb, or adverb form was selected that was most commonly used by attorneys.

Whenever a main heading has more than one usage it is divided into separate subheadings. For the convenience of the user, these subheadings are arranged alphabetically.

The book also provides an alphabetical listing of associated legal concepts under each main entry. In this way, writers will be able to find complete legal concepts when only a single, central word comes to mind.

Foreign phrases, which are used in the practice of law, are also included under each main heading. Most reference books list foreign phrases alphabetically under the first letter of the foreign word. This book, however, lists foreign phrases under their pivotal English concepts.

To assist the user in locating synonyms, in addition to the alphabetically arranged listings in the main entries, there is also a full index.

The author would welcome and appreciate suggestions of additional entries and changes for the expansion and improvement of the next edition.

William C. Burton, Esq.
Author

ACKNOWLEDGMENTS

I dedicate this twenty-fifth anniversary edition of my book in honor of my extraordinary and lovely wife, Michele, and my two delightful children, Brian and Marni. Together they are my greatest source of pride.

It is fitting that this fourth edition will arrive during the year that Brian graduates from law school at Penn Law and Marni graduates from college at Buffalo University. It is a major, positive step forward for each of us.

I gratefully acknowledge, with profound gratitude and affection, the assistance and motivation given by my loving parents Martin and Ellen Burton. I am forever indebted to them for providing me with the educational background and resources to undertake the initial compilation of this book. I was inspired by my father's writings and encouraged by my loving mother who exclaimed: "I'm not looking for a legal thesaurus in bookstores again. If you want the book, you'll have to write it yourself."

A special thank you to:

Melissa Bonventre, Associate Editor, McGraw-Hill, for being a pleasure to work with on promoting the concept of a new edition and then overseeing the project.

Scott Kurtz, Senior Editing Supervisor, McGraw-Hill, for his extreme expertise in editing this book.

USING THIS BOOK

Here are samples of the comprehensive, esay-to-use listings:

MAIN ENTRY

Definition
(when there is more than one meaning)

Parts of Speech

Synonyms

Associated Legal Concepts

Foreign Phrases and Translations
(keyed to concepts)

---

refutable, suspect, unsustainable

DUE *(Owed),* ***adjective*** chargeable, claimable, collectable, condign, *debitus,* delinquent, deserved, earned, in arrears, merited, outstanding, owing, to be paid, uncompensated, unpaid, unrewarded, unsettled
ASSOCIATED CONCEPTS: amount due, balance due, debt due, due bills, due date, due on demand, indebtedness due, justly due and owing, legally due, money due, payment due, rent due, taxes due
FOREIGN PHRASES: ***Nihil peti potest ante id tempus, quo per rerum naturam persolvi possit.*** Nothing can be demanded before the time when, in the nature of things, it can be paid.

DUE *(Regular),* ***adjective*** according to law, allowable, appropriate, authorized, befitting, correct, expedient, fit, lawful, legal, legislated, legitimate, licit, nomothetic, permitted, proper, rightful, sanctioned, statutory
ASSOCIATED CONCEPTS: due acknowledgment, due administration of justice, due and proper care, due and reasonable care, due care, due compensation, due consideration, due course, due course of business, due course of law, due diligence, due execution, due exercise of discretion, due process of law, due proof, due proof of death, due proof of loss, due regard, holder in due course

DUE, ***noun*** accounts collectable, accounts outstanding, arrears, balance to pay, charge, claim, compensation owed, *deberi,* debit, debt, deficit, droit, entitlement, favor owed, fee, indebtedness, lawful claim, liability, obligation accrued, outstanding debt, overdue payment, pledge, right, something owed, that which is owing, vested right

---

lead, mulct
play upon,
trap for, sp
fraud, take

DUPLICATE
double, ec
tion, imita
repetition,
ASSOCIATED

DUPLICITY
fulness, de
duplexity,
edness, fal,
fidy, sham,

DURABLE,
ranthine, c
tinual, cont
everlasting,
well, imm
pervious to
eradicable,
terminable,
irremovabl
enduring,
gevous, m
long durati
perpetual,
resistant, r
sound, *sta,*
substantial,

INDEX ENTRY

Synonym

(Main Entry under which the synonym is listed.)

Note Readable Type

(Sample Excerpts, Exact Size)

---

abandon nationality expatriate
abandoned dissolute, helpless *(defenseless),* licentious, obsolete, solitary, tainted *(corrupted),* uncurbed, vicious, void *(empty).* SEE MAIN ENTRY
abandoned child orphan
abandoned infant orphan
abandoned to vice profligate *(corrupt)*
abandoning cancellation
abandonment abdication, abjuration, absence *(nonattendance),* cancellation, capitulation, cessation *(termination),* cloture, dereliction, desertion, desuetude, disclaimer, disuse, estrangement, expense *(sacrifice),* halt, neglect, negligence, rejection, release, renunciation, rescision, resignation *(relinquishment),* waiver. SEE MAIN ENTRY
abandonment of a known right waiver
abandonment of a trademark SEE MAIN ENTRY
abandonment of allegiance desertion, infidelity
abase adulterate, betray *(lead astray),*

abbreviatory compact *(pithy)*
abbreviature abridgment *(condens* abstract, curtailment
abdere hide
abdicate abandon *(withdraw),* cede fect, demit, forfeit, leave *(depart),* q *(discontinue),* relinquish, renounce, r ate, resign, retire *(conclude a career* render *(give back),* vacate *(void),* wi draw, yield *(submit).* SEE MAIN ENTRY
abdicatio abdication, renunciation, nation *(relinquishment)*
abdication abandonment *(disconti ance),* renunciation, resignation *(relin quishment),* waiver. SEE MAIN ENTRY
abditus latent
abduce carry away
abduct carry away, hijack, kidnap. MAIN ENTRY
abduction taking. SEE MAIN ENTRY
abecedarian elementary, neophyte mentary
aberemurder SEE MAIN ENTRY
aberrance deviation, error, indirect

BURTON'S
LEGAL
THESAURUS

MAIN ENTRIES

A FORTIORI, *adverb*   above all, accordingly, all the more, by a stronger reason, by inference, certainly, chiefly, consequently, *ergo*, especially, even more, for a certainty, for a still stronger reason, in chief, in the main, mainly, over and above, paramountly, particularly, primarily, thus, with the greater force

A PRIORI, *adverb*   accordingly, as a consequence, as a result of, as is, because of this, by reason of, consequently, deducibly, deductively, derivatively, doubtlessly, *ergo, ex concesso*, for that reason, for this reason, for which reason, from a general law to a particular instance, from cause to effect, from that cause, from this cause, in consequence, inferentially, necessarily, on account of this, on that account, on that ground, proceeding from antecedent to consequent, thusly, to that end

A SAVOIR, *adverb*   below, details now to be provided, the following, hence, hereunder, hereupon, namely, next, now to be accounted for, now to be announced, now to be described, now to be enunciated, now to be itemized, now to be listed, now to be mentioned, now to be narrated, now to be presented, now to be read, now to be recited, now to be recounted, now to be reported, now to be set forth, now to be stated, now to follow, subsequently set down, the succeeding, that is, that is to say, to wit, *videlicet*

AB INITIO, *adverb*   *ab origine, ab ovo*, as a start, at first, at the beginning, at the start, chiefly, first, first and foremost, first of all, firstly, for a beginning, from its birth, from the beginning, in its infancy, in the beginning, in the first place, initially, mainly, originally, primarily, principally
ASSOCIATED CONCEPTS: *ab initio*, void

ABALIENATE, *verb*   assign, bequeath, convey, demise, grant, hand down, hand over, pass on, transfer, transfer by deed, transfer by will

ABALIENATION, *noun*   alienation, assignation, assignment, conferment, consignment, conveyance, deeding, deliverance, delivery, grant of conveyance, transfer, the transfer of title, transmission

ABANDON *(Physically leave),* **verb**   abscond, absent oneself, back out, be gone, be off, cast off, decamp, defect, depart from, desert, *destituere,* disappear, emigrate, evacuate, forsake, *hominem deserere,* leave behind, leave in the lurch, make one's exit, move off, quit, remove from, retreat,

run away, secede from, set off, slip away from, take leave, take one's departure, take one's leave, turn one's back on
ASSOCIATED CONCEPTS: abandoned husband, abandoned land, abandoned property, abandoned wife, desertion

ABANDON *(Relinquish),* **verb**   abjure, abstain, apostasize, cast aside, cast away, cast off, cease, cede, concede, demit, desert, desist, discard, discontinue, dispense with, dispose of, dispossess oneself of, disuse, divest oneself of, drop, forbear, forego, forsake, forswear, give away, give over, give up, give up claim to, go back on, jettison, lay aside, part with, put aside, quit, render up, renounce, repudiate, resign, sacrifice, set aside, surrender, tergiversate, throw away, throw off, turn away, yield
ASSOCIATED CONCEPTS: abandon a claim, abandon a crime, renunciate a claim, surrender propertyÁ

ABANDON *(Withdraw),* **verb**   *ab re desistere,* abdicate, back down, back off, back out, forsake, *omittere,* pull out, quit, *rem relinquere,* renege, retire, retract, retreat, stand aside, tender one's resignation, vacate office

ABANDONED, *adjective*   castaway, castoff, derelict, deserted, discontinued, disregarded, disused, forsaken, ignored, neglected, obsolete, occupantless, out of use, slighted, tenantless, unattended to, uncared for, uninhabited, unoccupied, unpopulated, untenanted
ASSOCIATED CONCEPTS: abandoned claims, abandoned evidence, abandoned husband or wife, abandoned leasehold, abandoned property, abandonment of pleadings

ABANDONMENT *(Desertion),* **noun**   abrogation, apostasy, cession, decampment, defection, demission, departure, dereliction, disaffection, disavowal, evacuation, flight, hasty departure, relinquishment, repudiation, retirement, vacating, withdrawal
ASSOCIATED CONCEPTS: abandonment of a child, abandonment of a husband, abandonment of a property, abandonment of a wife, abandonment of land, dissolution of marriage, Enoch Arden laws
FOREIGN PHRASES: *Occupantis fiunt derelicta.* Things abandoned become the property of the first who is the occupant.

ABANDONMENT *(Discontinuance),* **noun**   abdication, abrogation, cessation, *derelictio,* desistance, discontinuation, disjunction, disruption, relinquishment, surrender, suspension, withdrawal

1

ABANDONMENT

ASSOCIATED CONCEPTS: abandonment of a crime, abandonment of a pleading, abandonment of an easement, abandonment of assets in bankruptcy, abandonment of proscriptive rights

ABANDONMENT *(Repudiation),* **noun**   abnegation, cancellation, declination, denial, disapprobation, disapproval, disavowal, dismissal, disownment, rejection, renouncement, renunciation, reprobation, rescission

ABANDONMENT OF A TRADEMARK, *noun*   abjuration, disownment, disuse, divestiture, divestment, forfeiture, relinquishment, resignation, surrender

ABASE, *verb*   abuse, adulterate, belittle, bring down, brutalize, calumniate, debase, de-civilize, defame, deform, degrade, demean, demote, derogate, diminish, discredit, disgrace, dishonor, downgrade, humble, humiliate, lower, pervert, reduce, set down, shame, take down, vitiate, vituperate, warp

ABATE *(Extinguish),* **verb**   abolish, abrogate, annul, *cadere,* cancel, defeat, destroy, discontinue, dissolve, eliminate, exterminate, invalidate, nullify, obliterate, put an end to, quash, quell, repeal, rescind, revoke, terminate, void
ASSOCIATED CONCEPTS: abate a bequest, abate a cause of action, abate a debt, abate a devise, abate a legacy, abate an action

ABATE *(Lessen),* **verb**   alleviate, curtail, decline, decrease, *decrescere,* diminish, *imminui,* lighten, limit, mitigate, modify, palliate, reduce, relieve, *remittere,* suppress, temper
ASSOCIATED CONCEPTS: abate a nuisance, abate a tax

ABATEMENT *(Extinguishment),* **noun**   abolition, abrogation, annulment, cancellation, deadening, defeat, destruction, discontinuance, dissolution, elimination, extermination, invalidation, nonuse, nullification, obliteration, *remissio,* repeal, rescindment, revocation, termination, voidance
ASSOCIATED CONCEPTS: abatement by death, abatement of a bequest, abatement of a cause of action, abatement of a freehold, abatement of a legacy, abatement of an action, abatement of debts, abatement of taxes, plea in abatement
FOREIGN PHRASES: *Cassetur billa.* That the bill be quashed. *Cassetur breve.* That the writ be quashed.

ABATEMENT *(Reduction),* **noun**   alleviation, curtailment, declination, decline, decrease, decrement, *deminutio,* diminishing, diminution, lessening, lightening, limitation, mitigation, modification, palliation, reduction, relief, *remissio,* suppression, tempering
ASSOCIATED CONCEPTS: abatable nuisance, abatement of a tax

ABDICATE, *verb*   abandon, back out, be relieved, cede, demit, drop, forego, forfeit, give the reins to, give up, hand over, hold off, leave, let go, make way for, quit one's hold, relinquish, resign, retire, stand aside, surrender, unclench, vacate office, withdraw, yield

ABDICATION, *noun*   abandonment, *abdicatio,* abjuration, demission, departure, deposition, dethronement, *eiuratio,* leaving, quitting, relinquishment, renunciation, resignation, surrender, surrender of control, uncrowning, vacating, vacation, withdrawal
FOREIGN PHRASES: *Cessa regnare, si non vis judicare.* Cease to reign, if you don't wish to adjudicate.

ABDUCT, *verb*   carry away, convey away, decamp, denude, deprive, ensnare, impress, kidnap, pirate, purloin, ravish, shanghai, spirit away, subjugate, take away, take by force, take surreptitiously
ASSOCIATED CONCEPTS: kidnapping
FOREIGN PHRASES: *A piratis aut latronibus capti liberi permanent.* Persons taken by pirates or robbers remain free.

ABDUCTION, *noun*   child-stealing, impressment, kidnapping, overmastering, *raptus,* ravishment, shanghaiing, spiriting away, subjugation, taking away

ABEREMURDER, *noun*   assassination, carnage, dealing death, decimation, destruction of life, elimination, extermination, extinction, homicide, killing, killing with malice aforethought, liquidation, massacre, slaughter, slaying, taking of life, unlawful homicide

ABERRANCE, *noun*   aberration, abnormality, abnormity, anomaly, change, deviation, difference, distinguishing characteristics, erroneousness, error, individual characteristics, irregularity, out of the ordinary, peculiarity, perversion, unnaturalness

ABERRANCY, *noun*   aberration, abnormality, abnormity, anomaly, deviation, distinguishing characteristics, erroneousness, error, irregularity, peculiarity, perversion, speciality, unique characteristic, unnaturalness, unusual characteristic

ABERRANT, *adjective*   abnormal, amorphous, anomalistic, anomalous, astray, changeable, departing, deviative, devious, discursive, disordered, divergent, eccentric, errant, erratic, erroneous, excursive, indirect, irregular, nonuniform, rambling, stray, straying, unnatural, unpredictable, untrue, variable, wandering

ABERRATION *(Abnormality),* **noun**   alienation, declension, deflection, departure, derailment, deviation, digression, discrepancy, dislocation, disorientation, displacement, divergence, divergency, diversion, irregularity, lapse, misdirection, refraction, wandering, wrong course

ABERRATION *(Insanity),* **noun**   abnormality, amentia, delirium, delusion, dementedness, derangement, disordered intellect, frenzy, hallucination, loss of reason, lunacy, madness, mental derangement, mental incapacity, mental infirmities, mental instability, mental sickness, paranoia, unsound mind, want of reason

ABET, *verb*   *adiuvare,* advance, advocate, afford aid, aid, arouse, assist, back, contribute, cooperate with, embolden, encourage, endorse, facilitate, foment, foster, furnish aid, goad, help, incite, instigate, nourish, nurture, prompt, second, serve, spur, stimulate, succor, supply aid, support, urge
ASSOCIATED CONCEPTS: accessory, accomplice, aid and abet, co-conspirator, facilitation

ABETMENT, *noun*   advocacy, aegis, aid, auspices, backup, collusion, contribution, cooperation, countenance, encouragement, favor, fosterage, guidance, helpfulness, interest, patronage, plying, pressing, sponsorship, urging

ABETTING, *adjective*   ancillary, coaxing, concerted, conducing, encouraging, fostering, expediting, facilitating, indorsing, inspiring, promoting, prompting, urging
ASSOCIATED CONCEPTS: accessory after the fact, accessory before the fact, accomplice and accessories, aiding and abetting, principals

ABETTOR, *noun*   accessory, accomplice, accomplice in crime, actuator, adjutant, advocate, aide, aider, assistant,

associate, auxiliary, backer, coadjutor, collaborator, confederate, conspirator, cooperator, encourager, exponent, favorer, fomentor, helper, henchman, impeller, inducer, inspirer, instigator, mainstay, maintainer, motivator, *particeps criminis*, patron, promoter, prompter, protagonist, second, support, supporter, sustainer, upholder
ASSOCIATED CONCEPTS: aiding and abetting, conspiracy, renunciation

ABEYANCE, *noun* arrest, cessation, check, deadlock, delay, desistance, discontinuance, discontinuation, dormancy, halt, immobility, *in dubio esse,* inaction, inactivity, inertion, inertness, interim, interlude, intermission, *intermitti,* interregnum, interruption, interval, lapse, quiescency, recess, recumbency, *rem integram relinquere,* repose, reprieve, respite, rest, stalemate, stay, stillness, stoppage, suspension
ASSOCIATED CONCEPTS: contingency, escrow, fee held in abeyance, held in abeyance, in expectation

ABIDE, *verb* accept, acknowledge, acquiesce, adhere, agree, assent, carry into execution, comply, concur, conform, cooperate, endure, execute, follow, heed, obey, observe, perform, permit, respect, sanction, stare, submit, subscribe to, suffer, tolerate, yield
ASSOCIATED CONCEPTS: abiding conviction

ABIDING, *adjective* changeless, constant, continuing, durable, enduring, eternal, everlasting, fixed, immutable, inherent, lasting, long-lasting, long-lived, long-standing, of long duration or standing, perennial, permanent, persistent, persisting, remaining, stable, staying, steadfast, sustained, unaltered, unchanged, unchanging, unshifting, unvaried, unvarying

ABILITY, *noun* ableness, adaptability, adeptness, adequacy, aptitude, aptness, capability, capacity, competence, competency, enablement, *facultas,* faculty, fitness, fittedness, *ingenium,* mastership, mastery, potentiality, *potestas,* proficiency, prowess, skill, versatility, *vires*
ASSOCIATED CONCEPTS: ability to contract, ability to earn, ability to pay, ability to perform, ability to provide, ability to purchase, ability to support, capacity, financial ability, readiness, testamentary ability

ABJECT, *adjective* base, boorish, common, contemptible, corrupt, cowardly, craven, debased, degenerate, degraded, depraved, despicable, discreditable, dishonest, dishonorable, disreputable, ignoble, ignominious, inferior, inglorious, mean, penitent, plebeian, repentant, reproachful, scandalous, scurrilous, servile, sordid, wretched

ABJECTION, *noun* abasement, baseness, debasement, decadence, degeneracy, degradation, demoralization, dishonor, disrepute, humiliation, ignominy, meanness, servility, vileness

ABJECTNESS, *noun* abominableness, baseness, degradation, despicableness, contemptibleness, meanness, obsequiousness, odiousness, pettiness, shabbiness, shoddiness, smallness, sordidness, submissiveness, vileness, worthlessness, wretchedness

ABJUDGE, *verb* adjudicate, appraise, arbitrate, ascertain, assess, award, conclude, consider, decide, declare, decree, deduce, deem, derive, determine, discern, draw a conclusion, examine, find, hold, interpret, judge, prescribe, pronounce formally, rule

ABJURATION, *verb* abandonment, defection, denial, disaffirmation, disallowance, disavowal, disclaimer, disclamation, disownment, forswearing, recall, recantation, rejection, renouncement, renunciation, repudiation, retraction, revocation, revokement
ASSOCIATED CONCEPTS: abjuration of allegiance, law of sanctuary, oath of abjuration

ABJURE, *verb* abandon, abrogate, deny, disaffirm, disavow, discard, disclaim, disown, exclude, forgo, forswear, give up, recant, refuse to admit, reject, relinquish, renounce, repudiate, resign, retract, revoke, surrender, yield

ABLE, *adjective* accomplished, adept, adequate, adroit, apt, bright, clever, competent, deft, dexterous, dynamic, effective, effectual, efficacious, efficient, equal to, experienced, expert, facile, fit, fitted, forward, handy, ingenious, intelligent, inventive, learned, practical, practiced, proficient, qualified, quick, resourceful, sagacious, shrewd, skillful, strong, talented, versed, viable, worthy

ABLENESS, *noun* ability, adequacy, caliber, capability, capacity, competence, efficacy, efficiency, faculty, lucidity, normalcy, normality, normalness, proficiency, quality, rationality, reason, reasonability, saneness, sound mind, soundness of mind, sufficiency

ABNEGATE, *verb* abjure, contravene, decline, deny, disavow, disclaim, disown, drop, forbear, gainsay, let go, negate, quit one's hold, rebuff, recall, refuse, refute, reject, relinquish, renounce, repudiate, repulse, retract, say no, spurn, surrender, unclench

ABNEGATION, *noun* abandonment, abjuration, declination, denial, disallowance, disavowal, disclaimer, forbearance, moderation, negation, nonacceptance, noncompliance, nonconsent, refusal, rejection, renouncement, renunciation, surrender, temperance, unwillingness

ABNORMAL, *adjective* aberrant, amorphous, anomalous, bizarre, curious, deviative, disordered, divergent, eccentric, erratic, exceptional, freakish, frenetic, idiocratic, idiosyncratic, irregular, monstrous, odd, outlandish, peculiar, preternatural, strange, unconformable, unconventional, unheard of, unhinged, unnatural, unusual

ABNORMALITY, *noun* aberration, anomaly, curiosity, deformity, deviation, divergence, erraticism, exception, idiosyncrasy, irregularity, malformation, nonconformity, oddity, peculiarity, perversion, singularity, strangeness, unconformity, unconventionality, unnaturalness, variation

ABNORMITY, *noun* aberrance, aberration, abnormality, anomalism, anomalousness, anomaly, deviation, divergence, erraticism, irregularity, non-conformity, quirk, subnormality, unnaturalness

ABODE, *noun* address, domicile, *domus,* dwelling, dwelling place, fixed residence, *gîte,* habitancy, habitat, habitation, home, homestead, house, inhabitancy, inhabitation, living place, place of dwelling, residence, residency
FOREIGN PHRASES: ***Constitutum esse eam domum unicuique nostrum debere existimari, ubi quisque sedes et tabulas haberet, suarumque rerum constitutionem fecisset.*** It is established that the home of each of us is considered to be the place of his abode and books, and where he may have made an establishment of his business.

3

ABOLISH, verb abate, *abolere,* abrogate, annihilate, annul, cancel, declare null and void, *delere,* delete, deprive of force, destroy, disannul, discontinue, disestablish, dispense with, dispose, dissolve, eliminate, eradicate, *exstinguere,* exterminate, extinguish, extirpate, invalidate, negate, nullify, obliterate, override, overrule, overturn, prohibit, quash, raze, render null and void, repeal, repudiate, rescind, retract, revoke, set aside, squelch, *subvertere,* supersede, supplant, suppress, terminate, *tollere,* undo, vacate, vitiate, void, withdraw
ASSOCIATED CONCEPTS: repeal by amendment

ABOLISHMENT, noun abatement, annulment, cancellation, cessation, close, completeness, conclusion, culmination, discontinuance, dissolution, elimination, end, expiration, extinguishment, finality, finish, termination

ABOLITION, noun abolishment, abrogation, annihilation, annulment, cancellation, defeasance, deposal, destruction, desuetude, discontinuance, *dissolutio,* dissolution, disusage, disuse, elimination, eradication, extermination, extinction, extinguishment, extirpation, invalidation, nonuse, nullification, obliteration, recantation, recision, repeal, repudiation, rescindment, rescission, retraction, revocation, revokement, vacation, voidance
ASSOCIATED CONCEPTS: abolition of a remedy, abolition of an action, abolition of office, abolition of slavery, express abolition, implied abolition
FOREIGN PHRASES: *Cujus est instituere, ejus est abrogare.* Whoever may institute, his right it is to abrogate.

ABORTION (Feticide), noun aborticide, abortio, expulsion of a fetus, termination of a pregnancy

ABORTION (Fiasco), noun blunder, clumsiness, dereliction, disablement, disaster, failure, folly, frustration, inability, incapacity, incompetence, incompetency, ineffectuality, inefficacy, ineptitude, inexpertness, insufficiency, nonfulfilment, quackery, unskillfulness, vain attempt, vain effort, want of success

ABOVE-MENTIONED, adjective as contained above, as referred to previously, first, former, precedent, preceding, previous, previously named, previously specified, previously stated, prior

ABOVE-NAMED, adjective above-mentioned, as contained above, as referred to previously, first, former, precedent, preceding, previous, previously named, previously specified, previously stated, prior

ABOVE SUSPICION, adjective above reproach, absolved, blameless, clean, clear, exculpable, faultless, free from guilt, free from wrong, guilt-free, guiltless, impeccable, incorrupt, inculpable, innocent, irreprehensible, moral, sinless, taintless, unblamable, unblemished, uncensurable, uncorrupted, unreproached, unsoiled, unsullied, upright, vindicated

ABRIDGE (Divest), verb attach, deprive of, dispossess of, disseise, divest of, expropriate, limit, restrict, seize, strip, take away, usurp, wrest from

ABRIDGE (Shorten), verb abbreviate, bate, boil down, capsulize, *circumcidere,* compress, condense, contract, *contrahere,* curtail, cut down, decrease, diminish, epitomize, foreshorten, give the sum and substance, lessen, *praecidere,* reduce, shrink, sketch, subtract, summarize, synopsize, take away, telescope, trim, whittle

ABRIDGED, adjective abbreviated, brief, capsulized, compact, compressed, condensed, contracted, curtailed, decreased, diminished, elliptic, epitomized, foreshortened, laconic, lessened, minimal, reduced, shortened, shrunk, summarized, synopsized, telescoped

ABRIDGMENT (Condensation), noun abbreviation, *abbreviature,* abstract, *aperçu,* brief, capsule, compendium, compression, consolidation, conspectus, contraction, curtailment, digest, epitome, epitomization, extract, *précis,* reduction, sketch, summary, synopsis
ASSOCIATED CONCEPTS: abridgment of time

ABRIDGMENT (Disentitlement), noun abatement, curtailment, deprivation, deprivement, dispossession, divestiture, limitation, loss, privation, restriction
ASSOCIATED CONCEPTS: abridgment of rights

ABROGATE (Annul), verb abjure, abnegate, abolish, *abrogare,* cancel, contradict, contravene, declare null and void, disannul, disapprove, dissolve, eliminate, impair, invalidate, make void, negate, nullify, obstruct, prohibit, quash, rebuff, refuse, reject, renounce, repudiate, retract, reverse, undo, void
FOREIGN PHRASES: *Cujus est instituere, ejus est abrogare.* Whose right it is to institute anything may abrogate it. *Non impedit clausula derogatoria, quo minus ab eadem potestate res dissolvantur a qua constituuntur.* A derogatory clause does not prevent things from being dissolved by the same power by which they were originally created.

ABROGATE (Rescind), verb abolish, annul, bar, cancel, countermand, declare null and void, deprive of power, destroy, disannul, eliminate, exclude, invalidate, not accept, nullify, omit, override, overrule, prohibit, recall, recant, repeal, repudiate, *rescindere,* retract, reverse, revoke, set aside, supersede, terminate, vacate, void, waive
ASSOCIATED CONCEPTS: abrogating an appeal, express abrogation
FOREIGN PHRASES: *Clausula quae abrogationem excludit ab initio non valet.* A clause which precludes repeal is void from the beginning. *Perpetua lex est nullam legem humanam ac positivam perpetuam esse, et clausula quae abrogationem excludit ab initio non valet.* It is a perpetual law that no human and positive law can be perpetual, and a clause which precludes the power of abrogation or repeal is void from the beginning.

ABROGATED, adjective abolished, annulled, barred, countermanded, declared null and void, defunct, deprived of power, eliminated, excluded, inactive, invalid, invalidated, nullified, overridden, set aside, superseded, terminated, vacated, waived

ABROGATION, noun abolishment, abolition, annihilation, annulment, canceling, cancellation, countermand, counterorder, defeasance, dissolution, invalidation, nullification, overriding, overruling, recall, recantation, renege, repeal, repudiation, rescission, retraction, reversal, revocation, suppression, undoing, voidance, vacation, vacatur, withdrawal

ABSCIND, verb amputate, break, cancel, cleave, clip, cut, decapitate, delete, detach, disconnect, disengage, disjoin, dismember, dispart, dissever, dissociate, disunite, divide, erase, excise, extirpate, mutilate, part, partition, rend, rive, rupture, segregate, separate, sever, shear, split, sunder, tear

ABSCOND, verb absent oneself, avoid, bolt, decamp, *delitescere,* depart, desert, disappear, dodge, elude, emigrate, escape, eschew, evade, expatriate oneself, flee, hide, *latere,* leave, levant, make off, *occultari,* remove, run, run away, steal away, take flight, withdraw, withdraw clandestinely

ASSOCIATED CONCEPTS: abscond on bail, absconding debtor, attachment, fugitive, *quasi in rem jurisdiction*

ABSENCE (Nonattendance), **noun** abandonment, *absentia,* abstention, avoidance, defection, desertion, nonappearance, nonpresence, removal, truancy, withdrawal

ASSOCIATED CONCEPTS: absence from the state, absent creditors, absent debtor, absent defendant, absent from a jurisdiction, leave of action

FOREIGN PHRASES: *Absentem accipere debemus eum qui non est eo loci in quo petitur.* We must consider absent he who is not in that place in which he is sought.

ABSENCE (Omission), **noun** deficiency, deprivation, disappearance, hiatus, inadequacy, lack, need, negation, nonbeing, nonexistence, shortage, unavailability, void, want

ASSOCIATED CONCEPTS: absence of counsel, absence of fraud, absence of funds, absence of heirs, absence of issue, absence of negligence, absence of notice, absence of wrongdoing

ABSENT, adjective absorbed, abstracted, astray, away, bare, bemused, blank, deficient, devoid, elsewhere, faraway, flown, gone, heedless, lost, missing, not present, nowhere to be found, null and void, preoccupied, removed, vacant, vacuous, wanting

ASSOCIATED CONCEPTS: absent intent, absent malice, absent the elements of a crime, new trial based on absence of an accused, counsel, evidence, absent witness

ABSOLUTE (Complete), **adjective** *absolutus,* blanket, comprehensive, downright, entire, exhaustive, final, finished, full, sheer, total, unbounded, unconditional, unconstrained, unlimited, unqualified, unreserved, unrestrained, unrestricted, unstinted, utter, whole, without qualification

ASSOCIATED CONCEPTS: absolute acceptance, absolute admission, absolute assignment, absolute bequest, absolute control, absolute deed, absolute devise, absolute fee, absolute gift, absolute immunity, absolute insuror, absolute owner, absolute power of alienation, absolute power of disposition, absolute sale, absolute transfer, fee simple absolute

ABSOLUTE (Conclusive), **adjective** accurate, actual, axiomatic, beyond doubt, categorical, certain, clear, clearly defined, decided, decisive, definite, definitive, determinate, exact, explicit, express, final, fixed, inalienable, indisputable, indubitable, obvious, positive, precise, real, settled, straightforward, true, unconditioned, undoubted, unequivocal, unerring, unimpeachable, unmistakable, unmitigated, unmixed, unquestionable, veritable, well-defined

ASSOCIATED CONCEPTS: absolute certainty, absolute conviction, absolute discretion, absolute duty, absolute liability, absolute moral certainty, absolute pardon, absolute privilege, absolute right, absolute title

ABSOLUTE (Ideal), **adjective** best, beyond compare, champion, consummate, crowning, defectless, excelling, exemplary, faultless, flawless, highest, immaculate, impeccable, incomparable, matchless, model, *ne plus ultra,* paramount, peerless, perfect, preeminent, pure, spotless, stainless, superior, superlative, supreme, taintless, unblemished,

unequaled, unexcelled, unrivaled, unsurpassed, untainted, untarnished

ABSOLUTION, noun acquittal, amnesty, clearance, deliverance, discharge, dismissal, dismissal of an accusation, exculpation, exoneration, forgiveness, forgiveness of sins, grace, liberation, pardon, purgation, release, release from punishment, remission, reprieve, vindication

ABSOLVE, verb *absolvere,* acquit, adjudge innocent, clear, discharge, exculpate, excuse, exonerate, find not guilty, forgive, free, let off, *liberare,* liberate, pardon, prove innocent, prove not guilty, *purgare,* purge, release from imputation, remit, reprieve, set free, vindicate

ASSOCIATED CONCEPTS: absolve of blame

ABSOLVED, adjective acquitted, adjudged blameless, clear, cleared, discharged, exculpated, excused, exempt, exonerated, forgiven, found not guilty, free, immune, innocent, let off, liberated, pardoned, proven innocent, reprieved, set free, vindicated

ABSTAIN, verb avoid, be loath, be neutral, by-pass, cease, decline, defer, desist, discontinue, dispense with, do without, eschew, forebear, forgo, hold back, keep away, keep off, let alone, not use, not vote, refrain voluntarily from, refuse, restrain oneself, shirk, shun, spare, stand aside, take no sides, turn aside from, waive, withhold

ABSTENTION, noun abstainment, abstemiousness, abstinence, abstinence from action, avoidance, elusion, eschewal, evasion, forbearance, holding off, inaction, nonparticipation, refrainment

ASSOCIATED CONCEPTS: abstention awaiting the state court's decision, abstention based on deferral, abstention based on state issues, doctrine of abstention

ABSTRACT, noun abbreviation, abbreviature, abridgment, analect, brief, capsule, compendium, compilation, compression, condensation, consolidation, conspectus, contraction, digest, *epitoma,* epitome, extract, pandect, precis, reduction, summary, synopsis

ASSOCIATED CONCEPTS: abstract idea, abstract of a record, abstract of judgment, abstract of title, abstract proposition of law, abstracts of evidence, marketable title acts, title search

ABSTRACT (Separate), **verb** detach, disengage, disjoin, dissociate, disunite, isolate, remove, take out of context

ABSTRACT (Summarize), **verb** abbreviate, abridge, capsulize, compact, compress, condense, contract, epitomize, reduce, shorten, synopsize, telescope

ABSTRUSE, adjective abstract, ambiguous, attenuated, cloudy, complex, difficult to understand, elusive, enigmatic, esoteric, hidden, incomprehensible, indefinable, indefinite, inexplicable, mysterious, nebulous, obscure, profound, puzzling, rarefied, recondite, remote, subtle, technical, unclear, unfathomable, vague

ABUSE (Corrupt practice), **noun** baseness, breach of trust, deviation from rectitude, dishonesty, distortion, erroneous use, excessive use, exploitation, fraudulency, ill usage, ill use, improper usage, improper use, jobbery, malfeasance, malversation, misapplication, misappropriation, misdirection, misemployment, mishandling, mismanagement, misrepresentation, misstatement, misusage, misuse, perversion, *usus perversus,* violation, want of principle, wrong use

ABUSE

ASSOCIATED CONCEPTS: abuse of a mandate, abuse of a proceeding, abuse of authority, abuse of discretion, abuse of executive authority, abuse of legal process, abuse of power, neglect
FOREIGN PHRASES: *Ab abusu ad usum non valet consequentia.* A conclusion as to the use of a thing from its abuse is invalid. *Confirmat usum qui tollit abusum.* He confirms a use who removes an abuse. *Omnium rerum quarum usus est, potest esse abusus, virtute sola excepta.* There may be an abuse of everything of which there is a use, virtue alone excepted.

ABUSE *(Physical misuse)*, **noun**   atrocity, bad treatment, damage, debasement, defilement, dishonor, dishonoring, hurt, ill treatment, ill usage, ill use, impairment, indecent assault, injury, maltreatment, mishandling, mistreatment, misusage, molestation, outrage, persecution, victimization, violation
ASSOCIATED CONCEPTS: abuse of a child, wife-beating

ABUSE *(Misuse)*, **verb**   *abuti*, ill-use, injure, make excessive use of, make improper use of, maltreat, manhandle, misapply, misappropriate, misemploy, mishandle, mistreat, pervert, use improperly, use wrongly
ASSOCIATED CONCEPTS: abuse of a minor

ABUSE *(Victimize)*, **verb**   injure, maltreat, manhandle, mistreat, molest, oppress

ABUSE *(Violate)*, **verb**   debauch, defile, degrade, dishonor, harm, ill-use, persecute, pollute, profane, wrong

ABUSED, *adjective*   aggrieved, debased, defamed, defiled, degraded, disparaged, execrated, exploited, illtreated, ill-used, injured, maltreated, mistreated, misused, oppressed, persecuted, victimized, vilified, wronged
ASSOCIATED CONCEPTS: abused children

ABUSIVE, *adjective*   detracting, insulting, maledictory, menacing, quarreling, reviling, threatening, ungracious
ASSOCIATED CONCEPTS: abusive language, abusive letter, abusive manner

ABUT, *verb*   *aboutir*, adjoin, attach, be adjacent to, be contiguous, border on, bound, butt, conjoin, connect, end at, extend to, join, lean against, meet, reach, *rei adiacere, rem attingere*, touch, verge on
ASSOCIATED CONCEPTS: abutting land, abutting on the improvement, abutting owner, abutting property owner

ABUTMENT, *noun*   abutment, abuttal, adhesion, adjacency, adjoinment, appendage, apposition, appurtenance, attachment, buttress, conjunction, connection, contact, contiguity, joint, junction, juxtaposition, union
ASSOCIATED CONCEPTS: abutting owners

ACCEDE *(Concede)*, **verb**   abide by, accept, accord, acknowledge, acquiesce, admit, agree to, approve, assent, back down, capitulate, comply, concur, conform, consent, deign, give assent, give in, grant, obey, permit, submit, subscribe to, succumb, surrender, vouchsafe, yield, yield assent

ACCEDE *(Succeed)*, **verb**   assume, attain, become heir to, come after, come next, displace, follow in order, inherit, reach, replace, supersede, supplant, take the place of

ACCELERATED JUDGMENT, *noun*   accelerated decision, expedited determination, expedited judgment, facilitated decision, speeded adjudication

ACCELERATION, *noun*   dispatch, expedition, expeditious performance, hastening, hurrying, increase of speed, quickening, shortening of time, speedup, spurt, stepping up a pace
ASSOCIATED CONCEPTS: acceleration clause, acceleration doctrine, acceleration of a testamentary gift, acceleration of payments, acceleration of remainders

ACCENTUATE, *verb*   accent, deepen, emphasize, heighten, highlight, intensify, italicize, make clear, point up, pronounce, punctuate, reaffirm, spearhead, star, strengthen, stress, underline, underscore

ACCEPT *(Admit as sufficient)*, **verb**   accede to, acquiesce, admit as satisfactory, agree to, allow, comply, confirm

ACCEPT *(Assent)*, **verb**   accede to, acquiesce, affirm, agree to, allow, authorize, comply, confirm, endorse, ratify, sanction, tolerate
ASSOCIATED CONCEPTS: accept a contract, ratification

ACCEPT *(Embrace)*, **verb**   adopt, consider as true, embrace, internalize

ACCEPT *(Recognize)*, **verb**   accord recognition to, acknowledge, allow, honor
ASSOCIATED CONCEPTS: accept a bill, accept a check, accept a draft

ACCEPT *(Take)*, **verb**   *accipere*, acquire, obtain, receive, receive with approval, secure, take control of, take hold of, take possession of
ASSOCIATED CONCEPTS: accept a bribe, accept gainful employment

ACCEPTABLE, *adjective*   adequate, admissible, advisable, agreeable, allowable, applicable, appropriate, attractive, becoming, comfortable, commensurate, conventional, decent, desirable, eligible, entitled, enviable, expedient, fair, felicitous, fit, gratifying, inviting, justifiable, likable, mediocre, moderate, opportune, palatable, passable, pleasant, pleasing, presentable, proper, qualified, respectable, satisfactory, seemly, suitable, tenable, timely, tolerable, unobjectionable, viable, welcome
ASSOCIATED CONCEPTS: acceptable compromise, acceptable contract, acceptable settlement, accord and satisfaction, performance

ACCEPTANCE, *noun*   accedence, *acceptio*, accession, accordance, acknowledgment, acquiescence, adoption, agreement, allowance, approbation, approval, assent, assurance, compliance, *comprobatio*, concordance, consent, endorsement, ratification, receipt, receptiveness, resignation, sanction, tolerance, toleration
ASSOCIATED CONCEPTS: acceptance by a grantee to a deed, acceptance by conduct, acceptance in a sale, acceptance of a bill of exchange, acceptance of a bribe, acceptance of a check, acceptance of a contract, acceptance of a draft, acceptance of a gift by a donee, acceptance of an insurance application, acceptance of an offer, acceptance of an order, acceptance of benefits, acceptance of employment, acceptance of goods, acceptance of risk, blank acceptance, conditional acceptance, constructive acceptance, conversion by acceptance, implied acceptance
FOREIGN PHRASES: *Cum in corpore dissentitur, apparet nullam esse acceptionem.* When there is a disagreement in the substance of a thing, it appears that there is no acceptance.

ACCESS (Opening), **noun**   accessibility, approachability, availability, chance, means, occasion, open position, opportunity, possibility, unfilled place, vacancy

ACCESS (Right of way), **noun**   *accessus, adit, aditus,* admission, admittance, approach, course, direct approach, entrance, entrance way, entry, ingress, inlet, means of access, means of approach, opening, passage, passageway, path, right of entry, road, route, way, way in, way of approach, way through

ACCESSIBLE, **adjective**   achievable, amenable, approachable, assailable, attainable, available, communicative, convenient, obliging, open, open-minded, penetrable, pervious, reachable, receptive, responsive

ACCESSION (Annexation), **noun**   *accessio,* addition, adherence, adhesion, adjoining, affixation, annexing, appendage, attachment, binding, cementation, cohesion, combination, combining, conjoining, consolidation, coupling, fastening, fusion, inclusion, incorporation, joining, merger, putting together, securing, subjoining, subjunction, supplementation, unification, union, uniting
ASSOCIATED CONCEPTS: accession of fixtures, accession of property

ACCESSION (Enlargement), **noun**   accretion, accrual, accumulation, acquisition, addition, advance, aggrandizement, amplification, appreciation, attainment, augmentation, broadening, burgeoning, development, elaboration, enhancement, expansion, extension, gain, growth, increase, multiplication, progress, progression, supplementation, swelling
ASSOCIATED CONCEPTS: accession of property, accretion, acquisition of title by accession, doctrine of accession, permanent accession, riparian accession

ACCESSORY, **noun**   abettor, accomplice, accomplice in crime, advisor, aider, assistant, coconspirator, codirector, collaborator, confederate, *confrère, conscius,* consociate, cooperator, copartner, coworker, *culpae socius,* encourager, fellow conspirator, helper, helpmate, partaker, *particeps criminis,* participant, participator, partner, partner in crime, planner, *socius criminis*
ASSOCIATED CONCEPTS: accessory after the fact, accessory before the fact, accessory contract, accessory during the fact, accessory obligation, accessory to a crime, accessory to an offense, aiding and abetting, principal
FOREIGN PHRASES: *Accessorium non ducit, sed sequitur suum principale.* That which is the accessory or incident does not lead, but follows its principals. *Accessorius sequitur naturam sui principales.* An accessory follows the nature of his principal, thus, an accessory cannot be found guilty of a greater crime than his principal. *Cujus juris est principale, ejusdem juris erit accessorium.* He who has jurisdiction of the principal thing also has jurisdiction of the accessory. *Nullus dicitur accessorius post feloniam, sed ille qui novit principalem feloniam fecisse, et illum receptavit et comfortavit.* No one is called an "accessory" after the fact but the one who knew the principal had committed a felony, and who received and comforted him. *Omne principale trahit ad se accessorium.* Every principal thing draws the accessory to itself. *Quae accessionum locum obtinent, extinguuntur cum principales res peremp tae fuerint.* When the principal thing is destroyed, those things which are accessory to it are also destroyed. *Res accessoria sequitur rem principalem.* An accessory follows the principal. *Ubi non est principalis, non potest*

esse accessorius. Where there can be no principal, there cannot be an accessory.

ACCIDENT (Chance occurrence), **noun**   adventitiousness, befalling, blind chance, casus, circumstance, fortuitous event, fortuity, happening, hazard, incident, inevitable occurrence, sudden happening, unanticipated event, undesigned occurrence, unexpected misfortune, unexpected occurrence, unforeseen occurrence
ASSOCIATED CONCEPTS: accidental cause, accidental loss, accidental means
FOREIGN PHRASES: *Casus fortuitus non est sperandus, et nemo tenetur devinare.* A fortuitous event is not to be foreseen, and no one is bound to expect it. *Casus fortuitus non est supponendus.* A fortuitous happening is not to be presumed.

ACCIDENT (Misfortune), **noun**   adversity, affliction, calamity, casualty, *contretemps,* disaster, injurious occurrence, misadventure, miscarriage, mischance, mishap, unfortunate event
ASSOCIATED CONCEPTS: accident arising out of the course of employment, accidental bodily injury, accidental fires, collision, disability caused by an accident, expectable loss, external, foreseeable loss, violent and accidental means

ACCIDENTAL, **adjective**   adventitious, casual, chance, coincidental, extrinsic, fortuitous, inadvertent, incidental, indeterminate, undesigned, undetermined, unexpected, unforeseen, unintended, unintentional, unpremeditated, unwitting
ASSOCIATED CONCEPTS: accident and health insurance, accidental loss, accidental means, disability, life insurance, negligence

ACCOMMODATE, **verb**   accept, *accommodare,* adapt, adjust, administer to, agree, aid, arrange, assist, attune, be capable of holding, benefit, bring into consistency, bring to terms, comfort, compose, contain, convenience, defer, do a favor for, do a service for, favor, fit, furnish, gratify, harmonize, have, have capacity for, help, hold, meet the wants of, minister to, oblige, provide, render a service, serve, settle, settle amicably, suit, supply the wants of, support, yield

ACCOMMODATING, **adjective**   accepting, adjustable, affable, agreeable, amiable, attentive, benevolent, benignant, charitable, civil, complaisant, compliant, conciliatory, considerate, cordial, courteous, decent, deferential, fair, favorable, friendly, generous, gracious, heedful, helpful, indulgent, kind, kindly, mindful, neighborly, obliging, pliable, polite, solicitous, thoughtful, unselfish, warm-hearted, well-intentioned, well-meaning, yielding

ACCOMMODATION (Adjustment), **noun**   accordance, adaptation, agreement, arrangement, *compositio,* composition of differences, compromise, friendly agreement, harmonization, mutual understanding, obliging, provision, readjustment, *reconciliatio,* rectification, settlement

ACCOMMODATION (Backing), **noun**   assistance, assurance, championing, cooperation, endorsement, guarantee, seconding, security, sponsorship, succor, support, surety
ASSOCIATED CONCEPTS: accommodated endorser, accommodated party, accommodated payee, accommodation acceptance, accommodation bill, accommodation endorsement, accommodation guarantor, accommodation maker, accommodation note, accommodation paper, accommodation signer, *cautio fidejussoria*

ACCOMPANY, verb associate with, coexist, commingle, consort, convoy, join, keep, keep company with

ACCOMPANYING, adjective accessory, associated, associated with, attendant, attending, coactive, coexistent, collateral, commingled, concomitant, concurrent, co-operant, cooperative, fellow, incidental, joined, joint, synergetic

ACCOMPLICE, noun abettor, accessory, accessory after the fact, accessory before the fact, advisor, aid, aider, aider and abettor, assistant, associate, associate in crime, associate in guilt, coactor, coconspirator, codefendant, codirector, collaborator, comate, confederate, *confrère, conscius,* consociate, contriver, cooperator, coworker, *culpae socius,* encourager, fellow conspirator, helper, helpmate, partaker, *particeps criminis,* participant, participator, partner, partner in crime, partner in wrongdoing, planner, principal, *socius criminis,* supporter
ASSOCIATED CONCEPTS: accomplice witness, aiding and abetting, complicity, inchoate crimes, mens rea, vicarious liability, Wharton's rule
FOREIGN PHRASES: **Agentes et consentientes pari poena plectentur.** Acting and consenting parties are liable to the same punishment.

ACCOMPLISH, verb achieve, attain, bring about, complete, consummate, discharge, dispatch, effect, enact, execute, finish, fulfill, realize, succeed

ACCORD, noun accommodation, accordance, adjustment, agreement, arrangement, compromise, concession, concord, concordance, mutual understanding, settlement, understanding
ASSOCIATED CONCEPTS: accord and satisfaction, disputed claims, executed accord, executory accord, novation, payment of a debt, release, satisfaction, substituted agreement, unliquidated claim
FOREIGN PHRASES: **Concordare leges legibus est optimus interpretandi modus.** To reconcile laws with other laws is the best method of interpreting them.

ACCORDANCE (Compact), **noun** accommodation, accord, adjustment, agreement, arrangement, conciliation, concord, concordance, concurrence, consonance, contract, *entente cordiale,* pact, reconcilement, reconciliation, settlement, unison, unity

ACCORDANCE (Understanding), **noun** accommodation, adjustment, agreement, amity, assent, assonance, common view, communion, compatibility, compliance, concinnity, concurrence, conformance, conformity, consensus, consentience, consonance, consonancy, harmonization, harmony, meeting of minds, rapport, reconcilement, reconciliation, unanimity, understanding

ACCORDING TO LAW, adjective allowable, allowed, authorized by law, conformable to law, conformable with the law, constitutional, de *jure,* due, established, in accordance with the law, in compliance, inviolable, jural, law abiding, lawful, legal, legalized, legitimate, licit, permissible, proper, rightful, statutory, valid, within the law

ACCORDINGLY, adverb a fortiori, a priori, agreeably, as a matter of course, as a result, because of this, by reason of that, compatibly, compliantly, conformably, consequently, consistently, correspondingly, hence, in due course, inevitably, it follows that, naturally, necessarily, then, thereafter, therefore, thus, wherefore

ACCOST, verb address, *adoriri,* affront, ambush, approach, assail, assault, assault belligerently, attack, beset, *compellare,* confront, draw near, fall upon, rise in hostility before, set upon, strike at, thrust at, waylay

ACCOUNT (Evaluation), **noun** appraisal, assessment, *compte rendu,* enumeration, financial statement, ledger, list of receipts and payments, *ratio,* register, statement, statement of debits and credits, statement of pecuniary transactions, tally, valuation
ASSOCIATED CONCEPTS: accounts payable, accounts receivable, account rendered, account stated, bank account, joint account, liquidated account, open account, totten trust account

ACCOUNT (Report), **noun** brief, description, history, memoir, *memoria, narratio,* narration, presentation, recapitulation, recital, record, review, saga, summary, summation

ACCOUNTABILITY, noun amenability, blame, burden, charge, commitment, dueness, duty, exposure, incumbency, liability, obligation, onus, responsibility, the decent thing, the proper thing, the right thing, trustworthiness, vulnerability

ACCOUNTABLE (Explainable), **adjective** construable, deducible, definable, describable, determinable, explicable, inferential, interpretable, renderable, translatable

ACCOUNTABLE (Responsible), **adjective** answerable, beholden, bound, chargeable, devolving on, liable, obligated, obliged, owing, under obligation
ASSOCIATED CONCEPTS: held accountable for one's actions

ACCOUNTANT, noun bookkeeper, calculator, certified public accountant, chartered accountant, clerk, reckoner, recorder, registrar, statistician

ACCOUNTING, noun auditing, bookkeeping, complete report, computation, full report, fully detailed analysis, reckoning
ASSOCIATED CONCEPTS: account stated, accounting officer, accounts receivable

ACCREDIT, verb accept, affirm, approve, authenticate, authorize, certify, confirm, endorse, ratify, sanction, validate, vouch for
ASSOCIATED CONCEPTS: accredited law school, accredited representative

ACCRETION, noun addition, advance, annexation, augmentation, enlargement, extension, gain, growth, increment

ACCROACH, verb appropriate, arrogate, assume, break bounds, encroach, impose upon, infringe, interlope, intrude, invade, obtrude, overstep, presume on, take over, transgress, trespass, usurp

ACCRUE (Arise), **verb** acquire, be derived, become due, become enforceable, become present, come, develop, emanate, ensue, eventuate, fall due, flow, follow, inure, issue, mature, occur, originate, proceed, progress, result from, rise from, spring, yield
ASSOCIATED CONCEPTS: accrual accounting method, accrual of a cause of action, accrued benefit, accrued claims against a municipal corporation, accrued debt, accrued rights, statute of limitations, tolls

FOREIGN PHRASES: *Confirmare nemo potest prius quam jus ei acciderit.* No one can confirm a right before the right accrues to him.

ACCRUE (Increase), **verb** accumulate, acquire, add on, advance, aggrandize, amass, amplify, annex, appreciate, augment, become added, become greater, become larger, branch out, broaden, build, build up, collect, enlarge, escalate, expand, extend, further, gain, gather, greaten, grow, heighten, improve, intensify, mount, multiply, raise, redouble, supplement, swell, widen
ASSOCIATED CONCEPTS: accrual accounting method, accrual of compensation, accrual of taxes, accrued basis, accrued costs, accrued dividend, accrued earnings, accrued income, accrued interest, accrued overtime, accrued taxes

ACCRUED, adjective accumulated, added to, annexed, grew, increased, mounted, multiplied
ASSOCIATED CONCEPTS: accrued debts, accrued depreciation, accrued dividends, accrued income, accrued installments, accrued interest, accrued rent, accrued rights, accrued taxes

ACCUMULATE (Amass), **verb** *accumulare,* agglomerate, aggregate, assemble, bring together, *coacervare,* collect, collect into a mass, collect together, colligate, combine, compile, concentrate, cumulate, garner, gather, gather into a mass, gather together, gather up, hoard, mass, pile up, stockpile, store up, unite
ASSOCIATED CONCEPTS: accumulate dividends, accumulate funds, accumulate income, accumulated damages, accumulated deductions, accumulated earnings, accumulated profits, accumulated reserve, accumulated sick leave, accumulated surplus, accumulation in a trust, accumulative judgment, accumulative sentence, consecutive sentence

ACCUMULATE (Enlarge), **verb** accrue, add to, aggrandize, amplify, augment, broaden, build up, enlarge in size, *exaggerare,* expand, extend, gain, greaten, grow, grow larger, increase, make greater, multiply, redouble, reinforce, spread, swell
FOREIGN PHRASES: *Alienatio rei praefertur juri accrescendi.* The law prefers the alienation of property rather than accumulation.

ACCUMULATION, noun abundance, accession, accretion, accruement, agglomeration, aggregation, amassing, amassment, amplification, appreciation, assemblage, augmentation, batch, centralization, collection, compilation, concentration, conglomeration, cumulation, deposit, development, gain, gathering, great quantity, growth, harvest, increase, increment, plenty, plethora, sufficiency
ASSOCIATED CONCEPTS: accumulation of income, accumulation of property, trusts, wills

ACCURATE, adjective actual, authentic, bona fide, careful, clear-cut, conscientious, correct, defect-free, dependable, direct, errorless, exact, executed with care, explicit, factual, faithful, faultless, free of error, genuine, inerrant, literal, meticulous, minute, particular, perfect, precise, proper, punctilious, realistic, reliable, right, rigorous, scrupulous, thorough, true, trustworthy, truthful, unambiguous, unchallenged, uncolored, undenied, undeviating, undisguised, undisputed, undistorted, unerring, unimpeachable, unmistaken, unperjured, unquestioned, unrefuted, unvarnished, valid, veracious, verbatim, verifiable, well-defined

ACCUSATION, noun accusal, *accusatio,* allegation, ascription, assertion, attribution, bill of indictment, charge, citation, *crimen, criminatio,* crimination, delation, filing of charges, formal charge, imputation, imputation of blame, incrimination, inculpation, indictment, information, preferring of charges, true bill, true charge
ASSOCIATED CONCEPTS: accusatory instrument, complaint, grand jury report, indictment, information, presentment, warrant
FOREIGN PHRASES: *Accusare nemo se debet, nisi coram deo.* No one is bound to accuse himself, except before God.

ACCUSATORY, adjective contemptuous, decrying, deprecatory, derogative, derogatory, disparaging, disapproving, incriminatory, inculpatory, pejorative
ASSOCIATED CONCEPTS: accusatory instrument, grand jury, indictment, prosecution

ACCUSE, verb *accusare, arguere,* attack, blame, bring a charge, bring accusation, bring in a true bill, charge with, *citare,* cite, complain against, criminate, denounce, expose, fix blame, impeach, implicate, incriminate, inculpate, indict, lodge a complaint, prefer charges, prosecute, report against
ASSOCIATED CONCEPTS: accusatory instrument

ACCUSE OF WRONGDOING, verb accuse, allege, arraign, bring a charge, charge with, cite, criminate, denounce, expose, fix blame, impeach, implicate, incriminate, inculpate, indict, prefer charges, prosecute
ASSOCIATED CONCEPTS: felony complaint, grand jury, indictment, malicious prosecution

ACCUSED (Attacked), **verb** attacked, defamed, imputed, maligned, reproached, reproved

ACCUSED (Charged), **verb** arraigned, brought charges, charged, complained of, filed charges, have charges against, held responsible, impeached, indicted

ACCUSER, noun accusant, accusatrix, challenger, complainant, delator, denouncer, impeacher, incriminator, indictor, informer, libelant, litigant, party to a suit, petitioner, prosecutor

ACCUSTOMED (Customary), **adjective** *adsuetus,* common, commonplace, confirmed, consuetudinal, consuetudinary, conventional, established, fixed, habitual, normal, ordinary, prevailing, regular, routine, *solitus,* traditional, usual
ASSOCIATED CONCEPTS: accustomed practice, accustomed use

ACCUSTOMED (Familiarized), **adjective** acclimated, acclimatized, acquainted, adapted, addicted, adjusted, conditioned, familiar, familiar through use, given to, habituated, in the habit of, ingrained with

ACHIEVE (Acquire), **verb** acquire, arrive, attain, bring about, build, carry, close, complete, conclude, construct, consummate, decide, determine, discharge, earn, evoke, function, gain, get, implement, obtain, operate, originate, prevail, procure, reach, realize, reap, recover, win

ACHIEVE (Perform), **verb** accomplish, actualize, carry out, compass, contrive, create, dispatch, effect, effectuate, encompass, execute, finish, fulfill, perfect, perform, produce, succeed, terminate, transact

ACKNOWLEDGE (Declare), **verb** admit, affirm, ascribe, assert, asseverate, attest to, avow, bear witness, certify, depone, depose, disclose, endorse, express, implicate oneself, state, swear

9

ACKNOWLEDGE *(Respond)*, **verb** accede, agree, answer, be responsive, concur, ratify, rejoin, remark, reply, signify assent

ACKNOWLEDGE *(Verify)*, **verb** admit, admit a right, admit the charge, concede, confess, confirm, defer to, recognize, recognize authority of, testify, yield
ASSOCIATED CONCEPTS: acknowledge a document, acknowledge the signatures on a will

ACKNOWLEDGED, *adjective* accepted, acquiesced, admitted, approved, avowed, conceded, confessed, conventional, correct, customary, established, familiar, formal, granted, immemorial, inveterate, long-standing, orthodox, popular, prescriptive, professed, public, putative, received, recognized, rooted, time-honored, traditional, understood, undisputed, unquestioned, usual, warranted
ASSOCIATED CONCEPTS: acknowledged actions, acknowledged certificates, acknowledged consideration, acknowledged debt, acknowledged evidence, acknowledged indebtedness, acknowledged instruments, acknowledged liability, acknowledged parties, acknowledged payments, acknowledged pleadings, acknowledged set-off of a claim, acknowledged signatures, acknowledged statements, authority, false certification, recitals

ACKNOWLEDGMENT *(Acceptance)*, **noun** accession, acquiescence, admittance, agreement, answer, assent, compliance, concession, concurrence, endorsement, ratification, recognition, replication, reply, response, verification
ASSOCIATED CONCEPTS: acknowledgment to an offer

ACKNOWLEDGMENT *(Avowal)*, **noun** admission, affirmation, assertion, asseveration, authentication, avowance, certification, *confessio,* confession, confirmation, declaration, formal declaration, statement, validation
ASSOCIATED CONCEPTS: acknowledgment in a deposition, acknowledgment of a conveyance, acknowledgment of a debt, acknowledgment of a deed, acknowledgment of a mortgage, acknowledgment of a will, acknowledgment of an illegitimate child, acknowledgment of indebtedness, acknowledgment of liability, certificate of acknowledgment, public acknowledgment

ACQUAINTED, *adjective* advised, apprised, attuned to, awakened, aware of, briefed, *cognitus,* cognizant of, conscious of, conversant with, enlightened, informed, instructed, introduced to, knowledgeable, notified, *notus, peritus,* posted, primed, told

ACQUIESCE, **verb** abide, accede, accept, acknowledge, admit, agree, agree to, allow, assent, be willing, bow to, comply, concede, concur, conform, consent, cooperate, defer to, give in, grant, obey, observe, ratify, receive, recognize, relent, resign oneself, sanction, submit, subscribe to, succumb, suffer, surrender, tolerate, yield

ACQUIESCENCE, *noun* accedence, acceptance, accession, accordance, acknowledgment, *adsensus,* agreement, allowance, assent, compliance, concession, concordance, concurrence, consent, grant, implied consent, nonresistance, observance, passive agreement, passive consent, permission, permittance, resignedness, sanction, subjection, submission, submissiveness, submittal, sufferance, tacit assent, willingness
ASSOCIATED CONCEPTS: acquiescence in judgment, acquiescence to a breach of contract, acquiescence to a breach of covenant, acquiescence to boundaries, acquiescence to the terms of a contract, ratification by acquiescence

FOREIGN PHRASES: *Agentes et consentientes pari poena plectentur.* Acting and consenting parties are liable to the same punishment. *Longa patientia trahitur ad consensum.* Long sufferance is interpreted as consent.

ACQUIRE *(Receive)*, **verb** accept, achieve, *adipisci,* adopt, be given, come into possession of, derive, gain, glean, obtain, reap, take in, win

ACQUIRE *(Secure)*, **verb** *adquirere,* annex, appropriate, assume, assume ownership, attain, exact, extort, extract, force from, gain, get, make one's own, obtain by any means, procure, purchase, realize, steal, take, take possession, wrest from
ASSOCIATED CONCEPTS: acquire a business, acquire by fraud, acquire by gift, acquire by inheritance, acquire by will, acquire for resale, acquire ownership
FOREIGN PHRASES: *Incorporalia bello non adquiruntur.* Things incorporeal are not acquired in war.

ACQUISITION, *noun* acceptance, acceptation, acquirement, appropriation, assumption, attainment, find, gain, gleaning, intaking, obtainment of property, possession, procuration, procurement, realization, receival, receiving, reception, recipience, stealing, taking
ASSOCIATED CONCEPTS: acquisition by purchase, acquisition of assets, acquisition of property, acquisition value
FOREIGN PHRASES: *Qui acquirit sibi acquirit haeredibus.* He who acquires for himself acquires for his heirs.

ACQUIT, **verb** absolve, *absolvere,* clear, compurgate, declare innocent, discharge, discharge from accusation, exculpate, excuse, exempt, exonerate, find not guilty, give a favorable verdict, grant remission, let off, *liberare,* liberate, make free, pardon, pronounce not guilty, prove innocent, *purgare,* release, remit, reprieve, set at liberty, set free, vindicate
ASSOCIATED CONCEPTS: acquittal in fact, acquittal in law

ACQUITTAL, *noun* *absolutio,* absolution, acquitment, acquittance, amnesty, clearance, compurgation, discharge, dismissal, exculpation, exoneration, favorable verdict, letting off, *liberatio,* liberation, pardon, purgation, quittance, release, remission, reprieve, restoration, verdict of not guilty, vindication
ASSOCIATED CONCEPTS: acquittal by a jury
FOREIGN PHRASES: *Paribus sententiis reus absolvitur.* When the opinions are equal, where the court is equally divided, the defendant is acquitted.

ACQUITTED, *adjective* cleared, exculpated, exonerated, freed of wrongdoing, let go, let off, not guilty, proved innocent, vindicated

ACRIMONIOUS, *adjective* acerb, acerbic, acrid, astringent, biting, bitter, blistering, captious, caustic, censorious, choleric, corrosive, cross-tempered, cruel, cutting, cynical, embittered, envenomed, gruff, harsh, hostile, huffy, ill-natured, inimical, irascible, irritable, malevolent, malicious, malignant, negative, peevish, pejorative, petulant, rancorous, resentful, rough, rude, sarcastic, scathing, severe, sharp, snappish, snarling, sour, spiteful, stinging, tart, testy, touchy, vicious, virulent, vitriolic, waspish

ACT *(Enactment)*, **noun** *acte,* administration, bill, code, deed, dictate, edict, law, legislation, legislative decree, *lex,* mandate, ordinance, precept, prescript, *règlement,* regulation, resolution, rule, ruling, statute, written law
ASSOCIATED CONCEPTS: Congressional act, legislative act

FOREIGN PHRASES: *Actus legis nemini est damnosus.* The act of the law shall prejudice no one.

ACT *(Undertaking),* **noun** accomplishment, achievement, action, commission, course, dealing, deed, doing, effectuation, enterprise, execution, feat, implementation, maneuver, manipulation, measure, method, move, operation, performance, perpetration, step, stratagem, task, transaction
ASSOCIATED CONCEPTS: act in official capacity, act of bankruptcy, act of commission, act of cruelty, act of embezzlement, act of flight, act of God, act of infringement, act of insolvency, act of larceny, act of law, act of misfeasance, act of necessity, act of omission, act of ownership, act of providence, act of reckless disregard, act of violence, act of war, *actus reas,* judicial act, mala prohibita act, overt act
FOREIGN PHRASES: *Actus me invito factus non est meus actus.* An act done by me, against my will, is not my act. ***Actus non facit reum, nisi mens sit rea.*** An act does not render a person guilty, unless the mind is guilty. ***Idem est facere, et non prohibere cum possis.*** It is the same thing to commit an act as not to prohibit it, when it is in your power. ***Facta sunt potentiora verbis.*** Acts or deeds are more powerful than words.

ACT AS AGENT, *verb* act as intermediary, act as substitute, act as surrogate, act for, act in place of, answer for, appear for, designate to represent, front for, intercede, represent, serve in one's stead, stand for, stand in the stead of

ACT ILLEGALLY, *verb* be derelict, be illegal, be perfidious, be recalcitrant, break the law, commit a crime, disobey the law, not comply, refuse to obey, repudiate, resist, transgress, traverse, trespass, violate, violate the law

ACT IN CONCERT, *verb* act jointly, agree, be in collusion with, collude, combine, concur, connive, conspire, cooperate, federate, form a coalition, involve, join, participate, pool, unite

ACT OF GOD, *noun* accident, chance occurrence, fortuitousness, fortuity, random luck

ACT ON *(Complete),* **verb** agree, answer, choose, choose a course of action, come to a conclusion, come to an agreement, conclude, decree, determine, draw a conclusion, elect, establish, finalize, find, form a judgment, form a resolution, form an opinion, make a choice, make a decision, make a selection, ok, opt, pronounce, reach a decision, react, reply, resolve, respond

ACT ON *(Rule),* **verb** adjudge, adjudicate, arrive at a judgment. ascertain, award, come to a decision, compromise, conclude, decree, determine, finalize, find, judge, make a decision, pronounce, reach a decision, reach a verdict, resolve, rule, sentence, settle
ASSOCIATED CONCEPTS: act on a motion, act on an application, act on case, act on evidence, act on information provided by an informant, act on petition

ACTING, *adjective* adjutant, deputative, deputy, functioning, holding legal rights conferred by another, impermanent, replacing, representative, representing, short-term, speaking by delegated authority, standing in the place of, substituting for, temporary, transient
ASSOCIATED CONCEPTS: acting illegally, acting in a boisterous manner, acting in concert with others, acting in good faith, acting judge, acting mayor, acting officer, acting within the course of employment, acting within the scope of employment

ACTION *(Performance),* **noun** accomplishment, achievement, administration, carrying out, concrete results, consummation, course of conduct, discharge, doing, effectuation, enforcement, execution, *factum,* implementation, line of action
FOREIGN PHRASES: *Non quod dictum est, sed quod factum est inspicitur.* Not what is said, but what is done, is to be regarded. ***Factum cuique suum, non adversario, nocere debet.*** A man's own acts should prejudice himself, not his adversary. ***Factum infectum fieri nequit.*** A thing which has been done cannot be undone. ***Les lois ne se chargent de punir que les actions exterieures.*** Laws do not assume to punish other than overt acts.

ACTION *(Proceeding),* **noun** *actio,* action at law, case, cause, cause in court, court proceeding, formal prosecution, hearing, hearing on the merits, judicial contest, judicial proceeding, lawsuit, legal action, legal contest, legal proceeding, *lis,* litigation, litigation of the charges, prosecution, suit, suit at law, suit in law, trial, trial of a case, trial of the issues
ASSOCIATED CONCEPTS: abatement, action arising under the laws of the United States, action at law, action brought, action by one party against another, action ex delicto, action ex parte, action for a declaratory judgment, action for bodily injury, action for breach of a contract, action for damages, action for deceit, action for disparagement, action for dissolution, action for divorce, action for fraud, action for injury to property, action for liquidated damages, action for misrepresentation, action for money damages, action for recovery of chattel, action for rescission and restitution, action in assumpsit, action in conversion, action in detinue, action in ejectment, action in equity, action in interpleader, action in personam, action in quantum meruit, action in rem, action in replevin, action in tort, action in trespass, action in trover, action of foreclosure, action of garnishment, action on a contract, action on a debt, action on account rendered, action on contract, action quasi in rem, action to quiet title, action to remove a cloud, affirmative action, cause of action, chose in action, civil action, class action, commence an action, consolidation, continuance of action on submitted facts, criminal action, cross action, derivative action, independent actions, joinder of actions, joint action, legal action, local actions, main action, multiplicity of actions, pending action, right of action, severance of actions, stockholders' action, third-party action
FOREIGN PHRASES: *Ex nudo pacto non oritur nascitur actio.* No action arises on a contract without a consideration. ***Cum actio fuerit mere criminalis, institui poterit ab initio criminaliter vel civiliter.*** When an action is merely criminal, it can be instituted either criminally or civilly at the outset. ***In rem actio est per quam rem nostram quae ab alio possidetur petimus, et semper adversus eum est qui rem possidet.*** An action in rem is one by means of which we seek our property which is owned by another, and is always against him who possesses the property. ***Actio quaelibet it sua via.*** Every action proceeds in its own course. ***Secta est pugna civilis; sicut actores armantur actionibus, et, quasi, gladiis accinguntur, ita rei muniuntur exceptionibus, et defenduntur, quasi, clypeis.*** A suit is a civil battle; for as the plaintiffs are armed with actions, and as it were, girded with swords, so the defendants are fortified with pleas, and defended, as it were, by shields. ***Remoto impedimento, emergit actio.*** The impediment being removed, the action emerges. ***Omnis quereia et omnis actio injuriarum limita est infra certa tempora.*** Every complaint and every action for injuries is limited within certain times. ***Omnes actiones in mundo infra certa tempora habent limitationem.*** All actions in the world are

limited within certain periods of time. *In haeredes non solent transire actiones quae poenales ex maleficio sunt.* Penal actions arising from anything of a criminal nature do not pass to heirs. *Actio personalis moritur cum persona.* A personal action dies with the person. *Ex tupi causa non oritur actio.* No cause of action arises out of an immoral or illegal consideration.

ACTIONABLE, adjective accountable, amenable, answerable, bound, causidical, chargeable, controvertible, disputable, justiciable, liable to prosecution, litigable, litigant, litigious, pertaining to litigation, remediable by an action at law, *res cuius actio est,* responsible, suable, under legal obligation, under obligation, unexempt from
ASSOCIATED CONCEPTS: actionable cause of action, actionable charges, actionable claim, actionable words, actionable wrongdoing

ACTIONS, noun bearing, behavior, behavior pattern, comportment, conduct, dealings, demeanor, deportment, doings, guise, manner, mien, mode of action, *modus vivendi,* policy, practice, presence, procedure, ways
ASSOCIATED CONCEPTS: abandonment, abatement, action at law, actions in equity, appeals, arbitrations, bankruptcy, civil actions, collateral estoppel, consolidation, construction, criminal, declaratory judgments, easements, employment, federal actions, fidelity actions, frivolous actions, garnishment, habeas corpus, labor law, landlord and tenant, *lis pendens,* mandamus, marital actions, municipal actions, removal of actions, replevin, *res judicata,* severance of an action, splitting a cause of action, state actions, summary proceedings, supplemental proceedings, venue

ACTIVATE, verb accelerate, actuate, animate, boost, drive, empower, energize, enliven, excite, excite to action, impel, initiate, intensify, launch, maintain, motivate, originate, prompt, quicken, step up, stimulate, stir, urge

ACTIVE, adjective assiduous, at work, busily employed, busily engaged, busy, effective, effectual, efficacious, efficient, energetic, enterprising, functioning, *impiger,* in a state of action, in actual process, in operation, in practice, industrious, *industrius, navus,* operant, operating, performing, sedulous, trenchant, vigorous, working
ASSOCIATED CONCEPTS: active concealment, active negligence, active participant, active tort feasor, active trust, active wrongdoing, passive negligence, passive tort feasor

ACTIVITIES, noun actions, acts, affairs, arrangements, dealings, deals, doings, exchange, interests, matters, measures, policy, practice, proceedings, relations, transactions, understandings, undertakings

ACTIVITY, noun assignment, campaign, cause, crusade, drive, endeavor, enterprise, function, interest, movement, operation, pursuit, undertaking, venture, work

ACTOR, noun *actor,* aggrieved party, complainant, intervener, litigant, malcontent, man with a grievance, operator, participant, party, performer, person, petitioner, plaintiff, *qui facit*
ASSOCIATED CONCEPTS: an actor as a witness in a prosecution, an actor in a legal proceeding

ACTS *(Conduct),* **noun** actions, bearing, behavior, demeanor, manners, mien, observance, pattern

ACTS *(Legislation),* **noun** enactments, laws, provisions of the law, statutes

ASSOCIATED CONCEPTS: acts in emergencies, acts of Congress, acts of insolvency, bills, case law, local ordinances, ordinances, statutes

ACTUAL, adjective absolute, accurate, as represented, ascertained, authentic, authenticated, *bona fide,* categorical, categorically true, certain, concrete, correct, *de facto,* decided, defined, definite, demonstrable, demonstrated, determinate, essential, exact, existent, existing, factual, faithful, genuine, honest, in fact, *ipse,* literal, nonabstract, not fictitious, not imaginary, not merely supposed, objective, official, palpable, positive, precise, present, real, realistic, right, rightful, specific, substantial, substantive, tangible, true, true to the facts, true to the letter, truthful, unerring, unerroneous, unfallacious, unfalse, unimagined, unimpeachable, unmistaken, unrefuted, unsupposed, valid, veracious, veritable, *verus,* well-founded, well-grounded
ASSOCIATED CONCEPTS: actual authority, actual bailment, actual book value, actual case or controversy, actual cash receipts, actual cash value, actual damages, actual delivery, actual earnings, actual eviction, actual expense, actual force, actual fraud, actual income, actual intent, actual intent to defraud, actual knowledge, actual loss, actual malice, actual market value, actual notice, actual occupancy, actual possession, actual residence, actual use, actual value, actual waste, actually engaged in business, actually occupied, actually owing, actually owning, actually receive, fair, fair reasonable cash price, reasonable cash price

ACTUARY, noun calculator of insurance risks, compiler of tables of mortality, insurance adviser, statistician
ASSOCIATED CONCEPTS: actuarial bureaus, actuarial solvency, actuarial tables

ACTUS REUS, noun actions, at fault, bearing, behavior, blamable, blameworthy, censurable, chargeable, condemnable, convicted, criminal, criminous, culpable, delinquent, demeanor, deserving, deserving of blame, deserving reproof, erring, external element of a crime, guilty act, imputable, in error, in the wrong, incriminated, indictable, manners, mien, observance, of punishment, pattern, peccant, reprehensible, reproachable, reprovable, to blame, transgressing

ACUMEN, noun acuity, astuteness, caliber, cleverness, common sense, comprehension, discernment, discretion, discrimination, foresightedness, ingenuity, insight, intelligence, intuition, judgment, keenness, mental acuteness, mental capacity, perception, perspicacity, reason, sagacity, sense, sharpness, shrewdness, smartness, subtlety, wisdom

ACUTE, adjective *acer,* acuminate, *acutus,* alert, apt, astute, aware, clear-sighted, critical, crucial, cutting, discerning, fine, foreseeing, intense, intuitive, keen, keenly sensitive, knowledgeable, penetrating, perceptive, perspicacious, *perspicax,* piercing, pointed, prompt, provident, prudent, quick-witted, *sagax,* sapient, sharp, sharp-edged, sharp-witted, *subtilis,* trenchant, vivid

AD DAMNUM CLAUSE, noun claim for damages, demanded damages, fixed amount of damages, monetary clause, provision for damages

AD HOC, adjective extemporaneous, for the sake of, for this case alone, improvised, in consideration of, on account of, special
ASSOCIATED CONCEPTS: ad hoc appointment, ad hoc committee

AD INFINITUM, *adverb* boundlessly, endlessly, eternally, illimitably, immeasurably, incalculably, incomprehensibly, indefinitely, indeterminately, innumerably, interminably, limitlessly, measurelessly, to infinity, without end

AD INTERIM, *adverb* at the same time, during, during the interval, *en attendant,* for a time, for the time being, in the course of, in the interim, in the intervening time, in the meantime, in the meanwhile, meantime, meanwhile, pending, throughout, till, until, when, while
ASSOCIATED CONCEPTS: ad interim copyright, ad interim restraining order

AD VALOREM, *adjective* according to value, appraised, appraisement, assessable, assessment, charge, chargeable, charged, dutiable, duty, evaluated, excisable, imposition, leviable, levy, ratable, taxation, valorization, value added tax, valued at
ASSOCIATED CONCEPTS: ad valorem tax

ADAMANT, *adjective* callous, firm, frozen, hard-hearted, immovable, immutable, implacable, inelastic, inexorable, inflexible, intractable, irreconcilable, merciless, obdurate, persistent, pertinacious, resolute, rigid, stationary, stiff, stubborn, tough, unaffected, unalterable, unbending, uncompassionate, uncompromising, unfeeling, unmalleable, unmoved, unpliable, unpliant, unrelenting, unyielding

ADAPT, *verb* acclimatize, accommodate oneself, adjust, alter, *aptare,* arrange, change, comply with, conform, convert, correlate, fashion, fit, make conformable, make suitable, modify, modulate, readjust, reconcile, regularize, render accordant, revise, standardize, temper, transform, work a change

ADAPTABLE, *adjective* accommodating, accommodative, acquiescent, adaptive, adjustable, adroit, ambidextrous, amenable, applicable, bendable, buoyant, comformable, complaisant, compliant, corrigible, deft, disposable, docile, ductile, elastic, fitting, flexible, governable, idoneous, in accord, in keeping, in line, in step, limber, lissome, lithe, malleable, manageable, moldable, obedient, open to, plastic, pliable, pliant, practical, resilient, sequacious, serviceable, stretchable, submissive, suitable, suited, supple, tractable, tractile, usable, utilizable, versatile

ADAPTED, *adjective* able, absorbed, acclimated, acclimatized, accommodating, accordant, accustomed, adaptable, adequate, adjustable, adjusted, agreed, apposite, appropriate, apt, becoming, befitting, capable, centralized, combined, complaisant, compliant, conditioned, conformable, congruous, consonant, correct, correlative, deft, effective, embodied, familiarized, fit, fitting, flexible, harmonious, integrated, malleable, opportune, pertinent, pliant, proper, qualified, seemly, suitable, suited, tempered, unified

ADD (*Calculate*), *verb* account, appraise, assess, audit, compute, count, enumerate, estimate, evaluate, figure, measure, modify, reckon, suffix, sum, tally, total, valuate

ADD (*Combine*), *verb* adjoin, affix, agglutinate, aject, alter, annex, append, attach, cement, clip to, conjoin, connect, couple, fuse, glue, innovate, match, mix, pair, put with, subjoin, superpose, tack on, unite, weld
ASSOCIATED CONCEPTS: add a paragraph to a complaint, add a party to action

ADD (*Heighten*), *verb* broaden, contribute, enhance, expand, extend, greaten, grow, increase, inflate, insert, widen

ADD (*Interject*), *verb* express, include, inject, insert, inset, interpose, introduce, intromit, mention, state, supplement

ADDENDUM, *noun* additament, addition, adjunct, affix, annex, annexation, *annexe,* appanage, appendage, appendix, attachment, codicil, complement, concomitant, inclusion, insertion, postscript, rider, subscript, supplement, supplementation
ASSOCIATED CONCEPTS: addendum to a contract, pocket part

ADDICT, *noun* adherent, ardent admirer, believer, creature of habit, devotee, disciple, enthusiast, fan, fanatic, fancier, follower, frequenter, partisan, practitioner, pursuer, votary, zealot

ADDICTED, *adjective* accustomed, attached, fanatic, given over, habituated, imbued with, in the habit, indulgent, obsessed with, prone to, *rei deditus,* surrendered to, under the influence of, wedded to
ASSOCIATED CONCEPTS: addicted to alcohol, addicted to drugs, addicted to pills

ADDITION, *noun* *accessio,* accession, accessory, addend, addendum, additament, additive, *adiectio,* adjunct, adjunction, annex, annexation, attachment, augmentation, complement, enlargement, extension, increase, increment, joining, pendant, subjunction, supplement
ASSOCIATED CONCEPTS: addition to a structure

ADDITIONAL, *adjective* accessory, added, additive, *additus, adiectus,* another, appended, auxiliary, collateral, extra, further, included, joined, more, other, superadded, supervenient, supplemental, supplementary, ulterior
ASSOCIATED CONCEPTS: additional assured, additional burden, additional charges, additional compensation, additional consideration, additional coverage, additional duties, additional insured, additional relief, additional servitude

ADDITIONALLY, *adverb* along with, also, as well as, besides, by the same token, conjointly, ditto, further, furthermore, in addition, in conjunction with, including, more than that, moreover, over and above, plus, similarly, then again, together with, together with that, too

ADDITIVE, *noun* accrual, addendum, addition, adjunct, appurtenance, attachment, augmentation, enhancement, extension, increment, supplement

ADDITUR, *noun* assessment of damages, increase of damages, increase of jury award

ADDRESS, *noun* abode, box number, domicile, dwelling, dwelling place, habitation, headquarters, home, inhabitancy, *inscriptio,* legal residence, *locus,* lodging, lodging place, lodgment, place of business, residence, seat, street number
ASSOCIATED CONCEPTS: business address, last known address, local address, office address, post office address, residence

ADDRESS (*Direct attention to*), *verb* apply oneself to, approach, be occupied with, bring to attention, bring to notice, call attention to, call to notice, concern oneself with, devote oneself to, direct to, occupy oneself with

ADDRESS (*Petition*), *verb* appeal, call upon, enter a plea, enter a suit for, plead, prepare a complaint, prepare a formal request, prepare a petition, seek redress
ASSOCIATED CONCEPTS: address the court

13

ADDRESS *(Talk to),* **verb** deliver a talk, discourse, discuss, give a speech, harangue, *hominem adloqui,* lecture, orate, preach, *se rei dedere,* sermonize, speak to

ADDUCE, **verb** *adducere,* advance, allege, allude, assert, assign, aver, bring to the fore, claim, declare, disclose, divulge, evidence, evince, furnish, give, indicate, introduce, manifest, mention, offer, place in the foreground, plead, present, produce, *producere, proferre,* proffer, propound, reveal, show, state
ASSOCIATED CONCEPTS: adduce evidence, adduce testimony

ADDUCED, *adjective* acknowledged, added, advanced, advocated, alleged, alluded, asserted, averred, avouched, avowed, brought forth, certified, cited, claimed, contended, declared, divulged, enunciated, imparted, insisted, introduced, maintained, presented, proclaimed, stated, supplemented
ASSOCIATED CONCEPTS: evidence adduced at trial

ADEEM, **verb** abnegate, abolish, abrogate, annul, avoid, cancel, declare null and void, deny, deprive of, disinherit, disseise, divest, make void, negate, nullify, obliterate, offset, remove, render null and void, render void, repeal, repudiate, rescind, retract, revoke, take away, take back, take from, vacate, void, withdraw
ASSOCIATED CONCEPTS: adeem a bequest, adeem a devise, adeem a gift, adeem a legacy

ADEMPTION, *noun* abnegation, abolishment, abolition, abrogation, annulment, cancellation, cancellation of a legacy, contravention, disclamation, discontinuance, disownment, dissolution, extinction, invalidation, negation, nullification, recall, renouncement, renunciation, repeal, repudiation, rescindment, rescission, retraction, revocation, revokement, vacation, *vacatur,* voidance, withdrawal, withdrawment
ASSOCIATED CONCEPTS: ademption of a bequest, ademption of a devise, ademption of a gift, ademption of a legacy, operation of law, satisfaction

ADEPT, *adjective* able, accomplished, adroit, apt, artful, capable, clever, competent, deft, dexterous, experienced, expert, gifted, handy, ingenious, masterful, masterly, practiced, professional, proficient, qualified, sharp, skillful, smart, sound, talented, trained, versed, well-skilled

ADEQUACY, *noun* ability, ableness, acceptability, admissibility, caliber, capability, capacity, competence, competency, completeness, contentment, deftness, efficacy, efficiency, employability, fitness, proficiency, qualification, satisfaction, satisfactoriness, sufficiency, utility, wherewithal, usefulness
ASSOCIATED CONCEPTS: adequacy of contents of pleadings, adequacy of proof, competency

ADEQUATE, *adjective* able, acceptable, *accommodatus,* ample, *aptus,* availing, capable, commensurate, competent, effectual, enough, equal to the need, fair, fit, fully sufficient, *idoneus,* proportionate, reasonable, reasonably sufficient, satisfactory, satisfying, serving, sufficient, sufficient for the purpose, sufficing, suitable, valid
ASSOCIATED CONCEPTS: adequate administrative review, adequate care, adequate cause, adequate consideration, adequate notice, adequate remedy at law, adequate support, fair and adequate consideration

ADEQUATE NOTICE, *noun* ample notice, commensurate notice, fair notice, good notice, satisfactory notice, sufficient notice, suitable notice, valid notice

ASSOCIATED CONCEPTS: adequate care, adequate compensation, adequate remedy at law, adequate security

ADEQUATE PROOF, *noun* adequate evidence, burden of going forward, burden of proof, legal responsibility, obligation of going forward, sufficient corroboration, sufficient evidence in a case, sufficient evidence to establish a case, sufficient proof, sufficient proof of facts, validation of proof of a case, verification of proof of a case
ASSOCIATED CONCEPTS: cause of action or claim, evidence, evidential burden, failure to sustain, preponderance of the evidence, prima facie case, rebuttal
FOREIGN PHRASES: *Onus probani,* Burden of proof.

ADHERE *(Fasten),* **verb** agglutinate, anchor, attach, band together, cement, clamp, clasp, cling to, coalesce, cohere, compound, fuse, glue, hold fast, hold firmly, *inhaerere,* join, latch, secure, stick to, stick together, tighten, unite

ADHERE *(Maintain loyalty),* **verb** abide by, act in support, advocate, argue for, back, be devoted, be faithful, be loyal, be partisan, be steadfast, be true, champion, comply, conform, *deditum esse,* defend, devote oneself, espouse, follow, give support, keep faith, obey, pay allegiance, preserve, show devotion, stand by, *studere,* support, uphold

ADHERE *(Persist),* **verb** abide, be constant, be devoted, be obstinate, be steadfast, be steady, be unyielding, carry on, cling tenaciously, continue, endure, go to any lengths, go to the limit, have tenacity, hold on, hold tight, *in re stare,* keep going, keep on, maintain, *manere,* persevere, persist in, pursue, show determination, stand firm, stick to, sustain, work unceasingly
ASSOCIATED CONCEPTS: adhere to the Constitution, adhere to the terms of a contract

ADHERE TO, **verb** acknowledge, comply, conform, fulfill, have regard to, head, keep, make a practice of, obey, observe, pay attention to, pursue, regard, respect

ADHERENCE *(Adhesion),* **noun** attachment, bond, cementation, coherence, cohesion, cohesiveness, concretion, conglutination, connectedness, firmness, fixedness, holding together, sticking together, tenaciousness, tenacity, tie

ADHERENCE *(Devotion),* **noun** allegiance, attachment, *bona fide,* bond, compliance, constancy, dedication, devotedness, faithfulness, fealty, fidelity, homage, loyalty, obedience, observance, steadfastness, tenaciousness, tenacity, tie, troth
ASSOCIATED CONCEPTS: adherence to a contract, adherence to the principles of the Constitution

ADHERENT, *adjective* adhering, clinging, coherent, cohesive, gluey, glutinous, gummy, mucilaginous, sticking, sticky, tenacious, viscid, viscous

ADHERENT, *noun* abettor, accessory, accomplice, acolyte, advocate, aider, ally, approver, backer, champion, companion, confederate, dependent, devotee, disciple, follower, helper, partisan, partner, patron, protégé, satellite, seconder, supporter, upholder

ADHESION *(Affixing),* **noun** adherence, adhesiveness, agglomeration, agglutination, aggregation, attachment, cementation, clinging, close contact, coadunation, coagulation, coherence, cohesion, cohesiveness, concretion,

condensation, congelation, conglomeration, conglutination, conjunction, connection, consolidation, fusion, glutinosity, gumminess, gummosity, inseparability, inseparableness, iron grip, junction, prehension, solidification, stickiness, union, unity, viscidity, viscosity
ASSOCIATED CONCEPTS: contract of adhesion, unequal bargaining power

ADHESION (Loyalty), **noun** adherence, adherence to duty, allegiance, alliance, ardor, association, attachment, attention, *bona fide*, bond, close identification, commitment, conscientiousness, consecration, constancy, dependability, devotedness, devotion, devoutness, dutifulness, earnestness, faithfulness, fealty, fidelity, firmness, homage, incorruptibility, integrity, obedience, reliability, resolution, scrupulousness, sense of duty, sense of responsibility, service, servitude, single-mindedness, staunchness, steadfastness, strong connection, submission, submissiveness, subservience, support, tenaciousness, tenacity, tie, troth, trueness, trustiness, trustworthiness, union, unswerving fidelity, vote of confidence, willingness, zeal

ADHESIVENESS, noun adhesion, coherence, cohesiveness, glutinosity, gumminess, stickiness, stick-to-itiveness, tackiness, toughness, viscidity, viscosity

ADJACENT, adjective abutting, adjoining, alongside, beside, bordering, conterminous, contiguous, *contiguus,* continuous, convergent, *finitimus,* juxtaposed, meeting, neighboring, next to, proximal, touching, verging on, vicinal, *vicinus*
ASSOCIATED CONCEPTS: adjacent county, adjacent land, adjacent owners, adjacent property

ADJECTIVE LAW, noun legal course to adhere to, legal methods, procedural law

ADJOIN, verb abut on, *adiacere,* appose, *attingere,* be adjacent to, be contiguous to, be joined to, border on, cohere, conjoin, connect, converge, juxtapose, juxtaposit, lie beside, lie near to, meet, neighbor, place side by side, reach to, stand by, *tangere,* touch

ADJOINER, noun addition to, appendage, attachment, conjoiner, connection, convergence, subjoiner

ADJOURN, verb *ampliare,* continue, defer, delay, hold in abeyance, hold over, intermit, keep pending, postpone, prorogue, put off, recess, reserve, stop, suspend, terminate
ASSOCIATED CONCEPTS: adjourn a case, adjourn a proceeding, adjourn for a session of the court, adjourn for the term of the court, adjourn on consent, adjourned term

ADJOURNMENT, noun adjournal, break, continuation, deferment, *dilatio,* discontinuation, extension, hold-over, intermission, interruption, moratorium, postponement, prolongation, prorogation, protraction, recess, reservation, respite, stay, suspension, termination
ASSOCIATED CONCEPTS: adjournment for a session, adjournment for the term, adjournment in contemplation of dismissal, adjournment of a hearing, adjournment of a trial, adjournment of the court, *sine die*

ADJUDGE, verb *addicere, adiudicare,* adjudicate, arbitrate, award, conclude, decide, decree, deem, deliver judgment, determine, dispense, dispense judgment, exercise judgment, find, give an opinion, hold, judge, judicate, judicially determine, make a decision, order, pass judgment, pronounce formally, rule, sentence, settle, sit in judgment

ASSOCIATED CONCEPTS: adjudge bankrupt, adjudge guilt, adjudge incompetent, adjudge innocence, adjudge insolvent, adjudge liability
FOREIGN PHRASES: Res judicata pro veritate accipitur. A thing which is adjudicated is accepted or received for the truth.

ADJUDICATE, verb adjudge, arbitrate, award, award judgment, conclude, decide, decree, deem, deliver judgment, determine, determine finally, exercise judicial authority, find, give judgment, hear, hear the case, hold court, judge, make a decision, mediate, order, pass judgment, pass sentence, pronounce, referee, render judgment, rule, rule upon, settle, sit in judgment, try, try the cause
ASSOCIATED CONCEPTS: adjudicate a juvenile delinquent, adjudicate a youthful offender, adjudicate an incompetent, adjudicate bankruptcy, adjudicate guilt, adjudicate innocence, adjudicate insolvency, adjudicate jurisdictional questions, adjudicate liability
FOREIGN PHRASES: *Cessa regnare, si non vis judicare.* Cease to reign, if you don't wish to adjudicate. *In propria causa nemo judex.* No one can be a judge in his own cause.

ADJUDICATION, noun act of judgment, adjudgment, arbitrage, arbitrament, arbitration, authoritative decision, award, conclusion, decision, declaration, decree, deliberate determination, determination, determination of issues, disposition, edict, final determination, final judgment, finding, irrevocable decision, judgment, judgment on facts, judicial decision, opinion, order, order of the court, proclamation, pronouncement, reasoned judgment, *res judicata,* resolution, result, ruling, sentence, settled decision, verdict
ASSOCIATED CONCEPTS: adjudication of a court of competent jurisdiction, adjudication of bankruptcy, adjudication of guilt, adjudication of incompetency, adjudication of innocence, adjudication of insolvency, adjudication of liability, adjudication on the merits, adjudication under law, adjudicative facts, judicial assessment
FOREIGN PHRASES: *Novum judicium non dat novum jus, sed declarat antiquum; quia judicium est juris dictum et per judicium jus est noviter revelatum quod diu fuit velatum.* A new adjudication does not promulgate a new law, but declares the old; because adjudication is the utterance of the law, and by adjudication the law is newly revealed which was for a long time hidden. *Res judicata pro veritate accipitur.* A thing which is adjudicated is accepted or received for the truth.

ADJUNCT, adjective accessory, addendum, additament, addition, appanage, appendage, augmentation, auxiliary, branch, complement, component, corollary, extension, subordinate part, supplement
FOREIGN PHRASES: *Sublato principali, tollitur adjunctum.* By the removal of the principal thing, the adjunct is taken also.

ADJURATION, noun affirmation, attestation, averment, avouchment, avowal, avowance, declaration, legal pledge, oath, pledge, solemn avowal, swearing, sworn statement, testimony, vouching, vow

ADJURE, verb administer an oath, affirm, appeal to, ask, attest, beseech, bid, bind, call, charge, command, conjure, declare, enjoin, entreat, enunciate, exhort, express, formulate, implore, imprecate, petition, plead, pray, prescribe, press, pressure, promise, pronounce, request, require, set down, solicit, state, swear, swear by, swear in, take a pledge, take oath on, urge, witness to

ADJUST

ADJUST *(Regulate),* **verb** *accommodare,* accommodate, adapt, *aptare,* attemper, balance, calibrate, coordinate, establish equilibrium, even, methodize, moderate, normalize, reset, restore equilibrium, stabilize, standardize, strike a balance, systematize, temper, tune
ASSOCIATED CONCEPTS: adjust differences, adjusted, adjusted cost basis, adjusted gross income

ADJUST *(Resolve),* **verb** accord, amend, arrange, bring to agreement, change, clarify, complete, conclude, conform, correct, curb, emendate, fix, mitigate, rectify, redress, remedy, set, settle, solve, treat
ASSOCIATED CONCEPTS: adjust a claim

ADJUSTER, *noun* arbitrater, interagent, interceder, intercessor, interlocutor, intermediary, intermediate, intermediator, intermedium, intervener, mediator, negotiant, negotiator, reconciler

ADJUSTMENT, *noun* abatement of differences, *accommodatio,* accommodation, accord, accordance, adaptation, agreement, arrangement, attunement, bargain, binding agreement, coaptation, compact, composition, compromise, concurrence, conformance, conformation, conformity, congruence, congruity, consistency, contract, coordination, correction, covenant, disposition, harmony, mutual concession, mutual understanding, negotiation, pact, reconcilement, reconciliation, rectification, regulating, settlement, stipulation, terms, understanding, uniformity
ASSOCIATED CONCEPTS: adjusted basis, adjusted reserves, adjustment of contracts, adjustment of loss, adjustments in wills

ADJUVANT, *adjective* accessory, aiding, ancillary, assistant, assisting, auxiliary, cooperative, helpful, helping, ministerial, obliging, serving, subservient, subsidiary

ADJUVANT, *noun* acolyte, adjutant, aid, aide-de-camp, ancillary, assistant, attendant, auxiliary, backer, coactor, coadjutant, colleague, confederate, copartner, help, helper, helpmate, participant, partner, second, servant, subsidiary

ADMEASURE, *verb* administer, allocate, allot, apportion, bestrew, broadcast, circulate, classify, diffuse, dispense, dispose, disseminate, distribute, divide, dole, issue, measure, mete, parcel out, partition, propagate, radiate, set apart, share, sow, spread, systematize, tabulate

ADMINISTER *(Conduct),* **verb** administrate, carry out, control, direct, dispose of, effect, effectuate, enforce, engineer, govern, guide, handle, have executive charge of, manage, mastermind, minister, officiate, operate, overlook, oversee, pilot, prescribe, preside over, procurare, put in force, regulate, *rem administrare, rempublicam gubernare,* settle, steer, superintend, supervise
ASSOCIATED CONCEPTS: administer a bankrupt's assets, administer an estate, administer the law

ADMINISTER *(Tender),* **verb** accord, afford, bestow on, confer, deal out, disburse, dispense, disperse, distribute, dole out, extend, give, impart, issue, measure out, mete out, offer, procurare, provide with, render
ASSOCIATED CONCEPTS: administer drugs, administer oaths

ADMINISTRATE, *verb* administer, captain, command, conduct, control, direct, govern, head, lead, manage, officiate, operate, preside, regulate, render, sit in judgment, stand over, superintend, supervise

ADMINISTRATION, *noun* administratio, care, conduct, control, direction, dispensation, disposal, disposition, distribution, execution, executive charge, guardianship, guidance, handling, keeping, management, ministration, oversight, performance of executive duties, practical management, *procuratio,* regulation, settlement of an estate, superintendence, supervision
ASSOCIATED CONCEPTS: administration of a bankrupt's estate, administration of an estate, administration of expenses, administration of the laws, fair administration of justice, trust administration
FOREIGN PHRASES: *Nihil infra regnum subditos magis conservat in tranquilitate et concordia quam debita legum administratio.* Nothing better preserves in tranquillity and concord those subjected to the same government than the due administration of the laws.

ADMINISTRATIVE, *adjective* directorial, guiding, managerial, managing, ministerial, regulative, superintending, supervising, supervisory
ASSOCIATED CONCEPTS: administrative act, administrative action, administrative agency, administrative board, administrative body, administrative capacity, administrative discretion, administrative function, administrative hearings, administrative judges, administrative law, administrative procedures, administrative proceeding, administrative process, administrative regulations, administrative remedy, administrative rulings

ADMINISTRATOR, *noun* administrative head, chief executive, curator, custodian, director, executive, guardian, head of affairs, intendant, leader, legal representative, manager, officer of the court, overseer, personal representative, supervisor, supervisor of an estate, trustee
ASSOCIATED CONCEPTS: *administrator cum testamento annexo, administrator de bonis non, administrator de bonis non cum testamento annexo,* administrator executor, administrator general, *administrator pendente lite,* administrator's bond, administratrix, administratrix general, ancillary administrator, *executrix administrator ad prosequendum,* legal representative, supervisor of an estate

ADMISSIBILITY, *noun* acceptability, adequateness, allowableness, applicability, appositeness, appropriateness, aptness, eligibility, fitness, justifiability, legality, legitimacy, permissibility, presentability, propriety, reasonability, sanctionability, sanctionableness, sufficiency, suitability, tolerability, unexceptionability, unobjectionability, warrantability, warrantableness
ASSOCIATED CONCEPTS: affirmative evidence, confessions, decedent's statements, extrajudicial statements, hearsay, objections, secondary evidence

ADMISSIBLE, *adjective* à *propos,* acceptable, *aequus,* allowable, allowed, applicable, appropriate, authorized, eligible, justifiable, legal, legitimate, licensed, passable, permissible, permitted, presentable, proper, qualified, sanctionable, sanctioned, suitable, tolerable, unexceptionable, unforbidden, unobjectionable, unprohibited, warrantable, warranted
ASSOCIATED CONCEPTS: admissions of party-opponent, confessions, declarations against interest, limited admissibility, McNabb-Mallory rule, Miranda rule, nolo contendere, offer of proof, probative value, requests for admissions, secondary evidence

ADMISSIBLE EVIDENCE, *noun* acceptable evidence, creditable evidence, legal evidence, permissible evidence

ADMISSION (*Disclosure*), **noun** acknowledgment, assertion, attestation, avowal, communication, *concessio,* concession, confession, declaration, divulgence, enlightenment, exposure, expression, profession, revealment, revelation, statement, testimonial averment, testimony, unmasking, unveiling, voluntary acknowledgment

ASSOCIATED CONCEPTS: acknowledged adversary's claim, admission against interest, admission against pecuniary interest, admission as an exemption to the hearsay rule, admission by conduct, admission by flight, admission implied from silence, admission in a pleading, admission in an answer from a failure to deny, admission of a debt, admission of a fact, admission of a party, admission of guilt, admission of liability, admission to a crime, admission to bail, admissions by a representative, declaration against interest, direct admissions, expression admissions, extrajudicial admissions, implied admission, incidental admissions, inconsistent statement, judicial admissions, oral admissions, plenary admissions, written admissions

FOREIGN PHRASES: *Qui non negat fatetur.* He who does not deny admits.

ADMISSION (*Entry*), **noun** access, admittance, avenue, course, entrance, entryway, ingress, inlet, opening, passage, passageway, path, road, roadway, route, way

ASSOCIATED CONCEPTS: admission to bail, admission to practice law, admission to the bar

ADMISSION OF GUILT, noun avowal, concession, confession, confessional, contrition, culpability, disclosure, *mea culpa,* owning up, penance, penitence, remorse, repentance, sinfulness

ASSOCIATED CONCEPTS: admissibility, coerced confession, traditional admissions

ADMIT (*Concede*), **verb** accede, accept, acknowledge, acquiesce, affirm, agree, assent, *concedere,* concur, confess, confirm, declare, disclose, divulge, enlighten, expose, *fateri,* grant, recognize, relate, reveal, unmask, unveil

ASSOCIATED CONCEPTS: admit fault, admit in a reply, admit in an answer, admit liability, admit to probate

ADMIT (*Give access*), **verb** *adeundi copiam, admittere,* allow entrance, create an opening, give right of entry to, inaugurate, induct, initiate, install, institute, invest, open a passage, open a path, open a road, open a route, open an entryway, open an inlet, recipere, throw open, vest, yield passage to

ASSOCIATED CONCEPTS: admit to bail, admit to practice

ADMITTANCE (*Acceptance*), **noun** admission, confirmation, designation, entrance, entree, entry, inclusion, induction, initiation, permission

ADMITTANCE (*Means of approach*), **noun** access, admission, approach, avenue, course, entrance, entry, entryway, ingress, inlet, liberty of approach, opening, passage, passageway, path, portal, road, route, way

ADMITTED, adjective accepted, acknowledged, allowed, approved, avowed, believed, conceded, confessed, credited, granted, prescriptive, professed, received, recognized, trusted, undoubted, unquestioned

ASSOCIATED CONCEPTS: admitted and marked as an exhibit, admitted culpability, admitted into evidence, admitted wrongdoing

ADMITTEDLY, adverb acceptedly, allowedly, assuredly, authentically, authoritatively, avowedly, certainly, concededly, confessedly, doubtlessly, genuinely, incontestably, incontrovertibly, indisputably, indubitably, irrefragably, irrefutably, surely, truly, undeniably, undoubtedly, unquestionably, validly, veritably

ADMIXTURE, noun amalgam, amalgamation, blend, coalescence, combination, commixture, composite, composition, compound, integration, intermingling, intermixture, melange, mingling, mixture, pastiche

ASSOCIATED CONCEPTS: confusion of goods

ADMONISH (*Advise*), **verb** *admonere,* advocate, alert, call attention to, charge, correct, counsel, enjoin, exhort, give advice, give counsel, give notice, inform, instruct, notify, offer counsel, prescribe, propound, recommend, submit, suggest, urge

ADMONISH (*Warn*), **verb** address a warning to, administer a rebuke, advise against, caution, censure, com-*monere,* counsel against, dehort, deprecate, exhort, expostulate, forebode, forewarn, give warning, *monere,* objurgate, premonish, prewarn, rebuke, remonstrate, reprehend, reprimand, reprove, warn against

ADMONITION, noun admonishment, advance notice, advice, alarm, animadversion, caution, *caveat,* censure, commonition, contraindication, contrariety, contrary advice, counsel, dehortation, deprecation, dissuasion, exhortation, expostulation, foreboding, forewarning, hindrance, increpation, indication, instruction, intimidation, judicial reprimand, monition, notice, notification, object lesson, objection, protest, rebuke, reminder, remonstrance, reprimand, reproach, reprobation, reproof, signal, stricture, warning

ADOLESCENCE, noun *adulescentia,* immaturity, juniority, juvenility, minority, nonage, puberty, pubescence, puerility, youth

ADOLESCENT, noun junior, juvenile, minor, teenager, young person, youngling, youngster, youth

ADOPT, verb accept, *ad sententiam,* admit, *adoptare,* affiliate, annex, appropriate, arrogate, assimilate, assume, attach oneself to, avail oneself of, borrow, choose, co-opt, conform to, *constituere,* denizenize, elect, embrace, endenizen, espouse, exercise one's option, follow, foster, imitate, make one's own, naturalize, raise, seize, select, select as one's own, take, take on, take possession of, take up, try, usurp, utilize, vote to accept

ASSOCIATED CONCEPTS: adopt a child, adopt a law, adopt a philosophy, legitimation, support

ADOPTION (*Acceptance*), **noun** acknowledgment, admission, approbation, approval, assimilation, assumption, attachment to, choice, co-optation, election, embracement, espousal, favorable reception, ratification, reception, recognition, sanction, selection

ASSOCIATED CONCEPTS: adoption by estoppel, adoption of a contract, adoption of a proposal, adoption of domicile, arrogation

ADOPTION (*Affiliation*), **noun** *adoptio,* custody, fosterage, guardianship, parentage, protection, protectorship, wardship

ASSOCIATED CONCEPTS: adoption decree, adoption petition, custody, foster care, foster parent, inheritance by adoption, intestate succession, legitimation, legitimation of child, parental rights, paternity proceedings, support, wards of the juvenile court

ADOPTIVE, *adjective*   *adoptivus,* appointive, choosing, discretional, elective, preferential, selective
ASSOCIATED CONCEPTS: adoptive father, adoptive mother, adoptive parent, foster care, inheritance by adoptive parents, inheritance from adoptive parents, intestate succession, parental rights, wards of the juvenile court

ADULATE, *verb*   acclaim, admire, applaud, approbate, approve, celebrate, commend, compliment, eulogize, exalt, express, extol, flatter, glorify, idolize, laud, lionize, overpraise, pay tribute to, praise, salute

ADULATION, *noun*   admiration for, appreciation, approbation, blandishment, compliment, encomium, eulogy, fawning, flattery, glorification, homage, honor, idolatry, laudation, praise, sycophancy, toadyism

ADULT, *noun*   *adultus,* elder, fully developed person, fully grown person, grown-up person, mature person, one who has attained legal majority, person of age, person of voting age, *pubes,* senior
ASSOCIATED CONCEPTS: adult male, adult person, adult woman, age of majority

ADULTERATE, *verb*   abase, *adulterare,* change for the worse, contaminate, *corrumpere,* corrupt, debase, debilitate, defile, degrade, denature, depreciate, deteriorate, devalue, devitalize, impair, infect, lessen, lower the standard, make impure, make lower in quality, mar, pervert, pollute, render spurious, spoil, taint, tamper with, *vitiare,* vitiate, weaken

ADULTERATED, *adjective*   artificial, contaminated, corrupted, debased, defiled, degraded, deteriorated, devalued, fraudulent, impaired, impure, infected, perverted, polluted, spoiled, spurious, tainted, weakened

ADULTERATION, *noun*   contamination, corruption, defilement, degradation, deterioration, fraudulence, impairment, infection, perversion, pollution, spuriousness, weakness
ASSOCIATED CONCEPTS: drugs, food, purity of food

ADULTERY, *noun*   *adulterium,* criminal unchastity, cuckoldry, extramarital promiscuity, extramarital relations, illicit intercourse, illicit love, illicit sexual intercourse, infidelity, marital infidelity, sexual unfaithfulness of a married person, unfaithfulness, unlawful carnal connection, unlawful carnal knowledge, unlawful carnality, violation of the marriage vows
ASSOCIATED CONCEPTS: adultery by collusion, adultery by connivance, condonation of adultery, criminal conversation, dissolution of marriage, recrimination of an action of adultery

ADUMBRATION, *noun*   blurry image, darkening, dim representation, dimming, faint resemblance, imperfect portrayal, obfuscation, obscuration, uncertainty, vague outline

ADUMBRATIVE, *adjective*   bleary, blurry, cloudy, dim, foggy, hazy, ill-defined, indefinite, indistinguishable, misty, nebulous, obscure, reflexive, shadowy, shrouded, uncertain, unclear, unknown, unspecified, vague

ADVANCE (Allowance), *noun*   accommodation, anticipated loan, cash payment, compensation, credit, defrayment, disbursement, emolument, expenditure, fee, giving beforehand, installment, investment, pay, payment beforehand, remuneration, subscription

ASSOCIATED CONCEPTS: advance as against profits, advancement from an estate grant, future advances

ADVANCE (Increase), *noun*   amplification, augmentation, elaboration, enhancement, enlargement, enrichment, expansion, extension, improvement, increase, increment, intensification, prolongation, protraction

ADVANCE (Progression), *noun*   elevation, expedition, facilitation, forward motion, forward movement, forwarding, headway, progress, progression, *progressus,* promotion, upsurge
ASSOCIATED CONCEPTS: advance payment, advance sheets, anticipatory repudiation, contract breached in advance

ADVANCED (Elderly), *adjective*   aged, along in years, ancient, old, senior, venerable

ADVANCED (Progressive), *adjective*   contemporary, far ahead, forward-looking, modern, present-day, sophisticated, up-to-date, up-to-the-minute

ADVANCED NOTICE, *noun*   announcement, declaration, dispatch, forewarning, intelligence, notice, notification, prediction, preliminary, pronouncement, prophecy, prospectus, publication, publicity, warning

ADVANCEMENT (Improvement), *noun*   aggrandizement, amplification, betterment, development, elaboration, elevation, emendation, enlargement, expansion, furtherance, gain, *gradus amplior,* growth, increase, progress, progression, promotion, rise

ADVANCEMENT (Loan), *noun*   accommodation, advance, allowance, anticipation, concession, consideration, investment, realization in advance
ASSOCIATED CONCEPTS: intestate succession, statute of distribution

ADVANTAGE, *noun*   accommodation, aid, approval, ascendancy, asset, assistance, authority, avail, behoof, benefit, choice, convenience, dominance, easement, edge, eminence, expedience, favor, favorable opportunity, favoring circumstance, gain, good, head start, help, hold, improvement, influence, lead, leverage, mastery, odds, patronage, plus, position, power, precedence, predominance, preeminence, preference, prestige, primacy, privilege, profit, protection, resources, sake, sanction, success, superior situation, superiority, support, supremacy, sway, upper hand, utility, welfare, worth

ADVENTITIOUS, *adjective*   accidental, acquired, casual, circumstantial, external, extraneous, extrinsic, extroverted, foreign, fortuitous, incidental, outward, outward-looking, random, subordinate, subsidiary, transcendent, unintentional, unwitting

ADVENTURE, *noun*   endeavor, enterprise, episode, exercise, experience, exploit, happening, happenstance, operation, quest, undertaking, venture
ASSOCIATED CONCEPTS: detour and adventure

ADVENTURE, *verb*   chance, endanger, hazard, imperil, jeopardize, risk, run the risk, stake, take a chance, venture

ADVERSARY, *adjective*   *adversarius,* adverse party, antagonist, competitor, contender, contestant, contester, corival, disputant, dissentient, enemy, foe, litigant, opponent, opposer, opposing party, oppositionist, oppugnant, resister, rival

ASSOCIATED CONCEPTS: adversary parties, adversary proceeding

ADVERSE (Hostile), **adjective**   antagonistic, antagonistical, deprecatory, disagreeable, discordant, disinclined, disobedient, dissuasive, fractious, inauspicious, indisposed, *infensus*, inimical, intolerant, opposed, recalcitrant, renitent, repugnant, resistive, restive, uncooperative, unfriendly, unpropitious, unreconciled, untoward, unwilling
ASSOCIATED CONCEPTS: adverse claim, adverse effect, adverse enjoyment of property, adverse interest, adverse possession, adverse use, adverse user, adverse witness
FOREIGN PHRASES: *Longa possessio parit jus possidendi, et tollit actionem vero domino.* Long possession creates the right of possession, and ripens into a right of action against the real owner.

ADVERSE (Negative), **adjective**   afflictive, calamitous, catastrophic, corrosive, deleterious, destructive, detrimental, dire, disadvantageous, disastrous, disserviceable, dreadful, harmful, hurtful, injurious, insalubrious, malefic, maleficent, prejudicial, ruinous, scatheful, unadvisable, unfavorable, unfortunate
ASSOCIATED CONCEPTS: adverse determination of the court, adverse effect, adverse holding of the court, adverse interest

ADVERSE (Opposite), **adjective**   *adversus,* antipodal, antipodean, antithetical, antonymous, at variance, conflicting, conflictive, contradictory, contradistinct, contrapositive, contrariant, contrarious, *contrarius,* contrary, contrastable, converse, counter, counteractive, diametrically opposite, inverse, irreconcilable, obverse, reverse
ASSOCIATED CONCEPTS: adverse action, adverse party

ADVERSE CIRCUMSTANCE, noun   disadvantage, plight, predicament, regrettable occurrence, unfavorable development, unfortunate situation
ASSOCIATED CONCEPTS: agreements, contracts, impossibility

ADVERSE EVENT, noun   adversity, calamity, casualty, catastrophe, debacle, detriment, infliction, misfortune, plight, tragedy, trouble, unpropitious turn of events

ADVERSE POSSESSION, noun   acquisition, appropriation, assumption, attainment, obtainment, ownership, procurement, proprietorship, recovery, seizure
ASSOCIATED CONCEPTS: adverse claim, adverse holding, adverse interest, adverse party, adverse user, adverse verdict, adverse witness

ADVERSE TO (Hostile), **adjective**   abhorrent to, against, antagonistic to, antipathetic to, at odds with, clashing, conflicting with, contra, contrary to, different, discordant to, hostile to, inimical to, opposed to, repugnant to

ADVERSE TO (Unfavorable), **adjective**   calamitous, catastrophic, disastrous, harmful, inopportune, unfortunate, unlucky, unpropitious

ADVERSELY AFFECTED, adjective   aggrieved, damaged, endamaged, harmed, hurt, ill-treated, impaired, inflicted with injury, injured, wronged

ADVERSITY, noun   adverse circumstances, adverse fortune, affliction, bale, *calamitas,* calamity, catastrophe, *contretemps,* difficulty, disaster, distress, hardship, injuriousness, injury, misadventure, mischance, *miseria,* misfortune, mishap, oppression, perdition, *res adversae,* ruination, ruinousness, setback, suffering, tragedy, visitation

ADVERT, verb   affirm, articulate, assert, asservate, aver, comment, communicate, convey, declare, express, heed, mark, mention, mind, note, notice, recite, recognize, reconsider, remark, review, speak, take cognizance of, take into consideration, tell, utter, verbalize, vocalize, voice

ADVERTENCE, noun   assertion, attention, averment, comment, commentary, declaration, diligence, exclamation, expression, interjection, mention, note, notice, observation, pronouncement, recitation, regard, thought, utterance, word

ADVERTISE, verb   advise, announce, apprise, attract, broadcast, circularize, circulate, communicate, describe, disseminate, divulge, exhibit, expose, feature, flourish, focus the attention, headline, herald, inform, notice, notify, placard, post, proclaim, proffer, promote, promulgate, publish, push, report, rumor, spotlight, spread, throw the spotlight on, transmit, trumpet, warn, whisper
ASSOCIATED CONCEPTS: deceptive advertising practices, false advertisement, unfair trade practices

ADVICE, noun   advisement, advocacy, communication of knowledge, *consilium,* counsel, direction, guidance, information, instruction, legal counsel, notice, notification, opinion, prompting, proposal, proposition, recommendation, rede, suggestion, view, warning
ASSOCIATED CONCEPTS: advice of counsel, privilege
FOREIGN PHRASES: *Incivile est, nisi tota lege perspecta, una aliqua particula ejus proposita, judicare, vel respondere.* Unless the entire law has been examined, it is improper to pass judgment upon a single portion of it. *Nemo ex consilio obligatur.* No one is obligated as a consequence of giving advice. *Simplex commendatio non obligat.* A mere recommendation is not binding.

ADVICE OF COUNSEL, noun   advice of legal counsel, communication of legal knowledge, recommendation of counsel, rendering of legal advice, representation

Generally: advisement, consultation, direction, guidance, opinion

ADVISABLE, adjective   acceptable, advantageous, advisory, appropriate, becoming, befitting, commendable, congruous, desirable, expedient, favorable, feasible, fit, fitting, judicious, opportune, profitable, proper, prudent, recommendable, seemly, sensible, suitable, wise, worthy

ADVISE, verb   advocate, alert, apprise, *auctorem esse,* caution, coach, communicate, confer with, *consiliari, consilium dare,* consult with, convey, counsel, direct, enlighten, express, familiarize, forewarn, give advice, give an opinion, give counsel, give information, give notice, give one to understand, give suggestions, give warning, guide, *homini suadere,* impart, inform, intimate, make known, mention, notify, offer an opinion, offer counsel, opine, prescribe, propose, recommend, remind, represent, reprove, submit, suggest, warn
ASSOCIATED CONCEPTS: advisory opinion, declaratory judgment
FOREIGN PHRASES: *Consilia multorum quaeruntur in magnis.* The advice of many are required in affairs of magnitude.

ADVISORY, adjective   cautionary, communicatory, consulting, counselling, directing, enlightening, expressive of opinion, guiding, inducive, instructing, recommendatory, suggesting
ASSOCIATED CONCEPTS: advisory board, advisory opinion, advisory referendum

ADVOCACY, *noun* active espousal, advancement, advice, aid, approbation, approval, assistance, auspices, backing, championship, constructive criticism, countenance, defense, encouragement, endorsement, forceful persuasion, furtherance, guidance, help, intercession, interest, patronage, plea, praise, promotion, recommendation, sanction, seconding, sponsorship, subscription, suggestion, support, vindication, vouching, warranting

ADVOCATE *(Counselor)*, ***noun*** adviser, apologist, attorney, attorney-at-law, barrister, barrister-at-law, champion, counsel learned in the law, counselor-at-law, defender, friend at court, friend in court, interagent, interceder, intercessor, interlocutor, intermediary, intermediate, intermediate agent, intermediator, intermedium, internuncio, intervener, interventionist, interventor, jurisconsult, jurist, justifier, lawyer, learned counsel, legal adviser, legal practitioner, legal representative, legate, legist, maintainer, man of law, mediator, medium, member of the legal profession, mover, negotiant, negotiator, one called to the bar, paraclete, patron, *patronus,* pleader, proctor, prompter, protector, representative, seconder, solicitor, spokesman, spokeswoman, suasor, upholder, votary

ADVOCATE *(Espouser)*, ***noun*** abettor, adherent, apologist, *auctor,* backer, champion, countenancer, defender, encourager, exponent, expounder, favorer, maintainer, partisan, patron, promoter, propagandist, propagator, proponent, seconder, sectary, spokesman, spokeswoman, support, supporter, sympathizer, upholder, votary
ASSOCIATED CONCEPTS: advocate the abolishment of the death sentence, advocate the commission of a crime, advocate the overthrow of government

ADVOCATE, *verb* advise, allege in support, approve, argue for, assert, back, champion, commend, consent, contend for, counsel, defend, endorse, espouse, exhort, favor, give advice, plead for, plead in favor of, plead one's case, plead one's cause, prescribe, promote, prompt, propose, propound, recommend, sanction, second, speak in favor of, *suadere,* subscribe to, suggest, support, uphold, urge
ASSOCIATED CONCEPTS: advocate the commission of a crime, advocate the overthrow of government

AEGIS, *noun* advocacy, aid, auspices, backing, care, championship, countenance, custody, defense, encouragement, fosterage, guaranty, guard, guidance, influence, interest, patronage, protection, safeguard, safekeeping, shelter, shield, sponsorship, support, surety, tutelage

AESTHETIC, *adjective* artistic, cultured, discriminative, ornamental, refined, tasteful

AFFAIR, *noun* activity, adventure, avocation, circumstance, duty, employment, enterprise, event, function, happening, incident, interest, matter, occasion, occupation, occurrence, profession, pursuit, subject, transaction, undertaking, work

AFFAIRS, *noun* activities, concerns, interests, matters, proceedings, pursuits, topics, transactions

AFFECT, *verb* act on, *adficere,* bear upon, cause to alter, cause to vary, change, *commovere,* conduce, exert influence, have an effect upon, have influence, impress, induce, influence, introduce a change, make a change, play a direct part, prevail upon, produce a change, produce an effect, superinduce, *tangere,* transfigure, work a change, work upon

ASSOCIATED CONCEPTS: affect an action, affected with public interest, affecting a substantial right

AFFECTING, *adjective* affected, agitating, altering, changing, emended, exciting, inviting, modifying, moving, potent, provocative, provoking, stirring, touching, transforming

AFFECTION, *noun* admiration, adoration, amorousness, ardor, attachment, closeness, devotion, enchantment, endearment, excitation of feeling, fancy, feeling, fervency, fervor, firm attachment, fondness, fullness of heart, inclination, infatuation, kindness, love, mutual attraction, partiality, passion, penchant, *pietas,* popular regard, predisposition, proneness, regard, sentiment, sentimental attachment, sentimentality, state of excitement, tender feeling, tender passion, tenderness, understanding, warmth, zealous attachment
ASSOCIATED CONCEPTS: alienation of affection

AFFIANT, *noun* attestant, attester, deponent, signer, subscriber, swearer, testifier, voucher

AFFIDAVIT, *noun* affirmation under oath, assertory oath, attested statement, averment, avouchment, avowal, avowance, confirmation under oath, declaration under oath, evidence on oath, instrument in proof, solemn affirmation, statement, statement under oath, sworn evidence, sworn statement, testification under oath, *testimonium per tabulas datum,* voluntary attestment under oath, written declaration upon oath, written statement under oath
ASSOCIATED CONCEPTS: affidavit of defense, affidavit of demand, affidavit of judicial power, affidavit of merit, affidavit of service, affidavit to advise the court of a right or on an issue, affidavit to hold to bail, affirmation, verified deposition, verified pleading

AFFILIATE, *noun* arm, assistant, associate, auxiliary, branch, branch organization, chapter, colleague, component, division, offshoot, subdivision, subsidiary, wing

AFFILIATE, *verb* ally, associate, attach, belong to, bring into close connection, bring into close relation, cement a union, confederate, connect, consociate, embrace, federalize, federate, form a connection, join, join forces, join together, make common cause, pertain to, relate to, unite

AFFILIATED, *adjective* allied, associated, closely allied, closely related, confederated, connected, coupled, federated, incorporated, intimately allied, intimately related, joined with, leagued, linked, related, united
ASSOCIATED CONCEPTS: affiliated association, affiliated company, affiliated corporation, affiliated firm, affiliated organization

AFFILIATION *(Amalgamation),* ***noun*** aggregation, alliance, association, centralization, coalition, combination, confederacy, confederation, consortium, corporation, embodiment, federation, fusion, integration, league, merger, unification, union, unity, voluntary association

AFFILIATION *(Bloodline),* ***noun*** agnation, ancestry, apparentation, blood relation, blood relationship, common derivation, consanguinity, descent, family, family connection, family tie, filiality, filiation, heredity, kindred, kinfolk, kinship, kinsmen, line of descent, lineage, next of kin, origin, parentage, relation, relationship, ties of blood, ties of race

ASSOCIATED CONCEPTS: affiliation proceedings, paternity proceedings

AFFILIATION (Connectedness), **noun**   alignment, appositeness, apposition, association, band of union, bond, coaction, coadjuvancy, coalition, colleagueship, combination, concert, conjunction, connection, consociation, copartnership, coworking, friendly association, implication, inclusion, intimate connection, involvement, joint enterprise, link, linkage, membership, participation, partnership, relation, relationship

AFFINITY (Family ties), **noun**   affiliation, ancestry, blood relative, brethren, clan, cognatio, cognation, common ancestry, coniunctio, connection, consanguinitas, consanguinity, family, family connection, filiation, heritage, kindred, kinship, lineage, linkage, necessitudo, offspring, parentage, propinquitas, relation, relation by blood, relationship, tribe
ASSOCIATED CONCEPTS: challenge to a prospective juror based on affinity
FOREIGN PHRASES: *Affinis mei affinis non est mihi affinis.* One who is related by marriage to a person who is related to me by marriage has no affinity to me.

AFFINITY (Regard), **noun**   affection, attachment, attraction, closeness, concern, devotion, fondness, friendliness, friendship, good will, inclination, liking, love, natural liking, partiality, predilection, proclivity, propensity, sympathy, tenderness

AFFIRM (Claim), **verb**   assert, asseverate, aver, declare to be fact, enunciate, establish, express, make a positive statement, make an assertion, proclaim, profess, pronounce, state, state positively, state with conviction

AFFIRM (Declare solemnly), **verb**   asseverate, attest, aver, avouch, avow, depone, depose, give oral evidence, give sworn evidence, give verbal evidence, make a solemn declaration, make an asseveration, make an attestation, make an averment, pronounce, take one's oath, testify, vouch
ASSOCIATED CONCEPTS: affirm a contract
FOREIGN PHRASES: *Affirmanti, non neganti incumbit probatio.* The proof is borne by the person who affirms, rather than the person who denies. *Affirmantis est probare.* He who is affirming must prove. *Ei incumbit probatio, qui dicit, non qui negat; cum per rerum naturam factum negantis probatio nulla sit.* The burden of proof lies upon him who asserts it, not upon him who denies; since, by the nature of things, he who denies a fact cannot produce any proof of it.

AFFIRM (Uphold), **verb**   adfirmare, approve, authenticate, certify, confirm, confirmare, endorse, establish, make firm, ratify, substantiate, support, sustain, validate, verify, vouch for, warrant
ASSOCIATED CONCEPTS: affirm a judicial decision, affirm on appeal, affirmed in part, affirmed in whole

AFFIRMANCE (Authentication), **noun**   acknowledgment, assertion, assurance, attestation, certification, confirmation, countersignature, declaration, endorsement, establishment, predication, pronouncement, ratification, substantiation, validation, verification
ASSOCIATED CONCEPTS: affirmance of a contract, confirmation of a judgment, ratification of a voidable contract
FOREIGN PHRASES: *Posito uno oppositorum, negatur alterum.* By the establishment of one of two opposite propositions, the other one is denied.

AFFIRMANCE (Judicial sanction), **noun**   acceptance, acquiescence, assent, concord, concordance, countersignature, endorsement, legal approval, legal authorization, legal ratification, subscription
ASSOCIATED CONCEPTS: affirmed without opinion, en banc affirmance, unanimous affirmance

AFFIRMANCE (Legal affirmation), **noun**   absolute assertion, adjuration, assertory oath, asseveration, attestation, averment, avouchment, avowal, evidence on oath, legal evidence, legal pledge, oral evidence, positive declaration, positive statement, pronouncement, proposition, solemn averment, solemn avowal, statement on oath, sworn evidence, testimony, verbal evidence, written evidence
ASSOCIATED CONCEPTS: affirmation of a statement

AFFIRMANT, noun   affirmer, apprizer, attestant, attestator, attester, confirmist, deponent, one who testifies under oath, testifier, voucher
ASSOCIATED CONCEPTS: affidavit, affirmation, deponent, oath, perjury

AFFIRMATION, noun   absolute assertion, acknowledgment, acquiescence, adfirmatio, adjurement, affirmance, approval, assertion, assertory oath, asseveration, attest, attestation, authentication, averment, avouchment, avowal, certification, confirmation, declaration, deposition, endorsement, establishment, factual statement, formal declaration, legal evidence, legal pledge, oath, oath-giving, oath-taking, positive statement, predication, profession, pronouncement, ratification, solemn affirmation, solemn averment, solemn avowal, solemn declaration, statement, statement on oath, substantiation, swearing, sworn evidence, sworn statement, testification, testimonial, testimonium, testimony, validation, verification
ASSOCIATED CONCEPTS: affirmation of fact, affirmation to a will, attorney's affirmation
FOREIGN PHRASES: *Affirmatio unius exclusio est alterius.* The affirmance of one thing is the exclusion of the other.

AFFIRMATION UNDER OATH, noun   affidavit, attestation, authentication, avouchment, certification, declaration, deposition, sworn evidence, verification
ASSOCIATED CONCEPTS: perjury, sworn affidavit

AFFIRMATIVE, adjective   absolute, affirmatory, categorical, certain, confirmative, confirmatory, convinced, decided, persuaded, positive, sure, undoubting, unqualified
ASSOCIATED CONCEPTS: affirmative action, affirmative action for past discrimination, affirmative action in hiring, affirmative allegation, affirmative authorization, affirmative charge, affirmative covenant, affirmative defense, affirmative easement, affirmative negligence, affirmative plea, affirmative proof, affirmative relief, affirmative showing, affirmative statute, affirmative warranty, affirmative wrongdoing

AFFIRMATIVE ACTION, noun   effort to correct past injustices, means to right the wrongs of the past, plan to make up for unfairness in the past, positive steps to correct past discrimination
Generally: fairness, just treatment, opportunities, remedial change
Specifically: plan for increased representation for minorities, plan for increased representation for women, racial quotas

AFFIX, verb   add, adfigere, adhere, adjoin, adligare, adnectere, agglutinate, annex, append, attach, bind, cohere,

combine, conjoin, connect, couple, enclose, fasten, fix, incorporate, insert, join, link, put together, secure, subjoin, supplement, unite
ASSOCIATED CONCEPTS: affix a seal to an instrument, affix a signature, affix exhibits to a pleading, affix process to the door

AFFLICT, verb   agonize, anguish, assault, bruise, burden, chasten, discommode, discompose, disquiet, distress, grate, harm, hurt, impair, infect, inflict, irritate, mistreat, pain, plague, punish, rasp, sicken, smite, strike, victimize

AFFLICTION, noun   adversity, agony, bereavement, burden, calamity, casualty, catastrophe, curse, destruction, deterioration, disability, disease, disorder, encumbrance, evil, hardship, illness, indisposition, infirmity, misadventure, mischance, misfortune, mishap, ordeal, suffering, tragedy, trouble, unhappiness

AFFRAY, noun   agitation, altercation, battle, brabble, brawl, brush, clash, combat, commotion, conflict, contestation, disturbance, embroilment, encounter, fight, fisticuffs, fracas, fray, free fight, hand-to-hand fight, *melee*, passage at arms, *pugna, rixa,* row, scrimmage, scuffle, set-to, skirmish, sortie, squabble, struggle, tumult, *tumultuous* assault, *tumultus,* turmoil, tussle, violence

AFFRONT, verb   afflict, aggrieve, antagonize, be offensive, be rude, cause dislike, cause offense, chafe, disconcert, disdain, disoblige, disquiet, distress, disturb, embitter, encounter, gall, give offense to, grieve, hurt the feelings, ill-treat, insult, irritate, make angry, offend, pique, rankle, scorn, slight, snub, sting, vex, wound the feelings, wrong

AFOREDESCRIBED, adjective   above-mentioned, antecedent, anterior, before-mentioned, inaugural, preceding, precursory, preliminary, prior

AFOREGOING, adjective   above-mentioned, antecedent, anterior, before-mentioned, earlier, inaugural, last referred to, preceding, precursory, preliminary, previous, prior

AFOREHAND, adjective   above-mentioned, antecedent, anterior, before-mentioned, inaugural, last referred to, preceding, precursory, preliminary, prior

AFOREMENTIONED, adjective   above-mentioned, antecedent, anterior, before-mentioned, inaugural, last referred to, last said, preceding, precursory, preliminary, prior

AFORESAID, adjective   above-mentioned, aforecited, aforedescribed, aforegiven, aforegoing, aforementioned, aforenamed, aforestated, already mentioned, already said, antecedent, anterior, before-mentioned, beforesaid, foregoing, forenamed, former, introductory, mentioned, mentioned previously, named, precedent, preceding, precursive, precursory, preexistent, preluding, prelusory, prevenient, previous, previously specified, prior, recited, said, said in a preceding part, specified

AFORESTATED, adjective   above-mentioned, antecedent, anterior, before-mentioned, inaugural, last referred to, last said, preceding, precursory, preliminary, prior

AFORETHOUGHT, adjective   beforehand, calculated, contrived, contrived in advance, deliberate, designed, intended, planned, planned beforehand, prearranged, preconceived, preconsidered, predeliberated, predetermined, premeditated, prepared, prepense, preresolved, previously in mind, purposed, purposive, reflective, studied, well-considered, with forethought
ASSOCIATED CONCEPTS: malice aforethought

AFRAID, adjective   affrighted, alarmed, anxious, apprehensive, cautious, distrustful, dreading, fearful, frightened, haunted by fear, leery, nervous, scared, shrinking, terrified, terror-stricken, timid, timorous, uneasy

AFTERMATH, noun   after-effect, aftergrowth, by-product, consequence, development, effect, end, event, gleanings, issue, offshoot, outcome, outgrowth, result, sequel, subsequence, succession, turnout, upshot

AGAINST ONE'S WILL, adjective   against, coerced, commanded, compelled, constrained, enforced, extorted, forced, imperative, imposed, inescapable, inevitable, inexorable, levied, mandatory, obligatory, opposed, preemptory, prescriptive, prescriptory, pressured, required, unavoidable, unconsenting, unwilling

AGE, noun   *aetas,* date, duration of existence, eon, epoch, era, interval of years, longevity, maturity, period, seniority, stage of life, term of life, time of life, vintage, years
ASSOCIATED CONCEPTS: age of consent, age of majority, legal age, statutory age

AGENCY (Commission), **noun**   administration, authority, bureau, charge, command, committee, control, delegation, department, office
ASSOCIATED CONCEPTS: administrative agency, governmental agency

AGENCY (Legal relationship), **noun**   activity, appointment, assignment, authority, care, charge, command, commission, conduct, conduct of affairs, control, delegation, deputation, derivative authority, direction, dominion, duty, employ, employment, function, governance, handling, instrumentality, intermediation, intervention, jurisdiction, management, mandate, mission, procuracy, procuration, proxy, quest, representation, responsibility, role, service, services, superintendence, supervision, task, trust
ASSOCIATED CONCEPTS: actual agency, agency by estoppel, agency coupled with an interest, agency of necessity, deed of agency, exclusive agency, express agency, general agency, implied agency, scope of the agency, undisclosed agency, vicarious liability
FOREIGN PHRASES: *Actus me invito factus non est meus actus.* An act done against my will is not my act. *Qui facit per alium facit per se.* He who acts through another acts himself. *Qui mandat ipse fecissi videtur.* He who orders or commands is deemed to have done the thing himself. *Quod per me non possum, nec per alium.* What I cannot do myself, I cannot do through the agency of another. *Vicarius non habet vicarium.* A vicar has no deputy.

AGENDA, noun   blueprint, business, business affairs, business on hand, calendar, docket, items of business, legal program, main business, matters to be attended to, order, order of the day, plan, planning, procedure, program of business, program of operation, proposal, proposed action, proposition, schedule, schedule of affairs, scheme

AGENT, noun   alternate, appointee, assistant, delegate, emissary, envoy, functionary, go-between, intermediary, intermediate, intermedium, mediary, medium, middleman, negotiant, negotiator, procurator, proxy, representative, solicitor, substitute

ASSOCIATED CONCEPTS: agent to accept process, authorization of an agent, bailee, common agent, employee, escrow agent, general agent, implied agent, independent contractor, insurance broker, joint venture, managing agent, master-servant relationship, owner-operator relationship, partnership, principal-agent relationship, real estate agent, real estate broker, special agent, subagents, undisclosed agency, warranty of authority

FOREIGN PHRASES: *Idem agens et patiens esse non potest.* A person cannot be at the same time the person acting and the person acted upon. *Delegatus non potest delegare.* A representative cannot delegate his authority. *Qui facit per alium facit per se.* He who acts by or through another acts for himself.

AGGLOMERATION, *noun*   accumulation, agglomerate, agglutination, aggregate, aggregation, amassment, assemblage, cluster, coagulation, collection, congeries, conglomerate, conglomeration, consolidation, cumulation, glomeration, mass, pile, solidification

AGGRANDIZEMENT, *noun*   accession, advancement, amplification, augmentation, boom, broadening, deification, dignification, elevation, embellishment, eminence, enablement, enhancement, enlargement, enshrinement, enthronement, exaggeration, exaltation, expansion, extension, gain, glorification, greatness, growth, heightening, honor, inflation, immortalization, largeness, lionizing, magnification, overstatement, preferment, promotion, widening

AGGRAVATE *(Annoy),* *verb*   acerbate, aggrieve, annoy, bother, cause pain, chafe, dismay, disturb, enrage, envenom, exasperate, excite, give pain, hurt, incense, inflame, infuriate, injure, irk, irritate, madden, miff, nettle, offend, pain, pique, provoke, rankle, ruffle, sour, sting, trouble, vex

ASSOCIATED CONCEPTS: aggravating circumstances

AGGRAVATE *(Exacerbate),* *verb*   add to, add weight to, amplify, augment, complicate, deepen, deteriorate, further, heighten, impair, increase, intensify, magnify, make more offensive, make more serious, make more severe, make worse, render less excusable, render less tolerable, render worse, worsen

ASSOCIATED CONCEPTS: aggravated assault, aggravating circumstances

AGGRAVATION *(Annoyance),* *noun*   complication, difficulty, distress, frustration, grievance, harassment, inconvenience, irritant, irritation, nuisance, ordeal, pressure, provocation, strain, stress

AGGRAVATION *(Exacerbation),* *noun*   agitation, amplification, augmentation, deepening, enlargement, excitation, fomentation, heightening, increase, inflammation, intensification, magnification, stimulation, worsening

ASSOCIATED CONCEPTS: aggravated assault, aggravation of a crime, aggravation of damages, aggravation of injury, aggravation of the disability

FOREIGN PHRASES: *Omne crimen ebrietas et incendit et detegit.* Drunkenness both inflames or aggravates, and uncovers every crime.

AGGREGATE, *noun*   agglomerate, aggregation, amount, assemblage, assembly, body, collection, conglomeration, entire number, entire quantity, entirety, gross, gross

amount, indissoluble entity, indivisible entity, mass, sum, sum total, total, totality, whole

ASSOCIATED CONCEPTS: aggregate corporation, aggregate income, combine

AGGREGATE, *verb*   accumulate, acquire, add together, agglomerate, aggroup, amass, amount to, assemble, bring together, build up, clump, cluster, collect, collect into a mass, colligate, compile, conglomerate, cumulate, gather, gather together, group, integrate, join, mass, total, unite

ASSOCIATED CONCEPTS: aggregate claims

AGGREGATION, *noun*   accumulation, adhesion, affiliation, agglomeration, aggregate, amassment, body, collection, combination, company, compilation, composite, composition, concentration, conglomeration, congregation, consolidation, corpus, cumulation, force, gathering, group, hoard, incorporation, mass, multitude, organization, selection, totality

AGGRESSION, *noun*   aggressiveness, antagonism, assault, attack, beleaguerment, bellicosity, belligerence, belligerency, besiegement, combativeness, contentiousness, drive, enterprise, fight, foray, hostility, hustle, illapse, incursion, infringement, initiative, injury, inroad, intrusion, invasion, irruption, jingoism, martiality, militancy, offense, onset, onslaught, outbreak, provocation, pugnacity, push, pushiness, raid, sally, sortie, storming, transgression, trespass, unprovoked attack, warlikeness

AGGRESSOR, *noun*   antagonist, assailant, assailer, assaulter, attacker, belligerent, besieger, combatant, contender, criminal, fighter, foe, initiative seizer, invader, militant, prime mover, provocator, ravager, ruffian, stormer, violator

AGGRIEVED *(Harmed),* *adjective*   abused, afflicted, anguished, bilked, damnified, deprived of legal rights, distressed, grieved, having suffered invasion of legal rights, hurt, ill-treated, incommoded, injured, misused, pained, preyed upon, provoked, swindled, tyrannized, vexed, wounded

ASSOCIATED CONCEPTS: aggrieved heirs, aggrieved party, aggrieved person

AGGRIEVED *(Victimized),* *adjective*   adversely affected, cheated, damaged, defrauded, fleeced, harrassed, harried, ill-used, imposed upon, injured, justly complaining, misserved, offended, oppressed, persecuted, taken advantage of, wronged

AGITATE *(Activate),* *verb*   actuate, arouse, coax, electrify, energize, excite, exhort, ferment, foment, goad, impel, incite, induce, inflame, influence, inspire, inspirit, instigate, irritate, kindle, persuade, prompt, provoke, roil, rouse, spur, stimulate, stir up, urge on

AGITATE *(Perturb),* *verb*   alarm, concern, discomfort, disconcert, dismay, displease, disquiet, disturb, fluster, fret, jar, perplex, perturbate, shake up, throw into confusion, trouble, unsettle, upset, worry

AGITATE *(Shake up),* *verb*   convulse, disarrange, dishevel, disorder, impart motion to, mix, mix up, put in motion, ruffle, stir, throw out of order, tousle, tumble

AGREE *(Comply),* *verb*   accede, accept, accommodate, accord, acknowledge, acquiesce, adapt, adjust differences,

adopt, allow, approve, assent, avow, be accordant, be at one with, be in harmony with, be in unison, be willing, coincide, come to an understanding, come to terms, comply with, *componere*, concede, *concinere*, concord, concur, confirm, *congruere*, consent, cooperate, correspond, fit, give assent, give consent, homologate, ratify, reconcile, settle, subscribe to, suit, understand, unite, yield assent
ASSOCIATED CONCEPTS: agreed case, agreed order, agreed statement of facts

AGREE *(Contract)*, **verb** adjust differences, arrive at a settlement, bargain, bring into concord, come to an agreement, come to an understanding, come to terms, compromise, consent, *consentire, constituere,* cooperate, covenant, engage, give assurance, make a bargain, make an agreement, make terms, mutually assent, pacisci, pact, pledge, promise, settle, settle by covenant, stipulate, undertake

AGREE TO, *verb* accede, accept, accommodate, acknowledge, acquiesce, adopt, allow, approve, assent, authorize, certify, come to terms, comply, comply with, concur, confirm, cooperate, countenance, covenant, embrace, pass, permit, ratify, sanction, sign, submit, subscribe to, yield
ASSOCIATED CONCEPTS: agreed to contract, agreed to judgment, agreed to stipulation, execution of a contract

AGREEABLE *(Amenable)*, **adjective** acceptable, accommodating, accordant, acquiescent, amiable, apropos, appropriate, charming, coexistent, compatible, complaisant, compliant, concordant, conformable, congenial, congruous, consensual, consenting, cordial, courteous, delightful, enjoyable, fitting, flexible, friendly, genial, gratifying, likable, malleable, pleasant, pliant, prone, sapid, savory, sociable, suitable, willing

AGREEABLE *(Palatable)*, **adjective** acceptable, adequate, admissible, allowable, applicable, apposite, appropriate, apt, attractive, becoming, comfortable, commensurate, conventional, desirable, eligible, expedient, fair, felicitous, fit, good, gratifying, inviting, justifiable, likable, opportune, passable, pleasing, proper, qualified, satisfactory, seemly, suitable, tenable, tolerable, unobjectionable, viable

AGREED *(Harmonized)*, **adjective** accordant, adapted, appeased, arbitrated, arranged, balanced, coherent, compromised, conceded, conciliated, concordant, conforming, correlative, correspondent, counterbalanced, equable, equal, equalized, equivalent, matching, mediated, negotiated, parallel, propitiated, reconciled, settled, suited
ASSOCIATED CONCEPTS: agreed case, agreed price, agreed statement of facts, agreed submission of a case, agreed upon price, agreed value
FOREIGN PHRASES: *Ad quod curia concordavit.* To which the court agreed.

AGREED *(Promised)*, **adjective** affirmed, approved, arranged, assured, attested, avowed, committed, confirmed, contracted, covenanted, declared, endorsed, guaranteed, insured, pledged, stipulated, sworn, warranted
ASSOCIATED CONCEPTS: agreed price, agreed value

AGREEMENT *(Concurrence)*, **noun** accord, amity, arrangement, assent, common assent, common consent, common view, community of interests, concord, concordance, conformance, congruence, congruency, congruity, consent, consentaneity, consentaneousness, consentience,

consonance, cooperation, good understanding, harmony, meeting of the minds, mutual assent, mutual promise, mutual understanding, oneness, reciprocity of obligation, settlement, unanimity, understanding, uniformity, unison, unity
FOREIGN PHRASES: *Aggregatio mentium.* Meeting of the minds. *Bona fides exigit ut guod convenit fiat.* Good faith demands that what is agreed upon shall be done. *Consensus ad idem.* An agreement of parties for the same thing; a meeting of minds without which no contract exists. *Conventio privatorum non potest publico juri derogare.* An agreement of private parties cannot derogate from public right. *Conventio vincit legem.* The agreement of parties controls the law. *Modus et conventio vincunt legem.* Custom, convention, and agreement of the parties overrule the law. *Ratihabitio mandato aequiparatur.* Ratification is equivalent to an express command. *Quando verba et mens congruunt, non est interpretationi locus.* When the words and the mind agree, there is no room for interpretation. *Privatorum conventio juri publico non derogat.* The agreement of private persons cannot derogate from public law. *Modus et conventio vincunt legem.* Custom and agreement control the law. *Non differunt quae concordant re, tametsi non in verbis iisdem.* Those matters do not differ which agree in substance, though not in the same words.

AGREEMENT *(Contract)*, **noun** alliance, arrangement, bargain, binding promise, bond, commitment, compact, concordat, *concordia,* contractual statement, convention, covenant, deal, engagement, legal document, mutual pledge, obliga, obligation, pact, pledge, settlement, stipulation, transaction, understanding, undertaking
ASSOCIATED CONCEPTS: abrogate an agreement, agency agreement, agreement implied in fact, agreement of sale, agreement to answer for the debt of another, agreement to purchase, agreement under seal, agreements in contemplation of marriage, antenuptial agreement, area-wide agreement, articles of agreement, articles of impeachment, articles of incorporation, articles of partnership, articles of war, express agreement, illusory agreement, implied agreement, implied agreement in law, sale agreement, settlement agreement, support agreement
FOREIGN PHRASES: *Contractus ex turpi causa, vel contra bonds mores nullus est.* A contract founded on an evil consideration, or against good morals, is void. *Contractus legem ex conbentione accipiunt.* Contracts take their law from the agreement of the parties. *Ex pacto illicito non oritur actio.* An action will not lie on an agreement to do something unlawful. *Ex maleficio non oritur contractus.* No contract is born of wrongdoing. *Nudum pactum est ubi nulla subest causa praeter conventionem; sed ubi subest causa, fit obligatio, et parit actionem.* A naked contract is where there is no consideration except the agreement; but, where there is a consideration, an obligation is created and gives rise to a right of action. *In stipulationibus cum quaeritur quid actum sit verba contra stipulatorem interpretanda sunt.* In the construction of agreements words are interpreted against the person offering them. *Ea quae dari impossibilia sunt, vel quae in rerum natura non sunt, pro non adjectis habentur.* Those things which cannot be given, or which are not in existence, are regarded as not included in the contract. *Conventio facit legem.* The agreement creates the law; i.e., the parties to a binding contract must keep their promises. *Ex nudo pacto non oritur actio.* No action arises on a contract without a consideration. *Ea quae, commendandi causa, in venditionibus dicuntur, si palam appareant,*

venditorem non obligant. Those things which are said as praise of the things sold, if they are openly apparent do not bind the seller. *In contrahenda venditione, ambiguum pactum contravenditorem interpretandum est.* In a contract of sale, an ambiguous agreement is to be interpreted against the seller. *In conventionibus, contrahentium voluntas potius quam verba spectari placuit.* In contracts, it is the rule to regard the intention of the parties rather than the actual words. *Ome jus aut consensus fecit, aut necessitas constituit aut firmavit consuetudo.* All right is either made by consent, constituted by necessity, or confirmed by custom. *Pacta conventa quae neque contra leges neque dolo malo inita sunt omni modo observanda sunt.* Agreements which are not contrary to the laws nor entered into with a fraudulent design must be observed in all respects. *Pacta dant legem contractui.* Stipulations constitute the law for the contract. *Pacta quae contra leges constitutionesque, vel contra bonos mores fiunt, nullam vim habere, indubitati juris est.* It is unquestionably the law that contracts which are made contrary to the laws or against good morals, have no force in law. *Pacta quae turpem causam continent non sunt observanda.* Contracts which are based on unlawful consideration will not be enforced. *Quae dubitationis tollendae causa contractibus inseruntur, jus commune non laedunt.* Those clauses which are inserted in agreements to avoid doubts and ambiguity do not offend the common law. *Nuda pactio obligationem non parit.* A naked agreement does not effect an otherwise binding obligation. *Privatis pactionibus non dubium est non laedi jus caeterorum.* There is no doubt that private contracts cannot prejudice the rights of others.

AGREEMENT BETWEEN PARTIES, *noun*   alliance, arrangement, bargain, bilateral contract, binding agreement, compact, contract, covenant, mutual pledge, pact, promise, stipulation, understanding

AID (Help), *noun*   abetment, accommodation, advance, advocacy, aidance, assistance, auspices, backing, benefit, coadjuvancy, cooperation, countenance, endorsement, espousal, facilitation, furtherance, guidance, help, helpfulness, maintenance, ministration, ministry, patronage, promotion, reinforcement, relief, rescue, service, sponsorship, subscription, subsidy, subsistence, succor, support, sustainment, sustenance, tutelage, willing help
ASSOCIATED CONCEPTS: aid and abet, aid and comfort

AID (Subsistence), *noun*   benefaction, benefit, charity, compensation, endowment, humanitarianism, maintenance, ministration, ministry, patronage, relief, subsidy, support, sustainment, sustenance

AID, *verb*   abet, advance, assist, augment, avail, be auxiliary to, be of service, benefit, collaborate, cooperate with, facilitate, further, give aid, give support, help, minister to, nurture, oblige, promote, provision, reinforce, relieve, render help, rescue, second, serve, service, strengthen, subserve, succor, supplement, support, sustain, uphold
ASSOCIATED CONCEPTS: aid and abet, aid and comfort

AIDE, *noun*   abettor, acolyte, adjutant, aider, assistant, attendant, coadjutant, consociate, contributor, helper, helpmate, second, support, supporter, upholder

AIR POLLUTION, *noun*   contamination, defilement, impure air, unhealthy air

AKIN (Germane), *adjective*   affiliated, alike, allied, analogous, appertaining, applicable, apropos, associated, closely related, collateral, connected, correlative, correspondent, corresponding, interchangeable, like, linked, parallel, pertinent, related, relating, relevant, resembling, similar

AKIN (Related by blood), *adjective*   affiliated, connate, consanguine, consanguinean, consanguineous, consanguineus, fraternal, kindred, of the same stock

ALACRITY, *noun*   agreeableness, anxiety, briskness, celerity, compliance, dispatch, eagerness, enthusiasm, expedition, facility, haste, immediacy, immediateness, industry, promptitude, promptness, punctuality, quickness, readiness, speed, speediness, spontaneity, swiftness, zeal

ALCOHOL, *noun*   alcoholic beverage, inebriant, intoxicant, intoxicating liquor, liquor, potation, spirits

ALEATORY (Perilous), *adjective*   adventurous, beset with perils, dangerous, endangered, exposed, exposed to risk, fraught with danger, full of risk, hazardous, imperiled, minatory, ominous, parlous, precarious, riskful, risky, treacherous, unsafe, venturesome, venturous

ALEATORY (Uncertain), *adjective*   alterable, ambiguous, capricious, changeable, changeful, depending, dubious, equivocal, in question, incalculable, indefinite, mutable, not fixed, open, permutable, protean, undecided, unsettled, unstable, unsure, variable
ASSOCIATED CONCEPTS: aleatory contract

ALERT (Agile), *adjective*   alive, animated, expeditious, nimble, quick, spirited, sprightly, spry

ALERT (Vigilant), *adjective*   active, alive, attentive, guarded, observant, on guard, prepared, wary, watchful

ALERT, *verb*   advise, alarm, arouse, caution, give notice, notify, put on one's guard, sound the alarm, warn

ALIAS, *adverb*   acknowledged elsewhere as, a.k.a., alias dictus, also, also acknowledged as, also acknowledging the name of, also answering to, also called, also known as, also known by, also known under the name of, also recognized as, at other times known as, elsewhere known as, known elsewhere as, known elsewhere by, known elsewhere under the name, known otherwise as, known previously as, known variously as, *nomen alienum,* otherwise called, otherwise known as, otherwise known by, otherwise named, previously called, variously called, variously known as
ASSOCIATED CONCEPTS: alias execution, alias process, alias subpoena, alias summons, alias writ, assumed name

ALIBI, *noun*   corroborative excuse, declaration, defense, defensive evidence, defensive plea, exculpatory excuse, excuse, explanation, justifiable excuse, justification, justificatory excuse, plausible excuse, plea in being elsewhere, proof of absence, verifiable excuse, verificative excuse
ASSOCIATED CONCEPTS: affirmative defense, notice of intention to introduce alibi defense, traverse of indictment

ALIEN (Foreign), *adjective*   coming from another land, external, extrinsic, foreign-born, from abroad, immigrant, imported, not domestic, not indigenous, not native, not naturalized, of foreign origin, outside, unnaturalized

ALIEN (Unrelated), **adjective**   detached, different, digressive, disconnected, disjoined, disrelated, dissociated, from nowhere, inappropriate, independent, insular, irrelated, no relation, not comparable, of external origin, outside, unaffiliated, unallied, unassociated, unconnected, ungermane, unrelated, without context, without relation

ALIEN, **noun**   advena, alienigena, emigrant, étranger, expatriate, foreigner, immigrant, interloper, intruder, noncitizen, one excluded from some privilege, outlander, outsider, peregrinus, person coming from a foreign country, person from foreign parts, refugee, stranger

ALIENATE (Estrange), **verb**   abalienare, aggravate, antagonize, avertere, be hateful, be unfriendly, bear malice, break off, cause dislike, cause loathing, come between, destroy goodwill, detach, disaffect, disunite, divide, embitter, enrage, envenom, fall out, harden the heart, incense, make averse, make indifferent, make inimical, make unfriendly, part, pit against, provoke hatred, repel, separate, set against, set at odds, set at variance, sow dissension, take umbrage, turn away, turn off, wean, withdraw the affections of
ASSOCIATED CONCEPTS: alienation of affections, alienation of power

ALIENATE (Transfer title), **verb**   abalienare, abalienate, assign, barter, consign, convey, deed, deliver over, demise, devolve, enfeoff, part with, pass, pass over, remise, sign away, sign over, substitute, surrender, transfer ownership, turn over
ASSOCIATED CONCEPTS: alienation of property
FOREIGN PHRASES: **Regulariter non valet pactum de re mea non alienanda.** It is a rule that an agreement not to alienate my property is not binding.

ALIENATION (Estrangement), **noun**   abhorrence, abomination, acrimony, alienatio, animosity, antagonism, antipathy, aversion, bitterness, breach, break, deflection, disaffection, disfavor, disruption, division, enmity, execration, hostility, implacability, loathing, malevolence, malice, odium, rancor, rift, rupture, schism, separation, split, umbrage, unfriendliness, variance, withdrawal
ASSOCIATED CONCEPTS: alienation of affections, alienation of power
FOREIGN PHRASES: **Alienatio rei praefertur juri accrescendi.** Alienation is favored by the law rather than accumulation.

ALIENATION (Transfer of title), **noun**   abalienatio, abalienation, assignation, assignment, cession, conferment, conferral, consignation, consignment, conveyance, conveyancing, deeding, deliverance, delivery, demise, enfeoffment, limitation, nonretention, selling, surrender, transference, transmission
ASSOCIATED CONCEPTS: alienation clause, alienation of property

ALIGHT, **verb**   climb down, depart, descend, descendere, disembark, dismount, egress, evacuate, exit, get down, get off, ground oneself, land, leave, part, set down, step down

ALIGN, **verb**   accommodate, adapt, adjust, ameliorate, amend, attune, change, collimate, conform, correct, cure, improve, level, line up, make uniform, modify, normalize, pattern, perfect, readjust, rectify, regularize, remedy, revise

ALIKE, **adjective**   accordant, akin, allied, analogous, cognate, comparable, copied, correspondent, corresponding, duplicate, equable, equal, equivalent, even, identical, indistinguishable, interchangeable, kindred, matched, mated, parallel, resemblant, resembling, same, selfsame, similar, synonymous, undiscriminated, uniform

ALIKE, **adverb**   akin, analogously, both, close to, coincidentally, comparably, correspondently, correspondingly, equally, identically, in common, likewise, similarly, synonymously, together

ALIMONY, **noun**   allotment, allowance, care, dispensation, emolument, grant, income, maintenance, maintenance allowance, pecuniary aid, pecuniary assistance, personal allowance, provision, recompense, remuneration, separate maintenance, separation money, settlement, stipend, subsidization, subsidy, subvention, support, sustenance, sustentation, upkeep
ASSOCIATED CONCEPTS: alimony award, alimony judgment, alimony penpendente lite, division of property, divorce, necessaries, permanent alimony, separation, support, temporary alimony

ALL, **adjective**   complete, each and every, full, global, integral, nothing but, only, perfect, the sum of, total, undivided, universal, wholly

ALL, **noun**   aggregate, all and sundry, allness, assemblage, collectiveness, completeness, complexus, ensemble, entireness, entirety, everyone, everything, fullness, gross amount, indivisibility, intactness, integer, integrality, one and all, sum, sum total, total, totality, undividedness, universality, whole, wholeness

ALLAY, **verb**   abate, alleviate, appease, assuage, blunt, calm, cause to be still, cause to subside, check, compose, constrain, control, curb, curtail, deaden, decrease, diminish, dull, hush, lenire, lessen, lighten, lull, minimize, mitigare, mitigate, moderate, mollify, pacify, palliate, qualify, quell, quench, quiet, reduce, reduce in severity, relieve, repress, restrain, sedare, silence, slake, smooth, soften, soothe, still, subdue, suppress, temper, tone down, tranquilize

ALLEGATION, **noun**   adfirmatio, assertion, averment, bill of complaint, charge, claim, complaint, crimination, declaration, denunciation, formal averment, imputation, inculpation, ipse dixit, plea, positive assertion, positive declaration, positive statement, pronouncement, statement
ASSOCIATED CONCEPTS: allegation of fact, allegation of law, allegation of wrongdoing

ALLEGE, **verb**   adduce, advance, affirm, announce, annunciate, assert, asseverate, attest, aver, avouch, charge, cite, claim, contend, declare, enunciate, express, maintain, make an assertion, plead, present, profess, pronounce, propound, recite, relate, say, set forth, state, state as true, urge as a reason
ASSOCIATED CONCEPTS: allege a crime

ALLEGE UNDER OATH, **verb**   adjure, assert as true, attest, authenticate, avouch, avow, bear witness, certify, confirm, declare, declare true, depose, give evidence, guarantee, maintain under oath, make solemn affirmation, state, swear, take an oath, vouch, vow

ALLEGED, **adjective**   acknowledged, adduced, advanced, advocated, affirmed, announced, argued, asserted, asserted formally, asseverated, assured, averred, avouched, avowed, certified, cited, claimed, contended, declared, divulged, enunciated, imparted, imputed, insisted, introduced, maintained, positively declared, presented, proclaimed, produced, professed, promulgated, pronounced, propounded, put forward, reported, set forth, stated, stressed, testified to, uttered with conviction, vouched

ALLEGIANCE, noun   adherence, adherence to duty, attachment, bounden duty, call of duty, case of conscience, commitment, constancy, deference, devotedness, devotion, duteousness, dutifulness, faith, faithfulness, fealty, fidelity, *fides*, homage, imperative duty, inescapable duty, loyalty, matter of duty, moral obligation, obedience, obligation, obsequiousness, observance, observance of obligation, onus, pledge, promise, responsibility, sense of duty, steadfastness, subjection, submission, subordination, support, trueness

FOREIGN PHRASES: *Nemo patriam in qua natus est exuere, nec ligeantiae debitum ejurare possit.* No man can renounce his native country nor adjure his obligation of allegiance. *Ligeantia est quasi legis essentia; est vinculum fidei.* Allegiance is the essence of law; it is the bond of faith.

ALLEVIATE, verb   abate, *adlevare*, allay, appease, assuage, attenuate, blunt, calm, check, commute, compose, console, curb, dampen, diminish, disburden, disencumber, divert, dulcify, dull, ease, ease the burden, extenuate, free, help, hush, lessen, lighten, lull, mitigate, moderate, modulate, nullify, obtund, pacify, palliate, qualify, quell, quiet, redress, reduce, relieve, remedy, remit, restrain, salve, slacken, slow down, smooth, soften, solace, soothe, still, subdue, succor, tame, temper, tranquilize, unburden, unload, weaken

ALLIANCE, noun   accordance, adhesion, affiliation, agreement, alignment, amalgamation, association, band, bloc, cartel, centralization, chain, coalescence, coalition, combination, combine, compact, company, concert, concordant, confederacy, conformity, conjunction, connection, connivance, consolidation, consortium, contract, contribution, convention, cooperative, corporation, covenant, federation, fusion, integration, junction, league, merger, organization, pact, partnership, peace, pool, rapprochement, relationship, sodality, syndicate, treaty, trust, understanding, union

ALLIED, adjective   affiliated, affinitive, akin, associated, bonded, confederate, connected, federate, kindred, leagued, related

ALLOCATE, verb   administer, allot, appoint, apportion, appropriate, arrange, assign, assort, cast, class, classify, collocate, consign, deal, deal out, designate, destine, detail, dispense, disperse, dispose, distribute, divide, divide and bestow in shares, dole out, earmark, fix, give out, grant, group, hand out, intend, line up, locate, marshal, mete, parcel out, place, portion off, portion out, prescribe, prorate, ration, render, set apart, set aside, set out, share, situate, specify

ASSOCIATED CONCEPTS: allocate funds, special allocatur

ALLONGE, noun   addendum, additament, addition, adjunct, affix, appendage, appendix, attachment, complement, postscript, rider, supplement

ALLOT, verb   addicere, administer, *adsignare*, allocate, appoint, apportion, assign, deal, delimit, demarcate, designate, dispense, disperse, dispose, *distribuere,* distribute, divide, dole, earmark, indicate, measure, mete, mete out, parcel out, partition, portion out, prorate, ration, share, specify

ALLOTMENT, noun   adsignatio, allocation, annuity, appointment, apportionment, appropriation, arrangement, assignment, assignment by share, designation, dispensation, disposal, disposition, distribution, distribution by lot, dole, ordering, partition, portion, proportion, ration

ASSOCIATED CONCEPTS: allotment certificate, allotment note, allotment system

ALLOW (Authorize), verb   accredit, acknowledge, approve, certify, charter, commission, empower, enable, endorse, enfranchise, entitle, give, give authority, give leave, give permission, grant, grant permission, invest, legalize, legitimatize, license, permit, privilege, qualify, sanction, support, sustain, vouchsafe, warrant

ASSOCIATED CONCEPTS: allow to bail, allowable debt, allowable loss, allowed by law, allowed claim

FOREIGN PHRASES: *Est quiddam perfectius in rebus licitis.* There is something more perfect in things permitted.

ALLOW (Endure), verb   abide, accede, accept, accord, acquiesce, afford, agree, approve, assent, be answerable, be indulgent of, bear, brook, carry on under, concede, consent, countenance, forbear, permit, submit to, suffer, suffer to occur, sustain, take patiently, tolerate, undergo, withstand, yield

FOREIGN PHRASES: *Tout es que la loi ne defend pas est permis.* Everything which the law does not forbid is permitted.

ALLOWABLE, adjective   acceptable, accepted, admissible, approvable, approved, authorized, excusable, granted, justifiable, lawful, legal, legalized, legitimate, licit, not impossible, not improper, not objectionable, pardonable, passable, permissible, proper, right, sanctionable, sanctioned, sufferable, suffered, suitable, tolerable, tolerated, unforbidden, unobjectionable, unprohibited, venial, warrantable

ASSOCIATED CONCEPTS: allowable claims

ALLOWED, adjective   acceptable, accepted, acknowledged, admissible, admitted, allowable, approvable, approved, authorized, certified, chartered, commissioned, conceded, consented, eligible, empowered, endorsed, enfranchised, granted, justified, lawful, legal, legalized, legitimate, licensed, licit, passed, permissible, permissioned, permitted, ratified, recognized, rightful, sanctioned, sanctioned by the law, suitable, supported by authority, tolerable, tolerated, unforbidden, unprohibited, valid, validated, vouchsafed, warranted, within the law

ASSOCIATED CONCEPTS: allowed claim, allowed into evidence

FOREIGN PHRASES: *Est quiddam perfectius in rebus licitis.* There is something more perfect in things permitted.

ALLUDE, verb   advert, *attingere*, bring to mind, cite, connote, convey, *designare*, evince, hint, imply, import, indicate, infer, insinuate, leave an inference, make indirect reference, mention, point to, refer to, relate, *significare*, signify, suggest, touch upon

ALLUSIVE, adjective   allusory, ambiguous, clandestine, connotative, covert, eclipsed, evasive, imperspicuous, implicational, implicative, indicative, indirect, inferential, inferred, notional, obscure, screened, suggestive, tacit, vague, veiled

ASSOCIATED CONCEPTS: evasive contempt

ALLUVION, noun   batture, deposit, deposition, residuary, sediment, settlement, settlings

ASSOCIATED CONCEPTS: accretion, alluvial accretion, alluvial land, riparian lands, riparian rights

ALMOST, *adverb*   approximately, close to, nearly, on the brink of, on the verge of, scarcely, within sight of

ALONE (Solitary), ***adverb***   apart, detached, in solitude, independently, insular, isolated, privately, removed, separate, solo

ALONE (Unsupported), ***adverb***   unabetted, unaccompanied, unaided, unassisted, unattended, unseconded

ALONG, *adverb*   coupled with, forward, in company with, in conjunction with, lengthwise, side by side, together, with

ALSO, *adverb*   additionally, as well, besides, extra, furthermore, in addition, including, likewise, moreover, over and above, plus, similarly, then again, together with, too

ALSO KNOWN AS, *noun*   alias, also called, also identified as, also named, also referred to, assumed name, called, identification, identity, otherwise called, otherwise known, pseudonym

ALTER, *verb*   adapt, adjust, amend, change, commutare, commute, convert, deviate, *immutare*, innovate, invert, make innovations, metamorphose, moderate, modify, modulate, *mutare*, qualify, rearrange, recast, reconstruct, reorganize, temper, transform, transmogrify, transmute, turn, variegate, vary
ASSOCIATED CONCEPTS: alter a document, alter a will, forgery, fraud

ALTER EGO, *noun*   alternate, counterpart, double, living image, match, other, other half, other person, other self, perfect substitute, second self, shadow, stand-in, twin
ASSOCIATED CONCEPTS: agent, alter ego doctrine, corporate alter ego, piercing the corporate veil, separate corporate entity

ALTERATION, *noun*   adjustment, conversion, correction, difference, diversity, innovation, modification, modulation, reform, rehabilitation, reorganization, repair, revision, transition, transposition, variability, variance, variation
ASSOCIATED CONCEPTS: alteration of a contract, alteration of a license, alteration of a pleading, alteration of an instrument, restoration of an instrument

ALTERCATION, *noun*   affray, *altercatio*, angry dispute, argument, bickering, broil, commotion, conflict, contestation, controversy, disaccord, disputation, dispute, disturbance, feud, fight, fracas, heated debate, *iurgium*, jangle, jangling, melee, noisy quarrel, quarrel, *rixa*, row, scuffle, snarl, squabble, strife, wrangle, wrangling
FOREIGN PHRASES: **Veritas nimium altercando amittitur.** Truth is lost by too much altercation.

ALTERNATE (Fluctuate), ***verb***   be periodic, be unsettled, oscillate, pendulate, show indecision, vacillate, vary, waver

ALTERNATE (Take turns), ***verb***   act interchangeably, *alternare, alterner*, change by alternation, follow one another interchangeably, follow one another reciprocally, interchange, interchange regularly, interchange successively, perform by turns, perform reciprocally, perform responsively, permute, substitute, switch
ASSOCIATED CONCEPTS: alternate causes of action, pleading in the alternate

ALTERNATIVE (Option), ***noun***   alternate choice, choice, conclusion, decision, determination, discernment, discretion, discrimination, distinction, election, embracement, espousal, free selection, judgment, pick, recourse, remaining course, selection, voluntary decision
ASSOCIATED CONCEPTS: alternative conditions

ALTERNATIVE (Substitute), ***noun***   change, other choice, replacement, succedaneum, superseder, supplanter
ASSOCIATED CONCEPTS: alternative conditions, alternative contract, alternative covenant, alternative judgment, alternative legacy, alternative obligation, alternative plea, alternative pleading, alternative relief, alternative remedies, alternative writs

ALTERNATIVE DISPUTE RESOLUTION, *noun*   alternative litigation resolution, alternative means to litigation, alternative method of resolving a dispute, arbitration, litigation substitute, means to resolve a dispute, mediation, pretrial mediation
Specifically: arbitration, mediation, pretrial mediation

ALWAYS (Forever), ***adverb***   all the time, all the while, at all times, for all history

ALWAYS (Without exception), ***adverb***   by and large each and every time, invariably, universally

AMALGAMATE, *verb*   admix, bind, blend, centralize, coadunate, coalesce, combine, commingle, commix, conflate, consolidate, fuse, inosculate, join, meld, merge, mix, solidify, syndicate, unify, unite
ASSOCIATED CONCEPTS: amalgamated labor organizations

AMANUENSIS, *noun*   clerk, recorder, recording secretary, scribe, scrivener, secretary, writer

AMASSED, *adjective*   aggregated, amalgamate, amalgamated, blended, collective, compact, complex, composite, compound, compounded, conglomerate, fused, manifold, medley, mingled, mixed, mosaic, multiform, multiple, variegated

AMATEUR, *adjective*   inept, unaccomplished, unadroit, undextrous, unfit, ungifted, unskilled, untalented

AMATEUR, *noun*   apprentice, aspirant, beginner, disciple, entrant, fledging, freshman, inexperienced person, initiate, layman, neophyte, novice

AMBIGUITY, *noun*   abstruseness, *ambiguitas*, bafflement, bewilderment, confounded meaning, confused meaning, confusion, disconcertion, doubtful meaning, doubtfulness, dubiety, dubiousness, duplexity in meaning, equivocalness, equivocation, incertitude, indefinite meaning, indefiniteness, indeterminacy, obscure meaning, obscurity, puzzlement, reconditeness, uncertainty of meaning, unintelligibility, vagueness
ASSOCIATED CONCEPTS: ambiguity upon the factum, latent ambiguity, patent ambiguity
FOREIGN PHRASES: **Cum in testamento ambigue aut etiam perperam scriptum est benigne interpretari et secundum id quod credibile est cogitatum credendum est.** Where an ambiguous, or even an erroneous, expression occurs in a will, it should be interpreted liberally, and in accordance with the intention of the testator. **Ambiguitas verborum latens verificatione suppletur; nam quod ex facto oritur ambiguum verificatione facti tollitur.** A latent verbal ambiguity may be removed by evidence; for whatever ambiguity arises from an extrinsic fact may be explained by

extrinsic evidence. ***Ambiguum placitum interpretari debet contra proferentem.*** An ambiguous plea ought to be interpreted against the party entering it. ***Quae cubitationis tollendae causa contractibus inseruntur, jus commune non laedunt.*** Those clauses which are inserted in agreements to avoid doubts and ambiguity do not offend the common law. ***Quoties in verbis nulla est ambiguitas, ibi nulla expositio contra verba fienda est.*** Whenever there is no ambiguity in the words, then no exposition contrary to the words should be made. ***Quum in testamento ambigue aut etiam perperam scriptum est, benigne interpretari et secundum id quod credibile et cogitatum, credendum est***. When an ambiguous or even an erroneous expression occurs in a will, it should be construed liberally and in accordance with what is thought the probable meaning of the testator. ***Ubi jus incertum, ibi jus nullum.*** Where the law is uncertain, there is no law. ***Verbis standum ubi nulla ambiguitas.*** Where there is no ambiguity, one must abide by the words.

AMBIGUOUS, *adjective*   abstruse, *ambiguus,* ambivalent, confused, difficult to comprehend, doubtful, dubious, equivocal, having a double meaning, indefinite, indistinct, inexact, lacking clearness, not clear, not plain, obscure, open to various interpretations, uncertain, unintelligible, vague
ASSOCIATED CONCEPTS: ambiguous language
FOREIGN PHRASES: ***Ambigua responsio contra proferentem est accipienda.*** An ambiguous answer is to be taken against him who offers it. ***In ambigua voce legis ea potius accipienda est significatio quae vitio caret, praesertim cum etiam voluntas legis ex hoc colligi possit.*** In an ambiguous expression of law, that interpretation is to be preferred which is consonant with equity, especially where it is in conformity with the purpose of the law. ***In ambiguis orationibus maxime sententia spectanda est ejus qui eas protulisset.*** In ambiguous expressions, the intent of the person using them is particularly to be regarded. ***In ambiguo sermone non utrumque dicimus sed id duntaxat quod volumus.*** In ambiguous discourse, language is not used in a double sense, but in the sense in which it is meant.

AMBIT, *noun*   border, boundary, boundary line, bounds, circumference, contour, delineation lines, domain, dominion, furthest extent, furthest point, jurisdiction, limit, lines, orbit, outline, outer limit, pale, perimeter, periphery, province, realm, sphere
ASSOCIATED CONCEPTS: ambit of a statute, within the ambit of the law

AMBIVALENCE, *noun*   dubiety, dubitancy, equivocalness, hesitation, incertitude, indecision, indecisiveness, indeterminacy, indetermination, irresoluteness, irresolution, mental reservation, prevarication, uncertainty, undecidedness, undetermination, vacillation

AMBULATORY, *adjective*   able to be altered, alterative, amendable, amendatory, changeable, emendable, emendatory, modifiable, movable, mutable, not fixed, permutable, renunciatory, repudiative, repudiatory, reversible, reversional, revisional, revisory, revocable, revocatory, subject to change, variable
ASSOCIATED CONCEPTS: ambulatory deed, ambulatory patient, ambulatory will
FOREIGN PHRASES: ***Ambulatoria est voluntas defuncti usque ad vitae supremum exitum.*** The will of a deceased person is ambulatory until the latest moment of life.

AMBUSH, *verb*   assail, assault, attack, attack from a concealed position, bait a trap, catch by perfidy, ensnare, entrap, lay a trap for, lie in wait for, set a trap for, snare, trap, waylay

AMELIORATE, *verb*   advance, allay, better, change for the better, correct, *corrigere,* cultivate, develop, ease, elevate, enhance, forward, fructify, help, improve, make better, make progress, meliorate, mend, mitigate, palliate, promote, raise, rectify, reform, upgrade
ASSOCIATED CONCEPTS: ameliorating facts and circumstances, ameliorating waste

AMENABILITY, *noun*   accessibleness, accommodativeness, acquiescence, adaptability, agreeableness, compliance, compliancy, conformability, docility, ductility, flexibility, flexibleness, inclination, influenceability, malleability, manageability, mansuetude, obligingness, persuasibility, placability, plasticity, pliability, pliancy, readiness, receptiveness, responsiveness, servility, submission, submissiveness, tractability, versatility, willingness, yieldingness

AMENABLE, *adjective*   accessible, acquiescent, agreeable, amiable, available, compliant, *dicto oboediens,* flexible, impressionable, influenceable, movable, obedient, open to suggestions, persuadable, persuasible, pervious, pliable, pliant, reasonable, responsible, suasible, tractable, yielding
ASSOCIATED CONCEPTS: amenable to process

AMEND, *verb*   add to, adjust, alter, ameliorate, better, change, correct, *corrigere,* edit, emend, *emendare,* emendate, enhance, enrich, improve, mend, modify, perfect, polish, rectify, refashion, refine, reform, remedy, remove faults, renew, revamp, revise, rework, rewrite, upgrade
ASSOCIATED CONCEPTS: amend a certificate of incorporation, amend a law, amend a pleading, amend a statute, amend a will

AMENDMENT *(Correction),* *noun*   adjustment, amelioration, betterment, change, *correctio,* elaboration, *emendatio,* emendation, enhancement, improvement, melioration, modification, perfection, refinement, reformation, remedy, revampment, revisal, revision, supplement
ASSOCIATED CONCEPTS: amendment in a statute, amendment to a will

AMENDMENT *(Legislation),* *noun*   act, bill, clause, legislation, legislative act, legislative bill, measure, modification of the law, rider, supplement
ASSOCIATED CONCEPTS: amendment to a charter, amendment to the Constitution, Bill of Rights

AMENITIES, *noun*   civilities, convention, correctness, decency, decorousness, decorum, elegances, etiquette, formalities, gentilities, manners, prescribed code of conduct, propriety, protocol, seemliness, social code, standards

AMENITY, *noun*   accommodation, agreeable manner, agreeable way, agreeableness, allure, *amoenitas,* appeal, attractive feature, attractive quality, attractiveness, civility, delightfulness, desirable feature, grace, invitingness, lure, mildness, niceness, pleasantness, pleasingness, refinement

AMERCEMENT, *noun*   damages, fine, forfeit, forfeiture, pecuniary penalty, penalty

AMICABLE, *adjective*   affable, amiable, cordial, friendly, genial, harmonious, sociable, unhostile

AMICUS CURIAE, *noun*   advocate, champion, exponent, friend in court, intercessor, intervening party, intervenor, party, representative, speaker
ASSOCIATED CONCEPTS: amicus brief, amicus motion to intervene

AMMUNITION, *noun*   *apparatus belli,* armament, armature, arms, ballistics, cartridges, charge, defense, deterrent, explosive, firearms, gunnery, gunpowder, materials of combat, means of attack, muniment, munition, panoply, propellants, provisions, weapons

AMNESTY, *noun*   absolution, acquittance, act of grace, act of mercy, conciliation, condonation, discharge, disculpation, exculpation, exoneration, forgiveness, general pardon, grace, *ignoscere,* pardon, quittance, release, reprieve, universal forgiveness of past offenses, *venia*
ASSOCIATED CONCEPTS: express amnesty, implied amnesty, presidential pardon

AMONG, *adverb*   amid, amidst, between, in the middle of, parenthetically

AMORTIZATION, *noun*   clearance, defrayal, defrayment, disbursement, discharge, extinction of a debt, extinguishment of claim, liquidation of a debt, payment, remittance, satisfaction
ASSOCIATED CONCEPTS: amortization contract, amortization of a mortgage, amortize a loan

AMOUNT *(Quantity),* ***noun***   aggregate, bulk, count, extent, magnitude, mass, measure, measurement, net quantity, number, numeration, strength, substance, sum, summa, total, whole
ASSOCIATED CONCEPTS: amount of evidence, amount of loss
FOREIGN PHRASES: **Major numerus in se continet minorem.** The greater number contains in itself the lesser.

AMOUNT *(Result),* ***noun***   conclusion, consequence, effect, end result, full effect, import, net quantity, outcome, outgrowth, product, purport, resultant, sum, sum total, upshot

AMOUNT *(Sum),* ***noun***   account, count, rate, reckoning, statement, summation, tally, value, worth
ASSOCIATED CONCEPTS: amount allowed, amount due, amount in controversy, amount in dispute, amount of loss, amount recovered, jurisdictional amount

AMPLE, *adjective*   abounding, abundant, adequate, bountiful, broad enough, capacious, commodious, comprehensive, copious, expansive, extensive, generous, large enough, liberal, many, plenteous, satisfactory, sufficient

AMPLIFICATION, *noun*   accession, accretion, accrual, accumulation, advance, advancement, aggrandizement, aggravation, augmentation, broadening, clarification, deepening, development, dilation, elaboration, enhancement, enlargement, expansion, explanation, extension, furtherance, gain, growth, heightening, increasing, increment, intensification, magnification, progression, restatement, rewording

AMPLIFY, *verb*   add to, augment, delineate, develop, elaborate, enlarge, expand, extend, increase, specify, specify in greater detail

ANACHRONISTIC, *adjective*   antedated, antiquated, archaic, archaizing, behind the times, ill-advised, ill-judged, ill-timed, incongruous, misdated, misjudged, non-contemporary, obsolete, outdated, outmoded, previous, untimely, Victorian

ANACOLUTHON, *noun*   broken thread, disconnectedness, discontinuity, lost connection, non sequitur, unwarranted conclusion

ANALOGOUS, *adjective*   akin, alike, allied, analogical, associated, coequal, cognate, comparable, correlative, correspondent, corresponding, equipollent, equivalent, homologous, kindred, like, matching, parallel, related, resembling, same, similar, *similis*

ANALOGY, *noun*   affinity, agreement, close relation, close resemblance, common feature, comparability, comparison, congruity, correlation, correspondence, equivalence, homology, like quality, likeness, logical relation, parallel relation, parallelism, parity, partial similarity, point in common, point of resemblance, points of comparison, relation, relativeness, relativity, resemblance, semblance, similar appearance, similar form, similar relation, similarity, similitude, *similitudo,* symmetry
FOREIGN PHRASES: **De similibus ad similia eadem ratione procedendum est.** Proceeding in similar matters we are to proceed by the same rule.

ANALYSIS, *noun*   ascertainment, assay, audit, canvassing, close inquiry, consideration, critical examination, critique, delineation, dissection, examination, exhaustive inquiry, *explicatio,* exploration, inquiry, investigation, perusal, probe, research, review, scrutinization, scrutiny, searching inquiry, sifting, strict inquiry, study, survey, treatment
ASSOCIATED CONCEPTS: chemical analysis, lab analysis

ANALYTICAL, *adjective*   deductive, demonstrative, diagnostic, demonstrative, experimental, fact-finding, investigative, logical, mathematical, probing, rational, reasoning, resolvent, searching, separative, solvent

ANALYZE, *verb*   anatomize, audit, canvass, conduct an inquiry, consider, delineate, delve into, dissect, examine, examine critically, explore, hold an inquiry, inquire into, institute an inquiry, investigate, make an analysis, make an inquiry, probe, question, reason, research, review, scan, scrutinize, set up an inquiry, sift, study, subject to examination, survey

ANARCHY, *noun*   absence of authority, breakdown of administration, chaos, confusion, discord, disobedience, disorder, disorderliness, disorganization, disregard, disunion, indiscipline, insubordination, insurgence, insurrection, interregnum, irresponsibility, lawlessness, *licentia,* misgovernment, misrule, mob law, mob rule, nihilism, political disorder, rebellion, revolution, riot, sedition, terrorism, tumult, turmoil, unruliness, uprising
ASSOCIATED CONCEPTS: criminal anarchy

ANCESTOR, *noun*   ascendant, *auctor generis, auctor gentis,* forebear, forefather, foregoer, forerunner, genitor, grandsire, parent, patriarch, precursor, predecessor, primogenitor, procreator, progenitor
ASSOCIATED CONCEPTS: ancestral estate, ancestral property, descendant, immediate ancestor, inheritance, lineal ancestor, maternal ancestor, paternal ancestor

ANCESTRY, noun affiliation, ascendants, blood, blood relationship, blood tie, bloodline, cognation, connection, consanguinity, derivation, descent, family, family connection, family tree, filiation, forebears, forefathers, former generations, genealogy, genesis, *genus*, heredity, history, kinship, line, lineage, origin, origination, *origo*, parentage, parents, patriarchs, pedigree, predecessors, procreators, stirps, strain
ASSOCIATED CONCEPTS: ancestral estate, ancestral property

ANCILLARY *(Auxiliary)*, **adjective** abetting, accessory, added, additional, adjunct, adjuvant, advantageous, aidful, aiding, assistant, attendant, beneficial, coadjuvant, collateral, completing, conducive, contributory, cooperative, extra, helpful, in addition, ministrant, more, other, serving as an adjunct, serving as an aid, spare, supernumerary, supplemental, supplementary, supporting
ASSOCIATED CONCEPTS: ancillary acts, ancillary agreements, ancillary attachment, ancillary covenants, ancillary jurisdiction, ancillary proceeding, ancillary relief, ancillary remedies

ANCILLARY *(Subsidiary)*, **adjective** complementing, dependent, derivational, derivative, ensuing, following, lesser, resultant, resulting, secondary, sequential, subaltern, subordinate

ANCILLARY RELIEF, noun accessory relief, additional relief, adjunct relief, an added judgment, attendant relief, beneficial relief, collateral relief, complementing relief, extra relief, other relief, resultant relief, resulting relief, secondary relief, sequential relief, spare relief, subordinate relief, supplemental relief, supplementary relief, supporting relief
ASSOCIATED CONCEPTS: ancillary administration, ancillary attachment, ancillary bill, ancillary jurisdiction, ancillary proceeding

ANEW, adverb afresh, again, another time, newly, once more, over again

ANGUISH, verb ache, aggrieve, agonize, desolate, disturb, excruciate, grieve, harry, make miserable, pain, prostrate, rack, suffer, torment, torture, trouble, writhe
ASSOCIATED CONCEPTS: mental anguish, non-economic loss, pain and suffering

ANIMADVERSION, noun admonition, adverse comment, aspersion, blame, censorious remark, censure, chiding, condemnation, correction, criticism, deprecation, disapprobation, disapproval, discredit, fault-finding, impeachment, impugnation, imputation, obloquy, rebuke, reflection, remark, remonstrance, reprehension, reprimand, reproach, reprobation, reproof, revilement, stricture

ANIMAL, noun *animans,* beast, beast of burden, beast of the field, brute, brute creation, created being, creature, pet, wild being
ASSOCIATED CONCEPTS: animals of a base nature, domestic animals, wild animal
FOREIGN PHRASES: *Animalia fera, si facta sint mansueta et ex consuetudine eunt et redeunt, volant et revolant, ut cervi, cygni, etc., eo usque nostra sunt, et ita intelliguntur quamdium habuerunt animum revertendi.* Wild animals, if they are tamed, and are accustomed to leave and return, fly away and fly back, as stags, swans, etc., are considered to belong to us so long as they have the intention of returning to us.

ANIMUS, noun bent, character, decision, deliberateness, design, determination, disposition, fixed purpose, inclination, intendment, intent, intention, intentionality, mind, motive, nature, penchant, predetermination, predilection, predisposition, propensity, purpose, resolution, resolve, set purpose, settled purpose, temper, tendency, volition, will
ASSOCIATED CONCEPTS: *animus derelinquendi, animus et factum, animus furandi, animus revertendi, animus testandi,* anti-union animus

ANNEX *(Add)*, **verb** affix, append, attach, bind, bring together, combine, conjoin, connect, consolidate, fasten, fix, hold together, incorporate, interlink, intertwist, join, merge, put together, subjoin, supplement, unite
ASSOCIATED CONCEPTS: annex an exhibit, annex court papers, annex to a pleading, annexed writing, fixtures

ANNEX *(Arrogate)*, **verb** accroach, appropriate, assume, assume ownership, confiscate, convert, disseise, distrain, expropriate, impound, seize, take over, take possession, take summarily, usurp
ASSOCIATED CONCEPTS: annex a territory

ANNIHILATE, verb abolish, annul, blast, cancel, consume, crush, cut down, decimate, demolish, destroy, devour, dismantle, dissolve, efface, eliminate, end, eradicate, expunge, exterminate, extinguish, extirpate, invalidate, kill, liquidate, massacre, negate, nullify, obliterate, overthrow, quench, ravage, remove, render null and void, revoke, ruin, slaughter, slay, snuff out, stifle, subvert, undo, vitiate, wipe out, wreck

ANNOUNCE, verb acquaint, advertise, advise, affirm, allege, annunciate, apprise, assert, asserverate, aver, broadcast, bruit, bulletin, circulate, communicate, contend, convey, declare, disabuse, disclose, disseminate, enunciate, foretell, give out, herald, inform, maintain, make manifest, mention, notify, observe, post, proclaim, profess, prognosticate, promulgate, pronounce, propound, publish, relate, report, reveal, set forth, signal, speak, specify, state, tell, transmit, trumpet, utter

ANNOY, verb acerbate, affront, aggravate, badger, bedevil, bother, chafe, cross, discommode, discompose, displease, disquiet, distress, disturb, enrage, exasperate, fester, fret, gall, get on the nerves of, grate, grieve, harass, harm, harry, heckle, hector, importune, incommode, inconvenience, infest, irk, irritate, nag, needle, offend, pain, pester, pique, plague, provoke, rankle, roil, ruffle, thwart, torment, trouble, upset, vex

ANNUITY, noun allotment, allowance, *annua pecunia,* annual allowance, earnings, income, pension, remuneration, retirement income, return, specified income payable for life, stipend, subsidy, subvention, yearly payment
ASSOCIATED CONCEPTS: annuity by a trust, annuity by will, annuity contract, annuity policy, antenuptial annuity, life insurance annuity, verifiable annuity
FOREIGN PHRASES: *Annua nec debitum judex non separat ipsum.* A judge does not divide annuities nor debt.

ANNUL, verb abnegate, *abolere,* abolish, *abrogare,* abrogate, annihilate, avoid, call back, cancel, cancel out, contradict, contravene, countermand, counterorder, deny, destroy, discontinue, disestablish, efface, end, expunge, exterminate, extinguish, invalidate, make illegal, make void, negate, nullify, obliterate, overrule, put an end to, recall, reduce to nothing, reduce to nought, relinquish, render null and void, render void, renege, repeal, repudiate, rescind, retract, reverse, revoke, set aside, *solvere*, strike out, supersede, terminate, unmake, vitiate, void, withdraw

ASSOCIATED CONCEPTS: annul a marriage, annul a statute, nol-pros

ANNULMENT, *noun* abolishment, abolition, abrogation, cancellation, contravention, decree of nullity, deletion, discontinuance, disestablishment, dissolution, effacement, invalidation, negation, nullification, obliteration, rasure, rescindment, retraction, reversal, revocation, revokement, undoing, vitiation, voidance

ASSOCIATED CONCEPTS: alimony, annulment of a marriage, dissolution of marriage, divorce, separation, voidable marriage

ANNUM, *noun* age, *annus*, continuum of days, cycle, fifty-two weeks, full round of the seasons, period, time, twelve months, year

ANNUNCIATE, *verb* advise, affirm, announce, apprise, assert, aver, communicate, convey, declare, dispatch news, disseminate, enunciate, explain, express, get across, get through, give notice, impart, inform, keep posted, make known, make known publicly, make proclamation, notify, pass on, pass on information, post, proclaim, profess, promulgate, pronounce, propound, publicize, publish, report, specify, state, tell, transmit

ANOMALOUS, *adjective* aberrant, abnormal, anomalistic, atypical, awry, breaking with tradition, deranged, deviating from the common rule, deviative, disarranged, disjunct, dislocated, disordered, disorganized, divergent, eccentric, erratic, in disorder, in the wrong place, inconsistent, irregular, misplaced, nonstandard, nonuniform, not conforming to the usual, out of keeping, out of order, out of the ordinary, peculiar, solecistic, uncommon, unconventional, uncustomary, unnatural, unrepresentative, untypical, unusual

ANOMALY, *noun* aberration, abnormality, amorphism, curiosity, departure, deviation, discrepancy, divergence, eccentricity, exception, incongruity, inconsistency, irregularity, monstrosity, nonconformity, oddity, peculiarity, quirk, singularity, subnormality, unconformity, unnaturalness, variance

ANONYMOUS, *adjective* authorless, bearing no name, having no acknowledged name, incognito, innominate, nameless, of unknown authorship, secret, *sine nomine*, unacknowledged, unclaimed, undesignated, unidentified, unknown, unnamed, unsigned, unspecified, without a name, without the name of the author

ASSOCIATED CONCEPTS: anonymous donor

ANSWER *(Judicial response)*, **noun** confutation, contradictory evidence, countercharge, counterclaim, counterevidence, counterreply, counterstatement, defense, denial, legal argument, negation, negative evidence, official reply, opposite evidence, plea, plea in rebuttal, rebuttal, rebutting evidence, recrimination, refutation, rejoinder, replication, reply to a charge, surrebuttal, surrebutter, surrejoinder

ASSOCIATED CONCEPTS: amended answer, appearance by an answer, frivolous answer, general appearance, notice of appearance, responsive answer, sham answer, supplemental answer

FOREIGN PHRASES: *Ambigua responsio contra proferentem est accipienda.* An ambiguous answer is to be taken against him who offers it.

ANSWER *(Reply)*, **noun** acknowledgment, denial, negation, reaction, rebuttal, refutal, rejoinder, repartee, replication, respondence, response, retort, return, riposte

ASSOCIATED CONCEPTS: argumentative answer, irrelevant answer, nonresponsive answer, responsive answer

ANSWER *(Solution)*, **noun** cause, elucidation, explanation, finding, outcome, reason, resolution, result, revelation, verdict

ANSWER *(Be responsible)*, **verb** be accountable, be answerable, be bound, be chargeable, be compelled, be liable, be obligated, be obliged, be subject, be surety, be under legal obligation, undertake responsibility

ANSWER *(Reply)*, **verb** acknowledge, act in response to, be responsive, confute, contend, contest, contradict, contravene, controvert, counter, counterclaim, debate, defeat, defend, deny, disclaim, disprove, dispute, forswear, impugn, make a rejoinder, oppose, oppugn, plead, rebut, refute, rejoin, repudiate, *rescribere*, respond, *respondere*, retaliate, retort, return, riposte, say in reply, *se defendere*, traverse

ASSOCIATED CONCEPTS: answer in the alternative, argumentative answer

ANSWER *(Respond legally)*, **verb** contest, controvert, counterblast, countercharge, counterclaim, defend, plead, rebut, recriminate, rejoin, reply, surrejoin

ASSOCIATED CONCEPTS: appearance by an answer, argumentative answer, supplemental answer

ANSWER FOR *(Act for)*, **verb** act on behalf of, appear for, be accepted for, be attorney for, be proxy for, be regarded as, be responsible for, be taken as, be the equivalent of, count for, front for, go as, pass as, pass for, represent, serve as, stand for, stand in place for, stand in place of, substitute for, take responsibility for, take the blame

ANSWER FOR *(Sponsor)*, **verb** champion, commit, contract, defend, endorse, ensure, favor, guarantee, indemnify, insure, promote, protect, support, sustain, undertake, uphold

ANTAGONIZE, *verb* act in opposition to, aggress, alienate, cause dislike, cause offense, cause umbrage, compete with, conflict with, contend against, counteract, cross, destroy good will, disaffect, displease, embitter, envenom, estrange, excite hate, go against, incur the hostility of, irritate, make an antagonist of, make unfriendly, offend, oppose, provoke, render inimical, repel, rival, run counter to, set against, set at odds, show ill will, spite, take issue with, take one's stand against, turn against, work against

ANTECEDE, *verb* antedate, forerun, go before, have precedence, precede, predate, prevene

ASSOCIATED CONCEPTS: ancestor, antecedent creditor, antecedent debt, antecedent encumbrance, antecedent fraud, antecedent promise

ANTECEDENT, *adjective* *antecedens*, anterior, earlier, first, fore, foregoing, forerunning, former, going before in time, inaugural, introductory, precedent, preceding, precursive, precursory, pre-existent, prefatory, preliminary, prelusive, preparatory, prevenient, previous, prior

ASSOCIATED CONCEPTS: antecedent creditors, antecedent debt, preexisting debts, preexisting liabilities

ANTECEDENT, noun ancestor, ancestry, before mentioned, derivation, forerunner, former, last, lineage, original, patriarch, pedigree, pioneer, precedent, precursor, predecessor, preliminary, premise, primogenitor, progenitor, stock

ANTEDATE, verb affix an earlier date, anachronize, assign to an earlier date, date back, date before the true date, date before the true time, date earlier than the fact, foredate, predate, set an earlier date, transfer to an earlier date

ANTENUPTIAL AGREEMENT, noun agreement before marriage, concord before marriage, contract before marriage, legal arrangement before marriage, pact before marriage, understanding before marriage

ANTICIPATE (Expect), **verb** antevertere, assume, be ready for, calculate on, consider in advance, contemplate, count on, forearm, get the start on, guard against, have in prospect, hold in view, intuit, make preparations, plan on, preconceive, predispose, prepare for, suppose, surmise, wait for
ASSOCIATED CONCEPTS: anticipated profits, anticipating defenses, anticipation notes, anticipatory breach, anticipatory repudiation, anticipatory warrant, duty to anticipate in negligence

ANTICIPATE (Prognosticate), **verb** announce in advance, augur, auspicate, betoken, conjecture, divine, forebode, forecast, foreknow, foreshow, forespeak, harbinger, have a presentiment, herald, look forward to, omen, portend, praevertere, preannounce, precognize, predetermine, predict, premonish, presage, prophesy, vaticinate

ANTICIPATION (Expectation), **noun** apprehension, contemplation, divination, forecast, foreseeing, foresight, imminence, insight, intuition, preconception, prediction, preparation, prescience, presentiment, prolepsis, second sight

ANTICIPATION (Likelihood), **noun** contemplation, expectancy, foreboding, forecast, hope, outlook, possibility, preconception, preoccupation, presumption, prevision, probability, prospect
ASSOCIATED CONCEPTS: anticipation of income, anticipation of injuries

ANTIPATHETIC (Distasteful), **adjective** abhorrent, bitter, disagreeable, disgusting, displeasing, hateful, loathsome, odious, offensive, repellent, repugnant, repulsive, undesirable, uninviting, unsatisfactory, virulent

ANTIPATHETIC (Oppositional), **adjective** adverse, alien, alienated, antagonistic, antipodean, antithetic, antithetical, at cross-purposes, averse, conflicting, constitutionally opposed, contradictory, contradistinct, contrapositive, contrary, contrasted, converse, counter, diametrically opposite, having a natural contrariety, inimical, negatory, opposed, opposing, opposite, oppositive, oppugnant, resistant, reverse, unfriendly, unpropitious

ANTIPATHY, noun abhorrence, abomination, alienation, animosity, antagonism, anathema, antipode, aversion, clashing, collision, conflict, contradiction, contrariness, detestation, deviation, difference, disagreement, disapprobation, disfavor, disgust, disinclination, dislike, enmity, execration, hatred, horror, hostility, ill will, incompatibility, inimicalness, loathing, malice, odium, opposition, rancor, reluctance, repugnance, repulsion, unfriendliness

ANTIPODE, noun absolute difference, adverseness, adversus, antimony, antipathy, antipodes, antipole, antithesis, collision, conflict, contradiction, contradistinction, contraindication, contraposition, contrariety, contrariness, contrary, contrast, converse, counteraction, countermeaning, counterpart, counterpole, direct opposite, disagreement, inconsistency, inverse, inversion, negation, obverse, opposite, opposite extreme, opposite pole, opposite side, oppositeness, opposition, other extreme, polarity, repugnance, reverse, vis-à-vis

ANTIQUATED, adjective aged, anachronistic, ancient, antediluvian, antique, archaic, disused, fossilized, moribund, obsolescent, obsolete, old, olden, old-fashioned, ossified, outdated, outmoded, out-of-date, outworn, passé, pre-historic, primitive, quaint, retired, rundown, superannuated, timeworn, unfashionable

ANTIQUE, adjective ancient, antedeluvian, archaic, bygone, old, old-fashioned, older, superannuated, time worn, venerable

ANTITHESIS, noun absolute difference, adverseness, antipode, balanced contrast, conflict, contentio, contradiction, contradistinction, contraposition, contrariety, contrarium, contrary, contrast, converse, counterpart, counterpole, direct opposite, disagreement, divergence, incompatibility, inverse, irreconcilability, mutual exclusiveness, opposite, opposite pole, opposition, other extreme, polarity, reverse, strong contrast

ANTITRUST ACT, noun against fair trade, against free commerce, against free mercantilism, against free trade, against open business, against open markets, contrary to good business

APART, adjective alien, alone, asunder, detached, disconnected, disengaged, disjoined, disjoint, disjointed, disjunct, disrelated, dissociated, distare, disunited, diversus, foreign, having independent qualities, having unique features, having unique qualities, independent, irrelative, isolated, no relation, removed, separare, separate, separated, solo, solus, unaffiliated, unallied, unassociated, unattached, unconnected, unjoined
ASSOCIATED CONCEPTS: living apart

APARTMENT, noun home, place of residence, premises, residence
ASSOCIATED CONCEPTS: condominium, cooperative apartment

APATHETIC, adjective aloof, bored, callous, careless, casual, cold, cold-blooded, cursory, disinterested, dragging, dull, frigid, heartless, heedless, impassive, inactive, inattentive, incurious, indifferent, indolent, inert, inexpressive, insensible, insentient, insouciant, lackadaisical, languid, lax, lethargic, lifeless, listless, lukewarm, nonchalant, obtuse, otiose, passionless, passive, perfunctory, phlegmatic, sluggish, soulless, spiritless, stoical, stolid, stony, supine, torpid, unaffected, unanimated, unemotional, unenthusiastic, unfeeling, unimpassioned, uninquisitive, uninterested, unmoved, unsusceptible

APLOMB, noun assurance, backbone, balance, boldness, calmness, composure, confidence, constancy, correctness, decorum, demeanor, deportment, dignity, elegance, equanimity, equilibrium, grit, intrepidity, levelheadedness, poise, presence of mind, resolution, restraint, security, self-possession, self-reliance, solidity, stability, stature, steadiness

APOLOGIST, noun advocate, arguer in defense, champion, defender, *defensor,* disputant, excuser, exponent, expositer, expounder, favorer, justifier, pleader, proponent, protector, supporter, upholder

APPALLING, adjective abhorrent, abominable, atrocious, beneath contempt, contemptible, deplorable, despicable, detestable, dreadful, foul, frightening, frightful, ghastly, ghoulish, gruesome, harrowing, hateful, heinous, horrendous, horrid, horrifying, loathsome, obnoxious, odious, offensive, outrageous, pathetic, pitiful, repellent, reprehensible, repulsive, revolting, shameful, shocking, terrible, terrifying, unspeakable, vile, villainous
ASSOCIATED CONCEPTS: appalling conduct, contempt of court, harassment

APPARENT (Perceptible), **adjective** able to be seen, clear, conspicuous, definite, detectable, discernible, distinct, easily seen, evident, explicit, exposed, express, *fictus,* identifiable, in sight, in view, indubitable, known, manifest, *manifestus,* noticeable, notorious, obvious, open, open to view, overt, palpable, patent, perceivable, plain, real, recognizable, self-evident, showing, *species,* tangible, uncovered, undisguised, *videor,* viewable, visible
ASSOCIATED CONCEPTS: apparent ability, apparent agency, apparent authority, apparent cause, apparent danger, apparent defect, apparent easement, apparent from the record, apparent necessity, apparent ownership, apparent partnership, apparent risk, apparent scope of authority, apparent use

APPARENT (Presumptive), **adjective** appearing, assumptive, conjectural, contemplated, evidential, expected, hopeful, intended, likely, logical, manifest, ostensible, plausible, premised, presumable, probable, proposed, propositional, prospective, seeming, suggestive, supposable, supposed, suppositional, suppositionary, suppositive, taken for granted, to be supposed
ASSOCIATED CONCEPTS: apparent heir, apparent validity
FOREIGN PHRASES: *Quod constat clare non debet verificari.* What is clearly apparent is not required to be proved. ***Quod constat curiae opere testium non indiget.*** That which appears to the court needs not the help of witnesses.

APPEAL, noun appellate review, *appellatio,* application for retrial, application for review by a higher tribunal, bid, complaint to a superior court, *obtestatio,* petition, *provocatio,* reconsideration, recourse to some higher power, reexamination, rehearing, reopening, request for another decision, request for retrial, request for review, resort to superior authority, retrial, review
ASSOCIATED CONCEPTS: appellate courts, appellate jurisdiction, *certiorari*
FOREIGN PHRASES: *De fide et officio judicis non recipitur quaestio, sed de scientia, sive sit error juris, sive facti.* The good faith and honesty of a judge are not to be questioned, but his knowledge, whether it be in error of law or fact, may be.

APPEAL, verb *appelare,* apply for a reexamination of a case, apply for a retrial, apply for a review of a case to a higher tribunal, bid, bring new evidence, claim, consider again with a view to a change or action, contest, contest a case by asking for review, *homini placere, obsecrare,* reconsider, reexamine, refer to, rehear, reopen, request another decision, request reexamination, request reopening of a case, retry, review, seek reexamination, seek reference of a case from one court to another, seek review of a case, sue

ASSOCIATED CONCEPTS: appeal as a matter of right, appeal bond, appeal in forma pauperis, appealable interest, appealable judgment, appealable order, appealed from an order of the court, discretionary appeal, perfect on appeal

APPEAR (Attend court proceedings), **verb** *adesse,* answer, be in attendance, be manifest, be present, be present to answer, come formally before a tribunal, come into court, *comparere,* enter an appearance, *in iudicium venire,* make an appearance, present an answer, present oneself, put in an appearance, submit oneself to
FOREIGN PHRASES: *Idem est non esse, et non apparere.* Not to exist is the same thing as not to appear.

APPEAR (Materialize), **verb** *apparere,* arise, be in sight, be manifest, become visible, come into sight, come into view, come to light, *conspici, emerge,* exsistere, manifest itself, occur, present to the view

APPEAR (Seem to be), **verb** be patent, convey the impression, create the impression, give the effect, give the impression, have a certain semblance, have every indication, look, look as if, present the appearance, resemble, seem like, strike one as being, take on the aspect, take on the manner, *videri,* wear the aspect

APPEARANCE (Coming into court), **noun** answer, entrance in a case, presence in court, response to an action, submission to a court's jurisdiction
ASSOCIATED CONCEPTS: compulsory appearance, general appearance, limited appearance, special appearance, specific appearance, voluntary appearance

APPEARANCE (Emergence), **noun** *adventus,* arrival into view, coming, evincement, introduction, manifestation, occurrence, rise

APPEARANCE (Look), **noun** air, aspect, *aspectus,* complexion, demeanor, embodiment, external aspect, face, form, guise, likeness, manner, mien, outward look, outward show, personal presence, physiognomy, posture, pretense, *rem simulare,* show, sight, *species*
ASSOCIATED CONCEPTS: appearance of authority, appearance of validity

APPEASEMENT, noun accommodation, adjustment, allayment, amends, assuagement, calming, conciliation, deadening, détente, dulcification, dulling, mitigation, mollification, pacification, placation, propitiation, rapprochement, reconcilement, reconciliation, salving, satisfaction, softening, soothing, submission, tranquilization

APPELLANT, noun aggrieved party, appealer, *appellator,* contender, delator, litigant, objector, party, party to a suit, petitioner, suitor
ASSOCIATED CONCEPTS: appellee, respondant

APPELLATE COURT, noun court of appellate jurisdiction, court of review, higher court, senior court
ASSOCIATED CONCEPTS: appellate division, appellate jurisdiction, appellate term

APPELLATION, noun alias, appellative, assumed name, call, calling, characterization, cognomen, definition, denomination, description, designation, eponym, identification, label, moniker, name, namesake, nickname, nomenclature, nomination, patronym, pen name, pseudonym, sobriquet, style, surname, term, title

APPEND, verb add, *addere, adiungere,* affix, annex, attach, augment, conjoin, connect, extend, fasten, include, insert, join, subjoin, supplement

APPENDIX (Accession), **noun** accessory, additament, *adiungere,* annexation, appendage, attachment, complement, extension, inclusion, insertion, pendant

APPENDIX (Supplement), **noun** accessio, *addendum, addere,* addition, adjunct, appendage, attachment, codicil, continuation, excursus, rider
ASSOCIATED CONCEPTS: pocket part

APPERCEPTION, noun acumen, appreciation, astuteness, awareness, cognition, cognizance, conception, discernment, foresight, insight, intellect, judgment, knowledge, mentality, penetration, perception, perspicacity, psyche, realization, reason, reasoning power, recognition, sagacity, sense, understanding

APPERTAIN, verb affect, allude to, apply to, associate, be akin, be applicable, be characteristic of, be concerned with, be congruent, be connected with, be dependent upon, be incident to, be intrinsic, be part of, be pertinent, bear on, belong as a part, belong as an attribute, concern, deal with, depend upon, have reference, have relation, inhere, interest, involve, link, pertain, refer, regard, relate, touch

APPLIANCE, noun accessory, adjunct, apparatus, appurtenance, attachment, commodity, contrivance, convenience, device, equipment, facility, implement, instrument, *instrumentum,* labor-saving device, machine, means, mechanism, piece of apparatus, precision tool, tool, utensil, utility
ASSOCIATED CONCEPTS: fixtures

APPLICABILITY, noun adequacy, application, apposition, aptitude, aptness, availability, efficacy, efficiency, expediency, felicity, pertinence, practicability, propriety, qualification, regard, relativity, relevancy, serviceability, usability, usefulness, utility, utilizability

APPLICABLE, adjective à propos, acceptable, adaptable, adapted to, appertaining, appliable, appropriate, apt, befit, befitting, belonging, fit, fitting, germane, pertinent, proper, relevant, right, sortable, suitable, to the point, usable, useful, utilizable
ASSOCIATED CONCEPTS: applicable law, applicable local law

APPLICANT (Candidate), **noun** aspirant, bidder, candidate under consideration, entrant, inquirer

APPLICANT (Petitioner), **noun** claimant, moveant, party, petitioner, solicitant

APPLICATION, noun advancement, bid, motion, *petitio,* petition, presentation, proposal, proposition, request, requisition, requisition to the court, submission
ASSOCIATED CONCEPTS: application duly made, application for a change of venue, application for a discharge, application for a review, application for adjournment, application of payments, application to the court, insurance application, motion
FOREIGN PHRASES: *Contemporanea expositio est optima et fortissima in lege.* A contemporaneous construction is the best and strongest in the law.

APPLY (Pertain), **verb** affect, be applicable, be concerned with, be connected with, be pertinent, be proper to, be relevant, bear upon, belong to, concern, deal with, have

a connection to, have bearing on, have reference, have relation, involve, *pertinere ad,* refer, regard, relate, touch

APPLY (Put in practice), **verb** adapt, adjust, *admovere,* adopt, carry out, convert to use, employ, execute, exercise, exert, put in action, put in operation, put to use, use, utilize

APPLY (Request), **verb** ad hominem confugere, ask, *hominem adire,* make formal request, petition, pray, seek, solicit
ASSOCIATED CONCEPTS: motion

APPOINT, verb approve, assign, authorize, charge, charter, choose, commission, confirm, *constituere, creare,* create, delegate, depute, designate, *destinare, dicere,* direct, employ, empower, engage, enlist, entrust, establish, *facere,* give a mandate, license, name, pick, pick out, proclaim, require, sanction, select
ASSOCIATED CONCEPTS: appoint to fill a vacancy, appoint under a will, appointing officer, appointing power, appointive office, public officers

APPOINTED COUNSEL, noun appointed attorney, appointed co-counsel, appointed counsel, appointed counsel representing a party, appointed legal adversary, appointed legal counsel, appointed legal opponent, appointed legal representative, appointed litigating attorney, appointed litigating counsel, appointed litigation attorney, appointed litigation counsel, appointed litigator

APPOINTMENT (Act of designating), **noun** allocation, allotment, assignment, authorization, certification, charter, choice, decree, delegation, deputation, designation to office, dispensation, distribution, installation, naming, nomination, order, ordination, placing in office, requirement, selection
ASSOCIATED CONCEPTS: agency, delegation, limited power of appointment

APPOINTMENT (Meeting), **noun** agreement as to time and place of meeting, date, engagement, interview, rendezvous, tryst, visit

APPOINTMENT (Position), **noun** capacity, chargeship, employment, function, incumbency, job, living, occupation, office, post, profession, sphere of occupation, station, undertaking, vocation, work
ASSOCIATED CONCEPTS: agency, authority

APPORTION, verb administer, *adsignare,* allocate, allot, assign, assort, award, carve up, classify, deal out, delimit, demarcate, dispense, *dispertire,* disseminate, *distribuere,* distribute, distribute proportionately, divide, divide according to rule, divide into shares, divide proportionately, divide up, dole out, measure out, mete, mete out, parcel out, partition, place in order, portion out, portion out equitably, prorate, set in order, share, split, subdivide

APPORTIONED, adjective administered, allocated, allotted, appropriated, assigned, carved up, dealt, dispensed, distributed, divided, divvied up, doled out, measured, meted, parceled out, portioned, proportioned, pro rata, prorated, rationed, split up
ASSOCIATED CONCEPTS: apportioning assessment, apportioning compensation, apportioning damages, apportioning liability, apportioning taxes

APPORTIONMENT, noun administration, allocation, allotment, allowance, assignment, assignment in proportion, consignment, disposition, distribution, division, division in proportion, doling out, issuance, just division, measuring out, meting out, partition, partitionment, proportionment

ASSOCIATED CONCEPTS: apportionment of blame, apportionment of damages, apportionment of liability, apportionment of taxes, comparative negligence, doctrine of apportionment, *pro tanto*

APPOSITE, *adjective* accordant, *ad rem,* adapted, affiliated, affinitive, allied, applicable, applying to, appropriate, appurtenant, apropos, apt, associated, associative, bearing upon, befitting, belonging to, cognate, comparable, compatible, congeneric, congenerous, congenial, connatural, connected, consistent, consonant, correlated, correlative, correspondent, corresponding, fit, fitting, germane, in accordance with, in conjunction with, *in loco,* in relation with, pertinent, reconcilable, relating to, relative, relevant, seasonable, suitable, suited, timely, to the point, to the purpose, well-adapted, with reference to

APPOSITION, *noun* abutment, abuttal, adjacency, admissibility, affiliation, applicability, application, appropriateness, aptitude, aptness, bearing, concern, conjunction, connection, contiguity, felicity, fitness, function, interconnection, interest, junction, juxtaposition, mutual relation, nearness, pertinence, placing, propinquity, propriety, proximity, reference, regard, relation, relativeness, relativity, relevance, respect, side by side, state of suitability, union

APPRAISAL, *noun* appraisement, assessment, calculation, computation, determination, estimate, estimated value, estimation, evaluation, examination, fixing a price, measurement, quantification, reckoning, setting a price, setting the value, survey, valuation

ASSOCIATED CONCEPTS: appraisal at actual value, appraisal at estimated value, appraisal at market value, appraisal value

APPRAISE, *verb* appreciate, assess, balance, calculate, compare, conjecture, consider, diagnose, differentiate, discriminate, distinguish, estimate, evaluate, excise, fathom, gauge, judge, measure, opine, ponder, price, rank, rate, reckon, size up, sort out, sound, sum up, survey, take stock, value, weigh

ASSOCIATED CONCEPTS: appraise value of property, criminal record, misconduct

APPRECIABLE, *adjective* appraisable, ascertainable, assessable, calculable, capable of being perceived, cognizable, computable, concrete, considerable, conspicuous, countable, detectable, determinable, discernible, discoverable, distinguishable, estimable, evident, fathomable, gaugeable, knowable, manifest, material, measurable, mensurable, mensural, meterable, notable, noticeable, observable, palpable, patent, perceivable, perceptible, perspicuous, ponderable, prominent, recognizable, seeable, sizable, substantial, substantive, surveyable, tangible, visible, weighable

ASSOCIATED CONCEPTS: appreciable damages, appreciable losses

APPRECIATE *(Comprehend),* *verb* acknowledge, apprehend, be aware of, be cognizant of, be conscious of, conceive, discern, know, notice, perceive, realize, recognize, take into consideration, take notice, understand

ASSOCIATED CONCEPTS: appreciate a risk, appreciate the danger

APPRECIATE *(Increase),* *verb* advance, become greater, become more numerous, become of greater value, enhance the degree of, gain in worth, grow in value, improve, increase the market price of, make of greater value, rise, rise in value

ASSOCIATED CONCEPTS: appreciate in value

APPRECIATE *(Value),* *verb* adequately perceive, *aestimare,* esteem, perceive the worth of, realize the worth of, recognize the worth of

APPRECIATION *(Increased value),* *noun* accrual, accruement, accumulation, added monetary worth, addition, advance in worth, gain, gain in worth, growth, growth in value, increase, increased price, increment, realization, rise, rise in value

APPRECIATION *(Perception),* *noun* apperception, appraisal, appraisment, assessment, awareness, clear perception, cognition, cognizance, comprehension, consciousness, correct valuation, discernment, estimation, full appraisal, just estimation, measurement, recognition, valuation

APPREHEND *(Arrest),* *verb* capture, catch, commit, *comprehendere,* confine, constrain, detain, detain by legal process, fetter, hold, legally restrain, place under arrest, put in restraint, put under arrest, restrain, seize, send to prison, take, take by authority, take captive, take into custody, take prisoner

APPREHEND *(Perceive),* *verb* appreciate, be acquainted with, be apprized of, be aware of, be cognizant of, be conscious of, be under the impression, become aware of, cognize, come to know, comprehend, *comprehendere,* conceive of, detect, discern, discover by observation, fathom, have an impression, have an understanding of, have cognizance of, have knowledge of, ken, know entirely, know of, know well, learn, master, realize, recognize, regard as, see, sense, surmise, understand, view

APPREHENSIBLE, *adjective* accountable, cognizable, coherent, comprehensible, conceivable, discoverable, explicable, fathomable, intelligible, knowable, penetrable, perceivable, perceptive, realizable, recognizable, scrutable, understandable, unmistakable

APPREHENSION *(Act of arresting),* *noun* arrest, caption, capture, catch, confinement, detention, holding in custody, imprisonment, incarceration, internment, restraint, retention, seizure, taking, taking hold

APPREHENSION *(Fear),* *noun* agitation, alarm, anticipation of adversity, anxiety, apprehensiveness, care, concern, consternation, distrust, foreboding, misdoubt, misgiving, mistrust, overanxiety, perturbation, phobia, presentiment, qualm, sense of danger, suspicion, threat, trepidation, uneasiness, worry

APPREHENSION *(Perception),* *noun* cognition, cognizance, comprehension, conception, discernment, grasp, idea, image, impression, intellection, judgment, knowledge, mastery, mental capacity, notion, observation, opinion, recognition, reflection, sense, thought, understanding, view

APPREHENSIVE, *adjective* afraid, agitated, alarmed, anticipative of evil, anxious, aware, bothered, cognizant, concerned, conscious, disquieted, distrustful, expectant, fearful, hesitant, leery, mindful, mistrustful, nervous, perceptive, pusillanimous, qualmish, qualmy, sagacious, shrewd, solicitous, suspicious, terrified, timid, tremulous, troubled, uneasy, vigilant, wise, worried

APPRENTICE, *noun* beginner, learner, novice, novitiate, probationer, worker

APPRISE, *verb* acquaint, advise, alert, announce, brief, communicate, convey knowledge, counsel, describe, disclose, divulge, enlighten, familiarize, give information, give notice, impart knowledge, inform, instruct, let know, make aware, make cognizant, make known, notify, orient, point out, publish, report, reveal, tell, warn
ASSOCIATED CONCEPTS: apprise of the facts

APPROACH, *verb* *accedere,* accost, advance, *adventare, appropinquare,* be in proximity, be in sight of, be in the neighborhood of, be in the vicinity of, be near, come forward, come near, confront, converge upon, draw near, edge close to, get near, go near, move near, move toward, pursue, stalk, step up to, verge on

APPROACHES, *noun* accesses, avenues, channels, entrances, entranceways, entryways, gates, highways, ingresses, inlets, intakes, means of access, passages, routes, ways

APPROBATE, *verb* accept, accredit, acquiesce, admire, adopt, advocate, agree with, applaud, approve, assent, authorize, back, commend, concur, confirm, consent, countenance, endorse, esteem, favor, laud, license, pass, praise, prize, ratify, recognize, recommend, salute, sanction, support, validate, value

APPROBATION, *noun* acceptance, acclamation, acquiescence, admiration, adoption, advocacy, agreement, applause, appreciation, approval, assent, attestation, commendation, compliment, concurrence, congratulation, consent, countenance, encomium, encouragement, endorsement, esteem, eulogy, honor, laudation, leave, license, mention, permit, praise, ratification, recognition, recommendation, regard, respect, sanction, satisfaction, support

APPROPRIATE, *adjective* *accommodatus,* accordant, accurate, adapted to, admissible, applicable, apposite, apropos, apt, aptus, befitting, concordant, condign, conformable, *congruens,* congruous, consistent, consonant, correct, correspondent, exact, expedient, fine, fit, fitting, germane, good, harmonious, likely, meet, opportune, pertinent, practicable, precise, proper, relevant, right, rightful, seemly, suitable, suited, timely, well-suited
ASSOCIATED CONCEPTS: appropriate bargaining unit, appropriate cause of action, appropriate remedy

APPROPRIATE, *verb* acquire, adopt, annex, arrogate, assume, assume ownership, borrow, capture, claim, possess, take, take over

APPROPRIATION (Allotment), ***noun*** allocation, allowance, apportionment, budget, budgeting, concession, designation of use, dispensation, distribution, setting apart
ASSOCIATED CONCEPTS: appropriation bill, appropriation for public use, appropriation of money, budgetary appropriation

APPROPRIATION (Donation), ***noun*** benefaction, bestowal, contribution, disbursement, endowment, funding, gift, grant, guerdon, meed, sponsorship

APPROPRIATION (Taking), ***noun*** accroachment, acquisition, adoption, annexation, apprehension, assumption, capture, confiscation, conversion, dispossession, disseisin, divestment, expropriation, impoundment, impropriation, seizure, snatching, taking possession

ASSOCIATED CONCEPTS: appropriation from revenues, appropriation of land, appropriation of payment

APPROVAL, *noun* acceptance, accord, acknowledgment, acquiescence, adoption, affirmance, affirmation, agreement, allowance, *approbatio,* approbation, assent, assurance, authentication, authorization, *comprobatio,* concordance, concurrence, confirmation, consent, countenance, encouragement, endorsement, expression of satisfaction, favor, license, nod of approbation, permit, ratification, recognition, sanction, support, toleration, validation, verification
ASSOCIATED CONCEPTS: acceptance by a bank, approved endorsed note, sale on approval
FOREIGN PHRASES: *Qui non improbat, approbat.* He who does not disapprove, approves. ***Quod approbo non reprobo.*** That which I approve I do not later reject.

APPROVE, *verb* accede to, accept, acquiesce in, adopt, advocate, affirm, agree to, allow, *approbare,* approbate, assent to, authenticate, authorize, be in favor of, be satisfied with, certify, *comprobare,* concur in, confirm, consent to, countenance, endorse, favor, make valid, *probare,* ratify, sanction, second, support, sustain, uphold, validate

APPROVED (Agreed), ***adjective*** acknowledged, admitted, allowable, allowed, arranged, completed, contracted for, decided, eligible, formal, meritorious, permissible, settled, stipulated

APPROVED (Authoritative), ***adjective*** accepted, accredited, authentic, authoritative, conceded, conventional, established, fixed, granted, legal, official, prescriptive, proper, right, standard, unimpeachable, warranted
ASSOCIATED CONCEPTS: approve a claim, approve a public contract, approve a stipulation, approve a transcript, approved adoption, approved the findings of the court, settle on order

APPROXIMATE, *adjective* alike, almost, approaching, close, comparable, estimated, imprecise, in the vicinity of, inexact, like, much the same, nearly accurate, nearly correct, nearly equal, nearly perfect, nearly resembling, nigh, not perfectly accurate, *propinquus,* proximal, proximate, similar, surmised, uncertain, unprecise
ASSOCIATED CONCEPTS: approximate value

APPROXIMATE, *verb* *accedere ad,* advance near to, approach, approach closely, approach in amount, be in the vicinity of, be near, border on, closely resemble, come close in estimation, come close to, come near, come near in position, compare with, draw near, nearly equal, nearly rival, resemble

APPROXIMATION, *noun* approach, calculation, computation, contiguity, correspondence, estimate, estimation, inexactitude, inexactness, interpolation, likeness, measure, nearness, neighborhood, parity, propinquity, proximity, reckoning, resemblance, rough closeness, rough equivalent, sameness, semblance, similitude, tally, unpreciseness, vicinity

APPURTENANCE, *noun* accession, accessory, accompaniment, addendum, additament, addition, adjunct, annex, annexation, *annexe,* appanage, appendage, appendant, appendix, attachment, auxiliary, concomitant, dependency, extension, incidental, pendant, something added, subsidiary, supplement

ASSOCIATED CONCEPTS: accession, appurtenance to realty, appurtenant right, conveyance of property, covenants, deeds of conveyance, easement appurtenant, easements, fixture

APPURTENANT, *adjective* accessory, adjunct, ancillary, annexed, appended, appertaining, attached, auxiliary, belonging, connected, dependent on, incident, necessarily connected, subsidiary, used with another thing
ASSOCIATED CONCEPTS: appurtenant passage of air, appurtenant passage of light, appurtenant to land, appurtenant watercourse, *causa rei,* dominant land, servient land

APROPOS, *adjective* akin, applicable, apposite, appropriate, apt, belonging, concerning, connected, felicitous, fit, germane, linked, pertaining to, pertinent, related, relevant, suitable

APT *(Appropriate),* ***adjective*** applicable, apposite, appropriate, apropos, artful, comely, concordant, congruous, consonant, correct, deft, expedient, expert, felicitous, fit, germane, given to, harmonious, inclined, liable, likely, opportune, pertinent, practiced, presumable, probable, prone, proper, qualified, quick, ready, relative, relevant, resourceful, right, seemly, subject to, subtle, suitable, timely, verisimilar, viable, well chosen

APT *(Gifted),* ***adjective*** able, accomplished, adroit, alert, bright, clever, competent, dexterous, expert, fitted, gifted, handy, proficient, sharp, skillful, smart

APTITUDE, *noun* ability, applicability, bent, endowment, faculty, fitness, flair, gift, inclination, innate ability, intelligence, learning, propensity, propriety, suitability, talent, tendency

ARBITER, *noun* adjudicator, advisor, *arbiter,* arbitrator, determiner, *disceptator,* final authority, interagent, interceder, intercessor, intermediary, intermediate, intermediator, intervener, mediator, moderator, negotiant, negotiator, prescriber, recommender, reconciler, referee
ASSOCIATED CONCEPTS: arbitrament, final arbiter

ARBITRARY, *adjective* according to desires, capricious, contrary to reason, determined by no principle, done at pleasure, fanciful, illogical, independent of law, independent of rule, *infinitus,* injudicious, irrational, *libidinosus,* nonrational, perverse, unaccountable, unjustified, unreasonable, unreasoned, without adequate determining principle, without consideration, without reason, without substantial cause
ASSOCIATED CONCEPTS: arbitrary act, arbitrary action, arbitrary and capricious, arbitrary classification, arbitrary determination, arbitrary standards, arbitrary verdict

ARBITRARY AND CAPRICIOUS, *adjective* absolute, authoritative, baseless, dictatorial, dogmatic, fanciful, groundless, impetuous, motiveless, purposeless, restrictive, unduly, whimsical, willful

ARBITRATE *(Adjudge),* ***verb*** adjudicate, arrange, arrive at a conclusion, ascertain after reasoning, assess, conciliate, decide, decide between opposing parties, decree, decree authoritatively, determine, determine a controversy, determine a point at issue, *dijudicare,* end by a decision, fix conclusively, give judgment, judge, judicate, lead to a decision, make a decision, mete out, order, pass judgment, pronounce formally, pronounce judgment, resolve, rule, settle, settle by authoritative decision, sit in judgment
ASSOCIATED CONCEPTS: mediate

ARBITRATE *(Conciliate),* ***verb*** accord, adjust differences, arrange, bring into agreement, bring into harmony, bring to terms, bring together, *disceptare,* harmonize, intercede, intervene, make compatible, make peace between, moderate, negotiate, prevail with, propitiate, put in accord, reconcile, referee, regulate, render compatible, render concordant, render no longer opposed, restore harmony, settle, settle differences

ARBITRATION, *noun* adjudgment, adjustment, apportionment, appraisal, arbitrage, *arbitrium,* assessment, conciliation, decision, decree, determining of a controversy, finding, intercession, interjacence, intermediation, interposition, intervention, judgment, *rapprochement,* resolution, settlement
ASSOCIATED CONCEPTS: advisory arbitration, arbitrability, arbitration agreement, arbitration and award, arbitration award, arbitration clause, arbitration provision, arbitrators, binding arbitration, compulsory arbitration, grievance arbitration, interest arbitration, proceeding to confirm arbitration award, voluntary arbitration

ARBITRATOR, *noun* adjudicator, arbiter, determiner, *disceptator,* interagent, interceder, intercessor, intermediary, intermediate, intervenor, interventionist, judicator, moderator, negotiant, negotiator, reconciler, referee, referendary, ruler
ASSOCIATED CONCEPTS: arbitration and award, arbitrator's authority, arbitrator's award, board of arbitrators, scope of arbitrator's authority

ARCANE, *adjective* esoteric, incomprehensible, inexplicable, inscrutable, mysterious, recondite, unaccountable, unfathomable, unintelligible, unrecognizable

ARCHAIC, *adjective* ancient, antediluvian, antiquated, extinct, fossilized, medieval, obsolescent, obsolete, old, old-fashioned, old-world, outdated, outmoded, passé, prehistoric, primitive, superannuated, time-worn

ARCHITECT, *noun* *architectus,* artificer, author, begetter, builder, composer, constructor, contriver, creator, designer, deviser, draftsman, enterpriser, founder, framer, generator, introducer, inventor, maker, organizer, originator, planner, prime mover, projector, schemer

ARDENT, *adjective* active, ambitious, animated, aspiring, assiduous, burning, devoted, eager, earnest, enthusiastic, excitable, excited, fanatical, fervent, fervid, feverish, fierce, fiery, glowing, hearty, heated, high-spirited, impassioned, impatient, impetuous, industrious, inflamed, intense, intensive, intent, keen, passionate, ready, sedulous, serious, sincere, spirited, true, vehement, zealous

ARDOR, *noun* ardency, *ardor,* drive, eagerness, effusiveness, *élan,* emotion, energy, enthusiasm, excitation of feelings, excitement, exhilaration, fanaticism, fervency, fervidness, fervor, feverishness, fire, force, forcefulness, furor, impassionedness, intense desire, liveliness, magniloquence, passion, passionateness, perfervor, spirit, state of excitability, *studium,* verve, vigor, vigorousness, vitality, vivacity, warmth of feeling, zeal

ARDUOUS, *adjective* backbreaking, burdensome, difficult, exhausting, fatiguing, formidable, grueling, hard, hard-earned, hard-fought, intricate, irksome, laborious, lofty, onerous, operose, oppressive, painful, precipitous, punishing, rugged, severe, strenuous, tiresome, toilsome, tough, troublesome, trying, wearisome

AREA (Province), **noun**   area, arena, bounds, confines, demesne, domain, expanse, field, jurisdiction, limits, location, orbit, place, premises, purview, range, realm, region, scope, sphere, territory, vicinage, vicinity, zone
ASSOCIATED CONCEPTS: area variance, specific areas of the law

AREA (Surface), **noun**   amount of surface, dimensions, expanse, expansion, extent of surface, measured size, measurements, plane surface, proportions, real size, *superficies,* true dimensions

ARGUABLE, adjective   at issue, contestable, controversial, controvertible, debatable, disputable, in dispute, in question, up for discussion
ASSOCIATED CONCEPTS: arguable claim, arguable contention

ARGUE, verb   advance, affirm, allege, *argumentari,* assert, challenge, claim, confute, *conligere,* contend, contend in argument, contest, controvert, *de re disserere,* debate, disagree, dispute, elucidate, emphasize, enunciate, establish, explain, expostulate, express, maintain, make an assertion, oppose, present reasons against, present reasons for, proclaim, pronounce, propose, propound, put forth, reason upon, remonstrate, set forth, show, state with conviction, stress, submit, urge
ASSOCIATED CONCEPTS: *a posteriori, a priori, ab inconvenienti, ad hominem, arguendo*

ARGUENDO, adverb   for mere discussion only, for the sake of argument, hypothetically

ARGUMENT (Contention), **noun**   altercation, antagonism, belligerency, bickering, breach, clashing, conflict, contentiousness, controversy, cross-purposes, debate, difference of opinion, disaccord, disagreement, discord, disputatio, disputation, dispute, dissension, dissent, dissidence, disunion, disunity, division, divisiveness, feud, hard feelings, hostility, ill feeling, ill will, lack of concord, misunderstanding, opposition, oral contention, polemics, quarrel, quarreling, strife, variance, verbal conflict, war of words, wrangle, wrangling
ASSOCIATED CONCEPTS: *a posteriori, a priori, apex juris*
FOREIGN PHRASES: *In rebus manifestis, errat qui auctoritates legum allegat; quia perspicua vera non sunt probanda.* In clear cases, he errs who cites legal authorities because obvious truths are manifest and do not have to be proved. *Argumentum ab inconvenienti est validum in lege; quia lex non permittit aliquod inconveniens.* An argument drawn from what is inconvenient is good in law, because the law will not permit any inconvenience.

ARGUMENT (Pleading), **noun**   argument at the bar, counterstatement, course of reasoning, defense, demonstration, discourse designed to convince, disputation, expression of opinion for or against, plea, pleading, rationale, rebuttal, refutation, statement of defense, statement offered in proof, statement tending to prove a point, submission
ASSOCIATED CONCEPTS: argument submitted to the court, closing argument, equittable argument, legal argument, opening argument, oral argument, preargument statement
FOREIGN PHRASES: *In rebus manifestis, errat qui auctoritates legum allegat; quia perspicua vera non sunt probanda.* In clear cases, he errs who cites legal authorities because obvious truths are manifest and do not have to be proved.

ARGUMENTATION, noun   analysis, argument, bickering, conflict, contention, contentiousness, controversy, critical examination, dialectic, dialogue, disaccord, disagreement, disceptation, discord, disputation, dispute, dissension, logical synthesis, pattern of reasoning, polemics, quarrelsomeness, ratiocination, wrangling
ASSOCIATED CONCEPTS: instructions to the jury, reargument, rebuttal, summation, surrebuttal

ARGUMENTATIVE, adjective   belligerent, characterized by argument, combative, contentious, dialectical, discordant, disputatious, dissentient, eristic, eristical, factious, given to controversy, litigious, logomachic, logomachical, petulant, pilpulistic, polemic, polemical, pugnacious, quarrelsome
ASSOCIATED CONCEPTS: argumentative denial

ARISE (Appear), **verb**   become manifest, become noticeable, become visible, come forth, come in sight, come in view, come to light, come to notice, emerge, make an appearance, manifest itself, present itself, reveal itself, show itself
ASSOCIATED CONCEPTS: arise under an obligation, arise under the laws of the United States, arising out of a contract, arising out of and in the course of employment, arising out of employment, arising under federal law, arising under the Constitution, arising upon contract, cause of action arising, counterclaim arising out of the plaintiff's claim

ARISE (Occur), **verb**   become operative, come about, come to pass, eventuate, get under way, happen, proceed, take place, transpire

ARISE (Originate), **verb**   accrue, be born, be derived, become, begin, come from, come into action, come into being, come into existence, come to be, emanate, ensue, eventuate, evolve, flow, follow, grow out of, have origin, initiate, issue forth, proceed from, spring forth, spring up, start, start out, take birth, take origin

ARMED, adjective   *armatus,* bristling with arms, equipped with arms, fortified, furnished with weapons, in arms, issued weapons, panoplied, provided with arms, supplied with arms, under arms, well-armed
ASSOCIATED CONCEPTS: armed burglary, armed felony, armed forces, armed guards
FOREIGN PHRASES: *Arma in armatos sumere jura sinunt.* The laws permit the taking up of arms against armed persons. *Ligna et lapides sub "armorum" appellatione non continentur.* Sticks and stones are not included within the definition of "arms."

ARRAIGN, verb   *accusare,* accuse, accuse of wrong, blame, brand, brand with reproach, bring accusation, bring before a court, bring to trial, bring up for investigation, bring up on charges, call before a court, call to account, charge, *citare,* cite, complain against, criminate, denounce, denunciate, formally accuse, formally charge, formally criminate, formally incriminate, implicate, incriminate, inculpate, *postulare,* prefer charges, prosecute

ARRAIGNMENT, noun   accusation, accusation in court, allegation of criminal wrongdoing, crimination through law enforcement, delation by criminal charges, formal accusal, imputation from criminal proceeding, incrimination, inculpation by prosecution, judicial charge, prosecution
ASSOCIATED CONCEPTS: arrest, bail, felony hearing, indictment

ARRANGE *(Methodize),* **verb** adapt, adjust, allocate, apportion, bring into order, bring to terms, collocate, come to an agreement, come to terms, *componere, constituere,* coordinate, determine, devise, *digerere,* direct, fix, fix the order, group, manage, marshal, order, *ordinare,* organize, place in order, program, put in readiness, reduce to order, regulate, resolve, schematize, set in order, settle, size, space, straighten out, systematize

ARRANGE *(Plan),* **verb** blueprint, calculate, contrive, design, devise, engineer, formulate, frame, make arrangements, make preparations, mark out a course, prepare, program, project, schedule, shape a course, sketch out

ARRANGED *(Agreed),* **adjective** aligned, assorted, classified, contractual, cut and dried, definite, disposed, fixed, formal, graded, grouped, marshaled, orderly, organizational, placed, precise, ranked, regular, settled, stated, systematic, uniform

ARRANGED *(Planned),* **adjective** contrived, designed, devised, established, harmonious, organized, plotted, projected, prospective, schematic, set, ready

ARRANGEMENT *(Ordering),* **noun** adaption, arraying, collocation, *compositio,* composition, conformation, *conlocatio,* formation, method, regularity, schematism, symmetry, systematization, uniformity

ARRANGEMENT *(Plan),* **noun** conception, concoction, contrivance, course of action, ground plan, layout, master plan, method, outline, program of action, schema, scheme, system
ASSOCIATED CONCEPTS: arrangement for the benefit of creditors

ARRANGEMENT *(Understanding),* **noun** abatement of differences, accommodation, accord, accordance, adjustment, adjustment by agreement, agreement, compact, compromise, concord, contract, entente, harmonization, mutual agreement, mutual assent, mutual promise, mutual undertaking, pact, proviso, reconciliation, restoration of harmony, settlement, terms
ASSOCIATED CONCEPTS: arrangement through a marital settlement

ARRANT, **adjective** abominable, atrocious, bad, base, blameworthy, contemptible, crass, damnable, despicable, disgraceful, disreputable, egregious, evil, execrable, flagitious, flagrant, foul, heinous, ignominious, immoral, infamous, lawless, low, mean, monstrous, nefarious, notorious, obnoxious, odious, outrageous, peccant, scandalous, shameful, shameless, shocking, sinful, sinister, unmitigated, unscrupulous, vicious, vile, wicked, wrong

ARRANT *(Definite),* **adjective** clear, complete, confirmed, conspicuous, consummate, identifiable, obvious, palpable, plain, recognizable, salient, striking, through, uncontestable, unmistakable, utter

ARRAY *(Jury),* **noun** body of jurors, good men and true, jurors, jurymen, panel, trier, trier of the facts
ASSOCIATED CONCEPTS: challenge to the array, jury panel, venire

ARRAY *(Order),* **noun** arrangement, assemblage, classification, collocation, composition, comprehensiveness, course, design, display, disposition, disposure, distribution, due order, fixed order, formation, gamut, good order, gradation, layout, logical order, marshaling, method, methodicalness, methodology, multiplicity, multitude, ordering, organization, parade, pattern, perspective, placing, progression, range of choices, range of view, regularity, rule, schematic arrangement, scope, sequence, series, show, sight, state of order, strict order, subordination, system, systematization, unbroken order, uniformity

ARRAY, **verb** accouter, arrange, attire, deploy, display, dispose, draw up, enhance, enrich, file, fix, group, marshal, orchestrate, order, rank, sequence, set in order, sort

ARREARS, **noun** arrearage, back payments, balance due, debit, debt, debt unpaid though due, default, deferred payment, deficit, delinquency, indebtedness, indebtment, liability, obligation, outstanding debt, overdue bill, overdue payment, payments past due, *pecuniae residuae,* state of indebtedness, unpaid bill, unpaid debt
ASSOCIATED CONCEPTS: arrears in taxes, arrears of alimony, arrears of assessment, arrears of dues, arrears of interest, arrears of premiums, arrears of rent, arrears of taxes, judgment on arrears

ARREST, **noun** apprehension, capture, confinement, custodial detention, imprisonment, incarceration, internment, prehension, restraint, restriction, retention, seizure
ASSOCIATED CONCEPTS: extradition, rendition

ARREST *(Apprehend),* **verb** arrêt, capture, cast into prison, catch, commit, commit to an institution, commit to prison, *comprehendere,* confine, constrain, *deprehendere,* deprive of liberty, detain, detain by criminal process, entrammel, give in custody, hold, immure, imprison, *in custodiam dare,* incarcerate, intern, jail, lay under restraint, legally restrain, make captive, make prisoner, place in confinement, put in durance, put in duress, put under restraint, restrain, secure, seize, seize by legal warrant, send to jail, shackle, take by authority, take captive, take charge of, take into custody, take into preventive custody, take into protective custody, take prisoner, throw into prison
ASSOCIATED CONCEPTS: arrest warrant, false arrest, false imprisonment, illegal arrest, prior arrest, probable cause, resisting arrest, search incident to an arrest, warrant of arrest

ARREST *(Stop),* **verb** avert, block, bring to a standstill, bring to a stop, check, countercheck, curb, curtail, delay, detain, deter, end, enjoin, foil, foreclose, forestall, frustrate, hinder, hold, hold back, impede, inhibit, interfere, interrupt, keep back, obstruct, prevent, quell, repel, restrain, stall, stay, stifle, subdue, suppress, suspend, thwart, withhold
ASSOCIATED CONCEPTS: arrest of inquest, arrest of judgment

ARRESTED *(Apprehended),* **adjective** captured, caught, collared, committed, confined, constrained, detained, held, held in custody, immurred, imprisoned, incarcerated, interned, jailed, kept in custody, legally restrained, made captive, made prisoner, remanded, remanded into custody, restrained, seized, sent to prison, taken by force by the authorities, taken into custody, taken prisoner, under arrest
ASSOCIATED CONCEPTS: arrest warrant, body execution, civil arrest, detention and custody, false arrest, false imprisonment, habeas corpus, imprisonment, malicious prosecution, probable cause to arrest, resisting arrest, restraint of liberty, search incident to an arrest, unlawful arrest

ARRESTED *(Checked),* **adjective** adjourned, blocked, bridled, circumscribed, contained, controlled, curbed, deferred, delayed, deterred, discouraged, encumbered, governed, hampered, held back, hindered, impeded, inhibited, interrupted, limited, obstructed, postponed, prescribed, prevented, repressed, restrained, restricted, retarded, slowed down, stayed, stopped, suppressed, suspended, withheld

ARRIVE, verb accomplish, achieve, advance, alight, appear, approach, attain, befall, betide, come to, consummate, culminate, emerge, enter, eventuate, gain, get to, happen, join, land, make good, occur, reach, show up, supervene, turn up, visit

ARROGATE, verb accroach, adopt, annex, appropriate, ascribe falsely, assume, assume command, attach, collect, commandeer, convert, demand, deprive, expropriate, harass, hijack, impress, infringe, invade, preempt, preoccupy, prepossess, seize, sequester, stake a claim, take, take charge, take command, take over, take possession, usurp, wrest

ARROGATION, noun accession, adoption, application, appropriation, ascription, assignation, assignment, assumption, attachment, attribution, impropriation, placement, requisition, seizure, taking, usurpation

ARSENAL, noun accumulation, agglomeration, ammassment, conglomeration, depository, garnering, repository, reservoir, storage, treasury

ARSON, noun criminal setting of fires, deliberate burning of property, destruction of property by fire, fire-raising, firing, incendiarism, malicious burning of property, pyromania, set conflagration, willful burning of property

ARTFUL, adjective able, acute, adept, adroit, apt, artistic, astute, astutus, aware, calculating, callidus, canny, capable, characterized by art, clever, contriving, crafty, cunning, deft, devious, dexterous, done with skill, experienced, facile, gifted, imaginative, ingenious, intriguing, knavish, Machiavellian, masterly, plotting, proficient, quick, rascally, ready, resourceful, scheming, serpentine, sharp, sharp-witted, shrewd, skillful, sly, stealthy, subtle, talented, versatile, versutus, vulpine, well-planned, wily

ARTICLE (Commodity), noun effect, item, lifeless object, material, material object, matter, object, particular object, res, subject, substance, thing

ARTICLE (Distinct section of a writing), noun chapter, clause, contractual clause, division, item, portion, provision, proviso, res, section, subject, term of reference
ASSOCIATED CONCEPTS: article in a statute, paragraph of a statute, subdivision of a statute

ARTICLE (Precept), noun canon, caput, condicio, dictated term, dogma, mandate, maxim, principle, requirement, rubric, set of terms, tenet
ASSOCIATED CONCEPTS: articles of incorporation

ARTICULATE, verb avow, clarify, communicate, converse, convey, enunciate, express, observe, phrase, pronounce, recite, recount, remark, speak, utter

ARTIFICE, noun artful contrivance, artfulness, artificiality, beguilement, charlatanry, cheating, chicanery, circumvention, cleverness, concealment, connivance, contrivance, cover, cozenage, craftiness, crafty device,

cunning, cunningness, deceit, deception, delusion, design, device, disguise, distortion, dodgery, duplicity, espieglerie, evasion, expediency, fabrication, false claim, false pretensions, falsification, feint, finesse, forgery, fraudulence, guile, hoax, illusion, impersonation, imposture, ingenuity, insidiousness, insubstantiality, intrigue, jobbery, knavery, Machiavellianism, machination, maneuvering, mendacity, misrepresentation, perfidy, pettifoggery, ploy, pretense, pretension, pretext, rascality, ruse, scheme, sham, sharp practice, slyness, snare, stratagem, subterfuge, tactics, trap, trick, trickery, wile, wiliness, wrinkle

ARTIFICIAL, adjective adulterine, artificiosus, assumed, casuistic, concocted, counterfeited, deceptive, ersatz, faked, false, feigned, fictitious, forged, illusory, imaginary, imagined, imitation, imitative, man-made, not natural, pretended, simulated, simulative, spurious, superficial, unauthentic, ungenuine, unnatural, unreal
ASSOCIATED CONCEPTS: artificial boundaries, artificial ingredients, artificial monuments, artificial person, artificial pond, artificial presumption, artificial watercourse

ARTISAN, noun artifex, artificer, craftsman, craftworker, faber, handicraftsman, journeyman, laborer, machiner, master craftsman, master workman, mechanic, mechanician, one engaged in a manual enterprise, one skilled in an industrial art, one trained in a mechanic trade, operator, opifex, skilled laborer, skilled worker, technician, tradesman, worker, workingman, workingwoman, workman, workwoman
ASSOCIATED CONCEPTS: artisan lien

AS A CONSEQUENCE, adverb a priori, accordingly, as a result, as matters stand, because, because of this, by reason of, by the same token, consequently, deductibly, derivatively, doubtlessly, for reasons given, for that reason, hence, in conclusion, in consequence, in that case, in that event, in which case, inferentially, necessarily, on account of, to that end

AS A MATTER OF RIGHT, adverb be entitled to, by right, correctly, duly, fitting, properly, rightfully, with authority

AS A RULE, adverb as a matter of course, by and large, chiefly, commonly, customarily, for the most part, generally, generally speaking, in general, in most cases, in the main, in the usual course of things, mainly, most frequently, most often, mostly, normally, on the whole, ordinarily, principally, regularly, substantially, to all intents and purposes, usually

AS AGREED UPON, adverb according to contract, according to the agreement, according to the bargain, according to the contract, as agreed to, as arranged by the agreement, as contracted for, as negotiated for, as pledged, as promised, as settled upon, consistent with the agreement, corresponding to the contract, in accordance with the contract, in correspondence with the contract, in obedience to the agreement

AS IS, adjective as it is, as it stands, as offered, as presented, as represented, as seen, as shown, as things are, in its present condition, in its present form, in its present state, in the same way, just the same, without warranty
ASSOCIATED CONCEPTS: as is contract, caveat emptor, without covenants or warranties

AS PROVIDED BY LAW, *adverb* as contained in the statutes, as set forth by law, as specified in the law, as delineated in the law

AS SO DEFINED, *adverb* as contained, as delineated, as explained, as set forth, as specified

AS SOON AS FEASIBLE, *adverb* as soon as possible, as soon as reasonably possible, at the first opportunity, at the first possible moment, expeditiously, forthwith, promptly, without delay

ASCENDANCE, *noun* authority, command, dominance, domination, dominion, hegemony, predominance, preponderance, prevalence, primacy, sovereignty, superiority, supremacy, upper hand

ASCENDANT, *noun* ancestor, antecedent, forebear, forefather, forerunner, genitor, *praestare,* precursor, predecessor, procreator, progenitor, sire, *summus, superior*

ASCERTAIN, *verb* acquire information, acquire intelligence about, adjudge, arrive at a conclusion, assure oneself, become acquainted with, certify, clear from obscurity, clear of doubt, clear of obscurity, *cognoscere,* come to a conclusion, come to know, *comperire,* conclude, confirm, decide, decipher, deduce, derive, descry, determine, discover, disentangle, draw a conclusion, establish, establish with certainty, *explorare,* fathom, ferret out, figure out, find, find out, find out exactly, find the answer, find the solution, learn about, make certain, make oneself acquainted with, make sure, prove, ravel, reassure oneself, remove doubt, render certain, render definite, resolve, satisfy oneself, solve, unearth, unravel, unriddle, unscramble, untangle, verify
ASSOCIATED CONCEPTS: ascertain loss, ascertained by law

ASCERTAINABLE, *adjective* answerable, certifiable, cognizable, comprehensible, confirmable, decipherable, definable, demonstrable, determinable, discernible, discoverable, distinguishable, evincible, explainable, fixable, knowable, learnable, perceptible, recognizable, understandable, verifiable
ASSOCIATED CONCEPTS: ascertainable consequences, ascertainable damages, ascertainable debt, ascertainable loss

ASCERTAINED, *adjective* absolute, actual, authoritative, axiomatic, certain, clear, cogent, cognizable, common, conclusive, definite, definitive, evident, factual, genuine, incontrovertible, indisputable, indubious, irrefutable, positive, real, reliable, sound, stated, sure, true, trustworthy, unambiguous, unconfuted, undeniable, undoubting, unequivocal, unerring, unmistakable, unqualified, unquestionable, unquestioned

ASCRIBE, *verb* accord, accredit, *adsignare,* affiliate, allege to belong, apply, appropriate, *ascribere,* assign, attach, *attribuere,* attribute, charge with, connect with, credit with, derive from, filiate, give, impute, point to, predicate, refer to, trace to
ASSOCIATED CONCEPTS: ascribe a motive

ASCRIPTION, *noun* accusal, accusation, alleging, animadversion, appropriation, aspersion, assignment, attribution, blame, citation, complaint, charge, derivation, imputation, innuendo, insinuation, obloquy, reference, reflection, reproach, slur, stigmatization, stricture

ASPECT, *noun* appearance, *aspectus,* condition, element, facet, factor, feature, *forma,* look, mien, part, peculiar feature, perspective, phase, position, posture, regard, relative position, salient characteristic, situation, slant, *spectare,* state, view, viewpoint, visage, vista

ASPECTS, *noun* attributes, character, characteristics, color, difference, features, individual qualities, nature, particularities, parts, peculiarities, perspectives, properties, qualities, segments, traits, unique qualities

ASPERSION, *noun* abuse, affront, *calumnia,* calumniation, calumny, censure, condemnation, contumely, defamation, denigration, denunciation, derision, derogatory criticism, detraction, dishonor, disparagement, envenomed tongue, execration, imputation, insult, invective, libel, malediction, objurgation, obloquy, *opprobrium,* railing, rebuke, reproach, reproof, reviling, scurrility, slander, slight, slur, stricture, traducement, vilification, vituperation

ASPORTATION, *noun* criminal ablation, criminal remotion, criminal removement, criminal transmission, delocalization, felonious abreption, felonious removal, felonious transference, felonious translocation, furtive removal, illegal amotion, illegal carriage, illegal subduction, illegal transmittance, illegal transplantation, illegal transshipment, wrongful displacement, wrongful removal, wrongful transfer
ASSOCIATED CONCEPTS: burglary, conversion and trover, larceny, robbery

ASSAIL, *verb* accost, *adgredi, adoriri,* advance against, advance upon, aggress, assault, assault belligerently, attack, beset, encounter, fall upon, invade, mug, oppugn, *oppugnare,* rush upon, savage, set upon, set upon with violence, storm, thrust at, waylay
ASSOCIATED CONCEPTS: assailant

ASSAILABLE, *adjective* accessible, attacked, beatable, censurable, conquerable, criticized, defenseless, exposed, impugnable, indefensible, open to attack, penetrable, pregnable, ridiculed, scorned, sensible, surmountable, vincible, vulnerable, weak

ASSAILANT, *noun* accoster, aggressor, antagonist, assailer, assaulter, attacker, bludgeon man, criminal, felon, invader, obstructionist, *qui oppugnat,* ravager, terrorist, thug, violator

ASSASSINATION, *noun* annihilation, *caedes,* destruction, dispatching, execution, homicide, killing, liquidation, murder, murder by stealth, slaying, treacherous killing, unlawful homicide
ASSOCIATED CONCEPTS: *aestimatio capitis,* conspiracy, murder, political assassination

ASSAULT, *noun* act of hostility, aggression, aggressive action, assailment, attack, besiegement, encounter, *impetus,* incursion, *incursus,* injury, intrusion, irruption, offense, onset, onset with force, onslaught, *oppugnatio,* siege, strike, sudden attack, violation of another's rights
ASSOCIATED CONCEPTS: aggravated assault, assault and battery, assault with a deadly weapon, assault with intent to commit a felony, assault with intent to commit murder, assault with intent to maim, assault with intent to rape, assault with intent to rob, battery, felonious assault, simple assault

ASSAULT, *verb*   accost, accost bellicosely, *adgredi, adriri,* affront hostilely, aggress, *appetere,* assail, assault belligerently, attack, attack physically, attempt violence to, besiege, deal a blow, harm, oppugn, set upon, set upon with force, set upon with violence, strike, thrust at

ASSAY, *noun*   analysis, ascertainment, assessment, breakdown, calculation, computation, diagnosis, examination, experiment, exploration, measurement, probation, probe, test, test case, verification

ASSAY, *verb*   analyze, ascertain, assess, calculate, compute, diagnose, endeavor, evaluate, experiment, measure, research, test, try, verify, weigh

ASSEMBLAGE, *noun*   accumulation, acervation, agglomeration, aggregation, amassment, array, *assemblage,* assembly, association, audience, bale, band, batch, bevy, body, bolt, bulk, bunch, bundle, caucus, claque, clump, cluster, collection, colligation, combination, committee, company, compilation, concentration, conclave, concourse, confluence, conflux, congeries, conglomerate, conglomeration, congregation, congress, convention, convocation, corps, coven, cumulation, drove, ensemble, flock, flood, gang, gathering, group, heap, horde, ingathering, legion, lot, lump, mass, mass meeting, medley, meeting, miscellany, mob, multitude, outfit, pack, packet, party, pile, queue, rally, réunion, series, set, sheaf, squad, stack, string, swarm, symposium, thicket, throng, tribe, troop, troupe, union
ASSOCIATED CONCEPTS: disorderly assemblage, unlawful assemblage

ASSEMBLY, *noun*   aggregation, assemblage, body, caucus, collection, company, conclave, concourse, conference, congregation, *consilium, contio,* convention, conventus, convocation, crowd, gathering, group, mass, meeting, multitude

ASSENT, *noun*   acceptance, accord, accordance, acknowledgment, acquiescence, *adsensio, adsensus,* affirmance, affirmation, agreement, approbation, approval, authorization, compliance, concord, concordance, concurrence, confirmation, consent, consentaneity, consonance, endorsement, permission, ratification, recognition, sanction, submission, willing consent, willingness
ASSOCIATED CONCEPTS: legal assent
FOREIGN PHRASES: *Nemo videtur fraudare eos qui sciunt et consentiunt.* No one is considered as deceiving those who know and consent to his acts. ***Non refert an quis assensum suum praefert verbis, aut rebus ipsis et factis.*** It is immaterial whether a man gives assent by his words or by his acts and deeds.

ASSENT, *verb*   accede, accept, accord, acknowledge, acquiesce, *adnuere, adsentari,* agree, allow, approve, authorize, comply, concede, concur, confirm, conform to, consent, embrace an offer, endorse, express concurrence, favor, give consent, homologate, permit, ratify, recognize, sanction, subscribe to
ASSOCIATED CONCEPTS: assent by acts, assent by gestures, assent by silence, express assent, implied assent, judicial assent, mutual assent
FOREIGN PHRASES: *Qui non prohibet id quod prohibere potest assentire videtur.* He who does not forbid what he is able to prevent, is deemed to assent. ***Qui tacet consentire videtur, ubi tractatur de ejus commodo.*** He who is silent is deemed to consent.

ASSERT, *verb*   *adfirmare,* advance, affirm, allege in support, announce, annunciate, argue for, assever, asseverate, attest, aver, avouch, avow, certify, claim, *confirmare,* contend, declare, depose, *dicere,* emphasize, enunciate, espouse, express, insist upon, maintain, plead one's case, plead one's cause, profess, pronounce, propound, recite, relate, set forth, state, state as true, stress, urge, urge reasons for

ASSERTION, *noun*   *adfirmatio,* affirmation, allegation, announcement, asseveration, attestation, averment, avouchment, avowal, declaration, *defensio,* disclosure, enunciation, expression, insistence, insistence on a claim, insistence on a right, *ipse dixit,* positive declaration, positive statement, predication, profession, pronouncement, representation, statement, *vindicatio*
ASSOCIATED CONCEPTS: admission, confession, criminal accusation, false accusation

ASSERTIVE, *adjective*   authoritative, confident, dogmatic, influential, potent, powerful, self-assured, strong

ASSESS *(Appraise),* ***verb***   *aestimare,* apprize, ascertain, calculate, calibrate, compute, consider, count, determine, estimate, evaluate, fix the value, gauge, judge, measure, mensurate, mete, rate, reckon, set, valuate, value, weigh
ASSOCIATED CONCEPTS: assess a penalty, assess damages, assessed valuation

ASSESS *(Tax),* ***verb***   affix an impost, charge with one's share, demand a payment, demand toll, exact a charge, exact a toll, excise, fix a valuation, impose a charge, impose a levy, lay an impost, levy
ASSOCIATED CONCEPTS: assess taxes

ASSESSMENT *(Estimation),* ***noun***   *aestimatio,* appraisal, appraisement, calculation, determination, estimate, measure, mensuration, rating, reckoning, survey, valuation
ASSOCIATED CONCEPTS: assessment of damages

ASSESSMENT *(Levy),* ***noun***   amount assessed as payable, capitation, census, cess, charge, charge levied, exaction, exactment, imposition, impost, rate, tallage, tax, toll
ASSOCIATED CONCEPTS: assessed valuation, assessment and collection of taxes, assessment district, assessment for benefits, assessment for special improvements, assessment insurance, assessment lien, assessment of property, assessment roll, assessor, equalized assessment, improvements, municipal improvements, public improvements, special assessment, tax assessment, valuation of property

ASSESSOR, *noun*   *censor,* charger, collector, exciseman, official receiver, one who exacts, one who imposes a charge, one who levies, tax collector, tax gatherer, tax man, tax receiver, tax taker, taxer
ASSOCIATED CONCEPTS: tax assessor

ASSETS, *noun*   available means, belongings, *bona,* capital, chattels, effects, estate, funds, goods, holdings, inventories, money, pecuniary resources, personal effects, personal resources, possessions, principal, property, reserves, resources, riches, valuables, wealth, wherewithal
ASSOCIATED CONCEPTS: assets of a trust corpus, assets of an estate, capital assets, concealment of assets, contingent assets, corporation's assets, depletion of assets, disposal of assets, equitable assets, fixed assets, foreign assets, fraudulent transfer of assets, liquid assets, partnership assets, personal assets, real assets, sale of assets, testamentary assets

ASSEVERATION, *noun* acknowledgment, adjuration, affirmance, affirmation, assertion, attestation, averment, avouchment, avowal, certification, confirmation, declaration, emphatic assertion, legal pledge, oath, positive declaration, positive statement, profession, pronouncement, solemn averment, solemn avowal, solemn declaration, sworn statement, vow

ASSIGN (*Allot*), *verb* allocate, apportion, appropriate, attribuere, deal out, dispense, distribute, divide in portions, dole out, give out, mete out, partition, portion out, *rem homini adsignare*, share
ASSOCIATED CONCEPTS: assign a cause of action, assign a chose in action, assign a lease, assign over, assign without recourse, assignable interest, assigned counsel, assigned risk, sublease

ASSIGN (*Designate*), *verb* appoint, ascribe, attribute, authorize, charge, commission, commit powers to another, delegate, depute, detail, empower, entrust, invest, name, prescribe, put in commission, set, specify
FOREIGN PHRASES: *Assignatus utitur jure auctoris.* An assignee is clothed with the right of his principal.

ASSIGN (*Transfer ownership*), *verb* abalienate, alienate, commit to another's trust, consign, convey, deliver, devolve upon, dispose of, endorse over, entrust, grant, make over to another, negotiate, refer, release, relegate, sign over, surrender to another, transfer to another, transmit

ASSIGNABLE, *adjective* consignable, conveyable, deliverable, devisable, disposable, exchangeable, grantable, negotiable, transferable, transmissible, transmittable
ASSOCIATED CONCEPTS: assignable contract, assignable interest

ASSIGNATION, *noun* application, arrogation, ascription, assignment, attribution, blame, charge, imputation, placement

ASSIGNEE, *noun* accipient, allottee, donee, grantee, receiver, recipient, transferee
ASSOCIATED CONCEPTS: lessee
FOREIGN PHRASES: *Assignatus utitur jure auctoris.* An assignee has the rights of his principal.

ASSIGNMENT (*Allotment*), *noun* allocation, allowance, apportionment, appropriation, assignation, dispensation, distribution, division, partition, portion
ASSOCIATED CONCEPTS: assignment of choses in action

ASSIGNMENT (*Designation*), *noun* appointment, authorization, commission, delegation, deputation, mandate, nomination, placing in office, prescription, selection, signification, specification, stipulation
ASSOCIATED CONCEPTS: assignment of error

ASSIGNMENT (*Task*), *noun* business, charge, chore, commission, duty, function, mission, part, pursuit, responsibility, role, stint, work

ASSIGNMENT (*Transfer of ownership*), *noun* abalienation, alienation, assignation, cession, conferment, conferral, consignation, consignment, conveyance, conveyancing, delivery, demise, devolvement, disposition, distribution, grant, impropriation, mutual transfer, nonretention, relegation, transfer, transference, transmission, transmittal

ASSOCIATED CONCEPTS: assignment by operation of law, assignment for the benefit of creditors, assignment for value, assignment of a cause of action, assignment of a chose in action, assignment of an account, assignment of claim, assignment of dower, assignment of lease, assignment of rents and profits, assignment of wages, consignment, general assignment, lease, license, partial assignment, promise to make assignment, voluntary assignment
FOREIGN PHRASES: *Assignatus utitur jure auctoris.* An assignee is clothed with the right of his principal.

ASSIST, *verb* abet, accommodate, act as assistant to, administer to, afford aid, aid, *auxiliari*, back, be of help, be of use, come to the aid of, cooperate with, do a service, endorse, foster, furnish aid, further, give a hand, give aid, give support, help, help along, intercede for, minister to, nurture, oblige, *opitulari*, participate, promote, reinforce, relieve, second, serve, stand by, subserve, subsidize, *subvenire*, succor, supply aid, support, take part with
ASSOCIATED CONCEPTS: accessory, aiding and abetting, complicity

ASSISTANCE, *noun* accommodation, *adiumentum*, adjuvancy, advocacy, aid, *auxilium*, benefit, benevolence, championship, cooperation, furtherance, help, helpfulness, intercession, participation, reinforcement, subsidy, succor, support
ASSOCIATED CONCEPTS: able assistance of counsel, writ of assistance

ASSISTANT, *noun* abettor, accessory, accomplice, *adiutor, adiutrix*, adjutant, adjuvant, advocate, agent, aide, *aide-de-camp*, aider, apprentice, associate, backer, champion, clerk, coadjutor, coaid, collaborator, colleague, confederate, *confrère*, cooperator, copartner, coworker, deputy, employee, helper, helpmate, partner, right-hand man, second, seconder, subaltern, subordinate, supporter, underling, underworker
ASSOCIATED CONCEPTS: accessory, accomplice, coconspirator

ASSOCIATE, *noun* adjunct, aid, aide-de-camp, assistant, auxiliary, coadjutant, coadjutor, coadjuvant, cohelper, cohort, collaborator, colleague, comate, companion, compeer, confederate, confidante, confrere, cooperator, copartner, coworker, fellow worker, friend, partner, *socius, sodalis*
ASSOCIATED CONCEPTS: associates in a law office, confederacy, partner, union

ASSOCIATED, *adjective* affiliated, agnate, akin, allied, closely allied, closely related, coactive, coadunate, combined, concerted, confederated, conjoint, conjunct, connate, connected, cooperant, cooperative, coupled, coworking, federate, federated, incorporated, inosculated, interallied, joined, leagued, linked, related, synergetic, united
ASSOCIATED CONCEPTS: associated companies

ASSOCIATION (*Alliance*), *noun* affiliation, amalgamation, coalition, combination, combine, company, confederacy, confederation, *conlegium*, corporation, coterie, federation, guild, league, syndicate, union
ASSOCIATED CONCEPTS: articles of association, bar associations, beneficial associations, convenant of associations, joint stock associations, mutual benefit associations, professional associations, unincorporated associations, voluntary associations

ASSOCIATION (*Connection*), *noun* bond, coadjuvancy, coalition, colleagueship, combination, conjunction, *conlegium,* connectedness, consociation, copartnership, coworking, involvement, joint enterprise, link, linkage, organization, participation, partnership, relatedness, relation, relationship, *societas,* working in concert

ASSUAGE, verb abate, allay, alleviate, appease, attemper, blunt, chasten, check, comfort, compose, curb, diminish, ease, lessen, *levare, mitigare,* mitigate, moderate, mollify, obtund, pacify, palliate, quell, quench, reduce, relieve, remedy, salve, sate, satiate, satisfy, *sedare,* slake, smother, soften, solace, soothe, still, temper, tranquilize

ASSUME *(Seize),* **verb** accroach, adeem, adopt, *adsumere,* annex, appropriate, arrogate, commandeer, confiscate, dispossess, distrain, expropriate, help oneself to, make free with, *occupare,* possess oneself of, *rem sibi adrogare,* take as one's own, usurp

ASSUME *(Simulate),* **verb** act as, counterfeit, dissemble, dissimulate, don, feign, impersonate, make believe, outwardly seem, pass for, personate, play the part, pose as, pretend to be, profess, put on deceitfully, represent as, take the part of, take the semblance of

ASSUME *(Suppose),* **verb** be inclined to think, be of the opinion, conclude, conjecture, consider, deduce, deem true, divine, draw the inference, find probable, gather, have an idea that, hold the opinion, infer, predicate, premise, presume, presuppose, suspect, take for granted, take without proof, theorize, think credible, think likely, think probable

ASSUME *(Undertake),* **verb** accept, accept an obligation, attempt, attend to, be willing to bear, become responsible for, begin, broach, commit oneself, contract, contract for, embark upon, engage, enter upon, incur a duty, manage, proceed to, pursue, set about, shoulder, *suscipere,* take care of, take charge, take on oneself, take up, venture upon
ASSOCIATED CONCEPTS: assume a debt, assume a lease, assume a mortgage, assume responsibility, assumed name, assumed risk

ASSUMED *(Feigned),* **adjective** adopted, apocryphal, bogus, contrived, counterfeit, deceptive, delusive, disguised, fabricated, factitious, fake, false, fictitious, fraudulent, invented, manufactured, misleading, misrepresented, pretended, pretexted, spurious, synthetic, unauthentic, ungenuine, unreal
ASSOCIATED CONCEPTS: allegation of fact, allegation of law, alleged fact, material allegation, pleading, responsive allegation, specific allegation

ASSUMED *(Inferred),* **adjective** accepted, conjectured, connoted, considered true, given, granted, hypothesized, implicit, indicated, insinuated, intimated, posited, postulated, presumed, presupposed, stated, supposed, suppositional, taken for granted, understood

ASSUMPTION *(Adoption),* **noun** acceptance, acquisition, receiving, reception, recipience, selection, taking on, undertaking
ASSOCIATED CONCEPTS: *assumpsit on quantum meruit,* assumption agreement, assumption of debt, assumption of facts, assumption of indebtedness, assumption of jurisdiction, assumption of liability, assumption of mortgage, assumption of obligation, assumption of risk

ASSUMPTION *(Seizure),* **noun** annexation, appropriation, arrogation, dispossession, encroachment, exaction, expropriation, impropriation, infringement, usurpation

ASSUMPTION *(Supposition),* **noun** basis, belief, conjecture, foundation, ground, hypothesis, hypothesization, impression, notion, opinion, personal judgment, postulate, premise, presumption, presupposition, *sumptio,* supposal, surmise, theory, thinking, view

ASSURANCE, noun adjuration, affirmation, assuredness, attestation, averment, avow, avowal, avowance, commitment, confidence, confidentness, *confirmatio,* covenant, declaration, earnest declaration, engagement, *fiducia,* guaranty, oath, obligation, pact, paction, pledge, promise, reassurance, security, solemn assertion, solemn promise, surety, voucher, vow, warranty
ASSOCIATED CONCEPTS: assurance of title, covenant of future assurances

ASSURE *(Give confidence to),* **verb** buoy up, cause to feel certain, cheer, comfort, confirm in conviction, console, convince, deliver from uncertainty, dismiss all doubt, embolden, encourage, enhearten, free from doubt, free from uncertainty, give hope, hearten, inspire, inspire hope, lead to believe, make certain, make confident, offer assurances to, persuade, put at ease, raise expectations, reassure, render certain, restore one's faith, satisfy, set at ease, solace

ASSURE *(Insure),* **verb** affirm, agree to indemnify for loss, answer for, asseverate, attest, aver, avouch, avow, certify, confirm, endorse, espouse, give security, guarantee, make a promise, make certain, make sure, pledge, profess, promise, render certain, render safe, secure against loss, solemnly promise, subscribe to, swear, underwrite, verify, vouch for, vow, warrant

ASTRAY, adjective aberrant, adrift, afield, amiss, awry, circuitous, deviating, errant, erratic, indirect, lost, misguided, misled, off-center, out of one's bearings, out of one's reckoning, random, round-about, straying, undirected, unguided

ASTRINGENT, adjective acid, acrid, acrimonious, *adstrictorius,* austere, bitter, caustic, dour, exigent, harsh, mordant, rough, severe, stern, strict, stringent, tart

ASYLUM *(Hiding place),* **noun** covert, exile, haven, inviolable refuge, place of immunity, place of refuge, refuge, retreat, safehold, sanctuary, *sanctum sanctorum,* secure retreat, shelter, temporary refuge

ASYLUM *(Hospital),* **noun** lazaretto, mental hospital, mental institution, nursing home, psychiatric hospital, psychiatric ward, sanitorium, shelter for the afflicted, state hospital, state institution

ASYLUM *(Protection),* **noun** freedom from danger, refuge, safeguard, safety, sanctuary, security, shelter
ASSOCIATED CONCEPTS: granted asylum

AT FAULT, adverb culpable, erring, in error, guilty, liable, responsible for, wrong

AT ISSUE, adverb being analyzed, in contemplation, in dispute, in question, on the agenda, under advisement, under consideration, under examination

AT RISK, adverb at peril, capable of loss, involved, potentially liable

AT WILL EMPLOYMENT, *noun*   at the will of the employer, discretionary employment without the necessity of reasons, employment at will, freedom to discharge, freedom to discharge without grounds, freedom to discharge without reasons, freedom to fire

ASSOCIATED CONCEPTS: just cause employees, morally reprehensive reasons, morally wrong reasons

ATMOSPHERE, *noun*   air, airspace, ambience, aura, background, circumambience, climate, climatic condition, element, environing influence, environment, medium, milieu, mood, setting, space, surroundings, weather

ASSOCIATED CONCEPTS: clouding the atmosphere, polluting the atmosphere

ATROCITY, *noun*   abomination, abuse, act of ferocity, atrocious crime, *atrocitas*, barbarity, deed of savagery, ferity, ferocity, fiendishness, flagitious villainy, flagitiousness, flagrancy, gross offense, heinousness, holocaust, infamy, inhumanity, iniquity, malevolence, maltreatment, mercilessness, monstrosity, nefariousness, *nefas, res atrox*, ruthlessness, savagery, truculence, victimization, villainy, wantonly wicked conduct, wickedness

FOREIGN PHRASES: ***Patria potestas in pietate debet, non in atrocitate, consistere.*** Paternal power should consist of affection not of atrocity.

ATTACH *(Join)*, ***verb***   add, add as an accessory, *adfigere*, adhere, adjoin, *adligare*, affix, agglutinate, annex, append, assemble, bind, cohere, combine, conjoin, connect, consolidate, couple, embody, embrace, fasten, fasten together, incorporate, insert, link, make one, merge, put together, secure, subjoin, supplement, unite

ASSOCIATED CONCEPTS: attach exhibits

ATTACH *(Seize)*, ***verb***   adeem, annex, appropriate, arrogate, confiscate, disseise, distrain, distress, exact, expropriate, garnish, impound, impress, levy, overcome, preempt, press, replevy, retake, secure, seize summarily, sequester, sequestrate, take, take over, take possession of, take summarily, usurp

ASSOCIATED CONCEPTS: attach property, provisional remedy

ATTACHED *(Annexed)*, ***adjective***   added, affixed, agglutinated, appendant, appended, *aptus*, bound, conjoined, connected, fastened, fixed, joined, paired, subjoined, united

ATTACHED *(Seized)*, ***adjective***   adeemed, annexed, appropriated, arrogated, confiscated, disseised, distrained, expropriated, foreclosed, forfeited, garnisheed, impounded, levied, replevied, sequestered, usurped

ASSOCIATED CONCEPTS: provisional remedy

ATTACHMENT *(Act of affixing)*, ***noun***   adjunction, affixation, annexation, annexion, attaching, binding, bond, cohesion, confixation, conjunction, connection, fastening, fixing, insertion, joinder, joining, junction, ligation, nexus, subjunction, that which attaches, tie

ASSOCIATED CONCEPTS: attachment of a security interest, garnishment, in rem jurisdiction, provisional remedy, quasi in rem jurisdiction

ATTACHMENT *(Seizure)*, ***noun***   annexation, apprehending, confiscation, deprivation, deprivement, disownment, dispossession, distrainer, distraint, distress, divestment, *embargo*, execution, expropriation, foreclosure, garnishment, impoundage, impoundment, impressment, seizing, sequestration

ASSOCIATED CONCEPTS: ancillary attachment, attachment execution, attachment of persons, attachment of property, attachment proceedings, attachment to obtain jurisdiction, attachment upon mesne process, body attachment, execution, extraordinary remedy, lien or incumbrance, proceeding in rem, property subject to attachment, provisional remedy, sequestration, writ of attachment, wrongful attachment

ATTACHMENT *(Thing affixed)*, ***noun***   accessory, addendum, additum, adjunct, affixture, annex, appendage, appendix, appurtenance, fixture, postfix, supplement, supplementary device

ATTACK, *verb*   abuse, *adgredi, adoriri*, advance upon, aggress, assail, assault, assume the offensive, bear down upon, beat, begin hostilities against, beleaguer, beset, besiege, bombard, charge, combat, commit hostilities, descend on, engage in hostilities, fall upon, fight offensively, fly at, force, hit, impugn, invade, *invehi in*, lay hands on, lay into, make an onset against, open fire upon, oppugn, oppugnare, pitch into, pounce upon, raid, revile, run at, rush upon, set upon with force, shoot at, spring upon, start a fight, start a war, storm, strike, strike the first blow, tackle, take offensive action, take the initiative, take the offensive, tear into, throw oneself upon, waylay

ASSOCIATED CONCEPTS: assault, attack on credibility, collateral attack, direct attack, impeach, provocation of attack

ATTAIN, *verb*   accomplish, achieve, acquire, *adsequi*, arrive at, be successful, bring about, bring off successfully, bring to pass, carry through, come by, come to, complete, *consequi*, consummate, earn, effect, effectuate, finish, gain, gain one's end, get, get by effort, get done, get possession of, obtain, perfect, procure, put through, reach, reach one's goal, realize, reap, score a success, secure, succeed, succeed in reaching

ATTAINT, *noun*   abasement, bad name, bad reputation, bad repute, brand, debasement, defilement, degradation, derogation, deviation from rectitude, disapprobation, discredit, disesteem, disgrace, dishonor, disreputability, disrepute, disrespect, humiliation, ignominy, ill fame, ill favor, ill repute, improbity, imputation, infamy, ingloriousness, loss of reputation, mark, obloquy, odium, opprobrium, reproach, shame, smear, smirch, stain, stigma, taint, tarnish, tarnished honor

ASSOCIATED CONCEPTS: attainder, *autrefois attaint*, bill of attainder, civil death

ATTEMPT, *verb*   aim at, assay, be at work, be in action, bid for, carry on, *conari*, do one's best, do the needful, drive at, employ oneself, endeavor, essay, exert oneself, go after, go all out for, intend, labor for, make a bid, make an effort at, make the effort, ply one's task, pursue, put forth an effort, quest, seek to, set out to, strive, take on, *temptare*, test, try, try hard, try one's best, undertake, use one's best endeavors, venture

ASSOCIATED CONCEPTS: attempt to commit a crime, attempt to defraud, attempt to prove, conspiracy, failure of intended act, preparatory acts, renunciation

FOREIGN PHRASES: ***Affectus punitur licet non sequatur effectus.*** The intention is punished although the intended result does not follow. ***Non officit conatus nisi sequatur effectus.*** An attempt does not harm unless a consequence follows. ***In maleficiis voluntas spectatur, non exitus.*** In criminal offenses, the intention and not the result must be regarded. ***Officit conatus si effectus sequatur.*** The attempt becomes of consequence, if the effect follows.

ATTEND (Accompany), *verb*   be associated with, be connected with, go along with

ATTEND (Be present at), *verb*   frequent, go to, visit

ATTEND (Heed), *verb*   be attentive to, give heed to, listen, mark, mind, note, notice, take notice of

ATTEND (Take care of), *verb*   be attendant on, care for, guard, minister to, see to, serve, wait upon, watch over

ATTENDANCE, *noun*   accompaniment, ministration, presence

ATTENUATE, *verb*   attenuare, bate, constrict, constringe, contract, curtail, debilitate, decrease, deflate, devitalize, diminish, diminish in effect, *extenuare,* extenuate, lessen, lighten, make thin, narrow, reduce, reduce in intensity, reduce in strength, render threadlike, taper, weaken, weaken in force
ASSOCIATED CONCEPTS: attenuation between a cause and the result, proximate cause, remote cause

ATTEST, *verb*   adjure, affirm, assert, authenticate, aver, bear out, bear witness to, certify, confirm, corroborate, declare, declare the truth of, depone, depose, endorse, evince, ratify, *rem testari,* speak on oath, subscribe, substantiate, support, swear, take one's oath, *testem facere, testificari,* testify to, validate, verify, vouch for, witness
ASSOCIATED CONCEPTS: affidavit, interrogatory

ATTESTATION, *noun*   act of bearing witness, adjuration, affirmation, allegation, assertion, asseveration, attest, attesting declaration, authentication, averment, avouchment, avowal, certification, declaration, endorsement, oath, solemn averment, solemn avowal, solemn declaration, statement, substantiation, swearing, sworn evidence, *testificatio,* testification, *testimonium,* testimony, validification, verification, witnessing
ASSOCIATED CONCEPTS: acknowledgment, attestation clause, attestation of chattel mortgage, attestation of deed, attestation of note, attestation of will, attesting witnesses

ATTORN, *verb*   allot, assign, cede, confer, confer ownership, consign, convey, deliver, demise, devise, devolve upon, dispose of, give, grant, impart, let, part with, pass down, relinquish, transfer, turn over

ATTORNEY, *noun*   advocate, attorney-at-law, barrister, counsel, counselor, counselor-at-law, jurisconsult, jurisprudent, jurist, lawyer, learned counsel, legal adviser, legal practitioner, legist, member of the bar, officer of the court, pleader, practitioner, procurator, publicist, solicitor
ASSOCIATED CONCEPTS: attorney of record, staff attorney
FOREIGN PHRASES: *Consilia multorum quaeruntur in magnis.* The advice of many is required in affairs of magnitude.

ATTORNEY-CLIENT PRIVILEGE, *noun*   confidential relationship, confidentiality, fiduciary privilege, immunity from divulging confidences, non-disclosable relationship, private relationship, privileged relationship
Generally: protected relationship
Specifically: confidential communications
ASSOCIATED CONCEPTS: privileged communications

ATTORNEY IN FACT, *noun*   alternate, legal appointee, legal representative, proxy, surrogate

ATTORNMENT, *noun*   agreement, arrangement, commitment, compact, condition, deal, liability, prerequisite, provision, proviso, requisite, stipulation, understanding

ATTRACTIVE, *adjective*   adorable, agreeable, alluring, appealing, attracting, attrahent, beauteous, beautiful, beckoning, becoming, beguiling, bewitching, captivating, catching, catchy, charming, comely, delightful, desirable, drawing, elegant, enchanting, engaging, enthralling, enticing, entrancing, exquisite, fair, fascinating, fetching, glamorous, interesting, intriguing, inviting, likeable, luring, magnetic, pleasant, pleasing, prepossessing, pretty, ravishing, seductive, sightly, sweet, tasteful, tempting, titillating, to one's liking
ASSOCIATED CONCEPTS: attractive nuisance doctrine

ATTRACTIVE NUISANCE, *noun*   allure, bait, dangerous conditions, draw, endangerment, enticement, inducement, lure, seducement, unprotected
ASSOCIATED CONCEPTS: attractive nuisance doctrine, specific conditions

ATTRIBUTE, *verb*   accredit with, *adsignare,* ascribe, assign, charge with, connect with, consider as belonging to, impute, point to, predicate, set down to, *tribuere*
ASSOCIATED CONCEPTS: attribute a cause to an individual

ATTRIBUTION, *noun*   accounting, acknowledgment, affirmation, allusion, ascription, assignation, assignment, association, connection, implication, imputation, incrimination, indication, insinuation, mention, quotation, reference, relation

ATTRITION, *noun*   decrease, disintegration, dwindling, erosion, fading, falling off, lessening, waning, wearing away

ATTUNE, *verb*   acclimatize, accommodate, accord, adapt, adjust, attemper, be harmonious, blend, bring into accord, bring into agreement, fit for a purpose, harmonize, make accordant, make adjustments, make agree, readapt, readjust, rectify, regulate, render accordant, resolve a discord, restore harmony, set right

ATYPICAL, *adjective*   aberrant, abnormal, anomalous, dissimilar, diverse, exceptional, never the same, non-uniform, unalike, unrepresentative, variable

AUCTION, *noun*   auctio, auctione vendere, public sale, public sale of property, sale by bid, sale by outcry, sale to the highest bidder, *sub hasta vendere,* vendue
ASSOCIATED CONCEPTS: auction license, auction sale, auctioneer, highest bidder, public sale

AUDACITY, *noun*   audacia, audaciousness, bold front, boldness, bravado, brave face, bravura, confidence in one's powers, daring, defiance of danger, derring-do, hardihood, intrepidity, nerve, overboldness, overdaring, *protervitas,* rashness, recklessness, scorn of the consequences, temerity, undauntedness, want of caution

AUDIO RIGHTS, *noun*   audio cassette rights, audio reproduction rights, compact disc rights, sound recording rights
Generally: secondary rights, subsidiary rights

AUDIT, *verb*   bring into question, certify, check, check on, conduct an inquiry, examine, examine financial accounts, examine the accounts officially, go through the books, hold an inquiry, inspect, inspect accounts officially, investigate, monitor, probe, pursue an inquiry, *rationes dispungere,* reexamine, research, review, scrutinize, search, study, subject to examination

ASSOCIATED CONCEPTS: allowance of claim, audit of account, audited claims, auditor, auditor's report, disallowance of claim, fraudulent audit

AUGMENTATION, noun *accessio,* accessory, accrual, accruement, accumulation, adding, advance, advancement, aggrandizement, *amplificatio,* amplification, appreciation, appurtenance, broadening, build-up, cumulative effect, cumulativeness, development, enhancement, enlargement, enlarging, expansion, extension, gain, growth, improvement, increase, increasing, increment, intensification, magnification, progress, proliferation, redoubling, reinforcement, rise, something added, spread, supplement, widening
ASSOCIATED CONCEPTS: augmentation of assets, augmentation of estate

AUSPICES, noun abetment, aegis, assistance, *auspicium,* authority, backing, benign favor, care, charge, countenance, custody, encouragement, favor, favoring influence, fosterage, guardianship, guidance, management, oversight, patronage, protection, protectorship, recommendation, safeguard, sponsorship, superintendence, supervision, support, tutelage, wardenship, wardship
ASSOCIATED CONCEPTS: under governmental auspices

AUSPICIOUS, adjective betokening success, encouraging, favorable, favored by fortune, favoring, felicitous, *felix,* fortunate, good, hopeful, inspiriting, lucky, of good omen, of promise, opportune, portending happiness, presaging good fortune, promising, propitious, *prosper,* providential, roseate, successful

AUSTERITY, noun abstemiousness, *austeritas,* bare subsistence, chariness, closed purse, economicalness, economy, frugality, frugalness, good management, husbandry, lack of luxury, meagerness, scantiness, scrimping, self-denial, self-restraint, severe discipline, *severitas,* severity, stinginess, stint, strictness, stringency, subsistence level, temperance, thrift, thriftiness, unwastefulness
ASSOCIATED CONCEPTS: austerity budget

AUTHENTIC, adjective accordant with the facts, according to the facts, accredited, accurate, actual, as represented, attested, authoritative, bona fide, *certus,* credible, demonstrated, dependable, documented, entitled to acceptance and belief, factual, faithful, founded on fact, from competent sources, from the original data, genuine, genuine in origin, honest, inartificial, legitimate, literal, not apocryphal, not false, not fictitious, not spurious, not tampered with, of the origin reputed, original, positive, pure, real, reliable, solid, sound, true, trusted, trustworthy, unadulterated, uncounterfeited, undisguised, undistorted, unexaggerated, unfabricated, unfaked, unfeigned, unfictitious, unplagiarized, unquestionable, unsimulated, unspecious, unspurious, unsynthetic, valid, verifiable, veritable, *verus,* well-based, well-founded, well-grounded, worthy of belief
ASSOCIATED CONCEPTS: authentic act, authenticate, forgery, notaries

AUTHOR (Originator), noun architect, *auctor,* begetter, causer, composer, contriver, creator, deviser, discoverer, effecter, fabricator, founder, generator, inaugurator, initiator, innovater, institutor, introducer, inventor, maker, manufacturer, occasioner, organizer, parent, prime mover, producer, sire
ASSOCIATED CONCEPTS: copyright
FOREIGN PHRASES: Culpa tenet suos auctores. Fault binds its own authors.

AUTHOR (Writer), noun compiler, composer of a literary work, drafter, essayist, literary person, man of letters, person who writes, *scriptor,* verse maker
ASSOCIATED CONCEPTS: copyright, plagiarism

AUTHORITIES, noun administration, commanders, directors, executives, government, heads, *magistratus,* management, officeholders, officials, persons in office, persons of commanding influence, *potestates,* powers that be, rulers, those holding power, those in command, those in control, those of influence, those who rule
ASSOCIATED CONCEPTS: competent authorities, governmental authorities, lawful authorities, local authorities, municipal authorities, port authorities, turnpike and toll authorities

AUTHORITY (Documentation), noun authoritative example, authoritative rule for future similar cases, court rule, decision, judgment, judicial decision establishing a rule, judicial precedent, legislative precedent, order, precedent, precept, prior instance, *ratio decidendi,* ruling, sanction, statute
ASSOCIATED CONCEPTS: established authority

AUTHORITY (Legal expert), noun able, acomplished, acquainted, adept, adroit, all-knowing, apt, artful, capable, clever, cognizant, competent, conversant, deft, dexterous, effective, efficient, encyclopedic, experienced, facile, finished handy, ingenious, knowing, knowledgeable, learned, masterful, masterly, omniscient, practiced, prepared, professional, proficient, qualified, seasoned, skilled, skillful, trained, tried, versed, veteran, well-qualified, wise
ASSOCIATED CONCEPTS: forensic expert

AUTHORITY (Power), noun *auctoritas,* authoritativeness, control, dominance, domination, force, governance, importance, influence, position of influence, position of power, powers that be, seniority, source, supremacy, sway
ASSOCIATED CONCEPTS: abuse of authority, acting under authority, actual authority, agency, apparent authority, authority by estoppel, authority coupled with an interest, authority of law, authority of the court, colorable authority, constituted authority, de facto authority, delegation of authority, express authority, general authority, implied authority, incidental authority, indicia of authority, lawful authority, legislative authority, limited authority, local authority, municipal authority, naked authority, parental authority, power of attorney, proxy, public authority, real authority, scope of authority, special authority, under cover of authority, unlimited authority, want of authority, written authority
FOREIGN PHRASES: Argumentum ab auctoritate est fortissimum in lege. An argument drawn from authority is the strongest in the law. **Majus dignum trahit ad se minus dignum.** The greater authority appropriates to itself the lesser authority. **Nihil tam proprium imperio quam legibus vivere.** Nothing is so becoming to authority as to live in conformity with the laws. **Non debet cui plus licet, quod minus est non licere.** He who is given a greater authority ought not to be forbidden that which is less. **Ubi non est condendi auctoritas, ibi non est parendi necessitas.** Where there is no authority for establishing a rule, there is no need for obeying it. **Firmior et potentior est operatio legis quam dispositio hominis.** The operation of the law is more firm and more powerful than the will of man. **Fortior et potentior est dispositio legis quam hominis.** The disposition of the law has greater force and stronger effect than that of man. **Judici officium suum excedenti non paretur.** No obedience is to be given to a judge exceeding

his office or jurisdiction. *Legitime imperanti parere necesse est.* One who commands lawfully must be obeyed. *In maxima potentia minima licentia.* In the greatest liberty there is the least freedom. *Semper praesumitur pro legitimatione puerorum.* The presumption always is in favor of the legitimacy of children.

AUTHORITY *(Right), noun*   jurisdiction, legal power, legitimacy, prerogative, right to adjudicate, right to command, right to determine, right to settle issues, rightful power
FOREIGN PHRASES: *Omnis ratihabitio retrotrahitur et mandato priori aequiparatur.* Every ratification relates back and is taken to be the equal of prior authority. *Nullius hominis auctoritas apud nos valere debet, ut meliora non sequeremur si quis attulerit.* No man's influence ought to prevail upon us, that we should not follow better opinions should anyone present them. *Nemo potest facere per obliquum quod non potest facere per directum.* No man can do indirectly that which he cannot do directly. *In rebus manifestis, errat qui auctoritates legum allegat; quia perspicua vera non sunt probanda.* In clear cases, he errs who cites legal authorities because obvious truths are manifest and do not have to be proved.

AUTHORIZE, *verb*   accord, accredit, acquiesce in, admit, advocate, affirm, agree to, allow, appoint, approve, assent to, assign, auctor esse, be favorable to, be in favor of, certify, charge, charter, commission, concede, confer a privilege, confer a right, confirm, confirm officially, consent to, consign, countenance, credit, declare lawful, delegate to, depute, empower, enable, endorse, endow, endow with power, enfranchise, entitle, entrust, establish, formalize, formally sanction, give a right, give authority, give leave, give permission, give power, go along with, grant, grant claims, grant permission, have no objection, homologate, interpose no obstacles, invest with power, legalize, legislate, legitimate, legitimatize, legitimize, license, maintain, make legal, make valid, permit, *potestatem facere,* prescribe, privilege, pronounce legal, put in force, put up with, recognize, recommend, release, restore permission, sanctify, sanction, sanction a claim, sign, subscribe to, suffer to occur, support by authority, sustain, sustain by authority, tolerate, underwrite, validate, vest with a title, vouch for, vouchsafe, warrant
ASSOCIATED CONCEPTS: agency, delegation
FOREIGN PHRASES: *Semper qui non prohibet pro se intervenire, mandare creditur.* He who does not prohibit the intervention of another in his behalf is deemed to have authorized it.

AUTONOMOUS *(Independent), adjective*   detached, existing as an independent entity, free, free to choose, self-contained, self-reliant, self-sufficient, self-supporting, uncoerced, uncompelled, unconstrained, uncontrolled, unrestricted

AUTONOMOUS *(Self governing), adjective*   at liberty, autarchic, autonomic, enfranchised, free, politically independent, self-determined, self-directing, self-ruling, sovereign

AVAIL *(Be of use), verb*   aid, assist, assist in accomplishing a purpose, be good to, be of service, be of value, be profitable, be useful, benefit, bestead, bring to bear, confer a benefit on, do service, have efficacy, help, perform a function, *prodesse,* promote, serve, service, subserve, succor, suit one's purpose, *valere*

AVAIL *(Bring about), verb*   accomplish, bear fruit, bring forth, cause, conduce, effect, effectuate, engender, evolve, generate, give origin to, give rise to, have force, meet the demand, occasion, produce, profit, provide, *re uti,* realize, render, succeed, suffice

AVAILABLE, *adjective*   accessible, approachable, at hand, at one's disposal, attainable, convenient, fit, handy, obtainable, on call, on the market, open, reachable, ready, receptive, securable, suitable, to be had, unfilled, untaken, usable, vacant, willing, within reach
ASSOCIATED CONCEPTS: available remedies

AVENUE *(Means of attainment), noun*   approach, course, course of action, customary way, definite procedure, formula, manner, manner of working, means of access, method, method of attack, mode, mode of operation, procedure, process, scheme, standard procedure, system, tack, technique, way, ways and means

AVENUE *(Route), noun*   approach, boulevard, channel, corridor, course, egress, entrance, entry, ingress, passage, passageway, path, principal thoroughfare, road, roadway, street, way

AVERAGE *(Midmost), adjective*   center, centermost, intermediate, mean, mean proportioned, medial, median, mediate, medium, mid, middle, middle class, middle grade, middlemost, middling
ASSOCIATED CONCEPTS: average annual earnings or wages, average capital, average charges, average daily attendance, average daily balance, average daily wage, average price, average speed, average value, average weekly wage, general average, gross average, income averaging, particular average, petty average, simple average

AVERAGE *(Standard), adjective*   common, commonplace, conventional, fair, mediocre, moderate, normal, normative, ordinary, passable, prosaic, stock, typical, unexceptional, unnoteworthy, usual
ASSOCIATED CONCEPTS: average man, average person, average quality

AVERMENT, *noun*   adjuration, adjurement, affirmance, affirmation, announcement, assertion, assertment, assertory oath, asseveration, attest, attestation, avouchment, avowal, confirmation, declaration, formulation, instrument in proof, positive declaration, positive statement, profession, pronouncement, solemn affirmation, statement of facts, statement on oath, swearing, testification, vouching, written statement
ASSOCIATED CONCEPTS: averment of facts, descriptive averment, general averment, material averment, negative averment, particular averments, pleading, unnecessary averments

AVERSE, *adjective*   adverse, *alienus,* antagonistic, antipathetic, *aversus,* disinclined, disliking, hostile, indisposed, inimical, loath, opposed, reluctant, repelled, repugnant, revolted, undesirous, unfavorable, unwilling

AVERT, *verb*   *amovere,* arrest, *avertere,* avoid, change the course of, check, counteract, deflect, deter, divert, fend off, forestall, head off, intercept, make possible the avoidance of, parry, prevent, *prohibere,* shove aside, shunt, stave off, thwart, turn, turn aside, turn away, turn to the side, ward off
ASSOCIATED CONCEPTS: averting danger

AVOID *(Cancel), verb*   annul, defeat, destroy the efficacy of, invalidate, make inoperative, make of no effect, make void, make wholly without effect, refute, vacate, void

AVOID (*Evade*), *verb*   abstain from, avert, balk at, decline, depart from, dodge, elude, escape, eschew, flee from, forbear, forsake, have nothing to do with, hold back, keep at a distance from, keep away from, keep clear of, make off, part company, refrain from, retreat, shun, shy away from, *vitare*

AVOIDANCE (*Cancellation*), *noun*   abrogation, annulling, annulment, cancelling, cessation, discontinuation, dismissal, invalidation, making useless, nullifying, quashing, removal, rendering void, rescission, setting aside, vacating, vacation, voidance
ASSOCIATED CONCEPTS: avoidable preference, avoidance of contract, avoidance of will
FOREIGN PHRASES: *Falsa demonstratione legatum non perimi.* A legacy is not nullified by an erroneous description.

AVOIDANCE (*Evasion*), *noun*   bypass, detour, deviation, dodge, elusion, eschewment, evasion, evasive action, parrying, refraining, retreat, shunning, sidestep
ASSOCIATED CONCEPTS: avoidable consequences, avoidance by the courts of question of constitutionality, avoidance of consequences, avoidance of risk, confession and avoidance, last clear chance, pleading in avoidance

AVOUCH (*Avow*), *verb*   acknowledge, affirm, affirm with confidence, allege, allege as a fact, assert, assert peremptorily, assert positively, assert under oath, asseverate, attest, aver, bear witness, certify, confirm, confirm by oath, contend, declare, declare openly, declare with positiveness, depose, maintain, make an assertion, make open affirmation, make solemn affirmation, proclaim, profess, pronounce, propound, put in an affidavit, reaffirm, reassert, solemnly affirm, state, state as true, state with conviction, swear, swear an oath, swear the truth, testify, vouch, vow

AVOUCH (*Guarantee*), *verb*   assume responsibility for, assure, authenticate, back, be answerable for, be surety for, certify, endorse, ensure, give assurance, insure, pledge, pledge one's word, sponsor, underwrite, verify, vouch for, warrant

AVOUCHMENT, *noun*   acknowledgment, adjuration, affirmance, affirmation, assertion, asseveration, assurance, attest, attestation, averment, avowal, avowance, declaration, formulation, oath, open statement of affirmation, positive assertion, positive statement, proclamation, pronouncement, public declaration, solemn averment, solemn avowal, solemn declaration, statement of facts, swearing, testification, vouch, vow
ASSOCIATED CONCEPTS: affidavit

AVOW, *verb*   acknowledge, admit, admit frankly, affirm, allege as a fact, articulate, assert, assert on oath, assert peremptorily, assert under oath, asseverate, attest, authenticate, aver, avouch, be bound, bear witness, certify, commit oneself, confess, confirm, *confiteri*, contend, declare, declare openly, declare positively, declare the truth of, depose, enunciate, express, *fateri*, formulate, maintain, make a statement, make an assertion, postulate, predicate, proclaim, profess, *profiteri*, pronounce, propound, protest, set down, speak, state, state as true, state with conviction, swear, take one's oath, testify, vouch, vow, witness

ASSOCIATED CONCEPTS: affidavit, testimony

AVOWAL, *noun*   acknowledgment, adjurement, affirmance, affirmation, assertion, asseveration, attestation, authentication, averment, *aveu*, avouchment, avowance, *confessio*, confession, confirmation, contention, corroboration, declaration, endorsement, legal pledge, open declaration, positive statement, profession, pronouncement, protestation, statement, statement on oath, testimony, validation, verification

AVULSION, *noun*   divulsion, evulsion, forcible extraction, plucking out, ripping out, tearing away, tearing off, violent separation, wresting
ASSOCIATED CONCEPTS: accretion, erosion, riparian rights

AWARD, *noun*   act of judgment, action, adjudgment, adjudication, authoritative decision, decision, decree, determination, edict, finding, grant, judication, judicial decision, judicial sentence, opinion, order, order of the court, pronouncement, pronouncement by a court, recorded expression of a formal judgment, resolution, result, ruling, ruling of the court, verdict, warrant
ASSOCIATED CONCEPTS: arbitration and award, award of damages, compensatory award, confirmation of an award, monetary award, punitive award

AWARD, *verb*   act on, *addicere, adiudicare,* adjudge, adjudge to be due, adjudicate, bestow by judicial decree, bring in a verdict, conclude, decide, decree, decree by deliberate judgment, decree to be merited, deliver judgment, determine, establish, find, fix, ordain, order, pass judgment, pass sentence, pass upon, pronounce, pronounce judgment, pronounce on, rule, settle

AWAY, *adjective*   at a distance, distant, far, far away, far-off, further away, in the background, in the distance, inaccessible, long distance, long range, out of range, out of reach, out of sight, outlying, remote, removed, separated, unapproachable, uncommunicative, unresponsive

AWFUL, *adjective*   abhorrent, abominable, atrocious, beneath contempt, contemptible, deplorable, despicable, detestable, dreadful, drive, foul, frightening, frightful, ghastly, ghoulish, gruesome, harrowing, hateful, heinous, horrendous, horrid, horrifying, indefensible, loathsome, macabre, obnoxious, odious, offensive, outrageous, pathetic, pitiful, repellent, reprehensible, repulsive, revolting, shameful, shocking, terrible, terrifying, unspeakable, vile, villainous, wholly inadequate
ASSOCIATED CONCEPTS: deplorable conditions

AXIOMATIC, *adjective*   a priori, absolute, aphoristic, apodictic, apparent, ascertained, assured, beyond all question, beyond dispute, categorical, certain, decided, decisive, definite, determinate, doubtless, incontestable, incontrovertible, indubious, indubitable, irrefutable, manifest, positive, questionless, self-evident, sententious, solid, sure, unambiguous, unchallengeable, uncontested, undeniable, undisputed, undoubted, unequivocal, unimpeachable, unmistakable, unquestionable, unquestioned, well-founded

B

BABY, *noun*   bairn, changeling, child, fledgling, infant, juvenile, kid, minor, toddler, young innocent, youngling
ASSOCIATED CONCEPTS: abortion, adoption, baby act, illegitimacy

BACK *(In arrears),* *adjective*   behind, behind time, belated, deferred, delayed, detained, earlier, elapsed, expired, fore, forgotten, former, in abeyance, late, long-delayed, overdue, past, prior, tardy, unpunctual, unready
ASSOCIATED CONCEPTS: back pay, back taxes, back time doctrine, back wages

BACK *(In reverse),* *adjective*   backward, hindermost, hindmost, hindward, posterior, rearmost, rearward, retrogressive, retrospective, reversed, turned around
ASSOCIATED CONCEPTS: back lands

BACKBONE, *noun*   ardor, audacity, boldness, cornerstone, courage, dependency, determination, earnestness, embodiment, endurance, firmness, fortitude, gist, ground, indefatigability, intestinal fortitude, main point, mainstay, marrow, mettle, nerve, pillar, pith, pluck, quality, resoluteness, resolution, resolve, spine, steadfastness, strength, substance, support, tenacity, underpinning, valor, vigor, will

BACKER, *noun*   abettor, adherent, adjunct, adjutant, adjuvant, advocate, aider, ally, assister, auxiliary, benefactor, champion, coadjutant, coadjutor, coadjuvant, defender, endorser, ensurer, exponent, fautor, guarantor, helper, investor, lender, mainstay, maintainer, mortgatee, partisan, patron, promoter, protagonist, protector, reliever, second, seconder, sectary, sponsor, subsidizer, supporter, sustainer, sympathizer, upholder, warrantor

BACKING, *noun*   advocacy, aegis, aid, approval, assistance, auspices, bolstering, championing, charity, comfort, commendation, cooperation, coverage, defense, encouragement, favor, financing, furtherance, guarantee, guidance, help, indorsement, interest, investment, loan, maintenance, patronage, promotion, protection, reinforcement, relief, seconding, security, service, sponsorship, strengthening, subsidy, succor, support, sustenance, warranty

BACKSLIDING, *verb*   about face, adoption, afterthoughts, change like a chameleon, change of heart, change of mind, conversion, defection, diametrically opposed stance, divergence, diversion, flip-flop, 180 degree about face, qualification, realignment, regression, restructuring, reversal, reversion, temporizer, tergiversation, turn of the tide, turnabout
ASSOCIATED CONCEPTS: flip-flop on a political stance

BACKWARD, *adjective*   arrested, behindhand, belated, dallying, defected, delayed, delaying, dilatory, impeded, late, mentally deficient, overdue, procrastinating, regressive, retarded, retroactive, retrograde, reversed, slow, subnormal, tardy, untimely

BAD *(Inferior),* *adjective*   adultered, base, decaying, defective, degenerative, degraded, deleterious, deplorable, deteriorated, detrimental, dreadful, faulty, foul, fulsome, imperfect, impure, injurious, malignant, *malus,* noxious, objectionable, ruined, undesirable, unfit, unsound, unsuitable
ASSOCIATED CONCEPTS: bad bargain, bad check, bad title

BAD *(Offensive),* *adjective*   abhorrent, abominable, accusable, amoral, arrant, atrocious, baleful, baneful, base, contemptible, corrupt, cruel, debauched, degenerate, degraded, demoralized, deplorable, depraved, derogatory, despicable, destructive, detrimental, diabolic, dire, disastrous, disgraced, disgusting, dishonorable, disreputable, evil, execrable, flagitious, flagrant, fulsome, heinous, ignoble, immoral, *improbus,* improper, indecent, infamous, iniquitous, injurious, insidious, loathsome, maleficent, malevolent, malific, *malus,* miscreant, monstrous, nasty, nefarious, *nequam,* nocuous, objectionable, obnoxious, odious, offensive, onerous, oppressive, opprobrious, peccant, perfidious, pernicious, reprehensible, reprobate, repugnant, repulsive, retrogressive, revolting, ruined, ruinous, scandalous, sinful, sinister, treacherous, troublous, turpitudinous, undesirable, unfit, unsuitable, unvirtuous, venal, vicious, vile, villainous, virtueless, wicked
ASSOCIATED CONCEPTS: bad behavior, bad character, bad faith, bad influence, bad motive, bad reputation, bad repute
FOREIGN PHRASES: *In facto quod se habet ad bonum et malum, magis de bono quam de malo lex intendit.* In an act or deed which may be considered as both good and bad, the law directs its attention more to the good than the bad.

BAD CHARACTER, *noun*   bad name, bad reputation, bad repute, baseness, discredit, discreditableness, disesteem, disfavor, disgrace, dishonor, dishonorableness, disreputability, disrepute, ignobility, ignominy, ill favor, ill repute, infamy, lowness, reproachability, undesirability, unrespectability
ASSOCIATED CONCEPTS: character evidence, credibility, impeachment of credibility, imputation of character, reputation, slander

51

BAD CHECK, noun   deceptive check, defective check, forged check, fraudulent check, inutile check, invalid check, nugatory check, returned check, rubber check, suppositious check, unmarketable check, unserviceable check, unsound check, useless check, valueless check, void check, worthless check

ASSOCIATED CONCEPTS: criminal charge of worthless check-writing

BAD DEBT, noun   dishonored bill, inconvertible bill, irredeemable bill, irretrievable debt, loss, outstanding debt, protested bill, uncollectible debt, write-off

ASSOCIATED CONCEPTS: bad debt loss, bad debt tax deduction

BAD FAITH, noun   abjection, abjectness, abscondence, apostasy, artifice, base conduct, betrayal, betrayment, breach of faith, broken faith, broken promise, collaboration, collusion, complicity, connivance, cozenage, debasement, deceit, deceitfulness, deception, defalcation, defection, delusion, delusiveness, dereliction, dereliction of duty, deviation from rectitude, deviousness, disaffection, disavowal, dishonesty, dishonor, disingenuousness, disloyalty, disobedience, disrepute, double-dealing, duplicity, fallaciousness, false pretenses, false pretension, false swearing, falseheartedness, falseness, forswearing, fraud, fraudulency, furtiveness, guile, hypocrisy, ignominy, improbity, indiscretion, infidelity, infraction, insidiousness, insincerity, inveracity, lack of conscience, lack of fidelity, lack of principle, lack of probity, *mala fides,* malversation, mendaciousness, mendacity, meretriciousness, misfeasance, misrepresentation, obliquity, peculation, perfidiousness, perfidy, pettifoggery, pretense, pretext, punic faith, recantation, recreancy, reprobacy, sedition, seditiousness, spuriousness, subterfuge, subversion, subversive activity, suppression of truth, surreptitiousness, suspiciousness, traitorousness, treacherousness, treachery, truthlessness, turpitude, unauthenticity, unconscientiousness, underhand dealing, unfairness, unfaith, unfaithfulness, unfaithworthiness, ungenuineness, unloyalty, unscrupulousness, unsteadfastness, untrueness, untrustiness, untrustworthiness, untruthfulness, unveraciousness, unveracity, unverity, venality, violation of allegiance, violation of duty

ASSOCIATED CONCEPTS: fraud

BAD JUDGMENT, noun   aberrancy, aberration, blunder, distortion, errancy, erroneousness, error, fallacy, falseness, faultiness, inattention, indiscretion, inexactness, misapplication, miscalculation, misconception, misestimation, misinterpretation, misjudgment, misreckoning, mistake, perversion, wrong verdict

ASSOCIATED CONCEPTS: bad behavior, bad faith, bad judgment, bad motives

BAD REPUTE, noun   abasement, abjection, abjectness, abomination, allegation, amoralism, amorality, animadversion, antagonism, aspersion, attaint, bad character, bad influence, bad name, betrayal, calumniation, calumny, castigation, censoriousness, censure, charge, condemnation, confutation, contemptibility, contumely, corruption, criminality, crimination, criticism, debasement, decrial, defilement, degeneracy, degradation, delinquency, demoralization, denigration, denunciation, depravity, deprecation, derision, derogation, despicability, despicableness, detraction, deviation from rectitude, deviation from virtue, deviousness, disapprobation, discommendation, discountenance, discredit, disesteem, disfavor, disgrace, disgracefulness, dishonor, dishonorableness, disparagement, displacency, disreputability, disreputableness, disrepute, disrespectability, disrespectfulness, excoriation, exposure, flagitiousness, flagrancy, fraud, fraudulence, ignobility, ignominiousness, ignominy, ill repute, immorality, impaired reputation, improbation, improbity, impropriety, impugnation, increpation, inculpation, indecorum, infamousness, infamy, infidelity, insolence, irreverence, lack of integrity, laxity, loss of honor, loss of reputation, low regard, low standard, maculation, malevolence, malignity, malversation, misbehavior, moral degeneracy, moral turpitude, notoriety, objurgation, obliquity, obloquy, obnoxiousness, obtrectation, odiousness, odium, opprobrium, peccability, peculation, perfidiousness, perfidy, perversity, prodition, profligacy, public reproach, rapacity, rebuke, reflection, reprehension, reprimand, reproach, reprobation, reproof, revilement, scurrility, sedition, shame, shamefulness, slight, stigma, stricture, suspiciousness, taint, traducement, transgression, turpitude, unacceptableness, unrespectability, unscrupulousness, venality, vice, vilification, vilipendency, want of principle

ASSOCIATED CONCEPTS: character evidence, credibility of witness, moral turpitude, reputation

BADGER, verb   abuse, afflict, aggravate, aggrieve, annoy, annoy excessively, assail, bait, beset, bother, bully, chafe, discomfort, discommode, discompose, disconcert, disquiet, distress, disturb, disturb keenly, exasperate, excruciate, fret, goad, grate, harass, harrow, harry, heckle, hector, hound, importune, incommode, irk, irritate, mortify, nettle, oppress, perplex, persecute, perturb, pester, pique, plague, provoke, rile, roil, ruffle, taunt, tease, torment, torture, trouble, try one's patience, vex, worry

BAFFLE, verb   balk, befog, beguile, bewilder, bluff, bother, check, circumvent, complicate, confound, confuse, cross, defeat, discomfort, disconcert, dismay, disrupt, evade, flummox, fool, frustrate, fuddle, hoax, hinder, impede, incommode, inconvenience, irk, muddle, mystify, nonplus, obfuscate, obstruct, outwit, perplex, perturb, puzzle, stall, stymie, swindle, thwart, trick, upset

BAIL, noun   assurance, bond, caution money, collateral, earnest, gage, guaranty, indemnity, *pignus,* pledge, security, surety, undertaking

ASSOCIATED CONCEPTS: admission to bail, bail bond, bail piece, bonds, cash bail, common bail, excessive bail, execute on bail, forfeiture of bail, *ne exeat,* recognizance, reduction of bail, release on bail, revocation of bail, special bail, straw bail

BAILIWICK, noun   area, arena, authority, circle, department, district, domain, dominion, enclave, field, haunt, jurisdiction, orbit, precinct, province, purlieu, realm, region, specialty, sphere, sway, territory, ward

BAILMENT, noun   giving up, held in pledge, in escrow, transferred, under control

BAIT (Harass), **verb**   afflict, affront, aggravate, aggrieve, agitate, agonize, anger, annoy, arouse, attack, badger, be malevolent, be offensive, beset, besiege, bother, browbeat, cause resentment, chafe, compel, deride, detract, discommode, displease, distract, distress, disturb, dragoon, embitter, enflame, enrage, envenom, exasperate, excite, excite indignation, exhort, give offense to, give umbrage to, goad, grate, harry, haze, heckle, hector, hound, impel, importune, incense, incite, incommode, inconvenience, inflame, inflict, infuriate, instigate, insult, intimidate, irk, irritate, macerate, make wrathful, malign, maltreat, menace, offend, oppress, outrage, peeve, perplex, persecute, perturb, pique, plague, prey upon, provoke, pursue, put out of countenance, put pressure on, raid, rankle, rile, rouse, solicit insistently, spur, taunt, tease, terrorize, threaten, torment, trouble, try one's patience, tyrannize, urge, vex, victimize, worry

BAIT *(Lure)*, **verb** actuate, allure, appeal to, attract, bamboozle, befool, beguile, bias, chouse, compel, cozen, deceive, decoy, delude, dispose, draw, dupe, enlist, enmesh, ensnare, entangle, entice, entrap, entreat, entreaty, evoke, excite, exert pressure, exhort, forelay, gammon, goad, hold out allurement, impel, importune, incite, induce, influence, inveigle, lead astray, lead into temptation, lobby, persuade, predispose, press, prevail upon, provoke, seduce, snare, solicit, stimulate, suborn, swindle, take advantage of, tantalize, tease, tempt, titillate, trap, trepan, trick, urge
ASSOCIATED CONCEPTS: bait advertising, entrapment

BALANCE *(Amount in excess)*, **noun** carry-over, excess, extra, leftover, margin, oddments, overflow, overmeasure, overplus, overrun, oversupply, plus, *reliquus,* remainder, remaining portion, remains, remnant, residual, residual portion, residue, residuum, spare, superfluity, superfluousness, superplus, surfeit, surplus, surplusage
ASSOCIATED CONCEPTS: balance due

BALANCE *(Equality)*, **noun** analagousness, commensurability, comparability, comparableness, comparativeness, correspondence, equalization, equation, equilibration, equilibrium, equipoise, equipollence, equiponderance, equivalence, equivalency, homeostasis, level, *libro,* neutralization of forces, parity, stabilization, stable equilibrium, state of equilibrium, symmetrical scales, symmetry
ASSOCIATED CONCEPTS: balance account, balance of convenience, balance of hardship, balance sheet, balancing equities

BALANCED, *adjective* cadenced, cadent, coextensive, consonant, consistent, constant, equable, equal, equiponderant, equitable, even, evenhanded, fair, firm, fluent, harmonious, just, level, measured, on an even keel, orderly, poised, proportionate, proportioned, rational, regular, sane, square, symmetrical, uniform
ASSOCIATED CONCEPTS: balance of convenience, balance of power, balance of the equities

BALD, *adjective* arrant, artless, austere, bare, bawdy, blank, blunt, colorless, disclosed, dull, evident, exact, exposed, factual, flagrant, flat, glaring, insipid, laconic, literal, manifest, mere, obvious, open, outright, overt, plain, raw, revealed, ribald, severe, simple, stark, straightforward, tame, unabstructed, unadorned, undisguised, unembellished, unembroidered, ungarnished, uninteresting, unmistakable, unmitigated, unqualified, unsupported, unvarnished, vapid

BALEFUL, *adjective* bad, baneful, calamitous, damaging, dangerous, deadly, deleterious, despiteful, destructive, detrimental, dire, disadvantageous, evil, harmful, heinous, hurtful, ill-omened, inauspicious, insalubrious, lethal, malefic, malevolent, malicious, malignant, mischievous, nocuous, noxious, ominous, pernicious, pestilent, poisonous, portentous, prejudicial, sinister, spiteful, unpropitious, venomous, virulent

BALK, *verb* avert, baffle, bar, be obstructive, block, check, counter, counteract, countercheck, curb, defeat, delay, detain, *eludere,* estop, foil, forefend, forestall, *frustrari,* frustrate, give trouble, halt, hamper, hinder, hold in check, hold back, impede, impedite, interlope, interrupt, keep in check, nullify, obstruct, obturate, obviate, occlude, prevent, put in check, restrain, stall, stand in the way, stay, stop, stop short, stultify, stymie, suspend, thwart, traverse

BAN, *verb* abrogate, banish, bar, block, censor, check, declare illegal, deny, disallow, disqualify, embargo, enjoin, estop, exclude, forbid, foreclose, forfend, interdict, obstruct, outlaw, prevent, prohibit, proscribe, refuse, refuse permission, repress, restrain, say no to, shut off, shut out, stay, stop, suppress, taboo, veto, withhold permission
ASSOCIATED CONCEPTS: ban on Sunday sales

BANAL, *adjective* colorless, common, commonplace, conventional, deadly, drab, dreary, dull, hackneyed, familiar, flat, insipid, lifeless, matter of fact, mediocre, mundane, ordinary, pedestrian, platitudinous, simple, stale, stereotyped, stuffy, tedious, timeworn, traditional, trite, unimaginative, uninteresting, unoriginal, usual, vapid, worn

BAND, *noun* alliance, army, array, association, bevy, body, cabal, coalition, collection, combination, confederation, congregation, corps, coterie, covey, crew, detail, force, gang, *grex,* group, horde, league, legion, movement, outfit, pack, panel, phalanx, squad, team, tribe, troop, troupe, *turba,* unit

BANEFUL, *adjective* bad, baleful, corrosive, damaging, dangerous, deadly, deleterious, destructive, detrimental, disadvantageous, disastrous, disserviceable, evil, fatal, harmful, heinous, hostile, hurtful, insalubrious, injurious, lethal, malevolent, malignant, mischievous, noisome, noxious, pernicious, pestilent, poisonous, prejudicial, ruinous, sinister, threatening, toxic, unwholesome, venomous, virulent

BANISH, *verb* abandon, ban, bar, cast out, condemn, deport, dismiss, dispel, disperse, displace, drive out, eliminate, exclude, excommunicate, exile, expatriate, expel, export, extradite, isolate, ostracize, oust, outlaw, prohibit, proscribe, reject, remove, renounce, seclude, transport, turn out

BANISHMENT, *noun* deportation, discharge, dismissal, displacement, ejection, eviction, excommunication, exile, exilement, expatriation, expulsion, extradition, *interdictio aquae et ignis,* involuntary exile, ostracism, ostracization, ousting, outlawry, *relegatio,* removal

BANK, *noun* bursary, cash box, coffer, depository, monetary reservoir, money box, pecuniary resource, promptuary, public treasury, repository, reserve, safe, safe-deposit vault, storehouse, strongroom, till, vault
ASSOCIATED CONCEPTS: bank account, bank bill, bank certificate, bank check, bank collections, bank deposit, bank draft, bank examiner, bank money order, bank note, bank of deposit, bank of issue, bank robber, bank stock, bank transaction, bank withdrawal, bankbook, banker's acceptance, banker's lien, banking hours, banking powers, banking privileges, commercial bank, savings bank

BANKRUPT, *adjective* bereft, broke, broken, *decoctor,* defaulting, destitute, failed, impecunious, impoverished, in receivership, in the hands of receivers, incapable of discharging liabilities, indigent, insolvent, left in penury, moneyless, out of funds, out of money, pauperized, penniless, poverty-stricken, ruined, unable to make both ends meet, unable to pay matured debts, unable to satisfy creditors, unmoneyed
ASSOCIATED CONCEPTS: bankruptcy, bankruptcy court, discharge in bankruptcy, estate of the bankrupt

BANKRUPTCY, *noun* defaulting, destituteness, destitution, failure, financial disaster, financial failure, financial ruin, impecuniosity, inability to pay, indigence, insolvency, involuntary liquidation, loss, loss of fortune, pauperism, penury, privation, ruin, ruination

ASSOCIATED CONCEPTS: adverse claims, arrangement for the benefit of creditors, bankruptcy act, bankruptcy assets, bankruptcy court, bankruptcy estate, bankruptcy proceedings, composition in bankruptcy, composition proceedings, discharge in bankruptcy, foreclosure, fraudulent conveyance, fraudulent transfers, involuntary bankruptcy, preferences, priorities, provable debts, receivers in bankruptcy, referees in bankruptcy, reorganization proceedings, sale of assets, schedules, trustee in bankruptcy, valuation, void preference, voidable transfer

BAR (Body of lawyers), **noun**   advocates, attorneys, attorneys-at-law, barristers, counsel, counselors, counselors-at-law, jurists, lawyers, the legal fraternity, legal profession, legists, solicitors
ASSOCIATED CONCEPTS: bar association, member of the bar

BAR (Court), **noun**   assize, bench, court of justice, court of law, curia, forum, judicature, judiciary, seat of justice, sessions, tribunal
ASSOCIATED CONCEPTS: bar of justice

BAR (Obstruction), **noun**   balk, ban, barricade, barrier, block, blockage, circumscription, constraint, curb, difficulty, embargo, enjoining, estoppel, exclusion, forbiddance, foreclosure, forestalling, hindrance, hurdle, impediment, impedition, infarction, injunction, interdict, interference, limit, limitation, nonadmission, noninclusion, obstacle, preclusion, prevention, prohibition, proscription, refusal, rejection, restraint, stoppage, stopper, stumbling block, suppression
ASSOCIATED CONCEPTS: bar by former judgment, estoppel

BAR (Exclude), **verb**   ban, blacklist, circumscribe, debar, deny, disallow, except, exile, forbid, interdict, keep out, leave out, limit, lock out, occlude, omit, ostracize, outlaw, preclude, prevent, prohibit, refuse, reject, relegate, restrict, shut out, spurn, suspend

BAR (Hinder), **verb**   avert, barricade, block, blockade, bolt, bridle, choke, choke off, curb, embar, enjoin, erect a barrier, estop, fasten, fence, forbid, foreclose, frustrate, hamper, impede, inhibit, interfere with, obstruct, obviate, occlude, preclude, prevent, prohibit, proscribe, put an embargo on, put one's veto upon, repress, restrain, retard, seal, secure, shut off, stand in the way, stay, stop, thwart, trammel

BAR SINISTER, **noun**   bastardism, bastardization, bastardy, baton, birth out of wedlock, champain, illegitimacy, illegitimateness, illegitimation, illicit procreation, misbegetting, unlawful begetting

BARE, **verb**   admit, air, announce, appear, be disclosed, be public, bring into view, bring out in evidence, bring to light, confess, declare, denude, disclose, display, divulgate, divulge, evince, evulgate, exhibit, expose, expose to view, lay bare, lay open, make apparent, make evident, make known, make manifest, make public, manifest, open, open up, publicize, represent, reveal, set forth evidence, show, surface, tell the truth, uncloak, unclothe, unconceal, uncover, uncurtain, undisguise, undrape, unfold, unfurl, unmask, unscreen, unseal, unsheathe, unshield, unshroud, unveil, unwrap, vent, ventilate

BARGAIN, **noun**   accord, accordance, agreement, arrangement, collective agreement, compact, compromise, concord, concordance, concordat, contract, convention, covenant, entente, mutual agreement, mutual pledge, mutual understanding, mutual undertaking, pact, pactio, settlement, stipulation, treaty, understanding

ASSOCIATED CONCEPTS: arm's-length bargain, bargain and sale deed, bargain and sale in a conveyance, bargain collectively, bargain in good faith, bargain in restraint of trade, bargaining agent, bargaining unit, benefit of the bargain rule, collective bargaining, collective bargaining agreement

BARGAIN FOR, **verb**   agree to, anticipate, assume, bank on, buy, calculate on, come to terms, contemplate, contract for, count upon, covenant, expect, figure on, foresee, incur, look for, plan on, prepare for, reckon on, specify, stipulate, surmise, think likely

BAROMETER, **noun**   climate, conclusion, criterion, feeling, gauge, measure, model, norm, outcome, pattern, result, rule, scale, sounding board, standard, test, touchstone, type, yardstick

BARRAGE, **noun**   artillery fire, assault, attack, blare, blast, blitz, bombardment, bombings, boom, broadside, burst, cannonade, clamor, concentration, covering fire, cross fire, explosions, fire, gunfire, protective fire, roar, salvo, shelling, shower, siege, spray, storm, storming, thunder, verbal assault, volley

BARRED, **adjective**   banned, debarred, disallowed, excepted, excluded, precluded, prohibited, proscribed, shut out

BARREN, **adjective**   arid, bare, childless, desolate, disused, empty, fallow, fruitless, functionless, idle, impotent, inactive, inane, infecund, infertile, insufficient, issueless, nonfertile, nonproducing, nonproductive, profitless, scarce, shallow, sparse, stagnating, sterile, teemless, unable to yield, unfertile, unfruitful, ungerminating, unprocreant, unproductive, unprofitable, unprolific, unrewarded, unrewarding, unsalable, unyielding, vacant, vacuous, valueless, void, void of contents, waste, wasteful, without issue, worthless
ASSOCIATED CONCEPTS: barren land

BARRICADE, **noun**   bar, barrier, blockade, bulwark, damper, dike, embankment, fortification, impediment, obstacle, obstruction, protection, rampart, restraint, stockade, wall

BARRICADE (Hinder), **verb**   bar, block, check, deter, enjoin, halt, hamper, impede, lock, obstruct, occlude, shut, stop

BARRICADE (Protect), **verb**   bolt, close, close off, confine, constrict, contain, dam up, defend, dig in, enclose, entrench, fasten, fence in, fortify, lock up, picket, secure, shut out

BARRIER, **noun**   bar, barricade, bound, boundary, bulwark, check, confines, enclosure, encumbrance, fence, fortification, hindrance, hurdle, impediment, interference, limit, obstacle, obstruction, partition, prevention, preventive, prohibition, protective device, rampart, restraining device, restraint, restriction, safeguard, stay, stop, stumbling block, termination, wall

BARRISTER, **noun**   advocate, attorney, attorney-at-law, counsel, counselor, counselor-at-law, jurisconsult, jurisprudent, jurist, lawyer, learned counsel, legal adviser, legal practitioner, legist, member of the bar, procurator, publicist, solicitor

BARTER, **verb**   bargain, buy and sell, deal, dicker, exchange, give and take, give in exchange, haggle, interchange, make exchanges, market, merces mutare, merchandise, peddle, rem pro re pacisci, rem re mutare, strike a bargain, swap, switch, trade, trade by exchange, trade off, traffic by exchange, vend

BASE (Bad), *adjective*   contemptible, cowardly, despicable, despised, disreputable, heinous, immoral, odious, virtueless, wicked

BASE (Inferior), *adjective*   abject, cheap, common, dilapidated, dirty, lowly, mean, menial, poor

BASE (Foundation), *noun*   basis, cause, pivotal argument, starting point, support

BASE (Place), *noun*   abode, center, central headquarters, headquarters, place, station

BASED ON, *adverb*   bear upon, built on, contingent upon, dependent on, founded on, grounded on, relying on, rested on

BASELESS, *adjective*   bottomless, empty, erroneous, false, foundationless, gratuitous, groundless, having no foundation, idle, ill-founded, illogical, nonactual, not well-founded, rootless, unbased, uncaused, uncorroborated, unfounded, ungrounded, unjustifiable, unprincipled, unreasonable, unsound, unsubstantial, unsubstantiated, unsupportable, unsupported, unsustainable, unsustained, untenable, unwarranted, vain, without base, without basis, without cause, without reality, without reason

BASIC, *adjective*   a priori, aboriginal, central, elementary, essential, fundamental, implicit, indispensable, initial, innate, integral, intrinsic, material, monolithic, native, necessary, organic, original, practical, primary, prime, primitive, primordial, requisite, rudimentary, simple, substantial, substantive, ultimate, underlying, virtual, vital
ASSOCIATED CONCEPTS: basic patent, basic understanding of the law

BASIC FACTS, *noun*   essentials, the case, the facts in the matter, the facts of the case, the whole story

BASIS, *noun*   assumption, authority, background, base, cause, essence, foundation, fulcrum, fundamentals, *fundus,* ground, groundwork, hypothesis, justification, motive, origin, premise, principle, proposition, purpose, *raison d'être,* rationale, reason, root, source, support, underlying principle, warrant
ASSOCIATED CONCEPTS: basis of cost, basis of keeping accounts, basis of the bargain, cash basis, contingency basis, cost-plus basis

BASTARD, *noun*   adulterine, bantling, child born before marriage, child born out of wedlock, illegitimate child, nothus, *nullius filius,* spurious issue
ASSOCIATED CONCEPTS: acknowledgment, bastardy proceeding, illegitimate, inheritance, legitimacy support, putative father
FOREIGN PHRASES: **Bastardus non potest habere haeredem nisi de corpore suo legitime procreatum.** A bastard cannot have an heir unless he is one lawfully begotten of his own body. **Bastardus nullius est filius, aut filius populi**. A bastard is the son of no one, or the son of the people. **Non est justum aliquem antenatum post mortem facere bastardum qui toto tempore vitae suae pro legitimo habebatur.** It is not just to make anyone a bastard after his death, who during his lifetime was regarded as legitimate. **Qui nascitur sine legitimo matrimonio, matrem sequitur.** He who is born out of lawful matrimony succeeds to the condition of his mother. **Partus ex legitimo thoro non certius noscit matrem quam genitorem suum.** The offspring of a legitimate marriage knows not his mother more certainly than his father.

Qui ex damnato coitu nascuntur inter liberos non computentur. They who are born of an illicit union should not be reckoned among the children.

BASTION, *noun*   asylum, bulwark, castle, citadel, defense, fort, fortification, fortress, mainstay, parapet, rampart, sanctuary, security, stronghold, tower

BATTERY, *noun*   assault, attack, beating, harmful physical contact, injurious force, offensive action, onslaught, thrashing, unlawful hitting, unlawful striking, unlawful touching
ASSOCIATED CONCEPTS: assault and battery, simple battery

BATTLE (Dispute), *noun*   action, affair, affray, argument, campaign, clash, collision, conflict, confrontation, contention, contest, crusade, discord, dispute, dissension, encounter, engagement, hostilities, ordeal, resistance, row, showdown, strife, struggle

BATTLE (Fight), *noun*   affray, altercation, armed conflict, bout, brawl, combat, conflict, fracas, fray, free-for-all, melee, quarrel, rift, scuffle, skirmish, tussle, war, warfare

BATTLE (Dispute), *verb*   altercate, argue, attack, bicker, campaign, clash, compete, contend, contest, debate, disagree, dissent, encounter, engage, grapple, litigate, oppose, resist, strike at, struggle, take on, wrangle

BATTLE (Fight), *verb*   assault, attack, combat, come to blows, physically assault, pummel, resist, skirmish

BEAR (Adduce), *verb*   acknowledge, acknowledge openly, adjure, admit, affirm, afford proof of, allege, allude to, argue, ascertain, assent, assert, assert absolutely, asseverate, assure, attest, authenticate, aver, avouch, avow, bring forward, bring to light, bring up, call to mind, certify, circumstantiate, cite, claim, contend, corroborate, declare, declare to be fact, demonstrate, denote, depone, depose, display, divulge, document, elucidate, emphasize, endorse, establish, evidence, evince, exemplify, exhibit, expose, express, formulate, furnish evidence, give evidence, give information, give one's word, give witness, guarantee, have evidence, illustrate, imply, indicate, inform, introduce, invoke, involve, maintain, make a statement, make an assertion, make evident, make reference to, make solemn, manifest, name, plead, pledge, point out, point to, present, proclaim, produce, produce the evidence, profess, promulgate, propound, prove, publish, ratify, refer to, represent, show, signify, stand firm, state as fact, state on oath, stipulate, submit, subscribe, substantiate, sustain, swear, take one's oath, testify, validate, verify, vindicate, vouch for, vow, warrant, witness to
ASSOCIATED CONCEPTS: bear false witness, bear witness

BEAR (Support), *verb*   abet, aid, ally, assist, back, back up, bolster, brace, bulwark, buoy up, buttress, carry, champion, contribute to, cradle, cushion, *ferre,* finance, fortify, fortress, foster, furnish assistance, furnish support, furnish sustenance, garrison, *gestare,* give base, give foundation, give ground, give support, hold a brief for, hold up, justify, lend support, maintain, nourish, oblige, plead for, *portare,* promote, prop, provide for, rally to, reinforce, safeguard, sanction, second, shoulder, steady, strengthen, succor, supply aid, supply support, sustain, truss, upbear, uphold, vindicate
ASSOCIATED CONCEPTS: bear the expense, bear weight

BEAR (Tolerate), *verb*   abide, accede to, accept, acquiesce, adhere to, allow, approve, be lenient, be patient, be subjected to, brave, carry on, concede, condone, continue, endure, experience, forbear, go through, keep on, keep one's countenance, labor under, live through, meet with, obey, observe, *pati,* permit, persevere, persist in, plod, put up with, recognize, resign oneself, sanction, show forbearance, spare, stand, stand the strain, submit to, suffer, suffice, support, sustain, *sustinere,* take patiently, *tolerare,* treat with indulgence, undergo, weather

BEAR *(Yield),* **verb**   accrue, afford, aggrandize, allot, assign, augment, bestow, breed, bring about, bring forth, bring in a supply, cause, confer, contribute, convey, create, deliver, develop, dispense, earn, effectuate, emit, endow, engender, enlarge, equip, evolve, fructify, fund, furnish, gain, generate, give, give increase, grant, impart, make payment, make provision, manifest, minister to, multiply, offer, *parere,* pay back, procreate, produce, profit, proliferate, propagate, provide, provision, purvey, reinforce, remit, render, replenish, reproduce, restore, return, supply, surrender, transfer
ASSOCIATED CONCEPTS: bear interest

BEAR FALSE WITNESS, verb   abrogate, affirm the contrary, apostatize, be deceitful, be devoid of truth, be dishonest, be erroneous, be faithless, be fallacious, be false, be forsworn, be fraudulent, be insincere, be mendacious, be perfidious, be perjured, be spurious, be untruthful, belie, betray, break faith, contradict, deny, deviate from the truth, distort, falsely testify, falsify, forswear, go back on one's word, impugn, lie, miscite, misreport, perjure oneself, pervert, prevaricate, revoke, speak falsely, swear falsely, take back, tell a lie, utter a falsehood
ASSOCIATED CONCEPTS: false swearing, perjury

BEAR THE EXPENSE, verb   bear the cost, compensate, defray, defray expenses, defray the cost, discharge, expend, give money, incur costs, incur expenses, indemnify, make compensation, make expenditure, make payment, make restitution, meet the bill, outlay, pay an indemnity, pay compensation, pay damages, pay for, pay in full, pay on demand, pay the bill, pay the costs, pay wages, recompense, refund, reimburse, remit, remunerate, render, repay, restitute, stand the cost

BEAR UPON, verb   advocate, affect, apply, apply to, cause, coax, concern, connect, have to do with, influence, insist, interest, involve, pertain, pertain to, press, pressure, recommend, refer, regard, relate, relate to, respect, rest on, tie in with, touch, urge
ASSOCIATED CONCEPTS: to bear upon a witness' credibility, to bear upon guilt or innocence, to bear upon the evidence, to bear upon the outcome of a case

BEAR WITNESS, verb   acknowledge, attest, authenticate, avouch, avow, certify, corroborate, give evidence, inform on, promise, seal, sell out, speak, substantiate, swear, take the stand, tell on, testify, turn informer, turn state's evidence, vouch, witness
ASSOCIATED CONCEPTS: bear witness to a crime, bear witness to an accident, bear witness to an incident

BEARER, noun   acceptor, carrier, casher, check holder, draft holder, grantee, holder, possessor, receiver, recipient, taker, transferee
ASSOCIATED CONCEPTS: bearer check, bearer instrument, bearer note, bearer paper, negotiable instruments

BEAT *(Defeat),* **verb**   be superior, be supreme, be victorious over, bring to terms, checkmate, claim a victory, conquer, crush, dash, discomfit, excel, get the best of, get the

better of, have the advantage, hold the advantage, lay waste, obtain a victory, outclass, outdo, outflank, outmaneuver, outplay, outpoint, outrange, outrival, overbear, overbid, overcome, overmaster, overmatch, overpower, override, overtake, overthrow, overtrump, overwhelm, predominate, preponderate, prevail over, put to rout, quell, ravage, reduce, repulse, rout, seize the advantage, subdue, subjugate, succeed in winning, *superare,* suppress, surmount, surpass, take precedence, thwart, trample upon, transcend, triumph over, undo, upset, vanquish, *vincere,* win the battle

BEAT *(Pulsate),* **verb**   alternate, come and go, convulse, ebb and flow, falter, flicker, flitter, fluctuate, flutter, move up and down, oscillate, palpitate, pass and repass, pendulate, pound, pulse, quake, quaver, quiver, reciprocate, seesaw, shake, shiver, shuffle, strike, sway, swing, teeter, throb, thump, toss, tremble, undulate, vacillate, vibrate, wave, waver, writhe

BEAT *(Strike),* **verb**   abuse, afflict, attack, baste, bastinado, batter, bruise, buffet, *caedere,* club, concuss, contund, contuse, cudgel, cuff, *ferire,* fight, flagellate, flail, flog, fustigate, give a blow, give a thrashing, hit, inflict, kick, knock down, lambaste, land a blow, lash, lunge at, maul, pelt, *percutere,* pound, *pulsare,* pummel, punch, punish, rap, slam, slap, slug, smack, smite, swing, thrash, thresh, trounce, truncheon, *verberare,* whip
ASSOCIATED CONCEPTS: assault, assault and battery, battery

BECOME *(Arise),* **verb**   befall, come about, come into being, come into existence, commence, ensue, germinate, happen, materialize, occur, proceed, result, succeed

BECOME *(Develop),* **verb**   adorn, alter, arise, befit, behoove, benefit, beseem, change into, come to be, comport, convert, enhance, enrich, evolve, ferment, fit, garnish, harmonize with, heighten, mature, ornament, please, ripen into, satisfy, spring up, suit, take its course, turn into, turn out to be

BEFORE MENTIONED, adjective   above, above-cited, above-mentioned, above-named, above-stated, aforehand, aforestated, antecedent, anterior, earlier, foregoing, forementioned, forenamed, former, latter, named, precedent, preceding, precursive, precursory, preexistent, prefatory, preliminary, prepositive, prevenient, previous, prior

BEFOREHAND, adverb   ahead of, already, antecedent to, as a precursor to, before now, earlier, early, in advance of, in anticipation, on the eve of, preparatory to, previous to, previously, prior to

BEGIN, verb   arise, assume, broach, come into existence, commence, conceive, create, dawn, develop, embark, enter, establish, found, generate, go ahead, inaugurate, incept, initiate, institute, introduce, launch, maintain, open, originate, pave the way, pioneer, preface, prepare, promote, provoke, spring, start, start up, stem, tackle, take on, take shape, undertake, unfold, unveil

BEGINNING, noun   birth, causative, commencement, conception, creation, derivation, early derivation, elementary, embryo, emergence, foundation, fountain, fountainhead, genesis, inauguration, inception, incipience, infancy, initial, kick-off, nascence, onset, opening, origin, origination, overture, preamble, precursor, preface, preliminary, prelude, prime, source, spring, stage, start, starting point

BEHALF, noun account, advantage, advocacy, aid, aidance, assistance, auspices, avail, behoof, benefaction, benefit, benevolence, betterment, boon, contribution, countenance, defense, endowment, expedience, favor, furtherance, gift, good, help, improvement, increment, interest, ministration, opportunity, preferment, profit, promotion, propriety, protection, sponsorship, stead, support, sustenance, utility, welfare
ASSOCIATED CONCEPTS: agency, representative capacity

BEHAVIOR, noun actions, air, bearing, beliefs, carriage, character, comportment, conduct, consuetude, course, course of conduct, course of life, decorum, demeanor, deportment, habits, habituation, habitude, inveteracy, line of conduct, manner, manner of life, manners, matter of course, mien, mode of action, *mores*, personal bearing, presence, propriety, ritual, ritualism, routine, way of acting, way of life
ASSOCIATED CONCEPTS: bad behavior, contemptuous behavior, good behavior, indecent behavior
FOREIGN PHRASES: *Ad vitam aut culpam.* For life, or until guilty of misbehavior. *De bono gestu.* For or during good behavior.

BEHOLD, verb catch sight of, clap eyes on, consider, descry, detect, discern, discover, distinguish, espy, examine, eye, gaze at, glimpse, heed, inspect, look, look at, look upon, make out, mark, notice, observe, perceive, pierce, recognize, regard, remark, scan, scrutinize, see, see at a glance, sight, spy, stare at, survey, take in, view, watch, witness

BEING (Core), noun actuality, center, character, complexion, constituent, entity, essence, identity, individuality, inherence in, intellect, lifeblood, mind, monad, nature, occurrence, presence, psyche, quiddity, reality, root, spirit, substance, truth, veracity

BEING (Person), noun body, creature, existence, individual, inhabitant, life, living, man, mortal, object, organism, personality, somebody, someone, subsistence, thing, woman

BELAUD, verb compliment, eulogize, exalt, extol, glorify, laud, make much of, pay tribute, praise, sing the praises of

BELIEF (Something believed), noun canon, conclusion, conviction, credo, creed, doctrinal statement, doctrine, dogma, expectation, maxim, persuasion, precept, principle, rule, tenet
ASSOCIATED CONCEPTS: beyond reasonable doubt, presumption

BELIEF (State of mind), noun absoluteness, assurance, assuredness, certainty, certitude, conclusion, confidence, conviction, credence, credulity, definiteness, expectation, intuition, judgment, *opinio*, opinion, persuasio, positiveness, sanguineness, understanding, unequivocalness
ASSOCIATED CONCEPTS: good faith belief, suspicion
FOREIGN PHRASES: *Cuilibet in arte sua perito est credendum.* Credence should be given to one skilled in his particular art. *Cuique in sua arte credendum est.* Everyone is to be believed in reference to his own art or profession. *Testibus deponentibus in pari numero, dignioribus est credendum.* When the number of testifying witnesses is equal on both sides, the more worthy are to be believed.

BELIEVABLE, adjective conceivable, convincing, credential, credible, creditable, dependable, incontestable, incontrovertible, indisputable, indubitable, irrefragable, irrefutable, likely, persuasive, plausible, presumable, probable, reliable, sure, tenable, trustworthy, trusty, undeniable,

unimpeachable, unquestionable, verisimilar, well-founded, well-grounded
ASSOCIATED CONCEPTS: evidence of trustworthiness

BELIEVE (Presume), verb admit, apprehend, assert, assume, be assured, be certain, be convinced, conceive, conjecture, consider, declare, deduce, deem, divine, expect, fancy, feel, guess, hold, imagine, infer, judge, know, maintain, opine, perceive, postulate, presuppose, realize, regard, rely on, suppose, surmise, suspect, swallow, theorize, think, trust in, understand

BELIEVE (Trust), verb accept, accredit, acknowledge, be confident of, be sure of, buy, count on, credit, entrust with, give credence to, have confidence in, have faith in, hope, rely upon, swear by
ASSOCIATED CONCEPTS: believe a witness, liable, making a false statement, perjury, slander

BELLIGERENCY, noun affray, aggression, aggressiveness, altercation, animosity, antagonism, assault, attack, battling, bellicosity, belligerance, clashing, combat, combativeness, conflict, contentiousness, contestation, controversy, disagreement, discord, disputation, dissension, disturbance, embroilment, encounter, enmity, feud, fighting, fracas, hostility, impugnation, impugnment, inimicality, malevolence, martiality, melee, militancy, opposition, oppugnancy, oppugnation, pugnaciousness, pugnacity, resort to arms, revengefulness, riot, rivalry, scuffle, siege, sparring, state of siege, state of war, strife, time of war, tumult, tussle, unpeacefulness, violence, warfare, warlikeness, wartime, wrangle
ASSOCIATED CONCEPTS: adverse possession, belligerency de facto, international law, national defense

BENCH, noun bar, bar of justice, board, cabinet, chamber, circuit, council, court, court of justice, court of law, forum, forum of justice, judge, judgment seat, judicatory, judicature, judicial assembly, judicial forum, judicial tribunal, judiciary, *judicium*, justice, justice seat, law court, legal administration, magistracy, magistrate, magistrature, open court, panel of judges, privy council, seat of judgment, seat of justice, tribunal
ASSOCIATED CONCEPTS: at the bench, bench docket, bench notes, bench warrant

BENCHMARK, noun bookmark, critical point, crucial point, crux, essence, essential matter, fundamental part, gist, gravamen, heart, key point, linchpin, main point, material point, milestone, pivotal point, prime issue, salient point, substance, substantive point, turning point

BENEATH CONTEMPT, adjective abhorrent, abominable, appalling, atrocious, contemptible, deplorable, despicable, detestable, dreadful, foul, frightening, frightful, ghastly, ghoulish, gruesome, harrowing, hateful, heinous, horrendous, horrid, horrifying, loathsome, obnoxious, odious, offensive, outrageous, pathetic, pitiful, repellent, reprehensible, repulsive, revolting, shameful, shocking, terrible, terrifying, unspeakable, vile, villainous
ASSOCIATED CONCEPTS: appalling conduct, contempt of court, harassment

BENEFACTOR, noun abettor, advocate, aid, aider, ally, altruist, assister, backer, beneficent friend, benefiter, champion, contributor, defender, donor, favorer, free giver, friend, giver, Good Samaritan, help, helper, humanitarian, kind person, maintainer, ministrant, patron, philanthropist, promoter, protector, redeemer, rescuer, seconder, succorer, supporter, sustainer, upholder, well-doer

BENEFICIAL, *adjective* advantageous, aidful, aiding, anodyne, availing, beneficent, benign, benignant, conducive, constructive, contributive, contributory, convenient, cooperative, edifying, efficacious, favorable, fertile, for one's good, for one's interest, functional, gainful, good for one's advantage, helpful, helping, improving, invaluable, obliging, of general utility, of service, of value, paying, practicable, practical, productive, proficuous, profitable, prolific, promoting, propitious, prosperous, remunerative, salubrious, *salutaris,* salutary, salutiferous, serendipitous, to one's advantage, usable, useful, *utilis,* utilitarian, valuable, worthwhile
ASSOCIATED CONCEPTS: beneficial association, beneficial enjoyment, beneficial estate, beneficial gift, beneficial interest, beneficial owner, beneficial power, beneficial purposes, beneficial use

BENEFICIARY, *noun* *bènèficiare,* donee, grantee, heir, heiress, inheritor, legatee, one who receives, payee, receiver, recipient, usufructuary
ASSOCIATED CONCEPTS: beneficiary of a trust, beneficiary under a will, *cestui que trust*

BENEFIT *(Betterment),* ***noun*** accommodation, advantage, assistance, avail, behoof, benefaction, comfort, convenience, enjoyment, expediency, gain, good, gratification, improvement, interest, pleasure, profit, promotion, relief, return, satisfaction, solace, success, succor, usufruct, utility, utilization, welfare, well-being, worth
ASSOCIATED CONCEPTS: beneficial use, benefit of clergy, benefit of counsel, benefit of creditors, benefit of estate, benefit of the bargain, benefit of third person
FOREIGN PHRASES: *In favorabilibus magis attenditur quod prodest quam quod nocet.* In things favored, what is beneficial is more regarded than what is harmful. *Privatum incommodum publico bono pensatur.* Private inconvenience is compensated for by public benefit.

BENEFIT *(Conferment),* ***noun*** aid, award, benefaction, beneficence, benevolence, bequest, bestowal, bonus, boon, charity, compensation, contribution, courtesy, devise, dispensation, donation, endowment, favor, gift, good turn, gratuity, kindness, largess, legacy, liberality, oblation, offering, offertory, philanthropy, present, presentation, remittance, reward, subsidy, subvention
ASSOCIATED CONCEPTS: benefit certificate
FOREIGN PHRASES: *Invito beneficium non datur.* A benefit is not conferred upon a person against his will. *Privilegium est beneficium personale, et extinguitur cum persona.* A privilege is a personal benefit, and is extinguished with the death of the person. *Omnes licentiam habere his quae pro se indulta sunt, renunciare.* All are free to renounce those privileges which have been allowed for their benefit.

BENEVOLENCE *(Act of kindness),* ***noun*** assistance, benefaction, beneficence, *benevolentia,* boon, charitable effort, charity, favor, good deed, good treatment, good turn, helpfulness, kind office, kind treatment, philanthropy, relief, service, succor, support

BENEVOLENCE *(Disposition to do good),* ***noun*** affection, agreeableness, altruism, amiability, amicableness, beneficence, benignancy, bountifulness, brotherliness, charitableness, charity, clemency, compassion, consideration, cordiality, courtesy, forbearance, friendliness, friendship, generosity, good disposition, good intention, good nature, good will, goodness, goodness and mercy, graciousness, helpfulness, humaneness, humanism, humanity, indulgence, kindheartedness, kindliness, kindness, liberality, mercy, munificence, obligingness, philanthropy, placability, Samaritanism, softheartedness, solicitousness, solicitude, tenderness, thoughtfulness, tolerance, understanding, unselfishness, warmheartedness

BENEVOLENT, *adjective* accommodating, affable, agreeable, altruistic, amiable, amicable, bearing good will, beneficient, *benevolus,* benign, big-hearted, bounteous, bountiful, charitable, complacent, condolent, considerate, cooperative, cordial, decent, disposed to good, doing good, eleemosynary, empathetic, freehanded, friendly, full of good will, generous, genial, good-humored, good natured, gracious, helpful, hospitable, humane, humanitarian, indulgent, kind, kindhearted, kindly, kindly disposed, liberal, magnanimous, merciful, munificent, neighborly, obliging, openhanded, philanthropic, softhearted, solicitous, supportive, sweet-tempered, sympathizing, tender, thoughtful, tolerant, understanding, ungrudging, unselfish, unsparing, unstinting, warm, warmhearted, well-intentioned, well-meaning, well-meant
ASSOCIATED CONCEPTS: benevolent and charitable organization, benevolent and charitable purposes, benevolent association, benevolent corporation, benevolent institution, benevolent use, charitable corporation

BEQUEATH, *verb* administer to, afford, allow, assign dower, bestow upon, cede, change hands, contribute, deliver to, demise, devise, devolve upon, dispense, dispose of, distribute, donate, endow with, enfeoff, furnish, give, give away at death, give by will, grant, hand down, hand on, hand over to, interchange, invest, leave, leave a legacy, leave by will, leave to, make a bequest, make a present of, make legacies, pass on to, pass over to, provide, put in possession, remit, render, transfer ownership, vest in, will to
ASSOCIATED CONCEPTS: bequest
FOREIGN PHRASES: *Da tua dum tua sunt, post mortem tunc tua non sunt.* Give that which is yours while it is yours, after death it is not yours.

BEQUEST, *noun* bequeathal, birthright, demise, devisal, devise, endowment, entail, gift, heirdom, heirloom, hereditament, heritable, heritage, inheritance, legacy, *legatum,* patrimony, testamentary disposition, testamentary gift
ASSOCIATED CONCEPTS: bequest by implication, bequest for life, bequest in trust, devise, gift, inheritance
FOREIGN PHRASES: *Nemo plus commodi haeredi suo relinquit quam ipse habuit.* No one leaves a greater advantage for his heir than he himself had.

BESPEAK, *verb* argue, attest, call, connote, convey, denote, express, imply, import, indicate, mean, purport, signify, speak of, suggest, tell of, testify

BEST, *adjective* above the average, beyond compare, brought to perfection, chief, choice, crowning, distinguished, exceptional, exemplary, extraordinary, faultless, favorite, first-class, first-rate, flawless, foremost, greater, highest, impeccable, incomparable, inimitable, matchless, maximum, most desirable, most excellent, optimal, *optimus,* outstanding, paramount, peerless, perfect, preeminent, quintessential, record-breaking, *sans pareil,* second to none, select, superfine, superior, superlative, supernormal, supreme, surpassing, top-level, top-notch, topmost, transcendent, unapproached, unequaled, unparalleled, unrivaled, uppermost, without comparison
ASSOCIATED CONCEPTS: best ability, best and highest use, best bid, best efforts, best energies, best evidence, best interests, best interests of a child, best interests of the public, best

judgment, best quality, best skill and discretion or judgment, best testimony

BESTIALITY, noun animalism, barbarity, barbarousness, beastliness, bloodthirstiness, brutality, brutishness, cruelty, ferociousness, ferocity, fiendishness, fierceness, grossness, inhumanity, monstrousness, savagery, unnaturalness, viciousness

BESTOW, verb accord, accredit, address, administer, afford, allot, allow, appoint, apportion, *attribuere,* authorize, award, be favorable to, be prodigal, bequeath, cater, cede, charter, commission, communicate, *conferre,* concede, confer, confer a privilege, confer distinction, consent, contribute, convey, deal, deign, deliver, dignify, dispense, dispose of, distribute, dole, donate, empower, endow, enfranchise, enrich, entitle, equip, extend, facilitate, facultate, favor with, finance, foster, fund, furnish, give, give a present, give approval, give assent, give away, give back, give clearance, give consent, give dispensation, give freely, give leave, give one's hand to, give out, give out in shares, give permission, give power, give up, grant, grant a boon, grant a request, grant permission, gratify, hand out, hand over, heap upon, help to, honor with, impart, *impertire,* indulge, install, invest, issue, *largiri,* lavish, lend, let, license, maintain, make a benefaction, make a loan, make a present of, make provision for, mete, minister to, oblige, ordain, part with, pay tribute, permit, philanthropize, present, proffer, promise, provide, provision, ratify, recognize, recommend, reflect honor upon, release, relinguish, remit, render, replenish, restore, sanction, serve, show favor, shower upon, spare, spend, sponsor, submit, supply, tender, transmit, vest, vouchsafe, yield
ASSOCIATED CONCEPTS: bestow a present upon, gifts

BET, verb adventure, ante, ante up, cast lots, chance, chance the odds, draw, draw lots, encounter the risk, flip a coin, gamble, game, hazard, incur the risk, lay a wager, lay even money, lay money down, lay odds, leave to chance, parlay, play, play a long shot, play for, punt, put money down, raffle, rely on fortune, risk, run the risk, speculate, sport, stake, stand the hazard, take a chance, take the chances of, toss up, trust to chance, try one's fortune, try one's luck, venture, wager
ASSOCIATED CONCEPTS: betting on horse races, betting on numbers, bettor, gambling, lottery

BETRAY (Disclose), verb acknowledge, admit, air, aperire, avow, bare, bear witness against, bring into the open, bring to light, come clean, confess, declare, detegere, divulge, double-cross, expose, give away, give utterance to, impart, inform, inform against, inform on, lay bare, let slip, make a clean breast, make known, make public, own up, prodere, report, reveal, sell out, show, tattle, tell, tell on, turn informer, uncover, unearth, unfold, unmask, violate a confidence
ASSOCIATED CONCEPTS: confidences, privileges, professional secrets, trade secrets, trusts, wrongful disclosure

BETRAY (Lead astray), verb abandon, abase, bamboozle, be dishonest, be false to, befool, beguile, bluff, break faith with, break one's promise, cheat, circumvent, corrupt, cozen, debauch, deceive, deceive by treachery, decoy, defile, defraud, deliver up, delude, dupe, enmesh, ensnare, entice, entrap, fleece, forswear, fraud, gammon, give over to the foe, give up treacherously, hoax, hoodwink, inveigle, let down, lure, misinform, mislead, outwit, overreach, play false, prostitute, put on, put something over on, ruin, seduce, sell out, swindle, take in, trick, undo, victimize, violate

BETTERMENT, noun accommodation, adjustment, advance, advancement, alteration, amelioration, amendment, bettering, breakthrough, change, change for the better, changeover, constructive change, deviation, difference, divergence, enhancement, enrichment, improvement, increase, lift, melioration, modification, progress, progression, progressive change, redesign, reform, reformation, reshaping, restoration, restructuring, transition, tweaking, upgrade
ASSOCIATED CONCEPTS: financial betterment, improvement in real estate value
FOREIGN PHRASES: Nul ne doit s'enrichir aux despens des autres. No man should enrich himself at the expense of others.

BETTOR, noun better, gambler, gamester, gentleman of fortune, hazarder, piker, player, player for stakes, plunger, punter, risk-taker, sharper, speculatist, speculator, venturer, wagerer

BEWARE, verb be careful, be cautious, be chary, be circumspect, be forewarned, be guarded, be on one's guard, be on the alert, be on the lookout, be on the watch, be prepared, be prewarned, be prudent, be warned, be wary, have a care, keep out of harm's way, look about one, look out, mind, receive notice, stop look and listen, take care, take heed, take precautions, take warning, think twice, watch out

BIAS, noun bigotry, disinclination, disposition, favoritism, foregone conclusion, *inclinatio,* inclination, intolerance, jaundice, partiality, partisanism, partisanship, penchant, preapprehension, preconceived idea, preconception, predetermination, predilection, predisposition, preference, prejudgment, prejudication, prejudice, prenotion, proclivity, proneness, *propensio animi,* propensity, susceptibility, tendency, trend, undetachment, undispassionateness
ASSOCIATED CONCEPTS: actual bias, bias of mind

BICAMERAL, adjective bifurcated, bipartite, bisected, divided, dual chambered, multipartite, separated

BICKER, verb agitate, altercate, argue, argue to no purpose, bandy words, battle, be at loggerheads, be at variance, be discordant, brabble, brangle, brawl, cavil, clash, conflict, contend, contest, controvert, differ, disaccord, disagree, dispute, dissent, disunite, embroil, entangle, equivocate, fall foul of, fall out, fence, fight, have an altercation, have it out, have words, jar, join issue, nag, parry, pick a quarrel, pull different ways, quarrel, scrap, spar, spat, split hairs, squabble, take sides, tiff, tilt, wrangle
ASSOCIATED CONCEPTS: bicker over the terms of an agreement, bicker over trivial provisions in a contract

BID, noun advance, approach, estimate, *licitatio,* offer, offered price, overture, presentation, price, proffer, proposal, proposition, quotation, quoted price, submission, tender
ASSOCIATED CONCEPTS: auction sale, bid bond, bid in, bid off, bidder, biddings, by-bidding, competitive bidding, proposal, upset bid, with reserve, without reserve

BID-RIGGING, noun conspiracy to fix a bid, contrived bidding, criminal act regarding a bid, criminal contrivance in a bid, fixing a bid, fraudulence in a bid, illegal accommodation in a bid, illegal act regarding a bid, illegal action regarding a bid, illegal agreement regarding a bid, illegal arrangement in a bid, illegal contrivances in a bid, illegal consortium, illegal efforts to fix a bid, illegal maneuvering in a bid, illegal means to fix a bid, illegal measures to fix a bid, trumped-up provisions in a bid
ASSOCIATED CONCEPTS: competitive bidding, procurement policies

BIFURCATE, verb bisect, branch, branch off, branch out, cleave, cut in two, dichotomize, dimidiate, divaricate, diverge, divide into two, fork, form a fork, furcate, halve, part, partition, ramify, separate, split, sunder
ASSOCIATED CONCEPTS: bifurcated trial

BIFURCATED TRIAL, noun bisection of a case, segmentation in a case, segregation in a case, separate liability and damage phases, separate quilt and insanity defense phases, separation in a case, severance in a case, split in a case, split trial, two or more hearings held, two-part trial
ASSOCIATED CONCEPTS: punitive damages

BIGAMY, noun unlawful marriage, illegal marriage, multiple illegal marriages, multiple spouses, marrying multiple partners, marrying multiple wives, marrying multiple husbands

BIGOT, noun die-hard, doctrinaire, dogmatic theorist, dogmatist, dogmatizer, energumen, extremist, fanatic, illiberal, infatuate, intolerant, *ipse dixit,* know-all, know-it-all, monomaniac, opinionated person, opinionist, persecutor, ranter, redneck, rigorist, stickler, stubborn person, zealot

BILATERAL, adjective bi-facial, dual, two-sided
ASSOCIATED CONCEPTS: bilateral contract, bilateral option, bilateral record

BILIOUS, adjective bileful, choleric, dyspeptic, jaundiced, spiteful, spleenful

BILK, verb appropriate fraudulently, bait, bamboozle, befool, beguile, betray, bluff, cheat, chisel, circumvent, cozen, cully, deceive, defraud, delude, dupe, elude, embezzle, ensnare, entangle, evade, exploit, foist upon, fool, fraud, hoax, hoodwink, humbug, inveigle, levant, misapply, misappropriate, misinform, mulct, peculate, purloin, put something across, put something over, shuffle, swindle, take advantage of, take in, trick, use for one's own needs, utilize for profit, victimize

BILL (Formal declaration), **noun** allegation of facts, claim, contractual obligation, customs documents, formal petition, indictment, itemized specification, legislative declaration, petition, promissory obligation, specification of details, statement of facts, written certificate, written complaint
ASSOCIATED CONCEPTS: bill for discovery, bill for fraud, bill for new trial, bill in equity, bill in nature of interpleader, bill of attainder, bill of entry, bill of exceptions, bill of health, bill of indictment, bill of instructions, bill of interpleader, bill of particulars, bill of review, Bill of Rights, bill to quiet title, no true bill, true bill

BILL (Invoice), **noun** account, accounts payable, amount due, audit, balance due, charges, check, cost, deferred payment, demand for payment, expenditures, expenses, figure, itemized account, list, manifest, postponed payment, reckoning, record, report, request for payment, score, statement, statement of indebtedness, *syngrapha,* tally
ASSOCIATED CONCEPTS: bank bill, bill book, bill for account, bill of costs, bill of credit, bill of exchange, bill of lading, bill of sale, bill payable, bill receivable, bond, creditor's bill

BILL (Proposed act), **noun** draft, legislation, measure, projected law, proposal, proposed enactment, proposed law, proposed regulation, proposed rule, proposed statute, protocol, resolution, *rogatio*

ASSOCIATED CONCEPTS: act of legislature, law, omnibus bill, private bill, revenue bill

BIND (Obligate), **verb** adstringere, burden, charge, compel, confirm, conscript, constrain, drive, encumber, exact, force, impose, indent, indenture, obligare, oblige, pledge, promise, require, sanction, set a task, warrant
ASSOCIATED CONCEPTS: bind a deal, binding authority, binding instruction, binding receipt, binding transaction
FOREIGN PHRASES: *Nuda ratio et nuda pactio non ligant aliquem debitorem.* Naked intention and naked promise do not bind any debtor. *Quodque dissolvitur eodem modo quo ligatur.* A thing is unbound in the same manner that it is made binding.

BIND (Restrain), **verb** block, check, compel, confine, constrain, encumber, fetter, fix, hamper, hinder, immobilize, impede, inhibit, limit, repress, secure, shut in
ASSOCIATED CONCEPTS: bind over

BINDER, noun assurance, caution money, collateral, collateral security, deposit, earnest, escrow, expense outlay, gage, guaranty, handsel, indemnity, installment, investment, payment, pledge, receipt, receipt for payment, recognizance, security, stake, token, token payment
ASSOCIATED CONCEPTS: binder receipt, insurance binder, real estate binder

BINDING, adjective coercive, compelling, compulsory, confining, constraining, *de rigueur,* final, hampering, hindering, imperative, incumbent, inhibiting, limiting, mandatory, necessary, obligatory, obliging, required, requisite, restrictive
ASSOCIATED CONCEPTS: binding agreement, binding instruction, binding offer, binding over, binding receipt, binding sale

BIOETHICS, noun ethical study of drug research, ethical study of genetic engineering, ideals of genetic engineering and drug research, moral study of drug research, moral study of genetic engineering, morality for genetic engineering, probity for drug research, proper conduct in genetic engineering and drug research, proper moral behavior on genetic engineering, proper moral judgment on drug research, proper moral philosophy on genetic engineering, proper moral principles for drug research, rectitude for genetic engineering, study of ethics in biomedical advances, system of morals for genetic engineering, the ethics of biological medicine, the ethics of biological science
ASSOCIATED CONCEPTS: cloning

BIPARTITE, adjective apart, being in two corresponding parts, bicameral, bifurcated, bifurcous, bisected, detached, dichotomous, disconnected, disengaged, disjoined, disjointed, disjunct, disunited, divaricate, divided, furcate, furcular, halved, in two, partitioned, separate, separated, severed, subdivided

BIRTH (Beginning), **noun** animation, arrival, commencement, creation, debut, embarkation, establishment, *exordium,* genesis, inauguration, inception, incipience, incipiency, incunabula, infancy, introduction, nascency, onset, origin, origination, *ortus,* vitalization
ASSOCIATED CONCEPTS: *ante natus*

BIRTH (Emergence of young), **noun** arrival, childbirth, delivery, nativity, parturition, vivification
ASSOCIATED CONCEPTS: birth certificate, birth control, issue, pretermission

FOREIGN PHRASES: *Non nasci, et natum mori, paria sunt.* Not to be born, and to be born dead, are the same.

BIRTH *(Lineage),* **noun** ancestry, bloodline, derivation, descent, extraction, heredity, heritage, inheritance, line, line of descent, parentage, provenance, succession
ASSOCIATED CONCEPTS: birth certificate, legitimacy
FOREIGN PHRASES: *Qui in utero est pro jam nato habetur, quoties de ejus commodo quaeritur.* He who is in the womb is regarded as already born, whenever a question arises for his benefit.

BIRTHRIGHT, **noun** absolute right, ancestry, droit, due, entitlement, heritage, heritance, indefeasible right, inheritance, inherited rights, interest, legal right, one's due, *patrimonium,* patrimony, prerogative, primogeniture, privilege, right, rights and privileges, vested interest, vested right

BITTER *(Acrid tasting),* **adjective** absinthal, absinthian, acerbate, acerbic, *acerbus,* acid, acidulous, *acidus,* acrid, *asper,* biting, caustic, cutting, disagreeable, distasteful, pungent, sharp, sour, soured, sourish, tart, unappetizing, unpalatable, unpleasant, unsavory, unsweet, vinegarish

BITTER *(Penetrating),* **adjective** acrimonious, afflictive, astringent, austere, bilious, biting, brutal, burning, choleric, constringent, corrosive, cutting, double-edged, dyspeptic, harsh, incisive, keen, mordant, nasty, piercing, poignant, pricking, scathing, scorching, severe, smarting, sore, stabbing, stern, stinging, trenchant, venomous, virulent, withering

BITTER *(Reproachful),* **adjective** acrimonious, antipathetic, biting, caustic, cross, despiteful, embittered, envenomed, hostile, hurtful, indignant, piqued, provoked, rancorous, resentful, sarcastic, sardonic, scornful, sorrowful, sour-tempered, spiteful, splenetic, unamiable, unhappy, venomous, vexed, vitriolic

BLACKMAIL, **noun** exaction, extortion, hush money, illegal compulsion, oppressive exaction, protection, ransom, shakedown, taking by undue exercise of power

BLAME *(Culpability),* **noun** accusal, accusation, blameworthiness, castigation, censurability, censurableness, censure, chargeability, condemnation, crimination, criticism, *culpa,* culpableness, damnation, decrial, delation, delinquency, denouncement, denunciation, dereliction, deviation from rectitude, disapproval, disparagement, dispraise, excoriation, expostulation, exprobation, fault, guilt, guiltiness, incrimination, inculpation, malfeasance, misconduct, neglect, objurgation, obloquy, opprobrium, peccability, rebuke, remonstrance, *reprehensio,* reprehension, reproach, reprobation, reproof, *vituperatio,* wrong
ASSOCIATED CONCEPTS: culpable negligence, *mens rea*
FOREIGN PHRASES: *Culpa caret qui scit sed prohibere non potest.* One is clear of blame who knows, but cannot prevent.

BLAME *(Responsibility),* **noun** accountability, ascription, assignation, assignment, attribution, charge, implication, imputation, liability
ASSOCIATED CONCEPTS: allocation of blame, blameworthy, culpability, placing the blame

BLAME, *verb* abhor, accuse, administer a rebuke, admonish, anathematize, animadvert, arraign, ascribe to, assign to, attribute to, berate, call to account, carp, cast a slur on, castigate, cavil, censure, charge, chastise, chide, cite, complain against,

condemn, criminate, criticize, *culpare,* denounce, deplore, deprecate, depreciate, detract, disapprove, discommend, discountenance, disparage, dispraise, execrate, expostulate, fault, find fault, hold no brief for, hold responsible, hold up to reprobation, impeach, implicate, impugn, impute to, incriminate, inculpate, indict, lodge a complaint, objurgate, rebuke, recriminate, remonstrate, reprehend, *reprehendere,* reprimand, reproach, reprobate, reprove, revile, show disapproval, upbraid, vilipend, *vituperare*

BLAMEFUL, *adjective* abject, accusable, at fault, blamable, blameworthy, censorious, censurable, censured, chargeable, compunctious, condemnable, condemned, contemptible, contemptuous, corrupt, criminal, criminous, criticized, culpable, damnatory, decried, delinquent, deplorable, deplored, despicable, disapproved, discommendable, discreditable, discredited, dishonorable, disowned, dispraised, disreputable, disreputed, errant, exceptionable, execrable, faulty, flagitious, found guilty, found wanting, guilty, heinous, held in contempt, ignominious, illaudable, immeritorious, impeachable, imputable, in the wrong, indefensible, indictable, inexcusable, iniquitous, insalubrious, liable, liable to prosecution, nefarious, neglectful, negligent, objectionable, objurgatory, open to criticism, opprobrious, out of favor, peccable, peccant, reprehensi-ble, reprimanded, reproachable, reproachful, reprobate, reprobative, reprovable, responsible, unacceptable, uncommendable, unjustifiable, unpardonable, unpraiseworthy, unworthy, venal, vile, without defense, without excuse, wrongful

BLAMELESS, *adjective* above reproach, above suspicion, absolved, acquitted, clean, clear, condonable, entirely defensible, exculpable, exculpated, exonerated, faultless, free from guilt, free from wrong, guilt-free, guiltless, immaculate, impeccable, incensurable, incorrupt, inculpable, innocent, innocuous, inoffensive, irreprehensible, irreproachable, irreprovable, moral, not guilty, not liable, not tainted, offenseless, perfect, pure, reprieved, rightful, sinless, stainless, taintless, unblamable, unblameworthy, unblemished, uncensurable, uncondemned, uncorrupt, uncorrupted, unculpable, undefiled, unfallen, unguilty, unimpeachable, uniniquitous, unobjectionable, unoffending, unreproachable, unreproached, unreproved, unsoiled, unspotted, unsullied, untainted, upright, vindicated, virtuous, without blame, without fault, without reproach

BLAMEWORTHY, *adjective* abject, accusable, answerable, arrant, at fault, beneath contempt, blamable, blameful, censurable, chargeable, condemnable, condemnatory, condemned, contemned, contemptible, contemptuous, contumelious, convicted, corrupt, criminal, criminous, criticized, culpable, damnatory, delinquent, deplorable, depraved, despicable, devious, discreditable, discredited, disdainful, dishonorable, disreputable, disrespectable, errant, erring, execrable, flagitious, flagrant, *flagrante delicto,* found guilty, guilty, ignominious, illaudable, impeachable, in fault, in the wrong, indefensible, indictable, infernal, inglorious, iniquitous, injurious, insalubrious, irremediable, justiciable, liable, liable to prosecution, nefarious, negligent, not honorable, not respectable, not to be recommended, objectionable, obnoxious, odious, of no repute, open to criticism, opprobrious, peccable, peccant, questionable, reprehensible, reprimanded, reproachable, reprobate, reprobative, reprovable, responsible, ribald, scandalous, sentenced, sinister, tainted, transgressing, uncommendable, unjustifiable, unpraiseworthy, unrespected, unrighteous, unvirtuous, unworthy, venal, without defense, woeful, wrong, wrongful

BLANK *(Emptiness),* **noun** absence, barrenness, cipher, hiatus, hollowness, inexistence, insubstantiality, nil, *non-esse,* nonexistence, nonsubsistence, nonentity, nothing, nothingness, nullity, *tabula rasa,* unsubstantiality, vacancy, vacuousness, vacuum, *vacuus,* void, zero
ASSOCIATED CONCEPTS: blank acceptance, blank bond, blank check, blank endorsement, blank instrument, blank verdict, endorsement in blank, signed in blank

BLANK *(Form),* **noun** data sheet, document, dossier, instrument, legal document, paper, questionnaire

BLASPHEMY, **noun** apostasy, blasting, cursing, derogation of religion, desecration, disrespect, epithet, execration, expletive, heresy, iconoclasm, impiety, impious utterance, impiousness, imprecation of evil, irreverence, irreverent behavior, lack of piety, lack of reverence, malediction, profanation, profane oath, profaneness, revilement of religion, sacrilege, sacrilegiousness, sanctimoniousness, solemn mockery, swearing, unholiness, unorthodoxy, unsacredness
ASSOCIATED CONCEPTS: freedom of religion, libel and slander
FOREIGN PHRASES: *Nec veniam, l'aeso numine, casus habet.* Where the divinity is insulted the case cannot be pardoned.

BLATANT *(Conspicuous),* **adjective** apparent, celebrated, clear, discernible, exposed, famous, manifest, noticeable, notorious, observable, obvious, outstanding, overt, patent, perceivable, plain, prominent, public, sensational, well-known

BLATANT *(Obtrusive),* **adjective** bellowing, boisterous, braying, clamorous, coarse, common, crass, crude, crying, flaring, flaunting, gaudy, glaring, gross, harsh, ill-behaved, ill-bred, ill-mannered, improper, indecorous, indelicate, loud, noisy, obstreperous, offensive, offensively assertive, offensively obtrusive, raffish, ribald, rough, rowdy, rude, screaming, scurrilous, tawdry, ululant, uncivil, uncouth, uncultured, undignified, ungenteel, ungentlemanly, ungracious, unladylike, unpolished, unpresentable, unrefined, unseemly, vociferous, vulgar, vulgarian

BLEAK *(Exposed and barren),* **adjective** bare, barren, blank, cold, deserted, desolate, exposed, unpopulated, unsheltered, waste

BLEAK *(Not favorable),* **adjective** dark, depressing, disheartening, dismal, distressing, forbidding, gloomy, grave, grim, inauspicious, joyless, ominous, somber, sombrous, unfavorable

BLEAK *(Severely simple),* **adjective** austere, cheerless, cold, comfortless, depressing, dismal, dour, drear, dreary, dull, gloomy, grim, joyless, somber, sombrous, uninviting

BLEMISHED, **adjective** besmirched, blistered, bruised, chipped, damaged, defaced, defective, deformed, dented, deteriorated, discolored, discredited, disfigured, disgraced, dishonored, faded, faulty, flawed, imperfect, impure, injured, malformed, marred, misshapen, pitted, pock-marked, soiled, spotted, stained, sullied, tainted, tarnished

BLIND *(Concealed),* **adjective** buried, camouflaged, covered, covert, dim, disguised, hidden, imperceptible, inconspicuous, indiscernible, latent, masked, obscure, out of view, private, screened, secreted, shadowy, sheltered, shrouded, unapparent, undetected, unexposed, unknown, unobserved, unperceived, unrevealed, unseen, unsuspected

BLIND *(Impassable),* **adjective** barred, barricaded, blanked, blockaded, blocked, closed, dead-end, leading nowhere, obstructed, sealed, shut, shut-off, stopped-up, without exit

BLIND *(Not discerning),* **adjective** benighted, careless, deluded, headlong, heedless, inadvertent, inattentive, incognizant, inconsiderate, indifferent, indiscriminate, indiscriminating, insensible, insensitive, led astray, mindless, misled by deception, nescient, obtuse, *oculis captus,* rash, thoughtless, unacquainted, unapprised, uncomprehending, unconscious, unconversant, undiscerning, unenlightened, uninformed, unknowing, unlucid, unmindful, unobservant, unobserving, unperceiving, unreflecting, unseeing, unversed, without insight
ASSOCIATED CONCEPTS: blind allegiance, blind amendments

BLIND *(Sightless),* **adjective** caecus, deprived of sight, dim-sighted, eyeless, feeble-eyed, groping, in darkness, unseeing, visionless, weak-eyed

BLIND *(Deprive of sight),* **verb** blight one's optical powers, destroy one's perception, extinguish visual discernment, make eyeless, make sightless, make unable to see, obstruct one's vision, render eyeless, render sightless, render visionless, ruin one's eyesight, strike sightless, strike visionless

BLIND *(Obscure),* **verb** adumbrate, becloud, becurtain, bedim, befog, bemask, benight, blanket, blear, blur, blur the outline, camouflage, cloak, cloud, conceal, conceal from sight, cover, cover up, curtain, dim, eclipse, ensconce, enshroud, envelop, hide, hide away, hide the identity of, hide underground, keep clandestine, keep out of sight, make inconspicuous, make indiscernible, make unapparent, make unperceptible, muddle, obfuscate, occult, overcloud, put in concealment, put out of sight, render dim, render invisible, render uncertain, screen, screen from observation, screen from sight, seclude, secrete, shade, shadow, shield, shroud, veil, veil the brightness

BLOCK, **verb** arrest, avert, ban, bar, barricade, blockade, bridle, check, choke, clog, close, cohibit, constrict, cramp, curb, dam, debar, delay, encumber, estop, exclude, fend off, forbid, foreclose, frustrate, halt, hamper, hinder, hobble, impede, intercept, interdict, interfere with, jam, leave out, limit, obstruct, occlude, oppose, parry, plug up, preclude, prevent, prohibit, proscribe, repulse, restrain, restrict, retard, shut off, shut up, snag, stall, stand in the way, stay, stem, stop, stop up, thwart, trammel, wall up

BLOCKADE *(Barrier),* **noun** bar, barricade, block, blockage, bottleneck, cordon, curb, impediment, obsessio, *obsidio,* obstacle, obstruction, stop, stumbling block

BLOCKADE *(Enclosure),* **noun** circumjacence, circumscription, circumvallation, compass, containment, encincture, encirclement, enclosing, encompassment, envelopment, framing, girdling, sealing off, surrounding
ASSOCIATED CONCEPTS: capture and prize, commercial blockade

BLOCKADE *(Limitation),* **noun** compression, confinement, contraction, debarring, exclusion, obturation, occlusion, preclusion, restriction, shutdown, stoppage, strangulation

BLOOD, **noun** affinity, agnation, ancestry, breed, brethren, brood, children, clan, cognation, common ancestry, consanguinity, derivation, descent, ethnic group, extraction, family connection, family relationship, family tie, family tree, filiation, genealogical tree, genealogy, gentility, *genus,* heredity, heritage, issue, kind, kindred, kinsfolk, kinship, kinsman, kinsmen, kinswoman, line, lineage, nationality, next of kin, offspring, one's people, parentage, pedigree, propinquity, relations, *sanguis,* stock, strain, ties of family, tribe

ASSOCIATED CONCEPTS: blood heirs, blood issue, blood relatives, full blood, half blood, mixed blood

FOREIGN PHRASES: *Consanguineus est quasi eodem sanguine natus.* A person related by consanguinity is, as it were, one born from the same blood. *Pueri sunt de sanguine parentum, sed pater et mater non sunt de sanguine puerorum.* Children are of the blood of their parents, but the father and mother are not of the blood of their children.

BLOODLINE, *noun* affiliation, ancestry, birth, blood, caste, derivation, descent, dynasty, extraction, family, family tree, genealogy, heredity, history, line, line of ancestors, lineage, origin, parentage, pedigree, progeniture, root, stem, stock, strain, succession

ASSOCIATED CONCEPTS: pedigree

BLUE SKY LAW, *noun* canons regarding securities, precepts on securities, securities law, securities oversight, securities rules, securities statutes

BLUEPRINT, *noun* design, detailed plan, diagram, draft, ground plan, map, master plan, mechanical drawing, outline, plan, scheme, sketch

BLUSTER *(Commotion),* *noun* boisterousness, brawl, disturbance, embroilment, eruption, flare-up, fracas, frenzy, hubbub, maelstrom, melee, outbreak, outburst, pandemonium, racket, rampage, riot, row, rumpus, scramble, storm, tempest, temptestuousness, tumult, tumultuousness, turbulence, turmoil, upheaval, uproar

BLUSTER *(Speech),* *noun* boast, bragging, *declamatio,* ebullition, ranting, raving, swaggering, talking big

BOARD, *noun* bureau, cabinet, commission, *conlegium,* consistory, consultative body, council, court, *curia,* department, directorate, directorship, governing body, judicatory, management, presidium, tribunal

ASSOCIATED CONCEPTS: advisory boards, board of aldermen, board of arbitrators, board of directors, board of education, board of elections, board of equalization, board of examiners, board of finance, board of health, board of medical examiners, board of public works, board of review, board of special inquiry, board of supervisors, board of trade, board of trustees, de facto boards, draft board, local board, maritime board, qualification board, revenue board, welfare board, zoning board

BODILY, *adjective* carnal, corporal, corporeal, corporeous, *corporeus,* de facto, embodied, existent, existing, human, incarnate, living, manifest, material, materiate, natural, organic, palpable, perceptible, physical, solid, somatic, somatical, tactile, tangible, visible

ASSOCIATED CONCEPTS: bodily condition, bodily contact, bodily function, bodily harm, bodily heirs, bodily infirmity, bodily injury, bodily issue, bodily pain or suffering

BODY *(Collection),* *noun* aggregation, assemblage, batch, colligation, community, company, compilation, congeries, conglomeration, entity, gathering, host, mass, multitude, plenum, polity, sodality, troupe, wholeness

ASSOCIATED CONCEPTS: body corporate, body politic, governmental body, reviewing body

BODY *(Main part),* *noun* core, *corpus,* essential part, exposition, figure, form, greater part, hub, main part, major part, principal part, shape, structure, substance

ASSOCIATED CONCEPTS: body of an instrument

BODY *(Person),* *noun* anatomy, cadaver, carcass, carrion, corporality, corporalness, corporeality, *corpse,* corpus, embodiment, entity, human being, material existence, personage, physical being, physique

ASSOCIATED CONCEPTS: body attachment, body execution, body heirs

BOGUS, *adjective* affected, artificial, counterfeit, false, phony, sham, spurious, unauthentic, ungenuine, unreal, untrue

ASSOCIATED CONCEPTS: bogus ceremony, bogus certificate, bogus check

BOILER PLATE, *adjective* accepted, after the same pattern, common, commonplace, consonant, conventional, customary, dictated, formulary, habitual, homogeneous, patterned, prescribed, regulation, standardized, stereotyped, stock, typical, undeviating, uniform, universal, unvaried, wonted

ASSOCIATED CONCEPTS: boiler plate clause, boiler plate language

BOLSTER, *verb* aid, back, buoy up, lift, prop, shore up, shoulder, succor, support, sustain, underpin, uphold

BOMB, *noun* ammunition, armament, blockbuster, bombshell, charge, detonator, dynamite, explosive, explosive device, fireball, grenade, gunpowder, hand grenade, high explosive, infernal machine, instrument of warfare, mine, missile, Molotov cocktail, munitions, petard, shell, T.N.T., torpedo, weapon

BOMBAST, *noun* affectation, boastfulness, boasting, braggery, chatter, declamation, diatribe, embellishment, empty talk, enlargement, euphemism, exaggeration, expansion, flatulence, floridness, fustian, garnishing, grandiloquence, grandiosity, harangue, high coloring, high-sounding words, hyperbole, idle speeches, inanity, inflation, loftiness, magnification, magniloquence, oration, ornamentation, orotundity, ostentation, overstatement, polysyllabic profundity, pomposity, pompous prolixity, prate, preciosity, preciousness, pretentiousness, rant, raving, rhetoric, rhetoricalness, rodomontade, sesquipedalian words, sesquipedalism, sesquipedality, superlative, swelling utterance, swollen diction, tirade, tumidity, tumidness, turgescence, turgidity, vainglory, verbiage

BOMBSHELL, *noun* astonishment, bewilderment, blow, consternation, eye opener, inexpectation, jolt, nonexpectation, shock, startler, stupefaction, sudden attack, sudden burst, surprisal, surprise, surprise package, thunderbolt, thunderclap, unawaited event, unexpected event, the unforeseen

BONA FIDE, *adjective* aboveboard, accurate, actual, as represented, candid, faithful, forthright, genuine, honest, honorable, in good faith, ingenuous, intended, just, legitimate, meant, open, plain-speaking, principled, real, reliable, rightful, scrupulous, straightforward, trustworthy, unaffected, uncounterfeited, undisguised, undissembling, undistorted, unexaggerated, unfaked, unfeigned, unperfidious, unperjured, unpretended, unpretentious, unreserved, unsimulated, unspecious, unspurious, veracious, veridical

ASSOCIATED CONCEPTS: bona fide assignment, bona fide belief, bona fide business purpose, bona fide claimant, bona fide controversy, bona fide creditors, bona fide domicile, bona fide holder, bona fide holder for value, bona fide holder in due course, bona fide labor dispute, bona fide members, bona fide operation, bona fide purchaser in good faith, bona fide sale, bona fide seller

BOND, *noun* assurance, certificate of debt, certificate of indebtedness, *chirographum,* debenture, evidence of a debt, government paper, guarantee, guaranty, indenture, obligation, promise, promissory note, real security, security, surety, *syngrapha,* voucher, warrant, warranty

ASSOCIATED CONCEPTS: back bond, bearer bond, bond discount, bond for costs, bond for deed, bond for title, bond holder, bond issue, bond of matrimony, bond premium, bonded indebtedness, bondsman, cash bond, construction bond, coupon bond, defense bond, delivery bond, fidelity bond, governmental bond, indemnity bond, interest-free bond, municipal bond, *ne exeat,* serial bond, state bond, supersedeas bond, tax-exempt bond

FOREIGN PHRASES: *Eodem ligamine quo ligatum est dissolvitur.* A bond is released by the same formalities by which it was made binding.

BOND *(Hold together),* **verb** attach, blend, cement, coagulate, coalesce, cohere, combine, conglutemate, connect, consolidate, couple, fix, fuse, glue, interlock, join, merge, secure, stick, unite

BOND *(Secure a debt),* **verb** agree, assure, certify, confirm, contract, covenant, endorse, ensure, give security, guarantee, hypothecate, indenture, insure, pledge, post, promise, secure, stake, underwrite, warrant

BONDAGE, *noun* abject slavery, arrest, bond of slavery, bonds, captivity, chains, coarctation, compulsory service, confinement, constraint, constraint by force, custodianship, custody, detention, durance, enslavement, entombment, fetters, forced confinement, forced labor, forcible restraint of liberty, guardianship, guarding, helotry, immuration, immurement, impoundment, imprisonment, incarceration, internment, involuntary servitude, loss of freedom, manacles, penal restraint, penal servitude, prison, refusal of bail, reins, remand, restraint, restriction, restriction on movement, servitude, slavery, slavishness, subduing, subjection, subjugation, subordination, subservience, surveillance, thralldom, yoke

ASSOCIATED CONCEPTS: involuntary servitude, kidnapping

BONUS, *noun* additive, benefit, *boni,* boon, bounty, dividend, donation, extra, gift, gratuity, honorarium, incentive, perquisites, *pourboire,* premium, *prime,* reward, something over and above, surplus, surplusage, tip

ASSOCIATED CONCEPTS: bonus stock

BOOK, *verb* accuse, arrest, chronicle, docket, engage, enter, enumerate, file, index, inscribe, insert, list, log, make an entry, mark down, note, order, post, prefer charges, record, register, report, schedule, seize legally, tabulate, take into custody, write down

BOOM *(Increase),* **noun** acceleration, accretion, accrual, accruement, accumulation, additament, addition, additory, advance, advancement, amplification, amplitude, annexation, appreciation, appurtenance, attachment, augment, augmentation, boost, broadening, burgeoning, complement, deepening, development, distension, doubling, duplication, enhancement, enlargement, escalation, expansion, extension, gain, growth, heightening, hike, improvement,

increasement, increasing, increment, intensification, interest, magnification, production, progress, progression, proliferation, prolongation, protraction, raise, reinforcement, reproduction, rise, spread, spreading, sprouting, strengthening, supplement, swell, swelling, upgrowth, upsurge

BOOM *(Prosperity),* **noun** abundance, accomplishment, accumulation, achievement, acquisition, advance, advancement, affluence, aggrandizement, amelioration, amplitude, attainment, augmentation, auspiciousness, avails, benefaction, booming economy, bountifulness, burgeoning, capital gains, copiousness, cornucopia, development, earnings, economic prosperity, escalation, excess, exorbitance, exorbitancy, expansion, expediency, favorable trade balance, flourishing condition, gain, good fortune, great quantity, growth, impetus, improvement, increment, inflation, lucre, mutual profit, opulence, opulency, outgrowth, outpouring, plentifulness, plentitude, prevalence, production, productivity, profit, profit making, profluence, profluency, profuseness, profusion, progress, progression, progressiveness, proliferation, prosperous issue, prosperous outcome, prosperousness, recovery, remuneration, revenue, richness, rising prices, spiral inflation, superabundance, superfluity, surplus, thriving conditions, thriving economy, upgrading, upgrowth, upsurge, upward curve, upward trend, weal, wealth, welfare, well-being

BOOTLEGGER, *noun* black marketeer, contrabandist, gunrunner, illicit dealer, moonshiner, runner, smuggler

ASSOCIATED CONCEPTS: prohibition, sale of intoxicating liquor

BORDER, *noun* ambit, borderland, boundary, bounds, brim, brink, circumference, circumjacence, confine, contiguity, edge, edging, end, enframement, extremity, flange, frame, fringe, frontier, hem, ledge, limit, line of demarcation, marge, margin, outline, outpost, outside, outskirts, pale, perimeter, periphery, purlieus, rim, selvedge, side, skirt, terminal, termination, verge

ASSOCIATED CONCEPTS: border search

BORDER *(Approach),* **verb** abut upon, adjoin, align convergently, approximate, be in the vicinity of, be near, close on, come close, come to a point, concentrate, converge, draw near, encroach, gravitate toward, join, juxtapose, juxtaposit, lie near, meet, move toward, near, neighbor, place in juxtaposition, place near, place parallel, proximate, put along side, skim, skirt, unite, verge, verge upon

BORDER *(Bound),* **verb** abut upon, adiacere, adjoin, appose, attach, *attingere,* be adjacent to, be circumjacent to, be conterminous, be contiguous, be in conjunction with, be in contact with, be juxtaposed, butt, cincture, circumpose, circumvalate, circumvent, close in, confine, conjoin, connect, contain, corral, cut off, define, delimit, delimitate, delineate, demarcate, edge, embrace, encase, enchase, encircle, enclose, enclose within bounds, encompass, ensphere, envelop, environ, extend to, flank, frame, gird, hem in, impinge, join, juxtapose, juxtaposit, lean against, lie contiguous to, lie next to, limit, mark off, meet end to end, meet with, outline, place limitations, proscribe, restrain, restrict, shut in, specify limits, stake out, surround

BORN *(Alive),* **adjective** animated, begotten, breathing, enlivened, live, living, quick, vital, vitalized

BORN *(Innate),* **adjective** congenital, connate, connatural, fundamental, genetic, hereditary, immanent, in the blood, inborn, inbred, incarnate, indigenous, ingrained, inherited, instinctive, instinctual, intrinsic, inwrought, native, natural, organic

BORROW, verb accept the loan of, apply for a loan, ask for credit, get on credit, get temporary use of, *mutuari,* obtain a mortgage, obtain the use of, take an advance, take on credit, take on loan
ASSOCIATED CONCEPTS: borrowed capital, borrowed employees, borrowed servant, borrowing statute
FOREIGN PHRASES: *In satisfactionibus non permittitur amplius fieri quam semel factum est.* In settlements more must not be received than was received once for all.

BORROWING LIMIT, noun breaking point of debt, debt ceiling, debt limit, greatest limit of debt, largest debt, largest loan, maximum amount of debt, maximum debt, maximum funds to be loaned, maximum loan outer limit of debt, outer line of credit
ASSOCIATED CONCEPTS: bankruptcy, fraudulent debt, insolvency, interrogation, solvency

BOUND, adjective accountable, answerable, beholden, called by duty, chargeable, committed, compelled, constrained, destined, engaged, forced, having no alternative, impelled, liable, necessitated, obligated, obliged, pledged, pressed by duty, required, responsible, restrained, tied, under a vow, under compulsion, under necessity, under obligation
FOREIGN PHRASES: *Naturale est quidlibet dissolvi eo modo quo ligatur.* It is natural for a thing to be unbound in the same way in which it was made binding. *Nemo tenetur ad impossibile.* No one is bound to do an impossibility. *Quo ligatur, eo dissolvitur.* By the same means by which a thing is bound, it is released.

BOUNDARY, noun border, borderline, bound, circumscription, compass, configuration, confine, confinement, contour, delimitation, delineation, division line, edge, enclosure, extremity, *finis,* limit, limitation, limits, line of circumvallation, line of demarcation, lineaments, lines, outline, perimeter, periphery, radius, rim, *terminus,* verge
ASSOCIATED CONCEPTS: adjoining landowners, boundary line, boundary of a water course, boundary suit, metes and bounds, surveys and surveyors, trespass to try title, zoning

BOUNTY, noun award, benefaction, benevolence, bonanza, bonus, boon, cadeau, conferment, emolument, favor, gift, grant, gratification, gratuity, guerdon, hand sel, honorarium, largess, *largitas, liberalitas,* perquisite, *pourboire,* premium, prize, reward, reward for service, tip, token, tribute
ASSOCIATED CONCEPTS: bounty lands

BOWDLERIZE, verb censor, curtail, cut, cut out, delete, edit out, emasculate, eviscerate, excise, expunge, expurgate, extirpate, remove
ASSOCIATED CONCEPTS: censorship, freedom of speech

BOYCOTT, noun abstention from buying, abstention from using, avoidance, ban, banning, black-listing, blackballing, debarring, embargo, exclusion, ostracism, proscription, refusal to do business, rejection, shunning, strike, withholding of patronage
ASSOCIATED CONCEPTS: primary boycott, secondary boycott

BRAND, noun badge, colophon, copyright label, disgrace, earmark, emblem, hallmark, identification mark, identification tag, impress, imprint, insignia, label, mark, *nota,* owner's mark, owner's sign, *piste,* seal, sigil, sign, signet, smirch, stain, stamp, sticker, stigma, stigmatism, tag, taint, ticket, token, trade name, trademark, watermark
ASSOCIATED CONCEPTS: brand name

BRAND *(Mark),* **verb** autograph, blaze, distinguish by mark, earmark, emblaze, emboss, endorse, engrave, identify, impress, imprint, inscribe, label, *notam homini inurere, notare,* print, put a mark on, put an indication on, seal, sign, stamp, tag

BRAND *(Stigmatize),* **verb** asperse, attaint, besmear, besmirch, bespatter, blacken, blot, bring into discredit, cast a slur upon, cast aspersions at, corrupt, debase, decry, defame, defile, deride, derogate, dirty, discredit, disgrace, dishonor, disparage, excite disapprobation, hold up to shame, impugn, involve in shame, malign, pillory, put to shame, reflect upon, slur, smear, smirch, smudge, soil, stain, sully, taint, tar, tarnish, throw dishonor upon, vilify, vilipend
ASSOCIATED CONCEPTS: libel, reputation, slander

BRANDISH, verb dangle before the eyes, display, draw one's sword, exhibit, flap, flaunt, flourish, gesture, rattle the saber, shake, show, swing, threaten, *vibrare,* wag, waggle, wave, wield
ASSOCIATED CONCEPTS: harassment, menacing

BRAVE, adjective adventurous, audacious, bold, bold as a lion, bold-spirited, chivalric, chivalrous, courageous, daring, dauntless, fearless, foolhardy, gallant, heroic, hero-like, high-spirited, intrepid, knightly, lionhearted, rash, reckless, soldierly, stalwart, stout, stouthearted, unafraid, unalarmed, undaunted, valiant, valorous, virile

BRAWL, noun altercation, brangle, breach of the peace, broil, commotion, deafening row, din, dispute, disturbance, embranglement, embroilment, feud, fight, fisticuffs, fracas, fray, hubbub, imbroglio, jangle, *jurgium, mêlée,* noisiness, outbreak, pandemonium, quarrel, racket, rampage, riot, *rixa,* row, rowdiness, ruction, scramble, scrimmage, scuffle, squabble, tumult, turmoil, uproar, wrangle
ASSOCIATED CONCEPTS: disorderly conduct

BRAWL, verb altercate, be noisy, bicker, brangle, break the peace, broil, clamor, create a disturbance, create a riot, dispute angrily, fight, have a row, have words with, jangle, make a commotion, make a racket, make an uproar, quarrel noisily, rampage, riot, *rixari,* row, run riot, scrap, scrimmage, scuffle, set to, spat, squabble, tiff, wrangle
ASSOCIATED CONCEPTS: disorderly conduct

BRAZEN, adjective arrogant, assuming, audacious, aweless, barefaced, blatant, bluff, bold, boldfaced, brash, conscienceless, daring, defiant, disrespectful, familiar, flagrant, flaunting, flippant, forward, immodest, immoral, impertinent, *impudens,* impudent, indecent, indecorous, insolent, malapert, obtrusive, of loose morals, outspoken, pert, petulant, presumptuous, *risqué,* rude, saucy, shameless, unabashed, unashamed, unblushing, unembarrassed, unmannerly, unmodest, unreserved, unseemly

BREACH, noun break, contravention, default, delinquency, dereliction, *discutere,* disobedience, disregard, dissension, dissentience, encroachment, enmity, failure, illegal evasion, illicitness, impropriety, infidelity, infraction, infringement, inobservance, neglection, nonadherence, noncompletion, nonconformity, nonfulfilment, nonobservance, nonperformance, omission, perfidy, *perfringere,* rejection, repudiation, retraction, shortcoming, tergiversation, transgression, trespass, unconformity, undueness, unduteousness, undutifulness, unfaithfulness, unobservance, violation, violation of law

ASSOCIATED CONCEPTS: anticipatory breach, breach of bond, breach of contract, breach of covenant, breach of duty, breach of faith, breach of lease, breach of marriage promise, breach of promise, breach of the close, breach of the covenant of warranty, breach of the peace, breach of trust, breach of warranty, constructive breach, continuing breach, material breach, partial breach, total breach

BREAK *(Fracture),* **verb**   burst, cave in, comminute, cut, destroy, fissure, fragment, hew, interpenetrate, *interrumpere,* penetrate, pierce, pulverize, puncture, rend, rupture, scatter, shatter, shiver, smash, splinter, stave in
ASSOCIATED CONCEPTS: breakage, breaking a close, breaking and entering, burglary, forcible entry and detainer

BREAK *(Separate),* **verb**   cleave, crack, detach, disband, disconnect, disengage, disentangle, disintegrate, disjoin, dislocate, dismantle, dispart, disperse, dissociate, disunite, divaricate, force apart, force open, get free, get loose, incise, lop, open, part, rive, sever, split, split off, subdivide, sunder, take apart, take to pieces, unbind, unchain, unclinch, uncouple, unfetter, unknot, unloose, untie
ASSOCIATED CONCEPTS: break in occupancy, break in the chain of events

BREAK *(Violate),* **verb**   abscind, be derelict, be guilty of infraction, breach, defy, disobey, disregard, infringe, invade, neglect, trample upon, transgress, trespass

BREVET, *noun*   authorization, charge, charter, declaration, decree, edict, fiat, grant, law, license, mandate, manifesto, ordinance, ordination, *placet,* precept, prescription, rule, sanction, warrant, writ

BRIBE, *noun*   corrupt money, corrupt offering, graft, hush money, illegal donation, illegal incentive, illegal incitation, illegal inducement, illegal lure, illegal offer, illegal offering, illegal present, illegal reward, offering, *pretium,* protection money, sop, unlawful bait, unlawful compensation, unlawful gift, unlawful gratuity
ASSOCIATED CONCEPTS: acceptance of a bribe, bribe-giving for public office, bribe-receiving, bribery, bribing a witness, corruption, obstructing justice, offer to bribe, official misconduct, rewarding official misconduct, solicitation of a bribe, unlawful gratuities

BRIBERY, *noun*   allurement, baiting, blandishment, breach of faith, bribing, cajolement, cajolery, collusion, complicity, connivance, corrupt inducement, corrupt payment, corruptibility, corruption, crime, criminality, enticement, illegal incitation, illegal inducement, improbity, inducement, inveiglement, jobbery, lawbreaking, luring, misdealing, opportunism, perfidy, pettifoggery, plying, pressure, prodition, seducement, snaring, tantalization, temptation, tempting, unlawful encouragement, venality
ASSOCIATED CONCEPTS: commercial bribery, obstruction of justice, official misconduct, public bribery

BRIEF, *adjective*   abbreviated, abridged, aphoristic, bare, brisk, close, cometary, compact, compendious, compressed, concise, condensed, contracted, cursory, curtailed, cut short, elliptical, ephemeral, epigrammatic, epitomized, exact, fading, fleeting, hasty, hurried, laconic, limited, meteoric, momentary, not protracted, passing, pauciloquent, pithy, precise, quick, reduced, sententious, short, short-term, slight, small, sparing of words, speedy, succinct,

sudden, summarized, summary, swift, temporary, to the point, transient, transitory, trenchant, unprolonged, volatile
ASSOCIATED CONCEPTS: brief description, brief statement, brief summary

BRIEF, *noun*   abridgment, account, argument, capsule, compendium, condensation, conspectus, depiction, description, digest, extract, legal abstract, legal document, legal epitome, legal memorandum, memorandum, memorandum of law, outline, outline on the law, profile, representation, resume, sketch, statement of the case, summary, summary on the law, synopsis, thumbnail sketch, vignette
ASSOCIATED CONCEPTS: *amicus curiae,* appellate brief, brief of evidence, points and authorities, reply brief, responsive brief

BRING TO LIGHT, *verb*   disclose, discover, educate, elucidate, enlighten, expose, get out in the open, impart, inform, knowledge, leak out, reveal, shed light on, shed new light, show, take the lid off of, take the wraps off, uncover, unearth, unfold, unmask
ASSOCIATED CONCEPTS: confidentiality, secrecy

BROAD, *adjective*   ample, amplitudinous, *amplus,* blanket, collective, comprehensive, covering all cases, deep, diffuse, encyclopedic, expansive, extended, extending, extensive, far-flung, far-reaching, far-spread, full, general, generalized, generic, immense, inclusive, indefinite, indeterminate, indiscriminate, large, large-scale, latitudinous, *latus,* liberal, liberalistic, nonspecific, outspread, outstretched, pervasive, representative, spacious, spreading, standard, sweeping, synoptic, typical, ubiquitous, unbiased, unconfined, unspecified, vague, wide, widespread
ASSOCIATED CONCEPTS: broad appeal, broad definition, broad interpretation, broad meaning, broad sense, broad spectrum

BROKEN *(Fractured),* **adjective**   crumbled, damaged, defective, destroyed, disintegrated, dismembered, divided, fractional, fragmentary, injured, lacerated, mangled, mutilated, pulverized, riven, ruptured, sectional, separated, severed, shattered, shivered, slivered, splintered

BROKEN *(Interrupted),* **adjective**   checked, deranged, desultory, disarranged, disconnected, discontinuous, disjunct, disordered, divided, erratic, fitful, halting, hindered, incomplete, inconstant, intermittent, irregular, obstructed, spasmodic, sporadic, stopped, suspended, unequal, uneven, unsteady, unsuccessive, variable

BROKEN *(Unfulfilled),* **adjective**   contravened, delinquent, derelict, disloyal, disobedient, disregarded, disregardful, dutiless, encroached upon, infringed, infringing, inobservant, insubordinate, lawless, nonadhering, nonobservant, repudiated, transgressed, uncompliant, undutiful, unfaithful, unlawful, unloyal, unobservant, untrue, violated, violative

BROKER, *noun*   agent, bargaining agent, commission agent, commission merchant, customers' man, dealer, deputy, factor, go-between, intermediary, intermedium, internuncio, *interpres,* link, matchmaker, mediator, medium, middleman, monger, negotiant, negotiator, realtor, regrater, representative, trader
ASSOCIATED CONCEPTS: brokerage, broker's commission, exchange broker, insurance broker, merchandise broker, note-broker, pawnbroker, real estate broker, stockbroker

BROKERAGE, *noun*   agio, charge, charges, commission, compensation, discount, emolument, factorage, fee, recompense, remuneration

ASSOCIATED CONCEPTS: agents, brokerage business, brokerage commission, brokerage contract, brokers, commissions

BROOD, verb agonize, be dejected, cogitate, consider, contemplate, deliberate over, despair, despond, dwell upon, fret, grieve, *incubare,* meditate on, mope, morbidly meditate, mull over, muse, ponder, reflect, ruminate, study, sulk, think anxiously, think over, weigh

BROWBEAT, verb abash, badger, beat down, bully, chide, cow, daunt, deflate, discourage, dishonor, domineer, dress down, drive, exert pressure on, frighten, give one a talking to, goad, harass, humble, humiliate, intimidate, make nervous, make one feel small, nag, overawe, overbear, override, petrify, prevail upon, push into, put in fear, put pressure on, raise apprehensions, reprove, scare, set down, shame into, subdue, trounce

BRUTAL, adjective atrocious, barbarous, bearish, beastly, bestial, bloody, brute-like, brutish, churlish, coarse, cruel, despotic, domineering, excessive, extreme, fell, ferocious, *ferus,* fierce, flint-hearted, grim, gross, gruff, hardhearted, harsh, *immanis,* inexorable, inhuman, *inhumanus,* mean, merciless, oppressive, overharsh, overbearing, persecuting, pitiless, primitive, remorseless, rough, rugged, ruthless, sadistic, savage, severe, stonyhearted, truculent, tyrannical, tyrannous, uncivilized, unfeeling, ungentle, unmerciful, unrelenting, untamed, vicious, violent

BRUTALITY, noun act of inhumanity, barbarity, bestiality, brutalness, brutilization, brutishness, cruelness, cruelty, grossness, hardness, hardness of heart, harshness, heart of stone, heartlessness, *immanitas,* inhumanity, lack of feeling, mercilessness, moral insensibility, pitilessness, ruffianism, ruthlessness, savageness, savagery, truculence, truculency, unfeelingness, violence

ASSOCIATED CONCEPTS: cruel and inhuman treatment, cruel and unusual punishment

BRUTALIZE, verb barbarize, be pitiless, be vicious to, be wicked to, brutify, bully, corrupt, decivilize, deform one's character, dehumanize, demoralize, hurt, injure, lead astray, make insensitive, make wicked, maltreat, mislead, molest, oppress, persecute, pervert, render evil, run down, seduce, teach wickedness, tyrranize

ASSOCIATED CONCEPTS: assault, cruel and inhuman punishment

BUDGET, noun accountancy, accounts, allocation, allotment, allowance, appropriation, balance sheet, balance statement, distribution, estimated expenditures, planned disbursement, profit and loss account, provision, ration, statement, statement of account

ASSOCIATED CONCEPTS: appropriations, budget bill, budget notes, itemized budget, municipal budget, public debt limitations

BUFFER ZONE, noun added protection, bulkhead, bulwark, insulation, medium, rampart, screen, territory for defense

BUILD (Augment), verb add to, aggrandize, amplify, develop, elevate, enhance, enlarge, expand, extend, grow, heighten, increase, lift, magnify, make higher, make larger, parlay, pyramid, raise, rise, swell

BUILD (Construct), verb achieve, assemble, carpenter, cast, compile, compose, construct, contrive, create, devise, elevate, engineer, erect, establish, evolve, fabricate, fashion, figure, form, found, frame, lay the foundation,

make, manufacture, model, originate, produce, put up, raise, set up, shape, superstruct, upbuild

BUILDING (Business of assembling), noun *aedificatio,* amalgamation, architecture, arrangement, assembling, causation, collocation, compilation, composition, compounding, conformation, conjunction, constitution, construction, contriving, craftsmanship, creating, design, development, devising, effectuation, efformation, engineering, establishment, fabrication, fashioning, formation, formulation, foundation, framing, grouping, handiwork, implementation, incorporation, industry, installation, institution, interrelation, making, manufacture, organization, origination, plan, prefabrication, preparation, production, shaping, structuring, synthesis

ASSOCIATED CONCEPTS: building for a particular use

FOREIGN PHRASES: *Aedificare in tuo proprio solo non licet quod alteri noceat.* It is not lawful to build upon one's own land what may injure another.

BUILDING (Structure), noun abiding place, abode, address, *aedificium,* boardinghouse, construction, domicile, *domus, dulce domum,* dwelling, dwelling place, edifice, elevation, erection, establishment, fabric, frame, framework, habitat, habitation, headquarters, home, homestead, house, institute, living quarters, lodging, lodging house, lodging place, lodgings, lodgment, piece of architecture, place, place of habitation, premises, quarters, residence, shelter, site, station, superstructure

ASSOCIATED CONCEPTS: building and construction contracts, building code, building contract, building inspector, building laws, building lien, building lines, building loan, building loan mortgage, building material, building or other improvement, building permit, building purposes, building restriction, building site, building superintendent, building trades

BULK, noun abundance, accumulation, a commanding portion, amount, *amplitudo,* batch, block, chief part, clump, cluster, corpus, greatest part, heap, lot, magnitude, *magnitudo,* main part, major part, majority, mass, *moles,* overwhelming part, predominant part, principal part, quantity, quantum, size, stack, substance, substantial number, substantial part, substantial quantity, volume

ASSOCIATED CONCEPTS: bulk assignments, bulk cargo, bulk price, bulk property, bulk sale, bulk sales, bulk sales act, bulk sales laws, bulk shipment, bulk storage, bulk transaction, stored in bulk

BULK TRANSFER, noun large asset transfer, main asset transfer, major business asset transfer

BULWARK, noun abutment, asylum, barricade, barrier, bastion, battlement, buffer, bulkhead, buttress, citadel, defense, embankment, fort, fortification, fortress, guard, haven, insulation, insulator, palladium, parapet, preservation, *propugnaculum,* protection, rampart, refuge, safeguard, sanctuary, security, shelter, shield, stockade, stronghold, support

BUMPER CROP, noun a sufficiency, affluence, ampleness, amplitude, an ample amount, an ample supple, avalanche, bonanza, bounteousness, bountifulness, copiousness, flood, full measure, fullness, generosity, generousness, glut, great abundance, landslide, lavishness, much, outpouring, overbrim, overbrimming, overburden, overcharge, overflow, overload, plenty, plethora, profuseness, profusion, saturation, superabundance, surfeit

BUMPTIOUS, *adjective* audacious, contumelious, forward, obtrusive, procacious

BUNKO, *noun* bamboozlement, cheating, chicanery, con game, confidence trick, defraudation, double-dealing, dupery, ensnarement, flimflam, gyp, hoax, legal chicanery, pettifogging, racket, ruse, skulduggery, *supercherie*, swindle, trick, victimization, wile
ASSOCIATED CONCEPTS: bunko men, bunko steering, confidence game, fraud, gambling, larceny, wagering

BURDEN, *noun* accountability, adversity, affliction, anxiety, assignment, bother, botheration, bounden duty, brunt, call of duty, care, charge, chore, cumbrance, *devoir*, difficulty, drawback, duty, encumbrance, engagement, errand, handicap, hardship, hindrance, impediment, imposition, job, liability, line of duty, load, mandate, necessity, obligation, onus, oppression, ordeal, pains, requirement, requisite, responsibility, strain, task, tribulation, trouble, undertaking, vexation, weight, work
ASSOCIATED CONCEPTS: burden of covenant, burden of easement, burden of going forward with evidence, burden of loss, burden of persuasion, burden of proof, burden upon commerce, shifting of burden
FOREIGN PHRASES: *Non debet alteri per alterum iniqua conditio inferri.* A burdensome condition ought not to be imposed upon one man by the act of another. *Cum par delictum est duorum, semper oneratur petitor et melior habetur possessoris causa.* When there is equal fault on both sides, the burden is always placed on the plaintiff, and the cause of the possessor is preferred. *Actus curiae neminem gravabit.* An act of the court shall prejudice no one. *Probandi necessitas incumbit illi qui agit.* The necessity of proving lies with the person who sues. *Qui sentit onus sentire debet et commodum.* He who assumes the burden ought to derive the benefit.

BURDEN OF GOING FORWARD, *noun* adequate evidence, adequate proof legally presented at trial, burden of proof, legal responsibility, obligation of going forward, sufficient corroboration, sufficient evidence in a case, sufficient evidence to establish a case, sufficient proof, sufficient proof of facts, validation of proof of a case, verification of proof of a case
ASSOCIATED CONCEPTS: cause of action or claim, evidence, evidentiary burden, failure to sustain, preponderance of the evidence, prima facie case, rebuttal
FOREIGN PHRASES: *Onus probani.* Burden of proof.

BURDEN OF PROOF, *noun* adequate evidence, adequate proof legally presented at trial, burden of going forward, legal responsibility, obligation of going forward, sufficient corroboration, sufficient evidence in a case, sufficient evidence to establish a case, sufficient proof, sufficient proof of facts, validation of proof of a case, verification of proof of a case
ASSOCIATED CONCEPTS: cause of action or claim, evidence, evidential burden, failure to sustain, preponderance of the evidence, prima facie case, rebuttal, weight of evidence
FOREIGN PHRASES: *Onus probani.* Burden of proof.

BUREAU, *noun* administration, administrative unit, agency, authority, board, branch, commission, committee, department, division, ministry, office, specialized administrative unit, specialized unit

BUREAUCRACY, *noun* administration, agency, authorities, delegated authority, departmentalization, governance, government, government by bureaus, government office, governmental procedure, governmental system for decision-making, inflexible routine, management, ministration, official procedure, officialdom, officiation, organization, powers that be, process of governing, red tape, regulation, reins of government, rigid routine, rule, service, sovereignty, state management, strict procedure, system

BURGLAR, *noun* bandit, bank robber, criminal, despoiler, filcher, gangster, holdup man, *homo trium literarum,* housebreaker, larcener, marauder, pilferer, pillager, plunderer, prowler, raider, rifler, robber, safebreaker, safecracker, second-story thief, sneak thief, spoiler, stealer, stickup man, thief
ASSOCIATED CONCEPTS: burglar's tools, criminal trespass

BURGLARY, *noun* breaking and entering, crime, *effractura,* felony, filching, forcible entry, *furtum,* housebreaking, illegality, larceny, lawlessness, looting, marauding, pilfering, pillaging, plunderage, plundering, prowling, purloinment, raiding, robbery, robbing, spoiling, stealing, theft, thievery, unlawful act, unlawful breaking and entering, unlawfulness
ASSOCIATED CONCEPTS: burglar's tools, burglary insurance, common law burglary, receiving stolen goods, robbery, statutory burglary

BURN, *verb* blaze, blister, brand, burn to a cinder, burst into flame, catch fire, cauterize, char, conflagrate, consume, cremate, deflagrate, enkindle, fire, flame up, flare, gut, ignite, incandesce, incendiarize, incinerate, inflame, kindle, light up, melt, overheat, parch, relume, scald, scorch, scorify, sear, seethe, singe, sizzle, smelt, smolder, strike a light, vesicate
ASSOCIATED CONCEPTS: arson, revocation of wills

BUSINESS (Affair), ***noun*** activity, concern, duty, interest, matter, mission, proceeding, proposition, responsibility, task, undertaking
FOREIGN PHRASES: *Aliena negotia exacto officio geruntur.* The business of another is to be carried out with particular care. *Constitutum esse eam domum unicuique nostrum debere existimari, ubi quisque sedes et tabulas haberet, suarumque rerum constitutionem fecisset.* It is established that the home of each of us is considered to be the place of his abode and books, and where he may have made an establishment of his business. *In suo quisque negotio hebetior est quam in alieno.* Everyone is more dull in his own business than in that of another.

BUSINESS (Commerce), ***noun*** barter, buying and selling, commercial intercourse, dealings, exchange, industry, intercourse, merchandising, merchantry, production, trade, trading, traffic, transaction, ventures
ASSOCIATED CONCEPTS: business address, business agent, business corporation, business crimes, business district, business done in state, business enterprise, business expenses, business hours, business interruption insurance, business invitees, business license, business losses, business name, business paper, business purposes, business records, business restrictions, business secrets, business situs, business trust, business venture, business visitor, doing business, good will of business, in the course of business, interference with business, ordinary course of business, transacting business
FOREIGN PHRASES: *Ea quae raro accidunt non temere in agendis negotiis computantur.* Those things which rarely happen are not to be taken into account in the transaction of business without sufficient reason.

BUSINESS (Commercial enterprise), ***noun*** cartel, combine, company, concern, corporation, establishment, firm, industry, manufacture, organization, private enterprise, shop, store, syndicate, venture

BUSINESS *(Occupation)*, **noun**   activity, avocation, calling, career, craft, duty, employment, endeavor, following, function, handicraft, job, line, livelihood, living, means of support, mission, office, practice, profession, pursuit, specialty, trade, undertaking, vocation, walk of life, work

BUY, verb   acquire by purchase, acquire ownership of, bargain for, complete a purchase, contract, get in exchange, make a purchase, make one's own, *mercari,* obtain, order, pay a price for, pay cash for, pay for, procure, procure title to, purchase, redeem, secure, secure for a consideration, trade

ASSOCIATED CONCEPTS: buy and sell agreement, buy in the ordinary course of business, buy long, buy out, buy short, buyer beware, buyer's needs, buyer's option, buyer's risk, buying a note or a bill, buying and receiving stolen goods, buying broker

FOREIGN PHRASES: *Caveat emptor, qui ignorare non debuit quod jus alienum emit.* Let a purchaser beware since he ought not to be ignorant that he is purchasing whatever rights another has. *Emptor emit quam minimo potest, venditor vendit quam maximo potest.* The buyer purchases for the least he can; the seller sells for the most he can. *In pretio emptionis et venditionis, naturaliter licet contrahentibus se circumvenire.* In respect to the price, in buying and selling, it is naturally permitted to the contracting parties to overreach one another.

BYLAW, noun   canon, charter, code, municipal regulation, ordinance, prescript, prescription, *reglement,* regulation, rubric, rule, standard

ASSOCIATED CONCEPTS: amendment of bylaws, authorization for bylaws, enactment of bylaws, interpretation of bylaws, repeal of bylaws

BYSTANDER, noun   apprizer, attestant, attester, audience, beholder, corroborator, earwitness, enlightener, eyewitness, indicator, informant, informer, insider, listener, looker, looker-on, monitor, observer, one who bears witness, onlooker, passer-by, reporter, seer, spectator, swearer, teller, testifier, tipster, tout, undercover man, viewer, viewership, watcher, witness, witness, witness to a crime, witness as to character

ASSOCIATED CONCEPTS: accessory, disinterested party, Good Samaritan, innocent bystander, third persons

CABAL, noun   band, camarilla, clique, coalition, collusion, combination, complicity, complot, confederacy, connivance, conspiracy, council, design, *factio,* faction, gang, intrigue, junta, league, machination, plot, ring, scheme, secret group, secret plot, *societas clandestina,* union

CACHE *(Hiding place)*, **noun**   *abri,* ambuscade, backroom, confinement, hideaway, inmost recesses, place of concealment, protectory, refuge, safe place, safe retreat, secret place, shelter, undercover

CACHE *(Storage place)*, **noun**   depository, place of deposit, place of safety, promptuary, repertory, repository, reservoir, safe, safe place, secret storehouse, stockroom, storage, store of provisions, storehouse, storehouse for safekeeping, storeroom, warehouse

CADAVER, noun   carcass, corpse, corpus delecti, dead body, victim

CADUCITY, noun   decadence, decay, decline, decrepitude, degeneracy, deterioration, dotage, feebleness, infirmity of old age, senility, weakness

CAITIFF, adjective   abject, afraid, base, baseborn, brutish, churlish, craven, currish, dastardly, despicable, faint-hearted, fear-stricken, ignoble, ignominious, low, lowborn, mean-spirited, of low extraction, of low origin, of mean extraction, of mean origin, poltroonish, pusillanimous, raffish, recreant, rude, scared, spiritless, uncivilized, uncourageous, unpolished, vile, vulgar, weak-minded

CAJOLE, verb   allure, bait, coax, entice, importune, lure, ply, pressure, push, tease, tempt, urge

CALAMITY, noun   act of God, adverse fortune, adversity, affliction, bad fortune, blight, *calamitas,* cataclysm, catastrophe, *clades,* destruction, disaster, evil fortune, evil lot, evil luck, grievous harm, hardship, ill fortune, loss, major misfortune, mischance, misery, misfortune, stroke, tragedy

ASSOCIATED CONCEPTS: calamity bonds

CALCULATE, verb   account, appraise, ascertain mathematically, assess, average out, cast accounts, cipher, *computare,* compute, consider, count, design, determine, devise, enumerate, estimate, evaluate, figure, figure out, form an estimate, furnish an estimate, gauge, make a computation, make an estimate, measure, mete, number, place a value on, plan, predict, quantify, rank, rate, reckon, score, set a value on, size, suit, take an account of, take into account, take stock, take the dimensions, tally, think out, totalize, valorize, valuate, value, work out

CALENDAR *(List of cases),* ***noun*** agenda, cases ready for argument, court's log, docket, enumeration of causes arranged for trial, list of cases set down for hearing, list of causes arranged for trial, list of causes instituted in court, list of causes ready for trial, motion docket, order of cases, record, register, register of cases, schedule, systematic arrangement of cases, table of cases, timetable, trial list
ASSOCIATED CONCEPTS: calendar practice, court calendar, *fasti*

CALENDAR *(Record of yearly periods),* ***noun*** agenda, almanac, annals, chronicle, chronology, daybook, diary, docket, established division of time, history, journal, list of appointments, list of events, log, logbook, memoranda, menology, order of business, plans, program, record, record of yearly periods, register, schedule, schedule of events, sequence of events, system of reckoning time, table, tabular register of the year, timetable
ASSOCIATED CONCEPTS: calendar day, calendar month, calendar week, calendar year, Gregorian calendar

CALIBER *(Measurement),* ***noun*** amount, amplitude, area, breadth, broad gauge, broadness, compass, cross dimension, cross measurement, degree, diameter, diameter of a cylindrical body, dimensions, expanse, extent, full size, gauge, girth, grade, magnitude, mass, measure, measured size, measurement across, proportion, scale, size, thickness, width

CALIBER *(Mental capacity),* ***noun*** ability, ableness, acumen, acuteness, adequacy, aptitude, arguteness, attainment, capability, capableness, capacity, competence, comprehension, depth, discernment, discrimination, efficacy, efficiency, endowment, faculty, genius, gift, good judgment, instinct, intellect, intellectual power, intelligence, judgment, knowledge, mentality, perspicacity, proficiency, qualification, reach of mind, sagacity, sapience, specialty, talent, understanding, wisdom

CALIBER *(Quality),* ***noun*** attribute, capability, character, distinctiveness, eminence, excellence, grade, importance, merit, potency, rate, standing, state, station, status, value, virtue, worth

CALL *(Appeal),* ***noun*** address, adjuration, application, beseechment, bid, cry, earnest request, entreaty, impetration, imploration, importunity, insistent demand, instance, invocation, invocatory plea, invocatory prayer, motion, obsecration, obtestation, petition, plea, prayer, request, requirement, requisition, solemn entreaty, solicitation, suit, supplication, *vox*
ASSOCIATED CONCEPTS: adjournment of a term of the court subject to call, calendar call, call contract, call prior to maturity, calls for more margin, dismissal for failure to answer a call

CALL *(Option),* ***noun*** alternative, choice, decision, demand made on a stock holder, discretion, discretionary order, freedom of choice, liberty of action, opportunity, requirement, requisition, right of put and call, stock agreement
ASSOCIATED CONCEPTS: "call" option on stock or assessments, calls and assessments, "puts" and "calls" as options in a contract

CALL *(Title),* ***noun*** agnomen, alias, antonomasia, appellation, appellative, application, baptism, byword, caption, cognomen, cognomination, compellation, convertible terms, description, designation, epithet, eponym, expression, given name, head, indication, matronymic, name, namesake, naming, nomenclature, patronymic, praenomen, prenomen, proper name, sign, signature, sobriquet, style, surname, synonym, term, trope

CALL *(Appeal to),* ***verb*** address a petition, address a request, address oneself to, adjure, appeal, apply to, ask, ask for, be a suppliant, beg a favor, beg leave, beseech, bespeak, call for aid, call for help, call upon, *clamare,* cry, cry to, entreat, impetrate, implore, importune, invite, invoke, make a petition, make a request, make a requisition, make appeal, make application, make bold to ask, make earnest entreaty, petition, plead for, plead with, prefer a petition, prefer a request, prefer an appeal, press, put to, put up a request, request, solicit, sue, supplicate, turn to, urge

CALL *(Demand),* ***verb*** ask for with authority, assert a right to, claim, claim as a right, clamor for, command, cry for, demand, *deposcere,* exact, *flagitare,* insist on, lay claim to, make a demand, make an authoritative request, make claims upon, make requisition, necessitate, oblige, order, prescribe, present an ultimatum, present one's claim, press, put in a claim for, render necessary, require, require of others, requisition, send an order for

CALL *(Summon),* ***verb*** advocare, ask to come, assemble, assemble by summons, beckon, bid come, command to appear, convene, convocare, convocate, convoke, desire the presence of, gather, group, invite, invoke, issue an invitation, mobilize, muster, muster up, page, rally, request the presence of, reunite, send for, serve with a writ, subpoena, summon forth, unite
ASSOCIATED CONCEPTS: call as a witness, call for trial, called in question, called to testify, calling the docket

CALL (Title), ***verb*** characterize, christen, classify, define, denominate, designate, determine, *dicere,* differentiate, discriminate, distinguish, entitle, give a name, identify, identify by name, individualize, label, name, *nominare,* personalize, provide with nomenclature, specify, supply with an epithet, tag, term, *vocare*

CALLING, ***noun*** activity, business, career, chosen work, concern, craft, employment, endeavor, enterprise, field, function, industry, job, learned profession, lifework, line, line of achievement, line of business, line of work, livelihood, living, means of earning a living, metier, mission, *munus,* occupation, office, operation, position, post, practice, profession, pursuit, specialization, specialty, sphere of activity, task, trade, undertaking, vocation, walk of life, work
ASSOCIATED CONCEPTS: trade or calling, unlawful calling

CALLOUS, ***adjective*** adamant, adamantine, brutal, *callosus,* cold, cold of heart, coldblooded, coldhearted, *durus,* hard, hard of heart, hardened, hardhearted, heartless, impassive, impenetrable, impenitent, imperturbable, impervious, implacable, inclement, indifferent, indisposed to mercy, indurate, indurated, inexcitable, inexorable, inflexible, infrangible, insensate, insensible, insensitive, insentient, intolerant, obdurate, persecuting, pitiless, relentless, remorseless, rigorous, seared, severe, shock-proof, steeled against, stubborn, tearless, thick-skinned, toughened, unbending, unblushing, uncaring, uncomforting, uncompassionate, uncondoling, unconsoling, unfeeling, unforgiving, unimpressed, unimpressible, unimpressionable, unmelting, unmerciful, unmoved, unpardoning, unpitying, unrelenting, unruffled, unstirred, unsusceptible, unsympathetic, unsympathizing, unyielding

CALUMNIOUS, adjective abusive, blackening, calumniatory, castigatory, caustic, censorious, comminatory, compromising, condemnatory, contemptuous, contumelious, criminatory, *criminosus,* damaging, damnatory, decrying, defamatory, denigratory, denunciatory, deprecatory, depreciative, depreciatory, derisive, derogatory, detractory, disapproving, discreditable, disparaging, disrespectful, evil-speaking, ignoble, ignominious, imprecative, imprecatory, imputative, injurious, insinuating, insolent, insulting, libelous, maledictory, malevolent, obloquial, obloquious, offensive, opprobrious, pejorative, scandalous, scurrile, scurrilous, slanderous, slighting, smearing, stigmatizing, unflattering, vilifying, vituperative

ASSOCIATED CONCEPTS: contempt of court, defamation

CAMOUFLAGE, verb adumbrate, alter the appearance of, assume a mask, be concealed, becloud, becurtain, bedim, befog, bemask, blanket, blind, bury, change the face of, cloak, close the curtain, cloud, color, conceal, couch, cover, cover up, curtain, deceive, deform, disguise, dissemble, distort, draw the veil, dress up, embellish, embroider, ensconce, enshroud, envelop, fake, gild, give a color to, give a false appearance, give a false coloring, hide, hide away, hide one's identity, keep from sight, keep from view, keep in the dark, keep in the shade, keep out of view, keep secret, make unrecognizable, mask, masquerade, miscolor, obfuscate, obscure, occultate, pervert, put in concealment, reshape, screen, screen from observation, screen from sight, seclude, secrete, shade, shroud, suppress, throw a veil over, twist, twist the meaning of, veil

ASSOCIATED CONCEPTS: fraudulent misrepresentation

CAMPAIGN, noun action, activism, activity, cause, course of action, course of conduct, course of proceeding, crusade, design, drive, effort, emprise, endeavor, enterprise, exercise, exertion, expedition, hard task, implementation, large undertaking, line of action, line of conduct, line of proceeding, maneuvering, maneuvers, measures, method, mobilization, motion, movement, operation, organization, plan, plan of offensive, plot, procedure, program, project, proposal, proposition, quest, scheme, self-imposed task, steps, *stipendium,* stratagem, strategy, struggle, tactics, task, undertaking, voluntary work, warfare

ASSOCIATED CONCEPTS: campaign committee, campaign contributions, campaign expenditures, campaign expenses, campaign funds, election campaign, political campaign

CANARD, noun deceit, deception, fabrication, false report, false rumor, false statement, falsehood, falsification, fiction, fraud, groundless story, hoax, lie, report intended to delude, roorback, rumor, ruse, trick, unfounded story, untruth, untruthful report

CANCEL, verb abolish, abort, abrogate, annihilate, annul, avoid, countermand, counterorder, counterpoise, declare invalid, declare null and void, *delere,* deny, deprive of force, discard, disclaim, discontinue, disestablish, dismiss, dissolve, drop, end, eradicate, excise, expunge, exterminate, extinguish, *inducere,* invalidate, make void, negate, not proceed with, nullify, obliterate, override, overrule, put an end to, quash, quell, quench, recall, recant, remove, render invalid, render useless, render void, renege, repeal, repudiate, rescind, restrain, retract, reverse, revoke, set aside, suspend, terminate, *tollere,* vacate, void, withdraw

ASSOCIATED CONCEPTS: cancel a contract, cancel a debt, cancel an instrument, cancel an order, obsolete, rescission, termination, void

CANCELLATION, noun abandoning, abandonment, abolishing, abolishment, abolition, abrogation, abscission, annulling, annulment, cassation, circumduction, countermand, counterorder, deletion, discontinuance, dismissal, dissolution, dissolving, disuse, elimination, eradication, erasure, excision, expunction, extinction, invalidating, invalidation, liquidation, moratorium, negation, nonuse, nullification, nullifying, overruling, rasure, recall, recalling, recantation, relinquishment, renunciation, repeal, repudiation, rescinding, rescindment, rescission, retracting, retraction, reversal, reversing, revocation, revokement, revoking, supersession, surrender, suspension, termination, unmaking, vacation, vacatur, voidance, voiding, waiver, withdrawal, withdrawing

ASSOCIATED CONCEPTS: abatement, cancellation of a contract, cancellation of a lease, cancellation of a mortgage, cancellation of a will, cancellation of an insurance policy, cancellation of bills, cancellation of certificate of registration, cancellation of instruments, cancellation of judgment, cancellation of notes, judicial cancellation

CANDID, adjective aboveboard, *apertus sincerus,* apparent, blunt, *candidus,* categorically true, creditworthy, direct, explicit, express, forthright, frank, frankhearted, honest, ingenuous, *liber,* not lying, objective, open, outright, outspoken, overt, realistic, reliable, scrupulous, *simplex,* sincere, straightforward, substantially true, true, true to scale, true to the facts, trustworthy, truthful, unconstrained, undisguised, undissembling, undistorted, uninhibited, unperfidious, unperjured, unreserved, unshaded, untreacherous, veracious, veridical, veritable, *verus*

CANDIDATE, noun applicant, aspirant, aspirer, *candidatus,* challenger, competitor, contender, contestant, designee, desirer, entrant, hopeful, job seeker, nominee, office hunter, office seeker, petitioner, political aspirant, political contestant, runner, seeker, struggler

ASSOCIATED CONCEPTS: candidate for election, candidate for political office, candidate for public office, judicial candidate, legislative candidate, political candidate

CANDOR (Impartiality), noun detachment, disinterestedness, disinterestness, dispassionateness, equitableness, equity, even-handedness, evenness, fair treatment, fairness, justness, liberality, neutrality, nonpartisanship, objectivity, probity, unbias, unprejudicedness

CANDOR (Straightforwardness), noun bluntness, candidness, directness, forthrightness, frankness, genuineness, guilelessness, honesty, ingenuousness, openness, outspokenness, reliability, sincerity, unaffectedness, unpretentiousness, uprightness

CANNABIS, noun arouser, bhang, cannabis sativa, drug, grass, hash, hashish, hemp, marijuana, narcotic, opiate, pot, weed

ASSOCIATED CONCEPTS: drug laws

CANON, noun act, behest, citation, code, command, commandment, criterion, decree, demand, dictate, dictation, dictum, direction, edict, established principle, fiat, fundamental principle, general rule, imperative, imposition, instruction, interdiction, law, legislation, *lex,* mandate, manifesto, *norma,* order, ordinance, precept, prescript, prescription, proclamation, pronunciamento, public announcement, *regula,* regulation, requirement, requisition, rescript, rule, rule of conduct, ruling, standard, statute, test, ultimatum, warrant, word, writ

ASSOCIATED CONCEPTS: canon law, canons of construction, canons of ethics, canons of judicial ethics, canons of justice, professional canon, rule of construction

CANVASS, verb *ambire,* analyze, ask, ask earnestly, audit, bring in question, carry on an inquiry, conduct an inquiry, count, delve into, dig into, discuss, dissect, examine, examine searchingly, explore, follow up an inquiry, hold an inquiry, inquire, inquire into, inspect, institute an inquiry, investigate, look about for, look into, make a survey, petition, poll, preexamine, probe, pursue an inquiry, question, report, request, research, review, scan, scrutinize, search, set up an inquiry, study, subject to examination, survey, take up an inquiry, throw open to inquiry
ASSOCIATED CONCEPTS: canvass a jury, canvass the members of a class

CAP, noun ceiling, greatest amount, lid, limit, maximum amount

CAP, verb complete, conclude, end, finish, finish off, get done, get through with, perfect, terminate

CAPABLE, adjective able, accomplished, adept, adequate, adroit, *aptus,* competent, deft, effective, effectual, equal to, expert, facile, fit, fitted, gifted, *idoneus,* masterly, potent, proficient, qualified, skillful, suited, worthy
ASSOCIATED CONCEPTS: capable of assisting with one's defense, capable of contracting, capable of inheriting, capable of taking and holding property, capable to inherit, capable to marry, competence capable of distinguishing right from wrong

CAPACIOUS, adjective able to contain a great deal, ample, big, broad, capable of holding much, colossal, commodious, comprehensive, deep, expanded, expansive, extended, extensive, generous, gigantic, great, huge, immense, large, massive, roomy, spacious, substantial, vast, vasty, voluminous, wide

CAPACITY (Aptitude), noun ability, ableness, aptness, capability, capableness, competence, competency, effectuality, faculty, giftedness, potentiality, power, proficiency, qualification, range, reach, scope, skill, talent
ASSOCIATED CONCEPTS: full capacity, lack of capacity, legal capacity, lessened capacity, mental capacity, private capacity, proprietary capacity, quasi-judicial capacity, representative capacity, testamentary capacity, want of capacity
FOREIGN PHRASES: *Sola ac per se senectus donationem testamentum aut transactionem non vitiat.* Old age does not alone and of itself vitiate a will, gift, or transaction. *Furiosus stipulare non potest nec aliquid negotium agere, qui non intelligit quid agit.* An insane person who knows not what he is doing, cannot contract nor transact any business. *Furiosus nullum negotium contrahere potest.* An insane person can make no contract. *Furiosi nulla voluntas est.* A madman has no will. *Homo potest esse habilis et inhabilis diversis temporibus.* A man is capable and incapable at different times.

CAPACITY (Authority), noun accordance, allowance, authorization, certification, charter, consent, control, dispensation, droit, enablement, jurisdiction, justification, leave, legal capacity, liberty, license, permission, permit, power, prerogative, privilege, qualification, right, sanction, sovereignty, stature, supremacy, warrant
ASSOCIATED CONCEPTS: capacity to sue

CAPACITY (Job), noun assignment, function, occupation, position, role, situation, task

CAPACITY (Maximum), noun ampleness, amplitude, breadth, compass, comprehensiveness, containing power, extent, full complement, full extent, full volume, fullness, greatest amount, greatest extent, greatest size, holding ability, largeness, limit, limit of endurance, limitation, measure, physical limit, plenitude, reach, room, scope, spaciousness, stretch, tankage, upper limit, volume

CAPACITY (Sphere), noun ambit, area, arena, boundaries, bounds, division, domain, extent, field, jurisdiction, limits, orbit, pale, province, reach, realm, region, scope, specialty, stretch, territory

CAPITAL, noun assets, available means, balances, bank annuities, belongings, *caput,* cash supplies, credits, economic resources, finances, financial provision, financial resources, funds, funds for investment, funds in hand, holdings, income, investment portfolio, investments, line of credit, liquid assets, money, pecuniary resources, property, ready cash, receipts, reserves, resources, revenue, savings, *sors,* working assets
ASSOCIATED CONCEPTS: authorized capital, capital account, capital assets, capital budget, capital case, capital construction, capital contribution, capital crime, capital expenditure, capital gains, capital gains tax, capital improvement, capital in a corporation, capital investment, capital loss, capital of a state, capital offense, capital outlay, capital paid-in, capital project, capital punishment, capital reserve, capital stock, capital surplus, circulating capital, distribution of capital, equity capital, fixed capital, floating capital, impairment of capital, reduction of capital, return of capital, stated capital, working capital
FOREIGN PHRASES: *Excusat aut extenuat delictum in capitalibus quod non operatur idem in civilibus.* That excuses or extenuates a wrong in capital cases which would not have the same effect in civil suits.

CAPITAL PUNISHMENT, noun dealing death, death, death sentence, execution, extreme penalty, judicial murder, killing
ASSOCIATED CONCEPTS: cruel and unusual punishment

CAPITALIZE (Provide capital), verb advance, afford aid, afford support, aid, aid with a subsidy, back, back up, bring aid, contribute, extend credit, favor, finance, fund, furnish aid, furnish foundations, furnish support, give aid, give support, help, invest, lend, lend one's aid, lend support, loan, *pecuniam mutuam* dare, pension, promote, provide capital for, provide for, provide funds for, provide money for, set up, set up in business, sponsor, subsidize, supply aid, supply support, supply with a subsidy, support, venture capital
ASSOCIATED CONCEPTS: capitalization of income, capitalization of net income, capitalization of stabalized income, capitalize earning

CAPITALIZE (Seize the chance), verb avail oneself of, benefit, convert to use, create an opening, employ, exploit, find one's advantage in, make an opening, make the most of, make use of, manipulate, profit, put in operation, put to advantage, put to service, reap the benefit of, render useful, take advantage of, take the opportunity, turn to good account, turn to one's advantage, utilize, utilize for profit

CAPITULATION, noun abandonment, acquiescence, assent, compliance, consent, docility, giving way, nonresistance, obedience, passiveness, passivity, recedence, recession, relinquishment, resignation, resignedness, self-abnegation, submission, submissiveness, submittal, surrender, unresistingness, yielding

ASSOCIATED CONCEPTS: confession, nolo contendere, plea of guilty

CAPRICIOUS, *adjective* apt to change suddenly, changeable, changeful, changing, erratic, everchanging, fanciful, fantasied, fantastical, fickle, flighty, fluctuating, frivolous, giddy, *inconstans,* inconstant, irresolute, irresponsible, *levis,* mercurial, reversible, uncertain, uncontrolled, undisciplined, unmethodical, unreliable, unrestrained, unstable, unsystematic, vacillating, vagarious, variable, wavering, whimsical, without rational basis
ASSOCIATED CONCEPTS: arbitrary and capricious, arbitrary, capricious and unlawful, review of administrative determination

CAPSULE, *noun* abbreviation, *abrégé,* abridgment, abstract, analysis, brief, capitulation, compend, compendium, compression, condensation, conspectus, contents, digest, epitome, essence, minute, note, outline, pandect, precis, recapitulation, reduction, resumé, review, skeleton, sketch, substance, sum and substance, summary, syllabus, synopsis

CAPTION, *noun* annotation, banner, banner head, banner line, characterization, clause, description, designation, display line, head, heading, headline, headnote, imprint, indication of contents, inscription, legend, mark of identification, notes, preface, rubric, section head, specification, statement, subhead, subheading, subtitle, superscription, title, topic
ASSOCIATED CONCEPTS: caption of a petition, caption of a pleading, caption of indictment

CAPTIVE, *noun* bondman, bondsman, *captivus,* captured person, *captus,* convict, felon, helot, hostage, imprisoned person, incarcerated person, inmate, internee, one held in captivity, one held in confinement, one held in subjegation, pawn, person under arrest, prisoner, slave, subject, thrall, victim

CAPTIVITY, *noun* bondage, *captivitas,* commitment, committal, confinement, constraint, custody, detention, durance, duress, enslavement, entombment, immuration, immurement, impoundment, imprisonment, incarceration, internment, jail, prison, quarantine, quarantine station, restraint, slavery, subjection, subjugation, term of imprisonment
ASSOCIATED CONCEPTS: domestic animals in captivity

CAPTURE, *verb* apprehend, arrest, *capere,* carry away, catch, *comprehendere,* confine, hold captive, hold in captivity, immure, impress, imprison, incarcerate, jail, lock up, make an arrest, make prisoner, net, repress, restrain, restrict, seize, subdue, take by assault, take by force, take captive, take into custody, take possession of, take prisoner
ASSOCIATED CONCEPTS: capture of a criminal defendant, capture of wild animals, captured property

CARDINAL (Basic), ***adjective*** apical, basal, capital, central, chief, controlling, elemental, elementary, essential, first, foremost, fundamental, indispensable, key, main, material, necessary, overruling, pivotal, *praecipuus,* preponderant, primal, primary, prime, *primus,* principal, rudimentary, strategic, substantial, substantive, summital, underlying, undermost, uppermost, utmost, vital
ASSOCIATED CONCEPTS: cardinal rule

CARDINAL (Outstanding), ***adjective*** absolute, all powerful, best, central, chief, commanding, controlling, crowning, dominant, eventful, excellent, finest, foremost, greatest, greatest possible, highest, incomparable, inimitable, insurmountable, key, leading, major, maximal, momentous,

most important, notable, paramount, *praecipuus,* predominant, preeminent, preponderant, prevailing, prime, *primus,* second to none, supereminent, superlative, supreme, top, unequaled, unexcelled, unparalleled, unsurpassed, uppermost, utmost

CARE (Be cautious), ***verb*** be cautious, be concerned, bear in mind, beware, consider, *curare,* give heed to, guard, have regard, heed, look out for, mind, pay attention to, protect, take precautions, watch out for, watch over
ASSOCIATED CONCEPTS: care and caution, care and skill, careful, careless, degree of care, due care, extraordinary care, great care, lack of care, ordinary care, slight care, want of care

CARE (Regard), ***verb*** administer to, attend, attend to, be concerned, be concerned for, become involved, bother, *curare,* foster, mind, minister to, nurture, pay attention to, protect, serve, supervise, support, sustain, tend, watch over
ASSOCIATED CONCEPTS: care and custody, care and maintenance, custody or control

CAREER, *noun* activity, avocation, business, calling, chosen work, craft, *curriculum, cursus,* employment, field, job, lifework, line, livelihood, metier, occupation, office, position, post, profession, pursuit, situation, skilled occupation, specialty, trade, vocation, work

CAREFUL, *adjective* *accuratus,* alert, attentive, *attentus,* cautious, circumspect, concerned, *diligens,* discreet, foresighted, guarded, heedful, judicious, meticulous, mindful, on one's guard, on the alert, overcautious, painstaking, precautious, provident, prudent, regardful, scrupulous, thoughtful, unadventurous, unenterprising, vigilant, watchful, wide-awake
ASSOCIATED CONCEPTS: careful and prudent manner, caution, diligence, due care, protection, prudence, reasonable care

CARELESS, *adjective* casual, cursory, disregardful, forgetful, hasty, heedless, hurried, impetuous, improvident, imprudent, impulsive, inadvertent, inattentive, incautious, inconsiderate, indifferent, indiscreet, injudicious, insouciant, irresponsible, lackadaisical, lax, loose, neglectful, *neglegens,* negligent, nonchalant, oblivious, overhasty, perfunctory, pococurante, precipitant, precipitate, rash, reckless, regardless, remiss, slack, slipshod, sloppy, superficial, temerarious, thoughtless, unapprehensive, uncalculating, uncircumspect, unconcerned, unguarded, unmindful, unobservant, unthinking, unwary, wasteful
ASSOCIATED CONCEPTS: careless and imprudent manner, careless and negligent manner, grossly careless, negligence, recklessly careless, standard of care, wantonly careless

CARETAKER (One caring for property), ***noun*** archivist, attendant, *concierge,* convoy, curator, custodian, governor, guard, guardian, keeper, lookout, overseer, porter, sentry, sexton, steward, superintendent, supervisor, warden, watchman

CARETAKER (One fulfilling the function of office), ***noun*** administrator, collector, commissioner, controller, director, district officer, government servant, grand vizier, high official, key person, magistrate, manager, minister, officeholder, officer, officer in charge, officer of state, overseer, person in charge, public servant, state servant, superintendent

CARGO, *noun* baggage, boatload, bulk, capacity, carload, cartload, charge, commodities, consignment, contents, conveyance, freight, freightage, furnishings, goods, haul, impedimenta, lading, lading of a ship, load, luggage,

merchandise, *onus,* pack, packages, payload, produce, provisions, shipload, shipment, shipping, stock, tonnage, trainload, transfer, truckload, vanload, ware, wares
ASSOCIATED CONCEPTS: carriers, delivery contract, hot cargo, risk of loss of cargo

CARICATURE, noun apery, cartoon, characterization, depiction, exaggerated likeness, exaggeration, farce, graphic treatment, grotesque portrayal, grotesque rendition, hyperbole, imitation, lampoon, mimicking, mimicry, mockery, overcoloring, overdrawing, overestimation, parody, personation, portrayal, satire, travesty

CAROUSE, verb be a drunkard, be convivial, be drunk, be immoderate, be intemperate, carry to excess, celebrate, *comissari,* commit a debauch, debauch, dissipate, drink, drink to excess, enervate oneself, exceed, feast, frolic, go on a spree, imbibe, indulge in dissipation, indulge oneself, lack self-control, live dissolutely, lose control, overindulge, *potare,* quaff, revel, spree, tipple, wallow
ASSOCIATED CONCEPTS: breach of peace, disorderly conduct, disturbing the peace

CARRIAGE, noun affreightment, airfreight, carrying, cartage, conveyance, drayage, portage, porterage, shipment, shipping, transfer, transference, translocation, transportation, transshipment, truckage, *vehiculum*
ASSOCIATED CONCEPTS: affreightment, carriage of goods, Carriage of Goods by Sea Act

CARRIER, noun conveyor, dispatcher, express shipper, ferrier, shipper, steamship company, transferor, transport company
ASSOCIATED CONCEPTS: air carriers, baggage, carrier by air, carrier engaged in interstate commerce, carrier for hire, carrier of goods, carrier of passengers, carrier's lien, common carriers, forwarding carriers, initial carriers, motor vehicle carrier, operating carriers, private carriers, public carriers, railroad carriers

CARRY (Succeed), **verb** accomplish, achieve, attain, be victorious, bring to pass, cause to happen, complete, culminate, effect, effectuate, gain, prevail, score, succeed, triumph, win
ASSOCIATED CONCEPTS: carry a vote

CARRY (Transport), **verb** bear, bring, cart, convey, convoy, haul, move, take, tote, transport
ASSOCIATED CONCEPTS: carry a concealed weapon, carry a weapon, carry back, carry on a business, carry on trade, carrying charges, carrying on a trade or business, carrying on any trade or business, carrying on business, larceny, take and carry away

CARRY AWAY, verb abduce, abduct, capture, carry off, commandeer, convey away, drag away, expropriate, kidnap, make off with, overcome, overpower, purloin, ravish, remove, remove bodily, run off with, seize, shanghai, spirit away, steal, take away, take by assault, take by stealth, take captive, take forcibly, take prisoner, thieve, waylay
ASSOCIATED CONCEPTS: abduction, asportation, kidnapping, theft
FOREIGN PHRASES: ***Cepit et asportavit.*** He took and carried away.

CARTEL, noun accord, accordance, affiliation, agreement, alliance, amalgamation, association, bloc, body corporate, coadjuvancy, coalition, colleagueship, combination, combine, common consent, community of interest, compact, concert, concord, concordance, concordat, concurrence, confederation, conjunction, consensus, consociation, consonancy, consort, consortium, contract, cooperation, covenant, federation, fusion, group, joint concern, league, merger, mutual understanding, organization, pact, sodality, syndicate, trust, union, unity
ASSOCIATED CONCEPTS: business cartel, international cartel

CASE (Example), **noun** demonstration, exemplification, illustration, instance, model, occurrence, paradigm, representative, representative selection, sample, specimen, type

CASE (Lawsuit), **noun** action, cause, claim, contention, controversy, court action, dissension, judicial contest, legal argument, legal dispute, legal issue, legal proceedings, litigation, matter, matter for judgment, proceedings, suit, suit at law
ASSOCIATED CONCEPTS: case arising under laws of the United States, case arising under the Constitution, case at common law, case in equity, case law, case of fraud, case on appeal, case or controversy, criminal case, dismissal of a case, divorce case, equity case, homicide case, injunction case, judicial case, jury case, justiciable case, law case, law of the case, leading case, meritorious case, pending case, prima facie case, sufficient case for jury, trespass on the case
FOREIGN PHRASES: **Secta est pugna civilis; sicut actores armantur actionibus, et, quasi, a ccinguntur gladiis, ita rei muniuntur exceptionibus, et defenduntur, quasi c lypeis.** A suit is a civil battle; for as the plaintiffs are armed with actions, and, as it were, girded with swords, so the defendants are fortified with pleas, and are defended, as it were, with shields. **In consimili casu, consimile debet esse remedium.** In similar cases, the remedy should be similar. **Ubi non est directa lex, standum est arbitrio judicis, vel procedendum ad similia.** Where there is no direct law, the decision of the judge is to be taken, or references to be made to similar cases. **Certa debet esse intentio, et narratio, et certum fundamentum, et certa res quae deducitur in judicium.** The intention, declaration, foundation, and matter brought to the court to be tried ought to be certain.

CASE (Set of circumstances), **noun** affairs, arrangement, background, circumstance, condition, conjuncture, context, course of events, existing state, factors, grounds, juncture, milieu, occurrence, place, plight, point, position, posture, predicament, set of facts, setting, situation, standing, state, state of affairs, status, terms

CASH, noun available means, bill, capital, coin, coin of the realm, coinage, currency, dollar currency, finances, funds, hard money, legal tender, medium of exchange, monetary unit, money, moneys, pecunia praesens, pecuniary resources, principal, ready money, reserve, resources, riches, specie, treasure, working assets
ASSOCIATED CONCEPTS: cash and securities, cash assets, cash bail, cash bond, cash dividend, cash down, cash method, cash on delivery, cash on hand, cash surrender value, cash value

CAST (Register), **verb** assert, ballot, commit oneself, deposit formally, effect, establish, exercise one's choice, exercise one's options, give a vote, go to the polls, hold up one's hand, make a choice, make a decision, make a selection, make an entry, make one's choice, make one's selection, mark down, place on record, poll, put down, put on record, record, register one's vote, select, tabulate, vote
ASSOCIATED CONCEPTS: votes cast

CAST (Throw), **verb** bestrew, catapult, *conicere,* disseminate, distribute, eject, emit, fling, force, hurl, *iactare,* impart, impel, launch, let off, *mittere,* project, propel, put into motion, radiate, send forth, send off, shed, spread, toss

CAST LIGHT ON, *verb*   illuminate, inform, light, light up, lighten up, radiate, throw light upon, throw sunlight on

CASTIGATE, *verb*   admonish, be severe, berate, call to account, *castigare,* caution, censure bitterly, chasten, chastise, chide, criticize severely, deal retributive justice, discipline, excoriate, execrate, expostulate, objurgate, rebuke, remonstrate, reprehend, reprimand, reproach, reprove, scold, take to task, upbraid, vituperate
ASSOCIATED CONCEPTS: judicial censure

CASUAL, *adjective*   aimless, apathetic, blase, causeless, cursory, designless, desultory, fortuitous, haphazard, inattentive, incidental, indeterminate, indifferent, indiscriminate, informal, insouciant, irregular, nonchalant, occasional, orderless, perfunctory, pococurante, purposeless, superficial, thoughtless, unarranged, uncertain, unconcerned, uncritical, undetermined, undirected, unexacting, unfixed, unmethodical, unmeticulous, unmindful, unordered, unorganized, unparticular, unprecise, unpunctilious, unstudied, unsystematic, unweighed
ASSOCIATED CONCEPTS: casual act, casual employment, casual transaction

CASUALTY, *noun*   accident, adversity, affliction, backset, bad fortune, blight, calamity, catastrophe, contretemps, *débâcle,* disaster, emergency, hardship, ill fortune, ill hap, incident, infliction, injury, misadventure, mischance, misfortune, mishap, serious accident, setback, tragedy, unforeseen accident, unfortunate accident, unfortunate occurence
ASSOCIATED CONCEPTS: casualty insurance, casualty loss

CASUISTRY, *noun*   behaviorism, deontology, empiricism, ethical philosophy, ethology, idealism, moral science, perfectionism, sophistry, utilitarianism

CATACHRESIS, *noun*   distortion, exaggeration, false coloring, false construction, false reading, garbling, incorrect usage, misapplication, misapprehension, miscitation, misconception, misconstruction, misexplanation, misexplication, misexposition, misinterpretation, misjudgment, misquotation, misreading, misrendering, misrepresentation, mistake, mistranslation, misunderstanding, misusage, solecism, strained sense, wrong interpretation, wrong usage

CATACLYSM, *noun*   alluvion, avalanche, convulsion, crash, debacle, deluge, disaster, disturbance, earthquake, eruption, extensive flood, flood, holocaust, inundation, overflow, overflowing, overrunning, quake, storm, temblor, tidal wave, tremor, upheaval, violent upheaval
ASSOCIATED CONCEPTS: act of God, state of emergency

CATALYST, *noun*   abettor, activator, active element, active partisan, active reformer, actuator, *agacerie,* agent *provocateur,* agitator, animator, catalytic agent, cause, encouragement, encourager, excitant, exciter, ferment, force, goad, impeller, impetus, impulse, incentive, incitation, incitement, inducement, inspiration, inspirer, instigator, maneuverer, modifying cause, motivating force, motivation, mover, moving spirit, planner, popular ringleader, power, prompter, *provocateur,* provocation, provocative, spur, stimulant, stimulator, strategist, suggester

CATASTROPHE, *noun*   accident, adversity, affliction, *calamitas,* calamity, cataclysm, collapse, contretemps, *débâcle,* decimation, desolation, destruction, devastation, disaster, downfall, emergency, eradication, extinction, great misfortune, hardship, havoc, holocaust, infliction, misadventure, mischance, misfortune, mishap, notable disaster, obliteration, ravage, ruin, ruination, scourge, serious calamity, tragedy
ASSOCIATED CONCEPTS: act of God, natural catastrophe, state of emergency

CATCHALL, *noun*   container, depository, holder, receiver, receptacle, repository
ASSOCIATED CONCEPTS: catchall clause to a contract

CATCHWORD, *noun*   adage, byword, catch phrase, clew, cliché, clue, colloquialism, common saying, cue word, key, maxim, mot, password, pithy saying, saying, shibboleth, slogan, stock saying, tag, vogue word, watchword
ASSOCIATED CONCEPTS: trademarks

CATEGORICAL, *adjective*   absolute, apodictic, assured, authoritative, beyond a shadow of doubt, beyond all question, clear-cut, complete, conclusive, confident, convinced, convincing, decided, decisive, definite, definitive, *definitus,* distinct, dogmatic, doubtless, emphatic, evidential, final, forceful, incontestable, incontrovertible, indisputable, indubitable, inevitable, irrefragable, irrefutable, past dispute, positive, settled, *simplex,* strong, total, ultimate, unambiguous, unassailable, unchangeable, unconditional, unconditioned, uncontested, undeniable, undisputed, unequivocal, unhesitating, unmitigated, unqualified, unquestionable, unquestioning, vehement, without a shade of doubt, without appeal, without reserve

CATHARSIS, *noun*   abreaction, acting out, deliverance, detersion, discharge of emotions, emotional release, outlet, purgation, purge, release, riddance, ventilation

CAUCUS, *noun*   assemblage, *assemblée,* assembly, *attroupement,* body of partisans, committee, conclave, concourse, conference, consultation, convention, convergence, convocation, council, council meeting, discussion, foregathering, gathering, ingathering, mass meeting, meet, meeting, meeting of political leaders, policy-fixing meeting, political confluence, *pourparler,* rally, session, subcommittee, summit, top-level meeting
ASSOCIATED CONCEPTS: congressional caucas, legislative caucus

CAUSAL, *adjective*   causative, compelling, conductive, constitutive, creative, determinant, determinative, effective, effectual, formative, generating, generative, inception, inducing, influential, institutive, instrumental, originating, originative, productive
ASSOCIATED CONCEPTS: causal connection, causal negligence, causal relationship

CAUSATIVE, *adjective*   beginning, causal, caused, constitutive, constructive, creative, determinant, directive, dominant, formative, generative, impelling, inceptive, induced, inducing, inductive, influential, inspired, institutive, original, originative, pivotal, predominant, primary, procreative, productive, responsible, stimulating

CAUSE *(Lawsuit),* *noun*   action, action in court, case, legal action, legal proceedings, litigation, proceedings, subject of dispute, suit, suit at law, trial
ASSOCIATED CONCEPTS: accrual of a cause of action, adversary cause, cause of action, cause pending, meritorious cause, trial of a cause

CAUSE *(Reason),* *noun*   agent, aim, allurement, base, basis, *causa,* causation, consideration, derivation, design, determinative, end, enticement, factor, foundation, generator, genesis, goal, ground, impulse, incitement, inducement, influence, instigation, intent, intention, mainspring, motivation, motive, object, objective, origin, prompting, purpose, rationale, root, source, spur, stimulant, stimulation, stimulus, temptation, underlying principle

ASSOCIATED CONCEPTS: accidental cause, adequate cause, cause and consequence, cause and effect, cause for removal, cause of death, cause of loss, cause of the injury, cause shown, challenge for cause, compelling cause, concurrent cause, contributing cause, controlling cause, dependent cause, direct cause, discharged for cause, dominant cause, due cause, effective cause, efficient cause, external cause, for cause, good cause, immediate cause, independent cause, initial cause, intervening cause, just cause, justifiable cause, legal cause, meritorious cause, natural cause, nature of the cause, originating cause, primary cause, probable cause, proper cause, proximate cause, reasonable cause, related concepts, remote cause, removal for cause, resulting cause, show cause, sole cause, sufficient cause, superseding intervening cause, supervening cause, unforeseen cause, without cause, without just cause

CAUSE, verb be responsible, be the author of, breed, bring, bring about, bring down, bring into existence, bring on, bring to pass, causa, compel, conduce to, contribute to, contrive, create, cultivate, develop, direct, effect, effectuate, elicit, engender, engineer, evoke, foment, generate, give occasion for, give origin to, give rise to, inaugurate, incite, induce, influence, initiate, inspire, institute, launch, lay the foundations, lead to, make, motivate, occasion, originate, precipitate, produce, prompt, provoke, sow the seeds of, start, stimulate, superinduce

ASSOCIATED CONCEPTS: causa causans, causa remota, causa *sine qua non*

FOREIGN PHRASES: *Causa et origo est materia negotii.* The cause and its origin are the essence of a transaction. *Causa proxima non remota spectatur.* The direct and not the remote cause is regarded. *Causa vaga et incerta non est causa rationabilis.* A vague and uncertain cause is not a reasonable cause. *Cessante causa, cessat effectus.* The cause ceasing, the effect ceases. *Effectus sequitur causam.* The effect follows the cause. *Eventus est qui ex causa sequitur; et dicitur eventus quia ex causis evenit.* An event is that which follows from the cause, and is called an "event" because it eventuates from causes. *Malum non habet efficientem, sed deficientem, causam.* Evil has not an efficient, but a deficient, cause. *Scire proprie est rem ratione et per causam cognoscere.* To know properly is to know a thing by its cause and its reason. *Ubi lex aliquem cogit ostendere causam, necesse est quod causa sit justa et legitima.* Where the law compels a man to show cause, it is necessary that the cause be just and legal. *Causae dotis, vitae, libertatis, fisci, sunt inter favorabilia in lege.* Causes of dower, life, liberty, revenue are among the things favored in law.

CAUSE-IN-FACT, noun actual cause, causation, derivation, immediate legal basis, sufficiently legal basis, sufficiently legal cause, sufficiently legal factor, sufficiently legal genesis, sufficiently legal inducement, sufficiently legal source

CAUSE OF ACTION, noun action, action at law, basis for relief, cause, claim, claim for relief, demand, enforceable claim, ground, issue, just claim, lawful cause, legal assertion, reason for legal pursuit, reason for relief, reasonable claim, redressible wrong, right, right of action, right of recovery, right to relief

ASSOCIATED CONCEPTS: accrual of a cause of action, capacity to institute a cause of action, collateral estoppel, derivative cause of action, facts giving rise to a cause of action, facts sufficient to constitute a cause of action, inconsistent claims, joint interest in a cause of action, limitation of actions, meritorious cause of action, relief splitting a cause of action, res judicata, venue

CAUSEWAY, noun acceleration lane, access road, *agger,* approach road, arterial, arterial highway, artery, avenue, by-passage, causey, concourse, crossroad, drive, driveway, express, express highway, expressway, freeway, highroad, highway, lane, motor road, motorway, parkway, paved road, paved way, post road, raised path, raised road, road, roadway, service road, side road, speed track, speedway, state highway, street, superhighway, thoroughfare, through road, thruway, trunk road, turnpike

CAUSTIC, adjective abrasive, abrupt, *acerbus,* acrid, acrimonious, acute, astringent, austere, biting, brash, burning, corroding, corrosive, cruel, curt, cutting, derisive, derisory, envenomed, erosive, excoriating, excruciating, harsh, hurtful, insulting, invidious, irritating, lashing, malevolent, malicious, malignant, mocking, mordacious, *mordax,* mordent, piercing, pungent, pyrotic, rancorous, rude, scalding, severe, sharp, short, stinging, tart, tormenting, tortuous, trenchant, ungentle, unkind, venomous, virulent

CAUTION (Vigilance), **noun** attention, attentiveness, care, carefulness, *cautio,* circumspection, concern, conscientiousness, consideration, *cura,* diligence, exactitude, exactness, forethought, guardedness, heed, heedfulness, meticulousness, mindfulness, prudence, *prudentia,* regard, thoroughness, wariness, watchfulness

ASSOCIATED CONCEPTS: due caution, ordinary caution

CAUTION (Warning), **noun** admonition, alarm, alert, augury, caveat, exhortation, foreboding, foretelling, forewarning, monition, notice, omen, portent, precursor, prefiguration, presage, prognosis, prognostic

ASSOCIATED CONCEPTS: cautionary instructions

CAUTION, verb admonish, advise against, apprise, be vigilant, communicate to, counsel, dissuade, exhort, exhort to take heed, forearm, foreshow, forewarn, give advice, give fair warning, give intimation of impending evil, give notice, give warning, give warning of possible harm, inform, make aware, *monere,* notify of danger, persuade against, precaution, predict, prenotify, prepare for the worst, prescribe, presignify, prewarn, put on guard, remonstrate, serve notice, sound the alarm, spell danger, take precautions, urge, warn

ASSOCIATED CONCEPTS: due caution, ordinary caution, unusual caution

FOREIGN PHRASES: *Abundans cautela non nocet.* Extreme caution does no harm.

CAVEAT, noun admonishment, admonition, advance notice, advisement, alert, announcement, augury, bodement, caution, communication, direction, foretoken, forewarning, implication, indication, instruction, lesson, monition, notice, notification, order, portendance, portendment, portention, prefiguration, premonition, prewarning, telling, warning, warning sign

ASSOCIATED CONCEPTS: caveat emptor, caveat venditor

CAVEAT EMPTOR, noun at one's own risk, purchase without a guaranty, purchase without a warranty, purchased at one's risk, unassured purchase, uncovenanted purchase, unendorsed purchase, unguaranteed purchase, unwarranted purchase

CAVIL, verb attack, belittle, *calumniari,* carp, *carpere,* censure frivolously, complain frivolously, condemn, criticize frivolously, decry, denigrate, denounce, deprecate, deride, disapprove, discredit, disparage frivolously, faultfind, find fault with, haggle, object frivolously, protest frivolously, raise frivolous objection to, raise objections frivolously, raise specious objection to, reprehend, ridicule irresponsibly, upbraid, *vellicare*

CEASE, verb abate, abrogate, abstain from, adjourn, annul, arrest, be all over, be at an end, be silent, become void, bring to an end, cancel, cause to halt, check, close, come to a close, come to a standstill, come to an end, conclude, consummate, culminate, *desinere,* desist, *desistere,* discontinue, draw to a close, drop, end, expire, extinguish, finish, forbear, get through, give over, halt, hold off, intermit, interrupt, lapse, leave off, make an end of, pause, put a stop to, put an end to, quell, quit, refrain, relinquish, remain, run its course, stanch, stay, stem, stop, stop work, surcease, suspend, terminate, vacate, withdraw
ASSOCIATED CONCEPTS: cease and desist order, cease doing business, cease from occupying, cease to act, cease to do business
FOREIGN PHRASES: *Cessante causa, cessat effectus.* When the cause ceases, the effect ceases. ***Cessante ratione legis, cessat et ipsa lex.*** The reason of the law ceasing, the law itself also ceases.

CEDE, verb abalienate, abandon, abdicate, abjure, accede, alienate, assign, bequeath, concede, *concedere,* confer, consign, convey, deed, deliver, devolve, dismiss, donate, give, give away, give up, give up claim to, grant, part with, quitclaim, release, relinquish, remise, render, renounce, renounce claim to, resign, sign away, submit, succumb, surrender, tender, transfer, transmit, turn over, vouchsafe, yield
ASSOCIATED CONCEPTS: cede jurisdiction, cede territory

CEILING, noun acme, altitude, apex, apogee, climax, culmination, extreme, extremity, farthest point, height, highest degree, highest point, limit, maximum, optimum, peak, pinnacle, record, roof, summit, *tectum,* top, ultimate, utmost, utmost extent, utmost height, uttermost, vertex, zenith
ASSOCIATED CONCEPTS: maximum income ceiling, maximum rent ceiling

CELL *(Enemy combatants),* **noun** enemy group, extremist group, extremists, incendiaries, insurgents, rebel organization, revolutionaries, saboteurs, subversives, underground extremists
ASSOCIATED CONCEPTS: enemy combatants, justice courts, military tribunals, Patriotic Act, prison cells, sleeper cell, terrorism, terrorist cell

CELL *(jail),* **noun** cage, *cella,* chamber, compartment, confined room, confinement, cubicle, *cubiculum,* enclosed cage, incarceration, jailhouse, penitentiary, pound, prison, prison house, small cavity, small room, solitary abode

CEMENT, verb accouple, adhere, affix, agglomerate, agglutinate, amalgamate, annex, attach, bind, braze, coagulate, coalesce, cohere, combine, concrete, congeal, *conglutinare,* conglutinate, conjoin, connect, consolidate, couple, crystallize, fasten, fix, fix together, fuse, glue, harden, hold together, incorporate, join, make firm, merge, mortar, put together, secure, set, solder, solidify, stick, unite, weld

CENSOR, verb ban, bar, blot out, bowdlerize, cancel, *censor,* control, control the flow of news, cut, delete, disallow, disapprove, discountenance, dispense with, disqualify, eject, eliminate, enforce censorship, eradicate, erase, exclude, expunge, expurgate, forbid, impose a ban, inhibit, interfere, judge, keep within bounds, leave out, limit, not include, omit, oversee, pass under review, police, preclude, prevent, prevent publication, prohibit, proscribe, quash, refuse, refuse permission, reject, restrain, restrict, review, rub out, scratch out, sift, submerge, supervise communications, suppress, withhold permission
ASSOCIATED CONCEPTS: censorship, Federal Communications Act

CENSORSHIP, noun abolition, abridgment, bar, blackout, block, blockage, blue-penciling, bowdlerization, cancellation, control, curb, deprivation, elimination, expurgation, forbidding, governmental control, hindrance, impediment, imposition of veil of secrecy, inhibition, limitation, news blackout, obliteration, prohibition, repression, restraint, restriction, rigid control, seal of secrecy, stifling, suppression
ASSOCIATED CONCEPTS: censorship of books, censorship of films, censorship of First Amendment rights, censorship of mail, censorship of the theatre

CENSURE, verb administer a rebuke, admonish, animadvert upon, assail, attack, berate, blame, bring into discredit, cast a reproach, cast a slur upon, cast blame upon, cast reflection upon, castigate, chastise, chide, condemn, declaim against, decry, denigrate, denounce, denunciate, deprecate, depreciate, descant, disapprove, disparage, dispraise, exclaim against, excoriate, execrate, expostulate, expurgate, find fault with, *fronder,* fulminate against, hold up to execration, hold up to reprobation, impugn, inveigh against, not speak well of, objurgate, raise a hue and cry against, rebuff, rebuke, recriminate, remonstrate, reprehend, *reprehendere,* reprimand, reproach, reprobate, reprove, speak ill of, upbraid, view with disfavor, vilipend, *vituperare*
ASSOCIATED CONCEPTS: censure for improper conduct, censure for prejudicial conduct, letter of admonition, reprimand

CENSUS, noun account, calculation, *census,* ciphering, computation, count, counting, demography, enumeration, evaluation, figure-work, figures, figuring, list, listing, measurement, numbering, numeration, official count, official enumeration of inhabitants, official enumeration of the population, official reckoning, official registration, poll, reckoning, recount, registering, registration, score, statement, statistical inquiry, statistics, supputation, tables, tabulation, tally, valuation, vital statistics
ASSOCIATED CONCEPTS: federal census, representation based upon the last census

CENTER *(Central position),* **noun** axis, center of gravity, central point, convergence, converging point, core, epicenter, equidistance, eye, focal point, focus, focus of attention, fulcrum, half distance, halfway, media pars, medius, middle, middle distance, middle point, middle position, midmost point, midpoint, midst, point of convergence
ASSOCIATED CONCEPTS: center lane, center line, center of gravity, grouping of contacts doctrine

CENTER *(Essence),* **noun** base, basis, bedrock, cardinal point, central nature, chief part, constitutive principle, core, essential part, gist, gravamen, heart, hypostasis, important part, inmost nature, inmost substance, inner reality, main part, main point, nature, nucleus, pith, primary element, prime constituent, prime ingredient, principal part, quid, quiddity, quintessence, *sine qua non,* soul, substance, sum and substance, vital element, vital part

CENTER OF ATTENTION, noun   arena, center, center of activity, center of attraction, center of focus, center of interest, central point, centrality, converging point, focal point, heart, hub, pivotal point, point of convergence

CENTER OF FOCUS, noun   arena, center, center of activity, center of attention, center of attraction, center of interest, central point, centrality, converging point, focal point, heart, hub, pivotal point, point of convergence

CENTRAL (Essential), **adjective**   basal, basic, capital, cardinal, chief, crucial, dominant, elemental, first, foremost, foundational, fundamental, highly important, indispensable, intrinsic, intrinsical, key, main, major, necessary, paramount, pivotal, primal, primary, principal, requisite, ruling, significant, supreme, underlying, vital

CENTRAL (Situated near center), **adjective**   center, centermost, centric, centrical, equidistant, focal, halfway, inmost, inner, medial, median, mesial, middle, middlemost, midmost
ASSOCIATED CONCEPTS: central board of appeals, central filing, centralization center of gravity doctrine

CENTRALIZATION, noun   absorption, aggregation, alliance, amalgamation, amassing, assembling, association, bringing together, centering, centralism, coalescence, coalescing, coalition, combination, compacting, compilation, compression, concentralization, concentration, condensation, conglomeration, congregation, consolidation, convergence, converging, coordinate, focalization, fusion, gathering together, grouping, incorporation, massing, merging, narrowing, nucleation, organization, synthesis, systematization, unification, union, unity
ASSOCIATED CONCEPTS: centralization of administration, centralization of government, decentralization

CEREMONY, noun   caerimonia, celebration, commemoration, conventionality, festive occasion, festivity, formal occasion, formality, memorialization, observance, official reception, prescribed procedure, reception, rite, ritual, ritus, solemn observance, solemnity, solemnization, state occasion
ASSOCIATED CONCEPTS: ceremonial marriage, marriage ceremonies, testimentary ceremonies

CERTAIN (Fixed), **adjective**   absolute, assured, attested, certified, changeless, conclusive, confident, confirmed, decided, decisive, definite, determinate, determined, firm, guaranteed, incontestable, incontrovertible, indisputable, indubitable, inescapable, inevitable, infallible, irrefragable, irrefutable, official, positive, reliable, settled, stable, static, sure, unambiguous, unanswerable, unappealable, unavoidable, unchanging, undeniable, undisputed, unerring, unfailing, unmistakable, unpreventable, unquestionable, unquestioned
ASSOCIATED CONCEPTS: absolutely certain, capable of being rendered certain, certain powers and privileges, sum certain

CERTAIN (Particular), **adjective**   certus, distinct, especial, exact, exclusive, individual, marked, peculiar, precise, singular, special, specific, specified, unique

CERTAIN (Positive), **adjective**   absolute, actual, ascertained, assertive, assured, attested, authoritative, avoidless, axiomatic, beyond a shadow of doubt, beyond all dispute, beyond all question, capable of proof, certified, certus, changeless, clear, clear-cut, clearly known, cognizant, conclusive, concrete, confident, consistent, convinced, correct, credulous, decided, decisive, definite,

demonstrable, demonstrated, dependable, distinct, doubtless, ensured, established, evident, evidential, existing, factual, final, fully convinced, guaranteed, inalterable, inappealable, incommutable, incontestable, incontrovertible, inconvertible, indefeasible, indestructible, indisputable, indubitable, inerrant, inescapable, inevitable, inexorable, inextinguishable, infallible, inflexible, invariable, inviolate, invulnerable, irreducible, irrefragable, irrefutable, irresistible, irresoluble, irreversible, irrevocable, knowing, past dispute, persuaded, questionless, real, reliable, right, satisfied, secure, self-evident, settled, stated, sure, tangible, true to the facts, unaltered, unambiguous, unassailable, unavoidable, unchangeable, unconfuted, undeniable, undeviating, undisputed, undoubted, undoubtful, undoubting, unequivocal, unerring, unfailing, unhesitating, unimpeachable, unmistakable, unqualified, unquestionable, unquestioned, unrefuted, unshakable, unsusceptible of change, unvarying, unwavering, valid, veracious, verifiable, void of suspicion
ASSOCIATED CONCEPTS: capable of being rendered certain

CERTAIN (Specific), **adjective**   appropriate, ascertained, assigned, bounded, categorical, characteristic, choice, circumscribed, clear-cut, clearly defined, clearly stated, concrete, definite, designated, determinate, distinct, distinguished, esoteric, especial, exact, exclusive, explicit, express, expressed, fixed, individual, limited, marked, noteworthy, particular, peculiar, precise, prescribed, quidam, respective, restricted, select, settled, singular, special, specified, stated, well-defined

CERTAINTY, noun   absence of doubt, absolute confidence, absoluteness, assurance, assuredness, authoritativeness, certification, certitude, certus, complete conviction, conclusiveness, confidentness, conviction, corroboration, definiteness, firmness, firmness of belief, inability to doubt, incontestability, incontrovertibility, indisputability, indubitability, indubitableness, inerrability, inerrancy, inexorability, infallibility, irrefragability, irrefutability, knowledge, objective certitude, positiveness, quality of being certain, questionlessness, reassurance, reliability, secureness, security, solidity, soundness, stability, substantiality, sure presumption, sureness, surety, unconfutability, undeniability, unequivocalness, unimpeachability, unmistakability, unqualification, unquestionability, unquestionableness, verification, warranty
ASSOCIATED CONCEPTS: absolute certainty, certainty to a common intent, moral certainty, proof to a reasonable certainty, reasonable certainty
FOREIGN PHRASES: **Certum est quod certum reddi potest.** That is certain which is capable of being rendered certain. **Terminus annorum certus debet esse et determinatus.** A term of years ought to be certain and determinate.

CERTIFICATE, noun   affidavit, attestation, authentication, authorization, certification, charter, covenant, credentials, declaration, endorsement, guarantee, instrument, license, matter of record, muniment, official writing, paper, testament, voucher, warrant, writ, written contract, written evidence
ASSOCIATED CONCEPTS: allotment certificate, certificate of authority, certificate of deposit, certificate of incorporation, certificate of indebtedness, certificate of occupancy, certificate of probable cause, certificate of public convenience and necessity, certificate of reasonable doubt, certificate of stock, certificate under seal, death certificate, demand certificate, land certificate, marriage certificate

CERTIFICATION (Attested copy), **noun**   affirmation, assurance, attestation, attesting declaration, authenticated

confirmation, authentification, authoritative attestation, avouchment, confirmation, corroboration, declaration, documentary evidence, documentation, endorsement, evidence, instrument of proof, legal pledge, proof, ratification, reassurance, reassurement, solemn declaration, statement, substantiation, support, swearing, sworn evidence, testification, testimony, validation, verification, written evidence
ASSOCIATED CONCEPTS: audited and paid, certification of loss reserves, certification of stock, certified, certified according to law, certified check, false certification, fraudulent certification

CERTIFICATION (Certainness), **noun** absolute certainty, absolute confidence, ascertained fact, ascertainment, assurance, assuredness, authoritativeness, certain knowledge, certainty, certitude, complete conviction, conclusive proof, conclusiveness, confidence, conviction, dependability, freedom from error, incontestability, incontrovertibility, indisputability, indubitability, indubitable fact, inerrancy, inevitableness, infallibility, irrefragability, irrefutability, knowledge, matter of fact, objective certainty, positive fact, positiveness, proof, reliability, reliableness, rigorous proof, sureness, trustworthiness, unambiguity, unimpeachability, unquestionability, unquestionableness, utter reliability

CERTIFICATION (Certification of proficiency), **noun** affirmance, authority, authorization, citation, confirmation, copy, credential, credentials, declaration, documentation, entitlement, indorsement, letter of recognition, license, recognition
ASSOCIATED CONCEPTS: certification to practice law

CERTIFY (Approve), **verb** accede to, accept, accord, accord one's approval, accredit, acknowledge, admit, agree, agree to, allow, assent, assent to, authorize, charter, coincide, concur, concur in, confirm, confirm officially, consent, countenance, empower, endorse, entitle, establish, give assent, give clearance, give consent, give permission, indorse, legalize, license, make valid, permit, pronounce legal, ratify, sanction, uphold, validate, yield assent

CERTIFY (Attest), **verb** acknowledge, advance, advocate, affirm, affirm explicitly, affirm in an official capacity, allege, assert, assert formally, assert oneself, assert positively, assert under oath, asseverate, assure, attest, authenticate, aver, avouch, avow, be sworn, bear out, bear witness, bear witness to, bring forward, claim, confess, confirm, confirm as correct, *confirmare,* convenant, corroborate, countersign, declare the truth of, declare to be true, deliver as one's act and deed, depone, depose, document, endorse, ensure, evidence, evince, execute, fortify, give a guarantee, give one's word, guarantee, guaranty, insist, insure, issue a statement, make absolute, make certain, make one's oath, make sure, proclaim, pronounce, ratify, reaffirm, reassure, reinsure, set one's hand and seal to, solemnly affirm, state emphatically, state with conviction, stress, sustain, swear, swear an affidavit, take one's oath, testify, utter with conviction, validate, verify, vouch, vouch for, vouch for as genuine, warrant
ASSOCIATED CONCEPTS: certification of pleadings

CERTIORARI, **noun** appeal to a higher court, application for retrial, course of law, legal procedure, legal process

CERTITUDE, **noun** absolute certainty, absoluteness, ascertained fact, assurance, assuredness, attestation, certainness, certainty, certainty of meaning, conclusiveness, confidence, confidentness, conviction, dead certainty, definiteness, freedom from error, incontestability, incontrovertibility, indisputability, indubitability, indubitable fact, indubitableness, inerrability, inerrancy, inevitableness,

inexorability, infallibilism, infallibility, infallibleness, irrefragability, irrefutability, irrevocability, moral certainty, objective certainty, positiveness, sure assumption, sure presumption, sureness, surety, unambiguity, undeniability, unequivocalness, unimpeachability, unquestionableness
ASSOCIATED CONCEPTS: proof beyond a reasonable doubt

CESSATION (Interlude), **noun** abeyance, adjournment, armistice, arrest, break, ceasing, cloture, delay, desistance, discontinuance, discontinuation, dormancy, *embolium,* halt, hiatus, inaction, inactivity, interim, intermediate time, *intermissio,* intermission, interregnum, interruption, interval, intervening episode, intervening period, intervening space, intervening time, lapse, latency, lull, moratorium, pause, pendency, postponement, procrastination, quiescence, remission, respite, rest, standstill, stay, stop, suspension, temporary inaction, truce, wait

CESSATION (Termination), **noun** abandonment, climax, close, closing, closure, completion, conclusion, consummation, curtain, *dénouement,* determination, dissolution, end, ending, expiration, finale, *finis,* finish, fulfillment, *intermissio,* issue, outcome, realization, retirement, stoppage, surcease, terminus
ASSOCIATED CONCEPTS: cessation of business, cessation of hostilities, cessation of occupation, cessation of possession, cessation of work

CESSION, **noun** abalienation, allowance, assignment, award, bestowal, concession, conveyance, delivery, disposal, disposition, donation, gift, giving up, giving up claim to, grant, handing over, nonretention, parting with, presentation, release, relinquishing claim to, relinquishment, resignation, submittal, surrender, transfer, waiver, yielding

CHAIN (Nexus), **noun** act of coming together, act of coupling, act of joining, act of uniting, affiliation, affinity, alliance, association, attachment, attraction, bond, bond of union, bridge, conjunction, connectedness, connecting link, connecting medium, connection, correlation, interconnection, intermedium, interrelation, junction, kinship, liaison, ligament, ligature, link, linkage, privity, relatedness, relation, relationship, relativity, tie, union

CHAIN (Series), **noun** array, catena, catenation, classification, concatenation, connected series, consecution, constant flow, continuity, cordon, gradation, line, links, order, procession, progression, range, round, row, run, scale, sequence, *series,* set, succession, suit, suite, train, unbroken line, *vinculum*
ASSOCIATED CONCEPTS: chain of causation, chain of circumstances, chain of custody, chain of title

CHAIN OF CUSTODY, **noun** complete administration, custodianship, guardianship, preservation, preservation from harm, preservation from injury, proper accounting, proper administration, proper archiving, proper care, proper cataloguing, proper documentation, proper recording, proper records and management, proper registration, protection, safe case and control, safeguard, safekeeping, stewardship, trusteeship
ASSOCIATED CONCEPTS: appropriation, care and possession, search and seizure

CHAIN OF EVIDENCE, **noun** enemy group, extremist group, extremists, incendiaries, insurgents, rebel organization, revolutionaries, saboteurs, subversives, underground extremists

ASSOCIATED CONCEPTS: enemy combatants, justice courts, military tribunals, Patriotic Act, prison cells, sleeper cell, terrorism, terrorist cell

CHAIRMAN, noun chair, conductor, director, head, headman, key man, leader, master of ceremonies, moderator, monitor, overseer, person in authority, presider, presiding officer, principal, *qui conventui praeest*, speaker, supervisor, symposiarch

ASSOCIATED CONCEPTS: chairman of a committee, chairman of the board of directors

CHALLENGE, noun appeal, confront, confute, contradict, controvert, defy, denounce, differ, disagree, disapprove, dispute, dissent, enter an appeal, initiative, menace, negate, object to, oppose, opposition, protest, raise a question, raise objections, reject, remonstrate, repudiate, resist, show reluctance, stand up against, take exception to, threaten, wrangle

ASSOCIATED CONCEPTS: challenge an award of a bid, challenge an opponent, challenge to the law

CHALLENGE, verb *ad pugnam provocare*, affront, appeal, argue, bid defiance to, call out, call to answer, combat an opinion, confront, confute, contradict, controvert, cry out against, debate, defy, denounce, differ, disagree, disapprove, dispute, dissent, enter a protest, hurl defiance at, invite competition, invite to contest, menace, negate, negative, object to, oppose, protest, quarrel, query, question, raise a question, raise objections, raise one's voice against, reject, remonstrate, repudiate, resist, say no, show reluctance, stand up against, take exception to, threaten, wrangle

ASSOCIATED CONCEPTS: challenge for cause, challenge jurisdiction, challenge of ownership, challenge to a finding of a lower court, challenge to a Grand Jury's composition, challenge to sufficiency of pleading, challenge to the array, challenge to the panel, challenge to the venire, preemptory challenge

CHAMBER (Body), **noun** aggregation, *assemblée*, assembly, bench, bench of judges, board, body of judges, cabinet, caucus, collocation, committee, confederacy, confederation, conflux, congress, constituency, convocation, council, court, federation, forum, gathering, group, ingathering, institute, judicial branch, judicial department, judicatory, law-making body, lawmakers, league, legislative body, legislature, mass, meeting, members of the bar, organization, panel, panel of judges, parliament, plenum, representatives, session, society, tribunal, union

ASSOCIATED CONCEPTS: chamber of commerce

CHAMBER (Compartment), **noun** alcove, antechamber, anteroom, apartment, box, camera, cell, *chambre*, closet, court, cubicle, *cubiculum*, den, division, enclosure, hall, hold, hollow, hollow place, lodging, meeting hall, office, parlor, *pars interior*, partitioned space, reception room, retreat, room, *salle*, section, separate part, sitting room, stall, stateroom, *thalamus*

ASSOCIATED CONCEPTS: chambers of the court, judicial chambers, legislative chambers

CHANCE (Fortuity), **noun** advantage, befalling, casus, circumstance, event, favorable time, fortuitousness, good fortune, happening, occasion, opening, suitable circumstance, time

ASSOCIATED CONCEPTS: arise by chance, last clear chance

CHANCE (Possibility), **noun** aptitude, attainability, bare possibility, conceivability, conceivableness, contingency,

favorable prospect, hope, imaginability, indeterminacy, indeterminateness, liability, likelihood, possibleness, potential, potentiality, probability, prospect, *spes*, uncertainty, unexpectedness, unpredictability

ASSOCIATED CONCEPTS: chance verdict, games of chance

FOREIGN PHRASES: *Casus fortuitus non est supponendus.* A chance happening is not to be presumed. ***Casus fortuitus non est sperandus, et nemo tenetur devinare.*** A chance happening is not to be expected, and no one is bound to foresee it.

CHANCE HAPPENING, noun accident, blunder, bungle, chance good fortune, chance misfortune, chance occurrence, error, fluke, fortuity, lucky situation, miscalculation, misconception, misinterpretation, misjudgment, misreading, misunderstanding, one in a lifetime occurrence, random achievement, random luck, random mistake, random success, stroke of bad luck, stroke of misfortune

CHANGE, verb adapt, adjust, alter, be converted, be inconstant, be irresolute, convert, *convertere in*, deviate, displace, diverge, evolve, exchange, fluctuate, give in exchange, go through phases, *immutare*, innovate, interchange, make a transition, make different, make over, metamorphose, modify, modulate, permute, put in the place of, recast, recondition, reconstruct, reform, regenerate, remake, reorganize, replace, resolve into, restyle, revise, revive, revolutionize, show phases, subrogate, substitute, switch, switch around, transfigure, transform, transmogrify, transmute, transubstantiate, turn from, turn into, variegate, vary

ASSOCIATED CONCEPTS: additions and alterations, change in circumstances, change in conditions, change in occupancy, change in ownership, change in title, change of address, change of beneficiary, change of domicile, change of duties, change of name, change of ownership, change of parties, change of position, change of possession, change of venue, immaterial change, major change, minor change, permanent change, proposed change

CHANNEL (Avenue), **noun** arrangement, conduit, course, duct, expedient, facility, forum, instrument, instrumentality, means, medium, method, mode, outlet, passage, path, procedure, process, scheme, set up, strategy, tool, way

CHANNEL (Navigable water), **noun** body of water, canal, gully, moat, navigable river, navigable stream, stream, trench, trough, water, waterway

ASSOCIATED CONCEPTS: navigable waters of the United States, Navigation Acts

CHAOS, noun agitation, anarchy, bedlam, commotion, confusion, convulsion, disarray, discomposure, discord, disorder, disorderliness, disunion, embroilment, entanglement, ferment, flurry, fracas, furor, havoc, imbroglio, incoherence, irregularity, misrule, mob rule, muddle, pandemonium, panic, perturbation, racket, riot, shambles, stir, storm, tempest, tumult, turbulence, turmoil, unrest, unruliness, upheaval, uproar, upset

CHAOTIC, adjective aimless, anarchical, askew, awry, complex, confused, discordant, disordered, disorganized, fermenting, formless, frantic, frenzied, furious, haphazard, mixed-up, muddled, raging, scattered, shapeless, stormy, tempestuous, tumultuous, turbulent, unmethodical, unrestrained, unorganized, unruly, unsystematic, untidy

CHAPTER *(Branch),* **noun** affiliate, associate, branch member, branch office, bureau, component, department, division, local, local office, lodge, member, office, organ, section, subdivision, subsidiary

CHAPTER *(Division),* **noun** article, *caput,* clause, column, component, fragment, head, heading, paragraph, part, partition, passage, phrase, portion, section, sector, segment, separate part, subdivision, subgroup
ASSOCIATED CONCEPTS: chapter 10 reorganization, paragraphs, sections

CHARACTER *(An individual),* **noun** being, body, figure, human, human being, man, mortal, party, person, personage, personality, self-determined being, somebody, someone

CHARACTER *(Personal quality),* **noun** *animus,* aspects, attribute, bent, characteristic mood, constitution, description, disposition, dominant quality, essence, essential part, essential quality of one's nature, essentialness, ethos, features, fiber, frame of mind, grain, inclination, individualism, individuality, *ingenium,* inherited characteristics, inner nature, intellect, intrinsicality, intrinsicalness, kind, leaning, makeup, manner, marked traits, mental and spiritual makeup, mettle, mold, moral qualities, *mores, natura,* natural turn of mind, nature, peculiarity, personal traits, personality, predilection, prime ingredients, proclivity, proneness, propension, propensity, *proprietas,* psychological habits, qualities, quiddity, quintessence, slant, striking qualities, style, substantiality, susceptibility, temper, temperament, tendency, tone, trait

CHARACTER *(Reputation),* **noun** celebrity, credit, deference, distinction, eminence, esteem, estimation, *existimatio, fama,* fame, grandeur, high reward, honor, *locus standi,* name, nobility, notability, notice, notoriety, notoriousness, *opinio,* place, popular favor, popularity, position, position in society, preeminence, prestige, prominence, public esteem, publicly recognized standing, recognition, regard, renown, reputableness, repute, respect, respectability, standing, station, status
ASSOCIATED CONCEPTS: character evidence, character witness

CHARACTERISTIC, noun aspect, attribute, cast, constitution, differentia, differential, distinction, distinctive feature, distinguishing trait, essence, essential part, feature, humor, idiocrasy, idiosyncrasy, immanence, inclination, individuality, inherence, inhersion, leaning, liability, makeup, mannerism, marked feature, marked quality, nature, particularity, peculiar idiom, peculiarity, penchant, personal equation, point of difference, predilection, proclivity, proneness, propensity, property, *proprietas,* quality, quintessence, speciality, specialty, specific quality, tendency, trait, type, uniqueness
ASSOCIATED CONCEPTS: characteristic of and peculiar to business of an employer, characteristic of work performed by an employee

CHARACTERIZE, verb classify, construe, delineate, depict, descend to particulars, describe, *designare,* detail, diagram, differentiate, distinguish, draw, elucidate, exemplify, express precisely, formalize, give an account of, give precise meaning to, give the details of, identify, illustrate, individualize, individuate, interpret, make apparent, make clear, make vivid, mark, mark off, *notare,* outline, personify, picture, portray, profile, reflect, render precise, represent, set apart, set forth the character of, specify, specify the peculiarities of

CHARGE *(Accusation),* **noun** *accusatio,* allegation, arraignment, attack, blame, castigation, censure, citation, complaint, condemnation, count, countercharge, *crimen,* crimination, delation, denouncement, denunciation, disapprobation, formal complaint, impeachment, imputation, incrimination, inculpation, indictment, information, insinuation, objurgation, plaint, presentment, recrimination, reproach, reproof, summons
ASSOCIATED CONCEPTS: charge of a crime, charges of misconduct, criminal charge, indictment, offense charged, specifically charged

CHARGE *(Command),* **noun** call, commandment, commission, dictate, direction, imperative, imposition, injunction, instruction, mandate, *mandatum,* order, precept, proclamation, request, requirement, requisition, subpoena, summons, ultimatum, writ
ASSOCIATED CONCEPTS: charge with responsibility

CHARGE *(Cost),* **noun** assessment, debit, disbursement, due, dues, exaction, exactment, expenditure, expense, fee, obligation, outlay, payment, pecuniary burden, *pretium,* price, quotation, rate, rent, tax, toll, valuation, value, worth
ASSOCIATED CONCEPTS: charge against an estate, charge-off, chargeback, charging lien, deferred charges, minimum charge

CHARGE *(Custody),* **noun** administration, auspices, care, chaperonage, concern, control, *curare, custodia,* entrusted cause, entrusted object, guardianship, guidance, jurisdiction, keeping, object of responsibility, patronage, protection, safekeeping, superintendence, supervision, trust, trusteeship, *tutela,* tutelage, ward, wardship, watch

CHARGE *(Lien),* **noun** accountability, bond, burden, claim on property, commitment, debenture, duty, encumbrance, guarantee, guaranty, hold on property, hypothecation, indebtedness, liability, obligation, pecuniary burden, pignus *judiciale,* pledge, real security, right to dispose of property, security, security on property, tie, *vadium mortuum, vadium vivum*
ASSOCIATED CONCEPTS: charging lien, incumbrance

CHARGE *(Responsibility),* **noun** accountability, accountableness, allegiance, appointment, assignment, burden, commitment, engagement, function, imperative duty, inescapable duty, mission, obligation, one's duty, responsibleness, sense of duty, task, undertaking
ASSOCIATED CONCEPTS: public charge

CHARGE *(Statement to the jury),* **noun** address to the jury, adjuration, admonition, advice, declamation, definitions on the law, details on the law, direction, discourse, disquisition, exhortation, guidance, instructions, lecture, legal instructions
ASSOCIATED CONCEPTS: charge to the jury

CHARGE *(Accuse),* **verb** *accusare, arguere,* arraign, attack, blame, bring accusation, censure, challenge, cite, complain against, condemn, criminate, denounce, denunciate, expostulate, file a claim, hold responsible, impute, incriminate, inculpate, indict, issue a writ, lay responsibility upon, lodge a complaint, put the blame on, recriminate, reprehend, stigmatize
ASSOCIATED CONCEPTS: charged with crime

CHARGE *(Assess),* **verb** appraise, assess a tax upon, assess pro rata, assign, assign one's share to, bill, compute, demand payment, dun, estimate, exact, fix a charge, fix the price at, give a final notice, impose, incur a debt, invoice, lay a duty upon, levy, make claims upon, present an ultimatum, present one's claim, pricing, prorate, rate, send a final demand, tax, value

CHARGE (Empower), **verb**   appoint, assign, authorize, authorize formally, commission, confer power on, delegate, delegate authority to, deputize, emper, enable, endow, endow the power, engage, entrust, give authority to, give power to, grant, invest the power, invest with authoritative power, make able, mission, nominate, permit, put in care of, warrant

CHARGE (Instruct on the law), **verb**   admonish, advise, caution, counsel, detail the law, direct, exhort, give advice, give suggestions to, guide, inform, instruct, offer counsel, point out, prepare, prescribe the law, press advice on, propose legal instructions, recommend points of law, suggest, suggest conclusions of law, urge
ASSOCIATED CONCEPTS: charging a jury

CHARITABLE (Benevolent), **adjective**   almsgiving, altruistic, beneficent, *beneficus, benignus,* bounteous, eleemosynary, freehanded, generous, giving, gracious, greathearted, liberal, magnanimous, munificent, openhanded, philanthropic, princely, unselfish, unsparing, unstinting

CHARITABLE (Lenient), **adjective**   accommodating, acquiescent, beneficent, benevolent, benign, benignant, clement, compliant, condoning, considerate, empathetic, exorable, forbearing, forgiving, free from vindictiveness, gracious, helpful, humane, humanitarian, kind, kindhearted, liberal, *liberalis,* merciful, obliging, patient, permitting, sensitive, soft, softhearted, sympathetic, sympathizing, temperate, tolerant, understanding, warm, yielding

CHARITY, **noun**   active giving, aid, almsgiving, altruism, assistance, backing, benefaction, beneficentia, benevolence, benevolentness, bestowal, bounteousness, bountifulness, clemency, considerateness, consideration, contribution, donation, dotation, endowment, generosity, generous giving, gift, good will, grace, grant, help, hospitality, humaneness, humanitarianism, humanity, kindness, *liberalitas,* liberalness, magnanimity, munificence, patronage, philanthropic gift, philanthropy, relief, support, unselfishness, willing help
ASSOCIATED CONCEPTS: charitable and benevolent institution, charitable association, charitable bequest, charitable contributions, charitable corporation, charitable enterprise, charitable gift, charitable institution, charitable organization, charitable purposes, charitable trusts, charitable use

CHARTER (Declaration of rights), **noun**   announcement, constitution, decree, official announcement, proclamation, promulgation, pronouncement, public announcement, public statement, publication, writing
ASSOCIATED CONCEPTS: amendment of a charter, amendment to a charter, articles of incorporation, charter of a foreign corporation, charter of a municipal corporation, charter of an association, corporate charter, county charter, municipal charter, partnership charter, reform a charter, repeal of a charter, special charter, state charter

CHARTER (License), **noun**   authority, certificate, certificate of permission, dispensation, express permission, grant, imprimatur, instrument, muniment, official document, patent, permit, written permission
ASSOCIATED CONCEPTS: chartered bank, chartered by law, expiration of a charter, renewal of a charter

CHARTER (Sanction), **noun**   acceptance, acknowledgment, acquiescence, admission, allowance, approval, assent, authority, authorization, concurrence, confirmation, consent, countenance, delegation, empowerment, endorsement, enfranchisement, entitlement, franchise, grant, leave, liberty, license, permission, permit, pragmatic sanction, privilege, ratification, recognition, sufferance, support, tolerance, toleration, vested right
ASSOCIATED CONCEPTS: chartered by the law

CHASE, **verb**   endeavor to overtake, follow, go after, go in pursuit of, go in quest of, hunt, pursue, run after, run in pursuit, search, seek, track, trail, try to overtake

CHATTEL, **noun**   asset, belonging, commodity, effect, equipment, fortune, holding, movable article of property, movables, personal effect, personalty, possession, property, resource, trapping, valuable
ASSOCIATED CONCEPTS: action to recover a chattel, chattel interest, chattel mortgage, chattel trust, chattels real, conveyance of a chattel, household chattels, lien upon a chattel, personal chattels, personal property
FOREIGN PHRASES: *Catalla juste possessa amitti non possunt.* Chattels justly possessed cannot be lost. *Catalla reputantur inter minima in lege.* Chattels are considered in law of lesser importance.

CHEAT, verb   act dishonestly, be cunning, be dishonest, befool, beguile, betray, break faith, commit breach of trust, cozen, deceive, defalcate, defraud, deprive of dishonestly, dissemble, dupe, embezzle, *fraudare,* ignore ethics, inveigle, lack honesty, obtain money by false pretenses, peculate, pettifog, play false, practice chicanery, practice fraud, prevaricate, purloin, represent falsely, sharp, swindle
ASSOCIATED CONCEPTS: cheating by false weights and measures, false pretenses, larceny

CHECK (Bar), **noun**   abeyance, arrest, barricade, barrier, block, blockage, cessation, checkmate, control, curb, damper, deadlock, deadstop, delay, detainment, detention, disruption, drawback, embargo, estoppel, foil, frustration, full stop, halt, hindrance, impediment, *impedimentum,* impedition, injunction, interference, interruption, limitation, *mora,* obstacle, obstruction, opposition, preclusion, prohibition, proscription, rebuff, regulation, rejection, restraint, restriction, retardation, retardment, standstill, stop, stoppage, stopper, suspension, trammel

CHECK (Instrument), **noun**   bank paper, banknote, bill, bill of exchange, certificate, commercial instrument, commercial paper, debenture, draft, fiduciary currency, money order, negotiable paper, note, order on a bank, paper money, security, sight draft, treasury note
ASSOCIATED CONCEPTS: acceptance of a check, altered check, bad check, bank check, bearer check, bill of exchange, cashier's check, certified check, check payable on demand, conditional check, conversion of a check, delivery of a check, deposit of a check, dishonored check, drawee, drawer, endorsed check, endorsement, forged check, holder in due course of a check, insufficient funds, order check, pay check, payee, payment of a check, postdated check, presentment of a check, registered check, time check, unauthorized endorsement, worthless check

CHECK (Inspect), **verb**   audit, balance accounts, canvass, case, check up, examine, experiment, explore, go over, inquire into, inventory, investigate, keep watch, look for flaws, look into, look over, make a reconnaissance, make a trial run, monitor, observe, overhaul, overlook, oversee, peruse, probe, query, question, quiz, reconnoiter, reexamine, regard carefully, regulate, review, run checks on, run tests on, sample, scan, scrutinize, search into, see about, study, subject to scrutiny, superintend, supervise, survey, take stock, test, try, verify, watch

CHECK (Restrain), verb   abate, adjust, arrest, attemper, bate, block, bring to a standstill, call a halt, cause a stoppage, constrain, control, countercheck, curb, cut off, delay, detain, deter, diminish, discourage, dissuade, draw rein, encumber, estop, freeze, frustrate, halt, head off, hinder, hold in check, impair, impede, impedite, inhibit, intercept, interrupt, intervene, keep back, keep under control, lay under restraint, limit, obstruct, overpower, put a restraint upon, put a stop to, put an end to, put under restraint, restrain, restrict, retard, run counter, set back, slow, slow down, stalemate, stand in the way, stem, stop, stultify, suppress, thwart, undermine

CHIEF, noun   boss, captain, *caput,* chairman, chairperson, chief controller, chieftain, commandant, commander, directing head, director, *dux,* employer, foreman, foreperson, general, head, headman, headperson, highest ranking person, leader, manager, organizer, overlooker, overseer, person in authority, person in charge, president, primate, *princeps,* principal, principal person, senior, superior, supervising director
ASSOCIATED CONCEPTS: chief agent, chief counsel, chief deputy, chief examiner, chief executive, chief executive officer, chief fiscal officer, chief judge, chief justice, chief of fire department, chief of police, chief officer of a corporation or business, chief place of business

CHILD, noun   adolescent, boy, daughter, *filia, filius,* foster child, girl, grandchild, *infans,* infant, ingenue, issue, juvenile, lineal descendant, minor, newborn, offspring, progeny, *pueri,* scion, young, young boy, young descendant, young girl, youngling, youngster, youth
ASSOCIATED CONCEPTS: abandoned child, abortive child, adopted child, afterborn child, child born out of wedlock, child by future marriage, child custody, child labor, child support, childbirth, childcare, childhood, *en ventre sa mere,* foster child, illegitimate child, legitimate child, minor child, natural child, neglected child, orphan, posthumous child, pretermitted child, stepchild

CHILDREN, noun   babies, brood, descendants, heirs, infants, innocents, issue, lineage, minors, offspring, progeny, *pueri,* rising generation, seed, young people, younger generation, youngsters, youth
ASSOCIATED CONCEPTS: descendants, disinheriting, illegitimate children, legal heirs, legitimate children, limitation, purchase, surviving children

CHILLING EFFECT, adjective   benumbing, damaging, deterring, discouraging, effect, intimidating, paralyzing, threatening

CHINESE WALL, noun   barrier, detachment, disassociation, disconnection, disunion, dividing wall, division, grouping, impenetrable barrier, isolation, partition, protection, safeguard, secure separation, segmentation, separation, severance, shield, total separation
ASSOCIATED CONCEPTS: Chinese wall between clients, conflict of interest, conflicts of interests

CHOATE LIEN, noun   according to law, allowed, binding, brought to fruition, compulsory, consummated, enforceable, finished, lawful, legal, legalized, legitimate, legitimized, matured, obligatory, official, perfected, ratified, refined, validated

CHOICE (Alternatives offered), noun   *delectus,* discretion, discrimination, election, opportunities, option, pick, remaining courses, remaining options, selection, substitutes
ASSOCIATED CONCEPTS: alternative causes of action, counsel of one's own choosing, election of remedies, splitting a cause of action

CHOICE (Decision), noun   act of judgment, analysis, appraisal, assessment, conclusion, considered decision, *delectus,* designation, determination, disposition, election, finding, judgment, order, outcome, predilection, preferability, preference, pronouncement, resolution, resolve, selection, settlement
ASSOCIATED CONCEPTS: domicile of choice, freedom of choice

CHOOSE, verb   act on one's own authority, adopt, appoint, be disposed to, be resolute, be so minded, co-opt, commit oneself to a course, cull, decide, *deligere,* desire, determine, determine upon, discriminate, discriminate between, do of one's own accord, draw, elect, eliminate the alternatives, embrace, excerpt, exercise one's choice, exercise one's discretion, exercise one's option, exercise one's preference, exercise the will, have volition, make a decision, make one's choice, make one's selection, mark out for, opt for, pick, pick out, prefer, put to the vote, resolve, select, set apart, settle, side, support, take a decisive step, take one's choice, take up an option, use one's discretion, use one's option, will
ASSOCIATED CONCEPTS: election of remedies, freedom of choice, voluntary choice

CHRONIC, adjective   ceaseless, confirmed, constant, continual, continuing, continuous, cyclical, deep-rooted, deep-seated, drawn out, endless, enduring, entrenched, established, ever-present, everlasting, extended, forever, frequent, habitual, immedicable, incessant, inextinguished, invariable, lasting, lingering, long-continuing, long-lived, long-standing, longstanding, maintained, never-ceasing, never-stopping, not averruncated, not restorable, of long duration, often, ongoing, perdurable, perennial, permanent, perpetual, persevering, persistent, persisting, prolonged, protracted, recurrent, recurring, regular, repeating, repetitious, repetitive, resisting, returning, returning at intervals, serious, set, settled, steadfast, stubborn, sustained, tenacious, unalleviated, unceasing, uncorrectable, undestroyed, undying, unending, unerasable, unfading, unhealable, unintermitting, uninterrupted, unmitigated, unmitigating, unrelievable, unremedied, unremittent, unremitting, unshifting, unslackening, unstopped, unstopping, unsubsiding, unsuppressed, unvarying, unyielding, virulent, wearing

CHURN, verb   convulse, shake up, stir up, whip, work up

CIRCUIT, noun   ambit, area, *arrondissement,* bounds, *circuitus, circulus,* confines, district, domain, dominion, exclusive area, extent, field, hemisphere, jurisdiction, land, *locus, orbis,* orbit, pale, part, place, precinct, province, quarter, range, realm, region, section, site, situs, sphere, territory, zone
ASSOCIATED CONCEPTS: circuit court, circuit court of appeals, circuit judge, circuit officers, judicial circuits, riding circuit

CIRCUITOUS, adjective   ambagious, anfractuous, anguilliform, anguine, circumfluent, circumambulating, circumfluous, circumlocutory, complicated, contorted, convoluted, convolutional, crooked, curved, deviating, deviatory, devious, digressive, discursive, eel-shaped, eel-like, excursive, flexuous, helical, helicoid, helicoidal, indirect, intorted, labyrinthine, mazy, meandering, meandrous,

oblique, out of the way, rambling, roundabout, roving, serpentiform, serpentile, serpentine, serpentoid, sigmoid, sinuate, sinuous, skirting, snakelike, snaky, spiriferous, tortile, tortuous, turning, twining, twisting, undulate, undulated, undulating, undulative, undulatory, wandering, whorled, winding, zigzag
ASSOCIATED CONCEPTS: circuitous proceedings, circuitous route, circuity of action

CIRCULATE, verb acquire currency, announce, bandy, be public, be published, become public, bring before the public, bring out, broadcast, bruit abroad, change hands, change places, circuit, circularize, *circumagere*, come out, communicate, convey, diffuse, *dispergere*, disperse, disseminate, distribute, *divulgare*, divulgate, divulge, flow, get abroad, give currency to, give forth, give out, give to the world, go forth, have currency, issue, lay before the public, make known, make public, make the round of, noise abroad, pass, pass current, pass from one to another, pass round, print, proclaim, promulgate, propagate, publish, put about, put forward, put into circulation, radiate, reissue, repeat, reveal, rumor, rumor about, send forth, speak of, spread, spread a report, spread abroad, talk of, transmit, trumpet, ventilate, voice

CIRCULATION, noun allocation, allotment, branching out, *circumagere*, diffusion, dispensation, dispensing, *dispergere*, dispersal, dispersion, dissemination, distribution, divergence, *divulgare*, emanation, flow, flowing, flux, issuance, motion, movement, passage, passing, scattering, spread, spreading, transit, transition, transmigration, transmission

CIRCUMSCRIBE (Define), **verb** border, *circumscribere*, *definire*, delimit, delineate, demarcate, demark, determine, distinguish, establish, outline

CIRCUMSCRIBE (Surround by boundary), **verb** begird, belt, border, bound, circuit, circumvallate, cloister, close around, close in, compass, confine, contain, contour, delineate, determine boundaries, edge, embrace, encircle, enclose, encompass, engird, ensphere, envelop, fence in, fix bounds, fix limits, form a circle round, frame, gird, girdle, hedge in, hem in, include, keep in, mark off, mark out, outline, shut in, surround

CIRCUMSPECT, adjective alert, assiduous, astute, attending, attentive, careful, cautious, *cautus*, chary, circumspective, cognizant, conscientious, conscious, considerate, contemplative, deliberate, deliberative, diligent, discerning, discreet, discretionary, discriminating, discriminative, exacting, guarded, heedful, intent, introspective, judicious, meditative, meticulous, mindful, observant, observing, on guard, painstaking, particular, percipient, perspicacious, precautionary, precautious, precise, premeditative, prepared, *providus, prudens*, prudent, reflecting, reflective, regardful, scrutinizing, sensitive, thinking, thorough, thoroughgoing, thoughtful, vigilant, wary, watchful, well considered

CIRCUMSTANCES, noun accompanying events, attendant conditions, bases, changes, conditions, controlling factors, course of events, details, events, factors, facts, features, full particulars, governing factors, grounds, happenings, incidentals, instances, items, minutiae, occasions, occurrences, particulars, qualifying factors, situations, special points, state of affairs, surrounding facts, surroundings, terms imposed, vicissitudes
ASSOCIATED CONCEPTS: aggravating circumstance, change of circumstances, changed circumstance, circumstances beyond control, exceptional circumstances, extraordinary circumstances, like circumstances, mitigating circumstances, special circumstances, unusual circumstances

CIRCUMSTANTIAL, adjective accessory, *accuratus*, additional, adscititious, apparent, by inference, collateral, conditional, conjectural, construable, contingent, deduced, extraneous, founded on circumstances, implicational, implicative, implicatory, incidental, inconclusive, indecisive, indicative, indicatory, indirect, inessential, inferential, insinuatory, insubstantial, likely, nonessential, ostensible, presumable, presumptive, probable, second rank, secondary, subsidiary, suggestive, unnecessary, verisimilar
ASSOCIATED CONCEPTS: circumstantial errors, circumstantial evidence, circumstantial inference, corroborating evidence, inference

CIRCUMVENT, verb avoid doing, be cunning, be sly, beguile, bypass, *circonvenir, circumscribere, circumvenire*, cloak, conceal, confuse, contravene, contrive, counteract, counterwork, cover, deceive, defeat, defraud, delude, devise, disrupt, elude, escape, evade, foil, hoax, mislead, outmaneuver, outreach, outwit, pettifog, practice chicanery, prevaricate, proceed by stratagem, scheme, swindle, thwart, *tourner la loi*, traverse, trick
ASSOCIATED CONCEPTS: circumvent the law

CITATION (Attribution), **noun** ascription, assignment, credit, derivation, designation, mention, organization, parentage, quotation, reference, source
ASSOCIATED CONCEPTS: citation of authorities, citation of tables

CITATION (Charge), **noun** command to appear, decree, dictate, interpellation, legal process, mandate, mittimus, monition, notice, notice to appear, notification, official notice, ordination, precept, prescript, prescription, rescript, subpoena, ukase, warrant, writ, writ of summons
ASSOCIATED CONCEPTS: citation for a crime, citation for a violation, citation for contempt

CITE (Accuse), **verb** allege, blame, bring a charge, bring an action, call to account, censure, challenge, charge, complain, denounce, discredit, impeach, implicate, impute, incriminate, inform against, lodge a complaint, make a complaint

CITE (State), **verb** advance, attest, authenticate, bring forward, certify, circumstantiate, document, enunciate, establish, evidence, evince, exemplify, exhibit, express, give as example, illustrate, indicate, introduce as an example, maintain, make evident, make reference to, manifest, mention, name, point to, predicate, present as proof, prove, quote, recite, refer to, refer to legal authorities, set forth, show, show evidence, show proof, specify, substantiate, use in support of propositions of law
ASSOCIATED CONCEPTS: cite a case as precedence

CITIZEN, noun *civis,* denizen, dweller, habitant, *indigen,* indigene, indweller, inhabitant, inhabiter, inmate, native, occupant, occupier, residencer, resident, resider
ASSOCIATED CONCEPTS: adopted citizens, citizen of a state, citizen of the United States of America, citizens of different states, diversity of citizenship, domicile of a citizen, foreign citizen, native-born citizen, natural-born citizen, naturalized citizen, nonresident citizen, privilege and immunities of citizens, renunciation of citizenship
FOREIGN PHRASES: **Semel civis semper civis.** Once a citizen always a citizen.

CITY, *noun*   megalopolis, metropolis, metropolitan area, municipality, polis, urban district, urban place, urbanization, *urbs*
ASSOCIATED CONCEPTS: city attorney, city council, city court, city districts, city employee, city hall, city limits, city marshal, city officer, city purpose, municipal corporations

CIVIC, *adjective*   *civicus,* civil, *civilis,* common, communal, community, government, governmental, juridical, lawful, legal, metropolitan, municipal, neighborhood, official, political, public, regulatory, town, urban
ASSOCIATED CONCEPTS: civic affairs, civic enterprise, civic organizations

CIVIL *(Polite),* *adjective*   accommodating, affable, amiable, chivalric, chivalrous, civilized, cordial, courteous, courtly, cultivated, deferential, dignified, diplomatic, easy-mannered, fine-mannered, genial, genteel, gentlemanlike, gentlemanly, gracious, mannerly, mild, obliging, polished, refined, respectful, urbane, well-behaved, well-bred, well-brought up, well-mannered, well-spoken

CIVIL *(Public),* *adjective*   civic, civilian, communal, governmental, laic, laical, metropolitan, mundane, municipal, noncriminal, nonecclesiastical, nonmilitary, oppidan, political, secular, social, societal, temporal, unspiritual, urban, worldly
ASSOCIATED CONCEPTS: civil action, civil aeronautics board, civil arrest, civil authorities, civil case, civil cause, civil ceremony, civil contempt, civil contract, civil courts, civil damages, civil death, civil defense, civil disabilities, civil jurisdiction, civil law, civil liability, civil liberties, civil matters, civil officer, civil proceedings, civil rights, civil service, civil service commission, civil suit, civil unrest, civil war
FOREIGN PHRASES: *Cum actio fuerit mere criminalis, institui poterit ab initio criminaliter vel civiliter.* When an action is merely criminal, it can be instituted from the beginning either criminally or civilly.

CIVIL LIBERTIES, *noun*   First Amendment guarantees, First Amendment Rights, freedom of expression, freedom of press, freedom of religion, freedom of speech, freedom of thought, fundamental individual rights, guarantees from the Bill of Rights, human rights, individual rights, right to life, right to peacefully assemble, right to petition government for redress, right to privacy, right to property, right to worship
ASSOCIATED CONCEPTS: civil rights, protection against unwarranted governmental interference

CIVILIZATION, *noun*   accomplishments, acquired knowledge, advancement, advancement of knowledge, civilized life, civilized society, cultivation, culture, enlightenment, evolution, *humanitas,* illumination, level of education, national culture, progress, progression, refinement, social adjustment, social elevation, society, sophistication, state of refinement

CLAIM *(Assertion),* *noun*   affirmation, allegation, asseveration, averment, avouchment, avowal, declaration, position, predication, presentation, proposition, statement
ASSOCIATED CONCEPTS: claimed use, disputed claims, doubtful claims, false claim, fictitious claims, fraudulent claims
FOREIGN PHRASES: *Debitorum pactionibus creditorum petitio nec tolli nec minui potest.* The rights of creditors to sue cannot be prejudiced or diminished by agreements between their debtors.

CLAIM *(Legal demand),* *noun*   accusation, adjuration, bill of complaint, cause of action, challenge, command, complaint, counterclaim, declaration, exaction, obsecration, plea, postulate, *postulatio,* presentment, requirement, suit, ultimatum
ASSOCIATED CONCEPTS: allowed claim, claim against bankrupt estate, claim against estate, claim and demand, claim arising on contract, claim for alternative relief, claim for support, claim of a creditor, claim of interest, claim or defense notice of claim, claimed on appeal, claimed use, claims ex delicto, colorable claim, common law claim, compensation claim, conflicting claims, contingent claims, counter claim, court of claims, cross claim, disputed claims, doubtful claims, equitable claims, fictitious claims, fixed claims, fraudulent claims, frivolous claims, illegal claims, indeterminate claims, individual claim, insurance claim, just claim, lawful claim, money claim, moral claims, particular nature of claims, prior claim, proof of claim, provable claim, secured claim, settlement of claim, stale claim, subordination of claim, subsequent claims, undisputed claim, unliquidated claims, unmatured claims
FOREIGN PHRASES: *Rogationes, quaestiones, et positiones debent esse simplices.* Demands, questions, and claims ought to be simple.

CLAIM *(Right),* *noun*   beneficial interest, contingent interest, due, equitable interest, expectancy, heritage, interest, legacy, ownership, privilege, share, stake, title, vested interest
ASSOCIATED CONCEPTS: claim of ownership, claim of right, claim of title

CLAIM *(Demand),* *verb*   ask for, assert as one's own, assert as one's right, declare one's right, dun, exact as due, have a right, insist upon, make demands on, petition, press, pretend, reclaim, request, require, requisition, seek as due, sue, think one deserves, vindicate a right, vindicate a title
ASSOCIATED CONCEPTS: claim against an estate, claim and demand, claim arising from a contract, claim for relief, claim of right, claim of title, compensation claim, contingent claim, counterclaim, court of claims, fraud claim, insurance claim, money claim, ownership claim, valid claim

CLAIM *(Maintain),* *verb*   advocate, affirm, allege, assert, asseverate, attest, aver, avouch, avow, certify, charge, contend, declare, hold, insist, make a statement, make an assertion, predicate, profess, propound, put forward, say, stand firm, state, utter with conviction, vow, warrant
ASSOCIATED CONCEPTS: claimed use

CLAIMANT, *noun*   accusant, accuser, appellant, applicant, asserter, claimer, complainant, libelant, litigant, one who asserts a demand, one who claims a right, party to a suit, person who makes a claim, person with a grievance, petitioner, plaintiff, pleader, postulant, solicitant, solicitor, suitor
ASSOCIATED CONCEPTS: lien claimant, subsequent claimant, suit by claimant
FOREIGN PHRASES: *Semper necessitas probandi incumbit ei qui agit.* The burden of proof always lies upon the claimant.

CLANDESTINE, *adjective*   arcane, behind the scenes, camouflaged, *clandestinus,* cloaked, collusive, concealed, confidential, conspiring, covert, *cunning,* disguised, ensconced, evasive, furtive, *furtivus,* hidden, in the background, irrevealable, masked, obscure, screened, secluded, secret, secretive, shrouded, sneaking, stealthy, stifled, subterranean, suppressed, surreptitious, undercover, underground, underhand, underhanded, undisclosed, unknown, unrevealed, unseen, veiled, with secret design
ASSOCIATED CONCEPTS: clandestine adultery, clandestine importation, clandestine marriage, clandestine meeting

CLARIFICATION, noun amplification, apostil, clarification, commentary, deciphering, definition, delineation, demonstration, description, elimination of ambiguousness, elimination of complexity, elimination of complication, elucidation, enlightenment, epexegesis, erasure of ambiguity, exemplification, explanation, explication, exposition, illumination, illustration, increase of clarity, increase of clearness, increase of intelligibility, interpretation, making apparent, making distinct, making evident, making lucid, making perspicuous, making precise, making specific, making trenchant, presentation, refinement, rendering explicit, rendering incisive, rendering unequivocal, rendering unmistakable, scholium, simplification, specification

CLARIFY, verb articulate, bare, bring to light, clear up, comment upon, construe, decipher, define, delineate, *deliquare,* demonstrate, disentangle, elucidate, enlighten, exemplify, explain, explicate, expose, exposit, expound, free from ambiguity, free from confusion, illuminate, illustrate, interpret, lay open, make clear, make comprehensible, make explicit, make intelligible, make lucid, make understood, refine, render intelligible, shed light on, show, simplify, spell out, subtilize, unfold, unmask, unravel, unscramble, unveil
ASSOCIATED CONCEPTS: clarify and amplify a complaint, clarify the pleadings

CLASS, noun assortment, bracket, branch, brand, breed, caste, category, classification, *classis,* denomination, designation, division, echelon, genera, genre, *genus,* gradation, grade, group, grouping, hierarchy, ilk, kind, layer of society, order, *ordo,* place, position, rank, rating, sect, set, social rank, social status, sort, standing, station, status, stratum, subdivision, subgroup, suborder, subspecies, type, variety
ASSOCIATED CONCEPTS: class action, class gifts, class interest, class legislation, class suit, definite class, gift to a class
FOREIGN PHRASES: *Clausula generalis de residuo non ea complectitur quae non ejusdem sint generis cum iis quae speciatim dicta fuerant.* A general clause of remainder does not include those things which are not of the same kind as those which have been specially mentioned.

CLASS ACTION LAW SUIT, noun derivative action, directors' and officers' liability, group lawsuit, group litigation, law suit by large numbers of litigants with a common grievance, suit by multiple parties with common interest
ASSOCIATED CONCEPTS: representative action

CLASSIFICATION, noun allocation, allotment, analysis, apportionment, arrangement, assignment, assortment, cataloguing, categorization, category, class, codification, denomination, designation, disposition, distribution, division, gradation, group, grouping, identification, methodization, nomenclature, order, ordering, orderly arrangement, ordination, organization, placement, ranking, reducing to order, regulation by a system, specification, subgroup, syntaxis, systematization, taxis, type
ASSOCIATED CONCEPTS: arbitrary classification, illegal classification, unreasonable classification

CLASSIFY, verb allocate, allot, analyze, apportion, arrange, assort, brand, break down, catalogue, categorize, class, classify as, codify, collocate, coordinate, correlate, dispose, distinguish, distribute, divide, file, form into classes, grade, group, identify, *in genera describere,* index, introduce a system, label, list, marshal, methodize, name, organize, partition, pigeonhole, place in a category, place in order, put in array, put in order, range, rank, rate, reduce to order, segregate, separate, seriate, set in order, size, sort, specify, subsume, systematize, tag, type

ASSOCIATED CONCEPTS: arbitrary classification, illegal classification, unreasonable classification

CLAUSE, noun article, *caput,* condition, *conditiosine qua non,* contract, covenant, exception, exemption, limitation, *membrum,* paragraph, *pars,* passage, phrase, proposition, provision, proviso, qualification, section, sentence, specification, stipulation, term
ASSOCIATED CONCEPTS: commerce clause, commercial clause, enacting clause, escalation clause, forfeiture clause, grandfather clause, incontestable clause, loss payable clause, most favored nation clause, penalty clause, residuary clause, saving clause, specific clause, spendthrift clause, standard mortagagee clause, sunsetting clause
FOREIGN PHRASES: *Clausula generalis de residuo non ea complectitur quae non ejusdem sint generis cum iis quae speciatim dicta fuerant.* A general clause concerning the remainder does not include those matters which are not of the same kind with those which have been specially expressed. *Clausula generalis non refertur ad expressa.* A general clause does not refer to things expressly mentioned. *Clausula quae abrogationem excludit ab initio non valet.* A clause which forbids its abrogation is invalid from the beginning. *Clausula vel dispositio inutilis per praesumptionem remotam, vel causam ex post facto non fulcitur.* A useless clause or provision is not supported by a remote presumption, or by a cause that arises afterwards. *Clausulae inconsuetae semper inducunt suspicionem.* Unusual clauses always arouse suspicion.

CLEAN, adjective above suspicion, acquitted, angelic, blameless, bloodless, cleanhanded, cleanminded, clear, decent, entirely defensible, fair, faultless, free from guilt, free from impurities, free from sin, good, guileless, guiltless, highminded, high-principled, honest, honorable, immaculate, impeccable, in the clear, incorrupt, incorruptible, innocent, inviolable, inviolate, irreprehensible, irreproachable, irreprovable, lawabiding, lawful, moral, *mundus,* not guilty, not responsible, pure, pure-hearted, pure in heart, *purus,* right-minded, righteous, scrupulous, snowy, spotless, stainless, straight, strictly honest, taintless, unblamable, unblemished, unbribed, uncorrupted, unculpable, unerring, unexceptionable, unguilty, unimpeachable, uninvolved, unmuddied, unobjectionable, unoffending, unsoiled, unspotted, unstained, unsullied, untarnished, unviolated, upright, veracious, virtuous, white, wholesome, without a stain, without reproach
ASSOCIATED CONCEPTS: clean bill of lading, clean credit, clean docket receipt, clean hands doctrine, clean money

CLEAR (Apparent), **adjective** blunt, clarified, clear-cut, demonstrative, direct, distinct, downright, emphatic, *évident,* evident, exact, explicit, express, expressive, frank, glaring, graphic, identifiable, in bold relief, in evidence, in strong relief, intelligible, limpid, manifest, observable, outspoken, overt, patent, pellucid, perceivable, perceptible, perspicuous, plain, prominent, pronounced, pure, salient, self-evident, showing, shown, straightforward, striking, transparent, unadorned, unambiguous, unblurred, unclouded, uncovered, understood, undisguised, unequivocal, unevasive, unmistakable, visible, vivid, well-defined, well-marked, well-seen
ASSOCIATED CONCEPTS: clear and convincing danger, clear and present danger, clear-cut question of law, clear meaning, clear preponderance, clear proof, clearly ascertainable, last clear chance

CLEAR (Certain), **adjective** absolute, actual, ascertained, authoritative, beyond a shadow of a doubt, beyond all dispute, categorical, cogent, conclusive, definite, definitive, doubtless, free from doubt, incontestable, incontrovertible, indefeasible, indisputable, indubitable, irrefragable, irrefutable, positive, questionless, settled without appeal, sure, unassailable, unchallengeable, unconfutable, uncontested, uncontroversial, undeniable, undisputed, undoubted, unequivocal, unerring, unhesitating, unimpeachable, unmistakable, unqualified, unquestionable, unquestioned, unrefutable

ASSOCIATED CONCEPTS: clear legal right, clear right, clearly erroneous

CLEAR (*Free from criminal charges*), **adjective** absolved, acquitted, at liberty, cleared, condoned, delivered, disburdened, discharged, disculpated, dismissed, exculpated, excused, exempted, exonerated, forgiven, freed, guiltless, immune, justified, manumitted, nonliable, not guilty, pardoned, purged, released, remitted, reprieved, spared, unburdened, uncensurable, unchastised, uncondemned, unpunished, vindicated

CLEAR (*Unencumbered*), **adjective** disburdened, disencumbered, exempt, free, free from burden, free from encumbrance, free from hindrance, free from impediment, free from limitation, free from obstruction, not answerable, not responsible, unaccountable, unbound, unbridled, unburdened, unconstrained, uncurbed, unfettered, unhampered, unhindered, unobstructed, unrestrained, untrammeled

ASSOCIATED CONCEPTS: clear title

CLEAR, verb absolve, acquit, amnesty, deliver, disburden, discharge, disembroil, disencumber, disentangle, dismiss, exculpate, excuse, exempt, exonerate, *explicare,* extricate, find not guilty, forgive, free, give a reprieve, give absolution, grant a reprieve, grant amnesty, grant remission, let go, let off, liberate, pardon, pronounce not guilty, prove innocent, purge, quash the conviction, release, render free, reprieve, rescue, set at large, set at liberty, set free, shrive, vindicate

ASSOCIATED CONCEPTS: clear and convincing evidence, clear and convincing standard of proof, clear and present danger, clear title, last clear chance doctrine

CLEAR UP, verb answer, ascertain, brighten, clarify, complete, construe, consummate, decipher, decode, die away, disentangle, dispatch, dispose of, elucidate, explain, exposit, expound, fathom, figure out, interpret, lift, light, make sense, resolve, settle, simplify, solve, strike, unlock, unravel, unriddle, unscramble, untangle, wind up, work out

ASSOCIATED CONCEPTS: clear up inconsistencies in testimony, clear up misconceptions

CLEARED, adjective absolved, acquitted, condoned, disburdened, discharged, dismissed, exculpated, excused, exempted, exonerated, forgiven, freed, guiltless, immune, justified, not guilty, overturned, pardoned, purged, released, reprieved, reversed and overturned, spared, unburdened, vindicated

ASSOCIATED CONCEPTS: Appeals Court, cleared in a probe, DNA, habeas corpus, reversal

CLEARLY DEFINED, adjective absolute, blunt, candid, categorical, certain, clear, clearly formulated, comprehensible, decisive, definite, definitive, determinate, direct, distinct, distinctly stated, exact, explanatory, explicit, frank, lucid, obvious, perceptible, plain, pointed, positive, precise, specific, straightforward, unambiguous, unconditional, unequivocal, unmistakable, vivid, well developed

CLEMENCY, noun absolution, amnesty, benefaction, beneficence, benevolence, benignity, charity, *clementia,* clementness, commutation, compassion, consideration, decency, disposition to mercy, disposition to pardon, excuse, exemption, extenuation, forbearance, forgiveness, forgivingness, generosity, generousness, gentleness, good will, grace, humaneness, humanity, indemnity, indulgence, kindness, lenience, leniency, lenity, liberality, magnanimity, magnanimousness, *mansuetuda,* mercifulness, mercy, obligingness, pardon, pardoning, purgation, release, reprieve, respite, temperance, tolerance, toleration, willingness to forgive

ASSOCIATED CONCEPTS: clemency by the Governor, clemency by the President of the United States, Executive clemency

CLERICAL, adjective accessory, *ad administrationem pertimens,* administrating, administrative, assistant, assisting, attendant, attending, auxiliary, *ex officio,* helping, instrumental, intermediary

ASSOCIATED CONCEPTS: clerical acts, clerical duties, clerical errors, clerical mistakes, clerical omissions

CLERK, noun archivist, chronicler, copyist, court employee, court official, court scribe, judicial administrator, judicial assistant, judicial recorder, judicial secretary, office holder, office worker, official, prothonotary, recorder, record keeper, registrar, *scriba,* scribe, scrivener, secretary

ASSOCIATED CONCEPTS: clerk of the county, clerk of the court, county clerk, papers filed with the clerk, town clerk

FOREIGN PHRASES: Errores scribentis nocere non debent. An error made by a clerk ought not to prejudice.

CLERK, verb aid a judge, assist a judge, help a judge, work for a judge

CLIENT, noun business contact, buyer of labor, *cliens, consultor,* consumer, customer, employer of legal advice, hirer, offerer, patron, patron of professional servies, patronizer, person employing advice, person represented, person represented by counsel, purchaser, retainer of counsel

ASSOCIATED CONCEPTS: attorney-client privilege, attorney-client relationship

CLIMATE, noun atmosphere, aura, *caelum,* circumambiency, clime, condition, environment, environmental conditions, feeling, forces of nature, influences, mood, prevailing attitudes, prevailing conditions, prevailing standards, surrounding influence, surroundings

CLINICAL, adjective analytical, detached, dispassionate, impersonal, imperturbable, unemotional, unimpressionable

CLOAK, verb beguile, belie, blind, bluff, bury, camouflage, cloud, conceal, conceal the truth, construe falsely, couch, cover, cover up, curtain, deceive, decoy, disguise, dissemble, *dissimulare,* dissimulate, distort, divert, dress up, dupe, eclipse, embellish, embroider, ensconce, enshroud, envelop, exaggerate, fake, falsify, feign, forswear, garble, give a false coloring, gloss over, go undercover, hide, hide away, keep a secret, keep hidden, keep in ignorance, keep secret, keep undercover, mask, miscolor, misinform, mislead, misrepresent, muffle, obscure, obstruct the view of, occult, pretend, put out of sight, render invisible, screen, seclude, secrete, shade, shadow, sham, shelter, shroud, sneak, stifle, suppress, swear falsely, tegere, veil

ASSOCIATED CONCEPTS: cloaked with authority

CLOG, verb arrest, astrict, bar, barricade, be obstructive, block, block up, bridle, burden, checkmate, choke, close,

close off, constrict, cumber, dam, deadlock, detain, exclude, forbid, foreclose, forestall, frustrate, hamper, handicap, hinder, hold back, hold in check, hold up, impede, *impedire,* impedite, intercept, interfere, keep out, obstruct, occlude, place limitations, plug, plug up, preclude, prevent, prevent passage, prohibit, put a stop to, repress, restrain, restrict, retard, shut off, stall, stand in the way of, stay, stifle, stop, stop short, stop up, stultify, stymie, suppress

CLONE, noun a carbon copy created by genetic engineering, a copy created by genetic engineering, a double created by genetic engineering, a facsimile created through genetic engineering, an exact copy created through genetic engineering, duplication created by genetic engineering, production of a copy, production of a copy through genetic engineering, production of multiple identical copies, propagation asexually, propagation from a clone cell, replication created by genetic engineering, replication through genetic engineering, reproduction asexually

ASSOCIATED CONCEPTS: bioethics, computer clone, embryo splitting, human clone

CLONING, noun copy, counterpart, double, duplication, embodiment, exact copy, genetically identical copy, genetically identical individual, genetically identical reproduction, producing, replica, reproduction

Generally: duplicating, manifestation, match

CLOSE *(Intimate),* **adjective** allied, bosom, brotherly, confidential, dear, devoted, faithful, familiar, fast, fraternal, friendly, inseparable, strongly attached

ASSOCIATED CONCEPTS: close corporation, closely held

CLOSE *(Near),* **adjective** adjacent, adjoining, approaching, approximate, at hand, bordering, close at hand, close by, coming, contiguous, forthcoming, handy, imminent, impending, in close proximity, in the area, in the neighborhood, in the vicinity, near at hand, nearby, neighboring, nigh, *propinquus,* proximal, proximate, tangent, touching, vicinal

ASSOCIATED CONCEPTS: close confinement, close proximity

CLOSE *(Rigorous),* **adjective** assiduous, attentive, careful, conscientious, diligent, earnest, exact, hard, harsh, intense, keen, meticulous, *parcus,* precise, punctilious, relentless, rigid, scrupulous, severe, sharp, stiff, strict, stringent, *tenax,* uncompromising, unremitting, unsparing

CLOSE *(Conclusion),* **noun** adjournment, cessation, closing, closure, completion, *conclusio,* consummation, discontinuance, discontinuation, end, ending, expiration, finale, *finis,* finish, last part, last stage, omega, peroration, shutdown, stoppage, termination, *terminus,* windup

ASSOCIATED CONCEPTS: the close of a trial, the closing on a real estate transaction

CLOSE *(Enclosed area),* **noun** compound, confine, court, courtyard, enclosure, grounds, pen, precinct, square, yard

ASSOCIATED CONCEPTS: breaking the close

CLOSE *(Agree),* **verb** accept an offer, arrive at an agreement, bargain, come to an arrangement, come to an understanding, come to terms, consent, endorse, enter into a contractual obligation, establish by agreement, execute, finalize, finalize an agreement, fix by agreement, give assurance, go to contract, guarantee, make a bargain, make an agreement, negotiate, *pacisci,* seek accord, settle, strike a bargain, subscribe, undertake, underwrite

ASSOCIATED CONCEPTS: close a business transaction, close a real estate transaction

CLOSE *(Terminate),* **verb** apply the closure, break off, bring to an end, call a halt, cause a stoppage, cease, *claudere,* come to a stop, come to an end, complete, conclude, consummate, discontinue, dispatch, dispose of, eliminate, end, expire, finish, finish up, fulfill, halt, have run its course, interrupt, make an end of, make inactive, *operire,* prosecute to a conclusion, put a stop to, run out, shut down, stop, surcease, suspend, suspend operation, wind up

ASSOCIATED CONCEPTS: close a bank account, close a case, close a grand jury investigation, close an investigation

CLOSING ARGUMENTS, noun closing, closing statements at trial, summation at trial, summing up a case

Generally: recapitulation, reiteration, renumeration, restatement, review

CLOTHE, verb accouter, *amicire,* appoint, arm, array, attire oneself, bedeck, bedrape, cloak, conceal, costume, cover, cover up, disguise, drape, dress, embroider, empower, enable, encase, endow, endue, enfold, enrobe, envelop, enwrap, equip, fit out, frock, furnish, garb, gear, *induere sibi vestem,* invest, invest with power, outfit, provide, put in uniform, robe, suit, supply, uniform, *vestire,* wrap

ASSOCIATED CONCEPTS: clothe with authority to act, clothe with indicia of ownership

CLOTURE, noun abandonment, abeyance, adjournal, adjournment, arrest, break, cease, cessation, check, closing, closure, desistance, discontinuance, discontinuation, halt, interruption, lapse, letup, lull, noncontinuance, prorogation, recess, standstill, stay, stop, stoppage, suspension, withdrawal

CLOUD *(Incumbrance),* **noun** burden, charge, claim, claim on property, commitment, debt, hold on property, hypothecation, indebtedness, indebtment, liability, mortgage, obligation, obstruction, outstanding debt, *pignus judiciale, pignus legale,* pledge, prescription, real security, restraint, security, security on property, state of indebtedness, *vadium mortuum*

ASSOCIATED CONCEPTS: a cloud on personalty, a cloud on real property

CLOUD *(Suspicion),* **noun** apprehension, apprehensiveness, consternation, contestability, controvertibility, deniability, disbelief, disputability, distrust, distrustfulness, doubt, fear, hesitation, incredulity, incredulousness, intimation, lack of certainty, lack of confidence, lack of faith, misdoubt, misgiving, mistrust, mistrustfulness, *onus probandi,* perplexity, puzzlement, questionability, refusal to believe, refutability, reluctance to believe, skepticism, trepidation, unbelief, uncredulousness, want of certainty, want of confidence, want of faith

CLOUT, noun authoritative power, authority, consequence, controlling power, directing power, dominancy, dominion, eminence, force, hegemony, importance, influence, influentiality, leverage, mastership, notability, potency, power, power of impelling, predominancy, prestige, prominence, puissance, significance, weight

CLUE, noun data, evidence, finding, guide, hint, idea, index, indication, indicator, information, inkling, insinuation, intimation, key, lead, mark, reason to believe, scent, sign, signal, token

COACTION, noun alliance, association, coalition, cohesion, collaboration, colleagueship, collective action, collusion, combined effort, common effort, complicity, concert of action, concourse, concurrence, confederacy, cooperancy, cooperation, cooperativeness, coworking, federation, fellowship, fraternity, fusion, joint effort, joint participation, league, mutual assistance, mutuality, partnership, solidarity, teamwork, union, union of action, united action, working together

COACTOR, noun abettor, accessory, accessory after the fact, accessory before the fact, accomplice, accomplice in crime, acolyte, adjunct, adjutant, adjuvant, advocate, aid, aide-de-camp, aider, aider and abettor, ally, assistant, associate, attendant, auxiliary, coadjutant, coadjutor, cohelper, collaborationist, collaborator, colleague, colluder, confederate, consociate, consort, conspirator, conspirer, contriver, cooperator, copartner, coworker, deviser, fellow conspirator, helper, henchman, joint-operator, partner, partner in crime, planner, plotter, promoter, promotor, schemer, strategist, supporter

COADJUTANT, noun abettor, accessory, accomplice, adjutant, adjuvant, aid, aide, aider, ally, apprentice, assistant, associate, attendant, auxiliary, coadjutor, collaborator, colleague, confederate, consociate, cooperator, coworker, deputy, fellow worker, follower, help, helper, henchman, lieutenant, mate, partner, subordinate, supporter, teammate, underling

COADUNATE, adjective adherent, adhering, adhesive, agglomerate, aggregate, aggregated, allied, amalgamative, assembled, associated, centralized, clinging, coagulated, coagulative, coalesced, coalescent, cohering, cohesive, combined, compact, concerted, confluent, conglomerate, conglomeratic, congregated, conjoined, conjoint, conjugate, conjunct, connected, consolidated, cooperative, fused, incorporated, integrated, interlinked, interlocked, interrelated, joined, leagued, linked, related, unified, united

COALESCENCE, noun abutting, accordance, adherence, adhesion, admixture, affiliation, agglomeration, agglutination, alliance, amalgamation, annexation, annexing, assemblage, association, attachment, binding, bond, centralization, closeness, coadunation, coagulation, coalition, coherence, cohesion, cohesiveness, combination, commixture, compound, concrescence, concurrence, confederacy, confederation, confluence, conglomeration, conglutination, conjugation, conjunction, connection, consociation, consolidation, contact, convergence, converging, coupling, federation, fusing, fusion, immixture, incorporation, interconnection, interfusion, joining, junction, league, linkage, merger, merging, mixture, solidification, symbiosis, synthesis, unification, union

COALITION, noun affiliation, alliance, amalgamation, association, binding, bond, cartel, combination, combine, coming together, community, concurrence, confluence, conglomerate, congress, conjoining, *conjunctio,* conjunction, conjuncture, connection, consociation, consolidation, consortium, *conspiratio,* convergence, cooperation, federation, fellowship, fusing, fusion, fusion of interests, group, integration, interlocking, joint concern, joint endeavor, junction, league, meeting, merger, merging, mixture, mutual concern, partnership, society, sodality, syndicate, unification, union, union of factions, unity

COAX, verb allure, appeal, attract, bait, blandish, bribe, cajole, captivate, convince, encourage, engage, enlist, ensnare, entice, evoke, exert pressure, exhort, *hominem permulcere, homini blandiri,* impel, incite, induce, influence,

insist, inspire, intrigue, inveigle, keep in countenance, lead, lure, manipulate, motivate, offer an inducement, persuade, press, prevail, prevail upon, procure, prod, prompt, provoke, rally, recommend, rouse, spellbind, stimulate, suborn, suggest, sway, tempt, urge

COCONSPIRATOR, noun abettor, accessory, accessory after the fact, accessory before the fact, accomplice, adjunct in crime, adjutant in crime, adjuvant in crime, aide in crime, aide in wrongdoing, aider in wrongdoing, ally in crime, ally in wrongdoing, assistant, associate in crime, associate in guilt, auxiliary in crime, coactor in crime, coadjutor, coaider in crime, collaborator, colleague in crime, colluder, companion in crime, comrade in crime, comrade in wrongdoing, confederate, consociate in crime, cooperator in crime, copartner in crime, coworker in crime, fellow conspirator, fellow machinator, fellow plotter, fellow schemer, fellow strategist, fellow traiter, partner, partner in crime, partner in wrongdoing, supporter

CODE, noun arrangement of statutes, body of laws, bylaw, canon, capitulary, charter, civil code, codification, codified law, collection, collection of laws, collection of statutes, compilation, compilation of law, compilation of laws, constitution, *corpus juris,* digest, enactment, enactment of rules, established law, established order, firm principle, formulary, formulation, guide, guideline, laws, legal code, legislation, *lex,* maxim, model, norm, ordinance, precedent, precept, precepts, prescript, prescription, principles, regulation by law, regulation by statute, regulations, rubric, rules, ruling, settled law, standard, statute, statute book, statute law, subsidiary law, system of law, system of rules, written constitution, written law
ASSOCIATED CONCEPTS: building code, civil code, code of criminal procedure, code of ethics, code of fair competition, Code of Hammurabi, code of judicial conduct, code of law, code of procedure, code of professional responsibility, code pleading, criminal code, ethics code, Napoleonic code, penal code, probate code
FOREIGN PHRASES: *Ad ea quae frequentius accidunt jura adaptantur.* Laws are adapted to those cases which most commonly occur.

CODICIL, noun accessory, accompaniment, addendum, additament, addition, addition to a will, additive, additum, adjunct, affixation, affixture, annex, annexation, appanage, appendage, appendix, attachment, augmentation, complement, epilogue, insertion, postscript, sequel, sequela, subscript, suffix, supplement, supplement to a will, testament, will addendum, will supplement
ASSOCIATED CONCEPTS: will

CODIFICATION, noun act, arrangement of laws, arrangement of rules, arrangement of statutes, authoritative law, bill, bylaws, canon, capitulary, categorization of laws, collection of statutes, commandment, compendium, compilation, decree, doctrine, enactment, formalization of laws, formulation of laws, lawmaking, legislation, ordinance, precept, prescription, regulation, rule, rules and regulations, rulings, sanctions, scheduling, scheme, set of rules, standardization of laws, statute, statute book, statute law, system, system of laws, system of regulations, systematic arrangement of laws, systematization of laws, tabulation, written law
ASSOCIATED CONCEPTS: codification act, codification of statutes

CODIFY, verb accumulate, arrange, assemble, assort, break down, bring into order, catalog, categorize, classify, collect, compile, coordinate, *digerere,* divide, formalize, formulate, group, index, introduce order, list, methodize,

organize, rank, reduce to a code, reduce to a digest, reduce to order, regularize, sort, subdivide, systematize, systemize, tabulate
ASSOCIATED CONCEPTS: codifying act

COEQUAL, *adjective* *aequalis,* agreeing, analogous, as great as another, coextensive, coincident, commensurate, comparable, congruent, coordinate, correlative, correspondent, corresponding, equal, equibalanced, equipollent, equiponderant, equivalent, even, homologous, identical in value, interchangeable, level, like in degree, like in quantity, matching, neither more nor less, of equal dignity, of equal power, of like rank, of the same rank, on a footing with, on a level with, on a par, on a par with, on the same footing, parallel, reciprocal, symmetrical, synonymous, tantamount, uniform, up to the mark

COERCE, *verb* apply pressure, bear down, bludgeon, bring pressure to bear, coercere, command, compel, conscript, constrain, demand, dictate, dominate, draft, dragoon, drive, elicit by threat, enjoin, enthrall, exact, exhort, extort, foist, force, impel, impose, impose restrictions, impress, induce, insist, interdict, intimidate, issue threats, necessitate, oblige, oppress, order, press, pressure, prod, push, put pressure on, put under restraint, require, rule, subjugate, suppress, terrorize, threaten, use force upon, wrest from
ASSOCIATED CONCEPTS: duress, harassment
FOREIGN PHRASES: *Ejus nulla culpa est cui parere necesse sit.* No guilt attaches to him who is compelled to obey.

COERCION, *noun* blackmail, bondage, brute force, *coercitio,* command, compulsion, constraint, constraint by force, control, dictation, duress, exaction, exigency, extortion, force, forcing, illegal compulsion, impelling, inducement, insistence, intimidation, moral compulsion, necessity, negative compulsion, oppression, oppressive exaction, pressure, prevailing, prohibition, repression, restraint, strong arm tactics, threat, undue influence, unlawful compulsion
ASSOCIATED CONCEPTS: coercive conduct, duress, extortion, coercion of employees
FOREIGN PHRASES: *Extortio est crimen quando quis colore, officii extorquet quod non est debitum, vel supra debitum, vel ante tempus quod est debitum.* Extortion is a crime when, by color of office, any person extorts that which is not due, or more than is due, or before the time when it is due. *Nihil consensui tam contrarium est quam vis atque metus.* Nothing is so opposed to consent as force and fear. *Vis legibus est inimica.* Force is inimical to the laws.

COEXTENSIVE, *adjective* agreeing, aligned, analogous, balanced, coequal, coextending, collateral, comparable, concentric, concurrent, congruent, coordinate, correlative, correspondent, corresponding, equable, equal, equal in scope, equal in space, equal in time, equalized, equidistant, equilateral, equipollent, equiponderant, equipondious, equivalent, even, even-sided, homologous, in equilibrium, lined up, matched, parallel, proportioned, symmetrical, synonymous
ASSOCIATED CONCEPTS: coextensive with rights under the United States Constitution

COFFER, *noun* *arca,* bank, *cista,* container, depository, holder, locker, money chest, receptacle, safe, safe deposit box, storage, strongbox, till, treasury, vault

COGENT, *adjective* appealing conclusively, appealing forcibly, authoritative, commanding, compelling, conclusive, convincing, definite, definitive, demonstrable, demonstrating, determinative, effective, effectual, efficacious, evidential, forceful, forcible, incontestable, incontrovertible, indubitable, inducive, influential, irrefragable, irrefutable, irresistible, logical, meritorious, of consequence, past dispute, persuasive, potent, powerful, proving, puissant, reliable, solid, sound, strong, suasive, substantial, telling, to the point, trenchant, trustworthy, unanswerable, unconfuted, undeniable, undoubtable, undoubted, unequivocal, unquestionable, valid, veridical, weighty, well-founded, well-grounded

COGITATIVE, *adjective* contemplative, deliberate, deliberative, ideative, introspective, meditative, museful, pensive, philosophical, pondering, reflective, ruminant, ruminative, speculative, thinking, thoughtful

COGNATE, *adjective* affiliated, affined, agnate, akin, alike, allied, analogical, analogous, appertaining, appurtenant, associated, bearing upon, belonging, close, closely allied, closely related, coordinate, commensurate, common, comparable, comparative, compared, complementary, concurrent, congeneric, congenerous, congenial, connected, consanguine, consanguineous, correlated, correlative, correspondent, corresponding, entwined, equal, equivalent, germane, homogeneous, homologous, in common with, in the same category, interchangeable, interdependent, interrelated, intimately allied, intimately related, like, linked, mutual, near, of that kind, of that sort, parallel, proportionable, reciprocal, related, relating to, relative, same, serial, sharing, similar, something like, synonymous

COGNITION, *noun* acquaintance, apperception, appreciation, apprehension, awareness, *cognitio,* cognitive process, cognizance, comprehension, conception, consciousness, discernment, enlightenment, familiarity, grasp, illumination, insight, intellection, ken, knowledge, mastery, perception, percipience, realization, recognition, sensibility, understanding, wisdom

COGNIZABLE, *adjective* accountable, apprehensible, ascertainable, ascertained, capable of being examined, capable of being tried in the court, clear, comprehensible, decipherable, definite, discernible, discoverable, distinct, distinguishable, explicable, explicit, familiar, fathomable, intelligible, jurisdictionally sound, knowable, known, lucid, luminous, meaningful, pellucid, penetrable, perceived, perceptible, perspicuous, readable, realizable, realized, recognizable, scrutable, straightforward, unblurred, understandable, understood, unequivocal, unevasive, uninvolved, unmistakable, well-written
ASSOCIATED CONCEPTS: cognizable by the courts

COGNIZANT, *adjective* accomplished, acquainted, alert, apperceptive, apprehensive, apprised, astute, aware, clear-sighted, cognitive, comprehending, conscious, *conscius,* conversant, discerning, discriminating, educated, endowed with consciousness, endowed with reason, enlightened, erudite, expert, familiar, informed, keen, knowing, knowledgeable, learned, lettered, mindful, perceptive, percipient, perspicacious, possessed of knowledge, posted, practiced, proficient, regardful, sagacious, sage, sensible to, sharp, understanding, versed, well-advised, well-educated, well-grounded, well-informed, well-read, well-versed, wise

COGNOMEN, *noun* appelation, appellative, byname, byword, denomination, designation, name, nickname, sobriquet, style

COGNOVIT, noun acknowledged judgment, adjudication, admitted judgment, conceded judgment, confessed judgment, confirmed judgment, decision, declaration, decree, determination, disclosed judgment, finding, legal decision

COHABIT, verb abide together, be intimate, conjugate, *consuescere*, copulate, couple, dwell together, live in sexual intimacy, live together, live with, lodge together, reside together, room together, share an address, share bed and board, stay together
ASSOCIATED CONCEPTS: cohabit as husband and wife

COHABITATION (*Living together*), **noun** abiding together, act of dwelling together, alliance, living together in sexual intimacy, lodging together, lodging together as husband and wife, occupying the same domicile, residing together, rooming together
ASSOCIATED CONCEPTS: cohabiting in a state of adultery, fornication, illicit cohabitation, lewd and lascivious cohabitation
FOREIGN PHRASES: *Nuptias non concubitus sed consensus facit.* Not cohabitation but consent makes the valid marriage.

COHABITATION (*Married state*), **noun** act of living together as husband and wife, act of pairing, bond of matrimony, conjugal bliss, conjugality, connubiality, coverture, domestication, legal relation of spouses to each other, legal union of a man and a woman, marriage, married status, matrimony, nuptial bond, nuptial tie, state of matrimony, union, *vinculo matrimonii*, wedded state, wedded status, wedlock
ASSOCIATED CONCEPTS: bigamous cohabitation, cohabiting in a state of adultery, matrimonial cohabitation, polygamous cohabitation
FOREIGN PHRASES: *Nuptias non concubitus sed consensus facit.* Not cohabitation but consent makes the marriage.

COHERE (*Adhere*), **verb** affix, agglomerate, agglutinate, attach, be dense, be tacked together, become solid, cement, clasp, cleave, cling, clot, coagulate, coalesce, *cohaerere*, combine, come together, compress, congeal, conjoin, consolidate, fasten, grasp, grow together, hang on, harden, hold fast, hold on, hold together, hold up, mass, quadrate with, solidify, stay, stick, stick close, stick on to, stick together, unify, unite

COHERE (*Be logically consistent*), **verb** accord, agree, be a sound argument, be accordant, be clear, be coherent, be congruous, be intelligible, be logical, be lucid, be rationally connected, be reasonable, be understandable, *cohaerere*, comport with, conform, correspond, hang together, harmonize, hold together, make sense

COHERENCE, noun adherence, adhesion, adhesiveness, agreement, apprehensibility, attachment, blending, cleavage, coherency, cohesion, cohesiveness, comprehensibility, concert, congruence, congruity, conjunction, connectedness, connection, consistency, consolidation, consonance, *contextus*, continuity, *convenientia*, correspondence, correspondency, firm hold, fusion, harmony, holding together, intelligibility, interrelation, rationality, sticking together, understandability, union, unity

COHERENT (*Clear*), **adjective** adapted to the understanding, apparent, apprehensible, articulate, audible, clear-cut, cogent, cognizable, *cohaerens*, comprehensible, concise, *congruens*, decipherable, defined, definite, direct, discernible, distinct, easily understood, easy to grasp, easy to understand, evident, exact, exoteric, exoterical, explained, explanatory, explicable, explicatory, explicit, express, expressive, fathomable, forthright, graphic, illuminated, in evidence, intelligible, interpreted, knowable, legible, logical, logically appealing, logically consistent, lucid, luminous, making sense, manifest, meaningful, obvious, palpable, pellucid, penetrable, perceivable, perceptible, perspicuous, plain, precise, realizable, recognizable, scrutable, self-evident, simple, straightforward, unambiguous, unblurred, unconfused, understandable, understood, undisguised, unequivocal, unmistakable, visible, vivid, well-defined, well-marked

COHERENT (*Joined*), **adjective** accreted, accretive, adherent, adhering, adhesive, agglutinate, agglutinative, allied, amalgamative, cleaving, cleaving together, clinging, close, coadunate, coagulate, coagulated, coalescent, *cohaerens*, cohering, cohesive, combined, composite, compressed, congealed, conglomerate, conglomeratic, *congruens*, conjoined, conjunct, connected, consolidated, *contextus*, coupled, fused, holding together, incorporated, indivisible, inseparable, interlinked, interlocked, interrelated, sticking, sticking together, united, viscous

COHESIVE (*Compact*), **adjective** close, compressed, concentrated, concise, concrete, conjacent, conjunct, consolidated, dense, firm, hard, impenetrable, impermeable, indivisible, inseparable, pressed together, solid, strong, substantial, terse, thick, tight, to the point, well-knit

COHESIVE (*Sticking*), **adjective** adherent, adhering, adhesive, agglutinate, agglutinative, attached, cementitious, cleaving, clinging, coherent, cohering, conglutinative, connected, consistent, glutinous, holding together, resisting, sticking, tenacious, tied, united

COHORT, noun abettor, accessory, accomplice, aider and abettor, ally, assistant, associate, attendant, auxiliary, coadjutor, cohelper, *cohors*, collaborator, colleague, comate, companion, comrade, confederate, consociate, cooperator, coworker, faithful companion, fellow, fellow conspirator, follower, friend, helper, *particeps criminis*, partner, *socius criminis*, stalwart, supporter

COINCIDE (*Concur*), **verb** accede, accept, accord, acquiesce, agree, approve, arrive at an agreement, arrive at an understanding, arrive at terms, assent, be accordant, be at one with, be of the same mind, be one with, come to an agreement, come to an understanding, come to terms, conform to, consent, correspond, endorse, give assent, go along with, harmonize, meet, merge, nod assent to, subscribe to, synchronize, unite, yield assent

COINCIDE (*Correspond*), **verb** accompany, be concomitant, be congruent, be contemporaneous, be identical, be simultaneous, coexist, *concurrere*, conform to, *congruere, convenire*, exist together, fall exactly together, fill identical times, fit exactly, go with, happen together, match

COINCIDENTAL, adjective accidental, accompanying, at the same time, by circumstance, casual, chance, circumstantial, coexistent, coexisting, coincident, coinciding, coinstantaneous, concomitant, concurrent, conjunctional, contemporaneous, corresponding, fortuitous, *fortuitus*, occurring simultaneously, occurring together, simultaneous, surprising, unexpected, unplanned

COLD-BLOODED, adjective aloof, barbarous, brutal, brutish, calculated, calculating, callous, cold, cold-hearted, cruel, cruel hearted, deliberate, demoniac, devilish, diabolic, dispassionate, feelingless, fiendish, frigid, hard, hard-hearted, hardened, heartless, imperturbable, impervious,

indifferent, indurate, indurated, inhumane, insensitive, malevolent, malicious, malign, obdurate, passionless, pitiless, pococurante, relentless, remorseless, ruthless, savage, soulless, truculent, uncaring, unconcerned, unemotional, unfeeling, unimpressible, uninterested, unkind, unmerciful, unmindful, unmoved, unperturbed, unrelenting, unresponsive, unsolicitous, unsusceptible, unsympathetic, untouched, untroubled, without heart, without warmth
ASSOCIATED CONCEPTS: cold-blooded murder

COLLATERAL *(Accompanying),* **adjective**   accessory, additional, affiliated, ancillary, appertaining, associated, attendant, auxiliary, belonging, closely related, concomitant, concurrent, conjoined, connected, correlated, correspondent, corresponding, coupled with, entwined, interrelated, parallel, related, simultaneous, supplemental, supplementary
ASSOCIATED CONCEPTS: collateral action, collateral agreement, collateral attack, collateral contract, collateral estoppel, collateral note, collateral powers, collateral proceeding, collateral promise, collateral source rule, collateral undertaking, collateral warranties

COLLATERAL *(Immaterial),* **adjective**   being of no importance, extraneous, impertinent, inapplicable, inappropriate, incidental, inconsequential, indifferent, insignificant, insubstantial, irrelevant, meaningless, minor, negligible, nonessential, nugatory, of little moment, peripheral, secondary, trifling, trivial, unconnected, unessential, unimportant
ASSOCIATED CONCEPTS: collateral evidence, collateral facts, collateral fraud, collateral impeachment, collateral inquiry, collateral issue, collateral matter, collateral question, collateral testimony
FOREIGN PHRASES: *Frustra probatur quod probatum non relevat.* It is useless to prove that which when proved is irrelevant.

COLLATERAL RELIEF, **noun**   accessory relief, additional relief, adjunct relief, an added judgment, ancillary relief, attendant relief, beneficial relief, complementing relief, extra relief, other relief, resultant relief, resulting relief, secondary relief, sequential relief, spare relief, subordinate relief, supplemental relief, supplementary relief, supporting relief
ASSOCIATED CONCEPTS: ancillary administration, ancillary attachment, ancillary bill, ancillary jurisdiction, ancillary proceeding

COLLATION, **noun**   analogical procedure, analogy, appositeness, ascertainment, balance, check, checking, comparability, comparative estimate, comparison, confirmation, *conlatio,* contrast, correlation, cross-check, determination, differentiation, examination, juxtaposition, relation
ASSOCIATED CONCEPTS: collation of seals, collation of the property in an estate

COLLEAGUE, **noun**   abettor, accessory, accompanier, accomplice, adjunct, adjutant, adjuvant, advocate, aider and abettor, ally, assistant, associate, attendant, auxiliary, backer, brother, champion, coadjutant, coadjutor, coadjutress, coadjutrix, coadjuvant, coaid, codirector, cohelper, collaborator, comate, companion, compeer, comrade, confederate, *confrère, conlega,* consociate, consort, cooperator, coworker, fellow, fellow companion, fellow conspirator, fellow worker, helper, mate, *particeps criminis,* participator, partner, seconder, *socius criminis,* stalwart, stand-by, votary

COLLECT *(Gather),* **verb**   accumulate, acquire, add to, aggregate, amalgamate, amass, assemble, bring to a common center, bring to a point of union, bring together, compile,

concentrate, *conferre, congerere,* conglomerate, consolidate, convene, *convocare,* draw together, embrace, gain, garner, gather together, group, incorporate, join, mass, muster, pile, put together, reunite, roll into one, unify, unite
ASSOCIATED CONCEPTS: collect rent, collect special assessments

COLLECT *(Recover money),* **verb**   accept, acquire, appropriate, arrogate, assume, be given, be paid, collect payment, demand and obtain payment, exact payment, execute, gain, get back, get money, get possession of, levy, obtain payment, profit, raise, raise contributions, raise funds, reacquire, realize, receive money, receive payment, reclaim, recompense, recoup, recover, redeem, regain, retrieve, secure, secure payment, sequester, settle accounts with, take back again, take possession
ASSOCIATED CONCEPTS: collect a debt, collect on delivery, collect taxes, collecting bank

COLLECTION *(Accumulation),* **noun**   accession, accretion, acervation, *acervus,* acquisition, addition, agglomeration, aggregate, aggregation, amassment, amount accrued, compilation, concentration, *congestus,* conglomerate, conglomeration, convergence, cumulation, group, growth by addition, heap, hoard, mass, obtainment, pile, stockpile, store
ASSOCIATED CONCEPTS: collection of trust funds

COLLECTION *(Assembly),* **noun**   aggregation, assemblage, association, audience, colligation, collocation, company, conflux, congregation, conventicle, convention, con*ventus,* crowd, forgathering, gathering, group, ingathering, meet, meeting, multitude, muster, rally, reassembly, reunion, throng
ASSOCIATED CONCEPTS: freedom of assembly

COLLECTION *(Payment),* **noun**   acquittance, adjustment, amends, bearing the cost, cash payment, clearance, compensatio, compensation, contribution, defrayal, defrayment, disbursement, discharge, enforcement of judgment, expenditure, fulfillment, full satisfaction, guerdon, indemnification, indemnity, installment, making amends, money paid, paying for, payment, price, propitiation, *quid pro quo,* quittance, receipted payment, recompense, rectification, redress, reimbursement, remission, remittance, remuneration, reparation, repayment, requital, restitution, restoration
ASSOCIATED CONCEPTS: collecting bank, collection agencies, collection agent, collection and payment, collection attorney, collection districts, collection of money, collection of taxes, collection officer, for collection only endorsements

COLLECTIVE, **adjective**   accumulated, accumulative, aggregate, aggregated, amalgamated, amassed, assembled, associated, broad, brought together, combined, compiled, composite, compound, comprehensive, concentrated, concerted, concurrent, confederate, congregate, congregational, congregative, considered together, consolidated, corporate, cumulative, each and every, encyclopedic, entire, every, federative, gathered, general, grouped, integrated, integrative, joined, leagued, massed, mutual, of the same mind, total, unified, united, universal, unspecified, whole, widespread
ASSOCIATED CONCEPTS: collective bargaining, collective bargaining agreement

COLLECTIVE BARGAINING, **noun**   abatement of differences, adjustment, arbitrage, arbitrament, arbitration, bargaining, compromise, conciliation, conference, intercession, intermediation, interposition, intervention, mediation,

mediatorship, negotiation, package bargaining, pattern bargaining, umpirage
ASSOCIATED CONCEPTS: collective bargaining unit

COLLECTIVELY, adverb altogether, as a group, as a whole, as one, en banc, en bloc, en masse, fully, in a body, in all, in conjunction, in its entirety, integrally, in the aggregate, in toto, mutually, together, totally, unitedly, wholly, withal

COLLIDE (Clash), **verb** altercate, antagonize, argue, be antagonistic, be at cross-purposes, be at variance, be contrary, be discordant, be in antagonism, be incompatible, be inimical, be mutually opposed, conflict with, confront, contend, contradict, contrast with, contravene, controvert, counter, counteract, countervail, counterwork, differ, differ in opinion, differ violently, disaccord, disagree, dispute, dissent, embroil, encounter, entangle, feud, go contrary to, go in opposition to, hold opposite views, interfere with, join issue, object, oppose, oppugn, quarrel, resist, run afoul of, run against, run at cross-purposes, run counter to, run foul of, show hostility, smash up, take issue, traverse, vary, withstand, work against, wrangle

COLLIDE (Crash against), **verb** bump, bump into, butt against, come in contact, come into collision, come together, *confligere*, converge, crash into, crash together, drive against, drive into, encounter with a shock, enter into collision, hit, hurtle against, impinge, knock against, knock into, make contact, make impact, meet, run into each other, run together, slam into, smash into, strike, strike against, strike at, strike forcibly against each other

COLLISION (Accident), **noun** concussion, contact, convergence, crash, encounter, impact, impingement, jar, jolt, meeting, percussion, pileup, shock, striking together, sudden contact, violent contact
ASSOCIATED CONCEPTS: avoidable collision, collision auto insurance, collisions by carriers

COLLISION (Dispute), **noun** affray, altercation, antagonism, battle, clash, combat, *concursio, concursus,* conflict, contention, contradiction, contrariety, counteraction, disagreement, discord, disputation, embroilment, encounter, fight, fracas, fray, friction, hostility, interference, *mêlée,* opposition, resistence, skirmish

COLLUDE, verb abet, calculate, combine, conceive, confederate, connive, conspire, contrive, cooperate, design, devise, engineer, foment, frame, incite, intrigue, involve, machinate, maneuver, plan, plot, prearrange, predetermine, scheme
ASSOCIATED CONCEPTS: collusion between husband and wife, collusion to circumvent the law, collusive action, fraudulent conveyances

COLLUSION, noun abetment, act of working together, agreement, agreement for fraud, alliance, association, cabal, chicanery, coadjuvancy, coagency, collaboration, combination for fraud, combined operation, complicity, complot, concert, concord, concurrence, confederacy, conjunction, *conlusio,* connivance, conspiracy, contrivance, contriving, cooperation, cooperation for fraud, counterplot, covin, deceit, deceitful agreement, deceitful compact, deceitfulness, deception, double-dealing, duplicity, foul play, fraud, fraudulence, guile, hoax, illegal pact, intrigue, intriguery, joint effort, joint planning, junction, knavery, league, liaison, participation, participation in fraud, perfidy, plotting, *praevaricatio,* schemery, scheming, secret association, secret fraudulent understanding, secret understanding, secret understanding for fraud, synergism, synergy, treachery, trickery, underhand dealing, underplot, union

ASSOCIATED CONCEPTS: collusion in divorcing a spouse, collusion in obtaining the grounds of a divorce, collusion in procurement of a judgment, collusion to create diversity of citizenship, collusive action, collusive effort, collusive suit, connivance, conspiracy

COLLUSIVE, adjective artful, beguiling, calculating, clandestine, confidential, connivant, conniving, conspirational, conspirative, conspiratorial, conspiring, covinous, cunning, deceitful, deceptive, defrauding, designing, fraudulent, furtive, guileful, illicitly covert, indirect, insidious, intriguing, obreptitious, perfidious, plotting, schemeful, scheming, subreptitious, surreptitious, treacherous, undercover, underhanded, wily
ASSOCIATED CONCEPTS: collusion as a divorce defense, collusive claim, collusive suit, conspiracy, fraud and collusion

COLOR (Complexion), **noun** apparent character, aspects, attribute, bearing, character, characteristics, component, constitution, denomination, description, designation, distinction, endowment, faculty, features, fettle, figure, flavor, form, hue, image, inclination, kind, likeness, lineament, make, manner, mark, nature, particularity, peculiarities, posture, principle, quality, shape, *species,* style, temperament, tendency, tone, trim, type, variety
ASSOCIATED CONCEPTS: the color of a case

COLOR (Deceptive appearance), **noun** act of dissembling, affectation, allegation, alleged motive, apparent right, appearance, cloak, concealment, cunning, deceit, deception, deceptive covering, device, disingenuousness, display, dissemblance, dissimulation, distortion, equivocalness, equivocation, evasion, exaggeration, external appearance, false appearance, falseness, falsification, feint, gloss, guile, guise, impression, misrepresentation, misstatement, outward appearance, *praetextus,* pretense, pretext, representation, show, *simulacrum,* simulation, subterfuge, *suggestio falsi, suppressio veri*
ASSOCIATED CONCEPTS: color a cause of action, color of authority, color of claim, color of interest, color of jurisdiction, color of law, color of office, color of right, color of state law, color of title, color of title in adverse possession, under color of, under color of law

COLORABLE (Plausible), **adjective** *ad captandum,* alleged, apparent, apparently right, ben trovato, conceivable, conjecturable, convincing, credible, feasible, *in posse,* logical, ostensible, persuasive, presumable, presumptive, rational, reasonable, seeming, seemingly fair, seemingly sound, seemingly valid, sensible, supposable, surmisable, tenable, thinkable, *verisimilis,* warrantable
ASSOCIATED CONCEPTS: colorable authority, colorable cause, colorable claim, colorable invocation of jurisdiction, colorable title

COLORABLE (Specious), **adjective** appearing, artful, crafty, deceitful, deceiving, deceptive, delusive, delusory, factitious, false, feigned, fraudulent, sham, trumped up, untrue

COMAKER, noun certifier, coapplicant, coborrower, coobligor, coratifier, cosignatory, cosigner, endorser, party to an instrument

COMBINATION, noun affiliation, aggregate, aggregation, amalgamation, arrangement, assemblage, bringing together, coadjutorship, coalescence, coalition, collection, composition, compound, *coniunctio,* congregation, conjugation, conjunction, consolidation, fusion, incorporation, joining, junction, merger, pool, *societas,* unification, union
ASSOCIATED CONCEPTS: combination in restraint of trade, combination

patent, combination to restrict competition and commerce, combination trademark, combined offense, combined property, illegal combination, patentable combination

COMBINE *(Act in concert),* **verb** act as one, act jointly, affiliate with, ally, associate, band together, coact, collaborate, collude, concert, confederate, conspire, cooperate, coordinate, enlist with, enter into partnership with, federate, form a union, harmonize, join forces, join with, league with, make common cause with, marry, pair with, participate with, pool, rally, syncretize, syndicate, take part, team up with, unite, work in unison, work together
ASSOCIATED CONCEPTS: Anti-Monoply Act, antitrust

COMBINE *(Join together),* **verb** admix, affix, agglutinate, amalgamate, annex, append, attach, bind, blend, coalesce, cohere, colligate, commingle, commix, compound, concatenate, conglomerate, conglutinate, *coniungere,* conjoin, connect, *consociare,* consolidate, couple, entwine, fasten, form a union, fuse, glue, group, immix, inosculate, interblend, interfuse, interlink, intermix, intertwine, intertwist, interweave, intwine, link, make a mixture, meld, merge, mingle, *miscere,* mix, paste, piece together, secure, splice, stick together, tack together, tie, unify, unite
ASSOCIATED CONCEPTS: combined offense, combined property

COMITY, *noun* accommodation, accord, affability, agreeableness, amenity, amiability, amity, benevolence, camaraderie, civility, compliance, concord, considerateness, consideration, cordiality, courtesy, courtly politeness, deference, disposition to please, fellow feeling, friendliness, general reciprocity, gentility, good-fellowship, good will, graciousness, harmony, mansuetude, mutual consideration, mutual respect, neighborliness, obligingness, politeness, *prévenance,* reciprocity, respect, respectfulness
ASSOCIATED CONCEPTS: comity between courts, comity in conflict of laws, comity of nations, comity of states

COMMAND, *verb* adjure, authorize, bid, call for, call upon, charge, compel, constrain, decree, demand, direct, direct imperatively, enact, exact, exercise authority, force, give directions, give orders, govern, have control, *hominem iubere facere, homini imperare, homini praecipere ut faciat, imminere,* impose, instruct, issue a command, issue a decree, issue an order, lead, mandate, ordain, order, order with authority, prescribe, proclaim, promulgate an order, require, rule, state authoritatively, take charge, take the lead
FOREIGN PHRASES: *In maleficio, ratihabitio mandato comparatur.* In tort, a ratification is regarded as a command. *Qui mandat ipse fecisse videtur.* He who gives an order is held to be the doer. *Ratihabitio mandato aequiparatur.* Ratification is equivalent to an express command. *Remissius imperanti melius paretur.* He who commands more gently is better obeyed.

COMMENCE, *verb* arise, auspicate, begin, bring, broach, come into existence, come into the world, embark on, engage in, enter upon, inaugurate, incept, *incipere,* initiate, install, institute, introduce, launch, lay the foundations, make one's debut, open, originate, pioneer, put in execution, rise, set forth, set in operation, start, take the initiative, undertake, venture on
ASSOCIATED CONCEPTS: commence a prosecution, commence a suit, commence by filing, commence by summons, commencement of a proceeding, commencement of a suit, commencement of a trial, commencement of action, duly commenced

COMMENSURABLE, *adjective* analagous, analogical, coequal, coextensive, coherent, commensurate, comparable, concordant, concurrent, conformable, congruous, consistent, consonant, coordinate, correspondent, equal, equivalent, even, identical in size, level, matching, of an equal size, of equal length or volume, parallel, proportional, proportionate, relative, similar

COMMENSURATE, *adjective* acceptable, accordant, adequate, agreeing, analogous, appropriate, coequal, coextensive, commeasurable, commensurable, comparable, concordant, congruent, congruous, consistent, corresponding, equal in extent, equal in measure, equal to, equivalent, fitted, having a common measure, in accord, in agreement, in exact agreement, matching, of equal duration, of equal extent, of equal rank, on a par, on a proper scale, on a suitable scale, on even terms, paralleling, proportional, proportionate, relative, similar, sufficient, sufficing, suitable, synchronal

COMMENT, *noun* animadversion, annotation, assertion, averment, *censeo,* clarification, commentary, dictum, elucidation, enucleation, example, exegesis, exemplification, explanation, explanatory note, explication, exposition, expounding, expression, finding, footnote, gloss, illumination, illustration, interpretation, marginal annotation, mention, notation, note, note of explanation, observation, postulate, reflection, remark, report, scholium, statement, utterance, word of explanation
ASSOCIATED CONCEPTS: comment on defendant's failure to testify, comment on evidence, comment on witness' credibility, comment upon the testimony, comments on the weight of evidence

COMMENT, *verb* allege, animadvert, annotate, assert, bring out, *censere,* clarify, clear, criticize, declare, define, descant, dilate upon, discourse upon, discuss, elucidate, enlighten, enucleate, exemplify, expand on, explain, explicate, exposit on, expound, express, give a sense to, gloss, illuminate, illustrate, interject, interpose, interpret, make clear, make notes, make observations, make remarks, mention, note, notice, observe, opine, pass on, point out, posit, postulate, put a meaning on, rationalize, remark, remark upon, render intelligible, reprove, review, say, *sententiam dicere,* shed light upon, spell out, state, touch upon, treat, utter
ASSOCIATED CONCEPTS: comment on defendant's failure to testify, comment on evidence, comment on witness' credibility, comment upon the testimony, comments on the weight of evidence, prosecutor's comments on evidence

COMMENTARY, *noun* analysis, annotation, clarification, comment, critique, discourse, discussion, dissertation, editorial, elucidation, exegesis, explanation, explication, exposition, illumination, illustration, interpretation, marginalia, notation, note, notice, observation, proposal, remark, report, review, scholium, thesis
ASSOCIATED CONCEPTS: commentaries to the statutes

COMMERCE, *noun* interstate commerce, bargaining, barter, bartering, business, business affairs, business deals, business intercourse, business transactions, buying and selling, chaffering, commercial intercourse, *commercium,* dealing, exchange, fiscal exchange, industry, industry and trade, interchange, interchange of commodities, interchange of goods, intercourse, marketing, mercantile business, mercantile relations, mercantilism, *mercatura,* merchandising, merchantry, monetary exchange, multilateral trade, negotia, negotiation, private enterprise, production and distribution, reciprocal trade, system of exchanges, trade, trading, traffic, traffic of commodities, transportation of commodities, transportation of goods

ASSOCIATED CONCEPTS: affect commerce, affect interstate commerce, arising under a law regulating commerce, commerce among the several states, commerce clause, commerce power, commerce with foreign nations, commercial code, commercial paper, industry affecting commerce, international commerce, intrastate commerce, law regulating commerce, navigation and commerce, regulate commerce, restraint of commerce

FOREIGN PHRASES: *Commercium jure gentium commune esse debet, et non in monopolium et privatum paucorum quaestum convertendum.* Commerce, by the law of nations, ought to be common, and not converted into monopoly and the private gain of a few persons. *Jus accrescendi inter mercatores, pro beneficio commercii, locum non habet.* The right of survivorship does not exist between merchants for the benefit of commerce.

COMMERCIAL, *adjective* business, businesslike, *commercium,* economic, engaged in commerce, financial, fiscal, in the market, industrial, jobbing, manufactured for sale, mercantile, merchandising, monetary, pecuniary, pertaining to business, pertaining to merchants, pertaining to trade, prepared for sale, skilled in commerce, supplying, trade, trading

ASSOCIATED CONCEPTS: commercial agency, commercial bank, commercial bribery, commercial business, commercial consumption, commercial endorsement, commercial frustration, commercial insolvency, commercial law, commercial letter of credit, commercial loan, commercial mark, commercial partnership, commercial purpose, commercial use, commercial zone

COMMERCIAL RIGHTS, *noun* business rights, economic rights, industrial rights, merchandizing rights, product rights, trade rights

COMMINGLE, *verb* admix, alloy, amalgamate, assemble, associate, band, bind together, blend, bring in contact with, coalesce, *commiscere,* combine, commix, compound, conglomerate, conjoin, connect, consolidate, consort with, couple, cross with, embody, entwine, fasten, fuse, harmonize, hybridize, immix, incorporate, interbreed, interlace, interlard, intermingle, intermix, involve together, join, league, link, lump together, merge, mix, mix together, pair with, piece, put together, run together, scramble, stir, unite

ASSOCIATED CONCEPTS: commingling of assets, commingling of funds by an agent, commingling of property

COMMISSION *(Act),* *noun* accomplishment, achievement, actualization, actuation, attainment, carrying out, completion, consummation, discharge, dispatch, doing, effecting, effectuation, enactment, enforcement, execution, exercise, exercising, fruition, fulfilment, implementation, inflicting, infliction, making, *mandatum,* operation, perpetration, realization, transaction

ASSOCIATED CONCEPTS: commission of crime

COMMISSION *(Agency),* *noun* advisory group, appointed group, board, board of inquiry, body of commissioners, body of delegates, body of deputies, bureau, cabinet, consultants, convocation, council, delegation, deliberative group, embassy, executive committee, investigating committee, planning board, representatives, standing committee, trustees

ASSOCIATED CONCEPTS: advisory body, Federal Trade Commission, Municipal Commission, Public Service Commission

COMMISSION *(Fee),* *noun* allotment, allowance, bonus, compensation, consideration, defrayment, disbursement, dividend, earnings, emolument, extra compensation, increment, interest, pay, pay-off, payment, percentage, percentage compensation, portion, proceeds, profit, recompense, reimbursement, remuneration, repayment, return, reward, salary, share of profits, stipend, subsidy, wage

ASSOCIATED CONCEPTS: broker's commission, commission merchant, compensation, fees, finder's commission, profits

COMMIT *(Entrust),* *verb* allot, assign, authorize, charge, charge with, commission, confer a trust, confide, consign, convey, delegate, employ, empower, engage, grant authority to, invest, invest with power, make responsible for, put an obligation upon, put in the hands of, relegate to, trust, turn over to, vest in

ASSOCIATED CONCEPTS: commit to a writing

COMMIT *(Institutionalize),* *verb* arrest, confine, consign, constrain, deliver into custody, enthrall, hold in constraint, hold in restraint, immure, impound, imprison, incarcerate, intern, jail, lock up, place in confinement, put in custody, recommit to custody, remand to custody, remit to custody, restrain, send to an asylum, send to jail, send to prison

ASSOCIATED CONCEPTS: commit to a hospital, commit to a mental institution, commit to prison, committing magistrate

COMMIT *(Perpetrate),* *verb* accomplish, achieve, act, act on, administer, apply oneself to, be a participator in, be a party to, be an accomplice, be engaged in, be engrossed in, bring about, bring to pass, carry into execution, carry on, carry out, carry through, complete, consummate, discharge, discharge the duties of, effect, employ oneself, execute, finish, fulfill, go through with, inflict, occupy oneself with, operate, participate in, perform, realize, transact

ASSOCIATED CONCEPTS: commit an offense against the United States

COMMIT TO WRITING, *verb* affirm, assert, assure, attest, authenticate, be bound, certify, circumstantiate, commemorate, contract, covenant, document, guarantee, inscribe, insure, make a statement, note, ratify, set down, sign a pact, stipulate, subscribe, underwrite, validate, warrant

ASSOCIATED CONCEPTS: agreements, contracts, holographic will

COMMITMENT *(Confinement),* *noun* committal, confining, constraint, detention, durance, handing over into custody, holding in constraint, holding in restraint, immuring, impoundment, imprisonment, incarcerating, incarceration, interning, internment, jailing, legal confinement, legal constraint, locking up, mittimus, placing in confinement, putting in custody, remanding to custody, remitting to custody, restraint, restriction, sending to jail, sentencing

ASSOCIATED CONCEPTS: commitment to an institution, commitment to jail

COMMITMENT *(Responsibility),* *noun* accountability, accountableness, agreement, allegiance, assignment, assurance, burden, call of duty, charge, conscience, contract, covenant, devoir, duty, engagement, faithfulness, incumbency, mission, obligation, onus, pledge, promise, sense of duty, solemn declaration, trust, undertaking, vow, warrant

COMMITTEE, *noun* advisory group, agency, alliance, appointed group, association, board, body, body of consultants, bureau, cabinet, commission, confederacy, confederation, congregation, *consilium,* council, delegation,

federation, fellowship, group of delegates, league, organization, organized group, representatives, staff, syndicate, trustees
ASSOCIATED CONCEPTS: campaign committee, committee of the whole, political committee, standing committee

COMMODITIES, noun   articles, articles of commerce, articles of merchandise, articles of trade, assets, chattels, goods, holdings, items, merchandise, merx, movables, objects, possessions, produce, produced materials, products, properties, raw materials, res, specialties, staples, stock, stock in trade, vendibles, wares
ASSOCIATED CONCEPTS: agricultural commodity, commodity rate, horticultural commodity, public utility commodity, stocks and bonds

COMMON (Customary), **adjective**   accepted, ascertained, commonplace, conventional, current, currently perceived, established, everyday, familiar, frequent, generally known, natural, normal, often met with, ordinary, popular, prevailing, prevalent, publicly known, received, recognized, repeatedly recognized, traditional, typical, universally known, usual, usually understood, well-known, widely known, widespread
ASSOCIATED CONCEPTS: common assault, common-law, common-law burglary, common-law contempt, common-law copyright, common-law crime, common-law forgery, common-law jurisdiction, common-law larceny, common-law lien, common-law marriage, common-law misdemeanor, common-law murder, common-law nuisance, common-law remedy, common-law trademark, common-law trust, common-law wife, common liability, common peril, common question of law or fact, common seal, common source of title, common stock, common thief, common use

COMMON (Shared), **adjective**   belonging equally to, belonging to all, belonging to many, collective, communal, communis, commutual, conjoint, cooperative, for the use of all, in partnership, joint, mutual, owned jointly, participating, participatory, pertaining to the whole community, pooled, popular, public, publicus, reciprocal, shared among several, shared by two or more, universal, used by all
ASSOCIATED CONCEPTS: common adventure, common belief, common boundary line, common carrier, common council, common directors, common disaster, common driveway, common enemy doctrine, common enterprise, common good, common interest, common jurisdiction, common knowledge, common labor, common lands, common necessity, common plan, common plea courts, common property, common recovery, common rights, common scheme, common stock, common wall, common walls

COMMON KNOWLEDGE, noun   accepted fact, acknowledgment, announcement, annunciation, avowance, declaration, disclosure, dissemination, experience, exposé, familiarity, general information, history, learning, manifestation, notoriety, patefactio, public disclosure, public knowledge, public notice, publicness, state of being public

COMMON SENSE, noun   acumen, astuteness, balanced judgment, calmness, clear thinking, composure, experience, experienced view, good judgment, good sense, intelligence, intuition, judgment, level-headedness, logic, mental poise, native reason, natural sagacity, ordinary judgment, ordinary sense, plain sense, plausibility, practical discernment, practical knowledge, practicality, presence of mind, prudence, rational faculty, rationality, reason, reasonableness, resourcefulness, sagacity, sapience, savoir faire, sensibleness, sober-mindedness, sobriety, solidity, sound

perception, sound sense, sound understanding, unbiased impulse, understanding, unemotional consideration, wisdom, worldly wisdom
ASSOCIATED CONCEPTS: commonsense reading of a statute, commonsense ruling

COMMOTION, noun   affray, agitatio, agitation, altercation, brawl, clamor, clash, conflict, confusion, convulsion, disorder, disorderliness, disorganization, disquiet, disquietude, disturbance, ebullition, embroilment, encounter, entanglement, eruption, excitement, ferment, fermentation, fight, fomentation, fracas, fray, furor, imbroglio, inquietude, insurgence, insurrection, maelstrom, mayhem, mêlée, moil, motus, noisy strife, overthrow, pandemonium, perturbation, public disturbance, quarrel, racket, rampage, rebellion, restlessness, rising insubordination, row, ruction, scuffle, skirmish, stir, struggle, tempest, tumult, tumultus, turba, turbulence, turmoil, tussle, unruliness, upheaval, uprising, uproar, violence, welter, whirl

COMMUNICATE, verb   acquaint, advertise, advise, announce, apprise, articulate, assert, bandy words, breathe, bring word, broadcast, commerce with, commune, communicare, confabulate, converse, convey, correspond, deal with, declare, demonstrate, disclose, discourse with, divulge, engage in a conversation, enlighten, enunciate, express, familiarize, find words to express, give an account, give expression, give notice, give notification, give one to understand, give the facts, give tongue, give utterance, give voice, have intercourse, impart, inform, instill, instruct, interchange thoughts, intercommunicate, lay before, let know, let out, make known, mention, narrate, notify, parley, present facts, proclaim, pronounce, publicize, put forth, put in words, relate, reveal, say, send word, serve notice, set forth, signify, sound, speak one's mind, speak, specify, talk, teach, tell, traffic with, transmit, utter, verbalize, vocalize, voice, write

COMMUNICATE EFFECTIVELY, verb   broadcast, clarify, communicate, convey, decipher, decode, define, deliver, demonstrate, demystify, descramble, disambiguate, disseminate, elucidate, enlighten, enunciate, explain, explain in plain language, explicate, get across, get through to, illuminate, impart, make crystal clear, particularize, simplify, spell out, tell

COMMUNICATION (Discourse), **noun**   collocution, colloquy, communicatio, communiqué, conference, conversation, correspondence, dialogue, dissertation, exchange, interchange, intercommunication, intercourse, interlocution
ASSOCIATED CONCEPTS: attorney and client communication, conditionally privileged communication, confidential communication, husband and wife communication, physician and patient communication, privileged communication, telegraph communication, telephonic communication, verbal communication, written communication

COMMUNICATION (Statement), **noun**   announcement, annunciation, declaration, disclosure, dissemination, divulgement, information, message, news, notification, proclamation, report, revelation, utterance, writing

COMMUNITY, noun   body, body politic, borough, citizenry, city, civilization, civitas, commonalty, commonwealth, commune, group, inhabitants, kinship, locality, municipality, neighborhood, partnership, people, polity, populace, population, respublica, society, town
ASSOCIATED CONCEPTS: community estate, community interest, community of right or interest, community property

COMMUTE, verb abate, abbreviate, abridge, allay, alleviate, alter, ameliorate, bate, change, change penalties, curtail, cut, decrease a punishment, dilute, diminish, ease, exchange, exchange penalties, lessen, lighten, limit, make less extreme, make less harsh, make less intense, make less rigorous, make less rough, make less severe, make lighter, make milder, meliorate, minimize, mitigate, modify sentence, palliate, reduce, reduce a punishment, reduce in asperity, relax severity, relieve, render less difficult, shorten, shrink, slacken, slash, soften, substitute, temper, tone down, trim, truncate
ASSOCIATED CONCEPTS: commute a sentence

COMPACT (Dense), **adjective** arranged within a small space, bunched, close, close-knit, close-set, close together, closely united, clustered, cohesive, compacted, compressed, concentrated, condensed, consolidated, constricted, constringed, contracted, crammed, crowded, densified, economical of space, firm, firmly united, forced into smaller space, hard, massed, massive, packed, populous, pressed into smaller compass, pressed together, rammed, serried, solid, solidified, space saving, squeezed together, stuffed, thick, tight, tightly knit

COMPACT (Pithy), **adjective** abbreviated, abbreviatory, abridged, abstracted, aphoristic, aphoristical, apothegmatic, apothegmatical, brief, compendious, concise, condensed, contracted, crisp, curt, digested, direct, epigrammatic, epitomized, expressed concisely, gnomic, gnomical, laconic, meaty, outlined, pointed, recapitulated, sententious, short, shortened, shrunk, straightforward, succinct, summarized, summary, summed up, synoptic, telescoped, terse, tidy, to the point, trim

COMPACT, noun agreement, agreement between parties, arrangement, bargain, cartel, commitment, compromise, concord, concordat, contract, contractual obligation, contractual statement, convention, *conventus,* covenant, deal, entente, *entente cordiale,* indenture, mutual pledge, mutual promise, obligation, pact, *pactio, pactum,* pledge, promise, stipulation, treaty, understanding
ASSOCIATED CONCEPTS: interstate compact
FOREIGN PHRASES: *Pacta privata juri publico derogare non possunt.* Private compacts cannot derogate from public right. *Re, verbis, scripto, consensu, traditione, junctura vestes sumere pactasolent.* Agreements usually take their clothing from the thing itself, from words, from writing, from consent, from delivery.

COMPANY (Assemblage), **noun** aggregation, assembled body, *assemblée,* assembly, *attroupement,* caucas, coalition, conclave, conference, confluence, conflux, congregation, congress, convention, convergence, convocation, crowd, gathering, group, ingathering, league, meeting, mustering, *societas*

COMPANY (Enterprise), **noun** association, body corporate, business, business establishment, coetus, combination, commercial enterprise, concern, confederacy, consociation, copartnership, corporate body, corporation, establishment, federation, firm, *grex,* guild, institute, joint concern, organization, partnership
ASSOCIATED CONCEPTS: affiliated company, company union, construction company, corporation, holding company

COMPARABLE (Capable of comparison), **adjective** akin, alike, analogous, analogical, approximate, associated, close, cognate, commensurable, *comparabilis,* congeneric, correlative, homogeneous, homologous, kindred, like, much the same, parallel, related, resembling, similar

COMPARABLE (Equivalent), **adjective** coequal, commensurate, equable, equal in value, equipollent, even, identical, interchangeable, matched, matching, on par, tantamount, undeviating, uniform, unvarying, without distinction

COMPARATIVE, adjective analagous to, comparable, comparativus, connected with, contrastive, correlative, corresponding to, estimated by comparison, in connection with, in proportion to, in relation to, in relation with, in respect to, in the same category, judged by comparison, matching, metaphorical, pertaining to, pertinent to, referable to, referential, referring, relating to, relational, relative, rivaling, similar to, similitudinous, vying with, with reference to, with regard to, with relation to
ASSOCIATED CONCEPTS: comparative injury, comparative negligence, comparative rectitude

COMPARE, verb aequiperare, analogize, balance against, bring into comparison, bring into meaningful relation with, bring into relation, *comparare, componere, conferre,* contrast, correlate, differentiate, discriminate between, distinguish between, draw a parallel, equate, estimate relatively, exercise critical judgment, identify with, juxtapose, liken, match, measure, note the similarities and differences, parallel, parallelize, place in juxtaposition, put alongside, relate, represent as resembling, set side by side, show correspondence, show to be analagous, show to be similar, weigh
ASSOCIATED CONCEPTS: comparative negligence, comparing equities

COMPARISON, noun alikeness, analogical procedure, analogy, association, balance, *comparatio,* comparative estimate, *conlatio,* contrast, correlation, equation, measurement, nearness, parallel, *rapprochement,* relative estimate, relative estimation, resemblance
ASSOCIATED CONCEPTS: comparison of negligence of opposing parties

COMPATIBILITY, noun acclimation, accommodation, accord, accordance, adjustment, affiliation, agreement, amity, attunement, balance, coexistence, comity, common view, companionship, compliance, concord, concordance, concurrence, conformity, congeniality, congruity, congruousness, *consensus omnium,* consent, consentaneity, consistency, consonance, cooperation, coordination, *entente,* equanimity, harmony, mutual understanding, rapport, reconciliation, unanimity, union, unity
ASSOCIATED CONCEPTS: incompatibility

COMPEL, verb bear down against, bear hard upon, blackmail, bring pressure to bear upon, burden, cause, coerce, *cogere,* command, *compellere,* constrain, control, decree, demand, dictate, distrain, drive, elicit, employ force, enforce, exact, force, impel, impose, impose a duty, inflict, insist, leave no option, limit, necessitate, obligate, oblige, obtrude on, order, press, pressure, put under obligation, require, restrict, *subigere,* subject, take no denial, threaten, urge, urge forward
ASSOCIATED CONCEPTS: compel accused to give evidence against himself, compel by legal process, compel to testify under a grant of immunity

COMPELLING, adjective absolute, assertive, authoritative, binding, categorical, coercive, commanding, compulsive, compulsory, constraining, decisive, dominant, driving, emphatic, enforcing, forcible, *gravis,* great, impelling, imperative, incisive, inducive, influential, involuntary, irresistible, necessary, obligatory, obsessing, obsessional, obsessive, of necessity, omnipotent, overpowering, overriding, overruling, overwhelming, peremptory, potent, predominant, preeminent, preponderant, pressing, propulsive, puissant, strong, thrustful, trenchant, unavoidable, *validus, vehemens,* vigorous, weighty

ASSOCIATED CONCEPTS: compelling interest, compelling necessity, compelling need

COMPENDIUM, *noun* abbreviation, abridgment, abstract, breviary, brief, capsule, compend, concise treatment, condensation, conspectus, contraction, digest, *epitoma,* epitome, essence, extract, outline, pandect, precis, recapitulation, review, summary, survey, syllabus, synopsis

COMPENSATE (*Counterbalance*), **verb** act against with equal force, allow for, atone, balance, be equivalent, *compensare,* correspond, counteract, counterpoise, countervail, counterweigh, equalize, equate, equilibrate, even, furnish an equivalent, level off, make equal, make level, make steady, make up for, neutralize, offset, oppose, produce equilibrium, restore to equilibrium, set off, square, stabilize, strike a balance

COMPENSATE (*Remunerate*), **verb** allow for, defray, discharge a debt, give equal value, give satisfaction for damage, give satisfaction for injury, honor, indemnify, make payment, make restitution, pay damages, pay for, pay in full, pay the equivalent, pay the value, pay wages, recompense, redress, refund, reimburse, remit, *remunerari,* remunerate for injury, repay, repay for a loss, return, reward, reward for a loss, reward for an injury, salary, satisfy, settle accounts with

ASSOCIATED CONCEPTS: compensation for expenses, compensation for goods sold and delivered, compensation for hospital bills, compensation for injuries, compensation for out-of-pocket expenses, compensation for pain and suffering, compensation for the negligent acts of another, compensation for wrongdoing, costs, fair and reasonable compensation, fees, penalties, reimbursement, wages, workmen's compensation

COMPENSATION, *noun* amends, atonement, commutation, *compensatio,* consideration, damages, defrayal, defrayment, earnings, emolument, equivalent given for injury, equivalent given for loss sustained, fee, financial remuneration, guerdon, indemnification, indemnity, meed, monetary remuneration, pay, payment, payment of damages, quittance, reclamation, recompensation in value, recompense, recoupment, recovery, rectification, reimbursement, remuneration, remuneration for injury, reparation, repayment, requital, restoration, retainer, retaining fee, retrieval, return, reward, reward for injury, reward for loss, reward for service, salary, satisfaction, satisfaction for damage, satisfaction for injury, settlement, solatium, wages

ASSOCIATED CONCEPTS: adequate compensation, adjusted compensation, agreement for compensation, compensatory damages, fair and reasonable compensation, full compensation, just and adequate compensation, payments of compensation, reasonable compensation

FOREIGN PHRASES: ***Corporalis injuria non recipit aestimationem de futuro.*** A personal injury cannot be compensated for by later acts.

COMPENSATORY, *adjective* atoning, balancing, compensating, compensative, equivalent, expiating, expiatory, in compensation, indemnificatory, paying, propitiating, recompensive, redemptive, refunding, reimbursing, remitting, remunerative, reparative, repaying, restitutive, restitutory, retributive, rewardful, rewarding, satisfying, unindebted

ASSOCIATED CONCEPTS: compensatory damages, compensatory penalties

COMPETE, *verb* battle, be a candidate, be in the running, certare, challenge, clash, combat, contend, contest, *cum homine contendere,* duel, employ stratagem, encounter, engage in a contest, enter, enter competition, joust, match strength with, match wits with, oppose, participate in, rival, spar, strive, struggle, take part, tilt, vie with, wrestle

COMPETENCE (*Ability*), **noun** adequacy, adroitness, aptitude, capability, capacity, conversance, dexterity, effectiveness, effectuality, efficacy, eligibility, enablement, endowment, equipment, experience, facility, faculty, fitness, flair, forte, gift, grasp, intelligence, legal competence, legal fitness, mastery, potency, proficiency, qualifications, responsibility, skill, skillfulness, sufficiency, suitability, talent, training

ASSOCIATED CONCEPTS: competency of a witness, competent and intelligent waiver of counsel, competent authority, competent jurisdiction, legally competent

FOREIGN PHRASES: ***Homo potest esse habilis et inhabilis diversis temporibus.*** A man may be capable and incapable at different times. ***Nemo praesens nisi intelligat.*** One is not present unless he understands. ***Nullus idoneus testis in re sua intelligitur.*** No person is deemed to be a competent witness in his own behalf. ***Pupillus pati posse non intelligitur.*** An infant is not considered able to do an act to his own prejudice. ***Sola ac per se senectus donationem testamentum aut transactionem non vitiat.*** Old age alone and of itself will not vitiate a will or gift.

COMPETENCE (*Sanity*), **noun** capability, clearmindedness, coherence, healthy mindedness, lucidity, mental balance, mental capacity, mental equilibrium, mental health, normalcy, normality, normalness, rationality, reason, reasonability, sanemindedness, saneness, sense, senses, sound mind, soundmindedness, soundness, soundness of mind

ASSOCIATED CONCEPTS: age of maturity, competency of a witness, competent and intelligent waiver of counsel, age of maturity, infancy, legally competent, mental competence, *non compos mentis*

FOREIGN PHRASES: ***Furiosi nulla voluntas est.*** A madman has no will.

COMPETENCY (*Capacity*), **noun** ability, clear-mindedness, coherence, efficiency, faculty, fitness, lucidity, mental capacity, mental equilibrium, qualification, reasonableness

ASSOCIATED CONCEPTS: competency of a guarantor, competency of a guardian, competency of an executive, competency of counsel, competency of jurors to serve on a panel, competency of parties to testify, competency of trustees, competency of witnesses, competency to stand trial, competency to testify, incompetence, objections raised over the competency of a witness, withdrawal from serving in designated capacity due to a lack of competency

COMPETENCY (*Sufficiency*), **noun** abundance, adequacy, applicability, capability, craft, dexterity, efficacy, effectiveness, mastery, proficiency, prowess, satisfactoriness, skill

ASSOCIATED CONCEPTS: competency to stand trial, competency to testify, competency of witnesses

COMPETENT, *adjective* able, accomplished, adept, adequate, adroit, artful, capable, *competere,* conversant,

credible, deft, dexterous, effective, effectual, efficacious, efficient, enterprising, excellent, experienced, expert, fit, good, ingenious, learned, masterful, masterly, mentally capable, practiced, prepared, proficient, properly qualified, qualified, ready, resourceful, responsible, satisfactory, skilled, skillful, sufficient, suitable, trained, versed, well fitted
ASSOCIATED CONCEPTS: *capax negotii,* competent and intelligent waiver of counsel, competent authority, competent court, competent evidence, competent jurisdiction, competent witness, legally competent, mentally competent

COMPETITION, *noun* attempt to equal, bout, challenge, combat, conflict, *contentio,* contest, corrivalry, encounter, engagement, open contest, opposition, outrivalry, pitting of strength, pitting of wits, race, rivalry, scramble, strife, striving for superiority, struggle for superiority, trial of superiority, vying for ascendance
ASSOCIATED CONCEPTS: competitive bidding, competitive class, competitive examination, fair competition, free and open competition, unfair competition, unreasonable interference with competition

COMPETITIVE (Antagonistic), ***adjective*** adverse, at issue, at variance, challenging, clashing, colliding, combatant, combative, combatting, competing, competitory, conflicting, contending, contentious, contrary, counteractive, decided by competition vying, discordant, disputatious, dissident, emulative, in competition, opposing, oppugnant, rival, rivaling, striving, vying
ASSOCIATED CONCEPTS: competitive bidding, competitive class, competitive examination, unfair competition

COMPETITIVE (Open), ***adjective*** accessible to all, common, comprehensive, equal, free, free to all, general, nonexclusive, not partial, not privileged, open to the public, popular, public, unbounded, unclosed, unconfined, universal, unrestrained, unrestricted
ASSOCIATED CONCEPTS: fair competition, free and open competition, unreasonable interference with competition

COMPILATION, *noun* accretion, accumulation, agglomeration, aggregation, anthology, arrangement, assemblage, classification, codification, collection, colligation, collocation, combination, conglomeration, consolidation, gathering, incorporation, miscellany, selection
ASSOCIATED CONCEPTS: Official Compilation of Codes Rules, and Regulations

COMPILE, *verb* accumulate, agglomerate, aggregate, amass, anthologize, arrange, arrange materials for publication, assemble, bring together, bunch, bunch together, cluster, collect, combine, *componere,* compose, conglomerate, cull, cumulate, draw together, draw up, extract from other works, garner, gather, gather together, glean, group, group together, lump together, make up, mass, prepare, recapitulate, select, select and arrange, unite, write

COMPLACENT, *adjective* at ease, carefree, complaisant, compliable, compliant, composed, content, contented, fulfilled, gratified, peaceful of mind, placid, pleased, *qui sibi placet,* reposeful, resigned, satisfied, self-content, self-satisfied, serene, smug, *suffisant,* tranquil, unvexed

COMPLAIN (Charge), ***verb*** *accusare,* accuse, arraign, blame, bring a suit, bring an action, bring charges, bring proceedings against, bring up on charges, censure, challenge, charge with, cite, criminate, declaim against,

delate, denounce, denunciate, file a charge, file a claim, file a suit, implicate, impute, incriminate, inculpate, inform against, institute a lawsuit, lay an information, lay blame upon, lay responsibility on, lay the blame on, lodge a complaint, make an accusation, prefer charges, prosecute, reprehend, reproach, reprobate, start an action, state a grievance, sue, take action
ASSOCIATED CONCEPTS: complain of a criminal act, complain of a tortious act

COMPLAIN (Criticize), ***verb*** accuse, admonish, animadvert, asperse, assail, be critical, be dissatisfied, berate, blame, carp, cast aspersions, castigate, cavil, censure, chastise, chide, condemn, *conqueri de rem,* contravene, decry, defy, denounce, deprecate, differ, disagree, disapprove, disparage, faultfind, find fault, find fault with, malign, object, object to, oppose, protest, rebuke, remonstrate, repine, reprehend, reprimand, reproach, reprove, speak ill of, take exception, take exception to, upbraid

COMPLAINANT, *noun* accusant, accuser, aggrieved party, challenger, charger, claimant, complaining party, delator, denouncer, impeacher, incriminator, indicter, indictor, libelant, litigant, one instigating an action, opposing party, party, party to a suit, petitioner, petitioner for legal redress, plaintiff, preferror of charges, prosecution, prosecutor, public prosecutor, relator, suitor
ASSOCIATED CONCEPTS: complainant's costs, complaining witness

COMPLAINT, *noun* accusal, accusation, allegation, bill of indictment, case, case for the prosecution, charge, citation, count, crimination, criticism, denouncement, denunciation, expostulation, first pleading, formal allegation, gravamen of a charge, grievance, incrimination, indictment, information, information against, litigation, main charge, objection, particular charge, petition, plaint, plaintiff's initiatory pleading, pleading in a civil action, preferment of charges, prosecution, protest, protestation, *querimonia,* remonstrance, statement of the plaintiff's cause, substance of a charge
ASSOCIATED CONCEPTS: bill of complaint, petition, cross complaint, verified complaint

COMPLEMENT, *noun* companion, *complementum,* completion, congener, coordinate, correlate, correspondent, corresponding part, counterpart, pendant, reciprocal, remainder, rest, supplement

COMPLETE (All-embracing), ***adjective*** absolute, all, all-comprehending, all-comprehensive, all-covering, all inclusive, all-pervading, all-sufficing, blanket, broad-based, capacious, comprehensive, consummate, developed, encyclopedic, entire, exhaustive, expansive, extensive, full, global, inclusive, of great scope, overall, plenary, sweeping, thorough, thoroughgoing, total, unconditional, undiminished, undivided, unimpaired, unqualified, unreduced, unreserved, unrestricted, unsevered, utter, very thorough, wide-embracing, with no exception, without omissions
ASSOCIATED CONCEPTS: complete abandonment, complete and adequate remedy at law, complete contract, complete coverage, complete delivery, complete jurisdiction, complete liquidation, complete ownership, complete record, complete relief, complete remedy, complete title, completed instrument

COMPLETE (Ended), ***adjective*** accomplished, achieved, at an end, brought to a conclusion, carried through, closed, completed, completive, concluded, conclusive, consummated, culminated, decided, definitive, disposed of, done, effected, effectuated, executed, final, finished, over, performed, realized, set at rest, settled, terminated, terminational, terminative, through

COMPLETE, verb accomplish, achieve, apply a closure, bring to a close, bring to an end, bring to conclusion, bring to maturity, bring to perfection, carry out, carry through, carry to completion, clinch, close, conclude, consummate, determine, discharge, dispatch, dispose of, draw to a close, end, finalize, finish, follow through, fulfill, perfect, polish, realize, seal, succeed, terminate, wind up
FOREIGN PHRASES: *Extincto subjecto, tollitur adjunctum.* When the substance is extinguished, the incident ceases.

COMPLETION, noun accomplishment, achievement, attainment, climax, close, commission, conclusion, consequence, consummation, course, crowning, culmination, denouement, discharge, dissolution, effectuation, end, ending, entirety, execution, expiration, extremity, fait accompli, finale, finality, finish, fulfillment, maturity, outcome, perfection, performance, realization, sequel, settlement, sufficiency, termination, terminus, transaction, windup
ASSOCIATED CONCEPTS: bankruptcy, completion of a trial, dissolution

COMPLEX, adjective abstruse, bewildering, chaotic, circuitous, complicated, confused, convoluted, difficult, elaborated, enigmatic, entangled, flexuous, impenetrable, implicated, inextricable, inscrutable, interlaced, interwoven, intricate, involuted, involutional, involved, irreducible, jumbled, kaleidoscopic, knotted, labyrinthine, mingled, muddled, *multiplex,* obscure, perplexing, recondite, sinuous, snarled, tangled, tortuous, unarranged, unclassified, undecipherable, unfathomable, unorganized, varied
ASSOCIATED CONCEPTS: complex issues to be tried

COMPLEX (Development), **noun** aggregate, aggregation, association, collectivity, compages, composite, compound, conglomerate, conglomeration, group, network, organization, structure, system, totality, unity
ASSOCIATED CONCEPTS: building complex, industrial complex, residential housing complex

COMPLEX (Entanglement), **noun** clutter, complexus, complication, confusion, convolution, derangement, difficulty, disarrangement, disarray, disorder, disorganization, enmeshment, imbroglio, intricacy, involution, involvement, jumble, labyrinth, maze, muddle, *multiplex,* snag, snarl, tangle, twist

COMPLEXION, noun apparent character, apparent state, appearance, aspect, carriage, character, *color,* contour, demeanor, display, disposition, external appearance, facet, fashion, favor, feature, figure, form, guise, image, impression, look, manifestation, manner, mien, nature, outline, outward appearance, port, posture, presence, quality, regard, respect, semblance, shape, slant, spirit, style, temper, tenor, tone, view, visage
ASSOCIATED CONCEPTS: complexion of the case

COMPLIANCE, noun accedence, acceptance, accommodation, accord, accordance, acquiescence, adaptability, adherence, agreeability, agreement, assent, bowing, compliancy, concession, concord, concurrence, conformability, conformance, conformity, consent, consonance, consonancy, cooperation, dutifulness, harmony, keeping, nonresistance, obedience, *obsequium,* observance, pliancy, submission, tractability, tractableness, willingness to comply, yielding, yieldingness

ASSOCIATED CONCEPTS: compliance with the law, in compliance with statute, strict compliance, substantial compliance
FOREIGN PHRASES: *Impotentia excusat legem.* The impossibility of performing a legal duty is an excuse from the performance. *Obedientia est legis essentia.* Obedience is the essence of the law.

COMPLIANT, adjective accepting, accommodating, acquiescent, agreeable, amenable, assenting, charitable, collaborative, concordant, concurring, conformable, conforming, consensual, consenting, docile, facile, favorable, indulgent, loyal, malleable, obedient, obeisant, obliging, obsequious, passive, patient, permissive, pliable, pliant, servile, submissive, toadying, tractable, uncomplaining, unreluctant, willing, yielding

COMPLICATE, verb aggravate, bedevil, befoul, confound, confuse, dislocate, disorganize, embroil, encumber, entangle, exacerbate, implicate, intensify, involve, jumble, knot, make intricate, make worse, mix up, muddle, obfuscate, obscure, perplex, perturb, snarl, tangle

COMPLICATION, noun aggravation, bafflement, barrier, complexity, complexness, complexus, complicated state, confusion, development, difficulty, dilemma, entanglement, hindrance, imbroglio, impediment, *implicatio,* incomprehensibility, inextricability, inscrutability, intricacy, intrigue, involution, involved state, involvement, labyrinth, obscurity, obstacle, obstruction, perplexity, predicament, puzzle, quandary, sinuosity, stumbling block, unforeseen circumstance

COMPLICITY, noun abetment, alliance, artifice, association, bad faith, collaboration, collusion, collusiveness, complexity, concert, concurrence, confederacy, connivance, conspiracy, contribution, contrivance, corruption, criminal participation, entanglement, guilt, implication, intricacy, intrigue, mutual assistance, league, plot, scheme
ASSOCIATED CONCEPTS: complicity to commit a crime

COMPLY, verb abide by, accede to, accept, accommodate, acknowledge, acquiesce in, adhere to, agree with, assent to, attend to orders, be faithful to, be willing, carry into effect, carry into execution, carry out, cease resistance, complete, *concedere,* concur, conform to, consent to, cooperate with, defer to, fall in with, fit, fulfill, give consent to, go along with, harmonize with, *morem gerere,* not resist, obey, observe, *parere,* perform, relent, resign oneself to, respect, satisfy, stoop, submit to, succumb, yield to
ASSOCIATED CONCEPTS: compliance with statutes

COMPONENT, noun aspect, basic substance, complement, component part, constituent, constituent part, content, division, element, elementary unit, factor, feature, fragment, fundamental part, ingredient, installment, integral part, item, material part, one of the contents, part, particular part, physical element, piece, portion, principle part, section, sector, segment, subdivision, unit, unit of composition
ASSOCIATED CONCEPTS: component parts

COMPORT (Agree with), **verb** accord with, attune, be accordant, be applicable, be apposite, be appropriate, be apt, be consistent, be consonant, be in accordance with, be in keeping, be in tune with, be suitable, become, befit, belong, chime in with, click, cohere, coincide, concur, conform, correspond, fall in with, fit, fit in, fit together, harmonize, jibe, match, mesh with, quadrate, reconcile, render accordant, square with, suit, tally

COMPORT *(Behave)*, *verb*   acquit, act, appear, conduct, demean, deport, discipline, manage, perform, present oneself, quit, represent, seem, show manner, show mien
ASSOCIATED CONCEPTS: demeanor of a witness

COMPOSE, *verb*   accomplish, achieve, actualize, arrange, author, be responsible, be the agent, be the cause of, be the reason, bring about, bring into being, bring into effect, bring into existence, build, call into being, call into existence, carry into execution, cause, cause to be, cause to exist, chalk out, compile, *componere*, conceive, construct, contrive, develop, devise, draft, draw out, draw up, effect, *efficere*, efform, engineer, envisage, execute, express, fashion, form, formulate, frame, generate, give rise to, imagine, improvise, invent, orchestrate, organize, originate, pattern, produce, shape, use one's imagination, visualize, work out, work up, write

COMPOSITE, *adjective*   accompanied, admixed, agglomerate, aggregate, aggregated, all-embracing, alloyed, amalgamated, amassed, assembled, assorted, blended, clustered, collected, collective, combined, commixed, complex, *compositus,* compound, compounded, conglomerate, conjoint, conjunct, conjunctive, connected, coupled, diversified, fused, gathered, gathered into a whole, glomerate, heterogeneous, incorporated, integrated, intermixed, joined, medley, miscellaneous, mixed, mosaic, motley, multifarious, multiple, *multiplex,* scrambled, sundry, united, unseparated, varied, variegated, wedded
ASSOCIATED CONCEPTS: composite class, composite facts, composite instrument, composite knowledge, composite statements

COMPOSITION *(Agreement in bankruptcy)*, *noun*   agreement, arrangement, clearance, compact, compromise agreement, contract, discharge, liquidation, mutual agreement, mutual concession, payment in lieu, reciprocal concession, release, settlement, settlement by mutual agreement, settlement on account
ASSOCIATED CONCEPTS: composition agreement, composition in bankruptcy, contract of composition, reorganization

COMPOSITION *(Makeup)*, *noun*   arrangement, array, combination, compilation, *compositio,* compounding, comprisal, concoction, conformation, constitution, construction, contents, creation, design, efformation, embodiment, establishment, fabrication, formation, formulation, inclusion, manufacture, nature, organization, preparation, production, structure, synthesis, union

COMPOSURE, *noun*   *aequus animus,* aplomb, balance, calm, calmness, command of one's faculties, command of temper, complacence, constraint, content, contentment, control, equability, equanimity, equilibrium, evenness, forbearance, fortitude, harmony, imperturbability, imperturbation, indisturbance, inexcitability, moderation, patience, peace, peace of mind, peacefulness, placidity, placidness, poise, presence of mind, quiescence, quietude, repose, reserve, rest, restraint, sedateness, self-assurance, self-command, self-possession, self-restraint, serenity, stability, tolerance, tranquil mind, *tranquillitas,* tranquillity

COMPOUND, *adjective*   aggregate, aggregated, amalgamated, assimilated, associated, blended, combined, commixed, complex, complicated, composite, *compositus,* conglomerate, congregated, conjoint, conjugate, conjunct, connected, convoluted, elaborate, embodied, entangled, fused, hybridized, incorporated, infused, inseparable,

integrated, interlaced, intermingled, interwoven, intricate, involved, manifold, merged, mingled, mixed, mosaic, motley, multifarious, multiform, multiple, *multiplex,* solid, tangled, tied, united, varied, variegated, woven
ASSOCIATED CONCEPTS: compound a crime, compound interest, compound larceny, compounding a felony
FOREIGN PHRASES: *Aestimatid praeteriti delicti ex postremo facto nunquam crescit.* The weight of an offense committed in the past is never increased by a subsequent fact.

COMPOUND, *verb*   accrue, add to, advance, aggrandize, aggravate, amount, *ampliare, amplificare,* annex, append, *augere,* be augmented, be numerous, become greater, become larger, branch out, build up, burgeon, contribute to, develop, *dilatare,* dilate, distend, elaborate, enhance, enlarge, enrich, exacerbate, exaggerate, exalt, expand, extend, fill in, fill out, fortify, further, gain ground, gain strength, get ahead, give strength to, glorify, greaten, grow larger, heighten, increase, increase the numbers, inflate, intensify, lend force to, lengthen, magnify, make greater, make larger, multiply, open out, parlay, pile up, prolong, protract, raise, refine, reinforce, restrengthen, spread out, strengthen, subjoin, superadd, supplement, widen
ASSOCIATED CONCEPTS: compounding a crime, compounding a debt, compounding a felony, compounding penalty
FOREIGN PHRASES: *Aestimatio praeteriti delicti ex postremo facto nunquam crescit.* The weight of a past crime is never increased by a subsequent fact.

COMPOUNDED, *adjective*   amalgamated, blended, coalesced, combined, complicated, composite, conglomerate, consolidated, convoluted, elaborate, entangled, fused, incorporated, inextricable, inseparable, integrated, intermingled, intricate, manifold, merged, mingled, mixed, mosaic, motley, multifarious, multiform, solidified, tangled, united, variegated
ASSOCIATED CONCEPTS: compounded crime, compounded larceny, compounded offenses

COMPREHEND *(Include)*, *verb*   be composed of, be comprised of, be made up of, circumscribe, compass, comprise, consist of, constitute, contain, cover, embody, embrace, encircle, encompass, envelop, incorporate, involve, possess, span, take in
ASSOCIATED CONCEPTS: comprehensive zoning

COMPREHEND *(Understand)*, *verb*   absorb, appreciate, apprehend, assimilate, be acquainted, be apprized, be aware, be cognizant, be conscious, be conversant with, be in possession of the facts, be informed, cognize, come to understand, *comprehendere,* conceive, descry, detect, discern, fathom, gain insight, grasp, grow aware, ken, know, master, perceive, realize, recognize, see, take in, understand fully
ASSOCIATED CONCEPTS: comprehend the nature and consequences of an act, intent, scienter

COMPREHENSIBLE, *adjective*   apprehensible, articulate, ascertainable, clear, clear-cut, cognizable, cognoscible, comprehendable, conceivable, decipherable, defined, disclosed, easily understood, easy to understand, evident, exoteric, explicable, explicit, express, fathomable, graphic, graphical, intelligible, knowable, legible, lucid, luculent, manifest, obvious, overt, palpable, patent, pellucid, penetrable, perceivable, perceptible, perspicuous, *perspicuus,* plain, realizable, recognizable, revealed, self-evident, self-explanatory, simple, unambiguous, unclouded, unconcealed, unconfused, understandable, unhidden, unmistakable, unobscure, unveiled

COMPREHENSION, noun ability to know, alertness, appreciation, apprehension, attentiveness, awareness, awareness of, capability, capacity to understand, cognition, cognizance, command of thought, *comprehensio,* conception, consciousness, discernment, enlightenment, erudition, expertise, familiarity, grasp, imagination, information, insight, intellect, intellectual power, intellectualism, intellectuality, *intellegentia,* intuition, keeness, knowledge, learning, mastery of thought, mental capacity, mental grasp, mentality, mind, mindfulness, observation, penetration, perception, perspicaciousness, power to grasp ideas, power to understand, rationality, reach of mind, realization, reason, recognition, sagacity, sageness, sense, understanding, wisdom

COMPREHENSIVE, adjective all-covering, all-embracing, all-inclusive, all-pervading, broad, capacious, compendious, complete, completive, comprising, consummate, containing, copious, discursive, encircling, encyclopedic, exhaustive, expansive, extended, extensive, far-reaching, full, fully realized, having no limit, inclusive, intensive, late patens, overall, panoramic, sweeping, synoptic, thorough, thoroughgoing, total, unconditional, unexclusive, universal, unmitigated, unqualified, unreserved, unrestricted, wide, wide-reaching, widespread
ASSOCIATED CONCEPTS: comprehensive coverage, comprehensive findings, comprehensive plan, comprehensive police power, comprehensive statute, comprehensive zoning

COMPREHENSIVENESS, noun blanket, breadth, capacity, comendiousness, completeness, complex, copiousness, coverage, ensemble, entireness, entirety, exhaustiveness, expansion, extensiveness, full realization, fullness, great scope, inclusiveness, integrality, integrity, omnibus, oneness, substantiality, thoroughness, totality, universality, voluminiousness, wholeness, width

COMPRISE, verb aggregate, amount to, be composed of, be formed of, be made of, consist of, constitute, contain, embody, embrace, encapsulate, encompass, hold, include, incorporate, involve, subsume, total
ASSOCIATED CONCEPTS: comprising a cause of action

COMPROMISE, noun abatement of differences, adaptation, adjustment, agreement, bargain, commutation, composition, concession, deal, happy medium, middle ground, mutual concession, negotiation, peacemaking, settlement, terms
ASSOCIATED CONCEPTS: accord and satisfaction, compromise a claim, compromise agreement, compromise and settlement, compromise of a claim, compromise verdict, discharge or release, novation, offer of compromise
FOREIGN PHRASES: Compromissum ad similitudinem judiciorum redigitur. A compromise is brought into affinity with judgments.

COMPROMISE *(Endanger),* **verb** bring into danger, expose to danger, hazard, imperil, jeopardize, make liable to danger, make vulnerable, place in a dubious position, put at hazard, put in jeopardy, put under suspicion, risk, stake, venture

COMPROMISE *(Settle by mutual agreement),* **verb** accommodate, adjust, agree, arrange by mutual concession, bargain, come to an agreement, come to an understanding, come to terms, *compromittere,* concede, conciliate, find a middle ground, harmonize, maintain a middle position, make a compromise, make a deal, make an adjustment, make concessions, mediate, meet halfway, negotiate, reconcile, settle, settle differences, strike a balance

ASSOCIATED CONCEPTS: accord and satisfaction, compromise a claim, compromise agreement, compromise verdict, discharge, discontinuance, negotiation, novation, offer of compromise, quotient verdict, settlement, substitute contract

COMPTROLLER, noun accountant, auditor, banker, bookkeeper, bookkeeping expert, bursar, business manager, cashier, chartered accountant, chief accounting officer, depositary, examiner of business accounts, financial officer, inspector of accounts, inventory expert, manager, purser, reckoner, registrar, supervisor of accounts, treasurer, trustee
ASSOCIATED CONCEPTS: city comptroller, state comptroller

COMPULSION *(Coercion),* **noun** application of force, constraint, constraint to obedience, constriction, demand, dictation, domination, duress, duty, employment of force, enforcement, force, forcible inducement, forcible urging, forcing, high pressure methods, imposition, impressment, limitation, *necessitas,* necessity, objective necessity, obligation, oppression, physical force, pressure, requirement, restraint, restriction, spur of necessity, stress, subjection to force, urgency, urging by force, urging by moral constraint, urging by physical constraint, *vis*
ASSOCIATED CONCEPTS: compulsion of law, compulsory act, compulsory contributions, compulsory demand, compulsory liquidation, compulsory nonsuit, compulsory payment, compulsory process, compulsory sale

COMPULSION *(Obsession),* **noun** ardor, besetting idea, craze, drive, earnestness, enchantment, engrossment, enthusiasm, fanaticism, fancy, fascination, fervency, fetish, fixation, fixed conviction, fixed idea, infatuation, intentness, irresistible impulse, mania, need, one-track mind, possession, predilection, preoccupation, prepossession, quirk, zeal

COMPULSORY, adjective against one's will, authoritative, binding, coactive, coercive, commanded, compelling, constraining, decretive, demanded, enforced, exigent, forced, forcible, imperative, incumbent upon, indefeasible, indispensable, inescapable, irresistible, irrevocable, mandatory, necessary, obligatory, peremptory, prerequisite, prescriptive, pressing, required, requisite, restraining, restrictive, stringent, unable to be evaded, unavoidable, unpreventable, urgent, vital, without choice
ASSOCIATED CONCEPTS: compulsory arbitration, compulsory counterclaim, compulsory education, compulsory insurance, compulsory joinder of parties, compulsory performance of duties, compulsory testimony

COMPURGATION, noun absolution, acquittal, acquittance, alibi, benefit of doubt, clearance, defeat of the prosecution, defense, dismissal, exculpation, excuse, exoneration, favorable verdict to the defendant, innocence, just cause, justification, legal defense, liberation, nonprosecution, pardon, reprieve, verdict of not guilty, vindication, withdrawal of the charge

COMPUTATION, noun account, accountancy, accounting, adding, amount computed, appraisal, appreciation, assessment, audit, bookkeeping, calculation, count, counting, deduction, enumeration, estimate, estimation, evaluation, figure work, figuring, measurement, numeration, reckoning, score, statistic, sum, summation, tally, total, valuation

CONATUS, noun attempt, choice, conation, conative will, desire, determination, direction, disposition, drift, endeavor, fancy, inclination, intention, leaning, mind, natural impulse, natural tendency, nisus, option, penchant, predilection, predisposition, preference, proclivity, proneness, propensity, temperament, tendency, trend, trial, unprompted will, volition, voluntariness, voluntary activity, want, will, wish

CONCEAL, verb camouflage, cloak, confine, cover, cover up, curtain, disguise, eclipse, enshroud, entomb, envelop, harbor, hide, keep clandestine, keep from, keep out of sight, keep secret, keep to oneself, keep underground, make inconspicuous, make indiscernible, make unapparent, make unperceptible, mask, not reveal, obscure, *occulere*, protect, render invisible, screen, seclude, secrete, shade, shadow, shield, shroud, store, suppress, throw a veil over, veil, withdraw from observation, withold, withold information
ASSOCIATED CONCEPTS: conceal assets, conceal information, conceal material facts
FOREIGN PHRASES: *Fraus est celare fraudem.* It is fraud to conceal a fraud.

CONCEALED (*Confidential*), **adjective** abstruse, clandestine, cloaked, covert, cryptic, delitescent, disguised, evasive, furtive, impalpable, latent, lurking, obscure, private, privy, recondite, secret, secreted, shrouded, stealthy, surreptitious, ulterior, unbeknown, undisclosed, unheard, unknown, unrecognized, unsaid, unspoken, untold, veiled
ASSOCIATED CONCEPTS: concealed weapon, concealment of a crime

CONCEALED (*Covered*), **adjective** blanketed, buried, camouflaged, disguised, hidden, imperceptible, inconspicuous, invisible, masked, screened, sheltered, unapparent, unexposed, unperceived, unseen
ASSOCIATED CONCEPTS: concealed weapon

CONCEALMENT, noun camouflage, confinement, cover, deceitfulness, disappearance, disguise, disguisement, duplicity, evasion, furtiveness, hiding, incognito, inconspicuousness, invisibility, nonappearance, obfuscation, obscurity, obsuration, privacy, seclusion, secrecy, secretion, secretiveness, silence, stealthiness, subterfuge, suppression, suppression of the truth
ASSOCIATED CONCEPTS: concealment of assets, concealment of information, concealment of material fact, concealment voiding an insurance policy, concealment with intent to defraud creditors, evasive contempt
FOREIGN PHRASES: *Aliud est celare, aliud tacere.* To conceal is one thing; to be silent is another. *Suppressio veri, suggestio falsi.* The suppression of truth is equivalent to the suggestion of what is false.

CONCEDE, verb abide by, accede, accept, acknowledge, acquiesce, affirm, agree, agree in principle, allow, arrive at an agreement, assent, be persuaded, come to terms, comply with, *concedere*, consent, endorse, endure, give in, grant, impart, permit, *permittere*, profess, recognize, respect, sanction, settle, submit, submit to, succumb, tolerate, withdraw one's objections, yield
ASSOCIATED CONCEPTS: conceded facts
FOREIGN PHRASES: *Qui concedit aliquid, concedere videtur et id sine quo concessio est irrita, sine quo res ipsa esse non potuit.* He who concedes anything is considered as conceding that without which his concession would be idle, without which the thing itself is worthless.

CONCEIVE (*Comprehend*), **verb** absorb, accept, appreciate, apprehend, assimilate, conceptualize, conjure up, digest, discern, envisage, envision, fathom, figure out, form

a conception, grasp, have an idea, ideate, image, imagine, know, perceive, picture, realize, see, understand, visualize

CONCEIVE (*Invent*), **verb** begin, bring into being, bring into existence, coin, compose, *concipere*, concoct, con-trive, create, design, develop, devise, draft, dream up, excogitate, fabricate, formulate, frame, generate, give birth to, hatch, inchoate, initiate, innovate, make up, originate, plan, prepare, start
ASSOCIATED CONCEPTS: conceive a criminal plan

CONCENTRATE (*Consolidate*), **verb** accumulate, agglomerate, aggregate, amass, assemble, bring into a small compass, bring toward a central point, center, centralize, cluster, coalesce, collect, combine, compact, compress, concenter, condense, congest, conglomerate, congregate, conjoin, *conligere*, constrict, *contrahere*, converge, crowd together, densify, focalize, focus, gather, make firm, make solid, mass, strengthen, unite

CONCENTRATE (*Pay attention*), **verb** *animum attendere*, apply the mind, attend, attend minutely, be engrossed in, consider closely, contemplate, direct the mind upon, examine closely, fix one's attention, focus, focus attention on, give attention to, give heed, hearken, listen, meditate, muse, occupy the mind with, occupy the thoughts with, peruse carefully, ponder, put one's mind to, regard carefully, ruminate, scrutinize, study deeply, think intensely

CONCENTRATION (*Centralization*), **noun** agglomeration, aggregation, assemblage, collection, combination, compilation, confluence, contemplation, cumulation, density, horde, immersion

CONCENTRATION (*Compression*), **noun** absorption, accumulation, agglomeration, amassment, cluster, coagulation, compactness, conflux, congestion, conglomeration, consolidation, convergence, densification, intensification, mass, multitude, press, solidification, throng

CONCENTRATION (*Emphasis*), **noun** application, condensation, deepening, devotion, focus, heightening, intensification, interest, observation, regard, strength, strengthening

CONCEPT, noun abstract idea, abstraction, appraisal, appreciation, apprehension, assessment, assumption, belief, conception, conclusion, conjecture, consideration, deduction, doctrine, estimate, evaluation, fancy, feeling, formative notion, guess, idea, image, impression, intellectualization, judgment, knowledge, mental image, mental impression, mental representation, notion, observation, opinion, percept, perception, persuasion, picture, point of view, postulate, presumption, reflection, representation, supposition, surmise, tenet, theory, thought, understanding, view, visualization
ASSOCIATED CONCEPTS: legal concept

CONCEPTION (*Beginning*), **noun** concept, design, idea, ingenuity, invention, notion, original plan, origination, plan, thought

CONCEPTION (*Insemination*), **noun** beginning of life, fecundation, fecundity, fertilization, impregnation, inception of pregnancy, pregnancy, superimpregnation

CONCERN (*Business establishment*), **noun** business, company, corporation, establishment, firm, house, institution, organization
ASSOCIATED CONCEPTS: partnership, proprietorship

CONCERN

CONCERN *(Interest)*, **noun** anxiety, attention, care, concernment, consequence, consideration, disquietude, importance, regard, solicitude, *sollicitudo*, uneasiness, worry

CONCERN *(Care)*, **verb** administer to, attend, attend to, be mindful, be vigilant, be watchful, check, consider, *curare*, devote oneself to, direct the attention to, examine intently, foster, give attention, give one's attention, keep, look after, mind, minister to, pay attention to, regard, respect, safeguard, take care of, take into consideration, take note of, tend, watch

CONCERN *(Involve)*, **verb** absorb, affect, appertain to, apply, *attinere*, be a factor, be applicable to, be interdependent with, be involved, be one of, be pertinent to, be related to, be relevant, deal with, embody, embrace, enclasp, entail, have a bearing on, have a connection, have a reference, have a relation, have interrelationship with, immerse, influence, interest, pertain to, *pertinere*, refer to, regard, relate to, respect, stand in relation, *versari in re*
ASSOCIATED CONCEPTS: concerned in interest, concerning a matter of law, general state concern, local concern

CONCERT, **noun** accord, accordance, agreement, alliance, coaction, coadjument, coadjuvancy, coagency, coalition, coefficiency, collaboration, combination, combined action, combined effort, compatibility, complicity, concord, concordance, concurrence, concurrency, confederation, conjunction, consentaneity, consonance, cooperation, fusion of interests, harmony, joint action, joint operation, merger, mutual assistance, pool, rapport, synergy, teamwork, unanimity, unison, unity
ASSOCIATED CONCEPTS: acting in concert

CONCERTED, *adjective* abetting, accordant, agreed, agreeing, aiding and abetting, aligned, amalgamated, assenting, blended, bonded, coacting, coactive, coadjutant, coadjuvant, coalescent, coeval, coexistent, coexisting, cohesive, coincident, coinciding, collaborating, colluding, combined, combining, commixed, composite, concordant, concurrent, concurring, conformable, conforming, congruent, congruous, conjoined, conjoint, conjunct, connective, conniving, consensual, consentaneous, consentient, consenting, consistent with, consolidated, consonant, contributing, converging, cooperating, cooperative, corresponding, coworking, fused, harmonious, harmonized, in accord, in accordance with, in agreement, in alliance, in unison, interactive, joined, joint, merging, mutually agreed, parallel, simultaneous, sympathetic, synergic, united, uniting

CONCESSION *(Authorization)*, **noun** allowance, authority, authorization, bestowal, clearance, *concessio*, conferment, conferral, endowment, giving, grant, impartment, leave, license, permission, permit, presentation, privilege, sanction, vouchsafement, warrant

CONCESSION *(Compromise)*, **noun** acceptance, accord, acknowledgment, acquiescence, admission, admitting, agreement, allowance, assent, capitulation, concurrence, giving in, grant, granting, recognition, recognizance, reconciliation, relinquishment, settlement, submission, surrender, yielding

CONCILIATION, **noun** abatement of differences, accommodation, accord, accordance, adaptability, adjustment, agreement, appeasement, arrangement, bipartisanship, compact, compliance, compromise, concert, concession, *conciliatio*, concord, concurrence, conformability, conformity, consonance, cooperation, entente, harmony, league, mediation, mutual accord, mutual agreement, mutual concession, mutual understanding, negotiation, pacification, peacemaking, placation, propitiation, reconcilement, reconciliation, reunion, satisfaction, settlement, settlement of differences, solidarity, submission, truce, unanimity, understanding, uniformity, union, unity
ASSOCIATED CONCEPTS: conciliation in a marriage

CONCILIATORY, *adjective* accommodative, agreeable, amiable, atoning, bland, civil, compassionate, compatible, concordant, cordial, courteous, deferential, expiatory, forgiving, friendly, gracious, harmonious, magnanimous, mediatory, nonmilitant, obeisant, pacific, pacifying, peacemaking, penitent, persuasive, placable, polite, propitiating, propitiatory, reconcilable, reconciliatory, reconciling, respectful, unresentful

CONCISE, *adjective* abbreviated, abridged, abstracted, brief, capsule, capsulized, compact, compacted, compendious, compressed, condensed, contracted, curtailed, curtate, epigrammatic, epitomized, laconic, pithy, short, shortened, succinct, summarized, summary, synoptic, to the point, trenchant

CONCLUDE *(Complete)*, **verb** abort, adjourn, break off, bring to a close, bring to an end, bring to rest, carry to completion, cease, climax, close, *conficere*, consummate, culminate, discharge, discontinue, dispose of, end, execute, exhaust, finalize, *finire*, finish, fulfill, halt, make an end of, make complete, maturate, prosecute to a conclusion, render complete, seal, set at rest, settle, shut down, stop, surcease, terminate
ASSOCIATED CONCEPTS: conclude a hearing, conclude a trial

CONCLUDE *(Decide)*, **verb** choose, come to a determination, concludere, *conligere*, decide upon, declare, decree, decree by judicial authority, deduce, deem, deliver judgment, determine, end by a decision, find, form a judgment, form a resolution, form an opinion, give a ruling, give an opinion, give judgment, hold, infer, judge, make a decision, make a resolution, make terms, make up one's mind, pass judgment, pronounce a judgment, resolve, rule, seal, settle, settle in one's mind, settle upon, take a decisive step
ASSOCIATED CONCEPTS: conclusion of guilt, findings

CONCLUDED, *adjective* abandoned, all over, ceased, closed, completed, conclusive, consummated, crowned, culminated, decided, determinative, discharged, discontinued, dispatched, done, ended, expired, final, finished, fulfilled, halted, lapsed, last, matured, perfected, settled, terminated, through, ultimate

CONCLUSION *(Determination)*, **noun** adjudication, arbitrament, ascertainment, assessment, authoritative opinion, *conclusio*, consideration, decision, declaration, decree, deduction, derived principle, discernment, estimation, evaluation, final judgment, finding, inference, judgment, observation, opinion, persuasion, pronouncement, realization, reasoned judgment, report, resolution, resolve, result, result ascertained, result of judicial inquest, ruling, settling, solution, surmise, valuation, verdict, view
ASSOCIATED CONCEPTS: conclusion as to intent, conclusion as to motive, conclusion of a trial, conclusion of guilt, conclusion of innocence, conclusion of law, conclusion of mixed law and fact

CONCLUSION *(Outcome)*, **noun** cessation, close, closure, completeness, completion, *conclusio*, consequence, consequent, consummation, culmination, denouement, effect, effectuation, end, end product, end result, ending, eventuality, final result, finale, finalty, *finis,* finish, fulfillment, last stage, outcome, outgrowth, product, repercussion, result, resultance, resultant action, termination, upshot

FOREIGN PHRASES: *Ab abusu ad usum non valet consequentia.* A conclusion as to the use of a thing from its abuse is invalid. *Inclusio unius est exclusio alterius.* The inclusion of one is the exclusion of another. *In propria causa nemo judex.* No one can be judge in his own cause. *Negatio conclusionis est error in lege.* The denial of a conclusion is in error in law.

CONCLUSIVE *(Determinative),* **adjective** absolute, apparent, ascertained, assured, categorical, certain, conspicuous, definite, demonstrated, evident, final, guaranteed, immutable, incommutable, incontestable, incontrovertible, indefeasible, indisputable, indubitable, infallible, irrefragable, irrefutable, irrepealable, irrevocable, mandatory, obligatory, positive, tested, tried, ultimate, unambiguous, unchallengeable, unchangeable, uncontested, undeniable, undoubted, unequivocal, unimpeachable, unmistakable, unquestionable

ASSOCIATED CONCEPTS: conclusive admission, conclusive beyond a reasonable doubt, conclusive evidence, conclusive judgment, conclusive presumption, conclusive presumption of validity, conclusive proof

CONCLUSIVE *(Settled),* **adjective** ascertained, beyond dispute, *certus,* clear, closing, complete, completed, completing, completive, conclusory, confirming, culminating, decided, decisive, definitive, determining, evidential, extreme, final, finished, finishing, terminal, terminative, ultimate

ASSOCIATED CONCEPTS: conclusive adjudification, conclusive as to the facts

CONCOMITANT, *adjective* accompanying, aligned, allied, associated, attendant, attending, coincident, complemental, concurrent, conjoint, conjunctional, conjunctive, contemporaneous, contemporary, correlative, correspondent, corresponding, coupled, joint, parallel, simultaneous, synergic

FOREIGN PHRASES: *Principia data sequuntur concomitantia.* Given principles are followed by their concomitants.

CONCORDANCE, *noun* accord, accordance, agreement, amity, assent, coaction, coincidence, common assent, communion, compact, concert, concord, concurrence, concurrence in opinions, conformance, conformity, congeniality, congruence, congruency, conjunction, consensus, consent, consentaneity, consentaneousness, consistency, consonance, cooperation, correspondence, fraternity, friendship, harmony, likemindedness, neighborliness, oneness, peace, rapport, sympathy, understanding, unity

CONCORDANT, *adjective* accommodative, accordant, agreeable, agreeing, aligned, allied, assenting, assentive, at one, banded together, blending, bonded, cemented, coexistent, coexisting, coinciding, combinative, compatible, complementary, compliant, *concors,* concurrent, concurring, conformable, conforming, congruent, congruous, conjoined, conjunctional, consensual, consentaneous, consenting, consistent, consonant, coordinate, correlated, correlative, correspondent, corresponding, fusing, harmonious, in accord, in agreement, in concert, in conjunction, in harmony, in rapport, in unison, joint, merged, merging, mutual, of the same mind, reconcilable, sympathetic, unanimous, uniform, united, uniting

CONCRESCENCE, *noun* adherance, amalgamating, blending, coalescence, combining, consolidation, fusion, making one, mingling, mixing, symphysis, uniting

CONCRETE, *adjective* bodily, certain, cognizable, definite, demonstrable, determinate, distinct, embodied, existent, existing, explicit, firm, material, palpable, particular, perceptible, physical, real, solid, solidified, *solidus,* specific, substantial, substantive, tangible

ASSOCIATED CONCEPTS: concrete cause of action, concrete idea, concrete interest

CONCUR *(Agree),* **verb** accede to, accept, accord, accredit, acknowledge, acquiesce, act in concert, affirm, allow, approbate, approve, assent to, band together, come to an agreement, come to an understanding, come to terms, come together, comply, condone, conform with, consent, cooperate, countenance, defer to, echo, endorse, favor, give credit, go along with, harmonize, hold with, homologate, jibe, join forces, join in, join together, join with, league together, meet, operate jointly, ratify, sanction, say yes, second, side with, signify assent, subscribe to, suit, support, sustain, sympathize with, unite efforts, unite with, uphold, work jointly, yield

ASSOCIATED CONCEPTS: concurring opinion

CONCUR *(Coexist),* **verb** accompany, be concomittant, be contemporaneous, be contemporary, be parallel, coincide, exist together, happen at the same time, happen simultaneously, happen together, keep pace with, occur at the same time, occur concurrently

ASSOCIATED CONCEPTS: concurrent acts, concurrent causes, concurrent conditions, concurrent contracts, concurrent covenants, concurrent jurisdiction, concurrent negligence, concurrent power, concurrent sentences, consecutive sentences

CONCURRENT *(At the same time),* **adjective** accompanying, associated, at the same instant, attendant, attending, coacting, coactive, coetaneous, coeval, coexistent, coexisting, coincident, coinstantaneous, collateral, concerted, concomitant, conjunctive, contemporaneous, contemporary, convergent, converging, coupled, occurring at the same time, parallel, synchronal, synchronistic, synchronistical, synchronous

ASSOCIATED CONCEPTS: concurrent actions, concurrent findings, concurrent legislation, concurrent remedies, concurrent sentences, concurrent stipulations

CONCURRENT *(United),* **adjective** abetting, accordant, acquiescent, acting in conjunction, agreeing, aiding, allied, amalgamated, assenting, associating, assonant, banded together, binding, blended, bonded, cemented, centralized, coacting, coactive, coalitional, cohesive, collaborative, combinative, combined, common, communal, commutual, compatible, complementary, concerted, concordant, concurring, confederated, conforming, conjoined, connected, consentaneous, consolidated, consonant, contributing, cooperative, coupled, coworking, *en rapport,* fused, harmonizing, in accord, in agreement, in unison, interallied, joined, joint, leagued, linked, meeting, merged, of one accord, paired, participating, shared, synergic, undivided, unified, united, wedded, well-matched

CONCURRENT CAUSE, *noun* a second legal basis, accompanying legal basis, additional legal basis, another legal basis, another legal basis in concert, coexistent legal basis, coexisting legal basis, coincident legal basis, coinstantaneous legal basis, concomitant legal basis, contemporaneous legal basis

CONDEMN *(Ban)*, **verb** abhor, abnegate, abrogate, banish, bar, blackball, block, boycott, call a halt, cancel, cast aside, cast out, censor, check, counter, debar, deny, deprive, disallow, disapprove, discommode, discountenance, disfavor, disown, disqualify, embargo, enjoin, exclude, excommunicate, expel, forbid, forestall, frustrate, halt, hamper, impede, interdict, interrupt, keep in bounds, keep out, keep within bounds, lay an embargo on, limit, make impossible, object, obstruct, oppose, ostracize, outlaw, preclude, prevent, prohibit, proscribe, put a stop to, put an embargo on, put an end to, put one's veto to, put under an injunction, put under an interdiction, put under prohibition, quash, quell, refuse, reject, repress, reprobate, restrain, restrict, restrict access, retard, seclude, shut out, stop, suppress, thwart, *vetare*, withhold

CONDEMN *(Blame)*, **verb** accuse, anathematize, animadvert, asperse, assail with censure, attack, berate, bring into discredit, call to account, cast blame upon, castigate, charge, chide, *condemnare*, criticize, *culpare*, declaim against, decry, denigrate, denounce, deprecate, derogate, disapprove, discountenance, disdain, disparage, dispraise, execrate, find guilty, fulminate against, impeach, implicate, impugn, incriminate, indict, inveigh against, pass censure on, publicly accuse, rebuke, reprehend, reproach, reprove, repudiate, revile, take to task, upbraid, vilify, *vituperare*, vituperate

CONDEMN *(Punish)*, **verb** adjudge, administer correction, bring to account, carry out a sentence, convict, *damnare*, deal retributive justice, discipline, doom, exact a penalty, exact retribution, execute a sentence, execute justice, impose a penalty, impose penalty, inflict penalty, inflict punishment, pass sentence on, penalize, prescribe punishment, pronounce judgment, pronounce sentence, *punire*, reprimand, reprove, sentence, subject to penalty, take disciplinary action

CONDEMN *(Seize)*, **verb** accroach, acquire, appropriate, arrogate, assume, assume ownership, attach, compulsorily acquire, confiscate, declare to be forfeited, deprive of corporal possession, deprive of ownership, disentitle, dispossess, disseise, distrain, divest of property, expropriate, foreclose, impound, impropriate, municipalize, nationalize, *publicare*, sequestrate, take for public use, take over, take possession, usurp
ASSOCIATED CONCEPTS: eminent domain

CONDEMNATION *(Blame)*, **noun** accusation, animadversion, ascription, attack, castigation, censure, charge, chastening, chastisement, chiding, complaint, *condemnatio*, criticism, denigration, denunciation, deprecation, derogation, disapprobation, disapproval, discountenance, discredit, disdain, disfavor, disparagement, dispraise, execration, expostulation, impeachment, implication, imputation, incrimination, inculpation, invective, objection, objurgation, opposition, rebuke, recrimination, reprehension, reprimand, reproach, reprobation, reproof, repudiation, stricture, vilification, vituperation

CONDEMNATION *(Punishment)*, **noun** conviction, disciplinary action, exaction of penalty, execration, finding of guilty, guilty verdict, infliction, judgment, justice, penalization, penalty, punishing experience, punishment, punition, retribution, retributive justice, sentence

CONDEMNATION *(Seizure)*, **noun** abrogation, acquisition by right of eminent domain, appropriation, arrogation, assumption, commandeering, compulsory acquisition, confiscation, deprivation, dispossession, distraint, distress, divestment, expropriation, forced sale, forcible seizure, foreclosure, impounding, impropriation, municipalization, nationalization, prehension, takeover, taking of property for public use, taking possession
ASSOCIATED CONCEPTS: condemnation of land for public use, condemnation proceedings, reverse condemnation, title by condemnation

CONDENSE, **verb** abbreviate, abridge, abstract, capsulize, compress, consolidate, contract, curtail, cut short, detruncate, digest, epitomize, foreshorten, make brief, make concise, make denser, make terse, outline, precis, reduce, render more compact, shorten, shrink, summarize, sum up, synopsize, truncate

CONDESCEND *(Deign)*, **verb** accommodate oneself, accord, be courteous, be gracious, descend, *descendere*, disregard prestige, grant, humble oneself, lower oneself, sacrifice pride, *se submittere*, stoop, tolerate, unbend, vouchsafe, waive privilege, yield

CONDESCEND *(Patronize)*, **verb** assume a patronizing air, be contemptuous, be overbearing, belittle, care nothing for, consider beneath notice, contemn, disdain, disparage, disrespect, hold in contempt, hold in disrespect, look down on, look with scorn upon, spurn, talk down to

CONDIGN, **adjective** appropriate, befitting, *debitus*, deserved, due, earned, fit, fitting, just, justified, merited, *meritus*, right, suitable, warranted, well-deserved, well-earned, worthy

CONDITION *(Contingent provision)*, **noun** article, clause, *condicio*, contractual terms, desideratum, essential provision, exception, final terms, limitation, obligation, pact, postulate, postulation, prerequirement, prerequisite, prescription, presumption, presupposition, promise, provision, proviso, qualification, regulation, requirement, requisite, reservation, restriction, rule, ruling, specification, stated term, stipulation, supposal, supposition, term, ultimatum, uncertain event
ASSOCIATED CONCEPTS: cause, condition implied in law, condition of employment, condition precedent, condition running with the land, condition subsequent, conditions and exceptions, conditions and restrictions, express condition, implied condition, sale on condition, terms and conditions, warranties
FOREIGN PHRASES: *Ea quae dari impossibilia sunt, vel quae in rerum natura non sunt, pro non adjectis habentur.* Those things which can not be given, or which are not in the nature of things, are regarded as not included in the agreement. *Conditiones quaelibet odiosae; maxime autem contra matrimonium et commercium.* Any conditions are odious, but especially those which are in restraint of marriage and commerce. *Proviso est providere praesentia et futura, non praeterita.* A proviso is to provide for the present and the future, not the past. *Conditio illicita habetur pro non adjecta.* An unlawful condition is deemed not to be annexed. *Conditio praecedens adimpleri debet prius quam sequatur effectus.* A condition precedent must be fulfilled before the effect can follow. *Conditio dicitur, cum quid in casum incertum qui potest tendere ad esse aut non esse, confertur.* It is called a "condition", when something is given on an uncertain event, which may or may not come into existence. *Conditio beneficialis, quae statum construit, benigne secundum verborum intentionem est interpretanda; odiosa autem. quaestatum destruit, stricte secundum berborum proprietatem accipienda.* A beneficial condition, which creates an estate, ought to be interpreted favorably, according to the intention of the

words; but a condition which destroys an estate is odious, and ought to be construed strictly according to the letter.

CONDITION (State), **noun**   appearance, aspect, character, circumstance, complexion, *condicio*, crasis, grade, habitude, look, plight, position, posture, predicament, quality, rank, shape, situation, state of being, station, *status*, temperament, tenor
ASSOCIATED CONCEPTS: dangerous condition, emergency condition, financial condition, good operating condition, physical condition

CONDITIONAL, **adjective**   alterable, changeable, conditioned, containing stipulations, contingent on, dependent on, depending on, depending on a future event, determined by, equivocal, granted on certain terms, hypothetical, imposing a condition, indefinite, indeterminable, indeterminate, liable to, limitative, limited, modified by conditions, negotiable, not absolute, not certain, not sure, pending, possible, provisional, provisionary, provisory, qualified, regulated by, restricted, specified, stipulative, subject to, subject to chance, subject to change, subject to terms, suspenseful, tentative, unassured, uncertain, undecided, under the control of, undetermined, unpositive, unpredictable, unsettled, unsure
ASSOCIATED CONCEPTS: conditional acceptance, conditional agreement, conditional bequest, conditional bill of sale, conditional bond, conditional charge, conditional consent, conditional contract, conditional conveyance, conditional delivery, conditional devise, conditional endorsement, conditional estate, conditional execution, conditional fee, conditional gift, conditional guaranties, conditional judgment, conditional lease, conditional legacy, conditional liability, conditional limitation, conditional obligations, conditional pardon, conditional payment, conditional promise, conditional release, conditional revocation of a will, conditional rights, conditional sale, conditional sales act, conditional sales contract, conditional subscription, conditional will

CONDONATION, noun   absolution, accommodation, acquittal, allowance, amnesty, cancellation, charity, clearance, clemency, compassion, conciliation, concord, discharge, dismissal, disposition to pardon, disregard, excusal, exemption, exoneration, expiation, extenuation, extrication, forgiveness, full pardon, grace, impunity, indemnity, indulgence, lenience, magnanimity, mercy, nonliability, overlooking, pardon, reconcilement, reprieve, sympathy, vindication, willingness to forgive
ASSOCIATED CONCEPTS: condonation as grounds for a dissolution of a marriage

CONDONE, verb   absolve, accept, allow, assoil, be lenient, be merciful, be reconciled, be tolerant, bear with, blot out, clear, countenance, dismiss, disregard, excuse, exempt, exonerate, forbear, forget, forgive, free, give a reprieve, give absolution, give amnesty, grant amnesty, grant immunity, let pass, make allowance, overlook, overlook an offense, palliate, pardon, pass over, permit, recommend to pardon, refrain from punishing, release, relent, remit, reprieve, set free, show mercy, spare, tolerate, vindicate, waive punishment, yield

CONDUCE, verb   abet, advance, aid, assist, augment, bring about, bring on, cause, *conducere*, contribute toward, cooperate, effect, encourage, expedite, favor, foment, foster, incline to, increase the chances, influence, lead to, make probable, predispose to, promote, put ahead, put forward, tend to, work toward

CONDUCT, noun   actions, acts, address, air, aspect, attitude, bearing, behavior, behavior pattern, breeding, carriage, code, compliance, comportment, conformance, correctness, course of behavior, dealings, decorum, deeds, demeanor, deportment, established practice, ethics, etiquette, fashion, guise, habits, management, manner, manners, method, mien, mode of action, mode of behavior, morals, operation, performance, personal bearing, port, posture, practice, presence, procedure, propriety, public manners, role, seemliness, social behavior, social graces, style, way, way of acting, ways, wise
ASSOCIATED CONCEPTS: coercive conduct, course of conduct, disorderly conduct, good conduct, immoral conduct, improper conduct, inequitable conduct, justifiable conduct, reasonable conduct, standard of conduct, unprofessional conduct

CONDUCT, verb   administer, *administrare*, administrate, assume responsibility, carry on, carry out, command, control, deal with, direct, direct affairs, discharge, dispatch, do, enact, execute, *gerere*, guide, handle, have control, lead, look after, manage, officiate at, operate, oversee, *perducere*, pilot, preside over, proceed with, regulate, run, superintend, supervise, take care of, take charge of, transact, usher
ASSOCIATED CONCEPTS: conduct a business, conduct a sale, conducted for profit, conducting business
FOREIGN PHRASES: *Melius est recurrere quam malo currere.* It is better to recede than to proceed in error.

CONDUIT (Channel), **noun**   agency, artery, avenue, contrivance, course, device, instrument, machinery, manner, means, medium, method, mode, path, process, route, way
ASSOCIATED CONCEPTS: intermediary and accomplice to a crime

CONDUIT (Intermediary), **noun**   advocate, agent, delegate, deputy, emissary, envoy, functionary, go-between, intermedium, mediary, mediator, medium, middleman, negotiator, proxy, representative, substitute, surrogate

CONFEDERACY (Compact), **noun**   affiliation, alignment, alliance, association, body, cartel, coalition, combination, combine, concurrence, confederation, confraternity, consolidation, coterie, federation, fellowship, *foedus*, fusion, guild, league, *pactum*, set, *societas*, society, solidarity, syndicate, trust, unification, union

CONFEDERACY (Conspiracy), **noun**   cabal, collusion, complicity, complot, *coniuratio*, connivance, criminal agreement, illegal agreement, illegal compact, intrigue, plot, schemery, treasonable alliance

CONFEDERATE, noun   abettor, accessory, accomplice, adjunct, adjutant, adjuvant, aid, aider, ally, assistant, associate, auxiliary, coactor, coadjutant, coadjutor, collaborator, colleague, colluder, comate, companion, comrade, confidant, confrere, consociate, conspirator, conspirer, cooperator, coworker, fellow, friend, helper, helpmate, intrigant, participator, partner, support, supporter

CONFER (Consult), **verb**   advise, compare opinions, confide in, consult with, *consultare*, counsel, deliberate, discuss, exchange observations, exhort, give advice, hold a conference, hold a consultation, interchange views, negotiate, palaver, parley, refer, seek advice, take counsel, talk over
ASSOCIATED CONCEPTS: confer with a client, confer with an associate

CONFER *(Give),* **verb** accord, adjudge, administer, award, bestow, cede, *conferre,* convey, deliver, dispense, endow, give, grant, hand down, impart, invest, issue, pass down, present, relinquish, tender, transfer, transmit, yield
ASSOCIATED CONCEPTS: confer authority, confer jurisdiction, conferred powers

CONFERENCE, *noun* assembly, colloquy, conclave, confabulation, consultation, consultation meeting, convention, conversations, convocation, deliberation, dialogue, discussion, exchange, forum, gathering, interchange of opinions, interlocution, meeting, negotiation, negotiations, palaver, parlance, parley, premeditation, seminar, symposium, talks

CONFESS, *verb* acknowledge, acknowledge one's guilt, admit, admit guilt, bare, come forth, compurgate, concede, *confiteri,* declare, disburden one's conscience, disclose, divulge, expose, *fateri,* give evidence, inculpate, lay open, make a confession, make solemn affirmation, own up, purge oneself, reveal, tell all, turn state's evidence, utter, yield
ASSOCIATED CONCEPTS: confess guilt, confess judgment, confess participation
FOREIGN PHRASES: *Qui tacet non utique fatetur, sed tamen verum est eum non negare.* He who is silent does not confess, but it is nevertheless true that he does not deny.

CONFESSION, *noun* acknowledgment, acknowledgment of guilt, acquiescence, admission, admission of fault, admission of guilt, assertion, avowal of guilt, confirmation, declaration, disclosure, disclosure of fault, divulgement, divulgence, exclamation, exomologesis, incriminating statement, inculpatory statement, pronouncement, purgation, revealment, self-accusation, self-condemnation, statement, utterance
ASSOCIATED CONCEPTS: confessed judgment, confession and avoidance, confession of error, extrajudicial confessions, implied confession, involuntary confession, judgment by confession, judicial confession, voluntary confession, written confession
FOREIGN PHRASES: *Confessus in judicio pro judicato habetur, et quodammodo sua sententia damnatur.* A person confessing his guilt in court is deemed to have been found guilty, and is, in a manner, condemned by his own sentence. *Cum confitente sponte mitius est agendum.* One making a voluntary confession is to be dealt with more leniently.

CONFIDE *(Divulge),* **verb** disclose, disclose something secret, discuss private affairs, divulgate, entrust with private information, let know, make known, reveal something private, share secrets, tell a secret, tell with assurance of secrecy, trust to keep secret

CONFIDE *(Trust),* **verb** believe in, commit, consign, deliver to the care of, entrust, feel sure of, give in trust, have confidence in, have faith in, hold responsible for, place reliance on, put faith in, put in care of, rely on, rely upon
ASSOCIATED CONCEPTS: attorney-client privilege, confidential creditor, confidential informant, confidential relation, fiduciary relationship, husband-wife privilege, physician-patient privilege, priest-penitant privilege, privileged against self-incrimination, privileged communications

CONFIDENCE *(Faith),* **noun** affiance, aplomb, assurance, boldness, certainty, certitude, cocksureness, confidentness, conviction, courage, credence, credulity, fearlessness, *fides, fiducia,* firm belief, heart, intrepidity, morale, nerve, optimism, poise, positiveness, reliance, sanguineness, security, sureness, surety, trust
FOREIGN PHRASES: *Multa fidem promissa levant.* Many promises lessen confidence. *Fides servanda est.* Good faith must be observed.

CONFIDENCE *(Relation of trust),* **noun** assurance of secrecy, classified communication, concealment, confidential communication, confidential matter, intimacy, personal matter, privacy, private, private affair, privileged communication, secrecy, secret, secret communication
ASSOCIATED CONCEPTS: attorney-client confidence, confidential communications, husband-wife confidence, physician-patient confidence, priest-penitent confidence

CONFIDENTIAL, *adjective* arcane, *arcanus,* auricular, classified, concealed, *fidus,* hidden, imparted in secret, irrevealable, not for publication, not to be communicated, not to be disclosed, not to be quoted, not to be spoken of, off the record, private, restricted, secret, spoken in confidence, told in confidence, top-secret, undercover, unmentionable, unrevealed
ASSOCIATED CONCEPTS: confidential communication, confidential information, confidential proceeding, confidential relationship, fiduciary relationship, privilege

CONFIDENTIAL COMMUNICATION, *noun* acquired facts which cannot be revealed, acquired knowledge which cannot be revealed, compilations which cannot be revealed, concealed documents, knowledge of facts which cannot be revealed, knowledge which cannot be revealed, learning which cannot be revealed, not for publication, not to be communicated, not to be disclosed, not to be quoted, not to be spoken about, private, privileged communication, protected communication, restricted, secret, spoken in confidence, told in confidence, top-secret
ASSOCIATED CONCEPTS: attorney-privileged, doctor-patient, priest-penitent, spousal immunity

CONFIDENTIALITY, *noun* classified, concealed, hidden, not for publication, not to be communicated, not to be disclosed, not to be quoted, not to be spoken of, privacy, private, protected, restricted, revealed in confidence, secrecy, secret, spoken in confidence, told in confidence, top-secret, unmentionable, unrevealed
ASSOCIATED CONCEPTS: affirmative defense, need to know principle, nondisclosure agreement, secrecy

CONFIGURATION *(Confines),* **noun** borders, boundary, bounds, circumscription, contour, delineation, dimensions, edges, extent, framework, frontiers, limitations, limits, line of demarcation, outline, perimeter

CONFIGURATION *(Form),* **noun** anatomy, appearance, arrangement, body, cast, character, composition, conformation, constitution, construction, contour, design, external form, features, figuration, figure, format, formation, frame, framework, *galbe,* layout, lines, look, makeup, outline, outward form, pattern, physique, profile, rough outline, scheme of arrangement, shape, silhouette, skeleton, structural composition, structural design, structure

CONFINE, *verb* arrest, barricade, bind, bound, cage, capture, circumscribe, *coercere, cohibere,* commit, commit to prison, constrain, contain, control, detain, enchain, enclose, enthrall, fence in, harness, hold, hold as a hostage, hold back, hold captive, hold in captivity, hold in check, hold in thrall, hold prisoner, immure, impound, imprison, incarcerate, *includere,* institutionalize, intern, jail, keep in custody, keep under control, keep within bounds, limit, lock up, pen in, place in durance, place under protective custody, put into isolation, put under arrest, put under restraint, quarantine, recommit, remand, repress, restrain, restrict, restrict access, seclude, send to jail, shut in, subdue, subjugate, suppress, take into custody, take prisoner, trammel

ASSOCIATED CONCEPTS: actual confinement, confine to an asylum, confinement to a jail, false imprisonment, kidnapping, solitary confinement

CONFINES, noun borders, boundaries, boundary lines, bounds, compound, confinements, curbs, curtilages, division lines, edges, enclosures, ends, environs, extents, extremities, fringes, limitations, limits, lines of demarcation, metes, outer edges, outlines, perimeter, precincts, restraints, skirts

ASSOCIATED CONCEPTS: within the confines of the law

CONFIRM, verb accede, accord, accredit, acknowledge, acquiesce, add strength to, adhere, agree to, agree with, ally, approve, assent, attest, authenticate, authorize, avow, charter, commend, *comprobare,* concede, concur, consent, corroborate, countersign, document, endorse, establish, fortify, give one's word for, give security, guarantee, homologate, join in a compact, legalize, license, make firm, make valid, pass, permit, prove, ratify, recognize, *sancire,* sanction, seal, second, support, sustain, uphold, validate, verify, vote for, vouch for

FOREIGN PHRASES: *Confirmare nemo potest prius quam jus ei acciderit.* No one can confirm a right before it accrues to him. *Confirmare est id firmum facere quod prius infirmum fuit.* To confirm is to make firm that which had been infirm. *Confirmat usum qui tollit abusum.* He confirms a use who removes an abuse.

CONFIRMATION, noun acceptance, accord, accordance, acknowledgment, acquiescence, admission, affidavit, affirmance, affirmation, approval, assent, assertion, assurance, attestation, authentication, authorization, averment, avouchment, certification, corroboration, corroborative statement, declaration, deposition, documentation, endorsement, legal pledge, oath, proof, ratification, sanction, seal, solemn averment, solemn avowal, solemn declaration, stamp of approval, subscription, substantiation, support, swearing, validation, verification, *visé,* warrant

ASSOCIATED CONCEPTS: confirmation of judgment, confirmation of sale

FOREIGN PHRASES: *Non valet confirmatio, nisi ille, qui confirmat, sit in possessione rei vel juris unde fieri debet confirmatio; et eodem modo, misi ille cui confirmatio fit sit in possessione.* Confirmation is not valid unless he who confirms is either in possession of the thing itself or of the right of which confirmation is to be made, and, in like manner, unless he to whom confirmation is made is in possession. *Confirmatio est nulla ubi donum praecedens est invalidum.* Confirmation is a nullity where the preceding gift is invalid. *Confirmatio omnes supplet defectus, licet id quod actum est ab initio non valuit.* Confirmation supplies all defects, though that which had been done was not valid at the beginning.

CONFISCATE, verb adeem, annex, appropriate, appropriate to public use, assume, attach, cause to be forfeited, compulsorily acquire, condemn, condemn to public use, deprive, deprive of, disentitle, disinherit, dispossess, disseise, distrain, divest, expropriate, foreclose, forfeit, impound, impress,

levy, *publicare,* seize, seize and appropriate, seize as forfeited to the public treasury, seize by authority, sequester, sequestrate, take away from, take over, take possession of, take summarily, wrench away from, wrest away from, wring away from

ASSOCIATED CONCEPTS: condemn, eminent domain, exercise the right of

CONFISCATORY, adjective acquisitive, appropriating, attaching, capturing, commandeering, conquering, deprivative, depriving, disseizing, distraining, divesting, exacting, expropriatory, extortionary, foreclosing, forfeiting, garnishing, impounding, rapacious, requisitory, seizing, sequestrating, taking, usurpatory

ASSOCIATED CONCEPTS: confiscatory orders, confiscatory rates

CONFLAGRATION, noun blaze, bonfire, deflagration, destructive fire, devastation, devouring element, fire, general fire, *ignis,* incendiarism, *incendium,* sheet of flame, wall of flame, wholesale destruction, wildfire

CONFLICT, noun adverseness, affray, altercation, animosity, antagonism, antipathy, argument, argumentation, battle, belligerency, breach, challenge, clash, clash of arms, collision, combat, competition, conflict of opinion, contention, contentiousness, contest, contradiction, contraposition, contrariety, contrariness, contrast, contravention, controversy, corrivalry, counteraction, debate, defiance, difference, disaccord, disagreement, disapprobation, discord, discordance, discrepancy, disharmony, dislike, dispute, disputed point, dissensio, dissension, dissent, dissidence, dissonance, disunion, disunity, divergence, divergent opinions, division, embroilment, encounter, engagement, enmity, faction, failure to agree, fight, fighting, firm opposition, friction, hatred, hostilities, hostility, incompatibility, incongruence, incongruity, inconsistency, infringement, inharmoniousness, inimicality, interference, irreconcilability, mismatch, misunderstanding, opposing causes, opposition, oppugnancy, polarity, quarrel, quarreling, question at issue, rencounter, renitency, resistance, rivalry, subject of dispute, tension, turmoil, unharmoniousness, variance, want of harmony, wrangle

ASSOCIATED CONCEPTS: center of gravity theory, conflict of interest, conflict of laws, conflicting clauses, conflicting evidence, conflicting findings, conflicting jurisdiction, conflicting provisions, irreconcilable conflict

CONFLICT, verb ablude, argue, be at cross purposes, be at variance, be contrary, be different, be discordant, be inconsistent, be inharmonious, be opposed, be opposed to, be unwilling, change, clash, collide, combat, come into collision, contend, contest, contradict, contrast, controvert, counteract, cross, debate, defy, depart from, deviate, differ, differ in opinion, disaccord, disagree, disapprove, *discrepare,* dislike, dispute, dissent, *dissentire,* divaricate, diverge from, go contrary to, go in opposition to, have differences, hinder, hold opposite views, interfere with, not abide, not accept, not conform, not have any part of, object, oppose, play at cross purposes, protest, quarrel, refute, *repugnare,* resist, revolt, rival, run against, run at cross purposes, run counter to, run in opposition to, schismatize, set oneself against, strike back, strive against, struggle, take exception, vary, wrangle

ASSOCIATED CONCEPTS: conflicting claim, conflicting clauses, conflicting evidence, conflicting findings, conflicting interests, conflicting jurisdiction, conflicting provisions

CONFLICT OF INTEREST, noun conflict, divergent interests between clients, ethical breach, prohibiting acceptance or retention of a case, variance of interest between clients

109

CONFORM

ASSOCIATED CONCEPTS: code of professional responsibility, disqualification

CONFORM, verb abide by, accede, accept, acclimatize, accommodate, accord, adapt, adhere to, adjust, agree, align, approve, arrive at terms, assimilate, attend to instructions, attune, be at one with, be in harmony, be in keeping, be regulated by, become like, become similar, bend, come round, comply, concede, concur, conventionalize, coordinate, correlate, correspond, equalize, fall in, fall into line, fit, fit in, follow, follow precedent, follow routine, go along with, join the majority, keep to, liken, make uniform, match, measure up to, obey, obey orders, obey regulations, obey rules, observe, observe discipline, *obtemperare*, reconcile, render accordant, side with, stand together, standardize, submit, suit, support, synchronize, systematize, tailor, yield, yield assent
ASSOCIATED CONCEPTS: conformed copies, conformed to the law

CONFORMITY (Agreement), **noun** accommodation, accord, accordance, acquiescence, adjustment, affinity, agreement, alliance, assent, coincidence, collaboration, combined operation, compatibility, concert, concinnity, concord, concurrence, concurrent opinion, conformance, conformation, congeniality, congruence, congruency, congruity, conjunction, consensus, consent, consonance, *convenientia*, convention, cooperation, correspondence, harmony, joint effort, joint planning, league, likeness, oneness, similarity, uniformity, union
ASSOCIATED CONCEPTS: conformity in pleadings

CONFORMITY (Obedience), **noun** adherence, assimilation, association, close observance, compliance, conformance, conformation, consent, consistency, conventionality, dutifulness, faithfulness, fidelity, full observance, obeisance, observance, submission, submissiveness, subordination, willingness, yielding

CONFOUND, verb abash, astonish, astound, baffle, be uncertain, becloud, bewilder, bring into disorder, complicate, *confundere*, confuse, dumbfound, embrangle, embroil, entangle, involve, make havoc, mingle confusedly, mislead, muddle, mystify, nonplus, obfuscate, obscure, ob-*stupefacere, per miscere*, perplex, put into disorder, puzzle, scramble, throw into confusion

CONFRONT (Encounter), **verb** accost, brave, breast, come across, come face to face with, come in contact, face, meet, stand facing, stand opposite

CONFRONT (Oppose), **verb** act in opposition to, argue against, assail, be against, be at cross-purposes, be opposite, challenge, come in conflict with, contend against, contend with, contradict, contrapose, contrast with, contravene, controvert, count against, counteract, counterattack, counterwork, cross, defy, deny, disagree with, disapprove, dispute, engage in conflict with, go against, mark against, match against, meet in conflict, object, offer resistance, oppugn, protest, put in opposition, rebuff, recalcitrate, repel, resist, rise against, rival, run counter, run counter to, *se opponere*, set oneself against, skirmish, stand firm, stem, strike back, struggle, take exception to, turn against, wrangle, wrestle with
ASSOCIATED CONCEPTS: right of cross-examination, right to confront witnesses

CONFRONTATION (Act of setting face to face), **noun** act of facing, approach, audience, colloquy, coming together, conference, consultation, dialogue, discussion, encounter, engagement, interview, meeting, parley, rencounter
ASSOCIATED CONCEPTS: right of confrontation, right of cross-examination, right to confront witnesses

CONFRONTATION (Altercation), **noun** affray, argument, battle, bout, brawl, brush, clash, collision, combat, conflict, confrontment, contention, contestation, disagreement, discord, dispute, engagement, fight, fracas, fray, hostile contest, hostile encounter, *mêlée*, opposition, opposure, quarrel, rencounter, row, scuffle, skirmish, squabble, struggle, velitation, wrangle

CONFUSE (Bewilder), **verb** abash, addle, astonish, baffle, befog, befuddle, bemuddle, confound, *confundere*, daze, discompose, disconcert, distract, embarrass, flurry, fluster, fog, jumble, mislead, mix up, muddle, mystify, nonplus, obfuscate, *permiscere*, perplex, *perturbare*, puzzle, rattle, render uncertain, stump, stupefy, throw into confusion, unhinge, unsettle

CONFUSE (Create disorder), **verb** clutter, derange, disarrange, disarray, disorder, disorganize, displace, disturb, embroil, entangle, intermingle, jumble, mess, mess up, mingle, mix up, muddle, snarl, throw into confusion, throw into disorder, unsettle
ASSOCIATED CONCEPTS: mistake, mistake of fact, mistake of law

CONFUSION (Ambiguity), **noun** agitation, amorphousness, astonishment, brouhaha, complex, complexity, complication, confusion, congestion, convulsion, disarrangement, disarray, discomposure, dislocation, disorganization, distraction, doubt, enigma, ferment, fog, fracas, fuzziness, haze, hodgepodge, imbroglio, intricacy, involution, jumble, labyrinth, maze, melee, mix-up, opacity, panic, paraphrenia, patchwork, perplexity, rumpus, scramble, skein, stupefaction, to-do, tumult, turbulence, uncertainty, uproar, vagueness
ASSOCIATED CONCEPTS: confusion of goods, confusion of issues, confusion of rights

CONFUSION (Commotion), **noun** chaos, dilemma, disorder, disturbance, embroilment, entanglement, havoc, imbroglio, irregularity, medley, muddle, pandemonium, shambles, snarl, tangle, turmoil

CONFUSION (Consternation), **noun** befuddlement, chagrin, confoundment, disconcertion, disorientation, distress, fear, fluster, fright, mortification, mystification, perturbation, quandary, suffusion, trepidation

CONFUSION (Turmoil), **noun** anarchy, chaos, clamor, clutter, commotion, complexity, *confusio*, congestion, demoralization, difficulty, disarrangement, disarray, discord, disorder, disorderliness, disorganization, disquiet, disquietude, distraction, disturbance, entanglement, farrago, ferment, frenzy, havoc, imbroglio, inseparable intermixture, muddle, pandemonium, *perturbatio*, rampage, shapelessness, tumult, turbulence, unrest, unsettlement, upheaval, uproar

CONFUTATION, noun abjurement, challenge, condemnation, contradiction, contrariety, contrary assertion, contravention, countercharge, counterevidence, counterstatement, disavowal, disproof, effective rejoinder, evidence against, evidence on the other side, negation, plea in rebuttal, rebuttal, rebutter, redargution, refutation, rejoinder, renunciation, reply, repudiation, retort, surrejoinder

CONFUTE, *verb*   answer, argue, challenge, confound, contradict, contravene, controvert, counter, counteract, countercharge, countervail, debate, defeat, demolish, deny, disagree, disavow, disown, disprove, dispute, dissent, fight, gainsay, impeach, impugn, invalidate, negate, oppose, parry, quash, quibble, rebut, refute, reply, repudiate, retort, riposte, set aside, squelch, subvert, upset, vanquish
ASSOCIATED CONCEPTS: confute a witness' testimony

CONGEALMENT, *noun*   act of hardening, coagulation, cohesion, compactness, concreteness, concretion, condensation, congelation, consistence, consolidation, crystallization, gelatinization, gelling, hardness, impenetrability, impermeability, incompressibility, indivisibility, jellification, petrification, precipitation, solidification, solidity, solidness, thickening, thickness

CONGLOMERATE, *adjective*   accumulated, agglomerate, aggregate, amalgamated, amassed, assembled, blended, brought together, collected, collectivized, combined, complex, composite, compound, compounded, congregate, congregated, cumulated, gathered into a round mass, glomerate, indiscriminate, inseparable, mass, mingled, miscellaneous, mixed, united, varied

CONGLOMERATION, *noun*   accumulation, agglomeration, aggregate, aggregation, amassment, array, assembly, assortment, collection, compilation, consolidation, cumulation, forgathering, glomeration, group, ingathering, lot, mass, miscellany, multitude, quantity

CONGREGATE, *verb*   accumulate, aggregate, aggroup, amass, assemble, bring together, bring together in a crowd, bunch, cluster, collect, collect into a focus, come in contact, come together, compile, concentrate, conglomerate, *congregari,* convene, converge, convocate, crowd together, gather, get together, group, herd together, ingather, join, mass, meet, meet in a body, rally, receive, throng, unite
ASSOCIATED CONCEPTS: breach of the peace, congregate in a public place

CONGREGATION, *noun*   aggregate, aggregation, amassment, assemblage, assembly, assembly of persons, association, audience, batch, *coetus,* collection, conclave, conference, congregated body, convention, *conventus,* convergence, convocation, crowd, forgathering, gathering, getting together, horde, ingathering, mass, mass meeting, meeting, multitude, reunion, session

CONGRESS, *noun*   advisory body, assemblage, assembly, consultive body, council, governmental body, legislative body, legislature, political body

CONGRUENCE, *noun*   accord, accordance, acquiescence, adjustment, affinity, agreement, coherence, coincidence, common feature, compatibility, compliance, concert, concordance, conformance, conformity, congeniality, congruity, consensus, consistency, correspondence, harmony, identification, likeness, oneness with, parallelism, relevance, resemblance, similarity, understanding, uniformity, unison, unity

CONGRUOUS, *adjective*   accordant, acquiescent, adapted, agreeable, agreed, akin, analogical, analogous, applicable, apposite, appropriate, assenting, coexistent, coexisting, coincident, coinciding, combining, commendable, commensurate, compatible, concordant, concurrent, conformable, conforming, congruent, consensual, consentaneous, consentient, consistent with, consonant, consubstantial, correlative,

correspondent, corresponding, equal, equivalent, fit, fitting, germane, harmonious, harmonized, identified with, in accord, in accordance with, in harmony with, in point, in rapport, in unison with, like, matching, near, parallel, proportional, proportionate, reconcilable, relevant, representative, representing, resembling, similar, similative, suiting, synchronized, synchronous, synonymous

CONJECTURAL, *adjective*   abstract, allusive, apparent, assumed, circumstantial, debatable, disputable, doubtful, hypothetical, ideal, imagined, impractical, notional, postulated, presumptive, propositional, putative, referential, reputed, speculative, speculatory, suppositional, suppositive, surmised, theoretical, uncertain, undetermined, unsettled
ASSOCIATED CONCEPTS: conjecture as an objection to a witness' testimony

CONJECTURE, *noun*   assumption, belief, guess, guesswork, hypothesis, imputation, inference, opinion, postulate, postulation, presumption, presupposition, presurmise, speculation, supposal, supposition, surmise, suspicion, theory, thesis, unverified supposition
FOREIGN PHRASES: *In claris non est locus conjecturis.* In matters which are obvious there is no room for conjecture.

CONJOIN, *verb*   accumulate, add, add to, ally, amass, annex, assemble, attach, be joined, blend, bring together, cement, clap together, clasp together, coalesce, cohere, collect, combine, compound, connect, consolidate, entwine, fuse, gather, hold together, incorporate, interlace, interlock, intertwist, interweave, join together, make one, mass, merge, mix, reunite, unify, unite
ASSOCIATED CONCEPTS: conjoint legacy, conjoint robbery, conjoint wills

CONJOINT, *adjective*   affiliated, affixed, agreed, allied, amalgamated, assimilated, associated, attached, banded together, blended, bound together, cemented, coalescent, coalitional, cohesive, collective, combined, common, commutual, compact, compatible, composite, concerted, concomitant, concurrent, confederate, confederated, congruent, conjunct, conjunctive, connected, consolidated, corporate, coupled, coworking, *en rapport,* fastened together, federated, federative, fused, in alliance, in common, in conjunction, in league, incorporated, indivisible, inseparable, integrated, interclasped, interdependent, interfused, intermixed, joined, joined together, joint, leagued, linked, locked, merged, mixed, paired, partnered, pieced together, pooled, reciprocally attached, spliced, tied together, together, unified, united, wedded, welded
ASSOCIATED CONCEPTS: conjoint legacy, conjoint robbery, conjoint wills

CONJUGAL, *adjective*   betrothed, bridal, cojugate, coniugalis, connubial, coupled, espoused, marital, married, matched, mated, matrimonial, nuptial, paired, partnered, united, wedded
ASSOCIATED CONCEPTS: conjugal rights

CONJUNCT, *adjective*   allied, amalgamated, associated, binding, coadunate, coalescent, coherent, cohesive, combined, complex, composite, concerted, conjoint, connected, consensual, consolidated, contiguous, cooperative, correlative, incorporated, indissoluble, indivisible, inextricile, inseparable, integrated, joined, joint, matched, merged, paired, partnered, participant, symbiotic, unified, united

ASSOCIATED CONCEPTS: conjunctive denials, conjunctive obligations, conjunctive of averments, conjunctive relief
FOREIGN PHRASES: *Conjunctim et divisim.* Jointly and severally

CONJUNCTION, *noun* adjacency, agreement, alliance, association, compliance, concatenation, concert, concomitance, concord, concurrence, concurrent opinion, conformity, conjoining, connection, cooperation, harmony, joint effort, junction, network, union, united action

CONJURE, *verb* call to mind, conceive, conceptualize, contemplate, create, devise, dream up, envisage, *excogitare,* excogitate, fabricate, fancy, *fingere,* form an image, formulate, frame, give play to the imagination, have a vision, imagine, improvise, invent, *machinari,* make up, nurture, originate, perceive, produce, realize, represent to oneself, think of, think up, visualize
ASSOCIATED CONCEPTS: conjure up a cause of action

CONJURE UP, *verb* call to mind, conceive, create, devise, dream, envisage, envision, evoke, excogitate, fancy, ideate, imagine, invent, invoke, objectify, occur, picture, recall, recollect, remember, summon, summon up, visualize

CONNECT *(Join together),* *verb* *adligare,* amalgamate, annex, append, assemble, attach, band, band together, bind, blend, bridge, bring in contact with, cement, coalesce, cohere, combine, conjoin, *connectere,* consolidate, couple, entwine, fasten together, fuse, gather, graft, harness together, hook, hyphenate, interlink, interlock, intertwine, interweave, *iungere,* join, knit, lace, league, link together, lock, marry, match, meet, merge, pair, partner, put together, solder, subjoin, tie, touch, unite, verge on, wed

CONNECT *(Relate),* *verb* affiliate, ally, appertain to, associate, bracket, bridge, cohere, consociate, correlate, draw a parallel, group, integrate, interconnect, interrelate, link together, make relevant, match, pertain to, relate, show a relationship, show affinity, show as cognate, show as kindred, show relation, show resemblance, show similarity, span
ASSOCIATED CONCEPTS: connect the suspect to the crime

CONNECTED, *(Affiliated),* *adjective* affinitive, allied, amalgamated, apposite, appurtenant, attached, bracketed, coadunate, cognate, coherent, communicating, compact, confederate, congenerous, congenial, conjoint, connatural, consanguineous, consecutive, consolidated, contiguous, continual, continuous, corporate, coupled, federate, germane, homogenous, inseparable, joined, kindred, knit, leagued, related, spliced, unbroken, undivided, united
ASSOCIATED CONCEPTS: connected causes of action, connected counterclaims, connected subjects contained in a bill

CONNECTED *(Apropos),* *adjective* akin, applicable, appropriate, associated, collateral, combined, consonant, continued, correlative, linked, pertinent, relevant, uninterrupted

CONNECTION *(Abutment),* *noun* abuttal, border, contact, contiguousness, junction, juxtaposition, nearness, tangency, union

CONNECTION *(Fastening),* *noun* attachment, binder, bond, bridge, catch, catenation, cohesion, combination, concatenation, conjunction, consolidation, copula, couple, fastener, hitch, holdfast, interconnection, joiner, joint, junction, juncture, knot, liaison, ligature, link, linkage, nexus, splice, tie, unifier, union

CONNECTION *(Relation),* *noun* affiliation, alliance, analogy, applicability, application, association, bearing, coalition, coherence, coherency, common denominator, common reference, consanguinity, consociation, correlation, identification, interrelation, kinship, league, liaison, linkage, match, parallel, pertinence, propinquity, rapport, reference, relatedness, relationship, relevance, tie
ASSOCIATED CONCEPTS: connection between a suspect and a crime

CONNIVANCE, *noun* act of maneuvering, act of scheming, alliance, association, chicanery, coagency, coincidence, collaboration, collusion, combined operation, complicity, complot, concert, concord, concurrence, concurrent opinion, confederacy, conjunction, conspiracy, contrivance, cooperation, corrupt agreement, corrupt collusion, corrupt consent, corrupt consenting, corrupt cooperation, implied assent, *indulgentia,* intrigue, joint effort, joint planning, junction, league, liaison, machination, manipulation, participation, plot, scheme, secret approval, underhand participation, underhanded complicity, underplot, voluntary oversight, working together
ASSOCIATED CONCEPTS: connivance as a defense to a divorce

CONNIVE, *verb* act in concert, be a party to, be in collusion with, collude, combine, complot, concert, conspire, cooperate, cooperate with secretly, countermine, counterplot, engineer, *in re connivere,* intrigue, join forces, join with, machinate, make an agreement with, maneuver, participate, participate surreptitiously, plot, *rem dissimulare,* scheme

CONNOTATION, *noun* allusion, application, bearing, broad meaning, coloring, comprehension, construction, context, denotation, derivation, drift, essence, essential meaning, expression, force, general meaning, gist, hint, idea, impact, implication, import, inference, information, innuendo, insinuation, intent, intention, interpretation, literal interpretation, literal meaning, literal sense, literality, meaning, natural meaning, object, obvious interpretation, obvious meaning, obvious sense, original meaning, plain meaning, point of, primary meaning, purport, range of meaning, real interpretation, real meaning, real sense, reference, scope, secondary implied meaning, sense, significance, signification, simple meaning, source, spirit, substance, substantial meaning, suggestion, symbolization, tenor, true meaning, unstrained meaning, worth

CONNOTE, *verb* allude to, carry a suggestion, communicate, convey, denote, designate, evidence, express, give indirect information, hint, imply, indicate, infer, insinuate, intimate, involve, make indirect suggestion, mean, point to, refer to, represent, signify, speak of, stand for, suggest, symbolize, tell of, touch on

CONSANGUINEOUS, *adjective* affiliated, agnate, akin, allied, ancestral, blood related, closely allied, closely related, cognate, collateral, congenerous, connatural, consanguine, distantly related, family related, fraternal, hereditary, intimately related, kindred, maternal, matrilineal, nearly allied, nearly related, of the blood, of the same family, of the same kind, paternal, patriarchal, patrilinear, related, relative
ASSOCIATED CONCEPTS: lineal consanguinity

CONSCIENCE, *noun* categorical imperative, code of duty, code of honor, compunction, *conscientia,* conscientiousness, ethical judgment, ethical philosophy, ethical self, ethics, high ideals, high standards, honesty, honor, ideals, inner voice, integrity, inward monitor, mind, moral consciousness, moral faculty, moral obligation, moral principles, moral sense, principle, probity, professional ethics, rectitude, scruples, sense of duty, sense of moral right, sense of right and wrong, standards, superego, uprightness

ASSOCIATED CONCEPTS: conscientious objector

FOREIGN PHRASES: *Fides est obligatio conscientiae alicujus ad intentionem alterius.* A trust is an obligation of conscience of one to the will of another. *Judex habere debet duos sales—sales, salem sapientiae, ne sit insipidus; et salem conscientiae, ne sit diabolus.* A judge ought to have two salts-the salt of wisdom, lest he be insipid; and the salt of conscience, lest he be devilish. *La conscience est la plus changeante des regles.* Conscience is the most changeable of rules.

CONSCIENTIOUS, *adjective*   assiduous, attentive, careful, diligent, duteous, dutiful, exacting, faithful, fastidious, heedful, honest, honorable, incorruptible, just, meritorious, meticulous, minute, moral, observant, painstaking, particular, precise, principled, punctilious, regardful, reliable, *religiosus,* reputable, righteous, *sanctus,* scrupulous, strict, thorough, trustworthy, trusty, uncorrupt, upright, virtuous

CONSCIOUS *(Awake), adjective*   able to recognize, active, acute, alert, alive, animate, astir, breathing, endowed with life, enlivened, existent, existing, extant, imbued with life, in existence, inspirited, live, living, mortal, vivified

CONSCIOUS *(Aware), adjective*   acquainted with, apperceptive, appreciative, apprehending, apprised, attentive, cognizant, comprehending, *conscius,* discerning, heedful, informed, knowing, mindful, observant, perceptive, percipient, rational, regardful, sensible, sentient, undeceived, understanding, vigilant, watchful

ASSOCIATED CONCEPTS: conscious act, conscious disregard for others, conscious indifference, conscious reaction

CONSECUTIVE, *adjective*   chronological, coming after, connected, consequent, *continens,* continual, continuing, continuous, cumulative, ensuing, following in a series, in a line, in a row, in order, in regular order, in sequence, in turn, in unbroken sequence, in uninterrupted succession, nonstop, one after another, one after the other, perennial, recurrent, repeated, repetitive, running, sequent, sequential, serial, serialized, seriate, seriatim, steady, subsequent, succeeding, successive, unbroken, uninterrupted, uninterrupted in course, unremitting

ASSOCIATED CONCEPTS: consecutive sentences

CONSENSUAL, *adjective*   accordant, acquiesced in, acquiescent, agreeable, agreed upon, approving, assented, at one with, attuned to, carried, coherent, coincident with, collaborating, compatible, compliant, conceded, concomitant, concordant, concurred in, concurrent, confirming, conforming to, congruent, conjunct, consentaneous, consentient, consistent with, cooperative, endorsed, granted, harmonious, harmonized, in agreement, in alliance, joint, like-minded, mutually agreeable, mutually understood, of one accord, of one mind, of the same mind, parallel, popularly believed, reconciled, sympathetic, synergic, unanimous, unchallenged, uncontested, uncontradicted, uncontroversial, uncontroverted, understood, undisputed, united, unopposed, unquestioned, voted

CONSENSUS, *noun*   acclamation, accord, acknowledgment, affirmance, affirmation, agreement, assonance, attonement, bipartisanship, common consent, compact, compatibility, concent, concentus, concert, concinnity, concord,

concordance, concurrence, conformance, conformation, conformity, congruence, consentaneity, consentaneousness, consentience, consistency, consonance, cooperation, correspondence, general agreement, harmony, mutual agreement, mutual sympathy, mutual understanding, reconcilement, solid vote, synchronization, unanimity, uniformity, union, unison

ASSOCIATED CONCEPTS: consensus of opinion, per curiam opinion

CONSENT, *noun*   accedence, acceptance, accord, acknowledgment, acquiescence, admission, adoption, affirmance, affirmation, agreement, allowance, approbation, approval, assent, assurance, authentication, authority, authorization, certification, commendation, compliance, concession, concord, concordance, concurrence, confirmation, *consensus,* corroboration, countenance, empowering, endorsement, entitlement, grace, grant, guarantee, harmony, indulgence, leave, legalization, license, permission, permit, ratification, sanction, stipulation, subscription, sufferance, support, tolerance, toleration, unison, unity, validation, verification, vouchsafement, warrant, warranty, willingness

ASSOCIATED CONCEPTS: consent decree, consent in writing, consent judgment, consent of adoptive parents, consent of owner, consent of parties, consent to a taking, consent to an act, consent to search, express consent, implied consent, legal consent, limited consent, mutual consent, parental consent, qualified consent, removal of an action by consent, voluntary consent, without consent

FOREIGN PHRASES: *Consensus non concubitus facit nuptias vel matrimonium et consentire non possunt ante annos nubiles.* Consent, not cohabitation, constitutes nuptials or marriage, and persons cannot consent before marriageable years. *Consensus voluntas multorum ad quos res pertinet, simul juncta.* Consent is the united will of several interested in one subject matter. *Consentientes et agentes pari poena plectentur.* Persons who consent and those who perform are subject to the same penalties. *Longa patientia trahitur ad consensum.* Long sufferance is construed as consent. *Itelius estomnia mala pati quam malo consentire.* It is better to suffer every ill than to consent to evil. *Nihil consensui tam controrium est quam vis atque metus.* Nothing is as much opposed to consent as force and fear. *Non consentit qui errat.* He who makes a mistake does not consent. *Non refert an quis assensum suum praefert verbis aut rebus ipsis et factis.* It matters not whether a man gives his consent by his words or by his acts and deeds. *Non videntur qui errant consentire.* Those who err are not deemed to consent. *Non videtur consensum retinuisse si quis ex praescripto minantis aliquid immutavit.* He does not appear to have retained consent who has changed anything through menaces. *Nuptias non cuncubitus sed consensus facit.* Not cohabitation but consent makes the marriage. *Omne jus aut consensus fecit, aut necessitas constituit aut firmavit consuetudo.* Consent created, necessity established, or custom has confirmed every law. *Omnis consensus tollit errorem.* Every consent removes error. *Qui tacet, consentire videtur.* He who is silent, is deemed to consent. *Actus me invito factus non est meus actus.* An act done against my will is not my act. *Agentes et consentientes pari poena plectentur.* Acting and consenting parties are liable to the same punishment. *Consensus est voluntas plurium ad quos res pertinet, simul juncta.* Consent is the conjoint will of several persons to whom the thing belongs. *Consensus facit legem.* Consent makes the law. *Consensus tollit errorem.*

Consent removes or obviates mistake. ***Quod meum est sine me auferri non potest.*** What is mine cannot be taken away without my consent. ***Volenti non fit injuria.*** He who consents cannot receive an injury.

CONSENT, verb accede, accept, accord, acquiesce, *adsentire,* affirm, agree, allow, approve, assent, authorize, be in favor of, be willing, come to terms, comply, concur, *consentire,* endorse, give approval, give consent, give permission, grant, gratify, have no objection, indicate willingness, license, permit, ratify, sanction, suffer, support, tolerate, warrant, yield
ASSOCIATED CONCEPTS: consent to an adjournment, consent to jurisdiction

CONSENT DECREE, noun an order accepted by the parties, an order acquiesced by the parties, an order agreed to by the parties, an order approved by the parties, an order consented to by the parties, an order endorsed by the parties, an order supported by the parties, an order with the accord of the parties, consent order
ASSOCIATED CONCEPTS: consent rule

CONSENT ORDER, noun an order accepted by the parties, an order acquiesced by the parties, an order agreed to by the parties, an order approved by the parties, an order consented to by the parties, an order endorsed by the parties, an order supported by the parties, an order with the accord of the parties, consent decree
ASSOCIATED CONCEPTS: consent rule

CONSENTING, adjective accommodating, accordant, acquiescent, acquiescing, agreeable, agreeing, allowing, approving, assentient, assenting, assentive, compliable, compliant, concordant, consentaneous, consentient, favorably inclined, in accord, in agreement, in harmony with, inclined to assent, likeminded, marked by consent, of one accord, permitting, voluntary, willing, yielding
ASSOCIATED CONCEPTS: abetting, consenting to be adjudged a bankrupt, permitting, ratifying

CONSEQUENCE (Conclusion), noun aftereffect, aftergrowth, aftermath, climax, completion, conclusion, *consecutio,* consummation, culmination, decision, deduction, denouement, derivation, derivative, determination, development, effect, emanation, ensual, eventuality, execution, final result, finale, finding, finish, fruition, illation, induction, logical result, offshoot, outcome, outgrowth, product, reaction, resolution, response, result, resultant action, settlement, upshot, verdict
ASSOCIATED CONCEPTS: consequential benefits, consequential contempt, consequential contracts, consequential damages, consequential injuries, consequential loss
FOREIGN PHRASES: ***Consuetudo non trahitur in conseqentiam.*** Custom is not drawn into consequence. ***Non officit conatus nisi sequatur effectus.*** An attempt does not harm unless a consequence follows. ***Officit conatus si effectus sequatur.*** The attempt becomes of consequence, if the effect follows.

CONSEQUENCE (Significance), noun accent, *auctoritas,* base, basis, core, distinction, effect, essence, essential quality, force, germ, heart, import, importance, influence, magnitude, marrow, materialness, meaning, merit, nature, notable feature, nucleus, point, primary element, principle, prominence, purport, quintessence, relevance, self-consequence, self-importance, seriousness, signification, soul, substance, usefulness, vital part

CONSEQUENTIAL (Deducible), adjective derivative, following, inferential, resultant, sequential
ASSOCIATED CONCEPTS: consequential contempt, consequential damages

CONSEQUENTIAL (Substantial), adjective authoritative, considerable, eminent, great, important, influential, momentous, powerful, self-important, significant, weighty

CONSEQUENTLY, adverb accordingly, as a consequence, as a matter of course, as a result, as matters stand, as the case may be, because, by reason of, by the same sign, by the same token, *ergo,* finally, for reasons given, for that cause, for that reason, for this reason, for which reason, from that cause, hence, *igitur,* in accordance therefore, in conclusion, in that case, in that event, in which case, it follows that, *itaque,* logically then, naturally, necessarily, of course, of necessity, on account of this, on that account, on this account, such being the case, that being so, that being the case, therefore, thus, thusly, to that end, under the circumstances, wherefore

CONSERVATION, noun economy, fostering, guarding, harboring, keeping, maintaining, maintenance, nourishing, nursing, preservation, preserving, protecting, protection, providing sanctuary, safeguarding, safekeeping, saving, sheltering, shielding, sparing, storage, support, sustaining, sustentation, upholding, upkeep
ASSOCIATED CONCEPTS: conservation of assets, conservation of property

CONSERVATIVE READING, noun accurate meaning, correct meaning, defined meaning, definition, distinct meaning, exact meaning, explanation, explicit meaning, express meaning, faithful meaning, inflexible meaning, literal meaning, methodical meaning, meticulous meaning, narrow meaning, not subject to interpretation, ordinary meaning, plain meaning, precise meaning, prescribed meaning, rigid meaning, rigorous meaning, sharply defined, significance, specific meaning, strict meaning, unbending meaning, uncompromising meaning, unequivocal meaning
ASSOCIATED CONCEPTS: construction, literal contract, literal proof plain meaning rule, rules of statutory, soft plain meaning rule, textualism

CONSERVE, verb avoid using, conservare, expend gradually, expend slowly, guard, keep, keep from loss, keep in existence, keep safe, keep unimpaired, maintain, omit using, preserve, prolong, protect, refrain from using, refuse to waste, safeguard, save, save from loss, secure, *servare,* shield, spare, store up, sustain, treasure, use carefully, use frugally, use sparingly, use thriftily

CONSIDER, verb advert to, analyze, appraise, assess, be attentive, cerebrate, cogitate, confer, *considerare,* consult, contemplate, debate, deliberate, devote attention to, digest, evaluate, examine, *expendere,* gauge, heed, inspect, investigate, mark, meditate on, mull over, muse, notice, observe, pay attention to, ponder, pore over, probe, reckon, reflect upon, regard, *respicere,* ruminate, scrutinize, study, take into account, think about, turn over in one's mind, weigh
ASSOCIATED CONCEPTS: adjudge, consider on its merits

CONSIDERABLE, adjective abundant, ample, cardinal, commanding, compelling, consequential, dominant, estimable, a good deal of, *gravis,* great, important, impressive, influential, large, *magnus,* marked, material, momentous, not to be overlooked, notable, noteworthy, of importance, of note, overruling, plentiful, potent, powerful, predominant, puissant, reasonable, remarkable, respectable, significant, sizable, special, substantial, tolerable, valuable, worthy of consideration

ASSOCIATED CONCEPTS: considerable damage, considerable provocation, considerable time

CONSIDERATION (Contemplation), *noun*   advertency, advisement, attention, attentiveness, cogitation, *consideratio,* examination, forethought, heed, judgment, meditation, pondering, premeditation, reckoning, reflection, review, rumination, serious thought, speculation, study

ASSOCIATED CONCEPTS: due consideration

CONSIDERATION (Recompense), *noun*   accommodation, benefits, bounty, compensation, defrayment, disbursement, emolument, fees, financial assistance, gratuity, guerdon, incentive, indemnification, indemnity, inducement, largess, payment, pecuniary aid, prize, reckoning, refund, reimbursement, remittance, remuneration, reparation, repayment, requital, restitution, return, reward, satisfaction, settlement, solatium, something of value, stipend, subsidy, sum

ASSOCIATED CONCEPTS: adequate consideration, collateral consideration, complete failure of consideration, consideration for a contract, due consideration, failure of consideration, fair and valuable consideration, fictitious consideration, founded on a consideration, fraud in consideration, full and adequate consideration, good and sufficient consideration, illegal consideration, illusory consideration, immoral consideration, lack of consideration, legal consideration, meritorious consideration, moral consideration, mutual consideration, new consideration, nominal consideration, partial failure of consideration, past consideration, pecuniary consideration, present consideration, sufficiency of consideration, valid consideration, want of consideration

FOREIGN PHRASES: *Ex turpi causa non oritur actio.* No cause of action arises out of an immoral or illegal consideration. *In omnibus contractibus, sive nominatis sive innominatis, permutatio continetur.* In all contracts, whether nominate or innominate, there is implied an exchange. *L'obligation sans cause, ou sur une fausse cause, ou sur cause illicite, ne peut avoir aucun effet.* An obligation without consideration, or with a false one, or with an unlawful one, cannot have any effect. *Nuda pactio obligationem non parit.* A naked promise does not create a binding obligation. *Nudum pactum est ubi nulla subest causa praeter conventionem; sed ubi subest causa, fit obligatio, et parit actionem.* A naked contract is where there is no consideration for the undertaking or agreement; but where there is a consideration, an obligation is created, and an action arises. *Pacta quae turpem causam continent non sunt observanda.* Agreements founded upon an immoral consideration are not to be enforced.

CONSIDERATION (Sympathetic regard), *noun*   accommodation, attentiveness, beneficence, benevolence, benignity, care, chivalry, civility, clemency, compassion, complaisance, concern, considerateness, cordiality, courteousness, courtesy, courtliness, deference, delicacy, diplomacy, esteem, estimation, friendliness, gallantry, generosity, geniality, gentleness, good manners, graciousness, helpfulness, humanity, kindheartedness, kindliness, kindness, mercy, neighborliness, obligingness, politeness, regard, respect, solicitousness, solicitude, tact, tenderness, thought, thoughtful regard, thoughtfulness, understanding, unselfishness, willingness to please

CONSIGN, *verb*   abalienate, assign to, authorize, charge, commit, commit to another's trust, *committere,* convey, deliver, deliver formally, deliver over, deposit with, entrust, give in trust, hand over, have conveyed, send, ship, transfer, transfer for sale, transmit, transplant, transport, turn over

ASSOCIATED CONCEPTS: bailment, conditional sale, consignment contract of goods

CONSIGNMENT, *noun*   allocation, allotment, appropriation, assignation, assignment, cession, concession, consignation, conveyance, conveyancing, delivering to, dispatchment, distribution, expressage, goods shipped, interchange, merchandise sent, sending, shipment, shipping, transfer, transference, transferring, transmission

ASSOCIATED CONCEPTS: consignment for sale, consignment shipper

CONSIST, *verb*   add up to, amount to, be composed of, be comprised of, be contained in, be formed of, be made of, be made up of, comprise, *consistere,* constitute, contain, cover, embody, encompass, enfold, entail, envelop, form, has as a component, have as its foundation, hold, in essence is, in nature is, in substance is, include, incorporate, involve, is composed of, is essentially, make up, occupy, synthesize

CONSISTENT, *adjective*   accordant, agreeing, alike, coherent, cohering, compatible, compliable, concordant, conformable, congruent with, congruous, consonant, *constans, conveniens,* correspondent, equable, equal, harmonious, logical, not contradictory, regular, self-consistent, unchanging, undeviating, uniform

ASSOCIATED CONCEPTS: consistent cases, consistent causes of action, consistent construction of sales contracts, consistent decisions, consistent defenses, consistent interpretation of the Constitution, consistent precedence, consistent with the public interest

CONSOCIATE, *noun*   abettor, accessory, accomplice, adherent, adjunct, adjutant, aide, ally, assistant, associate, attendant, auxiliary, coadjutor, cohelper, cohort, collaborator, colleague, comate, companion, comrade, confederate, confidant, confrere, consort, cooperator, copartner, coworker, fellow companion, fellow conspirator, fellow worker, follower, helper, helpmate, intimate, mate, participator, partner, retainer, side-partner

ASSOCIATED CONCEPTS: accomplice

CONSOLIDATE (Strengthen), *verb*   add to, amass, bind, blend, bring together, build up, coalesce, cohere, combine, compact, compound, compress, concatenate, concentrate, condense, congeal, conjoin, conjoint, connect, contract, crystallize, densify, fortify, fuse, harden, intensify, make firm, make solid, mass, mix, put together, render solid, settle firmly, solidify, squeeze together, unify

CONSOLIDATE (Unite), *verb*   accumulate, affiliate, ally, amalgamate, amass, band, become one, bring together, centralize, coact, coadjuvate, coalesce, combine, compound, compress, concentrate, concert, confederate, congeal, conglomerate, conjoin, connect, cooperate, couple, cowork, draw together, federate, fuse, gather together, incorporate, interblend, interfuse, intertwine, join, join forces, join forces with, league, link, lump together, make one, meet, melt into one, merge, mix, mobilize, piece together, put together, roll into one, shade into, solidify, stay together, stick together, synthesize, unionize, work together

ASSOCIATED CONCEPTS: consolidate actions

115

CONSOLIDATION, *noun* affiliation, aggregation, amalgamation, assemblage, association, centralization, coadunation, combination, compact, confederation, conjunction, conjuncture, consortium, federation, fusion, incorporation, integration, junction, league, merger, mixture, pool, solidification, strengthening, unification, union

ASSOCIATED CONCEPTS: consolidated laws, consolidated school district, consolidation of actions, consolidation of stock

CONSONANCE, *noun* accord, accordance, agreement, assent, assonance, attunement, chorus, coherence, coincidence, compatibility, compliance, concert, conciliation, concord, concordance, concurrence, conformity, consensus, consistency, continuity, correspondence, equability, harmony, homogeneity, persistence, rapport, unanimity, uniformity, union, unison, unity

CONSONANT, *adjective* accordant, adapted, agreeing, alike, answerable, appropriate, apt, arranged, at one, attuned, balanced, becoming, coherent, coincident, commensurate, compatible, concerted, concordant, concurrent, conformable, conforming, congenial, *congruens,* congruent, congruous, consentaneous, consentaneus, consentient, consequent, consistent, *conveniens,* cooperating, correspondent, corresponding, equable, equal, fit, fitting, harmonious, in accord, in agreement, in concord, in harmony, in rapport, in unison, logically consistent, parallel, reconcilable, related, self consistent, similar, suitable, synchronal, synchronized, unchangeable, unchanged, unchanging, undeviating, undiscordant, unified, uniform, unisonant, unisonous

CONSORT, *noun* accompanier, associate, colleague, comate, *comes,* companion, compeer, comrade, *confrère,* conjugal partner, copartner, escort, fellow, fellow companion, helpmate, husband, marital partner, *maritus,* marriage partner, mate, partner, *socius,* spouse, wife

ASSOCIATED CONCEPTS: alienation of affections, criminal conversation, loss of consortium

CONSORTIUM *(Business cartel),* *noun* association, business agreement, business combine, business entente, cartel, coalition, combination, combination of financial institutions, confederacy, consolidation, league, merger, monopoly, partnership, pool, syndicate, trust, union

CONSORTIUM *(Marriage companionship),* *noun* accommodation, affiliation, affinity, alliance, assistance, association, attachment, closeness, comfort, compact, companionship, compliance, comradeship, concordance, congruity, congruousness, consociation, consortship, correspondence, familiarity, friendship, help, intercommunion, intimacy, league, marriage accord, marriage compatibility, marriage concord, partnership, reciprocal feeling, understanding

ASSOCIATED CONCEPTS: loss of consortium

CONSPICUOUS, *adjective* apparent, *clarus,* clear, clearcut, *conspicuus,* definite, discernible, discoverable, distinct, distinguishable, distinguished, evident, exposed, exposed to view, flagrant, in bold relief, in evidence, in plain sight, in the foreground, in view, manifest, *manifestus,* marked, notable, noticeable, notorious, observable, obvious, open, overt, patent, perceivable, perceptible, plain, pointed, preeminent, prominent, pronounced, public, recognizable, remarkable, renowned, self-evident, spectacular, standing out, striking, tending to attract attention, unblurred, unclouded, uncovered, undisguised, unhidden, unmistakable, visible, well-defined, well-marked, well-seen

ASSOCIATED CONCEPTS: conspicuous places

CONSPIRACY, *noun* abetment, abetting, acting in combination, acting in concert, acting in harmony, agreeing with another or others, agreement to accomplish an unlawful end, agreement to commit a crime, aiding another or others, an agreement with another or others, associate with another, banded together, coalescence, coalition, colluding together, collusion, combination, combination of operations, combine to perform a crime, combine to plan a crime, combine to plan an unlawful act, combine to plan secretly, combine together, combined operation, combining, combining for a criminal purpose, compact, compliance, complicity, composition, concert, confederacy, connivance, connive jointly, contrivance, contrive jointly, cooperation with, corrupt agreement, countermine, counterplot, criminal arrangement, design jointly, devise jointly, duplicitous agreement, in concert with, intrigue, intriguery, join forces with, join together with, joint effort, joint planning, maneuvering, plan, plot, plot together, proposal, scheme, scheme together, take part in a crime together, take part with another in crime, treasonable alliance, underplot, unlawful combination, unlawful contrivance, unlawful plan, unlawful scheme

ASSOCIATED CONCEPTS: conspiracy charges, conspiracy in restraint of interstate trade, conspiracy in restraint of trade, conspiracy to commit felony, conspiracy to defraud, conspiracy within the Scherman Antitrust Act, continuing conspiracy, criminal conspiracy, entered into a conspiracy, felony murder, furtherance of the conspiracy, overt act

CONSPIRATOR, *noun* abettor, colluder, complotter, confederate, coniuratus, conniver, deceiver, intrigant, intriguer, machinator, plotter, schemer, spy, strategist

CONSPIRE, *verb* abet, act in combination, act in concert, act in harmony, agree, aid, associate, be banded together, be stealthy, cabal, calculate, coact, cohere, collude, combine, combine for some evil design, combine operations, concert, concoct a plot, concur, confederate, confederate for an unlawful purpose, *coniurare,* conjoin, connive, *conspirare,* contribute toward, contrive, cooperate, countermine, counterplot, cowork, design, devise, devise treachery, form a coalition, form plots, frame, hatch a plot, hold together, intrigue, join, join forces, league together, league with, machinate, make an agreement with, make secret arrangements, maneuver, participate in an unlawful scheme, plan, plan a crime, plan an unlawful act, plan secretly, plan to commit a crime, plot, plot an action in advance, plot craftily, plot together, scheme, take part in, take part with, unify, unite

ASSOCIATED CONCEPTS: conspire to commit a crime, conspire to defraud the United States Government

CONSPIRER, *noun* abettor, accessory, accessory after the fact, accessory before the fact, accomplice, accomplice in crime, adjutant, agent provocateur, aid, aider, aider and abettor, assistant, associate, coactor, coadjutant, coadjutor, cohelper, collaborationist, collaborator, colleague, colluder, confederate, consociate, conspirator, contriver, cooperator, counterpart, fellow conspirator, helper, helpmate, intrigant, intriguer, partner, partner in crime, planner, plotter, promoter, saboteur, schemer, strategist, subversive, traitor

ASSOCIATED CONCEPTS: accomplice

CONSTANCY, *noun* adherence, allegiance, application, attachment, backbone, constance, continuity, decision, determination, devotion, diligence, faithfulness, firmness, fortitude, grit, industry, loyalty, permanence, perpetuity, perseverance, persistence, regularity, reliability, resoluteness, resolution, steadfastness, steadiness, tenacity, uniformity

CONSTANT, *adjective* abiding, aeonian, certain, changeless, chronic, consistent, *constans,* continual, continually recurring, continuing, continuous, dependable, durable, endless, enduring, entrenched, eternal, faithful, firm, *firmus,* fixed, habitual, immortal, immutable, imperishable, inalterable, incessant, inconvertible, indeciduous, indelible, indestructible, indissoluble, inextinguishable, inflexible, invariable, invariant, inveterate, lasting, loyal, perdurable, perennial, permanent, perpetual, regular, reliable, sempiternal, *stabilis,* stable, steadfast, steady, sure, sustained, unchanging, undeviating, undying, unequivocal, uninterrupted, unrelenting, unshaken, unswerving, unvarying, unwavering

CONSTANT, *noun* certainty, conformity, consistency, constancy, *constans,* convention, firmness, *firmus,* fixation, form, immutability, inextricability, invariability, invariable, invariant, inveteracy, maxim, pattern, permanence, prescribed form, procedure, prototype, regularity, reliability, rule, sameness, *stabilis,* stability, standard, standard practice, standard procedure, staunchness, steadfastness, steadiness, symmetry, unchangeableness, uniformity

CONSTERNATION, *noun* affright, agitation, alarm, anxiety, anxious concern, anxiousness, apprehension, apprehensiveness, aversion, boding, despair, dismay, disquiet, disquietude, disturbance, dread, fear, fearfulness, fright, horror, inquietude, *pavor,* perturbation, sudden fear, trepidation

CONSTITUENCY, *noun* affiliates, associates, body of members, chapter, collective members, community, constituents, delegation, district, division, electorate, electors, enrollment, faction, group, interest group, lobby, members, membership, partisanship, party, polity, voters, voting district, voting list

CONSTITUENT *(Member),* *noun* associate, colleague, constituency, fellow resident, resident, resident of the same district, resident voter, voter

CONSTITUENT *(Part),* *noun* balloter, component, component part, division, element, *elementum,* factor, feature, fraction, fragment, included, ingredient, installment, integral part, integrant, integrant part, one of, *pars,* part, part and parcel, particle, piece, section, sector, segment, subdivision
ASSOCIATED CONCEPTS: constituent elements, constituent members, constituent parts

CONSTITUTE *(Compose),* *verb* be a feature, be inherent, be part of, belong, belong intrinsically, classify as, *componere,* comprise, consist of, contain, create, *efficere,* embody, embrace, encompass, form, include, incorporate, inhere in, involve, make up, produce, put together

CONSTITUTE *(Establish),* *verb* bring about, bring about by legislation, charter, codify, commission, constituere, create, create by law, declare lawful, decree, *designare,* determine, develop, devise, effect, effect by legislation, effectuate, empower, enact, endorse, engender, formulate, formulate by law, give legal form to, inaugurate, install, institute, invest, legalize, legislate, legitimate, legitimatize, legitimize, license, make legal, ordain, organize, originate, pass, prescribe, prescribe by law, put in force, sanction, set up, *statuere,* validate
ASSOCIATED CONCEPTS: constitute a cause of action, constitute a crime, constitute a fraud, constitute an obstruction
FOREIGN PHRASES: *Eodem modo quo quid constituitur, dissolvitur.* A thing is discharged in the same way in which it was created.

CONSTITUTION, *noun* act, body of law, body of rules of government, canon, charter, civil law, *civitatis,* code of laws, codification, codified law, collection of laws, compact to govern, compilation of law, dictate, edict, enactment, fundamental law, law, legal code, maxim, organic law, pandect, paramount law, precept, prescription, principles of government, regulation, rubric, statute, supreme law, written law
ASSOCIATED CONCEPTS: action arising under Constitution or laws, Amendment to the Constitution, Constitutional Amendment, Constitutional Convention, Constitutional court, Constitutional officer, Constitutional question, Constitutional right

CONSTRAIN *(Compel),* *verb* actuate, apply pressure, assert oneself, bring about by force, bring pressure to bear upon, burden, cause to, charge, coerce, cogere, command, command influence, compel, *compellere,* decree, demand, dominate, drive, enforce, enforce obedience, exact, exert influence, force, goad, have influence, impel, impose, impose a duty, induce, insist, insist on, issue a command, leave no option, make necessary, move, move to action, necessitate, obligate, oblige, order, press, pressure, prevail upon, prod, propel, push, put pressure on, put under obligation, require, secure by force, squeeze, subject, take no denial, tell, urge, urge forward, work upon

CONSTRAIN *(Imprison),* *verb* arrest, bind, bridle, chain, circumscribe, commit, commit to an institution, commit to prison, confine, confine forcibly, detain, enclose, enthrall, entomb, harness, hold, hold as hostage, hold back by force, hold captive, hold in restraint, immure, impound, incarcerate, institutionalize, intern, isolate, jail, keep as captive, keep in custody, keep in detention, keep prisoner, limit, manacle, put in a cell, put under arrest, put under restraint, restrain, restrict, send to prison, shackle, take captive, take into custody, trammel

CONSTRAIN *(Restrain),* *verb* ban, bar, block, bridle, censor, chain, check, control, curb, debar, deny, disallow, forbid, hamper, harness, hinder, hold back, hold back by force, hold down, hold in, hold in check, impede, impose restrictions, inhibit, keep back, keep in check, lay under restraint, limit, obstruct, oppress, preclude, prevent, prohibit, proscribe, put a stop to, put under restraint, refuse, refuse to grant, repress, restrain, restrict, restrict access, subdue, subjugate, suppress, withhold

CONSTRAINT *(Imprisonment),* *noun* act of keeping in, apprehension, arrest, bondage, bonds, bounds, captivity, care, charge, commitment, confinement, containment, control, custodianship, custody, detainment, detention, encincture, enclosure, enthrallment, fetter, immuration, immurement, impoundment, incarceration, internment, keeping, legal restraint, preventive custody, preventive detention, prison, prohibition, protective custody, quarantine, remand, restriction

CONSTRAINT *(Restriction),* *noun* act of forestalling, act of hampering, act of quelling, act of stifling, act of strangling, act of thwarting, astriction, bar, circumscription, coercion, compulsion, constriction, curb, deprivation, detainment, deterrent, disallowance, disapprobation, duress, encumbrance, enthrallment, fetter, forbiddance, force, hindrance, impediment, inhibition, interdict, interdiction, limitation, muzzle, obstruction, obstructionism, preclusion, pressure, prevention, prohibition, proscription, rein, repression, restraint, restrictive practice, strangulation, stultification, suppression, temperance, trammel
ASSOCIATED CONCEPTS: estoppel

CONSTRICT *(Compress)*, **verb** abbreviate, abridge, astringe, bind, capsulize, cause to contract, clench, coarct, compact, concentrate, condense, consolidate, constringe, contract, cram, cramp, crowd, crush, draw together, make brief, make dense, make smaller, narrow, pack tightly, pinch, press, press together, ram, reduce, reduce volume, restrict in area, shorten, shrink, squeeze, telescope, tighten

CONSTRICT *(Inhibit)*, **verb** arrest, astrict, barricade, be an impediment, be an obstacle, block, check, choke, close, constrain, control, curb, dam, delay, detain, deter, estop, fetter, foil, frustrate, halt, hamper, handicap, hinder, hold back, impede, interfere, keep, keep back, limit, obstruct, occlude, rein in, repress, restrain, restrict, retard, set back, set limitations, set limits, slow, stall, staunch, stay, stem, stifle, stop, strangulate, stymie, suppress, thwart, tie up, withhold

CONSTRUCTION, *noun* clarification, comment, commentary, configuration, conformation, constitution, construability, construal, deduction, definability, definition, delineation, description, diagnosis, exegesis, exemplification, explanation, explicability, explication, exposition, expounding, form, formulation, frame, framework, illumination, inference, interpretability, *interpretatio,* interpretation, meaning, rationale, sense, significance, structure, substance, translation, understanding, version

ASSOCIATED CONCEPTS: construction of a contract, construction of a statute, construction of a writing, construction of will, contemporaneous construction, liberal construction, rule of construction, statutory construction, strict construction

FOREIGN PHRASES: *Contemporanea expositio est optima et fortissima in lege.* Contemporaneous exposition is the best and most powerful in the law. *Quum in testamento ambigue aut etiam perperam scriptum est, benigne interpretari et secundum id quod credible et cogitatum, credendum est.* When an ambiguous or even an erroneous expression occurs in a will, it should be construed liberally and in accordance with what is thought the probable meaning of the testator. *Copulatio verborum indicat acceptationem in eodem sensu.* The coupling of words indicates that they are to be taken in the same sense. *Cum duo inter se pugnantia reperiuntur in testamento, ultimum ratum est.* When two repugnant matters are found in a will, the last will be confirmed. *Curiosa et captiosa interpretatio in lege reprobatur.* A curious and captious interpretation is disapproved. *Verbis standum ubi nulla ambiguitas.* Where there is no ambiguity, one must abide by the words. *Designatio unius est exclusio alterius, et expressum facit cessare tacitum.* The designation of one is the exclusion of the other, and that which is expressed prevails over that which is implied. *In ambigua voce legis ea potius accipienda est significatio quae vitio caret, praesertim cum etiam voluntas legis ex hoc colligi possit.* In an ambiguous expression of law, that interpretation is to be preferred which is consonant with equity, especially where it is in conformity with the purpose of the law. *Non aliter a significatione verborum recedi oportet quam cum manifestum est, aliud sensisse testatorem.* The ordinary meaning of the words ought not to be departed from unless it is evident that the testator intended otherwise. *Non est novum ut priores leges ad posteriores trahantur.* It is not novel that prior statutes should give place to later ones. *Non in legendo sed in intelligendo legis consistunt.* The laws consist not in being read, but in being understood. *Omnis definitio in lege periculosa.* All definition in law is dangerous. *Omnis interpretatio si fieri potest ita fienda est in instrumentis, ut omnes contrarietates amoveantur.* Every interpretation of instruments is to be made, if they will admit of it, so that all contradictions may be removed. *In ambiguo sermone non utrumque dicimus sed id duntaxat quod volumus.* In ambiguous discourse, we do not use language in a double sense, but in the sense in which we mean it. *Benedicta est expositio quando res redimitur a destructione.* Blessed is the exposition when a thing is saved from destruction. *Benignior sententia in verbis generalibus seu dubiis, est praeferenda.* The more favorable construction is to be placed on general or doubtful expressions. *Benignius leges interpretandae sunt quo voluntas earum conservetur.* Laws are to be liberally construed, in order that their intent may be preserved. *Lex non exacte definit, sed arbitrio boni viri permittit.* The law does not define exactly, but trusts to the judgement of a good man. *Lex posterior derogat priori.* A later statute takes away the effect of a prior one. *Magis de bono quam de malo lex intendit.* The law favors a good rather than a bad interpretation. *Maledicta est expositio quae corrumpit textum.* It is a cursed construction which corrupts the text. *Mandata licita strictam recipiunt interpretationem, sed illicita latam et extensam.* Lawful commands receive a strict interpretation, but unlawful commands a broad and extended one. *Neque leges neque senatus consulta ita scribi possunt ut omnis casus qui quandoque in sedriunt comprehendatur; sed sufficit ea quae plaerumque accidunt contineri.* Neither laws nor acts of a legislature can be so written as to include all actual or possible cases; it is sufficient if they provide for those things which frequently or ordinarily may happen. *In stipulationibus cum quaeritur quid actum sit verba contra stipulatorem interpretanda sunt.* In the construction of agreements words are interpreted against the person offering them. *Omne majus minus in se complectitur.* Every greater thing embraces within itself the less. *Partem aliquam recte intelligere nemo potest, antequam totum, iterum atque iterum, perlegerit.* No one can rightly understand any part until he has read the whole over again. *Quamvis lex generaliter loquitur, restringenda tamen est, ut, cessante ratione, ipsa cessat.* Although a law speaks generally, yet it is to be restrained, so that when its reason fails, it should cease also. *Quotiens idem sermo duas sententias exprimit, ea potissimum accipiatur, quae rei gerendae aptior est.* Whenever the same words express two meanings, that is to be adopted which is the better fitted for carrying out the proposed end. *In ambiguis orationibus maxime sententia spectanda est ejus qui eas protulisset.* In ambiguous expressions, the intent of the person using them is particularly to be regarded. *Statutum generaliter est intelligendum quando verba statuti sunt specialia, ratio autem generalis.* When the words of a statute are special, but the reason general, the statute is to be understood generally. *Tortura legum pessima.* The torture or wresting of laws is the worst. *Verba accipienda sunt secundum subjectam materiam.* Words are to be understood with reference to the subject-matter. *Verba chartarum fortius accipiuntur contra proferentem.* The words of a grant are to be taken most strongly against the person offering them. *Verba generalia generaliter sunt intelligenda.* General words are to be understood generally. *Verbis standum ubi nulla ambiguitas.* Where there is no ambiguity, the words are adhered to. *Semper sexus masculinus etiam femininum sexum continet.* The masculine sex of gender always includes the feminine also. *Semper specialia generalibus insunt.* Special expressions are always included in general ones. *Si nulla sit conjectura quae ducat alio, verba intelligenda sunt ex proprietate, non grammatica sed populari ex usu.* If there be no inference which leads to a different conclusion, words are to be understood according to their proper meaning, not according to a grammatical usage but to a popular and ordinary one. *Statuta pro publico commodo late interpretantur.* Statutes enacted for the public good ought to be liberally construed. *Quando charta continet generalem clausulam, posteaque descendit ad verba specialia quae clausulae generali sunt consentanea, interpretanda est charta secundum verba specialia.* When a deed contains a general clause, and afterwards descends to special words which are consistent with the general clause, the deed is to be interpreted according to the special words. *Quando lex est specialis, ratio autem generalis, generaliter lex est intelligenda.* When the law is special, but its reason is general, the law is to be understood generally. *Quando licet id quod majus videtur et licere id quod minus.* When the greater is allowed, the less is to be deemed to be allowed also. *Quod in minori valet valebit in majori; et quod in majori non valet nec valebit in minori.* That which is valid in the greater shall be valid in the less; and that which is not valid in the greater shall not be valid in the less. *Quum in testamento ambigue aut etiam perperam scriptum est, benigne interpretari et secundum id quod credible et cogitatum, credendum est.* Where an ambiguous or even an erroneous expression occurs in a will, it should be construed liberally and in accordance with what is thought the probable meaning of the testator. *Semper in dubiis benigniora praeferenda sunt.* In doubtful cases, the more liberal constructions are always to be preferred. *Transgressione multiplicata, crescat poenae inflictio.* Upon the multiplication of the transgression, let the infliction of punishment increase. *Ex tota materia emergat resolutio.* The construction should arise out of the whole subject-matter. *Expressio unius est exclusio alterius.* The expression of one thing is the exclusion of another. *Generale dictum generaliter est interpretandum.* A general expression is to be construed generally. *Generale nihil certum implicat.* A general expression implies nothing certain. *In dubio haec legis constructio quam verba ostendunt.* In a doubtful case, that construction which the words indicate should be adopted. *In expositione instrumentorum, mala grammatica, quod fieri potest, vitanda est.* In the drafting of instruments, bad grammar is to be avoided as much as possible. *In his enim quae sunt favorabilia animae, quamvis sunt damnosa rebus, fiat aliquando extentio statuti.* In matters that are favorable to the spirit, though injurious to property, an extension of the statute should sometimes be made. *In rebus quae sunt favorabilia animae, quamvis sunt damnosa rebus, fiat aliquando extensio statuti.* In matters that are favorable to the spirit, though injurious to things, an extension of a statute should sometimes be made. *In stipulationibus cum quaeritur quid actum sit verba contra stipulatorem interpretanda sunt.* In the construction of agreements terms are interpreted against the person using them. *In verbis non verba, sed res et ratio, quaerenda est.* In the construction of words, not the mere words, but the thing and the meaning, are to be inquired into. *Injustum est, nisi tota lege inspecta, de una aliqua ejus particula proposita judicare vel respondere.* It is unjust to give judgement or advice concerning any particular clause of a law without having examined the whole law. *Interpretatio fienda est ut res magis valeat quam pereat.* Construction should be such that the transaction may be effective rather than fall. *Interpretare et concordare leges legibus, est optimus interpretandi modus.* To interpret and harmonize laws with laws is the best mode of interpretation. *Interpretatio talis in ambiguis semper fienda est ut evitetur inconveniens et absurdum.* In ambiguous things, such a construction should be always made that the inconvenient and absurd

may be avoided. *Legis constructio non facit injuriam.* The construction of law does no wrong. *Generalis clausula non porrigitur ad ea quaeantea specialiter sunt comprehensa.* A general clause is not extended to include those things that have been previously provided for specially. *Leges posteriores priores contrarias abrogant.* Subsequent laws repeal prior laws that are repugnant to them. *Id quod est magis remotum, non trahit ad se quod est magis junctum, sed e contrario in omni casu.* That which is more remote does not draw to itself that which is nearer, but the contrary in every case. *In ambigua voce legis ea potius accipienda est significatio quae vitio caret, praesertim cum etiam voluntas legis ex hoc colligi possit.* In an ambiguous expression of law, that signification is to be preferred which is consonant with equity, especially when the spirit of the law can be collected from that. *In obscuris, inspici solere quod verisimiltus est, aut quod plerumque fieri solet.* In obscure cases, we usually regard what is most probable or what is done. *In obscuris, quod minimum est sequimur.* In obscure or doubtful cases, we follow that which is the least. *In poenalibus causis benignius interpretandum est.* In penal causes or cases, the more liberal interpretation should be adopted. *In re dubia, benigniorem interpretationem sequi, non minus justius est quam tutius.* In a doubtful matter, to follow the more liberal interpretation is no more just than it is the more safe. *Generale tantum valet in generalibus, quantum singulare in singulis.* That which is general prevails in general matters, as that which is particular prevails in particular matters. *In ambiguo sermone non utrumque dicimus sed id duntaxat quod volumus.* In ambiguous language, we do not use it in a double sense, but in the sense in which we mean it. *Generalia specialibus non derogant.* General words do not derogate from special. *Generalia sunt praeponenda singularibus.* General things are to be put before particular things. *Generalia verba sunt generaliter intelligenda.* General words are to be understood generally in a general sense. *Generalibus specialia derogant.* Special words derogate from the meaning of general ones. *Verba posteriora propter certitudinem addita, ad priora quae certitudine indigent, sunt referenda.* Subsequent words, added for the purpose of certainty, are to be referred to the preceding words which are need of certainty. *Verbis standum ubi nulla ambiguitas.* One must abide by the words where there is no ambiguity. *Generalia praecedunt, specialia sequuntur.* Things general precede, things special follow. *In ambiguis orationibus maxime sententia spectanda est ejus qui eas protulisset.* When there are ambiguous expressions, the intentions of the person who uses them is chiefly to be regarded. *A verbis legis non est recendendum.* From the words of a statute, there must be no departure. *Aliud est distinctio, aliud separatio.* Distinction is one thing; separation is another.

CONSTRUCTIVE (Creative), *adjective* advantageous, applicable, causative, contributive, convenient, cooperative, desirable, developmental, effective, effectual, efficient, fabricative, favorable, formative, generative, helpful, important, improving, instrumental, invaluable, operative, originative, practical, productive, profitable, resultant, serviceable, significant, stimulating, suitable, usable, useful, valuable, worthy, yielding

CONSTRUCTIVE (Inferential), *adjective* apparent, assumable, conceivable, connoted, constructional, implicative, implicatory, implicit, implied, implied in law, in effect, in essence, in practice, indicated, indirect, indirectly meant, inferable, inferred, inferred in law, insinuated, involved, parallel, potential, pragmatic, presumable, presumed,

CONSTRUE

probable, seeming, suggested, supposable, tacit, tacitly assumed, tantamount to, understood, virtual

ASSOCIATED CONCEPTS: constructive contempt, constructive contract, constructive control, constructive conversion, constructive delivery, constructive desertion, constructive escape, constructive eviction, constructive force, constructive fraud, constructive gift, constructive intent, constructive knowledge, constructive malice, constructive mortgage, constructive notice, constructive possession, constructive receipt, constructive total loss, constructive trespass, constructive trust, constructively present

CONSTRUE (Comprehend), **verb** *accipere,* analyze, apprehend, ascertain the meaning of, assimilate, be aware of, be given to understand, cognize, conceive of, conclude, conclude from evidence, consignify, decipher, decode, deduce, deduce by interpretation, deduce the meaning of, deduct, derive by reasoning, determine, determine exactly, discern, disentangle, divine, draw an inference, draw as an implication, explain, fathom, figure out, find out the meaning of, form an opinion, gather, glean, grasp mentally, grow aware, infer, interpret, judge, ken, make deductions, master, opine, perceive, ratiocinate, realize, reason, represent, see through, seize, show the meaning of, solve, take one's meaning, understand, understand by, understand the meaning of

CONSTRUE (Translate), **verb** analyze, assign a meaning to, characterize, characterize precisely, clarify, clear up, connote, convey, decipher, decode, define, delineate, demonstrate, denote, depict, describe, disclose, elucidate, enlighten, enunciate, explain, explicate, exposit, expound, express, give explanation to, give sense to, illuminate, illustrate, indicate, inform, interpret, *interpretari,* literalize, make intelligible, of, outline, paraphrase, put a meaning on, put an interpretation, put in other words, render, render intelligible, rephrase, restate, retranslate, reveal, reword, signify, transfuse the sense, unfold, unravel

ASSOCIATED CONCEPTS: construe the law

CONSULT (Ask advice of), **verb** advise with, ask, ask advice, ask an opinion, ask for recommendations, ask for suggestions, call in, confer, *consultare,* deliberate, discuss, exchange observations, interchange views, parley, question, seek counsel, seek guidance, seek the opinion of, take counsel, talk over, turn to, ventilate

ASSOCIATED CONCEPTS: consult with counsel

CONSULT (Seek information from), **verb** check a reference, check a source, examine a source, inquire of, look up information in, refer to, refer to for information, search for an answer, seek facts from

CONSUME, **verb** *absumere,* annihilate, burn up, *consumere,* demolish, destroy, devour, disappear, drain, dwindle, eat, empty, eradicate, evaporate, exhaust, expend, spend, squander, swallow, use up, utilize, waste, wear away, wear out

CONSUMER, **noun** buyer, buyer of labor, client, clientele, coemptor, customer, emptor, leaser, lessee, obtainer, patron, procurer, purchaser, purchaser of goods, shopper, transferee, vendee

ASSOCIATED CONCEPTS: consumer action, consumer credit, consumer fraud, consumers sales tax, ultimate consumer

CONSUMMATE, **verb** accomplish, achieve, actualize, attain, attain the goal, bring to a close, bring to effect, carry into effect, carry out, carry through, carry to completion, complete, conclude, *conficere, consummare,* do thoroughly,

effect, effectuate, end, execute, finalize, finish, follow through, fulfill, implement, leave nothing to be desired, perfect, *perficere,* prosecute to a conclusion, reach the goal, realize, render complete, terminate, to bring to completion

ASSOCIATED CONCEPTS: consummate dower, consummation of a marriage, consummation of an agreement, constructive service

FOREIGN PHRASES: *Omne testamentum morte consummatum est.* Every will is consummated by death.

CONSUMPTION, **noun** *confectio, consumptio,* decay, decomposition, decrement, depletion, desolation, destruction, devastation, diminishment, diminution, dissipation, exhaustion, expenditure, loss, ravage, ruin, ruination, squandering, usage, use, using up, utilization, wastage, waste, wastefulness, wear, withering

ASSOCIATED CONCEPTS: business consumption, consumption in interstate commerce, consumption of goods, consumption of intoxicating liquors, for use and consumption

CONTACT (Association), **noun** accord, acquaintanceship, affiliation, alliance, bond, camaraderie, close union, cooperation, coalition, combination, commerce, communication, community, companionship, conjunction, connection, consanguinity, consociation, consortium, cooperation, dealings, exchange, federation, fellowship, interchange, intercommunication, intercommunion, intercourse, interrelation, intimacy, kinship, liaison, link, linkage, mutual intercourse, participation, rapport, relation, relationship, tie, transmission, union

ASSOCIATED CONCEPTS: contacts theory in conflicts of law, grouping of contacts

CONTACT (Touching), **noun** abutment, abuttal, adhesion, adjacency, coherence, *contactus,* connection, connective, contiguity, contiguousness, contingence, convergence, impact, joining, junction, junction of bodies, juncture, juxtaposition, meeting, nexus, taction, tangency, union

CONTACT (Communicate), **verb** call, consociate, *contactus,* correspond, establish connection, get through to, get to, have an exchange, have dealings with, inform, interchange, intercommunicate, make connection, meet with, notify, reach, relate, serve notice, signal

CONTACT (Touch), **verb** abut, adjoin, annex, attach, be contiguous, border, border on, bridge, butt against, cohere, collide with, come together, conjoin, connect, converge, embrace, encounter, establish connection, graze, hit, impinge, inosculate, interconnect, join, lie adjacent to, link, meet, osculate, overlap, reach, rub, strike, unite, verge upon

CONTAGIOUS, **adjective** catching, communicable, contaminating, conveyable, epidemic, impartible, infectious, infective, pathogenic, pestiferous, spreading, transferable, transmissible, transmissive

CONTAIN (Comprise), **verb** be composed of, be compounded of, be constituted of, be formed of, capere, *comprehendere,* consist of, embody, embrace, enfold, envelop, hold, include, incorporate, number, reckon among, subsist of

ASSOCIATED CONCEPTS: containing facts sufficient to constitute a cause of action

CONTAIN (Enclose), **verb** beleaguer, belt, bind, blockade, border, close in, confine, *continere,* embox, embrace, encapsulate, encase, encincture, encircle, enclasp, encompass, engird, ensphere, envelop, enwrap, fence in, frame, immure, incase, inclose, infold, keep in, quarantine, seal up, shut in, surround

CONTAIN *(Restrain),* **verb** arrest, barricade, bind, block, bridle, cage, chain, check, commit to prison, confine, constrain, control, curb, detain, enchain, encumber, enjoin from, fetter, forfend, hinder, hold back, hold in check, hold in custody, impede, impound, imprison, incarcerate, inhibit, jail, keep in captivity, keep in check, keep prisoner, keep under arrest, keep under control, lock up, manacle, obstruct, pinion, place in durance, prohibit, quash, quell, repress, restrict, shackle, stave off, stop, subdue, suppress, thwart, trammel, ward off

CONTAMINATE, *noun* abomination, adulteration, befoulment, contagion, defilement, infection, poisoning, pollution, taint, vitiation

CONTAMINATE, *verb* adulterate, befoul, corrupt, debase, defile, degenerate, degrade, denaturalize, desecrate, disease, impair, infect, mar, poison, pollute, profane, sully, tamper with, taint, tarnish, vitiate

CONTAMINATION, *noun* adulteration, corruption, debauchment, decay, defilement, degradation, despoilment, impureness, impurity, infection, pollution, vitiation

CONTEMN, *verb* abhor, abominate, accuse, asperse, be contemptuous of, belittle, besmirch, calumniate, cast aspersions, censure, criticize, debase, debauch, decry, defile, denigrate, denounce, depreciate, deride, derogate, desecrate, despise, detest, disapprove, discredit, disdain, disesteem, dishonor, disparage, disprize, disrate, disregard, disrespect, execrate, expose, exprobate, feel contempt for, flout, hold in contempt, hold in despite, inveigh against, loathe, malign, misprize, not respect, objurgate, oppress, overlook, rebuff, reject, reproach, repudiate, repulse, resent, revile, ridicule, scandalize, scoff at, scorn, slight, slur, smear, spurn, taint, vilify, vilipend, vituperate

CONTEMPLATION, *noun* absorption, aim, attention, brooding, calculation, cerebration, cogitation, concentration, consideration, *contemplatio,* deliberateness, deliberation, design, determination, engrossment, envisagement, envisionment, examination, excogitation, expectance, expectation, forethought, goal, inspection, intellectualization, intent, intention, introspection, musing, observance, pensiveness, plan, pondering, preoccupation, prospect, purpose, ratiocination, reasoning, reflection, resolve, reverie, review, rumination, scrutiny, seriousness, speculation, study, surveillance, thought, thoughtfulness, weighing
ASSOCIATED CONCEPTS: contemplation of assignment, contemplation of bankruptcy, contemplation of insolvency, contemplation of marriage, contemplation of parties, in contemplation of death

CONTEMPORANEOUS, *adjective* coeval, coexistent, coexisting, coincident, coinciding, coinstantaneous, concomitant, concurrent, concurring, contemporary, correspondent, corresponding, *quod eodem tempore est,* simultaneous, synchronal, synchronistic, synchronous
ASSOCIATED CONCEPTS: contemporaneous agreement, contemporaneous declaration, contemporaneous exposition, contemporaneous forgeries, contemporaneous memorandum, contemporaneous transaction

CONTEMPORARY, *adjective* co-existent, latest, modern, new, present day, up to date, up to the minute

CONTEMPT *(Disdain),* **noun** abhorrence, abomination, animosity, arrogance, aspersion, aversion, condemnation,

contemptuousness, *contemptus,* contumely, debasement, defilement, denigration, denunciation, deprecation, depreciation, derision, derogation, detestation, detraction, disapprobation, disapproval, disdainfulness, disesteem, disfavor, disgust, dislike, disparagement, dispraise, disregard, disrepute, disvaluation, *fastidium,* imprecation, incivility, indignant aversion, infamy, insolence, malediction, misprision, objurgation, obloquy, odium, opposure, opprobrium, rebuff, reproach, reprobation, reproof, reproval, repugnance, revilement, revulsion, ridicule, scorn, scurrility
FOREIGN PHRASES: **Qui contemnit praeceptum contemnit praecipientem.** He who contemns a precept contemns the party who gives it.

CONTEMPT *(Disobedience to the court),* **noun** audacity, contemptuous resistance, contumaciousness, contumacy, contumely, defiance of orders, deprecation, dereliction, disaffection, disobedience, disposition to resist, disregard of orders, disrespect, disrespectfulness, dissension, encroachment, fractiousness, impertinence, improbity, impudence, indiscipline, indocility, infringement, inobservance, insolence, insubmission, insubordination, intractableness, irreverence, nonadherence, noncompliance, noncooperation, nonobservance, obstinacy, obstructionism, perverseness, recalcitrance, recusancy, refractoriness, refusal to obey orders, reproach, repudiation, repulsion, resistance, resistance to authority, restiveness, rudeness, undutifulness, unobservance, unruliness, unsubmissiveness, unwillingness, violation of orders, willful disregard
ASSOCIATED CONCEPTS: aggravated contempt, civil contempt, common-law contempt, constructive contempt, contempt of court, continuing contempt, criminal contempt, evasive contempt, judicial contempt, obstruction of justice, summary contempt

CONTEMPTIBLE, *adjective* abhorrent, *abiectus,* abject, abominable, atrocious, base, blameworthy, censurable, condemnable, condemnatory, contemned, *contemnendus, contemptus,* contumelious, corrupt, culpable, damnable, deplorable, depraved, despicable, despised, detestable, discreditable, disgraceful, disgusting, dishonorable, disreputable, egregious, evil, execrable, foul, fulsome, hateful, heinous, horrendous, horrible, ignominious, infamous, inglorious, insidious, insufferable, loathsome, nefarious, noxious, objurgatory, odious, offensive, opprobrious, perfidious, repellent, reprehensible, reproachful, reprobative, repugnant, repulsive, shameful, shameless, unworthy, vile, villainous, wicked, worthless
ASSOCIATED CONCEPTS: contemptible criminal act

CONTEMPTUOUS, *adjective* abasing, abject, abominable, abusive, accusatory, arbitrary, arrogant, base, brazen, bumptious, calumniating, calumniatory, calumnious, challenging, compromising, contemptible, contumelious, damaging, decrying, defamatory, defiant, defying, denigratory, denunciatory, depreciating, depreciative, derisive, derisory, derogative, derogatory, detestable, detracting, disapproving, discourteous, disdainful, dishonorable, dishonoring, dislikable, disparaging, disregardful, disrespectful, execrable, expressing disdain, flouting, forward, harsh, hateful, ignominious, impertinent, impudent, indignant, infamous, injuring, injurious, insinuating, insolent, insulting, irreverent, libelous, maledicent, malevolent, malicious, malignant, maligning, manifesting contempt, nefarious, objectionable, obnoxious, obtrusive, offensive, opprobrious, repellent, reproachful, reproaching, repugnant, repulsive, reviling, rude, scandalous, scornful, slighting, spiteful, uncivil, vile, vituperative

CONTEND (Dispute), **verb** altercate, argue, battle, be discordant, bicker, brawl, carry on an argument, challenge, clash, combat, compete, conflict, *contendere,* contest, contradict, *decernere,* differ, disaccord, disagree, discept, discord, dissent, encounter, engage, fight, gainsay, have an altercation, have words with, impugn, litigate, make an issue, oppose, *pugnare,* quarrel, reluct, rival, skirmish, spar, spat, squabble, strike at, strive, struggle, take on, vie with, war, wrangle

CONTEND (Maintain), **verb** *adfirmare,* advance, affirm, argue, assert, asseverate, assure, attest, aver, avow, claim, claim to know, *confirmare, contendere,* declare, emphasize, express, hold, hold the opinion, insist, make a statement, make an assertion, predicate, profess, say, set forth, state, state emphatically, stress, utter with conviction, vouch, warrant

CONTENDER, noun adversary, adverse party, antagonist, appellant, applicant, arguer, aspirant, campaigner, candidate, challenger, charger, claimant, combatant, competitor, complainant, contestant, contester, controversialist, corrival, debater, denouncer, disputant, entrant, examinee, feuder, fighter, foe, libelant, litigant, litigator, nominee, office-seeker, opponent, opposer, opposition, oppositionist, party, party to a suit, petitioner, polemist, the prosecution, pugilist, respondent, rival, striver, suitor

CONTENT (Meaning), **noun** accepted meaning, aim, basis, bearing, cardinal point, chief constituent, chief part, denotation, design, drift, emphasis, essence, essential matter, essential meaning, essential part, exegesis, explanation, explication, exposition, force, general meaning, gist, gravamen, impact, implication, import, intent, intention, interpretation, literal interpretation, literal meaning, literal sense, literality, main point, matter, matter of cognition, meaningfulness, motif, nature, object, obvious interpretation, obvious meaning, obvious sense, plain meaning, point, *prima facie,* primary element, primary meaning, purport, purpose, quiddity, quintessence, salient point, scope, sense, *sensus, sententia,* significance, significant part, signification, *significatio,* spirit, subject, subject matter, substance, substantial meaning, sum, sum and substance, tenor, text, theme
ASSOCIATED CONCEPTS: content contained in an instrument, content of a contract, content of a note

CONTENT (Structure), **noun** anatomy, arrangement of parts, body, combination, complement, composite, composition, configuration, conformation, constitution, construction, contexture, core, design, form, format, formation, framework, interrelation, makeup, nature, organization, pattern, plan, setup, style of arrangement

CONTENTION (Argument), **noun** allegation, area of disagreement, argumentation, cause, conflict, contest, controversy, debate, discord, *disputatio,* disputation, dispute, disputed point, ground, issue, legal dispute, legal issue, plea, point, polemic, proposition, reason, root of dissension

CONTENTION (Opposition), **noun** antagonism, challenge, clashing, combat, competition, competitiveness, conflict, contentiousness, contest, contestation, contrariety, contravention, controversy, counteraction, cross purposes, debate, difference, disaccord, disagreement, discord, disharmony, disputation, dispute, dissension, dissent, dissidence, dissonance, divergence, enmity, faction, factiousness, feud, fight, friction, hostility, inimicality, irreconcilability, protest, protestation, quarrel, quarreling, quarrelsomeness, recrimination, resistance, rivalry, schism, strife, struggle, unappeasability, velitation, wrangling

CONTENTIOUS, adjective aggressive, argumentative, bellicose, belligerent, cantankerous, captious, caviling, combative, competitive, contrary, contumacious, cross, discordant, disputatious, dissentious, factious, inimical, irascible, litigious, militant, noncooperating, nonpacific, obstinate, perverse, polemical, pugnacious, *pugnax,* quarrelsome, recalcitrant, schismatic, stubborn, uncooperative, unfriendly, unpacific, unpeaceful, wrangling

CONTENTS, noun components, constituents, details, drift, essence, gist, items, meaning, parts, pith, scope, sense, subject, subject matter, subject of thought, substance, text, themes, thesis, topics
ASSOCIATED CONCEPTS: contents of a chose in action, contents of a note

CONTEST (Competition), **noun** bout, *certamen, certatio,* challenge, clash, corrivalry, emulation, encounter, engagement, game, match, opposition, pitting of strengths, race, rivalry, rivalship, sport, sporting event, struggle, test of endurance, tournament, tourney, trial
ASSOCIATED CONCEPTS: election contest

CONTEST (Dispute), **noun** action, altercation, antagonism, argument, battle, bickering, brawl, challenge, clash, combat, contention, controversion, controversy, debate, difference of opinion, disaccord, disagreement, disceptation, discord, disharmony, disputation, dispute, dissension, dissent, dissonance, embroilment, encounter, failure to agree, feud, fight, fracas, fray, impugnation, impugnment, inharmony, litigation, monomachy, noncomformity, obstinacy, opposition, oppugnancy, polemics, quarrel, recalcitrance, recusancy, resistance, revolt, skirmish, squabble, strained relations, strife, variance, verbal contention, verbal engagement, war, war of words, wrangle
ASSOCIATED CONCEPTS: notice of contest, will contest

CONTEST, verb altercate, argue, battle, call to answer, challenge, combat, conflict, contend, *contendere,* contradict, contravene, controvert, counter, debate, defy, disaffirm, disagree, dispute, fight, gainsay, grapple with, impugn, object, oppose, oppugn, quarrel over, question, refuse to accept, refuse to admit, resist, struggle, take exception to, traverse, vie with
ASSOCIATED CONCEPTS: contest a will, contest an election, contest an insurance policy, contested case

CONTESTABLE, adjective at issue, close, competing, confutable, controversial, controvertible, debatable, deniable, disputable, questionable, refutable

CONTESTANT, noun adversary, adverse party, aemulus, antagonist, appellant, battler, belligerent, candidate, challenger, claimant, combatant, complainant, contender, contester, corrival, disputant, foe, libelant, litigant, opponent, opposer, opposing party, opposition, oppositionist, participant, party to a suit, *petitor,* rival, suitor
ASSOCIATED CONCEPTS: contestant to a will

CONTEXT, noun *argumentum,* background, circumstance, coloring, connection, connotation, extended meaning, force, gist, implication, import, main meaning, meaning, mode of expression, purport, range of meaning, scope, sense, subject matter, sum and substance, surroundings, tenor, text, topic
FOREIGN PHRASES: ***Nemo enim aliquam partem recte intelligere possit antequam totum iterum atque iterum perlegerit.*** No one can rightly understand one part before he has again and again read the whole.

CONTIGUOUS, adjective abutting, adjacent, adjoining, against, at close quarters, beside, bordering, bounding, close, *confinis,* conjoining, conjunct, connected, conterminous, *continens,* convergent, coupled, edging, end to end, fringing, in close proximity, in common boundaries with, in contact, joined, meeting, near, neighboring, next to, on the confines of, on the edge of, proximal, proximate, side by side, touching, verging

ASSOCIATED CONCEPTS: contiguous lands, contiguous municipalities, contiguous property, contiguous territory

CONTINENCE, noun abstainment, abstention, abstinence, asceticism, chastity, conservatism, *continentia,* eschewal, forbearance, moderateness, moderation, prudence, renunciation, restraint, self-command, self-control, self denial, self-discipline, self-restraint, sobriety, stoicism, temperance, *temperantia,* temperateness

ASSOCIATED CONCEPTS: continuance of a law suit

CONTINGENCY, noun accident, befalling, casus, chance, circumstance, circumstantial event, coincidence, conditional event, contingence, contingent, contingent event, dependent event, doubtful event, fortune, hap, happening, inadvertence, incident, luck, occurrence, possibility, uncertain event, uncertainty, unforeseen occurrence, unintentional happening

ASSOCIATED CONCEPTS: contingency contract, double contingency, unavoidable contingency, unforeseen contingency, unusual or extraordinary contingencies

FOREIGN PHRASES: ***Casus fortuitus non est sperandus, et nemo tenetur devinare.*** A fortuitous event is not to be expected, and no one is bound to foresee it.

CONTINGENT, adjective attributed to, coincidental, conditioned, consequential, dependent, dependent on, dependent on circumstances, depending, due to, in a state of uncertainty, incident to, possible, provisional, resulting from, subject to, subject to terms, subsidiary

ASSOCIATED CONCEPTS: contingent basis, contingent claim, contingent contract, contingent debt, contingent demand, contingent estate, contingent event, contingent expectancy, contingent fee, contingent fund, contingent gift, contingent interest, contingent legacy, contingent liability, contingent life estate, contingent obligation, contingent remainder, contingent right, contingent use, contingent will

CONTINUAL (Connected), **adjective** constant, constantly recurring, continued, continuing, *continuus,* nonstop, of regular recurrence, perennial, persistent, proceeding without cessation, proceeding without interruption, regular, steadfast, steady, sustained, unbroken, unceasing, unchanging, unintermitted, uninterrupted, unremitting, unstopped

CONTINUAL (Perpetual), **adjective** *adsiduus,* boundless, ceaseless, continuous, endless, eternal, everlasting, incessant, infinite, interminable, never-ending, permanent, *perpetuus,* sempiternal, unceasing, unending, unstopped, unvarying

CONTINUANCE, noun abiding, adjournment of a cause, adjournment of a proceeding, admission of postponement, *adsiduitas, continuatio,* continuation, endurance, extension, lasting, lengthening, perpetuation, *perpetuitas,* perseverance, persistence, postponement, prolongation, protraction, stay, sustained action

ASSOCIATED CONCEPTS: continuance in office, continuance of a nonconforming use, continuance of a partnership, continuance of a proceeding, continuance of criminal case, presumption of continuance

CONTINUATION (Prolongation), **noun** addition, adherence, *adsiduitas,* augmentation, continuance, *continuatio,* extension, lengthening, maintenance, perpetuation, *perpetuitas,* perseverance, persistence, preservation, protraction, stretching, sustaining, sustenance

ASSOCIATED CONCEPTS: continuation of a business, continuation of a condition, continuation of a fact, continuation of a lien, continuation of an easement, continuation of service

CONTINUATION (Resumption), **noun** carrying on, continuance, fresh start, new beginning, new start, proceeding, reestablishment, recommencement, recurrence, reinstatement, reinstitution, renewal, reopening, restoration, return, reversion, supplementation

ASSOCIATED CONCEPTS: continuation of a proceeding, continuation of a suit

CONTINUE (Adjourn), **verb** arrest temporarily, defer, delay, discontinue, hold over, interrupt, keep pending, lay aside, lay over, postpone, prorogue, put over, put over to a future date, recess, respite, restrain, set for a later time, shelve, stall, stay, suspend, table, tide over

ASSOCIATED CONCEPTS: continue an action, grant of a continuance

CONTINUE (Persevere), **verb** abide, be durable, be permanent, bide, exist, forge ahead, go on, keep, last, linger, maintain, move ahead, *pergere, perseverare, persevere,* persist, *persistere,* press onward, prevail, progress, promote, pursue, stay on, subsist, sustain

ASSOCIATED CONCEPTS: continuing application, continuing contracts, continuing nuisance, continuing offer, continuing trespass, continuing wrong

CONTINUE (Prolong), **verb** arrange in succession, drag out, draw out, *durare,* extend, extend in duration, lengthen, maintain, maintain continuity, perpetuate, preserve, protract, retain, *stare,* sustain, uphold

ASSOCIATED CONCEPTS: continue in force and effect, continue in office, continue to carry on business, continued and uninterrupted use, continued concealment, continued good health, continued possession, continuing accumulation, continuing affirmative act, continuing and subsisting trust, continuing body, continuing conspiracy, continuing contempt, continuing crime, continuing duty, continuing guaranty, continuing jurisdiction, continuing loan, continuing obligation, continuing offense, continuing offer, continuing proceeding, continuing representation, continuing right, continuing tort, continuing trust

CONTINUE (Resume), **verb** begin again, begin over, carry on, carry over, go back to, make a new beginning, proceed, reestablish, rebegin, recommence, reinstate, reinstitute, renew, *renovare,* reopen, restore, return to, take up again

CONTINUITY, noun coherence, connectedness, connection, consecution, consecutiveness, consistency, constancy, continualness, continuance, *continuatio,* continuation, continuousness, continuum, incessancy, permanence, *perpetuitas,* perpetuity, progression, protraction, sequence, succession, successiveness, unintermittedness, uninterrupted connection, uninterruptedness, uninterruption

CONTINUOUS, adjective ceaseless, consecutive, constant, continual, continuing, endless, extended, following, incessant, never ending, perennial, perpetual, progressive, prolonged, repeated, running, sequential, steady, sustained, unbroken, unceasing, unending, unfaltering, unintermittent, unintermitting, uninterrupted, unremitting, unstopped, without cessation, without interruption

ASSOCIATED CONCEPTS: continuous absence, continuous account, continuous activity, continuous adverse possession, continuous and unbroken, continuous and uninterrupted use, continuous course of business, continuous crime, continuous disability, continuous easement, continuous guaranty, continuous injury, continuous nuisance, continuous possession, continuous residence, continuous servitude, continuous tort, continuous use, continuous wrong, continuously carry on, continuously confined, continuously disabled, continuously employed

CONTORT, verb bend, bend out of shape, deform, depravare, *detorquere*, dislocate, *distorquere*, distort, knot, misshape, pervert, turn, twine, twist, twist and turn, wind, wrench, wrest, wrinkle, writhe

CONTOUR (Outline), **noun** ambit, bounds, circle, circuit, circumference, circumscription, configuration, delineation, diagram, figuration, figure, form, frame, framework, laterality, *lineamenta,* lines, main features, outside, perimeter, periphery, picture, plan, profile, relief, rough sketch, silhouette, skeleton, sketch, structure, *tournure*

CONTOUR (Shape), **noun** configuration, conformation, feature, *figura,* figuration, figure, form, *forma,* formation, frame, lines, profile, relief, sculpture, silhouette, structure, substance, substantial form, turn

CONTRA, adverb adverse to, against, con, contrarily, contrariwise, contrawise, conversely, counter, in conflict with, in contrast to, in opposition to, inversely, loathe to, on the contrary, on the other hand, opposed to, opposite, oppositely, otherwise, *per contra,* quite the contrary, to the contrary, vice versa, *versus*

CONTRA, noun antipode, antithesis, antonym, contrary, converse, counter, extreme, inverse, obverse, offset, opposite, reverse, the other side

CONTRA, preposition adverse to, against, at cross purposes, athwart, contrariwise, counter, in conflict with, in opposition to, opposed to, opposite to, over against, versus, vis-à-vis

CONTRABAND, noun banned goods, bootlegged commerce, bootlegged goods, bootlegged trade, bootlegged traffic, captured goods, confiscated goods, confiscated property, embargoed goods, goods exported illegally, goods imported illegally, goods subject to confiscation, goods subject to seizure, illegal property, illegal traffic, illegally exported goods, illegally imported goods, illicit gains, merces vetitae, poached trade, poached traffic, prohibited articles, prohibited import, restricted goods, seized articles, seized goods, smuggled commerce, smuggled goods, smuggled trade, smuggled traffic, stolen article, stolen goods, swag
ASSOCIATED CONCEPTS: contraband articles, contraband goods

CONTRACT, noun accord, accordance, agreement, arrangement, articles of agreement, assurance, avouchment, avowal, bargain, binding agreement, bond, charter, collective agreement, commitment, compact, compromise, concordat, *condicio, conductio,* confirmation, *conventio,* covenant, deal, embodied terms, engagement, *entente,* guarantee, instrument evidencing an agreement, ironclad agreement, legal document, mutual agreement, mutual pledge, mutual promise, mutual undertaking, negotiated agreement, obligation, pact, paction, *pactum,* pledge, pledged word, private understanding, promise,

ratified agreement, set terms, settlement, stated terms, stipulation, terms for agreement, understanding, undertaking, warranty, written terms
ASSOCIATED CONCEPTS: acceptance of a contract, accessory contract, action on contract, adhesion contract, aleatory contract, alteration of a contract, alternative contract, anticipatory breach of contract, assent to a contract, assignment of a contract, bilateral contract, breach of a contract, breach of contract, cancellation of a contract, claim arising on contract, collateral contract, collective agreement, commercial contract, concurrent contracts, conditional acceptance of a contract, conditional agreement, conditional contract, consideration in a contract, constructive contract, contingency contract, continuing contract, contract action, contract carrier, contract for an option, contract implied in fact, contract obligation, contract of agency, contract of carriage, contract of employment, contract of guaranty, contract of hire or hiring, contract of indemnity, contract of insurance, contract of record, contract of sale, contract of subscription for stock, contract of suretyship, contract price, contract rights, contract to lease, contract to purchase, contract to sell, contracting out work, de facto contract, divisible contract, endowment contract, enforceable contract, exclusive contract, executed contract, executory contract, express contract, fictitious contract, fiduciary contract, formal contract, fraudulent contract, future contract, general contract, government contract, gratuitous contract, guaranty contract, illegal contract, illusory contract, immoral contract, impairing the obligation of contract, implied contract, indivisible contract, inequitable contract, installment contract, joint contract, liberty of contract, lump sum contract, marriage contract, material alteration of contract, material breach of contract, obligation of contract, optional contracts, oral contract, parol agreement, parties to a contract, passive breach of contract, performance of a contract, pre-existing contracts, private contract, privity of contract, public contract, quasi contract, reformation of a contract, release from a contract, renunciation of a contract, repudiation of a contract, requirements contract, rescission of a contract, restitution on a contract, revival of a contract, right to contract, sealed contract, separable contract, service contract, severable contract, specialty contract, subcontract, surety contract, third-party beneficiary contract, unconditional contract, unconscionable contract, unenforceable contract, unilateral contract, unlawful contract, valid contract, verbal contract, void contract, written contract

FOREIGN PHRASES: *Vox emissa volat; litera scripta manet.* Words spoken vanish; the written letter remains. *Qui cum alio contrahit, vel est, vel debet esse non ignarus condicionis ejus.* He who contracts with another is not, or ought not to be ignorant of his condition. *Praescriptio et executio non pertinent advalorem contractus, set ad tempus et modum actionis instituendae.* Prescription and execution do not affect the validity of the contract, but the time and manner of instituting an action. *Ex turpi contractu actio non oritur.* From an immoral contract an action does not arise. *Dolo malo pactumse non servaturum.* An agreement induced by fraud is not valid. *Pacto aliquod licitum est, quid sine pacto non admittitur.* By agreement, things are allowed which are not otherwise permitted. *Nulla pactione effici potest ne dolus praestetur.* By no agreement can it be effected that a fraud shall be maintained. *In contractibus, benigna, in testamentis, benignior; inrestitutionibus, benignissima interpretatio facienda est.* In contracts, the interpretations should be liberal, in wills, more liberal; in restitutions, most liberal. *Scientia utrinque par pares contrahentesfacit.* Equal knowledge on both sides makes the contracting parties equal. ***Pacta conventa quae neque contra leges, neque dolo malo inita sunt, omni modo observanda sunt.*** Agreements which are not contrary to the laws, nor fraudulently entered into, are in all respects to be observed. ***Pactis privatorum juri publico non derogatur.*** Private contracts do not derogate from public law. ***In stipulationibus cum quaeritur quid actum sit verba contrasti pulatorem interpretanda sunt.*** In agreements, when the question is what was agreed upon, the terms are to be interpreted against the party offering them. ***Privatis pactionibus non dubium est non laedi jus caeterorum.*** There is no doubt that the rights of others cannot be prejudiced by private agreements. ***In omnibus contractibus, sive nominatis sive innominatis, permutatio continetur.*** In all contracts, whether nominate or innominate, an exchange, i.e., a consideration, is implied. ***Pacta quae contra leges constitutionesque vel contra bonos mores fiunt, nullam vim habere, indubitati juris est.*** It is unquestionably the law that contracts which are made contrary to the laws or against good morals, have no force in law. ***Nemo tenetur ad impossibile.*** No one is bound to an impossibility. ***Pacta dant legem contractui.*** Stipulations constitute the law for the contract. ***Pacta que turpem causam continent non sunt observanda.*** Contracts which are based on an unlawful consideration will not been forced. ***Conventio vincit legem.*** The agreement of parties controls the law. ***Contractus ex turpi causa, vel contra bonos mores, nullus est.*** A contract founded on a base consideration, or one against good morals, is null. ***Nudum pactum est ubi nulla subest causa praeter conventionem; sed ubi subest causa, fit obligatio, et parit actionem.*** A naked contract is where there is no consideration for the agreement; but, where there is a consideration, an obligation is created and gives rise to a right of action. ***Modus et conventio vincunt legem.*** Custom, convention and an agreement of the parties overrule the law. ***Conventio facit legem.*** An agreement creates the law, i.e. the parties to a binding contract will be held to their promises. ***Ex nudo pacto non oritur actio.*** No action arises on a contract without a consideration. ***Contractus legem ex conventione accipiunt.*** Contracts receive legal sanction from the agreement of the parties. ***Naturale est quidlibet dissolvi eo modo quo ligatur.*** It is natural for a thing to be unbound in the same way in which it was made binding. ***Nihil tam conveniens est naturali aequitati quam unumquodque dissolvi eo ligamine quo ligatum est.*** Nothing is so agreeable to natural equity as that a thing should be dissolved by the same means by which it was bound. ***In conventionibus, contrahentium voluntas potius quam verba spectari placuit.*** In contracts, it is the rule to regard the intention of the parties rather than the actual words. ***Ex maleficio non oritur contractus.*** No contract is born of wrongdoing. ***Ex pacto illicito non oritur actio.*** From an unlawful agreement, no action will lie. ***In contrahenda venditione, ambiguum pactum contra venditorem interpretandum est.*** In the negotiation of a sale, an ambiguous agreement is to be interpreted against the seller. ***In contractibus, rei veritas potius quam scriptura perspici debet.*** In contracts, the truth of the matter ought to be regarded as more important than the writing. ***In contractibus, tacite insunt quae sunt moris et consuetudinis.*** In contracts, matters of custom and usage are tacitly implied. ***Incerta quantitas vitiat actum.*** An uncertain quantity vitiates the act. ***Legem enim contractus dat.*** The contract makes the law. ***Nuda pactio obligationem non parit.*** A naked promise does not create a binding obligation. ***Eisdem modis dissolvitur obligatio quae nascitur ex contractu, vel quasi, quibus contrahitur.*** An obligation which arises in contract, or quasi contract, is dissolved in the same ways in which it is contracted.

CONTRACT, *verb* accept an offer, agree, *contrahere*, covenant, engage, enter into, *locare*, make a bargain, make terms, obligate oneself, pledge, promise, undertake, undertake by contract
ASSOCIATED CONCEPTS: contract to perform services

CONTRACT OBLIGATION, *noun* avowal, bond, commitment, compact, concordant, condition, covenant, guarantee, indenture, issue, liability, pact, pledge, promise, provision, proviso, specific obligation, specific term, term, warranty

CONTRACT PROVISION, *noun* arrangement, article of agreement, clause, condition, limitation, obligation, postulation, prerequisite, proviso, qualification, requisite, restriction, specification, stipulation, term

CONTRACTOR, *noun* architect, artificer, builder, constructor, designer, deviser, engineer, maker, planner, worker
ASSOCIATED CONCEPTS: artisan's lien, independent contractor, general contractor, materials lien, mechanic's lien, subcontractor

CONTRACTUAL, *adjective* accordant, agreed, agreed to, arranged, binding, collectively agreed, committed, consensual, consentient, in accord, in accordance with, in conformity, negotiated, obligated, obligatory, pledged, promised, settled, signed, signed and sealed, stipulated, understood
ASSOCIATED CONCEPTS: contractual agreement, contractual assumption of risk, contractual consideration, contractual liability, contractual obligation, contractual relationship, contractual right, contractual status

CONTRADICT, *verb* *ab re discrepare*, abrogate, affirm the contrary, annul, answer back, argue, assert the contrary, assert the opposite, challenge, clash, come in conflict with, conflict, confute, *contradicere*, contrast, contravene, controvert, counter, counteract, countervail, counterwork, deny, differ, disagree, disclaim, disprove, dispute, dissent, give denial to, go against, go contrary to, go counter to, go in opposition to, impugn, *inter se repugnare*, negate, negative, oppose, oppugn, prove the contrary, quarrel, rebut, refuse to accept, refute, repudiate, reverse, run counter to, take issue with, traverse
ASSOCIATED CONCEPTS: contradiction by a witness on the stand

CONTRADICTION, *noun* adverseness, antipathy, antithesis, assertion of the contrary, assertion of the opposite, conflict, conflicting evidence, confutation, contradistinction, contraindication, contraposition, contraries, contrariety, contrariness, contrary assertion, contrast, contravention, controversion, controversy, counteraccusation, counteraction, counterargument, countercharge, counterevidence, counteroath, counterstatement, defiance, denunciation, difference of opinion, direct opposite, disaccord, disagreement, discord, *discrepantia*, disproof, dispute, dissension, dissent, divergence, divergent opinion, incongruity, inconsistency, negation, negative evidence, opposite extreme, oppositeness, opposites, opposition, other extreme, rebuttal, rebutting evidence, refutal, refutation, rejoinder, *repugnantia*, variance
ASSOCIATED CONCEPTS: contradiction in terms, contradiction of a witness, contradiction of a writing, impeachment of a witness

CONTRADICTORY, *adjective* abjuratory, absonant, adversative, adverse, antagonistic, antithetical, asserting the contrary, asserting the opposite, at odds, at variance, clashing, conflicting, confutative, confuting, contradicting, contradistinct, contraindicating, contrapositive, contrarious, *contrarius,* contrary, contrary to reason, contrasted, contravening, converse, counter, counteractant, countervailing, counterworking, denying, diametrically opposite, disagreeing, disclaiming, discordant, discrepant, dissentient, dissenting, *diversus,* in the opposite scale, inconsistent, inverse, irreconcilable, negating, negatory, obverse, opponent, opposed, opposing, opposite, oppositional, oppositive, rebutting, refutative, refutatory, refuting, *repugnans,* repugnant, reverse, *tout au contraire,* unreconciled

ASSOCIATED CONCEPTS: contradiction of a writing, contradictory evidence, contradictory findings, contradictory instructions, contradictory statement

FOREIGN PHRASES: *Allegans contraria non est audiendus.* One making contradictory allegations is not to be heard. *Cum duo inter se pugnantia reperiuntur in testamento, ultimum ratum est.* When two things repugnant to each other are found in a will, the last shall be confirmed.

CONTRADISTINCTION, noun antagonism, antithesis, clashing, contradiction, contradictoriness, contrariety, contrast, counterpoint, departure from, difference, disparity, dissimilarity, distinction, distinctness, divergence, oppositeness, opposition

CONTRAPOSITION, noun antagonism, antithesis, confrontation, confrontment, contradiction, contradistinction, contrariety, contrast, converse, counterpart, disagreement, disparity, dissimilarity, incompatibility, obverse, odds, opposite, opposite side, opposition, otherness, placement against, placement opposite, reverse, unlikeness

CONTRARY, adjective abnegative, adversative, adverse, *adversus,* answering, antagonistic to, antipathetic, antithetic, antithetical, at cross purposes, at issue, at variance, averse, captious, conflicting, confutative, confuting, contradicting, contradictory, contradistinct, contraindicating, contrapositive, *contrarius,* contrasted, contrasting, contraway, converse, counter, counteracting, countervailing, denying, diametrically opposite, different, disaffirming, disagreeing, disavowing, discordant, in opposition to, inverse, negative, negatory, obverse, opposed, opposing, opposite, opposite in character, opposite in nature, oppositional, oppugnant, rebutting, refutative, refutatory, refuting, *tout le contraire,* vis-à-vis

ASSOCIATED CONCEPTS: contrary intent, contrary to evidence, contrary to good morals, contrary to law, contrary to public interest, contrary to statute

CONTRARY, noun antilogy, antipode, antithesis, conflict, contradiction, contradistinction, contrast, converse, incompatibility, inconsistency, opposite, opposition, other extreme, reverse, vice versa

ASSOCIATED CONCEPTS: contrary to the law

CONTRARY TO FACT, adjective aberrant, deceptive, delusory, dishonest, distorted, erroneous, fallacious, false, fraudulent, inexact, questionable, solecistical, specious, unfactual, untrue

CONTRARY TO LAW, adjective criminal, false, felonious, illegal, illegitimate, improper, inaccurate, incorrect, inexact, lawless, malefactory, malfeasant, outlawed, prohibited, proscribed, tortious, unauthorized, unlawful, unlicensed, wrong

ASSOCIATED CONCEPTS: contrary to the evidence

CONTRAST, verb appose, bring into comparison, *comparare,* compare by observing differences, compare to, compare with, confront, differ, differentiate, *discrepare,* discriminate, distinguish, distinguish between, draw a comparison, exhibit the differences between, institute a comparison, make a comparison, oppose, place against, place in juxtaposition, set in opposition, set off against, set off by opposition, stand out in opposition

CONTRAVENE, verb balk, be contrary to, be in conflict with, clash, conflict with, contest, contradict, counteract, cross, defeat, defy, deny, disagree, dispute, disregard, foil, frustrate, gainsay, go against, impugn, infringe, negate, nullify, oppose, rebut, refute, run counter to, thwart, transgress, traverse, violate

ASSOCIATED CONCEPTS: contravene a statute, contravene the law

CONTRAVENTION, noun antagonism, argument, breaking an obligation, clash, conflict, confrontation, contention, contest, contradiction, controversion, counteraction, countervail, debate, denial, disagreement, discord, dissent, dissidence, disunion, disunity, divisiveness, friction, gainsaying, infringement, lack of concord, negation, opposing, opposition, oppugnancy, quarrel, rebuttal, resistance, transgression, traversal, variance, violation, vying with, wrangle

ASSOCIATED CONCEPTS: contravention of a contract, contravention of a statute, contravention of an agreement

CONTRIBUTE (Assist), verb abet, accommodate, *adiuvare,* advance, advise, afford aid, aid, assist, assist substantially, be a party to, be helpful, be of service, bear a part, bring aid, conduce, cooperate, encourage, enter into, furnish aid, give aid, help, intercede for, join in, lend assistance, minister, partake, partake of, participate, *prodesse,* render help, serve, stand by, subscribe to, succor, support, take an active part in, tend

ASSOCIATED CONCEPTS: contributing cause, contributing to delinquency of a minor, contributing to support a dependent

CONTRIBUTE (Indemnify), verb compensate, give back, indemnity, make compensation, make reparation, make restitution, pay back, pay damages, recompense, reimburse, remit, remunerate, restore, return, satisfy, tender

CONTRIBUTE (Supply), verb accord, add, administer, afford, allot, assign, award, bequeath, bequest, bestow, cede, commit, confer, consign, convey, deed, deliver, demise, devote, dispense, dispose of, dole out, donate, endow, enrich, equip, furnish, give, give away, grant, hand over, impart, invest, mete out, pass down, pay, present, proffer, relinquish, remit, render, share, subsidize, supply, tender, transmit, will

ASSOCIATED CONCEPTS: contributed capital, contributing fault, contributing negligence, contributing proximate cause

CONTRIBUTION (Donation), noun alms, assistance, award, benefaction, benefit, bequest, bestowal, bestowment of a share, bonus, boon, bounty, charity, conferment, *conferre, contribuere,* dispensation, endowment, generosity, gift, grant, grant of a share, gratuity, honorarium, lagniappe, largesse, offering, present, presentation, provision, remembrance, subsidy, subvention, succor, sustenance, tribute

CONTRIBUTION (Indemnification), noun compensation, guerdon, indemnity, need, offsetting, paying back, payment, quittance, reckoning, recompense, redress, reimbursement, remuneration, reparation, repayment, requital, requitement, restitution, restoration, return, satisfaction, substitution

ASSOCIATED CONCEPTS: contribution among joint tort feasors, subrogation

CONTRIBUTION *(Participation)*, *noun* abetment, aid, alliance, assistance, association, coaction, coalition, collaboration, collusion, combination, complicity, comradeship, concert, confederation, consent, cooperation, coordination, encouragement, federation, fellowship, harmony, help, interest, league, partnership, pool, shareholding, sharing, teamwork, union

ASSOCIATED CONCEPTS: accumulated contributions, contributing to the injury, contribution to capital, contributory fault, contributory infringer, contributory negligence, indemnity

CONTRIBUTOR *(Giver)*, *noun* almoner, almsgiver, altruist, assignor, benefactor, bestower, donator, donor, granter, grantor, investor, patron, philanthropist, presenter, subscriber, supplier, supporter, testator, vouchsafer

CONTRIBUTOR *(Contributor)*, *noun* abettor, accessory, accomplice, aide, ally, assistant, associate, auxiliary, coadjutor, cohelper, collaborator, colleague, compeer, comrade, confederate, confrere, consort, cooperator, copartner, coworker, fellow, helper, helpmate, mate, participant, participator, partner, party, peer, shareholder, sharer, teammate, teamworker, workfellow

CONTRIBUTORY, *adjective* accessory, additional, aiding, assisting, auxiliary, beneficial, conducive, contributing, determining, helpful, helping, influential, instrumental, lending assistance, salutary, secondary, tributary, useful

ASSOCIATED CONCEPTS: contributory cause, contributory negligence

CONTRITE, *adjective* apologetic, broken in spirit, chastened, compunctious, conscience-smitten, conscience-stricken, desirous of forgiveness, full of regrets, full of remorse, guilty, humble, humbled, *paenitet*, penitent, penitential, regretful, regretting, remorseful, repentant, rueful, self-accusing, self-condemnatory, self-convicted, self-denunciatory, self-reproachful, sorrowful, sorry, soul-searching

CONTRIVANCE, *noun* artifice, collusion, complicity, connivance, craft, deception, design, designing power, device, dodge, engineering, *excogitatio*, intrigue, *inventio*, invention, inventiveness, machination, maneuver, manipulation, means to an end, mechanism, method, plan, plot, scheme, stratagem, strategics, subterfuge, tactics, wile, wily device

CONTRIVE, *verb* arrange, cause, collude, compose, conceive, concoct, connive, consider, conspire, counterplot, design, develop a course, devise, draft, effect, *excogitare*, fabricate, fashion, forecast, form, frame, imagine, improvise, induce, intrigue, *invenire*, invent, lay plans, *machinari*, machinate, make up, maneuver, mine, organize, pattern, plan, plot, predesign, preestablish, prepare, procure, project, provoke, scheme, shape out a course, sketch, systematize

ASSOCIATED CONCEPTS: contrive a cause of action

CONTROL *(Restriction)*, *noun* blockade, brake, check, constraint, curb, deterrence, deterrent, disallowance, exclusion, inhibition, limitation, moderation, prevention, prohibition, qualification, rationing, repression, restraint, restrictive practice, subdual, suppression

ASSOCIATED CONCEPTS: institution of controls, price control

CONTROL *(Supervision)*, *noun* administration, auspices, authority, care, charge, command, custody, direction, discipline, dominance, domination, dominion, government, guardianship, guidance, jurisdiction, keeping,

management, managership, mastery, ministry, *moderatio*, oversight, patronage, power, proctorship, protectorship, *regimen*, regulation, stewardship, superintendence, *temperantia*, ward, wardenship, wardship

ASSOCIATED CONCEPTS: absolute control, circumstances beyond control, complete control, constructive control, exclusive control, immediate control, indirect control, joint control, loss of control, mutuality of control, parental control, reasonable control

CONTROL *(Regulate)*, *verb* administer, administrate, check, *coercere*, command, conduct, direct, dominate, engineer, govern, guide, handle, have charge of, have in one's charge, have the direction of, have under control, instruct, lead, look after, maintain, manage, manipulate, *moderari*, operate, order, overlook, oversee, pilot, preside over, regiment, rule, superintend, supervise, take care of

ASSOCIATED CONCEPTS: Bureau of Control and Accounts, control board, controlled corporation, controlled substance, controlling clause, controlling influence, controlling interest, controlling issues, controlling question of law or fact

CONTROL *(Restrain)*, *verb* arrest, confine, constrain, *continere*, guard, hamper, hinder, hold back, hold in check, impede, inhibit, keep in check, keep under control, limit, obstruct, prohibit, put under restraint, restrict, retard, subdue, suppress, *temperare*, trammel

ASSOCIATED CONCEPTS: controlled substance

CONTROLLED *(Automatic)*, *adjective* contrived, devised, machine like, mechanical, mechanistic

CONTROLLED *(Restrained)*, *adjective* aloof, calm, conditioned, constrained, cool, detached, disciplined, disengaged, distant, guarded, impassive, imperturbable, in check, inhibited, moderate, obedient, passionless, reflex, restrained, self-controlled, steady, stoical, temperate, unconcerned, undemonstrative, unemotional, unexcitable, unruffled

CONTROVERSIAL, *adjective* arguable, at issue, at odds, at variance, confutable, contestable, *controversus*, controvertible, debatable, dialectic, disputable, doubtful, dubious, dubitable, eristic, exhibiting pros and cons, factious, in dispute, in question, not axiomatic, open to discussion, open to doubt, open to question, polemical, problematical, questionable, refutable, speculative, suspect, uncertain, uncertified, undecided, under inquiry, unsure, unverifiable

CONTROVERSY *(Argument)*, *noun* *altercatio*, altercation, antagonism, argumentation, brawl, break, broil, clashing, conflict, conflict of opinion, contention, contest, contestation, *controversia*, debate, difference of opinion, disaccord, disagreement, *disceptatio*, disceptation, discongruity, discord, discordance, disharmony, disputation, dispute, disputed point, disputed question, dissension, dissidence, dissonance, disunion, disunity, divergence, divergent opinions, embroilment, failure to agree, feud, friction, impugnation, inaccordance, incongruence, inconsistency, inharmoniousness, inharmony, jangle, lack of concord, opposition, polemics, quarrel, question at issue, rupture, set-to, split, squabble, strife, subject of dispute, unconformity, variance, wrangle

ASSOCIATED CONCEPTS: arbitrable controversy, matters in controversy, submission of a controversy

CONTROVERSY *(Lawsuit)*, *noun* action, case, case at law, cause, contest, judicial contest, legal action, legal argument, legal proceeding, legal process, litigation, matter for judgment, process in law, suit in law

ASSOCIATED CONCEPTS: actual present controversy, amount in controversy, case or controversy, controversies in bankruptcy, controversy arising under Constitution, controversy arising under laws of the United States, controversy at law or in equity, controversy between citizens of a state and a foreign country, controversy between citizens of different states, controversy over claim, justiciable controversy, real controversy, settlement of controversy in bankruptcy, subject of controversy, sum in controversy

CONTROVERT, verb abjure, abnegate, abrogate, answer, answer conclusively, argue, argue the case, argue the point, attack, confute, contend against in discussion, contest, contradict, contradict absolutely, contravene, counter, debate, defeat, deny, disaffirm, disagree with, disallow, disavow, disclaim, discuss, dismiss, disprove, dispute, give denial to, make a rejoinder, negate, oppose, overwhelm, rebuff, rebut, *refellere, refutare,* refute, repudiate
ASSOCIATED CONCEPTS: controverted question of fact, controverting plea

CONTUMACIOUS, adjective anarchistic, cantankerous, contemptuous, *contumax,* defiant, defying lawful authority, disobedient, *entêté,* factious, fractious, headstrong, indocile, indomitable, insolent, insolently disobedient, insubordinate, intractable, mutinous, not compliant, obstinate, *pertinax,* perverse, rebellious, recalcitrant, recusant, refractory, refusing to obey, renitant, repulsive, resistant, resisting authority, resisting control, restive, stubbornly disobedient, stubbornly rebellious, uncomplying, ungovernable, unmanageable, unreasonable, unsubmissive, willfully disrespectful
ASSOCIATED CONCEPTS: contumacious conduct, contumacious witness

CONTUMELY, noun abuse, affront, arrogance, aspersion, berating, castigation, contempt, contemptuous treatment, contemptuousness, *contumelia,* derision, despite, despiteful treatment, discourtesy, disdain, disdainfulness, dishonor, disrespect, effrontery, haughtiness, humiliating rudeness, humiliation, indignity, insolence, insult, invective, objurgation, obloquy, opprobrium, presumptuousness, reproach, revilement, rudeness, scornful insolence, scornful treatment, scornfulness, scurrility, vilification, vituperation

CONVENE, verb accumulate, aggroup, amass, assemble, bring together, call, call together, call up, collect, congregate, consolidate, converge, convocare, convoke, draw together, gather, gather together, group, hold a meeting, hold a session, meet, mobilize, muster, rally, reunite, round up, summon, unite
ASSOCIATED CONCEPTS: convene a session of a court, convene a term of the court

CONVENIENT, adjective acceptable, accessible, accommodatus, advantageous, agreeable, applicable, appropriate, available, befitting, beneficial, carefree, commodious, conducive, desirable, easily accessible, easily done, easy, effortless, eligible, expedient, fitted, fitting, *habilis,* helpful, *idoneus,* opportune, presenting few difficulties, requiring no effort, serviceable, suitable, suited, useful
ASSOCIATED CONCEPTS: balance of convenience, certificate of public convenience and necessity, convenience and necessity, convenience of parties, enforcement in convenience, greatest convenience, public convenience, reasonably convenient, rule of convenience
FOREIGN PHRASES: Non solum quid licet, sed quid est conveniens, est considerandum; quia nihil quod est inconveniens est licitum. Not only that which is lawful, but that which is convenient is to be considered, because nothing which is inconvenient is lawful.

CONVENTIONAL, adjective acceptable, accepted, accustomed, approved, classical, common, conformable, conforming, conforming to accepted standards, customary, established, established by general consent, everyday, familiar, fitting, fixed, general, habitual, in established usage, long-established, natural, normal, of long standing, ordinary, orthodox, permanent, prevalent, regular, routine, standard, time-honored, tradition-bound, traditional, *translaticius,* typical, usual, widely used, wonted
ASSOCIATED CONCEPTS: conventional interest, conventional life estate, conventional mortgage, conventional obligation, conventional sequestration, conventional subrogation, conventional trust

CONVERGE, verb approach, approach one another, assemble, blend, bring into focus, bring near, bring together, center upon, centralize, close in upon, coalesce, *coire,* come closer, come to a focus, come to a point, come together, concenter, concentralize, concentrate, congregate, consolidate, convene, convocate, draw gradually together, draw in, focalize, focus, gather, *in unum vergere,* incline toward each other, interfuse, join together, meet, merge, taper, unite

CONVERSATION, noun articulation, *causerie,* chat, collocution, colloquial discourse, colloquy, communication, confabulation, *conloquium,* consultation, conversing, deliberation, dialogue, discourse, discussion, dissertation, exchange, exchange of views, familiar discourse, imparting of thoughts, inquiry, interchange, interchange of information, interchange of opinions, interchange of speech, interchange of thoughts, intercommunication, interlocution, interview, oral communication, parley, questioning, speaking, talk, telling, verbal intercourse
ASSOCIATED CONCEPTS: confidential conversations, criminal conversation, wiretapping conversations

CONVERSE, verb address, advise, allocute, answer, articulate, attest to, carry on a conversation, comment on, commune with, communicate with, confabulate, confer with, *conferre,* consult with, debate, descant, discourse, discuss, dissertate, exchange ideas, exchange views, have dialogue, have verbal intercourse, hold conference, impart thoughts, inform, interchange ideas, interchange information, interchange opinions, interchange thoughts, interview, make a rebuttal, make a speech, make a statement, parley, perorate, recite, recount, relate, relate ideas, relay ideas, say, speak with, state, talk, utter

CONVERSION (Change), **noun** alteration, interchange, metamorphosis, passage, reconstruction, shift, switch, transformation, transition, transmutation
ASSOCIATED CONCEPTS: conversion of a security

CONVERSION (Misappropriation), **noun** appropriation, defraudation, deprivation, embezzlement, fraud, larceny, malfeasance, misapplication, misappropriation of funds, misemployment, misuse, peculation, theft, thievery, unauthorized assumption of property, unlawful appropriation, unlawful use of another's property, wrongful assumption, wrongful exercise of dominion
ASSOCIATED CONCEPTS: action for conversion, attachment, constructive conversion, conversion by assertion of ownership, conversion of goods, conversion of property, conversion of stock, detinue, fraudulent conversion, innocent conversion, involuntary conversion, larceny by conversion, technical conversion, trover, wrongful conversion

CONVERT (Change use), **verb** alter, amend, become, change, change into, change over, commute, *convertere,*

denature, develop, diversify, emend, evolve, exchange, interchange, make into, make over, metabolize, metamorphose, modify, mutate, permute, rearrange, recast, reconstitute, reconstruct, refashion, reform, regenerate, remake, remodel, remold, render different, renovate, reorganize, replace, reshape, restyle, revamp, revise, shift, substitute, switch, transfer, transfigure, transform, transmogrify, transmute, transpose, transshape, transubstantiate, turn, vary
ASSOCIATED CONCEPTS: basic converter, convert bonds, innocent converter

CONVERT (*Misappropriate*), **verb** apply dishonestly, appropriate wrongfully, assume unlawful rights of ownership, embezzle, expropriate, misapply, misdirect, misemploy, mismanage, misuse, peculate, put to a wrong use, steal, take illegally
ASSOCIATED CONCEPTS: convert to one's own use, fraudulently convert

CONVERT (*Persuade*), **verb** align, brainwash, bring around, convince, enlist, induce, influence, lead to believe, prevail, propagandize, proselytize, reform, sway, talk into, win an argument, win over

CONVERTIBLE, **adjective** capable of being exchanged, changeable, commutable, commutative, complementary, compromisable, correlative, counterchangeable, exchangeable, interchangeable, mutable, permutable, reciprocative, reversible, substitutive, transformable, transmutable, transposable
ASSOCIATED CONCEPTS: convertible bond rule, convertible bonds, convertible coupon bonds, convertible securities

CONVEY (*Communicate*), **verb** acquaint, advise, affirm, announce, annunciate, apprise, articulate, assert, aver, avow, bare, become known, broadcast, comment, confide, contact, declare, describe, detail, direct the attention to, disclose, disseminate, divulgate, divulge, educate, elucidate, enlighten, evince, explain, expose, express, get across, get in touch, give an account, give notice, impart, indicate, inform, instruct, keep posted, make acquainted, make aware, make known, make public, manifest, mention, narrate, notify, pass on, point out, post, proclaim, promulgate, pronounce, publish, recite, recount, relate, remark, render an account, report, represent, reveal, share, signify, speak, specify, state, suggest, teach, tell, transmit, uncover, vent

CONVEY (*Transfer*), **verb** abalienate, alienate, assign, award, bequeath, carry, cede, consign, contribute, deed, deliver, deliver over, demise, devolve, dispense, donate, endow, enfeoff, give, grant, hand down, hand out, impart, lease, pass, pass down, pass title, present, relinquish, shift, transfer title, transmit, transport, transpose
ASSOCIATED CONCEPTS: lawfully convey, quitclaim and convey

CONVEYANCE, **noun** alienation, alienation of property, assignation, assignment, bestowal, bestowment, conferment, consignation, consignment, delivery, demise, devise, devolution, disposal, sale, shift, testamentary disposition, tranmission, transfer, transfer of property, transfer of title, transference, transmission, transmittal
ASSOCIATED CONCEPTS: absolute conveyance, conveyance by deed, encumbrance, fraudulent conveyance, involuntary conveyance, presumptive conveyance
FOREIGN PHRASES: *Transit terra cum onere.* Land passes subject to any encumbrances affecting it. *Nihil tam conveniens est naturali aequitati quam voluntatem domini rem suam in alium transferre ratam habere.* Nothing is more conformable to natural equity than to confirm the intention of an owner who desires to transfer his property.

CONVICT, **noun** accused, accused person, bad example, captive, condemned person, condemned prisoner, criminal, crook, culprit, defaulter, defendant, delinquent, desperado, desperate criminal, escapee, evildoer, felon, first offender, fugitive, guilty man, guilty person, inmate, internee, jail inmate, lawbreaker, malefactor, malevolent, malfeasant, malfeasor, miscreant, misdemeanant, misfeasor, offender, outlaw, parolee, prisoner, prisoner at the bar, prisoner behind bars, prisoner of state, public enemy, recidivist, recreant, reprobate, rogue, scoundrel, sinner, thief, transgressor, villain, wrongdoer
ASSOCIATED CONCEPTS: certificate of relief from disabilities

CONVICT, **verb** attaint, bring to justice, call to account, cast blame upon, censure, condemn, condemn after judicial investigation, declare guilty of an offense, denounce, denunciate, doom, find against, find guilty, find liable, give a guilty verdict, hold liable, hold responsible, impose a penalty on, inflict a penalty on, inflict punishment, pass censure on, pass sentence on, penalize, prescribe punishment, pronounce judgment, pronounce sentence, punish, put the blame on, sentence, utter judicial sentence against
ASSOCIATED CONCEPTS: convict of a crime, convict of wrongdoing, sentence

CONVICTION (*Finding of guilt*), **noun** adjudgment, adjudication, aspersion, avengement, blame, censure, charge, condemnation, criminality, culpability, *damnatio,* damnation, decision, decree, decrial, denouncement, denunciation, determination, exaction of penalty, execution of sentence, final condemnation, finding, hostile verdict, imposition, judgment, passing judgment, penalization, penalty, prescribed punishment, proof of guilt, punishment, punition, reprehension, reprisal, reprobation, reproof, retribution, retributive justice, ruling, sentence, sentencing, unfavorable verdict, verdict
ASSOCIATED CONCEPTS: certificate of conviction, criminal conviction, felony conviction, final conviction, guilty verdict, nolo cotendere plea, record of conviction, sentencing

CONVICTION (*Persuasion*), **noun** ascertained principle, assumption, assurance, assured belief, attitude, avowal, certainty, certitude, concept, conception, conclusion, consideration, credence, creed, declaration of faith, doctrine, dogma, faith, firm belief, fixed opinion, impression, inclination, judgment, leaning, mind, *opinio,* opinion, outlook, personal judgment, point of view, position, positiveness, postulation, posture, predilection, predisposition, presupposition, principle, proclivity, profession, propensity, rooted belief, *sententia,* sentiment, settled belief, settled judgment, standpoint, staunch belief, supposition, sureness, tenet, theory, thinking, understanding, unshakable opinion, view, viewpoint, way of thinking, well-founded opinion

CONVINCE, **verb** allure, argue into, assure, bring to reason, carry conviction, clinch an argument, compel, compel belief, convert, dispose, enlist, exert influence, extort belief, gain the confidence of, impel, impress, incline, indoctrinate, induce, influence, inspire, inveigle, lead to believe, make confident, make realize, outweigh, overcome by argument, overweigh, persuade, persuade by argument, *persuadere,* predispose, prevail upon, produce conviction, prompt, propagandize, prove, prove one's point, satisfy, satisfy by evidence, satisfy by proof, suborn, sway, win over

CONVINCING, **adjective** absolute, *ad persuadendum accommodatus,* assured, assuring, attestable, authentic, believable, believed, believing, bona fide, categorical, certain, cogent, coherent, commanding, compelling, conclusive, confirmable, confirmatory, confirming, convictive, corrobo-

rating, corroborative, credal, credible, creditable, decisive, deducible, demonstrable, documentary, documented, establishable, established, evident, evincible, forceful, genuine, influential, irrefragable, irrefutable, likely, logical, maintaining, moving, persuasive, plausible, positive, possible, potent, powerful, practiced, prevailing, profound, provable, proving, rational, real, reasonable, reliable, secure, self-evident, stated, strong, suasive, substantial, supportable, sustainable, swaying, tenable, to be believed, tried, true, trusted, trusting, trustworthy, unconfutable, undeniable, undisputed, unrefutable, valid, verifying, well-founded, well-grounded, worthy of credence
ASSOCIATED CONCEPTS: clear and convincing proof, convincing proof

COOPERATE, verb act in concert, act jointly, act together, *adiuvare,* ally, amalgamate, associate, be a party to, cabal, coact, cofunction, collaborate, collude, combine, combine forces, concert, concord, concur, confederate, conjoin, connive, conspire, contribute, cowork, federate, fraternize, go along with, go into partnership, join forces, join in, join with, league, lend one's support to, lend oneself to, make an agreement with, make common cause with, partake in, participate, pool, pull together, rally round, share in, side with, stand together, take part in, take part with, unite ones efforts, unite with, work as a team, work side by side with, work together

COOPERATIVE, noun alliance, association, collective, communal business establishment, communal society, commune, concurrent effort, federation, guild, joint action, joint operation, joint possession, partnership, teamwork, union

COORDINATE, verb adjust, arrange, assimilate, balance, combine, equalize, harmonize, homologize, integrate, methodize, organize, proportion, regularize, regulate, schematize, set in order, synchronize, systematize

COPARTNER *(Business associate),* **noun** adjuvant, associate, auxiliary, coadjutant, cohelper, collaborator, colleague, comate, companion, compeer, *confrère,* consociate, consort, cooperator, coworker, fellow, fellow worker, helper, mate, partner, peer, *personnel,* sharer

COPARTNER *(Coconspirator),* **noun** abettor, accessory, accessory after the fact, accessory before the fact, accompanier, accomplice, accomplice in crime, adjunct, adjutant, adjuvant, aid, aide-de-camp, aider and abettor, assistant, associate, attendant, *camarade,* coadjutant, coadjutor, coadjutress, co-aid, co-helper, cohort, collaborator, colluder, comate, companion, comrade, confederate, *confrère,* consociate, conspirer, cooperator, copartner in crime, helper, helpmate, *intrigant,* intriguer, machinator, *particeps criminis,* partner in crime, socius criminis, supporter
ASSOCIATED CONCEPTS: joint adventure, joint enterprise, tenant in copartnership

COPIOUS, adjective abounding, abundant, ample, bountiful, considerable, *copiosus,* countless, extravagant, exuberant, filled, flowing, full, generous, gigantic, great, in profusion, inexhaustible, innumerable, large, lavish, liberal, luxuriant, massive, more than enough, numerous, of great extent, opulent, overflowing, plenteous, plentiful, populous, producing abundantly, productive, profitable, profuse, profusive, prolific, replete, rich, streaming, superabundant, supernumerary, teeming, unlimited, unmeasured, unrestricted, unsparing, unstinting, voluminous, well-provided, well-stocked, wide, yielding abundantly

COPY, noun cast, counterfeit, counterpart, duplicate, duplication, ectype, facsimile, fake, forgery, image, imitation,

impress, impression, imprint, likeness, offprint, personation, print, reissue, repetition, replica, representation, reprint, reproduction, simulation, tracing, transcript, transfer
ASSOCIATED CONCEPTS: certified copy, conformed copy, correct copy, true copy

COPY, verb adopt, ape, approximate, assume, borrow, caricature, cartoon, cheat, conform, depict, ditto, do like, double, draw, duplicate, echo, emulate, falsify, follow, follow suit, follow the example of, forge, give an encore, *imitari,* imitate, impersonate, infringe copyright, iterate, make a duplicate of, make a transcript of, make a replica, mirror, mock, model, parrot, pattern after, personate, pirate, plagiarize, portray, pretend, print, rebuild, recapitulate, reconstruct, recreate, reduplicate, reecho, reestablish, refashion, rehash, reiterate, remake, repeat, replicate, represent, reprint, reproduce, republish, restate, retell, retrace, revive, rewrite, simulate, take after, trace, transcribe
ASSOCIATED CONCEPTS: counterfeit, impersonate, infringe

COPYRIGHT, noun authority, authorization, certificate of invention, certification, concession, enfranchisement, entitlement for a term of years, exclusive privilege of publication, exclusive privilege of publication and sale, exclusive right of production, grant, license, permit, privilege to publish, privilege to reproduce, right of literary property, sanction
ASSOCIATED CONCEPTS: copyright license, patent

CORE, noun backbone, bedrock, body, center, consequence, content, cornerstone, corpus, epitome, essence, fundamentals, gist, gravance, heart, main point, meat, nave, nub, nucleus, prime ingredient, principle, quiddity, quintessence, soul, substance, sum and substance, summary
ASSOCIATED CONCEPTS: core of a case, core of a claim, core of an accusation, core of an allegation, core of testimony

CORNERSTONE, noun backbone, base, body, cardinal point, core, corpus, critical point, crucial point, crux, essence, essential matter, exigency, foundation, frame of reference, fundamental, gravamen, groundwork, heart, highlight, key, keynote, keystone, landmark, main body, main element, main point, main thing, mainstay, major event, major part, material point, matter of concern, matter of importance, milestone, nucleus, pedestal, pivot, principal part, principle, purport, purpose, quintessence, rudiment, salient point, *sine qua non,* standard, substance, substantiality, support, *terra firma,* threshold

COROLLARY, noun addition, adjunct, appurtenance, complement, correlation, correspondence, deduction, derivation, derived principle, logical sequence, offshoot, outcome, outgrowth, propinquity, sequent, supplement, syllogism

CORPORAL, adjective bodily, corporeal, fleshy, incarnate, material, not spiritual, palpable, physical, somatic, substantial, tangible
ASSOCIATED CONCEPTS: corporal imbecility, corporal oath, corporal punishment

CORPORAL PUNISHMENT, noun beating, branding, caning, capital punishment, conviction, death penalty, death sentence, death warrant, denouncement, denunciation, doom, excommunication, flogging, guilty verdict, hitting, mutilation, punishment, spanking, whipping
FOREIGN PHRASES: *Corporalis injuna non recipit a estimationem de futuro.* A personal injury is not satisfied by the outcome of a future proceeding.

CORPORATE *(Associate),* **adjective** affiliate, allied, banded, federative, incorporate, leagued, partnered
ASSOCIATED CONCEPTS: corporate act, corporate assets, corporate authorities, corporate body, corporate bonds, corporate commission, corporate conduct, corporate dividends, corporate existence, corporate franchise, corporate name, corporate officer, corporate powers and privileges, corporate property, corporate purpose, corporate rights, corporate seal, corporate securities, corporate stock

CORPORATE *(Joint),* **adjective** associated, coincident, compact, concurrent, conjoint, conjunct, correal

CORPORATE GOVERNANCE, *noun* code of conduct, corporate canons, corporate dictates, corporate direction, corporate mandates, corporate norms, corporate principles, corporate regulation, corporate restrictions, corporate standards, corporate tenets, directives, guidelines, laws of governance, model of propriety, oversight, rules of conduct, standards, supervision
ASSOCIATED CONCEPTS: affiliated person, audit committee, board committees, board compensation review, board composition, board independence, ethics, executive officers, independent directors, retirement ages selection process, term limits

CORPORATION, *noun* affiliate, affiliation, agglomerate, alliance, artificial entity, artificial person, associate, association, body, body corporate, business, business association, business establishment, coalition, combination, combine, commercial enterprise, company, concern, confederacy, conglomerate, *conlegium,* consociation, consolidation, corporate body, enterprise, establishment, federation, firm, foundation, holding company, industry, institute, institution, joint concern, legal body, legal entity, operating company, organization, sodality, stock company, syndicate, union
ASSOCIATED CONCEPTS: alter ego, business trust, cartel, closed corporation, closely held corporation, consolidation, corporate charter, corporate officers dissolution, corporate structure, de facto corporation, de jure corporation, derivative action, directors, dissolution, domestic corporation, fictitious corporations, foreign corporation, joint stock associations, limited partnerships, membership corporation, merger, municipal corporation, officers, parent corporation, public corporation, partnership, proxies, self-dealing, shareholders, sole proprietorship, stockholders, subsidiaries, voting trusts
FOREIGN PHRASES: *Jus quo universitates utuntur est idem quod habent privati.* The law which governs corporations is the same as that which governs individuals. *Corporatio non dicitur aliquid facere nisi id sit collegialiter deliberari, etiamsi major pars id faciat.* A corporation is not said to do anything unless it be deliberated upon collectively, although the majority should do it.

CORPOREAL, *adjective* actual, appreciable, bodily, *bona fide,* certain, concrete, corporal, definite, demonstrable, embodied, existent, firm, fleshly, having substance, in existence, incarnate, material, palpable, physical, real, solid, substantial, substantive, tangible, temporal, unspiritual
ASSOCIATED CONCEPTS: corporeal hereditaments
FOREIGN PHRASES: *Haereditas, alia corporalis, alia incorporalis; corporalis est, quae tangi potest et videri; incorporalis quae tangi non potest nec videri.* An inheritance is either corporeal or incorporeal; corporeal is that which can be touched and seen; incorporeal, that which can neither be touched nor seen.

CORPSE, *noun* body, *cadaver,* carcass, carrion, casualty, corpus, dead body, dead person, deceased, departed,

individual, lifeless body, mortal remains, murder victim, organic remains, remains, victim
ASSOCIATED CONCEPTS: *corpus delicti*

CORPUS, *noun* aggregate, aggregation, amassment, assemblage, body, bulk, chief part, collection, collectivity, colligation, compages, compilation, complexus, comprehensiveness, concentration, concretion, confluence, conglomerate, core, cornerstone, corporality, corporeity, cumulation, distillation, embodiment, ensemble, essence, fullness, grand total, gross amount, grouping, import, importance, inclusiveness, integrality, integration, keynote, legal body, legal entity, main body, main part, major part, mass, materiality, materialization, matter, pith, plenum, principal, principle, quantity, quintessence, res, signification, solid substance, solidarity, structure, substance, substantiality, sum, sum and substance, sum total, summation, total, totality, weight, whole, wholeness
ASSOCIATED CONCEPTS: *corpus delicti, corpus juris,* corpus of a trust

CORRECT *(Actual),* **adjective** accepted, accurate, appropriate, approved, becoming, certain, comely, conscientious, convenable, convenial, customary, decent, decorous, definite, due, established, exact, exacting, factual, faultless, fitting, flawless, fussy, gracious, impartial, impeccable, in perfect order, infallible, judicious, just right, literal, meticulous, neat, perfect, polite, precise, proper, punctilious, reasonable, redressed, reformed, regulated, remedied, repaired, restored, revised, right, scrupulous, seemly, strict, stylish, suitable, tasteful, tidy, traditional, trim, true, unerring, unmistaken, valid

CORRECT *(Honest),* **adjective** equitable, ethical, fair, having a code of conduct, having been brought up properly, having good upbringing, having values, just, moral, official, orthodox, proper, reputable, rightful, scrupulous, true, upright

CORRECT *(Adjust),* **verb** alter, ameliorate, amend, appropriate, better, cure, doctor, disabuse, improve, meliorate, mend, reclaim, rectify, redress, reform, remedy, repair, touch up

CORRECT *(Admonish),* **verb** berate, castigate, chasten, chastise, chide, disabuse, disenchant, disillusion, enlighten, lecture, objurate, penalize, perfect, punish, put right, rebuke, redress, reprehend, reprimand, reprove, scold, set right, take to task, upbraid

CORRECT *(Review),* **verb** amend, change, convert, edit, emend, expostulate, help, regulate, revise

CORRECTION *(Change),* **noun** adjustment, alteration, amelioration, amending, amendment, betterment, *correctio,* curative, cure, *emendatio,* emendation, improved version, improvement, melioration, mending, modification, qualification, readjustment, reconstruction, rectification, redaction, reform, reformation, rehabilitation, remedy, removal of errors, renovation, repair, repairing, replacement, rescript, restoration, retraction, revampment, revisal, revised edition, revision, rewrite, righting
ASSOCIATED CONCEPTS: corrective action, corrective procedures

CORRECTION *(Punishment),* **noun** amercement, *animadversio,* animadversion, *castigatio,* castigation, censure, chastening, chastisement, condemnation, corrective measure, disciplinary action, discipline, infliction, invective, lesson, payment, penal retribution, penal servitude, penalization, penalty, punition, reprobation, reproval, retribution, retributive justice, scourging, stricture

CORRECTIVE

ASSOCIATED CONCEPTS: board of corrections, correctional facility, house of correction

CORRECTIVE (*Progressive*), **adjective**   alternative, amendatory, analeptic, antidotal, assuasive, counteractive, curative, emendatory, healing, improving, medicinal, modifying, palliative, progressive, rectifying, reformative, reformatory, remedial, remonstrative, restorative, revisional, salubrious, salutary, sanative, sanatory, therapeutic
ASSOCIATED CONCEPTS: corrective treatment

CORRECTIVE (*Punitive*), **adjective**   avenging, castigatory, disciplinary, inflictive, medicinal, palliative, penal, penalizing, punishable, punishing, punitory, recriminatory, retaliative, retaliatory, retributive, revengeful, vengeful, vindictive

CORRELATE, noun   affiliate, agnate, ally, analogue, associate, cognate, companion, comparison, complement, complemental term, congener, coordinate, correspondent, counterpart, double, duplicate, equal, equivalent, fellow, like, match, mate, parallel, pendant, reciprocal, reciprocator, relation, similitude, supplement, twin

CORRELATION, noun   analogy, chain, collation, comparison, connection, corollary, correspondence, counterpart, equivalence, functionality, interchange, interconnection, interdependence, likeness, mutual, mutuality, parity, proportion, quid pro quo, reciprocation, reciprocity, relation, relativeness, relativity, resemblance, similarity, similitude, transmutation
ASSOCIATED CONCEPTS: correlation between fact and fiction

CORRELATIVE, adjective   accordant, adapted, affiliate, affiliated, affined, affinitive, agnate, agreeing, akin, allied, amalgamated, analogous, anent, applicable, apposite, appropriate, associated, associative, belonging, cognate, coinciding, collateral, commensurable, commensurate, commutual, comparable, comparative, compatible, complemental, complementary, concerning, concordant, concurrent, conformable, congeneric, congenerous, congruent, congruous, conjoint, conjunct, conjunctive, connate, connatural, connected, connective, consentaneous, consociate, consonant, conspecific, contingent, coordinate, correspondent, corresponding, dependent, equivalent, exchangeable, fellow, fitting, germane, homological, interacting, interdependent, interlinked, interrelated, joined, linked, matched, mutual, mutually related, paired, parallel, pertaining, proportionate, reciprocal, reconcilable, related, relating to, relative, relevant, resembling, similar, suitable, suited
ASSOCIATED CONCEPTS: correlative rights doctrine

CORRESPOND (*Be equivalent*), **verb**   adapt to, agree, answer the purpose, appertain, approach, approximate, be accordant, be akin, complement, be complemental, be congruent, be related, bear resemblance, belong, border on, bring into relation with, cohere, coincide, compare, comply with, comport with, concur, conform, *congruere*, conjoin, coordinate, copy, correlate, deal with, dovetail, draw a parallel, equal, harmonize, have a comparison, have a connection, have a relation, homologate, homologize, join, liken, match, parallel, pertain, reciprocalize, reconcile, relate, resemble, run parallel to, support an analogy, tie in with, to be similiar, touch, unite
ASSOCIATED CONCEPTS: corresponding tax

CORRESPOND (*Communicate*), **verb**   acknowledge, contact, disseminate, epistolize, exchange letters, notify, publicize, relate, reply, respond, send a message, transmit, write

CORRESPONDENCE (*Communication by letters*), **noun**   communication, dispatches, *epistulae*, exchange of letters, letter writing, letters, *litterae*, mail, missives, writings

CORRESPONDENCE (*Similarity*), **noun**   accord, agreement, analogy, comparability, conformity, congruence, *congruentia*, congruity, correlation, equivalence, harmony, likeness, parity, resemblance, sameness, semblance, similitude, symmetry, uniformity

CORRESPONDENT, adjective   adapted, agreeable, agreed, akin, analogous, answerable, apposite, appropriate, belonging, coequal, coextensive, cognate, coincidental, coinciding, collateral, comfortable, comparable, commensurable, complementary, concomitant, concordant, congruous, consistent, consonant, contemporaneous, correlative, corresponsive, counterpart, counterposed, equal in effect, equal in force, equal in significance, equal in value, equivalent, fit, fitted, germane, harmonious, homologous, mutual, pendent, reciprocal, related, relative, relevant, similar, suitable, suited, synonymous, uniform

CORRESPONDENT, noun   analogue, complement, coordinate, correlative, counterpart, duplicate, equal, equivalent, obverse, pendant, reciprocator, similitude

CORRESPONDING, adjective   accordant, agreeing, akin, analogous, answerable, apposite, coequal, coextensive, cognate, coincidental, coinciding, collateral, commensurate, comparable, compatible, concerted, concomitant, concordant, conformable, congenial, congruous, consonant, contemporaneous, convertible, correlative, equivalent, harmonious, identical, indistinguishable, like-minded, matching, mutual, parallel, pendent, proportionate, reciprocal, reconcilable, relative, similar, synonymous, tantamount

CORRIGIBLE, adjective   able to improve, adaptable, alleviative, alterative, ameliorable, amenable, amendable, beneficial, controllable, correctable, curable, developmental, emendable, extricable, fixable, functional, governable, improvable, manageable, mendable, perfectible, progressive, reclaimable, recoverable, rectifiable, redeemable, reformable, reformational, reformatory, remediable, renewable, repairable, reparable, replaceable, rescuable, resilient, restorable, resurgent, retrievable, revisable, revisional, salvageable, subject to revisal, submissive to correction, tameable, teachable, tractable

CORROBORATE, verb   acknowledge, adduce evidence, advocate, affirm, assent, assure, attest, authenticate, aver, avouch, bear out, bear witness, bolster up, buttress, call to witness, certify, circumstantiate, *comprobare*, confirm, countersign, defend, document, endorse, fortify, guarantee, justify, maintain, manifest, prove, ratify, reassure, reinforce, sanction, strengthen, subscribe, substantiate, support, sustain, testify to, undersign, uphold, uphold in evidence, validate, verify, vouch for, warrant
ASSOCIATED CONCEPTS: corroborating evidence, corroborating witness

CORROBORATION, noun   acknowledgment, affirmation, assurance, attestation, authentication, averment, avouchment, bearing out, certification, circumstantiation, conclusive evidence, conclusive proof, confirmation, demonstrability, demonstration, documentation, endorsement, establishment, establishment of proof, evidence, exemplification, fortification, legal evidence, presentation of evidence, proof, ratification, strengthening, substantiation, support, supportability, supporting evidence, sustaining, testification,

testimony, upholding, validation, validification, verifiability, verification, vindication, voucher, witness
ASSOCIATED CONCEPTS: corroborating circumstances, corroborating evidence, corroborative proof, corroborative testimony

CORROBORATIVE, *adjective* affirmatory, agreeing, ascertained, assenting, attested, borne out, certified, confirmatory, confirmed, confirming, convincing, corroborating, deductible, determined, established, evidential, evidentiary, prima facie, proved, substantiated, testificatory, valid, validated, verified, vindicatory
ASSOCIATED CONCEPTS: corroborating circumstances, corroborating evidence, corroborating information

CORRUPT, *verb* adulterate, befoul, bribe, cause to be dishonest, contaminate, corrode, *corrumpere,* debase, debauch, decay, defraud, degenerate, *depravare,* deprave, devalue, distort, lead astray, misdirect, mislead, pervert, pollute, prostitute, seduce, spoil, suborn, subvert, taint, undermine, *vitiare,* vitiate, vulgarize, warp
ASSOCIATED CONCEPTS: corrupt a minor

CORRUPTION, *noun* abuse of public trust, act of bribing, act of profiteering, baseness, breach of faith, breach of trust, bribery, complicity, conduct involving graft, corrupt inducement, *corruptela,* corruptibility, *corruptio,* crime, criminality, debasement, deception, *depravatio,* deviation from rectitude, deviousness, disgrace, dishonesty, dishonor, disloyalty, disrepute, feloniousness, fraudulence, fraudulency, graft, illegality, improbity, indirection, injustice, jobbery, knavery, lack of conscience, lack of principle, lack of probity, malignancy, obliquity, perfidiousness, perfidy, perversion of integrity, scoundrelism, turpitude, unscrupulousness, venality, villainousness, villainy, want of principle, wickedness
ASSOCIATED CONCEPTS: corruption in public office
FOREIGN PHRASES: Corruptio optimi est pessima. The corruption of the best is worst. **Maledicta est expositio quae corrumpit textum.** It is a cursed interpretation which corrupts the text.

COSIGN, *verb* accredit, answer for, approve, assure, authorize, back, be surety for, certify, confirm, countersign, endorse, give assurance, give one's signature, guarantee, indorse, insure, promise, ratify, secure, support, undersign, underwrite, validate, vouch for
ASSOCIATED CONCEPTS: accommodation indorser, accommodation party

COST *(Expenses), noun* business expense, charge, disbursement, expenditure, legal expense, money expended, obligation incurred, outgo, outlay, overhead, payment, running expense
ASSOCIATED CONCEPTS: awarding costs, bill of costs, costs and disbursements

COST *(Penalty), noun* amercement, bereavement, damage, damages, fine, forfeiture, harm, impairment, injury, loss, penal retribution, penalization, penance, privation, punishment, sacrifice, unfortunate consequence
ASSOCIATED CONCEPTS: court costs, treble costs

COST *(Price), noun* appraisal, asking price, assessment, carrying charge, charge, consideration, expensiveness, face value, high worth, *impensa,* mark up, marked price, purchase price, quotation, quoted price, reckoning, sum asked for, valuation, value
ASSOCIATED CONCEPTS: accrued costs, actual cost, all costs, cost basis, cost of administration, cost of doing business, cost of materials, cost of repair, cost of replacement,

cost-plus contract, costs and expenses, costs of suit, disbursements, fixed costs, full costs, legal costs, legitimate cost, marginal cost, operating costs, sheriff's costs, total cost, wholesale cost

COSTS, *noun* burden of expenditure, charges, damages, disbursement, expenditure, expenses, outlay, out-of-pocket expenses, payment, penalty
ASSOCIATED CONCEPTS: award of costs in an action, awards for pain and suffering, bill of costs, certification of costs, damages, fees, fines, payment of costs, penalties, punitive awards, remittiture

COTENANT, *noun* another addressee, another denizen, another dweller, another inhabitant, another inhabiter, another leaseholder, another lessee, another lodger, another occupant, another occupier, another paying guest, another possessor, another renter, another resident, another residentiary, coaddressee, codenizen, codweller, cohouseholder, coinhabitant, coinhabiter, coleaseholder, colessee, cooccupant, cooccupier, copossessor, corenter, coresident, coresidentiary

COUNCIL *(Assembly), noun* advisory board, board, committee, conclave, conference, forum, judicature, palaver, parley, parliament, synod, tribunal

COUNCIL *(Consultant), noun* advocate, counselor, deliberation

COUNSEL, *noun* adviser, advocate, attorney, attorney-at-law, barrister, barrister-at-law, *consilium,* counselor, counselor-at-law, jurisconsult, jurist, lawyer, legal adviser, legal practitioner, legist, member of the bar, member of the legal profession, officer of court, pleader, solicitor
ASSOCIATED CONCEPTS: advice of counsel, aid of counsel, assigned counsel, assistance of counsel, attorney's fees, benefit of counsel, counsel in a cause, counsel of record, denial of counsel, effective counsel, Escobedo Rule, of counsel, opposing counsel, sixth amendment, waiver of counsel
FOREIGN PHRASES: Consilia multorum quaeruntur in magnis. The advice of many is required in great affairs. Praepropera consilia raro sunt prospera. Rash counsels are rarely prosperous.

COUNSEL, *verb* advise, advocate, caution, coach, commend, confer, consult, direct, discuss, dissuade, encourage, exchange observations, expostulate, forewarn, give a recommendation, give advice, give suggestions to, guide, instruct, offer an opinion to, opine, persuade, prescribe, prompt, propose, reason with, recommend, seek advice, seek to persuade, submit, suggest, suggest a proposed claim, suggest a proposed contention, urge, warn

COUNSELOR, *noun* advisor, advocate, attorney, attorney-at-law, barrister, barrister-at-law, counsel, counselor-at-law, individual admitted to the bar, instructor, intercessor, jurisconsult, jurist, lawyer, legal adviser, legal defender, legal practitioner, legal representative, legist, member of the bar, member of the legal profession, officer of court, one called to the bar, solicitor
ASSOCIATED CONCEPTS: counselor at law, of counsel

COUNT, *noun* accusation, allegation, assertion, averment, case for the prosecution, charge, citation, claim, comes, condemnation, countercharge, crimination, declaration, delation, denunciation, distinct statement, imputation, inculpation, indictment, item, item in the indictment, main charge, particular charge, statement of a cause of action

ASSOCIATED CONCEPTS: count in an accusatory instrument, omnibus count

COUNTENANCE, verb   abet, accede to, accredit, acquiesce in, adjust oneself to, advocate, affirm, agree to, aid, allow, *approbare,* approbate, approve, approve of, assent to, assist, back, be in favor of, charter, commend, concur in, confirm, consent to, corroborate, empower, endorse, favor, forward, further, give one's blessing, go along with, help, hold with, homologate, license, make allowances for, make valid, *permittere,* ratify, recognize, recommend, sanction, stand by, subscribe to, support, sustain, view with favor

COUNTER, verb   act against, act in opposition to, agitate against, antagonize, avert, be at cross purposes, be contrary, be inimical, be obstructive, bid against, challenge, clash, collide, come in conflict with, compete with, conflict with, confute, contend, contradict, contravene, counteract, countercheck, countermand, countervail, cross, deflect, defy, disapprove, fend, fight against, fight off, foil, frustrate by contrary action, go against, go contrary to, go in opposition to, hinder, hold at bay, hold off, hold out against, impede, inhibit, interfere, make a stand against, militate against, negate, not support, object, obstruct, oppose, pit against, play against, prevent, prohibit, protest, protest against, put in check, raise objections, rebuff, repel, resist, run in opposition to, set against, side against, stand against, strike back, suppress, take a stand against, take evasive action, take issue with, thwart, ward off, work against, work at cross purposes

COUNTERACT, verb   act in opposition to, agitate against, annul, antagonize, be at cross purposes, be contrary, bid against, cancel out, clash, collide, come in conflict with, conflict with, confute, contend, contradict, counter, counterbalance, countermand, countermine, counterpoise, countervail, counterwork, cross, deactivate, defeat, defy, destroy the effect of, disconcert, disrupt, equalize, equiponderate, fight against, find a remedy, foil, frustrate, frustrate by contrary action, go against, go in opposition to, hinder, inhibit, interfere with, make a stand against, match against, militate against, negate, neutralize, nullify, offset, oppose, oppugn, pit against, play against, play at cross purposes, prevent, protest, protest against, rebuff, repress, resist, *resistere,* reverse, rival, run against, run counter, run counter to, run in opposition to, set against, set at naught, side against, squelch, stand against, take issue with, take one's stand against, traverse, undo, withstand, work against

COUNTERARGUMENT, noun   answer, *audi alteram partem,* challenge, confutation, contradiction, contraremonstrance, contravention, controversion, counteraccusation, countercharge, counterclaim, counterprotest, counterreply, counterstatement, defense, denial, disproof, gainsaying, invalidation, negation, opposition, plea, plea in rebuttal, proof, rebuttal, rebutter, *reductio ad absurdum,* refutation, rejoinder, replication, reply, response, retort, subversion, surrebuttal, surrebutter, surrejoinder, traversal, upset

COUNTERATTACK, noun   counteraction, counterassault, counterblast, counterblow, countermeasure, countermovement, counteroffensive, counterplot, counterpush, counterstrike, counterstroke, counterthrust, cross fire, reprisal, retaliation, retort, retortion, revenge, riposte

COUNTERCHARGE, verb   abnegate, answer, answer back, be respondent, be responsive, confute, contradict, counter, defend, negate, oppose by contrary proof, provide the answer, rebut, rebut the charge, recriminate, refute, refute

by argument, rejoin, reply, respond, respond conclusively, retort, riposte, say in reply
ASSOCIATED CONCEPTS: counterclaim, cross-claim

COUNTERCLAIM, noun   action to defeat plaintiff's demand, assertion against the plaintiff, cause against an opposing party, cause of action in favor of defendants, claim advanced by defendant, claim for relief by defendant, claim presented by defendant, contraremonstrance, counteraction, counterapplication, countercharge, counterdeclaration, counterdemand, countermotion, counterpetition, counterpostulation, counterproposal, counterreclamation, counterrequest, countersuit, cross-action, cross-bill, opposing suit, rejoinder, set-off
ASSOCIATED CONCEPTS: compulsory counterclaim, cross-complaint, cross-demand, cross-petition, equitable counterclaim, permissive counterclaim, set-off, sham counterclaim

COUNTERFEIT, noun   act of copying, bogus, copy, criminal imitation, deception, ersatz, fabrication, fake, false copy, false duplication, false representation, false reproduction, falsehood, falseness, falsification, falsity, *falsus,* forged copy, forgery, fradulent copy, fraudulent imitation, imitation, plagiarism, plagiary, pretense, simulation, unauthorized copy
ASSOCIATED CONCEPTS: counterfeit bill, counterfeited written instrument

COUNTERINTELLIGENCE noun   bugging, cloak-and-dagger work, counterespionage, discover, electronic surveillance, espial, espionage, examine, fish out, follow, following, gumshoe, heel, hound, hunt, intelligence, intelligence agency, intelligence work, look for, meddle, military intelligence, observation, observe, peer, pry, scout, scrutinize, search, secret police, secret service, set a watch on, shadowing, sleuth, spot, spy upon, spying, stakeout, tagging, tailing, take note, trail, trailing, turn over, 24-hour surveillance, watch, wiretap, wiretapping

COUNTERMAND, noun   abolishment, abolition, abrogation, annulment, ban, cancellation, counterorder, defeasance, disallowance, invalidation, nullification, prohibition, recall, recantation, repeal, repudiation, rescindment, rescission, retraction, reversal, revocation, revocation of orders, revokement, suppression, vacation, veto, voidance, withdrawal
ASSOCIATED CONCEPTS: countermand an order

COUNTEROFFER, noun   *casus foederis,* contractual terms, counterbid, counterclause, counterconditions, counterexception, counterlimitation, countermeasure, counterplan, counterpresentation, counterproposal, counterproposition, counterprovision, counterqualification, counterrecommendation, counterrequest, counterreservation, counterstipulation, countersuggestion, hard bargaining, negotiation, new offer, part of the bargain, responsive offer, set of terms, terms proposed

COUNTERPART (Complement), noun   alter ego, analogue, brother, coequal, congener, coordinate, correlate, correlation, correlative, correspondent, *doppelganger,* homologue, mate, obverse, pendant, reciprocal, reverse

COUNTERPART (Parallel), noun   carbon, carbon copy, copy, corresponding part, double, duplicate, duplication, *effigies,* effigy, equal, equivalent, image, likeness, match, replica, reproduction, *res simillima,* twin

COUNTERSIGN, verb   certify, confirm, corroborate, endorse, execute, ratify, sanction, second, support

COUNTERTERRORISM, *noun* counterespionage, counterintelligence, espionage, intelligence, intelligence agency, intelligence work, spying, surveillance

ASSOCIATED CONCEPTS: enemy combatants, justice courts, military tribunals, national security profiling, Patriotic Act, racial profiling, war on terrorism

COUNTERVAIL, *verb* abrogate, act against with equal force, agitate against, alter, avail against, balance, be contrary, cancel, cancel out, check, conflict with, confute, contradict, contravene, counter, counteract, counterpoise, cross, damage, destroy, equiponderate, go counter to, hinder, inhibit, interfere, match, militate against, negate, neutralize, offset, oppose, outbalance, prevent, rebut, refute, resist, run counter to, set off, suppress, thwart, traverse, undermine, weaken, weigh against, work against

COUPON, *noun* allocation, card, certificate, check, cheque, credit, credit check, detachable part of a certificate, detachable portion, dividend, interest certificate, interim dividend, negotiable instrument, note, premium bond, premium certificate, redeemable part, redemption slip, separable part of a certificate, separate ticket, share-out, slip, stub, ticket, token, voucher, written instrument

ASSOCIATED CONCEPTS: coupon bond, coupon book, coupon interest, coupon note

COURSE, *noun* act, act of pursuing, action, activity, advance, approach, arrangement, attack, campaign, completion, conduct, customary manner of *procedure,* delivery, design, direction, effectuation, effort, employment, endeavor, evolution, execution, exercitation, furtherance, handling, implementation, interaction, *iter,* line of action, line of conduct, management, manner, measures, method, mode, mode of management, mode of procedure, *modus operandi,* motion, movement, operation, order, particular manner of proceeding, performance, perpetration, plan, policy, positive action, practice, praxis, prescribed system, procedure, process, program, pursuance, pursuit, road, route, scheme, succession of acts, system

ASSOCIATED CONCEPTS: arising out of and in course of employment, course of business, course of conduct, course of dealings, course of employment, courses and distances, direct course, general course, water course

FOREIGN PHRASES: *In dubio, pars mitior est sequenda.* In doubt, the safer course is to be followed.

COURT, *noun* bar, bar of justice, *basilica,* bench, forum for adjusting disputes, forum of justice, *iudicium,* judgment seat, judicial assembly, judicial forum, judicial tribunal, justice, justice seat, lawcourt, magistrates, place where justice is administered, tribunal

ASSOCIATED CONCEPTS: adjournment of the court, appearance in court, application addressed to the court, civil court, clerk of court, competent court, contempt of court, county court, court-appointed receiver, court below, court calendar, court costs, court in banc, court martial, court of appeals, court of bankruptcy, court of chancery, court of claims, court of common pleas, court of competent jurisdiction, court of first instance, court of general jurisdiction, court of inquest, court of justice, court of last resort, court of limited jurisdiction, court of probate, court of record, court's own motion, court's own witness, criminal court, district court, family court, federal court, fraud upon the court, inferior courts, inherent right of court, jurisdiction of a court, leave of court, legislative courts, local court, municipal courts, opinion of the court, order of the court, power of the court, probate court, proceedings in court,

state court, Supreme Court, tax court, term of court, United States courts

FOREIGN PHRASES: *Actus curiae neminem gravabit.* An act of the court shall prejudice no man. *Cursus curiae est lex curiae.* The practice of the court is the law of the court. *Ea quae in curia nostra rite acta sunt debitae executioni demandari debent.* Those things which are properly transacted in our court ought to be committed to a due execution. *Nihil habet forum ex scena.* The court has nothing to do with what is not before it. *Nulla curia quae recordum non habet potest imponere finem neque aliquem mandare carceri; quia ista spectant tantummodo ad curias de recordo.* No court which has not a record can impose a fine or commit any person to prison; because those powers belong only to courts of record.

COURTESY, *noun* affability, amenity, amiability, chivalry, civility, *comitas,* comity, complaisance, consideration, cordiality, courteous conduct, courteousness, courtliness, deference, elegance of manners, etiquette, excellence of behavior, friendliness, gallantry, geniality, gentility, good behavior, good breeding, good manners, graciousness, manners, *officium,* polished manners, polite act, politeness, refinement, respect, reverence, suavity, tact, thoughtfulness, *urbanitas,* urbanity

COURTROOM, *noun* court, lawcourt, part, room in which a court of law is held, room in which a lawcourt is held, room used for the application of the laws, room used for the public administration of justice, room where justice is administered

COVENANT, *noun* agreement, arrangement, avowal, binding agreement, collective agreement, commitment, compact, concordat, contract, contractual obligation, contractual statement, *conventio,* convention, engagement, guarantee, mutual understanding, oath, *pacisci, pact, pactio, pactum,* pledge, promise, stipulation, understanding, undertaking, warranty, written agreement, written pledge

ASSOCIATED CONCEPTS: breach of covenant, collateral covenants, concurrent covenants, covenant against incumbrances, covenant appurtenant to the land, covenant for quiet enjoyment, covenant not to institute suit, covenant in praesenti, covenant not to convey, covenant of future assurance, covenant of general warranty, covenant of title, covenant of warranty, covenant running with the land, covenant to pay, dependent covenant, doctrine of implied covenants, joint covenant, negative covenants, restrictive covenant

COVER *(Pretext),* *noun* alleged reason, camouflage, claim, disguise, excuse, guise, mask, *obtegere, operire,* pretense, profession, screen, sham, subterfuge, *velare*

COVER *(Protection),* *noun* blanket, coating, covering, coverture, guard, integument, safeguard, sheath, shelter, shield, veneer

COVER *(Substitute),* *noun* alternate, alternative, equivalent item, exchange, replacement, similar item, stand-in, substitution

COVER *(Conceal),* *verb* becloud, befog, bury, camouflage, cloak, curtain, disguise, enshroud, hide, keep out of sight, mask, obscure, put out of sight, screen, seclude, secrete, shroud, veil, *velare*

ASSOCIATED CONCEPTS: cover one's assets

COVER *(Guard),* ***verb***   care for, defend, ensure, harbor, insure, keep in safety, keep safe from harm, keep under close watch, make safe, protect, safeguard, secure, sheathe, shelter, shield, take care of, watch over, wrap

COVER *(Provide for),* ***verb***   compensate for, counterbalance, insure, make compensation, make provision for, offset, pay, recompense, replace, substitute, suffice to defray
ASSOCIATED CONCEPTS: buyer's right to cover

COVERAGE *(Insurance),* ***noun***   act of promise-making, amount for which anything is insured, assurance, backing, bond, covenant, guarantee, guaranty, indemnity, obligation, pledge, promise, promise to pay, protection, reassurance, reinsurance, safeguard, security against loss, support, surety, undertaking, underwriting, warrant, warranty
ASSOCIATED CONCEPTS: blanket coverage, casualty coverage, comprehensive coverage, extended coverage, fire coverage, theft coverage

COVERAGE *(Scope),* ***noun***   accommodation, act of compassing, act of comprehending, act of containing, act of embracing, act of encircling, act of encompassing, act of engrossing, act of spanning, act of subsuming, act of surrounding, ambit, bounds, capacity, circulation, circumscription, composition, comprehension, comprehensiveness, comprisal, domain, dominion, embodiment, embrace, enclosure, encompassment, envelopment, expanse, extent of view, fact of comprehending, field, formation, grasp, inclusion, inclusiveness, inclusivity, incorporation, latitude, measure, participation, province, purview, range, range of view, reach, realm, region, room, space, sphere, spread, sweep, that which is comprehended, view, volume, wide currency, zone

COVERT, *adjective*   clandestine, cloaked, concealed, covered, cryptic, cryptical, dark, delitescent, disguised, furtive, hidden, insidious, invisible, latent, muffled, mysterious, mystic, mystical, nonapparent, occult, out of sight, private, screened, secluded, secret, sheltered, shrouded, sly, sneaky, stealthy, surreptitious, tacit, undercover, underground, underhand, undisclosed, unknown, unobtrusive, unseen, unsuspected, veiled

COVERTURE, *noun*   condition of a married woman, conjugality, legal status of a married woman, living as man and wife, marriage lines, married state, married tie, matrimony, matronage, matronhood, matronship, nuptial bond, state of a married woman, state of matrimony, union, wedded state, wifedom

CREATE, *verb*   be responsible, be the agent, be the author, be the cause of, be the reason, beget, bring about, bring into being, bring on, bring out, bring to effect, bring to pass, build, carve, cause, cause to exist, chisel, compose, conceive, concoct, constitute, construct, contribute, contrive, *creare,* develop, devise, effect, engender, engineer, erect, establish, fabricate, fashion, *fingere,* forge, form, formulate, found, frame, generate, give birth to, give origin to, give rise to, ideate, improvise, inaugurate, induce, initiate, institute, invent, kindle, launch, lay the foundations, make, make up, occasion, organize, originate, pattern, procreate, produce, put together, set going, set up, shape, spawn, start, think up
ASSOCIATED CONCEPTS: create a debt, create a liability, create a lien, created by fraud, created by law

CREATION, *noun*   arrangement, artistic effort, authorship, beginning, birth, bringing forth, building, causation, composition, concoction, constituting, construction, contriving, defiance of precedent, designing, development, devising, endeavor, engenderment, establishment, expression, fabrication, fashioning, formation, forming, formulation, formulation of a mental image, formulation of a principle, formulation of an idea, foundation, framing, fruition, imagination, *initium,* invention, manufacture, molding, new departure, original work, origination, patterning, preparation, procreation, producing, production, productiveness, productivity, realization, shaping

CREDENCE, *noun*   acceptance, act of believing, assurance, belief, certainty, complete trust, confidence, conviction, credit, dependence on, faith, firm belief, fixed belief, full assurance, full belief, implicit belief, instinctive belief, persuasion, reliance, subjective belief, sureness, surety, suspension of disbelief, trust, unshaken belief, view
FOREIGN PHRASES: ***Culbet in arte sua perito est credendum.*** Credence should be given to one skilled in his peculiar profession.

CREDENTIALS, *noun*   authorization, certificates, certification, documents, identification, papers, passport, proof of authority, recommendations, records, references, testimonials, vouchers

CREDIBILITY, *noun*   appearance of truth, *auctoritas,* believability, believableness, credibleness, faithfulness, *fides,* integrity, plausibility, probity, rectitude, reliability, tenability, tenableness, trustworthiness, truthfulness, uprightness, veracity, verisimilitude
ASSOCIATED CONCEPTS: credibility of a witness, impeachment of credibility

CREDIBLE, *adjective*   assured, believable, commanding belief, commanding confidence, convincing, *credibilis,* creditworthy, dependable, deserving belief, deserving of confidence, faithful, faithworthy, frank, honest, incorruptible, indisputable, indubitable, ingenuous, irrefutable, not improbable, of repute, reliable, reputable, scrupulous, sound, straightforward, to be depended on, to be relied upon, true, trusted, trustworthy, truth telling, truthful, uncorrupt, uncorruptible, undeniable, unequivocal, unfailing, unfalse, upright, veracious, verisimilar, void of suspicion, well-grounded, worthy of belief, worthy of confidence, worthy of credence
ASSOCIATED CONCEPTS: attack on credibility, credible evidence, credible person, credible witness

CREDIBLE EVIDENCE, *noun*   admitted testimony, believable proof, believable testimony, confirmed proof, convincing proof, corroborated proof, credible documents, credible exhibits, credible proof, creditworthy proof, dependable proof, documented proof, honest proof, indisputable proof, indubitable proof, irrefutable proof, legitimate proof, legitimate proof of facts, proof worthy of belief, proof worthy of credence, tested testimony, testimony which is above reproach, trustworthy proof, truthful proof, truthful testimony, validated proof, verified proof
ASSOCIATED CONCEPTS: attack on credibility, credible evidence, credible person, credible witness

CREDIT *(Recognition),* ***noun***   commendation, consideration, distinction, esteem, fame, favorable opinion, good name, high regard, honor, merit, power, prestige, rank, regard, reputableness, reputation, repute, respect, standing, status, worth
FOREIGN PHRASES: ***Judiciis posterioribus fides est adhibenda.*** Faith or credit is to be given to the more recent decisions.

CREDIT *(Delayed payment)*, **noun** advance, chance to borrow money on time, confidence, future payment, installment buying, loan, opportunity to obtain goods on time, permission to defer payment, purchase on time, purchase on trust, reliance

ASSOCIATED CONCEPTS: confirmed credit, consumer credit, contingent creditors, credit agreement, credit association, credit bureau, credit rating, credit union, creditor and debtor, creditor-beneficiary, creditor of bankrupt, creditor of estate, creditor's bill, creditor's committee, creditor's reference, creditor's suits, establishment of credit, extension of credit, general creditors, judgment creditors, junior creditors, letter of credit, line of credit, paper credit, personal credit, preferred creditors, renewal of credit, secured creditors, unconditional credit

CREDITOR, noun backer, debtee, investor, lender, mortgagee, pledgee, seller, sponsor

FOREIGN PHRASES: *Debitorum pactionibus creditorum petitio nec tolli nec minui potest.* The rights of creditors to sue cannot be prejudiced or diminished by agreements between their debtors.

CREDULITY, noun belief, blind faith, *credulitas,* credulousness, deceivability, disposition to believe, easiness of belief, foolishness, gullibility, gullibleness, impressibility, innocence, lack of doubt, lack of dubiety, lack of dubiousness, lack of skepticism, lack of sophistication, lack of suspicion, naiveness, naivete, overtrustfulness, persuasibility, pliability, pliancy, readiness to believe, simpleness, simplicity, suggestibility, susceptibility, susceptivity, tractability, trust, trustfulness, uncritical acceptance, unquestioning belief, unsophistication, unsuspectingness, unsuspiciousness

CREDULOUS, adjective believing, *credulus,* deceivable, disposed to believe, easily convinced, easily deceived, easily duped, easily taken in, green, gullible, misjudging, naive, overly trustful, persuasible, prone to believe, simple, trusting, undoubting, unquestioning, unsophisticated, unsuspecting, unsuspicious

CRIME, noun act prohibited by law, breach of law, contravention, corruption, criminal activity, criminal offense, delict, *delictum,* delinquency, dereliction, deviation from rectitude, encroachment, *facinus,* felony, flagitiousness, infringement, graft, gross offense against law, guilty act, illegality, indictable offense, infringement, jobbery, *maleficium,* malfeasance, malversation, misconduct, misdealing, misdeed, misdemeanor, misdoing, misfeasance, misprision, noncompliance with law, nonobservance of law, nonfeasance, obliquity, offence, offense, offense against the law, offense against the state, official misconduct, omission prohibited by law, public wrong, serious infraction of the law, violation of law, wrong

ASSOCIATED CONCEPTS: accessory to crime, acquittal of crime, antecedent crime, attempted crime, capital crime, commission of a crime, common-law crimes, compounding a crime, concealment of a crime, convicted of a crime, crime against law of nations, crime against nature, crime involving moral turpitude, crime mala in se, crime mala prohibita, crime of violence, *crimen falsi,* element of the crime, guilt, implement a crime, imprisonment, indictable crime, infamous crime, necessarily included crime, pary to crime, proceeds of crime, prosecution for a crime, punishment for a crime, quasi crime, victim

FOREIGN PHRASES: *Crescente malitia crescere debet et poena.* Punishment ought to be increased as malice increases. *Aestimatio praeteriti delicti ex postremo facto nunquam crescit.* The weight of a past crime is never increased by a subsequent fact. *Receditur a placitis juris, potius quam injuriae et delicta maneant impunita.* Settled rules of law will be departed from rather than that crimes should remain unpublished. *Peccata contra naturam sunt gravissima.* Crimes against nature are the most heinous. *Nemo punitur pro alieno delicto.* No one is to be punished for the crime of another. *Ubi culpa est, ibi poena subesse debet.* Where a crime is committed, there punishment should be inflicted. *Impunities semper ad deteriora invitat.* Impunity always invites to greater offenses. *Melior est justitia vere praeveniens quam severe puniens.* Truly preventive justice is better than severe punishment. *Multiplicata transgressione crescat poenae inflictio.* The infliction of punishment should be increased in proportion to the repetition of the offense. *Poena non potest, culpa perennis erit.* Punishment cannot be everlasting, but crime will be. *In atrocioribus delictis punitur affectus licet non sequatur effectus.* In the more atrocious crimes the intent is punished, although an effect does not follow. *Crimen laesae majestatis omnia alia crimina excedit quoad poenam.* The punishment for treason exceeds that for all other crimes. *Crimen omnia ex se nata vitiat.* Crime vitiates all which springs from it. *Crimina morte extinguuntur.* Crimes are extinguished by death. *Culpae poena par esto.* Let the punishment fit to the crime. *Venia facilitas incentivum est delinquendi.* Facility of pardon is an incentive to crime. *Voluntas et propositum distinguunt maleficia.* The will and purpose distinguish offenses. *Multiplicata transgressione crescat poenae inflictio.* The infliction of punishment should be increased in proportion to the repetition of the offense. *In criminalibus, voluntas reputabitur pro facto.* In criminal cases, the intent will be taken for the deed. *In maleficiis voluntas spectatur, non exitus.* In offenses, the intention is regarded, not the result. *In omnibus poenalibus judiciis, et aetatl et imprudentiae succurritur.* In all penal judgments, allowance is made for youth and lack of prudence. *In criminalibus, sufficit generalis malitia intentionis, cum facto paris gradus.* In crimes, a general malicious intent suffices where there is an act of equal degree. *Interest reipublicae quod homines conserventur.* It is in the interest of the state that men be preserved.

CRIMINAL, noun bandit, blackguard, buccaneer, burglar, convict, defrauder, evildoer, extortionist, felon, filcher, fugitive, gangster, grafter, guilty person, gunman, hardened offender, juvenile delinquent, kidnapper, killer, knave, lawbreaker, malefactor, malfeasant, manslayer, marauder, misdemeanant, murderer, offender, outlaw, pilferer, pillager, pirate, plunderer, public enemy, recidivist, recreant, reprobate, *reus,* robber, *sceleratus,* smuggler, sneak thief, swindler, terrorist, thief, transgressor, underworld character, villain, worker of iniquity, wrongdoer

ASSOCIATED CONCEPTS: convicted criminal, criminal action, criminal attempt, criminal capacity, criminal case or cause, criminal charge, criminal code, criminal conduct, criminal conspiracy, criminal contempt, criminal conviction, criminal courts, criminal information, criminal intent, criminal judgments, criminal jurisdiction, criminal motive, criminal negligence, criminal offense, criminal procedure, criminal process, criminal prosecution, criminal responsibility, criminal sanctions, criminal solicitation, criminal statute, criminal syndicalism, criminal transaction, criminal trial, habitual criminal, known criminals

FOREIGN PHRASES: *Frustra legis auxilium invocat qui in legem committit.* He vainly seeks the aid of the law who transgresses the law.

CRIMINALITY, noun blameworthy conduct, corruptness, criminal attitude, criminal conduct, crookedness, culpability, culpable conduct, felonious conduct, feloniousness, fraudulence, guilt, heinous conduct, illegality, illicitness, infamous conduct, infamous misbehavior, lawlessness, malversation, misdoing, official misconduct, outlawry, transgression, unlawfulness, wrongdoing
ASSOCIATED CONCEPTS: criminal culpability, criminal intent

CRIMINOUS, adjective blameful, blameworthy, censurable, condemnable, corrupt, criminal, culpable, degenerate, dishonest, errant, evil, felonious, flagitious, flagrant, fraudulent, guilty, illegitimate, illicit, immoral, inexcusable, infamous, iniquitous, irregular, law-breaking, lawless, malefactory, malfeasant, nefarious, peccant, recreant, reprehensible, sinful, unpardonable, vile, villainous, wicked

CRITERION, noun barometer, basis, code, custom, design, discipline, example, exemplar, form, formula, foundation, frame of reference, gauge, ground rules, guide, ideal, law, measure, model, norm, *obrussa*, pattern, point of comparison, precedent, prescribed form, principle, regulation, rule, rules and regulations, shape, standard, standard of comparison, standard of criticism, standard of judgment, test, test case, type, yardstick

CRITICAL (Crucial), **adjective** acute, *anceps*, chief, climacteric, climactic, commanding, considerable, deciding, decisive, determining, *dubius*, essential, eventful, exigent, far-reaching, fateful, foremost, grave, imperative, important, imposing, key, major, material, momentous, never to be forgotten, notable, of decisive importance, of great consequence, of importance, of vital importance, outstanding, overruling, overshadowing, paramount, pivotal, pressing, primary, principal, prominent, serious, significant, solemn, strategic, substantial, turning, urgent, vital, weighty
ASSOCIATED CONCEPTS: critical stage of a trial

CRITICAL (Faultfinding), **adjective** accusing, blaming, captious, carping, castigating, caustic, caviling, censorious, censuring, chiding, choleric, comminatory, condemnatory, condemning, criminative, criminatory, criticizing severely, cynical, damnatory, defamatory, denunciatory, derogatory, disapproving, *elegans*, exacting, hard upon, hardhitting, hypercritical, inclined to judge with severity, nagging, objecting, objurgatory, overcritical, rebuking, recriminative, reprehensive, reproachful, reprobative, reproving, scarifying, scathing, scolding, severe, taunting, ultracritical, uncomplimentary, upbraiding

CRITICAL POINT, noun benchmark, bookmark, critical point, crux, essence, essential matter, fundamental part, gist, gravamen, heart, key point, linchpin, main point, material point, milestone, pivotal point, prime issue, salient point, substance, substantive point, turning point

CRITICISM, noun abuse, accusation, admonition, adverse comment, analysis, animadversion, aspersion, blame, carping, caviling, censure, charge, chiding, commentary, complaining, complaint, condemnation, contravention, critical examination, critical remarks, critique, denunciation, deprecation, depreciation, derogation, detraction, disapproval, discommendation, disdain, disparagement, dispraise, disvaluation, exception, expostulation, fault-finding, grievance, grumbling, imputation, indictment, insinuation, *iudicium*, lecture, objection, obloquy, odium, opposition, opprobrium, protestation, reflection, rejection, remonstrance, reprehension, reprimand, reproach, reproof, review, revilement, scolding, upbraiding

ASSOCIATED CONCEPTS: fair and honest criticism, freedom of speech, privileged criticism

CRITICIZE (Evaluate), **verb** adjudge, appraise, assess, consider, examine, gauge, *iudicare*, judge, measure, rank, rate, reckon, review, scrutinize, sum up, take stock of, value, weigh

CRITICIZE (Find fault with), **verb** animadvert, berate, blame, castigate, censure, chide, complain, condemn, *culpare*, decry, deprecate, depreciate, disapprove, disparage, dispraise, express dissatisfaction, find cause to blame, impugn, object to, objurgate, rebuke, reprehend, *reprehendere*, reprimand, reproach, reprobate, reprove, upbraid

CROSS (Disagree with), **verb** act in opposition to, argue, be opposed to, collide, conflict with, confront, confute, contend, contest, contradict, contravene, controvert, debate, defy, dispute, gainsay, *homini obsistere*, make a stand against, neutralize, oppose, protest, refuse to conform, refute, repudiate, resist, run counter to, speak against, take exception, traverse
ASSOCIATED CONCEPTS: cross action, cross-appeal, cross-claim, cross-complaint, cross-demand, cross-examination, cross-interrogatories, cross libels, cross-motions, cross-petition, cross-remainders, cross section, cross-suit, crosswalk

CROSS (Intersect), **verb** bisect, braid, crisscross, crosscut, cut across, divide, go across, halve, intercross, interrupt, intersect, lie across, move across, section, segment, separate, split, traverse

CROSS-EXAMINATION, noun asking questions, challenge, checking, cross interrogation, cross questioning, enquiry, evidence-seeking, examination, exploration, formulating questions, grilling, inquest, inquiry, inquisition, interpellation, interrogation, investigation, leading inquiry, minute examination, probe, prosecution, query, quest, questioning, reexamination, scrutiny, search, search into facts, searching inquiry, trial
ASSOCIATED CONCEPTS: right to cross-examine, scope of cross-examination

CROSS-EXAMINE, verb ask questions, catechize, challenge, check, cross interrogate, cross question, examine, ferret out, grill, inquire of, interpellate, interrogate, petition, probe, query, question, quiz, reexamine, subject to examination
ASSOCIATED CONCEPTS: cross-examination limited to the scope of the direct examination, direct examination, impeachment, right to cross-examine

CROSS-PURPOSES, noun adverseness, antonym, at variance, clashing, contention, contradiction, difference of opinion, difficulty, disagreement, discord, disparity, in opposition, misunderstanding, odds, variance
ASSOCIATED CONCEPTS: at cross-purposes with the intent of the law

CROSS-QUESTIONING, noun close inquiry, cross examination, cross-interrogation, exploration, inquiry, inspection, interrogation, investigation, probe, query, questioning, reexamination, review, scrutiny

CROSS SECTION, noun average, characterization, composite representation, embodiment, epitome, example, exemplar, *exempli gratia*, exemplification, *exemplum*, fair sample, *locus classicus*, norm, part exemplifying a mass, part exemplifying a number, profile, random sample, representation, representative sampling, representative section, representative selection, sample

CROSSROAD (*Intersection*), **noun**   confluence, conjuncture, cross-way, crossing, crossways, four corners, interchange, intercrossing, intersecting road, intersection, joining road, junction, vertex

CROSSROAD (*Turning point*), **noun**   calm before a storm, climacteric, climax, conjuncture, crisis, critical moment, critical period, critical point, crossways, crowning point, crucial moment, culmination, decisive moment, dividing point, eleventh hour, floodgate, hinge, hour of decision, juncture, landmark, line of demarcation, meeting of events, milestone, pivot, point of no return, relapse, turn, turn of the tide, watershed, well-chosen moment, well-timed initiative

CROWNING (*Best*), **adjective**   absolute, capping, cardinal, chief, definitive, dominant, foremost, heading, leading, main, master, paramount, pre-eminent, preponderant, prevailing, prime, principal, stellar, super, superlative, supreme, surmounting, topping, ultimate

CROWNING (*Ending*), **adjective**   climaxing, closing, concluding, consummatory, culminating, final, finishing, last, terminating

CRUCIAL, **adjective**   acute, climacteric, conclusive, consequential, critical, deciding, decisive, definitive, determining, essential, exigent, final, grave, imperative, important, influential, instant, material, momentous, of moment, of note, of supreme importance, pivotal, pressing, severe, significant, supreme, urgent, valuable, vital

CRUCIAL POINT, **noun**   conclusive point, conclusory point, convincing point, cornerstone, crisis, critical moment, crossroads, definitive point, determinative point, determining point, hour of decision, impelling point, juncture, key point, landmark, main point, optimum point, proof positive, turning point

CRUEL, **adjective**   acrimonious, agonizing, atrocious, barbarous, blood-thirsty, brutal, cold, cold-blooded, cold-hearted, *crudelis,* demoniacal, devilish, diabolical, distressing, evil-minded, ferocious, fiendish, fierce, hard, hard-hearted, harsh, heartless, hellish, ill-intentioned, ill-natured, ill-willed, implacable, indifferent to suffering, inhuman, inhumane, insensitive, malevolent, malicious, malign, malignant, merciless, oppressive, painful, pitiless, punishing, relentless, remorseless, ruthless, sadistic, satanic, savage, severe, spiteful, tortuous, treacherous, tyrannical, unbenevolent, uncompassionate, unfeeling, unkind, unmerciful, unnatural, unpitying, unrelenting, unsympathetic, unsympathizing, vicious
ASSOCIATED CONCEPTS: cruel and abusive treatment, cruel and barbarous treatment, cruel and inhuman punishment, cruel and inhuman treatment, cruel and unusual punishment, cruel disposition, cruel treatment

CRUELTY, **noun**   atrocity, austerity, barbarity, barbarousness, bloodthirstiness, brutality, brutalness, brutishness, *crudelitas,* cruel act, cruel conduct, deliberate malice, deviltry, enmity, ferity, ferociousness, ferocity, fierceness, harshness, heartlessness, ill-nature, ill-usage, ill-will, infliction of pain, inhumanity, intolerance, malice, malice aforethought, malice prepense, maliciousness, malignance, malignancy, malignity, mercilessness, oppression,

outrage, persecution, rancor, relentlessness, remorselessness, ruthlessness, savageness, savagery, severity, spite, sternness, torture, tyranny, uncompassionateness, unkindness, unremorsefulness, viciousness, victimization, violence
ASSOCIATED CONCEPTS: cruelty of treatment, cruelty to animals, cruelty to children, extreme cruelty, habitual cruelty, mental cruelty, unneccessary cruelty

CRYSTALLIZE, **verb**   accumulate, amalgamate, arrange itself, assume a pattern, assume definite characteristics, be solid, become a reality, become definite, become delineated, become firm, become settled, become solid, become visible, bring together, cement, coagulate, cohere, combine, come together, compact, compress, condense, conglomerate, consolidate, develop, eventuate, fall into line, fashion, form, form a core, formulate, set, shape up, solidify, take form, take on character, take order, take shape, thicken, unfold, unify

CUDGEL, **noun**   arm, *baculum,* bar, bastinado, bat, battering ram, billy, blackjack, bludgeon, cane, club, cosh, deadly device, deadly weapon, deterrent, ferule, *fustis,* instrument for use in combat, instrument of war, lethal instrument, lethal weapon, mallet, means of offense, night stick, pole, shillelagh, staff, stick, truncheon, war hammer, weapon
ASSOCIATED CONCEPTS: deadly weapons

CULL, **verb**   accumulate, amass, *carpere,* choose, collect, *decerpere,* gather, glean, *legere,* make a selection, pick, pick out, pluck, round up, select, separate, sift, single out, sort out, winnow

CULMINATE, **verb**   accomplish, cap, climax, close, complete, conclude, consummate, crown, effect, end, execute, finish, reach a peak, reach the highest point, reach the zenith, terminate, top

CULMINATION, **noun**   acme, apex, apogee, cap, climax, crest, crown, crowning touch, head, height, highest point, peak, pinnacle, summit, top, topmost point, utmost height, zenith

CULPABILITY, **noun**   blame, blameworthiness, censurableness, chargeableness, criminality, delinquency, dereliction, failure in duty, fault, guilt, guiltiness, improbity, misbehavior, misconduct, misdoing, peccability, peccancy, remissness, reprehensibility, reproachableness, transgression, wrongdoing
ASSOCIATED CONCEPTS: culpable recklessness, culpably negligent

CULPABLE, **adjective**   accusable, at fault, blamable, blameworthy, censurable, chargeable, condemnable, convictable, criminal, criminous, *culpandus,* delinquent, deserving blame, deserving censure, discreditable, dishonest, disorderly, dissolute, encroaching, felonious, guilty, having violated the law, improper, in error, in the wrong, indictable, indiscreet, lawbreaking, lawless, meriting censure, meriting condemnation, misdemeanant, peccant, punishable, responsible, transgressing, unrighteous, worthy of blame, wrong

CULTIVATE, **verb**   advance, *colere,* develop, elevate, enrich, farm, forward, foster, further, garden, improve, make better, nourish, nurture, polish, prepare for crops, promote, rarefy, refine, till, train, work

CUMULATION, **noun**   accession, accretion, accruement, accumulation, acervation, acquisition, addition, agglomerate, agglomeration, aggregate, aggregation, amassment, amount accrued, assemblage, assembly, *attroupement*, augmentation, bringing together, build up, bulk, collection, compilation, concentration, conglomerate, conglomeration, congregation, glomeration, growth by addition, mass, pile, reserve, stock, stockpile, storage, store, supply

CUMULATIVE (Increasing), *adjective*   accruing, accumulative, added together, additional, additive, additory, advancing, becoming greater, becoming larger, broadening, continually increasing, enlarging, ever-widening, expanding, flourishing, growing, growing by successive additions, incremental, lengthening, multiplying, on the increase, piling up, strengthening, successively gaining in force, successively waxing in force, swelling, thriving, widening
ASSOCIATED CONCEPTS: cumulative criminal acts, cumulative sentences, cumulative voting

CUMULATIVE (Intensifying), *adjective*   accelerating, aggravative, amplifying, augmentative, becoming more intense, boosting, concentrating, deepening, enhancing, escalating, exaggerating, extending, heightening, intensive, magnifying, maximizing, multiplying, quickening, sharpening, strengthening

CURATIVE, *adjective*   analeptic, corrective, emendatory, healing, relieving, remedial, reparative, restorative, therapeutic

CURB, *verb*   arrest, brake, check, control, delay, detain, govern, harness, hinder, hold back, hold in check, hold up, impede, inhibit, keep within limits, limit, mitigate, moderate, muzzle, obstruct, prohibit, repress, restrain, retard, snub, stay, suppress, temper, throttle down, trammel, yoke

CURE, *noun*   antidote, antipoison, antitoxin, assuager, balm, catholicon, corrective, counteractant, elixir, emollient, healing agent, medical treatment, medicament, medicine, method of treatment, palliative, panacea, recovery, recuperation, redress, relief, remedy, restoration to health, restorative, salve, *sanatio*, successful remedial treatment, therapeutic, tonic

CURE, *verb*   ameliorate, apply a remedy, correct, doctor, effect a cure, heal, improve, make well, make whole, mederi, medicate, meliorate, mend, minister to, nurse, palliate, recall to life, reclaim, recover, rectify, recuperate, redeem, redress, regenerate, rehabilitate, rejuvenate, relieve, relieve of something detrimental, remedy, renew, repair, restore, resuscitate, revive, revivify, right, salve, *sanare*, soothe, treat
ASSOCIATED CONCEPTS: cured by verdict, curing defect, curing error, curing title, opportunity to cure

CURRENCY, *noun*   bank notes, bills, cash, circulating medium, coin, government notes, hard cash, legal tender, medium of exchange, *moneta*, money, money in actual use, notes, paper money, ready money, specie
ASSOCIATED CONCEPTS: lawful currency

CURRENT, *adjective*   being done, belonging to the time, concurrent, contemporaneous, contemporary, customary, existent, existing, *hic*, immediate, in fashion, in style, in the fad, in vogue, instant, latest, latter day, new, occurring, of the moment, of the present, of this date, of todays date, popular, present, present day, prevailing, prevalent, recent, revised, stylish, topical, up to date, up to the minute, *usitatus*, widespread
ASSOCIATED CONCEPTS: current account, current assets, current basis, current business expenses, current debts, current

events, current expenditures, current market value, current obligations, current operating expenses, current rate of exchange, currently distributable

CURRICULUM, *noun*   agenda, compendium, course, course of study, discipline, plan, program, prospectus, schedule, seminar, study, syllabus
ASSOCIATED CONCEPTS: continuing legal education

CURSORY, *adjective*   apathetic, brief, careless, casual, desultory, hasty, heedless, hurried, immethodical, inattentive, incautious, indifferent, lax, offhand, passing, perfunctory, quick, rapid, regardless, shallow, short, slapdash, slipshod, speedy, summary, superficial, surface, thoughtless, undiscerning, unmindful, unthorough
ASSOCIATED CONCEPTS: cursory examination

CURTAIL, *verb*   abate, abbreviate, abridge, clip, coartare, cut, cut down, cut short, decrease, diminish, halt, lessen, lop, make smaller, *minuere*, pare, pare down, reduce, retrench, shorten, subtract, trim

CURTAILMENT, *noun*   abatement, abbreviation, abbreviature, abridgment, compression, condensation, constriction, contraction, cut-back, cutting down, cutting off, declension, decline, decrease, decrescence, depression, deprivation, diminishment, diminution, divestment, elimination, lessening, minimization, modification, privation, reduction, retrenchment, shortening, shrinkage, subduction, subtraction, trimming

CURTILAGE, *noun*   court, courtyard, enclosure, fenced, garden, land, yard

CUSTODIAL, *adjective*   cared for, carefully watched, caretaking, keeping, protected, protecting, protective, restraining, safe, screened, sheltering, shielding, tutelary, watched
ASSOCIATED CONCEPTS: custodial interference

CUSTODIAN (Protector), *noun*   champion, curator, defender, guardian, keeper, manager, overlooker, overseer
ASSOCIATED CONCEPTS: custodian of assets, gratuitous custodian
FOREIGN PHRASES: *Nemo alienae rei, sine satisdatione, defensor idoneus intelligitur.* No one is considered a competent defender of another's property, without security.

CUSTODIAN (Warden), *noun*   caretaker, jailer

CUSTODIANSHIP, *noun*   captivity, care, charge, confinement, constraint, custody, detention, durance, guardianship, incarceration, restraint, retention, safekeeping

CUSTODY (Incarceration), *noun*   arrest, arrestment, bondage, bounds, captivity, circumscription, commitment, confinement, constraint, detention, durance, enthrallment, fetter, holding, immuration, immurement, impoundment, imprisonment, limitation, restraint, restriction, safekeeping, thralldom
ASSOCIATED CONCEPTS: arrest, bail, constructive custody, hold in custody, parole, probation
FOREIGN PHRASES: *Fortior est custodia legis quam hominis.* The custody of the law is stronger than that of man. ***In custodia legis.*** In the custody of the law.

CUSTODY (Supervision), *noun*   act of protecting, administration, aegis, auspices, *carcer*, care, charge, control, custodia, custodianship, direction, guardianship, guidance, jurisdiction, keeping, management, preservation, preservation from harm, preservation from injury, protection, regulation, safeguard, safekeeping, stewardship, superintendence, trusteeship, wardship, watch

ASSOCIATED CONCEPTS: custody and control, custody decree, custody of children, custody of property, custody order, custody proceeding, guardianship

CUSTOM, *noun*   ceremony, characteristic way, common usage, consuetude, convention, conventionalism, conventionality, course of business, dictates of society, established way of doing things, etiquette, familiar way, fashion, fashionableness, formality, habit, habit of a majority, habitual activity, habitual practice, habituation, habitude, institution, manner, matter of course, observance, ordinary manner, practice, prescribed form, prevailing taste, prevalence, rite, ritual, routine, routine procedure, social usage, style, tradition, traditionalism, traditionality, unwritten law, usage, usual manner, vogue, wont, wontedness

ASSOCIATED CONCEPTS: custom of merchants, custom or practice, custom or usage, general custom, local customs, usual course and custom, waiver by custom

FOREIGN PHRASES: *Servanda est consuetudo loci ubi causa agitur.* The custom of the place where the action is brought should be observed. *In contractibus, tacite insunt quae sunt moris et consuetudinis.* In contracts, matters of custom and usage are tacitly implied. *Consuetudo tollit communem legem.* Custom supersedes the common law. *Consuetudo non trahitur in consequentiam.* Custom is not drawn into consequence. *Consuetudo manerii et loci observanda est.* Custom of a manor and a locality is to be observed. *Consuetudo est optimus interpres legum.* Custom is the best interpreter of the laws. *Consuetudo est altera lex.* Custom is another law. *Consuetudo contra rationem introducta potius usurpatio quam consuetudo appellari debet.* A custom introduced contrary to reason ought rather to be called a usurpation than a custom. *Ratio est formalis causa consuetudinis.* Reason is the source and cause of custom. *Quae praeter consuetudinem et morem majorum fiunt neque placent neque recta videntur.* Things which are done contrary to the custom and manner of our ancestors neither please nor appear right. *Optimus interpres rerum usus.* Usage is the best interpreter of things. *Optima est legis interpres consuetudo.* Custom is the best interpreter of the law. *Omne jus aut consensus fecit, aut necessitas constituit aut firmavit consuetudo.* Every right is either derived from consent, established by necessity, or is confirmed by custom. *Minime mutanda sunt quae certam habuerunt interpretationem.* Those matters which have had a certain interpretation are to be altered as little as possible. *Obtemperandum est consuetudini rationabili tanquam legi.* A reasonable custom is to be obeyed like law. *Malus usus abolendus est.* A bad custom is to be abolished. *Consuetudo volentes ducit, lex nolentes trahit.* Custom leads the willing, the law compels the unwilling. *Consuetudo vincit communem legem.* Custom overrules the common law. *In consuetudinibus, non diuturnitas temporis sed soliditas rationis est consideranda.* In customs, not lapse of time, but the soundness of reason should be considered. *Consuetudo semel reprobata non potest amplius induci.* Custom once disallowed cannot again be invoked. *Consuetudo praescripta et legitima vincit legem.* A prescriptive and lawful custom prevails over the law. *Consuetudo neque injuria oriti neque tolli potest.* Custom can neither arise from nor be abolished by a wrongful act. *Consuetudo loci observanda est.* The custom of a locality is to be observed. *Consuetudo, licet sit magnae auctoritatis,*

nunquam tamen, praejudicat manifestae veritati. A custom, though it be of great authority, should never be prejudicial to manifest truth. *Consuetudo ex certa causa rationabili usitata privat communem legem.* A custom, based on a certain and reasonable cause, supersedes the common law. *Consuetudo et communis assuetudo vincit legem non scriptam, si sit specialis; et interpretatur legem scriptam, si lex sit generalis.* Custom and common usage override the unwritten law, if it be special; and interprets the written law, if the law be general.

CUSTOMARY, *adjective*   accustomed, acknowledged, boiler plate, common, commonplace, consuetudinary, continued, conventional, current, daily, established, everyday, expected, favorite, fixed, formal, frequent, general, habitual, inveterate, long-standing, natural, normal, ordinary, orthodox, popular, prescriptive, prevailing, prevalent, pro forma, recognized, regular, repeated, right, routine, standard, stipulated, stock, systematic, time-honored, traditional, typical, understood, universal, usual, wonted

ASSOCIATED CONCEPTS: customary despatch, customs and usages, customs court

CUSTOMER, *noun*   acceptor, bargainer, bidder, business contact, buyer, buyer of labor, client, consumer, *emptor,* investor, leaser, lessee, one of the clientele, one of the purchasing public, patron, prospect, purchaser, purchaser of goods from another, redeemer, share buyer, shopper, taker, user, vendee

ASSOCIATED CONCEPTS: buyer in the ordinary course of business, cash customer, customer in ordinary course of business, duty to customers, interference with customers, loss of customers, occasional customer, solicitation of customers

CY PRES, *adverb*   as near as may be, as near as practicable, as near as possible

CYBERCRIME, *noun*   a criminal offense on the Web, a criminal offense regarding the Internet, a violation of law on the Internet, an illegality committed with regard to the Internet, breach of law on the Internet, computer crime, contravention through the Web, corruption regarding Internet, criminal activity on the Internet, disrupting operations through malevolent programs on the Internet, e-crime, electric crime, Internet crime, sale of contraband on the Internet, stalking victims on the Internet, theft of identify on the Internet

ASSOCIATED CONCEPTS: copyright theft through cybercrime, cyber laws, cyber-stalking, hacking, privacy

CYCLE, *noun*   age, alternation, circle, circuit, *circulus,* consecution, course, eon, epoch, era, flow, period, progression, recurrence, recurring period, regular return, regularity of recurrence, repetitiveness, revolution, rotation, round, sequence, succession

CYNICAL, *adjective*   acrimonious, apt to distrust, arrogant, caustic, cavalier, censorious, condemnatory, contemptuous, contumelious, critical, decrying, defamatory, defeatist, denunciatory, derisive, derogative, derogatory, despising, disapproving, disdainful, disillusioned, disparaging, disposed to doubt, distrustful, distrusting the motives of others, doubtful, doubting, dubious, fault finding, haughty, holding a low opinion of mankind, inconvincible, indisposed to believe, misanthropic, mistrustful, mocking, *mordax,* pessimistic, questioning, ridiculing, sarcastic, sarcastical, sardonic, scoffing, scornful, skeptical, sneering, supercilious, suspecting, suspicious, unbelieving, untrustful

D

DAILY, *adjective* accustomed, common, diurnal, established, habitual, ordinary, quotidian, *quotidie,* regular, routine, usual

ASSOCIATED CONCEPTS: daily attendance, daily balance, daily occupation, daily output, daily publication, daily rate of pay, daily wages

DAMAGE, *noun* adversity, affliction, aggravation, casualty, declination, decline, decrement, depravation, depreciation, destruction, deterioration, detriment, dilaceration, diminution, disrepair, exacerbation, grievance, hardship, harm, hurt, impairment, infliction, injury, loss, ruin, ruination, spoiling, vexation, vitiation, weakening, wreck, wrong

ASSOCIATED CONCEPTS: actual loss, ad damnum clause, aggravation of damages, business damage, conjectural damages, consequential damages, contingent damages, damages actually sustained, damages by fire, damages by the elements, damages in contemplation of party, damages to land, damages to person, damages to property, damages to realty, *damnum absque injuria,* excessive damages, exemplary damages, future damages, general damages, incidental damages, *injuria absque damno,* limitation of liability, liquidated damages, measure of damages, minimizing damages, nominal damages, personal injury, property damage, punitive damages, remote damages, special damages, treble damages, unliquidated damages, unusual or extraordinary damage

FOREIGN PHRASES: ***Nemo damnum facit, nisi qui id fecit quod facere jus non habet.*** No one is considered as doing damage, except he who does that which he has no right to do. ***Nul sans damage avera error ou attaint.*** No one shall have error or attaint unless he has suffered damage. ***Ubicunque est injuria, ibi damnum sequitur.*** Wherever there is a wrong, there damage follows. ***Quod quis ex culpa sua damnum sentit non intelligitur damnum sentire.*** He who incurs a damage by his own fault is not held to suffer damage. ***Damnum sine injuria esse potest.*** There can be damage or injury inflicted without any act of injustice. ***Actus legis nemini est damnosus.*** An act of the law shall prejudice no one.

DAMAGE, *verb* abase, abuse, blemish, blight, break, break down, bruise, cause detriment, cause injury, cause mischief, cheapen, contaminate, corrupt, cripple, crush, debase, deface, defile, deform, degrade, demolish, destroy, devalue, devastate, diminish, disable, disfigure, disparage, disrupt, disserve, do disservice to, do violence to, harm, hurt, impair,

incapacitate, injure, lacerate, lay waste, maim, make unsound, malign, maltreat, mangle, mar, mutilate, pervert, pollute, prejudice, ravage, ruin, sabotage, scathe, spoil, stain, taint, tamper with, trample on, traumatize, vandalize, violate, vitiate, weaken, wound, wreck, wrong

ASSOCIATED CONCEPTS: damage from negligence, damage to goods, destruction, estimated damage, latent damage, loss, mitigation of damages, opportunity to repair, patent damage, permanent damage, recovery for damage, water damage

DAMAGES, *noun* amends, compensation, costs, expenses, expiation, fine, indemnification, indemnity, injury, just compensation, legal costs, legal liability, loss, penalty, recompense, recovery, reimbursement, remuneration for injury suffered, reparation, repayment for injury sustained, repayment for loss, restitution, restoration

ASSOCIATED CONCEPTS: actual loss, addamnum clause, additur, aggravation of damages, amercement, apportionment of damages, assessment of damages, civil damages, claim for damages, compensatory damages, conjectural damages, consequential damages, contingent damages, continuing damages, damages accrued, damages actually sustained, damages to person, damages to property, damages to realty, *damnum absque injuria,* direct damages, division of damages, duty to minimize damages, estimated damages, excessive damages, exemplary damages, future damages, general damages, incidental damages, intervening damages, irreparable damages, irreparable injury, lawful damages, limitation of liability, liquidated damages, measure of damages, minimizing damages, mitigation of damages, nominal damages, ordinary damages, pecuniary damages, pecuniary loss, permanent damages, presumptive damages, property damage, prospective damages, proximate damages, punitive damages, reasonable certainty of damages, remote damages, special damages, speculative damages, substantial damages, treble damages, unliquidated damages

FOREIGN PHRASES: ***Ubi damna dantur, victus victori in expensis condemnari debet.*** Where damages are given, the losing party ought to be condemned to pay costs to the victor.

DAMAGING, *adjective* baneful, calamitous, calumnious, caustic, contemptuous, corrosive, deleterious, destructive, detrimental, disadvantageous, disastrous, grievous, harmful, hurtful, incriminatory, inculpatory, inimical, injurious, insalubrious, malefic, malevolent, malignant, mischievous, mordacious, noisome, noxious, outrageous,

pejorative, pernicious, pestilent, poisonous, prejudicial, ruinous, scathing, unfavorable, virulent, wanton, wasting
ASSOCIATED CONCEPTS: damaging testimony

DAMPEN, *verb*   abate, allay, alleviate, assuage, blunt, chasten, chill, constrain, control, cool, cushion, deaden, decrease, deject, depress, deter, diminish, discourage, dishearten, dispirit, dull, lessen, mitigate, moderate, modulate, muffle, mute, palliate, quench, reduce, repress, restrain, smother, sober, soften, stifle, subdue, suppress, tame, temper, weaken

DAMPER *(Depressant),* *noun*   backset, bleakness, cheerlessness, chill, cloud, crushed spirits, depressing influence, discouragement, disheartener, downheartedness, feeling of dejection, feeling of depression, gloom, glumness, heaviness, heaviness of spirit, joylessness, lack of spirit, lack of warmth, letdown, low spirits, pessimism, sadness, setback, shadow, unhappiness

DAMPER *(Stopper),* *noun*   bar, barricade, barrier, block, blockage, bridle, check, clog, control, cork, curb, delay, determent, deterrent, difficulty, disadvantage, discouragement, encumbrance, hamper, hindrance, hitch, impediment, impedition, inhibition, interference, interruption, limitation, muffler, obstacle, obstruction, occlusion, oppilation, plug, preclusion, prevention, rein, restraint, restriction, retardation, snag, stoppage, stopper, stopple

DANGER, *noun*   assailability, crisis, defenselessness, *discrimen,* exposure to harm, hazard, helplessness, imperilment, jeopardy, lack of protection, lack of safety, liability to injury, menace, nonimmunity, penetrability, *periculum,* peril, perilousness, precariousness, pregnability, risk, susceptibility, threat, unguardedness, vincibility, vincibleness, vulnerability
ASSOCIATED CONCEPTS: apparent danger, appreciation of danger, assumption of risk, avoidance of danger, clear and present danger, danger invites rescue doctrine, danger signal, danger zone, foreseeable dangers, hidden danger, imminent danger, impending danger, inherent danger, intrinsic danger, knowledge of danger, known danger, latent danger, obvious danger, obvious risks, patent danger, unavoidable danger, unnecessary exposure to danger, zone of apprehendable danger
FOREIGN PHRASES: *Periculosum existimo quod bonorum virorum non comprobatur exemplo.* I think that dangerous which is not approved by the example of good men.

DANGEROUS, *adjective*   alarming, assailable, attended with risk, baleful, baneful, beset with danger, breakneck, causing danger, deadly, destructive, disastrous, explosive, exposed to risk, fearsome, fraught with danger, fraught with peril, full of risk, harmful, hazardous, hurtful, injurious, involving risk, likely to harm, maleficent, malignant, menacing, minatory, ominous, perilous, pestiferous, risky, serious, threatening, treacherous, unprotected, unreliable, unsafe, unsheltered, unstable, unsteady, unstrengthened, untrustworthy, venomous, vicious, viperine, viperous, virulent
ASSOCIATED CONCEPTS: attractive nuisance, danger to the community, dangerous animal, dangerous business, dangerous condition, dangerous contraband, dangerous defect, dangerous drug, dangerous employment, dangerous instrument, dangerous instrumentality, dangerous machinery, dangerous occupation, dangerous or defective condition, dangerous place, dangerous premises, dangerous propensities, dangerous structures, dangerous to health, dangerous to life, dangerous trap, dangerous weapon, deadly weapon

DANGEROUS CONDITION, *noun*   crisis, dangerous situation, emergency, endangerment, hazard, imperilment, jeopardy, menace, ominousness, peril, pitfall, precariousness, predicament, razor's edge, threat, unhealthy situation
ASSOCIATED CONCEPTS: dangerous drugs, dangerous instrumentality, dangerous per se, dangerous substance, dangerous weapon, dangers of the sea, known and obvious dangers

DARING, *adjective*   adventurous, audacious, blunt, brave, brazen, challenging, chivalrous, courageous, dauntless, defiant, disregardful, doughty, enterprising, fearless, flagrant, foolhardy, forthright, gallant, hardy, heroic, hot-blooded, impulsive, intrepid, lionhearted, mettlesome, outspoken, plucky, presumptuous, rash, reckless, revealing, resolute, self-reliant, shameless, showy, Spartan, spirited, stalwart, unabashed, unblushing, undaunted, unflinching, valiant, valorous, venturesome, virile

DARING, *noun*   adventurousness, audaciousness, audacity, backbone, boldness, bravado, bravery, bravura, chivalry, defiance, disregard, élan, enterprise, fearlessness, firmness, foolhardiness, fortitude, gallantry, grit, heart, heroism, mettle, nerve, overboldness, presumption, prowess, rashness, spirit, spunk, valor

DARK *(Devoid of light),* *adjective*   absent of light, bereft of light, black, darkened, darkish, dim, drab, ill-lighted, poorly lit, shaded, somber, sunless, unlighted, without light

DARK *(Dismal),* *adjective*   cheerless, clouded, dejected, depressed, dim, disconsolate, doleful, dolorous, grim, joyless, melancholy, sad, solemn, somber, sorrowful, sullen

DARK *(Evil),* *adjective*   base, demoniac, demonic, deplorable, diabolical, immoral, inexorable, infamous, iniquitous, mean, mean spirited, menacing, peccant, pernicious, sinfully malevolent, sinister, terrifying, untoward, vicious, vile, villainous, wicked

DATA, *noun*   back-up, documents, evidence, facts, grounds, information, logic, papers, proof, specifics

DATABASE, *noun*   catalogue, computer base of information, computer file, computer storage, memory *Generally:* cyberspace, record, records, registry

DATE, *noun*   assigned time, day, day of the week, *dies,* marked time, moment, particular point of time, period, period of time, point of time, specified period of time, *tempus,* time, time during which anything occurs
ASSOCIATED CONCEPTS: antedating, certainty of date, date certain, date of acceptance, date of acknowledgment, date of application, date of appointment, date of availability, date of award, date of birth, date of commencement of action, date of death, date of default, date of enactment, date of execution, date of final judgment, date of injury, date of issue, date of loss, date of maturity, date of notice, date of publication, date of sale, date of taking, date on which a cause of action accrues, delivery date, due date, effective date, expiration date, filing date, future date, publication date, return date, termination date
FOREIGN PHRASES: *In omnibus obligationibus in quibus dies non ponitur, praesenti die debetur.* In all obligations in which no time is designated for their payment, the obligation is due immediately.

DATE, *verb*   affix a date to, appoint the time of, ascertain the time of, assign a time to, calendar, chronologize, fix the date, fix the time, furnish with a date, mark the time of, note the time of, reckon from some point in time, record, register, *rem tempore tribuere, rem tempori adsignare,* set the date, time

ASSOCIATED CONCEPTS: post date

DATE RAPE, *noun* acquaintance rape, committing a rape while on a date, forced sexual intercourse on a date, forceful penetration while on a date, forcible rape on a date, sexual assault and rape while on a date

ASSOCIATED CONCEPTS: consent, incapacitation, marital rape, physical resistance, sexual assault

DATED (Antiquated), ***adjective*** ancient, antiquated, antique, archaic, discontinued, not modern, obsolete, past, preexisting, stale, superannuated, timeworn, used, vintage, waning, weathered, worn, worn out

DATED (Date-stamped), ***adjective*** checked-in, embossed, imprinted, logged-in, marked, recorded, sealed, stamped-in

ASSOCIATED CONCEPTS: a date certain, acknowledgment, date of injury, date of issue

FOREIGN PHRASES: ***Datum.*** A date. ***A datu.*** From the date. ***A die confectionis.*** From the date of the making (action taken). ***A die datus.*** From the day of the actual date.

DAY (Morning), ***noun*** broad daylight, daylight, daylight hours, daytime, full day, full sun, light of day, sunlight hours

DAY (24 Hours), ***noun*** date, during a 24-hour cycle, period from dawn to dark, solar day, time between sunrise and sunset, twenty-four hours

ASSOCIATED CONCEPTS: calendar day, day certain, day fixed for trial, day in court, day of trial, day rule, day writ, grace day, judicial day, natural day, work day

DAY IN COURT, *noun* action, case, complete lawsuit, full chance, hearing, legal action, legal contest, legal trial, litigation, occasion, opportunity, proceeding, trial

DE FACTO, *adjective* absolutely, actual, actually, as a matter of fact, authentic, *bona fide,* certain, demonstrable, determinate, existent, existing, existing in fact, factual, genuine, in existence, in fact, in point of fact, in reality, positively, present, real, substantive, tangible, true, truly, unquestionable, valid, veritable, well-founded, well-grounded, with validity

ASSOCIATED CONCEPTS: de facto administrator, de facto admissions, de facto apprenticeship, de facto appropriation, de facto authority, de facto board, de facto board of directors, de facto contract, de facto contract of sale, de facto corporation, de facto court, de facto director, de facto dissolution, de facto districts, de facto domicile, de facto government, de facto guardian, de facto judge, de facto officer, de facto trust, de facto trustee

DE JURE, *adjective* according to law, authorized, authorized by law, by law, by order, by right of law, by statute, in accordance with law, in accordance with the ordinance, in accordance with the statute, in the eyes of the law, lawful, lawfully, legal, legally, legitimate, legitimately, licit, licitly, nomothetical, of right, sanctioned by law, within the law

ASSOCIATED CONCEPTS: de jure board, de jure corporation, de jure director, de jure dissolution, de jure election, de jure judge, de jure marriage, de jure office, de jure officer, de jure sovereignty, de jure title

DE MINIMUS, *adjective* inconsequential, insignificant, meager, moderate, modest, negligible, of minor importance, of no account, paltry, petty, obscure, scanty, slight, trifling, trivial, unworthy of serious consideration

DE NOVO, *adverb* afresh, again, anew, another time, encore, freshly, from the beginning, new, newly, once more, over, over again, revived, second time

ASSOCIATED CONCEPTS: de novo proceeding, hearing de novo, trial de novo

DEACTIVATE, *verb* change, decommission, defuse, demobilize, disarm, disband, disengage, dismantle, fix, undo, withdraw

DEAD, *adjective* at rest, bereft of life, breathless, buried, cadaverous, deceased, defunct, demised, departed, departed this life, deprived of life, destitute of life, devoid of life, dormant, ended, exanimate, expired, extinct, extinguished, inactive, inert, lifeless, long gone, no longer living, not possessing life, passed away, still, terminated, without a sign of life, without life, without the appearance of life

ASSOCIATED CONCEPTS: dead-born, next of kin, presumed dead, surviving spouse, wrongful death

FOREIGN PHRASES: Cadaver nullius in bonis. A dead body is no one's property.

DEAD, *noun* corpse, the deceased, decedent, the defunct, the departed, *exanimis, exanimus,* fatal casualty, fatality, the late, the late lamented, *mortuus*

ASSOCIATED CONCEPTS: autopsy, dead-born, dead man's statute, decedent's estates, next of kin, presumed dead, surviving spouse, wrongful death

FOREIGN PHRASES: ***Extra legem positus est civiliter mortuus.*** He who is placed outside the law is civilly dead.

DEAD SET, *adjective* ardent, decided, determined, devout, dogged, dutiful, earnest, faithful, fervent, firm, fixed, fixed in purpose, intransigent, obdurate, passionate, purposeful, relentless, resolute, resolved, settled, steadfast, tenacious, uncompromising, unfaltering, unswerving, unyielding, zealous

ASSOCIATED CONCEPTS: dead set against changes in the law

DEADLOCK, *noun* block, blockage, check, checkmate, dead end, dead heat, dilemma, draw, drawn battle, drawn game, frustration, impasse, insoluble difference, no decision, obstruction, paralysis, predicament, quandary, stalemate, stand off, standstill, state of inaction, state of indecision, state of inertia, state of neutralization, stoppage, stumbling block, tie

ASSOCIATED CONCEPTS: deadlock breaking instructions, deadlocked corporation, jury deadlocked, tie vote

DEADLY, *adjective* aiming to destroy, aiming to kill, annihilating, attended with death, baleful, calamitous, capital, cataclysmic, consuming, dangerous, dangerous to life, death-bringing, death-dealing, deathful, deathly, destroying, destructive, disastrous, envenomed, *exitialis,* fatal, feral, grave, homicidal, incurable, internecine, killing, lethal, lethiferous, malignant, mephitic, miasmic, mortal, *mortifer,* mortiferous, murderous, noxious, *perniciosus,* pernicious, pestiferous, poisoned, poisonous, ruinous, sanguinary, seriously dangerous, slaughterous, steeped in poison, stifling, suffocating, tending to cause death, toxic, toxicant, unhealthy, unsafe, venomous

ASSOCIATED CONCEPTS: armed with a deadly weapon, assault with a deadly weapon, deadly attack, deadly force, deadly weapon, possession of a deadly weapon

DEAL, *noun* agreement, arrangement, bargain, business transaction, commerce, commercial transaction, compromise, contract, exchange, merchantry, negotiation, operation, pact, pledge, purchase, trade, transaction, understanding

ASSOCIATED CONCEPTS: agreement to sell or exchange, dealer, dealings, lump sum deal, trade deals

DEAL, verb bargain, barter, buy and sell, carry on negotiations, commercialize, do business, do business with, drive a trade, exchange, export and import, handle, have business relations, have commerce, have dealings with, have to do with, make arrangements, market, merchandise, negotiate, open a trade, open an account with, sell, trade, trade with, traffic, traffic in, turn over

ASSOCIATED CONCEPTS: agreement to sell or exchange, cessation of dealing, dealer, dealing and trading, dealing at arm's length, dealing in, dealing in goods, dealing in property, dealing in securities, dealings, trade deals, transacting business

DEALER, noun agent, broker, businessman, businessperson, chandler, changer, *colporteur,* commission agent, commission man, conduit, consigner, exporter, factor, hawker, huckster, jobber, local representative, man of business, *mercator,* merchandiser, merchant, middleman, monger, *negotiator,* one engaged in buying and selling, operator, packman, packwoman, peddler, retailer, salesman, salesperson, saleswoman, seller, shipper, shopkeeper, shopman, shopperson, shopwoman, storekeeper, street vendor, trader, tradesman, tradesperson, tradeswoman, trafficker, vendor, wholesale trader, wholesaler

ASSOCIATED CONCEPTS: agent, authorized dealer, broker-dealer, dealer at retail, dealer in goods, dealer in real estate, dealer in securities, dealer's talk, established dealer, merchant, retail vendor or dealer, wares and merchandise, wholesale dealer

DEALINGS, noun actions, activities, acts, affairs, arrangements, barter, business, business intercourse, business transaction, buying and selling, commerce, commercial enterprise, commercial intercourse, contracts, deals, deeds, doings, exchange, executions, intercourse, interests, manner of conduct, matters, method of business, practice, proceedings, relations, trade, traffic, transactions, understandings, undertakings

ASSOCIATED CONCEPTS: commercial dealings, continuous dealings, direct dealings, mutual dealings, unfair dealings

FOREIGN PHRASES: *Scire debes cum quo contrahis.* You ought to know with whom you are dealing.

DEARTH, noun absence, *caritas,* deficiency, destitution, exiguity, exiguousness, impoverishment, inadequacy, inadequateness, incompleteness, indigence, *inopia,* insufficiency, lack, leanness, littleness, meagerness, need, paucity, *penuria,* penury, pinch, poorness, poverty, privation, rareness, scantiness, scantness, scarceness, scarcity, short supply, shortage, smallness of number, sparsity, want, wantage

DEATH, noun cessation of life, decease, demise, departure from life, dying, ebb of life, end of life, expiration, extinction, extinguishment, failure of vital functions, fatality, loss of life, mortality, passing away, termination of life

ASSOCIATED CONCEPTS: accidental death, capital punishment, *causa mortis,* cause of death, civil death, Dead Man's Statute, death action, death benefits, death by accidental means, death by natural causes, death by violence, death certificate, death gamble, death penalty, death resulting from accident, death resulting from injury, death sentence, death tax, death trap, death warrant, death without issue, deathbed will, homicide, in contemplation of death, injuries resulting in death, instantaneous death, last illness, life expectancy, likely to produce death, mortality tables, natural death, penalty of death, presumption of death, presumptive death, proof of death, registration of death, right to die, simultaneous death, sudden death, time of death, transfer in contemplation of death, unreasonable risk of death, wrongful death

FOREIGN PHRASES: *Crimina morte extinguuntur.* Crimes are extinguished by death. *Actio personalis moritur cum persona.* A personal action dies with the person.

DEATH PENALTY, verb capital punishment, corporal punishment, death sentence, death warrant, punishment by execution, ultimate penalty

ASSOCIATED CONCEPTS: cruel and unusual punishment, death warrant, Eighth Amendment, life in prison

DEATH SENTENCE, verb capital punishment, condemnation, corporal punishment, death penalty, death warrant, verdict of guilty

ASSOCIATED CONCEPTS: cruel and unusual punishment, death warrant, Eighth Amendment, life in prison

DEBACLE, noun adversity, blow, breakdown, calamity, cataclysm, catastrophe, collapse, contretemps, crash, defeat, demolishment, demolition, destruction, devastation, disaster, disruption, dissolution, downfall, emergency, failure, fall, fiasco, havoc, misadventure, mischance, misfortune, mishap, overthrow, overturn, ravage, reverse, rout, ruin, ruination, setback, smash, tragedy, upset, wreck

DEBAR, verb abrogate, arrest, astrict, ban, bar, barricade, block, cancel, check, confine, constrain, countermand, curb, detain, deter, disallow, discourage, dispose of, dissuade, eliminate, embargo, enjoin, estop, exclude, *excludere,* excommunicate, forbid, forestall, gainsay, halt, hamper, hinder, hold back, impede, inhibit, interdict, interfere, limit, obstruct, occlude, outlaw, paralyze, preclude, prevent, *prohibere,* prohibit, proscribe, refuse, remove, restrain, restrict, retard, revoke, shut out, stall, stifle, stop, stymie, suppress, suspend, trammel, veto, ward off, withdraw, withhold

DEBASE, verb abase, adulterate, bastardize, befoul, cheapen, coarsen, contaminate, *corrumpere,* corrupt, debauch, defile, degrade, dehumanize, demoralize, deprave, depreciate, depress, desecrate, deteriorate, discredit, disgrace, dishonor, downgrade, foul, humble, humiliate, impair, impair in worth, injure, lower, lower in value, pervert, pollute, profane, reduce in quality, soil, stain, taint, tarnish, *vitiare,* vitiate, vulgarize, weaken

DEBATABLE, adjective admitting of doubt, ambiguous, arguable, at issue, baffling, capable of being debated, changeable, confutable, conjecturable, conjectural, contentious, contestable, controversial, controvertible, cryptic, deniable, disposed to question, disputable, disputatious, doubtable, doubtful, dubious, dubitable, dubitative, enigmatic, eristic, hard to believe, hypothetical, in dispute, in issue, in question, inconceivable, incredible, indecisive, indefinite, indeterminate, nebulous, obscure, open to debate, open to discussion, open to dispute, open to doubt, open to question, open to suspicion, paradoxical, perplexing, possible, precarious, problematic, problematical, puzzling, questionable, refutable, speculative, subject to argument, subject to contention, subject to contravention, subject to controversy, suppositious, suspect, suspicious, theoretical, unaffirmed, unascertained, unbelievable, uncertain, unconfirmed, undecided, undemonstrable, undemonstrated, under discussion, under examination, undetermined, unfixed, unpredictable, unproven, unreliable, unresolved, unsettled, unsure, unsustainable, unsustained, unverifiable, up for discussion, up in the air, vague

ASSOCIATED CONCEPTS: debatable issue, debatable question

DEBATE, verb agitate, altercate, argue, argue pros and cons, attempt to disprove, bandy, battle verbally, canvass, confer with, confute, consider, consult with, contend, contest, controvert, deliberate, disagree, discept, discuss, dispute, engage in oral controversy, examine a question, examine by argument, moot, negotiate, ponder, present reasons for and against, present varied opinions, ratiocinate, reason, refute, weigh, wrangle

ASSOCIATED CONCEPTS: debates of Constitutional Convention, freedom of debate, legislative debate

DEBAUCH, verb   abuse, be intemperate, *corrumpere,* corrupt, debase, degenerate, degrade, *depravare,* deprave, despoil, dissipate, lead astray, molest, pervert, ruin, stuprate, sully, violate, *vitiare,* vitiate

DEBAUCHERY, noun   bacchanalia, debauchment, dissipation, dissoluteness, excess, excessiveness, grossness, immoderation, impudicity, incontinence, intemperance, lasciviousness, lechery, lewdness, libertinage, libertinism, licentiousness, lust, obscenity, orgy, profligacy, salacity, seduction, *stuprum,* unrestraint

DEBAUCHMENT, noun   defilement, defloration, deflowering, perversion, seduction, violation, vitiation

DEBENTURE, noun   bond, negotiable instrument, paper money, pledge, title deed

DEBILITATE, verb   cripple, denature, deprive of strength, devitalize, emasculate, enervate, enfeeble, eviscerate, exhaust, impair, incapacitate, injure, lessen, make feeble, make languid, reduce, render weak, sap the strength of, undermine, weaken

DEBIT, noun   amount due, amount payable, arrears, bills, commitment, debt, deferred payment, *expensum,* indebtedness, liability, obligation, pecuniary due, sum owing, that which is owed

ASSOCIATED CONCEPTS: debit agent, debit and credit system, debit life insurance

FOREIGN PHRASES: *Perjuri sunt qui servatis verbis juramenti decipiunt aures eorum qui accipiunt.* They are perjured, who, by preserving the words of an oath, deceive the ears of those who receive it. *Non decipitur qui scit se decipi.* A person is not deceived who knows she is being deceived. *Fraus et dolus nemini patrocinari debent.* Fraud and deceit should not excuse anyone.

DEBRIEF, noun   examine, gain information, gain knowledge, get briefing, inquire, interrogate, investigate, question, quiz, scrutinize

ASSOCIATED CONCEPTS: counterintelligence, espionage, interrogation, terrorism

DEBT, noun   account outstanding, account owing, *aes alienum,* amount due, amount owing, arrearage, arrears, balance owed, balance to pay, bill, debit, deferred payment, deficit, encumbrance, indebtedness, liability, money due, money owed, nonpayment, obligation, sum owed

ASSOCIATED CONCEPTS: action for debt, admission of debt, antecedent debt, bad debt, bad debt loss, bona fide debt, bonded debt, book debt, business debt, common debt, contingent debt, continuing debt, contract debts, corporate debt, creating a debt, creation of a debt, debt against estate, debt arising on contract, debt by contract, debt by loan, debt discharged, debt due, debt founded on contract, debt incurred, debt instruments, debt not yet due, debt of another, debt of bankrupt, debt of municipality, debt of record, debt owed, debt provable in bankruptcy,

debt which is to become due, debtor and creditor, debts of deceased, dischargeable debt, equitable debt, evidence of debt, evidence of indebtedness, existing debt, fiduciary debt, fixed debt, floating debt, fraudulent debt, funded debt, holder of debt, imprisonment for debt, inability to pay debts as they mature, just debt, lawful debt, liquidated debt, moral debt, mutual debts, nonpayment of debt, partnership debt, pecuniary debt, preexisting debt, promise to pay, provable debt, public debt, public debt limitations, recovery of debt, secured debt, simple debt, situs of indebtedness, unliquidated debt, unsecured debt, worthless debt

FOREIGN PHRASES: *Debita sequuntur personam debitoris.* Debts follow the person of the debtor. *Debitor non praesumitur donare.* A debtor is not presumed to make debts. *Reprobata pecunia liberat solventem.* Money refused releases the debtor. *Nemo potest sibi debere.* No one can be indebted to himself. *Incendium aere alieno non exuit debitorem.* A fire does not discharge a debtor from his debt. *Id solum nostrum quod debitis deductis nostrum est.* That only is ours which remains to us after deduction of our debts. *Chirographum non extans praesumitur solutum.* An evidence of debt not existing is presumed to have been paid. Chirographum apud debitorem repertum praesumitur solutum. An evidence of debt found in the debtor's hands is presumed to be paid. *Annua nec debitum judex non separat ipsum.* A judge does not divide annuities nor debt. *In satisfactionibus non permittitur amplius fieri quam semel factum est.* In settlements more must not be received than was received once for all. *Minus solvit, qui tardius solvit; nam et tempore minus solvitur.* He does not pay who pays too late; for, from the lapse of time, he is judged not to pay. *In omnibus obligationibus in quibus dies non ponitur, praesenti die debetur.* In all obligations in which no time is fixed for their fulfillment, the obligation is due immediately.

DEBT LIMIT, noun   borrowing limit, breaking point of debt, debt ceiling, greatest limit of debt, largest debt, largest loan, maximum amount of debt, maximum debt, maximum funds to be loaned, maximum loan, outer limit of debt, outer line of credit

ASSOCIATED CONCEPTS: bankruptcy, fraudulent debt, insolvency, interrogation, solvency

DEBT SERVICE, noun   carrying cost, charge, cost of the loan, obligation, overhead payment, repayment

ASSOCIATED CONCEPTS: bankruptcy, fraudulent debt, insolvency, interrogation, solvency, usury

DEBTOR, noun   borrower, borrowing party, debtor, defaulter, loanee, mortgagor, obligor, pledgor, responsible party

ASSOCIATED CONCEPTS: accord and satisfaction, account stated, assignment, bankruptcy, collection, compromise and settlement, debtor and credit, debtor and creditor relationship, execution, financial transactions, garnishment, reorganization

DEBUNK, verb   cast doubt upon, decry, deflate, derogate, detract, disabuse, disdain, disenchant, disillusion, disparage, expose, puncture, set right, undeceive

DECADENT, adjective   breaking down, cankered, corrosive, corrupt, crumbling, debauched, decaying, declining, decomposing, decrepit, degenerate, degenerating, depraved, deteriorated, deteriorating, dilapidated, disintegrating, effete, failing, falling, falling into ruin, feeble, immoral, in decadence, in decline, moldering, moribund, on the wane, regressive, retrograde, retrogressive, rotting, shabby, sinking, spoiled, spoiling, unprogressive, wasting, wasting away, weakened, withering, worn out

DECAY, verb addle, atrophy, be reduced in worth, become enfeebled, become lower in quality, become putrescent, blight, break down, break up, canker, consume, corrode, corrupt, crumble, decline, decompose, decompound, degenerate, depreciate, deteriorate, dilapidate, disintegrate, fade, fail, fall apart, fall to pieces, grow worse, languish, molder, putrefy, render putrid, retrograde, retrogress, rot, ruin, shrivel, sink, spoil, waste away, wear away, wither, worsen

DECEASE, verb cease existing, cease living, cease to be, cease to exist, cease to live, come to an end, demise, depart, depart from life, die, end one's life, expire, lose life, meet death, pass away, pass on, perish, succumb
ASSOCIATED CONCEPTS: decedent's estate

DECEASED, adjective bereft of life, dead, defunct, demised, departed, deprived of life, destitute of life, devoid of life, exanimate, former, late, lifeless, no longer living, passed away, passed on, perished
ASSOCIATED CONCEPTS: dead man's statute, deceased child, deceased debtor, deceased persons, estate of deceased person, transaction or communication with deceased person, transaction with person since deceased
FOREIGN PHRASES: *Cadaver nullius in bonis.* A dead body is no one's property.

DECEDENT, noun dead man, dead person, deceased, deceased person, demised, departed, he who has passed away, intestate individual, she who has expired, testator
ASSOCIATED CONCEPTS: decedent's estate, obligation of the decedent, transaction with decedent

DECEIT, noun beguilement, camouflage, cheating, collusion, cozenage, craftiness, cunning, deceitfulness, deception, deceptiveness, delusiveness, dissembling, dissimulation, *dolus,* double-dealing, duplicity, equivocation, fabrication, *fallacia,* fallaciousness, falseheartedness, falsehood, falseness, falsification, falsity, forgery, fraud, fraudulence, *fraus,* furtiveness, indirection, insidiousness, insincerity, jugglery, lying, mendacity, misrepresentation, perfidy, perjury, pretense, prevarication, sham, sneakiness, subreption, surreptitiousness, treachery, trickery, underhanded practice, underhandedness, untruth, untruthfulness
ASSOCIATED CONCEPTS: action for fraud or deceit, discovery of the fraud or deceit, fraud or deceit, misrepresentation

DECEIVE, verb befool, beguile, belie, blind, cheat, chicane, circumvent, cog, cozen, decoy, defraud, delude, dissemble, dissimulate, dupe, ensnare, entrap, *fainaigue,* fake, falsify, fool, forswear, gull, hoax, hoodwink, humbug, intrigue, inveigle, lie, misdirect, misguide, misinform, mislead, misrepresent, mulct, practice chicanery, practice deception, prevaricate, snare, sneak, swindle, take advantage, trap, trick, victimize

DECENTRALIZATION, noun apportionment, branching out, breakdown, delegation, diffusion, disbandment, disintegration, disjoining, disjunction, dispersal, dispersion, dissipation, dissolution, distribution, division, fragmentation, partition, scattering, scission, section, separation, severance, subdivision

DECEPTION, noun artifice, beguilement, blind, bluff, camouflage, charlatanry, cheat, chicane, chicanery, circumvention, con, counterfeit, cozenage, craft, craftiness, cunning,

deceit, decoy, defraudation, defraudment, delusion, device, disguise, dishonesty, dissimulation, dodge, double-dealing, dupery, duplicity, equivocation, fabrication, fake, false appearance, false front, falsehood, falseness, falsification, feint, forgery, fraud, fraudulence, fraudulency, guile, hoax, humbuggery, illusion, imposition, imposture, indirection, indirectness, insincerity, intrigue, knavery, legerdemain, lie, machination, masquerade, mendacity, mirage, misrepresentation, obliquity, pretext, prevarication, rascality, roguery, ruse, sham, simulacrum, snare, stratagem, subterfuge, swindle, trap, trepan, trick, trickery, trickiness, trumpery, untruth, untruthfulness, unveracity, wile
ASSOCIATED CONCEPTS: confusion, deception doctrine
FOREIGN PHRASES: *Non decipitur qui scit se decipi.* He is not deceived who knows that he is being deceived. *Decipi quam fallere est tutius.* It is safer to be deceived than to deceive.

DECEPTIVE, adjective artificial, beguiling, bogus, calculated to give a false impression, camouflaged, cheating, collusive, counterfeit, covinous, crafty, cunning, deceitful, deceiving, delusive, delusory, designing, disguised, dishonest, disingenuous, double dealing, fallacious, false, feigned, fraudulent, illusive, illusory, impostrous, indirect, insidious, insincere, knavish, lying, mendacious, misleading, mock, oblique, obliquitous, pretended, prevaricating, scheming, seeming, sham, slippery, sly, sneaky, sophistic, sophistical, specious, spurious, subdolous, tricky, underhanded, untrue, wily
ASSOCIATED CONCEPTS: deceptive acts, deceptive advertising, deceptive practice, deceptively misdescriptive, deceptively similar

DECIDE, verb adjudge, adjudicate, adjust, agree, arbitrate, arrive at a judgment, ascertain, award, choose, choose a course of action, choose an alternative, choose an option, come to a conclusion, come to an agreement, come to terms, commit oneself, conclude, *constituere, decernere,* decree, determine, diagnose, *diiudicare,* dispose of, elect, end, establish, finalize, find, fix, form a resolution, form an opinion, hold, judge, make a choice, make a decision, make a selection, make up one's mind, opt, ordain, pass, pass judgment, pass sentence, pick, pronounce, reach a decision, reach a verdict, referee, resolve, rule, select, sentence, settle, sit in judgment, terminate, umpire, vote
ASSOCIATED CONCEPTS: decide a case, decide a motion, decided adversely, decided as a matter of law, decided on the merits, decided upon legal principles, jurisdiction to decide

DECIDED, adjective absolute, categorical, certain, clear, conclusive, decisive, definite, definitive, demonstrated, evident, explicit, indefeasible, indisputable, infallible, irrefutable, manifest, obvious by an overwhelming number, palpable, proven, self-evident, solid, unassailable, undeniable, undisputed, unequivocal, unimpeachable, unmistakable, unqualified, unquestionable, unreserved
ASSOCIATED CONCEPTS: decided litigation advantage

DECISION *(Election),* **noun** choosing, judgment, pick, selection, will
ASSOCIATED CONCEPTS: appellate decision, decision upon the merits, lower court decision

DECISION *(Judgment),* **noun** choice, decree, determination, placitum, resolution, verdict

DECISIVE, adjective absolute, assured, authoritative, beyond all dispute, beyond all question, categorical, certain, characterized by decision, clear, clearly defined, commanding, compelling, conclusive, conclusory, consequential,

critical, crucial, culminating, definite, definitive, determinant, determinative, determining, effectual, ernest, final, forceful, impelling, imperative, important, incontestable, indubious, inflexible, influential, intent upon, irresistible, irrevocable, momentous, of great consequence, peremptory, pivotal, positive, powerful, purposeful, questionless, resolute, resolved, significant, summary, thrustful, undoubted, unequivocal, unhesitating, unqualified, unquestionable, unquestioned, without doubt, without question
ASSOCIATED CONCEPTS: decisive proof

DECLAIM, *verb* address, deliver oratorically, descant, dilate, discourse, dissertate, expand, expatiate, expound, give a formal speech, harangue, hold forth, lecture, make a speech, orate, perorate, preach, prelect, proclaim, rant, recite, rhetorize, sermonize, speak, speak publicly, speak rhetorically, talk

DECLAMATION, *noun* address, allocution, art of speaking, *declamatio*, discourse, elocution, grandiloquence, harangue, lecture, oration, oratorical display, oratory, orotundity, *pronuntiatio*, public speaking, reading, recital, recitation, rhetoric, screed, sermon, speech, speechification, talk, tirade

DECLARANT, *noun* affiant, affirmant, complainant, one who affirms, one who asserts, one who proclaims, person who makes allegations, proclaimor, witness

DECLARATION, *noun* admission, affirmation, announcement, annunciation, assertion, attestation, bulletin, communication of knowledge, *communiqué, declaratio,* decree, decreement, *dictum,* edict, *edictum,* explicit utterance, exposition, expression, fiat, formal assertion, formal notice, *ipse dixit,* notice, notification, official bulletin, positive statement, *praedicatio,* presentation, proclamation, profession, promulgation, pronouncement, public announcement, public notice, publication, recitation, resolution, revelation, solemn averment, solemn avowal, statement, statement of facts, transmission of knowledge, ukase
ASSOCIATED CONCEPTS: declaration against interest, declaration against pecuniary interest, declaration against penal interest, declaration of candidacy, declaration of deceased person, declaration of dividends, declaration of estimated tax, declaration of homestead, declaration of independence, declaration of intent, declaration of intention, declaration of law, declaration of parties, declaration of public necessity, declaration of rights, declaration of trust, declaration of value, declaration of war, dying declarations, extrajudicial declaration, judicial declaration, narrative declaration, *res gestae,* self-serving declaration, spontaneous declaration

DECLARATORY, *adjective* annuciative, annunciatory, assertative, assertive, communicative, declarative, decretal, decretive, decretory, demonstrative, elucidating, enunciative, enunciatory, explanatory, expository, express, expressive, notificatory, proclamatory, promulgatory, serving to declare
ASSOCIATED CONCEPTS: declaratory act, declaratory action, declaratory decree, declaratory judgment, declaratory order, declaratory statute

DECLARATORY JUDGMENT, *noun* affirmation, announcement, declaration, enunciation, judgment of the court, non-executory judgment

DECLARE, *verb* advance, affirm, announce, assert, asseverate, assure, aver, avow, bruit, claim, come out, communicate, contend, *declarare,* disclose, divulge, enounce, enunciate, herald, inform, maintain, make a declaration, make a statement, make known, praedicare, predicate, proclaim, profess, *profiteri,* pronounce, put forward, reveal, say, set forth, state, tell, utter
ASSOCIATED CONCEPTS: declare a nullity, declare insolvent, declare null and void

DECLARER, *noun* affiant, author, compiler, composer, declarant, drafter, party, scriptor, sworn declarant, undersigned, writer
ASSOCIATED CONCEPTS: accommodation endorser, accommodation maker, dying declaration

DECLINATION, *noun* abnegation, denial, disavowal, disclaimer, negation, nonacceptance, noncompliance, nonconsent, refusal, refusal of consent, rejection, renunciation, repudiation, unwillingness

DECLINE, *noun* abatement, act of crumbling, act of dwindling, act of falling away, act of lessening, act of losing ground, act of shrinking, act of slipping back, act of wasting away, act of weakening, act of worsening, atrophy, backward step, cheapening, collapse, consumption, contraction, corrosion, corruption, decadency, decay, decrease, decrement, decrepitude, decurrence, deflation, degeneracy, degenerateness, degeneration, *deminutio,* depreciation, descension, descent, deterioration, devaluation, dilapidation, diminishing, dissolution, downfall, downgrade, downhill, downtrend, downturn, downward inclination, downward incline, downward trend, drop, ebb, enfeeblement, erosion, failing, fall, falling away, falling-off, gradual crumbling, gradual impairment, lessening, loss, loss of value, lowering, marcescence, pejoration, period of decrease, plunge, recession, regress, regression, relapse, retreat, retroaction, retrocession, retrogradation, retrogression, reversion, ruin, setback, shrinkage, sinkage, sinking, slump, subsidence, wane
ASSOCIATED CONCEPTS: spoilage, waste

DECLINE *(Fall),* **verb** come down, decay, degenerate, deteriorate, drop, drop in strength, ebb, fall, lapse, stoop, trend downward, wane, wither
ASSOCIATED CONCEPTS: decline in price

DECLINE *(Reject),* **verb** abnegate, abstain, eschew, excuse oneself, hold back, rebuff, *recusare,* refuse, refuse to accept, renounce, *renueve,* repel, repudiate, resist, spurn, turn away, turn down, veto
ASSOCIATED CONCEPTS: decline an appointment, decline to accept an offer

DECOMMISSION, *verb* change, deactivate, defuse, demobilize, disarm, disband, disengage, dismantle, fix, undue, withdraw

DECONTAMINATE, *verb* absterge, antisepticize, clean, cleanse, depurate, deterge, disinfect, fumigate, hygienize, lustrate, make aseptic, make disease-free, make germ-free, make healthful, make hygienic, make innoxious, make pure, make salubrious, make wholesome, purge, purify, rarefy, refine, remove pollutants, remove unhealthy agents, render harmless, render sanitary, render sterile, sanitize, scour, scrub, sterilize, unadulterate, uncorrupt, unpollute, untaint

DECORUM, *noun* act demanded by social custom, amenability, amenableness, amenities, appropriate behavior, appropriateness, best behavior, best of taste, *bienséance,* civility, civilized behavior, code of what is fitting, conduct, conformity, consideration, *convenance,* convention, conventionality, conventions, conventions of society, correctness, courtesy, cultivated taste, custom, decencies, decency, decorousness, *decorum,* delicacy, demeanor, dictates of society, dignity, discrimination, etiquette, fastidiousness, fittingness, form, formalities, formality, gentility, gentlemanliness, good form, good manners, good taste, goodness, grace, mannerliness, manners, modesty, mores, natural courtesy, nice appreciation, nicety, orderliness, point of etiquette, poise, polish, polished manners, politeness, prescribed code of conduct, proper thing to do, properness, propriety, protocol, punctilio, punctiliousness, refined manners, refined taste, refinement, requirement of polite society, respect, respectability, respectful deportment, right note, right thing to do, rules of conduct, sedateness, seemliness, social code, social conduct, social graces, social procedures, social usage, standard, suitability, suitableness, tact, tastefulness, that which is proper

DECOY, noun allure, allurement, ambush, attraction, bait, blind, camouflage, deception, disguise, diversion, enticement, imitation, inducement, *inlex,* inveiglement, misleader, simulation, trap, trick
ASSOCIATED CONCEPTS: entrapment

DECREASE, noun abatement, abbreviation, abridgment, alleviation, attenuation, constriction, contraction, curtailment, cut, cutback, deceleration, declension, declination, decline, decline and fall, decrement, decrescence, deduction, deflation, *deminutio,* depreciation, depression, deterioration, devaluation, diminishment, diminution, dissipation, downtrend, downturn, downward trend, drop, dwindling, ebb, fall, falling-off, getting less, *imminutio,* lessening, loss, loss of value, lowering, making less, mitigation, narrowing, reduction, reflux, restriction, retrenchment, shortening, shrinkage, shrinking, sinking, slowing down, slump, subduction, subsidence, subtraction, wane, waning, weakening
ASSOCIATED CONCEPTS: decrease in payment, decrease in price, decrease in value, decreased capacity, decreased cost, decreased earning capacity, decreased or diminished mental capacity

DECREASE, verb abate, abbreviate, abridge, allay, attenuate, bate, be consumed, become smaller, blunt, cause to diminish, coarctate, compact, compress, concentrate, condense, constrict, constringe, contract, curtail, cut, cut back, cut down, cut off, cut short, dampen, decelerate, decline, deduct, deflate, *deminuere,* depreciate, depress, detract from, die down, diminish, drain, drop, dwindle, ebb, emaciate, extenuare, fall, fall behind, fall below, fall off, go downhill, grow less, *imminuere,* lessen, level off, lower, make brief, make less, make smaller, mark down, melt away, minimize, mitigate, narrow, pare, prune, quell, rake off, recede, reduce, render less, retrench, roll back, run down, scale down, shave, shorten, shrink, sink, slacken, slash, slump, strike off, subduct, subside, subtract, suffer loss, take away, take off, taper, trim, wane
ASSOCIATED CONCEPTS: decrease in payment, decrease in price, decrease in value, decreased capacity, decreased cost, decreased earning capacity, decreased or diminished mental capacity

DECREE, noun adjudgment, adjudication, authoritative decision, award, command, commandment, decision, declaration, *decretum,* dictate, direction, edict, *edictum,* fiat, final judgment, finding, imperative, interdiction, judgment, judicial decision, mandate, opinion, order, order of the court, *placitum,* proclamation, pronouncement, *pronunciamiento,* resolution, ruling, ruling of the court, *senatus consultum,* sentence, standing order, ukase, verdict

ASSOCIATED CONCEPTS: alimony decree, annulment decree, bankruptcy decree, consent decree, declaratory decree, decree for payment of money, decree for possession of property, decree *nisi,* decree of a court of competent jurisdiction, decree of court of record, decree of dismissal, decree of distribution, decree of nullity, decree of support, decree *pro confesso,* default decree, deficiency decree, divorce decree, entry of decree, final decree, foreclosure decree, foreign decree, interlocutory decree, joint decree, judicial decree, summary decree, supplemental decree

DECREE, verb adjudge, adjudicate, award, charge, command, deliver judgment, dictate, direct, establish, exact, find, give judgment, give orders, impose, instruct, issue a fiat, issue a proclamation, issue a ukase, issue an edict, judge, order, pass judgment, prescribe, proclaim, promulgate, pronounce, require, rule, sanction
ASSOCIATED CONCEPTS: alimony decree, annulment decree, bankruptcy decree, consent decree, decree by confession, *decree nisi,* decree of dismissal, *decree pro confesso,* default decree, deficiency decree, divorce decree, entry of decree, final decree, foreclosure decree, foreign decree, interlocutory decree, summary decree, supplemental decree

DECREMENT, noun abatement, abridgment, contraction, curtailment, cut, damage, declension, decrease, decrescence, deduction, deficit, depletion, diminishment, diminution, dissipation, drain, erosion, exhaustion, expenditure, leak, leakage, lessening, loss, shortcoming, shortening, shrinkage, spoilage, subtraction, wastage, waste, wear and tear

DECRETAL, adjective binding, commanded, commanding, decreed, decretive, decretory, demanded, directive, instructive, jussive, law-giving, mandatory, nomothetic, ordered, preceptive, prescriptive
ASSOCIATED CONCEPTS: decretal paragraph

DECRY, verb admonish, be unable to respect, belittle, berate, bring discredit on, bring into disrepute, censure, censure as faulty, clamor against, condemn, condemn as worthless, contemn, criticize, cry down, cry out against, declaim against, degrade, denigrate, denounce, deny respect, deprecate, depreciate, depreciate publicly, deride, derogate, despise, detract, detract from, disapprove, disapprove of, discredit, disdain, disesteem, dismiss, disparage, dispraise, disprize, disrespect, fail to appreciate, fault, feel utter contempt for, find fault, find nothing to praise, have no regard for, have no respect for, have no use for, hold cheap, hold in contempt, inveigh against, make little of, malign, not respect, not speak well of, *obtrectare,* protest against, raise a hue and cry against, raise one's voice against, reject, remonstrate against, reprehend, revile, ridicule, scorn, set at nought, set no value on, speak disparagingly of, speak ill of, speak slightingly of, spurn, vilify, vilipend, *vituperare*

DEDICATE, verb address to, award, bestow, confer, confer honor on, *consecrare,* consecrate, convey, *dedicare,* devote, do honor, donate, endow, enshrine, give, give a prize, give earnestly, give honor, hallow, honor, immortalize, inscribe, offer to give, pay honor, philanthropize, present, reflect honor on, render honor to, set apart, set apart for special use, set aside, vest

DEDICATION, noun bestowal, celebration, consecration, devotion, endowment, enshrinement, giving, gratuity, honoring, immortalization, inscription, offering, ordination, philanthropy, presentation, presentment, setting apart, setting aside for a particular purpose, solemn appropriation

149

DEDUCE

ASSOCIATED CONCEPTS: act of dedication, actual dedication, appropriation for a public use, appropriation of a charitable use, common-law dedication, constructive dedication, dedication by estoppel, dedication of property for public use, dedication to a charitable use, dedication to a public use, express dedication, implied dedication, irrevocable dedication, manner of dedication, private dedication, public dedication, public easement, revocation of offer of dedication, statutory dedication, unaccepted dedication

DEDUCE, verb   apply reason, arrive at a conclusion, ascertain, assume, calculate, come to a conclusion, conclude, conjecture, consider probable, construe, deduct, deem, derive, determine, divine, draw a conclusion, educe, extract, gather, guess, infer, judge, ratiocinate, rationalize, reason, suppose, surmise, think, think likely, trace, understand

DEDUCT *(Conclude by reasoning)*, **verb**   apply reason, arrive at a conclusion, ascertain, assume, calculate, come to a conclusion, conclude, conjecture, consider probable, construe, deduce, deem, derive, determine, divine, draw a conclusion, educe, extract, gather, guess, infer, judge, rationalize, ratiocinate, reason, suppose, surmise, think, think likely, trace, understand

DEDUCT *(Reduce)*, **verb**   abate, attentuate, bate, cheapen, cut, cut down, decrease, deflate, deplete, depreciate, devaluate, dilute, diminish, discount, downgrade, dwindle, lessen, lower, make less, make smaller, mark down, remove, render few, shrink, slash, strike off, strip, subduct, subtract, take away, take off, trim, truncate, withdraw
ASSOCIATED CONCEPTS: tax credit, tax deduction

DEDUCTIBLE *(Capable of being deducted from taxes)*, **adjective**   able to be subducted, able to be subtracted for tax purposes, allowable, capable of being deducted, capable of being rebated, discountable, likely to decrease taxes, recoupable, removable
ASSOCIATED CONCEPTS: deductible business expense, deductible debt, deductible expense, deductible loss, deductible policy

DEDUCTIBLE *(Provable)*, **adjective**   able to be confirmed, able to be shown, ascertainable, based on evidence, based on proof, capable of being figured out, capable of being proved, conclusible, corroborative, deducible, demonstrable, derivable, documentable, expectable, following, illative, inferable, inferential, likely, presumed, presumptive, probable, ratiocinative, substantiable, supportable, sustainable, testable, traceable, valid, verifiable

DEDUCTION *(Conclusion)*, **noun**   assumption, calculation, divination, hypothesis, illation, implication, logical process, logical sequence, opinion, postulate, postulation, ratiocination, rationalization, reasoned judgment, supposal, supposition, surmise, theory, thesis

DEDUCTION *(Diminution)*, **noun**   abatement, abridgment, attenuation, cut, decline, decrease, decrement, decrescence, *deductio, deminutio,* discount, dwindling, elimination, lessening, lowering, making less, minimization, reduction, removal, shortening, shrinkage, subduction, subtraction, withdrawal
ASSOCIATED CONCEPTS: allowable deduction, business deductions, deduction directed by law, deduction from purchase price, deduction of cost, deduction of expense, deductions from account, deductions from salary, income tax deductions, marital deduction, special deduction

DEDUCTIVE, adjective   analytic, analytical, deducible, evidential, following, inferable, inferential, logical, rational, reasoned, resultant

DEED, noun   assignment, authentication, certificate, charter, conveyance, covenant, document, document which passes a present interest, instrument, instrument which transfers title to realty, muniments, record, release, signed and delivered instrument, transfer, transference
ASSOCIATED CONCEPTS: ancient deed, bargain and sale deed, commissioner of deeds, contract for deed, deed by way of mortgage, deed duly registered, deed for a nominal sum, deed in fee simple, deed in the nature of a mortgage, deed of assignment, deed of conveyance, deed of covenant, deed of gift, deed of land, deed of trust, deed with covenant of warranty, estoppel by deed, executed deed, general warranty deed, gift deed, good and effectual deed, good and sufficient deed, joint deeds, mineral deed, quitclaim deed, recorded deed, registers of deeds, rescission of deed, reservation in a deed, sheriff's deed, simultaneous deeds, special warranty deed, tax deed, trust deed, void or voidable deeds, warranty deed
FOREIGN PHRASES: *Interpretatio chartarum benigne facienda est, ut res magis valeat quam pereat.* The construction of deeds should be liberal in order that the transaction may be effective rather than fail. *Traditio loqui facit chartam.* Delivery gives voice to the words of a deed. *Mala grammatica non vitiat chartam; sed in expositione instrumentorum ma la grammatica quo ad fieri possit evitanda est.* Bad grammar does not vitiate a deed; but, in the drafting of instruments, bad grammar should, as far as possible, be avoided. *Grammatica falsa non vitiat chartam.* False grammar does not vitiate a deed. *Charta de non ente non valet.* A deed of a thing not in being is invalid. *Facta tenent multa quae fieri prohibentur.* Deeds contain many things which are prohibited to be done. *Allegatio contra factum non est admittenda.* An allegation contrary to the deed is not admissible.

DEEM, verb   account, adjudge, adopt an opinion, assume, be inclined to think, be of the opinion, be under the impression, believe, believe on consideration, call, conceive, conclude, consider, decide, determine, embrace an opinion, esteem, feel, form a judgment, form an opinion, have an opinion, have the impression, hazard an opinion, hold, hold an opinion, hold in belief, imagine, judge, look upon, opine, perceive, presume, pronounce judgment, regard, suppose, surmise, suspect, take for, take it to be, think, view as
ASSOCIATED CONCEPTS: deemed advisable, deemed to be in the best interests of the child

DEEMPHASIZE, verb   attach little importance to, belittle, declassify, deprecate, depreciate, detract from, disregard, downplay, dwarf, give little weight to, make light of, make little of, marginalize, minify, minimize, moderate, play down, take no account of, think little of, think nothing of, tone down, underplay
ASSOCIATED CONCEPTS: declassification

DEEP *(Down)*, **adjective**   at the lowest point, below, below floor level, below ground level, below the floor, below the ground, beneath, under grade, under the ground, underground, underneath
ASSOCIATED CONCEPTS: declaration against interest, declaration of a dividend, declaration of a trust, in deep trouble with the law, searching deep into the evidence of a case, self-serving declaration

DEEP (Profound), **adjective**   abstruse, astute, complicated, erudite, esoteric, intellectual, intellectually profound, penetrating, perceptive, philosophical, recondite, reflective, sagacious, sage, scholarly, thoughtful, wise
ASSOCIATED CONCEPTS: deep constituted interpretation

DEEP POCKETS, noun   abounding wealth, abundance, abundant wealth, bounteous wealth, bountiful material wealth, riches, source of sufficient funds, substantial assets, substantial support, substantial wealth, wealth, wealthy, well-off, well-provided, well-situated, well-stocked, well-to-do
ASSOCIATED CONCEPTS: insurance, predatory pricing

DEEP-ROOTED, adjective   deeply engrained, deeply implanted, deeply manifest, engrained, ensconced, established, impeded, imprinted, indoctrinated, injected, instilled, manifest
ASSOCIATED CONCEPTS: common law, precedence deep-rooted in the law

DEEP-SEATED, adjective   deep, deeply felt, embedded, engraved, established, fixed, implanted, instilled, manifest
ASSOCIATED CONCEPTS: malicious prosecution, motive

DEFACE, verb   begrime, blacken, blemish, blot, blot out, blotch, blur, cover up, crack, cross out, damage, deform, *deformare,* delete, deprive of form, despoil, destroy, destroy form, disfigure, distort, efface, erase, expunge, flaw, *foedare,* foul, hurt, impair, impair the legibility of, impair the looks of, injure, make illegible, make ugly, make unsightly, mangle, mar, mar the appearance of, mark, misshape, mutilate, obliterate, render illegible, rub off, rub out, scar, scratch, scratch out, smear, smudge, soil, spoil, spoil the look of, spot, stain, strike out, sully, tarnish, unshape, warp, wipe away
ASSOCIATED CONCEPTS: cancellation by defacing, defacing public property

DEFACEMENT, noun   blemish, blot, blotch, blotting out, crack, damage, defect, deformation, deformity, destruction, discoloration, disfiguration, disfigurement, distortion, effacement, erasure, fault, flaw, impairment, injury, injury to outward appearance, marring, mutilation, obliteration, scar, scratch, smear, smudge, soiling, splotch, spot, stain, tarnish, unsightliness, vandalism, wear and tear, wrecking activities
ASSOCIATED CONCEPTS: defacement of ballots, defacement of documents, defacement of labels, defacement of monuments, defacement of public property

DEFALCATE, verb   appropriate to one's own use, cheat, defraud, divert funds, embezzle, falsify accounts, misapply funds, misappropriate money, misemploy funds, misuse entrusted monies, obtain money under false pretenses, peculate, purloin, rob, steal, swindle, take by fraud, thieve

DEFAMATION, noun   abuse, aspersion, calumniation, calumny, denigration, derogation, detraction, discommendation, disparagement, disrepute, false accusation, false publication, false report, imputation, infamy, insinuation, insult, invective, libel, obloquy, scandal, slander, slur, smear, smirch, traducement, untruth
ASSOCIATED CONCEPTS: defamation against title, defamation of business or profession, defamation of character, defamation per quod, defamation per se, defamatory publication, defamatory upon its face, defamatory words, injury to character or reputation, injury to profession or business
FOREIGN PHRASES: **Inveniens libellum famosum et non corrumpens punitur.** A person who finds a libel and does not destroy it is punished.

DEFAME, verb   accuse, accuse falsely, anathematize, asperse, assail, belittle, berate, besmear, besmirch, bespatter, blacken, blemish, brand, bring disrepute upon, call names, *calumniari,* calumniate, cast aspersions on, censure, charge, condemn, criticize, damage one's reputation, decry, degrade, denigrate, denounce, depreciate, destroy one's reputation, discredit, disgrace, dishonor, disparage, dispraise, falsify, fulminate, gibbet, give a bad name, impeach, indict, injure the good name of, injure the good reputation of, inveigh against, lessen one's reputation, libel, lower, malign, objurgate, *obtrectare,* ostracize, pillory, put in a bad light, reprehend, revile, run down, scandalize, shame, slander, slur, smear, smirch, spatter, speak evil, speak ill, speak ill of, speak of slightingly, stain the character of, stigmatize, sully, taint, tarnish, traduce, vilify, vilipend, vituperate
ASSOCIATED CONCEPTS: defamation, defamation per quod, defamation per se, defamatory per se, defamatory upon its face, defamatory words, disparagement, injury to character or reputation, injury to profession or business, libel, slander

DEFAULT, noun   abrogation, ad *vadimonium non venire,* arrear, avoidance, bankruptcy, breach, breach of orders, delinquence, delinquency, dereliction, dereliction of duty, dishonoring, disregard, evasion of duty, failure of credit, failure of duty, failure to answer, failure to appear, failure to meet one's obligations, failure to pay, financial disaster, insolvency, insufficient funds, neglect, nonfulfillment, nonobservance, nonperformance, omission, pretermission, refusal to pay, repudiation, *vadimonium deserere,* violation of duty
ASSOCIATED CONCEPTS: date of default, declaration of default, default decree, default in payment, default of issue, default or misconduct in office, excusable default, failure to pay money due, failure to perform duty, judgment by default, material default, motion for default, motion to open default, motion to vacate default judgment, willful default

DEFAULT, verb   ad vadimonium non venire, avoid, be deficient, be delinquent, be derelict, be faithless, be in arrears, be in debt, be neglectful, be negligent, be remiss, be unfaithful, become unable to meet obligations, breach the agreement, break one's trust, break the contract, desert, dishonor, disregard one's duty, disregard one's obligations, dodge, elude, evade, fail, fail in duty, fail to act, fail to answer, fail to appear, fail to meet financial engagements, fail to pay, fail to perform, forsake, ignore one's obligations, lapse, lose by failure to appear, neglect one's duty, not pay, omit what is due, renege, repudiate, shirk, shirk one's duty, shun, stop payment, *vandimonium* deserere, withhold payment
ASSOCIATED CONCEPTS: date of default, default decree, default in office, default in payment, default of issue, default or misconduct in office, excusable default, judgment by default, motion for default, motion to open default, motion to vacate default judgment, opening of default, willful default

DEFEASANCE, noun   abolishment, abolition, abrogation, annulment, breakup, canceling, cancellation, cassation, cessation, close, conclusion, deprivation, disallowance, discharge, discontinuance, disendowment, disestablishment, dissolution, end, end of the matter, ending, expiration, finish, invalidation, limit, negation, nullification, ousting, recall, removal, repeal, replacement, rescindment, rescission, retractation, retraction, reversal, reversion, revocation, revokement, stoppage, supersession, suppression, undoing, vacation, voidance, windup, withdrawal
ASSOCIATED CONCEPTS: condition, defeasance clause, defeasance of contract, defeasance of title, defeasible estate

DEFEASIBLE, *adjective* confutable, dismissible, disprovable, dissoluble, *functus officio,* nullifiable, refutable, removable, revocable, subject to being abrogated, subject to being annulled, subject to being cancelled, subject to being divested, subject to being invalidated, subject to being repealed, subject to being retracted, subject to being revoked, subject to being taken away, subject to being withdrawn, terminable, voidable
ASSOCIATED CONCEPTS: defeasible deed, defeasible estate, defeasible fee, defeasible interest, defeasible remainder, defeasible title, determinable fee

DEFEAT, *noun* beating, breakdown, collapse, confutation, default, destruction, disappointment, downfall, failure, invalidation, loss, nonfulfillment, overthrow, refutation, *repulsa,* ruin, ruination, setback, thwarting, undoing, vanquishment
ASSOCIATED CONCEPTS: defeat a cause of action, defeat the purpose, defeat the rights, defeated candidate, defeated party

DEFEAT, *verb* beat, block, checkmate, confound, conquer, contravene, crush, demolish, drub, foil, frustrate, gain control over, halt, master, outwit, overcome, overmaster, overpower, overthrow, overwhelm, prevail over, put down, quell, refute, rout, smash, squelch, subdue, subjugate, *superare,* suppress, surmount, thwart, triumph over, trounce, upset, vanquish, *vincere,* victimize
ASSOCIATED CONCEPTS: defeat a cause of action, defeat a will, defeat or impair jurisdiction, defeat the purpose, defeat the rights

DEFECT, *noun* blemish, blot, damage, deficiency, deformity, demerit, deviation, drawback, failing, fault, faultiness, flaw, foible, frailty, impairment, imperfection, impotency, inadequacy, incompleteness, incompletion, infirmity, insufficiency, lack, *mendum,* mistake, mutilation, shortcoming, weakness
ASSOCIATED CONCEPTS: actionable defect, concealed defect, cure of defects, dangerous defect, defect appearing upon face of record, defect in description, defect in form, defect in material or workmanship, defect in title, defect of parties, defect of substance, hidden defects, immaterial defects, inherent defect, jurisdictional defect, knowledge of defect, latent defect, legal defect, material defect, mental defect, obvious defect, open and obvious defect, patent defect, products liability, structural defects

DEFECT, *verb* abandon allegiance, abdicate, abscond, apostasize, back out, be disloyal, betray, break away, break fealty, break with, cast off, change sides, default, demit, depart, desert, disavow, disobey, disown, forsake, leave, leave unlawfully, mutiny, prove treacherous, quit, rebel, reject, renege, renounce, repudiate, resign, revolt, run away, secede, tergiversate, transfer, violate one's oath, withdraw one's support

DEFECTIVE, *adjective* amiss, awry, below par, below standards, beneath standards, blemished, broken, bruised, crippled, damaged, deficient, deformed, distorted, falling short, faultful, faulty, flawed, impaired, imperfect, *imperfectus,* inadequate, incomplete, incondite, incorrect, infirm, injured, inoperative, insufficient, lacking, lame, marred, mutilated, out of order, unfinished, unsound, wanting, warped, weak
ASSOCIATED CONCEPTS: defective and unsafe condition, defective condition, defective construction, defective in form, defective in substance, defective instrumentality, defective machinery, defective materials, defective or dangerous condition, defective product, defective service of process, defective title, defective workmanship or material, defective writ, mentally defective, products liability

DEFEND, *verb* advocate, allege in support, argue for, champion, espouse, guard, justify, maintain, plead for, plead one's cause, promote a cause, propound, protect, safeguard, shield, stand up for, support, sustain, uphold, urge reasons for
ASSOCIATED CONCEPTS: effectiveness of counsel, opportunity to defend

DEFENDANT, *noun* the accused, accused litigant, accused party, charged party, party against whom a complaint is lodged, party against whom charges are pending, party who is sued, respondent
ASSOCIATED CONCEPTS: codefendant, defendant's rights, indispensable party defendant, necessary party defendant, nominal defendant, party defendant, principal defendant, proper party defendant, third party defendants
FOREIGN PHRASES: **Favorabiliores rei potius quam actores habentur.** The condition of the defendant is to be favored rather than that of the plaintiff. **Reus excipiendo fit actor.** The defendant by his pleading may make himself a plaintiff. **Melior est conditio possidentis, et rei quam actoris.** The condition of the possessor and that of the defendant is better than that of the plaintiff. **Habemus optimum testem, confitentem reum.** We have the best witness, a confessing defendant. **Melior est conditio defendentis.** The position of the defendant is the better one.

DEFENSE, *noun* confutation, counterargument, espousal, justification, parry, preservation, protection, rebuttal, resistance against attack, support, warding off
ASSOCIATED CONCEPTS: affirmative defense, alibi defense, anticipating a defense, assist in his own defense, coercion as a defense, complete defense, defense of a third person, defense of action, defense of estoppel, defense of insanity, defense on the merits, defensive pleading, equitable defense, frivolous defense, ground of defense, incomplete defense, inconsistent defenses, legal defenses, meritorious defense, motion to strike defense, negative defense, new defense, partial defense, personal defense, self-defense, sham defense, special defense
FOREIGN PHRASES: **Peccatum peccato addit qui culpae quam facit patrocinium defensionis adjungit.** He adds one offense to another who connects a wrong which he has committed with his defense. **Vani timoris justa excusatio non est.** A frivolous fear is not a lawful excuse. **Nemo prohibetur pluribus defensionibus uti.** No one is prohibited from making use of several defenses. **Impotentia excusat legem.** Performing a legal duty excuses from the performance. **Quodcunque aliquis ob tutelam corporis sui fecerit, jure id fecisse videtur.** Whatever any one does in defense of his person, that he is deemed to have done legally. **Vim vi repellere licit. modo fiat moderamine inculpatae tutelae, non ad sumendam vindictam, sed ad propulsandam injuriam.** It is lawful to repel force by force, provided it be done with the moderation of blameless defense, not for the purpose of taking revenge, but to repel injury.

DEFENSIBLE, *adjective* armed, believable, condonable, credible, defendable, exculpatory, excusable, impregnable, invincible, invulnerable, justifiable, justified, maintainable, pardonable, plausible, prepared, sound, supportable, tenable, unassailable, unattackable, vindicable, vindicatory, warrantable

DEFER *(Put off),* ***verb*** adjourn, arrest, be dilatory, bide, delay, detain, *differre,* discontinue, extend, file, forbear, forestall, gain time, hesitate, hinder, hold back, hold in abeyance, hold off, hold up, impede, interfere, interrupt, intervene, keep pending, lay aside, linger, *obsequi,* obstruct,

pause, pigeonhole, postpone, pretermit, procrastinate, prolong, prorogue, put aside, recess, respite, retard, set aside, shelve, stall, stave off, stay, suspend, table, wait, withhold
ASSOCIATED CONCEPTS: deferred charges, deferred compensation, deferred dividend, deferred income, deferred legacy, deferred payments, deferred premiums, deferred sentence, deferred wage

DEFER *(Yield in judgment)*, **verb**   abide by, abstain, accede, accept, accord, accord superiority to, acknowledge, acquiesce, agree, assent, capitulate, cede, comply, conform to, consent, do honor to, esteem, fall in with, give assent, give consent, give in, give way, go along with, hearken, hold in esteem, honor, *obsequi,* pay respect to, regard, respect, show courtesy, show respect, submit, submit for determination, submit in judgment to, subscribe to, venerate, yield, yield in opinion to
ASSOCIATED CONCEPTS: defer to an administrative agency's decision

DEFERENCE, noun   acquiescence, assent, complaisance, compliance, consideration, courtesy, esteem, honor, nonresistance, obedience, politeness, regard, respect, respectfulness, submission, submissiveness, submittal, willingness

DEFERMENT, noun   adjournment, cunctation, dalliance, deferral, delay, dilatoriness, extension, extension of time, interruption, moratorium, postponement, procrastination, prolongation, prorogation, putting off, respite, stoppage, suspension, tabling, tarrying, wait
ASSOCIATED CONCEPTS: deferment of action, draft deferment

DEFIANCE, noun   affront, challenge, contumacy, dare, daring, disobedience, disregard, disregard of orders, gage, impudence, impudency, insolence, insubmission, insubordination, insurgence, insurgency, insurrection, invitation to combat, mutiny, noncompliance, noncooperation, opposition, oppugnation, *provocatio,* rebellion, rebelliousness, recalcitrance, recalcitrancy, recalcitration, recusancy, resistance, revolt, revolution, sedition, strike, stubbornness, unruliness, uprising
ASSOCIATED CONCEPTS: in defiance of the law

DEFICIENCY, noun   absence, dearth, defect, deficit, deprivation, destitution, failing, failure to comply, falling short, fault, faultiness, flaw, foible, impairment, imperfection, inadequacy, inadequateness, incompleteness, incompletion, infirmity, insufficiency, lack, loss, meagerness, need, noncompletion, nonfulfillment, nonperformance, omission, paucity, penury, poverty, privation, scarcity, short supply, shortage, shortcoming, sparsity, ullage, want, weakness
ASSOCIATED CONCEPTS: deficiency assessment, deficiency bill, deficiency decree, deficiency judgment, deficiency tax, income tax deficiency, liability for deficiency, mental deficiency, notice of deficiency, recovery of deficiency, tax deficiency

DEFICIENT, adjective   attenuated, barren, below par, blemished, defective, depleted, devoid, disappointing, discontenting, empty, falling short, faulty, few, flawed, hollow, impaired, imperfect, impoverished, in arrears, inadequate, incompetent, incomplete, inferior, *inops,* insubstantial, insufficient, jejune, lacking, less than necessary, *mancus,* marred, meager, missing, not enough, not satisfying, not up to normal, not up to par, paltry, partial, poor, scant, scanty, scarce, short, shy, sketchy, skimpy, slight, small, sparing, sparse, starved, substandard, thin, too little, unample, uncompleted, undeveloped, unequal to, unfinished, unfulfilled, unfurnished, unnourishing, unprovided, unsatisfactory, unsound, unsufficing, unsupplied, void of, wanting, weak

DEFICIT, noun   absence, arrears, balance to pay, dearth, default, deficiency, financial shortage, inadequacy, incompleteness, insufficiency, lack, loss, meagerness, omission, overdraft, paucity, scantiness, scarcity, shortage, shortcoming, shortness

DEFILEMENT, noun   abomination, adulteration, besmirching, blackening, contamination, corruption, corruption of purity, debasement, debauchment, deflowering, degradation, demoralization, denigration, depravation, desecration, despoilment, devastation, dirtiness, disgrace, dishonor, filthiness, foulness, impairment, indignity, insult, *macula,* outrage, ravagement, ruination, shamefulness, smearing, sullying, turpitude, uncleanliness, uncleanness, violation

DEFINE, verb   characterize, characterize precisely, *circumscribere,* clarify, construe, *definire,* delineate, denominate, depict the essential qualities of, describe, describe the properties of, designate, determine the essential qualities of, determine with precision, differentiate, elucidate, enumerate, establish, exemplify, explain, explain the nature of, expound, fix, fix the meaning, fix with precision, formalize, formulate, give the meaning, identify, illustrate, individualize, individuate, interpret, label, limit, make clear, mark the limits, name, prescribe, render, render precise, specify, spell out, state the meaning of, state the meaning precisely, tell the meaning, term, throw light upon, translate
ASSOCIATED CONCEPTS: defined by law, defined by statute

DEFINED *(Clear),* **adjective**   clear-cut, coherent, comprehensible, concrete, conditional, confining, conterminable, conterminate, cramped, crystal clear, definite, determinable, determined, distinct, distinguishable, evident, exact, explicit, express, fixed, in focus, manifest, narrow, obvious, patent, perceptible, plain, precise, qualified, quantified, recognizable, specific, straightened, unambiguous, unequivocal, unmistakable

DEFINED *(Determined),* **adjective**   actual, bound, bounded, determined, finite, fixed, limited, precise, restricted, specific, stated
ASSOCIATED CONCEPTS: defined crime, defined nature of an offense, defined offense, defined within a statute

DEFINED MEANING, noun   accurate meaning, correct meaning, definition, distinct meaning, exact meaning, explanation, explicit meaning, express meaning, faithful meaning, inflexible meaning, literal meaning, methodical meaning, meticulous meaning, narrow meaning, not subject to interpretation, ordinary meaning, plain meaning, precise meaning, prescribed meaning, rigid meaning, rigorous meaning, sharply defined, significance, specific meaning, strict meaning, unbending meaning, uncompromising meaning, unequivocal meaning
ASSOCIATED CONCEPTS: construction, literal contract, literal proof, plain meaning rule, rules of statutory, soft plain meaning rule, textualism

DEFINITE, adjective   absolute, accurate, actual, allowed, ascertained, assured, attested, authoritative, axiomatic, beyond all dispute, beyond all question, bound, bounded with precision, categorical, certain, certified, *certus,* clear, clearcut, conclusive, confident, *constitutus,* convinced, correct, decided, decisive, *definitus,* demonstrable, determinate, determined, distinct, doubtless, ensured, established, evident, evidential, exact, existing, express, firm, fixed, fully convinced, granted, guaranteed, having fixed limits, immutable, inappealable, incommutable, incontestable, indefeasible, indisputable, indubious, indubitable, inescapable, inevasible, inevitable, inexorable, inflexible, insured, intransmutable, invariable, inviolate, irrefragable, irrefutable, irresistible, irreversible, irrevocable, persuaded, positive, precisely bounded, quantified, questionless, real, reliable, resolute, satisfied, secure, settled, stated, strictly defined, tested, true, unchanging, unconfuted, uncontested, undeniable, undisputed, undoubting, unequivocal, unerring, unfailing, unfaltering, unhesitating, unimpeachable, univocal, unmistakable, unqualified, unquestioned, unrefuted, unshaken, unsuspecting, unsuspicious, unwavering, veritable, well-defined, well-marked

ASSOCIATED CONCEPTS: definite and certain, definite class, definite description, definite failure of issue, definite interest, definite location, definite period, definite quantity, definite sentence, definite term

DEFINITION, noun   clarification, decipherment, decoding, delimitation, delineation, demarcation, description, elucidation, equivalent meaning, exact meaning, exact statement, explanation, explication, expressed meaning, formulation, identification, illumination, interpretation, making intelligible, meaning, representation, simplification, statement of meaning, synonym, translation

FOREIGN PHRASES: **Omnis definitio in jure civili periculosa est, parum est enim ut non subverti possit.** Every definition in the law is dangerous, because there is little that cannot be subverted.

DEFINITIVE, adjective   absolute, accurate, ascertained, authentic, authenticated, authoritative, beyond a doubt, beyond all dispute, closing, complete, completed, conclusive, conclusory, confirmative, consummate, crowning, decided, decisive, definite, determinate, determinative, determining, exact, exhaustive, final, fixed, incontestable, incontrovertible, indisputable, indubitable, irrefutable, last, most complete, most precise, perfect, supreme, terminational, terminative, thorough, ultimate, unassailable, uncontested, undeniable, undisputed, undoubted, unimpeachable, unquestionable, without doubt, without question

ASSOCIATED CONCEPTS: definitive decree, definitive judgment, definitive order

DEFLAGRATE, verb   blaze, burn, burn fiercely, burn up, burst into flame, conflagrate, consume, cremate, fire, flame, flame up, flare, flare up, flash, ignite, incandesce, incinerate, inflame, reduce to ashes, scorch, sear, singe, torrefy

DEFRAUD, verb   befool, beguile, bilk, cheat, cheat out of money, *circumscribere*, commit breach of trust, cozen, deceive, *defraudare*, delude, deprive dishonestly, dupe, embezzle, fleece, fool, hoax, inveigle, levant, mislead, mulct, obtain money on false pretenses, peculate, practice chicanery, practice fraud upon, swindle, take advantage of, take by fraud, take in, trick

ASSOCIATED CONCEPTS: conspiracy to defraud, intent to defraud, use of mails to defraud

DEFRAY, verb   adjust, bear the cost, bear the expense, compensate, contribute, disburse, discharge, expend, foot the bill, give compensation for, honor a bill, indemnify, liquidate, make payment, make repayment, make restitution, meet the bill, pay, pay an indemnity, pay compensation, pay for, pay one's way, pay reparations, pay the costs, redeem, refund, reimburse, remit,

remunerate, repay, requite, satisfy a claim, solvere, spend, stand the cost, *suppeditare*

ASSOCIATED CONCEPTS: defraying cost, defraying expenses

DEFRAYAL, noun   collection, compensation, defrayment, disbursement, expenditure, expense, pay, payment, pay-off, quittance, recovery, reimbursement, remittance, remuneration, satisfaction, settlement of charges

DEFT, adjective   able, accomplished, adept, adroit, agile, apt, canny, capable, clever, competent, cunning, dexterous, efficient, expert, facile, flexible, gifted, good at, handy, ingenious, light, masterful, masterly, nimble, nimble-fingered, practiced, proficient, qualified, quick, resourceful, sharp, skilled, skillful, slick, smooth, talented

DEFUNCT, adjective   abrogated, all gone, all over with, annulled, cancelled, dead, deceased, demised, departed, devoid of life, ended, exanimate, expired, extinct, finished, gone, gone out of existence, inactive, inefficacious, inoperative, lifeless, *mortuus*, no longer living, no more, not endowed with life, not existing, not in action, not in force, obsolete, old-fashioned, out of fashion, passed away, past, perished, terminated, unknown, unobserved, unused, vanished, void, without life

ASSOCIATED CONCEPTS: defunct business, defunct corporation

DEFY, verb   affront, assume a fighting attitude, battle, beard, brave, breast, buck, challenge, conflict with, confront, dare, disobey, disregard, flout, front, mutiny, oppose, outface, *provocare*, rebel, resist, resist openly, stand up against, withstand

ASSOCIATED CONCEPTS: defy a court order

DEGENERATE, noun   corrupt person, debased person, debauchee, decadent person, degraded person, depraved person, derelict, disreputable person, immoral person, pervert, rapscallion, recreant, scamp, scapegrace, transgressor, wastrel, worthless person

DEGENERATE, verb   atrophy, be destroyed, be reduced in worth, be worse, become depraved, become deteriorated, become enfeebled, become impaired, become lower in quality, become notably worse, become perverted, become tainted, become worse, break up, canker, come down, consume, corrupt, crumble, debase, debase in quality, debauch, decay, decline, decompose, *degenerare*, degrade, deprave, derange, deteriorate, dilapidate, disband, disintegrate, disorder, dissolve, ebb, erode, fall apart, fall away, fall into decay, fall off, fall to pieces, get worse, go bad, go to pieces, grow weak, grow worse, languish, lapse, lessen in worth, lose morale, make inferior in value, make lower in character, make worse, moulder, poison, pollute, putrefy, render chaotic, retrogress, rot, run down, shrivel, sicken, sink, sink to a lower condition, taint, vitiate, wane, waste, wear, wear away, wither, worsen

DEGRADATION, noun   abasement, abjection, baseness, debasement, decadence, decadency, declension, declination, decline, *dedecus*, degeneratess, degeneration, demotion, deprival of honor, deterioration, discredit, disgrace, dishonor, dismissal from office, disrepute, fall from repute, humiliation, *ignominia*, ignominy, ingloriousness, obloquy, odium, opprobrium, reduction in rank, retrogradation, retrogression, shame

DEGREE *(Academic title)*, **noun**   academic honor, award, certificate, collegiate distinction, credentials, credit, dignification, diploma, distinction, graduation certificate, qualification, title, title of honor

DEGREE *(Kinship)*, **noun** affiliation, blood relation, blood relationship, cognation, connation, connection, consanguinity, extraction, family connection, family relationship, family tie, filiation, line of descent, proximity of blood, relatedness, relationship between persons, ties of blood
ASSOCIATED CONCEPTS: degree of descent, degree of kindred

DEGREE *(Magnitude)*, **noun** amount, amplitude, caliber, consequence, dimension, enormity, expanse, extent, greatness, import, importance, intensity, largeness, measure, measurement, might, moment, proportions, range, reach, scope, seriousness, significance, strength, tenor, value, vastness, volume, weight
ASSOCIATED CONCEPTS: degree of care, degree of certainty, degree of crime, degree of disability, degree of offense, degree of proof, degrees of criminality, highest degree of care, lesser included offenses
FOREIGN PHRASES: *Quae sunt minoris culpae sunt majoris infamiae.* Those things which are less culpable may be more infamous.

DEGREE *(Station)*, **noun** classification, echelon, gradation, grade, *gradus,* level of development, manner, mark, *ordo,* plane, point, position, rank, ranking, relative position, rung, situation, stage, stage of advancement, standing, status, step, tier

DEIGN, *verb* allow, allow with condescension, be so good as to, condescend, descend, favor, grant, patronize, stoop, vouchsafe

DELAY, *noun* *cunctatio,* cunctation, dalliance, deceleration, deferment, demurral, detainment, detention, dilatoriness, impediment, intermission, interruption, lag, lateness, *cessatio, mora,* moratorium, pause, postponement, procrastination, prolongation, prorogation, putting off, retardation, setback, slowness, stall, stay, suspension, tardiness, tarriance, wait
ASSOCIATED CONCEPTS: dilatory motions
FOREIGN PHRASES: *De morte hominis nulla est cunctatio longa.* When the death of a human being may be concerned, no delay is considered long. *Justitia non est neganda non differenda.* Justice is neither to be denied nor delayed. *Dilationes in lege sunt odiosae.* Delays are odious to the law.

DELAY, *verb* adjourn, arrest, arrest temporarily, be dilatory, block, bring to a standstill, curb, defer, detain, *detinere,* hamper, hinder, hold, hold back, hold in abeyance, hold over, hold up, impede, impede the progress of, interfere, intermit, keep back, keep from proceeding, keep one waiting, keep pending, lay over, linger, loiter, make inactive, obstruct, postpone, prevent, prolong, protract, put off, remit, retard, set back, shelve, slacken, slow, slow down, slow up, stall, stall for time, stand in the way, stay, stop, stymie, table, *tardare,* tarry, temporize
ASSOCIATED CONCEPTS: accidental delays, damages for delay, delay beyond the seller's control, delay occasioned by the defendant, delayed compensation, dilatory delay, excusable delay, excuse for delay, hinder and delay, inexcusable delay, justifiable delay, laches, unavoidable delay, unreasonable delay, without delay

DELAYED *(Arrested)*, **adjective** adjourned, belated, contained, deferred, dilatory, late, lingering, overdue, postponed, protracted, remanded, restrained, set back, stopped, suspended, tabled, tardy, unpunctual, untimely

DELAYED *(Lagging)*, **adjective** arrested, behindhand, delinquent, detained, impeded, in abeyance, in arrears, late, overdue, sluggish
ASSOCIATED CONCEPTS: dilatory action, dismissal due to delay, expedited proceedings, motion to accelerate the proceedings, prejudice due to delay, right to a speedy trial, unusual delay

DELEGATE, *verb* accord, accredit, allocate, allot, appoint, appoint as agent, appoint as representative, assign, assign a duty, assign power of attorney to, assign to a position, authorize, authorize formally, authorize to represent, award, bestow, call upon, charge, charge with an errand, charter, choose, commission, commit, commit powers to another, commit to the hands of, *committere,* confer power on, confide, confide for care, confide for use, consign, convey, *credere, delegare,* deliver, deliver in trust, deliver over, deposit with, depute, designate, designate to a post, despatch, detail, devolve on, dispatch, employ, empower, empower to act for another, enable, engage, entitle, entrust, entrust to the care of another, give, give a mandate, give a responsibility to, give authority to, give employment, give in charge, give in trust, give power, give power of attorney, give to, hand over, hire, hold responsible, impose a duty, impower, instate, intitle, intrust, invest, invest with authoritative power, license, make someone a trustee of, make someone guardian of, *mandare,* name, name to fill an appointment, nominate, oblige, offer a job to, offer a post, order, parcel out to, place in an office, place in charge of, place trust in, put in commission, put in one's hands, put in safekeeping, qualify, refer, relegate, sanction, select, send, send as deputy, send on a commission, send on a mission, send on an errand, send out, substitute, swear in, transfer, transmit, trust with, turn over to, vest in, warrant
ASSOCIATED CONCEPTS: delegated legislative function, delegated power, delegated state function, delegation of authority

DELEGATION *(Assignment)*, **noun** agency, agentship, appointment, authorization, charge, commission, commissioning, consigning, consignment, delegating, deputation, deputization, designation, devolution, entrusting, entrustment, giving over, investing with authority, investiture, license, mandate, ordination, procuration, proxyship, reference, referring, warrant
ASSOCIATED CONCEPTS: delegation of authority, delegation of duty, delegation of governmental power, delegation of judicial power, delegation of legislative functions, delegation of legislative power, delegation of power
FOREIGN PHRASES: *Vicarius non habet vicarium.* A deputy cannot have a deputy. *Quod per me non possum, nec per alium.* What I cannot do myself, I cannot do through another. *Delegatas potestas non potest delegari.* A delegated power cannot be further delegated. *Delegatus non potest delegare.* A representative cannot delegate his authority.

DELEGATION *(Envoy)*, **noun** body of delegates, body of representatives, commission, committee, delegates, deputies, embassy, legation, mission, people delegated, procuracy, representatives

DELETE, *verb* blot out, cancel, censor, cross off, cross out, cut, cut out, dele, discard, do away with, drop, edit out, efface, elide, eliminate, eradicate, erase, excise, expel, expunge, extirpate, get rid of, leave out, modify by excisions, obliterate, omit, remove, rub out, rule out, scratch out, strike off, strike out, take out, weed, wipe out

DELETERIOUS, *adjective* adverse, bad, baleful, baneful, consuming, corroding, corrosive, damaging, deadly, disadvantageous, disserviceable, envenomed, fatal, foul, harmful, injurious to health, insalubrious, lethal, malefic, maleficent, malignant, miasmal, morbiferous, morbific, nocuous, noisome, noxious, *noxius*, pernicious, pestilential, poisonous, ruinous, septic, toxic, unadvantageous, unfavorable, unhealthful, unhealthy, unsatisfactory, venomous, virulent, wasting
ASSOCIATED CONCEPTS: deleterious drug, deleterious substance

DELIBERATE, *adjective* advised, aimed, attentive, calculated, careful, carefully considered, carefully weighed, cautious, characterized by reflection, cogitative, *cogitatus,* conscious, *consideratus,* considered, contemplated, contemplative, controlled, deliberative, designed, determined, dispassionate, done on purpose, excogitative, fixed, full of thought, given due consideration, gradual, intended, intentional, judged, leisurely, maturely considered, measured, meditated, meditative, outlined beforehand, planned, planned in advance, plotted, pondered, prearranged, preconsidered, predeliberated, predesigned, predetermined, premeditated, prepense, *prudens,* prudent, purposed, purposeful, reasoned, reflective, resolved, slow, slow-moving, slow-paced, sober, speculative, studied, thought-out, thoughtful, unhasty, unhurried, volitient, volitional, volitive, voluntary, wary, weighed, well-considered, willed, willful, with forethought
ASSOCIATED CONCEPTS: deliberate act, deliberate and premeditated killing, deliberate and premeditated malice, deliberate and premeditated murder, deliberate and willful misconduct, deliberate assumption of risk, deliberate killing, deliberate or intentional wrongdoing, deliberate speed, deliberately and with premeditation, deliberative body

DELIBERATE, *verb* advise together, advise with, analyze, brood, cerebrate, cogitate, confer formally, consider, consider attentively, consider carefully, consider pro and con, *considerare,* consult, *consultare,* contemplate, debate, *deliberare,* discourse about, discuss, examine, examine carefully, excogitate, go into, hold a consultation, hold conclave, investigate, judge, meditate, mull over, negotiate, parley, ponder, ponder over, ponder reasons for and against, ratiocinate, reason, reason out, reason the point, reflect, reflect over, reflect upon, regard upon, review, ruminate, sit in conclave, sit in council, study, take counsel with oneself, take into consideration, take under consideration, think carefully, think over, weigh, weigh in the mind

DELIBERATE OMISSION, *noun* abandonment, abnegation, ban, bar, boycott, breach, declination, defalcation, default, delinquency, disregard, elision, exception, exclusion, failure of duty, intentional omission, laches, laxity, leaving out, lockout, neglect, negligence, noncompliance, nonfulfillment, noninclusion, nonperformance, preclusion, relinquishment, renunciation, repudiation, waiver
ASSOCIATED CONCEPTS: obstruction of justice, perjury

DELIBERATION, *noun* advisement, analysis, brooding, calculation, careful consideration, carefulness, caution, cautiousness, cerebration, circumspection, close attention, close study, cogitation, conscious purpose, consideration, *consultatio,* contemplation, contemplativeness, counsel, debate, *deliberatio,* determination prepense, discussion, distinct intention, examination, excogitation, forethought, heed, heedfulness, inquiry, inspection, intellection, judgment, level-headedness, logical discussion, mature consideration, mature reflection, meditation, pondering, premeditation, prudence, ratiocination, reflection, rumination,

sobriety, study, taking counsel, thinking out, thought, thoughtfulness, unhurriedness, wariness, watchfulness, weighing

DELICT, *noun* corruption, crime, *delictum,* dereliction of duty, duty unfulfilled, felony, injurious act, injury, malefaction, malfeasance, malversation, misdemeanor, misfeasance, misprision, neglect of duty, negligent act of injury, negligent offense, negligent wrongdoing, nonfeasance, obligation repudiated, offense, official misconduct, tort, violation, violation of a duty, wrong
ASSOCIATED CONCEPTS: quasi delict

DELIMIT, *verb* allot, bound, circumscribe, confine, define, demarcate, determine, draw the line, edge, encircle, enclose, encompass, fix, lay out a boundary, mark limits, mark off, mark out, measure, surround

DELINEATE, *verb* *adumbrare,* block out, blueprint, circumscribe, construct a figure, contour, convey an impression of, define, depict, *depingere,* describe, *describere,* detail, determine, diagram, draft, draw, draw a picture, engrave, etch, figure, frame, give the details of, illuminate, illustrate, itemize, limn, make a likeness, make apparent, make clear, make vivid, map, mold, outline, paint, paint a picture, particularize, picture, picturize, plot, portray, portray in words, profile, recite, recount, relate, report, represent, represent by diagram, represent by outlines, represent pictorially, set forth, shape, silhouette, sketch, sketch in outline, sketch out, specify, specify the particulars of, survey, tell vividly, trace, trace out, trace the outline of, traverse the outline of

DELINEATION, *noun* abstract, account, act of setting forth, the act of tracing, *adumbratio,* blueprint, chart, circumscription, configuration, contour, *débauche,* depiction, depiction of essential features, *descriptio,* description, design, diagram, enumeration of the essential qualities, facsimile, form, framework, graph, line drawn round, map, outline, pattern, plan, plot, portrayal, profile, recital, recitation, relation, rendition, report, representation, representation by words, rough draft, shape, silhouette, skeleton plan, sketch, specification, statements that describe, structure, tracing, verbal portraiture, word picture

DELINQUENCY (Failure of duty), ***noun*** breach, breach of a promise, carelessness, default, dereliction of duty, error, failure, failure of obligation, failure to act, incompletion, indifference to act, inobservance, lapse in conduct, malpractice, misprision, neglect, neglect of obligation, negligence, noncompletion, noncompletion of a task, nonfulfillment, nonobservance, nonperformance, omission, omission of duty, omission of obligation, oversight, repudiation of one's duty, slight, slip, unfulfillment of an assignment, unfulfillment of duty

DELINQUENCY (Misconduct), ***noun*** atrocity, badness, baseness, breach of the law, corruption, crime, criminality, culpability, decadence, degeneracy, *delictum,* depravity, dereliction, devilishness, dissoluteness, evil, evil behavior, fault, *flagrante delicto,* foulness, heinousness, immorality, improbity, impropriety, indiscretion, infraction, infraction of the law, infringement, iniquity, lawbreaking, lawlessness, malefaction, malfeasance, *malum,* malversation, misbehavior, misdeed, misdoing, misstep, nefariousness, obliquity, offense, outrage, peccability, peccancy, prodigality, profligacy, reprobacy, tort, transgression, trespass, turpitude, unvirtuousness, viciousness, vileness, villainousness, villainy, violation, wantonness, waywardness, wickedness, wrong, wrongdoing

ASSOCIATED CONCEPTS: contributing to delinquency, delinquency proceeding, juvenile delinquency

DELINQUENCY (Shortage), **noun** arrearage, arrears, dearth, debt, default, deficiency, deficit, depletion, inability to pay, inadequacy, indebtment, insufficiency, lack, late payment, liability, nonfulfillment, nonpayment, obligation, outstanding debt, paucity, scantiness, scarcity, short measure, short supply, shortage, shortness, sparseness, sparsity, unpaid amount

ASSOCIATED CONCEPTS: delinquency assessment, delinquency charges

DELINQUENT (Guilty of a misdeed), **adjective** accusable, at fault, bad, blamable, blameful, blameworthy, censurable, condemnable, conscienceless, corrupt, criminal, culpable, derelict, dishonest, disreputable, erring, evil, evildoing, evil-minded, flagrant, guilty, *homo maleficus,* immoral, improper, in error, in fault, in the wrong, incorrigible, iniquitous, irredeemable, lawbreaking, maleficent, malevolent, malfeasant, misbehaving, monstrous, nefarious, negligent, offending, peccant, profligate, punishable, remiss, reprehensible, reproachable, reprobate, scandalous, sinful, to blame, transgressing, unjust, unlawful, unprincipled, unscrupulous, unseemly, unvirtuous, unworthy, vicious, villainous, virtueless, wicked, worthless

ASSOCIATED CONCEPTS: delinquent child, delinquent minors

DELINQUENT (Overdue), **adjective** back, behind, behindhand, chargeable, defaultant, defaulting, deficient, due, failing in duty, in arrears, lacking, missing, neglectful of obligation, not discharged, not met, not paid on time, outstanding, owed, owing, past due, payable, receivable, remiss, short, to be paid, undefrayed, unliquidated, unpaid, unsatisfied, unsettled, wanting

ASSOCIATED CONCEPTS: delinquent assessments, delinquent debtor, delinquent lands, delinquent payment, delinquent premiums, delinquent property, delinquent taxes, delinquent taxpayer

DELINQUENT, noun criminal, culprit, dangerous person, evildoer, guilty man, *homo maleficus,* insolvent debtor, lawbreaker, malefactor, malfeasor, mischief-maker, miscreant, misdemeanant, misdoer, misfeasor, neglector of duty, nonpayer, offender, recidivist, recreant, reprobate, rogue, ruffian, scofflaw, swindler, transgressor, trouble maker, undesirable, worker of iniquity, wrongdoer

ASSOCIATED CONCEPTS: delinquent child, delinquent neglected and dependent children, delinquent premiums, delinquent taxes, juvenile delinquent

DELIRIOUS (Incoherent), **adjective** bereft of reason, crazed, crazy, deranged, hallucinating, insane, lunacy, mad, mentally ill, rabid, ranting, raving, sick, unsound

ASSOCIATED CONCEPTS: criminally insane, insanity defense, involuntary commitment

DELIRIOUS (Wildly happy), **adjective** ardent, blissful, carried away, ebullient, elated, electrified, enamored, excited, fanatical, feverish, frantic, frenzied, happy, hectic, impassioned, intoxicated, thrilled, tumultuous

DELIVER, verb carry, cart, commit, communicate, convey, dedere, delegate, entrust, forward, give into another's keeping, give out, hand, hand down, haul, impart, make over, pass on, place in the possession of, *prodere,* put into the hands of, relay, remit, send, ship, surrender, *tradere,* traject, transfer by deed, transfer property, transfer right, transfuse, translate, translocate, transmit, transplant, transport, turn over

ASSOCIATED CONCEPTS: agreement to deliver, constructively delivered, deliver himself up, deliver in trust, deliver possession, deliver up, delivered for shipment, executed and delivered, sold and delivered, writing signed and delivered

DELIVERY, noun *actio,* conveyance, conveyancing, deliverance, *dictio, elocutio,* impartment, mutual transfer, remittance, rendering, sending, shipment, surrender, transfer, transference, transferral, transmission, transmittal, transmittance, transposal, transposition

ASSOCIATED CONCEPTS: absolute delivery, acceptance, acknowledgment of delivery, actual delivery, complete delivery, conditional delivery, constructive delivery, contingent delivery, delivery and acceptance, delivery bond, delivery f.o.b., delivery in escrow, delivery of a deed, delivery of an instrument, delivery of deed, delivery of freight, delivery of goods, delivery of instrument, delivery of mail, delivery of possession, delivery terms, delivery to a third person, failure of delivery, failure to make delivery, immediate delivery, improper delivery, misdelivery, nondelivery, partial delivery, personal delivery, prompt delivery, proper delivery, sale and delivery, sale for future delivery, substituted delivery, symbolic delivery, tender of delivery, unconditional delivery, valid delivery

FOREIGN PHRASES: **In traditionibus scriptorum, non quod dictum est, sed quod gestum est, inspicitur.** In the delivery of writings, not what is said, but what is done, is regarded. **Periculum rei venditae, nondum traditae, est emptoris.** The risk of a thing sold, but not yet delivered, is the purchaser's. **Traditio nihil amplius transferre debet vel potest, ad eum qui accipit, quam est apud eum qui tradit.** Delivery ought to, and can, transfer nothing more to him who receives than is in possession of him who makes the delivery. **Traditio loqui facit chartam.** Delivery makes the deed speak.

DELUDE, verb be cunning, befool, beguile, bluff, cause error, cheat, cozen, create a false impression, cully, dazzle, deceive, decoy, defraud, *deludere,* dissemble, dupe, falsify, fool, give a false idea, give a false impression, gull, hoax, hoodwink, illude, inveigle, lead astray, lead into error, make a fool of, misdirect, misguide, misinform, mislead, misrepresent, misstate, mystify, persuade to believe error, play a trick on, practice chicanery, practice fraud upon, practice upon one's credulity, swindle, take advantage of, take in, trick

DELUSIVE, adjective artful, beguiling, bogus, chimerical, crafty, cunning, deceitful, deceiving, deceptive, deluding, delusory, dreamy, elusive, fallacious, *fallax,* false, *falsus,* fancied, fanciful, fantastic, fantastical, feigned, fraudulent, guileful, hallucinative, hallucinatory, illusionary, illusive, illusory, imaginary, imagined, insubstantial, make-believe, misleading, mock, notional, phantasmal, pretended, sham, sleightful, specious, spurious, tricky, unactual, unfounded, unreal, unsubstantial, untrue, *vanus,* visionary, wily

DELVE, verb ask for, burrow, carry on intensive research, conduct an inquiry, dig down into, dig into, examine, explore, fathom, ferret out, *fodere,* follow the trail, go deep into, go in pursuit of, go in search of, go through, hold an inquiry, hunt for, hunt through, inquire for, inquire into, institute an inquiry, investigate, look around for, look behind the scenes, look for, look into, look through, make inquiry, peer, penetrate, poke, probe, probe to the bottom, prosecute an inquiry, pry, pursue, quest, research, rummage, search, search for, search laboriously, search through, seek, seek a clue, set up an inquiry, track, trail, unearth

DEMAGOGUE, *noun*   agitator, charismatic leader, declaimer, exciter, factionary, factioneer, factious leader, fanatic, firebrand, fomenter, haranguer, incentor, inciter, inflamer, instigator, leader, mob swayer, *plebicola, plebis dux,* politician, popular agitator, provocator, provoker, rabble-rouser, radical, ranter, rebel, revolutionary, ringleader, rouser, troublemaker, unprincipled politician, unscrupulous agitator, unscrupulous haranguer, urger

DEMAND, *noun*   asking for what is due, assertion of legal right, authoritative request, behest, bidding, call, claim, command, emphatic inquiry, exigency, imperative request, imposition, legal claim, notice of claim, order, peremptory claim, request to perform, requirement, requisite, statement of claim, ultimatum

ASSOCIATED CONCEPTS: actual demand, cross demand, demand and refusal, demand certificates, demand deposits, demand for payment, demand for relief, demand instruments, demand note, excessive demands, legal demand, notice and demand, on demand, presentment and demand, unreasonable demand

FOREIGN PHRASES: *Rogationes, quaestiones, et positiones debent esse simplices.* Demands, questions, and claims ought to be simple.

DEMAND, *verb*   arrogate, ask, ask for with authority, assert a right to, assert one's rights, call for, claim, claim as one's due, command, direct, enjoin, exact, give notice, impose, insist, make application, order, present one's claim, press, request, require, urge

ASSOCIATED CONCEPTS: actual demand, cross demand, demand and refusal, demand certificates, demand deposits, demand for payment, demand for relief, demand instruments, demand note, excessive demands, legal demand, notice and demand, on demand, presentment and demand, unreasonable demand

FOREIGN PHRASES: *Nihil peti potest ante id tempus quo per rerum naturam persolvi possit.* Nothing can be demanded before the time when, in the nature of things, it can be paid. *Judex non reddit plus quam quod petens ipse requirit.* A judge should not render judgments for a larger sum than the plaintiff demands.

DEMARCATE, *verb*   allocate, allot, apportion, assign, border, bound, circumscribe, compass, confine, contradistinguish, define, delimit, delimitate, demark, determine, determine boundaries, differentiate, discriminate, distinguish, disunite, divide, enclose, encompass, establish boundaries, fence off, fix limits, lay down limits, limit, mark, mark limits, mark out, outline, partition, rope off, segregate, separate, set apart, set bounds to, set off, stake out, zone

DEMEAN (Deport oneself), ***verb***   acquit, act, appear, bear, behave, carry, comport, conduct, convey the impression, create the impression, function, have the mien, leave the impression, look, manage, present oneself, present the appearance, quit, represent oneself, resemble, seem, seem to be, show, take on the manner

DEMEAN (Make lower), ***verb***   abase, belittle, bring down, bring into disrepute, bring low, cheapen, conquer, crush, debase, deflate, degrade, depreciate, derogate, descend, detract from, diminish, discredit, disgrace, dishonor, disparage, humble, humiliate, lower, make ashamed, make lowly, mortify, put down, reduce, shame, stain, take down, tarnish, vanquish

DEMEANOR, *noun*   appearance, aspect, attitude, bearing, behavior, carriage, comportment, conduct, countenance, deportment, expression, guise, look, manner, mien, physical appearance, poise, posture, presence, way

ASSOCIATED CONCEPTS: demeanor of witnesses

DEMESNE, *noun*   acquest, chattels real, domain, dominion, empire, estate, freehold, hereditament, holding, land, landed estate, landed property, manor, one's own land, property, real estate, real property, realm, realty

ASSOCIATED CONCEPTS: demesne lands

DEMISE (Conveyance), ***noun***   abalienation, alienation, bequeathal, cession, conferment, conferral, conveyancing, deeding, deliverance, delivery, testamentary disposition, transfer, transference, transmission, transmittal

DEMISE (Death), ***noun***   annihilation, cessation of life, decease, departure, end of life, expiration, extinction, extinguishment, loss of life, mortality, necrosis, passing away

DEMISE, *verb*   award, bequeath, bestow by will, confer by will, convey, deliver over, devise, devolve upon, endow, give by will, grant by will, hand down, leave, leave a legacy, leave by will, make a bequest, make a legacy, make testamentary disposition, pass by will, pass down, transfer by will, transfer ownership, transmit, will

ASSOCIATED CONCEPTS: demise and grant, demise for a term of years, demise for life, demised premises

DEMIT, *verb*   abdicate, give up, go into retirement, hand in one's resignation, lay down one's office, leave, make way for, quit, relinquish, renounce, resign, retire, retire from office, stand aside, stand down, tender one's resignation, vacate office, vacate one's seat, withdraw

DEMOBILIZE, *noun*   cure, curtail, deactivate, demilitarize, disarm, disband, disengage, fix, limit, reduce, remedy, sever, stop

ASSOCIATED CONCEPTS: demobilize forces involved in an armed conflict

DEMONSTRABLE, *adjective*   absolute, apparent, assured, beyond a question, beyond all doubt, clear, clear-cut, conclusive, decided, definite, dependable, determinate, doubtless, established, evident, incontestable, indisputable, indubitable, not to be disputed, positive, stable, trustworthy, unambiguous, unequivocal, unimpeachable, unmistakable, unqualified, unquestionable, valid, veracious, without doubt, workable

DEMONSTRATE (Establish), ***verb***   authenticate, circumstantiate, clarify, confirm, corroborate, display, elucidate, evince, exemplify, exhibit, illuminate, illustrate, indicate, instruct, lay out, make clear, make evident, make plain, manifest, perform, point out, prove, set forth, show, show by example, substantiate, support, sustain, teach by example, uphold, validate, verify

DEMONSTRATE (Protest), ***verb***   challenge, clamor, complain publicly, contravene, controvert, counter, counteract, cry out against, declare opposition, demur, denounce, dissent, expostulate, express disagreement, express disapproval, express dissatisfaction, impugn, inveigh, march, negate, object, oppose, parade, picket, rail, reject, reluct, remonstrate, resist, show disagreement, show disapproval, show opinion publicly, show opposition, spurn, state opposition, storm, traverse

DEMONSTRATIVE (Expressive of emotion), ***adjective*** communicative, effusive, emotional, emotive, excitable, expressive, fanatical, fervent, feverish, fierce, fiery, free in expression, furious, histrionic, maudlin, overflowing, overwrought, passionate, prone to display of feeling, prone to emotional display, talkative, temperamental, unrestrained, vehement, violent, without reserve

DEMONSTRATIVE (*Illustrative*), *adjective* affording proof, allegorical, analytical, annotative, characteristic, clarifying, confirmative, confirmatory, confirming, connotative, corroborating, declarative, delineative, depictive, descriptive, elucidative, enlightening, exegetic, exegetical, explanatory, explicative, explicatory, explicit, expository, expressive, graphic, illuminating, illuminative, informative, informing, interpretative, interpretive, representative, revealing, showing, substantiative, suggesting, suggestive, supportive, telling, typical, verificative, verifying
ASSOCIATED CONCEPTS: demonstrative bequest, demonstrative evidence, demonstrative gift, demonstrative legacy, demonstrative words

DEMOTE, *verb* abase, belittle, bring down, bring low, cashier, cause to descend, cause to sink, debase, decrease in importance, dedecorate, deflate, degrade, demean, depose, depreciate, deprive, dethrone, diminish, discrown, dismiss from favor, dispossess, disrate, divest, downgrade, drop, humble, impose a penalty, lessen importance of, lower, lower in rank, make less important, otherwordly, penalize, reduce, reduce to inferior rank, reduce to the ranks, relieve, remove from office, strip, take down, unseat
ASSOCIATED CONCEPTS: demotion in rank, demotion in salary, demotion of employee

DEMUR, *verb* beg to differ, challenge, contradict, contravene, controvert, deny, differ, disagree, disapprove, disavow, dissent, enter a demurrer, *exceptionem facere*, not confirm, object, oppose, protest, raise objections, reject, repudiate, scruple, take exception, traverse, withhold assent

DEMURRAGE, *noun* compensation for delay, payment for delay, penalty for delay, remittance for delay

DEMURRER, *noun* be at variance, challenge, challenge to the sufficiency of the pleading, confutation, denial of the allegations, denial of the pleading, denial of the statements, exception, exception to a pleading, general denial, negation of allegations, objection, objection to a pleading, opposition to allegations, refusal to answer, refutation, repudiation of the allegations, take exception to the allegations, take issue with, traversal
ASSOCIATED CONCEPTS: argumentative demurrer, demurrer to a pleading, demurrer to evidence, demurrer to interrogatories, frivolous demurrer, general demurrer, special demurrer

DENATURE, *verb* adulterate, alter, attemper, bemingle, blend, change, cheapen, convert, corrupt, deform, denaturalize, devalue, dilute, disguise, distort, doctor, impair, infuse, intermix, introduce changes, invalidate, make impure, make lower in quality, mask, mix, pervert, pollute, sophisticate, tamper with, transfigure, transform, transmute, vitiate, water down, weaken
ASSOCIATED CONCEPTS: denatured food

DENIAL, *noun* abjuration, abnegation, abridgment, challenge, confutation, contradiction, contrary assertion, contravention, deprivement, disaffirmation, disallowance, disavowal, disclaimer, disclamation, disentitlement, dissent, divestment, gainsaying, *negatio,* negation, negative answer, nonacceptance, nonconsent, objection, privation,

prohibition, protest, protestation, rebuttal, recantation, refutation, rejection, relinquishment, renouncement, renunciation, *repudiatio,* repudiation, retraction, revocation, spurning, swearing off
ASSOCIATED CONCEPTS: argumentative denial, denial of admittance, denial of civil rights, denial of claim, denial of counsel, denial of due process, denial of equal protection, denial of knowledge or information, denial of liability, denial of motion, denial of relief, general denial, specific denial
FOREIGN PHRASES: ***Per rerum naturam, factum negantis nulla probatio est.*** It is the nature of things that a person who denies a fact is not bound to give proof. ***Justitia non est neganda, non differenda.*** Justice is neither to be denied nor delayed. ***Qui non negat fatetur.*** He who does not deny, admits. ***Posito uno oppositorum negatur alterum.*** One of two opposite positions being established, the other is denied. ***Semper praesumitur pro negante.*** A presumption is always in favor of the person who denies.

DENIGRATE, *verb* abase, accuse, asperse, attack, attaint, belittle, besmear, besmirch, bespatter, blacken, blacken one's good name, blemish, brand, call names, calumniate, cast aspersions, charge, compromise, condemn, criticize, decry, defame, degrade, delate, denounce, depreciate, deride, dishonor, expose, gibbet, give a bad name, humiliate, implicate, incriminate, inculpate, insult, libel, lower, malign, pillory, put in a bad light, put to shame, reflect poorly upon, reproach, reprove, revile, run down, shame, slander, smear, smirch, sneer at, soil, speak ill of, stain, stigmatize, sully, tarnish, taunt, traduce, vilify, vilipend, vituperate

DENIZEN, *noun* burgher, citizen, dweller, habitant, *incola,* indweller, inhabitant, inmate, occupant, occupier, oppidan, resident, residentiary, sojourner, tenant, townsman

DENOMINATE, *verb* call, call by name, christen, classify, coin, *denominare,* denote, designate, distinguish by name, dub, entitle, give a name to, give title to, label, name, phrase, signify, specify, style, term, title

DENOMINATION, *noun* appellation, association, band, branch, brotherhood, caption, categorization, category, characterization, class, classification, clique, community, coterie, description, designation, differentiation, distinction, division, faction, genre, group, grouping, heading, identification, kind, label, movement, name, nomenclature, order, organization, party, persuasion, religious order, sect, section, species, subdivision, term, terminology, title, trademark, type, variety
ASSOCIATED CONCEPTS: denomination of money, denominational institution, denominational school, religious denomination

DENOTE, *verb* be a name for, be a sign of, be an indication of, bespeak, betoken, convey a meaning, denominate, denotate, depict, depicture, *designare,* designate, express, imply, *indicare,* indicate, label, mark, mean, note, point out, portray, refer to, represent, show, signal, *significare,* signify, stand for, suggest, symbolize, tell the meaning of, token
ASSOCIATED CONCEPTS: denoting ownership, denoting possession

DENOUEMENT, *noun* apodosis, climax, close, closing, closure, completion, conclusion, consummation, *dénouement,* determination, development, disclosure, disentanglement, dissolution, end, ending, epilogue, eventuation, *fait accompli,* final happening, final statement, final touch, *finale,* finalization, finis, finish, finishing stroke, fruition,

159

issue, last act, outcome, outgrowth, *quietus,* realization, resolution, result, settlement, solution, summation, termination, *terminus,* unfolding, unraveling, unraveling of plot, unveiling, upshot, windup

DENOUNCE *(Condemn),* **verb** anathematize, animadvert, asperse, assail, assail with censure, assault, attack, be censorious, belittle, berate, besmear, besmirch, blackball, blacken, blacklist, brand, bring into discredit, bring to account, call to account, calumniate, cast a slur upon, cast aspersions, cast reflection upon, cast reproach upon, castigate, cavil, censure, challenge, chastise, chide, cite, comminate, condemn openly, contemn, criminate, criticize, criticize severely, cry down, cry out against, declaim against, decry, defame, deflate, degrade, denigrate, denunciate, deprecate, depreciate, derogate, destroy, detract, disapprove, discommend, discountenance, discredit, dishonor, disparage, dispraise, disvalue, dress down, excite disapprobation, exclaim against, excoriate, execrate, find fault with, frown upon, fulminate against, gibbet, impugn, inculpate, inveigh, lash, malign, ostracize, pass censure on, pillory, protest against, publicly accuse, put in a bad light, rebuke, recriminate, reflect upon, remonstrate, reprehend, reprimand, reproach, reprobate, revile, scold, slur, smear, speak ill of, stigmatize, take exception to, take to task, traduce, upbraid, vilify, vilipend, vituperate

DENOUNCE *(Inform against),* **verb** accuse, arraign, bear witness against, blame, bring accusation, bring charges, charge, complain against, divulge, hold accountable, hold responsible, impeach, implicate, impute, incriminate, inculpate, incur blame, indict, inform, inform on, involve, lay blame upon, lay charges against, lodge a complaint, make charges against, make formal accusation against, name, point at, publicly accuse, report against, turn informer

DENSITY, *noun* closeness, compactness, concentration, concretion, intransparency, opacity, opaqueness, palpability, solidity, thickness

DENUDE, *verb* bare, bring to light, defoliate, denudate, disclose, disfurnish, disrobe, divest, doff, exhibit, expose, flay, lay bare, lay open, lay waste, make naked, make public, manifest, open, pare, peel, present to view, publicize, reveal, shed, show, shuck, skin, slough, strip, tear off, uncase, uncloak, unclothe, uncover, uncurtain, undo, undrape, undress, unfold, unfrock, unrobe, unscreen, unsheathe, unshroud, unveil, unwrap, vent

DENUNCIATION, *noun* accusal, *accusatio,* accusation, anathema, aspersion, backbiting, blame, calumny, carping, castigation, censure, charge, chiding, commination, complaint, condemnation, contumely, *coup de bec,* criticism, damnation, decrial, defamation, *delatio,* delation, denigration, denouncement, deprecation, depreciation, derogation, detraction, diatribe, disapprobation, disapproval, discommendation, discountenance, disparagement, dispraise, excoriation, execration, *exposé,* faultfinding, fulmination, incrimination, inculpation, indictment, informing against, invective, malediction, objurgation, obloquy, opprobrium, philippic, plaint, rebuke, recrimination, reprehension, reprimand, reproach, reprobation, reproof, revilement, severe censure, slur, smear, stigmatization, stricture, tirade, tongue-lashing, traducement, upbraiding, utter disapproval, vehement condemnation, vilification, vituperation

DENY *(Contradict),* **verb** contravene, controvert, declare to be false, declare to be untrue, disaffirm, disagree, disallow, disavow, disclaim, disown, dispute, dissent, forswear, gainsay, *infitias ire, negare,* negate, refuse to acknowledge, refuse to admit, refuse to allow, reject as erroneous, repudiate, traverse

FOREIGN PHRASES: *Ei incumbit probatio, qui dicit, non qui negat; cum per rerum naturam factum negantis probatio nulla sit.* The burden of proof lies upon him who asserts it, not upon him who denies; since, by the nature of things, he who denies a fact cannot produce any proof of it.

DENY *(Refuse to grant),* **verb** abnegate, forbid, keep from, *negare,* prohibit, refuse to allow, refuse to bestow, refuse to give, refuse to permit, refuse to supply, reject, renege, renounce, withhold

ASSOCIATED CONCEPTS: deny a claim, deny a motion, deny a right, deny due process, deny liability

DEPART, **verb** abscond, absent oneself, be gone, decamp, desert, deviate, differ, digress, disappear, disassociate, *discedere,* disengage, disjoin, dissociate, diverge, divorce, emigrate, evacuate, exit, expatriate oneself, fade, flee, forsake, issue forth, leave, make an exit, march off, part, recede, resign, retire, set out, start out, swerve, vacate, vanish, vary from, withdraw

ASSOCIATED CONCEPTS: depart from scope of employment, depart from terms of a trust, depart from the state, departure in pleading, material departure

DEPARTMENT, *noun* agency, area, assignment, branch, bureau, categorization, category, chapter, class, classification, designation, district, division, domain, field, field of activity, jurisdiction, ministry, *munus, pars,* part, precinct, province, *provincia,* realm, section, sector, specialty, sphere, station, subdivision, subsection, zone

ASSOCIATED CONCEPTS: department of government, department of state, department rules and regulations, executive department, judicial department, legislative department, municipal department

DEPENDABLE, *adjective* assured, certain, conscientious, constant, devoted, faithful, guaranteed, incorrupt, loyal, proved, proven, reliable, reputable, responsible, solid, stable, staunch, steadfast, steady, sure, tested, tried, true, trustable, trusted, trustworthy, trusty, unchanging, unfailing, upright, veracious

ASSOCIATED CONCEPTS: dependable evidence

DEPENDENT, *adjective* ancillary, conditional, conditioned, contingent, controlled by, derivative, derived from, due to, evolved from, granted on certain terms, helpless, imposing a condition, incident to, limited, minor, modified by conditions, needing outside support, *obnoxius,* pendent, provisory, qualified, regulated by, reliant, restricted, resulting from, servile, subject, subject to, subordinate, subservient, sustained by, unable to exist without, weak

DEPENDENT, *noun* charge, child, helpless person, individual under guardianship, juvenile charge, minor, minor under guardianship, minor under protectorship, pensioner, person under guardianship, vassal, ward

ASSOCIATED CONCEPTS: actual dependent, dependent and neglected child, dependent person, dependent wife, lawful dependent, legal dependent, minor dependent, partial dependency, total dependency

DEPICT, *verb* characterize, communicate, connote, convey, delineate, *depingere,* describe, *describere,* detail, diagram, draw, *effingere,* embody, enunciate, evince, evoke, exemplify, exhibit, explain, explicate, express, give an account, give expression to, illuminate, illustrate, indicate, limn, manifest, outline, particularize, personify, picture, portray, recite, recount, relate, render an account, report, represent, reveal, set forth, show, signify, sketch, specify, symbolize, tell, tell vividly, typify

DEPLETE, *verb*   beggar, bleed, consume, decrease, dissipate, drain, drain of resources, dry up, eliminate, empty, empty out, evacuate, exhaust, expend, finish, impoverish, lessen, lose, pauperize, purge, reduce, render insufficient, run down, spend, unload, use up, void, waste, weaken, wear out

DEPLORABLE, *adjective*   afflicted, appalling, atrabilious, atrocious, bad, black, calamitous, catastrophic, demoralizing, depressing, depressive, despicable, dire, disagreeable, disastrous, disheartening, dismal, displeasing, distasteful, distressing, doleful, dolorous, dreadful, dreary, *flebilis,* frightful, ghastly, grievous, horrible, horrid, horrific, horrifying, insufferable, intolerable, lamentable, *miserabilis,* miserable, outrageous, pathetic, piteous, pitiable, pitiful, poor, regrettable, sad, shocking, sorrowful, sorry, terrible, tragic, tragical, unbearable, undesirable, unfortunate, unhappy, unpleasant, unpleasing, unsatisfactory, untoward, vile, wretched

DEPLORE, *verb*   be sorry for, bemoan, bewail, brood over, complain, cry over, *deflere, deplorare,* express deep grief for, fret over, grieve for, groan, lament, moan, mourn, regard with sorrow, regret, regret profoundly, repine, rue, shed tears over, show concern for, sigh for, sorrow over, view with regret, weep over

DEPLOY, *verb*   assign to battle stations, assign to positions, branch out, broaden, diffuse, *dilatare,* distribute, diverge, expand, *explicare,* extend, fan out, outspread, place, radiate, scatter, splay, spread, spread out in battle formation, stretch out, thin out, unfold, unfurl, widen

DEPONENT, *noun*   affiant, apprizer, attestant, attestator, attester, attestor, communicant, communicator, compurgator, enlightener, indicator, informant, informer, one who attests, one who bears witness, one who gives evidence, one who makes an affidavit, one who testifies under oath, party making an affidavit, reporter, swearer, teller, testifier, voucher, witness, witness who gives testimony
ASSOCIATED CONCEPTS: witness

DEPORT *(Banish), verb*   bar, cast out, dislodge, dismiss, displace, drive away, drive out, eject, evict, exclude, exile, expatriate, expel, extradite, force out, oust, outlaw, remove, send away, thrust out, transfer, transport, turn out

DEPORT *(Conduct oneself), verb*   acquit, act, bear oneself, behave, carry oneself, comport oneself

DEPORTATION, *noun*   banishment, casting out, dislocation, dismissal, displacement, driving out, ejection, ejectment, elimination, eviction, exclusion, exile, exilement, expatriation, expulsion, extradition, extrusion, forced departure, forced leave taking, ouster, purge, removal, riddance, sending away, thrusting out

DEPORTMENT, *noun*   actions, address, air, appearance, aspect, attitude, bearing, behavior, breeding, carriage, comportment, conduct, decorum, demeanor, dignity, guise, *habitus,* look, manner, mien, personal bearing, poise, port, posture, practice, presence, propriety, way, ways

DEPOSE *(Remove), verb*   cast away, cast out, demote, deprive of rank, dethrone, discard, discharge, discharge from office, disemploy, disentitle, disestablish, dislodge, dismiss, displace, dispossess, divest, drive out, drop, eject, evict, exile, expel, fire, impeach, *loco movere,* oust, oust from office, put out, put out of possession, recall, reduce, turn away, turn out, unseat, usurp

DEPOSE *(Testify), verb*   adduce, affirm, affirm under oath, asseverate, attest, aver, avouch, avow, bear witness to, certify, declare under oath, depone, give a solemn declaration, give an account of, give evidence, give proof, give proof by a witness, give sworn testimony, make an affidavit, make deposition, plead, profess, promise, relate, say under oath, swear, swear under oath, *testari, testificari,* verify, vouch, vouch for, witness
ASSOCIATED CONCEPTS: depose a witness

DEPOSIT, *noun*   accumulation, collateral, collateral security, *depositum,* down payment, earnest pledge, forfeit, gage, guarantee, installment, money in bank, part payment, pawn, payment, pledge, retainer, security, stake, surety
ASSOCIATED CONCEPTS: binder, certificate of deposit, earnest money, escrow, interpleader, savings deposit, security deposit, time deposit

DEPOSIT *(Place), verb*   *deponere,* dump, install, lay, locate, lodge, place in a receptacle, plant, put, quarter, reposit, rest, set, settle, situate, stash, store, stow

DEPOSIT *(Submit to a bank), verb*   bank, commit, enter into an account, entrust, invest, keep an account, lay by, present money for safekeeping, put at interest, save
ASSOCIATED CONCEPTS: interpleader, stake

DEPOSITION, *noun*   compurgation, declaration under oath, disclosure, documentation, oral evidence, oral statement under oath, proof by a witness, solemn declaration, statement on oath, statement under oath, sworn evidence, testification, testimonial, *testimonium,* testimony, transcript of testimony, vouching, written declaration under oath

DEPOSITORY, *noun*   *apotheca,* archives, bunker, cache, catchall, coffer, collection, container, depot, hold, holder, magazine, place for safe keeping, place of deposit, receptacle, *receptaculum,* repertory, repository, reservoir, safe, safe-deposit box, storage, store, storehouse, vault, warehouse
ASSOCIATED CONCEPTS: depository box, legal depository, reservoir

DEPRAVED, *adjective*   abominable, bad, base, base-minded, contemptible, corrupt, debased, debauched, degenerate, degraded, deteriorated, disreputable, dissipated, dissolute, evil, execrable, flagitious, foul, gross, heinous, horrendous, immeritorious, immoral, indecent, iniquitous, lecherous, lewd, licentious, low, low-minded, obscene, perverted, profligate, rank, ruined, salacious, shameful, shameless, sinful, unprincipled, unscrupulous, vile, vitiated, vulgar, warped, wicked
ASSOCIATED CONCEPTS: depraved act, depraved indifference, depraved mind

DEPRECATE, *verb*   *abominari,* asperse, belittle, berate, cast aspersions, charge, decry, demean, denigrate, denounce, deplore, derogate, detract, disapprove, disclaim, discommend, discredit, disdain, disfavor, dislike, disparage, dispraise, disvalue, excoriate, exprobate, fault, find fault, impugn, inculpate, object, objurgate, oppose, protest, reject, repudiate, traduce, view with disfavor, vilipend

DEPRECIATE, verb atrophy, attenuate, become deteriorated, become of less worth, belittle, censure, cheapen, contemn, corrode, cut, debase, debilitate, decay, decline, decrease, decry, deduct, defame, deflate, degenerate, degrade, denigrate, denounce, depress, deride, derogate from, deteriorate, detract from, *detrectare,* devaluate, devalue, dilute, diminish the price of, diminish the value of, discount, discredit, disesteem, disgrace, disparage, dispraise, drop, dwindle, ebb, enervate, enfeeble, erode, fall, fault, find fault with, get worse, grow less, grow worse, impoverish, lessen, lessen the price of, lose value, lower, lower in price, lower in reputation, lower in value, lower the value of, make little of, malign, minimize, misprize, *obtrectare,* readjust downward, reduce the purchasing value of, reduce the strength of, retrograde, run down, shrink, sink, slight, slur, soil, spoil, stain, sully, taint, take away, tarnish, traduce, underestimate, underpraise, underprize, underrate, underreckon, undervalue, weaken, wear, worsen
ASSOCIATED CONCEPTS: depreciate a loss, obsolescence

DEPREDATION, noun foray, havoc, marauding, raid, rapine, ravaging, sack, spoliation

DEPRESS, verb abase, bring down, bring low, cause to sink, cheapen, dampen, darken, decline, decrease, deflate, deject, depreciate, deteriorate, devaluate, devalue, diminish, discourage, dispirit, drop, ebb, flatten, indent, lessen, lower, make despondent, make sad, plunge, press down, reduce, sadden, shrink, sink, slump, squash, weaken

DEPRESSION, noun debasement, decline, deflation, dejection, depreciation, despondence, despondency, disheartenment, dispiritedness, dolefulness, economic decline, gloom, lowering, lowness, *maeror,* sinking, slump, *tristitia*
ASSOCIATED CONCEPTS: economic depression

DEPRIVE, verb arrogate, attach, bereave, capture, commandeer, confiscate, convert, denude, despoil, disendow, disentitle, disherit, disinherit, disown, dispossess, disseize, distrain, divest, expropriate, extort, fleece, foreclose, impound, impoverish, leave destitute, mulct, pauperize, purloin, rob, seize, sequester, sequestrate, steal, strip, take away, tear away, usurp, wrench, wrest
ASSOCIATED CONCEPTS: deprivation of liberty, deprivation of property, deprivation of right, deprive of employment, deprive of life, deprived of liberty, deprived of substantial right
FOREIGN PHRASES: **Privatio praesupponit habitum.** A deprivation presupposes something possessed.

DEPUTATION (Delegation), **noun** agents, body of delegates, body of representatives, commissaries, commission, committee, consulate, delegates, delegation, emissaries, envoys, factors, *legati, legatio,* legation, mission, plenipotentiaries, proxies, representation, representatives

DEPUTATION (Selection of delegates), **noun** appointing, appointment, assignment, authorization, authorizing, commission, conferment, delegation, deputization, designation, devolution, empowering, entrustment, installation, investiture, investment, nomination, procuration

DEPUTY, noun agent, alternate, ambassador, appointee, assignee, broker, commissary, commissioner, delegate, emissary, envoy, factor, intermediary, *legatus,* lieutenant, minister, plenipotentiary, proctor, procurator, proxy, representative, second, secondary, substitute, surrogate, vicar, vicarius, vicegerent

ASSOCIATED CONCEPTS: de facto deputy, deputy commissioner, deputy marshal, deputy officer, deputy sheriff, general deputy, special deputy
FOREIGN PHRASES: **Vicarius non habet vicarium.** A deputy cannot have a deputy.

DERANGED, adjective bereft of reason, confused, *demens,* demented, disarranged, disconcerted, disjointed, dislocated, disordered, disorganized, displaced, dissonant, distraught, frenetic, frenzied, in disorder, incompetent, inconsistent, insane, *insanus,* insensate, mad, maddened, maniacal, of unsound mind, rabid, reasonless, unbalanced, unsettled

DERELICT (Abandoned), **adjective** adrift, avoided, cast aside, cast off, castaway, deserted, desolate, discarded, disowned, dispensed with, excluded, forgotten, forlorn, forsaken, friendless, given up, helpless, homeless, ignored, isolated, jettisoned, left, lonely, lonesome, neglected, on the fringe of society, outcast, rejected, relinquished, repudiated, scorned, scrapped, set adrift, shunned, solitary, thrown overboard, uncared for, unclaimed, unfortunate, unfriended, unowned, unpossessed, unwanted, wretched, written off
ASSOCIATED CONCEPTS: derelict property

DERELICT (Negligent), **adjective** careless, delinquent, disregardful, dutiless, failing in duty, faithless, faulty, heedless, improvident, inattentive, inconsiderate, indifferent, lax, neglectful, neglecting, regardless, remiss, slack, thoughtless, uncircumspect, unconcerned, unfaithful, unheedful, unheeding, uninterested, unmindful, unobservant, unwatchful

DERELICT, noun displaced person, drifter, exile, fugitive, ne'er-do-well, outcast, pariah, scamp, tramper, vagrant, wanderer, wastrel

DERELICTION, noun abandonment, breach, carelessness, *culpa,* default, defection, delinquency, desertion, disregard, dutilessness, evasion, failure in duty, faithlessness, heedlessness, indifference, laxity, laxness, misprision, neglect, neglectfulness, negligence, noncooperation, nonfeasance, nonobservence, nonperformance, omission, relinquishment, remissness, truancy, unconcern, unfaithfulness
ASSOCIATED CONCEPTS: dereliction of duty, moral dereliction

DERIVATION, noun ancestor, ancestry, antecedent, author, authority, base, basis, begetter, beginning, birth, birthplace, causality, causation, cause, commencement, creator, descent, determinant, extraction, family, first cause, first occasion, foundation, fount, fountainhead, generator, genesis, ground, head, inception, issue, line, lineage, mainspring, origin, origination, parent, parentage, prime motive, primogenitor, producer, progenitor, provenance, provenience, reference, root, source, source material, spring, springhead, starting point, stem, stock, tracing back, ultimate cause

DERIVATIVE, adjective ascribable, attributable, caused, coming from, consequent, consequential, derivate, derivational, derived, deriving, descendant, descended, ensuing, evolved, following, hereditary, imitative, resultant, resulting, secondary, sequent, subordinate, subsequent, subsidiary, vicarious
ASSOCIATED CONCEPTS: derivative action, derivative authority, derivative deed, derivative jurisdiction, derivative liabilities, derivative powers, derivative rights, derivative stockholder's suit, derivative title

DERIVATIVE WORK, *noun*   consequential work, corollary work, ensuing work, resulting work, secondary work, subsequent work

DERIVE *(Deduce)*, *verb*   conclude, construe, *deducere*, draw a conclusion, draw an inference, extract, infer, make a deduction, obtain by reasoning, reason, theorize, trace

DERIVE *(Receive)*, *verb*   acquire, come into possession, draw from, extract, get, glean, obtain, procure, secure, take, *trahere*

DEROGATE, *verb*   abase, asperse, be derogatory, belittle, besmirch, bespatter, blacken, blot, brand, bring down, bring into discredit, bring low, bring shame upon, calumniate, cast a slur upon, cast aspersions, debase, decry, defame, demean, demote, denigrate, depreciate, depress, deprive, *derogare*, detract, *detrahere*, diminish, discredit, disgrace, dishonor, disparage, dispraise, disprize, disrate, humble, incur disgrace, lessen, lessen the reputation of, lower, make ashamed, make little of, make lowly, make smaller, malign, misprize, not do justice to, pull down, put down, reduce, revile, ridicule, run down, scoff, shame, smirch, sneer at, speak evil of, speak ill of, speak slightingly of, stain, subtract from, sully, taint, take something from, tarnish, traduce, underestimate, underrate, underreckon, undervalue, vilify, vilipend, weaken
ASSOCIATED CONCEPTS: derogation of common law, derogation of deed, derogation of right

DEROGATORY, *adjective*   belittling, calumniatory, calumnious, censorious, condemnatory, contumelious, defamatory, denunciatory, deprecatory, depreciative, depreciatory, detracting, detractory, disapprobatory, disapproving, discrediting, disdainful, dishonoring, disparaging, faultfinding, injurious, lessening, libelous, objurgatory, pejorative, slanderous, slighting, uncomplimentary, unfavorable, unflattering
ASSOCIATED CONCEPTS: derogatory statements
FOREIGN PHRASES: *Quae legi communi derogant stricte interpretantur.* Those things which derogate from the common law are strictly interpreted. *Quae legi communi derogant non sunt trahenda in exemplum.* Those things which derogate from the common law are not to be drawn into precedent.

DESCEND, *verb*   bequeath, bestow, come down by transmission, come down lineally, deed, demise, *descendere*, endow, entrust, give, give by will, grant, hand down, hand on, leave a legacy, make a bequest, make a legacy, pass by devise, pass by inheritance, pass by operation of law, pass by succession, pass down from generation to generation, pass on, settle upon, transmit, will, will and bequeath

DESCENDANT, *noun*   child, family, future generation, heir, issue, kin, lineage, offshoot, offspring, posterity, progeny, scion, succeeding generation, successor
ASSOCIATED CONCEPTS: descendants of the line, direct descendant, lawful descendants, lineal descendant or heir, lineal descendants

DESCENT *(Declination)*, *noun*   change from higher to lower, comedown, coming down, downrush, droop, drop, falling, going down, inclination downward, lapse, settlement, sinking, subsidence

DESCENT *(Lineage)*, *noun*   ancestry, birth, birthright, blood, bloodline, breed, clan, derivation, dynasty, extraction, family tree, filiation, genealogy, heredity, heritage, kin, line, line of ancestors, origin, parentage, paternity, pedigree, race, stock, strain
ASSOCIATED CONCEPTS: ancestors, collateral descent, descendants, line of descent, right and interest by descent, title by descent

DESCRIBE, *verb*   annotate, be specific, characterize, clarify, define, delineate, depict, *depingere, describere*, detail, elucidate, explain, *explicare*, expound, give an account, identify, illuminate, illustrate, itemize, make clear, make plain, make vivid, outline, paint, particularize, picture, portray, portray in words, represent by words, specify, spell out
ASSOCIATED CONCEPTS: falsely describe

DESCRIPTION, *noun*   account, characterization, definition, delineation, depiction, *descriptio*, details, *enarratio*, explanation, *expositio*, formulation, narrative, outline, particulars, portrayal, profile, sketch, specification
ASSOCIATED CONCEPTS: correct description, description in a will, description of goods, description of land, description of persons, description of property, specific description
FOREIGN PHRASES: *Veritas demonstrationis tollit errorem nominis.* In all penal judgments, allowance is made for youth and lack of prudence. *Falsa demonstratione legatum non perimi.* A legacy is not nullified by an incorrect description. *Praesentia corporis tollit errorem nominis; et veritas nominis tollit errorem demonstrationis.* The presence of the body cures an error in the name; and the accuracy of the name cures an error of description. *Non accipi debent verba in demonstrationem falsam, quae competunt in limitationem veram.* Words ought not to be taken to import a false description which may be taken to describe a true limitation.

DESCRIPTIVE, *adjective*   characterizing, circumstantial, classificatory, clear, definitional, definitive, delineative, designating, detailed, eloquent, explanatory, explicatory, expositive, expository, graphic, identifying, illuminating, illuminative, illustrative, interpretive, lifelike, narrative, particularized, photographic, pictorial, realistic, representational, representative, revealing, specific, true to life, vivid, well-drawn
ASSOCIATED CONCEPTS: descriptive calls, descriptive term, descriptive trade name, descriptive trademark, descriptive word

DESEGREGATE, *verb*   admix, agglomerate, amalgamate, assimilate, associate, band, be mixed, blend, coalesce, combine racially, combine with, commingle, commix, compound, confederate, conglomerate, conjoin, connect, consolidate, eliminate racial segregation, fuse, incorporate, institute commingling of races, integrate, interblend, interfuse, interlace, interlard, intermingle, intermix, join together, make no racial distinctions, mass, meld, merge, merge in, mingle, mix, promote racial harmony, promote racial mixing, to bring together, unify, unite

DESERTION, *noun*   abandonment, abandonment of allegiance, abjuration, absence without leave, act of forsaking, apostasy, AWOL, defection, departure, *derelictio*, disaffection, disloyalty, flight, forsaking, forswearing, leaving, mutiny, quitting, recreancy, renouncement, renunciation, repudiation, resignation, secession, unlawful departure, willful abandonment
ASSOCIATED CONCEPTS: constructive desertion, willful desertion

DESIDERATUM, *noun*   aim, ambition, aspiration, desideration, desire, essential object of desire, exigency, goal, necessary, necessity, need, objective, requirement, requisite, requisition, want

DESIGN *(Construction plan)*, ***noun***   blueprint, chart, conception, delineation, depiction, *descriptio*, diagram, draft, drawing, *forma*, graph, layout, *lineamenta*, map, model, outline, picture, plan, preliminary drawing, projection, proof, rendering, representation, rough cast, rough copy, rough representation, skeleton, sketch, treatment

DESIGN *(Intent)*, ***noun***   aim, ambition, animus, approach, aspiration, bent, *consilium, consulto*, contemplation, course of action, desire, destination, determination, direction, end, end in view, expectation, fixed purpose, forethought, goal, hope, inclination, intention, intentionality, meaning, mission, motive, object, objective, plan, plan of attack, predetermination, projected goal, proposed action, proposed sequence of action, purport, purpose, purpose in view, pursuit, resolve, scheme, set purpose, settled purpose, stratagem, strategy, target, ultimate end, view, way of doing things, will
ASSOCIATED CONCEPTS: common design, formed design, premeditated design

DESIGNATE, *verb*   appoint, assign, authorize, be specific, characterize, choose, commission, declare, define, denominate, denote, *designare*, detail, determine, discriminate, earmark, enter into detail, entitle, express, fix, formulate, indicate, itemize, mark, mark out, mention, name, *nominare*, nominate, *notare*, note, particularize, pinpoint, point out, select, set, set apart, set aside, show, signify, specify, stipulate
ASSOCIATED CONCEPTS: designate as a beneficiary, designate as an agent, designate as an executor

DESIGNATION *(Naming)*, ***noun***   appellation, appointment, approval, assigning, assignment, authorization, calling, categorization, choosing, commissioning, delegating, delegation, denomination, denotation, deputation, description, *designatio*, fixing, identification, indication, installation, label, ordainment, ordination, particularization, placing in office, pointing out, selection, signification, specification, stipulation
ASSOCIATED CONCEPTS: designated agent, designated document, designation of beneficiary

DESIGNATION *(Symbol)*, ***noun***   badge, cipher, distinguishing mark, earmark, emblem, hallmark, identification mark, indicator, indicium, initial, insignia, label, mark, name, representation, sign, standard, title, token, totem, trademark, type

DESIRABLE *(Pleasing)*, ***adjective***   enjoyable, gratifying, pleasant, pleasurable, pleasureful, welcome

DESIRABLE *(Qualified)*, ***adjective***   acceptable, eligible, entitled, qualified, recommendable, suitable, worthy

DESIRE, *noun*   ambition, appetency, appetite, *appetitio*, ardent impulse, ardor, aspiration, attraction, avidity, bent, concupiscence, covetousness, craving, *cupiditas*, cupidity, *desiderium*, eagerness, fancy, fondness, hankering, hunger, impulse, inclination, liking, longing, lust, motive, predilection, proclivity, propensity, rapaciousness, thirst, urge, want, will, wish, yearning, yen
ASSOCIATED CONCEPTS: precatory words

DESIRE, *verb*   apply for, ask, ask for, aspire, be after, be bent upon, be eager, beg a favor, call for, clamor for, covet, crave, cry out for, cupere, desiderare, desiderate, entreat, *expetere*, express a wish to obtain, have a proclivity, have a yearning, have an appetite, have an impulse, have designs on, have one's heart set on, hope for, incline, like to, long for, make a request for, make application for, press, pursue, put in a claim for, request, solicit, supplicate, urge, want, wish for
ASSOCIATED CONCEPTS: precatory words

DESIST, *verb*   abstain, arrest, be quiescent, call off, cease, check, *desinere, desistere*, discontinue, end, finish, forbear, freeze, halt, hold, intermit, interrupt, leave off, make inactive, put a stop to, refrain, repose, rest, stand, stay, stop, surcease, suspend, terminate
ASSOCIATED CONCEPTS: cease and desist order

DESPISE, *verb*   abhor, abominate, be hostile to, be inimical toward, bear malice toward, detest, disfavor, dislike, execrate, feel hostile toward, hate, have an aversion toward, have animus toward, have aversion to, have contempt for, have ill will toward, loathe, resent

DESPOIL, *verb*   assail, attack, bereave, consume, denude, deplume, depredate, deprive, desolate, devastate, devour, dispossess, divest, forage, foray, impoverish, invade, lay waste, leave destitute, loot, make off with, maraud, overrun, pilfer, pillage, plunder, purloin, raid, ransack, ravage, raven, rifle, rob, ruin, ruinate, sack, seize, spoliate, steal, strip, take, take by force, thieve, wreck

DESPONDENT, *adjective*   aggrieved, beaten, defeated, defeatist, dejected, depressed, desolate, despairing, disconsolate, dismal, dispirited, dolorous, downcast, dreary, gloomy, hopeless, in despair, inconsolable, joyless, listless, lugubrious, melancholic, melancholy, moody, mournful, pessimistic, rueful, sad, sluggish, somber, sorrowful, sullen, unhappy, unhopeful

DESTINATION, *noun*   aim, aspiration, bourn, conclusion, consummation, debarkation point, destiny, end, end result, ending, finish, goal, intent, intention, journey's end, last stop, object, objective, planned place of arrival, point of cessation, point of disembarkation, port, purpose, resting place, result, stop, stopping-place, target, terminal, terminal point, termination, terminus
ASSOCIATED CONCEPTS: destination contracts, final destination, place of destination, point of destination

DESTITUTE, *adjective*   bankrupt, beggarly, bereft, depleted, deprived, distressed, impecunious, impoverished, indigent, *inops*, insolvent, lacking funds, moneyless, necessitous, needful, needy, out of money, penniless, poor, poverty-stricken, reduced in means, short of money, squalid, unmoneyed, wanting, without resources
ASSOCIATED CONCEPTS: destitute children, destitute of means of support, destitute of property, destitute persons

DESTROY *(Efface)*, ***verb***   abort, annihilate, blast, blight, blot out, break to pieces, bring to ruin, burn, consume, corrode, deal destruction, decimate, deface, demolish, desolate, destruct, *destruere*, devastate, devour, *diruere*, disintegrate, dissolve, do away with, eliminate, eradicate, erase, expunge, exterminate, extinguish, extirpate, gut, incinerate, kill, lay waste, level, liquidate, murder, mutilate, obliterate, overthrow, overturn, *perdere*, pulverize, put to death, quell, ravage, raze, reduce to nothing, rend, root out, rub out, ruin, ruinate, scratch out, slay, subvert, uproot, waste, wipe out, wreck

ASSOCIATED CONCEPTS: destroy a will, fraudulently destroyed, lost or destroyed

DESTROY *(Void)*, **verb**   abolish, annul, break up, bring to naught, completely end, dismantle, extinguish, invalidate, make null, nullify, put an end to, render ineffective, terminate, unmake

ASSOCIATED CONCEPTS: destruction of contingent remainders

DESTRUCTIBLE, adjective   accessible, assailable, breakable, delicate, depletable, destroyable, dissolvable, eradicable, exhaustible, extinguishable, ruinable, scissile, unsafe, vulnerable

DESTRUCTION, noun   abolition, annihilation, breaking down, collapse, consumption, decimation, decomposition, demolishment, demolition, devastation, dissolution, eradication, extinction, extirpation, nullification, obliteration, perdition, ruin, ruination, tearing down, undoing, unmaking

ASSOCIATED CONCEPTS: destruction of business, destruction of records, total destruction, willful destruction

FOREIGN PHRASES: *Res perilt domino.* A thing which has been destroyed is lost to its owner.

DESTRUCTIVE, adjective   annihilating, baleful, damaging, destroying, detrimental, feral, harmful, injurious, internecine, malign, miasmal, miasmatic, miasmic, pernicious

DESUETUDE, noun   abandonment, abeyance, abrogation, absence, abstention, archaism, arrest, cancellation, cessation, desistance, *desuetudo,* discarding, discontinuance, disusage, disuse, dormancy, failure to use, halt, idleness, impotence, inaction, inactivity, inanimation, inertia, inusitation, inutility, neglect, nonavailability, nonobservance, nonretention, nonuse, obsolescence, obsoleteness, omission, relinquishment, stagnation, standstill, state of being unused, stop, stoppage, stoppage of use, surrender, suspension, termination

DESULTORY, adjective   broken, deviating, diffuse, digressive, disarranged, disconnected, discontinuous, discursive, disjoined, disjunct, dispersed, erratic, inconsistent, *inconstans,* inconstant, interrupted, lacking continuity, nonrecurrent, nonuniform, rambling, random, spasmodic, uncohesive, unconnected, unmethodical, unrepeated, unsuccessive, unsystematic, varying

DETACH, verb   break off, cleave, disconnect, disengage, disentangle, *disiungere,* disjoin, dispart, dissever, dissociate, disunite, divide, divorce, part, remove, *seiungere, separare,* separate, sever, split, uncouple, unfasten, unlink, unplug, unstick

ASSOCIATED CONCEPTS: detached dwelling houses, detached pages in a will

DETAIL, noun   aspect, circumstance, circumstantiality, component, component part, division, element, feature, fractional part, fragment, individual part, ingredient, instance, integral part, integrant, item, minor part, minute part, part, particular, particularity, piece, point, portion, section, *singula,* special point, specification, subdivision, technicality, trivia

DETAIL *(Assign)*, **verb**   allocate, appoint, authorize, bid, call, charge, command, commission, compel, consign,

decree, delegate, demand, depute, designate, devolve, dictate, distribute, empower, enjoin, entrust, impose, obligate, oblige, order, prescribe, relegate

DETAIL *(Particularize)*, **verb**   amplify, analyze, be precise, catalogue, chronicle, circumstantiate, clarify, delineate, depict, describe, draw, elucidate, enumerate, explain, give an account, give details, go into the particulars, illuminate, illustrate, individualize, itemize, make clear, make vivid, narrate, particularize, picture, portray, recite, recount, relate, report, set forth, show, specify, tell, tell details, tell fully, tell particulars

DETAILED, adjective   accounted, accurate, all-inclusive, annotated, complete, comprehensive, delineated, described, descriptive, elaborated, enumerated, exact, exhaustive, explicit, full of details, graphic, inclusive, itemized, meticulous, minute, particular, particularized, plenary, precise, punctilious, replete, representational, specific, thorough, total, vivid, whole

ASSOCIATED CONCEPTS: detailed account, detailed audit, detailed report, detailed statement

DETAILS, noun   circumstances, contents, counts, description, distinct parts, fine points, intelligence, items, minor circumstances, minutiae, niceties, particulars, special points, specifics, trivialities

DETAIN *(Hold in custody)*, **verb**   apprehend, arrest, capture, commit, confine, contain, control, enthrall, guard, hold, hold captive, hold in check, hold in preventive custody, hold in thrall, hold under duress, immure, impound, imprison, incarcerate, intern, isolate, jail, keep in custody, keep in detention, keep under arrest, keep under control, keep within bounds, lock up, mure, pen, place in durance, put under arrest, put under restraint, quarantine, remand, retain, secure, shut in, surround, take captive, take into custody, take prisoner, trammel

ASSOCIATED CONCEPTS: detained in custody, detained in jail

DETAIN *(Restrain)*, **verb**   arrest, bind, bound, chain, check, circumscribe, confine, constrain, contain, control, curb, delay, encumber, fetter, filibuster, forestall, gyve, halt, hamper, hinder, hold back, hold up, impede, inhibit, keep, keep back, keep under control, keep within bounds, lay under restraint, limit, manacle, obstruct, prevent, rein in, restrict, *retinere,* shackle, stall, stay, stop, suppress, *tenere, trammel*

ASSOCIATED CONCEPTS: unlawfully detained

DETAINER, noun   detainment, illegal custody, illegal detention, illegal restraint, illegal withholding, unlawful detention, unlawful restriction, unlawful retention, wrongful impoundment, wrongful keeping

DETECT, verb   be conscious of, become aware of, behold, bring to light, decipher, deduce, descry, determine, diagnose, diagnosticate, discern, discover, disinter, distinguish, divine, educe, espy, expose, extract, feel, ferret out, find, find out, gain knowledge, identify, learn, locate, make out, notice, observe, *patefacere,* perceive, realize, recognize, *rem invenire, reperire,* reveal, see, sense, sight, spot, trace, track, uncover, unearth, unmask, unravel, unveil, view

DETECTION, noun   apprehension, ascertainment, disclosure, discovery, exposure, finding, learning, perception, sighting, spotting, unearthing, unfolding

DETECTIVE, noun agent, criminologist, espier, examinant, examiner, indagator, inquirer, inquiry agent, inquisitor, inspector, investigator, prober
ASSOCIATED CONCEPTS: police detectives, private detective

DETENTION, noun arrest, captivity, circumscription, committal, commitment, confinement, constraint, control, *custodia,* custodianship, custody, detainment, durance vile, fetter, guardianship, immuration, immurement, impoundment, imprisonment, incarceration, internment, keeping, keeping back, keeping in, keeping in custody, legal restraint, limitation, preventive custody, prison, protective custody, quarantine, restraint, restriction, restriction on movement, retentio
ASSOCIATED CONCEPTS: detention facility, detention of property, illegal detention, lawful detention, preventive detention
FOREIGN PHRASES: Furtum non est ubi initium habet detentionis per dominium rei. It is not theft where the commencement of the detention arises through the consent of the owner.

DETER, verb *absterrere,* avert, avoid, ban, bar, barricade, block, blunt, caution, check, chill, circumscribe, constrict, cow, cramp, cumber, dampen, deflect, deny access, *deterrere,* detour, discommode, discountenance, discourage, disenchant, disencourage, dishearten, disincline, dismay, dissuade, divert, divert from, fend, fend off, fetter, foil, forbid, foreclose, forestall, forefend, frustrate, hamper, hamstring, hinder, hold back, hold up, impede, incommode, indispose, inhibit, interclude, interfere with, intimidate, keep back, keep from, keep off, limit, nip in the bud, obstruct, obturate, obviate, overawe, persuade against, put a stop to, put off, quell, quench, remonstrate, render averse, repel, repress, reprove, restrain, restrict, rule out, set one back, shake one's faith, stave off, stop, stultify, thwart, turn aside, undermine one's belief, ward off, warn
ASSOCIATED CONCEPTS: deter from crime

DETERIORATE, verb adulterate, aggravate, atrophy, become worse, collapse, corrode, *corrumpere,* corrupt, debase, debauch, debilitate, decay, decline, decompose, decrease, defile, degenerate, degrade, demoralize, denature, *depravare,* depreciate, devalue, dilapidate, downgrade, ebb, lapse, lower, pervert, pollute, prostitute, regress, retrograde, retrogress, spoil, taint, vitiate, wane, waste, weaken, worsen
ASSOCIATED CONCEPTS: deteriorating building, deteriorating goods

DETERIORATION, noun abasement, abrasion, atrophy, caducity, consumption, corrosion, corruption, debasement, decadence, decay, declension, declination, decomposition, decrepitude, degradation, demission, depreciation, destruction, *deterior condicio,* dilapidation, disintegration, disrepair, emaciation, erosion, gradual decline, gradual impairment, impairment, irrepair, putrefaction, putridity, reduction, retrogradation, retrogression, ruin, ruination, senescence, spoliation, unrepair
ASSOCIATED CONCEPTS: property deterioration

DETERMINABLE *(Ascertainable),* **adjective** accountable, admitting of decision, amenable to measurement, appraisable, appreciable, assessable, capable of decision, certifiable, cognizable, computable, construable, countable, decipherable, deducible, definable, detectible, discernible, discoverable, distinguishable, estimable, explainable, explicable, fathomable, fixable, gaugeable, interpretable, judicable, knowable, measurable, mensurable, noticeable, observable, perceivable, perceptible, resolvable, solvable, subject to measurement, surveyable, that may be determined, translatable, verifiable, workable
ASSOCIATED CONCEPTS: determinable period of usefulness
FOREIGN PHRASES: Terminus annorum certus debet esse et determinatus. A term of years ought to be certain and determinate.

DETERMINABLE *(Liable to be terminated),* **adjective** approaching an end, approaching the finish, coming to an end, drawing to a close, having the possibility of termination, liable to be completed, liable to be discontinued, liable to be dropped, liable to be ended, liable to come to an end, liable to expire, nearing completion, subject to be concluded, subject to cancellation, subject to discontinuance, subject to termination, terminable, with the end in sight
ASSOCIATED CONCEPTS: determinable fee, determinable interest, determinable remainder in fee

DETERMINANT, noun agent, authority, background, base, basis, consideration, constitutive element, contributing force, contributor, decisive factor, determining circumstance, determining element, determining influence, driving force, element, factor, fomentor, generator, genesis, impetus, inducement, instigation, justification, leaven, means, medium, motivation, motive, object, origin, prime mover, producer, root, source, ultimate cause, ultimate motive

DETERMINATION, noun adjudgment, adjudication, appraisal, appraisement, appreciation, apprisement, apprizement, *arbitrium,* ascertainment, assessment, authoritative estimate, authoritative opinion, award, conclusion, consideration, considered opinion, *consilium,* conviction, court decision, decision, declaration, decree, diagnosis, evaluation, final assessment, finding, *institutum, iudicium,* judgment, judgment on facts, opinion, order, pronouncement, reasoned judgment, reckoning, recommendation, resolution, resolve, result, result ascertained, ruling, sentence, settlement, solution, verdict
ASSOCIATED CONCEPTS: actual determination, determination of a suit, determination of claims, determination of fact, determination of guilt, final determination, judicial determination, official determination, review a determination, self-determination
FOREIGN PHRASES: Judicia in deliberationibus crebro maturescunt, in accelerato processu nunquam. Judgments frequently mature by deliberations, never by hurried process. **De audiendo et terminando.** To hear and determine. **In propria causa nemo judex.** No one can be judge in his own case.

DETERMINATION OF DAMAGES, noun adjudication, assessment, award, award judgment, compensation, finding, grant, inquest, judgment, penalization, penalty, relief, remuneration

DETERMINATIVE, adjective authoritative, conclusive, convincing, deciding, decisive, decretal, definitive, directing, *ex parte,* final, important, judgmatic, judicious, limiting, limitive, persuasive, shaping, significant, telling, weighty

DETERMINE, verb adjudge, adjudicate, arrive at a conclusion, ascertain, award, bring in a verdict, bring to an end, bring to justice, choose, come to a conclusion, come to a decision, come to a determination, conclude, confirm, *constituere, decernere,* decide, decide upon, declare, decree, decree by judicial authority, deduce, delimit, deliver judgment, direct, draw a conclusion, end by a decision, estimate, exercise the judgment, find, fix upon, form a judgment, form a resolution, give a ruling, give an opinion, give judgment, hold, infer, interpret, judge, limit, make a decision, make a resolution, make one's choice, make terms, make up one's mind, opine, pass an opinion, pass judgment, pass sentence, prescribe punishment, pronounce, pronounce a judgment, pronounce guilty, reckon, referee, regulate, remain firm, resolve, rule, seal, seal the doom of, settle, settle in one's mind, settle upon, sit in judgment, *statuere*, stipulate, take a decisive step, utter judicial sentence against, weigh, will

ASSOCIATED CONCEPTS: determine the nature of the loss, finally determined, legally determine the rights of the parties to an action

DETERMINED (Certain), *adjective*   ascertained, attested, authenticated, certified, conditioned, confined, confirmed, definite, established, finite, firm, fixed, indomitable, industrious, inexorable, inflexible, intentional, peremptory, positive, prescriptive, qualified, set, settled, substantial, unalterable, uncompromising, validated

DETERMINED (Strong-willed), *adjective*   decided, deliberate, dogged, earnest, obdurate, obstinate, persistent, pertinacious, purposeful, relentless, resolute, resolved, serious, Spartan, staunch, steadfast, stubborn, unfaltering, unflinching, unwavering, unyielding

DETERMINING, *adjective*   absolute, acute, binding, cardinal, certain, complete, conclusive, contributory, critical, crucial, deciding, decisive, definitive, determinate, fateful, final, important, key, momentous, pivotal, prevailing, primary, ultimate

DETERRENCE, *noun*   abridgment, active discouragement, admonition, barrier, block, blockade, caveat, check, compulsion, constraint, constriction, contraindication, *contretemps,* control, curb, detainment, deterrent, discouragement, disincentive, dissuasion, extinguishment, forestalling, frustration, halt, hindrance, hurdle, impediment, impedition, inhibition, interference, intimidation, legal restraint, limitation, means of restraint, monition, obstacle, obstruction, opposition, preclusion, prevention, prohibition, prophylaxis, proscription, quashing, repression, resistance, restraint, restriction, stop, striction, stumbling block, suppression, thwarter

ASSOCIATED CONCEPTS: deterrence of crime

FOREIGN PHRASES: *Nemo prudens punit ut praeterita revocentur, sed ut futura praeveniantur.* No wise man punishes in order that past things may be revoked, but that future wrongs may be prevented. *Poena ad paucos, metus ad omnes perveniat.* If punishment be inflicted on a few, a fear comes to all.

DETERRENT, *noun*   admonishment, admonition, barrier, barring, block, caution, caveat, constraint, constriction, contraindication, counteraction, counterpressure, curb, damper, deactivation, determent, deterrence, discouragement, disincentive, dissuasion, forestalling, hampering, hinderer, hindrance, hurdle, impedance, impeder, inhibition, inhibitor, insuperable obstacle, interference, interposition, intimidation, legal restraint, limitation, means of restraint, monition, obstacle, obstructer, obstruction, obstructive, obtrusion, occlusion, opposition, preclusion, prevention, proscription, repression, restraint, restriction, retardation, suppression, thwarter, warning

DETOUR, *noun*   alternate route, by-pass, by-passage, circuitous route, deflection, departure, deviation, deviation from a direct course, digression, diversion, excursion, indirect path, loop, roundabout course, temporary route, wrong course

ASSOCIATED CONCEPTS: detour from course of employment, frolic and detour

DETOUR, *verb*   *aberrare,* alter one's course, avoid, bypass, change direction, change the bearing, circuit, circumambulate, deflect, depart from, depart from one's course, deviate, deviate from a direct course, *digredi,* digress, diverge, divert, divert from its course, drift, encircle, excurse, go around, go out, go out of one's way, go out of the path, go out of the way, go round about, make a circuit, meander, perform a circuit, ramble, sidestep, skirt, stray, swerve, take a circuitous route, take a roundabout course, take a temporary route, take an alternate highway, take an alternate route, take an indirect way, turn aside, vary, veer

ASSOCIATED CONCEPTS: detour from course of employment, frolick and detour

DETRACT, *verb*   abate, belittle, blacken, blame, decrease, decry, defame, denigrate, depreciate, derogate, deteriorate, diminish, discommend, discount, disparage, distract, divert, draw away, lessen, lower, malign, minimize

DETRIMENT, *noun*   adulteration, adversity, affliction, aggravation, atrophy, bane, bedevilment, blemish, blow, collapse, contamination, corrosion, corruption, cost, crippling, damage, *damnum,* decadence, decay, deformation, degeneration, demolishment, deprivation, destruction, deterioration, detraction, *detrimentum,* dilapidation, disability, disablement, disadvantage, disintegration, disorder, disturbance, erosion, evil, forfeit, forfeiture, handicap, hardship, harm, hurt, impairment, impotence, inadequacy, inadvisability, *incommodum,* inconvenience, ineffectualness, inefficiency, inexpedience, inexpediency, injuriousness, injury, insufficiency, laming, liability, loss, misfortune, mutilation, obstacle, poisoning, pollution, prejudice, privation, ruin, ruination, undesirability, undoing, unprofitability, weakness

ASSOCIATED CONCEPTS: legal detriment

DETRIMENTAL, *adjective*   adverse, afflicting, bad, corrupting, crippling, damaging, deleterious, destructive, disadvantageous, disastrous, discommodious, distressing, disturbing, dreadful, extirpative, fulsome, grievous, harmful, hindering, hurtful, ill-advised, ill-contrived, impolitic, inappropriate, inimical, *iniquus,* injurious, inopportune, insalubrious, insidious, internecine, malefic, malignant, noisome, noxious, oppressive, *perniciosus,* pernicious, pestilential, prejudicial, toxic, treacherous, undermining, unfit, unhealthy, unhelpful, unprofitable, unpropitious, unsatisfactory, unsuitable, untoward, unwholesome, unwise

ASSOCIATED CONCEPTS: actively detrimental, detrimental to the best interests of the child, detrimental to the public interest

DEVALUE, *verb*   adulterate, belittle, cheapen, contaminate, corrupt, damage, debase, debauch, defile, degenerate, degrade, denature, depreciate, depress, deteriorate, dilute, disable, disparage, impair, pollute, reduce, taint

DEVASTATE, *verb*   demolish, depopulate, depredate, desolate, despoil, destroy, gut, lever, overwhelm, pillage, plunder, raid, ransack, ravage, raze, ruin, sack, wreck

DEVELOP, *verb*   accrue, *adolescere,* advance, advance in successive gradation, *alere,* amplify, arise from, *augeri,* augment, become, become apparent, begin from, bring forth, bring into being, bring to a complete condition, bring to a more advanced state, bring to light by degrees, broaden, build up, cause to expand, cause to grow, change into, come gradually into existence, come to be, come to maturity, *crescere*, cultivate, derive from, descend from, detail, *educare*, elaborate, emanate, emerge, enlarge, enlarge upon, enter into detail, evolve, *excolere*, expand, expand upon, extend, fill in, fill out, further, germinate, give being to, give forth, give rise to, go into detail, grow, grow better, grow from, improve, increase the strength of, infuse, intensify, invigorate, magnify, make headway, make progress, mature, meliorate, mend, perfect, proceed, produce, progress, promote, raise, reach manhood, refine, reinforce, revive, ripen, shape up, show improvement, stimulate, strengthen, stretch, swell, take form, take shape, unfold, widen, work out in detail

DEVELOPER, noun builder, building entrepreneur, creator, designer, enterpriser, establisher, land developer, organizer, originator, planner, promoter
ASSOCIATED CONCEPTS: commercial developer, residential developer

DEVELOPMENT (Building), **noun** commercial building, construction, creation of housing project, development of industrial sites, erection, house-building program, housing, industrial area, industrial building, institution of commercial sites, residential building, urbanization

DEVELOPMENT (Outgrowth), **noun** accomplishment, achievement, aftergrowth, aftermath, attainment, by-product, conclusion, consequence, consequent, derivation, effect, emanation, ending, ensual, event, eventuality, eventuation, occurrence, offshoot, outcome, product, realization, result, resultant, sequel, side issue, upshot

DEVELOPMENT (Progression), **noun** accretion, accumulation, advance, advancement, amelioration, ampliation, amplification, anabasis, *auctus*, betterment, change, cultivation, effectuation, elaboration, enhancement, enrichment, evolution, evolvement, expansion, *explicatio*, extension, furtherance, gain, germination, gradual evolution, growth, improvement, increase in size, lengthening, melioration, modernization, progress, progress to maturity, progressive growth, *progressus*, promotion, refinement, reform, reformation, regeneration, remodeling, renovation, reorganization, revision, stimulation, strengthening, supplementation, transfiguration, transformation, unfolding, unravelment, upgrowth, uptrend
ASSOCIATED CONCEPTS: development costs

DEVIANT, adjective aberrant, abnormal, adverse to, against the rules, atypical, clashing, contrary, counter to, departing from, desultory, deviating, discordant, discrepant, dissident, dissonant, divergent, eccentric, errant, heretical, in violation of, irregular, nonconformist, nonuniform, oblique, out of order, out of step, recalcitrant, stray, unconventional, unfashionable, unorthodox, variant
ASSOCIATED CONCEPTS: deviant behavior

DEVIATE, verb *aberrare*, alter course, angle off, be at variance, be different, be distinguished from, be oblique, bear no resemblance, bear off, branch out, break bounds, break the pattern, change direction, clash, clash with, conflict with, contrast, *declinare*, deflect, *degredi*, depart from, depart from one's course, differ, digress, disagree, divaricate, diverge, divert from its course, drift, err, fall into error, fly off at a tangent, get off the subject, glance off, go adrift, go amiss, go astray, go awry, go off on a tangent, go out of one's way, go round about, go wrong, infringe a law, infringe custom, make a detour, meander, not conform, perform a circuit, show variety, slip, stand apart, step aside, stray, swerve, take a different course, turn, turn aside, turn out of one's way, vary, veer, wander from the subject

DEVIATE FROM THE TRUTH, verb alter one's course, deceive, depart from a norm, digress, diverge, drift, fabricate, fake, go astray, lie, maunder, meander, mislead, misrepresent, misstate, prevaricate, skew, stray, struggle, swerve, take a different course, wander

DEVIATING, adjective aberrant, astray, circuitous, departing, deviative, devious, different, differing, digressive, discursive, disparate, dissimilar, divergent, diverse, diversified, errant, erratic, indirect, labyrinthine, meandering, nonconforming, peculiar, perverse, separate, shifting, sinuous, undirected, vagrant, variant, varying, wandering, widely apart

DEVIATING FROM THE NORM, verb alter one's course, depart from a norm, digress, diverge, drift, go astray, maunder, meander, skew, slew, straggle, stray, swerve, take a different course, wander

DEVIATION, noun aberrance, aberrancy, aberration, abnormality, alteration, anomalousness, anomaly, antipathy, antithesis, branching off, breach of practice, change of direction, change of position, contrast, *declinatio*, defiance of custom, departure, departure from usage, difference, *digressio*, disaccord, disaccordance, disagreement, discongruity, discontinuity, discord, discrepancy, disharmony, disparity, dissidence, dissimilarity, dissonance, distinctness, divagation, divergence, diverseness, diversion, incongruity, inconsistency, inconsonance, inharmoniousness, irregularity, nonconformism, nonconformity, nonimitation, nonobservance, nonuniformity, straying, swerve, swerving, unconformity, unlikeness, unorthodoxy, variability, variance, variation
ASSOCIATED CONCEPTS: deviation doctrine, deviation from scope of employment, deviation from the norm

DEVIATION FROM RECTITUDE, noun abuse, bad faith, bad repute, blame, corruption, crime, disgrace, dishonor, guilt, malfeasance, misconduct, misdoing, misfeasance, misprision

DEVICE (Contrivance), **noun** artifice, circumvention, craft, design, gimmick, *machina*, machination, maneuver, means to an end, method, plan, program of action, project, resort, ruse, scheme, setup, stratagem, subtle maneuver, system, trick, wile, working plan, working proposition

DEVICE (Distinguishing mark), **noun** badge of office, design, designation, earmark, emblem, ensign, hallmark, identification mark, indicant, *inscriptio*, insignia, label, mark that designates, sign, symbol, token, trademark

DEVICE (Mechanism), **noun** apparatus, appliance, equipment, facility, fixture, gadget, gear, implement, instrument, invention, mechanical aid, tool, utensil
ASSOCIATED CONCEPTS: safety device

DEVIOUS, adjective aberrant, ambagious, artful, circuitous, crafty, crooked, cunning, deceitful, designing, deviating, deviative, *devius*, errant, excursive, foxy, indirect, insidious, labyrinthine, roundabout, scheming, serpentine, sinuous, sly, sneaking, tortuous, tricky, uncandid, unstraightforward, wily

DEVISE *(Give)*, **verb**   allot, assign, bequeath, bestow, confer, convey, endow, give, give and bequeath, give away, give by will, grant, leave, leave by will, make a bequest, make testamentary dispositions, transfer, transmit, transmit by will, will and bequeath, will to

ASSOCIATED CONCEPTS: absolute devise, alienation, bequest, conveyance, demonstrative devise, executory devise, general devise, legacy, testamentary disposition

FOREIGN PHRASES: *Nemo plus commodi haeredi suo relinquit quam ipse habuit.* No one leaves a greater benefit to his heir than he had himself. *Da tua dum tua sunt, post mortem tunc tua non sunt.* Give that which is yours while it is yours; after death it is not yours. *Quando aliquis aliquid concedit, concedere videtur et id sine quo res unon potest.* When anyone grants anything, he is deemed to grant also that without which the thing granted cannot be used.

DEVISE *(Invent)*, **verb**   arrange, calculate, compose, conceive, construct, contrive, create, design, draw up, engineer, erect, evolve, *excogitare,* fabricate, fashion, find a way, form, formulate, frame, have an idea, imagine, improvise, *invenire,* lay down a plan, lay out, make a plan, make arrangements, make up, maneuver, manufacture, map out, piece together, plan, plan out, prearrange, predetermine, prepare, proceed by stratagem, put together, schematize, scheme, set up, shape, sketch out, take steps, work out

DEVISEE, *noun*   acceptor, beneficiary, donee, grantee, heir, inheritor, legatee, recipient, successor, transferee

DEVOID, *adjective*   bare, barren, bereft of, blank, bleak, deficient, denuded of, deprived of, deserted, desolate, destitute of, empty, empty of, found wanting, ill-furnished, ill-provided, ill-stored, impotent, in default of, in the absence of, in want of, incomplete, insufficient, lacking, missing, out of, poor, *re vacuus,* scant of, short, short of, sparing, stinted, tenantless, unacquired, unexisting, uninhabited, unmanned, unoccupied, unofficered, unpeopled, unpossessed of, unprovided, unreplenished, unstaffed, unsupplied, untenanted, vacant, vacuous, void of, wanting, without, without content, without resources

DEVOID OF TRUTH, *adjective*   corrupt, criminal, deceitful, dishonest, disingenuous, fallacious, false, false-hearted, forsworn, fraudulent, immoral, insidious, knavish, lying, mendacious, perfidious, perjured, shameless, unconscientious, unconscionable, unethical, unprincipled, unscrupulous, untruthful, unveracious, wicked

DEVOLUTION, *noun*   assignment, bequeathal, bequest, change of hands, change-over, conveyance, delegation, delegation of duties, deliverance, delivery, demise, devise, interchange, nonretention, reversion, substitution, succession, succession of property rights, transfer, transfer of property, transference, transmission

ASSOCIATED CONCEPTS: devolution of liability, devolution of property

DEVOLVE, *verb*   be handed down to, be handed over, be transferred, bequeath, cause to pass to another, cede, change from one to another, change ownership, confer ownership, convey, *deferre,* delegate upon another, deliver, deliver over to a successor, descend by inheritance,

descend upon, fall by inheritance, fall by succession, give, grant, interchange, invest with, leave to, make over, *mandare,* pass to, *permittere,* put in possession, sign away, substitute, trade, transfer, transfer ownership, transfer to, transmit, turn over

ASSOCIATED CONCEPTS: devolution of a lease

DEVOTE, *verb*   allot, apply, apportion, appropriate, assign, attend, be absorbed in, be attentive, be engrossed in, concentrate, concern, *consecrare,* consecrate, contemplate, *dedere,* dedicate, *devovere,* direct attention, focus, give attention, heed, meditate upon, occupy oneself with, pay attention, pay heed, set apart, set aside, think about, turn attention

ASSOCIATED CONCEPTS: devote attention, devote to a public use

DEVOTED *(Faithful)*, **adjective**   affectionate, attached, close, consecrated, constant, dedicated, dependable, devout, earnest, fond, inseparable, loving, loyal, obedient, partisan, passionate, purposeful, reliable, stanch, staunch, steadfast, tender, tried and true, true, unyielding

DEVOTED *(Zealous)*, **adjective**   ardent, assiduous, dutiful, fanatical, fast, fervent, firm, sedulous, serious, sincere

DEVOTION, *noun*   addiction, adhesion, admiration, affection, affinity, allegiance, application, ardor, attachment, concentration, constancy, dedication, deference, determination, devoutness, diligence, discipline, earnestness, enchantment, engagement, faithfulness, fastness, fealty, fervor, fidelity, firmness, fondness, homage, honor, immersion, inclination, industry, infatuation, involvement, love, loyalty, passion, preoccupation, regard, reverence, sanctity, stanchness, staunchness, yearning, zeal

DIABOLIC, *adjective*   accursed, amoral, amoralistic, bad-hearted, brutal, brutalized, callous, conscienceless, cruel, cursed, deadly, dehumanized, demoniac, demonic, devil-like, devilish, evil, evil-doing, evil-minded, execrable, fiendish, fiendlike, full of sin, god-forsaken, guilty, heinous, hellish, hopeless, horrible, immoral, impious, infernal, inhuman, iniquitous, irredeemable, irreligious, maleficent, malevolent, malignant, Mephistophelian, merciless, monstrous, murderous, nefarious, outrageous, pitiless, possessed, profane, ruinous, ruthless, sadistic, Satanic, sinladen, sinful, sinister, sinning, transgressing, unnatural, unprincipled, unredeemed, unrighteous, unscrupulous, unvirtuous, vicious, virtueless, wicked

DIAGNOSE, *verb*   analyze, appraise, classify, compare critically, discern, distinguish, estimate, examine critically, have insight, identify, judge, make a judgment, recognize, see the difference, sort out, specify, weigh

DIAGNOSIS, *noun*   analysis, appreciation of differences, assay, breakdown, careful appreciation, categorization, category, classification, classificatory description, conclusion, critical appraisal, critical scrutiny, critique, designation, differentiation, discernment, discretion, discriminating judgment, discrimination, estimation, interpretation, judgment, perception of difference, scientific determination, specification, symptomatology

ASSOCIATED CONCEPTS: faulty diagnosis, malpractice

DIALECTIC, *noun*   applied logic, apprehension, argumentation, brainwork, cerebration, chain of reasoning, cogitation, concluding, consideration, contemplation, deducing, deduction, deliberation, deriving, discursive reasoning, drawing conclusions, force of argument, induction, inferring, judgment, logic, logic of discursive argument, logical argumentation, logical discussion, logical process, logical sequence, mode of reasoning, ratiocination, rationalism, rationalization, rationalizing, reasoning, reflection, rumination, thinking

DIALOGUE, noun bull session, causerie, chat, colloquy, communication, communion, confabulation, conference, confrontation, conversation, debate, discourse, disputation, exchange, formal discourse, give and take, interlocution, interview, palaver, parley, powwow, question and answer, script, swapping opinions, symposium, talk, talkfest, verbal intercourse

DIATRIBE, noun abuse, abusive harangue, abusive language, accusation, act of berating, admonition, adverse comment, animadversion, backbiting, bitter harangue, bitter words, blame, carping, castigation, censure, chiding, complaining, condemnation, countercharge, *coup de bec*, criticism, cutting words, denunciation, deprecation, depreciation, discommendation, disparagement, disparage, dressing down, faultfinding, gainsaying, harangue, hostile attack, hostile criticism, hostile eloquence, hypercriticism, inculpation, indictment, insult, invective, long vehement speech, objurgation, obloquy, oration, prolonged outburst of denunciation, railing, rebuke, remonstrance, reprehension, reprimand, reproach, reproof, revilement, reviling, sarcasm, scolding, scurrility, sermon, stinging words, strain of invective, stream of abuse, tirade, tongue-lashing, upbraiding, verbal onslaught, vilification, vituperation

DICHOTOMIZE, verb apportion, bifurcate, bisect, branch, cleave in two, cut in halves, cut in two, detach, disconnect, disjoin, dissect, dissever, disunite, divaricate, diverge, divide, fragment, furcate, halve, keep apart, part, partition, rend, rive, section, sectionalize, segment, separate, separate in two, sever, split, subdivide, transect

DICHOTOMY, noun bifurcation, bipartition, bisection, dissection, divarication, division, halving, separation, severance, split, subdivision

DICKER, verb adjust differences, arbitrate terms, argue price, arrange terms, arrive at a price, bargain, barter, bicker, bid for, come to terms, confer on price, contend, deal, drive a bargain, give terms, haggle, have dealings, make terms, negotiate, put through a deal, state one's terms, strike a bargain, trade, transact, wrangle
ASSOCIATED CONCEPTS: dicker over terms of a contract

DICTATE, noun act, authoritative suggestion, behest, charge, command, commandment, commission, decree, demand, direction, edict, enactment, fiat, imperative, imperious direction, injunction, instruction, judgment, law, mandate, order, ordinance, ordination, precept, prescript, prescription, proclamation, regulation, requirement, rescript, rubric, rule, ruling, ultimatum

DICTATE, verb bid, charge, command, compel, decree, demand, direct, enjoin, exercise authority, give orders, impose an order, instruct, issue a command, issue an order, oblige, ordain, order, prescribe, require, require authoritatively, rule

DICTATOR, noun absolute leader, absolute ruler, autarch, autocrat, autocratic master, despot, despotic commander, despotic master, dictatorial mogul, disciplinarian, imperious commandant, inquisitor, martinet, oppressive taskmaster, oppressor, repressive governor, strict disciplinarian, totalitarian, tyrannical leader, tyrant

DICTATORIAL, adjective absolutistic, arbitrary, arrogant, authoritarian, authoritative, autocratic, censorious, commanding, compelling, controlling, despotic, *dictatorius,* dogmatic, domineering, enslaving, exacting, fanatic, fascist, highhanded, imperative, *imperiosus,* imperious, inexorable, inquisitorial, intimidating, ironhanded, lordly, masterful, monocratic, officious, oppressive, overbearing, peremptory, pompous, power-crazed, power-hungry, power-mad, relentless, repressive, severe, suppressive, supreme, totalitarian, tyrannical, tyrannous, uncompromising, undemocratic, unlimited, unrelenting, unrestricted, with an iron hand

DICTUM, noun announcement, assertion, authoritative assertion, declaration, extrajudicial opinion, finding, gratuitous remark, illustrative statement, incidental opinion, judicial assertion, judicial comment, judicial remark, observation, opinion, pronouncement, recommendation, remark, statement, statement by way of illustration
ASSOCIATED CONCEPTS: judicial dictum, obiter dictum

DIDACTIC, adjective academic, adapted to teach, curricular, edifying, educating, educational, educative, enlightening, enriching, erudite, expository, fitted to teach, informational, informative, instructional, instructive, intended for instruction, intended for teaching, learned, pedagogic, propaedeutic, scholarly, scholastic, teaching, tutorial

DIE, verb be no more, breathe one's last, cease living, cease to exist, decease, demise, depart, end one's life, expire, lose one's life, meet one's death, *mori, mortem obire,* part with life, pass away, pass on, perish, relinquish life, rest in peace, succumb to death, suffer death, *vita decedere*
ASSOCIATED CONCEPTS: die at any time without issue surviving, die by his own hand or act, die in performance of duty, die intestate, die leaving issue, die seised and possessed, die simultaneously, die without children or issue, die without heirs, die without issue, die without lawful issue, testamentary dispositions

DIFFER (Disagree), verb be discordant, be incongruent, be inharmonious, bicker, cavil, clash, conflict with, contend, contradict, dispute, divide on, hold different views, object, oppose, protest, raise objections, reject, repudiate, take exception, take issue, think differently, withhold assent

DIFFER (Vary), verb argue, be at cross purposes, be at variance, be contrary, be dissimilar, be distinct, be distinguished from, be inharmonious, be opposite, be unique, be unlike, bear no resemblance, contrast, depart from, deviate from, digress, disaccord, disaccord with, disagree, discept, *discrepare,* dissent, *dissentire, dissidere,* divaricate from, diverge from, diversify, have a dissimilar opinion, lack resemblance, not agree, not compare with, not conform, not equate, show contrast, show variety, take exception, take issue, think differently, vary, withhold assent
FOREIGN PHRASES: *Non differunt quae concordant re, tametsi non in verbis iisdem.* Those matters do not differ which agree in substance, though not in the same words.

DIFFERENCE, noun adverseness, antipathy, antithesis, antitheticalness, asymmetry, atypicality, breach, change, clash of temperament, clashing, conflict of opinion, contradiction, contradistinction, contraposition, contrariety, contrariness, contrast, controversy, counterpoint, departure, departure from, deviation, differentiation, disaccord, disagreement, discongruity, disconnection, discontinuity, discord, discordance, discrepancy, *discrepantia,* discrimination, disequilibrium, disharmony, disjunction, disparity, disproportion, dissemblance, dissension, dissimilarity, dissimilitude, dissonance, distinction, distinctness, distortion, divergence, diverseness, *diversitas,* diversity, failure to agree, heterogeneity, imbalance, imparity, inaccordance, incommensurability, incongruence, incongruity, incongruousness, inconsistency, inconsonance, individuality, inequality, inharmoniousness, inharmony, irreconcilability, irrelation, lack of connection, lack of resemblance, misunderstanding, multifariousness, mutual exclusiveness, nonconformity, nonimitation, nonuniformity, nuance, oppositeness, opposition, schism, separateness, state of being different, unconformity, unequalness, uniqueness, unlikeness, unrelatedness, variance, variation, variegation, *varietas,* variety

ASSOCIATED CONCEPTS: difference in degree, difference in kind, difference in the nature and elements of a crime, difference in value, difference of opinion, settling of differences

DIFFERENT, *adjective* alien, *alius,* altered, antagonistic, antithetic, atypical, changed, clashing, contradictory, contradistinct, contradistinctive, contrary, contrasting, contrastive, deviating, diametric, discordant, *discrepans,* discrepant, disparate, dissimilar, dissonant, distinct, distinctive, divergent, diverse, diversiform, *diversus,* foreign, heterogeneous, idiosyncratic, in disagreement, incommensurable, incomparable, incompatible, incongruous, individual, inharmonious, mismatched, mismated, nonidentical, not the same, novel, opposed, other than, out of the ordinary, peculiar, separate, set apart, singular, unidentical, unique, unlike, unmatched, unrelated, unusual, unwonted, variant, varied, varietal, various, varying

ASSOCIATED CONCEPTS: different causes of action, different offenses

DIFFERENTIAL, *noun* attribute, characteristic, constituting a difference, contrasting quality, delicate distinction, difference of degree, differentiating trait, distinction, distinctive feature, distinguishing feature, feature, gradation, grade, graduation, nuance, particularity, peculiarity, property, proportion, quality, rate, ratio, relative quantity, scale, shade of difference, singularity, subtle difference, trait, variant

ASSOCIATED CONCEPTS: wage differential

DIFFERENTIATE, *verb* characterize, classify, contrast, demarcate, discern between, discriminate, distinguish, diversify, draw the line, exercise discrimination, make a distinction, make distinctive, mark off by differences, mark out, particularize, perceive clearly, recognize as separate, segregate, separate as different, set apart as different, set off, show a difference, single out, sort out, subtilize, tell apart, tell from

DIFFERENTIATION, *noun* contrast, definition, demarcation, denomination, description, despecification, difference, discrepancy, discrimination, disequalization, distinction, distinguishment, diversification, division, individualization, modification, nuance, particularization, segregation, separation, severance, specialization, specification, variation

DIFFERING, *adjective* at odds, at variance, clashing, conflicting, deviative, different, disagreeing, discordant,

discrepant, discriminatory, disparate, disproportionate, dissenting, dissident, dissimilar, distinct, distinctive, distinguished, divergent, diverse, diversified, incompatible, incongruous, inconsonant, inharmonious, irreconcilable, jarring, nonconforming, peculiar, recusant, separate, unequal, unrelated, variant

ASSOCIATED CONCEPTS: differing accounts, differing claims, differing testimony

DIFFICULT, *adjective* arduous, attended by obstacles, awkward, beset with difficulty, beyond one's reach, bothersome, burdensome, complex, complicated, convoluted, *difficile, difficilis,* encompassed with difficulties, enigmatic, entangled by difficulties, fatiguing, grueling, hard, hard to deal with, hard to manage, hard to understand, impassable, *impeditus,* impenetrable, incomprehensible, insoluble, insurmountable, intractable, involved, labored, laborious, labyrinthine, obscure, obstinate, offering a problem, operose, out of reach, painstaking, perplexing, perverse, problematic, puzzling, recondite, refractory, strenuous, stubborn, surrounded by difficulties, too hard, troublesome, unachievable, unapproachable, unavailable, uncertain, unclear

ASSOCIATED CONCEPTS: difficult and extraordinary action, difficult and extraordinary case or proceeding

DIFFIDENT, *adjective* abashed, awestricken, awestruck, bashful, blushful, blushing, cautious, demure, deprecating, deprecative, *diffidens,* embarrassed, fainthearted, faltering, hesitating, humble, humbled, lacking self-confidence, modest, overanxious, overapprehensive, overshy, qualmish, quiet, reserved, retiring, self-conscious, self-effacing, shaky, shameful, sheepish, shrinking, shy, timid, timorous, treading warily, tremulous, unambitious, unassuming, unboastful, unheard, unimposing, unobstrusive, unostentatious, unpretentious, unpushing, unsure of oneself, *verecundus,* wary, without vanity

DIFFUSE, *verb* bespread, besprinkle, bestrew, break up, broadcast, cast forth, circulate, circumfuse, commingle, deal out, decentralize, *diffundere, diffundi,* disband, disintegrate, disperse, dispread, disseminate, dissipate, distribute, effuse, go in different directions, go in many directions, intermix, intersperse, mix, overspread, *permeare,* permeate, pervade, promulgate, propagate, put into circulation, radiate, scatter, send abroad, send forth, sow, spatter, spread, spread about, spread abroad, spread around, spread far and wide, spread widely, strew, unloose

DIGAMY, *noun* finding another mate after the death of the first spouse

DIGEST, *noun* abbreviation, abridgment, abstract, analysis, anthology, arrangement, brief, capsule, code, collection, compendium, compilation, condensation, consolidation, conspectus, contraction, epitome, essence, extract, outline, pandect, recapitulation, review, summary, synopsis

ASSOCIATED CONCEPTS: digest of cases, digest of laws

DIGEST *(Comprehend), verb* absorb, analyze, appreciate, assimilate, cognize, consider, contemplate, fathom, grasp, incorporate, ken, know, muse, register, think about, understand, weigh

DIGEST *(Summarize), verb* abbreviate, abridge, abstract, capsulize, catalogue, classify, codify, condense, cut down, edit, excerpt, make a summary of, make brief, make concise, outline, recapitulate, reduce, select, shorten, sum up, survey

DIGRESS, verb *aberrare,* alter course, be diffuse, branch out, change direction, depart, detour, deviate, *digredi,* divagate, divaricate, diverge, divert, drift, expatiate, fly off at a tangent, go astray, meander, ramble, rove, shift, sidestep, sidetrack, skirt, stray, swerve, turn, veer, wander

DIGRESSION, noun aberrancy, aberration, alteration, break, change, circuity, convolution, departure, detour, deviation, *digressio,* divagation, divarication, divergence, diversion, drift, excursus, misdirection, periphrasis, roundabout way, shift in topic, sideslip, sidestep, swerve, variance, variation
ASSOCIATED CONCEPTS: dictum

DILAPIDATED, adjective altered for the worse, condemned, damaged, decomposed, decrepit, fallen into ruin, far-gone, frayed, friable, impaired, imperfect, marred, mouldering, *obsoletus,* on the wane, ramshackle, ruined, shabby, stale, tabid, timeworn, used, weatherbeaten, wilted, withering, worn, worn out
ASSOCIATED CONCEPTS: depreciation, obsolescence

DILATORY, adjective after time, behind time, belated, deferring, delayed, delaying, deliberately slow, eleventh hour, inclined to delay, indolent, intended to bring about delay, intended to defer decision, intended to gain time, lackadaisical, last minute, late, overdue, pausing, procrastinating, procrastinative, procrastinatory, remiss, tardy, unpunctual
ASSOCIATED CONCEPTS: dilatory defense, dilatory exceptions, dilatory motion, dilatory plea, dilatory practice

DILEMMA, noun awkward predicament, awkward situation, baffle, bafflement, confoundment, confusion, decision, difficult choice, difficulty, imbroglio, impasse, indecision, limited choice, perplexity, predicament, puzzle, puzzlement, puzzling alternative, quandary, uncertainty, unfair choice, vexed question

DILIGENCE (Care), noun absorption of mind, active application, active attention, active study, active thought, *adsiduitas,* advertence, advertency, alertness, application, attention, attention to detail, carefulness, caution, check-up, circumspection, close application, close attention, close study, close thought, concern, consideration, contemplation, deep application, deep attention, deep study, deep thought, deliberate application, deliberate attention, deliberate study, deliberate thought, diligent application, diligent attention, diligent study, diligent thought, *diligentia,* earnestness, exactitude, exactness, exclusive application, exclusive attention, exclusive study, exclusive thought, fastidiousness, foresight, guard, heed, heedfulness, *industria,* inquisitive attention, inspection, intense application, intense study, intense thought, intentness, meticulousness, mindfulness, minute application, minute attention, minute study, minute thought, minuteness, observation, orderliness, painstaking, particularity, pedantry, preparedness, profound application, profound attention, profound study, profound thought, prudence, rapt attention, readiness, regard, review, scrutiny, seriousness, single-mindedness, studiousness, study, thoroughgoingness, thoroughness, undivided attention, utmost care, vigilance, wakefulness, wariness, watchfulness, whole attention, whole mind
ASSOCIATED CONCEPTS: due diligence, lack of diligence, ordinary diligence, reasonable diligence, utmost diligence

DILIGENCE (Perseverance), noun application, ardor, assiduity, assiduousness, constancy, continuance, determination, devotedness, devotion, doggedness, earnestness, endurance, firmness of purpose, fixity of purpose, habitual devotion, indefatigability, industriousness, insistence, intentness, intrepidity, meticulosity, patience, persistence, persistency, persistent exertion, pertinacity, purposefulness, relentlessness, resolution, restlessness, sedulity, sedulousness, singleness of purpose, staying power, steadfastness, steadiness, steady application, strength of will, stubbornness, tenaciousness, tenacity, tirelessness, undauntedness, undivided attention, vigilence, vigor, zeal, zealousness
ASSOCIATED CONCEPTS: diligence in prosecution

DILIGENT, adjective assiduous, attentive, busily intent, businesslike, busy, conscientious, constant, dependable, *diligens,* dogged, enduring, exact, faithful, fastidious, hardworking, heedful, indefatigable, industrious, *industrius,* never idle, never tiring, operose, painstaking, perseverant, persevering, persistent, pertinacious, punctilious, relentless, reliable, resolute, responsible, scholarly, sedulous, steadfast, studious, tenacious, thorough, thoroughgoing, tireless, trustworthy, undaunted, unfaltering, unrelenting, unremitting, untiring, unwavering, unwearying, watchful
ASSOCIATED CONCEPTS: diligent creditor, diligent efforts, diligent inquiry, diligent prosecution, diligent search, diligent use, due diligence

DILUTE, verb abbreviate, add water, attenuate, bate, belittle, cheapen, combine with water, depreciate, detract from, *diluere,* extenuate, lessen the strength of, make less concentrated, make more fluid, make more liquid, make thin, make weak, minimize, mitigate, reduce the strength of, render weak, subtract, take away, thin, thin out, thin with liquid, water, weaken

DIMENSION, noun area, boundaries, configuration, conformation, measure, outline, proportions, shape, size, square measure, surface, territorial shape

DIMINISH, verb abate, abbreviate, abrade, abridge, alleviate, assuage, bate, become smaller, belittle, bound, cause to be smaller, cause to taper, cheapen, compress, consume, contract, curb, curtail, cut back, cut down, damp down, dampen, decelerate, decimate, decrease, deduct, deflate, delete, *deminuere,* depopulate, depreciate, depress, deprive, derogate, detract, detract from, dilute, divest, do subtraction, dock, drain, drop off, dull, dwindle, eat away, ebb, economize, empty, erode, excise, expurgate, extenuate, fade away, fall away, grow less, lessen, lighten, limit, lower, make less, make smaller, make thin, minify, minimize, *minuere,* mitigate, pare, prune, quell, quiet, recede, reduce, relieve, remit, render few, render smaller, restrain, retard, retrench, roll back, rub away, run down, run low, scale down, shave off, shorten, shrink, slow down, step down, stifle, subdue, subside, subtract, take away, take from, take off, taper, thin, thin out, tone down, tune down, unload, use up, wane, waste, waste away, weaken, wear away, wear down, wear out, weed out, whittle, withdraw, wither
ASSOCIATED CONCEPTS: diminished responsibility, diminished use, diminishing returns

DIMINUTION, noun abatement, abbreviation, contraction, decrease, deduction, deflation, diminishment, lessening, let up, lowering, mitigation, reduction, remission, shrinkage

DINT, noun ableness, authority, control, effectiveness, effectuality, efficacy, force, forcefulness, greatness, influence, might, mightiness, potence, potency, power, powerfulness, prepotency, pressure, puissance, strength, superiority, sway, vigor, weight

DIPLOMATIC, *adjective* adept, artful, cautious in dealing, cunning, deft, dexterous, discreet, graceful, polite, politic, prudent, scheming, skillful in handling others, smoothly, strategic, tactful
ASSOCIATED CONCEPTS: diplomatic immunity, diplomatic recognition, diplomatic relations, diplomatic status

DIPSOMANIA, *noun* acute alcoholism, addictedness, addiction, alcoholic addiction, alcoholism, bibacity, cacoethes, chronic alcoholism, compulsion, crapulence, craving for drink, drunkenness, ebriosity, excessive drinking, excessiveness, inebriation, inebriety, insobriety, intemperance, intoxication, obsession, potation

DIRE, *adjective* annihilative, appalling, awful, baleful, calamitous, cataclysmic, catastrophic, catastrophical, deadly, demolishing, destroying, destructive, devastating, direful, disastrous, dismal, dreaded, dreadful, eradicative, exterminative, extirpative, extirpatory, extreme, fatal, fearful, fell, frightening, grave, grievous, grim, horrible, horrid, horrifying, ill-boding, ill-omened, inauspicious, lethal, ominous, portentous, ruinous, serious, sinister, terrible, tragic, tragical, unfortunate, unlucky, unpropitious, woeful, worst

DIRECT *(Forthright),* ***adjective*** aboveboard, blunt, candid, clear, explicit, face to face, forthright, frank, genuine, guileless, honest, ingenuous, open, outspoken, plain, pointblank, pointed, *rectus,* sincere, straightforward, summary, transparent, truthful, unaffected, unambiguous, unassuming, unconstrained, undeceitful, undeceiving, undeceptive, undesigning, undisguising, unfeigning, unpretending, unpretentious, unreserved, unrestrained, veracious, veridical

DIRECT *(Straight),* ***adjective*** aimed, guided, immediate, linear, rectilineal, steered, straightaway, true, unbent, unbroken, undeflected, undeviating, undistorted, unswerving, unturned, unwarped, without a bend, without circumlocution, without divergence
ASSOCIATED CONCEPTS: direct and proximate cause, direct attack, direct benefit, direct cause, direct contempt, direct control, direct damages, direct descendants, direct evidence, direct interest, direct knowledge, direct loss, direct result, direct route, direct tax, direct testimony, direct trust

DIRECT *(Uninterrupted),* ***adjective*** connected, consecutive, continual, continuous, progressive, steady, straight, successive, unbroken, unending, unfaltering, unstopped

DIRECT *(Order),* ***verb*** adjure, bid, call upon, charge, command, decree, demand, dictate, enjoin, give a directive, give an order, give directions, give instructions, give orders, govern, instruct, issue a command, issue a decree, issue an order, ordain, prescribe, rule, set a task, signal, tell
ASSOCIATED CONCEPTS: directed verdict

DIRECT *(Show),* ***verb*** conduct, designate, guide, *homini viam monstrare,* indicate, instruct, lead, navigate, point, point out, steer

DIRECT *(Supervise),* ***verb*** administer, *administrare,* administrate, assign, be master, boss, coach, command, conduct, control, *dirigere,* dominate, educate, engineer, exercise authority, exercise supervision, govern, guide, head, lead, look after, manage, mastermind, oversee, preside,

preside over, *regere,* regulate, rule, stage, steer, superintend, take command

DIRECT CAUSE, *noun* immediate cause, immediate legal basis, immediate legal cause, immediate legal genesis, legitimate legal cause, legitimate legal reason, prime cause, sufficient legal basis, sufficient legal cause, sufficient legal factor, sufficient legal genesis, sufficient legal inducement, sufficient legal source, true justification, true legal basis, true legal cause, true legal inducement, true legal source
ASSOCIATED CONCEPTS: concurrent clause, just cause, sufficient combined causes

DIRECTION *(Course),* ***noun*** aim, approach, bearing, bent, blueprint, course of action, *cursus,* design, draft, drift, heading, inclination, line, map, master plan, method, outline, plan, policy, procedure, program, range, *regio,* route, scheme, strategy, tactics, tendency, trend, *via,* way

DIRECTION *(Guidance),* ***noun*** administration, admonition, advice, advocacy, auspices, care, charge, coaching, conduct, *consilium,* counsel, design, directorship, education, enlightenment, exhortation, governorship, *gubernatio,* headship, information, injunction, instruction, jurisdiction, leadership, management, managership, ministration, officiation, oversight, pilotage, preparation, protection, recommendation, regulation, steerage, superintendence, supervision, surveillance, teaching, training, tuition, tutelage, tutoring
ASSOCIATED CONCEPTS: directions of donor, under the direction of

DIRECTION *(Order),* ***noun*** adjudication, canon, charge, citation, command, commandment, decree, demand, dictate, directive, *edico,* edict, enactment, fiat, imperative, *imperium,* injunction, instructions, *iubeo,* judgment, mandate, ordinance, precept, prescript, prescription, proscription, regulation, rescript, rubric, rule, subpoena, summons, warrant, writ
ASSOCIATED CONCEPTS: direction of verdict, express direction, specific direction of court

DIRECTIVE, *noun* behest, bidding, charge, command, commandment, declaration, decree, decretal, demand, dictate, direction, edict, enjoinment, fiat, hest, imperative, instruction, mandate, notification, order, ordinance, precept, prescript, prescription, proclamation, requirement, rescript, ukase, writ

DIRECTOR, *noun* administrator, boss, chief, curator, executive, executor, foreman, governor, guide, inspector, intendant, leader, manager, overseer, presiding officer, principal, proctor, procurator, superintendent, supervisor
ASSOCIATED CONCEPTS: board of directors, de facto director, de jure director, director's liability, dummy director, interlocking directorates

DIRECTORY, *noun* catalogue, guidebook, handbook, index, manual, reference book, reference work

DISABILITY *(Legal disqualification),* ***noun*** disablement, impairment, invalidation, invalidity, legal incapacity, unfitness, unqualification, unqualifiedness, unsuitability, unsuitableness, unsuitedness, want of legal capacity, want of legal qualification
FOREIGN PHRASES: ***Contra non valentem agere nulla currit praescriptio.*** No prescription runs against a person who is unable to act.

DISABILITY *(Physical inability),* **noun** affliction, ailment, debilitation, debility, deterioration, disablement, disorder, disqualification, feebleness, frailty, handicap, helplessness, illness, impairment, impotence, impotency, inability, inability to work, inadequacy, incapability, incapacitation, incapacity, incompetence, incompetency, indisposition, ineffectiveness, ineffectuality, ineffectualness, inefficacy, inefficiency, infirmity, insufficiency, malady, powerlessness, sickness, unfitness, unsoundness, weakness

ASSOCIATED CONCEPTS: complete disability, continuous disability, disability benefits, disability compensation, disability insurance, general disability, medical disability, mental disability, partial disability, physical disability, proof of disability, temporary disability, total disability

DISABLE, *verb* annul, bar, becripple, break, cancel, cripple, crush, damage, deactivate, debar, *debilitare,* debilitate, deflate, deprive of power, deprive of strength, devalue, devitalize, disarm, disassemble, disenable, disenfranchise, disfranchise, dismantle, disqualify, emasculate, endamage, *enervare,* enervate, enfeeble, exhaust, harm, hinder, hurt, impair, inactivate, incapacitate, indispose, injure, invalidate, lame, maim, make inactive, make incapable, make unfit, make useless, mangle, mutilate, neutralize, nullify, paralyze, preclude, prostrate, put out of action, render helpless, render impotent, render incompetent, render powerless, render unfit, ruin, sabotage, scathe, sicken, spoil, stultify, take to pieces, undermine, unnerve, vitiate, weaken, wound, wreck

ASSOCIATED CONCEPTS: disabled from holding office, disabled vehicle, disabled veterans, disabled worker, partially disabled, wholly disabled, workmen's compensation

DISABLED *(Deprived of legal right),* **adjective** disenabled, disqualified, helpless, impotent, incapacitated, ineffectual, inoperative, invalid, invalidated, legally incapable, unable, unendowed, unfit, unqualified, untenable

DISABLED *(Made incapable),* **adjective** bedridden, crippled, debilitated, decrepit, defenseless, deprived of strength, devitalized, disarmed, disenabled, enfeebled, handicapped, helpless, *hors de combat,* impaired, impotent, incapacitated, incompetent, indisposed, ineffective, inefficacious, inept, invalid, maimed, paralytic, paralyzed, pregnable, shattered, unendowed, unfit, unfitted, unfortified, unqualified, useless, vincible

ASSOCIATED CONCEPTS: veterans' rights

DISABLING, *adjective* crippling, damaging, debilitating, enfeebling, harming, hurting, impairing, incapacitating, injuring, maiming, paralyzing, weakening

DISABUSE, *verb* acquaint, admonish, advise, air, announce, apprise, awaken, brief, clear the mind, communicate, convey, correct, debunk, direct the attention to, disclose, disillusion, divulge, edify, educate, enlarge the mind, enlighten, *eripere,* expose, fill with information, free from a mistaken belief, free from error, give to understand, illumine, impart, indicate, inform, instruct, lay open, let know, make known, manifest, notify, open the mind, point out, prove, put right, put straight, recount, rectify, relate, remedy, remove falsehood, report, reveal, rid of deception, set right, set straight, specify, state, straighten out, teach, tell the truth, unbeguile, unblindfold, uncover, undeceive, unfold, unfool, unmask, unveil, vent

DISACCORD, *noun* affray, animosity, antagonism, argument, argumentation, brawl, broil, caviling, clashing, cleavage, conflict, conflict of opinion, confrontation, contention, contradiction, contrariety, contrariness, controversy, cross-purposes, debate, difference, disaffection, disagreement, discongruity, discord, discordance, discordancy, discrepancy, disharmony, disparity, disputation, dispute, disruption, dissension, dissent, dissidence, dissonance, disunion, disunity, divergence, diversity of opinion, division, embranglement, embroilment, enmity, faction, failure to agree, falling out, feud, fracas, friction, heterodoxy, imbroglio, incompatibility, incongruence, incongruity, inconsistency, inconsonance, inharmoniousness, inharmony, maladjustment, misalliance, nonagreement, nonconformity, noncooperation, odds, opposition, polemics, protest, quarrel, rift, row, schism, skirmish, split, squabble, strained relations, strife, tension, unconformity, variance

DISACCORD, *verb* ablude, altercate, argue, be at variance, bicker, brabble, brangle, break with, challenge, clash, conflict, contend, contradict, contravene, controvert, debate, deny, deviate, differ, differ in opinion, disaffirm, disagree, disapprove, disavow, discept, disclaim, discredit, disharmonize, dispute, dissent, disunite, divaricate, diverge, divide, fall out, gainsay, have differences, have words with, hold opposite views, impugn, join issue, lack harmony, negate, object, oppose, protest, quarrel, rebut, redargue, refuse assent, refuse to accept, refuse to acknowledge, refuse to admit, refuse to consent, refute, reject, remonstrate, repudiate, repugn, resist, run counter to, split, squabble, take exception, traverse, vary, withhold approval, withhold assent, wrangle

DISADVANTAGE, *noun* adverse circumstance, adversity, block, blockade, blockage, burden, check, curb, damage, defect, deficiency, detainment, determent, deterrence, deterrent, detriment, difficulty, disability, disablement, discommodity, discouragement, drawback, embarrassment, encumbrance, failing, fault, frailty, hamper, handicap, harm, hindrance, holdback, impediment, imperfection, imperfectness, imposition, inadequacy, inaptitude, *incommodum,* inconvenience, inexpedience, inferiority, infirmity, inhibition, *iniquitas,* injury, insalubriousness, insufficiency, interference, lack, liability, limitation, loss, nuisance, objection, obstacle, obstruction, penalty, prejudice, prevention, problem, repression, resistance, restraint, restriction, retardation, retardment, setback, shortcoming, stifling, stumbling block, suppression, taint, unfavorable circumstance, unfavorableness, weak point, weakness

FOREIGN PHRASES: ***Cujus est commodum ejus debet esse incommodum.*** He who receives a benefit should also bear the disadvantage.

DISADVANTAGE, *verb* astrict, baffle, balk, bridle, burden, cause problems, check, circumscribe, constrain, cramp, cumber, curb, damage, deprive of advantage, disaccommodate, discommode, encumber, foil, frustrate, hamper, handicap, harm, hinder, hold back, hold in check, impair, impede, impedite, incommode, *incommodum,* inconvenience, inhibit, injure, interfere with, limit, muzzle, obstruct, overburden, overload, prejudice, put out, rein, repress, restrict, retard, saddle, shackle, stall, stymie, suppress, thwart, trammel, weaken, weigh down

DISADVANTAGED, *adjective* burdened, deprived, handicapped, impeded, prejudiced, retarded, weakened

DISADVANTAGEOUS, *adjective* adverse, baleful, baneful, biased, corrosive, counteractant, damaging, deleterious, destructive, detrimental, disapproved, disserviceable, gain-less, harmful, hindering, hurtful, impolitic, inadvisable, *in-commodus,* injurious, inopportune, insalubrious, malefic, maleficent, malignant, negative, pernicious, prejudicial, prof-itless, thwarting, unadvisable, unavailing, unfavorable, un-fruitful, unhealthy, unhelpful, unprofitable, unpropitious, un-wise

DISAFFECT, verb alienate, antagonize, cause a rift, cause dislike, cause hostility, come between, destroy the affection of, disenchant, disfavor, disillusion, disoblige, dis-satisfy, disunite, divide, envenom, estrange, incense, irri-tate, make discontented, make disloyal, make hostile, make inimical, make less friendly, make unfaithful, mislike, pro-voke hatred against, render averse, rile, separate, set against, set at odds, sow dissension, turn away, wean away, withdraw the affections of

DISAFFECTION, noun abandonment, alienation, ani-mosity, antagonism, antipathy, aversion, bad blood, bad faith, bitterness, breach, break, contempt, coolness, defec-tion, dereliction, desertion, disagreement, discomfort, dis-content, discord, discordance, disfavor, disgust, disillusion, disinclination, dislike, disloyalty, displeasure, dissatisfac-tion, dissension, dissent, dudgeon, dyspathy, enmity, es-trangement, falling-out, falseness, feud, grudge, hatred, hostility, ill will, implacability, infidelity, malaise, malice, mutiny, odium, offense, pique, rancor, rebellion, reluc-tance, resentment, revenge, schism, secession, sedition, spleen, split, umbrage, unfriendliness, withdrawal

DISAFFIRM, verb abjure, abnegate, abolish, challenge, conflict with, contravene, controvert, defy, demur, deny, differ, disaffiliate, disagree, disallow, disavow, disclaim, disown, dispute, disregard, dissent, forswear, gainsay, im-pugn, negate, object, oppose, oppugn, overrule, overturn, protest, raise objections, rebut, recant, refuse, refute, re-ject, renounce, repudiate, resist, retract, reverse, run counter to, traverse

ASSOCIATED CONCEPTS: disaffirmance of contract

DISAFFIRMATION, noun abjuration, abjurement, con-tradiction, contravention, contraversion, declination, denial, disallowance, disavowal, disclaimer, disclamation, disown-ing, disownment, forswearing, negation, refusal, rejection, renunciation, repudiation, traversal

DISAGREE, verb argue, battle, be at variance, be con-trary, be discordant, be disunited, be in opposition, be of different opinions, be opposed, bicker, break with, cavil, challenge, clash, collide, conflict, confute, contest, contra-dict, contravene, controvert, create strife, debate, defy, demonstrate, demur, deny, depart, deviate, differ, differ in opinion, disapprove, discord, *discrepare,* dispute, dissent, *dissentire, dissidere,* dissociate oneself, divaricate, diverge, divide, fight, gainsay, have dissension, hold opposite views, lack harmony, not accept, object, oppose, oppugn, protest, quarrel, raise objections, refuse assent, refuse to agree, refute, remonstrate, repudiate, repugn, revolt, split, take a stand against, take exception, take issue, think dif-ferently, traverse, vary, wrangle

DISAGREEMENT, noun altercation, argument, argu-mentation, challenge, conflict, conflict of interest, conflict of opinion, contention, contradiction, contraposition, contrari-ety, contrariness, contravention, controversy, debate, de-murral, difference, difference of opinion, disaccord, dis-cord, discordance, discordancy, discrepancy, *discrepantia,*

disharmony, disputation, *dissensio,* dissension, dissent, dissidence, *dissidium,* dissimilitude, dissonance, disunion, disunity, divergent opinions, diversity of opinion, excep-tion, faction, failure to agree, feud, gainsaying, incompati-bility, inconsonance, inharmoniousness, negation, noncon-sent, objection, odds, opposition, oppugnancy, polemics, quarrel, rebuttal, recusancy, strife, unconformity, variance

FOREIGN PHRASES: ***Cum in corpore dissentitur, apparet nul-lam esse acceptionem.*** Where there is a disagreement on the substance, it appears that there is no acceptance.

DISALLOW, verb abjure, abnegate, abrogate, contra-dict, contravene, controvert, deny, disaffirm, disagree, dis-approve, disavow, disclaim, discredit, disown, dispute, dis-sent, impugn, negate, not accept, not comply, not confirm, object, oppose, protest, rebuff, rebut, refuse, refuse to ac-knowledge, refuse to allow, refuse to corroborate, refuse to grant, refute, reject, renunciate, repudiate, repulse, resist, spurn, vetare, withhold approval

ASSOCIATED CONCEPTS: disallow a claim, notice of disal-lowance

DISALLOWANCE, noun abjuration, abjurement, cen-sorship, compliance, contradiction, contravention, counter-mand, declination, defeasance, denial, disaffirmation, dis-approval, disavowal, disclaimer, disownment, embargo, interdiction, nonconsent, nonforbiddance, obstacle, ob-struction, prohibition, proscription, refusal, rejection, re-nunciation, repudiation, restraint, traversal, veto

DISANNUL, verb abolish, abrogate, annul, cancel, countermand, declare null and void, disclaim, disown, dis-solve, invalidate, nullify, overrule, quash, recall, recant, re-nege, repeal, repudiate, rescind, retract, reverse, revoke, set aside, vacate, vitiate, void, withdraw

DISAPPEAR, verb *abire,* abscond, be effaced, be erased, be lost to view, become extinct, become imper-ceptible, decamp, dematerialize, dissipate, dissolve, es-cape, evanesce, *evanescere,* evaporate, exit, extinguish, fade, fade away, flee, leave, leave no trace, melt away, pass out of sight, recede from view, retreat, take flight, take wing, undergo eclipse, vacate, vanish, vaporize

ASSOCIATED CONCEPTS: unexplained disappearance

DISAPPEARANCE, noun absence, concealment, dema-terialization, departure, desertion, dispersal, dissipation, eclipse, erosion, escape, evanescence, evaporation, exit, exodus, fading, flight, obscuration, occultation, retirement, vanishment, withdrawal

ASSOCIATED CONCEPTS: disappearance of evidence

DISAPPOINT, verb break one's promise to, cause dis-content, dash one's expectation, *deicere,* discourage, dis-enchant, disgruntle, dishearten, disillusion, disillusionize, displease, dissatisfy, fail, *frustrari,* hinder, let down, make dissatisfied, ruin one's prospects, *spe depellere*

DISAPPOINTED, adjective crestfallen, dashed, de-feated, dejected, despondent, discontented, discouraged, disenchanted, disgruntled, disillusioned, displeased, dissat-isfied, distressed, foiled, forlorn, frustrated, let down, put out, successless, thwarted, unsatisfied, unsuccessful

DISAPPROBATION, noun abhorrence, admonishment, adverse comment, animadversion, aspersion, ban, bar, cavil-ing, censure, chiding, commination, complaint, condemna-tion, contumely, criticism, damnation, decrial, denouncement, denunciation, deprecation, depreciation, derogation, detraction, diatribe, disagreement, disapproval, discommendation, discontent, discountenance, disdain, disesteem, disfavor, dislike, disparagement, displeasure, dispraise, disrespect, dissatisfaction, dissent, dissidence, exclusion, excoriation, execration, expostulation, gainsaying, imputation, indictment, lamentation, negation, nonapproval, objection, objurgation, opposition, opprobrium, protest, protestation, rating, rebuke, rejection, remonstrance, remonstration, reprehension, reprimand, reproach, reproof, reproval, repudiation, repugnance, repugnancy, revilement, revulsion, scurrility, shunning, vilipendency, vitriol

DISAPPROVAL, *noun*   abhorrence, adverse comment, animadversion, censure, complaining, complaint, condemnation, contradiction, contravention, criticism, demurrer, demurring, denial, denouncement, denunciation, deprecation, detraction, difference, difference of opinion, disagreement, disallowance, disapprobation, discommendation, discordance, discountenance, disdain, disesteem, disfavor, dislike, disparagement, displeasure, dissatisfaction, dissent, dissentience, dissidence, exception, faultfinding, *improbatio,* low opinion, negation, nonacceptance, nonapproval, nonconsent, objection, opposition, protestation, refusal, rejection, remonstrance, remonstration, reprehension, reproach, repudiation, resistance, shunning, traversal, unacceptance, veto

FOREIGN PHRASES: ***Qui non improbat, approbat.*** He who does not disapprove, approves.

DISAPPROVE *(Condemn), verb*   admonish, animadvert, belittle, berate, brand, call to account, cast aspersions on, cast blame upon, castigate, cavil, censure, chastise, chide, criticize, debase, declaim against, decry, denounce, denunciate, deprecate, discommend, discountenance, discredit, disfavor, dislike, disparage, dispraise, dress down, exclaim against, excoriate, find fault with, fulminate against, hold up to execration, hold up to reprobation, impeach, impugn, malign, muckrake, not take kindly to, object to, objurgate, pass censure upon, pass unfavorable judgment upon, rebuff, rebuke, regard as wrong, regard with blame, remonstrate, reprehend, reprimand, reproach, reprobate, reprove, repudiate, revile, run down, scold, set oneself against, sully, take a dim view of, take exception to, take to task, think ill of, think reprehensible, think wrong, upbraid, view with disfavor, vilipend

DISAPPROVE *(Reject), verb*   abnegate, be against, be contrary, be opposed to, boycott, come in conflict with, *condemnare,* confute, contradict, contravene, controvert, debunk, decline to sanction, demur, deny, deprecate, disaccord with, disagree with, disallow, disavow, disclaim, dispute, gainsay, go against, negate, negative, not abide, not accept, not admit, not approve, not consider, not countenance, not have any part of, not support, object, oppose, pass up, protest, rebuff, refuse, refuse assent to, refuse consent, refuse to confirm, refuse to ratify, refuse to receive, refuse to sanction, reject as inadmissable, renounce, repel, repudiate, resist, scorn, set aside, shun, side against, speak against, spurn, stand against, take exception, take exception to, turn away, turn down, turn from, veto, vote against, vote down, withhold approval from, withhold one's assent, withhold permission

DISARM *(Divest of arms), verb*   *arma homini adimere,* attenuate, cripple, deactivate, debilitate, decimate, deescalate, demilitarize, demobilize, deprive of arms, deprive of means of defense, deprive of power, deprive of strength,

deprive of weapons, devitalize, dilute, disable, disenable, disinvigorate, enervate, enfeeble, *hominem armis exuere,* incapacitate, invalidate, make inactive, make useless, muzzle, neutralize, paralyze, put out of combat, reduce forces, reduce in strength, reduce the armament, render harmless, render innocuous, render powerless, render weak, strip, unarm, undermine, weaken

DISARM *(Set at ease), verb*   allay fears, allay mistrust, appease, assuage, assure, beguile, bring around, bring over, conciliate, content, divest of suspicion, gain over, gain the confidence of, make friendly, mollify, pacify, placate, propitiate, quell suspicion, reconcile, remove suspicion, restore harmony, satisfy, smooth over, subdue, touch, tranquilize, win over

DISARRANGE, *verb*   confuse, derange, discompose, dislocate, disorder, disorganize, disorient, displace, disrupt, disturb, jumble, mismanage, ruffle, scatter, scramble, unsettle, upset

DISASSOCIATE, *verb*   cut off, detach, disconnect, disengage, disjoin, dissociate, disunite, divide, divorce, isolate, part, remove, seclude, separate, set apart, sever, uncouple, withdraw

DISASSOCIATION, *noun*   breach, break, breakdown, detachment, dichotomy, discerption, disconnection, discontinuation, disengagement, disjointure, disjunction, dismemberment, disruption, disseverance, dissociation, dissolution, disunion, divarication, divergence, division, divorce, divorcement, interruption, partition, rift, rupture, schism, segmentation, separation, severence, split, sunderance

DISASTER, *noun*   adversity, affliction, bale, bane, blight, blunder, breakdown, *brutum fulmen, calamitas,* calamity, casualty, cataclysm, catastrophe, *clades,* collapse, *contretemps,* crushing reverse, *déabacle,* devastation, downfall, emergency, extremity, failure, fell stroke, fiasco, great misfortune, great mishap, hard blow, harm, holocaust, misadventure, miscarriage, misery, misfortune, misventure, nasty blow, ravage, ruin, ruination, ruinousness, scourge, setback, sudden misfortune, terrible accident, tragedy, travail, trouble, undoing, unfortunate event, upheaval, upset, woe

ASSOCIATED CONCEPTS: common disaster

DISASTROUS, *adjective*   all-destroying, annihilative, appalling, bad, baneful, blighting, *calamitosus,* calamitous, cataclysmal, cataclysmic, catastrophic, crushing, damaging, deadly, deleterious, demolishing, desolating, destroying, destructive, detrimental, devastating, dire, disheartening, distressing, dreadful, eradicative, exterminating, exterminatory, extirpative, fell, fraught with harm, frightful, *funestus,* grievous, grim, harmful, harrowing, heartbreaking, horrendous, horrible, horrid, hurtful, ill-omened, injurious, malefic, malign, oppressive, perilous, *perniciosus,* pernicious, ravaging, ruining, ruinous, sinistrous, tragic, tragical, unfavorable

DISAVOW, *verb*   abnegate, back down, back out, call back, declare not to be true, decline, deny, deny absolutely, deny connection with, deny emphatically, deny entirely, deny peremptorily, deny responsibility for, deny wholly, *diffiteri,* disaffirm, disbelieve, discard, disclaim, discredit, disdain, disown, dispense with, dissent, dissociate oneself, forswear, *infitiari, infitias ire,* invalidate, negate, negative, not accept, not admit, not approve, not confirm, not maintain, not pass, nullify, pass up, protest, recall, recant, refuse, refuse credence, refuse to accept, refuse to acknowledge, refuse to admit, refuse to corroborate, reject, relinquish, renounce, repel, repudiate, repulse, rescind, retract, revoke, scorn, send back, set aside, set at naught, shun, spurn, take back, traverse, turn away from, turn back, turn from, veto, withdraw

DISBAND, *verb* break apart, break the association of, break up, cut off, deactivate, demobilize, detach, *dimittere,* discharge, disconnect, disembody, disengage, disjoin, disjoint, dislocate, dismember, dismiss, dismiss from service, disorganize, dispel, disperse, dissever, dissociate, dissolve by dismissal, disunite, divorce, *exauctorare,* go apart, go different ways, go separate ways, let go, let out, part, part company, release, scatter, separate, sever, sunder, unbind, uncouple, withdraw from association

DISBAR, *verb* disbench, dismiss from the bar, dismiss from the legal profession, disqualify as an attorney, divest of legal office, drum out of the legal profession, exclude from the profession of law, expel from the bar, expel from the legal profession, invalidate an attorney's license, remove from legal office, remove from the practice of law, remove from the roll of attorneys, render an attorney's license null and void, rescind an attorney's license to practice, revoke one's license to practice law, strike off the roll of lawyers, suspend from the practice of law, suspend from the profession of law, void the license of an attorney
ASSOCIATED CONCEPTS: disbarment proceedings

DISBELIEVE, *verb* be doubtful, be incredulous, be skeptical, be unconvinced, challenge, consider implausible, consider not to be true, consider unproven, consider untrue, discredit, dispute, distrust, doubt, give no credence to, give no credit to, harbor doubts, harbor suspicions, have doubts, have qualms, have reservations, hold not to be true, lack faith, mistrust, *non credere,* not accept, not believe, not find tenable, question, refuse credence, refuse to admit, refuse to believe, refuse to credit, reject, reject as untrue, remain unconverted, set no store by, suspect, take no stock in, withhold assent

DISBURSE *(Distribute),* *verb* administer, allocate, allot, apportion, assign, circulate, deal out, diffuse, discharge, dispense, disseminate, divide, dole out, give, give away, give out, hand out, make available, make distribution of, mete, parcel out, pass out, prorate, ration, scatter, share, spread

DISBURSE *(Pay out),* *verb* bear the cost of, bear the expense of, compensate, defray, defray the cost, *dissolvere,* endure the cost of, expend, *exsolvere,* give money, give out in payment, incur costs, incur expenses, lay out, make expenditure, make payment, meet charges, meet the bill, meet the expense of, outlay, pay, pay off, recompense, reimburse, remunerate, render payment, repay, requite, reward, *solvere,* spend, stand the cost of, support the expense of, tender payment, undergo the cost of, undergo the expense of

DISBURSEMENT *(Act of disbursing),* *noun* alloting, allotment, apportioning, apportionment, assigning by lot, compensating, dealing out, dispersal, disposal, disseminating, dissemination, dividing, handing out, laying out, outgo, outlay, parceling out

DISBURSEMENT *(Funds paid out),* **noun** allowance, compensation, costs, defrayal, defrayment, emolument, expenditure, expense, fees, money going out, moneys expended, moneys paid out, outgo, outlay, pay, payment, recompense, redress, reimbursement, remittance, remuneration, repayment, restitution, spendings
ASSOCIATED CONCEPTS: disbursements necessarily paid or incurred, legal disbursements, necessary disbursements

DISCARD, *noun* castaway, castoff, debris, *déclassé,* derelict, detritus, *évacué,* foundling, leaving, oddment, *proscrit,* reject, remainder, remnant, waste

DISCERN *(Detect with the senses),* **verb** appreciate, apprehend, apprehend clearly, ascertain, awake to, become acquainted with, become apprized, become aware of, become informed, behold, cast eyes on, catch sight of, cognize, command a view of, comprehend, descry, detect, discover, espy, examine, experience, fathom, have in sight, inspect, know, lay eyes on, look at, look on, look upon, make out, mentally appreciate, note, notice, observe, perceive, realize, recognize, regard, scrutinize, see, see at a glance, set eyes on, sight, spot, spy, view, visualize, witness

DISCERN *(Discriminate),* **verb** detect differences, differentiate, distinguish, exercise discretion, have insight, judge, keep in perspective, make distinctions, note the distinctions, recognize as distinct, see as distinct, see the difference

DISCERNIBLE, *adjective* apparent, beholdable, cognizable, detectable, evident, in sight, knowable, manifest, observable, perceivable, perceptible, recognizable, seeable, self-evident, viewable, visible, visual

DISCERNING, *adjective* acute, astute, circumspect, clever, cognizant, conscious, critical, discreet, discriminating, discriminative, incisive, intelligent, judicious, juridical, keen-sighted, knowing, lucid, omniscient, penetrating, perceptive, perspicacious, provident, rational, reasonable, responsive, sagacious, sage, sapient, sensible, sensitive, sharp, shrewd, subtle, understanding, wise
ASSOCIATED CONCEPTS: discern right from wrong

DISCERNMENT, *noun* acuity, acumen, acuteness, apperception, appreciation, ascertainment, astuteness, clairvoyance, cleverness, cognition, comprehension, conclusion, conspection, diagnosis, discovery, discretion, discrimination, farsightedness, good sense, ingenuity, insight, intelligence, intuition, judgment, ken, knowledge, observance, penetration, perception, perspicacity, profundity, realization, reason, sense, sensibility, sharpness, shrewdness, subtlety, understanding

DISCHARGE *(Annulment),* **noun** abolishment, abolition, abrogation, canceling, cancellation, cessation, defeasance, discontinuance, dissolution, invalidation, negation, nullification, recall, repeal, repudiation, rescission, retractation, reversal, revocation, voidance

DISCHARGE *(Dismissal),* **noun** dimissio, displacement, ejection, elimination, eviction, expulsion, firing, ouster, ousting, removal, removal from employment, replacement, unseating
ASSOCIATED CONCEPTS: cause for discharge, conditional discharge, discharge from army, discharge from employment, discharge of employee, discriminatory discharge, improper discharge

DISCHARGE

DISCHARGE *(Liberation),* **noun** absolution, acquittal, clearance, deliverance, disenthrallment, emancipation, exculpation, exemption, exoneration, extrication, legal release from confinement, loosing, release, release from custody, reprieve, salvation, setting free

DISCHARGE *(Payment),* **noun** acquitment, acquittal, acquittance, amortization, amortizement, annulment of debt, clearance, compensation, defrayal, defrayment, full satisfaction, liquidation, paying off, recompense, redemption, refund, reimbursement, remittance, reparation, repayment, restitution, retirement of a debt, return, satisfaction, settlement, settlement on account

DISCHARGE *(Performance),* **noun** accomplishment, achievement, attainment, carrying through, commission, completion, conclusion, consummation, culmination, dispatch, effectuation, enforcement, execution, fruition, fulfillment, implementation, observance, perpetration, production, realization, termination
ASSOCIATED CONCEPTS: discharge of duty, faithful discharge of official duties

DISCHARGE *(Release from obligation),* **noun** abolition, abrogation, absolution, acquittal, cancellation, defeasance, deliverance, delivery, dismissal, dispensation, emancipation, exception, exculpation, excuse, exemption, exoneration, extrication, invalidation, loosing, nullification, pardon, repeal, reprieve, rescission, revocation, voidance

DISCHARGE *(Shot),* **noun** blast, blasting, bombardment, burst, *coniectio, coniectus,* crash, detonation, emanation, *emissio,* emmission, explosion, firing, firing a charge, flare, flash, fulguration, fulmination, fusillade, igniting, salvo, spray, volley

DISCHARGE *(Dismiss),* **verb** cashier, cast, cast loose, depose, deprive of office, *dimittere,* disbar, discard, disemploy, displace, drop, eject, exclude, expel, fire, get rid of, give notice, impeach, let go, let loose, *missum facere,* put on the retired list, release, relieve, remove, remove from office, replace, retire, shut out, strike off the roll, suspend, throw out, turn loose, turn out, unseat
ASSOCIATED CONCEPTS: discharged for cause, lawfully discharged, reinstatement

DISCHARGE *(Liberate),* **verb** absolve, acquit, bail out, clear, deliver, emancipate, exculpate, excuse, exonerate, extricate, forgive, free, let go, let loose, let out, let out of prison, loose, pardon, parole, purge, release, relieve, render free, set at liberty, set free, turn loose
ASSOCIATED CONCEPTS: discharge from imprisonment, discharge from prison

DISCHARGE *(Pay a debt),* **verb** adjust, amortize, clear, hand over, honor, liquidate, make reparation, make restitution, meet, pay in full, pay off, pay up, recompense, redeem, refund, repay, satisfy, satisfy in full, settle, settle accounts, square accounts, strike a balance, take up
ASSOCIATED CONCEPTS: discharge from obligation

DISCHARGE *(Perform),* **verb** accomplish, achieve, act on, adjust, administer, attain, bring about, bring to pass, carry into effect, carry into execution, carry out, carry through, complete, comply, concern oneself with, conclude, consummate, culminate, devote oneself to, dispatch, dispose of, do, effect, effectuate, enforce, execute, fulfill, go about, go through with, implement, *munus obire,*

proceed with, produce, realize, render, resolve, succeed, transact
ASSOCIATED CONCEPTS: properly discharge one's responsibilities

DISCHARGE *(Release from obligation),* **verb** abolish, abrogate, absolve, annul, cancel, declare null and void, discontinue, dismiss, dissolve, excuse, exempt, exonerate, forgive, invalidate, make void, nullify, quash, recall, relieve, relieve of responsibility, remove, render void, repeal, rescind, retract, reverse, revoke, set aside
ASSOCIATED CONCEPTS: discharge of a debt
FOREIGN PHRASES: *Eodem modo quo oritur, eodem modo dissolvitur.* It is discharged in the same manner in which it was created.

DISCHARGE *(Shoot),* **verb** blast, burst, deliver a charge, detonate, emit, expel, explode, fire, fire at, fulminate, ignite, launch, *mittere,* open fire, send forth
ASSOCIATED CONCEPTS: discharge of a weapon

DISCIPLE, **noun** accepter, adherent, admirer, advocate, ally, apostle, apprentice, *auditor,* backer, believer, condisciple, devotee, *discipulus, élève,* favorer, follower, hanger-on, imitator, learner, loyalist, promoter, protegé, pupil, receiver, recruit, scholar, student, supporter, sympathizer, true believer, truster, votary

DISCIPLINARY *(Educational),* **adjective** academic, cultural, didactic, didactical, doctrinal, educative, informational, informative, instructional, instructive, paedeutic, pedagogic, pedagogical, preceptive, preceptoral, scholarly, scholastic, training, tuitionary, tutorial

DISCIPLINARY *(Punitory),* **adjective** amercing, castigatory, chastening, corrective, inflictive, penal, penological, punishing, punitive, reformational, reformative, reformatory, regulatory, retaliatory, retributive, talionic
ASSOCIATED CONCEPTS: disciplinary action, disciplinary hearing, disciplinary power, disciplinary proceeding

DISCIPLINE *(Field of study),* **noun** area of education, area of learning, branch of instruction, branch of knowledge, course, curriculum, doctrine, education, field of interest, field of learning, learning, lore, teaching

DISCIPLINE *(Obedience),* **noun** acquiescence, compliance, constancy, constraint, control, curb, deference, devotion, *disciplina,* dutifulness, faithfulness, fidelity, limitation, loyalty, malleability, nonresistance, obsequiousness, observance, pliancy, repression, restraint, self-command, self-conquest, self-denial, self-direction, self-mastery, self-regulation, self-restraint, servility, stoicism, strength of character, strength of will, submission, submissiveness, subordination to rules, will power
ASSOCIATED CONCEPTS: disciplinary proceeding

DISCIPLINE *(Punishment),* **noun** amercement, castigation, chastening, chastisement, correction, deprivation, infliction, judgment, just deserts, penal retribution, penalty, penance, penology, reprimand, reproof, retribution, retributive justice, scourge, suffering, trial

DISCIPLINE *(Training),* **noun** coaching, conditioning, conduct, cultivation, development, diligent exercise, diligent practice, drill, drilling, exercise, grooming, guidance, inculcation, indoctrination, initiation, instruction, practice, preparation, qualification, readying, regulation, rehearsal, schooling, system of drill, systematic training

DISCIPLINE *(Control)*, **verb**   administer, bridle, bring to a state of obedience, bring under subjection, check, command, curb, direct, dominate, exercere, exercise direction over, govern, govern strictly, harness, hold in leash, hold in line, limit, make toe the line, manage, muzzle, oversee, pull in, regulate, rein in, restrain, restrict, stand over, subjugate, superintend, supervise

DISCIPLINE *(Punish)*, **verb**   administer correction, bring to retribution, call to account, carry out a sentence, castigate, chasten, chastise, correct, deal retributive justice, exact a penalty, exact retribution, execute a sentence, execute judgment, execute justice, get even with, give one his deserts, impose a penalty, inflict penalty, inflict penance upon, make an example of, penalize, reprove, scourge, sentence, subject to punishment, take to task, visit punishment

ASSOCIATED CONCEPTS: deterrence, disciplinary proceeding, isolation, rehabilitation, retribution

DISCIPLINE *(Train)*, **verb**   accustom, break in, bring up, coach, condition, cultivate, direct, educate, enlighten, form, foster, give directions, give instructions, give lessons in, groom, guide, habituate, impress upon the mind, inculcate, indoctrinate, infuse, instill, *instituere,* instruct, nurture, prepare, put through paces, qualify, raise, ready, rear, school, show, train by instruction

DISCLAIM, verb   abandon, abnegate, abrogate, annul, cancel, declare null and void, deny, deny any knowledge of, desert, disaffirm, disannul, disavow, disbelieve, discard, discharge, discountenance, disown, dispense with, divest oneself of, forego, forsake, forswear, give up, not accept, not admit, recant, reject, renounce, *repudiare,* repudiate, rescind, retract, set aside, spurn, take back, take exception to, turn away, unsay

DISCLAIMER, noun   abandonment, abjuration, abjurement, annulment, denial, disaffirmation, disallowance, disavowal, disclamation, disownment, dissociation, negation, nullification, recantation, refusal, rejection, relinquishment, renouncement, renunciation, repudiation, revocation

ASSOCIATED CONCEPTS: disclaimer of interest, disclaimer of knowledge, disclaimer of liability, disclaimer of title, disclaimer of warranties, innocent bystanders, liability to third parties, third parties

DISCLOSE, verb   acknowledge, acquaint, admit, advise, air, allude to, announce, *aperire,* apprise, bare, blazon, bring into the open, bring into view, bring out, bring to light, circulate, communicate, confess, declare, describe, *detegere,* dismask, disseminate, divulge, enlighten, evidence, evince, exhibit, expose, give utterance to, impart, *indicare,* indicate, inform, lay bare, make known, make public, mention, notify, present, proclaim, promulgate, publish, report, reveal, speak out, speak the truth, tell, uncover, unearth, unfold, unmask, unscreen, unseal, unshroud, unveil, utter, vent, voice

ASSOCIATED CONCEPTS: disclose assets, disclose the location of a debtor's residence, disclose wrongdoing, disclosed principal, disclosure of public information

DISCLOSURE *(Act of disclosing)*, **noun**   admission, advisement, announcement, appraisal, assertion, communication, concession, confession, declaration, disclosing, dissemination, divulgation, divulgement, divulgence, enlightenment, enumeration, exposition, exposure, informing, making aware, making public, mention, notification, patefactio, presentation

to view, proclamation, production, profession, publication, recital, recitation, relation, representation, revealing, revealment, showing, telling, uncovering, uncovery, unfolding, unfoldment, unmasking, unveiling, uttering

ASSOCIATED CONCEPTS: disclosure device, disclosure of assets, disclosure of interest, duty of disclosure, false disclosure, nondisclosure, right to disclosure, voluntary disclosure

FOREIGN PHRASES: *Suppressio veri, suggestio falsi.* The suppression of truth is equivalent to the suggestion of what is false.

DISCLOSURE *(Something disclosed)*, **noun**   acknowledgement, admission, affirmation, announcement, answer, assertion, averment, avowal, communication, concession, confession, confirmation, declaration, deposition, discovery, divulgence, enunciation, explanation, exposé, exposition, expression, *indicium,* information, inside information, knowledge, manifestation, message, news, notice, notification, presentation, proclamation, profession, publication, recital, remark, report, revealment, revelation, statement, testimony, utterance, word

DISCOMMEND, verb   asperse, attack, belittle, bring into discredit, censure, clamor against, condemn, contemn, criticize, decry, denigrate, denounce, deprecate, depreciate, deride, derogate, detract, disapprove, discredit, disfavor, disparage, dispraise, disvalue, fault, find fault, malign, reflect discredit upon, revile, ridicule, scoff at, slight, slur, sneer at, speak ill of, speak slightingly of, spurn, traduce, underrate, undervalue, view with disfavor, vilify, vilipend

DISCOMMODE, verb   afflict, affront, aggravate, agitate, annoy, arouse, astound, badger, beset, bother, chafe, contravene, counteract, disaccommodate, disadvantage, disconcert, dishearten, disoblige, displease, disquiet, distress, disturb, exasperate, grieve, harry, hinder, impede, impose upon, incommode, inconvenience, irk, irritate, make uneasy, oppress, perplex, perturb, pique, plague, provoke, put to inconvenience, trouble, undermine, unnerve, upset, vex, worry

DISCOMPOSE, verb   addle, afflict, aggravate, agitate, annoy, appall, astound, badger, bedazzle, bedevil, befuddle, bewilder, bring into disorder, browbeat, carp at, chafe, confound, confuse, convulse, cross, daze, dazzle, dement, demoralize, derange, disarrange, discomfit, discomfort, discommode, disconcert, dishevel, dislocate, dismay, disorder, disorganize, displace, disquiet, distemper, disturb, disturb the composure of, embitter, enrage, envenom, exasperate, excite, ferment, fluster, fog, fret, goad, gripe, harass, harry, heckle, hurt the feelings, incense, inflame, infuriate, irk, irritate, jar, jolt, jumble, make uneasy, mix up, mortify, muddle, nettle, nonplus, perplex, perturb, pester, pique, plague, provoke, put out, rattle, rile, roil, ruffle, shake, shake up, shatter, stir, taunt, tease, throw into confusion, torment, tousle, trouble, try the patience, unbalance, unhinge, unsettle, upset, vex, worry

DISCONCERT, verb   abash, agitate, alarm, annoy, appall, astound, bedazzle, bedevil, cause discontent, chagrin, confound, confuse, discomfit, discomfort, discompose, discountenance, dismay, disquiet, disrupt, disturb, fluster, give cause for alarm, *percellere,* perplex, perturb, *perturbare,* puzzle, ruffle, startle, throw into confusion, upset

DISCONNECTED, adjective   abstracted, adrift, apart, asunder, broken, broken off, cut apart, cut in two, detached, disassociated, discontinuous, discrete, disembodied, disjoined, disjointed, disjunct, disjunctive, disparate, disunited, divergent, divorced, incoherent, inconsistent, interrupted, irrational, irrelative, isolated, jumbled, loose, noncohesive, partitioned, put asunder, scattered, separate, separated, set apart, set asunder, severed, sundered, switched off, unaffiliated, unallied, unannexed, unassociated, unattached, uncohesive, unconnected, uncoupled, unintelligible, unjoined, unlinked, unrelated

DISCONSOLATE, _adjective_ afflicted, anguished, atrabilious, bereaved, brokenhearted, burdened, careworn, cast down, cheerless, comfortless, crestfallen, crushed, dejected, depressed, desolate, despairing, despondent, discouraged, disheartened, dismal, dispirited, distressed, doleful, dolorous, downcast, downhearted, elegiac, encumbered, forlorn, funereal, gloomy, glum, grief-stricken, grieved, grieving, heartbroken, heartsick, heavy-laden, hopeless, hurt, in despair, in heavy spirits, inconsolable, infelicitous, joyless, lachrymose, lamenting, languishing, lost, low spirited, _maestus,_ melancholic, melancholy, miserable, moody, morose, mournful, mourning, overcome, pained, pathetic, pessimistic, plaintive, sad, saturnine, sober, somber, sorrowful, spiritless, stricken, tearful, _triste,_ troubled, unconsolable, unhappy, unnerved, wan, weeping, woebegone, woeful, wretched

DISCONTINUANCE (_Act of discontinuing_), **noun** abeyance, abolishment, abolition, adjournment, breaking off, cancellation, cancelling, cessation, defeasance, desistance, discontinuation, dismissal, disruption, disuse, interruption, interval, invalidation, nonuse, nullification, pause, postponement, recess, remission, stop, stoppage, suspension, termination, withdrawal

DISCONTINUANCE (_Interruption of a legal action_), **noun** ampliation, cessation, desistance, discontinuation, dismissal, moratorium, termination, withdrawal

DISCONTINUE (_Abandon_), **verb** abolish, abort, abrogate, abstain, annul, apostatize, arrest, break, break off, bring to a close, bring to an end, call off, cancel, cause a discontinuance, cease, cease using, check, close, complete, conclude, consummate, demit, desist, desist from, destroy, discard, disconnect, disjoin, dismiss, dissever, dissolve, disunite, drop, end, expire, finish, forfeit, forsake, give up, halt, have done with, invalidate, leave, leave off, let lapse, play out, put an end to, quit, relinquish, renounce, repeal, resign, retire, revoke, separate, sever, shut down, stop, sunder, surrender, suspend, terminate, vacate, void, waive, withdraw
ASSOCIATED CONCEPTS: discontinuance of an action, dismissal, judgment of discontinuance, lack of prosecution, nonsuit, voluntary discontinuance

DISCONTINUE (_Break continuity_), **verb** adjourn, arrest, balk, break, break off, bring to a standstill, check, cut, cut short, dam up, defer, delay, disconnect, disengage, disjoin, disrupt, dissever, dissolve, disturb, disunite, divide, foil, frustrate, hesitate, hinder, hold in abeyance, intercept, interfere with, interject, intermit, interpose, interrupt, intervene, intrude, leave off, obstruct, part, postpone, punctuate, recess, remit, retard, separate, sever, sunder, suspend, thwart, wait, waive

DISCORD, _noun_ animosity, antagonism, argumentation, bickering, clashing, conflict, contention, controversy, difference, disaccord, disaccordance, disagreement, discongruity,

discordance, _discordia,_ discrepancy, disharmony, disparity, dispute, _dissensio,_ dissension, dissent, dissentience, dissidence, _dissidium,_ dissimilarity, dissonance, disunion, disunity, divergent opinions, diversity, division, divisiveness, enmity, faction, failure to agree, friction, hostility, ill feeling, ill will, incompatibility, incongruence, incongruity, lack of concord, nonagreement, opposition, quarreling, schism, split, strained relations, strife, unharmoniousness, variance, wrangling

DISCORDANT, _adjective_ adverse, antagonistic, antipathetical, antithetical, antonymous, at cross purposes, at variance, cacophonous, clashing, colliding, conflicting, conflictory, contradictory, contradistinct, contrarious, contrary, counter, differing, disaccordant, disagreeing, _discors, discrepans,_ discrepant, dissentient, dissenting, dissident, dissimilar, dissonant, _dissonus,_ divergent, diverse, hostile, in disagreement, inaccordant, incompatible, incongruent, incongruous, inconsistent, inconsonant, inharmonious, inimical, inverse, irreconcilable, opposed, opposing, opposite, oppositional, oppugnant, out of accord, strident, unagreeing, variant

DISCOUNT, _noun_ abatement, allowance, amount deducted, bargain, _decessio,_ decrease, decrement, _deductio,_ deduction, diminution, lower price, markdown, reduction, special price, subtraction
ASSOCIATED CONCEPTS: discount a loan, discount bills, discount notes, trade discount

DISCOUNT (_Disbelieve_), **verb** be indifferent to, belittle, brush aside, _decessio, deductio,_ depreciate, discountenance, discredit, disdain, disesteem, disparage, disregard, distrust, doubt, gloss over, harbor suspicions, ignore, make light of, misprize, mistrust, pass over, pay no attention, pay no heed, pay no mind, question, slight, spurn, suspect

DISCOUNT (_Minimize_), **verb** abate, abbreviate, abridge, allay, attenuate, condense, curtail, deflate, detract, diminish, lessen, minimalize, pare, reduce, render less, scale down, shorten, underestimate, understate, undervalue

DISCOUNT (_Reduce_), **verb** abate, allow a margin, cut, decrease, deduct from, depreciate, detract, lower, lower the sale price, make allowance for, mark down, rebate, reduce the mark-up, sell below par, slash prices, strike off, subduct, subtract, take from, take off, underprice, undersell, undervalue

DISCOURAGE, _verb_ advise against, affright, _animum frangere,_ argue against, avert, cast down, cause discontent, cause dislike, cause doubt, caution, contraindicate, convince to the contrary, dampen, daunt, deflect, dehort, deject, demoralize, deprecate, depress, deprive of courage, destroy confidence, deter, _deterrere,_ disaffect, discountenance, disenchant, disgruntle, dishearten, disillusion, disincline, disinterest, dismay, dispirit, dissuade, divert, expostulate, forestall, frighten away, give one pause, hinder, impose difficulties, indispose, inspire fear, intimidate, keep back, keep from, lessen the self-confidence of, lower the courage of, obstruct by opposition, oppose, persuade against, put a damper on, quench, remonstrate, render averse, repel, reprove, restrain, sadden, scare, set against, thwart, turn aside, turn from, unnerve, upset, warn, weaken the resolution of

DISCOURSE, _noun_ address, allocution, argument, argumentation, commentary, conference, _conlocutio, conloquium,_ conversation, declamation, dialogue, discussion, disquisition, dissertation, elucidation, exchange of views, excursus, exhortation, exposition, expression of views, formal discussion, interchange of views, interlocution, language, lecture, oral communication, oration, prelection, recital, recitation, rhetorical presentation, *sermo*, speech, talk, verbal communication, verbal exposition, verbal intercourse

DISCOURSE, verb address, comment, commune with, communicate orally, confabulate, confer, *conloqui*, converse, debate, deliver a speech, deliver a talk, deliver an address, dilate, discuss, dissertate, exchange observations, expatiate, explain, expound, give a speech, give a talk, give an address, hold a conference, lecture, make a speech, orate, *orationem facere, orationem habere*, parley, perorate, prelect, recite, sermonize, speak, talk, talk over, talk together

DISCOVER, verb ascertain, awake to, become informed, behold, bring to light, chance upon, *cognoscere*, collect knowledge, come to know, come upon, *comperire*, deduce, descry, detect, determine, diagnose, discern, divine, elicit, encounter, expose, ferret out, find out, get a glimpse of, identify, *invenire*, investigate, learn, learn for a certainty, learn of, locate, manifest, observe, perceive, pinpoint, realize, see, turn up, uncover, understand, unearth, unravel
ASSOCIATED CONCEPTS: discover facts and information known by an adverse party, discovered negligence, doctrine of discovered peril, proceeding to discover assets

DISCOVERY, noun acquisition of knowledge, ascertainment, checking, declaration, descrial, detection, discernment, disclosure, disclosure proceedings, distinguishing, divulgence, espial, examination for the purpose of ascertaining facts, exploration, exposition, exposure, finding out, first sight, identification, inquiry, inspection, investigation, investigation to uncover facts, observation, perception, perusal, pretrial examination proceedings, quest, reconnoitering, revealment, revelation, scrutiny, sighting, surveying, uncovering, unearthing
ASSOCIATED CONCEPTS: discovery of deceit, discovery of facts, discovery of fraud, discovery of loss, discovery of mistake, discovery proceeding, discovery which can be patented, doctrine of discovered peril

DISCREDIT, noun animadversion, aspersion, attaint, baseness, castigation, censure, condemnation, contumely, criticism, debasement, *dedecus*, degradation, denunciation, derogation, disapprobation, disapproval, disbelief, disesteem, disfavor, disgrace, dishonor, disparagement, dispraise, disreputability, disrepute, distrust, *ignominia*, ignominy, impaired reputation, imputation, incredulity, *infamia*, infamy, ingloriousness, lack of confidence, lack of esteem, loss of belief, loss of credence, loss of credit, loss of repute, mistrust, odium, opprobrium, *probrum*, reflection, remonstrance, reprehension, reproach, reprobation, repudiation, revilement, scandal, shame, slur, stain, stigma, stricture, taint, tarnish, turpitude
ASSOCIATED CONCEPTS: discredit a witness

DISCREDIT, verb *abrogare*, asperse, besmirch, brand, bring disgrace upon, bring into disfavor, bring reproach upon, cast aspersions on, cast shame upon, debase, decry, degrade, denigrate, deprecate, depreciate, deprive of credit, *derogare*, derogate from, discount, disgrace, dishonor, disparage, downgrade, hold up to shame, impair the reputation of, impute shame to, injure the credit of, involve

in shame, make distasteful, malign, reflect dishonor upon, reprehend, scandalize, stain, stigmatize, taint, tarnish
ASSOCIATED CONCEPTS: discredit a witness, discredited witness

DISCREET, adjective astute, calculating, careful, cautious, *cautus*, chary, circumspect, *consideratus*, deliberate, diplomatic, discerning, discretional, discretionary, discriminate, discriminating, discriminative, distinguishing, forethoughtful, guarded, intelligent, judicious, mindful, perceptive, polite, politic, precautious, prepared, *prudens*, prudent, refined, reflecting, regardful, reserved, reticent, sensible, sensitive, subtle, thoughtful, vigilant, watchful, well-advised, wise

DISCREPANCY, noun aberration, anomaly, asymmetry, clash, conflict, contradiction, contrast, departure, deviation, difference, differential, differentiation, disaccord, disagreement, discongruity, discord, discordance, disharmony, disparity, disputed point, dissimilarity, dissimilitude, dissonance, divergence, failure to correspond, ground of argument, inaccordance, incompatibility, incongruence, incongruency, incongruity, inconsistency, inequality, irreconcilability, lack of accord, lack of agreement, lack of concert, lack of conformity, lack of congruence, lack of congruity, lack of consonance, lack of resemblance, matter of disputation, nonagreement, nonconformity, nonuniformity, split, subject of controversy, subject of dispute, unconformity, unlikeness, variance, variation

DISCREPANT, adjective at variance, clashing, conflicting, conflictory, contradictory, contrary, deviant, different, differing, disagreeing, discordant, disparate, disproportionate, dissenting, dissident, dissimilar, dissonant, distinct, divergent, diverse, divided, divisive, factious, ill-matched, ill-mated, inapplicable, inapposite, incommensurate, incongruent, incongruous, inconsistent, inconsonant, inimical, jarring, opposite, peculiar, quarreling, schismatic, unconformable, unrelated, variant

DISCRETE, adjective apart, asunder, cut off, detached, different, disassociated, disconnected, *discontinu*, discontinuous, discretive, disengaged, disjoined, disjoint, disjunct, dissociated, distinct, distinguished, disunited, divided, individual, isolated, noncontinuous, parted, removed, separate, separated, sundered, unannexed, unassimilated, unassociated, unattached, unconnected, unfastened, unjoined

DISCRETION (Power of choice), **noun** analysis, appraisal, assessment, choice, consideration, contemplation, decision, designation, determination, discrimination, distinction, election, evaluation, examination, free decision, free will, freedom of choice, liberty of choosing, liberty of judgment, license, option, optionality, permission, pick, power of choosing, review, right of choice, sanction, selection, self-determination, suffrage, suo *arbitrio*, volition, will
ASSOCIATED CONCEPTS: absolute discretion, abuse of discretion, administrative discretion, arbitrariness, capriciousness, certiorari, judicial discretion, legal discretion, mandemus, prohibition, unreasonableness
FOREIGN PHRASES: *Optima est lex quae minimum relinquit arbitrio judicis; optimas judex qui minimum sibi.* That is the best system of law which leaves the least to the discretion of the judge; that judge is the best who leaves the least to his own discretion. *Optimam esse legem, quae minimum relinquit arbitrio judicis; id quod certitudo ejus praestat.* That law is the best which leaves the least discretion to the judge; this is an advantage which results from its certainty. *Optimus judex, qui minimum sibi.* He is the

best judge who leaves the least to his own discretion. ***Quam longum debet esse rationabile tempus non definitur in lege, sed pendet ex discretione justiciariorum.*** How long a reasonable time ought to be is not defined by law, but is left to the discretion of the judges. ***Quam rationabilis debet esse finis, non definitur, sed omnibus circum stantiis inspectis pendet ex justiciariorum discretione.*** What a reasonable fine ought to be is not defined, but is left to the discretion of the judges, all the circumstances being considered.

DISCRETION (*Quality of being discreet*), **noun** ability to get along with others, acuteness, aesthetic judgment, appreciation, appreciativeness, art of negotiating, artful management, artfulness, artistic judgment, attention, care, carefulness, caution, cautiousness, chariness, circumspection, circumspectness, cleverness, competence, concern, considerateness, consideration, craft, deftness, deliberation, delicacy, diplomacy, discernment, discreetness, discriminating taste, discrimination, discriminatory powers, distinction, expertness, facility, finesse, good sense, guardedness, heed, heedfulness, insight, intuition, *iudicium,* judiciousness, mature responsibility, maturity, mindfulness, nicety, particularness, perception, perspicacity, polish, precaution, presence of mind, providence, prudence, *prudentia,* qualification, quick judgment, refined discrimination, refinement, regardfulness, resourcefulness, safeguard, sagacity, sagesse, *savoir faire,* sensitiveness, sensitivity, sharpness, shrewd diagnosis, shrewdness, skill, sound judgment, sound reasoning, statesmanship, strategy, subtlety, sympathetic perception, tact, tactfulness, taste, technique, thoughtfulness, wariness, watchfulness, wisdom

ASSOCIATED CONCEPTS: absolute discretion, abuse of discretion, administrative discretion, discretion to set aside a judgment, improper exercise of discretion, judicial discretion, prosecutorial discretion, sound discretion

FOREIGN PHRASES: ***Discretio est scire per legem quid sit justum.*** Discretion consists in knowing through the law what is just.

DISCRETIONARY, *adjective* conative, discretional, discriminative, elective, left to discretion, left to individual judgment, optional, selective, volitional, volitive

ASSOCIATED CONCEPTS: discretionary authority, discretionary damages, discretionary power of the court, discretionary trusts

DISCRIMINATE (*Distinguish*), **verb** characterize, classify, compare, contrast, designate, determine the essentials, differentiate, *diiudicare, discernere, distinguere,* divide, draw the line, individualize, *internoscere,* label, make a choice, make a distinction, make a selection, mark, mark the difference between, note differences, point out, recognize as separate, see the difference, separate, set apart, set off, sift, sort out, tell apart

DISCRIMINATE (*Treat differently*), **verb** avoid, be partial, be predisposed, bear a grudge against, bear malice, disapprove of, disfavor, favor, have an affection for, have ill feelings toward, incline toward, lean toward, look down upon, make a distinction, object to, prefer, reject, show an aversion, show bias, show preference, show prejudice, shun, tend toward

ASSOCIATED CONCEPTS: age discrimination, discriminate against an employee, discriminate in price, discriminatory tax, equal protection, invidious discrimination, race discrimination, religious discrimination, sex discrimination, unlawful discrimination

DISCRIMINATING (*Distinguishing*), **adjective** contradistinct, contrasting, diacritical, differentiating, differentiative, differing, discriminate, distinctive, inconsistent, individualizing, selective, separative

ASSOCIATED CONCEPTS: discrimination because of race, discrimination in hiring, discriminatory practices, equal protection, illegal discrimination, invidious discrimination, racial discrimination, reverse discrimination

DISCRIMINATING (*Judicious*), **adjective** appraising, astute, clear-sighted, critical, discerning, dispassionate, fastidious, impartial, judgmatic, keen, knowing, meticulous, perceptive, perspicacious, rational, reasonable, sagacious, sapient, selective, sober, sound, thoughtful, unbiased, well-advised, wise

DISCRIMINATION (*Bigotry*), **noun** bias, blind zeal, class prejudice, favoritism, illiberality, intolerance, opinionativeness, preference, race hatred, race prejudice, racialism, racism, unfairness, want of forbearance

ASSOCIATED CONCEPTS: blacklist, civil rights act, compelling state interest, discrimination based on sex, discrimination in hiring and tenure, due process clause, equal protection, illegal discrimination, invidious discrimination, overwhelming state interest, prejudicial discrimination, race discrimination, rational basis, reasonable classification, unjust discrimination

DISCRIMINATION (*Differentiation*), **noun** analysis, appraisal, appreciation, assessment, comprehension, consideration, contemplation, contrasting, demarcation, *discrimen,* disequalization, *distinctio,* distinction, distinguishment, division, estimation, examination, evaluation, individualization, segregation, separation, setting apart, weighing

ASSOCIATED CONCEPTS: compelling state interest, equal protection

DISCRIMINATION (*Good judgment*), **noun** acumen, acuteness, circumspection, discernment, discreetness, discretion, good sense, insight, *intellegentia,* intelligence, intuition, *iudicium,* judiciousness, knowledge, perception, perspicacity, perspicuity, prudence, *prudentia,* rationality, reason, sagacity, shrewdness, sound reasoning, thoughtfulness, understanding

DISCRIMINATORY, *adjective* biased, bigoted, favoring, inequitable, influenced, iniquitous, jaundiced, one-sided, partisan, preconceived, predilected, predisposed, prejudging, prejudiced, selective, separate, slanted, undispassionate, unjust, unjustified, warped

ASSOCIATED CONCEPTS: discriminatory action, discriminatory implementation, discriminatory laws, selective enforcement

DISCURSIVE (*Analytical*), **adjective** a fortiori, a posteriori, a priori, analytic, argumentative, deductive, dialectic, disquisitional, epagogic, inductive, inferential, interpretative, logical, ratiocinative, ratiocinatory, rational, rationalistic, reasoning

DISCURSIVE (*Digressive*), **adjective** aimless, circuitous, desultory, deviating, deviative, devious, disconnected, drifting, errant, indirect, meandering, rambling, random, ranging, roaming, roundabout, roving, shifting, straying, undirected, unsystematic, *vagus, varius,* wandering

DISCUSS, *verb* *agitare,* air, analyze, argue for and against, argue the case, argue the point, bandy words, carry on a conversation, comment, comment upon, confabulate, confer, confer with, consider, consult, contend in words, contest, converse, debate, deliberate upon, dialogize, *disceptare,* discourse, discourse about, *disputare, disserere,* dissertate, engage in a conversation, engage in conversation, engage in oral controversy, exchange observations, exchange opinions, explain, have a conference on, hold conclave, hold conference, hold conversations, hold intercourse, indulge in argument, interchange views, join in a conversation, negotiate, parley, partake in a symposium, present varied opinions, reason about, reason with, recite, review, speak of, speak on, take into account, take up in conference, talk about, talk it over, talk of, talk out, talk over, talk together

ASSOCIATED CONCEPTS: confidential information, privileged information

DISDAIN, noun abhorrence, abjuration, abnegation, act of despising, act of discrediting, act of loathing, act of scorning, act of shunning, act of spurning, act of taunting, airs, arrogance, contempt, *contemptio,* contemptuousness, contumeliousness, declination, denial, derision, detestation, detraction, disapprobation, disapproval, disavowal, disclamation, discountenancing, disesteem, disfavor, dislike, disownment, disregard, disrespect, *fastidium,* haughtiness, haughty contempt, haughty indifference, *hauteur,* icy aloofness, indignant aversion, insolence, nonacceptance, nonrecognition, opprobrium, proud contempt, rebuff, rejection, renunciation, reprobation, repudiation, repulse, repulsion, revilement, scoff, scorn, scornfulness, scorning, sneer, spurning, superciliousness, supreme contempt, unutterable contempt, utter contempt

DISDAIN, verb abhor, *aspernari,* avoid, be contemptuous of, belittle, brush aside, care nothing for, consider beneath notice, consider beneath oneself, consider unworthy of regard, contemn, decline, decry, deem unbecoming, deem unsuitable, deride, *despicere,* despise, detest, disavow, discard, disclaim, disesteem, disown, disparage, disregard, esteem of no account, esteem of small account, *fastidire,* feel contempt for, feel utter contempt for, flout, gibe, have no use for, hold cheap, hold in contempt, ignore, jeer, laugh at, loathe, look down on, look with scorn on, misprize, mock, not accept, not consider, not respect, pass by, pass over, rebuff, recoil from with pride, regard with proud contempt, reject, renounce, repudiate, repulse, ridicule, scoff, scorn, shun, slight, sneer at, snub, *spernere,* spurn, think nothing of, think unworthy of notice, treat with contempt, turn one's back upon, turn to scorn, view with a scornful eye

DISDAINFUL, adjective aloof, arrogant, audacious, bumptious, cavalier, cold, condescending, contemptuous, contumelious, cynical, deprecating, derisive, despising, disapproving, discourteous, disrespectful, distant, *fastidiosus,* filled with pride, flouting, full of contempt, haughty, high, icy, imperious, indifferent, indignant, insolent, insulting, intolerant, jeering, lordly, mocking, overbearing, overweening, proud, ridiculing, rude, sardonic, scornful, sneering, snobbish, snobby, snooty, supercilious, superior, unapproachable, uncivil, unmannerly, unsociable

DISEASE, noun affliction, ailment, attack, bodily deviation from health, bout of sickness, breakdown, chronic disability, collapse, condition, contagion, defect, deterioration, disability, discomfort, disorder, distemper, epidemic, handicap, ill health, illness, indisposition, infection, infirmity, insalubrity, invalidism, loss of health, malady, *morbus,* physical derangement, plague, scourge, sickness, taint, unhealthiness, unsoundness, unwholesome condition, virus, weakness

DISENCUMBER, verb alleviate, cast off, clear, clear away, deliver from a hindrance, disburden, disembroil, disengage, disentail, disentangle, disjoin, ease, ease the burden, emancipate, exonerate, extract, extricate, free, free from encumbrance, liberate, lighten the labor, loose, loosen, release, relieve, remove, remove a hindrance, remove a restraint, remove an impediment, rescue, save from, set at large, set free, unbar, unbind, unburden, unchain, unclog, unfasten, unfetter, unhamper, unharness, unload, unlock, unloose, unshackle, untie, untrammel, unyoke

DISENDOW, verb confiscate, cut off, denude, deprive, dethrone, discrown, disentitle, disinherit, disown, dispossess, divest, expropriate, strip, uncrown, unsaddle, unseat, wrest from

DISENGAGE, verb *avocare,* become detached, break the connection with, cut loose, cut off, decontrol, deliver, detach, disconnect, disembroil, disencumber, disentangle, disenthrall, disjoin, dislodge, dispart, displant, dissever, dissociate, disunite, divorce, draw off, emancipate, expedire, extricate, free, free from engagement, free from pledge, free from vow, let out, *liberare,* liberate, liberate from connection, lift controls, loose, make free, manumit, part, release, release from attachment, relieve of obligation, separate, set at liberty, set free, sever, *solvere,* sunder, unattach, unbar, unbind, unbolt, unbuckle, unchain, unclasp, undo, unfasten, unfetter, unfix, unglue, unhamper, unhitch, unhook, unknot, unlace, unlatch, unlock, unloose, unpin, unravel, unscrew, unshackle, unsnap, unstick, unstrap, untie, withdraw

DISENTANGLE, verb arrange, clear, detach, disburden, disconnect, disembroil, disencumber, disengage, disinvolve, disjoin, ease, *expedire, explicare, exsolvere,* extricate, free, liberate, loosen, methodize, organize, release, relieve, relieve of complication, separate, set free, straighten out, unfasten, unfetter, unhamper, unknot, unloose, unravel, untie, untwist

DISENTHRALL, verb bail out, deliver, deliver from bondage, discharge, disengage, emancipate, enfranchise, extricate, free, free from bondage, free from thralldom, give liberty to, let go, let loose, let out, let out of prison, liberate, liberate from oppression, loosen, make free, manumit, redeem, release, release from bondage, release from restraint, render free, rescue, rescue from imprisonment, rescue from oppression, rescue from slavery, set at large, set at liberty, set free, turn loose, unbar, unbind, unchain, unfetter, unlock, unmanacle, unshackle, untie

ASSOCIATED CONCEPTS: Emancipation Proclamation

DISFAVOR, verb avoid, be loath, deny respect, despise, disaffect, disapprove, discountenance, discredit, disdain, dishonor, dislike, disregard, disrespect, frown on, have no regard for, have no respect for, have no use for, hold cheap, *invidia,* look askance at, look down on, misprize, not care for, not like, not respect, object to, *offensa,* rebuff, regard unfavorably, reject, repel, repulse, turn away, turn from, view with disfavor

DISFRANCHISE, verb deprive, forfeit, illegalize, limit, make illegitimate, outlaw, prohibit, restrict

DISGRACE, noun abasement, abjectness, abomination, attaint, bad character, bad name, bad report, bad reputation, bad repute, badge of infamy, baseness, blemish, blot, brand, cause of reproach, cause of shame, comedown, condition of infamy, contempt, debasement, defame, defilement, deflation, degradation, derogation, detestation, deviation from rectitude, disapprobation, disapproval, discredit, disesteem, disfavor, dishonor, disparagement, disreputability, disrepute, disrespect, embarrassment, exclusion from favor, humbled pride, humbling, humiliation, *ignominia,* ignominy, ill-favor, ill-repute, imputation, indignity, *infamia,* infamy, ingloriousness, loss of honor, loss of reputation, mortification, notoriety, obloquy, odium, opprobrium, reproach, scandal, sense of shame, setdown, shame, shamefacedness, shameful notoriety, slur, smear, smirch, stain, stigma, taint, tarnish, tarnished honor, *turpitudo*

ASSOCIATED CONCEPTS: character evidence, reputation

DISGRACE, verb abase, abash, affect dishonorably, attaint, be a reproach to, be unable to respect, besmear, blacken, blot, brand, bring down, bring into discredit, bring reproach upon, bring shame upon, cast a slur upon, cast dishonor upon, cast reproach upon, corrupt, debase, debunk, *dedecorare, dedecori esse,* defile, deflate, defrock, degrade, *dehonestare,* demean, demoralize, deny respect, depress, deride, derogate, diminish, disbar, discredit, dishonor, dismiss from favor, disrespect, downgrade, embarrass, fling dishonor upon, have no respect for, hold up to shame, humiliate, impute shame to, involve in shame, lower, make unclean, mock, mortify, pillory, pollute, reflect discredit upon, reflect dishonor upon, reflect shame upon, ridicule, scandalize, shame, slur, smirch, soil, stain, stigmatize, sully, taint, tarnish, throw dishonor upon, treat with disfavor

DISGRACEFUL, adjective abominable, atrocious, base, beneath one's dignity, blameworthy, censurable, compromising, contemptible, damaging, deflated, degrading, demeaning, demoralizing, deplorable, derogatory, deserving reproach, despicable, detestable, discreditable, dishonest, dishonorable, disreputable, *flagitiosus,* flagitious, flagrant, foul, heinous, horrible, humiliating, humiliative, ignoble, ignominious, improper, indecent, infamous, inglorious, *inhonestus,* iniquitous, odious, opprobrious, outrageous, peccant, *probrosus,* recreant, reprobate, scandalous, shameful, shocking, sinful, tarnished, *turpis,* unseemly, unworthy, vile, worthy of contempt

DISGUISE, noun artifice, camouflage, caricature, cloak, concealment, counterfeit, cover, covering, deception, deceptive covering, dissimulation, facade, faking, false appearance, false colors, false copy, false front, guise, hiding, imitation, mask, masquerade, pose, posture, pretense, pretension, pretext, representation, screen, semblance, sham, shield, *simulacrum, simulatio,* simulation, smoke screen, veneer, *vestis mutata*

DISGUISE, verb alter the appearance of, becloud, belie, bemask, camouflage, change the appearance of, change the face of, change the guise of, cloak, conceal, counterfeit, cover, curtain, deceive, dissemble, dissimulate, distort, dress to conceal, dress up, fake, falsify, feign, give a false coloring, give color to, hide, hide one's identity, make unrecognizable, mask, masquerade, misrepresent, muffle, obscure, *occultare,* pass off for, put a false appearance upon, *rem dissimulare,* screen, shield, shroud, simulate, veil

DISHONEST, adjective beguiling, bogus, cheating, conniving, conscienceless, contrary to fact, corrupt, corruptible,

counterfeit, cunning, deceitful, deceiving, deceptive, delusive, delusory, designing, destitute of good faith, destitute of integrity, devoid of truth, discreditable, dishonorable, disingenuous, disposed to cheat, disreputable, double-dealing, faithless, fake, faked, fallacious, false, false-hearted, falsified, feigned, fraudulent, *fraudulentus,* guileful, hypocritical, immoral, *improbus,* iniquitous, insidious, insincere, lying, *malus,* meretricious, misleading, nefarious, not honest, not true, perfidious, perjured, scheming, shameless, shifty, spurious, surreptitious, treacherous, truthless, unauthentic, undependable, underhanded, unethical, unfaithful, ungenuine, unprincipled, unreal, unreliable, unscrupulous, untrue, untrustworthy, untruthful, unveracious, unvirtuous, void of truth, wanting in probity, without probity, without truth

ASSOCIATED CONCEPTS: dishonest act, dishonest practice, fraudulent or dishonest acts

DISHONESTY, noun bad faith, cheating, chicane, chicanery, corruption, corruptness, cozenage, deceit, deceitfulness, deception, deviation from probity, dishonor, disingenuousness, disposition to deceive, disposition to defraud, disposition to lie, duplicity, faithlessness, false swearing, falseheartedness, falsehood, falseness, falsification, falsity, fraudulence, fraudulency, *fraus,* furtiveness, *improbitas,* improbity, infidelity, insincerity, inveracity, knavery, knavishness, lack of conscience, lack of honesty, lack of integrity, lack of principle, lack of probity, lying, mendaciousness, mendacity, perfidiousness, perfidy, perjury, prevarication, surreptitiousness, thievishness, treacherousness, trickiness, truthlessness, undependability, underhand dealing, underhandedness, unreliability, unscrupulousness, unstraightforwardness, untrustworthiness, untruth, untruthfulness, violation of trust, want of integrity, wiliness

ASSOCIATED CONCEPTS: criminal acts, dishonest acts, fraudulent acts

DISHONOR (Nonpayment), noun breach of faith, breach of promise, declination, default, delinquency, disregard, failure, improbity, inability to pay, inattention, inobservance, insolvency, nonacceptance, nonadherence, noncompletion, noncompliance, nonfeasance, nonfulfillment, nonobservance, nonpayment at maturity, omission, refusal to accept, refusal to pay, rejection, repudiation of payment

ASSOCIATED CONCEPTS: dishonor of checks, dishonor of negotiated instruments, notice of dishonor

DISHONOR (Shame), noun abasement, abjection, abjectness, aspersion, attaint, bad character, bad favor, bad name, bad reputation, bad repute, badge of infamy, baseness, blemish, blot, brand, calumny, contempt, contumely, debasement, decrial, defamation, defilement, degradation, depravity, derogation, detraction, deviation from rectitude, disapprobation, discredit, disesteem, disfavor, disgrace, disparagement, disreputability, disrepute, disrespect, humiliation, ignobility, *ignominia,* ignominy, ill-fame, ill-favor, ill-repute, improbity, imputation, indignity, *infamia,* infamy, ingloriousness, lack of conscience, lack of honor, lack of principle, lack of probity, loss of reputation, low estimation, mockery, no repute, no standing, notoriety, obloquy, opprobrium, outrage, public disgrace, reproach, ridicule, scandal, scorn, shamefulness, slur, smear, stain, stigma, taint, tarnish, tarnished honor, traducement, turpitude, *turpitudo,* vileness, vilification, wickedness

DISHONOR (Deprive of honor), verb abase, asperse, attaint, besmear, besmirch, blot, brand, bring into discredit, bring shame upon, cast a slur on, cast aspersions, cast reproach upon, contemn, debase, debauch, *dedecorare,* defame, defile, deflower, degrade, *dehonestare,* denigrate, denounce, deride, desecrate, despise, discredit, disgrace, disparage, expose, malign, pillory, reflect discredit upon, reproach, slur, smear, smirch, speak ill of, stain, stigmatize, *stuprare,* taint, tarnish, vilify

DISHONOR *(Refuse to pay),* **verb** decline to pay, decline to redeem, disallow payment, disregard, evade, not observe, not pay, refuse payment, refuse to honor, repudiate, stop payment, withhold payment
ASSOCIATED CONCEPTS: dishonor a check, notice of dishonor

DISINCENTIVE, noun averseness, check, constraint, curb, damper, determent, deterrence, deterrent, discouragement, disinclination, dissuasion, hindrance, indisposition, lack of allurement, lack of charm, lack of desire, lack of enticement, lack of impetus, lack of incentive, lack of inducement, lack of motivation, lack of stimulus, lack of temptation, reluctance, restraint, unprovocativeness, unwillingness

DISINCLINED, adjective adverse, against, antagonistic, antipathetic, antipathetical, averse, *aversus,* balking, contrary, counter, demurring, disaffected, dissenting, dissident, faltering, grudging, hesitant, indisposed, laggard, loath, noncooperating, not in the mood, opposed, qualmish, recalcitrant, refusing, reluctant, restive, shirking, shrinking from, slow to, squeamish, unaccommodating, unconsenting, uncooperative, unenthusiastic, uninclined, unpersuadable, unpersuaded, unreconciled, unwilling, unzealous

DISINGENUOUS, adjective artful, artificial, conscienceless, counterfeit, crafty, cunning, deceitful, deceiving, deceptive, delusive, delusory, designing, devious, dishonest, dodging, evasive, false, false hearted, feigned, fraudulent, hypocritical, insidious, insincere, lacking frankness, lying, mendacious, misdealing, misleading, *parum candidus,* perfidious, prevaricating, scheming, shifty, sly, spurious, surreptitious, tricky, truthless, uncandid, underhanded, unethical, ungenuine, unprincipled, unscrupulous, unstraightforward, untrustworthy, untruthful, wanting in candor, wily, without truth

DISINHERIT, verb abandon, abrogate, annul, cast out, cut off, cut off from inheritance, cut out of one's will, deprive, deprive of hereditary succession, disaffirm, discard, disclaim, disendow, disentitle, disherit, disown, dispossess of hereditary right, divest, exclude from inheritance, *exheredare,* forfeit, forsake, nullify, oust, quash, recall, recant, renounce, replace, repudiate, rescind, retract, revoke, supersede, take away from, turn out, withdraw, withhold
ASSOCIATED CONCEPTS: disinherit a husband, disinherit a wife, disinherit an adopted child, disinherit pretermitted children

DISINTEGRATE, verb break up, crumble, decay, decompose, diffuse, disband, disperse, dissolve, disunite, fall to pieces, fragment, shatter, split up

DISINTER, verb bare, bring from obscurity into view, bring out, deracinate, detect, dig out, dig up, dig up out of the earth, discover, disentomb, disinhume, display, draw forth, draw out, educe, *effodere,* elicit, eruere, evince, evoke, evulse, excavate, exhibit, exhume, expose, expose to view, extract, extricate, ferret out, find, find out, lay open, make known, manifest, present to view, pull out, pull up, remove, resurrect, reveal, root out, root up, show, take out of the place of interment, turn up, unbury, uncover, unearth, unroot, unsepulcher, untomb, unveil, withdraw

DISINTEREST *(Lack of interest),* **noun** aloofness, apathy, boredom, callousness, carelessness, coolness, detachment, disdain, disinterestedness, disregard, heedlessness, inappetance, inappetancy, inattention, inattentiveness, inconsideration, incuriosity, incuriousness, indifference, insensitivity, insouciance, lack of attention, lack of concern, langour, languidness, laxity, listlessness, mindlessness, neglect, neglectfulness, negligence, nonchalance, noninvolvement, obliviousness, perfunctoriness, phlegm, pococurantism, spiritlessness, supineness, tepidity, thoughtlessness, unconcern, unmindfulness, unsolicitousness, want of attention, want of interest

DISINTEREST *(Lack of prejudice),* **noun** broadmindedness, candor, catholicity, detachment, dispassion, dispassionateness, equitableness, equity, evenhandedness, fair play, fair treatment, fairness, freedom from bias, freedom from prejudice, freedom from self-interest, impartiality, impartialness, impersonality, indiscrimination, justice, justness, liberality, neutrality, noninvolvement, nonpartisanship, objectivity, open-mindedness, tolerance, toleration, unbiasedness, unprejudice, unselfishness, unslantedness
ASSOCIATED CONCEPTS: disinterested judge, disinterested party, disinterested persons, disinterested witness, without pecuniary interest

DISINVOLVE, verb clear, disconnect, disembarrass, disentangle, disjoin, extricate, loosen, separate, unbind, unfold, unknot, unravel, unscramble, untangle, untie

DISJOIN, verb break, cut, cut off, demobilize, depart, detach, dichotomize, disband, disconnect, discontinue, disembody, disencumber, disengage, disentangle, disjoint, dislocate, dismember, dispart, dissect, dissociate, disunite, divide, divorce, excise, extricate, free, insulate, interrupt, isolate, keep apart, loosen, luxate, part, partition, quarter, remove, rend, rive, rupture, segregate, separate, sever, split, subdivide, uncouple, unhitch, unplug

DISJOINT, adjective apart, detached, disassembled, disassociated, disconnected, disengaged, disjunct, dismantled, displaced, dissected, disunited, divaricated, divided, far between, in two, isolated, removed, rent, riven, sectioned, separate, separated, severed, split, subdivided, sundered, unassociated, unattached, unconnected, unhinged, unjoined, unloosened

DISJOINT, verb break apart, break up, carve, cleave, cut up, detach, disarticulate, disassemble, disassociate, disband, disconnect, disengage, disjoin, dislocate, dismantle, dismember, dispart, displace, dissect, dissever, dissociate, disunite, divaricate, divide, divorce, luxate, part, quarter, rend, rive, section, segment, separate, sever, split, subdivide, sunder, take apart, tear apart, uncouple, unfasten, unhinge, unjoint, unloosen

DISJOINTED, adjective aimless, confused, deranged, desultory, disarranged, disassociated, discerpted, discordant, disjunctive, disordered, disorderly, disorganized, erratic, in disarray, in disorder, incoherent, *incompositus,* incongruent, incongruous, indiscriminate, interrupted, jumbled, lacking order, nonuniform, orderless, out of order, spasmodic, unclassified, uncohesive, unsorted, unsuccessive, unsystematic

DISJUNCTIVE *(Alternative),* **adjective** alternate, discretional, discretionary, elective, equivalent, having the privilege to choose, interchangeable, noncompulsory, nonobligatory, not compulsory, open to choice, optional, selective, subject to preference, substitute, substitutional, substitutive

ASSOCIATED CONCEPTS: disjunctive allegations, disjunctive covenants, disjunctive relief, disjunctive words of a statute

DISJUNCTIVE *(Tending to disjoin),* **adjective** broken, desultory, detached, disarticulated, disconnected, discrete, disjoined, disjoint, disjointed, dismembered, distinct, disunited, divided, divorced, erratic, fitful, inconsistent, individual, insular, intermittent, intermitting, interrupted, irregular, isolated, loose, noncontinuous, not cohesive, not integrated, parted, partitioned, periodic, punctuated, separate, severed, spasmodic, successive, suspended, unannexed, unassociated, unconnected, unjoined, unsuccessive

DISLIKE, noun abhorrence, abomination, animosity, animus, antagonism, antipathy, aversion, contempt, detestation, disaffection, disapprobation, disapproval, discomfort, disdain, disfavor, disgust, disinclination, disparagement, displeasure, dissatisfaction, distaste, enmity, hatred, hostility, ill will, incompatibility, inimicality, intolerance, loathing, malevolence, malice, objection, odium, prejudice, rancor, rejection, reluctance, renitence, repugnance, repulsion, revulsion, umbrage, unfriendliness, unwillingness

DISLIKE, verb abhor, abominate, antipathize, condemn, deprecate, detest, disapprove, discountenance, disesteem, disfavor, disrelish, distaste, execrate, loathe, mind, not care for, not like, object to, resent, scorn

DISLOCATE, verb agitate, cast out, complicate, confound, confuse, derail, derange, disarrange, disconnect, disjoin, disjoint, dislodge, disorder, disorganize, disorient, displace, disturb, disunite, eject, evacuate, evict, expel, luxate, mislay, misplace, move, oust, remove, scatter, throw into confusion, throw out of joint, throw out of order, unseat, unsettle, upset

DISLODGE, verb banish, carry off, cart away, cashier, cast out, *deicere,* delocalize, demote, *depellere,* deport, depose, deracinate, dethrone, detrude, disbar, discharge, disemploy, disenthrone, disestablish, dislocate, dismiss, displace, displant, dispossess, disturb, divest of office, eject, eliminate, evacuate, evict, exclude, exile, expatriate, expel, *expellere,* expropriate, extract, force out, lay off, oust, overthrow, push out, put out, relegate, remove, retire, rid, send away, supersede, supplant, take away, throw away, throw out, thrust out, turn out, unload, unseat, uproot, usurp

DISLOYALTY, noun apostasy, barratry, betrayal, betrayal of trust, breach, breach of faith, breach of promise, breach of trust, broken promise, contumacy, defection, dereliction of allegiance, desertion, disobedience, faithlessness, falseness, falsity, fickleness, improbity, inconstancy, *infidelitas,* infidelity, insincerity, insubordination, insurgency, insurrection, lack of fidelity, lack of loyalty, malfeasance, mutineering, mutinousness, mutiny, perfidiousness, perfidy, rebellion, recreancy, revolt, sabotage, sedition, seditiousness, subversion, subversive activity, traitoriousness, treachery, treason, treasonable activities, unfaithfulness, unsteadfastness, venality, violation of allegiance, violation of trust, want of loyalty

DISMAL, adjective black, bleak, cheerless, cloudy, comfortless, dark, deplorable, depressing, despairing, despondent, dim, dingy, dire, disagreeable, disconsolate, dreary, dull, dusky, flat, foggy, gloomy, gray, joyless, lam-

entable, lifeless, lowering, lugubrious, obscure, overcast, pessimistic, sad, saturnine, shadowy, solemn, somber, sombrous, tedious, umbrageous, uncomfortable, unconsoling, unhappy, unilluminated, uninviting, unpleasant, unrelieved

DISMAY, noun affright, agitation, alarm, anxiety, apprehension, chagrin, consternation, discomfort, discomposure, discouragement, disheartenment, disquiet, doubt, dread, fret, inquietude, intimidation, misgiving, mistrust, perturbation, pique, qualm, scare, shock, trepidation, uneasiness, worry

DISMAY, verb abash, aggravate, agitate, alarm, appall, bewilder, bother, confound, daunt, deter, discomfort, discompose, disconcert, discourage, disquiet, disturb, embarrass, harrow, horrify, intimidate, panic, perturb, startle, take aback, unnerve

DISMISS *(Discharge),* **verb** cashier, cast out, demobilize, depose, deprive of force, disemploy, dispatch, dispense with, displace, dispossess, eject, expel, fire, lay off, oust, purge, release, remove, remove from office, send away, send off, set free, suspend, turn away, turn out, unseat, vacate

ASSOCIATED CONCEPTS: dismiss a cause of action, dismissal because of laches, dismissed for cause, dismissed with prejudice, dismissed without prejudice, motion to dismiss, motion to dismiss for failure to state a claim, motion to dismiss for lack of jurisdiction, nonsuit

DISMISS *(Put out of consideration),* **verb** brush aside, decline, deny, disallow, disavow, discountenance, disregard, ignore, lay aside, not hear of, pass over, pay no regard to, put out of mind, refuse, reject, rule out, set aside, take no notice, think no more of

DISMISS CHARGES, verb absolve, acquit, clear, discharge, exculpate, exonerate, forgive, grant amnesty to, palliate, pardon, prove innocent, release, reprieve, restitute, vindicate

DISMISSAL *(Discharge),* **noun** cashiering, deposition, *dimissio,* discharge from employment, disemployment, dislodgment, displacement, ejection, elimination, exclusion, expulsion, firing, layoff, ouster, release from employment, removal from a job, removal from a position, removal from office, severance

DISMISSAL *(Termination of a proceeding),* **noun** annulment, cancellation, conclusion of a proceeding, conclusion of an action, discontinuance, disposal, ending of a proceeding, ending of an action, invalidation, nonsuit, quashing, rejection, removal of a cause out of court, termination of an action

ASSOCIATED CONCEPTS: dismissal for cause, dismissal for failure to prosecute, dismissal for want of jurisdiction, dismissal for want of substantial federal question, dismissal of a cause for want of prosecution, dismissal of a charge, dismissal of an action with prejudice, dismissal of an appeal, dismissal of an employee, dismissal of proceedings, dismissal on the merits, dismissal without prejudice

DISMISSED, adjective acquitted, clear, discarded, discharged, dispensed, exculpated, forgiven, free, obsolete, pardoned, rejected, released, vindicated

ASSOCIATED CONCEPTS: automatic dismissal, dismiss due to improper venue, dismiss for failure to answer, dismiss for improper parties, dismiss for insufficient evidence, dismiss for want of jurisdiction, dismiss for want of prosecution, dismissal with prejudice, dismissed case, dismissed case due to delay, dismissed charges, failure to prosecute, harmless error, involuntary dismissal, irregularities, judgment of dismissal, voluntary dismissal

DISOBEDIENT, adjective apostatizing, arbitrary, averse, contrary, contumacious, culpable, defiant, delinquent, derelict, disloyal, disorderly, disregarding, disrespectful, fractious, froward, headstrong, hostile, ill-behaved, incorrigible, indisposed, insubordinate, insurgent, insurrectional, intractable, irascible, irresponsible, lawbreaking, lawless, licentious, loath, misbehaving, mutinous, neglectful, negligent, *non obsequi,* noncompliant, obdurate, objecting, obstinate, obstreperous, opposed, opposing, perfidious, perverse, rebellious, recalcitrant, recusant, refractory, reluctant, remiss, renitent, resistant, resistive, restive, riotous, stubborn, traitorous, transgressive, treasonous, trespassing, truant, uncompliant, uncomplying, unconsenting, uncooperative, undependable, undisciplined, undutiful, unfaithful, ungovernable, unmanageable, unmindful, unreliable, unruly, unsubmissive, unwilling, unyielding, violating, violative, wayward, wild, willful
ASSOCIATED CONCEPTS: disobedience to lawful mandate of court, lawful disobedience, willful disobedience

DISOBEY, verb act illegally, arise, be derelict, be disloyal, be insubordinate, be mutinous, be negligent, be perfidious, be recalcitrant, be recusant, be treasonous, be undisciplined, be unruly, betray, break a law, break a rule, break the law, commit a crime, contravene, cross, defy, deviate, disregard, fail to comply, go counter to, ignore, infringe, insurrect, misbehave, mutiny, negate, neglect, not comply, not cooperate, not heed, not listen, not mind, not obey, oppose, pay no attention to, rebel, recalcitrate, refuse, refuse to obey, reject, repudiate, resist, revolt, revolutionize, rise, shirk, transgress, traverse, trespass, violate
ASSOCIATED CONCEPTS: disobedience, disobedience to a lawful mandate of the court, failure to comply, willful disobedience

DISOBLIGE, verb act contrary, affront, antagonize, balk, be unaccommodating, be unwilling, cause displeasure, debase, decline, degrade, demur, denigrate, denounce, deprecate, disaccommodate, discommode, disdain, dishonor, disparage, disregard, fail to accommodate, fail to comply with, give offense to, ignore, incommode, incur disapproval, insult, malign, maltreat, neglect to obey, not accept, not comply with, not obey, offend, *offendere,* put out, rebuff, refuse, refuse to oblige, reject, repel, repudiate, scorn, shrink, slight, spite, spurn, traduce, treat with indignity, turn down, vilipend, withhold consent

DISORDER (Abnormal condition), **noun** affliction, ailment, complaint, condition, disability, disease, distemper, handicap, illness, indisposition, infirmity, malady, malfunction, sickness

DISORDER (Lack of order), **noun** anarchism, anarchy, breach of peace, chaos, commotion, confusion, derangement, disarrangement, disarray, discomposure, disharmony, dishevelment, disorderly conduct, disorganization, disturbance, fracas, irregularity, lack of regular order, lawlessness, muddle, pandemonium, racket, riot, slipshodness, tumult, tumultuousness, turbulence, turmoil, unrest, uproar
ASSOCIATED CONCEPTS: breach of the peace, disorderly conduct

DISORDERED, adjective aberrant, abnormal, agitated, amiss, anarchical, anomalous, askew, atypical, awry, bedraggled, bemuddled, capricious, changeable, changeful, chaotic, confused, deviating, disarranged, discomposed, discontinuous, disheveled, disjunct, dislocated, disorganized, divergent, diverse, entangled, heterogeneous, illogical, immethodical, impetuous, in chaos, in disarray, in hysterics, incoherent, inconsistent, incontrollable, inverted, involved, jumbled, lawless, messy, nonuniform, not belonging, orderless, out of order, out of place, patternless, random, raveled, shapeless, tangled, tumultuary, tumultuous, turbulent, twisted, unarranged, unassembled, unclassified, uncoordinated, undisciplined, uneven, unkempt, unmanageable, unmethodical, unorganized, unpatterned, unruly, unsystematic, untidy, without method

DISORDERLY, adjective aberrant, aggressive, agitated, anarchic, anarchical, anarchistic, barbaric, barbarous, bellicose, blustering, blustery, boisterous, brutal, careless, churlish, confused, contumacious, defiant, deranged, destructive, disagreeable, disarranged, discomposed, discontinuous, discourteous, disgraceful, disheveled, disjointed, disobedient, disorganized, dissolute, disturbed, explosive, fitful, fluctuating, froward, heinous, ill-mannered, immethodical, immoderate, impolite, improper, incendiary, incorrigible, indecorous, inflammatory, insolent, insurrectionary, intemperate, irregular, lawbreaking, lawless, licentious, loud, mannerless, misbehaved, misbehaving, mutinous, nihilistic, nonobservant, obstreperous, orderless, out of order, outrageous, quarrelsome, rackety, raging, rampant, random, rebellious, recalcitrant, refractory, resisting, restive, revolutionary, riotous, rough, rowdy, rude, ruffianly, savage, scampish, scandalous, slovenly, stormy, strong, tangled, tempestuous, tumultuary, tumultuous, turbulent, unauthorized, unbridled, uncivil, uncivilized, uncommendable, uncontrolled, uncourtly, uncurbed, undisciplined, uneven, ungenteel, ungentle, ungentlemanlike, ungentlemanly, ungoverned, unladylike, unmanageable, unmannered, unmannerly, unmethodical, unmitigated, unquelled, unregulated, unrepressed, unruly, unseemly, unsettled, unsteady, unsubmissive, unsystematic, untidy, untrained, uprisen, uproarious, violent, warlike, wayward, wild
ASSOCIATED CONCEPTS: breach of the peace, disorderly conduct, disorderly houses, disorderly persons, disturbance of the public peace

DISORGANIZE, verb abolish the organization of, agitate, bedevil, befog, befuddle, bewilder, bother, clutter, come to pieces, complicate, confound, *confundere,* confuse, daze, deactivate, decompose, deform, demobilize, deprive of organization, derange, destroy the form of, deteriorate, disarrange, disband, discompose, disconcert, dishevel, disintegrate, disjoin, dismantle, disorder, disorientate, dispel, disperse, disrupt, dissipate, dissolve, distract, disturb, embrangle, entangle, interrupt, invert, liquidate, make havoc, misarrange, *miscere,* misplace, muddle, obfuscate, obscure, perplex, perturb, *perturbare,* play havoc with, put out of order, ravel, render uncertain, revert, scatter, scramble, separate, tangle, tear up, throw into confusion, throw into disorder, throw out of order, tumble, twist, unbalance, undo, unmake, unsettle, upset

DISORIENT, verb abash, baffle, befuddle, bewilder, confound, dement, derange, disarrange, discompose, disconcert, dislocate, dislodge, disorder, disorganize, distract, disturb, fluster, impair, invert, make havoc, misdirect, mislay, mislead, misplace, muddle, mystify, nonplus, obfuscate, obscure, overturn, perturb, render uncertain, ruffle, scramble, throw into confusion, throw into disorder, throw out of order, trouble, unbalance, unsettle, upset

DISOWN (*Deny the validity*), **verb** abjure, abnegate, affirm the contrary, annul, call in question, challenge, confute, contest, contradict, contravene, controvert, countermand, demur, deny, deny absolutely, deny peremptorily, deny the possibility, deny wholly, disaffirm, disagree, disallow, disannul, disavow, disbelieve, disclaim, disprove, disregard, dissent, forswear, hold no brief for, impugn, *infitiari,* invalidate, negate, negative, not accept, not admit, not confirm, not maintain, nullify, object, oppose, overrule, protest, rebut, recant, refuse credence, refuse to accept, refuse to admit, refuse to corroborate, refute, reject, render null and void, *repudiare, repudiate,* rescind, retract, reverse, revoke, set aside, set at nought, stand up to, take issue with, traverse, undo, vacate, void

DISOWN (*Refuse to acknowledge*), **verb** abandon, abjure, alienate, cast away, cast off, cede, cut off, cut out of one's will, deprive of hereditary succession, deprive of the right to inherit, disaffiliate, disallow, disclaim, disclaim the responsibility for, disdain, disendow, disinherit, dispense with, dispossess, dispossess of hereditary right, dissociate oneself, divest, divorce, forsake, get rid of, give up, have nothing to do with, *infitiari,* jettison, let go, not maintain, oust, part with, rebuff, refuse to recognize, relinquish, renounce, *repudiare,* repudiate, repulse, scorn, spurn
ASSOCIATED CONCEPTS: disown a child

DISPARAGE, verb affront, asperse, be insolent, be rude, belittle, bemock, besmear, bespatter, blacken, blot, bring reproach upon, calumniate, cavil, censure, cheapen, condemn, contemn, criticize, debase, decry, defame, deflate, degrade, denigrate, depreciate, deride, derogate, detract, *detrectare,* discount, discredit, disesteem, disfavor, disgrace, dishonor, disregard, disrespect, downgrade, *elevare, extenuare,* find fault with, frown upon, gibe, humiliate, imitate insultingly, insult, jeer, lampoon, laugh at, look down on, lower the estimation of, make fun of, make light of, make sport of, malign, minimize, misprize, mock, play down, reflect poorly upon, ridicule, run down, scoff, scorn, shame, slander, slight, slur, smear, sneer, speak ill of, stain, stigmatize, sully, taint, tarnish, taunt, think little of, traduce, underrate, undervalue, vilify, vilipend
ASSOCIATED CONCEPTS: disparage a name, disparage a product

DISPARAGEMENT, noun accusation, act of berating, act of running down, admonishment, adverse criticism, aspersion, bad review, belittlement, belittling, blame, brand, castigation, complaint, condemnation, confutation, contempt, criticism, damnation, decrial, denigration, *dénigrement,* denouncement, denunciation, deprecation, depreciation, derogation, destructive criticism, detraction, disapprobation, disapproval, discontent, discourtesy, disesteem, disfavor, dishonor, disillusionment, dislike, displeasure, disrepute, disrespect, disrespectfulness, exception, faultfinding, hostile criticism, hypercriticism, impeachment, impugnation, imputation, indignation, insinuation, invective, irreverence, low estimation, low opinion, low valuation, mockery, muckraking, nonapproval, objection, objuration, obloquy, *obtrectatio,* outcry, overcriticalness, poor opinion, protest, rebuke, rejection, reprehension, reprimand, reproach, reprobation, reproof, revilement, ridicule, rude reproach, rudeness, scant respect, scolding, scorn, slighting language, stigma, tirade, uncomplimentary remark, vilification, vilipendency, vituperation, want of respect

ASSOCIATED CONCEPTS: disparagement of goods, disparagement of property, disparagement of title

DISPARAGING, adjective abusive, blameful, calumnious, censorious, condemnatory, contemptuous, contumelious, damnatory, defamatory, denunciatory, deprecative, derogatory, detractory, disrespectful, incriminatory, inculpatory, injurious, invective, inveighing, libelous, maledictory, objurgatory, pejorative, reproachful, reprobative, reviling, scandalous, scurrile, scurrilous, slanderous, unfavorable, vilifying, vituperative
ASSOCIATED CONCEPTS: disparagement of goods, disparagement of name, disparagement of products, libel, slander

DISPARATE, adjective aberrant, atypical, clashing, conflicting, contradictory, contrasting, departing from, deviating, different, differentiated, differing, digressive, disagreeing, discordant, discrepant, disproportionate, dissimilar, distinct, distinguished, divaricating, divergent, essentially different, ill-matched, incommensurable, incongruent, incongruous, inconsistent, inconsonant, independent, irreconcilable, irregular, nonuniform, not comparable, not the same, out of proportion, separate, unconformable, unequal, uneven, unlike, unmatched, varied
ASSOCIATED CONCEPTS: disparate award, disparate relief

DISPARITY, noun argument, asymmetry, conflict of opinion, contradiction, contradistinction, contraposition, contrast, controversy, deviation, difference, disaccord, disagreement, discord, discordance, discrepancy, disequilibrium, disharmony, dissimilitude, *dissimilitudo,* dissonance, disunity, divergence, diversity, failure to agree, imbalance, incommensurability, incompatibility, incongruence, incongruity, inequality, inharmoniousness, irreconcilability, irrelation, lack of relation, lack of symmetry, nonagreement, nonconformity, nonuniformity, unconformity, unlikeness, variance, variation

DISPASSIONATE, adjective aloof, ascetic, *blasé,* calm, *calme,* cold, cold-blooded, cold-hearted, collected, composed, controlled, cool-headed, detached, disengaged, disinterested, even-handed, even-tempered, fair, heartless, immovable, impartial, impassive, impersonal, imperturbable, indifferent, inexcitable, inscrutable, neutral, nonchalant, objective, open-minded, passionless, peaceful, phlegmatic, *placatus, placidus,* sang-froid, self-controlled, selfless, steady, stoical, stolid, subdued, temperate, tolerant, tranquil, *tranquillus,* unaffected, unbiased, uncorrupted, undemonstrative, undisturbed, unemotional, unexcited, unfeeling, ungrudging, unimpassioned, unimpressible, unimpressionable, uninfluenced, uninvolved, unirritable, unjealous, unmindful, unnervous, unoffended, unpassionate, unperturbed, unprejudiced, unprepossessed, unresponsive, unruffled, unsentimental, unshaken, unstirred, unsusceptible, unswayed, untouchable, without nerves, without warmth

DISPATCH (*Act of putting to death*), **noun** act of killing, act of slaying, assassination, bloodshed, death by violence, deathblow, destruction, disposal, doing away with, execution, extermination, homicide, killing, liquidation, massacre, murder

DISPATCH (*Message*), **noun** aviso, bulletin, circular, communication, *communiqué,* correspondence, enlightenment, epistle, *epistula,* information, instruction, letter, *litterae,* mail, missive, monition, news, note, notice, notification, official correspondence, postal communication, report, statement, stream of correspondence, telegram

DISPATCH (*Promptness*), **noun**   alacrity, briskness, bustle, celerity, dash, *dépêche, diligence,* excitation, expediousness, *expédition,* expeditious performance, fast rate, fastness, *festinatio,* feverish haste, flurry, haste, hastiness, hurry, immediateness, impetuosity, inability to wait, instantaneity, liveliness, lively pace, movement, nimbleness, precipitance, precipitancy, precipitation, precipitousness, *promptitude, properatio,* punctuality, punctualness, quick discharge, quick riddance, quickness, rapidity, readiness, rush, scramble, scurry, speed, speediness, speedy completion, speedy disposition, speedy transaction, spurt, suddenness, summariness, swift execution, swift rate, timeliness, urgency
ASSOCIATED CONCEPTS: with all possible dispatch

DISPATCH (*Dispose of*), **verb**   absolvere, accomplish, achieve, attain, bring about, bring off, bring to a conclusion, bring to an end, bring to pass, carry out, carry through, carry to completion, close, complete, conclude, *conficere,* consummate, deal with definitely, do the deed, effect, effectuate, execute, finish, fulfill, implement, make an end of, make final disposition of, *perficere,* perform, realize, see through, set at rest, succeed, work out

DISPATCH (*Put to death*), **verb**   assassinate, bring down, commit murder, *coup de grâce,* cut down, deal a deathblow, deprive of life, destroy, dispose of, do away with, end, end life, execute, exterminate, give the deathblow, hasten one's end, *interficere, interimere,* kill, liquidate, make away with, massacre, murder, put an end to, put down, put out of the way, put to death, remove from life, slaughter, slay, take life, take one's life away

DISPATCH (*Send off*), **verb**   address, detail, direct, expedite, fling, forward, get under way, hasten, hasten on, have conveyed, hurry, hurry along, hurry on, impart motion, impel, *mittere,* mobilize, move on, post, propel, push, push through, put in motion, remit, rush, rush off, send, send away, send forth, send through the mail, set going, ship, speed, speed along, speed on its way, transfer, transmit
ASSOCIATED CONCEPTS: with all due dispatch

DISPEL, verb   banish, bestow, bestrew, break up, broadcast, cast adrift, cast off, cast out, deal out, diffuse, discharge, *discutere,* disintegrate, dismiss, *dispellere,* disperse, disperse completely, disseminate, *dissipare,* dissipate, dissolve, do away with, drive away, drive away by scattering, drive off in various directions, eject, expel, fling off, get rid of, loose, push away, put into circulation, radiate, release, remove, rout, scatter, send, send flying, send home, set abroach, set aside, set asunder, shake off, spread, strew, string out, throw away, throw off, turn adrift, utterly disperse
ASSOCIATED CONCEPTS: dispel an inference

DISPENSABLE, adjective   disposable, excusable, expendable, extraneous, futile, gratuitous, in excess, inconsequential, ineffectual, minor, needless, negligible, non-essential, of no avail, otiose, pardonable, petty, redundant, replaceable, severable, sparable, spendable, superfluous, supernumerary, unavailing, unessential, unimportant, unnecessary, unrequired

DISPENSATION (*Act of dispensing*), **noun**   accommodation, administration, allocation, allotment, appointment, apportionment, assignment, bestowal, bestowment, conferment, conferral, dispersal, dispersion, disposal, disposition, dissemination, distribution, division, fair sharing, impartation, impartment, issuance, partition, presentation, presentment, provision, repartition, share, subvention, transfer

DISPENSATION (*Exception*), **noun**   absolution, acquiescence, allowance, amnesty, approval, authorization, *carte blanche,* certificate of exemption, clearance, *congé,* consent, deliberate omission, escape-clause, exception, exception in favor of, exclusion, exculpation, excuse, exemption, exemption from law, exoneration, forgiveness, freedom, grace, grant, immunity, indulgence, leave, liberty, license, noninclusion, nonliability, nonresponsibility, omission, pardon, permission, permit, privilege, relaxation of law, release from obligation, sanction, special privilege, sufferance, tolerance, toleration, warrant
ASSOCIATED CONCEPTS: concession, franchise, special dispensation

DISPENSE, verb   administer, allocate, allot, appoint, apportion, appropriate, assign, bestow, bestow upon, confer, deal, deal to, detail, *dimittere,* dispense, disperse, dispose of, disseminate, *distribuere,* distribute, divide in portions, do away with, do without, dole out, donate, give out, grant, hand out, issue, mete, parcel out, portion out, proportionate, provide, ration, *re carere,* render, scatter, serve, share, tender
ASSOCIATED CONCEPTS: dispense with

DISPENSE WITH, verb   abandon, abjure, abolish, abstain, cede, censor, disavow, disclaim, dismiss, disown, dispose of, do without, except, exclude, excuse, exempt, extinguish, forbear, forgo, forswear, give up, jettison, not use, pass over, refrain, refuse, relinquish, renounce, sell off, set aside, spare, waive, yield
ASSOCIATED CONCEPTS: dispense with the testimony

DISPERSE (*Disseminate*), **verb**   administer, allocate, apportion, assign, bestow in shares, bestrew, cast forth, cast off, circulate, consign, convey, deal, deal out, dispense, dispose, distribute, divide, dole, dole out, give away, give out among a number, issue, mete out, parcel out, partition, pass out, pay dividends, pay out, portion out, propagate, scatter abroad, spread, spread abroad, spread out, strew
ASSOCIATED CONCEPTS: disperse public information

DISPERSE (*Scatter*), **verb**   asunder, decentralize, depart, diffuse, disband, disintegrate, disjoin, dispart, dispel, *dispellere, dispergere, dissipare,* dissipate, dissolve, disunite, divide, go different ways, go in different directions, go separate ways, part, partition, rend, rive, scatter abroad, separate, split up, spread widely

DISPERSION, noun   allocation, decentralization, diffraction, diffusion, disjunction, dispensation, dispersal, dissemination, dissipation, distribution, divergence, division, emanation, parting, radiation, refraction, scattering, separation, spread

DISPLACE (*Remove*), **verb**   banish, carry away, cart away, cast out, change the place of, clear away, convey, delocalize, deport, detach, discard, discharge, dislocate, dislodge, dismiss, dispatch, disperse, dispossess, disturb, eject, evict, exclude, exile, expatriate, expel, export, expropriate, *loco suo movere,* move, not retain, oust, purge, put out, send, send away, shift from its place, take away, throw out, transfer, turn out, unhouse, unjoint, unseat
ASSOCIATED CONCEPTS: displaced person, displaced worker

189

DISPLACE *(Replace)*, **verb**   act for, act the part of, answer for, change for, count for, double for, exchange, fill another's position, fill in for, interchange, make a shift with, make way for, offer in exchange, pass for, put in the place of, replace with, stand in for, substitute, succeed, supersede, supplant, switch, take another's place, take in exchange, take over another's duties, take the place of, transfer, transpose, understudy for

DISPLAY, **verb**   brandish, bring to light, demonstrate, disclose, divulge, evidence, evince, exhibit, express, flaunt, flourish, illustrate, indicate, parade, present, reveal, show, wave

DISPLEASE, **verb**   affront, agitate, anger, annoy, antagonize, bait, chafe, chagrin, disaffect, disappoint, discommode, discontent, disenchant, disgruntle, dishearten, dislike, disoblige, dissatisfy, disturb, embitter, exasperate, excite, fret, grate, harrow, harry, inflame, irritate, offend, pique, plague, provoke, repel, rile, sour, vex, worry

DISPOSABLE, **adjective**   adaptable, advantageous, available, consumable, dispensable, employable, expendable, exploitable, fit for use, free for use, helpful, movable, of service, of use, on call, open to, pervious, procurable, reachable, ready for use, realizable, salable, securable, serviceable, spendable, suitable, to be had, usable, useful, utilitarian, utilizable, within reach
ASSOCIATED CONCEPTS: disposable assets

DISPOSE *(Apportion)*, **verb**   deal out, distribute, dole out, fix, mete out, parcel out, place

DISPOSE *(Incline)*, **verb**   affect, arrange, bend, bias, decide, determine, incline, induce, influence, put, sway, tend, verge
ASSOCIATED CONCEPTS: disposing mind and memory

DISPOSITION *(Determination)*, **noun**   adjustment, conclusion, decision, disposal, final settlement of a matter, finding, order, pronouncement, putting in order, resolution, settlement, solution
ASSOCIATED CONCEPTS: disposition of a case

DISPOSITION *(Final arrangement)*, **noun**   adjustment, administration, arrangement, array, *conlocatio*, control, direction, dispensation, disposal, *dispositio*, distribution, grouping, management, marshaling, method, order, ordering, *ordinatio*, organization, placement, regulation, settlement
ASSOCIATED CONCEPTS: conditional disposition, final disposition, fraudulent disposition, power of disposition, testimentary disposition
FOREIGN PHRASES: ***Cujus est dare, ejus est disponere.*** Whoever has the right of giving a thing, has the right of any disposition of it.

DISPOSITION *(Inclination)*, **noun**   aptitude, bent, bias, cast, character, characteristic, characteristic mood, constitution, frame of mind, grain, humor, idiosyncrasy, inclination, individualism, *indoles, ingenium,* leaning, liking, makeup, mental constitution, mold, mood, native character, *natura,* natural fitness, natural tendency, nature, penchant, personality, predilection, predisposition, preference, proclivity, proneness, propensity, spirit, temper, temperament, tendency, turn of mind
FOREIGN PHRASES: ***Impunitas continuum affectum tribuit delinquendi.*** Impunity confirms the disposition of a delinquent.

DISPOSITION *(Transfer of property)*, **noun**   alienation, arrangement for disposal, assignment, conveyance, conveyancing, deliverance, delivery, dispensation, disposal, distribution, giving, manner of disposal, release, relinquishment, relinquishment by gift, sale, surrender, transfer, transference, vouchsafement, yielding
ASSOCIATED CONCEPTS: dispose of and convey, disposition by will, final disposition, fraudulent disposition, power of disposition, sale or other disposition, testamentary disposition
FOREIGN PHRASES: ***Cujus est dare, ejus est disponere.*** He who has a right to give, has the right to dispose of the gift.

DISPOSSESS, **verb**   cause to forfeit, declare forfeit, depose, deprive, deprive of occupancy, *deturbare*, disendow, disentitle, dislodge, displace, disseise, disseize, divest, eject from possession, evict, expel, expropriate, foreclose, oust, *possessione depellere,* relieve of, remove, turn out
ASSOCIATED CONCEPTS: dispossess a tenant, eviction, foreclosure, summary proceedings

DISPOSSESSION, **noun**   abridgment, assumption, bereavement, condemnation, confiscation, dislodgment, disownment, disqualification, distrust, divestment, ejection, eviction, expropriation, expulsion, foreclosure, forfeiture, ouster, privation, removal, taking, usurpation
ASSOCIATED CONCEPTS: adverse possession, ejection, landlord-tenant, wrongful dispossession, wrongful eviction

DISPRAISE, **noun**   blame, castigation, censure, condemnation, criticism, decrial, denunciation, depreciation, detraction, disapprobation, disapproval, discommendation, discredit, disgrace, dishonor, disparagement, dissatisfaction, disvaluation, ignominy, malediction, obloquy, onus, opprobrium, rebuke, reprimand, reprisal

DISPRAISE, **verb**   blame, castigate, censure, condemn, criticize, damn, decry, defame, denounce, deprecate, depreciate, derogate, disapprove, discommend, discountenance, discredit, dishonor, disparage, disvalue, fault, inveigh, lessen, malign, reprimand, rebuke

DISPROPORTIONATE, **adjective**   assymetrical, at odds, at variance, conflicting, contrary to reason, disaccordant, discordant, discrepant, disparate, divergent, excessive, ill-adapted, ill-matched, ill-proportioned, ill-sorted, ill-suited, illogical, *impar,* improperly proportioned, *inaequalis,* inapplicable, inapposite, inappropriate, incommensurable, incommensurate, incompatible, inconformable, incongruent, incongruous, inconsequent, inconsistent, inconsonant, infelicitous, inharmonious, inordinate, irrational, irreconcilable, lacking proportion, mismatched, not following, not in keeping, out of joint, out of keeping, out of place, out of proportion, overcharged, overmuch, poorly adapted, superfluous, too much, unapt, unbalanced, unbefitting, uncalled for, unconformable, undeserved, undeserving, undue, unequal, uneven, unfitting, unjustifiable, unreasonable, unseemly, unsuitable, unsymmetrical, untoward, unwarrantable, unwarranted, wanting in proportion
ASSOCIATED CONCEPTS: disproportionate penalty, disproportionate to the value, punishment disproportionate to the crime

DISPROVE, **verb**   belie, confute, contravene, controvert, counteract, countervail, deny, discredit, dispel, find unfounded, invalidate, negate, nullify, oppugn, prove false, prove the contrary, prove to be wrong, prove to the contrary, rebut, *redarguere, refellere,* refute, show the fallacy of, show to be false, traverse

DISPUTABLE, *adjective* admitting of doubt, ambiguous, apocryphal, appealing to reason, arguable, arguing, argumentative, at issue, confutable, conjectural, contestable, controversial, controvertible, cryptic, debatable, deniable, disputatious, doubtable, doubtful, doubting, dubious, dubitable, dubitative, enigmatic, equivocal, eristic, fallible, hard to believe, hypothetical, improbable, in dispute, in doubt, in issue, in question, incredible, indefinite, indeterminate, *infamis,* not axiomatic, not to be believed, of doubtful certainty, open to debate, open to discussion, open to doubt, open to question, open to suspicion, paradoxical, perplexing, polemic, problematic, questionable, refutable, speculative, subject to argument, subject to controversy, suppositional, suspect, suspicious, theoretical, to be decided, unaffirmed, unascertained, unbelievable, uncertain, unconfirmed, undecided, undemonstrable, undemonstrated, under discussion, undetermined, unfixed, unknown, unlikely, unproven, unreliable, unresolved, unsettled, unsure, unsustainable, unsustained, unverifiable, vague
ASSOCIATED CONCEPTS: disputable presumption

DISPUTANT, *noun* adversary, adverse party, antagonist, argumentative person, assailant, belligerent, caviler, combatant, contender, contestant, controversialist, controvertist, discussant, dissenter, litigant, objector, obstructionist, opponent, opposer, oppositionist, polemicist, resister, rival, wrangler

DISPUTATIOUS, *adjective* argumentative, bickering, cantankerous, captious, competitive, contentious, contrary, controversial, debatable, dialectic, discordant, discrepant, disputable, disputative, dissenting, dissentious, divided, fractious, hostile, litigious, logomachical, moot, petulant, polemic, pugnacious, quarrelsome, querulous, remonstrative, schismatic, testy

DISPUTE, *noun* aggressive argument, *altercatio,* altercation, argument, bickering, challenge, clash of opinions, conflict, conflict of opinion, contention, *controversia,* controversy, debate, *démêlé,* difference, difference of opinion, disaccord, disagreement, *disceptatio,* discord, dissension, dissentience, dissidence, disturbance, disunity, divergence, divergent opinions, embranglement, embroilment, failure to agree, feud, imbroglio, impugnation, legal battle, litigation, nonagreement, opposition, polemic, remonstrance, remonstration, strife, variance, verbal contention, verbal controversy, verbal engagement, wrangle
ASSOCIATED CONCEPTS: amount in dispute, dispute as to the amount, dispute concerning terms or conditions of employment, jurisdictional dispute, labor dispute, matter in dispute, undisputed claim

DISPUTE (Contest), *verb* *altercari,* altercate, argue against, argue vehemently, be at cross purposes, be at variance, bring in question, call in question, challenge, clash, collide, combat, compete, *concertare,* conflict, confute, contend, contend for, contradict, contravene, controvert, deny, deny absolutely, deny emphatically, deny entirely, deny flatly, deny peremptorily, deny the genuineness of, differ, disagree with, dissent from doubt, gainsay, give denial to, have a feud, have an altercation, have differences, have words with, impugn, negative, not agree, object to, oppose by argument, quarrel over, query, question the truth of, recriminate, refute, *rixari,* strive against, struggle against, take exception, take issue with, traverse
ASSOCIATED CONCEPTS: disputed claim, disputed demand, disputed issue, disputed question of fact, disputed writing, labor dispute

FOREIGN PHRASES: ***Non est certandum de regulis juris.*** There is no disputing about rules of the law.

DISPUTE (Debate), *verb* *ambigere,* argue, argue a case, argue a point, argue in opposition, argufy, bandy words, be contrary, bicker, carry on an argument, confute, contend in argument, contradict, controvert, differ, disagree, discept, *disceptare, disputare,* dissent, divide on, have a verbal controversy over, hold an argument, indulge in argument, make a rejoinder, not agree, parry, rebut, refute, wrangle

DISPUTE RESOLUTION, *noun* alternative dispute resolution, judicial alternative, means to conclude an action, means to gain a decision, means to gain a determination, means to gain an outcome, means to obtain findings, means to resolve an action
ASSOCIATED CONCEPTS: alternative dispute resolution

DISPUTED POINT OF LAW, *noun* at issue, bone of contention, contention, debatable point, desideratum, development, difficulty, in question, issue, issue under consideration, matter in dispute, outgrowth, point, point in question, problem, question at issue, sticking point, under advisement, under examination

DISQUALIFICATION (Factor that disqualifies), *noun* defect, disability, disablement, failure, handicap, inability, inadequacy, inaptitude, incapability, incapacitation, incapacity, incompetence, incompetency, ineptitude, inexpertness, insufficiency, invalidation, invalidity, lack of dexterity, lack of proficiency, lack of qualification, shortcoming, unaptness, undeftness, undesirability, unfitness, unfittedness, unpreparedness, unproficiency, unqualifiedness, unskillfulness, unsuitability, want of ability, want of skill

DISQUALIFICATION (Rejection), *noun* banishment, deposal, deprivation, dethronement, disapprobation, disbarment, discharge, disentitlement, disfavor, disfranchisement, dislodgment, dismissal, displacement, dispossession, ejection, elimination, eviction, exclusion, expulsion, forfeiture, inadmissibility, ineligibility, invalidation, loss of right, nonadmission, noninclusion, ouster, preclusion, rejecting, rejection, repudiation, throwing out
ASSOCIATED CONCEPTS: disqualification to hold office, legal disqualification

DISQUALIFY, *verb* bar, block, check, counteract, debar, deny, deprive of power, disable, disarm, disenable, disentitle, disfranchise, dispossess of right, divest of right, *excipere,* exclude, incapacitate, inhibit, interfere, invalidate, make impossible, make useless, neutralize, preclude, prevent, prohibit, reject, render impotent, render unfit, restrain, restrict, rule out, stop, strip of right, undermine, unfit
ASSOCIATED CONCEPTS: disqualified for interest, disqualified to act, disqualifying interest, disqualifying opinion, permanently disqualified

DISREGARD (Lack of respect), *noun* affront, aloofness, bad manners, belittlement, callousness, contempt, contemptuousness, contumely, depreciation, discourtesy, disdain, disesteem, disfavor, dishonor, disobedience, disregardfulness, disrespect, heedlessness, impoliteness, impudence, inappreciation, inattentiveness, incivility, inconsiderateness, inconsideration, indifference, insensitivity, insolence, insult, low estimation, outrage, regardlessness, rudeness, scoffing, scorn, slight, snub, thoughtlessness, underestimation, undervaluation, unheedfulness, unmindfulness, want of thought

DISREGARD *(Omission)*, **noun** breach of orders, default, delinquency, dereliction of duty, disregardfulness, failure to carry out, infraction, infringement, malefaction, malpractice, misbehavior, misconduct, neglect, neglectfulness, noncompliance, nonobservance, preterition, pretermission, refusal to obey, regardlessness, remissness, transgression, trespass, violation

DISREGARD *(Unconcern)*, **noun** carelessness, disinterest, disinterestedness, disregardfulness, exclusion, heedlessness, improvidence, imprudence, inattention, inattentiveness, incaution, inconsideration, indifference, inobservance, insouciance, lack of care, lack of consideration, lack of interest, lack of observation, leaving out, mindlessness, neglect, neglectfulness, negligence, nonobservance, oblivion, obliviousness, overlooking, oversight, regardlessness, unconsciousness, unheedfulness, unmindfulness, unthinkingness, unwariness, unwatchfulness, want of notice, want of thought

DISREGARD, *verb* be incurious, be indifferent, be insensitive, dismiss, fail to notice, fail to observe, feel no concern, give no heed, ignore, leave out, leave out of consideration, neglect, *neglegere,* not bother with, not consider, not hear, not heed, not include, not listen, not think about, not think of, not trouble oneself, *omittere,* overlook, *parvi facere,* pass by, pay no attention, pay no regard to, pretermit, refuse to hear, refuse to know, refuse to regard, snub, spurn, take no account of, take no interest, take no note of, take no notice of, think little of, think nothing of, treat without due respect
ASSOCIATED CONCEPTS: disregard for the law, instruct the jury to disregard testimony, reckless disregard

DISREPAIR, *noun* collapse, corrosion, damage, decadence, decadency, decay, decrepitude, degeneration, deterioration, dilapidation, impaired condition, impairment, lack of maintenance, neglect, ruination

DISREPUTABLE, *adjective* abominable, arrant, bad, base, beastly, being in ill repute, characterless, cheap, coarse, conscienceless, contemptible, corrupt, crass, degraded, demoralizing, deplorable, despicable, despised, detestable, devious, discreditable, discredited, disgraced, disgraceful, dishonest, dishonorable, disliked, disrespectable, dissolute, dreadful, foul, hateful, having a bad reputation, heinous, held in contempt, horrendous, horrid, ignoble, ignominious, immoral, improper, impure, in disgrace, indecent, indecorous, indelicate, inelegant, *infamis,* infamous, inglorious, iniquitous, insincere, knavish, licentious, loathsome, meretricious, misdealing, nefarious, not reputable, not respectable, not thought much of, notorious, objectionable, obnoxious, odious, of bad character, of ill fame, opprobrious, prevaricating, profligate, recreant, rejected, reprehensible, reproached, ribald, shameful, shameless, spurious, suspicious, tasteless, undignified, unethical, unprincipled, unrefined, unrespectable, unsavory, unscrupulous, untrustworthy, untruthful, unworthy

DISREPUTE, *noun* abasement, abjectness, abominableness, bad character, bad reputation, bad repute, baseness, beastliness, brand, contemptibility, debasement, degradation, despicability, despicableness, discreditableness, disesteem, disgracefulness, dishonor, dishonorableness, disparagement, disreputability, disreputableness, disrespect, execrableness, heinousness, ignobility, ignominiousness, ignominy, ill-fame, ill-favor, ill-repute, *infamia,* infamousness, infamy, ingloriousness, loathsomeness, loss of honor,

loss of reputation, monstrousness, nefariousness, no reputation, no repute, obloquy, obnoxiousness, odiousness, odium, opprobrium, shady reputation, shame, shamefulness, shoddiness, stain, taint, turpitude, vileness, want of esteem, wickedness, wretchedness

DISRESPECT, *noun* abruptness, affront, arrogance, audacity, bluntness, brashness, brazenness, brusqueness, cavalierness, condescension, contempt, contemptuousness, contumacy, contumely, curtness, defiance, depreciation, derision, derisiveness, detraction, discourteousness, discourtesy, disdain, disesteem, dishonor, disobedience, disparagement, disregard, disrespectfulness, effrontery, flippancy, flout, impertinence, impoliteness, impudence, incivility, indecorum, insolence, *insolentia,* insubordination, insult, inurbanity, irreverence, lack of consideration, lack of courteousness, lack of courtesy, lack of politeness, lack of respect, mockery, offense, pertness, presumption, presumptuousness, rebuff, ridicule, rude behavior, rudeness, sauciness, scoffing, scorn, shortness, slight, sneer, snub, spurn, superciliousness, tactlessness, uncourtliness, ungallantness, ungentlemanliness, ungraciousness, unmannerliness, unmannerly conduct, unpoliteness, vilification, vilipendency, want of esteem
ASSOCIATED CONCEPTS: disrespect to flag

DISRUPT, *verb* agitate, annoy, break apart, cause chaos, cause confusion, cause scission, confuse, create a disturbance, create disorder, derange, disarrange, discompose, discontinue, dishevel, disjoin, disorder, disorganize, disquiet, dissociate, distract, disturb, embroil, fluster, get in the way, hinder, impede, infringe, intercept, interfere, intermit, interrupt, intervene, intrude, meddle, mess up, mix up, obstruct, overturn, perturb, prevent, rend asunder, ruffle, rupture, split up, stir up, stop, sunder, suspend, thwart, unsettle, upset

DISSATISFACTION, *noun* annoyance, chagrin, complaint, dejection, disaffection, disagreement, disappointment, disapprobation, disapproval, discomfort, discontent, discontentedness, discontentment, discouragement, disesteem, disfavor, disgruntlement, disgust, dislike, displeasure, disquiet, dissatisfiedness, dissent, distaste, fault-finding, grievance, grudge, inquietude, irritation, *molestia,* nonapproval, nonfulfillment of one's hopes, *offensa, offensio,* opposition, pique, querulousness, regret, state of not being satisfied, umbrage, uncomfortableness, uneasiness of mind, unhappiness, unhappiness with one's lot, unsatisfaction, vexation
ASSOCIATED CONCEPTS: express dissatisfaction

DISSEISIN, *noun* arrogation, assuming ownership, attachment, capture, commandeering, compulsory acquisition, confiscation, deprivation, deprivation of possession, disendowment, displacement of rightful owner, dispossession, distraint, distress, divestment, exclusion of entitled owner, expropriation, forcible seizure, foreclosure, impropriation, ouster, prehension, privation of seisin, seizure, sequestration, take-over, taking, taking possession, taking without compensation, wrongful dispossession
ASSOCIATED CONCEPTS: adverse possession, disseisin by election

DISSEMINATE, *verb* announce, annunciate, apprise, broadcast, bruit, carry a report, circulate, communicate, convey, deal out, diffuse, dispatch news, dispense, *dispergere,* disperse, *disseminare,* distribute, impart, inform, issue, make public, notify, promulgate, propagate, publicize, publish,

publish abroad, radiate, relay, report, *spargere,* spread a report, spread far and wide, strew, transmit, utter
ASSOCIATED CONCEPTS: publication of a libel

DISSENSION, noun angry disagreement, argumentation, bickering, *brouillerie,* caviling, clashing, conflict, conflict of opinion, contention, controversy, difference of opinion, differences, disaccord, disaffection, disagreement, discord, discordance, *discordia,* disharmony, dispute, dissent, dissentience, dissidence, dissonance, disunion, disunity, divergence, divergent opinions, diversity of opinion, division, friction, lack of harmony, nonagreement, nonassent, nonconcurrence, protest, protestation, quarrel, refusal of agreement, remonstrance, resentment, rift, schism, strife, strong dissension, violent disagreement, wrangling

DISSENT *(Difference of opinion),* **noun** apostasy, argument, caviling, challenge, clash, confirmed opposition, conflict, conflict of opinion, contraposition, demur, disaccord, disagreement, discord, discordance, disharmony, disparity, dissensio, dissension, dissentience, dissidence, dissonance, divergence, diversity of opinion, expostulation, failure to agree, friction, lack of harmony, nonagreement, noncompliance, objection, oppositeness, opposition, schism, unconformity, variance

DISSENT *(Nonconcurrence),* **noun** contrariety, disagreement, disapproval, disavowal, disclaimer, discontent, dissatisfaction, dissension, dissentient voice, disunity, nonagreement, nonassent, nonconformity, nonconsent, nonobservance, objection, opposition, repudiation, variance
ASSOCIATED CONCEPTS: dissenting opinion, dissenting vote

DISSENT *(Differ in opinion),* **verb** argue, be at variance, be contrary, be of contrary sentiment, bicker, clash, collide, conflict, confute, contradict, differ, differ in sentiment, disagree, disagree in opinion, dispute, *dissentire, dissidere,* not agree, oppose, quarrel, take exception, take issue with
ASSOCIATED CONCEPTS: dissenting fiduciary, dissenting stockholders

DISSENT *(Withhold assent),* **verb** be unwilling, challenge, decline, decline to agree, defy, demur, disallow, disapprove, negate, negative, nonconsent, not accept, not approve, not consider, not defend, not hold with, object, oppose, prohibit, protest, raise objections, raise one's voice against, rebuff, refuse, refuse assent, refuse to admit, reject, repudiate, repulse, resist, spurn
ASSOCIATED CONCEPTS: dissent from the majority opinion

DISSENTING, adjective arguing, argumentative, at cross-purposes, at issue, at loggerheads, at odds, at variance, caviling, clashing, conflicting, conflictive, conflictory, contentious, contradicting, controverting, debating, declining to agree, demurring, denying, differing, disaccordant, disagreeing, disapproving, discordant, discrepant, disharmonious, disputatious, disputative, disputing, dissentient, dissentious, dissident, dissonant, disunited, divergent, divided on, factious, going contrary to, in conflict, in disagreement, incongruous, inconsistent, inharmonious, irreconcilable, not abiding, not accepting, not agreeing, not conforming, objecting, opposing, polemical, protesting, quarreling, quarrelsome, questioning, recusant, refusing to admit, refusing to agree, refuting, repudiating, repugning, resisting, running counter to, taking exception, taking issue with, unconsenting, varying, withholding approval, withholding assent, wrangling

ASSOCIATED CONCEPTS: dissenting judges, dissenting opinion, dissenting shareholders

DISSERVICE, noun bad turn, damage, detriment, *detrimentum,* harm, ill turn, *incommodum,* injury, injustice, malfeasance, mischief, misdeed, misdoing, mistreatment, outrage, unkindness, wrong

DISSIDENCE, noun argument, bickering, clashing, conflict, contradiction, contrariety, controversy, contumaciousness, difference, disaccord, disagreement, discongruity, discord, discordance, discordancy, disharmony, dissension, dissent, dissonance, disunion, disunity, divergence, faction, incongruence, incongruity, inharmoniousness, noncompliance, nonconcurrence, nonconformity, opposition, quarrel, recusancy, schism, strife, unconformity, variance, wrangle

DISSIDENT, adjective antagonistic, at odds with, at variance with, challenging, clashing, contrary, differing, disagreeing, discontented, discordant, discrepant, disinclined, disobedient, dissatisfied, dissentient, dissenting, dissentious, divergent, divided, factious, inaccordant, inacquiescent, incompatible, inconsistent with, irreconcilable, loath, malcontent, noncompliant, nonconforming, nonconformist, nonobservant, not consenting, objecting, opposing, protestant, protesting, quarreling, rebellious, recalcitrant, recusant, refusing, resistant, unassenting, unconformable, unconsenting, unwilling

DISSIMILAR, adjective aberrant, asymmetrical, atypical, clashing, contrary, contrasted, contrasting, deviating, different, differing, disagreeing, discordant, discrepant, *dispar,* disparate, *dissimilis,* divergent, divers, diverse, diversified, heterogeneous, incongruent, irregular, irrelative, mismatched, mixed, multiform, nonidentical, nonuniform, not comparable, not similar, odd, of a different kind, of all sorts, of many kinds, unalike, unconformable, unidentical, unlike, unmatched, unpaired, unrelated, unresembling, unsame, unsimilar, untypical, varied, variegated, variform, various
ASSOCIATED CONCEPTS: dissimilar condition

DISSIPATE *(Expend foolishly),* **verb** abuse, be extravagant, be immoderate, be intemperate, be prodigal, burn up, consume, consume one's substance, deny oneself nothing, deplete, drain, empty, exhaust, expend, indulge in extravagance, indulge oneself, live idly, misspend, misuse, overdraw, overspend, overstrain, practice extravagance, prodigalize, spend, spend lavishly, spend wastefully, use up, waste
ASSOCIATED CONCEPTS: dissipation of assets, dissipation of property, waste

DISSIPATE *(Spread out),* **verb** bestrew, break up, cast forth, cease, cease to be, dematerialize, diffuse, disappear, disintegrate, disperse, disseminate, *dissipare,* dissolve, diverge, evanesce, fade, fade away, overspread, radiate, scatter, scatter thinly, scatter to the winds, scatter widely, sow, spread, spread over, sprinkle, strew, vanish

DISSOCIATE, verb break up, cut adrift, cut off, demobilize, detach, disassociate, disband, disconnect, disencumber, disengage, disjoin, dispart, disperse, displace, dissever, disunite, divide, divorce, free, have no concern with, isolate, keep apart, liberate, loosen, part, release, remove, scatter, segregate, separate, set free, sever, sunder, take leave, unbind, unchain, uncouple, undo, unlock, unloose, unyoke, withdraw

DISSOLUTE, *adjective* abandoned, base-minded, carnal, concupiscent, corrupt, corrupted, debased, debauched, decadent, degenerate, degraded, depraved, dissipated, *dissolutus,* evil-minded, free-living, graceless, immoderate, immoral, impure, incontinent, incorrigible, indecent, indulgent, iniquitous, intemperate, lascivious, libertine, libidinous, licentious, low-minded, lustful, *luxuriosus,* perverted, polluted, prodigal, profligate, prurient, rakish, reprobate, salacious, satyric, sensual, shameless, unashamed, unbridled, unchaste, uncurbed, unprincipaled, unrestrained, unvirtuous, warped, wayward
ASSOCIATED CONCEPTS: dissolute person

DISSOLUTION (Disintegration), ***noun*** adulteration, atomization, atrophy, breaking up, corrosion, corruption, crumbling, decay, decomposition, demolition, deterioration, dilapidation, disassembly, disbanding, dismantlement, disorganization, dispersal, disruption, dissipation, erosion, rotting, separation, spoilage, spoliation, undoing

DISSOLUTION (Termination), ***noun*** abolishment, abolition, abrogation, annihilation, annulment, breaking up, cancellation, cancelling, cessation, close, closing, completion, conclusion, death, defeasance, demise, destruction, discontinuance, dismissal, *dissolutio,* disuse, effacement, elimination, end, ending, eradication, erasure, expiration, expunction, extinction, extinguishment, extirpation, finis, finish, invalidation, liquidation, nullification, obliteration, overthrow, prorogation, repeal, rescission, revocation, revokement, ruin, ruination, suppression, voidance
ASSOCIATED CONCEPTS: corporate dissolution, de facto dissolution, de jure dissolution, dissolution of marriage, dissolution of partnership, dissolution proceeding
FOREIGN PHRASES: **Nihil tam naturale est, quam eo genere quidque dissolvere, quo colligatum est.** Nothing is so natural as to dissolve anything in the way in which it was made binding. **Nihil tam conveniens est naturali aequitati quam unumquodque dissolvi eo ligamine quo ligatum est.** Nothing is so agreeable to natural equity as that a thing should be dissolved by the same means by which it was bound. **Nihil est magis rationi consentaneum quam eodem modo quodque dissolvere quo conflatum est.** Nothing is more consonant to reason than that a thing should be dissolved in the same way in which it was created.

DISSOLVE (Disperse), ***verb*** atomize, decompose, diffuse, disintegrate, dispel, dissipate, *dissolvere,* evanesce, intersperse, *liquefacere,* melt away, radiate, scatter, spread

DISSOLVE (Separate), ***verb*** break apart, break up, decentralize, demobilize, detach, disband, disconnect, disengage, disjoin, dismantle, dispart, dissever, dissociate, disunite, divide, divorce, part, set asunder, sever, split up, sunder, take apart, uncouple, undo

DISSOLVE (Terminate), ***verb*** abort, abrogate, break up, bring to an end, bring to conclusion, call off, cancel, cease, conclude, desist, destroy, disband, discontinue, dispose of, draw to a close, efface, effect a dissolution, end, erase, expire, finish, halt, neutralize, nullify, obliterate, quash, render inert, revoke, split up, stop, undo, vitiate, wipe out
ASSOCIATED CONCEPTS: dissolving an injunction
FOREIGN PHRASES: **Eddem modo quo quid constituitur, dissolvitur.** Anything is dissolved in the same manner in which it is made binding.

DISSUADE, *verb* abash, advise against, argue against, attempt to divert, attempt to prevent, cause doubt, caution, convince to the contrary, daunt, *dehortari,* deter from

one's purpose, *deterrere,* discourage, disenchant, dishearten, disillusion, dispirit, *dissuadere,* divert by appeal, divert from, exhort against, frighten away, raise apprehension, remonstrate, render averse, stave off, talk out of, turn from a purpose, urge not to

DISTANT (Detached), ***adjective*** afar, far, far away, far-off, in the distance, out of distance, out of range, out of reach, out of sight, outlying, remote, removed
ASSOCIATED CONCEPTS: distant relative, trust and estates, wills

DISTANT (Far), ***adjective*** aloof, coif, remote, removed, standoffish, unapproachable, uncommunicative, unfriendly, unresponsive, unsociable, withdrawn

DISTILL, *verb* boil down, clarify, concentrate, condense, decoct, *destillare,* draw forth, draw out, draw out the essence, drop, expel, extract, filtrate, filter, free from extraneous matter, press out, purify by removing the foreign and nonessential, reduce to extreme purity and strength, separate, squeeze out, *stillare,* strain, strain out, take out, trickle, vaporize and condense, wring
ASSOCIATED CONCEPTS: distilled liquor, distilled spirits, distilling apparatus, distilling the essence out of a case

DISTINCT (Clear), ***adjective*** apparent, *clarus,* clear-cut, clear to the mind, clear to the senses, clearly defined, concrete, conspicuous, crystal clear, definite, *distinctus,* distinguishable, easily perceived, easily understood, eidetic, evident, explicit, exposed to view, express, for all to see, glaring, graphic, in full view, indubitable, intelligible, lucid, manifest, noticeable, obvious, palpable, particular, pellucid, perceivable, perceptible, *perspicuus,* positive, precise, pronounced, recognizable, self-evident, sharp, striking, unambiguous, unclouded, uncovered, undisguised, undistorted, unequivocal, unhidden, visible, visualized, vivid, well-defined, well-drawn, well-marked
ASSOCIATED CONCEPTS: clear and distinct, distinct action

DISTINCT (Distinguished from others), ***adjective*** characteristic, contrasted, contrasting, decidedly different, departing from, different, differing, disassociated, discrepant, discrete, discriminate, dissimilar, distant, distinctive, *distinctus,* distinguished by nature, distinguished by station, divergent, diverse, divorced, idiosyncratic, incongruent, incongruous, individual, marked, nonuniform, not identical, not the same, observably different, out of the ordinary, particular, peculiar, poles apart, removed, separate, *separatus,* set apart, singular, special, standing apart, uncommon, unconfused, unimitated, unique, unlike, unlike others, unusual
ASSOCIATED CONCEPTS: distinct entity, distinct interests

DISTINCT MEANING, *noun* accurate meaning, correct meaning, defined meaning, definition, exact meaning, explanation, explicit meaning, express meaning, faithful meaning, inflexible meaning, literal meaning, methodical meaning, meticulous meaning, narrow meaning, not subject to interpretation, ordinary meaning, plain meaning, precise meaning, prescribed meaning, rigid meaning, rigorous meaning, sharply defined, significance, specific meaning, strict meaning, unbending meaning, uncompromising meaning, unequivocal meaning
ASSOCIATED CONCEPTS: construction, literal contract, literal proof, plain meaning rule, rules of statutory, soft plain meaning rule, textualism

DISTINCTION (Difference), ***noun*** antithesis, characteristic difference, contrariety, contrast, differentia, differential, differentiation, disaccord, disagreement, discongruity, discrepancy, *discrimen,* discrimination, disharmony, disparity, dissension, dissonance, *distinctio,* distinguishing characteristic, distinguishing quality, diverseness, earmark, individuality, irrelation, nonuniformity, peculiarity, perceivable dissimilarity, point of difference, special marking, unconformity, unique feature, uniqueness, unlikeness, variance, variant, variation

ASSOCIATED CONCEPTS: substantial distinction

DISTINCTION (Reputation), **noun**   account, *aura popularis,* brilliance, celebrity, credit, *dignitas,* dignity, eminence, exaltation, fame, grandeur, greatness, honor, illustriousness, immortality, importance, loftiness, marked superiority, name, nobility, notability, note, noteworthiness, popular favor, prestige, prominence, public esteem, renown, reputability, repute, respectability, significance, special favor, superiority

DISTINCTIVE, adjective   characteristic, conspicuous, contrasting, diacritical, different, differentiating, differentiative, differing, discriminating, distinct, distinguishing, exclusive, idiomatic, idiosyncratic, indicating difference, indicative, individualistic, individualizing, marked, noteworthy, noticeable, particular, peculiar, *proprius,* salient, separative, serving to distinguish, singular, special, uncommon, unimitated, unique, unlike

ASSOCIATED CONCEPTS: distinctive characteristic, distinctive name

DISTINGUISH, verb   ascertain, characterize, classify, contradistinguish, define, demarcate, differentiate, discern, discriminate, *distinguere,* divide, draw a distinction, exercise discretion, exercise discrimination, individualize, *internoscere,* judge, make distinctions, mark out, note differences, particularize, perceive clearly, point out an essential difference, recognize as different, *secernere,* separate, set apart, specify, winnow

ASSOCIATED CONCEPTS: distinguish between right and wrong, distinguishing cases, distinguishing characteristics, distinguishing mark

FOREIGN PHRASES: *Ubi lex non distinguit, nec nos distinguere debemus.* Where the law does not distinguish, we ought not to distinguish. *Qui bene distinguit bene docet.* He who distinguishes well, teaches well.

DISTINGUISHABLE, adjective   able to draw a distinction, able to exercise discretion, ascertainable, capable of being judged, capable of making distinctions, classifiable, definable, demarcation, differentiation, discernment, essentially different, individualized, particularized, recognized as different, separated, set apart, specified

ASSOCIATED CONCEPTS: distinguishable case law, distinguishable mark, distinguishable precedence

DISTORT, verb   bend, camouflage, caricature, change out of recognition, change the face of, conceal, contort, corrupt, deform, disguise, disproportion, dissemble, *distorquere,* exaggerate, falsify, give a false idea, give a false impression, give a strained meaning, give a turn, give twist, inflate, make unlike, miscite, miscolor, misconstrue, misdescribe, misdirect, miseducate, misestimate, misexplain, misexpress, misinform, misinstruct, misinterpret, mislead, misquote, misread, misreckon, misreport, misrepresent, misshape, misteach, mistranslate, overdo, overdramatize, overstate, palter with the truth, paralogize, parody, pervert, play upon words, put a false construction on, put a false sense on, put an erroneous construction on, reshape, strain, strain the meaning, strain the sense, strain the

truth, stretch, stretch the meaning, transfigure, transform, turn awry, twist, twist the meaning, twist the sense, twist the words, understate, warp, wrench, wrench the meaning, wrench the sense

ASSOCIATED CONCEPTS: distort the truth

DISTORT THE MEANING, verb   belie, bias, contort, deform, distort, falsify, garble, interpret incorrectly, manipulate, misapply, misapprehend, miscolor, misconceive, misconstrue, misdirect, misinterpret, misjudge, misread, misrender, misreport, misstate, mistranslate, misuse, pervert, put a false construction on, twist, warp

ASSOCIATED CONCEPTS: distort the meaning of a decision, distort the meaning of a statute, distort the truth

DISTORTION, noun   anamorphosis, camouflage, caricature, contortion, convolution, deception, deformation, deformity, disguise, disparity, disproportion, dissemblance, dissimilarity, dissimilitude, *distortio,* embroidery, enlargement, exaggeration, expansion, false coloring, false construction, false copy, false reading, falsification, gloss, hyperbole, illusion, imbalance, irrelation, magnification, misapplication, misconstruction, misdirection, misexplanation, misinformation, misinstruction, misinterpretation, misquotation, misrendering, misrepresentation, mistranslation, misusage, misuse of words, one-sided conception, one-sided view, over-coloring, overstatement, perversion, *pravitas,* satire, simulacrum, strained sense, stretch, travesty, twist, unlikeness, warped judgment, wrong interpretation

DISTORTION OF THE TRUTH, noun   deceitfulness, deception, exaggeration, fabrication, faking, falsehood, falsification, falsity, garbling, lie, lying, mendacity, misconception, misconstruction, misinterpretation, misrepresentation, mythomania, perfidy, perversion, sophistry, spuriousness, untruthfulness

ASSOCIATED CONCEPTS: perjury, uttering a false statement

DISTRAIN, verb   annex, appropriate, assume ownership, attach, bear away, carry away, carry off, compulsorily acquire, confiscate, deprive of, divest, garnish, *hominis bona vendere,* hurry off with, impound, impress, lay hold of, levy, levy a distress, make away with, possess oneself of, preempt, replevy, seize, sequester, sequestrate, take away, take into custody, take over, take possession of

DISTRAINT, noun   annexation, appropriation, attachment, capture, confiscation, dispossession, distress, divestment, execution, expropriation, forcible seizure, garnishment, impoundage, impoundment, levy, obtainment, securement, seizure and appropriation, seizure to procure satisfaction of a debt, sequestration

ASSOCIATED CONCEPTS: distraint for rent, process of distraint

DISTRESS (Anguish), **noun**   agitation, agony, anxiety, anxiousness, blight, depression, desolation, despair, despondency, difficulty, discomfort, discomposure, disquiet, disquietude, dissatisfaction, infelicity, inquietude, mental agony, misery, pain, perturbation, sadness, sorrow, suffering, torment, trial, tribulation, trouble, uneasiness, unhappiness, vexation, woe, worry, wretchedness

ASSOCIATED CONCEPTS: distress for rent, distress warrant, mental distress, unreasonable distress, warrant of distress

DISTRESS (Seizure), **noun**   acquirement, acquisition, adoption, annexation, appropriation, arrogation, assumption, attachment, capture, confiscation, deprivation, deprivement, dispossession, disseisin, distraint, divestment, expropriation, impoundage, impoundment, impress, impressment, impropriation, levy, removal, seizing, sequestration, snatching, taking, usurpation

DISTRESS, verb afflict, aggravate, aggrieve, agitate, agonize, annoy, bedevil, bother, cause suffering, chagrin, discompose, disgust, disquiet, disturb, exacerbate, grieve, harass, harrow, harry, hurt, irk, irritate, make miserable, make sorrowful, make unhappy, molest, offend, pain, perturb, sadden, subject to strain, torment, trouble, upset, vex, worry

DISTRIBUTE, verb admeasure, administer, allocate, allot, appropriate, arrange, array, assign, assign places to, assort, class, classify, deal, decentralize, dispense, *dispertire*, disseminate, *distribuere*, divide, *dividere*, dole, file, give out, mete, parcel out, portion out, prorate, ration, scatter, set in order, share, sort, sow, space, spread, sprinkle, systematize
ASSOCIATED CONCEPTS: distributed among creditors, distributed because of liquidation, distribution of an estate

DISTRIBUTION (Apportionment), **noun** allocation, allotment, appropriation, assignment, dealing out, dispensation, disposal, dissemination, division, dole, handing out, issuance, parceling out, partition, placement, proporting, rationing, repartition, sharing
ASSOCIATED CONCEPTS: capital distribution, distribution by operation of law, distribution of assets, distribution of capital, distribution of corporate assets, distribution of earnings or profits, distribution of powers and functions, distribution of proceeds, distribution points, just and equal distribution, partial distribution, per capita distribution, per stirpes distribution, pro rata distribution, ratable distribution

DISTRIBUTION (Arrangement), **noun** assemblage, categorization, classification, collocation, disposition, disposure, formation, gradation, graduation, grouping, management, marshaling, ordering, organization, placement, regimentation, serialization, systematization

DISTRICT, noun *ager*, area, circuit, constituency, department, domain, locale, locality, neighborhood, pale, precinct, province, quarter, realm, *regio*, region, section, sphere, *terra*, territorial division, territory, tract, ward, zone
ASSOCIATED CONCEPTS: business district, collection district, election district, federal district, improvement district, judicial district, school district, tax district

DISTRICT ATTORNEY, noun accuser, attorney for the people, attorney representing the state's interest, law enforcement agent, the people, prosecuting attorney, the prosecution, prosecutor, public attorney, public pleader, public prosecutor, the state, state's attorney
ASSOCIATED CONCEPTS: attorney general, county attorney, prosecuting attorney, state's attorney

DISTURB, verb agitate, alarm, annoy, arouse, badger, bedevil, befuddle, bewilder, bother, churn, *commovere*, confound, confuse, *conturbare*, derange, disarrange, discomfit, discompose, disconcert, dishevel, dislocate, dislodge, dismay, disorder, disorganize, disorientate, displace, displant, displease, disquiet, distemper, distract, distress, enrage, exasperate, ferment, fluster, havoc, incommode, interfere, interrupt, intrude, irk, make uneasy, meddle, molest, nettle, nonplus, outrage, overturn, perplex, perturb, *perturbare*, pique, plague, puzzle, rearrange, roil, rouse,

ruffle, shake, shake up, startle, stir up, subvert, tamper, trouble, unbalance, unnerve, unseat, unsettle, upset, vex, worry
ASSOCIATED CONCEPTS: disturbing the peace, right to quiet enjoyment

DISTURBANCE, noun affray, agitation, annoyance, anxietude, anxiety, anxiousness, commotion, confusion, disarrangement, discomfiture, discomposure, disconcertion, discontinuity, dishevelment, dislocation, disorder, disorganization, displacement, disquiet, disquietude, embroilment, eruption, faction, ferment, fomentation, fracas, fuss, hindrance, inquietude, interruption, intrusion, maelstrom, misarrangement, misgiving, molestation, *motus*, perturbation, quandary, rebellion, restiveness, restlessness, revolt, revolution, state of disorder, trepidation, tumult, *tumultus*, *turbatio*, turbulence, turmoil, unrest, unruliness, unsettlement, uprising, uproar
ASSOCIATED CONCEPTS: creating a disturbance, disorderly conduct, disturbance of court, disturbance of possession, disturbance of quiet possession, disturbing the peace, nuisance

DISUSE, noun abandonment, abolishment, abolition, abstinence, archaism, cessation of use, decay, desuetude, discontinuance, discontinuation, disregard, disusage, failure to use, ignorement, inattention, inusitation, neglect, nonemployment, nonuse, obsolescence, staleness, suspension, unemployment

DIVERGENT, adjective aberrant, bifurcate, bifurcated, branching, departing, deviating, deviative, deviatory, different, differing, discrepant, disharmonious, disparate, dissimilar, divaricating, diverging, diverse, diversified, eccentric, factional, factious, forking, furcate, furcated, incompatible, inconsistent, nonuniform, parting, radiating, ramified, separating, straying, taking different courses, unconventional, untraditional, variant, varying
ASSOCIATED CONCEPTS: divergent interests

DIVERSE, adjective *alius*, assorted, contrastive, deviative, different, differing, disagreeing, discrepant, *dispar*, disparate, dissimilar, distinct, distinguishable, divergent, divers, diversified, diversiform, *diversus*, heterogeneous, incomparable, manifold, miscellaneous, mixed, motley, multifarious, multiform, several, sundry, unidentical, unlike, unmatched, variant, varied, variegated, various, varying
ASSOCIATED CONCEPTS: diverse citizenship, diverse interests, diversity jurisdiction

DIVERSIFICATION, noun alteration, assortment, change, contrast, deviation, difference, differentiation, heterogeneity, multifariousness, multiformity, separation, shift, variation
ASSOCIATED CONCEPTS: diversification of investments

DIVERSITY, noun assortment, discongruity, *discrepantia*, dissimilarity, dissimilitude, diverseness, *diversitas*, heterogeneity, inconformity, irregularity, manifoldness, medley, miscellany, mixture, multifariousness, multiformity, multiplicity, nonuniformity, unconformity, unevenness, unlikeness, variability, variation, variegation, variety, variousness
ASSOCIATED CONCEPTS: diversity jurisdiction, diversity of citizenship

DIVERT, verb avertere, cause to bend, cause to curve, cause to deviate, cause to turn from, change the course of, deducere, deflect, *derivare,* deter, deviate, distract, draw aside, draw away, misappropriate, misdirect, mislead, parry, pull aside, push aside, put off the track, redirect, shift, shunt, sidetrack, swerve, turn aside, veer

ASSOCIATED CONCEPTS: diversion of assets, diversion of corporate funds, diversion of proceeds, diversion of public funds to a private purpose, diversion of trust funds, illegal diversion, unlawful diversion

DIVEST, verb attach, confiscate, depose, deprive, despoil, discharge, disendow, disentitle, dislodge, displace, dispossess, disrobe, disseize, distrain, drive out, evict, expel, expropriate, forfeit, lay bare, lay open, oust, reduce, relieve, remove, seize, strip, take away, uncover, unseat

ASSOCIATED CONCEPTS: divesting of title, divestiture of rights

DIVIDE *(Distribute),* **verb** admeasure, administer, allocate, allot, apportion, appropriate, assign, carve, consign, dispense, disperse, dispose, *distribuere, dividere,* dole, dole out, endow, give out, issue, mete, mete out, parcel out, pass out, pay out, portion out, prorate, ration, serve, share

DIVIDE *(Separate),* **verb** bisect, cleave, cut, demarcate, detach, disconnect, disengage, *disiungere,* disjoin, dismember, dispart, dissever, dissociate, disunite, *dividere,* divorce, fractionize, fragment, halve, part, partition, section, sectionalize, segment, segregate, *separare,* separate, sever, split, sunder, tear, unbind, uncouple

ASSOCIATED CONCEPTS: divide and distribute, divided according to law, divided court, divided equally, divided share and share alike

DIVIDEND, noun advantage, allotment, benefit, distribution of earnings, distribution of profits, gain, increment, interest, net profit, profit, return, share

ASSOCIATED CONCEPTS: cumulative dividends, dividend accumulations, dividend additions, dividend earned or declared, dividend in liquidation, dividend in scrip, dividend payable in stock, dividend-paying corporation, dividends paid, guaranteed dividends, life insurance dividend, liquidation dividend, participating dividend, preferential dividend, preferred dividend, regular dividend, stock dividend, taxable dividend, unauthorized dividends, unpaid dividends

DIVISIBLE, adjective apportionable, bisectable, breakable, capable of being divided, cleavable, detachable, disconnectable, dissectible, disseverable, dividable, dividual, fissile, fissionable, partible, scissile, separable, severable, subdivisible, susceptible of apportionment, susceptible of division, tearable

ASSOCIATED CONCEPTS: divisible contract, divisible covenant, divisible divorce, divisible guaranty, divisible offense

DIVISION *(Act of dividing),* **noun** allocation, allotment, apportionment, breaking, breakup, cleavage, cut, cutting, departmentalization, detachment, disaccord, disagreement, disassociation, disbandment, disconnection, discord, disengagement, disharmony, disjunction, disjuncture, dismemberment, dispersal, dispersion, dissemination, dissension, disseverance, dissipation, dissociation, dissonance, distribution, disunion, disuniting, disunity, *divisio,* divorce, faction, noncooperation, opposition, parcelling, parting, *partitio,* partition, portioning, rationing, schism, scission, section, segmentation, segregation, sejunction, separation, severance, sharing, split, splitting, spread, sunderance, tearing, uncoupling, untying

ASSOCIATED CONCEPTS: division of costs, division of damages, division of governmental powers, division of property, equitable division, final division and distribution, political subdivision

DIVISION *(Administrative unit),* **noun** area, branch, cadre, canton, category, chapter, class, classification, department, district, group, grouping, province, region, ward, zone

DIVISIVE, adjective bisected, causing disagreement, causing disassociation, causing disjunction, causing separation, cleavable, creating dissension, creating disunity, creating hostility, discordant, discrepant, disengaging, disjoined, disjunctive, dissentient, dissident, dissonant, diverging, dividing, divisible, factious, fragmentable, inharmonious, partible, schismatic, separable, severable, split, subdivisive

DIVORCE, noun annulment of marriage, broken marriage, conclusion, decree of nullity, *discidium,* dissolution of marriage, dissolution of the marriage bond, disunion, *divortium,* finality, judgment dissolving a marriage, judicial separation of a husband and wife, legal dissolution of marriage, legal nullification of marriage, legal termination of marriage, repudiation of a marriage, *repudium*

ASSOCIATED CONCEPTS: absolute divorce, alimony, annulment of marriage, comparative rectitude, custody of children, decree for divorce, divisible divorce, divorce action, divorce proceeding, divorce suit, foreign divorce, grounds for divorce, judgment of divorce, legal separation, limited divorce

DIVORCE, verb annul, annul a marriage, detach, disjoin, dissociate, dissolve of the bonds of matrimony, dissolve the marriage of, disunite, legally discard a spouse, nullify a marriage, part, put asunder, put out of matrimony, put out of wedlock, release from matrimonial status, release from matrimony, release from wedlock, sever, split up, sunder, uncouple, unmarry, unyoke

ASSOCIATED CONCEPTS: separation

DIVULGATION, noun disclosure, dissemination, divulgement, divulgence, evulgation, making public, proclamation, promulgation, spreading abroad

DIVULGE, verb acquaint, advertise, air, apprise, bare, blurt out, break news, breathe, bring to light, broadcast, communicate, confide, disclose, divulgate, enlighten, evince, expose, impart, inform, lay bare, lay open, leak, let drop, let slip, make known, make public, manifest, noise abroad, proclaim, promulgate, publicize, publish, relate, report, reveal, spread abroad, squeal, tattle, tell, unbosom, uncover, unmask, unveil, voice

ASSOCIATED CONCEPTS: divulge or publish

DNA, noun authentication, certification, confirmation of identity, proof of identity, scientific evidence, scientific means of designation, scientific means of identity, scientific means to distinguish a person, scientific method to reveal identity, substantiation, validation of identity, verification of identity, deoxyribonucleic acid

ASSOCIATED CONCEPTS: appeal of a case, DNA fingerprint, DNA polymerase, forensics, overturning a case, reversal of a case

DOCKET, noun agenda, calendar, catalog, entry book, enumeration, list, list of cases, listing, order of the day,

197

program, record, record of proceedings, register, registry, roll, schedule, slate

ASSOCIATED CONCEPTS: bench docket, court docket, docket book, docket entry, docketing a judgment, docketing cases

DOCTOR-ASSISTED SUICIDE, *noun* active euthanasia, euthanasia, medically assisted suicide, mercy killing, physician-assisted suicide

ASSOCIATED CONCEPTS: passive euthanasia

DOCTRINE, *noun* belief, canon, credendum, credo, creed, dogma, formulated belief, gospel, maxim, orthodoxy, philosophy, precept, principle, professed belief, rule, system, system of belief, teaching, teachings, tenet, universal principle

ASSOCIATED CONCEPTS: added risk doctrine, avoidable consequences doctrine, beneficial consideration doctrine, collateral source doctrine, cy pres doctrine, de facto doctrine, doctrine of abstention, doctrine of assumed risk, doctrine of avoidable consequences, doctrine of last clear chance, doctrine of recrimination, doctrine of relation back, doctrine of res judicata, doctrine of subrogation, doctrine of the law of the case, doctrine of unclean hands, doctrine of unjust enrichment, emergency doctrine, exclusive control doctrine, exhaustion of remedies doctrine, humanitarian doctrine, imminent peril doctrine, last clear chance, main purpose doctrine, res ipsa loquitur doctrine, rescue doctrine

DOCUMENT, *noun* book, certificate, confirmation, diploma, evidence, evidentiary record, instrument, *instrumentum, litterae,* official publication, paper, proof, record, recorded material, register, report, *tabula,* verification, writ, written material

ASSOCIATED CONCEPTS: allograph, ancient documents, cancellation of document, document of a public nature, document of title, integrated document, legal documents, public document

DOCUMENT, *verb* assemble the facts, authenticate, back, bear out, buttress, circumstantiate, collect evidence, confirm, corroborate, demonstrate, establish, evidence, exhibit, fortify, give references, justify, make certain, make evident, manifest, prove, provide with documents, provide with proof, show, strengthen, substantiate, support, sustain, uphold, validate, verify

DOCUMENTARY, *adjective* accredited, accurate, actual, attested, authentic, authoritative, certified, chronicled, correct, described, documental, documented, evidential, factual, founded on fact, genuine, in writing, not fictitious, on record, real, recorded, reported, true, valid, veracious, veritable, written

ASSOCIATED CONCEPTS: defense based upon documentary evidence, documentary evidence, documentary stamp

DOCUMENTATION, *noun* annals, authentication, authority, basis, certification, circumstantiation, confirmation, corroboration, data, evidence, evidential record, evidentiary record, exhibit, factual basis, grounds, grounds for belief, medium of proof, proof, record, recorded material, reference, source, substantiation, support, supporting evidence, validation, verification

DOCUMENTS, *noun* case history, chronicle, credentials, data, documentation, evidence, exhibits, file, instruments, legal instruments, manuscript, moving papers, official writing, papers

ASSOCIATED CONCEPTS: ancient documents, attorney-client privilege, attorney's work product, documentary evidence, production of documents, public documents, subpoena, traditional documents

DOGMA, *noun* article of faith, axiom, belief, canon, conviction, credendum, credo, creed, declaration of faith, dictum, doctrinaire opinion, doctrine, *dogma,* doxy, maxim, orthodoxy, persuasion, *placitum,* precept, principle, professed belief, rule, tenet

DOGMATIC, *adjective* absolute, arrogant, assertive, assertory, assured, authoritarian, authoritative, canonical, categorical, certain, confident, creedal, decided, definite, definitive, dictatorial, doctrinaire, doctrinal, domineering, emphatic, fanatical, forceful, imperious, insistent, intolerant, magisterial, narrow-minded, opinionated, opinionative, orthodox, overbearing, pedantic, peremptory, positive, positivistic, sure, tenacious, unequivocal, unshakable, unyielding

DOLE, *verb* admeasure, allocate, allot, allow, apportion, appropriate, assign, award, bestow, contribute, deal, deliver, dispense, distribute, divide, furnish, give, give away, give out, grant, hand out, hand over, issue, measure out, mete, mete out, parcel out, pay out, portion, present, ration, share, spare, supply

DOMAIN *(Land owned),* ***noun*** alodium, demesne, estate, freehold, hereditament, holding, land, manor, possessio, property, real estate, real property, realty, seigniory, tenure

ASSOCIATED CONCEPTS: eminent domain

DOMAIN *(Sphere of influence),* ***noun*** bailiwick, department, dominion, jurisdiction, kingdom, province, realm, region, seigniory, territory

ASSOCIATED CONCEPTS: private domain, public domain

DOMESTIC *(Household),* ***adjective*** belonging to the house, domiciliary, family, home, homemaking, household, housekeeping, internal, pertaining to one's household, pertaining to the family, pertaining to the home, relating to the family, relating to the home

ASSOCIATED CONCEPTS: domestic animals, domestic duties, domestic employment, domestic fixtures, domestic purposes, domestic relations, domestic servants, domestic service, domestic status, domestic use

DOMESTIC *(Indigenous),* ***adjective*** endemic, home, homemade, local, national, native, native grown, not foreign, not imported

ASSOCIATED CONCEPTS: domestic commerce, domestic corporation, domestic judgment

DOMICILE, *noun* abiding place, abode, accommodations, address, billet, *domicilium, domus,* dwelling, habitance, habitancy, habitat, habitation, home, house, inhabitance, inhabitancy, living quarters, lodging, lodgment, place of occupancy, place of residence, quarters, residence, residency, tabernacle

ASSOCIATED CONCEPTS: abandonment of domicile, acquisition of domicile, bona fide domicile, change of domicile, de facto domicile, family domicile, legal domicile, matrimonial domicile, plural domiciles

FOREIGN PHRASES: *Uxor sequitur domicilium viri.* The wife follows the domicile of her husband. ***Domus sua cuique est tutissimum refugium.*** Everyone's home is his safest refuge.

DOMICILIARY, _noun_ citizen, denizen, dweller, habitant, indweller, inhabitant, inhabiter, native, occupant, occupier, resident, settler

DOMINANCE, _noun_ ascendance, ascendancy, authority, control, dominancy, domination, dominion, eminence, force, governance, hold, importance, influence, mastery, mightiness, power, predominance, predominancy, prepollence, prepollency, preponderance, prepotency, primacy, sovereignty, supremacy, sway, weight

DOMINANT, _adjective_ ascendant, authoritative, cardinal, chief, commanding, controlling, eminent, first, foremost, governing, hegemonical, influential, leading, main, master, overshadowing, paramount, predominant, predominating, preeminent, preponderant, prepotent, prevailing, prevalent, primary, prime, principal, regnant, ruling, sovereign, superior, supreme, unsurpassed, weighty
ASSOCIATED CONCEPTS: dominant aspect rule, dominant estate, dominant land, dominant party, dominant right, dominant tenant, serviant land

DOMINATE, _verb_ administer, carry authority, command, compel, control, dictate, domineer, govern, have power, hold down, influence, keep subjugated, lead, manage, master, oppress, overrule, predominate, preponderate, preside over, prevail, reign over, repress, rule, rule over, subdue, subject, subjugate, sway, tame, tyrannize

DOMINATION, _noun_ administration, ascendancy, authority, command, control, dictation, dictatorship, dominance, dominion, force, hegemony, hold, influence, jurisdiction, mastery, monopoly, oppression, potency, power, predominance, preponderance, prevalence, primacy, reign, rule, sovereignty, superiority, supremacy, suzerainty, transcendence

DOMINION (Absolute ownership), **_noun_** claim, control, deed, demesne, domain, freehold, holding, interest, lawful possession, manor, ownership, possession, possessorship, power of disposal, property, proprietorship, right, right of possession, right to property, rightful possession, seignorage, seisin, stake, territory, title
ASSOCIATED CONCEPTS: act of dominion

DOMINION (Supreme authority), **_noun_** ascendancy, authority, command, control, _dicio,_ dominance, dominancy, domination, eminent domain, empery, government, grip, hegemony, hold, _imperium,_ jurisdiction, lordship, management, mastery, _potestas,_ power, primacy, regency, reign, rule, sovereignty, supremacy, sway

DONATION, _noun_ alms, benefaction, bequest, bestowment, bounty, charity, contribution, dispensation, _donum,_ dotation, endowment, gift, grant, gratuity, handout, impartation, impartment, largess, munificence, offering, philanthropy, present, presentation, provision, subsidy, subvention
ASSOCIATED CONCEPTS: charitable donation, donation deed, donation _causa mortis,_ donation of land, gratuitous donation, special donation

DONATIVE, _adjective_ aiding, awarding, beneficent, benevolent, bestowing, bountiful, charitable, conferring, contributing, contributory, conveying, dispensing, eleemosynary, endowing, freehanded, furnishing, generous, given away, giving, granting, gratuitous, imparting, openhanded, philanthropic, presenting, providing, supplying
ASSOCIATED CONCEPTS: donative intent, donative trust

DONEE, _noun_ acceptor, beneficiary, devisee, grantee, legatee, recipient

DONOR, _noun_ aider, almsgiver, altruist, assignor, backer, benefactor, benefactress, bequeather, bestower, cheerful giver, conferrer, consignor, contributor, deliverer, devisor, distributor of largess, donator, free giver, generous giver, giver, Good Samaritan, grantor, helper, humanitarian, patron, patroness, philanthropist, presenter, rewarder, subscriber, vouchsafer
FOREIGN PHRASES: **_Voluntas donatoris in charta doni sui manifeste expressa observetur._** The will of the donor which is clearly expressed in his deed of gift should be observed.

DORMANT, _adjective_ abeyant, asleep, at rest, becalmed, deactivated, hibernating, _iacere,_ in abeyance, in suspense, inactive, inert, inoperative, latent, passive, quiescent, quiet, resting, sleeping, slumbering, smoldering, static, still, suspended, torpid, unaroused, unawakened, undeveloped, unwakened
ASSOCIATED CONCEPTS: dormant case, dormant corporation, dormant judgment, dormant partner, dormant powers, dormant season

DOSSIER, _noun_ archive, brief, case history, data, document, documentation, facts, file, journal, papers, portfolio, record, recorded information, recorded material, resumé

DOUBLE JEOPARDY, _noun_ double prosecution, double punishment, re-charged, re-litigated, re-prosecuted, re-tried, tried for the same crime

DOUBT (Indecision), **_noun_** ambiguity, anxiety, apprehension, apprehensiveness, confusion, _dubitatio, dubito,_ faltering, feeling of uncertainty, hesitancy, improbability, inability to decide, incertitude, indefiniteness, indeterminateness, indetermination, infirmity of purpose, insecurity, instability, irresolution, lack of certitude, lack of confidence, lack of conviction, lack of faith, matter of dubitation, misgiving, perplexity, precariousness, qualification, qualm, qualmishness, quandary, question, reluctance, reservation, reserve, self-doubt, state of suspense, suspended judgment, suspense, uncertain state, uncertainness, uncertainty, undecidedness, undeterminedness, unsettled opinion, unsettlement, unsteadiness, unsureness, vacillation, vagueness, want of confidence, want of faith, wavering
ASSOCIATED CONCEPTS: beyond a reasonable doubt standard, rational doubt, reasonable doubt
FOREIGN PHRASES: **_Nobiliores et benigniores praesumptiones in dubiis sunt praeferendae._** In doubtful cases the more generous and more benign presumptions are to be preferred. **_Ambiguitas verborum latens verificatione suppletur; nam quod ex facto oritur ambiguum verificatione facti tollitur._** A latent verbal ambiguity may be removed by evidence; for whatever ambiguity arises from an extrinsic fact may be explained by extrinsic evidence. **_Quae dubitationis tollendae causa contractibus inseruntur, jus commune non laedunt._** Those clauses which are inserted in agreements to avoid doubts and ambiguity do not offend the common law.

DOUBT (Suspicion), **_noun_** apprehension, chariness, consternation, critical attitude, disbelief, discredit, dismay, distrust, distrustfulness, doubtfulness, dubiety, dubiousness, dubitation, faithlessness, hesitation, improbability, incredibility, incredulity, incredulousness, lack of confidence, lack of faith, lack of trust, matter of dubitation, misdoubt, misgiving, mistrust, mistrustfulness, qualm, qualmishness, question in one's mind, refusal to believe, reluctance to believe, skepticalness, skepticism, *suspicio,* suspiciousness, unbelief, uncredulousness, want of confidence, want of faith, want of trust, wariness

DOUBT *(Distrust),* **verb**   awake a suspicion, be apprehensive, be doubtful, be dubious, be incredulous, be nervous, be skeptical, be suspicious, be uncertain, challenge, disbelieve, discredit, dispute, entertain doubts, entertain suspicions, feel distrust, find hard to believe, give no credence to, greet with skepticism, half believe, harbor doubts, harbor suspicions, have doubts, have fears, have misgivings, have questions, have suspicions, impugn, lack confidence in, misbelieve, misdoubt, misgive, mistrust, not admit, not believe, object, query, question, raise a question, raise a suspicion, refuse to believe, refuse to trust, regard with suspicion, suspect, withhold reliance
ASSOCIATED CONCEPTS: doubt the credibility of a witness

DOUBT *(Hesitate),* **verb**   be in a quandary, be irresolute, be puzzled, be uncertain, be undecided, be undetermined, debate, delay, deliberate, demur, dubitate, equivocate, falter, feel unsure, fluctuate, have qualms, have reservations, hold off, pause, ponder, push aside, put off a decision, puzzle over, scruple, stop to consider, table, think it over, vacillate, waver, withhold judgment
ASSOCIATED CONCEPTS: beyond a reasonable doubt, beyond a shadow of a doubt, free from all doubt

DOUBTFUL, *adjective*   arguable, at issue, conditional, conjectural, contestable, controvertible, debatable, disbelieving, disposed to question, disputable, distrustful, doubtable, doubting, dubious, dubitable, *dubius,* equivocal, implausible, improbable, in a dilemma, in a quandary, in dispute, in doubt, in question, in suspense, inconceivable, inconvincible, incredible, indecisive, indistinct in character or meaning, irresolute, misbelieving, mistrustful, mistrusting, of uncertain issue, open to doubt, open to question, open to suspicion, problematic, questionable, questioning, speculative, suppositional, unbelievable, unconvincing, unlikely, unresolved, unsettled in opinion, unsolved, unsure, unsustainable, untenable
ASSOCIATED CONCEPTS: doubtful cases, doubtful credit, doubtful debts, doubtful title

DOUBTING, *adjective*   cynical, disbelieving, disputable, distrustful, doubtful, dubious, hesitant, inconvincible, incredulous, indecisive, irresolute, jealous, leery, misbelieving, mistrustful, mistrusting, questioning, skeptical, suspicious, uncertain, unconvinced, undetermined, unresolved, unsure, vacillating, wary

DOWER, *noun*   allotment, allowance, appanage, award, bequest, bestowal, bestowment, dos, dotation, effects, endowment, estate, inheritance, jointure, legacy, remainder, settlement, widow's estate, widow's portion
ASSOCIATED CONCEPTS: consummated right of dower, curtesy, dower interest, dower right, election of dower, estate in dower, inchoate right of dower, right of dower, widow's dower
FOREIGN PHRASES: *Favorabilia in lege sunt fiscus, dos, vita, libertas.* Favorites of the law are the treasury, dower, life, and liberty.

DOWN *(Dejected),* **adjective**   depressed, despondent, disconsolate, discouraged, downcast, gloomy, glum, somber sorrowful, sullen, unhappy, upset, weary,

ASSOCIATED CONCEPTS: capacity, mental illness, incompetency

DOWN *(Lowest Point),* **adjective**   below, beneath, depressed, far below, lower, lowest, rock-bottom, under, underground, underneath
ASSOCIATED CONCEPTS: interest rates down, trip and fall, slip and fall

DOWN PAYMENT, *noun*   collateral, deposit, installment, payment, retainer, stake, surety

DOWNFALL, *noun*   abasement, adversity, breakdown, calamity, casualty, cataclysm, catastrophe, collapse, debacle, decline, defeat, demotion, destruction, disaster, disgrace, failure, fall, fatality, humiliation, miscarriage, misfortune, perdition, prostration, reverse, ruin, ruination, setback, slump, undoing

DOWNGRADE, *verb*   debase, decline, deduct, deflate, defrock, degrade, demote, depreciate, deprive, deteriorate, discredit, disgrace, disparage, humiliate, mock, pillory, reduce, supersede, suspend, unfrock

DOXOLOGY, *noun*   adulation, compliment, glorification, hero worship, idolatry, laudation, overpraise, paean, praise

DRACONIAN, *adjective*   austere, exacting, extreme, fanatical, formalistic, harsh, inflexible, insensitive, intolerant, precise, punctilious, puritanical, relentless, rigid, rigorous, ruthless, severe, Spartan, stiff, strict, stringent, unbending, uncompassionate, uncompromising
ASSOCIATED CONCEPTS: Draconian laws

DRAFT, *noun*   acceptance bill, bank check, bank note, bank paper, bill, bill of exchange, cashier's check, check, commercial paper, debenture, letter of credit, *lettre de change,* money order, negotiable instrument, negotiable paper, note, order, order for payment, promissory note, voucher, warrant
ASSOCIATED CONCEPTS: bill of exchange, check, overdraft, sight draft

DRAFT A BRIEF, *noun*   draft a synopsis of the salient legal points, draft support for the position espoused, pen an explanation of the law, prepare a legal document, prepare a summary on the law, prepare justification, write a legal memorandum, write a memorandum of law

DRAFT A DOCUMENT, *noun*   complete a contract, complete an agreement, finish an instrument, prepare a negotiable instrument, prepare materials, write an instrument

DRAFT A WILL, *noun*   pen a testamentary instrument, prepare a last will and testament, prepare a testamentary document, prepare a will for a testator, write a testamentary disposition

DRAMATIC RIGHTS, *noun*   dramatizing rights, live stage rights, performance rights, stage presentation rights, stage rights, theatrical rights

DRAMATICALLY OPPOSED, *verb*   about face, adoption, afterthoughts, change like a chameleon, change of heart, change of mind, conversion, defection, divergence, diversion, flip-flop, 180-degree about face, qualification, realignment, regression, restructuring, reversal, reversion, temporizer, tergiversation, turn of the tide, turnabout

ASSOCIATED CONCEPTS: flip-flop on a political stance

DRASTIC, *adjective* acting with force, desperate, dire, exceeding, excessive, extreme, fanatic, fanatical, forceful, harsh, immoderate, improper, inordinate, intemperate, intense, outrageous, powerful, radical, severe, strict, strong, undue, unmitigated, unreasonable, vigorously effective, violent
ASSOCIATED CONCEPTS: drastic remedy, extraordinary remedy

DRAW *(Attendance),* ***noun*** frequence, level of attendance

DRAW *(Attraction),* ***noun*** attractiveness, enticement, force, gravity, influence, magnetism, pull

DRAW *(Tie),* ***noun*** dead heat, deadlock, impasse, stalemate, standoff

DRAW *(Depict),* ***verb*** delineate, describe, picture, portray, represent, sketch

DRAW *(Extract),* ***verb*** concentrate, condense, derive, pull, receive

DRAW THE LINE, *noun* ascertained boundary, bound, boundary, delineate the boundary, determination, fix the boundary, fix the guideline, guideline, limit, limitation, outer limit, outer perimeter, perimeter, prescribed limit, prescribed limitation, restriction, set the parameter

DRAWBACK, *noun* damage, decremental, defect, disadvantage, discount, fault, flaw, harm, hurt, impediment, inconvenience, injury, liability, objection, obstacle, prejudice, protest, protestation, qualification, set-off

DROIT, *noun* appurtenance, authority, authorization, birthright, certification, claim, due, dueness, easement, eligibility, empowerment, entitlement, faculty, franchise, just claim, legal power, legal right, legal title, license, licitness, power, prerogative, prescriptive right, pretension, privilege, right, sanction, vested right, warrant
ASSOCIATED CONCEPTS: right

DROP A CASE, *verb* bring to a close a case, bring to an end a case, cancel an action, cause a discontinuance, cease litigation by a plaintiff, conclude litigation by a plaintiff, discontinue an action, end prosecutor by a prosecutor, stop litigating by a plaintiff, stop prosecuting by a prosecutor, terminate a case by a plaintiff, terminate a case by a prosecutor

DRUG, *noun* alterant, analgesic, anesthetic, anesthetic agent, anodyne, antibiotic, chemical substance, curative preparation, medical preparation, medicament, *medicamentum,* medication, medicinal component, medicinal ingredient, narcotic preparation, narcotic substance, nepenthe, opiate, painkiller, palliative, physic, prescription, remedy, sedative, soporific, stimulant, stupefacient
ASSOCIATED CONCEPTS: adulterated drugs, dangerous drugs, drug addiction, habit-forming drug, influence of drugs, labeling of drugs, poisonous drugs or chemicals, possession of drugs, preparation of drugs, prescription drugs, regulation of drugs, sale of drugs

DRUG, *verb* administer, anesthetize, anoint, apply a remedy, benumb, cure, deaden, desensitize, dose, dull, heal, inject, *medicare,* medicate, narcotize, numb, palliate, physic, poultice, prescribe, put to sleep, stun, stupefy, treat
ASSOCIATED CONCEPTS: drug addicts

DRUNK, *adjective* *ebrius,* inebriated, intemperate, intoxicated, overcome, overcome by liquor, riotous, saturated, sottish, *temulentus,* uncontrolled, under the influence of liquor, unsober
ASSOCIATED CONCEPTS: alcoholism, delirium tremens, driving while intoxicated, drunkometer test, intoxication, voluntary intoxication

DUBIOUS, *adjective* ambiguous, *anceps,* arguable, chancy, conditional, confusing, confutable, contestable, contingent, controversial, controvertible, debatable, dependent, disputable, doubtful, dubitative, *dubius,* equivocal, fallible, hazy, in dispute, in doubt, in question, *incertus,* insecure, moot, perplexing, provisional, questionable, refutable, shadowy, skeptical, speculative, suppositional, unascertained, unassured, unauthentic, unauthenticated, unauthoritative, uncertain, uncertified, unconfident, unconfirmed, undemonstrated, undetermined, unexplained, unlikely, unreliable, unresolved, unsound, unsure, unverifiable, vacillating, vague, wavering

DUBITATIVE, *adjective* contestable, controversial, controvertible, deniable, disputable, doubtable, doubtful, dubious, dubitable, in doubt, open to question, questionable, refutable, suspect, unsustainable

DUE *(Owed),* ***adjective*** chargeable, claimable, collectable, condign, *debitus,* delinquent, deserved, earned, in arrears, merited, outstanding, owing, to be paid, uncompensated, unpaid, unrewarded, unsettled
ASSOCIATED CONCEPTS: amount due, balance due, debt due, due bills, due date, due on demand, indebtedness due, justly due and owing, legally due, money due, payment due, rent due, taxes due
FOREIGN PHRASES: ***Nihil peti potest ante id tempus, quo per rerum naturam persolvi possit.*** Nothing can be demanded before the time when, in the nature of things, it can be paid.

DUE *(Regular),* ***adjective*** according to law, allowable, appropriate, authorized, befitting, correct, expedient, fit, lawful, legal, legislated, legitimate, licit, nomothetic, permitted, proper, rightful, sanctioned, statutory
ASSOCIATED CONCEPTS: due acknowledgment, due administration of justice, due and proper care, due and reasonable care, due care, due compensation, due consideration, due course, due course of business, due course of law, due diligence, due execution, due exercise of discretion, due process of law, due proof, due proof of death, due proof of loss, due regard, holder in due course

DUE, *noun* accounts collectable, accounts outstanding, arrears, balance to pay, charge, claim, compensation owed, *deberi,* debit, debt, deficit, droit, entitlement, favor owed, fee, indebtedness, lawful claim, liability, obligation accrued, outstanding debt, overdue payment, pledge, right, something owed, that which is owing, vested right
ASSOCIATED CONCEPTS: due and payable, due in full, due on demand, having become due, payable upon sight

DUE PROCESS, *noun* due process of law, legal fairness, legal safeguards, protection against deprivations, protection guarantees, protection of deprivation of accepted legal principles
Generally: fundamental fairness
Specifically: Fifth Amendment, Fourteenth Amendment

ASSOCIATED CONCEPTS: procedural due process, right to confront accuser, substantive due process

DULY, *adverb*   accurately, as required, correctly, deservedly, fairly, legitimately, rightfully
ASSOCIATED CONCEPTS: duly adjudged, duly allowed, duly appointed, duly assigned, duly awarded, duly certified, duly commenced, duly commissioned, duly completed, duly convened, duly directed, duly enacted, duly entered into, duly established, duly executed, duly filled, duly found, duly given, duly issued, duly made, duly organized, duly presented, duly prosecuted, duly qualified, duly recorded, duly rendered, duly served, duly shown, duly summoned, duly sworn, duly verified

DUN, *noun*   bill of accounts, bill of costs, claim, demand, entreaty, exaction, final demand, final notice, forcible demand, *fuscus,* impetration, importunity, insistence, insistent demand, levy, notice, obsecration, obtestation, peremptory demand, reckoning, request, requisition, solicitation, statement, strong request, *suffuscus,* threat, ultimatum, warning notice

DUN, *verb*   beseige, beset, clamor for payment, demand, demand payment, demand with threats, exact, *exposcere, flagitare,* give final notice, importune, insist, make claims upon, make demands on, plague, press a claim, request, require

DUPE, *verb*   befool, beguile, bilk, cheat, circumvent, counterfeit, cozen, create a false impression, cully, deceive, defraud, delude, ensnare, entrap, fleece, fool, gull, hoax, inveigle, *lactare,* make a fool of, misdirect, misguide, mislead, mulct, outmaneuver, outsmart, outwit, play a trick, play upon, practice chicanery, put something over, set a trap for, sport with, swindle, take advantage of, take by fraud, take in, trap, trick, victimize

DUPLICATE, *noun*   carbon, carbon copy, copy, ditto, double, ectype, *exemplar, exemplum,* facsimile, gemination, imitation, likeness, match, photostat, reenactment, repetition, replica, representation, reproduction, twin
ASSOCIATED CONCEPTS: duplicate copy, duplicate original

DUPLICITY, *noun*   artifice, casuistry, chicanery, deceitfulness, deception, dissimulation, double-dealing, duality, duplexity, equivocation, evasion, false conduct, falseheartedness, falseness, fraud, guile, hypocrisy, insincerity, perfidy, sham, trickery, two-facedness

DURABLE, *adjective*   abiding, aeonian, ageless, amaranthine, ceaseless, changeless, chronic, constant, continual, continuing, endless, enduring, established, eternal, everlasting, firm, *firmus,* fixed, hard, hardy, holding up well, immortal, immovable, immutable, imperishable, impervious to change, incessant, indeciduous, indelible, ineradicable, inerasable, inexhaustible, inexpungeable, interminable, intransmutable, invariable, inveterate, inviolate, irremovable, lasting, lifelong, living, long-continuing, long-enduring, long-lasting, long-lived, long-standing, longevous, maintained, never-ending, not easily worn out, of long duration, of long standing, perdurable, permanent, perpetual, persevering, persistent, persisting, remaining, resistant, robust, rocklike, sempiternal, settled, *solidus,* sound, *stabilis,* stable, staying, steadfast, strong, sturdy, substantial, surviving, sustained, tenacious, timeless, tough, unaltered, unceasing, unchangeable, undying, unending, unfading, unfailing, unintermitting, uninterrupted, unyielding, without end

DURANCE, *noun*   arrest, bondage, bonds, captivity, commitment, confinement, custody, detention, forced confinement, forcible detention, immurement, incarceration, internment, legal restraint, *lettre de cachet,* quarantine, restraint, restriction on movement, thrall, thralldom

DURATION, *noun*   age, continuance, continuance in time, continuation in time, course, epoch, era, extension in time, extent, interregnum, interval, lasting period, length of time, limit, period, period of time, phase, season, space of time, span, spell, stage, stretch, *temporis spatium,* tenancy, tenure, term, time, while
ASSOCIATED CONCEPTS: duration of any office, duration of contract, duration of emergency, duration of liability, duration of possession, duration of use, duration of war

DURESS, *noun*   bondage, captivity, coaction, coercion, compulsion, confinement, constraint, control, dominance, enforcement, exaction, force, high pressure, impressment, necessitation, obligation, press, pressure, repression, requirement, restriction, stress, subjection, subjugation, threat
ASSOCIATED CONCEPTS: actionable duress, business compulsion, defense of duress, duress of goods, duress of property, legal duress, moral duress, payment under duress, undue influence
FOREIGN PHRASES: *Vani timores sunt aestimandi, qui non cadunt in constantem virum.* Those fears are to be regarded as groundless which do not affect an ordinary man. *Nihil consensui tam contrarium est quam vis atque metus.* Nothing is so contrary to consent as force and fear. Vani timoris justa excusatio non est. A frivolous fear is not a lawful excuse.

DURING, *preposition*   all along, all the while, as, at the same time as, at the time, for the time being, in the course of, in the interim, in the meanwhile, in the middle of, meanwhile, through, throughout, throughout the course, throughout the duration, when, while, while pending, while waiting
ASSOCIATED CONCEPTS: during good behavior, during normal work hours, during the heat of passion, during the trial

DUTY (Obligation), **noun**   accountability, allegiance, answerability, assignment, burden, charge, chore, commission, commitment, debt, dictate of conscience, engagement, *fides,* function, indebtedness, liability, moral necessity, moral obligation, *munus,* obedience, office, *officium,* pledge, promise, responsibility, role, task, work
ASSOCIATED CONCEPTS: absolute duty, breach of duty, conditional duty, continuing duty, delegation of duty, duty enjoined by law, duty of support, equitable duty, imperative duty, in performance of duty, in the line of duty, lawful duty, legal duty, ministerial duty, moral duty, neglect of duty, nondelegatable duty, nondiscretionary duty, official duty, on duty, private duty, public duty, relief from duty, scope of servant's duties, statutory duty, unfit for duty, violation of duty
FOREIGN PHRASES: *Qui jussu judicis aliquod fecerit non videtur dolo malo fecisse, quia parere necesse est.* He who does anything by command of a judge will not be deemed to have acted from an improper motive, because it was necessary to obey. *Judicis officium est opus diei in die suo perficere.* It is the duty of a judge to finish the day's work within that day. *Judicis est judicare secundum allegata et probata.* It is the duty of a judge to decide according to the allegations and proofs.

DUTY (Tax), **noun**   assessment, burden, capitation, charge, exaction, exactment, excise, imposition, impost,

levy, onus, rate, revenue, tallage, tariff, task, tax on demand, taxation, toll, tribute, *vectigal*
ASSOCIATED CONCEPTS: duty on exports, duty on imports

DWARF, verb control, dominate, minimize, overshadow, rise above, stunt, tower over
ASSOCIATED CONCEPTS: federal government's laws dwarfing state laws, supremacy clause

DWELL *(Linger over),* **verb** accent, accentuate, brood over, continue, emphasize, extend, harp upon, impress, *in re commorari,* insist, intensify, point up, prolong, prolongate, reiterate, *rem longius prosequi,* stress

DWELL *(Reside),* **verb** abide, be located, be present, be settled, be situated, be stationed, billet, bunk, denizen, domicile, domiciliate, *domicilium, habere, habitare,* have a habitation, have one's address at, indwell, inhabit, live, lodge, make one's home, occupy, populate, quarter, re-

main, reside, room, settle, sojourn, stay, stop, take up one's abode, take up residence, tarry, tenant
ASSOCIATED CONCEPTS: citizenship

DWELLING, noun abode, camp, domicile, *domicilium, domus,* dormitory, edifice, habitation, homestead, house, living quarters, lodging, lodging place, lodgment, place of residence, quarters, residence, *sedes,* shelter, tabernacle
ASSOCIATED CONCEPTS: dwelling house purposes, inhabited dwelling house, multiple dwelling, principal dwelling place, private dwelling

DYNAMITE CHARGE, noun Allen charge, command to arrive at findings, dynamite admonition, dynamite instruction, order to arrive at findings, shotgun charge, shotgun instruction, third-degree charge

DYSEPTIC, adjective bilious, bitter, choleric, embittered, jaundiced, sour, sour-tempered, spiteful

EACH, pronoun each one, each other, every last one, every one, individually, one, one after another, one and all, one another, one by one, the individual one, the particular one
ASSOCIATED CONCEPTS: each ground of a complaint, joint and several liability

EAGER, adjective agressive, alacritous, ambitious, anxious, appetent, ardent, aspiring, assiduous, athirst, avid, *avidus,* bent upon, covetous, craving, desirous, diligent, disposed, earnest, enthusiastic, excited, fanatic, fanatical, fervent, *fervidus,* forward, full of enterprise, full of enthusiasm, full of initiative, impassioned, impatient, inclined, industrious, intense, interested, keen, longing, passionate, perfervid, pushy, ravenous, ready, spirited, tantalized, tempted, unable to resist, vehement, voracious, willing, wishful, yearning, zealous, zestful

EARLY, adjective antecedent, earlier, first, former, introductory, past, precedent, preceding, precursory, preexistent, prefatory, preliminary, preparatory, previous, seminal
ASSOCIATED CONCEPTS: early payment of principle

EARMARK, noun brand, cachet, designation, distinguishing mark, emblem, identification, indication, label, mark, mark of identification, mark of identity, sign, symbol

EARN, verb achieve, achieve by continued effort, acquire by service, attain, be deserving, be entitled to, be successful, be worthy, clear, deserve, gain, gain by labor, gain by service, get a profit, get by effort, have a right to,

merere, merit, merit as compensation, net, obtain a victory, procure by effort, profit, prosper, realize, reap, receive compensation, secure, succeed in reaching, win
ASSOCIATED CONCEPTS: ability to earn, earned commissions, earned income, earned premiums, earned surplus, earned wages, a sum earned and unpaid

EARN OUT, verb bring to a zero balance, bring up to date, defray the expenses, lend, loan, paid back, pay back after an advance, repayment, used up
Generally: indemnify, recoupment, reimburse, remit, remunerate

EARNEST, adjective assiduous, bent upon, concentrating, conscientious, determined, devoted, diligent, eager, *enixus,* enthusiastic, fervent, firm, grave, *gravis,* impassioned, intent, *intentus,* purposeful, resolute, serious, set upon, sincere, sober, solemn, staid, strong-willed, thoughtful, zealous

EARNEST MONEY, noun collateral, collateral security, deposit, down payment, earnest, earnest payment, earnest pledge, guarantee, installment, pledge, security, stake

EARNINGS, noun balance, commission, compensation, earned income, emolument, fruit of labor, gains, income, *lucrum,* money earned, pay, payment, personal gain, proceeds, profit, profits, profits from employment, *quaestus,* rate, receipts, recompense, remuneration, returns, revenue, reward, reward of labor, reward of office, salary, takings, wages, winnings

ASSOCIATED CONCEPTS: accrued earnings, annual earnings, corporate earnings, earning capacity, future earnings, gross earnings, individual earnings, loss of earnings, net earnings, profits, rents, surplus earnings, total earnings

EASE, verb abate, alleviate, ameliorate, bate, calm, comfort, console, cushion, disburden, disencumber, ease the burden, expedite, extenuate, facilitate, free from anxiety, give repose, give rest, help along, lessen, let up, lighten, loosen, make comfortable, make easy, mitigate, moderate, *otium,* pacify, *quies,* quiet, reduce tension, relax, release from pressure, relieve, render less difficult, slacken, soften, *tranquillitas,* unburden, unload, unstrain

EASEMENT, noun advantage in land, convenience, gateway, interest in land, liberty of use, privilege, right of passage, right of use, right of way, serviceway, way over land
ASSOCIATED CONCEPTS: affirmative easement, apparent easement, appurtenance, appurtenant easement, discontinuing easement, dominant and servient estates, easement by grant, easement by necessary implication, easement by prescription, easement in gross, easement of access, easement of convenience, easement of necessity, equitable easement, implied easement, implied reservation of easement, incorporeal hereditament, incumbrance, intermittent easement, irrevocable license, license in nature of easement, natural easement, necessary easement, negative easement, noncontinuous easement, prescription, private easement, profit a prendre, public easement, quasi easement, right of way, right of way in gross, secondary easement, servitude, visible easement
FOREIGN PHRASES: *Iter est jus eundi, ambulandi hominis; non etiam jumentum agendi vel vehiculum.* A way is the right of going or walking by man, and does not include the right of driving a beast of burden or a vehicle.

EASILY *(By far),* **adverb** beyond question, certainly, definitely, doubtlessly, easy, far and away, indisputably, indubitably, naturally, obviously, unquestionably, without a doubt, without any question
ASSOCIATED CONCEPTS: claims easily preventable, laws easily circumvented

EASILY *(Without trouble),* **adverb** accessible, adroitly, apparent, dexterously, effortless, effortlessly, elementary, facilely, handily, manageable, not burdensome, nothing to it, obvious, requiring no effort, simply, skillfully, smoothly, uncomplicated, undemanding, with ease, with no trouble at all, without even trying

EASY *(Effortless),* **adjective** effortless, facile, not burdensome, not complicated, not difficult, push over, quick and easy, simple, soft, straightforward, uncomplicated
ASSOCIATED CONCEPTS: easy access to the courts, simple contract

EASY *(Lenient),* **adjective** accommodating, benevolent, easy, forbearing, indulgent, lax, loose, permissive, pushover, relaxed, soft, unburdensome, undemanding, understanding, unexacting, unoppressive

EASY *(Obvious),* **adjective** apparent, axiomatic, clear, distinct, evident, indisputable, manifest, obvious, plain, readily comprehensible, readily learnable, simple, straightforward, totally comprehensible, totally learnable, uncomplicated, undemanding
ASSOCIATED CONCEPTS: easy construction of a legal document

EAVESDROP, verb hearken, intercept, listen, listen stealthily, overhear, tap the lines, wiretap

ASSOCIATED CONCEPTS: eavesdropping device, search warrant, suppression hearing, wiretapping

EBB, verb crumble, decay, decline, decrease, degenerate, deteriorate, drop, drop off, dwindle, fade away, fail, fall, fall away, fall off, move back, recede, *recedere,* retire, retreat, shrink, sink, slide, slip, slip back, subside, wane, waste away, withdraw

EBULLIENT, adjective bubbling, bubbly, effervescent, filled with personality, outward, sparkling

ECCENTRIC, adjective aberrant, anomalous, bizarre, contrary, curious, departing from the usual course, deviant, deviating, deviative, different, differing, divergent, erratic, extraordinary, idiosyncratic, independent, individual, *inusitatus,* irregular, *mirus,* nonconforming, nonconformist, *novus,* odd, out of the common run, out of the ordinary, outlandish, peculiar, quaint, queer, singular, strange, uncommon, unconforming, unconventional, unfashionable, unimitative, unique, unorthodox, unusual, wayward

ECHO, verb copying, duplication, imitation, reecho, reflect, repeat, repetition, resound, return, reverberate, reverberation
ASSOCIATED CONCEPTS: a circuit court decision echoing another circuit of the US Court of Appeals

ECLIPSE, verb adumbrate, becloud, block, by far exceed, by far outweigh, cloak, cloud, conceal, cover, dwarf, enshroud, exceed, far exceed, far outweigh, hide, obfuscate, overshadow, shade, shadow, surpass

ECOLOGY, noun antipollution project, bioecology, bionomics, conservation, environmental science, environmental studies, human environment, maintenance, management of natural resources, natural science, nature study, pollution control, preservation, protection, study of ecosystems, study of environs, study of surroundings, support, survival studies, sustainment, sustenance

ECONOMIC, adjective cost effective, cost reducing, economical, labor saving, money saving, time saving, thrifty
ASSOCIATED CONCEPTS: economic activity, economic conditions, economic depression, economic groups, economic factors, economic interest, economic policy, economic segregation, economic status, economic value

ECONOMICAL, adjective *attentus,* avoiding extravagance, careful, chary of expense, cheap, cost-reducing, *diligens,* economizing, efficient, financially prudent, forehanded, free from waste, frugal, *frugi,* inexpensive, labor-saving, money-conscious, money-saving, niggardly, parsimonious, provident, prudent, saving, sparing, thrifty, time-saving, unlavish, unwasteful

ECONOMY *(Economic system),* **noun** administration, administration of economics, administration of resources, economic science, management, management of resources, regulation of finances, system of distributing wealth, wealth

ECONOMY *(Frugality),* **noun** avoidance of waste, careful management, carefulness, carefulness in outlay, chariness, cheapness of operation, economicalness, forehandedness, freedom from extravagance, frugalness, good management, husbanding of resources, management, paring, *parsimonia,* prevention of waste, providence, prudence, restriction, saving, scheduling, sound stewardship, sparing, thrift, thriftiness

ECSTATIC, *adjective* approving, beatific, beside oneself, blissful, carried away, delighted, delirious with joy, dithyrambic, elated, elevated, emotional, enchanted, enraptured, enthusiastic, entranced, excited, exultant, felicitous, full of feeling, glad, happy, heartfelt, joyful, joyous, jubilant, overjoyed, overpowered with emotion, passionate, radiant, rapt, rapturous, rhapsodical, thrilled, tingling, transported

EDGE *(Advantage)*, *noun* advantageous position, benefit, favorable position, head start, jump, lead, odds, superiority, upper hand, vantage

EDGE *(Border)*, *noun* bank, boundary, bounds, brim, brink, confines, corner, demarcation line, dividing line, edging, extremity, *fimbriae*, frame, fringe, frontier, limit, lip, margin, *margo*, molding, *ora*, outer edge, outline, outskirts, periphery, point, rim, side, skirts, tip, verge

EDICT, *noun* authoritative command, canon, command, *consultum*, declaration, decree, *decretum*, dictate, *edictum*, enactment, fiat, judgment, law, legislation, mandate, order, ordinance, precept, pronouncement, regulation, regulation by law, regulation by statute, rule, ruling, statute

EDIFICATION, *noun* acquirement, advancement, advantage, attainment, avail, benefit, betterment, direction, education, educational clarification, educational knowledge, enlightenment, gain, guidance, improvement, information, instruction, knowledge, learning, mental cultivation, preparation, profit, progress, schooling, spiritual upbuilding, teaching, training, tuition, tutelage, uplifting

EDIFICE, *noun* architectural monument, building, building of imposing appearance, construction, high structure, imposing building, piece of architecture, public building, skyscraper, structure, tower

EDIFY, *verb* brief, coach, direct, discipline, *docere*, educate, enlarge the mind, enlighten, guide, improve, inform, instruct, prime, school, show, strengthen, teach, train, tutor, upbuild, uplift

EDIT, *verb* alter, amend, annotate, arrange, choose, comment on, correct, cross out, cut, dele, delete, emend, emendate, erase, expunge, improve, *librum edere*, make corrections, make improvements, make ready for publication, modify by excisions, polish, prepare for publication, put right, rearrange, rectify, redact, redraft, refine, remove errors, revamp, revise, rework, rewrite, select, strike out, trim, weed, write notes for

EDITORIAL, *adjective* analytical, critical, editing, elucidative, elucidatory, enlightening, explaining, explanatory, explicatively, explicatory, expositive, expository, illuminative, illustrative, journalistic, reportorial, technical
ASSOCIATED CONCEPTS: law review, plain language

EDITORIALIZE, *verb* articulate a personal position, elucidate on, examine an issue, issue a policy statement, issue a position statement, opine on, personal analysis, prepare critical analysis, present a perspective, write a column, write a commentary, write an analytical piece, write an article, write an opinion piece
ASSOCIATED CONCEPTS: broadcasting law, free speech, First Amendment

EDUCATE, *verb* brief, bring up, civilize, coach, cultivate, direct, discipline, drill, edify, *educare*, enlighten, *erudire*, explain, familiarize, give lessons, guide, implant, inculcate, indoctrinate, inform, initiate, *instituere*, instruct, interpret, nurture, preach, prepare, prime, rear, school, show, teach, train, tutor, wipe out illiteracy

EDUCATION, *noun* accomplishments, acquirements, acquisition of knowledge, body of knowledge, coaching, cultivation, culture, direction, edification, elucidation, enlightenment, erudition, explanation, general information, guidance, imparting of skill, improvement of the mind, inculcation, indoctrination, instruction, intellectuality, knowledge, learning, letters, literacy, pedagogy, preparation, propaedeutics, qualification, scholarship, schooling, science of teaching, store of knowledge, studies, system of knowledge, systematic training, teaching, training, tuition, tutelage, tutoring, upbringing
ASSOCIATED CONCEPTS: board of education, educational corporation, educational facilities, educational institution, educational purposes, educational trust, educational uses

EDUCE, *verb* bring forth, bring out, bring to light, call forth, deduce, derive, discover, draw, draw forth, draw out, elicit, evoke, evolve, extract, extricate, ferret out, infer, lay open, make obvious, obtain, procure, pull, pull out, secure, summon forth, unearth, unfold, unveil
ASSOCIATED CONCEPTS: educe evidence

EFFACE, *verb* abolish, annihilate, black out, blot out, cancel, decimate, delete, demolish, destroy, destruct, devour, discontinue, disintegrate, dissolve, do away with, eliminate, end, eradicate, erase, expel, expunge, exterminate, extinguish, liquidate, obliterate, quell, ravage, raze, remove, root out, ruin, scratch out, stop, terminate

EFFECT, *noun* accomplishment, achievement, aftermath, *consecutio*, consequence, development, effectuation, *effectus*, end product, end result, eventuation, *eventus*, final result, fruit, fruition, impact, issue, outcome, outgrowth, payoff, product, reaction, repercussion, response, result, resultant, resultant action, sequel, termination, upshot
ASSOCIATED CONCEPTS: cause and effect, chilling effect, effective procuring cause, force and effect, natural effect, personal effects
FOREIGN PHRASES: *Effectus sequitur causam.* The effect follows the cause. *Verba accipienda sunt cum effectu, ut sortiantur effectum.* Words are to be received with effect, so that they may be productive of effect. *Cessante causa, cessat effectus.* The cause ceasing, the effect must cease. *Cum quod ago non valet ut ago, valeat quantum valere potest.* When that which I do is of no effect as I do it, it shall be as effective as it can (otherwise) be made. *Nova constitutio futuris formam imponere debet non praeteritis.* A new law ought to affect the future, not what is past. *Non efficit affectus nisi sequatur effectus.* The intention amounts to nothing unless some effect follows. *Verba accipienda ut sortiantur effectum.* Words should be taken so that they may have some effect. *Cuicunque aliquis quid concedit concedere videtur et id, sine quo res ipsa esse non potuit.* Whoever grants anything to another is supposed to grant that also without which the grant itself would be of no effect. *Juris affectus in executione consistit.* The effectiveness of a law lies in its execution. *Quando quod ago non valet ut ago, valeat quantum valere potest.* When that which I do does not have effect as I do it, let it have as much effect as it can. *Cessante ratione legis, cessat et ipsa lex.* Where the reason for a law ceases, the law itself also ceases. *Officit conatus si effectus sequatur.* The attempt becomes of consequence, if the effect follows.

EFFECTIVE *(Efficient)*, **adjective**   able, adapted, adequate, advantageous, capable, competent, convenient, effectual, efficacious, *efficax*, equal to, expedient, fit, functional, handy, helpful, implemental, instrumental, of service, of use, practicable, practical, pragmatic, productive, proficient, profitable, serviceable, skillful, successful, to the purpose, unerring, up to, useful, utilitarian, valid

EFFECTIVE *(Operative)*, **adjective**   active, at work, effectual, fit for use, having legal force, in action, in effect, in force, in operation, operational, ready for use, usable, valid, working
ASSOCIATED CONCEPTS: effective assignment, effective at death, effective date, effective dissolution

EFFECTS, noun   assets, belongings, *bona,* chattel property, chattels, contents, estate, goods, holdings, legal estate, means, movable property, paraphernalia, personal property, personalty, possessions, property, *res,* resources, things, wealth, worldly substance
ASSOCIATED CONCEPTS: household effects, personal effects, personal property, personalty

EFFECTUAL, adjective   achieved, authoritative, binding, effective, efficacious, efficient, end result, eventuation, final result, impact, outcome, outgrowth, response, result, resultant, resultant action, rewarding, upshot, valuable, worthwhile

EFFECTUATE, verb   accomplish, achieve, attain, bring to maturity, bring to pass, carry into effect, carry into execution, carry through, cause, cause to happen, complete, effect, enact, enforce, execute, fulfill, manage, perform, produce, put in force, realize, succeed, work

EFFICIENCY, noun   ability, ableness, adeptness, adroitness, capability, capableness, command, competence, competency, deftness, dexterity, dexterousness, effectiveness, efficacy, *efficientia,* excellence, expertness, handiness, helpfulness, mastery, potency, productiveness, proficiency, prowess, quickness, resourcefulness, skill, skillfulness, vis

EFFICIENT, adjective   able, adroit, capable, competent, deft, dexterous, effective, effectual, expedient, expeditious, expert, functional, *habilis,* mighty, potent, powerful, practical, productive, proficient, puissant, skilled, skillful
ASSOCIATED CONCEPTS: efficient cause, efficient intervening cause

EFFORT, noun   applied energy, arduousness, assiduity, assiduousness, attempt, *conatus, contentio,* endeavor, essay, exertion, expenditure of energy, hard work, industry, laboriousness, *opera,* pains, strain, strenuousness, struggle, toil, travail, trial, vigor, vigorousness

EFFORTLESS *(Accomplished)*, **adjective**   a natural, deft, dexterous, docile, practiced, skilled, skillful, talented

EFFORTLESS *(Easy)*, **adjective**   deft, dexterous, easily done, easy, nothing to it, readily mastered, simple
ASSOCIATED CONCEPTS: simplified court system, simplified procedures for uncontested divorce

EFFUSE, verb   deal out, diffuse, disperse, disseminate, distribute, exude, flow, flow out, give clemency to, issue, notify, outpouring, pour out, promulgate, publicize, publish, radiate, spill, transmit

EFFUSIVE, adjective   building up, complimentary, complimenting, delighted with, demonstrative, ebullient, emotional, emotive, enthusiastic, exuberant, fervent, gushing with compliments, gushy, heaping praise, overflowing, praising, profuse

EGO, noun   character, conceit, egoism, egotism, feelings, identity, image of oneself, individuality, person, personality, pride, pride in administration by others, pride in place in society, pride in reputation, pride in status, self, self-concept, self-esteem, self-identity, self-image
ASSOCIATED CONCEPTS: alter ego

EGREGIOUS, adjective   absurd, appalling, arrant, bizarre, excessive, extravagant, flagrant, glaring, immoderate, inordinate, intemperate, outrageous, outré, remarkable, uncomfortable

EGRESS, noun   departure, discharge, doorway, egression, *egressus,* emergence, emersion, emigration, escape, evacuation, exit, *exitus,* exodus, gate, gateway, leavetaking, means of exit, opening, outlet, parting, passage out, place of exit, way out, withdrawal

EITHER, adjective   alternative, both, choice, each, either alternate, either item, either one, either or, either particular one, either possibility, either potentiality, on the one hand, one, one of two, one or the other, the one and the other
ASSOCIATED CONCEPTS: either case law or common law, either party to a marriage, either state law or federal, pleading in the alternative

EJECT *(Evict)*, **verb**   cast out, *deicere,* dislodge, displace, dispossess, divest, expel, get rid of, oust, put out, put out of possession, remove, remove from premises, rid, summarily dispossess, throw out, thrust out, turn out, turn out of possession

EJECT *(Expel)*, **verb**   cast forth, cast out, detrude, discard, discharge, disgorge, dismiss, *eicere,* eliminate, eruct, eructate, exclude, *expellere, extrudere,* force out, jettison, oust, push away, push out, remove, throw out, thrust out

ELABORATE, adjective   baroque, beautified, bedecked, complex, complicated, daedal, decorated, deluxe, detailed, developed minutely, done with thoroughness, *elaboratus,* embellished, executed with exactness, fancy, festooned, flamboyant, flashy, garnished, grandiose, highly wrought, intricate, intricately wrought, involute, involved, labored, marked by excessive effort, ornamented, ornate, ostentatious, painstaking, palatial, perfected, rich, showy, studied, sumptuous, wrought with labor

ELABORATE, verb   add to, amplify, augment, be more specific, detail, develop, elaborare, enlarge upon, enrich, expand, give additional information, go into detail, improve upon, magnify, perfect, refine, state something in detail

ELAPSE, verb   cease, cease to be, close, come to an end, conclude, disappear, discontinue, draw to a close, end, expire, finish, go, go by, happen, lapse, occur, pass, pass by, run out, slip away, stop, succumb, take place, terminate, transpire, vanish
ASSOCIATED CONCEPTS: time elapsing for an appeal, time elapsed to challenge a ruling

ELATED, adjective   blissful, delighted, ecstatic, euphoric, exalted, excited, exhilarated, exultant, happy, in paradise, joyful, jubilant, overjoyed, pleased, rejoicing, thrilled, triumphant

ELDER, *noun* adult, advanced in years, ancestor, ancient, antiquated, antique, archaic, early, elderly, matured, older man, older woman, one of the older generation, original, senior, senior citizen, superannuated, veteran, vintage
ASSOCIATED CONCEPTS: elder care, medicare, social security

ELDERLY, *adjective* advanced in years, aetate *provectus,* aged, along in years, hoary, matured, old, seasoned, senescent

ELECT (Choose), ***verb*** *creare,* decide, *deligere,* determine in favor of, distinguish by special selection, *eligere,* eliminate the alternatives, exercise an option, exercise discretion, make a choice, make a selection, name, opt for, pick, select, settle on, will
ASSOCIATED CONCEPTS: election of remedies, election of rights, election under a will, equitable election, right of election

ELECT (Select by a vote), ***verb*** appoint by vote, cast the majority of ballots for, choose for office, designate for office by vote, place in office, select for office, vote into office
ASSOCIATED CONCEPTS: election by ballot, election contest, election day, election district, election laws, election returns, electioneering, elective office, general election, notice of election, popular election, primary election, public election, regular election, special election

ELECTION (Choice), ***noun*** appointment, choice between alternatives, cooptation, decision, deliberate choice, designation, determination, *electio,* option, pick, preference, selection, *suffragia,* volition
ASSOCIATED CONCEPTS: election between inconsistent remedies, election of remedies, election of rights, election under a will, equitable election, estoppel by election
FOREIGN PHRASES: ***Consecratio est periodus electionis; electio est praeambula consecration is.*** Consecration is the termination of election; election is the preamble of consecration. ***Electio est interna libera et spontanea separatio unius rei ab alia sine compulsione, consistens in animo et voluntate.*** Election is an internal, free, and spontaneous separation of one thing from another, without compulsion, consisting of intention and will. ***Electio semel facta, et placitum testatum non patitur regressum.*** An election once made, and the intent shown, cannot be recalled. ***Electiones fiant rite et libere sine interruptione aliqua.*** Elections should be made in due form, and freely, without any interruption.

ELECTION (Selection by vote), ***noun*** appointment by vote, balloting, choosing by vote, plebiscite, poll, referendum, representation, selection for office by vote, vote-casting
ASSOCIATED CONCEPTS: ballots, caucus, election contest, election district, election law, election petitions, election returns, general election, primary election, referendum, regular election, special election

ELECTIVE (Selective), ***adjective*** alternative, bestowed by ballot, by vote, choosing, cooptive, disjunctive, on approval, open to choice
ASSOCIATED CONCEPTS: elective franchise, elective office

ELECTIVE (Voluntary), ***adjective*** appointive, discretionary, gratuitous, not required, optional, spontaneous

ELECTORATE, *noun* American voters, body politic, constituency, constituents, general election voters, registered voters, voters
ASSOCIATED CONCEPTS: electoral college, elector

ELECTROCUTION, *noun* capital punishment, condemnation by death, conviction of death sentence, death penalty, death sentence, death warrant, execution, first degree murder with death sentence, give the chair, judgment of death, put to death, ultimate sentence
ASSOCIATED CONCEPTS: death by legal injection, Eighth Amendment, gas chamber

ELECTRONIC RIGHTS, *noun* all media and technology rights, electronic data, electronic product rights, electronic publishing rights, interactive media rights, multimedia rights, non-linear display rights

ELEGANT, *adjective* aesthetic, beautiful, chic, deluxe, dignified, distinguished, *elegans,* exquisite, fashionable, gorgeous, graceful, grand, handsome, in good taste, lovely, magnificent, proportioned, refined, sophisticated, splendid, stately, stylish, tasteful, unmeretricious

ELEMENT, *noun* cantle, component, component part, constituent, content, detail, *elementum,* essential part, factor, feature, fraction, fragment, fundemental part, ingredient, integral part, item, member, part, particle, piece, portion, rudiment, section, segment, substance
ASSOCIATED CONCEPTS: elements of a cause of action, elements of a crime, elements of recovery

ELEMENTAL, *adjective* basic, beginning, crude, delineated in basic terms, easy, easy to understand, foundational, fundamental, inceptive, initiatory, introductory, obvious, plain, precursory, prefatory, primal, primary, primitive, rudimental, rudimentary, simple, simplified, sophomoric, starting, uncomplicated, understandable, unsophisticated

ELEMENTARY, *adjective* abecedarian, apparent, basal, basic, beginning, crude, easy, easy to understand, elemental, foundational, fundamental, inceptive, initiatory, introductory, obvious, plain, precursory, prefatory, primary, primitive, *primus,* proemial, rudimental, rudimentary, simple, simplified, starting, uncomplex, uncomplicated, understandable, unraveled, unsophisticated
ASSOCIATED CONCEPTS: elementary canon of interpretation

ELEVATE, *verb* advance, aggrandize, *attollere,* beatify, boost, build up, canonize, cause to rise, confer an honor, consecrate, deify, dignify, distinguish, erect, exalt, glorify, heave up, heft, heighten, hoist, hold aloft, hold up, honor, improve, jack up, *levare,* lift, make higher, pick up, pitch, promote, prop, put on a pedestal, raise, raise aloft, raise to a higher position, sanctify, sublimate, upgrade, uplift, upraise

ELEVATION, *noun* advancement, aggrandizement, altitude, canonization, consecration, coronation, deification, dignification, *elatio,* elevated place, eminence, eminency, erection, exaltation, height, high land, highness, lift, loftiness, promotion, rise, sanctification, stature, steepness, tallness, uplift, upright distance

ELICIT, *verb* arouse, author, awaken, beget, bring about, bring forth, bring forward, bring out, call forth, cause, draw forth, draw out, *eblandiri,* educe, effect, effectuate, *elicere, evocare,* evoke, extract, generate, initiate, make manifest, stimulate, summon forth

ELIDE, *verb* abate, abolish, annul, cancel, countermand, declare null and void, delete, discard, dismiss, dispel, dissolve, end, eradicate, extinguish, extirpate, invalidate, leave out, nullify, obliterate, omit, overrule, overturn, put an end to, quell, quench, repeal, repress, rescind, reverse, stop, subdue, suppress, terminate, vacate, withdraw

ELIGIBLE, adjective acceptable, appropriate, approved, befitting, capable, desirable, *dignus,* employable, fit, fit for appointment, fit for election, fit for selection, fit to be chosen, fitting, *idoneus,* legally qualified, *opportunus,* proper, qualified, right, satisfactory, suitable, usable
ASSOCIATED CONCEPTS: eligible to hold public office

ELIMINATE *(Eradicate),* **verb** abolish, annihilate, blot out, cancel, clear out, consume, cut out, decimate, delete, demolish, deracinate, desolate, destroy, devour, dispatch, dispose of, dissolve, do away with, efface, end, erase, evacuate, expunge, expurgate, exterminate, extirpate, get rid of, kill, lay waste, liquidate, nullify, obliterate, overthrow, purge, put a stop to, put an end to, quash, quell, raze, remove, render useless, slaughter, stamp out, strike out, suppress, sweep away, tear out, terminate, uproot, void, weed out, wipe out

ELIMINATE *(Exclude),* **verb** ban, banish, bar, blockade, cashier, cast out, censor, count out, debar, deport, disallow, disbar, discard, disdain, dismiss, disqualify, disregard, do away with, eject, elide, evacuate, evict, except, exclude, excommunicate, exempt, exile, expatriate, expel, keep out, leave out, lock out, omit, ostracize, oust, outlaw, preclude, prevent, prohibit, proscribe, put aside, rebuff, reject, remove, renounce, repulse, rule out, set aside, shed, shut out, spurn, throw out, thrust out, turn out, weed

ELIMINATION, noun abatement, abolition, annihilation, cancellation, curtailment, depletion, destruction, discardment, discharge, disposal, disposition, disqualification, dissolution, ejection, emptying, end, eradication, evulsion, exclusion, excretion, exhaustion, expulsion, extermination, extinction, extinguishment, extirpation, extrusion, exudation, nullification, obliteration, omission, prohibition, proscription, purge, rejection, removal, renunciation, riddance, separation, voidance
ASSOCIATED CONCEPTS: censorship, elimination of rights

ELITE, noun aristocracy, best part, best people, choice group, chosen few, cream of society, fashionable society, gentry, high society, most carefully selected group, nobility, optimates, privileged class, select body, select few, superior group, top people, upper circles, upper classes

ELONGATION, verb add to, aggrandize, amplify, augment, compound, continue, continuing, drag out, draw out, enlarge, enlarge upon, expand, extend, grow longer, increase, lengthen, linger, make larger, meandering, never-ending, prolong, protract, spread, stretch, supplement, sustain

ELOQUENT, adjective articulate, calculated to stir, communicative, compelling, convincing, *disertus,* effective, *eloquens,* expressive, flowing, fluent, forceful, full of feeling, full of meaning, full of substance, graceful, impassioned, impressive, incisive, informative, meaningful, mellifluous, moving, movingly expressive, persuasive, pithy, pointed, powerful, powerfully expressive, pregnant, rich, spellbinding, striking, telling, trenchant, vivid

ELSEWHERE, adverb absent, another place, away, further away, gone, in a distant place, in a foreign location, in a foreign place, in a foreign setting, in another place, in some other place, not present, not under consideration, outside, remote, removed

ELUCIDATE, verb annotate, ascertain, bring out more clearly, cast light upon, clarify, clear of obscurity, clear up, comment upon, commentate, construe, decipher, decode, define, demonstrate, describe, detail, determine, disentangle, enlighten, enucleate, exemplify, explain, *explanare,* explicate, *exponere,* exposit, expound, find a clue, give an explanation, give an interpretation, illuminate, illustrate, interpret, *interpretari,* lay open, make apparent, make clear, make intelligible, make less confusing, make lucid, make plain, make sense of, make simple, make understandable, manifest, paraphrase, popularize, put in other words, ravel, rephrase, restate, shed light upon, simplify, solve, spell out, teach, throw light upon, translate, unfold, unravel, unriddle, unscramble, untangle

ELUDE, verb abscond, avoid, baffle, be concealed, break away, break loose, dodge, *eludere,* escape, escape by artifice, escape detection, escape notice, evade, *evitare,* flee, get away, hide, keep aloof, keep out of sight, make an escape, mystify, outmaneuver, outwit, parry, remain hidden, remain undiscovered, shun, slip away, slip out, steal away, take evasive action

ELUSIVE, adjective abstruse, apt to flee, baffling, difficult, difficult to catch, difficult to comprehend, difficult to understand, eluding clear perception, elusory, enigmatic, equivocal, escaping, evanescent, evasive, fleeting, fugitive, hard to define, hard to express, hard to grasp, hard to maintain, hard to understand, impalpable, intangible, liable to disappear, mysterious, nebulous, obscure, occult, puzzling, runaway, shadowy, shunning, slippery, tending to elude, tending to escape, tending to slip away, uncertain, unclear, vanishing

ELUSORY, adjective abstract, complex, convex, deceptive, elusive, enigmatic, evanescent, evasive, fleeting, furtive, hard to grasp, hazy, illusive, impalpable, imponderable, intangible, mysterious, oblique, obtruse, recondite, transient
ASSOCIATED CONCEPTS: illusory agreements, illusory statutes

EMANATE, verb arise from, come forth, come from, debouch, derive from, descend from, *effundi,* effuse, eject, *emanare,* emerge, emit, ensue from, exude, fall out, flow forth, *fluere,* follow from, go out of, grow from, grow out of, issue, originate in, pour out of, proceed, project, radiate, result, spring from, stream out

EMANCIPATION, noun acquittal, deliverance, deliverance from bondage, discharge, enfranchisement, extrication, freedom, *liberatio,* liberation, liberty, *manumissio,* manumission, pardon, possession of full rights, release, release from custody, reprieve, salvation, setting free, unshackling
ASSOCIATED CONCEPTS: complete emancipation, emancipation of minors, Emancipation Proclamation, express emancipation, implied emancipation, partial emancipation

EMASCULATION, noun castration, debilitation, debility, decrepitude, depleted, enervation, expurgation, fault, helplessness, infirmity, impotence, languor, unmanning, weakness

EMBARGO, noun authoritative stoppage of trade, ban, bar, control of trade, debarment, denial, detention of ships, disallowance of trade, exclusion from commerce, forbiddance, freeze, governmental order of prohibition, halt, interference, legal restraint, preclusion, prohibition, restraint, restriction, stop, stoppage
ASSOCIATED CONCEPTS: embargo of commerce, embargo of goods, embargo of products

EMBARK, verb auspicate, begin, commence, conscendere, engage in an enterprise, enter, enter upon, get under way, go into, inaugurate, initiate, institute, launch, make a beginning, originate, plunge into, *rationem inire,* set out, start, start out, take on, take the first step, take up, undertake, venture

EMBARRASS, verb abash, annoy, baffle, bedevil, beset, bewilder, bother, burden, cause confusion, cause discomfort, cause to feel ill at ease, chagrin, confuse, *conturbare,* discomfit, discomfort, discompose, disconcert, disquiet, distress, disturb, encumber, fluster, *impedire,* incommode, make self-conscious, make uncomfortable, mortify, nonplus, perturb, plague, put at a disadvantage, render flustered, render ill at ease, shame, trouble, upset, vex, worry

EMBARRASSMENT, noun abashment, awkward situation, awkwardness, bafflement, chagrin, confusion, constraint, discomfiture, discomfort, discomposure, disturbance, fluster, humiliation, *implicatio,* mortification, perturbation, pudency, *scrupulus,* self-consciousness, shame, uneasiness

EMBASSY, noun ambassadorial function, ambassadorial office, ambassadorial residence, commission, consulate, delegation, deputation, diplomatic corps, embassage, establishment of an ambassador, legateship, *legatio,* legation, mission, mission of the ambassador, official headquarters of an ambassador, official mission
ASSOCIATED CONCEPTS: consular and diplomatic officers

EMBED, verb bury, deposit, engraft, entrench, fix, fix firmly, implant, impress, imprint, infix, ingrain, insert, lodge, plant, press in, root, seat, set, set firmly, settle, stamp

EMBELLISH, verb add details, adorn, array, beautify, bedeck, bedizen, bejewel, beribbon, bespangle, better, blazon, chase, dandify, deck, *decorare,* decorate, dizen, dress up, elaborate, emblazon, emboss, embroider, encrust, enhance, enrich, *exornare,* fix up, frill, garnish, gild, glamorize, grace, illuminate, illustrate, improve, make beautiful, make elaborate, make improvements, make resplendent, meliorate, ornament, polish, rubricate, smarten, spangle, spruce up, stretch, tool, touch up, trim, varnish

EMBEZZLE, verb appropriate fraudulently, appropriate to one's own use, *avertere,* commit larceny, defalcate, defraud, divert to one's own use, filch, *intercipere, intervertere,* misapply, misappropriate, misappropriate funds, misappropriate intrusted funds, misuse, pilfer, purloin, swindle, take by fraud, take feloniously, thieve
ASSOCIATED CONCEPTS: convert

EMBEZZLEMENT, noun appropriation, breach of trust, cheating, defalcation, fraud, fraudulent appropriation, fraudulent appropriation of money, fraudulent conversion, larceny, malversation, misappropriation, peculation, pilfering, purloining, stealing, swindle, theft, theft of money entrusted to one's care, theft of money entrusted to one's management, thievery, wrongful appropriation
ASSOCIATED CONCEPTS: conversion, corporate embezzlement, embezzlement of public funds, larceny, misappropriation, theft by means of embezzlement

EMBEZZLER, noun cheater, criminal, crook, culprit, defalcator, defrauder, evildoer, *interceptor,* lawbreaker, malefactor, one who commits larceny, peculator, *pecuniae aversor,* pilferer, purloiner, swindler, thief

EMBLEM, noun allusion, badge, banner, chevron, coat of arms, colors, crest, crown, escutcheon, figure, flag, hallmark, identification, image, indicium, insignia, keepsake, logo, mark, medal, monogram, motto, pennant, regalia, seal, sign, signet, standard, symbol, token
ASSOCIATED CONCEPTS: brand, emblem law, logo, mark, registration, trademark

EMBLEMATIC, adjective allusive, denotative, indicant, indicative, representational, representative, suggestive, symbolic, typical

EMBODIMENT, noun actualization, bodily presentation, bodily representation, concrete expression, corporeity, definite form, *effigies,* form, formation, incarnation, manifestation, material figuration, material representation, materialization, personification, realization, representation, *simulacrum,* substantiality, synthesis, tangibility, tangible form, visible form
ASSOCIATED CONCEPTS: embodied in a contract, embodied in the instrument

EMBODY, verb actualize, constitute, corporealize, exhibit in visible form, express in concrete form, form, give concrete form to, give definite form to, give tangible form to, incarnate, *includere,* incorporate, integrate, interblend, interfuse, intermix, invest with a body, invest with matter, make corporeal, make visible, manifest, materialize, personify, put into bodily form, substantialize, syncretize, synthesize

EMBOLDEN, verb abet, animate, assure, bolster, buoy, cheer, encourage, enhearten, foment, give confidence, hearten, impel, incite, inspire, inspirit, instigate, invigorate, nerve, press, promise, rally, reassure, rouse, stimulate, strengthen, urge

EMBRACE *(Accept),* **verb** adopt, advocate, affiliate, agree to, assume, be in favor of, concur in, consent to, countenance, endorse, espouse, favor, make one's own, ratify, sanction, seize, subscribe to, support, take to oneself, take up, welcome

EMBRACE *(Encircle),* **verb** begird, belt, cincture, circumscribe, compass, *complecti, comprehendere,* contain, cover, encincture, enclose, encompass, enfold, engird, envelop, gird, girdle, hold, include, incorporate, integrate, invest, involve, lap, receive, skirt, surround, take in

EMBROILMENT, noun affray, agitation, brawl, breach, broil, chaos, clash, combat, commotion, complication, conflict, confusion, contention, contest, derangement, difference of opinion, disarrangement, disorder, disquiet, dissension, dissentience, disturbance, embranglement, encounter, engagement, entanglement, ferment, fracas, fray, imbroglio, involvement, mix-up, muddle, odds, outbreak, pandemonium, quarrel, riot, row, rupture, squabble, strife, struggle, tumult, turbulence, turmoil, unrest, uproar, violence

EMBRYO, noun basis for development, beginning, bud, commencement, earliest stage, fetus, first stage, genesis, germ, immature stage, inchoation, incipience, incipient organism, origin, origination, partus, rudiment, rudimentary state, seed, source, start, starting point, undeveloped stage
ASSOCIATED CONCEPTS: abortion

EMEND, verb adjust, alter, ameliorate, amend, better, change, correct, *corrigere,* do over, *emendare,* emendate, fix, help, improve, make better, make corrections, make improvements, make repairs, meliorate, mend, put in order, put right, reconstruct, rectify, redo, refine, reform, remedy, remodel, remove errors, render better, reorganize, repair, restore, retouch, revamp, revise, rework, rewrite, rid of defects, right, set right, set straight, touch up, work over

EMERGE, verb appear, arise, arrive, become apparent, become manifest, become plain, become visible, break through, burst forth, come forth, come forward, come into notice, come into view, come out, come out of hiding, come to light, crop up, dawn, emanate, *emergere,* enter the picture, exit, expose, issue, loom, make an appearance, manifest, materialize, put in an appearance, rise, show, show up, surface, turn up

EMERGENCE, noun appearance, arrival, commencement, development, evidence, initiation, issue, manifestation, materialization, notice, now apparent, show, start, viewed
ASSOCIATED CONCEPTS: emergent law, the emergence of law

EMERGENCY, noun accident, *casus,* climacteric, condition of insufficiency, crisis, critical point, crucial period, difficulty, dilemma, *discrimen,* exigency, extremity, insufficiency of service, last minute need, necessitousness, need, need for action, needfulness, plight, predicament, pressing necessity, pressing need, strait, sudden peril, *tempus,* trouble, unexpected happening, unforeseen condition, unforeseen occurrence, urgency
ASSOCIATED CONCEPTS: Emergency Court of Appeals, Emergency Defense Act, emergency employment doctrine, Emergency Price Control Act, private necessity, public emergency, public necessity

EMINENCE, noun aggrandizement, *amplissimus gradus,* authority, celebrity, consequence, dignity, distinction, elevated rank, elevation, esteem, exaltation, fame, *fastigium,* glory, grandeur, great station, greatness, height, high position, high rank, high station, honor, importance, important station, influence, loftiness, majesty, mark, mightiness, nobility, notability, note, noteworthiness, *praestantia,* preeminence, prestige, prominence, renown, repute, standing, supereminence, superiority, supremacy, weight

EMINENT DOMAIN, noun annex for public use, assume for public use, take possession for public use, usurp for public use

EMIT, verb beam, cast out, discharge, eject, *emittere,* eructate, erupt, exhale, exhaust, expel, expend, exude, give forth, give off, give out, gush, hurl, issue, jet, let out, pour forth, pour out, put forth, radiate, secrete, send forth, send out, shed, shoot, spurt, squirt, throw, throw off, throw out

EMOLUMENT, noun advance, allowance, benefit, bonus, commission, compensation, consideration, disbursement, earnings, fee, income, indemnification, pay, payment, profit, recompense, remuneration, requital, restitution, return, revenue, reward, salary, stipend, tribute, wage

EMOTION, noun affect, agitation, *animi motus,* ardor, eagerness, ebullition, enthusiasm, ferment, fervor, furor, great feeling, mood, passion, reaction, response, sensation, sensitiveness, sentiment, spirit, stir, turmoil, verve, zeal

EMPANEL, verb calendar, docket, enlist jurors, enroll, enter those names designated as jurors, insert names on a register, list for jury duty, list jurors, place upon a list, register, schedule, select jurors, sign in
ASSOCIATED CONCEPTS: empanel a jury

EMPATHIZE, verb be compassionate, be in tune, be sorry for, be understanding, comfort, commiserate, condole, express sympathy, feel for, grieve for, have pity for, identify with, pity, project, react, relate to, respond, share grief, share sorrow, show solace, show tenderness, soothe, sympathize, understand

EMPHASIS, noun accent, accentuation, affirmation, attention, concentration, consequence, consideration, distinction, distinctness, eminence, *emphasis,* energy, exclamation, force, force of expression, force of voice, forcibleness, highlight, ictus, importance, impressiveness, inflection, insistence, intensity of expression, moment, most important point, notability, note, outstanding feature, positiveness, pressure, primacy, prominence, salience, saliency, significance, special attention, special concern, special intonation, special significance, strength, stress, thrust, underlining, underscoring, value, vigorous enunciation, vociferation, weight, worth

EMPHASIZE, verb accent, accentuate, affirm, argue, articulate, assert, bear, contend, dwell, enforce, enhance, feature, heighten, highlight, insist, intensify, iterate, magnify, mark, plead, point up, pronounce, protest, punctuate, reaffirm, repeat, spearhead, spotlight, stress, underline, underscore, vociferate

EMPHATIC, adjective absolute, categorical, clear, compelling, decided, dogmatic, energetic, explicit, express, forceful, forcible, graphic, insistent, overt, positive, reiterative, resounding, strong, telling, vehement, vivid

EMPIRICAL, adjective analytical, based on evidence of the senses, based on observation, derived from experience, diagnostic, guided by experiment, provisional

EMPLOY (Engage services), verb add to the payroll, appoint, assign, authorize, commission, contract, delegate, *detineri,* empower, engage, enlist, enroll, entrust with a task, entrust with management, fill a position, fill a vacancy, fill an opening, find help, furnish occupation for, give a job to, give a position to, give a post to, give employment, give work to, hire, keep in service, *occupatum,* place, put to work, recruit, retain, retain the services of, secure, set to work, sign up, staff, take into employ, take into service, use another's services, use as an agent, *versari*
ASSOCIATED CONCEPTS: actual employment, customarily employed, dangerous employment, employed in hazardous work, employed in interstate commerce, lawfully employed, legally employed, permanently employed

EMPLOY (Make use of), verb apply, avail oneself of, capitalize upon, exercise, exploit, have recourse to, manipulate, mobilize, operate, ply, practice, profit by, put in action, put in operation, put to service, put to use, resort to, take advantage of, turn to account, turn to use, use, utilize, wield, work

EMPLOYEE, noun agent, apprentice, assistant, attaché, factotum, hand, help, helper, hired hand, hireling, jobholder, laborer, mercenary, personnel, representative, salaried worker, servant, staff person, subordinate, toiler, wage earner, worker, workman
ASSOCIATED CONCEPTS: agent, bona fide employee, borrowed employee, casual employee, de facto employee, independent contractor, joint adventurer, loaned employee, part-time employee, permanent employee, provisional employee, servant, subcontractor

EMPLOYER, noun administrator, boss, chief, controller, director, executive, head, leader, management, manager, master, overseer, owner, patron, proprietor, superintendent, superior, supervisor, taskmaster
ASSOCIATED CONCEPTS: employers' liability acts

EMPLOYMENT, noun activity, appointment, assignment, avocation, berth, billet, business, calling, capacity, career, commission, craft, duty, employ, engagement, enterprise, field, function, incumbency, industry, job, labor, lifework, line, livelihood, living, means of livelihood, means of support, *negotium,* occupation, office, position, post, practice, profession, pursuit, retainment, service, situation, specialty, task, trade, vocation, work
ASSOCIATED CONCEPTS: abandonment of employment, arising out of and in course of employment, available for employment, casual employment, conditions of employment, contract of employment, course of employment, covered employment, dangerous employment, duration of employment, during term of employment, engaged in employment, exempt employment, extrahazardous employment, extraordinary employment, general employment, grade of employment, injury arising in course of employment, permanent employment, place of employment, private employment, professional employment, public employment, scope of employment, seasonal employment, temporary employment, tenure of employment

EMPLOYMENT DISCRIMINATION, noun bias in the workplace, prejudice in an employment environment
Generally: differentiation, disequalization, inequality, injustice, unfairness

EMPOWER, verb accredit, activate, aggrandize, allow, appoint, arm, assign, authorize, capacitate, commission, confer power on, delegate, depute, deputize, enable, endow, energize, entrust, franchise, give ability, give authority, give permission, give power, give right, grant, grant authority, grant power, *homini rei,* impart power to, implement, invest, license, make able, make capable, make potent, permit, potentiate, *potestatem facere,* privilege, qualify, render competent, sanction, strengthen, train, vest, warrant

EMPTY (Nothing left), **adjective** all gone, bare, blank, depleted, devoid, drained, exhausted, hollow, nothing left inside, unfilled, vacuous, void, without contents
ASSOCIATED CONCEPTS: empty judgment, empty law

EMPTY (Vacant), **adjective** abandoned, available, barren, deserted, fruitless, idle, no one home, not inhabited, unclaimed, uninhabited, unoccupied, untenanted, up for grabs
ASSOCIATED CONCEPTS: empty premises

EMPTY (Without substance), **adjective** devoid of merit, inconsequential, ineffective, ineffectual, insignificant, insubstantial, meaningless, meritless, unavailing, unimportant, unreal, unsatisfying, useless, vain, valueless, without substance, worthless
ASSOCIATED CONCEPTS: an empty threat, veiled threat of law suit

EMULOUS, adjective admiring, competing, competitive, contending, copying, envious, follow the example of, following, imitative, jealous, rival

EN BANC, adverb all together, as a unit, as a whole, collectively, *en bloc, en masse,* entirely, in a body, in a mass, in sum, *in toto,* one and all

EN MASSE, adverb all together, as a body, as a group, as a whole, as one, at the same time, collectively, *en bloc,* ensemble, in assembly, in mass, in the aggregate, together

EN ROUTE, adverb along the way, bound, during the journey, during travel, in passage, in progress, in transit, midway, on the journey, on the road, on the way

ENABLE, verb abet, aid, allow, approve, arm, assist, authorize, capacitate, confer, consent, emancipate, empower, endow, facilitate, *facultatem facere,* give ability, give authority, give means, give permission, give power, grant, help, *homini rei,* implement, indulge, invest, let, liberate, license, make able, make capable, make possible, make practicable, permit, privilege, provide, provide means, qualify, release, remove a disability, render assistance, render competent, sanction, strengthen, supply with means, support
ASSOCIATED CONCEPTS: enabling act, enabling legislation, enabling statute

ENABLING LEGISLATION, noun establishing legislation, first initiative, law giving authority, law giving power, law granting authority, law granting license, law investing power, original ordinance, seminal measure, underlying act, underlying legislative pronouncement
ASSOCIATED CONCEPTS: enacting clause

ENACT, verb adopt a measure, appoint by act, codify, command, declare, decree, dictate, enjoin, establish, establish by law, give legislative sanction, institute by law, issue a command, legislate, make into a statute, make laws, ordain by law, order, pass, *perferre,* prescribe, put in force, put into effect
ASSOCIATED CONCEPTS: enacting clause
FOREIGN PHRASES: *Non obligat lex nisi promulgata.* A law is not obligatory unless it is promulgated. *Ejus est interpretari cujus est condere.* It is for him who enacts anything to give it interpretation.

ENACTMENT, noun act, bill, charter, codification, decree, dictate, edict, establishment, fiat, law, legislation, *lex,* measure, ordinance, *plebiscitum,* regulation, rule, ruling, *sanctio,* statute, statutory law
FOREIGN PHRASES: *Leges suum ligent latorem.* Laws should bind their own proposer. *Jus constitui oportet in his quae ut plurimum accidunt non quae ex inopi nato.* Laws ought to be made with a view to those cases which occur most frequently, and not to those which are of rare or accidental occurrence. *Leges figendi et refigendi consuetudo est periculosissima.* The practice of making and remaking the laws is a most dangerous one. *Quod populus postremum jussit, id jus ratum esto.* What the people have last enacted, let that be the settled law.

ENCLOSE, verb blockade, bound, bracket, capture, *cingere,* circumscribe, circumvallate, close in, compass, confine, contain, embrace, encase, encincture, encircle, encompass, enfold, envelop, environ, fence in, gird, girdle, hem in, immure, impound, imprison, incarcerate, *includere,* insert in a wrapper, insert in an envelope, keep behind bars, keep in, keep in custody, limit, pen, put a barrier around, put into a receptacle, restrain, restrict, retain, ring, *saepire,* shut in, surround, take into custody, trammel, wall in

ENCLOSURE, noun arena, barrier, blockade, border, boundary, bracket, cincture, circle, circumjacence, circumscription, circumvallation, confine, confinement, container, containment, custody, edge, embrace, encasement, encirclement, enclosed space, encompassment, enfoldment, envelopment, fence, fenced in area, girdle, immurement, impoundment, imprisonment, incarceration, insertion, limit, limitation, perimeter, pound, receptacle, restriction, trammel, walled in area, wrapper, zone

ENCOMPASS (Include), **verb**   adscribere, complecti, comprise, consist of, contain, continere, cover, embrace, hold, incorporate, span, subsume, take in
ASSOCIATED CONCEPTS: encompass a broad cross section of the law

ENCOMPASS (Surround), **verb**   be circumjacent, begird, belt, border, bound, cincture, cingere, circle, circuit, circumcludere, circumplecti, circumscribe, compass, corral, edge, encase, encincture, encircle, enclose, enclose on all sides, engird, enring, ensphere, envelop, enwrap, fence in, form a circle round, gird, girdle, hem in, immure, keep in, pen in, ring, shut in, wall in, wrap

ENCOURAGE, verb   back, back up, boost, embolden, endorse, hearten, inspire, support

ENCROACH, verb   breach, commit an infraction, enter by stealth, enter upon the domain of another, enter wrongfully, impinge, infiltrate, infringe, ingress wrongfully, interfere, interlope, intrude, intrude illegally, invade, invade unlawfully, invadere, irrupt, make an incursion, make inroads, obtrude, occupare, overstep, penetrate, raid, transgress, trespass, violate

ENCROACHMENT, noun   breach, entrance by stealth, entrance upon the domain of another, illegal intrusion, impingement, imposition, incursion, infiltration, infraction, infringement, iniuria, inroad, interference, interloping, intrusion, invasion, irruption, obtrusion, overlap, overstepping, penetration, prying, raid, real estate trespass, transgression, trespass, unlawful invasion, violation, wrongful entry, wrongful ingress
ASSOCIATED CONCEPTS: adverse possession, common nuissance, easements, public nuissance

ENCUMBER (Financially obligate), **verb**   assess, burden, charge, hold liable, impedire, impose a charge, impose a lien, make accountable for, make responsible for, mortgage, obligate, onerare, place a cloud on, praegravare, subject to a charge, subject to a liability
ASSOCIATED CONCEPTS: mortgage

ENCUMBER (Hinder), **verb**   block, block up, burden, charge, cramp, cumber, disadvantage, discommode, entangle, entrammel, frustrate, hamper, hinder movement, hold back action, hold up, impede, impose, incommode, inconvenience, inflict, inhibit, interfere, interrupt, keep back, lade, limit, obstruct action, render difficult, retard, saddle, shackle, slow down, strain, tax, thwart, tie up, trammel, trouble, weaken, weigh down

ENCUMBRANCE, noun   burden, charge, claim, curb, difficulty, disadvantage, drawback, hampering, hindering, hindrance, hitch, hurdle, impediment, impedimentum, imposition, inconvenience, infliction, interference, liability, lien, lien on an estate, load, mortgage, obstacle, obstruction, onus, oppression, pressure, restriction, retardation, stay, stop, stoppage
ASSOCIATED CONCEPTS: easements, mortgage
FOREIGN PHRASES: **Transit terra cum onere.** Land passes subject to any encumbrances affecting it.

END (Intent), **noun**   aim, ambition, aspiration, bourn, consilium, desideration, desideratum, design, desire, desired result, destination, dream, expectation, goal, guiding principle, hope, idea, intended result, intendment, intention, mission, motivating idea, motivation, motive, object, objective, purpose, reason, target, wish
ASSOCIATED CONCEPTS: ends of justice

END (Termination), **noun**   accomplishment, achievement, adjournment, attainment, border, borderline, bound, boundary, cessation, close, closing piece, closure, completion, concluding part, conclusion, consummation, culmination, curtain, death, decease, decline, demise, denouement, departure, destination, destiny, determination, dissolution, edge, elimination, ending, estoppage, exitus, expiration, expiry, extinction, extinguishment, extreme, extreme point, extremity, fate, final event, final state, finale, finality, finis, finish, fulfillment, furthermost part, halt, last of a series, last part, limit, limitation, omega, outcome, point, pole, realization, remnant, result, resultant, retirement, stop, stoppage, tail, terminal, terminal point, termination, terminus, tip, upshot, wane

ENDANGER, verb   abuse, be careless with, be malevolent, bring into peril, bully, compromise, damage, dare, expose, expose to danger, expose to injury, expose to loss, harm, hazard, hurt, impair, imperil, in discrimen, in periculum, injure, jeopardize, leave defenseless, leave unprotected, make insecure, make liable to danger, make liable to injury, make unsafe, make vulnerable, maltreat, menace, misuse, molest, peril, persecute, prey upon, put in hazard, put in jeopardy, risk, risk exposure to harm, speculate with, stake, subject to loss, terrify, terrorize, threaten, torment, torture, victimize, violate
ASSOCIATED CONCEPTS: endanger life, endanger safety

ENDEAVOR, noun   achievement, aim, application, assiduity, attempt, bid, campaign, cause, conatus, contentio, deed, effort, emprise, enterprise, essay, exercise, exertion, experiment, exploit, feat, labor, nisus, pains, project, pursuance, pursuit, quest, scheme, search, strain, strenuous effort, struggle, sustained trial, task, toil, travail, trial, try, undertaking, venture, work

ENDEAVOR, verb   address oneself to, aim, apply oneself to, aspire, assay, assume, attempt, attempt strenuously, be resolute, bestir oneself, bid, compete for, conari, contendere, do all one can, do one's best, do one's utmost, engage in, eniti, essay, exert effort, exert oneself, experiment, labor, make a bid, make an attempt, make an effort, persevere, pursue, put oneself out, resolve, risk, seek, set about, spare no effort, spare no pains, strain, strive, struggle, tackle, take a crack at, take action, take on, take pains, take up, take upon oneself, test, toil, trouble oneself, try, undertake, venture, vie for, work at

ENDLESS, adjective   boundless, ceaseless, continual, continuous, countless, endless, enduring, eternal, everlasting, illimitable, immeasurable, incalculable, incessant, indefinite, indeterminable, inexhaustible, infinite, innumerable, interminable, limitless, measureless, never-ending, nonstop, perpetual, recurring, unbounded, unceasing, unchecked, unconditional, unconfined, uncontrolled, undying, unending, unfathomable, uninterrupted, universal, unlimited, unmeasured, unremitting, unrestrained, unrestricted, untold, vast, without end, without number
ASSOCIATED CONCEPTS: endless case law, endless punishment, endless torments, endless violence

ENDORSE, verb approve, attest, authenticate, back, certify, commend, confirm, ratify, sanction, second, support, validate

ENDORSEMENT (Backing), **noun** advertisement, advocacy, approval, assistance, assurance, attestation, authorization, commendation, encouragement, imprimatur, license, patronage, recommendation, sanction, signature, stamp of approval, support, testimonial, testimony, vouch, word
ASSOCIATED CONCEPTS: political endorsement

ENDORSEMENT (Signature), **noun** acceptance, approval, authorization, autograph, confirmation, countersignature, execution, go-ahead, passage, permission, ratification, sanction, seal, signet, signing, sponsorship, stamp of approval, support, underwriting, warrant
ASSOCIATED CONCEPTS: endorsement to an insurance policy

ENDORSER, noun attestant, attester, backer, certifier, confirmer, cosigner, countersigner, guarantor, proponent, ratifier, signatory, sponsor, subscriber, surety, undersigned, underwriter

ENDOW, verb aid, allot, allow, award, bequeath, bestow, contribute, donate, endue, enrich, fund, furnish, give, grant, hand down, hand out, hand over, help, *hominem, instruere,* make pecuniary provision, pass down, present, provide, put in the hands of, subsidize, supply, supply with means

ENDOWMENT, noun aid, allotment, allowance, appropriation, assistance, award, benefaction, benefit, bequeathal, bequest, bestowal, bestowment, boon, bounty, contribution, donation, dowry, enrichment, fund, funding, gift, grant, present, presentation, presentment, provision, stipend, subsidy
ASSOCIATED CONCEPTS: annuity, endowment fund, endowment policy in insurance

ENDUE, verb accord, allot, allow, apportion, arm, assign, award, bestow, confer, dispense, donate, empower, enable, endow, enrich, entrust, fortify, furnish, give, grant, hand out, invest, invigorate, make provision for, present, provide, strengthen, supply

ENDURE (Last), **verb** abide, be constant, be durable, be firm, be permanent, be preserved, be prolonged, be protracted, be timeless, carry on, continue, continue to be, continue to exist, *durare,* exist, exist uninterruptedly, exist without break, extend, forge ahead, go on, hang on, have duration, have no end, hold one's ground, hold out, keep, linger on, live on, maintain, move ahead, outlast, outlive, perdure, *permanere,* persevere, persist, press onward, prevail, progress, refuse to give up, refuse to yield, remain, remain alive, remain valid, stand, stand fast, stay, subsist, survive, sustain, wear, weather, withstand

ENDURE (Suffer), **verb** accustom oneself to, be subjected to, bear, bear pain, bear up under, bear without resistance, bide, brave, brook, continue under pain, countenance, encounter, experience, experience unpleasantly, face, feel, forbear, go through, make the best of, meet, pass through, *perferre,* put up with, receive, resign oneself to, stand, stomach, submit to, suffer pain, sustain, *sustinere,* swallow, take, take patiently, tolerare, tolerate, undergo, weather, withstand

ENEMY, noun adversary, antagonist, arch rival, assailant, betrayer, foe, nemesis, opponent, opposer, opposition, rival, sworn opponent, the other side

ASSOCIATED CONCEPTS: alien enemy, tending to aid a public enemy

ENEMY ALIEN, noun adventitious, adversary, adverse, antagonist, antagonistic, assailant, attacker, barbarian, competitor, conflicting, contender, contestant, contradictory, contrary, contrasting, counteracting, differing, dissimilar, distant, emigrant, exotic, external, extrinsic, faraway, foe, foeman, foreign, foreigner, hostile, hostile nation *or* state, hostile party, immigrant, inimical, newcomer, nonterrestrial, opponent, opposed, opposer, opposite, outlander, outlandish, outsider, outward, remote, rival, Satan, strange, stranger, the adversary, the archenemy, the devil, the enemy, the opposition, the other side, them, tramontane, transalpine, transatlantic, transmarine, transmontane, transpacific, ultramarine, ultramontane, ultramundane, unearthly, unlike, unnaturalized, unnaturalized citizen, vier, wetback

ENEMY COMBATANT, noun active combatant in the foreign theater of conflict, an enemy force, anarchist, assailant, assassin, attacker, combatant, demoniac force, destroyer, detainee, enemy alien, enemy operation, faction at war, fanatic, foreign assailant, hostile force, insurgent, internees, murderer, opponent, radical, rebel, revolutionary, revolutionist, rival force, subversive force, terrorist
ASSOCIATED CONCEPTS: alien enemies, detainees, justice courts, military tribunals, Patriotic Act, prisoners of war, public enemies, terrorism, treason

ENERGETIC, adjective active, aggressive, alive, ambitious, animated, brisk, busy, chipper, committed, determined, devoted, diligent, driving, dynamic, eager, effective, effectual, efficacious, efficient, electric, emphatic, enterprising, enthusiastic, excited, exerting effort, exertive, forceful, forcible, full of energy, full of life, hardworking, industrious, jumping, laborious, lively, mighty, physical, potent, powerful, pushing, ready to go, robust, snappy, spirited, vibrant, vigorous, vital, wholeheartedly supporting, zealous

ENERGIZE, verb activate, agitate, animate, augment, boost, charge, dynamize, elate, electrify, empower, encourage, enliven, excite to action, exhilarate, galvanize, give life to, goad, imbue with life, incite, inflame, inspire, intensify, invigorate, kindle, labor, liven, magnetize, pep up, quicken, reinforce, restore, spur, stimulate, strain, strengthen, struggle, toil, vitalize, vivify

ENERGY, noun activation, activity, animation, ardor, brawn, dash, drive, dynamism, enterprise, ferment, fervor, fire, force, forcefulness, go, hustle, impetus, industry, intensity, labor, life, liveliness, lustiness, main force, might, mightiness, momentum, muscle, potency, potentiality, power, pressure, puissance, punch, push, sinew, spirit, stamina, steam, stir, strength, strenuousness, verve, vigor, virility, vitality, vivacity, zeal

ENERVATE, verb adulterate, attenuate, debase, debilitate, defeat, deplete, deprive of strength, devitalize, dilute, diminish, disable, drain, enfeeble, fatigue, handicap, impair, incapacitate, invalidate, lessen, lower, minimize, paralyze, reduce, sap, strain, thin, tire, undermine, water down, weaken

ENFORCE, verb administer, bring to pass, carry into effect, carry into execution, carry out, carry through, coerce, compel, compel obedience, *confirmare,* dictate, drive, effect, effectuate, employ force, exact, execute, *exsequi,* force, have executed, impel, implement, impose, insist on, insist upon, make compulsory, make effective, necessitate, obtain

213

by compulsion, obtain by force, press, put in action, put in force, put in operation, put into effect, put into execution, put pressure on, require, strengthen, subject to pressure

ASSOCIATED CONCEPTS: enforce a contract, enforce a judgment, enforce a lien, enforce provisions of the law, enforce sanctions, enforcement proceedings

ENFORCEMENT, noun administration, carrying into effect, carrying out, coaction, compulsion, compulsory execution, constraint, dictation, effectuation, exaction, execution, force, forcible urging, implementation, imposition, insistence, insistence upon, necessitation, necessity, obligation, obligement, pressure, requirement, strengthening, support

ASSOCIATED CONCEPTS: enforcement of a contract, enforcement of a judgment, enforcement of a lien, enforcement of a right, enforcement proceeding

FOREIGN PHRASES: *Pacta conventa quae neque contra leges neque dolo mala inita sunt omni modo observanda sunt.* Agreements which are not contrary to the laws nor entered into with a fraudulent design must be observed in all respects. *Executio juris non habet injuriam.* The execution of law does no injury. *Scire leges non hoc est verba earum tenere, sed vim ac potestatem.* To know the laws is not to observe their words alone, but their force and power. *Interest reipublicae ne maleficia remaneant impunita.* It concerns the state that crimes do not go unpunished. *Ex nudo pacto non oritur nascitur actio.* No action arises on a contract without a consideration. *Nemo jus sibi dicere potest.* No one can declare the law for himself.

ENFRANCHISE, verb *accipere,* admit to citizenship, *adsciscere,* affranchise, allow, authorize, disenthrall, emancipate, empower, endow with political privilege, franchise, free, free from political disabilities, give liberty to, give political privileges to, give the right to vote, grant, liberate, license, manumit, permit, permit to vote, qualify, *recipere,* release, restore to liberty, sanction, set at liberty, set free

ENGAGE (Hire), verb appoint, arrange for the services of, arrange for the use of, bind, book, charter, commission, *conducere,* contract for, employ, enlist, enlist in one's service, fill a position, give a job to, give a situation to, give employment to, lease, let, obtain, procure, put to work, put under contract, reserve, retain, secure, set to work, staff with, take into one's employ, take into service

ASSOCIATED CONCEPTS: engage the services of an employee

ENGAGE (Involve), verb absorb, assail, associate, attack, battle, become involved, bring into conflict, busy, carry on hostilities, combat, compete, connect, contend, contest, draw in, encounter, engross, enmesh, entangle, enter into, enter into conflict with, entertain, fight with, fill one's time, gear with, hold the interest of, *incipere,* interest, interlock, join battle with, link, meet, mesh together, occupy, oppose, partake, participate, share, struggle, take on, take part, tangle, undertake, wage war, war with

ASSOCIATED CONCEPTS: doing business, engaged in agriculture, engaged in commerce, engaged in doing business, engaged in interstate commerce, engaged in manufacture, engaged in transacting business, primarily engaged, principally engaged

ENGAGE IN, verb accept, apply oneself to, assume, be occupied with, carry on, commence, commit to, concern oneself with, conduct, contract, devote oneself to, embark on, employ, endeavor, execute, exercise, follow, labor, manage, operate, participate, ply, practice, prosecute, pursue, take up, touch, undertake, use, venture on, work

ENGAGEMENT (Appointment), noun adventure, application, assignation, assurance, commitment, competition, contract, covenant, duty, encounter, enlistment, enterprise, interaction, interaffiliation, interplay, interview, involvement, meeting, obligation, pursuit, responsibility, undertaking

ENGAGEMENT (Confrontation), noun altercation, argument, battle, brawl, clash, collision, combat, conflict, confrontation, contention, disagreement, discord, dispute, embroilment, fight, fracas, fray, skirmish, squabble, struggle, wrangle

ENGENDER, verb arouse, author, be the cause of, bear, beget, begin, breed, bring about, bring forth, bring into being, bring into existence, call forth, call into being, cause, cause to exist, create, develop, effect, effectuate, excite, execute, furnish, *generare,* generate, *gignere,* give rise to, hatch, help, induce, incite, induce, initiate, institute, lead to, manufacture, occasion, originate, plant, produce, provoke, spawn, start, stir up, take birth, yield

ASSOCIATED CONCEPTS: engender a settlement

ENGINE, noun apparatus, appliance, contraption, contrivance, convenience, device, facility, generator, implementation, locomotive, machine, machinery, means, mechanical aid, mechanical device, mechanism, method, motor, muscle power, power plant, powerhouse, source of power, tool, transducer, transformer, turbine, utensil, utility

ENGINEER, noun architect, artificer, contractor, contriver, creator, framer, instigator, inventor, machinist, maker, manager, mechanic, originator, producer

ENGINEER, verb arrange, assemble, brew, build, cause, collude, compose, conspire, construct, contrive, control, create, devise, direct, erect, finagle, handle, hatch, intrigue, jockey, machinate, manage, maneuver, manipulate, manufacture, militate, negotiate, operate, originate, oversee, pioneer, plan, plot, produce, program, raise, regulate, run, scheme, wangle

ENGROSS (Copy), verb address, assimilate, inscribe, inscroll, record, scribe, scroll, superscribe, transcribe, write, write out

ENGROSS (Monopolize), verb absorb, busy, obsess, consume, corner, devour, drink in, employ, engage, haunt, have all to oneself, immerse, impropriate, occupy, preoccupy, take up

ENGULF, verb absorb, annihilate, bury, consume, deluge, destroy, devour, drown, entomb, exterminate, immerse, inundate, liquidate, overcome, overwhelm, submerge, submerse, swallow up

ENHANCE, verb add to, advance in value, aggrandize, *amplificare,* amplify, appreciate, *augere,* augment, better, boost, brighten, cultivate, deepen, develop, elaborate, elevate, emphasize, enlarge, enrich, escalate, exaggerate, expand, extend, heighten, improve, increase the value of, intensify, lift, magnify, make better, make improvements, make more attractive, make more valuable, maximize, perfect, polish, promote, raise, refine, reinforce, retouch, sharpen, strengthen, touch up, upgrade, uplift, upraise

ASSOCIATED CONCEPTS: enhanced in value

ENHANCEMENT (Exaggeration), noun aggrandizement, elaboration, embellishment, exaggeration, exaltation, hyperbole, magnification, overstatement, superlative

ENHANCEMENT *(Increase),* **noun** accession, advance, aggrandizement, amelioration, amendment, amplification, augmentation, betterment, boom, deepening, development, enlargement, enrichment, exaltation, heightening, improvement, intensification, melioration, progress, raising, reform, renewal, revaluation, strengthening

ENIGMA, noun *aenigma, ambages,* ambiguous saying, arcanum, bewilderment, braintwister, complexity, confusing statement, confusion, difficulty, inexplicable statement, inscrutable person, knotty point, mystery, obscure question, obscure statement, paradox, perplexity, poser, problem, puzzle, puzzling problem, question, riddle, secret, stumper, teaser

ENIGMATIC, adjective ambiguous, baffling, bewildering, bothering, confounding, confusing, conjectural, cryptic, disconcerting, esoteric, hard to understand, hidden, inexplicable, mysterious, mystifying, nebulous, obscure, of hidden meaning, perplexing, perturbing, puzzling, secret, veiled

ENJOIN, verb abate, ban, bar, barricade, bid, block, blockade, bring to a standstill, cause to halt, charge, command, constrain, curb, decree, dictate, direct, disallow, disapprove, discountenance, embargo, exact, exhort, foil, forbid, forbid by law, forestall, frustrate, give orders, hamper, hinder, hold in check, impede, impose, impose a ban, impose a duty, impose a task, impose with authority, inhibit, insist on, instruct, interdict, issue an order, keep from happening, keep in bounds, lay under embargo, limit, make unlawful, not countenance, not permit, oblige, order, place under interdiction, place under the ban, positively direct, preclude, prevent, prohibit, prohibit by legal injunction, prompt, proscribe, put a stop to, put an end to, put under an injunction, put under an interdiction, put under embargo, put under the ban, quash, quell, repress, require, restrain, restrain by injunction, restrict, retard, rule, stem, stop, suppress, thwart
ASSOCIATED CONCEPTS: permanent injunction, preliminary injunction, temporary injunction

ENJOYMENT *(Pleasure),* **noun** amusement, bliss, delectation, delight, diversion, ecstasy, entertainment, exhilaration, *fructus,* gaiety, *gaudium,* gratification, gusto, merriment, recreation, refreshment, rejoicing, relaxation, relish, satisfaction, thrill, treat, zest
FOREIGN PHRASES: Omnis privatio praesupponit habitum. Every privation presupposes a former enjoyment.

ENJOYMENT *(Use),* **noun** avail, disposal, employment, habitation, occupancy, occupation, ownership, possession, prerogative, proprietorship, retention, seisin, tenancy, tenure, usuage, utilization
ASSOCIATED CONCEPTS: adverse enjoyment, covenant of quiet enjoyment

ENLARGE, verb add to, aggrandize, *amplificare,* amplify, annex, *augere,* augment, broaden, build, build up, develop, *dilatare,* dilate, distend, elaborate, enhance, escalate, exaggerate, expatiate, extend, fatten, fill out, grow, increase, inflate, intensify, lengthen, magnify, make greater, make larger, multiply, progress, protract, raise, spread, stretch, supplement, swell, widen
ASSOCIATED CONCEPTS: materially alter, repair

ENLARGEMENT *(Addition),* **noun** accession, advance, advancement, aggrandizement, aggravation, augmentation, broadening, expatiation, explication, extension, fullness, growth, increment, intensification, multiplication, proliferation, spreading, tumefaction, widening

ENLARGEMENT *(Exaggeration),* **noun** amplification, blow-up, development, distortion, enhancement, expansion, increase, inflation, magnification, overstatement

ENLIGHTEN, verb account for, acquaint, apprise, clarify, disclose, divulge, edify, educate, elucidate, enable to comprehend, enable to see, enucleate, explain, explicate, expound, free from ignorance, free from prejudice, free from superstition, give reason for, illuminate, illumine, illustrate, impart, inform, *inluminare, inlustrare,* instruct, interpret, make aware, make clear, make known, notify, report, reveal, shed light upon, simplify, spell out, teach, tutor

ENLIGHTENMENT, noun appreciation, awakening, clarification, cognition, cognizance, comprehension, direction, disabusal, disclosure, edification, education, elucidation, enucleation, experience, explication, explanation, familiarity, illumination, insight, instruction, intelligence, knowledge, learning, mention, monition, objectivity, perception, publication, rationalism, realization, recognition, refinement, sense, teaching, tip, understanding

ENLIST, verb activate, admit, attract, call up, conscript, draft, employ, engage, enroll, get, impress, induce, induct, initiate, inscribe, join, mobilize, muster, procure, recruit, register, retain, sign up
ASSOCIATED CONCEPTS: conscription, enlist into a voluntary army, enlist support of witnesses, enlistment

ENMITY, adjective acrimony, alienation, anger, animosity, animus, antagonism, antipathy, aversion, bitterness, contention, despise, dislike, estrangement, hard feelings, hate, hatred, hostility, ill will, invidiousness, loathe, malevolence, malice, malignity, odium, opposition, rancor, repugnance, venom

ENNOBLE, verb a higher position, adorn, advance, aggrandize, bestow honor upon, boost, build up, canonize, confer an honor, consecrate, deify, dignify, distinguish, elevate, erect, exalt, glorify, grace, heighten, hold aloft, honor, knight, lift, lionize, look up to, magnify, praise, promote, prop, put on a pedestal, raise, sanctify, uplift

ENORMITY, noun complexity, enormous size, enormousness, immense scope, immensity, vast size
ASSOCIATED CONCEPTS: enormity of a crime

ENORMOUS, adjective colossal, excessive, gigantic, huge, immense, large, mammoth, massive, tremendous, vast
ASSOCIATED CONCEPTS: enormous burden of proof to overcome

ENOUGH, noun a satisfactory amount, a substantial amount, a sufficient amount, a suitable amount, abundance, acceptable amount, adequacy, adequate amount, ample amount, complete amount, copious amount, full amount, just amount, minimal amount, plenteous amount, plenty
ASSOCIATED CONCEPTS: enough evidence, imprisonment, tough enough laws

ENRAGE, verb acerbate, agitate, anger, enflame, exacerbate, exasperate, fire up, incense, inflame, infuriate, irk, irritate, lash into, madden, provoke, rile
ASSOCIATED CONCEPTS: provocation, self-defense

ENRICHMENT, noun adornment, advancement, aggrandizement, appreciation, beautification, betterment, cultivation, decoration, development, embellishment,

endowment, enhancement, furtherance, improvement, ornamentation, refinement, reward
ASSOCIATED CONCEPTS: unjust enrichment, unlawful enrichment

ENROLL, *verb* accept as a member, *adscribere,* book, catalogue, docket, draft, enlist, enter, enter on a list, enter on a record, enter on a register, file, induct, initiate, inscribe, join, list, make a member, make a record, record, recruit, register, sign up, subscribe

ENSCONCE, *verb* blanket, camouflage, cloak, cloud, conceal, cover, cover up, curtain, disguise, eclipse, encase, enclose, enshield, enshroud, envelop, enwrap, guard, hide, hide away, hide from view, hide securely, keep from danger, keep guarded, keep hidden, keep safe, keep secret, keep under cover, mask, obscure, preserve, protect, safeguard, screen, seclude, secrete, secure, shade, shadow, sheathe, shelter, shield, shroud, suppress, veil, watch over, wrap

ENSCONCED, *adjective* deep-rooted, deeply engrained, deeply implanted, deeply manifest, engrained, established, impeded, imprinted, indoctrinated, injected, instilled, manifest
ASSOCIATED CONCEPTS: precedence deep-rooted in the law, common law

ENSHROUD, *verb* blanket, camouflage, case, cloak, cloud, conceal, cover, curtain, disguise, eclipse, encase, enclose, ensconce, envelop, enwrap, guard, hide, hood, invest, keep clandestine, keep from notice, keep from view, keep hidden, keep out of sight, keep under cover, mantle, mask, obscure, obstruct the view of, prevent from being discovered, prevent from being seen, protect, render invisible, screen, seclude, secrete, shade, sheathe, shelter, shield, shroud, surround, swathe, veil, visor, wrap

ENSNARE, *verb* allure, ambuscade, ambush, apprehend, bait, bamboozle, beguile, bilk, bluff, *capere,* capture, catch, catch unprepared, cheat, cozen, deceive, decoy, defraud, delude, dupe, enmesh, entangle, entice, entrap, fool, gull, hoax, hoodwink, hook, *inlicere, inretire,* lay a trap for, lead astray, lead on by artifice, lure, misdirect, misguide, mislead, net, outmaneuver, outwit, play one false, set a trap for, snare, take advantage of, take by craft, take by stratagem, trap, trepan, trick, victimize, waylay
ASSOCIATED CONCEPTS: entrapment

ENSUE, *verb* arise, attend as consequence, be caused by, be due to, be subsequent, be the effect of, come after, come afterward, come next, derive, develop, eventuate, flow, follow, follow as a consequence, follow in a train of events, grow out of, issue, occur, proceed, result, spring, succeed, supervene, transpire

ENSUING, *adjective* after, following, later, next, posterior, resultant, resulting, subsequent, succeeding, successive, sequential

ENSURE, *verb* ascertain, assure, certify, check, clinch, confirm, corroborate, dismiss doubt, endorse, give security, give surety, guarantee, indemnify against loss, insure, keep from harm, keep safe, make certain, make sure, offer collateral, promise, protect, safeguard, secure, underwrite, verify, warrant

ENTAIL, *verb* *adferre,* call for, demand, force, impel, include as a necessary consequence, *inferre,* involve, make

essential, make incumbent, make inescapable, make necessary, make requisite, make unavoidable, necessitate, need, obligate, occasion, require

ENTANGLEMENT *(Confusion),* **noun** agitation, chaos, commotion, complexity, complication, confusedness, derangement, disarrangement, disarry, disorder, disorganization, embroilment, enmeshment, ferment, imbroglio, intricacy, irregularity, jumble, maze, mix-up, snag, snarl, tumult

ENTANGLEMENT *(Involvement),* **noun** dilemma, entrapment, fix, *implicatio,* implication, incrimination, inculpation, predicament, scrape, strait

ENTER *(Go in),* **verb** arrive, board, come in, cross the threshold, effect an entrance, gain admittance, gain entry, go into, *inire, intrare, introire,* make an entrance, pass into, set foot in, step in, walk in
ASSOCIATED CONCEPTS: breaking and entering, forcible entry, immigration, lawful entry, open and peaceable entry, trespass

ENTER *(Insert),* **verb** implant, infuse, inject, intercalate, interject, interpose, introduce, intromit, place into, put in, stick in

ENTER *(Penetrate),* **verb** bore, cut into, cut through, drill, empierce, gore, impale, infiltrate, interpenetrate, invade, lance, perforate, pervade, pierce, prick, puncture, sink into, stab, transpierce

ENTER *(Record),* **verb** catalogue, check in, chronicle, enroll, file, inscribe, inscroll, jot down, list, log, make an entry, mark down, note, place in the record, post, put down, put in writing, put on record, *referre,* register, report, set down, tabulate, take down, transcribe, write down, write in
ASSOCIATED CONCEPTS: entered on the record, entry of a judgment

ENTERPRISE *(Economic organization),* **noun** business, business establishment, commercial establishment, company, concern, corporate body, corporation, firm, house, industry, syndicate
ASSOCIATED CONCEPTS: commercial enterprise, free enterprise, private enterprise

ENTERPRISE *(Undertaking),* **noun** activity, adventure, attempt, campaign, cause, effort, endeavor, engagement, *inceptum,* job, occupation, operation, opus, plan, program, project, pursuit, scheme, task, undertaking, venture
ASSOCIATED CONCEPTS: mutual enterprise

ENTERTAINMENT, *noun* amusement, cabaret, carnival, celebration, cheer, concert, delight, enjoyment, exhibition, extravaganza, festival, firm industry, frolic, fun, gaiety, gala, gratification, jollity, joviality, lark, merriment, merrymaking, movie industry, party, pastime, performance, pleasure, presentation, production, reception, recreation, regalement, relaxation, show, spectacle, treat
ASSOCIATED CONCEPTS: entertainment law

ENTHUSIASM, *noun* animation, bounce, buoyancy, delight, determination, devotedness, devotion, eagerness, ebullience, ecstasy, elation, emotion, energy, excitement, exhilaration, exuberance, feeling, fervor, fever, fire, force, frenzy, furor, fury, glow, gusto, heat, intensity, intentness, interest, joy, keenness, liveliness, mania, passion, rage, rapture, relish, snap, spirit, vehemence, verve, vigor, vim, vitality, zeal, zealousness, zest, zip

ENTHUSIAST, verb addict, adherent, admirer, aficionado, angel, backer, believer, booster, champion, collector, devotee, disciple, fan, fanatic, fiend, follower, hound, lover, maniac, partisan, promoter, supporter, zealot

ENTHUSIASTIC, adjective absorbed, all fired up, all worked up, animated, anxious, ardent, attracted, avid, burning, chomping at the bit, charged up, crazed, delighted, demonstrative, desiring, desirous, dying to, eager, earnest, ebullient, ecstatic, effervescent, effusive, emotive, energetic, enraptured, enthused, excited, exhilarated, expressive, exuberant, fanatical, fascinated, fervent, fervid, fevered, feverish, fiery, gushing, impassioned, impatient, intent, interested, keen, keen about, longing, passionate, spirited, thrilled, vehement, vigorous, vivacious, wholehearted, zealous

ENTICE, verb allure, bait, cajole, coax, decoy, divert, induce, inveigh, lure, seduce, tempt

ENTICEMENT, noun wrongful allure, wrongful allurement, wrongful appeal, wrongful attraction, wrongful attractiveness, wrongful bait, wrongful decoy, wrongful draw, wrongful glamour, wrongful inducement, wrongful invitation, wrongful lure, wrongful seduction, wrongful solicitation, wrongful temptation
ASSOCIATED CONCEPTS: coercion and enticement, illegal enticement

ENTIRE, adjective absolute, across the boards, aggregate, all-inclusive, complete, complete gamut, complete universe, comprehensive, entire universe, exhaustive, extensive, full, full-fledged, gross, inclusive, in-depth, integral, plenary, sound, sweeping, thorough, total, unabated, unabridged, unalloyed, unbounded, undiminished, undividable, unequivocal, unimpaired, unimpeded, unitary, universal, unlimited, unmitigated, unmodified, unqualified, unrestricted, whole, widesweeping
ASSOCIATED CONCEPTS: entire act, entire benefit, entire contract, entire estate, entire use

ENTIRETY, noun accumulation, aggregate, all, amount, assemblage, collectiveness, collectivity, completeness, completion, comprehensiveness, congeries, ensemble, entire amount, entireness, everything, exhaustiveness, fullness, gross, gross amount, inclusiveness, indiscerptibility, indiscerptibleness, intactness, lot, lump, mass, sum, total, totality, totalness, *totus*, undiminished quantity, undividedness, whole, wholeness
ASSOCIATED CONCEPTS: entirety clause, tenants by the entirety, tenants in common

ENTITLED, adjective allowed, authorized, deserved, deserving, desirable, due, earned, eligible, empowered, fit, having the right, justified, labeled, legalized, licensed, merited, ordained, permitted, privileged, qualified, sanctioned, suitable, warranted, worthy

ENTITY, noun actuality, being, body, character, corpus, creature, embodiment, existence, individual, item, life, living thing, matter, module, object, oneness, organism, separate existence, single item, single piece, specimen, tangible object, unit, unit of being
ASSOCIATED CONCEPTS: corporate entity, distinct entity, legal entity, separate entity

ENTRANCE, noun access, adit, *aditus*, admission, anteroom, approach, door, entry, entryway, foyer, gangway, gate, gateway, illapse, infiltration, influx, ingress, inlet, inroad, insertion, introgression, *introitus*, invasion, lobby, means of access, means of entering, mouth, opening, *ostium*, passage, passageway, penetration, place of entry, portal, reception, threshold, vestibule, way in
ASSOCIATED CONCEPTS: forcible entrance, public entrance

ENTRAP, verb allure, bait, beckon, befool, beguile, bring unawares into danger, bring unawares into evil, capere, catch, catch by artifice, deceive, decoy, draw as by a lure, draw by artful inducements, draw in, dupe, enmesh, ensnare, entangle, entice, fool, hold out allurement, hold out temptation, *inlicere, inretire,* inveigle, lay a snare for, lay a trap for, lead astray, lead by inducement, lead into danger by artifice, lead into temptation, lead on, lure, lure into a compromising act, set a snare for, set a trap for, snare, take in, tempt, trap, trip up
ASSOCIATED CONCEPTS: predisposition to commit a crime

ENTREATY, noun adjuration, appeal, beseechment, call, cry, earnest request, impetration, imploration, importunity, invocation, *obsecratio*, obsecration, *obtestatio*, petition, plea, prayer, *preces*, request, solicitation, suit, supplication

ENTRENCH, verb advance, barricade, brace, bulwark, buttress, defend, embattle, embed, encroach, establish, fortify, immerse in, immersed in, infiltrate, invade, make inroads, overrun, protect, reinforce, shore up, solidify, surround, wall
ASSOCIATED CONCEPTS: entrench leadership, entrench power

ENTREPRENEUR, noun administrator, baron, business leader, businessman, businessperson, businesswoman, director, employer, enterpriser, exec, executive, financier, industrialist, magnate, man of commerce, owner, producer, top executive, tycoon
ASSOCIATED CONCEPTS: entrepreneur law, free trade

ENTRUST, verb appoint, assign, assign the care of, authorize, charge with a duty, charge with a trust, commit, *committere, concredere,* consign, delegate, depute, deputize, devolve, elect, empower, give a mandate, give a responsibility to, invest empower, license, make someone guardian of, *mandare,* place in the protection of, put in charge, trust, turn over for safekeeping
ASSOCIATED CONCEPTS: entrust goods, entrust personal property
FOREIGN PHRASES: *Securius expediuntur negotia commissa pluribus, et plus vident oculi quam oculus.* Matters which are entrusted to several persons are executed more surely, because eyes see more than an eye.

ENTRY (Entrance), **noun** access, adit, admission, entrance, immigration, ingress, ingression, passage
ASSOCIATED CONCEPTS: entry on land, forcible entry, lawful entry, trespass

ENTRY (Record), **noun** account, bulletin, chronicle, deposition, file, information preserved in writing, inscription, item, memo, memorandum, minute, *nomen*, note, recorded item, registration, report, statement recorded in a book, writing, written record
ASSOCIATED CONCEPTS: entry by court, entry in regular course of business, entry of an appeal, entry of an appearance, entry of an order, entry of judgment, writ of entry

ENUMERATE, verb be specific, catalog, count, designate, detail, differentiate, enroll, *enumerare*, index, inventory, itemize, keep count, list, make a list, mention, mention one by one, mention specifically, name expressly, name one by one, number, numerate, point out, specify, tabulate

ASSOCIATED CONCEPTS: descriptive enumeration, enumerated counts, enumerated motions

FOREIGN PHRASES: *Enumeratio infirmat regulam in casibus non enumeratis.* Enumeration disaffirms the rule in cases which are not enumerated.

ENUNCIATE, *verb*   accent, affirm, announce, annunciate, apprise, articulate, assert, asseverate, aver, declaim, declare, *edicere*, emit, enounce, explain, express, give expression, give utterance, *indicare*, inform, intonate, intone, make an announcement, mouth, notify, phonate, proclaim, profess, promulgate, pronounce, pronounce distinctly, pronounce in a distinct manner, *pronuntiare,* publish, put in words, say, speak, speak clearly, state, stress, tell, utter, verbalize, vocalize, voice

ENVELOP, *verb*   beleaguer, beseige, beset, blanket, box, cage, case, *circumfundere*, circumscribe, cloak, cloister, close in, clothe, compass, completely cover, conceal, confine, corral, cover, curtain, edge, embox, embrace, encapsulate, encase, encircle, enclose, encompass, enfold, enshroud, ensphere, environ, enwrap, fence in, frame, go around, hedge in, hem in, hide, hood, *involvere,* mask, *obducere,* obscure, overlay, protect, screen, sheathe, shelter, shield, shroud, surround, swaddle, swathe, veil, wall in, wrap, wrap around, wrap up

ENVELOPMENT, *noun*   clothe, concealment, cover, embracement, encasement, enclosement, hood, overlay, protection, screen, sheathe, shelter, shield, shroud, surroundings

ENVIRONMENT, *noun*   atmosphere, aura, circumstances, context, environs, locality, milieu, situation, surroundings

ENVIRONMENTAL CONSERVATION, *noun*   maintenance of the environment, maintenance of the habitat, preservation of the environs, protection of the environment

EPHEMERAL, *adjective*   *brevis,* brief, caducous, *caducus,* continuing for a short time, deciduous, disappearing, elusive, enduring only a very short time, ephemerous, evanescent, existing for a short time, fleeting, fugacious, fugitive, hurried, impermanent, lasting a very short time, meteoric, meteorical, momentary, mortal, nondurable, not lasting, passing, perishable, short, short-lived, temporal, temporary, transient, transitory, unenduring, *unius diei,* unstable, vanishing, volatile

EPHEMERALLY, *adverb*   a condition of short duration, a passing condition, a situation of finite duration, brief condition, evanescence, fading condition, fleeting condition, fluffiness, insubstantiality, light overview, momentary condition, nonsubstantial perspective, short-lived condition, temporary situation, transience, transitory situation

EPIC, *adjective*   chronicle, classic, colossal, descriptive, detailed, elevated, exalted, fabulous, fantastic, grand, grandiose, great, heroic, high-flown, high-sounding, historic, historical, history, impressive, inflated, legend, legendary, lofty, majestic, major, momentous, monumental, narrative, on a grand scale, saga, significant, story, superhuman, tremendous, vast

EPIDEMIC (Disease), *noun*   ailment, contagion, disease, endemic, illness, infection, malady, pandemic, plague, scourge, sickness

ASSOCIATED CONCEPTS: antiepidemic law, epidemic law, pandemic

EPIDEMIC (Large scale), *noun*   a far-reaching occurrence, a rampant situation, a universal situation, a widespread situation, acceleration, an omnibus situation, burgeoning number, comprehensiveness, extensiveness, flurry, increasing number, mounting number, upsurge, upswing, upturn

ASSOCIATED CONCEPTS: class action

EPIPHANY, *noun*   comprehension, contemplation, creation, disclosure, divine inspiration, divine revelation, expression, innovation, manifestation, meaning, mystical experience, mystical intuition, prophecy, prophetic, remarkable idea, revelation, revolutionary idea, revolutionary solution, understanding

EPISODE, *noun*   chapter, circumstance, event, experience, happening, incident, occasion, occurrence, sequel, short-lived event, sudden event

EPITOME, *noun*   characteristic part, core, embodiment, essence, exemplification, model, representative, standard, *summarium,* typical component, typical part, typification

EQUAL, *adjective*   abreast, *aequalis, aequus,* alike, balanced, coequal, coextensive, coordinate, democratic, equable, equalized, equally divided, equidistant, equilateral, equipollent, equitable, even, evenhanded, fair, fairminded, homologous, identical in amount, identical in quantity, identical in size, identical in value, impartial, just, like, like in degree, like in quantity, matched, of the same degree, of the same rank, on a par, on even terms, on the same level, same, similar, symmetric, symmetrical, tantamount, tied, to the same degree, unbiased, unchanging, undeviating, unfluctuating, uniform, unprejudiced, unvaried, unvarying

ASSOCIATED CONCEPTS: equal before the law, equal in degree, equal in value, equal protection of laws, equal taxation, equally divided, separate but equal

EQUATE, *verb*   analyze, assess, balance, compare, coordinate, counterbalance, determine, equalize, judge, match, measure against

ASSOCIATED CONCEPTS: equate law with morality, equating law with justice

EQUIPMENT, *noun*   accouterment, apparatus, appointment, material, provisioning, supplies

ASSOCIATED CONCEPTS: equipment trust agreement, equipment trust certificate

EQUIPOISE, *noun*   balance, counterbalance, counterpoise, counterweight, equal distribution of weight, equality of force, equality of weight, equilibration, equilibrium, equiponderance, even balance, evenness, match, offset, parity, stability, symmetry

EQUITABLE, *adjective*   *aequus,* deserved, detached, disinterested, dispassionate, distributing justice, equal, evenhanded, exhibiting equity, existing in equity, fair, fairminded, giving each his due, honest, honorable, impartial, incorrupt, incorruptible, *iustus,* just, merited, *meritus,* neutral, objective, principled, proper, reasonable, right, righteous, scrupulous, unbiased, unbigoted, unchallengeable, unprejudiced, upright

ASSOCIATED CONCEPTS: equitable assignment, equitable charge, equitable claim, equitable conversion, equitable counterclaim, equitable defenses, equitable estate, equitable estoppel, equitable interest, equitable lien, equitable life estate, equitable mortgage, equitable rate of interest, equitable recission, equitable recoupment, equitable relief, equitable remedy, equitable rights, equitable set-off, equitable title, fair and equitable value

EQUITY *(Justice),* **noun** *aequitas, aequum,* chancery, evenhandedness, fair-mindedness, fair treatment, fairness, honesty, ideal justice, impartial justice, *iustitia,* justice, justice as distinguished from conformity to enactments or statutes, justice ascertained by natural reason, justice under the law, justness, natural right, quality of being equal and fair, reasonableness, recourse to the principles of natural justice, redress, remedial justice, right dealing, righteousness, rightfulness, spirit of the law, unwritten law, uprightness

ASSOCIATED CONCEPTS: balance of equities, chancery, equitable right, equity action, equity jurisdiction, existing equities, suit in equity

FOREIGN PHRASES: *Nihil tam conveniens est naturali aequitati quam unumquodque dissolvi eo ligamine quo ligatum est.* Nothing is so agreeable to natural equity as that a thing should be dissolved by the same means by which it was bound. *Lex aequitate gaudet; appetit perfectum; est norma recti.* The law delights in equity; it grasps at perfection; it is a rule of right. *In fictione juris semper aequitas existit.* In a fiction of law, equity is always present. *Equitas sequitur legem.* Equity follows the law. *Lex respicit aequitatem.* The law regards equity. *Ratio in jure aequitas integra.* Reason in law is impartial equity. *Nulli vendemus, nulli negabimus, aut differemus rectum vel justitian.* We will sell to none, we will deny to none, we will delay to none, either equity or justice. *Judex ante oculos aequitatem semper habere debet.* A judge ought always to have equity before his eyes. *Aequitas supervacua odit.* Equity abhors superfluous things. *Aequitas uxoribus, liberis, creditoribus maxime favet.* Equity favors wives and children, creditors most of all. *Aequitas est quasi aequalitas.* Equity is as it were equality. *Aequum et bonum est lex legum.* That which is equitable and right is the law of laws. *In omnibus quidem, maxime tamen injure, aequitas spectanda sit.* In all matters, but especially in law, equity should be regarded. *Prima pars aequitatis aequalitas.* The prime element of equity is equality. *Nemo allegans suam turpitudinem audien dus est.* No one should be permitted to testify as a witness to his own baseness or wickedness. *Nemo ex suo delicto meliorem suam conditionem facere potest.* No one can improve his condition by his own misdeed. *Jure naturae aequum est neminem cum alterius detrimento et injuria fieri locupletiorem.* According to the laws of nature, it is just that no one should be enriched by the detriment and injury of another. *Nihil iniquius quam aequitatem nimis intendere.* Nothing is more unjust than to extend equity too far. *Judex aequitatem semper spectare debet.* A judge ought always to regard equity. *Bonus judex secundum aequum et bonum judicat, et aequitatem stricto juri praefert.* Good judges decide according to what is just and right, and prefer equity to strict law. *Si aliquid ex solemnibus deficiat, cum aequitas poscit, subveniendum est.* If anything is deficient in formal requisites, where equity requires it, it should be supplied. *Aequitas nunquam contravenit legis.* Equity never counteracts the laws. *Aequitas non facit jus, sed juri auxiliatur.* Equity does not make law, but assists law. *Aequitas ignorantiae opitulatur, oscitantiae non item.* Equity assists ignorance, but not carelessness.

Vigilantibus et non dormientibus jura subveniunt. The laws aid the vigilant and not those who slumber. *Aequitas agit in personam.* Equity acts upon the person. *Jure naturae aequum est neminem cum alterius detrimento et injuria fieri locupletiorem.* By natural law it is not just that any one should be enriched by the detriment or injury of another. *Hoc quidem perquam durum est, sed ita lex scripta est.* This indeed is exceedingly hard, but such is the written law. *Nemo debet aliena jactura locupletari.* No one ought to gain by another's loss. *Frustra legis auxilium quaerit qui in legem committit.* He vainly seeks the aid of the law who transgresses the law. *Commodum ex injuria sua non habere debet.* No person ought to derive any advantage by his own wrong. *Nemo ex proprio dolo consequitur actionem.* No one acquires a right of action from his own fraud.

EQUITY *(Share of ownership),* **noun** allotment, apportionment, claim, division, interest, investment, part, portion, right, stake, vested interest

EQUIVALENT, adjective alike, as good as, balancing, coequal, comparable, compensatory, equal, equal in effect, equal in force, equal in power, equal in significance, equal in value, equalized, equipollent, even, identical, identical in size, identical in value, interchangeable, like, of equal force, of equal value, of equal weight, on a par with, parallel, *pro re valere,* reciprocal, same, similar, substitutable, synonymous, tantamount, without difference

ASSOCIATED CONCEPTS: equivalent acts, fair equivalent, substantially equivalent

EQUIVOCAL, adjective ambiguous, *ambiguus,* ambivalent, amphibological, amphibolous, *anceps,* bewildering, cloudy, confusing, controversial, debatable, deceptive, dim, disputable, doubtful, *dubious,* dubius, enigmatic, enigmatical, equivocating, equivocatory, hard to understand, hazy, imperspicuous, imprecise, indecisive, indefinite, indeterminate, misleading, moot, nebulous, obscure, of doubtful meaning, of uncertain significance, open, open to question, perplexing, possessing double meaning, prevaricating, puzzling, questionable, recondite, shadowy, uncertain, unclarified, unclear, undecided, undefined, undetermined, unexplained, unintelligible, unplain, unresolved, unsolved, unsure, untransparent, vague, veiled

FOREIGN PHRASES: *Verba aequivoca, ac in dubio sensu posita, intelliguntur digniori et potentiori sensu.* Equivocal words and those which are used in a doubtful sense are to be understood in their more worthy and effective sense.

EQUIVOCATE, verb avoid a straight answer, be ambiguous, be false, be unclear, be untruthful, be vague, deceive, disguise, dissemble, dissimulate, dodge, elude, evade, fence, hedge, lie, misguide, misinform, mislead, misrepresent, misstate, mystify, palter, parry, prevaricate, quibble, shift, shuffle, *tergiversari,* tergiversate

ERADICATE, verb abolish, annihilate, annul, black out, blot out, cause to cease, deal destruction, delete, demolish, deracinate, destroy, destroy thoroughly, displace, dispose of, dissolve, do away with, do away with completely, efface, eject, eliminate, *eradere,* erase, *evellere, excidere,* expunge, expurgate, exstirpare, exterminate, extinguish, extirpate, extract, lay waste, leave no trace of, leave no vestige of, liquidate, obliterate, purge, remove, remove utterly, stamp out, strike out, subtract, sweep away, unroot, uproot, void, weed out

ERASE, verb abolish, annihilate, annul, blot out, deal destruction, delete, demolish, destroy, dispose of, dissolve, do away with completely, efface, eliminate, exceed the record, expunge, exterminate, extinguish, leave no vestige of, obliterate, purge, remove, rewrite the records, stamp out, strike out, terminate, uproot, void, wipe out

ASSOCIATED CONCEPTS: distribution of evidence, erase debt through bankruptcy, tampering with evidence

ERODE, verb abrade, break down, consume, decay, decrease, deteriorate, diminish, disintegrate, dissolve, file, gradually eat away, grind, lessen, lose, make thin, rasp, recede, reduce, rub away, scrape, shrink, strip, waste, weaken, wear, wear away, wear down, wear down by friction, weather

ASSOCIATED CONCEPTS: erode the credibility of a witness

EROSION, noun abrasion, attrition, breakdown, consumption, crumbling, decay, decrease, decrement, deterioration, detrition, diminishment, diminution, disappearance, disintegration, dissolution, gradual eating away, gradual wearing away, grinding, lessening, loss, recession, reduction, rubbing away, shrinkage, thinning out, waste, wear, wearing away, wearing down by friction

ERR, verb be deceived, be erroneous, be in the wrong, be misguided, be misled, be mistaken, blunder, cause error, commit an error, delude oneself, *errare,* fall into error, *falli,* go amiss, go astray, go wrong, labor under a misapprehension, make a mistake, misapprehend, miscalculate, miscompute, misconstrue, misinterpret, misjudge, misreckon, mistake, misunderstand, receive a false impression, slip, *vagari*

ERRANT, adjective aberrant, amiss, astray, at fault, awry, deviant, deviating, deviatory, erring, erroneous, fallacious, faultful, faulty, imperfect, incorrect, misdirected, mistaken, not right, peccant, wrong

ERRATIC, adjective aberrant, abnormal, bizarre, capricious, changeable, changeful, eccentric, extraordinary, inconsistent, inconstant, intermittent, irregular, mercurial, not consistent, odd, outlandish, peculiar, random, sporadic, strange, unconventional, unfixed, unique, unorthodox, unpredictable, unsettled, unsteady, unusual, volatile, wandering

ASSOCIATED CONCEPTS: erratic behavior, erratic law enforcement, insanity

ERRONEOUS, adjective aberrant, amiss, blundering, containing error, counterfeit, devoid of truth, erring, fallacious, false, *falsus,* faulty, fictitious, groundless, illogical, inaccurate, incorrect, inexact, mistaken, spurious, unfounded, ungrounded, unreal, unsound, unsubstantial, unsustainable, untrue, wrong

ASSOCIATED CONCEPTS: erroneous assessment, erroneous decision, erroneous judgment, erroneous law, erroneous order, erroneous tax

ERROR, noun aberrance, aberrancy, aberration, *corrigendum,* delusion, deviation, distorted conception, distortion, *erratum,* erroneous statement, *error,* false conception, false impression, fault, flaw, inaccuracy, incorrect belief, inexactness, injustice, lapse, malapropism, misbelief, miscalculation, miscarriage of justice, miscomputation, misconception, misconjecture, miscount, misguidance, misinterpretation, misjudgment, misprint, misreckoning, misstatement, mistake, mistaken belief, mistaken judgment, mistranslation, misunderstanding, misuse of words, oversight, *peccatum,* poor judgment, slip, unfactualness, wrong course, wrong impression, wrongness

ASSOCIATED CONCEPTS: assignment of error, clerical error, confession of error, coram nobis, cross-errors, error apparent on the record, error of fact, error of judgment, error of law, fatal errors, fundamental error, harmful error, immaterial error, judicial error, legal error, manifest error, obvious error, plain error, prejudicial error, presentation of error, reversible error, substantial error, technical error, writ of error

FOREIGN PHRASES: *De fide et officio judicis non recipitur quaestio, sed de scientia, sive sit error juris, sive facti.* The good faith and honesty of a judge are not to be questioned, but his knowledge, whether it be in error of law or fact, may be. *Praesentia corporis tollit errorem nominis; et veritas nominis tollit er rorem demonstrationis.* The presence of the body cures an error in the name; and the accuracy of the name cures an error of description. *Veritas nominis tollit errorem demonstrationis.* Correctness of the name cures error in the description. *Veritas demonstrationis tollit errorem nominis.* Correctness of the description cures the error of the name. *Error qui non resistitur approbatur.* An error which is not resisted or opposed is waived. *Error fucatus nuda veritate in multis est probabilior; et saepenumero rationibus vincit veritatem error.* Error artfully disguised is, in many instances, more probable than naked truth; and frequently error overwhelms truth by argumentation. *Non videntur qui errant consentire.* Those who err are not deemed to consent. *Falsa orthographia, sive falsa grammatica, non vitiat concessionem.* Bad spelling or grammar does not vitiate a deed. *Vitium clerici nocere non debet.* Clerical errors ought not to prejudice. *Communis error facit jus.* Common error makes the law. *Tutius erratur ex parte mitiori.* It is safer to err on the side of leniency. *In generalibus versatur error.* Error thrives on generalities. *Error juris nocet.* An error of law works an injury. *Nihil facit error nominis cum de corpore constat.* An error in the name is of no consequence when there is certainty as to the person. *Tutius semper est errare acquietando, quam in puniendo; ex parte miseric ordiae quam ex parte justitiae.* It is always safer to err in acquitting than in punishing; on the side of mercy rather than on the side of justice. *Negatio conclusionis est error in lege.* The denial of a conclusion is error in law. *Errores ad sua principia referre, est refellere.* To refer errors to their sources is to refute them.

ESCAPE, verb abscond, achieve liberty, avoid, avoid arrest, avoid capture, avoid peril, become free, bolt, break from prison, break loose, break out, circumvent, decamp, depart custody, depart unlawfully, desert, disappear, *elabi,* elude, evade, *evadere,* find freedom, flee, *fugere,* gain liberty, get to safety, levant, make a getaway, run away, slip away, sneak off, steal away, take flight

ASSOCIATED CONCEPTS: extradition, flight, forcible escape

ESCAPE HATCH, noun alternative, choice, clause, condition, contingency, contrivance, definition, device, escape clause, escape valve, evasion, exception, excuse, expedient, given, grounds, loophole, means of escape, means to escape, mechanism for evasion, opening, outlet, saving clause, technicality, vehicle of escape, way of escape, way out

ASSOCIATED CONCEPTS: contracts

ESCHEAT, verb be forfeited back, cede back, go back, *hereditas caduca,* obstruct the course of descent, recede, regress, relapse, retrocede, retrovert, return, reverse, revert, revert to the state, slip back, turn back

ASSOCIATED CONCEPTS: forfeiture

ESCHEATMENT, noun act of reverting, confiscation, conversion to the government, deprivation, descent by forfeiture, forfeiture, reversion to the government, reversion to the state

ESCHEW, verb abstain, avoid, back away from, boycott, bypass, deny oneself, do without, elude, evade, flee from, forbear, forswear, give a wide berth, have nothing to do with, keep at a distance, keep away, keep clear of, keep out of the way, make unwelcome, neglect, recoil from, refrain, reject, shrink from, shun, stand aloof, stand clear, turn aside, turn away from, *vitare,* withdraw from

ESCROW, noun conditional deed held in trust, conditional instrument, contingent deed held in trust, entrustment, instrument held until the performance of a condition, written instrument of contingency

ESOTERIC, adjective abstruse, acroamatic, acroamatical, acroatic, arcane, cabalistic, cabalistical, concealed, confidential, confined to a select circle, covert, cryptic, deep, designed for the initiated, difficult to comprehend, enigmatic, enigmatical, esoterical, for a select few, hidden, involved, mysterious, mystic, mystical, obscure, occult, private, profound, puzzling, recondite, secret, shrouded, shrouded in mystery, understood by a select few, understood by the initiated, undisclosed, undivulged, untold, veiled

ESPIONAGE, noun espial, intelligence, obtaining national defense secrets, obtaining of classified information, practice of spying on others, search made for useful military information, secret observation, secret watching, spying, subversive activity, surveillance, systematic secret observation of the words and conduct of others, undercover work
ASSOCIATED CONCEPTS: espionage act, treason

ESPOUSE, verb abet, accept, adopt, advocate, aid, ally, argue for, assist, associate with, back, become a participator, become a partisan, champion, choose, contribute to, cooperate, defend, embrace, endorse, enter into, favor, help, join, lend oneself to, opt, participate, side with, sponsor, stand behind, stand up for, subscribe to, support, take part in, take up, uphold

ESQUIRE, noun adviser, advocate, *armiger,* attorney, attorney-at-law, barrister, counsel, counselor, counselor-at-law, jurisconsult, jurisprudent, jurist, lawyer, legal adviser, legal practitioner, legist, member of the bar, member of the legal profession, officer of the court, practitioner, solicitor
ASSOCIATED CONCEPTS: advice of counsel, assigned counsel, assistance of counsel, attorney of record, attorney's fees, benefit of counsel, Code of Professional Responsibility, counsel of record, denial of counsel, effective counsel, of counsel, Sixth Amendment, waiver of counsel

ESSENCE, noun basic part, core, embodiment, essential part, fundamental part, gist, heart, hypostasis, inmost nature, inner being, meaning, *natura,* nature, pith, quiddity, quintessence, soul, substance, *vis*
ASSOCIATED CONCEPTS: essence of a contract, essence of testimony by a witness

ESSENTIAL (Inherent), adjective basal, basic, basilar, basilary, elemental, fundamental, immanent, implicit, integral, intrinsic, intrinsical, main, primary

ESSENTIAL (Required), adjective basic, binding, called for, chief, compulsory, critical, crucial, demanded, exigent, fundamental, important, incumbent upon, indispensable, lacking, mandatory, material, necessary, needed, needful, obligatory, of vital importance, pressing, primary, *proprius,* requisite, urgent, *verus*
ASSOCIATED CONCEPTS: essential duties, essential governmental duties, essential parties, essential services, essential terms of a contract

ESTABLISH (Entrench), verb cause to endure, *confirmare,* fix deeply, fix permanently, implant firmly, ingrain, make durable, make firm, make lasting, make permanent, make stable, make steadfast, perpetuate, plant, put on a firm basis, root, situate, solidify, *stabilire,* stabilitate, stabilize, steady, strengthen

ESTABLISH (Launch), verb begin, bring about, bring into being, bring into existence, build, charter, *constituere,* constitute, construct, create, develop, form, found, give rise to, inaugurate, inchoate, initiate, *instituere,* institute, introduce, lay the foundations, open, organize, originate, prepare, put in motion, set going, set in operation, set up, start, *statuere*
FOREIGN PHRASES: *Cujus est instituere, ejus est abrogare.* Whoever may institute, his right it is to abrogate.

ESTABLISH (Show), verb ascertain, attest, authenticate, certify, circumstantiate, cite evidence, confirm, corroborate, demonstrate, document, manifest, *probare,* prove, substantiate, testify to, uphold, uphold in evidence, validate, verify, *vincere*
ASSOCIATED CONCEPTS: conclusively establish, establish beyond a reasonable doubt, establish by a fair preponderance of the credible evidence, establish to a clear certainty, established by law, legally established

ESTATE (Hereditament), noun bequest, birthright, devise, gift by succession, heritage, heritance, inheritance, legacy, patrimony
ASSOCIATED CONCEPTS: beneficial estate, charge against an estate, claim against an estate, distribution, estate tax, residue

ESTATE (Property), noun acres, *ager,* assets, assets and liabilities, belongings, chattels, chattels real, chose in action, collective assets, earthly possessions, effects, equity, freehold, goods, grounds, hereditament, holdings, intangible assets, interest in land, land and buildings, lands, liquid assets, material assets, material things which are owned, personalty, piece of landed property, *possessio,* possessions, real estate, realty, resources, right, title and interest in land, tangible assets, tangibles, tenement, territory, valuables, *villa*
ASSOCIATED CONCEPTS: absolute estate, conditional estate, defeasible estate, equitable estate, estate at sufferance, estate at will, estate by entirety, estate by purchase, estate for life, estate for years, estate from period to period, estate from year to year, estate in common, estate in expectancy, estate in land, estate in remainder, estate in reversion, estate lands, estate on a conditional limitation, estate pour autre vie, estate tail, estate upon a limitation, executory estate, fee-simple estate, fee-tail estate, forfeiture of an estate, freehold, joint estate, landed estate, life estate, limited estate, next eventual estate, qualified estate, vested estate
FOREIGN PHRASES: *Post executionem status lex non patitur possibilitatem.* After the execution of the estate the law suffers not a possibility.

ESTATE PLANNING, *noun* arrangements for succession, proper testamentary scheme, testamentary planning, will planning
Generally: tax planning

ESTIMATE *(Approximate cost),* *noun* admeasurement, *aestimatio,* appraisal, appraisement, approximate calculation, approximate judgment of value, approximate value, approximation, assessment, calculation, charge, computation, considered guess, educated guess, estimation, evaluation, gauge, market price, measurement, quotation, rate, rating, reckoning, rough calculation, rough guess, statement of the costs, valuation, value, worth
ASSOCIATED CONCEPTS: fraudulent estimates

ESTIMATE *(Idea),* *noun* assumption, belief, conjecture, consideration, deduction, determination, guess, guesswork, impression, *iudicium,* judgment, observation, opinion, perception, personal judgment, reaction, reckoning, speculation, supposal, supposition, surmisal, surmise, understanding, view

ESTIMATE, *verb* *aestimare,* appraise, budget, calculate approximately, *censere,* conjecture, evaluate, figure, figure costs, form an opinion, gauge, give an approximate value, guess, judge, place a value on, put an approximate price on, rank, rate, reckon, set a price on, set a value on, suppose, survey, value, weigh
ASSOCIATED CONCEPTS: estimated tax, estimated cash value, estimated cost, estimated revenue, final estimate

ESTIMATION *(Calculation),* *noun* admeasurement, appraisal, appraisement, approximate calculation, approximate judgment of value, approximation, assessment, assumption, computation, conjecture, considered guess, deduction, educated guess, estimate, evaluation, gauge, guess, guesswork, judgment, measurement, mensuration, opinion, rating, reckoning, rough calculation, rough guess, speculation, supposal, supposition, surmisal, surmise, valuation, weighing

ESTIMATION *(Esteem),* *noun* admiration, appreciation, approbation, approval, commendation, credit, deference, favor, favorable opinion, favorable recognition, favorable repute, fondness, good opinion, good reputation, good standing, high opinion, high regard, homage, honor, praise, regard, respect, reverence, veneration

ESTOP, *verb* avert, ban, bar, barricade, bind, block the way, block up, blockade, bring to a stop, create a stoppage, cut off, encumber, fend off, forbid, forestall, halt, hamper, handicap, hinder, impede, inhibit, interfere, interrupt, intervene, not allow, obstruct, obviate, preclude, prevent, prohibit, put a stop to, put an end to, restrain, restrict, shackle, stand in the way, stay, stop, stop the progress of, stop the way, stymie, thwart, turn aside, ward off
ASSOCIATED CONCEPTS: change in position

ESTOPPEL, *noun* ban, bar, bar to an allegation, barrier, barring, blockage, disallowance, forbiddance, hindrance, impediment, inhibition, legal restraint, obstruction, preclusion, preclusion by act, preclusion by conduct, prohibition, restraint, restriction
ASSOCIATED CONCEPTS: agency by estoppel, collateral estoppel, equitable estoppel, estoppel by concealment, estoppel by conduct, estoppel by deed, estoppel by judgment, estoppel by laches, estoppel by matter in pais, estoppel by matter of accord, estoppel by recital, estoppel by record,

estoppel by silence, estoppel by suppression, estoppel by verdict, estoppel letter, judicial estoppel, partnership by estoppel, ratification, stare decisis, waiver
FOREIGN PHRASES: *Nemo contra factum suum venire potest.* No man can contradict his own act or deed. *Un ne doit prise advantage de son tort demesne.* One ought not to take advantage of his own wrong.

ESTRANGE, *verb* *abalienare,* alienate, avoid, be disjoined, break with, cut off, disaffect, disband, disconnect, dispart, dissever, dissociate, disunite, divert from original use, divert from the original possessor, divide, draw apart, drive apart, exclude, fall out, isolate, keep aloof, keep apart, keep at a distance, leave out, offend, part, part company, segregate, separate, set against, set apart, set at variance, sever, sunder
ASSOCIATED CONCEPTS: separation of spouses

ESTRANGEMENT, *noun* abalienation, abandonment, *alienatio,* alienation, alienation of affection, breach, break, cleavage, conflict, detachment, difference, disaffection, disagreement, disassociation, *discidium,* disconnection, discord, disengagement, disfavor, disharmony, disjunction, disloyalty, disruption, dissevering, dissociation, dissonance, disunion, disunity, division, divorce, divorcement, dudgeon, enmity, hostility, ill will, incompatibility, loss of affection, parting, riddance, rift, rupture, schism, segregation, separate maintenance, separation, severance, severance of relations, split, sundering, termination of cohabitation, unfriendliness, variance, withdrawal

ET AL., *adverb* and all, and everyone, and more of the same, and other parties, and other things, and others, and the rest

ETHICAL, *adjective* above board, conforming to moral standards, conforming to professional conduct, decent, good, honest, honorable, idealistic, in accord with ethics, in accordance with the rules for right conduct, in accordance with the standards of a profession, just, law-abiding, legitimate, moral, *moralis,* principled, professional, relating to moral action, respectable, right, righteous, straight, uncorrupt, uncorrupted, unimpeachable, upright, virtuous
ASSOCIATED CONCEPTS: Code of Judicial Conduct, Code of Professional Responsibility

ETHICS, *noun* casuistry, code, code of morals, code of right and wrong, conduct, good conduct, goodness, honesty, honor, ideals, integrity, justice, laws of a profession, moral behavior, moral conduct, moral judgment, moral obligation, moral philosophy, moral practice, moral principles, moral rectitude, moral strength, moral tone, morality, morals, *philosophia moralis,* principles, principles of morality, probity, professional standards, rectitude, righteousness, sense of right and wrong, standards, standards of conduct, standards of professional behavior, system of morals, uprightness, values, virtue, virtuous conduct, virtuousness
ASSOCIATED CONCEPTS: legal ethics, professional delinquency, professional ethics

EUTHANASIA, *noun* assisted dying, authorization to end life for humane reasons, early death for humane reasons, grant permission to terminate life for humane reasons, grant to terminate life for humane reasons, legalized killing for humane reasons, legalized taking of life for humane reasons, license to take life for humane reasons, loss of life for humane reasons, means to die sanctioned, permission to terminate life for humane reasons, permit to terminate life for humane reasons, permitting to die for humane reasons

ASSOCIATED CONCEPTS: involuntary euthanasia, physician-assisted suicide, voluntary euthanasia

EVACUATE, *verb*   abscond, absent oneself, break camp, clear out, decamp, depart, disappear, empty, escape, exit, flee, leave, leave empty, *locum vacuefacere,* make a departure, march out, move out, quit, remove, retreat, run away, send away, take flight, vacate, vanish, withdraw

EVADE *(Deceive), verb*   avoid, be evasive, beguile, circumvent, defraud, delude, dissemble, dodge, equivocate, falsify, fool, hedge, hoax, lie, mislead, misrepresent, outwit, palter, pretend, prevaricate, shuffle, sophisticate, trick

EVADE *(Elude), verb*   avoid, dodge, escape, escape notice, flee, get away from, hide from, keep clear of, slip out

ASSOCIATED CONCEPTS: evade execution of a judgment, evade the law

EVALUATE, *verb*   appraise, ascertain the amount of, assess, calculate, class, criticize, determine the worth of, estimate, express an opinion, figure costs, find the value of, form an opinion, gauge, give an estimate, give an opinion, judge, measure, place a value on, prepare an estimate, price, rank, rate, reckon, review, set a figure, set a price on, set a value on, value

ASSOCIATED CONCEPTS: evaluate the evidence

EVASION, *noun*   *ambages,* artful dodge, artifice, avoidance, camouflage, chicane, chicanery, circumvention, concealment, covering up, craftiness, cunningness, deceit, deceitfulness, deception, device, disingenuousness, distortion, dodge, elusiveness, equivocation, escape by cleverness, escape by trickery, fabrication, flight, guile, knavery, *latebra,* maneuver, masquerade, misrepresentation, obfuscation, partial truth, perversion of the truth, pretext, prevarication, ruse, secrecy, secretiveness, secretness, sham, slyness, sophistical excuse, stealth, stealthiness, subterfuge, subtlety, *tergiversatio,* tergiversation, trick, underhand dealing

ASSOCIATED CONCEPTS: evasion of taxation, evasive contempt, evasive pleading

EVASIVE, *adjective*   *ambiguus,* ambivalent, artful, avoiding, beguiling, clandestine, concealed, covert, covinous, crafty, deceitful, deceiving, deceptive, delusive, eluding, elusive, elusory, equivocating, feigned, fictitious, fictive, furtive, guileful, hedging, hypocritical, in disguise, misleading, misrepresentative, mysterious, perfidious, pretended, scheming, secluded, secretive, seeking to avoid, seeking to elude, seeking to evade, shifty, sleightful, slippery, sneaky, stealthy, surreptitious, tending to evade, tricky, truthless, untruthful, unveracious, unwilling, using evasion, vague

ASSOCIATED CONCEPTS: evasive argument, evasive contempt, evasive pleading, evasive witness

EVENHANDED, *adjective*   detached, disinterested, dispassionate, equal, equitable, fair, fair-minded, impartial, indifferent, just, neutral, objective, proper, scrupulous, unbiased, unbribed, unchallengeable, uncorrupt, uncorrupted, unprejudiced, upright, virtuous

EVENT, *noun*   adventure, affair, development, episode, *eventus, exitus,* experience, *factum,* hap, happening, incident,

marked occurrence, milestone, occasion, occurrence, proceeding, transaction

ASSOCIATED CONCEPTS: contingent event, fortuitous event, future event, person interested in the event, unforseen event, witness to an event

FOREIGN PHRASES: *Casus fortuitus non est sperandus, et nemo tenetur devinare.* A fortuitous event is not to be forseen, and no one is bound to expect it. *Casus fortuitus non est supponendus.* A fortuitous happening is not to be presumed.

EVICT, *verb*   *depellere,* deprive of possession, *detrudere, deturbare,* dislodge, displace, dispossess, disturb, eject, expel, jettison, kick out, oust, put out of house by legal process, recover property, remove, take possession, thrust out, turn adrift, turn out, turn out of doors, turn out of house and home, uproot, wrest property from

ASSOCIATED CONCEPTS: actual eviction, constrictive eviction, partial eviction, total eviction, unlawful eviction

EVICTION, *noun*   act of driving out, act of throwing out, deprivation of possession, dislodgment, dispossession, divestment, ejection, ejectment, entry under paramount title, *evictio,* expulsion, extrusion, forcible expulsion from property, intentional exclusion of lessee, ouster, ouster by paramount title, recovery of property from another's possession, removal, take-over of property

ASSOCIATED CONCEPTS: abandonment of possession, actual eviction, breach of covenant of quiet enjoyment, constructive eviction, eviction by paramount title, partial eviction, total eviction, unlawful eviction

FOREIGN PHRASES: *Sive tota res evincatur, sive pars, habet regressum emptor in venditorem.* The purchaser who has been evicted totally or in part has an action against the vendor.

EVIDENCE, *noun*   admitted testimony, body of facts on which belief is based, circumstances in a case, confirmation, corroboration, document, documentation, documents, exhibit, exhibits submitted to jury, facts, facts admitted at trial, facts judicially noted, facts which bear on the point in question, facts which establish the point in issue, factual matter, ground of proof, grounds for belief, *indicium,* instrument of proof, matter legally submitted to the jury, matters of fact, means of proof, means of proving a fact, medium of proof, persuasive facts, probative matter, proof, proof legally presented at trial, proof of facts, record, relevant fact, relevant material, species of proof, substantiation, *testimonium,* that which furnishes proof, that which tends to prove, validation, verification

ASSOCIATED CONCEPTS: acceptance of evidence, admission of evidence, affirmative evidence, after-discovered evidence, against the weight of the evidence, all the evidence favorable to the plaintiff, best evidence, burden of going forward, burden of persuasion, burden of proof, character evidence, circumstantial evidence, clear and convincing evidence, clear preponderance of the evidence, collateral evidence, competent evidence, conclusive evidence, conflicting evidence, corroborating evidence, credible evidence, cumulative evidence, demonstrative evidence, destruction of evidence, direct evidence, documentary evidence, evidence of title, exclusion of evidence, expert evidence, extrinsic evidence, fabricated evidence, fair preponderance of evidence, favorable evidence, foundation for evidence, hearsay evidence, immaterial evidence, impeaching evidence, incompetent evidence, incredible evidence, inculpatory evidence, independent evidence, indispensable evidence, insufficient evidence, intrinsic evidence, introduction of evidence, irrelevant evidence, judicial evidence, legal evidence, material evidence, newly discovered evidence, objection to evidence, offering in evidence, opinion evidence, parol evidence, persuasive evidence, positive evidence, preponderance of evidence, presumptive evidence, prima facie evidence, primary evidence, probative evidence, real evidence, rebutting evidence, receiving evidence into the record, record evidence, reliable evidence, res gestae, rules of evidence, satisfactory evidence, scintilla of evidence, secondary evidence, state's evidence, substantial evidence, substantive evidence, sufficient evidence, sufficient evidence to support the verdict, supporting evidence, suppression of evidence, sworn evidence, taking evidence, testimony, visible evidence, weight of evidence, written evidence

FOREIGN PHRASES: *Ponderantur testes, non numerantur.* Witnesses are weighed, not counted. *Principia probant, non probantur.* Principles prove, they are not proved. *Praesumptiones sunt conjecturae ex signo verisimili ad probandum assumptae.* Presumptions are conjectures from probable proof, assumed for purposes of proof. *Testimonia ponderanda sunt, non numeranda.* Evidence is to be weighed, not counted. *De non apparentibus, et non existentibus, eadem est ratio.* The law is the same respecting things which do not appear and those which do not exist. *Non potest probari quod probatum non relevat.* That may not be proved which, if proved is irrelevant.

EVIDENCE, verb attest, authenticate, avouch, bear out, bear witness to, bring to light, bring to view, certify, circumstantiate, confirm, declare to be genuine, declare to be true, demonstrate, denote, disclose, display, establish, evince, exemplify, expose, give indication of, illustrate, imply, indicate, *indicium,* infer, instance, lay bare, make obvious, make plain, manifest, reveal, signify, suggest, swear, tell of, tend to show, *testimonium,* uncover, unsheathe, verify

ASSOCIATED CONCEPTS: proof evidencing a crime occurred

EVIDENT, adjective *apertus,* apparent, appearing, axiomatic, axiomatical, bald, clear, conspicuous, discernible, disclosed, distinct, easily seen, easy to perceive, easy to see, *evidens,* explicit, exposed, express, glaring, in evidence, in full view, in sight, in view, indisputable, indubitable, lucid, manifest, *manifestus,* noticeable, obvious, open, open to the vision, open to view, ostensible, overt, palpable, patent, perceivable, perceptible, perspicuous, plain, pronounced, revealed, salient, showing, standing out, standing out clearly, transparent, unconcealed, undeniable, undisguised, unequivocal, unhidden, unmistakable, unquestionable, visible

ASSOCIATED CONCEPTS: evident mistake, proof of guilt being evident

EVIDENTIARY, adjective admissible circumstances in a case, admitted testimony, corroboration, documentation with evidentiary value, documents which play a role in a trial, documents which tend to prove the outcome, exhibits, exhibits submitted to jury, facts admitted, facts judicially noted, facts proving the outcome of a trial, facts which bear on the point in question, facts which establish the point in issue, grounds for belief, having confirmatory effect, information which furnishes proof, instrument of proof, means of proof in a case, means of proving a fact at trial, medium of proof, proof, proof legally presented at trial, proof of facts, relevant documents, relevant information, relevant matters, substantiation, validation, verification

ASSOCIATED CONCEPTS: evidentiary facts, evidentiary importance, evidentiary law, rules of evidence, the law of evidence

EVINCE, verb bespeak, betoken, bring into view, demonstrate, denote, display, evidence, exhibit, furnish evidence, illustrate, indicate, make clear, make evident, make manifest, make plain, manifest, *ostendere,* point to, *praestare, probare,* prove, show, show signs

EVISCERATE, verb cut out, damage, debilitate, deprive of essential parts, deprive of force, deprive of vital parts, devitalize, dig out, disembowel, dismantle, embowel, enervate, enfeeble, exenterate, exsect, extract, gut, harm, impair, injure, mar, pick out, pluck, pull out, remove an essential part, rip out, sap, spoil, take away an essential part, tear out, weaken

EVOKE, verb accomplish, achieve, arouse, be the cause of, bring about, bring forth, bring out, bring to pass, call forth, call up, cause, cause to happen, draw forth, draw out, educe, effect, effectuate, *elicere,* elicit, *evocare,* excite, *excitare,* extract, generate, give rise to, hasten, incite, induce, initiate, inspire, instigate, motivate, obtain, occasion, precipitate, procure, produce, prompt, provoke, rouse, secure, stimulate, summon, summon forth, summon up

EVOLVE, verb advance, arise from, become, change into, come from, come to be, derive from, descend from, develop, emerge, *evolvere, explicare,* follow, grow from, have a common origin, issue, originate from, progress, result, spring from, take form, take shape, turn into, undergo evolution, unfold

EVULSION, noun avulsion, deracination, disengagement, displacement, drawing out, ejection, elicitation, elimination, eradication, excavation, exsection, extirpation, extraction, extrication, plucking out, pull, pulling out, removal, ripping out, separation, unravelment, unrooting, uprooting, withdrawal

EX OFFICIO, adverb authoritarian, by divine right, by law, by right, de jure, duly, empowered, in authority, in charge, in control, in office, official

EX PARTE, adjective by one party, done by one person, for one party, in behalf of one party, on one side only, on the application of one party, one-sided, unilateral

ASSOCIATED CONCEPTS: ex parte application, ex parte decree, ex parte hearing, ex parte motion, ex parte proceeding

EX PARTE, adverb biased, in the interest of one party, one sided, partial, partisan, prejudiced, relating to one side only, unilateral

ASSOCIATED CONCEPTS: ex parte affidavit, ex parte appointment, ex parte certificate, ex parte commission, ex parte declaration, ex parte experiment, ex parte investigation, ex parte motion and order, ex parte petition, ex parte presentment, ex parte proceedings, ex parte settlement, ex parte statement

EX POST FACTO, adjective affecting a previous act, after, after the act is committed, after the fact, afterward, at a later period, at a later time, at a subsequent period, at a succeeding time, directly after, following in time, later, later in time, retroactive, thereafter

ASSOCIATED CONCEPTS: ex post facto law

EXACERBATE, verb aggravate, arouse, augment, deteriorate, enrage, *exacerbare,* excite, heighten, incense, incite, increase, inflame, infuriate, intensify, irritate, make more severe, make worse, provoke, render worse, worsen

EXACT, *adjective* accurate, admitting of no deviation, allowing no departure from the standard, careful, clear cut, close, correct, defined, detailed, *diligens, exactus,* explicit, express, faithful, literal, meticulous, minute, particular, plain, precise, punctilious, punctual, right, rigid, scrupulous, specific, strict, *subtilis,* true to fact, undeviating, unerring, unexaggerated, verbatim, with no mistake, without error

ASSOCIATED CONCEPTS: exact copy

EXACT, *verb* ask for, assess, call for, charge, claim, clamor for, coerce, compel, constrain, cry for, demand, demand payment, demand toll, draw from, dun, elicit, enforce, enjoin, extort, force, force payment, impel, impose, impose a duty, impose a tax, insist upon, lay a duty on, lay claim to, levy, make an authoritative request, make demands, make obligatory, make pay, make requisition, mulct, necessitate, obligate, oblige, order, press, require, require authoritatively, requisition, squeeze, task, tax, threaten, toll, urge, wrench, wrest, wring

ASSOCIATED CONCEPTS: certified copy, exact copy

EXAGGERATION, *noun* addition, aggrandizement, augmentation, boast, brag, caricature, disproportion, distortion, embellishment, embroidery, enlargement, excess, excessiveness, exorbitance, exorbitancy, expansion, extravagance, extravagant statement, extremes, gasconade, histrionics, hyperbole, immoderacy, immoderateness, immoderation, inaccuracy, inexactitude, inexactness, inflation, inordinacy, inordinateness, intemperance, intemperateness, intensification, magnification, misleading enlargement, outrageousness, overassessment, overemphasis, overenthusiasm, overpraise, overstatement, overvaluation, rodomontade, sensationalism, stretch, superfluity, superfluousness, *superlatio,* superlative, *traiectio,* undueness, unreasonable amplification

ASSOCIATED CONCEPTS: deceit, fraud, misrepresentation

EXAMINATION *(Study),* ***noun*** active study, analysis, audit, careful noting of details, check, close inquiry, close observation, consideration, deliberation, diligent attention, exhaustive inquiry, exploration, inquest, *inquisitio,* inquisition, inspection, *investigatio,* investigation, observation, perquisition, perusal, reconnaissance, research, review, scrutiny, search, strict inquiry, survey

ASSOCIATED CONCEPTS: cross-examination, direct examination of a witness, examination before trial, examination in chief, examination of records, examination of title

EXAMINATION *(Test),* ***noun*** interrogation, interview, probation, questioning under oath, quiz, set of questions

ASSOCIATED CONCEPTS: blood tests, board of examiners, civil service examination, entrance examination, health examination, medical examiners, mental examination, motor vehicle examination, physical examination, professional examinations, title examination

EXAMINE *(Interrogate),* ***verb*** catechize, challenge, inquire, *inquirere, inspicere,* interpellate, interview, *investigare,* probe, put questions to, query, question, question under oath, quiz, subject to questioning

ASSOCIATED CONCEPTS: examine a witness

EXAMINE *(Study),* ***verb*** analyze, anatomize, audit, canvass, check, conduct research on, contemplate, delve into, dissect, explore, go over, inquire into, inspect, investigate, keep under surveillance, look for flaws, look into, look over, look through, make an analysis, monitor, observe, peer at,

peruse, probe, pry into, reconnoiter, regard carefully, research, review, scrutinize, study systematically, subject to analysis, subject to scrutiny, survey, take stock of, watch closely

ASSOCIATED CONCEPTS: examine books and records

EXAMPLE, *noun* archetype, case, case in point, demonstration, *documentum,* exemplar, exemplification, *exemplum,* exponent, guide, ideal, illustration, instance, metaphor, model, norm, paradigm, pattern, point of comparison, representation, representative, representative selection, sample, simile, something to be imitated, specimen, standard, standard of comparison, typical instance

FOREIGN PHRASES: ***Nil agit exemplum litem quod lite resolvit.*** A precedent which settles a controversy with a question does no good. ***Plus exempla quam peccata nocent.*** Examples do more harm than crimes.

EXCEPT *(Exclude),* ***verb*** count out, deduct, delete, differentiate, discount, discriminate, dismiss, disregard, eliminate, *excipere,* exempt, *eximere,* extract, leave out, make an exception, omit, pick out, put aside, remove, separate, set apart, single out, subduct, subtract, take out, treat as a special case

EXCEPT *(Object),* ***verb*** be at variance, call in question, challenge, come in conflict with, contradict, contravene, cry out against, decry, demur, denounce, deplore, differ, disapprove, discountenance, dispute, dissent, entreat against, express disapproval, feel disapproval, find fault, gainsay, go contrary to, impeach, impugn, make objection, object to, oppose, protest, refuse to accept, repudiate, run counter to, take exception

EXCEPTION *(Exclusion),* ***noun*** apartness, breach of practice, contrariety, defiance of custom, departure from usual, detachment, deviation, disconformity, disruption, *exceptio,* exemption, expulsion, inconsistency, infraction of rule, irregularity, nonconformity, noninclusion, nonuniformity, oddity, omission, preclusion, rarity, removal, segregation, separation, severance, special case, subtraction, unconformity, unconventionality, withdrawal

ASSOCIATED CONCEPTS: exception in a deed, proviso, reservation, statutory exception

EXCEPTION *(Objection),* ***noun*** adverse criticism, challenge, charge, clamor, complaint, contradiction, contravention, criticism, demurrer, disapprobation, disapproval, discommendation, discontent, dislike, disparagement, displeasure, dispraise, dispute, dissatisfaction, dissent, grievance, improbation, impugnation, lack of agreement, lack of conformity, nonagreement, nonapproval, offense, opposition, outcry, protest, protest against a ruling, protestation, rebuke, rejection, remonstrance

ASSOCIATED CONCEPTS: bill of exceptions, formal objection, general exception, peremptory exception, special exception

FOREIGN PHRASES: ***Exceptio firmat regulam in contrarium.*** An exception affirms the rule to be the contrary. ***Omnis regula suas patitur exceptiones.*** Every rule is subject to its own exception. ***Exceptio semper ultima ponenda est.*** An exception is always to be placed last. ***Exceptio quoque regulam declarat.*** An exception also declares the rule. ***Exceptio quae firmat legem, exponit legem.*** An exception which confirms the law expounds the law. ***Omnis exceptio est ipsa quoque regula.*** Every exception is itself also a rule. ***Ubi quid generaliter conceditur, inest haec exceptio, si non aliquid sit contra jus fasque.*** Where anything

225

is granted generally, this exception is implied: that nothing shall be contrary to law and right. ***Exceptio firmat regulam in casibus non exceptis.*** An exception confirms the rule in cases not excepted. ***Exceptio probat regulam de rebus non exceptis.*** The exception proves the rule concerning things not excepted.

EXCERPT, *noun* citation, clipping, excerption, extract, part, passage, passage taken from a book, portion, quotation, quote, quoted passage, reference, representative selection, select passage, selection

ASSOCIATED CONCEPTS: redact portions of a confession

EXCESS, *adjective* excessive, exorbitant, extra, extravagant, extreme, immoderate, inordinate, lavish, more than enough, needless, *nimium,* overabundant, overflowing, overmuch, profuse, recremental, recrementitial, recrementitious, redundant, spare, superabundant, supererogative, supererogatory, superfluous, supernumerary, surplus, undue, unnecessary, unneeded

ASSOCIATED CONCEPTS: excess fees, excess of jurisdiction, excess profits tax

EXCESSIVE, *adjective* characterized by excess, disproportionate, exaggerated, exceeding, exceeding what is usual, exorbitant, extra, extravagant, extreme, fanatical, fulsome, gross, immoderate, *immoderatus, immodicus,* inordinate, intemperate, needless, *nimius,* nonessential, out of bounds, outrageous, overflowing, overmuch, plethoric, preposterous, profuse, rank, redundant, spare, superabundant, supererogatory, superfluous, supernumerary, surplus, unbounded, uncalled for, unconscionable, undue, unnecessary, unneeded, unreasonable

ASSOCIATED CONCEPTS: excessive assessment, excessive bail, excessive damages, excessive sentence, excessive tax, excessive verdict

EXCHANGE, *noun* bargain, barter, bazaar, bourse, business intercourse, buying and selling, change, commerce, commutation, conversion, deal, interchange, intercourse, market, mart, merchantry, *permutatio,* permutation, rearrangement, reciprocation, reciprocity, replacement, reprisal, requital, retaliation, shift, shuffle, stock market, substitute, substitution, supplanting, swap, trade, traffic, transaction, transfer, transposal, transposition

ASSOCIATED CONCEPTS: bill of exchange, exchange of property, reciprocal exchange, reciprocal transfers

EXCISE, *noun* assessment, capitation, charge, custom, demand, duty, exaction, exactment, fee, imposition, impost, levy, liability, obligation, tariff, tax, taxation, toll

ASSOCIATED CONCEPTS: direct tax, excise tax, fee, gift tax, license tax, privilege tax

EXCISE *(Cut away), **verb*** abscind, clip, cut, cut out, deduct, delete, detruncate, diminish, disjoin, dissever, divest, eradicate, expunge, expurgate, extract, pare, pluck out, remove, separate, sever, subduct, subtract, take away, take out, tear out, thin, truncate, weed, withdraw

EXCISE *(Levy a tax), **verb*** appraise, assess, charge, charge duty, claim, collect, compel payment, demand, demand payment, demand toll, enforce payment, exact, force payment, impose a duty on, impost, lay a duty on, lay claim to, levy, levy an excise on, oblige, raise, require a tax, requisition, take, tax

ASSOCIATED CONCEPTS: direct tax, franchise tax, gift tax, indirect tax, privilege tax, succession tax

EXCLUDE, *verb* avoid, ban, banish, bar, block, blockade, boycott, cast out, censor, count out, debar, deny entry, deport, deprive, disallow, disbar, discount, disdain, dismiss, disown, displace, disqualify, disregard, eject, eliminate, eradicate, except, *excludere,* excommunicate, excuse, exempt, exile, *eximere,* expatriate, expel, force out, forswear, have nothing to do with, ignore, impose a ban, isolate, keep from entering, keep out, lay aside, leave out, leave unregarded, liberate, make an exception, neglect, omit, ostracize, oust, outlaw, overlook, pass over, place out of bounds, preclude, prevent, *prohibere,* prohibit, proscribe, put aside, put out, quarantine, rebuff, refuse to admit, refuse to consider, refuse to include, refuse to see, reject, remove, renounce, repel, repudiate, repulse, restrict, rule out, scorn, segregate, sequester, set apart, set aside, shut out, spurn, taboo, take out, throw out, thrust out, treat as a special case, turn away, turn out, uproot, veto, weed

ASSOCIATED CONCEPTS: exclude from a will, exclude from employment

EXCLUSION, *noun* apartheid, avoidance, ban, bar, blackball, boycott, debarment, denial, denial of entry, deportation, disbarment, discard, dislodgment, dismissal, disownment, displacement, ejection, *exclusio,* exemption, exile, expatriation, expulsion, immunity, intolerance, isolation, monopoly, nonacceptance, nonadmission, nonconsideration, noninclusion, omission, ostracism, preclusion, prejudice, privilege, prohibition, purge, refusal, rejection, removal, repudiation, riddance, seclusion, segregation, separation, voidance

ASSOCIATED CONCEPTS: Escobedo rule, exception, exclusion from a will, exclusion of a juror, exclusionary clause, exclusionary rule, Miranda rule, systematic exclusion

FOREIGN PHRASES: ***Inclusio unius est exclusio alterius.*** The inclusion of one is the exclusion of another. ***Expressio unius est exclusio alterius.*** The expression of one thing is the exclusion of another.

EXCLUSIVE *(Limited), **adjective*** biased, bigoted, choice, clannish, cliquish, esoteric, exclusionary, exclusory, illiberal, preclusive, prejudiced, prohibitive, restricted, restrictive, select, selective, snobbish, snobby, uncharitable

ASSOCIATED CONCEPTS: exclusive agency, exclusive control, exclusive franchise, exclusive immunity, exclusive jurisdiction, exclusive license, exclusive ownership, exclusive possession, exclusive remedy, exclusive right, exclusive use

EXCLUSIVE *(Singular), **adjective*** distinct, especial, isolated, lone, one, only, separate, single, sole, solitary, special, unique

EXCLUSIVE RIGHTS, *noun* distinctiveness, exclusive right, limited territory, restrictive territory, restrictiveness, selectiveness, singularity, sole and undivided right, specialization, uniqueness

ASSOCIATED CONCEPTS: covenant not to compete

EXCULPATE, *verb* absolve, absolve of fault, absolve of wrongdoing, acquit, clear, clear from a charge, clear from alleged guilt, clear from imputation of fault, declare guiltless, declare not guilty, dismiss, *excusare,* excuse, exonerate, free, free from blame, give absolution to, justify, liberate, pardon, prove guiltless, prove not guilty, set free, vindicate, vindicate from unjust reproach

ASSOCIATED CONCEPTS: exculpatory clause, exculpatory evidence, exculpatory statement, mitigation of damages

EXCULPATORY, *adjective*   absolve, absolve of fault, absolve of liability, absolve of wrongdoing, acquit, clear, clear from, clear from a charge, clear from imputation of fault, clear from liability, clear of blame, clear of guilt, clearing, declare not guilty, excuse, exonerate, free, free from blame, justify, liberate, tending to absolve, tending to clear, tending to pardon, tending to prove guiltless, tending to prove not guilty, tending to set free, tending to vindicate
ASSOCIATED CONCEPTS: exculpatory clause, exculpatory evidence

EXCULPATORY CLAUSE, *noun*   absolution from liability, clear from a charge, clear from alleged guilt, clear from imputation of fault, condition to clear of liability, contract to clear of liability, covenant to clear of liability, declaration to clear of liability, exception to liability, excuse against the imposition of liability, exemption from liability, exemption from liability, means to absolve of liability, means to clear of liability, out clause, provision to absolve of liability, proviso to absolve of liability, vindication from liability
ASSOCIATED CONCEPTS: contracts, trusts and estates, wills

EXCUSE, *noun*   alibi, allowance, defense, dispensation, exculpation, *excusatio,* exemption, exoneration, explanation for some delinquency, extenuation, justification, mitigation, ostensible reason, pretense, pretext, rationalization, reason, subterfuge
ASSOCIATED CONCEPTS: excusable assault, excusable homicide, excusable neglect, legal excuse
FOREIGN PHRASES: *Impotentia excusat legem.* The impossibility of performing a legal duty is an excuse from the performance. *A l'impossible nul n'est tenu.* No one is bound to do what is impossible.

EXCUSE, *verb*   absolve, acquit, allow for, bear with, clear, condone, discharge, exculpate, excusare, exempt, exonerate, *expurgare,* extenuate, forgive, free, give absolution to, give dispensation, grant amnesty to, judge with indulgence, justify, let off, liberate, make allowances for, overlook, pardon, pass over, pronounce innocent of wrong, provide with an alibi, regard indulgently, release, release from obligation, relieve, remit, reprieve, shrive, vindicate
ASSOCIATED CONCEPTS: affirmative defense, alibi, defense, just cause, justification, lawful excuse, legitimate excuse, reasonable excuse
FOREIGN PHRASES: *Impotentia excusat legem.* The impossibility of performing a legal duty is an excuse from the performance. *Injuria non excusat injuriam.* One wrong does not excuse another. *Ignorantia excusator, non juris sed facti.* Ignorance of fact may excuse, but not ignorance of law. *Ignorantia eorum quae quis scire tenetur non excusat.* Ignorance of those things which a person is deemed to know is no excuse. *Vani timoris justa excusatio non est.* A frivolous fear is not a lawful excuse. *Ignorantia juris non excusat.* Ignorance of the law is no excuse. *Regula est, juris quidem ignorantiam cuique nocere, facti vero ignorantiam non nocere.* The rule is that a person's ignorance of the law may prejudice him, but that his ignorance of fact will not.

EXECUTE *(Accomplish),* *verb*   achieve, act, act upon, attain, bring about, bring to pass, carry into effect, carry into execution, carry out, commit, complete, discharge, do, effect, effectuate, *efficere,* enact, fulfill, manage, perform, perpetrate, put in action, put in force, realize, see through, succeed, take action, transact
ASSOCIATED CONCEPTS: execute a contract, execute a note, execute a promise, execute a warrant, execute after entry of a judgment, execute an agreement, execute an instrument, execute an obligation, execute an order, execute the laws, executed consideration, executed contract, executed estate, executed fine, executed remainder, executed trust, execution creditor, execution debtor, execution lien, execution sales, garnishment, tax execution

EXECUTE *(Sentence to death),* *verb*   condemn, condemn to death, deprive of life, dispatch, end life, inflict capital punishment, kill, punish with death, put to death, put to death according to law, slay, *supplicium*
ASSOCIATED CONCEPTS: execute pursuant to a death sentence, execution of a sentence, sentence

EXECUTIVE, *adjective*   administrative, directing, high level, legislative, managing, ministerial, officiating, presiding
ASSOCIATED CONCEPTS: executive acts, executive branch, executive clemency, executive committee, executive council, executive department, executive director, executive duties, executive officer, executive order, executive powers, executive records, executive session

EXECUTIVE, *noun*   administrator, employer, industrialist, key man, key person, key woman, manager

EXECUTIVE PRIVILEGE, *noun*   classified, concealed, confidential, confidentiality with other branches of government, confidential relationship, Executive Department's immunity, Executive Department's privilege, executive immunity, hidden, imparted in secret, not for publication, not to be communicated, not to be disclosed to other branches of government, President's staff's nondisclosures, private with other branches of government, protected communication from other branches of government, protected relationship, restricted from other branches of government, secret, spoken in confidence, told in confidence, top-secret, unmentionable, unrevealed
Generally: freedom from testifying, nondisclosable information, nondisclosure, refusal to disclose
ASSOCIATED CONCEPTS: invoking executive privilege

EXECUTOR, *noun*   administrator, administrator of a will, administrator of the decedent's estate, administratrix, custodian, delegate, fiduciary, legal representative, person in charge, person in responsibility, person named to carry out the provisions of a will, personal representative, representative of the decedent, trustee
ASSOCIATED CONCEPTS: administor, administrix, ancillary executor, custodian, executor named in a will, executorship expenses, executrix, guardian, independent executors, probate court, surrogate's court

EXECUTORY, *adjective*   contingent, *imperfectus, infectus,* not yet carried into operation, unaccomplished, unadministered, uncompleted, unexecuted, unfinished, unfulfilled, unperformed
ASSOCIATED CONCEPTS: executory accord, executory bequest, executory consideration, executory contract, executory devise, executory estate, executory gift, executory instrument, executory interest, executory limitation, executory remainder, executory treaty, executory trust

EXEMPLAR, *noun*   apotheosis, archetype, example, *exemplum,* exponent, frame of reference, good example, guide, height of perfection, hero, ideal, model, model of virtue, nonesuch, nonpareil, paradigm, paragon, pattern, person of repute, prize, prototype, replica, shining example, specimen, standard, standard for comparison, standard for imitation, standard of perfection, superior individual, the epitome of virtue, the finest example, the paragon of virtue, the perfect example, the prime example, the summit

EXEMPLARY, adjective excellent, honorable, ideal, illustrative, in point, laudable, meritorious, model, normal, normative, paradigmatic, personifying, praiseworthy, precedential, representative, sample, serving as a deterrent, serving as a model, serving as a pattern, serving as a sample, serving as a warning, serving as an instance, typifying, used as a deterrent, used as a model, used as a specimen, worthy, worthy of imitation

ASSOCIATED CONCEPTS: exemplary damages

EXEMPLIFY, verb act the part of, actualize, be taken for, be the equivalent of, betoken, cite, connote, convey an impression, delineate, demonstrate, denote, depict, display, elucidate, embody, enucleate, evidence, evince, exhibit, explicate, express, give an example, give an instance, give concrete form to, illuminate, illustrate, indicate, instance, make clear by examples, make evident, make manifest, make obvious, make plain, manifest, picture, point to, portray, portray by example, produce an instance, render manifest, represent, show by example, signify, stand for, symbolize, typify

ASSOCIATED CONCEPTS: exemplified copies

EXEMPT, adjective absolved, at liberty, cleared, discharged, excluded, excused, exempted, favored, free, free of binding obligation, freed from, immune, *immunis, liber,* liberated, not answerable, not liable, not responsible, not restricted, not subject to, outside, possessed of immunity, privileged, protected, released, relieved from liability, set apart, shielded, *solutus,* unaffected, unbound, unchecked, unconfined, uncontrolled, unencumbered, unimpeded, unrestrained, unrestricted, waived

ASSOCIATED CONCEPTS: exempt from attachment, exempt from execution, exempt from sale, exempt from taxation, exempt property

EXEMPTION, noun allowance, discharge, disengagement, exception, freedom, freedom from duty, freedom from liability, freedom from obligation, freedom from requirements, freedom from service, *immunitas,* immunity, liberation, liberty, license, permit, privilege, release, release from liability, release from obligation, special privilege, va- *catio, vacuitas*

ASSOCIATED CONCEPTS: exemption from jury service, exemption from sale, exemption statute, homestead exemption, personal exemption, tax exemption

EXERCISE (Discharge a function), verb act, administer, carry into execution, carry on, carry out, conduct, do duty, *efficere,* engage in, execute, *exercere, facere,* officiate, perform, practice, pursue, put in motion, put into action, put into effect, put into practice, serve as, translate into action, wage

ASSOCIATED CONCEPTS: authority exercised under the United States Constitution, exercise an option, exercise jurisdiction, exercise of judicial discretion

FOREIGN PHRASES: *Cui jurisdictio data est, ea quoque concessa esse videntur, sine quibus jurisdictio explicari non potest.* To whomsoever jurisdiction is given, those things also are supposed to be granted, without which the jurisdiction cannot be exercised. *Frustra est potentia quae nunquam venit in actum.* A power is a vain one if it is never exercised.

EXERCISE (Use), verb apply, avail oneself of, bring into play, bring to bear, draw on, employ, make use of, manipulate, operate, practice, put in action, put in practice, put to use, put to work, turn to account, utilize, wield

ASSOCIATED CONCEPTS: exercise a right to vote, exercise an option, exercise discretion, exercise dominion, exercise due care, exercise of power

EXERT, verb apply, bring into operation, bring into play, bring to bear, *contendere,* employ, exercise, expend, *intendere,* make use of, manipulate, operate, put forth, put in action, set to work, spend, strain, strive, try, use, utilize, wield, work

EXHAUST (Deplete), verb *absumere, conficere,* consume, consume completely, *consumere,* debilitate, deflate, deprive of strength, devitalize, dissipate, drain, draw, draw out, empty, enervate, enfeeble, expend, fatigue, overtire, reach the end of, run through, sap, spend, strain, tax, tire, use, use up, waste, weaken, wear out, weary

ASSOCIATED CONCEPTS: exhaust all available assets

EXHAUST (Try all possibilities), verb carry to completion, complete, *exhaurire,* finish, follow through, litigate completely, treat thoroughly, use up available remedies

ASSOCIATED CONCEPTS: exhaustion of administrative remedies, exhaustion of remedies, exhaustion of state remedies

EXHIBIT, noun disclosure, display, document produced as evidence, evidence, exhibition, exposition, item of evidence, object produced as evidence, object submitted in proof of facts, presentation, revelation, showing

EXHIBIT, verb bring forward, bring to light, bring to notice, bring to view, demonstrate, disclose, display, evidence, evince, *exhibere, exponere,* expose, express, feature, illustrate, indicate, lay bare, lay open, make clear, make known, make obvious, make plain, manifest, offer for inspection, open up, point out, present, present for consideration, present to view, produce, *proponere,* reveal, reveal to public notice, set forth, show, submit in evidence, uncover, unveil

ASSOCIATED CONCEPTS: exhibit in evidence

EXHORT, verb *adhortari,* adjure, admonish, advise, advocate, animate, arouse, beg, beseech, caution, charge, coax, command, counsel, encourage, enjoin, entreat, goad, impel, implore, importune, incite, induce, influence, inspire, inspirit, instigate, instruct, offer advice, persuade, plead, press, prevail upon, prompt, push, recommend, rouse, spur, stimulate, talk into, urge, warn

EXIGENCY, noun crisis, critical situation, difficulty, exigence, imperativeness, necessity, need, press, pressing necessity, pressure, requirement, urgency, urgent need, want

ASSOCIATED CONCEPTS: public exigency

EXIGENT, adjective acute, badly needed, clamant, compelling, compulsory, critical, crucial, crying, demanding, essential, grave, high priority, imperative, important, indispensable, inescapable, insistent, mandatory, necessary, necessitous, needed, needful, not to be delayed, not to be overlooked, pressing, required, requiring immediate attention, requiring immediate care, requiring prompt action, serious, unavoidable, urgent, vital

ASSOCIATED CONCEPTS: exigent circumstances

EXIST, verb be, be alive, be in effect, be in present force, breathe, come into existence, continue, continue to

be, continue to live, endure, *esse, exsistere, exstare,* go on, have being, have existence, have life, inhere, last, live, live on, persist, remain, remain alive, stay, stay alive, subsist, survive
ASSOCIATED CONCEPTS: corporate existence, existing creditors, existing debt, existing estate, existing law, existing liability, existing lien, existing rights, existing use

EXONERATE, verb absolve, absolve of a charge, acquit, clear, clear of an imputation of guilt, declare blameless, declare innocent, declare not guilty, discharge, discharge of responsibility, exculpate, excuse, forgive, free from accusation, free from blame, give absolution, grant a reprieve, grant amnesty, liberare, *liberate,* pardon, pronounce free from guilt, prove blameless, prove not guilty, purge, release from an obligation, release from liability, relieve, relieve from accusation, relieve of blame, relieve of liability, remit a penalty, set free, vindicate
ASSOCIATED CONCEPTS: indemnify

EXONERATION, noun absolution, absolution of a charge, acquittal, acquittance, act of indemnity, amnesty, bill of indemnity, clearance, clearing, discharge, dismissal of charges, dispensation, exculpation, excuse, forgiveness, freedom, freedom from accusation, freedom from guilt, freeing from blame, liberation, pardon, release, relief from, remission, reprieve, vindication, withdrawal of the charge
ASSOCIATED CONCEPTS: exoneration clause in a will, exoneration of bail, pardon

EXORBITANT, adjective dear, enormous, excessive, expensive, extortionate, extravagant, extreme, fabulous, greedy, gross, high-priced, huge, immense, immoderate, *immodicus,* inordinate, intemperate, outrageous, overmuch, preposterous, uncalled-for, unconscionable, undue, unreasonable, unwarranted

EXPAND, verb accumulate, add to, advance, aggrandize, aggravate, amplify, ascend, augment, balloon, be augmented, be distended, become broad, become greater, become larger, blow up, branch out, broaden, build up, burgeon, deepen, develop, develop in greater detail, *dilatare,* dilate, distend, elaborate, elevate, enhance, enlarge, enlarge on, enter into detail, escalate, exacerbate, exaggerate, expatiate on, express in fuller form, extend, *extendere,* fan out, fatten, fill out, further, gain, gain strength, go into detail, greaten, grow, grow larger, heighten, increase, increase in bulk, increase in extent, increase the capacity of, inflate, intensify, *lazare,* lengthen, magnify, make greater, make larger, make more comprehensive, maximize, multiply, outspread, outstretch, progress, prolong, raise, redouble, render broad, render larger, shoot upward, sprawl, spread, spread out, spread over, step up, stretch, stretch out, supplement, swell, unfold, wax, widen

EXPATRIATE, verb abandon nationality, banish, cast out, change national allegiance, deport, drive from one's native land, eject, exclude, exile, expel, leave one's country, outlaw, renounce citizenship, renounce rights of citizenship, send away, transport, withdraw from one's native land
ASSOCIATED CONCEPTS: aliens, citizenship, deportation

EXPECT (Anticipate), verb await, bargain for, be certain, be confident, be prepared, calculate upon, count on, *expectare,* have in prospect, look for, look forward to, plan on, prepare for, provide for, reckon on, *sperare,* wait for, watch for
ASSOCIATED CONCEPTS: contingent expectancy, expectancy of heir, expectant estate, expectant interest, expectant right, life expectancy

EXPECT (Consider probable), verb apprehend, assume, believe, conclude, conjecture, consider likely, divine, envision, fancy, forecast, foresee, gather, guess, have a hunch, have a presentiment, imagine, infer, judge, predict, presume, prognosticate, prophesy, regard likely, suppose, surmise, suspect, think, think likely

EXPECTATION, noun anticipation, assurance, awaiting, calculation, contemplation, expectance, expectancy, *exspectatio,* foreboding, forefeeling, foreknowledge, foresight, hope, intention, misgiving, *opinio,* preconception, presentiment, presumption, presurmise, prevenience, probability, promise, prospect, prospection, prospicience, *spes,* suspense, trust, waiting
ASSOCIATED CONCEPTS: expectant estates, expectant heir, expectant right, reasonable expectation

EXPEDIENCE, noun acceptability, advantageousness, appropriateness, aptness, commendableness, convenience, discrimination, expediency, favorableness, feasibility, felicitousness, fitness, fittingness, meetness, opportuneness, practicality, pragmatism, profitableness, propitiousness, propriety, prudence, reasonableness, rightness, seemliness, sense, sensibleness, sound judgment, suitability, suitableness, timeliness, usefulness, *utilitas,* utility, worthiness

EXPEDIENT, noun agency, alternative, apparatus, appliance, arrangement, artifice, auxiliary, campaign, *consilium,* contributing force, contrivance, convenience, course, design, device, equipment, formula, implement, instrument, invention, *machina,* machination, machine, makeshift, maneuver, material, means, means to an end, measure, mechanism, medium, method, mode of procedure, plan, practice, procedure, proceeding, process, *ratio,* resort, resource, ruse, scheme, shift, step, stopgap, stratagem, strategy, stroke, subterfuge, suggestion, tactic, technique, tool, treatment, trick, undertaking, utensil, vehicle, way, wherewithal

EXPEDITE, verb accelerate, accomplish promptly, advance, aid, assist, clear the way, dispatch, drive on, ease, encourage, *expedire,* facilitate, forward, foster, further, give a start, hasten, help, hurry, maturare, move up, pave the way, precipitate, promote, push ahead, push forward, push through, put into action, quicken, rush, set in motion, smoothe, speed, speed up, stimulate, support, urge forward, urge on

EXPEDITIOUS, adjective accelerated, accomplished efficiently, active, alacritious, brisk, *celer,* done quickly, done with expedition, efficient, express, fast, fleet, hasty, immediate, instant, *maturus,* prompt, *promptus,* punctual, quick, rapid, ready, snappy, speedy, spirited, swift, with alacrity, with dispatch, with speed

EXPEL, verb banish, cut out, deport, discard, discharge, dislodge, dismiss, disown, dispose of, dispossess, drive out, *eicere,* eject, eliminate, emit, evict, exclude, excommunicate, *exigere,* exile, expatriate, *expellere,* extrude, force away, force out, get rid of, kick out, ostracize, oust, outlaw, purge, put out, reject, remove, rout out, throw out, thrust out, turn out, weed out

EXPEND (Consume), verb apply, avail oneself of, burn, deplete, devour, dissipate, employ, exert, exhaust, finish, lessen, reduce, spend, turn to account, use, use up, waste

EXPEND (Disburse), verb allocate, allot, apportion, assign, bear the cost of, bear the expense of, distribute, erogare, expendere, give money, impendere, incur an expense, incur costs, make an expenditure, make payment, meet the expense of, pay, pay out, render payment, spend, support the expense of

EXPENDABLE, adjective   accessory, added, additional, auxiliary, dispensable, disposable, duplicate, excess, excessive, expletive, extra, extraneous, functionless, futile, gratuitous, impotent, inapplicable, inconsequential, ineffectual, inessential, inoperative, insignificant, inutile, irrelevant, leftover, needless, negligible, nonessential, nonfunctional, nugatory, of no account, overplus, peripheral, purposeless, redundant, replaceable, spare, substitutable, superabundant, supererogatory, superfluous, supernumerary, supplemental, supplementary, surplus, trifling, unavailing, uncalled-for, unessential, unimportant, unnecessary, unneeded, unprofitable, unrequired, unusable, unused, useless, valueless, worthless

EXPENDITURE, noun   amount, cash paid, charge, cost, cost incurred, defrayal, defrayment, disbursement, discharge, expense, expenses, funds paid out, investment, money expended, outgo, outlay, payment, price, remittance, spendings, sum
ASSOCIATED CONCEPTS: actual expenditure, capital expenditure, extraordinary expenditure, good faith expenditure, lawful expenditure, legitimate expenditure, ordinary expenditure

EXPENSE (Cost), **noun**   amount, appraisal, appraisement, assessment, budgeted items, buying price, charge, consideration, cost incurred, costliness, debit, defrayal, defrayment, discharge of a debt, dispendium, drain on resources, due, exaction, exactment, expenditure, fair value, fee, impendium, impensa, market price, monetary value, money expended, obligation, outgo, outlay, overhead, payment, price, rate, remittance, sum, sum charged, valuation, value, worth
ASSOCIATED CONCEPTS: accrued business expense, actual expenses, capital expense, collection expense, contingent expense, current expenses, deductible expense, disbursements, expenditures of an estate, expenses in bringing an action, expenses incurred, expenses of administration, expenses of condemnation, expenses of receivership, extraordinary expenses, general operating expense, incidental expenses, legitimate expense, maintenance expense, mandatory expense, necessary and regular expense, necessary business expense, nonbusiness expense, office expenses, operating expenses, ordinary expenses, personal expenses, proper expenses, reasonable expenses, unusual expenses, witness expenses

EXPENSE (Sacrifice), **noun**   abandonment, casualty, cession, concession, consumption, costliness, damage, decline, deprival, deprivation, deterioration, detriment, disadvantage, disposal, dissipation, dissolution, drain, drain on resources, erosion, forfeit, forfeiture, harm, hurt, ill fortune, impairment, injury, loss, penalty, privation, relinquishment, renunciation, surrender

EXPERIENCE (Background), **noun**   acquaintance, adroitness, apprenticeship, cognizance, competence, competency, cosmopolitanism, education, empiricism, enlightenment, experientia, expertise, expertness, familiarity, instruction, judgment, ken, know-how, knowledge, learning, mastery, maturity, peritia, perspicaciousness, practical knowledge, practical wisdom, practice, preparation, proficiency, qualification, schooling, seasoning, skill, skillfulness, sophistication, teaching, training, tuition, understanding, wisdom, worldliness

FOREIGN PHRASES: **Experientia per varios actus legem facit. Magistra rerum experientia.** Experience by various acts makes law. Experience is the mistress of things. **Per varios actus legem experientia facit.** By various acts experience makes the law.

EXPERIENCE (Encounter), **noun**   adventure, befalling, circumstance, confrontation, episode, escapade, event, happening, incident, occasion, occurrence, pass, phenomenon, presentation, proceeding, situation, transpiration, venture

EXPERIMENT, noun   assay, attempt, dry run, endeavor, essay, examination, experimentum, first attempt, investigation, organized observation, periculum, research, search, test, testing program, trial, tryout, venture, verification

EXPERT, adjective   able, accomplished, acquainted, adept, adroit, all-knowing, apt, artful, callidus, capable, clever, cognizant, competent, conversant, deft, dexterous, effective, efficient, encyclopedic, experienced, facile, finished, handy, ingenious, knowing, knowledgeable, learned, masterful, masterly, omniscient, practiced, prepared, professional, proficient, qualified, sciens, seasoned, skilled, skillful, trained, tried, versed, veteran, well-qualified, wise
ASSOCIATED CONCEPTS: expert evidence, expert opinion, expert witness, handwriting expert

EXPERT, noun   authority, connoisseur, experienced hand, experienced person, experienced personnel, genius, knowing person, man of erudition, man of learning, master, master hand, mastermind, paragon, practiced hand, practitioner, professional, proficient person, qualified person, sage, savant, scholar, skilled hand, skilled practitioner, sophisticate, specialist, specializer, specially trained person, strategist, technician, trained person, trained personnel, veteran, virtuoso
ASSOCIATED CONCEPTS: expert testimony, expert witness

EXPIATION, noun   acknowledgement, adjustment, amends, apology, atonement, compensation, damages, expiatio, full satisfaction, guerdon, indemnification, indemnity, pacification, paying back, payment, piaculum, poena, propitiation, punishment, quittance, reckoning, recompense, reconciliation, recoupment, recovery, repayment, requital, restitution, satisfaction, settlement, solatium

EXPIRATION, noun   cessation, close, closing, closure, completion, conclusion, consummation, death, discontinuance, discontinuation, dissolution, dying, end, ending, expiry, exspiratio, finish, limit, period, retirement, running out, stop, stoppage, term, termination
ASSOCIATED CONCEPTS: expiration of a charter, expiration of a contract, expiration of a franchise, expiration of a grant, expiration of a lease, expiration of a license, expiration of a patent, expiration of a period of redemption, expiration of a sentence, expiration of a term of office, expiration of a trademark, expiration of an insurance policy, expiration of an option to buy, expiration of credit

EXPIRE, verb   animam edere, become void, cease, cease to be, close, come to a close, come to an end, conclude, decease, depart, die, die away, die out, disappear, discontinue, draw to a close, elapse, end, exspirare, fade away, finish, go, lapse, pass, pass away, perish, run out, stop, succumb, surcease, terminate, vanish, wear away, wind up

EXPLAIN, verb   account for, annotate, assign a meaning to, cause to be understood, clarify, clear of obscurity, clear up, decipher, define, demonstrate, describe, disentangle, elucidate, enlighten, enucleate, exemplify, *expedire, explanare,* explicate, *exponere,* expound, give reason for, illuminate, illustrate, increase clarity, interpret, make clear, make evident, make explicit, make manifest, make plain, manifest, offer an explanation, paraphrase, point out, popularize, put across, put in other words, rephrase, restate, reveal, shed light upon, show, simplify, solve, specify, spell out, teach, tell how, throw light upon, translate, unfold, unravel, unscramble, untangle

EXPLANATION, *noun* amplification, annotation, clarification, commentary, deciphering, defense, definition, delineation, demonstration, description, elucidation, enucleation, exegesis, exemplification, *explanatio, explicatio,* explication, exposition, expounding, illumination, illustration, *interpretatio,* interpretation, justification, key, meaning, plain interpretation, rationale, rendering, rendition, showing, simplification, solution, strict interpretation, translation, unfolding
ASSOCIATED CONCEPTS: commentary to a statute, explanatory expressions in a will

EXPLANATORY, *adjective* annotative, apodictal, clarifying, commentarial, demonstrational, demonstrative, descriptive, elucidative, enlightening, evincive, exegetic, exegetical, exemplificative, explicative, explicatory, explicit, expository, expressive, illustrative, informative, informatory, interpretative, justificatory, revealing, revelatory

EXPLETIVE, *noun* addition, anathema, bad language, blaspheming, curse, denunciation, ecphonesis, embellishment, execration, foul invective, foul language, imprecation, injection, insertion, interjection, interpolation, irreverence, malediction, outcry, profane interjection, rhetorical phrase, rhetorical word, scurrility, strong language, swearing, unnecessary addition, unnecessary inclusion

EXPLICABLE, *adjective* accountable, apprehensible, ascribable, cognizable, coherent, comprehensible, conceivable, constructable, deducible, determinable, discoverable, easily understood, explainable, fathomable, intelligible, interpretable, knowable, penetrable, scrutable, understandable

EXPLICATE, *verb* clarify, define, describe, detail, develop, elucidate, enlighten, *enodare,* enucleate, explain, *explicare,* expound, give a detailed explanation, illuminate, illustrate, interpret, *interpretari,* make clear, make explicit, make plain, render clear, reveal, shed light upon, simplify, spell out, throw light upon, translate, unfold, unfold the meaning of, unfold the sense of, unriddle, untangle

EXPLICATORY, *adjective* analytical, clarifying, coherent, commentarial, demonstrative, descriptive, elucidative, enlightening, evincive, exegetic, exemplificative, explanatory, explicative, expository, illustrative, informative, informatory, interpretative, revealing, revelatory

EXPLICIT, *adjective* absolute, accurate, *apertus,* beyond doubt, categorical, certain, clear, clearly defined, clearly expressed, clearly formulated, clearly stated, comprehensible, crystal-clear, decided, definite, *definitus,* determinate, direct, distinct, distinctly expressed, distinctly stated, easy to understand, evident, evincive, exact, explanatory, express, expressed outright, forthright, indisputable, intelligible, lucid, manifest, obvious, open, outspoken, patent, perspicuous, plain, pointed, positive, precise, recognizable, specific, straightforward, strict, sure, to the point, transparent, unambiguous, unconfusing,

understandable, undisguised, unequivocal, unmistakable, well-developed
ASSOCIATED CONCEPTS: explicit notice, explicit power

EXPLOIT *(Make use of),* **verb** apply, avail oneself of, bring into play, capitalize on, consume, employ, exercise, fall back on, find useful, implement, make the most of, manipulate, operate, profit by, put in practice, put into action, put into operation, put to service, put to use, put to work, resort to, set in motion, set to work, take advantage of, turn to account, use, utilize, wield, work

EXPLOIT *(Take advantage of),* **verb** abuse, do an injustice to, ill-treat, ill-use, maltreat, manipulate, milk, misapply, misappropriate, misdirect, misemploy, misgovern, mishandle, mismanage, mistreat, misuse, oppress, overburden, overtask, overtax, overuse, overwork, persecute, put to wrong use, turn selfishly to one's own account, use badly, use improperly, use selfishly, use wrongly, victimize

EXPLOITATION, *noun* employ, misapplication, misuse, overcharge, profiteering, turning to account, unethical use, use, usury, utilization, utilization for profit

EXPONENT *(Explainer),* **noun** definer, exegete, explicator, expositor, expounder, interpreter

EXPONENT *(Representative),* **noun** abettor, advocate, apologist, backer, demonstration, emblem, embodiment, example, exemplar, exemplifier, illustration, indicant, indication, proponent, proxy, sample, specimen, substitute, symbol, token, type

EXPOSE *(Disclose),* **verb** abandon, advertise, air, bare, bring into the open, bring to light, cast out, *coarguere,* defame, denounce, denude, deprive of protection, descry, detect, *detegere,* dig up, disclose, discover, display, divest, divulge, emerge, endanger, evince, exhibit, *exponere,* feature, find, give away, hazard, hold up to public ridicule, hunt down, imperil, indicate, inform on, issue, jeopardize, lay bare, lay open, lay open to harm, locate, make liable, make visible, manifest, muckrake, open to view, present, produce, publish, put in a conspicuous place, put in danger, put in peril, put in view, report, reveal, risk, shame, show, show off, smoke out, strip, strip of disguise, subject, turn out, uncloak, unconceal, uncover, undrape, undress, unearth, unfold, unmask, unsheathe, unveil, unwrap, vent
ASSOCIATED CONCEPTS: expose to disease, expose to harm, expose to obloquy, expose to ridicule, expose to the elements

EXPOSE *(Incriminate),* **verb** abase, accuse, betray, brand, denounce, dishonor, endanger, hazard, impeach, imperil, implicate, impugn, inform, jeopardize, refute, stigmatize

EXPOSIT, *verb* account for, clarify, clear up, elucidate, enlighten, enucleate, explain, explicate, expound, give a lesson, give reason for, hold forth, illuminate, make clear, make lucid, make plain, make simple, make understandable, present, set forth, shed light upon, simplify, spell out, state, throw light upon, unfold

EXPOSITORY, *adjective* clarifying, commentarial, declarative, declaratory, demonstrative, descriptive, didactic, discursive, discursory, disquisitional, dissertational, divulgatory, elucidative, enlightening, exegetical, exemplary, exemplificative, explanatory, explicative, explicatory, graphic, illuminating, illuminative, illustrative, informative, informatory, instructive, narrative, realistic

231

EXPOSTULATE, verb   admonish, advise against, animadvert upon, appeal against, argue, attempt to divert, cast reproach upon, castigate, caution, chastise, chide, convince to the contrary, correct, declaim against, dehort, deter, disapprove, discourage, disincline, dissuade, divert by appeal, divert by persuasion, enjoin, exclaim against, exhort against, find fault with, gainsay, give advice against, object, objurgate, oppose, premonish, protest, reason earnestly against, recommend against, remonstrate, repugn, take exception, talk out of, turn aside, urge against, view with disfavor, withhold assent

EXPOSTULATION, noun   admonition, altercation, blame, caution, complaint, condemnation, confirmed opposition, contention, contrary advice, criticism, dehortation, deprecation, difference, disapprobation, disapproval, dissidence, dissent, dissuasion, expostulation, guidance, objection, objuration, protest, protestation, rebuke, remonstrance, remonstration, reproach, reproof

EXPOSURE, noun   danger, discernibility, discovery, divulgation, exposé, exposition, hazard, jeopardy, laying open, liability, manifestation, openness, perceptibility, peril, presentation, publication, publicity, revelation, risk, susceptibility, susceptivity, unfolding, unmasking, unveiling, visibility, vulnerability
ASSOCIATED CONCEPTS: exposure to asbestos, exposure to toxic chemical, insurance coverage and exposure

EXPOUND, verb   clarify, clear of obscurity, clear up, comment upon, commentate, construe, define, delineate, develop, elucidate, enucleate, explain, explicate, exposit, illustrate, interpret, make clear, make plain, present the meaning of, reveal, set forth, simplify, solve, spell out, state fully, state in detail, unfold, unriddle
ASSOCIATED CONCEPTS: expound the law

EXPRESS, adjective   advised, aforethought, calculated, categorical, certain, clear, clearly indicated, clearly stated, conscious, decided, defined, definite, deliberate, determinate, direct, distinct, distinctly indicated, distinctly stated, emphatic, especially prepared, exact, explicit, fixed, intended, intended for a specific purpose, intentional, meant, not accidental, not by chance, outlined beforehand, outspoken, particular, peculiar, plain, planned, planned in advance, positive, prearranged, precise, predetermined, premeditated, purposeful, purposive, single, specially prepared, specific, specified, unambiguous, unequivocal, willful, with forethought
ASSOCIATED CONCEPTS: express abrogation, express agreement, express authority, express condition, express contract, express covenant, express malice, express notice, express permission, express promise, express terms, express trust, express warranty

EXPRESS, verb   affirm, air, allege, articulate, assert, asseverate, aver, breathe, comment, communicate, convey, couch in terms, *declarare,* declare, denote, describe, disclose, enumerate, enunciate, *exprimere,* find words for, formulate, give expression to, give vent to, give voice to, impart, indicate, make a statement, make an assertion, make explicit, make known, make plain, manifest directly, mouth, observe, phrase, predicate, present, proclaim, pronounce, put in words, remark, say, set down, set forth, set forth in words, show, *significare,* speak, state, state directly, state with conviction, tell, utter, vent, verbalize, voice
FOREIGN PHRASES: *Quoties in verbis nulla est ambiguitas, ibi nulla expositio contra verba fienda est.* Whenever there is no ambiguity in the words, then no exposition contrary

to the words should be made. *Tacita quaedam habentur pro expressis.* Certain things, though unexpressed, are considered as explicit. *Expressio unius est exclusio alterius.* Expression of one thing is the exclusion of another. *Expressio eorum quae tacite insunt nihil operatur.* The expression of those things which are tacitly implied has no effect.

EXPRESSION (Comment), **noun**   articulation, assertion, asseveration, cliché, communication, declaration, expressed opinion, formula, formulation, idiom, indication, locution, maxim, mention, motto, profession, remark, representation in language, saying, *sententia,* set phrase, setting forth in words, statement, verbalism, verbum, vocal embodiment of thought, voicing, *vox*
ASSOCIATED CONCEPTS: construction, interpretation
FOREIGN PHRASES: *Expressio unius est exclusio alterius.* The expression of one thing is the exclusion of another.

EXPRESSION (Manifestation), **noun**   appearance, demonstration, disclosure, display, emergence, evidence, evincement, exhibit, exhibition, exposition, exposure, illustration, indication, instance, mark, presentation, presentment, revealment, revelation, show, showing, sign, token, uncovering

EXPRESSIVE, adjective   animated, artistic, clear, coherent, declaratory, demonstrative, depictive, descriptive, ebullient, effervescent, eloquent, emphatic, exhibitive, expositive, expository, forceful, forcible, fraught with meaning, graphic, imaginative, indicative, informative, irrepressible, lively, meaningful, momentous, moving, natural, pithy, significant, spirited, strong, substantial, suggestive, telling, unaffected, vital, vivacious, vivid, weighty

EXPROPRIATE, verb   abridge, annex, appropriate, arrogate, assume, carry away, commandeer, confiscate, convert, deprive, dislodge, displace, dispossess, divest, hijack, impress, occupy, plagiarize, seize, take over, take possession of, transfer, usurp

EXPROPRIATION (Divestiture), **noun**   attachment, confiscation, deprivation, dislodgment, dispossession, disseisin, distraint, distress, divestment, ejection, eviction, expulsion, forcible seizure, foreclosure, removal, sequestration

EXPROPRIATION (Right of eminent domain), **noun** compulsory purchase, condemnation, condemnation for public use, government appropriation of private land, seizure of private property for public use, seizure of property by the government, seizure of property in the public interest, taking for public use, taking of private land by the government

EXPULSION, noun   ban, banishment, debarment, deportation, deprivation, detrusion, disbarment, discharge, disgorgement, dislodgment, dismissal, displacement, dispossession, disqualification, driving out, effusion, ejection, ejectment, elimination, enforced withdrawal, eruption, eviction, *exactio,* excision, exclusion, excommunication, exile, expatriation, expelling, *expulsio,* extradition, extrusion, isolation, ostracism, ouster, outlawing, permanent exclusion, purge, putting out, rejection, removal, segregation, separation, suspension, termination of membership, throwing out

EXPUNGE, verb   abrade, annul, black out, blot out, cancel, cause to disappear, censor, cross off, cross out, *delere,* delete, destroy, dispose of, do away with, edit out, efface,

eradicate, erase, excise, extinguish, extirpate, *inducere*, leave no trace, nullify, obliterate, *oblitterare*, put an end to, quash, quell, raze, remove, remove all sign of, remove all trace of, render illegible, rub out, scratch out, strike out, take out, wipe away, wipe off, wipe out
ASSOCIATED CONCEPTS: expunge the record

EXPURGATE, *verb*   abridge, amend by removing, blue-pencil, bowdlerize, cancel, censor, clean up, cleanse, conceal, cross out, cut, cut out, delete, depurate, efface, eliminate, enforce censorship, erase, expunge, *expurgare*, free from objectionable content, make better, purge, purify, refine, strike out, suppress, weed

EXPURGATED, *adjective*   bowdlerized, censored, clarified, cleansed, diminished, disinfected, edited, emasculated, excised, excluded, pure, purged, purified, refined

EXTANT, *adjective*   alive, current, currently existing, existent, existing, exstare, in being, in current use, in existence, living, not extinct, not lost, present, standing, still existing, still to be found, subsistent, surviving, undestroyed, visible

EXTEND (Enlarge), ***verb***   add, aggrandize, amplify, *augere*, augment, broaden, build up, carry beyond the limit, carry further, cause to grow, continue, deepen, develop, dilate, distend, draw out, elongate, enlarge the scope of, expand, extendere, increase, increase the length of, inflate, lengthen, magnify, make larger, make more comprehensive, *propagare*, protract, spread out in area, stretch, stretch out, supplement, swell, widen
ASSOCIATED CONCEPTS: extended lease, extension of a contract, extension of credit, extension of time for good cause

EXTEND (Offer), ***verb***   advance, give, hold out, introduce, place at one's disposal, present, present an opportunity, present for acceptance or rejection, proffer, propose, provide an opportunity, put forth, put forward, put forward for consideration, submit, tender

EXTENSION (Expansion), ***noun***   addition, aggrandizement, amplification, augmentation, broadening, dilatation, dilation, distention, enlargement, growth, increase, increase of size, increment, magnification, *prolatio, propagatio*, spreading, stretching, supplementation, widening

EXTENSION (Postponement), ***noun***   abeyance, added time, additional time, adjournment, break, continuance, continuation, deferment, deferral, delay, extra time, further time, intermission, moratorium, more time, pause, prolongation, recess, respite, rest, stall, stay, suspension, suspension of activity, temporary stop, temporary suspension
ASSOCIATED CONCEPTS: extension for good cause, extension of payment, extension of renewal of note, extension of time

EXTENSIVE, *adjective*   ample, *amplus*, big, branching, broad, broad-based, capacious, commodious, comprehensive, considerable, covering a wide area, deep, diffuse, diffusive, embracing a large area, encompassing a wide area, expanded, expansive, extended, extending, far-flung, far-ranging, far-reaching, great, inclusive, large, large-scale, latus, liberal, *magnus*, prevalent, spread-out, spreading, sweeping, vast, wide, wide-reaching, widely extended, widespread
ASSOCIATED CONCEPTS: extensive damage

EXTENT, *noun*   amount, area, borders, bounds, breadth, circuit, compass, comprehensiveness, coverage, degree, dimensions, distance, expanse, gauge, *hactenus*, length, limit, limitation, magnitude, measure, quantity, range, reach, scope, size, space, spaciousness, span, stretch, sweep, width
ASSOCIATED CONCEPTS: extent of injury, extent of loss

EXTENUATE, *verb*   absolve, acquit, allow for, attemper, attenuate, clear, condone, debilitate, deprive of strength, dilute, diminish, enervate, enfeeble, exculpate, excuse, exonerate, forgive, justify, lessen, *levare*, lighten, make allowance for, make excuses for, make less serious, *minuere, mitigare*, mitigate, moderate, palliate, pardon, qualify, reduce, reduce in strength, soften, temper, thin, vindicate, weaken

EXTENUATING CIRCUMSTANCES, *noun*   alleviating circumstances, consideration, exception, extenuation, mitigating circumstances, mitigation, palliation, palliative circumstances, partial excuse, qualification, qualifying reasons, softening circumstances

EXTINGUISH, *verb*   abolish, abort, annihilate, annul, assassinate, blot out, bring to an end, butcher, cancel, choke, crush, cut out, deaden, deal destruction, demolish, deracinate, destroy, devastate, dismantle, dispel, dispense with, do away with, drown out, efface, end, eradicate, erase, expunge, exterminate, *extinguere*, extirpate, finish off, hold down, keep down, kill, kill by suffocation, lay waste to, liquidate, murder, nullify, obliterate, put an end to, put out, put to death, quash, quell, quench, raze, reduce to nothing, repress, *restinguere*, ruin, shatter, slaughter, slay, smother, squash, squelch, stifle, strangle, subdue, suffocate, suppress, terminate, wipe out
ASSOCIATED CONCEPTS: extinguish a debt, extinguish a legacy, extinguish a right
FOREIGN PHRASES: ***Resoluto jure concedentis resolvitur jus concessum.*** When the right of the grantor is extinguished the right granted is extinguished. ***Extincto subjecto, tollitur adjunctum.*** When the substance is extinguished, the incident ceases.

EXTIRPATE, *verb*   abolish, annihilate, annul, blast, blot out, bring to ruin, cancel, consume, cut down, deal destruction, demolish, deracinate, desolate, destroy, devastate, devour, dissolve, do away with, efface, eliminate, end, *eradicare*, eradicate, erase, *excidere, exstirpare*, exterminate, extinguish, get rid of, gut, lay waste, level, liquidate, nullify, obliterate, overturn, pluck out, pull out, pull up by the roots, purge, put an end to, quash, quell, ravage, raze, remove, render null, rid, root out, rub out, sacrifice, shatter, smash, stamp out, tear out, tear to pieces, unmake, uproot, weed out, wipe out

EXTORT, *verb*   blackmail, coerce, compel, compel by intimidation, compel by threat, constrain by force, draw out by compulsion, draw out by force, elicit by threat, exact, exact by force, *exprimere, extorquere*, force, gain by wrongful methods, gain wrongfully, obtain by compulsion, obtain in an unlawful manner, obtain unlawfully, victimize, wrest, wring
ASSOCIATED CONCEPTS: kidnapping
FOREIGN PHRASES: ***Accipere quid ut justitiam facias, non est tam accipere quam extorquere.*** The acceptance of anything as a reward for doing justice is extorting rather than accepting.

EXTORTION, *noun*   blackmail, coercion, compulsion, corrupt demanding, exaction, exaction by oppression, illegal compulsion, obtaining by force, obtaining by threat, oppression, oppressive exaction, rapaciousness, rapacity, *res repetundae*, taking by undue exercise of power, unlawful taking, wrenching, wresting, wresting money by force, wringing, wrongful exaction
ASSOCIATED CONCEPTS: kidnapping

FOREIGN PHRASES: *Extortio est crimen quando quis colore officii extorquet quod non est debitum, vel supra debitum, vel ante tempus quod est debitum.* Extortion is a crime when anyone under color of office extorts that which is not due, or more than is due, or before the time when it is due.

EXTORTIONIST, noun   blackmailer, compeller, corrupt demander, demander, exacter, illegal exacter, illegal taker, taker, unlawful obtainer, wrester
ASSOCIATED CONCEPTS: coercion, kidnapping, larceny

EXTRACT, verb   abridge, abstract, bring forth, choose, cite, collect, cull, deduce, derive, dig out, distill, draw, draw forth, draw out, educe, elicit, epitomize, *evellere,* eviscerate, evoke, excavate, *excerpere,* excerpt, *extrahere,* gather, glean, make a selection, mine, obtain, pick, pick out, pull, pull out, quarry, quote, remove, select, separate, single out, summarize, take out, withdraw

EXTRADITION, noun   apprehension and transfer, capture and deportation, change of place, deportation, seizure and transference, sending to another state for trial, surrender of an individual, transfer to another authority, transference, translocation, turning over to a foreign state
ASSOCIATED CONCEPTS: habeas corpus, rendition

EXTRANEOUS, adjective   additional, alien, *alienus,* aside from the point, coming from without, derived from without, dispensable, extra, extraneus, extrinsic, extrinsical, foreign, impertinent, inapplicable, inapposite, incidental, inconsequent, inconsequential, irrelative, irrelevant, needless, noncompulsory, nonessential, nonpertinent, optional, peripheral, pleonastic, redundant, strange, subsidiary, superfluous, supervenient, supplementary, unaffiliated, unallied, unassociated, uncalled for, unessential, unnecessary, unneeded, unrelated
ASSOCIATED CONCEPTS: extraneous evidence

EXTRAORDINARY, adjective   above average, amazing, beyond the ordinary, curious, different, especial, exceeding the usual, exceptional, *extraordinarius,* infrequent, *inusitatus,* irregular, notable, noteworthy, *novus,* out of the ordinary, out of the regular order, outstanding, peculiar, phenomenal, rare, remarkable, singular, special, supernormal, unaccustomed, uncommon, uncustomary, unequalled, unexampled, unfamiliar, unheard of, unique, unordinary, unparalleled, unprecedented, unusual, worthy of attention, worthy of regard
ASSOCIATED CONCEPTS: extraordinary care, extraordinary circumstances, extraordinary expenses, extraordinary grand jury, extraordinary peril, extraordinary prerogative writ, extraordinary purpose, extraordinary remedy, extraordinary risks, extraordinary services, extraordinary session
FOREIGN PHRASES: *Ubi cessat remedium ordinarium, ibi decurritur ad extraordinarium.* Where an ordinary remedy fails, than resort must be made to an extraordinary one. *Recurrendum est ad extraordinarium quando non valet ordinarium.* Resort must be made to the extraordinary when the ordinary does not succeed. *Nunquam decurritur ad extraordinarium sed ubi deficit ordinarium.* Resort is never made to the extraordinary until the ordinary fails.

EXTREME (Exaggerated), **adjective**   aggrandized, amplified, beyond the limit, drastic, enlarged, exceeding, exceeding the bounds of moderation, excessive, exorbitant, fanatical, flagrant, going to the utmost lengths, going too far, gross, hyperbolic, immoderate, inordinate, intemperate, magnified, out of bounds, out of proportion, outrageous, overboard, overdone, overstated, overzealous, rabid, radical, undue, unreasonable, unwarranted, violent

EXTREME (Last), **adjective**   at the edge, at the utmost point, concluding, conclusive, definitive, determinative, ending, endmost, *extremus,* farthest, farthest removed, final, finishing, furthest, hindermost, hindmost, last, most distant, most remote, outermost, situated at the farthest limit, *summus,* terminal, terminative, ultimate, *ultimus,* utmost, uttermost
ASSOCIATED CONCEPTS: extreme cases
FOREIGN PHRASES: *Probatis extremis, praesumuntur media.* The extremes having been proved, those things which lie between are presumed.

EXTREMITY (Death), **noun**   cessation of being, cessation of existence, cessation of life, close, completion, conclusion, demise, departure, discontinuance, discontinuation, dissolution, end, end of life, expiration, extinction, extinguishment, finish, passing, quietus, stoppage, termination

EXTREMITY (Furthest point), **noun**   border, borderline, boundary, brink, edge, end, extreme limit, *extremitas,* farthest end, farthest point, farthest reach, final point, fringe, frontier, limit, margin, outer edge, outside, pole, tail end, terminal point, termination, terminus, tip, ultimate point, utmost point, verge

EXTRICATE, verb   clear, cut loose, deliver, deobstruct, detach, disburden, discharge, disembarrass, disembroil, disencumber, disengage, disentangle, disenthrall, disjoin, dislodge, disprison, enlarge, exonerate, *expedire,* exsolvere, free, let loose, *liberare,* liberate, loosen, make free, ransom, redeem, release, release from restraint, relieve, rescue, save, set at large, set at liberty, set free, tear loose, unbind, unfetter, unhamper, unharness, unknot, unloose, unloosen, unravel, unshackle, untie

EXTRINSIC, adjective   accessory, added, additional, alien, apart, applied from without, collateral, contingent, derived from without, exterior, external, extra, extraneous, extrinsical, foreign, incidental, irrelevant, nonessential, outside, peripheral, secondary, separate, strange, subordinate, subsidiary, supplemental, unessential
ASSOCIATED CONCEPTS: extrinsic agreements, extrinsic ambiguity, extrinsic circumstances, extrinsic evidence, extrinsic facts, extrinsic fraud, extrinsic mistake

EXUDE, verb   bleed, discharge, disembogue, drain, drip, drop, effuse, eliminate, emit, escape, excrete, find outlet, find passage, find vent, flow out, give off, gush, issue, leak, *manare,* ooze, pass, release, run, secrete, seep, spout, trickle, vent, weep

EYEWITNESS, noun   arbiter, attestant, attester, bystander, compurgator, corroborator, giver of evidence, identifier, informant, informer, looker-on, observer, one who obtains evidence first hand, one who personally observes an occurrence, one who testifies to what he has seen, onlooker, seer, spectator, spectator et *testis,* testifier, viewer, watcher

F

FABRICATE *(Construct),* ***verb***   assemble parts, bring into being, bring into existence, build, call into being, cast, cause to be, cause to exist, complete, compose, create, devise, erect, establish, execute, *fabricari,* fashion, form, generate, make, manufacture, mold, organize, piece together, produce, put together, set up, shape, structure, turn out

FABRICATE *(Make up),* ***verb***   be untruthful, beguile, counterfeit, deceive, delude, devise falsely, dissemble, dissimulate, distort, fake, falsify, feign, fictionalize, forswear, invent, lie, misguide, misinform, mislead, misrepresent, misstate, palter, perjure oneself, pretend, prevaricate, sham, stretch the truth, tell a falsehood, tell a lie, trump up
ASSOCIATED CONCEPTS: fabricated evidence

FACE AMOUNT, ***noun***   exact amount, precise amount, sum, sum shown, sum stated, total

FACE VALUE *(First blush),* ***noun***   appearance, emanation, manifestation, semblance, visual impact

FACE VALUE *(Price),* ***noun***   price charged, quoted price, sum, total, worth

FACILE, ***adjective***   accomplished, amenable, attainable, compliable, compliant, conquerable, deft, dexterous, docile, easily done, easily influenced, easily persuaded, easy, easygoing, effortless, *facilis,* flexible, flowing, fluent, impressionable, malleable, manageable, moldable, performable, pliable, pliant, practiced, quick, readily mastered, ready, simple, skilled, skillful, smooth, tractable, undemanding, within reach, yielding

FACILITATE, ***verb***   accelerate, advance, aid, assist, assist the progress, clear, clear the way, deobstruct, disburden, disencumber, disentangle, ease, enable, encourage, *expedire,* expedite, forward, foster, free from difficulty, free from hindrance, free from impediment, free from obstruction, further, give clearance, hasten, help, lend a hand, lessen the labor, lift a ban, lighten, make a path for, make easy, make possible, open the way for, pave the way, promote, push forward, quicken, *rem faciliorem reddere,* render a task easier, render assistance, render less difficult, simplify, smooth, speed up
ASSOCIATED CONCEPTS: accomplice, aiding and abetting, facilitation

FACILITATION, ***noun***   advancement, aid, assistance, cleared the way, ease, encouragement, expedience, expedition, furtherance, help, involvement, lubrication, open the doors, play a positive role, promotion, quickening, support
ASSOCIATED CONCEPTS: criminal facilitation, facilitation of a crime, facilitation of a felony

FACILITY *(Easiness),* ***noun***   ability, adeptness, adroitness, capability, competence, deftness, dexterity, ease, effortlessness, expertise, expertness, *facilitas,* flexibility, fluency, freedom from difficulty, grace, gracefulness, proficiency, quickness, readiness, ready ability, skill, smoothness

FACILITY *(Institution),* ***noun***   agency, bureau, *conlegium,* establishment, foundation, institute, organization, organized society, *sodalitas*
ASSOCIATED CONCEPTS: reinsurance facility

FACILITY *(Instrumentality),* ***noun***   agency, apparatus, appliance, channel, *consilium,* contrivance, device, *facultas,* implement, instrument, machinery, manner, means, mechanism, medium, method, technique, tool, *via,* way

FACSIMILE, ***noun***   copy, duplicate, exact copy, mold, molding, oneness, replica, reproduction, sameness, semblance

FACT, ***noun***   absolute certainty, absolute reality, actual occurrence, actual reality, actuality, authenticated incident, certainty, documented event, established matter, established phenomenon, event, existent thing, experience, *factum,* incontrovertible incident, indisputable event, palpable episode, perceived happening, real episode, real experience, reality, *res,* substantiated incident, tangible proof, true incident, truth, verifiable happening
ASSOCIATED CONCEPTS: conceded facts, established fact, facts in issue, facts of a case, facts pleaded, facts presented, facts which constitute a cause of action, question of fact, stipulated facts, uncontroverted facts, undisputed facts
FOREIGN PHRASES: ***Ubi factum nullum, ibi fortia nulla.*** Where there is no principal in fact, there can be no accessory. ***Regula est, juris quidem ignorantiam cuique nocere, facti vero ignorantiam non nocere.*** The rule is that a person's ignorance of the law may prejudice him, but that his ignorance of fact will not. ***Ex facto jus oritur.*** Law arises out of facts. ***Ad quaestionem facti non respondent judices; ad quaestionem juris non respondent juratores.*** Judges do not answer to a question of fact; jurors do not answer to a question of law. ***Facta sunt potentiora verbis.*** Facts are more powerful than words.

FACT FINDING, *noun*   ascertainment of facts, authentication of facts, certification of facts, conclusion based on facts, confirmation of facts, decision based on facts, declaration based on facts, decree based on facts, determination based on facts, draw a conclusion on the facts, evidence based on facts, finding on facts, form a resolution on facts, incontrovertible determination based on facts, investigation of the facts, resolution based on facts, substantiation of the facts, tangible proof of the facts, verification based on facts

FACTION, *noun*   cabal, camarilla, clique, conspiracy, contentious group, disaccord, disagreeing party, discord, dissension, dissent, division, *factio, pars,* partisan conflict, partisanship, pressure group, side, splinter party, united body

FACTIOUS, *adjective*   argumentative, at loggerheads, at odds, bellicose, cantankerous, combative, contentious, controversial, contumacious, disagreeing, discordant, disputatious, dissenting, dissident, divergent, divided, divisive, hostile, implacable, inimical, insubordinate, irascible, militant, mutinous, negative, polemic, pugnacious, quarrelsome, schismatic, turbulent, uncooperative, unilateral

FACTITIOUS, *adjective*   assumed, contrived, counterfeited, faked, false, feigned, fictitious, forged, imaginary, imagined, imitative, pretended, simulated, simulative, unauthentic

FACTOR (Commission merchant), ***noun***   agent, broker, commercial agent, delegate, deputy, envoy, interagent, intermediary, manager, medium, middleman, one who sells for factorage, proctor, *procurator,* representative
ASSOCIATED CONCEPTS: consignee, factors' lien

FACTOR (Ingredient), ***noun***   additive, agent, aid, aspect, cause, component, constituent, constitutive element, content, contributing force, determinant, element, elementary unit, feature, integral part, part, portion, segment, unit

FACTUAL, *adjective*   accurate, actual, ascertained, attested, authentic, authoritative, correct, definite, definitive, dependable, disinterested, errorless, exact, faithful, genuine, honest, incontestable, incontrovertible, infallible, irrefutable, literal, objective, official, precise, real, realistic, reliable, right, rigid, scrupulous, strict, true, trustworthy, unbiased, uncolored, undeniable, undeviating, undisguised, undisputed, undistorted, unerring, unerroneous, unexaggerated, unfabricated, unimagined, unimpeachable, unmistakable, unprejudiced, unquestionable, unrefuted, unspurious, valid, veracious, veridical

FACULTY (Ability), ***noun***   ableness, adroitness, aptitude, capability, capacity, cleverness, competence, competency, cunning, deftness, dexterity, enablement, endowment, equipment, expertise, expertness, fitness, flair, gift, handiness, knack, know-how, potency, power, proficiency, qualification, readiness, skill, skillfulness, strength, talent, *vis*
ASSOCIATED CONCEPTS: the faculty to comprehend

FACULTY (Teaching staff), ***noun***   body of professors, instructional corps, instructional personnel, instructors, lecturers, literati, mentors, officers of instruction, professorate, professors, teachers, teaching body, teaching personnel, tutors

FADE, *verb*   abate, becoming, blanch, bleach, blench, cease, cloud, decay, decline, decrease, degenerate, deliquesce, deteriorate, die, die out, dim, diminish, disappear, discolor, dissolve, drop off, ebb, etiolate, evaporate, fail, faint, falloff, flag, flicker, grow dimmer, grow duller, languish, lessen, let up, lose brightness, lose luster, neutralize, obsolesce, pale, perish, reduce, sag, shrivel, sink, slacken, subside, taper off, tarnish, tone down, turn colorless, turn dull, vanish, wane, wash out, waste away, weaken, wilt, wither

FAIL (Lose), ***verb***   be defeated, be demoted, be unsuccessful, become bankrupt, become insolvent, botch, bungle, *cadere,* collapse, come short, come to naught, come to nothing, *concidere,* crash, decline, *deficere,* deteriorate, disappoint, dishonor, err, fall short, flunk, fold, go out of business, go under, lose, miscarry, miss the mark, not succeed, prove inadequate, prove unsatisfactory, prove useless, succumb

FAIL (Neglect), ***verb***   abandon, avoid, break one's promise, break one's word, desert, evade, forsake, ignore, leave, let one down, mismanage, miss, miss an opportunity, omit, prove unreliable, shirk
ASSOCIATED CONCEPTS: fail to act, fail to appear, fail to comply

FAILING, *noun*   asthenia, atony, blemish, cachexia, collapse, debilitation, decadence, decay, decline, decrepitude, defeat, deficiency, delinquency, disadvantage, failure, fallibility, fault, fiasco, flaw, foible, frailty, imperfection, inadequacy, infirmity, insufficiency, misconduct, perfunctoriness, nonfulfillment, shortcoming, unworthiness, vice, weakness, weak point

FAILURE (Bankruptcy), ***noun***   commercial failure, default, discontinuance of business, economic downfall, failure to maintain solvency, financial disaster, financial loss, financial ruin, inability to maintain solvency, inability to meet financial obligations, insolvency, insufficiency of funds, lack of funds, suspension of business
ASSOCIATED CONCEPTS: failure to meet one's obligations, insolvency

FAILURE (Falling short), ***noun***   *defectio,* defectiveness, deficiency, delinquency, dereliction, inability, insufficiency, lack, loss of strength, noncompletion, nonfulfillment, nonobservance, nonperformance, omission, oversight, pretermission, shortcoming, slip, want
ASSOCIATED CONCEPTS: failure of consideration, failure of evidence, failure of heirs, failure of issue, failure of proof, failure of purpose, failure of title, failure of trust, failure to act, failure to bargain collectively, failure to comply, failure to file a return, failure to give notice, failure to make delivery, failure to perform, failure to prosecute, law office failures, partial failure

FAILURE (Lack of success), ***noun***   aborted attempt, beating, botch, breakdown, collapse, debacle, defeat, disappointment, downfall, drubbing, error, fall, fiasco, fruitless effort, frustration, ineffectualness, labor in vain, loss, miscarriage, misfortune, mistake, ruin, unsuccessful attempt, vain attempt

FAILURE TO COMPLY, *noun*   contravention, default, defiance, deficiency, deliquency, dereliction, disobedience, disregard, evasion, ignoring, inexecution, infringement, laxity, mutiny, neglect, neglect to obey, negligence, nonfeasance, nonfulfillment, nonobservance, omission, rebellion, recalcitrance, refusal to obey, resistance, revolt, transgression, violation

FAILURE TO UNDERSTAND, *noun*   error, laboring under a misapprehension, misapprehension, miscalculation, misconception, misconstruance, miscount, misguidance, misinterpretation, misjudgment, misread, misreckon, mistake, misunderstanding

FAIR *(Just)*, *adjective* *aequus,* affording no undue advantage, appropriate, balanced, deserved, detached, dispassionate, equal, equitable, evenhanded, fair-minded, fitting, honest, honorable, impartial, merited, objective, scrupulous, sporting, sportsmanlike, square, suitable, unbiased, uncolored, uncorrupted, uninfluenced, unprejudiced, unswayed, upright

ASSOCIATED CONCEPTS: fair and impartial trial, fair hearing, fair on its face, fair preponderance of evidence, fair representation, fair trade, fair trial, fair wages

FAIR *(Satisfactory)*, *adjective* acceptable, adequate, bearable, decent, good enough, mediocre, medium, middling, moderate, moderately good, passable, reasonable, reasonably good, respectable, *secundus,* sufficient, suitable, tolerable, unexceptional, unobjectionable

ASSOCIATED CONCEPTS: fair aggregate value, fair and equitable value, fair and reasonable compensation, fair and reasonable market value, fair and reasonable value, fair cash value, fair consideration, fair equivalent, fair market value, fair preponderance, fair return on investment, fair use, fair valuation, fair value

FAIR TRADE AGREEMENT, *noun* trade agreement on set prices, trade alliance on set prices, trade binding promise on set prices, trade commitment on set price, trade compact on set prices, trade concordat on set prices, trade deal on set prices, trade obligation on set prices, trade pact on set prices, trade pledge on set prices, trade understanding on set prices

FAIRLY *(Clearly)*, *adverb* absolutely, *aperte,* certainly, *clare,* completely, conspicuously, decidedly, decisively, definitely, discernibly, *distincte,* distinctively, distinctly, distinguishably, doubtlessly, evidently, explicitly, fully, indubitably, intelligibly, irrefragably, irrefutably, legibly, lucidly, manifestly, markedly, noticeably, obviously, openly, palpably, perceptibly, plainly, pointedly, positively, prominently, recognizably, surely, tangibly, unambiguously, unconfusedly, undeniably, understandably, undoubtedly, unequivocally, unmistakably, unquestionably, visibly, vividly, with assurance, with certainty, with confidence

FAIRLY *(Impartially)*, *adverb* *aeque,* benevolently, disinterestedly, dispassionately, equably, equally, equitably, evenhandedly, evenly, free from prejudice, honestly, honorably, impersonally, in a fair manner, *iuste,* justly, lawfully, legally, morally, properly, righteously, rightfully, rightly, scrupulously, tolerantly, unbiasedly, with justice, without bias, without distinction, without favor, without prejudice

ASSOCIATED CONCEPTS: adjudicate a case fairly

FAIRLY *(Moderately)*, *adverb* acceptably, adequately, decently, *mediocriter,* mildly, modestly, not badly, passably, presentably, pretty well, rather well, satisfactorily, somewhat, to a degree, to a limited extent, to some extent, tolerably, up to standard, well enough, within bounds, within reason

FAIRNESS, *noun* *aequitas,* appropriateness, balance, detachment, disinterestedness, dispassionateness, equality, equitable treatment, equitableness, equity, evenhanded justice, evenhandedness, fair-mindedness, fair play, fair treatment, honesty, impartiality, integrity, *iustitia,* just dealing, justice, justness, lack of corruption, lack of prejudice, objectivity, open-mindedness, probity, reasonableness, rectitude,

right, rightfulness, rightness, scrupulousness, unbiasedness, uprightness

FAIT ACCOMPLI, *noun* accomplished fact, accomplishment, achievement, actuality, actualization, attainment, carrying through, certainty, completeness, completion, consummation, deed done, effectuation, execution, fact, finished product, fruition, fulfillment, implementation, matter of fact, reality, realization, undeniable fact, work done

FAITH, *noun* acceptance, allegiance, assurance, assured expectation, belief, certainty, certitude, confidence, constancy, conviction, credence, deep-rooted belief, dependence, fidelity, *fides,* firm belief, freedom from doubt, hope, implicit belief, implicit confidence, loyalty, *opinio,* optimism, *persuasio,* reliance, sanguine expectation, sanguineness, staunch belief, staunch loyalty, steadfast belief, steadfastness, sureness, surety, troth, trust, unquestioning acceptance, unshakable trust

FOREIGN PHRASES: *Fides servanda est.* Faith must be observed. *Judiciis posterioribus fides est adhibenda.* Credit should be given to the more recent decisions. *Ligeantia est quasi legis essentia; est vinculum fidei.* Allegiance is the essence of law; it is the bond of faith.

FAITHFUL *(Diligent)*, *adjective* assiduous, attentive, careful, conscientious, constant, dogged, exacting, *fidelis, fidus,* indefatigable, industrious, laborious, meticulous, mindful, painstaking, particular, persevering, persistent, pertinacious, relentless, sedulous, thorough, tireless, unflagging, unrelenting, unremitting, untiring, unwavering

ASSOCIATED CONCEPTS: faithful discharge of duty, faithful performance bond, faithful service

FAITHFUL *(Loyal)*, *adjective* constant, dependable, devoted, devout, duteous, dutiful, firm, incorruptible, obedient, patriotic, reliable, resolute, sincere, singlehearted, staunch, steadfast, true, trustworthy, unfailing, unwavering, zealous

FAITHFUL *(True to fact)*, *adjective* accurate, adhering to an original, close, conformable, correct, corresponding, equivalent, exact, faultless, genuine, honest, like, literal, perfect, precise, real, realistic, strict, true

FAITHFULLY, *adverb* absolutely, accurately, acquiescently, closely, compliantly, conscientiously, consistently, constantly, devotedly, diligently, duteously, dutifully, earnestly, exactly, expressly, *fideliter,* firmly, honestly, honorably, in every respect, in good faith, incorruptibly, literally, loyally, meticulously, obediently, observantly, precisely, punctiliously, reliably, religiously, resolutely, responsibly, rigidly, scrupulously, sincerely, stanchly, steadfastly, steadily, strictly, submissively, to the letter, truly, trustingly, trustworthily, truthfully, undeviatingly, unerringly, unswervingly, uprightly, veraciously, verbatim, virtuously, with allegiance, with constancy, with fealty, with fidelity, with good faith, word for word

ASSOCIATED CONCEPTS: faithfully discharge the duties of office, faithfully perform, perform duties faithfully, serve faithfully

FAITHFULNESS, *noun* adherence, allegiance, attachment, commitment, conformity, constancy, credibility, deference, devotion, discipline, fidelity, firmness, homage, integrity, loyalty, meticulousness, rectitude, responsibility, trustworthiness, veracity

FAITHLESS, *adjective* apostatizing, changeable, corrupt, corruptible, deceitful, derelict, disaffected, dishonest,

dishonorable, disloyal, double-dealing, false, falsehearted, fickle, fluctuating, hypocritical, inconstant, indifferent, *infidelis,* insincere, mutable, *perfidiosus,* perfidious, *perfidus,* recreant, shifting, traitorous, treacherous, treasonable, treasonous, trothless, two-faced, undependable, unfaithful, unloyal, unpatriotic, unreliable, unscrupulous, unstable, unsteadfast, untrue, untrustworthy, vacillating, variable, wavering
ASSOCIATED CONCEPTS: divorce

FAKE, *noun* charlatan, copy, counterfeit copy, emulation, fabrication, facsimile, false representation, falsehood, falsification, feigned copy, forged duplicate, forgery, fraud, fraudulent replica, hoax, imitation, imposter, pretender, quack, replica, reproduction, ruse, simulation, unauthorized reproduction
ASSOCIATED CONCEPTS: counterfeit, forgery

FAKE, *verb* act, act falsely, adulterate, affect, alter with intent to deceive, be deceitful, beguile, belie, bluff, cheat, claim falsely, counterfeit, cover up, cozen, deceive, decoy, defraud, delude, disguise, dissemble, dissimulate, distort, dupe, fabricate, falsify, feign, foist off, forge, go through the motions, hoax, hoodwink, imitate, lie, make a show of, make believe, malinger, mislead, misrepresent, pass off, plagiarize, portray falsely, pose as, prepare something specious, pretend, put on an act, put up a front, render spurious, sham, simulate, swindle, trick
ASSOCIATED CONCEPTS: false pretenses

FALLACIOUS, *adjective* abounding in error, beguiling, contrary to fact, deceitful, deceiving, deceptive, delusive, delusory, devoid of truth, distorted, erroneous, *fallax,* false, faultful, faulty, faulty in logic, fraudulent, groundless, guileful, illusive, illusory, in error, inaccurate, incorrect, invalid, miscalculated, misconstructed, misfigured, misleading, misrepresentative, mistaken, paralogistic, sophistical, truthless, unfounded, ungrounded, unsound, untrue, *vanus,* wrong

FALLACIOUSNESS, *noun* aberrancy, aberration, bad faith, casuistry, deceit, deception, deceptiveness, defectiveness, delusion, deviation, distortion, equivocation, erroneousness, fallacy, falseness, faultiness, faulty reasoning, fraudulence, illogic, illogicalness, illusion, inaccuracy, misapplication, self-contradiction, sophism, sophistry, speciousness

FALLACY, *noun* *captio,* deception, deceptive belief, delusion, deviation from truth, distortion, erroneous reasoning, erroneousness, error, fallacious argument, false appearance, falseness, falsity, faultiness, faulty reasoning, flaw in reasoning, illusion, inaccuracy, misapprehension, misbelief, miscalculation, misconception, misconstruction, misinterpretation, misjudgment, misleading notion, mistake, mistaken idea, paralogism, sophism, sophistry, unsound argument, *vitium,* worthless argument

FALLIBLE, *adjective* deficient, errable, errant, erring, *errori obnoxius,* faulty, flawed, imperfect, liable to be erroneous, liable to mistake, not perfect, prone to error, prone to inaccuracy, uncertain, undependable, unpredictable, unreliable, unstable, unsure, untrustworthy, weak

FALLOUT, *noun* a bleak outcome, a deleterious outcome, a deleterious outgrowth, a malignant scenario, an extremely unfortunate sequence of events, deleterious aftermath, deleterious developments, deleterious effects, deleterious results, grave consequences, important and significant effects

FALSE (Disloyal), *adjective* apostatizing, corrupt, deceitful, disaffected, dishonest, dishonorable, double-dealing,

double-tongued, faithless, false hearted, fickle, hypocritical, inconstant, insincere, knavish, perfidious, *perfidus,* recreant, roguish, tergiversating, traitorous, treacherous, treasonable, treasonous, trothless, two-faced, undependable, underhanded, unfaithful, unprincipled, unreliable, unscrupulous, unsteadfast, untrue, untrustworthy

FALSE (Inaccurate), *adjective* abounding in error, concocted, contrary to fact, deceiving, deceptive, delusive, devoid of truth, distorted, erroneous, fallacious, faulty, fictitious, groundless, improper, in error, incorrect, invalid, mendacious, misleading, mistaken, truthless, unfounded, ungrounded, unreliable, unsound, untrue, unveracious, wrong
ASSOCIATED CONCEPTS: altered, false advertising, false and malicious, false and misleading, false arrest, false check, false entry, false imprisonment, false information, false instrument, false oath, false personation, false pretense, false reports, false representation, false statement, false swearing, false testimony, false writing, knowingly false, materially false

FALSE (Not genuine), *adjective* artificial, assumed, beguiling, bogus, copied, counterfeit, deceitful, deceptive, delusory, designed to deceive, factitious, fake, feigned, *fictus,* forged, fraudulent, given to deceit, imitation, intentionally untrue, make believe, misrepresentative, mock, pretend, pseudo, sham, simulated, spurious, *subditus,* substitute, synthetic, unreal
ASSOCIATED CONCEPTS: false checks, false claim, false pretenses, false representation, false statement, false swearing, false witness

FALSE ALARM, *noun* deception, fabrication, fake, false alert, false arrest, false danger signal, false notice, false notification, false signal, false warning, fraud, misrepresentation, sham

FALSE ARREST, *noun* bogus arrest, illegal detainment, illegal placement in confinement, improper arrest, improper captivity, improper commitment to prison, improper confinement, improper constraint, improper deprivation of liberty, improper imprisonment improper incarceration, improper legal restraint, improper placement into protective custody, improper restraint, improper seizure, wrong capture, wrongful placement into custody

FALSE PRETENSE, *noun* act, affectation, affectedness, artifice, artificiality, assumed basis, bogus purpose, bogus reason, chicane, chicanery, circumvention, circumvention of truth, cozenage, deceit, deceitful purpose, deceitfulness, deceptive reason, deceptive representation of fact, delusion, designed misrepresentation, device, disguise, dishonesty, dissemblance, dissimulation, dupery, duplicity, evasion of truth, fabrication, facade, factitious reasons, fake, fake reasons, false representation of fact, falsehood, falseness, falsification, falsity, *falsus,* feigned basis, feint, *fictus,* forgery, fraud, fraudulence, fraudulency, guise, hoax, impetus, imposture, improper, improper basis, improper intent, improper intention, improper motivation, improper motive, improper pretensions, intentional untruths, invention, lie, mask, masquerade, mendacity, misinformation, misrepresentation, misstatement, perfidy, perversion of truth, pettifoggery, pretense, pretext, prevarication, ruse, sham, simulated basis, simulation, *simulatus,* sleight, spurious reasons, spuriousness, stratagem, subterfuge, suppression of truth, surreptitiousness, swindle, treacherousness, treachery, trick, trumped-up basis, trumped-up reasons, underhandedness, unnaturalness, untruth, untruthfulness, unveracity, wile, wrong foundation, wrong incentive

ASSOCIATED CONCEPTS: cheating by false pretenses, false representation, larceny, obtaining property by false pretenses, under false pretenses

FALSEHOOD, noun canard, *commentum,* deception, dissimulation, distortion, distortion of truth, equivocation, evasion, fabrication, false assertion, false statement, falsification, falsity, *falsum,* fiction, flam, fraud, fraudulence, inaccuracy, intentional misstatement, invention, inveracity, lie, *mendacium,* misrepresentation, misstatement, nonconformity to fact, perversion of truth, pretense, pretext, prevarication, story, tale, untrue declaration, untruth

FOREIGN PHRASES: Lex punit mendacium. The law punishes mendacity.

FALSIFICATION, noun beguilement, *corrumpere,* counterfeit, deceit, deceitfulness, deception, disguise, dissimulation, distortion, dupery, duplicity, exaggeration, fabrication, fake, fibbing, flimflam, forgery, forswearing, fraud, hoax, imposture, indirection, insincerity, *interpolare,* invention, lying, mendacity, misconstruction, misquotation, misrepresentation, misstatement, mockery, perjury, phoniness, pretense, prevarication, trickery, trumpery, untruthfulness, *vitiare*

ASSOCIATED CONCEPTS: falsification of evidence, falsification of records, falsification of testimony, perjury

FALSIFY, noun deceive, disguise, distort, dupe, duplicity, fabricate, fake, forge, fraudulent, invent, lie, misrepresent, misstate, prevaricate

ASSOCIATED CONCEPTS: falsify a record, falsify reports, falsify tax returns

FOREIGN PHRASES: Falsus in uno, falsus in omnibus. False in one thing, false in everything.

FALSIFY, verb adulterate, alter, alter fraudulently, belie, camouflage, color, *corrumpere,* dissemble, distort, doctor, embellish, embroider, exaggerate, fabricate, fake, feign, garble, *interpolare,* lie, make false statements, miscite, miscolor, misquote, misreport, misrepresent, misstate, pervert, represent falsely, stretch, tamper with, tell a falsehood, twist, violate the truth, *vitiare*

ASSOCIATED CONCEPTS: falsify records

FAMILIAR (Customary), adjective accepted, accustomed, acknowledged, clichéd, common, commonplace, consuetudinary, conventional, current, established, everyday, *familiaris,* frequent, general, generally seen, habitual, hackneyed, homely, household, humble, inveterate, natural, normal, *notus,* ordinary, popular, prevailing, prevalent, recognized, regular, regulation, routine, standard, stereotyped, stock, time-honored, traditional, typical, understood, unexceptional, universal, universally recognized, unoriginal, usual, well-known, well-trodden, widespread, wonted

ASSOCIATED CONCEPTS: custom and usage

FAMILIAR (Informed), adjective accomplished, acquainted, advised, apprised, aware of, briefed, capable, certified, closely acquainted, cognitive, cognizant, competent, conscious, conversant, counseled, deft, dexterous, educated, enlightened, erudite, experienced, expert, fit, fitted, *gnarus,* instructed, intimate, knowing, knowledgeable, learned, lettered, literate, mindful, on intimate terms, *peritus,* practiced, prepared, privy to, proficient, qualified, schooled, *sciens,* sensible, skilled, skillful, trained, tutored, used to, versed, well-acquainted, well-educated, well-versed

ASSOCIATED CONCEPTS: familiar with the facts sufficient to sign an affidavit

FAMILY (Common ancestry), noun ancestry, antecedents, birth, blood connection, clan, common extraction, common forebears, common lineage, common parentage, consanguinity, descent, dynasty, ethnic group, ethnicity, extraction, filiation, folk, genealogy, house, kin, kindred, kinship, kinsmen, line, line of ancestors, line of descent, lineage, origin, parentage, people, same line of descent, same strain, sept, stirps, stock, strain, tribe

FAMILY (Household), noun brood, domestic circle, domestic establishment, *familia,* family unit, home circle, issue, offspring, progeny

ASSOCIATED CONCEPTS: adoption, curtesy, dependent, domestic relation, dower, Family Court, family law, family purpose doctrine, head of household, heirs, next of kin, surviving spouse

FAMOUS, adjective acclaimed, applauded, *celeber,* celebrated, celebrated in public, conspicuous, distinguished, elevated, eminent, esteemed, exalted, fabled, famed, foremost, glorified, glorious, held in high esteem, highly reputed, holding public interest, honored, illustrious, important, in the limelight, in the public eye, in the spotlight, *inlustris,* known, leading, legendary, memorable, notable, noted, noteworthy, notorious, outstanding, popular, preeminent, prominent, public, recognized, remarkable, renowned, sung, talked of, universally recognized, well-known

ASSOCIATED CONCEPTS: libel, public figure, right to privacy, slander

FANATICAL, adjective ardent, burning, devoted, dogmatic, enthusiastic, excessive, extreme, fanatic, *fanaticus,* fervent, immoderate, impassioned, inordinate, obsessed, obsessive, overemotional, overenthusiastic, overzealous, passionate, phrenetic, phrenetical, possessed, rabid, radical, resolute, ultrareligious, unreasonable, unreasonably resolute, unyielding, zealous

FANTASTIC, adjective beyond anything ever experienced, celebrated, clever, colossal, compelling, dignified, distinguished, elevated, eminent, enormous, esteemed, exalted, excellent, expert, extensive, extraordinary, far-reaching, first-rate, glorious, grand, huge, immense, important, in another dimension, inconceivable, incredible, inexplicable, leading, lofty, major, massive, mastered, mighty, momentous, monstrous, noted, outrageous, outstanding, paramount, perfect, potent, powerful, preeminent, remarkable, renowned, skillful, splendid, strong, substantial, superior, supreme, unequaled, unparalleled

FAR, adjective back, beyond the eye, beyond the horizon, distant, far away, far back, far off, further, in the distance, inaccessible, miles away, out of reach, out of sight, out of the way, outlying, remote, removed, too distant, too far, too far away, too far removed, unapproachable

ASSOCIATED CONCEPTS: far apart for purposes of settlement

FAR FETCHED, adjective concocted, doubtable, doubtful, implausible, impossible, improbable, inconceivable, incredible, long odds against being correct, not probably correct, only remotely possible, poor prospect of truth, questionable, remote, small chance, unbelievable, unimaginable, unlikely

FAR REACHING, adjective boundless, comprehensive, considerable, endless, enormous, epidemic, extended, extensive, far-flung, far-ranging, great, having a significant impact, huge, immeasurable, immense, infinite, large scale, limitless, of great extent, of great scope, prodigious, spread out, substantial, sweeping, tremendous, uncircumscribed, unending, unlimited, vast, wide, widespread

FARCE, noun absurdity, burlesque, comedy, dry humor, dry wit, humor, imitation, jest, joke, lampoon, mockery, nimble wit, nonsense, parody, pleasantry, pretense, quick wit, satire, slapstick, spoof, wit
ASSOCIATED CONCEPTS: judgment a farce, travesty of justice, verdict a farce

FARE, noun carfare, charge, charge for carriage of passengers, charge for conveyance of a person, cost of commutation, cost of conveyance, cost of transportation, expense, expense of transportation, fee, hire, money paid for passage, *naulum,* passage, passage money, payment for the right of carriage, portage fee, price, price of a ticket, price of passage, sum paid for carrying a passenger, tariff, ticket, toll, transportation charge, transportation fee, *vectura*
ASSOCIATED CONCEPTS: rates, fares and charges of carrier

FASCINATE, verb allure, appeal to, attract, beguile, bewitch, captivate, capture, charm, coax, compel, delight, enamor, enchant, engage, engross, enrapture, enthrall, excite, grab, grip, hold attraction for, hold interest, hold spellbound, hypnotize, infatuate, influence, interest, intoxicate, intrigue, invite, kindle, mesmerize, overpower, overwhelm, pique, please, provoke, seize, stimulate, stir, transfix, win over

FAT CAT, noun affluent contributor, contributor with deep pockets, moneyed contributor, rich backer, rich contributor, wealthy campaign contributor, wealthy contributor, wealthy donor, wealthy supporter
ASSOCIATED CONCEPTS: campaign finance laws, election laws, limits on campaign contributions, publicly funded campaigns

FATAL, adjective annihilative, calamitous, catastrophic, causing death, causing destruction, consumptive, deadly, death-dealing, deathly, deleterious, demolishing, destroying, destructive, devastating, dire, disastrous, eradicative, *exitialis,* exterminative, extirpative, fateful, fell, feral, *funestus,* harmful, hurtful, injurious, involving death, involving ruin, killing, lethal, lethiferous, malignant, mortiferous, murderous, noisome, noxious, *perniciosus,* pernicious, poisonous, ruining, ruinous, slaughterous, toxic, tragic, venomous, virulent, wasting
ASSOCIATED CONCEPTS: fatal consequences, fatal defect, fatal errors, fatal injury, fatal to a cause of action, fatal variance

FATALITY, noun accidental death, calamity, casualty, *casus,* cataclysm, catastrophe, deadliness, deadly accident, death, death by accident, destruction, disaster, downfall, fatal accident, fatal casualty, fatal mishap, lethality, liability to disaster, malignance, malignancy, malignity, mischance, misfortune, mortality, perniciousness, ruin, subjection to fate, sudden death, tragedy, violent death, virulence, virulency

FATE (Destiny), **noun** certainty, destination, destined lot, fate-to-be-predetermined events, fortune, future, future course of events, future state, inevitability, inevitableness, lot, luck, outcome, power to predetermine events, predestination, predetermination, sureness, ultimate future, what is destined to happen, what is doomed to occur, what is fated to occur, what is written, what looms
ASSOCIATED CONCEPTS: fortuitous event, insurance, the defendant's fate is with the jury
FOREIGN PHRASES: *Fatum.* Fate.

FATE (Termination), **noun** apocalypse, bad luck, bane, bitter end, catastrophe, collapse, conclusion, curtain, cut-off, death, death knell, death warrant, deathblow, debacle, destruction, disaster, doom, downfall, end, end of the world, final blow, final event, final curtain, final result, finale, *finis,* finish, ill luck, last act, misfortune, payoff, quietus, ruin, ruination, terminus, tough luck, undoing, windup

FATED, adjective certain, destined, determined, doomed, foredoomed, in the cards, inescapable, inevitable, ordained, predestinated, predestined, predetermined, preordained, sure, unavoidable, written

FATUOUS, adjective absurd, absurdly foolish, addled, asinine, brainless, deficient in reason, destitute of reason, dumb, fatuitous, *fatuus,* foolish, idiotic, ill-advised, illogical, imbecilic, inane, incapable of managing one's own affairs, inept, *ineptus,* irrational, ludicrous, moronic, nonsensical, obtuse, ridiculous, scatterbrained, senseless, shallow, silly, simple, stupid, thoughtless, unintelligent, unreasoning, unthinking, unwise, vacuous, witless
ASSOCIATED CONCEPTS: fatuous claim

FAULT (Mistake), **noun** aberration, blunder, bungling, erratum, error, error of judgment, failing, false step, flaw, impropriety, inaccuracy, miscalculation, misjudgment, misstep, misunderstanding, omission, oversight, slip
FOREIGN PHRASES: *Imperitia culpae adnumeratur.* Unskillfulness is considered as negligence. *Quod quis ex culpa sua damnum sentit non intelligitur damnum sentire.* He who suffers a damage by his own fault is not considered to have suffered damage. *Culpa tenet suos auctores.* A fault binds its own authors. *Magna negligentia culpa est; magna culpa dolus est.* Gross negligence is fault; gross fault is equivalent to a fraud.

FAULT (Responsibility), **noun** accountability, answerability, blame, cause for blame, *culpa,* culpability, *delictum,* delinquency, dereliction, liability, malefaction, misbehavior, misconduct, misdeed, misfeasance, negligence, *peccatum,* transgression
ASSOCIATED CONCEPTS: comparative fault, contributory fault, contributory negligence, gross fault, with all faults, without fault
FOREIGN PHRASES: *Culpa est immiscere se rei ad se non pertinenti.* A person is at fault who intermeddles in matters not concerning him. *Ejus nulla culpa est, cui parere necesse sit.* No guilt attaches to a person who is compelled to obey. *In pari delicto potior est conditio possidentis, defendentis.* Where the parties are equally guilty of wrongdoing, the defendant holds the stronger position.

FAULT (Weakness), **noun** debility, defect, deficiency, delicacy, devitalization, drawback, emasculation, failing, feebleness, flaw, foible, frailty, impairment, imperfection, impotence, impuissance, inadequacy, incapacity, infirmity, instability, insufficiency, lack of strength, loss of strength, powerlessness, shortcoming, vitiation, vulnerable point, weak point

FAULT, verb *accusare,* accuse, admonish, animadvert, attack, berate, blame, bring into discredit, cast a slur upon, cast blame upon, castigate, censure, charge, chastise, chide, condemn, criticize, *culpare,* declaim against, de-cry, denigrate, denounce, deprecate, depreciate, disapprove, discommend, discountenance, disparage, dispraise, dress down, hold to blame, impeach, impugn, impute, remonstrate, reprehend, reprimand, reprove, scold, take to task, upbraid

FAULTLESS (Infallible), **adjective** above suspicion, absolute, accurate, best, chaste, correct, finished, flawless, ideal, immaculate, impeccable, incorruptible, indefectible, intact, irreproachable, letter-perfect, literal, irreprehensible, perfect, precise, pure, sinless, stainless, unadulterated, unblemished, uncontaminated, unimpeachable, untainted, virtuous, whole, without reproach

FAULTLESS (Not guilty), **adjective** blameless, free from guilt, free from moral wrong, guiltless, inculpable, innocent, lawful, legitimate, pardonable, sinless, unblamable, unoffending, upright, virtuous, without harm, without offense

FAULTY, adjective aberrant, amiss, awry, below par, blemished, damaged, defective, deficient, distorted, errant, erroneous, fallacious, false, flawed, found wanting, full of faults, impaired, imperfect, imprecise, improper, inaccurate, inadequate, incorrect, inferior, injured, invalid, lacking, less than perfect, malformed, mendosus, mistaken, not ideal, out of order, solecistic, solecistical, unfit, unprecise, unsatisfactory, unsound, vitiosus, wanting, warped, wrong

FAVOR (Act of kindness), **noun** accommodation, act of generosity, act of grace, benefaction, beneficium, benefit, benevolence, benignity, boon, bounty, charity, courtesy, friendly turn, good deed, good service, good turn, grace, indulgence, kind act, philanthropy

FAVOR (Partiality), **noun** approval, attachment, attraction, bent, bias, disposition, favoritism, fondness, inclination, kind regard, leaning, liking, partisanship, penchant, predilection, preference, preferential treatment, prejudice, proclivity, proneness, propensity
ASSOCIATED CONCEPTS: challenge to the favor, favored legislation, favored treatment

FAVOR (Sanction), **noun** abetment, advancement, advocacy, aegis, aid, approbation, approval, assistance, auspices, backing, benefaction, championship, cooperation, countenance, encouragement, endorsement, espousal, fosterage, furtherance, good opinion, help, leave, patronage, permission, sponsorship, subscription, support

FAVOR, verb advance, advocate, afford advantages, aid, approve, assist, back, be biased, be favorable to, be indulgent toward, be partial to, be prejudiced, befriend, benefit, bolster, boost, champion, countenance, deal with gently, ease, encourage, endorse, facilitate, fancy, favere, further, grant favors to, gratify, help, make easier, prefer, promote, regard with favor, regard with kindness, sanction, show consideration for, show favor to, show unfair bias, studere, succor, suffragari, support, treat differently, treat with partiality
ASSOCIATED CONCEPTS: favored beneficiary

FAVORABLE (Advantageous), **adjective** advisable, appropriate, auspicious, becoming, befitting, beneficial, commodus, conducive, convenient, desirable, encouraging, expedient, felicitous, fit, fitting, fortunate, full of promise, good, helpful, opportune, politic, profitable, promising, propitious, prosperus, providential, salutary, seasonable, suitable, timely, useful, wise
ASSOCIATED CONCEPTS: favorable decision

FAVORABLE (Expressing approval), **adjective** acclamatory, acquiescent, admiring, agreeable, approbative, approving, assenting, benign, commending, compliant, cooperative, encomiastic, encouraging, eulogistic, eulogistical, favorably prejudiced, favoring, generous, gracious, helpful, kind, laudatory, obliging, panegyrical, praising, reassuring, recommendatory, responsive, uncritical, willing

FAVORABLE DECISION, noun advisable outcome, an outcome which followed precedence, appropriate determination, auspicious determination, becoming outcome, befitting outcome, beneficial outcome, correct decree, desirable outcome, fair result, fit determination, fitting outcome, fortunate result, good result, impartial determination, judicious determination, just resolution, just result, just verdict, opportune determination, propitious result, providential result, reasonable outcome, right choice, salutary solution, Solomon-like determination, suitable result, the correct decision, the right decision, the right pronouncement, victory, win, wise resolution
FOREIGN PHRASES: *Favorabilia in lege sunt fiscus, dos, vita, libertas.* Things favorable considered within the law are the treasury, dower, life, and liberty.

FAVORABLE POSITION, noun advantage, edge, favorable opportunity, handicap, head start, high road, inside track, point of vantage, strategic advantage, superior situation, upper hand, winning position
FOREIGN PHRASES: *Favorabilia in lege sunt, fiscus, dos, vita, libertas.* Things which are favorably considered in law are the treasury, dower, life, and liberty. *Favorabiliores rei, potius quam actores, habentur.* The condition of the defendant shall be favored, rather than that of the plaintiff.

FAVORITISM, noun attachment, bias, discrimination, fondness, inequality, inequity, leaning, one-sidedness, partialism, partiality, partisanship, penchant, preference, prejudice, proclivity, proneness, slant

FEALTY, noun allegiance, compliance, constancy, deference, devotion, duteousness, duty, faith, faithfulness, fidelity, homage, humble service, loyalty, obedience, respect, reverence, servility, steadfastness, support, veneration

FEAR, noun affright, alarm, anxiety, apprehension, apprehension of danger, apprehension of harm, apprehension of injury, apprehension of punishment, apprehensiveness, awe, concern, consternation, cowardice, cowardliness, cravenness, diffidence, dismay, disquietude, dread, faintheartedness, fearfulness, foreboding, fright, horror, intimidation, metus, misgiving, panic, pavor, phobia, presentiment, pusillanimity, qualm, scare, state of anxiety, terror, timidity, timor, timorousness, trepidation, uneasiness, want of confidence
ASSOCIATED CONCEPTS: duress, mental anguish
FOREIGN PHRASES: *Nihil consensui tam contrarium est quam vis atque metus.* Nothing is so opposed to consent as force and fear. *Vani timoris justa excusatio non est.* A frivolous fear is not a lawful excuse. *Vani timores sunt aestimandi, qui non cadunt in constantem virum.* Those fears are to be regarded as groundless which do not affect an ordinary, steady man.

FEAR, verb anticipate danger, anticipate injury, apprehend, apprehend danger, apprehend harm, apprehend punishment, be a coward, be afraid, be alarmed, be anxious, be apprehensive, be concerned, be cowardly, be daunted, be fearful, be frightened, be horrified, be in awe, be intimidated, be nervous, be overawed, be petrified, be scared, be startled, be terrified, be timid, cower, dare not, dread, feel terror, fret, have qualms, live in terror, lose courage, metuere, stand aghast, stand in awe, take alarm, take fright, timere, vereri, worry

FEARFULNESS, noun affright, agitation, alarm, anxiousness, apprehension, consternation, distrust, faint-heartedness, fear, fright, intimidation, misgiving, nervousness, pusillanimousness, shyness, stress, suspicion, superstition, terror, timidity, timorousness, tremulousness, trepidation, unease

FEARLESS, adjective adventurous, audacious, bold, brave, confident, courageous, daring, dauntless, gallant, heroic, indomitable, intrepid, resolute, self-reliant, Spartan, spirited, stout-hearted, unabashed, unafraid, unawed, undaunted, unfearing, unflinching, unfrightened, unscared, unshakable, unterrified, valiant

FEASIBILITY, noun achievability, advantageousness, attainability, expedience, expediency, feasibleness, likelihood, opportuneness, performability, possibility, potentiality, practicability, practicableness, practicality, profitableness, reasonableness, usefulness, utility, viability, workability, workableness
ASSOCIATED CONCEPTS: feasibility study

FEATURE (Appearance), **noun** aspect, countenance, external appearance, form, lineament, *lineamentum,* lines, look, outward appearance, physiognomy, shape, visage

FEATURE (Characteristic), **noun** aspect, attribute, component, constituent, detail, distinction, distinctive trait, element, factor, idiosyncrasy, individuality, ingredient, mark, notability, outstanding property, part, particular, peculiarity, point, *proprietas,* quality, salient point, salient quality, singularity, trait

FEATURE (Special attraction), **noun** featured attraction, highlight, lead item, main attraction, main item, outstanding item, principal item, special attraction, specialty, star

FEDERAL, adjective allied, associated, banded, central, combined, confederate, federate, federative, *foederatus, foedere sociatus,* governmental, joined in a union, joint, leagued, merged, national, united
ASSOCIATED CONCEPTS: federal aid, federal common law, federal Constitution, federal courts, federal government, federal jurisdiction, federal law, federal offense, federal question, federal regulation, federal rights

FEDERALIZE (Associate), **verb** act in concert, affiliate, ally, amalgamate, associate, band in a federation, band together, centralize, collaborate, combine, confederate, consociate, consolidate, cooperate, federate, form a cartel, form a union, go into partnership, incorporate, join, join forces, league, make a common cause with, merge, organize, participate, pool, syncretize, team up, unify, unionize, unite, unite in a league, work as a team, work together

FEDERALIZE (Place under federal control), **verb** assume authority, exercise federal authority over, exert authority, exert federal control, place under federal administration, place under federal rule, seize from private control, seize from state control, seize power, take command, take control

FEDERATE, verb act in concert, affiliate, ally, amalgamate, assemble, associate, band, collaborate, combine, concert, confederate, conjoin, consociate, join, join forces, league, merge, organize, participate, pool one's interests, unify, unionize, unite, unite by compact, unite in a federation, unite in a league

FEDERATION, noun affiliation, alliance, amalgamation, association, centralization, coalition, combination, combine, concert, confederacy, confederation, cooperation, federal union, integration, league, merger, organized body, pool, syndicate, unification, union
ASSOCIATED CONCEPTS: labor federation, unincorporated association

FEE (Charge), **noun** charge for services, compensation, compensation for labor, compensation for professional service, consideration, cost, disbursement, dues, emolument, exactment, expenditure, expense, fare, fixed charge, *merces,* payment, price, recompense, remuneration, reward, toll, wage
ASSOCIATED CONCEPTS: attorney's fee, counsel fees, reasonable fee, splitting a fee

FEE (Estate), **noun** absolute inheritance, absolute interest in realty, corporal hereditament, feod, feud, fief, freehold, hereditament, holding, interest, land, landed estate, landed property, lands, legal estate, property, real estate, real property, realty, right of possession, title, unconditional inheritance, unlimited inheritance, unrestricted inheritance, vested interest in land
ASSOCIATED CONCEPTS: absolute fee, base fee, conditional fee, contingent fee, defeasible estate, determinable fee, fee simple, fee tail, limited fee, qualified fee
FOREIGN PHRASES: *Feodum est quod quis tenet ex quacunque causa sive sit tenementum sive redditus.* A fee is that which any one holds from whatever cause, whether it be tenement or rent.

FEE FOR SERVICES, noun direct-bill the patient, direct payment, direct payment to a doctor for care provided, entire payment, full payment, independent rates, nondiscounted rate, payment by a patient to a doctor for medical services, payment for medical services to a practitioner, payment in full for services provided, payment of the entire bill, payment without accepting any insurance, payment without insurance, payment without regard to health insurance payments
ASSOCIATED CONCEPTS: health care, HMOs, PPOs

FEE SIMPLE, noun absolute interest in realty, estate in fee simple, estate in land, fee simple absolute, holding, legal estate, ownership in property, ownership in real estate, ownership in real property, ownership in realty, ownership interest, real estate ownership, right in real property, title to property, title to real property, unlimited right to property ownership, unrestricted right to property ownership, vested interest in land
ASSOCIATED CONCEPTS: allodial title, concurrent estate, defeasible estate, fee simple determinable, fee tail, future estate, leasehold estate, life estate

FEEDBACK, noun acknowledgment, alternative view, answer, clarification, comments, criticism, elucidation, explanation, illumination, input, interpretation, positive input, reaction, reply, response, sense, sentiment, translation
ASSOCIATED CONCEPTS: negative feedback, polling, positive feedback

FEEL, verb appreciate, be informed of, believe, comprehend, conceive, conclude, deduce, glean, grasp, internalize, know, labor under, learn, note, observe, perceive, sense, share, sustain, sympathize, understand
ASSOCIATED CONCEPTS: feel positive about the outcome of a case, feel the defendant is guilty or innocent

FEELING (Compassion), **noun** aesthetic sense, affect, affection, appreciation, ardor, capacity, chord vibration, commiseration, delicacy, discernment, discrimination, echo, emotion, empathy, faculty, fellow feeling, fervor, heart, identification, intuition, judgment, keenness, passion, pathos, pity, refinement, response, sensibility, sentiment, sentimentality, sharpness, soul, spirit, susceptivity, sympathy, taste, tenderheartedness, tenderness, vibe, warmth

FEELING (Consciousness), **noun** activity, awareness, consideration, contractibility, discrimination, enjoyment, excitability, excitation, excitement, feel, feeling in one's bones, flash, foreboding, forefeeling, funny feeling, galvanism, gut feeling, hunch, impressibility, impression, innervation, intimation, intuition, intuitive impression, motility, motor response, perception, perceptiveness, perceptivity, preapprehension, premonition, presentiment, reaction, receptivity, reflex, responsiveness, sensation, sense, sensibility, sensitiveness, sensitivity, sensory response, sensuality, sentience, shrinking, susceptibility, suspicion, synesthesia, tact, tactfulness, titillation, vague feeling, voluptuousness

FEELING (Premonition), **noun** attitude, conception, emotions, estimation, feeling sensibilities, foreboding, gut reaction, hunch, idea, inkling, notion, opinion, outlook, passions, point of view, position, posture, sentiment, stance, susceptibilities, sympathies, theory, thought, viewpoint, way of thinking

FEELING (Suspicion), **noun** assumption, belief, common belief, concept, conclusion, conjecture, consideration, estimation, hunch, idea, impression, inkling, intuition, judgment, notion, observation, opinion, premonition, presumption, prevailing belief, prevailing sentiment, reaction, response, sensation, sense, sentiment, stance, supposition, theory, thinking, thought, vague feeling, view, viewpoint

FEELING (View), **noun** air, atmosphere, attitude, belief, character, characteristic, conception, emotions, estimation, feeling sensibilities, idea, mood, notion, opinion, outlook, passions, point of view, position, posture, sentiment, stance, susceptibilities, sympathies, theory, thought, viewpoint, way of thinking
ASSOCIATED CONCEPTS: feeling about the outcome of a case

FEIGN, **verb** affect, beguile, belie, cheat, concoct, counterfeit, create a false appearance, deceive, delude, disguise, dissemble, dissimulate, distort the truth, fabricate, falsify, *fingere,* imagine, imitate deceptively, impersonate, lack candor, lie about, make a false show of, make believe, make up, mislead, misreport, misrepresent, misstate, palter, personate, pretend, prevaricate, represent fictitiously, sham, *simulare,* simulate, speak falsely
ASSOCIATED CONCEPTS: feigned accomplice, feigned disability, feigned dispute, feigned issue

FEIGNED, **adjective** apocryphal, artificial, assumed, bogus, colorable, counterfeit, deceptive, delusive, disguised, dishonest, disingenuous, evasive, fabricated, factitious, faked, false, fictitious, forged, fraudulent, hypocritical, illusory, imaginary, insincere, lying, make-believe, mendacious, mock, mythical, pretended, pseudo, sham, simulated, spurious, supposititious, trumped up, unauthentic, untrue, ungenuine
ASSOCIATED CONCEPTS: feigned accomplice, feigned action, feigned issue

FEINT, **noun** ambush, artifice, camouflage, chicanery, counterfeit, deception, device, disguise, dodge, dupery,

duplicity, fakery, false appearance, false pretense, gimmick, illusion, legerdemain, maneuver, mask, masquerade, pass, ploy, prestidigitation, pretext, ruse, sham, sleight, stratagem, subterfuge, swindling, trap, trick, trickery, wile

FELICITOUS, **adjective** accordant, adapted, agreeing, applicable, apposite, appropriate, apropos, apt, becoming, befitting, concinnous, concordant, conformable, congruous, consonant, desirable, effective, excellent, fit, fitting, fortunate, germane, happy, harmonious, ideal, in place, inspired, joyful, joyous, meet, opportune, perfect, pertinent, relevant, rightful, seemly, successful, suitable, suiting, tasteful, timely, to the point, to the purpose, *venustus,* well-chosen, well-expressed, well-timed

FELLOW (Cohort), **noun** adjunct, attendant, colleague, companion, comrade, confederate, consort, contributor, co-partner, correlative, individual, mate, member, participant, partner, peer, person

FELLOW (Complement), **noun** associate, co-equal, counterpart, equal, equipollent, like, match, obverse, parallel, reciprocal, similitude

FELLOW SERVANT, **noun** associate worker, employee, fellow employee, participatory employee, worker
ASSOCIATED CONCEPTS: common service, concurrent negligence, delegation of duty, invitees, master and fellow servant, superintending, superior servant, vice principal, workers' compensation

FELON, **noun** convict, criminal, culprit, delinquent, evildoer, guilty person, lawbreaker, malefactor, *nefarius,* offender, outlaw, recidivist, recreant, reprobate, *sceleratus, scelestus,* transgressor, wrongdoer
ASSOCIATED CONCEPTS: convicted felon
FOREIGN PHRASES: *Nullus dicitur felo principalis nisi actor, aut qui praesens est, abettans aut auxilians ad feloniam faciendam.* No one is called a principal felon except the party actually committing the felony, or the person who is present, aiding and abetting in its commission.

FELONIOUS, **adjective** against the admonition of law, against the law, against the rules, base, condemnable, contrary to law, criminal, criminous, culpable, dishonest, dissolute, done with intent to commit crime, evildoing, extralegal, fraudulent, illegal, illegitimate, immoral, in violation of law, *inlicitus,* lawbreaking, lawless, malfeasant, malicious, nefarious, *non legitimus,* nonlegal, of the quality of a felon, offending, outlawed, outside the law, perfidious, transgressing, unallowed, unauthorized, unlawful, unlicensed, unpardonable, unwarrantable, *vetitus,* villainous, wicked, wrong, wrongful
ASSOCIATED CONCEPTS: felonious act, felonious arson, felonious assault, felonious homicide, felonious intent, felonious purpose, feloniously taking

FELONY, **noun** capital crime, crime graver than a misdemeanor, criminal activity, criminal offense, gross offense, heinous crime, heinous misconduct, illegality, indictable offense, misdeed punishable by imprisonment, offense, offense punishable by imprisonment, transgression, violation of law, wrongdoing
ASSOCIATED CONCEPTS: assault with intent to commit felony, capital felony, common law felony, compounding a felony, felonious intent, felony conviction, felony murder, substantive felony
FOREIGN PHRASES: *Felonia, ex vi termini significat quodlibet capitale crimen felleo animo perpetratum.* Felony by force

of the term, signifies any capital crime perpetrated with a criminal mind. ***Felonia implicatur in qualibet proditione.*** Felony is implied in every treason.

FEMALE, *noun*　　female being, female gender, female sex, gender, girl, her, herself, lady, miss, mrs., ms., she, woman
ASSOCIATED CONCEPTS: women's rights
FOREIGN PHRASES: ***Feme, Femme.*** A woman. ***Feme covert.*** A married woman. ***Feme sole.*** A single woman.

FENCE, *noun*　　buyer of stolen goods, buyer of stolen property, disposer of stolen goods, purchaser of stolen goods, purchaser of stolen property, receiver, receiver of stolen goods, receiver of stolen property, recipient of stolen goods, recipient of stolen property, vendor of stolen goods, vendor of stolen property
ASSOCIATED CONCEPTS: burglary, robbery, theft

FEOFFEE, *noun*　　acceptor, assignee, devisee, donee, donee of a corporeal hereditament, grantee, legatee, one to whom a fee is conveyed, one to whom seisin passes, one to whom title is passed, one who is enfeoffed, receiver, recipient of a fee, transferee

FEOFFMENT, *noun*　　assignation of title, cession of a fee, conferral of a fee, conferment of title, conveyance of realty, conveyancing, conveying title, delivery of title, gift of a freehold interest, investiture of title, livery of seisin, passing of seisin, transfer of property, transmission of title

FEOFFOR, *noun*　　assignor, bequeather, bestower, devisor, donor, giver, grantor, one who enfeoffs another, one who gives a corporeal hereditament, one who transfers property by deed, one who transfers real property to another, person making a feoffment, person who conveys a fee, transferor

FERMENT, *verb*　　agitate, arouse, create a disturbance, create turbulence, excite, fervid, flame, foment, impassion, incense, incite, inflame, instigate, kindle, pique, stir, stir-up

FEROCITY, *noun*　　agitation, commitment, excitement, extreme emotion, ferociousness, fierceness, raging, ranting, raving, ravished, roaring, viciousness, violence, zealousness

FERRET, *verb*　　bring to light, dig out, discover, disinter, elicit, find, fish out, hunt, look for, *rimari,* root out, search, seek, trace, track down, unearth
ASSOCIATED CONCEPTS: ferret out a crime

FERTILE, *adjective*　　arable, bearing offspring freely, creative, fecund, *fecundus,* feracious, *ferax, fertilis,* flowering, fructiferous, fructuous, fruitful, imaginative, ingenious, inventive, lush, luxuriant, original, originative, parturient, philoprogenitive, procreant, procreative, productive, profitable, progenerative, prolific, rank, rich, yielding
ASSOCIATED CONCEPTS: fertile octogenarian rule, presumption of fertility

FERVENT, *adjective*　　active, all out, animated, *ardens,* ardent, avid, committed, dedicated, devoted, devout, eager, earnest, enthusiastic, excited, feeling, *fervens,* fervid, *fervidus,* feverish, fierce, fiery, hearty, hectic, impassioned, in earnest, intense, keen, passionate, perfervid, resolute, serious, sincere, spirited, vehement, zealous, zestful
ASSOCIATED CONCEPTS: testator's fervent desire

FERVID, *adjective*　　agitate, ardent, create a disturbance, create a turbulence, devoted, devout, earnest, earnestly, excite, faithful, fervent, impassioned, instigate, intense, intent, passionate, perfervid, serious, sincere, spirited, stir, stir-up, zealous

FETTER, *noun*　　bond, bridle, catena, chain, check, *compes,* confinement, constraint, control, curb, detention, deterrence, deterrent, disadvantage, encumbrance, gyve, hamper, handicap, hindrance, impediment, imprisonment, incarceration, inhibition, interference, iron, limitation, lock, manacle, means of restraint, obstacle, obstruction, prevention, prohibition, rein, repression, restraint, restriction, shackle, strap, suppression, tie, trammel, *vinculum,* yoke

FETTER, *verb*　　bind, *catenas,* chain, check, confine, curb, enchain, enclose, entrammel, gyve, hamper, handcuff, handicap, hinder, immobilize, impede, *impedire,* impose restraint, inhibit motion, inhibit movement, keep in check, lock up, make captive, make prisoner, manacle, paralyze, prohibit, put in irons, put under restraint, restrain, restrain motion, restrain movement, restrict, secure, secure with chains, shackle, shut in, suppress, tie, tie down, trammel, *vincula*

FETUS, *noun*　　baby, embryo, genesis, immature stage, life, origination, seed, source, starting point, unborn young

FEUD, *noun*　　alienation, altercation, animosity, animus, antagonism, bitterness, breach, clash, conflict, contention, controversy, difference, disaccord, disagreement, discord, dispute, dissension, enmity, estrangement, faction, grudge, hereditary enmity, hostility, ill will, incompatability, inimicality, *inimicitia,* intolerance, inveterate hatred, inveterate strife, malevolence, mutual aversion, odds, open breach, open quarrel, opposition, private war, quarrel, rancor, rupture, *simultas,* split, strain, strife, tension, variance, vendetta

FEVER (Excitement), *noun*　　agitation, ardor, arousing, delirium, desire, disquiet, eagerness, enthusiasm, excitation, exhilaration, fervency, fever pitch, feverish excitement, feverishness, fire, fomentation, frenzy, galvanization, heat, intensity, panic, passion, provocation, stimulation, stirring up, tizzy, turmoil, upset, working up, zeal, zealousness, zest
ASSOCIATED CONCEPTS: proceedings reaching a fever pitch

FEVER (Illness), *noun*　　affliction, ailment, burning-up, elevated temperature, feverishness, has a disorder, has a malady, has an affliction, has an ailment, ill health, illness, in poor health, infirmity, not healthy, sickness, temperature
ASSOCIATED CONCEPTS: fee services, health care, HMO

FEVER PITCH, *noun*　　boil, boiling point, crescendo, excitement, extreme enthusiasm, fermentation, fervency, fever of excitement, feverishness, fire, flap, flurry, fluster, frenzy, fuming, furor, fuss, heat, intensity, maelstrom, nervousness, passion, rage, restlessness, roil, turbulence, turmoil, unrest, upset, zeal, zealousness

FEW, *adjective*　　a few, a handful of, a small number of, a sprinkling of, excess of two, few and far between, hardly any, inconsequential, inconsiderable, infrequent, insignificant, least, less, little, littlest, low, lowest, meager, minimal, minimum, more than two, negligible, not many, not too many, occasional, of small number, petty, picayune, precious few, rare, scant, scarce, scarcely any, seldom, several, slightest, small, smallest, some, sparse, straggling, superficial, too few, trifling, unimportant

FEW AND FAR BETWEEN, adjective an inconsiderable amount, few, hard to come by, hardly any, infrequent, less, meager, negligible, not many, not much, not too many, one-shot, one-time, piddling, scant, scanty, scarce, scarcely any, seldom, seldom met with, seldom seen, slim, slow, small number of, some, sparse, sporadic, spotty, unique, unprecedented, unusual

FIAT, noun authoritative order, authorization, command, decree, decree having the force of law, dictate, direction, directive, edict, enactment, hest, *imperium*, imposition, injunction, instruction, *iussum*, judgment, mandamus, *mandatum*, order, prescript, prescription, pronouncement, regulation, rescript, rule, sanction, ukase, warrant

FICTION, noun canard, *commentum*, concoction, fable, fabrication, *fabula*, false statement, falsehood, falsification, fancy, fantasy, feigned story, figment, invention, legend, lie, myth, perjury, prevarication, product of imagination, *res ficta*, untruth, untruthful report
FOREIGN PHRASES: Fictio legis inique operatur alieni damnum vel injuriam. Fiction of law is wrongful if it works loss or harm to anyone. **Fictio juris non est ubi veritas.** A fiction of law will not exist where the fact appears. **Les fictions naissent de la loi, et non la loi des fictions.** Fictions arise from the law, and not law from fictions. **Fictio cedit veritati. Fictio juris non est ubi veritas.** Fiction yields to truth. Where truth is, fiction of law does not exist.

FICTITIOUS, adjective apocryphal, arbitrarily invented, artificial, chimerical, *commenticius*, concocted, counterfeit, deceiving, delusive, erroneous, fabled, fabricated, fake, faked, false, fancied, fanciful, feigned, fictional, fictive, *fictus*, figmental, forged, founded on fiction, illusive, illusory, imaginary, imagined, invented, legendary, make-believe, mendacious, misleading, misrepresentative, mythic, mythical, mythological, nonexistent, notional, phony, pretended, sham, spurious, trumped-up, unfounded, unhistorical, unreal, untrue
ASSOCIATED CONCEPTS: fictitious address, fictitious claims, fictitious corporation, fictitious debts, fictitious name, fictitious parties, fictitious payee, fictitious person, fictitious statements

FIDELITY, noun allegiance, conscientiousness, constancy, *constantia*, devotedness, devotion, dutiful adherence, dutifulness, faith, faithfulness, fealty, *fidelitas, fides*, good faith, homage, loyalty, stanchness, steadfastness, trueness, trustiness, trustworthiness
ASSOCIATED CONCEPTS: fidelity bond, fidelity guaranty, fidelity insurance

FIDUCIARY, adjective commanding belief, commanding confidence, confidential, deserving belief, fiducial, founded in confidence, reliable, sound, trusted, trustworthy, worthy of belief, worthy of credence
ASSOCIATED CONCEPTS: fiduciary bequest, fiduciary bond, fiduciary capacity, fiduciary relation

FIDUCIARY, noun agent, caretaker, custodian, executor, guardian, one who handles property for another, one who transacts business for another, person entrusted with property of another, trustee
ASSOCIATED CONCEPTS: escrow, trust

FIEND (Addict), noun abuser, drug abuser, drug addict, drug user, narcotics addict, person hooked on something, user

FIEND (Enthusiast), noun admirer, adorer, buff, crazed fan, devotee, disciple, fan, fanatic, idolizer, individual with a one track mind, individual with a single minded dogma, infatuate, lover, worshiper, zealot

FIERCE (Ferocious), adjective battling, blustering, blusterous, blustery, by force, clamorous, contentions, destructive, devastating, distracted, feral, fighting, frantic, frenzied, frightening, furious, gladiatorial, militant, possessed, rabid, raging, rampant, ranting, raving, ravished, rip-roaring, roaring, tempestuous, thunderous, torrential, truculent, turbulent, uncontrollable, uncontrolled, unrestrained, warlike, warring
ASSOCIATED CONCEPTS: fierce criticism, fierce debate, fierce fight

FIERCE (Intense), adjective abandoned, acute, aggressive, amok, angry, animal, animated, ardent, avid, awful, barbarous, bellowing, berserk, beside oneself, bestial, bloodthirsty, bloody, blue in the face, bold, brutal, brutish, carried away, cruel, dangerous, deep, delirious, demoniacal, demonic, desperate, distracted, eager, earnest, ecstatic, enraged, enraptured, enthusiastic, fanatical, fearsome, feral, ferocious, fervent, fervid, fiery, frantic, frenzied, frightening, frothing, fulminating, furious, grim, haggard, hard, hard-boiled, hearty, high-spirited, hog-wild, hostile, howling, hysterical, impassioned, impetuous, in a transport or ecstasy, in hysterics, insane, intoxicated, irate, keen, mad, madding, malevolent, malign, maniac, maniacal, menacing, merciless, monstrous, mouth, murderous, orgasmic, orgiastic, out of one's wits, passionate, possessed, primitive, rabid, raging, ramping, ranting, ravening, raving, ravished, roaring, rough, running mad, ruthless, sanguinary, savage, sense, spirited, storming, terrible, tigerish, tough, transported, truculent, unbridled, unchecked, uncivilized, uncontrollable, uncontrolled, uncurbed, unrestrained, untamed, venomous, vicious, violent, virulent, wild, wild-eyed, wild-looking, wrathful, zealous

FIERI FACIUS, noun authorization to seize, authorization to seize chattels, authorization to take, execution on property, judicial authorization to remove chattels, judicial authorization to remove goods, levy on goods to pay a judgment, means to pay a judgment, order to seize, permission to seize, remedy, writ of execution, writ to seize

FIFTH AMENDMENT (Double jeopardy), noun protection against being tried twice for the same offense, protection against multiple punishment, protection against multiple punishment for the same offense

FIFTH AMENDMENT (Self-incrimination), noun protection against exposing one's self to prosecution, protection against incriminating one's self, protection against testifying against one's self
Generally: due process protection
Specifically: right to remain silent
ASSOCIATED CONCEPTS: full immunity, Miranda Warnings, transactional immunity, use and derivative immunity, use immunity

FIGHT (Argument), noun altercation, bickering, broil, *certamen*, clash, conflict, confrontation, contest, controversy, debate, difference, disagreement, discord, disputation, dispute, dissension, embroilment, estrangement, expression of contrary opinions, imbroglio, logomachy, oral contention, polemics, *pugna*, quarrel, row, schism, squabble, strife, variance, verbal contest, war of words, wrangle

FIGHT (Battle), noun action, affray, appeal to arms, armed action, assault, attack, bloodshed, bout, brawl, clash of arms, combat, contest, encounter, engagement, exchange of blows, fracas, fray, hostile encounter, *pugilatio,* rencounter, resistance, scuffle, skirmish, struggle, tussle, war, warfare

FIGHT (Battle), **verb**   act in opposition, altercate, appeal to arms, assail, assault, assume the offensive, attack, bandy with, be violent, break the peace, campaign, carry on war, challenge, close with, combat, come to blows, commit hostilities, compete with, confront, contend, contest, declare war, dispute, duel, engage, exchange blows, exchange fisticuffs, face danger, go to war, grapple with, have words with, joust, make war, oppose, *proelium committere,* pummel, rebel, reluct, resist, resort to arms, revolt, scrimmage, scuffle, set to, skirmish, spar, squabble, stand up to, strike, struggle against, take on, take the offensive, take up arms, tourney, tussle, vie with, wage war, wrestle with

FIGHT (Counteract), **verb**   act in opposition to, be at cross-purposes, be contrary, be obstructive, confound, confute, contradict, counter, countermine, counterpose, counterwork, cross, debar, defy, disapprove, foil, frustrate, hinder, impede, inhibit, interfere, make a stand against, negate, object, obstruct, oppose, preclude, prevent, protest, rebuff, reject, repulse, resist, run against, run counter to, side against, spurn, stand against, stand up to, thwart, traverse, vote down, work against
ASSOCIATED CONCEPTS: fight passage

FIGMENT, **noun**   canard, chimera, concoction, creation of the mind, deception, delusion, fabrication, falsehood, falsification, fancy, fantasy, feigned story, fiction, fiction of the mind, flight of fancy, hallucination, idle fancy, illusion, imagined thought, inaccuracy, invention, lie, mirage, myth, product of the imagination, reverie, romance, story, unreality, untruth

FIGURATIVE, **adjective**   allegoric, allegorical, anagogic, anagogical, depictive, descriptive, emblematic, emblematical, evidential, exhibitive, expressive, figural, illustrating, illustrational, illustrative, imagistic, imitative, implicative, indicative, indicatory, metaphoric, metaphorical, pictographic, pictorial, portraying, representational, representative, representing, satirical, signifying, simulative, standing for, suggestive, symbolic, symbolical, symbolizing, symptomatic, typical, typifying, vivid

FIGURE (Form), **noun**   art form, configuration, conformation, design, device, diagram, drawing, figuration, formation, illustration, layout, model, picture, prototype, representation, representation in art, representative, shape, symbol

FIGURE (Individual), **noun**   head, human being, leader, mortal, official, overseer, person, somebody, someone, supervisor

FIGURE (Numeral), **noun**   aggregate, amount, Arabic numerals, charge, expenditure, expense, number, price, quotation, rate, Roman numerals, sales price, sum, total, value

FIGURE (Conclude), **verb**   ascertain, decide, determine, estimate, infer, opine, suppose, think

FILE, **noun**   archive, card index, catalogue, classified index, docket, dossier, entry, folder, information, list, notebook, orderly arrangement of papers, record, record of the court, recorded information, register, registry, report, roll
ASSOCIATED CONCEPTS: duly filed, file a brief, file a complaint, file a lien, file a mortgage, file a reply, file a reply brief, file a summons, file papers, filed in open court, filing fee, filing of a claim, reporting act

FILE (Arrange), **verb**   align, arrange methodically, array, assign places to, bring into order, catalogue, categorize, class, classify, codify, collocate, coordinate, distribute, fix the order, grade, graduate, group, *limare,* line up, make orderly, marshal, organize, pigeonhole, place in order, position, put in array, put in order, range, rank, reduce to order, regulate, set in order, set to rights, sort, subdivide, systematize

FILE (Place among official records), **verb**   book, calendar, chronicle, deliver an instrument, deposit among records of the court, docket, document, enroll, enter, inscribe, list, place an instrument in a place of deposit, place in official custody of the clerk, place on record, preserve permanently as a public record, put on record, receive an instrument officially, register, store in the archives
ASSOCIATED CONCEPTS: docket, filing fee, filing of a deed, filing of a suit, filing of claims, filing of papers, filing of pleadings, late filing, time to file

FILIATION, **noun**   affiliation, assignment of paternity, blood relationship, cognation, determination of a child's paternity, family connection, fatherhood, fathership, kinship, lineage, parentage, paternity, relationship, ties of blood
ASSOCIATED CONCEPTS: filiation proceeding
FOREIGN PHRASES: *Semper praesumitur pro legitimatione puerorum.* The presumption always is in favor of the legitimacy of children. *Filiatio non potest probari.* Filiation cannot be proved. *Pater est quem nuptiae demonstrant.* He is the father whom the marriage points out.

FILIBUSTER, **noun**   attempt to obstruct legislation, blockage, cunctation, delay, delay in legislation, dilatory obstruction, hindrance, impediment, interference, obstruction, obstruction to congressional action, prevention of congressional action, protraction, retardation, retardment, stalling, stoppage

FILL (Pervade), **verb**   diffuse, extend throughout, imbue, infuse, leave no void, occupy, penetrate, perfuse, permeate, saturate, spread throughout

FILL (Sell out), **verb**   bulged, fill to capacity, fill to overflowing, fill to the brim, fill up, jam in, overfill, pack in, stuff in, supply, swell with a crowd

FILL (Supply), **verb**   appoint, choose, elect, furnish, lay in *or* by, name, outfit, provide, refill, renew, replenish, restock, stock, store
ASSOCIATED CONCEPTS: fill an order under the Uniform Commercial Code

FILTER, **noun**   classification, means to rectify, means to refine, purification, purifier, refinery, screen, sieve, sifter, strainer

FILTER, **verb**   clarify, clean, clear, distill, filtrate, find, leach, pass through, percolate, purify, rectify, refine, screen, strain
ASSOCIATED CONCEPTS: filter the evidence through the jury

FINAL, **adjective**   closing, completing, concluding, conclusive, conclusory, crowning, decisive, definitive, determinative, end, ending, extreme, *extremus,* finishing, irrevocable, last, rearmost, supreme, terminal, terminating, terminational, terminative, ultimate, *ultimus,* unappealable, without appeal
ASSOCIATED CONCEPTS: final accounting, final adjudication, final and conclusive, final award, final conviction, final decision, final decree, final determination, final disposition, final finding, final hearing, final judgment, final offer, final order, final settlement, final submission

FINAL APPEAL, *noun* appeal of last resort, appeal to the ultimate power, appeal to U.S. Supreme Court or Court of Appeals, application for concluding appeal, conclusive appeal, decisive appeal, definitive appeal, determinative appeal, extreme appeal, finishing appeal, irrevocable decision, last appeal, last appellate stage, last decision, last hearing, last recourse, last reexamination, resort to the highest tribunal, review by a highest tribunal, review by highest authority, review by the highest court
ASSOCIATED CONCEPTS: Court of final appeal, final adjudification

FINALITY, *noun* accomplishment, achievement, cessation, close, closure, completeness, completion, conclusion, consummation, definitiveness, denouement, determination, end, ending, entireness, entirety, execution, expiration, expiry, extremity, finish, fulfillment, fullness, halt, implementation, maturation, maturity, performance, stop, stoppage, term, terminal, termination, terminus, totality, wholeness

FINALIZE, *verb* achieve, cap, clinch, close, complete, conclude, consummate, crown, decide, draw to a close, effect, end, finish, get done, get it over with, perfect, perfect in detail, put the finishing touches on, seal, settle, terminate, wind up

FINALLY (Conclusively), ***adverb*** absolutely, assuredly, beyond the shadow of a doubt, certainly, convincingly, decisively, definitely, in the end, in the long run, irrevocably, permanently, ultimately, when all is said and done

FINALLY (Ultimately), ***adverb*** after a time, after all, at the end, at the final point, at the last moment, belatedly, eventually, in conclusion, in consequence, in the end, inevitably, lastly, necessarily, therefore, when all is said and done

FINANCE, *noun* accounts, *aerarium,* art of monetary relations, budget, business science, commercial theory, economics, exchange, expenditure, financial affairs, financial resources, *fiscus,* funds, income, investments, management of money, monetary theory, money, money dealings, money-making, money matters, *pecuniaria,* pecuniary management, public economy, public revenue, resources, revenue, science of monetary relations, science of wealth, theory of business, theory of fiscal relations, wealth, working capital

FINANCE, *verb* advance, aid, assist, back, capitalize, float, fund, invest, lend, loan, patronize, pay for, provide capital, provide funds, provide money, provide subvention, put up the money, set up in business, sponsor, subsidize, supply money, support, sustain

FINANCIAL, *adjective* *ad aerarium pertinens,* budgetary, bursal, fiscal, monetary, nummary, pecuniary, sumptuary
ASSOCIATED CONCEPTS: financial institution, financial loss, financial responsibility, financial worth

FIND (Adjudge), ***verb*** adjudicate, ascertain, award, conclude, confirm, decide, declare a verdict, decree, detect, determine, encounter, experience, hear of, hold, judge, learn, observe, perceive, pronounce, rule, sentence, settle, sit in judgment

FIND (Determine), ***verb*** adjudge, adjudicate, announce a conclusion, arrive at a conclusion, arrive at a verdict, ascertain, ascertain and declare, ascertain by judicial inquiry, calculate, come to a conclusion, compromise, conclude, decide, decide a question of fact, decide upon, declare a verdict, deduce, deliver judgment, determine a controversy,

determine after judicial inquiry, determine an issue, draw a conclusion, establish as facts, give an opinion, give judgment, hold, judge, make a decision, pass an opinion, pass judgment, pronounce as an official act, resolve, rule, set a question at rest, sit in judgment
ASSOCIATED CONCEPTS: findings of fact

FIND (Discover), ***verb*** acquire information about, answer, apprehend, ascertain, attain by effort, bare, become acquainted with, become apprised of, become informed, bring into the open, catch a glimpse of, chance upon, *cognoscere,* come upon, create, decipher, decode, detect, discern, disclose, disentangle, disinter, divine, divulge, elicit, encounter, explore, expose, fathom, ferret out, figure out, gather knowledge, get to the bottom of, glimpse, happen upon, hit upon, identify, *invenire,* invent, ken, know, learn, light upon, locate, make certain, meet with, notice, observe, obtain by search, perceive, realize, recognize, reveal, run across, solve, strike, stumble on, trace, uncloak, unconceal, uncover, understand, unearth, unfold, unlock, unmask, unravel, unscramble, unscreen, unshroud, unveil, verify

FIND (Locate), ***verb*** achieve, attain, collect, descry, dig up, discover, disinter, espy, expose, furnish, gain, gather, procure, provide the wherewithal, recover, repossess, resolve, retrieve, spot, supply, uncover, unearth

FINDING, *noun* ascertainment, award, conclusion, decision, decree, determination, judgment, judicial conclusion, judicial outcome, judicial verdict, opinion, opinion of the court, order, outcome, precedent, pronouncement, report, resolution, resolution of the court, result, ruling, sentence, solution, verdict, verdict after judicial inquiry
ASSOCIATED CONCEPTS: administrative finding, erroneous finding, evidence sufficient to support a finding, evidentiary finding, finding of a referee, finding of fact, finding of guilt, general findings, implied findings, inconsistent findings, special finding, supplemental findings

FINDING OF GUILT, *noun* adjudication, award, censure, condemnation, conviction, conviction of guilt, criminal conviction, decision, decree, decrial, denunciation, determination, judgment, judgment of guilt, pronouncement, ruling, sentence, unfavorable verdict, verdict

FINE, *noun* amercement, compulsory payment, forfeit, forfeiture, legal liability, liability, mulct, *multa,* payment for misconduct, pecuniary penalty, pecuniary punishment, penalty, prescribed punishment, sconce
ASSOCIATED CONCEPTS: excessive fine, forfeitures, penalties
FOREIGN PHRASES: *Quam rationabilis debet esse finis, non definitur, sed omnibus circumstantiis inspectis pendet ex justiciariorum discretione.* What a reasonable fine ought to be is not defined, but is left to the discretion of the judges, all the circumstances being considered. ***Mulcta damnum famae non irrogat.*** A fine does not impose a loss of reputation.

FINE, *verb* amerce, exact a penalty, exact retribution, impose a forfeiture, impose a mulct, impose a penalty, impose payment for misconduct, impose pecuniary punishment, inflict a penalty upon, mulct, *multare,* penalize, punish, punish by pecuniary penalty, subject to a pecuniary penalty, tax

FINE PRINT, *noun* boiler plate, detailed clauses, detailed conditions, detailed contingencies, detailed grounds, express conditions, intricate notice of conditions, limitations, limiting conditions, precise conditions, prerequisites,

247

provisions, provisos, requisites, small pica font, small print, specific warnings, specification, specified warnings, terms
ASSOCIATED CONCEPTS: contract

FINESSE, noun acuteness, adeptness, adroitness, artful management, artfulness, artifice, astuteness, canniness, cunning, deception, deftness, delicacy, elegance, grace, guile, maneuver, nicety, polish, prowess, refined discrimination, refinement, ruse, *savoir-faire*, science, shrewdness, skill, slyness, stratagem, subterfuge, subtleness, tact, taste, trickery, wile, wiliness, worldly wisdom

FINESSE, adjective ability, acuteness, adeptness, adroitness, astuteness, brilliance, cageyness, canniness, capability, capacity, cleverness, competence, craftiness, cunningness, deftness, dexterousness, expertness, facility, faculty, foxiness, handiness, ingeniousness, ingenuity, judiciousness, know-how, marksmanship, mastership, mastery, proficiency, prowess, resourcefulness, savvy, sharpness, shrewdness, skill, skillfulness, technical mastery, technical skill, technique, virtuosity, workmanship

FINGERPRINTS, noun identification, identification records, impression, impression of fingers, imprint, marks, marks left by a person's finger, means of identification, prints

FINISH, verb accomplish, achieve, arrive at the end of, bring to a close, bring to an end, bring to completion, cap, carry out, carry through, cease, close, come to a close, come to an end, complete, conclude, *conficere, consummare*, consummate, discontinue, end, finalize, halt, perfect, put a stop to, put an end to, stop, *terminare*, terminate, wind up
FOREIGN PHRASES: *Extincto subjecto, tollitur adjunctum.* When the substance is extinguished, the incident ceases.

FINISHED (Complete), **adjective** absolute, choice, classic, complete, completed, concluded, conclusive, consummated, defunct, elegant, ended, entire, extinct, faultless, final, flawless, full, ideal, immaculate, impeccable, irredeemable, perfect, perfected, prime, primed, refined, shapely, skilled, sound, thoroughgoing, trained, whole

FINISHED (Gone), **adjective** consumed, decided, defunct, done with, elapsed, irrecoverable, lapsed, no-more, obsolete, passé, passed, settled, through, used up

FIRE (Burn), **verb** conflagrate, deflagrate, heat, ignite, incandesce, inflame, kindle, light, scorch, singe, warm
ASSOCIATED CONCEPTS: Fire Act, Firefighter's Rule, Fireman's Rule, invitees

FIRE (Discharge), **verb** depose, dismiss, expel, lay off, remove, stimulate, terminate, torrefy

FIRE (Stimulate), **verb** animate, arouse, electrify, enliven, excite, foster, goad, incite, inspirit, quicken, rouse, spur, stir

FIRM, adjective anchored, balanced, confirmed, durable, established, fast, fastened, *firmus*, fixed, immobile, immotile, immovable, indissoluble, inflexible, irremovable, moored, motionless, rigid, rooted, secure, secured, securely fixed, set, settled, solid, *solidus*, sound, *stabilis*, stable, stanch, stationary, steadfast, steady, stout, strong, sturdy, substantial, taut, unalterable, unbending, unmovable, unmoving, unyielding
ASSOCIATED CONCEPTS: firm offer

FIRM, noun association, bureau, business, business establishment, business house, commercial enterprise, commercial house, company, concern, enterprise, establishment, holding company, house, industry, institution, joint concern, office, organization, partnership
ASSOCIATED CONCEPTS: corporation, law firm, professional corporation

FIRMNESS, noun adherence, assurance, backbone, calosity, certainty, compactness, confidence, constancy, courage, determination, durability, endurance, fixedness, force, fortitude, hardness, high morale, immutability, inexorability, inflexibility, intransigence, intrepidity, obdurateness, obstinacy, pertinacity, prowess, purpose, reliability, renitence, resoluteness, resolution, resolve, rigidity, rigor, secureness, security, solidity, soundness, spirit, stability, stanchness, staunchness, steadfastness, steadiness, stiffness, stoutness of heart, strength, substantiality, surety, temper, tenacity, toughness, unyieldingness
FOREIGN PHRASES: *Firmior et potentior, est operatio, legis quam dispositio hominis.* The operation of law is firmer and more powerful than the will of man.

FIRST (Earlier), **adjective** aboriginal, anterior, earlier, earliest, embryonic, inaugural, incipient, introductory, previous, primeval, primitive, prior
ASSOCIATED CONCEPTS: at first impression, first lien, first reading, first stages of litigation, on first blush

FIRST (Superior), **adjective** antecedent, authentic, capital, cardinal, central, chief, crowning, dominant, foremost, highest, important, initial, leading, maiden, main, original, paramount, precessional, precursory, preeminent, preferred, premier, primary, prime, primordial, principal, second to none, starting, stellar, superior, supreme, unprecedented, vital
ASSOCIATED CONCEPTS: first-degree offense

FIRST, adverb *ab initio*, at first, at the outset, before, chiefly, first and foremost, firstly, formerly, from the beginning, initially, in the beginning, in the front, originally, primarily, principally

FIRST AMENDMENT (Free speech), **noun** freedom of expression, freedom of right to assemble, freedom of speech, freedom of the right to petition, freedom to amass, freedom to express an opinion, right of free speech
ASSOCIATED CONCEPTS: Bill of Rights, slander

FIRST AMENDMENT (Freedom of right to assemble), **noun** freedom to amass, freedom to collect, freedom to gather

FIRST AMENDMENT (Freedom of the press), **noun** freedom to express an opinion, freedom to print, freedom to publish, freedom to write
ASSOCIATED CONCEPTS: libel

FIRST AMENDMENT (Freedom of the right to petition), **noun** freedom of the right to challenge, freedom of the right to oppose, freedom of the right to speak out

FIRST APPEARANCE, noun appearance, debut, inauguration, initial, gambit, opening

FIRST IMPRESSION, noun earliest reaction, early reaction, first blush reaction, first ever impression, first reaction, first sight impression, first stage, initial reaction, original reaction, primary reaction, prime reactive

ASSOCIATED CONCEPTS: case of first impression, first impression of the defendant on the jury

FIRST OFFENSE, noun first charge, first crime, first criminal violation, first violation

FIRST POSITION, adjective antecedent place, anterior place, beginning place, best place, cardinal place, crowning place, earliest place, first-class place, first-rate place, foremost place, grade a place, greatest place, highest place, leading place, main place, major place, original place, paramount place, precedent place, preceding place, predominant place, preeminent place, premier place, prevailing place, primal place, primary place, prime place, primeval place, principal place, supreme place, uppermost place
ASSOCIATED CONCEPTS: bankruptcy, filings, recording statutes

FIRST STEP, noun beginning, birth, commencement, debut, embarkment, embryo, genesis, inauguration, inception, inchoation, incipiency, initiation, introduction, nascency, onset, opener, opening, origin, origination, outset, point of departure, start, starting point, unveiling

FIRSTHAND, adjective absolute, admissible, attestative, authentic, certain, conclusive, decisive, determinative, documented, empirical, eyewitness, factual, incontrovertible, indisputable, irrefutable, overwhelming, reliable, sure, valid
ASSOCIATED CONCEPTS: firsthand knowledge of a crime

FISCAL, adjective budgetary, bursal, economic, financial, *fiscalis,* monetary, pecuniary, pertaining to financial matters, pertaining to government finances, pertaining to monetary receipts and expenditures, pertaining to the public revenues, pertaining to the public treasury, relating to accounts, relating to money matters, relating to the management of revenue
ASSOCIATED CONCEPTS: fiscal affairs, fiscal year

FISHING EXPEDITION, noun careless inquisition, careless probe, comprehensive research, comprehensive study, comprehensive survey, fundamental research, investigation with reckless abandon, reckless inquiry, reckless investigation, reckless pursuit, wanton examination, wanton exploration, wanton inquest, widespread scrutiny, widespread search, wild inquest
ASSOCIATED CONCEPTS: prosecutorial misconduct

FIT, adjective able, acceptable, accommodated, adapted, adequate, adjusted, advantageous, advisable, applicable, apposite, appropriate, apropos, apt, *aptus,* becoming, befitting, capable, *commodus,* compatible, competent, concordant, conformable, congruous, consistent, consonant, correspondent, eligible, fitted, fitting, harmonious, *idoneus,* in keeping, in place, legitimate, matched, opportune, pertinent, prepared, primed, proper, qualified, ready, relevant, right, seasonable, seemly, sortable, suitable, suited, tailor-made, tasteful, to the purpose, well-fitted, well-qualified, well-suited, well-timed, wise, workable, worthy
ASSOCIATED CONCEPTS: fit for use, fitness for a particular purpose, implied warranty of fitness, reasonably fit for the purpose intended

FITNESS (Ability), noun admissibility, applicability, appositiveness, appropriateness, aptitude, aptness, competence, expedience, faculty, felicity, instinct, propriety, seemliness, skill, suitableness

FITNESS (Relevancy), noun acceptability, admissibility, advisability, capability, capacity, compatibility, competency, congruity, correctness, correspondence, desirability, due, efficiency, eligibility, expedience, pertinence, propriety, qualification, worthiness
ASSOCIATED CONCEPTS: fitness for a particular purpose under product liability theories

FITTING, adjective adapted, appropriate, auspicious, becoming, convenient, correct, desirable, expedient, favorable, geared to, likely, opportune, proper, propitious, providential, seasonable, seemly, suitable, suited, relevant, timely

FIX (Arrange), verb adjust, align, array, assign places to, assort, bring into order, catalogue, class, classify, codify, collocate, *constituere,* coordinate, distribute, divide, establish, file, form, grade, graduate, group, index, introduce order into, line up, list, marshal, methodize, *ordinare,* organize, place, place in order, prepare, put in order, put in proper order, range, rank, regulate, set in order, sort, sort out, sort systematically, straighten out, systematize, tabulate
ASSOCIATED CONCEPTS: fix prices

FIX (Make firm), verb attach, confirm, consolidate, embed, entrench, establish, fasten in position securely, fasten securely, ground, harden, implant, infix, ingraft, ingrain, lock, lodge, make fast, make rigid, pin, place permanently, plant, ratify, render solid, root, secure, set, solidify, stabilize, stiffen, tether
ASSOCIATED CONCEPTS: fix compensation, fix rates

FIX (Repair), verb adjust, alter, ameliorate, amend, correct, do repairs, emend, freshen, freshen up, heal, improve, improve upon, invigorate, make corrections, make over, make restoration, make sound, make whole, meliorate, mend, overhaul, patch, patch up, purify, put in condition, put in good condition, put in order, put in repair, put in shape, rebuild, reclaim, recondition, reconstruct, rectify, redintegrate, redress, refashion, *reficere,* refit, reform, refurbish, regenerate, rehabilitate, reinvigorate, rejuvenate, remake, remedy, remove the errors, renew, renovate, *reparare, restituere,* restore, retouch, return to the original state, revamp, revive, revivify, right, service, set aright, set right, straighten, touch up

FIX (Settle), verb agree, arrange, arrive at a conclusion, arrive at an agreement, ascertain, come to a determination, come to a resolution, come to an agreement, conclude, *constituere,* decide, *definire,* determine, establish, make a decision, resolve, seal, set, *statuere,* straighten out, work out

FIXATION, noun compulsion, delusion, fascination, fixedness, fixity, infatuation, intoxication, lodgment, monomania, obsession, predilection, preoccupation, prepossession

FIXED (Securely placed), adjective anchored, *certus,* fast, fastened, firm, firmly established, firmly implanted, firmly seated, firmly set, immovable, irremovable, made fast, permanent, rendered stable, rigid, secure, set, solid, sound, stable, steadfast, steady, tethered, tight

FIXED (Settled), adjective arranged, changeless, closed, decided, definite, determined, entrenched, established, not fluctuating, not varying, permanent, predetermined, prescribed, rooted, unchangeable, unchanging, unshifting, unvarying, unwavering, well established
ASSOCIATED CONCEPTS: fixed asset, fixed by law, fixed capital, fixed costs, fixed income, fixed liability, fixed salary, fixed term, fixed time

FIXING A BID, verb bid-rigging, conspiracy to fix a bid, contrived bidding, criminal act regarding a bid, criminal contrivance in a bid, fraudulence in a bid, illegal accommodation in a bid, illegal act regarding a bid, illegal action regarding a bid, illegal agreement regarding a bid, illegal arrangement in a bid, illegal contrivances in a bid, illegal consortium, illegal efforts to fix a bid, illegal maneuvering in a bid, illegal means to fix a bid, illegal measures to fix a bid, trumped-up provisions in a bid

FIXTURE, noun addition to realty, affixed to realty, attachment to realty, permanent attachment to real property, something constructively affixed to real property, something immovable from realty, something physically annexed to realty
ASSOCIATED CONCEPTS: appurtenance, domestic fixtures, equipment, irremovable fixtures, machinery, permanent fixtures, removal of fixtures, trade fixtures

FLAGITIOUS, adjective abominable, accursed, amoralistic, arrant, atrocious, bad, base, blameworthy, criminal, decadent, degenerate, depraved, diabolical, disgraceful, dissolute, egregious, evil, execrable, facinorous, felonious, flagrant, grievous, heinous, ignominious, immoral, impious, incarnate, inexcusable, inexpiable, infernal, iniquitous, monstrous, nefarious, outrageous, profligate, reprehensible, reprobate, scandalous, shameful, shocking, sinister, unprincipled, unrighteous, unscrupulous, vile, villainous, wicked

FLAGRANT, adjective aiming for effect, apparent, arrant, audacious, blatant, bold, brazen, clear, conspicuous, daring, done for effect, enormous, flagitious, flaming into notice, flashy, flaunting, glaring, gross, immodest, *impudens,* infamous, loud, manifest, *manifestus,* monstrous, nefarious, noticeable, notorious, obtrusive, obvious, open, outrageous, outstanding, plain, prominent, pronounced, scandalizing, scandalous, screaming, shameless, shocking, showy, striking, striving for effect, visible, wanton
ASSOCIATED CONCEPTS: flagrant abuse of the law

FLAIR, noun a way with, ability, acuity, acumen, acuteness, adequacy, adroitness, aptitude, aptness, astuteness, caliber, capability, capableness, capacity, competence, competency, deftness, dexterity, discernment, efficacy, efficiency, endowment, enthusiasm, equipment, expertness, facility, faculty, felicity, fitness, flamboyance, gift, inclination, innate ability, innate aptitude, instinct, keenness, knack, leaning, liveliness, long suit, natural gift, panache, perception, percipience, perspicacity, potential, potentiality, power, proclivity, proficiency, propensity, qualification, qualities, sagaciousness, sagacity, savvy, sharpness, showiness, shrewdness, skill, skillfulness, smartness, spirit, strength, strong flair, strong point, strong suit, style, sufficiency, susceptibility, talent, talents, tendency

FLAMBOYANT, adjective affected, baroque, brave, braw, bright, colorful, dazzling, elaborate, extravagant, fancy, flaming, flashy, flowery, frilled, frilly, fussy, garish, gaudy, glitzy, grandiose, high-flown, high-flying, lofty, ornate, orotund, ostentatious, overdone, pompous, pretentious, sensational, sensationalistic, showy

FLATULENT, adjective bombastic, bombastical, declamatory, fustian, garrulous, grandiloquent, high-flown, inflated, long-winded, mouthy, oratorical, orotund, pompous, pretentious, prolix, rhetorical, talkative, tumid, turgid, verbose, wordy

FLAUNT, verb air, be conspicuous, be ostentatious, be showy, boast, brag, brandish, display, display oneself boldly, display with effrontery, exhibit, exhibit boastfully, flash, flourish, gloat, *lactare,* make a gaudy display, make a show of, make a showy appearance, make a spectacle, make a splash, make a splurge, *ostentare,* parade, parade conspicuously, put forth, put forward, shake, show, show off, sport, spotlight, strut, swagger, vaunt, wave, wave brazenly, wave conspicuously, wave ostentatiously, wear

FLAVOR (Essence), **noun** attributes, character, characteristic, configuration, core, distinctive features, essential meaning, expertise, feature, figure, gist, good point, heart, impression, mannerism, mark, material issues, meaning, mold, nature, particularity, peculiarity, point of character, property, quality, quintessence, redeeming feature, savor, shape, signature, singularity, sole, substance, sum and substance, taste, trait
ASSOCIATED CONCEPTS: the flavor of a holding, the flavor of an argument, the flavor of an issue

FLAVOR (Taste), **noun** appreciation, deliciousness, favor, like, palate, salty taste, savor, sense of taste, sharp taste, sour taste, sourness, spicy taste, sweet taste, sweetness, taste in the mouth

FLAW, noun blemish, blot, breach, crack, defacement, defect, deficiency, deformity, demerit, disfigurement, error, failing, failure, fault, foible, frailty, gap, imperfection, imperfectness, inferiority, infirmity, injury, limitation, loophole, maculation, marring feature, *mendum,* omission, patch, rift, shortcoming, stain, unevenness, vice, *vitium,* weak point, weak spot, weakness
ASSOCIATED CONCEPTS: latent defect

FLAWED, adjective below par, blemished, damaged, defective, deficient, fallible, faulty, impaired, imperfect, inadequate, incomplete, incorrect, inexact, insufficient, lacking, marred, peccable, sinister, soiled, vicious, deformed, defaced, scarred, unfinished, unsound, vulnerable, wanting
ASSOCIATED CONCEPTS: flawed argument

FLAWLESS, adjective absolute, best, complete, consummate, defectless, faultless, immaculate, impeccable, infallible, intact, irreproachable, one hundred percent, perfect, precise, pure, sound, spotless, unblemished, untainted, without blemish

FLEE, verb abandon, abscond, absent oneself, clear out, decamp, desert, disappear, *effugere,* escape, evacuate, evade, fly, *fugam petere,* hasten away, hide, make an escape, make off, play truant, remove oneself, retire, retreat, run, run away, run off, take flight, take to one's heels, withdraw
ASSOCIATED CONCEPTS: flee from creditors, flee from justice, unlawful flight to avoid prosecution

FLEXIBLE, adjective adaptable, adjustable, bendable, bending, capable of conforming to new situations, capable of responding to changing situations, disposed to yield, ductile, easily bent, easily managed, elastic, *facilis, flexibilis,* flexile, formable, *lentus,* limber, lissome, lithe, malleable, manageable, moldable, plastic, pliable, pliant, responsive, responsive to change, soft, stretchable, supple, tractable, unexacting, unstrict, waxen, wieldy, willing to yield to influence of others, willowy, yielding

FLIGHT, noun absconding, avoidance, decampment, departing, departure, desertion, disappearance, *effugium,* elusion, escaping, evacuation, evasion, exodus, fleeing, *fuga*, hasty departure, hegira, leaving, removal, retreat, running away

ASSOCIATED CONCEPTS: flight from justice, fugitive from justice, unlawful flight to avoid prosecution

FLIMFLAM, noun   a pack of lies, artifice, bamboozlement, befooling, bluffing, calculated deception, circumvention, conning, deceiving, deception, deceptiveness, defrauding, delusion, delusiveness, dupery, empty talk, enmeshment, ensnarement, fallaciousness, falseness, falsity, fiction, fooling, fraud, illusion, legal fiction, mirage, pretense, prevarication, trickery, trumped-up story, willful misconception

ASSOCIATED CONCEPTS: bunco, confidence games, fraud

FLIP-FLOP, verb   about face, adoption, afterthoughts, backsliding, change like a chameleon, change of heart, change of mind, conversion, defection, diametrically opposed stance, divergence, diversion, 180-degree about face, qualification, realignment, regression, restructuring, reversal, reversion, temporizer, tergiversation, turn of the tide, turnabout

ASSOCIATED CONCEPTS: flip-flop on a political stance

FLOAT, verb   announce, attempt, buoy, buoy up, instigate, issue, launch, offer, present, project, promote, propel, sell, set in motion, try

ASSOCIATED CONCEPTS: float a bond, float an idea or concept

FLOOD (Abundance), **noun**   a sufficiency, affluence, ampleness, amplitude, an ample amount, an ample supple, avalanche, bonanza, bounteousness, bountifulness, bumper crop, copiousness, full measure, fullness, generosity, generousness, glut, great abundance, landslide, lavishness, much, outpouring, overbrim, overbrimming, overburden, overcharge, overflow, overload, plenty, plethora, profuseness, profusion, saturation, superabundance, surfeit

FLOOD (Deluge), **noun**   avalanche, burst of rain, catastrophe, cloudburst, downfall, downpour, drenching rain, driving rain, groundwater, heavy rain, heavy shower, inundation, massive amounts of rain, massive amounts of raising groundwater, pelting rain, pouring rain, rainfall, rainstorm, rainwater, raising water, sheets of rain, spurt of rain, storm, streams of rain, thundershower, thunderstorm, torrent of rain, torrential downpour, torrential rain

ASSOCIATED CONCEPTS: FEMA, National Flood Insurance Program

FLOODGATE, noun   allow in massive problems, avoidance, circumvention, colossal opening, door, escape, evasion, exhaust, exit, inundation, means, moat, open faucet, open flood-hatch, open gate, opening, outlet, overflow, provide a wide opening, release, safety valve, spout, vent

ASSOCIATED CONCEPTS: immigration, open the floodgates

FLOOR, noun   base, basis, bedrock, bottom, flooring, foundation, fundamental basis, girder, ground, groundwork, jumping off point, premise, principle, rudiment, starting point, support, supporting structure, underlying principle, underpinning basis

ASSOCIATED CONCEPTS: floor plan in zoning and construction laws, hacking the floor in parliamentary procedure, minimum wage

FLOUT, verb   affront, be contemptuous of, be disrespectful, be scornful, care nothing for, *cavillari*, contemn, defy, deride, despise, disdain, disregard, esteem slightly,

feel contempt for, fleer, gibe, hold in contempt, hold in derision, hold in disrespect, hold up to scorn, insult, jeer, laugh at, *ludificari*, mock, outrage, rail at, revile, ridicule, scoff, scorn, set no store by, show contempt for, slight, sneer, spurn, take no account of, treat with contempt, treat with disdain, view with a scornful eye

FLOW, verb   become, develop, go, journey, meander, move, pass, proceed, progress, roam, run, travel, turn into, voyage

FLUCTUATE, verb   alter, alternate, be changeful, be intermittent, be periodic, be unsteady, change, change continuously, *fluctuare*, intermit, move in waves, pendulate, rise and fall, shift, show variety, swing, vary, wave, waver

FLUFF, noun   elusive support, ephemeral content, fleeting analysis, immaterial substance, inadequate analysis, momentary analysis, no substance, passing consideration, smoke and mirrors, support that is vaporizing, temporal consideration, thin content, trifle, triviality

FLUID, adjective   able to adapt, adaptable, adjustable, alterable, alterative, continuous, flexible, fluent, impermanent, inconstant, liquid, malleable, mobile, modifiable, movable, ongoing, resilient, solvent, transient, transitory

ASSOCIATED CONCEPTS: cash flow

FLUKE, noun   accident, blunder, bungle, chance good fortune, chance happening, chance misfortune, chance occurrence, error, fortuity, lucky situation, miscalculation, misconception, misinterpretation, misjudgment, misreading, misunderstanding, once in a lifetime occurrence, random achievement, random luck, random mistake, random success, stroke of bad luck, stroke of misfortune

FLUVIAL, adjective   along the river banks, coursing, diffluent, eddying, flowing, fluent, fluid, fluidic, fluviatic, fluviatile, fluvicoline, from the river, riparian, riverine, rivery, rolling, running, streaming, streamy, surging

FOCAL POINT, noun   arena, center, center of activity, center of attention, center of attraction, center of focus, center of interest, central point, centrality, converging point, heart, hub, pivotal point, point of convergence

FOCUS, noun   arena, center, center of activity, center of attention, center of attraction, center of consciousness, center of interest, central point, centrality, convergence, converging point, focal point, gathering place, goal, heart, hub, objective, point of concentration, point of convergence

ASSOCIATED CONCEPTS: target of an investigation

FOCUS, verb   attend, attend minutely, bring into focus, bring the mind to bear upon, bring together, center, centralize, come to a point, concenter, concentrate on, concentrate the mind, concentrate the thoughts, direct one's thoughts to, direct toward one object, examine closely, fix on, fix the thoughts upon, give attention, give the mind to, look to, meditate upon, occupy the thoughts with, regard carefully, render central

ASSOCIATED CONCEPTS: focus an investigation on a suspect

FOE, noun   *adversarius*, adversary, adverse party, antagonist, armed enemy, assailant, attacker, belligerent, bitter enemy, combatant, competitor, contender, contestant, detractor, disputant, enemy, fighter, foeman, hostile person, *hostis, inimicus,* one who is unfriendly, one who opposes, open enemy, opponent, opposer, opposing party, opposite camp, opposite side, other side, outlaw, public enemy, public opponent, rival, sworn enemy

FOIBLE, noun blemish, defect, deficiency, demerit, failing, failure, fault, flaw, frailty, frailty of character, human weakness, imperfection, lack, limitation, moral weakness, need, problem, room for improvement, shortcoming, vice, *vitium*, want, weak point, weak side, weakness, weakness of character

FOIL, verb baffle, balk, be obstructive, bring to naught, cause to be nugatory, check, confound, counter, counteract, countermine, cripple, crush, dash, dash one's hopes, defeat, disable, disappoint, disrupt, *eludere*, frustrate, get in the way of, hamper, hinder, impede, intercept, keep from being successful, nip, obstruct, override, prevent, render vain, restrain, retard, ruin, spoil, stultify, subdue, thwart, undermine, upset, vanquish
ASSOCIATED CONCEPTS: foil a crime

FOIST, verb apply pressure, beguile, coerce, compel, compel to accept, constrain, deceive, fob off on, force, force upon, gull, impose, impose by fraud, inflict, insert surreptitiously, palm off, palm off fraudulently, pass off as genuine, put in slyly, put in stealthily, *subdere, supponere,* thrust upon surreptitiously, trick

FOLLOW *(Be behind),* **verb** be after, bring up the rear, chase, come after, fall back, fall behind, fall behind, follow after, follow up, get behind, go after, go behind, harass, hound, hunt, lag behind, on the footsteps of, on the heels of, pursue, search, seek, shadow, straggle, succeed, track, trail
ASSOCIATED CONCEPTS: follows the property, priorities in bankruptcy, recording statutes

FOLLOW *(Conform),* **verb** abide by, accept as an authority, accord, adhere to, adopt, ape, attend to, be consistent with, be guided by, be in keeping, comply, comply with, copy, copy after, copycat, do as, do like, echo, emulate, follow in the footsteps of, follow in the steps of, follow in the wake of, follow like sheep, follow suit, follow the example of, give allegiance to, harmonize, heed, hold fast, imitate, jump on the bandwagon, match, mimic, mind, mirror, model after, model on, note, obey, observe, pattern after, pattern on, play follow the leader, put oneself in another's shoes, reflect, regard, shape after, simulate, string along, take a leaf out of one's book, take after, take as a model, walk in the shoes of, yield to
ASSOCIATED CONCEPTS: follow precedence, follow the dictates of the court

FOLLOW THROUGH, verb accomplish, achieve, act, attain, be instrumental, bring to fruition, conclude, decide, determine, discharge, effectuate, enforce, execute, find a method, find the means, find the way, fulfill, gain, gain results, get, obtain, perform, produce, realize, take the necessary measures
ASSOCIATED CONCEPTS: attach, contempt, execution, filing a judgment, filing an appeal, order of the court

FOLLOW-UP, noun by-product, completion, consequence, result, sequel

FOLLOW-UP, verb accomplished, be thorough, carry through, complete, conduct, develop, discharge, end, execute, finalize, finish, follow through, gain a determination, gain finality, gain results, go through with, handle, manage,

oversee, perform, prosecute to a conclusion, pursue, scrutinize closely, see through, supervise, transact

FOLLOWING, adjective ensuing, next, resulting, subsequent, succeeding, successive
ASSOCIATED CONCEPTS: following form doctrine

FOLLY, noun absurdity, absurdness, act of folly, blooper, blunder, eccentricity, excessiveness, extravagance, foolery, foolishness, frivolity, frivolousness, gaffe, humor, humorousness, indiscretion, ineptitude, insanity, laughableness, ludicrousness, lunacy, madness, mindlessness, nonsense, nonsensicality, nonsensicalness, oddity, oddness, senselessness, shallowness, strangeness, stupidity, thoughtlessness, triviality

FOMENT, verb abet, agitate, aid, arouse, awaken, call forth, encourage, engender, enkindle, excite, ferment, fire, foster, *fovere,* galvanize, goad, impassion, incite, infect, inflame, infuse life into, inspirit, instigate, kindle, promote, provoke, rouse, set astir, stimulate, stir, stir up, urge, wake up, waken, work up

FOOLISH, adjective absurd, beyond belief, bizarre, crazy, illogical, improper, inappropriate, incorrect, incredible, ludicrous, monstrous, not advisable, not smart, outlandish, outrageous, preposterous, ridiculous, senseless, unfitting, unseemly, unsuitable, unwise, weird, wrong

FOR, conjunction as, as a result of, associated with, because of, by reason of, caused by, concerning, due to, for the sake of, in consideration of, in contemplation of, in favor of, in furtherance of, in pursuance of, in spite of, in support of, in the direction of, in the interest of, instead of, on account of, on behalf of, on the part of, to the extent of, toward, with a view to, with regard to, with respect to

FOR CAUSE, adverb for legitimate reason, for just reason, with cause, with justification

FORAY, noun aggression, armed attack, attack, brigandage, depredation, drive, hostile invasion, incursion, inimical descent, inroad, invasion, looting, maraud, offense, offensive, pillaging, plundering, predatory incursion, push, raid, ransack, razzia, sack, sudden attack, thrust

FORBEAR, verb abstain, be patient, be temperate, be tolerant, bear with, break off, cease, decline, delay enforcing rights, deny oneself, desist from, dispense with, do without, endure, forgo, hold back, hold in abeyance, hold off, keep back, keep from, leave off, not proceed with, *parcere,* put up with, refrain, refrain from action, renounce, restrain, sacrifice, stop, submit, submit without complaint, suffer, *supersedere, temperare,* tolerate, treat with indulgence, wait, waive, withhold, withhold action
ASSOCIATED CONCEPTS: forbearance as consideration

FORBID, verb ban, bar, block, check, command not to do, debar, declare illegal, deny, deny permission, deprive, deter, disallow, disapprove, discountenance, discourage, enjoin, exclude, forfend, hinder, impede, inhibit, *interdicere,* interdict, make forbidden, not allow, obstruct, oppose, order not to do, outlaw, preclude, prevent, prohibit, proscribe, put under an injunction, refuse, refuse approval, refuse consent, refuse to allow, refuse to authorize, refuse to give permission, refuse to permit, render impossible, restrain, restrict, stop, taboo, *vetare,* veto, withhold consent, withhold permission
ASSOCIATED CONCEPTS: disallow a claim, mala prohibita, prohibit by an administrative agency, prohibition

FOREIGN PHRASES: *Qui non prohibet id quod prohibere potest assentire videtur.* He who does not forbid what he is able to prevent, is deemed to assent.

FORCE *(Compulsion),* **noun**   arbitrary power, authority, coaction, coercion, command, compulsion, constraining power, constraint, constriction, control, demand, dictation, discipline, drive, duress, enforcement, exaction, impelling, imposition, impressment, inducement, insistence, martial law, necessitation, necessitude, necessity, need, oppression, persuasion, pressure, prevailing, repression, restraint, restriction, sanction, spur of necessity, stress, strict control, subjection, subjugation, urgency, vehemence
ASSOCIATED CONCEPTS: ejectment by force, forced merger, forced payment, forced sale
FOREIGN PHRASES: *Vis legibus est inimica.* Force is inimical to the laws. *Quod alias bonum et justum est, si per vim vel fraudem petatur, malum et injustum efficitur.* What otherwise is good and just, becomes bad and unjust if it is sought by force and fraud. *Non videtur vim facere, qui jure suo utitur et ordinaria actione experitur.* He is not considered to use force who exercises his own right, and proceeds by ordinary action. *Ejus nulla culpa est, cui parere necesse sit.* No guilt attaches to a person who is compelled to obey. *Nihil consensui tam contrarium est quam vis atque metus.* Nothing is so opposed to consent as force and fear.

FORCE *(Legal efficacy),* **noun**   authorized might, lawful power, lawful vigor, legal vitality, legitimate puissance, rightful strength, sanctioned effectiveness, sanctioned potency, statutory cogency, valid potentiality

FORCE *(Strength),* **noun**   ability, ableness, ascendancy, authoritativeness, brawn, capability, cogency, command, competence, consequence, control, domination, dominion, effectiveness, effectuality, efficacy, empowerment, enablement, endurance, energy, firmness, forcefulness, hardiness, impact, *impetus,* importance, influence, influentiality, intensity, *manus,* mastery, might, mightiness, omnipotence, physical power, potence, potency, power, powerfulness, predominance, pressure, primacy, proficiency, stamina, supremacy, sway, vigor, vigorousness, virulence, *vis,* vitality
ASSOCIATED CONCEPTS: armed force, constructive force, excessive force, intervening force, physical force, superior force, threats of force, unnecessary force, unreasonable force
FOREIGN PHRASES: *Vim vi repellere licet, modo fiat moderamine inculpatae tutelae, non ad sumendam vindictam, sed ad propulsandam injuriam.* It is lawful to repel force by force, provided it be done with the moderation of blameless defense, not for the purpose of taking revenge, but to repel injury.

FORCE *(Break),* **verb**   batter, breach, crack, disjoint, fissure, *inrumpere,* invade, pry, rend, rive, rupture, shatter, smash, split, strain, tear asunder, wrench

FORCE *(Coerce),* **verb**   apply pressure, cause to yield, command, compel, constrain, control, demand, enforce, enforce obedience, enjoin, enslave, enthrall, exercise power over, *exprimere, extorquere,* extort, impose, insist, make obligatory, necessitate, obligate, oblige, order, overpower, overwhelm, press, push, put under obligation, require, tax, urge, use violence

FORCIBLE, *adjective*   aggressive, authoritative, binding, brought about by force, coercive, commanding, compelling, compulsory, controlling, convincing, dominant, done by

force, drastic, emphatic, energetic, enforced, forceful, full of power, full of strength, having a strong effect, having force, having great strength, impelling, impressive, incumbent, influential, intense, invincible, oppressive, *per vim factus,* powerful, predominant, prepotent, prevailing, producing a powerful effect, required, resistless, strong, vehement, vigorous, violent, wielding power
ASSOCIATED CONCEPTS: defilement, forcible detainer, forcible dispossession, forcible entry, forcible repossession, forcible trespass, rape, sodomy

FOREBODING, *adjective*   anxiety filled, anxiousness, apprehension, apprehensiveness, concerning, dark, disquieting, disquietude, distressing, disturbing, dreading, fearful, foreshadowed, ill-omened, inauspicious, intimidating, menacing, nervous, ominous, perturbing, portentous, premonitory, tension provoking, threatening, troubling, unfavorable, unpropitious, upsetting, vexatious, warning

FORECAST, *noun*   actuarial prediction, all beforehand, anticipation, augur, augury, conjecture, consideration, contemplation, design, determine, discretion, divination, envisagement, envisionment, estimate, estimation, farseeingness, farsightedness, feeling, figure out, forebode, foreboding, forecasting, foreglance, foregleam, foreglimpse, forehandedness, foreknowing, foreseeing, foresight, foresightedness, foretelling, forewarn, fortunetelling, gauge, guess, guesswork, guestimation, hunch, improbability, inference, longsightedness, looking ahead, omen, plan, plan ahead, portend, prediction, prefiguration, prefigurement, prefiguring, preparation, prepublication, presage, presaging, presentiment, preshowing, presignifying, presigning, preview, prevision, probability, prognosis, prognostication, prophesy, prophesying, prospect, prospection, sagacity, soothsaying, statistical prediction

FORECLOSE *(Action to seize property),* **verb**   enforcement of a lien through the judiciary, extinguish rights through the judiciary, extinguish the equity of redemption through the judiciary, remove rights through the judiciary, seize by judicial process, transfer ownership by judicial process, transfer ownership rights by judicial process, transfer title by judicial process
ASSOCIATED CONCEPTS: deed in lieu of foreclosure

FORECLOSE *(Extinguish),* **verb**   bar, deprive, destroy equity of redemption, disentitle, divest, forfeit, halt, remove, shut out, stop, terminating rights
ASSOCIATED CONCEPTS: foreclosure opportunity, statute of limitations, statutory foreclosure, strict foreclosure

FORECLOSURE, *noun*   confiscation, deprivation, disentitlement, dislodgment, dispossession, distraint, distress, divestment, enforcement of mortgage, eviction, expropriation, expulsion, forfeiture, legal enforcement of a lien, privation, process of extinguishment of rights, removal, suit to extinguish the equity of redemption
ASSOCIATED CONCEPTS: ejectment, foreclosure decree, foreclosure of a lien, foreclosure of a mortgage, foreclosure of collateral, foreclosure proceedings, foreclosure sale, redemption by purchaser

FOREGO, *verb*   abandon, abdicate, abjure, abstain, avoid, cease, cede, deny oneself, desist from, dispense with, disposed of, do without, drop, eschew, fast, forbear, forfeit, forgo, forswear, give up, give up on, go without, hold back, hold off, lay down, leave off, let alone, make do without, not use, pass up, refrain, release, relinquish, renounce, reserve, resign, sacrifice, shun, surrender, waive, withhold, write off, yield, yield up

ASSOCIATED CONCEPTS: forego interest owed, forego opportunity

FOREGOING, adjective above, above-mentioned, afore-mentioned, antecedent, before-mentioned, earlier, early, first, former, last, latter, named, older, precedent, preceding, pre-existent, preliminary, previously referred to, previously stated, prior, referred to above, referred to earlier, referred to previously, senior

FOREGONE CONCLUSION, noun forejudgment, foreordination, inevitable result, onesidedness, partiality, preconceived idea, preconclusion, predecision, pre-designed conclusion, predetermination, predetermined conclusion, predilection, predisposition, prejudged conclusion, prejudgment, prejudice, prejudiced view, prenotion, preordination, prepossession, presentiment, presupposal, presupposition, presurmise

FOREIGN, adjective adventicius, alien, attached to another jurisdiction, belonging to another country, detached, different, disconnected, dissociated, distant, externus, extraneous, extrinsic, independent, nonresident, not indigenous, not native, outside, peregrine, peregrinus, remote, separate, strange, subject to another jurisdiction, unaffiliated, unallied, unassociated, unconnected, unfamiliar, unrelated, unusual, without connection

ASSOCIATED CONCEPTS: foreign bills, foreign commerce, foreign corporation, foreign divorce, foreign judgment, foreign jurisdiction, foreign laws, foreign notes, foreign patents, foreign state

FOREIGN LANGUAGE RIGHTS, noun foreign interpretation rights, foreign translation rights, nonresidential translation rights

FOREJUDGE, verb assume, be prejudiced, be rash, decide in advance, determine in advance, have a bias, have a prejudice, have a prepossession, judge beforehand, judge in advance, jump to a conclusion, preconceive, preconclude, predecide, predetermine, prejudge, prejudicate, prepossess, presume, presuppose, presurmise

FOREMAN, noun chairman of a jury, chief, commander, director, head, leader, manager of the jury, master, member of the jury, overseer, presiding juryman, superintendent, supervisor

ASSOCIATED CONCEPTS: grand jury foreman, petit jury foreman, trial jury foreman

FOREMOST, adjective best, cardinal, central, chief, commanding, critical, crowning, dominant, eminent, essential, famous, first, important, in the forefront, influential, initial, leading, main, major, notable, noteworthy, original, outstanding, paramount, preceding, predominant, preeminent, premier, preponderant, prevailing, primal, primary, prime, principal, professional, prominent, rated, renowned, ruling, salient, stellar, superior, superlative, uppermost, vital

FORENSIC, adjective adapted to argumentation, arguable, argumentative, barristerial, belonging to courts of justice, belonging to debate, capable of being debated, concerning the law, contentious, contestable, controversial, controvertible, discursive, disputable, disputative, fitted for legal argumentation, fitted for public argumentation, forensis, in the field of public debate, iudicialis, iuridicialis, judicatory, judicial, jural, juridic, juridical, jurisdictional, jurisprudential, juristic, lawful, learned in the law, legal, legalistic, litigious, open to discussion, pertaining to the courts, pertaining to the law, polemical, proper to public debate, solicitorial, statutory, subject to contention, subject to controversy

ASSOCIATED CONCEPTS: forensic medicine

FORERUNNER, noun ancestor, antecedent, antecessor, auspice, forebear, harbinger, herald, leader, messenger, omen, pioneer, portent, praenuntius, precedent, precursor, predecessor, preface, prefigurement, presage, progenitor, scout, sign, vanguard, warning

FORESEE, verb anticipate, augur, await, be clairvoyant, be provident, conjecture, contemplate, divine, envisage, envision, expect, forecast, forebode, foretell, look ahead, look forward, preconceive, predict, presage, prognosticate, promise, prophesy, show foresight, surmise, vaticinate

ASSOCIATED CONCEPTS: foreseeability as proximate cause

FORESEEABLE, adjective anticipatable, anticipated, calculable, contemplated, counted upon, expected, forecasted, foreknowable, foreseen, foretellable, known in advance, looked for, perceived, planned, praesciens, predictable, predicted, probable, prophesied, reasonably anticipated, to be expected, vaticinal

ASSOCIATED CONCEPTS: duty to anticipate, forseeability in considering proximate cause, forseeable dangers, forseeable injury, forseeable risk, last clear chance

FOREIGN PHRASES: *Nemo tenetur divinare.* No man is bound to foretell, or to have foreknowledge of, a future event. *Rerum progressus ostendunt multa, quae in initio praecaveri seu praevide ri non possunt.* In the course of events, many problems arise which at the beginning could not be guarded against or foreseen.

FORESEEN, adjective anticipated, awaited, expected, forecast, foretold, looked for, predicted, presaged, presumed, promised, prophesied

FORESHADOW, verb adumbrate, augur, auspicate, betoken, bode, divine, forebode, forecast, forewarn, herald, point to, portend, precurse, predestine, predict, prefigure, premonstrate, presage, preshow, presignify, prognosticate, promise, prophesy, threaten, vaticinate, warn

FORESIGHT, noun acumen, anticipation, astuteness, boding, clairvoyance, diligence, discernment, discretion, expectation, forecast, forethought, insight, omen, perception, perspicacity, portent, precaution, precognition, preconception, prediction, premeditation, premonition, prenotion, preparation, presagement, prescience, presentiment, prevision, prognosis, prognostication, prospect, providence, prudence, sagacity, second sight, sense, shrewdness, vaticination, vision, wisdom

FORESTALL, verb act in advance, antevertere, anticipate, arrest, avert, avoid, await, be armed, be forewarned, bring to a standstill, cancel, censor, check, counteract, deter, disallow, enjoin, estop, filibuster, forbid, forefend, frustrate, halt, hinder, hold back, impede, inhibit, intercept, interfere, intervene, look forward to, make provisions, obstruct, obviate, praecipere, praevenire, preclude, prepare for, prevent, prohibit, provide against, stave off, stay, stifle, stop, stymie, suppress, suspend, take precautions, thwart, veto, wait for, ward off

ASSOCIATED CONCEPTS: forestall an action

FORETHOUGHT, noun advance planning, aim, anticipation, calculation, circumspection, consideration, consideration in advance, contemplation, deliberate intention, deliberation, design, direction, distinct purpose, fixed purpose, intent, intention, plan, planned course of action, planning ahead, plot, preconsideration, predeliberation, predetermination, premeditation, previous consideration, previous design, previous reflection, prior planning, prior thought, *providentia*, provision, purpose, resolution, resolve, scheme, shrewdness, strategy, thought beforehand, thoughtfulness, volition, will, willfulness

ASSOCIATED CONCEPTS: malice

FOREWARN, verb admonish beforehand, advise, advise against, advise beforehand, alarm, alert, alert to danger, augur, caution, caution against danger, caution beforehand, caution in advance, counsel, deter, discourage, dissuade, exhort, expostulate, forbid, forebode, forecast, foreshadow, foreshow, give fair warning, give intimation of impending evil, give notice, give previous notice to, give previous warning to, give warning of possible harm, inform, make acquainted with, make aware, notify, offer a word of caution, ominate, portend, *praemonere*, predict, prefigure, premonish, prepare, presage, preshow, prewarn, prognosticate, prophesy, put on guard, signal, threaten, urge against, urge to take heed, vaticinate, warn, warn beforehand, warn in advance

ASSOCIATED CONCEPTS: abandon a crime, forseeability, notice

FORFEIT, verb abandon, abdicate, abjure, alienate by breach of condition, be deprived of, capitulate, cede, concede, default, deliver up, demit, disgorge, escheat, fail to keep, fail to retain, forgo, forswear, give away, give up, give up claim to, give up the argument, give up the point, incur a loss, let go, let slip, lose, lose an opportunity, lose by breach of condition, lose by default, lose by failure to appear, meet with a loss, part with, put aside, quit, *re multari*, relinquish, *rem amittere*, renounce, repudiate, sacrifice, surrender, waive, withdraw, yield

ASSOCIATED CONCEPTS: forfeit a bond, forfeit a deposit, forfeit bail

FORFEITURE *(Act of forfeiting)*, **noun** confiscation, deprivation, deprivation of a right, destruction of a right, disenfranchisement, disentitlement, dispossession, divestiture of property, divestment, eviction, exaction, expropriation, forcible seizure, foreclosure, involuntary loss of right, loss of right, punishment, seizure, seizure of a privilege

ASSOCIATED CONCEPTS: action for forfeiture, forfeiture clause, forfeiture of bail, forfeiture of bond, forfeiture of deposit, forfeiture of office, forfeiture provision, redemption of property forfeited, relief from forfeiture, right of forfeiture, tax forfeiture

FOREIGN PHRASES: *Nullus jus alienum forisfacere potest.* No man can forfeit the right of another.

FORFEITURE *(Thing forfeited)*, **noun** amercement, cost, fine, loss, loss consequent to a default, mulct, pecuniary penalty, penal retribution, penalization, penalty, punishment

FORGE *(Counterfeit)*, **verb** commit forgery, copy fraudulently, fake, falsify, feign, imitate, imitate falsely, imitate fraudulently, issue counterfeit money, make a spurious copy of, produce counterfeit money, reproduce fraudulently, simulate, *subicere, supponere*

ASSOCIATED CONCEPTS: forged check, forged instrument

FORGE *(Produce)*, **verb** actualize, bring into being, bring into existence, build, cause, compose, concoct, construct, contrive, create, develop, devise, efform, evolve, fabricate,

fashion, form, formulate, frame, hammer out, invent, make, manufacture, model, mold, originate, put together, shape

FORGERY, noun copy, counterfeit, counterfeiting, deception, fake, false fabrication, falsification, fraud, fraudulence, fraudulent document, imitation, imposition, imposture, misrepresentation, sham, *subiectio*

ASSOCIATED CONCEPTS: alteration of instruments, false entry, forged check, forged instrument, fraud

FORGIVE, verb absolve, acquit, bear no malice, cancel, clear, *condonare*, condone, exculpate, excuse, exempt, exonerate, forget, give absolution, grant amnesty, grant pardon, *ignoscere*, overlook, palliate, pardon, reprieve, shrive, vindicate

ASSOCIATED CONCEPTS: executive pardon, forgiveness of debt

FORGO, verb abandon, abjure, abnegate, abstain from, avoid, bypass, cast aside, cast off, cease, decline, desist from, *dimittere*, discard, discontinue, dismiss, dispense with, dispose of, do without, eliminate, eschew, forbear, forsake, forswear, give up, give up claim to, give up the right to, keep aloof from, keep away from, keep from, lay aside, leave, let pass, omit, part with, pass, quit, refrain from, refuse, reject, relinquish, renounce, renounce claim to, resign, rid oneself of, shun, sign away, stop, surrender, swear off, throw aside, waive, withdraw from, yield

FORM *(Arrangement)*, **noun** array, ceremony, class, classification, custom, design, distribution, efformation, established practice, *facies*, fashion, *figura, forma*, formality, format, formation, formula, formulary, grouping, kind, manner, method, mode, model, order, organization, outline, pattern, plan, procedure, regimentation, regularity, rite, ritual, scheme, shape, sort, style, system, systematization, type, way

ASSOCIATED CONCEPTS: form of action, objections to form

FOREIGN PHRASES: *Si aliquid ex solemnibus deficiat, cum aequitas poscit, subveniendum est.* If anything is deficient in formal requisites, where equity requires it, it should be supplied. *Forma legalis forma essentialis.* Legal form is essential form. *Forma non observata, infertur adnullatio actus.* If form is not observed, it is inferred that the act is a nullity.

FORM *(Document)*, **noun** blank, card, copy, data sheet, information blank, instrument, muniment, questionary, questionnaire, record, reference form, register, registry, report, standard letter, written document

ASSOCIATED CONCEPTS: legal forms, standard form

FORM, verb arrange, assemble, build, compose, *conformare*, construct, contrive, create, design, devise, embody, establish, *fabricari*, fabricate, fashion, *figurare*, forge, formulate, frame, give shape to, initiate, make, manufacture, materialize, mold, organize, produce, put together, shape, structure

ASSOCIATED CONCEPTS: form a corporation

FORMAL, adjective accepted, according to established form, affected, approved, businesslike, ceremonial, ceremonious, confirmed, conventional, customary, decorous, fixed, following established custom, following established form, following established rules, *formalis*, formalistic, in accordance with conventional requirements, inflexible, mannered, observant of form, official, polite, pompous, prescriptive, prim, proper, reserved, rigid, ritual, ritualistic, set, starched, stiff, stilted, systematic, traditional, unbending, uncompromising

ASSOCIATED CONCEPTS: formal acceptance, formal charges, formal defect, formal party

FORMALITY, noun ceremonial rite, ceremoniousness, ceremony, convention, conventionality, correctness, custom, decorum, established mode, etiquette, formalness, observance of form, outward form, prescribed form, propriety, punctilio, rigidity, rigidness, rite, ritual, *ritus,* rule of proceeding, set form, settled method, solemnity, stiffness, stiltedness

ASSOCIATED CONCEPTS: formalities in executing a will

FORMALIZE, verb conventionalize, form, give form to, give formal approval to, give formal status to, legalize, legitimate, legitimatize, make formal, make official, make valid, ritualize, shape, solemnize, validate

ASSOCIATED CONCEPTS: formalize an agreement

FORMAT, noun anatomy, appearance, arrangement, blueprint, completed form, composition, configuration, conformation, contents, contour, creation, design, figuration, finished form, form, layout, look, makeup, mode, model, plan, shape, sketch, structure, structuring, style, type, variety

FORMATION, noun arrangement, array, coinage, composition, concoction, configuration, *conformatio,* conformation, construction, creation, efformation, establishment, fabrication, figuration, *forma,* format, foundation, generation, genesis, institution, invention, layout, manufacture, order, organization, origination, production, structure, synthesis, systematization

FORMER, adjective antecedent, bygone, earlier, erstwhile, foregoing, late, past, preceding, preexistent, previous, prior, *pristinus,* quondam, retired, whilom

ASSOCIATED CONCEPTS: former adjudication, former conviction, former jeopardy, former marriage, former trial, former will

FORMIDABLE, adjective alarming, appalling, arduous, awe-inspiring, awesome, dangerous, deterring, difficult, disturbing, dreadful, exciting fear, fear-inspiring, fearful, fierce, *formidolosus,* frightening, frightful, hard to overcome, horrible, horrifying, huge, indomitable, menacing, overpowering, overwhelming, redoubtable, terrible, terrifying, threatening, unconquerable, unnerving, unyielding

FORMULA, noun avenue, axiom, canon, code, criterion, expedient, fixed expression, form, formulary, maxim, method, mode, model, phrase, postulate, prescribed procedure, prescription, principle, proposition, recipe, rubric, rule, standard, theorem, usage

ASSOCIATED CONCEPTS: formula instruction

FORMULATE, verb arrange, compose, devise, draft, draw up, efform, express in a formula, express in a systematic way, express in precise form, fabricate, fashion, forge, form, formularize, formulize, frame, give form to, hammer out, indite, produce, put into shape, put together, redact, reduce to a formula, set down, shape, state systematically, turn out

FORMULATION, noun composition, construction, creation, definition, delineation, description, determination, elaboration, expression, fashioning, formation, forming, framing, preparation, rule

FORSWEAR, verb abandon, abhor, abjure, abnegate, avoid, break off, cast aside, cast away, cast off, decline, deny, desert, disaccustom, discard, disclaim, discontinue, discountenance, disdain, dispense with, divest oneself, do without, drop, eschew, forego, forsake, give up, lay aside, leave, let alone, omit, part with, proscribe, quit, refrain from, refuse, reject, relinquish, renounce, repel, repudiate, sacrifice, scorn, shun, spurn, toss aside, waive, withdraw from, yield

FORTHCOMING, adjective about to happen, advancing, anticipated, approaching, at hand, awaited, close at hand, coming, coming soon, destined, drawing near, due, ensuing, eventual, expected, fated, following, foreseeable, future, imminent, impending, inescapable, inevitable, in store, looming, near, nearing, nigh, on the agenda, on the docket, on the horizon, oncoming, pending, planned, predestined, predicted, projected, promised, prospective, scheduled, to come, ultimate, unavoidable, upcoming, yet to be

ASSOCIATED CONCEPTS: expectancy under a will

FORTHRIGHT, adjective blunt, bona fide, candid, direct, downright, emphatic, exact, explicit, factual, frank, genuine, honest, ingenuous, outspoken, plain-spoken, positive, scrupulous, simple, sincere, straight, straightforward, unadorned, unaffected, unambiguous, unembroidered, unequivocal, unmistakable, unvarnished, upright

FORTHWITH, adverb as soon as can be reasonably expected, at once, immediately, instantaneously, instantly, promptly, quickly, straightaway, with all reasonable speed, with reasonable dispatch

FORTIFY, verb assure, augment, authenticate, bolster, brace, buoy, buttress, cheer, confirm, comfort, document, embolden, encourage, endue, entrench, harden, hearten, help, inspirit, invigorate, make safe, nurture, protect, prop, ratify, reaffirm, reassure, reinforce, secure, shore up, stand by, stiffen, stimulate, strengthen, supplement, sustain, uphold

FORTUITOUS, adjective accidental, adventitious, casual, chance, circumstantial, coincidental, designless, *forte oblatus, fortuitus,* haphazard, happening by chance, involuntary, lucky, occurring by chance, providential, random, spontaneous, surprise, surprising, uncalculated, undesigned, undirected, unexpected, unforeseen, unintended, unintentional, unlooked for, unmeant, unmotivated, unplanned, unpredicted, unpremeditated, unrehearsed

ASSOCIATED CONCEPTS: fortuitous event

FORTUITY, noun accident, accidentalness, adventitiousness, adventure, casualness, casualty, chance, chance occurrence, coincidence, contingence, fluke, fortuitousness, happenstance, hazard, occurrence, opportunity, quirk, random luck, randomness, speculation, uncertainty

ASSOCIATED CONCEPTS: fortuitous collision, fortuitous event

FORTUNATE (Accomplished), adjective booming, doing quite well, flourishing, fortuitous, halcyon, happy, moneyed, of adequate means, on top of the world, prosperous, successful, thriving, triumphant, wealthy, well-heard, well-off

FORTUNATE (Opportune), adjective advantageous, auspicious, encouraging, favorable, fortuitous, hopeful, just in time, lucky, of promise, optimistic, perfect timing, prevailing, promising, propitious, providential, timely, triumphant, victorious, well-timed, winning

FORUM (Court), noun assize, the bench, court of justice, court of law, courtroom, *forum,* judicatory, judicature, judicial tribunal, panel of judges, session of the court, tribunal

ASSOCIATED CONCEPTS: *forum non conveniens,* law of the forum

FORUM *(Medium)*, **noun**   agency, agent, channel, instrument, intermediary, means, means of expression, mechanism, method of communication, method of expression, mode of communication, vehicle

FORUM NON CONVENIENS, noun   better alternative forum available, better choice of jurisdictions, in appropriate forum, inconvenient forum, more appropriate court, more convenient court

ASSOCIATED CONCEPTS: forum shopping, *lex fori, lis alibi pendens*

FORWARD, verb   abet, accelerate, actuate, adjuvate, advance, aid, assist, drive, encourage, expedite, facilitate, favor, foster, further, hasten, help, impel, influence, inure, meliorate, move, nurture, precipitate, promote, propel, put in motion, quicken, subserve, succor, support

FOSTER, verb   abet, advance, advocate, aid, *alere,* assist, befriend, breed, bring up, care for, cherish, coach, countenance, cultivate, encourage, favor, forward, further, harbor, help, hold dear, indulge, look after, minister to, nourish, nurse, nurture, *nutrire,* patronize, promote, protect, raise, rear, safeguard, stimulate, subserve, succor, support, sustain, take care of, tend, train, treasure, watch over, work for

FOUL PLAY, noun   artifice, attack, chicanery, collusion, connivance, crime, deception, dishonesty, double-dealing, duplicity, fraud, guile, improper conduct, injustice, knavery, machination, misconduct, misdoing, perfidiousness, perfidy, transgression, treacherousness, treachery, trickery, underhanded dealing, unfair conduct, unfairness, violation

FOUND *(Decided)*, **adjective**   adjudged, agreed, approved, ascertained, command, confirmed, decreed, determined, determined on its merits, dictated, finalized, held, judged, mandated, mandatory, opined, ordained, ordered, prescribed, propounded, required, resolved, ruled, specified

FOUND *(Recovered)*, **adjective**   apparent, appeared, disclosed, discovered, dug-up, exposed, furnished, gained, gathered, procured, retrieved, revealed, seen, spotted, supplied, surfaced, uncovered, unearthed

ASSOCIATED CONCEPTS: bailment

FOUNDATION *(Basis)*, **noun**   base, bedrock, beginning, cornerstone, frame, framework, *fundamenta,* fundamental principle, groundwork, keystone, origin, premise, root, rudiment, *sedes,* skeleton, substructure, support, supporting structure, underlying principle, underpinning

ASSOCIATED CONCEPTS: foundation for evidence, foundation of a claim, foundation of a lien, laying a foundation for a document

FOUNDATION *(Organization)*, **noun**   association, charitable institution, charity, *conlegium,* eleemosynary corporation, endowed institution, endowment, establishment, fund invested for a charitable purpose, institute, institution, organization to aid the needy, organized body for charity, philanthropic institution, *sodalitas*

ASSOCIATED CONCEPTS: charitable foundation, not-for-profit organization

FOURTEENTH AMENDMENT, noun   due process of law, legal fairness, legal safeguards, protection against deprivations, protection guarantees, protection of deprivation of accepted legal principles

ASSOCIATED CONCEPTS: procedural due process, right to confront accuser, substantive due process

FRACAS, noun   affray, altercation, battle, bickering, blows, brawl, breach of the peace, broil, clash, commotion, conflict, contention, disagreement, discord, dispute, dissension, disturbance, fight, fray, fuss, jangle, jar, melee, noisy quarrel, outbreak, quarrel, riot, row, rowdiness, ruction, scramble, scuffle, set-to, squabble, squall, trouble, tumult, turmoil, tussle, uproar, wrangle

ASSOCIATED CONCEPTS: disorderly conduct, disturbing the peace

FRACTIOUS, adjective   apt to quarrel, bad-tempered, bearish, bickering, cantankerous, captious, carping, caviling, choleric, churlish, complaining, contentious, contrary, crabby, cranky, cross, cross-grained, crusty, *difficilis,* difficult, disposed to cavil, disputatious, exceptious, excitable, faultfinding, fretful, grouchy, hot-tempered, ill-tempered, impatient, inclined to anger, indocile, inflammable, irascible, irritable, moodish, moody, *morosus,* peevish, perverse, pettish, petulant, quarrelsome, querulous, rebellious, recalcitrant, refractory, restive, sharp-tempered, short-tempered, shrewish, snappish, spleenful, spleeny, splenetic, stubborn, surly, temperamental, testy, touchy, unmanageable, unruly, untractable, waspish

FRAILTY, noun   blemish, breakability, brittleness, debility, defect, defectiveness, deficiency, delicacy, demerit, destructibility, enervation, failing, failure, failure of strength, fallibility, fault, feebleness, flaw, flimsiness, foible, *fragilitas,* fragility, human weakness, imperfection, imperfectness, impotence, inadequacy, *infirmitas,* infirmity, instability, liability to err, loss of strength, peccability, proneness to error, shortcoming, unsoundness, unworthiness, vulnerability, vulnerableness, want of moral strength, weak point, weak side, weakness

ASSOCIATED CONCEPTS: human frailty

FRAME *(Mood)*, **noun**   animus, attitude, bent, character, condition, constitution, cue, disposition, fiber, grain, heart, makeup, mental constitution, mettle, mind, nature, proclivity, proneness, propensity, spirit, state of feeling, state of mind, streak, temper, temperament

FRAME *(Structure)*, **noun**   build, building, chassis, *compages,* construction, fabric, framework, groundwork, shell, skeleton, support

FRAME *(Charge falsely)*, **verb**   accuse falsely, accuse unfairly, accuse unjustly, bear false witness, blame falsely, blame unfairly, blame unjustly, charge unfairly, charge unjustly, conspire against, criminate falsely, criminate unfairly, criminate unjustly, denounce falsely, denounce unfairly, denounce unjustly, fabricate evidence, fake charges against, falsely call to account, hatch a plot against, impeach falsely, impeach unfairly, impeach unjustly, implicate falsely, implicate unfairly, implicate unjustly, incriminate unjustly, inculpate falsely, inculpate unfairly, inculpate unjustly, lay a plot, lie against, make false statements, perjure oneself, prearrange fraudulently, swear falsely, tell falsehoods about, tell lies about, trump up a charge, unfairly call to account, unjustly call to account, unjustly involve

FRAME *(Construct)*, **verb**   block out, build, carpenter, coin, compose, concoct, constitute, contrive, create, design, devise, draft, draw up, enframe, erect, fabricate, fashion, fit together, forge, form, formulate, hammer together, make, manufacture, map out, mold, organize, originate, piece together, plan, prepare, produce, put together, raise, set up, shape, sketch, systematize, write

ASSOCIATED CONCEPTS: frame an issue

FRAME (Formulate), **verb** arrange, cast, *componere*, conceive, *concipere*, concoct, contrive, create, design, devise, draft, draw up, excogitate, express, fashion, forge, form, formalize, hatch, invent, lay plans, make arrangements, map out, organize, originate, plan, produce, pull into shape, put into shape, scheme, set up, shape, sketch, take measures, take steps, think up, work up

ASSOCIATED CONCEPTS: frame a complaint

FRAME (Prearrange), **verb** arrange, charge falsely, conspire against, contrive, contrive a result, ensure a result, fake, fake the evidence, incriminate unjustly, lie against, plan, plant the evidence, prearrange, prearrange fraudulently, predesign, predetermine, trump up, use false evidence

ASSOCIATED CONCEPTS: framed evidence, framed testimony, perjury

FRAME UP, noun baseless charge, cabal, conspiracy, counterfeit evidence, faked charge, false charge, false evidence, false information, foul play, frame, hoax, intrigue, machination, perjured testimony, plant, trap, trickery, trumped-up charge, trumped-up story

ASSOCIATED CONCEPTS: perjury

FRANCHISE (License), **noun** allowance, assent, authorization, charter, concession, consent, dispensation, droit, exemption, favor, grace, grant, immunity, indulgence, leave, monopoly, pass, permission, permit, prerogative, privilege, recognition, right, sanction, sufferance, tolerance

ASSOCIATED CONCEPTS: corporate franchise, federal franchise, franchise tax, grant of a franchise, irrevocable franchise, license, municipal franchise, perpetual franchises, personal franchise, public franchise, secondary franchise, special franchise

FRANCHISE (Right to vote), **noun** ballot, choice, discretion, enfranchisement, freedom of choice, liberty of choice, liberty to vote, option, prerogative, privilege, right of choice, right of representation, suffrage, vote, voting power

FRANK, adjective aboveboard, blunt, candid, clear, clear-cut, crystal clear, decent, direct, distinct, evident, explicit, express, forthright, honest, ingenuous, manifest, obvious, on the up and up, open, open and aboveboard, open and sincere, open and genuine, sincere, straight, straightforward, straight-out, unequivocal, unreserved, upfront

ASSOCIATED CONCEPTS: franking privilege

FRAUD, noun artfulness, artifice, beguilement, charlatanism, charlatanry, cheating, chicane, chicanery, *circumscriptio*, collusion, covin, cozenage, craftiness, crookedness, cunning, deceit, deceitful practice, deceitfulness, deception, deceptiveness, delusiveness, dishonesty, dissembling, dissimulation, double-dealing, dupery, duplicity, fabrication, *fallacia*, fallaciousness, false conduct, false representation, falseness, falsification, falsity, fraudulence, *fraus*, furtiveness, guile, improbity, insidiousness, intentional deception, intrigue, lack of probity, mendacity, misrepresentation, outwitting, perfidy, pretense, prevarication, quackery, ruse, sham, sneakiness, subreption, surreptitiousness, swindling, treachery, trickery, trickiness, underhandedness, unscrupulousness, untruthfulness, wiliness

ASSOCIATED CONCEPTS: action for fraud, actionable fraud, bad faith, collateral fraud, collusion, constructive fraud,

debt created by fraud, deceit, discovery of fraud, extrinsic fraud, false representation, fraudulent misrepresentation, fraudulent representation, implied fraud, intrinsic fraud, mail fraud, material fraud, misrepresentation, positive fraud, presumptive fraud, public fraud, statute of frauds

FOREIGN PHRASES: *Qui per fraudem agit frustra agit.* What a man does fraudulently he does vainly. *Vendens eandem rem duobus falsarius est.* He is fraudulent who sells the same thing to two persons. *Dolus auctoris non nocet successori.* The fraud of a predecessor does not prejudice the successor. *Fraus latet in generalibus.* Fraud lies hidden in general expressions. *Fraus est odiosa et non praesumenda.* Fraud is odious and will not be presumed. *Fraus et jus nunquam cohabitant.* Fraud and justice never dwell together. *Nulla pactione effici potest ut dolus praestetur.* It cannot be provided in any contract that fraud can be practiced. *Nemo ex dolo suo proprio relevetur, aut auxilium capiat.* No one is relieved or gains an advantage by his own fraud. *Nemo videtur fraudare eos qui sciunt et consentiunt.* No one is considered as deceiving those who know and consent to his acts. *Lata culpa dolo aequiparatur.* Gross fault or negligence is equivalent to fraud. *Ex dolo malo non oritur actio.* No right of action can arise out of fraud. *Non decipitur qui scit se decipi.* A person is not deceived who knows he is being deceived. *Fraus et dolus nemini patrocinari debent.* Fraud and deceit should not excuse anyone. *Dolus et fraus nemini patrocinentur; patrocinari debent.* Deceit and fraud shall excuse or benefit no man; they themselves need to be excused. *Dolum ex indiciis perspicuis probari convenit.* Fraud should be established by clear showings of proof. *Aliud est celare, aliud tacere.* To conceal is one thing, to be silent is another. *Dolus circuitu non pergator.* Fraud is not purged by circuity. *Quod alias bonum et justum est, si per vim vel fraudem petatur, malum et injustum efficitur.* What otherwise is good and just, becomes bad and unjust if it is sought by force and fraud. *Megna negligentia culpa est; magna culpa dolus est.* Gross negligence is fault; gross fault is equivalent to a fraud. *Dolo malo pactumse non servaturum.* An agreement induced by fraud is not valid. *Fraus est celare fraudem.* It is fraud to conceal a fraud.

FRAUDULENT, adjective beguiling, bogus, cheating, conniving, contrary to fact, corrupt, counterfeited, crafty, crooked, cunning, deceitful, deceiving, deceptive, delusive, delusory, designing, destitute of good faith, destitute of integrity, devoid of truth, discreditable, dishonest, dishonorable, disingenuous, disreputable, *dolosus*, double-dealing, fake, faked, fallacious, false, falsified, feigned, finagling, forsworn, *fraudulentus*, furtive, guileful, iniquitous, insidious, meretricious, misleading, not honest, not true, perfidious, perjured, phony, scheming, sham, shifty, sneaky, spurious, surreptitious, treacherous, trickish, tricky, truthless, unauthentic, underhanded, unethical, unfaithful, ungenuine, unreal, unreliable, unscrupulous, untrue, untrustworthy, untruthful, unveracious, unvirtuous, void of truth, wanting in probity, wily, without probity, without truth

ASSOCIATED CONCEPTS: fraudulent concealment, fraudulent conveyance, fraudulent intent, fraudulent misrepresentation, fraudulent practice, fraudulent preferences, fraudulent representation, fraudulent transfer

FOREIGN PHRASES: *Dolosus versatur in generalibus.* A fraudulent person takes refuge in generalities.

FRAY, noun affray, battle, brabble, brawl, broil, clash, combat, commotion, contention, contest, disagreement, dispute, dissension, disturbance, fight, fracas, jangle, melee, *pugna*, quarrel, row, ruction, rumpus, scramble, scrimmage, scuffle, skirmish, strife, tumult, turmoil, uproar

FREE *(At no charge),* **adjective** complimentary, costing nothing, costless, expenseless, for nothing, given, given away, gratis, gratuitous, *gratuitus,* not charged for, provided without charge, unbought, uncharged, unpaid, untaxed, without cost

ASSOCIATED CONCEPTS: free on board

FREE *(Enjoying civil liberty),* **adjective** autonomic, autonomical, autonomous, democratic, emancipated, enfranchised, enjoying liberty, exempt from external authority, franchised, freed, independent, liberated, manumitted, not enslaved, not in bondage, not subject to regulation, removed from bondage, saved from bondage, self-directing, self-governing, self-ruling, sovereign, *sua sponte, sua voluntate,* unenslaved, unenthralled, unsubjected

ASSOCIATED CONCEPTS: free access, free press, free speech
FOREIGN PHRASES: *A piratis aut latronibus capti liberi permanent.* Persons taken by robbers remain free.

FREE *(Not restricted),* **adjective** at large, at liberty, cast loose, clear from, disengaged, immune from restriction, independent, let out, *liber,* liberated, loose, privileged, *solutus,* unattached, unbound, unbridled, uncaught, unchained, unchecked, uncoerced, unconfined, uncurbed, unentangled, unfastened, unfettered, unfixed, unhampered, unhindered, unimpeded, unobstructed, unpent, unprevented, unqualified, unreined, unrestrained, unshackled, unstopped, untied, untrammeled

ASSOCIATED CONCEPTS: free and voluntary, free enterprise, free from encumbrances, free press, free speech

FREE *(Relieved from a burden),* **adjective** absolved, acquitted, clear, cleared, delivered, disburdened, discharged, disembarrassed, disencumbered, disengaged, disentangled, dismissed, excused, exempted, exonerated, *immunis,* liberated, pardoned, paroled, quit of, ransomed, *re liber,* released, relieved, reprieved, rescued, rid, saved, set free, spared, unburdened, unencumbered, unimpeded, *vacuus*

ASSOCIATED CONCEPTS: free and clear, free from fault

FREE, verb absolve, acquit, affranchise, clear, come to the rescue, deliver, deliver from bondage, disburden, discharge, disembroil, disencumber, disengage, disentangle, disenthrall, dismiss, emancipate, enfranchise, exculpate, excuse, exempt, *eximere,* exonerate, extricate, forgive, franchise, give a reprieve, give absolution, grant a reprieve, grant amnesty, grant pardon, let escape, let go, let loose, let out, let out of prison, *liberare,* liberate, manumit, pardon, parole, privilege, purge, ransom, redeem, release, release from restraint, relieve, remit, rescue, save, set at large, set at liberty, set free, *solvere,* turn loose, unbind, unburden, unchain, unfasten, unfetter, unfix, unimprison, unleash, unmanacle, unshackle, untie, vindicate

FREE ENTERPRISE, noun at liberty, business enterprise, business immune from restriction, capitalism, capitalistic policies, capitalistic system, deregulation of business enterprise, free competition, free economy, free enterprise economy, free enterprise system, free trade, *laissez-faire* public policy, laissez-fairism, noninterference, nonintervention, noninvolvement, open market, private enterprise, private ownership, self-regulating market, unbound economic policy, unimpeded free competition, unobstructed free competition

FREE HAND, noun absolute discretion, authority, blank check, carte blanche, complete liberty, discretion, every option, freedom, full authority, full delegated authority, full power, full range, latitude, leeway, maneuvering space, total discretion, unbridled authority, unbridled discretion, unhampered authority

FREE TRADE, noun absence of government control, autonomous business, business at liberty, capitalism, decontrolled marketplace, democratic business environment, deregulated business, deregulation, economic autonomy, emancipated business place, fair trade, free business dealings, free commercial enterprise, free competition, free enterprise, free interchange of goods, free intercourse of goods, free market, free mercantile business, free mercantile relations, free movement of goods, free multilateral trade, immune from restriction, independent, *laissez-faire,* noninterference in trade, nonintervention in trade, noninvolvement in trade, open market, reciprocal trade, trade liberalism, unbounded trade, unbridled trade, unconstrained trade, uncurbed trade, unfettered commerce, unfettered commercial affairs, unfettered merchandising, unhampered trade, unhindered trade, unimpeded trade, unobstructed trade, unregimented trade, unregulated trade, unrestrained business intercourse, unrestrained trade, unrestricted trade, unshackled trade, without trade barriers

ASSOCIATED CONCEPTS: balanced trade, comparative advantage, international barter, protectionism

FREEDOM, noun affranchisement, *arbitrium,* autonomy, civil liberty, decontrol, deliverance, discharge, disengagement, disenthrallment, disimprisonment, emancipation, empowerment, enfranchisement, entitlement, exemption, exemption from external control, exemption from restraint, extrication, franchise, franchisement, independence, latitude, leave, leeway, legal right, liberation, *libertas,* liberty, license, *licentia,* noninterference, permit, political independence, prerogative, privilege, redemption, relaxation of control, release, right to decide, room, self-determination, self-government, self-rule, unconstraint, unfettering, uninhibitedness, unrestraint

ASSOCIATED CONCEPTS: freedom from fault, freedom of action, freedom of assembly, freedom of conscience, freedom of contract, freedom of press, freedom of religion, freedom of speech, freedom of thought, freedom of trade, freedom of worship

FOREIGN PHRASES: *Impius et crudelis judicandus est qui libertati non favet.* He should be adjudged impious and cruel who does not favor liberty. *Libertas non recipit aestimationem.* Freedom does not admit a valuation. *Libertas est naturalis facultas ejus quod cuique facere libet, nisi quod de jure aut vi prohibetur.* Liberty is a person's natural power which permits one to do as he pleases. *Libertas inestimabilis res est.* Liberty is a thing of inestimable value.

FREEDOM OF ASSOCIATION, noun authority, authorization, autonomy, blanket permission, choice, civil liberty, constitutional freedom, decontrol, emancipation, free will, freedom of affiliation, freedom of alignment, freedom of alliance, inclusion, incorporation, independence, *laissez-faire,* latitude, liberation, liberty, license, openness, participation, privilege, self-determination, self-direction, unconditional authority, unconstrained use, unrestricted use

ASSOCIATED CONCEPTS: First Amendment protection, individual freedoms, individual liberties

FREEDOM OF CHOICE, noun alternatives, artistic license, authority, blanket permission, call, carte blanche, civil liberty, decontrols, deregulation, discretion, emancipation, franchise, free choice, free will, lack of censorship, *laissez-faire,* latitude, liberation, liberty, license, noninterference, nonintervention, openness, option, permission, prerogative, privilege, pre-abortion, pre-choice, right of choice, right of selection, rights, self-determination, self-direction, unbridled discretion, unconditional authority, unconstraint, unrestraint, unrestricted use

FREEDOM OF INFORMATION REQUEST, noun ask for information, communication requesting information, disclosure request, elicit information, FOIL request, formal demand for information, request for data, request for documents, request for information, request for records, request for specifics

FREEDOM OF PRESS, noun authority of the press, autonomy of the press, blanket permission for the press, broadcast freedom, civil liberty, commentators, communications, communications industry, constitutional freedom, contributors, correspondents, First Amendment rights, free commentary, free journalism, free public communication, freedom of expression, freedom to publish, freedom to write, full franchise of expression, lack of censorship, liberty, license, noninterference, nonintervention, openness, privilege, self-determination of the press, unbridled freedom to publish, unrestricted freedom of expression, unrestricted freedom of the press

FREEDOM TO DISCHARGE, noun at the will of the employer, at will employment, discretionary employment without the necessity of reasons, employment at will, freedom to discharge without grounds, freedom to discharge without reasons, freedom to fire
ASSOCIATED CONCEPTS: just cause employees, morally reprehensive reasons, morally wrong reasons

FREEHOLD, noun acres, domain, estate, estate for life, estate in fee, fee simple, feud, fief, hereditament, *immune,* interest in real property, land, landed estate, landed property, life estate, *praedium liberum,* property, real property, realty, territory, vested interest in land

FREIGHT, noun article of commerce, cargo, carload, consignment, freightage, goods, lading, load, merchandise, *onus,* packages, pay load, shipment

FRENETIC, adjective berserk, crazed, crazy, deranged, excited, feverish, frantic, frenzied, *furens,* furibund, hysterical, *insanus,* maniacal, overwrought, perturbed, possessed, raving, restless, unsettled, *vesanus,* worked up, wrought up

FREQUENCY, noun common occurrence, commonness, continuity, *crebritas,* cycle, frequence, *frequentia,* periodicity, prevalence, rate, recurrence, regularity, regularity of recurrence, repetition, repetitiveness, succession, usualness

FREQUENT, adjective accustomed, common, consuetudinal, consuetudinary, *creber,* customary, familiar, *frequens,* habitual, numberless, numerous, oft-repeated, often done, persistent, prevalent, reiterative, repeated, repetitive, usual

FRICTION, noun abrasion, antagonism, antipathy, attrition, chafing, clash, clashing, collision, conflict, contention, contravention, controversy, counteraction, disaccord, disagreement, discord, disharmony, dissension, dissent, dissonance, erosion, fretting, friction, grating, grinding, hostility, inflammation, interference, irritation, jangle, lack of harmony, opposition, polarity, quarrel, renitency, resistance, strained relations, strife, tension, ulceration, unharmoniousness

FRIEND, noun acquaintance, adherent, advocate, ally, associate, backer, benefactor, cohort, colleague, companion, comrade, confidant, confederate, confrère, crony, defender, faithful companion, favorer, friend-in-need, partisan, partner, patron, proponent, supporter, sympathizer
ASSOCIATED CONCEPTS: *Amicus curiae,* friend of the court

FRIENDLY, adjective accessible, affable, affectionate, agreeable, amiable, amicable, auspicious, benevolent, close, companionable, compatible, congenial, cooperative, cordial, devoted, empathetic, encouraging, familiar, fast, favorable, favorably disposed, firm, fond, fraternal, generous, genial, gracious, harmonious, hearty, helpful, homey, hospitable, kind, kind-hearted, loyal, obliging, openhearted, peaceable, pleasant, receptive, sociable, staunch, sympathetic, warm-hearted, welcoming

FRIGHT, noun affright, agitation, alarm, anxiety, apprehension, consternation, cowardice, dismay, disquietude, dread, extreme fear, fear, fear of danger, horror, intimidation, misgiving, panic, *pavor,* phobia, scare, sudden terror, *terror,* trepidation

FRIGHTEN, verb affright, alarm, browbeat, bully, bullyrag, cow, daunt, deter, disquiet, *exterrere,* fright, give cause for alarm, horrify, intimidate, menace, panic, petrify, raise apprehension, scare, shock, shock with sudden fear, startle, strike with overwhelming fear, terrify, terrorize, threaten, unnerve

FRIGHTFUL, adjective abhorrent, abominable, appalling, atrocious, awful, contemptible, deplorable, despicable, detestable, disastrous, dreadful, foul, frightening, ghastly, ghoulish, harrowing, heinous, hideous, horrendous, horrid, horrifying, loathsome, macabre, monstrous, nauseating, obnoxious, odious, offensive, outrageous, regrettable, repellent, reprehensible, repulsive, revolting, shameful, shocking, terrible, terrifying, vile, villainous

FRINGE, noun border, brink, edge, extremity, fimbriation, frontier, furthest point, furthest reach, limit, margin, outskirt, parameter, penumbra, periphery, skirt, verge

FRISK, verb check, conduct a search, examine, examine closely, examine intently, explore, hunt, hunt through, inspect, investigate, *lascivire,* look into, look over, look through, peer into, poke into, probe, pry into, rake through, review, *salire,* scan, scour, scrutinize, search one's pockets, search through, seek, subject to scrutiny
ASSOCIATED CONCEPTS: reasonable belief that safety requires a patting down, search, stop and frisk

FRIVOLOUS, adjective childish, flighty, flimsy, flippant, giddy, immaterial, *inanis,* insignificant, *levis,* light, light-minded, meaningless, minor, *nugax,* of little weight, of no account, paltry, petty, senseless, shallow, silly, slight, superficial, trifling, trivial, unimportant, unserious, unworthy of serious notice, worthless
ASSOCIATED CONCEPTS: frivolous answer, frivolous appeal, frivolous cause of action, frivolous claims, frivolous pleading

FROLIC, noun amusement, antic, caper, carousal, drollery, entertainment, escapade, fun, gaiety, gambol, jocoseness, jollity, joviality, lark, merriment, merrymaking, mirth, play, pleasantry, recreation, rollick, romp, vagary
ASSOCIATED CONCEPTS: detour and frolic

FROLIC, verb act up, amuse oneself, caper, carouse, cavort, dance, disport, enjoy oneself, frisk, gambol, have a good time, have fun, joke, paint the town red, play, revel, rollick, romp, sport

FRONT (Anterior), **noun**   area in foreground, beginning, closest area, designated area in the foreground, exterior, facade, face, foreground, forepart, frontage, frontal area, head
ASSOCIATED CONCEPTS: road frontage, street frontage

FRONT (Concealed criminal operation), **noun**   alter ego, concealed business, cover, cover up, criminal operation, disguise, felonious operation, fraudulent operation, illegitimate operation, illicit operation, lawless operation, masked operation, pretense, sham, sham device, sham means, sham vehicle, unlawful operation, unlicensed operation, untoward operation
ASSOCIATED CONCEPTS: illegal fencing operation

FRONTAGE, noun   border along the road, border of the property, edge of the property, front boundary of the land, front of a lot, front of a tract of land, front of the land, front of the property, land at the street, outer limits of a property, outskirts of the property, periphery of a property, property at the curb, side of a property along the periphery, side of a property at the front, the outer line of a tract of land
ASSOCIATED CONCEPTS: zoning

FRONTIER, noun   ambit, border, borderland, bound, boundary, boundary line, circumjacencies, compass, confinium, demarcation line, edge, faubourg, finis, fringe, limit, limitations, line of demarcation, march, outer district, outer edge, outer part, outlines, outlying area, outlying borders, outlying districts, outpost, outskirts, perimeter, periphery, remote district, rim, termination

FROWARD, adjective   cantankerous, captious, contrary, contumacious, contumax, cross, crusty, difficilis, difficult, disobedient, fractious, headstrong, indocile, insubmissive, insubordinate, intractable, irascible, irritable, moody, obstinate, peevish, pertinax, perverse, petulant, querulous, rebellious, refractory, restive, splenetic, stubborn, surly, troublesome, unaccommodating, uncooperative, ungovernable, unmanageable, unruly, unyielding, wayward, willful, willfully contrary

FRUCTIFY, verb   ameliorate, bear, bear fruit, beget, blossom, bring forth, conceive, cultivate, enrich, fatten, fecundate, fertilize, flourish, generate, impregnate, inseminate, irrigate, make fruitful, make productive, pollinate, procreate, produce, proliferate, propagate, reproduce, spermatize, thrive

FRUGAL, adjective   abstemious, careful, cautious, chary, cheap, conservative, economical, economy-minded, frugi, parcus, parsimonious, penny-conscious, provident, prudent, restrained, sparing, spartan, stinting, thrifty, unwasteful

FRUGALITY, noun   abstention, abstinence, austerity, carefulness, chariness, economizing, economy, frugalness, moderation, parsimoniousness, parsimony, plain living, prudence, retrenchment, scrimping, skimping, sparingness, temperance, thrift, thriftiness, unwastefulness

FRUITION, noun   accomplishment, achievement, attainment, consummation, effectuation, execution, flowering, fructus, fulfillment, gratification, implementation, performance, production, realization, satisfaction, success
ASSOCIATED CONCEPTS: accrual of a cause of action, maturity of a debt

FRUSTRATE, verb   abort, ad inritum redigere, ad vanum, annul, baffle, balk, be obstructive, bring to nought, cancel, check, checkmate, confound, counter, counteract, cripple, defeat, disappoint, disconcert, discourage, foil, forestall, frustrari, hinder, invalidate, let down, mar, neutralize, nullify, obstruct, oppose, outwit, override, prevent, render invalid, render null and void, spoil, stultify, stymie, thwart, undermine, undo
ASSOCIATED CONCEPTS: frustrate performance of a contract, frustration of purpose

FRUSTRATION, noun   abortive attempt, defeat, failure, foil, futile effort, hindrance, impediment, inability of performance, inability to be completed, incapacity, interference, interruption, noncompletion, nonfulfillment, nonperformance, obstruction, prevention, prevention of accomplishment, thwarted expectation, thwarting, unsatisfied hopes, unsuccessfulness
ASSOCIATED CONCEPTS: commercial frustration, frustration of purpose, frustration under a contract, impossibility of performance

FUGITIVE, noun   absconder, avoider, defaulter, deserter, escaped prisoner, escapee, escaper, evader, fleer, fugitivus, hunted person, levanter, one who flees, person who flees justice, prisonbreaker, profugus, refugee prisoner, renegade, runagate, runaway
ASSOCIATED CONCEPTS: fugitive from justice, fugitive warrant

FULFILL, verb   abide by, accomplish, achieve, adhere to, answer, be faithful to, be sufficient, bring about, bring to completion, bring to pass, carry into effect, complete, comply with, consummate, discharge, do, effect, effectuate, efficere, execute, explere, fill, finish, follow, heed, implere, keep, live up to, make good, meet, obey, observe, perfect, perform, realize, redeem, satisfy, serve, suffice
ASSOCIATED CONCEPTS: fulfillment of trust purpose

FULL, adjective   abounding, abundant, affluent, baggy, brimful, brimming over, charged, chock-full, cloyed, complete, comprehensive, crammed, detailed, entire, entirely occupied, exhaustive, filled, filled to utmost capacity, flowing, flush, fraught, glutted, gorged, imbued, integer, laden, loaded, mature, maximum, occupied, overflowing, packed, plenary, plenus, plethoric, replete, repletus, resonant, rich, sated, satiated, satisfied, saturated, soaked, stuffed, surfeited, swollen, teeming, total, unabridged, unstinted, well-provided, well-stocked, well-supplied, whole
ASSOCIATED CONCEPTS: full amount, full and true value, full cash value, full consideration, full control, full faith and credit, full hearing, full opportunity to be heard, full payment, full performance, full satisfaction, full settlement, full-time employment

FULL-FLEDGED, adjective   all-encompassing, all-inclusive, all-out, broad, complete, comprehensive, entire, every possible combination, extensive, liberal, maximum, thorough, total, unabridged, unbridled, unrestrained, vast, voluminous, whole, without abridgment, without limitation, without reduction, without restraint

FULL-SCALE, adjective   all-encompassing, all-inclusive, broad, complete, entire, extensive, jealously, maximum, total, unbridled, unrestrained, vigorously, whole, with every concentrated effort, with every effort, with force, without control, without reduction, without restraint

FULL THROTTLE, adjective   act on, all out, as fast as possible, at full speed, commence, continued at maximum, flow, following at full throttle, forging ahead, gathering steam, get in high gear, going forward, in full gear, in high gear, making headway, making progress, maximum strength, moving ahead, pressing on, progressing, pushing on, rolling on, springing from, streaming

FULLY EXECUTED *(Consummated)*, *adjective*   completed, discharged, fulfilled, realized

FULLY EXECUTED *(Signed)*, *adjective*   authenticated, authorized, binding, completed, executed, legitimized

FULLY SECURED, *adjective*   backed-up, bonded, certified, covered, guaranteed, hypothecated, insured, pledged, mortgaged, warranted

FULMINATE, *verb*   blame, blast, bluster, burst, cast blame, censure, condemn, criticize harshly, decry, denounce, denunciate, detonate, disapprove of, discharge, disfavor, erupt, explode, go off, not approve, object to, oppose, potent, reprehend, thunder, trigger, upbraid

FUNCTION, *noun*   appropriate activity, assignment, business, chore, design, duty, employment, exploitation, mission, *munus,* occupation, office, *officium,* performance, purpose, pursuit, responsibility, role, task, usage, use, utility, work
ASSOCIATED CONCEPTS: discretionary function, executive function, government function, judicial function, legislative function, political function, quasi-judicial function

FUNCTION, *verb*   achieve, act, act effectively, answer a purpose, avail, be effective, be in operation, be useful, benefit, carry on, carry out, effectuate, execute, have effect, manage, operate, perform, render a service, run, serve, work

FUNCTIONAL, *adjective*   adequate, advantageous, applicable, applied, convenient, effective, effectual, efficacious, efficient, employable, expedient, fit for use, gainful, handy, helpful, in action, in operation, in order, instrumental, invaluable, operable, operant, operational, operative, practicable, practical, pragmatic, profitable, sensible, serviceable, suitable for use, usable, useful, utile, utilitarian, utilizable, valuable, workable, working
ASSOCIATED CONCEPTS: functional claim, functional depreciation, functional disability

FUNCTIONARY, *noun*   administrator, bureaucrat, commissary, commissioner, delegate, dignitary, office holder, officer, official, representative, syndic

FUND, *noun*   accumulation, assets, capital, *copia,* endowment, foundation, fount, hoard, investment, mine, nest egg, *pecunia,* pool, reserve, reservoir, resources, savings, spring, stock, store, sum of money, supply, well
ASSOCIATED CONCEPTS: available fund, cash funds, commingling of funds, contingent fund, endowment fund, escrow fund, guaranty fund, insurance fund, joint fund, misapplication of funds, misappropriation of funds, permanent funds, reserve fund, residuary fund, trust fund

FUND, *verb*   accommodate, accumulate, afford, allot, amass, apportion, bank, be a benefactor, bestow, cache, collect, conserve, contribute, deposit, dispense, dole, donate, endow, endue, equip, finance, furnish, garner, give, give money, grant, hand out, hoard, invest money, keep, keep in reserve, lay in store, lay up, maintain, pay, pay for, present, present money, preserve, provide, provide for, provide money, provide the wherewithal, provision, purvey, reserve, retain, save, save up, settle upon, spare, stock, stockpile, store, subsidize, supply, sustain, treasure, yield

FUNDAMENTAL, *adjective*   basal, basic, basilar, basilary, cardinal, central, constitutional, elemental, elementary, essential, inchoative, indispensable, key, necessary, needed, organic, primary, *primus,* principal, *principalis,* required, requisite, rudimentary, structural, underlying, vital
ASSOCIATED CONCEPTS: fundamental change, fundamental error, fundamental issue, fundamental law, fundamental question, fundamental right

FUNDS, *noun*   assets, bank account, capital, cash, currency, economic success, finance, income, liquid assets, lucre, means, money, pecuniary resources, pelf, personalty, possessions, principal, proceeds, property, revenue, specie, stocks and bonds, substance, treasure, wealth, wherewithal
ASSOCIATED CONCEPTS: Social Security Fund, Unemployment Compensation Fund, Welfare Fund, Workers' Compensation Fund

FURLOUGH, *noun*   absence, *commeatus,* holiday, leave, leave of absence, leisure, liberty, recess, respite, rest, suspension of work, time off, vacation

FURNISH, *verb*   accommodate, accouter, afford, appoint, apportion, arm, bestow, contribute, enable, endow, endue, equip, fit out, gear, give, grant, indulge, *instruere,* lavish, outfit, praebere, present, produce, provide, provision, purvey, rig, stock, *suppeditare,* supply, yield
ASSOCIATED CONCEPTS: furnish proof, labor furnished, material furnished, work furnished

FUROR, *noun*   ado, agitation, broil, clamor, commotion, craze, disruption, disturbance, eruption, excitement, ferment, ferocity, fervency, fever, flare-up, fracas, fray, frenzy, fury, fuss, hysteria, madness, maelstrom, mania, outbreak, outburst, pandemonium, passion, pother, rabidity, rage, rumpus, stir, storm, tempest, tumult, turbulence, turmoil, upheaval, uproar, wildness

FURTHER, *adverb*   a greater extent, additionally, at a further point, at a more distant point, besides, beyond, else, extra, farther, furthermore, in addition, more, plus, supplementary, to a greater extent
ASSOCIATED CONCEPTS: continuance, further consideration, further conveyance, further hearing, further notice, further proceeding, further security, further waste, furtherance

FURTHER, *verb*   advance, contribute to, facilitate, favor, forward, foster, impel, motivate, move, promote

FURTHERANCE, *noun*   advancement, advocacy, aid, amelioration, assistance, behalf, betterment, championship, change for better, cooperation, course, defense, development, favor, gain, growth, headway, help, improvement, lift, longevity, preferment, progress, progression, promotion, reinforcement, raise, rise, succor, uptrend
ASSOCIATED CONCEPTS: furtherance of a crime, in the furtherance of the business of the employer, in the furtherance of the discharge of duties

FURTHERMORE, *adverb*   additionally, along with, also, at the same time, besides, beyond, by the same token, in addition, in conjunction with, likewise, moreover, over and above, then again, together with, too, what's more

FURTIVE, *adjective*   backstair, catlike, clandestine, cloaked, concealed, covert, crafty, cunning, deceitful, evasive, feline, *furtivus,* hangdog, hidden, indirect, insidious, masked, mysterious, private, secret, secretive, shady, shifty, shrouded, sly, sneaking, sneaky, stealthy, subtle, surreptitious, thievish, undercover, underground, underhand, undisclosed, unobtrusive, unrevealed, unseen, veiled

FUSE, verb adhere, admix, agglutinate, amalgamate, assimilate, band together, blend, blend together, bond, cement, coadunate, coalesce, combine, combine together, commingle, compile, compound, condense, confederate, conglomerate, conjoin, connect, consolidate, embody, federate, flux, galvanize, incorporate, interfuse, intermix, join, league, lock, lump together, meld, melt together, merge, mingle, mix, refine, run, smelt, solder, unify, unite, weld

FUSTIAN, adjective bombastic, declamatory, flatulent, *gausape*, grandiloquent, grandiose, high-flown, high-sounding, inflated, mouthy, orotund, pompous, pretentious, ranting, swollen, tumid, turgid

FUSTIAN, noun affectation, altiloquence, bombast, bombastic language, bombastry, declamation, empty talk, euphuism, *gausape*, high-sounding words, idle speech, inflated language, inflated speech, inflated style, magniloquence, orotundity, pomposity, pretentious speech, rant, rhetoric, rodomontade, sesquipedalianism, swollen language, turgid language, verbiage, verbosity, wordiness

FUTILE, adjective abortive, barren, bootless, feckless, fruitless, *futilis*, gainless, hopeless, *inanis*, ineffective, ineffectual, inefficacious, insignificant, inutile, nugatory, otiose, profitless, resultless, unavailing, unfruitful, unimportant, unproductive, unprofitable, unsubstantial, unsuccessful, useless, vain, valueless, *vanus*, wasted, worthless

ASSOCIATED CONCEPTS: failure to exhaust a futile remedy

FOREIGN PHRASES: *Lex neminem cogit ad vana seu inutilia peragenda.* The law compels no one to do futile or useless things. *Lex nil facit frustra, nil jubet frustra.* The law does not do anything nor commands anyone to do anything which would be futile.

FUTURE, adjective advancing, anticipated, approaching, arriving, close, close at hand, coming, designate, destined, ensuing, eventual, expected, fated, following, foreseeable, forthcoming, *futurus*, imminent, impending, inevitable, later, likely, looked toward, looming, near, near at hand, next, nigh, pending, planned, planned for, possible, *posterus*, predestined, predicted, probable, prospective, scheduled, sequent, subsequent, succeeding, to be, to come, ultimate, upcoming

ASSOCIATED CONCEPTS: after acquired property, future acquired property, future advances, future contingency, future damages, future debt, future earnings, future estates, future expectancy, future interests, future loss of earnings, future payments, future profits, future services

GAG RULE, noun judicial bar of communication, judicial cessation of communication, judicial preclusion of communication, judicial prevention of communication, judicial prohibition of communication, judicial prohibition of expression, judicial suspension of communication, judicial termination of communication, order of silence

GAIN, noun accomplishment, accretion, accrual, achievement, advancement, amplification, appreciation, attainment, augmentation benefit, betterment, enlargement, expansion, growth, heightening, improvement, increase, increment, master, obtainment, procurement, productiveness, profit, success, upturn, winning

ASSOCIATED CONCEPTS: gain derived from capital, gain derived from profits, net gain

GAIN, verb accept, accomplish, achieve, acquire, adopt, advance, assume, attain, avail, bag, be better for, be improved by, benefit, *capere*, capture, cash in on, clear, collect, come by, come into, *consequi,* derive, draw, earn, extract, flourish, gather, get, get possession of, glean, grasp, harvest, improve, learn, *lucrari,* make, make a profit, make capital, make money, master, move forward, net, obtain, pick up, procure, profit, prosper, realize, reap, reap profits, reap rewards, reap the benefit of, receive, secure, succeed, take, thrive, turn to account, win, yield returns

ASSOCIATED CONCEPTS: accrued gain, activity for gain, annual gain, business gain, capital gains, economic gain, gainful employment, long term capital gain, net gain, pecuniary gain, private gain, short term capital gain

FOREIGN PHRASES: *Nemo debet aliena jactura locupletari.* No one ought to gain by another's loss.

GAINFUL, adjective advantageous, beneficial, fertile, fruitful, lucrative, *lucrosus*, money-making, paying, productive, profitable, *quaestuosus*, remunerative, rewarding, useful, valuable, well-paying, worthwhile

ASSOCIATED CONCEPTS: gainful employment

GAINSAY, verb act against, be contrary, conflict with, contest, contradict, contravene, controvert, counter, deny, disaffirm, disagree, disallow, disavow, disclaim, dispute, dissent, forbid, impugn, negate, oppose, oppugn, protest, rebut, refuse to admit, refute, reject, repudiate, speak against, take exception to, take issue with, traverse

GALVANIZE, verb animate, arouse, astonish, astound, confound, dumbfound, electrify, enkindle, excite, fluster, foment, impress, infuse new life into, inspire, inspirit, overwhelm, petrify, put about, quicken, shock, spur on, stagger, startle, stimulate, stir, strike dumb, stun, stupefy, thrill, turn one's head, wake

GAMBLE, verb *alea ludere*, bet, chance, lay a wager, lay money on, play for money, play for stakes, practice gaming, risk, speculate, stake, take a chance, try one's luck, wager
ASSOCIATED CONCEPTS: bookmaking, gambling apparatus, gambling device, gambling houses

GAMUT, noun breadth, circuit, compass, complete sequence, complete series, extent, length, limit, progression, range, reach, scope, span, stretch, sweep, vastness, whole range, width

GARBLE, verb bewilder, befuddle, blur, cloud, complicate, confound, confuse, discombobulate, fog, jumble, mix-up, muddle, mystify, nonplus, obfuscate, obscure, perplex, scramble
ASSOCIATED CONCEPTS: plain language

GARISH, adjective bedizened, blatant, blinding, cheap, cheaply magnificent, coarse, crude, dazzling, flamboyant, flashy, flaunting, gaudy, glaring, glittering, in bad taste, indelicate, loud, obtrusive, ostentatious, pompous, pretentious, showy, spangled, tawdry, vivid, vulgar

GARNER, verb accumulate, acquire, aggregate, amass, assemble, bank, bring together, cache, collect, compile, *condere*, deposit, fund, gather, group, hoard, keep in reserve, muster, reserve, save, stock, stockpile, store, stow, treasure

GARNISH, verb appropriate, attach, commandeer, confiscate, *decorare*, distrain, execute, *exornare*, impound, *instruere*, levy upon, seize, seize and appropriate, sequester, sequestrate

GARNISHMENT, noun annexation, appropriation, confiscation, dispossession, distraint, distress, divestiture, execution, expropriation, impoundment, levy, seizure
ASSOCIATED CONCEPTS: attachment, enforcement of judgments, equitable garnishment, execution, garnishment of a debt, lien

GARRULOUS, adjective babbling, chattering, chatty, communicative, declamatory, effusive, eloquent, gabby, glib, gossiping, gossipy, indiscreet, leaky, long-winded, loquacious, prattling, talkative, tattling, verbose, wordy

GATHER (Accumulate), **verb** accrue, aggregate, assume, batch, collect, compile, concentrate, congregate, conjoin, connect, convene, cull, deduce, deduct, extract, gain, garner, gather, harvest, hold, join, mass, obtain, pick, pluck, procure, read, reap, secure, store

GATHER (Compile), **verb** amass, assemble, bring together, cluster, glean, group, harvest, hoard, marshal, meet, mobilize, muster, pick, pluck, rally, secure, stockpile

GATHERING, noun accumulation, aggregate, aggregation, amassment, assemblage, assembly, caucus, chamber, collection, company, compilation, concentration, conclave, conference, confluence, conflux, congregation, convention, convergence, convocation, cumulation, forgathering, gang, ingathering, mass, meet, meeting, mob, mobilization, multitude, muster, pack, rendezvous, selection, throng, turnout

GAUGE, verb adjudge, appraise, appreciate, arrive at a conclusion, ascertain, assess, calculate, calibrate, class, compute, consider, decide, deduce, determine, draw an inference, estimate, evaluate, exercise judgment, fathom, form an estimate, form an opinion, imagine, judge, make an estimation, measure, *metiri*, opine, rank, rate, set a value on, size up, suppose, surmise, survey, valorize, valuate, value, weigh

GAVEL, noun club, device to gain order, hammer, instrument of control, means of control, symbol of office, mallet, wooden mallet
ASSOCIATED CONCEPTS: parliamentary procedure

GAY, noun homoerotic, homophile, homosexual, lesbian, life partner, same sex partner
ASSOCIATED CONCEPTS: gay marriage

GAY MARRIAGE, adjective homosexual, homosexually bonded, homosexually joined, homosexually married, lesbian bonded, lesbian joined, lesbian married, same sex, same sex wedded
ASSOCIATED CONCEPTS: gay rights

GENDER, noun female, category, class, classification, delineation, kind, male, neuter, sex, sexuality, type
ASSOCIATED CONCEPTS: gender law

GENDER BIAS, noun gender prejudice, one-sidedness, partiality, partisanship, prejudice, sexual discrimination, unequal treatment, unfair treatment, unfairness, unlawful treatment of a protected class
ASSOCIATED CONCEPTS: employment law

GENDER DISCRIMINATION, noun favoritism, gender bias, gender prejudice
Generally: intolerance, one-sidedness, partiality, partisanship, sexual discrimination, unfairness

GENERAL, adjective accepted, average, broad, catholic, characteristic, common, common to many, *communis*, customary, ecumenical, epidemic, extensive, *generalis*, habitual, illustrative, inclusive, not partial, not select, open to all, ordinary, pandemic, popular, prevailing, prevalent, regular, relevant to all, representative, rife, standard, sweeping, typical, undisputed, universal, unrestricted, usual, vast, widespread
ASSOCIATED CONCEPTS: general agency, general agent, general appearance, general applicability, general assignment for the benefit of creditors, general bequest, general brokerage, general circulation, general creditor, general damages, general denial, general election, general issue, general jurisdiction, general legacy, general lien, general obligation, general power of appointment, general release, general statute, general strike, general verdict, general welfare
FOREIGN PHRASES: *Generale tantum valet in generalibus, quantum singulare in singulis.* That which is general prevails in general matters, as that which is particular prevails in particular matters. *Generalibus specialia derogant.* Special words derogate from the meaning of general ones. *Generalis regula generaliter est intelligenda.* A general rule is to be understood generally. *Generalis clausula non porrigitur adea quaeantea specialiter sunt comprehensa.* A general clause is not extended to include those things that have

been previously provided for specially. ***Statutum generaliter est intelligendum quando verba statuti sunt specialia, ratio autem generalis.*** When the words of a statute are special, but the reason general, the statute is to be understood generally. ***Generalia praecedunt, specialia sequuntur.*** General matters precede, special matters follow. ***In generalibus versatur error.*** Error thrives in generalities. ***Fraus latet in generalibus.*** Fraud lies hidden in general expressions.

GENERAL AGREEMENT, noun acclamation, accord, acquiescence, affirmance, affirmation, common consent, concord, concordance, concurrence, consensus, consent, consenteity, consentience, harmony, like-mindedness, meeting of minds, unanimousness, understanding, union, universal agreement

ASSOCIATED CONCEPTS: bilateral agreement, conditioned agreement, executory agreement, express agreement, implied agreement, parole agreement

GENERAL MEANING, noun connotation, content, cornerstone, drift, essence, essential matter, essential part, gist, idea, implication, import, important part, main point, marrow, meat, principle, purport, quintessence, sense, significance, substance, sum and substance, tenor

GENERAL PRINCIPLES, noun approach, course of action, line of action, mode of management, *modus operandi*, overall approach, policy, procedure, strategy

GENERALITY *(Bulk),* **noun** better part, biggest part, body, common run, greater part, greatest number, largest part, main body, main part, majority, mass, predominant part, preponderance, preponderancy, preponderation, principal part, universality

GENERALITY *(Vague statement),* **noun** abstraction, broad statement, general law, general principle, general rule, general statement, generalization, imprecision, inexactitude, inexactness, loose statement, principle, simplistic statement

GENERALIZATION, noun appraisal, assumption, attitude, broad statement, conclusion, estimate, estimation, general statement, generality, guide, hypothesis, illation, imprecise statement, inexact statement, inference, observation, postulate, postulation, premise, presumption, presupposition, supposal, supposition, theorization, theory

GENERALIZE, verb assume, conclude, deal in generalities, discuss in the abstract, draw inferences, *generatim,* hypothesize, ignore distinctions, *loqui,* make a generalization, suppose, surmise, theorize, universalize, *universe*

GENERALLY, ad verb as a rule, chiefly, commonly, customarily, extensively, for the most part, habitually, in general, in most cases, in the main, in the usual course of things, mainly, most frequently, most often, naturally, normally, on the whole, ordinarily, principally, regularly, usually, without particularizing

GENERALSHIP, noun administration, administratorship, authority, captainship, care, charge, command, direction, directorate, directorship, *ductus,* guidance, headship, intendance, intendancy, jurisdiction, lead, leadership, management, managership, mastership, stewardship, superintendency, supervision, supervisorship

GENERATE, verb animate, author, be the cause, beget, begin, breed, bring about, bring forth, bring into being, bring into existence, call into being, call into existence, cause, cause to be, conduce, construct, contrive, create, develop, do, effect, effectuate, elicit, engender, evoke, execute, fabricate, father, form, formulate, found, frame, *generare, gignere,* give life to, give rise to, inaugurate, induce, initiate, institute, invent, kindle, launch, lay the foundation of, make, manufacture, occasion, open, originate, *parere,* produce, provoke, set in motion, sire, start, undertake, vitalize, vivify

GENERIC, adjective applicable to a class, blanket, broad, collective, common, comprehensive, general, indeterminate, inexact, nonexclusive, nonspecific, not particular, not special, sweeping, universal, unspecified, wide

ASSOCIATED CONCEPTS: generic name, trade name, trademark

GENEROUS, adjective altruistic, beneficent, benevolent, big-hearted, bountiful, capacious, charitable, chivalrous, copious, decent, donative, gracious, humane, kind, kindly, magnanimous, meritorious, munificent, noble, philanthropic, unselfish, warm-hearted

GENESIS, noun beginning, birth, commencement, cradle, creation, dawn, derivation, exordium, formation, foundation, inception, inchoation, incipience, incipiency, incunabula, initiation, introduction, launching, nativity, onset, origin, origination, outset, provenance, rise, root, source, start

GENETIC, adjective atavistic, congenital, hereditary, incarnate, ingrained, inherited, innate

GENETIC ENGINEERING, noun a carbon copy created by genetic engineering, a copy created by genetic engineering, a double created by genetic engineering, a facsimile created through genetic engineering, an exact copy created through genetic engineering, clone, duplication created by genetic engineering, production of a copy, production of a copy through genetic engineering, production of multiple identical copies, propagation asexually, propagation from a clone cell, replication created by genetic engineering, replication through genetic engineering, reproduction asexually

ASSOCIATED CONCEPTS: bioethics, computer clone, embryo splitting, human clone

GENIUS, noun aptitude, brilliant intellect, cognition, creative power, endowment, expert, gift, ingenuity, insight, inspiration, intellect, intelligence, mastermind, natural gift, perception, percipience, prodigy, propensity, sagacity, science, sense, specialty, talent, wisdom

GENOCIDE, noun annihilation, bloodbath, butchery, carnage, decimation, extermination, liquidation, mass destruction, mass execution, mass extermination, mass murder, mass slaying, slaughter, wholesale murder

ASSOCIATED CONCEPTS: Geneva Convention, War Crimes Commission

GENRE, noun breed, category, character, class, classification, denomination, description, designation, division, form, generic class, genus, group, nature, species, specific category, specific class, specific type, type, variety

GENUINE, adjective accurate, actual, ascertained, authentic, authenticated, bona fide, demonstrable, exact, factual, forthright, frank, *germanus,* guileless, honest, inartificial, legitimate, *merus,* natural, official, original, plain, pure, purebred, real, rightful, simple, sincere, *sincerus,* sterling, tested, true, unadulterated, unaffected, unalloyed, uncolored, uncounterfeited, undisguised, undistorted, unfabricated, unfaked, unfeigned, unfeigning, unfictitious, unimitated, unimpeachable, uninvented, unpretended, unpretending, unpretentious, unquestionable, unsimulated, unspurious, unsynthetic, unvarnished, valid, veridical, veritable

ASSOCIATED CONCEPTS: genuine issue

GERMANE, *adjective* accordant, *adfinis*, affinitive, allied, applicable, applying to, apposite, appropriate, appurtenant, apropos, apt, associated, bearing upon, belonging to, cognate, concerning, congruent, congruous, connected, correlated, correspondent, fitting, important, pertaining to, pertinent, referring, related, relating, relative, relevant, to the point

GERMINATE, *verb* become, bud, burgeon, develop, emerge, evolve, flourish, gemmate, generate, *germinare*, grow, produce, progress, pullulate, sprout, thrive, vegetate, yield

GET, *verb* accumulate, achieve, acquire, appropriate, attain, capture, collect, earn, elicit, gain, gain possession of, gather, harvest, obtain, possess, procure, realize, receive, recover, secure, seize, take, take over, take possession of

ASSOCIATED CONCEPTS: devices and bequests under a will, laws of intestacy

GET ACROSS, *verb* broadcast, clarify, communicate, communicate effectively, convey, decipher, decode, define, deliver, demonstrate, demystify, descramble, disambiguate, disseminate, elucidate, enlighten, enunciate, explain, explain in plain language, explicate, get through to, illuminate, impart, make crystal clear, particularize, simplify, spell out, tell

GET AWAY WITH (Let off), *verb* absolved, be under the radar, escape, escape punishment, escape without any penalty, found not guilty, get off, get off easy, get off lightly, get off with a slap on the wrist, go free, lack evidence to accuse, lack proof to accuse, let loose, pardon, walk away unscathed

ASSOCIATED CONCEPTS: getting away with murder

GET AWAY WITH (Put over on), *verb* accomplish without difficulty, carry off, escape notice, get by without any downside, succeed without a problem

GET EVEN WITH, *verb* avenge, even the score, exact a price, exact revenge, get back, get justice, get revenge, make reprisals, pay back, reciprocate, reckon with, repay, requite, respond in kind, retaliate, revenge, settle a score, strike back at

GIFT (Flair), *noun* ability, adeptness, adroitness, aptitude, capability, capacity, cleverness, competence, cunning, deftness, dexterity, dextrousness, endowment, expertise, expertness, facility, faculty, felicity, forte, genius, handiness, inborn aptitude, ingeniousness, ingenuity, innate ability, innate quality, instinct, knack, mastery, *natura et ingenium*, natural ability, natural quality, proficiency, qualification, quality, readiness, skill, skillfulness, special ability, special endowment, talent, turn

GIFT (Present), *noun* allowance, award, benefaction, bestowment, contribution, dispensation, donation, donative, *donum*, endowment, favor, grant, gratuity, legacy, *munus*, present, presentation, tribute

ASSOCIATED CONCEPTS: absolute gift, acceptance of a gift, bequest, charitable gift, class gift, conditional gift, contingent gift, delivery of a gift, devise, donative intent for a gift, executory gift, expectation of a gift, future gift, gift causa mortis, gift for a public purpose, gift in contemplation of death, gift in praesenti, gift to take effect at death, illusory gift, incomplete gift, intervivos gift, qualified gift, revocable gift, testamentary gift, unconditional gift, verbal gift

FOREIGN PHRASES: ***Invito beneficium non datur.*** A benefit is not conferred upon a person against his will. ***Modus legem dat donationi.*** Custom gives validity to the gift. ***Ubi et dantis et accipientis turpitudo versatur, non posse repeti dicimus; quotiens autem accipientis turpitudo versatur, repeti posse.*** Where there is turpitude by both the giver and receiver, we say it cannot be recovered back; but whenever the turpitude is in the receiver only, it can be recovered. ***Non valet donatio nisi subsequatur traditio.*** A gift is invalid unless accompanied by possession. ***Nemo dare potest quod non habet.*** No one is able to give that which he has not. ***Nemo praesumitur donare.*** No one is presumed to have made a gift. ***Inter alias causas acquisitionis, magna, celebris, et famosa est causa donationis.*** Among other methods of acquiring property, there is a great, frequently used and famous means, that of gift. ***Cujus per errorem dati repetitio est, ejus consulto dati donatio est.*** That which, when given through mistake can be recovered back, when given deliberately is a gift. ***Cujus est dare, ejus est disponere.*** He who has a right to give, has the right to dispose of the gift. ***Nul charter, nul vente, ne nul done vault perpetualment, si le donor n'est seise al temps de contracts de deux droits, sc. del droit de possession et del droit de propertie.*** No grant, no sale, no gift, is valid forever, unless the donor, at the time of contract, has two rights, namely, the right of possession, and the right of property. ***Sola ac per se senectus donationem testamentum aut transactionem non vitiat.*** Old age alone and of itself will not vitiate a will or gift. ***Qui sciens solvit indebitum donandi consilio id videtur fecisse.*** One who knowingly pays what is not due is deemed to have done it with the intention of making a gift. ***Legatum morte testatoris tantum confirmatur, sicut donatio inter vivos traditione sola.*** A legacy is confirmed by the death of a testator, in the same manner as a gift, as between living persons is confirmed by delivery alone. ***Donatio perficitur possessione accipientis.*** A gift is perfected by the possession of the receiver. ***Confirmatio est nulla ubi donum praecedens est invalidum.*** A confirmation is a nullity, where the preceding gift is invalid. ***Dans et retinens, nihil dat.*** A person who gives and retains possession, gives nothing. ***Donari videtur, quod nullo jure cogente conceditur.*** That is considered to be given which is transferred under no legal compulsions. ***Donator nunquam desinit possidere, antequam donatorius incipiat possidere.*** A donor never ceases to possess until the donee begins to possess. ***Donatio non praesumitur.*** A gift is not presumed to have been made. ***Dona clandestina sunt semper suspiciosa.*** Clandestine gifts are always open to suspicion.

GIMMICK, *noun* artifice, contrivance, deception, design, device, flimflam, gadget, invention, maneuver, method, plan, ploy, ruse, scheme, secret device, snag, stratagem, strategy, subterfuge, trap, trick

ASSOCIATED CONCEPTS: false advertising

GIST (Ground for a suit), *noun* alleged reason, base, basis, basis of argument, basis of litigation, cardinal point, cause, cause of action, essential ground, essential matter, essential part, focal point of the complaint, foundation of a suit, gravamen, gravamen of a charge, gravamen of the complaint, great point, ground, important point, keystone, main charge, main point, object of the action, outstanding feature, pith of a matter, point, principal part, principal point, reason, reason for which suit is commenced, salient point, substance, substantial part of a complaint, sum and substance, ultimate cause

ASSOCIATED CONCEPTS: gist of a cause of action, gist of an offense, gist of the complaint

GIST (Substance), **noun**   backbone, basis, broad meaning, connotation, core, drift, essence, essential meaning, essential part, fundamentals, general meaning, idea conveyed, implication, import, *index,* intrinsic nature, marrow, matter, meaning, pith, primary meaning, purport, quiddity, quintessence, real content, reality, root, sense, spirit, substantial meaning, sum and substance, tenor, true meaning, vital principle

GIVE (Grant), **verb**   accord, administer, afford, allot, assign, award, bequeath, bestow, cede, commit, concede, confer, consign, contribute, deal, deed, deliver, devise, devote, dispense, dispose of, distribute, donate, endow, entrust, equip, furnish, impart, indulge, leave, make a gift, make a presentation, pass, present, *prodere,* proffer, provide, remit, submit, supply, surrender, transfer, transmit, turn over, vouchsafe, will

ASSOCIATED CONCEPTS: bequeath, convey, deliver, devise, dispose, give judgment, give notice

FOREIGN PHRASES: *Praesentare nihil aliud est quam praesto dare seu offere.* To present is no more than to give or offer forthwith.

GIVE (Yield), **verb**   abate, become flexible, become less rigid, become pliant, collapse, compromise, concede, crumble, *deponere,* ease, loosen, retreat, sag, soften, surrender

GIVE AND TAKE, noun   accommodation, an exchange of ideas, arguments, banter, barter, bicker, collaboration, communication, compromise, contention, conversation, dialogue, disagreement, discussion, discussion of positions, ideas bandied about, interaction, interchange, negotiation, back and forth, quibbling, repartee, sparring, squabbling, thrashing out of ideas

ASSOCIATED CONCEPTS: collective bargaining

GLANCE, verb   behold, briefly observe, catch a brief look at, catch a glimpse of, glimpse, look, peek, picture, scan, see, skim, snatch a glimpse, sneak a look at, sneak a peek at, view quickly, watch, witness

GLARING, adjective   apparent, blatant, bright, brilliant, clear, conspicuous, crude, distinct, downright, egregious, evident, extreme, flagrant, flamboyant, flashy, flaunting, garish, glittering, intense, loud, manifest, noticeable, notorious, obtrusive, obvious, open, ostentatious, outrageous, outright, overt, patent, penetrating, perceivable, perceptible, piercing, prominent, pronounced, salient, self-evident, sensational, spectacular, stark, striking, unequivocal, vivid, vulgar

GLEAN, verb   accumulate, aggregate, amass, assemble, batch together, bring together, collect, cull, cumulate, draw together, extract, *facere,* garner, gather, harvest, lay in store, obtain, pick up, procure, save, scrape together

GLOBAL, adjective   all-embracing, all-inclusive, complete, comprehensive, extensive, far-reaching, international, non-sectarian, omnipresent, overall, pandemic, prevailing, prevalent, total, universal, widespread, world-wide

GLOOM, noun   affliction, anguish, apprehension, bitterness, blackness, chagrin, cheerlessness, cloud over, darkness,

dejection, depression, desolation, despair, despondency, dimness, distress, doldrums, dolor, dullness, dumps, foreboding, gloominess, grief, heaviness, low spirits, malaise, melancholia, melancholy, misery, misgiving, morbidity, moroseness, mortification, mourning, obscurity, oppression, overcast, pensiveness, pessimism, sadness, shade, shadow, sorrow, sullenness, the blues, the doldrums, vexation, weariness, woe

GLORIFY, verb   adore, aggrandize, apotheosize, beatify, bless, brighten, canonize, celebrate, deify, elevate, ennoble, enshrine, enthrone, exalt, extol, glamorize, honor, idolatrize, idolize, immortalize, laud, magnify, make illustrious, overestimate, panegyrize, praise highly, raise, recommend, regard, revere, uplift, venerate

GLORIOUS, adjective   admirable, august, awe inspiring, beautiful, blissful, brilliant, captivating, celebrated, celestial, charming, commanding, conspicuous, delectable, delightful, dignified, distinguished, ebullient, ecstatic, elated, elevated, eminent, enchanting, enjoyable, enraptured, entranced, esteemed, estimable, exalted, excellent, exemplary, exultant, fabulous, famed, famous, far-famed, festive, glorified, grand, gratifying, grave, great, halcyon, heavenly, heroic, honorable, honored, illustrious, immortal, immortalized, imperial, impressive, jubilant, lofty, magnificent, majestic, marked, marvelous, memorable, meritorious, named, noble, notable, noted, notorious, overjoyed, peerless, praiseworthy, preeminent, prestigious, princely, regal, remarkable, renowned, royal, serene, spectacular, splendid, stately, striking, sublime, successful, superb, superior, supreme, surpassing, surprising, time-honored, towering, transcendent, triumphant, unique, unrivaled, victorious, well-known, winning, wonderful, wondrous, worthy

GLUTTONOUS, adjective   crapulent, crapulous, debauched, edacious, excessive, greedy, immoderate, inabstinent, incontinent, indulgent, inordinate, insatiable, intemperate, omnivorous, orgiastic, ravenous, unrestrained, voracious

GO, verb   abandon, advance, amble, budge, decamp, decease, demise, depart, disappear, emigrate, evacuate, flit, gain ground, hie, hike, journey, leave, make a journey, make off, make progress, march, meander, migrate, move, pace, part, part company, pass away, peregrinate, perish, proceed, promenade, quit, retreat, ride, roam, rove, set out, slip away, steal off, stride, strut, succumb, take flight, take wing, traipse, travel, tread, trek, trudge, walk, wander, wend, withdraw

GO (Start), **verb**   begin, carry on, commence, continue, embark upon, inaugurate, initiate, keep going, maintain, originate, persist, proceed

GO (Travel), **verb**   get away, go to, jet to, journey, journey to, leave, take a cruise to, take a plane to, tour, travel by car to, travel to, vacation to

GO-AHEAD, noun   acceptance, accord, affirmance, affirmation, agreement, approval, assent, authorization, compliance, confirmation, consent, endorsement, green light, imprimatur, leave, liberty, license, nod, okay, permission, ratification, sanction, say-so, sign-off, special permission, validation, willingness

GO ALONG WITH, verb   accede to, acquiesce to, affiliate with, agree to, agree in opinion, agree on, agree with, allow, amalgamate with, approve, arrive at an agreement, assent, associate, band, coadunate, cohere, collaborate, collude,

combine, come to an agreement, come to an understanding, come to terms, comply, concur, confederate, conform, conform to, conjoin, consent, consolidate, conspire, cooperate, correspond, countenance, echo, give in to, go with, grant, harmonize, join forces with, league with, merge with, pull together, ratify, sanction, side with, stand together, submit to, unite efforts with, work together with, yield to
ASSOCIATED CONCEPTS: settlement

GO-BETWEEN, *noun* agent, appeaser, arbiter, arbitrator, broker, buffer, *conciliator,* connecting link, connection, contact, contractor, dealer, delegate, diplomat, interagent, interceder, intercessor, intermediary, intermediate, intermediate agent, intermediator, *interpres,* judge, liaison, link, mediary, mediator, middleman, moderator, negotiator, ombudsman, pacifier, peacemaker, procurer, propitiator, reconciler, referee, representative, spokesman, umpire, vehicle
ASSOCIATED CONCEPTS: arbitration, conduit, court system, mediation

GO TO CONTRACT, *verb* close, come to an agreement, conclude, covenant, enter into an agreement, make terms, obligate oneself, pledge, settle with

GO UP AGAINST, *verb* act in opposition to, argue against, attack, battle, be at cross purposes, be contrary to, be on the opposite side of, be on the other side of, challenge, collide, combat, confront, confute, contend, contest, contradict, contravene, controvert, counter, counteract, counterattack, counterbalance, countermine, counterpoise, countervail, counterweigh, counterwork, debate, defy, demur, deny, disaffirm, disagree, disapprove, dispute, encounter, go contrary to, join issue, land into, negate, object, obstruct, offer resistance, oppose, oppugn, prevent, prohibit, protest, put in opposition, rebut, refute, reject, remonstrate, repel, resist, set against, stand firm against, stand on the other side of, take a stand against, take exception to, take issue with
ASSOCIATED CONCEPTS: litigation

GOAD, *noun* catalyst, encouragement, fillip, impetus, incentive, incitement, inducement, instigation, lash, pique, pressure, prick, prod, provocation, spur, stimulant, stimulus, thorn, tickler

GOAD, *verb* abet, agitate, annoy, arouse, badger, bait, bring pressure to bear on, browbeat, constrain, discompose, egg on, exhort, foment, harass, hector, hustle, impel, incite, inflame, instigate, invite a quarrel, irritate, jab, lash, motivate, needle, nudge, pique, poke, press, pressure, push, prod, prompt, propel, shove, spur, stimulate, sting, stir up, taunt, tease, torment, urge, vex, whip, worry

GOAL, *noun* aim, ambition, aspiration, design, destination, determination, end, fixed purpose, hope, intent, intention, mark, mission, object, objective, plan, predeliberation, predetermination, premeditation, purpose, resolution, resolve, scheme, set purpose, target

GONE *(Dead),* ***adjective*** bygone, deceased, defunct, demised, exanimate, expired, extinct, lifeless, passed, passed on

GONE *(Finished),* ***adjective*** accomplished, achieved, at an end, brought to a conclusion, completed, concluded, consumed, consummated, culminated, disposed of, done, done with, ended, executed, final, over with, past, realized, settled, spent, terminated, through

GONE *(Irretrievable),* ***adjective*** abrogated, absent, annulled, away, canceled, departed, disappeared, flown, gone away, inefficacious, irrecoverable, irredeemable, irretrievable, irreversible, left, lost, no more, not present, null, over, used up, vanished, void

GONE *(Unremembered),* ***adjective*** ancient, distant, elapsed, forgotten, lapsed, not recalled, not remembered, old, out of sight, over, unrecalled, unrecollected

GOOD *(Favorable),* ***adjective*** admirable, ample, apt, auspicious, beneficial, capital, choice, clean, cordial, correct, estimable, ethical, excellent, fair, favorable, fine, first-rate, genial, healthful, innocent, legitimate, palatable, praiseworthy, preferable, proper, propitious, reliable, replete, responsible, right, rightful, salubrious, salutary, savory, select, seemly, serviceable, solid, sound, sterling, sufficient, unsullied, untainted, wholesome, worthy

GOOD *(Nice),* ***adjective*** apt, agreeable, bona fide, chaste, commendable, conscientious, cordial, decent, decorous, devout, dutiful, estimable, ethical, exemplary, genial, genuine, honest, honorable, human, just, kind, likeable, meritorious, moral, pious, proper, pure, reliable, righteous, sapid, seemly, sincere, solid, sufficient, toothsome, upright, valid, valuable, virtuous, well-behaved, wholesome, worthy
ASSOCIATED CONCEPTS: Good Samaritan

GOOD *(Skilled),* ***adjective*** competent, correct, first-rate, fit, proficient, right, select, skilled, tiptop
ASSOCIATED CONCEPTS: a licensed practitioner in good standing

GOOD *(Benefit),* ***noun*** advantage, benefit, blessing, enjoyment, excellence, favor, gain, happiness, improvement, item, kindness, prize, profit, prosperity, service, weal, well-being, windfall

GOOD *(Virtue),* ***noun*** caliber, character, ethics, honesty, integrity, merit, probity, rectitude, righteousness, value, veracity, weal, worth

GOOD CAUSE SHOWN, *noun* legitimate basis proven, proper cause demonstrated, reasonable basis shown, substantial cause shown, substantial factors proven, sufficient foundation shown, sufficient grounds
ASSOCIATED CONCEPTS: temporary restraining orders

GOOD FAITH, *noun* bona fide, goodness, honest effort, probity, rectitude, sanctity, uprightness
ASSOCIATED CONCEPTS: good faith attempt, good faith estimate, good faith purchaser, offer in good faith

GOOD SAMARITAN, *noun* aide, aider, altruist, assistant, assister, befriender, benefactor, deliverer, donor, giver, helper, helping hand, humanitarian, kind person, one who gives assistance, one who helps another, one who renders aid, patron, philanthropist, redeemer, rescuer, succorer, unselfish person
ASSOCIATED CONCEPTS: Good Samaritan Law

GOOD STANDING, *noun* admiration, appreciation, approbation, approval, enviable reputation, esteem, estimation, favorable repute, high regard, prestige, respect, reverence, veneration

GOODWILL, *noun* altruism, amity, benefaction, beneficence, benevolence, brotherhood, charity, cheerful consent, cheerful willingness, commercial advantage, cordiality, countenance, customer approval, customer encouragement, earnestness, established patronage, established popularity, established reputation, favor, favorable disposition, favorable regard, friendly disposition, geniality, good name, good nature, good reputation, helpfulness, humanity, kindness, known name, munificence, patronage, philanthropy, proven name, public favor, public support, sponsorship, support, sympathy, tolerance, willingness

ASSOCIATED CONCEPTS: impairment of good will, sale and transfer of good will

GOODS, *noun* appurtenances, articles of commerce, assets, belongings, chattels, commodities, consumer durables, durables, effects, items, materials, paraphernalia, personal estate, possessions, produce, products, property, resources, staples, stock, stock-in-trade, supplies, things for sale, vendibles

ASSOCIATED CONCEPTS: bulk sale, chattels, foreign goods, goods and chattels, goods sold and delivered, personalty, sale of goods, special goods, tangible goods

GOVERN, *verb* administer, administrate, assume command, be in power, *coercere*, command, conduct, control, dictate, direct, dominate, enact, exercise authority, exercise power over, exert authority, give orders, guide, have authority, have executive charge of, have jurisdiction over, head, hold authority, hold office, hold sway, lead, legislate, manage, officiate, order, oversee, pilot, prescribe, preside over, prevail on, *regere*, regulate, reign, restrain, rule, steer, superintend, supervise, take charge, take command, wield authority

ASSOCIATED CONCEPTS: governing authority, governing body, governing law

FOREIGN PHRASES: *Minor minorem custodire non debet, alios enim praesumitur male regere qui seipsum regere nescit.* A minor ought not to be guardian to a minor, for a person who knows not how to govern himself is presumed to be unfit to govern others. *Mitius imperanti melius paretur.* The more gently a person commands, the better he is obeyed.

GOVERNANCE, *noun* administration, agency, authority, bureaucracy, control, dictation, dominance, domination, dominion, executive power, government, hegemony, influence, jurisdiction, management, mightiness, power, regime, reins of government, rule, supremacy, sway

ASSOCIATED CONCEPTS: corporate governance

GOVERNING PRINCIPLE, *noun* allowance, autarky, freedom, doctrine, dogma, guideline, limitation, maxim, mode of management, permission, policy, precepts, procedure, prohibition, protocol, restraint, rule, strategy, tactics, tenet

GOVERNMENT *(Administration)*, ***noun*** *administratio*, authorization, command, control, decision making, direction, dominion, governance, *gubernatio*, guidance, jurisdiction, management, power, *procuratio*, regnancy, regulation, reign, rule, rulership, state management, statecraft, statesmanship, stewardship, superintendence, sway

GOVERNMENT *(Political administration)*, ***noun*** administration, agency of the state, authority, body of office holders, congress, delegates, *ii qui reipublicae praesunt*, lawgivers, lawmakers, legislators, ministers, *penes quos est reipublica*, political community, political leaders, political regime, politicians, politicos, polity, public servants, representatives, ruling power, sovereign, state managers, statemongers, statesmen

ASSOCIATED CONCEPTS: de facto government, de jure government, democratic government, federal government, governmental agency, governmental body, governmental function, governmental immunity, powers of government, provisional government

FOREIGN PHRASES: *Privilegium non valet contra rempublicam.* A privilege is of no avail against the state.

GOVERNOR, *noun* caretaker, director, elected official, executive, executive leader, government official, highest state official, politician, potentate, public official, statesman

ASSOCIATED CONCEPTS: executive branch of government

GRACE, *noun* absolution, clemency, concession, excuse, favor, forbearance, forgiveness, indulgence, pardon, reprieve

GRACE PERIOD, *noun* concession, exemption, leniency, pardon, period of allowance, period of indulgence, period of tolerance, reprieve

GRADATION, *noun* class, classification, continuity, continuum, course, degree, differential, grade, gradual advance, gradualism, graduation, hierarchy, intensity, measure, order, rank, rate, regular progression, sequence, step, succession, series, stage, standard, variation

GRADE *(Accomplishment)*, ***noun*** achievement, acquirement, attainment, conquest, cut, fulfillment, measurement, pass muster, pass scrutiny, stand the test, success

GRADE *(Rating)*, ***noun*** achievement, marks, category, evaluation, measurement, merit, performance, rank, ratio, results, standing, station, status, success, value

GRADUAL *(Slow)*, ***adjective*** by degrees, continuous, creeping, gradational, graduated, in steps, leisurely, measured, methodical, orderly, paced, progressive, regular, slow, step-by-step, systematic

GRAFT, *noun* blackmail, bribery, corruption, exploitation, fraudulent income, hush money, illegal profit, illicit profit, illicit revenue, *inserere*, kickback, money illegally acquired, political corruption, profiteering, property illegally acquired, unjust acquisition, unlawful gain

ASSOCIATED CONCEPTS: bribery, corruption, official misconduct

GRAND, *adjective* august, capacious, compendious, comprehensive, dignified, distinguished, elegant, elevated, eminent, exalted, excellent, famous, first-rate, glorious, good, grandiose, great, illustrious, imperial, important, impressive, leading, lofty, magnificent, majestic, mighty, momentous, noble, palatial, paramount, pompous, preeminent, princely, prodigious, prominent, proud, renowned, splendid, stately, stellar, sublime, superb, superior, supreme, very magisterial, wide-reaching

GRAND LARCENY, *noun* crime, crime graver than a misdemeanor, crime greater in value than petit larceny, criminal offense, felony, gross offense, illegality, larceny of property which exceeds petit larceny, misdeed, offense, theft, transgression, violation of law, wrongdoing

GRANDILOQUENCE, *noun* abstruse language, bloated wording, bombastic wording, complex legalese, convoluted wording, inflated wording, legal jargon complexities, legalese, legalism, long winded jargon, orotund language, ostentatious wording, pedantic verbiage, pompous wording, sophisticated legal term, sophisticated legal verbiage, swollen wording, technical language, technical term, technical wording, turgid wording

GRANDIOSE, adjective affected, boastful, bombastic, enormous, exorbitant, flamboyant, flashy, flaunting, fustian, grandiloquent, high-sounding, huge, immense, inflated, lofty, magniloquent, mighty, ornate, orotund, ostentatious, pompous, pretentious, showy, stupendous, theatrical, tumid, turgid, vainglorious

GRANT, noun acknowledgment, allotment, allowance, appanage, award, benefaction, benefit, bequeathal, bequest, bestowal, boon, bounty, concession, devise, dispensation, donation, *donum*, douceur, endowment, favor, gift, gratuity, handsel, indulgence, lagniappe, largess, largesse, legacy, legal cession, libation, oblation, present, reward, subscription, subsidy, subvention

ASSOCIATED CONCEPTS: express grant, grant and convey, grant by implication, grant of power, legislative grant, license, private land grant, public grant

FOREIGN PHRASES: *Resoluto jure concedentis resolvitur jus concessum.* When the right of the grantor is extinguished the right granted is extinguished. *Ubi aliquid conceditur, conceditur et id sine quo res ipsa esse non potest.* When anything is granted, that also is granted without which it could not exist. *Quando aliquis aliquid concedit, concedere videtur et id sine quo res uti non potest.* When anyone grants anything, he is deemed to grant also that without which the thing cannot be used. *Quod sub certa forma concessum vel reservatum est non trahitur ad valorem vel compensationem.* That which is granted or reserved under a certain form cannot be twisted into a valuation or compensation. *Qui concedit aliquid concedit omne id sine quo concessio est irrita.* He who grants anything is considered to grant everything without which the grant is worthless. *A gratia.* By grace, not by right. *Cuicunque aliquis quid concedit concedere videtur et id, sine quo res ipsa esse non potuit.* Whoever grants a thing is presumed also to grant that without which the grant of the thing itself would be of no use. *Quaelibet concessio fortissime contra donatorem interpretanda est.* Every grant is to be interpreted most strictly against the grantor. *Concessio versus concedentem latam interpretationem habere debet.* A grant ought to have a liberal interpretation against the grantor. *Nul charter, nul vente, ne nul done vault perpetualment, si le donor n'est seise al temps de contracts de deux droits, sc. del droit de possession et del droit de propertie.* No grant, no sale, no gift, is valid forever, unless the donor, at the time of the contract, has two rights, namely, the right of possession and the right of property.

GRANT *(Concede),* **verb** accede, accept, accord, acknowledge, acquiesce, admit, agree, allow, approve, assent, authorize, be persuaded, cede, *concedere,* concur, confer a privilege, consent, *dare,* empower, enable, express concurrence, favor, give, give authority, give clearance, give consent, give leave, give permission, gratify, have no objection, indulge, let, license, permit, *permittere,* privilege, recognize, sanction, support, vouchsafe, warrant, yield, yield assent

ASSOCIATED CONCEPTS: grant a franchise, grant a mistrial, grant a motion, grant a right of way, grant a right to a jury trial, grant an adjournment, grant an easement, grant an injunction, grant or allowance, granting clause

FOREIGN PHRASES: *Cui jus est donandi, eidem et vendendi et concedendi jus est.* One who has a right to give has also a right to sell and to grant.

GRANT *(Transfer formally),* **verb** assign, award, bequeath, bestow, bestow voluntarily, cede, change ownership, *concedere,* confer, confer formally, confer ownership, consign, convey, convey by deed, deed, deliver, demise, devise, devolve upon, give, give away, give over to, impart, make a present, make conveyance of, make over, pass, pass over, *permittere,* present, put in possession, sign over, transfer, transfer by writing, transfer ownership, transmit

ASSOCIATED CONCEPTS: grant a license, grant a privilege, grant a right of way, grant of easement, grant by implication, grant by necessity, grant in gross, grant in praesenti, land grant, proprietary grant

FOREIGN PHRASES: *Quaelibet concessio fortissime contra donatorem interpretanda est.* Every grant is to be interpreted most strictly against the grantor.

GRANT AUTHORITY TO, verb accredit, allow, appoint, assign, authorize, commission, confer a right, consent, delegate, depute, deputize, empower, endow, enfranchise, entrust, give a mandate to, give permission, give power, invest, invest with power, license, nominate, ordain, sanction, vest, warrant

ASSOCIATED CONCEPTS: agent

GRANT OF RIGHTS, noun authorization, bestowal of authority, ceding of authority, conveyance of authority, conveyance of rights, grant of authority, transfer of rights

GRANTEE, noun acceptor, beneficiary, devisee, donee, recipient, taker

ASSOCIATED CONCEPTS: grantee of power

GRANTOR, noun assignor, bequeather, bestower, conferrer, contributor, devisor, donator, giver, investor, presenter, rewarder, testator

ASSOCIATED CONCEPTS: grantor of a power

GRAPHIC, adjective clear, cogent, coherent, comprehensible, decorative, delineatory, demonstrative, descriptive, detailed, distinct, effective, energetic, explicatory, explicit, expressive, illustrative, imaginative, lively, lucid, lurid, pictorial, precise, realistic, representing, scenic, sharp, striking, strong, suggestive, telling, unequivocal, vivid, well-delineated

GRAPPLE, verb attack, battle, clasp, clinch, close, close with, clutch, combat, come in conflict with, compete with, confront, contest, do battle with, encounter, engage with, fasten upon, fight, get hold of, grasp, grip, hang on, hold, hold fast, oppose, seize, struggle, tackle, take hold of, take on, tussle, vie with, wrestle

GRASP *(Mastery),* **noun** ability, apprehension, clasp, cognition, compass, competence, comprehension, conception, embrace, grip, handle, hold, judgment, ken, knowledge, mastery, perception, purchase, range, reach, retention, savvy, scope, seizure, sense, stretch, sweep, thorough understanding, understanding

GRASP *(Possession),* **noun** clench, clutch, de facto possession, embracement, grip, hold, purchase, taking hold

GRASP, verb apprehend, capture, clasp, clinch, clutch, cohere, comprehend, conceive, digest, discern, fathom, gain, get to the bottom of, grab, grapple, grip, hold, hold firmly, ken, penetrate, realize, recognize, retain, seize, seize the meaning, sense, snatch, take, understand

GRASS-ROOTS, adjective basic elements, collective, common, comprehensive, extensive, far-reaching, from the bottom up, general, general public, global, groundswell, large-scale, omnibus, ordinary, popular, prevalent, rank and file, substantial, sweeping, the masses, total, universal
ASSOCIATED CONCEPTS: grass-roots political support

GRATIFICATION, noun beatitude, benefit, bliss, cheer, comfort, delectation, delight, elation, enchantment, enjoyment, exhilaration, felicity, fruition, gladness, glee, happiness, indulgence, joy, jubilation, merriment, pleasure, rapture, relish, satisfaction, savor, stimulus, thrill, titillation, transport, well-being

GRATIS, adjective as a favor, complimentary, costless, expenseless, for nothing, free, free of charge, free of cost, free of expense, *gratiis*, *gratuito*, unbought, unpaid for, unrecompensed, voluntary, without charge, without consideration, without monetary inducement, without monetary reward, without pecuniary gain, without recompense, without reward

GRATITUDE, noun acknowledgment, appreciation, appreciativeness, deepest appreciation, expression of appreciation, genuine appreciation, grace, gratefulness, praise, recognition, responsiveness, sense of indebtedness, sense of obligation, sincere appreciation, thankfulness, thanks

GRATUITOUS (Given without recompense), **adjective** bestowed, by way of gift, chargeless, charitable, complimentary, contributory, costless, donated, expenseless, for nothing, free, free of cost, free of expense, given, given away, gratis, not charged, not charged for, not subject to a payment, provided without charge, unbought, unpaid, unpaid for, unrecompensed, voluntary, without charge, without compensation, without consideration
ASSOCIATED CONCEPTS: gratuitous agency, gratuitous allowance, gratuitous bailment, gratuitous contract, gratuitous guest, gratuitous invitee, gratuitous licensee, gratuitous service, gratuitous undertaking, gratuitous use

GRATUITOUS (Unwarranted), **adjective** additional, baseless, causeless, dispensable, excessive, extraneous, *gratuitus*, groundless, inapposite, inappropriate, inessential, irrelative, irrelevant, needless, nonpertinent, not fitting, not following, not necessitated, not pertinent, superfluous, uncalled for, unconnected, undesirable, undue, unessential, unfounded, unjustified, unnecessary, unneeded, unprovoked, unrelated, unsuitable, unsuited, without basis, without foundation
ASSOCIATED CONCEPTS: gratuitous remarks during an examination of a witness

GRATUITY (Bribe), **noun** corrupting gift, corruption, graft, hush money, illegal gain, influence by a gift, jobbery, kickback, price, price of corruption, protection, rakeoff, sop, subornation
ASSOCIATED CONCEPTS: bribe receiving, emolument, illegal gratuity, official misconduct, tampering with a witness

GRATUITY (Present), **noun** award, benefaction, bonus, charity, contribution, dispensation, dole, donative, extra, favor, gift, grant, handout, offering, perquisite, premium, presentation, reward, tip, unearned increment

GRAVAMEN, noun burden of a charge, cardinal point, center, central point, content, core, cornerstone, crux, essence, essence of a grievance, essential matter, essential part, essential point, focal point, gist, gist of a charge, grievance, key, keystone, main point, material part, material point, nucleus, pith, pivotal point, principal part, root, salient point, *sine qua non*, spirit, substance, substantial cause, substantial part of a complaint, sum and substance, thrust
ASSOCIATED CONCEPTS: gravamen of a complaint

GRAVE (Important), **adjective** chief, consequential, critical, essential, exigent, *gravis*, imperative, indispensable, pressing, serious, *serius*, substantial, *tristis*, urgent, weighty

GRAVE (Solemn), **adjective** cheerless, dolorous, frowning, grim, heavy, humorless, joyless, pensive, sad, saturnine, serious, sober, somber, sorrowful, spiritless, uncheerful, uncheery, unlively
ASSOCIATED CONCEPTS: grave consequences for illegal acts

GRAVE CONSEQUENCES, noun a bleak outcome, a deleterious outcome, a deleterious outgrowth, a malignant scenario, an extremely unfortunate sequence of events, deleterious aftermath, deleterious developments, deleterious effects, deleterious results, important and significant effects, severe fallout
ASSOCIATED CONCEPTS: punishment

GRAVITATE, verb approach, be attracted, be prone to, draw near, draw toward, have a proclivity for, have a propensity for, head toward, incline, lean, move toward, tend, tend toward, trend
ASSOCIATED CONCEPTS: gravitate to a life of crime

GRAVITY, noun attraction, attractiveness, concern, consideration, draw, enormity, greatness, heaviness, heft, import, importance, interest, magnetism, magnitude, materiality, momentousness, ponderosity, ponderousness, pull, pulling power, severity, significance, solemnity, weight
ASSOCIATED CONCEPTS: gravity of a crime

GRAY AREA, noun ambiguous, blind, borderline, chance, complex, cryptic, contingent, dark, enigmatic, equivocal, esoteric, foreign, gamble, hidden, indeterminate, mysterious, never experienced before, new, novel, obscure, open question, puzzling, questionable, secret, strange, unascertained, uncalculated, uncertain, undecided, undefined, undesignated, undetermined, undisclosed, undiscovered, unexplored, unfamiliar, unfixed, unidentified, uninvestigated, unknown, unset, unsettled, unstudied, untold, untraced
ASSOCIATED CONCEPTS: statutory construction

GREAT (Major), **adjective** able, absolute, adroit, august, big, bulky, capacious, celebrated, chief, clever, colossal, commanding, compelling, complete, consequential, crackerjack, critical, dandy, dignified, distinguished, elevated, eminent, enormous, esteemed, exalted, excellent, expert, extensive, extraordinary, extreme, fabulous, famous, far-reaching, fine, first-rate, gigantic, glorious, grand, high-minded, huge, illustrious, immense, important, influential, inordinate, large, leading, lofty, magnanimous, main, majestic, major, massive, master, maximum, meritorious, mighty, momentous, monstrous, noble, notable, noted, outstanding, paramount, perfect, potent, powerful, preeminent, prime, principal, prodigious, proficient, profound, puissant, remarkable, renowned, respectable, serious, sizable, skillful, solid, splendid, strong, sublime, substantial, superior, supreme, topflight, unconditional, vast, very good, weighty

GREAT *(Many)*, **adjective**   abundant, ample, boundless, considerable, copious, countless, excessive, generous, illimitable, inexhaustible, manifold, many, multitudinous, numerous, unlimited, voluminous

GREED, *noun*   acquisitiveness, appetency, avarice, avariciousness, *avaritia, aviditas,* avidity, covetousness, crapulence, *cupiditas,* cupidity, desire to hoard wealth, eagerness, edacity, excess, gluttonous appetite, gluttony, greediness, gulosity, incontinence, indulgence, inordinate desire, inordinate desire to gain, insatiability, insatiableness, intemperance, intense desire, lust for money, omnivorousness, overindulgence, possessiveness, ravenousness, selfishness, voraciousness, voracity

GRIEF, *noun*   adversity, affliction, agony, anguish, anxiety, bereavement, bitterness, broken heart, burden, calamity, casualty, catastrophe, chagrin, concern, contrition, desolation, despair, despondency, disaster, discomfort, discontent, displeasure, dole, dolor, failure, gloom, grievance, hardship, heartache, heavy heart, ill-fortune, malaise, melancholy, misadventure, mischance, misery, misfortune, mishap, ordeal, pain, remorse, reverse, ruin, sadness, sorrow, sorrowfulness, strain, tension, tragedy, tribulation, trouble, vexation, woe, worry

GRIEVANCE, *noun*   affliction, annoyance, burden, cause of sorrow, charge, complaint, criticism, discontent, disservice, foul play, grounds for complaint, hardship, iniquity, *iniuria,* injury, injustice, objection, oppression, problem, *querela, querimonia,* reason to complain, trial, trouble, unfairness, vexation, wrong
ASSOCIATED CONCEPTS: arbitration, exhaustion of contractual remedies, grievance committee

GRIEVE, *verb*   ache, aggrieve, anguish, be anguished, be sad, bemoan, bewail, complain, cry, cut to the quick, desolate, discommode, distress, feel regret, fret, groan, harass, lament, languish, moan, mourn, pain, pine, repine, rue, sadden, sorrow, suffer, take to heart, torment, wail, weep

GRIEVOUS, *adjective*   afflicting, afflictive, agonizing, appalling, arrant, atrocious, bad, base, bitter, burdensome, cataclysmic, catastrophic, crushing, cutting, deplorable, detrimental, dire, disastrous, distressing, doleful, dolorous, dreadful, execrable, glaring, grave, grim, gross, horrible, iniquitous, insufferable, intense, intolerable, lamentable, mournful, nefarious, oppressive, outrageous, pitiable, piteous, plaintive, raw, rueful, ruinous, sad, severe, shameful, sharp, sorrowful, terrible, torturous, tragical, unbearable, vile, violent, woeful
ASSOCIATED CONCEPTS: grievous crime

GROSS *(Flagrant)*, **adjective**   absolute, aggravated, atrocious, big, colossal, considerable, deplorable, dire, disgusting, dreadful, easily seen, egregious, enormous, evident, extreme, fulsome, gigantic, glaring, grave, great, grievous, heinous, horrible, huge, immense, indelicate, lamentable, large, manifest, massive, monstrous, obvious, odious, offensive, outrageous, reprehensible, shameful, shocking, terrible, unmitigated, utter
ASSOCIATED CONCEPTS: gross fraud, gross inadequacy, gross misconduct, gross neglect, gross negligence, gross unfairness

GROSS *(Total)*, **adjective**   aggregate, all-inclusive, complete, comprehensive, entire, exhaustive, full, inclusive, *incredibilis,* intact, inviolate, lacking nothing, *magnus,*
nimius, plenary, unabridged, unbroken, uncut, undeducted from, undeleted, undiminished, undivided, unexpurgated, unreduced, unshorn, unshortened, whole, without deductions
ASSOCIATED CONCEPTS: easement in gross, gross earnings, gross estate, gross income, gross profit, gross receipts, gross sales, gross value

GROSS REVENUES, *noun*   aggregate income, all encompassing revenues, comprehensive earnings, gross income, income without deductions, total proceeds

GROUND, *noun*   assumption, backbone, base, basis, *causa,* cause, cause for complaint, cause for protest, complaint, criticism, data, evidence, fact, footing, foundation, grave injustice, gross wrong, inequity, infliction, iniquity, injury, injustice, justification, motive, objection, oppression, oppressive act, origin, outrage, premise, principle, proof, purpose, *ratio,* rationale, reason, resentment, root, support, supposition, unjust deed, unjustness, wrong
ASSOCIATED CONCEPTS: cause of action, general grounds, good and sufficient grounds, ground for complaint, ground of action, grounds of belief, meritorious grounds, reasonable grounds

GROUNDLESS, *adjective*   baseless, empty, erroneous, fallacious, false, ill-founded, inaccurate, paralogistic, unfounded, unjustifiable, unreal, unreasonable, unsound, unsubstantiated, unsupported, unsustainable, unsustained, untenable, untrue, unwarranted, vain, without foundation, without reality

GROUNDS *(Cause)*, **noun**   arguments, base, basis, case, circumstances, data, determinant, documentation, elements, evidence, factors, facts, foundation, fundament, justification, medium of proof, motive, occasion, principles, proof, pros and cons, provisions, rationale, reason to believe, terms
ASSOCIATED CONCEPTS: grounds to convict of a crime, grounds to impeach, grounds to indict

GROUNDS *(Property)*, **noun**   area, estate, land, lot, premises, parcel, parcel of land, property, real property, realty, section

GROUP, *noun*   affiliation, aggregate, array, assemblage, assembly, association, band, bracket, branch, category, circle, class, classification, clique, coalition, collection, community, conglomeration, constituency, corps, crowd, denomination, faction, family, force, galaxy, gathering, genus, guild, horde, league, membership, nomination, order, organization, representation, sect, section, segment, sodality, species, subdivision, team, throng, troupe, sector, unit, variety

GROUP, *verb*   adjust, align, allocate, arrange, array, assemble, catalogue, categorize, class, classify, cluster, codify, collect, combine, compile, compose, congregate, connect, convene, coordinate, form into ranks, gather, index, intertwine, line up, marshal, match, organize, place, put together, rank, register, screen, size, sort, subdivide

GROW *(Enlarge)*, **verb**   accrue, accumulate, advance, amplify, appreciate, augment, burgeon, dilate, earn interest, expand, gain, increase, inflate, intensify, magnify, mellow, multiply, progress, propagate, pullulate, spread, stem, strengthen, swell, thrive, wax, widen

GROW *(Mature)*, **verb**   blossom, build, develop, engender, evolve, expand, germinate, increase, maturate, nurture, progress, pullulate, ripen

GROWTH (Evolution), **noun**   advancement, development, evolvement, expansion, flowering, fruition, germination, improvement, maturation, movement toward adulthood, movement toward maturity, progress, ripening, sprouting, unfolding

GROWTH (Increase), **noun**   accumulation, addition, advancement, aggrandizement, amplification, *auctus,* augmentation, distention, enlargement, escalation, expansion, extension, heightening, increment, *incrementum,* inflation, intensification, multiplication, rise, spread, surge, swell, swelling

GRUELING (Difficult), **adjective**   complex, complicated, difficult, extreme, formidable, hard, harsh, involved, labyrinthine, obscure, onerous, opaque, operose, trying

GRUELING (Weakening), **adjective**   debilitating, devitalizing, enervating, enfeebling, exhausting, fatiguing, onerous, operose, painful, punishing, sapping, tiresome, tiring, weakening, wearying

GUARANTEE, verb   answer for, assume responsibility, assure, back, be responsible for, become liable, become surety for, certify, commit oneself, ensure, *fides,* give assurance, give one's word, guard, hypothecate, impignorate, insure, make oneself answerable for, obligate, pledge, promise, safeguard, secure, *sponsio,* sponsor, stake, support, underwrite, *vadimonium,* vouch for, warrant
ASSOCIATED CONCEPTS: guarantee a title, guarantee against breakage, guarantee payment

GUARANTEED (Definite), **adjective**   agreed, assured, attested, certain, certified, committed, conclusive, definite, dependable, ensured, indubious, inevitable, pledged, promised, reliable, safe, secure, secured, solid, sure

GUARANTEED (Insured), **adjective**   assured, covenanted, ensured, promissory, warranteed

GUARANTOR, noun   approver, attester, backer, cosignatory, cosigner, endorser, guarantee, guaranty, insurer, obligator, sponsor, subscriber, supporter, surety, warrantor
ASSOCIATED CONCEPTS: commercial transactions

GUARANTY, noun   assurance, backing, bond, certification, commitment, endorsement, gage, guard, hypothecation, indemnity, insurance, pact, pledge, promise to pay another's debt, recognizance, safeguard, security, stake, support, surety, token, voucher, warrant, warranty
ASSOCIATED CONCEPTS: absolute guaranty, collateral guaranty, continuing guaranty, fidelity guaranty, guaranty company, guaranty fund, guaranty insurance, guaranty of payment, indemnity bond, limited guaranty, special guaranty, suretyship

GUARD (Guardian), **noun**   bodyguard, custodian, defender, defense, keeper, monitor, palladium, panoply, peace officer, protector, security, sentinel, sentry, surveillance, ward, warden, watchman

GUARD (Safeguard), **noun**   palladium, protection, protector, refuge, safe-conduct, safeguard, safekeeping, shield, veil

GUARD, verb   be vigilant, beware, care, conserve, control, cover, defend, detain, ensconce, enshroud, ensure, escort, harbor, keep, keep under surveillance, maintain, make safe, monitor, patrol, preserve, protect, safeguard, save, secure, shelter, shield, supervise, sustain, uphold

GUARD AGAINST, verb   be on the vigil for, be there for, champion, defend, insulate, look out for, overlook, oversee, preserve, protect, safeguard, secure, shield, stand by the side of, stand guard over, superintend, take care of, take measures for, take steps for, watch over
ASSOCIATED CONCEPTS: guard against crime, guard against fraud

GUARDED, adjective   alert, attentive, awake, aware, careful, cautious, *cautus,* chary, circumspect, *circumspectus,* conservative, defended, discreet, fenced, heedful, in custody, noncommittal, protected, prudent, reserved, reticent, safe, safeguarded, secured, sheltered, shielded, shy, suspicious, under surveillance, vigilant, wary, watched over, watchful

GUARDIAN, noun   argus, attendant, bodyguard, caretaker, champion, chaperon, conductor, conservator, curator, custodian, *custos,* defender, *defensor,* escort, gatekeeper, guard, keeper, overseer, patron, *praeses,* preserver, protector, safeguard, safekeeper, sentinel, sentry, sponsor, superintendent, supervisor, trustee, tutelar, warden, warder, watchman
ASSOCIATED CONCEPTS: de facto guardian, domestic guardian, general guardian, guardian ad litem, guardian by statute, guardian de son tort, guardian of the person, legal guardian, special guardian, testamentary guardian
FOREIGN PHRASES: *Tuta est custodia quae sibimet creditur.* That guardianship is secure which trusts to itself alone. *Lucrum facere ex pupilli tutela tutor non debet.* A guardian ought not to make money out of the guardianship of his ward. *Custos statum haeredis in custodia existentis meliorem, non deteriorem, facere potest.* A guardian can make the estate of an existing heir under his guardianship better, but not worse. *Minor minorem custodire non debet, alios enim praesumitur male regere qui seipsum regere nescit.* A minor ought not to be guardian to a minor, for a person who knows not how to govern himself is presumed to be unfit to govern others.

GUARDIANSHIP, noun   adoption, auspices, care, charge, control, custody, patronage, preservation, protection, protectorship, safekeeping, trust

GUESS, verb   assume, *augurari,* be of the opinion, believe, conjecture, deem, *divinare,* divine, estimate, forejudge, form an estimation, gather, have a hunch, hypothesize, imagine, infer, judge, judge at random, judge with uncertainty, *opinari,* opine, postulate, presume, presuppose, reckon, speculate, suppose, surmise, suspect, take for granted, theorize, think, think likely
ASSOCIATED CONCEPTS: speculative testimony

GUEST, noun   boarder, confidante, friend, frequenter, houseguest, inmate, lodger, patron, regular, renter, sharer, traveler, visitor
ASSOCIATED CONCEPTS: guest statute

GUIDANCE, noun   admonition, advice, advisement, advocacy, backing, bidding, briefing, coaching, *consilium,* consultation, counsel, criticism, cue, direction, directive, *ductus,* edification, education, encouragement, enlightenment, exhortation, expostulation, fosterage, help, hint, inculcation, indoctrination, information, instruction, lead, leadership, lesson, management, monition, opinion, orientation, patronage, pedagogy, persuasion, precept, prescription, prompting, recommendation, reference, schooling, sponsorship,

273

steering, suggestion, supervision, teaching, training, tuition, tutelage, tutoring

ASSOCIATED CONCEPTS: advisory opinion, assistance of counsel, declaratory judgment

GUIDE, noun advisor, archetype, bellwether, code, conductor, criterion, director, educator, example, exemplar, generalization, indication, instructor, marshal, master, maxim, mentor, model, monitor, paradigm, paragon, pattern, pedagogue, pilot, precedent, precept, preceptor, precursor, prototype, rule, sample, specimen, standard, symptom, teacher

GUIDE, verb advise, attend, command, conduct, control, convoy, counsel, direct, dispose, engineer, escort, familiarize with, go ahead, go in the van, inculcate, indicate, indoctrinate, inform, instill, instruct, lead, light the way, manage, maneuver, marshal, motivate, officiate, orientate, overlook, oversee, predominate, prescribe, preside, prevail, rear, recommend, regulate, rule, shepherd, show, steer, superintend, teach

GUIDELINE, noun advisory limitation, aspect, bench mark, borderline indication, boundary, confinement, dictate, dimension, direction, formula, gauge, general guideline, guide, idea, instruction, key, limitation, margin, marker, measure, outer limits, parameter, perimeter, restraint, restriction, rule, specific, standard, yardstick

GUILT, noun blame, blameworthiness, breach of law, censurability, corruption, crime, criminal activity, criminal deed, criminal offense, criminality, criminousness, *culpa,* culpability, delict, delinquency, deviation from rectitude, dishonesty, fault, felonious conduct, ill conduct, immorality, impeachability, improbity, improper conduct, iniquity, law-breaking, malefaction, malfeasance, malpractice, malversation, misbehavior, misconduct, misdeed, misdemeanor, misdoing, misfeasance, misprision, *noxia,* offense, offense against the law, offensiveness, official misconduct, peccadillo, peccancy, reprehensibility, reproach, sin, sinfulness, transgression, turpitude, unlawful practice, unrighteousness, vice, viciousness, violation, violation of law, *vitium,* wrong, wrongdoing

ASSOCIATED CONCEPTS: admission of guilt, finding of guilt, guilt beyond a reasonable doubt, guilt by association, *nolo contendre,* presumption of innocence

FOREIGN PHRASES: *Cum par delictum est duorum, semper oneratur petitor et melior habetur possessoris causa.* When there is equal fault on both sides, the burden is always placed on the plaintiff, and the cause of the possessor is preferred. *Quae sunt minoris culpae sunt majoris infamiae.* Those things which are less culpable may be more infamous. *Poenae suos tenere debet actores et non alios.* Punishment belongs to the guilty, and not others. *Excusat aut extenuat delictum in capitalibus quod non operatur idem in civilibus.* That excuses or extenuates a wrong in capital cases which would not have the same effect in civil suits.

GUILTY, adjective at fault, blamable, blameworthy, censurable, chargeable, condemnable, convicted, criminal, criminous, culpable, delinquent, deserving of blame, deserving of punishment, deserving reproof, erring, imputable, in error, in the wrong, incriminated, indictable, peccant, reprehensible, reproachable, reprovable, *sceleratus,* to blame, transgressing

ASSOCIATED CONCEPTS: bail, conviction, find the defendant guilty, guilty as charged, guilty knowledge, guilty of the crime charged, guilty of wrongdoing, innocence, insanity, parole, plea of guilty, qualified plea of guilty, sentencing, verdict

GUILTY PLEA, noun acceptance of criminal wrongdoing, admission of blame, admission of guilt, admission of punishment, admission of the charges as read, at fault, blameworthiness, conviction, culpable plea, plea of guilt

ASSOCIATED CONCEPTS: Fifth Amendment, plea of nolo contendere, right against self-incrimination torture

GUN, noun armament, arms, carbine, firearm, lethal instrument, munition, piece, pistol, repeater, revolver, rifle, shotgun, *tormentum,* weapon

ASSOCIATED CONCEPTS: concealed weapon, deadly weapon

GUN CONTROL, noun check on the sale of guns, control of armaments, control of arms, control of firearms, control over weapons, prohibition on green sales, prohibition on sale of firearms, regulation on gun sales, regulation on use of weapons, restrictions on sale of arms

ASSOCIATED CONCEPTS: Brady law, gun control, National Rifle Association, right to bear arms, Second Amendment

HABEAS CORPUS, noun appeal, application for discharge, application for liberty, collateral review of detention, collaterial review, complaint to a higher court, examination, extraordinary remedy, extraordinary writ, judicial reexamination, petition for release, redress, remedy, review, writ, writ for deliverance from illegal confinement, writ to gain freedom
ASSOCIATED CONCEPTS: coram nobis, exhaustion of state remedies, federal writ of habeas corpus, prerogative writ, special proceeding, state writ of habeas corpus, writ of inquiry

HABIT, noun acquired mode of behavior, attitude, characteristic behavior, characteristically repeated action, common practice, confirmed way, consuetude, *consuetudo,* convention, conventionality, course of conduct, custom, customary action, customary conduct, disposition, fashion, frequently repeated act, *habitus,* inclination, inveterate practice, leaning, mannerism, mode, *mos,* observance, particularity, pattern, peculiarity, practice, predisposition, proclivity, propensity, recurrence, repetition, routine, rule, second nature, style, tendency, tradition, trait, usual procedure, way
ASSOCIATED CONCEPTS: confirmed habits, continued habits, custom and usage, temperate habits

HABITABLE, adjective adequate, appropriate for residence, capable of being inhabited, comfortable, fit for dwelling, fit for habitation, fit to be occupied, fit to live in, *habitabilis,* inhabitable, livable, occupiable, residential, suitable, suitable for living in, tenantable
ASSOCIATED CONCEPTS: warranty of habitability

HABITANT, noun abider, boarder, denizen, domiciliary, dweller, *habitator, incola,* indweller, inhabitant, inhabiter, inmate, lodger, occupant, occupier, resident, residentiary, resider, settler, sojourner, squatter, tenant, townsman, villager
ASSOCIATED CONCEPTS: residency laws

HABITATION (Act of inhabiting), **noun** abiding, continuance, dwelling, habitancy, inhabitance, inhabitancy, inhabitation, lodgment, occupancy, occupation, possession, remaining, residence, residing, settlement, sojourn, sojournment, tenancy

HABITATION (Dwelling place), **noun** abiding place, abode, accommodations, address, domicile, *domicilium, domus,* dwelling, habitat, headquarters, home, homestead, house, housing, living quarters, lodging, lodgment, nest, place, place of abode, place of residence, quarters, residence, settlement, site, tabernacle, *tectum*

HABITUAL, adjective according to habit, accustomary, accustomed, automatic, chronic, common, commonplace, confirmed, constant, consuetudinary, continual, customary, daily, established, expected, familiar, fixed, frequent, general, ingrained, inveterate, *inveteratus,* natural, normal, ordinary, periodic, periodical, perpetual, prevalent, recurrent, recurring, regular, repeated, rooted, routine, set, standard, sustained, traditional, typical, *usitatus,* usual, wonted
ASSOCIATED CONCEPTS: habitual cohabitation, habitual criminal, habitual cruel and inhuman treatment, habitual insanity, habitual intemperance, habitual intoxication, habitual offender, habitual use, habitual violator, predicate felon, recidivist

HABITUATION, noun acclimation, acclimatization, accustoming, adaptation, adjustment, conditioning, confirmed habit, customariness, familiarization, inurement, inveteracy, inveterate habit, inveterateness

HACKING INTO, verb breaking in on, breaking into, breaching, cut in on, force into, gaining access, gaining by force, interfere, interlope, interrupt, intervene, intrude on, penetrate
ASSOCIATED CONCEPTS: cybercrime, identity theft

HAGGLE, verb argue, bargain, beat down, bid for, chaffer, deal, dicker, dispute, drive a bargain, higgle, make terms, negotiate, palter, quibble, stickle, underbid, wrangle
ASSOCIATED CONCEPTS: arm's-length bargaining, bickering over price

HALLMARK, noun champion, example, exemplar, good example, height of perfection, ideal, model, model of virtue, paramount example, specimen, standard, standard for comparison, summit, the best
ASSOCIATED CONCEPTS: hallmark law

HALLOWED, adjective adored, blessed, consecrated, divine, glorified, holy, honored, regarded as holy, respected, revered, sacred, sanctified, venerated, worshiped
ASSOCIATED CONCEPTS: hallowed law

HALT, noun abandonment, abeyance, armistice, arrest, block, break, breathing spell, cessation, check, close, closing,

deadlock, delay, desistance, detention, deterrent, discontinuance, discontinuation, end, ending, estoppage, estoppel, hesitation, impasse, impediment, inactivity, *intermissio*, intermission, interruption, lapse, lull, obstruction, pause, prevention, prohibition, recess, remission, respite, rest, shutdown, stalemate, standstill, stay, stop, stopover, stoppage, suspension, termination, time out, truce, wait
ASSOCIATED CONCEPTS: freeze, injunction, restraining order

HALT, *verb* adjourn, arrest, balk, bar, bar someone's way, barricade, block, blockade, break, break off, bring to a standstill, call a halt, cease, check, come to a stop, *consistere*, counteract, curb, cut short, dam, deadlock, debar, defeat, desist, deter, disallow, discontinue, end, estop, foil, forbid, frustrate, hamper, hinder, hold, impede, inhibit, interrupt, make inactive, obstruct, pause, preclude, prevent, prohibit, put an end to, quell, quit, remain, rest, restrain, restrict, stand, stand still, stay, stem, stop, stop an advance, stop short, subdue, *subsistere*, suspend, terminate, thwart, wait
ASSOCIATED CONCEPTS: abandon a crime, discontinue an action, injunction, stop and frisk laws

HAMPER, *verb* arrest, balk, bar, barricade, bind, block, brake, bridle, burden, check, choke, clog, confine, counteract, cramp, curb, debar, delay, deter, encumber, estop, fetter, foil, frustrate, handicap, hinder, hold back, impede, *impedire*, impedite, *implicare*, inhibit, intercept, interfere, interrupt, limit, manacle, muzzle, obstruct, oppose, preclude, prevent, rein, repress, resist, restrain, restrict, retard, shackle, smother, stymie, suppress, thwart, trammel, undermine, withhold
ASSOCIATED CONCEPTS: hamper a prosecution

HANDCUFF, *noun* bond, bridle, chain, collar, fastener, fetter, harness, manacle, *manicae*, padlock, pinion, shackle, trammel

HANDCUFF, *verb* belay, bind, bridle, chain, enchain, entrammel, fasten, fetter, gyve, hamper, hold, lash, leash, make fast, manacle, pinion, put in irons, render powerless, rope, secure, shackle, strap, string, tether, tie, tie one's hands, tie the hands of, tie up, trammel

HANDICAP, *noun* affliction, barrier, blemish, bridle, burden, defect, deficiency, detriment, difficulty, disability, disadvantage, discommodity, drawback, encumbrance, faultiness, hindrance, hurdle, impairment, impediment, *impedimentum*, imperfection, inconvenience, inferiority, insufficiency, interference, limitation, obstacle, obstruction, onus, remora, restraint, shortcoming, stumbling block

HANDLE *(Manage)*, *verb* administer, be master of, command, conduct, control, deal with, direct, dominate, execute, exercise authority, exercise direction over, exercise power over, exert authority, govern, guide, have authority, have charge of, have the care of, have the direction of, have under control, hold authority, keep in order, keep order, keep under control, look after, manipulate, officiate, operate, possess authority, preside over, regulate, reign over, rule, see to, superintend, supervise, use, wield, wield authority

HANDLE *(Trade)*, *verb* auction, barter, bring to market, carry, carry on a trade, carry on business, carry on commerce, carry on negotiations, chaffer, conduct business, deal in, do business, drive a bargain, effect a sale, exchange, exchange in commerce, have commerce, have for sale, hawk, interchange, make a bargain, make a sale, market, merchandise, offer for sale, peddle, put up for sale, sell, sell at the market, trade, trade in, traffic in, transact business, vend

HANDLING, *noun* administration, carrying out, conduct, control, direction, discipline, disposition of, effective management, effectuation, enforcement, governing, guidance, have charge of, management, mastermind, oversight, pilot the project, preside over, regulation, rule over, superintendence over, supervision over
ASSOCIATED CONCEPTS: handling of a case, handling of an issue, handling of litigation, handling stolen goods, safe patient handling law

HANDSEL, *noun* deposit, down payment, earnest money, first installment, first payment, first receipts, installment, payment, security, stake money

HANDWRITING, *noun* autography, calligraphy, *chirographum*, chirography, cursive writing, hand, longhand, *manus*, pencraft, penmanship, script, scription, style of penmanship, writing
ASSOCIATED CONCEPTS: forgery, handwriting expert, handwriting sample, holographic wills

HANG, *verb* condemn to death, corporal punishment, deprive of life, dispose of by death, end the life of a condemned, inflict capital punishment, inflict mortal punishment, kill, murder, punish by death, punish with death, put to death, put to death according to law, slay, snuff out the life of, terminate the life of
ASSOCIATED CONCEPTS: death by lethal injection, death penalty, electric chair, gas chamber, right to life

HAPHAZARD, *adjective* accidental, adventitious, arbitrary, capricious, casual, chance, chaotic, confused, designless, desultory, determined by chance, disordered, disorderly, fitful, immethodical, indiscriminate, irregular, nonsystematic, orderless, planless, promiscuous, random, systemless, unaimed, unarranged, unconsidered, undirected, unforeseen, unguided, unintended, unintentional, unmethodical, unorganized, unplanned, unpredictable, unpremeditated, unsorted, unsystematic, without order

HAPPEN, *verb* appear, arise, arrive, become, become a fact, become known, befall, bring to light, come into being, come into existence, crop up, develop, emerge, ensue, eventuate, issue, materialize, occur, proceed, recur, result, take effect, take its course, take place, transpire, turn up, uncover, unearth

HAPPENING, *noun* action, affair, *casus*, chance event, course of events, development, episode, event, experience, incident, matter, occasion, occurrence, phenomenon, proceeding, transpiration, unfolding
ASSOCIATED CONCEPTS: unforeseen happening

HAPPENSTANCE, *noun* accident, accidental occurrence, casualty, chance, chance happening, circumstance, coincidence, fate, fortuitousness, fortuity, inexpectation, involuntariness, random luck, serendipity, unexpected occurrence, unforeseen occurrence, unpredictability

HAPPY, *adjective* animated, at peace, blissful, bright, bubbling over, buoyant, carefree, celebrating, cheerful, cheery, chipper, contented, convivial, delighted, delirious, ecstatic, elated, enchanted, enraptured, euphoric, exhilarated, exuberant, exultant, favorable, felicitous, festive, flourishing, full of cheer, fun-loving, genial, glad, good-humored, intoxicated, jocund, joking, jovial, joyful, jubilant, laughing, merry, of good cheer, on top of the world, overjoyed, peaceful, pleased as punch, positive, prosperous, radiant,

rapturous, rejoicing, smiling, sparkling, spirited, thrilled, thriving, untroubled, upbeat, vivacious, zestful
ASSOCIATED CONCEPTS: happy outcome to litigation

HARANGUE, noun abusive speech, bombast, *contio*, declamation, declamatory speech, diatribe, disquisition, effusion, exhortation, expatiation, invective, lecture, prelection, tirade, vehement speech
ASSOCIATED CONCEPTS: harassment

HARASS, verb acerbate, afflict, aggrieve, agitate, agonize, alarm, alienate, anger, annoy, arose, arrogate, assail, badger, bagger, be malevolent, bedevil, beset, besiege, bludgeon, bother, browbeat, burden, coerce, confound, convulse, discomfort, discompose, disconcert, dismay, dispirit, disquiet, distress, disturb, enrage, envenom, *ex-agitare*, exasperate, excite, excruciate, fret, goad, grieve, harbor a grudge, harrow, harry, haunt, heckle, hurt, ill-treat, ill-use, importance, incense, incommode, infest, inflame, infuriate, injure persistently, intimidate, intrude upon, irk, irritate, malign, maltreat, miff, misuse, mock, obsess, offend, oppress, outrage, overburden, overdrive, overrun, overstrain, overtax, overwork, perplex, pester, pique, plague, prey upon, provoke, rankle, shake up, *sollicitare*, spite, strain, terrorize, torment, trouble, tyrannize, unsettle, upbraid, upset, vex, *vexare*, victimize, wear down, weigh on
ASSOCIATED CONCEPTS: barratry, employment law, harassing a witness, workplace sexual harassment

HARASSMENT, noun alarm, annoyance, bother, discomfort, disconcertedness, dismay, disregard, disturbance, enragement, excitement, injury, offense, outrageous behavior, outrageous conduct pain, provocation, rankle
ASSOCIATED CONCEPTS: employment law, sexual harassment, workplace violation

HARBINGER, noun announcer, annunciator, *antecursor*, augur, augury, auspice, courier, crier, forerunner, foretoken, forewarning, herald, informer, intelligencer, messenger, omen, portent, *praenuntius*, precursor, premonitory sign, presage, proclaimer, prognostic, publicizer, sign, teller, usher, warning

HARBOR, verb afford sanctuary, aid, cache, care for, cloak, conceal, cover, defend, ensconce, give refuge, grant asylum, guard, haven, hide, insure, keep, keep out of sight, keep safe, keep secret, lodge, look after, maintain, preserve, protect, provide refuge, provide safety, provide sanctuary, quarter, safeguard, screen, seclude, secrete, secure, shelter, shield, shroud, stow away, sustain, watch
ASSOCIATED CONCEPTS: accessory after the fact, alienation of affections, assisting escape, harbor and secrete, harboring a criminal, harboring a fugitive, harboring an animal

HARD, adjective arduous, beyond one's reach, bothersome, burdensome, complex, complicated, convoluted, demanding, difficult, enigmatic, grueling, impassable, impenetrable, incomprehensible, insoluble, insurmountable, involved, involving obstacles, overwhelming, perplexing, problematic, puzzling, vigorous, strenuous, stubborn, troublesome, unachievable, unavailable
ASSOCIATED CONCEPTS: hard and fast law, hard choices, hard lessons learned from law

HARDCORE, adjective adamant, constant, decided, dedicated, determined, devoted, enduring, firm, fixed, hard, immobile, immovable, inexorable, inflexible, intractable,

intransigent, invariable, obdurate, obstinate, opinionated, persevering, persistent, recalcitrant, relentless, resolute, rigid, set, settled, solid, stanch, steadfast, steady, stern, stiff, strong, stubborn, tenacious, unbending, unchangeable, uncompromising, uncontrollable, undeviating, unwavering, zealous
ASSOCIATED CONCEPTS: pornography

HARDENED, adjective calculated, calculating, callous, cold, cold-hearted, cruel, cruel-hearted, deliberate, diabolic, dispassionate, fiendish, hard, imperturbable, impervious, indifferent, insensitive, passionless, remorseless, ruthless, uncaring, unconcerned, unemotional, unfeeling, uninterested, unkind, unmerciful, unmoved, unperturbed, unrelenting, unresponsive, unsympathetic, untouched
ASSOCIATED CONCEPTS: hardened criminal

HARDLY, adverb almost, almost all, barely, deficient, few, inadequately, incomplete, inconsiderably, insufficiently, limited, little, meagerly, not abundant, not plentiful, not quite, paltry, rarely, scantly, scarcely, seldomly, sparingly, sparsely, thinly scattered

HARDSHIP, noun adversity, affliction, misfortune, suffering, travail

HARM, noun aggravation, balefulness, bedevilment, damage, *damnum*, deadliness, detriment, *detrimentum*, disablement, disservice, evil, hurt, hurtfulness, ill consequence, ill-treatment, impairment, injury, malignance, malignancy, malignity, mischief, misfortune, mutilation, noxiousness, perniciousness, ruin, scathe, scourge, virulence
ASSOCIATED CONCEPTS: accidental harm, bodily harm, foreseeable harm, irreparable harm, unreasonable risk of harm

HARM, verb abuse, adulterate, afflict, aggravate, attack, be malevolent, bruise, cause pain, corrode, corrupt, cripple, damage, debase, deface, demolish, devastate, disadvantage, disfigure, disserve, do evil, do mischief, do violence, endamage, exacerbate, hurt, ill-treat, ill-use, impair, incapacitate, infect, inflict injury, injure, *laedere*, maim, maltreat, mar, misuse, mutilate, *nocere*, pervert, plague, pollute, ravage, ruin, scathe, scourge, smite, spoil, subvert, worsen, wound, wrong
ASSOCIATED CONCEPTS: accidental harm, bodily harm, foreseeable harm, irreparable harm, unreasonable harm
FOREIGN PHRASES: *Error scribentis nocere non debit.* An error made by a clerk ought not to prejudice. *Qui jure suo utitur, nemini facit injuriam.* One who exercises his legal rights, injures no one.

HARMFUL, adjective afflicting, bad, baleful, baneful, calamitous, cataclysmic, catastrophic, consuming, consumptive, corrosive, costly, crippling, cruel, crushing, damaging, dangerous, deleterious, destructive, detracting, detrimental, devouring, dire, disadvantageous, disastrous, disserviceable, evil, fell, fiendish, foul, hurtful, illintentioned, inexpedient, infectious, injurious, insalubrious, insidious, internecine, malefic, maleficent, malicious, malign, mephitic, merciless, miasmal, mischievous, morbific, nasty, *nocens*, nocent, nocuous, noisome, noxious, *noxius*, pernicious, pestiferous, pestilential, pitiless, poisonous, polluted, ruinous, spiteful, subversionary, subversive, toxic, treacherous, troublous, unfavorable, unfortunate, unhealthy, unlucky, unpropitious, unsafe, unwholesome, venomous, vicious, wicked, wounding
ASSOCIATED CONCEPTS: harmful consequences from an overt act, harmful products

HARMLESS, adjective benign, blunt, gentle, hurtless, impotent, *innocens,* innocent, innocuous, *innocuus,* innoxious, *innoxius,* inoffensive, nonmalignant, nonpoisonous, nontoxic, nonvenomous, nonviolent, nonvirulent, powerless, tame, trustworthy, unaggressive, unhazardous, uninjurious, unmilitant, unthreatening, weak, without risk
ASSOCIATED CONCEPTS: harmless beyond a reasonable doubt, harmless error, hold harmless

HARMONIOUS, adjective accordant, acquiescent, adapted, adjusted, agreeable, agreeing, allied, amicable, apposite, apt, arranged, assenting, becoming, blended, bonded, *canorus,* coexistent, coexisting, combined, compatible, concinnous, concordant, *concors,* conforming, congenial, *congruens,* congruent, congruous, consentaneous, consentient, consistent, consonant, cooperative, coordinated, correlative, correspondent, corresponding, equable, fraternal, frictionless, friendly, halcyon, joint, leagued, matching, pacific, peaceful, pleasant, pleasing, proportional, proportionate, sociable, suitable, suiting, unanimous, united, unstrained, untroubled

HARNESS, verb control, command, constraint, curb, direct, dominate, get one's hands around, get the entire picture on, govern, guide, handle, instruct, lead, limit, maintain, manage, operate, overlook, oversee, pilot, rule, superintend, supervise
ASSOCIATED CONCEPTS: harness and control energy, seat belt harness laws

HARP, verb accentuation, attention, beat into the ground, drill into someone's head, bother, disturb, dwell on, emphasize, force, go over and over, hammer into someone's head, harass, harp on, hassle, persist in, pester, pound into someone's head, push, reiterate, repeat, state repeatedly

HARROW, verb aggrieve, agitate, alarm, annoy, appall, assail, badger, bedevil, beset, besiege, bother, browbeat, bully, chafe, chagrin, cross, discompose, disconcert, dismay, displease, disquiet, disturb, *excruciare,* fret, give pain, harass, harm, harry, hurt, ill-treat, ill-use, inflict pain, injure, irritate, lacerate, lancinate, maltreat, misuse, molest, needle, outrage, persecute, perturb, pique, plague, provoke, spite, tease, torment, *torquere,* try, upset, vex, *vexare,* wrong

HARRY (Harass), **verb** aggrieve, annoy, badger, bait, be offensive, be rude, beleaguer, beset, bother, browbeat, bully, *cruciare,* deride, discompose, disconcert, displease, distress, disturb, fluster, fret, haze, heckle, hound, importune, irritate, needle, offend, oppress, persecute, pester, pique, plague, provoke, rile, ruffle, tease, torment, *torquere,* try, vex, *vexare,* worry

HARRY (Plunder), **verb** assail, attack, create havoc, despoil, forage, foray, invade, lay waste, maraud, pillage, raid, ransack, ravage, rob, sack, seize, spoliate, strip

HARSH, adjective acerb, acerbic, acid, acrid, acrimonious, ascetic, astringent, austere, biting, bitter, brusque, brutal, burning, caustic, corrosive, crude, cruel, despiteful, discordant, disrespectful, draconian, drastic, excessive, extreme, feral, ferine, ferocious, grating, grim, grueling, gruff, ill-natured, incisive, inclement, inharmonious, inhuman, inhumane, intense, merciless, mordacious, mordant, noisome, noxious, oppressive, piercing, pitiless, punishing, rancorous, rigorous, rough, ruthless, savage, scathing, severe, sharp, stern, stinging, strident, stridulous, stringent,

surly, truculent, uncomforting, unconsoling, unfeeling, unflattering, ungentle, ungracious, unkind, unkindly, unmerciful, unmitigated, unpitying, unsympathetic, untender, virulent, vituperative, withering
ASSOCIATED CONCEPTS: cruel and unusual punishment, harsh penalty, harsh rule

HASTE, noun acceleration, alacrity, briskness, celerity, dash, dispatch, eagerness to act quickly, expedition, expeditiousness, *festinatio,* flurry, frenzy, hurriedness, hurry, hustle, inability to wait, precipitance, precipitancy, precipitation, precipitousness, *properantia, properatio,* quick-ness, rapidity, rashness, rush, speed, swiftness, urgency, velocity
ASSOCIATED CONCEPTS: speedy trial
FOREIGN PHRASES: *Festinatio justitiae est noverca infortunii.* The hastening of justice is the stepmother of misfortune.

HASTEN, verb accelerare, accelerate, advance, *contendere,* dash, dispatch, drive forward, expedite, facilitate, forward, help along, hurry, hurry along, hustle, incite, lose no time, make haste, *maturare,* move fast, move quickly, move speedily, precipitate, press, pressure, promote, *properare,* push on, put on speed, race, rouse, rush, rush through, speed along, spur, urge on

HATE, noun abhorrence, abomination, anger, animosity, animus, antagonism, antipathy, aversion, bias, detestation, enmity, hostility, ill feeling, ill will, intolerance, loathing, malevolence, prejudice, revulsion
ASSOCIATED CONCEPTS: hate crimes

HATE CRIME, noun offense involving animosity toward others, offense involving antagonism toward others, offense involving discrimination, offense involving enmity toward others, offense involving hate, offense involving hatred, offense involving intolerance, offense involving malevolence toward others, offense involving prejudice, offense involving victim's color of skin, offense involving victim's ethnicity, offense involving victim's gender, offense involving victim's national origin, offense involving victim's race, offense involving victim's religion, offense involving victim's sexual orientation

HATRED, noun abhorrence, abomination, animosity, animus, antagonism, antipathy, aversion, defamation, detestation, dislike, enmity, hostility, ill feeling, ill will, intolerance, loathing, malevolence, odium, prejudice, revulsion

HAVEN, noun anchorage, asylum, citadel, cove, harbor, hideout, landing, place of safety, port, *portus,* protection, refuge, resting place, retreat, sanctuary, shelter
ASSOCIATED CONCEPTS: diplomatic immunity

HAVING NO FOUNDATION, adjective baseless, empty, erroneous, false, foundationless, gratuitous, groundless, idle, ill-founded, illogical, nonactual, rootless, unbased, uncorroborated, unfounded, ungrounded, unjustifiable, unreasonable, unsound, unsubstantial, unsubstantiated, unsupportable, unsustainable, untenable, unwarranted, without basis, without cause, without foundation, without reality, without reason

HAVOC, noun anarchy, carnage, cataclysm, chaos, chaotic state, confusion, depredation, derangement, desolation, destruction, devastation, disorder, disorganization, dispersion, disruption, holocaust, overturning, pillage, plundering, ravage, ruin, ruination, sack, scattering, shambles, spoliation, *strages,* turmoil, upheaval, *vastatio,* violence, waste

ASSOCIATED CONCEPTS: disorderly conduct, disturbing the peace

HAZARD, noun *casus,* cause for alarm, chance, danger, dangerous course, dangerous situation, endangerment, *fors,* gamble, imperilment, insecurity, jeopardy, liability to injury, menace, *periculum,* peril, pitfall, precariousness, risk, source of risk, threat, uncertainty, unsafe object, unsureness
ASSOCIATED CONCEPTS: dangerous hazard, extreme hazard, hazardous business, hazardous condition, hazardous employment, hazardous undertaking, inherent hazard, latent hazard, moral hazard, patent hazard, private hazard, public hazard, undue hazard

HAZARDOUS *(Dangerous),* **adjective** adverse, chancy, dangerous, fraught with danger, full of danger, insalubrious, insecure, noxious, ominous, perilous, precarious, risky, shaky, threatening, toxic, unprotected, unreliable, unsafe, unsound, unsteady
ASSOCIATED CONCEPTS: hazardous materials, hazardous substances, hazardous waste

HAZARDOUS *(Imprudent),* **adjective** aleatory, chancy, full of risk, menacing, riskful, speculative, threatening, venturesome, venturous
ASSOCIATED CONCEPTS: aleatory contract

HEAD *(Chairperson),* **noun** acme, apex, beginning, cap, capital, chairman, chief, commandant, commencement, conclusion, crest, crisis, crown, crowning event, director, employer, end, flowering, fructification, fruition, heading, height, inception, issue, leader, manager, master, overseer, person in control, prime, principal, realization, ruler, section, superior, supervisor, top, ultimate, upper part, windup, zenith

HEAD *(Culmination),* **noun** conclusion, consummation, finality, finish, paramount, pinnacle, summit

HEAD *(Initiate),* **verb** incept, instigate, introduce, lead, lead the way, originate, pioneer, precurse, set in motion, spearhead, take the lead

HEAD *(Oversee),* **verb** command, control, determine, direct, govern, guide, inaugurate, incept, introduce, manage, officiate, originate, preside, preside over, regulate, spearhead, superintend, supervise

HEAD-ON, adjective contrary to in direct opposition, convergence in direct opposition, crash, encounter, impact, meeting, percussion, striking together, sudden contact, violent contact

HEADING, noun banner, caption, head, headline, label, proper title, section, superscription, title, topic

HEADQUARTERS, noun base, base camp, base of authority, base of operations, center, center of authority, center of operations, central station, chief office, distributing center, home base, home office, main office, manager's office, *praetorium,* residence, seat, supply base
ASSOCIATED CONCEPTS: nerve center of a corporation

HEADSTRONG, adjective audacious, bullheaded, cantankerous, contrary, contumacious, disobedient, foolhardy, forward, headlong, hot-blooded, impetuous, incautious, inexorable, inflexible, intractable, irresponsible, obdurate, obstinate, pertinacious, perverse, pigheaded, precipitate,

rash, recalcitrant, reckless, resolute, restive, self-assured, self-willed, strong-willed, stubborn, uncontrollable, ungovernable, unhesitating, unmanageable, unruly, untoward, unyielding, vehement, wanton

HEADWAY, noun advance, ascent, betterment, climb, development, forward motion, furtherance, gain, ground gained, growth, improvement, momentum, progress, progression, promotion, upswing

HEAL, verb alleviate, ameliorate, attend to, be on the mend, convalesce, cure, cure medically, disinfect, doctor, effect a cure, fix, fix up, get better, get well, grow better, help to get well, improve, make better, make right, make well, make whole, meliorate, mend, minister to, mitigate, nurse, on tract, palliate, rebuild, reconstruct, recover, recuperate, regenerate, rehabilitate, reinvigorate, rejuvenate, relieve, remedy, renew, repair, restore, restore to health, resuscitate, revitalize, revive, set straight, set right, show improvement, take care of, treat, work a cure

HEALTH, noun condition, fitness, freedom from ailment, freedom from disease, haleness, hardiness, heartiness, physical condition, robustness, ruggedness, salubriousness, salubrity, *salus, sanitas,* soundness, soundness of body, stamina, state of health, strength, sturdiness, *valetudo,* vigor, vitality, well-being, wholesomeness
ASSOCIATED CONCEPTS: bill of health, board of health, dangerous to health, department of health, health care, health education and welfare, health insurance, impairment of health, mental health, public health and safety, public health law, sanitary code

HEALTH CARE, noun coverage, health coverage, health insurance, health protection, medical coverage, medical insurance, medical plan, plan

HEALTH MAINTENANCE ORGANIZATION, noun closed medical organization, closed medical panel, controlled medical coverage, HMO, supervised medical care
Generally: group health care coverage, health maintenance coverage

HEAR *(Give a legal hearing),* **verb** adjudicate, *causam, cognoscere,* conduct a trial, decide, examine judicially, examine the witnesses, give a formal hearing to, give a judicial hearing to, give an official hearing to, hold court, inquire into, investigate judicially, judge, preside over, put on trial, referee, sit in judgment, try, try a case, try the cause
ASSOCIATED CONCEPTS: arbitrate, hear and report, mediate

HEAR *(Give attention to),* **verb** accept advice, accipere, acknowledge, advert, attend to, audition, ausculate, be attentive, be guided by, *cognoscere,* comply, defer to, give audience, give way, heed, listen, mind, note, obey, pay attention, regard, submit, subscribe, succumb, yield

HEAR *(Perceive by ear),* **verb** *auribus,* become aware of, become conscious of, detect, discern something audible, make out, notice, perceive something audible, *percipere,* receive information aurally, recognize, take cognizance of

HEARING, noun action, case at law, close inquiry, *cognitio,* contest, examination, exhaustive inquiry, formal proceeding, formal questioning, inquest, inquiry, inquisition, interrogation, investigation, judicial examination, judicial investigation, legal proceedings, legal trial, litigation, presentation of arguments and evidence, presentation of testimony, probe, public inquest, public proceeding, searching inquiry, strict inquiry, trial, trial at the bar, trial by jury, trial in court

ASSOCIATED CONCEPTS: adjudicative hearing, adversary hearing, de novo hearing, default hearing, due process, fair and impartial hearing, fair hearing, final hearing, formal hearing, full hearing, hearing on damages, hearing on the merits, interlocutory hearing, judicial hearing, notice of hearing, preliminary hearing, public hearing, statutory hearing, suppression hearing, traverse

FOREIGN PHRASES: *Qui aliquid statuerit, parte inaudita altera, aequum licet dixerit, haud aequum fecerit.* He who decides anything without hearing both sides, although he may decide correctly, has by no means acted justly.

HEARING OFFICER, *noun* adjudicator, arbitrator, administrative officer, final authority, hearing examiner, intermediary, intervener, mediator, moderator, negotiator, reconciler

ASSOCIATED CONCEPTS: administrative law judge, chief administrator hearing officer, staff hearing officer

HEARSAY, *noun* *auditio,* evidence from impersonal knowledge, gossip, groundless rumor, indirect evidence, popular report, report, *rumor,* secondary evidence, secondhand evidence, unconfirmed account, unconfirmed report, unverified comments, unverified news

ASSOCIATED CONCEPTS: admission, ancient writings, business records, declarations against pecuniary interest, declarations against penal interest, dying declarations, exceptions to hearsay rules, hearsay evidence, records of past recollection, reputation as to pedigree, res gestae, spontaneous declarations

HEART *(Essential part),* **noun** core, essence, fundamental, marrow, nerve, nucleus, pith, sum and substance

ASSOCIATED CONCEPTS: heart of the case, heart of the pleadings

HEART *(Fortitude),* **noun** ardor, backbone, doughtiness, fearlessness, fervor, focus, gallantry, intestinal fortitude, mettle, spirit, substance, toleration, valor

HEART *(Kindness),* **noun** altruism, benevolence, charity, clemency, compassion, gentleness, grace, humanity, kind offices, kind treatment, leniency, magnanimity, mercifulness, mercy, pity, sympathy, temperament, tenderness

HEARTENING, *adjective* assuring, auspicious, bright, cheerful, comforting, consoling, encouraging, favorable, felicitous, fortunate, full of promise, halcyonian, halcyonic, hopeful, opportune, optimistic, promising, propitious, providential, reassuring, roseate, salubrious, salutary

HEARTLESS, *adjective* apathetic, brutal, callous, cold, cold-blooded, cruel, disdainful, disinterested, dispassionate, hardened, hard-hearted, impervious, indifferent, insensible, insensitive, insouciant, insusceptible, iron-hearted, obdurate, passionless, pitiless, remorseless, ruthless, sinister, soulless, spiritless, stony, unaffected, uncaring, unconcerned, unemotional, unfeeling, unforgiving, unmoved, unpitying, unrelenting, unresponsive, unsusceptible, unsympathetic, untouched, without compunction

HEAVEN, *noun* abode of God, abode of God and angels, abode of spirits, abode of the saints, aerosphere, afterworld, bliss, canopy of heaven, celestial city, celestial sphere, city of God, divine abode, ecstasy, eternal home, Garden of Eden, glory, God's kingdom, great beyond, heavenly city, heavenly home, heavenly kingdom, hereafter, holy city, home of the Gods, kingdom of God, kingdom of heaven, life everlasting, next world, paradise, rapture, supreme happiness, the abode of saints, the hereafter, throne of God, utopia, Valhalla, world to come

HEAVY *(Burdened),* **adjective** benumbing, careworn, clumsy, dejected, depressed with sorrow, dull, dulled, gloomy, languid, leaden, serious, sluggish, somber, stolid, tempestuous, tiresome, torpid, violent, weary

ASSOCIATED CONCEPTS: heavy burden to fulfill in order to prove a case

HEAVY *(Important),* **adjective** commanding, eventful, immense, noteworthy, overwhelming, prominent, significant, solemn, vast

HEAVY *(Onerous),* **adjective** afflictive, burdensome, consequential, critical, cumbersome, difficult, excessive, grave, grievous, hard, imposing, intense, intolerable, momentous, notable, oppressive, striking, severe, substantial, trying, unbearable, unpleasant, unwieldy, wearying

HEAVY *(Ponderous),* **adjective** careful, deliberate, ominous, profound, serious, weighty

HEAVY-HANDED, *adjective* crushing, determined, firm, forceful, forcible, hard, harsh, inflexible, intense, perseverant, persevering, persistent, persuasive, potent, powerful, puissant, resolute, rugged, staunch, steadfast, steady, tenacious, unremitting, unyielding, vigorous

HECTOR, *verb* badger, bait, beset, bluster, bother, browbeat, bully, cow, distress, disturb, fret, gibe, goad, harass, harrow, harry, heckle, hound, insult, intimidate, irritate, jeer, menace, molest, nag, nettle, offend, persecute, pester, plague, pother, provoke, roil, tease, threaten, torment, treat with insolence, trouble, vex, worry

HEDGE, *noun* caution, circumspection, course of protection, equivocation, hesitancy, hesitation, instrumentality of protection, means of protection, method of protection, prevention against loss, prevention of downside, protection, protection against loss, safeguard

ASSOCIATED CONCEPTS: hedge laws, hedges encroaching on another, hedge against inflation, notice of appeal as hedge against loss, person's property

HEDGE, *verb* be careful, be cautious, border, bound, circle, circumscribe, compass, conceal, cover, delimit, delimitate, delineate, demarcate, divide, dodge, edge, encircle, enclose, encompass, ensphere, evade, fence, flank, girdle, guard, hide, limit, mark off, outline, play safe, protect, render safe, ring, safeguard, screen, shelter, shield, surround

HEED, *verb* attend to, be attentive, be aware, be careful, be cautious, be conscious of, be guided by, check, comply, consider, *curare,* follow, hark, hear, hearken to, listen to, look to, mark, mind, note, notice, obey, *observare,* observe, *parere,* pay attention, recognize, regard, respect, take care, take cognizance of, take into account, take note, take notice, watch

ASSOCIATED CONCEPTS: heed counsel's advice

HEEDLESS, *adjective* blind, careless, deaf, disregardful, hasty, improvident, imprudent, impulsive, inattentive, incautious, *incautus,* insouciant, irresponsible, mindless, neglectful, *neglegens,* negligent, nonobservant, oblivious, off guard, precipitate, rash, reckless, *temerarius,* thoughtless, unaware, uncaring, unconcerned, undiscerning, unhearing, unheedful, unheeding, unmindful, unnoticing, unobservant, unperceiving, unseeing, unsolicitous, unthinking, unwary, unwatchful, without consideration

ASSOCIATED CONCEPTS: recklessness

HEGEMONY, noun   ascendance, ascendancy, authority, command, control, directorship, dominance, domination, dominion, governance, headship, importance, influence, lawful authority, leadership, lordship, mastery, paramountcy, power, predominance, predominating influence, prepollence, regency, reign, rule, superiority, supremacy, sway

HEIGHT (Maximum), **noun**   culmination, end, extreme, extremity, high point, limit, maximum, perfection, supremacy, top, utmost, zenith

HEIGHT (Measurement), **noun**   altitude, angular measurement, ceiling, distance upward, elevation, expanse, extent, extent upward, highest part, length, tallness, upright distance, vertex

ASSOCIATED CONCEPTS: height restrictions in construction

HEIGHTEN (Augment), **verb**   add, advance, aggravate, *amplificare,* amplify, *augere,* build up, enhance, enlarge, exacerbate, *exaggerare,* expand, greaten, improve, increase, intensify, magnify, make higher, make larger, multiply, promote, raise, reinforce, strengthen, vivify

HEIGHTEN (Elevate), **verb**   *altior,* build up, hold up, lift up, make higher, pick up, raise, raise aloft, uplift, upraise

HEINOUS, adjective   abhorrent, abominable, arrant, atrocious, awful, bad, baleful, baneful, base, beastly, black, confounded, contemptible, damnable, deplorable, despicable, *detestabilis,* detestable, devilish, diabolic, dire, disgraceful, disgusting, distasteful, dreadful, egregious, evil, execrable, facinorous, flagitious, flagrant, foul, fulsome, ghastly, gross, hateful, hellish, horrendous, horrible, horrid, infamous, infernal, iniquitous, invidious, loathsome, low, malefic, mean, monstrous, *nafarius,* nasty, *nefandus,* nefarious, noisome, objectionable, obnoxious, odious, offensive, opprobrious, outrageous, pernicious, reprehensible, reptilian, repugnant, revolting, rotten, satanic, shameful, shocking, sickening, sinister, terrible, unprincipled, vicious, vile, villainous, wicked, wretched, wrong

ASSOCIATED CONCEPTS: heinous crime

HEIR, noun   acceptor, after-comer, after-generations, allottee, *bénéficiaire,* beneficiary, consignee, descendant, devisee, donee, inheritor, inheritrix, legatee, one who inherits, parcener, payee, possessor of descent, posterity, receiver, recipient, scion, successor, survivor, transferee

ASSOCIATED CONCEPTS: adopted heir, aggrieved heir, bodily heir, coheir, collateral heir, distributee, eligible heir, expectant heir, heir apparent, heirs at law, heirs in fee simple, illegitimate heir, immediate heir, intestate succession, issue, legal heir, legitimate heir, lineal heir, living heir, natural heir, natural offspring, next of kin, presumptive heir, pretermitted heir, Rule in Shelley's Case, surviving heir, unknown heir

FOREIGN PHRASES: *Haeres est aut jure proprietatis aut jure representationis.* A person is an heir either by right of property or by right of representation. *Haeredum appellatione veniunt haeredes haeredum in infinitum.* Under the name heirs come the heirs of heirs without limit. *Cohaeredes una persona censentur, propter unitatem juris quod habent.* Coheirs are regarded as one person because they own under unity of right. *In haeredes non solent transire actiones quae poenales ex maleficio sunt.* Actions which are penal and which arise out of anything of a criminal nature do not pass to the heirs. *Posthumus pro nato habetur.* A posthumous child is regarded as born before the death of the parent. *Nemo est haeres viventis.* No one can be the heir of a living person. *Haeres minor uno et viginti annis non respondebit, nisi in casu dotis.* A minor heir under twenty-one years of age is not answerable, except in the matter of dower. *Filius est nomen naturae, sed haeres nomen juris.* Son is the natural name, but heir is a name of law. *Nemo potest esse dominus et haeres.* No one can be both owner and heir. *Haeres est pars antecessoris.* An heir is a part of his ancestor.

HELM, noun   administration, auspices, authority, care, charge, command, custody, direction, discipline, dominance, domination, dominion, government, guardianship, guidance, jurisdiction, keeping, leadership, management, oversight, power, regulation, stewardship, superintendence, ward

HELP, noun   abetment, accommodation, advantage, advice, aid, assist, assistance, *auxilium,* avail, backing, benefaction, benefit, benevolence, boon, care, charity, contribution, cooperation, cure, deliverance, encouragement, expedient, facilitation, favor, fosterage, furtherance, good turn, guidance, hand, helpfulness, humanitarianism, kindness, ministration, patronage, philanthropy, redress, reinforcement, relief, remedy, rescue, resource, seconding, service, stead, strengthening, *subsidium,* subvention, succor, support, sustenance, use, utility

ASSOCIATED CONCEPTS: Good Samaritan

HELP, verb   abet, accommodate, advance, advise, aid, alleviate, ameliorate, apply a remedy, assist, avail, back, be benevolent, be of use, benefit, better, boost, come to the aid of, contribute, cooperate, correct, cure, do a service, ease, encourage, expedite, facilitate, fix, fortify, forward, furnish assistance, further, heal, improve, intercede for, lend a hand, lend aid, lend support, make easy, oblige, patronize, promote, prop, put right, rally, reinforce, relieve, remedy, render assistance, second, serve, smooth, speed, stand by, stead, strengthen, *subvenire,* succor, *succurrere,* support, sustain, work for

ASSOCIATED CONCEPTS: aid and abet, facilitation, rescue doctrine

HELPLESS (Defenseless), **adjective**   abandoned, aidless, conquerable, deserted, exposed, expugnable, forsaken, friendless, guardless, in danger, *inermis, inops,* open to attack, pregnable, resourceless, shelterless, unaided, unarmed, unarmored, unbefriended, uncovered, undefended, unfortified, unguarded, unprotected, unsheltered, unshielded, unstrengthened, unsupported, untenable, vincible, vulnerable, without aid, without succor

ASSOCIATED CONCEPTS: last clear chance

HELPLESS (Powerless), **adjective**   crippled, debilitated, dependent, disabled, enervated, feeble, impotent, incapable, incompetent, invalid, paralyzed, prostrate, strengthless, unable, weak, without force

ASSOCIATED CONCEPTS: disability, incompetency

HENCE, adverb   accordingly, as a consequence, as a result, before, consequently, earlier, finally, formerly, in consequence, in that event, necessarily, previous to, prior to, then too, therefore

HENCEFORTH, *adverb* from here on in, from now on, from this day forward, from this day on, from this moment in time on, from this point forward, from this point in time forward, hereafter, immediately, in the future, starting tomorrow, subsequently, thereafter
ASSOCIATED CONCEPTS: plain language

HENCHMAN, *noun* aide, ally, assassin, backer, champion, colleague, confidante, enforcer, follower, hatchet man, heavy, hired gun, hit man, right-hand man, supporter, thug, tool, trigger-man

HERALD, *verb* advertise, air, announce, apprise, augur, betoken, blazon, circulate, communicate, cry, disseminate, enlighten, enunciate, forecast, forerun, foreshow, foretell, foretoken, gazette, give tidings, harbinger, inform, introduce, make known, notify, omen, presage, proclaim, prognosticate, promulgate, publicize, publish, report, spread, tell, tip, trumpet, usher in, warn
ASSOCIATED CONCEPTS: *nuntiare*

HERE *(At a specific point)*, ***adverb*** at this juncture, at this place, at this point, at this point in time, at this spot, at this time, at this very moment, now, now precisely at this point, precisely at a point, quickly, right away, right here, within reach, without delay

HEREABOUTS, *adverb* around here, here, in the area, in the direction of, in the general vicinity, in the locale, in the vicinity, near here, somewhere close, somewhere near
ASSOCIATED CONCEPTS: plain language

HEREAFTER *(Eventually)*, ***adverb*** at a fixed time, later, ultimately
ASSOCIATED CONCEPTS: hereafter acquired, hereafter built

HEREAFTER *(Henceforth)*, ***adverb*** afterwards, from here on, from now on, from this time on

HEREBY, *adverb* by means of, by the aid of, by virtue of, through, through the medium of, whereby

HEREDITAMENT, *noun* bequest, devise, heirloom, heritable, heritage, heritance, inheritable property, inheritance, patrimony, personal property capable of being inherited, property which may descend to an heir, real property capable of being inherited
ASSOCIATED CONCEPTS: corporeal hereditament, easement, incorporeal hereditament

HEREDITARY, *adjective* ancestorial, ancestral, ancient, congenital, connatal, connate, constitutional, genealogical, genetic, hereditable, *hereditarius*, heritable, inborn, inbred, indigenous, ingenerate, inherited, innate, instinctive, instinctual, lineal, native, passed down, *paternus*, traditional, transmissible
ASSOCIATED CONCEPTS: hereditary disease, hereditary insanity, hereditary succession

HEREIN, *adverb* in, inside, inwardly, therein, wherein, within

HEREINAFTER, *adverb* after this, after today, afterwards, beginning now, commencing immediately, from here on in, from here on out, from now on, from now on in, from this day forward, from this day on, from this moment on, from this point on, from this time forward, from this time on, hereafter, immediately, immediately following today, in a subsequent part of the statement, in a subsequent part of this document, in future, in the future, looking ahead, subsequently
ASSOCIATED CONCEPTS: plain language

HEREOF, *adverb* about this, concerning this, in this regard, on this subject, regarding this, relating to this, with reference to, with specific reference to, with specific regard to
ASSOCIATED CONCEPTS: plain language

HERETIC, *noun* apostate, dissenter, dissentient, dissident, *haereticus*, iconoclast, infidel, misbeliever, nonconformist, protestant, schismatic, sectarian, separatist, skeptic, unbeliever

HERETOFORE, *adverb* before now, earlier, formerly, from the start, historically speaking, in the past, previous to, previously, prior to, retrospectively, up to this time

HEREWITH, *adverb* added to, along with this, appended to, attached to, by these means, connected to, enclosed with, fastened to, inside with, joined with, together with
ASSOCIATED CONCEPTS: plain language

HERITABLE, *adjective* alienable, assignable, bequeathable, bestowable, consignable, conveyable, devisable, exchangeable, givable, hereditable, hereditary, inheritable, negotiable, testamentary, transferable, transmissible
ASSOCIATED CONCEPTS: bequest, curtesy, devise, dower, intestate succession laws, legacy, testamentary gift

HERITAGE, *noun* ancestry, bequest, birthright, descent, expectations, future possession, hereditament, *hereditas, heredium,* heritance, incorporeal hereditament, inheritance, inherited lot, inherited portion, legacy, lineage, *patrimonium*, patrimony, portion, reversion
ASSOCIATED CONCEPTS: descendants

HERO, *noun* brave person, celebrity, champion, combatant, conquering hero, conqueror, decorated hero, deity, demigod, fearless soldier, fighter, folk hero, god, goddess, great man, great woman, guardian, heroine, highest type, ideal type, idol, immortal, luminary, man of courage, man of valor, martyr, master, megastar, model, notable, paragon, perfect type, person who serves as a shining example, phoenix, pillar of the community, protector, soldier, stalwart, star, superhero, superstar, tiger, valiant knight, warrior
ASSOCIATED CONCEPTS: Good Samaritan laws

HEROIC, *adjective* bold, brave, courageous, daring, dauntless, doughty, fearless, *fortis, fortis et invictus,* gallant, herolike, intrepid, lionhearted, noble, resolute, soldierly, stalwart, stout, stouthearted, unblenching, undaunted, unflinching, unshrinking, valiant, valorous
ASSOCIATED CONCEPTS: Good Samaritan

HESITANT, *adjective* averse, balking, balky, cautious, dallying, debating, deliberate, demurring, diffident, doubtful, doubting, equivocal, faltering, fluctuating, groping, half-hearted, hesitating, hesitative, indecisive, irresolute, lacking confidence, loath, pausing, qualmish, reluctant, shrinking, shy, slow, tentative, timid, unassured, uncertain, unconfident, undecided, unresolved, unsettled, unsure, vacillating, wavering
ASSOCIATED CONCEPTS: hestitant buyer, hestitant reluctant seller

HESITATE, verb balk, be dilatory, be dubious, be irresolute, be tentative, be uncertain, *cunctari*, dally, debate, delay, deliberate, demur, doubt, *dubitare*, equivocate, falter, fluctuate, *haerere*, have reservations, hold back, oscillate, pause, ponder, procrastinate, question, quibble, reluctant, scruple, shift, slow, stop, think twice, vacillate, wait, waver

HESITATION, noun caution, *cunctatio*, delay, diffidence, doubt, dubiety, *dubitatio*, dubitation, equivocation, faltering, fluctuation, *haesitatio*, hesitancy, holding back, incertitude, indecision, irresolution, nervousness, oscillation, overcaution, qualm, reluctance, scruple, second thoughts, slowness, tentativeness, uncertainness, uncertainty, unsureness, unwillingness, vacillation, wavering

HETEROGENEOUS, adjective assorted, different, disparate, dissimilar, *dissimilis*, diverse, diversified, diversiform, *diversus*, incongruous, irrelative, miscellaneous, mixed, motley, multiform, nonuniform, unalike, unequal, unlike, unmatched, unrelated, variant, varied, variegated, variform, various, varying, without relation

HIATUS, noun abeyance, adjournment, break, cessation, chasm, delay, disconnection, discontinuity, disjunction, disunion, fracture, gap, gulf, halt, *hiatus*, incompleteness, interference, interim, interlude, intermission, interregnum, interruption, interstice, interval, intervening period, lacuna, lapse, lull, moratorium, opening, pause, recess, respite, rest, rift, separation, spell, standstill, stop, stoppage, suspension, temporary stop

HIDDEN, adjective *absconditus*, abstruse, ambushed, arcane, blind, buried, camouflaged, clandestine, cloaked, close, clouded, concealed, covered, covert, cryptic, dark, delitescent, disguised, eclipsed, enigmatical, enshrouded, esoteric, hieroglyphic, indiscernable, invisible, latent, lurking, masked, mysterious, mystic, mystical, obscure, obscured, occult, *occultus*, out of sight, out of view, perdu, puzzling, recondite, screened, secluded, secret, secreted, shrouded, suppressed, surreptitious, unapparent, uncomprehended, undeciphered, undercover, underground, underhanded, undetected, undisclosed, undivulged, unexplained, unexposed, unknown, unobserved, unperceived, unrevealed, unseen, untold, veiled
ASSOCIATED CONCEPTS: attractive nuisance, duty to discover, hidden assets, hidden danger, hidden defects, hidden traps, latent defects, patent defects

HIDE, verb *abdere*, abscond, *abscondere*, be clandestine, become indiscernible, become unapparent, bury, cache, camouflage, *celare*, cloak, closet, cloud, conceal, conceal from knowledge, conceal from sight, cover, cover up, curtain, deceive, disguise, dissemble, eclipse, ensconce, enshroud, envelop, fail to reveal, harbor, hush up, keep out of sight, keep out of view, keep secret, keep to oneself, keep under cover, mask, obscure, protect, put out of sight, render invisible, screen, seclude, secrete, shade, shadow, shelter, shield, shroud, smuggle, store, stow away, suppress, veil, withhold, wrap
ASSOCIATED CONCEPTS: hide assets, hide behind the law, hide fraud, terrorist cells

HIDEOUS, adjective abhorrent, abominable, appalling, atrocious, contemptible, deplorable, despicable, detestable, dreadful, foul, frightening, frightful, ghastly, gruesome, heinous, horrendous, horrid, horrifying, macabre, monstrous, obnoxious, odious, offensive, pathetic, pitiful, regrettable, repellent, reprehensible, repulsive, revolting, scary, shameful, shocking, terrible, terrifying, unspeakable, vile

HIERARCHY (Arrangement in a series), noun arrangement, categorization, chain, classification, collocation, distribution, gradation, grouping, order, order of succession, progression, range, run, seriation, series, succession, system

HIERARCHY (Persons in authority), noun administrators, authorities, bureaucracy, commanders, controllers, dictators, directors, government, heads, leadership power, management, managers, masters, officials, persons in power, powers, regency, regime, rulers, sovereignty

HIGH-MINDED, adjective admirable, conscientious, estimable, ethical, fair, firm in principle, high-principled, honest, honorable, incorrupt, incorruptible, meritorious, moral, noble, principled, reputable, respectable, right-minded, righteous, scrupulous, sterling, trustworthy, uncorrupt, uncorrupted, upright, upstanding, virtuous, worthy

HIGH-POWERED, adjective aggressive, all-powerful, authoritative, commanding, compelling, connected, dominant, dynamic, effective, efficient, forceful, highest, important, in control, indomitable, influential, mighty, omnipotent, overpowering, potent, powerful, ruling, supreme
ASSOCIATED CONCEPTS: high-powered law firm, high-powered lobbyist

HIGH PROBABILITY, noun almost certainly, favorable prospect, in all likelihood, in most instances, with a high degree of certainty
ASSOCIATED CONCEPTS: high probability of chance, high probability of risk, high probability of success

HIGH TECHNOLOGY, noun best scientific advancement, highest standard of technology, most advanced discipline, most advanced technology, most developed technology, most perfected design, most up-to-date technology, newest advancement, newest design, newest development, newest invention

HIGHEST (Gravest), adjective altissimo, apical, best, capital, chief, critical, crown, crucial, crying, deep, desperate, earnest, essential, far-reaching, forcible, head, heavy, intense, intensified, maximal, maximum, momentous, most, of great force, of great number, overmost, paramount, potent, preeminent, pressing, principal, serious, sharp, strong, superlative, supreme, telling, tiptop, top, topmost, top-notch, urgent, vigorous, violent, vital, weighty, zenithal
ASSOCIATED CONCEPTS: highest degree of care, highest proved value

HIGHEST (Most Important), adjective best, capital, cardinal, chief, crowning, distinguished, eminent, exalted, first, foremost, greatest, important, leading, main, major, maximal, maximum, most, most august, most celebrated, most consequential, most considerable, most dominant, most influential, most memorable, most momentous, most notable, most prominent, most remarkable, most significant, noble, notable, paramount, preeminent, primary, prime, principal, superlative, supreme, uppermost
ASSOCIATED CONCEPTS: highest court, highest decision, highest law in the land

HIGHEST (Tallest), adjective best, biggest, colossus-sized, giant-sized, grandest, greatest, largest, lofty, mammoth-sized, maximal, maximum, most considerable, most elevated, most sizable, most substantial, most towering, paramount, preeminent, soaring, steepest, supreme

HIGHLIGHT, noun central point, cynosure, distinctive feature, focal point, high spot, important event, keynote, memorable part, outstanding feature, prominent detail, prominent part, salient point, significant feature, striking part

HIGHLY, adverb abundantly, appreciatively, certainly, chiefly, clearly, considerably, decidedly, enormously, entirely, exceedingly, extraordinarily, extremely, greatly, hugely, immensely, in great measure, largely, mostly, noticeably, obviously, overwhelmingly, predominantly, prominently, significantly, substantially, vastly
ASSOCIATED CONCEPTS: highly immoral, highly qualified, highly specialized area of the law

HIJACK, verb abduct, appropriate, arrogate, assume command, bear away, capture, carry away, carry off, commandeer, convey away, dispossess, expropriate, force, help oneself to, impress, intercept, lay hold of, make off with, make prisoner, overcome, overpower, overwhelm, pirate, plunder, secure, seize, snatch, take, take away, take by assault, take by force, take captive, take prisoner
ASSOCIATED CONCEPTS: air piracy

HINDER, verb annoy, arrest, barricade, be an impediment, be an obstacle, block, bother, check, clog, constrain, cramp, cripple, curb, detain, discommode, discourage, encumber, fetter, get in the way, halt, hamper, hamstring, handicap, hold back, impair, impede, *impedire*, incommode, inconvenience, inhibit, intercept, interfere, interrupt, keep back, obstruct, occlude, prevent temporarily, *prohibere*, render difficult, restrain, restrict, retard, *retardare*, set back, shackle, slow down, stand in the way, trammel, traverse, work against
ASSOCIATED CONCEPTS: interference with a contract, interference with a lawful order, obstructing justice

HINDRANCE, noun annoyance, arrest, barrier, blockade, bother, check, complication, constriction, detention, deterrent, detriment, difficulty, disadvantage, discouragement, drawback, embargo, encumbrance, hamper, handicap, holdback, impediment, *impedimentum*, inconvenience, inexpedience, inhibition, interference, interposition, interruption, obstacle, obstruction, preclusion, problem, restraint, restriction, retardation, retardment, setback, shackle, striction

HINDSIGHT, noun act of looking backward, afterthought, consideration, contemplation, contemplation of past events, contemplation of the past, deliberation, later meditation, later thought, looking back, meditation, memory, musing, recall, recollection, reconsideration, reexamination, reflection, remembrance, retrospect, retrospection, review, review of things past, rumination, second thoughts, second view, subsequent meditation, subsequent reflection, survey of time past, thoughts of the past

HINGE, verb arise from, around, center, center on, critical moment, critical period, critical point, crossways, crowning point, crucial moment, culmination, decisive moment, depend on, derive from, emanate from, ensue from, evolve from, generate from, hang, issue from, juncture, pivot, turn out
ASSOCIATED CONCEPTS: case hinging on circumstances, outcome hinges on the evidence

HINT, noun adumbration, allusion, clue, connotation, covert allusion, cue, faint outline, faint suggestion, foreshadowing, idea, implication, indication, indirect suggestion, inference, inkling, insinuation, intimation, *significatio*, slight indication, slight mention, suggestion, trace, vague impression, vague suggestion

HINT, verb adumbrate, advert, allude, clue, connote, cue, give an inkling, imply, indicate, infer, insinuate, intimate, make an allusion, prompt, refer, *significare*, signify, *subicere*, suggest
ASSOCIATED CONCEPTS: disclosure

HIRE, verb add to the payroll, appoint, assign to a position, authorize, commission, *conducere*, contract for, delegate, depute, designate to a post, employ, engage, enlist, fill a position, fill a vacancy, furnish occupation for, give a job to, give employment to, give work to, induct, install, place in office, procure, put on payroll, put to work, recruit, retain, secure the services of, set to work, staff, take into service, take on
ASSOCIATED CONCEPTS: bailee for hire, carriage, contract for hiring, discrimination in hiring, employment contract

HISTORY (Background), **noun** account, adventures, all aspects, all sides, delineation, depiction, each and every detail, entire universe, epic, episodes, events, experiences, explanation, exposition, facts, information, intelligence, narration, narrative, recapitulation, recital, record, representation, retelling, review, saga, series of incidents, story, summary

HISTORY (Past), **noun** annals, archives, bygone era, chronicle, days of old, earlier point in time, historical times, old days, prior point in time, prior time, record, schedule, the past, times gone by, tradition, yesterday
ASSOCIATED CONCEPTS: Legal history

HISTRIONIC, adjective affected, aiming for effect, artificial, dramatic, embroidered, exaggerated, exhibitionistic, insincere, mannered, melodramatic, orotund, ostentatious, overacted, pretentious, *scaenicus*, self-conscious, showy, stagy, stilted, striving for effect, theatric, theatrical, unnatural

HISTRIONICS, noun acting, affectation, affectedness, airs, *ars ludicra*, artificial behavior for effect, display, dramatic art, dramatic representation, dramaturgy, emotional display for effect, exaggeration, false show, fanfaronade, melodramatics, orotundity, ostentation, overacting, overemphasis, parade, performance, pretense, *scaenicus*, show, showmanship, stagecraft, theatrecraft, theatricalism, theatricality, theatricalness

HIT, verb accost, assail, assault, attack, batter, beat, besiege, damage, deal a blow, harm, hurt, inflict harm, inflict injury
ASSOCIATED CONCEPTS: battery, hit and run

HIT AND RUN, noun accident, breaking the law, commission prohibited by law, crime, criminal matter, departure, felony, flight, hasty departure, illegality, knockdown, leaving the scene of an accident, malfeasance, motor vehicle matter, nonobservance of law, offense, offense against the law, serious infraction of the law, wrong, wrongdoing

HOARD, noun accumulation, *acervus*, aggregation, amassment, cache, collection, *copia*, cumulation, fund, heap, mass, repository, reserves, riches, saving, stack, stock, stockpile, store, supply, treasure

HOARD, verb accrue, accumulate, acquire, agglomerate, aggregate, aggroup, amalgamate, amass, augment, bank, batch together, bring together, build up, bunch, cache, cluster, *coacervare*, collect, *conligere*, conquirere, cumulate, deposit, draw together, garner, garner up, gather for oneself, gather in, gather up, get together, group, hang on to, have in store, heap, hide, hide away, hive, hold back, husband, husband one's resources, keep, keep back, keep in reserve, lay by, lay in store, lay up, load up, lump together, pack away, pile, pile up, preserve, provide, put aside, reposit, reserve, retain, save up, set apart, set aside, set by, stock up, stockpile, store, store secretly, store up, stow, stow away, treasure up, withhold

HOAX, noun artifice, beguilement, canard, cheat, chicanery, circumvention, counterfeit, cozenage, deceit, deception, defraudation, delusion, device, dupery, duplicity, fabrication, fake, false alarm, false report, falsification, fraud, fraudulence, fraudulency, guile, imposition, imposture, knavery, lie, *ludificatio,* machination, masquerade, misrepresentation, pettifogging, practical joke, pretense, ruse, scheme, sham, shift, stratagem, subterfuge, swindle, trick, trickery, wile
ASSOCIATED CONCEPTS: false representation, forgery, fraud, impersonation

HOIST, noun burglary, felonious taking, fraudulent taking, larceny, misappropriation, pilferage, pilfering, purloining, robbery, stealing, swindling, theft, thievery, wrongful taking

HOLD (Decide), **verb** adjudge, adjudicate, ascertain, come to a conclusion, conclude, decide legally, decree, determine, find, fix, judge, make a decision, pass judgment, propound, resolve, rule, settle

HOLD (Possess), **verb** assume authority, assume command, be accorded, be heir to, be in possession of, be master of, be offered, be possessed of, be proffered, be vouchsafed, bear the responsibility of, care for, cling to, collect, command, conserve, control, devolve upon, direct, dominate, exercise direction over, fill a post, gather, get control, get possession of, grasp, *habere,* have, have a firm grip on, have a title to, have absolute disposal of, have as property, have by inheritance, have by tenure, have claim upon, have in hand, have in one's possession, have inherited, have rights to, have the care of, have the charge of, have the direction of, have title to, have under control, hold fast, hold in one's grasp, impropriate, inherit, keep, keep as one's own, keep for, keep in hand, keep in readiness, keep in reserve, keep on, keep prepared, lay aside, lay away, not dispose of, not part with, occupy, own, *possidere,* preserve, receive, recover, retain, save, secure, set apart, set aside, take authority, take command, take over, *tenere,* wield restraint over
ASSOCIATED CONCEPTS: adverse holding, hold in due course, hostile holding

HOLD ACCOUNTABLE, verb accuse, blame, brand, bring to account, castigate, charge, condemn openly, convict, criminate, denounce, expose, incriminate, implicate, impugn, inculpate, inveigh against, rebuke, reprehend, reprimand, reproach, reprobate, revile, take to task, upbraid, vilify, vituperate

HOLD IN ABEYANCE, verb adjourn, defer, delay, discontinue, forbear, give ground, give way, hold up, lay over, postpone, procrastinate, prolong, protract, retard, shelve, suspend, table, temporize

HOLD OFF, verb abandon, abdicate, abjure, abstain, avoid, cease, cede, deny oneself, desist from, dispense with, disposed of, do without, drop, eschew, fast, forbear, forfeit, forego, forgo, forswear, give up, give up on, go without, hold back, lay down, leave off, let alone, make do without, not use, pass up, refrain, release, relinquish, renounce, reserve, resign, sacrifice, shun, surrender, waive, withhold, write off, yield, yield up

ASSOCIATED CONCEPTS: forego interest owed, forego opportunity

HOLD OUT (Deliberate on an offer), **verb** make overtures, offer, place at ones disposal, present, proffer, *promittere,* propone, propose, put forward, submit, suggest, urge, volunteer

HOLD OUT (Resist), **verb** balk, be unwilling, hold fast, hold one's own, make a resolute stand, not budge, not compromise, not give up, not submit, not weaken, not yield, offer resistance, oppugn, persevere, *persist,* refuse, refuse consent, remain firm, repel, *resistere,* stand fast, stand firm, withhold assent, withhold consent, withstand

HOLD RESPONSIBLE FOR, verb accuse, ascribe to, attribute to, blame, call to account, censure, charge, charge with, cite, convict, criticize, denounce, deprecate, execrate, fix the responsibility for, impeach, implicate, impugn, impute to, incriminate, inculpate, indict, reprehend, upbraid

HOLD UP (Delay), **verb** adjourn, arrest, arrest temporarily, be dilatory, block, brake, bring to a standstill, call a halt, call off, cause a stoppage, cause to arrive late, cause to move with undue slowness, cause to put off to a later time, check, contain, control, cumber, curb, decelerate, defer, detain, deter, *detinere,* encumber, filibuster, gain time, halt, hamper, hinder, hold in abeyance, impede, impede the progress of, incommode, inconvenience, inhibit, interfere, interrupt, intervene, keep one waiting, keep pending, lay aside, lay under restraint, obstruct, pigeonhole, postpone, procrastinate, prolong, protract, push aside, put a stop to, put aside, put off, put off to a future time, put under restraint, repress, reserve, resist, restrain, retard, *retinere,* set aside, set one back, shelve, slow up, stall, stand in the way, stave off, stop, suppress, suspend, table, *tardare,* thwart, undermine, upset, withhold

HOLD UP (Rob), **verb** abscond with, abstract, appropriate, carry away, carry off, commit robbery, *compilare,* deprecate, despoil, divert, *eripere, expilare,* impress, make off with, maraud, misappropriate, pickeer, pilfer, pillage, pirate, plunder, poach, purloin, reave, reive, remove, rob, run off with, sack, spirit away, spoil, stick up, take away, take by theft, take dishonestly, take feloniously, take possession of, take wrongfully, thieve, walk off with, withdraw

HOLD UP TO SCORN, verb belittle, condemn, deride, disdain, disesteem, disparage, feel contempt for, flout, hold in contempt, hold in derision, hold up to obloquy, insult, jape, jeer, laugh at, mock, rail at, revile, ridicule, scoff, scorn, slight, sneer at, taunt

HOLDBACK, noun kept in reserve, reservation, reserved rights, withheld, withholding

HOLDBACK, verb check, constrain, contain, control, curb, curtail, desist, detain, enjoin, forbear, hesitate, hinder, hold, hold at bay, hold fast, hold up, impede, inhibit, keep back, keep from, keep in check, not proceed, not use, obstruct, prevent, prohibit, proscribe, put the brakes on, refuse, regress, repress, restrain, restrict oneself, retain, retard, slow down, smother, stay, stop, suppress, withhold
ASSOCIATED CONCEPTS: holdback in construction law, retention on construction contracts

HOLDER, noun endorsee, individual in possession, keeper, owner, payee, person in possession, *possessor,* receiver, recipient

ASSOCIATED CONCEPTS: bona fide holder, holder for value, holder in due course, holder in good faith, holder of a lien, joint holder, legal holder, license holder, negotiable instruments, original holder, policyholder, property holder, shareholder, stockholder

HOLDING *(Property owned)*, **noun**   asset, belonging, chattel, domain, effect, estate, exclusive possession, interest, land, landed estate, legal estate, *possessio*, possession, property, real estate, real property, realty, resource, seisin, share, stake

ASSOCIATED CONCEPTS: holding a lien, holding a position of authority, holding company, holding for value, holding in due course, holding office, holding over

HOLDING *(Ruling of a court)*, **noun**   act of judgment, action, adjudication, ascertainment, conclusion, conclusion of the matter, considered opinion, decision, decree, *decretum*, deduction, deliverance, determination, dictate, final judgment, finding, *iudicium*, judgment, judgment on facts, judicial decision, law, law of the case, maxim, opinion, order, order of the court, outcome, precedent, precept, professional advice, professional decision, pronouncement, pronouncement by a court, recommendation, recorded expression of a formal judgment, report, resolution, result, sentence, *sententia*, settled decision, settlement by authoritative decision, that which is decided, upshot, verdict, written order

ASSOCIATED CONCEPTS: decision en banc, holding of the court, opinion per curiam

HOLDOVER, noun   carry over, individual who stays on, one who remains, one who stays on, relic, remainder, remaining portion

ASSOCIATED CONCEPTS: eviction, holdover tenant

HOLE noun   absence, abyss, aperture, cave, cavern, cavity, chamber, chasm, cleft, depression, depth, excavation, fracture, hollow, incision, indentation, opening, orifice, pit, rupture, shaft, tunnel, vacuum, void

HOLIDAY, noun   celebration, day of festivities, day off, *dies festus, feriae*, festival, fête, furlough, gala, jubilee, leave, leisure, lull, recess, rest, time off, vacation

ASSOCIATED CONCEPTS: general holiday, legal holiday

HOLLOW, noun   bare, bereft of, carved out, clear, deficient, deprived, destitute of, devoid, devoid of, empty, lacking, short of, vacant, vacuous, void, wanting, without

ASSOCIATED CONCEPTS: hollow victory

HOLOGRAPHIC, adjective   cursive, graphic, handwritten, in black and white, in longhand, in print, in writing, inscribed, inscriptional, longhand, manuscript, on paper, penned, printed, scribbled, scriptorial, scriptural, under one's hand, written

ASSOCIATED CONCEPTS: execution of a will, nuncapative will, Probate Court, Surrogates Court, will formalities

HOMAGE, noun   allegiance, attention, compliance, consideration, constancy, court, *cultus*, deference, devotedness, devotion, esteem, estimation, exaltation, faithfulness, fidelity, glorification, high regard, honor, humility, loyalty, obedience, obeisance, *observantia*, regard, respect, reverence, service, servility, servitude, subjection, submission, submissiveness, subservience, veneration, *verecundia*

HOME *(Domicile)*, **noun**   abode, apartment, cottage, *domicilium, domus*, dormitory, dwelling, dwelling place, fireside, fixed residence, habitat, habitation, haven, homeland, homestead, house, household, living quarters, locality, lodging, lodging place, native environment, permanent legal address, place of abode, place of dwelling, place of existence, place of one's domestic affections, place of refuge, place of residence, place of rest, place to live in, place where one lives, quarters, refuge, residence, resting place

ASSOCIATED CONCEPTS: home office, home rule domicile, home site

FOREIGN PHRASES: *Constitutum esse eam domum unicuique nostrum debere existimari, ubi quisque sedes et tabulas haberet, suarumque rerum constitutionem fecisset.* It is established that the home of each of us is considered to be the place of his abode and books, and where he may have made an establishment of his business.

HOME *(Place of origin)*, **noun**   birthplace, country, country of origin, fatherland, homeland, mother country, motherland, native ground, native hearth, native land, native soil, place of birth

HOME INVASION, noun   act prohibited by law, breach of law, contravention, crime, criminal activity, criminal offense, encroachment, felony, illegality, infringement, offense, offense against the law, robbery, serious infraction of the law

ASSOCIATED CONCEPTS: break in, breaking and entering, burglary, housebreaking, robbery, trespassing

HOME RULE, noun   autonomy, enfranchisement, franchise, freedom from domination, freedom from interference, freedom of action, freedom of choice, independence, individualism, noninterference, nonintervention, political independence, self-containment, self-derived power, self-determination, self-direction, self-government, self-legislation, self-reliance, self-subsistence, self-sufficiency, self-support, sovereignty, unlimited sovereignty

HOMEMADE, adjective   amateurish, coarse, crude, do-it-yourself, domestic, domestically manufactured, handcrafted, home-born, homegrown, home-manufactured, home-produced, home-raised, homespun, home-woven, indigenous, internal, locally made, locally manufactured, locally produced, made at home, made locally, manufactured, native-grown, native-raised, natural, personally made, produced domestically, self-made, simple, unskilled

ASSOCIATED CONCEPTS: homemade law, homemade wills

HOMESTEAD, noun   abode, acreage, acres, country house, domicile, dwelling, dwelling place, edifice, estate, farm, farm land, farmplace, farmstead, grounds, habitation, home, house, household, living quarters, lodging, lodging place, manor, messuage, place of residence, place of settlement, quarters, residence

ASSOCIATED CONCEPTS: homestead laws

HOMICIDE, noun   annihilation, assassination, butchery, *caedes*, capital crime, capital murder, carnage, crime, destruction of life, elimination, extermination, felony, felony murder, killing, liquidation, manslaughter, massacre, murder, removal, slaughter, slaying, termination of life, violent death

ASSOCIATED CONCEPTS: assault with intent to murder, *corpus delicti*, criminally negligent homicide, culpable homicide, excusable homicide, felonious homicide, felony murder, infanticide, involuntary manslaughter, justifiable homicide, manslaughter, premeditated homicide, voluntary homicide

FOREIGN PHRASES: *Maihemium est homicidium inchoatum.* Mayhem is unfinished homicide.

HOMOSEXUAL, adjective gay, gay person, homo-erotic, homophile, lesbian
ASSOCIATED CONCEPTS: gay marriage, gay rights

HONEST, adjective aboveboard, accurate, actual, artless, as represented, authentic, bald, blunt, candid, clean, conscientious, correct, creditable, decent, downright, earnest, equitable, erect, estimable, ethical, evenhanded, exact, factual, fair, fair-dealing, forthright, frank, free from fraud, genuine, guileless, historical, honorable, impartial, impeccable, inartificial, incapable of deceit, incorrupt, incorruptible, ingenuous, innocent, inviolate, irreproachable, just, laudable, law-abiding, legal, legitimate, licit, literal, moral, open, outspoken, plain-speaking, principled, *probus*, proper, pure, reliable, reputable, respectable, right, scrupulous, *simplex*, sincere, *sincerus*, sound, stainless, sterling, straightforward, true, true to the facts, truehearted, trustworthy, truthful, unadulterated, unaffected, unassumed, unassuming, unbiased, unbribable, uncolored, uncopied, uncounterfeited, undiluted, undisguised, undisguising, undissembling, undissimulating, undistorted, unembroidered, unexaggerated, unfabricated, unfaked, unfeigned, unfeigning, unfictitious, ungarbled, uninvented, unperjured, unpretended, unpretending, unpretentious, unsimulated, unsophisticated, unspecious, unspurious, unsynthetic, unvarnished, valid, veracious, veridical, veritable, well-principled
ASSOCIATED CONCEPTS: honest belief, honest claim, honest dispute

HONESTY, noun accuracy, artlessness, authenticity, baldness, bluntness, candidness, candor, conscientiousness, estimableness, exactitude, factualness, fairness, fidelity, *fides*, frankness, genuineness, guilelessness, high character, high-mindedness, high principles, honorableness, impartiality, inartificiality, incorruptibility, ingenuousness, integrity, legitimacy, openness, plainness, plainspeaking, principles, *probitas*, probity, reality, realness, reputability, repute, respectability, rightness, sanctity, scrupulosity, scrupulousness, simplicity, *sinceritas*, sincerity, soundness, stainlessness, trustworthiness, truth, truthfulness, unadulteration, unaffectedness, unconstraint, undeceitfulness, undeceptiveness, unreserve, unrestraint, unspeciousness, unspuriousness, unvarnished truth, uprightness, upstandingness, validity, veraciousness, veracity, veridicality, verity, virtue, worthiness
ASSOCIATED CONCEPTS: character evidence, reputation for honesty

HONOR (Good reputation), noun character, *dignitas*, *existimatio*, *fama*, good name, good opinion, goodness, high regard, incorruptibility, integrity, moral rectitude, principle, probity, purity, rectitude, regard, reliability, reputability, repute, respectability, righteousness, scrupulousness, sense of responsibility, standing, status, trustiness, trustworthiness, uprightness, virtue
ASSOCIATED CONCEPTS: reputation evidence

HONOR (Outward respect), noun acclaim, admiration, adulation, aggrandizement, appreciation, approbation, approval, commendation, consideration, courtesy, credit, deference, devotion, distinction, esteem, estimation, exaltation, favor, glorification, glory, high regard, homage, laud, laudation, obeisance, praise, prominence, regard, reverence, tribute, veneration, worship

HONOR, verb acclaim, accredit, advance, aggrandize, applaud, belaud, bepraise, canonize, *celebrare*, celebrate, cheer, cite, *colere*, commemorate, commend, compliment, confer distinction on, congratulate, consecrate, crown, *decorare*,

decorate, defer to, distinguish, elevate, ennoble, esteem, eulogize, exalt, extol, glorify, hail, hold in esteem, idolize, laud, lionize, look up to, make important, memorialize, pay deference, pay homage, pay respects, pay tribute, praise, prize, promote, put on a pedestal, raise, raise to distinction, regard, respect, revere, reverence, salute, set store by, show respect, toast, value, venerate
ASSOCIATED CONCEPTS: honorary trust

HONORABLE (Honest), adjective beyond reproach, blameless, chaste, Christian, clean, creditable, decent, erect, esteemed, estimable, ethical, excellent reputation, fair, full of integrity, good, held in esteem, high-minded, high-principled, highly regarded, highly reputed, highly respectable, honored, immaculate, in favor, in good order, in high favor, in one's good books, inviolate, irreproachable, just, law-abiding, law-loving, law-revering, manly, meritorious, moral, much esteemed, noble, of repute, prestigious, principled, pure, reputable, respectable, respected, revered, reverend, right, right-minded, righteous, sinless, spotless, squeaky-clean, stainless, sterling, straight-arrow, true-blue, true-dealing, true-devoted, true-disposing, truehearted, true-souled, true-spirited, unblemished, uncorrupt, uncorrupted, undefiled, unimpeachable, unsmirched, unspotted, unstained, unsullied, untarnished, upright, uprighteous, upstanding, venerable, venerated, virtuous, well-thought-of, worshipful, worth one's salt, worthy, yeomanly

HONORABLE (Judge), adjective acclaimed, adjudger, adjudicator, administrator of justice, admired, applauded, arbiter, arbitrator, assessor, celebrated, chancellor, distinguished, elected, eminent, esteem, esteemed, exalted, eximious, favor, held, held in esteem or high, held in respect, her honor, high, highly considered, highly regarded, highly reputed, his honor, honorable justice, honorary, honored, honorific, illustrious, in favor, in high, in high regard, intercessor, interpreter, jurist, justice, justicer, magistrate, marked, moderator, much admired, negotiator, noble, notable, noted, of mark, of note, one who dispenses justice, praetor, preeminent, prestigious, prominent, quaestor, referee, respected, revered, surrogate, the court, umpire, venerable, well-thought-of, widely acclaimed, your honor

HONORABLE (Upright), adjective august, awe-inspiring, dignified, estimable, ethical, high-minded, high-principled, honest, incorruptible, legitimate, moral, noble-minded, principled, respected, time-honored, to be trusted, tried and true, true, trustworthy, truth-loving, uncorrupted, upstanding, venerable

HONORARIUM, noun acknowledgment, arrangement, compensation, consideration, earnings, emolument, fee, financial remuneration, gratuity, guerdon, income, indemnity, installment, meed, payment, quittance, recompense, reimbursement, remuneration, requital, retainer, reward for service, salary, settlement, stipend

HONORARY, adjective commemorative, commendatory, dedicatory, enshrining, hallowing, honorific, honorifical, in memory of, in tribute, kept in remembrance, memorial, perpetuating, recalling to mind, serving to commemorate
ASSOCIATED CONCEPTS: honorary degree, honorary officer, honorary trust

HONORED, adjective acclaimed, admired, adored, applauded, appreciated, approved, celebrated, cheered, commended, complimented, considered, distinguished, ennobled, esteemed, eulogized, exalted, extolled, fabled, famed, famous, far-famed, glorified, hailed, held in highest esteem, held in highest regard, held in highest respect, highly regarded, honored, idolized, lauded, lionized, much-acclaimed, much-admired, mythical, notable, noted, notorious, of mark, praised, prized, renowned, respected, revered, saluted, sought-after, time-honored, valued, well-considered, well-known, well-thought-of, world-class, worshiped

HOODLUM, noun agitator, bandit, blackguard, brigand, burglar, convict, criminal, embezzler, evildoer, felon, firebrand, gunman, holdup man, knave, larcener, larcenist, lawbreaker, malefactor, malevolent, malfeasant, malfeasor, miscreant, mobster, oppressor, outlaw, peculator, pickpocket, purloiner, rogue, roisterer, rough, ruffian, scoundrel, stealer, thief, villain, wrongdoer
ASSOCIATED CONCEPTS: juvenile delinquent, multiple offender, predicate felon, youthful offender

HOODWINK, verb be dishonest, befool, beguile, blind, blindfold, cheat, cozen, deceive, defraud, delude, dupe, *fallere,* hoax, *inludere,* inveigle, *ludificari,* make a fool of, misinform, mislead, mystify, outwit, puzzle, swindle, trick
ASSOCIATED CONCEPTS: deception, fraud, misrepresentation

HOPE, verb assume, expect, feel sure, give credence to, have faith in, have no doubt, have no reservations, look forward to, place reliance in, pray for, presume, put confidence in, rely on
ASSOCIATED CONCEPTS: hopelessly insolvent

HORIZON, noun border, boundary, field of view, field of vision, prospect, range, range of vision, realm, skyline, view, vista

HORNBOOK, noun abstract on the law, analysis, analyzation, annotated text, capitulation, capsule, commentary, compendium, condensation, desk book, digest of the law, discourse on the law, dissection, dissertation on the law, encyclopedia, excursus, exposition, manual, manual of instruction, pandect, primer, recapitulation, review, run-through, study, study book, text, textbook, topical outline, treatise, treatise on the law

HORRENDOUS, adjective abominable, appalling, atrocious, awful, contemptible, deplorable, despicable, detestable, disgusting, dreadful, foul, frightening, frightful, ghastly, ghoulish, gruesome, harrowing, heinous, hideous, horrible, horrid, horrifying, loathsome, macabre, monstrous, obnoxious, odious, offensive, pathetic, pitiful, reprehensible, repulsive, revolting, shameful, shocking, terrible, terrifying, unspeakable, vile, villainous

HORRIBLE, adjective abhorrent, abominable, appalling, atrocious, awful, contemptible, deplorable, despicable, detestable, disgusting, dreadful, foul, frightening, frightful, ghastly, ghoulish, gruesome, harrowing, heinous, hideous, horrendous, horrid, horrifying, loathsome, macabre, monstrous, obnoxious, odious, offensive, pathetic, pitiful, reprehensible, repulsive, revolting, shameful, shocking, terrible, terrifying, unspeakable, vile, villainous

HORRIFY, verb abash, alarm, appall, become reprehensible, consternate, disgust, dismay, distress, disturb, frighten, intimidate, nauseate, offend, outrage, petrify, repel, repulse, scare, scare to death, shock, sicken, startle, stun, stupefy, terrify

ASSOCIATED CONCEPTS: horrifying a jury to evoke a desired response

HORROR, noun abhorrence, abomination, anguish, aversion, awfulness, detestation, disgust, fright, frightfulness, ghastliness, gruesomeness, hideousness, horribleness, horridness, loathing, loathsomeness, lunacy, odiousness, offense, outrage, rancor, repugnance, repulsion, revulsion

HORTATIVE, adjective admonitory, advising, advisory, consultative, didactic, exhortative, exhortatory, expostulative, expostulatory, full of exhortation, full of urgency, *hortans,* hortatory, *monens,* monitorial, persuading, persuasive, remonstrative, suasive, warning

HOST *(Multitude),* **noun** a many, a mass of, aggregation, an abundance of, army, array, assembly, body, cloud, cluster, company, congregation, crowd, crush, flood, galaxy, group, herd, horde, jam, large amount, litter, nest, no end of, numbers, pack, panoply, quantities, school, scores, slew, storm

HOST *(Owner),* **noun** barkeeper, bartender, hostess, hotel keeper, innkeeper, inviter, owner, owner of an establishment, party-giver, proprietor, restaurant owner, restaurateur, saloon keeper, serving liquor, tavern keeper
ASSOCIATED CONCEPTS: host liability statute

HOSTAGE, noun bond, captive, collateral, guarantee, internee, *obses,* pledge, political prisoner, prisoner, real security, security
ASSOCIATED CONCEPTS: false imprisonment, kidnapping, ransom

HOSTILE, adjective abusive, acrimonious, actively opposed, adverse, aggressive, alienated, antagonistic, antipathetic, antipodal, antithetic, antithetical, antonymous, arguing, argumentative, assaulting, at odds, at variance, baneful, battling, besetting, bitter, bristling, calamitous, cantankerous, challenging, clashing, combative, competitive, conflicting, contentious, contesting, contradictory, contrariant, contrarious, contrary, counteracting, counteractive, destructive, disaffected, disagreeing, disastrous, discordant, disdainful, disloyal, disputatious, dissentient, dissenting, dissentious, dissident, divided, dreadful, embittered, estranged, factious, frictional, full of hate, full of malice, harmful, harsh, ill-disposed, ill-willed, in opposition, inacquiescent, incompatible, inconsistent with, *infensus, infestus,* inimical, *inimicus,* irreconcilable, malevolent, noncooperating, opposed, opposing, opposite, oppositional, oppugnant, polarized, pugnacious, rancorous, reactionary, refractory, renitent, reverse, schismatic, spiteful, truculent, unapproving, unconsonant, uncooperative, unharmonious, vicious, vis-à-vis, wrangling
ASSOCIATED CONCEPTS: hostile fire, hostile intent, hostile party, hostile possession of property, hostile witness

HOSTILE WITNESS, noun adverse testifier, adverse witness, antithetical witness, challenger, contrary witness, disagreeing witness, dissenting witness, dissentious witness, dissident, harmful witness, opposing witness, traitor, turncoat, witness in opposition
ASSOCIATED CONCEPTS: cross examination, leading questions

HOT-BLOODED, adjective aggressive, amorous, athirst, avid, barbarous, bold, brutal, burning, careless, danger-loving, daredevil, daring, desirous, desperate, eager, excessive, excitable, extreme, febrile, fervent, fervid, feverish, fiery, flaming, foolhardy, frantic, hasty, headstrong, heated, heedless, high-spirited, high-strung, hot-headed, hot-tempered, immoderate, impatient, impractical, imprudent, inattentive, incautious, inflamed, inflammatory, insuppressible, intemperate, intense, intent, irrepressible, lustful, madcap, oversensitive, passionate, piquant, quenchless, quick-tempered, rampant, rash, reckless, risk-taking, savage, sensitive, short-tempered, strong-willed, temerarious, thoughtless, torrid, turbulent, unadvised, unbridled, uncircumspect, uncontrollable, ungentle, ungovernable, unmitigable, unquelled, unquenched, unrepressed, unwary, vehement, venturesome, violent, wanton, willful, zealous

ASSOCIATED CONCEPTS: heat of passion, manslaughter, temporary insanity

HOUSE, noun abode, accommodations, *aedes*, business establishment, business firm, clan, commercial establishment, company, concern, domicile, *domicilium, domus*, dwelling, dwelling place, family, firm, habitation, home, homestead, household, kin, kindred, lineage, living place, living quarters, lodging, place of habitation, quarters, residence, shelter, tribe

ASSOCIATED CONCEPTS: House of Representatives

HOUSE ARREST, noun confinement at home, confinement to a residence, custodial detention, domestic restraint, house confinement, imprisonment, punishment at home, restraint at home, restriction at home, retention at home, serving a sentence at home, serving time at home

HOUSEBREAKING, noun appropriation, breaking and entering, burglarizing, burglary, felony, filching, forcible entry, larceny, looting, pilfering, plundering, raiding, robbery, stealing, theft, thievery, trespassing

HOUSEHOLD (Domestic), **adjective** at home, *domesticus*, domiciled, domiciliary, domiciliated, family, fond of home, having home interests, home, home-loving, home-owning, homemaking, housekeeping, in residence, *lares, penates*, pertaining to home, pertaining to the family, residential, residentiary

ASSOCIATED CONCEPTS: household articles, household effects, household goods, household member, household servant

HOUSEHOLD (Familiar), **adjective** accustomed, celebrated, cognized, common, commonly known, commonplace, conventional, customary, everyday, famous, habitual, ordinary, plain, popular, prevalent, recognized, regular, renowned, simple, standard, stock, talked-about, talked-of, universally recognized, usual, well-known, well-recognized, widely known, widespread, workaday

HOUSEHOLD, noun domestic circle, domestic domicile, domestic establishment, domus, establishment, *familia*, family, family abode, family circle, family dwelling place, habitation, home, homestead, lodging, parents and children, place of abode, residence

ASSOCIATED CONCEPTS: homestead

FOREIGN PHRASES: *Domus sua cuique est tutissimum refugium.* Everyone's home is his safest refuge. *Debet sua cuique domus esse perfugium tutissimum.* Every man's home should be a perfectly safe refuge.

HUMAN, noun being, body, character, human being, individual, living soul, man, member of the human race, one, particular one, party, person, woman

ASSOCIATED CONCEPTS: human rights law, United Nations Declaration of Human Rights

HUMANE, adjective altruistic, beneficent, benevolent, benign, bounteous, brotherly, charitable, *clemens*, clement, considerate, decent, fraternal, generous, helpful, hospitable, humanitarian, *humanus*, kind, kindhearted, kindly, merciful, *misericors*, philanthropic, unselfish, warm-hearted

ASSOCIATED CONCEPTS: gift for a humane purpose

HUMANITY (Humaneness), **noun** altruism, beneficence, benevolence, benignancy, benignity, charitableness, clemency, *clementia*, compassion, feeling, gentleness, good will, *humanitas*, kindheartedness, kindness, lenience, leniency, lenity, mercifulness, mercy, mildness, *misericordia*, sympathy, understanding, unselfishness

ASSOCIATED CONCEPTS: crimes against humanity, humanitarian doctrine, humanitarian laws, last clear chance

HUMANITY (Mankind), **noun** generations of man, *gens humana, hominum generis,* homo sapiens, human beings, humankind, *humanum genus*, man, mortals, people, peoples of the earth, persons

ASSOCIATED CONCEPTS: crimes against humanity

HUMILIATE, verb abase, abash, affront, befool, bespatter, blackball, blacken, brand, bring shame upon, cast a slur upon, cast down, contemn, cow, crush, debase, defame, deflate, degrade, demean, demote, depreciate, deride, derogate, discredit, disgrace, dishonor, disparage, disrank, disrate, downgrade, embarrass, expose to infamy, fill with shame, give offense to, hold in derision, hold in disrespect, humble, incur blame, insult, laugh at, lower, make a fool of, make lowly, malign, misprize, mock, mortify, offend, put down, put out of countenance, put to shame, reduce to the ranks, render humble, ridicule, scoff, scorn, shame, show disrespect, slight, sneer, snub, spurn, stain, stigmatize, sully, taint, tarnish, treat with disrespect, treat with indignity, undervalue, vanquish, vilify

ASSOCIATED CONCEPTS: mental anguish

HUMILIATION, noun chagrin, defamation, degradation, disgrace, dishonor, disparagement, disrespect, embarrassment, ignominy, insult, malign, mortification, obloquy, ridicule, scoff, scorn, shame, shame, slander, slight, sneer, snub, spurn, taint, treat with indignity

ASSOCIATED CONCEPTS: defamation, frivolous law suit with sanctions, libel, slander

HUNT, verb burrow, chase, chase after, conduct a search, *consectari*, delve for, ensnare, explore, fasten oneself upon, ferret, follow, follow close upon, follow the trail, forage, give chase, go after, go in pursuit of, go in search of, grope for, gun for, hawk, hound, inquire for, look for, probe, prowl after, pry, pursue, quest, root, run after, search for, search out, seek, set a trap for, snare, stalk, trace, track down, trail, trap, try to find, *venari*

ASSOCIATED CONCEPTS: extradition, hunt for a fugitive, rendition, search and seizure, search warrant

HURDLE, noun barricade, barrier, block, constraint, curb, detainment, difficulty, drawback, hamper, handicap, hindrance, impediment, inconvenience, limitation, obstacle, obstruction, prohibition, restraint, restriction, stumbling block, wall

HURRICANE, noun adversity, calamity, catastrophe, disaster, flood, natural disaster, rain, rain and wind storm, rainstorm, serious calamity, storm, tragedy, upheaval

ASSOCIATED CONCEPTS: FEMA

HURRY, verb accelerate, conclude, create, demand more, develop, drive faster, drive harder, engender, expedite, get more productivity, go faster, hasten, in high gear, pick up the pace, precipitate, press, press forward, push, quicken, quicken the pace, speed-up, spur, to go full throttle

ASSOCIATED CONCEPTS: expedited trial, speedy trial

HUSH MONEY, noun blackmail, blood money, bribe, bribe money, corrupt money, cover-up, criminal payoff, enticement, graft, gratuity, illegal bribe, illegal funds, illegal gratuity, illegal money, illegal payoff, illegal pay-out, inducement, payoff, payoff for corruption, payoff for silence, payoff to quash testimony, prize, slush fund, suppression of evidence

ASSOCIATED CONCEPTS: bribery, public officials' code of conduct

HYPERBOLE, noun aggrandizement, amplification, enhancement, enlargement, exaggeration, extravagance, magnification, overemphasis, overenlargement, overstatement

HYPERBOLIC, adjective blown-up, distorted, elaborated, embellished, enhanced, enlarged, exaggerated, expanded, expressed to an excess, expressed to an extreme, grandiloquent, heightening, inflated, intensified, magnified, maximization, over amplified, overdoing, overemphasized, puffing up, sensationalized, stretched, stretched to the imagination, swelled

HYPOCRISY, noun artfulness, charlatanism, charlatanry, deceit, deceitfulness, deception, dishonesty, dissembling, *dissimulatio*, double-dealing, duplicity, false profession, falsification, fraud, fraudulence, *fraus*, front, guile, hollow pretense, imposture, improbity, insincerity, perjury, pharisaism, pretense, pretense of virtue, pretension, quackery, sanctimoniousness, sanctimony, show, trickery

HYPOTHECATION, noun collateral, contract of mortgage, contract of pledge, creation of a lien, guarantee, lien, mortgage, pledge, security

ASSOCIATED CONCEPTS: hypothecated property

HYPOTHESIS, noun assertion, assignment of cause, assumption, conclusion drawn from accepted truths, *coniectura*, conjecture, deduction, guess, inference, postulate, postulation, speculation, suggestion, supposal, supposition, surmise, tentative explanation, tentative law, theory, thesis, unproved theory

HYPOTHETICAL, adjective assumed, conjectural, hypothetic, imaginary, make-believe, *opinabilis*, pretended, speculative, supposed, suppositional, suppositive, unreal, unverifiable

ASSOCIATED CONCEPTS: hypothetical controversy, hypothetical facts, hypothetical issue, hypothetical pleading, hypothetical question, speculation

IDEA, noun abstraction, aim, appraisal, apprehension, assessment, belief, calculation, *cogitatio*, conceit, concept, conception, conjecture, conviction, doctrine, dogma, estimate, estimation, evaluation, excogitation, fancy, guess, hypothesis, impression, inference, intent, intention, judgment, *notio*, notion, object, opinion, percept, perception, persuasion, plan, point of view, presupposition, product of imagination, purpose, reflection, sentiment, supposition, surmise, suspicion, tenet, theory, thought, train of thought, valuation, view, viewpoint

IDEAL, adjective absolute, abstract, advantageous, archetypical, best, complete, consummate, dreamy, excellent, exemplary, fancied, fantastic, faultless, fictitious, idealistic, legendary, optimum, supreme, utopian

IDENTICAL, adjective alike, coequal, comparable, congeneric, congenerous, consimilar, consubstantial, duplicate, equal, equivalent, exact, exactly alike, exactly the same, faithful, homogeneous, *idem*, indistinguishable, interchangeable, like, matching, resembling, similar, synonymous, tantamount, twin, uniform, without distinction

ASSOCIATED CONCEPTS: identical issue, identical real estate

IDENTIFICATION, noun appellation, ascertainment, association, certification, characterization, classification, cognizance, comparison, corroboration, definition, delineation, denomination, description, designation, detection, discernment, disclosure, ID, identity classification, identity comparison, identity verification, label, proof of domicile, proof of identity, proof of residency, recognition, recognizance, recollection, signature, signification, substantiation, verification

ASSOCIATED CONCEPTS: extrajudicial identification, laws, national identification cards, lineup, voter identification

FOREIGN PHRASES: **Ex multitudine signorum, colligitur identitas vera.** The true identity of a thing is shown from a number of signs. **Nihil facit error nominis cum de corpore constat.** An error in the name is of no consequence when there is certainty as to the person.

IDENTIFY, verb analyze, ascertain, attest, authenticate, call, catalogue, certify, classify, confirm, corroborate, delineate, denominate, denote, describe, descry, designate, detect, determine, discriminate, distinguish, espy, establish, give a name to, give an appellation to, know, label, locate,

name, perceive, pick out, pinpoint, place, point a finger to, prove, provide with nomenclature, recognize, recollect, select, specify, spot, style, substantiate, term, uncover, verify
ASSOCIATED CONCEPTS: DNA, identity theft

IDENTIFY WITH, *verb*   associate with, compare, connect with, empathize with, equate with, relate to, understand, look up to, hold in highest regard

IDENTITY *(Individuality),* **noun**   being, characteristic, difference, dissimilarity, distinction, distinctive feature, distinctiveness, distinctness, distinguishing characteristic, distinguishing quality, idiosyncrasy, individualism, mannerism, oneness, originality, particularity, peculiarity, perceivable dissimilarity, personal characteristic, personality, personship, quality of being singular, self, selfhood, selfness, singleness, singularity, speciality, specialty, specific quality, specificity, uniqueness, unlikeness
ASSOCIATED CONCEPTS: duty to ascertain identity, proof of identity
FOREIGN PHRASES: *Nihil facit error nominis cum de corpore constat.* An error in the name is of no consequence when there is certainty as to the person. *Ex multitudine signorum, colligitur identitas vera.* The true identity of a thing is shown from a number of signs. *Nomina sunt mutabilia, res autem immobiles.* Names are mutable, but things are immutable.

IDENTITY *(Similarity),* **noun**   agreement, alikeness, closeness, coequality, comparability, conformability, consimilarity, consimilitude, consimility, duplication, equality, equipollence, equipollency, equivalence, homogeneity, identicalness, interchangeability, likeness, match, oneness, parallelism, parity, resemblance, sameness, semblance, similarity, similitude, synonymity, uniformity, unity

IDENTITY THEFT, *noun*   crime through impersonation, criminal theft through impersonation, embezzlement through impersonation, felonious deception, felonious taking through impersonation, fraudulent deception, fraudulent taking through impersonation, grand larceny by impersonation, illegal deception, larcenous deception, larceny by impersonation, misappropriation through impersonation, petit larceny by impersonation, pilferage by impersonation, pilfering by impersonation, stealing by deception, stealing through impersonation, swindling by deception, swindling through impersonation, taking illegally through impersonation, theft by impersonation, thievery by impersonation, thievery by imposed deception, wrongful deception

IDLE, *adjective*   disengaged, fallow, fruitless, futile, *ignavus,* inactive, indolent, inert, jobless, lazy, listless, motionless, *otiosus,* shiftless, slothful, still, uncultivated, unemployed, unoccupied, unprofitable, unused, vacant, *vacuus,* workless

IDLE THREAT, *noun*   deficient threat, empty threat, harmless threat, ineffectual threat, meaningless threat, menacing, mere notice, mere talking, mere warning, only words, saber-rattling, subtle intimidation, testing, trial balloon, veiled threat

IGNOBLE, *adjective*   abject, base, baseborn, beggarly, below par, boorish, common, contemptible, corrupt, cowardly, craven, debased, degenerate, degraded, depraved, despicable, discreditable, disgraceful, dishonest, dishonorable, disreputable, humble, *humilis,* ignominious, indecent, infamous, inferior, inglorious, *inhonestus, inliberalis,* insignificant,

low, lowborn, lowly, mean, menial, of humble birth, of low character, of low extraction, of low station, peasant, plebian, proletarian, raffish, reproachful, scandalous, scrubby, scurrilous, servile, shameful, sorry, subaltern, unchivalrous, uncouth, uncultivated, underbred, ungenteel, unmanly, unrespectable, untitled, unworthy, vile, vulgar, wicked, worthless

IGNOMINY, *noun*   abasement, abjection, abjectness, attaint, bad name, bad reputation, bad repute, badge of infamy, blot, brand, chagrin, condemnation, contempt, contemptibility, contemptibleness, culpability, culpableness, debasement, dedecoration, degradation, demotion, denunciation, derision, derogation, despisedness, disapprobation, disapproval, discommendation, discredit, discreditableness, disesteem, disfavor, disgrace, dishonor, dishonorableness, dislike, disparagement, dispraise, disreputability, disreputableness, disreputation, disrepute, disvaluation, embarrassment, faded reputation, humiliation, ignobility, *ignominia,* ignomy, ill favor, ill-repute, imputation, *infamia,* infamy, ingloriousness, irreverence, lack of respect, loss of honor, loss of reputation, loss of respect, low standing, mortification, obloquy, odium, opprobrium, ostracism, poor reputation, reproach, scandal, sense of disgrace, sense of shame, shame, slur, smirch, stain, stigma, taint, tarnish, tarnished honor, *turpitudo,* unrespectability

IGNORANCE, *noun*   benightedness, bewilderment, blindness, darkness, denseness, fog, foolishness, greenness, haze, illiteracy, illiterateness, *imprudentia,* incapacity, incognizance, incomprehension, ineptitude, inerudition, inexperience, innocence, *inscientia, inscitia,* insensibility, lack of education, lack of knowledge, lack of learning, maze, nescience, obtuseness, perplexity, rawness, simpleness, simplicity, unacquaintance, unawareness, unconsciousness, unenlightenment, unfamiliarity, unintellectuality, unintelligence, unknowingness, unlearnedness, unscholarliness, untaught state, unworldliness, vagueness, want of knowledge
ASSOCIATED CONCEPTS: culpable ignorance, essential ignorance, ignorance of law, involuntary ignorance, plead ignorance, voluntary ignorance
FOREIGN PHRASES: *Ignorantia praesumitur ubi scientia non probatur.* Ignorance is presumed where knowledge is not proved. *Ignorantia legis neminem excusat.* Ignorance of the law excuses no one. *Regula est, juris quidem ignorantiam cuique nocere, facti vero ignorantiam non nocere.* The rule is that a person's ignorance of the law may prejudice him, but that his ignorance of fact will not. *Ignorantia juris sui non praejudicat juri.* Ignorance of one's right does not prejudice the right. *Ignorantia excusator, non juris sed facti.* Ignorance of fact may excuse, but not ignorance of law. *Ignorantia juris quod quisque tenetur scire, neminem excusat.* Ignorance of law, which everyone is bound to know, excuses no one. *Nemo tenetus informare qui nescit, sed quisquis scire quod informat.* No one who is ignorant of a thing is bound to give information about it, but everyone is bound to know that concerning which he gives information.

IGNORANCE OF LAW, *adjective*   blindness, devoid of knowledge of the law, have no idea of the specifics of the law, incognizance, incomprehension, ineptitude, lack of knowledge of legal requirements, lack of learning of legal requirements, no knowledge of legal constraints, not schooled in the law, obtuseness, unawareness of rules, unawareness of rules of conduct, unawareness of standards which are imposed, unawareness of statutory requirements, unfamiliarity, unfamiliarity with established rule of law, unfamiliarity with laws, unfamiliarity with legal requirements, vagueness on the specifics in the law

ASSOCIATED CONCEPTS: defenses, due process, notice

FOREIGN PHRASES: *Ignorantia, legis neminem, excusat.* Ignorance of the law excuses no one. *Ignorantia, praesumitur, ubi scientia non probatur.* Ignorance is presumed where knowledge has not been proven.

IGNORANT, *adjective* dense, devoid of knowledge, devoid of learning, devoid of understanding, failing to comprehend, illiterate, in a daze, in a fog, incapable, inept, inexperienced, lacking education, lacking knowledge, lacking learning, lacking the ability to comprehend, lacking understanding, not being aware, not capable of comprehending, not capable of learning, obtuse, perplexed, raw, simple, unaware, unconscious, unenlightened, unknowing

ASSOCIATED CONCEPTS: ignorance of the law, ignorant of the rule of law

IGNORE *(Disbelieve),* **verb** be indifferent to, brush aside, discountenance, disregard, gloss over, make light of, pass over, pay no attention to, pay no heed to, pay no mind to, turn a deaf ear to

IGNORE *(Disregard),* **verb** be indifferent to, belittle, brush aside, depreciate, discountenance, discredit, disesteem, disparage, disregard, distain, distrust, doubt, gloss over, harbor suspicions, make light of, misprize, mistrust, pass over, pay no attention, pay no heed, pay no mind, question, slight, spurn, suspect

ILL *(Bad),* **adjective** adverse, antagonistic, baleful, bellicose, belligerent, calamitous, cantankerous, corrupt, crabbed, crabby, cross, damaging, degenerate, deleterious, depraved, destructive, detrimental, evil, fell, fractious, harm, harmful, hostile, hurtful, immoral, inauspicious, infelicitous, iniquitous, injurious, insult, irascible, irritable, low, mean, mischief, misfortune, nefarious, nocuous, pernicious, ruinous, sinful, snappish, snappy, sullen, trouble, unfavorable, unfriendly, unkind, unkindly, unlucky, unpromising, unpropitious, wicked, wrong

ILL *(Sick),* **adjective** afflicted, ailing, bedridden, confined, diseased, feeble, feverish, has a medical condition, in the hospital, indisposed, infirm, laid up, malady, not feeling well, not up to snuff, not well, on the sick list, out of commission, under the weather, weak

ASSOCIATED CONCEPTS: fee for service, health care, HMO

ILL-ADVISED, *adjective* counterproductive, disadvantageous, falsely construed, foolish, hasty, ill-considered, ill-contrived, ill-judged, impolitic, imprudent, inadvisable, inappropriate, inconsiderate, *inconsultus,* inconvenient, inexpedient, infelicitous, injudicious, inopportune, interpreted incorrectly, irresponsible, labored over under a misapprehension, misadvised, miscalculated, misconstrued, miscounseled, misestimated, misguided, misinformed, misinterpreted, misjudged, misled, mistaken, misunderstood, rash, reckless, senseless, shortsighted, *temerarius,* unconsidered, undesirable, unfit, unpolitical, unreasonable, unseemly, unsuitable, unwise

ILL-CONCEIVED, *adjective* deceived, distorted, estimated incorrectly, failed to understand, impolitic, inexpedient, laboring under a misapprehension, misapprehended, miscalculated, misconstrued, misestimated, misguided, misinformed, misinterpreted, misjudged, misled, mistake, mistaken, misunderstood, perverted the meaning of, reasonless, received a false impression of, received a wrong impression of, senseless, thoughtless, valued incorrectly

ASSOCIATED CONCEPTS: ill-conceived decision by the count

ILL-CONSIDERED, *adjective* adverse, against, antagonistic, antipathetic, averse, badly assessed, contrary, disadvantageous, discordant, disturbing, fractious, hasty, hostile, ill-advised, ill-judged, impolitic, imprudent, inadvisable, inappropriate, infelicitous, inhospitable, injudicious, misadvised, misguided, offensive, opposed, pugnacious, reckless, senseless, shortsighted, unconsidered, undesirable, unfit, unfriendly, unpleasant, unreasonable, unseemly, unsuitable, unsympathetic, unwise

ASSOCIATED CONCEPTS: ill-considered opinion or course of action

ILL-CONCEIVED, *adjective* deceived, impolitic, inexpedient, misguided, misinformed, misled, mistaken, distorted, estimated incorrectly, failed to understand, laboring, under a misapprehension, mistake, misapprehended, miscalculated, misconstrued, misestimated, misinterpreted, misjudged, misunderstood, perverted the meaning of, reasonless, received a false impression of, received a wrong impression of, senseless, thoughtless, valued incorrectly

ASSOCIATED CONCEPTS: ill-conceived decision by the count

ILL-CONTRIVED, *adjective* counterproductive, falsely construed, foolish, ill-advised, imprudent, inadvisable, inexpedient, injudicious, interpreted incorrectly, misadvised, miscalculated, misconstrued, misestimated, misguided, misinformed misinterpreted, misjudged, misled, mistaken, misunderstood, to labor under a misapprehension, unpolitical

ILL-DISPOSED, *adjective* acrimonious, against, antagonistic, anti, antipathetic, apprehensive, averse, belligerent, considering, contentious, contra, contrary, crusty, discordant, disdainful, disputatious, epugnant to, fractious, hostile, hostile to, ill-intentioned, ill-natured, ill-willed, inhospitable, inimical, malevolent, malicious, mean, on the fence, opposed to, opposing, quarreling, rancorous, reluctant, repellent, resentful, resistant, resistive, sinister, spiteful, testy, unaligned, unfavorable, unfriendly to, unpropitious, unsympathetic, unsympathetic to

ILL-FOUNDED, *adjective* apocryphal, baseless, empty, erroneous, fallacious, false, fanciful, groundless, inaccurate, incorrect, insubstantial, sophistic, sophistical, suppositional, trumped up, unbased, unconfirmed, unfounded, ungrounded, unsubstantial, unsupportable, unsupported, unsustainable, untenable, unwarranted, without basis, without foundation, without sound basis, without substance

ILL-JUDGED, *adjective* acting without due consideration, against reason, blind, careless, hasty, headstrong, heedless, ill-advised, ill-chosen, ill-considered, ill-contrived, illogical, impatient, imprudent, inconsiderate, inept, inexact, inexpedient, injudicious, irrational, lacking discretion, misadvised, miscalculated, rash, reckless, shortsighted, showing poor judgment, thoughtless, unconsidered, undiscerning, unenlightened, unguided, unreasonable, unreasoning, unsensible, unsound, unthinking, unthoughtful, unwise, wild

ILL-NATURED, *adjective* abject, acrimonious, antipathetic, arrant, base, cantankerous, coarse, contemptible, contentious, contrary, crusty, despicable, disobliging, disputatious, froward, hostile, ignoble, ignominious, ill-disposed, ill-tempered, inhospitable, knavish, mean, nervous, objectionable, pusillanimous, scandalous, servile, snappish, testy, unaccommodating, vicious, vile, villainous, virulent

ILL-REPUTE, *noun* bad name, bad repute, baseness, contemptibility, contemptibleness, degradation, disapproval, disesteem, disfavor, disgrace, dishonor, dislike, disreputability, disreputation, disrespectability, improperness, impropriety, infamy, notoriety, questionability, questionableness, rascality, shadiness, shame, unpopularity

ILL-REPUTE, adjective berated, censured, contemptible, debased, defamed, degraded, denunciated, discredited, disesteemed, disfavored, disgraced, dishonored, disparaged, disrespected, has a bad reputation, having a stigma, lewd, reviled, scorned, shamed, vilified
ASSOCIATED CONCEPTS: discrediting a witness

ILL-TREATMENT (Misuse), **noun** ill-usage, ill-use, maltreatment, mishandling, mistreatment, misusage

ILL-TREATMENT (Oppression), **noun** abuse, bullying, intimidation, malice, outrage, persecution, tyranny, viciousness, victimization
ASSOCIATED CONCEPTS: ill-treatment of prisoners

ILL-USE, verb abuse, abuti, afflict, be hurtful, be malevolent, bruise, buffet, castigate, cause evil, damage, deal hard measure to, do an injustice to, do evil, do harm to, do violence, do wrong, flagellate, grind, harm, hurt, ill-treat, injure, knock about, malign, maltreat, manhandle, manipulate, mishandle, mistreat, misuse, oppress, overdrive, persecute, plague, show ill will, torment, torture, treat cruelly, treat unfairly, treat unkindly, use badly, use wrongly, vicitimize
ASSOCIATED CONCEPTS: contributory negligence, misuse of a product

ILL-WILL, noun acerbity, acute dissatisfaction, adverseness, alienation, animosity, animus, antagonism, antipathy, aversion, bad intent, belligerency, bitter feelings, bitterness, chagrin, conflict, contrariety, coolness, deliberate malice, detestation, disaffection, discontent, dislike, disquiet, dissatisfaction, enmity, hard feelings, hostility, ill disposition, ill-feeling, ill-intent, incompatibility, inimicality, intolerance, malevolence, malevolentia, malice, maliciousness, malignance, malignancy, odium, opposition, rancor, resentment, spite, spitefulness, strain, tension, unfriendliness, unfriendly feeling, unkindness, unpopularity, wrath

ILLEGAL, adjective actionable, against the law, banned, contrary to law, criminal, exceeding the law, felonious, forbidden, illegitimate, illicit, impermissible, improper, inlicitus, invalid, lawless, not according to law, not allowed, not approved, not authorized by law, not covered by law, not permitted, not valid, outlawed, outside the law, prohibited, prohibited by law, proscribed, punishable, quod contra leges fit, unauthorized, unchartered, unconstitutional, unjustified, unlawful, unsanctioned, unwarrantable, unwarranted, vetitus, without authority, wrongful
ASSOCIATED CONCEPTS: illegal acts, illegal business, illegal combination, illegal contract, illegal detention, illegal discrimination, illegal force, illegal operation, illegal picketing, illegal possession, illegal practice, illegal purpose, illegal restraint, illegal sale, illegal search and seizure, illegal statute, illegal taking, illegal tax, illegal trade, illegal transaction, illegal use, mala in se, mala prohibita

ILLEGALITY, noun corruptness, criminality, illegitimacy, impropriety, infraction, infringement, lawlessness, malefaction, misdeed, transgression, unauthorization, underhandedness, unfitness, unlawfulness, violation of the law
ASSOCIATED CONCEPTS: ultra vires
FOREIGN PHRASES: **Pacta quae contra leges constitutionesque vel contra bonos mores fiunt nullam vim habere, indubitati juris est.** It is unquestionably the law that contracts which are made contrary to the laws or against good morals, have no force in law.

ILLEGALLY, adverb contrary to law, criminally, feloniously, illegitimately, illicitly, impermissibly, improperly, in violation of law, tortiously, unlawfully, without legal authority, without legal sanction, wrongfully
ASSOCIATED CONCEPTS: acting illegally, illegally assessed, illegally obtained, illegally procured, illegally sold

ILLEGITIMATE (Born out of wedlock), **adjective** adulterine, base-born, bastard, misbegot, misbegotten, nothus, of illicit union, unlawfully begotten, unnatural
ASSOCIATED CONCEPTS: illegitimate children, legitimation, paternity proceeding, presumption of legitimacy
FOREIGN PHRASES: **Parentum est liberos alere atiam nothos.** It is the duty of parents to support their children even when illegitmate. **Qui nascitur sine legitimo matrimonio, matrem sequitur.** He who is born out of lawful matrimony succeeds to the condition of his mother. **Non est justum aliquem antenatum post mortem facere bastardum qui toto tempore vitae suae pro legitimo habebatur.** It is not just to make anyone a bastard after his death, who during his lifetime was regarded as legitimate. **Justum non est aliquem antenatum mortuum facere bastardum, qui pro tota vita sua pro legitimo habetur.** It is not just to make a bastard after his death one elder born who all his life has been accounted legitimate. **Qui ex damnato coitu nascuntur inter liberos non computentur.** They who are born of an illicit union should not be reckoned among the children.

ILLEGITIMATE (Illegal), **adjective** against the law, banned, contrary to law, criminal, forbidden, illicit, impermissible, improper, interdicted, lawbreaking, malfeasant, non legitimus, not according to law, not permitted, outlawed, outside the law, prohibited, prohibited by law, proscribed, unallowed, unauthorized, unlawful, unlicensed, unsanctioned, wrongful

ILLIBERAL, adjective avaricious, avarus, biased, bigoted, churlish, close, close-fisted, conservative, covetous, dogmatic, fanatical, grasping, greedy, grudging, hidebound, inhospitable, inliberalis, intolerant, mean, mercenary, miserly, narrow, narrow-minded, niggardly, one-sided, opinionated, parochial, parsimonious, partial, penurious, persecuting, petty, prejudiced, reactionary, selfish, sordidus, sparing, stingy, stinting, tight, tightfisted, uncharitable, unchivalrous, ungenerous, ungentlemanly

ILLICIT, adjective accusable, actionable, against the law, banned, censored, contrary to law, criminal, exceeding the law, felonious, forbidden, forbidden by law, guilty, illegal, illegitimate, immoral, impermissible, improper, infamous, iniquitous, injudicial, inlicitus, interdicted, lawless, nonconstitutional, nonlegal, not according to law, not allowed, not approved, not covered by law, not permitted, out of bounds, outlawed, outside the law, prohibited, proscribed, punishable by law, quod contra leges fit, taboo, tortious, triable, unallowed, unauthorized, unconstitutional, under ban, unlawful, unlegalized, unlegislated, unprincipled, unsanctioned, unseemly, unwarrantable, unwarranted, vetitus, wicked, without authority, wrong, wrongful
ASSOCIATED CONCEPTS: illicit cohabitation, illicit relations, illicit relationship, illicit trade

ILLITERACY, noun ineducation, inerudition, unintellectualism, unlearnedness, unscholarliness

ILLNESS, noun affliction, ailing, ailment, complaint, defect, disability, disease, disorder, infirmity, malady, prostration, sickness

ASSOCIATED CONCEPTS: mental illness, terminal illness, Unemployment Compensation, Workers' Compensation Law

ILLOGICAL, adjective absurdus, contradictory, contrary to reason, contrary to the rules of logic, fallacious, faulty, groundless, inconsistent, indefensible, irrational, logically unsound, mistaken, nonscientific, paralogistic, self-contradictory, sophistic, sophistical, unfounded, ungrounded, unscientific, unsound, unsustainable, untenable, without basis, without foundation
ASSOCIATED CONCEPTS: arbitrary and capricious

ILLUDE, verb be cunning, befool, beguile, cheat, chouse, circumvent, cozen, deceive, decoy, defraud, delude, deride, dupe, ensnare, fool, gerrymander, gull, hoax, inveigle, lead astray, lead into error, make a fool of, misdirect, misguide, misinform, mislead, mock, outmaneuver, outwit, play false, practice chicanery, put something over, ridicule, scorn, swindle, take advantage of, take in, trick, victimize

ILLUMINATE (Brighten), **verb** cast light upon, light, light up, lighten up, radiate, throw light upon, throw sunlight on

ILLUMINATE (Inform), **verb** acquaint, advise, apprise, cast light upon, clarify, clear up, convince, counsel, define, delineate, demonstrate, disabuse, edify, elaborate, elucidate, embellish, enlighten, enucleate, explain, expound, familiarize with, give insight to, illustrate, impart, inspire, instill, instruct, lecture, make aware, make clear, make explicit, notify, stimulate, unfold

ILLUMINATION, noun clarification, cognition, cognizance, comment, construction, definition, education, elucidation, explanation, explication, illustration, information, instruction, intellectual enlightenment, learning, realization, recognition, simplification, solution

ILLUSION (Deception), **noun** aberration, distortion, fallacy, false impression, misbelief, misconception, prestidigitation

ILLUSION (Impression), **noun** apparition, artifice, chimera, daydream, deception, delusion, dream, figment, hallucination, masquerade, mirage, myth, optical illusion, phantasm, phantasmagoria, phantom, semblance, specter, spirit, unreality, vision, wraith

ILLUSORY, adjective casuistic, casuistical, chimerical, conjuring, counterfeit, deceiving, deceptive, deluding, delusive, fabricated, fallacious, false, falsus, fancied, fanciful, fatuitous, feigned, fictitious, hatched, illusive, imaginary, imagined, insidious, insubstantial, invented, make-believe, misleading, mythic, mythological, not true, notional, phantasmal, pretended, sophistic, sophistical, suppositional, tenuous, tricky, unactual, unauthentic, unreal, unsubstantial, unsupportable, vanus, visionary
ASSOCIATED CONCEPTS: illusory agreement, illusory appointment, illusory contract, illusory promise, illusory transfer, illusory trust
FOREIGN PHRASES: *Judicium non debet esse illusorium; suum effectum habere debet.* A judgment ought not to be illusory; it ought to have its proper effect.

ILLUSTRATE, verb cite, clarify, define, demonstrate, display, elucidate, enlighten, exemplify, exhibit, explain, expound, furnish an example, give an instance, illuminate, *inlustrare,* instance, interpret, make evident, make plain, make vivid, manifest, produce an example, represent, show, show by example, teach by examples
ASSOCIATED CONCEPTS: illustrative questions

ILLUSTRATION, noun case in point, clarification, depiction, depictment, display, elucidation, enucleation, example, exemplar, exemplification, *exemplum,* explanation, explication, exponent, exposition, illumination, instance, manifestation, model, practical demonstration, relevant instance, representation, sample, showing, simplification, specimen

ILLUSTRATIVE, adjective annotative, clarifying, definitive, delineatory, depictive, descriptive, elucidative, evincive, exemplary, explanatory, expository, figurative, general, graphic, illuminative, indicative, inferential, interpretative, narrative, picaresque, representative, symbolic, typical

ILLUSTRIOUS, adjective acclaimed, *amplus,* applauded, bright, brilliant, celebrated, conspicuous, distinguished, eminent, excellent, eximious, famed, famous, glorious, grand, great, heroic, honored, important, *inlustris,* known, memorable, noble, notable, noted, popular, prominent, radiant, remarkable, renowned, resplendent, shining, signal, splendid, *splendidus,* splendorous, sublime, talked of, time-honored, transplendent, well-known, widely known

IMAGE, noun appearance, apprehension, aspect, color, complexion, concept, conception, copy, counterpart, duplicate, embodiment, fancy, fantasy, form, guise, impression, likeness, living picture, look, material representation, mental image, model, percept, perception, phase, phenomenon, physiognomy, picture, portrait, presence, reflection, reproduction, resemblance, semblance, symbol, vision

IMAGINATION, noun conceive, concept, conception, conceptualization, creation, creative power, creativity, formulation, idea, illusion, image, imaginative faculty, imaginativeness, innovativeness, inventiveness, perception, presumption, vision
ASSOCIATED CONCEPTS: perjury, trumped-up charges

IMAGINATIVE, adjective clever, constructive, creative, ingenious, innovative, inventive, original, productive, resourceful, visionary

IMAGINE, verb apprehend, assume, believe, compose, conceive, conclude, conjure, conjure up, contrive, create, deduce, delineate, depict, devise, dream, envision, expect, fabricate, fancy, gather, guess, ideate, improvise, infer, invent, judge, make up, opine, originate, picture, plan, presume, pretend, profess, regard, scheme, speculate, suppose, surmise, suspect, think, visualize

IMBALANCE, noun difference, disequilibrium, disparity, disproportion, dissimilarity, distortion, diversity, inconstancy, inequality, irregularity, unevenness, unjust distribution, variableness

IMBROGLIO, noun babel, bedlam, broil, chaos, commotion, complexity, complicated misunderstanding, complication, confusing situation, confusion, difficult situation, difficulty, dilemma, disagreement, disorder, disturbance, embarrassing situation, embranglement, embroilment, entanglement, fracas, impasse, intricate involvement, intricate plot, involved situation, jam, jungle, labyrinth, maze, melee, mess, muddle, perplexing state of affairs, pickle, plight, predicament, quandary, riot, row, rumpus, scrape, stew, stymie, tight spot, tumult, turmoil, uproar, welter

IMBUE, verb bathe, drench, fill, *imbuere,* implant, impress upon the mind, inculcate, indoctrinate, *inficere,* influence, infuse, inject, inspire, instill, leaven, permeate, pervade, pour in, saturate, soak, *tingere*

IMITATE, verb adopt, be like, caricature, clone, copy, counterfeit, duplicate, echo, emulate, fabricate, fake, follow, follow as an example, follow suit, forge, impersonate, look like, make a copy, match, mimic, mirror, model after, pattern after, parrot, plagiarize, portray, pose, pretend, reflect, repeat, replicate, represent, reproduce, simulate
ASSOCIATED CONCEPTS: counterfeit, identity theft

IMITATION, adjective artificial, bogus, burlesque, copied, counterfeit, deceptive, dummy, *effigies,* ersatz, factitious, faked, false, feigned, imitated, imitative, make-believe, mock, phony, pretended, pseudo, quasi, sham, simulacrum, simulated, spurious, substitute, synthetic, unauthentic, ungenuine
ASSOCIATED CONCEPTS: forgery

IMMACULATE, adjective above suspicion, blameless, chaste, clean, faultless, flawless, impeccable, incorrupt, inculpable, innocent, irreproachable, perfect, pure, refined, sinless, spotless, spotlessly clean, unblemished, undefiled, unflawed, unimpeachable, unpolluted, unsoiled, unstained, unsullied, untainted, untarnished, virginal, virtuous

IMMATERIAL, adjective baseless, beside the point, beside the question, bodiless, chimerical, diminutive, ethereal, *expers corporis,* extraneous, groundless, impertinent, inapplicable, inappreciable, inappropriate, inconsequential, incorporeal, inessential, insignificant, insubstantial, intangible, irrelevant, lightweight, meaningless, minor, nominal, nonessential, nonphysical, not connected with, not important, not pertaining to, not pertinent, *nullius momenti,* of little account, of no consequence, of no essential consequence, of no importance, of no moment, of no significance, off the point, off the topic, other wordly, out of place, out-of-the-way, outside the question, pointless, remote, sine corpore, spectral, trivial, unessential, unimportant, unrelated, unsubstantial, vaporous, without depth, without substance, without weight, worthless
ASSOCIATED CONCEPTS: immaterial allegations, immaterial alteration, immaterial averment, immaterial breach, immaterial facts, immaterial issues, immaterial testimony, immaterial variance, incompetent evidence, irrelevant evidence

IMMATERIALITY, noun inconsequence, incorporeality, inessentiality, insignificance, insubstantiality, insufficiency, intangibility, irrelevance, irrelevancy, lack of depth, lack of substance, lightness, meagerness, nonessentiality, otherworldliness, paltriness, pettiness, pointlessness, shallowness, spirituality, spiritualness, thinness, triviality, unimportance, unnoteworthiness, unsubstantiality, worthlessness

IMMATURE, adjective callow, crude, green, gullible, ignorant, inexperienced, jejune, juvenile, naive, puerile, raw, rudimental, rudimentary, undeveloped, unfinished, unfledged, unformed, unmellowed, unprepared, unripe, unseasoned, unsophisticated, young, youthful

IMMEASURABLE, adjective boundless, countless, endless, extending forever, extensive, great, illimitable, immerse, indeterminate, inexhaustible, infinite, innumerable, interminable, large, limitless, measureless, never-ending, unbounded, undeterminable, undetermined, unfathomable, unlimited, untold, vast
ASSOCIATED CONCEPTS: immeasurable harm

IMMEDIACY, noun availability, closeness, confines, convenience, environs, hear, immediateness, instantaneousness, nearness, simultaneousness, neighborhood, now, occurrence, occurring at the present time, precinct, presence, propinquity, proximity, simultaneity, vicinage, vicinity
ASSOCIATED CONCEPTS: statute of limitations

IMMEDIATE *(At once),* **adjective** flash, instant, instantaneous, *praesens,* prompt, quick, speedy, sudden, unhesitating, with reasonable dispatch, without delay

IMMEDIATE *(Imminent),* **adjective** about to happen, anticipated, approaching, at hand, close, close at hand, coming, drawing near, expected, following, foreseen, forthcoming, impendent, impending, in the offing, in view, looked for, momentary, near at hand, nearing, next, nigh, prospective, to come, upcoming

IMMEDIATE *(Not distant),* **adjective** abutting, adjacent, adjoining, at hand, bordering, bounding, close, close at hand, conjoining, conterminous, contiguous, handy, juxtapositional, near, near by, neighboring, next to, proximate, verging
ASSOCIATED CONCEPTS: immediate beneficiaries, immediate benefit, immediate cause, immediate consequences, immediate control, immediate damage, immediate delivery, immediate irreparable harm, immediate legatees, immediate need, immediate transferor

IMMEDIATELY *(In the proximity),* **adverb** alongside, around, at close quarters, at close range, close by, close to, closely, directly, in the area of, in the neighborhood of, in the vicinity of, near, nearby, next door, promptly, proximately, without an interval of time
ASSOCIATED CONCEPTS: proximate cause

IMMEDIATELY *(Instantly),* **adverb** at once, at the same time, at this moment, concurrently, in a moment, in an instant, instaneously, instantly, now, posthaste, promptly, pronto, quickly, rapidly, right away, shortly, simultaneously, speedily, straight off, suddenly, this very moment

IMMENSE, adjective boundless, broad, bulky, capacious, colossal, endless, enormous, exorbitant, extremely large, far-reaching, gigantic, grandiose, gross, huge, illimitable, immeasurable, innumerable, mammoth, massive, monumental, mountainous, myriad, outrageous, prodigious, stupendous, titanic, tremendous, vast

IMMERSE *(Engross),* **verb** absorb, attend, be attentive, bury, engage, enthrall, fascinate, grip, hold, hold spellbound, interest, involve, monopolize, occupy, overwhelm, preoccupy, submerge, take up

IMMERSE *(Plunge into),* **verb** bathe, cover with water, deluge, dip, douse, drench, drown, duck, dunk, engulf, flood, insert, inundate, place under a liquid, plunge into a liquid, put under water, send to the bottom, sink, soak, souse, steep, submerge, submerse, swamp, thrust under

IMMIGRANT, noun alien, expatriate, foreigner, incomer, migrant, naturalized citizen, newcomer, resident alien, settler
ASSOCIATED CONCEPTS: immigration law

IMMIGRATION, noun admission of foreigners, *adventus,* change of national location, colonization, entry of aliens, establishment of foreign residence, expatriation, foreign influx, incoming population, ingress, migration, movement of population, transmigration
ASSOCIATED CONCEPTS: issuance of visas, passports

IMMINENT, adjective about to be, about to happen, alarming, approaching, at hand, brewing, closing in, coming, destined, drawing near, expected, following, forecasted, forthcoming, future, *imminere,* impendent, *impendere,* impending, in store, in the offing, in the wind, in view, instant, likely to happen, looming, menacing, minatorial, minatory, near, near at hand, nearing, next, ominous, on the way, oncoming, overhanging, portentous, *praesens,* predicted, prospective, threatening, threatening harm, upcoming
ASSOCIATED CONCEPTS: imminent danger, imminent irreparable harm, imminent peril

IMMOBILIZE, adjective fixed, have no freedom, have no mobility, immovable, impassive, inactive, inexpressive, inflexible, like a statue, motionless, paralyzed, rigid, riveted, rooted, stationary, staunch, steadfast, still, transfixed, unmoving

IMMODERATE, adjective exaggerated, excessive, exorbitant, extravagant, extreme, inordinate, intemperate, not balanced, not fair, overblown, preposterous, self-indulgent, squandering, unbalanced, unconscionable, uncontrolled, uncurbed, unlimited, unreasonable, unrestrained, unwarranted
ASSOCIATED CONCEPTS: immoderate punishment, immoderate use

IMMORAL, adjective amoral, arrant, bad, base, conscienceless, corrupt, criminal, debauched, degenerate, depraved, dishonest, dishonorable, disreputable, dissipated, dissolute, evil, exploitative, false, flagitious, graceless, heinous, ignoble, illaudable, illegal, illicit, improper, impure, indecent, iniquitous, knavish, lacking morals, lecherous, lewd, libidinous, licentious, *male moratus,* miscreant, nefarious, objectionable, *perditus,* pernicious, perverted, pettifogging, *pravus,* profligate, promiscuous, prurient, reprobate, roguish, salacious, shameless, shocking, sinful, unchaste, unconscionable, unethical, unjustifiable, unlawful, unmoral, unprincipled, unrighteous, unscrupulous, unvirtuous, unwholesome, wicked, without integrity, wrong
ASSOCIATED CONCEPTS: immoral act, immoral agreement, immoral conduct, immoral consideration, immoral contract, obscenity
FOREIGN PHRASES: *Ex turpi causa non oritur actio.* No cause of action arises out of an immoral or illegal consideration.

IMMORALITY, noun atrocity, bad repute, carnality, concupiscence, contamination, corruption, criminality, delinquency, demoralization, depravity, dissoluteness, evil, indecency, iniquity, knavery, lechery, lewdness, licentiousness, loose morals, misdoing, obscenity, perversion, profligacy, salacity, sexual promiscuity, sin, turpitude, vice, wantonness, wickedness, wrong
ASSOCIATED CONCEPTS: adultery, bribery, criminal conversation, immoral conduct, immoral contracts, lewdness

IMMORTAL, adjective always, canonizing, commemorating, continuity, continuous, endless, endlessness, eternal, everlasting, forever, imperishable, indestructible, lasting, never dying, permanent, perennial, undying, unfading

IMMORTALITY (Deathlessness), **noun** athanasy, canonization, commemoration, continuity, deathlessness, endless life, endlessness, eternal continuance, eternity, everlastingness, imperishability, indestructibility, infinity, perpetuation, perpetuity, undying repute, unlimited existence

IMMORTALITY (Distinction), **noun** commemoration, enshrinement, immortal name, imperishability, lasting fame

IMMOVABLE, noun affixed property, fixed assets, fixed chattel, fixed property, fixture, *immobilis, immotus,* land, property permanently affixed to the realty, real estate, real property, *stabilis*

IMMUNE, adjective absolved, armored, clear, excused, exempt, free, granted amnesty, *immunis,* immunized, impregnable, inaccessible, inexpugnable, inviolable, invulnerable, not accountable, not answerable, not liable, not responsible, not subject, possessed of immunity, privileged, protected, released, safe, screened, sheltered, shielded, spared, unaccountable, unaffected by, unanswerable, unassailable, unattackable, under shelter, unencumbered, unexposed, unliable, unpunishable, unrestrained, unrestricted, unsubject, unsusceptible, unthreatened, untouchable, untouched, without risk
ASSOCIATED CONCEPTS: immune from prosecution

IMMUNITY, noun absolution, acquittal, charter, commutation, discharge, exception, exculpation, exemption, exemption from punishment, franchise, freedom, freedom from exemption, freedom from obligation, freedom from prosecution, *immunitas,* liberation, liberty, license, nonliability, privilege, protection, release, release from charge, release from duty, relief, reprieve, respite, safety from prosecution, special privilege, *vacatio*
ASSOCIATED CONCEPTS: absolute immunity, complete immunity, derivative immunity, full transactional immunity, full waiver, governmental immunity, immunity from arrest, immunity from prosecution, immunity from service of process, limited immunity, limited waiver, partial immunity, privileges and immunities, qualified immunity, state immunity, transactional immunity, use and derivative immunity, use immunity, waiver of immunity

IMMUNIZE, verb counterbalance, countervail, free, grant immunity, guard against, inoculate, make safe, neutralize, not affected by, offset, preserve, privileged, protect, resist, safeguard, shield, shield from damage, shield from danger, shield from injury, unsusceptible to, vaccinate against

IMMURE, verb cast into prison, commit to an institution, commit to prison, confine, constrain, detain, encage, enclose, enclose within walls, entomb, gate, hold, hold captive, hold in captivity, hold in check, hold within bounds, impound, imprison, incarcerate, *includere,* isolate, keep in, keep in captivity, keep in check, keep in custody, keep in detention, keep prisoner, keep under arrest, keep within bounds, lay under restraint, lead into captivity, lock in, lock up, make captive, put under arrest, quarantine, restrain, seal up, seclude, send to prison, shelter, shut up, take captive, take into custody, throw into prison, wall up

IMMUTABLE, adjective adamant, ageless, confirmed, constans, constant, continual, continuous, durable, eternal, firm, fixed, immovable, *immutabilis,* implacable, incontrovertible, indestructible, inexorable, inflexible, intractable, invariable, irremovable, irrevocable, never changing, never varying, nonelastic, not to be changed, not to be moved, obstinate, perennial, permanent, perpetual, persistent, relentless, riveted, rooted, settled, *stabilis*, static, steadfast, steady, stiff, unaging, unalterable, unbending, unchangeable, unchanging, uncompromising, undeviating, undying, unending, unmalleable, unpliable, unrelenting, untractable, unyielding, vested

ASSOCIATED CONCEPTS: immutable principle of law

FOREIGN PHRASES: *Nomina sunt mutabilia, res autem immobiles.* Names are mutable, but things are immutable.

IMPACT *(Effect), noun* aftermath, bearing, cogency, concern, conclusion, consequence, deduction, full effect, germaneness, import, interest, materiality, meaning, outcome, outgrowth, pertinency, preference, reaction, relevance, repercussion, result, reverberation, upshot, value

IMPACT *(Importance), noun* consequence, end result, force, gravity, greatness, import, magnitude, mark, merit, meaning, moment, net result, noted value, portent, pronounced impression, reaction, result, significance, signification, substance, value, weightiness

ASSOCIATED CONCEPTS: impact from a landmark decision of the court

IMPACT, verb compress, cram, crowd, drive, drive firmly in, fill, fill to capacity, force, force together, hammer in, inject, insert, jam, load, overburden, overcrowd, overload, pack, pack close, pack in, pack together, press, press together, push, push together, ram, shove, squeeze, strike, thrust in, wedge

IMPAIR, verb adulterate, affect injuriously, blight, blunt, contaminate, cripple, crumble, damage, *debilitare*, debilitate, decrease in excellence, demolish, deplete, deprive of power, desecrate, devalue, dilapidate, diminish, diminish in quality, dissipate, disturb, dull, enervate, enfeeble, erode, *frangere*, harm, hinder, hurt, *imminuere*, injure, lessen in power, lessen in value, make inroads on, make worse, mar, obtund, paralyze, pollute, put out of commission, reduce, relax, render feeble, ruin, sap, stifle, taint, undermine, unhinge, waste, weaken, wear out, worsen

ASSOCIATED CONCEPTS: impairing the obligation of contracts, impairment of capital, impairment of good will, impairment of memory, impairment of powers, impairment of security

IMPAIRED CONDITION, noun atrophy, caducity, collapse, corrosion, damage, decadence, decadency, decay, decrepitude, degeneration, deterioration, detriment, dilapidation, disrepair, fault, impairment, impediment, injury, lack of maintenance, neglect, ruination, weakness, wear and tear

ASSOCIATED CONCEPTS: driving while impaired, impairing the rights of contract

IMPAIRMENT *(Damage), noun* detriment, disrepair, harm, hurt, injury, loss

ASSOCIATED CONCEPTS: impairment of vision

IMPAIRMENT *(Disability), noun* affliction, ailment, debilitation, debility, deterioration, disablement, disorder, disqualification, feebleness, frailty, handicap, helplessness, illness, impairment, impotence, impotency, inability, inability to work, inadequacy, incapability, incapacitation, incapacity, incompetence, incompetency, indisposition, ineffectiveness, ineffectuality, ineffectualness, inefficacy, inefficiency, infirmity, insufficiency, malady, powerlessness, sickness, unfitness, unsoundness, weakness

ASSOCIATED CONCEPTS: complete disability, continuous disability, disability benefits, disability compensation, disability insurance, general disability, medical disability, mental disability, partial disability, proof of disability, temporary disability, total disability

IMPAIRMENT *(Drawback), noun* detriment, disadvantage, inability, liability, limitation

ASSOCIATED CONCEPTS: impairment of funds, impairment of security

IMPALPABILITY, noun abstraction, bodilessness, flimsiness, immateriality, immaterialness, imperceptibility, inappreciability, incorporality, incorporealism, incorporeality, incorporeity, insubstantiality, intangibility, lack of substance, unconcreteness, unsolidity, unsubstantialness

IMPALPABLE, adjective attenuated, barely seen, concealed, covered, covert, delicate, difficult to feel, difficult to perceive, difficult to see, doubtable, dubitable, equivocal, fine, hidden, immateriate, imperceptible, inappreciable, inapprehensible, incapable of being perceived, inconspicuous, incorporeal, indefinite, indistinct, infinitesimal, intangible, invisible, little, microscopic, minute, nonmaterial, not manifest, not readily discerned, obscure, *quod tangi non potest,* screened, shaded, shadowy, shrouded, slight, small, subtle, tiny, unapparent, unclear, undiscernable, unevident, unexplicit, unnoticeable, unobservable, unobvious, unpatent, unperceivable, unplain, unpronounced, unreal, unrecognizable, unrevealed, unsubstantial, untouchable, vague, veiled, very fine

IMPANEL, verb catalog, enter, enumerate, itemize, list, record, register, schedule

ASSOCIATED CONCEPTS: impanel a jury

IMPART, verb accord, acquaint, advise, apprise, be indiscreet, bestow, brief, *communicare*, communicate, confer, confide, convey, deliver, disclose, dispense, donare, educate, endow, enlighten, enrich, favor with, *impertire*, inform, instruct, issue, make known, mention, point out, present, provide, relate, reveal, teach, tell, transfer, transmit

IMPARTIAL, adjective aequabilis, aequus, broadminded, detached, disinterested, dispassionate, equitable, even, evenhanded, evenly balanced, fair, fair-minded, free from bias, free to choose, honest, honorable, impersonal, incorrupt, *incorruptus*, independent, indifferent, *integer*, judicious, just, lacking prejudice, neutral, nonpartisan, not biased, not partial, objective, open, open-minded, reasonable, scrupulous, unaffected, unbiased, unbigoted, unbought, unbribed, uncolored, uncommitted, uncompelled, uncorrupt, uncorrupted, undecided, uninfluenced, unjaundiced, unopinionated, unopinioned, unprejudiced, unprepossessed, unswayed, untouched, without a preference, without favoritism

ASSOCIATED CONCEPTS: fair and impartial, impartial hearing officer, impartial judge, impartial jury, impartial trial

FOREIGN PHRASES: *Nemo potest esse simul actor et judex.* No one can be at the same time judge and suitor. *Judex non potest injuriam sibi datam punire.* A judge cannot punish a wrong done to himself. *Judex non potest esse testis in propria causa.* A judge cannot be a witness in his own case.

IMPASSE, noun abruption, bar, block, blockade, blockage, cessation, check, complete standstill, complexity, *cul-de-sac,* dead end, dead stop, deadlock, desistance, deterrence, difficulty, dilemma, discontinuance, discontinuance of activity, discontinuation, end, halt, hopelessness, impediment, impossibility, impossible task, inextricability, insoluble difference, insuperability, insuperable obstacle, nonresumption, obstacle, obstruction, perplexity, preclusion, predicament, problem, quagmire, quandary, stalemate, stall, standstill, state of inaction, state of no progress, stop

ASSOCIATED CONCEPTS: impasse in negotiations

IMPASSION, verb affect, agitate, arouse the emotions, electrify, encourage, enkindle, excite, incite, infect, inspire, kindle, move, provoke, rouse, spirit, spur, stir, stir the feelings, stir up

IMPATIENCE, adjective agitation, anger, annoyance, anxiety, disquiet, eager, excitable, excited, have a short temper, hotheadedness, in impetuosity, intolerance, irascibility, nervousness, possess a quick temper, prickly, quick tempered, short, snappish

IMPEACH, verb *accusare,* accuse, accuse of maladministration, accuse of misconduct, admonish, animadvert, attack, attaint, blame, bring a charge, bring charges, bring into discredit, bring to account, bring to justice, bring up for investigation, call in question, call to account, cast an imputation upon, cast blame upon, castigate, censure, challenge, challenge the credibility of, charge, charge to, charge with, complain against, condemn, confute, criticize, declaim against, decry, denigrate, denounce, denunciate, disapprove, discredit, disparage, dispute, expose, fault, file a claim, find an indictment against, hold at fault, implicate, impugn, impute fault to, inculpate, incur blame, indict, indict for maladministration, prefer a claim, prefer charges, put on trial, put the blame on, rebuff, recriminate, reprimand, reproach, reprove, ridicule, take to account, upbraid, vituperate

ASSOCIATED CONCEPTS: impeach a government official, impeach a witness

IMPEACHABILITY, noun blame, blameworthiness, censurability, chargeability, culpability, discredit, dishonor, disrepute, grave culpability, guiltiness, liability, peccability

IMPEACHMENT, noun accusal, *accusatio,* accusation, act of discrediting, admonition, animadversion, arraignment, attack, blame, castigation, censure, challenge, charge, complaint, condemnation, countercharge, criminal proceeding, crimination, criticism, denigration, denouncement, denunciation, disapproval, discommendation, exposure, hostile criticism, imputation of dereliction, imputation of fault, indictment, questioning integrity, questioning witness's veracity, rebuke, reprimand, reproach, reproof, vilification

ASSOCIATED CONCEPTS: articles of impeachment, character evidence, collateral impeachment, impeachment of a governmental officer, impeachment of a verdict, impeachment of a witness, impeachment of credibility, moral terpitude, prior inconsistent statement, reputation evidence

IMPECCABLE, adjective above reproach, absolutely ravishing, absolutely the finest, beautiful, complete, delightful, excellent, exemplary, faultless, finished, flawless, glorious, ideal, immaculate, incredible, irreproachable, perfect, refined, spotless, stylish, superb, unblemished, virtuous

IMPECUNIOUS, adjective bankrupt, beggared, beggarly, broke, cleaned out, destitute, distressed, embarrassed, flat, flat broke, hard up, impoverished, in need, in straitened circumstances, in the red, in want, indigent, insolvent, necessitous, needy, not well off, out of money, pauperized, penniless, penurious, pinched, poor, poorly off, poverty-stricken, short, short of cash, short of funds, short of money, strapped, unable to make ends meet, unmoneyed, unprosperous, without funds, without money

IMPEDE, verb annul, arrest, barricade, be a drag on, be an obstacle to, be in the way, block, blockade, bolt, bother, brake, bring to a standstill, burden, cause to delay, check, circumscribe, confine, cramp, cumber, curb, dam up, deadlock, decelerate, delay, detain, deter, disable, drag, embarrass, encumber, erect a barrier, estop, fetter, foreclose, frustrate, hamper, handicap, hinder, hold back, hold in check, hold up, impair, *impedire,* incommode, inconvenience, inhibit, interfere, interrupt, keep back, keep in check, limit, load, mar, obstruct, paralyze, postpone, preclude, press, prevent, quell, restrain, restrict, retard, *retardare,* set one back, shackle, slacken, slow down, stalemate, stand in the way, stay, stop, stop in progress by hindrances, suffocate, suspend, thwart, trammel, turn aside

ASSOCIATED CONCEPTS: impede negotiations

FOREIGN PHRASES: *Ubi aliquid impeditur propter unum, eo remoto, tollitur impedimentum.* Where anything is impeded by one single cause, with the removal of it, the impediment is removed.

IMPEDIMENT, noun bar, barrier, block, blockade, blockage, brake, burden, censorship, check, clog, complication, constraint, counteraction, damper, delay, deterrence, difficulty, disability, disadvantage, discouragement, drawback, encumbrance, estoppel, fetter, frustration, hamper, hampering, handicap, hindrance, holdback, *impedimentum,* impasse, imposition, inconvenience, inhibition, interference, interruption, limitation, load, objection, obstacle, obstruction, obtrusion, opposition, preclusion, predicament, prevention, prohibition, resistance, restraint, restriction, retardation, retardment, setback, shackle, snag, stop, stoppage, stumbling block, trammel

ASSOCIATED CONCEPTS: absolute impediment, detrimental impediment, impediment to a legal remedy, legal impediment, prohibitive impediments, relative impediments

FOREIGN PHRASES: *Non valet impedimentum quod de jure non sortitur effectum.* An impediment which has no effect in law is of no force. *Remoto impedimento, emergit actio.* The impediment being removed, the action comes to life.

IMPEDITIVE, adjective burdensome, conditional, cumbrous, deterrent, difficult, hindering, inhibitive, inhibitory, labyrinthine, limitative, limiting, onerous, preclusive, preventive, prohibitive, proscriptive, repressive, restrictive, suppressive

IMPEL, verb actuate, agitate, arouse, catapult, cause, drive forward, drive onward, encourage, fling, give an impetus, heave, hurl, impart momentum, impart motion, *incitare,* incite, incite to action, induce, instigate, jaculate, launch, mobilize, motivate, move forward, precipitate, press on, prod, project, prompt, propel, push, put in motion, rouse, send headlong, set going, set in motion, set moving, shove, spur, start, stimulate, throw, urge, urge forward, *urgere*

IMPEND, verb approach, be at hand, be forthcoming, be imminent, be in store, be near, be near at hand, draw near, *imminere, impendere,* loom, menace, promise ill, threaten

ASSOCIATED CONCEPTS: impending danger, impending death, impending peril

IMPENDING, *adjective* about to happen, approaching, brewing, close, forthcoming, future, hanging, immediate, inevitable, in prospect, instant, in the offing, looming, near at hand, necessary, oncoming, pending, projecting, prospective, proximate, suspended, threatening, unavoidable
ASSOCIATED CONCEPTS: impending indictment

IMPENETRABLE, *adjective* adamantine, closed, complex, crass, difficult, dull, enigmatic, hidden, impassable, impermeable, imperviable, impervious, inaccessible, inapprehensible, incomprehensible, indefinable, inexplicable, inexpressive, inexpugnable, insoluble, insurmountable, mysterious, obscure, obtuse, opaque, past comprehension, pathless, recondite, shut, snug, solid, stolid, tight, unfathomable, unopened, unreachable, untrodden

IMPERATIVE, *adjective* compulsory, critical, crucial, demanding, essential, exigent, *impero,* indispensable, mandatory, necessary, needful, obligatory, pressing, required, requiring immediate attention, requisite, unavoidable, urgent
ASSOCIATED CONCEPTS: imperative power, imperative statute, imperative trust

IMPERCEPTIBLE, *adjective* blurred, concealed, dim, enshrouded, faint, hazy, hidden, ill-defined, impalpable, inappreciable, inaudible, indiscernible, indistinct, inscrutable, intangible, invisible, minuscule, minute, nebulous, obscure, scant, screened, shadowy, unapparent, unappreciable, undiscernible, unnoticeable, unseeable, unseen, vague, veiled, very slight, very subtle

IMPERFECT, *adjective* abortive, average, bad, below par, blemished, broken, corrupt, crippled, crude, damaged, decrepit, defective, deficient, deteriorated, disfigured, failing, fair, faulty, feeble, flawed, fragmentary, frail, garbled, harmed, hurt, impaired, *imperfectus,* inadequate, incomplete, indifferent, inelegant, inexact, inferior, infirm, injured, insufficient, lacking, lame, limited, marred, mediocre, middling, moderate, mutilated, ordinary, out of order, partial, passable, peccable, poor, raw, rickety, rough, ruined, scanty, short, tainted, tolerable, uncompleted, uncultured, undeveloped, unfinished, unpolished, unsatisfactory, unsound, unsuitable, wanting, warped, weak
ASSOCIATED CONCEPTS: imperfect description, imperfect grant, imperfect performance, imperfect title

IMPERFECTION, *noun* blemish, defect, defectiveness, deficiency, deformity, disfigurement, drawback, error, failing, fault, faultiness, flaw, foible, frailty, imperfectness, inadequacy, incompleteness, infirmity, liability, limitation, malformation, misdeed, offense, omission, shortcoming, taint, transgression, vice, weak point, weakness
ASSOCIATED CONCEPTS: allergic user

IMPERIAL, *adjective* arbitrary, august, authoritarian, authoritative, chief, commanding, despotic, dictatorial, dogmatic, dominant, domineering, grand, imperatorial, imperious, imposing, kinglike, kingly, lofty, lordly, magisterial, magnificent, majestic, mandating, masterful, monarchal, paramount, peremptory, predominant, preeminent, princely, regal, royal, ruling, sovereign, splendid, stately, supreme, tyrannical
ASSOCIATED CONCEPTS: imperial law

IMPERIL, *verb* compromise, endanger, expose, expose to danger, hazard, jeopardize, put in danger, put in peril, risk, stake

IMPERIOUS, *adjective* arbitrary, assertive, authoritative, autocratic, bumptious, commanding, compelling, critical, despotic, dictatorial, dogmatic, domineering, haughty, heavy-handed, high-and-mighty, high-handed, imperative, overbearing, peremptory, powerful, requisite, tyrannical
ASSOCIATED CONCEPTS: imperious law

IMPERMEABLE, *adjective* airtight, close, compact, dense, hermetic, impassable, impenetrable, impervious, imporous, incompressible, nonporous, shut, solid, unpenetrable, unpierced

IMPERMISSIBLE, *adjective* actionable, against the law, banned, black-market, contraband, contrary to law, criminal, disallowed, disapproved, felonious, forbidden, illegal, illegitimate, illicit, iniquitous, irregular, nonlegal, objectionable, out of bounds, outlawed, outside the law, prohibited, proscribed, punishable, unallowable, unauthorized, unchartered, unconstitutional, under ban, unentitled, unlawful, unlicensed, unsanctioned, vetoed, wicked, wrong, wrongful
ASSOCIATED CONCEPTS: impermissible grounds for divorce

IMPERSONAL *(Dispassionate), **adjective*** candid, cold, cold-blooded, detached, disinterested, dispassionate, frigid, general, impartial, indefinite, insensible, neuter, nonsubjective, objective, passionless, undetermined, unfeeling, unforthcoming, unjaundiced, unselfish, unspecified, without warmth

IMPERSONAL *(Unbiased), **adjective*** uninfluenced, unprejudiced, unswayed

IMPERSONATE, *verb* act a part, act out, act the part of, ape, assume a character, copy, double for, dress as, enact, *hominem imitari,* imitate, masquerade as, mime, mimic, mirror, parrot, *partes hominis agere,* pass for, personate, personify, portray, pose as, pretend to be, represent, represent oneself to be, take the part of
ASSOCIATED CONCEPTS: fraud, impersonation of a governmental officer

IMPERTINENT *(Insolent), **adjective*** abusive, arrogant, assuming, audacious, bellicose, bold, brash, brazen, cavalier, churlish, coarse, contempt, contemptuous, contumacious, contumelious, defiant, derisive, discourteous, disdainful, disrespectful, flippant, forward, fresh, haughty, hostile, ill-mannered, impolite, improper, impudent, *insolens,* insubordinate, insulting, intrusive, irreverent, malapert, offensive, pert, presumptuous, procacious, provocative, rebellious, rough, rude, saucy, scoffing, shameless, surly, unabashed, uncivil, uncouth, ungracious, unmannerly, unpolished, unrefined, vulgar

IMPERTINENT *(Irrelevant), **adjective*** alien, beside the mark, beside the point, beside the question, disconnected, extraneous, gratuitous, immaterial, inadmissible, inapplicable, inapposite, inappropriate, inapropos, incidental, incongruous, inconsequent, independent, irrelative, malapropos, off the subject, out of place, *quod nihil ad rem est,* remote, separate, unallied, unapt, unconnected, unrelated, without connection
ASSOCIATED CONCEPTS: impertinent questioning

IMPERTURBABLE, *adjective* callous, calm, cold-blooded, collected, composed, cool, dispassionate, even-tempered, impassive, impervious, inexcitable, inexpressive, inured, levelheaded, nonchalant, patient, peaceable, philosophical, placid, resolute, sedate, serene, stable, steady, stoic, tranquil, unflappable, unmoved, unruffled, unworried, unworrying

IMPERVIOUS, adjective adrogans, airtight, blind to, blocked, buffered, callous, closed, deaf to, dense, detached, hard, hard to convince, hardened, hermetic, impassable, impassive, *impeditus, impenetrabilis,* impenetrable, imperforate, *imperiosus,* impermeable, impersuadable, impersuasible, imperturbable, imperviable, *impervious,* imporous, inaccessible, incapable of being affected, incapable of being impaired, incapable of being influenced, incapable of being injured, indifferent, indurate, indurated, insensate, insensitive, inured, invious, locked, not permitting passage, not permitting penetration, obstinate, obstructed, obtuse, opaque, pachydermatous, pathless, protected, safe, sealed, seared, shielded, shut, steeled, stubborn, thick, thick-skinned, tight, unaffected, unamenable, uninfluenceable, uninfluenced, unmovable, unmoved, unnavigable, unopened, unpassable, unperforated, unpierceable, unreachable, unreceptive, unresponsive, unswayable, unventilated, unyielding, waterproof, watertight

IMPETUOUS, adjective abrupt, capricious, careless, changeable, dashing, disordered, emotional, excitable, fervid, fickle, foolhardy, hasty, headstrong, heedless, hotblooded, hotheaded, ill-conceived, impatient, impulsive, incautious, intense, mercurial, overhasty, overzealous, precipitate, quick, rash, reckless, slapdash, spirited, spontaneous, spur-of-the-moment, stormy, stubborn, sudden, swift, thoughtless, uncontrollable, uncontrolled, unexpected, ungovernable, ungoverned, unstable, vehement, volatile, zealous
ASSOCIATED CONCEPTS: impetuous employee

IMPETUS, noun actuation, boost, call, drive, encouragement, energy, force, goad, impellent, impelling force, impulse, impulsion, incentive, influence, instigation, jog, jolt, kick, momentum, motive, moving force, pressure, propellant, propulsion, propulsive force, purpose, push, reason, shove, spur, start, stimulus, thrust, urge, vis

IMPIETY, noun apostasy, backsliding, desecration, disregard, disrespect, iniquity, irreligion, irreverence, malediction, noncomformity, offense, profaneness, profanity, recusancy, reprobation, sacrilege, sacrilegiousness, sinfulness, transgression, undutifulness, unrighteousness, unspirituality, violation, wickedness

IMPINGE, verb advance upon, aggress, attack, bang, barge in, break bounds, break in on, bump, butt against, collide, come into collision, contact, dash against, encroach, entrench on, fall against, foray, force oneself in, hit, *impingi,* impose, *incidere,* infringe, interlope, intrude, invade, knock, knock against, make impact, make inroads, obtrude, overrun, overstep, overstep boundaries, pommel, raid, run into, strike, tap, thrust, touch, transgress established bounds, trench upon, trespass, violate

IMPIOUS, adjective amoral, blasphemous, desecrative, diabolic, heretical, immoral, iniquitous, irreligious, irreverent, nefarious, offensive, peccant, perverted, profane, recusant, reprobate, sacrilegious, satanic, sinful, sinister, undevout, undutiful, unethical, ungodly, unrighteous
FOREIGN PHRASES: Impius et crudelis judicandus est qui libertati non favet. He is judged to be impious and cruel who does not favor liberty.

IMPLACABLE, adjective adamant, immovable, *implacabilis, inexorabilis,* inexorable, inexpiable, inflexible, intransigent, irreconcilable, obdurate, obstinate, pitiless, relentless, unappeasable, unbending, uncompromising, unforgiving, unpacifiable, unpropitiating, unrelenting, unyielding, vindictive

IMPLANTED, adjective deep-rooted, deep-seated, embedded, engraved, entrenched, established, etched, impressed, inculcated, indoctrinated, ingrained, injected, well-established, well-founded

IMPLAUSIBLE, adjective beyond belief, contrary to experience, doubtable, doubtful, dubitable, hard to believe, hardly possible, improbable, inconceivable, incredible, open to doubt, open to suspicion, questionable, suspicious, unbelievable, unconvincing, unheard of, unimaginable, unlikely, unsubstantiated, untenable, unthinkable

IMPLEAD, verb add as a third party, bring in as a third party, commence proceedings against a third party, *in ius vocare,* institute an action against a third party, join as a third party, make one a third party, plead a cause against a third party, sue a third party
ASSOCIATED CONCEPTS: counterclaim, crossclaim, third party defendant, third party plaintiff, third party practice

IMPLEMENT, verb accomplish, achieve, actualize, bring about, bring off, bring to pass, carry into effect, carry into execution, carry out, carry through, complete, consummate, discharge, do, effect, effectuate, enact, enforce, execute, fulfill, give force to, give validity to, make a reality, make active, make valid, perform, provide the means, put in force, put in practice, put into effect, realize, see through, set in motion, succeed, take action, work out
ASSOCIATED CONCEPTS: implement the agreement of the parties, implement the order of the court

IMPLEMENTATION, noun accomplishment, achievement, act, action, attainment, commission, consummation, course, discharge, effectuation, enforcement, execution, *fait accompli,* finality, fruition, fulfillment, instrumentation, means, mechanism, method, performance, procedures, production, realization, result, rules, upshot

IMPLICATE, verb accuse, *admiscere,* allege to be guilty, associate, brand, bring into connection with, charge, connect, criminate, delate, denounce, draw in, embroil, engage, enmesh, entangle, expose, hold responsible, *implicare,* impute, include, incriminate, inculpate, infer, inform against, *inligare,* interlace, intertwine, involve, link, lodge a complaint, make a party to, point to, suggest, tangle
ASSOCIATED CONCEPTS: implicate a codefendant, implicate an accomplice, implicate in a crime

IMPLICATION (Incriminating involvement), noun complicity, connection, crimination, culpability, enmeshment, entanglement, inculpation, link
ASSOCIATED CONCEPTS: implication of a codefendant

IMPLICATION (Inference), noun allusion, broad meaning, coloring, connotation, hidden meaning, hint, import, indication, innuendo, insinuation, intimation, overtone, signification, suggested meaning, suggestion, tacit inference
ASSOCIATED CONCEPTS: easement by implication, gift by implication, grant by implication, necessary implication
FOREIGN PHRASES: Omissio eorum quae tacite insunt nihil operatur. The omission of those things which are tacitly expressed is unimportant.

IMPLICATIVE, adjective allusive, assumed, circumstantial, hinting, implicational, implicatory, incriminatory, inculpatory, indicative, inferential, inferring, leading, presumed, provocative, provoking, referential, suggestive, supposed

IMPLICIT, adjective absolute, allusive, basic, implied, implied rather than expressly stated, inherent, innate, intrinsic, not declared openly, not expressed, not plainly apparent, suggested, suggestive, tacit, *tacitus*, understood, unexpressed, unpronounced, unsaid, unspoken, unvoiced
ASSOCIATED CONCEPTS: implicit in the facts of a case, implicit powers

IMPLIED, adjective alluded to, allusive, assumed, connoted, expressed indirectly, implicit, indicated, inferential, inferred, insinuated, meant, signified, suggested, tacit, undeclared, understood, unspoken
ASSOCIATED CONCEPTS: implied acceptance, implied acquiescence, implied admission, implied agency, implied agreement, implied authority, implied contract, implied covenant, implied dedication, implied malice, implied notice, implied powers, implied promise, implied ratification, implied trust, implied warranty

IMPLODE, verb bankrupt, blow-up, cave, cave in, close, collapse, deflate, decommissioned, disintegrate, dismantled, end, ended abruptly, fold, fold up, terminate

IMPLORE, verb appeal to, beseech, besiege, call, call upon, entreat, evoke, exhort, importune, invoke, obsecrate, obtest, petition, plead, pray, press, pressure, request, solicit, solicitate, supplicate, urge

IMPLY, verb advert, allude to, carry a suggestion, connote, denote, drop a hint, give a hint, give indirect information, hint at, include by implication, *indicare*, indicate, indirectly state, infer, insinuate, intimate, involve, leave an inference, make an allusion to, point to, show indirectly, *significare*, state in nonexplicit terms, suggest, whisper
ASSOCIATED CONCEPTS: implied acceptance, implied agency, implied authority, implied consent, implied contract, implied dedication, implied easement, implied in law, implied knowledge, implied license, implied malice, implied notice, implied permission, implied power, implied promise, implied ratification, implied trust, implied warranty
FOREIGN PHRASES: *In omnibus contractibus, sive nominatis sive innominatis, permutatio continetur.* In all contracts, whether nominate or innominate, there is implied an exchange. *Expressio eorum quae tacite insunt nihil operatur.* The expression of those things which are tacitly implied has no effect.

IMPOLITIC, adjective careless, foolish, harebrained, hasty, headlong, heedless, ill-advised, ill-considered, ill-judged, *imprudens*, imprudent, inadvisable, incautious, inconsiderate, *inconsultus*, indiscreet, inexpedient, injudicious, rash, reckless, senseless, stupid, temerarious, thoughtless, undiplomatic, unreasonable, unsensible, unsound, untactful, unthinking, unwary, unwise

IMPONDERABLE, adjective immaterial, immateriate, impalpable, imponderous, impossible to calculate, impossible to measure, impossible to weigh, incalculable, incapable of being evaluated, incomputable, inestimable, intangible, subtile, unsubstantial, unweighable, vague

IMPORT, noun connotation, consequence, drift, essence, gist, gravity, idea, importance, matter, meaning, meaningfulness, moment, pith, point, purport, sense, seriousness, significance, *significatio*, signification, substance, sum, tenor, *vis*, weight, weightiness

IMPORTANCE, noun concern, concernment, consequence, distinction, eminence, emphasis, essentiality, fame, grandeur, gravity, greatness, import, influence, irreplaceability, magnitude, mark, materiality, materialness, memorability, memorableness, merit, moment, momentousness, *momentum*, notability, note, noteworthiness, outstanding quality, paramountcy, *pondus*, precedence, prestige, primacy, priority, prominence, relevance, repute, salience, seriousness, significance, solemnity, substance, substantiality, superiority, supremacy, urgency, usefulness, value, *vis*, weight, weightiness

IMPORTANT (Significant), **adjective** big, capital, chief, commanding, consequential, considerable, crucial, dignified, distinguished, esteemed, famous, far-reaching, first, foremost, formidable, grand, grave, *gravis*, high-level, illustrious, imposing, impressive, influential, leading, *magnus*, main, majestic, major, marked, material, mattering much, memorable, mighty, momentous, notable, noteworthy, of great consequence, of great magnitude, of great weight, of high standing, of high station, of importance, outstanding, overshadowing, paramount, portentous, powerful, preeminent, primary, prime, principal, prominent, relevant, remarkable, salient, serious, signal, solemn, substantial, superior, supreme, valuable, weighty, well-known

IMPORTANT (Urgent), **adjective** acute, called for, clamant, clamorous, cogent, compelling, critical, crucial, crying, demanding attention, driving, essential, exigent, high-priority, impelling, imperative, importunate, in demand, indispensable, inescapable, instant, necessary, necessitous, needed, prerequisite, pressing, requested, required, requisite, unavoidable, vital, wanted

IMPORTUNE, verb adjure, appeal, apply to, ask urgently, badger, beg, beseech, beset, besiege, bother, cajole, call upon, clamor for, coax, cry to, demand, dun, entreat persistently, *fatigare*, harass, hound, impetrate, implore, insist, inveigle, make bold to ask, nag, obsecrate, obtest, pester, petition, plague, plead, ply, pray, press, press by entreaty, push, *rem hominem flagitare*, request, requisition, solicit, solicit earnestly, solicit insistently, sue, supplicate, urge

IMPOSE (Enforce), **verb** bid, bind, burden, charge, coerce, command, compel, conscript, constrain, decree, demand, dictate, direct, drive, enact, encumber, enjoin, exact, execute, extort, force upon, impel, *imponere, iniungere*, insist upon, lay upon, leave no option, make, make obligatory, necessitate, oblige, obtain by force, ordain, order, prescribe, press, put in force, require, require compliance, tax
ASSOCIATED CONCEPTS: impose by law

IMPOSE (Intrude), **verb** encroach, enter unlawfully, entrench, force an entrance, force oneself in, impose, infringe, insinuate, intercede, interfere, interlope, interpose, intervene, invade, obtrude, overreach, overstep, poach, thrust oneself in, transgress, trespass, violate

IMPOSE (Subject), **verb** bring under rule, coerce, compel, constrain, control, domineer, effect, enslave, force, make submissive, master, oblige, overcome, require, subdue, subject to authority, subject to control, subject to dependence, subject to influence, subjugate, subordinate

IMPOSE A PENALTY, verb bring to account, discipline, exact a penalty, execute a sentence, fine, inflict punishment, levy, penalize, punish, rebuke, reprimand, subject to penalty, subject to punishment
ASSOCIATED CONCEPTS: judgment, sentence

IMPOSITION (Excessive burden), **noun** encroachment, encumbrance, excessive demand, extraordinarily burdensome requirement, hindrance, impediment, infliction, infringement, interference, onus, unjust burden, unjust requirement

IMPOSITION (Tax), **noun** charge, duty, excise, levy, penalty, tariff, toll

IMPOSSIBILITY, noun difficulty, failure, futility, hopelessness, impossibleness, impracticability, impracticality, inaccessibility, inconceivability, infeasibility, inoperability, insuperability, insuperableness, insurmountability, lack of possibility, lack of potentiality, unachievability, unattainability, unfeasibility, unattainable, unavailability, unobtainability, unobtainableness, unperformability, unpracticability, unthinkability, unworkability
ASSOCIATED CONCEPTS: frustration of purpose, impossibility of performance, legal impossibility, rescission, supervening impossibility
FOREIGN PHRASES: *Lex non intendit aliquid impossibile.* The law does not intend anything impossible. *Lex non cogit ad impossibilia.* The law does not require the performance of the impossible. *Impotentia excusat legem.* The impossibility of performing a legal duty excuses from the performance. *A l'impossible nul n'est tenu.* No one is bound to do what is impossible. *Argumentum ab impossibili valet in lege.* The argument from impossibility is of great force in law. *Impossibilium nulla obligatio est.* One cannot be obliged to perform impossible tasks.

IMPOSSIBLE, adjective absurd, contrary to reason, hopeless, impassable, impracticable, improbable, inaccessible, incapable of being done, incapable of existing, incapable of happening, inconceivable, incredible, infeasible, innavigable, insuperable, insurmountable, *nullo modo fieri potest,* out of the question, paradoxical, preposterous, *quod fieri non potest,* self-contradictory, unachievable, unattainable, unbelievable, unfeasible, unimaginable, unlikely, unmanageable, unobtainable, unreasonable, unthinkable, unworkable, unyielding, visionary

IMPOSTURE, noun cheat, chicane, counterfeit, craft, cunning, deceit, deception, dodge, duplicity, fake, *fallacia,* false conduct, forgery, fraud, fraudulence, *fraus,* guile, hoax, hollow pretense, imitation, knavery, pretense, ruse, sham, sleight, subterfuge, swindle, swindling, trap, trick, trickery, wile

IMPOTENCE, noun debilitation, debility, defenselessness, failure, feebleness, forcelessness, helplessness, *imbecillitas,* impotency, impuissance, inability, inadequacy, incapability, incapacitation, incapacity, incompetence, incompetency, ineffectiveness, ineffectuality, ineffectualness, inefficaciousness, inefficacy, inefficiency, ineptitude, *infirmitas,* insufficiency, lack of power, lack of strength, powerlessness, strengthlessness, unfitness, weakness

IMPOTENT, adjective barren, disabled, inadequate, ineffective, inept, infertile, innocuous, powerless, spent, sterile, unproductive, unprofitable, unsuccessful, useless, vain, valueless, weak, without power, worthless

IMPOUND, verb appropriate, attach, confiscate, deprive of, distrain, hold in legal custody, remove, retain in custody, seize, sequester, sequestrate, take, take into custody, take into legal custody, take over, take possession of
ASSOCIATED CONCEPTS: impounding a jury, impounding property

IMPRACTICABLE, adjective beyond control, difficult, hard to deal with, hopeless, impassable, impossible, impractical, inapplicable, incapable of being accomplished, inconceivable, inoperable, insuperable, insurmountable, out of the question, *quod fiere non potest,* thorny, too hard, unachievable, undoable, unemployable, unfeasible, unfunctional, unhandy, unmanageable, unperformable, unrealizable, unreasonable, unserviceable, unsuitable for practical use, unusable, unviable, unwieldy, unworkable, useless

IMPRECATION, noun abuse, anathema, aspersion, bad wishes, blasphemy, commination, curse, damnation, denunciation, execration, expletive, *exsecratio,* foul language, fulmination, ill wishes, invocation of evil, malediction, malison, objuration, obsecration, *preces,* profanity, swearing, vilification, vindictive oath, vituperation

IMPRESS (Affect deeply), **verb** absorb, amaze, arouse, astound, awe, electrify, galvanize, have a strong effect, hit, influence, inspire, intrigue, make an impact upon, make an impression on, move, move strongly, *movere,* penetrate, pierce, reach, rouse, smite, stir, strike, strike hard, strike home, stun, touch

IMPRESS (Procure by force), **verb** acquire, appropriate, arrogate, attach, deprive, disentitle, disseise, expropriate, garnish, impound, impropriate, levy, seize, sequester, sequestrate, take, take possession of

IMPRESSION, noun *animi motus,* apprehension, belief, concept, conception, consciousness, consideration, effect, feeling, general notion, guiding conception, image, image in the mind, impact, imprint, indirect influence, influence, inward perception, mark, mental attitude, mental image, mental view, notion, *opinio,* opinion, organizing conception, outward perception, perception, print, *putare,* reaction, reflection, remembrance, response, sensation, sense, sense perception, sensory perception, subconscious perception, trace, visible effect
ASSOCIATED CONCEPTS: case of first impression, impression on the minds of the jurors

IMPRESSIVE, adjective absorbing, assuring, awe-inspiring, commanding, considerable, electrifying, eloquent, enthusiastic, exciting, fervent, formidable, grand, important, imposing, influential, magnificent, majestic, major, memorable, momentous, moving, notable, noteworthy, outstanding, overpowering, paramount, persuasive, pervading, potent, prodigious, profound, prominent, proud, rapturous, remarkable, sapid, satisfactory, satisfying, sensational, solemn, spectacular, stellar, striking, strong, telling, weighty

IMPRISON, verb bring into custody, cast into prison, circumscribe, commit to an institution, commit to prison, confine, constrain, deprive of freedom of movement, deprive of liberty, detain, detain in custody, enclose, entomb, hold captive, hold in captivity, hold in restraint, immure, *in carcerem, in custodiam,* incarcerate, *includere,* intern, jail, keep as captive, keep behind bars, keep in captivity, keep in custody, keep in detention, keep under arrest, lock in, lock up, mew, place in confinement, put behind bars, put in a cell, put in irons, put into a cage, put under lock and key, put under restraint, refuse bail, restrain, send to jail, send to prison

ASSOCIATED CONCEPTS: false imprisonment, habeas corpus, imprison at hard work, imprison for a term of years, parole, term of imprisonment

IMPRISONMENT, noun commitment to an institution, commitment to prison, confinement, custody, detainment, detainment in custody, held in captivity, held in restraint, in captivity, in custody, in jail, incarceration, internment, keep behind bars, kept as captive, kept in captivity, kept in custody, kept in detention, kept under arrest, locked up, put behind bars, put in a cell, put under restraint, sent to jail, sent to prison

ASSOCIATED CONCEPTS: false imprisonment, habeas corpus

IMPROBABILITY, noun bare possibility, doubt, doubtfulness, implausibility, impossibility, inexpectation, infrequency, little chance, long odds, non verisimilis, nonexpectation, poor chance, poor prospect, questionability, rare occurrence, rarity, small chance, small hope, uncertainty, unlikelihood, unlikeliness

ASSOCIATED CONCEPTS: inherently improbable evidence, inherently improbable testimony

IMPROBABLE, adjective a distant chance, barely a possibility, defying logic, doubtful, dubious, hardly possible, implausible, little chance, little hope, little likelihood, long odds, not likely, not likely to occur, not probable, poor chance, poor prospect, questionable, rare, remote possibility, uncertainty, unexpected, unlikelihood, unlikely

IMPROBITY, noun artfulness, breach of trust, corruption, craftiness, crookedness, deceit, deceitfulness, deviousness, dishonesty, disingenuity, disingenuousness, duplic-ity, falsehood, falseness, falsity, fraud, fraudulence, fraudulency, furtiveness, graft, guile, indirection, insidiousness, insincerity, inveracity, jobbery, knavery, lack of conscience, lack of integrity, lack of principle, lying, mendaciousness, mendacity, obliquity, rascality, roguery, shadiness, surreptitiousness, treacherousness, trickiness, truthlessness, undependability, underhandedness, unreliability, unscrupulousness, unstraightforwardness, untrustworthiness, untruthfulness

IMPROMPTU, adjective ad-lib, extemporaneous, extemporary, extemporized, immediate, improvised, makeshift, not arranged, not planned, offhand, off-the-cuff, spontaneous, spur-of the-moment, unprompted, unrehearsed

IMPROPER, adjective amiss, awkward, contrary to decency, contrary to good taste, discordant, discrepant, erroneous, false, forbidden, gross, ill-adapted, ill-founded, ill-timed, illicit, illogical, immodest, immoral, inaccurate, inadmissible, inapplicable, inapposite, inappropriate, inapt, incongruous, incorrect, indecent, indecorous, indecorus, indelicate, indignus, inept, inexact, infelicitous, inharmonious, inopportune, irrelevant, mistaken, naughty, not pertinent, not right, not suitable, objectionable, off-color, off the mark, out of place, prohibited, risque, unadapted, unallowable, unauthorized, unbecoming, unbefitting, uncharacteristic, undesirable, undue, unfit, unfitting, unmeet, unreasonable, unrefined, unseasonable, unseemly, unsound, unsuitable, unsuited, untimely, unwarrantable, wide of the mark, wrong, wrongful

ASSOCIATED CONCEPTS: improper act, improper conduct, improper discharge, improper influence, improper joinder of

actions, improper motive, improper performance, improper practice, improper use

IMPROPER VENUE, noun improper court location, improper location, incorrect court location, incorrect location, not suitable location, unauthorized location, unsuitable location, wrong judicial location

ASSOCIATED CONCEPTS: local venue, waiver of venue

IMPROPRIATE, verb accroach, adopt, annex, apply to one's own uses, appropriate, arrogate, assume, assume ownership, avail oneself of, bear away, carry away, claim, claim unduly, confer ownership on oneself, convert, disseise, embezzle, employ, help oneself to, lay hold of, make one's own, make use of, misappropriate, peculate, pirate, possess, purloin, rob, seize, steal, take as one's own, take for oneself, take over, take possession of, take to oneself, thieve, use, usurp

IMPROPRIETY, noun bad taste, improper action, improper behavior, imprudence, inappropriate behavior, inappropriateness, incongruousness, incorrectness, indecency, indecorousness, indecorum, indelicacy, indiscretion, inelegance, inexpedience, inexpediency, inopportuneness, lack of good taste, misbehavior, peccadillo, quod indecorum est, tactlessness, unaptness, unfitness, unfittingness, unseemliness, unsuitability, unsuitable action, unsuitableness, untimeliness, want of caution, want of circumspection

ASSOCIATED CONCEPTS: crime, violation

IMPROVE, verb advance, ameliorate, amend, appreciate, beautify, correct, cultivate, cure, develop, doctor, edify, edit, elaborate, elevate, embellish, emend, enhance, ennoble, enrich, fix, flourish, gain, gain strength, heighten, help, increase, modernize, modify, mollify, nurture, perfect, progress, promote, prosper, rectify, recuperate, redeem, redress, refine, reform, rehabilitate, relieve, remedy, repair, restore, retouch, revise, supplement

IMPROVEMENT, noun amelioration, betterment, change for the better, melioration, recovery, rehabilitation

ASSOCIATED CONCEPTS: improvement bond, improvement district

IMPROVIDENT, adjective brash, careless, dissipated, extravagant, happy-go-lucky, hasty, headlong, heedless, improvidus, imprudens, imprudent, impulsive, incautious, incautus, indiscreet, injudicious, lacking foresight, lax, losel, neglectful, negligent, prodigal, profligate, rash, reckless, remiss, shiftless, spendthrift, squandering, temerarious, thoughtless, thriftless, uneconomical, unfrugal, unguarded, unpreparing, unproviding, unthrifty, unwary, wasteful, without foresight

IMPROVISE, verb adept, ad-lib, compose, concoct, create, devise, extemporize, fabricate, invent, invent offhand, make up, originate, play by ear, ride with the waves, utilize, without preparation

IMPRUDENCE, noun blunder, carelessness, heedlessness, impetuosity, impolicy, improvidence, inadvisability, incautiousness, inconsiderateness, inconsideration, indiscreetness, indiscretion, injudiciousness, irrationality, irresponsibility, neglect, negligence, recklessness, senselessness, temerity, thoughtlessness, unreasonableness, unwiseness, witlessness

ASSOCIATED CONCEPTS: imprudent act, imprudent advice

IMPRUDENT, adjective adventurous, brash, careless, foolhardy, foolish, hasty, hazardous, heedless, hot-headed, ill-advised, ill-considered, ill-judged, impolitic, improvident, impulsive, inadvisable, incautious, inconsiderate, *inconsultus,* indiscreet, inexpedient, injudicious, inopportune, lacking caution, lacking judgment, lacking prudence, neglectful, overhasty, precipitate, rash, reckless, short-sighted, temerarious, *temerarius,* thoughtless, unadvised, uncalculated, uncircumspect, undesirable, unguarded, unwary, unwise, venturesome, venturous, wanting discretion, wanton

ASSOCIATED CONCEPTS: negligence

IMPUDENCE, noun arrogance, audacity, boldness, brashness, brazenness, contempt, defiance, disdain, disregard, disrespect, disrespectfulness, effrontery, flippancy, forwardness, gall, impertinence, insolence, nerve, overbearance, pertness, rudeness, temerity

IMPUGN, verb assail, assail by argument, attack, attack by words, be skeptical, call in question, cast doubt, cast reflection upon, challenge as false, confute, contest, contradict, controvert, criticize, denounce, disbelieve, discredit, disprove, dispute, doubt the truth of, find fault with, impeach, *improbare, impugnare,* inveigh against, involve in suspicion, negate, oppose, oppose as false, *oppugnare,* overcome by argument, query, question, raise a hue and cry against, raise a question as to, raise one's voice against, raise questions, rebut, refuse credence, refute, render suspect, take issue with, throw doubt upon, undermine one's belief

ASSOCIATED CONCEPTS: defamation, impugn the integrity of a witness

IMPUGN A WITNESS, verb assail, attack, call in question, cast doubt, cast doubt on testimony of a witness, cast doubt on the integrity of a witness, challenge, confute, contest, contradict, controvert, criticize, denounce, discredit, disprove, dispute, find fault with, impeach, involve in suspicion, oppose as false, question a witness, raise questions regarding the integrity of a witness, rebut, refute, reveal, undermine confidence in a witness, undermine the credibility of

ASSOCIATED CONCEPTS: discrepancies, impeachment, impugn a witness's competency or credibility, rules of evidence

IMPUGNATION, noun adverse comment, adverse criticism, animadversion, antagonism, attack, censure, challenge, condemnation, conflict, confrontation, contradiction, contrariety, contrariness, contravention, counteraction, counterwork, criticism, decrial, defiance, difference, disagreement, disapprobation, disapproval, discord, disfavor, disputation, dispute, dissent, faultfinding, gravamen, grievance, hostile attack, hostility, impugnment, lack of harmony, nonacceptance, nonagreement, noncompliance, nonconsent, noncooperation, obstruction, opposition, oppugnancy, protest, protestation, rejection, reprehension, reprobation, repudiation, resistance, rivalry, traversal, want of harmony

IMPUISSANCE, noun caducity, debility, decrepitude, disability, disablement, exhaustion, failure, feebleness, frailty, helplessness, impotence, inability, inaptitude, incapability, incapacity, incompetence, inefficacy, inefficiency, ineptitude, infirmity, invalidity, lack of force, lack of might, lack of power, lack of strength, lack of vigor, powerlessness, prostration, strengthlessness, weakness

IMPULSE, noun actuation, drive, encouragement, impelling force, *impetus, impulsio,* impulsion, *impulsus,* incentive, motivation, motive, pressure, push, spontaneity, spontaneous inclination, stimulant, sudden desire, sudden force, thrust

ASSOCIATED CONCEPTS: heat of passion, impulsive acts, irresistible impulse, uncontrollable impulse

IMPULSIVE *(Impelling),* **adjective** activating, actuating, animating, compelling, driving, dynamic, dynamical, energizing, impellent, kinetic, moving, prompting, propulsive, pushing, stimulating, urging

IMPULSIVE *(Rash),* **adjective** abrupt, adventurous, bold, breakneck, careless, daring, emotional, extemporaneous, extemporary, foolhardy, hasty, heedless, hotheaded, hurried, ill-considered, impetuous, impromptu, improvised, imprudent, incautious, indeliberate, injudicious, offhand, passionate, precipitant, precipitate, precipitous, quick, rapid, reckless, risk-taking, risky, snap, spontaneous, sudden, swift, temerarious, thoughtless, unadvised, unanticipated, uncalculating, unchary, uncircumspect, unconsidered, uncontrolled, unexpected, unmindful, unpremeditated, unprepared, unprompted, unthinking, venturesome, venturous, without prudence, without thought

IMPUNITY, noun absolution, acquittal, amnesty, condonation, dispensation, escape, exemption, exemption from judgment, exemption from penalty, exemption from punishment, freedom, freedom from judgment, freedom from penalty, freedom from punishment, immunity, *impunitas,* liberation, license, nonliability, nonprosecution, pardon, prerogative, privilege, protection, reprieve

IMPURE *(Adulterated),* **adjective** alloyed, contaminated, degraded, diluted, hybrid, mixed, perverted, polluted, sullied, tainted, tampered with, unclean, unrefined, watered down

IMPURE *(Debased),* **verb** amoral, base, contaminated, defiled, degenerate, degraded, depraved, immodest, immoral, improper, indecent, lascivious, licentious, passionate, poisoned, profligate, promiscuous, shameless, sinful, sullied, unchaste

IMPUTATION, noun abuse, accusal, accusation, adverse criticism, allegation, animadversion, arrogation, ascription, aspersion, attaint, attribution, blame, brand, calumny, censure, challenge, charge, condemnation, criticism, defamation, denouncement, detraction, disapprobation, discredit, disgrace, dishonor, disparagement, disrepute, exprobration, fault-finding, ignominy, ignomy, incrimination, inculpation, insinuation, obloquy, onus, opprobrium, reference, reproach, slur, stain, stigma, stigmatization, stricture, traducement, vilification

ASSOCIATED CONCEPTS: imputation of a crime, imputation of negligence, imputation of payment

IMPUTE, verb *adsignare,* apply, ascribe, *ascribere,* assign, attach, *attribuere,* attribute, attribute vicariously, blame, charge to, charge upon, credit, fix the burden of, fix the responsibility for, fix upon, place the blame on, place the responsibility for, put

ASSOCIATED CONCEPTS: imputed consent, imputed guilt, imputed intent, imputed knowledge, imputed liability, imputed negligence, imputed notice

IN ACCORDANCE WITH, adjective accordant, affiliated, affinitive, allied, applicable, apposite, appropriate, appurtenant, apropos, apt

ASSOCIATED CONCEPTS: bearing upon, befitting, belonging to, cognate, comparable, congeneric, congruous, connected, correspondent, germane, in conjunction with, pertinent, pursuant to, relevant, with reference to

IN ADDITION, *adverb* added to, additionally, also, as well, besides, furthermore, moreover, over and above, plus, taken together with, then again, then too, too
ASSOCIATED CONCEPTS: alternative relief

IN AGREEMENT, *adjective* affirmed, approved, arranged, assented, assured, attested, avowed, committed, concurred, confirmed, consented, contracted, covenanted, declared, endorsed, guaranteed, having a meeting of the minds, in consonance with, pledged, promised, stipulated, subscribed, sworn, understood, undertaken, warranted

IN ALL LIKELIHOOD, *preposition* apparently, conceivably, expectedly, feasibly, for the most part, indubitably, likely, logically, ostensibly, plausibly, possibly, practicably, predominately, presumably, presumptively, promisingly, reasonably, seemingly, supposedly, unquestionably, with considerable certainty, with direct certainty, with realistic certainty

IN ALL RESPECTS, *preposition* absolutely, all-comprehensively, all-inclusively, broad-based, capaciously, comprehensively, consummately, developed, encyclopedically, entirely, exhaustively, expansively, extensively, fully, globally, in all regards, inclusively, overall, sweepingly, thoroughly, totally, unconditionally, undividedly, universally, unreduced, utterly, very thoroughly, with every aspect considered, with no exception, without omissions,
ASSOCIATED CONCEPTS: inadequate in all respects, insufficient in all respects

IN BETWEEN, *adjective* affiliated with, allying with, amid, amidst, among, around, associating with, at intervals, between, bounded by, centrally located, coached in between, enclosed by, halfway, halfway from both, in the middle, in the middle of, in the midst of, inserted between, intermediate to, intervening, linking, located in the area of, located in the proximity of, lodged between, mid, midst, midway, nestled between, situated between, within
ASSOCIATED CONCEPTS: distinctions in law

IN CAMERA, *noun* confidential, confidentially, in antechambers, in chambers, in judge's chamber, in judicial chamber, in private, in secrecy, out of public view

IN CONCLUSION, *adverb* as a completion, as closure, as the finale, as the outcome, finally, at the outgrowth, in closing, in consequence, in culmination, in ending, in finishing, in fulfillment, in the final result, lastly, the result, the upshot is
ASSOCIATED CONCEPTS: conclusion to a memorandum, summation to the jury

IN CONSPIRACY WITH, *preposition* abet with, act in combination with, act in concert with, act in harmony with, agree with, aid with, associate with, be banded together with, collude with, combine for some evil design with, combine operations with, combine with, concert with, concoct a plot with, conjoin with, connive with, contrive with, cooperate with, design with, devise treachery with, devise with, form a coalition with, form a plot with, in complicity with, join forces with, join with, participate for an unlawful purpose with, plan a crime with, plan secretly with, plan to commit a crime, plan to perform an unlawful act with, plan with, plot an action in advance with, plot craftily with, plot together with, plot with, scheme with, take part with
ASSOCIATED CONCEPTS: conspiracy theory

IN CUSTODY, *adverb* behind bars, captive, confined, detained, held, imprisoned, in prison, incarcerated, jailed, kept in prison, maintained in prison, under arrest, under lock and key

IN DUE COURSE, *adverb* eventually, in good time, in the long run, in time, presently, shortly, soon, ultimately

IN EXTREMIS, *adjective* approaching death, at one's end, at the conclusion of life, at the last stage, at the point of death, at the termination of life, during the last moments of life, dying, expiring, in one's last moments, in the final moments of life, in the jaws of death, moribund, near death, near one's end, on one's deathbed, passing away, terminally ill, under a sense of impending death
ASSOCIATED CONCEPTS: dying declaration, gift causa mortis

IN FULL FORCE, *adjective* functioning, high powered, in full effect, mighty, omnipotent, operating, overpowering, potent, puissant, strong, with full effect, with full force

IN FULL GEAR, *adjective* act on, all out, as fast as possible, at full speed, at full throttle, commence, continued at maximum, flow, following at full throttle, forging ahead, gathering steam, get in high gear, going forward, in high gear, making headway, making progress, maximum strength, moving ahead, pressing on, progressing, pushing on, rolling on, springing from, streaming

IN FURTHERANCE, *preposition* for, for the sake of, in favor of, in the name of, in the service of, on account of, on behalf of

IN GENERAL, *adverb* accepted, average, broad, common to many, customary, extensive, generally, habitual, in common, inclusive, most of the time, overall, popular, prevailing, prevalent, representative, sweeping traditionally, typical, universal, usually, widespread
ASSOCIATED CONCEPTS: summation before a jury

IN GOOD FAITH, *adverb* bona fide, constantly, devotedly, fairly, faithfully, honestly, legitimately, steadily, truly
ASSOCIATED CONCEPTS: good faith effort, presented in good faith, written in good faith

IN HARMONY, *adjective* accordant, adapted, agreeing, alike, appropriate, apt, arranged, at one with, attuned, balanced, becoming, coincident, commensurate, compatible, concerted, concordant, concurrent, conformable, conforming, congruent, congruous, consentient, consistent, cooperating, correspondent, corresponding, equable, equal, fit, fitting, harmonious, in accord, in agreement, in concert, in tandem with, in unison, parallel, related, similar, suitable, synchronized, unchanged, unchanging, undeviating, unified, uniform
ASSOCIATED CONCEPTS: conspiracy, contractual obligations

IN HARMONY WITH, *preposition* accordant with, agreeing with, alike with, at one with, attuned to, balanced with, coincident with, commensurate with, compatible with, concerted with, concordant to, concurrent with, conforming to, congruent with, congruous with, consistent with, cooperating with, correspondent with, corresponding

to, equably with, equally with, fitting with, harmoniously with, in accordance with, in agreement with, in concord with, in rapport with, in unison with, logically consistent with, parallel with, reconcilably, related to, similarly with, suitably with, uniformly with
ASSOCIATED CONCEPTS: co-conspirators

IN LIEU OF, *preposition* as a substitute for, as an alternative, as proxy for, by proxy, for, in place of, instead of, on behalf of, rather than, representing
ASSOCIATED CONCEPTS: in lieu of payment

IN LIGHT OF, *preposition* because of, by way of explanation, considering, even considering, in consideration of, in view of, taken in relation to, taken together with, taken with regard to, to clarify, to clear up, to simplify, with knowledge of, with regard to, with specific reference to
ASSOCIATED CONCEPTS: in light of precedence, in light of the circumstances

IN PART, *adverb* in installments, in some measure, incompletely, not wholly, partially, partly, somewhat, to a certain extent, to a degree, to a limited extent

IN PERSON, *adverb* bodily, in one's own person, individually, personally, privately

IN SOLIDO, *noun* aggregate, each and every, in whole, joint and several, one and all, sum total, the entirety, total, totality

IN STRICT CONFORMITY, *adverb* in accordance with, in keeping with, in line with, in obedience with, in strict compliance with, predominantly the same

IN TERROREM, *adjective* alarmed, apprehensive, concerned, filled with anxiety, fraught with apprehension, frightened, horrified, in a state of anxiety, in fear, intimidated, mortified, scared, timorous, uneasy, with an apprehension of danger, with an apprehension of harm, with an apprehension of injury, with an apprehension of punishment, with consternation, with fright, with panic, with timidity, with trepidation
ASSOCIATED CONCEPTS: *in terrorem* clauses, *in terrorem* letters

IN THE HEAT OF, *verb* during extreme emotion, in the emotion of, in the excitement of, in the fervor of, in the fury of, in the passion of, while caught-up in emotion, while caught-up in the moment, while excited, while extremely emotional, while overcome with emotion, while passionately involved, without thinking
ASSOCIATED CONCEPTS: in the heat of the commission of a crime

IN TOTO, *adverb* absolutely, all in all, altogether, as a whole, collectively, completely, comprehensively, entirely, fully, in all, in all respects, in full, in its entirety, in the aggregate, in the whole, *omnino*, on all counts, *plane, prorsus*, thoroughly, totally, unabridgedly, unanimously, undividedly, unreservedly, utterly, wholly, without omission

IN TRUST, *adverb* held in pledge, held in trust, in escrow, under fiduciary control

IN WRITING, *adverb* expressed in writing, in black and white, on paper, recorded, reduced to a writing, scriptory, stated in a writing, stated in writing

INABILITY, *noun* disability, disablement, disqualification, failure, helplessness, impotence, impuissance, inadequacy, incapability, incapacitation, incapacity, incompetence, incompetency, ineffectualness, inefficacy, inefficiency, ineptitude, ineptness, *infirmitas,* infirmity, *inopia,* insufficiency, lack of ability, lack of competence, lack of power, powerlessness, shortcoming, undeftness, unfitness, unproficiency, unskillfulness, want of ability, want of capacity, want of power, want of skill
ASSOCIATED CONCEPTS: inability to meet an obligation, inability to pay a debt as it matures, inability to pay arrears, inability to work

INABILITY, *adjective* defect, disability, disablement, failure, feebleness, frailty, handicap, helplessness, inadequacy, inaptitude, inaptness, incapability, incapableness, incapacitation, incapacity, incompetence, incompetency incomprehension, ineligibility, ineptitude, ineptness, infirmity, insufficiency, lack of ability, shortcoming, unfitness, unsuitability, unsuitableness
ASSOCIATED CONCEPTS: disability and inability to serve under the Twenty-Fifth Amendment

INACCESSIBLE, *adjective* beyond reach, distant, elusive, far, far away, far off, impossible to reach, *inaccessus,* inapproachable, out of reach, out of touch, *rari aditus,* remote, removed, separated, unaccessible, unachievable, unacquirable, unapproachable, unattainable, unavailable, unobtainable, unprocurable, unreachable, unrealizable, unsecurable
ASSOCIATED CONCEPTS: inaccessibility of property, inaccessible to service of process, inaccessible witness

INACCURACY, *noun* aberration, blunder, canard, deception, delusion, erratum, erroneousness, error, exaggeration, fallacy, falsehood, falsification, fault, illusion, imprecision, impropriety, incorrectness, inexactitude, inexactness, miscalculation, misconstruction, misestimation, misinterpretation, misjudgment, misprint, misrepresentation, misstatement, mistake, obliquity, oversight, unpreciseness

INACCURATE, *adjective* amiss, approximate, blundering, broad, careless, erring, erroneous, fallacious, false, *falsus,* faulty, garbled, general, generalized, groundless, imprecise, improper, incorrect, *indiligens,* inexact, loose, misreported, misstated, mistaken, slipshod, unconscientious, unfactual, unfounded, unfussy, unpainstaking, unreal, unsound, unstrict, untrue, untrustworthy, wrong

INACTION, *noun* abeyance, abrogation, abstinence from action, *cessatio,* cessation, dormancy, failure to act, idleness, immobility, impotence, indolence, inertness, inoccupation, languor, latency, motionlessness, *otium,* paralysis, passiveness, passivity, *quies,* quiescence, rest, sloth, sluggishness, stagnation, stillness, suspended animation, suspension, torpidity, torpor, unemployment, unprogressiveness, vegetation

INACTIVE, *adjective* abeyant, abolished, abrogated, apathetic, canceled, comatose, destroyed, disabled, dormant, idle, *ignavus,* inanimate, indifferent, indolent, *iners,* inert, inoperative, insentient, invalid, languid, latent, lazy, lethargic, lethargical, listless, motionless, nugatory, null, obsolete, otiose, pococurante, powerless, *quietus,* recumbent, reposing, resting, sedentary, slothful, sluggish, spiritless, stagnant, static, supine, suspended, torpid, unbusied, unemployed, unexercised, unmoving, unspirited, unstirred, vegetative, void, weak
ASSOCIATED CONCEPTS: inactive account, inactive trust

INADEPT, *adjective* artless, awkward, feckless, feeble, impotent, incapable, incompetent, ineffective, ineffectual, inefficacious, inefficient, inept, inexpert, insufficient, lacking, lame, poor, unable, unaccomplished, unadroit, unapt, unclever, undeft, undexterous, unendowed, unequal to, unfacile, unfit, unfitted, ungifted, unproficient, unqualified, unskillful, unsuccessful, untalented, wanting, without dexterity

INADEQUATE, *adjective* assailable, deficient, depleted, disabled, disappointing, displeasing, emasculate, exhausted, feckless, feeble, helpless, impaired, *impar*, impotent, incapable, incompetent, incomplete, indefensible, ineffective, ineffectual, inefficacious, inept, inferior, inoperative, insubstantial, insufficient, lacking, not enough, not up to expectation, nugatory, perfunctory, poor, powerless, scant, short, unable, unapt, undeveloped, unempowered, unequal to, unfit, unfitted, unreplenished, unsatisfactory, unsufficing, untenable, useless, vincible, vulnerable, wanting, weak
ASSOCIATED CONCEPTS: inadequate consideration, inadequate damages, inadequate remedy at law, inadequate representation

INADMISSIBILITY, *noun* debarment, disqualification, exclusion, impropriety, inappositeness, inappropriateness, inaptitude, inaptness, ineligibility, misalliance, nonadmission, objectionability, preclusion, rejection, unacceptability, undesirability, unfitness, unqualification, unsuitability
ASSOCIATED CONCEPTS: challenges, inadmissibility of evidence

INADMISSIBLE, *adjective* banned, barred, disallowed, disapproved, excepted, excluded, improper, inapplicable, inapposite, inappropriate, incompetent, ineligible, *inlicitus*, irrelevant, not admitted, not allowed, not capable of being introduced as evidence, not included, not receivable as evidence, not receivable in evidence, not to be admitted, not to be allowed, not wanted, objectionable, prohibited, refused, rejected, suppressed, undue, unfit, unfitted, unqualified, unreceivable, unsuitable, wrong
ASSOCIATED CONCEPTS: inadmissible evidence, inadmissible statement, inadmissible testimony, incompetent testimony

INADVERTENCY, *noun* carelessness, dereliction, disregard, inattention, inattentiveness, indifference, laxity, miscue, mistake, neglect, negligence, nonobservance, omission, oversight, thoughtlessness, unmindfulness

INADVERTENT, *adjective* accidental, blind, careless, disregardful, heedless, *imprudens*, inattentive, neglectful, negligent, oblivious, regardless, thoughtless, undesigned, undiscerning, unheedful, unheeding, unintended, unintentional, unmeant, unmindful, unnoticing, unobservant, unperceptive, unpremeditated, unseeing, unthinking
ASSOCIATED CONCEPTS: neglect, negligence

INADVISABLE, *adjective* adverse, deleterious, detrimental, disadvantageous, disapproved, harmful, hurtful, ill-advised, ill-considered, ill-judged, impolitic, imprudent, inappropriate, inexpedient, infelicitous, injudicious, injurious, inopportune, insalubrious, misadvised, misguided, nocuous, objectionable, pernicious, undesirable, unfavorable, unfitting, unhealthy, unhelpful, unprofitable, unsatisfactory, unsensible, unsound, unsuitable, untoward, unwise, wrong

INAFFABLE, *adjective* bad-natured, bad-tempered, bellicose, belligerent, cantankerous, contrary, difficult, discourteous, disrespectful, fractious, impolite, intractable, obstreperous, offensive, perverse, petulant, pugnacious, rude, touchy, troublesome, truculent, unaccommodating, unapproachable, uncivil, uncomplaisant, uncooperative, uncourtly, ungallant, ungracious, unmannerly, untoward, unyielding, vexatious

INALIENABLE, *adjective* incapable of being conveyed, incapable of being sold, incapable of being transferred, nontransferable, not able to be conveyed, *quod abalienari non potest,* secured by law, unable to be bought, unable to be disposed of, unforfeitable, untouchable
ASSOCIATED CONCEPTS: inalienable lands, inalienable rights

INANE, *adjective* absurd, asinine, fatuous, foolish, imbecile, incogitant, inept, insipid, irrational, ludicrous, nonsensical, ridiculous, senseless, shallow, thought-free, thoughtless, unintelligent, unreasoning, unthinking, vacuous, vain

INAPPEALABLE, *adjective* absolute, beyond all dispute, beyond all question, beyond question, clear, conclusive, decided, decisive, definite, definitive, established, final, finally settled, fixed, impregnable, incapable of being reviewed, incontestable, incontrovertible, indisputable, irrefutable, irrevocable, not to be disputed, past dispute, peremptory, *quod refutari non potest,* unassailable, unchangeable, uncontroversial, unimpeachable, unrefutable, without power of appeal

INAPPLICABLE, *adjective* alien, at variance, clashing, disagreeing, discordant, discrepant, divergent, foreign, ill-adapted, impertinent, improper, inadmissible, inapposite, inappropriate, inapt, incommensurable, incompatible, incongruent, incongruous, inconsistent, infelicitous, irrelevant, jarring, malapropos, misapplied, mismatched, misplaced, *non valere,* out of keeping, out of place, unapt, uncalled for, unconformable, unconsonant, unfit, unfitted, unfitting, ungermane, unharmonious, unqualified, unsuitable, unsuited, unusable, wrong

INAPPOSITE, *adjective* alien, aside from the point, at variance, beside the mark, beside the point, clashing, disagreeing, discordant, discrepant, disproportionate, dissonant, extraneous, far-fetched, foreign, ill-adapted, ill-timed, illogical, immaterial, impertinent, improper, inaccordant, inadmissible, inapplicable, inappropriate, inapt, incidental, incompatible, incongruent, incongruous, inconsequent, inconsequential, inconsistent, inept, inessential, infelicitous, inharmonious, inopportune, insignificant, irreconcilable, irrelative, irrelevant, isolated, jarring, lacking importance, lacking relevance, malapropos, negligible, *non idoneus,* of little importance, pointless, remote, trivial, unallied, unapt, unbecoming, unbefitting, unconformable, uncongenial, unconnected, unconsonant, undue, unessential, unfavorable, unfit, unfitting, ungermane, unharmonious, unimportant, unnoteworthy, unrelated, unseasonable, unsuitable, unsuited, untimely, untoward, wrong

INAPPRECIABLE, *adjective* beneath consideration, beneath notice, disregarded, impalpable, imperceptible, inconsequential, inconsiderable, infinitesimal, insignificant, insubstantial, intangible, irrelevant, little, marginal, meager, mean, *minimus,* minor, negligible, of little account, of little importance, paltry, petty, scant, scanty, slight, small, trifling, unimportant, unworthy of consideration, unworthy of notice

INAPPREHENSIBLE, *adjective* abstruse, acroamatic, acroamatical, acroatic, ambiguous, beyond comprehension, beyond understanding, enigmatic, enigmatical, hidden, impenetrable, impossible to understand, incognizable, incomprehensible, indistinct, inexplicable, inexpressible, inscrutable, mysterious, mystic, mystical, obscure, opaque, past comprehension, puzzling, recondite, unaccountable, undecipherable, undefinable, undiscoverable, unexplainable, unfathomable, unintelligible, unknowable, unreadable, unrecognizable, vague

INAPPROPRIATE, *adjective* alien, amiss, clashing, disagreeing, discordant, discrepant, disproportionate, dissonant, divergent, forced, gratuitous, impertinent, impolitic, improper, in bad taste, inadmissible, inapplicable, inapposite, inapt, incompatible, incongruent, incongruous, inconsistent, indecorous, ineligible, inessential, inexpedient, infelicitous, inopportune, irrelevant, maladjusted, malapropos, misapplied, misbecoming, misdirected, misplaced, *non idoneus,* objectionable, odd, out of character, out of keeping, out of place, remote, unadvisable, unapt, unbecoming, unbefitting, uncalled for, uncommendable, unconformable, unconsonant, undesirable, undignified, undue, unfit, unfitted, unfitting, ungermane, unharmonious, unmeet, unseasonable, unseemly, unsuitable, unsuited, untimely, untoward, wrongly timed

INAPT, *adjective* at variance, clashing, discordant, discrepant, disproportionate, dissonant, ill-adapted, ill-suited, ill-timed, impolitic, improper, inaccordant, inadmissible, inadvisable, inapplicable, inapposite, inappropriate, incompatible, incongruent, incongruous, inconsistent, inexpedient, infelicitous, inharmonious, inopportune, irreconcilable, jarring, malapropos, mismatched, misplaced, objectionable, out of character, out of keeping, out of place, out of proportion, unapt, unbecoming, unbefitting, uncongenial, unconsonant, undesirable, undue, unfit, unfitting, unmeet, unqualified, unseasonable, unseemly, unsuitable, untimely, untoward, unwise

INARTICULATE, *adjective* abstruse, abysmal, close, defective, deficient, deprived of speech, fumbling, garbled, guarded, inadequate, inaudible, incommunicative, incomprehensible, inconversable, indiscernible, indistinct, indistinguishable, ineffective, inelegant, inferior, laconic, monosyllabic, muffled, mute, nebulous, not able to vocalize a position, not fluent, not glib, not polished, not smooth, opaque, *parum distinctus,* poor, reserved, reticent, silent, sparing of words, taciturn, tongue-tied, unclear, unfathomable, unintelligible, unplain, unrefined, untrained, unvocal, vague, withdrawn

INATTENTIVE, *adjective* absent-minded, absorbed, apathetic, blind, careless, casual, cursory, dazed, derelict, disregardful, distracted, forgetful, heedless, inadvertent, incogitant, inconsiderate, indifferent, lax, mercurial, neglectful, negligent, oblivious, off guard, perfunctory, preoccupied, reckless, remiss, thoughtless, unaware, undiscerning, unguarded, unmindful, unobservant, unresponsive, unsuspecting, wandering

INAUDIBLE, *noun* abstruse, acroamatic, acroamatical, acroatic, ambiguous, beyond comprehension, concealed, dark, deep, difficult to comprehend, dim, dull, enigmatic, enigmatical, esoteric, faint, fathomless, gentle, hard to hear, hard to make out, hard to understand, hidden, impenetrable, imperceptible, impossible to hear, impossible to understand, inapprehensible, incalculable, incogniscible, incoherent, inconceivable, indefinite, indistinct, inexplicable, inscrutable, insoluble, insolvable, intricate, low, meaningless, metaphysical, miraculous, muffled, mumbled,

murmured, mute, muted, muttered, mysterious, mystic, mystical, nebulousness, noiseless, not heard, obscure, occult, out of earshot, puzzling, quiet, recondite, silent, soft, stifled, still, unaccountable, unclear, unfathomable, unimaginable, unintelligible, unknowable, unrecognizable, unthinkable, vague, whispered

INAUGURAL, *adjective* commencing, embryonic, exploratory, foundational, inceptive, incipient, initial, initiative, initiatory, introductory, nascent, original, precursory, prefatory, preliminary, premier, preparatory, primal, primary, prime, prior, rudimentary

INAUSPICIOUS, *adjective* adverse, boding, disadvantageous, ill-timed, inadvisable, inexpedient, *infelix,* inopportune, mistimed, *nefastus,* ominous, presageful, problematic, problematical, unfavorable, unlucky, unpromising, unpropitious, untimely, untoward

INBRED, *adjective* absorbed, acquired, born, congenital, connate, deep-rooted, engrafted, genetic, hereditary, implicit, inborn, inculcated, indigenous, ingenerate, ingrained, inherent, inherited, innate, instilled, integral, intrinsic, native, natural

INCALCULABLE, *adjective* aleatory, boundless, countless, endless, enormous, equivocal, illimitable, immeasurable, immense, imponderable, incomprehensible, incomputable, indefinite, indeterminate, inestimable, inexhaustible, infinite, innumerable, innumerous, interminable, limitless, measureless, multitudinous, myriad, numberless, unaccountable, unbounded, uncertain, uncountable, unfathomable, unlimited, unmeasured, unnumbered, unpredictable

INCAPABLE, *adjective* crippled, disabled, feeble, impuissant, inadequate, incompetent, ineffective, ineffectual, inept, *inhabilis,* insufficient, not equal to, unable, unempowered, unequipped, unfit, unpowerful, unqualified, unskillful, unsuitable, unsuited, useless, weak
ASSOCIATED CONCEPTS: incapable of conducting his own affairs, incapable of intended use, incapable party, legal incapacity, physically incapable, total incapacity
FOREIGN PHRASES: *Contra non valentem agere nulla currit praescriptio.* No prescription runs against a person who is unable to act. ***Nemo admittendus est inhabilitare seipsum.*** No one is allowed to incapacitate himself.

INCAPABLE OF KNOWING RIGHT FROM WRONG, *adjective* bereft of reason, crazy, defective, demented, insensate, legally insane, mentally deficient, mentally deranged, mentally ill, *non compos mentis,* not of sound mind, unsound

INCAPACITATION, *noun* affliction, caducity, calamity, debility, disability, disablement, handicap, inability to work, incapacity for work, infirmity, misfortune, sickness

INCAPACITY, *noun* adynamy, anility, caducity, disability, disablement, disenablement, disqualification, dotage, failure, feebleness, helplessness, impotence, impuissance, inability, inadequacy, inaptitude, incapability, incapacitation, incompetence, incompetency, incomprehension, inefficacy, inefficiency, ineptitude, infirmity, *inscitia,* lack of capacity, lack of fitness, lack of power, morosis, unfitness, unproficiency, unskillfulness, weakness
ASSOCIATED CONCEPTS: disability, incapacity for work, incapacity to sue, legal incapacity, mental incapacity, permanent incapacity, physical incapacity, total incapacity

INCARCERATE, verb cast into prison, commit to prison, confine, constrain, hold in captivity, hold in custody, immune, imprison, institutionalize, intern, jail, lock in, lock up, place in confinement, put behind bars, put under lock and key, put under restraint, remand, restrain, restrict, send to prison, shut in, take into custody, throw in the brig
ASSOCIATED CONCEPTS: incarcerate an inmate, penal reform, prison conditions, prisoners' rights

INCARCERATED PERSON, noun captive, convict, convicted person, criminal, felon, hostage, inmate, internee, lawbreaker, prisoner, transgressor, wrongdoer

INCARCERATION, noun arrest, bondage, captivity, carcer, commitment, confinement, confinement by public authority, confinement in a jail, confinement in a penitentiary, confinement under legal process, constraint, custodia, custodianship, custody, detention, immurement, impoundment, imprisonment, internment, legal restraint, restraint, restriction, restriction on personal liberty, vincula
ASSOCIATED CONCEPTS: deterrence, habeas corpus, isolation, parole, rehabilitation, retribution, sentencing

INCENDIARY (Aggravating), **adjective** accelerant, agitating, angering, arousing, distressing, disturbing, enraging, fomenting, ignition, inciter, inciting, inflaming, inflammatory, infuriating, instigating, instigator, irking, provoking, stirring, turbulent, vexing

INCENDIARY (Burning), **adjective** aggravating, agitator, angering, ardent, arousing, arsonist, blazing, building-burner, burnable, combustible, criminal, electrifying, enraging, exasperating, exciting, fiery, firebrand, firebug, fire-setter, flammable, fomenting, hot, ignitable, incensing, inciter, inciting, inflaming, inflammatory, infuriating, instigating, instigator, insurgent, maddening, mischief-maker, mutineer, organizer, outraging, piquing, provocative, pyromaniac, rabble-rouser, rebel, revolutionary, ringleader, smoldering, stimulating, stirring, thrilling, torch, troublemaker
ASSOCIATED CONCEPTS: incendiary bomb, incendiary device, incendiary explosive

INCENSE, verb accendere, aggravate, agitate, anger, antagonize, arouse, arouse ire, arouse resentment, cause dislike, cause loathing, cause resentment, chafe, discompose, disquiet, embitter, embroil, enkindle, enrage, envenom, exacerbate, exasperate, excite, excite hatred, excite indignation, harass, incendere, inflame, inflame with wrath, infuriate, irritate, kindle one's wrath, madden, make one lose one's temper, nettle, pique, provoke, provoke hatred, provoke ire, push too far, put into a temper, raise anger, rile, ruffle, vex, work into a passion
ASSOCIATED CONCEPTS: heat of passion, incense the jury, mistrial, prejudice, provocation

INCENTIVE, noun actuation, allure, allurement, appeal, attraction, bait, causality, causation, cause, cause of action, consideration, driving force, encouragement, enticement, goad, impetus, impulse, impulsion, incitamentum, incitement, inducement, influence, irritamentum, inspiration, instigation, lure, motivation, motive, persuasion, prompting, provocation, provocative, reason, spur, stimulant, stimulus, tantalization, temptation
ASSOCIATED CONCEPTS: incentive contract

INCEPTION, noun beginning, birth, commencement, dawn, debut, derivation, embarkation, exordium, genesis, inauguration, inceptum, inchoation, incipience, incipiency,

initiation, initium, onset, opening, origin, origination, outbreak, outset, rise, source, start, starting point

INCERTITUDE, noun ambiguity, bewilderment, changeableness, dilemma, doubt, doubtfulness, dubiety, dubiosity, dubiousness, dubitancy, dubitation, fog, haze, hesitancy, hesitation, indecision, indetermination, insecurity, irresolution, misgiving, perplexity, quandary, question, uncertainness, uncertainty, unsureness, vacillation, vagueness

INCESSANT, adjective adsiduus, ceaseless, constant, continual, continuous, continuus, endless, eternal, everlasting, frequent, indefatigable, infinite, interminable, interminate, iterative, long-lasting, never-ending, nonstop, perennial, perpetual, perpetuus, persistent, recurrent, reiterative, repeated, repetitious, returning, steady, sustained, timeless, unbroken, unceasing, undying, unending, unintermittent, unintermitting, uninterrupted, unremitting, untiring, unwearying, without ceasing, without interruption, without stopping

INCEST, noun abnormal cohabitation, abnormal relationship, brother-sister relationship, carnal abuse, degenerate behavior, degenerative behavior, depraved, father-daughter relationship, illegal relationship, illicit relationship, immoral family relationship, immoral relationship, inbreeding, incestuous relationship, interbreeding, lewdness, mother-son relationship, perversion, sex crime, sexual abnormality, sexual abuse, sexual deviance, sexual deviation, sexual offense, sexual perversion, unlawful sexual intercourse
ASSOCIATED CONCEPTS: incest laws

INCESTUOUS, adjective banned family relationships, criminal family relationships, forbidden family relationships, illegal family relationships, immoral family relationships, improper family relationships, inbred, interbred, perversion, prohibited relationship, sexual abnormality, sexual deviance, sexual deviation, sexual offense, sexual perversion, unlawful family relationships
FOREIGN PHRASES: Incestuousi. Those offspring of incestuous relationships.

INCHOATE, adjective anticipatory, basic, beginning, budding, commencing, developing, early, elemental, elementary, embryonic, fragmentary, fundamental, half-begun, half-done, hardly begun, immature, imperfect, in its infancy, inaugural, inceptive, incipient, incohatus, incomplete, infant, infant stage, initial, initiatory, introductory, just begun, maiden, nascent, newborn, not completely formed, not fully executed, not fully formed, original, out of order, partial, prefatory, preliminary, preparatory, primal, primary, prime, primeval, primitive, primordial, rudimental, rudimentary, semiprocessed, sketchy, starting, uncompleted, undeveloped, unexecuted, unfinalized, unfinished, unprocessed
ASSOCIATED CONCEPTS: attempt, conspiracy and solicitation, inchoate contract, inchoate crimes, inchoate gift, inchoate interest, inchoate lien, inchoate right, inchoate title, inchoate will

INCIDENCE, noun amount, degree, embodiment, experience, exposure, extent, frequency, measure, number, number of times occurred, prevalence, range of occurrence, rate, representative number, representative selection, sample, scope
ASSOCIATED CONCEPTS: causation, incidence of a crime, incidence of drug abuse, incidence rate

INCIDENT, *adjective* accessory, affiliated, allied, appertaining to, apropos, associated, bearing upon, belonging, circumstantial, collateral, connected, contextual, contingent, correlative, dependent on, following upon, implicated, in connection with, in relation to, inherent in, pertaining to, related to, relating to, relative to, subject to, subsidiary
ASSOCIATED CONCEPTS: customarily incident, necessary and incident to

INCIDENT, *noun* affair, case, *casus,* contingency, episode, event, experience, happening, occasion, occurrence, pass, proceeding

INCIDENTAL, *adjective* accessory, accidental, accompanying, added, additional, allied, associated, attendant, extrinsic, *forte oblatus,* minor, not vital, parenthetic, secondary, subordinate, subsidiary, supervenient, supplemental, supplementary
ASSOCIATED CONCEPTS: incidental authority, incidental benefits, incidental consequence, incidental damages, incidental expenses, incidental jurisdiction, incidental power, incidental relief, incidental to employment, incidental use, incidental work

INCINERATE, *verb* blaze, burn, burn to a cinder, burn up, burning to ashes, catch fire, conflagrate, deflagrate, fire, ignite, incandesce, inflame, kindle, light up, melt down, roast, scald, scorch, sear, singe, smolder, strike a light
ASSOCIATED CONCEPTS: EPA

INCIPIENT, *adjective* aboriginal, beginning, budding, commencing, elemental, elementary, embryonic, foundational, fundamental, immature, inceptive, inchoate, inchoative, incunabular, infant, initial, initiatory, introductory, maiden, nascent, original, precursory, prefatory, primal, primary, primeval, primitive, proemial, rudimental, rudimentary, starting, uncompleted

INCISIVE, *adjective* acute, biting, brisk, caustic, cutting, discerning, effective, electric, galvanic, harsh, keen, mordacious, mordant, *mordax,* moving, penetrating, piercing, piquant, pointed, powerful, pungent, sarcastic, sarcastical, satiric, satirical, scathing, sententious, severe, sharp, slashing, stinging, telling, trenchant, vehement

INCITE, *verb* advise, advocate, agitate, animate, arouse, arouse to action, awaken, bring about, bring on, call forth, cause, counsel, drive, encourage, energize, enthuse, excite, exert influence, exert pressure, exhort, foment, give advice, give impetus, goad, impart momentum, impassion, *incitare,* induce, influence, initiate, inspire, inspirit, *instigare,* instigate, kindle, launch, move, persuade, press, prevail upon, prompt, provoke, push, rally, recommend, rouse, set in motion, spur on, start, stimulate, stir, stir up, urge, wake
ASSOCIATED CONCEPTS: incite a riot

INCIVILITY, *noun* acerbity, acrimony, boorishness, discourteousness, discourtesy, disrespect, ill-breeding, impertinence, impoliteness, impropriety, inappropriateness, indecency, indecorum, indelicacy, inelegance, insult, misbehavior, provocation, rudeness of manner, slight, snub, tactlessness, unbecoming conduct, uncouthness, uncultivation, unrefinement, urbane, vulgarity
ASSOCIATED CONCEPTS: professionalism

INCLEMENT, *adjective* arctic, astringent, austere, biting, bitter, bleak, blustery, cold, crisp, cruel, freezing, frigid, glacial, grim, gusty, harsh, icy, inexorable, merciless, nasty, nipping, penetrating, piercing, rainy, rigorous, rough, rugged, ruthless, severe, sharp, stone-cold, stormy, stringent, tempestuous, unrelenting, unsparing, violent, wintry

INCLINATION, *noun* affinity, aptitude, aptness, bent, bias, cast, direction, fondness, *inclinatio,* leaning, liking, partiality, penchant, predilection, predisposition, preference, prejudice, proclivity, proneness, propensity, readiness, slant, *studium,* tendency, *voluntas*
FOREIGN PHRASES: *Judicium redditur in invitum, in praesumptione legis.* In presumption of law, a judgment is given against one's inclination. ***Favores ampliandi sunt; odia restringenda.*** Favorable inclinations should be encouraged, animosities should be restrained.

INCLINED, *adjective* acquiescent, affected, agreeable, amenable, apt, assenting, bent, consenting, content, delighted, desirous, disposed, dispositioned, eager, favorable, glad, happy, leaning, liable, moved, partial to, pleased, predisposed, prepared, *proclivis,* prompted, prone, *propensus,* ready, receptive, slanted, stimulated, tending, trending, well-disposed, willing

INCLUDE, *verb* absorb, *adscribere,* be composed of, be formed of, be made up of, begird, boast, bound, bracket, circumscribe, classify, close in, combine, compass, *complecti,* comprehend, *comprehendere,* consist of, consolidate, contain, cover, embody, embrace, encircle, encompass, engird, envelop, girdle, hold, incorporate, involve, merge, put a barrier around, span, subsume, surround, take in, unify, unite
FOREIGN PHRASES: *In eo quod plus sit semper inest et minus.* The less is always included in the greater. ***Inclusio unius est exclusio alterius.*** The inclusion of one thing is the exclusion of another.

INCLUSION, *noun* all acceptance, all-embracing universe, all-encompassing universe, all facets, blanket analysis, broad analysis, compendious amount, comprehensive number, diverse mix, diverse mixture, every facet, every side, exhaustive approach, extensive analysis, full vision, mainstreaming everyone, sweeping analysis, total number, total scope, umbrella, universe, unlimited acceptance
ASSOCIATED CONCEPTS: inclusion of children with disabilities, inclusionary approach

INCLUSIVE, *adjective* all-embracing, broad, comprehensive, comprising, consisting of, containing, embodying, embracing, encircling, enclosing, exhaustive, extensive, full, general, inclusory, sweeping, total, vast, wide

INCOGNITO, *adjective* alias, anonymous, assumed name, camouflaged, charade, clandestine, concealed, confidential agent, confidentially, cover, discreetly, disguise, disguised, false identity, isolated, mask, masked, masquerade, mysterious, mysteriously, mystery man, nameless, privacy, private, privately, privileged, protected, quietly, recluse, retired, screen, secluded, seclusion, secrecy, secret, secret agent, secreted, secretive, secretiveness, secretly, sheltered, shielded, under an assumed name, under cover, undisclosed, unidentified, unknown, unnamed, unrecognized, unrevealed, unspecified, veiled, with circumspection, without a name, without fanfare

INCOGNIZANT, *adjective* benighted, blind, clueless, deaf, heedless, ignorant, insensible, mystified, nescient, oblivious, unacquainted, unadvised, unapprized, unaware, unconscious, unenlightened, unfamiliar, uninformed, uninstructed, unknowing, unmindful, unrealizing, unseeing, unsuspecting, unwitting

INCOHERENCE, noun absence of meaning, chaos, disconnection, discontinuity, disjunction, disorder, illegibility, imperspicuity, inapprehensibility, incomprehensibility, lack of clarity, meaninglessness, randomness, ranting, raving, unclearness, undecipherability, unevenness, unintelligibility, wandering
ASSOCIATED CONCEPTS: commitment to an institution, guardian, insanity, lack of capacity

INCOHERENT, adjective babble, confused, deranged, deviating, digressive, disconnected, discontinuity, discordant, disjointed, illogical, inarticulate, irrational, jumbled, lacking clarity and cohesion, mixed-up, muddled, scrambled, unfit, unintelligible, variant, wandering
ASSOCIATED CONCEPTS: chromatic coherence, experience incoherence, insanity defense, intent and coherence, polarization coherence, rehabilitations, spatial coherence, temporal coherence, waive equation

INCOME, noun allowance, annuity, business profits, commercial profits, compensation, consideration, earnings, emoluments, fees, financial remuneration, financial resources, fringe benefits, gain derived from capital, gain derived from labor, gains, gross, gross income, gross return, increase in amount of wealth, livelihood, means, money coming in, net return, pay, payment, *pecunia*, pension, periodic returns from property or labor, proceeds, profit from conversion of assets, profit from sale, profits, profits of commerce, *quaestus*, receipts, recompense, remuneration, return in money, return on capital, returns, revenue, salary, sale proceeds, something produced by capital, stipend, subsidy, value received, *vectigal*, wage, wages, wealth
ASSOCIATED CONCEPTS: accumulated income, actual income, affordable housing, aggregate income, annual net income, current income, deferred income, division of income, employment law, estimated income, garnishment of income, gross income, income-bearing property, income execution, income tax, income tax evasion, income yield, legacy, life income, low income, minimum wage, net income, retirement income, social security income

INCOMING, adjective about to be received, approaching, arriving, coming, entering, homeward, homeward-bound, in transit, inbound, incoming, mailed, receiving, sent, shipped, soon to be received

INCOMMENSURABLE, adjective at variance, cannot be compared to, cannot be weighed against, discordant, discrepant, disproportionate, dissimilar, greatly dissimilar, ill-balanced, incomparable, incongruent, inconsistent, inconsonant, inharmonious, lopsided, mismatched, out of proportion, unbalanced, unequal
ASSOCIATED CONCEPTS: incommensurable goods, incommensurable values

INCOMMENSURATE, adjective at variance, discordant, discrepant, disproportionate, inaccordant, incommensurable, inconsistent, mismatched, out of keeping, out of proportion, short, unconformable, unequal

INCOMMUNICABLE, adjective be silent, confidential, immutable, inexpressible, keep quiet, keep silent, not speak, not speaking, not talking, silent, top-secret

INCOMPARABLE, adjective beyond, beyond comparison, beyond imitation, beyond words, excellent, exceptional, exquisite, extraordinary, incredible, matchless, peerless, perfect, rare, superior, superlative, supreme, unapproachable, unequaled, unique, unmatchable, unparalleled, unrivaled, unsurpassed, unusual, without equal

INCOMPATIBLE, adjective antipathetical, clash, conflict, contradictoriness, contrariety, contrast, controversy, disaccord, disagreement, discord, discordance, dispute, dissension, dissent, dissidence, disunion, disunity, divergence, faction, fight, hatred, hostility, incongruous, inimicality, intolerance, not agreeing, not compatible, not harmonizing, opposition, repelling, repugnance, variance
ASSOCIATED CONCEPTS: doctrine of incompatibility, incompatibility, incompatibility of public offices

INCOMPATIBILITY (Difference), noun animosity, antagonism, antipathy, clash, conflict, contradictoriness, contrariety, contrast, controversy, disaccord, disagreement, discord, discordance, dislike, dispute, dissension, dissent, dissidence, disunion, disunity, divergence, division, faction, fight, hatred, hostility, inimicality, intolerance, intransigence, intransigency, irreconcilability, irreconcilable difference, irreconcilableness, lack of agreement, misunderstanding, nonagreement, opposition, quarrel, repugnance, unfriendliness, variance, want of adaptation, want of agreement
ASSOCIATED CONCEPTS: divorce for incompatibility

INCOMPATIBILITY (Inconsistency), noun antithesis, clash, conflict, contrast, disagreement, disconformity, discongruity, discord, discordance, discordancy, discrepancy, disharmony, disparity, dissimilarity, dissimilitude, dissonance, divergence, incongruity, inconsonance, inequality, inharmoniousness, inharmony, lack of agreement, lack of harmony, nonconformity, nonuniformity, unconformity, unlikeness, unsuitableness, variance, want of agreement
ASSOCIATED CONCEPTS: incompatible use of land

INCOMPETENCE, noun illegitimacy, inadequacy, incapability, incapacity, inefficiency, inexpertness, insufficiency, mismanagement, negligence, undeftness, unendowment, unfitness, unprofessional conduct, unproficiency, unqualifiedness
ASSOCIATED CONCEPTS: incompetence of counsel, incompetence of representation, incompetent evidence

INCOMPETENT, adjective amateurish, awkward, bungling, clumsy, deficient, disqualified, floundering, gauche, gawky, ignorant, improficient, inadequate, incapable, incapacitated, ineffective, ineffectual, inefficient, inept, inexperienced, inexpert, *inhabilis, inscitus,* insufficient, *inutilis,* lacking qualification, maladroit, raw, stumbling, stupid, unable, unadapted, unapt, unequal, unequipped, unfit, unfitted, ungainly, unhandy, uninitiated, unqualified, unskilled, unskillful, unsuitable, untrained, useless, without adequate ability
ASSOCIATED CONCEPTS: incompetence of counsel, incompetent evidence, incompetent witness

INCOMPLETE, adjective defective, deficient, devoid, disappointing, failing, faulty, fragmentary, half-done, imperfect, imperfected, inaccurate, inadequate, inchoate, insufficient, lacking, left undone, less than perfect, not completed, outstanding, partial, perfunctory, rough, sketchy, truncated, unaccomplished, uncompleted, undeveloped, unexecuted, unfinished, unsatisfactory, wanting

INCOMPREHENSIBLE, *adjective* abstruse, acroamatic, acroamatical, acroatic, ambiguous, beyond comprehension, concealed, dark, deep, difficult to comprehend, dim, enigmatic, enigmatical, esoteric, fathomless, hard to understand, hidden, impenetrable, impossible to understand, inapprehensible, incalculable, incognoscible, incoherent, inconceivable, indefinite, inexplicable, inscrutable, insoluble, insolvable, *intellegi non potest,* intricate, meaningless, metaphysical, miraculous, mysterious, mystic, mystical, nebulousness, obscure, occult, puzzling, *quod comprehendi,* recondite, unaccountable, unclear, unfathomable, unimaginable, unintelligible, unknowable, unrecognizable, unthinkable, vague

INCOMPREHENSIVE, *adjective* abstract, abstruse, ambiguous, beyond comprehension, beyond understanding, complex, complicated, deep, difficult, difficult to comprehend, enigmatic, esoteric, hard to understand, impenetrable, impossible to understand, inapprehensible, incoherent, indecipherable, inexplicable, intricate, involved, jumbled, metaphysical, muddled, mysterious, mystic, mystical, nebulous, oblique, obscure, perplexed, profound, recondite, unclear, undecipherable, unexplainable, unfathomable, unimaginable, unintelligible, vague

INCONCEIVABLE, *adjective* disputable, doubtful, excluded, extraordinary, hard to believe, implausible, impossible, impracticable, inapprehensible, incogitable, incomprehensible, incredible, inexplicable, infeasible, marvelous, miraculous, not understandable, out of the question, overwhelming, portentous, prodigious, questionable, rare, staggering, stupendous, surprising, suspect, suspicious, unbelievable, uncanny, unconsidered, undreamed, unexplainable, unimaginable, unreasonable, unthinkable, unthought of, unusual

INCONCLUSIVE, *adjective* doubtful, flimsy, indecisive, ineffective, not final, *quo nihil efficitur,* subject to verification, unascertained, uncertain, unconfirmed, uncorroborated, undemonstrated, unestablished, unproved, unproven, unsettled, unsubstantiated, unsupported, unsupported by evidence, unsure, untested, untried, unverified, weak
ASSOCIATED CONCEPTS: inconclusive account, inconclusive evidence

INCONGRUENT, *adjective* contradictory, different, disagreeing, discordant, discrepant, disjointed, disparate, disproportionate, dissimilar, distinct, diverse, ill-assorted, ill-matched, improper, inapplicable, inapposite, inappropriate, inapt, incompatible, incongruous, inconsistent, inconsonant, inept, inharmonious, inopportune, malapropos, peculiar, unalike, unconformable, unequal, unfortunate, unmatched

INCONGRUITY, *noun* abnormality, absurdity, absurdness, contradiction, contradictoriness, contrariety, contrariness, deviation, difference, disagreement, discordance, discordancy, discrepancy, disharmony, disparity, dissimilarity, dissimilitude, dissonance, impropriety, inapplicability, inappropriateness, incompatibility, incongruousness, inconsistency, inconsonance, inharmoniousness, lack of consonance, lack of harmony, ludicrousness, misalliance, mismatch, nonconformity, *repugnantia,* ridiculousness, unconformity, unfitness, unfittingness, unlikeness, unsuitability, variance

INCONGRUOUS, *adjective* alien, *alienus,* at odds, at variance, clashing, conflicting, contradictory, contrary, disaccordant, disagreeing, discordant, discrepant, disharmonious, disproportionate, dissonant, divergent, ill-matched, illogical, improper, inaccordant, inapplicable, inapposite, inappropriate, incompatible, inconformable, *incongruens,* incongruent, inconsequent, inconsistent, inconsonant, inharmonious, irreconcilable, irregular, jarring, lacking agreement, lacking harmony, misjoined, mismatched, mismated, *non aptus,* out of character, out of keeping, out of place, strange, unbecoming, uncongenial, uncoordinated, unfit, unfitting, unsuitable

INCONSEQUENCE, *noun* disassociation, disconnection, disjunction, dissociation, immateriality, impertinence, impertinency, inapplicability, inappositeness, inconsequentiality, inconsiderableness, inconsistence, inconsistency, insignificance, irrelevance, irrelevancy, negligibility, paltriness, smallness, triviality, unimportance, unnoteworthiness, unrelatedness

INCONSEQUENTIAL, *adjective* dispensable, flimsy, frivolous, immaterial, impertinent, inapplicable, inappreciable, inappropriate, inconsequent, inconsiderable, inessential, insignificant, invalid, irrelevant, minor, niggling, nonessential, not vital, nugatory, of minor importance, of no account, of no consequence, paltry, petty, picayune, remote, slight, superficial, trifling, trivial, unconnected, unessential, ungermane, unimportant, unnecessary, unrelated, unsound, unwarranted, worthless
ASSOCIATED CONCEPTS: irrelevant evidence

INCONSIDERABLE, *adjective* beneath notice, *exiguus,* immaterial, inappreciable, inconsequential, insignificant, insubstantial, irrelevant, *levis,* meager, mean, minor, minute, modest, negligible, nominal, nonessential, not worth considering, not worthy of notice, nugatory, of no consequence, of no moment, paltry, petty, piddling, slight, small, *tenuis,* trifling, trivial, unessential, unimportant, unworthy of consideration, unworthy of notice, worthless

INCONSIDERATE, *adjective* blind, blunt, brusque, careless, cavalier, censorious, churlish, derelict, disobliging, disregardful, flippant, harsh, heedless, ill-advised, ill-judged, impolitic, imprudent, inattentive, incautious, indifferent, indiscreet, injudicious, intolerant, neglectful, negligent, oblivious, reasonless, reckless, remiss, rude, self-centered, selfish, severe, tactless, thoughtless, uncharitable, unconsidered, ungracious, unheeding, unkind, unmindful, unobliging, unobservant, unpolitic, unthoughtful, unwary

INCONSIDERATION, *noun* carelessness, cruelty, disregard, disrespect, disrespectfulness, foolhardiness, forgetfulness, hastiness, heedlessness, impetuosity, improvidence, imprudence, impulsiveness, inadvertence, inadvertency, inattention, inattention to consequences, incaution, incautiousness, incircumspection, inconsiderateness, indiscretion, injudiciousness, irresponsibility, lack of care, lack of caution, lack of consideration, lack of respect, lack of reverence, meanness, neglect, negligence, oversight, precipitance, precipitancy, prodigality, rashness, recklessness, regardlessness, thoughtlessness, unkindness, unpremeditation, unwariness

INCONSISTENCY, *noun* antilogy, antinomy, capriciousness, changeableness, contradiction, contradictoriness, contrariety, deviation, difference, disaccord, disagreement, discord, discordance, discordancy, discrepancy, disparity, dissimilarity, dissimilitude, dissonance, divergence, diversity, fitfulness, flightiness, inapplicability, inappropriateness, incompatibility, incongruity, incongruousness, inconsonance, inconstancy, *inconstantia,* inequality, inharmony, instability, lack of accord, mercurialness, *mutabilitas,* nonconformity, unconformity, unlikeness, unsteadiness, unsuitableness, vacillation, variance, volatility, want of harmony

INCONSISTENT, *adjective* at variance, capricious, changeable, conflicting, contradictory, *contrarius,* contrary, different, disagreeing, discordant, discrepant, dissonant, divergent, erratic, fickle, fitful, flighty, illogical, incompatible, incongruous, inconsonant, *inconstans,* inconstant, irreconcilable, jarring, lacking accord, lacking harmony, mercurial, moody, mutable, notional, paradoxical, unstable, unsteady, unsuitable, vacillating, variable, volatile
ASSOCIATED CONCEPTS: alternative pleadings, inconsistent causes of action, inconsistent defenses, inconsistent statements, inconsistent verdict

INCONSPICUOUS, *adjective* barely seen, blurred, concealed, covert, dim, faint, feeble, fuzzy, half-seen, half-visible, hazy, hidden, ill-defined, ill-marked, imperceptible, indefinite, indiscernible, indistinct, indistinguishable, invisible, merely visible, misty, modest, nebulous, obscure, *obscurus,* out of sight, *parum insignis,* poorly defined, poorly seen, quiet, retiring, shadowy, shrouded, subtle, suppressed, unapparent, unclear, undefined, undiscernible, unevident, unnoticeable, unnoticed, unobserved, unobtrusive, unobvious, unostentatious, unperceivable, unpretentious, unpronounced, unrecognizable, unseeable, unseen, vague, veiled, viewless

INCONTESTABILITY, *noun* impregnability, incontrovertibility, indefeasibility, indisputability, indubitableness, irrefragibility, irrefutability, unassailability, undeniability, unequivocalness, unimpeachability, unquestionability, unrefutability
ASSOCIATED CONCEPTS: incontestability clause, incontestable policy

INCONTESTABLE, *adjective* absolutely clear, beyond all question, clear, conclusive, impregnable, inappealable, incontrovertible, indefeasible, indisputable, indubious, indubitable, irrefragable, irrefutable, noncontroversial, past dispute, unambiguous, unassailable, uncontradictable, undeniable, unequivocal, unimpeachable, unquestionable
ASSOCIATED CONCEPTS: incontestable claim

INCONTESTABLY, *adverb* admittedly, assuredly, authoritatively, certainly, clearly, conclusively, incontrovertibly, indisputably, indubiously, indubitably, infallibly, irrefutably, irresistibly, obviously, palpably, patently, plainly, reliably, self-evidently, unambiguously, unassailably, uncontradictably, uncontroversially, undeniably, unequivocally, unimpeachably, unmistakably, unquestionably

INCONTROVERTIBLE, *adjective* absolute, apodictic, ascertained, assured, authoritative, beyond a shadow of a doubt, beyond contradiction, capable of proof, certain, clear-cut, conclusive, definite, demonstrable, established, factual, inappealable, incontestable, indisputable, indubious, indubitable, irrefragable, irrefutable, noncontroversial, past dispute, positive, questionless, *quod refutari non potest,* settled, sure, testable, true, unambiguous, unanswerable, unchallengeable, unconfutable, uncontradictable, undeniable, unequivocal, unimpeachable, unmistakable, unquestionable, unshakable, veracious
ASSOCIATED CONCEPTS: incontrovertible fact, incontrovertible proof

INCONVENIENCE, *verb* annoy, be obstructive, be uncooperative, bother, disadvantage, discommode, displace, disturb, encumber, give trouble, hamper, hinder, impede, impose hardship, incommode, irritate, obstruct, stall, stand in the way, stymie, thwart, trouble, unsettle, vex
ASSOCIATED CONCEPTS: forum non conveniens, public inconvenience
FOREIGN PHRASES: ***Privatum incommodum publico bono pensatur.*** Private inconvenience is compensated by public benefit. ***Argumentum ab inconvenienti est validum in lege; quia lex non permittit aliquod inconveniens.*** An argument drawn from what is inconvenient is good in law, because the law will not permit any inconvenience. ***Quod est inconveniens aut contra rationem non permissum est in lege.*** What is inconvenient or contrary to reason is not permitted in the law.

INCONVENIENT, *adjective* bother, disadvantage, discommode, displace, disturbance, encumbering, hamper, hinder, impede, impose hardship, incommode, irritate, obstruct, stand in the way, stymie, thwart, trouble, unsettle, vex
ASSOCIATED CONCEPTS: forum non conveniens

INCONVINCIBLE, *adjective* cynical, disbelieving, disposed to doubt, distrustful, doubtful, doubting, dubious, given to suspicion, hard to convince, inclined to suspect, incredulous, indisposed to believe, questioning, skeptical, slow to believe, suspecting, suspicious, unbelieving, uncertain, unwilling to accept, wary, without faith

INCORPORATE *(Form a corporation),* **verb** affiliate, begin a corporation, charter, confer a corporate franchise upon, confer corporate status upon, create a corporation, establish a corporation, form a company, initiate a corporation, *inserere,* organize a corporation, start a corporation
ASSOCIATED CONCEPTS: certificate of incorporation

INCORPORATE *(Include),* **verb** absorb, alloy, become a component, become an ingredient, bring together, centralize, coalesce, combine, compound, consolidate, contain, couple, cover, embody, embrace, encircle, encompass, fuse, interblend, interfuse, interlace, intermix, involve, join, meld, merge, mix, put together, take in, unite, weave, yoke
ASSOCIATED CONCEPTS: incorporate by reference

INCORPORATION *(Blend),* **noun** aggregation, amalgamation, assimilation, centralization, coalescence, combination, commixation, compound, consolidation, fusion, infusion, interfusion, interlacement, intermixture, minglement, mixture, unification, union
ASSOCIATED CONCEPTS: incorporation by reference
FOREIGN PHRASES: ***Verba relata hoc maxime operantur per referentiam, ut in eis inesse videntur.*** Words incorporated by reference have as great an effect through reference, as they are deemed to be inserted.

INCORPORATION *(Formation of a business entity),* **noun** association, chartering, coalition, *coniunctio, cooptatio,* establishment of a firm, formation of a company, formation of a corporation, formation of an organization, organization of a commercial concern, organization of a company, unification, union
ASSOCIATED CONCEPTS: certificate of incorporation, dissolution of a corporation

INCORPOREAL, *adjective* asomatous, bodiless, ethereal, immaterial, immateriate, impalpable, incorporal, intangible, nonphysical, not of material nature, spiritual, unbodied, unembodied, unfleshly, unsubstantial, unworldly, without body, without substance

313

ASSOCIATED CONCEPTS: incorporeal chattels, incorporeal hereditament

FOREIGN PHRASES: *Haereditas, alia corporalis, alia incorporalis; corporalis est, quae tan gi potest et videri; incorporalis quae tangi non potest nec videri.* An inheritance is either corporeal or incorporeal; corporeal is that which can be touched and seen; incorporeal is that which can neither be touched nor seen.

INCORRECT, adjective amiss, awry, erring, erroneous, fallacious, false, *falsus,* faulty, flawed, imperfect, imprecise, *improbus,* improper, inaccurate, inappropriate, inexact, miscalculated, misconstrued, misfigured, misjudged, misleading, mistaken, *perversus,* solecistic, solecistical, sophistic, sophistical, unfactual, ungrounded, unsound, untrue, unveracious, wrong

INCORRIGIBLE, adjective beyond help, beyond reform, chronic, cureless, hardened, hopeless, impenitent, incapable of correction, incurable, intractable, intransigent, inveterate, irreclaimable, irrecoverable, irredeemable, irreformable, irremediable, irreparable, lost, obdurate, obstinate, past cure, past hope, *perditus,* recalcitrant, recidivous, refractory, remorseless, reprobate, stubborn, toughened, unapologizing, uncontrite, uncontrollable, ungovernable, unmanageable, unreformable, unregretful, unregretting, unrepentant, unsubmissive, wicked

ASSOCIATED CONCEPTS: incorrigible child, incorrigible juvenile delinquent, multiple offender

INCORRUPTIBLE, adjective above suspicion, blameless, dependable, ethical, faultless, guiltless, having integrity, high-principled, honest, honorable, impeccable, *incorruptus,* inculpable, *integer,* irreproachable, just, meritorious, moral, reliable, reputable, respectable, *sanctus,* scrupulous, sinless, stanch, trustable, trustworthy, trusty, unable to be bought, unblemished, unbribable, uncorrupt, unerring, unimpeachable, untarnishable, untreacherous, unvenal, upright, virtuous

INCREASE, verb abound, accrue, accumulate, add on, add to, aggrandize, *amplificare,* amplify, annex, appreciate, augere, augment, become larger, become greater, boost, branch out, broaden, build, burgeon, *crescere,* develop, *dilatare,* dilate, enlarge, escalate, expand, extend, flourish, gain, gain ground, *gliscere,* greaten, grow, inflate, lengthen, make greater, make larger, maximize, mount, multiply, progress, proliferate, prolong, protract, pullulate, raise, rise, skyrocket, spread, step up, stretch, supplement, surge, swell, thrive, widen

ASSOCIATED CONCEPTS: increase in value, increased cost, increased hazard, increased risk, increased valuation

INCREDIBLE, adjective absurd, beyond belief, doubtful, hard to believe, hardly credible, implausible, impossible, improbable, inconceivable, *incredibilis,* nonsensical, open to doubt, open to suspicion, preposterous, ridiculous, staggering, suspect, suspicious, unbelievable, unconvincing, unimaginable, unlikely, unthinkable

ASSOCIATED CONCEPTS: incredible statements, incredible testimony

INCREDULITY, noun amazement, denial, disbelief, discredit, distrust, distrustfulness, doubt, doubtfulness, dubiety, dubiousness, faithlessness, inability to accept, inability to believe, inconvincability, incredulousness, indisposition to admit, indisposition to believe, lack of belief, lack of faith, mistrust, mistrustfulness, question, reluctance to believe, skepticalness, skepticism, suspicion, suspiciousness, uncertainty, unwillingness to believe, want of faith

INCREDULOUS, adjective disposed to doubt, distrustful, doubtful, doubting, dubious, hard to convince, *incredulus,* indisposed to believe, mistrustful, questioning, skeptical, slow to believe, suspecting, suspicious, unbelieving, unconvinced, untrusting, unwilling to accept, without belief, without faith, wondering

INCREMENT, noun accretion, addition, augmentation, boost, enlargement, expansion, extension, gain, growth, increase, *incrementum,* raise, rise, supplement, surge

ASSOCIATED CONCEPTS: unearned increment

INCRIMINATE, verb accuse, allege, ascribe, ascribe blame, assign, attribute, blame, bring accusation, bring charges against, bring proceedings against, bring up on charges, cast blame upon, charge, charge with a crime, charge with an offense, complaint against, condemn, connect with a crime, criminate, denounce, draw in, enmesh, entangle, expose, find fault with, hold accountable, hold responsible, impeach, *impedire, implicare,* implicate, impute, impute guilt to, inculpate, indict, inform against, insinuate, involve, involve in criminal proceedings, involve in guilt, lay blame upon, lodge a complaint, make a party to, place the blame on, point the finger at, prefer charges, prosecute, providing evidence, providing information of a crime, proving, proving guilt, recriminate, stigmatize, *suspectum reddere*

ASSOCIATED CONCEPTS: Fifth Amendment, incriminating admission, incriminating circumstance, incriminatory statement, Miranda warnings, self-incrimination

INCRIMINATION, noun accusal, accusation, assignation, attribution, blame, calling to account, censure, charge, complaint, crimination, decrial, denouncement, impeachment, implication, imputation, imputation of wrongdoing, inculpation, indictment, recrimination, reproach, reproachful accusation

ASSOCIATED CONCEPTS: Fifth Amendment, incriminating admission, incriminating circumstance, incriminating statement, privilege against self-incrimination, privileges and immunities, self-incrimination

FOREIGN PHRASES: *Accusare nemo se debet.* No one is bound to accuse himself.

INCRIMINATORY, adjective accusatory, accusing, blaming, charging with guilt, condemnatory, condemning, convicting, criminative, criminatory, damaging, damnatory, damning, defamatory, denunciatory, disparaging, establishing guilt, harming, implicating, implicative, implicatory, imputative, imputing blame, inculpatory, involving in guilt

ASSOCIATED CONCEPTS: incriminatory admission, incriminatory statement, incriminatory testimony

INCUBATE, verb appear, arise, become distinct, breed, develop, give form to, grow, materialize, mature, nurture, produce, take form, transforming

INCULCATE, verb convince, direct, discipline, educate, guide, imbue, implant, impress, impress by repeated statement, impress upon the mind, imprint, *inculcare,* indoctrinate, infix, infuse, inspire, instill, instruct, lecture, plant, preach, prelect, press, propagandize, sermonize, teach, train, urge

INCULPABLE, adjective above suspicion, blameless, entirely defensible, exculpable, faultless, free from fault, free from guilt, guiltless, impeccable, *innocens*, innocent, *integer,* irreprehensible, irreproachable, not blamable, not guilty, pure, *sanctus,* sinless, unblamable, unblameworthy, uncorrupt, unerring, unimpeached, unreproached, unreproved, virtuous

INCULPATE, *verb* accuse, arraign, blame, bring to justice, charge, cite, criminate, impeach, implead, implicate, imply guilt, impute, incriminate, indict, institute proceedings, involve in blame, lodge a complaint, press charges, prosecute, recriminate

INCULPATION, *noun* accusation, blame, charging with fault, charging with guilt, condemnation, crimination, denunciation, faultfinding, implication, imputation, incrimination
ASSOCIATED CONCEPTS: confessions, exculpatory statements, inculpatory statements

INCULPATORY, *adjective* accusative, accusatory, accusing, blaming, charging with guilt, condemnatory, condemning, convicting, criminative, criminatory, damaging, damnatory, damning, denouncing, denunciatory, disparaging, establishing guilt, implicating, implicative, implicatory, imputative, imputing blame, incriminating, incriminatory, inculpating, injuring, involving in guilt
ASSOCIATED CONCEPTS: inculpatory admission, inculpatory evidence, inculpatory facts, inculpatory statements

INCUMBENT, *noun* bureaucrat, commissioner, dignitary, functionary, holder of an office, job holder, minister, occupant of an office, officebearer, officeholder, officer, official, person in authority
ASSOCIATED CONCEPTS: de facto incumbent, incumbent officer

INCUMBRANCE *(Burden), **noun*** deadweight, disadvantage, handicap, impediment, load, millstone, onus, oppression, weight

INCUMBRANCE *(Lien), **noun*** commitment, liability, imposition, obligation, restraint, title impairment
ASSOCIATED CONCEPTS: artisan's lien, encumbrance upon property, materialman's lien

INCUR, *verb* acquire, assume, bargain for, become liable for, become responsible for, bring on, bring upon oneself, contract, enter into, expose onself to, fall into, get, *incurrere,* lay oneself open to, meet with, run the chance, suscipere, undertake
ASSOCIATED CONCEPTS: claim incurred, incur a debt, incur a liability, incur an obligation, incurred risk, incurring indebtedness, penalty incurred

INCUR COSTS, *verb* acknowledge the costs, answer for, assume liability for, be answerable for, be liable for, be responsible for, bear the expense, disburse, expend, lay out for, outlay, pay the costs
ASSOCIATED CONCEPTS: assessment of costs, bill of costs, inquest

INCUR EXPENSES, *verb* assume liability for, be responsible for, bear the expense, disburse, expend, outlay, pay for, pay the costs, pick up the tab

INCURABLE, *adjective* beyond hope, beyond remedy, deadly, difficult, fatal, grave, hopeless, inoperable, irredeemable, irremediable, irreparable, irretrievable, irreversible, little hope, malignant, no hope, past hope, serious, terminal, terminal case, unsalvageable

INCURSION, *noun* advancement, aggression, assault, attack, breach, encroachment, entrance, foray, forced entry, hostile entrance, *incursio,* infiltration, influx, infringement, ingress, ingression, inroad, introgression, intrusion, invasion, irruption, onslaught, overrun, overstepping, penetration, raid, rushing in, sortie, storm, violation

INDAGATION, *noun* analysis, audit, careful search, careful study, challenge, check, close inquiry, dissection, examination, exhaustive inquiry, exhaustive study, exploration, exploratory examination, inquest, inquiry, inquisition, inspection, interrogation, investigation, minute investigation, narrow search, observation, perquisition, perscrutation, perusal, probe, quest, questioning, research, review, rigorous search, scrutation, scrutiny, search, searching investigation, strict examination, strict inquiry, strict search, study, systematic search, test, trial

INDEBTED, *adjective* beholden, bound, bounden, devoted, encumbered, in arrears, in debt, legally obliged to repay, obaeratus, obligated, *obligatus,* obliged, owing, short of funds, thankful, unable to pay, under obligation
ASSOCIATED CONCEPTS: involuntary indebtedness, voluntary indebtedness

INDECENCY, *noun* impropriety, indecorousness, indelicacy, obnoxiousness, tastelessness, unseemingliness, untastefulness, vulgarity
ASSOCIATED CONCEPTS: indecent assault, indecent exposure, indecent liberties, indecent publications, lewd and lascivious conduct

INDECENT, *adjective* abusive, course, debauched, degenerate, depraved, dissolute, distasteful, foul, immoral, improper, inappropriate, inelegant, lascivious, lecherous, lewd, libertine, libidinous, licentious, lickerish, loose, lubricous, lurid, lustful, offensive, outrageous, perverted, profane, profligate, promiscuous, repulsive, ribald, risqué, salacious, scandalous, scurrilous, shameful, shameless, suggestive, tawdry, unacceptable, unapt, unbecoming, unbefitting, unfitting, unseemly, unsuitable, vile, vulgar
ASSOCIATED CONCEPTS: indecent act, indecent assault, indecent behavior, indecent broadcasts, indecent communications, indecent exhibition, indecent exposure, indecent liberties, obscenity laws

INDECIPHERABLE, *adjective* abstract, abstruse, arcane, baffling, blurred, complex, complicated, concealed, cryptic, difficult, effaced, enigmatic, erased, esoteric, illegible, impenetrable, incomprehensible, indistinct, indistinguishable, inexplicable, inextricable, inscrutable, intricate, involved, mysterious, nebulous, oblique, obscure, puzzling, recondite, tangled, unclear, undecipherable, undistinguishable, unexplainable, unfathomable, unrecognizable, vague, veiled

INDECISION, *noun* changeableness, dilemma, doubt, doubtfulness, dubiety, dubiousness, dubitancy, *dubitatio,* dubitation, equivocalness, fickleness, fluctuation, *haesitatio,* hesitancy, hesitation, inability to decide, incertitude, *inconstantia,* indetermination, infirmity of purpose, instability, irresoluteness, irresolution, lack of certainty, lack of decision, oscillation, quandary, tendency to change the mind, tendency to waver, uncertainty, unsettled opinion, unsteadiness, unsureness, vacillation

INDECISIVE, *adjective* careful, cautious, changeable, circumspect, dubious, equivocal, fickle, hesitant, irresolute, lacking leadership, noncommitted, oscillating, prudent, unable to act, unable to decide, uncertain, uncertainty, uncommitted, unsure, vacillating

INDEED, adverb above all, absolutely, actually, admittedly, affirmative, all the more, as a matter of fact, assuredly, by all manner of means, by all means, certainly, chiefly, clearly, decidedly, decisively, definitely, demonstrably, distinctly, dominantly, especially, first of all, for certain, for the most part, in chief, in effect, in fact, in point of fact, in reality, in the first place, in the main, in truth, indeed, mainly, manifestly, most assuredly, most certainly, mostly, noticeably, observably, obviously, particularly, positively, precisely, predominantly, primarily, principally, surely, to be sure, truly, unequivocally, unmistakably, unquestionably, without a doubt

INDEFEASIBLE, adjective binding, confirmed, entrenched, established, immutable, imperishable, imprescriptible, in perpetuum ratus, inalienable, incapable of being defeated, incapable of being revoked, incontestable, incontrovertible, indestructible, indissoluble, indubitable, ineradicable, inextinguishable, insusceptible of change, intransmutable, invariable, inviolable, irrefragable, irremovable, irreversible, irrevocable, nonreversible, not forfeitable, not to be abrogated, not to be annulled, not to be made void, permanent, reverseless, settled, unalterable, unchallengeable, unchangeable, undefeatable, undeniable, undisputable, unquestionable
ASSOCIATED CONCEPTS: indefeasible estate, indefeasible interest, indefeasible title, indefeasibly vested

INDEFENSIBLE, adjective accessible, assailable, capable of being conquered, capable of being overcome, conquerable, defenseless, exposed, helpless, inexcusable, inexpiable, insupportable, pregnable, quod defendi non potest, unfortified, unguarded, unjustifiable, unprotected, untenable, unwarrantable, vincible, vulnerable

INDEFINABLE, adjective abstruse, beyond expression, confusing, cryptic, difficult to explain, difficult to translate, difficult to understand, enigmatic, enigmatical, hard to explain, hard to translate, hard to understand, impenetrable, impossible to explain, impossible to translate, impossible to understand, incomprehensible, indescribable, inexplicable, inexpressible, inscrutable, mysterious, obscure, opaque, perplexing, puzzling, unaccountable, unclear, unfathomable, unplain, untranslatable

INDEFINITE, adjective alterable, ambiguous, ambiguus, amorphic, amorphous, barely seen, blurred, blurry, boundless, broad, changeable, cloudy, controvertible, cryptic, debatable, dim, doubtful, dubious, dubius, enigmatic, enigmatical, equivocal, evasive, faint, formless, ill-defined, imperspicuous, imprecise, in doubt, incertus, indecisive, indeterminate, indistinct, indistinguishable, inexact, inexplicit, mysterious, nondescript, nonspecific, not positive, not sharp, obscure, opaque, open to question, oracular, questionable, shapeless, subject to change, suppositional, theoretical, unascertained, unbounded, uncertain, unclear, undecided, undefined, undetermined, undiscernible, unexact, unintelligible, unlimited, unresolved, unsettled, unspecified, unstable, unsure, untold, vague
ASSOCIATED CONCEPTS: indefinite contract, indefinite failure of issue, indefinite liability, indefinite sentence

INDELIBLE, adjective changeless, deep, deep-felt, durable, enduring, fadeless, fast, firm, fixed, fixed in the mind, haunting, immovable, immutable, imperishable, impressed on the mind, incapable of being deleted, indefeasible, indelibilis, indestructible, indissoluble, ineffaceable, ineradicable, inerasable, inextinguishable, ingrained, insoluble, irremovable, irreversible, irrevocable, keen, lasting, memorable, nagging, never to be erased from the mind, never to be forgotten, nonperishable, penetrating, permanent, persevering, persistent, persisting, pervading, pervasive, piercing, plaguing, poignant, profound, recurrent, reverseless, rooted, sempiternus, stable, stamped on one's memory, steadfast, unalterable, unchangeable, undestroyable, unerasable, unfading, unforgettable, unforgotten, unyielding, vivid
ASSOCIATED CONCEPTS: indeligible public interests in property, indeligible ruse

INDEMNIFICATION, noun amends, compensation, indemnity, monetary remuneration, payment, recompense, redemption, reimbursement, remuneration, reparation, repayment, requital, requitement, restitution, restoration, return, satisfaction

INDEMNIFY, verb answer for, compensate, compensate for injury, compensate for loss, compensate for loss sustained, damnum restituere, damnum sarcire, give back, give satisfaction, grant monetary compensation, guarantee, insure, make good, make good against anticipated loss, make reparation, make restitution, make up, offer compensation, offer reparation, offer satisfaction, pay, pay back, pay compensation, pay reparations, recompense, recompense for past loss, redeem, refund, reimburse, remunerate, repay, requite, restore, return money paid out, save harmless, secure against damage, secure against loss
ASSOCIATED CONCEPTS: subrogate

INDEMNITY, noun act of holding harmless, amends, assurance against loss, compensation, full satisfaction, indemnification, lex oblivionis, payment, protection against loss, recompense, recoupment, redemption, refund, reimbursement, remuneration, repayment, requitement, restitution, restoration, return, security, security against damage, security against loss, setoff, vindication
ASSOCIATED CONCEPTS: contract of indemnity, covenant of indemnity, indemnity against liability, indemnity against loss, indemnity agreement, indemnity bond, indemnity insurance, indemnity mortgage, indemnity policy, indemnity reinsurance, limitation of indemnity, subrogation

INDEMONSTRABLE, adjective containing variables, doubting, equivocal, incalculable, indecisive, inexplicit, irresolute, irresponsible, not ascertainable, not provable, skeptical, uncertain, unconfirmable, unconvinced, uncountable, unprovable, unsure, unverifiable
ASSOCIATED CONCEPTS: indemonstrable principles

INDENTURE, noun agreement, agreement to work, apprenticeship agreement, arrangement, commitment, compact, contract, contract to work, contractual obligation, contractual statement, covenant, deed of agreement, instrument, mutual agreement, mutual undertaking, pact, pactum, stipulation, undertaking

INDENTURED, adjective apprenticed, articled, bound by agreement, bound by contract, contracted, engaged, enslaved, obligated, obliged, promised, tied down, under obligation
ASSOCIATED CONCEPTS: indentured apprentice

INDEPENDENCE, noun authority, authorization, autonomy, delegation, disassociation, disconnection, emancipation, freedom, liberty, license, not controlled, prerogative, privilege, self-determination, self-direction, sovereignty, unencumbered, unrestraint, unshackled

INDEPENDENT, *adjective*   autarkic, autonomous, detached, disconnected, dissociated, free, freelance, irrelative, *liber,* masterless, neutral, nonpartisan, self-governing, self-reliant, self-subsistent, self-supporting, *solutus,* sovereign, unaffiliated, unallied, unassociated, unattached, unbound, unbridled, unchecked, uncommitted, unconnected, unconquered, uncontrolled, uncurbed, unencumbered, unenslaved, unenthralled, unfettered, unhindered, uninfluenced, unreined, unshackled, unsubjected, unvanquished
ASSOCIATED CONCEPTS: independent advice, independent agreement, independent cause, independent contractor, independent covenant, independent duty, independent negligence, independent tortfeasor, independently established
FOREIGN PHRASES: *Illud quod alteri unitur extinguitur neque amplius per se vacare licet.* That which is united to another is extinguished, nor can it be independent.

INDESCRIBABLE, *adjective*   astonishing, astronomical, beyond words, dazzling, delightful, extraordinary, incommunicable, inconceivable, incredible, indefinite, inexpressible, miraculous, nondescript, off the charts, remarkable, striking, stunning, unheard of, unspeakable, unusual, wonderful, wondrous

INDESTRUCTIBILITY, *noun*   *aplomb,* ceaselessness, changelessness, constancy, continuance, continuity, durability, durableness, endlessness, endurance, eternalness, everlastingness, immortality, immutability, imperishability, indefeasibility, indelibility, indissolubility, ineradicableness, inerasableness, insusceptibility to change, interminability, lastingness, permanence, perpetuity, stability, steadiness, unalterability, unchangeability
ASSOCIATED CONCEPTS: indestructible trust

INDESTRUCTIBLE, *adjective*   abiding, durable, endless, enduring, everlasting, fadeless, hardy, imperishable, indefeasible, indelible, indissoluble, ineffaceable, inerasable, inextinguishable, insusceptible, invulnerable, irrevocable, lasting, nonperishable, perennial, permanent, perpetual, *perpetuus,* persevering, persisting, *quod everti non potest,* reliable, sturdy, tenacious, tough, undestroyable, undying, unfading, unyielding
ASSOCIATED CONCEPTS: indestructible trust

INDETERMINATE, *adjective*   ambiguous, *anceps,* boundless, cryptic, *dubius,* endless, equivocal, featureless, fluctuant, fluid, formless, hazy, ill-defined, immeasurable, in a state of uncertainty, in doubt, inarticulated, incalculable, *incertus,* inconclusive, indefinite, indistinct, infinite, interminable, limitless, measureless, nonspecific, not ascertained, not designated, not fixed, not fixed in extent, not made certain, not particularly designated, not precise, not settled, obscure, open, open to question, shapeless, speculative, termless, unbounded, uncertain, unclear, undecided, undefined, unfathomable, unfixed, unlimited, unmeasured, unordered, unresolved, unsettled, unspecified, vague, without bound, without end, without limit, without measure
ASSOCIATED CONCEPTS: indeterminate damages, indeterminate penalty, indeterminate punishment, indeterminate sentence

INDETERMINATION, *noun*   ambiguousness, blurred line, blurry line, borderline decision, boundless variables, clouded choices, confusion, doubtfulness, equivocalness, immeasurable choices, imprecise, in a state of uncertainty, in

doubt, inconclusiveness, indefiniteness, indefinity, indeterminateness, indistinctness, inexactness, inexplicitness, infiniteness, interminableness, lacking specificity, limitlessness, nebulousness, obscurity, speculation, uncertainness

INDEX *(Catalog), noun*   earmark, enumeration, indicant, indicator, list, listing, listing of contents, mark, sign

INDEX *(Docket), verb*   categorize, codify, file, submit

INDEX *(Gauge), noun*   measure, guide, scale

INDEX *(Relate), verb*   catalog, class, classify, document, enumerate, group, inventory, itemize, list, specify, record, supply or furnish with reference

INDICANT, *noun*   augury, auspice, badge, beacon, brand, caution, characteristic, cipher, clue, cue, diagnostic, emblem, ensign, example, exponent, figure, flag, foretoken, hint, implication, index, indication, indicator, landmark, manifestation, mark, note, omen, pointer, portent, presage, prognostic, representation, representative, sign, signal, signature, signboard, stamp, suggestion, symbol, symptom, token, trademark, visible token, watchword

INDICATE, *verb*   advert to, allude to, augur, be a sign of, be a token of, bespeak, betoken, brief, call attention to, connote, convey, direct, direct attention to, evidence, evince, express briefly, express generally, foretoken, give a signal, guide, highlight, hint, imply, index, *indicare,* insinuate, intimate, make necessary, make needed, mark out, point out, point to, portend, presage, show, signal, signalize, *significare,* signify, sketch, stand for, suggest, touch on

INDICATION, *noun*   allusion, augury, auspice, badge, brand, clue, connotation, cue, emblem, evidence, evincement, exponent, foretoken, guide, hint, implication, index, indicant, indicator, *indicium,* innuendo, insinuation, intimation, mark, marker, mention, monition, note, omen, pointer, portent, premonitor, premonitory sign, presage, prognostic, prompt, reference, sign, signal, *significatio,* signpost, suggestion, symbol, symptom, token, trace, *vestigium,* warning

INDICATOR, *noun*   attestant, attester, augury, auspice, badge, beacon, clue, cue, emblem, ensign, flag, foreshadowing, harbinger, herald, hint, index, informant, informer, landmark, mark, note, pointer, precursor, prognostic, semaphore, sign, stamp, symbol, symptom, token, warning, witness

INDICIA, *noun*   characteristic marks, characteristics, evidence, expressions, features, hints, indications, manifestations, marks, means of recognition, signs, symbols, tokens
ASSOCIATED CONCEPTS: indicia of ownership

INDICT, *verb*   accusare, accuse, blame, bring a formal accusation against, call to account, charge, charge with offense, charge with the commission of a crime, formally charge, formally charge with a crime, implicate, incriminate, inculpate, lodge a complaint, make formal accusation against, *nomen deferre,* prefer charges

INDICTMENT, *noun*   accusal, *accusatio,* accusation, allegation, castigation, charge, complaint, *crimen,* delation, denunciation, formal accusation, grand jury's accusation, *libellus,* main charge, presentment, reproach, written accusation

ASSOCIATED CONCEPTS: arraignment, counts of an indictment, felony complaint, felony information, grand jury, indictable offense, motion to quash, no true bill, plea, presentment, true bill

INDIFFERENCE, noun aloofness, apathy, blankness, coldness, coolness, detachment, disinterestedness, disregard, impassiveness, imperturbability, inattention, inconsideration, insouciance, laxity, lukewarmness, neglect, negligence, nonchalance, nonobservance, unconcern

INDIFFERENT, adjective aloof, callous, casual, derelict, disinterested, dispassionate, distant, fair, faithless, heedless, impartial, impassible, imperfect, impervious, inactive, inappreciable, inattentive, inconsequential, incurious, insensate, insignificant, insipid, insouciant, languid, lax, listless, marginal, mediocre, middling, moderate, negligent, neutral, nonchalant, not caring, obdurate, oblivious, ordinary, otiose, passable, passive, perfunctory, phlegmatic, poor, reckless, remiss, slipshod, thoughtless, tolerable, unbiased, unconcerned, uninquisitive, uninterested, unjaundiced, unmindful, unprejudiced, unresponsive, usual, vapid
ASSOCIATED CONCEPTS: disinterested party, impartiality

INDIGENCE, noun bare subsistence, dearth, destitution, egestas, embarrassment, impecuniosity, impoverishment, *inopia,* insolvency, insufficiency, insufficient income, *mendicitas,* narrow means, necessitousness, need, neediness, needy circumstances, pauperism, pennilessness, penury, poor circumstances, poorness, poverty, privation, scarcity, want

INDIGNATION, adjective adversarial, adverse, antithetical, at odds, averse, dead set against, differing, disagreeing, disinclined, fractious, hesitant, hostile, not feeling like, not in favor of, not in the mood, not inclined, obdurate, opposed, queasy, recalcitrant, reluctant, resistant, righteousness, squeamish, unwilling
ASSOCIATED CONCEPTS: inequality and indignation, moral indignation, righteous indignation

INDIRECT, adjective allusive, ambagious, backhanded, circuitous, circumambulating, circumlocutory, covert, crooked, desultory, deviating, deviatory, devious, *devius,* digressing, digressive, excursive, hidden, implicit, labyrinthine, meandering, *non rectus,* oblique, *obliquus,* out of the way, periphrastic, periphrastical, rambling, roundabout, serpentine, sidelong, sinuous, tacit, tortuose, turning, twisting, understood, unexpressed, vagrant, wandering, winding, zigzag
ASSOCIATED CONCEPTS: indirect benefit, indirect evidence, indirect interest, indirect notice, indirect result, indirect tax, indirect testimony

INDIRECTION (Deceitfulness), **noun** concealment of truth, cozenage, craft, craftiness, cunning, deceit, deception, deviousness, dishonesty, disingenuity, disingenuousness, dissimulation, duplicity, falsehood, falseness, fraud, fraudulency, guile, hypocrisy, improbity, insincerity, intrigue, lack of candidness, lack of conscience, lack of probity, mendaciousness, mendacity, obliqueness, obliquity, perfidiousness, perfidy, perversion of truth, pretense, prevarication, slyness, underhandedness, unstraightforwardness, untrustworthiness, untruthfulness

INDIRECTION (Indirect action), **noun** aberrance, aberrancy, circuitous action, circuitous route, circuitousness, circuity, circumflexion, circumlocution, crookedness, departure, deviation, deviousness, digression, divagation, obliquation, obliqueness, obliquity, periphrasis, roundabout action, roundaboutness, straying, swerve, unstraightforward action, zigzag

INDISCERNIBLE, adjective camouflaged, concealed, delitescent, disguised, evanescent, hidden, impalpable, imperceptible, inconspicuous, indistinguishable, invisible, screened, unapparent, unbeholdable, undiscoverable, unnoticeable, unperceivable, unrecognizable, unregarded, unseeable, veiled

INDISCREET, adjective careless, culpable, hasty, heedless, ill-judged, impetuous, impolitic, improvident, imprudent, impulsive, incautious, inconsiderate, indiscriminating, inexpedient, injudicious, inopportune, lacking prudence, misadvised, precipitate, thoughtless, uncritical, undiscerning, unpolitic, unprofessional, unreflecting, unselective, unsensible, unsound, unthinking, unwise

INDISCRETION, noun blunder, carelessness, error, ill judgment, impoliticness, imprudence, *impudentia,* incaution, incautiousness, incircumspection, injudiciousness, lack of circumspection, lack of consideration, lack of judgment, misconduct, misjudgment, misstep, mistake, offense, *os impudens,* poor judgment, rashness, recklessness, slip, tactlessness, thoughtlessness, uncircumspection, unwariness, unwiseness

INDISCRIMINATE, adjective blanket, broad, comprehensive, designless, haphazard, immethodical, not choosy, not selective, orderless, promiscuous, *promiscuus,* random, systemless, unaimed, uncritical, undifferentiating, undirected, unmethodical, unorganized, unparticular, unspecific, unsystematic

INDISPENSABLE, adjective basic, called for, cardinal, central, compulsory, critical, crucial, dictated, essential, exigent, fundamental, high-priority, imperative, important, imposed, integral, irreplaceable, key, main, major, mandatory, *necessarius,* necessary, necessitated, needed, obligatory, of importance, pivotal, pressing, primary, required, requisite, significant, unavoidable, urgent, vital, wanted
ASSOCIATED CONCEPTS: indispensable evidence, indispensable parties

INDISPENSABLE PARTY, noun added party, compulsory defendant, compulsory party, critical added party, essential party, imperative party, mandatory party, obligatory party, required party, requisite party, vital party
ASSOCIATED CONCEPTS: indispensable party to an action, motion to dismiss for failure to join an indispensable party

INDISPOSED, adjective adverse, antipathetic to, at loggerheads to, at odds, averse, dead set against, differing, disagreeing, disinclined, fractious, hesitant, hostile, loath, obdurate, opposed, out of commission, out of order, out of sorts, recalcitrant, reluctant, resistant

INDISPUTABLE, adjective absolute, apodictic, assured, authoritative, axiomatic, believable, beyond a shadow of a doubt, beyond dispute, categorical, certain, clear, conclusive, decided, decisive, definite, definitive, demonstrable, demonstrated, determinate, evident, explicit, factual, impregnable, inappealable, incontestable, incontrovertible, indefeasible, indisputable, indubious, indubitable, infallible, irrefutable, manifest, obvious, official, palpable, positive, proven, real, reliable, self-evident, solid, unassailable, unconditional, undeniable, undisputed, undoubting, unequivocal, unimpeachable, unmistakable, unmitigated, unqualified, unquestionable, unrefutable, unreserved, unshakable, well-founded

INDISTINCT, *adjective* ambiguous, blurred, blurry, cryptic, delitescent, dim, dusky, enigmatic, enigmatical, faded, faint, filmy, foggy, half-seen, hazy, ill-defined, illegible, imperceptible, inaudible, incomprehensible, indistinguishable, lacking clarity, lacking precision, misty, muffled, mysterious, nebulous, nubilous, *obscurus,* out of focus, *parum clarus, perplexus,* smoky, unclear, undecipherable, undefined, unintelligible, unplain, unrecognizable, vague, weak

INDISTINCTNESS, *noun* blur, blurriness, delitescence, delitescency, dimness, dullness, faintness, filminess, fog, fogginess, fuzziness, gloom, grayness, haziness, imperceptibility, inaudibility, indefiniteness, indistinguishability, mistiness, murkiness, mysteriousness, nebulosity, obscuration, obscurity, opacity, paleness, poor visiblity, shadow, shadowiness, smokiness, unclearness, unplainness, vagueness

INDISTINGUISHABLE, *adjective* alike, balanced, coequal, coincident, coinciding, collateral, comparable, corresponding, duplicate, equal, equivalent, exact, exactly alike, exactly the same, hard to make out, homogeneous, identical, indiscernible, interchangeable, like, matching, similar, uniform, without distinction

INDIVIDUAL, *adjective* detached, deviating, different, differentiated, discrete, disjoined, disjunct, distinct, distinctive, distinguishable, exceptional, extracted, extraordinary, independent, individualized, isolated, nonconforming, nonuniform, particular, *proprius,* rare, separate, separated, single, singular, *singularis,* sole, solitary, special, unallied, unannexed, unassimilated, unassociated, unattached, unclassifiable, uncommon, unconnected, unconventional, unimitated, unique, unjoined, unrelated, unusual
ASSOCIATED CONCEPTS: individual capacity, individual causes of action, individual damages, individual debts, individual liability

INDIVIDUAL, *noun* autonomous being, being, body, character, distinct indivisible entity, human being, individuality, integer, monad, monas, one, organism, particular one, party, person, person full of character, personage, personality
ASSOCIATED CONCEPTS: individual capacity, individual liability, individual property, individual rights

INDIVIDUAL RIGHTS, *noun* authority, authorization, basic rights, civil rights, constitutional rights, fundamental rights, inalienable rights, just claims, justification, legal power, power, privilege, right, sanction, vested interest
ASSOCIATED CONCEPTS: freedom, individualism, Libertarianism

INDIVIDUALISM, *noun* attribute, badge, brand, character, characteristic, credentials, differential, disposition, distinctive feature, earmark, feature, identity, idiosyncrasy, independence, individuality, leaning, lineament, mark, nature, originality, particularity, peculiarity, personality, property, quality, self-determination, self-identity, singularity, specialty, temperament, tendency, trait, type

INDIVIDUALITY, *noun* being, character, characteristic, curiosity, definiteness, diagnostic, difference, distinction, eccentricity, entity, feature, identity, idiosyncrasy, individual, integrality, mannerism, nonconformity, oneness, originality, particularity, peculiarity, person, personality, property, quirk, singleness, singularity, specialty, specific quality, temperament, trait, uniqueness

INDIVISIBLE, *adjective* close, impartible, incapable of being divided, incapable of being separated, indiscerptible, *individuus,* inseparable, inseverable, nondivisible, one, tenacious, unbreakable, undividable, united, unsunderable
ASSOCIATED CONCEPTS: indivisible contract, indivisible injury, indivisible ownership of property

INDOCTRINATE, *verb* beat into, beat into the head, brainwash, brainwash with propaganda, convert, convince, drill into, drum into, get into the head of, imbue, implant, impregnate, impress upon the mind, inculcate, indoctrinate, infect, infix, influence, infuse, ingrain, instill, persuade, pound into head, program, subvert, train, urge, win over
ASSOCIATED CONCEPTS: indoctrinating jurors

INDOLENT, *adjective* apathetic, cunctative, *deses,* dilatory, idle, *ignavus,* inactive, indifferent, indisposed to action, *iners,* lackadaisical, lacking vigor, laggard, languid, lax, lazy, leaden, lethargic, listless, loafing, motionless, negligent, otiose, passive, phlegmatic, procrastinative, shiftless, slack, slothful, sluggish, stagnant, supine, torpid, unenterprising

INDOMITABLE, *adjective* bold, brave, courageous, dauntless, defiant, determined, doughty, energetic, fearless, firm, forceful, forcible, formidable, hardy, impregnable, incapable of being subdued, indefatigable, indocile, *indomitus,* inextinguishable, insuperable, insurmountable, intractable, *invictus,* invincible, irrepressible, irresistible, masterful, omnipotent, overpowering, overwhelming, persevering, plucky, potent, powerful, puissant, quenchless, recalcitrant, redoubtable, refractory, resisting, resistless, resolute, resolved, solid, sound, stable, stalwart, stanch, stiff, stout, strong, stubborn, tough, unbeatable, unconquerable, undaunted, unflinching, ungovernable, unmanageable, unquenchable, unruly, unshrinking, unsubduable, unsubmissive, unwavering, unyielding, valiant, vigorous

INDORSE, *verb* accredit, acquiesce in, advocate, affirm, allow, assent to, assist, authenticate, authorize, certify, commend, concur in, confirm, confirm officially, consent to, *consignare,* cosign, countenance, countersign, encourage, guarantee, initial, inscribe one's signature, lend one's name to, make valid, *praestare,* ratify, recommend, sanction, second, sign, sign one's name on, stand by, subscribe to, support, sustain, undersign, underwrite, uphold, validate, vouch for
ASSOCIATED CONCEPTS: indorse a check, indorse a note, indorse a warrant, indorse an instrument

INDORSEMENT, *noun* acceptance, accord, acquiescence, *adfirmatio,* affirmance, agreement, approbation, approval, assent, authorization, backing, certification, championship, compliance, *comprobatio,* concurrence, *confrmatio,* confirmation, consent, encouragement, esteem, favor, liking, partisanship, permission, ratification, sanction, sponsorship, stamp of approval, support, warrant
ASSOCIATED CONCEPTS: conditional indorsement, indorsement for collection, indorsement in blank, indorsement in due course, indorsement of an instrument, indorsement without recourse, subsequent indorsement

INDUBIOUS, *adjective* absolute, ascertained, assured, attested, certain, confident, convinced, definite, demonstrable, demonstrated, doubtless, factual, foolproof, guaranteed, incontestable, irrefutable, official, past dispute, positive, safe, satisfied, sure, tested, tried, uncontested, undeniable, undoubtful, unequivocal, unshakable, verifiable, without doubt, without question

INDUCE, verb actuate, *adducere,* affect, be responsible, begin, bring, bring about, bring on, bring to pass, call forth, cause, coax, conduce, convince, create, develop, drive, effect, effectuate, encourage, enlist, entice, exercise influence over, generate, goad, hasten, impel, *impellere,* incite, *inducere,* influence, inspire, instigate, inveigle, kindle, lead one to, lure, motivate, move, obtain, occasion, originate, persuade, precipitate, prevail on, prevail upon, produce, prompt, propel, provoke, rouse, spur, stimulate, sway, talk into, urge

ASSOCIATED CONCEPTS: fraud in inducement, induce to sign a contract, inducement, inducing a breach of contract, inducing perjury, inducing trade, libel, material inducement, undue influence

INDUCEMENT, noun allurement, attraction, blandishment, *causa,* cause, consideration, drive, encouragement, enticement, exhortation, fillip, goad, *incitamentum,* incitation, incitement, influence, *inlecebra,* inspiration, instigation, persuasion, persuasiveness, pressure, prompting, provocation, provocative, stimulant, stimulater, stimulation, stimulative, stimulus, urging

ASSOCIATED CONCEPTS: fraud in the inducement, inducement to purchase, material inducement

INDUCT, verb admit, appoint, assign, bring in, call up, commission, conscript, delegate, employ, engage, give entrance to, impress, *inaugurare,* inaugurate, initiate, install, instate, introduce, introduce into office, invest, license, name, nominate, ordain, place in office, post, prepare, recruit, start up, usher in

INDULGE, verb accommodate, acquiesce, allow, bear with, do a favor, do service for, endure, entertain, favor, flatter, fulfill, give in to, give license to, go along with, humor, jumps into, minister to, pamper, pander to, permit, satiate, satisfy, spoil, tolerate, yield to

INDULGENCE, noun accordance, acquiescence, allowance, approval, benevolence, *benignitas,* clearance, clemency, compassion, favor, forgiveness, generosity, generousness, grant, gratification, gratification of desire, humoring, inabstinence, *indulgentia,* leave, lenience, leniency, lenity, license, magnanimity, obligingness, pampering, pardon, patience, permission, quarter, sanction, sufferance, tolerance, toleration, *venia,* vouchsafement

INDURATE, adjective become fixed, become hardened, calcify, callous, chilled, cold, concrete, conditioned, hard, harden, hardened, ossified, petrified, rigid, toughen, unyielding, vitreous, vitrify

INDUSTRIAL, adjective automated, commercial, engaged in business, engaged in traffic, factory-made, industrialized, machine-made, manufactural, manufactured, manufactured for sale, mass-produced, mechanical, mechanized, mercantile, relating to traffic, standardized, technical, technological

ASSOCIATED CONCEPTS: industrial accident, industrial board, industrial commission, industrial disease, industrial dispute, industrial insurance, industrial uses

INDUSTRIOUS, adjective active, *adsiduus,* aggressive, ardent, assiduous, busily engaged, busy, dedicated, determined, devoted, diligent, eager, earnest, energetic, enthusiastic, hard working, indefatigable, *industrius,* intent, laborious, never idle, operose, painstaking, persevering, persistent, purposeful, sedulous, *sedulus,* sleepless, steadfast, steady, studious, tenacious, thorough, tireless, unceasing, undeviating, unfaltering, unflagging, unrelaxing, unremitting, unsleeping, unswerving, untiring, unwavering, unyielding, zealous

INDUSTRY *(Activity),* **noun** *adsiduitas,* alacrity, application, ardor, assiduity, assiduousness, attention, bustle, busyness, constancy, determination, devotedness, devotion, diligence, *diligentia,* drive, dynamism, eagerness, earnestness, effort, employment, endeavor, endurance, energy, enterprise, enthusiasm, exertion, hard work, indefatigability, *industria,* intentness, labor, laboriousness, occupation, perseverance, persistence, pursuance, pursuit, sedulity, sedulousness, steadfastness, stir, strenuousness, tenacity, toil, vigor, vim, work, zeal, zealousness

INDUSTRY *(Business),* **noun** enterprise, establishment, manufacture, mercantile business, métier, production, profession, pursuit, trade, undertaking, work

ASSOCIATED CONCEPTS: engage in industry, industrywide contract

INEBRIATION, noun alcoholism, bacchanalianism, bibulosity, bibulousness, dipsomania, drunkenness, ebrietas, inebriety, influence of liquor, insobriety, intemperance, intoxication, potation

ASSOCIATED CONCEPTS: driving while intoxicated, drunken driving, under the influence of alcohol

INEFFABLE, adjective amazing, astounding, awe-inspiring, awesome, beyond expression, beyond words, fearful, great, impossible to describe, impossible to express, incommunicable, inconceivable, incredible, *incredibilis,* indefinable, indescribable, inexpressible, *infandus,* marvelous, miraculous, mysterious, nameless, not explainable, not expressible, not to be spoken, overwhelming, sacred, splendid, staggering, strange, terrific, unable to be expressed, unable to be spoken, undefinable, unheard, unimaginable, unmentionable, unnamable, unpronounceable, unspeakable, untranslatable, unutterable

ASSOCIATED CONCEPTS: ineffable accident

INEFFECTIVE, adjective abortive, barren, disabled, effete, emasculated, feckless, feeble, figurehead, fruitless, futile, gainless, good for nothing, impotent, inadequate, incompetent, indecisive, ineffectual, inefficacious, inept, inoperative, insufficient, inutile, *inutilis,* invalid, *invalidus,* lame, neutralized, nugatory, null, powerless, profitless, sterile, unauthoritative, unavailing, unfruitful, uninfluential, unoperative, unproductive, unprofitable, unserviceable, unsuccessful, useless, vain, void, weak, withered, without effect, without weight, worthless

ASSOCIATED CONCEPTS: ineffective restriction

INEFFECTUAL, adjective abortive, barren, effete, emasculated, feckless, feeble, figurehead, fruitless, futile, gainless, good for nothing, idle, impotent, inadequate, incompetent, indecisive, ineffective, inefficacious, inept, inoperative, insufficient, inutile, *inutilis,* invalid, *invalidus,* lame, neutralized, nugatory, null, powerless, profitless, sterile, unauthoritative, unavailing, unempowered, unfruitful, uninfluential, unoperative, unproductive, unprofitable, unserviceable, unsuccessful, useless, vain, void, weak, withered, without effect, without weight, worthless

INEFFICACIOUS, adjective barren, feeble, for naught, futile, idle, impotent, inadequate, incapable, incompetent, ineffective, ineffectual, inefficient, inept, infertile, inutile, profitless, sterile, to no avail, to no purpose, unavailing, unproductive, unprofitable, unrewarding, unsuccessful, unyielding, valueless, weak, worthless

INEFFICACY, noun disability, disablement, failure, feebleness, forcelessness, helplessness, impotence, inability, inadequacy, incapability, incapacitation, incapacity, incompetence, incompetency, ineffectiveness, ineffectuality, ineffectualness, inefficaciousness, inefficiency, insufficiency, lack of power, lack of strength, powerlessness, unfruitfulness, unskillfulness, weakness

INELEGANT, adjective awkward, base, boorish, churlish, cloddish, coarse, common, crass, crude, earthy, graceless, gross, homely, homespun, ill-bred, ill-mannered, improper, in bad taste, indecorous, indelicate, *inelegans, inurbanus, invenustus,* lacking elegance, lacking good taste, lacking grace, lacking refinement, low, offensive, ribald, rough, rude, rustic, tasteless, uncourtly, uncouth, uncultivated, uncultured, undignified, ungainly, ungenteel, ungraceful, unkempt, unmannerly, unpolished, unrefined, unseemly, untasteful, vulgar, without taste

INELIGIBLE, adjective cast out, disallowed, disapproved, disentitled, disqualified, eliminated, excluded, expelled, improper, inadmissible, inappropriate, inapt, *inopportunus,* kept out, not considered, not eligible, objectionable, out of the question, outcast, rejected, unacceptable, unadapted, unchosen, undesirable, unentitled, unequipped, unfit, unfitted, unfitting, unqualified, unsuitable, unsuited, unwanted

ASSOCIATED CONCEPTS: disability, ineligible to run for political office

INEPT (Inappropriate), **adjective** absurd, at variance, bizarre, clashing, discordant, discrepant, disproportionate, dissonant, ill-adapted, ill-advised, ill-suited, ill-timed, illogical, impolitic, improper, imprudent, inaccordant, inadmissible, inadvisable, inapplicable, inapposite, inapt, incompatible, incongruent, incongruous, inconsistent, indecorous, inexpedient, infelicitous, inharmonious, injudicious, inopportune, insagacious, irreconcilable, jarring, ludicrous, malapropos, mismatched, misplaced, objectionable, out of character, out of keeping, out of place, out of proportion, outrageous, preposterous, ridiculous, silly, unapt, unbecoming, unbefitting, uncongenial, unconsonant, undesirable, undue, unfit, unfitting, unmeet, unqualified, unseasonable, unseemly, unsuitable, unsuited, untimely, untoward, unwise

INEPT (Incompetent), **adjective** awkward, blundering, bungling, clumsy, disqualified, foolish, ignorant, ill-qualified, impotent, inadept, inadequate, inapt, incapable, incompetent, ineffective, ineffectual, inefficacious, inefficient, *ineptus,* inexpert, lacking dexterity, lacking dexterousness, lacking skill, maladroit, powerless, puerile, raw, unable, unadroit, unapt, unclever, undeft, unfacile, ungainly, unhandy, unproductive, unproficient, unqualified, unskillful, useless

ASSOCIATED CONCEPTS: incompetency of counsel, incompetent to contract, insanity, under the age of majority

INEPTITUDE, noun fatuity, futility, impotence, impropriety, impuissance, inability, inadequacy, inanity, inaptitude, inappropriateness, incapacity, incompetence, inefficacy, inefficiency, inutility, stupidity, unfitness, uselessness, worthlessness

ASSOCIATED CONCEPTS: inadequacy of counsel, ineffective counsel

INEQUALITY, noun asymmetry, bias, contrast, deviation, difference, disaccord, disagreement, discrepance, discrepancy, disparity, disproportion, disproportionateness, dissimilarity, dissimilitude, *dissimilitudo,* dissonance, distinction, divergence, diversity, imbalance, imparity, *inaequalitas,* incompatibility, incongruity, incongruousness, inconsistency, inconsonance, injustice, irregularity, lack of equality, lack of symmetry, nonconformity, nonuniformity, partiality, prejudice, unbalance, unconformity, unevenness, unfairness, unlikeness, ununiformity, variance, variation

INEQUITABLE, adjective discriminatory, favoring, one sided, partial, partisan, prejudiced, unbalanced, uneven, unfair, unjust, weighted

INEQUITY, noun bias, biased judgment, bigotry, discrimination, disproportion, favor, favoritism, foregone conclusion, foul play, inequitableness, injustice, intolerance, leaning, miscarriage of justice, one-sidedness, partiality, partisanism, partisanship, preapprehension, preconceived idea, preconceived notion, preconception, predilection, preference, preferential treatment, prejudgment, prejudice, prenotion, prepossession, presentiment, presumption, undetachment, undispassionateness, undueness, unfairness, unjust decision, unjustness

INERTIA, noun apathy, dormancy, dullness, firmness, immobility, immobilization, immovability, inability to act, inaction, inactivity, indecision, indisposition to move, indolence, inertness, inexcitability, irresolution, lack of activity, lack of motion, lack of movement, languor, lassitude, laziness, lethargy, lifelessness, motionlessness, negligence, oscitancy, paralysis, passiveness, passivity, quiescence, resistance to change, rest, sloth, sluggishness, stagnation, stupor, supineness, torpor, vegetation, want of activity, weariness

INESCAPABLE, adjective absolute, cannot be avoided, certain, destined, fated, fateful, for sure, inevasible, inexorable, necessary, predestined, sure, unalterable, unavoidable, uncontrollable, uneluctable, unpreventable, unstoppable, unyielding

ASSOCIATED CONCEPTS: inescapable law, inescapable truths

INESTIMABLE, adjective above all price, above all value, above appraisal, beyond price, choice, costly, immeasurable, immensurable, *inaestimabilis,* incalculable, infinite, inimitable, invaluable, irreplaceable, matchless, measureless, peerless, precious, priceless, rare, select, unequalled, unique, unmatched, unparalleled, unsurpassable, valuable, without equal, without price

INEVITABLE, adjective about to happen, approaching, assured, at hand, brewing, certain, decided, definite, destined, determined, fated, fixed, following, foreordained, forthcoming, guaranteed, imminent, impending, in store, in the offing, ineluctable, ineludible, inescapable, inevasible, *inevitabilis,* looming, near, *necessarius,* next, ordained, predestined, preordained, sure, sure to happen, to come, unalterable, unavoidable, unchangeable, unfailing, unpreventable, unquestionable

ASSOCIATED CONCEPTS: inevitable accident, inevitable casualty, inevitable occurrence

INEXACT, adjective ambiguous, approximate, approximative, broad, careless, crude, erroneous, estimated, faulty, flawed, general, guessed, *haud accuratus,* hazy, imperfect, imprecise, inaccurate, incorrect, loose, miscalculated, misfigured, misinterpreted, misreported, misstated, mistranslated, more or less, nearly accurate, nearly correct, rough, surmised, unclear, unmeticulous, unrevised, unscientific, unspecified, vague, without precision

INEXCUSABLE, *adjective*   atrocious, blameworthy, brutal, condemnable, cruel, disgraceful, flagitious, heinous, immoral, incapable of being justified, incorrigible, indefensible, inexpiable, irremissible, monstrous, objectionable, outrageous, *quod nihil excusationis habet,* reprehensible, reprobate, shameful, unallowable, unatonable, unforgivable, unjustifiable, unpardonable, unprincipled, unreasonable, unwarrantable, unwarranted, vicious, without defense, without excuse

ASSOCIATED CONCEPTS: inexcusable conduct, inexcusable delay, inexcusable neglect

INEXCUSABLE DELAY, *noun*   default, dereliction, dilatoriness, disregard, failure of duty, indifference, inobservance, lack of diligence, laggardness, laxity, laxness, malfeasance, neglect, neglectfulness, negligence, noncompliance, nonfeasance, nonobservance, nonperformance, prejudicial delay, procrastination, remissness, unconscionable delay, undue delay, unexplained delay, unnecessary prolongation, unreasonable delay

ASSOCIATED CONCEPTS: failure to litigate, laches

INEXCUSABLE NEGLECT, *noun*   breach of trust, careless abandon, carelessness, delinquency, dereliction, disregard, failure to care, heedlessness, idleness, inaction, inattention, inattentiveness, indifference, inexcusable carelessness, malfeasance, malignant oversight, nonfeasance, nonperformance, omission, reckless absentmindedness, recklessness, severe laxity, severe laxness, thoughtlessness, unforgivable abandonment

ASSOCIATED CONCEPTS: inexcusable neglect of duty, latches, malpractice

INEXORABLE, *adjective*   adamant, convinced, decided, determined, dogged, firm, headstrong, immovable, immutable, implacable, indomitable, *inexorabilis,* inflexible, intractable, merciless, obdurate, obstinate, opinionated, opinionative, persevering, persistent, persisting, pertinacious, pitiless, positive, relentless, resistant, resolute, resolved, set, severe, steadfast, steady, sternly just, strong-minded, strong-willed, stubborn, tenacious, unalterable, unbending, unchanging, uncompassionate, uncompromising, uncontrollable, unfaltering, unimpressible, unmanageable, unmerciful, unmovable, unmoved by entreaties, unpersuadable, unrelenting, unshaken, unwavering, unyielding, willful

INEXPEDIENCE, *noun*   disadvantage, disadvantageousness, folly, foolishness, imprudence, inadvisability, inappropriateness, inexpediency, infelicity, injudiciousness, inopportuneness, *inutilitas,* ludicrousness, rashness, senselessness, undesirability, undesirableness, unfitness, unfittingness, unprofitability, unsensibleness, unsoundness, unsuitability, unthoughtfulness, untimeliness, unwiseness

INEXPERIENCED, *adjective*   amateur, artless, beardless, callow, green, *ignarus,* ignorant, ill-qualified, immature, *imperitus,* inapt, inept, inexpert, innocent, lacking experience, lacking proficiency, lacking skill, naive, new, poorly qualified, raw, *rudis,* sophomoric, unaccustomed, unacquainted, unadapted, unbusinesslike, unconversant, undeveloped, undisciplined, undrilled, unfamiliar, unfledged, unhabituated, uninformed, uninitiated, unlicensed, unpracticed, unqualified, unripe, unschooled, unseasoned, unskilled, unsophisticated, untrained, untried, untutored, unused, unversed, unworldly, verdant, without experience, without knowledge, young, youthful

INEXPIABLE, *adjective*   base, blameworthy, censurable, condemnable, disgraceful, evil, facinorous, flagitious, heinous, indefensible, inexcusable, *inexplicabilis,* infamous, nefarious, reprehensible, scandalous, shameful, unallowable, unatonable, unforgivable, unjustifiable, unpardonable, unreasonable, vicious, villainous, virtueless, wicked, without defense, without excuse

INEXPLICABLE, *adjective*   abstruse, acroamatic, acroamatical, acroatic, baffling, concealed, enigmatic, enigmatical, esoteric, hard to understand, hidden, impenetrable, inapprehensible, incapable of being explained, incomprehensible, indefinable, *inexplicabilis,* inscrutable, insoluble, insolvable, mysterious, mystic, mystical, obscure, occult, paradoxical, puzzling, recondite, shrouded in mystery, strange, unaccountable, undecipherable, undiscoverable, unexplainable, unfamiliar, unintelligible, unknowable, unknown, unrecognizable

INEXPRESSIVE, *adjective*   apathetic, blank, characterless, cold, deadpan, devoid of expression, dim, dull, empty, enigmatic, enigmatical, expressionless, hardened, impassive, impenetrable, imperturbable, impervious, incomprehensible, inexplicable, inscrutable, lackluster, listless, meaningless, nebulous, nonsensical, obtuse, pokerfaced, puzzling, senseless, spiritless, stupid, trite, unaffected, unanimated, undecipherable, unemotional, unfathomable, unintelligible, unmoved, vacant, vacuous, vague, void

INEXPUGNABLE, *adjective*   defensible, formidable, hardy, immune, impenetrable, imperdible, impregnable, indomitable, *inexpugnabilis,* inextinguishable, insuperable, insurmountable, invincible, inviolable, invulnerable, irresistible, mighty, potent, powerful, protected, puissant, redoubtable, resistless, safe, secure, secure from capture, strong, sturdy, tenable, unassailable, unattackable, unbeatable, unbreakable, unchallengeable, unconquerable, unsubduable, unyielding

INEXTRICABLE, *adjective*   adhering, attached, bound, cohesive, combined, complex, complicated, compounded, confused, conjunct, connected, convoluted, embrangled, entangled, fast, fixed, immovable, impacted, indissoluble, indivisible, *inexplicabilis, inextricabilis,* inseparable, inseverable, insoluble, intricate, involute, involuted, involved, irreducible, irremovable, jammed, joined, knotted, labyrinthine, matted, mazy, mixed, raveled, snarled, stuck, tangled, tangly, tied, turbid, twisted, wedged

INFALLIBLE, *adjective*   assured, *certus,* continuing, defectless, dependable, enduring, errorless, everlasting, exhaustless, faithful, faultless, flawless, foolproof, free from imperfection, free from mistake, *haud dubius,* imperishable, incapable of error, incontestable, incontrovertible, indefatigable, indefectible, indefective, indomitable, inerrable, inerrant, inexhaustible, irrefragable, irreproachable, lasting, never-failing, perfect, reliable, secure, stable, stainless, stanch, staying, steady, sure, tenacious, trustworthy, trusty, unassailable, unbeatable, unchanged, unchanging, unconquerable, undestroyable, undying, unerring, unfading, unfailing, unfaltering, unflagging, unimpeachable, unquestionable, unquestioned, unspotted, unstoppable, unsurpassed, untainted, unwavering, unyielding, without blemish

INFAMOUS, *adjective*   abominable, arrant, atrocious, bad, base, contemptible, contemptuous, despicable, detestable, discreditable, disgraceful, dishonorable, disreputable, egregious, execrable, felonious, flagitious, flagrant, heinous, ignoble, ignominious, illicit, inexpiable, inglorious, iniquitous, Machiavellian, malevolent, maleficent, monstrous, nefarious, notorious, odious, opprobrious, outrageous, peccant, perfidious, profligate, reprehensible, reprobate, scandalous, scurrilous, shameful, shameless, shocking, sinister, unprincipled, unrespectable, villainous

INFAMY, *noun*   abasement, aspersion, bad name, bad reputation, baseness, blot, brand, contempt, defamation, degradation, derision, detestableness, disapprobation, disapproval, discredit, disesteem, disfavor, disgrace, dishonor, disrepute, disrespect, evil fame, humiliation, ignobility, *ignominia,* ignominiousness, ignominy, ill repute, *infamia,* infamousness, ingloriousness, loss of reputation, notoriety, obloquy, odium, opprobrium, *probrum,* public reproach, reproach, scandal, scorn, shame, stain, stigma, taint, tarnish
ASSOCIATED CONCEPTS: infamous acts, infamous crime, infamous offense, infamous punishment, infamy from conviction of a crime
FOREIGN PHRASES: *Quae sunt minoris culpae sunt majoris infamiae.* Those things which are less culpable may be more infamous.

INFANT, *noun*   baby, child, *infans,* innocent, juvenile, little one, minor, nursling, one who has not come of age, one who has not reached his majority, person under the age of majority, person under 18 years old, person who is not of full age, toddler, tot, young person, youngster, youth
ASSOCIATED CONCEPTS: adoption, after-born child, age of minority, best interests of the child, child abuse, child labor, child support, custody, delinquent child, emancipation, filiation proceeding, foster child, guardian, guardian ad litem, illegitimate children, incompetency to contract, infanticide, juvenile delinquency, neglected child, pretermitted child, ratification of an infant's contract, visitation
FOREIGN PHRASES: *In omnibus poenalibus judiciis, et aetatl et imprudentiae succurritur.* In all penal judgments, allowance is made for youth and lack of prudence. *Infans non multum a furioso distat.* An infant does not differ much from an insane person. *In judiciis, minori aetati succurritur.* In judicial proceedings, infancy is aided. *Qui in utero est pro jam nato habetur, quoties de ejus commodo quaeritur.* He who is in the womb is regarded as already born, whenever a question arises for his benefit. *Pupillus pati posse non intelligitur.* An infant is not considered able to do an act to his own prejudice.

INFEASIBLE, *adjective*   absurd, impossible, impracticable, inaccessible, inconceivable, out of reach, out of the question, unachievable, unattainable, unimaginable, unlikely, unobtainable, unrealistic, unreasonable, unthinkable, unworkable, visionary

INFECT, *verb*   adulterate, befoul, besmirch, blight, canker, cause illness, *contaminare,* contaminate, corrupt, debase, defile, dirty, empoison, envenom, foul, harm, impair, make ill, make impure, pervert, poison, pollute, putrefy, render unclean, smirch, soil, spoil, stain, sully, taint, tarnish, transmit disease, vitiate, *vitiis* inficere

INFER, *verb*   conclude, conclude from evidence, concludere, conjecture, *conligere,* consider probable, construe, deduce, derive, derive by reasoning, draw a conclusion, draw an inference, extract, gather, glean, guess, hint, imply, indicate, insinuate, intimate, judge from premises, posit, postulate, presume, reach a conclusion, reason, reckon, suppose, surmise, suspect, understand
ASSOCIATED CONCEPTS: infer guilt from the evidence

INFERABLE HARM, *noun*   aggravation, balefulness, bedevilment, damage, deadliness, detriment, disablement, disservice, evil, hurt, hurtfulness, ill consequence, illtreatment, impairment, injury, malignance, malignancy, malignity, mischief, misfortune, mutilation, noxiousness, perniciousness, ruin, scathe, scourge, virulence

INFERENCE, *noun*   allusion, assumption, *conclusio,* conclusion, *coniectura,* conjecture, deduction, guess, guesswork, hint, hypothesis, illation, implication, impression, inkling, judgment, observation, postulate, postulation, postulatum, premise, presupposal, presupposition, speculation, supposal, supposition, surmise, suspicion, theorem, theory, thesis, understanding
ASSOCIATED CONCEPTS: evidentiary inference, favorable inference, legal inference, legitimate inference, presumption
FOREIGN PHRASES: *Expressa nocent, non expressa non nocent.* Things expressed may be prejudicial; that which is not expressed will not.

INFERIOR (Lower in position), *adjective*   accessory, auxiliary, *deterior,* governed by, in the power of, insignificant, junior, less powerful, lesser, lower, lower in authority, lower in rank, lower in the scale, lowly, menial, minor, of less importance, puisne, reduced, secondary, subaltern, subject, subjugated to, subordinate, subservient, subsidiary, tributary, under, unimportant
ASSOCIATED CONCEPTS: inferior courts

INFERIOR (Lower in quality), *adjective*   adulterated, amateurish, awful, bad, badly made, base, below, below par, blemished, bush, bush-league, cheap, contemptible, crude, damaged, defective, deficient, displeasing, faulty, flimsy, imperfect, inadequate, incompetent, indifferent, inelegant, inferior grade, inferior to, insignificant, insipid, insufficient, junior, less than, less valuable, lesser, lousy, low, low-grade, lower, lower than, lowly, malformed, mediocre, menial, middling, minor, miserable, not as good as, not the quality of, not up to par, paltry, passable, pedestrian, petty, poor, rank, second-class, second-fiddle, second-rate, secondary, servile, shabby, shoddy, slipshod, subordinate, subordinate to, subservient, subsidiary, substandard, trashy, unacceptable, undesirable, unsatisfactory
ASSOCIATED CONCEPTS: in bankruptcy, inferior bargaining position, inferior position, inferior products, inferior quality, inferior services

INFERRED IN LAW, *adjective*   apparent, conceivable, connoted, constructive, implicative, implicatory, implied, implied in law, in effect, in essence, in practice, indirectly meant, inferable, insinuated, presumable, presumed, tantamount to, understood, virtual

INFIDELITY, *noun*   abandonment of allegiance, apostasy, bad faith, betrayal, betrayal of oath, betrayal of trust, breach of faith, breach of promise, breach of trust, broken faith, broken word, cuckoldry, deceitfulness, defection, desertion, disaffection, dishonor, disloyalty, double-dealing, dutilessness, evasion of duty, faithlessness, falseheartedness, falsity, fickleness, inconstancy, *infidelitas,* lack of faith, lack of loyalty, mutiny, *perfidia,* perfidiousness, perfidy, rebellion, recreancy, revolt, sedition, seditiousness, traitorousness, treachery, treason, undutifulness, unfaithfulness, violation of oath
ASSOCIATED CONCEPTS: adultery

INFINITE, *adjective*   boundless, ceaseless, countless, endless, enduring, eternal, everlasting, exhaustless, illimitable, immeasurable, imperishable, incalculable, indestructible, inexhaustible, *infinitus,* innumerable, interminable, lasting, limitless, measureless, numberless, perdurable, permanent, perpetual, persistent, sempiternal, termless, timeless, unbounded, unceasing, undying, unending, unlimited, unmeasured, unnumbered, without end, without limit, without measure, without number

INFINITY, adjective boundless, ceaseless, complete, continual, continually, endless, enormous, eternal, everlasting, expansively, great, huge, immense, immortal, indefinite, infinite, innumerable, interminable, perfect, permanent, perpetual, unbounded, unceasing, undeterminable, uninterrupted, unlimited

INFIRM (Irresolute), adjective changeable, easily led, faint-hearted, faltering, fickle, inconstant, indecisive, insecure, pliable, precarious, undecided, undetermined, unreliable, unresolved, unstable, unsteady, untrustworthy, vacillating, wavering

INFIRM (Weak), adjective ailing, debilitated, defective, deteriorated, enfeebled, failing, feeble, flimsy, fragile, frail, frangible, helpless, imperfect, impotent, insecure, insubstantial, languid, nonsubstantial, powerless, sickly, unsound, wasted, weakened, withered, worn

INFLAME, verb aggravate, agitate, anger, arouse, convulse, deflagrate, discompose, electrify, embitter, energize, enliven, enrage, envenom, exacerbate, exasperate, excite, foment, galvanize, goad, harass, ignite, impassion, incense, incite, infuriate, intensify, invigorate, irritate, kindle, madden, nettle, offend, perturb, pester, pique, provoke, rouse, stimulate, stir up, taunt, vex
ASSOCIATED CONCEPTS: inflame the jury

INFLAMMATORY, adjective combustible, dissentious, explosive, fomenting, heated, immoderate, incendiary, incitive, inciting, inflammable, intemperate, offensive, provocative, scorching, unbridled, volcanic
ASSOCIATED CONCEPTS: inflammatory statements, inflammatory testimony

INFLATE, verb aggrandize, amplify, balloon, bloat, blow up, broaden, cause to bulge, dilate, distend, enlarge, escalate, exaggerate, expand, extend, fatten, fill out, fill with air, grow, increase, increase dimensions, *inflare,* magnify, make greater, make larger, make swollen, make tumid, pad, puff up, pump up, raise above the proper value, rise, spread, stretch, sufflate, surge, swell, upsurge, wax

INFLATED (Bombastic), adjective altiloquent, altisonant, artificial, declamatory, flatulent, fustian, grandiloquent, high-flown, high-sounding, *inflatus,* magniloquent, mouthy, oratorical, ostentatious, overblown, pedantic, pompous, pretentious, rhetorical, stilted, tumid, *tumidus,* turgid, vainglorious, verbose

INFLATED (Enlarged), adjective amplified, augmented, ballooned, bloated, blown up, dilated, distended, enlarged by swelling, expanded, extended, filled, *inflatus,* puffed, puffed up, puffy, spread, stretched, swelled, swollen, tumid, *tumidus,* turgid, *turgidus*

INFLATED (Overestimated), adjective aggrandized, amplified, embellished, enlarged, exaggerated, exaggerative, excessive, heightened, hyperbolic, magnified, miscalculated, overdrawn, overpraised, overpriced, overprized, overrated, overstated, overstressed, overvalued

INFLATED (Vain), adjective arrogant, boastful, braggart, bumptious, conceited, condescending, contemptuous, disdainful, egocentric, egoistic, egoistical, egotistic, egotistical, grandiose, haughty, immodest, impressed with oneself, lordly, overbearing, overproud, overweening, patronizing, pleased with oneself, pompous, pretentious, prideful, proud, scornful, self-applauding, self-centered, self-glorifying, self-important, self-lauding, self-satisfied, showy, strutting, superior, swaggering, vaporing, vauntful

INFLATION (Decrease in value of currency), noun boost in prices, currency devaluation, decrease in purchasing power, high prices, hike in prices, jump in prices, price increase, substantial rise of prices, undue expansion of currency, upturn in prices

INFLATION (Increase), noun aggrandizement, amplification, bloatedness, blowing up, dilation, distension, elevation, enlargement, escalation, exaggeration, expansion, extension, growth, increase, *inflatio,* rise, spread, sufflation, surge, swell, swelling, turgescence, turgidity, turgidness, upsurge, waxing
ASSOCIATED CONCEPTS: inflation of damages, inflation of value

INFLECTION, noun accent, accentuation, cadence, emphasis, expression, intonation, modulation, pitch, stress, tone, voice change
ASSOCIATED CONCEPTS: demeanor of a witness, polygraph test

INFLEXIBLE, adjective adamant, cantankerous, changeless, contumacious, decided, determined, dogged, firm, fixed, hard, hardened, headstrong, immobile, immovable, immutable, impersuadible, impersuasible, indocile, indomitable, inelastic, inexorable, intractable, intransigent, invariable, mulish, nonelastic, obdurate, obstinate, obstinatus, opinionated, opinionative, persevering, pertinacious, *pertinax,* refractory, relentless, resolute, resolved, rigid, rigidus, rigorous, solid, steadfast, stiff, strict, stringent, strong-willed, stubborn, tenacious, unalterable, unamenable, unbending, unchangeable, uncompromising, unmalleable, unmanageable, unmovable, unpliable, unpliant, unrelenting, unswayable, unyielding, willful
ASSOCIATED CONCEPTS: inflexible bargaining position

INFLICT, verb administer a penalty, administer punishment, agitate, agonize, apply, beset, bring about, bring upon, burden, cause, cause to suffer, coerce, commit, deal, disquiet, distress, enforce, force, force upon, give pain, harass, harm, hurt, *imponere,* impose, impose punishment, *inferre, infligere,* injure, maltreat, mete out, perform, produce injury, punish, put into force, strike, torment, torture, wound, wreak
ASSOCIATED CONCEPTS: inflict pain and suffering, inflict punishment

INFLICTION, noun abuse, application, blow, castigation, commission, commitment, execution, force, harassment, imposition, *incommodum,* injury, maltreatment, misfortune, oppression, ordeal, penalty, performance, perpetration, persecution, plague, punishment, torment, torture, trial, violence, wound

INFLOW, noun approach, arrival, coming in, entrance, entry, immigration, importation, incoming, incursion, induction, infiltration, influx, ingoing, ingress, ingression, initiation, inpour, inpouring, inroad, inrush, insertion, introduction, introgression, inundation, invasion, irruption, penetration, progress

INFLUENCE, noun ascendance, ascendancy, authority, command, consequence, control, dominance, domination, dominion, effect, effectiveness, effectuality, eminence,

encouragement, forcefulness, governance, hegemony, hold, importance, incitation, incitement, inspiration, instigation, leadership, leverage, masterfulness, mastery, might, mightiness, omnipotence, paramountcy, *pondus,* potency, *potentia,* power, powerfulness, predominance, predominancy, prepollence, prepollency, prepotency, prestige, provocation, puissance, reign, rule, sovereignty, superiority, supremacy, sway, urging, vis, weight
ASSOCIATED CONCEPTS: coercion controlling influence, improper influence, influence peddling, political influence, undue influence

INFLUENCE, *verb* actuate, arouse, brainwash, bring pressure to bear, cajole, carry weight, convince, direct, form, guide, impel, *impellere,* impress, incite, induce, inspire, inveigle, lead, militate, modify, mold, motivate, move, *movere,* persuade, prejudice, pressure, prevail upon, prompt, pull strings, shape, stimulate, sway, talk into, urge, work upon
ASSOCIATED CONCEPTS: bribery, control, duress, improper influence, under the influence of alcohol, undue influence, wrong influence

INFLUENCED, *adjective* biased, decided, induced, inequitable, interested, one-sided, partial, partisan, persuaded, prejudiced, prepossessed, swayed, undetached, undispassionate, unfair
ASSOCIATED CONCEPTS: unduly influenced

INFLUENTIAL, *adjective* authoritative, cogent, commanding, consequential, controlling, convincing, determinative, distinguished, dominant, domineering, effective, effectual, efficacious, eminent, empowered, esteemed, foremost, governing, *gravis,* hegemonic, hegemonical, honored, illustrious, imperious, important, impressive, leading, mighty, multipotent, notable, noteworthy, omnipotent, paramount, potens, potent, powerful, predominant, preeminent, prepollent, preponderant, prepotent, prevailing, prevalent, prominent, puissant, recognized, reigning, renowned, reputable, respectable, respected, ruling, strong, supreme, well-known, well-recognized, well-regarded, worthy of notice

INFORM *(Betray),* **verb** accuse, announce, bear witness against, betray the secret, break faith, break trust, charge, communicate, confess, declare, denounce, disclose, disclose intentionally, disclose secrets, divulge, expose, give over to the foe, *hominis nomen deferre,* impart, impeach, implicate, incriminate, inculpate, lay bare, lay open, make known, report against, reveal, tell secrets, testify against, uncover, unmask, violate a confidence, violate the confidence of

INFORM *(Notify),* **verb** acquaint, advertise, advise, an**noun**ce, annunciate, apprise, blazon, brief, carry tales, communicate, confide, describe, detail, disabuse, disclose, divulge, *docere,* educate, enlighten, explain, familiarize, give a report, give an account, give notice, give out information, give the facts, give tidings, herald, impart, instruct, keep posted, let know, level with, make known, mention, narrate, notify, *nuntiare,* orient, outline, point out, post, present information, proclaim, promulgate, publish, recite, recount, relate, report, reveal, send word, set right, set straight, signify, state, tattle, teach, tell, testify, tip, tout, trumpet, undeceive, warn

INFORMAL, *adjective* casual, common, congenial, cursory, extemporaneous, extempore, familiar, natural, nonchalant, offhand, ordinary, perfunctory, relaxed, spontaneous, unceremonial, unceremonious, unconventional, uncustomary, unmethodical, unofficial, unorthodox, unrestrained, unstereotyped, unstrict, without ceremony, without formality
ASSOCIATED CONCEPTS: informal charges, informal contract, informal hearing, informal proceeding

INFORMALITY, *noun* absence of ceremony, affability, casualness, ease, easiness, easygoingness, extemporaneousness, familiarity, fellowship, flexibility, freedom, freedom from affectation, friendliness, inexactitude, inexactness, informalness, ingenuousness, inobservance, irregularity, latitude, laxity, liberty, license, lightness, looseness, naturalness, noncompliance, nonconformity, nonobservance, offhandedness, plainness, relaxation, simplicity, slackness, unaffectedness, unassumingness, unceremoniousness, unconstraint, unconventionality, unorthodoxy, unrigorousness, want of formality

INFORMANT, *noun* accuser, adviser, announcer, annunciator, appriser, *auctor,* communicant, communicator, delator, dispatcher, divulger, enlightener, envoy, harbinger, herald, information giver, informer, intelligencer, narrator, notifier, proclaimer, relator, reporter, source, spy, stool pigeon, talebearer, tipper, tipster, witness
ASSOCIATED CONCEPTS: paid informant, reliable informants, undercover informant

INFORMATION *(Charge),* **noun** accusal, accusation, allegation, charge, criminal accusal, formal accusation, formal averment, formal charge, formal criminal charge, formal criminal complaint, official criminal charge, prosecutorial complaint, written accusation
ASSOCIATED CONCEPTS: felony information, misdemeanor information

INFORMATION *(Facts),* **noun** communiqué, data, exact data, figures, news, notice, notification, specifics, statistics

INFORMATION *(Knowledge),* **noun** acquired facts, acquired knowledge, available facts, book learning, collected writings, communication, communiqué, compilations, comprehension, education, enlightenment, erudition, experience, familiarity, grasp, intelligence, intelligent grip, knowledge, knowledge of facts, known facts, learning, lore, mental grasp, revelation, understanding, wisdom
ASSOCIATED CONCEPTS: duty to ascertain information, privileged information, upon information and belief, withholding information
FOREIGN PHRASES: *Nemo tenetur informare qui nescit, sed quisquis scire quod informat.* No one who is ignorant of a thing is bound to give information about it, but everyone is bound to know that concerning which he gives information.

INFORMATIONAL, *adjective* advisory, communicative, documentary, edifying, educational, educative, enlightening, enriching, explanatory, explicative, illuminating, informatory, instructional, instructive, narrative, revealing, revelatory, telling

INFORMATIVE, *adjective* advisory, communicative, communicatory, didactic, disclosing, edifying, educational, educative, enlightening, enriching, explanatory, explicative, explicatory, explicit, expositive, expository, expressive, homiletic, homiletical, hortative, hortatory, illuminating, instructional, instructive, newsy, pedagogic, preceptive, propaedeutic, propaedeutical, revealing, scholastic

INFORMATORY, *adjective* acquainting, admonitory, advising, advisory, chatty, clarifying, communicative, descriptive, disclosing, doctrinal, documentary, educational, elucidatory, enlightening, explanatory, explicative, explicatory, expositive, expository, gossipy, hortative, hortatory, illuminating, informational, informative, instructive, monitory, newsy, notifying, presenting information, reporting, revealing, revelatory, teaching, telling

INFORMED (Educated), **adjective**   accomplished, conversant with, cultured, enlightened, erudite, expert, instructed, knowledgeable, learned, lettered, literate, prepared, proficient, schooled, taught, trained, versed, well-educated, well-grounded, well-read, well-rounded, well-versed, widely read

INFORMED (Having information), **adjective**   abreast, acquainted, advised, apprized, briefed, enlightened, familiar, familiarized, forewarned, notified, posted, primed, set straight, tipped, told, undeceived, warned
ASSOCIATED CONCEPTS: informed decision, informed opinion

INFORMER (One providing criminal information), **noun**   accuser, auctor, complainant, criminal information supplier, impeacher, indicter, informant, information supplier, one who supplies criminal information to the police, police tipper, squealer, tipster, witness against
ASSOCIATED CONCEPTS: corroboration, reliable informer

INFORMER (A person who provides information), **noun**   adviser, an**noun**cer, annunciator, communicant, communicator, courier, crier, delator, divulger, envoy, harbinger, herald, intelligencer, messenger, notifier, proclaimer, relater, reporter, source, spokesman, teller, tipper, tipster, warner

INFRACTION, noun   breach, breach of faith, breach of law, breach of orders, breach of privilege, breach of promise, breach of the peace, breach of trust, breaking, contravention, crime, default, defiance, defiance of orders, disobedience, encroachment, evasion of duty, failure, failure of duty, immunitio, infringement, inobservance, noncompliance, nonobservance, nonobservance of rules, offense, omission, overstepping, refusal to obey, transgression, trespass, violatio, violation, violation of law, violation of orders, wrong
ASSOCIATED CONCEPTS: infraction of rules, infraction of the law, traffic infraction

INFRANGIBLE, adjective   cohesive, durable, everlasting, firm, hallowed, holy, indestructible, indiscerptible, indissoluble, indissolvable, indivisible, inseparable, insoluble, inviolable, invulnerable, lasting, perdurable, resistant, sacred, sacrosanct, secure, solid, strong, unbreakable, unchangeable, united, unshakeable, unshatterable

INFREQUENT, adjective   atypical, discontinuous, erratic, exceptional, extraordinary, few, inconstant, inhabitual, intermittent, irregular, limited, occasional, outstanding, periodic, phenomenal, rare, rarus, scarce, seldom happening, seldom occurring, seldom seen, singular, sparse, sporadic, uncommon, uncustomary, unfrequent, unsteady, untypical, unusual

INFRINGE, verb   abuse a privilege, abuse one's rights, advance stealthily, aggress, arrogate, breach, break, break bounds, break in upon, break into, commit a breach, frangere, impinge, impose, infract, interfere, interlope, intrude, invade, meddle, overstep, rumpere, seize wrongfully, take liberties, transgress, trespass, use wrongfully, usurp, violare, violate, violate a contract, violate a law, violate a privilege, violate a regulation

ASSOCIATED CONCEPTS: infringe on a copyright, infringe on a trademark

INFRINGEMENT, noun   abuse of privilege, aggression, arrogation, breach, contravention, disfranchisement, disobedience, dispossession, entrance upon domain of another, force, illegality, immunitio, incursion, infraction, injustice, interference, intrusion, invasion, invasion of a right, misdoing, misfeasance, nonobservance, repudiation, seizure, surpassing, trangression, transcendence, transcending, trespass, trespassing, usurpation, violatio, violation, violation of a contract, violation of a law, violation of a privilege, violation of a regulation, violence, wrong, wrongdoing, wrongfulness
ASSOCIATED CONCEPTS: copyright infringement, license infringement, patent infringement, trademark infringement

INFUSE, verb   imbrue, imbue, implant, impregnate, inculcate, incutere, infundere, ingrain, inicere, inject, insert, inspire, inspirit, instill, introduce

INFUSION, noun   imbruement, imbuement, implantation, impregnation, inculcation, infiltration, infusio, injection, insertion, instillation, introduction, penetration, permeation

INGENUOUS, adjective   aboveboard, apertus, artless, blunt, candid, childlike, devoid of dissimulation, downright, forthright, frank, free from reserve, genuine, guileless, honest, honorable, inartificial, innocent, liber, naive, natural, open, outspoken, plain, rustic, simple, simplex, sincere, spontaneous, straightforward, transparent, trustworthy, truthful, unaffected, unconstrained, undesigning, undisguised, unforced, unreserved, unrestrained, unselfconscious, unsophisticated, unstudied, unsuspicious, veracious, with simplicity, without guile

INGRAIN, verb   embed, engrave, establish, fix, imbue, implant, impregnate, impress, imprint, inculcate, indoctrinate, infix, influence, infuse, inject, inspire, instill, introduce, invest, permeate, train

INGRAINED, adjective   confirmed, deep, deep-seated, embedded, engrafted, entrenched, essential, established, firmly established, firmly fixed, fixed, habitual, implanted, inborn, inbred, indelible, indwelling, ineffaceable, infixed, ingrown, inherent, innate, insitus, intrinsic, inveterate, inveteratus, inwrought, permanent, rooted, set, settled, thorough, well-established

INGRATITUDE, adjective   animus ingratus, heedlessness, inappreciation, inconsiderateness, inconsideration, insensibility, lack of appreciation, lack of consideration, lack of gratitude, respectlessness, rudeness, thanklessness, thoughtlessness, unappreciativeness, unfeelingness, ungratefulness, unthankfulness, want of consideration

INGREDIENT, noun   aspect, component, component part, constituent, constituent part, content, element, essential part, factor, feature, fragment, fundamental part, integral part, member, membrum, pars, part, section, sector, unit, unit of composition, vital part

INGRESS, noun   access, admission, admittance, approach, entrance, entry, incoming, incursion, ingoing, ingression, ingressus, inlet, inroad, liberty to enter, means of access, means of entry, passage, power of entrance, right of entry, right to enter, way in, way to
ASSOCIATED CONCEPTS: easement, license, right of access

INHABIT, verb abide, be established in, be resident in, board, colonize, domicile, dwell in, dwell permanently, habitare, have quarters, *incolere,* keep house, live, lodge, occupy, remain, reside in, room, sojourn, squat, stay, take up residence, tenant, visit

INHABITANT, noun abider, addressee, boarder, citizen, cohabitant, denizen, dweller, habitant, *habitator, homo,* householder, *incola,* indweller, inhabiter, inmate, lodger, native, occupant, occupier, permanent resident, resident, residentiary, settler, sojourner, tenant
ASSOCIATED CONCEPTS: citizenry, residency

INHABITATION *(Act of dwelling in),* **noun** dwelling, habitancy, habitation, inhabitancy, living, lodging, lodgment, occupancy, occupation, sojourn, stay, tenancy, tenantry

INHABITATION *(Place of dwelling),* **noun** abode, asylum, domicile, *domicilium,* dwelling, dwelling place, edifice, establishment, home, house, living quarters, living space, lodging, lodging place, lodgment, place, place of abode, place of residence, quarters, refuge, residence, residency, sedes, *tectum*

INHARMONIOUS, adjective at odds, clashing, conflicting, contradictory, derived at variance, differing, disagreeable, discordant, disharmonious, dissonant, factious, harsh, incompatible, inharmonic, irreconcilable, opposing, unharmonious

INHERENT, adjective connate, deep-rooted, essential, fixed, immanent, implicit, inborn, inbred, ineffaceable, ingrained, ingredient, innate, *innatus, insitus,* instinctive, integral, internal, intrinsic, native, natural, proprius, subsistent
ASSOCIATED CONCEPTS: inherent defect, inherent power, inherently dangerous

INHERIT, verb accede to, acquire, acquire from ancestors, be granted a legacy, be the heir of, come into possession as an heir, derive from, fall heir to, gain, have succession as an heir, obtain, receive, receive a legacy, receive an endowment, receive as right, receive by bequest, receive by devise, receive by law of descent, receive by succession, receive property as an heir, *rem hereditate accipere,* succeed to, take, take as an heir, take by descent, take by inheritance, take by succession

INHERITANCE, noun appanage, benefaction, bequest, devise, dispensation, endowment, gift, *hereditas,* heritage, inherited property, legacy, presentation, property obtained by descent, property obtained by devise, provision, seisin, succession of property
ASSOCIATED CONCEPTS: coparcenary, curtesy, descent, distribution, dower, inheritance estate, inheritance tax, intestate succession, patrimony, wills
FOREIGN PHRASES: *Hereditas, alia corporalis, alia incorporalis; corporalis est, quae tangi potest et videri; incorporalis quae tangi non potest nec videri.* An inheritance is either corporeal or incorporeal; corporeal is that which can be touched and seen; incorporeal is that which can neither be touched nor seen. *Feodum simplex quia feodum idem est quod hereditas, et simplex idem est quod legitimum vel purum; et sic feodum simplex idem est quod hereditas legitima vel hereditas pura.* A fee-simple is so called because fee is the same as inheritance, and simple is the same as lawful or pure; and so fee-simple is the same as a lawful inheritance or pure inheritance. *Filius est nomen naturae, sed haeres nomen juris.* Son is the natural name, but heir is a

name of law. *Haeredum appellatione veniunt haeredes haeredumin infinitum.* Under the name heirs come the heirs of heirs without limit. *Haereditas est successio in universum jus quod defunctus habuerit.* Inheritance is the succession to every right which the deceased had possessed. *Haereditas nihil aliud est, quam successio in universum jus, quod defunctus habuerit.* An inheritance is nothing other than the succession to all the rights which the deceased had. *Si quis praegnantem uxorem reliquit, non videtur sine liberis decessisse.* If a man dies, leaving his wife pregnant, he is considered as having died childless. *Major haereditas venit unicuique nostrum a jure et legibus quam a parentibus.* A greater inheritance comes to each one of us from justice and the laws than from our parents.

INHIBIT, verb arrest, ban, bar, bridle, check, choke, constrain, control, curb, debar, delay, disallow, enjoin, estop, extinguish, forbid, frustrate, gag, govern, harness, hinder, hold back, hold in, impede, intercept, *interdicere,* interdict, interrupt, keep in, leash, muzzle, obstruct, paralyze, prevent, prohibit, proscribe, pull in, quench, refuse to allow, rein in, repress, restrain, restrict, retard, smother, stifle, stop, strangle, suppress, suspend, taboo, veto, withhold

INIMICAL, adjective adverse, alienated, antagonistic, antipathetic, antipathetical, at variance, at war with, bellicose, belligerent, contrary, cool, cross, disaffected, estranged, harmful, hostile, hurtful, *inimicus,* irreconcilable, malevolent, mean, noxious, on bad terms, opposed, opposing, pernicious, repugnant, unfavorable, unfriendly, unpropitious, up in arms, warlike

INIQUITOUS, adjective accursed, atrocious, bad, base, black, corrupt, criminal, culpable, depraved, dishonest, disreputable, dissolute, evil, facinorous, felonious, flagitious, foul, gross, heinous, immoral, *improbus,* improper, incorrigible, inequitable, infamous, *iniquus, iniustus,* irreclaimable, knavish, lawless, malevolent, miscreant, naughty, nefarious, objectionable, peccant, pernicious, profligate, recreant, reprehensible, reprobate, scandalous, scurvy, shameful, sinful, sinning, unfair, unjust, unjustifiable, unprincipled, unrighteous, vicious, vile, villainous, wicked, wrong
FOREIGN PHRASES: *Nullum iniquum est praesumendum in jure.* Nothing iniquitous is to be presumed in law.

INITIAL, adjective basic, beginning, commencing, early, elementary, embryonic, first, fundamental, inaugural, inceptive, inchoate, incipient, initiative, initiatory, introductory, leading, maiden, nascent, opening, original, prefatory, premier, primal, primary, *primus,* pristine, rudimentary, starting
ASSOCIATED CONCEPTS: initial carrier, initial fault, initial license, initial loss, initial payment, initial pleading, initial stage of a proceeding

INITIATE, verb admit, begin, break ground, bring into use, broach, commence, conceive, direct, discover, enlighten, enter upon, familiarize, found, give entrance to, *imbuere,* implant, inaugurate, inchoate, *incipere,* inculculate, indoctrinate, induct, inform, *initiare,* install, instill, institute, instruct, introduce, invent, launch, lay the foundation, lead, lead the way, open, originate, pioneer, plant, preinstruct, prepare, present, prime, prompt, propose, set afoot, set going, set up, start, take the initiative, take the lead, teach, think of, train, undertake, usher in
ASSOCIATED CONCEPTS: initiate an action

INJECT, verb drive in, force in, imbed, imbue, implant, impregnate, infix, *infundere,* infuse, inoculate, insert, instill,

327

interjaculate, interject, interpolate, interpose, introduce, intromit, pierce, place into, press in, put into, ram in, saturate, shoot, thrust in, transfuse, vaccinate

INJUDICIOUS, adjective   blind, disadvantageous, hasty, heedless, ill-advised, ill-judged, impolitic, impolitical, improvident, imprudent, inappropriate, incautious, inconsiderate, *inconsideratus, inconsultus,* indiscreet, inexpedient, inopportune, insufficiently considered, irrational, lacking discretion, misguided, needless, negligent, objectionable, precipitate, reckless, showing lack of judgment, showing poor judgment, temerarious, temerarius, thoughtless, unadvisable, uncalculating, unconsidered, undesirable, undiscerning, unfit, unprofitable, unreasoned, unsound, unsuitable, unwary, unwise

INJUNCTION, noun   ban, bidding, command, command to undo wrong, denial, enjoinder, imperative, *imperium,* interdiction, *iussum,* judicial order to refrain from an act, *mandatum,* order, precept, prescript, prohibition, proscription, restraining order, restraint, restriction, stay order, warrant
ASSOCIATED CONCEPTS: cease and desist order, dissolution of an injunction, interlocutory injunction, modification of injunction, order to show cause, permanent injunction, preliminary injunction, temporary injunction, temporary restraining order

INJURE *(Harm),* **verb**   abuse, aggravate, blemish, bruise, brutalize, cripple, damage, debase, debilitate, deface, disable, disfigure, do harm to, endanger, eviscerate, harrow, hit, hurt, ill treat, ill use, impair, inflict, inflict pain, lacerate, maim, maltreat, mangle, mar, mishandle, mistreat, misuse, molest, mutilate, spoil, violate, vitiate, wound

INJURE *(Persecute),* **verb**   affront, annoy, asperse, blacken, calumniate, defame, denigrate, disadvantage, disparage, insult, libel, malign, offend, oppress, prejudice, slander, subvert, traduce, vilify, wrong

INJURIOUS *(Derogatory),* **adjective**   abusive, calumnious, contemptuous, contumelious, corrupt, defamatory, detractory, detrimental, disadvantageous, inadvisable, insulting, invidious, libelous, malevolent, mischievous, pejorative, pernicious, prejudicial, scurrilous, slanderous, unfavorable

INJURIOUS *(Harmful),* **adjective**   abusive, adverse, bad, baneful, calamitous, corrosive, corrupt, damaging, dangerous, deleterious, destructive, depraved, destructive, detrimental, disadvantageous, disastrous, facinorous, fatal, felonious, grievous, harmful, hurtful, inequitable, iniquitous, insalubrious, insidious, lethal, malefic, malignant, nefarious, noisome, noxious, offensive, outrageous, peccant, pernicious, perverse, pestiferous, pestilent, ruinous, sinister, unjust, vicious, virulent, wrongful

INJURY, noun   abuse, adversity, bane, breakage, damage, *damnum,* deprivation, detriment, *detrimentum,* disservice, harm, harmful act, hurt, ill treatment, impairment, *incommodum,* invasion of a legal right, loss, offense, physical hurt, prejudice, privation, violence, wrong
ASSOCIATED CONCEPTS: accidental injury, cause of injury, comparative injury, compensable injury, contributory negligence, direct injury, efficient cause, future injury, indirect injury, indivisible injury, injury to business, injury to property, injury to reputation, intentional injury, irreparable injury, malicious injury, permanent injury, personal injury, previous injury, proof of injury, *res ipsa loquitur,* serious injury suffered, wanton injury

FOREIGN PHRASES: *Quid sit jus, et in quo consistit injuria, legis est definire.* What constitutes right, and what injury, it is the business of the law to define. *Non omne damnum inducit injuriam.* Not every loss produces an injury. *Neminem laedit qui jure suo utitur.* He who stands on his own rights injures no one. *Jus est norma recti; et quicquid est contra normam recti est injuria.* Law is the rule of right; and whatever is contrary to the rule of right is an injury. *Melius est in tempore occurrere, quam post causam vulneratum remedium quaerere.* It is better to meet a thing in time, than to seek a remedy after an injury has been inflicted. *Prohibetur ne quis faciat in suo quod nocere possit alieno.* It is forbidden for anyone to do on his own property what may injure another's. *Lex nemini facit injuriam.* The law works injury to no one. *Paci sunt maxime contraria vis et injuria.* Violence and injury are especially hostile to peace. *Res inter alios judicatae nullum aliis praejudicium faciunt.* Transactions between strangers ought not to injure those who are not parties to them. *Volenti non fit injuria.* No injury is done where the person injured consents. *Corporalis injuria non recipit aestimationem de futuro.* A personal injury cannot be compensated for by later acts. *Fictio legis inique operatur alieni damnum vel injuriam.* Fiction of law is wrongful if it works loss or harm to anyone. *Privatis pactionibus non dubium est non laedi jus caeterorum.* There is no doubt that private contracts cannot prejudice the rights of others. *Damnum sine injuria esse potest.* There can be damage or injury inflicted without any act of injustice. *Ab assuetis non fit injuria.* No injury is done by things long acquiesced in. *Consuetudo neque injuria oriti neque tolli potest.* A custom can neither arise nor be abolished by an injury. *Aedificare in tuo proprio solo non licet quod alteri noceat.* It is not lawful to build upon one's own land what may injure another. *Factum unius alteri nocere non debet.* The act of one person should not prejudice another. *Injuria non praesumitur.* A wrong is not presumed. *Lex nemini operatur iniquum, nemini facit injuriam.* The law never works an injury, or does a wrong.

INJUSTICE, noun   abuse, bias, bigotry, breach, crime, damage, denial of justice, discrimination, disparity, encroachment, error of the court, evil, fault of the court, favoritism, illegality, imposition, improbity, inequality, inequitable action, inequity, infraction, infringement, infringement on one's rights, iniquity, *iniuria, iniustitia,* injury, malfeasance, maltreatment, miscarriage, miscarriage of justice, misfeasance, mistake of the court, mistreatment, offense, omission of a court, oppression, outrage, partiality, partisanship, persecution, prejudice, transgression, tyranny, unevenness, unfair action, unfairness, unjust treatment, unjustness, unlawfulness, unrighteousness, violation, violation of right, wrong, wrong verdict, wrongdoing
ASSOCIATED CONCEPTS: social injustice
FOREIGN PHRASES: *Fictio legis inique operatur alicui damnum vel injuriam.* Fiction of law is wrongful if it works loss or harm to any one. *Lex nemini operatur iniquum, nemini facit injuriam.* The law never works an injury, or does a wrong.

INMATE, noun   captive, *captus,* convict, dweller, habitant, inhabitant, lawbreaker, occupant, occupier, prisoner, resident, roomer
ASSOCIATED CONCEPTS: inmate at a correctional institution

INNATE, adjective   basic, congenital, constitutional, derived from within, essential, existing from birth, fundamental, hereditary, immanent, inborn, inbred, indigenous, infixed, ingrained, inherent, inherited, *innatus, insitus,* instinctive, intrinsic, intuitive, involuntary, native, natural, *proprius*

INNOCENCE, noun   absence of guilt, blamelessness, exculpation, exoneration, freedom from blame, freedom from guilt, freedom from illegality, guiltlessness, incorruption, innocency, *innocentia, integritas,* sinlessness
ASSOCIATED CONCEPTS: presumption of innocence
FOREIGN PHRASES: *Omnis indemnatus pro innoxis legibus habetur.* Every uncondemned person is regarded by the law as innocent. *Quisquis praesumitur bonus; et semper in dubiis pro reo respondendum.* Everyone is presumed to be good; and in doubtful cases it should be resolved in favor of the accused. *In favorem vitae, libertatis, et innocentiae, omnia praesumuntur.* Every presumption is made in favor of life, liberty, and innocence.

INNOCENT, adjective   blameless, *culpa vacuus,* faultless, free from guilt, guiltless, *innocens, insons,* sinless, unblamable, unoffending, upright, virtuous, without harm, without offense
ASSOCIATED CONCEPTS: innocent holder for value, innocent misrepresentation, innocent mistake, innocent purchaser, innocent third party, innocent trespass
FOREIGN PHRASES: *Minatur innocentibus qui parcit nocentibus.* He who spares the guilty threatens those who are innocent.

INNOCENT BYSTANDER, noun   attester, beholder, blameless witness, chance looker-on, corroborator, eyewitness, faultless witness, guiltless witness, informant, informer, observer, onlooker, passer-by, perceiver, spectator, testifier, viewer, watcher, witness, witness free from guilt

INNOCUOUS, adjective   harmless, hurtless, innocent, *innocuus,* innoxious, inoffensive, mild, nonirritating, nonmalignant, nontoxic, painless, safe, simple, uninjurious, unlikely to cause harm, unlikely to cause injury, unobjectionable, unobnoxious, unoffending, virtuous, without power to harm, without tendency to harm

INNOVATION, noun   adaptation, alteration, breaking of precedent, change, change in method, departure, digression, divergence, diversification, exchange of obligations, invention, modernization, modification, mutare, neoterism, new device, new idea, new method, new phase, *novare,* novelty, radically new measure, revision, revolution, shift, variation

INNUENDO, noun   accusation, allusion, aside, aspersion, charge, connotation, *denuntiatio,* hint, implication, implied indication, imputation, incrimination, indication, indirect allusion, inference, insinuation, mention, *nuntius,* oblique allusion, overtone, reference, reflection, *significatio,* suggestion
ASSOCIATED CONCEPTS: defamation, disparagement, libel, slander

INNUMERABLE, adjective   boundless, countless, endless, exhaustless, frequent, immeasurable, immense, incalculable, incapable of being counted, incomprehensible, incomputable, inexhaustible, infinite, *innumerabilis, innumerus,* interminable, legionary, limitless, many, more than one can tell, much, multitudinous, myriad, numberless, sumless, uncountable, uncounted, unfathomable, unlimited, unmeasured, unnumbered, untold

INOPERABLE (Impracticable), **adjective**   undoable, unfeasible, unworkable

INOPERABLE (Incurable), **adjective**   cureless, hopeless, immedicable, remediless

INOPPORTUNE, adjective   at the wrong time, badly calculated, badly timed, ill-chosen, ill-seasoned, ill-timed, inadvisable, inappropriate, inauspicious, inconvenient, inexpedient, *inopportunus,* malapropos, misjudged, mistimed, undesirable, unfavorable, unfit, unfortunate, unpropitious, unseasonable, unsuitable, unsuited, untimely, wrong

INORDINATE, adjective   crammed, exaggerated, exceeding, excessive, exorbitant, extortionate, extraordinary, extravagant, extreme, fanatical, gluttonous, great, immoderate, *immoderatus, immodicus,* inabstinent, intemperate, lavish, monstrous, needless, nimious, out of bounds, out of limits, outrageous, overcharged, overflowing, overmuch, preposterous, prodigal, profuse, prohibitive, redundant, superabundant, supererogatory, superfluous, supersaturated, unbridled, uncalled-for, unconscionable, uncurbed, undue, unlimited, unnecessary, unreasonable, unrestrained, wasteful, without restraint

INPUT (Data), **noun**   capture of information, communications, enumerated facts, facts, figures, files, information, numbers, raw data, specifics, statistics

INPUT (Thinking), **noun**   analysis, communication, contribution, enlightenment, expression, imparting knowledge, impartment of wisdom, involvement, partaking, participation, provide a prospective, provide expertise, provide information, provide knowledge, sharing thoughts, weigh-in

INQUEST, noun   determination of damages, examination, hearing, inquiry, interrogation, investigation, judicial inquiry, legal investigation, *quaestio,* quest, questioning, review, search, search into facts
ASSOCIATED CONCEPTS: assessment of damages, civil inquest, coroner's inquest

INQUIRE, verb   ask, catechize, conduct research, cross-examine, delve into, examine, explore, interrogate, investigate, look into, probe, propose a question, pry into, pursue, query, question, quiz, research, scrutinize, search, search into, seek information, solicit, sound out, study, subject to scrutiny, survey

INQUIRE INTO, verb   analyze, canvass, check, conduct an inquiry, consider, delve into, examine, explore, ferret out, hear, hold an inquiry, institute an inquiry, interrogate, investigate, monitor, probe, pry, pursue, query, question, reconnoiter, research, review, scrutinize, search, set up an inquiry, sound, study, unearth, want to know
ASSOCIATED CONCEPTS: Grand Jury Inquiry, special investigation

INQUIRY (Request for information), **noun**   examination, examination into facts or principles, exploration, hearing, inquisition, *interrogatio,* interrogation, investigation, *percontatio,* poll, probe, query, question, scrutiny, search, search for information, survey
ASSOCIATED CONCEPTS: duty to inquire, inquiry into title, reasonable inquiry, speculative inquiry
FOREIGN PHRASES: *Quaerere dat sapere quae sunt legitima vere.* Inquiry is the way to know what things are truly lawful. *Quaeras de dubiis legem bene discere si vis.* Inquire into doubtful matters if you wish to understand the law well. *Quaere de dubiis, quia per rationes pervenitur ad*

legitimam rationem. Inquire into doubtful matters, because by reasoning we arrive at legal reason.

INQUIRY (*Systematic investigation*), **noun** analyzation, asking, assay, canvassing, *cognitio,* conference, delving into evidence, disquisition, examination, exploration, fundamental research, hearing, hearing of evidence, inquest, *inquisitio,* inquisition, interrogation, investigation, legal trial, narrow search, overview, perusal, probe, pursuit, *quaestio,* question, research, scrutiny, search, study, survey, trial
ASSOCIATED CONCEPTS: Grand Jury Inquiry, judicial inquiry, public inquiry

INQUISITION, noun examination, harassment, infliction, inquest, inquiry, interrogation, oppression, persecution, scrutiny, unfair inquiry

INQUISITIVE, adjective *audiendi, cupidus, curiosus,* curious, eager for knowledge, fond of investigation, given to research, inquiring, interested, interrogative, investigative, questioning, quizzical, scrutinizing, searching, seeking, speculative

INROAD, noun access, advancement, aggression, assault, attack, charge, consumption, damage, detriment, entrance, havoc, impairment, incursion, infiltration, inflow, infraction, infringement, ingress, interference, interloping, intervention, invasion, intrusion, introgression, irruption, loss, offensive, onslaught, outrage, overrunning, overstepping, ravage, sally, transgression, trespass

INSALUBRIOUS, adjective baleful, baneful, calamitous, damaging, dangerous, deleterious, destructive, detrimental, disadvantageous, disastrous, fraught with danger, gravis, harmful, hazardous, hurtful, injurious, *insalubris,* lethal, lethiferous, malefic, maleficent, menacing, mephitic, miasmal, miasmatic, miasmatical, miasmic, morbific, morbifical, mortiferous, noisome, noxious, ominous, pathogenic, perilous, pernicious, pestiferous, *pestilens,* pestilent, pestilential, poisonous, risky, ruinous, threatening, toxic, unclean, unfavorable to health, unhealthful, unhealthy, unhygienic, unsafe, unsanitary, unwholesome, venomous, virulent

INSANE, adjective bereft of reason, certifiable, crazed, crazy, defected, delirious, demented, deranged, disordered, frenetic, frenzied, hysterical, incoherent, insensate, lunatic, mad, maniacal, manic, mental, mentally deranged, *non compos mentis,* of unsound mind, paranoiac, psychotic, raving, unsound, wandering, wild
ASSOCIATED CONCEPTS: insanity defense, insanity plea

INSANITY, noun aberration, aberration of mind, abnormality, alienation, alienation of mind, amentia, brain damage, craziness, daftness, delirium, delusion, dementedness, *dementia,* deranged intellect, derangement, diseased mind, disordered intellect, disordered mind, disordered reason, disorientation, frenzy, hallucination, *insania,* loss of reason, lunacy, madness, mental abnormality, mental alienation, mental decay, mental deficiency, mental derangement, mental disease, mental incapacity, mental infirmities, mental instability, mental sickness, mental unsoundness, paranoia, raving, unbalanced mind, unsound mind, unsoundness of mind, *vecordia,* want of comprehension, want of reason
ASSOCIATED CONCEPTS: adjudication of insanity, diminished capacity, habitual insanity, incompetency, insane delusion, insane impulse to act, insanity defense, insanity plea, irresistible impulse

FOREIGN PHRASES: *Furiosus nullum negotium contrahere potest.* An insane person can make no contract. *Furiosus stipulare non potest nec aliquid negotium agere, qui non intelligit quid agit.* An insane person who knows not what he is doing, cannot contract nor transact any business. *Furiosi nulla voluntas est.* A madman has no will. *Furiosus solo furore punitur.* A madman is punished by his madness alone. *Furor contrahi matrimonium non sinit, quia consensu opus est.* Insanity prevents a marriage from being contracted, because consent is required. *Ira furor brevis est.* Anger is short insanity. *Furiosus absentis loco est.* A madman is considered as a person who is absent. *Insanus est qui, abjecta ratione, omnia cum impetu et furore facit.* A person is insane who, deprived of reason, does everything with violence and rage.

INSATIABLE, adjective acquisitive, avaricious, covetous, craving, discontented, gluttonous, grasping, greedy, hoggish, incapable of being satisfied, *inexplebilis, insatiabilis,* intemperate, piggish, quenchless, rapacious, selfish, unappeasable, unfilled, unquenchable, unsated, unsatisfied

INSCRIBE, verb *ascribere,* commit to writing, *consignare,* engrave, enroll, enscroll, enter, imprint, *inscribere,* insert, letter, list, make an entry, mark, post, put in writing, put upon record, record, register, scribe, write

INSCRIPTION, noun autograph, caption, dedication, engraving, entry, *index, inscriptio,* legend, mark, record, superscription, *titulus,* written matter
ASSOCIATED CONCEPTS: inscribed securities, registration of a deed

INSCRUTABLE, adjective ambiguous, baffling, blank, cloudy, concealed, deadpan, enigmatic, expressionless, hidden, impassive, impenetrable, impossible to understand, inapprehensible, incognizable, incomprehensible, indiscernible, inexplicable, insoluble, mysterious, obscure, *obscurus,* occult, *occultus,* past comprehension, pokerfaced, puzzling, secret, *tectus,* unable to be investigated, unaccountable, unclear, undiscoverable, unfathomable, unintelligible, unknowable, unrevealed, unsearchable, vague

INSECURE, adjective adrift, borderline, changeable, changeful, dangerous, defenseless, dependent, endangered, exposed, exposed to risk, fragile, frail, fraught with danger, harborless, hazardous, helpless, *incertus,* infirm, *instabilis,* lacking stability, perilous, precarious, risky, shaky, slippery, speculative, subject to chance, subject to change, ticklish, tottering, treacherous, unassured, unbalanced, uncertain, unconfident, undependable, unfastened, unprotected, unreliable, unsafe, unsettled, unsheltered, unshielded, unsound, unstable, unsteadfast, unsteady, unsure, untrustworthy, venturesome, venturous, vulnerable
ASSOCIATED CONCEPTS: insecure obligation, insecurity clause

INSECURITY, noun ambiguity, bewilderment, danger, dilemma, doubt, doubtfulness, dubiousness, endangerment, exposure, fallibility, hazard, haziness, hesitation, incertitude, indecision, infirmity, instability, jeopardy, obscurity, peril, perplexity, precariousness, quandary, risk, suspicion, threat, uncertainty, undependability, unreliability, unsoundness, unsteadiness, unsureness, untrustworthiness, vacillation, vagueness, vulnerability

INSEMINATE, verb embed, implant, impregnate, inject, insert, introduce, plant, pollinate, pollinize, seed, sow

INSENSIBLE, adjective apathetic, benumbed, bewildered, blind, callous, clueless, comatose, dazed, deaf, deprived of sensation, dormant, drugged, dull, emotionless, exanimate, frigid, heedless, ignorant, imperceptive, impercipient, inanimate, incapable of feeling, incapable of perceiving, inexcitable, insensate, insensitive, insentient, *obdurescere,* passive, senseless, sensu carere, spiritless, stony, stupefied, supine, torporific, unacquainted, unaffected, unaroused, unaware, unconscious, undiscerning, unenlightened, unfeeling, unhearing, unknowing, unmindful, unmoved, unperceptive, unrealizing, unresponsive, unseeing, unsuspecting, untouched, unwitting, vegetating, void of feeling

INSENSITIVE, adjective blind, callous, cold-blooded, cruel, draconian, hard, impervious, indiscreet, insensate, insensible, insentient, numb, obtuse, ponderous, relentless, remorseless, ruthless, thick-skinned, unaffected, unfeeling, unimpressionable, unresponsive, unsusceptible

INSENTIENCE, noun absence of feeling, absence of sensation, blackout, blankness, immobility, inability to act, inability to perceive, inaction, inactivity, inanimateness, inanimation, incognizance, incomprehension, indifference, *inertia,* inertness, insensateness, insensibility, insensibleness, insensitivity, lack of awareness, lack of comprehension, lack of knowledge, lack of perception, lifelessness, nonrecognition, powerlessness, senselessness, stillness, stupor, suspension of consciousness, trance, unawareness, unconsciousness, unfamiliarity, unfeelingness, want of sensibility

INSEPARABLE, adjective attached, blended, cemented, close, combined, consolidated, constantly together, devoted, fast, firm, fused, glued, impartible, incapable of being parted, indiscerptible, indissoluble, indivisible, inextricable, infrangible, inseverable, insoluble, integrated, interdependent, intertwined, intimate, joined, locked, molded together, nondivisible, *perpetuo comitari,* tenacious, undissolvable, undividable, united, unsunderable, welded
ASSOCIATED CONCEPTS: inseparability of easement, inseparability of statutory provisions

INSERT, verb affix, append, attach, book, embed, enter, file, graft, imbed, imbue, immerse, implant, infuse, inject, inlay, inscribe, inscroll, inset, instill, interject, interpolate, interpose, intersperse, intervene, intrude, obtrude, penetrate, pierce, plant, set in, splice, thrust in

INSERTION, noun addendum, additament, addition, appendix, entry, extension, inclusion, inset, intercalation, interjection, interpolation, *interpositio,* introduction, parenthesis, penetration, plant, postscript, supplement, supplementation, transplantation
ASSOCIATED CONCEPTS: codicil, insertion of a clause to a contract, rider

INSEVERABLE, adjective bound up with, impartible, indiscerptible, indivisible, inextricable, infrangible, infusible, inseparable, insoluble, insunderable, irresolvable, joined, one, unbreakable, undividable, united

INSIDER TRADING, noun criminality, disclosure of confidential information, illegal disclosure, illegal use, illegal use of secret information, illegality, impropriety, infraction, infringement, misappropriate nonpublic information and material, prohibited use of confidential information, SEC violation, use of restricted information, violation of law
ASSOCIATED CONCEPTS: insiders, Rule 10b-5, Securities Exchange Act

INSIDIOUS, adjective artful, beguiling, cheating, conniving, covinous, crafty, cunning, deceitful, deceiving, deceptive, designing, devious, dishonest, disloyal, *dolosus,* ensnaring, *fallax,* false, false-hearted, foxy, fraudulent, furtive, guileful, hypocritical, inconstant, indirect, *insidiosus,* intriguing, lying, perfidious, plotting, scheming, serpentine, sly, stealthy, subtle, surreptitious, treacherous, tricky, underhanded, unscrupulous, vulpine, wily

INSIGHT, noun ability to understand, acuity, acumen, acuteness, apperception, astuteness, awareness, cleverness, *cognitio,* cognition, cognizance, comprehension, consciousness, discernment, discrimination, enlightenment, *intellegentia,* intuition, intuitiveness, *iudicium,* keenness, ken, noesis, penetration, perception, percipience, percipiency, perspicacity, realization, sagaciousness, sagacity, sensitivity, sharpness, shrewdness, understanding, wisdom

INSIGNIFICANCE, noun *exiguitas,* immateriality, inconsequence, inconsequentiality, inessentiality, insubstantiality, irrelevance, irrelevancy, momentariness, nominalness, paltriness, paucity, scantiness, scarceness, shallowness, smallness, sparseness, transientness, triviality, unimportance, unnoteworthiness

INSIGNIFICANT, adjective beneath consideration, collateral, expendable, frivolous, futile, ignoble, immaterial, inapposite, inappreciable, incidental, inconsequential, inconsiderable, indifferent, inferior, irrelevant, meager, meaningless, mediocre, minor, minute, moderate, modest, negligible, niggling, nominal, nonessential, nonsubstantial, nugatory, of little account, paltry, petty, picayune, remote, senseless, slight, small, tenuous, trifling, trivial, unessential, unimportant, unnoteworthy, usual, worthless

INSINCERE, adjective artificial, deceitful, deceptive, dishonest, disingenuous, disreputable, dissembling, dissimulating, evasive, faithless, false, false league, fraudu-lent, guileful, hollow, hypocritical, illegitimate, illusive, lying, mendacious, perfidious, shallow, specious, superfi-cial, treacherous, uncandid, unfrank, unnatural, untrue, untruthful

INSINUATE, verb allude to, curry favor with, hint, implant, imply, impress, indicate, infer, infuse, inject, insert, instill, interject, intimate, introduce, involve, mention, point to indirectly, presume, refer, suggest
ASSOCIATED CONCEPTS: sexual harassment

INSINUATION, noun allusion, aspersion, clue, hint, implication, indirect allusion, indirect comment, indirect implication, inference, innuendo, intimation, oblique hint, reference, *significatio,* suggestion, veiled observation, veiled remark

INSIPID, adjective banal, bloodless, boring, colorless, diluted, dreary, dull, feeble, flat, flavorless, *frigidus,* half-hearted, impotent, inactive, ineffective, *ineptus,* insubstantial, *insulsus,* irresolute, languid, limp, pointless, powerless, savorless, spiritless, tame, tasteless, torpid, unanimated, uncaptivating, undramatic, unelevated, unemphatic, unentertaining, unexciting, unimpassioned, uninspired, uninspiring, uninteresting, unsavory, unscintillating, unsparkling, unspiced, unspirited, unstrengthened, unvivid, vapid, void of taste, weak, without force, without taste

INSIST, verb accent, accentuate, argue, be obstinate, be peremptory, be resolute, bid, brook no denial, command, contend, demand, dictate, *efflagitare,* emphasize, enforce, enjoin, exact, exert pressure, exhort, *exposcere,* force upon, importune, impose, impress on, *instare,* lay stress on, order, override, persevere, persist, press, press earnestly, put pressure on, repeat, require, stand firm, stress, take no denial, underline, urge

ASSOCIATED CONCEPTS: insist on legal protections, insist on one's rights

INSISTENT, *adjective* argumentative, assertive, bent upon, clamorous, coactive, coercive, commanding, compelling, crying, demanding, disposed to insist, dogmatic, driving, emphatic, exigent, forceful, harping, impelling, imperative, importunate, incessant, insisting on notice, instant, intent upon, iterative, monotonous, peremptory, perseverant, persevering, persistent, persisting, pertinacious, pressing, recurrent, reiterative, repeated, repetitional, repetitionary, requesting, serious, striking, tenacious, urgent, vehement

ASSOCIATED CONCEPTS: coercion, improper influence, intimidation

INSOLENT, *adjective* abusive, arrogant, assuming, audacious, bellicose, bold, brazen, bumptious, contemptuous, contumacious, *contumax,* contumelious, defiant, derisive, discourteous, disdainful, disobedient, disobliging, disregardful, disrespectful, flippant, fresh, froward, haughty, hectoring, imperious, impertinent, impolite, *impudens,* impudent, *insolens,* insulting, intolerant, magisterial, malapert, nervy, offensive, opprobrious, outrageous, overbearing, pert, presumptuous, procacious, rude, sarcastic, saucy, shameless, supercilious, swaggering, toplofty, unabashed, unmannerly

ASSOCIATED CONCEPTS: contempt

INSOLVENT, *adjective* bankrupt, broke, defaulting, destitute, failed, impecunious, impoverished, in arrears, indebted, lacking funds, moneyless, out of funds, out of money, penniless, reduced, ruined, unable to pay

INSPECTION, *noun* appraisal, ascertainment, assessment, careful scrutiny, critical examination, critical viewing, critique, evaluation, examination, exploration, inquest, inquiry, inventory, observation, perusal, reconnaissance, review, scrutiny, study, surveillance, survey, trial, visual examination

ASSOCIATED CONCEPTS: audit, authority to inspect, inspection for patent or latent defects, inspection of premises, inspection of records, on sight inspection, subject to inspection

INSPIRE, *verb* actuate, animate, arouse, awaken, bring about, cause, convince, effect, effectuate, elicit, encourage, enkindle, enliven, evoke, *excitare,* exert influence, fill with enthusiasm, generate, give an impetus, imbue, impassion, impel, *incendere, incitare,* incite, induce, influence, instigate, kindle, launch, motivate, move, occasion, originate, persuade, precipitate, prevail upon, produce, prompt, provoke, set astir, stimulate, sway, underlie, urge, wake

INSTALL *(Build In),* **verb** construct, embed, emplace, ensconce, fit, fix, lodge, place, put in

INSTALL *(Induct),* **verb** consecrate, crown, embed, emplace, ensconce, enthrone, establish, inaugurate, initiate, instate, invest, ordain, put in, usher in

INSTALLATION, *noun* admission, ceremony of induction into an office, establishment, inauguration, induction, initiation, installment, instatement, institution, introduction, investiture, launching, ordination, placement, presentation

INSTALLMENT, *noun* advance, allotment, contract payment, deposit, disbursement, dividend, division, down payment, fraction, one of several parts, one of several payments, one of successive parts, parcel, *pars,* part payment, part payment of a debt, partial payment, *pensio,* periodic payment, *portio,* portion, remittance, section, segment, successive portion, token payment

ASSOCIATED CONCEPTS: installment contract, installment note, installment payments, installment plan, installment sale

INSTANCE, *noun* case, case in point, clarification, demonstration, elucidation, embodiment, ensample, example, exemplar, exemplification, *exemplum,* frame of reference, illustration, model, paradigm, representative, representative selection, sample, specimen, type

ASSOCIATED CONCEPTS: first instance, special instance, specific instance

INSTANT, *adjective* approaching, at once, at the present time, at this moment, close, close at hand, current, early, existent, forthcoming, forthwith, imminent, impending, in process, looming, near, near at hand, punctual, *punctum temporis,* ready, simultaneous, speedy, upcoming, without delay

ASSOCIATED CONCEPTS: instant case, instant motion

INSTANTANEOUS, *adjective* abrupt, expeditious, hasty, hurried, immediate, instant, occurring in an instant, *praesens,* prompt, quick, rapid, simultaneous, speedy, *subitus,* swift, without delay, without perceptible time lapse

INSTANTLY, *adverb* anon, at once, directly, expeditiously, *extemplo,* fast, forthwith, hastily, hurriedly, immediately, instantaneously, now, presently, promptly, quickly, rapidly, right away, right now, shortly, soon, speedily, *statim,* straightway, swiftly, with speed, without a wait, without any lapse of time, without delay, without hesitation, without notice

INSTATE, *verb* admit, appoint, *confirmare, constituere,* designate, endow, enlist, enroll, ensconce, entrust, establish, establish in an office, found, give admittance to, give entrance to, *inaugurare,* inaugurate, induct, *initiare,* initiate, install, *instituere,* introduce, introduce into office, invest, launch, lay the foundations, lead the way, name, nominate, place, place in office, plant, put in possession, receive, seat, set, *stabilire, statuere,* take in

INSTIGATE, *verb* abet, actuate, agitate, coax, embolden, encourage, enflame, enkindle, excite, fire, fire up, foment, generate, goad, impel, incite, induce, inflame, influence, initiate, inspire, inspirit, invigorate, lure, motivate, move, persuade, prevail upon, prod, prompt, provoke, push, spur, start, stimulate, stir up, thrust, urge

ASSOCIATED CONCEPTS: code of conduct for law enforcement officials, entrapment

INSTIGATION, *noun* actuation, agitation, animation, cajolery, causation, coaxing, easement, encouragement, excitation, exhortation, fomentation, goading, helpfulness, hortation, impetus, impulsion, incentive, incitation, incitement, inducement, influence, initiation, insistance, insistence, inspiration, invigoration, invitation, irritation, motivation, persuasion, perturbation, piquancy, pressure, prompting, provocation, solicitation, stimulation, *stimulus,* suasion, supporting, taunting, urging

ASSOCIATED CONCEPTS: accomplice, aiding and abetting a crime, instigation of a crime, promoting a crime

FOREIGN PHRASES: *Plus peccat author quam actor.* The originator or instigator of a crime is a worse offender than the actual perpetrator of it.

INSTILL, verb direct, educate, familiarize with, ground, guide, impart, impart gradually, implant, impress upon the mind, inculcate, indoctrinate, infix, inform, infuse, inject, *instillare*, instruct, prepare, propagandize, qualify, school, teach, train, tutor

INSTINCT, noun affinity, *appetitus*, aptitude, aptness, automatic reaction, bent, fitness, inborn proclivity, inclination, innate inclination, innate proclivity, intuition, involuntariness, native tendency, natural sense, natural tendency, predisposition, proclivity, proneness, propensity, reflex action, tendency, untutored intelligence

INSTITUTE, noun academy, association, coalition, college, concern, *conlegium*, educational institution, establishment, firm, foundation, guild, house, institution, institution of learning, lyceum, organization, place of education, school, society, *sodalitas*, syndicate, system, union, university

ASSOCIATED CONCEPTS: business institution, charitable institution, educational institution, financial institution, lending institution, literary institution, penal institution, philanthropic institution, private institution, public institution

INSTITUTE A LAWSUIT, verb bring suit, bring to litigation, commence an action, file a claim, institute an action at law, litigate, sue, take action

INSTITUTION (Commencement), **noun** beginning, inauguration, inception, initiation, installation, installment, open introduction

INSTITUTION (Custom), **noun** academy, alliance, association, bylaw, canon, code, custom, established usage, establishment, familiar practice, fraternity, institute, law, league, ordinance, organization, permanent rule, place of education, prevalent practice, regulation, union

INSTRUCT (Direct), **verb** advise, advocate, bid, brief, call upon, charge, coach, command, compel, counsel, decree, demand, dictate, enact, exact, give a directive, give a mandate, give an order, give authoritative instructions to, give the signal, give the word, give the word of command, guide, impose a duty, impose a task, issue a command, issue a decree, issue an order, lay down the law, make a decree, make an order, *mandare*, order, pass orders, praecipere, *praescribere*, prescribe, prescribe a task, prompt, promulgate a decree, promulgate an order, recommend, require, send an order, suggest, tell

ASSOCIATED CONCEPTS: instruct the jury

INSTRUCT (Teach), **verb** acquaint, comment upon, convey information, direct one's attention, docere, edify, educate, elucidate, enlighten, *erudire*, explain, expound, familiarize, fill with information, give by way of information, give lessons in, give to understand, guide, guide the studies of, illumine, impart, implant, impress upon the memory, impress upon the mind, inculcate, indoctrinate, inform, instill, *instituere*, lecture, make known, point out, prepare, present, prime, provide with information, put before, qualify, school, show, train, tutor

INSTRUCTION (Direction), **noun** advice, authoritative statement, bidding, categorical imperative, caveat, charge, command, commandment, commission, decree, edification, firm advice, guidance, jury charge, mandate, *mandatum*, order, *praescriptum*, precept, regulation, requirement, rule, word of command, written order

ASSOCIATED CONCEPTS: instruction to a jury, peremptory instruction, special instructions

FOREIGN PHRASES: *Matter en ley ne serra mise in bouche del jurors.* A matter of law shall not be put into the mouth of jurors.

INSTRUCTION (Teaching), **noun** detailed statement, discourse, *doctrina*, edification, education, *eruditio*, explanation, exposition, guidance, inculcation, indoctrination, *institutio*, lecture, pedagogy, preaching, preparation, recital, recitation, schooling, sermon, training, tutelage, tutoring, upbringing

INSTRUMENT (Document), **noun** bill, certificate, charter, deed, draft, evidential writing, executed and delivered writing, formal writing, official record, official writing, paper, record, solemn writing, *syngrapha*, *tabula*, writing, writing delivered as the evidence of an agreement, writing which gives formal expression to a legal act, written formal expression

ASSOCIATED CONCEPTS: allonge, instrument evidencing a debt, instrument of writing, negotiable instrument

FOREIGN PHRASES: *Mala grammatica non vitiat chartam, sed in expositione instrumentorum mala grammatica quoad fieri possit evitanda est.* Bad grammar does not vitiate a deed, but in the drafting of instruments, bad grammar should, as far as possible, be avoided. *Ubi nulla est conjectura quae ducat alio, verba intelligenda sunt ex proprietate, non grammatica, sed populari ex usu.* Where there is nothing which calls for another construction, words are to be understood according to their proper sense, not according to their strict grammatical meaning, but according to their popular sense. *Qui haeret in litera haeret in cortice.* He who adheres to the letter of an instrument goes but skin deep into its meaning.

INSTRUMENT (Tool), **noun** agency, agent, aid, apparatus, appliance, article, channel, contributing force, contrivance, device, equipment, facility, implement, *instrumentum*, machine, machinery, means, mechanical construction, mechanism, medium, utensil, utility, vehicle

ASSOCIATED CONCEPTS: instrument of fraud

INSTRUMENTAL, adjective advantageous, aiding, assisting, auxiliary, beneficial, conducive, contributory, helpful, indispensable, serviceable, useful, valuable

INSTRUMENTALITY, noun channel, device, equipment, expedient, implement, instrument, interagent, intermediary, intermediate, intermedium, machinery, manner, means, medium, method, mode, operation, process, resource, stratagem, technic, technique, tool, vehicle, way, wherewithal

ASSOCIATED CONCEPTS: dangerous instrumentality

INSUBORDINATE, adjective contumacious, defiant, disloyal, disobedient, dissident, fractious, froward, indocile, insubmissive, insurgent, insurrectionary, intractable, lawless, mutinous, noncompliant, rebellious, recalcitrant, recusant, refractory, resistive, restive, revolutionary, sansculottic, *seditiosus*, treacherous, treasonous, *turbulentus*, uncomplying, ungovernable, unruly, wayward

ASSOCIATED CONCEPTS: contempt, discharge

INSUBSTANTIAL, adjective airy, baseless, bodiless, chimerical, ephemeral, fanciful, feeble, flimsy, fragile, frail, groundless, hallucinatory, illusive, illusory, imaginary, imagined, immaterial, impalpable, inadequate, inconsequential, inconsiderable, incorporeal, infirm, insignificant, lacking firmness, lacking substance, lame, made poorly, modest, nonexistent, notional, of no consequence, paltry, petty, picayune, poor, powerless, scant, slender, slight, slim, spectral, superficial, tenuous, thin, trifling, trivial, unbased, unfirm, unfounded, ungrounded, unimportant, unreal, unsolid, unsound, unsubstantial, unsupportable, unsustainable, untenable, vague, visionary, weak, without basis, without foundation, without plausibility, without reality, wobbly, worthless

INSUFFERABLE, *adjective*   acute, agonizing, crushing, distressing, dreadful, excruciating, extreme, frightful, harrowing, harsh, hurtful, impossible, insupportable, *intolerabilis*, intolerable, *intolerandus*, painful, past bearing, past enduring, racking, searing, severe, torturous, unbearable, unendurable

INSUFFERABLE HARM, *noun*   disablement, evil, malignance, malignancy, malignity, massive injury, not corrected by monetary compensation, noxiousness, permanent harm, perniciousness, ruin, serious damage, serious illtreatment, significant detriment, significant ill consequence, significant impairment, unbearable aggravation, unbearable harm, virulence
ASSOCIATED CONCEPTS: Latham Act, Patent Act, permanent injunctions, preliminary injunctions, temporary restraining orders, Uniform Trade Secrets Act

INSUFFICIENCY, *noun*   absence, dearth, deficiency, deficit, depletion, emptiness, exhaustion, exiguity, exiguousness, falling short, fewness, inadequacy, inadequateness, incompetence, incompleteness, *inopia*, lack, meagerness, need, not enough, paucity, *penuria*, scantiness, scantness, scarcity, short fall, short measure, short supply, shortage, shortcoming, sparseness, stint, too few, want
ASSOCIATED CONCEPTS: insufficiency of evidence, insufficiency of law to support a verdict

INSUFFICIENT, *adjective*   bereft of, defective, deficient, denuded of, destitute of, devoid of, drained, failing, faint, feeble, *haud sufficiens, impar,* imperfect, in default, inadequate, incapable, incommensurate, incompetent, incomplete, inconsiderable, lacking, lean, meager, missing, negligible, not enough, not sufficient, paltry, poor, scant, scanty, scarce, short, shy, slender, slight, slim, spare, sparse, thin, too little, uncompleted, unequal, unfinished, unfit, unfitted, unqualified, unsound, unsufficing, unsuited, wanting, weak
ASSOCIATED CONCEPTS: insufficient evidence, insufficient funds, insufficient service, insufficient verdict

INSUFFICIENT EVIDENCE, *noun*   a negligible amount of evidence, absence of sufficient evidence, bereft of evidence, deficient amount of evidence, devoid of sufficient proof, failing proof, inadequate amount of persuasive facts, inadequate confirmation, inadequate facts to prove the point in question, inadequate means of proof, inadequate proof, inadequate proof of facts, inadequate substantiation, incomplete evidence, insufficient admitted testimony, insufficient body of facts, insufficient corroboration, insufficient facts to establish the point in issue, insufficient means of proving a fact, insufficient proof at trial, insufficient verification, lacking proof, lean on evidence, meager degree of evidence, paltry amount of evidence, scant testimony, slim proof, sparse proof, thin evidence, weak on evidence
ASSOCIATED CONCEPTS: dismissal of an action, woefully insufficient evidence

INSULAR, *adjective*   alone, apart, confined, detached, discrete, distinct, enisled, isolated, removed, self-sufficient, separate, solitary

INSULATE, *verb*   compartmentalize, cut off, detach, isolate, keep apart, quarantine, screen off, seclude, segregate, separate, sequester, set apart, zone

INSULT, *noun*   abuse, affront, aspersion, atrocity, defamation, defilement, derision, diatribe, disparagement, enormity, impertinence, incivility, indignity, insolence, mockery, offense, offensive remark, open disrespect, outrage, provocation, rebuff, revilement, ridicule, rudeness, slap in the face, slight, snub, uncomplimentary remarks, vulgarity

INSULT, *verb*   affront, be rude to, denigrate, deride, disoblige, disparage, display insolence toward, disregard, disrespect, flout, hector, hold in derision, humiliate, jeer, mock, offend, pique, provoke, raise one's dander, rebuff, ridicule, treat with contemptuousness, treat with discourtesy, treat with indignity

INSUPERABLE, *adjective*   beyond control, difficult, formidable, impassible, impervious, impossible, impracticable, impregnable, inaccessible, incapable of being overcome, incapable of being surmounted, indomitable, innavigable, insurmountable, *invictus*, invincible, invulnerable, out of reach, out of the question, unachievable, unassailable, unattackable, unattainable, unbeatable, unbridgeable, unconquerable, undefeatable, unfeasable, unmasterable, unobtainable, unovercomable

INSURABLE INTEREST, *noun*   acceptable insured, acceptable risk, capable of being insured, insurable ownership, insurable risk, insurable stake, legitimate interest, stake, sufficiently close relationships, vested interest
ASSOCIATED CONCEPTS: life insurance

INSURANCE, *noun*   agreement to pay, assurance against loss, bond against risk, compensation for injury, compensation for loss, contract against future loss, contract against unknown contingencies, guarantee against loss, indemnification, indemnity against loss, pledge, promise, protection against loss, security against loss, stipulation to compensate for loss, warranty against loss
ASSOCIATED CONCEPTS: accident insurance, binder, casualty insurance, claim, coinsurance, contract of insurance, contributing insurance, controlled insurance, endowment insurance, excess insurance, fidelity insurance, fire insurance, group insurance, guaranty insurance, health insurance, insurance agent, insurance application, insurance broker, insurance carrier, insured, insurer, liability insurance, life insurance, loss, marine insurance, nonforfeitable insurance, occupational disability insurance, ordinary insurance, paid-up insurance, policy of insurance, premium, property insurance, reinsurance, surety insurance, term insurance, title insurance, valued insurance, vehicle insurance, whole life insurance

INSURE, *verb*   cover against loss, gain indemnity against loss, guarantee against loss, have underwritten, obtain insurance, protect against loss, reassure, secure against loss, underwrite against loss

INSURER, *noun*   assurer, compensator, guarantee, guarantor, indemnifier, indemnitor, insurance company, recompenser, remunerator, surety, underwriter

ASSOCIATED CONCEPTS: absolute insurer, accident and health insurer, agent, broker, casualty insurer, liability insurer, life insurer

INSURGENCY, noun agitators, criminals, exciters, guerrillas, incendiaries, inducers, inspirers, insurrection, prompters, provokers, rebellion, rebels, revolutionaries, stimulators, uprising
ASSOCIATED CONCEPTS: counter insurgency strategy, global insurgency, quelling insurgency

INSURGENT, noun agitator, anarchist, demagogue, disrupter, insubordinate, insurrectionary, insurrectionist, mutineer, nihilist, radical, rebel, *rebellis*, reformer, renegade, revolter, revolutionary, revolutionist, rioter, seditionary, subverter, traitor

INSURMOUNTABLE, adjective beyond one's power, beyond one's reach, beyond the bounds of possibility, formidable, hardly possible, impassable, impenetrable, impossible, impracticable, impregnable, inaccessible, incapable of being done, incapable of being overcome, incapable of success, indomitable, inexpugnable, insoluble, insuperable, invincible, out of reach, out of the question, too difficult, too hard, unachievable, unassailable, unattackable, unattainable, unbeatable, unconquerable, undefeatable, unfeasible, unmasterable, unperformable, unrealizable, unsolvable, unsubduable, unsurmountable, unvanquishable, unviable, unworkable

INSURRECTION, noun anarchy, defiance, disobedience, disorder, disturbance, insubordination, insurgence, insurgency, *motus,* mutineering, mutiny, noncompliance, outbreak, overthrow, political upheaval, *rebellio,* rebellion, resistance to government, revolt, revolution, riot, rising, *seditio,* sedition, uprising

INSUSCEPTIBLE (Resistant), **adjective** able to withstand, capable of resisting, defended, fortified, having immunity, having resistance, immune, immunized, not sensitive to, protected, repellent, strengthened, strong, tough, unyielding

INSUSCEPTIBLE (Uncaring), **adjective** aloof, apathetic, blind, callous, capable of resisting, capable of withstanding, cold, cool, deaf, detached, devoid of feeling, distant, frigid, hard, hardened, heartless, impassive, impervious, incapable of caring, indifferent, indurate, indurated, inflexible, insensate, insensible, insensitive, insolicitous, insouciant, *insusceptire,* lacking feeling, numb, obdurate, obstinate, pachydermatous, pococurante, recalcitrant, regardless, removed, renitent, *sensu carere,* stubborn, tough, toughened, unaffected, unaroused, unbending, unconcerned, unemotional, unfeeling, ungiving, unimpassioned, unimpressible, uninterested, unmoved, unresponsive, unstirred, unsympathetic, untouched, unwilling to care, unyielding, without regard

INTACT, adjective all-embracing, all in one, all-inclusive, complete, comprehensive, entire, faultless, flawless, free from imperfection, full, in good order, in its original form, in one piece, in perfect condition, inclusive, *intactus, integer,* integral, inviolate, perfect, preserved, replete, safe, *salvus,* solid, sound, together, unabated, unabridged, unaffected by injury, unalloyed, unaltered, unblemished, unbroken, unbruised, uncensored, unchanged, uncut, undamaged, undecayed, undefaced, undemolished, undestroyed, undiminished, undivided, unedited, unexpurgated, unfaded, unharmed, unhurt,

unified, unimpaired, uninjured, unmarked, unmarred, unreduced, unscarred, unscathed, unscratched, unsevered, unshattered, unspoiled, unsullied, untainted, untorn, untouched, unworn, whole, with nothing missing, without loss
ASSOCIATED CONCEPTS: keeping a law intact

INTANGIBLE, adjective abstract, aerial, airy, amorphous, asomatous, bodiless, difficult to appraise, dim, discarnate, disembodied, ethereal, immaterial, impalpable, imperceptible, imponderable, inappreciable, inconspicuous, incorporal, incorporate, incorporeal, indefinite, indiscernible, infinitesimal, insensible, insubstantial, intactile, *intactilis,* invisible, nonphysical, nonsubstantial, not clear to the mind, not definite, shadowy, spiritual, theoretical, unapparent, unbeholdable, uncertain, unconcrete, undiscernible, unearthly, unfleshly, unperceivable, unphysical, unseeable, unsolid, unsubstantial, untouchable, vague, weightless, without form, without physical substance
ASSOCIATED CONCEPTS: intangible assets, intangible personalty, intangible property

INTANGIBLE, noun assignable rights of action, chose in action, incorporeal entity, *intactilis,* personal chattels which are not in possession, personal right not reduced to possession, right, right to personal things, right to recovery
ASSOCIATED CONCEPTS: intangible assets, intangible personalty, intangible property, intangible trust property

INTEGRAL, adjective basic, cardinal, central, component, constituent, elemental, essential, essential to completeness, fundamental, indispensable, integrant, irreplaceable, *necessarius,* necessary, needed, needful, prerequisite, primary, required, requisite, vital
ASSOCIATED CONCEPTS: integral part of a case

INTEGRATE, verb accommodate, adjust, aggregate, amass, assimilate, combine, complete, connect, constitute a whole, coordinate, desegregate, embody, embrace, fit, harmonize, join, make into a whole, proportion, relate, synchronize, systematize, unify

INTEGRATION (Amalgamation), **noun** admixture, affiliation, alliance, association, blend, blending, coadunation, coalition, coexistence, combination, confederation, consolidation, federalization, fusion, incorporation, intermixture, medley, merger, mingling, mix, unification, union
ASSOCIATED CONCEPTS: integration of the terms into a contract

INTEGRATION (Assimilation), **noun** agreement, alliance, association, coalition, coexistence, combination, confederation, consociation, cooperation, federation, fellowship, merger, mingling, participation, partnership, racial balance, racial harmonization, racial harmony, removal of discrimination, solidarity, togetherness, undividedness
ASSOCIATED CONCEPTS: Equal Protection, segregation

INTEGRITY, noun character, estimableness, fairness, faithfulness, fidelity, good faith, goodness, high character, high-mindedness, honesty, honor, honorableness, incorruptibility, *innocentia, integritas,* justness, moral soundness, moral strength, morality, nobleness, principle, *probitas,* probity, propriety, purity, rectitude, reputability, responsibility, righteousness, scruples, scrupulousness, self-respect, sincerity, sound moral principle, strict honesty, trustworthiness, truthfulness, upright moral character, uprightness, uprightness of character, upstandingness, veridicality, virtue, virtuousness, worthiness
ASSOCIATED CONCEPTS: character evidence, impugning the integrity of a witness, want of integrity

INTELLECT, noun ability to perceive, ability to reason, ability to understand, brain, brilliance, cerebration, cognition, cognitive faculty, comprehension, genius, intellectual powers, intellectuality, *intellegentia*, intelligence, *mens*, mental ability, mental acuteness, mental capacity, mental faculty, mentality, mind, power to reason, rational faculty, rationality, reach of mind, reason, reasoning faculty, reasoning power, sense, understanding

INTELLECTUAL PROPERTY RIGHTS, noun creative product protection, creative thinking protection, protection, protection of creativity, protection of writings
ASSOCIATED CONCEPTS: copyrights, patent trademarks

INTELLIGENCE (Intellect), **noun** acumen, aptitude, astuteness, brains, brilliance, cleverness, cognition, cognitive faculty, comprehension, genius, insight, intellectual faculty, intellectual power, intellectuality, *intellegentia*, keenness, *mens*, mental ability, mental acuteness, mental capacity, mental faculty, mentality, mind, power to reason, quickness of perception, rational faculty, rationality, reach of mind, reason, reasoning faculty, reasoning power, sagacity, sense, understanding, wisdom

INTELLIGENCE (News), **noun** account, acquired facts, aviso, communication, communiqué, data, details, dispatch, enlightenment, information, knowledge, known facts, message, monition, notice, *nuntius*, report, tidings, tip, warning, word

INTELLIGENT, adjective able, acute, astute, brainy, bright, capable, clever, discerning, enlightened, gifted, intellectual, judicious, knowing, knowledgeable, perspicacious, perceptive, percipient, sagacious, sapient, sciential, sensible, sharp-witted, shrewd, talented, understanding, well-informed, wise

INTELLIGIBLE, adjective apprehensible, articulate, clear, cognizable, cognizant, coherent, comprehensible, definite, descriptive, distinct, easily understood, evident, explicable, explicit, fathomable, graphic, knowable, lucid, manifest, obvious, palpable, pellucid, plain, plain-spoken, precise, realizable, scrutable, simple, solvable, unambiguous, understandable, unequivocal, unmistakable

INTEMPERATE, adjective exceeding, excessive, exorbitant, extravagant, extreme, immoderate, inabstinent, indulgent, inordinate, unbridled, unchecked, uncontrolled, uncurbed, uninhibited, unlimited, unmeasured, unreined, unrestrained, unruly, unsuppressed, untempered, wasteful

INTEND, verb aim, aspire to, be determined to, calculate, *cogitare*, design, desire, determine upon, drive at, elect, endeavor, expect, fix the mind upon, harbor a design, have in mind, have in view, *intendere*, mean, plan, premeditate, presume, propose, purpose, resolve, scheme, set as a goal
ASSOCIATED CONCEPTS: intended design, intended destination, intended purpose, intended to take effect upon death, precatory words

INTENSE, adjective *acer*, acrimonious, active, acute, aggressive, agonizing, all-consuming, ambitious, angry, animated, anxiety ridden, *ardens*, ardent, aspiring, assiduous, brisk, burning, close, concentrated, consuming, cutting, deep, determined, diligent, distressing, drastic, dynamic, earnest, emotional, emotive, energetic, enthusiastic, excessive, excitable, excited, extraordinary, extreme,

fervent, fervid, feverish, fierce, fiery, flaming, flaring, forceful, frantic, frenzied, grave, harrowing, harsh, head-strong, heated, heightened, high-pressure, hostile, hot-heated, hysterical, impassioned, impatient, impetuous, impulsive, industrious, inflamed, injurious, intensified, intensive, intent, *intentus*, keen, malicious, nervous, passionate, perfervid, powerful, profound, pungent, purposeful, rancorous, resolved, rigorous, serious, severe, sharp, single-minded, stinging, strenuous, strict, strong, tense, testy, undeviating, unwavering, vehement, vigorous, vivid, zealous
ASSOCIATED CONCEPTS: intense law enforcement focus, intense scrutiny

INTENSIFY, verb add to, aggravate, *amplificare, augere*, augment, boost, concentrate, deepen, emphasize, enhance, escalate, exacerbate, exaggerate, heighten, increase, inflame, magnify, redouble, sharpen, step up, strengthen

INTENSITY, noun acuteness, amplitude, ardor, brightness, brilliance, degree, devotion, eagerness, earnestness, energy, enthusiasm, extent, extreme degree, fervency, fervor, force, furiousness, high degree, high pressure, loudness, magnitude, main force, mightiness, passion, potency, power, pressure, puissance, rigor, severity, sharpness, spirit, strength, vehemence, vigor, vividness, warmth, zeal

INTENSIVE, adjective acute, ardent, concentrated, exhaustive, fervent, forceful, intense, *intentivus*, powerful, sharp, strenuous, strong, thorough, thoroughgoing, unmitigated, vehement, vigorous, zealous

INTENT, noun aim, *attentus*, choice, contemplation, design, determination, end, *erectus, intentus*, meaning, mind, motive, object, objective, plan, point, predetermination, purport, purpose, resolution, resolve, scheme, scope, view, volition
ASSOCIATED CONCEPTS: charitable intent, corrupt intent, criminal intent, felonious intent, fraudulent intent, general intent, implied intent, intent of parties to contract, intent of testator, intent to defraud, larcenous intent, malice, mutual intent, premeditation, presumed intent, specific intent, testamentary intent, transferred intent
FOREIGN PHRASES: *Quod factum est, cum in obscuro sit, ex affectione cujusque capit interpretationem.* When there is doubt about an act, it receives interpretation from the feelings or disposition of the actor. *Impunitas continuum affectum tribuit delinquendi.* Impunity confirms the disposition of a delinquent. *Intentio mea imponit nomen operi meo.* My intent gives a name to my act. *Non aliter a significatione verborum recedi oportet quam cum manifestum est, aliud sensisse testatorem.* The ordinary meaning of the words ought not to be departed from unless it is evident that the testator intended otherwise. *Quicunque jussu judicis aliquid fecerit non videtur dolo malo fecisse, quia parere necesse est.* Whoever does anything by the command of a judge is not deemed to have done it with an evil intent, because it is necessary to obey. *Voluntas et propositum distinguunt maleficia.* The will and purpose distinguish offenses. *In criminalibus, sufficit generalis malitia intentionis, cum facto paris gradus.* In crimes, a general malicious intent suffices where there is an act of equal degree. *In criminalibus, voluntas reputabitur pro facto.* In criminal cases, the intent will be taken for the deed. *Voluntas facit quod in testamento scriptum valeat.* The will of the testator gives validity to what is written in the will. *Actus non facit reum, nisi mens sit rea.* An act does not render a person guilty, unless the mind is guilty.

Impunitas continuum affectum tribuit delinquendi. Impunity confirms the disposition of a delinquent. *In atrocioribus delictis punitur affectus licet non sequatur effectus.* In the more atrocious crimes the intent is punished, although an effect does not follow. *Malitia est acida; est mali animi affectus.* Malice is sour; it is the quality of an evil mind. *Voluntas in delictis, non exitus spectatur.* In crimes, the intent, and not the result, is regarded.

INTENTION, noun aim, ambition, *consilium,* design, desire, destination, determination, direction, earnestness, end in view, end intended, fixed direction, fixed purpose, goal, *institutum,* mark, object, objective, plan, *propositum,* purpose, resolution, resolve, set purpose, settled determination, target, ultimate purpose

ASSOCIATED CONCEPTS: donative intention, implied intention, the intention of the parties, malicious intention

FOREIGN PHRASES: *In testamentis plenius voluntates testantium interpretantur.* In wills, the intentions of the testators should be fully regarded. *Non efficit affectus nisi sequatur effectus.* The intention amounts to nothing unless some effect follows. *In conventionibus, contrahentium voluntas potius quam verba spectari placuit.* In contracts, it is the rule to regard the intention of the parties rather than the actual words. *Culpa lata dolo aequiparatur.* Gross negligence is held equivalent to malice. *In maleficiis voluntas spectatur, non exitus.* In offenses, the intention is regarded, not the result. *Intentio inservire debet legibus, non leges intentioni.* The intention of a party ought to be subservient to the laws, not the laws to intentions. *Benigne faciendae sunt interpretationes, propter simplicitatem laicorum, ut res magis valeat quam pereat; et verba intentioni, non e contra, debent inservire.* Interpretations should be liberal, because of the lack of training of laymen, so that the subject matter should be valid rather than void; and words should be subject to the intention, not the intention to the words.

INTENTIONAL, adjective by design, calculated, *cogitatus,* conscious, *consideratus,* considered, contemplated, decided, deliberate, designed, determined, intended, knowing, *lentus,* meditated, outlined before hand, planned, pondered, prearranged, preconsidered, predesigned, predetermined, premeditated, purposed, purposeful, reasoned, resolved, studied, thought out, thoughtful, willful

ASSOCIATED CONCEPTS: intentional act, intentional homicide, intentional neglect, intentional tort

INTER VIVOS, noun conferment between the living, conveyance between the living, transfer among the living

ASSOCIATED CONCEPTS: inter vivos will

INTERAGENT, noun agent, broker, go-between, instrument, intermediary, intermediate, intermediate agent, intermediator, intervener, intervening agent, mediating agency, mediator, medium, middleman, negotiator, spokesman, vehicle

INTERCEDE, verb act as agent, act as go-between, act as mediator, arbitrate, bring into harmony, bring to an understanding, bring to terms, bring together, compose differences, conciliate, *deprecari,* interfere, intermeddle, intermediate, interpose, intervene, judge, make peace between, meddle, mediate, moderate, negotiate, petition for, plead, referee, settle, stand between, step in, umpire

INTERCEPT, verb avert, block, check, close with, come between, commandeer, confiscate, debar, detain, dispossess,

disrupt, foil, forestall, hamper, hinder, impede, impound, inhibit, interfere, interpose, interrupt, obstruct, occlude, parry, preclude, prevent, restrain, retard, stave, stay, stem, stop, thwart, wrest from

ASSOCIATED CONCEPTS: intercept criminal activity

INTERCESSION, noun arbitrage, arbitration, conciliation, *deprecatio,* diplomacy, instrumentality, interference, interjection, intermeddling, intermediation, interposition, intervention, mediation, negotiation, peacemaking, reconcilement, reconciliation, supplication

INTERCHANGE, noun alternation, barter, change, exchange, give and take, intercourse, *permutatio,* rearrangement, reciprocal exchange, reciprocation, requital, retaliation, swap, trade, transaction

INTERDICT, verb arrest, bar, block, check, debar, declare illegal, deny, deter, disallow, embargo, enjoin, forbid, halt, hinder, impede, inhibit, *interdicere,* obstruct, preclude, prevent, prohibit, proscribe, refuse permission, repress, restrain, restrict, stop, thwart, veto

INTEREST *(Concern),* **noun** absorption, admiration, anxiety, application, assiduity, attention, attention to detail, awe, care, close attention, concentration, conscientiousness, consequence, consideration, curiosity, curiousness, desire to know, diligent attention, disposition to inquire, eagerness, enthusiasm, esteem, excitement, gravity, heed, heedfulness, import, importance, inclination to ask questions, intentiveness, intentness, mark, meddling, meticulosity, mindfulness, minute attention, minuteness, moment, note, pertinence, preoccupation, prying, questioning, regard, regardfulness, relevance, reverence, salience, significance, solicitude, studiousness, *studium,* thoughtfulness, undivided attention, veneration, weight, weightiness, worry

ASSOCIATED CONCEPTS: conflict of interest, declaration against interest, direct interest, insurable interest, interest in the controversy, interested witness, legal interest, material interest, real party in interest, united in interest

INTEREST *(Ownership),* **noun** assets, belongings, claim, dominion, droit, holding, lawful possession, part, participation, percentage of ownership, portion, possession, property, proprietorship, right, right of ownership, rightful possession, seisin, share, stake, title

ASSOCIATED CONCEPTS: accounts bearing interest, assignable interest, beneficial interest, common interest, contingent interest, continuity of interest, controlling interest, future interest, interest in land, joint interest, legal interest, legal rate of interest, life interest, person interested in a will, property interest, qualified interest, remainder interest, remaining interest, transfer of interest, undivided interest

FOREIGN PHRASES: *Nemo plus juris ad alienum transferre potest quam ipse habet.* No one can transfer to another any greater right than he himself has.

INTEREST *(Profit),* **noun** accrual, advantage, dividend, earnings, *faenus,* gain, increment, monetary benefit, monetary gain, premium for the use of money, profit from money loaned, *usura*

ASSOCIATED CONCEPTS: legal rate of interest, usury

INTEREST, verb absorb, affect, arouse, arouse notice, arouse one's enthusiasm, attract, attract notice, beguile, catch the eye, concern, *delectare,* divert one's attention, engage the attention, engage the mind, engage the thoughts, engross, engross the mind, engross the thoughts, entangle, entertain, enthrall, entice, excite, fascinate, grip, hold the attention, inspire, involve, move, occupy, occupy the attention, pique, *placere,* rouse, stir, tantalize, tempt, tenere, titillate, touch, whet one's interest

INTERESTED, *adjective* affected, affiliated, associated, biased, concerned, connected, directly affected by the outcome of a controversy, having investments in, influenced, involved, one-sided, partial, partisan, prejudiced, prepossessed, solicitous, undetached
ASSOCIATED CONCEPTS: interested juror, interested party, interested witness

INTERFERE, *verb* arrest, bar, be an obstacle, block, break in, burden, check, clog, counteract, countervail, cramp, cripple, cross, curb, deter, disallow, disturb, encroach, encumber, entrammel, fetter, foil, forbid, hamper, handicap, hinder, impede, infringe, inhibit, intercede, intercept, interject, intermeddle, intermit, *interpellare,* interpose, interrupt, intervene, *intervenire,* intrude, invade, meddle, obstruct, preclude, prevent, prohibit, retard, stop, thwart, work against
ASSOCIATED CONCEPTS: interference with business relations, interference with contract rights, interference with interstate commerce, unreasonable interference
FOREIGN PHRASES: ***Forstellarius est pauperum depressor et totius communitatis et patriae publicus inimicus.*** A forestaller is an enemy of the poor, and a public enemy of the country. ***Nemo debet immiscere se rei ad se nihil pertinenti.*** No one should interfere with a thing that in no respect concerns him.

INTERFERE WITH THE LAW, *verb* bar to investigation, become an obstacle to prosecutors, block prosecution, counteract the smooth prosecution of the law, countervail instructions, disturb a prosecution, hamper prosecution, handicap prosecution, hinder prosecution, impede prosecution, infringe on a prosecution, inhibit prosecution, interrupt a prosecution, meddle in a prosecution, obstruct a prosecution, prevent a prosecution, prohibit an ongoing prosecution, retard an investigation, stop an investigation, thwart a criminal investigation, work at cross-purposes with an investigation
ASSOCIATED CONCEPTS: consent necessity, law enforcement, self defense, torts

INTERFERENCE, *noun* antagonism, antipathy, bar, barrier, censure, check, collision, conflict, contravention, damper, disapproval, disturbance, encumbrance, fetter, friction, frustration, hindrance, impediment, imposition, infringement, interception, intercession, intermediacy, interposition, interruption, intervention, intrusion, invasion, meddling, nuisance, obstruction, onus, opposition, prohibition, resistance, restraint, setback, stricture, stumbling block
ASSOCIATED CONCEPTS: contempt, frustration of contract, interference with contractual relations

INTERIM, *adjective* impermanent, intermediate, makeshift, provisional, provisory, temporary, *temporis intervallum,* tentative, transient, unfinished, unofficial
ASSOCIATED CONCEPTS: interim relief, interim stay, provisional remedies

INTERIOR, *adjective* inherent, innate, inner, innermost, internal, inward, private, secret

INTERIOR, *noun* center, core, essence, inland, inner part, inside, middle

INTERJECT, *verb* add, blurt, comment, exclaim, explain, express, force in, implant, include, incorporate, infiltrate, inject, insert, intercalate, *intericere,* interjaculate, intermingle, interpolate, *interponere,* interpose, interrupt, intervene, interweave, introduce, intromit, place into, put between, set forth, specify, state, thrust in, vociferate, work in

INTERLOCKING, *adjective* connective, correlative, interacting, interlinking, meshing
ASSOCIATED CONCEPTS: interlocking defenses, interlocking instruments, interlocking signal systems

INTERLOCUTORY, *adjective* interim, intermedial, intermediary, intervening, interventional, nonfinal, nonpermanent, not final, provisional, provisory, temporary, tentative, transient, transitory
ASSOCIATED CONCEPTS: interlocutory appeal, interlocutory costs, interlocutory decree, interlocutory injunction, interlocutory order, interlocutory rulings

INTERMEDIARY, *noun* agent, *arbiter,* arbitrator, buffer, *conciliator,* connecting link, connection, delegate, *deprecator,* diplomat, emissary, go-between, interceder, intercessor, link, mediary, mediator, medium, middleman, moderator, negotiant, negotiator, peacemaker, pleader, propitiator, reconciler, referee, representative, vehicle

INTERMEDIATE, *adjective* average, between, central, compromising, equidistant, halfway, inserted, instrumental, intercurrent, interjacent, intermediary, interposed, intervenient, intervening, mean, medial, median, mediatorial, mediatory, medium, *medius,* mesial, mesne, mid, middle, midmost, moderate, neutral, transitional
ASSOCIATED CONCEPTS: interlocutory order, intermediate appellate court, intermediate order
FOREIGN PHRASES: ***Extremis probatis, praesumuntur media.*** When the extremes have been proved, those things which are between them are presumed.

INTERMINABLE, *adjective* boundless, ceaseless, constant, continual, continuous, drawn-out, durable, endless, eternal, everlasting, extended, extensive, illimitable, immeasurable, incessant, indeterminate, inexhaustible, infinite, innumerable, limitless, long-drawn, long-winded, measureless, olamic, open-headed, permanent, perpetual, profuse, prolonged, protracted, stretched, tediously long, termless, unbounded, unending, unceasing, uninterrupted, unlimited, unremitting, wearisome, without limit or end

INTERMISSION, *noun* abeyance, adjournment, break, cessation, delay, discontinuance, discontinuity, halt, hiatus, interim, interlude, intermittence, interregnum, interruption, interval, intervention, leave, lull, pause, pendency, recess, remission, respite, rest, stoppage, suspense, suspension

INTERMITTENT, *adjective* alternate, broken, cyclic, cyclical, desultory, discontinuous, fitful, flickering, fluctuating, infrequent, intermitting, interrupted, irregular, nonuniform, occasional, periodic, recurrent, recurring, remittent, rhythmic, seasonal, serial, spasmodic, sporadic, termly, unregular, unsuccessive, wavering

INTERNAL, *adjective* absorbed, domestic, domesticus, enclosed, implanted, infixed, ingrained, inmost, innate, inner, innermost, inside, *interior, intestinus,* private, under the surface, within boundary lines
ASSOCIATED CONCEPTS: internal affairs, Internal Revenue

INTERNMENT, noun apprehension, arrest, bondage, captivity, confinement, constraint, custody, detention, durance, immuration, immurement, impoundment, imprisonment, imprisonment term, incarceration, preventive custody

INTERPOSE, verb be an obstacle to, block, break into, come between, force in, hinder, impede, infiltrate, infringe, inject, insert, intercalate, intercede, intercept, interfere, *intericere*, interject, intermeddle, intermediate, *interponere*, interrupt, intervene, introduce, intrude, mediate, obstruct, obtrude, parenthesize, penetrate, place between, prevent, put in, stand in the way, thrust in
ASSOCIATED CONCEPTS: interpose a claim, interpose a defense, interpose an objection

INTERPOSITION, noun arbitration, insertion, intercalation, intercession, intercurrence, interjacence, interjection, interlocation, intermediation, interpenetration, interposure, interruption, intervention, introduction, negotiation

INTERPRET, verb annotate, characterize, clarify, clear up, *conicere*, construe, convey the meaning of, decipher, decode, deduce, define, delineate, depict, describe, diagnose, explain, explain the meaning, *explanare*, explicate, expound, figure out, give one an idea of, give one an impression of, illuminate, illustrate, *interpretari*, make clear, make plain, make sense of, offer an explanation of, reveal, set forth the meaning, simplify, solve, throw light upon, translate, translate orally, understand, unfold, unravel, unscramble
ASSOCIATED CONCEPTS: construction, interpret a contract, interpret a will

INTERPRETATION, noun analysis, annotation, application, clarification, comment, commentary, connotation, construction, content, decipherment, definition, depiction, description, diagnosis, elucidation, exegesis, exemplification, explanation, explication, exposition, illustration, implication, inference, meaning, portrayal, prognosis, reading, rendering, rendition, resolution, revelation, scholium, sense, significance, signification, solution, translation, understanding, version
ASSOCIATED CONCEPTS: authentic interpretation, close interpretation, customary interpretation, exact interpretation, free and unrestricted interpretation, genuine interpretation, incorrect interpretation, legal interpretation, liberal interpretation, limited interpretation, predestined interpretation, restricted interpretation, rightful interpretation, unfair interpretation

INTERPRETIVE, adjective annotative, clarifying, constructive, definitive, elucidative, enlightening, explanatory, explicative, illuminating, interpretational

INTERRELATED, adjective affiliated, affinitive, agnate, akin, allied, analogous, associated, cognate, conjugate, connatural, connected, consanguineous, consociate, correlated, correlative, enmeshed, fraternal, germane, interaffiliated, interallied, interassociated, interconnected, interlinked, interwoven, joined, kindred, linked, of the same family, pertinent, related, relevant, sib, tied, united

INTERRELATION, noun chain, coherence, connection, contact, correlation, interaffiliation, interassociation, interconnection, interdependence, interrelationship, mutual dependence, mutuality, nexus, proportion, relationship

INTERROGATE, verb ask, badger, catechize, conduct an inquiry, cross-examine, delve into, grill, heckle, inquire, interpellate, investigate, pose, probe, prosecute an inquiry of, put questions to, question, quiz, require an answer

INTERROGATION, noun catechization, cross-examination, examination, exploration, formal questioning, grilling, inquest, inquiry, inquisition, inspection, *interrogatio*, investigation, *percontatio*, probe, *quaestio*, query, questioning, scrutiny, search, taking information
ASSOCIATED CONCEPTS: grand jury inquiry, interrogation of a party to an action, interrogation of a witness

INTERROGATIVE, adjective all-searching, diagnostic, exploratory, fact-finding, inquisitional, inquisitive, inquisitorial, interested, interrogational, *interrogativus*, investigative, penetrating, piercing, probing, prying, questioning, quizzical, scrutinizing, searching

INTERROGATORIES, noun demands, inquiries, pretrial inquiries, questioning, questions, written requests for information

INTERRUPT, verb arrest, balk, barge in, break, break in, butt in, cause to cease, cause to delay, cease, check, chime in, clog, come between, cut, delay, desist, disconnect, discontinue, disjoin, dissever, dissolve, distract, disturb, disunite, divide, foil, frustrate, get in the way, hinder, inhibit, intercept, interfere, intermit, *intermittere, interpellare*, interpose, intrude, leave off, meddle, obstruct, punctuate, put a stop to, put an end to, retard, separate, sever, stop, sunder, suspend, thwart
ASSOCIATED CONCEPTS: interrupt a separation, interrupt possession

INTERRUPTION, noun abeyance, armistice, arrest, bar, block, break, cessation, check, clog, deadlock, delay, disconnection, discontinuance, disjunction, dissolution, disunion, gap, halt, hiatus, hindrance, impediment, *intercapedo*, interception, interference, interim, interlude, *intermissio*, intermission, interstice, *intervallum*, intrusion, lull, obstacle, obstruction, pause, recess, respite, severance, standstill, stop, stoppage, sunderance, suspension, truce
ASSOCIATED CONCEPTS: business interruption insurance, interruption of adverse possession, interruption of service

INTERSECTION, noun *bivium*, concourse, conjunction, connection, crossing, crossing point, crosspoint, crossroad, crosswalk, cruciation, *decussatio*, decussation, interconnection, intercrossing, joining place, joint, junction, juncture, meeting place, meeting point, traversal, union

INTERSPERSE, verb diffuse, disseminate, distribute, *immiscere*, interfuse, interlard, intermingle, interpenetrate, interpolate, interpose, interweave, mix, pepper, put between, scatter, shake, sprinkle, work in

INTERTWINE, verb braid, crisscross, cross, enlace, enmesh, entangle, entwine, form a network, *innectere*, inosculate, interknit, interlace, interlink, intermix, interthread, intertwist, interweave, inweave, knot, lace, mesh, plait, plat, *redimire*, reticulate, splice, tangle, tie together, twine together, twist, web, wreathe

INTERVAL, noun abeyance, break, gap, halt, hiatus, interim, interlude, intermission, interregnum, interruption, interstice, *intervallum*, intervening time, lapse, lull, pause, recess, respite, rest, *spatium interiectum*, spell, truce

INTERVENE, verb become a party to an action, break in, come between, encroach, infringe, intercede, *intercedere*, interfere, intermeddle, interpose, interrupt, *intervenire*, intrude, meddle, obtrude, step in, *supervenire*

ASSOCIATED CONCEPTS: intervening act, intervening agency, intervening cause, intervening efficient cause, intervening estate, intervening force, intervening parties, intervening sufficient cause, intervening superceding cause, intervenor, intervention as of right, intervention by leave of court

INTERVENING CAUSE, noun act which breaks the chain of events, break in causation, break in liability, break in proximate cause, independent act, interceding cause, interfering cause, interrupting cause, intervening act, intruding cause, nullifying act or action, overriding act or action, overruling act or action, preclusion, superseding intervening cause
ASSOCIATED CONCEPTS: duty of care, intervening damages, intervening force, negligence, proximate cause, standard care, superseding cause, torts

INTERVENTION (Imposition into a lawsuit), **noun** entrance into a lawsuit, entrance of a third party, insertion, interference, interjection, interjection into a lawsuit, interposition, intrusion
ASSOCIATED CONCEPTS: intervention by leave of the court, intervention by right

INTERVENTION (Interference), **noun** intercalation, interception, intercession, interjacence, interjection, interloping, intermeddling, intermediation, interpolation, interposition, interruption, interventus, intrusion

INTERVIEW, noun audience, audition, colloquy, conference, congressio, conloquium, consultation, conversation, dialogue, discussion, exchange of views, hearing, meeting, mutual exchange, oral examination, question and answer, talk, verbal intercourse

INTIMATE, adjective allied, associated with, brotherly, close, closely acquainted, closely associated, confidential, confiding, coniunctus, consociated, faithful, familiar, familiaris, federate, fraternal, friendly, guarded, inmost, innermost, intimus, linked, on familiar terms, personal, private, secret, strongly attached, trusted
ASSOCIATED CONCEPTS: confidentiality, fiduciary relationship

INTIMATION, noun allusion, denuntiatio, hint, idea, implication, inference, inkling, innuendo, insinuation, mention, nuntius, overtone, reference, significatio, suggestion

INTIMIDATE, verb abash, affright, alarm, badger, browbeat, bully, coerce, cow, daunt, deterrere, dismay, dispirit, disquiet, duress, frighten, harass, hector, incutere, inicere, menace, overawe, petrify, put in fear, scare, shock, terrify, terrorize, threaten, unnerve
ASSOCIATED CONCEPTS: unlawful intimidation

INTOLERABLE, adjective impossible, insufferable, insupportable, unbearable, unendurable
ASSOCIATED CONCEPTS: intolerable cruelty, intolerable severity

INTOLERANCE, noun acerbitas, adrogantia, aversion, bias, bigotry, chauvinism, discrimination, dislike, hatred, illiberality, incapacity to endure, jaundice, jingoism, lack of toleration, narrow-mindedness, narrowness, one-sidedness, partiality, persecution, preconception, prejudgment, prejudice, racism, rejection, sectarianism, sectionalism, segregation, slant, subjectivity, superbia, want of forbearance, want of toleration
ASSOCIATED CONCEPTS: intolerable cruelty

INTOLERANT, adjective biased, bigoted, close-minded, closed, disobliging, dogmatic, fanatical, illiberal, inconsiderate, inhospitable, insensitive, insular, jaundiced, mean spirited, narrow, narrow-minded, not open, one-sided, opinionated, partial, prejudiced, racist, sexist, small-minded, uncharitable, unfriendly, ungenerousness, unreasonable, unsympathetic
ASSOCIATED CONCEPTS: bias crimes

INTONATION, noun accentuation, cadence, delivery, inflection, phonation, pitch, quality, resonance, sound, timbre, tonality, tone, tone of voice, vocalism, voice
ASSOCIATED CONCEPTS: demeanor

INTRACTABLE, adjective adamant, balky, beyond control, contrary, contumacious, defiant, difficilis, disobedient, dogged, firm, froward, headstrong, heedless, incorrigible, indocile, indocilis, indomitable, inflexible, insubordinate, insuppressible, irrepressible, mulish, not easily governed, not pliable, obdurate, obstinate, obstreperous, pertinacious, perverse, pervicacious, rebellious, recalcitrant, refractory, resistive, restive, stubborn, tenacious, unbending, uncontrollable, uncurbed, undisciplined, ungovernable, unmalleable, unmanageable, unruly, unsubmissive, unwilling, unyielding, wayward, willful

INTRICATE, adjective complex, complicated, delicate, difficult, elaborate, involved, tangled, tricky

INTRINSIC (Belonging), **adjective** implicit, inherent, native, pertinent
ASSOCIATED CONCEPTS: intrinsic fraud, intrinsic jury, intrinsic value

INTRINSIC (Deep down), **adjective** deep-seated, inner, internal, inward

INTRODUCE, verb bring in, enter, inducere, induct, inject, insert, interpose, introducere, invehere, offer, offer as an exhibit, place before, present, present formally, present to the court for acceptance, proffer, put, put forward, put forward for consideration, put in, submit, surrender, tender, usher in

INTRODUCE INTO EVIDENCE, verb offer as an exhibit, offer evidence, place into evidence, present evidence, present formally, put forward for consideration, submit as evidence, submit to the court
ASSOCIATED CONCEPTS: introduce into evidence exhibits, introduce into evidence prior testimony

INTRODUCTION, noun act of bringing in, admittance, formal presentation, inductio, induction, interposition, introductio, invectio, offering, offering as an exhibit, placing, presentation
ASSOCIATED CONCEPTS: introduction of evidence

INTROSPECTION, noun contemplation, innermost thoughts, introversion, ipsum se inspicere, looking within, meditation, musing, pensiveness, reflection, reverie, self-absorption, self-communion, self-counsel, self-examination, self-inspection, self-knowledge, self-scrutiny, self-study, thoughtfulness

INTRUDE, verb come uninvited, crash, encroach, enter uninvited, enter unlawfully, foist oneself, force oneself, horn in, impose, infringe, interfere, interlope, interrupt, invade, irrupt, obtrude, se interponere, thrust in, thrust oneself, trench on, trespass
ASSOCIATED CONCEPTS: invade privacy, trespass

INTRUSION, noun aggression, attack, encroachment, forced entrance, *importunitas,* imposition, incursion, infiltration, infringement, interference, interloping, interruption, invasion, irruption, meddling, obtrusion, overrunning, trespass, uninvited attendance, uninvited entry, unlawful entry, unwelcome suggestion

ASSOCIATED CONCEPTS: intrusion of rights, right of privacy, trespass

INTRUSIVE, adjective hindering, infringing, interfering, interloping, interruptive, invading, invasive, obtrusive, trespassing

INUNDATE, verb bury, deluge, drench, engulf, fill to superfluity, flood, flow over, glut, immerse, overflood, overflow, overspread, overwhelm, pour over, run over, rush upon, saturate, spill over, surge, swamp

INURE *(Accustom),* **verb** acclimate, acclimatize, accustom, acquaint, adjust, *adsuefacere,* condition, domesticate, familiarize, get used to, habituate, harden, make routine, naturalize, sanctify by custom, season, toughen

INURE *(Benefit),* **verb** accumulate, advance, advantage, aid, assist, avail, be of use, be profitable, bolster, contribute, enhance, enrich, forward, furnish aid, further, gain, help, improve, pay, profit, promote, render useful, serve, subserve, supply aid, turn to account, upgrade, yield gain, yield profit

INVADE, verb aggress, arrogate, assail, assault, attack, break in, encroach, enter hostilely, impinge, *incurrere, incursionem,* infringe, intrude, *invadere,* obtrude, overrun, overtake, penetrate, raid, run over, trespass, usurp, violate

ASSOCIATED CONCEPTS: invade the corpus of a trust, invade the province of the jury, invasion of privacy, invasion of property rights, invasion of rights

INVALID, adjective abrogated, baseless, canceled, fallacious, faulty, futile, having no force, inadequate, ineffective, ineffectual, inefficacious, *infirmus,* inoperative, *inritus,* lacking authority, lacking force, lacking strength, not binding, *nugatorius,* nugatory, null, quashed, unauthentic, untenable, untrue, useless, vain, void, weak, without legal efficacy

ASSOCIATED CONCEPTS: invalid delegation, invalid gift, invalid transfer, invalid will

FOREIGN PHRASES: Ab abusu ad usum non valet consequentia. A conclusion as to the use of a thing from its abuse is invalid.

INVALIDATE, verb abolish, abort, abrogate, annul, cancel, confute, deprive of legal effect, disannul, disprove, disqualify, erase, *inritum facere, labefactare,* make void, nullify, override, overrule, overthrow, quash, refute, repeal, repudiate, rescind, *rescindere,* retract, reverse, revoke, undermine, undo, vitiate, withdraw

ASSOCIATED CONCEPTS: invalidate a transfer, invalidate a will, invalidate an election

INVALIDITY, noun annulment, cancellation, disqualification, erroneousness, fallaciousness, fallacy, falseness, falsity, inadequacy, incompetence, ineffectiveness, nullity, unsoundness, untenableness, vitiation, voidness

ASSOCIATED CONCEPTS: declaration of invalidity

FOREIGN PHRASES: Pacta quae turpem causam continent non sunt observanda. Contracts which are based on an unlawful consideration will not be enforced. **Pacta quae contra**

leges constitutionesque, vel contra bonos mores fiunt, nullam vim habere, indubitati juris est. It is unquestionably the law that contracts which are made contrary to the laws or against good morals, have no force in law. **Quae ab initio non valent, ex post facto convalescere non possunt. Things** invalid from the beginning cannot be made valid by a subsequent act.

INVALUABLE, adjective beyond price, costly, expensive, *inaestimabilis,* incalculable, incapable of being appraised, inestimable, matchless, of inestimable value, peerless, precious, *pretiosissimus,* priceless, unequaled, unparalleled, valuable, without price

INVARIABLY, adverb always, as a rule, changelessly, commonly, constantly, conventionally, customarily, faithfully, fixedly, frequently, generally, habitually, immutably, in all cases, in every instance, normally, ordinarily, perpetually, regularly, repeatedly, rigidly, routinely, steadily, systematically, traditionally, unalterably, unchangeably, undeviatingly, uniformly, unvarying, usually, without exception

INVASION, noun aggression, assault, attack, attack on rights, breach, disobedience, encroachment, foray, hostile entry, *incursio,* incursion, infiltration, infraction, infringement, inroad, *inruptio,* interference, interloping, intervention, intrusion, overstepping, raid, siege, transgression, trespass, violation

ASSOCIATED CONCEPTS: invasion of a corpus, invasion of principal, invasion of privacy, invasion of rights, wrongful invasion

INVEIGH, verb attack, blast, cry out against, denounce, dispraise, exclaim against, fulminate, impugn, *incessere, increpare, insectari,* lash, protest against, rage against, rail, raise one's voice against, rate, revile, scold, score, storm against, thunder against, utter invective, vilify, vituperate

INVEIGLE, verb allure, attract, bait, bamboozle, befool, beguile, blandish, cajole, cheat, chouse, coax, cozen, deceive, decoy, defraud, delude, draw, ensnare, entangle, entice, entrap, fool, gull, illaqueate, importune, induce, influence, lay a trap, lead astray, lead on, lure, maneuver, mislead, persuade, seduce, snare, suborn, sway, tempt, trap, trick, urge, victimize, wheedle, win

INVENT *(Falsify),* **verb** *comminisci,* counterfeit, distort, embroider, exaggerate, fabricate, fake, falsify, feign, fib, fictionalize, humbug, lie, make believe, make up, misrepresent, misstate, pervert, pretend, prevaricate, sham, trump up, varnish

INVENT *(Produce for the first time),* **verb** author, bring into being, build, coin, come upon, compose, conceive, concoct, construct, contrive, create, design, devise, discover, draft, dream up, envisage, *excogitare,* excogitate, fabricate, fashion, find, forge, form, imagine, improvise, initiate, introduce, *invenire,* manufacture, originate, produce, realize, *reperire,* think of, think up, visualize

INVENTION, noun brain child, coinage, composition, concoction, contraption, contrivance, creation, creative effort, creative fabrication, discovery, fabrication, finding, formation, handiwork, improvisation, innovation, *inventum,* origination, product, *reperta*

INVENTORY, noun catalogue, checklist, contents, enumeration, index, itemization, itemized list, list, list of

properties, manifest, merchandise list, record, register, schedule of articles, stock book, stock list, stock sheet, *tabula,* tally sheet
ASSOCIATED CONCEPTS: inventory of assets

INVERSE, *adjective* antipodal, antipodean, antithetical, contrary, converse, *conversus,* diametrically opposite, *inversus,* inverted, opposite, reverse, reversed, transposed, turned about
ASSOCIATED CONCEPTS: inverse condemnation, inverse discrimination

INVEST *(Fund),* **verb** advance, back, buy into, buy stock, deal in futures, employ capital, finance, gamble, infuse funds, lay out, lend, lend on security, loan, make an investment, *occupare,* outlay, play the market, *ponere,* provide capital, provide money, put out at interest, put up, risk, risk one's money, sink, speculate, sponsor, support, venture
ASSOCIATED CONCEPTS: invest capital

INVEST *(Vest),* **verb** appoint, authorize, charge, charter, commission, confer power, *deferre,* delegate, depute, empower, enable, endow with authority, entrust, furnish with rank, give a mandate, give authority, give power, grant authority, grant power, inaugurate, induct, install, instate, institute, license, *mandare,* name, nominate, ordain, permit, privilege, put in commission, sanction

INVESTIGATE, *verb* analyze, ask, cognoscere, collect facts, conduct an inquiry, consider, deliberate upon, delve into, dig into, discuss, dissect, examine, examine in detail, examine the particulars, examine with care and accuracy, explore, go into, hold an inquiry, inquire into, inquire into systematically, inspect, interrogate, look into, peer into, *perscrutari,* probe, pursue an inquiry, *quaerere,* question, reconnoiter, review, scan, scrutinize, search into, seek information regarding, study in detail, survey, take evidence, track, track mentally
ASSOCIATED CONCEPTS: investigate a crime, investigate charges, investigate the merits of a case

INVESTIGATION, *noun* careful search, careful study, close inquiry, collection of facts, detailed examination, examination, exhaustive study, exploration, formal scrutiny, *indagatio,* inquire to ascertain facts, inquiry, *inquisitio,* interrogation, *investigatio,* legal inquiry, official inquiry, probe, questioning, research, scrutinization, scrutiny, search, searching inquiry, statistical inquiry, strict inquiry, systematic search
ASSOCIATED CONCEPTS: blanket investigation, criminal investigation, governmental investigation, judicial investigation, legislative investigation

INVESTMENT, *noun* backing, capital invested, capital outlay, employment of capital, endowment, financial backing, financing, invested capital, invested money, invested property, loan, loan at interest, outlay, speculation, venture
ASSOCIATED CONCEPTS: investment broker, investment contract, investment security, investment trust

INVETERATE, *adjective* accustomed, addicted, chronic, chronical, confirmed, customary, deep-rooted, entrenched, established, firmly established, fixed, frequent, habitual, habituated, hardened, ingrained, inured, *inveteratus,* longstanding, *penitus defixus, penitus insitus,* rooted, set, time-honored, wonted

INVIDIOUS, *adjective* abominable, calculated to provoke resentment, disagreeable, disliked, disobliging, harmful, hateful, hurtful, injurious, *invidiosus,* irksome,

likely to excite ill will, loathsome, malicious, objectionable, obnoxious, odious, offensive, plaguesome, rancorous, spiteful, troublesome, unacceptable, unaccommodating, ungracious, unkind, unpleasant, unwelcome, vexatious
ASSOCIATED CONCEPTS: invidious discrimination

INVIGORATING, *adjective* analeptic, animating, bracing, energizing, enlivening, exhilarating, healthful, invigorative, medicinal, nourishing, quickening, refreshing, remedial, reparative, restorative, salubrious, salutary, stimulating, vitalizing

INVINCIBLE, *adjective* all-powerful, ever-victorious, impossible to defeat, impossible to vanquish, incapable of being overcome, indestructible, indomitable, ineradicable, inexpugnable, *inexsuperabilis,* inextinguishable, inpermeable, insuperable, insurmountable, *invictus,* inviolable, invulnerable, irresistible, overpowering, overwhelming, resistless, secure from capture, unable to be overcome, unable to be quelled, unable to be subjugated, unassailable, unbeatable, unconquerable, unsubduable, unvanquishable, unyielding

INVIOLABILITY, *noun* immunity from assault, impenetrability, impregnability, incorruptibility, indestructibility, inexpugnability, inviolableness, invulnerability, protection, safety, *sanctitas,* security, security against violence, unassailability
ASSOCIATED CONCEPTS: inviolability of Constitutional rights, inviolability of contracts

INVIOLATE, *adjective* complete, consecrated, free from desecration, free from impairment, hallowed, intact, *intactus, integer, inviolatus,* pure, sacred, sanctified, scatheless, secure, sound, spotless, stainless, unaffected by injury, unaltered, unblemished, unbroken, uncorrupted, undefiled, undestroyed, undisturbed, unharmed, unhurt, unimpaired, uninjured, unpolluted, unprofaned, unscathed, unspotted, unstained, untouched, unviolated, whole

INVISIBLE *(Small),* **adjective** diminutive, imperceptible, inappreciable, inconspicuous, infinitesimal, microbic, microscopic, minuscule

INVISIBLE *(Veiled),* **adjective** cloaked, concealed, covert, enshrouded, evanescent, hidden, impalpable, indiscernible, intangible, latent, lost to view, masked, obscure, screened, suppressed, unapparent, undetected, undisclosed, undiscovered, undivulged, unexplained, unexposed, unnoticeable, unperceived, unrevealed, unseeable, unseen, untraced, veiled

INVITATION, *noun* advance, allurement, appeal, approach, attraction, bid, bidding, call, challenge, encouragement, enticement, incitement, inducement, *invitatio,* offer, overture, petition, plea, proffer, prompting, proposal, proposition, provocative, request, solicitation, summons, tender, urging
ASSOCIATED CONCEPTS: business invitation, invitation to bid, license by invitation

INVOICE *(Bill),* **noun** account, account rendered, note, reckoning, statement, statement of account, statement of obligations, statement particularizing debts due, tab

INVOICE *(Itemized list),* **noun** account of goods shipped, account of merchandise, bill of lading, check list, enumeration, inventory, itemized account, *libellus,* list of goods, list of items, list of items shipped, list of mercantile goods, merchandise specification, schedule, schedule of items and their respective prices
ASSOCIATED CONCEPTS: uniform commercial code

INVOKE, verb ask solemnly for, beg for, bid, call on for a blessing, call on for help, call up, conjure, entreat, *implorare*, implore, *invocare*, invoke, raise spirits, recite a spell, recite an incantation, summon, summon by incantation
ASSOCIATED CONCEPTS: invoke the authority of the court, invoke the Fifth Amendment

INVOLUNTARY, adjective against one's will, averse, coactus, coercive, compulsory, forced, independent of volition, *invitus*, mandatory, non *voluntarius*, obligatory, unassenting, unconscious, unintended, unintentional, unmeditated, unpremeditated, unthinking, unwilled, unwilling, without consent, without power of choice, without will
ASSOCIATED CONCEPTS: involuntary bailment, involuntary bankruptcy, involuntary confession, involuntary dismissal, involuntary manslaughter, involuntary payment, involuntary sale, involuntary servitude, involuntary statements, involuntary suretyship, involuntary trust, involuntary unemployment

INVOLUNTARY MANSLAUGHTER, noun accidental homicide, accidental killing, accidental murder, killing with criminal negligence, killing with reckless disregard, killing without caution, killing without circumspection, unintentional homicide, unintentional killing, unpremeditated killing
ASSOCIATED CONCEPTS: corporate manslaughter, murder

INVOLUTION, noun complexity, complication, confusion, convolution, embroilment, entanglement, imbroglio, *implicatio*, intricacy, involvement, knot, labyrinth, maze, puzzle, sinuation, sinuosity, sleave, snarl, tangle, torsion, tortility, tortuosity, tortuousness, twist, web

INVOLVE (Implicate), verb accuse, ally, associate, blame, brand, bring accusation, bring charges, cast a slur on, charge, connect, consociate, *continere*, criminate, delate, denounce, draw in, entangle, incriminate, inculpate, interconnect, interrelate, lay the blame on, link together, lodge a complaint, make a party to, make participator, prefer charges, prove to be a participant in, relate, show to be an abettor, stigmatize, tie in with
ASSOCIATED CONCEPTS: involve a codefendant

INVOLVE (Participate), verb act in concert, associate, be a part of, be a party to, be in league with, collaborate, collude, confederate, connect, contribute, cooperate, enter into, have a hand in, join forces, join in, lend oneself to, make common cause with, partake, play a part, relate, share, side with, strike in with, support, take part, take sides, team up, unite, work together
ASSOCIATED CONCEPTS: involve a case or controversy, involve a Constitutional question, involve life or liberty, involve the merits of a case, involve title to real property, involve wrongdoing

INVOLVED (A party to), adjective absorbed, absorbed with, added as a defendant, added as a party, caught up in, contributing, devoted to, engaged, engrossed in, immersed in, implied, intent, intent on, occupied, sued, taken up with

INVOLVED (Complex), adjective a party to, cloudy, complexed, complicated, compound, concerned, confounded, confused, constructive, convoluted, difficult, disordered, elaborate, esoteric, implicated, inextricable, interested, intricate, involute, involutional, labyrinthine, obscure, problematic, recondite, sinuous, tortuous, unclear

INVOLVEMENT (Association), noun incrimination, inculpation

INVOLVEMENT (Complex), noun affiliation, complex, complexness, complication, complicity, dilemma, embroilment, engagement, engrossment, enmeshment, entailment, entanglement, implication, inextricability, involution, participation, perplexity, personal involvement, quagmire, quandary, relation, relationship, sympathy, tanglement

INVOLVEMENT (Concentration), noun absorption, application, devotion, engagement, intentness, occupation, preoccupation

INVULNERABLE, adjective certain, defensible, entrenched, fortified, immune, impenetrable, impregnable, indestructible, indomitable, inexpugnable, infrangible, insuperable, invincible, inviolable, permanent, safe, scatheless, secure, tenable, unassailable, unattackable, unbreakable, unchallengeable, unconquerable, unsurmountable

IOTA, noun bit, crumb, dab, dash, drop, fragment, grain, jot, minute quantity, morsel, particle, scintilla, shred, small amount, small quantity, spark, tittle, trace, whit

IPSO FACTO, adverb absolutely, by the act itself, by the fact itself, by the mere fact, by the very fact, essentially, positively, truly

IRASCIBLE, adjective bad-tempered, belligerent, cantankerous, captious, choleric, churlish, contentious, cranky, cross, disobedient, disputatious, dissentious, easily riled, edgy, fiery, fractious, froward, hostile, huffy, ill-humored, ill-natured, impatient, ireful, irritable, moody, nettlesome, perverse, petulant, pugnacious, quarrelsome, querulous, quick-tempered, snappish, testy, thin-skinned, unamiable

IRK, verb aggravate, aggrieve, annoy, badger, chafe, discommode, discompose, distress, disturb, exasperate, exercise, harass, incommode, irritate, jade, nettle, offend, perturb, pique, plague, provoke, rile, roil, ruffle, trouble, try one's patience, wear upon

IRKSOME, adjective annoying, boresome, boring, bothersome, distressing, *gravis*, irritating, jejune, *molestus*, *odiosus*, tiresome, tiring, troublesome, weariful, wearing, wearisome, wearying

IRONCLAD, adjective covered, defended, difficult to alter, difficult to break, difficult to change, exacting, firm, immutable, impossible to alter, impossible to break, impossible to change, inexorable, inflexible, ironbound, irreversible, irrevocable, relentless, rigid, rigorous, strict, stringent, unalterable, unbending, unbreakable, unchangeable, unchanging, uncompromising, unmalleable, unpliant, unrelenting, unshakeable, unyielding

IRONCLAD AGREEMENT, noun binding contract, binding legal document, concrete provisions, definite commitment, exact and binding agreement, precise covenants, solid protections, strong provisions, substantial understanding

IRONIC, adjective cynical, ironical, paradoxical, quizzical, sarcastic, sarcastical, sardonic, satiric, satirical

IRONY, noun cynicism, *dissimulatio, ironia*, mockery, sarcasm, satire

IRRATIONAL, *adjective* absurd, *absurdus*, bizarre, brainless, contrary to reason, crazy, foolish, heedless, ill-advised, ill-considered, ill-judged, illogical, imprudent, injudicious, insensate, ludicrous, mindless, nonsensical, outrageous, preposterous, rationis expers, reasonless, ridiculous, senseless, *stultus*, stupid, thoughtless, unconsidered, unintelligent, unreasonable, unreasoned, unreasoning, unreflecting, unsensible, unsound, unthinking, unthoughtful, unwise, utterly illogical, void of reason, without judgment, without reason, without rhyme or reason, witless
ASSOCIATED CONCEPTS: irrational behavior

IRREBUTTABLE, *adjective* incontestable, indisputable, indubitable, irrefutable, unchallengeable, unimpeachable, unquestionable
ASSOCIATED CONCEPTS: irrebuttable evidence

IRRECLAIMABLE, *adjective* abandoned, beyond cure, beyond hope, hopeless, incurable, irredeemable, irremediable, irreparable, irretrievable, irreversible, irrevocable, lost, ruined, undone, unredeemed

IRRECONCILABILITY, *noun* absolute difference, conflict, contention, contrariety, difference, disagreement, discongruity, discrepancy, disinclination, disparity, enmity, hostility, implacability, incommensurability, incompatibility, incongruity, inconsistency, inconsonance, intransigence, irrelation

IRRECONCILABLE, *adjective* adamant, alienated, antagonized, at variance, *contrariae*, estranged, firm, hostile, immovable, immutable, *implacabilis*, implacable, implacably opposed, *inexorabilis*, inexorable, inexpiable, inflexible, inimical, intransigent, refusing to agree, refusing to harmonize, rigid, unable to be pacified, unadjustable, unaffected, unalterable, unappeasable, unbending, unchangeable, uncompromising, unconformable, unforgiving, unmoved, unreconciled, unyielding
ASSOCIATED CONCEPTS: irreconcilable conflict, irreconcilable differences

IRRECONCILABLE DIFFERENCES, *noun* adamantness, complete alienation, complete intractability, immovability, immovable resolution, immutability, incurableness, inexorable positions, intransigence, irreparableness, irreversibility, irrevocability, obduracy, rigidity, rigorism, ruined relationship, total inflexibility, unbendingness, unmoved positions, unyieldingness
ASSOCIATED CONCEPTS: divorce, no fault divorce

IRRECOVERABLE, *adjective* beyond recall, incorrigible, irredeemable, irreparable, irretrievable, irreversible, past hope

IRREDEEMABLE, *adjective* beyond remedy, consumed, cureless, dissipated, expended, finished, gone, gone to waste, hopeless, immitigable, incapable of being bought back, inconvertible, incorrigible, incurable, irreclaimable, irrecoverable, irreformable, irreparable, irretrievable, irreversible, irrevocable, lost, past cure, past hope, past mending, past recall, remediless, ruined, spent, squandered, unchangeable, undone, unpayable, used up, wasted, without hope

IRREFUTABLE, *adjective* axiomatic, axiomatical, beyond doubt, certain, *certus*, demonstrable, *firmus*, inappealable, incontestable, incontrovertible, indisputable, indubious, indubitable, irrefragable, past dispute, positive, proven, questionless, sure, testable, unanswerable, unchallengeable, unconfutable, uncontestable, uncontroversial, undeniable,

undoubtable, unequivocal, unimpeachable, unmistakable, unquestionable
ASSOCIATED CONCEPTS: irrebuttable presumption

IRREGULAR *(Improper)*, *adjective* against the rules, condemnable, criminal, criminous, dishonest, foul, illegal, illegitimate, illicit, immoral, nefarious, open to objection, out of place, prohibited, unauthorized, unwarranted, wicked, wrong, wrongful
ASSOCIATED CONCEPTS: irregular conduct, irregular indorsement, irregularity in proceeding, jurisdictional irregularity

IRREGULAR *(Not usual)*, *adjective* aberrant, abnormal, anomalistic, anomalous, asymmetric, asymmetrical, atypical, deviating from the general rule, deviating from the norm, deviating from the standard, deviative, divergent, eccentric, erratic, exceptional, extraordinary, freakish, heteroclite, *inaequabilis, insitatus*, odd, out of order, out of place, out of the ordinary, peculiar, queer, singular, strange, unconformable, unconventional, unique, unnatural, unsymmetric, unsymmetrical, unusual
ASSOCIATED CONCEPTS: irregular incorporation, irregular judgment

IRREGULARITY, *noun* aberrance, aberrancy, aberration, abnormality, abnormity, anomaly, asymmetry, breach, changeableness, confusion, crookedness, desultoriness, deviation, disarrangement, discontinuity, disorder, disorderliness, distortion, divergence, eccentricity, exception, fitfulness, idiosyncrasy, illegality, imperfection, improperness, inconsistency, infringement, intermittence, jaggedness, lack of order, lack of propriety, lack of symmetry, lawlessness, lumpiness, malformation, malfunction, mutability, nonconformity, oddity, oddness, peculiarity, rarity, roughness, singularity, solecism, strangeness, turbulence, unconformity, unevenness, uniqueness, unnaturalness, unorthodoxy, unpunctuality, unruliness, unsmoothness, unsteadiness, ununiformity, unusualness, variability, variableness, variation, violation, want of method, wildness

IRRELATIVE, *adjective* alien, apart, detached, impertinent, inapplicable, inapposite, independent, irrelevant, removed, separate, separated, strange, unaffiliated, unallied, unassociated, unattached, unconnected, unrelated, without connection, without relation

IRRELEVANT, *adjective* alien, *alienus*, aside from the point, beside the mark, beside the point, beside the question, deviating, extraneous, far from the point, foreign, gratuitous, immaterial, impertinent, inapplicable, inapposite, inappropos, inappropriate, inapt, incongruous, inconsequent, inconsequential, inessential, insignificant, irrelative, malapropos, *nihil ad rem pertinet*, not applicable, not on point, not pertaining to, not pertinent, not significant, not to the point, not to the purpose, not vital, off the subject, off the topic, out of order, out of place, out of the way, remote, unallied, unapt, unconnected, unessential, unimportant, unrelated, unsuitable, unwarranted, without reference to
ASSOCIATED CONCEPTS: irrelevant evidence, irrelevant pleading, irrelevant statement, irrelevant testimony

IRREMEDIABLE, *adjective* beyond correction, beyond cure, beyond hope, beyond recall, beyond redress, beyond remedy, cureless, deadly, hopeless, immedicable, immitigable, impossible to better, incurable, inevitable, inexpiable, irrecoverable, irredeemable, irreparable, irretrievable, irreversible, irrevocable, past cure, past help, past mending, remediless, ruined, unable to be corrected, unable to be fixed, unable to be remedied, unfixable, unimprovable

IRREPARABLE, *adjective* incurable, irrecoverable, irredeemable, irreversible, remediless, ruined, undone
ASSOCIATED CONCEPTS: irreparable damage, irreparable harm, irreparable injury

IRREPARABLE HARM, *adjective* beyond recall, incurable effect, irreclaimable damage, irrecoverable effect, irredeemable impairment, irretrievable effect, irretrievable injury, irreversible effect, irrevocable damage
ASSOCIATED CONCEPTS: Latham Act, Patent Act, permanent injunctions, preliminary injunctions, temporary restraining orders, Uniform Trade Secret Act

IRREPREHENSIBLE, *adjective* above suspicion, aboveboard, blameless, circumspect, exalted, faultless, free from fault, free of guilt, guiltless, honest, impeccable, incorruptible, inculpable, *innocens,* innocent, innoxious, inoffensive, irreproachable, irreprovable, not guilty, *sanctus,* sinless, spotless, stainless, straightforward, unassailable, unblamable, unblameworthy, unblemished, uncensurable, unchallengeable, undeserving of censure, unerring, unexceptionable, unfallen, unimpeachable, uninvolved, unobjectionable, unoffending, unsullied, upright, virtuous

IRRESISTIBLE, *adjective* cogent, compelling, forceful, forcible, formidable, impossible to overcome, impossible to resist, impossible to withstand, indomitable, *insuperabilis, invictus,* invincible, mighty, omnipotent, overpowering, overwhelming, potent, powerful, puissant, resistless, strong, superior, unbeatable, unconquerable, vigorous
ASSOCIATED CONCEPTS: irresistible force, irresistible impulse

IRRESOLUTE, *adjective* capricious, changeable, changeful, doubtful, doubting, *dubius,* erratic, faltering, fickle, fluctuating, frivolous, hesitant, hesitating, *incertus,* indecisive, infirm of purpose, lukewarm, mercurial, mutable, oscillating, spineless, timid, uncertain, undecided, undetermined, unfixed, unresolved, unsettled, unsteadfast, unsteady, vacillant, vacillating, vacillatory, volatile, wavering

IRRESPECTIVE, *adjective* despite, in spite of, regardless of, without reference, without respect or regard to

IRRESPONSIBLE, *adjective* arbitrary, capricious, changeable, disloyal, disobedient, dutiless, flighty, fluctuating, frivolous, inconstant, infirm of purpose, lawless, mutinous, perfidious, rash, rebellious, shiftless, thoughtless, treacherous, trustless, uncontrolled, uncurbed, undependable, undisciplined, undutiful, unfaithworthy, unreliable, unrestrained, unstable, unsteady, untrustworthy, untrusty, vacillating, wavering
ASSOCIATED CONCEPTS: incompetence, irresponsible actions

IRRETRIEVABLE, *adjective* dissipated, dissolved, forfeited, given up, gone, hopelessly lost, *inreparabilis,* irreclaimable, irrecoverable, irredeemable, irreparable, lost, past recall, spent, unrecoverable, untraceable, vanished

IRREVERSIBLE, *adjective* beyond remedy, cureless, entrenched, hopeless, immutable, impossible to change, impossible to reverse, incommutable, incurable, indefeasible, indissoluble, indissolvable, ineradicable, inextinguishable, irreclaimable, irrecoverable, irredeemable, irreformable, irremedial, irremovable, irreparable, irrepealable, irretrievable, irrevocable, lasting, nonreversible, not capable of annulment, permanent, remediless, reverseless, unalterable, unchangeable, unrestorable, unreturnable
ASSOCIATED CONCEPTS: irreversible damage, irreversible detriment

IRREVOCABLE, *adjective* beyond recall, binding, changeless, definite, final, firm, fixed, immitigable, immovable, immutable, impossible to change, incapable of revocation, incommutable, indefeasible, indelible, indestructible, indissoluble, indissolvable, ineluctable, ineradicable, inescapable, inevasible, inevitable, inextinguishable, inflexible, *irrevocabilis,* intransmutable, irreclaimable, irredeemable, irremediable, irremovable, irreparable, irrepealable, irretrievable, irreversible, lasting, nonreversible, permanent, persisting, remediless, reverseless, settled, stable, unable to be annulled, unalterable, unavoidable, unchangeable, unmodifiable, unrepealable, unrestorable, without appeal
ASSOCIATED CONCEPTS: irrevocable dedication, irrevocable gift, irrevocable grant, irrevocable license, irrevocable option, irrevocable pledge, irrevocable transfer, irrevocable trust

IRRITATE, *verb* affront, aggravate, agitate, anger, annoy, badger, bother, bully, chafe, discompose, displease, disturb, enrage, exacerbate, exasperate, excite anger, excite impatience, fret, gall, give offense, grate, harass, hector, incense, inflame, infuriate, *inritare,* irk, jar, madden, molest, nag, needle, nettle, offend, pain, peeve, persecute, pester, pique, plague, provoke, put out of humor, rankle, rasp, rile, rub the wrong way, ruffle, sting, stir to anger, tease, torment, torture, vex

ISOLATE, *verb* banish, blacklist, confine, cut off, detach, disconnect, disengage, disjoin, dislocate, dissever, dissociate, disunite, enisle, exclude, excommunicate, exile, insulate, island, keep apart, keep from contact with others, keep in solitude, maroon, ostracize, outlaw, part, place by itself, put aside, quarantine, refuse to associate with, rope off, secernere, seclude, segregate, *seiungere,* separate, sequester, set apart, set aside, sever, split, sunder
ASSOCIATED CONCEPTS: isolated occurrence, isolated transaction

ISSUANCE, *noun* announcement, broadcast, bulletin, communication, communiqué, culmination, debouchment, decree, delivery, discharge, dispatch, effluence, effluency, effusion, egress, egression, emanation, emergence, emission, escape, exit, final result, fruit, gush, issue, manifesto, message, notice, notification, outcome, outflow, outgo, outlet, outpour, proclamation, promulgation, pronouncement, pronunciamento, prospectus, public announcement, publication, publicity, release, report, rescript, result, statement, ultimate result, upshot
ASSOCIATED CONCEPTS: issuance of an insurance policy, issuance of execution, issuance of order, issuance of process, issuance of subpoena, issuance of summons

ISSUE *(Matter in dispute),* ***noun*** *causa,* cause, debatable point, disputed point of law, disputed question, fact put in controversy by the pleadings, field of inquiry, item on the agenda, material point, material point deduced by the pleadings, matter, matter in hand, matter in question, matter of contention, point, point in question, problem, proposition, question, question at issue, *res,* subject for inquiry, topic under consideration
ASSOCIATED CONCEPTS: bond issue, collateral issue, fundamental issue, genuine issue, immaterial issue, joining of issue, justiciable issue, labor issue, material issue, moot issue, note of issue, triable issue
FOREIGN PHRASES: ***Placita negativa duo exitum non faciunt.*** Two negative pleas do not make an issue.

ISSUE *(Progeny),* **noun** child, children, descendants, family, heirs, *liberi,* lineage, lineal descendants, offspring, *progenies, stirps*
ASSOCIATED CONCEPTS: adopted children, die without issue, failure of issue, last issue, legitimate issue
FOREIGN PHRASES: *Si quis praegnantem uxorem reliquit, non videtur sine liberis decessisse.* If a man dies, leaving his wife pregnant, he is considered as having died childless.

ISSUE *(Publish),* **verb** air, an**noun**ce, assert formally, bring into the open, broadcast, call public attention to, circulate, communicate, declare, disclose, dispense, disperse, disseminate, distribute, divulge, *edere,* enunciate, expose, give out, give public notice of, inform, lay before the public, make a public announcement, make known, notify, notify publicly, offer to the public, post, print, proclaim, promulgate, pronounce, *pronuntiare,* proponere, propound, publicize, put forth, put forward, put into circulation, put out, release, reveal, send out, set forth, spread, state, utter with conviction
ASSOCIATED CONCEPTS: issue a decision of the court, issue a judgment, issue an order

ISSUE *(Send forth),* **verb** break forth, burst forth, come forward, come onto the horizon, come out, come out in the open, *egredi,* egress, emanate, emerge, *erumpere, exire,* exit, exude, flow, flow out, make its appearance, manifest itself, pour forth, pour out, put in an appearance, spring up, stream, surface, surge, transmit
ASSOCIATED CONCEPTS: issue stock

ISSUE AN ORDER, *verb* command, declare, decree, determine, dictate, direct, find, hand down a judicial command, hand down a judicial instruction, instruct, make an authoritative command, mandate, prescribe, proclaim, pronounce, publish an order, rule

ISSUE OF FACT, *noun* debatable issue, disputed factual point, disputed question, inquiry into the truth, issue to be addressed, material disputed point, material point, matter in question, matter of contention, point at issue, point in question, point to be determined, question at issue, question for inquiry, question to be addressed, question to be determined, questionable issue
ASSOCIATED CONCEPTS: affidavit, disputed fact a law, evidence, issue of material fact, issues of disputed fact

ITEM, *noun* article, asset, commodity, component, constituent, count, detail, effect, element, entity, entry, feature, gadget, good, ingredient, merchandise, object, pars, part, particular, piece, piece of information, piece of news, point, possession, product, *res,* salable commodity, separate paragraph, singleton, specification, staple, story, unit, vendible, ware
ASSOCIATED CONCEPTS: item of appropriation, item on deposit, itemization of damages, itemized account

ITEMIZE, *verb* be specific, catalog, circumstantiate, count, designate, detail, document, enter into detail, enumerate, index, inventory, list, mention, mention in detail, note, number, particularize, point out, post, recapitulate, recount, register, set down, specify, state by items, tabulate
ASSOCIATED CONCEPTS: itemize an account, itemize damages, itemize expenses

ITERATIVE, *adjective* duplicative, echoing, harping, recurrent, recurring, redundant, reiterant, repeated, repetitious, repetitive, tautological

ITINERANT, *adjective* ambulant, ambulatory, passing, peripatetic, journeying, moving, traveling, wandering, wayfaring
ASSOCIATED CONCEPTS: itinerant dealer, itinerant merchant, itinerant trader, itinerant vendor

ITINERANT, *noun* drifter, peripatetic, traveler, rambler, roamer, rover, runabout, voyager, wanderer

JACTATION, *noun* boast, boastfulness, brag, braggadocio, braggardism, conceit, fanfaronade, gasconade, jactitation, ostentation, pretension, rodomontade, self-glorification, swagger, swank, vainglory, vanity, vaunt, venditation

JAIL, *noun* *carcer,* cell, detention cell, detention center, detention station, house of correction, house of detention, inclosure, keep, penal institution, penitentiary, place of confinement, prison, prisonhouse, reformatory, stockade

JAIL, *verb* apprehend, capture, cast into prison, commit to an institution, commit to prison, confine, constrain, detain, hold captive, hold in captivity, hold in custody, immure, impound, imprison, *in carcerem, in custodiam,* incarcerate, institutionalize, isolate, lock in, lock up, place inconfinement, put behind bars, put under restraint, restrain, restrict, send to prison, shut in, shut up, subjugate, take into custody

JAILBREAK, *noun* break, breakout by inmates, escape by inmates, flight by inmates, forcible escape by inmates, liberation, planned escape by inmates, prison break, revolt
ASSOCIATED CONCEPTS: overcrowding

JAPE, *verb* bemock, burlesque, caricature, chaff, flout, fool, gibe at, imitate insultingly, jeer, jest, joke, lampoon, laugh at, make fun of, mimic, mock, parody, play tricks upon, poke fun at, ridicule, satirize, scoff, taunt, tease, travesty, twit

JARGON *(Technical language),* *noun* argot, cant, code, coined words, language of a particular profession, legalese, neologism, neology, private language, professional language, professional vocabulary, specialized language, specialized terminology, specialized vocabulary
ASSOCIATED CONCEPTS: legal jargon

JARGON *(Unintelligible language),* *noun* babble, blabber, blather, confused language, confused talk, confusion, double talk, empty talk, foolishness, gibberish, inanity, incoherence, incoherent discourse, jabber, jumble, nonsense, nonsensical language, nonsensical talk, nonsensicalness, prattle, rambling talk, senseless talk, silly talk, unintelligible talk

JEALOUS, *adjective* begrudging, competitive, covetous, desiring, desirous, discontented, disposed to envy, dissatisfied, distrustful, doubting, envious, greedy, grudging, *invidus, lividus,* longing, possessive, rival, suspicious

JEER, *verb* *cavillari,* deprecate, depreciate, deride, deridere, disparage, disregard, disrespect, gibe, have no regard for, hold in derision, *inridere,* insult, laugh at, make fun of, mock, ridicule, scoff, sneer, speak derisively, speak slightingly, taunt, treat with insolence, twit

JEJUNE *(Dull),* *adjective* bleak, boresome, boring, colorless, common, commonplace, drearisome, dreary, dry, flat, flavorless, hollow, indifferent, insipid, monotonous, ordinary, plain, ponderous, prosaic, prosy, stolid, tame, tasteless, tedious, thin, tiresome, torpid, undramatic, unenlivened, unentertaining, unexciting, unimpassioned, uninspired, uninspiring, unlively, unpointed, unspirited, usual, vacuous, vapid, weak, wearisome

JEJUNE *(Lacking maturity),* *adjective* adolescent, babyish, callow, childish, immature, inexperienced, infantile, infantine, juvenile, puerile, unfledged, unlearned

JEOPARDIZE, *verb* endanger, expose to danger, imperil, in *periculum,* leave unprotected, menace, peril, place in danger, risk, stake, threaten

JEOPARDY, *noun* crisis, danger, dangerous situation, dangerousness, endangerment, hazard, imperilment, insecurity, instability, menace, peril, perilousness, precariousness, risk, threat, uncertainty, unsafety, vulnerability
ASSOCIATED CONCEPTS: double jeopardy, former jeopardy, placed in jeopardy
FOREIGN PHRASES: *Nemo bis punitur pro eodem delicto.* No one can be punished twice for the same offense.

JETTISON, *verb* cast overboard, discard, dispense with, dispose of, eject, eliminate, expel, get rid of, part with, rid oneself of, slough, throw away, throw overboard, toss out, toss overboard

JOB, *noun* assignment, avocation, billet, business, calling, chore, duty, employment, function, labor, mission, obligation, occupation, position, profession, responsibility, role, task, trade, undertaking, vocation, work

JOCULAR, *adjective* amusing, arch, comic, diverting, facetious, frisky, frivolous, frolicsome, full of fun, funny, gamesome, gay, given to joking, gleeful, gleesome, hilarious, humorous, *iocosus, iocularis,* jesting, jocose, jocund, joking, jolly, joshing, jovial, joyful, joyous, laughing, light, merry, merrymaking, mirth-loving, mirthful, playful, pleasant, *ridiculus,* roguish, rollicking, rompish, sportive, sprightly, tricksy, waggish, witty

JOIN *(Associate oneself with),* **verb**   act in concert, affiliate, align, ally, associate, band together, be united, become a member, become connected with, belong to, combine, confederate, consociate, consort, cooperate, enlist, enroll, enter, fraternize, league together, make an agreement with, mingle, participate, pool, register, *se coniungere,* side with, sign on, subscribe, take part, take up membership, team up with, unite

JOIN *(Bring together),* **verb**   accouple, accumulate, adhere, aggregate, aggroup, alloy, amalgamate, amass, annex, append, assemble, attach, band, bind, blend, bridge, bring in contact, coact, collect, colligate, collocate, combine, commingle, compound, concatenate, *conectere,* conglomerate, conglutinate, *coniungere,* conjoin, connect, consolidate, convene, *copulare,* couple, entwine, federalize, federate, fit together, fuse, gather, glue, group, harness, incorporate, inosculate, interlink, interlock, intertwine, intertwist, interweave, knit, link, marry, mass, match, meld, merge, mix, pair, piece together, pool, put together, rally, splice, subjoin, unify, unite, wed, weld, yoke
ASSOCIATED CONCEPTS: issue joined, joinder of parties

JOINDER, *adjective*   assemblage, bringing together, coalescence, combination, concatenation, conjugation, conjunction, connection, coupling, joining, junction, linkage, linking, unification, union
ASSOCIATED CONCEPTS: fraudulent joinder, improper joinder, joinder of issue, joinder of parties, misjoinder, permissive joinder, severance

JOINDER OF A PARTY, *noun*   adding a claimant, adding a complainant, adding a defendant, adding a party, adding a plaintiff, enlisting a party, joining a party, joining an opposing party, joining a petitioner, joining a plaintiff
ASSOCIATED CONCEPTS: compulsory joinder, indispensable party, joinder of additional defendants, joinder of an interested party, joinder of third parties, misjoinder, necessary joinder, nonjoinder, notice of joinder, permissive joinder

JOINT, *adjective*   allied, amalgamated, associated, coadunate, coalitional, collaborative, collective, combined, common, communal, *communis,* community, concerted, concordant, concurrent, confederate, conjoint, conjugate, conjunct, consolidated, cooperative, coordinated, corporate, correal, harmonious, inseparable, joined, leagued, merged, mixed, mutual, shared, synergetic, unified, united
ASSOCIATED CONCEPTS: joint account, joint action, joint adventure, joint and several liability, joint enterprise, joint interest, joint liability, joint negligence, joint ownership, joint resolution, joint tenancy, joint tort feasors

JOINT AND SEVERAL, *adjective*   absolute and individual, all-encompassing and individual, blanket and individual, complete, comprehensive and individual, each and every and individual, entire and individual, full and individual, global and individual, omnibus and individual, the sum of total and individual, undivided and individual, universal and individual, wholly and individual
ASSOCIATED CONCEPTS: tortfeasors

JOINT AND SEVERAL LIABILITY, *noun*   absolute, abstruse, across-the-board, aggregate, all-embracing, all inclusive, all-out, bewildering, chaotic, circuitous, clear, collective,

combined, complete, complicated, composite, comprehensive, confused, convoluted, difficult, downright, dyed-in-the-wool, elaborated, enigmatic, entangled, entire, exhaustive, explicit, express, extended, extensive, flexuous, full, full-fledged, gradely, gross, impenetrable, implicated, inclusive, in-depth, individually and collectively liable, individually and mutually liable, inextricable, inscrutable, integral, interlaced, interwoven, intricate, involuted, involutional, involved, irreducible, jumbled, kaleidoscopic, knotted, labyrinthine, mingled, muddied, multiplex, obscure, out-and-out, outright, perplexing, plenary, radical, rank, recondite, sheer, sinuous, snarled, straight-out, sweeping, tangled, teetotal, thorough, together or separate, tortuous, unambiguous, unarranged, unclassified, uncompromised, unconditional, undecipherable, unequivocal, unfathomable, universal, unmitigated, unmodified, unorganized, unqualified, unreserved, utter, varied, whole, widespread
ASSOCIATED CONCEPTS: ostensible principal, torts

JOINT CUSTODY, *noun*   custody shared equally by both parents, equal custody, joint care, joint guardianship, shared custody
Generally: cooperative care, shared responsibility

JOSTLE *(Bump into),* **verb**   bang into, buffet, bump, bump against, butt, collide, crash into, crowd, elbow, *fodicare,* graze against, hit against, hustle, jab, jar, jolt, knock, knock against, nudge, poke, press, prod, push, run against, shake, shove, strike against, strike together
ASSOCIATED CONCEPTS: disorderly conduct

JOSTLE *(Pickpocket),* **verb**   abscond with, convey away, lift, loot, misappropriate, pick one's pockets, pilfer, purloin, run away with, run off with, steal, take away, walk off with, waylay
ASSOCIATED CONCEPTS: larceny

JOURNAL, *noun*   *acta diurna,* biographical record, cashbook, chronicle, chronology, contemporary account, daily paper, daily register, daybook, diary, *ephemeris,* gazette, historical record, ledger, log, logbook, magazine, narrative, periodical, record, register, serial

JUDGE, *noun*   adjudger, adjudicator, administrator of justice, arbiter, arbitrator, assessor, chancellor, the court, her honor, his honor, honorable justice, intercessor, interpreter, *iudex,* jurist, justice, justicer, magistrate, moderator, negotiator, one who dispenses justice, *praetor, quaesitor,* referee, surrogate, umpire, your honor
ASSOCIATED CONCEPTS: administrative judge, appellate judge, chief judge, County Court Judge, Court of Appeals Judge, Court of Claims Judge, District Court Judge, Family Court Judge, inferior court judge, judge de facto, judge of a court of record, justice of the peace, Justice of the Supreme Court, law clerk, lay judge, magistrates, presiding judge, removal of a judge, superior court judge, Surrogate, town judge
FOREIGN PHRASES: *In propria causa nemo judex.* No one can be a judge in his own case. *Ignorantia judicis est calamitas innocentis.* The ignorance of a judge is the misfortune of the innocent. *Judex bonus nihil ex arbitrio suo faciat, nec propositione domesticae voluntatis, sed juxta leges et jura pronunciet.* A good judge should do nothing of his own arbitrary will, nor on the dictate of his personal wishes, but should decide according to law and justice. *Veritas habenda est in juratore; justitia et judicium in judice.* Truth should be possessed by a juror; justice and judgment by a judge. *Judicium a non suo judice datum nullius est momenti.* A judgment rendered by one who is not the

proper judge is of no force. ***Quicquid judicis auctoritati subjicitur, novitati non subjicitur.*** Whatever is subject to the authority of a judge is not subject to innovation. ***Sententia a non judice lata nemini debet nocere.*** A sentence or judgment rendered by a person who is not a judge ought not to harm anyone. ***Respiciendum est judicanti ne quid aut durius aut remissius constituatur quam causa deposcit; nec enim aut severitatis aut clementiae gloria affectan da est.*** It is a matter of import to a judge that nothing should be either more leniently or more severely construed than the cause itself demands; for the glory neither of severity nor clemency should be affected. ***Judicis est in pronuntiando sequi regulam, exceptione non probata.*** The judge in his decision ought to follow the rule, the exception not having been proved. ***Nemo potest esse simul actor et judex.*** No one can be at the same time judge and suitor. ***Praxis judicum est interpres legum.*** The practice of judges is the interpreter of the laws. ***Judex non potest injuriam sibi datam punire.*** A judge cannot punish a wrong done to himself. ***Boni judicis est ampliare justitiam.*** It is the duty of a good judge to make precedents which amplify justice. ***Quemadmodum ad quaestionem facti non respondent judices, ita ad quaestionem juris non respondent juratores.*** Just as judges do not answer questions of fact, so jurors do not answer questions of law. ***Boni judicis est judicium sine dilatione mandare executioni.*** It is the duty of a good judge to issue judgments without delay. ***De jure judices, de facto juratores, respondent.*** Judges decide questions of law, jurors, questions of fact. ***Ubi non est manifesta injustitia, judices habentur pro bonis viris, et judicatum pro veritate.*** Where there is no manifest injustice, judges are to be regarded as honest men, and their judgment as truth. ***Judex damnatur cum nocens absolvitur.*** A judge is condemned when a guilty person is acquitted. ***Nemo sibi esse judex vel suis jus dicere debet.*** No man ought to be his own judge, or to administer the law in cases involving his family. ***Judici officium suum excedenti non paretur.*** No obedience is to be given to a judge exceeding his office or jurisdiction. ***Non refert quid notum sit judici, si notum non sit in forma judicii.*** It matters not what is known to a judge, if it be not known in a judicial form. ***Judex debet judicare secundum allegata et probata.*** A judge ought to decide according to the allegations and the proofs. ***Judex non potest esse testis in propria causa.*** A judge cannot be a witness in his own case. ***In re propria iniquum admodum est alicui licentiam tribuere sententiae.*** It is unjust for anyone to assign to himself the privilege of deciding his own case. ***De fide et officio judicis non recipitur quaestio, sed de scientia, sive sit error juris, sive facti.*** The good faith and honesty of a judge are not to be questioned, but his knowledge, whether it be in error of law or fact, may be. ***Judex ante oculos aequitatem semper habere debet.*** A judge ought always to have equity before his eyes. ***Judices non tenentur exprimere causam sententiae suae.*** Judges are not bound to explain the reason for their sentences. ***Judex aequitatem semper spectare debet.*** A judge ought always to regard equity. ***Bonus judex secundum aequum et bonum judicat, et aequitatem stricto juri praefert.*** Good judges decide according to what is just and right, and prefer equity to strict law. ***Ad questiones facti non respondent judices; ad questiones legis non respondent juratores.*** Judges do not answer to a question of fact, jurors do not answer to a question of law. ***Qui aliquid statuerit, parte inaudita altera, aequum licet dixerit, haud aequum fecerit.*** He who decides anything without hearing both sides, although he may decide correctly, has by no means acted justly. ***Judex habere debet***

duos sales,-salem sapientiae, ne sit insipidus; et salem conscientiae, ne sit diabolus. A judge ought to have two salts,-the salt of wisdom, lest he be insipid; and the salt of conscience, lest he be devilish. ***Optimam esse legem, quae minimum relinquit arbitrio judicis; id quod cer titudo ejus praestat.*** That law is the best which leaves the least discretion to the judge; this is an advantage which results from its certainty. ***Optima est lex quae minimum relinquit arbitrio judicis; optimus judex qui minimum sibi.*** That is the best system of law which leaves the least to the discretion of the judge; that judge is the best who leaves the least to his own discretion. ***Optimus judex, qui minimum sibi.*** He is the best judge who leaves the least to his own discretion. ***Judicis officium est opus diei in die suo perficere.*** It is the duty of a judge to finish the day's work within that day. ***Judicis est judicare secundum allegata et probata.*** It is the duty of a judge to decide according to the allegations and proofs. ***Quam rationabilis debet esse finis, non definitur, sed omnibus circumstantiis inspectis pendet ex justiciariorum discretione.*** What a reasonable fine ought to be is not defined, but is left to the discretion of the judges, all the circumstances being considered.

JUDGE, verb adjudge, adjudicate, appraise, arbitrate, ascertain, assess, censere, conclude, condemn, consider, criticize, decide, decree, deduce, deem, derive, determine, discern, draw a conclusion, estimate, examine, find, hold, infer, interpret, *iudicare, iudicium exercere,* moderate, negotiate, pass sentence upon, pass under review, perceive, pronounce, reckon, referee, reprobate, resolve, review, rule on, sentence, settle, sit in judgment, try, try a case, umpire, value, weigh
FOREIGN PHRASES: ***Judicis est jus dicere, non dare.*** It is the duty of a judge to declare the law, not to make it. ***Judex est lex loquens.*** The judge is the law speaking; that is, he is the mouthpiece of the law. ***Boni judicis est ampliare jurisdictionem.*** It is the duty of a good judge to enlarge his remedial authority.

JUDGE'S CHAMBER, noun judge's antechamber, judge's anteroom, judge's court chamber, judge's private office, judicial chamber, judicial office, judicial room

JUDGMATIC, adjective calculating, circumspect, considerate, determinative, discriminating, discriminative, enlightened, fair-minded, impartial, judicative, judicatory, judicial, judicious, juridical, juristic, just, magisterial, non-partisan, percipient, perspicacious, politic, provident, prudent, reflecting, sagacious, thoughtful, tolerant, unbiased, unbigoted, unprejudiced, well-advised, well-judged

JUDGMENT (Discernment), **noun** ability to distinguish, acumen, acuteness, analysis, apperception, appraisal, assessment, astuteness, awareness, circumspection, close observation, cognitive faculties, cognitive powers, comprehension, conclusion, consideration, *consilium,* contemplation, critical faculty, critical spirit, criticalness, critique, decision, diagnosis, discrimination, discursive faculties, estimate, estimation, evaluation, examination, exhaustive inquiry, grasp, incisiveness, inquiry, insight, inspection, intellectual faculties, intellectual powers, intuition, *iudicium,* judiciousness, keenness, mental faculty, observation, opinion, penetration, perception, perceptiveness, percipience, perspicacity, perspicuousness, probing, quickness, ratiocination, rational faculty, rationality, reasoning, reasoning faculties, reasoning power, review, sagacity, sapience, sharpness of mind, understanding, weighing
ASSOCIATED CONCEPTS: failure to exercise reasonable judgment
FOREIGN PHRASES: ***Incivile est, nisi tota lege perspecta, una aliqua particula ejus proposita, judicare, vel respondere.***

JUDGMENT

Unless the entire law has been examined, it is improper to pass judgment upon a portion of it. *Judicia in deliberationibus crebro maturescunt, in accelerato processu nunquam.* Judgments frequently mature by deliberations, never by hurried process.

JUDGMENT (*Formal court decree*), **noun** adjudgment, adjudication, announcement, arbitrament, assessment, censure, conclusion, condemnation, consideration, decision, declaration, decree, determination, evaluation, finding, *iudicium,* judicature, judicial assertion, legal decision, opinion, order, precedent, pronouncement, recommendation, report, resolution, result, ruling, sentence
ASSOCIATED CONCEPTS: advisory judgment, collateral attack on a judgment, conditional judgment, confession by judgment, consent judgment, declaratory judgment, default judgment, deficiency judgment, docketing a judgment, enforcement of a judgment, execution of judgment, final judgment, foreign judgment, full faith and credit, interlocutory judgment, judgment by confession, judgment creditor, judgment debtor, judgment in rem, judgment lien, judgment non obstante veredicto, judgment roll, money judgment, opening a default judgment, personal judgment, relief from judgment, res judicata, satisfaction of a judgment, vacating a judgment
FOREIGN PHRASES: *Ubi eadem ratio ibi, idem jus; et de similibus idem est judicium.* Where there is the same reason, there is the same law; and where there are similar situations, the judgment is the same. *Respiciendum est judicanti ne quid aut durius aut remissius constituatur quam causa deposcit; nec enim aut severitatis aut clementiae gloria affectanda est.* It is a matter of import to a judge that nothing should be either more leniently or more severely construed than the cause itself demands; for the glory neither of severity nor clemency should be affected. *Non exemplis sed legibus judicandum est.* Judgment should not be rendered from examples, but by the law. *Res judicata pro veritate accipitur.* A thing which is adjudicated is accepted or received for the truth. *Judicium non debet esse illusorium; suum effectum habere debet.* A judgment ought not to be illusory; it ought to have its proper effect. *Judicium a non suo judice datum nullius est momenti.* A judgment by one who is not the proper judge is of no force. *Omnis conclusio boni et veri judicii sequitur ex bonis et veris praemissis et dictis juratorum.* Every conclusion of a good and true judgment arises from good and true premises, and the verdicts of jurors. *In praeparatoriis ad judicium favetur actori.* In those matters preceding judgment the plaintiff is favored. *Frustra agit qui judicium prosequi nequit cum effectu.* He sues vainly who cannot prosecute his judgment with effect. *Sacramentum habet in se tres comites,-veritatem, justitiam, et judicium; veritus habenda est in jurato; justitia et justicium in judice.* An oath has in it three components-truth, justice, and judgment; truth in the party swearing; justice and judgment in the judge administering the oath. *Veredictum, quasi dictum veritatis; ut judicium, quasi juris dictum.* A verdict is, as it were, the expression of the truth; as a judgment is the expression of the law. *Judicium semper pro veritate accipitur.* A judgment is always taken for truth. *Judiciis posterioribus fides est adhibenda.* Credit should be given in the more recent decisions. *Judex non reddit plus quam quod petens ipse requirit.* A judge should not render judgments for a larger sum than the plaintiff demands. *Parum est latam esse sententiam nisi mandetur executioni.* It is not enough that sentence should be given unless it be reduced to execution.

JUDGMENT ON THE FACTS, noun act of judgment, adjudication, authoritative decision, decision, deliberative determination, determination, disposition, final judgment, findings, holding, irrevocable decision, judicature, judicial decision, opinion, pronouncement, resolution, ruling, settled decision, verdict
ASSOCIATED CONCEPTS: a judgment or decree, appeals, directed verdict, pleadings, setting aside, summary judgment, supplementary proceedings

JUDICATORY, noun bar of justice, bench, court, court of justice, court of law, forum, institution where justice is rendered, judicature, judiciary, law court, place where justice is administered, *ratio iudiciorum,* tribunal
ASSOCIATED CONCEPTS: inferior judicatory

JUDICATURE, noun administration of justice, authority, bench, court, court of law, court's jurisdiction, extent of the court's authority, forum, *iurisdictio,* judicatory, jurisdiction, jurisdiction of the court, legal authority, legal power, tribunal

JUDICIAL, adjective considerate, disinterested, equitable, fair, forensic, impartial, *iudicialis,* judgelike, judgmatic, judicative, judicious, juridical, juristic, juristical, just, knowing, politic, prudent, prudential, rational, reasonable, reasoned, sagacious, sage, sapient, sensible, thoughtful, unbiased, unbigoted, uninfluenced, unprejudiced, unswayed, wise
ASSOCIATED CONCEPTS: critical state in a judicial proceeding, judicial act, judicial business, judicial circuit, judicial decision, judicial district, judicial function, judicial inquiry, judicial notice, judicial office, judicial opinion, judicial power, judicial proceeding, judicial review, judicial separation, judicial sequestration, judicial tribunal
FOREIGN PHRASES: *Officia judicialia non concedantur antequam vacent.* Judicial offices are not to be granted or appointed before they become vacant.

JUDICIAL CONTEST, noun action, case, lawsuit, legal action, legal dispute, legal matter, legal proceedings, legal recourse, litigation, judicial proceeding, judicial recourse, proceedings, suit, trial

JUDICIAL DETERMINATION, noun action, award, court resolution, court's finding, declaration, decree, decretal, findings of fact and conclusions of law, holding, opinion judgment, judicial fiat, judicial pronouncement, order, order of the court, pronouncement, ruling, sentence

JUDICIAL PROCEEDING, noun action, case, cause in court, court proceeding, hearing, hearing on the merits, judicial contest, judicial recourse, lawsuit, legal action, legal dispute, legal proceeding, legal recourse, legal remedy, litigation, prosecution, suit, suit at law, suit in law, trial, trial of a case, trial of the issues

JUDICIAL REVIEW, noun certirari, judicial analysis, judicial review, judicial scrutiny, legal analysis, legal review, legal scrutiny
Specifically: judicial scrutiny
ASSOCIATED CONCEPTS: appellate system, basis to appeal, grounds to appeal, judicial issue, jurisdiction, trial de novo

JUDICIARY, noun administration of justice, arm of the law, bar, bench, body of judges, courts, courts of justice, department of justice, explicators of the law, forum of justice, interpreters of the law, judicatory, judicature, judicial branch, judicial branch of government, judicial department, judicial forum, justices, law courts, legal forum, magistracy, tribunal
ASSOCIATED CONCEPTS: judiciary powers

JUDICIOUS, *adjective* apperceptive, astute, calculating, careful, cautious, considerate, considered, deliberate, diplomatic, discerning, discreet, discretionary, discriminating, enlightened, heedful, judgmatic, mindful, moderate, perceptive, percipient, perspicacious, politic, provident, *prudens,* prudent, prudential, rational, reasonable, reflecting, regardful, sagacious, sagax, sage, *sapiens,* sapient, sensible, shrewd, sound, tactful, temperate, thorough, thoughtful, undaring, well-considered, wise

JUDICIOUSNESS, *noun* astuteness, cautiousness, deliberation, diplomacy, discernment, discretion, discriminating judgment, discrimination, enlightenment, expedience, good judgment, judgment, moderation, perception, perspicacity, prudence, rationality, reason, reasonableness, restraint, sagaciousness, sagacity, sense, sensibility, shrewdness, soundness, tactfulness, temperance, thoughtfulness

JUMPING OFF POINT, *noun* base, basis, bedrock, bottom, floor, flooring, foundation, fundamental basis, girder, ground, groundwork, premise, principle, rudiment, starting point, support, supporting structure, underlying principle, underpinning basis
ASSOCIATED CONCEPTS: floor plan in zoning and construction laws, hacking the floor in parliamentary procedure, minimum wage

JUNCTION, *noun* accompaniment, adhesion, alliance, association, attachment, chain, coalescence, coalition, collusion, combination, concentration, concomitance, concourse, concurrence, confluence, conflux, conjugation, conjunction, connection, connivance, consolidation, contact, convergence, correlation, crossroad, coupling, encounter, focalization, hinge, intersection, joining, liaison, meeting, union

JUNCTURE *(Crisis),* ***noun*** contingency, critical moment, critical point, crux, dilemma, emergency, exigency, extremity, plight, predicament, quandary, strait

JUNCTURE *(Eventuality),* ***noun*** advent, assemblage, coadunation, coalescence, coincidence, concentration, concourse, concurrence, confluence, conflux, congregation, conjuncture, contingency, convergence, correlation, crisis, crossroad, event, eventuality, incident, intersection, meeting, moment, occasion, period, point, posture, situation, stage, union

JUNCTURE *(Stage),* ***noun*** correlation, eventuality, moment, opportunity, period, turning point

JURAL, *adjective* according to law, de jure, founded in law, judicatory, judicial, judiciary, juridical, juristic, legal, of law, pertaining to law, recognized by law, sanctioned by law, within the law

JURAT, *noun* accreditation, affirmation, asseveration, attestation, attesting statement, authentication, avouchment, avowal, certification, confirmation, documentation, endorsement, ratification, solemn declaration, statement which confirms information on an affidavit, substantiation, verification, verifying statement
ASSOCIATED CONCEPTS: affidavit, affirmation, notary public, oath

JURIDICAL, *adjective* according to law, adjudged, advising, advisory, authoritative, authorized, concerning the law, conformable with the law, discerning, discretionary, discriminating, discriminative, enlightened, equitable, fair,

forensic, impartial, in accordance with the law, in conformity to the law, *iuridicialis,* judgelike, judgmatic, judicative, judicatorial, judicatory, judicial, judiciary, judicious, jural, juridic, jurisprudential, juristic, just, justifiable, justified, lawful, legal, legalistic, legalized, magisterial, perceptive, percipient, perspicacious, politic, prescribed, principled, proper, provident, prudent, prudential, rational, reflecting, right, rightful, sagacious, sage, sanctioned, sapient, solicitorial, sound, unbiased, understanding, unprejudiced, warranted, well-advised, within the law

JURISDICTION, *noun* authority, authority to hear and decide a case, capacity to decide the matter in issue, capacity to hear the controversy, command, control, decision-making power over the case, domain, domination, dominion, extent of authority, grasp, *iurisdictio,* legal authority, legal power, legal power to decide a case, legal right, power, province, purview, range, reach, realm, reign, sovereignty, sphere, superintendence, supervision, territorial range of authority, territory
ASSOCIATED CONCEPTS: basis jurisdiction, civil jurisdiction, concurrent jurisdiction, court of competent jurisdiction, equity jurisdiction, exclusive jurisdiction, forum non conveniens, in personam jurisdiction, in rem jurisdiction, inherent jurisdiction, jurisdiction of the court, jurisdiction over the person, jurisdictional amount, jurisdictional defect, jurisdictional dispute, jurisdictional facts, jurisdictional plea, jurisdictional requirement, jurisdictional statement, lack of jurisdiction, limited jurisdiction, original jurisdiction, pendent jurisdiction, primary jurisdiction, quasi in rem jurisdiction, subject matter jurisdiction, submission to jurisdiction, venue, want of jurisdiction
FOREIGN PHRASES: *Est boni judicis ampliare jurisdictionem.* It is the duty of a good judge to extend the jurisdiction. *Extra territorium jus dicenti impune non paretur.* One exercising jurisdiction outside of his territorial limits cannot be obeyed with impunity. *Jurisdictio est potestas de publico introducta, cum necessitate juris dicendi.* Jurisdiction is a power introduced for the public good, on account of the necessity of administering justice. *Quaelibet jurisdictio cancellos suos habet.* Every jurisdiction has its own bounds. *Qui habet jurisdictionem absolvendi, habet jurisdictionem ligandi.* He who has jurisdiction to release, has jurisdiction to bind. *Rerum ordo confunditur si unicuique jurisdictio non servetur.* The order of things is confused if everyone does not give heed to his own jurisdiction. *Ubi est forum, ibi ergo est jus.* Where the forum is, there the law is accordingly. *Judici officium suum excedenti non paretur.* No obedience is to be given to a judge exceeding his office or jurisdiction. *Est boni judicis ampliare jurisdictionem.* It is the duty of a good judge to interpret his jurisdiction liberally. *In personam actio est, qua cum eo agimus qui obligatus est nobis ad faciendum aliquid vel dandum.* The action in personam is that in which we sue him who is under obligation to us to do something or give something. *In omni actione ubi duae concurrunt districtiones, videlicet, in rem et in personam, illa districtio tenenda est quae magis timetur et magis ligat.* In every action where two distresses concur, that is to say, in rem and in personam, that is to be chosen which is most dreaded, and which binds more firmly. *Cui jurisdictio data est, ea quoque concessa esse videntur, sine quibus jurisdictio explicari non potest.* Those things without which jurisdiction could not be exercised are held to be given to each to whom jurisdiction has been granted. *Debet quis juri subjacere ubi delinquit.* Everyone ought to be subject to the law of the place where he commits an offense. *Nihil habet forum ex scena.* The court has nothing

to do with what is not before it. *Judicium a non suo judice datum nullius est momenti.* A judgment rendered by one who is not the proper judge is of no force.

JURISDICTIONAL AMOUNT, *noun* amount involved in a case, domain, extent of authority, jurisdiction, jurisdictional authority, jurisdictional boundary, jurisdictional legal authority, jurisdictional legal power, jurisdictional monetary limit, jurisdictional monetary threshold, jurisdictional outer edge, jurisdictional perimeter, jurisdictional power, monetary amount that can be heard by a court, province, purview, range, sphere, territorial authority, territorial range, territory
ASSOCIATED CONCEPTS: amount in controversy, subject matter jurisdiction

JURISPRUDENCE, *noun* body of laws, corpus juris, doctrines of lawmaking, *iuris prudentia,* knowledge of law, legal code, legal learning, legal philosophy, legal practice, legal precedent, legal science, nomography, nomology, philosophy of law, science of law, science of legal relations, system of laws
FOREIGN PHRASES: *Scire leges non hoc est verba earum tenere, sed vim ac potestatem.* To know the laws is not to observe their words alone, but their force and power. *Cessante ratione legis, cessat et ipsa lex.* Where the reason for a law ceases, the law itself also ceases. *Jurisprudentia est divinarum atque humanarum rerum notitia, justi atque injusti scientia.* Jurisprudence is the knowledge of things divine and human, the science of what is just and unjust.

JURIST, *noun* advocate, attorney, attorney-at-law, barrister, bencher, counsel, counselor, counselor-at-law, intercessor, iuris consultus, *iuris peritus,* judge, jurisconsult, jurisprudent, justice, lawyer, learned counsel, legal adviser, legal expert, legal practitioner, legal representative, legalist, legist, magistrate, master of jurisprudence, member of the bar, member of the legal profession, one called to the bar, pleader, practicing lawyer, practitioner of the law, procurator, prosecutor, public attorney, solicitor
FOREIGN PHRASES: *Natura appetit perfectum, ita et lex.* Nature seeks perfection, and so does the law. *Non verbis sed ipsis rebus. leges imponimus.* We do not impose laws upon words, but upon the things themselves. *Leges naturae perfectissimae sunt et immutabiles; humani vero juris conditio semper in infinitum decurrit, et nihil est in eo quod perpetuo stare possit.* The laws of nature are the most perfect and immutable, but the condition of human law is unending and there is nothing in it which can continue perpetually.

JUROR, *noun* adjudger, adjudicator, appraiser, arbiter, assessor, assessor of liability and damages, estimator, evaluator, examiner, hearer, individual selected for jury service, *iudex,* jurat, juryman, member of a jury, one authorized to deliver a verdict, one of an adjudgment body, one sworn to deliver a verdict, reviewer, swearer, trier of fact
ASSOCIATED CONCEPTS: challenge for cause, competent juror, foreman, grand juror, peremptory challenge to the selection of a juror, petit juror
FOREIGN PHRASES: *Veritas habenda est in juratore; justitia et judicium in judice.* Truth should be possessed by a juror; justice and judgment by a judge. *Omnis conclusio boni et veri judicii sequitur ex bonis et veris praemissis et dictis juratorum.* Every conclusion of a good and true judgment arises from good and true premises, and the verdicts of jurors. *Triatio ibi semper debet fieri, ubi juratores meliorem possunt habere notitiam.* Trial ought always to be had where the jurors can have the best information.

Quemadmodum ad quaestionem facti non respondent judices, ita ad quaestionem juris non respondent juratores. Just as judges do not answer questions of fact, so jurors do not answer questions of law.

JURY, *noun* adjudgment body, adjudicators, arbiters, arbitrators, array, assessors, body of jurors, determiners, *iudices,* judges of the facts, jurymen, panel, reviewers of fact, talesmen, tribunal, triers of fact
ASSOCIATED CONCEPTS: acquittal by a jury, advisory jury, challenges, charge to the jury, empaneling a jury, fair and impartial jury, foreman of the jury, Grand Jury, hung jury, impartial jury, instructing the jury, invading the province of the jury, Petit Jury, polling a jury, right to trial by jury, Special Grand Jury, swearing of the jury
FOREIGN PHRASES: *Matter en ley ne serra mise in boutche del jurors.* A matter of law shall not be put into the mouth of jurors. *Paribus sententiis reus absolvitur.* When the opinions are equal, where the court is equally divided, the defendant is acquitted. *Nemo qui condemnare potest, absolvere non potest.* No one who can convict is unable to acquit. *Patria laboribus et expensis non debet fatigari.* A jury ought not to be troubled by labors and expenses. *De jure judices, de facto juratores, respondent.* Judges decide questions of law, jurors, questions of fact.

JURY DELIBERATIONS, *noun* chance verdict, common jury, compromised verdict, consideration by the jury, contemplation by the jury, jury analysis, jury review, panel determination
ASSOCIATED CONCEPTS: Grand Jury, jury verdict, Petit Jury, quotient verdict, special jury, special verdict, trial jury

JURY NULLIFICATION, *noun* common sense judgment, disregard of the law by a body of jurors, independence by judges of the facts, independence by jurymen, independence by reviewers of fact, independence of the law by jurors, jurors' disregard of the law, jurors' independence, paid jurors, professional jurors

JURY-RIGGING, *verb* accompany, adjudgment body, adjudicators, agree, alternative, arbiters, arbitrators, array, assessors, be in time, body of jurors, coexist, coextend, coincide, concur, contemporize, co-occur, determiners, emergency, expedient, fixing a jury, go along with, go hand in hand, impermanent, improvised, isochronize, judges of the facts, jurymen, keep in, keep pace with, keep time, makeshift, match, panel, provisional, put *or* be in phase, reviewers of fact, step, stop-gap, substitute, succedaneous, sync, synchronize, talesmen, temporary, time, tribunal, triers of fact
ASSOCIATED CONCEPTS: mistrial, peremptory challenges

JUST, *adjective* aboveboard, according to law, admissible, *aequus,* affording no undue advantage, appropriate, as it should be, authoritative, awarded deservedly, balanced, befitting, bona fide, cogent, condign, conscientious, constitutional, deserved, deserving, detached, direct, disinterested, dispassionate, due, equable, equitable, ethical, even-handed, exact, expected, express, fair, fair and square, fair-minded, fit, fitting, forceful, honest, honorable, impartial, incorruptible, *iustus,* judicious, juridical, justifiable, justified, lawful, legal, legitimate, licit, logical, merited, meritorious, *meritus,* moral, objective, open-minded, open to reason, owed, owing, precise, principled, proper, rational, reasonable, reputable, right, righteous, rightful, scrupulous, sincere, solid, sound, square, straight, straightforward, sufficient, suitable, unbiased, unbigoted, unbought, unbribable, unbribed, unchallengeable, uncolored, uncorrupt, uncorrupted, unimpeachable, uninfluenced, unprejudiced, unswayed, upright, upstanding, veracious, virtuous, weighty, wise, worthy

ASSOCIATED CONCEPTS: just and reasonable grounds, just cause, just claim, just compensation, just debts, just decision, just terms, just value in a case, without just cause **FOREIGN PHRASES:** *Ubi lex aliquem cogit ostendere causam, necesse est quod causa sit justa et legitima.* Where the law compels a man to show cause, it is necessary that the cause be just and legal.

JUST CLAIM, noun contingent interest, in accordance with legal provisions, legitimate cause of action, legitimate legal issues, overwhelming proof, proper issues, strong basis, substantiated complaint, verifiable complaint

JUSTICE, noun *aequitas,* equitableness, equity, fairmindedness, fair play, fair treatment, fairness, freedom from bias, impartiality, *justitia,* justness, objectivity, probity, propriety, reason, reasonableness, rectitude, reparation, retribution, right, righteousness, rightfulness, uprighteousness

ASSOCIATED CONCEPTS: due administration of justice, ends of justice, equity, fleeing from justice, fugitive from justice, in furtherance of justice, in the interests of justice, miscarriage of justice, obstructing justice, preventive justice, speedy justice, substantial justice

FOREIGN PHRASES: *Melior est justitia vere praeveniens quam severe puniens.* Truly preventive justice is better than severe punishment. *Justitia non est neganda non differenda.* Justice is neither to be denied nor delayed. *In re propria iniquum admodum est alicui licentiam tribuere sententiae.* It is unjust for anyone to assign to himself the privilege of deciding his own case. *Sacramentum habet in se tres comites,-veritatem, justitiam, et judicium; veritus habenda est in jurato; justitia et justicium in judice.* An oath has in it three components-truth, justice, and judgment; truth in the party swearing; justice and judgment in the judge administering the oath. *Justitia est constans et perpetua voluntas jus suum cuique tribuendi.* Justice is the constant and perpetual means to render to each one his rights. *Lex dilationes semper exhorret.* The law always abhors delays. *Boni judicis est ampliare justitiam.* It is the duty of a good judge to make precedents which amplify justice. *Discretio est scire per legem quid sit justum.* Discretion consists in knowing through the law what is just. *Justitia est duplex, viz., severe puniens et vere praeveniens.* Justice is double, that is to say punishing severely, and truly preventing. *Nulli vendemus, nulli negabimus, aut differemus rectum vel justitian.* We will sell to none, we will deny to none, we will delay to none, either equity or justice. *Justitia non novit patrem nec matrem; solum veritatem spectat justitia.* Justice knows neither father nor mother; justice looks to the truth alone. *Quod ad jus naturale attinet omnes homines aequales sunt.* All men are equal as far as the natural law is concerned. *Accipere quid ut justitiam facias, non est tam accipere quam extorquere.* The acceptance of a reward for doing justice is not so much an acceptance as an extortion. *Justitia nemini neganda est.* Justice is to be denied to no one. *Plena et celeris justitia fiat partibus.* Let full and speedy justice be done to the parties. *Jure naturae aequum est neminem cum alterius detrimento et injuria fieri locupletiorem.* According to the laws of nature, it is just that no one should be enriched by the detriment and injury of another. *Fiat justitia, ruat coelum.* Let right be done, though the heavens fall. *Nihil magis justum est quam quod necessarium est.* Nothing is more just than what is necessary.

Lex non deficit in justitia exhibenda. The law does not fail in dispensing justice. *Bonus judex secundum aequum et bonum judicat, et aequitatem stricto juri praefert.* Good judges decide according to what is just and right, and prefer equity to strict law. *Lex plus laudatur quando ratione probatur.* The law is most praiseworthy when it is consistent with reason. *Vigilantibus et non dormientibus jura subveniunt.* The laws aid the vigilant and not those who slumber. *Judex bonus nihil ex arbitrio suo faciat, nec propositione domesticae voluntatis, sed juxta leges et jura pronunciet.* A good judge should do nothing of his own arbitrary will, nor on the dictate of his personal wishes, but should decide according to law and justice. *Qui aliquid statuerit, parte inaudita altera, aequum licet dixerit, haud aequum fecerit.* He who decides anything without hearing both sides, although he may decide correctly, has by no means acted justly. *Fraus et jus nunquam cohabitant.* Fraud and justice never dwell together. *Festinatio justitiae est noverca infortunii.* The hastening of justice is the stepmother of misfortune. *Commodum ex injuria sua non habere debet.* No person ought to derive any advantage by his own wrong. *Veritas habenda est in juratore; justitia et judicium in judice.* Truth should be possessed by a juror; justice and judgment by a judge. *Jus est ars boni et aequi.* Law is the science of what is good and just. *Lex est dictamen rationis.* Law is the dictate of reason. *Lex est ratio summa, quae jubet quae sunt utilia et necessaria et contraria prohibet.* That which is law is the consummation of reason, which commands those things useful and necessary, while prohibiting the contrary. *Sequi debet potentia justitiam, non praecedere.* Power ought to follow justice, not precede it. *Summa caritas est facere justitiam singulis, et omni tempore quando necesse fuerit.* The greatest charity is to do justice to everyone, and at all times when it is necessary.

JUSTICE COURT, noun bar, bar of justice, bench, for adjusting disputes, forum, forum of justice, judgment seat, judicial assembly, judicial forum, judicial tribunal, justice, justice seat, lawcourt, magistrates, place where justice is administered, tribunal

JUSTICIABLE, adjective actionable, amenable to law, appropriate for a trial, arguable, capable of being decided by a court, capable of being litigated, capable of being tried, cognizable, disputable, enforceable, jurisdictional, legally enforceable, liable to prosecution, litigable, proper for judicial examination, proper to be examined in courts of justice, ripe to submit for judicial review, subject to a court case, subject to action of a court of justice, subject to being resolved in court, triable

ASSOCIATED CONCEPTS: justiciable controversy, justiciable disputes

JUSTIFIABLE, adjective acceptable, admissible, allowable, condonable, defendable, defensible, excusable, exemptible, expiable, forgivable, inculpable, *iustus,* justified, lawful, legal, legalized, legitimate, *legitimus,* licit, maintainable, merited, meritorious, pardonable, permitted, plausible, practicable, proper, rational, reasonable, sanctioned, sensible, sound, suitable, vindicable, warrantable, warranted, well-grounded, worthy

ASSOCIATED CONCEPTS: defense of justification, justifiable controversy, justifiable homicide

JUSTIFICATION, noun adjustment, allowance, clarifying statement, clearance, compurgation, defense, exculpation, *excusatio,* excuse, exonerating circumstance, exonerating fact, exoneration, explanation, exposition, extenuation, good excuse, ground for excusing, legal defense, mitigating circumstance, mitigation, palliation, *purgatio,* rationalization, reason, reasonable excuse, reasoning, statement of defense, vindication **ASSOCIATED CONCEPTS:** justification for committing an unlawful act, legal cause

JUSTIFIED, *verb* accounted for, championed, condoned, countenanced, defended, endorsed, espoused, exculpated, excused, exonerated, explained, forgiven, legitimatized, maintained, made excuses for, made legitimate, mitigated, offered in defense, plead one's cause, proven as warranted, proven the truth of, seconded, shown to be just, spoken in favor of, stood up for, supported, sustained, upheld, urged as reasons for, vindicated, warranted, with adequate reasons, with sufficient reasons
ASSOCIATED CONCEPTS: family court, justification, juvenile delinquency court, juvenile justice system, Megan's Law, moral justification, termination from employment, torture

JUSTIFY, *verb* absolve, account for, allege in support, allege in vindication, answer for, argue for, back, be answerable for, be apologist for, bear out, bolster, champion, condone, contend for, countenance, declare guiltless, defend, defend as conformable to law, defend as conformable to right, endorse, espouse, espouse the cause of, exculpate, *excusare,* excuse, exonerate, explain, forgive, give as an excuse, legitimate, maintain, maintain as conformable to duty, maintain as conformable to justice, make defense for, make excuses for, make explanation of, make legitimate, mitigate, offer in defense, palliate, plead for, plead one's cause, pragmatize, prove the truth of, prove warranted, *purgare,* second, show to be just, speak in favor of, stand up for, strengthen, support, sustain, uphold, urge reasons for, vindicate, warrant

JUVENILE, *adjective* callow, childish, childlike, immature, inexperienced, infantine, intended for youth, *iuvenilis,* minor, pubescent, *puerilis,* suited to youth, unadult, underage, undeveloped, unfledged, unseasoned, vernal, young, youthful
ASSOCIATED CONCEPTS: Juvenile Court, juvenile delinquent, Person in Need of Supervision, youthful offender

JUVENILE, *noun* adolescent, child, fledgling, immature person, inexperienced person, *iuvenilis,* junior, juvenal, minor, person under legal age, puerile person, *puerilis,* stripling, teen, teenager, ward, young person, youngling, youngster, youth
ASSOCIATED CONCEPTS: Juvenile Court, juvenile delinquent

JUVENILE DELINQUENT, *noun* blameworthy child, blameworthy minor, culpable youth, derelict adolescent, derelict inexperienced person, derelict junior, immature youngster, misbehaving teenager, miscreant, misguided teen, misguided young person, neglectful fledgling, offending immature person, violator under age, young wrongdoer

JUXTAPOSE, *verb* abut, adjoin, align, annex, appose, arrange side by side, border, bring near, bring together, connect, coordinate, interconnect, join, line up, make contiguous, make even, make uniform, neighbor, osculate, place close together, place near, place next to, place side by side, position together, put alongside, put beside, put close together, put side by side, range together, set side by side

JUXTAPOSITION, *noun* adjacency, apposition, collation, collocation, connection, contact, contiguity, contiguousness, propinquity

KEEN, *adjective* acute, aggressive, all fired-up, all out, ambitious, animated, anxious, ardent, assiduous, avid, brisk, burning, committed, deep, deep-felt, desirous, diligent, disposed, dynamic, eager, earnest, ebullient, energetic, enterprising, enthused, enthusiastic, excited, extreme, exuberant, fervent, fervid, feverish, fiery, flaming, full of enthusiasm, heartfelt, hearty, heated, intense, intent, obsessed, passionate, pliant, proactive, profound, prompt, quick, raring to, ready, receptive, responsive, robust, spirited, vibrant, vigorous, vital, vivacious, vivid, zealous, zestful

KEEP *(Continue), **verb*** be constant, be steadfast, carry forward, carry on, endure, extend, forge ahead, go on, keep going, last, lengthen, live on, maintain, move ahead, never cease, perpetuate, *perseverare,* persevere, persist,

press onward, progress, prolong, pursue, remain, run on, stay, stick to, support, survive, sustain, wear

KEEP *(Fulfill), **verb*** abide by, acknowledge, adhere to, be faithful to, be true to, carry out, celebrate, commemorate, complete, comply with, conform to, discharge, follow, heed, honor, live up to, make good, meet, *observare, observe,* perform, regard, respect, *retinere,* satisfy, solemnize, stand by

KEEP *(Restrain), **verb*** arrest, bar, block, cage, check, *cohibere,* confine, constrain, contain, control, curb, delay, deprive, detain, deter, enclose, foil, frustrate, halt, hamper, hinder, hold, hold back, hold in, hold up, impede, inhibit, obstruct, prevent, prohibit, restrict, retard, *retinere,* shut in, shut up, stay, stifle, stop, stymie, suppress, thwart, withhold

KEEP *(Shelter)*, **verb** accumulate, amass, bank, cache, care for, cause to endure, cause to last, cherish, cling to, *condere,* conserve, deposit, embrace, foster, guard, have, hold, husband, keep alive, keep safe, lay aside, lay away, look after, maintain, nurture, pile up, possess, preserve, protect, put aside, put away, reserve, retain, retard decay, safeguard, save, secure, shelter, spare, store, support, sustain, take care of, tend, treasure, watch over

KEEP GOING, verb carry on for, continue, don't give up, don't let up, endure, extend, fulfill, further keep administering to, keep advancing, keep at, keep attending to, keep on, maintain, maintain a course, manage, minister to, perpetuate, persevere, persist, press on, proceed, pursue, resume, retain, stay on top of, steadfastly persevere, stick to, stick with, support, sustain
ASSOCIATED CONCEPTS: tolling statute of limitations or appeals

KEEP IN CUSTODY, verb capture, cast into prison, catch, under lock and key, commit to a prison, commit to jail, confine, constrain, deprive of liberty, detain, encage, hold, hold captive, imprison, imprison by authority, incarcerate, jail, legally restrain, lock up, make a captive, make a prisoner, place in confinement, place in custody, place in preventive custody, place in protective custody, put under restraint, remain in confinement, restrain, restrict, secure, seize, seize by legal warrant, take captive, take prisoner
ASSOCIATED CONCEPTS: chain of custody, child custody, speedy trial, visitation

KEEP IN PERSPECTIVE, noun analyze correctly, correctly perceive, judiciousness keep as the center, keep as the center of attention, keep as the center of interest, keep as the central point, keep as the converging point, keep as the focal point, keep as the goal, keep as the heart of the matter, keep as the objective, organize, the law of perspective

KEEP THE PEACE, verb agreement not to disturb, alliance not to disturb, armistice, calm, calmness, coexistence, concord, cooperation, end of hostilities, end of unrest, end of violence, harmony, hush, lull, maintain quiet, neutrality, pact, quiet, quietness, rapport, reconciliation, serenity, silence, stillness, suspension of hostilities, tranquility, treaty, truce, unanimity, unity
ASSOCIATED CONCEPTS: curfews, law enforcement

KEN, noun 20/20 vision, appreciation, apprehension, awareness, comprehension, discernment, discrimination, farsightedness, field of view, field of vision, foresight, intelligence, know-how, knowledge, perception, percipience, peripheral field of vision, practical knowledge, range of vision, recognition, scope, sentience, understanding, vision, wisdom

KEY, adjective critical, crucial, decisive, fateful, important, influential, major, momentous, significant, weighty

KEY *(Passport)*, **noun** bar, pass, permit, ticket

KEY *(Solution)*, **noun** answer, method, resolution, way

KEY MAN, noun indispensable person, man of mark, officer, person of importance, person of repute, president, top person

KICKBACK, noun bribe, criminal gift, criminal share, graft, hush money, illegal commission, illegal compensation, illegal cut, illegal payment, illegal percentage paid, illegal recompense, illegal remuneration, payoff, payola, protection money
ASSOCIATED CONCEPTS: anti-kickback law, illegal kickback scheme, official corruption

KIDNAP, verb abduct, bear off, capture, carry off, convey away, ensnare, hold for ransom, impress, put under duress, run away with, run off with, seize, shanghai, snatch, spirit away, steal away, take away, take by force, unlawfully seize, waylay
ASSOCIATED CONCEPTS: false imprisonment
FOREIGN PHRASES: *A piratis aut latronibus capti liberi permanent.* Persons captured by pirates or robbers remain free.

KILL *(Defeat)*, **verb** abolish, abrogate, annul, arrest, beat, block, cancel, check, *conficere,* counteract, crush, destroy, devitalize, dispatch, extinguish, *interficere,* invalidate, nullify, overthrow, overturn, prevail over, put down, quash, quell, repress, repulse, revoke, squash, stop, surmount, thwart, triumph, *trucidare,* upset, vanquish
ASSOCIATED CONCEPTS: kill a legislative bill

KILL *(Murder)*, **verb** assassinate, *conficere,* deprive of life, destroy, dispatch, execute, exterminate, injure fatally, *interficere,* liquidate, massacre, *occidere,* put to death, slaughter, slay, smite
ASSOCIATED CONCEPTS: deliberate killing, intent to kill, justifiable killing, malicious killing, premeditated killing

KILLER, noun annihilator, assassin, assassinator, butcher, criminal, decapitator, destroyer, exterminator, gunman, hit man, liquidator, manslayer, mass-murderer, mass slayer, murderer, serial murderer, shooter, slayer, triggerman, villain
ASSOCIATED CONCEPTS: cop killer law, serial killer

KILLING, noun annihilation, assassination, bloody murder, decimation, destruction, elimination, execution, extermination, homicide, liquidation, massacre, murder, murderous assault, slaughter, slaughtering, slaying, violent death
ASSOCIATED CONCEPTS: criminally negligent homicide, intent to kill, justifiable killing, malicious killing, premeditation, self-defense, wrongful death

KIN, noun affiliation, blood relation, blood relative, descendant, distant relative, family, family ties, ilk, kindred, kinship, line, lineage, near relation, next of kin, relation, relation through ties of blood, relationship through consanguinity, relative, sibling, stock
ASSOCIATED CONCEPTS: next of kin

KIND, adjective accommodating, affable, affectionate, agreeable, amiable, amicable, assisting, beneficent, benevolent, benign, benignant, brotherly, charitable, chivalrous, class, compassionate, compliant, considerate, cordial, courteous, decent, delicate, diplomatic, easy-going, forbearing, forgiving, fraternal, friendly, gallant, generous, genial, gentle, giving, good, good-natured, gracious, grade, heedful, helpful, hospitable, humane, humanitarian, kindhearted, kindly, lenient, merciful, mild, nice, noble, noble-minded, obliging, patient, philanthropic, pleasant, sensitive, softhearted, solicitous, sort, sympathetic, sympathizing, tactful, temperate, thoughtful, tolerant, understanding, well-intentioned, well-meaning

KIND, noun breed, category, character, class, classification, denomination, designation, division, form, *forma,* generic class, *generis,* genre, genus, group, ilk, modus, nature, sort, species, type, variety
ASSOCIATED CONCEPTS: payment in kind

KINDHEARTEDNESS, noun act of kindness, affection, agreeableness, altruism, amiability, amicableness, benefaction, benefit, benevolence, blessing, charity, clemency, compassion, consideration, cordiality, courteousness, courtesy, decency, generosity, gentleness, goodness, good disposition, good intentions, good-hearted, good nature, good-natured, graciousness, heartfelt sympathy, humane, humanity, id, kindhearted, kindliness, kindly disposed, kindness, loving, merciful, mildness, nice, philanthropic, softhearted, sympathy, thoughtfulness, understanding, virtuous, warmheartedness

KINDLE, verb affect, begin, commence, create, embark, emerge, engender, enkindle, establish, evolve, give birth, inaugurate, incept, incite, induce, initiate, instigate, led, motivate, nourish, nurture, occasion, originate, procure, start, stoke

KINDNESS, noun act of charity, act of grace, act of humanity, advantageous, affability, affectionate, agreeableness, aid, altruism, amiability, amicability, amicableness, assistance, beneficence, beneficial, benevolence, big-heartedness, brotherhood, charitableness, chivalry, clemency, compassion, consideration, cordiality, courteousness, decency, delicacy, diplomacy, fair, favorable, fellowship, fraternal, friendliness, friendship, gailantry, generosity, good intentions, good nature, goodheartedness, goodness, goodwill, graciousness, helpfulness, hospitality, humaneness, kindheartedness, lovingness, magnanimous, mindfulness, niceness, philanthropy, solicitousness, succor, sympathy, thoughtfulness, understanding, warm-heartedness, warmth

KINDRED, noun ancestor, ancestral relation, blood relations, blood relatives, brethren, clan, clansmen, *cognati, consanguinei,* descendant, family, folk, kin, kinsfolk, kinsmen, kinspeople, lineage, *necessarii,* next of kin, relation by birth, relation by blood, relation by consanguinity, relations, relatives, stock
ASSOCIATED CONCEPTS: collateral kindred, degree of kindred

KING, noun authority, bigwig, boss, chief, chieftain, commander, czar, dictator, director, emperor, executive, governor, head, head honcho, high chief, imperator, leader, lord, magnate, majesty, master, monarch, overlord, paramount lord, patriarch, person who is reported to, potentate, power, royal personage, ruler, superior

KINGDOM, noun area of control, country, demesne, domain, holding, interest, land, manor, nation, ownership, possession, private domain, property, proprietorship, province, right of possession, rightful possession, seisin, territory

KINSHIP, noun affiliation, affinity, association, bond, brotherhood, closeness, cognation, connection, consanguinity, family, family connection, kindredship, link, propinquity, relation, relationship, tie

KLEPTOMANIAC, noun criminal, lawbreaker, lifter, offender, petty thief, pilferer, pillager, purloiner, stealer, thief, wrongdoer
ASSOCIATED CONCEPTS: shoplifting

KNAVERY, noun artfulness, artifice, beguilement, cheat, cheating, chicanery, circumvention, corruption, cozenage, craft, craftiness, criminality, cunning, cunningness, deceit, deceitfulness, deception, defraudation, deviousness, dishonesty, double-dealing, dupery, duplicity, foul play, fraud, fraudulence, *fraus,* guile, hoax, humbuggery, insincerity, knavishness, lack of principle, lack of probity, legerdemain, malfeasance, *malitia, nequitia,* pettifoggery, rascality, roguery, roguishness, scampishness, scoundrelism, shadiness, sharp practice, skulduggery, slyness, treachery, trick, trickery, trickiness, turpitude, underhand dealing, unreliability, untrustworthiness, villainousness, villainy, wiles, wrongdoing

KNOCKDOWN, verb accost, assault, attack, batter, be reckless in harming a person, beat, besiege, damage, deal a blow, harm, hit, hurt, inflict harm, inflict injury, injure, shruck off
ASSOCIATED CONCEPTS: assault, battery, dart out case, hit and run

KNOW, verb absorb, apperceive, appreciate, apprehend, assimilate, be apprised of, be informed, cognize, comprehend, conceive, conclude, conjecture, deduce, digest, discern, fathom, find, gather, glean, grasp, identify, infer, internalize, learn, master, perceive, pierce, read, realize, recognize, retain, understand

KNOW-HOW, noun ability, adeptness, adroitness, artfulness, artisanship, artistry, background, brilliance, capability, capableness, capacity, cleverness, command, competence, craft, craftsmanship, deftness, dexterity, execution, experience, expertise, expertness, faculty, flair, gift, grace, ingeniousness, ingenuity, intellect, knack, knowledge, mastery, proficiency, prowess, resourcefulness, savoir-faire, skill, skillfulness, style, tactfulness, talent, technical mastery, technique, touch, workmanship
ASSOCIATED CONCEPTS: specialization in law

KNOWING, adjective acquainted, acute, apperceptive, apprehending, apprised, astute, aware, cognitive, cognizant, comprehending, conscious, deliberate, designed, educated, heedful, informed, instructed, intended, intentional, knowledgeable, meant, mindful, perceptive, percipient, planned, posted, *prudens,* purposeful, schooled, *sciens,* taught, understanding, well-informed, well-posted, well-versed
ASSOCIATED CONCEPTS: knowing or conscious, knowingly aid, knowingly and willfully, knowingly possess, knowingly receive, knowingly suffer or permit

KNOWINGLY, adverb advisedly, deliberately, designedly, intentionally, learnedly, pointedly, purposefully, with knowledge, wittingly
ASSOCIATED CONCEPTS: knowingly and willfully, knowingly permit, knowingly suffer

KNOWLEDGE (Awareness), noun acquaintance, apperception, appreciation, appreciativeness, cognition, cognizance, comprehension, consciousness, discernment, enlightenment, familiarity, grasp, information, intellection, intelligence, ken, know-how, mindfulness, perception, perceptiveness, percipience, realization, recognition, understanding
ASSOCIATED CONCEPTS: actual knowledge, actual notice, common knowledge, constructive knowledge, discovery, full knowledge, guilty knowledge, implied knowledge, imputed knowledge, judicial notice, knowledge sufficient to form a belief, scienter

KNOWLEDGE (Learning), noun *cognitio,* command, *doctrina,* education, enlightenment, erudition, expertise, familiarity, familiarization, information, ken, know-how, mastery, proficiency, scholarship, *scientia,* skill, study, wisdom

Idem est scire aut scire debet aut potuisse. To be bound to know or to be able to know is the same as to know. *Lex neminem cogit ostendere quod nescire praesumitur.* The law compels no one to divulge that which he is presumed not to know. *Scienti et volenti non fit injuria.* A wrong is not done to a person who understands and consents. *Ignorantia praesumitur ubi scientia non probatur.* Ignorance is presumed where knowledge is not proved. *Ignorantia facti.* Ignorance of facts excuses; ignorance of law does not excuse. *Scientia utrimque par pares contrahentes facit.* Equal knowledge on both sides makes the contracting parties equal.

KNOWLEDGEABLE, *adjective* apperception, cognition, cognizance, comprehension, discernment, enlightenment, familiarity, grasp, intellection, intelligence, ken, know-how, understanding
ASSOCIATED CONCEPTS: knowledgeable experts

KNOWN, *(Established)* *adjective* appreciated, ascertained, catch on, celebrated, comprehended, computed, conceive, discerned, disclosed, discovered, established, familiar, famous, known, noted, notorious, popular, prevalent, prominent, prominently known, recognized, revered, well-known, well-received
ASSOCIATED CONCEPTS: earliest known uses, little known laws, nationally known

KNOWN, *(Obvious),* *adjective* accepted, acknowledged, admitted, advertised, aired, clear, come to light, confessed, declared, disclosed, discovered, established, evident, exposed, familiar, identified, manifest, obvious, patently known, proclaimed, publicized, published, realized, recognized, revealed, uncloaked, unconcealed, uncovered, undisguised, unmasked, well-known

KUDOS, *noun* acclaim, acclamation, accolade, applause, approbation, approval, commendation, compliment, congratulation, credit, distinction, endorsement, flattery, glory, honor, laudation, magnification, plaudits, popular favor, popularity, praise, prestige, recognition, renown, tribute

LABEL, *noun* brand, cachet, classification, description, docket, emblem, hallmark, identification, identification tag, insignia, mark, mark of identification, marker, sign, slip, stamp, sticker, superscription, tag, ticket
ASSOCIATED CONCEPTS: disclaimer on a label, misleading labels, trademark for a brand on a label, warning on a label

LABEL, *verb* betoken, brand, call, call by a distinctive title, characterize, classify, define, demarcate, denominate, denote, describe, designate, differentiate, distinguish by a mark, docket, earmark, entitle, identify, imprint, indicate, mark, name, provide with nomenclature, put a mark upon, set apart, single out, specify, stamp, tag, term, ticket, title

LABOR *(Exertion),* *noun* discipline, effort, endeavor, energy, enterprise, industry, mental toil, pains, strain, strife

LABOR *(Work),* *noun* advocation, assignment, calling, craft, duty, employ, employment, job, line of business, line of work, occupation, profession, pursuit, responsibility, task, toil, trade, undertaking, vocation
ASSOCIATED CONCEPTS: boycotts, closed shop, collective bargaining, labor arbitration, labor dispute, labor organization, labor relations, labor union, lockout, open shop, scope of employment, skilled labor, strikes, terms and conditions of employment, union labor, union shop, wildcat strike, workmen's compensation

LABOR, *verb* apply oneself, attend to business, be diligent, be employed, be industrious, *contendere,* devote oneself to, do a job, do work, drudge, endeavor, engage in, exercise, exert energy, exert oneself, follow one's vocation, *laborare,* plod, plug away, ply, ply one's trade, strain, strive, struggle, toil, travail, work, work hard

LABOR UNDER A MISAPPREHENSION, *verb* be deceived, be misguided, be misinformed, be misled, be mistaken, blunder, deceive oneself, delude oneself, estimate incorrectly, fail to understand, interpret incorrectly, make a mistake, misapprehend, miscalculate, misconstrue, misestimate, misinterpret, misjudge, misunderstand, put a false interpretation to, receive a false impression, receive a wrong impression

LABORIOUS, *adjective* arduous, assiduous, backbreaking, brutal, burdensome, busy, difficult, exacting, exertive, exhausting, fatiguing, grueling, Herculean, industrious, intensive, intricate, involved, onerous, oppressive, painstaking, relentless, rigorous, strenuous, tiresome, tough, troublesome, vigorous
ASSOCIATED CONCEPTS: a laborious task

LABYRINTH *(Complex),* *noun* complexity, complication, confused situation, difficulty, enigma, involvement, intricacy, intricate state, knotty problem, maze, mystery, problem, puzzle, riddle, tangle

LABYRINTH *(Winding course),* **noun**   circuitous course, complex course, complexity, complicated arrangement, complication, convolution, involvement, maze, meander, meanderings, problem, puzzle, tanglement, tortuousness course, winding path, windings and turnings

LACHES, *noun*   delay, delay attended by change of position, delay that results in disadvantage, dereliction, dereliction of duty, failure of duty, failure to litigate within reasonable period, improvidence, inattention, inexcusable delay, inexcusable delay in assertion of rights, inobservance, lack of diligence, laggardness, laxity, laxness, laziness, neglect, neglectfulness, negligence, nonfeasance, nonperformance, omission, prejudicial delay, procrastination, remissness, unconscionable delay, undue delay, unexcused delay, unexplained delay, unnecessary prolongation, unreasonable delay, want of duty
ASSOCIATED CONCEPTS: equity, estoppel by laches, statute of limitations
FOREIGN PHRASES: *Tempus enim modus tollendi obligationes et actiones, quia tempus currit contra desides et sui juris contemptores.* For time is a means of dissipating obligations and actions, because time runs against the slothful and careless of their own rights. *Vigilantibus et non dormientibus jura subveniunt.* The laws relieve the vigilant and not those who sleep on their rights.

LACK, *verb*   be bereft of, be deficient, be deprived of, be desirous, be destitute, be in need, be in want, be inadequate, be inferior, be insufficient, be needy, be poor, be wanting, be without, crave, desiderate, desire, fall short, feel a dearth, hunger for, long for, miss, need, require, suffer privation, want, wish for, yearn for
ASSOCIATED CONCEPTS: lack of capacity, lack of consideration, lack of due care, lack of good faith, lack of intent, lack of jurisdiction, lack of knowledge, lack of mutuality, lack of probable cause, lack of prosecution, lack of trustworthiness

LACK ABILITY, *adjective*   forceless, helpless, ill-qualified, impotent, inadequate, inapt, incapable, ineffective, ineffectual, inept, inferior, not able, not equal to, not up to the task, outgunned, outmanned, outmatched, powerless, unable, unequipped, unfit, unqualified, unsuitable, untalented
ASSOCIATED CONCEPTS: capacity, lack of legal ability to act

LACK AGREEMENT, *adjective*   at an impasse, at cross purposes, contrary, discord, discordance, disharmonious, disputing, dissenting, failed to agree, far apart, feuding, fixed, holding divergent opinions, intransigent, not arriving at a consensus, not gaining conformity, unable to reach a resolution, warring
ASSOCIATED CONCEPTS: meeting of the minds, spirit of an agreement

LACK CONFIDENCE IN, *noun*   doubtful thoughts, doubting feelings, equivocal feelings, hesitancy, hold a dubious belief, insecurity, lack assurance, lack certitude, lack faith, lack sureness, lack trust, problematic, skeptical conclusion, suspiciousness, tentativeness, uncertain of, uncertainty, unconvinced of the outcome, undecided in ascertaining the results, unsettledness, unsure of feelings, wavering in a determination
ASSOCIATED CONCEPTS: confidentiality, encryption

LACK CONVICTION, *adjective*   considering, have no opinion, have no view, hold no belief, lack assurance, lack belief, lack certainty, lack certitude, lack faith, lack of direction, mulling it over, not convinced, not resolute, not sold on, pondering, unable to persuade, undecided

LACK HONESTY, *adjective*   beguiling, bogus, cheating, conscienceless, corrupt, deceitful, deceiving, deceptive, devoid of honesty, dishonorable, disingenuous, faked, fallacious, false, false-hearted, fraudulent, guileful, immoral, iniquitous, insidious, insincere, lying, meretricious, nefarious, not honest, perfidious, shameless, treacherous, unauthentic, underhanded, unethical, unprincipled, unscrupulous, untrustworthy, untruthful, void of truth, without probity
ASSOCIATED CONCEPTS: lack of civility and honesty

LACK OF AWARENESS, *adjective*   blinded, heedless, ignorant, inattentive, incognizant, not heeding, off guard, surprised, unadvised, unapprised, unconscious, undiscerning, unenlightened, unfamiliar with, uninformed, unknowing, unmindful, unprepared, unsuspecting, unwarned, without any notice

LACK OF CARE, *adjective*   careless, casual, cavalier, disregardful, flippant, forgetful, heedless, inadvertence, inattention, inattentive, inconsiderate, indifferent, lackadaisical, lacking awareness, lacking concern, lax, neglectful, negligent, not affording protection, not attending to, not consciousness, not heeding, not looking after, reckless, unattended, uncaring, unconcerned, unheeding, unmindful, without heed, without prudence, without regard
ASSOCIATED CONCEPTS: manslaughter, negligence

LACK OF CERTAINTY, *noun*   ambiguity, ambivalence, confusion, contingency, darkness, dimness, doubt, doubtfulness, dubiousness, equivocation, hesitancy, hesitation, incertitude, indecision, indefiniteness, indetermination, irresolution, perplexity, precariousness, quandary, reluctance, undependability, unpredictability, unreliability, unsteadiness, vacillation, wavering

LACK OF CONTROL, *adjective*   disobedient, disorderly, fractious, frenzied, headstrong, hysterical, impetuous, incorrigible, indocile, insubordinate, insuppressible, insurgent, irrepressible, lawless, obstreperous, out of control, recalcitrant, refractory, riotous, tempestuous, uncontrollable, ungovernable, unmanageable, unruly, untoward, violent, wild

LACK OF PERSONAL JURISDICTION, *noun*   bereft of authority, deficient personal jurisdiction, inadequate personal jurisdiction, insufficient personal jurisdiction, lack of authority to hear and decide a case, lack of capacity to decide the matter in issue, lack of capacity to hear the controversy, lack of decision-making power over the case, lack of legal authority, lack of legal power to decide a case, lack of purview, want of personal jurisdiction, without personal jurisdiction

LACK OF SUBJECT MATTER, *noun*   bereft of authority, deficient subject matter jurisdiction, inadequate subject matter jurisdiction, insufficient subject matter jurisdiction, lack of authority to hear and decide a case, lack of capacity to decide the matter in issue, lack of capacity to hear the controversy, lack of decision-making power over the case, lack of legal authority, lack of legal power to decide a case, lack of purview, want of subject matter jurisdiction, without subject matter jurisdiction

LACONIC, *adjective*   abbreviated, abridged, *adstrictus,* brevis, brief, brusque, closemouthed, compendious, compressed, concise, condensed, contracted, curt, economical of words, epigrammatic, exact, mum, pauciloquent, pithy, pointed, precise, quiet, reserved, reticent, secretive, sententious, short, sparing of words, succinct, summarized, taciturn, telegraphic, terse, to the point, uncommunicative, ungarrulous, unloquacious, untalkative

LAG, verb dally, dawdle, decelerate, decrease, delay, diminish in pace, ebb, fail, fall back, fall behind, get behind, go leisurely, hold back, idle, lag behind, linger, lose strength, move slowly, procrastinate, put off, saunter, slow up, take one's time, trail, wane
ASSOCIATED CONCEPTS: implementation date

LAISSEZ FAIRE, noun abstinence from action, hands-off policy, nonhampering, noninfringement, noninterference, nonintermeddling, noninterruption, nonintervention, nonintrusion, nontampering, refraining from involvement, refusal to become involved

LAMENT, verb bemoan, bewail, commiserate, feel concern for, feel emotions for, feel for, feel remorse for, feel sensitive to, fret, grieve, grieve for, mourn, mourn for, pine, pity, regret, sympathize

LAMENTABLE, adjective awful, comfortless, deplorable, depressing, depressive, disheartening, dismal, distressful, distressing, doleful, dreadful, flebilis, grave, grievous, horrible, horrid, joyless, lamentabilis, low, lugubrious, melancholy, miserable, mournful, painful, pathetic, piteous, pitiable, pitiful, poor, regrettable, rueful, sad, saddening, sorrowful, sorry, terrible, tragic, uncomfortable, unfavorable, unfortunate, unhappy, woeful, wretched

LANCINATE, verb break through, cleave, cut, cut into, discerp, divide, empierce, fractionalize, fragment, gash, gore, impale, incise, knife, lacerate, lance, make an incision, penetrate, perforate, pierce, prick, puncture, rend, rip, rive, slash, slit, stab, stick, sunder, tear, transpierce

LAND, noun property, real estate, seisin, terrain, tract
ASSOCIATED CONCEPTS: abutting land, adjacent land, agreement to sell land, alienation of land, appurtenance to land, common lands, condemnation of land, contiguous land, contract of sale of land, convey an interest in land, covenants running with the land, easement, easement running with the land, equitable interest in land, high land, improvements upon land, interest in land, land contract, land grant, land tax, lease of land, lien on land, raw land, right of way, subdivision of land, suit to recover land, survey of land, title in land, title in fee, trespass on land tract, undivided land, unimproved land, vacant land, waste lands

LANDHOLDER, noun estate owner, freeholder, holder of legal title, landlord, landowner, leaseholder, one who has land, owner of an estate in land, owner of the fee, owner of the fee simple absolute, property holder, property owner, proprietor, real property holder, real property owner, titleholder

LANDLOCKED, adjective buried, completely surrounded, confined, contained, embedded, encased, encompassed, hemmed in, implanted, locked in, wedged in
ASSOCIATED CONCEPTS: easements, egress, landlocked states

LANDLORD, noun agrorum possessor, lessor, owner of an estate in land, owner of lands, owner of tenements, propietory owner, proprietor
ASSOCIATED CONCEPTS: ejectment proceeding, landlord's lien

LANDMARK (Conspicuous object), **noun** boundary marker, cairn, cynosure, direction post, familiar object, guidepost, lapis, marker, monument, prominent object, signpost, waymark
ASSOCIATED CONCEPTS: preservation of landmarks

LANDMARK (Significant change), **noun** cardinal point, critical happening, critical juncture, critical occasion, crucial point, decisive turn, event, high point, key point, material point, milestone, moment of change, salient point, significant event, significant occurrence
ASSOCIATED CONCEPTS: landmark decision

LANDOWNER, noun agrorum possessor, estate owner, freeholder, holder of legal title, landed proprietor, landholder, landlord, owner of an estate in land, owner of land, owner of real estate, owner of real property, owner of the fee, property holder, property owner, proprietor, real property holder, real property owner, titleholder
ASSOCIATED CONCEPTS: landowner's liability

LANDSLIDE (Avalanche), **noun** accident, adversity, affliction, bad luck, calamity, casualty, catastrophe, devastation, disaster, emergency, hardship, infliction, misery, misfortune, ravage, tragedy, trouble
ASSOCIATED CONCEPTS: catastrophe insurance

LANDSLIDE (Overwhelming support), **noun** conclusive, decisive, large, lopsided, many, overwhelming
ASSOCIATED CONCEPTS: landslide political victory

LANGUAGE, noun communication, composition, dialect, expression, faculty of speech, folk speech, form of expression, formulation, idiom, jargon, lingua, linguistics, means of communication, oral, oratio, parlance, phrasing, phraseology, rhetoric, sermo, speech, spoken expression, spoken word, talk, terminology, tongue, verbal intercourse, verbiage, vernacular, vocabulary, wordage, wording, written expression, written word
ASSOCIATED CONCEPTS: abusive language, ambiguous language, obscene language, precatory language

LANGUID, adjective adynamic, anemic, apathetic, apathetical, asthenic, drooping, dry, dull, empty, exanimate, exhausted, faint, fatigued, feeble, flagging, hebetudinous, impotent, inactive, indifferent, ineffective, inert, lackadaisical, languens, languorous, lassus, leaden, lethargic, lethargical, lifeless, limp, listless, lukewarm, lustless, lymphatic, passionless, passive, phlegmatic, phlegmatical, pithless, pluckless, powerless, prosaic, remissus, sapless, sickly, sinewless, slack, slow, sluggish, spunkless, stagnant, stale, strengthless, supine, tired, torpid, unaggressive, unanimated, unimpassioned, uninspired, uninterested, unrefreshed, unrestored, unspirited, unstrengthened, vapid, wan, weak, without animation, without force, without spirit

LANGUISH, verb ail, become disheartened, become ill, become weak, collapse, decay, decline, despair, despond, deteriorate, droop, drop, ebb, fade, fail, fail in health, fall ill, fall sick, flag, fret, go into a decline, grieve, grow weak, lament, languere, languescere, live under unfavorable conditions, lose heart, lose spirit, lose strength, pine, pine away, repine, sag, sicken, sink, slump, stagnate, succumb, suffer, tabescere, vegetate, waste away, weaken, wear away, wilt, wither

LANGUOR, noun apathy, debility, drowsiness, dullness, emasculation, enervation, fatigue, feebleness, heaviness, hebetude, helplessness, idleness, immobility, impotence, inaction, inactivity, indifference, indolence, inertness, inexcitability, lack of strength, languor, lassitude, laziness, lethargy, lifelessness, listlessness, oscitancy, passivity, phlegm, quiescence, sloth, slow motion, slow pace, slowness, sluggishness, somnolence, somnolency, stagnation, supineness, tiredness, torpidity, torpidness, torpor, vegetation, weakness, weariness

359

LAPSE (Break), **noun** *fuga*, hiatus, interlude, interruption, lull, pause, recess
ASSOCIATED CONCEPTS: devise, lapsed, legacy

LAPSE (Expiration), **noun** decline, default, delinquency, dereliction, *error*, error, expiry, failure, inconstancy, *lapsus*, misdeed, misstep, mistake, negligence, *peccatum*, recreancy, regression, relapse, retrogradation, retrogression, reversion, secession, shortcoming, slip, termination
ASSOCIATED CONCEPTS: lapsed bequest, lapsed devise, lapsed legacy, lapsed license, lapsed policy

LAPSE (Cease), **verb** abate, become forfeit, become void, come to an end, complete, conclude, discontinue, end, expire, pass to another, relinquish, *reverti*, run out, stop, terminate
FOREIGN PHRASES: *Accusator post rationabile tempus non est audiendus, nisi se bene de omissione excusaverit.* An accuser ought not to be heard after the lapse of a reasonable time, unless he can account satisfactorily for his delay.

LAPSE (Fall into error), **verb** be at fault, commit an error, deviate from the proper path, deviate from virtue, do wrong, err, *errare*, fail, fall from grace, go astray, go awry, misbehave, misstep, *peccare*, slip, slip from virtue, stray, transgress, trespass, weaken

LAPSE IN JUDGMENT, **noun** be at fault, commit an error, deviation from the proper path, deviation from virtue, error, failure to act properly, fated moment, gone astray, gone awry, improper action, improper decision, improper judgment, misbehavior, misstep, negligent determination, negligent interval, slip, transgression, wrong decision, wrong evaluation, wrongdoing
ASSOCIATED CONCEPTS: negligence, reckless

LAPSE IN TIME, **noun** loss of age, loss of chronology, loss of computation of time, loss of duration, loss of end of the matter, loss of era, loss of interim, loss of interlude, loss of interval, loss of period, loss of tenure, loss of term
ASSOCIATED CONCEPTS: latches

LARCENOUS, **adjective** brigandish, burglarious, criminal, dishonest, felonious, fraudulent, lawbreaking, piratic, piratical, plundering, plunderous, predaceous, predatory, privateering, rapacious, ravaging, thieving, thievish
ASSOCIATED CONCEPTS: larcenous intent

LARCENY, **noun** abstraction, appropriation, brigandage, embezzlement, felonious stealing, fraudulent taking, *furtum*, misappropriation, peculation, pickpocketing, pilferage, rapacity, rapine, swindle, swindling, theft, thievery, unlawful acquisition, unlawful conversion, unlawful taking, wrongful taking
ASSOCIATED CONCEPTS: compound larceny, conversion, embezzlement, fraud, grand larceny, larceny by device, larceny by false pretenses, larceny by fraud, larceny by trick, petit larceny, receiving stolen goods, simple larceny

LARGE, **adjective** abundant, all-embracing, all-inclusive, big, broad, capacious, colossal, comprehensive, considerable, endless, enlarged, enormous, excessive, exhaustive, expansive, extensive, gargantuan, giant, giant-size, grand, great, great big, huge, immeasurable, immense, infinite, king-size, lavish, limitless, lofty, massive, monstrous, of great scope, oversized, sizable, substantial, tremendous, unbounded, unlimited, vast, wide-ranging, wide-reaching
ASSOCIATED CONCEPTS: large law firms

LARGESS (Generosity), **noun** aid, almsgiving, altruism, assistance, benefaction, beneficence, benignancy, benignity, bounteousness, bountifulness, bounty, charitableness, charity, *congiarium*, free giving, freehandedness, freeness, generosity, generousness, graciousness, help, helpfulness, hospitableness, hospitality, indulgence, kindliness, kindness, *largitio*, lavishment, lavishness, liberality, liberalness, magnanimity, magnanimousness, munificence, openhandedness, philanthropy, prodigality, readiness to give, selflessness, thoughtfulness, unselfishness

LARGESS (Gift), **noun** alms, assistance, award, benefaction, benefit, bestowment, bonus, boon, bounty, charity, contribution, dole, donation, donative, dotation, endowment, favor, grant, gratuity, handout, handsel, help, offering, present, presentation, presentment, vail, voluntary conveyance

LASCIVIOUS, **adjective** bawdy, carnal, coarse, concupiscent, corrupt, debauched, depraved, dissipated, dissolute, erotic, fleshly, goatish, immodest, immoral, improper, *impurus*, indecent, *lascivus*, lecherous, lewd, libertine, *libidinosus*, libidinous, lickerish, lubric, lubricous, lustful, obscene, Paphian, pornographic, promiscuous, prurient, ribald, salacious, satyric, satyrical, sensuous, sex-ridden, shameless, unblushing, unchaste, unregenerate, wanton
ASSOCIATED CONCEPTS: indecent and lascivious, lewd and lascivious cohabitation, obscenity

LASH (Attack verbally), **verb** admonish, animadvert upon, assail, berate, betongue, blackguard, cast reproach upon, castigate, chastise, chide, criticize severly, decry, excoriate, exprobrate, flay, fulminate against, impugn, increpate, inveigh, objurgate, rave against, rebuke, reprehend, reprimand, reproach, reprove, revile, scarify, scathe, slate, take to task, upbraid, vilify, vilipend, vituperate

LASH (Strike), **verb** bastinado, batter, beat, birch, bruise, cudgel, deal a blow to, deal a stroke, drub, *flagellare*, flagellate, flay, flog, fustigate, give a beating, give a thrashing, hit, larrup, maul, pelt, pound, pummel, scourge, slap, smite, switch, thrash, trounce, truncheon, verb*erare*, whack

LAST (Final), **adjective** aftermost, climactic, climactical, closing, completive, completory, concluding, conclusive, conclusory, crowning, decisive, definitive, determinative, end, ending, endmost, extreme, farthest, final, finishing, furthest, hindermost, hindmost, outermost, permanent, rear, terminal, terminating, terminational, terminative, ultimate
ASSOCIATED CONCEPTS: last clear chance, last known address, last residence, last will and testament

LAST (Preceding), **adjective** above, above-cited, above-mentioned, above-named, above-stated, aforegoing, aforementioned, aforesaid, *antecedens*, antecedent, anterior, before mentioned, earlier, fore, foregoing, former, freshest, introductory, most recent, newest, past, precedent, precursory, prefatory, preliminary, preludial, preludious, prelusive, prelusory, previous, *prior*

LAST, **verb** be long-lived, be stable, be timeless, be unconsumed, be unexhausted, bide, carry on, continue, *durare*, endure, exist, hang on, hold on, hold out, hold up, keep up, linger, live on, outlive, perdure, *permanere*, persevere, persist, prevail, prolong, protract, remain, stand firm, stay, stay on, subsist, survive, sustain, wait, withstand

LASTING, **adjective** abiding, continuing, enduring, lingering, maintained, perpetuated, perseverant, persistent, persisting, preserved, remaining, standing, staying, surviving, sustained, undestroyed, uneradicated, unerased, unfailing, unremoved, unrepealed

LATE *(Defunct),* **adjective** dead, deceased, demised, demortuus, departed, erstwhile, former, once, one-time, passed on, perished, previous, then

LATE *(Tardy),* **adjective** after time, behind time, belated, deferred, delayed, detained, held up, lagging, moratory, overdue, past due, postponed, retarded, slow, unpunctual, unready
ASSOCIATED CONCEPTS: late filing

LATENCY, **noun** behind the scenes, below the surface, camouflaged, concealed, covered, hidden from view, not manifested, screened, submerged, unapparent, under the surface, underlying, undetected, undeveloped, undiscovered, unexposed, unnoticed, unrevealed, unseen, unsuspected, veiled
ASSOCIATED CONCEPTS: toll the statute of limitations

LATENT, **adjective** *abditus, absconditus,* arcane, behind the scenes, below the surface, camouflaged, concealed, covered, covert, delitescent, hidden from view, imperceptible, indiscernible, *occultus,* screened, submerged, unapparent, under the surface, underlying, undetected, undeveloped, undiscovered, unexposed, unmanifested, unnoticed, unrevealed, unseen, unspied, unsuspected, veiled
ASSOCIATED CONCEPTS: latent ambiguity, latent danger, latent defect, latent injury, latent liability

LATER, **adverb** after, after a time, after a while, after that, afterwards, at a future time, at a later date, at a later point in time, at a subsequent time, at some point in the future, before long, before too long, imminently, in days to come, in the aftermath, in the course of time, in the future, in the immediate future, in the sequel, later on, next, sequentially, subsequently, succeeding, successively, then, tomorrow

LATEST, **adjective** current, final, just completed, just done, just finished, last, most current, most recent, newest, recent, up-to-date, up-to-the-minute

LATITUDE, **noun** absence of restraint, accommodation, amplitude, autonomy, carte blanche, choice, discretion, ease of movement, exemption from control, expanse, expansion, extension, field, free course, free decision, free hand, free play, free thought, free will, freedom, freedom of action, full play, independence, indiscipline, largeness, leverage, liberalism, *libertas,* liberty, license, *licentia,* maneuverability, margin, noninterference, nonintervention, openness, opportunity, option, play, power of choice, power to choose, range, range of choice, right of choice, room, scope, space, unconstraint, uninhibitedness, unrestraint, unstrictness, will

LAUDABLE, **adjective** admirable, approvable, commendable, creditable, deserving, estimable, excellent, exemplary, hallowed, *laudabilis, laudatus, laude dignus,* matchless, meritorious, model, noble, peerless, praiseworthy, saintly, sterling, uncensurable, unimpeachable, virtuous, worthwhile, worthy, worthy of estimation

LAUDATION, **noun** benediction, blessing, doxology, encomium, eulogy, exaltation, glorification, honor, idolatry, invocation, magnification, praise

LAUNCH *(Initiate),* **verb** activate, begin, embark, establish, found, generate, handsel, inaugurate, induce, institute, introduce, lay the foundations, make active, open, originate, put in motion, set going, set in motion, start, take the first step, take the lead, touch off, trigger, undertake

LAUNCH *(Project),* **verb** cast, catapult, *contorquere,* eject, fling, heave, hurl, *immittere,* impel forward, jaculate, lance, pitch, precipitate, propel, push, send flying, send forth, send headlong, send off, set in motion, shoot, throw, thrust, toss

LAUNCH AN INQUIRY, **verb** conduct an investigation into, delve into, dig into, examine, explore, fact find, go into, inquire, investigate, look into, nose into, probe, pry into, scrutinize, search, search for information, search into
ASSOCIATED CONCEPTS: launch a public inquiry, launch an independent inquiry

LAVISH *(Opulent),* **adjective** abounding, abundant, affluent, ample, bounteous, bountiful, copious, costly, effusive, excess, extravagant, generous, immoderate, inordinate, liberal, luxurious, munificent, open-handed, opulent, overabundant, overflowing, overlavish, overluxuriant, oversufficient, plenteous, plentiful, profuse, rich, sumptuous, superabundant

LAVISH *(Wasteful),* **adjective** extravagant, immoderate, improvident, intemperate, overflowing, overlavish, overluxuriant, oversufficient, squandering, thriftless, unthrifty

LAVISH, **verb** being generous, being extravagant, be liberal, bestow, be thriftless, be wasteful, carry to excess, furnish, luxuriate, pour on, spare no expense, spend, spend freely, spend recklessly, squander

LAW, **noun** act, article, body of rules, canon, charter, code, command, decree, decree absolute, dictum, enactment, established rule, expressed command, fiat, firm principle, instruction, *ius,* jurisprudence, legal code, *lex,* mandate, maxim, norm, order, ordinance, precedent, precept, prescribed form, prescription, principle, pronouncement, *regula,* regulation, rescript, rubric, rule, rule of conduct, set of rules, settled principle, standard, standing order, statute, tenet
ASSOCIATED CONCEPTS: action at law, adequate remedy at law, adjective law, administrative law, allowed by law, amendatory law, antitrust laws, application of the law, appropriation law, arising under laws of the united states, at law and in equity, attorney-at-law, authorized by law, aviation law, bankruptcy law, blue sky law, breach of the law, by operation of law, change in the law, civil law, civil rights law, civil service law, color of law, color of state law, commercial law, common law, common-law marriage, common-law trust, compliance with laws, conclusion of law, constitutional law, contrary to law, controversy arising under the laws of the United States, corporate law, court of law, criminal law, declare the law, domestic relations law, due process of law, duties and liabilities imposed by law, election law, enjoined by law, entertainment law, environmental law, equal protection of the law, error of law, established by law, ex post facto, executed in accordance with law, existing laws, federal law, fixed by law, foreign laws, fundamental law, general law, governed by law, homestead law, ignorance of law, implied by law, inconsistent with law, instructions on the law, insufficient in law, insurance law, international law, issue of law, judgment founded upon a matter of law, knowledge of the law, labor law, law

and equity, law enforcement, law of the case, law of the land, limited by law, local law, maritime law, martial law, matter of law, military law, mistake of law, municipal law, natural heirs at law, not in accordance with law, obligation imposed by law, omnibus law, operation of law, ordinary course of law, organic law, patent and trademark law, penal law, practice of law, preexisting law, prescribed by law, presumption of law, procedural law, process of law, prospective law, provided by law, provided by state law, question of law, question of local law, question of state law, real estate law, regulated by law, remedy at law, securities law, session laws, special law, specially prescribed by law, specific law, standing laws, state law, substantive law, sufficient as a matter of law, suits at law, supreme law, surrender by operation of law, tax law, terminate by limitation of law, under color of law, unemployment compensation law, uniform operation of laws, unwritten law, without due process of law

FOREIGN PHRASES: *Ubi lex est specialis, et ratio ejus generalis, generaliter accipienda est.* Where the law is special, and the reason of it general, it ought to be construed generally. *Praxis judicum est interpres legum.* The practice of the judges is the interpreter of the laws. *Lex nemini operatur iniquum, nemini facit injuriam.* The law never works an injury, or does a wrong. *Lex est norma recti.* Law is the rule of right. *Lex est sanctio sancta, jubens honesta, et prohibens contraria.* Law is a sacred santion, commanding that which is right, and prohibiting the contrary. *Lex est tutissima cassis; sub clypeo legis nemo decipitur.* Law is the safest helmet; under the shield of the law no one is deceived. *Lex fingit ubi subsistit aequitas.* The laws feigns where equity subsists. *Lex intendit vicinum vicini facta scire.* The law presumes that one neighbor is cognizant of the acts of his neighbor. *Non est certandum de regulis juris.* There is no disputing about rules of the law. *Receditur a placitis juris, potius quam injuriae et delictamaneant impunita.* In order that crimes not go unpunished, the law will be departed from. *Res est misera ubi jus est vagum et incertum.* It is a sorry state of affairs when law is vague and mutable. *Salus populi est suprema lex.* The welfare of the people is the supreme object of the law. *Si a jure discedas, vagus eris, et erunt omniaomnibus incerta.* If you depart from the law, you will go astray, and everything will be in a state of uncertainty to everyone. *Ubi lex non distinguit, nec nos distinguere debemus.* Where the law does not distinguish, we ought not to distinguish. *Ubi non est lex, ibi non est transgressio, quo ad mundum.* Where there is no law, there is no transgression, so far as worldly concerns and matters. *Firmior et potentior est operatio legis quam dispositio hominis.* The operation of the law is more firm and more powerful than the will of man. *Non jus ex regula, sed regula ex jure.* The law does not arise from the rule but the rule comes from the law. *Non verbis sed ipsis rebus, leges imponimus.* We do not impose laws upon words, but upon the things themselves. *Quando abest provisio partis, adest provisio legis.* When a provision of the party is lacking, the provision of the law supplies it. *Quod naturalis ratio inter omnes homines constituit, vocatur jus gentium.* The rule which natural reason has established among all men is called the law of nations. *Ratio est legis anima; mutata legis ratione mutatur et lex.* Reason is the soul of law; the reason of law being changed, the law is also changed. *Ratio potest allegari deficiente lege; sed ratio vera et legaliset non apparens.* Where the law is deficient, the reason can be alleged, but it must be true and lawful and not merely apparent. *Non in legendo sed in intelligendo legis consistunt.* The laws consist not in being read, but in being understood. *Lex semper intendit quod*

convenit rationi. The law always intends what is agreeable to reason. *Lex spectat naturae ordinem.* The law regards the order of nature. *Lex succurrit ignoranti.* The laws assist the ignorant. *Lex succurrit minoribus.* The law assists minors. *Melius est jus deficiens quam jus incertum.* A deficient law is better than an uncertain one. *Multa in jure communi contra rationem disputandi, procommuni utilitate introducta sunt.* Many things have been introduced into the common law, which are contrary to the public good, which are inconsistent with sound reason. *Non exemplis sed legibus judicandum est.* Judgment should not be rendered from examples, but by the law. *Id possumus quod de jure possumus.* We may do only that which we are able to do lawfully. *Idem est non probari et non esse; non deficit jus, sed probatio.* What is not proved, and what is not, are the same; it is not a defect of the law, but a want of proof. *Jus civile et quod sibi populus constituit.* The civil law is that law which the people establish for themselves. *Lex prospicit, non respicit.* The law looks forward, not backward. *Lex rejicit superflua, pugnantia, incongrua.* The law rejects those matters which are superfluous, repugnant, or incongruous. *Lex semper dabit remedium.* The law always furnishes a remedy. *Contra legem facit qui id facit quod lex prohibit; in fraudem vero qui, salvis verbis legis, sententiam ejus circumvenit.* He who does what the law prohibits, acts in fraud of the law, the letter of the law being inviolate, cheats the spirit of it. *Les fictions naissent de la loi, et non la loi des fictions.* Fictions arise from the law, and not law from fictions. *Legem enim contractus dat.* The contract makes the law. *Ubi non est directa lex, standum est arbitrio judicis, vel procedendum ad similia.* Where there is no direct law, the decision of the judge is to be taken, or references to be made to similar cases. *Consuetudo ex certa causa rationabili usitata privatcommunem legem.* A custom, based on a certain and reasonable cause, supersedes the common law. *Jus vendit quod usus approbavit.* The law recommends what use or custom has approved. *La ley favour la vie d'un homme.* The law favors human life. *Actus legis nemini est damnosus.* The act of the law shall prejudice no one. Matter en ley ne serra mise in bouche del jurors. A matter of law shall not be put into the mouth of jurors. *Equitas sequitur legem.* Equity follows the law. *Non obligat lex nisi promulgata.* A law is not obligatory unless it is promulgated. *Lex respicit aequitatem.* The law regards equity. *Ignorantia juris non excusat.* Ignorance of the law is no excuse. *Executio juris non habet injuriam.* The execution of law does no injury. Ignorantia excusatur, non juris sed facti. Ignorance of fact may excuse, but not ignorance of law. *Scire leges non hoc est verba earum tenere. sed vim ac potestatem.* To know the laws is not to observe their words alone, but their force and power. *Perpetua lex est nullam legem humanam ab positivam perpetuamesse, et clausula quae abrogationem excludit ab initio non valet.* It is a perpetual law that no human and positive law can be perpetual, and a clause in a law which precludes the power of abrogationor repeal is void from the beginning. *Experientia per varios actus legem facit. magistra rerum experientia.* Experience by various acts makes law. experience is the mistress of things. *Nemo jus sibi dicere potest.* No one can declare the law for himself. *Lex aequitate gaudet; appetit perfectum; est norma recti.* The law delights in equity; it grasps at perfection; it is a rule of right. In fictione juris semper aequitas existit. In a fiction of law, equity is always present. *Optima est lex quae minimum relinquit arbitrio judicis; optimus judex qui minimum sibi.* That is the best system of law which leaves the least to the discretion of the judge; that judge is the best who leaves the least to his own discretion. *Jus quo universitates utuntur est idem quod habent privati.* The law which governs corporations is the same as that which governs individuals. *Ignorantia facti excusat, ignorantia juris non excusat.* Ignorance of fact excuses; ignorance of the law does not excuse. *Regula est, juris quidem ignorantiam cuique nocere, facti vero ignorantiam non nocere.* The rule is that a person's ignorance of the law may prejudice him, but that his ignorance of fact will not. *Per varios actus legem experientia facit.* By various acts experience makes the law. *Juris affectus in executione consistit.* The effectiveness of a law lies in its execution. *Cessante ratione legis, cessat et ipsa lex.* Where the reason for a law ceases, the law itself also ceases. *Fortior et potentior est dispositio legis quam hominis.* The disposition of the law has greater force and stronger effect than that of man. *Lex non curat de minimis.* The law does not regard small matters. *Hominum causa jus constitutum est.* Law is established for the benefit of mankind. *Judicis est jus dicere, non dare.* It is the duty of a judge to declare the law, not to make it. *Lex est dictamen rationis.* Law is the dictate of reason. *Lex est ratio summa, quae jubet quae sunt utilia et necessaria, et contraria prohibet.* That which is law is the consummation of reason, which commands those things useful and necessary, while prohibiting the contrary. *Nemo est supra leges.* No one is above the law. *Ubi jus incertum, ibi jus nullum.* Where the law is uncertain, there is no law. *Lex neminem cogit ad vana seu inutilia peragenda.* The law compels no one to do futile or useless things. *Ex facto jus oritur.* Law arises out of facts. *Ad quaestionem facti non respondent judicis; ad quaestionem juris non respondent juratores.* Judges do not answer to a question of fact; jurors do not answer to a question of law. *Constructio legis non facit injuriam.* A law properly interpreted creates no wrong. *Argumentum ab inconvenienti est validum in lege; quia lex non permittit aliquod inconveniens.* An argument drawn from what is inconvenient is good in law, because the law will not permit any inconvenience. *Injustum est, nisi tota lege inspecta, de una aliqua ejus particula proposita judicare vel respondere.* It is unjust to give judgement or advice concerning any particular clause of a law without having examined the whole law. *Cuilibet licet juri pro se introducto renunciare.* Any one may waive or renounce the benefit of a principle or rule of law that exists only for his protection. *Ignorantia legis neminem excusat.* Ignorance of law excuses no one. *Ipsae leges cupiunt ut jure regantur.* The laws themselves are desirous of being governed by what is right. *Exempla illustrant non restringunt legem.* Examples illustrate, but do not restrain, the law. *Obedientia est legis essentia.* Obedience is the essence of the law. *Consuetudo est altera lex.* Custom is another law. *Consuetudo vincit communem legem.* Custom overrules common law. *Consuetudo praescripta et legitima vincit legem.* A prescriptive and legitimate custom prevails over the law. *Consuetudo et communis assue tudo vincit legem non scriptam, si sitspecialis; et interpretatur legem scriptam, si lex sit generalis.* Custom and common usage override the unwritten law, if it be special; and interpret the written law, if the law be general. *Consuetudo est optimus interpres legum.* Custom is the best interpreter of the laws. *Conventio privatorum non potest publico juri derogare.* The agreement of private persons cannot derogate from public right. Conventio vincit legem. The express agreement of parties overcomes the law. *Quamvis lex generaliter loquitur, restringenda tamen est, ut, cessante ratione, ipsa cessat.* Although a law speaks generally, yet it is to be restrained, so that when its reason fails, it should cease also.

Processus legis est gravis vexatio, executio legis coronat opus. The process of the law is a grave vexation; the execution of the law crowns the work. *Ubi eadem ratio, ibi idem jus; et de similibus idem est judicium.* Where there is the same reason, there is the same law; and where there are similar situations, the judgment is the same. *Lex nil frustra facit.* The law does nothing in vain. *Lex non deficit in justitia exhibenda.* The law does not fail in dispensing justice. *Lex plus laudatur quando ratione probatur.* The law is most praiseworthy when it is consistent with reason. *Ubi lex aliquem cogit ostendere causam, necesse est quod causa sit justa et legitima.* Where the law compels a man to show cause, it is necessary that the cause be just and legal. *Ita semper fiat relatio ut valeat dispositio.* Let the interpretation be so made that the disposition stands. *Judex est lex loquens.* The judge is the law speaking; that is, he is the mouthpiece of the law. *Natura appetit perfectum; ita et lex.* Nature seeks perfection, and so does the law. *A verbis legis non est recedendum.* The words of the law must not be departed from. *Apices juris non sunt jura.* Legal niceties are not law. *Communis error facit jus.* A common error makes law. *Casus omissus et oblivioni datus dispositioni communis juris relinquitur.* A case omitted and forgotten is left to the disposal of the common law. *Contemporanea expositio est optima et fortissima in lege.* Contemporaneous exposition is the best and most powerful in the law. *Neque leges neque senatus consulta ita scribi possunt ut omnis casus qui quandoque in sediriunt comprehendatur; sed sufficit ea quae plaerumque accidunt contineri.* Neither laws nor acts of a legislature can be so written as to include all actual or possible cases; it is sufficient if they provide for those things which frequently or ordinarily may happen. *Jura eodem modo destituuntur quo constituuntur.* Laws are abrogated by the same means by which they are enacted. Jura naturae sunt immutabilia. The laws of nature are unchangeable. *Leges humanae nascuntur, vivunt, et moriuntur.* Human laws are born, live, and die. *Legibus sumptis desinentibus, lege naturae utendum est.* When laws imposed by the state fail, the laws of nature must be invoked. *Tortura legum pessima.* The torture or wresting of laws is the worst kind of torture. Leges suum ligent latorem. Laws should bind their own proposer. *Jus constitui oportet in his quae ut plurimum accidunt non quae ex inopinato.* Laws ought to be made with a view to those cases which occur most frequently and not to those which are of rare or accidental occurrence. *Nova constitutio futuris formam imponere debet, non praeteritis.* A new law ought to affect the future, not what is past. *Ad ea quae frequentius accidunt jura adaptantur.* Laws are adapted to those cases which most commonly occur. *Inde datae leges ne fortior omnia posset.* Laws were made lest the stronger might become all-powerful. *Ex malis moribus bonae leges natae sunt.* Good laws arise from evil morals. *Quando lex est specialis, ratio autem generalis, generaliter lex est intelligenda.* When a law is special, but its reason general, the law is to be understood generally. *Intentio inservire debet legibus, non legesintentioni.* The intention ought to be subservient to the laws, not the laws to intentions. *Legislatorum est viva vox, rebus etnon verbis, legem imponere.* The voice of the legislators is the living voice, to impose laws upon things, and not on words. *Optimam esse legem, quae minimum relinquit arbitrio judicis; id quod certitudo ejus praestat.* That law is best which leaves the least to the decision of the judge; this being an advantage which results from its certainty. *Leges posteriores priores contrariasabrogant.* Subsequent laws repeal prior laws that are repugnant to them. *Jus est ars boni et aequi.* Law is the science of what is good and just. *Nihil infra regnum subditos magis conservatin tranquilitate et concordia quam debitalegum administratio.* Nothing better preserves in tranquillity and concord those subjected to the same government better than one due administration of the laws. *Aequum et bonum est lex legum.* That which is equitable and good is the law of laws.

LAW-ABIDING, adjective according to law, acquiescent, *bene moratus,* careful to follow the law, complying, conforming, conforming to the laws, descent, dutiful, ethical, evenhanded, follows the law, follows the prescribed laws, high-minded, high-principled, honest, honorable, in conformity with the law, incorrupt, incorruptible, inviolate, irreproachable, law-revering, legal, legitimate, licit, moral, noble, not illegitimate, obedient, obsequious, observant, on the up and up, principled, proper, reputable, respectable, right-minded, righteous, scrupulous, statutable, statutory, sticks to the law, sticks to the letter of the law, straight, straightforward, trustworthy, trusty, unbribable, uncorrupted, unimpeachable, upright, upstanding, valid, virtuous, well-principled, within the law, within the limits of the law
ASSOCIATED CONCEPTS: law-abiding citizens

LAW COURT, noun bench, court of justice, forum for adjusting disputes, forum of justice, judicial forum, judicial tribunal, judiciary, justice court, place where justice is administered, tribunal

LAW FIRM, noun attorneys-at-law, business company, counselors-at-law, law office(s), legal practitioners, LLC, partnership, PLC
ASSOCIATED CONCEPTS: prominent law firm, white glove law firms

LAW OF THE CASE, noun conclusion, conclusion of the matter, decision, decree, determination, dictate, final judgment, finding, holding, judicial decision, maxim, opinion, order, order of the court, outcome, precedence, precedent, precept, principle, pronouncement, pronouncement by a court, resolution, result, settled holding, underlying basis, upshot, written order

LAWBREAKER, noun arsonist, convict, convicted felon, criminal, crook, defrauder, delinquent, embezzler, felon, fugitive, guilty person, hoodlum, *legis violator,* malefactor, malfeasor, miscreant, misdemeanant, misfeasor, murderer, offender, outlaw, racketeer, recidivist, thief, transgressor, vandal, violator, wrongdoer

LAWFUL, adjective according to fiat, according to law, allowable, allowed, authorized by law, conformable to law, conformable with the law, constitutional, established, in accordance with the law, in conformity to the law, inviolable, juridic, law-abiding, legal, legalized, legitimate, *legitimus,* licit, nomothetic, obedient, permissible, permitted, prescribed by law, proper, sanctioned, sanctioned by law, statutable, statutory, unprohibited, valid, warranted by law, within the law
ASSOCIATED CONCEPTS: lawful act, lawful age, lawful beneficiary, lawful business, lawful command, lawful custody, lawful damages, lawful entry, lawful heirs, lawful interest, lawful issue, lawful order, lawful possession, lawful process, lawful purpose, lawful representative, lawful use

LAWFUL AUTHORITY, noun agency of the law, authorized agent of the law, authorized officer, established authority, legitimate member of law enforcement, member of a law enforcement agency, member of the police force, officer sanctioned by law, officer with credentials, police, proper authority, rightful authority, sanctioned authority, security, valid member of law enforcement

LAWFUL POSSESSION, noun allowable retention, authorized proprietorship, authorized retention, lawful retention, legal retention, legitimate control over, legitimate ownership, legitimate retention, permissible control, permitted control, possession in accordance with the law, possession in conformity to the law, possession prescribed by law, proper bailment, proper ownership, proper title, retention sanctioned by law, retention warranted by law, right of retention, rightful control, rightful retention, sanctioned retention, valid retention
ASSOCIATED CONCEPTS: governmental authority, marshal law, rule of law

LAWFUL POWER, noun allowed authority, authority authorized by law, constitutional power, established power, force in power, lawful right, legal power, legalized authority, legitimate authority, legitimized power, permitted authority, power according to law, proper power, rightful authority, sanctioned power, valid power, warranted power
ASSOCIATED CONCEPTS: carrying of weapons

LAWFULLY, adverb absolutely according to law, absolutely within conformity to the law, allowably, conforming to the law, definitely reflected in statute, entirely established, entirely in accordance with the law, entirely sanctioned, entirely sanctioned by law, entirely warranted by law, entirely within the law, entirely within the prescriptions of the law, law-abidingly, legally, legitimately, obediently, permissibly, properly, validly
ASSOCIATED CONCEPTS: lawfully authorized electronic surveillance, lawfully engaged in an investigation

LAWLESS, adjective against the law, anarchic, anarchical, arrant, *audax,* capricious, contrarious, contumacious, corrupt, criminal, degenerate, difficult, disobedient, disobeyed, disobeying, disorderly, disreputable, *effrenatus,* felonious, heedless, ill-disciplined, illegal, immoral, in defiance of the law, incorrigible, insidious, insolent, insubordinate, intemperate, intractable, irresponsible, knavish, lawbreaking, licensed, mutinous, nonconformist, nonlegal, nonobservant, not observant of the law, outlaw, profligate, rascally, rebellious, recalcitrant, recreant, recusant, refractory, reinless, restive, revolutionary, riotous, seditious, subversive, transgressive, unaccountable, unbidden, uncompliant, uncomplying, unconformable, unconstrained, uncontrolled, uncurbed, undisciplined, unfettered, ungovernable, ungoverned, unprincipled, unreined, unrighteous, unscrupulous, unsubmissive, unsuppressed, untamed, untoward, unwarrantable, unwarranted, venal, violative, wayward, without law, wrongful

LAWLESSNESS, noun actions in defiance of the law, anarchy, criminal anarchy, disreputable conduct, felonious conduct, havoc, illegal conduct, insidious behavior, insubordination to the rule of law, irresponsible conduct, lawbreaking activity, mutinous conduct, outlawed conduct, rebellious conduct, recalcitrant conduct, revolutionary conduct, riotous behavior, seditious activity, subversive actions, uncontrolled actions, ungovernable actions, unlicensed behavior, unsuppressed conduct, untoward behavior, unwarrantable behavior, wrongful action
ASSOCIATED CONCEPTS: international law, rule of law

LAWMAKER, noun alderman, alderwoman, assemblyman, assemblywoman, bill drafter, congressman, congresswoman, councilman, councilwoman, formulator of laws, lawgiver, legislative draftsman, legislator, member of a legislature, member of Congress, member of the Assembly, member of the House, member of the Senate, politician, politico, proposer of a law, proposer of legistation, representative, representative in Congress, senator

ASSOCIATED CONCEPTS: Assembly, Congress, House of Representatives, Senate

LAWSUIT, noun action, action at law, case, case for decision, cause in court, claim, contention, contest, controversia, controversy, controversy before a court, court action, dispute, judicial contest, legal action, legal argument, legal contest, legal controversy, legal dispute, legal proceedings, *lis*, litigation, matter for judgment, proceeding, suit at law, suit in equity, trial

LAWYER, noun avocat, advocate, attorney, attorney-at-law, barrister, barrister-at-law, counsel, counselor, counselor-at-law, iurisconsultus, *iurisperitus, jurisconsult,* jurisprudent, jurist, legal advisor, legal advocate, legal consultant, legal practitioner, legist, member of the legal profession, solicitor

ASSOCIATED CONCEPTS: admission to bar, attorney-client privilege, bar association, character and fitness committee, code of professional conduct, grievance committee, work product

LAX, adjective absentminded, apathetic, careless, casual, derelict, disorganized, disregarding, *dissolutus,* feckless, forgetful, halfhearted, heedless, idle, imprecise, improvident, imprudent, inaccurate, inadvertent, inattentive, incautious, indifferent, indolent, inexact, lackadaisical, lazy, loose, mindless, neglectful, *neglegens,* negligent, nonaggressive, oblivious, perfunctory, pococurante, regardless, remiss, remissus, slack, slipshod, slothful, slovenly, sluggish, temerarious, thoughtless, unambitious, unapprehensive, unaspiring, unaware, uncaring, uncircumspect, unconcerned, undemanding, unenterprising, unguarded, unheeding, uninterested, unmindful, unobservant, unobserving, unprepared, unstrict, unthinking, unthorough, unthoughtful, untidy, unwary, unwatchful

LAXITY, noun amorality, apathy, carelessness, dereliction, disregard, heedlessness, imprecision, improvidence, inaccuracy, inadvertence, inadvertency, inattention, inattentiveness, indifference, indolence, inexactitude, inexactness, inobservance, lack of control, lack of interest, lack of thoroughness, laziness, looseness, neglect, neglectfulness, *neglegentia,* negligence, noncompletion, nonfeasance, nonfulfillment, nonperformance, oversight, perfunctoriness, remissness, slackness, sloppiness, sloth, slovenliness, thoughtlessness, unconcern, unpreparedness, unrigorousness, untidiness, unwatchfulness

LAY ASIDE, verb abandon, adjourn, cancel, continue, defer, delay, detain, discard, disclaim, discount, dismiss, disregard, drop, exclude, extend, forestall, forgo, hold, hold in abeyance, hold off, hold up, ignore, isolate, keep, keep pending, lay away, lay by, lay in a stock, not decide, over rule, pass over, pause, pick out, place on hold, postpone, preserve, pretermit, procrastinate, prolong, put aside, put in suspension, put off, put on hold, recess, reject, relinquish, remove, renounce, repudiate, retain, retard, scrap, segregate, select, separate, set apart, set aside, set by, shelve, shut out, spurn, stall, stave off, stay,

stockpile, store away, store up, suspend, table, turn over, wait, weed out, winnow, withdraw, withhold

LAY DOWN (Dictate the Law), noun ascertain, assert, declare, delineate, determine, maintain, proclaim, report, specify, state, state categorically

ASSOCIATED CONCEPTS: lay down the law

LAY DOWN (Give up), noun cede, declare defeat, quit, relinquish, submit, surrender, turn over, yield

LAY DOWN THE LAW, verb administer the law, carry into effect the law, carry into execution the law, carry out the law, compel obedience with the law, effectuate the law, enforce the law, enforce to the letter of the law, ensure compliance, execute the law, implement the law, impose the law, insist upon, make compulsory, mandate, necessitate, obtain by force, put into effect, put into execution, put pressure on, read the riot act, require, strictly regulate, subject to pressure

LAY THE BLAME ON, verb accuse, ascribe blame, blame, bring up on charges, cast blame upon, charge, charge with an offense, complain against, condemn, connect with a crime, criminate, denounce, expose, find fault with, hold accountable, implicate, impute guilt to, inculpate, indict, inform on, insinuate, involve, involve in criminal proceeding, lodge a complaint, place the blame on, prefer charges, prosecute

LAY WASTE, verb abolish, annihilate, deal destruction, deracinate, desolate, destroy, destroy thoroughly, devastate, efface, obliterate, ravage

LAYER, noun amount, band, belt, blanket, cloak, cover, coverage, covering, curtain, level, shell, stratum, thickness, tier, zone

LAYMAN, noun amateur, civilian, laic, nonprofessional, nonspecialist, one who has no specialized training, unskilled practitioner, untrained person

ASSOCIATED CONCEPTS: lay witness

LAYOFF, noun banishment, cashiering, cessation, desistance, discarding, discharge, discontinuance, discontinuation, disemployment, dismissal, displacement, ejection, ejectment, elimination, expulsion, firing, halt, idling, interruption, letting go, ouster, rejection, release, removal, retirement, riddance, stoppage, suspension of employment, temporary deprivation, temporary discharge, temporary suspension, termination, termination of employment

ASSOCIATED CONCEPTS: suspension, temporary layoff

LEAD (Introduction), noun connection, foreword, opening, preamble, preface, prelude, prologue, prompt

LEAD (Predominant), noun clue, direction, example, generalship, guidance, headline, indication, influence, leading role, leadership, precedence, precedent, predominance, primacy, priority, protagonist, sign

LEAD, verb assume mastery over, coax, command, conduct, control, direct, dominate, drive, gain ascendancy, govern, guide, handle, head, hold the reins, influence, initiate, introduce, manage, manipulate, marshal, motivate, officiate, originate, oversee, persuade, pilot, pioneer, precede, predominate, preside, prevail upon, prompt, regulate, rule, run, show the way, steer, superintend

ASSOCIATED CONCEPTS: leading questions, leading the witness

LEAD COUNSEL, noun   advocate in charge, commanding counsel, controlling counsel, counsel in charge, first counsel, supervising and controlling counsel

LEADER, noun   administrator, antecedent, captain, chairman, chief, commander, controller, demagogue, director, employer, forerunner, manager, mastermind, official, overseer, pathfinder, pioneer, precursor, predecessor, principal, protagonist, ruler, shepherd, supervisor

LEADERSHIP, noun   ascendancy, authority, captaincy, chieftainship, direction, directorate, directorship, domination, first place, generalship, governorship, guidance, influence, legal power, management, mastery, paramountcy, potency, primacy, predominance, premiership, prerogative, presidency, proctorship, puissance, reign, right, seigniory, sovereignty, statesmanship, steering, superintendency, superiority, supremacy, suzerainty, sway

LEADING (Guiding), **adjective**   controlling, directing, implicational, implicative, implicatory, inferential, insinuating, insinuative, instructional, instructive, referential, regulating, steering, suggestive, supervising, supervisory
ASSOCIATED CONCEPTS: leading a witness, leading question

LEADING (Ranking first), **adjective**   beyond compare, capital, cardinal, central, chief, dominant, dominating, finest, first, foremost, greatest, main, most influential, outstanding, paramount, predominant, preeminent, prevailing, *primarius*, primary, prime, *princeps*, principal, prominent, stellar, supreme, top, topmost, unequaled, unexcelled, unmatched, unparalleled, unrivalled, unsurpassed

LEADING CASE, noun   case dispositive on a salient point, case which is dispositive of an issue, decisive case in point, greatest precedence, highest case in a circuit, highest case of precedence, milestone, most critical case in a subject area, most major case in point, number one case in the area

LEAGUE, noun   accord, affiliation, agreement, alignment, alliance, association, axis, band, bloc, cartel, club, coalition, collaboration, combination, combine, compact, complicity, concord, concordat, concurrence, confederacy, confederation, conjunction, cooperation, copartnership, corporation, covenant, deal, federation, fellowship, foedus, fusion, gang, group, guild, mutual undertaking, network, organization, pact, *pactum*, participation, partnership, pool, ring, *societas*, society, sodality, treaty, trust, understanding, unification, union

LEANING, noun   attitude, bent, bias, conviction, disposition, favor, favorable predisposition toward, favoritism, feeling, gravitation, habit, idiosyncrasy, in disequilibrium, inclinatin, liking, partiality, penchant, predisposition, predisposition toward, prejudgment, prejudice, prepossession, proclivity, proneness, propensity, readiness, stand, standpoint, susceptibility, temperament, tendency, trend, unbalanced
ASSOCIATED CONCEPTS: judge's leaning toward issuing a decision

LEAP OF FAITH, verb   blind acceptance, blind accession, blind belief, blind confidence, blind intentions, misguided trust, quantum confidence in, unjustified belief, unjustified confidence, unjustified freedom from doubt, unquestioning acceptance, unshakable trust, unwarranted conviction, unwarranted credence, unwarranted loyalty, unwarranted progression, unwarranted reliance, unwarranted trust

LEARN, verb   acquire knowledge, analyze, become knowledgeable, comprehend, concentrate on, edify, educate, enlighten, experience, gain erudition, gain information, gain knowledge, pursue knowledge, study, understand

LEARNED, adjective   accomplished, acquainted with, acroatic, apprised of, aware, bibliophilic, bookish, cognizant, conversant, *doctus,* educated, enlightened, erudite, eruditus, experienced, expert, familiar, informed, instructed, knowing, knowledgeable, lettered, literate, *litteratus,* omniscient, pansophic, pedantic, pedantical, professional, professorial, proficient, profound, recondite, sagacious, sage, sapient, scholarly, schooled, skilled, studious, versant, versed, well-educated, well-informed, well-read, well-rounded, well-taught, well-trained, widely read, wise

LEARNING, noun   acquired knowledge, acquirements, acquisition of knowledge, analysis, attainment, body of knowledge, common knowledge, comprehension, discipline, edification, education, enlightenment, erudition, experience, extensive knowledge, information, instruction, mental cultivation, pedantry, practical learning, proficiency, pursuit of knowledge, quest, recall, recalling, recollection, remembering, remembrance, sagaciousness, sagacity, science, search, study

LEASE, noun   agreement, *conductio*, contract, contract for exclusive possession of lands, contract for possession and profits, conveyance in consideration of recompense, conveyance of interest in real property, conveyance of land for a designated period, grant, grant of realty, grant of use and possession, instrument, instrument granting possession of premises, legal agreement, permission to rent, tenant-landlord agreement, written agreement
ASSOCIATED CONCEPTS: assignment of lease, building lease, cancellation of a lease, concurrent lease, divisible lease, forfeiture of lease, implied lease, let premises, long-term lease, option to lease, parol lease, perpetual lease, renewal of lease, rent, sublease, term of lease, termination of lease, voidable lease

LEASE, verb   allow the use of, charter, contract for exclusive possession, contract for possession of land, contract for use and occupation, convey for a designated period, convey real property for a specified period, demise, engage, engage premises for a designated period, grant exclusive possession for a designated period, grant use and possession, lend on security, let, let premises for a designated period, *locare*, rent, rent out, sublet, subrent
ASSOCIATED CONCEPTS: assignment of a lease, cancellation of a lease, commencement of a lease, extension of a lease, forfeiture of a lease, joint lease, lease at will, lease for years, lease of premises, month to month tenancy, perpetual lease, renewable lease, sublease, tenacy, tenacy at sufferance, tenacy at will, term of a lease, termination of a lease, voidable lease

LEASEHOLD, noun   estate for a fixed term, estate for a fixed term of years, estate in realty, freehold, interest in real estate, interest of a lessee, land held by lease, land leased, property leased, real property subject to a lease, tenure by lease

LEAST (Inadequate), **adjective**   beneath, deficient, imperfect, incompetent, inferior, insufficient, lowest, mediocre, poorest

LEAST (Insignificant), **adjective**   bottom number of, fewest, infinitesimally low, littlest, lowest, microscopically small, minimal, minute, minutest, most trivial, next to nothing, slightest, small, smallest, trivial

LEAVE (Absence), **noun**   absentation, break, *commeatus*, departure, freedom from duty, furlough, holiday, inactivity, interlude, intermission, interval of rest, leisure, liberty, non-appearance, nonattendance, parting, pause, recess, recreation time, relaxation, removal, repose, respite, rest, retirement, retreat, suspension of work, vacation
ASSOCIATED CONCEPTS: leave of absence, sick leave

LEAVE (Permission), **noun**   accordance, acquiescence, agreement, allowance, approbation, approval, assent, authorization, certification, concurrence, consent, countenance, dispensation, endorsement, exemption, favor, grace, grant, imprimatur, indorsement, indulgence, legalization, liberty, license, *licentia, permissio,* permittance, sanction, sufferance, tolerance, vouchsafement, warrant
ASSOCIATED CONCEPTS: leave of court

LEAVE (Allow to remain), **verb**   cease, deposit, desist, discard, disuse, drop, forbear, forget, give up, let be, let continue, let go, let stand, neglect, permit, relinquish, renounce, repudiate, set aside, shun, stop, supersede, surrender, suspend, waive
ASSOCIATED CONCEPTS: leave no issue, leave the scene of an accident

LEAVE (Depart), **verb**   abandon, abdicate, abjure, abscond, be off, bid farewell, break away, decamp, defect, desert, disappear, *discedere,* drop out, embark, emigrate, escape, evacuate, *excedere,* exit, flee, fly, forsake, go, go away, go forth, migrate, move on, part, *proficisci,* pull out, quit, resign, retire, retreat, run away, secede, set out, slip away, take leave, tergiversate, vacate, vanish, withdraw

LEAVE (Give), **verb**   accord, allot, apportion, assign, award, bequeath, bestow, confer, consign, demise, devise, donate, endow, entrust, give by will, grant, hand down, impart, *legare,* make a bequest, make a testamentary disposition, present, *relinquere,* settle upon, transmit, will

LEAVE A LEGACY (Accomplish), **verb**   bring about, consummate, dedicate, enrich, fulfill, make a contribution to society, minister, pass down, realize, redound to, succeed

LEAVE A LEGACY (Bequeath), **verb**   allot, assign, bestow, demise, descend, devise, dispense, donate, endow, entrust, give, hand down, leave, leave by will, make a bequest, pass on, transmit by will, will, will to
ASSOCIATED CONCEPTS: bequeaths and devises, estates, gifts, wills

LEAVE A WILL, verb   compose a will, draw up a testament, prepare a last will and testament, prepare a testament, prepare an instrument, produce an instrument, write a document, write a testament

LECHEROUS, adjective   addicted to lewdness, bawdy, concupiscent, corrupt, debauched, depraved, desirous, dissipated, dissolute, erotic, erotical, fleshly, gluttonous, goatish, immoral, inclined to lewdness, lascivious, lewd, libertine, libidinous, licentious, lickerish, loose, lubric, lubricous, lustful, profligate, prurient, rakish, reprobate, ruttish, salacious, sexually indulgent, unbridled, unchaste, unregenerate, unrestrained, unspiritual, wanton

LECTURE (Speak), **verb**   address, comment, deliver an address, discuss, elucidate, give a talk on, instruction, prepare comments, prepare a disclosure on, present, present information on, remonstrate, speak on, talk on, teach
ASSOCIATED CONCEPTS: continuing legal education

LECTURE, (Admonish), **verb**   berate, chide, correction, discipline, dress down, excoriate, harangue, rebuke, remonstrate, reprimand, reproach, scold, teach, teach an example to, tear into, tongue-lash, upbraid

LEDGER, noun   account book, account of transactions, accounts, balance sheet, bankbook, book of accounts, book of records, books, calculation, cashbook, *codex accepti et expensi,* computation, daybook, diary, entries, file, index, log, logbook, passbook, profit and loss statement, record, record book, record of credits and debits, record of money transactions, register, registry, running account, statement

LEERY, adjective   afraid, apprehensive, careful, cautious, chary, circumspect, distrustful, doubtful, doubting, dubious, entertaining suspicion, frightened, guarded, heedful, hesitant, hesitating, in doubt, mistrustful, questioning, shy of, skeptical, suspect, suspecting, suspicious, unbelieving, uncertain, unconvinced, unsure, vigilant, wary, watchful, without belief, without faith

LEEWAY, noun   allowance, breathing room, breathing space, deviation, elbowroom, extra room, freedom, headroom, indulgence, latitude, liberty, license, margin, room to maneuver, room to move, room to operate, room to spare, slack, some play, space
ASSOCIATED CONCEPTS: federal sentencing guidelines, mandates

LEFT (Direction), **adjective**   left hand, left-hand side, left side, leftward, near, on the other side, over there, port, portside

LEFT (Liberal), **adjective**   communalistic, communistic, leftist leanings, leftwing, liberal, progressive, radical, revolutionary, socialistic

LEFT (Remaining), **adjective**   balance, continuing, extra, leftover, over, spare, staying, surplus, surplusage
ASSOCIATED CONCEPTS: no child left behind, remainder

LEFTOVER, noun   balance, carry-over, excess, extra, overage, remainder, remaining, remnants, residual, residue, residuum, rest, surplus, unused

LEGACY, noun   bequeathal, bequest, bestowal, conferment, dispensation, disposition, disposition of personalty, dotation, endowment, gift by will, gift of property by will, grant, heritance, impartment, inheritance, *legatum,* testamentary gift
ASSOCIATED CONCEPTS: absolute legacy, alternate legacy, charitable legacy, conditional legacy, contingent legacy, cumulative legacy, demonstrative legacy, general legacy, indefinite legacy, lapsed legacy, pecuniary legacy, residuary legacy, special legacy, specific legacy

LEGAL, adjective   according to the law, allowable, allowed, approved, authorized, authorized by law, cognizable in courts of law, constitutional, decreed, enforceable in a court of law, established by law, good and effectual in law, governed by law, in conformity with law, lawful, legalized, legitimate, *legitimus,* licit, permissible, permitted by law, prescribed, prescribed by law, proper, *quod ex lege,* recognized by the law, required by law, rightful, sanctioned, *secundum leges fit,* statutory, sufficient in law, valid, warranted, within the law
ASSOCIATED CONCEPTS: legal action, legal age, legal arrest, legal beneficiaries, legal capacity to sue, legal cause, legal claim, legal consideration, legal damages, legal detriment,

legal disability, legal duty, legal entity, legal heir, legal notice, legal obligation, legal presumption, legal proceedings, legal process, legal remedy, legal representative, legal tender, legal title

FOREIGN PHRASES: *Id possumus quod de jure possumus.* We may do only that which we are able to do lawfully.

LEGAL ACTION, *noun* action, action at law, cause, controversy, instituted proceedings, judicial proceedings, judicial recourse, lawsuit, legal process, legal recourse, litigation, matter, proceeding, process, prosecution, suit, suit in law

LEGAL AGREEMENT, *noun* binding agreement, binding compact, binding contract, formal conveyance of interest, formal document, understanding

LEGAL ARGUMENT, *noun* affirmation, allegation, argument, asseveration, attestation, belief, cause of action, claim, counter argument, course of reasoning, declaration, defending of a cause by argument, defense, defensive measures, doctrine, insistence on a right or claim, issue, justification, philosophy, pleading, position, positive declaration or statement, statement, statement offered in proof

LEGAL ASSISTANT, *noun* assistant, contract paralegal, freelance paralegal, independent paralegal, law assistant, legal document assistant, legal technician, paralegal, traditional paralegal

LEGAL CLAIM, *noun* action, allegation, bill of complaint, complaint, declaration, demand, lawsuit, legal process, right, suit, summons

ASSOCIATED CONCEPTS: affirmative defenses, counterclaim, cross-claims, defenses

LEGAL DISPUTE, *noun* action, action at law, action in court, aggressive argument, case, challenge in the courts, claim, conflict, confutation, contention, controversy, court action, disputation, field action, judicial contest, lawsuit, legal action, legal challenge, legal clash, legal contest, legal disagreement, legal feud, legal proceeding, litigation, proceeding, suit at law, suit in law, trial

ASSOCIATED CONCEPTS: dispute resolution

LEGAL DOCUMENTS, *noun* evidentiary records, exhibits, legal evidence, legal instruments, legal materials, legal papers, legal proof, legal record, legal reports, legally written materials, papers, recorded material, verifications

ASSOCIATED CONCEPTS: discovery, document management, legal forms, legal research

LEGAL EVIDENCE, *noun* admitted testimony, body of facts on which belief is based, circumstances in a case, confirmation, corroboration, document, documentation, documents, documents which tends to prove, exhibit, exhibits submitted to jury, facts, facts admitted at trial, facts judicially noted, facts which bear on the point in question, facts which establish the point in issue, factual matter, ground of proof, grounds for belief, instrument of proof, legal proof, legal validation, legal verification, matter legally submitted to the jury, matters of fact, means of proof, means of proving a fact, medium of proof, persuasive facts, proof legally presented at trial, proof of facts, record, relevant fact, relevant material, substantiation, testimony which furnishes proof

ASSOCIATED CONCEPTS: demonstrative evidence, digital evidence, documentary evidence, exculpatory evidence, physical evidence, rules of evidence, scientific evidence, testimony

LEGAL EXPERT, *noun* authority, experienced, expert witness, highly qualified individual, highly technical specialist, leading authority in the field, legal scholar, professional authority, qualified professional, scholar, specialist, specially trained person, technician, well-known authority

ASSOCIATED CONCEPTS: forensic witness, legal consultant

LEGAL DISPUTE, *noun* action, action at law, action in court, aggressive argument, case, challenge in the courts, claim, conflict, confutation, contention, controversy, court action, disputation, filed action, judicial contest, lawsuit, legal action, legal challenge, legal clash, legal contest, legal disagreement, legal feud, legal proceeding, litigation, proceeding, suit at law, suit in law, trial

ASSOCIATED CONCEPTS: dispute resolution

LEGAL ISSUE, *noun* affirmation, allegation, argument, asseveration, cause, concern arising from law, counter argument, debatable point, declaration, disputed point of law, disputed question, fact put in controversy by the pleadings, field of inquiry, finer legal pint, finer point of law, item, insistence on a right or claim, justification, legal contention, legal question, legality, material point, material point educed from the pleadings, matter, matter in hand, matter in question, matter of contention, overriding question to be researched, overriding question to be resolved, point, point in question, point of contention, position, positive declaration, positive statement, problem, question at issue, question of law, sticking point, subject for inquiry

ASSOCIATED CONCEPTS: issue named in a will

LEGAL PRACTITIONER, *noun* advocate, attorney, attorney-at-law, barrister, counsel, counselor, counselor-at-law, Juris Doctor, lawyer, legal professional, member of the bar, practitioner, professional, solicitor, specialist

LEGAL PRECEDENT, *noun* authoritative decision, authoritative principle of law, case law, controlling law, decree, established doctrine, legal doctrine, model, paradigm, ruling, standard

LEGAL PROCEEDING, *noun* action, action at law, case, cause, controversy, instituted proceedings, judicial recourse, lawsuit, legal process, legal recourse, litigation, matter, proceedings, suit

LEGAL PROCESS, *noun* summons, summons for a case, summons for a cause in court, summons for a controversy before a court, summons for a court action, summons for a judicial contest, summons for a legal action, summons for a legal contest, summons for a legal controversy, summons for a legal dispute, summons for a trial, summons for an action, summons for an action at law, summons for legal proceedings, summons for litigation, summons for suit at law, writ

ASSOCIATED CONCEPTS: means to compel attendance

LEGAL RECOURSE, *noun* action, action at law, case, case for decision, cause in court, claim, contention, contest, controversy, controversy before a court, court action, court proceedings, dispute, judicial contest, legal action, legal argument, legal contest, legal controversy, legal dispute, legal proceedings, litigation, matter for judgment, proceeding, suit at law, suit in equity, trial

LEGAL REPRESENTATIVE, *noun* administrator, adminstratrix, appointed representative, attorney-at-law, authorized individual, authorized representative, executor, executrix,

legal agent, legal proxy, legal spokesman, legal substitute, professional representative
ASSOCIATED CONCEPTS: personal representative

LEGAL RIGHT, noun authority, authorization, cause, claim, empowerment, entitlement, freedom, inalienable right, just claim, legitimate right, license, power, prerogative, vested right or interest
ASSOCIATED CONCEPTS: due process, freedom of the press, free speech, right against self-incrimination, right to assemble, right to petition

LEGALESE, noun language of the law, lawyer's language, legal language, legal parlance, legal usage, legal writing, the legal profession's language

LEGALISM (Conservative meaning of the law), noun according to the letter of the law, by the strict letter of the law, chapter and verse of, conforming precisely to the law, conservative interpretation, exactly according to the law, literal interpretation of the law, orthodox interpretation of the law, precise interpretation of the law, strict interpretation of the law

LEGALISM (Legalese), noun abstruse language, bloated wording, bombastic wording, complex legalese, convoluted wording, grandiloquent language, inflated wording, legal jargon complexities, long winded jargon, orotund language, ostentatious wording, pedantic verbiage, pompous wording, sophisticated legal term, sophisticated legal verbiage, swollen wording, technical language, technical term, technical wording, turgid wording
ASSOCIATED CONCEPTS: legal term, legal verbiage, technical language, technical term

LEGALITY, noun accordance with law, allowableness, authorization, conformity to law, conformity with the law, constitutionality, lawfulness, legalism, legitimacy, legitimateness, permissibleness, rightfulness, sanction, sanctionableness, validity, warrantableness
ASSOCIATED CONCEPTS: legality of consideration, legality of contract, legality of obligation, legality of purpose

LEGALIZATION, noun affirmation, approval, authorization, codification, confirmation, legislative sanction, legitimatization, passing into law, ratification, regulation by statute, sanction, validation

LEGALIZE, verb approve, authorize, bring into conformity with law, confirm, confirm by law, decree by law, enact by law, ferre, legislate, legitimate, legitimatize, make lawful, make legal, order by law, permit by law, pronounce legal, sanction, sanction by law, validate

LEGALLY BINDING, adjective compulsory, controlled for, controlling, effective, enforceable, final, fully executed, governing, has legal effect, has legal force, imperative, in effect, legally adopted, legally committed, legally compelled, legitimate, mandatory, necessary, obligated for, obligatory, operative, prescribed, required, signed, valid, validated
ASSOCIATED CONCEPTS: contracts, instrument, marriage

LEGALLY ENFORCEABLE, adjective authoritative, authorized, binding, compelling, compulsory, decreed valid, effective, established, formulate, has legal effect, has legal force, imposed, in effect, legally binding, legitimate, legitimatized, licensed, mandated, mandatory, necessary, operative, ordained, prescribed, put into force, put into operation, put into practice, required, sanctioned, valid, validated, warranted
ASSOCIATED CONCEPTS: legally enforceable rights

LEGALLY IN FORCE, adjective compulsory, controlled for, controlling, effective, enforceable, final, fully executed, governing, has legal effect, has legal force, imperative, in effect, legally adopted, legally binding, legally committed, legally compelled, legitimate, mandatory, necessary, obligated for, obligatory, operative, prescribed, required, signed, valid, validated
ASSOCIATED CONCEPTS: contracts, instrument, marriage

LEGATEE, noun beneficiary, devisee, distributee, donee, feoffee, grantee, heir apparent, heir at law, heiress, inheritor, legal heir, legatary, one who inherits, recipient, transferee
ASSOCIATED CONCEPTS: pecuniary legatee, remainderman, residuary legatee, sole legatee, specific legatee

LEGEND (Fable), noun adventure, chronicle, epic, epos, fable, fantasy, fiction, folklore, lore, myth, mythology, odyssey, romance, saga, story, tale, tradition, yarn

LEGEND (Inscription), noun abstract, annotation, brief, caption, chronicle, cipher, compendium, device, epitaph, heading, imprint, impression, narrative, record, rubric, superscription

LEGENDARY (Famous), adjective acclaimed, celebrated, distinguished, eminent, epic, esteemed, exalted, fabled, famed, famous, heroic, illustrious, memorable, notable, outstanding, renowned

LEGENDARY (Fictitious), adjective apocryphal, fabled, fanciful, fictional, figmental, idealistic, imagined, mythological, storied, uncanonical, unhistorical, unwritten

LEGISLATE, verb authorize, codify, constituere, create by law, decree, dictate, effect, enact, enact laws, establish, establish by law, exercise the function of legislation, formulate, institute, leges facere, make into law, make laws, make legal, order, originate, pass, pass laws, prescribe laws, put in force, rule, sanction, scribere, vote in

LEGISLATION (Enactments), noun acts, bills, body of laws enacted, canon, canons, codes, dictates, laws, measures, ordinances, prescripts, provisions of a law, regulations, rulings, statutes

LEGISLATION (Lawmaking), noun codification of laws, enacting laws, formulating rules for the future, legislative process, preparation of laws
FOREIGN PHRASES: **Leges figendi et refigendi consuetudo est periculosissima.** The practice of making and remaking the laws is a most dangerous one. **Jura eodem modo destituuntur quo constituuntur.** Laws are abrogated by the same means by which they are enacted. **Legislatorum est viva vox, rebus et non verbis, legem imponere.** The voice of the legislators is the living voice, to impose laws upon things, and not on words. **Neque leges neque senatus consulta ita scribi possunt ut omnis casus qui quandoque in sediriunt comprehendatur; sed sufficit ea quae plaerumque accidunt contineri.** Neither laws nor acts of a legislature can be so written as to include all actual or possible cases; it is sufficient if they provide for those things which frequently or ordinarily may happen.

LEGISLATIVE, adjective congressional, decreeing, enacting, lawgiving, lawmaking, legislating, ordained by legislation, ordaining, prescriptive, statutory
ASSOCIATED CONCEPTS: legislative enactment

369

LEGISLATIVE DECREE, noun act, article, canon, chapter of law, code, legislative command, legislative enactment, legislative established law, legislative fiat, legislative initiative, legislative law, legislative legal code, legislative mandate, legislative maxim, legislative order, legislative ordinance, legislative precedent, legislative precept, legislative prescription, legislative principle, legislative pronouncement, legislative rule, legislative sanction, legislative set of rules, legislative standard, legislative statute, legislative tenet

LEGISLATIVE ENACTMENT, noun canon, code, codification, codified law, dictate, edict, enactment, law, legal code, legislation, mandate, measure, order, ordinance, provision of the law, regulation, rubric, statute, written law

LEGISLATIVE MANDATE, noun legislative command, legislative decree, legislative directive, legislative fiat, legislative forced imperatives, legislative imposed standards, legislative order, legislative pronouncement, legislative rule, legislative tenet
ASSOCIATED CONCEPTS: unfunded mandates

LEGISLATOR, noun congressman, lawgiver, lawmaker, member of a governmental body, member of a legislative body, member of parliament, officer of state, official representative, one who formulates laws, one who gives or makes laws, one who helps to pass laws, parliamentarian, politician, public servant, representative, senator

LEGISLATURE, noun assembly, body of persons who formulate laws, congress, house of representatives, lawmaking body, law-making branch of government, lawgivers, lawmakers, legislative body, parliament, senate

LEGITIMACY, noun authorization, conformity to law, genuineness, justifiability, lawfulness, legality, legitimateness, legitimation, legitimization, licitness, originality, permissibility, realness, rightfulness, soundness, validity
ASSOCIATED CONCEPTS: illegitimacy, paternity proceeding
FOREIGN PHRASES: *Semper praesumitur pro legitimatione puerorum.* The presumption always is in favor of the legitimacy of children. *Cum legitimae nuptiae factae sunt, patrem liberi sequuntur.* Children of a lawful marriage follow the condition of the father. *Praesumitur pro legitimatione.* There is a presumption in favor of legitimacy. *Non est justum aliquem antenatum post mortem facere bastardum qui toto tempore vitae suae pro legitimo habebatur.* It is not just to make anyone a bastard after death, who during his lifetime was regarded as legitimate. *Pater est quem nuptiae demonstrant.* He is the father whom the marriage points out.

LEGITIMATE *(Lawfully conceived),* **adjective** born in wedlock, born of parents legally married, conceived of parents legally married, natural, of lawful parentage, sired in wedlock
ASSOCIATED CONCEPTS: legitimate issue

LEGITIMATE *(Rightful),* **adjective** according to law, allowed, authorized, constitutional, enacted, genuine, in accordance with law, in accordance with legal provisions, juristic, law-abiding, lawful, legal, legalized, legislated, licensed, licit, mandated, official, real, recognized by law, rightful, sanctioned, sanctioned by custom, sanctioned by law, sanctioned by legal authority, sound, statutable, statutory, valid, well-founded, well-grounded, within the law
ASSOCIATED CONCEPTS: legitimate business, legitimate heirs, legitimate purpose, legitimate title

LEGITIMATE, verb approve, authorize, certify, declare lawful, legalize, legitimatize, make lawful, make legal, make legitimate, sanction, validate

LEGITIMIZE, verb authorize, confirm, constitute, declare lawful, enact, legalize, legitimate, make legal, make legitimate, make proper, pass, ratify, sanction, validate

LEND, verb accommodate with, advance, afford, aid, allow credit, assist, *commodare,* entrust, extend credit, finance, furnish, furnish credit, give, give credit, give money over, grant, invest, loan, permit to borrow, provide, provide with, put up the money, sign over, supply, supply aid, turn over
ASSOCIATED CONCEPTS: lend credit, lend funds

LENGTH, noun breadth, continuance, dimension, distance, distance lengthwise, elongation, expanse, expansion, extensiveness, extent, lengthiness, limit, long-windedness, magnitude, measure, measurement, proportion, range, reach, size, span, stretch
ASSOCIATED CONCEPTS: length of memoranda of law, term limit

LENGTHEN, verb add to, aggrandize, amplify, augment, compound, continue, draw out, elongate, enlarge, enlarge upon, expand, extend, increase, keep, make larger, project, prolong, prolongate, protract, spin out, spread, stretch, supplement, sustain, temporize

LENGTHY *(Prolix),* **adjective** digressive, discursive, garrulous, long-winded, loquacious, talky, verbose

LENGTHY *(Prolonged),* **adjective** elongated, extensive, far-reaching, gaunt, lengthened, made to last, prosy, protracted, rangy, sesquipedalian, spare, sustained

LENGTHY *(Tedious),* **adjective** accented, boring, desultory, diffuse, drawn-out, elongated, endless, errant, extended, interminable, long-spun, roving, spun out, tiresome, wearisome, wordy

LENIENCE, noun acceptance, benevolence, charity, clemency, compassion, condonation, consideration, disposition to mercy, endurance, favor, flexibility, forbearance, forgiveness, forgivingness, freedom from vindictiveness, generousness, gentleness, grace, humanity, indulgence, kindness, lack of strictness, leniency, lenity, liberality, longanimity, mercifulness, mercy, mildness, moderation, pampering, patience, pity, placability, placableness, quarter, ruth, softheartedness, softness, sympathy, tolerance, toleration, understanding

LENIENCY, noun allowance, benevolence, charitableness, compassion, compassionateness, condonation, condoning, considerateness, easiness, easygoingness, endurance, forbearance, forgiveness, generosity, generousness, humaneness, humanity, indulgence, kindheartedness, kindness, lenience, liberality, liberalness, mercifulness, mercy, mildness, moderateness, moderation, pardon, patience, permissiveness, sympathy, temperance, temperateness, tolerance, willingness to forgive, yielding
ASSOCIATED CONCEPTS: leniency delays, leniency law, leniency policies, sentencing

LENIENT, noun allowing, benevolent, charitable, *clemens,* clement, compassionate, condoning, considerate, easy, easygoing, enduring, exorable, favoring, forbearing, forgiving, free from vindictiveness, generous, gentle, humane, humoring, indulgent, indulging, kind, kindhearted, *lenis,* liberal, long-suffering, longanimous, magnanimous, merciful, mild, *mitis,* moderate, pampering, pardoning, patient, pitying, placable, soft, softhearted, sparing, sympathetic, tolerant, undemanding, unstrict, willing to forgive, yielding

FOREIGN PHRASES: *Cum confitente sponte mitius est agendum.* One confessing voluntarily should be dealt with more leniently.

LESS *(Fewer),* **adjective**   a decreased number, a limited number, a reduced number, a restricted number of, a smaller number, curtailed, cutback, diluted, diminished, fewer, hardly any, in decline, lessened, lesser, limited, little, minus, not as many, not as much, pared down, reduced, slighter, smaller
ASSOCIATED CONCEPTS: concise legal writing, plain language

LESS *(Inferior),* **adjective**   attenuated, belittled, beneath, circumscribed, curtailed, cutback, declined, decreased, deemphasized, deficient, deflated, depressed, diluted, diminished, dissipated, downplayed, dropped, eroded, fallen, in decline, inferior, insignificant, junior, lessened, lesser, limited, lower, lowered, mediocre, minimized, minor, pared down, reduced, retrenched, scaled-down, secondary, second-rate, subordinate, watered-down, weakened

LESSEE, *noun*   boarder, *conductor,* holder of an estate by virtue of a lease, leaseholder, lodger, occupant, occupier, person in possession, possessor, property holder, rent payer, rentee, renter, resident, roomer, tenant

LESSEN, *verb*   abate, abbreviate, abridge, abstract, adulterate, allay, alleviate, assuage, attenuate, bate, belittle, boil down, calumniate, censure, check, compress, condense, contract, curb, curtail, cut, cut down, decimate, decline, decrease, decry, deduct, defame, deflate, degenerate, deliquesce, *deminuere,* deplete, depreciate, dequantitate, deride, derogate, deteriorate, detract, devaluate, die away, dilute, diminish, discommend, discount, discredit, disparage, dispraise, disvalue, dock, drop off, dull, dwarf, dwindle, ease, ebb, erode, evaporate, extenuate, *imminuere,* let up, lighten, lower, malign, melt away, minify, minimize, mitigate, moderate, modulate, palliate, pare, qualify, reduce, remit, run down, set at naught, shorten, shrink, slacken, slight, soothe, speak slightingly, stigmatize, stunt, subside, subtract, summarize, take away, taper, temper, thin, thin out, traduce, trim, underestimate, underrate, undervalue, vilify, vilipend, wane, waste away, water down, weaken, wear away, weed out

LESSEN IN VALUE, *verb*   abate, curtail, cut, decline, decrease, deflate, depreciate, depress, diminish, dropping, dwindling, eroding, lower, reduce, shrink, subside, wane
ASSOCIATED CONCEPTS: depreciation, residual value insurance

LESSER, *adjective*   ancillary, baser, diminished, humbler, inferior, junior, less considerable, lower, mediocre, minor, more modest, secondary, second-rate, shorter, simpler, slighter, smaller, subaltern, subordinate, subservient, under, unimportant
ASSOCIATED CONCEPTS: lesser charge, lesser included offense

LESSON *(Castigation),* **noun**   admonishment, censure, chastening, chastisement, chiding, correction, denunciation, disciplinary measure, discipline, infliction, punishment, punition, rebuke, reprimand, reproach, reproof, scolding, tongue-lashing, upbraiding

LESSON *(Example),* **noun**   advice, archetype, education, exemplary, gold standard, good example, ideal, illustration, instruction, learning experience, lecture, maxim, model, moral fable, noble action, paragon, preachment, precedent, precept, prototype, schooling, sermon, shining example, standard, teaching

LESSOR, *noun*   business owner, landlord, owner, property owner

LET *(Lease),* **verb**   allow the use of, charter, contract, convey, demise, grant, grant the occupancy of, hire, hire out, lend, loan, make available, rent, rent out

LET *(Permit),* **verb**   affranchise, allow, approve, assent, authorize, certify, commission, concede, *concedere,* consent, empower, enable, endorse, enfranchise, entitle, entrust, favor, franchise, give leave, give permission, grant, have no objection, indulge, liberate, license, make possible, oblige, *pati,* privilege, release, sanction, *sinere,* suffer, support, tolerate, vouchsafe, warrant, yield

LET DOWN *(Disappointing outcome),* **noun**   dash one's hopes, defeat one's expectations, disappointment, disconcertedness, disenchantment, disgruntlement, disheartenment, disillusionment, dissatisfaction, failure, failure to live up to expectations, fall, fallen short, feelings of failure, frustration, thwarted hopes

LET DOWN *(Rest),* **noun**   abatement, allayment, alleviation, diminution, drugging, easing, lessening, let up, lightening, loosening, mitigation, reduction, relaxation, relenting, slackening, slacking off

LET GO, *verb*   abandon, cede, clear, disband, discharge, do away with, free, give up, leave, leave hold of, liberate, release, relinquish, remit, surrender, terminate, yield, yield control of
ASSOCIATED CONCEPTS: release from bailment, release from custody

LET OUT *(Disclose),* **verb**   air, bare, break the news, communicated, divulge, expose, express audibly, impart, leak, let slip out, make known, remove the veil, reveal, shine light on, slip, take the lid off, take the wraps off, tell, uncloak, uncover, unfold, unfurl, unmask, unveil, unwrap, utter sounds
ASSOCIATED CONCEPTS: confidentiality, off officials, privilege

LET OUT *(Release),* **verb**   deliver, demobilize, discharge, dismiss, free, let go, let go free, let loose, let off, let out on bail, pardon, parole, release from custody, release from prison, unbridle, unchain, unfetter, unharness, unlatch, unleash, unlock, unshackle
ASSOCIATED CONCEPTS: appeal, habeas corpus

LET STAND, *verb*   affirm, approve, assent to, back, certify, confirm, consent to, corroborate, defend, endorse, establish, fortify, ratify, reaffirm, reinforce, sanction, substantiate, support, sustain, uphold, validate, verify, vindicate
ASSOCIATED CONCEPTS: let stand a ruling, let stand a verdict, let stand an award

LETHAL, *adjective*   annihilative, baleful, baneful, dangerous, deadly, death-bringing, death-dealing, deathly, destructive, evil, *exitialis,* fatal, fell, feral, *funestus,* harmful, hurtful, injurious, internecine, internecive, killing, lethiferous, malefic, maleficent, maleficial, malign, malignant, mortal, *mortifer,* mortiferous, murderous, nocent, nocuous, noxious, pernicious, pestiferous, pestilent, pestilential, poisonous, slaughtering, toxic, toxiferous, unhealthy, venomous, virulent
ASSOCIATED CONCEPTS: lethal weapon

LETTER OF CREDIT, *noun* credit account, credit note, guaranty, negotiable instrument, paper credit, security
ASSOCIATED CONCEPTS: financial guarantee, letter of delegation, letter of exchange, letter of introduction, letter of license, letters testamentary

LETTER OF THE LAW, *noun* according to the letter, an orthodox interpretation, by chapter and verse, conservative interpretation, exact words of the law, exactly as written, literal interpretation, literally interpreted, perfectly as written, precise interpretation, precisely as written, strict construction, strict interpretation
ASSOCIATED CONCEPTS: respecting the spirit and letter of the law

LEVEL *(Balance),* *noun* aligned, equal, equal on a plane, even, exact, in the same plane, matched, of the same height, same, standard, straight, uniform

LEVEL *(Grade),* *noun* advanced status, class, freshman, graduate, junior, lowerclassmen, program, senior, seniority, sophomore, status, underclassman, undergraduate, upperclassman, year, year of graduation, year of studies

LEVEL *(Plane),* *noun* bank, deep slope, distance upward, easy slope, elevation, equal, exact, flat, flat surface, flattened, flush, grade, gradient, inclination, incline, inclined plane, on a line, parallel, pitch, slope, steep slope

LEVERAGE, *noun* advantage, force, influence, potency, pressure, purchase, vantage

LEVIED, *adjective* assessed, attached, collected, commandeered, confiscated, conscripted, drafted, exacted, excised, extorted, imposed as an assessment, put a duty on, recruited, seized, taken by force, take possession of, taxed, tolled

LEVY, *noun* assessment, attachment, collection, confiscation, duty, exaction, exactment, excise, gathering, impost, impressment, seizure, setting aside of specific property, tariff, tax, taxation, toll

LEVY, *verb* affix, assess, attach, charge, collect, confiscate, conscript, demand, disseise, distrain, divest, enlist, exact, execute, force, garnish, gather, impose, inflict, lay on, muster, place, put on, raise, require, seize, set, take by force, take up, tax, usurp, wrest
ASSOCIATED CONCEPTS: levy a tax, levy an assessment, wrongful levy

LEWD, *adjective* bawdy, carnal, concupiscent, corrupt, depraved, dissolute, exhibiting lust, immodest, immoral, *impudicus,* impure, *impurus, incestus,* indecent, indelicate, lascivious, lecherous, libertine, libidinous, licentious, lubricous, lustful, morally impure, morally unrestrained, obscene, offensive, pornographic, profligate, prurient, publicly indecent, questionable, reprobate, ribald, risque, ruttish, rutty, salacious, scandalous, scarlet, scurrilous, sexually impure, sexually indecent, shameless, suggestive, unchaste, unclean, unvirtuous, vulgar, wanton
ASSOCIATED CONCEPTS: lewd and lascivious cohabitation, obscenity

LEX LOCI, *noun* enactment in the area, firm principles in the area, law of the locale, law of the locality, law of the region, legal code in the local area, local law, settled principles in the area, the law in the area, the law of the circuit, the law of the judicial circuit, the law of the place, the law of the site, the law of the territory, the law of the vicinity, the law of the zone
ASSOCIATED CONCEPTS: choice of law, domicile, forum selection, lex domicilii, lex loci arbitri, lex loci celebrations in marriage, lex loci contractus, lex loci delicti commissi, lex situs, lex tori
FOREIGN PHRASES: *Lex loci actus.* The law of the location where the act was done.

LIABILITY, *noun* accountability, accountableness, amenability, amenableness, answerability, aptness, bounden duty, burden, contract obligation, debit, debt, disadvantage, drawback, due, duty, duty to pay, encumbrance, handicap, hindrance, indebtedness, legal obligation, legal responsibility, obligation, onus, proclivity, proneness, responsibility, unliquidated claim, vulnerability
ASSOCIATED CONCEPTS: absolute liability, admission of liability, civil liability, contingent liability, criminal liability, denial of liability, existing liability, fixed liability, incurring a liability, joint liability, known liability, legal liability, liability imposed by law, liability insurance, liability without fault, limited liability, manufacturer's liability, original liability, pecuniary liability, potential liability, primary liability, secondary liability, several liability, statutory liability, strict liability, tort liability
FOREIGN PHRASES: *Quando de una et eadem re duo onerabiles existunt, unus pro insufficientia alterius, de integro, onerabitur.* When two persons are chargeable with one and the same thing, one of them is chargeable with the whole thing, upon the failure of the other.

LIABLE, *adjective* accountable, amenable, answerable, bound in equity, bound in law, bound to, bound to respond, chargeable, exposed to, exposed to penalty, in danger, justly responsible, legally bound, legally responsible, obligated, obliged, obliged in law, *obnoxius,* responsible, subject to, susceptible, under legal obligation, under obligation, vulnerable
ASSOCIATED CONCEPTS: jointly liable, liable for debts, liable in tort, liable to forfeiture, liable to penalty, liable to prosecution, liable to punishment, party liable, personally liable, secondarily liable

LIAISON, *noun* administrator, agent, bond, connection, contact, delegate, deputy, emissary, envoy, go-between, interagent, intercessor, intermediary, intermedium, lieutenant, link, linkage, manger, mediating agency, mediator, messenger, negotiant, negotiator, nexus, representative, spokesman, spokesperson, substitute, tie

LIBEL, *noun* accusation, aspersion, calumny, *carmen famosum,* censorious writing, defamation, defamatory writing, degradation, denigration, denunciation, disparagement, false accusation, false publication, false statement, falsehood, falseness, falsification, impairment of reputation, impeachment of virtue, injury to character, injury to one's reputation, invective, *libellus famosus,* malicious defamation, malicious falsehood, malicious publication, revilement, slur, smear, vilification, writing that discredits, written accusation
ASSOCIATED CONCEPTS: actionable libel, libel per quod, libel per se, publication of libel, slander

LIBEL, *verb* accuse falsely, accuse in writing, asperse, besmirch, calumniate, censure, condemn, debase, decry, defame, defame by a published writing, degrade, denigrate, denounce, derogate, discredit, discredit in writing, disparage, expose to public contempt, impair one's reputation, incriminate, injure another's reputation, injure by a published writing, injure one's reputation, maliciously defame, malign, publish a falsehood, revile, ridicule, scandalize, slander, slur, smear, traduce, vilify

ASSOCIATED CONCEPTS: absolute privilege, actionable libel, actual malice, criminal libel, defamation, defense of truth, disparagement, First Amendment, libel per quod, libel per se, privileged communication, publication, qualified privileged, republication, slander, trade libel

LIBELOUS, *adjective* abusive, acrimonious, aspersive, calumnious, condemnatory, contemptuous, damaging, damnatory, defamatory, denunciatory, derogatory, detracting, detractive, discreditable, discrediting, disgracing, dishonorable, dishonoring, disparaging, false and injurious, humiliating, ignominious, ill-willed, improficient, injurious, insulting, malevolent, malicious, malignant, odious, pejorative, scandalous, scurrile, scurrilous, traducing, vilifying, vituperative

LIBERAL *(Broad minded),* *adjective* adaptable to change, advanced, emancipated, fair-minded, flexible, freethinking, impartial, *liberalis,* liberated, neutral, nonpartisan, not narrow-minded, objective, open, open-minded, progressive, receptive, tolerant, unbiased, unbigoted, uninfluenced, unopinionated, unprejudiced, unswayed

LIBERAL *(Generous),* *adjective* abundant, almsgiving, altruistic, ample, beneficent, benevolent, bounteous, bountiful, charitable, copious, free, freely giving, generous, handsome, hospitable, humane, humanitarian, lavish, magnanimous, munificent, *munificus,* openhanded, openhearted, philanthropic, plentiful, princely, prodigal, profuse, selfless, stintless, ungrudging, unselfish, unsparing, unstinting

LIBERAL *(Not literal),* *adjective* broad, enlarged, extended, free from narrowness, general, imprecise, inexact, loose, open, unprecise, unrigorous, unstrict, wide, with license

ASSOCIATED CONCEPTS: liberal construction, liberal interpretation

LIBERALITY, *noun* benefaction, beneficence, benefit, benevolence, charitableness, chivalry, clemency, generosity, generous giving, generous offering, generousness, gratuity, habit of giving, kindness, lavishness, lenience, liberal-mindedness, magnanimity, munificence, open-heartedness, philanthropy, reward, tolerance, unselfishness

LIBERATE, *verb* acquit, affranchise, bail out, deliver, discharge, disembroil, disengage, disenthrall, disimprison, dislodge, dismiss, emancipate, enfranchise, exculpate, exonerate, extract, franchise, free, give freedom, give liberty to, let go, let loose, let out, *liberare,* loose, manumit, *manumittere,* open up, pardon, parole, redeem, release, release from custody, rescue, separate, set at large, set at liberty, set free, turn loose, unbind, unchain, undo, unfasten, unfetter, unloose, unshackle, untie, vindicate

LIBERATED, *adjective* absolved, acquitted, affranchised, cleared, delivered, discharged, disengaged, emancipated, exculpated, exonerated, extricated, free, freed, liberal, pardoned, paroled, redeemed, released, sovereign, unbound, vindicated

LIBERATION, *noun* absolution, achievement of liberty, acquittal, acquittance, affranchisement, deliverance, delivery, discharge, disembroiling, disengagement, disenthrallment, disimprisonment, dislodgment, dismissal, emancipation, enfranchisement, exculpation, exoneration, franchisement, freedom, freeing, *liberatio, manumissio,* manumission,

pardon, parole, redemption, release, releasing from custody, rescue, separation, unbinding, unchaining, unfettering, unshacking, untying, vindication

LIBERTY, *noun* absence of foreign rule, absence of restraint, absence of servitude, affranchisement, autonomy, choice, clearance, deliverance, emancipation, enfranchisement, exemption from control, exemption from external control, exemption from restraint, franchise, free will, freedom, freedom from captivity, freedom of action, freedom of choice, grant, independence, latitude, leave, *liber,* liberation from foreign restraint, *libertas,* license, *licentia,* noninterference, permission, political independence, power of choice, power to choose, prerogative, privilege, right, right of choice, sanction, self-determination, self-direction, self-government, unconstraint, uninhibitedness

ASSOCIATED CONCEPTS: abuse of liberty, civil liberty, deprivation of liberty, individual liberties, liberty of contract, liberty of free press, liberty of speech, personal liberty, political liberty, religious liberty

FOREIGN PHRASES: *Favorabilia in lege sunt fiscus, dos, vita, libertas.* Favorites of the law are the treasury, dower, life, and liberty. *Libertas inaestimabilis res est.* Liberty is a thing of inestimable value. *Libertas est naturalis facultas ejus quod, cuique facere libet, nisi quod de jure aut vi prohibetur.* Liberty is a person's natural power which permits one to do as he pleases. *Libertas non recipit aestimationem.* Freedom does not admit a valuation.

LICENSE, *noun* accordance, allowance, approbation, approval, assurance, authority, authorization, canation, certification, charter, clearance, confirmation, consent, *copia,* empowerment, endorsement, enfranchisement, entitlement, exception, fiat, formal permission, franchise, freedom, grant, imprimatur, leave, liberty, permission, permit, *potestas,* power, prerogative, privilege, right, sanction, special privilege, vouchsafement, warrant, written permission

ASSOCIATED CONCEPTS: assignment of a license, cancellation of license, easement, issuance of license, patent license, permanent license, renewal of a license, revocation of license, suspension of license

LICENSE, *verb* allow, approve, authorize, certify, charter, clothe with authority, clothe with power, confirm, empower, enable, endow, enfranchise, entitle, grant, invest, permit, sanction, strengthen warrant

ASSOCIATED CONCEPTS: license fee, license tax, licensed to practice law, professional licenses

LICENSEE, *noun* appointee, assignee, assignee in fact, consignee, donee, nominee, selectee, transferee

LICENSING OF RIGHTS, *noun* approval of rights, authority, formal authorization, formal permission, granting of rights, sanctioning of use, warranted use

LICENSOR, *noun* appointer, assignor, consignor, nominator, releasor, selector, transferor

LICENTIOUS, *adjective* abandoned, aberrant, bawdy, concupiscent, debauched, disorderly, dissipated, dissolute, *dissolutus,* free, freethinking, immoral, *impudicus,* impure, indecent, indelicate, lascivious, lewd, libertine, *libidinosus,* loose, lubricous, lurid, nonconforming, obscene, profligate, promiscuous, rakish, riotous, ruttish, scandalous, scarlet, unchaste, uncontrolled, unconventional, uncurbed, undisciplined, ungoverned, unreined, unrestrained, unruly, vulgar, wanton, wild

LICIT, adjective according to edict, according to law, admissible, allowable, allowed, authorized, chartered, constitutional, in accordance with the law, judicatory, judicial, juridic, jurisprudent, jurisprudential, just, law-abiding, lawful, lawlike, legal, legalized, legislated, legitimate, *legitimus,* licensed, mandated, obedient, permissible, permitted, prescribed, proper, *quod ex lege,* right, rightful, sanctionable, sanctioned, sound, statutable, statutory, unprohibited, upright, valid, warrantable, warranted, within the law

LID, noun cap, ceiling, cover, greatest number, limit, maximum, most quantity, outer limit, outer restriction, roof, stop, top, top number
ASSOCIATED CONCEPTS: caps on awards

LIE, noun calumny, deceit, deception, distortion, fabrication, false statement, falsehood, falsification, falsity, *falsum,* fiction, fraud, intentional distortion, intentional exaggeration, intentional misstatement, intentional untruth, invention, mendacity, *mendacium,* misrepresentation, misstatement, perversion, prevarication, untruth
ASSOCIATED CONCEPTS: defamation, libel, perjury, polygraph test, slander

LIE (Be sustainable), verb be allowable, be appropriate, be available, be established, be evident, be fitting, be permissible, be permitted, be possible, be proper, be suitable, be suited, be supportable, be warranted, exist, extend, stand

LIE (Falsify), verb be dishonest, be untruthful, bear false witness, belie, commit perjury, concoct, counterfeit, deceive, delude, deviate from the truth, dissimulate, equivocate, fable, fabricate, falsify, fib, fool, forswear, invent, *mentiri,* misguide, misinform, mislead, misrepresent, misstate, palter, perjure oneself, pervert, pretend, prevaricate, represent falsely, swear falsely, tell a falsehood, tell an untruth
ASSOCIATED CONCEPTS: false testimony, lie detector, perjury

LIEN, noun charge, charge imposed on specific property, claim, claim on property, debt, hold on property, hold upon the property of another, incumbrance, indebtedness, indebtment, liability, obligation, pledge, property right, real security, right to enforce charge upon property, security, security on property, stake
ASSOCIATED CONCEPTS: agricultural lien, artisan's lien, attorney's lien, builder's lien, carrier's lien, common-law lien, concurrent lien, contractor's lien, discharge of lien, equitable lien, factor's lien, general lien, judgment lien, junior lien, landlord's lien, mechanic's lien, possessory lien, prior lien, priority of a lien, statutory lien, superior lien, vendor's lien

LIFE (Period of existence), noun *anima,* continuance, cycle, duration, endurance, existence, lastingness, lifetime, period, period of survival, span, survival, term, term of activity, term of effectiveness, time, time from birth to death, *vita*
ASSOCIATED CONCEPTS: life annuity, life estate, life expectancy, life imprisonment, life insurance company, life interest, life tenant
FOREIGN PHRASES: **Non nasci, et natum mori, paria sunt.** Not to be born, and to be born dead, are the same. **La ley favour la vie d'un homme.** The law favors human life.

LIFE (Vitality), noun activeness, activity, *alacritas,* alertness, animation, ardor, breeziness, briskness, drive, dynamic quality, dynamism, eagerness, effervescence, energy, enthusiasm, exuberance, fieriness, fire, impassionedness, intensity, jocularity, jocundity, joviality, liveliness, lustiness, spirit, spiritedness, sprightliness, verve, vigor, vim, vis, vivacity, zeal, zest, zestfulness

LIFE SUPPORT, noun artificial maintenance of life, continuance of life through medical equipment, extension of life by technological means, sustenance of life by artificial means *Generally:* being kept alive, fostering of life, life retention, preservation of life, prolongation of existence

LIFEBLOOD, noun animus, arterial blood, basic, basic nutrition, driving force, essence of life, essential ingredient, force of life, foundation, fundamental, inspiration, inspiriting force, inspiriting power, life essence, moving force, raison d'etre, spirit, vital energy, vital flame, vital fluid, vital force, vital principle, vital spark, vital spirit

LIFELESS (Dead), adjective abrogated, annihilated, annulled, at rest, bereft of life, breathless, cadaveric, cadaverous, canceled, deceased, defunct, demised, departed, destitute of life, devoid of life, ended, exanimate, *exanimus,* expired, extinct, gone, impercipient, inanimate, insensate, insensient, irrecoverable, late, null, passed away, passed on, perished, pulseless, quashed, repealed, unanimated, unfeeling, unrevived, void, without life

LIFELESS (Dull), adjective apathetic, arid, banal, barren, benumbing, boring, characterless, colorless, commonplace, deactivated, deadened, debilitated, dismal, dormant, drearisome, dreary, dronish, dry, empty, *exsanguis,* feeble, flat, *frigidus,* hebetudinous, inactive, indolent, inert, inexcitable, insensible, insipid, insulse, lackadaisical, lackluster, laggard, languid, languourness, lazy, leaden, lethargic, lethargical, listless, lumpish, lusterless, monotonous, oscitant, passionless, passive, phlegmatic, pococurante, producing boredom, producing ennui, prosaic, quiescent, quiet, slothful, sluggish, somber, spiritless, stagnant, stale, stodgy, stupefied, supine, tame, tedious, tired, tiresome, torpescent, torpid, trite, unactivated, unaroused, uncaptivating, unenlivened, unenterprising, unentertaining, unenthusiastic, unfeeling, unfertile, unimaginative, unimpassioned, uninspired, uninspiring, uninteresting, uninventive, unlively, unoriginal, unresponsive, unsparkling, unspirited, unvivid, usual, vapid, vegatating, vegetative, weak, wearisome, wearying

LIFETIME, noun *aetas, aevum,* age, duration of life, epoch, era, generation, life, life span, life's duration, period of existence, period of life, period of survival, season, span, span of years, term, time, years of existence
ASSOCIATED CONCEPTS: life estate, per otra vie, rule against perpetuities

LIFT (Boost), noun accommodation, advancement, aid, assist, assistance, auspices, backing, betterment, bliss, elation, encouragement, enhancement, exaltation, furtherance, good turn, guidance, help, improvement, inspiration, maintenance, ministration, nurture, patronage, preferment, promotion, rapture, relief, succor, support, sustenance, transport

LIFT (Elevation), noun acclivity, advance, ascension, ascent, climb, crane, derrick, elevator, eminence, erection, escalator, heave, height, hill, hoist, pickup, promotion, raise, raising, rise, rising, slope, sphere, upgrade, upheaval, uplift, vantage point, winch

LIFT (Boost), verb advance, aggrandize, ameliorate, benefit, buoy, elate, ennoble, exalt, give one a lift, heighten, improve, inspire, inspirit, promote, soar, support, take the load off one's mind, uplift

LIFT (Decontrol), verb free, liberate, lighten, release, take off, unburden

LIFT *(Raise)*, **verb**   acquit oneself of, appropriate, ascend, build, clear, come up or off, dignify, do a good turn, elevate, enhance, erect, flush, grow, heave, help, hoist, leaven, liquidate, mount, pick up, pull, raise, rear, set on its feet, take, take off, take up, transport, tug, upraise, uprear

LIFT *(Steal)*, **verb**   pilfer, purloin, snatch, swipe, thieve

LIFT A BAN, **verb**   abate, abolish, alleviate, annihilate, cancel, clear, delete, eliminate, eradicate, free, obliterate, obviate, omit, release, relieve, remove, suspend, take away, withdraw
ASSOCIATED CONCEPTS: lift a ban on abortions, lift a ban on arms, lift a ban on funding, lift a ban on immigration

LIGHT *(Easy)*, **adjective**   breezy, carefree, cushy, debonair, effortless, facile, lighthearted, manageable, not burdensome, not complex, not complicated, not difficult, not involved, nothing to it, painless, plain, simple, smooth, straightforward, uncomplicated

LIGHT *(Entertaining)*, **adjective**   amusing, animated, beamish, bird-witted, blithe, blithesome, breezy, capricious, carefree, changeable, cheerful, cheery, comical, debonair, delighted, distracting, diverting, easygoing, elated, erratic, fickle, flighty, flyaway, free and easy, frivolous, gay, glad, gleeful, happy, happy as a lark, happy-go-lucky, humorous, impulsive, in good or high spirits, inconsequential, inconsiderable, inconstant, insouciant, irresponsible, jaunty, jocund, jolly, jovial, joyful, jubilant, laughing, lighthearted, lively, mercurial, merry, mirthful, optimistic, out in left field, out to lunch, petty, pleasing, pleasurable, positive, recreative, riant, scatterbrained, skittish, smiling, sportive, sunny, superficial, trifling, trivial, unimportant, untroubled, upbeat, volatile, whimsical, witty

LIGHT *(Weightless)*, **adjective**   airy, buoyant, diluted, feathery, floatable, floating, fluffy, light as a feather, light as air, lighter than air, slender, slight, superficial, thin, thin-bodied, unsubstantial, watered down

LIGHT *(Daylight)*, **noun**   crack of dawn, dawn, day, daybreak, daylight hours, daytime, starlight, sunbeam, sunlight, sunrise, sunshine, sunup, visibility

LIGHT *(Illumination)*, **noun**   beaming, brightness, brilliance, brilliancy, clearness, comprehension, effulgence, emanation, flood of light, fluorescence, glare, gleam, gleaming, glimmer, glitter, glow, glowing, incandescence, irradiation, knowledge, lambency, lightness, luminescence, luminosity, luminous energy, luminousness, luster, openness, publicity, radiance, radiation, sheen, shine, shining, sparkle, sunlight, understanding
ASSOCIATED CONCEPTS: evidence coming to light, shine the light of law

LIGHTEN, **verb**   allay, alleviate, assuage, cut down, decrease, disburden, disencumber, ease, ease up, have less weight, lessen, lessen the load, lessen the weight of, make less burdensome, make lighter, mitigate, reduce, reduce the load of, reduce weight of, relieve, remove, temper, unburden, unload

LIKE, **adjective**   akin, alike, allied to, analogous, approaching, approximate, close, cognate, common to, comparable, comparative, congeneric, congruous, equal, equivalent, identical, illustrative, imitative, implicatory, implying, inferential, near, not unlike, parallel, probable, related, relative, relevant, similar, resembling, suggestive of, symbolic, uniform, unique with

LIKE, **verb**   admire, affect, appreciate, be attracted to, be fond of, be partial to, befriend, care, care for, care to, choose, correlate, delight in, desiderate, desire, enjoy, esteem, fancy, feel inclined, find agreeable to one's taste, find convenient, have a mind to, hold in regard or affection, please, regard with favor, relish, savor, take a fancy to, take pleasure in, think fit, want, welcome, wish

LIKE-KIND, **adjective**   alike, analogous, another of similar quality, close copy, close imitation, close match, close reproduction, commensurable, comparable, comparative, comparison, correlative, correspondent, equal, equivalent, identical, like, near, of equal quality, parallel, related, relive, replicate, similar, sister, twin
ASSOCIATED CONCEPTS: exchanges of like-kind properties, property of like-kind, quality of like-kind

LIKELIHOOD, **noun**   anticipation, chance, conceivability, conceivableness, confident expectation, excellent prospect, expectance, expectancy, expectation, fair chance, fair prospect, favorable chance, favorable prospect, good chance, good prospect, likeliness, plausibility, possibility, possibleness, potential, potentiality, *probabilitas*, probability, prospect, reasonable chance, reasonable ground, reasonable presumption, reasonable prospect, *veri similitudo*, well-grounded hope, well-grounded possibility

LIKELY, **adverb**   by all odds, doubtless, doubtlessly, in all likelihood, in all probability, indubitably, more likely than not, most likely, no doubt, presumably, presumptively, probably, undoubtedly, very likely, with almost a certainty
ASSOCIATED CONCEPTS: likely to be reversed on appeal, likely to prevail, likely to uphold the law, likely violates the law

LIMIT, **noun**   ambit, border, bound, boundary, boundary line, *circumscriptio*, circumscription, extreme boundary, final point, *finis*, fringe, frontier, furthest point, line of demarcation, outer edge, outer line, outer point, perimeter, rim, *terminus*, verge
ASSOCIATED CONCEPTS: jurisdictional limit, territorial limit

LIMIT, **verb**   bind, bridle, check, circumscribe, *circumscribere*, confine, constrain, constrict, contain, curb, deter, enclose, *finire*, hamper, hem in, hinder, hold back, impede, leash, modulate, narrow, proscribe, repress, restrain, restrict, set bounds, suppress, *terminare*

LIMITATION, **noun**   barrier, block, *circumscriptio*, circumscription, clause, condition, constraint, curb, demarcation, *determinatio*, disallowance, prohibition, proscription, provision, qualification, reservation, restraint, restriction, specific confinement, specific curtailment, specification
ASSOCIATED CONCEPTS: alternative limitations, collateral limitation, conditional limitation, contingent limitation, conveyance upon a limitation, estate upon a limitation, executory limitation, limitation of actions, limitation of damages, limitation of liability, limitation of time, limitation of warranties, limitation over, public debt limitation, special limitation, statute of limitations, tax limitation, words of limitation

LIMITED, **adjective**   *angustus*, bounded, *brevis*, checked, circumscribed, circumscriptive, confined, confining, constricted, controlled, cramped, curbed, definite, enclosed, fixed, hampered, impeded, insular, narrow, *parvus*, prescribed, restrained, restricted, stinted

ASSOCIATED CONCEPTS: limited agency, limited by law, limited guaranty, limited jurisdiction, limited partnership, limited waiver of immunity, limited warranty

LIMITING, adjective checking, circumscribing, close fitting, confining, constricting, containing, curbing, hampering, hindering, impeding, repressing, restraining, restricting, restrictive, stinting, suppressing

LIMITS, noun amplitude, area, boundary, bounds, capacity, configuration, confines, dimensions, extremity, frontiers, limitations, metes and bounds, outlines, perimeters, premises, purview, range, reach, scope
ASSOCIATED CONCEPTS: basis jurisdiction, jurisdiction of the courts, limited jurisdiction, monetary jurisdiction

LINE (Ancestry), **noun** arrangement, avenue, beat, birth, blood, bloodline, channel, communication, course, derivation, descent, direction, dispatch, drift, epistle, family, stock, genealogy, heredity, idea, lane, letter, lineage, method, missive, nature, note, origin, parentage, path, progeny, race, railroad, road, route, scheme, sort, succession, system, tendency, track, trail, transportation, way
ASSOCIATED CONCEPTS: descendant, direct line, maternal line, paternal line

LINE (Business), **noun** activity, airline, avocation, bus line, calling, career, chain, employment, livelihood, merchandise, occupation, profession, pursuit, specialization, specialty, stock in trade, undertaking, vocation, work

LINEAGE, noun ancestors, ancestry, antecedents, blood relatives, bloodline, clan, descent, extraction, family, folk, forebears, forefathers, genealogy, gens, genus, line, line of descent, origin, origo, parentage, progenitors, stirps

LINEUP, noun arrangement, arrangement with a potential defendant, configuration with the defendant, file, formation with the defendant, grouping, line to identify the criminal, line with a potential defendant, line with the likely suspect, order, parade, police lineup, queue, showing, showing of criminal defendants, showing of criminals for inspection and identification, showing of possible suspects, showing of suspected criminals, stage arrangement containing the guilty party
ASSOCIATED CONCEPTS: double-blind lineup, prejudicial and overly suggestive lineup, show-up

LINK, noun affiliation, alliance, association, bond, bridge, chain, connection, connective, contact, coupler, coupling, go-between, interconnection, intermediary, intermedium, intersection, joint, juncture, kinship, liaison, linkage, medium, member, nexus, privity, propinquity, relation, relationship, tie, union, vinculum, weld

LINK, verb ally, anastomose, appertain, associate, attach, band, bind, bridge, combine, commingle, conjoin, connect, consolidate, contact, couple, engage, fasten, fuse, fix, identify with, implicate, inosculate, interconnect, join, knot, marry, merge, relate, unite, span, tie, touch, yoke

LINKAGE, noun affiliation, affinity, alliance, association, bond, coalescence, combination, concatenation, confluence, conjugation, conjunction, connection, coupling, hookup, interconnection, intersection, joinder, joining, junction, juncture, linking, marriage, meeting, relationship, tie, tie-up, union, weld
ASSOCIATED CONCEPTS: evidence, link to a crime

LIQUID (Changeableness), **noun** convertibleness, fluency, fluidity, fluidness, liquidness, ready to be converted
ASSOCIATED CONCEPTS: liquid debt, liquid funds

LIQUID (Fluid), **noun** damp solution, fluid, fluidic solution, liquefied solution, moist solution, solvent, watery substance, wet substance

LIQUIDATE (Convert into cash), **verb** cash in, change into cash, change into money, conclude, distribute assets, exchange for money, finish, realize in cash, redeem, sell, sell assets, terminate, terminate business affairs, turn into money
ASSOCIATED CONCEPTS: liquidated account, liquidating trust, liquidation of assets, trustees in liquidation

LIQUIDATE (Determine liability), **verb** adjust, ascertain liability, ascertain the amount of indebtedness, ascertain the balance due, assemble and apportion assets, cancel debts, determine the amount of indebtedness, discharge, discharge a liability, discharge debts, dispose of, extinguish indebtedness, make restitution, meet payments, pay, pay and settle, pay debts, satisfy, settle, settle accounts with the debtors and creditors
ASSOCIATED CONCEPTS: liquidated claim, liquidated damages, liquidated debt, liquidated demand

LIS PENDENS, noun filed notice, notice of an action, notice of pending suit, notice of right, notice on file

LIST, noun accounting, an account, archive, arrangement, catalog, directory, docket, enumeration, file, index, inventory, itemization, listing, manifest, overview, record, register, specific delineation, specific listing, summary, tally
ASSOCIATED CONCEPTS: court calendar, docket

LISTEN, verb ausculate, be attentive, concentrate on, give one's attention to, hark, hear, hearken, heed, intercept, listen in, monitor, obey, overhear, pick up

LISTLESS, adjective absent, abstracted, apathetic, benumbed, careless, despondent, disinterested, distant, dormant, dreamy, dull, exanimate, faineant, faint, heedless, idle, impassive, inactive, inanimate, inattentive, incurious, indifferent, indolent, inert, inexpressive, insipid, insouciant, lacking zest, lackadaisical, lackluster, laggard, languid, lethargic, lifeless, nonchalant, oblivious, otiose, pepless, phlegmatic, slack, sluggish, spiritless, stagnant, supine, torpid, unconcerned, uninterested

LITERAL, adjective accurate, authentic, careful, close, correct, exact, factual, faithful, faultless, meticulous, precise, rigid, scrupulous, strict, textual, to the letter, true, true to fact, truthful, unchanged, uncorrupted, undeviating, undistorted, unembroidered, unerring, unexaggerated, unfigurative, ungarbled, unmetaphorical, unvaried, unvarnished, veracious, verbatim, without exaggeration, word for word
ASSOCIATED CONCEPTS: literal interpretation

LITERAL MEANING, noun accurate meaning, correct meaning, defined meaning, definition, distinct meaning, exact meaning, explanation, explicit meaning, express meaning, faithful meaning, inflexible meaning, methodical meaning, meticulous meaning, narrow meaning, not subject to interpretation, ordinary meaning, plain meaning, precise meaning, prescribed meaning, rigid meaning, rigorous meaning, sharply defined, significance, specific meaning, strict meaning, unbending meaning, uncompromising meaning, unequivocal meaning

ASSOCIATED CONCEPTS: construction, literal contract, literal proof plain meaning rule, rules of statutory, soft plain meaning rule, textualism

LITERALLY, *adverb* correctly, definitely, distinctly, exactly, explicitly, expressly, precisely, rigidly, rigorous, similarly, specifically, unambiguously, uncompromisingly, unequivocally, unerringly
ASSOCIATED CONCEPTS: laws read literally, strict construction

LITERATE, *adjective* accomplished, apprised, aware, conversant, cultivated, cultured, disciplined, educated, enlightened, enriched, erudite, having formal education, informed, intellectual, knowing, knowledgeable, learned, lettered, literary, polished, practiced, proficient, qualified, sapient, scholarly, scholastic, schooled, skilled, studied, studious, trained, well-educated, well-informed, well-read, well-taught, widely read

LITERATURE, *noun* *belles lettres*, books, classics, information, letters, literary output, papers, printed word, publication, reading matter, store of knowledge, treatises, work, works, writings, written language, written word

LITIGABLE, *adjective* actionable, appealable, arguable, argumentative, capable of being debated, confutable, contestable, controversial, controvertible, disputable, in dispute, justiciable, refutable

LITIGANT, *noun* adversary, adverse party, appellant, appellee, claimant, complainant, contender, contestant, controversialist, correspondent, cross-complainant, cross-defendant, defendant, disputant, intervenor, legal adversary, legal opponent, litigationist, litigator, opponent, opponent in a lawsuit, party, party to a lawsuit, party to a legal action, party to a proceeding, party to a suit, party to an action, party to legal proceeding, petitioner, plaintiff, respondent, suitor, the defense
ASSOCIATED CONCEPTS: public interest litigant law, vexatious litigant law
FOREIGN PHRASES: *Litigare.* To litigate.

LITIGATE, *verb* altercate, appeal to the law, assert in court, bring action against, bring an action, bring suit, bring to the bar, bring to trial, carry on a lawsuit, contend, contest in court, contest in law, go into litigation, institute legal proceedings, *litigare,* prefer a claim, press in court, pursue in court, seek legal redress, start a lawsuit, start an action, sue, take to court, urge in court

LITIGATING COUNSEL, *noun* appointed counsel, attorney, co-counsel, counsel, counsel representing a party, legal adversary, legal counsel, legal opponent, legal representative, litigating attorney, litigation attorney, litigation counsel, litigator, retained counsel
ASSOCIATED CONCEPTS: vexatious litigation laws

LITIGATION, *noun* action, case, cause, controversy, disputation, dispute, judicial contest, lawsuit, legal action, legal battle, legal contest, legal dispute, legal matter, legal proceeding, legal remedy, matter, proceeding, suit, suit at law, trial, wrangling
ASSOCIATED CONCEPTS: appellate proceedings, civil proceedings, collateral proceedings, common law proceedings, criminal proceedings, frivolous litigation, plenary proceedings, special proceedings, summary proceedings, supplemental proceedings

LITIGATOR, *noun* appointed counsel, attorney, co-counsel, counsel, counsel representing a party, lead counsel, legal adversary, legal opponent, litigating attorney, litigation counsel, of counsel, opposing counsel, retained counsel

LITIGIOUS, *adjective* actionable, aggressive, antagonistic, arguing, argumental, argumentative, at variance, bellicose, belligerent, combative, conflicting, contentious, contested, contrary, controversial, controvertible, debatable, disagreeing, discordant, disposed to controversy, disputable, disputatious, disputative, dissentious, eristic, eristical, exceptious, fighting, given to disputation, hostile, inimical, irreconcilable, litigatory, *litigiosus,* militant, offensive, open to debate, open to question, opposing, polemic, polemical, pugnacious, quarrelsome, querulous, unpeaceful, warlike
ASSOCIATED CONCEPTS: barratry

LITTLE, *adjective* abbreviated, cursory, diminutive, few, fleeting, immaterial, inadequate, inappreciable, inconsequential, inconsiderable, inessential, inferior, insignificant, insubstantial, insufficient, Lilliputian, limited, meager, minor, minute, negligible, nonessential, paltry, petty, scant, slight, slim, sparse, superficial, trivial, unessential, unimportant, unimpressive
ASSOCIATED CONCEPTS: little known law, little law

LITTLE-KNOWN, *adjective* abstract, abstruse, arcane, concealed, cryptic, dark, enigmatic, esoteric, hidden, mysterious, mystic, mystical, nebulous, obscure, perplexing, profound, puzzling, recondite, secret, shrouded in mystery

LITTORAL, *adjective* beach, beachfront, coastal, coastland, lakeside, riparian, seaboard, seacoast, seashore, seaside, tidewater, waterfront, waterside

LIVE *(Conscious),* ***adjective*** animate, animated, breathing, endowed with life, existent, existing, full of life, growing, imbued with life, incarnate, living, mortal, quick, viable, vital

LIVE *(Existing),* ***adjective*** abiding, continued, continuing, enduring, existent, extant, intact, lasting, ongoing, perduring, persevering, persisting, progressing, remaining, staying, surviving, sustained, unceasing, unchecked, undestroyed, unended, unfading, unfailing, unreversed, unrevoked, unstopped
ASSOCIATED CONCEPTS: live cause of action

LIVELIHOOD, *noun* business, calling, career, craft, employment, enterprise, job, keep, line of work, living, maintenance, means, occupation, position, profession, pursuit, resources, situation, source of income, subsistence, support, sustainment, sustenance, trade, undertaking, venture, *victus,* vocation, work

LIVID, *adjective* angry, disgusted, enraged, frantic, frenzied, fuming, furious, hostile, inflamed, infuriated, ireful, offended, offensive, outraged, raging, storming, tempestuous, tumultuous, turbulent

LIVING *(Alive),* ***noun*** activity, animal existence, animation, being alive, breathing, existence, existing, having life, respiring, subsisting, surviving, vitality
ASSOCIATED CONCEPTS: assisted living laws, living and cohabitating together, living trust, living will

LIVING *(Occupation),* ***noun*** area, career, discipline, domain, field, livelihood, maintenance, means of living, niche, profession, province, realm, specialty sphere, subsistence, trade

LIVING WILL, noun an instrument prescribing care in life-threatening situations, an instrument preventing medical life support to sustain life, an instrument to refuse care through medical life support, instructions for care when the patient has a terminal illness, instructions for care when the patient has an incurable disease, instructions for care when the patient has an incurable illness, instructions for care when the patient has an incurable injury

ASSOCIATED CONCEPTS: durable power of attorney, euthanasia

LOAD, verb burden, cram, cumber, fill, fill up, flood, freight, inundate, lade, make heavy, mass, *onerare, onus imponere,* pack, pile, put aboard, put goods in, put on board, saddle, shower upon, stack, steeve, store, stow, stuff, take on cargo, weigh down, weight

LOAN, noun accommodation, advance, advancement, aid, allotment, assistance, backing, *commodare,* credit, dole, entrustment, extension of credit, financing, funding, grant, imprest, moneys borrowed, *mutuum,* pledge, res *commodata,* stake, stipend, subsidy, sum entrusted, sum of money borrowed, sum of money lent, temporary accommodation, time payment, trust

ASSOCIATED CONCEPTS: bond, building loan, construction loan, continuing loan, discount, excessive loan, forbearance, gratuitous loan, loan association, loan broker, loan value of a policy, mortgage, secured loan, simple loan, stock loan, temporary loan, unpaid loan, usurious loan, usury laws

FOREIGN PHRASES: *Creditorum appellatione non hi tantum accipiuntur qui pecuniam crediderunt, sed omnes quibus ex qualibet causa debetur.* Under the head of "creditors" are included, not only those who have lent money, but all to whom from any cause a debt is owing.

LOAN, verb accommodate, advance, allow, extend credit, furnish funds, give, lend, permit to borrow, supply funds

LOATHE, verb abhor, be repulsed by, detest, dislike, dislike intensely, harbor hostility toward, harbor ill will toward, hate, have a strong distaste toward, have animus toward, have antagonism toward, have antipathy toward, have aversion to, have enmity toward, have ill feeling toward, have malevolence toward, possess hostility toward

LOATHSOME, adjective abhorrent, abject, abominable, accursed, annoying, appalling, atrocious, base, below contempt, beneath contempt, blameworthy, contemptible, deplorable, despicable, detestable, disagreeable, disgusting, disliked, dissatisfactory, distasteful, distressing, dreadful, execrable, *foedus,* forbidding, foul, frightful, fulsome, ghastly, hateful, heinous, hellish, hideous, horrible, horrid, insufferable, intolerable, invidious, irritating, loathful, mean, nasty, nauseating, nauseous, objectionable, obnoxious, odious, offensive, opprobrious, painful, putrid, rancid, rank, repellent, repelling, reprehensible, repugnant, repulsive, revolting, shocking, sickening, *taeter,* terrible, ugly, unbearable, undesirable, unendurable, unpalatable, unpleasant, unsavory, vile

LOBBY, noun active partisans, active reformers, active supporters, activists, advocates, agitators, influencers, influential persons, persuaders, petitioners, pressure group, reformers, special interest group, special interests, zealous advocates

LOBBY, verb actively represent, actuate, advance, arouse, bring pressure to bear, defend, effect, encourage, enlist, espouse, exercise influence, exert influence, exert pressure, incline, induce, influence, inspirit, instigate, motivate, negotiate, personally solicit, persuade, press, pressure, procure, promote, provoke, pull strings, put pressure on, represent, request, solicit, solicit votes, sway, urge, use one's influence, work on

ASSOCIATED CONCEPTS: lobbyists, registration laws, special interest groups

LOBBYIST, noun active partisan for, active supporter, activist, advocate, agent, government affairs executive, government affairs representative, influencer, influential agent, legislative representative, peddler of influence, persuader, reformer, representative, retained agent, special interest representative

ASSOCIATED CONCEPTS: disclosure ethics, law disclosure, lobbyist law, lobbyist registration

LOCAL, adjective adjacent, adjoining, civic, close, district, divisional, domestic, limited, localized, municipal, native, near, nearby, neighborhood, provincial, regional, restricted, sectional, subdivisional, surrounding, territorial

ASSOCIATED CONCEPTS: local act, local action, local agent, local application, local assessment, local authorities, local bill, local concern, local improvement, local law, local rules

LOCALE, noun address, area, district, domain, domicile, environs, exact location, geographic location, geographic place, habitat, home, location, neighborhood, place, precise location, region, scene, seat, sector, site, spot, territory, venue

LOCALITY, noun address, area, bearings, demesne, district, domain, environment, environs, habitat, locale, location, *locus,* neighborhood, pale, place, position, province, purlieus, quarter, region, scene, seat, section, sector, site, situation, *situs,* spot, station, surroundings, terrain, territory, venue, vicinage, vicinity, whereabouts, zone

LOCATE, verb ascertain a position, assign to a place, bring to light, come upon, define limits, define location, delineate, demarcate, deposit, designate a place, detect, discern, discover, discover by search, discover by survey, discover the location of, discover the place of, establish, expose, ferret out, find, fix the position, house, install, lodge, make a place for, map out, move to, park, pinpoint, place, position, put, put in place, quarter, reveal, search out, select boundaries, set, set in place, settle, situate, station, stumble on, take up abode, trace, track down, uncover, unearth

LOCATION, noun area, demesne, district, environment, fixation, locale, locality, locus, neighborhood, place, placement, plot, point, position, post, purlieus, quarter, region, scene, section, site, spot, station, territory, vicinage, vicinity, zone

ASSOCIATED CONCEPTS: domicile, residency, venue

LOCK, verb arrest, attach, band, bar, barricade, block, blockade, bolt, cage, catch, cement, check, cinch, clasp, close, close fast, *concludere,* confine, connect, couple, curb, cut off, dam, encircle, enclose, enthrall, entwine, fasten, fuse, glue, grapple, hamper, hinder, hold, immobilize, immure, impede, impound, imprison, incarcerate, inhibit, intern, jail, join, link, lock up, make fast, make inseperable, *obserere,* obstruct, occlude, padlock, pen, prohibit, put

behind bars, restrain, restrict, seal, secure, shackle, shut out, shut up, stop, trap, unite, weld, yoke
ASSOCIATED CONCEPTS: lockout

LOCKOUT, *noun*   barring out, cessation of employment, cessation of the furnishing of work, close-out, coercive refusal to furnish work, employer work stoppage, exclusion of workers, nonadmission of employees, preclusion of work, refusal to furnish work, repudiation of employment, stoppage of work, temporary closing, work stoppage
ASSOCIATED CONCEPTS: strike

LOCO PARENTIS, *adverb*   as a substitute for a parent, as an alternative for a parent, in place of a parent, instead of a parent

LOCUS, *noun*   bailiwick, demesne, emplacement, environment, ground, locale, locality, location, place, placement, position, region, site, *situs,* territory
FOREIGN PHRASES: *Locus crontractus, locus criminis.* The place of the crime. *Locus delecti.* The place of the offense. *Locus partitus.* A place divided. *Locus reisitae.* A place where something is situated.

LODGE *(Bring a complaint),* **verb**   accuse, bring a case, bring a suit, bring accusation, bring an action against, bring charges against, bring proceedings against, bring to justice, bring to the bar, bring to trial, bring up on charges, call to account, cast blame upon, charge with, file a claim, file a suit, fix the blame for, incriminate, inculpate, place the blame for, prefer charges, prosecute
ASSOCIATED CONCEPTS: lodge a criminal complaint

LODGE *(House),* **verb**   afford sanctuary, assign to lodgings, bed, berth, domicile, find a place for, find room for, furnish room for, furnish with quarters, garrison, harbor, *hospitio excipere,* hostel, install, locate, make a place for, park, place, put, quarter, screen, shield, situate, station, supply accommodations for

LODGE *(Reside),* **verb**   abide, board, camp, *deversari, devertere,* domicile, dwell, encamp, establish oneself, inhabit, live, locate oneself, make one's home at, place, quarter, remain, reside, rest, set up housekeeping, settle, sleep at, sojourn, squat, station, stay, stop, take lodgings, take rooms, take up quarters, take up residence in, tarry, tenant

LODGE A COMPLAINT, *noun*   accuse, blame, bring a suit, bring an action, bring charges, bring proceedings against, bring up on charges, challenge, charge with, cite, complain of, criminate, file a charge, file a claim, file a suit, implicate, impose blame upon, impose responsibility on, impute, incriminate, inculpate, inform against, institute a lawsuit, make an accusation, prefer charges

LODGER, *noun*   addressee, boarder, denizen, *deversor,* dweller, habitant, indweller, inhabitant, inhabiter, inmate, *inquilinus,* leaseholder, lessee, occupant, occupier, possessor, rent payer, renter, resident, residentiary, resider, roomer, sojourner, tenant, termor, transient

LODGING, *noun*   abode, accommodation, address, apartment, asylum, berth, billet, chambers, *deversorium, deverticulum,* domicile, dormitory, dwelling, dwelling place, habitat, habitation, harbor, home, housing, inhabitance, inhabitancy, living place, lodging place, lodgment,

meritoria, place of residence, place of rest, protection, quarters, refuge, residence, rooms, shelter

LOFTY, *adjective*   august, cavalier, celebrated, celestial, dignified, distinguished, elevated, eminent, enhanced, esteemed, exalted, exalted ideal, fabled, famous, far-reaching, heavenly, heightened, high, high intellectual values, high score value, honorable, illustrious, immortal, kingly, leading, legendary, lordly, magisterial, magnificent, majestic, noble, notable, noted, predominant, preeminent, princely, prominent, raised, renowned, respected, revered, soaring, venerable
ASSOCIATED CONCEPTS: lofty goals, lofty ideals, lofty plans

LOGIC, *noun*   analytic, analytical, argument, argumentation, art of controversy, art of disputation a, chain of reasoning, cogent, common sense, course of argument, course of thought, deduction, dialectic, dialectical, dialectics, explanation, good sense, inference, line of reasoning, logical reasoning, method of reasoning, philosophical, philosophy, polemics, process of reasoning, ratiocination, rational, rationalization, reason, reasoned, reasoning, science of reasoning, sense, sound judgment, sound reasoning, thought process, wisdom
ASSOCIATED CONCEPTS: laws of logic, logical relevancy

LOGICAL, *adjective*   analytic, analytical, cogent, coherent, consistent, deductive, dialectic, dialectical, inductional, inductive, philosophical, ratiocinative, ratiocinatory, rational, reasonable, reasoned, sound

LOITER, *verb*   be idle, be vagrant, cessare, hang around, idle, linger, move aimlessly, pass time in idleness, poke, stand around, tarry, wander aimlessly
ASSOCIATED CONCEPTS: vagrancy

LONE, *adjective*   alone, deserted, exclusive, first and last, individual, isolated, lonesome, one and only, only, single, singular, sole, solitary, unique
ASSOCIATED CONCEPTS: lone dissenter

LONG *(Delayed),* **adjective**   continued, day after day, dilatory, dragged out, drawn out, endless, enduring, eternal, forever and a day, hour after hour, interminable, long drawn-out, marathon, overlong, perpetual, prolonged, protracted, sustained delay, unending delay, without end
FOREIGN PHRASES: *Longa possessio jus parit.* Long possessions begets what is right.

LONG *(Lengthy),* **adjective**   boundless, broad, continued, day after day, deep, distant, elongate, elongated, endless, enduring, eternal, expanded, expansive, extended, extensive, faraway, far-off, far-reaching, far-seeing, forever and a day, great, hour after hour, interminable, large, lasting, lengthened, limitless, lofty, outstretched, perpetual, remote, spread out, stretched out, stretching, sustained, unending, widespread, without end
ASSOCIATED CONCEPTS: long arm of the law, long term

LONG AND SHORT OF IT, *noun*   analysis, assessment bottom line, conclusion, essence, essential parts, evaluation, immediate answer, immediate assessment, pro or con, professional opinion, quick answer, quick assessment, quick determination, result, solution, upshot

LONG-DRAWN, *(Protracted)* **adjective**   delayed, dilatory, enduring, eternal, forever and a day, lengthy, lingering,

long, long-lived, long-winded, meandering, overlong, perpetual, prolonged, roundabout, tedious, unending, without end
ASSOCIATED CONCEPTS: long-drawn-out trials

LONG-DRAWN *(Verbose),* ***adjective*** garrulous, lengthy, lingering, long-winded, loquacious, meandering, orotund, overlong, prolix, prolonged, repetitious, roundabout, tedious, unending
ASSOCIATED CONCEPTS: plain language

LONGANIMITY, *noun* composure, control, endurance, forbearance, forgiveness, forgivingness, fortitude, imperturbation, indulgence, inexcitability, lenience, leniency, magnanimity, optimism, pardon, patience, patient endurance, perseverance, placability, placidity, refusal to be provoked, resignation, self-control, stamina, steadiness, stoicism, submission, sufferance, temperance, tenacity, tolerance, toleration, tranquility, understanding

LONGEVITY, *noun* advancement, age, continuance, continuation, durability, durableness, duration, elderliness, endurance, furtherance, great span of life, lastingness, length of life, long life, longlivedness, maintenance, old age, oldness, perpetuation, persistence, prolongation, protraction, seniority, survivorship, survival, survivance, years

LONGSTANDING, *adjective* abiding, acknowledged, admitted, aged, ancient, antique, chronic, constant, continuing, continous, customary, deep-rooted, deep-seated, durable, enduring, established, fixed, habitual, hallowed, handed down, immemorial, immutable, inborn, inbred, ingrained, inveterate, lasting, legendary, lingering, long-established, long-lasting, long-lived, long-term, of long duration, of long standing, perennial, perpetual, persistent, persisting, prolonged, protracted, recognized, recurring, remaining, rooted, steadfast, sustained, time-honored, traditional, tried and true, true-blue, unabating, unfading, venerable
ASSOCIATED CONCEPTS: longstanding law, longstanding policy

LOOK *(Complexion),* **noun** appearance, aspect, bearing, cast, color, complexion, condition, configuration, countenance, demeanor, deportment, fashion, feature, figure, front, general aspect, guise, idea, impression, manner, mien, presence, quality, seeming, semblance, shape, show, thought
ASSOCIATED CONCEPTS: first look

LOOK (Sight), **noun** contemplation, gaze, glimpse, glower, inspection, observance, reconnaissance, regard, survey, view, vision

LOOK, *verb* attend, be a spectator, be cautious of, be closely observant, be on guard, be on the lookout for, behold, contemplate, examine, explore, eye, gaze at, inspect, keep under observation, look at, monitor, note, notice, observe, pay attention to, peer, perceive, regard, scrutinize, see, sport, stare, stare at, study, superinted, survey, tend, view, visualize, watch, witness
ASSOCIATED CONCEPTS: a free look, cancellation in insurance

LOOK INTO, *verb* ask about, check, delve into, dig into, evaluate, examine, explore, inquire, inquire into, inspect, investigate, look up, observe, poke into, probe, pursue, research, review, scrutinize, search, search into, study
ASSOCIATED CONCEPTS: criminal investigation, grand jury investigation

LOOK OVER, *verb* analyze, check thoroughly, edit, examine, go over, inspect, make corrections, make improvements, provide suggested changes, provide suggested edits, recheck, reexamine, review, revise, reword, rewrite, scrutinize, to examine in a cursory way, to examine swiftly

LOOK UP, *verb* delve into, explore, ferret through, find, gain, go to see, inquire into, look into, pry, pursue, research, scrutinize, search for, search thoroughly, seek out, study, track down
ASSOCIATED CONCEPTS: legal research

LOOMING *(Becoming visible),* **adjective** appearing, ascending, ascertainable, becoming clear, coming into view, coming to light, coming to the fore, emerging, impending, materializing, menacing, mounting, noticeable, revealing itself, rising, showing itself, surfacing, threatening, towering, visible

LOOMING *(Menacing),* **adjective** admonitory, brewing, dangerously, foreboding, hanging over, hovering over, ill-omened, impending, ominous, portentous, precariously lingering, threatening, with a black cloud overhead
ASSOCIATED CONCEPTS: looming battle in Congress, looming lawsuits

LOOPHOLE, *noun* alternative, aperture, contrivance, device, escape clause, escape hatch, escape valve, evasion, exception, excuse, expedient, *foramen,* means of escape, mechanism for evasion, opening, outlet, saving clause, uncommunicativeness, vehicle for escape, way of escape, way out

LOOSE *(Disconnected),* **adjective** detached, free, freed, liberated, separate, suggestive, unattached, unbound, unchained, unclasped, unconnected, unfastened, unlatched, unlocked, unrestrained, untethered, untied

LOOSE *(Inexact),* **adjective** abstruse, careless, circuitous, confused, cursory, decumbent, deviative, disconnected, discursive, disjointed, erratic, free, heedless, inaccurate, indefinite, inexact, lax, lecherous, liberal, licentious, muddled, obscure, open-ended, perfunctory, promiscuous, rambling, salacious, unexacting, vague, weak

LOOSEN *(Ease up),* **verb** abate, allay, alleviate, assuage, decrease tension, diminish, ease, ease off, extricate, free, lessen, let loose, let up, lighten, mitigate, moderate, palliate, reduce, relax, release, relieve, soften, soften up, weaken
ASSOCIATED CONCEPTS: loosen a monopoly, loosen rules, loosen the law

LOOSEN *(Release),* **verb** cut loose, detach, disjoin, ease, free, let go, let loose, let up, loosen, relax, relieve tension, unbind, unbolt, unbridle, unbuckle, undo, unfasten, unfetter, unlatch, unlock, unloosen, unshackle, untie

LOOT, *verb* abscond with, appropriate, break into, burglarize, carry off, defalcate, depredate, despoil, embezzle, forage, harry, lay waste, make off with, maraud, peculate, pilfer, pillage, pirate, plunder, prey upon, purloin, raid, ransack, ravage, rifle, rob, sack, seize, spoil, spoliate, steal, strip, take, thieve

LOQUACIOUS, *adjective* babbling, blabbing, chattering, chatty, communicative, copious in speech, disposed to talk freely, effusive, exuberant, flatulent, fluent, gabby, garrulous, *garrulus,* glib, gushy, informative, jabbering, long-winded, longiloquent, *loquax*, noisy, prattling, profuse, prolix, rambling, talkative, talking, tonguey, verbal, verbose, verb*osus*, vociferous, voluble, windy, wordy

LOSE *(Be deprived of)*, **verb**   *amittere,* be deprived of, be impoverished, be without, become poorer by, experience a loss, fail to find, fail to keep, forfeit, forget, incur a loss, meet with a loss, mislay, misplace, miss, part with, *perdere,* sacrifice, squander, suffer a deprivation, suffer loss, waste

LOSE *(Undergo defeat)*, **verb**   be confounded, be defeated, be destroyed, be disappointed, be foiled, be frustrated, be humbled, be left behind, be outdistanced, be outvoted, be overthrown, be ruined, be thwarted, be unsuccessful, come in last, fail, fail to win, forfeit, go down in defeat, succumb, suffer by comparison, suffer defeat, take a beating, yield
ASSOCIATED CONCEPTS: lose a case

LOSE BY DEFAULT, **verb**   abrogate responsibilities, be delinquent, be derelict, fail to answer, fail to appear, fail to meet one's obligations, neglect, never answer the docket call, omission, violation of duty

LOSE GROUND, **verb**   backsliding, backtrack, fail, fail to keep up, fail to make progress, fail to progress, fall behind, lose footing, regression, return, reverse, slip, weaken a position

LOSS, **noun**   calamity, catastrophe, cost, *damnum,* decline, decrement, deprivation, *detrimentum,* disaster, failure, forfeit, forfeiture, *iactura,* ill fortune, ill luck, misfortune, privation, removal, ruin, sacrifice, waste
ASSOCIATED CONCEPTS: actual loss, allowable loss, business loss, capital loss, cause of loss, consequential loss, constructive total loss, damages, deductible, direct loss, financial loss, guaranty funds, indemnification, involuntary losses, irreparable loss, loss of bargain, loss of earnings, loss of life, loss of profits, loss of services, loss payable clause, loss reserves, measure of damages, net loss, operating loss, out-of-pocket loss, pecuniary loss, permanent loss, profit and loss, recovery of losses from bad debts, salvage loss
FOREIGN PHRASES: *Nemo debet locupletari ex alterius incommodo.* No one ought to gain by another's loss. *Fictio legis inique operatur alieni damnum vel injuriam.* Fiction of law is wrongful if it works loss or harm to anyone. *Non omne damnum inducit injuriam.* Not every loss produces an injury. *Lex citius tolerare vult privatum damnum quam publicum malum.* The law would rather tolerate a private loss than a public evil. *Officium nemini debet esse damnosum.* An office ought to be injurious to no one. *Non videntur rem amittere quibus propria non fuit.* Persons to whom a thing did not belong are not considered to have lost it.

LOSS OF AFFECTION, **noun**   cause of action, damages, deprivation of companionship, forfeiture of companionship, loss of care, loss of companionship, loss of consortium, loss of passion
ASSOCIATED CONCEPTS: alienation of affection

LOSS OF OPPORTUNITY, **noun**   cost of removing from use, deprivation, forfeiture, loss of availability, loss of productivity, loss of prospective benefit, loss of readiness, loss of use, privation, removal, sacrifice
ASSOCIATED CONCEPTS: interference with contractual relations, loss of opportunity doctrine

LOSS OF REPUTATION, **noun**   abasement, attaint, badge of infamy, bad reputation, bad repute, baseness, black eye, black mark, blemish, debasement, defilement, degradation, derogation, discredit, disesteem, disfavor, disgrace, dishonor, disparagement, disrepute, exclusion from favor, humiliation, ignominy, ill-repute, infamy, ingloriousness, obloquy, odium, opprobrium, reproach, scandal, shame, shameful notoriety, stain, stigma, tarnish, turpitude
ASSOCIATED CONCEPTS: libel, slander

LOSS OF VALUE, **noun**   contraction, debasement, declension, declination, decline, declivity, decrease, deflation, degeneration, depreciation, deterioration, devaluation, diminution, dwindling, losing ground, recession, regression, retrenchment, retrogression, shrinking
ASSOCIATED CONCEPTS: diminishment, inquest

LOST *(Disoriented)*, **adjective**   adrift, astray, baffled, befogged, befuddled, bemuddled, bewildered, confused, mystified, obfuscated, perplexed, puzzled, strayed, unable to find the way, wandering, without bearings

LOST *(Taken away)*, **adjective**   absent, annihilated, confiscated, depleted, destroyed, dissipated, effaced, eliminated, eradicated, exhausted, exterminated, extinguished, extirpated, forfeited, gone, gone to waste, hidden, irreclaimable, irrecoverable, irredeemable, irretrievable, irrevocable, mislaid, misplaced, missing, nowhere to be found, obliterated, obscured, out of sight, perished, sacrificed, squandered, taken, thrown away, vanished, wasted

LOST CAUSE, **noun**   a defeated cause, abortion, bankruptcy, bomb, defeat, dereliction, downfall, flop, frustration, hopeless situation, insolvency, losing game, malfunction, misadventure, miscarriage, misstep, nonperformance, nonstarter, nonsuccess, omission, terminal case, total loss, waste of energies, waste of time

LOT, **noun**   parcel, part, piece, piece of ground, plot, portion, small parcel of land, subdivision, tract
ASSOCIATED CONCEPTS: adjacent lots, block, building lot, contiguous lots, partition of lots, vacant lot

LOTTERY, **noun**   allotment by chance, bet, chance, draw, drawing, gamble, game of chance, lot, raffle, *sors, sortitio,* sweepstake, wager

LOUD *(Deafening)*, **adjective**   big-voiced, blaring, blatting, blustering, boisterous, booming, brawling, clattery, crashing, ear-piercing, ear-rending, ear-splitting, earthshaking, emphatic, fulminating, grinding, head-splitting, howling, intense, jarring, loud-sounding, noisy, obstreperous, penetrating, piercing, powerful, pulsating, pulsing, raucous, rebounding, reechoing, repercussive, resonant, resounding, roaring, roiling, roistering, rollicking, shouting, shrill, sounding, throbbing, thundering, thunderous, tumultuous, vociferous

LOUD *(Ostentatious)*, **adjective**   blinding, brash, conspicuous, extravagant, flagrant, flaring, flashy, flaunting, garish, gaudy, glaring, intrusive, jazzy, loudmouthed, lurid, meretricious, obtrusive, offensive, ornate, outlandish, out-of-place, outstanding, pronounced, rude, showy, snazzy, spectacular, splashy, striking, tasteless, tawdry, vulgar

LOVE *(Affection)*, **noun**   adoration, ardor, attachment, attraction, cherishing, closeness, craving, crush, desire,

LOVE

devotedness, devotion, emotion, enchantment, enjoyment, esteem, fancy, fervor, flame, fondness, friendship, infatuation, intimacy, like, liking, longing, mutual attraction, passion, rapture, regard, sentiment, tender passion, tenderness, true love, wanting, warmth, weakness, yearning **ASSOCIATED CONCEPTS:** marriage ceremonies, same-sex marriages

LOVE *(Penchant),* **noun**   affection, avocation, consuming interest, dedication, devotion, effort, inclination, interest, likening for an interest, passion, predilection, pursuit, relished interest, vocation, zest for an effort

LOW *(Ignoble),* **adjective**   deep, depraved, depressed, flat, heinous, ignoble, inelegant, lamentable, minimal, nominal, odious, offensive, outrageous, poor, prone, scandalous, scarce, scurrilous, servile, subaltern, tainted, unelevated

LOW *(Nominal),* **adjective**   inconsiderable, inferior, insignificant, meager, minimal, minimum, minute, modest, negligible, non-substantial, reduced, unimportant, unsubstantial

LOWER *(Below),* **verb**   bring down, bring low, decrease, de-escalate, demote, descend, detrude, down further, drop, go down, go under, immerse, incline, less, lessen, lesser, let down, lower level, push down

LOWER *(Reduce),* **verb**   cutback, declass, decrease, deflate, defrock, demote, depose, depreciate, devaluate, dilute, diminish, disbar, discount, dissipated, downgrade, downplay, dropped, lessen, lesser, lowered, modify, palliate, pared down, play down, quell, relieve, remove, retrench, scale down, smaller, soften, soothe, strip, subtract, take away

LOWEST *(Far below),* **adjective**   all the way down, entirely under, extremely far under, furthest down, inferior in position, rock-bottom, under, way down, way under

LOWEST *(Least),* **adjective**   fewest, littlest, minimal, shortest, slightest, smallest

LOYAL, *adjective*   allegiant, beholden, biddable, bound, bounden, committed, compliant, conscientious, constant, dedicated, dependable, devoted, duteous, dutiful, faithful, fast, *fidelis, fidus, filial,* firm, honorable, incorrupt, incorruptible, indebted, obedient, patriotic, pledged, reliable, resolute, slavish, staunch, steadfast, steady, tried, true, truehearted, trustworthy, trusty, unbetraying, unbought, unbribed, unchangeable, unchanging, undeviating, unfailing, unimpeachable, uninfluenced, unperfidious, unswayed, unswerving, untreacherous, unwavering, worthy of confidence **ASSOCIATED CONCEPTS:** duty of loyalty, faithful performance, loyalty oath, undivided loyalty

LOYALTY, *noun*   adherence, adherency, allegiance, attachment, bond, compliance, constancy, dedication, dependability, devotedness, devotion, duty, faithfulness, fealty, *fidelitas,* fidelity, *fides,* good faith, group feeling, incorruptibility, obedience, reliability, single-mindedness, singleness of heart, stanchness, steadfastness, submissiveness, support, troth, trueness, trustworthiness, zeal

LUCID, *adjective*   apparent, articulate, certain, clear, clear-cut, clear-minded, clear-thinking, clear-witted, clear-headed, comprehending, comprehensible, crystalline, diaphanous, discerning, discriminating, distinct, effulgent, evident, explicit, express, fulgid, illuminated, illumined, indisputable, intelligible, limpid, lucent, *lucidus,* luculent, manifest, nitid, obvious, overt, palpable, patent, pellucid, *pellucidus,* perceptive, perspicacious, perspicuous, perspicuus, plain, pronounced, rational, refulgent, responsible, sagacious, sage, sane, sensible, simple, sober, sound, straightforward, transparent, unambiguous, undeniable, understandable, understood, undisguised, unequivocal, unmistakable, unquestionable

LUCK, *noun*   advantageous outcome, chance, coincidence, destiny, fate, fortuity, gamble, good break, good fortune, good luck, opportunity, positive results, serendipity **ASSOCIATED CONCEPTS:** gaming laws, moral luck

LUCRATIVE, *adjective*   accumulative, advantageous, bearing revenue, beneficial, compensating, compensatory, contributive, fertile, fruitful, gainful, high-paying, invaluable, *lucrosus,* moneymaking, paying, productive, profitable, *quaestuosus,* remunerative, rewardful, rewarding, successful, useful, valuable, well-paying, worthwhile

LUDICROUS, *adjective*   absurd, amusing, asinine, at variance with the facts, barely possible, beyond belief, bizarre, comical, contrary to common sense, contrary to reason, crazy, derisible, doubtable, dubitable, eccentric, fallacious, fantastic, fantastical, farcical, fatuous, foolish, funny, hard to believe, humorous, idiotic, implausible, impossible, inane, incongruous, inconsistent, incredible, irrational, laugh-provoking, laughable, nonsensical, odd, open to doubt, outlandish, peculiar, preposterous, queer, questionable, ridiculous, risible, senseless, silly, staggering belief, strange, suspect, unbelievable, unconvincing, unheard of, unreasonable, untenable, unthinkable, wild, without reason

LUGUBRIOUS, *adjective*   cheerless, crestfallen, dark, dejected, depressing, despondent, disconsolate, discouraged, disheartened, dismal, dispirited, doleful, dolorous, downcast, dreary, elegiac, *flebilis,* forbidding, forlorn, funereal, gloomy, glum, grieving, heavy-hearted, joyless, low-spirited, *lugubris,* melancholy, miserable, morose, mournful, piteous, plaintive, sad, saturnine, somber, sorrowful, tearful, unhappy, weary, woebegone, woeful, wretched

LULL, *noun*   abatement, armistice, break, breather, breathing spell, breathing time, brief silence, calm, calmness, cessation, cessation of activity, cessation of sound, desistance, discontinuance, discontinuation, halt, hush, idleness, inactivity, interlude, intermission, interregnum, interruption, pause, peace, period of rest, quiescence, quiescency, quiet, recess, remission, repose, respite, rest, silence, soundlessness, standstill, stay, stillness, stop, stoppage, subsidence, suspension, temporary quiet, temporary stillness, tranquillity, truce

LULL, *verb*   allay, alleviate, assuage, calm, cause to relax, compose, cradle, dulcify, ease, encourage repose, hush, induce forgetfulness, make calm, mitigate, pacify, palliate, placate, put to rest, put to sleep, quell, quiet, quiet down, quieten, relax, remit, remove one's anxieties, remove one's fears, rock, *sedare,* settle, silence, soothe, still, stupefy, subdue, tranquilize

LUMP SUM PAYMENT, *noun*   aggregate, bulk payment, conglomerate, congregate, entire funds due, payment at once, payment for all due, payment in bulk, payment in mass, total outstanding payment, total payment

ASSOCIATED CONCEPTS: awards, disability, divorce, employment termination, lump sum settlement

LUMP TOGETHER, *verb* admix, amalgamate, annex, append, attach, bind, blend, coalesce, cohere, commingle, commix, compound, conglomerate, conglutinate, conjoin, connect, consolidate, couple, entwine, fasten, form a union, fuse, glue, group, interblend, interfuse, interlink, intermix, link, meld, merge, mingle, mix, paste, piece together, put together indiscriminately, splice, tie, unify, unite
ASSOCIATED CONCEPTS: classifications, drawing new congressional lines, gerrymandering, lumping sale, reapportionment, redistricting

LUNACY, *noun* craziness, delusion, dementia, derangement, disordered mind, folly, foolishness, frenzy, impairment of mental faculties, insaneness, insanity, instability of mental powers, madness, mania, mental aberration, mental abnormality, mental dissociation, mental illness, mental imbalance, mental sickness, unsoundness of mind

LUNATIC, *adjective* absurd, bereft of reason, crazed, crazy, daft, dementate, demented, deranged, disordered, foolish, frenetic, frenzied, insane, insensate, irrational, mad, maniacal, manic, mentally aberrant, mentally ill, mentally unbalanced, nonsensical, obsessed, of unsound mind, out of one's mind, out of one's senses, possessed, raging, ranting, raving, reasonless, senseless, touched, unhinged, unsettled, wandering, wild

LURE, *noun* allure, attractive nuisance, bait, dangerous conditions, draw, endangerment, enticement, inducement, seducement, unprotected
ASSOCIATED CONCEPTS: attractive nuisance doctrine, specific conditions

LURE, *verb* adlicere, allure, attract, bait, beguile, bewitch, bribe, cajole, captivate, charm, coax, court, decoy, draw on, entice, hold out allurement, hold out temptation, induce, inlicere, inveigle, pellicere, provoke desire, seduce, tantalize, tempt

LURID, *adjective* appalling, caliginosus, coarse, disgusting, exaggerated, extreme, fulsome, ghastly, glaringly vivid, graphic, gross, gruesome, harsh, horrible, horrifying, indelicate, luridus, obscurus, offensive, overwhelming, racy, repulsive, revolting, risque, salacious, scabrous, scrofulous, sensational, shocking, startling, uncensored, unexpurgated, unusual, vulgar

LURK, *verb* ambuscade, be stealthy, be unseen, conceal oneself, crouch, delitescere, ensconce oneself, escape detection, escape notice, escape observation, escape recognition, hide, keep out of sight, latere, latitare, lie concealed, lie hidden, lie in ambush, lie in wait, lie low, move furtively, prowl, seclude oneself, secrete oneself, skulk, slink, sneak, steal

LUXURY, *noun* accessory, added comfort, added convenience, added creature toy, added enjoyment, added pleasure, added state-of-the-art edition added technological advancement, advantage, delight, delightfulness, ease of comfort, extra, extravagance, frill, gadgetry, newest product, nicety, nonessential, option, physical pleasure
ASSOCIATED CONCEPTS: luxury tax

LUXATE, *verb* break, detach, disconnect, disengage, disjoin, disjoint, dislocate, dispart, displace, dissever, dissociate, disunite, eject, expel, part, put out of joint, put out of place, rend, rive, separate, sever, sunder, throw out of gear, unhinge, unjoint, wrench

LYING, *adjective* bluffing, covinous, cunning, deceitful, deceptive, delusive, delusory, devoid of truth, dishonest, disingenuous, dissembling, double-dealing, equivocating, fabricating, faithless, faked, false, feigned, fictitious, forsworn, fraudulent, mendacious, misleading, misrepresentative, perfidious, perjured, sneaky, spurious, treacherous, tricky, trumped up, truthless, uncandid, unfactual, untrue, untruthful, unveracious
ASSOCIATED CONCEPTS: perjury

LYNCH LAW, *noun* anarchy, blatant violation of law, breakdown of administration, disorderliness, flagrant abuse of the law, illegal infliction of punishment, lack of due process, lack of justice, lack of legal sanction, lawlessness, misgovernment, misrule, mob rule, mobocracy, nihilism, ochlocracy, outlawry, paralysis of authority, punishment without trial, reign of terror, summary punishment by mob, taking the law in one's own hands, terrorism, unruliness

MACABRE, *adjective* abhorrent, abominable, atrocious, awful, beneath contempt, contemptible, deplorable, despicable, detestable, dreadful, drive, foul, frightening, frightful, ghastly, ghoulish, gruesome, harrowing, hateful, heinous, horrendous, horrid, horrifying, indefensible, loathsome, obnoxious, odious, offensive, outrageous, pathetic, pitiful, repellent, reprehensible, repulsive, revolting, shameful, shocking, terrible, terrifying, unspeakable, vile, villainous, wholly inadequate

ASSOCIATED CONCEPTS: deplorable conditions

MACHIAVELLIAN, *adjective* arch, artful, base, cagey, calculating, canny, cheating, clever, collusive, collusory, conniving, conscienceless, contriving, corrupt, covinous, crafty, crooked, cunning, deceitful, deceiving, deceptive, delusive, designing, devious, dirty, dishonest, dishonorable, disingenuous, double-crossing, double-dealing, double-tongued, evasive, faithless, falsehearted, feline, foxy, fraudulent, guileful, hypocritical, ignoble, immoral, infamous, insidious, insincere, intriguing, knavish, mean, misdealing, opportunist, perfidious, plotting, rascally, roguish, scheming, shady, shameless, sharp, shifty, shrewd, slick, slippery, sly, smooth, sneaking, sneaky, stealthy, subdolous, tortuous, treacherous, trickish, tricky, two-faced, undependable, underhand, underhanded, unethical, unprincipled, unscrupulous, untrustworthy, untruthful, venal, vile, vulpine, wily

MACHINATION, *noun* artful dodge, artifice, cabal, collusion, conspiracy, contrivance, covin, crafty design, crafty device, crafty plan, design, dodge, *dolus,* foul play, intrigue, jugglery, *machina,* maneuver, manipulation, plot, ploy, ruse, scheme, stratagem, strategy, subterfuge, tactic, treachery, trick, underplot, wile, wily device

MACHINERY (Equipment), *noun* apparatus, appurtenances, effects, equipment, facilities, heavy equipment, mechanism, products

MACHINERY (Means), *noun* contrivance, devices, guns, inner workings, instruments, means to implement, mechanism, mechanization, methods, organization, power, system, tools, vehicle, wherewithal, workings

MAD (Absurd), *adjective* absent-minded, anserine, apish, asinine, befooled, beguiled, bemused, besotted, birdbrained, brainless, buffoonish, careless, childish, clueless, confused, crackbrained, crazy, credulous, daft, dangerous, dazed, derisible, dizzy, doting, driveling, dull-witted, dumb, excessive, extravagant, fatuitous, fatuous, feebleminded, fond, fool, fool headed, foolish, for the birds, fuddled, futile, gaga, giddy, groundless, gulled, harebrained, harum-scarum, idiotic, ill-advised, ill-considered, illogical, ill-suited, imbecile, imbecilic, immature, impractical, improper, imprudent, inane, inappropriate, incoherent, incongruous, inconsistent, indiscreet, inept, infatuated, injudicious, insane, insensate, irrational, irresponsible, laughable, light-headed, light-minded, ludicrous, maudlin, moronic, muddled, muddlepated, nonsensical, perilous, pointless, preposterous, puerile, rambling, rash, reckless, ridiculous, risible, scatterbrained, senseless, sentimental, short-sighted, silly, simple-minded, spastic, stupid, thoughtless, unfounded, unreasonable, unsafe, unsensible, unsound, unwary, unwise, wandering, wet, wild-eyed, witless

MAD (Insane), *adjective* bereft of reason, deluded, demented, deprived of reason, deranged, idiosyncratic, insane, irrational, lunatic, manic, mentally deficient, non compos mentos, not of a sound mind, reasonless, senseless, unbalanced, unsound

MAD (Irritated), *adjective* abandoned, amok, angry, annoyed, at the end of one's rope, bellowing, berserk, beside oneself, blue in the face, carried away, chafed, delirious, demoniacal, demonic, displeased, distracted, drive one mad, ecstatic, enrage, enraged, enraptured, fed up, feral, ferocious, fierce, fiery, flaming, flared up, flaring, flushed with anger, frantic, frenzied, frenzy, frothing at the mouth, fulminating, fuming, furious, galled, haggard, hogwild, howling, hysterical, in a huff, in a transport or ecstasy, in high dudgeon, in hysterics, incensed, indignant, inflamed, infuriate, infuriated, intoxicated, irate, ireful, lash into fury, madden, madding, make one's blood boil, maniac, maniacal, nettled, orgasmic, orgiastic, out of one's wits, peeved, piqued, possessed, rabid, raging, ramping, ranting, raving, ravished, ready to burst, red-hot, riled, roaring, running mad, storming, transported, uncontrollable, up in arms, vexed, violent, white-hot, wild, wild-eyed, wild-looking, work up into a passion, wrathful, wroth

MAGIC, *adjective* by chance occurrence, coincidental, fortunate, lucky, out of the ordinary, magical, miraculous, mystic, mystical, mysterious, occult, sorcery, supernatural, uncanny, under a charm, under a spell, unusual, wizardly, wonderful

MAGISTRATE, *noun*   arbitrator, assessor, judge, jurist, justice, legist, *magistratus,* moderator, officer, official

MAGNANIMOUS, adjective   altruistic, benevolent, big-hearted, brotherly, charitable, chivalrous, compassionate, exalted, fraternal, generous, generous to a fault, giving, great hearted, great spirited, high-minded, idealistic, kind, magnificent, noble, noble-minded, overly generous, philanthropic, princely, stately, sympathetic, unselfish
ASSOCIATED CONCEPTS: charitable organizations

MAGNATE, *noun*   aristocrat, aristocratic, baron, big businessman, big gun, big name, bigwig, capitalist, captain of industry, celebrity, dignitary, director, distinguished person, enterpriser, entrepreneur, financier, giant, industrialist, leading figure, lion, lord, luminary, man of distinction, man of eminence, manager, name, noble, nobleman, person of eminence, person of importance, person of influence, personality, pillar of society, power, power elite, star, superstar, top executive, tycoon, Very Important Person
ASSOCIATED CONCEPTS: industrial magnate

MAGNETIC, adjective   absorbing, alluring, appealing, arresting, attracting, attractive, beguiling, bewitching, captivating, charismatic, charming, compelling, dynamic, effective, electric, electrical, enchanting, engaging, engrossing, enthralling, enticing, entrancing, exciting, fascinating, glamorous, grabbing, gripping, hypnotic, interesting, intriguing, inviting, irresistible, magnetized, mesmeric, mesmerizing, persuasive, potent, powerful, provocative, spellbinding, tantalizing, tempting, winning

MAGNIFICATION (Enlargement), *noun*   amplification, augmentation, blow up, boost, buildup, elaboration, enhancement, enlargement, exaggeration, expansion, greatening, heighten, increase the size of, intensification, maximization, raising
ASSOCIATED CONCEPTS: magnification of damages

MAGNIFICATION (Exaggeration), *noun*   amplification, augmentation, broadening, elaboration, enhancement, enlargement, expansion, extension, extremism, glorification, heightening, hyperbole, hyperbolism, inflation, overstatement, superlative

MAGNIFICENT, adjective   august, awe-inspiring, beauteous, beautiful, brilliant, distinguished, elegant, exalted, excellent, exceptional, glorious, gorgeous, grand, great, handsome, imposing, impressive, lovely, luxurious, majestic, nice looking, out of this world, outrageous, plush, posh, pretty, princely, radiant, regal, resplendent, royal, splendid, splendiferous, stately, sublime, superb, terrific

MAGNIFY, verb   add to, aggrandize, *amplificare,* amplify, *augere,* augment, balloon, boost, broaden, build up, cause growth, deepen, emphasize, enhance, enlarge, *exaggerare,* exaggerate, exalt, expand, extend, glorify, heighten, idealize, increase, increase the size of, inflate, intensify, make great, make larger, make more important, maximize, overestimate, overprize, overrate, overstate, overstress, overvalue, play up, raise, spread, strengthen, stretch, stretch a point, swell, widen

MAGNITUDE, *noun*   amplitude, *amplitudo,* bearing, concern, consequence, consideration, degree, dimension, effect, eminence, enormity, essentiality, extension, extent, gauge, gravity, immensity, import, importance, *magnitudo,* mark, materiality, materialness, measure, measurement, momentousness, precedence, primacy, priority, proportions, range, reach, scale, scope, seriousness, significance, size, span, *spatium,* stature, stretch, value, vastness, volume, weight, weightiness, worth

MAIL, *noun*   envelope sent, formal communication sent, item sent, letter sent for delivery, message sent, note sent, package sent, package which is posted, postal matter, sent communication, sent correspondence, sent letter, sent packages, sent through regular means, sent through U.S. mail
ASSOCIATED CONCEPTS: mail matter

MAIM, *verb*   cripple, damage, deface, disable, hobble, hurt, impair, incapacitate, injure, lame, make useless, mutilate, wound

MAIN FOCUS, *noun*   cardinal feature, cardinal point, center, central idea, chief feature, chief issue, chief part, chief point, core, critical feature, critical point, crucial feature, crucial point, crux, essence, essential matter, essential part, essential point, essentialness, fundamental feature, fundamental part, fundamental point, gravamen, heart, implication, import, important feature, important part, important point, main force, main idea, major part, major portion, material point, meaning, nucleus, pivotal point, prime basis, prime ingredient, principal point, prominent aspect, prominent point, purport, quintessence, salient feature, salient point, significance, substance

MAIN FORCE, *noun*   aggressiveness, brute force, compulsion, controlling force, controlling power, dominant strength, duress, effort, energy, forcefulness, full force, intensity, matchless effort, maxim effort, might, potence, potency, power, powerfulness, pressure, puissance, push, sheer force, sheer power, strength, toughness, unrivaled effort, utter force, vigor

MAIN POINT, *noun*   backbone, base, basis, benchmark, *caput,* cardinal feature, cardinal point, center, central idea, chief feature, chief idea, chief issue, chief part, chief point, core, cornerstone, cream, crisis, critical feature, critical point, crucial feature, crucial point, crux, drift, elixir, essence, essential matter, essential part, essential point, essentialness, focal point, focus, force, fundamental feature, fundamental part, fundamental point, gist, gravamen, great point, heart, heart of the matter, implication, import, important feature, important part, important point, inner core, kernel, key, key point, keynote, keystone, lifeblood, main idea, main thing, major part, marrow, material point, meaning, nub, nucleus, outstanding feature, pith, pivotal point, prime constituent, prime ingredient, prime issue, principal point, prominent aspect, prominent point, purport, quiddity, quintessence, real issue, *res summa,* root, salient feature, salient point, sense, significance, substance, tenor, vital concern
ASSOCIATED CONCEPTS: the main point in a legal argument

MAINLY, adverb   above all, all in all, all things considered, chiefly, cardinally, consequentially, dominantly, effectively, essentially, exhaustive, first, foremost, in general, in the main, on balance, on the whole, overall, particularly, predominantly, preponderantly, prevailing, primarily, principally, usually

MAINSTAY, *noun*   anchor, assurance, backbone, backer, bastion, brace, bulwark, buttress, champion, chief reliance, cornerstone, crutch, deliverance, dependence, foundation, help, keystone, maintainer, nucleus, pillar, principal backer, principal maintainer, principal support, principal supporter, principal sustainer, prop, rampart, reinforcement, reliance, right arm, right hand, salvation, security, staff, stay, strength, stronghold, support, sustainer, sustenance, tower of strength, upholder

MAINTAIN (Carry on), **verb** adfirmare, confirmare, contendere, continue, follow up, go on, keep alive, keep going, keep on, keep up, perpetuate, persevere, persist, proceed with, prolong, pursue, shore up, stick to

MAINTAIN (Commence), **verb** activate, begin, embark upon, initiate, institute, introduce, launch, originate, set in motion, set in operation, start, undertake
ASSOCIATED CONCEPTS: maintain an action

MAINTAIN (Sustain), **verb** abet, adhere, advocate, aid, assist, attend, be firm, be firmly fixed, bear up against, bolster, buttress, care for, champion, come to the defense of, conserve, countenance, cover, defend, espouse the cause of, feed, finance, guard, hold up, justify, look after, make provision, make safe, nourish, nurse, nurture, oversee, preserve, protect, provide for, rally to, safeguard, save, screen, secure, see to, service, shelter, shield, shoulder, side with, stand by, stand firm, stand one's ground, stick to, subscribe to, subsidize, substantiate, supply, support, take care of, take charge of, uphold, vindicate, watch over, weather

MAINTENANCE (Support of spouse), **noun** aid, alimony, allowance, assistance, financial backing, financing, legal assistance, legal support, means of subsistence, monetary help, necessaries, necessities of life, preservation, provisions, subsidy, subsistence, sustenance, upkeep, victus
ASSOCIATED CONCEPTS: separate maintenance, support and maintenance

MAINTENANCE (Upkeep), **noun** care, carrying charge, conservatio, conservation, cost, disbursement, drain on resources, expenditure, expense, outlay, overhead, repair, running expenses, salus, service
ASSOCIATED CONCEPTS: ordinary maintenance and repair, reasonable maintenance

MAJOR, **adjective** big, chief, comprehensive, consequential, considerable, crucial, decisive, distinguished, enormous, essential, extensive, extraordinary, far-reaching, fateful, goodly, grave, great, high-level, important, imposing, impressive, intense, key, large, leading, massive, matchless, material, memorable, meritorious, moderately large, momentous, notable, noteworthy, outstanding, paramount, ponderous, pressing, prime, principal, remarkable, serious, significant, sizable, sober, solemn, substantial, supreme, top, top-level, tremendous, unparalleled, vital, weighty, worthy of consideration, worthy of remark

MAJORITY (Adulthood), **noun** age of discretion, age of majority, age of responsibility, full age, full legal age, legal age, legal competence, legal maturity, manhood, matureness, maturity, voting age, womanhood
FOREIGN PHRASES: *Minor ante tempus agere non potest in casu proprietatis nec etiam convenire.* A minor under age cannot act in a case of property.

MAJORITY (Greater part), **noun** better part, biggest share, body, bulk, generality, greater number, larger number, larger part, lion's share, main body, main part, *maior numerus, maior pars,* major part, mass, more than half, most, plurality, predominance, predominant part, preponderance, preponderation, principal part, weight of numbers
ASSOCIATED CONCEPTS: majority rule, majority vote, plurality, quorum, requisite majority

MAKE, **verb** accomplish, achieve, actualize, assemble, attain, author, beget, bring about, bring forth, bring into being, bring into existence, bring to effect, bring to pass, build, call into being, call into existence, carry into effect, carry into execution, cast, cause, cause to exist, coin, compel, complete, compose, compound, concoct, constitute, constrain, construct, contrive, *creare,* create, develop, devise, draft, draw up, effect, effectuate, efform, enact, enforce, engender, erect, establish, evolve, execute, *fabricari,* fabricate, *facere,* fashion, force, forge, form, formulate, frame, generate, give birth to, give origin to, give rise to, hammer out, hatch, have in production, improvise, initiate, institute, invent, kindle, machine, manufacture, model, mold, organize, originate, pattern, perform, piece together, prepare, produce, provide, put together, set up, shape, synthesize, think up, turn out, yield results
ASSOCIATED CONCEPTS: make a decision, make a demand, make a motion, make an agreement, make an offer

MAKE A DEMAND, **verb** announce a sum demanded, ask for recompense, assert a legal right for damages, conduct negotiations, demand compensation, impose a claim, impose a peremptory claim, impose a requirement, make a financial claim, make an authoritative request for damages, request compensation, serve an ultimatum, state a claim, state a requisite sum as damages, state an amount in question, state an imperative

MAKE A FINDING, **verb** adjudge, adjudicate, announce a conclusion, arrive at a conclusion, ascertain, ascertain by judicial inquiry, calculate, come to a conclusion, conclude, decide, deduce, deliver, determine, draw a conclusion, establish, hold, judge, make a decision, pass judgment, pronounce, resolve, rule

MAKE A MOTION, **verb** apply, ask for, make a formal application, make a request, make application, move, offer for more consideration, petition, propose formally, put forth, put forward, request, requisition, submit

MAKE A REBUTTAL, **verb** answer, argue, argue against, confute, contradict, contravene, controvert, countercharge, counterclaim, deny, disagree, disprove, dispute, join issue, negate, oppose, present arguments against, rebuff, rebut, refute, rejoin, reply, repudiate, respond, retaliate, retort, submit arguments against, surrebut, surrejoin, take a stand against
ASSOCIATED CONCEPTS: rebut an argument, rebuttal case, surrebuttal.

MAKE A STATEMENT, **verb** affirm, allege, argue, assert positively, asseverate, attest, authenticate, aver, avouch, avow, bear, certify, claim, confirm, contend, converse, declare, explain, express, formulate, maintain, present, proclaim, profess, pronounce, propose, purport, report, speak, state, validate, verify, warrant
ASSOCIATED CONCEPTS: closing statement, statement to the jury

MAKE AN ARGUMENT, **verb** advance, allege, argue, assert, challenge, claim, confute, contend, contest, controvert, debate, disagree, dispute, elucidate, emphasize, enunciate, establish, explain, expostulate, express, maintain, oppose, present arguments against, present arguments for, proclaim, pronounce, propose, propound, put forth, put forward, remonstrate, set forth, show, state with conviction, stress, submit, urge
ASSOCIATED CONCEPTS: arguments contained in a submission, oral argument

MAKE APPLICATION, *verb* appeal, appeal for, apply, bid, bid for, call for, demand, file for, make formal request, move, obsecrate, petition, petition for, put in for, request, seek, solicit

ASSOCIATED CONCEPTS: make application for a directed verdict, make application for costs, make application for substitution of counsel, make application for summary judgment

MAKE CERTAIN, *verb* accomplish, achieve, acquire, affect, attain, complete, conclude, consummate, determine, earn, effectuate, end, ensure, execute, finish, get done, get it over with, guarantee, influence, leave no stone unturned, make absolutely certain, make absolutely definite, make definite, make unequivocal, perfect in detail, procure, put the finishing touches on, realize, reap, seal, secure, settle, take every step necessary, take no conceivable chance, win

MAKE CLEAR, *verb* articulate, bare, bring to light, clear up, comment upon, construe, decipher, define, delineate, demonstrate, disentangle, elucidate, enlighten, exemplify, explain, explicate, expose, exposit, expound, free from ambiguity, free from confusion, illuminate, illustrate, interpret, lay open, make comprehensible, make explicit, make intelligible, make lucid, make understood, refine, render intelligible, shed light on, show, simplify, spell out, subtilize, unfold, unmask, unravel, unscramble, unveil

ASSOCIATED CONCEPTS: plain language

MAKE INROADS, *verb* ameliorate a situation, be light years ahead, become better, develop, enhance, enrich, expand, forge ahead, gain, gain ground, get strides ahead, go forward, grow, improve, increase, make advancements, make headway, make progress, make quantum leaps, meliorate, mend, move ahead, move onward, press on, proceed, prosper, push on, progress

ASSOCIATED CONCEPTS: investigations

MAKE KNOWN, *verb* acknowledge, admit, advise, affirm, announce, apprise, bare, blurt out, break the news, bring to light, circulate, communicate, concede, confess, confide, confirm, declare, describe, disabuse, disclose, display, disseminate, divulge, enlighten, evince, explain, expose, give currency to, give inside information, impart, indicate, inform, make public, make publicly known, manifest, mention, notify, off, open, promulgate, publish, set right, tell, uncloak, uncover, unearth, unfold, unmask, unseal, unveil, utter, vent, verify, voice

ASSOCIATED CONCEPTS: confidentiality, grand jury secrecy, privilege

MAKE LEGAL, *verb* approve by law, authorize by law, bring into conformity with the law, confirm by law, decree by law, enact by statute, enact into law, legalize, legislate, legitimatize by law, make lawful, order by law, pass into law, permit by law, pronounce by statute, ratify, sanction by common law, sanction by law, sanction by the judiciary, validate

MAKE NULL AND VOID, *verb* abolish, abrogate, annul, cancel, declare not binding, declare of no effect, declare of no legal authority, declare of no legal effect, declare of no legal force, declare of no validity, declare without legal authority, defeat, disestablish, end, eradicate, extinguish, fail to consummate, make defunct, negate, nullify, obliterate, omit, overrule, overturn, quash, render forceless, render impotent, render ineffective, render inefficacious, render inoperative, render invalid, repeal, rescind, reverse, revoke, set aside, supersede, suspend, terminate, vacate, void, withdraw

ASSOCIATED CONCEPTS: annulment, declare a marriage null and void, law superseded and null and void

MAKE PROGRESS, *verb* advance, ameliorate, approach, ascend, climb, complete, continue onward, develop, enhance, enrich, expand, finish, forge ahead, gain, gain ground, get ahead, get results, go forward, go on, grow, improve, increase, keep going, keep moving, make headway, meliorate, mend, mount, move on, press on, proceed, prosper, ripen, rise

MAKE RESTITUTION, *verb* atone, compensate, indemnify, make amends, make whole, pay, pay back, pay damages, provide legal redress, recompense, refund, reimburse, remit, remunerate, repay, return, reward, satisfy an obligation, settle

ASSOCIATED CONCEPTS: criminal restitution law, law of restitution, legal remedies

MAKE VOID, *verb* annul, cancel, declare not binding, declare null and void, declare of no force, declare useless, declare without legal force, determine not in force, extinguish, make ineffective, make ineffectual, make inoperative, make meaningless, nullify

ASSOCIATED CONCEPTS: void for vagueness, void where prohibited by law, voidable

MAKER, *noun* author, devisor, donor, initiator, producer

ASSOCIATED CONCEPTS: maker of a note, maker of an instrument

MALADMINISTRATION, *noun* bad job, blunder, botchery, bungling, default, dereliction of duty, evasion of duty, failure of duty, incompetency, inefficiency, inefficient management, malfeasance, malversation, misadministration, misapplication, misconduct, misdirection, misfeasance, misgovernment, misguidance, mishandling, mismanagement, misrule, neglect, negligence, poor administration, *prava rerum administratio,* unproficiency, want of duty

MALADY, *noun* abnormality, affliction, ailment, defect, deformity, desperate condition, disability, disease, disorder, handicap, health difficulty, health problem, illness, impairment, infirmity, medical condition, sickness, syndrome, weakness

MALCONTENT, *noun* agitator, anarchist, ardent champion of change, brawler, caviler, censurer, complainant, complainer, critic, crusader, demonstrator, detractor, diehard, disputer, dissenter, dissentient, dissident, extremist, fanatic, faultfinder, fighter, fretter, griper, grumbler, heretic, *homo rerum novarum cupidus,* instigator, insubordinate, insurgent, insurrectionist, kicker, mutineer, nihilist, nonconformist, noncooperator, objector, obstructionist, petitioner, political agitator, protester, rabble-rouser, radical, reactionary, reactionist, rebel, recusant, reformer, renegade, repiner, resister, revisionist, revolter, revolutionary, revolutionist, rioter, seditionary, seditionist, traitor, troublemaker, whiner, wrangler

MALEDICTION, *noun* abusive speech, anathema, curse, damnation, defamation, denunciation, *dirae,* dispraise, evil-speaking, execration, *exsecratio,* foul language, fulmination, ill wishes, imprecation, invective, malevolence, malison, obloquy, revilement, tongue-lashing, verbal abuse, verbal assault, verbal attack, vilification, vituperation

MALEFACTION, *noun* abomination, atrocity, breach, contravention, crime, encroachment, evil deed, felony, harm, horror, hurt, illegal act, infringement, malfeasance, malpractice, misdeed, offense, outrage, tort, transgression, violation, wrong, wrongdoing

MALEFACTOR, *noun* bandit, brigand, convict, criminal, culprit, delinquent, desperado, evildoer, felon, gangster, hardened criminal, *homo maleficus, homo sceleratus,* hoodlum, hooligan, lawbreaker, lawless individual, mischief-maker, miscreant, misdemeanant, offender, offender against the law, outlaw, racketeer, rapscallion, rascal, recidivist, reprobate, rogue, ruffian, scamp, scoundrel, transgressor, trespasser, villain, violator of laws, wrongdoer

MALEFICENT, *adjective* antagonistic, baleful, baneful, deleterious, detrimental, diabolic, evil, evil-disposed, evil-intentioned, evil-minded, harmful, heinous, hostile, hurtful, ill-natured, inimical, injurious, invidious, lethal, malefic, malevolent, malicious, malignant, merciless, noxious, obnoxious, odious, offensive, oppressive, perfidious, pernicious, ruthless, surly, vicious
FOREIGN PHRASES: *Maleficia propositis distinguuntur.* Evil deeds are to be distinguished from evil purposes.

MALEVOLENCE, *noun* acerbity, acrimony, actively opposed, adverse, aggressive, animosity, antagonism, antagonistic, antipathetical, belligerence, bitterness, cruelty, devilishness, diabolicalness, embitterment, enmity, evil, evil-mindedness, full of hate, full of malice, harshness, hatefulness, hostility, hurtfulness, iniquitousness, injuriousness, invidiousness, ire, lethalness, malice, maliciousness, malignance, malignity, mercilessness, perfidiousness, perniciousness, pitilessness, repugnance, resentfulness, resentment, treacherousness, venomousness, viciousness
ASSOCIATED CONCEPTS: sentencing

MALEVOLENT, *adjective* acrimonious, actively opposed, adverse, aggressive, antagonistic, antipathic, antipathetical, baleful, baneful, barbarous, bellicose, belligerent, bilious, bitter, bloodthirsty, brutal, churlish, cold, cold-blooded, conspiratorial, cruel, damaging, deadly, deleterious, demonic, demoniacal, demonial, despiteful, devilish, diabolic, diabolical, disaffected, disobliging, embittered, envenomed, evil, evil-minded, faithless, ferocious, feuding, fiendish, full of hate, full of malice, full of revenge, full of spite, galling, grim, grudgeful, grudging, hardhearted, harmful, harsh, hateful, heinous, hellish, hostile, hurtful, ill-disposed, ill-intentioned, ill-natured, ill-wishing, implacable, infamous, infernal, iniquitous, injurious, invidious, lethal, malefic, maleficent, *malevolus,* malicious, malign, malignant, mean, merciless, mischievous, oppugnant, perfidious, pernicious, pitiless, plotting, poisonous, rancorous, repugnant, resentful, retaliative, retaliatory, revengeful, ruinous, ruthless, satanic, savage, scatheful, sinister, snaky, spiteful, spleenful, treacherous, truculent, unamicable, unfeeling, unfriendly, unkind, venomous, vicious, villainous, vindictive, viperous, virulent, vitriolic, warlike, wicked

MALFEASANCE, *noun* bad conduct, corruption, dereliction, deviation from rectitude, ill conduct, illegal action, infringement, injurious action, misbehavior, misdeed, misdoing, misgovernment, mismanagement, overstepping, peccadillo, peccancy, transgression, unjust performance, unlawful action, wrongful action, wrongful conduct
ASSOCIATED CONCEPTS: malfeasance in office, malfeasance of a public officer, misconduct, misfeasance, nonfeasance

MALFEASANT, *noun* a corrupt person, a derelict person, a person with wrongful actions, a person with wrongful conduct, an actor with ill conduct, an individual whose conduct deviates from rectitude, an individual with bad conduct, an individual with illegal actions, an individual with misbehavior, an individual with unjust actions, an individual with unlawful actions, a person with misdeeds, a person with transgressions, criminal, defendant, felon, lawbreaker, malefactor, miscreant, offender, reprobate, rogue, transgressor, wrongdoer
ASSOCIATED CONCEPTS: impeachment, malfeasance in office

MALICE, *noun* acrimony, active ill will, animosity, animus, antagonism, antipathy, aversion, bad intent, bad intention, bitter animosity, conscious violation of law, contempt, culpable recklessness, detestation, disaffection, dislike, enmity, evil disposition, evil intent, hard feelings, hardheartedness, harmful desire, hate, hatred, hostility, ill feeling, ill will, intentional wrongdoing, *invidia,* invidiousness, loathing, malevolence, *malevolentia,* maliciousness, *malignitas,* malignity, odium, personal hatred, pique, pitilessness, rancor, rankling, repugnance, repulsion, resentment, spite, spitefulness, umbrage, venom, viciousness, violent animosity, wanton disregard, wrath
ASSOCIATED CONCEPTS: actual malice, constructive malice, implied malice, legal malice, malice aforethought, malice in fact, malice in law, malicious abandonment, malicious abuse of process, malicious arrest, malicious injury, malicious intent, malicious mischief, malicious prosecution, malicious use, malicious wrong, universal malice
FOREIGN PHRASES: *In criminalibus, sufficit generalis malitia intentionis, cum facto paris gradus.* In crimes, a general malicious intent suffices where there is an act of equal degree. *Malitia est acida; est mali animi affectus.* Malice is sour; it is the quality of an evil mind. *Maleficia propositis distinguuntur.* Evil deeds are distinguished by their evil purposes. *Malitiis hominum est obviandum.* The malicious designs of men must be thwarted. *Eum qui nocentem infamat, non est aequum et bonum ob eam rem condemnari; delicta enim nocentium nota esse oportet et expedit.* It is not just and proper that he who speaks ill of a bad man should be condemned on that account; for it is fitting and expedient that the crimes of bad men be made known. *Malum non praesumitur.* Evil is not presumed.

MALICIOUS, *adjective* acrimonious, antagonistic, brutal, cruel, demoniac, demoniacal, destructive, diabolic, diabolical, evil, evil-minded, feral, ferocious, harmful, hateful, hostile, ill-disposed, ill-natured, invidious, *invidus,* malefic, maleficent, maleficial, malevolent, *malevolus,* malignant, merciless, mischievous, ornery, pernicious, relentless, resentful, ruthless, savage, spiteful, treacherous, truculent, unfeeling, venemous, vicious, vindictive, virulent, wanton, wicked
ASSOCIATED CONCEPTS: malicious mischief, malicious prosecution
FOREIGN PHRASES: *Malitiis hominum est obviandum.* The malicious designs of men must be thwarted.

MALICIOUS PROSECUTION, *noun* indefensible prosecution, Kafka-like prosecution, malicious charges instituted by a prosecutor, malicious criminal enforcement, malicious pursuit by a law enforcement agency, prosecution maintained with venal intentions, prosecution without proper procedures, reprehensible prosecution, unconscionable prosecution, unconstitutional prosecution, underhanded prosecution, unfair prosecution, unjust and unfair pursuit of criminal charges, unjustifiable prosecution, unmerited prosecution, unprincipled prosecution, unscrupulous prosecution, unwarrantable prosecution, wrongful prosecution

MALIGN, *verb* abuse, anathematize, asperse, attack, attack the reputation of, besmirch, blaspheme, bring into discredit, calumniate, cast a slur upon, cast aspersions, curse, decry, defame, defile, denigrate, denounce, deprecate, derogate, disesteem, dishonor, dishonor by false reports, disparage, dispraise, falsify, fulminate against, impugn, libel, revile, ridicule, slander, slur, smear, smirch, speak evil of, speak ill of, spread an evil report, stain one's reputation, traduce, vilify, vilipend, vituperate

MALIGNANT, *adjective*   atrocious, baleful, baneful, barbarous, bitter, blackhearted, bloodthirsty, brutal, brutish, cancerous, caustic, cold-blooded, coldhearted, consuming, corrosive, cruel, damaging, dangerous, deadly, death-bringing, death-dealing, deathly, deleterious, demoniacal, despiteful, destructive, detrimental, devilish, diabolical, envenomed, evil, evil-minded, execrable, fatal, fell, feral, ferocious, fiendish, fiendlike, flint-hearted, foul, hard of heart, harmful, hateful, heinous, hellish, hostile, hurtful, ill-intentioned, infernal, inhuman, iniquitous, injurious, insalubrious, invidious, lethal, malefic, maleficent, malevolent, malicious, malign, marble-hearted, mephitic, miasmal, miasmatic, miasmatical, monstrous, morbid, morbiferous, morbific, morbifical, mordacious, murderous, nasty, nefarious, nocuous, noisome, noxious, oppressive, peccant, pernicious, persecuting, pestiferous, pestilential, poisonous, rancorous, resentful, revengeful, ruinous, ruthless, satanic, savage, scatheful, scurrilous, sinful, sinister, spiteful, spleenful, stonyhearted, tending to cause death, toxic, toxiferous, treacherous, truculent, unmerciful, venomous, vicious, vile, villainous, vindictive, violent, virulent, virulently inimical, vitriolic, wicked

MALLEABLE, *adjective*   accommodating, acquiescent, adaptable, adjustable, agreeable, amenable, amiable, bendable, compliant, conformable, conforming, controllable, deferential, docile, ductile, *ductilis,* easily bent, easily influenced, easily persuaded, easy, easygoing, elastic, flexible, flexile, following, formable, governable, impressionable, *lentus,* limber, lissome, lithe, lithesome, manageable, meek, moldable, moldable like putty, moldable like wax, *mollis,* obliging, plastic, pliable, pliant, soft, softened, spineless, stretchable, submissive, tame, teachable, tractable, twistable, usable, weak like putty, weak-minded, weak-willed, well-behaved, willing, yielding

MALPRACTICE, *noun*   breach of practice, breach of profession, carelessness, culpable professional neglect, dereliction of duty, improper professional action, improper professional conduct, injudicious treatment, injurious treatment by a professional, misconduct, professional error of judgment, professional laxness, professional misconduct, professional neglect, professional negligence, unprofessional conduct, unprofessional treatment, violation of professional code, violation of professional duty
ASSOCIATED CONCEPTS: legal malpractice, medical malpractice, professional malpractice

MALTREAT, *verb*   abuse, assail, ill-treat, ill-use, mishandle, mistreat, oppress, persecute

MAMMOTH, *adjective*   as high as the sky, astronomical, colossal, enormous, gargantuan, gigantic, great, huge, immense, large, massive, monstrous, mountainous, thundering, towering, tremendous, up to the sky, vast, walloping

MANAGE, *verb*   administer, *administrare,* administrate, be in power, boss, care for, carry on, command, conduct, control, cope with, dictate, direct, disburse, dominate, engineer, execute, exercise authority, govern, guide, handle, have control, have under command, head, keep in order,

lead, look after, maneuver, manipulate, master, mastermind, occupy the chair, officiate, operate, order, oversee, pilot, preside, preside over, *regere,* regiment, regulate, rule, run, see to, steer, subjugate, superintend, supervise, sway, take charge of, take over, *tractare,* transact, treat, wield authority, work

MANAGEABLE, *adjective*   able to be completed, able to be finished, controllable, capable of completing, capable of finishing, doable, operable, performable, under control, workable
ASSOCIATED CONCEPTS: judicially manageable standards

MANAGED CARE, *noun*   controlled medical panel, supervised medical care, supervised medical panel
Generally: health care system

MANAGEMENT *(Directorate),* *noun*   administration, administrators, advisers, authority, board, board of directors, bureau, bureaucracy, caretakers, central office, chair, chairmen, command, committee, controllers, custodians, decision-making body, directors, directorship, executive committee, executive office, executives, front office, generals, governing body, government, headmen, headquarters, leaders, leadership, officers, officials, party in power, power, presidency, presidium, regime, steering committee, stewards, strategists, superintendents, supervisors

MANAGEMENT *(Judicious use),* *noun*   conduct, cunning practice, dealing, disposal, economic use, employment, finesse, frugality, handling, manipulation, operation, prudent conduct, running, skillful treatment, steerage, thrifty use, treatment, usage, utilization

MANAGEMENT *(Supervision),* *noun*   administratio, administration, administrators, authority, board of directors, care, charge, command, control, controllers, *cura,* direction, directorate, directors, directorship, executive arm, executives, generalship, governance, guidance, leadership, managers, managership, oversight, pilotage, protectorship, regulation, steering, stewardship, superintendence, surveillance, *tractatio,* wardship
ASSOCIATED CONCEPTS: exclusive management, fraud in management, general management, management of one's affairs, management of property

MANDAMUS, *noun*   charge, command, decree, dictate, direct, legislate, order, rule
ASSOCIATED CONCEPTS: writ of mandamus

MANDATE, *noun*   authoritative command, authoritative order, behest, bid, canon, charge, command, command by the court, commandment, decree, decretal, dictate, dictation, direction, directive, edict, enactment, fiat, imperative, instruction, judicial command, judicial decree, judicial order, *mandatum,* order, precept, prescript, prescription, proscription, regulation, request, requirement, requisition, rule, ruling, ultimatum, written order
ASSOCIATED CONCEPTS: judicial mandate, legislative mandate, mandate of the court
FOREIGN PHRASES: *Rei turpis nullum mandatum est.* The mandate of an immoral thing is void. *Cui jurisdictio data est, ea quoque concessa esse videntur, sine quibus jurisdictio explicari non potest.* To whom jurisdiction is given, those things also are held to be granted, without which the jurisdiction cannot be exercised.

MANDATORY, *adjective*   binding, bounden, called for, coercive, commanded, commanding, compulsory, crucial, decreed, demanded, essential, exigent, imperative,

incumbent on, indispensable, involuntary, necessary, necessitated, necessitous, obligatory, ordained, peremptory, prerequisite, prescribed, pressing, required, requisite, unavoidable, urgent, vital, without appeal, without choice
ASSOCIATED CONCEPTS: mandatory injunction, mandatory relief, mandatory sentence, mandatory statutory provisions

MANEUVER *(Tactic)*, **noun** approach, course of conduct, *decursio, decursus,* device, line of action, management, manipulation, mode of procedure, move, operation, plan of attack, planned campaign, procedure, scheme, stratagem, strategy, stroke, undertaking

MANEUVER *(Trick)*, **noun** artful dodge, artifice, *artificium,* chicanery, circumvention, cozenage, crafty device, cunning contrivance, deception, decoy, design, device, dodge, *dolus,* feint, fraud, fraudulent expedient, hoax, legerdemain, machination, plot, ruse, scheme, sharp practice, sleight, stratagem, subterfuge, trap, underhanded act, wile

MANEUVER, verb arrange, be in collusion, brew, cabal, cheat, collude, complot, concoct, connive, conspire, contrive, countermine, counterplot, deploy, design, devise, engineer, *evagari,* form a plot, frame, intrigue, jockey, lay plans, machinate, make a plan, make arrangements, manage, move, plan, plan strategy, plot, prearrange, proceed by stratagem, scheme, shift, take steps, trick, work out

MANIC, adjective agitated, aroused, enraged, excited, frantic, frenzied, hyped-up, hyper, hyperactive, hysterical, incensed, inflamed, nervous, out of control, perturbed, stirred-up, worked-up, wrought-up
ASSOCIATED CONCEPTS: insanity defense

MANIFEST, adjective *apertus,* apparent, avowed, bald, bare, beholdable, blatant, clear, clear-cut, conspicuous, crying, crystal clear, defined, discernible, disclosed, distinct, easy to see, *evidens,* evident, explicit, exposed, express, eye-catching, flagrant, glaring, gross, identifiable, in bold relief, in evidence, in focus, in full view, in sight, in the foreground, in view, indisputable, indubitable, insuppressible, lucid, marked, naked, not concealed, not obscure, notable, noticeable, observable, obvious, open, ostensible, overt, palpable, patent, perceivable, perceptible, perspicuous, *perspicuus,* plain, prominent, pronounced, public, recognizable, revealed, salient, seeable, showable, standing out, sticking out, striking, tangible, transparent, unclouded, unconcealed, uncontestable, undisguised, unhidden, unmistakable, unquestionable, visible, well-defined, well-marked, well-seen
ASSOCIATED CONCEPTS: manifest danger, manifest error, manifest necessity, manifest peril

MANIFEST, verb air, *aperire,* attest, bare, be evidence of, bespeak, betoken, bring forth, bring forward, bring into the open, bring out, bring to light, bring to notice, bring to the front, bring to view, certify, *declarare,* declare, demonstrate, denote, designate, disclose, discover, display, divulge, evidence, evince, exhibit, explain, expose, expose to view, express, hold up, hold up to view, illuminate, illustrate, impart, indicate, lay bare, lay open, lay out, make clear, make conspicuous, make evident, make known, make obvious, make plain, make visible, mark, open, open up, patefacere, point out, present, proclaim, prove, publish, represent, reveal, set forth, set out, show, signify, speak out, testify, throw open, unconceal, uncover, uncurtain, undrape, unearth, unfold, unmask, unscreen, unshroud, unveil
FOREIGN PHRASES: *In rebus manifestis, errat qui auctoritates legum allegat; quia perspicua vera non sunt probanda.*

In clear cases, he mistakes who cites legal authorities; for obvious truths are not to be proved. *Manifesta probatione non indigent.* Manifest facts do not require proof.

MANIFESTATION, noun appearance, badge, *declaratio, demonstratio,* demonstration, disclosure, discovery, display, divulgence, emblem, emergence, evidence, evincement, exhibit, exhibition, expose, exposition, exposure, expression, indication, *indicium,* mark, materialization, production, representation, revelation, show, showing, sign, signal, signification, symbol, symptom, uncovering, unfolding, unmasking, unveiling
ASSOCIATED CONCEPTS: manifestation of intent

MANIFOLD, adjective assorted, considerable, divers, diverse, diversified, innumerable, many, miscellaneous, multifarious, multifold, multiform, multiple, *multiplex,* multiplicate, multitudinous, myriad, numerous, populous, profuse, several, sundry, teeming, variegated, various, *varius*

MANIPULATE *(Control unfairly)*, **verb** dominate, exploit, influence, manage, misuse, pull strings, pull wires, rig, rule, take advantage of, use

MANIPULATE *(Utilize skillfully)*, **verb** apply, command, conduct, control, direct, drive, employ, engineer, govern, guide, handle, lead, make use of, maneuver, operate, pilot, ply, put in action, put into operation, regulate, run, set in motion, set to work, steer, *tractare,* use, utilize, wield, work

MANIPULATION, noun change, control, dominate, employment, execution, exercise, exploitation, finagling, governance, handling, influence, machination, management, maneuvering, maneuvers, plotting, ploy, regulation, scheming, take advantage of
ASSOCIATED CONCEPTS: manipulation of security prices, market manipulation law

MANNER *(Behavior)*, **noun** actions, acts, address, air, appearance, approach, aspect, attitude, bearing, behavior pattern, carriage, comportment, conduct, consuetude, course of action, course of conduct, custom, customary procedure, decorum, demeanor, deportment, distinctive social attitude, etiquette, fashion, guise, habit, habitual practice, line of action, line of conduct, look, method, method of action, mien, mode, mode of proceeding, observance, operation, pattern, personal bearing, personal style, port, posture, practice, praxis, presence, procedure, proceeding, routine, stance, style, tactics, tone, usage, way, wise, wont

MANNER *(Kind)*, **noun** brand, categorization, category, class, classification, denomination, description, designation, division, fashion, form, grouping, ilk, kind, make, order, selection, sort, species, style, type, variety

MANSLAUGHTER, noun accidental homicide, homicide, *homicidium, hominis caedes,* killing, murder, reckless homicide, unintentional homicide, unintentional murder, unpremeditated murder
ASSOCIATED CONCEPTS: involuntary manslaughter, killing in the heat of passion, second degree manslaughter, voluntary manslaughter

MANUAL *(By hand)*, **adjective** by use of the hands, each one, hand-operated, not automated, not automatic, old fashioned, one-at-a-time, one-by-one, without technology
ASSOCIATED CONCEPTS: manual labor, manual rates

MANUAL *(Guidebook)*, **noun**   comprehensive book, exercise book, guidebook, handbook, how-to book, reference book, standard, step-by-step analysis, text, textbook
ASSOCIATED CONCEPTS: buyer's manual

MANUFACTURE, noun   assemblage, assembly, composition, construction, creation, development, execution, *fabrica*, fabrication, fashioning, forging, formation, forming, making, molding, origination, preparation, production, synthesis

MANUFACTURE, verb   assemble, build, compose, construct, contrive, create, devise, engineer, evolve, *fabricari*, fabricate, fashion, forge, form, formulate, generate, invent, make, make by mechanical industry, make up, mass produce, mold, originate, process, produce, put in production, put together, turn out, turn out by industrial process
ASSOCIATED CONCEPTS: manufacture goods, products liability involved in manufactured goods

MARATHON, adjective   extended, forever, interminable, lasting, lengthened, lingering, long, long-continued, long-continuing, long-drawn, long-drawn-out, long-winded, never-ending, overlong, prolonged, protracted, taking forever, time-consuming, unending

MARGIN *(Outside limit)*, **noun**   bank, border, boundary, bounds, brim, brink, circumference, curb, edge, frame, fringe, hem, ledge, limit, lip, outskirt, perimeter, periphery, portal, rim, shore, skirt, threshold, verge

MARGIN *(Spare amount)*, **noun**   amount reserved, clearance, elbowroom, extra amount for contingencies, extra amount for emergencies, headway, latitude, leeway, opening, reserve, reserved amount, room, room to spare, space
ASSOCIATED CONCEPTS: margin of profit

MARGINAL, adjective   average, bare, barely acceptable, barely adequate, below par, borderline, fair, humble, *in margine positus, in margine scriptus*, inappreciable, indifferent, low-quality, meager, mediocre, mere, middling, moderate, modest, passable, poor, scant, scanty, skimpy, tenuous, tolerable, trifling, undistinguished, wanting, weak

MARGINALIA, noun   commentary, entry, footnote, inscription, notation, note, memorandum, record, register

MARK, noun   autograph, badge, characteristic, check, cipher, countermark, emblem, identification, idiosyncrasy, imprint, indication, initials, manifestation, marker, particularity, proof, record, representation, sign, signature, stamp, symbol, token, trace, trademark, vestige

MARKED OFF THE CALENDAR, verb   deferred, delayed, extended, halted temporarily, held in abeyance, held off, in suspense, not heard, placed in oblivion, prolonged, put off indefinitely, shelved, stalled, stricken from the calendar, suspended, suspended until restored, tabled, unsettled

MARKET *(Business)*, **noun**   agora, bazaar, bourse, concern, department store, emporium, establishment, exchange, fair, financial center, general store, house, *macellum*, mart, *mercatus, nundinae*, open mart, place of business, place of buying and selling, place of commerce, place of trade, place of traffic, retail store, rialto, shop, shopping center, store, trade fair, trading house, trading post, variety store
ASSOCIATED CONCEPTS: actual market value, fair market price, market conditions, market place, market price, market value

MARKET *(Demand)*, **noun**   call, call for, consumer demand, desire, desire to buy, desire to obtain, earnest seeking, essentiality, heavy demand, indispensability, inquiry, insufficiency, interest, lack, mania, necessity, need, outlet, pressing requirement, pursuit, request, requirement, requisition, run, search, steady demand, strong demand, vogue, want, willingness to purchase, wish

MARKET PLACE, noun   agora, emporium, exchange, exposition, financial center, *forum*, open market, place of business, place of business traffic, place of buying and selling, place of commerce, place of trade, plaza, shopping center, square, trading place
ASSOCIATED CONCEPTS: public markets

MARKETABLE, adjective   commercial, exchangeable, fit for sale, merchantable, salable, tradable, *venalis*, vendible
ASSOCIATED CONCEPTS: marketable title

MARRED, adjective   blemished, blighted, bruised, cankered, contaminated, corrupted, crippled, damaged, defaced, defective, deformed, despoiled, disabled, discolored, disfigured, faulty, flawed, fouled, garbled, hamstrung, harmed, hurt, impaired, imperfect, impure, infected, injured, lamed, maimed, mangled, marked, mutilated, no longer in perfect condition, pitted, rotten, ruined, scarred, scathed, scratched, speckled, spoiled, spotted, stained, sullied, tainted, tarnished, wounded

MARRIAGE *(Intimate relationship)*, **noun**   accouplement, alliance, bond, close relationship, closeness, cohabitation, couplement, coupling, intimacy, joining, linkage, linking, tie, union
ASSOCIATED CONCEPTS: common-law marriage

MARRIAGE *(Wedlock)*, **noun**   bond of matrimony, cohabitation, *coniugium*, conjugal union, conjugality, connubiality, espousal, espousement, marriage tie, married life, married state, married status, *matrimonium*, matrimony, *nuptiae*, nuptial bond, nuptial tie, spousal, wedded state, wedding
ASSOCIATED CONCEPTS: adultery, annulment, bigamous marriage, consensual marriage, consummation of marriage, contract of marriage, coverture, curtesy, divorce, dower, marriage ceremony, marriage license, marriage promise, polygamous marriage, solemnize a marriage, void marriage, voidable marriage
FOREIGN PHRASES: *Nuptias non concubitus sed consensus facit.* Not cohabitation but consent makes the valid marriage. *Pater est quem nuptioe demonstrant.* He is the father whom the marriage points out. *Semper praesumitur pro matrimonio.* The presumption is always in favor of the validity of a marriage. *Subsequens matrimonium tollit peccatum praecedens.* A subsequent marriage removes a previous fault.

MARSHAL, noun   arm of the law, bailiff, county officer, court officer, *dux*, federal officer, law enforcement agent, minor officer of the law, officer, officer of the law, officer who carries out orders of the court, peace officer

MARSHAL, verb   allocate, allot, apportion, arrange, array, assign, bring to order, collocate, compose, coordinate, deal out, *disponere*, distribute, fix, form into ranks, group, guide, index, *instruere*, introduce order, lead, line up, manage, muster, organize, parcel out, place, place in order, position, put in order, rank, regiment, regulate, set in order, set up, systematize
ASSOCIATED CONCEPTS: marshaling assets, marshaling liens, marshaling remedies, marshaling securities

MASK (Cover), **noun**   camouflage, cloak, cover-up, deflection, device, disguise, excuse, facade, false front, feint, front, guise, lame excuse, masquerade, mere cosmetics, obscuration, pretense, pretension, pretext, professed motive, refuge, screen, sham, smoke screen, stalking-horse, stratagem, subterfuge, varnish, whitewash

MASK (Shield), **noun**   camouflage, deflection, disguise, false front, false identity, incognito, masquerade, pretense, shield, veil

MASS (Body of persons), **noun**   aggregate, assemblage, body, cluster, congregation, crowd, drove, flock, gathering, host, mob, multitude, *multitudo,* phalanx, plurality, swarm, throng, *vulgus*
ASSOCIATED CONCEPTS: mass market, mass picketing

MASS (Weight), **noun**   amplitude, bigness, body, bulk, density, dimension, extent, fullness, gauge, greatness, immensity, largeness, magnitude, measure, measurement, sizableness, size

MASTER, adjective   arch, authoritative, capital, central, chief, commanding, controlling, crowning, dictating, dominant, eminent, foremost, governing, great, head, hegemonic, hegemonical, incomparable, influential, leading, main, most important, outstanding, paramount, predominating, preeminent, prepotent, prevailing, prevalent, primary, prime, ranking, recognized, regnant, reigning, ruling, sovereign, star, stellar, supereminent, supreme, top-flight, well-known
ASSOCIATED CONCEPTS: agency, master and servant

MASTERFUL, adjective   ace, adept, adroit, apt, artistic, authoritarian, authoritative, brilliant, clever, crackerjack, cunning, slick, deft, dexterous, diplomatic, excellent, exemplary, expert, first-rate, ingenious, lordly, magical, model, polished, powerful, preeminent, professional, proficient, quintessential, refined, resourceful, statesmanlike, stylish, technically brilliant, the complete professional, the consummate professional, virtuoso
ASSOCIATED CONCEPTS: masterful arguments in court

MASTERMIND, noun   authority, creative genius, creator, expert, genius, intellect, intellectual, intellectual prodigy, leader, learned person, luminary, master, mental giant, mentor, person of intellect, prodigy, pundit, qualified person, sage, savant, specialist, strategist, tactician, thinker, wise man

MASTERY, noun   ability, accomplishment, achievement, acquirement, acquisition, adeptness, adroitness, artisanship, artistry, attainment, brilliance, chieftainship, cleverness, cognizance, command, competence, comprehension, craftsmanship, cunning, expertise, expertness, extensive knowledge, facility, finesse, grace, grasp, in-depth knowledge, influence, ingeniousness, ingenuity, knowledge, nobility, perfection, polish, practical ability, preeminence, premiership, proficiency, profound knowledge, skill, skillfulness, specialized knowledge, style, success, superiority, tact, tactfulness, technical brilliance, technical mastery, technical skill, technique, timing, total command, unique knowledge, victory over, virtuosity, wizardry

MATCH (Contest), **noun**   bout, championship, competition, fight, final game, game, games, joust, matching, meet, playoff game, test, tournament, tourney

MATCH (Duplicate), **noun**   clone, companion, copy, equal, exact copy, exact duplicate, exact likeness, facsimile, likeness, mate, mirror, mirror copy, model, perfect likeness, reflection, replica, resemblance, semblance, the image, twin

MATCH (Marriage), **noun**   alliance, arranged marriage, bed, bond, bridal bed, bridebed, cohabitation, common-law marriage, conjugal bliss, conjugal bond, conjugality, coverture, getting hitched, holy matrimony, holy wedlock, homosexual marriage, husbandhood, ill-assorted marriage, interfaith marriage, intermarriage, interracial marriage, lesbian, living as man and wife, marriage bed, marriage sacrament, married state *or* status, married status, matching, match-up, matrimonial union, matrimony, misalliance, miscegenation, mixed marriage, nuptial bond, one flesh, remarriage, sacrament of matrimony *or* marriage, splicing, spousehood, tying the knot, union, wedded bliss, wedded state, weddedness, wedding knot, wedlock, wifehood

MATERIAL (Important), **adjective**   basic, capital, cardinal, central, compelling, consequential, considerable, critical, crucial, decisive, effective, essential, extensive, far-reaching, fundamental, indispensable, influential, key, leading, main, major, memorable, momentous, necessary, paramount, pertinent, pivotal, prevalent, primary, principal, relevant, remarkable, salient, signal, significant, substantial, valuable, vital, weighty, worth considering
ASSOCIATED CONCEPTS: material allegation, material alteration, material amendment, material change in circumstances, material defect, material defendant, material departure from the truth, material error, material evidence, material fact, material false representation, material misrepresentation, material witness

MATERIAL (Physical), **adjective**   actual, bodily, concrete, corporeal, *corporeus, de facto,* earthly, mundane, nonspiritual, palpable, real, secular, solid, substantial, tactile, tangible, temporal, unspiritual, worldly
ASSOCIATED CONCEPTS: material furnished

MATERIAL POINT, noun   bench mark, cardinal point, center, central idea, chief point, core, cornerstone, critical point, crucial point, crux, essence, essential matter, essential part, essential point, focal point, focus, fundamental point, gist, gravamen, heart, heart of the matter, important issue, important part, inner core, kernel, linchpin, main idea, marrow, material point, meat, nitty-gritty, nucleus, pivotal point, prime feature, prime issue, quintessence, root, salient point, substance, substantive point
ASSOCIATED CONCEPTS: material point in an argument

MATERIALITY (Consequence), **noun**   caliber, distinction, eminence, gravity, greatness, import, importance, magnitude, materialness, matter, memorability, momentousness, notability, notableness, priority, prominence, purport, rank, relevance, salience, significance, substantiality, sum and substance, value, weight, weightiness, worth

MATERIALITY (Physical existence), **noun**   bodiliness, bodily existence, body, concreteness, corporality, corporeity, embodiment, entity, essential nature, existence, mass, material existence, materialness, matter, palpability, physical being, physical nature, physicalness, reality, solidity, substance, substantiality, substantialness, tangibility

MATERIALMAN, noun   artificer, builder, constructor, contractor, designer, deviser, engineer, outfitter, provider, supplier
ASSOCIATED CONCEPTS: materialman's lien

MATERNITY, *noun*   fertility, motherhood, motherliness, parenthood, propagation, reproduction

MATRIMONY, *noun*   alliance, cohabitation, conjugality, connubiality, consortium, espousal, espousement, joining, marriage, marriage tie, married life, married state, married status, match, mating, *matrimonium,* nuptial bond, nuptial state, nuptial tie, partnership, sacrament of marriage, spousal, union, wedded state, wedlock
ASSOCIATED CONCEPTS: matrimonial action, matrimonial cohabitation, matrimonial domicile, matrimonial res

MATTER *(Case), noun*   action, *causa,* cause, cause in court, claim, court action, dispute, inquiry, lawsuit, legal action, legal proceedings, litigation, pleadings, proceedings, suit, suit at law, trial
ASSOCIATED CONCEPTS: matter of record

MATTER *(Subject), noun*   business on hand, case, case in question, claim, concern, debatable point, dispute, field of inquiry, *institutum,* issue, item on the agenda, point, point at issue, point in question, problem, proposition, *propositum,* question, *res,* subject for inquiry, subject matter, topic, topic for discussion
ASSOCIATED CONCEPTS: immaterial matter, matter in controversy, matter in dispute, matter in issue, matter in pais, matter of fact, matter of form, matter of law, matter of record, matter of substance, matters pending
FOREIGN PHRASES: *Certa debet esse intentio, et narratio, et certum fundamentum, et certa res quae deducitur in judicium.* The intention, declaration, foundation, and matter brought to judgment ought to be certain. *Eventus varios res nova semper habet.* A new matter always holds the possibility of a different result. *Culpa est immiscere se rel ad se non pertinenti.* It is a fault for anyone to meddle in matters which do not concern him.

MATTER IN DISPUTE, *noun*   argument, bone of contention, case, concern, conclusion, conflict, contention, contentiousness, contestation, controversy, crux, debate, dialogue, disputation, disputatiousness, dispute, embroilment, essence of the dispute, feud, fight, fighting, focus of attention, formal argument, fracas, hostility, imbroglio, infighting, issue, item for the agenda, litigation, matter, matter being examined in depth, matter in hand, matter under investigation, open controversy, open quarrel, plot, point, point at issue, point in question, polemic, position, premise, pretext, problem, purport, quarrel, quarreling, question, question at issue, point at issue, rationale, reason, reasoning, refutation, result, stance, subject, subject matter, substance, text, thesis
ASSOCIATED CONCEPTS: subject matter of dispute

MATTER IN QUESTION, *noun*   argument, concern, conclusion, controversy, crux, dialogue, dispute, embroilment, focus of attention, formal argument, imbroglio, issue, item for the agenda, litigation, matter, matter being examined in depth, matter in controversy, matter in dispute, matter in hand, matter under investigation, plot, point, point at issue, point in question, polemic, position, premise, pretext, problem, purport, question, question at issue, rationale, reason, reasoning, refutation, result, stance, subject, subject matter, substance, text, thesis, underlying issue

MATTER OF COURSE, *noun*   common practice, common run, common state of affairs, customary procedure, general run, natural state, ordinary run of things, ordinary state, prescribed form, procedure, regular procedure, routine, routine event, routine happening, rule, set form, usual custom, usual occurrence, usual practice, usual procedure, usual thing

MATTER OF RECORD, *noun*   a material part of the record, a point in question, accounted for on the record, chronicled, documented on the record, entered into evidence, entered into testimony, entered into the record, introduced into evidence, introduced into testimony, on the record, part of the record, part of the recorded proceedings, part of the text of the record, part of the transcript, part of the transcription
ASSOCIATED CONCEPTS: court testimony, estoppel by matter of record

MATURE, *verb*   accrue, advance toward perfection, age, attain majority, attain maturity, become due, become fully developed, become payable, become perfected, become prime, become ripe, bring to full development, bring to its peak, bring to maturity, bring to perfection, come of age, consummate, coquere, culminate, develop, evolve, fall due, finish, grow up, *maturare,* maturate, nurture, perfect, ripen, season
ASSOCIATED CONCEPTS: matured account

MATURITY, *noun*   adulthood, completion, consummation, culmination, due date, evolution, falling due, fulfillment, full age, full development, full growth, majority, matureness, *maturitas,* perfected condition, perfection, preparedness, readiness
ASSOCIATED CONCEPTS: maturity of a debt, maturity of an obligation

MAXIM, *noun*   adage, aphorism, aphoristic expression, axiom, byword, canon, established principle, expression, gnomic saying, moralism, pithy saying, postulate, *praeceptum,* precept, principium, principle, proverb, proverbial saying, *regula,* rule, sage reflection, saw, saying, sententious saying, sententious utterance, statement of general truth, teaching, truth, wise saying

MAXIMUM *(Amplitude), noun*   ampleness, capacity, fullness, greatest, peak, plentitude, saturation, size, total, utmost

MAXIMUM *(Pinnacle), noun*   crown, culmination, limit, most, ne plus ultra, upper extremity

MAZE *(Confusion), noun*   complexity, confusion, convolution, intricacy, labyrinth, meandering, network, puzzle, snarl, tangle, twist, winding

MAZE *(Winding course), noun*   bafflement, befuddlement, bewilderment, complex, convolution, disorientation, entanglement, incomprehensibility, intricacy, labyrinth, meandering, morass, network, perplexity, puzzle, tangle, torsion, twist, winding

MEAGER, *adjective*   a cosmetic measure, a drop in the bucket, bare, bare-boned, cursory, deficient, depthless, inadequacy, inadequate, inconsequential, inconsiderable, infrequent, insignificant, insufficient, lacking, lean, measly, miserly, negligible, niggardly, not enough, not much, not plentiful, paltry, petty, picayune, piddling, pittance, rare, scant, scanty, scarce, seldom seen, shabby, shallow, skeletal, skimping, slender, slight, slim, small, spare, sparing, sparse, sprinkled, superficial, tenuous, too little, trifial, underfed, undernourished, undersized, underweight, unimportant, unsuitability, wanting

MEAN

MEAN *(Average)*, **adjective**   central, grouping, intermediary, medial, median, medium, mesial, middle, midmost, statistical average

MEAN *(Base)*, **adjective**   abject, brutal, contemptible, degrading, despicable, disgraceful, dishonorable, heinous, ignoble, ignominious, inappreciable, inconsiderate, inimical, intermediate, loathsome, low-grade, low-minded, Machiavellian, malevolent, mediocre, mercenary, miserly, nasty, niggardly, odious, paltry, penurious, perverse, petulant, questionable, servile, shady, shameful, spiteful, tightfisted, vicious, vile, villainous, wretched

MEAN, noun   average, balance, center, heart, mean proportion, median, mediocrity, medium, middle ground, middle state, normal, rule

MEAN, verb   affirm, allude to, bespeak, betoken, connote, convey, declare, denote, express, imply, import, indicate, intend, intimate, manifest, propose, purport, represent, signify

MEANING, noun   acceptation, connotation, content, definition, denotation, drift, explanation, idea, import, interpretation, purport, semantics, semasiology, sense, *sententia*, significance, *significatio*, signification, substance, tenor, text, *vis*
ASSOCIATED CONCEPTS: plain meaning, secondary meaning
FOREIGN PHRASES: *Primo excutienda est verbi vis, ne sermonis vitio obstruatur oratio, sive lex sine argumentis.* The force of a word should be ascertained in the beginning, lest the sentence be destroyed by the fault of expression, or the law be without reason. *Sensus verborum est anima legis.* The meaning of words is the spirit of the law. *In testamentis ratio tacita non debet considerari, sed verba solum spectari debent; adeo per divinationem mentis a verbis recedere durum est.* In wills an unexpressed intention ought not to be considered, but the words alone ought to be regarded; for it is difficult to recede from the words by guessing at their intention.

MEANINGLESS, adjective   absurd, asinine, empty, failed, failing, farcical, fatuous, foolish, frivolous, fruitless, futile, hollow, immaterial, inane, inapplicable, incomprehensible, inconsequential, inconsiderable, ineffective, ineffectual, inefficacious, insignificant, insubstantial, irrational, irrelevant, malfunctioning, minor, miscarried, miscarrying, negligible, nonsensical, not worth mentioning, of little account, of little consequence, of little effect, of little import, of little importance, of no concern, of no great weight, paltry, petty, picayune, piddling, pointless, purposeless, senseless, small, trivial, unessential, unfortunate, unimportant, unintelligible, unreasonable, unsubstantial, unsuccessful, useless, worthless
ASSOCIATED CONCEPTS: jury nullification, meaningless law, meaningless utterances, rendered meaningless

MEANS *(Funds)*, **noun**   assets, finances, resource, resources, wealth, wherewithal
ASSOCIATED CONCEPTS: means doctrine, means of knowledge, means of satisfaction, means of support

MEANS *(Opportunity)*, **noun**   application, capacity, devices, employment, fashion, form, guise, handiness, manner, measures, method, mode, serviceability, style, system, tone, usage, use, ways, wherewithal

MEASURE, noun   act, bill, caveat, declaration, decree, dictate, edict, enactment, law, legislation, legislative enactment, legislative mandate, legislative proclamation, mandate, piece of legislation, prescript, prescription, proposal, proposed act, proposition, regulation, rubric, rule, ruling, statute
ASSOCIATED CONCEPTS: appropriate measures, measure of benefit, measure of damages, measure of value, regulatory measure, remedial measures

MEASURE, verb   admeasure, appraise, ascertain dimensions, ascertain size, assess, bring into comparison, calculate, calibrate, compare, compute, correlate, *demetiri*, determine size, determine value, estimate, evaluate, fathom, form an estimate, form an opinion, gauge, grade, graduate, graph, judge, liken, make a comparison, make an estimate, mark off, match, *metari*, mete, meter, pace off, *permetiri*, portion out, quantify, rank, rate, reckon, rule, set a value on, size, span, survey, value, weigh
ASSOCIATED CONCEPTS: appropriate measure of damages

MEASURABLE, adjective   appraisable, appreciable, ascertainable, calculable, capable of being delineated, capable of being quantified, computable, considerable, determinable, estimable, fathomable, measured, numerable, perceptible, quantifiable, ratable
ASSOCIATED CONCEPTS: measurable pollutants

MEASUREMENT, noun   admeasurement, amount, analysis, appraisal, appraisement, assessment, bulk, calculation, capaciousness, capacity, computation, dimensions, estimate, estimation, extent, gauge, girth, greatness, largeness, limit, magnitude, mass, measure, *mensio, mensura*, mensuration, metage, meterage, quantification, quantity, rating, reckoning, size, span, survey, valuation, vastness
ASSOCIATED CONCEPTS: measurement of damages, measurement of liability

MECHANICS LIEN, noun   charge, charge imposed on specific property, claim on property, hold on property, right to enforce charge on property, security on property

MEDDLE, noun   barge in, be curious, be officious, break in on, bust in, chime in, crash the gates of, dabble in, encroach, encumber, horn in, impose, infringe, inquire, insert yourself into, interfere, interlope, intermeddle, interpose, interrupt, intervene, intrude, muscle into, obstruct, provide your two cents, pry, push in, tamper with, trespass
ASSOCIATED CONCEPTS: tampering with evidence

MEDIATE, verb   adjust, adjust difficulties, arbitrate, arrange differences, bring to an understanding, bring to terms, bring together, compromise, conciliate, effect an agreement, intercede, interfere, intervene, moderate, negotiate, *pacem conciliare*, parley, reconcile, referee, restore harmony, *se interponere*, settle, settle a dispute, settle by conciliation, settle differences, umpire, work out differences
ASSOCIATED CONCEPTS: arbitrate

MEDIATION, noun   adjustment, adjustment of difficulties, arbitration, conciliation, finding a middle course, intercession, interference, intervention, intervention to facilitate a compromise, negotiation, negotiation process, parley, reconciliation, settlement of difficulties, settlement of dispute
ASSOCIATED CONCEPTS: fact finding, mediation board

MEDICAID, noun   government-provided health insurance for the uninsured, health care for the underprivileged, health coverage for low income persons
Generally: health insurance, medical assistance, medical coverage, national health insurance, supplemental medical program

MEDICARE, noun government health insurance coverage, government program for hospitalization of persons of 65 years of age, government-provided health insurance for senior citizens
Generally: health care, health protection, national health insurance, supplemental medical program

MEDICINAL, adjective Aesculapian, alexipharmic, alleviative, analeptic, anodyne, antidotal, antifebrile, assuasive, balmy, beneficial, cleansing, corrective, curative, demulcent, depurative, emollient, febrifugal, healing, health-giving, helpful, invigorating, lenitive, medical, medicative, palliative, purifying, recuperative, recuperatory, reformative, remedial, restitutive, restorative, roborant, salubrious, salutary, salutiferous, sanative, sanatory, soothing, therapeutic, therapeutical, tonic, vulnerary

MEDIOCRE, adjective acceptable, adequate, all right, average, banal, colorless, common, commonplace, decent, everyday, fair, fairish, good enough, inconsequential, indifferent, inferior, inglorious, insignificant, lesser, lifeless, low-class, low-grade, low-quality, meager, mean, *mediocris,* medium, middle, middling, moderate, modest, normal, ordinary, passable, poor, prosaic, prosaical, run of the mill, satisfactory, second-rate, so-so, standard, tolerable, trite, trivial, typical, undistinguished, unexceptionable, unexciting, unimportant, uninspiring, uninteresting, unnoteworthy, unobjectionable, unremarkable, usual

MEDIOCRITY, noun acceptability, adequateness, average, averageness, baseness, common lot, commonness, commonplaceness, deficiency, fairness, inconsiderableness, inferiority, inferiorness, insignificance, low grade, low quality, mean, meanness, *mediocritas,* middle state, ordinariness, passableness, poorness, satisfactoriness, standardness, tolerability, tolerableness, triviality, unexceptionality, unimportance, unnoteworthiness, unremarkableness, unsatisfactoriness

MEDIUM, noun agency, agent, broker, channel, delegate, deputy, emissary, envoy, expedient, go-between, instrument, instrumentality, interagency, interagent, intermediary, intermediate, intermediate agent, intervener, link, machinery, means, mechanism, mediating agency, mediator, middleman, mouthpiece, negotiant, negotiator, spokesperson, tool, vehicle

MEET, verb amass, assemble, associate, band together, center around, cluster, collect, collide, come face to face, come together, concur, *concurrere, confluere,* congregate, convene, converge, convoke, encounter, flock, forgather, gather together, get together, group, hold a convocation, hold a meeting, hold a session, huddle, *inter se congredi,* join, mass, muster, parley, rally, rejoin, reunite, swarm, throng, unite

MEETING (Conference), noun assembly, caucus, colloquy, conclave, *concursus, congressio,* consistory, consultation, convention, *conventus,* convocation, discussion, encounter, exchange of views, forum, gathering, interchange of views, negotiation, open discussion, panel, parley, plenum, reunion, seminar, session, summit, symposium, synod
ASSOCIATED CONCEPTS: annual meeting of shareholders, meeting of creditors, organizational meeting, public meeting, regular meeting, special meeting

MEETING (Encounter), noun appulsion, clash, collision, concours, confrontation, contact, convergence, convergency, engagement, fusion, intersection, joining, junction, juncture, merger, rendezvous, unification, union
ASSOCIATED CONCEPTS: meeting of minds

MEETING OF THE MINDS, noun accordance, agreement, common assent, compatibility, complete accord, compliance, concert, concord, concordance, concurrence, consensus, consentaneity, harmony, like-mindedness, mutual understanding, rapport, unanimity, unanimousness, understanding, uniformity, unison, unity
ASSOCIATED CONCEPTS: bilateral contract, rescission of an agreement

MELANGE, noun admixture, amalgam, assortment, blend, cento, combination, commixture, composition, compound, confused mass, conglomeration, farrago, gallimaufry, hash, hodgepodge, intermixture, jumble, medley, minglement, miscellaneous collection, miscellany, mixture, olio, pastiche, patchwork, potpourri, union

MELIORATE, verb adorn, advance, ameliorate, amend, assuage, beautify, better, correct, cultivate, cure, doctor, elaborate, elevate, embellish, emend, enhance, enrich, forward, have a good influence, improve, invigorate, lard, make better, make improvements, mend, mitigate, modernize, palliate, polish, purify, raise, reclaim, rectify, reface, refine, reform, refresh, refurbish, regenerate, rehabilitate, reinvigorate, relieve, render better, renew, renovate, reorganize, repair, restore, revive, touch up, transfigure, transform, upgrade, uplift

MEMBER (Constituent part), noun article, branch, category, component, department, division, element, factor, feature, fraction, ingredient, integral part, item, link, part, piece, portion, section, segment, share, small part, subdivision, subordinate part, unit

MEMBER (Individual in a group), noun affiliate, associate, belonger, cardholder, committeeperson, comrade, confederate, constituent, cooperator, copartner, cosharer, enlistee, enrolled person, fellow, follower, guildsman, insider, participator, partner, patron, registered person, shareholder, sharer, stockholder, teammate

MEMBER OF THE LEGAL PROFESSION, noun advocate, attorney, attorney at-law, barrister, barrister-at-law, counsel, counselor, counselor-at-law, esquire, lawyer, legal advisor, legal advocate, legal consultant, legal practitioner, practitioner, solicitor

MEMORABLE, adjective celebrated, classic, consequential, descent, distinguishable, doable, dramatic, electrifying, elevated, eminent, esteemed, estimable, eventful, excellent, exceptional, exciting, extraordinary, famous, fantastic, favorable, fine, first-rate, formidable, historic, illustrious, important, inspiring, makes the cut-off, marked, momentous, notable, noteworthy, of mark, ordinary, outstanding, passes muster, passes the grade, prestigious, prominent, reasonably notable, remarkable, special, sublime, telling, thrilling, top-notch, top-ten, unique, unusual
ASSOCIATED CONCEPTS: memorable decision

MEMORANDUM, noun aide-memoir, annotation, brief, chronicle, memoir, notation, note, postnote, record, report
ASSOCIATED CONCEPTS: memorandum of law

MEMORANDUM OF LAW, noun brief, brief containing legal arguments, brief containing legal justification, compendium of law justifying a case, condensation of law supporting a case, extract of body of law justifying a position, legal abstract of law supporting a case, legal document, legal memorandum, memorandum, summary of case law supporting an action, summary of law supporting positions, summary on the law, supporting legal issues, supporting positions, synopsis of law, the legal arguments in favor of a case, the legal basis supporting the outcome of a case

ASSOCIATED CONCEPTS: memorandum of law in support, motion for a directed verdict, motion to dismiss

MEMORY *(Commemoration)*, **noun**   celebration, remembrance, writing

MEMORY *(Retention)*, **noun**   mind, recalling, recollection, reflection

MENACE, noun   commination, danger, dangerous situation, hazard, imminent danger, imperilment, intimidating force, intimidation, minacious force, minacity, peril, prognostic, threat

MENACE, verb   affright, alarm, cause alarm, comminate, direct a threat against, disconcert, disquiet, disturb, exhibit hostile intentions, frighten, impend, inspire fear, intimidate, put in bodily fear, put in fear, raise apprehensions, scare, show hostility, startle, strike with overwhelming fear, terrify, threaten, unnerve

MENDACIOUS, adjective   artful, clever in deception, collusive, concocted, counterfeit, covinous, cunning, deceitful, deceiving, devoid of truth, dishonest, distorted, embroidered, fabricated, false, falsified, feigned, fictitious, fraudulent, given to lying, incorrect, insincere, invented, lacking truth, lying, made up, make-believe, *mendax,* misrepresentative, misrepresented, misstated, not straightforward, perfidious, perjured, perverted, pretended, prevaricating, sham, sly, spurious, truthless, uncandid, ungenuine, untrue, untruthful, unveracious, unveridical, varnished, void of truth, wrong

MENDACITY, noun   deception, dishonesty, disingenuousness, distortion, exaggeration, fabrication, falsehood, falsification, guilefulness, inaccuracy, legal fiction, lie, lying, mendaciousness, misrepresentation, misstatement, not credible, overstatement, partial truth, prevarication, sketch, tale, untruth, untruthfulness

MENS REA, noun   criminal design, criminal guilt, criminal intent, criminal purpose, criminality, culpability, vice, wrong, wrongdoing

MENTALLY ILL, adjective   bereft of reason, certifiable, delirious, demented, deranged, disabled, disordered, frenetic, frenzied, hysterical, incoherent, maniacal, manic, mental, mentally deranged, neurotic, of unsound mind, paranoiac, phobic, psychotic, raving, suffering with schizophrenia, unsound

ASSOCIATED CONCEPTS: insanity

MENTION *(Reference)*, **noun**   allegation, allusion, assertion, commemoratio, comment, communication, enlightenment, expression, hint, implication, indication, indirect hint, inference, insinuation, intimation, *mentio,* note, passing word, recital, recitation, referent, relation, remark, report, statement, suggestion

MENTION *(Tribute)*, **noun**   acclaim, acclamation, adulation, applause, appreciation, approbation, approval, blandishment, celebration, citation, commendation, compliment, credit, decoration, esteem, eulogistic speech, eulogy, exaltation, expression of merit, flattery, glorification, high opinion, homage, honor, laud, laudation, mark of honor, official recognition, panegyric, plaudit, praise, public recognition, regard, respect

MENTION, verb   acquaint, adduce, advert to, affirm, allude to, announce, annunciate, apprise, assert, bring word, broach, cite, comment upon, communicate, confide to, convey information, convey knowledge, declare incidentally, denominate, direct the attention to, disclose, discuss, divulge, enlighten, enumerate, express, give a hint, give notice, give utterance, hint at, impart, indicate, inform, insinuate, intimate, let know, make allusion to, make known, name, note, notify, observe, point out, point to, recite, recount, refer to, remark on, report, reveal, speak of, specify, state, stipulate, suggest, talk about, tell, touch upon, utter, voice

MERCANTILE, adjective   business, commercial, economic, exchange, financial, fiscal, industrial, market, merchandising, monetary, trade

ASSOCIATED CONCEPTS: mercantile law, mercantile paper

MERCENARY, adjective   accessible to bribery, acquisitive, avaricious, bribable, *conductus,* corrupt, corruptible, covetous, exacting, exploitative, grasping, greedy, hired, hireling, leased, materialistic, *mercenarius,* money conscious, money hungry, motivated by a desire for money, motivated by greed, opportunistic, paid, possessive, profiteering, purchasable, rapacious, selfish, simoniacal, unidealistic, usurious, venal, *venalis*

MERCHANDISE, noun   articles, articles of commerce, assets, belongings, capital goods, cargo, chattel, commodities, consumer durables, consumer goods, contents, effects, freight, goods, goods for sale, items for sale, line, line of goods, manufactured goods, material assets, materials, *merx,* movables, possessions, produce, property, provisions, *res venales,* salable commodities, shop goods, specialty, staples, stock, stock in trade, store, supplies, tangible assets, vendibles, wares

MERCHANT, noun   businessperson, chandler, consigner, dealer, distributer, distributor, entrepreneur, handler, hawker, huckster, *mercator,* merchandiser, middleman, monger, peddler, retailer, salesperson, seller, shopkeeper, shopman, storekeeper, trader, tradesperson, vendor

FOREIGN PHRASES: *Jus accrescendi inter mercatores, pro beneficio commercii, locum non habet.* The right of survivorship does not exist between merchants for the benefit of commerce.

MERCILESS, noun   barbaric, barbarous, bestial, brutal, callous, cold-blooded, cold-hearted, cruel, ferocious, fierce, harsh, heartless, indifferent, inhuman, monstrous, murderous, pitiless, relentless, remorseless, ruthless, sanguinary, savage, severe, stony-hearted, unappeasable, uncaring, uncivilized, uncompassionate, unconcerned, unfeeling, unforgiving, unmerciful, unremorseful, unsparing, unsympathetic, untamed, unyielding, vicious, vindictive, without mercy

ASSOCIATED CONCEPTS: merciless law

MERE, adjective   bare, just, nothing but, only, plain, sheer, simple

ASSOCIATED CONCEPTS: mere assumption of title, mere glimmering of reason, mere license, mere possibility

MERETRICIOUS, adjective   artificial, bedizened, brummagem, cheap, counterfeit, deceitful, deceptive, delusive, fake, false, fraudulent, garish, gaudy, imitation, misleading, mock, ornate, sham, showy, speciously attractive, spurious, tawdry, theatrical, tinsel, vulgar

ASSOCIATED CONCEPTS: adultery, meretricious relationship

MERGE, noun alliance, amalgamation, amassing, association, blending, bringing together, buildup, coalescence, combination, coming together, compact, compound, compression, concentration, condensation, congealing, congealment, congelation, conglomeratization, conjoining, conjunction, conjuncture, connection, consolidation, contract, contraction, crystallization, fortification, fusion, hardening, intensification, joining, melding, mixing, mixture, solidification, supplement, unification, uniting

ASSOCIATED CONCEPTS: doctrine of merger in copyright law, doctrine of merger in estates, merge companies, merger doctrine

MERGE, verb absorb, ally, amalgamate, associate, band together, be one with, be swallowed up, blend, cement, combine, compound, conglomerate, conjoin, consolidate, entwine, fuse, harmonize, incorporate, intermingle, intermix, intertwine, join, join forces, lose identity, lose individuality, melt into one, mix, piece together, unify, unite, weld

MERGER, noun absorption, affiliation, alliance, amalgamation, assimilation, association, centralization, coalescence, coalition, combination, confederation, conflation, consolidation, federation, fellowship, fusion, incorporation, integration, joinder, joint concern, loss of identity, mixture, partnership, solidarity, syndicate, unification, union, united front, voluntary association

ASSOCIATED CONCEPTS: compulsory merger, conglomerate merger, consolidation, forced merger, horizontal merger, merger of estates, vertical merger

MERIT, noun character, concern, concernment, consequence, consideration, credit, desert, deservedness, *dignitas,* distinction, excellence, emphasis, good actions, good behavior, goodness, greatness, honor, import, importance, interest, meritoriousness, *meritum,* note, praiseworthy quality, quality, rectitude, richly deserving, righteousness, self-importance, significance, superiority, uprightness, value, virtue, *virtus,* worth, worthness

ASSOCIATED CONCEPTS: affidavit of merits, dismissal on the merits, merit system

MERIT, verb be deserving, be entitled to, be worthy of, deserve, due, earn, justify, richly deserve

MERITORIOUS, adjective above par, acceptable, admirable, approvable, approved, august, benevolent, better, charitable, chivalric, chivalrous, choice, commendable, commendatory, conscientious, credit-worthy, creditable, dazzling, decent, deserving, deserving of commendation, deserving of compliment, deserving of praise, deserving of reward, desirable, dignified, distinctive, distinguished, duteous, dutiful, edifying, elevated, eminent, entitled, enviable, estimable, ethical, excellent, exemplary, extraordinary, fine, first-rate, generous, glorious, good, good-quality, gracious, great, greathearted, guiltless, heroic, high-minded, high-principled, honest, honorable, idealistic, impeccable, incorrupt, incorruptible, irreproachable, just, *laudabilis,* laudable, laudatory, *laude dignus,* lofty, magnanimous, magnificent, marvelous, moral, noble, perfect, philanthropic, popular, possessing merit, praiseworthy, preeminent, prime, princely, principled, proper, quality, rare, refined, reliable, remarkable, reputable, right-minded, righteous, select, solid, sound, splendid, stainless, sterling, sublime, substantial, superb, superior, superlative, supreme, terrifc, tested, uncensurable, unimpeachable, unselfish, upright, valuable, virtuous, well-done, well-intentioned, wonderful, worth imitating, worthwhile, worthy, worthy of fame, worthy of praise

ASSOCIATED CONCEPTS: meritorious cause, meritorious cause of action, meritorious claim, meritorious defense, meritorious grounds

MESNE, adjective coming between, interfering, interjacent, intermediary, intermediate, intervenient, intervening, mean, median, middle, transitional

ASSOCIATED CONCEPTS: mesne attachment, mesne grant, mesne process, mesne profits

MESSAGE, noun account, billet, bulletin, cable, communication, disclosure, dispatch, intelligence, issuance, letter, missive, note, notice, notification, report, signal, statement, telegram, wire

METE, noun barrier, border, borderland, borderline, bound, boundary, boundary line, boundary mark, bounds, circumscription, confine, division line, end, limit, limitation, line of circumvallation, line of demarcation, margin, measure, outline, perimeter, periphery, rim, terminal, terminus

ASSOCIATED CONCEPTS: legal description, metes and bounds

METE, verb admeasure, administer, allocate, allot, apportion, apportion by measure, appropriate, assess, assign, bestow, consign, deal out, dispense, distribute, divide, dole out, give, give out, hand out, issue, measure, measure out, parcel out, pay out, present, ration, share out, split, weigh out

METHOD, noun arrangement, blueprint, classification, consistency, course, course of action, custom, discipline, established order, fixed order, formula, habit, layout, logical order, manner, master plan, means, mode, *modus,* operation, order, orderliness, orderly arrangement, orderly disposition, organization, plan, practice, procedure, process, program, program of action, *ratio,* reduction to order, regular arrangement, regularity, regularity of action, routine, rule, scheme of arrangement, sequence, settled procedure, setup, system, tactic, technique, uniformity, *via,* way, working plan

ASSOCIATED CONCEPTS: business methods, method of operations

METICULOUS, adjective alert, assiduous, attentive, careful, circumspect, clean, conscientious, considered, correct, *diligens,* diligent, exact, exacting, faithful, fastidious, finical, finicking, finicky, fussy, gingerly, heedful, industrious, mindful, minute, minutely careful, neat, orderly, overcareful, painstaking, particular, precise, punctilious, regardful, rigid, rigorous, scrupulous, strict, thorough, thoroughgoing, tidy, vigilant, watchful

MIDDLE, adjective average, axial, centermost, central, centric, centroidal, equidistant, halfway, interjacent, intermediary, intermediate, mean, medial, median, mediate, mediocre, medium, mid, midmost, midway, pivotal

MIDDLE, noun average, axis, center, centrality, central part, central point, central position, centrum, core, focal point, heart, hub, kernel, mean, medium, mesne, midpoint, midst, nucleus

MIGHT, noun authoritativeness, brawn, durability, efficacy, energy, force, greatness, influence, intensity, main force, mightiness, muscle, potency, potential, powerfulness, prowess, puissance, robustness, severity, sinew, strength, sturdiness, toughness, vigor, vitality

MIGRANT, noun colonist, gypsy, nomad, ranger, rover, settler, trekker, wanderer

MILD *(Affable)*, **noun**   amiable, calm, civil, compassionate, conciliatory, considerate, docile, easy, easy to get along with, easy-going, easy-natured, fair, forbearing, forgiving, genial, good-natured, good-tempered, gracious, halcyon, humane, inane, indulgent, insipid, judicious, kind, lenient, lukewarm, meek, mellow, merciful, moderate, mollifying, nonviolent, pacific, passive, peaceful, placid, pleasant, pretty, prudent, sensitive, serene, sober, subdued, submissive, sympathetic, tactful, tame, tepid, tractable, tranquil, unassertive, unassuming, uncomplaining

MILD *(Temperature)*, **noun**   bland, easy, flat, gentle, insipid, jejune, moderate, middle ground, neutral, passive, placid, pleasant, pretty, soft, subdued, tame, tasteless, temperate, tepid, tranquil, unexcessive, unflavored, weak

MILITARY TRIBUNAL, noun   armed services court, armed services court of law, armed services judiciary, army tribunal, judiciary of the army, military court, military court of law, military judiciary, military trial
ASSOCIATED CONCEPTS: Patriot Act

MILITATE, verb   act on, affect, agitate, bring about change, carry on, *contra rem facere,* contrive, control, deal with, direct, engineer, handle, have effect on, have influence on, influence, interfere, manage, maneuver, manipulate, meddle, mold, operate, perform on, *rei adversari, rei obstare,* shape, steer, take action, wield, work

MIND, noun   animus, attitude, brain, brains, comprehension, *conatus,* concept, conception, concern, conscience, consideration, contemplation, conviction, desire, estimation, expectation, frame, gray matter, intellect, intelligence, intent, judgment, memory, mentality, observation, personal judgment, pleasure, position, propensity, psyche, reason, theory, thinking, understanding, will, wish

MINDFUL, adjective   aware, be reminded of, bear in mind, call to mind, conjure up, do not forget, fix in the mind, have at your fingertips, heed, keep in mind, know, know once again, master, memorize, preserve, recall, recognize, recollect, remind oneself, retain, summon up, think back
ASSOCIATED CONCEPTS: mitigating factors in sentencing

MINIMAL, adjective   abbreviated, abridged, below the mark, brief, cut, deficient, diminished, diminutive, exiguous, fragmentary, impalpable, inappreciable, inconsiderable, infinitesimal, insufficient, lean, least, lesser, light, Lilliputian, limited, little, low, meager, minimum, minor, minute, moderate, modest, narrow, paltry, reduced, rudimentary, scant, scanty, scarce, short, shortened, slender, slight, slim, small, smallest, thin, tiny, under par, under the mark, undersized, unimportant
ASSOCIATED CONCEPTS: minimal jurisdictional contacts, minimal standards

MINIMIZE, verb   abbreviate, abridge, attach little importance to, attenuate, bedwarf, belittle, cheapen, clip, criticize, curtail, cut down, cut down to size, cut short, decimate, decrease, decry, deduct, deflate, degrade, demote, depreciate, derogate, detract, diminish, discount, disparage, disprize, dwarf, lessen, lower, make brief, make less, make little of, make smaller, make thin, misprize, overshadow, pare, pay little attention to, pay little heed to, prune, reduce, render less, ridicule, run down, scale down, scorn, set at naught, shave, shorten, show no respect, shrink, slash,

slight, slur over, sneer at, strip, subtract, thin, think little of, think nothing of, underestimate, underpraise, underprice, underrate, underreckon, understate, undervalue
ASSOCIATED CONCEPTS: minimize damage

MINIMUM, noun   bit, dash, drop, fragment, iota, jot, least amount, least part, least quantity, lowest quantity, minim, modicum, morsel, mote, *pars minima,* particle, piece, quorum, scantling, scintilla, shade, sliver, small amount, small quantity, sprinkling, sufficiency, sufficient amount, tincture, tinge, tittle, touch, trace, whit
ASSOCIATED CONCEPTS: minimum age, minimum charge, minimum fee schedule, minimum price, minimum wage

MINIMUM WAGE, noun   bare minimum wage, barely adequate income, least recompense, lowest acceptable wage, lowest lawful pay, lowest legal hourly rate of compensation, lowest permissible wage, lowest possible remuneration

MINISTERIAL, adjective   administrative, agential, attendant, attending, auxiliary, bureaucratic, effectual, functional, helpful, helping, implemental, instrumental, intermedial, intermediary, intermediate, intervening, managing, officiating, operative, practical, serviceable, useful
ASSOCIATED CONCEPTS: ministerial act, ministerial duty, ministerial officer

MINOR, adjective   accessory, cursory, dispensable, expendable, futile, immaterial, inappreciable, inconsequential, inconsiderable, ineffectual, inessential, inferior, insignificant, insubstantial, irrelevant, junior, less important, lesser, little, low-level, lower, meaningless, mere, minimal, minimum, minute, modest, negligible, nonessential, not vital, not worth mentioning, nugatory, obscure, of no account, of second rank, paltry, peripheral, petty, picayune, scant, secondary, slight, small, smaller, subaltern, subordinate, subsidiary, superficial, trifling, trivial, unessential, unimportant, uninfluential, unnecessary, unnoteworthy, unnoticeable
ASSOCIATED CONCEPTS: minor breach, minor defect, minor dispute, minor subdivision

MINOR, noun   adolescent, baby, child, dependent, *filius familias,* individual under age, individual under the age of majority, infant, junior, juvenile, one not legally competent, person under legal age, person under 18 years of age, person who is not of full age, pubescent, teenager, underage person, ward, young person, youngling, youngster, youth
ASSOCIATED CONCEPTS: emancipation of a minor, minor dependent, unemancipated minor
FOREIGN PHRASES: *Minor minorem custodire non debet, alios enim praesumitur male regere qui seipsum regere nescit.* A minor ought not to be guardian to a minor, for a person who knows not how to govern himself is presumed to be unfit to govern others. *Meliorem conditionem suam facere potest minor, deteriorem nequaquam.* A minor can make his own condition better, but by no means worse. *Succurritur minori; facilis est lapsus juventutis.* A minor is to be favored; youth errs easily. *Minor non tenetur respondere durante minori aetati, nisi, in causa dotis, propter favorem.* A minor is not held responsible during his minority, unless, by reason of favor, in the matter of dower.

MINORITY *(Infancy)*, **noun**   childhood, immaturity, inexperience, infant status, legal immaturity, legal incapacity, legal incompetence, nonage, period of being under legal age, period of being under statutory age, puerility, unripeness, youth, youthfulness

ASSOCIATED CONCEPTS: age of minority, incapacity to contract, voidable contracts

FOREIGN PHRASES: *Haeres minor uno et viginti annis non respondebit, nisi in casu dotis.* A minor heir under twenty-one years of age is not answerable, except in the matter of dower. *Minor ante tempus agere non potest in casu proprietatis nec etiam convenire.* A minor under age cannot act in a case of property.

MINORITY *(Outnumbered group),* **noun**   insignificant number, lesser group, lesser part, the outvoted, paltry few, peripheral group, powerless group, secondary group, small group, small number, small percentage, small proportion, small quantity, smaller group, smaller part, subordinate group, subsidiary group, uninfluential group, weak group
ASSOCIATED CONCEPTS: minority group, minority member, minority party, minority stockholders

MISADVISED, adjective   badly advised, fatuous, ill-advised, ill-considered, ill-judged, illogical, impolitic, imprudent, in error, inadvisable, incautious, indiscreet, inexpedient, infelicitous, injudicious, irrational, irresponsible, misconducted, misdirected, misguided, misinformed, misinstructed, misled, mistaken, poorly advised, reasonless, reckless, senseless, shortsighted, thoughtless, unconsidered, unreasonable, unreflecting, unsensible, unsound, unthinking, unthoughtful, unwary, unwise, wrongly advised

MISAPPLICATION, noun   abuse, corrupt use, dishonest application, dishonest use, distortion, errancy, error, extravagance, false construction, fraudulent application, idle expenditure, illegal application, improper use, impropriety, incorrect application, incorrect usage, incorrect use, irregularity, malapropism, malpractice, misappropriation, misconception, misconstruction, misemployment, misexplanation, misexplication, mishandling, misinterpretation, misjudgment, mismanagement, mistake, mistranslation, misunderstanding, misusage, misuse, misuse of funds, misuse of words, perversion, poor usage, prodigality, reckless expenditure, squandering, useless expenditure, usus perversus, waste, wasteful expenditure, wastefulness, wrong application, wrong interpretation, wrong usage, wrong use, wrongful use
ASSOCIATED CONCEPTS: misapplication of funds

MISAPPREHEND, verb   be deceived, be in error, be misled, be mistaken, blunder, confuse, distort, err, fail to understand, have the wrong impression, miscalculate, miscomprehend, misconceive, misconstrue, misdeem, misinterpret, misjudge, misreckon, mistake, misunderstand, receive a false impression, take amiss, take wrongly

MISAPPROPRIATE, verb   bilk, cheat, commit breach of trust, divert, embezzle, exploit, expropriate, misapply, misdirect, misemploy, mismanage, peculate, pilfer, purloin, rob, steal, swindle

MISAPPROPRIATION, noun   abuse, appropriation for a dishonest use, appropriation for a wrongful use, arrogation, breach of trust, conversion, defalcation, defraudation, diversion, embezzlement, fraud, fraudulent conversion, illegal use of property, larceny, malversation, misapplication, misemployment, misusage, misuse, peculation, pilferage, stealing, swindle, theft, thievery, wrongful conversion of property, wrongful use
ASSOCIATED CONCEPTS: conversion, misappropriation of funds

MISCALCULATE, verb   be erroneous, be in error, be misguided, be misled, be mistaken, be wrong, blunder, calculate wrongly, commit an error, deceive oneself, deviate, err, *errare,* estimate incorrectly, fall into error, *falli,* go amiss, go astray, go awry, have the wrong impression, labor under a misapprehension, labor under an error, make a mistake, *male computare,* miscompute, misconceive, misconjecture, misconstrue, miscount, misdeem, misestimate, misjudge, misreckon, mistake, receive a false impression, slip, slip up, stray, stumble, understand incorrectly

MISCARRIAGE, noun   abortion, abortive attempt, abortive effort, bad behavior, breakdown, *cadere,* collapse, default, defeat, disappointment, downfall, failure, fiasco, frustration, futile effort, hopeless failure, ineffectiveness, ineffectual attempt, loss, lost labor, misadventure, misbehavior, mischance, misconduct, misfire, mistake, negative result, noncompletion, nonfulfillment, nonperformance, nonsuccess, overthrow, *parum procedere,* perdition, rout, ruin, *secus procedere,* stoppage, successlessness, total loss, unlawful act, unproductivity, vain attempt, vain effort
ASSOCIATED CONCEPTS: miscarriage of justice

MISCELLANEOUS, adjective   admixed, aggregated, amalgamated, assorted, blended, collected, combined, commingled, commixed, composite, disparate, diverse, diversified, diversiform, *diversus,* eclectic, heterogeneous, inconsistent, indiscriminate, intermixed, jumbled, manifold, many, medley, merged, mixed, mosaic, motley, multifarious, multiform, multiplex, nonuniform, of every description, of mixed character, of various kinds, *promiscuus,* scrambled, sundry, unclassified, unselected, unsorted, varied, variegated, variform, various, *varius*

MISCHIEF, noun   annoyance, criminality, cruelty, damage, *damnum,* danger, detriment, devilment, deviltry, disservice, evil, evil conduct, fault, foul play, frolicsomeness, harm, harmful action, hurt, ill consequence, impishness, *incommodum,* infliction, injurious conduct, injuriousness, injury, injustice, knavery, maleficium, malicious action, malignity, maltreatment, meanness, misbehavior, misconduct, misdoing, misusage, molestation, nastiness, naughtiness, nuisance, outrage, playfulness, prankishness, puckishness, rascality, roguery, roguishness, ruin, transgression, trouble, vice, villainy, waggery, waggishness, wickedness, wrong, wrongdoing
ASSOCIATED CONCEPTS: malicious mischief

MISCONCEIVE, verb   be deceived, be misguided, be misinformed, be misled, be mistaken, blunder, deceive oneself, delude oneself, distort the meaning, err, estimate incorrectly, fail to understand, fall into error, guess wrong, interpret incorrectly, labor under a misapprehension, make a mistake, misapprehend, miscalculate, misconjecture, misconstrue, misdeem, misestimate, misinterpret, misjudge, misreckon, misunderstand, *perperam accipere,* pervert, put a false construction on, receive a false impression, receive a wrong impression, value incorrectly

MISCONDUCT, noun   bad conduct, bad management, crime, *delictum,* delinquency, dereliction, deviation from rectitude, dishonest management, disorderly conduct, error, failing, failure, fault, guilty act, ill management, illegality, improper conduct, impropriety, indiscretion, infamous conduct, maladministration, malfeasance, malpractice, malversation, misadministration, misbehavior, misdeed, misdemeanor, misdoing, misfeasance, misgovernment, misguidance, mismanagement, misprision, negligence, nonfeasance, offense, peccadillo, *peccatum,* tort, transgression, turpitude, unprofessional conduct, wrong, wrongdoing

ASSOCIATED CONCEPTS: discharge for misconduct, gross misconduct, misconduct in office, official misconduct

MISCONSTRUE, verb   be confused, be in error, be misled, be wrong, blunder, confuse, construe wrongly, distort, fail to understand, garble, get wrong, have an incorrect impression, make a mistake, misapprehend, misconceive, misinterpret, misjudge, misread, mistake, misunderstand, pervert, put a false sense on, receive a false idea, receive a false impression, twist the words, understand improperly

MISCUE, noun   bad idea, blunder, botch, bungle, clumsy performance, corrigendum, deviation, erratum, error, flaw, fumble, impropriety, inadvertence, inadvertency, irregularity, miscalculation, misjudgment, miss, misstatement, misstep, mistake, misunderstanding, omission, oversight, slip, stumble

MISDEED, noun   abomination, atrocity, bad behavior, blunder, crime, cruel act, culpable omission, delict, *delictum,* delinquency, dereliction, dutilessness, evil deed, fault, felony, guilty act, illegality, improper behavior, impropriety, infamous conduct, infraction, infringement, iniquity, injury, injustice, lapse, lawlessness, malefaction, *maleficium,* malfeasance, malpractice, malversation, misbehavior, misconduct, misdemeanor, misdoing, misfeasance, mistake, offense, outrageous act, peccadillo, peccancy, *peccatum,* scrape, sin, slip, transgression, trespass, villainy, violation, wicked action, wicked deed, wrong, wrongdoing

MISDEMEANOR, noun   act committed in violation of law, act of lawbreaking, breach of law, crime committed, criminal act, criminal activity, criminal offense, *delictum,* dereliction, guilty act, illegality, improbity, impropriety, indiscretion, infamous conduct, malfeasance, malversation, misdeed, misdoing, misfeasance, offense, offense against the law, peccadillo, punishable offense, transgression, violation of law, wicked deed, wrong
ASSOCIATED CONCEPTS: felony, high crimes and misdemeanors, misdemeanor complaint, petit misdemeanor, violation

MISDIRECT, verb   confound, confuse, create a false impression, give a false impression, instruct badly, involve in error, lead astray, lead into error, misaddress, misadvise, miseducate, misguide, misinform, misinstruct, mislead, misteach, put off the scent, throw into confusion

MISDOING, noun   badness, blunder, bungle, crime, cruel act, culpability, delinquency, deviation from rectitude, dishonesty, disorderly conduct, dutilessness, error, evildoing, fault, foul play, guilty act, illegality, immorality, improbity, impropriety, incorrectness, indiscretion, inexcusability, infamous conduct, injustice, irregularity, knavery, lawlessness, maladministration, malefaction, malpractice, malversation, misapplication, misbehavior, mischief, misconduct, misdeed, misdemeanor, misfeasance, mismanagement, misprision, offense, outrage, peccadillo, rascality, roguery, ruffianism, scrape, sharp practice, slip, transgression, trespass, turpitude, unrighteousness, unsuitability, vice, villainy, violation, wicked deed, wickedness, wrong, wrongfulness

MISDOUBT, verb   be apprehensive, be doubtful, be irresolute, be nervous, be skeptical, be uncertain, be undetermined, challenge, cherish doubts, disbelieve, distrust, doubt, entertain doubts, entertain suspicions, give no credence to, give no credit to, harbor suspicions, have doubts about, have fears, have no confidence in, have no faith in, have questions, have reservations, have suspicions, hesitate, hold questionable, lack confidence, lack conviction, lack faith, misbelieve, misgive, mistrust, pause, question, scruple, suspect, waver, withhold judgment

MISEMPLOY, verb   abuse, *abuti,* corrupt, defile, desecrate, dissipate, distort, divert, employ improperly, ill treat, ill use, maltreat, manipulate improperly, misapply, misappropriate, misconduct, misdirect, misdo, mishandle, mismanage, misrule, misspend, mistreat, misuse, molest, overtax, overwork, pervert, pollute, prostitute, ruin, spoil, squander, taint, use wrongly, violate, waste, wear out

MISESTIMATION, noun   bad judgment, distorted idea, distorted impression, erroneousness, error, fallaciousness, false idea, false impression, inaccuracy, inaccurateness, incorrect appraisal, incorrect evaluation, incorrect valuation, inexactitude, inexactness, misapprehension, miscalculation, miscomputation, misconception, misconjecture, misinterpretation, misjudgment, misreckoning, misstatement, mistake, misunderstanding, poor judgment, uncorrectness, unpreciseness, warped idea, warped impression, warped judgment, wrong impression

MISFEASANCE, noun   breach of law, civil wrong, dereliction, deviation from rectitude, improper action, improper performance, infringement, injurious exercise of lawful authority, injurious exercise of authority, misconduct, misdeed, misdoing, offense, offense against the law, official misconduct, peccadillo, transgression, unlawful use of power, violation of law, wrong, wrong arising from affirmative action, wrongdoing, wrongful performance of a normally legal act, wrongfulness
ASSOCIATED CONCEPTS: malfeasance, negligence, nonfeasance

MISFORTUNE, noun   accident, adverse event, adverse fortune, adverse lot, adverse luck, adversity, affliction, backset, bad fortune, bad luck, bale, blow, *calamitas,* calamity, casualty, cataclysm, catastrophe, comedown, destruction, disadvantage, disappointment, disaster, evil fortune, *fortuna adversa,* hardship, ill fortune, ill luck, *incommodum,* infelicity, misadventure, mischance, mishap, problem, reverse, ruin, setback, suffering, tragedy, trial, tribulation, trouble, unforeseen adversity, unfortunate occurrence, unlucky accident, unlucky happening, visitation
FOREIGN PHRASES: *Festinatio justitiae est noverca infortunii.* The hastening of justice is the stepmother of misfortune. *Negligentia semper habet infortunium comitem.* Negligence always has misfortune for a companion.

MISGIVING, noun   anxietude, anxiety, anxious concern, anxiousness, apprehension, apprehensiveness, concern, critical attitude, disquiet, distrust, doubt, doubtfulness, dubiety, fear, fearfulness, forbodement, foreboding, gaingiving, hesitation, inquietude, lack of certainty, lack of confidence, *metus timor,* mistrust, mistrustfulness, nervousness, objection, perturbation, *praesagium,* prediction of misfortune, premonition, presage, presentiment, qualm, reluctance, reservation, reserve, skepticalness, skepticism, *sollicitudo,* trepidation, uncertainty, uneasiness

MISGOVERN, verb   administer badly, administer improperly, administer poorly, govern badly, maladminister, male *administrare, male regere,* manage badly, misadminister, misdirect, misguide, mismanage, misrule, rule dishonestly

MISGUIDE, verb   befool, beguile, bewilder, cause a mistake, cause error, conceal, corrupt, create a false impression, deceive, delude, dissemble, distort, falsify, fool, *in*

errorum inducere, lead astray, lead into error, lie, maladminister, misadvise, misconduct, misdirect, miseducate, mishandle, misinform, misinstruct, mislead, mismanage, misrepresent, misstate, misteach, pervert, tell a falsehood, tell a lie, tell an untruth, trip

MISHANDLE (*Maltreat*), **verb** abuse, assail, assault, batter, defile, handle badly, ill treat, ill use, impose upon, injure, manhandle, maul, misemploy, misuse, molest, overburden, persecute, ravish, rough, treat abusively, treat ill, treat improperly, tyrannize, use dispiteously, use wrongly, victimize, violate, wrong

MISHANDLE (*Mismanage*), **verb** abuse, administer improperly, conduct dishonestly, conduct without efficiency, conduct without honesty, handle badly, maladminister, manage badly, misconduct, misdirect, misuse, squander, use wrongly, waste

MISINFORM, **verb** conceal, create a false impression, deceive, delude, distort, exaggerate, *falsa docere,* falsify, give a false impression, misadvise, miscolor, misdirect, miseducate, misguide, misinstruct, mislead, misrepresent, misstate, misteach, propagandize, report inaccurately

MISINTERPRET, **verb** be misled, blunder, confuse, distort, err, explain incorrectly, fail to understand, garble, jumble, make a mistake, make an error, *male interpretari,* misapprehend, miscalculate, misconceive, misconjecture, misconstrue, misdeem, misjudge, misread, misreckon, misrepresent, mistake, mistranslate, misunderstand, place a false construction on, place a wrong construction on, place an erroneous construction on, receive a false impression, receive a wrong idea, receive an incorrect impression, twist the meaning, understand incorrectly
ASSOCIATED CONCEPTS: bilateral mistake, mistake of fact, mistake of law, recission, reformation, unilateral mistake

MISJOINDER, **noun** bad match, incongruity, misalliance, misfit, mismatch
ASSOCIATED CONCEPTS: misjoinder of causes, misjoinder of parties

MISJUDGE, **verb** be bewildered, be perplexed, blunder, err, err in judgment, estimate incorrectly, fail to recognize, have a wrong impression, judge erroneously, judge inaccurately, judge wrongly, make a mistake, make an error, male *iudicare,* misapprehend, miscalculate, miscompute, misconceive, misconstrue, misdeem, misesteem, misestimate, misinterpret, misread, misreckon, mistake, misthink, misunderstand, rate incorrectly

MISJUDGMENT, **noun** bad judgment, error, fallacy, grave injustice, gross injustice, imposition, inaccuracy, inaccurateness, inequitableness, inequity, inexactitude, inexactness, injustice, misapprehension, miscalculation, miscarriage of justice, miscomputation, misconception, misconstruction, misestimation, misinterpretation, mistake, misunderstanding, poor judgment, unfair judgment, unfairness, unjust opinion, unpreciseness, wrong estimation

MISLABEL, **verb** brand incorrectly, classify incorrectly, deceive, defraud, describe incorrectly, designate incorrectly, docket incorrectly, falsely characterize, identify incorrectly, label incorrectly, lead astray, lead into error, mark incorrectly, misbrand, mischaracterize, misclassify, misdenominate, misdescribe, misdesignate, misdirect, misguide, misidentify, misinform, mislead, mismark, misname, misrepresent, misstate, misticket, mistitle, name incorrectly, represent incorrectly, stamp incorrectly, tag incorrectly, ticket incorrectly, title incorrectly
ASSOCIATED CONCEPTS: fraud

MISLEAD, **verb** bait, be dishonest, befool, beguile, cause error, cheat, corrupt, counterfeit, cozen, create a false impression, cully, deceive, *decipere,* decoy, defraud, delude, dissemble, distort, double-cross, dupe, ensnare, entrap, *fallere,* falsify, fib, fool, give a false idea, give a false impression, guide astray, guide into error, guide wrongly, *in errorem inducere,* lead astray, lead into error, lie, misadvise, misdescribe, misdirect, miseducate, misguide, misinform, misinstruct, misrepresent, misstate, misteach, pervert, practice deception, prevaricate, seduce, snare, sophisticate, swindle, take advantage of, take in, tell a falsehood, tell an untruth, trap, trick, varnish

MISMANAGE, **verb** act foolishly, act improperly, administer improperly, administer inefficiently, administer poorly, blunder, boggle, botch, bungle, confound, derange, disarrange, fail, flounder, fumble, ill-manage, maladminister, manage poorly, manage unskillfully, misadminister, misapply, misappropriate, misconduct, misdirect, misdo, misemploy, misgovern, misguide, mishandle, misrule, missend, misuse, neglect, pervert, reduce to chaos, spoil, violate rules
ASSOCIATED CONCEPTS: mismanage trust assets

MISNOMER, **noun** error in naming, misapplied name, miscalling, misnaming, misterm, wrong designation, wrong name

MISPRISION, **noun** contempt, delinquency, deviation from rectitude, malefaction, malfeasance, malpractice, malversation, misconduct, misdeed, misfeasance, neglect, negligence, obstruction of justice, offense, transgression, violation, wrongful action of a public official
ASSOCIATED CONCEPTS: clerical misprision, misprision of felony, misprision of treason

MISPRIZE, **verb** be contemptuous of, belittle, contemn, deprecate, depreciate, despise, disdain, disesteem, disparage, disprize, disregard, feel contempt for, hold cheap, hold in contempt, look down upon, make little of, make nothing of, minimize, misjudge, overlook, push aside, ridicule, run down, scorn, set at naught, slight, sneer at, speak slightingly of, underestimate, underprize, underrate, underreckon, undervalue

MISREAD, **verb** be deceived, be erroneous, be mistaken, blunder, confuse, distort, err, fall into error, garble, interpret incorrectly, make a mistake, misapprehend, misconstrue, misdeem, misidentify, misinterpret, mistake, mistranslate, misunderstand, pervert, put a false construction on, put a wrong construction on, read incorrectly, receive a false impression, receive a wrong impression, receive an incorrect impression, translate incorrectly, twist the meaning of, understand incorrectly

MISREPRESENT, **verb** assert incorrectly, be false, bear false witness, beguile, belie, betray, break faith, *calumniari,* camouflage, color, contort, deceive, defraud, delude, *depravare,* disguise, dissemble, dissimulate, distort, distort intentionally, dupe, embroider, equivocate, exaggerate, explain wrongly, fabricate, fake, falsify, feign, fool, give a false coloring, give a false representation, hoax, lie, malign, miscite, miscolor, misdescribe, misexplain, misguide, mislead, misquote, misreport, misrepresent, misstate, misteach, mock, overstate, palter, pass off for, perjure oneself, pervert, pretend, prevaricate, put a false appearance on, put a false

401

construction on, represent falsely, represent fraudulently, represent incorrectly, sham, simulate, slant, speak falsely, state an untruth, state falsely, tell a falsehood, tell lies, trick, trump up, twist the meaning of, understate, utter a falsehood
ASSOCIATED CONCEPTS: fraud, knowingly misrepresent, misrepresent a material fact

MISREPRESENTATION, *noun*   deceitfulness, deception, deceptive statement, deceptiveness, distortion, exaggeration, fabrication, false representation, false statement, falsehood, falsification, falsity, fraud, inaccuracy, incorrect assertion, intentional misstatement, lie, misapplication, misconstruction, misguidance, misquotation, misreport, misstatement, misstatement of fact, overstatement, untrue statement, untruth, untruthfulness, unveracity
ASSOCIATED CONCEPTS: actionable misrepresentation, deceit, false misrepresentation, fraudulent misrepresentation, innocent misrepresentation, material misrepresentation, misrepresentation of a material fact, negligent misrepresentation

MISRULE, *noun*   anarchism, anarchy, breakdown of administration, chaos, confusion, disorder, disorganization, impolicy, lawlessness, maladministration, malfeasance, misconduct, misdirection, misgovernment, misguidance, mishandling, mismanagement, turmoil, unruliness

MISS (Long for), ***verb***   desiderate, desire, pine for, regret the loss

MISS (Overlook), ***verb***   disregard, fail to accomplish, fail to attain, fail to catch, fail to hear, fail to perform, fail to receive, fail to see, fail to understand, fall short, gloss over, go amiss, go astray, ignore, lack, let slip, let the moment pass, lose, lose an opportunity, miscarry, miscue, misfire, miss a chance, miss the mark, not succeed, omit, overlook, pretermit, prove unsuccessful, skip

MISS THE MARK (Not convey properly), ***verb***   be off the mark, cause error, close to, commit an error, get an incorrect assessment, give a false impression, gloss over the significance, go amiss, go astray, go wrong, labor under a misapprehension, make a mistake, miss the importance, miss the most important issue, not be clear, not be germane

MISS THE MARK (Not on point), ***verb***   be deceived, be erroneous, be misguided, be misled, be mistaken, be wrong, commit an error, delude oneself, fall into error, labor under a misapprehension, make a mistake, misapprehend, miscalculate, miscompute, misconstrue, misinterpret, misjudge, misunderstand, receive a false impression
ASSOCIATED CONCEPTS: directed verdict, motion to dismiss

MISSION, *noun*   aim, appointment, assignment, business, calling, charge, commission, concern, delegation, design, duty, embassy, errand, goal, job, legation, mandate, objective, office, profession, purpose, pursuit, task, trust, undertaking, venture, vocation, work

MISSTATE, *verb*   be deceptive, be erroneous, deceive, delude, dissemble, distort, falsify, give a false impression, give a wrong idea, lead astray, lead into error, lie, misguide, misinform, mislead, misreport, misrepresent, pervert, prevaricate, state incorrectly, state misleadingly, tell a falsehood, tell a lie, tell an untruth, twist the meaning

MISSTATEMENT, *noun*   bad reporting, blunder, deceit, deception, deviation from truth, distortion, duplicity, erratum, error, false statement, falsehood, falsification, fiction,

imprecision, inaccuracy, incorrect statement, inexactitude, inexactness, insincerity, lie, mendacity, *mendacium,* misinformation, misrepresentation, mistake, perjury, perversion, pretense, slip, subreption, suppression of truth, untruth, untruthfulness, wrong statement
ASSOCIATED CONCEPTS: misstatement of fact

MISSTATEMENT OF FACT, *noun*   distortion, exaggeration, fabrication, false coloring, false statement, falsification, garbled version, misconstruction, misinformation, misinterpretation, misrepresentation, misstatement, perversion, untruth
ASSOCIATED CONCEPTS: perjury, subornation of perjury

MISTAKE, *verb*   be deceived, be erroneous, be in the wrong, be misguided, be misled, be mistaken, blunder, bungle, commit an error, confuse, err, fall into error, get wrong, go amiss, go astray, go wrong, identify incorrectly, *ignorare,* labor under a misapprehension, misapprehend, miscalculate, misconceive, misconstrue, misidentify, misinterpret, misjudge, misread, misunderstand, name inaccurately, put a false sense on, receive a false impression, receive a wrong impression, slip up, stumble
ASSOCIATED CONCEPTS: excusable mistake, harmless error, mistake of fact, mistake of law, mistaken identity, mutual mistake, unilateral mistake

MISTREAT, *verb*   abuse, afflict, aggrieve, annoy, assail, assault, attack, badger, be hurtful, be malevolent, be offensive, be pitiless, be rude, be violent, bear malice, berate, bother, bruise, bully, burden, cause evil, cause pain, create havoc, debase, desecrate, destroy, disoblige, distress, disturb, do an injustice to, do violence to, do wrong, force, give pain, harass, harm, harrow, harry, heckle, hurt, ill treat, ill use, impair, induce pain, inflict evil, inflict pain, injure, lay waste, lead into trouble, make mischief, malign, maltreat, manhandle, maul, misemploy, misgovern, mishandle, mismanage, misrule, misuse, molest, offend, oppress, overburden, overtask, overtax, overwork, persecute, pervert, plague, pollute, prostitute, provoke, run down, savage, show ill will, spite, strain, strike, torment, torture, trample on, tread on, treat badly, tyrannize, use dispiteously, use hard, use wrongly, vex, victimize, violate, waste, wear out, work evil, worry, wound, wrong

MISTRIAL, *noun*   abrogation, annulment, cancellation, collapse, disannulment, erroneous trial, failure, fruitless trial, ineffective trial, invalid trial, nonfulfillment, nonsuccess, nugatory trial, nullification, nullity, revocation, terminated trial, unproductive trial, unsuccessful trial, useless trial, void trial, worthless trial
ASSOCIATED CONCEPTS: deadlocked jury, declaration of a mistrial, prejudicial error

MISTRUST, *verb*   apprehend, be anxious, be apprehensive, be cautious, be doubtful, be dubious, be loath, be nervous, be skeptical, be uncertain, cherish doubts, distrust, doubt, dread, entertain doubts, entertain suspicions, fear, give no credit to, harbor doubts, harbor suspicions, have anxiety, have doubts, have fears, have misgivings, have no faith in, have no trust in, have qualms, have reservations, have suspicions, hesitate, hold back, lack belief in, lack confidence in, lack faith in, lack trust in, misdoubt, misgive, question, regard with suspicion, shrink from, shy from, suspect, treat with reserve

MISUNDERSTAND, *verb*   be confused, be ignorant, be in the wrong, be misguided, be misled, be mistaken, blunder, commit an error, confuse, delude oneself, distort, err, fail to understand, fall into error, jumble, labor under a misapprehension, lack information, make a mistake, misapprehend, miscalculate, misconceive, misconstrue, misdeem, misinterpret, misjudge, misperceive, misread, misreckon, mistake, *perperam,* pervert, put a false construction on, put a wrong construction on, put an erroneous construction on, receive a wrong impression, twist the meaning, understand wrongly

MISUSAGE, *noun*   abuse, bad treatment, corruption, debasement, defilement, degradation, desecration, distortion, diversion, exploitation, force, ill treatment, ill usage, improper usage, improper use, impropriety, maladministration, malapropism, malpractice, malversation, misapplication, misappropriation, misemployment, mismanagement, mispronunciation, misuse, peculation, perversion, pollution, prostitution, violation, wrong use

MISUSE, *noun*   abuse, degradation, erroneous use, ill treatment, ill usage, ill use, improper usage, improper use, incorrect usage, incorrect use, maladministration, malpractice, maltreatment, misapplication, misappropriation, misemployment, mishandling, mismanagement, mistreatment, misusage, perversion, solecism, *usus,* violation, wrong use
ASSOCIATED CONCEPTS: misuse of a product, misuse of an easement, misuse of funds, misuse of powers, misuse of property, patent misuse
FOREIGN PHRASES: *Expedit reipublicae ne sua re quis male utatur.* It is for the interest of the state that no one should make ill use of his property.

MITIGATE, *verb*   abate, abate in intensity, adjust, allay, alleviate, ameliorate, appease, assuage, check, control, curb, cushion, decrease, diminish, ease, give relief, *lenire,* lessen, lessen in force, lighten, make less severe, meliorate, *mitigare, mitiorem facere,* moderate, moderate in severity, mollify, palliate, reduce, regulate, relieve, restrain, soften, temper, unburden
ASSOCIATED CONCEPTS: duty to mitigate

MITIGATING, *adjective*   abating, alleviating, ameliorative, assuaging, calmative, diminishing, discounting, easing, exculpatory, excusing, extenuating, lessening, limiting, meliorative, modifying, palliative, qualifying, reducing, relieving, softening, subduing, tempering
ASSOCIATED CONCEPTS: duty to mitigate damages, mitigating circumstances

MITIGATION, *noun*   abatement, abridgment, adjustment, alleviation, assuagement, attenuation, comforting, decrease, diminishment, diminution, easing, lessening, *levamentum, levatio,* lightening, *mitigatio,* moderation, palliation, reduction, relaxation, relief, softening, soothing, weakening
ASSOCIATED CONCEPTS: mitigation of damages, mitigation of sentence

MITTIMUS, *noun*   authorization, command, command to incarcerate, court order of imprisonment, decree, decretal, direction to imprison, edict, legal order, mandate, official order, order, transcript of minutes of commitment, warrant of commitment, written precept of imprisonment
ASSOCIATED CONCEPTS: commitment

MIX, *verb*   amalgamate, associate, blend, combine, commingle, commix, compound, conjoin, consolidate, denature, desegregate, diffuse, fuse, incorporate, interfuse, intermingle, interpolate, intersperse, interweave, join, merge, mingle, pool, put together, unite

MOCK *(Deride),* ***verb***   chaff, *deridere,* disparage, fleer, flout, gibe, heckle, hold in derision, hold up to ridicule, hoot, *inridere,* insult, jeer, joke about, lampoon, laugh at, *ludibrio,* make a butt of, make a fool of, make fun of, poke fun at, rag, ridicule, satirize, scoff, scorn, sneer, snicker, snigger, spurn, taunt, tease, treat with contempt, treat with derision, treat with disrespect, treat with scorn, trifle with, twit

MOCK *(Imitate),* ***verb***   act, ape, assume the appearance of, burlesque, caricature, copy, counterfeit, do likewise, duplicate, echo, emulate, fake, feign, follow, follow suit, follow the example of, impersonate, mime, mimic, mirror, model after, pantomime, parody, parrot, pattern after, personate, play a part, portray, pretend, repeat, reproduce, satirize, simulate, take after, take off on, travesty

MODE, *noun*   convention, course, craze, custom, design, fad, fashion, form, formula, guise, habit, manner, means, method, *modus,* outline, practice, precedent, prevailing style, prevailing taste, prevalence, procedure, process, protocol, rage, *ratio,* regulations, routine, rule, rules, scheme, shape, style, system, taste, technique, tendency, tenor, trend, usage, *via,* vogue, way

MODE OF OPERATION, *noun*   approach, avenue, behavior, conduct, course, course of conduct, definite procedure, fashion, form, guise, line of action, manner of operating, means, method, methodology, mode, *modus operandi,* plan of action, practice, procedure, process, standard procedure, strategy, style, system, tactics, technique, usage, way, ways and means

MODEL, *noun*   antetype, archetype, copy, copy in miniature, design, example, *exemplar, exemplum,* facsimile, gauge, guide, ideal, image, imitation, miniature, mold, paradigm, paragon, pattern, plan, precedent, prototype, replica, representation, sample, specimen, standard
ASSOCIATED CONCEPTS: Model Code

MODERATE *(Preside over),* ***verb***   act as chairman, act as moderator, act as president, administer, be at the head of, be in authority, chair, command, control, direct, discipline, govern, have charge of, head, hold in check, hold sway over, hold the chair, lead, manage, master, officiate, oversee, pilot, police, regulate, run, stand over, steer, supervise, take charge of

MODERATE *(Temper),* ***verb***   abate, allay, alleviate, appease, assuage, attemper, blunt, calm, chasten, check, constrain, cool, curb, dampen, decelerate, decrease, diminish, dull, ease, hush, keep within bounds, lessen, lighten, limit, make less, mitigate, modify, mollify, mute, narrow, pacify, palliate, qualify, quell, quiet, reduce, repress, restrain, season, slacken, slow down, smooth, sober, soften, soothe, still, subdue, suppress, tame, tone down, tranquilize, weaken

MODERATION, *noun*   abstemiousness, abstinence, alleviation, assuagement, avoidance of extremes, balance, calmness, composure, conservatism, constraint, continence, *continentia,* control, coolness, deliberateness, diminution, dispassionateness, economy, equanimity, fairness, forbearance, frugality, gentleness, innocuousness, justice, lack of excess, lenience, leniency, lenity, limitation, mean, mildness, mitigation, moderateness, moderatism, modus, nonviolence, palliation, patience, quiet, reasonableness, reduction, regulation, restraint, restriction, sedateness, self-control, sobriety, steadiness, temperance, *temperantia,* temperateness, thrift, thriftiness

MODICUM, noun fraction, fragment, grain, insignificant amount, iota, minimum, minor amount, mite, particle, *paululum, paulum,* small amount, small quantity, trifle amount

MODIFICATION, noun adaptation, adjustment, alteration, change, correction, exception, limitation, partial change, qualification, reservation, restriction, slight change, variation
ASSOCIATED CONCEPTS: amendment, material modification, modification of a contract, modification of a decree, modification of a will, modification of an order, modification of judgment, reformation

MODIFY *(Alter),* **verb** adapt, adjust, affect, ameliorate, amend, change, *commutare,* convert, correct, effect a change, emend, emendate, give a new form to, improve, improve upon, introduce changes, make adjustments, make corrections, make improvements, meliorate, metamorphose, modernize, *mutare,* overhaul, qualify, readjust, rearrange, recast, reconstruct, rectify, refine, reform, regularize, remodel, remold, render in a better form, reshape, revamp, revise, rework, rewrite, touch up, transfigure, transform, transmute, transubstantiate, vamp, vary, work over
ASSOCIATED CONCEPTS: modify a contract, modify a decision, modify an order

MODIFY *(Moderate),* **verb** abate, allay, assuage, blunt, check, condition, curb, cushion, decrease, ease, extenuate, lessen, lighten, limit, lower, make less extreme, make less intense, make less severe, mitigate, *moderari,* mollify, qualify, reduce, regulate, restrict, soften, subdue, temper, *temperare,* tone down

MODUS OPERANDI, noun approach, behavior, conduct, course, course of conduct, definite procedure, line of conduct, manner, manner of operating, means, method, methodology, mode, mode of operation, mode of procedure, operation, order, pattern, procedure, process, routine, standard procedure, style, system, tactics, technique, way, ways and means

MODUS VIVENDI, noun interim agreement, manner of living, method of living, mode of living, nonpermanent agreement, nonpermanent arrangement, provisional settlement, temporary agreement, temporary arrangement, temporary settlement, transient arrangement, way of life, way of living, working arrangement

MOIETY, noun allotment, division, equal part, equal share, fifty percent, fraction, fragment, half, indefinite portion, indefinite share, measure, parcel, part, percentage, piece, portion, ration, section, segment, share

MOLEST *(Annoy),* **verb** anger, arouse, badger, bother, discommode, disquiet, disturb, harass, harm, harry, hound, hurt, incense, incommode, inconvenience, inflame, injure, interfere with, interrupt, irk, irritate, misuse, perturb, pester, pique, plague, provoke, ruffle, *sollicitare,* tease, torment, trouble, vex, *vexare,* worry

MOLEST *(Subject to indecent advances),* **verb** abuse, assault, attack, defile, rape, ravish, sexually abuse, sexually assault, violate

MOLESTATION, noun abuse, aggravation, annoyance, bother, disturbance, ill treatment, ill usage, inconvenience, interference, interruption, intrusion, irritation, maltreatment, meddling, mistreatment, nuisance, oppression, persecution, *vexatio,* vexation

MOLLIFICATION, noun abatement, allayment, alleviation, amelioration, appeasement, assuagement, calmness, check, conciliation, curb, deadening, decrease, diminishment, diminution, dulcification, easement, easing, lessening, lightening, lull, mediation, melioration, mitigation, pacification, palliation, placation, propitiation, reconciliation, reduction, relaxation, relief, slackening, softening, softness, soothing, tranquilization

MOLLIFY, verb abate, allay, alleviate, ameliorate, appease, assuage, attemper, blunt, calm, check, compose, conciliate, cool, curb, deaden, decrease, diminish, dulcify, dull, ease, give relief, hush, improve, *lenire,* lessen, lull, make better, mediate, meliorate, mellow, milden, *mitigare,* mitigate, moderate, *mollire,* pacificate, pacify, palliate, placate, propitiate, quell, quiet, reconcile, reduce, relax, relieve, restrain, smooth, soften, soothe, still, subdue, temper, tone down, tranquilize, weaken

MOMENTOUS, adjective big, consequential, critical, crucial, earthshaking, far-reaching, fateful, grand, grave, great, important, impressive, *magni momenti,* major, marked, material, memorable, notable, noteworthy, outstanding, prominent, remarkable, serious, signal, significant, special, stirring, substantial, uncommon, unordinary, unusual, weighty

MONETARY, adjective capital, financial, fiscal, minted, numismatical, nummulary, pecuniary, stamped
ASSOCIATED CONCEPTS: monetary damages, monetary relief

MONEY, noun aes, affluence, assets, bank note, bankroll, buying power, capital, cash, change, coin, coinage, currency, finances, fortune, funds, greenback, hard cash, income, legal tender, means, measure of value, medium of exchange, mintage, *nummus, pecunia,* property, resources, revenue, riches, specie, standard of value, substance, token, treasure, wealth, wherewithal, working capital
ASSOCIATED CONCEPTS: money award, money damages, money decree, money demand, money due and owing, money had and received, money judgment, money paid into court, moneyed corporation

MONITION *(Legal summons),* **noun** authoritative citation to appear, authoritative command, bidding, call, citation, command, commandment, decree, dictate, direction, edict, fiat, invitation, legal notice, mandate, notice to appear, notification, official call, official notice, order, requisition, rescript, subpoena, summons, summons to appear and answer, warrant, writ

MONITION *(Warning),* **noun** admonishment, admonition, advice, alarm, alert, caution, caveat, dehortation, enlightenment, exhortation, forewarning, hint, indication, information, notice, notification, prediction of danger

MONITOR, verb *admonitor,* attend, audit, check, conduct an inquiry, control, eavesdrop, examine, guard, inquire into, inspect, investigate, keep in sight, keep in view, listen, observe, overlook, oversee, review, scan, scrutinize, study, subject to examination, subject to scrutiny, survey, watch

MONOPOLIZE, verb absorb, appropriate, control, control market supply, control prices, control trade, corner, corner the market, dominate, engage, engross, enthrall, exercise exclusive rights, grip, have all to oneself, hold spellbound, hold the interest of, involve, keep entirely to oneself, obtain exclusive possession, occupy, own exclusively, retain exclusive control, retain exclusive possession, secure exclusive control, secure exclusive possession, stifle competition, suppress competition

ASSOCIATED CONCEPTS: conspiracy to monopolize, restraint of trade

MONOPOLY, *noun* control, control of the market, control of trade, domination, exclusive control, exclusive possession, exclusive privilege to carry on a traffic, exclusive right, *monopolium,* oligopoly, sole control of a commodity

ASSOCIATED CONCEPTS: antitrust laws, combination in restraint of trade, exemptions from antitrust laws, price fixing, trust

FOREIGN PHRASES: ***Commercium jure gentium commune esse debet, et non in monopolium et privatum paucorum quaestum convertendum.*** By the law of nations, commerce ought to be common and not converted into a monopoly and the private gain of a few persons. ***Monopolia dicitur, cum unus solus aliquod genus mercaturae universum emit, pretium ad suum libitum statuens.*** A monopoly is said to exist when one person alone buys up the whole of one kind of commodity, fixing a price at his own pleasure.

MONUMENT, *noun* achievement, cairn, cenotaph, cromlech, dolmen, lasting reminder, mark, memorial, *monumentum,* permanent structure, remembrance, reminder, shrine, testimonial

MOOT, *adjective* abstract, academic, actionable, arguable, contentious, contestable, contested, controversial, controvertible, debatable, disputable, disputatious, disputed, doubtful, dubious, hypothetical, in dispute, in issue, in question, open to discussion, open to question, problematical, questionable, questioned, speculative, subject to controversy, suppositional, theoretical, uncertain, undecided, under discussion, undetermined, unsettled, untried

ASSOCIATED CONCEPTS: academic question, moot appeal, moot case, moot controversy, moot court, moot question

MORAL, *adjective* aboveboard, *bene moratus,* bound by duty, commendable, conscientious, correct, creditable, decent, deserving, duteous, dutiful, estimable, ethical, exemplary, good, high-minded, high-principled, honest, *honestus,* honorable, idealistic, incorrupt, incorruptible, innocent, just, laudable, law-abiding, meritorious, noble, praiseworthy, principled, *probus,* proper, pure, reputable, respectable, responsible, right-minded, righteous, *sanctus,* scrupulous, spotless, truehearted, trustworthy, uncorrupt, uncorrupted, unerring, upright, upstanding, virtuous, well-conducted, worthy

ASSOCIATED CONCEPTS: moral certainty, moral character, moral consideration, moral dereliction, moral duty, moral obligation, moral turpitude

MORATORIUM, *noun* abeyance, break, cessation, close, deferral, delay, desistance, discontinuance, end, ending, halt, hold, interim, interval, leaving off, lull, pause, period, period of obligatory delay, postponement, recess, respite, rest, standstill, stop, stoppage, suspension, temporary halt, temporary relief, termination, wait, waiting period

ASSOCIATED CONCEPTS: moratorium acts, moratorium on repayment of debt

MORDACIOUS, *adjective* acerbic, acid, acrid, acrimonious, acute, biting, bitter, caustic, corrosive, cutting, harsh, incisive, knifelike, malicious, mordant, penetrating, piercing, pointed, pungent, rancorous, raw, rough, scathing, severe, sharp, slashing, spiteful, stinging, trenchant, uncharitable, unkind, virulent, vitriolic

MORTALITY, *noun* *condicio mortalis,* death, destruction, evanescence, extinction, fatality, fugaciousness, fugacity, human race, humanity, humanness, impermanence, man, mankind, *mortalitas,* mortalness, subjection to death, temporary existence, transientness, transitoriness

ASSOCIATED CONCEPTS: mortality tables

MORTGAGE, *noun* charge, collateral security, conditional conveyance of land, conditional property transfer, contractual obligation, encumbrance, engagement, indebtedness, loan transaction, obligation, *pignus,* pledge, pledge for the payment of a debt, pledge of security, real security, security, security for a debt, something owing, state of indebtedness, transfer of property as security for a debt, transfer of security

ASSOCIATED CONCEPTS: amortization of a mortgage, assignment of a mortgage, assumption of a mortgage, chattel mortgage, constructive mortgage, equitable mortgage, first mortgage, foreclosure of a mortgage, holder of a mortgage, lien, maturity of a mortgage, mortgage commitment, mortgagee in possession, mortgagee of record, mortgagor, purchase money mortgage, recording of a mortgage, redemption of a mortgage, second mortgage, subject to a mortgage

MOTIF, *noun* adornment, arrangement, beautification, composition, construction, decoration, design, detail, dominant theme, embellishment, figuration, figure, form, format, garnishment, illumination, main feature, ornament, ornamentation, overall theme, pattern, plan, prevailing idea, recurring theme, shape, structure, style, theme

MOTION, *noun* application, application for a ruling, application for an order, application for proposed relief, claim, demand, petition, proposal, proposed measure, proposition, request, *rogatio, sententia*

ASSOCIATED CONCEPTS: alternative motions, costs of a motion, ex parte motion, interlocutory motion, motion for a more definite statement, motion for a new trial, motion for a nonsuit, motion for a decree, motion for judgment, motion for judgment notwithstanding verdict, motion for reargument, motion for summary judgment, motion papers, motion to dismiss, motion to quash, motion to set aside judgment, motion to strike, motion to vacate a judgment, omnibus motion, premature motion, renewal of a motion, withdrawal of a motion

MOTIVATE, *verb* activate, actuate, adjure, advise, affect, allure, animate, appeal, arouse desire, attract, captivate, carry weight, cause, challenge, charge, command, compel, convince, direct, draw, encourage, exert influence, exhort, fill with longing, fire up, goad, guide, impel, incite, incline, induce, infect, inflame, influence, inspire, inspirit, instigate, interest, invite, lead, move, move to action, persuade, press, prevail upon, promote, prompt, provide with a motive, provoke desire, rouse, set in motion, spirit, spur, stimulate, stir up, sway, talk into, tempt, urge, work upon

MOTIVE, *noun* aim, *causa,* causation, compulsion, consideration, design, determination, driving force, encouragement, end, goal, impelling power, impulse, incentive, inducement, influence, inner drive, inspiration, moving cause, moving power, moving spirit, object, objective, personal reasons, persuasion, plan, point, proposal, prospect, provocation, purpose, *ratio,* rationale, reason, reason for action, stimulant, stimulation, stimulus

ASSOCIATED CONCEPTS: corrupt motive, intent

MOVABLE, noun *agilis*, chattels personal, effects, goods, *mobilis*, personal effects, personal property, personalty, possessions, transportables, transportable property
ASSOCIATED CONCEPTS: fixtures, movable goods, movable machinery
FOREIGN PHRASES: Mobilia non habent situm. Movables have no situs or local habitation.

MOVE (Alter position), **verb** abscond, alter the position, break camp, carry, change an abode, change place, change residence, come away, *commovere*, convey, depart, disperse, emigrate, exit, flee, go, go away, go forth, go from home, go on, go one's way, journey, leave, leave a place, migrate, move out, part company, progress, propel, push on, put in motion, remove, slip away, slip off, take flight, transfer, translocate, transport, transpose, vacate, walk away, walk off

MOVE (Judicially request), **verb** apply, ask for, introduce, make a demand, make a motion, make a petition, make a request, make a requisition, make application, make formal application, make one's submission, offer for consideration, petition, propose, propose a motion, propose an action formally, put forth, put forward, put up a petition, referre, request, requisition, submit, submit a formal request
ASSOCIATED CONCEPTS: motion practice, move the court

MOVEMENT (Activity), **noun** campaign, cause, crusade, mass movement, motion, operation, principle, series of actions directed towards a particular end, undertaking

MOVEMENT (Progress), **noun** action, agitation, campaign, circulation, course, denomination, effort, great cause, interest, issue, measure, outflow, performance, removal, shift, step, stir, stride, transition, transmittal, traveling

MOVEMENT (Shipment), **noun** cartage, conveyance, transit, transportation

MOVING (Evoking emotion), **adjective** absorbing, affecting, agitating, animating, arousing, arresting, astonishing, awakening, breathtaking, captivating, charming, dra'pping, impelling, imposing, impressive, inciting, inflaming, influencing, inspiriting, instigating, interesting, *miserabilis*, overpowering, overwhelming, persuading, piquant, poignant, prompting, provocative, provoking, rousing, sensational, sensitive, stimulating, stimulative, stirring, thrilling, touching, warm

MOVING (In motion), **adjective** active, ambulant, ambulative, ambulatory, changing, conveyable, detachable, drifting, fugitive, itinerant, journeying, kinetic, locomotive, meandering, mercurial, migratory, mobile, motile, motive, mundivagant, nomadic, passing, peripatetic, removable, restless, roaming, roving, separable, shifting, touring, transient, transitional, transmigratory, traveling, unattached, unfastened, unsettled, unstaid, unstationary, vacillating, vagabond, vagrant, voyaging, wandering, wavering, wayfaring
ASSOCIATED CONCEPTS: moving papers, moving party, moving violation

MUDDLE, verb addle, baffle, becloud, befog, befuddle, bewilder, botch, bungle, cloud, complicate, confound, *confundere*, confuse, daze, derange, disarrange, discompose, disconcert, disorder, disorganize, disturb, embrangle, entangle, fluster, fog, fuddle, ignore distinctions, jumble, make a mess of, make havoc, mismanage, mix up, obfuscate, *permiscere*, puzzle, scramble, stupefy, throw into confusion, throw out of order, *turbare*, unsettle, upset

MULCT (Defraud), **verb** cheat, deceive, embezzle, fudge, peculate, practice fraud, sharp, steal, swindle, trick

MULCT (Fine), **verb** amerce, deprive, distrain, exact a fine, impose a fine, penalize, punish

MULTIFARIOUS, adjective different, disparate, dissimilar, diverse, diversified, heterogeneous, irregular, manifold, many, miscellaneous, mixed, motley, multiform, multigenerous, multiplex, nonuniform, numerous, varied, variegated, various, *varius*

MULTIFOLD, adjective diversified, diversiform, manifold, many, multifarious, multiform, multigenerous, multiple, multiplex, multiplicate, multitudinous, numerous, varied, variegated, variform

MULTIPLE, adjective abundant, aggregate, ample, assorted, composed of several elements, considerable, different, divergent, diverse, diversified, generous, innumerable, many, miscellaneous, mixed, more than one, multifarious, multifold, multiplex, multitudinous, myriad, numerous, plenteous, plural, profuse, several, sundry, superabundant, uncounted, unnumbered, untold, varied, various
ASSOCIATED CONCEPTS: multiple claims, multiple damages, multiple dwelling, multiple offender, multiplicity of suits

MULTIPLICITY, noun many sidedness, multitudinous, numerousness, plurality

MULTITUDE, noun abundance, accumulation, aggregation, amassment, army, array, assemblage, assembly, band, bevy, body, cluster, collection, conglomeration, congregation, covey, crowd, cumulation, drove, flock, force, gathering, herd, horde, host, legion, magnitude, many-sidedness, mass, masses, multiplicity, numbers, numerosity, numerousness, plurality, populace, profusion, quantities, quantity, scores, swarm, throng, troupe, volume

MUNDANE, adjective accustomary, average, banal, bodily, carnal, common, commonplace, conventional, corporeal, customary, earthly, everyday, familiar, fleshly, frequent, habitual, hackneyed, homespun, irreligious, material, nonsacred, nonspiritual, ordinary, pedestrian, physical, plain, profane, prosaic, prosy, regular, routine, secular, sensual, simple, stale, standard, stereotyped, sublunar, sublunary, tedious, tellurian, telluric, temporal, terrene, terrestrial, trite, typical, undistinguished, uneventful, unexalted, ungodly, unhallowed, unholy, unimaginative, uninspired, uninteresting, unpoetical, unsacred, unsanctified, unspiritual, usual, wearisome, well-known, well-trodden, workday, worldly, worldly-minded

MURDER, noun act of killing, act of slaying, act of taking life, assassination, *caedes*, destruction, destruction of human life, destruction of life, destructiveness, elimination, genocide, homicide, intentional killing, killing, liquidation, massacre, *occisio*, taking of human life, unlawful killing, violent death
ASSOCIATED CONCEPTS: assault with intent to murder, attempted murder, felonious homicide, felony murder, first-degree murder, premeditated murder, second-degree murder, voluntary manslaughter, willful murder

MURDERER, noun annihilator, assassin, assassinator, butcher, contract killer, criminal, destroyer, eradicator, executioner, exterminator, gunman, hired gun, hired killer, hit man, killer, liquidator, slaughterer, slayer, sniper

MUSE, verb   be abstracted, be distracted, be in a reverie, be inattentive, be occupied in concentration, be occupied in study, bestow thought upon, brood, cerebrate, cogitate, comment, commune with oneself, concentrate, consider, contemplate, daydream, debate, deliberate, digest, disregard, examine, intellectualize, introspect, meditate, mull, note, ponder, reflect, remark, review, revolve, ruminate, speculate, study in silence, study quietly, take into consideration, take stock of, think, think about, think over, turn over, weigh

MUTABLE, adjective   alterable, capricious, changeable, changeful, commutable, fickle, fluctuating, inconstans, inconstant, irresolute, *mutabilis*, protean, subject to change, transient, uncertain, undecided, unreliable, unsettled, unstable, unsteadfast, unsteady, vacillating, variable, versatile, volatile, wavering
FOREIGN PHRASES: **Nomina sunt mutabilia, res autem immobiles.** Names are mutable, but things are immutable. **Res est misera ubi jus est vagum et incertum.** It is a sorry state of affairs when law is vague and mutable.

MUTE, adjective   close-lipped, closemouthed, dumb, hushed, inarticulate, incapable of speech, incommunicative, indisposed to talk, *mutus,* noiseless, pauciloquent, quiescent, quiet, refraining from utterance, reserved, reticent, silent, soundless, speechless, still, taciturn, tight-lipped, tongue-tied, unable to speak, unable to utter articulate sound, uncommunicative, unexpressive, unloquacious, untalkative, unvocal, unvocalizing, voiceless, wordless

MUTILATE, verb   amputate, batter, blemish, bruise, butcher, cripple, cut, damage, debilitate, deface, deform, deprive of an important part, disable, disfigure, dismantle, dismember, distort, gash, impair, incapacitate, injure, knock out of shape, lacerate, maim, mangle, mar, *mutilare,* render a document imperfect, render imperfect, tear, tear apart, truncare, truncate, twist, unshape, warp, wound, wreck

MUTINY, noun   defiance, disloyalty, disobedience, insubordination, insurgence, insurgency, insurrection, *motus,* opposition, oppugnancy, outbreak, rebellion, refusal to comply, resistance, revolt, revolution, *seditio,* sedition, subversion, treason, upheaval, uprising

MUTUAL (Collective), **adjective**   coadjutant, coadjutive, coadjuvant, coadunate, coalitional, collaborated, collaborative, combined, common, communal, communalistic, commutual, confederated, conjoint, cooperant, cooperative, federal, federate, federated, federative, general, in common, interdependent, joint, leagued, participatory, shared, unified, united
ASSOCIATED CONCEPTS: mutual benefit association, mutual enterprise, mutual insurance company, mutual savings bank

MUTUAL (Reciprocal), **adjective**   bilateral, commutative, complemental, complementary, concurrent, correlative, correspondent, corresponding, done reciprocally, equivalent, interactive, interchanged, interrelated, *mutuus,* parallel, reciprocating, reciprocative, two-sided, two-way
ASSOCIATED CONCEPTS: mutual consent, mutual covenants, mutual easements, mutual mistake, mutual promise, mutual wills

MUTUAL AGREEMENT, noun   acclamation, accord, accordance, affirmation, common consent, concord, concordance, concurrent agreement, consensus, consentaneity, consentience, contract, general agreement, likemindedness, meeting of the minds, mutual arrangement, mutual bargain, pact, unanimity, unison, universal agreement

MUTUAL UNDERSTANDING, noun   accord, agreement, alliance, amity, bilateral contract, common agreement, common understanding, communion, compact, concordance, concurrence, contract, correlative agreement, entente, interchangeable commitment, joint agreement, joint pact, meeting of minds, mutual promise, pact, reciprocal agreement, reciprocal commitment, treaty

MUTUALITY, noun   coequality, commonality, commutability, commutation, correlation, correlativeness, correlativity, correspondence, dependence, exchange, interaffiliation, interassociation, interchange, interchangeability, interconnection, interdependence, intermutation, interplay, interrelation, mutual dependence, mutual relation, permutation, reciprocality, reciprocalness, reciprocation, reciprocity
ASSOCIATED CONCEPTS: mutuality of consent, mutuality of contract, mutuality of obligation, mutuality of remedy

MYRIAD, adjective   boundless, countless, endless, illimitable, immense, incalculable, inexhaustible, infinite, innumerable, innumerous, limitless, manifold, many, measureless, multitudinous, numberless, numerous, sescenti, sumless, uncountable, uncounted, unending, unfathomable, unlimited, unnumberable, unnumbered, untold, without number

MYSTERIOUS, adjective   abstruse, arcane, *arcanus,* baffling, cabalistic, clandestine, cloaked, coded, concealed, covert, cryptic, dark, disguised, enigmatic, enigmatical, esoteric, furtive, hidden, impenetrable, incomprehensible, ineffable, inexplicable, inscrutable, magical, masked, mystic, mystical, mystifying, obscure, occult, *occultus,* oracular, perplexing, preternatural, privy, puzzling, recondite, runic, screened, secret, secretive, *secretus,* shadowy, sphinxian, sphinx-like, stealthy, strange, supernatural, supernormal, surreptitious, transcendental, umbrageous, unaccountable, uncanny, undeciphered, undercover, underhand, undisclosed, unexplainable, unexplained, unfathomable, unintelligible, unknown, unrevealed, untold, veiled, weird

MYSTERY, noun   abstruseness, arcanum, cabala, cabalism, concealment, enigma, hidden meaning, inexplicableness, inscrutability, inscrutableness, mysticism, obscurity, occultism, occultness, puzzle, *res occulta,* riddle, secrecy, secret, secretiveness, thaumaturgy, undiscoverability, unexplored ground, unfathomability, unfathomableness

MYTH, noun   absurd story, concoction, doubtful narrative, fable, fabrication, *fabula,* false story, falsehood, fantasy, fiction, fictitious story, figment, folklore, folktale, invention, legend, legendary story, story, tale, tall story, tradition, trumped up story, unreality, untrue story, untruth, yarn
ASSOCIATED CONCEPTS: legal fiction

N

NAIVE, *adjective* believing, callow, childish, childlike, credulous, deceivable, deludable, dupable, exploitable, foolable, green, gullible, immature, inexperienced, innocent, natural, open, plain, provincial, simple, *simplex,* trusting, unaffected, unfeigned, unschooled, unsophisticated, unsuspecting, unsuspicious, unworldly, void of suspicion

NAKED *(Lacking embellishment),* ***adjective*** bare, basal, basic, devoid of consideration, elementary, fundamental, laid bare, mere, plain, sheer, simple, stark, straight, unadorned, unadulterated, uncomplicated, undecorated, undisguised, unembellished, unexaggerated, unmasked, unornamented, unvarnished, unveiled
ASSOCIATED CONCEPTS: naked promise

NAKED *(Perceptible),* ***adjective*** apparent, brought to light, clear, cognizable, conspicuous, discernible, disclosed, discoverable, distinct, distinguishable, easy to see, evident, explicit, exposed, express, in plain view, made public, manifest, not obscure, noticeable, observable, obvious, open, ostensible, overt, patent, perceivable, plain, prominent, recognizable, revealed, unconcealed, unmistakable, visible

NAME, *noun* being, characteristic, difference, distinction, distinctiveness, distinctness, identifier, identifying characteristic, identity, individualism, oneness, originality, particularity, personage, personal characteristic, personality, quality of being singular, self, selfness, singleness, singularity, specialty, uniqueness
ASSOCIATED CONCEPTS: distinctive name, trade name

NAMED, *adjective* called, classified, delineated, denoted as, described as, designate as, determined as, discriminated as, distinguished as, identified as, known as, recognized as, referred to as, specified as
ASSOCIATED CONCEPTS: named in a caption

NARCOTIC, *adjective* anesthetic, anodyne, anodynous, assuaging, assuasive, calmant, calmative, deadening, depressant, dulling, hypnotic, mitigating, narcotical, opiate, pain-killing, palliative, paregoric, sedative, slumberous, somniferous, somnific, soothing, soporiferous, soporific, stupefactive, torporifc, tranquilizing

NARCOTIC, *noun* alleviative, alleviator, anesthetic, anodyne, assuasive drug, barbiturate, calmative, depressant, dope, drug, hypnotic, lenitive, medication, medicine, mitigative, opiate, pain reliever, painkiller, palliative, sedative, somnifacient, soother, soporific, stupefacient, tranquilizer

NARRATION, *noun* account, chronicle, delineation, depiction, depictment, description, descriptive account, discourse, disquisition, *expositio,* exposition, iteration, *narratio,* narrative, portrayal, recapitulation, recital, recitation, recountal, recounting, reiteration, relation, rendition, repetition, report, representation, restatement, retelling, review, setting forth, sketch, storytelling, summarization, summary, tale, tale telling

NARRATIVE, *adjective* anecdotal, communicative, declarative, declaratory, descriptive, detailed, disquisitional, epic, exegetic, exegetical, explanatory, explicative, explicatory, expositive, expository, graphic, illuminating, illuminative, illustrative, informational, informative, *narrare,* recounted, reported, sequential, storylike, told
ASSOCIATED CONCEPTS: narrative testimony

NARROW, *adjective* attenuated, bigoted, circumscribed, compressed, confined, constricted, contracted, *contractus,* cramped, crowded, defined, dogmatic, exact, fanatical, fine, illiberal, incapacious, inhibiting, intolerant, limited, literal, narrow-minded, opinionated, parochial, pinched, precise, prescribed, protected, provincial, qualified, registered, restricted, rigid, scant, scanty, simple, slender, strict, tapering, thin, tight
ASSOCIATED CONCEPTS: a narrowly written decision, narrow interpretation

NARROW MEANING, *noun* accurate meaning, correct meaning, defined meaning, definition, distinct meaning, exact meaning, explanation, explicit meaning, express meaning, faithful meaning, inflexible meaning, literal meaning, methodical meaning, meticulous meaning, not subject to interpretation, ordinary meaning, plain meaning, precise meaning, prescribed meaning, rigid meaning, rigorous meaning, sharply defined, significance, specific meaning, strict meaning, unbending meaning, uncompromising meaning, unequivocal meaning
ASSOCIATED CONCEPTS: construction, literal contract, literal proof, plain meaning rule, rules of statutory, soft plain meaning rule, textualism

NASCENCY, *noun* beginning, birth, commencement, creation, debut, development, emergence, entrance, entry, evolution, evolvement, first appearance, first stage, first step, formation, foundation, founding, genesis, inauguration, inception, inchoation, incipience, incipiency, incunabula, induction, infancy, initiation, introduction, invention, launching, nascence, nativity, onset, origin, origination, outset, rise, start, starting

NASCENT, adjective beginning, budding, early, elemental, elementary, embryonic, first, first ever, first of all, formative, foundational, fundamental, in its infancy, inaugural, inceptive, inchoate, incipient, incunabular, infant, infantile, initial, initiatory, introductory, inventive, original, prenatal, primal, primary, prime, primeval, primitive, rudimental, rudimentary, seminal

NATION, noun captive nation, commonweal, commonwealth, confederation, county, developed nation, domain, dominion, kingdom, land, nationality, possession, power, province, realm, territory
ASSOCIATED CONCEPTS: comity, free trade, international law

NATIONAL, adjective affecting the nation as a whole, common, country-wide, domestic, established by the federal government, federal, general, government, government-owned, governmental, public, publicly owned, societal, sovereign

NATIONALITY, noun allegiance, birth, body politic, citizenry, commonwealth, country, fatherland, habitancy, homeland, inhabitancy, inhabitation, nation, national group, national status, native land, nativity, origin, people, polity, populace, society, sovereign state, statehood, stock
ASSOCIATED CONCEPTS: immigration and naturalization

NATIONALIZE, verb appropriate for federal use, appropriate for government use, make national, make national in character, place under government control, remove from private ownership, seize for public use, seize for the government, socialize, transfer control to the government, transfer ownership to the government

NATIVE (Domestic), adjective aboriginal, autochthonal, autochthonic, autochthonous, domestic, enchorial, enchoric, endemic, endemical, home-grown, indigenous, local, locally born, not alien, not foreign, original, regional, unborrowed, vernacular

NATIVE (Inborn), adjective basic, born, congenital, connate, connatural, essential, fundamental, genetic, hereditary, inbred, indigenous, ingenerate, ingenit, ingrained, inherent, inherited, innate, instinctive, instinctual, intrinsic, natal, natural, organic, original

NATURAL, adjective artless, authentic, characteristic, connate, consistent, crude, free from affectation, fundamental, genuine, inborn, inbred, indigenous, ingenerate, ingrained, innate, *innatus*, instinctive, instinctual, lifelike, native, nativus, normal, organic, original, pure, real, realistic, regular, true to life, typical, unadulterated, unartificial, uncultivated, unsynthetic, untouched
ASSOCIATED CONCEPTS: natural law

NATURALIZE (Acclimate), verb accommodate, accustom, adapt, adjust, assimilate, become habituated, cultivate a habit, familiarize, fit the pattern, get used to, habituate, harmonize, inure, learn a habit, make easy, make natural, normalize, regularize

NATURALIZE (Make a citizen), verb accept as a citizen, admit citizenship, adopt, adopt as a citizen, adopt into a nation, assimilate, citizenize, confer privileges of a native citizen, confer rights of citizenship, denizenize, endow with rights of citizenship, extend citizenship to an alien, *homini civitatem dare,* nationalize, place in the condition of natural born subjects

NATURE (Kind), noun attribute, brand, breed, character, characteristic, description, designation, differentia, differential, distinctive feature, domain, feature, ilk, individualism, label, make, manner, mannerism, mark, model, mold, particularity, peculiarity, persuasion, quality, quirk, specialty, species, sphere, strain, style, taint, tang, taste, the like or likes of, token, trait, tribe, trick, type, variety
ASSOCIATED CONCEPTS: nature of an action, the nature of a case

NATURE (Naturalness), noun artlessness, inartificiality, intactness, natural man, natural state, nature in the raw, pristineness, state of nature, virginity
ASSOCIATED CONCEPTS: environmental law

NEAR (Close), adjective adjacent, adjoining, approaching, approximate, bordering, close by, contiguous, imminent, impending, in close proximity, in the area, in the neighborhood, in the vicinity, nearby, neighboring, next, next to, proximal, proximate to, surrounding, tangent, touching, vicinal
ASSOCIATED CONCEPTS: case near to being put on the trial calendar, case nearly ready for trial, cases near trial, completion, near competition, substantial completion

NEBULOUS, adjective abstruse, ambiguous, bleared, blurred, blurry, clouded, cloudy, confused, dim, dusky, faint, foggy, hazy, ill-defined, imperspicuous, indeterminate, indistinct, lacking clarity, nebulose, *nebulosus,* not clear, obfuscated, obscure, out of focus, pale, recondite, shadowed, shadowy, uncertain, unclear, undefined, undiscernible, unintelligible, vague
ASSOCIATED CONCEPTS: nebulous contract

NECESSARY (Inescapable), adjective avoidless, certain, choiceless, compelling, constraining, decided, decreed, designated, destined, expected, fated, fateful, fixed, foreordained, imminent, impending, ineluctable, ineludible, inevitable, inexorable, irresistible, irrevocable, ordained, sealed, settled, sure, unalterable, unavoidable, uncontrollable, undeniable, unevasible, unpreventable
ASSOCIATED CONCEPTS: necessary damages, necessary expenses, necessary implication, necessary inference, necessary injury

NECESSARY (Required), adjective all-important, basic, binding, bounden, chief, coercive, compelling, compulsory, critical, crucial, demanded, dictated, essential, exigent, expedient, fundamental, imperative, important, imposed, incumbent, indispensable, integral, key, mandatory, necessitated, necessitous, needed, obligatory, paramount, prerequisite, prescribed, prime, principal, requisite, requisitioned, significant, strategic, strategical, substantive, urgent, vital
ASSOCIATED CONCEPTS: necessary parties

NECESSARY, noun essence, essential, essentiality, indispensable thing, *necessitas,* necessities, necessitousness, necessitude, necessity, need, prerequirement, prerequisite, qualification, requirement, requisite, vitals
ASSOCIATED CONCEPTS: duty to provide necessaries, necessaries of life

NECESSARY PARTY, noun critical party who cannot be joined, crucial party who cannot be joined, integral defendant who cannot be joined, integral disputant who cannot be joined, integral party who cannot be joined, integral petitioner who cannot be joined, integral plaintiff who cannot be joined, integral respondent who cannot be joined, needed party who cannot be joined, party whose interests will be affected, prescribed party whose cannot be joined, significant party who cannot be joined, strategic party who cannot be joined, vital party who cannot be joined

ASSOCIATED CONCEPTS: indispensable party, proper party

NECESSITATE, verb call for, clamor for, coerce, *cogere*, compel, concuss, create a need, decree, demand, dictate, enjoin, exact, force, impel, impose, insist upon, leave no choice, leave no option, make indispensable, make inevitable, make necessary, make unavoidable, obligate, oblige, ordain, predetermine, raise a demand, render necessary, require

NECESSITY, noun absolute requisite, basic ingredient, central element, characteristic feature, compelling quality, compulsory detail, crucial part, *egestas*, elementary detail, essential, essential element, exigency, fundamental, fundamental principle, fundamental unit, highly important detail, imperative, indispensable, indispensable provision, inevitable, integral part, irreplaceable feature, irresistible compulsion, main ingredient, mandatory factor, necessary attribute, necessary component, *necessitas*, need, precondition, prerequirement, prerequisite, primary constituent, qualification, recognized condition, required item, requirement, requisite, rudiment, significant detail, strategic item, urgency, urgent requirement, vital part, vitals

ASSOCIATED CONCEPTS: compelling necessity, economic necessity, finding of necessity, prescription by necessity, public necessity, strict necessity

FOREIGN PHRASES: *Quod est necessarium est licitum.* That which is necessary is lawful. *Necessitas excusat aut extenuat delictum in capitalibus, quod non operatur idem in civilibus.* Necessity excuses or extenuates an offense in capital cases, but not in civil cases. *Necessitas est lex temporis et loci.* Necessity is the law of a particular time and place. *Lex judicat de rebus necessario faciendis quasi re ipsa factis.* The law judges of things which must necessarily be done as if they were actually done. *Necessitas inducit privilegium quoad jura privata.* Necessity gives a privilege with reference to private rights. *Necessitas publica major est quam privata.* Public necessity is greater than private.

NECTAROUS, adjective candied, cloying, delectable, delicious, dulcet, honeyed, luscious, melliferous, oversweet, rich, saccharine, sugary, sweet, tasty

NEED (Deprivation), noun absence, dearth, deficiency, deficit, demand, exigency, extremity, inadequacy, incompleteness, indigence, insufficiency, lack, necessitousness, necessitude, necessity, paucity, penury, privation, scantiness, scarcity, shortage, shortness of supply, thirst, vacuum, want, wantage

NEED (Requirement), noun compulsion, compulsory detail, crucial part, demand, desideration, desideratum, essential element, essentiality, essentialness, fundamental, highly important detail, indispensability, indispensable provision, integral part, irreplaceability, irreplaceable feature, mandatory factor, necessary, necessary attribute, necessary component, necessity, obligation, precondition, preliminary condition, prequisiteness, prerequirement,

proviso, required item, requisite, requisiteness, strategic item, urgency, urgent requirement, vital part, vitalness

NEED, verb claim, clamor for, crave, cry for, demand, desire, exact, feel the necessity for, feel the want of, find indispensable, find necessary, have an urge for, have need for, have occasion for, have use of, hunger for, long for, lust for, miss, require, thirst for, want, yearn for

NEEDLESS, adjective avoidable, beside the point, causeless, dispensable, excess, excessive, exorbitant, expendable, expletive, extra, extraneous, fruitless, futile, gratuitous, groundless, inordinate, irrelevant, *non necessarius*, noncompulsory, nonessential, optional, overabundant, overmuch, overplentiful, oversufficient, pleonastic, prodigal, redundant, spare, superabundant, supererogatory, superfluous, supernumerary, supervenient, surplus, unavailing, uncalled-for, undesirable, unessential, unnecessary, unneeded, unprofitable, unrequired, unrewarding, unwanted, useless, valueless, wanton, wasteful, worthless

NEFARIOUS, adjective abominable, arrant, bad, base, confounded, contemptible, corrupt, criminal, degenerate, deplorable, depraved, despicable, detestable, devilish, diabolical, discreditable, disgraceful, dishonorable, dissolute, dreadful, evil, execrable, felonious, flagitious, flagrant, foul, gross, hateful, heinous, horrible, ignoble, immoral, impious, improper, indecent, infamous, infernal, iniquitous, malignant, miscreant, monstrous, *nefarius*, obnoxious, odious, outrageous, peccant, pernicious, profligate, reprehensible, reprobate, scandalous, shameful, sinful, sinister, terrible, treacherous, unrighteous, vile, villainous, wicked, wrong

NEGATE, verb abnegate, abolish, abort, abrogate, annihilate, annul, cancel, confound, confute, contradict, contravene, controvert, counter, counteract, countermand, counterpoise, declare invalid, declare null and void, defeat, demur, deny, deprive of force, disaffirm, disallow, disavow, disclaim, discontinue, discredit, disprove, dispute, disregard, explain away, falsify, impugn, invalidate, negative, neutralize, nullify, object, obliterate, offset, oppose, override, overrule, overthrow, prohibit, protest, prove the contrary, quash, rebut, recant, refute, render null and void, renounce, repeal, repudiate, rescind, retract, reverse, revoke, rule out, set aside, suppress, suspend, traverse, vacate, veto

NEGATION, noun abjuration, abnegation, abolishment, abolition, abrogation, annulment, cancellation, cassation, confutation, contradiction, contravention, declination, declinature, defiance, denial, disaffirmation, disagreement, disapprobation, disapproval, disavowal, disclaimer, disproof, dissent, forswearing, gainsay, gainsaying, *infitiatio*, invalidation, *negatio*, nonacceptance, nonagreement, noncompliance, nonconsent, noncorroboration, nullification, objection, opposition, protest, protestation, recantation, refusal, refutation, rejection, repeal, repudiation, rescission, resistance, retractation, retraction, reversal, revocation, revokement, traversal

ASSOCIATED CONCEPTS: negation of warranty

NEGATIVE, adjective acrimonious, antagonistic, antipathetic, antipathetical, argumentative, at odds with, attacking, averse, belligerent, bickering, cantankerous, clashing, conflicting, confutative, contentious, contesting, contradictory, contrary, contrasted, contrasting, contravening, converse, counteractive, countering, demurring, denying, disaccordant, disavowing, discordant, disobliging, disputing, dissentient, dissident, factious, fractious, gainsaying, hostile, ill-willed, impugning, incompatible, inimical, inverse, *negans,* negatory, opposed, opposing, opposite, quarrelsome, rancorous, rebuffing, rebutting, refuting, rejecting, repudiating, repugnant, resistive, reverse, spurning, traversing, unaffirmative, unconverted, unconvinced

ASSOCIATED CONCEPTS: negative covenant, negative easement, negative evidence, negative testimony

NEGLECT, *noun* abandonment, absentmindedness, breach, bungling, careless abandon, carelessness, default, delinquency, dereliction, disregard, failure, heedlessness, idleness, improvidence, imprudence, inaction, inadvertence, inattention, inattentiveness, *incuria,* indifference, indiligence, *indiligentia,* inexecution, inexertion, laches, laxity, laxness, misprision, *neglegentia,* negligence, noncompletion, noncompliance, nonfeasance, nonfulfillment, nonobservance, nonperformance, omission, oversight, procrastination, prodigality, rashness, recklessness, remissness, slackness, slight, sloth, slovenliness, thoughtlessness, unactivity, unalertness, unconcern, unconscientiousness, unheedfulness, unmindfulness, unobservance, unwariness, unwatchfulness

ASSOCIATED CONCEPTS: culpable neglect, neglect of duty, neglect to act, neglect to prosecute, willful neglect

FOREIGN PHRASES: ***Magna culpa dolus est.*** Gross neglect is the equivalent of fraud.

NEGLECT, *verb* be careless, be inattentive, be lax, *deserere,* disdain, disregard, fail, forget, gloss over, ignore, *intermittere,* lay aside, leave alone, lose sight of, *neglegere,* not care for, not use, omit, overlook, pass by, pass over, pay no attention, pay no heed, pay no regard to, preterit, procrastinate, refuse to recognize, shirk, shun, skip, slight, take no note, take no notice

NEGLECTFUL, *adjective* careless, delinquent, derelict, disregardful, forgetful, heedless, inadvertent, inattentive, incautious, injudicious, inobservant, irresponsible, lax, mindless, neglectful, not diligent, not heedful, oblivious, reckless, remiss, thoughtless, unconcerned, unheeding, unmindful, unthinking, unwatchful

ASSOCIATED CONCEPTS: defendants neglectful of their duty, neglectful parents

NEGLIGENCE, *noun* abandonment, breach of duty, carelessness, culpa, delinquency, dereliction, disregard, failure, heedlessness, improvidence, imprudence, inadvertence, inadvertency, inattention, inattentiveness, incautiousness, incircumspection, inconsideration, *incuria,* indifference, *indiligentia,* inobservance, irresponsibility, lack of attention, lack of diligence, laxity, laxness, neglectfulness, *neglegentia,* obliviousness, omission, oversight, recklessness, regardlessness, remissness, slackness, unalertness, unconcern, unmindfulness, unwariness, unwatchfulness, want of thought

ASSOCIATED CONCEPTS: actionable negligence, active negligence, assumption of risk, causal negligence, comparative negligence, concurrent negligence, contributory negligence, criminal negligence, culpable negligence, estoppel by negligence, gross negligence, imputed negligence, last clear chance doctrine, malpractice, negligence per se, ordinary negligence, passive negligence, *res ipsa loquitur,* standard of care, supervening negligence, wanton negligence, willful negligence

FOREIGN PHRASES: ***Magna negligentia culpa est; magna culpa dolus est.*** Gross negligence is fault; gross fault is equivalent to a fraud. ***Culpa lata dolo aequiparatur.*** Gross negligence is equivalent to intentional wrong.

NEGLIGENT, *adjective* bungling, careless, delinquent, derelict, disregardant, disregardful, heedless, ill-considered, improvident, imprudent, inadvertent, inattentive, incautious, indifferent, *indiligens,* injudicious, inobservant, irresponsible, lax, mindless, neglectful, *neglegens,* oblivious, off guard, rash, reckless, regardless, remiss, *remissus,* slack, slipshod, slothful, slovenly, temerarious, temerous, thoughtless, unalert, uncalculating, uncircumspect, unconcerned, undiligent, unheedful, unheeding, unmindful, unthinking, unthorough, unwary, unwatchful

ASSOCIATED CONCEPTS: negligent act, negligent conduct, negligent injury

NEGLIGIBLE, *adjective* beneath notice, dispensable, expendable, immaterial, imperceptible, inappreciable, inconsequential, inconsiderable, insignificant, insubstantial, irrelevant, *levis,* light, little, meager, minor, minute, moderate, modest, nominal, nugatory, of little account, of little consequence, of little importance, of no moment, of no significance, paltry, picayune, poor, puny, scant, scanty, slight, small, *tenuis,* trifling, trivial, unessential, unimportant, unnoteworthy, unsubstantial, unworthy of regard, valueless

FOREIGN PHRASES: ***De minimis non curat lex.*** The law pays no attention to insignificant things.

NEGOTIABLE, *adjective* alienable, assignable, capable of being transferred, consignable, conveyable, exchangeable, interchangeable, maneuverable, marketable, salable, transferable, transmissible, transmittible, vendible

ASSOCIATED CONCEPTS: commercial paper, negotiable contract, negotiable instruments, promissory note

NEGOTIABLE INSTRUMENT, *noun* bank check, bank note, bank paper, bill, bill of exchange, cashier's check, check, commercial instrument, commercial paper, commercial transition, debenture, draft, negotiable paper, note, personal check, promissory note, secured

ASSOCIATED CONCEPTS: dishonor, named payee presentment

NEGOTIATE, *verb* accommodate, arbitrate, arrange for, bargain, bid for, bring to terms, come to terms, dicker, haggle, hurdle, intercede, intermediate, make peace, make terms, mediate, meet halfway, parley, referee, settle, settle disputes, straighten out, surmount, transact, umpire, work out

NEGOTIATION, *noun* arbitrament, arbitration, bargaining, compromise, conference, *conloquium,* consultation, contract talks, deliberation, dickering, diplomacy, discussion, exchange of views, haggling, mediation, parley, summitry, treaty-making

ASSOCIATED CONCEPTS: collective bargaining, preliminary negotiation

NEOPHYTE, *noun* abecedarian, amateur, apprentice, beginner, catechumen, debutant, entrant, fledgling, freshman, learner, newcomer, novice, prentice, pupil, student, tenderfoot, trainee, tyro

NEPOTISM, *noun* bias, corruptibility, corruption, family patronage, favor, favoritism, inequitableness, inequity, injustice, interest, leaning, partiality, partisanism, partisanship, patronage, preferential treatment, undetachment, unfairness, unjustness

NESCIENCE, *noun* blindness, darkness, greenness, ignorance, ignoration, incognizance, inexperience, lack of awareness, lack of knowledge, lack of learning, naivete, rawness, unawareness, uncomprehension, unenlightenment, uninformedness, unintelligence, unknowingness, unlearnedness

NET, adjective clear, irreducible, leftover, remaining, residual, residuary, surplus, surviving, unexpended, unspent
ASSOCIATED CONCEPTS: net assets, net balance, net capital stock, net earnings, net estate, net income, net loss, net premium, net price, net proceeds, net profit, net rents, net revenues, net value, net worth

NETWORK, noun body, combined system, complicated system, interface, intertwining system, laced system, systematic web, weave, weaving, web, webbing

NEUTRAL, adjective disengaged, disinterested, dispassionate, equitable, fair, fair-minded, impartial, impersonal, independent, indifferent, isolationist, *medius, neutrius* partis, nonaligned, nonbelligerent, noncombatant, noncommittal, noninterfering, noninterventionist, nonparticipant, nonparticipating, nonpartisan, objective, pacific, pacifistic, peaceable, peaceful, unaffected, unbiased, unbigoted, uncommitted, unconcerned, uninfluenced, uninvolved, unjaundiced, unprejudiced, unprepossessed, unswayed
ASSOCIATED CONCEPTS: neutral property

NEUTRALITY, noun aloofness, detachment, disinterest, disinterestedness, dispassionateness, impartiality, indifference, moderateness, neutralism, nonbelligerence, noncombatance, noninterference, nonintervention, nonparticipance, nonparticipation, nonpartisanship

NEUTRALIZE, verb annul, balance, cancel, cancel out, counterbalance, counterpoise, countervail, deactivate, deaden, demagnetize, destroy the effect of, disable, disenable, equalize, incapacitate, invalidate, make ineffective, negate, nullify, offset, render inert, render inoperative, render neutral, vitiate

NEW (Creative), adjective causative, conceived, conceptive, conceptual, constructive, created with a different approach, created with a different look, created with a fresh approach, created with a fresh look, effectuated, formative, imagined, ingenious, innovative, inventive, original, originated by, originative, produced, produced by someone blessed with talent, produced by someone capable, produced by someone talented, resourceful, talented, unique
ASSOCIATED CONCEPTS: patents

NEW (Initial), adjective beginning, chief, elementary, first, first ever, foremost, fundamental, inaugural, inceptive, inchoate, incipient, introductory, nascent, original, preliminary, primary, primary original, rudimentary, seminal, unique
ASSOCIATED CONCEPTS: new law

NEWS, noun broadcast news, coverage, current affairs, daily news, developments, happenings, hard news, information, intelligence, media, news gathering, news medium, news service, press, reportage, reporting, television, the fourth estate, the press, the press corps, word

NEXT (Near), adjective abutting, adjacent, adjoining, bordering, connecting, contiguous, immediate, in the neighborhood, in the vicinity, joined, juxtaposed, neighboring, tangential

NEXT (Noted), adjective acclaimed, applauded, celebrated, consequential, conspicuous, distinguished, eminent, exalted, extraordinary, famed, famous, foremost, great, honored, illustrious, important, known, leading, matchless, much touted, notable, noteworthy, notorious, outstanding, popular, preeminent, prominent, recognized, remarkable, reputable, singular, unexampled, unique, unparalleled, unprecedented, well-known

NEXT (Succeeding), adjective additional, consequent, ensuing, following, progressive, sequent, sequential, serial, subsequent, successive
ASSOCIATED CONCEPTS: next devisee, next estate, next of kin

NEXT OF KIN, noun blood kindred, blood relation, blood relative, close relative, collateral relative, consanguineal relations, family, family connection, family tie, individual's nearest relative, kin, kindred, kinsman, kinspeople, near relation, nearest blood relation, nearest relative by blood, related by affinity, relation by blood, relations, relatives
ASSOCIATED CONCEPTS: decedent's estate, heirs

NEXUS, noun affiliation, alliance, association, attachment, bond, bridge, connecting link, connection, connective, coupling, interconnection, intermedium, interrelation, kinship, liaison, link, privity, relation, relationship, thread, tie, union, vinculum

NOBLE, adjective aristocratic, august, courtly, dignified, distinguished, elevated, eminent, esteemed, estimable, exalted, famous, glorious, grand, held in esteem, heroic, highly esteemed, honorable, honored, inspiring, kingly, lauded, lofty, magisterial, magnificent, majestic, meritorious, outstanding, prestigious, princely, prominent, regal, renowned, reputable, respectable, respected, revered, royal, soaring, stately, superb, worthy

NOISE, noun ado, blare, blatancy, cacophony, charivari, clamor, clamorousness, clangor, clatter, cry, detonation, din, discord, fanfare, fracas, harsh sound, hubbub, hullabaloo, jangle, loudness, outcry, pandemonium, racket, ruckus, ruction, *sonitus,* sound, stir, *strepitus,* tumult, unpleasant sound, uproar, uproariousness, vociferance, vociferation
ASSOCIATED CONCEPTS: disturbing the peace, noise pollution, nuisance

NOISOME, adjective abhorrent, abominable, arrant, atrocious, awful, base, blameworthy, brutal, coarse, contemptible, crude, deplorable, despicable, detestable, disgusting, dreadful, egregious, execrable, fetid, foul, grievous, heinous, horrible, horrid, ignoble, infamous, monstrous, nefarious, noxious, objectionable, obnoxious, odious, offensive, repellent, reprehensible, repugnant, repulsive, revolting, rude, sad, shameful, shocking, sickening, terrible, vile, woeful, wretched

NOLLO CONTENDERE, noun acceptance of penalty, admission of the facts, plea, settlement

NOLLO PROSEQUI, noun abrogation, cancellation, counter order, countermand, reversal, reversion

NOMINAL, adjective cheap, cut-rate, hardly worth mention, honorary, in name only, inconsiderable, inexpensive, insignificant, little, low, low-priced, meager, meaningless, minimum, minute, moderate, modest, negligible, *nomine,* petty, reduced, scanty, simple, slight, small, superficial, symbolic, titular, titulary, token, trifling, trivial, unactual, unimportant, unsubstantial

ASSOCIATED CONCEPTS: nominal capital, nominal considera- tion, nominal damages, nominal defendant, nominal owner, nominal parties, nominal plaintiff, nominal value

NOMINATE, verb appoint, assign, call, choose, com- mission, constitute, denominate, *designare, designate,* designate for appointment, designate for election, *dicere,* draft, engage, entitle, install, label, name, name for office, *nominare,* ordain, ordinate, place in authority, place in command, place in office, propose, propose as a candi- date, put up, select, specify, style, suggest, tag, title, vote into office

NOMINATION, noun appointment, assignment, au- thorization, choice, choosing, delegation, denomination, deputization, *designatio,* designation, election, naming, *nominatio,* ordainment, ordination, proposal, selection

NOMINEE *(Candidate),* **noun** chosen representative, flag bearer, named representative, political representative, selection

NOMINEE *(Delegate),* **noun** appointee, consignee, li- censee, representative, selectee, trustee

NON COMPOS MENTIS, adjective abnormal, bereft of reason, crazed, crazy, declared insane, defective, de- mented, deprived of one's wits, deranged, dim-witted, dis- eased in mind, disoriented, distraught, dull-witted, feeble- minded, idiotic, insane, insanely deluded, lunatic, mad, maddened, manic, maniacal, mental, mentally deficient, mentally diseased, mentally ill, mentally sick, mentally un- sound, mindless, moronic, of unsound mind, out of one's mind, out of one's senses, out of one's wits, psychologi- cally abnormal, psychopathic, psychotic, raving, senseless, simple-minded, unbalanced, unsettled, unsettled in one's mind, unsound, unstable, utterly senseless
ASSOCIATED CONCEPTS: insanity, lack of capacity

NON SEQUITUR, noun anacoluthon, bad logic, circular reasoning, contradiction of terms, disconnectedness, dis- continuity, fallacious argument, fallacious reasoning, fallacy, false reasoning, flaw in the argument, illogical conclusion, illogical deduction, illogical result, inconsequence, irrational conclusion, irrelevancy, loose thinking, lost connection, nonsensicality, nonsensicalness, paralogism, sophism, sophistry, specious argument, specious reasoning, un- founded conclusion, unwarranted conclusion, wrong rea- soning

NONACCEPTANCE, noun abnegation, abridgment, at an impasse, confutation, contradiction, contrary assertion, contravention, disaffirmation, disallowance, disavowal, dis- clamation, dissent, negation, no agreement, no meeting of the minds, objection, protest, rebuttal, recantation, refuta- tion, rejection, renouncement, renunciation, retraction
ASSOCIATED CONCEPTS: presentment

NONAGE, noun adolescence, childhood, early stage, immaturity, infancy, legal immaturity, legal minority, mi- nority, period of legal immaturity, period of legal minority, tender age, youth

NONAPPEARANCE, noun absence without leave, absen- tation, absenteeism, concealment, default, failure to appear, hiding, imperceptibility, indiscernibility, inexistence, invisibil- ity, invisibleness, nonattendance, nonpresence, obscurity, tru- ancy, unperceivability, unseeableness, vanishment

NONCANCELLABLE, adjective abiding, durable, indeli- ble, ineffaceable, irrepealable, irreversible, lasting, nonabol- ishable, nonannullable, nonerasable, nonrescindable, non- retractable, nonreversible, permanent, unchangeable, undestroyable, unquashable, unvoidable
ASSOCIATED CONCEPTS: noncancellable clause

NONCHALANT, adjective *aequo animo,* apathetic, blase, calm, carefree, casual, collected, composed, cool, dis- passionate, easygoing, impassive, imperturbable, indiffer- ent, insouciant, inured, lacking enthusiasm, lacking interest, lacking warmth, lukewarm, offhand, passionless, pococu- rante, self-controlled, spiritless, studied, unaffected, unaroused, unblushing, uncaring, unconcerned, unenthusi- astic, unexcited, unfeeling, unflappable, unimpassioned, unimpressed, uninterested, unmindful, unmoved, unruffled, unshocked, unspirited, unstirred, untouched, unworried

NONCOMMITTAL, adjective careful, cautious, change- able, close, discreet, evasive, faltering, guarded, hedging, heedful, hesitant, hesitating, incommunicative, inconstant, indecisive, infirm of purpose, irresolute, irresolved, laconic, lukewarm, mutable, neutral, on guard, precautionary, pre- cautious, prudent, reserved, reticent, secretive, silent, taci- turn, unassured, uncertain, uncommitted, uncommunica- tive, undaring, undecided, unforthcoming, uninvolved, unresolved, unresponsive, unsettled, unsteadfast, un- steady, unsure, vacillating, vague, wary, watchful, wavering

NONCOMPETE CLAUSE, noun agreement not to com- pete, contract against competing, covenant not to compete, express promise not to compete, noncompete agreement, prohibition against competition, restrictive covenant not to compete, restrictive provisions against competing
ASSOCIATED CONCEPTS: golden handcuffs, per se violations of law, restrictive covenants, scope of geographical area, time period

NONCOMPLIANCE *(Improper completion),* **noun** defi- cient work, faulty work, inadequate final work, poor quality work, shabby work, wrong implementation
ASSOCIATED CONCEPTS: noncompliance with a judicial order

NONCOMPLIANCE *(Nonobservance),* **noun** defiance, disloyalty, disregard of orders, non occurrence, nonconfor- mity, refusal

NONCONFORMING, adjective aberrant, alien, at odds with, at variance with, Bohemian, contrary, defiant, deviat- ing, different, differing, disagreeing, disapproved, discor- dant, disobedient, dissentient, dissenting, dissident, dissimi- lar, distinct, distinguished, diversified, eccentric, exotic, heretical, incongruous, independent, irregular, lawless, non- adhering, noncompliant, nonobservant, nonuniform, original, out of line, out of step, peculiar, quaint, rare, remarkable, sin- gular, solitary, special, unaccountable, unaccustomed, un- adaptable, unadjustable, unclassifiable, uncommon, uncon- formable, unconventional, uncustomary, unexpected, unfashionable, unique, unordinary, unorthodox, unparal- leled, unprecedented, unsubmissive, unusual, unwonted
ASSOCIATED CONCEPTS: nonconforming use

NONCONFORMITY, noun aberration, abnormality, ab- normity, anomalousness, anomaly, apostasy, bizarreness, Bohemianism, change, contrast, defiance, departure, de- viation, difference, disagreement, disconformity, disobe- dience, disparity, dispute, dissent, dissidence, dissimilar- ity, distinctness, divergence, diverseness, diversity, eccentricity, exception, exceptionality, heresy, heterodoxy, heterogeneity, idiosyncrasy, incongruity, inconsistency, independence, individuality, irregularity, lack of agreement, nonagreement, nonconcurrence, nonuniformity, objection, originality, otherness, peculiarity, protest, protestation, recusancy, rejection, separateness, separatism, singularity, strangeness, unconformity, unconventionality, uniqueness, unlikeness, unorthodoxness, unorthodoxy, variance, variation, variety, veto

NONCONSENTING, adjective critical, declinatory, defiant, disapproving, discontented, disobedient, disparaging, dissentient, dissenting, dissident, faultfinding, hostile, inacquiescent, insubordinate, intractable, nonconformist, noncontent, objecting, overcritical, protesting, recalcitrant, recusant, refusing, resistant, seditious, unapproving, uncomplying, unconsenting, unsubmissive, unwilling

NONCONTESTABLE, adjective nonchallengeable, noncontrovertible, nondebatable, nondisputable, nonproblematical, nonquestionable, nonrefutable, undeniable, undoubtable, unquestionable
ASSOCIATED CONCEPTS: noncontestable clause

NONDESCRIPT, adjective average, boring, characteristic, common, commonplace, conventional, difficult to classify, difficult to describe, dull, everyday, familiar, hackneyed, homely, indescribable, insipid, mediocre, middling, not extraordinary, not odd, not singular, not special, not unique, ordinary, pedestrian, plain, prosaic, stock, trite, typical, unadorned, unclassifiable, undistinguished, unenlivened, unexceptional, unexciting, unidentifiable, uninteresting, unremarkable, usual

NONENTITY, noun blank, cipher, existenceless, figurehead, inexistence, insignificance, insignificancy, insubstantiality, matter of no consequence, matter of no importance, *nihil,* no one, nobody, nonbeing, nonexistence, nothing, nothingness, nought, nullity, *terrae filius,* unsubstantiality, unsubstantialness

NONESSENTIAL, adjective accessory, added, additional, adscititious, auxiliary, avoidable, beside the point, beside the question, dispensable, excess, expendable, extra, extraneous, extrinsic, extrinsical, frivolous, gratuitous, incidental, inconsequential, inessential, insignificant, minor, needless, negligible, of little consequence, of little importance, of no account, of no concern, of no consequence, of no importance, of no significance, of small importance, optional, parenthetic, parenthetical, peripheral, redundant, spare, supererogatory, superfluous, supervenient, supplemental, supplementary, trifling, trivial, uncalled for, unessential, ungermane, unimportant, unnecessary, unneeded, unnoteworthy, unrequired, unwarranted
ASSOCIATED CONCEPTS: nonessential services

NONEXISTENT, adjective chimerical, fancied, fantastic, fantastical, hallucinatory, hypothetical, ideal, illusory, imaginary, imagined, inexistent, legendary, notional, theoretical, unborn, uncreated, unexisting, unreal, visionary

NONFEASANCE, noun delinquency, dereliction, disregard, disregard of duty, failure, inattention, indifference, laxity, misprision, neglect of duty, negligence, nonfulfillment, nonperformance, omission

NONMILITANT, adjective accommodative, agreeable, amicable, appeasable, conciliable, conciliative, conciliatory, concordant, forgiving, gentle, halcyon, irenic, irenical, meek, neutral, nonaggresive, noncombatant, noncombative, nonviolent, pacificatory, pacifistic, peace-loving, peaceable, peaceful, placable, placative, propitiable, propitiatory, tolerant, unaggressive, unbellicose, unbelligerent, uncontentious, unhostile, unmilitant, unpugnacious, unwarlike

NONOBSERVANCE, noun arbitrary, averse, contrary, contumacious, defiant, delinquent, derelict, disloyal, disregarding, disrespectful, fractious, hostile, incorrigible, independent, indisposed, insubordinate, insurgent, intractable, irascible, irresponsible, lawbreaking, lawless, licentious, loath, mind of his or her own, misbehaving, mutinous, neglectful, negligent, noncompliant, nonconforming, obdurate, objecting, obstinate, obstreperous, opposed, opposing, perfidious, rebellious, recalcitrant, refractory, reluctant, remiss, resistant, resistive, restive, stubborn, uncooperative, undependable, undisciplined, undutiful, unfaithful, ungovernable, unmanageable, unmindful, unreliable, unruly, unwilling, unyielding, violating, wayward, wild, willful
FOREIGN PHRASES: **Non observata forma, interftur adnullatio actus.** Where form is not observed, the annulling of the act is implied or follows.

NONPARTISAN, adjective autonomous, broad-minded, detached, disengaged, equitable, evenhanded, fair, fair-minded, impartial, independent, judicious, latitudinarian, moderate, neutral, nonaligned, objective, self-determined, self-directing, self-governing, sovereign, unbiased, unbigoted, uncommitted, uncompelled, unforced, uninduced, uninfluenced, unprejudiced, unswayed, unwarped

NONPAYMENT, noun bad debt, balance due, default, deferred payment, delinquency, dishonor, dishonored bill, evasion, failure, failure to pay, lapse, neglect, outstanding debt, oversight, refusal to pay, repudiation, unpaid dues
ASSOCIATED CONCEPTS: nonpayment of rent

NONPERFORMANCE, noun avoidance, breach of promise, default, delinquency, dereliction of duty, disregard, dutilessness, evasion, evasion of duty, failure to perform, idleness, inactivity, inexecution, laxity, neglect, negligence, noncompletion, noncompliance, noncooperation, nonfeasance, nonfulfillment, nonpractice, omission, truancy, unduteousness, undutifulness, unfulfillment
ASSOCIATED CONCEPTS: nonperformance of a contract, nonperformance of a duty

NONPHASED, adjective addled, at a loss, at a nonplus, at a stand or standstill, at an impasse, at one's wit's end, baffled, bamboozled, bewildered, buffaloed, confounded, dazed, deadlocked, fuddled, in a dilemma, in suspense, muddled, mystified, nonplussed, on tenterhooks, on the horns of a dilemma, perplexed, puzzled, stuck and stumped, stymied

NONPROFIT, adjective altruistic, beneficent, benevolent, charitable, eleemosynary, humanitarian, munificent, philanthropic, public service
ASSOCIATED CONCEPTS: nonprofit corporation

NONRESIDENCE, noun absence, nondomicile, nonhabitancy, nonhabitation, noninhabitance, noninhabitancy, nonoccupance, nonoccupancy, nonoccupation, nonpresence, nontenancy

NONSECTARIAN, adjective all-comprehensive, all-embracing, all-including, all-inclusive, broad, broad-based, collective, comprehensive, ecumenical, general, global, interdenominational, mixed, undenominational, universal, unspecified, world-wide

NONSUBSTANTIAL *(Not sturdy)*, **adjective** adynamic, asthenic, attenuated, below par, breakable, brittle, defective, deficient, delicate, destructible, enervated, ephemeral, fallacious, feeble, flimsy, fragile, frail, frangible, ghostly, illogical, inadequate, infirm, intangible, lame, limp, mediocre, perishable, powerless, slight, sorry, strengthless, tenuous, unearthly, ungrounded, unsolid, unsound, unstable, unsturdy, unsubstantial, untenable, weak, weakly, without force, without foundation, wobbly

NONSUBSTANTIAL *(Not sufficient)*, **adjective** deficient, depleted, deprived, disappointing, drained, inadequate, incomplete, insignificant, insubstantial, lacking, low, meager, niggardly, paltry, scant, scanty, scarce, stingy, thin, too little, too small, unacceptable, ungratifying, unsatisfactory, unsatisfying, unsufficing, wanting

NONSUIT, **noun** defeat, directed verdict, failure to establish a cause of action, failure to make a case, failure to meet the burden of proof, failure to present sufficient evidence, hostile verdict, insufficiency as a matter of law, insufficient evidence, judgment for the defendant as a matter of law, termination of a case by inaction, termination of a judicial contest, termination of a lawsuit, termination of a lawsuit by failing to proceed, termination of a legal action, termination of a legal proceeding, termination of a proceeding, termination of a suit in law, termination of an action, termination of an action at law by failure to proceed, termination of an action by neglect, termination of litigation
ASSOCIATED CONCEPTS: compulsory nonsuit, demurrer, discontinuance, dismissal, involuntary nonsuit, motion for nonsuit, peremptory nonsuit, voluntary nonsuit

NONTOXIC, **adjective** benign, harmless, hurtless, innocent, innocuous, innoxious, inoffensive, nonfatal, nonirritating, nonlethal, nonmalignant, nonpoisonous, nonvenomous, nonvirulent, not baneful, not dangerous, not deadly, not deleterious, not pernicious, not toxiferous, safe, undestructive, unhazardous, uninjurious, unobjectionable, without risk

NONUSE, **noun** abeyance, absence, abstinence, desuetude, disusage, disuse, forebearance, neglect, nonemployment, nonutilization, suspension

NORM, **noun** average, general performance, generality, habit, median, midpoint, model, mold, ordinary run, pattern, point of comparison, regular performance, rule, standard, typical performance

NORMAL *(Regular)*, **adjective** according to rule, average, common, commonplace, conforming, conventional, customary, established, everyday, habitual, natural, orderly, ordinary, representative, routine, standard, standardized, true to form, typical, unexceptional, unvarying, usual
ASSOCIATED CONCEPTS: normal conditions, normal course of business, normal use

NORMAL *(Sane)*, **adjective** fit, logical, lucid, mentally sound, of sound judgment, rational, reasonable, responsible, sensible, sound, temperate

NOSCITUR A SOCIIS, **adverb** comprehended from accompanying words, perceived from accompanying words,

realized from accompanying words, recognized from accompanying words, understood from accompanying words

NOT ADMISSIBLE, **adjective** banned, barred, deemed improper, deemed inapplicable, disallowed, disapproved, excepted, excluded, inadmissible, inapposite, inappropriate, ineligible, irrelevant, not admitted in, not allowed as evidence, not allowed in, not allowed in evidence, not allowed to be admitted as evidence, not capable of being introduced as evidence, objectionable, prohibited, refused, rejected, suppressed, unfit, unqualified, unsuitable, wrong
ASSOCIATED CONCEPTS: evidence obtained by torture, hearsay, impeachment, not admissible into evidence

NOT COUNTENANCED, **adjective** disallowed, forbidden, illegitimate, improper, inappropriate, incorrect, not allowed, not approved, not blessed, not permitted, not proper, prohibited, proscribed, unapproved, uncertified, undue, unendorsed, unlawful, unlicensed, unsanctioned, unsuitable, unwarranted
ASSOCIATED CONCEPTS: a deception not countenanced, a substantial departure not countenanced by law, mistake not countenanced, not countenanced by the courts, practices not countenanced by the courts

NOT EQUITABLE, **adjective** biased, fraudulent, improper, inequitable, jaundiced, not balanced, not fair, not just, not proper, one-sided, prejudiced, unequal, uneven, unfair, unjust, unprincipled, unreasonable
ASSOCIATED CONCEPTS: not equitable process

NOT GUILTY, **adjective** above suspicion, blameless, clean-handed, exculpable, faultless, free from guilt, guilt-free, guiltless, impeccable, incorrupt, inculpable, innocent, not responsible, sinless, unblemished, unimpeachable, uninvolved
ASSOCIATED CONCEPTS: plea of not guilty

NOT HONORABLE, **adjective** conniving, conscienceless, corrupt, deceitful, deceiving, deceptive, delusive, delusory, discreditable, dishonorable, disingenuous, disreputable, faithless, fake, faked, false, false-hearted, falsified, fraudulent, guileful, immoral, iniquitous, insidious, insincere, lying, meretricious, misleading, nefarious, not fair, not honest, not just, not legitimate, not proper, not true, perfidious, shameless, shifty, spurious, surreptitious, treacherous, underhanded, unethical, unfaithful, unprincipled, unprofessional, unscrupulous, untrue, untrustworthy, untruthful, worthy of disbarment

NOT PERMITTED, **adjective** banished, banned, barred, blocked, checked, curbed, debarred, denied, disallowed, disqualified, enjoined, excluded, forbid, foreclosed, halted, hampered, hindered, illegal, impeded, inhibited, interdicted, interfered, limited, negated, obstructed, omitted, opposed, ordered stopped, precluded, prevented, proscribed, quashed, quelled, refused, refused permission, regulated, rejected, repressed, repudiated, restrained, restricted, revoked, shut out, smothered, stayed, stopped, suppressed, suspended, thwarted, vetoed
ASSOCIATED CONCEPTS: motion practice, not permitted to disclose confidences, not permitted to many, punitive damages in private lawsuits

NOT PERTINENT, **adjective** alien, discordant, discrepant, dissonant, gratuitous, improper, inadmissible, inapplicable, inapposite, incongruent, incongruous, inconsistent, ineligible, inessential, inopportune, irrelevant, misapplied, misdirected, misplaced, not appropriate, not germane, not related, objectionable, undue, unfit, unfitting, unharmonious, unsuitable, unsuited

ASSOCIATED CONCEPTS: evidence presented that is not pertinent, information requested that is not pertinent, not pertinent trait or character, objections

NOT SUBSTANTIATED, *adjective* baseless, controvertible, empty, flimsy, groundless, ill-conceived, ill-founded, inconclusive, insubstantial, not proven, poorly argued, unfounded, ungrounded, unproved, unsound, unsubstantial, unsupportable, unsupported, unsustainable, unverifiable, without a sound basis, without basis, without foundation

ASSOCIATED CONCEPTS: allegations not substantiated, arguments not substantiated, claims not substantiated, complaints not substantiated, motions not substantiated

NOT VALID, *adjective* abrogated, baseless, canceled, fallacious, faulty, futile, having no force, inadequate, ineffective, ineffectual, inefficacious, inoperative, invalid, lacking authority, lacking force, lacking strength, not binding, nugatory, null, quashed, spurious, unauthentic, untenable, untrue, useless, vain, void, without legal basis, without legal efficacy, without legal justification

ASSOCIATED CONCEPTS: objections, patents, recordation in copyright office, validity of claims, wills

NOTABLE, *adjective* above par, acclaimed, astonishing, atypical, awe-inspiring, awesome, celebrated, conspicuous, distinguished, eminent, exceptional, extraordinary, famed, famous, foremost, illustrious, important, impressive, leading, luminous, marked, memorable, momentous, momumental, newsworthy, *notabilis*, noted, noteworthy, outstanding, preeminent, prime, prominent, rare, remarkable, rememberable, renowned, salient, signal, significant, singular, special, striking, superior, talked of, top-rank, transcendent, unforgettable, worthy of notice, worthy of remark

NOTARIZE, *verb* accord one's approval, accredit, affirm, affix a legal signature, affix one's signature to, approve, attach a legal signature, attest to, authenticate, authorize, bear witness, certify, confirm, confirm officially, evidence, legalize, make valid, pronounce legal, seal, set one's hand and seal, sign, sign and seal, sign legally, subscribe, undersign, validate, witness

NOTARY PUBLIC, *noun* attestor of documents, clerk of the court, commissioner of oaths, functionary, indorser, notary, official, recorder, register, registerer, registrar, *scriba*, scribe, scrivener, subscriber

NOTATION, *noun* annotation, chronicle, comment, commentary, entry, footnote, inscription, marginalia, memorandum, minute, note, record, register

NOTE *(Brief comment)*, ***noun*** abstract, *adnotatio*, annotation, billet, brief, *codicilli*, comment, commentary, communication, dispatch, entry, *epistula*, exegesis, explanatory comment, explanatory remark, footnote, gloss, marginal annotation, memorandum, message, minute, missive, record, reminder, scholium, short letter, statement, word of explanation

ASSOCIATED CONCEPTS: note of issue

NOTE *(Written promise to pay)*, ***noun*** bond, check, debenture, draft, money order, negotiable instrument, negotiable paper, voucher

ASSOCIATED CONCEPTS: accommodation note, bank note, bearer notes, cognovit note, commercial paper, negotiable note, promissory note, treasury note

NOTE *(Notice)*, ***verb*** acknowledge, advert to, apperceive, appreciate, attend, be attentive, become aware, become conscious, cognize, direct attention to, discern, discover, fix attention on, give attention to, hearken to, heed, look at, make out, mark, mind, observe, pay attention to, pay heed to, perceive, realize, regard, see, take account of, take cognizance of, take notice, turn attention to, watch, witness

NOTE *(Record)*, ***verb*** *adnotare*, annotate, calendar, catalogue, chronicle, commit to writing, docket, document, enregister, enter, jot down, keep accounts, log, make a memorandum, make an entry, mark, mark down, pen, put in writing, put on paper, put on record, scribe, set down, take down, write, write down

NOTED *(Acknowledged)*, ***adjective*** accepted, admitted, cleared, declared, disclosed, discovered, established, evident, exposed, familiar, identified, manifest, obvious, patently known, proclaimed, realized, recognized, revealed, well-known

ASSOCIATED CONCEPTS: as noted, briefly noted, judicial notice

NOTED *(Well known)*, ***adjective*** acclaimed, applauded, celebrated, consequential, conspicuous, distinguished, eminent, exalted, extraordinary, famed, famous, foremost, great, honored, illustrious, important, known, leading, matchless, much touted, notable, noteworthy, notorious, outstanding, popular, preeminent, prominent, recognized, remarkable, reputable, singular, unexampled, unique, unparalleled, unprecedented

ASSOCIATED CONCEPTS: a noted authority

NOTEWORTHY, *adjective* above par, amazing, anomalous, astonishing, astounding, atypical, bizarre, breathtaking, celebrated, choice, commanding, considerable, conspicuous, curious, different, distinctive, distinguished, egregious, eminent, especial, excellent, exceptional, extraordinary, extreme, famous, fantastic, foremost, idiosyncratic, illustrious, important, impressive, incredible, individual, individualistic, infrequent, leading, main, marked, material, memorable, momentous, monumental, newsworthy, notable, noticeable, novel, odd, original, out of the ordinary, outstanding, paramount, peculiar, peerless, pertinent, phenomenal, preeminent, principal, prodigious, prominent, queer, rare, remarkable, renowned, salient, signal, significant, singular, special, standing out, stirring, strange, surprising, telling, uncommon, uncustomary, unequaled, unfamiliar, unforgettable, unheard of, unimitated, unique, unparalleled, unprecedented, unusual, wonderful, wondrous, worthy of notice, worthy of remark

NOTHING *(Void)*, ***noun*** blank, clean slate, emptiness, empty feeling, empty space, inanity, nothingness, vacuity, vacuum

ASSOCIATED CONCEPTS: nothing but the truth, nothing to hide

NOTHING *(Zero)*, ***noun*** naught, nil, none, not one iota, nothing at all, nothing whatever

NOTICE *(Announcement)*, ***noun*** bulletin, circular, communication, communique, declaration, decree, *denuntiatio*, disclosure, dispatch, enlightenment, enunciation, flier, information, memorandum, mention, message, news, note, notification, presentation, proclamation, *promulgatio*, pronouncement, publicity, release, reminder, report, revelation, statement

ASSOCIATED CONCEPTS: legal notice, notice of appeal, notice of appearance, notice of claim, notice of motion, notice of protest, public notice

FOREIGN PHRASES: *Notitia dicitur a noscendo; et notitia non debet claudicare.* Notice is named from a knowledge being had; and notice ought not to be imperfect.

NOTICE *(Heed),* **noun** absorption, advertence, advertency, alertness, *animadversio,* attention, attentiveness, care, careful attention, carefulness, cautel, caution, cautiousness, circumspection, cognizance, consideration, discernment, engrossment, guard, heedfulness, mindfulness, *notatio,* observance, observation, recognition, regard, regardfulness, scrutiny, surveillance, thought, vigil, vigilance, wariness, watch, watchfulness

ASSOCIATED CONCEPTS: judicial notice

FOREIGN PHRASES: *De minimis non curat lex.* The law is not concerned with trifling matters.

NOTICE *(Warning),* **noun** admonishment, admonition, caution, caveat, commination, communication, counsel, dehortation, *denuntiatio,* forewarning, monition, premonishment, prenotification, ultimatum

ASSOCIATED CONCEPTS: absence of notice, actual notice, adequate notice, constructive notice, due notice, explicit notice, express notice, implied notice, imputed notice, notice of disallowance, notice to appear, notice to vacate, proper notice, reasonable notice, requisite notice, timely notice, verified notice, written notice

NOTICE *(Give formal warning),* **verb** address a warning to, advise, apprise, communicate, convey knowledge to, *denuntiatio,* direct attention to, disclose, divulge, entrust with information, forewarn, formally advise, give fair warning, give information, give warning, impart knowledge of, impart to, inform, instruct, make a formal proclamation, make acquainted with, make an announcement, make known, make mention of, make public, notify, offer a word of caution, pass on information, *promulgatio,* publish, put on one's guard, reveal, warn

ASSOCIATED CONCEPTS: notice a deposition, notice a hearing

NOTICE *(Observe),* **verb** acknowledge, *animadvertere,* appreciate, ascertain, assess, attend to, be attentive, be conscious of, become aware of, become conscious of, behold, call attention to, cognize, comment, detect, discern, discover, distinguish, elucidate, examine closely, examine intently, give heed to, glance at, hear, heed, inspect, investigate, look, look at, mark, mention, *notatio,* note, observe, occupy oneself with, pass under review, pay attention, perceive, pore over, realize, recognize, regard, review, scrutinize, see, sight, spot, take cognizance, take into account, take into consideration, take stock of, view, watch, witness

NOTICE OF APPEARANCE, **noun** announcement of the lawyer in a case, entrance by counsel in a case, formal notification of counsel's presence, noted presence in court, notification of representation, official acknowledgment of counsel's presence, official appearance by counsel, official statement of representation, statement of counsel's appearance

ASSOCIATED CONCEPTS: court proceeding, notice of limited appearance

NOTIFICATION, **noun** announcement, annunciation, aviso, bulletin, caution, communication, communique,

declaration, *denuntiatio,* disclosure, dispatch, dissemination, divulgation, enlightenment, enunciation, evulgation, information, intelligence, intercommunication, knowledge, legal notice, mention, message, monition, news, notice, proclamation, *promulgatio,* promulgation, pronouncement, publicity, release, report, revelation, statement, transmission of knowledge, warning

ASSOCIATED CONCEPTS: due process, process of service, proper notification

NOTIFY, **verb** acquaint, advertise, advise, alert, announce, annunciate, apprise, break the news, brief, bring word, call attention to, caution, communicate, confide, contact, convey, counsel, declare, disclose, disseminate, divulge, enlighten, enunciate, exhort, forewarn, give notice, give the facts, give to understand, give warning, herald, impart, indicate, inform, instruct, issue a proclamation, issue a pronouncement, let know, make an announcement, make known, make public, mention, post, proclaim, promote, promulgate, propagate, publicize, publish, recount, relate, remind, report, reveal, serve notice, signal, signify, state, tell, tip off, transmit, warn

ASSOCIATED CONCEPTS: notify a defendant of charges pending, notify of an action pending

NOTION, **noun** abstraction, apprehension, belief, caprice, concept, conception, conviction, desire, estimation, fancy, feeling, humor, idea, impression, inclination, inkling, judgment, mental image, *notio,* opinion, sentiment, suggestion, supposition, *suspicio,* thought, understanding, vagary, view, whim

NOTORIETY, **noun** attaint, bad report, bad reputation, bad repute, bruit, celebrity, censure, conspicuousness, dedecoration, degradation, denunciation, disapprobation, discredit, disesteem, disfavor, disgrace, dishonor, disparagement, disreputability, disreputableness, disrepute, disrespect, distinction, eclat, eminence, *fama,* fame, famousness, flagrancy, ignominy, ignomy, ill repute, imputation, indignity, *infamia,* infamousness, infamy, ingloriousness, loss of honor, loss of reputation, name, notability, notedness, obloquy, odium, opprobrium, popular repute, popularity, prominence, public notice, publicity, recognition, renown, reproach, reputation, repute, scandal, shame, significance, slur, stigma, stigmatization, taint, unrespectability

NOTORIOUS, **adjective** arrant, blameworthy, celebrated, conspicuous, contemptible, degraded, deplorable, despised, discreditable, disgraceful, dishonorable, disreputable, disrespectable, egregious, famed, famous, flagrant, generally known, glaring, held in contempt, ignoble, ignominious, infamous, inglorious, *nobilis,* noted, *notus,* odious, of ill fame, of ill repute, opprobrious, outcast, outrageous, prominent, publicized, renowned, scandalous, shameful, shameless, shocking, unfavorably known, unrespectable, unseemly, unworthy of respect, villainous, without repute

ASSOCIATED CONCEPTS: notorious easement, notorious possession, open and notorious use

NOTWITHSTANDING, **preposition** all the same, although, despite, even, however, in any case, in any event, in spite of, nevertheless, none the less, still, yet

NOVATION, **noun** complete substitution, exchange, replacement, substitution

ASSOCIATED CONCEPTS: novation of a contract

NOVEL, **adjective** alien, anomalous, bizarre, different, distinctive, eccentric, exceptional, extraordinary, foreign, fresh, innovative, inusitate, irregular, modern, neoteric, neoterical, new, newly come, nonconformist, *novus,* odd, original, peculiar, quaint, rare, recent, singular, strange, uncharacteristic, uncommon, unconventional, uncustomary, unfamiliar, unheard of, unique, unordinary, unorthodox, unprecedented, untested, untried, unused, unusual, up-to-date, up-to-the-minute

ASSOCIATED CONCEPTS: novel question of law

NOVICE, *noun* amateur, apprentice, aspirant, beginner, catechumen, disciple, entrant, fledgling, freshman, hopeful, inexperienced person, initiate, learner, neophyte, new arrival, newcomer, probationer, pupil, recruit, rookie, *rudis,* student, trainee, tyro, unskilled person, untrained individual

NOW AND FOREVER, *adverb* evermore, for ever and ever, forever, forevermore

NOXIOUS, *adjective* adverse, bad, baleful, baneful, brutal, causing danger, contaminated, corrupting, damaging, dangerous, deleterious, destructive, detrimental, disadvantageous, fatal, fraught with danger, harmful, hazardous, hurtful, impairing, injurious, insalubrious, internecine, jeopardous, lethal, malefic, malicious, malignant, menacing, mischievous, nocent, noisome, offensive, perilous, pernicious, pestiferous, pestilent, poisonous, precarious, risky, ruinous, scatheful, threatening, toxic, unfavorable, unhealthy, unsafe, unwholesome, vicious, virulent

NUANCE, *noun* cast, degree, delicacy, difference, differentiation, discrimination, distinction, hidden meaning, implication, nicety, shade, shade of difference, shade of meaning, shadow, subtle difference, subtlety, suggestion, touch, variance

NUGATORY, *adjective* fatuous, frivolous, frothy, futile, immaterial, inadequate, inane, inapt, incompetent, inconsequential, ineffective, ineffectual, inefficacious, inept, inoperative, insignificant, insubstantial, inutile, invalid, irrelevant, jejune, *nugatorius,* null, null and void, otiose, paltry, petty, purposeless, slight, superficial, trifling, trivial, unavailing, unfruitful, unimportant, unproductive, unprofitable, unserviceable, useless, vain, valueless, void, worthless

NUISANCE, *noun* affliction, aggravation, annoyance, anxiety, bedevilment, bother, burden, cause of distress, devilment, difficult situation, difficulty, discomfort, displeasure, disturbance, grievance, handicap, harassment, hardship, hindrance, imposition, inconvenience, infliction, infringement, injurious interference, interference, intrusion, irritation, molestation, obstacle, ordeal, pain, pest, pestilence, plague, problem, scourge, trial, trouble, unlawful obstruction, unwarrantable intrusion, vexation, worry

ASSOCIATED CONCEPTS: abatement of a nuisance, attractive nuisance, common nuisance, continuing nuisance, nuisance at law, nuisance in fact, nuisance per se, public nuisance

FOREIGN PHRASES: *Aedificare in tuo proprio solo non licet quod alteri noceat.* It is not lawful to build upon one's own land what may injure another.

NUISANCE VALUE, *noun* cost to resolve a frivolous action, disposal value, number to dispose of a frivolous case, number to get rid of a frivolous action, number to make a case go away, price to resolve a frivolous case, quick settlement amount for a frivolous case, value to dispose of a frivolous law suit, walking money

ASSOCIATED CONCEPTS: frivolous law suit

NULL *(Insignificant), adjective* beneath notice, dispensable, disregarded, empty, expendable, immaterial, impuissant, inappreciable, inconsequential, inconsiderable, inessential, inferior, insubstantial, insufficient, irrelevant, meaningless, minor, negligible, nominal, nugatory, of no account, of no effect, of no moment, of no value, paltry, peripheral, petty, pointless, powerless, puny, secondary, small, superficial, tenuous, token, trifling, trivial, unavailing, unessential, unimportant, uninfluential, unmeaningful, unnecessary, unsubstantial, useless, valueless, without consequence, without meaning, without significance, without substance, worthless

NULL *(Invalid), adjective* abolished, abrogated, annulled, canceled, dead, defeated, defunct, deleted, disannulled, disestablished, effectless, extinct, extinguished, forceless, gone, impotent, ineffective, ineffectual, inefficacious, inoperative, *inritus,* negated, no longer law, not valid, nugatory, nullified, obliterated, of no binding force, of no effect, of no validity, of no weight, omitted, overruled, powerless, quashed, repealed, rescinded, reversed, revoked, set aside, strengthless, superseded, suspended, unauthorized, unsanctioned, useless, vacated, valueless, void, withdrawn, without authority, without legal effect, without legal force, without potency, without value, worthless

NULL AND VOID, *adjective* abolished, abrogated, annulled, canceled, defeated, defunct, disannulled, disestablished, effectless, extinct, extinguished, forceless, impotent, ineffective, ineffectual, inefficacious, inoperative, invalid, negated, no longer law, not valid, nugatory, nullified, obliterated, of no binding force, of no effect, of no legal weight, of no validity, omitted, overruled, quashed, repealed, rescinded, reversed, revoked, set aside, strengthless, superseded, suspended, unauthorized, unsanctioned, useless, vacated, valueless, void, withdrawn, without authority, without legal effect, without legal force, without potency, without value, worthless

NULLIFICATION, *noun* abolishment, absolute contradiction, annulment, cancel, cancellation, cancelling, contradiction, contrary assertion, contravention, countering, disaffirmation, disallowance, disavowal, disclaimer, disclamation, disproof, emphatic denial, flat denial, invalidation, recantation, refutation, renunciation, repeal, repudiation, rescinding, rescission, retraction, reversal, revocation, revoke, setting aside, striking down, suspension, voidance

ASSOCIATED CONCEPTS: antinullification, Constitution, state's rights, ultimate sovereign

NULLIFY, *verb* abolish, abrogate, *ad inritum redigere,* annul, cancel, cast aside, counteract, countermand, declare null and void, deprive of efficacy, deprive of legal force, disannul, dissolve, invalidate, make useless, make valueless, make void, negate, neutralize, obliterate, offset, outweigh, override, overrule, overturn, quash, recall, recant, render invalid, renege, repeal, repudiate, rescind, retract, reverse, revoke, suspend, vacate, vitiate, void

NULLITY, *noun* blankness, *inanitas,* inefficacy, inexistence, insignificance, invalidity, naught, nihility, nonbeing, nonentity, nonexistence, nothing, nothingness, oblivion, vacuity, *vanitas,* void

ASSOCIATED CONCEPTS: decision to overrule decision

NUMBER, *noun* account, accounting, aggregate, calculation, collection, complement, count, decimal, degree, estimate, exponent, figure, integer, integral, multitude,

overall amount, overall quantity, quantity, score, sum, symbol, tally, total
ASSOCIATED CONCEPTS: gaming

NUMEROUS, *adjective* abundance, ample, an excessive amount, bounteous, bountiful, copious, countless, ever so many, exhaustless, generous, lavish, liberal, many, much, multiple, myriad, not a few, overflowing, plentiful, plentious, plenty, rampant, too many

NUNC PRO TUNC, *noun* acknowledged, operative with respect to the past, ratified, reaffirmed, reconfirmed, reendorsed, reestablished, retroactive effect, retrospective effect, revalidated
ASSOCIATED CONCEPTS: nunc pro tunc order

NUNCUPATIVE, *adjective* articulated, conversational, conveyed orally, declared, dictated, enunciated, expressed in words, not written, oral, oral declaration, oral testimony, oratorical, parol, phonic, pronounced, spoken, stated, unwritten, uttered, verbal, vocal, voiced
ASSOCIATED CONCEPTS: nuncupative will

NUPTIAL, *adjective* allied, betrothed, bridal, conjugal, connubial, coupled, espoused, *genialis,* marital, married, mated, matrimonial, *nuptialis,* united, wedded
ASSOCIATED CONCEPTS: antenuptial agreement

NUPTIAL AGREEMENTS, *noun* contract regarding a marriage arrangement, contract regarding the bonds of matrimony, marriage agreement, marriage compact, marriage concordat, marriage understanding, marriage undertaking, matrimonial contract, pact, pledge, postnuptial agreement, prenuptial agreement, spousal agreement
ASSOCIATED CONCEPTS: domestic relations, family law, postnuptial agreements, prenuptial agreement

NURTURE, *verb* advance, aid, assist, back, bolster, bring to maturity, bring up, care for, cherish, coach, cultivate, develop, direct, educate, encourage, enrich, feed, fortify, forward, foster, further, give aid, harbor, help, improve, instruct, invigorate, maintain, make provisions for, make strong, mold, nourish, nurse, *nutrire,* patronize, prepare, promote, provide for, rear, render better, render strong, sponsor, strengthen, succor, supply aid, support, sustain, teach, train, tutor, victual

OATH, *noun* adjuration, affirmation, affirmation of truth, affirmation of truth of a statement, asseveration, attestation, avouchment, avowal, avowance, guarantee, *iusiurandum,* open declaration, pledge, promise, solemn affirmation, solemn avowal, solemn declaration, solemn invocation, swearing, sworn pledge, sworn promise, sworn statement, vow
FOREIGN PHRASES: *Repellitur a sacramento infamis.* An infamous person is denied the right to make an oath. *Sacramentum habet in se tres comites,-veritatem, justitiam, et judicium; veritus habenda est in jurato; justitia et justicium in judice.* An oath has in it three components-truth, justice, and judgment; truth in the party swearing; justice and judgment in the judge administering the oath. *Juramentum est indivisibile; et non est admittendum in parte verum et in parte falsam.* An oath is indivisible; it is not to be held as partly true and partly false. *Jusjurandum inter alios factum nec nocere nec prodesse debet.* An oath made between other parties ought neither to hurt nor profit. *Non est arctius vinculum inter homines quam jusjurandum.* There is no stronger bond between men than an oath. *Jurato creditur in judicio.* He who makes an oath is to be believed in a judicial proceeding. *Jusjurandi forma verbis differt, re convenit; hunc enim sensum habere debet: ut Deus invocetur.* The form of taking an oath differs in language, agrees in meaning; for it ought to have this meaning: that the deity is invoked. *Perjuri sunt qui servatis verbis juramenti decipiunt aures eorum qui accipiunt.* They are perjured, who, preserving the words of an oath, deceive the ears of those who receive it. *Omne sacramentum debet esse de certa scientia.* Every oath ought to be founded on certain knowledge. *Sacramentum si fatuum fuerit, licet falsum, tamen non committit perjurium.* A foolish oath, although false, does not give rise to perjury.

OBDURATE, *adjective* callous, cold, decided, determined, dogged, dogmatic, dogmatical, firm, hard, hardbitten, hardened, hardhearted, harsh, headstrong, heartless, immovable, immutable, impervious, impossible to influence, incorrigible, indifferent, indurate, indurated, inexorable, inflexible, insensitive, intractable, intransigent, invariable, iron-hearted, irreclaimable, merciless, mulish, obstinate, opinionated, opinionative, pertinacious, pervicacious, pig-headed, positive, recalcitrant, refractory, relentless, remorseless, resolute, stony, strong-minded, strong-willed, stubborn, tenacious, unalterable, unbending, uncaring, unchangeable, uncompassionate, uncompromising, unconcerned, uncontrollable, unfeeling, unforgiving, ungovernable, unmalleable, unmanageable, unmerciful, unpitying, unrelenting, unresponsive, unstirred, unsusceptible, unsympathetic, untouched, unyielding, willful

OBEDIENT, adjective acquiescent, amenable, attentive, behaved, biddable, complaisant, compliable, compliant, complying, conformable, conforming, controllable, dedicated, deferential, devoted, *dicto audiens*, docile, ductile, duteous, dutiful, faithful, governable, honoring, law-abiding, loyal, manageable, meek, obeisant, obliging, *oboediens*, observant, *obtemperans*, passive, pliant, regardful, respectful, reverential, rule-abiding, servile, submissive, subservient, supple, tame, tractable, unresisting, venerating, well-behaved, willing, yielding

FOREIGN PHRASES: *Ubi non est condendi auctoritas, ibi non est parendi necessitas.* Where there is no authority for establishing a rule, there is no need of obeying it. ***Ejus nulla culpa est cui parere necesse sit.*** No guilt attaches to a person who is compelled to obey. ***Quicunque jussu judicis aliquid fecerit non videtur dolo malo fecisse, quia parere necesse est.*** Whoever does anything by the command of a judge is not deemed to have done it with an evil intent, because it is necessary to obey. ***Prudenter agit qui praecepto legis obtemperat.*** He acts prudently who obeys the precept of the law. ***Obedientia est legis essentia.*** Obedience is the essence of the law. ***Legitime imperanti parere necesse est.*** One who commands lawfully must be obeyed.

OBEISANT, adjective affable, amiable, civil, complaisant, compliant, conciliatory, courteous, decorous, deferential, deferring, duteous, dutiful, eager to please, good-humored, good-natured, gracious, helpful, honorable, humble, meek, nonresisting, obedient, obliging, pliant, polite, respectful, reverent, reverential, self-abasing, showing homage, submissive, subservient, surrendering, unresisting, willing, yielding

OBEY, verb abide by, accede, accept, accommodate, acquiesce, act in accordance with orders, act on, adhere to, agree, answer to, assent, attend to, attend to orders, be devoted to, be faithful to, be governed by, be guided by, be loyal to, be obedient, be regulated by, be subject, behave, bend to, be ruled by, bow to, carry out, come at call, comply, conform, consent, defer to, do the will of, execute, fall in with, follow, follow orders, fulfill, fulfill the commands of, give allegiance to, give way, heed, humble oneself to, keep, kneel to, listen, live by, mind, *oboedire, obsequi*, observe, *parere*, perform, please, respect, respond, satisfy, serve, submit, succumb, surrender, take orders, yield

FOREIGN PHRASES: *Ejus nulla culpa est cui parere necesse sit.* No guilt attaches to a person who is compelled to obey.

OBFUSCATE, verb addle, adumbrate, baffle, becloud, bedim, befuddle, begloom, bemist, bewilder, blacken, blind, blur, cloak, cloud, complicate, conceal, confound, confuse, cover, curtain, darken, daze, dim, disconcert, disturb, dull, eclipse, fluster, fog, hide, keep one guessing, mist, mix up, muddle, mystify, nonplus, obscure, obumbrate, occult, overshadow, perplex, perturb, put off the track, puzzle, screen, shade, shield, shroud, stupefy, throw into confusion, throw off the scent, unsettle, upset, veil

OBJECT, noun aim, butt, commodity, concern, *consilium*, corporeal body, design, destination, end, final cause, *finis*, goal, item, material product, material substance, matter, point, *propositum*, purpose, subject, substance, target, ultimate purpose

OBJECT, verb attack, be at variance, be averse, call in question, challenge, complain, *contra dicere recusare*, contravene, controvert, criticize, demur, disagree, disapprove, dispute, dissent, enter a demurrer, enter a protest, except, express an objection, express disapproval, find fault, oppose, protest, put forward in opposition, quarrel, *repugnare*, resist, state by way of objection, state opposition, take exception

OBJECT LESSON, noun case in point, crowning example, demonstration, embodiment, epitome, example, exemplar, exemplification, explanation, heinous example, illustration, instance, most wretched instance, paragon, quintessence, relevant instance, representative, specimen, symbol, terrible, worst

OBJECT TO, verb absolutely differ with, be at variance with, be averse to, be diametrically opposed to, be on all fours with, call in question, challenge, complain, contravene, controvert, counter, criticize, deny, disagree with, disapprove, dispute, dissent, express an objection, express disapproval, find fault, oppose, protest, put forward in opposition, resist, state by way of objection, state opposition, take exception, undermine

ASSOCIATED CONCEPTS: evidence, rules of procedure

OBJECTION, noun adverse argument, adverse charge, adverse comment, adverse reason, challenge, *contradictio*, counterargument, countercharge, criticism, denunciation, difference, disagreement, disapprobation, disapproval, dissatisfaction, dissent, exception, expostulation, grievance, opposition, protest, *quod contra dicitur*, reason for disapproval, rebuke, rejection, remonstrance, reservation

ASSOCIATED CONCEPTS: frivolous objection, general objection, grounds for an objection, oral objection, overrule an objection, preservation of an objection, specific objection, sustain an objection, technical objection, waiver, written objection

OBJECTIONABLE, adjective abhorrent, abominable, annoying, antipathetic, base, deplorable, despicable, detestable, disagreeable, disgusting, dislikable, displeasing, distasteful, evil, exceptionable, execrable, filthy, foul, fulsome, gross, hateful, heinous, horrid, illaudable, impalatable, improper, inadvisable, inappropriate, inexpedient, insufferable, intolerable, invidious, loathsome, nasty, nefarious, noisome, noxious, obnoxious, obscene, odious, offensive, opprobrious, peccant, pernicious, repugnant, repulsive, revolting, scurvy, sickening, unacceptable, unappealing, unbearable, unbecoming, uncommendable, undesirable, unendurable, uninviting, unlikable, unpalatable, unpleasant, unpleasing, unsatisfactory, unsavory, unseemly, unsuitable, vile, wrong

ASSOCIATED CONCEPTS: objectionable conduct, objectionable material, objectionable question

OBJECTIVE, adjective actual, broad-minded, candid, concrete, corporeal, desired, detached, disinterested, dispassionate, equitable, factual, fair, fair-minded, impartial, impersonal, judicial, just, material, neutral, nonpartisan, nonsubjective, open-minded, real, reasonable, scientific, sober, unbiased, unbigoted, uncolored, uninfluenced, unjaundiced, unprejudiced, unslanted, unswayed, unwarped

OBJECTIVE, noun achievement, aim, ambition, aspiration, design, desire, desired object, destination, dream, end, expectation, final point, fixed purpose, formulated intention, goal, height of one's ambition, hope, idea, intent, intention, *locus qui petitur*, mark, mission, point, purpose, pursuit, set purpose, settled purpose, target, terminal point

ASSOCIATED CONCEPTS: lawful objectives

OBJECTIVITY, *noun* *aequitas,* broadmindedness, detachment, disinterest, disinterestedness, dispassion, dispassionateness, equitableness, equity, fair-mindedness, fair play, fairness, immovability, impartiality, impersonality, justice, justness, lack of bias, lack of jaundice, lack of prejudice, neutrality, noninvolvement, nonpartisanship, nonsubjectivity, open-mindedness

OBJURGATION, *noun* accusation, admonishment, admonition, berating, castigation, chiding, denunciation, expostulation, lecture, rebuke, reprehension, reprimand, reproach, reproof, reproval, scolding, sermon, upbraiding

OBLIGATE, *verb* agree to perform, agree to be burdened with, assume a duty, assume a moral responsibility for, assume responsibility for, assume the performance of, become legally responsible for, become obliged, charged with, committed to accomplish, compel, contracted, covenanted, indebted to, promise to do
ASSOCIATED CONCEPTS: contractual duties, implied obligations

OBLIGATION *(Duty),* *noun* agreement, burden, charge, commitment, compulsion, contract, covenant, debt, duty owed, *homini gratiam* debere, legal responsibility, moral responsibility, necessity, oath, obligement, officium, pact, performance owed, promise, responsibility, social responsibility, that which a person owes to another, that which is due from a person
ASSOCIATED CONCEPTS: alternative obligation, antecedent obligation, community obligation, conditional obligation, contingent obligation, contractual obligation, existing obligation, fiduciary obligation, impairment of obligation, joint obligation, legal obligation, moral obligation, mutual obligations, parental obligation, pecuniary obligation, personal obligation, privity of obligation, secured obligation, several obligations, statutory obligations, voluntary obligation
FOREIGN PHRASES: *Fides est obligatio conscientiae alicujus ad intentionem alterius.* A truth is an obligation of conscience of one to the wishes of another. *Nihil tam naturale est, quam eo genere quidque dissolvere, quo colligatum est; ideo verborum obligatio verbis tollitur; nudi consensus obligatio contrario consensu dissolvitur.* Nothing is so natural as to dissolve anything in the way in which it was made binding. *In omnibus obligationibus in quibus dies non ponitur, praesenti die debetur.* In all obligations in which no time is fixed for their fulfillment, the obligation is due immediately. *Eisdem modis dissolvitur obligatio quae nascitur ex contractu, vel quasi, quibus contrahitur.* An obligation which arises in contract, or quasi contract, is dissolved in the same ways in which it is contracted. *Idem est scire aut scire debet aut potuisse.* To be bound to know or to be able to know is the same as to know. *Nuda pactio obligationem non parit.* A naked agreement does not effect an otherwise binding obligation. *Impossibilium nulla obligatio est.* One cannot be obliged to perform impossible tasks. *Unumquodque dissolvitur eodem ligamine quo ligatur.* Every obligation is dissolved by the same manner with which it is created. *Omnia quae jure contrahuntur, contrario jure pereunt.* All contracts which are entered into under a law, become void under a contrary law. *Ignorantia eorum quae quis scire tenetur non excusat.* Ignorance of those things which a person is deemed to know is no excuse. *L'obligation sans cause, ou sur une fausse cause, ou sur cause illicite, ne peut avoir aucun effet.* An obligation without consideration, or upon a false consideration, or upon unlawful consideration, cannot have any effect. *Nudum pactum est ubi nulla subest causa praeter conventionem; sed ubi subest causa, fit*

obligatio, et parit actionem. A naked contract is where there is no consideration except the agreement; but, where there is a consideration, an obligation is created and gives rise to a right of action.

OBLIGATION *(Liability),* *noun* accountability, amount due, charge, debit, debt, duty to pay money, indebtedness, indenture, outstanding debt, that which is owing, unliquidated claim, unpaid debt

OBLIGATION OF GOING FORWARD, *noun* adequate evidence, adequate proof legally presented at trial, burden of going forward, burden of proof, legal responsibility, sufficient corroboration, sufficient evidence in a case, sufficient evidence to establish a case, sufficient proof, sufficient proof of facts, validation of proof of a case, verification of proof of a case
ASSOCIATED CONCEPTS: cause of action or claim, evidence, evidential burden, failure to sustain, preponderance of the evidence, prima facie case, rebuttal
FOREIGN PHRASES: *Onus probani.* Burden of proof.

OBLIGATORY, *adjective* binding, coactive, coercive, commanded, compelling, compulsatory, compulsive, compulsory, constrained, dictated, enforced, essential, exigent, forced, forcible, imperative, importunate, imposed, incumbent on, indispensable, inescapable, involuntary, leaving no choice, mandatory, necessary, necessitated, not to be avoided, not to be evaded, prerequisite, pressing, required, requisite, unavoidable, unforgoable, urgent, vital, with force of law, without appeal, without choice
ASSOCIATED CONCEPTS: obligatory advance, obligatory payment, obligatory writing

OBLIGE, *verb* bind, coerce, compel, dragoon, elicit, exact, force, impel, impose, make another accept a role, make another accept responsibility for, make another party perform, obligate, require

OBLIGEE, *noun* bestower, financier, grantor, lender, lessor, mortgage holder, mortgagee

OBLIGOR, *noun* borrower, debtor, drawee, loan applicant, loanee, mortgagor, pledgor
ASSOCIATED CONCEPTS: obligor on a note

OBLIQUE *(Evasive),* *adjective* ambivalent, backhanded, circuitous, circumlocutory, cloaked, concealed, devious, disingenuous, elusive, elusory, equivocal, equivocating, furtive, indeterminate, indirect, inexact, lacking clarity, prevaricating, recondite, roundabout, secretive, sinuous, unclear, underhand, underhanded, unstraightforward, vague, veiled

OBLIQUE *(Slanted),* *adjective* angled, askew, aslant, awry, diagonal, inclined, inclining, leaning, *obliquus,* slanting, sloping, steep, tilted, tipped, tipping

OBLITERATE, *verb* *abolere,* abolish, annihilate, annul, blot out, bring to nothing, cancel, conceal, consume, cover, cover up, defeat, *delere,* delete, demolish, deracinate, desolate, destroy, devastate, devour, disintegrate, dispel, dissipate, dissolve, efface, eliminate, erase, expunge, exterminate, extinguish, extirpate, gut, invalidate, level, liquidate, mask, mow down, nullify, obscure, omit, pull up by the roots, quash, quell, ravage, raze, remove, remove the traces, render illegible, render imperceptible, rub off, rub out, ruin, rule out, scratch out, screen, shroud, smash, snuff out, squash, stamp out, strike out, suppress, swallow up, sweep away, tear down, topple, unmake, wipe out, wreck, write off

OBLIVIOUS, *adjective* absent, absentminded, absorbed, abstracted, blank, careless, distracted, dreamy, faraway, forgetful, heedless, *immemor,* inattentive, inconsiderate, indifferent, insensible, mindless, neglectful, negligent, *obliviosus,* overlooking, preoccupied, remiss, thoughtless, unaware, uncaring, unconscious, undiscerning, unheeding, unmindful, unnoticing, unobservant, unrecognizing, without consideration

OBLOQUY, *noun* abasement, abuse, abusive language, accusation, animadversion, aspersion, berating, blame, castigation, censure, chastisement, chiding, contempt, criticism, debasement, defamation, degradation, denunciation, derision, derogation, diatribe, disapprobation, discredit, disesteem, disfavor, disgrace, dishonor, disparagement, disrepute, disrespect, dressing down, execration, exprobration, faultfinding, humiliation, ignominy, ill favor, ill repute, infamy, ingloriousness, invective, lashing, *maledictum,* objurgation, odium, opprobrium, reproach, revilement, scolding, shame, slur, stigma, stricture, tirade, tongue-lashing, traducement, verbal abuse, vilification, *vituperatio,* vituperation
ASSOCIATED CONCEPTS: defamation

OBNOXIOUS, *adjective* abhorrent, abominable, annoying, antagonizing, antipathetic, base, beastly, blameworthy, censurable, contemptible, deplorable, despicable, detestable, disagreeable, disgusting, displeasing, execrable, faulty, foul, fulsome, gross, hateful, heinous, hellish, horrible, horrid, impalatable, insufferable, intolerable, invidious, *invisus,* loathful, loathsome, nasty, nauseating, nefarious, noisome, noxious, *noxius,* objectionable, odious, offensive, opprobrious, pernicious, poisonous, rank, repellent, reprehensible, repugnant, repulsive, revolting, unbearable, unendurable, unpleasant, unpleasing, unwholesome, vile, villainous, vulgar, wretched

OBNUBILATE, *verb* adumbrate, becloud, bedim, blacken, blind, blur, cast a shadow, cloak, cloud, cloud over, conceal, cover, cover up, curtain, darken, dim, disguise, dull, eclipse, encompass with gloom, enshroud, fog, haze, hide, make indistinct, mask, obfuscate, obscure, occult, overcast, overcloud, overshadow, screen, shade, shadow, shroud, veil, wrap

OBSCENE, *adjective* bawdy, broad, debauched, foul, immodest, immoral, impure, indecent, indelicate, *inquinatus,* lascivious, lecherous, lewd, libidinous, licentious, lubricous, lurid, lustful, *obscenus,* offensive, offensive to decency, offensive to modesty, patently offensive, pornographic, profane, profligate, ribald, risque, salacious, scabrous, sensual, sexy, shameful, shameless, spicy, tending to excite lustful desires, *turpis,* unchaste, unwholesome, vile, vulgar, wanton

OBSCENITY, *noun* bawdiness, coarseness, dirtiness, immodesty, immorality, impropriety, indecency, indecorum, indelicacy, lechery, lewdness, lubricity, *obscenitas,* offensiveness, pornography, ribaldry, salaciousness, salacity, scurrillity, smut, smuttiness, *turpitudo,* unchastity, vileness, vulgarity

OBSCURATION, *noun* adumbration, blackout, blur, cloud, concealment, darkening, darkness, dimming, dimness, disappearance, faintness, fogginess, fuzziness, gloom, gloominess, indistinctness, obfuscation, obliteration, obscurity, occultation, opacity, opaqueness, overshadowing, privacy, retirement, seclusion, secrecy, shade, shading, shadowing, unclearness, unintelligibleness, vagueness

OBSCURE *(Abstruse), **adjective*** complex, cryptic, cryptical, deep, difficult, difficult to understand, enigmatic, enigmatical, esoteric, hidden, impalpable, incomprehensible, intricate, involved, mysterious, profound, recondite, transcendental, unapparent, unintelligible

OBSCURE *(Faint), **adjective*** blurred, blurry, concealed, dim, hard to see, hidden, impalpable, imperceptible, inconspicuous, indefinite, indiscernible, indistinct, invisible, murky, nebulous, pale, shadowy, subtle, unapparent, unclear, undistinguished, unplain, vague, veiled, weak

OBSCURE *(Remote), **adjective*** alien, distant, far, foreign, isolated, private, rare, removed, secluded, strange, unconnected, unknown, unrenowned
ASSOCIATED CONCEPTS: obscure meaning

OBSCURE, *verb* adumbrate, becloud, bedim, befog, begloom, benight, blacken, blind, blur, cast a shadow, cloak, cloud, conceal, cover, cover up, curtain, darken, darkle, dim, disguise, dull, dusk, eclipse, encloud, enshroud, fog, haze, hide, keep in the dark, make dim, make indistinct, mask, mislead, obfuscate, occult, overcast, overcloud, overshadow, screen, shade, shroud, suppress, veil, wrap
FOREIGN PHRASES: *Semper in obscuris quod minimum est sequimur.* In obscure matters the construction which is least obscure should always be applied.

OBSEQUIOUS, *adjective* compliable, compliant, concessive, crawling, cringing, crouching, deferential, docile, enslaved, fawning, flattering, groveling, humble, ingratiating, obedient, scraping, servile, slavish, spineless, submissive, subordinate, subservient, sycophantic, toadying, unassertive, yielding

OBSERVANCE, *noun* abidance, acquiescence, adherence, allegiance, attention, compliance, conformance, cooperation, faithful adherence, honor, performance, respect, satisfaction, regard, submission, submissiveness
ASSOCIATED CONCEPTS: freedom of religion

OBSERVATION, *noun* advertence, advertency, annotation, ascertainment, assertion, attention, attentiveness, check, cognition, cognizance, comment, commentary, concentration, conclusion, consideration, declaration, detection, *dictum,* discovery, espial, espionage, estimation, examination, expression of opinion, finding, heed, heedfulness, inspection, intentness, investigation, look, mention, mindfulness, *notatio,* note, notice, *observatio,* opinion, pronouncement, reconnaissance, reflection, regard, remark, report, scrutiny, statement, study, supervision, surveillance, survey, utterance, view, watch, watchfulness, witnessing
ASSOCIATED CONCEPTS: observation of the demeanor of a witness

OBSERVE *(Obey), **verb*** abide by, acquiesce, adhere to, attend, be faithful to, be guided by, be regulated by, be submissive to, bow to, carry out, cling to, comply with, conform, *conservare,* cooperate, discharge, do the will of, execute, follow, fulfill, heed, honor, keep, obey, *observare,* pay attention to, perform, respect, satisfy, show regard for, yield to
ASSOCIATED CONCEPTS: observe the laws

OBSERVE *(Remark), **verb*** announce, articulate, assert, aver, comment, communicate, couch in terms, declare, exclaim, express, give expression to, give tongue to, give utterance to, give voice to, impart, make a remark, make mention of, mention, muse, phrase, proclaim, put into words, say, state, tell, utter, vocalize, voice

OBSERVE *(Watch),* **verb** *animadvertere,* attend, be a spectator, be a witness, be attentive, be aware, be conscious, be vigilant, behold, command a view, descry, devote attention to, direct the eyes to, espy, examine, eye, follow, gaze at, give attention to, give heed to, have in sight, heed, hold in view, inspect, keep an eye on, keep in sight, keep in view, lay eyes on, look, look at, mark, mind, note, notice, *observare,* pay attention, pay heed, peer at, perceive, peruse, reconnoiter, regard, review, scan, scout, scrutinize, see, *spectare,* spy, survey, take cognizance of, take note, take notice, take stock, turn the attention to, turn the eyes on, view

ASSOCIATED CONCEPTS: eyewitness

OBSESS, **verb** agitate, annoy, bedevil, beset, besiege, bewitch, compel, control, craze, dement, derange, discompose, disconcert, distress, dominate, drive, enthrall, gnaw, haunt, hold captive, hound, infatuate, madden, nag, overpower, pervade, plague, possess, preoccupy, prey on the mind, seize, torment, trouble, unbalance, unhinge, vex, weigh on the mind

OBSESSION, **noun** absorption, application, attraction, compulsion, craze, crotchet, dominating action, engrossment, exclusive attention, fanaticism, fancy, fascination, fetish, fixation, fixed idea, immersion, infatuation, irresistible impulse, mania, monomania, passion, preoccupation, rapt attention, ruling passion, ruling whim, singlemindedness, undivided attention, whole attention

OBSOLETE, **adjective** abandoned, anachronistic, anachronous, ancient, antediluvian, antiquated, antique, archaic, archaistic, bygone, dated, dead, discarded, discontinued, dismissed, disused, early, expired, extinct, fallen into desuetude, fallen into disuse, no longer in use, obsolescent, *obsoletus,* old, old-fashioned, out-of-date, out of use, outdated, outmoded, outworn, past, primitive, rejected, retired, stale, timeworn, unfashionable, unmodern

ASSOCIATED CONCEPTS: obsolete covenant, obsolete records, obsolete restrictions

OBSTACLE, **noun** arrest, balk, barricade, barrier, block, bridle, catch, check, constraint, curb, dam, delay, detainment, difficulty, disallowance, drawback, embargo, enjoining, estoppel, fence, forbiddance, hamper, handicap, hindrance, hurdle, impediment, *impedimentum,* inconvenience, inhibition, injunction, limitation, obstruction, preclusion, prohibition, proscription, remora, restraint, restriction, snag, stop, stoppage, stopper, stumbling block, suppression, trammel

OBSTRUCT, **verb** bar, barricade, block, brake, bridle, bring to a standstill, check, choke, circumscribe, congest, countervail, cramp, cripple, curb, debar, delay, disable, embar, encumber, estop, forbid, frustrate, halt, hamper, hamstring, handicap, hinder, impede, impedite, inhibit, interfere with, interrupt, intervene, limit, occlude, oppilate, preclude, prevent, prohibit, restrain, retard, slow down, snag, stall, stand in the way, stay, stem, stop, stop up, stymie, suppress, suspend, terminate, thwart, trammel, trap

ASSOCIATED CONCEPTS: obstruct a lawful authority, obstruct an investigation, obstruct justice, obstructing governmental administration

OBSTRUCTION, **noun** balk, ban, bar, barricade, barrier, block, blockade, blockage, bridle, catch, check, clog, closure, congestion, constraint, constriction, cork, curb, dam, difficulty, disallowance, embargo, embarrassment, enjoining, fence, forbiddance, hamper, hindrance, hitch, hurdle,

impediment, *impedimentum,* impedition, injunction, interference, interruption, limitation, obstacle, obstructio, obstruent, obturation, occlusion, plug, preclusion, prevention, prohibition, proscription, remora, restraint, restriction, shackle, snag, stop, stopper, stricture, trammel

FOREIGN PHRASES: *Forstellarius est pauperum depressor, et totius communitatis et patriae publicus inimicus.* A forestaller is an enemy of the poor, and a public enemy of the county.

OBTAIN, **verb** accumulate, achieve, acquire, *adipisci,* appropriate, arrive at, attain, be in receipt of, capture, collect, come into possession, *consequi,* earn, enter into possession, gain, gain possession, gather, get, get hold of, get possession of, grab, hold, lay hands upon, *nancisci,* pick up, pocket, possess, procure, reach, realize, receive, recover, secure, seize, take, take over, take possession, win

ASSOCIATED CONCEPTS: obtain a judgment, obtain a search warrant

OBTRUDE, **verb** accroach, break in, burst in, butt in, encroach, force, impose, *inculcare,* infringe, *ingerere,* interfere, interlope, intermeddle, interpose, interrupt, intervene, intrude, invade, meddle, trespass

OBTRUSIVE, **adjective** aggressive, assuming, bold, brash, brazen, encroaching, forward, impertinent, insolent, interfering, interrupting, interruptive, intruding, intrusive, invasive, malapert, meddlesome, meddling, officious, presuming, presumptuous, prominent, protruding, protrusive, protuberant, prying, pushy, rude, saucy, self-assertive, unmannerly

OBTUND, **verb** abate, allay, alleviate, anesthetize, assuage, benumb, blunt, calm, deaden, desensitize, dull, ease, impair the force of, make blunt, make less violent, mitigate, moderate, modulate, numb, palliate, quell, quiet, reduce the edge, reduce the violence, soften, take the edge off, weaken

OBTURATE, **verb** block, clog, close, cork, hinder, interfere, obstruct, prevent, shut, stop up, stopper

OBTUSE, **adjective** asinine, blockish, blunt, blunt-witted, callous, dense, doltish, dronish, dull, dull-witted, hebes, idiotic, ignorant, imbecilic, imperceptive, impercipient, insensitive, lumpish, moronic, oafish, obtusus, opaque, phlegmatic, retusus, senseless, simple, simpleminded, slow, stupid, thick, thickheaded, torporific, uncaring, uncomprehending, undiscerning, unfeeling, unimaginative, unintelligent, witless

OBVIATE, **verb** abolish, annihilate, crush, decimate, defeat, demolish, destroy, eliminate, foil, invert, obliterate, overcome, overpower, overset, overthrow, overturn, overwhelm, quell, repress, reverse, ruin, subdue, subvert, suppress, topple, upend, uproot, upset, vanquish

ASSOCIATED CONCEPTS: obviate the terms of a contract

OBVIATION, **noun** abolition, abrogation, arresting, bar, blockage, cancellation, check, deterrent, elimination, forestalling, interdiction, prevention, removal, stoppage, turning aside

OBVIOUS, **adjective** accessible, *apertus,* apparent, axiomatic, axiomatical, bald, bright, clear, comprehensible, conspicuous, discernible, discoverable, distinct, distinguishable, evident, exoteric, exoterical, explicit, exposed, glaring, in evidence, in view, indisputable, intelligible, lucid, manifest, *manifestus,* notable, noticeable, observable, open, overt, palpable, patent, perceivable, perceptible, perspicuous, *perspicuus,* plain, prominent, pronounced, recognizable, revealed, standing out, striking, transparent, uncamouflaged, unconcealed, undeniable, understandable, undisguised, unhidden, unmasked, unmistakable, unquestionable, unscreened, visible, well-defined

ASSOCIATED CONCEPTS: obvious danger, obvious defect, obvious error, obvious risks

OCCASION, *noun* advent, affair, chance, conjuncture, episode, event, experience, happening, incident, instance, juncture, moment, occasio, occurrence, opening, opportunity, point, situation, suitable time, *tempus,* time

OCCASION, *verb* breed, bring about, cause, create, effect, generate, give cause for, induce, make, produce, provoke

OCCLUDE, *verb* arrest, bar, barricade, block, blockade, check, choke off, close, cork, cover, dam up, debar, deter, fasten, hamper, hedge in, hem in, hinder, impede, inhibit, intercept, interclude, interrupt, lock, obstruct, obturate, oppilate, plug, preclude, prevent, prohibit, restrain, restrict, retard, seal, shut, shut in, shut off, stanch, stop, stop up, throttle, thwart, trammel, trap

OCCUPANCY, *noun* actual possession, control, dominion, enjoyment, habitation, holding, inhabitancy, occupation, ownership, *possessio,* possession, proprietorship, residence, retention, temporary possession, tenure

ASSOCIATED CONCEPTS: certificate of occupancy, continuous occupancy, illegal occupancy, partial occupancy, physical occupancy, principal occupation, residency laws, right of occupancy

OCCUPANT, *noun* addressee, denizen, dweller, freeholder, habitant, householder, inhabitant, inmate, leaseholder, lessee, lodger, occupier, possessor, renter, resident, residentiary, resider, roomer, sojourner, tenant

ASSOCIATED CONCEPTS: bona fide occupant, illegal occupancy, lawful occupant, right of occupancy, tenant in occupancy

OCCUPATION (Possession), ***noun*** ascendancy, authority, charge, command, control, direction, domination, dominion, influence, inhabitation, jurisdiction, mastery, occupancy, *occupatio,* ownership, power, predominance, predominancy, proprietary rights, proprietorship, residence, retention, right to retain, rule, seizure, superintendence, tenure

OCCUPATION (Vocation), ***noun*** activity, avocation, business, calling, capacity, career, chosen work, craft, employment, enterprise, field, industry, job, line, livelihood, mission, *negotium,* office, position, profession, pursuit, situation, specialty, trade, undertaking, venture, work

OCCUPY (Engage), ***verb*** absorb, absorb the attention, absorb the mind, absorb the thoughts, address oneself to, amuse, apply oneself to, apply the attention to, apply the mind to, arrest the attention, attract the attention, attract the mind, attract the thoughts, be active with, be at work on, be concerned with, be employed, busy oneself with, captivate, catch the attention, claim one's thoughts, concentrate on, concern oneself with, devote, direct the attention to, direct the mind to, engage the attention, engage the mind, engage the thoughts, engross, engross the mind, engross the thoughts, entertain, enthrall, entrance, excite

the attention, fascinate, go about, immerse, *in re versari,* interest, invite the attention, involve, keep busy, monopolize, monopolize the thoughts, obsess, occupare, plunge into, ply, preoccupy, rivet the attention, rivet the mind, rivet the thoughts, set about, set to work, specialize in, spend one's time in, tackle, take employment, take on, take part, take up, *tenere,* turn the attention to, turn the mind to, undertake, work at

OCCUPY (Take possession), ***verb*** abide, acquire, annex, appropriate, assume, assume ownership, be possessed of, *capere,* capture, claim, colonize, command, conquer, control, denizen, dominate, dwell, dwell in, expropriate, have possession of, have rights to, have title to, help oneself to, hold, indwell, inhabit, invade, keep, keep hold of, keep house, live, live in, lodge, make one's home at, move into, obtain, *occupare,* own, possess, procure, recover, reside in, retain, seize, settle in, stay, take from, take over, take up residence in

ASSOCIATED CONCEPTS: actually occupy, lawfully occupy

OCCUR (Come to mind), ***verb*** be uppermost in the mind, become aware, become visible, come into view, conjure up, crop up, cross one's mind, emerge, enter the mind, enter the picture, manifest itself, pass in the mind, present itself, present itself to the mind, remember, reveal itself, show itself, *subit,* suggest itself

OCCUR (Happen), ***verb*** arise, become a fact, become known, come about, come into being, come into existence, come to pass, develop, emerge, *fieri, incidere,* materialize, proceed, recur, result, take effect, take its course, take place, transpire

OCCURRENCE, *noun* affair, *casus,* circumstance, contingency, episode, event, eventuality, experience, fortuity, happening, happenstance, incident, instance, occasion, phenomenon, predicament, proceeding, realization, *res,* situation, transaction, turn, venture

FOREIGN PHRASES: *Casus fortuitus.* A chance occurrence.

ODD (Numeral), ***adjective*** alternating number, every other number, symbol, uneven digit, uneven figure, uneven integer, uneven number

ODD (Strange), ***adjective*** alien, antagonistic, antithetic, atypical, changed, contradictory, contradistinctive, contrary, contrasting, contrastive, deviating, diametrically opposed, different, discordant, discrepant, disparate, dissimilar, dissonant, distinct, distinctive, divergent, diverse, foreign, idiosyncratic, in disagreement, incommensurable, incomparable, incompatible, incongruous, individual, inharmonious, mismatched, opposed, out of the ordinary, peculiar, set apart, unique, unlike, unmatched, unrelated, unusual, variant, varied, varying

ODDITY, *noun* aberrance, aberrancy, aberration, abnormality, anomalism, anomaly, bizarreness, caprice, capriciousness, curiosity, curiousness, deformity, deviancy, deviation, distinctiveness, divergence, eccentric, exception, fancifulness, fantasticality, grotesqueness, idiosyncrasy, incongruousness, individuality, irregularity, malformation, mannerism, maverick, misfit, oddness, original, peculiarity, quaintness, rarity, strangeness, uniqueness

ODIOUS, *adjective* abject, abominable, accursed, annoying, base, beastly, blameworthy, coarse, confounded, contemptible, corrupt, cursed, damnable, despicable, detestable, diabolic, dirty, disagreeable, disgraceful, disgusting, displeasing, evil, execrable, forbidding, foul, frightening, fulsome, grotesque, hateful, heinous, hideous, horrible, horrid, ignoble, ignominious, infamous, infernal, insufferable, intolerable, *invidiosus,* invidious, *invisus,* loathsome, low, mean, monstrous, nasty, objectionable, obnoxious, *odiosus,* offensive, rank, repellent, reprehensible, repugnant, repulsive, revolting, rotten, scurvy, shocking, sickening, sinister, tainted, ugly, unbearable, unendurable, unlovable, unpalatable, unpleasant, unpopular, unworthy, vile, vulgar

ODIUM, noun abhorrence, alienation, animosity, animus, antipathy, aversion, avoidance, bad feeling, blame, censure, contempt, criticism, debasement, degradation, derision, despite, detestation, disaffection, disapproval, disesteem, disfavor, disgrace, disgust, dishonor, dislike, displeasure, disrepute, distaste, dudgeon, enmity, execration, hate, hatred, horror, hostility, humiliation, ignobility, ignominy, ill will, infamy, inimicalness, loathing, malevolence, malice, maliciousness, obloquy, odiousness, opprobrium, rancor, rebuke, reproach, repugnance, repulsiveness, resentment, revulsion, scandal, scorn, shame, strong aversion, unpopularity, venom

OF GREAT IMPORT, adjective of major significance, of overwhelming significance, of serious import, of significant consequence, of significant importance, of significant meaning, of vast importance

OFFEND (Insult), **verb** abuse, affront, anger, annoy, be discourteous, be impolite, chagrin, displease, distress, disturb, embarrass, enrage, gall, horrify, hurt, incense, inflame, infuriate, injure, irk, irritate, *laedere,* madden, make angry, mortify, nettle, *offendere,* outrage, pain, pique, provoke, ridicule, rile, slight, snub, taunt, tease, treat with discourtesy, treat with indignity, vex, wound

OFFEND (Violate the law), **verb** break a law, break the law, commit a breach of the law, commit a crime, commit a fault, commit an infraction, commit offense, commit sin, contravene, disobey the law, disregard the law, err, infringe, infringe a law, misconduct oneself, *peccare,* transgress, trespass, *violare*

OFFENDER, noun aggressor, assailant, criminal, delinquent, evildoer, felon, lawbreaker, malefactor, malfeasant, one implicated in the commission of a crime, one who breaks the law, one who commits a crime, *peccans,* sinner, transgressor, violator, wrongdoer
ASSOCIATED CONCEPTS: first offender, multiple offender, youthful offender

OFFENSE, noun aggression, assault, attack, breach, breach of the law, breaking of the law, crime, criminal act, criminal deed, criminality, delict, *delictum,* delinquency, disobedience, encroachment, evil behavior, evil deed, failure, felony, illegal act, illegal conduct, illegality, impropriety, infraction, infringement, injury, inobservance, lawbreaking, lawlessness, malefaction, malfeasance, malpractice, malversation, misconduct, misdeed, misdemeanor, misdoing, misfeasance, misprision, noncompliance, nonobservance, *offensio,* official misconduct, omission, outrage, pecability, *peccatum,* transgression, umbrage, unlawful act, unrighteousness, violation, violation of law, violation of orders, wrong, wrongdoing, wrongfulness
ASSOCIATED CONCEPTS: bailable offense, capital offense, charged with an offense, compound offense, continuing offense, degree of offense, grave offense, lesser offense, minor offense, offense against public decency, offense at common law, petty offense, prior offense, public offense

FOREIGN PHRASES: *Peccata contra naturam sunt gravissima.* Crimes against nature are the most heinous.

OFFENSIVE (Offending), **adjective** abhorrent, abominable, abusive, annoying, antipathetic, beneath contempt, biting, blasphemous, coarse, contemptible, contumelious, detestable, disagreeable, discourteous, disdainful, disgusting, displeasing, disrespectful, distasteful, execrable, foul, gravis, harsh, hateful, heinous, hideous, horrible, horrid, ignoble, ill-bred, impertinent, impious, impudent, inaffable, indecent, inharmonious, insolent, insulting, intolerable, invidious, irritating, loathsome, low, malignant, monstrous, nasty, nauseating, noxious, objectionable, obnoxious, *odiosus molestus,* odious, offending, opprobrious, outrageous, peccant, putrid, reeking, repellent, repelling, reprehensible, repugnant, repulsive, revolting, ribald, rude, sarcastic, saucy, shocking, sickening, stinging, truculent, unbearable, uncivil, uncongenial, unendurable, ungracious, unmannered, unmannerly, unpalatable, unpleasant, unpleasing, unsavory, unspeakable, vile, wounding

OFFENSIVE (Taking the initiative), **adjective** aggressive, agitational, antagonistic, assailant, assailing, attacking, battling, bellicose, combative, contentious, disruptive, exciting, fighting, hostile, inciting, incursive, inflammatory, instigating, instigative, invading, invasive, militant, militaristic, provocative, provoking, unpacific, unpeaceful, warlike

OFFENSIVE WORK ENVIRONMENT, noun abhorrent workplace, abominable job environment at work, actionable workplace, execrable milieu at work, hostile workplace, repulsive workplace, unacceptable workplace

OFFER (Propose), **verb** bid, bring forward, hold forth, hold out, invite, lay before, make a bid, make a proposition, make an overture, *offerre,* pose, proffer, *profiteri,* propound, put forth, put forth for acceptance, put forth for consideration, put forward, put forward for consideration, recommend, submit, suggest, urge upon, venture

OFFER (Tender), **verb** advance, cede, extend, offer performance, pay, present, present for acceptance, produce, proffer, proffer payment, remit, render, submit, tender performance
FOREIGN PHRASES: *Praesentare nihil aliud est quam praesto dare seu offere.* To present is no more than to give or offer forthwith.

OFFICE, noun appointment, assigned task, berth, billet, bureau, business, capacity, charge, duty, employment, function, incumbency, job, *munus,* occupation, *officium, partes,* place of business, place of employment, position, post, profession, role, service, situation, station, trade, trust, work, work place
ASSOCIATED CONCEPTS: impeachment from public office, malfeasance in office, misconduct in office, misfeasance in office, neglect of duty, nonfeasance in office, removal from office, vacancy in office
FOREIGN PHRASES: *Officium nemini debet esse damnosum.* An office ought to be injurious to no one. *Nemo duobus utatur officiis.* No one should hold two offices at the same time. *Officia judicialia non concedantur antequam vacent.* Judicial offices are not to be granted or appointed before they become vacant.

OFFICER, noun elected representative, functionary, named representative, officeholder, official
ASSOCIATED CONCEPTS: officer of the court, officer of the law

OFFICER OF THE COURT, noun advocate, appointed official of the court system, attorney, attorney-at-law, barrister, barrister-at-law, counsel, counselor, counselor-at-law, designated official of the court system, judicial designate, judicial officer, judicial official, legal advisor, legal advocate, legal consultant, legal practitioner, member of the legal profession, official of the court

OFFICIAL, adjective accredited, approved, assured, attested, authenticated, authoritative, ceremonious, certain, certified, conclusive, correct, decided, definite, dependable, endorsed, established, formal, guaranteed, indisputable, insured, legitimate, licensed, magisterial, officiary, proper, proven, *publicus,* reliable, sanctioned, to be depended on, to be trusted, trustworthy, undeniable, unequivocal, unimpeachable, valid, verified, worthy of confidence
ASSOCIATED CONCEPTS: official act, official bond, official business, official misconduct, official notice, official proceeding, official record

OFFICIAL, noun administrative head, administrator, bureaucrat, executive, executive officer, functionary, head of government, leader, leader of affairs, office bearer, officeholder, officer, overseer, person in authority, person responsible, *praefectus,* public office holder, superintendent, supervisor
ASSOCIATED CONCEPTS: public official

OFFICIAL MISCONDUCT, noun criminal conduct by a public official, criminal conduct by an administration's member, dereliction of performance in office, deviation from rectitude, dishonest management, failing to uphold a sworn oath of office, failure in office, guilty act while a public official, illegal act, illegality by a public official, improper conduct by a public official, impropriety by a public official, maladministration by a public servant, malfeasance by a public servant, misadministration by a public servant, misconduct by a public official, misdeeds by a public official, misfeasance by a public official, misgovernment, misguidance by a public official, mismanagement by an office holder, misprision by an office holder, nonfeasance by an office holder, offenses while in office, transgressions by an office holder, turpitude by an office holder, wrongdoing, by a public official
ASSOCIATED CONCEPTS: unlawful gratuities

OFFICIATE, verb act, administer, carry out, command, conduct, direct, discharge a function, do duty, execute, exercise, fill an office, failure, function, govern, guide, head, hold an office, lead, manage, minister, moderate, occupy the chair, *officio fungi,* oversee, perform, pilot, preside, regulate, run, serve, steer, superintend, supervise, take the chair

OFFSET, noun allowance, balance, compensation, contrast, counter, counteractant, counteragent, counterbalance, counterblast, counterpoise, counterweight, equalization, equivalent, hedge, impedance, neutralizer, nullifier, opposite, opposition, preventative, satisfaction, set off, substitute

OFFSHOOT, noun addition, annex, branch, byproduct, derivative, descendant, development, division, extension, issue, member, offspring, outgrowth, satellite, scion, subdivision, subsidiary, supplement

OFFSPRING, noun brood, cadet, child, children, descendants, family, heir, issue, lineage, next generation, offshoots, posterity, *progenies,* progeny, *proles,* scion, spawn, *stirps,* successor, younger generation
ASSOCIATED CONCEPTS: illegitimate offspring, natural offspring

OFTEN, adjective accustomed, common, consistently, customary, familiar, frequent, habitual, numerous, occurring over again, often done, often repeated, over and over again, persistent, prevalent, repeated, repetitive, same, usual

OLD, adjective advanced in years, ancient, antiquated, antique, archaic, crumbling, decadent, decayed, declining, decrepit, deteriorated, dilapidated, discontinued, disintegrated, early, elderly, enfeebled, hoary, *inveteratus,* matured, no longer young, not modern, obsolete, olden, original, past, preceding, preexisting, run down, rusty, stale, superannuated, timeworn, used, *vetus, vetustus,* vintage, waning, weakened, weathered, worn, worn out
ASSOCIATED CONCEPTS: ancient records doctrine

OMINOUS, adjective adverse, alarming, augurial, auspicial, baleful, bodeful, dangerous, dark, depressing, dire, direful, disastrous, dismaying, dispiriting, disquieting, disturbing, divinatory, fatidic, fatidical, fear-inspiring, fearful, forbidding, forboding, frightful, gloomy, grim, hapless, haunting, hopeless, ill-boding, ill-fated, ill-omened, ill-starred, inauspicious, luckless, menacing, minacious, minatory, monitory, morbid, perilous, pessimistic, portending evil, portentous, precursive, precursory, premonitory, presageful, presaging, presentient, pythonic, sinister, somber, threatening, threatful, unfortunate, unlucky, unpromising, unpropitious, vatic, vaticinal

OMISSION, noun breach, carelessness, default, default in performance, delinquency, dereliction, disregard, excluding, exclusion, failure, failure to perform, inadvertence, laxity, laxness, leaving out, neglect, neglect to perform, negligence, nonfeasance, noninclusion, oversight, passing over, *praetermissio,* pretermission, remissness, slip
ASSOCIATED CONCEPTS: material omission, negligent omission, omission of duty, omission to act, willful omission
FOREIGN PHRASES: Omissio eorum quae tacite insunt nihil operatur. The omission of those things which are tacitly expressed is unimportant.

OMIT, verb abstain from inserting, bypass, cast aside, count out, cut out, delete, discard, dodge, drop, exclude, fail to do, fail to include, fail to insert, fail to mention, leave out, leave undone, let go, let pass, let slip, miss, neglect, *omittere,* pass by, pass over, *praetermittere,* skip, slight, transire
FOREIGN PHRASES: Casus omissus et oblivioni datus dispositioni communis juris relinquitur. A case omitted and forgotten is left to the disposal of the common law.

OMNIBUS, adjective all-embracing, all-inclusive, blanket, broad, catholic, collective, compendious, complete, composite, comprehensive, encyclopedic, encyclopedical, exhaustive, expansive, extensive, general, generic, generical, inclusive, inclusory, indiscriminate, limitless, miscellaneous, of great scope, overall, pandemic, sweeping, unlimited, unqualified, unrestricted, wide-reaching, widespread
ASSOCIATED CONCEPTS: omnibus law

OMNIPOTENT, adjective able, all-powerful, almighty, capable, dominant, dominating, effective, effectual, godlike, Herculean, illimitable, infinitely powerful, irresistible, mighty, *omnipotens,* overwhelming, plenipotent, plenipotentiary, possessing unlimited power, potent, powerful, predominant, prepotent, puissant, ruling, sovereign, strong, supreme, uncircumscribed, unlimited in power

OMNISCIENT, adjective all-knowing, all-seeing, all-wise, apperceptive, comprehending, deific, deifical, discerning, encyclopedic, farseeing, foreseeing, godlike, infinitely wise, informed, knowing, knowledgeable, oracular, Palladian, pansophic, pansophical, perceptive, percipient, predicting, prescient, sagacious, sapient, smart, understanding, well-informed, wise

ON BEHALF OF, *verb* act for, act vicariously, appearing for, as agent for, be deputy for, be envoy for, be spokesman for, be the authorized agent for, be the authorized representative for, by proxy, in behalf of, representing, stand in for, substitute for
ASSOCIATED CONCEPTS: notice of appearance, representation

ON OR ABOUT, *adverb* approximately, in the general time frame, in the immediate vicinity of, in the neighborhood of, more or less, somewhere about

ON PURPOSE, *adjective* by design, deliberately, having a mission, having an intended result, intended, purposeful, to a particular goal, to a specific end, to gain a desired result, with a plan, with a singleness of purpose, with an intended motive, with an intended objective, with intent, with perserverance, with persistence, with specific intent, with tenacity, with the will to gain an intended result
ASSOCIATED CONCEPTS: malice, public purpose

ON THE DOCKET, *noun* anticipated, approaching, arranged, case which is calendared, due, expected, filed with the court, forthcoming, high on the agenda, imminent, impending, listed on the calendar, litigation docket, on the calendar, pending, planned, projected, prospective, put down on the docket, scheduled, scheduled case, set, slated, upcoming
ASSOCIATED CONCEPTS: case ready for trial

ON THE GROUNDS, *adjective* argued, arising from, based on, brought as a result of, brought on account of, built on, contingent upon, dependent on, established by, founded on, grounded on, justified by, rationalized by, relying on, rested on, rooted in, settled upon
ASSOCIATED CONCEPTS: charges brought on the grounds that, grounds for divorce, legal grounds, on the grounds for appeal, on the grounds of prejudice, predicted on the grounds for dismissal

ON THE LEVEL, *adjective* aboveboard, credible, decent, dependable, fair, honest, legitimate, on the up-and-up, open, sincere, square, straight, trustworthy, truthful, up front

ON THE OTHER HAND, *adverb* alternatively, by way of opposition, contrarily, contrariwise, conversely, counter, in direct contraposition, in opposition, interchangeably, inversely, just the opposite, just the other way around, just the reverse, oppositely, otherwise, quite to other contrary, rather, to the contrary, to the other extreme, vice versa

ON THE RECORD, *noun* capable of being released, capable of being reported, documented, for attribution, for public consumption, for the record, not discrete but open, not private, not secret, officially, out in the open, preserved for the record, put in the minutes, recorded, reported to the public

ON THE WHOLE, *adverb* all considering, all in all, all things considered, by and large, chiefly, essentially, everything being equal, for all intents and purposes, for all practical purposes, for the most part, generally, having said that, in the long run, in the main, mainly, mostly, nearly, on

balance, on the average, overall, substantially, taking all things into consideration, taking everything into account, that being so, uncharacterized
ASSOCIATED CONCEPTS: the record taken as a whole

ONE-SIDED, *adjective* biased, colored, discriminatory, exparte, *impar, inaequalis,* influenced, *iniquus,* interested, jaundiced, narrow, narrow-minded, partial, partisan, prejudiced, prepossessed, sectarian, slanted, swayed, undetached, undispassionate, uneven, unfair, unjust, warped
ASSOCIATED CONCEPTS: one-sided contract

ONEROUS, *adjective* arduous, backbreaking, burdensome, crushing, cumbersome, difficult, exacting, excessive, fatiguing, formidable, *gravis,* grinding, grueling, hard, harrowing, harsh, heavy, Herculean, intolerable, laborious, oppressive, overbearing, overpowering, overtaxing, pressing, rigorous, severe, strenuous, taxing, tedious, toilsome, trying, unbearable, unwieldy, wearisome, weighty

ONGOING, *adjective* abiding, adjourned, continuous, enduring, extension, lasting, lengthening, perpetuating, persevering, persisting, postponed, prolonged, protracted, stayed, successively continued
ASSOCIATED CONCEPTS: labor law, ongoing negotiations

ONLY *(No more than),* *adjective* bare, mere, plain, simple

ONLY *(Sole),* *adjective* exclusive, first and last, individual, lone, singular, solitary, unique

ONLY *(Unrepeated),* *adjective* unmatched, unparalleled

ONLY, *adverb* alone, apart, at least, at the very least, exclusively, merely, plainly, purely, simply, singly, solely

ONLY, *conjunction* but, but for the fact that, excepting that, if it were not that

ONSET *(Assault),* *noun* advance, aggression, assailment, attack, barrage, blitzkrieg, bombardment, charge, dragonnade, encounter, foray, forced entrance, fusillade, incursion, intrusion, invasion, maraud, offense, offensive, onrush, onslaught, raid, seizure, siege, storm, strike, thrust

ONSET *(Commencement),* *noun* aurora, beginning, birth, coming, dawn, embarkation, entrance, establishment, exordium, fashioning, first appearance, first move, first step, forging, forming, foundation, genesis, inauguration, inception, inchoation, incipience, incunabula, infancy, initiation, introduction, launching, making, oncoming, opening, origin, origination, outbreak, outset, rise, source, start, starting point, threshold

ONUS *(Blame),* *noun* accusation, blameworthiness, charge, culpability, error, fault, flaw, guiltiness, misdeed, reprehension, responsibility, shortcoming, transgression

ONUS *(Burden),* *noun* affliction, burdensome requirement, charge, drawback, encumbrance, handicap, hindrance, impediment, inescapable duty, interference, load, obstruction, responsibility, struggle, unusual task, weary load, weight

ONUS *(Stigma),* *noun* badge, blemish, blot, blotch, brand, censure, condemnation, degradation, denunciation, discredit, disgrace, dishonor, dispraise, imputation, infamy, mark of Cain, reproach, scar, shame, slur, smirch, smudge, smutch, soil, spot, stain, taint, tarnish

427

OPACITY

OPACITY, noun   asininity, blockishness, confusion, darkness, denseness, density, dimness, doltishness, dull-wittedness, dullness, fatuity, hebetude, impenetrability, imperceptibility, inapprehensibility, incomprehensibility, indiscernibility, indistinctness, indistinguishability, inscrutability, lack of understanding, lumpishness, nebulosity, oafishness, obfuscation, obscuration, obscurity, obtuseness, opaqueness, simplicity, slow-wittedness, slowness, stolidity, stolidness, stupidity, stupidness, thickheadedness, thick-wittedness, thickness, unclarity, unclearness, unfathomableness, unintelligibility, unplainness, unsearchableness, vacuity, vagueness, vapidity, want of transparency

OPAQUE, adjective   addlebrained, addleheaded, addlepated, ambiguous, asinine, benighted, bewildering, birdbrained, blind, blockish, boeotian, brainless, cloddish, clouded, cloudy, concealed, confused, confusing, cryptic, dark, dense, difficult, difficult to comprehend, difficult to understand, dim, dimwitted, doltish, dull, dull-witted, duncelike, duncical, enigmatic, fatuitous, fatuous, featherbrained, foggy, hard to comprehend, hard to understand, hazy, ignorant, ill-defined, imbecilic, impenetrable, imperceptive, imperspicuous, impervious, incomprehensible, indistinct, inscrutable, lacking clarity, loutish, lumpish, mindless, misty, moronic, muddleheaded, muddy, nebulous, nescient, nontranslucent, oafish, obfuscated, obscure, obtuse, purblind, puzzling, recondite, senseless, shadowy, simple, simple-minded, slow in understanding, stolid, stupid, thick, thick-headed, thick-witted, turbid, unclarified, unclear, uncomprehending, unenlightened, unfathomable, unintelligent, unintelligible, unplain, unreasoning, unthinking, untransparent, vacuous, vague, witless

OPEN (Accessible), **adjective**   allowable, allowed, approachable, attainable, available, defenseless, fit for travel, free of access, free to all, insecure, navigable, obtainable, patere, permitted, pregnable, procurable, public, reachable, securable, susceptible, unbarred, unblocked, undefended, unenclosed, unfenced, unfortified, unguarded, unlocked, unobstructed, unoccupied, unrestricted, unsealed, unshielded, vacated, vulnerable, within reach
ASSOCIATED CONCEPTS: open account, open market, open shop

OPEN (In sight), **adjective**   aspertus, apparent, bare, beholdable, blatant, clarus, clear, conspicuous, discernible, discoverable, distinct, evident, exposed, exposed to view, eye-catching, glaring, in full view, manifest, manifestus, marked, noticeable, observable, obvious, outstanding, overt, patent, perceivable, perceptible, perspicuous, plain, prominent, pronounced, recognizable, revealed, salient, seeable, striking, transparent, unclouded, unconcealed, uncovered, undisguised, unhidden, unmistakable, unobstructed, unprotected, unsecluded, unsheltered, unshielded, visible
ASSOCIATED CONCEPTS: open and notorious possession, open court

OPEN (Persuasible), **adjective**   acquiescent, amenable, apertus, candidus, flexible, impressible, impressionable, inducible, influenceable, malleable, movable, open-minded, persuadable, pervious, receptive, respondent, responsive, sensitive, simplex, suasible, suggestible, susceptible, swayable, sympathetic, tractable

OPEN (Unclosed), **adjective**   adapertus, agape, ajar, coverless, dehiscent, gaping, lidless, patens, patulous, patulus, spacious, spread out, unclogged, uncorked, uncovered, unfastened, unfurled, unlatched, unlocked, unsealed, unshut, unstoppered, wide, yawning

OPEN AND OVERBOARD, adjective   aboveboard, blunt, candid, clear, clear-cut, crystal clear, decent, direct, distinct, evident, explicit, express, forthright, frank, honest, ingenuous, manifest, obvious, on the up and up, open, open and genuine, open and sincere, sincere, straight, straightforward, straight-out, unequivocal, unreserved, upfront
ASSOCIATED CONCEPTS: franking privilege

OPEN-ENDED, adjective   boundless, ceaseless, changing, continued, continuing, expansive, going on, illimitable, illimited, indecisive, indefinite, indeterminable, inexact, infinite, interminable, limitless, loose, measureless, modifiable, not particular, not specific, ongoing, termless, unbounded, unbridled, unceasing, unconfined, unconstrained, uncontrolled, undefined, unending, unlimited, unmeasured, unrestricted, vague, variable, wide-open, without limits, without specified limits

OPEN-MINDED, adjective   accessible, amenable, broad-minded, detached, disinterested, dispassionate, equitable, evenhanded, fair, fair-minded, impartial, independent, indifferent, judicial, just, latitudinarian, liberal, neutral, objective, open, persuadable, persuasible, reasonable, receptive, responsive, tolerant, unbiased, unbigoted, uncolored, undogmatic, unimpassioned, uninfluenced, unjaundiced, unprepossessed, unswayed, unwarped

OPENING (Initial presentation of a case), **noun**   beginning of a case, commencement of a case, counsel's initial statement, counsel's introductory statement, counsel's overview of a case, inception of litigation, initiation of a legal case, introduction of a case, introductory, presentation, start of a case
ASSOCIATED CONCEPTS: litigation, opening statement

OPENING (Opportunity), **noun**   availability, chance, means, moment, occasion, once-in-a-lifetime chance, place, possibility, presented with an opportunity

OPENING STATEMENT, noun   opening argument, presentation of basics, presentation of data, presentation of essentials, presentation of the documentation, presentation of the evidence, presentation of the facts

OPERATE, verb   accomplish, achieve, act, act upon, administer, administrate, assume responsibility, attain, bring about, caretake, carry into execution, carry on, carry out, cause, command, conduct, control, deal with, direct, discharge, do, drive, effect, effectuate, enforce, engage in, engineer, execute, exercise, exercise power over, exert, fulfill, function, govern, handle, have charge of, impel, implement, lead, look after, manage, maneuver, manipulate, mastermind, militate, minister, move, officiate, oversee, perform, perpetrate, pilot, practice, preside over, prevail over, put into effect, put into practice, regulate, rule, run, steer, superintend, supervise, take care of, take charge of, work
ASSOCIATED CONCEPTS: operate to the detriment of a party

OPERATION, noun   act, action, campaign, course of action, crusade, effectio, enterprise, execution, exploit, function, handling, management, move, movement, performance, practice, procedure, proceeding, process, production, pursuit, routine, step, stratagem, stroke, task, thrust, transaction, undertaking, venture

OPERATIVE, adjective   acting, active, adequate, advantageous, ample, applicable, at work, beneficial, capable, competent, effective, effectual, *efficax*, efficient, employed, fruitful, functional, functioning, helpful, in action, in effect, in force, in harness, in operation, in play, instrumental, on duty, operational, performing, potent, productive, serviceable, successful, sufficient, useable, useful, valid, workable, working, yielding

OPEROSE, *adjective* arduous, backbreaking, bothersome, burdensome, crushing, demanding, difficult, effortful, emasculating, embittering, enervating, exacting, exhausting, fagging, fatiguing, formidable, grinding, grueling, hard, hard to cope with, Herculean, irksome, laborious, onerous, painstaking, plodding, pressing, Sisyphean, straining, strenuous, tiresome, tiring, toilsome, troublesome, trying, uphill, vexatious, weakening, wearing, wearisome, wearying

OPINE, *verb* adjudge, appraise, *arbitrari*, assume, be convinced, be persuaded, be satisfied, believe, cherish a belief, conclude, conjecture, consider, dare say, deem, determine, diagnose, esteem, estimate, express an opinion, fancy, feel, guess, have a hunch, have an idea, have an opinion, have faith, have no doubt, hold, hypothesize, imagine, infer, judge, look upon, nurture a belief, *opinari*, postulate, preconceive, prejudge, presume, presuppose, pronounce judgment, reckon, regard, rest assured, speculate, stand, suppose, surmise, suspect, theorize, think, view, ween

OPINION (Belief), ***noun*** assumption, attitude, conclusion, conjecture, consideration, conviction, determination, estimate, estimation, evaluation, fancy, feeling, guess, hypothesis, idea, impression, *iudicium*, judgment, notion, outlook, perspective, persuasion, point of view, position, posture, preconception, presumption, presupposition, reaction, reflection, sentiment, speculation, stance, stand, supposition, surmise, suspicion, theory, thesis, thinking, thought, view, viewpoint

FOREIGN PHRASES: *Incivile est, nisi tota lege perspecta, una aliqua particula ejus proposita, judicare, vel respondere.* Unless the entire law has been examined, it is improper to pass judgement upon a portion of it. *Incivile est, nisi tota sententia inspecta, de aliqua parte judicare.* It is improper to pass an opinion on any part without examining the entire sentence. *Nullius hominis auctoritas apud nos valere debet, ut meliora non sequeremur si quis attulerit.* No man's influence ought to prevail upon us, that we should not follow better opinions, should any one present them. *Opinio est duplex, scilicet, opinio vulgaris, orta inter graves et discretos, et quae vultum veritatis habet; et opinio tantum orta inter leves et vulgares homines absque specie veritatis.* Opinion is of two fold, namely, common opinion, which springs up among grave and discreet persons, and which has the appearance of truth, and opinion which arises among foolish and ordinary men. *Opinio quae favet testamento est tenenda.* An opinion which favors a will is to be followed.

OPINION (Judicial decision), ***noun*** adjudication, ascertainment, assessment, authoritative statement, conclusion, conclusion of the matter, consideration, decision, declaration, decree, decreement, determination, final judgment, finding, formal statement, judgment, judgment on facts, order, position, pronouncement, report, resolution, rule, ruling, sentence, *sententia,* settlement by authoritative decision, solution

ASSOCIATED CONCEPTS: advisory opinion, concurring opinion, dissenting opinion, expert opinion, judicial opinion, legal opinion, majority opinion, memorandum opinion, minority opinion, opinion evidence, opinion of the court, per curiam opinion, professional opinion, written opinion

FOREIGN PHRASES: *Ubi non est directa lex, standum est arbitrio judicis, vel procedendum ad similia.* Where there is no direct law, the decision of the judge is to be taken, or references to be made to similar cases. *Judices non tenentur exprimere causam sententiae suae.* Judges are not bound to explain the reason for their sentences.

OPPONENT, *noun* *adversarius,* adversary, adverse party, challenger, combatant, contender, corrival, disputant, one who opposes, opposer, opposing litigant, opposing party, opposite, opposite side, opposition, other side

OPPORTUNE, *adjective* advantageous, appropriate, apt, auspicious, befitting, *commodus,* convenient, due, expedient, fit, fitting, *idoneus, opportunus,* propitious, providential, seasonable, suitable, suited, timely, well-timed

OPPORTUNITY, *noun* auspiciousness, chance, convenience, copia, fair chance, favorable chance, favorable time, fit time, fitting occasion, fitting time, fortuity, good chance, good fortune, hap, liberty, luck, *occasio,* occasion, opening, opportune moment, opportune time, possibility, potestas, proper occasion, proper time, propitiousness, prospect, readiness, reasonable chance, right time, ripeness, scope, suitable circumstance, suitable occasion, suitable time, time, turn

ASSOCIATED CONCEPTS: earliest practicable opportunity, opportunity to appear, opportunity to be heard

OPPOSE, *verb* act in opposition to, argue against, balk, battle, be at cross purposes, be contrary to, block, buck, challenge, collide, combat, come in conflict with, confront, confute, contend, contest, contradict, contravene, controvert, counter, counteract, counterattack, counterbalance, countermine, counterpoise, countervail, counterweigh, counterwork, debate, defy, demur, deny, disaffirm, disagree, disapprove, dispute, encounter, fight, go against, go contrary to, join issue, negate, not submit, not yield, object, obstruct, offer resistance, oppugn, prevent, prohibit, protest, put in opposition, rebut, recalcitrate, refute, reject, remonstrate, repel, repugn, repulse, resist, set against, stand firm against, strive, strive against, take a stand against, take exception to, take issue with, tourney

ASSOCIATED CONCEPTS: oppose a motion, opposing counsel, opposing interest, opposing parties

FOREIGN PHRASES: *Error qui non resistitur approbatur.* An error which is not resisted or opposed is waived.

OPPOSED TO, *verb* act in opposition to, argue against, balk, battle, be at cross purposes, be contrary to, block, challenge, collide, combat, come in conflict with, confront, confute, contend, contest, contradict, contravene, controvert, counter, counteract, counterattack, counterbalance, countermine, counterpoise, countervail, counterweigh, counterwork, debate, defend, defy, deny, disaffirm, disagree, disapprove, dispute, fight, go against, go contrary to, go up against, negate, not yield, object, obstruct, offer resistance, oppugn, prevent, prohibit, protest, put in opposition, rebut, refute, reject, remonstrate, repel, repulse, resist, stand firm against, take a stand against, take exception to, take issue with

ASSOCIATED CONCEPTS: picketing

OPPOSING COUNSEL, *noun* competitor's counsel, defendant's or plaintiff's counsel, disputant's attorney, opponent' attorney, opposing litigant's attorney, opposite counsel, the adversary's counsel, the appellant's or appellee's counsel, the opponent's lawyer, the other party's lawyer, the other side's counsel, the petitioner's or respondent's attorney

OPPOSING PARTY, noun adversary, appellant, appellee, challenger, claimant, complainant, contender, defendant, disputant, petitioner, plaintiff, respondent, the other party, the other side

ASSOCIATED CONCEPTS: adversarial system, litigation

OPPOSITE, adjective absonant, *adversarius*, adverse, antagonistic, antipodal, antipodean, antithetic, antithetical, clashing, conflicting, contradictive, contradictory, *contrarius*, contrary, contrasted, contrasting, converse, counter, diametrically opposed, disagreeing, discordant, facing, hostile, incompatible, inconsistent, inharmonious, inimical, inverse, inverted, mismated, mutually opposed, negative, opposed, opposing, oppugnant, perverse, resisting, resistive, reverse, reversed, wayward

OPPOSITION, noun antinomy, challenge, conflict, confutation, contention, contrariety, contrary action, contravention, counteraction, counterattack, counterplot, counterworking, denial, disagreement, disapprobation, disapproval, dissension, enmity, impugnation, impugnment, interference, objection, oppugnancy, oppugnation, protest, protestation, recalcitration, refutation, remonstrance, remonstration, resistance, running counter to, struggle, traversal, want of harmony

OPPRESSION, noun abuse, abusiveness, brutality, brute force, coercion, compulsion, cruelty, despotism, dictatorship, domination, enslavement, force, harassment, harshness, ill treatment, inhumanity, *iniuria*, injustice, iron rule, liberticide, maltreatment, misrule, mistreatment, misuse of power, persecution, reign of terror, repression, rule of might, ruthlessness, severity, subjection, subjugation, suppression, torment, totalitarianism, tyranny, *vexatio*, victimization

OPPRESSIVE, adjective afflictive, arduous, burdensome, confining, cruel, crushing, cumbersome, cumbrous, depressing, detrimental, devouring, difficult, difficult to bear, distressing, engulfing, exacting, exhausting, fatiguing, formidable, galling, grievous, grinding, hard, harmful, harsh, heavy, hurtful, imperious, inhuman, *iniquus*, intolerable, irksome, laborious, *molestus*, onerous, operose, overbearing, overpowering, overwhelming, painful, pernicious, ponderous, rigorous, severe, stifling, strenuous, suffocating, taxing, tiring, toilsome, troublesome, trying, tyrannical, unbearable, uncomfortable, unendurable, unreasonable, unyielding, upsetting, vexatious, wearing, wearisome, weighty

OPPROBRIUM, noun abasement, attaint, bad light, bad name, blot, brand, contempt, culpability, debasement, *dedecus*, defamation, degradation, derogation, disapprobation, discredit, disesteem, disgrace, dishonor, disrepute, disrespect, humiliation, ignobility, ignominiousness, ignominy, ill fame, ill repute, imputation, indignity, infamousness, infamy, ingloriousness, loss of honor, loss of reputation, loss of standing, notoriety, obloquy, odium, reproach, scandal, shady reputation, shame, slur, smirch, stain, stigma, taint, tarnish, vilification

OPPUGN, verb aggress, assault, attack, be contrary, buck, call in question, challenge, clash, combat, conflict, confront, contend, contradict, contravene, controvert, counter, countervail, counterwork, criticize adversely, cross, deal a blow, defy, denounce, descend upon, disagree, dispute, dissent, fall upon, fight, foil, gainsay, go against, hinder, hold out against, interfere with, militate against, object,

obstruct, oppose, outface, pounce upon, protest, reason against, recalcitrate, refute, reluct, reluctate, remonstrate, resist, run against, run counter to, set upon, side against, stand against, stand up to, strike at, strive against, take exception, take the offensive, thrust at, thwart, traverse, wrangle

OPT FOR, verb ascertain, choose, decide on, determine, elect, favor, lean toward, make a choice, pick, prefer, select, take

OPTION (Choice), noun alternate choice, alternative, choice, discretion, election, free decision, free selection, free will, freedom, freedom of choice, leave, liberty, opportunity, pick, power to choose, preference, right of choice, selection

ASSOCIATED CONCEPTS: election between options, exercise of option, options after default

OPTION (Contractual provision), noun acquired right, agreement, allowance, approval, authorization, consent, continuing offer, continuing offer to buy, favor, grant, guaranty, license, power, prerogative, privilege, proviso, right, right to buy or sell, sanction, stipulation, term, understanding

ASSOCIATED CONCEPTS: conditional option, continuing option, exercise of an option, first option, irrevocable option, option to buy, option to lease, option to purchase, option to renew, option to sell

OPTIONALLY, adverb alternatively, at the option of, discretionally, electively, preferably, selectively

OPULENT, adjective abounding in riches, affluent, comfortable, flourishing, flush, moneyed, opulentus, pecunious, propertied, prosperous, rich, richly endowed, rolling in riches, substantial, well-fixed, well-off, well provided for, well-situated, well-to-do, with means, worth a great deal

ORACULAR, adjective cryptic, divinatory, enigmatic, fatidic, fatidical, foreknowing, foretelling, knowing, mysterious, mystical, obscure, ominous, portentous, precursive, precursory, predicting, predictive, presaging, prognostic, prophetic, sage, sapient, sibylline, vatic, vaticinal, wise

ORAL, adjective announced, articulated, audible, by word of mouth, communicated, enunciated, expressed, expressed in words, phonic, said, said aloud, sounded, spoken, spoken out loud, told, unwritten, uttered, verbal, vocal, vocalized, voiced

ASSOCIATED CONCEPTS: nuncupative will, oral contract, oral testimony, statute of frauds

ORAL COMMUNICATION, noun dissemination, divulgement, information, message, news, notification, proclamation, report, revelation, utterance, verbal announcement, verbal annunciation, verbal declaration, verbal disclosure, writing

ASSOCIATED CONCEPTS: defamation, public official, right to privacy, slander

ORAL EVIDENCE, noun corroboration, document, documentary evidence, documentation, species of proof, substantiation, validation, verbal confirmation, verbal explanation of facts admitted at trial, verbal proof, verbal proof of facts, verbal proof presented at trial, verbal testimony, verbal testimony which is part of the record, verification

ASSOCIATED CONCEPTS: independent experts, transcripts, wiretaps

ORCHESTRATE, verb adapt, adjust, allot the parts, arrange, assemble, assign the parts, bring into order, bring together, compose, concert, conduct, construct, coordinate, harmonize, lay out, methodize, order, organize, preconcert, predetermine, put in order, put into a systematic form, reduce to order, regiment, regulate, set in order, set to music, standardize, symphonize, systematize

ORDER (Arrangement), **noun** adjustment, allocation, allotment, apportionment, array, catalogue, categorization, chronology, classification, composition, design, disposal, distribution, form, formation, gradation, grouping, layout, lineup, methodology, *ordo,* organization, pattern, placement, plan, procession, progression, rotation, sequence, setup, stratification, structure, system, systematization
ASSOCIATED CONCEPTS: order of creditors, order of priorities, order of proof

ORDER (Judicial directive), **noun** authoritative command, behest, command, commandment, court commandment, court instruction, declaration, decree, dictate, direction, directive, edict, *edictum,* fiat, imperative, instruction, *iussum,* judicial command, judicial instruction, mandate, *mandatum,* precept, prescript, prescription, proclamation, pronouncement, rescript, rule, ruling, ukase
ASSOCIATED CONCEPTS: appealable order, charging order, confinement order, decision, decretal order, entry of order, final order, interlocutory order, motion, nonappealable order, nunc pro tunc order, order granting a new trial, order of dismissal, order of the court, order staying execution, order to show cause, preliminary order, restraining order, selfexecuting order, settle order, suspension order

ORDER, verb adjure, call forth, call upon, cite, command, compel, decree, demand, dictate, direct, *edicere, imperare,* impose, impose a duty, impose a task, insist on, instruct, issue a decree, issue one's fiat, *iubere,* make a requisition, make demands on, oblige, ordain, prescribe, proscribe, require, rule, serve, tell, warrant
ASSOCIATED CONCEPTS: administrative order, amended order, appealable order, charging order, confinement order, contempt order, entry of judgment and order of the court, ex parte order, final order, interlocutory order, nunc pro tunc order, order granting a new trial, order of discontinuance, order of probate, order of proof, order of the court, order to show cause, restraining order, reviewable order, special order, stay order, suspension order, vacation of an order
FOREIGN PHRASES: *Quando aliquid mandatur, mandatur et omne per quod pervenitur ad illud.* When something is commanded, everything by which it can be accomplished is also ordered.

ORDER OF THE COURT, noun authoritative pronouncement, authoritative ruling, binding order, command, court command, declaration by the court, edict, fiat, imperative, judicial command, judicial decree, judicial dictate, judicial direction, judicial directive, judicial mandate, pronouncement
ASSOCIATED CONCEPTS: entered order

ORDINANCE, noun authoritative rule, canon, charter, code, command, decree, decretum, direction, edict, *edictum,* enactment, fiat, imperative, law, legal command, legislation, legislative decree, legislative edict, local law, local legislation, local rule, mandate, maxim, municipal code, municipal regulation, ordainment, order, ordination, prescript, proclamation, regulation, requirement, rule, statute
ASSOCIATED CONCEPTS: city ordinance, criminal ordinance, local

ordinance, municipal ordinance, regulatory ordinance, traffic ordinance, violation of an ordinance, zoning ordinance

ORDINARY, adjective accepted, accustomary, accustomed, average, banal, boring, bourgeois, bromidic, characteristic, colloquial, commonplace, *communis,* consuetudinary, conventional, customary, daily, drab, established, expected, familiar, fixed, frequent, general, generally practiced, habitual, hackneyed, homely, homespun, household, humdrum, insipid, known, mediocre, middling, normal, oft-repeated, pedestrian, philistine, platitudinous, plebeian, plentiful, popular, prevailing, prevalent, prosaic, prosaical, *quotidianus,* recognized, regular, regulation, repeated, representative, rife, simple, stale, standard, stereotyped, stock, taken for granted, traditional, *translaticius,* trite, typical, unassuming, undistinguished, unexceptional, unexciting, unimaginative, unoriginal, unvaried, usual, vernacular, wearisome, well-trodden, well-worn, widespread, wonted, workaday
ASSOCIATED CONCEPTS: necessary expenses, ordinary care and skill, ordinary course of business, ordinary course of trade, ordinary duty, ordinary expenses, ordinary income, ordinary loss, ordinary meaning, ordinary negligence, ordinary prudent person, ordinary reasonable man, ordinary risk, ordinary standard of care, ordinary use, ordinary wear and tear
FOREIGN PHRASES: *Recurrendum est ad extraordinarium quando non valet ordinarium.* Resort must be made to the extraordinary when the ordinary does not succeed.

ORDINARY WEAR AND TEAR, noun diminution, disrepair, normal damage, normal decline in value, normal deterioration, normal detriment, normal harm, normal impairment, normal loss
ASSOCIATED CONCEPTS: depreciation, residual value insurance

ORGAN, noun affiliate, agency, annex, appendage, arm, associate, branch, branch office, bureau, chapter, component, department, division, extension, instrument, instrumentality, local, lodge, means, member, newspaper, office, offshoot, part, periodical, post, ramification, section, subdivision, subsidiary, unit, wing

ORGANIC, adjective anatomical, basal, basic, constitutional, deep-rooted, derived from within, elemental, fundamental, implanted, inborn, inbred, indigenous, ingrained, inherent, innate, instinctive, intrinsic, intrinsical, native, natural, original, primary, primitive, rooted, rudimentary, structural, substantial, substantive, underlying

ORGANIZATION (Association), **noun** affiliation, aggregation, alliance, bloc, club, coalition, combination, community, company, corps, coterie, establishment, faction, federation, foundation, group, institute, institution, joint concern, league, *reipublicae forma,* school, sodality, syndicate, troupe
ASSOCIATED CONCEPTS: charitable organization, de facto organization, domestic organization, labor organization, nonprofit organization, political organization

ORGANIZATION (Structure), **noun** arrangement, build, classification, composition, configuration, conformation, constitution, construction, *descriptio,* design, figuration, figure, form, formation, framework, grouping, interrelation of parts, makeup, manner of construction, order, placement, plan, regularity, scheme, shape, style of arrangement, systematization, *temperatio*

ORGANIZE (Arrange), **verb** adjust, align, assort, catalogue, categorize, class, classify, combine, *componere,* correlate, establish guide lines, establish parameters, file, form into classes, get in formation, grade, group, introduce a system, introduce order, lay down guide lines, list, marshal, methodize, order, *ordinare,* place, place in order, put in array, put in order, put into shape, rank, rate, reduce to order, regiment, regulate, separate into categories, set guidelines, set in array, set in order, sort, standardize, straighten, systematize

ASSOCIATED CONCEPTS: organize a corporation, organized labor

ORGANIZE *(Unionize),* **verb**   affiliate, amalgamate, associate, band together, cement a union, centralize, collaborate, combine, confederate, consolidate, create, enlist employees in a labor union, enlist in a labor union, enter into a league, establish, federate, form, form a labor union, form into a body, formulate, incorporate, institute, join, join together, merge, mold, set up, unify, unite, unite for a common purpose

ASSOCIATED CONCEPTS: organized labor

ORGULOUS, *adjective*   affected, aloof, arrogant, assuming, blustering, boastful, boasting, bragging, conceited, condescending, contemptuous, disdainful, egocentric, egoistic, egoistical, egotistic, egotistical, fanfaronading, flaunting, gasconading, grand, grandiose, haughty, immodest, imperious, inflated, insolent, intolerant, lofty, lordly, narcissistic, overbearing, overproud, overweening, patronizing, pompous, presumptuous, prideful, scornful, self-applauding, self-centred, self-flattering, self-glorifying, self-important, self-lauding, self-magnifying, self-praising, self-satisfied, supercilious, thrasonical, vain, vainglorious, vaunting

ORIGIN *(Ancestry),* **noun**   ancestral descent, birth, bloodline, derivation, descent, dynasty, extraction, family, filiation, genealogical tree, genealogy, heritage, kith and kin, line, line of ancestors, line of descent, lineage, *origo,* parentage, parenthood, pedigree, race, stock, tribe

FOREIGN PHRASES: *Origine propria neminem posse voluntate sua eximi manifestum est.* It is evident that no one by his own will can renounce his own origin.

ORIGIN *(Source),* **noun**   beginning, birth, birthplace, cause, commencement, cradle, creation, dawn, derivation, *fons,* font, foundation, fountainhead, genesis, inception, initiation, nascency, nativity, onset, *origo, principium,* root, starting point, wellspring

FOREIGN PHRASES: *Ex facto jus oritur.* Law arises out of facts. ***Causa et origo est materia negotii.*** The cause and origin are the substance of the transaction.

ORIGINAL *(Creative),* **adjective**   artful, clever, daring, demiurgic, demiurgical, different, eccentric, envisioning, exceptional, fanciful, fecund, fertile, fictive, fresh, gifted, imaginal, imaginative, individual, ingenious, inimitable, inspired, inventive, nonconformist, novel, odd, originative, out of the ordinary, poetic, productive, rare, resourceful, singular, unborrowed, uncommon, unconformable, unconventional, uncopied, uncustomary, underived, unexampled, unexpected, unfashionable, unheard of, unimitated, unique, unmatched, unordinary, unorthodox, unparalleled, unusual, unwonted, visioned, visualizing, whimsical

ORIGINAL *(Initial),* **adjective**   antecedent, authentic, basal, basic, basilar, beginning, commencing, earliest, elemental, elementary, embryonic, first, formative, foundational, fundamental, germinal, inaugural, inauguratory, inchoate, inchoative, incipient, incunabular, infant, initial, initiative, initiatory, introductory, maiden, nascent, natal,

native, nonimitative, opening, precursory, preliminary, prelusive, prelusory, primal, primary, prime, primeval, primigenial, primitive, primordial, pristine, proemial, pure, rudimental, rudimentary, seminal, starting, underlying

ASSOCIATED CONCEPTS: best evidence rule, original action, original decree, original evidence, original holder, original issue, original jurisdiction, original stock, original undertaking, original writing

ORIGINATE, *verb*   activate, arouse, author, awaken, beget, begin, break ground, breed, bring about, bring into existence, bring on, bring to pass, cause, coin, commence, compose, conceive, concoct, contrive, create, devise, draft, effect, elicit, engender, engineer, establish, evoke, fabricate, father, forge, form, formulate, found, frame, generate, get going, get up, give birth to, give impulse to, give origin to, give rise to, handsel, improvise, inaugurate, induce, initiate, inspire, institute, introduce, invent, kindle, launch, lay the foundation for, lead, make, make up, manufacture, motivate, mount, open, pioneer, plan, precipitate, prepare, produce, promote, prompt, propagate, provoke, raise, set afloat, set going, set in motion, set up, sire, start, stimulate, take the first step, take the initiative, take the lead, think up, trigger, undertake, usher in

ORIGINATION, *noun*   ancestry, beginning, birth, causation, cause, coinage, commencement, composition, cradle, creation, dawn, derivation, discovery, emergence, etymology, exordium, fabrication, fomentation, font, foundation, fountain, fountainhead, genesis, inauguration, inception, inchoation, incipience, incipiency, incunabula, infancy, initiation, instigation, introduction, invention, motivation, motive, nascency, nativity, onset, opening, outset, parentage, production, provenance, provenience, rise, root, source, spring, start, starting point, stimulation, stimulus, wellspring

ORIGINATOR, *noun*   author, beginner, commencer, composer, conceiver, concocter, contriver, creator, deviser, engineer, establisher, father, formulator, founder, framer, generator, improviser, inaugurator, inducer, initiator, inspirer, introducer, inventor, leader, maker, manufacturer, motivator, pioneer, precipitator, preparer, producer, propagator, provoker, starter, stimulator, the first one to bring into existence, the one who broke ground, undertaker

ASSOCIATED CONCEPTS: origination on loan

OROTUND, *adjective*   affected, artificial, blustering, bombastic, clear, declamatory, elocutionary, flatulent, forceful, full, fustian, grandiloquent, grandiose, high-flown, histrionic, inflated, magniloquent, mellow, oratorical, pompous, presumptuous, pretentious, resonant, rhetorical, showy, sonorous, stilted, strong, stuffy, swelling, swollen, theatrical, tumid, turgescent, turgid, vainglorious, windy

ORPHAN, *noun*   abandoned child, abandoned infant, bereaved child, castaway, child without parents, foundling, homeless child, *orbus,* orphaned child, orphaned infant, parentless child, twice-bereaved child, waif, ward

ORTHODOX, *adjective*   accepting, according to custom, according to regulation, according to rule, according to the book, accustomed, acknowledged, approved, believing, bound by convention, canonical, common, commonplace, compliant, conformable, conforming, conservative, conventional, correct, customary, devoted to convention, doctrinal, established, formal, habitual, inflexible, literal, ordinary, *orthodoxus,* prescriptive, prevailing, proper, recognized, rigid, scrupulous, strict, traditional, typical, unbending, unchangeable, uncompromising, unheterodox, usual, wonted

OSCILLATE, verb   *agitari,* agitate, alternate, be doubtful, be indecisive, be irresolute, be uncertain, be undecided, be undetermined, be unresolved, be unsteady, be unsure, beat, bounce, debate, deliberate, falter, flap, fluctuate, flutter, fret, hesitate, librate, lurch, move in waves, move to and fro, pendulate, rock, rotate, seesaw, shift, sway, swerve, swing, turn, undulate, vacillate, vary, waver

OSMOSIS, noun   absorption, assimilation, diffusion, digestion, engulfment, infiltration, ingress, interpenetration, introgression, passage, penetration, permeation, saturation, seepage, transmission

OSSIFIED, adjective   bony, calcified, calloused, congealed, crystallized, dense, firm, fossilized, hard, hardened, incrassate, incrassated, indurated, lapidified, petrified, solid, solidified, stiff, stiffened, stony, thick, thickened, tough, toughened, turned to bone

OSTENSIBLE, adjective   able to be seen, apparent, appearing, assumable, assumed, avowed, believable, claimed, clear, colorable, conjecturable, credible, deceiving, deceptive, declared, deluding, delusional, delusive, delusory, discernible, evident, explicit, express, *fictus,* illusional, illusionary, illusive, illusory, indubitable, likely, manifest, misleading, noticeable, observable, obvious, outward, overt, patent, perceivable, perceptible, perspicuous, plain, plausible, presumable, pretended, professed, purported, reasonable, seeable, seeming, self-evident, shown, *simulatus,* so-called, specious, supposable, supposed, surface, surmisable, visible

OSTRACISM, noun   avoidance, ban, banishment, blackball, blacklist, blame, blockade, censure, condemnation, coventry, criticism, decrial, deportation, disbarment, dislodgment, dismissal, displacement, dissociability, distance, ejection, elimination, eviction, exclusion, excommunication, exile, exilement, expatriation, expulsion, extrusion, hostility, inhospitality, intolerance, isolation, lockout, nonadmission, noninclusion, obloquy, omission, preclusion, prejudice, prohibition, proscription, quarantine, refusal, rejection, reprobation, reproof, segregation, separation, shame, snub, stricture, suspension, unfriendliness, unsociableness

OTHERWISE, adverb   apart from this, besides, by way of opposition, contrarily, contrariwise, conversely, counter, excepting that, excluding that, in a different circumstance, in a different manner, in a different way, in opposition, in other respects, in other ways, on the other hand, oppositely, quite to the contrary, rather, regardless, the other way around, to just the opposite, to just the reverse, to the contrary, with this as an exception
ASSOCIATED CONCEPTS: otherwise law abiding

OTIOSE, adjective   abortive, apathetic, arid, barren, bootless, dallying, dilatory, disengaged, dispensable, disused, dormant, dried up, effete, exhausted, expendable, faineant, fallow, feckless, fruitless, futile, idle, impotent, impracticable, impractical, inactive, indolent, ineffective, ineffectual, inefficacious, inefficient, inert, infertile, inoperative, invalid, issueless, jejune, jobless, lackadaisical, laggard, lagging, lame, languorous, lazy, leaden, lethargic, lethargical, lifeless, listless, lymphatic, motionless, neglectful, nonfunctional, nonfunctioning, nonparticipating, nugatory, null and void, oscitant, passive, phlegmatic, powerless, resultless, slack, slothful, slow, sluggish, spiritless, stagnating, sterile,

supine, torpescent, torpid, unable, unadaptable, unavailing, uncalled-for, unemployed, unfertile, unfruitful, unnecessary, unneeded, unoccupied, unpersevering, unproductive, unprofitable, unprolific, unserviceable, unsubstantial, unsuccessful, unusable, unwanted, unworkable, useless, vain, valueless, wasted, weary, worthless

OUST, verb   banish, cast out, chase out, depose, deprive of office, dislodge, dismiss, displace, dispossess, divest of office, drive out, eject, expel, force out, purge, put out, remove, remove from office, repudiate, throw out, thrust out, turn out, unseat
ASSOCIATED CONCEPTS: impeachment, removal from public office

OUSTER, noun   deprivation, dislodgment, dispossession, ejection, elimination, eviction, exclusion, permanent exclusion, removal, repudiation

OUT OF BOUNDS, adjective   banned, barred, disallowed, forbidden, illegal, impermissible, improper, nonpermissible, not acceptable, not allowed, not appropriate, not proper, off limits, prohibited, ruled out, unauthorized, unlawful, unlicensed, unsanctioned

OUT OF ORDER, adjective   discordant, egregious, improper, indecent, indecorous, inharmonious, objectionable, out of place, outrageous, prohibited, shocking, unallowable, unauthorized, unbecoming, unbefitting, uncharacteristic, undesirable, unreasonable, unrefined, unruly, unseemly, unsound, wrong

OUT OF POCKET, adverb   compensation, costs, damages, expenses, just compensation, payment, recovery, remuneration, reparation for loss, repayment, restitution, restoration, retrieval, satisfaction
ASSOCIATED CONCEPTS: pocket expenses

OUT-OF-POCKET EXPENSES, noun   administrative reimbursable expenses, defrayal, defrayment, disbursement, entertainment expenses, expenses, individual expenses, itemized expenses, payments, recompense, recoupment, reimbursables, remittance, remuneration, repayment, travel expenses
ASSOCIATED CONCEPTS: out-of-pocket rule

OUTBALANCE, verb   be greater in value, be greater in weight, be superior, better, compensate, counteract, counterbalance, counterpoise, countervail, counterweigh, cover, dominate, eclipse, equalize, equiponderate, exceed, gain the ascendancy, get ahead of, have the advantage, have the edge on, hedge, indemnify, make compensation, make leeway, make up for, neutralize, offset, outdo, outpoint, outrival, outstrip, outvie, outweigh, overbalance, overcome, overmatch, overtop, overweigh, pass, predominate, preponderate, prevail, recoup, redeem, rise above, rival, set off, surpass, top, transcend, trump

OUTBREAK, noun   affray, aggression, agitation, assault, attack, bloodshed, blow up, brawl, breach, breach of the peace, burst, cataclysm, commotion, conflict, convulsion, declaration of war, disruption, disturbance, ebullition, eruption, explosion, ferocity, fit, flare-up, foment, fomentation, fracas, fray, fury, insurgence, insurrection, invasion, irruption, mayhem, mutinousness, mutiny, onslaught, outburst, overthrow of authority, paroxysm, proruption, quarrel, rage, raid, rebellion, revolt, revolution, riot, rising, rush, siege, spasm, strife, throe, thunder, torrent, unruliness, uprising, uproar, violent behavior, warfare

OUTBURST, noun affray, agitation, attack, blast, blaze, blowout, blowup, bluster, breach of the peace, burst, clamor, commotion, convulsion, detonation, discharge, disgorgement, disquiet, disquietude, disruption, disturbance, ebullition, ejaculation, emission, eruption, explosion, expulsion, fit, flare up, flurry, foment, fomentation, fray, frenzy, furor, fury, fuss, gush, hysteria, hysterical state, hysterics, impetuosity, insurgence, insurrection, irascibility, irascibleness, irruption, jet, mayhem, outbreak, outpour, paroxysm, proruption, rage, rampage, rebellion, restlessness, revolt, revolution, rising, rush, sally, spasm, spurt, stir, strife, sudden excursion, tempest, throe, thunder, torrent, unruliness, upheaval, uproar, vehemence, violence, volcano

OUTCOME, noun achievement, aftereffect, aftermath, answer, attainment, close, completion, consequence, consummation, creation, culmination, decision, denouement, development, effect, end, end product, ending, eventuality, eventuation, finding, finish, fruit, fruition, fulfillment, issue, judgment, offspring, outgrowth, product, production, realization, resolution, result, resultant, sequence, sequent, settlement, solution, upshot, yield

ASSOCIATED CONCEPTS: outcome-determinative test

OUTCRY, noun accusation, blame, brawl, broken silence, bruit, burst of sound, castigation, censure, charge, chiding, chorus, clamor, clamorousness, complaint, condemnation, *convicium,* criticism, cry, denunciation, diatribe, din, disapprobation, disapproval, discontent, dislike, dissatisfaction, dissent, disturbance, execration, explosion, fracas, furor, grievance, howl, hullabaloo, invective, lament, loud noise, loud protest, noise, objection, opposition, pandemonium, philippic, plaint, protest, protestation, racket, raised voice, rebuke, reprimand, reproach, reprobation, revilement, scolding, scream, shout, stricture, tumult, turmoil, upbraiding, uproar, vilification, vituperation, *voces, vociferatio,* vociferation, wail, weeping, yell

OUTDATED, adjective anachronistic, anachronous, ancient, antediluvian, antiquated, antique, archaic, behind the age, behind the times, bygone, dated, defunct, demode, discarded, disused, expired, extinct, fallen into desuetude, fallen into disuse, forgotten, former, gone by, gone out, grown old, no longer customary, no longer fashionable, no longer in style, no longer prevailing, no longer prevalent, no longer stylish, not current, not in vogue, not modern, obsolescent, obsolete, of a previous fashion, of a previous style, of great age, of old, of the old order, of the old school, old, old-fashioned, old-time, old-world, olden, out-of-date, out-of-fashion, out-of-use, outmoded, outworn, passe, past, primitive, quaint, rejected, stale, styleless, superannuated, superseded, unaccepted, uncontemporary, uncurrent, unfashionable, unpracticed, unstylish

OUTED, verb betrayed, confidentiality announced, confidentiality revealed, cover blown off, identity declared, identity disclosed, identity divulged, identity exposed, identity revealed, inform on the identity, leak the identity, make known, make public, promulgation, publication, release confidential information, reveal confidential information, secret identity brought out into the open, secret identity brought to light, tell everything, tell the identity, unburden the identity of, uncover, unmask, unveil

OUTFLOW, noun abatement, current, defluxion, discharge, disemboguement, drain, drainage, ebb, effluence, efflux, effusion, egression, emanation, emergence, emersion, emigration, eruption, escape, evacuation, exodus, expenditure, expense, export, exportation, expulsion, extravasation, extrusion, exudation, flood, flux, gush, issue, jet, leakage, movement, ooze, outburst, outgush, outpour, outstream, outward flow, outward sweep, overflow, recession, refluence, reflux, runoff, seep, shipments, spill, spout, spurt, stream, tide, transudation, wane, withdrawal

OUTGROWTH, noun aftereffect, aftermath, development, effect, end result, eventuality, eventuation, excrescence, fruit, issue, offshoot, offspring, repercussion, result, resultance, resultant, sequel, sprout, yield

OUTLAW, noun bandit, brigand, convict, criminal, delinquent, evildoer, felon, fugitive, fugitive from the law, habitual criminal, habitual offender, hardened criminal, lawbreaker, lawless individual, malefactor, miscreant, notorious criminal, offender, offender against society, *proscriptus,* public enemy, racketeer, recidivist, robber, swindler, thief, transgressor, underworld character, violator of the law

OUTLAW, verb *aqua et igni interdicere,* banish, bar, declare illegal, declare unlawful, exclude, expel, forbid by law, make unlawful, place outside the protection of the law, proscribe, *proscribere,* put beyond the protection of the law, reject, repel

OUTLAY, noun amount expended, budgeted items, charge, cost, disbursement, expenditure, expense, *impensa,* outgo, payment, spending, *sumptus*

OUTLET, noun access, aperture, avenue, channel, chute, conduit, demand, door, egress, *egressus, emissarium,* exhaust, exit, *exitus,* floodgate, gate, gateway, hatch, hole, market, means of escape, opening, passage out, path, portal, spout, vent, way out

OUTLINE *(Boundary),* **noun** ambit, border, bounds, bourn, brink, circuit, circumference, circumscription, compass, confine, contour, demarcation, edge, edging, external form, *extrema lineamenta,* extremity, frame, fringes, frontier, limitations, limits, line of demarcation, lineaments, margin, metes, pale, perimeter, periphery, profile, rim, skirt, threshold, tracing, verge

OUTLINE *(Synopsis),* **noun** abbreviation, abridgment, abstract, *adumbratio,* agenda, brief, compend, compendium, compression, condensation, conspectus, contents, contraction, core, digest, epitome, essence, minute, note, pandect, recapitulation, report, skeleton, sketch, summation, syllabus

OUTLOOK, noun angle, aspect, attitude, emotional tone, field of view, frame of mind, frame of reference, observation, perspective, point of observation, point of view, position, posture, regard, slant, stand, standpoint, viewpoint, way of thinking

OUTMODED, adjective anachronistic, anachronous, ancient, antediluvian, antiquated, antique, archaic, behind the age, behind the times, bygone, dated, demoded, desuete, disapproved, discarded, disused, expired, extinct, fallen into desuetude, fallen into disuse, forgotten, former, gone out, grown old, neglected, no longer conventional, no longer customary, no longer prevailing, not in vogue, obsolescent, obsolete, of a previous fashion, of a previous style, of the old school, old, old-fashioned, old-world, out-of-date, out of fashion, out of use, outdated,

434

outworn, passe, past, primitive, quaint, rejected, retired, stale, styleless, superannuated, superseded, unaccepted, uncurrent, unfashionable, unpracticed, unstylish

OUTPOUR, verb be effusive, be prolix, cascade, cast forth, decant, detrude, discharge, discourse at length, disembogue, disgorge, drain, effuse, eject, emit, empty, enlarge upon, eruct, eructate, evacuate, exhaust, expel, extravasate, harangue, inundate, let fall, pour forth, pour out, rant, send forth, send out, shed, spill, spout, spurt, stream, vent

OUTPUT, noun accomplishment, achievement, amount produced, avail, benefit, creation, crop, discharge, earnings, effectuation, emanation, end, end product, fruit, gain, harvest, issuance, issue, manufactured product, merchandise, outcome, proceeds, produce, product, production, profit, quantity produced, result, return, yield
ASSOCIATED CONCEPTS: output contract

OUTRAGE, noun abomination, absurdity, abuse, affront, atrocity, contempt, contumacious, cruelty, disgracefulness, dishonorableness, disrespect, harmfulness, hatefulness, horribleness, ignobleness, iniquitousness, injuriousness, intolerableness, malevolence, maliciousness, nefariousness, odiousness, offensiveness, perfidiousness, unreasonableness, wickedness
ASSOCIATED CONCEPTS: moral outrage

OUTRAGEOUS, adjective abominable, absurd, abusive, acrimonious, affronting, arrant, atrocious, barefaced, base, black, brazen, conspicuous, contemptible, *contumeliosus,* contumelious, corrupt, cruel, deplorable, despicable, despiteful, dire, disgraceful, dishonorable, disobliging, disrespectful, drastic, egregious, enormous, exaggerated, excessive, execrable, exorbitant, extreme, fanatic, fanatical, ferocious, flagitious, flagrant, foul, fulsome, galling, glaring, gross, grossly offensive, harmful, hateful, heinous, horrifying, hot-headed, hyperbolical, ignoble, *immanis,* immense, immoderate, *immoderatus,* infamous, infuriating, iniquitous, injurious, inordinate, insolent, insulting, intolerable, low, mad, madcap, malevolent, malicious, malign, malignant, maniacal, monstrous, nefarious, notorious, odious, offensive, opprobrious, overdone, perfidious, preposterous, questionable, rabid, radical, raging, reprehensible, scandalous, shameless, shocking, sinful, spiteful, tempestuous, unconscionable, undue, unpleasant, unreasonable, unwarranted, villainous, wanton, wicked, wild, wrongful
ASSOCIATED CONCEPTS: outrageous conduct

OUTRIGHT, adjective absolute, all-out, altogether, complete, comprehensive, consummate, downright, entire, exhaustive, flagrant, full, full-fledged, obvious, out-and-out, sheer, straightforward, straight out, sweeping, thorough, through and through, total, unconditional, undiminished, undivided, unequivocal, unmitigated, unqualified, utter
ASSOCIATED CONCEPTS: outright grant

OUTRUN, verb beat, catch up, catch up with, come up to, edge out, gain on, leave behind, leave standing, outdo, outmaneuver, outpace, outperform, outrange, outreach, outrival, outstrip, overtake, pass, prevail over, win

OUTSET, noun beginning, birth, commencement, dawn, embarkation, entrance, exordium, first move, first step, foundation, genesis, inauguration, inception, inchoation, incipience, incipiency, induction, infancy, initiation, *initium,* introduction, launching, onset, opening, origin, origination, outbreak, rise, start, starting point, threshold

OUTSOURCING, verb contracting with outside sources, disposing of, eliminating work, eliminating workers, going outside, hiring outside sources, retaining others, retaining outside sources, subcontracting

OUTSTANDING (Prominent), **adjective** august, celebrated, chief, consequential, conspicuous, distinctive, distinguished, elevated, eminent, especial, esteemed, exalted, excellent, excelling, exceptional, eximious, extraordinary, famed, famous, far-famed, foremost, great, honorable, honored, illustrious, important, imposing, impressive, incomparable, influential, known, luminous, lustrous, majestic, marked, memorable, nonpareil, notable, noted, noteworthy, paramount, peerless, preeminent, prestigious, princely, principal, ranking, recognized, remarkable, renowned, reputable, respected, revered, royal, salient, significant, special, starring, sublime, substantial, supereminent, superior, superlative, supreme, transcendent, unforgettable, unparalleled, venerable

OUTSTANDING (Unpaid), **adjective** delinquent, due, in arrears, overdue, owing, past due, payable, surviving, uncollected, ungathered, unliquidated, unrecompensed, unrequited, unsatisfied, unsettled

OUTSTANDING (Unresolved), **adjective** in suspense, incomplete, indefinite, irresolved, open, pending, unadjusted, unascertained, unconcluded, undecided, undetermined, unfinished, unsettled

OUTWEIGH, verb be of greater significance, beat, better, come first, dominate, eclipse, exceed, exceed in importance, exceed in value, excel, get ahead of, go beyond, outbalance, outdo, outrank, outrival, overbalance, overpoise, overpower, overshadow, overtop, overweigh, *potiorem,* predominate, preponderate, prevail, rise above, *superare,* surpass, take precedence over, top, transcend, *vincere,* weigh more than

OVER AGAIN, adjective do over, duplicate, give an encore, perform multiple times, recreate, recur, redo, reduplicate, re-enact, remake, renew, repeat, replicate, reproduce, resume, retrace
ASSOCIATED CONCEPTS: concurrent sentences, consecutive sentences

OVERAGE, noun avalanche, balance, deluge, excess, extra, glut, inundation, leftover, overabundance, overflow, overmeasure, overplus, oversupply, plenty, profusion, redundance, redundancy, remainder, remnant, repletion, residue, spare, supersaturation, surfeit, surplus, surplusage, too many, too much, undue amount

OVERALL, adjective all in one, all-embracing, all-encompassing, all-inclusive, blanket, complete, comprehensive, entire, extended, extensive, general, globally, inclusive, panoramic, sweeping, total, undivided, universal, whole, wholesale, with all sides considered, with every aspect

OVERCOME (Overwhelm), **verb** astonish, awe-strike, bewilder, bowl over, break down, burden, confound, crush, daze, deluge, discomfit, drown, encumber, engulf, flood, get the upper hand, glut, hamper, immerse, inundate, overlay, overload, overpower, overtax, prostrate, saddle, shatter, stagger, stun, submerge, swallow up, swamp, weigh down, whelm

OVERCOME (Surmount), **verb** beat, command, conquer, defeat, destroy, dominate, drub, eclipse, get the better

435

of, get the upper hand, master, outdo, outrival, outshine, outstrip, overmatch, overpower, overshadow, overthrow, prevail over, quash, quell, rise above, rout, subdue, subjugate, tower above, transcend, triumph over, vanquish
ASSOCIATED CONCEPTS: overcome a presumption

OVERDRAW, *verb* aes *alienum contrahere,* be debited with, be in debt, be prodigal, become bankrupt, become insolvent, deplete, dissipate, exhaust, incur a debt, overcharge, overextend, overspend, overstrain, overstretch, owe, owe money, run into debt, spend more than one has, squander
ASSOCIATED CONCEPTS: overdraw an account

OVERDUE, *adjective* behind time, belated, *debitus,* delayed, delinquent, due, in arrears, late, long-delayed, more than due, not on time, outstanding, past due, past the time for payment, remiss, tardy, unpaid, untimely

OVERESTIMATE, *verb* adulate, aggrandize, attach too much importance to, enlarge, estimate too highly, exaggerate, exalt, exceed, expand, extol, flatter, glorify, inflate, magnify, make too much of, maximize, misestimate, misjudge, misrepresent, overassess, overcalculate, overcount, overdo, overjudge, overlaud, overmeasure, overpraise, overprize, overrate, overstate, overvalue, set too high an estimate

OVEREXTEND, *verb* develop too fast, develop too much, distend, go too far, grow too fast, grow too much, overcommit, overdevelop, overexpand, spread too far, spread too thin, strain, stretch, stretch too far

OVERHEAD, *noun* budget, business expenses, charges, cost, cost incurred, cost of living, current expenses, disbursement, drain on resources, expenditures, expense, general expenses, liabilities, living expenses, money expended, operating expenses, outlay, payments, spendings, upkeep
ASSOCIATED CONCEPTS: overhead expenses

OVERHEAR, *verb* attend, become aware of, catch, detect, eavesdrop, *exaudire, excipere,* find out, glean knowledge of, hear, intercept, listen in on, listen stealthily, monitor, obtain knowledge of, pick up, receive information, receive knowledge of, *subauscultare*
ASSOCIATED CONCEPTS: eavesdropping, wiretapping

OVERINDULGE, *verb* be gluttonous, be greedy, be intemperate, be selfish, be voracious, carry to excess, carry too far, cater to excessively, coddle excessively, eat excessively, favor excessively, gratify to excess, humor excessively, lack self-control, overdo, overeat, overgorge, overgratify, pamper excessively, satiate to excess, satisfy to excess, spoil excessively

OVERLAP, *verb* adjoin, cover, encroach, exceed, extend beyond, go beyond, imbricate, *imminere, impendere,* impinge, infringe, invade, lap over, lie over, make contact, overgrow, overhang, overlay, overlie, override, overrun, overspread, project, protrude, reach over, run over, spread over, superimpose, touch

OVERLOAD, *verb* burden, choke, congest, cram, crowd, cumber, deluge, drench, encumber, flood, force, glut, gorge, inundate, load to excess, make heavy, oppress, overabound, overburden, overdo, overdose, overexert, overfeed, overfill, overstrain, overstuff, overtask, overtax, overuse, overweigh, overwhelm, overwork, pack, saddle, saturate, soak, strain, supercharge, supersaturate, surcharge, surfeit, weigh down, work to excess

OVERLOOK (Disregard), *verb* fail to appreciate, fail to observe, fail to see, forget, leave out, leave undone, let ride, miss, neglect, omit, pass over, take no notice

OVERLOOK (Excuse), *verb* condone, disregard, excuse, forgive, pardon

OVERLOOK (Superintend), *verb* administer, be at the helm, be inattentive to, command, command a view of, *condonare,* conduct, control, direct, examine, govern, guide, have charge of, hold the reins, ignore, *ignoscere,* inspect, look after, look out, look over, oversee, pilot, *praeterire,* preside, review, scrutinize, steer, study, supervise, survey, watch over

OVERPOWER (Defeat), *verb* attack, conquer, crush, get the upper hand, master, outmaneuver, overcome, overwhelm, prevail, rout, stun, stupefy, subdue, subjugate, surmount, vanquish

OVERPOWER (Overtake), *verb* beat, finish first, master, outmaneuver, outrace, overmaster, overmatch, overset, prevail over, trounce, upset, win

OVERREACH, *verb* accroach, annul, cheat, *circumscribere, circumvenire,* circumvent, deceive, defeat one's own purpose, defeat oneself by overdoing matters, defraud, dupe, encroach, exceed, extend beyond, extend over, fool, get the better of, have one's plans backfire, mislead, nullify one's gains, offset, outsmart, outwit, overact, overdo, overextend, overshoot, reach beyond, reach over, reach too far, thwart, trick, trip, undermine, undo
ASSOCIATED CONCEPTS: undue influence

OVERRIDE, *verb* act despite, annul, cancel, counteract, countermand, crush, defeat, discard, dismiss, disregard, do away with, dominate, flout, fly in the face of, ignore, invalidate, make ineffectual, make null and void, make void, neglect, nullify, outweigh, overcome, overpower, overrule, overturn, pass over, prevail over, quell, reverse, revoke, set aside, subdue, supersede, surpass, take no account of, take precedence, thwart, upset
ASSOCIATED CONCEPTS: override a veto, overriding state interest

OVERRULE, *verb* abrogate, annul, cancel, countermand, decide against, *gubernare,* invalidate, make null, make void, nullify, obviate, override, overturn, refuse to sustain, reject, reject by subsequent action, reject by subsequent decision, renounce, repeal, repudiate, rescind, retract, reverse, revoke, rule against, rule out, set aside, supersede, undo, upset, *vincere,* void
ASSOCIATED CONCEPTS: overrule a decision, overrule a motion, overrule an objection

OVERSEE, *verb* administer, attend to, be at the helm, be the guiding force, carry on, coach, command, conduct, control, dictate, direct, dominate, engineer, examine, execute, govern, guide, handle, have authority over, have charge of, have the direction of, head, instruct, lead, look after, manage, master, mastermind, navigate, officiate, pay attention to, pilot, *procurare,* reconnoiter, regiment, regulate, rein, rule, scrutinize, steer, superintend, supervise, watch, watch over
ASSOCIATED CONCEPTS: master servant relationship, principal agent relationship, respondeat superior

OVERSHADOW, *verb* cast into the shade, dominate, dwarf, eclipse, extinguish, obscure, outshine, overshadow, prevail over, reduce, rise above, run circles around, shroud, steal the spotlight from, surmount, take the glory out of, top, tower above, tower over, upstage

OVERSIGHT (Carelessness), **noun**   blunder, careless mistake, careless omission, *erratum,* error, failure, failure to notice, heedlessness, inadvertency, inattention, *incuria,* lapse, laxity, laxness, mistake, neglect, negligence, nonobservance, remissness, slip, supervision, thoughtlessness, unintentional mistake, unintentional omission
ASSOCIATED CONCEPTS: negligence

OVERSIGHT (Control), **noun**   management, overlooking, superintendence, supervision, watchful care, watchfulness

OVERSTATEMENT, noun   aggrandizement, amplification, boasting, coloring, distortion, elaboration, embroidery, enlargement, exaggerated statement, exaggeration, expansion, extravagance, extravagancy, falsification, hyperbole, hyperbolism, inflated statement, inflation, magnification, magniloquence, misjudgment, misrepresentation, misstatement, overestimation, puffery

OVERSTEP, verb   accroach, advance beyond proper limits, break in upon, encroach, entrench, exceed, go beyond, go over, go too far, impinge, infringe, interfere, intrude, invade, meddle, not observe, obtrude, overpass, overrun, run over, strain, stretch, transcend, transgress, trench on, trespass, usurp, violate

OVERT, adjective   *apertus,* apparent, clear, definite, disclosed, distinct, easily seen, evident, explicit, exposed, express, glaring, in full view, in plain sight, manifest, *manifestus,* noticeable, notorious, obvious, open, ostensible, palpable, patent, perceptible, perspicuous, plain, public, revealed, unconcealed, uncovered, undisguised, unhidden, visible

OVERT ACT, noun   action, beginnings, commencement, criminal act, dealings, deed, doings, intentional act, maneuver, manifest act, open act, outward act, start
ASSOCIATED CONCEPTS: conspiracy

OVERTHROW, verb   abolish, *adfligere,* be victorious over, break up, bring down, cast down, conquer, defeat, deicere, dethrone, *diruere,* disrupt, eradicate, exterminate, extirpate, fell, invert, master, nullify, obliterate, obviate, overmaster, overpower, overrun, overset, overturn, overwhelm, prostrate, quash, quell, ravage, refute, remove, reverse, revolt, revolutionize, shatter, subdue, subjugate, subvert, suppress, surmount, terminate, throw down, throw over, topple, turn upside down, uncrown, unseat, upend, uproot, upset

OVERTURE, noun   advance, approach, beginning, bid, condicio, exordium, foreword, initiative, introduction, invitation, motion, offer, opening of negotiations, preamble, preface, preliminary, preliminary negotiation, prelude, presentation, proem, proffer, proposal, proposition, tender

OVERTURN, verb   abolish, annihilate, conquer, crush, defeat, demolish, destroy, *evertere,* foil, invert, obliterate, overcome, overpower, overset, overthrow, overwhelm, quell, repress, reverse, ruin, subdue, subvert, *subvertere,* suppress, topple, upend, uproot, upset, vanquish
ASSOCIATED CONCEPTS: overturn a decision

OVERVIEW, noun   analysis, comprehensive analysis, detailed summary, examination, general outlook, introduction, iteration, outline, recap, recapitulation, recount, recounting, reiteration, statement, summary, summation, survey
ASSOCIATED CONCEPTS: law firm profile

OVERWHELM, verb   astonish, beat, besiege, bewilder, bury, confound, confuse, conquer, daze, defeat, deluge, *demergere,* destroy, discomfit, immerse, impress, inundate, master, obruere, *opprimere,* overcome, overpower, overrun, overthrow, quash, quell, shock, stun, subdue, subjugate, submerge, suppress, surmount, surprise, triumph over, vanquish, weigh down

OVERWHELMING, adverb   absolutely, astonishingly, astronomically, comfortably, completely, decisively, definitively, distinctly, dramatically, emphatically, immensely, overpoweringly, popularly, radically, significantly, strongly
ASSOCIATED CONCEPTS: overwhelmingly approved, overwhelming passing the legislature, overwhelmingly rejected, overwhelmingly supported

OWE, verb   be beholden, be bound, be due, be in debt, be indebted, be liable, be obligated, be under obligation, contract a debt, debere, have a loan, have an obligation, incur a debt
ASSOCIATED CONCEPTS: debt owed, debtor-creditor laws, legally owed, taxes owed

OWN, verb   be in possession of, be in receipt of, be master of, be possessed of, claim, command, contain, control, dominate, enjoy, *habere,* have, have a deed for, have a title to, have claim upon, have hold of, have in hand, have rights to, have to one's name, hold, keep, maintain, occupy, possess, *possidere,* retain, *tenere*
FOREIGN PHRASES: Id solum nostrum quod debitis deductis nostrum est. That only is ours which remains to us after deduction of our debts.

OWNER, noun   claimer, controller, holder, homeowner, householder, land owner, landlord, lessor, legitimate person entitled to, master, occupier, person holding ownership on record, possessor, property owner, proprietor, receiver, record-holder, retainer, title holder
ASSOCIATED CONCEPTS: beneficial owner, co-owner, equitable owner, general owner, gun owner, joint owners, owner of copyright, part owners, record owner, repeated owner

OWNERSHIP, noun   claim, control, dominion, *dominium,* holding, mastery, occupancy, possessorship, proprietary, proprietorship, right of possession, seisin, tenancy, tenure, title, use
ASSOCIATED CONCEPTS: absolute ownership, apparent ownership, certificate of ownership, change of ownership, exclusive ownership, incident of ownership, individual ownership, joint ownership, occupation, ownership rights, possession, proprietary interest, qualified ownership, silent partner, sole ownership, sole proprietor, tenancy by the entirety, transfer of ownership, unconditional ownership, undisclosed interest, unqualified ownership

P

PACIFY, verb accommodate, alleviate, appease, assuage, becalm, bring to terms, calm, *componere*, conciliate, dulcify, ease, *lenire*, make peace, mediate, mellow, mollify, pacificate, placare, placate, please, propitiate, quell, quiet, reconcile, relieve, restore harmony, restore to a state of peace, restore to a state of tranquillity, reunite, salve, satiate, satisfy, settle, settle differences, smooth, soothe, still, subdue, tranquilize

PACT, noun agreement, alliance, arrangement, assurance, bargain, bond, charter, coalition, compact, compromise, concord, concordance, concordat, consentaneity, consortium, contract, convention, cooperation, covenant, deal, entente, *foedus,* guarantee, indenture, league, mutual agreement, mutual pledge, mutual promise, *pactio,* paction, *pactum,* pledge, promise, reconciliation, settlement, stipulation, treaty, understanding, union, warranty

PAIN, noun ache, adversity, affliction, aggravation, agony, ailment, anguish, blight, calamity, disability, discomfort, disease, displeasure, distress, *dolor,* grief, grievous trouble, hurt, ill, infliction, injury, malady, malaise, misery, ordeal, pang, sickness, sore, soreness, sorrow, strong discomfort, suffering, torment, unease, woe, worry
ASSOCIATED CONCEPTS: pain and suffering

PAIN AND SUFFERING, noun award for permanent damage, award for serious damage, award for sustained damage, damages, damages for an injured party, damages for emotional distress, damages for mental distress, damages for physical distress, damages for the afflicted, damages for the impaired, grant for damages sustained, noneconomic damages
ASSOCIATED CONCEPTS: general damages, special damages

PAINFUL, adjective aching, afflictive, agonizing, anguishing, arduous, beset with difficulties, difficult, difficult to endure, discomforting, distressful, distressing, disturbing, excruciating, grievous, grueling, hard to endure, harmful, harrowing, hurtful, hurting, inflamed, insufferable, intolerable, irksome, irritating, laborious, smarting, sore, throbbing, tiresome, tormenting, torturous, troublesome, troubling, trying, unbearable, uncomfortable, unendurable, unpleasant, unsufferable, wearisome

PAINSTAKING, adjective assiduous, attentive, careful, conscientious, diligent, earnest, elaborate, energetic, exacting, hardworking, heedful, industrious, labored, laborious,

meticulous, never-tiring, operose, *operosus,* particular, persevering, plodding, precise, punctilious, regardful, scrupulous, sedulous, *sedulus,* sparing no pains, strenuous, strict, thorough, untiring, zealous

PALATABLE, adjective acceptable, agreeable, ambrosial, ambrosian, amenable, appetizing, becoming, causing pleasure, cibarious, comestible, congenial, delectable, delicate, delicious, delightful, drinkable, dulcet, *dulcis,* eatable, edible, enjoyable, epicurean, esculent, flavorful, flavorous, flavorsome, good, good-tasting, good to eat, gratifying, inviting, iucundus, likable, *luscious,* meeting standards, nectareous, nice, piquant, pleasant, pleasing, pleasurable, potable, prepossessing, refreshing, relishable, sapid, satisfactory, savory, scrumptious, *suavis,* succulent, tangy, tasteful, tasty, tempting, toothsome, unobjectionable, up to par, welcome

PALAVER, noun babble, balderdash, blather, chatter, empty words, foolishness, gab, idle chatter, idle talk, mere chatter, nonsense, prattle, twaddle, words

PALE, adjective anemic in comparison, become impotent, become tarnished, colorless in comparison, contrast, dim, dismal, drab, drained of color, dreary in comparison, fails in comparison, feeble in comparison, flat in comparison, flimsy in comparison, frail in comparison, ghastly, impotent, inadequate, incompetent, ineffective, insufficient, lackluster, languishing, lose their luster, lusterless, obfuscated, obscured, pallid

PALLIATE (Abate), verb allay, alleviate, appease, arrest, assuage, attemper, bate, bound, bring to a standstill, cease, check, circumscribe, curb, curtail, deactivate, decelerate, decrease, desist, diminish, discontinue, ease, eliminate, lenify, lessen, limit, make less severe, make mild, minimize, mitigate, moderate, modulate, obtund, pacify, qualify, quell, quiet, reduce, regulate, relieve, soften, still, stop, subdue, suppress, suspend, temper, terminate

PALLIATE (Excuse), verb absolve, acquit, adjudge innocent, allow for, assoil, be lenient, clear, condone, declare guiltless, defend, discharge, disculpate, dismiss charges, exculpate, exempt, exonerate, extenuate, forbear, forgive, give amnesty, give dispensation, grant absolution, grant amnesty, grant exemption, grant immunity, judge innocent, justify, let go, let off, liberate, license, make allowance for, overlook, pardon, permit, privilege, provide justification, release, release from obligation, remit the penalty, reprieve, rescue, set free, show mercy, shrive, spare, support, tolerate, vindicate

PALLIATIVE *(Abating),* **adjective** allaying, alleviating, alleviative, assuaging, assuasive, beneficial, calmative, consolatory, corrective, curative, easeful, helpful, lenient, drudge, mitigating, mitigative, modifying, modulatory, mollifying, pacifying, quelling, quieting, relieving, restorative, sedative, softening, soothing, stilling, subduing, tempering, therapeutic, tranquilizing

PALLIATIVE *(Excusing),* **adjective** apologetic, condonable, condoning, excepting, exculpable, exculpating, excusatory, exempting, expiating, extenuating, extenuative, forgiving, justificatory, justifying, pardoning, qualifying, vindicating, vindicative, vindicatory

PALPABLE, *adjective* able to be felt, able to be handled, able to be touched, apparent, bold, certain, clear, clear-cut, conspicuous, crystal clear, definite, detectable, discernible, disclosed, discoverable, distinct, easily perceived, easily seen, *evidens,* evident, exhibited, explicit, glaring, identifiable, in evidence, indisputable, indubitable, lucid, manifest, *manifestus,* marked, notable, noticeable, observable, obvious, overt, patent, perceivable, perceptible, perspicuous, plain, prominent, pronounced, readily perceived, readily seen, recognizable, revealed, salient, seeable, self-evident, stark, striking, tactile, tangible, touchable, *tractabilis,* unconcealed, uncontestable, uncovered, uncurtained, undisguised, undoubtable, unequivocal, unhidden, unmasked, unmistakable, unobscure, unobscured, unquestionable, unscreened, unshrouded, unveiled, visible

PALTER, *verb* act, act insincerely, be deceitful, be deceptive, be dishonest, be evasive, be false, be fraudulent, be hypocritical, be inconstant, be insincere, be mendacious, be perfidious, be uncandid, be untruthful, bear false witness, beguile, betray, bluff, break faith, cant, cheat, concoct, counterfeit, cozen, deal crookedly, deceive, defraud, delude, deviate, disguise, dissemble, dissimulate, distort, doctor, dodge, dupe, equivocate, evade, evade the truth, fabricate, fake, falsify, feign, fence, fool, forswear, gammon, hoax, inveigle, invent, lack candor, lead astray, lie, make false pretenses, make false statements, manufacture, masquerade, misdirect, misguide, misinform, mislead, misrender, misreport, misstate, perjure, pervert, playact, pose, pretend, prevaricate, profess, render lip service, represent falsely, shift, shuffle, talk insincerely, tergiversate, trifle, trump up, twist, use trickery, utter a falsehood, victimize

PALTRY, *adjective* below par, beneath contempt, beneath notice, cheap, contemptible, deficient, despicable, diminutive, humble, inadequate, incomplete, inconsequential, inconsiderable, insignificant, irrelevant, lacking, little, meager, mean, measly, mediocre, minute, *minutus,* miserable, modest, negligible, niggardly, nugatory, of little consequence, of little value, of no account, of small value, pathetic, petty, piddling, pitiful, poor, puny, *pusillus,* scant, scanty, scarce, shameful, slight, small, sorry, trifling, trivial, unappreciable, unimportant, unsatisfactory, unworthy of serious consideration, useless, valueless, vile, *vilis,* wanting, worthless, wretched

PANACEA, *noun* answer, assistance, balm, catholicon, correction, corrective, curative, cure, cure-all, cure for all ills, healing agent, improvement, medicament, medicine,

palliative, relief, remedy, restorative, restorative agent, solution, solution to difficulties, tonic, universal cure, universal remedy

PANDECT *(Code of laws),* **noun** body of law, canon, canon of laws, charter, code, codification, codified law, collection of laws, complete body of laws, digest, digest of law, enactment, legal code, principles, statute book

PANDECT *(Treatise),* **noun** analysis, article, commentary, compendium, complete digest, comprehensive digest, conspectus, data paper, digest, discourse, discussion, disquisition, dissertation, essay, excursus, exhaustive tract, explanation, exposition, formal discourse, formal essay, handbook, lucubration, manual, outline, paper, position paper, publication, study, summary, survey, syllabus, synopsis, tract, tractate, treatment

PANADEMIC, *noun* all-embracing epidemic, far-reaching disease, global epidemic, international dispose, universal disease, widespread disease, worldwide epidemic

PANDEMONIUM, *noun* affray, agitation, anarchy, bedlam, chaos, clamor, commotion, confusedness, confusion, convulsion, derangement, din, disarrangement, disarray, discomposure, disharmony, disorder, disorganization, disquietude, disruption, disturbance, embroilment, entanglement, ferment, fracas, frenzy, imbroglio, inquietude, jumble, lack of order, melee, mixup, noise, outcry, panic, racket, rampage, riot, roar, row, ruction, rumpus, stir, storm, trouble, tumult, turbulence, turmoil, unruliness, uproar, uproariousness, vociferation, want of method, wild uproar, wildness

PANDER, *verb* assist, attend, be instrumental, be of service, be servile, be subservient, be useful, cater, court favor, do service, furnish, give, gratify, help, humor, indulge, ingratiate oneself, make contented, make oneself useful, minister, obey, oblige, pamper, please, procure, provide, purvey, render service, satisfy, satisfy desires, serve, subserve, supply, tend, toady, truckle to, wait on, work in the service of

PANEL *(Discussion group),* **noun** advisory body, caucus, conference, *consilium,* council, deliberative body, exchange of views, forum, joint discussion, open discussion, open forum, round table, seminar, summit, symposium

PANEL *(Jurors),* **noun** body of jurors, body of persons summoned as jurors, body of persons sworn to render a verdict, group of jurors, jury, list of jurors, persons summoned to attend the court as jurymen, triers of fact
ASSOCIATED CONCEPTS: grand jury, panel en banc, petit jury

PANIC, *noun* affright, agitation, alarm, anxiety, awe, confusedness, confusion, consternation, cowardice, despair, discomposure, disorder, disquietude, disturbance, dread, fear, fearfulness, flutter, frenzy, fright, great fear, horror, hysteria, hystericalness, inquietude, irrational terror, nervousness, outcry, overpowering fright, pandemonium, pavor, perturbance, perturbation, phobia, sheer terror, stampede, state of terror, sudden fear, terror, trepidation, turmoil, unreasoning fear
ASSOCIATED CONCEPTS: heat of passion, manslaughter, temporary insanity

PANOPLY, *noun* armature, armor, armored protection, barrier, brigandine, buffer, covering, cuirass, defense, defensive arms, defensive clothing, defensive equipment, deterrent, envelopment, fender, fortification, full array, guard, means of protection, precaution, preservation, preventive measure, protection, protective covering, protective outfit, safeguard, screen, shelter, shield, targe

PAR *(Equality)*, **noun** *aequalis, aequus,* balance, equal footing, equal value, equal worth, equality, equalness, equipollence, equivalence, evenness, identicalness, identity, interchangeableness, likeness, sameness, similarity

ASSOCIATED CONCEPTS: above par value, at par value, par value of stock

PAR *(Face amount)*, **noun** amount, appraisal, appraisement, evaluation, face value, market price, price, rate, valuation, value, value in exchange, worth

PARADE, noun caravan, cavalcade, column, display, exhibit, exhibition, gala, grandeur, honorary march, honorary procession, march, motorcade, presentation, public procession, salute to, show, spectacle, stream of marchers, throngs of marchers, walk of marchers

ASSOCIATED CONCEPTS: parade law, permits

PARADIGM, noun archetype, example, exemplar, guide, ideal, model, norm, original, paradigma, pattern, prototype, sample, standard

PARADOX, noun antilogy, antinomy, contradiction, contrariety, disagreement, discrepancy, dissonance, enigma, incompatibility, incongruity, inconsistency, inconsonance, irreconcilability, lack of agreement, lack of harmony, perplexity, puzzle, *quod est admirabile contraque opinionem omnium,* seeming contradiction, self-contradiction

PARADOXICAL, adjective abnormal but true, absurd but true, ambiguous but true, bewildering, conflicting but true, confounding but true, contradictory but true, enigmatic but true, incompatible but true, incongruous but true, inconsistent but true, inconsonant but true

PARAGON, noun acme of perfection, champion, eminent person, example, exceller, exemplar, good example, great person, height of perfection, hero, ideal, man of mark, model, model of virtue, nonesuch, nonpareil, person of repute, prize, *specimen,* standard, standard for comparison, summit, superior individual

PARALEGAL, noun assistant, law assistant, legal administrative assistant, legal document assistant, legal assistant, legal technician

PARALLEL, adjective abreast, agreed, akin, aligned, analogous, coequal, coextending, coextensive, cognate, coincident, collateral, commensurable, comparable, comparing, comparison, concerted, concomitant, concurrent, congeneric, congenerous, congruous, consensual, consonant, correlative, correspondent, corresponding, equal, equidistant, equivalent, even, matched, matching, mutual, of a kind, opposite, proportioned, resembling, similar, symmetrical, tantamount, tied, uniform

PARALLEL, noun analogue, coequal, companion, compeer, complement, correspondent, counterpart, double, equal, equivalent, fellow, like, match, mate, peer, resemblance, same, twin

PARALLEL, verb associate, be comparable to, be equal with, be equivalent to, be parallel, coextend, compare, compare with, copy, correlate, correspond to, double, draw a parallel, duplicate, follow, go alongside, imitate, match, relate, run parallel to

PARAMOUNT, adjective arch, beyond compare, beyond comparison, cardinal, champion, chief, crowning, distinguished, extraordinary, first, foremost, grand, great, greatest, head, hegemonic, hegemonical, highest, incomparable, inimitable, leading, main, master, matchless, memorable, model, notable, peerless, preeminent, prepollent, prepotent, primary, prime, principal, prominent, regnant, reigning, remarkable, salient, second to none, significant, sovereign, *summus,* supereminent, superior, superlative, supreme, top, transcendent, transcendental, unapproached, unequaled, unexcelled, unmatched, unparalleled, unrivaled, unsurpassed, without parallel, worthy of notice, worthy of remark

PARANOIA, noun delusional insanity, delusions, diseased mind, disordered reason, insanity, lunacy, madness, mania, mental aberration, mental disease, phobia, unreasonable fear, unreasonable fright

PARAPHERNALIA *(Apparatus)*, **noun** accessories, accompaniments, accouterments, apparatus, appliances, articles, attachments, contrivances, conveniences, equipage, equipment, gear, impedimenta, implements, instruments, material, supplies, tools, utensils

PARAPHERNALIA *(Personal belongings)*, **noun** accessories, appointments, assets, chattels, effects, estate, goods, holdings, merchandise, movables, parcels, perquisites, personal effects, personal estate, personal property, personalty, possessions, property, resources, seisin, trappings

PARAPHRASE, noun abridgment, brief, citation, condensation, description, elucidation, enucleation, equivalent meaning, explanation, explication, free translation, free wording, indirect quotation, *interpretatio,* interpretation, loose rendering, loose translation, meaning, minute, nonliteral translation, paraphrasis, recapitulation, rendering, rendition, representation, restatement, rewording, simplification, summary, synopsis, translation, version

PARASITE, noun *adsecula,* barnacle, beggar, bloodsucker, borrower, burden, cadger, destructive agency, follower, leech, loafer, mendicant, nonworker, panhandler, scrounger, sponge, sycophant

PARCEL, noun acreage, area, block, district, enclave, enclosure, estate, field, ground, land, lot, property, patch, piece, piece of land, plot, plot of ground, plot of land, portion, real estate, region, section, sector, segment, square, terrain, territory, tract

ASSOCIATED CONCEPTS: conveyance, partition

PARCEL, verb administer, allocate, allot, appoint, apportion, appropriate, assign, award, bestow, carve, deal out, dispense, dispose of, *distribuere,* distribute, divide, divide into shares, *dividere,* dole out, give away, give out, grant, measure, mete, part with, *partiri,* partition, pass out, portion out, prorate, ration, sectionalize, segment, split up, subdivide

PARCEL OUT, verb allocate, allot, allow, apportion, appropriate, assign, award, bestow, contribute, dispense, distribute, divide, dole out, furnish, give, give away, give out, grant, hand out, hand over, issue, measure out, mete out, pay out, portion, present, ration, share, spare, supply

PARDON, noun absolution, acquittal, amnesty, clearance, clemency, compurgation, discharge, dismissal, dispensation, exemption from punishment, exoneration, forgiveness, leniency, obliteration of grievances, release,

release from penalty, release from punishment, relinquishment, reprieve, *venia*, vindication

ASSOCIATED CONCEPTS: amnesty, commutation, conditional pardon, parole, relief from disabilities, suspended sentence, unconditional pardon

FOREIGN PHRASES: *Veniae facilitas incentivum est delinquendi.* Facility of pardon is an encouragement to crime.

PARDON, verb acquit, cancel a punishment, cancel an offense, condone, deliver, discharge, emancipate, excuse, exonerate, expunge the record of, fail to exact a penalty, forgive, give absolution, grant amnesty, grant clemency, grant forgiveness, grant remission, let loose, liberate, overlook, purge, redeem, release, release from punishment, remission of guilt, reprieve, set at liberty, set free, suspend charges, vindicate

PARDONABLE, adjective admissible, allowable, blameless, condonable, defensible, *excusabilis*, excusable, expiable, faultless, forgivable, guiltless, innocent, inoffensive, justifiable, justified, passable, permitted, slight, unblamable, unculpable, understandable, unobjectionable, vindicable

PARENT, noun ancestor, author, author of one's existence, derivation, father, generator, mother, mover, originator, precursor, predecessor, primogenitor, procreator, progenitor, source

ASSOCIATED CONCEPTS: abusive parent, child welfare, neglect

PARENTAGE, noun ancestry, antecedents, birth, bloodline, derivation, descent, extraction, family, family connection, family tree, filiation, forebears, forefathers, foreparents, former generations, genealogical tree, genealogy, genesis, *genus*, house, line, line of ancestors, lineage, origin, paternity, pedigree, primogenitors, progenitors, source, stem, *stirps*, stock, tribe

ASSOCIATED CONCEPTS: determination of parentage, illegitimacy, legitimacy, paternity proceeding

PARENTHETICAL, adjective beside the mark, beside the point, beside the question, explanatory, explicative, expressive, external, extraneous, extrinsic, illustrative, incidental, inconsequent, inconsequential, inessential, inserted, intervening, nonessential, not at issue, not to the purpose, of interest, also an issue, also material, also on point

PARENTS, noun ancestor, begetter, creator, father, forebear, founder of the family, genitor, head of the household, immediate forebear, matriarch, mother, parens, patriarch, precursor, predecessor, procreator, progenitor

ASSOCIATED CONCEPTS: abandonment of child, adoptive parent, custody of children, duty to support, fitness of parent, foster parent, in loco parentis, natural parent, paternity proceeding, sole surviving parent

FOREIGN PHRASES: *Parentum est liberos alere etiam nothos.* It is the duty of parents to support their children even when illegitimate.

PARI MATERIA, noun in consonance, in harmony, on the same matter, read as one, read in tandem, read with respect of another, read together

PARIAH, noun castaway, deportee, derelict, exile, expatriate, fugitive, heretic, offender, outcast, outlaw, outsider, proscribed person, rebel, renegade, scab, sectarist, sectary, tergiversator

PARITY, noun alikeness, analogy, approximation, balance, close correspondence, coequality, comparability, comparison, correlation, correspondence, equability, equality, equation, equilibrium, equipoise, equivalence, equivalency, identical value, identicalness, likeness, parallelism, resemblance, sameness, semblance, similarity, similitude, state of being equal, symmetry, uniformity

ASSOCIATED CONCEPTS: wage parity

PARLANCE, noun address, allocution, choice of words, command of idiom, command of language, command of words, conference, conversation, delivery, diction, discourse, elocution, eloquence, expression, fashion, flow of language, flow of words, fluency, formulation, idiom, interlocution, locution, manner, manner of speaking, mode, oral communication, oratory, phraseology, recitation, rhetoric, sense of language, speech, spoken word, style, talk, terminology, tone, use of words, utterance, verbal intercourse, vocabulary, vocalization, wordage

PARLAY *(Bet),* **verb** ante, back, bet on, gamble, hazard, lay a wager, lay money on, make a bet, make book, play, risk, speculate, stake, take a chance, trust to chance, venture, wager

PARLAY *(Exploit successfully),* **verb** boost, broaden, build up, develop, elevate, escalate, exalt, expand, further, maximize, pyramid, raise, use

PARLEY, noun assembly, collocution, colloquy, communication, conclave, conference, congress, *conloqui*, consultation, convention, conversation, council, debate, deliberation, dialogue, diplomacy, *disceptare*, discussion, exchange of views, hearing, intercommunication, interlocution, interview, meeting, negotiation, oral communication, seminar, summit, summit conference, summit talk, symposiac, symposium, talk, verbal intercourse

PAROCHIAL, adjective biased, dogmatic, fanatical, hidebound, illiberal, insular, intolerant, jaundiced, limited, literal, narrow, narrow-minded, one-sided, opinionated, opinionative, orthodox, *parochialis*, partial, partisan, predisposed, prejudiced, prepossessed, provincial, regional, restricted to a small area, restricted to a small scope, sectarian, small-minded, unbending, uncatholic, unimaginative, unliberal, untolerating

PARODY, noun amphigory, apery, buffoonery, burlesque, caricature, cartoon, comical representation, distortion, exaggeration, farce, imitation, lampoon, ludicrous imitation, mime, mimicry, mockery, mummery, pasquinade, ridicula *imitatio*, ridicule, satire, squib, travesty

PAROL, adjective evidenced solely by speech, expressed, expressed solely by speech, lingual, not committed to writing, not expressed by writing, not written, nuncupative, oral, outspoken, told, unwritten, uttered, verbal, vocal, voiced

ASSOCIATED CONCEPTS: extrinsic evidence, parol agreement, parol assignment, parol contract, parol evidence rule, parol gift, parol lease

PAROLE, noun affirmation, conditional deliverance, conditional discharge, conditional disenthrallment, conditional disimprisonment, conditional emancipation, conditional freedom, conditional freedom from confinement, conditional independence, conditional liberation, conditional liberty, conditional release, conditional reprieve, declaration, deliverance, discharge, emancipation, freedom,

freeing from prison, granting freedom, liberation, liberty, release, release from prison, reprieve, setting free
ASSOCIATED CONCEPTS: commutation of sentence, conditions of parole, pardon, parole board, probation, release from dissabilities

PAROLE, *verb*   cast loose, conditionally release, conditionally release from imprisonment, deliver, discharge, disimprison, emancipate, free, let go free, let out of jail, let out of prison, liberate, make free, release, release conditionally, release from imprisonment, set at liberty, set free, turn loose, unbolt, uncage, unchain, unfetter, unharness, unshackle
ASSOCIATED CONCEPTS: commutation, commute, pardon, Parole Board, probation

PARRY, *verb*   avert, avoid, beat off, block, brush off, chase away, chase off, confute, counter, *defendere,* deflect, dodge, drive away, drive back, elude, escape, evade, fence, fend off, fight off, foil, force back, hedge, hold at bay, hold back, hold off, intercept, interfere, intervene, keep at bay, keep away, keep clear of, keep off, offer resistance, oppose, outface, prevent, *propulsare,* push away, put up a struggle, rebuff, refute, reluct, reluctate, repel, *repellere,* repulse, resist, sidestep, stave off, stop, stymie, take evasive action, thwart, turn aside, turn away, turn back, ward off, withstand

PARSIMONIOUS, *adjective*   acquisitive, avaricious, chary, cheap, close, closefisted, curmudgeonly, economical, excessively frugal, frugal, grasping, grudging, illiberal, mean, mercenary, miserly, niggardly, *parcus,* penny-pinching, penurious, petty, *restrictus,* scrimping, selfish, small-minded, sparing, stingy, stinting, tenax, thrifty, tight, uncharitable, ungenerous, unwilling to give, unyielding

PART *(Place),* *noun*   area, division, locale, location, premises, purlieus, quarter, room, section, site, spot
ASSOCIATED CONCEPTS: part in a courthouse

PART *(Portion),* *noun*   allocation, allowance, amount, bit, chip, chunk, collop, component, constituent, cutting, detachment, detail, division, excerpt, factor, fraction, fragment, helping, ingredient, interest, lump, measure, particle, percentage, piece, quantity, section, segment, serving, share, slab, slice, subdivision, subgroup
ASSOCIATED CONCEPTS: principal part

PART *(Role),* *noun*   burden, character, charge, chore, concern, function, impersonation, job, mimesis, *partes,* performance, portrayal, province, realm, representation, responsibility, task, undertaking

PART *(Leave),* *verb*   be gone, break away, defect, depart, escape, evacuate, get away from, go, go away, go forth, march off, migrate, move away, move out, quit, remove, retire, retreat, separate oneself from, set off, set out, take leave, take one's departure, tear oneself away, withdraw

PART *(Separate),* *verb*   be severed, be sundered, bifurcate, break, carve, compartmentalize, cut in two, detach, disassociate, disconnect, disengage, disentangle, disjoin, dismember, dissever, dissociate, dissolve, disunite, divide, *dividere,* fissure, halve, isolate, keep apart, parcel, *partiri,* partition, portion, section, *separare,* sever, sort out, split, stand between, subdivide, sunder, tear assunder, undo, unloose

PART WITH, *verb*   award, bequeath, bestow, cede, contribute, confer, depart, dispense with, dispose of, donate,

get away from, gift, give away, give up, grant, impart with, leave, separate from, pass, transfer, turn over, will

PARTAKE, *verb*   accept, be a party to, experience, have a hand in, have a portion of, have a share of, lend oneself to, participate, receive, sample, savor, share, share in, take, take a share of, take an active part in, take part in, taste

PARTIAL *(Biased),* *adjective*   bigoted, *cupidus,* discriminatory, favorably disposed, inclined, influenced, *iniquus,* interested, jaundiced, narrow-minded, one-sided, partisan, predisposed, prejudiced, prepossessed, prone, restricted, *studiosus,* subjective, swayed, unbalanced, unequal, uneven, unfair, unjust, unjustified, unreasonable
ASSOCIATED CONCEPTS: partial acceptance, partial delivery, partial performance, partial restraint, partial summary judgment

PARTIAL *(Part),* *adjective*   apart, confined, divided, divisible, factional, fragmentary, incomplete, limited, narrow, not complete, not completed, *partim,* sectional, split, uncompleted, unfinished, unperformed, wanting

PARTIAL *(Relating to a part),* *adjective*   abridged, deficient, divided, divisible, fractional, fragmentary, imperfect, incomplete, inexact, insufficient, limited, *partim,* scanty, sectional, segmental, sketchy, uncompleted, undeveloped, unfinalized, unfinished, unperformed, unthorough, wanting
ASSOCIATED CONCEPTS: partial payment, partial summary judgment

PARTIALITY, *noun*   affinity, attachment, attraction, bent, bias, biased judgment, discrimination, favor, favoritism, fondness, inclination, *iniquitas,* injustice, intolerance, leaning, liking, one-sidedness, partisanship, penchant, preconception, predilection, predisposition, preference, preferential treatment, prejudgment, prejudice, prepossession, proclivity, propensity, taste

PARTICIPANT, *noun*   abettor, accessory, accomplice, adjuvant, aid, ally, assistant, associate, attendant, auxiliary, coadjutor, collaborator, colleague, comate, companion, comrade, confederate, cooperator, copartner, coworker, fellow, fellow worker, helper, mate, partaker, *particeps,* participator, partner, party, shareholder, sharer
ASSOCIATED CONCEPTS: participant in a crime

PARTICIPATE, *verb*   act in concert, act together, affiliate with, aid, associate, be a party to, be in league with, be involved, become involved with, collaborate, compete, confederate, *consortem,* contribute, cooperate, engage, engage in, enter into, *esse participem,* get in the act, go along with, have a hand in, have a part in, have a part of, have a share of, join, join forces, join in, join in partnership with, partake, play a part in, share, share in, take a part in, take a part of, take an active part in, take an interest in, take part, undertake, unite efforts with, unite with, work together
ASSOCIATED CONCEPTS: participate in a business venture, participate in a conspiracy, participate in a crime, participate in a labor dispute

PARTICLE, *noun*   atom, bit, component part, crumb, cutting, fragment, grain, granule, hint, mite, modicum, moiety, molecule, morsel, piece, pittance, point, scintilla, snippet, speck, spot, suggestion, trace

PARTICULAR *(Exacting),* *adjective*   accurate, astringent, attentive, attentive to detail, careful, choosy, conscientious, critical, *delicatus,* demanding, difficult to please, discriminating, discriminative, *elegans,* epicurean, excessively critical, exigent, fastidious, faultfinding, finical, finicky, fussy, hairsplitting, hard to please, heedful, hypercritical, inflexible, meticulous, mindful, overconscientious, overcritical, overfastidious, overmeticulous, painstaking, persnickety, picky, precise, punctilious, quality-minded, querulous, regardful, rigid, rigorous, scrupulous, selective, stern, strict, stringent, thorough, thoroughgoing, uncompromising, unyielding

PARTICULAR (*Individual*), **adjective**   characteristic, definite, distinct, distinctive, distinguished, especial, exclusive, original, own, peculiar, personal, respective, separate, single, singular, special, specific, unique, unusual
ASSOCIATED CONCEPTS: particular gift, particular purpose
FOREIGN PHRASES: *Generale tantum valet in generalibus, quantum singulare in singulis.* That which is general prevails in general matters, as that which is particular prevails in particular matters.

PARTICULAR (*Specific*), **adjective**   characteristic, chosen, differential, differentiated, distinct, distinctive, distinguishable, distinguished, eccentric, especial, exceptional, express, extraordinary, idiosyncratic, individual, marked, noteworthy, odd, outstanding, peculiar, prominent, *proprius,* select, selected, separate, *separatus,* signal, single, singular, special, striking, uncommon, unique, unmistakable, unusual

PARTICULAR, **noun**   article, aspect, case, circumstance, detail, event, experience, fact, feature, incident, incidental, instance, item, item of information, matter, minutia, occasion, occurrence, particularity, piece of information, point, punctilio, respect, single case, special point, specific, specification
ASSOCIATED CONCEPTS: bill of particulars

PARTICULARITY, **noun**   care, carefulness, characteristic, characteristic quality, circumstantiality, conscientiousness, criticalness, detail, discriminatingness, discrimination, distinctive feature, exactingness, exactitude, exactness, fastidiousness, feature, finicality, finicalness, fussiness, individuality, item, lineament, mark, meticulousness, minute circumstance, minuteness, particularness, perfectionism, preciseness, precision, punctiliousness, rigidness, scrupulosity, scrupulousness, selectiveness, singleness, singularity, special point, specific quality, strictness, trait, uniqueness

PARTICULARLY, **adverb**   above all, chiefly, distinctly, eminently, especially, expressly, extraordinally, individually, inordinately, mainly, markedly, *maxime,* notably, observably, peculiarly, *praecipue, praesertim,* preeminently, primarily, principally, prominently, remarkably, signally, singularly, specially, specifically, strikingly, supremely, uncommonly, uncustomarily, unfamiliarly, uniquely, unusually

PARTISAN, **adjective**   biased, clannish, cliquish, denominational, devoted, factional, factionary, fanatic, *fautor, homo studiosus,* influenced, leagued, partial, predisposed, sectarian, swayed, undetached, undispassionate

PARTISAN, **noun**   adherent, advocate, ally, apostle, backer, believer, champion, comrade, confederate, copartner, coworker, defender, devotee, disciple, encourager, enthusiast, favorer, fellow worker, follower, friend, hanger on, mainstay, maintainer, participant, partner, party-liner, party member, patron, promoter, proselyte, satellite, seconder, sectarian, sectary, sponsor, support, supporter, sustainer, sympathizer, upholder, votary, zealot, zealotist
ASSOCIATED CONCEPTS: discrimination, partisan motives

PARTISANSHIP, **noun**   advocacy, blind allegiance, blind sponsor, blind support, blind sympathy, proselytism, sectarian allegiance, unfair allegiance, unjust allegiance, zealotry
ASSOCIATED CONCEPTS: election law

PARTITION, **verb**   allocate, allot, apportion, break up, carve, compartmentalize, cut up, dissect, distribute, divide, divide into distinct portions, divide into portions, divide into shares, divide proportionately, divide up, dole out, form into classes, group, mete, mete out, parcel out, pigeonhole, place in a category, portion, portion out, prorate, section, sectionalize, segment, sever, sever the unity of possession, share, split up, subdivide
ASSOCIATED CONCEPTS: partition property

PARTNER, **noun**   abettor, accessory, accomplice, adjutant, adjutor, adjuvant, aid, aider, ally, assistant, associate, coadjutant, coadjutor, cohelper, collaborator, colluder, comate, companion, compeer, confederate, consociate, cooperator, coowner, copartner, coworker, fellow worker, helper, member of a partnership, partaker, *particeps,* participant, participator, sharer, *socius,* teammate, teamworker, workfellow
ASSOCIATED CONCEPTS: equal partner, general partner, limited partner, managing partner, nominal partner, partner in crime, silent partner, surviving partner
FOREIGN PHRASES: *Cum aliquis renunciaverit societati, solvitur societas.* When any partner renounces the partnership, the partnership is dissolved. *Socii mei socius meus socius non est.* The partner of my partner is not my partner.

PARTNERSHIP, **noun**   alliance, association, coalition, combination, concord, confederacy, confederation, conjunction, connection, consociation, *consortio,* consortium, cooperation, cooperative society, copartnership, federation, fellowship, firm, guild, joint interest, league, legal entity, mutual company, participation, pool, *societas,* sodality, syndicate
ASSOCIATED CONCEPTS: commercial partnership, copartnership, corporation, dissolution of partnership, general partnership, joint enterprise, joint venture, limited partnership, partnership agreement, partnership assets, partnership at will, partnership debts, partnership for a single transaction, partnership property, professional partnership, silent partner, special partnership, voluntary association
FOREIGN PHRASES: *Nemo debet in communione invitus teneri.* No one should be retained in a partnership against his will. *Si alicujus rei societas sit et finis negotio impositus est, finitus societas.* If there is a partnership in any matter, and the business is concluded, the partnership is ended.

PARTY (*Litigant*), **noun**   adversary, appellant, appellee, challenger, charger, claimant, complainant, contender, contestant, controversialist, defendant, disputant, intervener, libelant, opposing party, petitioner, plaintiff, respondent, suitor
ASSOCIATED CONCEPTS: adverse party, defect in parties, disinterested party, indispensable party, jurisdiction of parties, material party, mutuality of parties, necessary parties, nominal party, nonjoinder of parties, opposing party, party-in-practice, prevailing party, proper party, real party in interest, substantial party
FOREIGN PHRASES: *Saepe constitutum est, res inter alios judicatas aliis non praejudicare.* It has often been decided that matters adjudged between others ought not to prejudice those who are not parties.

PARTY (*Participant*), **noun**   attendant, cooperator, member, partaker, participator, partisan, partner, sharer

ASSOCIATED CONCEPTS: accommodation party, competent party, guilty party, injured party, innocent party, real party in interest, third party

PARTY *(Political organization),* **noun** association, body, caucus, club, coalition, combine, confederation, faction, group, league, lobby, organized group, party machine, political machine

PASS *(Advance),* **verb** *abalienatio,* award, bequeath, cede, change, change ownership, communicate, confer ownership, continue, convey, cross, deliver over, devolve, endow, flow, go, go by, go on, go past, *praetervehi,* proceed, progress, relay, remise, transfer ownership, transfer title, *transgredi, transire,* transmit, transpire
ASSOCIATED CONCEPTS: pass by will, pass title

PASS *(Approve),* **verb** accede to, accept, acquiesce, adopt, advocate, affirm, agree to, allow, approbate, assent, authorize, be in favor of, carry, confirm, consent, declare lawful, decree, dictate, enact, endorse, establish, establish by law, favor, give approval, give legislative sanction to, institute, institute by law, iubere, legalize, legislate, legitimize, make into law, make legal, ordain, ordain by law, prescribe, put in force, put into effect, put through, ratify, sanction, support, sustain, uphold, validate, vote favorably, vote in
ASSOCIATED CONCEPTS: pass a law

PASS *(Determine),* **verb** announce, decide, declare, decree, deliver, deliver a judgment, determine, enunciate, give an opinion, impart, ordain, present, pronounce, pronounce judgment, put forth, render a decision, render a judgment, rule, set forth
ASSOCIATED CONCEPTS: pass judgment

PASS *(Satisfy requirements),* **verb** accomplish, achieve, *approbare,* attain, be accepted, be graduated, be promoted, be successful, be victorious, come up to the standard, conform to, conquer, do well, earn, finish, fulfill, get by, get through, make one's mark, master, meet requirements, prevail, qualify, reach, realize, satisfy requirements, stand the test, succeed, triumph

PASS JUDGMENT, **verb** adjudge, adjudicate, administrator, arbitrate, ascertain, assess, compromise, conclude, decide, decree, declare, deliver, determine, dispense justice, draw a conclusion, establish, find, hold, interpret, judge, moderate, negotiate, officially act, order, referee, resolve, rule, umpire

PASS UP, **verb** abandon, abdicate, abjure, abstain, avoid, cease, cede, deny oneself, desist from, dispense with, disposed of, do without, drop, eschew, fast, forbear, forego, forfeit, forgo, forswear, give up, give up on, go without, hold back, hold off, lay down, leave off, let alone, make do without, not use, refrain, release, relinquish, renounce, reserve, resign, sacrifice, shun, surrender, waive, withhold, write off, yield, yield up
ASSOCIATED CONCEPTS: forego interest owed, forego opportunity

PASSABLE, *adjective* acceptable, accessible, achievable, admissible, allowable, approachable, bearable, beaten, broad, capable of passing, clear, crossable, easy, fair, fit for travel, fordable, free, mediocre, middling, moderate, navigable, open, ordinary, penetrable, pervious, presentable, pretty good, reachable, realizable, receivable, serviceable, tolerable, travelable, traveled, traversable, unimpeded, unobstructed, usable, within reach

PASSION, *noun* agitation, anger, ardency, ardor, avidity, craze, desire, eagerness, ecstasy, emotion, eruption, excitability, excitement, explosion, fanaticism, feeling, ferment, fervency, fervor, fierceness, fire, frenzy, furor, fury, glow, gusto, heat, hunger, impetuosity, impulse, infatuation, intensity, intoxication, ire, irresistible urge, itch, lust, mania, rabidity, rage, rampage, rampancy, rapture, storm, strong feeling, temper, thrill, transport, vehemence, vehement desire, verve, violence, violent anger, wrath, zeal
ASSOCIATED CONCEPTS: heat of passion

PASSIVE, *adjective* acquiescent, amenable, apathetic, calm, compliable, compliant, complying, concessive, conformable, docile, dormant, duteous, dutiful, enduring, feeble, flexible, forbearant, heedless, indifferent, indolent, influenced, irresolute, lamblike, languorous, malleable, nonresistant, nonresisting, obedient, obeisant, obsequious, otiose, phlegmatic, pliable, pliant, quiescent, receptive, recumbent, resigned, resistless, restrained, sequacious, servile, subdued, subject, submissive, subordinate, subservient, supine, supple, tame, tractable, unassertive, undemonstrative, unopposing, unresistant, unresisting, yielding
ASSOCIATED CONCEPTS: passive negligence, passive tortfeasor

PAST, *adjective* ancient, antediluvian, antiquated, archaic, back, defunct, departed, elapsed, expired, forgotten, former, gone, gone by, historical, irrecoverable, lapsed, last, late, lost, no longer functioning, obsolete, old, outdated, outmoded, over, passed, previous, prior, quondam, retired, unrecollected, unremembered
ASSOCIATED CONCEPTS: past consideration, past recollection

PAST, *noun* ancient times, antecedence, anteriority, antiquity, history, former time, former times, long ago, past times, preexistence, previous time, previousness, retrospection, the past, times past

PAST DUE, *adverb* in arrears, in debt, in default, outstanding, overdrawn, overdue

PATENT, *adjective* *apertus,* apparent, *clarus,* clear, conspicuous, disclosed, discoverable, easy to be seen, evident, exposed, exposed to view, free to all, glaring, in full view, in view, individual, manifest, *manifestus,* noticeable, observable, obvious, open, ostensible, overt, perceivable, perceptible, perspicuous, plain, plain to be seen, prominent, public, published, revealed, standing out, uncamouflaged, unconcealed, undisguised, unhidden, unmasked, unobstructed, unshaded, unusual, visible, wide-open
ASSOCIATED CONCEPTS: patent ambiguity, patent danger, patent defect, patent error

PATENT, *noun* certificate of invention, *diplomatis,* exclusive license, exclusive privilege, exclusive right, exclusive title, governmental grant, grant, grant of authority, legal right, license, permit, privilege, right, right to profits accruing, use and title
ASSOCIATED CONCEPTS: assignment of a patent, infringement of a patent, patent license, patent right

PATERNAL, *adjective* ancestral, benevolent, benign, family, fatherlike, fatherly, kindly, parental, paternus, patriarchal, patrimonial, patrius, protective

PATERNITY, *noun* ancestry, derivation, descent, fatherhood, fathership, lineage, male parentage, origin, parentage, paternal parentage, progenitorship
ASSOCIATED CONCEPTS: paternity proceeding

FOREIGN PHRASES: *Filiatio non potest probari.* Filiation cannot be proved. *Pater est quem nuptiae demonstrant.* He is the father whom the marriage points out.

PATH, noun access, access path, access road, approach, avenue, channel, course, device, entrance, easement, footpath, ingress, means, method, passage, passageway, pathway, right of way, road, roadway, route, street, trail, walkway, way

PATIENCE (Composure), **noun** acceptance, calm, composure, condonation, ease, equanimity, even temper, forbearance, forgiveness, imperturbability, indulgence, lenience, leniency, longanimity, moderation, passiveness, passivity, placidity, poise, refusal to be provoked, resignation, self-control, self-possession, serenity, stoicism, sufferance, temperament, temperance, tolerance, tranquility, understanding

PATIENCE (Indefatigability), **noun** assiduousness, determination, diligence, firmness, persistence, pertinacity, quiet perseverance, sedulity, staying power, tenacity of purpose

PATIENT, adjective acquiescent, agreeable, assiduous, calm, compliant, composed, constant, continuing, controlled, decided, determined, diligent, docile, dogged, dutiful, easygoing, enduring, firm, forbearing, forgiving, hard working, imperturbable, indefatigable, indulgent, lamblike, levelheaded, long-suffering, longanimous, meek, mild, mild-tempered, nonresisting, pacific, passive, *patiens,* peaceable, perseverant, persevering, persistent, persisting, pertinacious, philosophic, placid, pliant, plodding, quiescent, quiet, quietly persevering, reconciled, relentless, resigned, resolute, resolved, restrained, sedulous, self-controlled, serene, steadfast, steady, stoic, stoical, submissive, sympathetic, tenacious, *tolerans,* tolerant, tractable, tranquil, unceasing, unchangeable, uncomplaining, uncompromising, undaunted, understanding, undeviating, undiscouraged, undisturbed, unfaltering, unflagging, unflinching, unmurmuring, unperturbed, unrelaxing, unrelenting, unremitting, unresisting, unruffled, unshaken, unswerving, untiring, unvexed, unwavering, unwearied, unwearying, unyielding, yielding

PATIENT, noun *aeger, aegrotus,* case, convalescent, convalescent case, hospital case, hospitalized person, ill individual, inmate, invalid, medical case, one seeking cure, one seeking relief, one undergoing therapy, one undergoing treatment, shut-in, sick individual, sick person, sickling, victim
ASSOCIATED CONCEPTS: doctor-patient privilege

PATROL, verb attend, be on the alert, be on the lookout, be on the watch, *circumire,* cover, cover a beat, go the rounds, guard, inspect, keep an eye on, keep guard, keep in view, keep vigil, keep watch, look out, march, monitor, observe, overlook, pace, perform sentry duty, police, protect, reconnoiter, safeguard, scan, scout, stand guard, stand sentinel, superintend, sweep through, traverse, walk, walk a beat, watch

PATRON (Influential supporter), **noun** advocate, backer, benefactor, champion, defender, endorser, favorer, financer, friend, guardian, helper, influential sponsor, investor, leader, patronus, philanthropist, promoter, sponsor, supporter, upholder

PATRON (Regular customer), **noun** business contact, buyer, client, *consultor,* consumer, customer, *emptor,* frequenter, patronizer, prospective buyer, purchaser, shopper, supporter, vendee

PATRONAGE (Power to appoint jobs), **noun** advantage, assistance, *auctoritas,* authority, backing, choice, control, controlling power, directing agency, dominance, domination, *favor,* good offices, *gratia, indulgentia,* influence, influentiality, *patrocinium,* persuasion, position of influence, power, *praesidium,* predominance, preference, right of choice, selection, sway

PATRONAGE (Support), **noun** aid, assistance, backing, care, commendation, commercial backing, cordial assistance, countenance, encouragement, favor, friendly interest, friendship, guardianship, guidance, help, influence, interest, protection, protectorship, recommendation, special privileges, sponsorship, support, tutelage

PATRONIZE (Condescend toward), **verb** assume a lofty bearing, deign, favor, grant, indulge, look down on, lower oneself, oblige, talk down to, treat in a condescending way, vouchsafe

PATRONIZE (Trade with), **verb** be a customer of, buy from, deal with, do business with, *favere,* favor with one's patronage, frequent, frequent as a customer, have dealings with, purchase from, shop at, shop with, support, traffic with, transact business with, transact with, use

PATTERN, noun antetype, archetype, basis, criterion, design, die, draft, example, *exemplar, exemplum,* form, guide, ideal, impression, layout, matrix, model, mold, norm, original, outline, paradigm, paragon, plan, precedent, prototype, rule, sample, shape, specifications, *specimen,* standard, standard of criticism, standard of judgment, template, tracing
ASSOCIATED CONCEPTS: pattern jury instructions

PAUCITY, noun absence, bare subsistence, dearth, deficiency, deprivation, destitution, drought, exigency, exiguity, famine, fewness, finite quantity, fraction, inadequacy, infrequency, insufficiency, lack, limited amount, minimum, minority, modicum, need, *paucitas,* pittance, poverty, privation, rareness, scantiness, scantness, scarceness, scarcity, shortage, small number, small quantity, sparseness, sparsity, thinness, trickle, trifle, uncommonness, want

PAUSE, noun abeyance, armistice, break, breather, breathing spell, cessation, deferment, delay, demur, demurral, disconnection, gap, halt, hesitance, hesitancy, hesitation, *intercapedo,* interim, interlude, *intermissio,* intermission, interruption, interval, *intervallum,* intervening period, lag, letup, lull, moratorium, procrastination, recess, relaxation, remission, respite, rest, rest period, space, standstill, stay, stillness, stoppage, suspension, time out, truce, vacation

PAUSE, verb be dubious, be irresolute, be uncertain, bide time, break, breathe, cast anchor, cease, come to a standstill, consider, dally, dawdle, delay, deliberate, demur, desist, discontinue, dwell, forbear, halt, hang back, hesitate, hold back, hold off, intermit, *intermittere,* interrupt, linger, loiter, mark time, *morari,* put off, reflect, repose, rest, slacken, stall, stand still, stay, stop and consider, straddle, suspend, take a breather, take time out, tarry, think over, think twice, vacillate, wait, waver, weigh

PAWN, verb bond, deposit, deposit as collateral, deposit as security, give as security, give in earnest, guarantee, hypothecate, impignorate, mortgage, offer collateral, oppignerare, *pignerare,* pledge, post, put at hazard, put at stake, put in pledge, risk, stake, wager

445

PAY

PAY, noun allowance, award, compensation, consideration, defrayal, defrayment, earnings, emolument, fee, grant, hire, income, indemnity, meed, *merces,* monetary return, payment, perquisite, profit, reckoning, recompense, reimbursement, remittance, remuneration, repayment, return, revenue, reward, salary, settlement, solatium, stipend, *stipendium,* support, wages

PAY, verb acquit, adjust, award, be a good investment, be profitable, bear the cost, clear, compensate, contribute, defray, deposit, disburse, discharge a debt, expend, exsolvere, finance, foot, give payment, hand over, honor, indemnify, liquidate, make a good return, make compensation, make good, make payment, make restitution, meet, *numerare, pendere,* present, quit, ransom, reckon with, recompense, reimburse, remunerate, render, reward, satisfy, settle, spend, square, square accounts, subsidize, support, tender

PAY DAMAGES, verb award damages, conclude, finalize, indemnify, make restitution, make whole, pay for injuries sustained, pay for losses sustained, pay for the losses, pay just compensation, pay the value of a case, recompense, remunerate, resolve, restitution, restoration, settle
ASSOCIATED CONCEPTS: pay damages for defrauding investors

PAYABLE, adjective collectable, due, justly claimable, mature, maturing, outstanding, owing, redeemable, uncollected, unpaid, unsatisfied, unsettled
ASSOCIATED CONCEPTS: accounts payable, bills payable, due and payable, payable to bearer, payable upon demand, sum payable

PAYEE, noun acceptor, assignee, consignee, devisee, donee, drawer, endorsee, grantee, recipient, taker, transferee

PAYMENT (Act of paying), **noun** acquittal, acquittance, amortization, amortizement, clearance, compensation, defrayal, defrayment, disbursement, discharge of a debt, expenditure, liquidation, outlay, quittance, receipt in full, reckoning, recompense, reimbursement, remittance, restitution, return, satisfaction, settlement, spending, subsidy

PAYMENT (Remittance), **noun** allotment, allowance, amount, charge, compensation, consideration, earnings, emolument, expenditure, expense, fee, gratuity, guerdon, honorarium, indemnification, indemnity, money, pay, premium, quittance, recompense, reimbursement, remittance, remuneration, reparation, restitution, salary, solatium, stipend, tribute, wage
FOREIGN PHRASES: *In satisfactionibus non permittitur amplius fieri quam semel factum est.* In settlements, more must not be received than was received once for all. *Reprobata pecunia liberat solventem.* Money refused releases the debtor. *Quicquid solvitur, solvitur secundum modum solventis; quicquid recipitur, recipitur secundum modum recipientis.* Whatever money is paid, is paid according to the direction of the payor, whatever money is received, is received according to that of the recipient. *Qui ignorat quantum solvere debeat, non potest improbus videre.* He who does not know how much he ought to pay, cannot seem dishonest. *Jus non patitur ut idem bis solvatur.* Law does not suffer the same thing to be twice paid. *Bona fides non patitur ut bis idem exigatur.* Good faith does not allow us to demand the payment of the same thing twice.

PAYOFF (Payment in full), **noun** discharge, pay-out, satisfaction in full, settlement

PAYOFF (Result), **noun** closure, conclusion, consummation, determination, end, finale, finish

PAYROLL, noun allowance, compensation, disbursement of salary, employees' earnings, employees' salaries, labor expense, list of paid employees, list of salaried employees, list of wages to be paid out, payment, payment for services, recompense, remuneration, salary, stipend, wages
ASSOCIATED CONCEPTS: certification payroll, payroll check-off system, payroll deduction, payroll tax

PEACE, noun accord, adjustment of differences, agreement, alliance, amity, armistice, brotherhood, calm, calmness, coexistence, community of interests, conciliation, concord, concordance, concordancy, *concordia,* consentaneity, consentaneousness, cooperation, end of hostilities, fellowship, fraternalism, freedom from war, friendliness, friendship, good will, harmoniousness, harmony, hush, law and order, lull, neutrality, oneness, order, orderliness, *otium,* pacification, pact, *pax,* quiescence, quiet, quietness, rapport, reconciliation, repose, serenity, silence, stillness, suspension of hostilities, tranquility, treaty, truce, unanimity, unity
ASSOCIATED CONCEPTS: breach of the peace, disturbing the peace, peace officer
FOREIGN PHRASES: *Paci sunt maxime contraria vis et injuria.* Violence and injury are especially hostile to peace.

PEACE OFFICER, noun arm of the law, civil officer, constable, custodian of the law, detective, guard, guardian of the peace, law enforcement agent, law officer, member of the police force, officer, officer of the law, patrolman, police, police constable, police officer, policeman, policewoman, protector, security officer, sheriff

PEACEABLE, adjective agreeable, amiable, amicable, bloodless, calm, composed, contented, disposed to peace, easygoing, equable, forgiving, free from war, friendly, gentle, good-tempered, halcyon, halcyonian, imperturbable, inoffensive, kindly, lamblike, mild, moderate, neutral, noncombative, orderly, pacific, pacificatory, pacifistic, patient, peace-loving, peaceful, peacelike, *placabilis,* placid, *placidus,* quiescent, quiet, reasonable, restrained, satisfied, sedate, serene, slow to take offense, sober, still, tame, temperate, tolerant, tranquil, unagitated, unanxious, unbellicose, unbelligerent, uncontentious, undisturbed, unexcitable, unexcited, unmilitant, unmoved, unpugnacious, unresisting, unruffled, untroubled, well-disposed

PECCABLE, adjective bad, below par, blamable, blameworthy, censurable, culpable, defective, erring, exceptionable, fallen, fallible, faulty, flawed, guilty, illaudable, imperfect, inadequate, iniquitous, lacking, lax, less than perfect, liable to err, liable to sin, objectionable, recreant, reprehensible, reprobate, tainted, twisted, unchaste, uncommendable, unheroic, unprincipled, unrighteous, unsound, unstable, unvirtuous, virtueless, warped, wayward

PECCANT (Culpable), **adjective** aberrant, accursed, accusable, amoral, astray, bad, base, blameful, blameworthy, censurable, chargeable, criminal, criminous, debauched, dishonest, erroneous, evil, execrable, faultful, fiendish, foul, full of mischief, guilty, guilty of transgression, heinous, illegal, immoral, impious, incorrigible, inexcusable, infamous, iniquitous, intolerable, maleficent, maleficial, meriting blame, mischievous, naughty, nefarious, offensive, *peccans,* reprehensible, reprobate, scandalous, shameful, sinful, transgressing, trespassing, unforgivable, unjust, unjustifiable, unpardonable, unprincipled, unrighteous, unscrupulous, unvirtuous, unworthy, vicious, vile, villainous, wicked, without excuse, wretched, wrong, wrongful

PECCANT (Unhealthy), **adjective** afflicting, contaminated, corroding, corrosive, dangerous, deadly, deleterious, detrimental, disadvantageous, diseased, disserviceable, envenomed, gravis, harmful, injurious, insalubrious, insalubris, lethal, malefic, maleficent, malignant, miasmal, morbid, morbific, nocuous, noisome, noxious, perilous, pestilent, poisoned, poisonous, septic, tainted, toxic, unfavorable to health, unhygienic, unwholesome, venomous, virulent

PECULATE, **verb** appropriate criminally, appropriate dishonestly, appropriate illegally, appropriate wrongfully, bilk, cheat, cozen, deceive, defraud, divert, embezzle, misappropriate, mulct, obtain money on false pretenses, obtain under false pretenses, pilfer, purloin, rob, steal, swindle

PECULIAR (Curious), **adjective** aberrant, abnormal, abnormous, alien, anomalistic, anomalistical, anomalous, astonishing, bizarre, breaking with tradition, eccentric, foreign, inexplicable, irregular, little-known, mysterious, mystifying, odd, out of place, out of the ordinary, out of the way, outlandish, perplexing, preternatural, puzzling, queer, rare, remarkable, signal, singular, startling, strange, supernatural, surprising, unaccountable, unaccustomed, unclassified, unconformable, unconventional, uncustomary, unexampled, unexpected, unfamiliar, unheard of, unimaginable, unnatural, unorthodox, weird

PECULIAR (Distinctive), **adjective** atypical, characteristic, contrasted, contrasting, contrastive, deviating, different, differentiated, differing, disagreeing, discordant, discrepant, disparate, dissimilar, dissonant, distinct, distinguishable, distinguished, divergent, exceptional, extraordinary, idiosyncratic, in a different class, inconformable, incongruent, incongruous, individual, marked, noteworthy, original, out of the ordinary, particular, separated, singular, special, uncommon, unconformable, unconforming, unequal, unimitated, unique, unlike, unusual, variant

PECULIARITY, **adjective** atypical, characteristic, contrasted, contrasting, contrastive, deviating, different, differentiated, differing, disagreeing, discordant, discrepant, disparate, dissimilar, dissonant, distinct, distinctive, distinguishable, distinguished, divergent, exceptional, extraordinary, idiosyncratic, in a different class, incongruent, incongruous, individual, marked, one-of-a-kind, original, particular, singular, special, uncommon, unconformable, unequal, unique, unlike all others, unusual, variant
ASSOCIATED CONCEPTS: peculiar susceptibilities

PECUNIARY, **adjective** budgetary, economic, economical, fiducial, fiduciary, financial, fiscal, monetary, numismatical, nummary, pecuniarius, sumptuary
ASSOCIATED CONCEPTS: pecuniary advantage, pecuniary damages, pecuniary gain, pecuniary injury, pecuniary interest, pecuniary legacy, pecuniary loss, pecuniary profit

PEDAGOGUE, **noun** academician, adviser, classmaster, don, educator, expounder, faculty member, governor, guide, headmaster, inculcator, instructor, learned man, lecturer, magister, man of letters, master, preceptor, professor, sage, scholar, schoolman, schoolmaster, schoolteacher, teacher, trainer, tutor

PEDANT, **noun** affecter, bluffer, closed-minded person, dogmatist, narrow-minded person, opinionated person, philosophaster, pretender, sciolist

PEDESTRIAN, **adjective** arid, banal, barren, boresome, boring, characterless, cold, colorless, commonplace, dead, deadly, diffuse, drab, drearisome, dreary, dry, dull, flat, graceless, hackneyed, heavy, humorless, inelegant, inferior, insipid, jejune, lifeless, meaningless, mediocre, monotonous, ordinary, plain, platitudinous, plodding, pointless, ponderous, prosaic, prosy, soporific, spiritless, stale, stodgy, stuffy, tame, tasteless, tedious, tiresome, trite, unamusing, uncaptivating, uncharming, unenlivened, unentertaining, unimaginative, uninspiring, uninteresting, uninventive, unlively, unoriginal, unpoetical, unreadable, unscintillating, unsparkling, unvaried, unvivid, unwitty, usual, wearisome

PEDESTRIAN, **noun** ambulator, foot passenger, foot traveler, marcher, peripatetic, roamer, rover, traveler afoot, walker

PEER, **noun** associate, coequal, companion, compeer, competitor, comrade, contemporary, contender, corrival, equal, equivalent, fellow, likeness, match, mate, opposite number, par, parallel, rival

PEJORATIVE, **adjective** abusive, acrimonious, belittling, blackening, calumnious, castigatory, censorious, critical, cynical, damaging, decrying, defamatory, denigrating, denunciatory, depreciative, depreciatory, derisive, derogative, derogatory, detracting, disapproving, discourteous, disdainful, disparaging, disrespectful, faultfinding, harsh, injurious, insulting, irreverent, scornful, severe, slighting, smearing, spiteful, uncomplimentary, underestimating, unflattering, venomous, vilifying, vituperative

PELLUCID, **adjective** apparent, clear, clear-cut, comprehensible, crystalline, diaphanous, disclosed, easy to understand, exoteric, explicit, express, hyaline, intelligible, limpid, lucid, manifest, obvious, overt, palpable, patent, pellucidus, plain, pure, recognizable, revealed, simple, straightforward, transparent, unambiguous, unconcealed, understandable, undisguised, unhidden, unquestionable

PENAL, **adjective** castigatory, containing a penalty, corrective, disciplinary, enacting punishment, inflictive, mulctuary, poenalis, prohibiting, punishing, punitive, punitory, relating to a penalty, retaliatory, retributive
ASSOCIATED CONCEPTS: penal action, penal bond, penal law, penal ordinances, penal statute
FOREIGN PHRASES: *In haeredes non solent transire actiones quae poenales ex maleficio sunt.* Actions which are penal and which arise out of anything of criminal nature do not pass to the heirs.

PENALIZE, **verb** amerce, avenge, bring to account, call to account, carry out a sentence, castigate, chastise, confiscate, correct, discipline, exact a penalty, exact retribution, execute a sentence, execute judgment, fine, forfeit, harm, hurt, impose a penalty, inflict a penalty, inflict punishment, mulct, punish, put at a disadvantage, rebuke, reprimand, reprove, retaliate, revenge, sentence, subject to a handicap, subject to penalty, subject to punishment, visit punishment

PENALTY, **noun** amercement, castigation, compulsory payment, cost, deprivation, disadvantage, disciplinary action, fine, forefeiture, forfeit, handicap, infliction, liability, loss, multa, onus, penal retribution, penance, poena, prescribed punishment, punishment, punishment fixed by law, punishment prescribed by law, reprisal, retributive justice, sconce, sentence

ASSOCIATED CONCEPTS: action for penalty, civil penalty, confiscatory penalty, criminal penalty, excessive penalty, penalty clause, penalty for forfeiture, subject to penalty

FOREIGN PHRASES: *Quod a quoque poenae nomine exactum est id eidem restituere nemo cogitur.* No one is compelled to restore that which has been exacted as a penalty.

PENCHANT, *noun* affinity, appetite, ardor, attachment, attraction, bent, bias, capacity, competence, direction, disposition, eagerness, enthusiasm, fancy, fondness, gravitation, inborn ability, *inclinatio*, inclination, innate ability, leaning, liking, partiality, particular aptitude, passion, polarity, predilection, predisposition, preference, prejudice, proclivity, proneness, *propensio*, propension, propensity, relish, specialty, specific aptness, specific quality, talent, tendency, weakness

PENDENCY, *noun* abeyance, adjournment, break, cessation, continuance, discontinuity, halt, hiatus, interim, interlude, intermediate time, intermission, interregnum, interruption, interval, intervening period, lapse, lull, moratorium, pause, postponement, recess, respite, suspense, suspension, temporary stop

ASSOCIATED CONCEPTS: pendency of an action, pendency of an appeal

PENDENT, *adjective* additional, adjunct, adscititious, affinitive, allied to, ancillary, appurtenant, auxiliary, close, closely connected, cognate, collateral, complementary, congeneric, congenerical, congenerous, connatural, correspondent, corresponding, equivalent, *instar omnium,* matching, much the same, quasi, secondary, similar, something like, subsidiary, supplemental

ASSOCIATED CONCEPTS: pendent claim, pendent jurisdiction

PENDING (Imminent), **adjective** about to happen, anticipated, approaching, at hand, close, close at hand, coming, eventual, expectant, fearful, foreseen, foreshadowing, forthcoming, immediate, impending, instant, looming, minacious, momentary, near, ominous, on the horizon, oncoming, overhanging, prospective, threatening, upcoming

ASSOCIATED CONCEPTS: pending action, pending case, pending cause, pending claim, pending proceeding

PENDING (Unresolved), **adjective** in a state of uncertainty, in abeyance, in question, indefinite, indeterminate, open to discussion, open to question, still in debate, suspenseful, unascertained, uncertain, unclear, unconcluded, undecided, under consideration, undetermined, unfixed, unsettled, unsolved

PENETRABLE, *adjective* able to be pierced, absorbent, accessible, agape, ajar, assailable, attackable, conquerable, dehiscent, foraminated, foraminous, gaping, open, opened, passable, *penetrabilis*, perforable, perforated, permeable, pervious, *pervius,* porous, pregnable, receptive, riddled, susceptible, unclosed, vincible, vulnerable, wide open, yawning

PENETRATE, *verb* absorb, bore, break into, burst in upon, cut through, empierce, enter, erupt, fill, filter in, flow in, force a passage, give entrance to, go through, gore, imbrue, impale, impregnate, infiltrate, inflow, inject, insert, interfuse, lance, leak into, leaven, make a passage, osmose, overspread, pass, *penetrare*, perforate, permeate, pervade, *pervadere,* pierce, pour in, prick, probe, puncture, riddle, run through, saturate, seep in, sink in, skewer, slip into, soak through, spear, spike, stab, suffuse, tincture, transpierce, tunnel

PENITENT, *adjective* apologetic, atoning, awakened, chastened, compunctious, conciliatory, conscience-smitten, conscience-stricken, contrite, expiatory, full of regrets, humble, making amends, penitential, piacular, plagued by conscience, propiatory, purgatorial, reformed, regenerate, regretful, remorseful, repentant, rueful, self-accusing, self-condemned, self-convicted, self-reproachful, sobered, sorrowful, sorry

PENITENT, *noun* confessor, conscience-smitten person, conscience-stricken person, contrite person, penance doer, reformed character, remorseful person, repentant person, shriver

ASSOCIATED CONCEPTS: priest-penitent privilege

PENITENTIARY, *noun* cell, detention camp, detention center, house of correction, house of detention, jail, jailhouse, lockup, penal colony, penal institution, penal settlement, place of confinement, place of detention, place of imprisonment, prison, prisonhouse, reformatory

PENSION, *noun* allotment, allowance, *annua,* annual allowance, annuity, compensation, emolument, endowment, fee, financial remuneration, grant, grant for support, grant in aid, payment, pecuniary aid, remittance, remuneration, retirement benefits, retirement income, specified income payable for life, stated maintenance, stipend, subsidization, subsidy, subvention, support

ASSOCIATED CONCEPTS: pension act, pension and benefit fund, pension benefits

PENSIVE, *adjective* absorbed, abstracted, attentive, calculating, concentrating, contemplative, deliberative, dreaming, dreamy, engrossed, full of thought, given to thought, *in cogitatione* defixus, introspective, meditative, museful, musing, obsessed, occupied, rapt, ratiocinative, ratiocinatory, reasoning, reflective, ruminant, ruminative, self-communing, serious, sober, speculative, studious, thoughtful, wistful

PENUMBRA, *noun* brink, cover, edge, fringe, margin, outskirt, reflection, shade, shadow

ASSOCIATED CONCEPTS: penumbra of a Constitutional Amendment

PENURIOUS, *adjective* chary, cheap, churlish, close, close-fisted, close-handed, frugal, greedy, grudging, illiberal, impoverished, in distress, in need, in want, indigent, mean, mercenary, miserly, needy, niggard, niggardly, nonpaying, parsimonious, penniless, petty, poverty-stricken, saving, selfish, shabby, sordid, sparing, stingy, tenax, ungenerous, unwilling to pay, venal

PEOPLE, *noun* citizenry, commonality, community, community at large, country, cultures, general public, humanity, inhabitants, multitude, nation, national group, nationality, persons, populace, population, race, society, state

PER ANNUM, *adverb* annually, at a fixed interval, on the anniversary, on the basis of a year, yearly

PER CAPITA, ad*verb* allocated, an equal percentage, each to each, per head, percentage, pro rata, proportionately, respectively, share and share alike, to each according to his share

PER DIEM, *preposition* per day, for each and every day, for each day, for every day

PERAMBULATE, verb amble, circle, circumambulate, course, cover, cross, go around, go for a walk, go on an outing, go on foot, hike, jaunt, journey, make rounds, march, meander, pace, pass, pass through, patrol, pedestrianize, *peragrare*, peregrinate, *perlustrare, pervagari,* promenade, prowl, ramble, range, reconnoiter, roam, rove, saunter, scour, stalk, step, stride, stroll, strut, sweep through, take a constitutional, take a walk, take an airing, tour, tramp, travel, traverse, tread, trek, trudge, walk, walk through, wander

PERCEIVABLE, adjective apparent, appearing, appreciable, apprehensible, before one's eyes, beholdable, bold, clear, cognizable, detectable, discernible, disclosed, discoverable, distinct, distinguishable, easy to see, evident, exoteric, explicit, exposed, exposed to view, express, glaring, in evidence, in full view, in plain sight, in sight, in view, knowable, macroscopic, manifest, naked, notable, noticeable, observable, obvious, open, open to view, overt, palpable, patent, perceptible, perspicuous, plain, plain to be seen, prominent, recognizable, remarkable, revealed, salient, seeable, showing, sighted, tangible, transparent, unclouded, unconcealed, unhidden, unmistakable, viewable, visible, visual, well-defined, well-marked
ASSOCIATED CONCEPTS: last clear chance, latent defect, patent defect

PERCEIVE, verb apperceive, appreciate, apprehend, awaken, be acquainted with, be apprized of, be attentive to, be aware of, be cognizant of, be conscious of, be informed of, be sensitive to, become aware of, become conscious of, cognize, *cognoscere,* come to know, comprehend, detect, discern, discover, discriminate, distinguish, espy, experience, externalize, familiarize oneself, feel, gain insight into, give attention to, have cognizance of, have knowledge of, ken, know, learn, make out, mark, note, notice, observe, *percipere,* react, realize, recognize, regard, see, sense, *sentire,* take notice, understand, witness
ASSOCIATED CONCEPTS: perceive a product defect, perceive danger

PERCENTAGE, noun allotment, commission, contingent, factorage, fraction, interest, moiety, part, percent, portion, proportion, quota, rate per hundred, ratio, ration, share

PERCEPTIBLE, adjective apparent, apprehensible, ascertainable, beholdable, clear, clearly defined, clearly marked, cognizable, comprehensible, defined, detectable, discernible, disclosed, discoverable, distinct, distinguishable, easy to be seen, evident, explicit, exposed, exposed to view, express, glaring, in bold relief, in evidence, in full view, in plain sight, in sight, in view, indubitable, knowable, macroscopic, manifest, *manifestus,* marked, naked, notable, noticeable, observable, obvious, open, open to view, overt, palpable, patent, perceivable, perspicuous, plain, prominent, recognizable, revealed, salient, seeable, showing, shown, sighted, tangible, unconcealed, understandable, unhidden, unmistakable, viewable, visible, visual, well-defined, well-marked

PERCEPTION, noun ability to make distinctions, acuity, acumen, acuteness, apperception, appraisal, appreciation, apprehension, ascertainment, assessment, astuteness, attention, awareness, clear sight, cleverness, cognition, cognizance, comprehension, consciousness, deduction, detection, determination, discernment, discovery, discriminating judgment, discrimination, espial, estimate, evaluation, field of vision, finding, grasp, idea, image, impression, inkling, insight, *iudicium,* judgment, keen sight,

keeness, mental image, mental impression, *mentis acies,* mindfulness, noesis, note, notice, notion, observation, penetration, percipience, perspicaciousness, perspicacity, point of view, quick sense, realization, recognition, regard, sagaciousness, sagacitas, sagacity, scrutiny, sense, sensibility, sensory experience, sharp sight, sharpness, shrewdness, sight, smartness, supposition, surmise, theory, understanding, view, viewpoint, visualization

PERCEPTIVE, adjective acute, apperceptive, apprehensive, astute, aware, cognitive, cognizant, comprehending, conscious, discerning, discriminating, discriminative, easily affected, feeling, impressible, impressionable, keen, knowing, mindful, percipient, perspicacious, quick of apprehension, receptive, responsive, sagax, sensible, sensitive, sentient, sharp, shrewd, understanding, wise

PEREMPTORY *(Absolute),* **adjective** actual, axiomatic, certain, complete, decided, decisive, definite, determinate, determined, express, final, imperious, implicit, incontrovertible, independent, overbearing, perfect, positive, real, resolute, resolved, self-existent, total, unalterable, unconditional, unconditioned, unequivocal, unlimited, unqualified, unquestioned, unrestricted, without limitation
ASSOCIATED CONCEPTS: peremptory adjournment, peremptory challenge, peremptory exception, peremptory plea, peremptory writ

PEREMPTORY *(Imperative),* **adjective** assertive, authoritative, commanding, compulsory, crucial, decisive, demanding, despotic, dictatorial, domineering, essential, exigent, firm, imperious, important, inexorable, inflexible, iron-handed, mandatory, necessary, obligatory, paramount, pressing, unavoidable, urgent
ASSOCIATED CONCEPTS: peremptory instruction

PEREMPTORY CHALLENGE, noun absolute challenge, arbitrary challenge, axiomatic challenge, certain challenge, challenge as of right, challenge within prerogative, conclusive challenge, decision challenge, discretionary challenge, final determining challenge, guaranteed challenge, objection as of right, positive challenge, rejection as of right, right to eliminate jurors, self-determined challenge, unperative challenge, unrestricted challenge
ASSOCIATED CONCEPTS: challenge for cause

PERFECT, verb *absolvere,* accomplish, bring to a conclusion, bring to an end, bring to completion, bring to fullness, carry out, complete, conclude, consummate, correct, culminate, *cumulare,* effectuate, execute, finish, follow to a conclusion, *perficere,* refine
ASSOCIATED CONCEPTS: perfect a security interest, perfect an appeal, perfect title

PERFECTION, noun accomplishment, achievement, attainment, climax, completeness, completion, consummation, correctness, crown, crowning point, culmination, development, effectuation, elaboration, entireness, exactitude, exactness, excellence, faultlessness, finish, flawlessness, fulfillment, fullness, goodness, height, highest degree of proficiency, idealization, impeccability, paragon, peak, pinnacle, pinpoint precision, preeminence, quintessence, realization, refinement, summit, superiority, transcendence, ultimate, wholeness
ASSOCIATED CONCEPTS: perfection of a lien

PERFERVID, adjective burning, exceedingly ardent, impassioned, on fire, overly passionate, too zealous

449

PERFIDIOUS, adjective base, betraying, cheating, conniving, corrupt, deceitful, deceiving, designing, dishonest, dishonorable, disloyal, disobedient, dissembling, double-crossing, double-dealing, faithless, false, falsehearted, fraudulent, guileful, hypocritical, inconstant, insidious, intriguing, knavish, lying, *perfidiosus, perfidus,* perjured, plotting, scheming, shifty, slippery, sneaking, sneaky, traitorous, treacherous, treasonable, treasonous, tricky, trothless, unconscionable, undependable, unfaithful, unprincipled, unreliable, unscrupulous, untrue, untrustworthy, untruthful, without honor

PERFORM *(Adhere to), verb* abide by, achieve, be faithful to, carry into execution, carry out, cling to, complete, comply with, conclude, consummate, enact, end, enforce, execute, finish, fulfill, keep, keep one's word, observe, obtain, practice, put in force, put in practice, respect, satisfy, transact
ASSOCIATED CONCEPTS: perform a contract

PERFORM *(Execute), verb* accomplish, achieve, bring into operation, bring to pass, carry into execution, complete, discharge, discharge a duty, do, effect, effectuate, employ oneself, enact, function, *perficere,* perpetrate, pursue a course, put in force, serve, serve in the capacity of, take action, take steps, work

PERFORMANCE *(Execution), noun* accomplished fact, accomplishment, achievement, act, action, attainment, carrying into effect, carrying through, commission, completion, consummation, culmination, deed, enactment, finished product, fulfilment, implementation, operation, perpetration, production, realization, rendition, work
ASSOCIATED CONCEPTS: full performance, impossibility of performance, partial performance, performance bond, prevention of performance
FOREIGN PHRASES: *Non quod dictum est, sed quod factum est inspicitur.* Not what is said, but what is done, is to be regarded. *Lex non cogit ad impossibilia.* The law does not require the performance of the impossible.

PERFORMANCE *(Workmanship), noun* ability, accomplishment, achievement, action, aptitude, aptness, *ars,* art, artfulness, *artificium,* attainment, caliber, capability, capacity, competence, competency, composition, construction, craft, craftsmanship, creation, dexterity, effort, endowment, exhibition, expertness, faculty, finesse, formation, forte, handicraft, handiness, handiwork, ingenuity, manipulation, manufacture, mastership, mastery, operation, opus, play, preparation, production, proficiency, qualification, quality of execution, quality of work, representation, show, skill, skillfulness, talent, technique, virtuosity, work, working ability

PERFUNCTORY, adjective absent-minded, abstracted, apathetic, below par, careless, casual, cursory, deficient, disinterested, dispassionate, disregardful, failing, formal, half-hearted, hasty, heedless, hollow, hurried, ill-done, imperfect, inadequate, inattentive, incautious, incomplete, indifferent, inexact, insubstantial, lacking, lax, lenient, lukewarm, mechanical, mindless, needing, neglectful, negligent, offhand, omitting, passionless, poor, poorly done, quick, regardless, remiss, requiring, routine, rushed, short, sketchy, speedy, substandard, superficial, thoughtless, unattended to, uncaring, unconcerned, undiscerning, unenthusiastic, unexamined, unfeeling, unguarded, unheeded, unheedful, unheeding, uninspired, uninterested, uninvolved, unmindful, unobservant, unregarded, unresponsive, unstudied, unthinking, unthorough, unthought of, unwatchful, unweighed, wanting, without concern, without enthusiasm

PERIL, noun approach of danger, crisis, danger, dangerous situation, desperate situation, emergency, endangerment, exposure to danger, exposure to destruction, exposure to harm, exposure to injury, exposure to loss, hazard, helplessness, hopelessness, imperilment, insecurity, jeopardy, liability to injury, parlous state, precariousness, predicament, risk, source of danger, source of risk, susceptibility, susceptibleness, susceptivity, threat, uncertainty, unhealthy situation, unsafety, unsureness, vulnerability, vulnerable point
ASSOCIATED CONCEPTS: common peril, discovered peril, doctrine of discovered peril, doctrine of last clear chance, manifest peril, unforseen peril

PERIMETER, noun ambit, border, borderline, boundary, bounds, brink, circuit, circumference, compass, configuration, confines, contour, curb, delineation, edge, enclosure, frontier, girdle, limit, limitations, margin, outline, outside edge, pale, periphery, purview, range, zone
ASSOCIATED CONCEPTS: adverse possession, constructive eviction, metes and bounds, trespassing

PERIOD, noun age, bout, continuance, course, diuturnity, duration, eon, epoch, era, hitch, interval, juncture, length of time, limited time, point, season, shift, span, spell, stage, stint, stretch, tenure, term, time, time interval, time stretch, tour, while
ASSOCIATED CONCEPTS: period of redemption

PERIODIC, adjective cadenced, cadent, continual, cyclic, cyclical, erratic, fluctuating, frequent, habitual, intermittent, measured, occasional, occurring again, oft-repeated, oftentime, patterned, perpetual, reappearing, recurrent, recurring, regular, regulated, remittent, repeated, returning, returning at intervals, rhythmic, rhythmical, seasonal, serial, *sollemnis,* spasmodic, sporadic, successive, systematic, variable

PERIPHERAL, adjective beside the point, circumferential, collateral, exterior, external, extraneous, farthest, fringe, impertinent, inconsequential, inessential, irrelevant, on the edge, outer, outermost, outland, outlying, outmost, outside, perimetric, perimetrical, secondary, trivial, ungermane, unimportant, without

PERIPHERY, noun ambit, border, borderland, bound, boundary line, circuit, circumambiency, circumference, circumscription, compass, confine, contour, delimitation, demarcation, edge, end, exterior, extreme edge, fringe, frontier, limit, limitation, line of demarcation, march, margin, mete, outer boundary, outer part, outline, outpost, outside, outside surface, outskirts, pale, perimeter, *perimetros,* purlieu, rim, skirts, surrounding area, surrounding space, terminus, verge

PERISH, verb be annihilated, be destroyed, be eradicated, be extinguished, be null and void, be ruined, become extinct, cease, cease living, cease to be, cease to exist, cease to live, come to an end, come to naught, come to ruin, crumble, depart, die, die away, die out, disappear, evanesce, evaporate, expire, fade, fade away, fade out, fail, go, *interire,* leave no trace, lose life, meet death, melt away, *occidere,* pass, pass away, pass on, *perire,* peter out, relinquish life, render null, sink away, succumb, surrender, vanish, wilt, wither

PERJURE, verb be false, be untruthful, bear false witness, break one's oath, break one's word, deviate from the truth, falsify, falsify testimony, feign, forswear, hide the truth, lie, misrepresent, palter, *periurare, periurium facere,* put a false construction upon, say less than the truth, speak falsely, strain the truth, stretch the truth, swear falsely, tell a falsehood, tell a lie, trump up, utter a falsehood

PERJURY, noun act of oath-breaking, distortion of the truth, false statement, false swearing, falsehood, falseness, falsification, intentional misstatement, invention of lies, misrepresentation, misstatement, *periurium,* perversion of truth, prevarication, untruth, violation of an oath, willful distortion of the truth, willful falsehood, willful telling of a falsehood, willful telling of a lie

ASSOCIATED CONCEPTS: subornation of perjury

FOREIGN PHRASES: *Lex punit mendacium.* The law punishes mendacity. *Perjuri sunt qui servatis verbis juramenti decipiunt aures eorum qui accipiunt.* They are perjured, who, preserving the words of an oath, deceive the ears of those who receive it. *Sacramentum si fatuum fuerit, licet falsum, tamen non committit perjurium.* A foolish oath, although false, does not give rise to perjury. *Qui non libere veritatem pronunciat proditor est veritatis.* He who does not freely speak the truth is a betrayer of the truth.

PERMANENT, adjective abiding, ageless, ceaseless, changeless, chronic, confirmed, constant, continued, continuing, dateless, deep-seated, durable, endless, enduring, engrafted, entrenched, established, eternal, everlasting, fast, fixed, immortal, immutable, imperishable, incommutable, indefatigable, indefeasible, indelible, indestructible, ineradicable, inextinguishable, infinite, ingrained, insusceptible to change, interminable, intransient, intransmutable, invulnerable, irremovable, irreversible, irrevocable, lasting, long-lasting, never-ceasing, never-ending, never-stopping, nonreversible, perdurable, perduring, perennial, *perennis,* perpetual, perpetuated, persevering, persistent, persisting, preserved, radicated, remaining, reverseless, rooted, secure, sempiternal, set, *stabilis,* stable, static, stationary, staying, steadfast, steady, surviving, sustained, tenacious, unalterable, unceasing, unchangeable, unchanging, unchecked, undestroyable, undying, unending, unerasable, unfading, unfailing, unflagging, uninterrupted, unmodifiable, unmovable, unrepealable, unshifting, unvarying, unwavering, unyielding, without end

PERMEATE, verb bathe, diffuse, drench, fill, go through, imbue, impregnate, infiltrate, infuse, inject, interpenetrate, leaven, osmose, overrun, overspread, pass through, penetrate, percolate, pervade, run through, saturate, seep, soak, souse, spread through, steep, suffuse, transfuse, wash, waterlog

PERMISSIBLE, adjective according to law, admissible, allowable, allowed, amenable to law, approvable, approved, authorized, constitutional, empowered, fitting, franchised, granted, lawful, legal, legally sound, legitimate, licensed, *licet,* licit, *licitus,* permitted, proper, sanctioned, sanctioned by law, stamped with approval, sufferable, tolerable, unchallenged, unforbidden, unprohibited, viable, warrantable, within the law

PERMISSION, noun acquiescence, allowance, approval, assent, authority, authorization, blessing, concurrence, consent, *copia,* countenance, *facultas,* formal consent, full authority, grace, leave, license, *potestas,* sanction, tolerance, visa

ASSOCIATED CONCEPTS: explicit permission, implied permission, permission of the court

FOREIGN PHRASES: *Tout ce que la loi ne defend pas est permis.* Everything which the law does not prohibit is allowed.

PERMISSIVE, adjective acquiescent, allowing, broadminded, complaisant, discretional, granting, indulgent, lenient, liberal, mild, nonprohibitive, tolerant, tolerating, volitive, yielding

ASSOCIATED CONCEPTS: permissive counterclaim, permissive joinder, permissive statute, permissive use

PERMIT, noun affirmation, approbation, approval, authority, authorization, *carte blanche,* certificate, charter, confirmation, document granting permission, fiat, grant, leave, legalization, license, pass, passport, patent, permission, privilege, sanction, ticket of leave, visa, voucher, warrant

ASSOCIATED CONCEPTS: license

PERMIT, verb accord one's approval, agree to, allow, approve, approve of, assent, authorize, award assent, be in favor of, be indulgent of, confer a privilege, consent, empower, enable, entitle, facilitate, give clearance, give consent, give leave, give opportunity for, give permission, give power, grant permission, have no objection, let, license, make possible, remove the obstacles, sanction, suffer, tolerate, warrant, yield assent

PERNICIOUS, adjective adverse, afflicting, baleful, baneful, brutal, calamitous, catastrophic, corrosive, crippling, cruel, damaging, deadly, death-bringing, death-dealing, deathful, deathly, deleterious, destructive, detrimental, devouring, diabolic, dire, disadvantageous, disastrous, disserviceable, distressing, envenomed, evil, *exitiosus,* extirpative, fatal, fell, fiendish, fraught with evil, fraught with harm, harmful, hurtful, inimical, injurious, insalubrious, insidious, killing, lethal, malefic, maleficent, maleficial, malevolent, malign, malignant, menacing, mephitic, mischievous, morbiferous, morbific, mortal, murderous, nocent, noisome, *noxious,* noxius, painful, *perniciosus,* pestiferous, pestilential, poisonous, ruinous, serious, sinister, tending to cause death, toxic, toxicant, toxiferous, treacherous, unhealthful, unhealthy, unkind, unpropitious, unwholesome, venomous, vicious, violent, virulent, wicked

PERORATION, noun address, bombast, declamation, discourse, *epilogus,* formal speech, grandiloquence, homily, lecture, magniloquence, monologue, oration, oratorical display, orotundity, *peroratio,* prelection, prepared speech, public address, recitation, rhetorical discourse, sermon, soliloquy, speech, talk

PERPETRATE, verb accomplish, achieve, be guilty of, bring about, bring to pass, carry into execution, carry off, carry on, carry out, carry through, commit, *committere,* do, effect, effectuate, execute, follow through, fulfill, implement, impose, inflict, maneuver, manipulate, perform, produce, put into action, put into effect, take measures, transact, work, work out

ASSOCIATED CONCEPTS: perpetrate a crime

PERPETUAL, adjective *adsiduus,* amaranthine, ceaseless, chronic, constant, continuous, deathless, endless, enduring, eternal, ever-abiding, everlasting, fixed, having no limit, immortal, imperishable, impossible to stop, incessant, indelible, indestructible, ineradicable, inexhaustible, infinite, interminable, intransient, lasting, never-ceasing, never-dying, never-fading, never-failing, never-stopping, perdurable, *perennis,* permanent, perpetuated, persistent, sempiternal, *sempiternus,* stable, surviving, unceasing, undestroyable, unending, unerasable, unfading, unfailing, uninterrupted, unlimited, unrepealable, without end

ASSOCIATED CONCEPTS: perpetual easement, perpetual franchise, perpetual injunction, perpetual lease, perpetual lien, perpetual succession

FOREIGN PHRASES: *Perpetua lex est nullam legem humanam ac positivam perpetuam esse, et clausula quae abrogationem excludit ab initio non valet.* It is a perpetual law that no human and positive law can be perpetual, and a clause in a law which precludes the power of abrogation or repeal is void from the beginning.

PERPETUATE, verb   carry forward, carry on, cause to be continued, cause to endure, cause to last, eternize, immortalize, keep alive, keep in existence, maintain, make eternal, make everlasting, make last, make permanent, make perpetual, preserve, prolong, render deathless, retain, save, sustain
ASSOCIATED CONCEPTS: perpetuate testimony

PERPETUITY, noun   boundlessness, ceaselessness, constancy, constant progression, continualness, continuance, continuation, continued existence, continuous time, continuousness, endless duration, endless time, endlessness, eternalness, eternity, everlasting, forever, incessancy, indefiniteness, infinite duration, infiniteness, infinity, interminability, never-endingness, perenniality, permanence, perpetualness, perpetuation, *perpetuitas,* time without end, timelessness, unintermitted continuance, uninterrupted existence, uninterruptedness
ASSOCIATED CONCEPTS: after-born children, in perpetuity, lives in being, period of perpetuities, restraint on alienation, rule against perpetuities

PERPLEX, verb   baffle, bedevil, bemuse, beset, bewilder, bother, complicate, confound, confuse, corner, discompose, disconcert, disorient, disquiet, *distrahere,* disturb, embarrass, encumber, entangle, fill with doubt, fog, involve, make difficult, make intricate, mix up, muddle, mystify, nonplus, perturb, pose, pother, puzzle, rattle, render uncertain, snarl, *sollicitare,* tangle, tease, trouble, unsettle, upset, vex, worry

PERQUISITE, noun   allowance, annuity, benefaction, bonus, compensation, consideration, donation, emolument, endowment, fee, financial remuneration, financial reward, gain, gift, gratuity, incidental profits, payment, premium, present, profit, recompense, remuneration, return, revenue, reward, reward for service, stipend, subsidy, tip, token, wage

PERSECUTE, verb   abuse, afflict, aggrieve, agonize, annoy, assail, attack, badger, be intolerant, be malevolent, be malicious, be offensive, be ruthless, bedevil, beset, bother, browbeat, bully, carp at, chevy, crucify, damage, distress, disturb, do an injustice to, do harm, do mischief, do violence, do wrong to, dragoon, endamage, enrage, harass, ill treat, ill use, inflict evil, injure, maltreat, manhandle, misemploy, mishandle, mistreat, misuse, offend, oppress, outrage, overburden, overtax, overwork, plague, provoke, refuse to tolerate, scathe, scourge, show no mercy, show no pity, torment, treat poorly, trouble, use dispiteously, *vexare,* victimize, wrong

PERSEVERANCE, noun   application, backbone, constancy, continuance, continuation, determination, devotion, diligence, doggedness, endurance, firmness of purpose, indefatigableness, industry, intransigency, obduracy, obduration, obstinacy, patience, persistence, pertinacity, purpose, resoluteness, resolve, single-mindedness, singleness of purpose, stamina, steadfastness, steadiness, stubbornness, tenacity, tolerance, will, zeal

PERSEVERE, verb   adhere, apply oneself, be constant, be determined, be obstinate, be resolute, be steadfast, be steady, be stubborn, be tenacious, be unyielding, carry on, cling, cling tenaciously, *constare,* continue, endure, exert oneself, follow up, go forward, go on, hang on, hold fast, hold on, hold out, keep driving, keep going, keep on, keep up, labor, last, maintain, maintain a course, outlast, perpetuate, persist, *persistere, perstare,* plod, plug away, prevail, prolong, pursue, refuse to give up, refuse to yield, remain, resist change, run on, spare no effort, stand fast, stand firm, stay, stick to, stop at nothing, struggle, survive, sustain, take no denial, toil, work unceasingly, work unflaggingly

PERSIST, verb   abide, be determined, be obstinate, be resolute, be steadfast, be steady, be tenacious, be unyielding, bide, carry on, cling to, continue, drag on, endure, go forward, go on, hold fast, hold on, hold out, insist, keep at, keep on, last, linger, live on, maintain, make headway, never cease, outlast, perdure, persevere, *persistere, perstare,* plod, plug away, prevail, progress, pursue relentlessly, refuse to give up, remain, remain unchanged, stay, stick to, survive, sustain, take no denial, toil unceasingly, work unceasingly, work unflaggingly

PERSISTENT, adjective   abiding, adamant, assiduous, chronic, continued, continuing, continuous, determined, diligent, dogged, durable, enduring, everlasting, faithful, indefatigable, insistent, lasting, obstinate, patient, perdurable, perseverant, persevering, pertinacious, purposeful, refusing to relent, relentless, remaining, repeated, resolute, resolved, sedulous, serious, set upon, staying, steadfast, steady, strong-willed, stubborn, sustained, tenacious, tireless, unallayed, unceasing, unchanging, unchecked, undaunted, undeviating, undiscouraged, undying, unfailing, unfaltering, unflagging, unrelaxing, unremitting, unstopping, unswerving, untiring, unvarying, unwavering, unwearying, unyielding

PERSON, noun   autonomous being, being, caput, chap, character, fellow, *homo,* human, human being, human creature, individual, living being, living soul, member of the human race, mortal, mortal body, *mortalis,* party, personage, somebody, someone, soul
ASSOCIATED CONCEPTS: adult person, artificial person, competent person, credible person, disorderly person, fictitious person, injured person, natural person, person aggrieved, person in need of supervision, poor person, third person, unauthorized person

PERSONAL *(Individual),* **adjective**   characteristic, differentiating, discriminative, distinct, distinguishing, idiosyncratic, own, particular, peculiar, private, select, specific
ASSOCIATED CONCEPTS: personal action, personal appearance, personal communication, personal covenant, personal effects, personal estate, personal exemption, personal expenses, personal goods, personal injury, personal judgment, personal jurisdiction, personal liability, personal obligation, personal privilege, personal property, personal representative, personal rights, personal safety, personal service of process, personal services, personal transaction, personally responsible

PERSONAL *(Private),* **adjective**   buried, clandestine, closed, concealed, confidential, covert, cryptic, hidden, intimate, *privatus,* privy, restricted, secret, singular, subjective, undisclosed, unrevealed, unshared, untold, veiled
ASSOCIATED CONCEPTS: personal articles, personal belongings

PERSONALITY, noun   attributes, being, character, characteristics, disposition, distinction, distinctiveness, egohood, identity, individualism, individuality, *ingenium,* makeup, nature, oneness, originality, particularity, peculiarities, personal identity, personal mark, predisposition, selfhood, selfness, singularity, soul, style, temperament, traits, type, uniqueness

PERSONALTY, noun assets, available means, belongings, chattels, effects, funds, holdings, investments, personal property, personal resources, possessions, property, resources, wealth

PERSONIFY, verb ascribe personal qualities to, be the embodiment, characterize, copy, embody, embrace, exemplify, humanize, incarnate, manifest, *orationem attribuere,* symbolize, treat as human, typify

PERSONNEL, noun assistants, band of employees, body of employees, cast, clerical staff, company, corps of employees, coworkers, crew, employees, factotums, fellow workers, help, labor supply, laborers, laboring force, manpower, members, office force, servantry, servants, staff, team of employees, work force, work party, workers, working people

PERSPECTIVE, noun angle of vision, attitude, conception, distance, eyereach, feeling, field of view, field of vision, framework, impression, inclination, leaning, line of sight, mental view, orientation, outlook, point of observation, point of view, position, range of view, range of vision, scope of vision, sense of proportion, situation, slant, standpoint, thought, vantage point, view, viewpoint, way of thinking

PERSPICACIOUS, adjective *acutus,* alert, apperceptive, argute, artful, astute, bright, canny, clear-sighted, clearheaded, clever, crafty, cunning, dioristic, discerning, discriminating, discriminative, farseeing, farsighted, foresighted, forethoughtful, hardheaded, informed, intelligent, judicious, keen, keen-eyed, keen-sighted, keen-witted, knowing, longsighted, nimble-witted, observant, penetrating, perceptive, percipient, *perspicax,* piercing, quick, quick-witted, sagacious, *sagax,* sage, sapient, sensible, sharp, sharpsighted, sharp-witted, shrewd, understanding, wise

PERSPICACITY, noun acuity, acumen, acute discernment, acuteness, astuteness, capacity, clear thinking, clear thought, clear vision, discernment, discretion, discrimination, farsightedness, insight, judgment, ken, perception, perceptiveness, sagacity, sense, sensitivity, sharpness of mind, shrewdness, tact, understanding

PERSPICUOUS, adjective accurate, apparent, appreciable, apprehensible, clear, cognizable, coherent, comprehensible, conceivable, definite, distinct, evident, exact, explicable, explicit, factual, forceful, genuine, intelligible, manifest, obvious, overt, palpable, patent, pellucid, perceivable, perceptible, real, transparent, truthful, unambiguous, understandable, unmistakable

PERSUADE, verb actuate, advise, align, bend to one's will, blandish, bring a person to his senses, bring around, bring over, bring to reason, cajole, coax, compel, convert, convince, counsel, enlist, exercise influence, exert influence, exhort, gain the confidence of, impel, importune, impress, indoctrinate, induce, influence, inveigle, lead, lead to believe, lure, make one's point, make oneself felt, motivate, move, prevail upon, prompt, propagandize, proselyte, proselytize, rouse, satisfy by evidence, satisfy by proof, seduce, sell, suborn, sway, urge, win over, woo

PERSUASION, noun actuation, advocacy, alignment, argument, blandishment, cajolement, cajolery, cajoling, coaxing, conversion, dissuasion, encouragement, enlistment,

enticement, exhortation, incitation, incitement, inducement, influence, insistence, inveiglement, motivation, pleading, pressure, prompting, propaganda, proselytism, salesmanship, solicitation, suasion, winning over

PERSUASIVE, adjective actuating, arousing, authoritative, coaxing, cogent, compelling, convictive, convincing, credible, effective, eloquent, forceful, hortative, hortatory, impelling, impressive, inductive, influential, inspiring, inviting, logical, moving, persuasory, plausible, pointed, potent, powerful, propagandistic, provocative, provoking, rousing, sound, strong, suasive, subornative, swaying, telling, tempting, tenable, touching, valid, weighty
ASSOCIATED CONCEPTS: persuasive arguments, persuasive authority, persuasive legal testimony

PERTAIN, verb appertain, be appropriate, be associated with, be concerned with, be connected to, be suitable, bear upon, befit, behoove, belong, concern, have implications for, have interrelationship with, have reference to, have relation to, have relevance, have significance for, refer, relate, stand in relation to, tie in with, touch upon

PERTINACIOUS, adjective adamant, adhering to a purpose, assiduous, bent, bullheaded, certain, continuing, decided, determined, diligent, dogged, earnest, enduring, exhibiting purpose, faithful, firm, hard to get rid of, headstrong, holding to a purpose, immovable, immutable, implacable, indefatigable, indomitable, industrious, inexorable, inflexible, insistent, intent, intractable, inveterate, mulish, never-tiring, never-wearying, obdurate, obstinate, *obstinatus,* painstaking, patient, persevering, persistent, persisting, *pertinax,* pervicacious, *pervicax,* pigheaded, plodding, purposeful, relentless, resolute, resolved, rigid, sedulous, self-willed, serious, set, single-minded, stalwart, stanch, steadfast, steady, strong-willed, stubborn, sure, tough, unbending, uncompromising, undaunted, undeviating, undistracted, undoubting, unfaltering, unflagging, unflinching, unmovable, unrelaxing, unrelenting, unremitting, unshakable, unshaken, unshrinking, unswerving, untiring, unwavering, unwearying, unyielding, willful, zealous

PERTINENT, adjective adapted, affinitive, appertaining, applicable, apposite, appropriate, appurtenant, apropos, apt, associated, associative, bearing on the question, belonging, concerning, connected, fit, fitting, germane, having direct bearing, having to do with, material, opposite, pertaining, referential, referring, regarding, related, relating, relational, relevant, suitable, to the point, to the purpose, with reference to
ASSOCIATED CONCEPTS: pertinent testimony, relevant evidence

PERTURB, verb abash, agitate, alarm, annoy, arouse, badger, baffle, bewilder, bother, bring into disorder, cause a fuss, cause agitation, cause alarm, cause confusion, cause disorder, cause upset, churn, complicate, confound, confuse, derange, disarrange, discomfit, discompose, disconcert, dismay, disorder, disquiet, distract, distress, disturb, embarrass, entangle, exasperate, excite, ferment, flurry, fluster, fret, frustrate, gall, give cause for alarm, grieve, harass, harry, inflame, infuriate, irk, irritate, jar, jolt, madden, make havoc, make uneasy, nonplus, outrage, pain, perplex, perturbate, *perturbo,* pester, pique, plague, pother, provoke, put out, rouse, ruffle, shake, shake up, shock, snarl, stir, stir up, throw into confusion, trouble, unnerve, unsettle, upset, vex, work up, worry

PERUSAL, noun analysis, attention, close reading, contemplation, discovery, examination, inquiry, inspection, investigation, reading, review, scrutiny, study, survey

PERUSE, verb analyze, browse, check, con, conduct research on, consider, contemplate, delve into, devote oneself to, examine, explore, feel out, glance over, glean information, go over, inquire into, inspect, investigate, look over, observe, overlook, pass under review, peer into, perlegere, pore over, probe, pry into, read, regard studiously, research, review, scan, scrutinize, search, study, subject to scrutiny, survey, take note of, take stock of, thumb, turn one's gaze upon, turn the leaves of, watch

PERVADE, verb affect entirely, bathe, be rife, diffuse, disseminated, drench, enter, extend through, fill, filter through, flow into, force a passage, go through, imbrue, imbue, implant, impregnate, infiltrate, infuse, inject, instill, interfuse, interpenetrate, intrude, invade, make an entrance, overspread, pass through, penetrate, perforate, permeate, pierce, radiate, run into, run through, saturate, seep in, soak, spread, spread through, steep, suffuse, transfuse

PERVERSE, adjective bad, bad-natured, bad-tempered, base, bellicose, belligerent, boorish, bumptious, cantankerous, captious, churlish, contemptible, contrary, contumacious, contumelious, corrupt, corrupted, crabbed, cranky, cross, crusty, debauched, degenerate, depraved, deviating, difficult, discourteous, disobedient, disorderly, evil, evil-minded, fractious, froward, hard to deal with, hard to manage, headstrong, ill-behaved, ill-natured, ill-tempered, impolite, improper, impudent, inaffable, incorrigible, inimical, insubordinate, insulting, intractable, irascible, mean, nasty, naughty, negative, negativistic, noncompliant, obstinate, obstreperous, peevish, persisting in error, persisting in fault, *perversus,* perverted, petulant, pugnacious, refractory, reprobate, resistive, rude, self-willed, snappish, snarling, spiteful, spleenful, spleeny, splenetic, stubborn, surly, testy, thoughtless, touchy, troublesome, truculent, unaccommodating, uncivil, uncomplaisant, uncompliant, uncooperative, unfriendly, ungallant, ungovernable, ungracious, unhelpful, unmanageable, unmannerly, unpolite, unreasonable, unruly, untoward, unyielding, venomous, vexatious, waspish, wayward, wicked, wrong, wrongheaded

PERVERSION, noun abasement, aberrance, aberrancy, aberration, abnormality, abomination, abuse, baseness, contamination, *corruptio,* corruption, debasement, debauchery, defilement, degradation, demoralization, *depravatio,* depravation, depravity, evil behavior, foulness, immorality, infraction, lewdness, looseness of morals, malefaction, misuse, pollution, prostitution, sophistication, turpitude, unnatural habit, violation, vitiation, want of principle, wickedness
ASSOCIATED CONCEPTS: deviant sexual behavior

PERVERT, verb abuse, canker, contaminate, *corrumpere,* corrupt, debauch, degenerate, demoralize, *depravare,* deprave, divert, falsify, infect, lead astray, lower, make corrupt, misapply, mislead, misrepresent, misuse, poison, pollute, prostitute, render evil, ruin, soil, sophisticate, spoil, stain, subvert, taint, tamper with, teach wickedness, vitiate, warp
FOREIGN PHRASES: *Quae ad unum finem loquuta sunt, non debent ad alium detorqueri.* Those words which are spoken to one end ought not to be perverted to another.

PESSIMISM, noun blighted hope, cheerlessness, cynicism, dashed hopes, defeatism, dejectedness, dejection, depression, despair, desperation, despondence, despondency, disconsolation, discouragement, disheartenment, dispiritedness, dolefulness, downcastness, downheartedness, faint hope, forlorn hope, gloom, gloominess, gloomy outlook, glumness, heaviness of heart, heaviness of spirit, hopelessness, joylessness, lack of enthusiasm, lack of expectation, low-spiritedness, low spirits, melancholia, melancholy, misery, sorrowfulness, uncheerfulness, unhappiness, wretchedness

PESSIMISTIC, adjective cheerless, crushed, cynical, defeatist, dejected, depressed, despairing, desperate, despondent, disconsolate, discouraged, disheartened, dismayed, dispirited, distrustful, downcast, downhearted, foreboding, forlorn, gloomy, glum, grieved, heavyhearted, hopeless, joyless, low-spirited, melancholic, melancholy, miserable, morbid, morose, sad, sorrowful, troubled, uncheerful, uncheery, unhappy, unjoyful, unpromising, wretched

PESTILENT, adjective baleful, baneful, contagious, damaging, dangerous, deadly, death-dealing, deathly, deleterious, destructive, disastrous, disease-ridden, diseased, epidemic, evil, fatal, feral, foul, harmful, hurtful, infectious, injurious, insalubrious, killing, lethal, lethiferous, malefic, maleficent, malign, malignant, mephitic, morbid, morbiferous, morbific, morbifical, mortal, murderous, nocent, nocuous, noisome, noxious, pernicious, *pestilens,* pestilential, plagueful, poisonous, tending to cause death, terrible, threatening, toxic, toxicant, toxiferous, unhealthful, unhealthy, venomous, violent, virulent

PETITION, noun adjuration, application, bid, call for aid, demand, earnest request, entreaty, formal writing embodying a request, formal written plea, formal written request, invocation, *libellus,* motion, plea, prayer, request, request for relief, requisition, solemn request, written application for relief
ASSOCIATED CONCEPTS: affidavit, cross-petition, ex parte petition, filing of petition, order dismissing a petition, petition for a name change, petition for divorce, verified petition, voluntary petition in bankruptcy

PETITION, verb adjure, advocate, appeal for, apply for, apply to, ask for, beseech, bid, call upon, clamor for, entreat, entreat earnestly, file for, formally urge, *implorare,* implore, make a requisition, make application, make demands, make written application, obtest, petere, plead, pray for, prefer a request to, request, requisition, *rogare,* seek, solemnly request, solicit, urge
ASSOCIATED CONCEPTS: petition for a rehearing, petition for a writ of certiorari, petition for a writ of mandamus, petition for a writ of prohibition, petition for redress, petition for removal, petition for review

PETITIONER, noun applicant, asker, litigant, movant, one who applies for relief, one who files an application for relief, one who requests relief, party, pleader, solicitant, solicitor, *supplex,* supplicant
ASSOCIATED CONCEPTS: aggrieved party

PETTIFOG, verb beguile, bluff, cavil, circumvent, connive, deceive, dodge, dupe, ensnare, evade, fence, mislead, outmaneuver, palter, prevaricate, split hairs, trick, trifle

PETTIFOGGERY, noun artfulness, artifice, bamboozlement, cheating, chicane, chicanery, circumvention, corruption, cozenage, craft, craftiness, cunning, deceit, deception, dishonesty, dodgery, duplicity, equivocation, evasion, foul play, fraud, fraudulence, fraudulency, fraudulent practice, guile, humbug, indirection, intrigue, jobbery, jugglery, juggling, knavery, petty dishonesty, sharp practice, treachery, trickery, trickiness, underhand dealing, underhand practice

PETTY, *adjective* beggarly, contemptible, diminutive, dispensable, expendable, fribble, frivolous, inappreciable, inconsequential, inconsiderable, insignificant, limited, little, marginal, meager, mean, minor, minute, *minutus*, negligible, nonessential, nugatory, of small account, of small moment, paltry, petit, picayune, piddling, puny, scant, scanty, skimpy, slight, small, sparse, *tenuis*, trifling, trivial, unessential, unimportant, unnotable, unworthy of regard, worthless

ASSOCIATED CONCEPTS: petty larceny, petty misdemeanor, petty offense

PETULANT, *adjective* acrimonious, annoyed, argumentative, bad-tempered, bearish, cantankerous, captious, carping, cavilling, censorious, choleric, churlish, contentious, crabbed, crabby, cranky, cross, cross-tempered, crusty, curmudgeonly, difficult, disagreeable, disputatious, fractious, fretful, froward, grouchy, growling, grumbling, grumbly, grumpy, hot-headed, hot-tempered, huffy, ill-humored, ill-tempered, impatient, indocile, iracund, irascible, irritable, liverish, mean, mean-tempered, moody, nagging, out of humor, out of sorts, peevish, perverse, pettish, *petulans*, piqued, pugnacious, quarrelsome, querulous, short, short-tempered, shrewish, snappish, snappy, snarling, sour, sour-tempered, spiteful, spleenful, splenetic, splenetical, surly, testy, touchy, vixenish, waspish, whiny

PHANTOM, *noun* airy spirit, apparition, appearance, banshee, chimera, creation of the imagination, creation of the mind, delusion, disembodied spirit, dream, eidolon, fiction, fictive creation, figment, figment of the imagination, ghost, ghostly form, hallucination, illusion, image, *imago*, incorporeal being, mental image, mirage, phantasm, poltergeist, revenant, shade, specter, spirit, sprite, unreality, vapor, vision, wraith

PHASE (Aspect), ***noun*** angle, consideration, facet, feature, part, point, portion, *ratio*, section, side, *status*

PHASE (Period), ***noun*** age, continuance, duration, epoch, era, measured time, moment, period of time, point, point of time, season, session, shift, space of time, span, spell, stage, state, step, stretch, tenure, term, time, tour

PHENOMENON (Manifestation), ***noun*** apparition, appearance, display, feature, figure, form, image, materialization, presence, realization, shape, show, sight, sign, spectacle, vision

PHENOMENON (Unusual occurrence), ***noun*** amazement, amazing thing, astonishing thing, astonishment, curiosity, exception, experience, freak occurrence, marvel, miracle, nonesuch, nonpareil, *ostentum*, portent, *prodigium*, rare occurrence, rarity, *res mira*, sight, special occurrence, spectacle, unusual circumstance, unusual happening, unusual incident, wonder, wonderment, wonderwork

PHILANTHROPIC, *adjective* accommodating, almsgiving, altruistic, beneficent, benevolent, benign, benignant, bighearted, bounteous, bountiful, brotherly, charitable, civic-minded, considerate, devoted to others, eleemosynary, free, freehanded, generous, giving, good-natured, good-hearted, gracious, helpful, hospitable, humane, humanitarian, *humanus*, indulgent, kind, kindhearted, kindly, lavish, liberal, magnanimous, munificent, obliging,

open-handed, princely, public-spirited, selfless, ungrudging, unselfish, unsparing, unstinting

PHILANTHROPY, *noun* almsgiving, altruism, beneficence, benevolence, *benevolentia*, benignancy, benignity, bounteousness, bountifulness, bounty, brotherhood, brotherliness, brotherly love, charitableness, charity, considerateness, consideration, devotion to others, fellow feeling, free giving, free-handedness, generosity, good-heartedness, good nature, good will, good works, graciousness, helpfulness, hospitableness, hospitality, humaneness, humanitarianism, *humanitas*, indulgence, kindliness, kindness, largess, lavishness, liberality, love of mankind, magnanimity, munificence, open-handedness, princeliness, public spirit, self-sacrifice, selflessness, ungrudgingness, unselfishness, unsparingness

PHILISTINE, *noun* artless person, conformist, conventionalist, nouveau riche, social climber, traditionalist

PHILLIPIC, *noun* abusive language, acrimony, aspersion, bitter language, bitter words, castigation, censure, chastisement, commination, contumely, defamation, denunciation, detraction, diatribe, disparagement, execration, harangue, invective, malediction, obloquy, reprobation, revilement, screed, tirade, tongue-lashing, verbal abuse, vilification, vituperation

PHLEGMATIC, *adjective* aloof, apathetic, bloodless, bovine, callous, calm, cold, coldblooded, comatose, cool, detached, disinterested, dispassionate, distant, dull, frigid, halfhearted, hebetudinous, impassive, imperturbable, indifferent, inert, insensible, lackadaisical, languid, languorous, lazy, *lentus*, lethargic, lethargical, lifeless, listless, lymphatic, oscitant, passionless, passive, *patiens*, phlegmatical, pluckless, sedate, serene, slow, sluggish, sober, spiritless, spunkless, staid, stoical, stolid, stony, stupefied, supine, tame, *tardus*, torpid, unagitated, unanxious, unapprehensive, uncaring, uncommunicative, unconcerned, undemonstrative, undisturbed, unemotional, unexcitable, unexcited, unfeeling, unflustered, unimpassioned, unperturbed, unresponsive, unruffled, unsusceptible, untroubled, unworried

PHOBIA, *noun* abhorrence, abject fear, alarm, antipathy, anxiety, apprehension, aversion, awe, detestation, dislike, distaste, disturbance, dread, fear, fright, horror, loathing, obsession, panic, repugnance, terror, trepidation, unreasoned alarm, unreasoned fear

PHRASE, *noun* adage, aphorism, apothegm, byword, caption, clause, dictum, figure of speech, formula, idiom, inscription, motto, peculiar expression, proverb, saw, saying, slogan, trite expression, turn of expression, utterance, watchword, word group

PHRASE, *verb* articulate, call, clothe in words, come out with, comment, communicate, convey, couch, declare, deliver, denominate, describe, designate, dub, entitle, enunciate, express, find words to express, formulate, give expression to, give tongue to, give utterance, give voice to, give words to, impart, make known, mouth, name, observe, present, pronounce, put, put into language, put into words, recite, relate, remark, say, sound, speak, state, style, talk, tell, term, utter, verbalize, vocalize, voice, word

PHRASEOLOGY, *noun* argot, cant, choice of language, choice of words, command of idiom, command of language, composition, dialect, *dicendi genus*, diction, expression,

expression of ideas, formulation, idiom, jargon, language, lingo, literary artistry, literary style, locutio, locution, manner of expression, mode of expression, mode of speech, oratory, parlance, patois, pattern of words, peculiarity of phrasing, phrasing, rhetoric, selection of words, speech, style, terminology, text, tone, turn of expression, usage, use of words, vein, vocabulary, wording

PHYSICAL, *adjective* actual, bodily, carnal, concrete, corporal, corporeal, corporeous, earthly, embodied, external, flesh and blood, fleshly, human, incarnate, material, materiate, mundane, natural, nonspiritual, organic, palpable, real, sensible, sensual, sensuous, somatic, substantial, substantive, systemic, tangible, temporal, unspiritual, worldly
ASSOCIATED CONCEPTS: physical assets, physical condition, physical contact, physical control, physical damage, physical delivery, physical depreciation, physical disability, physical force, physical impairment, physical injury, physical loss, physical property

PICKET, *verb* avoid, blackball, blockade, boycott, demonstrate, demonstrate against, demonstrate protest, dissuade from entering, persuade not to work, protest, repudiate, restrict access, take part in a demonstration
ASSOCIATED CONCEPTS: informational picketing, lawful picketing, mass picketing, organizational picketing, peaceful picketing, primary picketing, recognitional picketing, retaliatory picketing, secondary boycotts, situs picketing, sympathy strikes, unlawful picketing, violent picketing

PIECEMEAL, *adverb* by degrees, drop by drop, gradually, in installments, in small doses, in small quantities, inch by inch, little by little, partially
ASSOCIATED CONCEPTS: piecemeal zoning

PIERCE *(Discern), **verb*** appreciate, apprehend, be acquainted with, be apprized of, be aware of, be conscious of, be informed, behold, cognize, comprehend, descry, detect, discover, distinguish, fathom, glimpse, grasp, have in sight, have knowledge of, know, lay eyes on, make out, make sensible, note, notice, observe, perceive, realize, recognize, see, understand, view, witness

PIERCE *(Lance), **verb*** bore, *confodere,* cut through, drive into, empierce, gore, impale, insert, knife, penetrate, perforare, perforate, plunge in, poniard, prick, puncture, run through, skewer, spear, spike, spit, stab, stick, *transfigere,* transfix, transpierce
ASSOCIATED CONCEPTS: pierce the corporate veil

PIERCING OF THE CORPORATE VEIL, *noun* alter ego, finding of additional liability in a subsidiary, finding of additional liability in shareholders, finding of personal liability, lancing of the corporate veil, lifting of the corporate veil, piercing of a body corporate's liability, piercing of a corporate body's liability, piercing of an artificial entity's liability, piecing of limited liability

PIGEONHOLE, *verb* allocate, allot, arrange, assort, bracket, break down, catalogue, categorize, class, collocate, divide, docket, file, form into classes, grade, group, index, label, list, methodize, name, order, organize, place, place in a category, put in order, rank, rate, reduce to order, section, sort, subdivide, subsume, systematize, tabulate, tag, ticket, type

PILFER, *verb* abscond with, appropriate illegally, bilk, commit larceny, convert, deprive illegally, embezzle, filch,

furari, loot, make off with, misappropriate, pillage, poach, purloin, rob, seize, steal, *surripere,* take, thieve

PILLAGE, *noun* appropriation, booty, brigandage, depredation, deprivation, despoilment, despoliation, destruction, devestation, *direptio, expilatio,* foray, havoc, maraud, piracy, plunder, plunderage, prey, raid, ransack, rapacity, *rapina,* rapine, ravage, razzia, sack, spoliation, vandalism

PILLAGE, *verb* bring to ruin, burglarize, damage, depopulate, depredate, desolate, despoil, destroy, devastate, lay in ashes, lay in ruins, lay waste, level, loot, make a shambles, make havoc, maraud, pirate, plunder, raid, ransack, reave, rob, ruin, ruinate, sabotage, sack, spoil, spoliate, steal, strip, thieve, waste, wreck
ASSOCIATED CONCEPTS: larceny

PILLORY, *verb* accuse, asperse, attaint, befoul, belittle, berate, besmear, besmirch, bespatter, blacken, blot, brand, bring shame upon, calumniate, cast a slur upon, cast aspersions on, cause a scandal, damage a reputation, debase, defame, defile, degrade, denigrate, denounce, destroy a reputation, discredit, disgrace, dishonor, disparage, expose, expose to infamy, gibbet, give a bad name, hold up to ridicule, hold up to shame, impute shame to, lampoon, laugh at, lower, make fun of, malign, mock, put in a bad light, put to shame, ridicule, run down, scandalize, scorn, smear, smirch, soil, spatter, speak ill of, stain, stigmatize, sully, taint, tarnish, traduce, vilify, vituperate

PINNACLE, *noun* acme, apex, apogee, cap, ceiling, climax, consummation, crest, crown, crowning point, culmination, extremity, head, height, highest degree, highest point, meridian, peak, point, summit, tip, top, upper extremity, utmost extent, utmost height, zenith

PINPOINT, *verb* be specific, enumerate, fix in, focus, locate, place, quantify, site, situate, specify
ASSOCIATED CONCEPTS: pinpoint rule

PIONEER, *noun* adventurer, colonist, colonizer, discoverer, establisher, explorer, forerunner, founder, founding father, frontiersman, innovator, inventor, lead, leader, modernist, pacesetter, pathfinder, precursor, predecessor, ringleader, scout, settler, trail blazer, vanguard

PIQUE, *verb* affront, agitate, anger, annoy, arouse resentment, bait, bedevil, beset, bother, bully, bullyrag, cause resentment, discompose, disgust, dismay, displease, disquiet, distemper, disturb, enrage, exasperate, fret, gall, give offense, give umbrage, gnaw, goad, harass, harry, heckle, hurt, incense, incite, incommode, inflame, infuriate, instigate, insult, irk, irritate, kindle wrath, madden, make wrathful, molest, needle, nettle, offend, pain, persecute, perturb, pester, plague, pother, provoke, put out of countenance, rile, roil, rouse, ruffle, *sollicitare,* sting, stir up, taunt, tease, torment, torture, trouble, try the patience, upset, vex, *vexare,* work up, worry

PIRATE *(Reproduce without authorization), **verb*** adopt and pass off as one's own, appropriate, borrow dishonestly, copy, counterfeit, crib, help oneself to, make use of without permission, plagiarize, purloin, steal, take illegally

PIRATE *(Take by violence), **verb*** commit piracy, commit robbery, despoil, lay hold of, loot, pillage, plunder, ransack, rifle, rob, sack, seize, spoil, spoilate, steal, take by force, thieve

PITFALL, noun abyss, catch, chasm, danger, dangerous spot, exposure to danger, exposure to harm, *fovea*, hazard, imminent danger, obstacle, peril, predicament, problem, quagmire, risk, risks, snare, threat, trap

PITHY, adjective brief, compact, compendious, compressed, concise, condensed, epigrammatic, full of meaning, gnomic, incisive, juicy, laconic, meaningful, meaty, *medullosus,* packed, pointed, sententious, substantial, succinct, summary, terse, trenchant

PITTED AGAINST, verb act in opposition to, argue against, attack, battle, be at cross purposes, be contrary to, be on the opposite side of, be on the other side of, challenge, collide, combat, confront, confute, contend, contest, contradict, contravene, controvert, counter, counteract, counterattack, counterbalance, countermine, counterpoise, countervail, counterweigh, counterwork, debate, defy, demur, deny, disaffirm, disagree, disapprove, dispute, encounter, go contrary to, go up against, join issue, land into, negate, object, obstruct, oppose, oppugn, prevent, prohibit, protest, put in opposition, rebut, refute, reject, remonstrate, repel, resist, set against, stand firm against, stand on the other side of, take a stand against, take exception to, take issue with
ASSOCIATED CONCEPTS: litigation

PITY, noun commiseration, compassion, condolement, condolence, consolation, feeling, fellow feeling, fellow suffering, fellowship in sorrow, kindliness, lenience, leniency, lenity, mercifulness, mercy, *misericordia,* quarter, ruth, sympathy
ASSOCIATED CONCEPTS: amnesty, clemency, pardon

PIVOTAL POINT, noun center, center of activity, center of attention, center of attraction, center of interest, central point, centrality, converging point, critical point, crux, essence, focal point, gravamen, heart, hub, key issue, main issue, most important part, point of convergence

PLACABLE, adjective appeasable, benevolent, capable of being appeased, capable of being pacified, charitable, clement, compassionate, conciliatory, disposed to mercy, *exorabilis,* exorable, forbearant, forbearing, forgiving, generous, gracious, indulgent, lenient, longanimous, magnanimous, merciful, mild, pacifiable, *placabilis,* reasonable, reconcilable, reluctant to punish, ruthful, satisfiable, softhearted, sparing, understanding, unresentful, unrevengeful, unvindictive, willing to forgive

PLACATE, verb allay, appease, assuage, bring to terms, calm, conciliate, disarm, dulcify, heal the breach, humor, hush, make peace, mollify, pacificate, pacify, patch up a quarrel, *placare,* please, propitiate, quiet, reconcile, restore harmony, salve, satisfy, silence, smooth, soothe, still, tranquilize, win over

PLACE, noun area, city, community, country, district, division, environment, locale, locality, location, neighborhood, point, region, scene, section, site, spot, state, territory, town, vicinity, village, zone
ASSOCIATED CONCEPTS: jurisdiction, long-arm jurisdiction, place of domicile, place of employment, place of residence, place to be named with particularity in searches and seizures, short-arm jurisdiction, venue

PLACID, adjective at peace, balmy, calm, calmative, collected, composed, cool, easeful, easygoing, equable, even, gentle, halcyon, halcyonian, imperturbable, irenic, irenical, meek, mild, motionless, pacific, paradisiacal, pastoral, patient, peaceable, peaceful, *placidus,* quiescent, quiet, quietus, reposeful, restful, serene, smooth, soothing, still, stormless, subdued, tame, tranquil, *tranquillus,* unagitated, undemonstrative, undisturbed, unexcited, unimpassioned, unmoved, unruffled, unstirring, untroubled

PLAGIARISM, noun appropriation, appropriation of a literary composition, copying, copyright infringement, duplication, forgery, imitation, imitation of an original, infringement, literary forgery, literary piracy, literary theft, misappropriation, pilfering, reproducing, reproduction, simulation, stealing, taking, thievery, unauthorized borrowing
ASSOCIATED CONCEPTS: copyright

PLAGIARIZE, verb adopt as one's own, apply to one's own uses, appropriate, avail oneself of, borrow dishonestly, copy from, counterfeit, duplicate, expropriate, fabricate, falsify, follow as a model, forge, imitate, infringe, misappropriate, paraphrase, pass off another's ideas as one's own, pass off another's writings as one's own, pirate, reduplicate, steal

PLAGUE, verb afflict, aggravate, aggrieve, annoy, badger, bait, bedevil, beset, bother, browbeat, bullyrag, cross, devil, discommode, discompose, displease, disquiet, distress, disturb, *exagitare,* exasperate, *exercere,* fret, gall, gibe, grate, harry, haunt, heckle, hector, incommode, inflict pain on, irk, irritate, macerate, molest, mortify, nag, needle, nettle, offend, oppress, pain, persecute, pester, pique, pother, prey on, provoke, rack, roil, ruffle, scourge, smite, spite, taunt, tease, torment, torture, trouble, try the patience, vex, *vexare,* worry

PLAIN LANGUAGE, noun accepted language, clear language, cogent writing, concise writing, conventional language, correct English, exact writing, plain English, plain speaking, plain speech, precise expression, precise writing, specific writing, unambiguous legalese, understandable language
Generally: plain language laws
ASSOCIATED CONCEPTS: comprehensible writing, correct writing, effective writing, proper writing

PLAINT, noun agony, anguish, complaint, cry, dirge, discontent, displeasure, dissatisfaction, distress, expression of discontent, expression of grief, expression of pain, grief, grieving, groan, lament, *lamenta,* lamentation, moan, outcry, *querela, querimonia,* sigh, sorrow, wail, whine, woe

PLAINTIFF, noun accuser, adversary, claimant, complainant, individual who brings a lawsuit, litigant, one who brings an action, opponent, party to the suit, party who sues, petitioner, *petitor,* suitor
ASSOCIATED CONCEPTS: indispensable party plaintiff, nominal plaintiff, proper plaintiff, real plaintiff, third party plaintiff
FOREIGN PHRASES: Reus excipiendo fit actor. The defendant by pleading may make himself a plaintiff. **Melior est conditio possidentis ubi neuter jus habet.** The condition of the possessor and that of the defendant is better than that of the plaintiff. **Cum par delictum est duorum, semper oneratur petitor, et melior habetur possessoris causa.** When there is equal fault on both sides, the burden is always placed on the plaintiff, and the cause of the possessor is preferred. **In praeparatoriis ad judicium favetur actori.** In those matters preceding judgment the plaintiff is favored.

PLAN, noun agenda, alternative, ambition, arrangement, cabal, campaign, complot, conspiracy, course of action, curriculum, design, draft, expedient, forethought, hope, intendment, intent, intention, itinerary, plot, predeliberation, preparation, program, projection, proposal, proposed action, proposition, prospectus, readiness, resolve, schedule, scheme, strategem, strategy, suggestion, syllabus, tactic, undertaking

ASSOCIATED CONCEPTS: ecological plan, feasibility plan, plan for reorganization, planning board

PLAN, verb aim, arrange, block out, cabal, calculate, collude, complot, concoct, connive, conspire, contrive, counterplot, design, determine upon, devise, engineer, establish guidelines for, expect, figure, frame, harbor a design, have a policy, intend, intrigue, lay out, lay the foundation, look ahead, machinate, make arrangements, make preparations, make ready, map out, mark out a course, organize, outline, plot, prearrange, preconcert, precontrive, predesign, predetermine, premeditate, prepare, project, propose, provide for, purpose, resolve, schedule, scheme, set up, shape a course, take measures, think ahead, work out

PLANT (Covertly place), **verb** bury, cache, camouflage, cloak, cover up, disguise, hide away, keep clandestine, keep hidden, keep secret, mantle, mask, obscure, put in concealment, put out of sight, render invisible, screen, secrete, shade, shroud, veil, wrap

ASSOCIATED CONCEPTS: entrapment

PLANT (Place firmly), **verb** base, bed, deposit, embed, engraft, ensconce, establish, fix, ground, implant, impregnate, infix, inject, inlay, insert, inset, install, instill, lay the foundation, locate, make a place for, place, put, root, set, set firmly, set up, settle, situate, sow, station, stick in, thrust in

PLATFORM, noun assumed position, attitude, body of principles, campaign promises, course, course of action, declaration, declaration of policy, doctrine, line of conduct, outlook, party line, party planks, plan, plan of action, point of view, policy, position, precepts, principles, program, proposal, proposed action, proposition, rule of action, scheme, tenets, view

PLATITUDE, noun absence of meaning, banality, cliche, commonplace expression, commonplace idea, commonplace phrase, dearth of ideas, dull comment, flat saying, hackneyed expression, hackneyed idea, hackneyed phrase, hackneyed saying, inanity, insipid remark, meaningless saying, nonsense, reiteration, senseless prate, stale comment, stereotyped saying, threadbare phrase, trite expression, trite phrase, trite remark, trite saying, triviality, truism, vapid expression, want of originality

PLAUSIBLE, adjective accepted, apparent, arguable, believable, cogitable, colorable, commanding belief, conceivable, conjecturable, convincing, credible, defensible, demanding belief, deserving belief, feasible, grantable, imaginable, justifiable, legitimate, logical, maintained, ostensible, possible, presumable, probabilis, putative, rational, reasonable, seeming, seemingly worthy of acceptance, sensible, sound, supposed, suppositional, thinkable, verisimilis, within the realm of possibility, worthy of credence

PLEA, noun allegation, answer, arguments at the bar, assertion, claim, counterstatement, defendant's answer to charges, defense, exceptio, excusatio, legal argument, legal defense, petitio, pleading, pleadings, rebuttal, refutation, reply, response, retort, statement alleged in defense, statement alleged in justification, statement of defense, statement which answers the charges, statements on behalf of the defense

ASSOCIATED CONCEPTS: entering a plea, plea in abatement, plea in bar, plea in equity, plea of estoppel, plea of guilty, plea of insanity, plea of nolo contendere, plea of not guilty, plea of payment, plea of recoupment, plea of release, plea of self-defense, plea of setoff

FOREIGN PHRASES: *Ambiguum placitum interpretari debet contra proferentem.* An ambiguous plea ought to be interpreted against the party entering it. *Exceptio falsi omnium ultima.* A false plea is the worst of all. *Interdum evenit ut exceptio quae prima facie justa videtur, tamen inique noceat.* It sometimes happens that a plea which on its face seems just, nevertheless is injurious and inequitable.

PLEAD (Allege in a legal action), **verb** advance, affirm, affirm explicitly, allege, assert, assert formally, assert positively, attest to, bring forward, contend, emphasize, enunciate, maintain, make an affidavit, make an assertion, present, proclaim, put forth, put forward, put in an affidavit, reaffirm, reassert, set forth, state, state emphatically, stress, swear

ASSOCIATED CONCEPTS: plead a cause of action, responsive pleading

PLEAD (Argue a case), **verb** advocate, argue at the bar, argue the point, bring into court, *causam agere,* contend for, defend a case, maintain by arguments, prosecute one's case, put one's case, speak for, speak up for, stand up for, state one's case, urge reasons for, use arguments

PLEAD (Implore), **verb** address a request, beseech, call upon, charge, clamor for, entreat, importune, make a request, *obsecrare, orare,* petition, prefer a request, press, put up a request, request, solicit, supplicate, urge

PLEADING, noun accusation, allegation, allegation of facts, answer, argument, claim, complaint, counterstatement, defendant's answer to charges, defense, denial, formal assertion, formal averment, plaintiff's allegations, plea, rebuttal, reply, responsive allegations, statement of defense, written statement of defense, written statements of accusation

ASSOCIATED CONCEPTS: alternative pleading, amendment to a pleading, amplication of the pleadings, argumentative pleading, blind pleading, clarification of the pleading, defect in the pleading, demurrer, failure to state a cause of action, failure to state a claim, formal pleading, frivolous pleading, inconsistent pleadings, liberal construction of pleadings, motion to correct pleadings, motion to dismiss the pleading, petition, prejudicial pleading, privileged pleadings, responsive pleading, scandalous pleading, sham pleading, supplemental pleading, verified pleading

FOREIGN PHRASES: *Placita negativa duo exitum non faciunt.* Two negative pleas do not make an issue. *Qui non negat fatetur.* He who does not deny, admits. *Ambigua responsio contra proferentem est accipienda.* An ambiguous answer is to be taken against him who offers it.

PLEBISCITE, noun ballot, choice, election, mandate, poll, referendum, vote

PLEDGE (Binding promise), **noun** act of giving one's word, agreement, assurance, attestation, avowal, avowance, commitment, compact, contract, covenant, guarantee, oath, obligation, promise, promissory oath, *promissum,* solemn declaration, solemn word, statement on oath, undertaking, vow, warranty, word, word of honor

PLEDGE (Security), **noun** collateral, deposit, earnest, earnest payment, guarantee, installment, personal security, *pignus,* real security, security, stake, stake money, token payment

ASSOCIATED CONCEPTS: assignment, collateral security, pledge of securities, pledged personalty, pledged property, secured transactions

PLEDGE *(Deposit)*, **verb**   bond, give as a guarantee, give as security for a debt, give as security for an obligation, give as surety, give one's signature, give security, guarantee, hypothecate, impignorate, indorse, insure, offer collateral, post, put in pawn, put up, stake

PLEDGE *(Promise the performance of)*, **verb**   assert solemnly, assure, avow, be answerable for, become bound to, bind, bind oneself, commit oneself, contract an obligation, covenant, engage solemnly, engage to give, give a guarantee, give assurance, give one's word, guarantee, make a promise, *obligare, oppignerare,* promise solemnly, take upon oneself, undertake, warrant, vow

PLENARY, adjective   absolute, complete, comprehensive, entire, exhaustive, full, full-blown, full-charged, fully constituted, fully furnished, limitless, thorough, total, unconfined, undiminished, unlimited, unqualified, unrestricted, whole
ASSOCIATED CONCEPTS: plenary action

PLENIPOTENTIARY, noun   advocate, agent, ambassador, assistant, broker, chancellor, coagent, consul, delegate, deputy, diplomat, diplomatic agent, emissary, envoy, factor, internuncio, legate, lieutenant, messenger, official representative, proctor, provost, proxy, regent, representative, secondary, speaker, spokesman, spokesperson, substitute, surrogate, viceroy

PLETHORA, noun   abundance, accumulation, amplitude, congestion, deluge, engorgement, excess, exorbitance, exorbitancy, flood, full measure, fullness, glut, great quantity, heap, impletion, inundation, load, margin, nimiety, overabundance, overflow, overload, overplus, oversupply, plentifulness, plenty, profuseness, profusion, repleteness, repletion, richness, satiation, satiety, saturation, spate, superabundance, superfluity, superfluousness, supersaturation, surfeit, surplus, surplusage, swelling, turgescence, undue amount

PLIABLE, adjective   accommodating, acquiescent, adaptable, adaptive, adjustable, alterable, amenable, assenting, bendable, biddable, changeable, compliant, conformable, conforming, controllable, docile, ductile, easily bent, easily influenced, easily persuaded, easygoing, elastic, facile, fictile, *flexibilis,* flexible, flexile, formable, formative, governable, impressionable, inclined, lamblike, *lentus,* limber, lissome, lithe, lithesome, malleable, manageable, manipulable, meek, modifiable, moldable, mutable, nonresisting, obedient, obliging, persuadable, persuasible, pervious, plastic, pliant, protean, proteiform, receptive, responsive, sequacious, servile, slavish, stretchable, suasible, submissive, supple, swayable, teachable, tractable, tractile, variable, versatile, willing, yielding

PLIANT, adjective   accommodating, acquiescent, adaptable, agreeable, bendable, compliable, compliant, concessive, conformable, conforming, deferential, docile, ductile, easily bent, easily persuaded, elastic, flexible, formable, impressible, impressionable, indecisive, indulgent, influenceable, irresolute, *lentus,* limber, lithe, malleable, manageable, meek, moldable, *mollis,* movable, nonresisting, obedient, obeisant, passive, plastic, pliable, readily influenced, receptive,

responsive, sequacious, servile, slavish, soft, submissive, subordinate, subservient, suggestible, supple, susceptible, susceptive, swayable, tractable, tractile, unassertive, undecided, willing, yielding

PLIGHT, noun   adverse circumstance, adversity, awkward situation, case, circumstance, condition, corner, crisis, critical situation, difficulty, dilemma, embarrassing position, embarrassing situation, emergency, footing, hardship, imbroglio, lot, misfortune, muddle, pass, pinch, position, predicament, problem, quagmire, quandary, reverse, scrape, setback, situation, state, state of affairs, station, strait, trial, trouble

PLOT *(Land)*, **noun**   acreage, *agellus,* block, division, field, ground, lot, parcel of land, patch, piece of land, plat, property, tract

PLOT *(Secret plan)*, **noun**   cabal, chicane, collusion, complicity, complot, *coniuratio,* conspiracy, *conspiratio,* counterplot, deception, design, intrigue, manipulation, ploy, ruse, scheme, stratagem, tactic, trick

PLOT, verb   act in collusion, arrange, be in collusion, cabal, collude, *coniurare,* connive, consentire, conspirare, conspire, deal secretly, devise, engineer, form a plan, frame, have designs, intrigue, machinate, make a plan, make arrangements, make preparations, maneuver, organize, outline, plan mischief, plan secretly, prearrange, preconcert, premeditate, prepare, scheme, take measures, take steps, undermine, work out

PLOY, noun   action, artifice, contrivance, device, maneuver, mechanism, plan, ruse, scheme, stratagem, trick, way, wile

PLUNDER, noun   booty, depredation, devastation, foray, haul, ill-gotten goods, illicit gains, loot, maraud, pillage, *praeda,* raid, *rapina,* rapine, ravin, razzia, robbery, sack, seizure, spoils, spoliation, stolen articles, stolen goods, take, theft

PLUNDER, verb   buccaneer, carry off, *compilare,* deplume, depredate, desolate, despoil, displume, divest, *expilare,* flay, impoverish, lay in ruins, lay waste, loot, maraud, overthrow, pillage, pirate, *praedari,* prey on, purloin, raid, ransack, ravage, raze, reave, rifle, rob, ruin, sack, seize, spoliate, steal, strip, take away, thieve

PLURALITY, noun   advantage in votes cast, bulk, great number, host, large amount, large number, large quantity, lead, main part, majority, multitude, multitudo, preponderance, preponderancy, shoal, superiority in number, weight of numbers
ASSOCIATED CONCEPTS: majority, quorum

PLY, verb   busy oneself with, carry on, devote oneself to, do work with, employ, engage in, *exercere,* exercise, exploit, handle, make use of, manipulate, occupy oneself with, operate, persevere at, practice, pursue, put in practice, put into effect, tackle, take up, undertake, use, utilize, wage, wield, work

POACH, verb   appropriate, carry off, filch, *furtim feras intercipere,* make off with, misappropriate, peculate, pilfer, pirate, plunder by stealth, purloin, rifle, run off with, snatch, steal, take by illegal methods, take by unfair methods, take illegally, walk off with

POINT (*Item*), **noun**   argument, *caput*, consideration, designated ground, detail, feature, ground, issue, matter, particular, reason, *res*, specific, thought
ASSOCIATED CONCEPTS: point of law, point of order

POINT (*Period of time*), **noun**   conjuncture, exact moment, hour, instant, interval, juncture, moment, occasion, precise moment, second, specific moment, stage, time

POINT (*Purpose*), **noun**   aim, core, design, end, essence, goal, import, intent, intention, motive, object, objective, purport, reason, significance, substance

POINT OF VIEW, noun   angle, angle of vision, apprehension, attitude, belief, concept, conception, conviction, estimate, idea, opinion, outlook, perception, perspective, platform, position, posture, private opinion, respect, side, slant, stand, standpoint, viewpoint

POLARIZE, verb   break up into opposing factions, contrapose, contrast, oppose, pit against one another, put in opposition

POLEMIC, adjective   argumental, argumentative, conflicting, contentious, contestable, contradictory, controversial, debatable, dialectic, dialectical, discordant, discrepant, disputatious, dissentient, dissonant, divided, eristic, eristical, factious, inharmonious, open to debate, open to discussion, open to question, polemical, pugnacious, quarrelsome, schismatic, subject to controversy, unreconciled

POLICE, noun   arm of the law, constabulary, custodians of the law, detective force, forces of law and order, government officers, law enforcement agency, law enforcement agents, law enforcement body, officers, officers of the law, peace officers, police force, police officers
ASSOCIATED CONCEPTS: police action, police brutality, police power

POLICE, verb   care for, check, control, exercise authority, exert authority, have authority, have charge of, invigilate, keep guard, keep in order, keep in view, keep order, keep orderly, keep under control, keep vigil, keep watch, observe, overlook, oversee, patrol, preserve public order, preserve public tranquility, prevent crime, prevent offenses against the state, promote public health and safety, protect, regulate, render safe, restrain, restrict access, rule, safeguard, secure, stand guard, stand sentinel, superintend, supervise, systematize, use one's authority, watch, watch diligently

POLICY (*Contract*), **noun**   agreement, arrangement, contractual obligation, contractual statement, insurance contract, legal document, mutual agreement, mutual undertaking, obligation, pact, schedule, understanding
ASSOCIATED CONCEPTS: insurance policy

POLICY (*Plan of action*), **noun**   approach, *consilium*, course, course of action, course of conduct, doctrine, established order, fundamental principles, general guidelines, general principles, governing course of action, governing plan, governing principle, line, line of action, line of conduct, management, manner of proceeding, method, mode of management, party line, plan, plan of campaign, platform, polity, prescribed form, principles, procedure, program, proposal, proposed action, proposition, rule of action, scheme, stratagem, ways
ASSOCIATED CONCEPTS: public policy

POLITIC, adjective   acute, artful, artfully contrived, astute, *astutus*, brilliant, calculating, canny, careful, cautious, circumspect, clever, considerate, contemplative, crafty, cunning, deceitful, diplomatic, discreet, effective, efficacious, enlightened, expedient, farsighted, feline, foxy, guarded, heedful, ingenious, judicial, judicious, knowing, mindful, perceptive, practical, provident, *prudens*, prudent, prudential, prudently contrived, regardful, sagacious, sensible, sharp, shrewd, subtle, tactful, thoughtful, well-adapted, well-advised, well-devised, well-informed, well-judged, wily, wise

POLITICAL, adjective   administrative, bureaucratic, civic, *civilis*, governmental, partisan, public, *publicus*
ASSOCIATED CONCEPTS: political question

POLITICIAN, noun   campaigner, candidate, governmental leader, lawgiver, lawmaker, legislator, office seeker, officeholder, officer of state, official, partisan, party member, politico, public servant, representative, statesman

POLITICS, noun   campaigning, *civilis ratio*, electioneering, governance, government, matters of state, partisanism, party leadership, party politics, party system, political affairs, political influence, political involvement, political maneuvers, political methods, political partisanship, political process, political strategy, public service, state affairs, statesmanship
ASSOCIATED CONCEPTS: campaign financing laws, disclosure laws, election laws, lobbying laws, reporting laws
FOREIGN PHRASES: *Politiae legibus non leges, politiis adaptandae.* Politics should be adapted to the laws, not the laws to politics.

POLITY, noun   body politic, civil constitution, commonwealth, constitution, country, course, form of government, fundamental principles of government, line, nation, nationality, plan of action, platform, policy, principles, procedure, program, recognized principles, *reipublicae forma*, republic, sovereignty, state, system of government

POLL (*Canvass*), **noun**   capitation, catalogue of persons, census, census report, census return, count, enumeration, evaluation, inquiry, numbering, numeration, public opinion, questary, questionnaire, register, registration, return, statistic, survey, tabulation, tally

POLL (*Casting of votes*), **noun**   ballot, casting of ballots, choice, consensus, decision, determination, election, elective privilege, expression of will, formal expression of choice, plebiscite, popular decision, preference, referendum, selection, voice, vote
ASSOCIATED CONCEPTS: electioneering at poll, polling place

POLL, verb   ballot, call the roll, canvass, collect the vote, compute, conduct research on, count, enumerate, keep count of, keep score, list, make a survey, record the vote, register, run checks on, sample, score, survey, tabulate, take a census, take a roll call, tally, total

POLLUTE, verb   adulterate, alloy, befoul, begrime, bemire, besmirch, bespatter, contaminate, corrupt, debase, debauch, defile, degrade, denaturalize, deprave, desecrate, destroy, dirty, dishonor, filthify, foul, grime, impair, infect, maculate, make foul, mess, mire, muck, muddy, pervert, poison, profane, prostitute, render filthy, smirch, soil, spatter, spoil, stain, sully, taint, tarnish, undermine, unhallow, violate, vitiate
ASSOCIATED CONCEPTS: ecology, environmental conservation, environmental protection, nuisance

POLYGAMOUS, *adjective* engaging in bigamy, engaging in unlawful marriage, having multiple husbands, having multiple wives, having plurality of wives or husbands, practicing plural marriage
ASSOCIATED CONCEPTS: bigamy, monogamy

PONDER, *verb* analyze, apply the mind, appraise, brood over, cerebrate, cogitate, commune with oneself, concentrate upon, consider, *considerare,* contemplate, debate, deliberate, devote thought to, digest, evaluate, examine, excogitate, give thought to, intellectualize, introspect, meditate, mull over, muse, occupy the thoughts with, *ponderare,* premeditate, puzzle over, rack the brains, ratiocinate, rationalize, reason, reflect upon, review, revolve in the mind, ruminate, speculate, study, take account of, take under consideration, theorize, think deeply, think on, turn over in the mind, view from all sides, view with deliberation, weigh, wonder about

PONDERABLE, *adjective* appreciable, ascertainable, cognizable, comprehensible, considerable, discernible, discoverable, distinguishable, knowable, palpable, perceptible, real, recognizable, substantive, understandable, weighable

PONDEROUS, *adjective* awkward, big, boring, bulky, burdensome, clumsy, corpulent, cumbersome, cumbrous, dense, drearisome, dreary, droning, dull, elephantine, enormous, forced, *gravis,* hard to lift, heavy, hulking, labored, large, leaden, lifeless, lumbering, lumpish, lusterless, lymphatic, massive, monotonous, onerous, oppressive, overweight, *ponderosus,* prosaic, slow-moving, sluggish, stiff, stolid, stout, supine, tedious, unlively, unmanageable, unwieldy, wearisome, wearying, weighty

POOL, *noun* alliance, amalgamation, bank, cartel, coalition, collaboration, collective, collectivism, combination, combination of funds, combine, common fund, common ownership, community of possession, confederacy, confederation, consolidation, consortium, cooperation, copartnership, cosharing, federation, joint concern, joint ownership, joint possession, league, mutual ownership, partnership, syndicate, trust, unification, union
ASSOCIATED CONCEPTS: insolvency pool, involuntary market pool, mortgage pool, stock pool

POOL, *verb* affiliate with, ally, amalgamate, associate, band together, blend, collaborate, combine, confederate, conjoin, connect, consolidate, coordinate, enter into partnership with, federate, involve together, league, merge, mix, share, unify, unite
ASSOCIATED CONCEPTS: pooling of assets

POOR *(Inferior in quality),* **adjective** bad, badly made, barely passable, base, beggarly, below par, below standard, cheap, coarse, common, contemptible, crude, defective, deficient, dubious, faulty, flimsy, gimcrack, imperfect, inadequate, inartistic, indifferent, inferior, lacking in quality, low, low-grade, marred, meager, mean, mediocre, *mediocris,* miserable, ordinary, paltry, pitiful, rejected, scant, scrub, scrubby, scurvy, second best, second-rate, seedy, shabby, shoddy, sleazy, sordid, sorry, subgrade, substandard, tawdry, *tenuis,* trashy, under average, undergrade, unimpressive, unsatisfactory, unsightly, unworthy, valueless, vulgar, wanting, weak, worthless, wretched
ASSOCIATED CONCEPTS: poor condition

POOR *(Underprivileged),* **adjective** bankrupt, beggared, bereft of funds, depleted, deprived, destitute, dispossessed,

distressed, drained, *egens,* embarrassed, empty-handed, fortuneless, hard up, ill-provided for, impecunious, impoverished, in distress, in embarrassed circumstances, in narrow circumstances, in need, in penury, in pinched circumstances, in reduced circumstances, in straitened circumstances, in want, indigent, *inops,* insolvent, *mendicus,* moneyless, necessitous, needful, needy, out of cash, out of money, pauperized, penniless, penurious, poverty-stricken, reduced, reduced to beggary, ruined, short, short of money, starved, straitened, strapped, suffering privation, unable to make ends meet, unmoneyed, unprosperous, unprovided for, with meager funds, with scanty funds, without a penny
ASSOCIATED CONCEPTS: petition to proceed as a poor person

POPULACE, *noun* body politic, canaille, citizenry, common folk, common people, commonage, commonalty, commoners, community, crowd, folk, folks, general public, habitants, humanity, individuals, inhabitants, masses, multitude, nation, people, persons, *plebs,* population, proletariat, public, residents, society

POPULAR, *adjective* accepted, accredited, admired, asked for, attractive, beloved, celebrated, conventional, coveted, current, customary, demanded, desirable, desired, doted on, enjoyed, esteemed, estimable, fair-haired, famous, fashionable, favored, favorite, highly thought of, in demand, in favor, in high esteem, in high favor, in vogue, liked, loved, noted, orthodox, palatable, pet, pleasing, praised, preferred, prevailing, prevalent, received, requested, respected, sought after, stamped with approval, standard, stylish, venerable, wanted, well-liked, well-received, well thought of, winning
ASSOCIATED CONCEPTS: popular election, popular name, popular name for a statute, popular sense

POPULATION, *noun* body politic, citizenry, citizens, *civium,* commonalty, community, dwellers, folk, general public, habitancy, habitants, humanity, *incolarum numerus,* inhabitants, masses, nation, natives, number of people, people, persons, populace, populacy, public, residents, society

POPULOUS, *adjective* *celeber,* close, closely packed, compact, crammed, crawling with people, crowded, dense, *frequens,* full, inhabited, massed, multitudinous, numerous, occupied, packed, peopled, populated, rife, swarming, teeming, tenanted, thick, thickly settled, thronged, well-populated

PORNOGRAPHY, *noun* bawdiness, curiosa, erotica, filth, indecency, lewdness, lubricity, obscene art, obscene literature, obscenity, prurience, salaciousness, salacity, smut, vulgarity
ASSOCIATED CONCEPTS: censorship, First Amendment rights

PORTAL, *noun* access, aperture, approach, corridor, door, doorway, entrance, entranceway, entry, gate, gateway, ingress, inlet, means of access, opening, passageway, postern, pylon

PORTEND, *verb* adumbrate, announce, augur, augurate, auspicate, be an omen, be harbinger, betoken, bode, caution, divine, forebode, forecast, foreshadow, foreshow, foretell, foretoken, forewarn, give token, herald, indicate, indicate beforehand, menace, notify, omen, ominate, portendere, precurse, predict, prefigurate, prefigure, preindicate, premonish, premonstrate, presage, preshow, presignify, prognosticate, prophesy, put on guard, show promise, *significare,* signify, threaten, vaticinate, warn

PORTENTOUS (Eliciting amazement), **adjective**   amazing, astonishing, breathtaking, exceptional, extraordinary, great, inconceivable, incredible, indescribable, marvelous, memorable, miraculous, notable, noteworthy, novel, out of the ordinary, outstanding, phenomenal, prodigal, prodigious, rare, remarkable, shocking, singular, staggering, startling, stirring, striking, stupendous, superb, superlative, surprising, tremendous, uncustomary, unexampled, unheard of, unique, unparalleled, unprecedented, unusual, wonderful, wondrous

PORTENTOUS (Ominous), **adjective**   alarming, augural, augurous, baleful, black, bodeful, boding, cautionary, dark, dire, direful, divinatory, doomful, dread, dreadful, dreary, fateful, fatiloquent, fearful, forbidding, foreboding, foretelling, forewarning, forthcoming, frightening, frightful, gloomy, grim, haunting, heralding, ill-boding, ill-fated, ill-starred, inauspicious, indicative, intimidating, mantic, menacing, minacious, minatorial, minatory, monitory, ominous, oracular, perilous, portending evil, premonitive, premonitory, presageful, presaging, presentient, prophetic, prophetical, pythonic, sibylline, sinister, somber, suggestive, threatening, unpropitious

PORTFOLIO, **noun**   futures, holdings, investments, negotiables, scrinium, securities, stocks, stocks and bonds

PORTION, **noun**   allotment, amount, component, element, excerpt, fair share, fragment, installment, measure, moiety, part, percentage, piece, portion, quantity, quota, ration, section, sector, segment, share

PORTION, **verb**   allocate, allot, apportion, bequeath, bequest, break down into portions, break up into units, budget, disperse, divide into shares, dole, dole out, parcel, partition, prorate, ration, section, segment, separate, split up, split up into units, subdivide

PORTRAY, **verb**   act, adumbrate, characterize, convey a verbal image, convey an impression, delineate, depict, depicture, depingere, describe, detail, draw, express, give words to, illustrate, limn, outline, paint, particularize, picture, present, recreate, report, represent, represent in words, reproduce, set forth, show, sketch, specify, stage, tell vividly

POSE (Impersonate), **verb**   act as, act the part of, ape, assume the character of, assume the role of, copy, counterfeit, double for, emulate, imitate, masquerade as, mimic, mock, model oneself after, parody, pass for, personate, play a part, portray, pretend to be, simulate, take the part of

POSE (Propound), **verb**   advance, ask, assert, broach, declare, interrogate, introduce, lay before, lay down, make a motion, moot, move, offer, posit, postulate, predicate, present, proffer, propose, put forward, put to, puzzle, query, question, set before, state, submit, suggest, tender, throw out, volunteer
ASSOCIATED CONCEPTS: pose a question

POSIT, **verb**   acknowledge, advance, advocate, affirm, allege, announce, argue, assert, asseverate, assume, attest, aver, avouch, avow, bring forward, certify, cite, claim, contend, declare, enunciate, express, hypothesize, inform, insist, issue a statement, lay down, maintain, moot, pose, postulate, predicate, proclaim, profess, promulgate, pronounce, propose, propound, put forth, put forward, say, set forth, state, stipulate, submit, take a stand, tell, testify, utter with conviction, vouch

POSITION (Business status), **noun**   appointment, assignment, avocation, business, calling, career, concern, duty, echelon, employment, function, incumbency, job, line of business, line of work, means of livelihood, occupation, office, post, practice, profession, pursuit, responsibility, role, situation, specialty, sphere, station, trade, vocation, walk of life, work

POSITION (Point of view), **noun**   apprehension, attitude, bearing, bent, bias, conclusion, feeling, frame of mind, inclination, judgment, leaning, mental outlook, mind set, opinion, outlook, pose, posture, predilection, predisposition, preference, presumption, proclivity, proneness, propensity, sentiment, slant, standpoint, tendency, turn of mind, view, viewpoint, way of thinking

POSITION (Situation), **noun**   circumstances, condition, footing, ground, locus, place, plight, posture, predicament, spot, state, station, status

POSITIVE (Confident), **adjective**   assured, believing, certain, certus, convinced, decided, decisive, definite, determined, fully convinced, insistent, perfectly sure, persuaded, reassured, satisfied, secure, self-assured, self-confident, sure, trusting, undoubting, unhesitating, unquestioning, unshaken, untroubled, unwavering
ASSOCIATED CONCEPTS: positive identification

POSITIVE (Incontestable), **adjective**   absolute, ascertained, authentic, axiomatic, axiomatical, beyond all question, beyond doubt, categorical, certain, clear, conclusive, decided, definite, determinate, evident, explicit, final, inappealable, incontestable, incontrovertible, indisputable, indubitable, inescapable, infallible, irrefragable, irrefutable, past dispute, precise, reliable, sound, sure, true, trustworthy, unanswerable, unchallengeable, unconfutable, undeniable, unequivocal, unerring, unimpeachable, unmistakable, unqualified, unquestionable, unrefutable
ASSOCIATED CONCEPTS: positive proof

POSITIVE (Prescribed), **adjective**   assigned, binding, commanded, compulsory, decreed, demanded, dictated, enacted, enjoined, established, exacted, fixed, impera-tive, imposed, instituted, issued, laid down, legislated, mandatory, obligatory, ordained, required, requisite, ruled, set, stated authoritatively
ASSOCIATED CONCEPTS: positive law

POSSE, **noun**   arm of the law, armed band, band, band of armed men, band of men armed with legal authority, body of men armed with legal process, body of men summoned by a sheriff, civilian police, custodians of the law, detachment of police, detail, force armed with legal authority, group of deputies, group of persons organized with legal authorization, law enforcement body

POSSESS, **verb**   acquire, adfirmatio, assume ownership, be in possession of, be in receipt of, be seized of, come into possession of, command, control, devolve upon, enjoy, enter into possession, gain, gain for oneself, get, get as one's own, habere, have, have a deed for, have a title to, have absolute disposal of, have as property, have at one's command, have at one's disposal, have for one's own, have in hand, have rights to, hold, keep, maintain, monopolize, obtain, occupy, own, receive, retain, secure, seize, take possession, tenere
ASSOCIATED CONCEPTS: lawfully possess, seized or possessed
FOREIGN PHRASES: **Aliud est possidere, aliud esse in possessione.** It is one thing to possess; it is another to be in possession.

POSSESSION *(Ownership)*, **noun**　authority, custody, demesne, domination, dominion, exclusive right, lordship, occupancy, *possessio*, proprietorship, right, right of retention, seisin, supremacy, tenancy, title

ASSOCIATED CONCEPTS: action to recover possession, actual possession, adverse possession, chain of possession, constructive possession, continuity of possession, continuous possession, debtor in possession, estate in possession, holder in possession, hostile possession, lawful possession, mortgagee in possession, naked possession, notorious possession, open and notorious possession, party in possession, peaceable possession, person in possession, physical possession, purchaser in possession, quiet possession, right of possession, tenant in possession, undisturbed possession, uninterrupted possession, unlawful possession, wrongful possession

FOREIGN PHRASES: *Traditio nihil amplius transferre debet vel potest, ad eum qui accipit, quam est apud eum qui tradit.* Delivery ought to, and can, transfer nothing more to him who receives than is in possession of him who makes the delivery. *Jus triplex est,-propietatis, possessionis, et possibilitatis.* Right is threefold,-of property, of possession, and of possibility. *In aequali jure melior est conditio possidentis.* In a case of equal right the condition of the party in possession is the better. *Pro possessione praesumitur de jure.* A presumption of law arises from possession. *Nihil praescribitur nisi quod possidetur.* There is no prescription for that which is not possessed. *Privatio praesupponit habitum.* A deprivation presupposes something held or possessed. *Duorum in solidum dominium vel possessio esse non potest.* Sole ownership or possession cannot be in two persons. C*um de lucro duorum quaeritur, melior est causa possidentis.* When the question of gain lies between two persons, the cause of the possessor is the better. *Longa possessio parit jus possidendi, et tollit actionem vero domino.* Long possession creates the right of possession, and deprives the true owner of his right of action. *Aliud est possidere, aliud esse in possessione.* It is one thing to possess; it is another to be in possession. *Quod meum est sine facto meo vel defectu meo amitti vel in alium transferri non potest.* That which is mine cannot be transferred to another without my act or my default. *Quod meum est sine me auferri non potest.* What is mine cannot be taken away without my consent. *Nul charter, nul vente, ne nul done vault perpetualment, si le donor n'est seise al temps de contracts de deux droits, sc. del droit de possession et del droit de propertie.* No grant, no sale, no gift, is valid forever, unless the donor, at the time of the contract, has two rights, namely, the right of possession, and the right of property. *Donatio perficitur possessione accipientis.* A gift is perfected by the possession of the receiver. *Melior est conditio possidentis, et rei quam actoris.* The condition of the possessor and that of the defendant is better than that of the plaintiff. *In pari delicto melior est conditio possidentis.* When the parties are equally in the wrong, the condition of the possessor is the preferable one. *Longa possessio jus parit.* Long possession begets right. *Donator nunquam desinit possidere, antequam donatorius incipiat possidere.* A donor never ceases to possess until the donee begins to possess. *Non valet donatio nisi subsequatur traditio.* A gift is invalid unless accompanied by possession. *Nemo dare potest quod non habet.* No one is able to give that which he has not. *Terra manens vacua occupanti conceditur. Land remaining vacant is given to the occupant.* Non potest videri desisse habere qui nunquam habuit. A person who has never had cannot be deemed to have ceased to have it. *In pari causa possessor potior haberi debet.* In an equal cause he who has the possession has the

advantage. *Cum par delictum est duorum, semper oneratur petitor et melior habetur possessoris causa.* When there is equal fault on both sides, the burden is always placed on the plaintiff, and the cause of the possessor is preferred.

POSSESSION *(Property)*, **noun**　asset, belonging, bona, chattel, effect, goods, holding, item, item of personalty, money, movable, *possessio*, res, resource, treasure, valuable

FOREIGN PHRASES: *Non possessori incumbit necessitas probandi possessiones ad se pertinere.* It is not incumbent on the possessor of property to prove that his possessions belong to him.

POSSESSIONS, noun　assets, belongings, *bonorum,* capital, chattels, colonies, domain, dominions, earnings, effects, equity, estate, fortune, funds, goods, holdings, items of personalty, material wealth, movables, pecuniary resources, personal property, personalty, *possessio*, private property, property, *res*, resources, stock, stock in trade, territory, treasure, wealth, worldly belongings

POSSIBILITY, noun　achievability, anticipation, attainability, availability, chance, conceivability, conceivableness, expectance, expectancy, expectation, *facultas*, favorable opportunity, favorable prospect, feasibility, gamble, hope, likelihood, opportunity, plausibility, *posse*, potential, potentiality, *potestas*, probability, promise, prospect, suggestion, uncertainty, viability, viableness

FOREIGN PHRASES: *Jus triplex est-propietatis, possessionis, et possibilitatis.* Right is threefold-of property, of possession, and of possibility. *Ultra posse non potest esse, et vice versa.* What is beyond possibility cannot exist, and the reverse, what cannot exist is not possible.

POSSIBLE, adjective　achievable, anticipated, apt, attainable, believable, capable, cogitable, conceivable, credible, feasible, grantable, imaginable, liable, likely, obtainable, performable, plausible, potential, probable, promising, rational, realizable, reasonable, superable, supposable, surmountable, thinkable, unrealized, viable, within reach, within the range of possibility, within the realm of possibility, workable

POST, noun　appointment, berth, billet, business, capacity, career, charge, commission, department, employment, field, function, incumbency, job, line, *locus*, means of livelihood, *munus*, occupation, office, place, position, profession, pursuit, service, situation, station, task, undertaking, vocation, work

POST, verb　advertise, announce publicly, bestow, call public attention to, circulate, communicate, convey, deliver, dispose of, distribute, give away, give forth, give out, give public notice of, impart, issue, issue a statement, make known, make public, offer to the public, pay, present, print, proclaim, publish, put up a sign, report, spread, spread abroad

ASSOCIATED CONCEPTS: post a notice, post bail

POSTERITY, noun　bloodline, children, descendants, descent, family, future relatives, heirs, issue, later generations, line, lineage, offspring, *posteritas*, progeny, scion, seed, stock, succeeding generations, successors

POSTHUMOUS, adjective　after death, continuing after death, following death, occurring after death, post mortem

ASSOCIATED CONCEPTS: posthumous child

POSTPONE, verb　adjourn, arrest temporarily, defer, delay, *differre*, extend, gain more time, hold off, keep for

future action, lay aside, pigeonhole, *proferre,* prorogate, prorogue, push aside, put aside, put off, reprieve, set aside, shelve, stall, stave off, stay, suspend, table
ASSOCIATED CONCEPTS: postpone a case

POSTULATE, *noun* assertion, assumed truth, assumption, axiom, conjecture, foundation, hypothesis, premise, speculation, starting point, statement, suggestion, *sumptio,* supposal, supposition, surmise, theorem, thesis, truism

POSTULATE, *verb* advance, assume, conjecture, consider, contend, determine, guess, hazard a supposition, hypothesize, infer, posit, predicate, premise, presume, presuppose, propound, put forth, put forward, reason, regard as axiomatic, specify, speculate, start, suggest, surmise, take as an axiom, take for granted, theorize, venture a conjecture, venture a supposition

POSTURE *(Attitude),* ***noun*** air, aspect, bearing, bent, cast, demeanor, disposition, disposition of mind, feeling, inclination, leaning, lie, manner, nature, opinion, outlook, partisan outlook, philosophy, point of view, pose, position, presence, sentiment, standpoint, temper, temperament, view, viewpoint, way of thinking

POSTURE *(Situation),* ***noun*** circumstance, *condicio,* condition, conjuncture, context, existing state, footing, juncture, lot, pass, plight, point, position, predicament, setting, shape, standing, state, state of affairs, station, *status,* terms, turn

POTENCY, *noun* ability, authoritativeness, authority, brawn, caliber, capability, clout, command, competence, control, effect, effectiveness, efficacy, energy, faculty, force, function, influence, intensity, main force, might, mightiness, muscle, omnipotence, potential, potentiality, power, powerfulness, predominance, pressure, prestige, puissance, quality, stamina, strength, sway, validity, vigor, virility, virtue, weight

POTENT, *adjective* able, active, affecting, capable, cogent, commanding, compelling, convincing, dominant, dramatic, dynamic, effective, effectual, efficacious, efficient, energetic, forceful, forcible, formidable, generative, impelling, important, impressive, indefatigable, indomitable, influential, inspiring, inspiriting, intense, invincible, manly, masterful, mighty, moving, operative, penetrating, powerful, predominant, prepotent, prevailing, productive, puissant, ruling, stiff, strong, telling, trenchant, useful, valid, vigorous, virile, weighty

POTENTIAL, *adjective* accessible, achievable, allowable, allowed, anticipated, attainable, concealed, conceivable, covert, doable, dormant, expected, feasible, future, imaginable, latent, likely, obtainable, performable, permissible, permitted, possible, *potentialis,* practicable, realizable, thinkable, unapparent, undetected, undisclosed, undiscovered, unexposed, unexpressed, unmanifested, unrealized, unseen, workable
ASSOCIATED CONCEPTS: potential existence, potential interest

POTENTIAL, *noun* ability, aptitude, capability, capacity, chance, competence, dormant energy, endowment, feasibility, force, latent power, might, mightiness, possibility, possibleness, potency, *potentialis,* power, powerfulness, practicability, proficiency, promise, prospect, puissance, qualification, skill, strength, talent, workability
ASSOCIATED CONCEPTS: potential damages, potential loss

POVERTY, *noun* absence, bare subsistence, beggarliness, beggary, dearth, deficiency, deficit, depletion, destitution, difficulty, distress, embarrassed circumstances, exigency, famine, humbleness, impecuniosity, impecuniousness, impoverishment, indigence, insolvency, lack, leanness, loss of fortune, meagerness, mendicancy, mendicity, moneylessness, narrow means, necessitousness, necessity, need, neediness, needy circumstances, paucity, pauperism, paupertas, penniless, penury, poor circumstances, poorness, privation, reduced circumstances, scantiness, scantity, scantness, scarceness, scarcity, shortage, slender means, sparseness, starvation, straitened circumstances, straits, subsistence level, *tenuitas,* unprosperousness, want
ASSOCIATED CONCEPTS: proceed in forma pauperus

POWER, *noun* auspices, authority, command, competence, control, controlment, dominance, domination, dominion, eminence, facility, force, hold, importance, influence, jurisdiction, mastership, mastery, potency, potestas, predominance, prepollence, prepollency, pressure, prestige, primacy, puissance, reign, rule, supremacy, supremeness, sway, vis, warrant, weight
ASSOCIATED CONCEPTS: apparent power, appointing power, arbitrary power, capacity, concurrent power, contingent power, continuing power, delegated power, discretionary power, equitable power, exercise of power, extinguishment of power, extraordinary power, general power, implicit power, implied power, inchoate power, incidental power, inherent power, legislative power, limited power, mandatory power, necessary power, nonexclusive power of appointment, power coupled with an interest, power of alienation, power of appointment, power of attorney, power of disposition, power of sale, power of termination, release of power, retention of power, revocation of power, special power, taxing power, testamentary power
FOREIGN PHRASES: ***Nemo potest facere per obliquum quod non potest facere per directum.*** No man can do indirectly that which he cannot do directly. ***Sequi debet potentia justitiam, non praecedere.*** Power ought to follow justice, not precede it. ***Potentia non est nisi ad bonum.*** Power is not conferred but for the good. ***Fortior et potentior est dispositio legis quam hominis.*** The disposition of the law has greater force and stronger effect than that of man. ***Frustra est potentia quae nunquam venit in actum.*** A power is a vain one if it is never exercised. ***Potestas stricte interpretatur.*** Power should be strictly interpreted. ***Delegatus non potest delegare.*** A representative cannot delegate his authority.

POWERFUL, *adjective* able, able-bodied, armipotent, authoritative, autocratic, autocratical, brawny, cogent, commanding, compelling, consequential, controlling, deafening, dominant, dominating, dynamic, effective, effectual, efficacious, empowered, forceful, forcible, great, hard, hearty, hegemonic, hegemonical, Herculean, high-potency, impelling, imperious, important, impregnable, indomitable, influential, intense, invincible, irresistible, leonine, loud, lusty, magisterial, mighty, multipotent, muscular, obeyed, omnipotent, overpowering, overwhelming, physically strong, plenipotent, potent, powerpacked, prevailing, puissant, regnant, reigning, resounding, rugged, ruling, sinewy, sovereign, stalwart, stentorian, stout, strapping, striking, strong, telling, trenchant, unconquerable, unquenchable, unweakened, vehement, vigorous, weighty

POWERLESS, *adjective* abrogated, adynamic, asthenic, canceled, crippled, debilitated, decrepit, defenseless, deposed, disabled, disqualified, drooping, droopy, effete, emasculated, exhausted, faint, faintish, feeble, figurehead, flaccid, forceless, fragile, frail, futile, harmless, helpless, *impotens,* impotent, impuissant, inactive, inadequate, inapt, incapable, incapacitated, incompetent, indefensible, ineffective, ineffectual, inefficacious, inept, infirm, *infirmus,* inoperative, *invalidus,* languid, languishing, listless, lustless, marrowless, mightless, nerveless, nugatory, null and void, palsied, paralytic, paralyzed, pithless, pregnable, sapless, sickly, sinewless, spent, spineless, strengthless, submissive, superannuated, torpid, unable, unapt, unarmed, unavailing, unempowered, unendowed, unequipped, unfit, unfortified, uninfluential, unnerved, unqualified, unsteady, unstrengthened, unstrung, unsupported, useless, vigorless, vincible, weak, weaponless, without authority, without force, without vitality, yielding

PRACTICABLE, *adjective* achievable, attainable, capable of being done, doable, effectible, feasible, not too difficult, obtainable, operable, performable, possible, practical, realizable, reasonable, within reach, within the bounds of possibility, workable
ASSOCIATED CONCEPTS: as soon as practicable

PRACTICAL, *noun* adaptable, advantageous, aiding, all-purpose, applicable, assisting, beneficial, commodious, conducive, convenient, effective, effectual, efficacious, efficient, employable, expedient, expediential, fitting, functional, handy, helpful, implemental, instrumental, invaluable, of general utility, operational, operative, practicable, profitable, serviceable, suitable, to the purpose, useful, utilitarian, utilizable, valuable, workable

PRACTICE *(Custom),* *noun* behavior, common course, confirmed habit, consuetude, conventionality, course of action, course of conduct, customary course, established order, fixed ways, frequent repetition, general course, habit, habitual course, habituation, habitude, inveterate habit, line of action, line of proceeding, manner, matter of course, method, mode, mode of procedure, natural course, order of the day, ordinary course, pattern, prescription, procedure, routine, settled disposition, style, usage, use, usual custom, usual method, way
ASSOCIATED CONCEPTS: custom and usage, practice in the industry
FOREIGN PHRASES: *Cursus curiae est lex curiae.* The practice of the court is the law of the court. *Multa multo exercitatione facilius quam regulis percipies.* You will perceive many things much more easily by practice than by rule.

PRACTICE *(Procedure),* *noun* approach, arrangement, conduct, *consuetudo,* course, course of action, course of conduct, established order, *exercitatio,* form, general guidelines, governing course of action, governing plan, line of action, line of conduct, manner of proceeding, method, mode, mode of management, *mos,* observance, operation, order of the day, organization, outline, plan of action, policy, prescribed form, prescribed usage, process, program, protocol, required manner, routine, rule, rules of business, scheme, stratagem, strategy, system, tactics, treatment, usual way, *usus,* way, way of doing things
ASSOCIATED CONCEPTS: civil practice, criminal practice

PRACTICE *(Professional business),* *noun* avocation, business, calling, career, chosen career, chosen field, chosen profession, employment, life, life's work, line of business, line of work, occupation, pursuit, specialty, trade, undertaking, vocation
ASSOCIATED CONCEPTS: practice of law, practice of profession

PRACTICE *(Engage in),* *verb* be employed, carry on business, devote oneself to, employ, employ one's professional skill, employ oneself in, engage in, *exercere, facere, factitare,* follow a calling, follow a profession, follow as an occupation, labor at one's vocation, perform the duties of, perform the functions of, pursue, specialize, specialize in, undertake, work at
ASSOCIATED CONCEPTS: practice law

PRACTICE *(Train by repetition),* *verb* acquire the habit, apply one's self to, become familiar with, condition, cultivate a habit, discipline, do repeatedly, drill, exercise, familiarize with, learn a habit, *meditari,* perfect a routine, perform repeatedly, prepare, rehearse, school, take training, work at

PRACTICED, *adjective* able, accomplished, adept, adroit, apt, artful, canny, capable, clever, competent, conversant, crafty, deft, dextrous, efficient, effortless, equipped, experienced, expert, facile, gifted, habituated, handy, informed, initiated, knowing, learned, masterful, masterly, panurgic, prepared, proficient, qualified, resourceful, seasoned, shrewd, skilled, skillful, smooth, sophisticated, talented, trained, veteran, well-qualified

PRACTITIONER, *noun* artificer, artisan, artist, attorney, counselor, craftsman, creative worker, journeyman, lawyer, master worker, professional, solicitor, specialist, trained person
ASSOCIATED CONCEPTS: legal practitioner, single practitioner, sole practitioner

PRAGMATIC, *adjective* clear-thinking, expedient, feasible, matter-of-fact, practical, rational, realistic, reasonable, sensible, serviceable, sound, straight-thinking, unidealistic, unromantic, unsentimental, useful, utilitarian

PRAGMATISM, *noun* expedience, expediency, matter of factness, practical attitude, practicality, practicalness, rationality, realism, realistic attitude, realisticness, reasonableness, sensibility, sensibleness, sound thinking, unidealism, unsentimentality

PRAISE, *noun* acclaim, acclamation, accolade, admiration, adulation, advocacy, applause, appreciation, approbation, approval, celebration, commendation, compliment, congratulation, credit, deserved tribute, distinction, encomium, estimation, exaltation, fame, glorification, glory, homage, honor, kudos, laud, laudation, mention, panegyric, plaudit, prestige, recommendation, regard, remembrance, renown, repute, respect, testimonial, tribute

PRAISE, *verb* admire, adore, adulate, applaud, approbate, approve, celebrate, commend, compliment, congratulate, express admiration of, extol, flatter, glorify, hold in esteem, honor, idolize, indorse, laud, panegyrize, pay tribute, pay tribute to, recommend, regard, value, venerate

PRATTLE, *noun* blather, gabble, nonsensical talk, twaddle, verbiage

PRATTLE, *verb* babble, blather, chatter, gab, jabber, prate, prattle, talk nonsense

PRAY, *verb* address a request, adjure, appeal to, apply to, ask earnestly, beseech, bid, call upon, clamor for, cry for help, entreat, entreat persistently, impetrate, implore, importune, make a request, make earnest petition for, make supplication, obtest, *orare,* petition, plead, *precari,* prefer a petition, prefer a request, press, put up petitions, raise up

one's voice, requisition, *rogare,* solicit, supplicate, urge, urge persistently, urge repeatedly
ASSOCIATED CONCEPTS: pray for relief in a complaint

PRAYER, noun application, application for relief, beseechment, call, claim, earnest entreaty, earnest request, entreaty, humble entreaty, *imploratio,* imploration, importunity, invocation, motion, petition, plea, *precatio,* request, request for relief, request for the aid of the court, requisition, solemn entreaty, supplication, urgent request, *votum*
ASSOCIATED CONCEPTS: prayer for relief

PREAMBLE, noun beginning, *exordium,* foreword, foundation, introduction, introductory part, introductory statement, lead, opening, preface, prefatory note, prelude, prelusion, proem, prolegomenon, prologue
ASSOCIATED CONCEPTS: preamble to a constitution

PREARRANGE, verb agree to beforehand, arrange beforehand, arrange in advance, concoct, consider beforehand, ensure a result, forearm, foreordain, lay down a plan, map out, plan, plot, preconcert, precontrive, predesign, predestinate, predestine, predetermine, preestablish, premeditate, preorder, prepare, preresolve, project, resolve beforehand

PRECARIOUS, adjective alarming, chancy, changeable, critical, crumbling, dangerous, defenseless, delicate, doubtful, dubious, *dubius,* equivocal, exposed, fraught with danger, full of risk, guardless, hazardous, impermanent, *incertus,* infirm, insecure, jeopardous, menacing, perilous, riskful, risky, shaky, slippery, thorny, threatening, ticklish, tottering, treacherous, unassured, uncertain, undependable, unfaithworthy, unprotected, unreliable, unsafe, unsettled, unsheltered, unshielded, unsound, unstable, unsteadfast, unsteady, unsubstantial, unsure, untrustworthy, vulnerable

PRECATORY, adjective advisory, appealing, asking, beseeching, entreating, expressing entreaty, imploratory, imploring, importunate, pleading, suggesting, suggestive
ASSOCIATED CONCEPTS: precatory words

PRECAUTION, noun alertness, anticipation, attention, care, carefulness, caution, circumspection, forearming, foresight, forethought, guarantee, guardedness, heed, heedfulness, premunition, preventive measures, prior measure, protection, providence, provision, prudence, safeguard, security, solicitude, surveillance, timely care, vigil, vigilance, wariness, warning, watch, watchfulness
ASSOCIATED CONCEPTS: last clear chance doctrine, precautions to guard against injury, standard of care

PRECEDE, verb antecede, *antecedere,* antedate, *antegredi, anteire,* anticipate, be ahead of, come before, come first, forerun, go ahead of, go before, go in advance, go in front of, harbinger, herald, introduce, lead, lead the way, pave the way, pioneer, preexist, prepare the ground, scout, take the lead, usher in

PRECEDENCE, noun advantage, antecedence, authority, elevation, exaltation, importance, predominance, preeminence, preference, prestige, primacy, priority, rank, seniority, status, superiority, supremacy
ASSOCIATED CONCEPTS: recording statute

PRECEDENT, noun archetype, authoritative decision, authoritative example, authoritative principle of law, authoritative rule, authority, basis, criterion, example, *exemplum,* foundation, frame of reference, guide, judicial antecedent, justification, maxim, model, model instance, point of comparison, preceding instance, precept, precursor, predecessor, prior instance, rule, rule for future determinations, rule for future guidance, standard
ASSOCIATED CONCEPTS: collateral estoppel, condition precedent, controlling authority, precedent sub silentio, res judicata, stare decisis

PRECEDING, adjective above-mentioned, above-named, antecedent, anterior, before mentioned, earlier, first-named, former, inaugural, introductory, precedent, precessional, precursive, precursory, preexistent, prefatory, preliminary, preludial, prelusive, prelusory, preparatory, prevenient, previous, prior, superior

PRECEPT, noun axiom, canon, charge, code, command, commandment, decree, dictate, direction, doctrine, dogma, edict, fiat, guide, injunction, instruction, law, legal order, mandate, order, ordinance, *praeceptum, praescriptum,* prescript, principle, regulation, requirement, rubric, rule, statute, teaching, tenet, warrant, writ
ASSOCIATED CONCEPTS: legal precept

PRECIPITATE, adjective abrupt, breakneck, foolhardy, harebrained, hasty, headlong, headstrong, heady, hellbent, hot-headed, hurried, immediate, impetuous, imprudent, impulsive, *inconsultus,* indiscreet, injudicious, madcap, overconfident, overly hasty, *praeceps,* precipitant, precipitous, quick, rapid, rash, reckless, rushed, speedy, sudden, swift, *temerarius,* thoughtless, uncalculating, unexpected, unprepared for, violent, wild

PRECIPITATE (Hasten), verb *accelerare,* accelerate, advance, bring on, expedite, forward, further, hurry, make haste, *maturare, praecipitare,* quicken, rush, speed, speed up, spur, urge forward

PRECIPITATE (Throw down violently), verb catapult, chuck, *deicere,* discharge, drop, ejaculate, expel, fell, fling, fling downward, heave, hurl headlong, jaculate, launch, let fall, let fly, pitch, *praecipitare,* project, propel, send flying, send forth, send headlong, shoot, shy, throw down, throw headlong, toss

PRECISE, adjective accurate, careful, clean-cut, clear-cut, close, correct, critical, defined, definite, detailed, determinate, *diligens,* distinct, *elegans,* even, exact, explicit, express, faithful, fastidious, faultless, finical, finicky, flawless, fussy, inflexible, literal, methodical, meticulous, narrow, painstaking, particular, precisian, proper, punctilious, punctual, rigid, rigorous, scientific, scrupulous, severe, sharply defined, specific, stiff, strict, thorough, truthful, unambiguous, unbending, uncompromising, unequivocal, unerring, watchful, well-defined

PRECLUDE, verb ban, bar, bar from access, block, check, choke, control, cramp, cripple, curb, cut off, debar, defeat, detain, deter, discourage, encumber, estop, exclude, foil, forbid, foreclose, frustrate, handicap, hinder, impede, interfere with, interrupt, make impossible, obstruct, oppose, override, preempt, prevent, *prohibere,* prohibit, regulate, restrain, restrict, retard, stay, stop, thwart
ASSOCIATED CONCEPTS: estoppel, preclude from introducing into evidence

PRECLUSION, noun ban, bar, curb, exclusion, forestalling, interference, obstruction, obviation, opposition, override, preemption, prevention, prohibition, regulation, restraint, restriction
ASSOCIATED CONCEPTS: claim preclusion, issue preclusion, preclusion order, statutory preclusion

PRECOGNITION, *noun*   clairvoyance, foreboding, foreknowledge, foresight, forethought, perception, prenotion, presage, prescience, presentiment

PRECONCEIVE, *verb*   anticipate, assume, be biased, be jaundiced, be prejudiced, forejudge, foresee, have a bias, have foreknowledge, incline, intuit, judge beforehand, jump to a conclusion, *praeiudicare*, preapprehend, precognize, preconclude, predecide, predetermine, predict, predispose, prejudge, prepossess, presume, presuppose, presurmise, surmise

PRECONCEPTION, *noun*   anticipation, assumption, bent, bias, fixed idea, foregone conclusion, forejudgment, inclination, leaning, partiality, *praeiudicata opinio*, preapprehension, preconceived idea, preconclusion, predetermination, preestimate, prejudgment, prejudication, prejudice, prejudiced view, prenotion, prepossession, presentiment, presumption, presupposal, presupposition, presurmise

PRECURSOR, *noun*   advance guard, ancestor, announcer, antecedent, augury, avant-courier, forebearer, forefather, foregoer, forerunner, guide, harbinger, herald, omen, parent, pathfinder, patriarch, pioneer, portent, *praecursor*, *praenuntius*, precedent, predecessor, preparation, preparer, presage, preview, prodrome, prognostic, scout, sign, token, usher, vanguard, warning

PRECURSORY, *adjective*   advance, antecedent, beginning, earlier, exploratory, first, foregoing, forerunning, foreshadowing, forewarning, foundational, inaugural, inauguratory, initiatory, introductory, leading, *praecurrentia*, precedent, preceding, precursive, prefatory, preliminary, preludial, preludious, prelusive, prelusory, preparatory, prevenient, previous, prior, prognosticative

PREDATORY, *adjective*   bloodthirsty, carnivorous, depredatory, devouring, greedy, living by prey, lupine, pillaging, plundering, *praedabundus*, *praedatorius*, predacious, predative, raiding, rapacious, raptorial, ravaging, ravening, ravenous, spoliatory, voracious, vulturine, vulturish, vulturous, wolfish

PREDECESSOR, *noun*   ancestor, antecedent, antecessor, elder, forebearer, forefather, foregoer, foreparent, forerunner, former incumbent, former officeholder, founder, originator, patriarch, precursor, procreator, progenitor

PREDETERMINATION, *noun*   aim, bias, closed-mindedness, conclusion beforehand, conclusion in advance, decision beforehand, decision in advance, destined lot, destiny, fate, fixed future, force of circumstances, foredoom, foregone conclusion, forejudgment, foreordainment, forethought, fortune, goal, inevitability, inevitableness, inexorable fate, intention, jaundice, kismet, lot, object, objective, one-sidedness, partiality, preapprehension, preconception, preconclusion, predecision, predeliberation, predestination, predetermined course of events, prejudgment, prejudice, premeditation, prenotion, prepossession, preresolution, presumption, presupposal, presupposition, presurmise, purpose, resolve, undetachment, will

PREDETERMINE, *verb*   agree beforehand, be biased, be influenced, be jaundiced, be prejudiced, be prepossessed, be swayed, contrive a result, decide beforehand, decide in advance, destinate, destine, determine beforehand, determine in advance, doom, fate, forecast, forejudge, foreordain, foreordinate, intend, jump to a conclusion, map out, ordain, plan, *praefinire*, *praestituere*, prearrange, preconceive, preconclude, preconsider, predecide, predestinate, predestine, predispose, preestablish, prejudge, premeditate, preordain, preresolve, presume, presuppose, presurmise, project, reserve, resolve beforehand

PREDICAMENT, *noun*   adverse circumstances, adversity, *angustiae*, barrier, case, circumstance, complication, condition, conjuncture, corner, crisis, critical situation, danger, dangerous condition, *difficultas*, difficulty, dilemma, embarrassing position, embarrassment, emergency, entanglement, exigency, fix, hole, imbroglio, impasse, impediment, intricacy, jeopardy, mess, misfortune, obstacle, obstruction, occurrence, pass, perplexity, pinch, plight, position, posture, precariousness, pressure, quandary, scrape, situation, sorry plight, state, straits, tight situation, tight spot, trial, trouble, trying situation

PREDICT, *verb*   adumbrate, advise, announce in advance, anticipate, augur, auspicate, betoken, bode, divine, envision, forebode, forecast, foreknow, foresee, foreshadow, foreshow, forespeak, foretell, foretoken, forewarn, give notice, herald, indicate, indicate beforehand, make a prediction, make a prognosis, notify, omen, ominate, point to, portend, *praedicere*, preannounce, preindicate, premonish, premonstrate, presage, presignify, prognose, prognosticate, promise, prophesy, read, read the future, signify, soothsay, tell fortunes, tell the future, *vaticinari*, vaticinate, warn

PREDILECTION, *noun*   affection, affinity, appetence, appetency, appetite, attachment, bent, bias, choice, desire, disposition, fancy, favor, fondness, inclination, infatuation, leaning, liking, love, partiality, partisanship, penchant, predisposition, preference, prejudgment, prejudice, prepossession, proneness, propensity, *studium*, taste, tendency

PREDISPOSITION, *noun*   affection, appetence, appetency, appetite, aptitude, aptness, ardor, attachment, attraction, bent, bias, cast, character, desire, disposition, fancy, favor, favoritism, fondness, foregone conclusion, *inclinatio*, inclination, keenness, leaning, liking, longing, natural tendency, nature, partiality, penchant, preapprehension, preconception, preconclusion, preconsideration, predecision, predetermination, predilection, preference, prejudice, prepossession, *proclivitas*, proclivity, proneness, propenseness, propension, propensity, readiness, *studium*, susceptibility, taste, temperament, tendency, turn, warp, weakness, willingness, wish, yearning, zeal

PREDOMINANCE, *noun*   almightiness, ascendency, authority, command, control, controlling influence, dominance, domination, dominion, imperium, influence, jurisdiction, lead, leadership, mastery, mightiness, omnipotence, paramountcy, *potentia*, power, predominancy, predomination, prepollence, prepollency, prepotency, *principatus*, puissance, pull, regency, reign, rule, seniority, sovereignty, strength, superiority, supremacy, supreme authority, sway, upper hand, weight

PREDOMINANT, *adjective*   abundant, all-powerful, almighty, ascendant, authoritative, cogent, commanding, common, controlling, dominant, dominating, effective, efficacious, epidemic, extensive, forceful, foremost, general, governing, important, influential, mighty, omnipotent, overpowering, overruling, pandemic, paramount, potens, potent, powerful, *praepollens*, preponderant, prevailing, prevalent, principal, puissant, rampant, recognized, regnant, reigning, rife, ruling, sovereign, strong, superior, supervisory, supreme, weighty, widely recognized, widespread

PREDOMINATE *(Command),* **verb** administer, be sovereign, be supreme, carry weight, command, determine, direct, dominate, gain the upper hand, govern, guide, have influence, have sway, have the upper hand, hold dominion, hold office, influence, lead, manage, master, mastermind, override, overrule, oversee, overshadow, play a leading part, *praepollere,* prevail, pull the strings, reign, rule, rule over, *superare,* supervise, sway, take the lead, *vincere*

PREDOMINATE *(Outnumber),* **verb** be in the majority, be rife, be superior in number, eclipse, exceed, go beyond, outrank, outrival, outstrip, outweigh, overtop, *plures esse,* preponderate, rise above, surpass

PREEMPT, **verb** acquire beforehand, annex, appropriate, appropriate for use, arrogate to oneself, assume, capture, catch, exclude, force from, gain possession, impropriate, invade, obtain, occupy, preclude, preoccupy, seize, take, take over, take possession of, usurp
ASSOCIATED CONCEPTS: doctrine of federal preemption, preemption in filing, preemptive right, preemptive right of shareholders, right of preemption

PREEMPTION, **noun** appropriation, displacement, exclusion, preclusion, replacement, substitution, supersedence, supersession, supervention, supplanting
ASSOCIATED CONCEPTS: federal preemption, preemption doctrine

PREEXISTING, **adjective** antecedent, anterior, earlier, preexistent, previous, prior
ASSOCIATED CONCEPTS: preexisting condition, preexisting debt

PREFACE, **noun** beginning, commencement, exordium, foreword, introduction, introductory part, opening, overture, *praefatio,* preamble, prefatory note, preliminary comment, preliminary statement, prelude, prelusion, proem, prolegomenon, prolusion, *prooemium*

PREFACE, **verb** advance, begin, commence, head, herald, inaugurate, initiate, institute, introduce, launch, lead in, lead the way, make a start, open, place before, *praefari,* preamble, precede, prelude, put first, say in advance, set in motion, start, usher in

PREFER, **verb** adopt, advance, *anteponere,* approve, be fond of, be partial to, bring forward, choose, cling to, dignify, elect, elevate, embrace, espouse, fancy, favor, fix upon, further, graduate, grant favors to, have a fancy for, indulge one's fancy, lean toward, like better, move up, patronize, pick, pick out, play favorites, *praeoptare, praeponere,* prize, promote, pull strings for, put forward, raise, recommend, sanction, select, set above others, show preference, single out, take a fancy to, take to, tend, think better, treat with partiality, value

PREFERABLE, **adjective** above par, better, choice, chosen, deserving of preference, enjoyable, excellent, excelling, favorite, good, likable, *melior,* more advantageous, more desirable, more in demand, more pleasing, more popular, more select, picked, *potior,* preferred, relishable, selected, superior, surpassing, worthy of choice

PREFERENCE (Choice), **noun** bias, discretion, disposition, election, fancy, favorite, inclination, leaning, liking, option, partiality, preconceived liking, predilection, prejudice, proclivity, proneness, propensity, selection
ASSOCIATED CONCEPTS: preferred risk

PREFERENCE *(Priority),* **noun** advancement, advantage, benefit, favored treatment, front position, *praepositio,* precedence, preeminence, preferment, preferred standing, seniority
ASSOCIATED CONCEPTS: calendar preference, fraudulent conveyances, fraudulent preference, preferred stock, unlawful preference, voidable preference
FOREIGN PHRASES: *Qui prior est tempore potior est jure.* He who is first in time is first in right. ***Prior tempore potior jure.*** First in time, superior in right.

PREFERENTIAL, **adjective** advantageous, better, biased, choice, desired, discriminating, discriminative, distinguished, elite, exceptional, exclusive, extraordinary, favored, first-rate, high-grade, marked, outstanding, paramount, partial, partisan, preferred, priority, privileged, prize, recommended, select, selected, selective, special, superb, superior
ASSOCIATED CONCEPTS: preferential treatment

PREFERRED *(Favored),* **adjective** adopted, approved, choice, chosen, decided upon, elected, endorsed, especially liked, fancied, favorite, handpicked, liked, picked out, preferable, preferential, selected, set apart, settled upon, singled out, special, taken

PREFERRED *(Given priority),* **adjective** first, given preference, having priority, having seniority, placed in advance, preceding, prior
ASSOCIATED CONCEPTS: preferred stock, voidable preference

PREFERRED PROVIDER ORGANIZATION, **noun** care plan, comprehensive health plan, controlled medical coverage, discounted health membership group, discounted provider network, network of medical care providers, organization of medical providers, PPO
Generally: supervised medical services, plan organization
Specifically: employer-sponsored plan

PREJUDGE, **verb** condemn beforehand, forejudge, judge before hearing, judge beforehand, judge in advance, jump to a conclusion, *praeiudicare,* preconceive, preconclude, precondemn, preconsider, predecide, predetermine, preestimate, prejudicate, presume, presuppose, presurmise, resolve beforehand, rush to conclusion

PREJUDICE *(Injury),* **noun** damage, detriment, *detrimentum,* disadvantage, harm, hurt, impairment, injustice, irreversible damage, loss, unfairness, wrong
ASSOCIATED CONCEPTS: absence of prejudice, dismissal with prejudice, dismissal without prejudice, prejudice to a party's rights, prejudicial error

PREJUDICE *(Preconception),* **noun** bent, bias, discrimination, favoritism, forejudgment, inclination, intolerance, leaning, narrow-mindedness, one-sidedness, *opinio praeiudicata,* partiality, partisanship, personal bias, preconceived idea, preconceived notion, preconception, predetermination, predilection, predisposition, preference, prejudgment, prepossession, provincialism, slant, subjectivity, unreasonable bias
ASSOCIATED CONCEPTS: disqualification for bias

PREJUDICE *(Influence),* **verb** affect, bear upon, bend to one's will, bias, bring pressure to bear, carry weight, color, convince, distort, exercise influence over, exercise influence upon, exert influence, gain over, give an inclination, have influence over, have influence upon, influence against,

jaundice, persuade, predetermine, predispose, prejudge, prepossess unfavorably, present with bias, prevail over, slant, sway, turn, twist, warp, win over
ASSOCIATED CONCEPTS: prejudice the trier of fact

PREJUDICE (Injure), **verb**   affect detrimentally, cause damage to, cause detriment, cause pain, damage, demolish, destroy, devastate, disadvantage, disservice, exacerbate, harm, hurt, impair, inflict injury, maim, mar, play havoc with, ravage, ruin, spoil, taint, weaken, wound, wreck, wrong
ASSOCIATED CONCEPTS: prejudicial error

PREJUDICIAL, *adjective*   biased, colored, damaging, *damnosus,* deleterious, destructive, detrimental, directed against, disadvantageous, disserviceable, harmful, hostile, hurtful, inimical, injurious, *nocens, noxius,* opinionated, partisan, pernicious, preconceived, preconceptual, predecisive, predispositional, prepossessed, slanted, tending to impair, tending to obstruct, unfavorable, unjust
ASSOCIATED CONCEPTS: prejudicial error

PRELIMINARY, *adjective*   aforementioned, antecedent, anterior, beginning, coming before, early, exordial, foregoing, former, inaugural, incipient, initial, initiatory, introductory, opening, original, preceding, precursive, precursory, preexisting, prefatory, preludial, prelusive, prelusory, preparative, preparatory, prevenient, previous, primary, prior, proemial, starting, trial
ASSOCIATED CONCEPTS: preliminary agreement, preliminary hearing, preliminary injunction, preliminary notice, preliminary plea, preliminary relief, preliminary restraining order

PRELUDE, *noun*   beginning, commencement, exordium, foreword, inauguration, inception, induction, initiation, introduction, opening, outset, overture, preamble, preface, preliminary part, prelusion, preparation, proem, prologue, *prooemium,* start

PREMATURE, *adjective*   ahead of time, anticipatory, before time, embryonic, green, hasty, ill-considered, ill-timed, *immaturus,* inchoate, inopportune, mistimed, overhasty, *praematurus,* precipitate, rash, raw, sooner than due, sooner than intended, too early, too soon, unanticipated, underripe, undeveloped, unformed, unmatured, unprepared, unready, unripe, unseasonable, untimely
ASSOCIATED CONCEPTS: exhaustion of remedies, premature action

PREMEDITATED, *adjective*   aforethought, calculated, conscious, considered, deliberate, deliberately intended, foreordained, intended, intentional, maturely considered, outlined beforehand, planned, planned beforehand, planned in advance, plotted, prearranged, preconsidered, precontrived, predeliberated, predesigned, predetermined, predetermined, predevised, preresolved, reasoned, studied, thought out, well-considered, well-devised, willful, with forethought
ASSOCIATED CONCEPTS: intent, malice aforethought, premeditated crime, premeditated murder

PREMEDITATION, *noun*   advance planning, aforethought, deliberate intent, deliberate intention, design, distinct purpose, forethought, machination, *praemeditatio,* prearrangement, preconsideration, predeliberation, predetermination, preresolution, previous deliberation, previous reflection, prior determination
ASSOCIATED CONCEPTS: intent

PREMISES (Buildings), **noun**   aedificium, bounds, domiciles, *domus,* dwellings, edifices, grounds, homes, house with the grounds belonging to it, land, limits, lodgings, piece of land, place, property, quarters, real estate, residences, structures, tract of land
ASSOCIATED CONCEPTS: premises liability

PREMISES (Hypotheses), **noun**   affirmations, assertions, assumed positions, axioms, bases, foundations, grounds, positions, postulates, *principia,* terms, theorems, theses

PREMIUM, *adjective*   best, capital, choice, desirable, elect, estimable, excellent, fine, finest, first-class, first-rate, grade A, high-grade, high-quality, incomparable, inimitable, matchless, peerless, precious, prime, quality, second to none, select, specially selected, splendid, superb, superfine, superior, superlative, top-notch, unbeatable, unequaled, unmatched, unparalleled, unrivaled, unsurpassed, very fine, worthy

PREMIUM (Excess value), **noun**   amount over par, bonus, bounty, charge beyond normal, charge to excess, excessive charge, extra, incentive, increased value, overcharge, prize

PREMIUM (Insurance payment), **noun**   amount paid periodically, annual commitment, annual encumbrance, annual fee, annual installment, annual liability, annual obligation, annual payment, annual rate of insurance, annual remittance, contract payment, periodic payment, yearly payment
ASSOCIATED CONCEPTS: assessment of a premium, earned premiums, gross premium, net premium, reduction of premium

PREMONITION, *noun*   augury, auspice, boding, caution, divination, evil adumbration, feeling, foreboding, forefeeling, foreshadowing, foretoken, forewarning, hunch, intimation, misgiving, *monitio, monitum,* omen, portent, prediction, premonishment, prenotification, presage, presentiment, presurmise, prevision, prewarning, sign, warning

PREOCCUPATION, *noun*   absorbed interest, absorption, abstraction, attentiveness, concentration, daydreaming, deep study, depth of thought, devotion, distraction, dreaminess, engrossment, enthrallment, fascination, fixation, fixed idea, *idée fixe,* immersion, intentness, involvement, musing, obsession, pensiveness, *praeoccupatio,* prepossession, profound thought, rapt attention, reverie, study, trance

PREORDAIN, *verb*   appoint beforehand, appoint in advance, decide in advance, decree beforehand, destine, determine beforehand, enact beforehand, establish beforehand, fix beforehand, foredoom, forejudge, foreshadow, preconceive, preconclude, preconsider, predecide, predeliberate, predestine, predetermine, preestablish, prejudge, preresolve, resolve beforehand

PREPARATION, *noun*   anticipation, apprenticeship, arrangement, background, basis, building, development, education, equipment, establishment, evolution, foresight, forethought, foundation, groundwork, initiation, instruction, making ready, neophytism, novitiate, plan, precaution, preliminaries, preliminary step, premunition, prior measure, probation, providence, provision, prudence, qualification, readiness, readying, rehearsal, safeguard, teaching, training
ASSOCIATED CONCEPTS: preparation for trial, preparation of a crime

PREPARATORY, adjective anticipatory, beginning, early, expectant, foundational, inaugural, inceptive, incipient, initial, initiative, initiatory, introductory, opening, precautionary, precedent, preceding, precursory, prefa-tory, preliminary, preludial, prelusive, prelusory, preparative, prepositional, prior, proemial, provident, qualifying, starting
ASSOCIATED CONCEPTS: preparatory acts

PREPAY, verb defray in advance, discharge in advance, give compensation for in advance, make payment in advance, meet the bill ahead of time, pay in advance, presettle, satisfy in advance, settle in advance, tender in advance
ASSOCIATED CONCEPTS: prepayment clause

PREPONDERANCE, noun dominance, domination, majority, outweighing, paramountcy, plurality, predominance, predomination, preeminence, prepollence, prepollency, preponderancy, preponderation, prevalence, superiority
ASSOCIATED CONCEPTS: preponderance of the credible evidence

PREREQUISITE, noun condition, demand, essential desideratum, exigency, fundamental, groundwork, indispensable item, necessary condition, necessary item, necessity, need, needed item, precondition, preliminary condition, pressing need, prior condition, proviso, requirement, requisite, specification, stipulation, vital part
ASSOCIATED CONCEPTS: condition precedent, jurisdictional prerequisite

PREROGATIVE, noun advantage, authority, authorization, benefit, charter, claim, droit, due, exclusive privilege, exclusive right, franchise, freedom, grant, inalienable right, legal power, liberty, license, perquisite, power, preference, prior right, priority, privilege, right, rightful power, sanction, special right, title, vested right, warrant
ASSOCIATED CONCEPTS: managerial prerogative, prerogative writ

PRESAGE, verb adumbrate, advise, announce in advance, anticipate, augur, *augurari,* augurate, auspicate, betoken, bode, divine, envision, forebode, forecast, foreknow, foresee, foreshadow, foreshow, foretell, foretoken, forewarn, have a presentiment, impend, indicate beforehand, indicate in advance, judge the future, make a prediction, omen, ominate, point to, portend, *portendere, praesagire,* predict, prefigurate, prefigure, preindicate, premonstrate, preshow, presignify, prewarn, prognosticate, promise, prophesy, signify, soothsay, threaten, vaticinate, warn

PRESAGEFUL, adjective augural, augurial, auspicial, foreboding, monitory, ominous, portentous

PRESCRIBE, verb administer, advocate, bid, charge, command, conduct, control, decide, decree, demand, designate, dictate, direct, enjoin, exact, exercise authority, give a directive, give a mandate, give an order, give directions, guide, impose, instruct, issue an order, lay out, lead, mandate, mark out, ordain, order, pilot, *praescribere,* prevail over, proclaim, regulate, require, set, steer, superintend, write a prescription
ASSOCIATED CONCEPTS: prescribe remedies, prescribed by law

PRESCRIPTION (Claim of title), **noun** authority, claim, inalienable right, interest, license, prerogative, right, vested interest, vested right
ASSOCIATED CONCEPTS: adverse possession, easement by prescription, right by prescription, title by prescription
FOREIGN PHRASES: *Praescriptio et executio non pertinent ad valorem contractus, set ad tempus et modum actionis*

instituendae. Prescription and execution do not affect the validity of the contract, but the time and manner of instituting an action. *Usucapio constituta est ut aliquis litium finis esset.* Prescription was established so that there be an end to lawsuits. *Nihil praescribitur nisi quod possidetur.* There is no prescription for that which is not possessed. *Interruptio multiplex non tollit praescriptionem semel obtentam.* Frequent interruptions do not defeat a prescription once obtained. *Praescriptio est titulus ex usu et tempore substantiam capiens ab auctoritate legis.* Prescription is a title by authority of law, deriving its force from use and time.

PRESCRIPTION (Custom), **noun** convention, conventional usage, fashion, habit, institution, observance, practice, precedent, tradition, usage, use

PRESCRIPTION (Directive), **noun** act, authority, axiom, canon, charge, command, decree, dictate, direction, doctrine, edict, enactment, formula, formulary, injunction, instruction, law, maxim, measure, order, ordinance, precept, prescript, principle, proposal, regulation, rubric, rule, ruling, statute, theorem

PRESCRIPTIVE, adjective accepted, acknowledge, acknowledge through possession, acknowledge through use, admitted, binding, commanded by long use, commanding, compulsory, customary, decretal, determined, dictated, established, fixed, legalized, long-established, longstanding, obligatory, ordained by custom, popular, preceptive, prescribed, recognized, recognized because of continued possession, recognized through use, required by custom, rooted, set, settled, time-honored, traditional, traditive, understood, unwritten, usual, vested, wonted
ASSOCIATED CONCEPTS: prescriptive rights

PRESENCE (Attendance), **noun** being, nearness, *praesentia,* proximity, sojournment, visitation

PRESENCE (Poise), **noun** air, appearance, aspect, bearing, behavior, carriage, comportment, conduct, decorum, demeanor, deportment, gentility, guise, image, look, manner, mien, ostent, outward show, personality, posture, presentation, refinement, semblance, style, visage, way, ways
ASSOCIATED CONCEPTS: demeanor of a witness

PRESENT (Attendant), **adjective** accessible, accounted for, adjacent, at close quarters, at hand, available, close, close at hand, close by, convenient, handy, in attendance, in the company of, in the presence of, in the vicinity, in view, near at hand, nearby, nigh, on hand, on the spot, *praesens,* proximate, unremoved, vicinal, within reach

PRESENT (Current), **adjective** at hand, at this moment, at this time, attendant, available, contemporaneous, contemporary, current, existent, existing, extant, going on, here, immediate, in view, instant, latest, living, modern, near, near in time, nigh, on the spot, *praesens,* present-day, present-time, prevalent, ready, recent, topical, ubiquitary, ubiquitous, unremoved, up-to-date, up-to-the-minute
ASSOCIATED CONCEPTS: clear and present danger, present ability, present consideration, present controversy, present enjoyment, present gift, present interest, present transfer

PRESENT (Introduce), **verb** demonstrate, disclose, display, exhibit, expose to view, give an introduction, *introducere,* make acquainted, make an introduction, make known, offer, offer evidence, open to view, propose, put forth, set forth, show, suggest, uncover, unveil
ASSOCIATED CONCEPTS: present a case, present evidence

PRESENT *(Make a gift),* **verb**   accord, allot, award, bequeath, bestow, confer, contribute, convey, deed, deliver, dispense, dole out, *donare,* donate, endow, extend, furnish, give, give as a gift, give over, grant, hand, hand over, impart, let have, make over, mete out, *munerari,* offer, place at one's disposal, proffer, provide, remit, render, supply, tender, vouchsafe

PRESENT *(Prefer charges),* **verb**   accuse, blame, charge, cite, criminate, fix the responsibility, implicate, impute, incriminate, lodge a complaint, prefer charges
ASSOCIATED CONCEPTS: present an indictment

PRESENTMENT, *noun*   accusation, arraignment, charge, citation, imputation, indictment, information

PRESERVATION, *noun*   care, cherishing, conservatio, conservation, curing, custody, defense, eternization, freedom from danger, guardianship, guarding, immortalization, maintenance, nourishment, nurture, perpetuation, protection, protective custody, safeguarding, safekeeping, safety, salvation, sanctuary, saving, security, shielding, storage, support, *tuitio,* upkeep, ward, wardship

PRESERVE, *verb*   attend to, bolster, care for, champion, cherish, *condire,* conservare, conserve, continue, cure, defend, economize, ensconce, ensure, favor, foster, give support, guard, harbor, haven, hoard, house, husband, insure, keep, keep alive, keep from harm, keep intact, keep safe, keep sound, keep under cover, keep up, keep watch over, lend support, look after, maintain, mind, minister to, nourish, patronize, perpetuate, prolong, promote, protect, protect from injury, provide for, provide sanctuary, put away, reinforce, rescue, safeguard, save, screen, secure, *servare,* shelter, shield, shield from danger, shield from injury, spare, stand behind, support, sustain, *sustinere,* take care of, tend, treasure, *tueri,* uphold, watch, watch over
ASSOCIATED CONCEPTS: preserve one's rights, preserve records, preserve the peace

PRESIDE, *verb*   act as chairman, act as president, administer, administrate, assume command, be at the head of, be in authority, be in charge, be in the chair, be the chairman, chair, command, control, direct, exercise supervision, govern, guide, have authority over, have control, head, hold a position of authority, hold authority, hold sway, hold the chair, keep order, lead, manage, occupy the chair, officiate, overlook, oversee, pilot, *praesidere,* regulate, reign, rule, steer, superintend, supervise, sway, take care of, take charge, take over, wield authority
ASSOCIATED CONCEPTS: preside over a hearing, preside over court, presiding justice, presiding officer

PRESS, *noun*   authors, columnists, commentators, contributors, correspondents, editors, interviewers, journalistic writers, journalists, literary publications, media, members of the media, members of the press, news business, news gatherers, newsmen, newspaper world, newspaperman, newspapers, newswriters, publicists, publishers, reporters
ASSOCIATED CONCEPTS: censorship, First Amendment, freedom of speech, freedom of the press

PRESS *(Beseech),* **verb**   adjure, appeal, ask earnestly, beg, call upon, enjoin, entreat, exhort, impetrate, implore, importune, petition, plead, request, supplicate, urge, *urgere*

PRESS *(Constrain),* **verb**   bear down on, bind, bring pressure to bear, coerce, command, compel, decree, demand, drive, enforce, exact, extort, force, impel, impose, insist, make, make necessary, necessitate, obligate, oblige, order, put pressure on, put under obligation, require, take no denial, urge forward, wring

PRESS *(Goad),* **verb**   aggravate, agonize, annoy, badger, beset, bother, browbeat, carp at, disquiet, drive, harry, heckle, hector, hound, incite, *instigare,* instigate, irritate, molest, persecute, pester, plague, prod, provoke, put pressure on, stir up, taunt, tease, torment, trouble, vex, worry

PRESSING, *adjective*   acute, cogent, compelling, compulsory, constraining, critical, crucial, demanded, demanding, driving, essential, exacting, exigent, forceful, grave, high priority, impelling, imperative, important, importunate, indispensable, major, mandatory, necessary, needed, obligatory, operose, peremptory, prerequisite, relentless, required, requisite, serious, urgent, vital

PRESSURE, *noun*   anxiety, anxiousness, brunt, brute force, burden, coercion, compulsion, constraining force, constraint, controlling power, crisis, drive, duress, encumbrance, exertion, exhortation, exigency, force, hardship, heaviness, hindrance, importunateness, influence, influentiality, insistence, intensity, intimidation, load, necessity, need, obligation, oppression, persuasion, *pondus,* power, power of directing, power of impelling, press, pull, push, strain, stress, sway, tension, undue influence, urgency, *vis,* weight
ASSOCIATED CONCEPTS: undue influence

PRESSURE, *verb*   adjure, advocate, bear down, beg, beseech, blandish, cajole, coax, coerce, command, compel, constrain, drive, entreat, exhort, force, goad, implore, induce, influence, insist, intimidate, oppress, persuade, plead, press, prod, push, request, solicit, stress, urge
ASSOCIATED CONCEPTS: coercion, duress, intimidation, undue influence

PRESTIDIGITATION, *noun*   conjuring, deluding, illusion, juggling, legerdemain, magic, palming, sleight of hand, sorcery, trickery

PRESTIGE, *noun*   ascendance, ascendency, aura, authority, celebrity, consequence, control, credit, dazzle, degree, dignity, distinction, *éclat,* eclat, eminence, esteem, estimation, exaltation, *fama,* fame, famousness, favor, force, glamor, *gloria,* glory, good repute, grandeur, greatness, high honor, high repute, honor, illustriousness, import, importance, influence, influentiality, luster, majesty, mark, name, nobility, *nomen,* notability, note, noteworthiness, notoriety, paramountcy, place, position, potency, power, precedence, predominance, predomination, preeminence, primacy, prominence, public favor, rank, regard, renown, reputation, repute, respect, significance, splendor, standing, station, status, superiority, sway, weight, worth

PRESUME, *verb*   anticipate, apprehend, assume, believe, come to a hasty conclusion, conceive, conclude, conjecture, consider as true, consider probable, contemplate, count upon, *credere,* dare say, deduce, deem, derive, divine, estimate, expect, forejudge, form an opinion, gather, guess, hazard a guess, hypothesize, infer, judge, jump to conclusions, opine, perceive as true, posit, postulate, preconceive, prejudge, presuppose, presurmise, regard as axiomatic, speculate, *sumere,* suppose, surmise, suspect, take for granted, take without proof, theorize, think, think likely, understand, venture
ASSOCIATED CONCEPTS: presume innocence

PRESUMPTION, noun anticipation, assumption, belief, conception, *coniectura,* conjecture, deduction, ground for believing, hypothesis, inference, likelihood, *opinio,* opinion, postulate, predilection, predisposition, premise, presupposition, probability, reasonable supposition, required assumption, required legal assumption, speculation, strong probability, supposition, surmise

ASSOCIATED CONCEPTS: conclusive presumption, disputable presumption, presumption against suicide, presumption of authority, presumption of constitutionality, presumption of continuance, presumption of death, presumption of delivery, presumption of innocence, presumption of knowledge, presumption of law, presumption of legitimacy, presumption of regularity, rebuttable presumption, statutory presumption

FOREIGN PHRASES: *Cuicunque aliquis quid concedit concedere videtur et id, sine quo res ipsa esse non potuit.* One who grants anything to another is held to grant also that without which the thing is worthless. *Lex judicat de rebus necessario faciendis quasi re ipsa factis.* The law judges of things which must necessarily be done as if they were actually done. *Novatio non praesumitur.* A novation is not presumed. *Nemo praesumitur malus.* No one is presumed to be wicked. *Nemo praesumitur ludere in extremis.* No one is presumed to be jesting while at the point of death. *Nihil nequam est praesumendum.* Nothing wicked should be presumed. *Semper praesumitur pro legitimatione puerorum.* The presumption always is in favor of the legitimacy of children. *Stabit praesumptio donec probetur in contrarium.* A presumption stands until the contrary is proven. *Praesumptiones sunt conjecturae exsigno verisimili ad probandum assumptae.* Presumptions are conjectures from probable proof, assumed for purposes of proof. *Fraus est odiosa et non praesumenda.* Fraud is odious and will not be presumed. *Donatio non praesumitur.* A gift is not presumed to have been made. *Nemo praesumitur donare.* No one is presumed to have made a gift. *Favorabiliores rei, potius quam actores, habentur.* The condition of the defendant is to be favored rather than that of the plaintiff. *Nobiliores et benigniores praesumptiones in dubiis sunt praeferendae.* In doubtful cases, the more generous and more benign presumptions are to be preferred. *Nullum iniquum est praesumendum in jure.* Nothing iniquitous is to be presumed in law. *Quisquis praesumitur bonus; et semper in dubiis pro reo respondendum.* Everyone is presumed to be good; and in doubtful cases it should be resolved in favor of the accused. *Praesumitur pro legitimatione.* There is a presumption in favor of legitimacy. *Semper praesumitur pro matrimonio.* The presumption is always in favor of the validity of a marriage. *Malum non praesumitur.* Evil is not presumed. *Pro possessione praesumitur de jure.* A presumption of law arises from possession. *Praesumptio violenta, plena probatio.* Strong presumption is full proof. *Semper qui non prohibet pro se intervenire, mandare creditur.* He who does not prohibit the intervention of another in his behalf is deemed to have authorized it. *Probatis extremis, praesumuntur media.* The extremes having been proved, those things which lie between are presumed. *In favorem vitae, libertatis, et innocentiae, omnia praesumuntur.* Every presumption is made in favor of life, liberty and innocence. *Nulla impossibilia aut inhonesta sunt praesumenda; vera autem et honesta et possibilia.* No things that are impossible or dishonorable are to be presumed; but things that are true and honorable and possible. *Omnia praesumuntur legitime facta donec probetur in contrarium.* All things are presumed to be lawfully done, until the contrary is proven. *Lex neminem cogit ostendere quod nescire praesumitur.* The law compels no one to divulge that which he is presumed not to know. *Injuria non praesumitur.* A wrong is not presumed.

PRESUMPTION OF INNOCENCE, noun assumption of innocence, belief of innocence, criminal standard of guilt, innocent until proven guilty, predisposition of innocence, premise rested on innocence, presupposition toward innocence, reasonable supposition of innocence, required assumption of innocence, required legal assumption of innocence, supposition of innocence

ASSOCIATED CONCEPTS: fundamental rights

PRESUMPTIVE, adjective anticipated, apparent, assumed, assumptive, believable, circumstantial, conceivable, conjecturable, conjectural, conjectured, credible, easy to believe, evidential, feasible, hypothesized, imagined, inferable, inferred, likely, plausible, possible, postulated, postulational, presumable, presumed, presupposed, probable, putative, seeming, speculative, speculatory, supposed, suppositional, suppositious, suppositive, surmisable, suspect, theoretical, well-founded, well-grounded

ASSOCIATED CONCEPTS: presumptive damages, presumptive evidence, presumptive grant, presumptive notice, presumptive ownership, presumptive possession

PRESUMPTUOUS, adjective *adrogans,* arrogant, assuming, audacious, bold, brash, brazen, cavalier, conceited, contumelious, daring, dictatorial, discourteous, disdainful, disrespectful, domineering, egoistic, egotistic, egotistical, excessively bold, excessively confident, familiar, flippant, foolhardy, forward, haughty, ill-bred, ill-mannered, imperious, impertinent, impolite, impudent, insolent, insulting, intrusive, irreverent, lacking respect, lofty, lordly, magisterial, malapert, offensive, outrageous, overbearing, overconfident, overfamiliar, overly bold, overly confident, overweening, pert, pompous, presuming, provocative, rash, rude, saucy, shameless, supercilious, unabashed, unceremonious, uncourtly, ungenteel, vain

PRESUPPOSE, verb assume, be biased, be inclined to think, be jaundiced, be prejudiced, believe, conjecture, count upon, decide beforehand, decide in advance, deduce, deem, determine beforehand, determine in advance, divine, draw an inference, estimate, expect, forejudge, gather, guess, have a bias, hypothesize, imagine, infer, intuit, judge, judge in advance, jump to a conclusion, opine, persuade oneself, posit, postulate, preconceive, preconclude, predecide, predetermine, preestimate, prefigurate, prefigure, prejudge, presume, presurmise, reckon, regard, rush to a conclusion, speculate, suppose, surmise, suspect, take for granted, theorize, think, trow, understand

ASSOCIATED CONCEPTS: presuppose a fact not in evidence

PRETEND, verb act, affect, assume, be deceitful, be hypocritical, beguile, bemask, bluff, cheat, claim falsely, counterfeit, cozen, deceive, delude, disguise, dissemble, *dissimulare,* dissimulate, dupe, fake, falsify, feign, *fingere,* fool, give a false appearance, hide under a mask, hoodwink, imagine, imitate, impersonate, lie, make a pretext of, make a show, make believe, malinger, mask, masquerade, mimic, mislead, misrepresent, pass off, perform, play, play act, play false, portray, present falsely, prevaricate, profess, purport, put on, put on a false front, seem, sham, *simulare,* simulate, twist the truth

PRETENSE *(Ostentation),* **noun** affectation, affectedness, airs, artificiality, blatancy, bravado, demonstration, display, empty show, false appearance, false show, fanfaronade, flagrancy, flashiness, flourish, fuss, garishness, gaudiness, glare, glitter, grandiosity, histrionics, impressive effect, inflation, insincerity, loftiness, mockery, obtrusiveness, *ostentatio,* ostentatiousness, outward show, panache, parade, pomp, pomposity, pompousness, pose, pretension, pretentiousness, sham, show, showiness, splash, splurge, theatricality, unnaturalness, window-dressing

PRETENSE *(Pretext),* **noun** appearance, beguilement, bluff, camouflage, cheat, claim, cloak, color, cover, deceit, deception, disguise, duplicity, empty words, excuse, fabrication, false appearance, false plea, false show, falsehood, falseness, falsification, feint, forgery, fraud, fraudulence, guise, hoax, hypocrisy, imitation, invention, lie, mask, mendacity, misrepresentation, ostensible purpose, ostensible reason, plea, *postulatio,* professed purpose, ruse, semblance, sham, show, simulation, *simulatione,* subterfuge, trick, trickery, untruth
ASSOCIATED CONCEPTS: false pretense, fraudulent pretense, larceny by false pretense

PRETENTIOUS *(Ostentatious),* **adjective** adorned, artificial, bespangled, brassy, conspicuous, decorated, embellished, flamboyant, flashy, fulgent, fulgid, garish, gaudy, *iactans,* meretricious, ornamented, ornate, *ornatus,* overly decorated, showy, superficial, tawdry

PRETENTIOUS *(Pompous),* **adjective** affected, arrogant, boastful, boasting, bombastic, braggardly, braggart, conceited, extravagant, full of affectation, *gloriosus,* grandiloquent, grandiose, haughty, *iactans,* immodest, inflated, *inflatus,* opinionated, overdramatized, prideful, prim, self-admiring, self-applauding, self-esteeming, self-glorifying, self-important, self-satisfied, smug, snobbish, stilted, swollen, *theatralis,* tumid, *tumidus,* turgescent, turgid, vain, vainglorious

PRETERMIT, **verb** abandon, avoid, bypass, cast aside, disregard, forget, gloss over, ignore, lay aside, leave, leave out, leave undone, let pass, miss, neglect, not care for, omit, overlook, pass, pass over, pay no attention to, pay no regard to, put aside, put off, shelve, skip, slight, suspend
ASSOCIATED CONCEPTS: pretermitted heir

PRETEXT, **noun** affectation, alibi, alleged purpose, alleged reason, camouflage, charade, claim, cover, deception, defense, disguise, evasion, excuse, fabrication, false appearance, false ground, false motive, false pretense, false reason, false show, falsification, feint, fraud, guise, insincerity, invention, justification, lie, make-believe, mask, misrepresentation, misstatement, obfuscation, ostensible motive, ostensible purpose, ostensible reason, *praetextum,* pretense, pretension, professed purpose, profession, ruse, semblance, sham, shift, show, *simulatio,* simulation, *species,* stratagem, subterfuge, trick, trickery, untruth, wile
FOREIGN PHRASES: *Praetextu liciti non debet admitti illicitum.* That which is illegal ought not to be permitted under a pretext of legality.

PREVAIL *(Be in force),* **verb** be in general use, control, dictate, direct, dominate, domineer, exist widely, govern, guide, have authority over, have charge of, have dominion over, have force, have superiority over, predominate, preponderate
ASSOCIATED CONCEPTS: prevailing rate of interest, prevailing rate of wages

PREVAIL *(Persuade),* **verb** actuate, argue into, bring around, cajole, carry weight with, coax, convert, convince, enlist, gain the confidence of, guide, have effect, impel, incite,

indoctrinate, induce, influence, inspire, inveigle, lure, motivate, move, *persuadere,* prompt, propagandize, seduce, sway, urge, wear down, win over, woo

PREVAIL *(Triumph),* **verb** be a winner, be effective, be efficacious, be in control, be in general use, be in the ascendant, be prevalent, be successful, be the victor, be triumphant, be victorious, carry authority, command, conquer, control, dominate, exceed, excel, gain a victory, gain the advantage, gain the upper hand, get the upper hand, have mastery, have superiority, lead, master, meet with success, overcome, predominate, preponderate, prosper, quell, reign, rule, subdue, succeed, *superare,* suppress, surmount, surpass, take over, thrive, transcend, *vincere,* win
ASSOCIATED CONCEPTS: prevail in a court of law, prevailing party

PREVAIL UPON, **verb** affect, be influential, beseech, bring over, bring to reason, carry weight with, coax, convince, encourage, enlist, entice, entreat, exercise influence over, exercise influence upon, exercise influence with, exhort, *exorare,* have influence over, have influence upon, have influence with, impel, importune, induce, influence, lead, motivate, move, move by persuasion, overcome another's resistence, persuade, *persuadere,* predispose, spur, sway, talk into, urge, wield influence, win over

PREVAILING *(Current),* **adjective** abundant, accepted, accustomary, accustomed, all-embracing, bourgeois, catholic, characteristic, colloquial, common, commonplace, comprehensive, conformable, contemporary, conventional, current, customary, diffuse, dominant, epidemic, established, everyday, extensive, familiar, frequent, general, generally accepted, global, habitual, in vogue, latest, natural, normal, pandemic, popular, predominant, prevalent, rampant, regular, rife, stock, sweeping, typical, universal, up-to-date, usual, vernacular, well-known, widely accepted, widespread, wonted, workaday, worldwide
ASSOCIATED CONCEPTS: prevailing conditions, prevailing rate, prevailing rate of interest

PREVAILING *(Having superior force),* **adjective** ascendant, authoritative, chief, commanding, conquering, controlling, defeating, determining, directing, dominant, dominating, effective, effectual, efficacious, forceful, governing, heading, hegemonic, hegemonical, influential, leading, mighty, moving, operative, overcoming, overruling, paramount, persuasive, potent, powerful, predominant, predominating, preponderant, preponderating, *puissant, régnant,* ruling, strong, successful, supreme, triumphal, triumphant, unvanquished, victorious, weighty, winning
ASSOCIATED CONCEPTS: prevailing party

PREVALENT, **adjective** abundant, accepted, accustomary, accustomed, all-embracing, ascendant, catholic, characteristic, chief, colloquial, common, commonplace, conformable, conventional, current, customary, dominant, epidemic, established, everyday, extensive, familiar, frequent, frequently met, general, generally accepted, global, habitual, household, normal, ordinary, pandemic, pedestrian, *pervulgatus,* popular, predominant, preponderant, prevailing, rampant, regular, rife, run of the mill, set, standard, stock, sweeping, typical, universal, vernacular, well-known, widely accepted, widely known, widespread, worldwide

PREVARICATE, **verb** be dishonest, be evasive, be untruthful, bear false witness, beg the question, belie, conceal the truth, concoct, counterfeit, deceive, defraud, delude,

deviate, deviate from the truth, dissemble, dissimulate, distort, dodge, dupe, elude, equivocate, evade, evade the truth, fabricate, falsify, feign, fence, fergiversate, fib, forswear, gloss over, hedge, hoodwink, invent, lie, make believe, mince the truth, misguide, misinform, mislead, misrepresent, misstate, palter, parry, perjure, pervert, pretend, put on, quibble, sham, shift, shuffle, sophisticate, speak falsely, stretch the truth, tell a falsehood, tell a lie, tell an untruth, *tergiversari,* tergiversate, twist the truth
ASSOCIATED CONCEPTS: false swearing, perjury

PREVENT, verb   arrest, avert, avoid, baffle, balk, bar, block, check, checkmate, circumvent, contest, counter, counteract, countercheck, cut off, debar, defeat, deflect, delay, detain, deter, discourage, estop, fend off, foil, forbid, foreclose, forestall, forfend, frustrate, halt, hamper, handicap, hinder, hold back, impede, *impedire,* inhibit, intercept, interfere, interrupt, keep from, keep from happening, limit, muzzle, neutralize, *obstare,* obstruct, obviate, oppose, override, overrule, paralyze, parry, preclude, *prohibere,* prohibit, repress, restrain, restrict, retard, rule out, stave off, stay, stop, thwart, tie, turn aside, turn away, veto, ward off
ASSOCIATED CONCEPTS: prevent competition, prevent waste, prevented by law, prevention of performance
FOREIGN PHRASES: *Qui non prohibet id quod prohibere potest assentire videtur.* He who does not forbid what he is able to prevent, is deemed to assent.

PREVENTION, noun   bar, barrier, constraint, constriction, control, damper, determent, deterrence, deterrent, disadvantage, fetter, hindrance, impediment, inhibition, interference, obstacle, obstruction, obtrusion, obviation, preclusion, predisposition, presumption, prohibition, restraint, restriction, retardation, stoppage, thwarting

PREVENTIVE, adjective   alert, antidotal, antiseptic, arresting, aseptic, averting, blocking, careful, cautious, checking, counteractant, counteracting, defensive, deterrent, deterring, disinfectant, forestalling, germicidal, guarded, guarding, hindering, hygienic, impedimental, impeding, impeditive, inhibitive, inhibitory, interfering, judicious, neutralizing, obstructive, opposing, precautionary, preclusive, preservative, preventative, prohibitive, prophylactic, protecting, protective, provident, regardful, resistive, restraining, restrictive, retardant, safeguarding, shielding, thwarting, warding off, watchful

PREVENTIVE MEASURE, noun   adequate plans, adequate procedures, adequate steps, buffer, defense, forearming, immunization, inoculation, precaution, preservation, protection, safeguard, screen, security, shield
ASSOCIATED CONCEPTS: preventive justice

PREVIOUS, adjective   above-cited, above-mentioned, above-named, aforementioned, aforesaid, already indicated, antecedent, anterior, earlier, early, erstwhile, first, fore, foregoing, foregone, forementioned, forerunning, former, initial, initiatory, introductory, one-time, past, precedent, preceding, precursive, precursory, preexistent, prefatorial, prefatory, preliminary, prelusive, prelusory, preparatory, prevenient, previously mentioned, prior
ASSOCIATED CONCEPTS: previous conviction, previous disability, previous injury, previous order, previously considered, previously determined, prior conduct, prior conviction, prior injury

PREVIOUSLY NAMED, adjective   above-mentioned, as stated earlier, as stated earlier in this document, beforementioned, forenamed, former, previously referred to

PREY, verb   commit violence, consume, depredate, despoil, destroy, devour, eat, extort, fatten upon, feast upon, feed upon, fleece, forage, foray, grab, gut, harass, harrow, hunt, kill, loot, maraud, oppress, parasitize, pillage, pirate, plague, plunder, *praedari,* profit by cheating, profit by swindling, raid, ransack, ravage, raven, ravish, rob, seize, spoil, spoliate, strip, torment, torture, victimize, waste

PRICE, noun   amount, appraisal, appraisement, charge, compensation, cost, disbursement, due, estimate, estimation, exaction, exchange value, expenditure, expense, fare, fee, figure, outlay, payment, premium, *pretium,* purchase money, quotation, rate, recompense, selling price, toll, valuation, value, worth
ASSOCIATED CONCEPTS: abatement of price, contract price, established price, fair price, inadequacy of price, market price, market value, price adjustment, price control fee schedules, price discrimination, price fixing, reasonable price, retail price, stipulated price
FOREIGN PHRASES: *Emptor emit quam minimo potest, venditor vendit quam maximo potest.* The buyer purchases for the least he can; the seller sells for the most he can.

PRICELESS, adjective   beyond price, commanding a high price, costly, dear, expensive, extraordinary, high, high-priced, *inaestimabilis,* incalculable, incomparable, inestimable, invaluable, irreplaceable, matchless, peerless, precious, *pretiosissimus,* rare, sterling, unequaled, valuable, without price

PRIDE, noun   affectation, affected manner, affectedness, airs, boastfulness, braggadocio, braggartism, cockiness, condescension, coxcombry, dandyism, egoism, egotism, foppishness, haughtiness, hubris, immodesty, lordliness, narcissism, pomposity, satisfaction, self-admiration, self-applause, self-approval, self-esteem, self-exaltation, self-glorification, self-importance, self-satisfaction, smugness, snobbery, superciliousness, superiority, swagger, toploftiness, vain pretensions, vainglory, vanity

PRIMA FACIE *(Legally sufficient),* **adjective**   adequate, lawfully sufficient, legally adequate, satisfactory, sufficient on its face, sufficient on the pleadings, sufficient to make out a case, sufficiently strong, suitable
ASSOCIATED CONCEPTS: prima facie case, prima facie claim, prima facie evidence, prima facie negligence, prima facie nuisance, prima facie proof, prima facie tort

PRIMA FACIE *(Self-evident),* **adjective**   apparently, at first glance, at first sight, at first view, at sight, before further examination, by all appearances, on presentation, on the face of the matter, on the first view, ostensibly, presumably, seemingly, to all appearances

PRIMACY, noun   ascendancy, authority, command, consequence, control, domination, dominion, eminence, excellency, first place, greatness, headship, hegemony, height, high position, hold, importance, influence, jurisdiction, lead, leadership, paramountcy, power, predominancy, predomination, preeminence, prestige, rule, seniority, sovereignty, supereminence, superiority, supremacy, supremeness, sway, weight

PRIMARY, adjective   basal, basic, central, chief, constitutive, determining, dominant, earliest, elemental, elementary, essential, first, formative, fundamental, greatest, highest, important, inaugural, initial, key, leading, main, nascent, necessary, nonpareil, original, overriding, overruling, paramount, predominant, preeminent, prime, *primus,* principal, *principalis,* prominent, requisite, ruling, second to none, supereminent, supreme, topmost, transcendent, underlying, unsurpassed, uppermost, utmost, vital

ASSOCIATED CONCEPTS: primary boycott, primary evidence, primary insurance, primary jurisdiction, primary liability, primary picketing, primary purpose, primary right, primary surety, primary tort feasor

PRIMARY, *noun*   ballot, choice, contest, contestation, election, election contest, exclusive competition, exclusive contest, exclusive election, exclusive political competition, exclusive political contest, first competition, first contest, first election, first political competition, first political contest, inaugural competition, inaugural contest, inaugural election, inaugural political competition, inaugural political contest, nomination contest, nominative competition, nominative contest, nominative election, partisan competition, partisan contest, partisan election, party competition, party contest, party election, political competition, political contention, political election, political rivalry, poll, preference, selection, vote

ASSOCIATED CONCEPTS: primary evidence, primary responsibility

PRIMARY RIGHTS, *noun*   direct rights, first publication rights, first rights, original rights, print publication rights, printing rights, publishing rights

PRIME *(Most valuable),* **adjective**   best, beyond all praise, beyond compare, capital, cardinal, champion, chief, choice, crowning, dominant, eminent, excelling, exceptional, exemplary, exquisite, finest, first-class, first in quality, first-rate, foremost, front, greatest, head, highest, important, leading, matchless, nonpareil, of highest excellence, of the best quality, optimas, paramount, peerless, predominant, preeminent, preponderant, prevailing, priceless, principal, prize, prominent, remarkable, select, specially selected, splendid, superb, supereminent, superior, superlative, supreme, top, transcendant, unequaled, unmatched, unparalleled, unrivaled, unsurpassable, unsurpassed, utmost, without comparison

PRIME *(Original),* **adjective**   aboriginal, authentic, basal, basic, beginning, dawning, earliest, early, elemental, elementary, embryonic, first, formative, fossil, fundamental, generative, genuine, germinal, inaugural, inceptive, incipient, initial, institutive, introductory, native, oldest, originative, primal, primary, primeval, primitive, primordial, *primus,* rudimentary, starting

PRIMOGENITOR, *noun*   ancestor, ancestral relation, ancestral relative, antecedent, ascendant, elder, father, forebear, forefather, forerunner, founder of the family, grandsire, *origo,* parent, patriarch, precursor, predecessor, procreator

PRIMORDIAL, *adjective*   aboriginal, archetypal, basal, basic, beginning, creative, elemental, elementary, first, fundamental, original, primal, primary, prime, primeval, primigenial, primitive, pristine, protogenic, prototypal, rudimentary, underived

PRINCIPAL, *adjective*   cardinal, chief, controlling, dominant, essential, first, foremost, hegemonic, hegemonical, highest, leading, main, most considerable, most important, most powerful, outstanding, paramount, predominant, preeminent, prevailing, primal, primary, prime, *primus, princeps, principalis,* prominent, ruling, stellar, supereminent, supreme

ASSOCIATED CONCEPTS: principal activity, principal contract, principal contractor, principal obligation, principal place of business, principal sum, principal wrongdoing

FOREIGN PHRASES: *Omne principale trahit ad se accessorium.* Every principal thing draws the accessory to itself. *Quae accessionum locum obtinent, extinguuntur cum principales res peremptae fuerint.* When the principal thing is destroyed, those things which are accessory to it are also destroyed. *Sublato principali, tollitur adjunctum.* By the removal of the principal thing, the adjunct is also taken.

PRINCIPAL *(Capital sum),* **noun**   assets, assets in hand, capital, caput, circulating capital, economic resources, fixed capital, fund, funds, gross amount, holdings, invested sum, main body, material assets, money, *nummi,* original sum, principal part, property, resources, sors, sum, sum total, tangible assets, totality, wealth, whole, working capital

PRINCIPAL *(Director),* **noun**   boss, chief, chief actor, chief authority, chief executive, chief party, chieftain, commandant, commander, controller, directing head, director, employer, engager of services, executive, executive officer, foreperson, governor, head, headperson, *magister,* manager, master, overlooker, overseer, owner, person in authority, person in charge, proprietor, senior, superintendent, superior, supervisor, taskmaster

ASSOCIATED CONCEPTS: partially disclosed principal, principal in the first degree, undisclosed principal

FOREIGN PHRASES: *Nullus dicitur accessorius post feloniam, sed ille qui novit principalem feloniam fecisse, et illum receptavit et comfortavit.* No one is called an "accessory" after the fact but the one who knew the principal had committed a felony, and who received and comforted him. *Nullus dicitur felo principalis nisi actor, aut qui praesens est, abettans aut auxilians ad feloniam faciendam.* No one is called a principal felon except the party actually committing the felony, or the person who is present, aiding and abetting in its commission. *Res accessoria sequitur rem principalem.* An accessory follows the principal. *Qui per alium facit per seipsum facere videtur.* He who acts through another is deemed as having acted himself. *Ubi non est principalis, non potest esse accessorius.* Where there can be no principal, there cannot be an accessory.

PRINCIPLE *(Axiom),* **noun**   accepted belief, adage, admitted maxim, article of belief, article of faith, assertion, assurance, basic doctrine, basic law, basic rule, basic truth, belief, canon, conviction, credo, declaration of faith, *decretum,* doctrine, dogma, established rule, form, formula, formulated belief, foundation, fundamental doctrine, fundamental law, fundamental rule, gospel, *institutum,* instruction, intuitive truth, law, law of conduct, maxim, model, philosophy, policy, position, postulate, postulate of reason, precept, professed belief, profession of faith, proposition, provision, received maxim, recognized maxim, regula, regulation, reliance on, rubric, rule, rule of action, sage maxim, self-evident proposition, self-evident truth, settled principle, standard, statement of belief, statement of position, tenet, theorem, truism, way of thinking

ASSOCIATED CONCEPTS: equitable principle, legal principle

FOREIGN PHRASES: *Principia data sequuntur concomitantia.* Given principles are followed by their concomitants. *Principia probant, non probantur.* Principles prove, they are not proved. *Unumquodque principiorum est sibimetipsi fides; et perspicua vera non sunt probanda.* Every general principle is its own evidence, and plain truths need not be proved.

PRINCIPLE *(Virtue),* **noun**   character, conviction, ethics, goodness, honesty, honor, honorableness, incorruptibility, *integritas,* integrity, justice, moral excellence, moral rectitude, morality, nobleness, probity, rectitude, righteousness, rightfulness, scrupulousness, trustworthiness, truth, uprightness, virtuousness

PRIOR, adjective antecedent, anterior, earlier, first, foregoing, former, inaugural, introductory, late, lead, leading, old, past, precedent, preceding, precursory, preexistent, prefatory, preliminary, preludial, prelusive, preparatory, prevenient, previous, proemial, quondam, *superior*
ASSOCIATED CONCEPTS: prior approval, prior conviction, prior lien, prior restraint

PRIORITY, noun advantage, antecedence, commanding position, essential status, exigency, first place, importance, necessity, needfulness, precedence, preeminence, preference, primacy, prior right, requisiteness, right-of-way, right to precedence, right to preference, seniority, superiority, supremacy, urgency, vitalness
ASSOCIATED CONCEPTS: priority of claim, priority of lien, priority statute
FOREIGN PHRASES: *Qui prior est tempore potior est jure.* He who is first in time is first in right. *Prior tempore potior jure.* First in time, superior in right.

PRISON, noun bastille, *carcer,* cell, facility, house of correction, house of detention, house of reform, incarceration facility, jail, penal colony, penal institution, penitentiary, prison house, reformatory
ASSOCIATED CONCEPTS: prison term
FOREIGN PHRASES: *Carcer ad homines custodiendos, non ad puniendos, dari debet.* A prison should be used for the custody of men, and not for their punishment.

PRISONER, noun captive, confined individual, convict, criminal, detainee, felon, hostage, incarcerated person, individual held in custody, individual jailed, inmate, internee, jailed person, person under arrest

PRIVACY, noun concealment, confidentiality, confidentialness, delitescence, disassociation, dissociation, evasion, evasiveness, intimacy, isolation, obscurity, penetralia, privateness, quietude, retirement, retreat, seclusion, secrecy, secretiveness, separateness, separation, solitariness, solitude, *solitudo,* voluntary exile, withdrawal
ASSOCIATED CONCEPTS: invasion of privacy, right of privacy

PRIVATE *(Confidential),* **adjective** abstruse, arcane, arcanus, clandestine, closet, concealed, covert, cryptic, cryptical, dark, esoteric, esoterical, hidden, intimate, inviolable, mysterious, off-the-record, personal, privy, recondite, secret, undercover, undisclosable, undivulgable, unrevealable
ASSOCIATED CONCEPTS: private papers, private writings

PRIVATE *(Not public),* **adjective** closed, confined, exclusive, individual, individualized, limited, nonofficial, nonpublic, not open, personalized, *privatus,* reserved, restricted, select, unofficial
ASSOCIATED CONCEPTS: private action, private agreement, private bill, private carrier, private corporation, private detective, private dwelling, private employment, private enterprise, private grant, private institution, private investigator, private nuissance, private property, private purposes, private sale, private statute, private trust, private use
FOREIGN PHRASES: *Privatum incommodum publico bono pensatur.* Private inconvenience is compensated for by public benefit. *Pactis privatorum juri publico non derogatur.* Private contracts do not derogate from public law. *Jura publica anteferenda privatis.* Public rights are to be preferred to private rights.

PRIVATE *(Secluded),* **adjective** apart, cloistered, hidden, inaccessible, insular, isolated, out-of-the-way, quiet, remote, removed, seclusive, separate, solitary, unfrequented

PRIVATION, noun absence, attachment, bad fortune, bad luck, bankruptcy, beggary, bereavement, confiscation, dearth, deprivation, deprivement, destitution, dispossession, dissipation, distress, divestment, egestas, exhaustion, famine, financial straits, hardship, impecuniosity, impecuniousness, indigence, *inopia,* insufficiency, lack, loss, loss of fortune, mendicancy, mendicity, narrow means, necessitude, necessity, need, neediness, pauperism, penury, pinch, poverty, reduced circumstances, riddance, sequestration, starvation, straitened means, want

PRIVILEGE, noun advantage, affranchisement, allowance, authority, authorization, *beneficium,* benefit, chance, charter, dispensation, enfranchisement, entitlement, exemption, favor, franchise, freedom, grant, honor, *immunitas,* immunity, indulgence, liberty, license, opportunity, permission, perquisite, prerogative, priority, release, right, sanction, title, tolerance, vouchsafement, warrant
ASSOCIATED CONCEPTS: executive privilege, immunity, privilege against self-incrimination, privileged communications, privileged statement, privileges and immunities, qualified privilege
FOREIGN PHRASES: *Privilegium est beneficium personale, et extinguitur cum persona.* A privilege is a personal benefit, and is extinguished with the death of the person. *Privilegium non valet contra rempublicam.* A privilege is of no avail against the state. *Necessitas inducit privilegium quo ad jura privata.* Necessity gives a privilege with reference to private rights.

PRIVILEGED, adjective allowed, authorized, chartered, empowered, entitled, excepted, excluded, excused, exempt, exempted, favored, franchised, free of, immune, *immunis,* immunized, licensed, not accountable, not subject, permitted, sanctioned, specially provided for, unrestrained
ASSOCIATED CONCEPTS: privileged communications, privileged information, privileged matter

PRIVILEGED COMMUNICATION, noun attorney's work product, closed conversation, confidential communication, confidential discussion, non-disclosable communication, private communication, private interchange, privileged discussion, privileged writing
ASSOCIATED CONCEPTS: attorney-client relationship, doctor-patient privilege, husband-wife privilege, physician-patient privilege, priest-penitent privilege, waiver

PRIVITY, noun affiliation, attachment, connecting medium, connection, contractual bond, derivative interest, interconnection, legal relationship, link, mutual relationship, mutuality of interest, nexus, relation, relationship, successive relationship, tie
ASSOCIATED CONCEPTS: privity of contract, privity of estate, privity of possession

PRIVY, adjective acquainted with, arcane, auricular, buried, clandestine, cognizant of, concealed, confidential, covert, cryptic, cryptical, dark, exclusive, furtive, hidden, inmost, limited, murky, mysterious, nonpublic, obscure, personal, private, recondite, reserved, restricted, secret, sequestered, stealthy, surreptitious, undisclosed, unrevealed

PRIVY, noun contracting party, interested party, partaken, participant, party
ASSOCIATED CONCEPTS: parties and privies

PRIZE, *noun* accolade, advantage, award, blue ribbon, bonus, booty, bounty, capture, catch, cordon, cup, decoration, distinction, find, first place, gain, guerdon, honor, inducement, jackpot, loot, medal, meed, payment, pillage, plum, plunder, *praemium,* premium, prey, privilege, recompense, reward, spoil, title, token, trophy, winning

PRO FORMA, *adjective* as a matter of form, by course of conduct, by custom, by habit, by past practice, by trade and usage, by usage, ceremoniously, common, customary, for the sake of appearances, for the sake of form, formally, in due form, in set form, ritualistically, ritually, standard, superficially, usual

ASSOCIATED CONCEPTS: pro forma decree, pro forma judgment, pro forma order

PRO RATA, *adjective* alloted, apportioned, appropriately, distributed, equivalently, in proportion, on even terms, proportionate

ASSOCIATED CONCEPTS: apportionment, pro rata share

PRO RATA, *adverb* each to each, in equal shares, proportionately, respectively, to each according to his share

PRO TEMPORE, *adverb* briefly, for a time, for the moment, for the present occasion, for the time being, momentarily, pro tem, provisionally, temporarily, transitorily

PROBABILITY, *noun* anticipation, appearance of truth, believability, chance, conceivability, credibility, credibleness, expectation, fair chance, fair expectation, favorable chance, liability, liableness, likelihood, likeliness, odds, ostensibility, plausibility, possibility, presumption, promise, prospect, reasonable chance, reasonableness, susceptibility, tendency, *veri similitudo,* verisimilitude

PROBABLE, *adjective* apparent, apt, believable, conceivable, conjectural, credible, feasible, foreseeable, full of promise, indubitable, liable, likely, logical, ostensible, plausible, possible, practicable, presumable, presumptive, promising, reasonable, seeming, supposed, surmisable, to be expected, unquestionable, *veri similis,* verisimilar, verisimilous

ASSOCIATED CONCEPTS: probable cause

PROBABLE CAUSE, *noun* adequate legal basis, ample legal basis to pursue, just and adequate basis, just evidence, just meritorious evidence, just qualified evidence, legally adequate basis to proceed, legally compelling basis, legally competent evidence, legally sufficient cause, satisfactory legal basis, sufficient evidence, sufficient legal basis

ASSOCIATED CONCEPTS: plain-view doctrine, reasonable suspicion

PROBATE, *noun* authentication of a will, authentication proceeding, judicial validation of a will, proof of the validity of a will, proof of the will, validation of a testament, validity proceedings, will validation proceeding, will verification proceeding

PROBATE, *verb* adjudge the validity of a will, adjudicate the validity of a will, authenticate a will, certify a will, confirm the validity of a will, establish the authenticity of a will, establish the genuineness of a will, establish the validity of a will, prove the validity of a will, substantiate, validate a will, verify a testament

ASSOCIATED CONCEPTS: probate a will, probate court, probate proceeding

PROBATION, *noun* conditional suspension of sentence, exemption, freedom, liberation, parole, period of testing, period of trial, *probatio,* release

ASSOCIATED CONCEPTS: parole, probation term, probationary employee, revocation of probation

PROBATIONER *(One being tested),* *noun* apprentice, beginner, candidate, entrant, initiate, learner, neophyte, newcomer, novice, novitiate, tiro

PROBATIONER *(Released offender),* *noun* criminal released at large, criminal under suspension of sentence, lawbreaker under suspension of sentence, malefactor under suspension of sentence, offender under suspension of sentence, parolee, released convict, released criminal, released felon, released lawbreaker, released malefactor, released prisoner, released transgressor, released wrongdoer, wrongdoer released from prison

PROBATIVE, *adjective* demonstrative, empiric, empirical, evidential, evidentiary, experimental, exploratory, offering evidence, probatory, providing evidence, providing proof, verificative

ASSOCIATED CONCEPTS: probative evidence, probative facts, probative value, probative weight

PROBE, *noun* analysis, careful search, critical examination, deep study, examination, exhaustive study, exploration, exploratory examination, indagation, inquiry, inspection, investigation, perquisition, perscrutation, pursuit, quest, research, review, rigorous search, *rimari, scrutari,* scrutiny, search, searching examination, strict examination

PROBE, *verb* check over, conduct an inquiry, conduct research on, consider attentively, delve into, dig into, dissect, examine, explore, follow up, indagate, inquire into, inspect, institute an inquiry, interrogate, investigate, look into, make an examination, make inquiries, observe, peruse, plumb, poke into, pry into, pursue an inquiry, put to the test, question, review, *rimari,* run checks on, scan, *scrutari,* scrutinize, search into, seek, seek information regarding, study, study in detail, subject to scrutiny, take up an inquiry, unearth

PROBITY, *noun* candidness, candor, conscience, dependability, deservingness, equitableness, equity, fair play, fairness, faith, frankness, good faith, goodness, guilelessness, high principles, honesty, honor, honorableness, impartiality, incorruptibility, ingenuousness, integrity, justice, merit, moral excellence, morality, morals, principle, *probitas,* rectitude, reputability, righteousness, scrupulousness, sincerity, straightforwardness, trustiness, trustworthiness, truth, truthfulness, undeceptiveness, uprightness, veraciousness, veracity, virtue

PROBLEM, *noun* anxiety, bafflement, bone of contention, care, cause for concern, complexity, complication, crisis, difficulty, dilemma, enigma, exercise, matter in dispute, moot point, mystery, obstacle, plight, point in dispute, point to be settled, predicament, puzzle, quandary, question, riddle, source of perplexity, stumper, subject of dispute, tight situation, trouble, vexed question

PROBLEMATIC, *adjective* ambiguous, complex, complicated, contestable, controversial, controvertible, cryptic, cryptical, debatable, difficult, disputable, doubtful, dubious, *dubius,* enigmatic, enigmatical, equivocal, imperspicuous, *incertus,* insoluble, involved, knotty, moot, mysterious,

477

open to doubt, paradoxical, perplexing, problematical, puzzling, questionable, raveled, shrouded in mystery, snarled, tangled, tentative, troublesome, uncertain, unconvincing, undecided, undemonstrable, undetermined, unsettled, vague, worrisome

PROCEDURAL, *adjective*   adjective, directive, functional, methodical, operative, relating to method, relating to the mechanics of a lawsuit, relative to the manner of proceeding, systematic
ASSOCIATED CONCEPTS: procedural defect, procedural due process, procedural law, procedural matter, procedural question, procedural right, procedural rule of law, procedural statute

PROCEDURE, *noun*   act, action, adjective law, behavior, common practice, conduct, course, course of action, custom, established method, habit, line of action, manner of proceeding, manner of working, matter of course, measure, method, methodology, mode, mode of operation, mode of use, modus operandi, motion, order, particular course of action, plan, plan of action, policy, practice, proceeding, process, program, proscribed form, routine, rule, scheme, set form, set format, step, strategy, system, tactics, usage, way, way of operation
ASSOCIATED CONCEPTS: civil procedure, criminal procedure, judicial procedure, pretrial procedure, rule of procedure
FOREIGN PHRASES: **Cursus curiae est lex curiae.** The practice of the court is the law of the court.

PROCEED *(Continue), verb*   begin again, begin where one left off, carry on, get back to work, get on, recommence, reinstate, renew, resume, return, take up again

PROCEED *(Go forward), verb*   act, advance, arise, emanate, ensue, extend, flow, follow, follow a course, gain ground, get ahead, get on, go, go ahead, go forth, issue, keep going, keep moving, make headway, make progress, make rapid strides, move ahead, move forward, pass on, press on, progress, propel oneself, push ahead, push on, roll on, spring, take steps
ASSOCIATED CONCEPTS: proceed with a case, proceed with due diligence

PROCEEDING, *noun*   actio, action, action at law, case, cause, conduct of a lawsuit, course of an action at law, dispute, hearing, lawsuit, legal action, legal procedure, litigation, matter, performance, prescribed method of action, prescribed mode of action, procedure, process, prosecution, series of events, step, steps in the prosecution of an action, suit, suit at law, transaction, trial, undertaking
ASSOCIATED CONCEPTS: abandonment of a proceeding, annulment proceeding, arbitration proceeding, bankruptcy proceeding, bastardy proceeding, certiorari proceeding, commencement of a proceeding, condemnation proceeding, contempt proceeding, criminal proceeding, custody proceeding, discontinuance of a proceeding, enforcement proceeding, equitable proceeding, extraordinary proceeding, filiation proceeding, garnishment proceeding, guardianship proceeding, habeas corpus proceeding, in personam proceeding, in rem proceeding, judicial proceeding, lawful proceeding, legal proceeding, liquidation proceeding, mandamus proceeding, official proceeding, partition proceeding, pending proceeding, plenary proceeding, probate proceeding, public proceeding, quasi in rem proceeding, special proceeding, supplementary proceeding, testamentary proceeding, void proceeding

PROCEEDS, *noun*   avails, balance, benefit, earnings, effect, end result, gain, gross profit, income, money coming in, net profit, produce, product, profit, receipts, *reditus,* renumeration, result, returns, revenue, sum derived from a sale, value received, yield
ASSOCIATED CONCEPTS: proceeds of a crime, proceeds of a sale, proceeds of an insurance policy

PROCESS *(Course), noun*   action, conduct, continued movement, continuing development, handling, line of action, manner, means, method, methodology, mode of operation, operation, performance, plan, policy, procedure, progressive course, *ratio,* regular proceeding, ritual, routine, scheme, series of measures, strategy, system, tactics, transaction, treatment, way, ways and means
ASSOCIATED CONCEPTS: due process, judicial process

PROCESS *(Summons), noun*   authoritative citation to appear before a court, authoritative command, behest, bidding, citation, command, direction, instruction to appear, legal call, *lis,* official call, official notice, requirement to appear, signal by which one is summoned, subpoena, writ
ASSOCIATED CONCEPTS: abuse of process, compulsory process, defective process, irregular process, return of process, service of process

PRO-CHOICE, *noun*   abortion advocate, accepting abortion, approving abortion, endorsing abortion, in favor of abortion, pro-abortion, sanctioning abortion, supporting legalized abortion, supportive of abortion
Generally: self-determination
ASSOCIATED CONCEPTS: abortion on demand, legalized abortion, spontaneous abortion, voluntary abortion

PROCLAIM, *verb*   advertise, air, announce, annunciate, assert, asseverate, blare, blaze abroad, broach, broadcast, bruit, call out, circulate, communicate, cry, *declarare,* declare, disseminate, divulge, enounce, exclaim, gazette, give notice of, give out, hawk about, herald, inform, make a proclamation, make known, make public, noise abroad, *praedicare,* promulgate, *pronuntiare,* propagate, publicize, publish, release, report, set forth, sing out, sound forth, spread abroad, state, tell, thunder forth, trumpet, utter, ventilate

PROCLAMATION, *noun*   announcement, annunciation, declaration, decree, decretal, edict, *edictum,* exclamation, fiat, mandate, manifesto, message, notification, official publication, promulgation, pronouncement, public announcement, public avowal, public notice, publication, recitation, rescript, statement

PROCLIVITY, *noun*   ability, appetence, appetency, aptitude, aptness, bent, bias, disposition, facility, gift, gravitation, inclination, inherent ability, innate disposition, innate sense, instinct, leaning, liking, natural sense, partiality, penchant, predilection, predisposition, prejudice, *proclivitas,* proneness, propensity, readiness, talent, tendency, turn

PROCRASTINATE, *verb*   adjourn, be dilatory, be idle, be inert, be neglectful, block, dally, dawdle, defer, delay, *differre,* dilly dally, do nothing, filibuster, gain time, hang back, hesitate, hold back, hold up, idle, keep one waiting, kill time, lag, let slide, let slip, let the matter stand, linger, loaf, loiter, neglect, pause, pigeonhole, play for time, postpone, *procrastinare,* prolong, prorogue, protract, push aside, put off, retard, shelve, stall, stave off, suspend, table, tarry, wait, waste time

PROCTOR, noun advocate, agent, appointee, broker, caretaker, delegate, deputy, functionary, instrument, lawyer, lieutenant, manager, minister, monitor, officer, procurator, proxy, representative, second, steward, surrogate, vicar

PROCURATOR, noun administrator, adviser, agent, appointee, assistant, broker, business representative, caretaker, conductor, *curator,* delegate, deputy, director, emissary, envoy, executor, factor, go-between, intendant, intermediary, intermediate, intermedium, *legatus,* lieutenant, manager, middleman, *moderator,* monitor, overseer, proctor, prolocutor, proxy, representative, solicitor, spokesman, steward, substitute, superintendent, supervisor, syndic, viceregent

PROCURE, verb accomplish, accumulate, achieve, acquire, appropriate, attain, bag, bring, buy, capture, cause, come by, commandeer, *comparare,* dig up, earn, effect, enlist, fetch, find, force from, gain, gather, get, glean, help oneself to, hire, lay hands on, make a purchase, obtain, pick up, provide, purchase, realize, reap, receive, secure, seize, take, take possession of

PRODIGAL, adjective careless, dissipated, dissipative, excessive, extravagant, heedless, immoderate, improvident, imprudent, intemperate, lavish, liberal, profligate, reckless, spendthrift, squandering, thriftless, unbridled, uncurbed, uneconomical, unfrugal, unrestrained, unthrifty, wanton, wasteful

PRODIGIOUS (Amazing), **adjective** abnormal, anomalous, astonishing, astounding, bizarre, curious, dumbfounding, exceptional, extraordinary, fantastic, freakish, grotesque, impressive, inconceivable, incredible, indescribable, marvelous, miraculous, noteworthy, out of the common run, out of the ordinary, outlandish, overwhelming, peculiar, phenomenal, queer, remarkable, renowned, singular, startling, strange, striking, supernormal, surprising, unaccountable, unaccustomed, uncommon, unconventional, uncustomary, unexampled, unfamiliar, unheard of, unimaginable, unique, unprecedented, unthinkable, weird, wonderful, wondrous

PRODIGIOUS (Enormous), **adjective** astronomical, big, colossal, cyclopean, elephantine, gargantuan, giant, gigantic, grand, great, Herculean, huge, *immanis,* immense, *ingens,* large, leviathan, mammoth, massive, mighty, monster, monstrous, monumental, sizable, stupendous, substantial, terrific, thumping, titanic, towering, tremendous, vast, whopping

PRODUCE (Manufacture), **verb** accomplish, achieve, assemble, bear, beget, breed, bring about, bring forth, bring into being, bring into existence, bring to pass, build, coin, compose, conceive, concoct, construct, contrive, create, devise, draw up, effect, effectuate, engender, erect, execute, fabricate, fashion, form, formulate, furnish, generate, give birth to, give rise to, hatch, institute, invent, make, make up, originate, prepare, procreate, propagate, provide, raise, realize, result in, turn out, yield

ASSOCIATED CONCEPTS: producing cause

PRODUCE (Offer to view), **verb** air, bring forward, bring into view, bring out, bring to light, bring to the fore, bring to the front, demonstrate, disclose, display, divulge, dramatize, evidence, evince, exhibit, expose, give a performance, hold up to view, impart, lay bare, lay out, make

known, make visible, manifest, parade, present, put on display, put on the stage, reveal, set out, show, uncover, unfold, unmask, unscreen, unveil

ASSOCIATED CONCEPTS: failure to produce, notice to produce, produce a witness, produce evidence

PRODUCT, noun accomplishment, article, article of merchandise, article of trade, commodity, creation, crop, effect, emanation, end result, final outcome, fruit, handiwork, harvest, invention, issue, item, merchandise, offspring, *opus,* outcome, output, proceeds, produce, result, salable commodity, stock in trade, yield

ASSOCIATED CONCEPTS: product defect, product patent, products liability

PRODUCTION (Operation), **noun** execution, industry, manifestation, manufacture

PRODUCTION (Output), **noun** accomplishment, attainment, business, compilation, composition, constitution, construction, consummation, creation, discharge, disclosure, dispatch, effectuation, establishment, fabrication, formation, fruition, fulfillment, implementation, lengthening, manifestation, organization, origination, outcome, output, performance, preparation, presentation, realization, work

ASSOCIATED CONCEPTS: production of a witness, production of documents, production of evidence

PRODUCTIVE, adjective advantageous, causative, constructive, creational, creative, demiurgic, demiurgical, efficient, fecund, ferax, fertile, formative, fructiferous, fructuous, fruitful, gainful, imaginative, industrial, inventive, life-giving, luxuriant, manufacturing, original, originative, paying, potent, pregnant, profitable, proliferative, proliferous, prolific, rank, remunerative, resourceful, rich, teeming, *uber,* useful, valuable, worthwhile, yielding

PRODUCTS, noun articles of commerce, assets, chattels, commodities, consumer durable, durables, effects, goods, holdings, items, line of goods, manufactured goods, merchandise, produce, produced materials, resources, staples, stock in trade, supplies, vendibles

ASSOCIATED CONCEPTS: products liability insurance

PROFANE, adjective bad, blasphemous, coarse, common, damnatory, dirty, disrespectful, evil, execrative, faithless, foul-spoken, foulmouthed, godless, impious, *impius,* imprecative, imprecatory, improper, impure, indelicate, irreligious, irreverant, laic, laical, lay, maledictive, maledictory, miscreant, mundane, peccable, peccant, polluted, *profanus,* sacrilegious, secular, shameless, sinful, smutty, temporal, transient, transitory, unblest, unconsecrated, undevout, ungodly, unhallowed, unholy, unprintable, unreligious, unsacred, unsaintly, unsanctified, unspeakable, unvirtuous, vice-ridden, virtueless, vulgar, wicked, worldly

PROFANITY, noun billingsgate, blasphemy, cursing, denunciation, derisive language, desecration, disparagement, disrespect, execration, foul language, foul talk, *impietas,* invective, malediction, obloquy, profanation, profane language, profaneness, swearing, vilification, vituperation, vulgarity

ASSOCIATED CONCEPTS: censorship, obscenity

PROFESS (Avow), **verb** acknowledge, admit, advocate, affirm, announce, assert, asseverate, assure, attest, aver, avouch, contend, declare, disclose, divulge, hold out, lay bare, lay open, maintain, make a statement, make an assertion, make clear, make evident, make known, own, pledge, proclaim, pronounce, put forth, put forward, reveal, set forth, state, subscribe to, tell, utter

PROFESS *(Pretend),* **verb**   affect, claim, concoct, counterfeit, create a false impression, disguise, dissemble, dissimulate, fabricate, feign, give a false impression, imagine, make a show of, make believe, pass for, posture, practice chicanery, put a false construction upon, represent fictitiously, sham, simulate

PROFESSION *(Declaration),* **noun**   affirmation, announcement, assertion, assurance, attestation, averment, avowal, claim, confession, declaration of faith, disclosure, enunciation, notification, oath, pledge, presentation, *professio,* pronouncement, representation, statement, troth, vow, word, word of honor

PROFESSION *(Vocation),* **noun**   association, avocation, business, calling, career, chosen work, concern, craft, employment, endeavor, engagement, field, job, learned profession, lifework, line of work, manus, occupation, office, position, practice, pursuit, role, specialty, trade, undertaking, vocation, walk of life, work
ASSOCIATED CONCEPTS: professional corporation

PROFESSIONAL *(Stellar),* **adjective**   admirable, businesslike, choice, commendable, excellent, exemplary, foremost, highest quality, illustrious, incomparable, laudable, model, paramount, praiseworthy, preeminent, prime, principal, sterling, superb, superior, unequaled, unexcelled, unrivaled, unsurpassed, well done

PROFESSIONAL *(Trained),* **adjective**   able, adept, career, competent, established, experienced, expert, learned, proficient, qualified, skilled, skillful, specialized, trained, well-qualified
ASSOCIATED CONCEPTS: professional capacity, professional corporation, professional ethics, professional misconduct, professional opinion, professional skill and judgment

PROFESSIONAL, **noun**   accomplished practitioner, adept practitioner, adroit practitioner, authority, competent practitioner, experienced person, expert, master, practiced individual, practitioner, proficient practitioner, qualified practitioner, skilled practitioner, skilled technician, specialist, trained person
ASSOCIATED CONCEPTS: professional opinion

PROFFER, **verb**   adduce, advance, advertise, bid, bring forward, donate, extend, give, hold out, invite, lay before, make a bid, make a motion, make an offer, make an overture, make possible, move, offer, prefer, present, promise, *promittere,* propose, propound, put forward, put up, render, set forth, submit, suggest, tender, volunteer

PROFICIENT, **adjective**   able, accomplished, adept, adequate, adroit, advanced, capable, clever, competent, conversant, cunning, deft, dexterous, effective, efficacious, efficient, equal to, excellent, experienced, expert, facile, good, habilitated, handy, ingenious, knowing, masterful, *peritus,* practiced, qualified, quick, ready, *sciens,* skilled, skillful, talented, trained, up to, well-qualified, well-versed

PROFIT, **noun**   accruance, accumulation, acquisition, advancement, advantage, augmentation, avails, benefaction, benefit, clearance, compensation, dividend, earnings, emolument, financial reward, *fructus,* fruits, gain, growth,

harvest, improvement, incentive, income, increase, increment, interest, *lucrum,* meed, output, pay, payment, premium, prize, proceeds, produce, *quaestus,* realization, receipts, remuneration, return, revenue, reward, service, take, utility, value received, windfall, winnings, yield
ASSOCIATED CONCEPTS: accumulated profits, anticipated profits, capital, carrying on business for profit, distributable profits, excessive profits, excess profits tax, gross profit, loss of profits, margin of profit, net profit, not for profit, pecuniary profits, profit a prendre, profit sharing, prospective profit, remote profits, secret profits, speculative profits, surplus profits, underwriting profits, undistributed profits
FOREIGN PHRASES: *Ubi periculum, ibi et lucrum collocatur.* He who risks a thing, should receive the profits arising from it.

PROFIT, **verb**   acquire, advance, assist, avail, be better for, be improved by, be of use, benefit, cash in on, clear, confer a benefit on, contribute, draw profit from, edify, gain, gain advantage, harvest, help, improve, learn a lesson from, make capital out of, make good use of, make improvement, make money by, make use of, obtain a return, produce a good effect, produce a good result, *proficere,* put to use, realize, reap, reap the fruits, turn to account, use, utilize, yield returns

PROFITABLE, **adjective**   advantageous, advisable, aiding, assisting, beneficial, desirable, edifying, emolumental, expedient, favorable, *fructuosus, frugifer,* fruitful, gainful, helpful, invaluable, lucrative, money-making, paying, productive, remunerative, rewarding, salutary, serviceable, successful, useful, *utilis,* valuable, well-paying, worthwhile

PROFLIGATE *(Corrupt),* **adjective**   abandoned to vice, base, corrupted, debauched, degenerate, depraved, disgraceful, disreputable, dissipated, dissipative, dissolute, evil, evil-minded, fallen, flagitious, foul, heinous, immoral, indecent, infamous, iniquitous, lacking decency, lacking principle, lacking shame, lawless, lost to principle, lost to virtue, morally evil, nefarious, offensive, peccant, *perditus,* rascally, rotten, scampish, shameful, shameless, sinful, unethical, unprincipled, unredeemable, unregenerate, unrepentant, vice-ridden, vicious, vile, vitiated, wicked

PROFLIGATE *(Extravagant),* **adjective**   economically imprudent, immoderate, improvident, intemperate, overly liberal, prodigal, *profligatus,* reckless, spendthrift, squandering, thriftless, unrestrained, unthrifty, wasteful

PROFOUND *(Esoteric),* **adjective**   abstruse, acroamatic, acroamatical, acroatic, astute, complicated, erudite, esoteric, gnostic, intellectual, intellectually deep, knowing, learned, oracular, penetrating, perceptive, philosophical, recondite, reflective, sagacious, sage, scholarly, thoughtful, wise

PROFOUND *(Intense),* **adjective**   abysmal, acute, bottomless, deep, deeply felt, fathomless, great, heart-stirring, heartfelt, heavy, impressive, indelible, intense, moving, penetrating, piercing, sharp, soul-stirring, strong, touching, unfathomable, vivid

PROFUSE, **adjective**   abounding, abundant, affluent, ample, boundless, bounteous, bountiful, copious, countless, crowded, diffuse, discursive, *effusus,* endless, excessive, exorbitant, extravagant, exuberant, flush, full, garrulous, generous, illimitable, immeasurable, immoderate, improvident, incalculable, inexhaustible, infinite, innumerable, inordinate, intemperate, interminable, lavish, liberal, limitless, long-winded, loquacious, luxuriant, measureless, multitudinary, multitudinous, munificent, myriad, number-less, numerous, overabounding, overflowing, overgener-ous, padded, plentiful, prodigal, profligate, *profusus,* pro-lific, prolix, protracted, rambling, reckless, redundant, replete, rich, rife, spendthrift, squandering, sumptious, su-perfluous, surplus, swarming, teeming, thriftless, unbridled, uncurbed, unnumbered, unsparing, unstinted, unstinting, unthrifty, unwarranted, verbose, wanton, wasteful, without bound, without end, without limit, without stint, wordy

PROGENITOR, noun   ancestor, antecedent, antecessor, begettor, forebear, forefather, foregoer, forerunner, genitor, origin, *parens,* parent, precursor, predecessor, primogeni-tor, procreator, sire, source

PROGENY, noun   bloodline, brood, children, descen-dants, family, fruit, heirs, issue, line, lineage, offspring, pos-terity, *progenies,* scions, seed, sons, stock, succeeding generations, tribe, young

PROGNOSIS, noun   conjecture, estimate, foreboding, forecast, foreknowledge, foresight, foretelling, guess, opin-ion, preannouncement, prediction, prefiguration, prefigure-ment, premonition, prenotice, presage, presagement, presumption, prognostication, promise, prophesy, supposi-tion, vaticination

PROGNOSTICATE, verb   advise, augur, augurate, auspi-cate, betoken, bode, conjecture, counsel, divine, forebode, forecast, foresee, foresee the future, foreshadow, foreshow, foretell, foretoken, herald, indicate beforehand, indicate in advance, look ahead to, look forward to, make a prediction, ominate, portend, preannounce, predict, premonish, pre-monstrate, presage, presignify, presume, promise, proph-esy, signify, soothsay, speculate, spell, surmise, tell for-tunes, theorize, vaticinate

PROGRAM, noun   agenda, arrangement, blueprint, cal-endar, campaign, catalogue, course, curriculum, design, docket, draft, list, order, outline, plan, policy, presentation, project, proposal, prospectus, schedule, series of events, set of tactics, strategy, syllabus, system

PROGRAM, verb   arrange, block out, book, budget, cal-endar, design, determine, devise, direct, docket, draft, en-gineer, *excogitare,* form a plan, frame, lay a plan, lay out, list, make an agenda, make arrangements, manage, map out, organize, outline, plan, plot, preconcert, predeter-mine, preestablish, project, register, schedule, scheme, sketch, slate, work out

PROGRESS, noun   accomplishment, achievement, ad-vance, advancement, amelioration, augmentation, better-ment, change, development, emendation, enhancement, enrichment, flow, furtherance, gain, growth, headway, im-provement, increase, increment, march, melioration, move-ment, movement forward, onward motion, passage, perfec-tion, preferment, progression, *progressus,* promotion, reclamation, recovery, redemption, reform, rehabilitation, reorganization, restoration, rise, steady advance, success

PROGRESS, verb   advance, ameliorate, approach, as-cend, become better, climb, continue onward, convalesce, develop, enhance, enrich, expand, forge ahead, gain, gain ground, get ahead, go ahead, go forward, go on, grow, grow better, grow up, improve, increase, keep going, keep moving, make headway, make progress, maturate, mature, meliorate, mend, mount, move ahead, move on,

move onward, press on, press onward, proceed, *proficere, progredi,* prosper, push on, recuperate, ripen, rise

PROGRESSIVE *(Advocating change),* **adjective**   ad-vanced, corrective, emendatory, enterprising, forward looking, improvement-minded, liberal, modern, open-minded, reformational, reformative, reformatory, remedial, up to date

PROGRESSIVE *(Going forward),* **adjective**   advancing, consecutive, continuous, dynamic, endless, forward, for-ward moving, growing, moving, ongoing, proceeding, profluent, rising, serial, successive, transitional, traveling, uninterrupted

PROHIBIT, verb   ban, banish, bar, block, check, circum-scribe, control, counteract, curb, debar, deny, disallow, dis-qualify, embargo, enjoin, exclude, forbid, foreclose, forfend, gainsay, halt, hamper, hinder, impede, inhibit, interdict, in-terfere, limit, make illegal, negate, negative, obstruct, omit, oppose, preclude, prevent, proscribe, protest, quash, quell, refuse, refuse permission, regulate, reject, repress, repudi-ate, restrain, restrict, revoke, shut out, smother, stay, stop, suppress, suspend, thwart, traverse, veto

ASSOCIATED CONCEPTS: prohibited action, prohibited by law, prohibited form, prohibited practice

FOREIGN PHRASES: ***Contra legem facit qui id facit quod lex prohibit; in fraudem vero qui, salvis verbis legis, senten-tiam ejus circumvenit.*** He who does what the law pro-hibits, acts in fraud of the law; the letter of the law being in-violate, cheats the spirit of it. ***Cui licet quod majus, non debet quod minus est non licere.*** He who is allowed to do the greater ought not to be prohibited from doing the less. ***Idem est facere, et nolle prohibere cum possis.*** It is the same thing to commit an act as not to prohibit it when it is in your power.

PROHIBITION, noun   ban, banishment, bar, barrier, block, check, circumscription, constraint, counterorder, curb, debarment, denial, determent, deterrence, deter-rent, disallowance, discouragement, disqualification, elimination, embargo, enforced abstention, enjoining, eradication, estoppel, exclusion, forbiddance, hindrance, illegality, illegitimacy, impediment, inhibition, injunction, interdict, interdiction, *interdictum,* interference, limit, lim-itation, negation, nonadmission, noninclusion, obstacle, obstruction, ostracism, outlawry, preclusion, prevention, proscription, refusal, rejection, repression, repudiation, re-straint, restriction, stay, stop, stoppage, suppression, taboo, traversal, unconstitutionality, unlawfulness, veto

ASSOCIATED CONCEPTS: injunctions, restraining orders, statu-tory prohibition, writ of prohibition

FOREIGN PHRASES: ***Semper qui non prohibet pro se inter-venire, mandare creditur.*** He who does not prohibit the intervention of another in his behalf is deemed to have au-thorized it. ***Quando aliquid prohibetur ex directo, prohi-betur et per obliquum.*** When anything is prohibited di-rectly, it is also prohibited indirectly.

PROHIBITIVE *(Costly),* **adjective**   exorbitant, expensive, extortionate, extravagant, high-priced, immoderate, inordi-nate, preposterous, unconscionable, undue, unreasonable, unwarranted

PROHIBITIVE *(Restrictive),* **adjective**   deterrent, disal-lowing, disqualifying, exclusive, exclusory, hindering, impeding, impossible, inhibitive, inhibitory, injunctive, interdictive, interdictory, interfering, limitative, limiting, obstructive, preclusive, preventing, preventive, prohibitory, proscriptive, repressive, restraining, suppressive

PROJECT, noun activity, aim, ambition, assignment, attempt, *consilium,* contrivance, deal, design, determination, device, employment, end, endeavor, engagement, enterprise, essay, fixed intention, goal, idea, *inceptum,* intent, intention, job, object, objective, occupation, outline, plan, projected campaign, projected scheme, proposal, proposition, *propositum,* purpose, pursuit, resolution, scheme, set purpose, task, undertaking, venture

PROJECT *(Extend beyond),* **verb** arch, bulge, hang over, jut, jut out, lengthen, overhang, protrude, protuberate, stand out, stick out, widen

PROJECT *(Impel forward),* **verb** cast, discharge, drive, eject, emit, expel, fling, hurl, launch, let fly, propel, push, send, send off, shoot forward, sling, throw, thrust, traject

PROLEPSIS, noun apriorism, assumption, hypothesis, postulation, presupposition

PRO-LIFE, noun against abortion, antiabortion, antithetic to abortion, diametrically opposed to abortion, hostile to abortion, in favor of barring abortion, in favor of life, in favor of prohibiting abortion, in opposition to abortion, inimical to abortion, opposed to abortion, pro-human life, right-to-life advocate
ASSOCIATED CONCEPTS: consistent life ethic, human rights, partial birth abortions, pro-choice, pro-life movement, unborn child

PROLIFERATE, verb abound, be fruitful, be numerous, be plentiful, blossom, breed, bud, burgeon, fecundate, fecundify, flourish, flower, grow, grow in number, have offspring, have progeny, increase the number of, make manifold, *multiplicare,* multiply, mushroom, produce rapidly, propagate, reproduce, reproduce in kind, reproduce rapidly, spawn, spread, sprout, swell, thrive, wax

PROLIFIC, adjective abundant, breedy, copious, creative, fecund, feracious, fertile, fruitbearing, fruitful, generative, philoprogenitive, procreative, productive, profuse, progenitive, proliferative, proliferous, rich, teeming, verbose, wordy, yielding

PROLIX, adjective bombastic, boresome, boring, circumlocutory, copious, diffuse, discursive, drearisome, extended, full of verbiage, lengthy, long, long-spun, long-winded, *longus,* maundering, monotonous, padded, pleonastic, pleonastical, prolonged, prosy, protracted, rambling, redundant, repetitive, spread out, spun out, tedious, tiresome, unconcise, uneconomical, verbose, *verbosus,* wandering, wearisome, wordy

PROLIXITY, noun effusion, long windedness, loquacity, redundancy, verbiage, verbosity, wordiness

PROLONG, verb be steadfast, continue, drag out, draw out, extend, *extendere,* hold over, increase, keep, lengthen, linger, maintain, make longer, perpetuate, persevere, preserve, *prorogare,* protract, retain, slow down, spin out, stretch, sustain, tarry, *trahere*

PROMINENCE, noun brilliancy, celebrity, character, clout, consequence, consideration, conspicuousness, cedit, distinction, eminence, emphasis, honor, fame, grandeur, greatness, height, illustriousness, import, importance, influence, majesty, notability, notoriety, paramountcy, popularity, prestige, projection, protuberance, reputation, respectability, significance, splendor, status, superiority, weight

PROMINENT, adjective apparent, bold, brilliant, celebrated, consequential, conspicuous, credited, dignified, discernible, distinct, distinctive, distinguished, elevated, eminent, evident, exalted, extended, famous, flagrant, foremost, glaring, honored, illustrious, important, imposing, influential, jutting, known, leading, lofty, main, manifest, marked, memorable, noble, notable, noticeable, notorious, obtrusive, obvious, outstanding, powerful, predominent, preeminent, principal, projecting, *prominens,* pronounced, protruding, protrusive, protuberant, raised, recognizable, relieved, remarkable, renowned, respected, rising, salient, showy, significant, striking, upmost, visible, weighty, well-known, well-marked, well-seen

PROMISCUOUS, adjective alloyed, amalgamated, blended, carnal, casual, chaotic, commingled, composite, confused, conjoined, crossbred, crossed, debauched, dissolute, diverse, easy, free, fused, heterogeneous, immodest, immoral, incontinent, indiscriminate, indiscriminative, indistinguishable, intemperate, interlarded, intermixed, interwoven, joined, jumbled, lax, lewd, licentious, loose, mingled, miscellaneous, mixed, profligate, *promiscuus,* scrambled, unchaste, uncritical, undiscerning, undiscriminating, unselective, unvirtuous, variegated, wanton, wild

PROMISE, noun affirmation, agreement, asseveration, assurance, avowal, bond, commitment, compact, consent, contract, covenant, declaration, engagement, *fides,* guarantee, oath, obligation, pact, paction, pledge, *promissum,* stipulation, treaty, understanding, vadium, vow, warranty, word
ASSOCIATED CONCEPTS: bilateral promises, consideration, contract, gift, unilateral promise
FOREIGN PHRASES: *Ea quae, commendandi causa, in venditionibus dicuntur, si palam appareant, venditorem non obligant.* Those things which are said as praise of the things sold, if they are openly apparent do not bind the seller. *Nudum pactum est ubi nulla subest causa praeter conventionem; sed ubi subest causa, fit obligatio, et parit actionem.* A naked contract is where there is no consideration except the agreement; but where there is a consideration, an obligation is created and gives rise to a right of action. *Nuda pactio obligationem non parit.* A naked agreement does not effect an otherwise binding obligation. *Nuda ratio et nuda pactio non ligant aliquem debitorem.* Naked intention and naked promise do not bind any debtor.

PROMISE *(Raise expectations),* **verb** augur well, betoken, bid fair, cheer, embolden, encourage, enhearten, excite expectation, forebode, forecast, foreshadow, foreshow, foretell, forewarn, foster hope, give expectation, give hope, inspirit, lead one to expect, make a prediction, portend, predict, presage, prognosticate, prophesy, quicken, raise hopes, set astir, show signs of, signify, stimulate, suggest, threaten

PROMISE *(Vow),* **verb** accept a liability, accept an obligation, accept responsibility, adjure, affirm, affirm positively, agree, assert, assert an oath, assert positively, assert solemnly, assert under oath, asseverate, assure, attest, aver, avouch, avow, be answerable for, bear witness, become bound, bind, bind by a pledge, bind oneself, bind oneself by oath, certify, commit oneself, consent, contract, contract

an obligation, covenant, declare, engage, engage in solemn manner, give assurance, give one's honor, give one's word, give one's word of honor, give security, guarantee, hypothecate, incur a duty, insure, make a solemn resolution, make an avowal, make an engagement, make an oath, make oneself answerable, obligate oneself, pledge, pledge one's credit, pledge one's honor, pledge one's word, pledge oneself, plight, plight one's honor, plight one's word, *polliceri*, stake one's credit, stipulate, swear, swear an oath, take a vow, take an oath, take upon oneself, testify, undertake, underwrite, vouch, vow, warrant
ASSOCIATED CONCEPTS: breach of promise, nude promise, promise to answer for the debt of another, promise to pay

PROMISSORY, *adjective* committed to payment, consisting of a guarantee, consisting of a pledge, containing a pledge, containing an assurance, guaranteed, on oath, on one's word, on one's word of honor, promising, promising to underwrite, under oath, vouched for
ASSOCIATED CONCEPTS: promissory estoppel, promissory note

PROMOTE (*Advance*), *verb* advocate, advance in rank, aggrandize, better, dignify, elevate, encourage, exalt, favor, forward, further, graduate, help, magnify, move up, pass, prefer, *producere, promovere, provehere,* push up, raise, upgrade

PROMOTE (*Organize*), *verb* abet, advertise, advocate, aid in organizing, assist, avail, back, befriend, benefit, bestead, bolster, build up, carry on, champion, come to the aid of, contribute to, cooperate, cultivate, develop, encourage, facilitate, foster, further, help, hold up, lend a hand, maintain, nourish, nurse, nurture, patronize, propagandize, push, render a service to, sanction, second, serve, speak for, speed, sponsor, stir up, subscribe to, subserve, support, sustain, uphold, urge

PROMOTER, *noun* *adiutor,* advocate, aider, auctor, backer, benefactor, encourager, enterpriser, *fautor,* financial backer, financier, founder, organizer, organizer of business enterprises, organizer of commercial enterprises, patron, planner, prime mover, publicist, sponsor, supporter

PROMOTION (*Advancement*), *noun* advance, amelioration, betterment, elevation, elevation in rank, exaltation, forwarding, graduation, headway, improvement, increase, lift, passing, preferment, progress, progression, raise, rise, uplift

PROMOTION (*Encouragement*), *noun* abetting, advertising, aid, *amplificatio,* assistance, backing, benefit, boosting, campaign, cultivation, fostering, furtherance, help, maintenance, publicity, service, sponsorship, upkeep

PROMPT, *adjective* businesslike, eager, early, efficient, expeditious, immediate, instant, instantaneous, on time, precise, *promptus,* punctual, quick, ready, seasonable, speedy, spontaneous, summary, swift, timely, unhesitating, without delay
ASSOCIATED CONCEPTS: prompt judicial action

PROMPT, *verb* activate, actuate, advise, alert, animate, arouse, cause, dispose, encourage, excite, exhort, goad, hint, hound, impel, incite, incline, induce, influence, initiate, inspire, instigate, lead, motivate, move, occasion, persuade, press, prod, promote, provoke, push, recommend, remind, rouse, spur on, stimulate, stir, suggest, tempt, urge
ASSOCIATED CONCEPTS: leading a witness, subornation

PROMULGATE, *verb* air, announce, annunciate, blaze, blazon, bring into the open, broadcast, bruit, circulate,

communicate, declare, disclose, disseminate, divulge, emit, enounce, give currency, give notice of, give publicity to, hawk about, herald, issue, make known, notify, proclaim, *promulgare,* propagate, publicize, publish, report, reveal, set forth, spread, spread abroad, vent
ASSOCIATED CONCEPTS: promulgate a law, promulgate a rule
FOREIGN PHRASES: *Non obligat lex nisi promulgata.* A law is not obligatory unless it is promulgated.

PRONE, *adjective* agreeable, apt, bent, biased, compliant, disposed, eager, easily persuaded, favorable, given, inclined, liable, likely, minded, partial, predisposed, *proclivis, pronus,* propense, ready, tending, well-disposed, willing

PRONOUNCE (*Pass judgment*), *verb* adjudge, adjudicate, an*noun*ce authoritatively, conclude, decide, declare to be, decree, deliver judgment, determine, find, give a ruling, give an opinion, give judgment, judge, officially utter, pass sentence upon, prescribe punishment, *pronuntiare,* rule, utter formally, utter judicial sentence

PRONOUNCE (*Speak*), *verb* accent, accentuate, announce, announce authoritatively, announce officially, articulate, assert, break silence, communicate, declare, deliver, deliver an address, deliver formally, *dicere,* emit, emphasize, enounce, enunciate, *enuntiare,* express, form, frame, present, proclaim, recite, say, sound, speak formally, state, stress, tell, utter, utter formally, utter forth, verbalize, vocalize, voice

PRONOUNCEMENT, *noun* affirmation, announcement, annunciation, assertion, asseveration, authoritative statement, averment, comment, decision, declaration, decree, deliverance, dictum, edict, enunciation, expression, fiat, formal statement, imperative, judgment, manifesto, notice, notification, observation, opinion, predication, profession, promulgation, pronunciamento, publication, remark, report, ruling, statement, utterance

PROOF, *noun* argumentum, assurance, attestation, averment, certainty, certification, clear demonstration, clear indication, conclusiveness, confirmation, data, demonstration, documentation, establishment, evidence, evident demonstration, facts, *indicium,* manifestation, process of proving, proved strength, ratification, records, satisfaction, satisfactory evidence, showing, substantiation, sufficient evidence, *testimonium,* testimony, verification, warrant
ASSOCIATED CONCEPTS: adequate proof, affirmative proof, burden of proof, clear and convincing proof, collateral proof, failure of proof, final proof, furnish proof, legal proof, positive proof, proof beyond a reasonable doubt, proof evident, proof of claim, proof of death, proof of disability, proof of payment, proof positive, quantum of proof, satisfactory proof
FOREIGN PHRASES: *Semper necessitas probandi incumbit ei qui agit.* The burden of proof always lies upon the claimant. ***Non possessori incumbit necessitas probandi possessiones ad se pertinere.*** It is not incumbent on the possessor of property to prove that his possessions belong to him. ***Affirmanti, non neganti incumbit probatio.*** The burden of proof is on the party who affirms, not upon one who denies. ***Facultas probationum non est angustanda.*** The right of offering proof is not to be narrowed. ***In criminalibus, probationes debent esse luce clariores.*** In criminal cases, the proofs ought to be clearer than light. ***Quod per recordum probatum, non debet esse negatum.*** That which is proved by record ought not to be denied. ***Quod constat curiae opere testium non indiget.*** That which is clear to the court needs not the help of witnesses. ***Qui melius probat melius habet.*** He who proves most recovers most.

Praesumptio violenta, plena probatio. Strong presumption is full proof. *Perspicua vera non sunt probanda.* Evident facts need not be proved. *Per rerum naturam factum negantis nulla probatio est.* It is in the nature of things that a person who denies a fact is not bound to give proof. *Probandi necessitas incumbit illi qui agit.* The necessity of proving lies with the person who sues. *Frustra probatur quod probatum non relevat.* It is useless to prove that which when proved is irrelevant. *Principia probant, non probantur.* Principles prove, they are not proved. *Praesumptiones sunt conjecturae ex signo verisimili ad probandum assumptae.* Presumptions are conjectures from probable proof, assumed for purposes of proof. *Reus excipiendo fit actor.* The defendant by pleading may make himself a plaintiff. *Idem est non probari et non esse: non deficit jus, sedprobatio.* What is not proved, and what is not, are the same; it is not a defect of the law, but a want of proof. *Factum negantis nulla probatio sit.* No proof is required of him who denies a fact. *Quod constat clare non debet verificari.* What is clearly apparent is not required to be proved. *Semper necessitas probandi incumbit ei qui agit.* The claimant is always bound to prove; the burden of proof lies on the actor. *Ei incumbit probatio, qui dicit, non qui negat; cum per rerum naturam factum negantis probatio nulla sit.* The burden of proof lies upon him who asserts it, not upon him who denies; since, by the nature of things, he who denies a fact cannot produce any proof of it.

PROPAGANDA, *noun* *arrière pensée,* brainwashing, conditioning, conversion, distortion, false teaching, implantation, inculcation, indoctrination, initiation, inoculation, misinstruction, misleading, persuasion, preaching, promotion, teaching

PROPAGATE *(Increase), verb* be fruitful, bear, beget, breed, bring into being, continue, create, engender, father, fecundate, generate, *gignere,* give birth, multiply, originate, procreare, procreate, produce, progenerate, proliferate, pullulate, reproduce, sire, spawn, teem

PROPAGATE *(Spread), verb* advertise, air, blaze, blazon, broadcast, circulate, diffuse, disseminate, enunciate, evulgate, hawk about, herald, issue, make known, make public, noise abroad, notify, proclaim, promote, promulgate, publicize, publish, repeat, report, serere, spread abroad, tell, transmit, trumpet, vent, ventilate, *vulgare*

PROPEL, *verb* actuate, cast, catapult, constrain, discharge, dispatch, drive, drive forward, eject, emit, force, goad, heave, hurl, impel, launch, move, pitch, precipitate, prod, project, provoke, push, push forward, send, set in motion, spirit, start, stimulate, thrust, urge

PROPENSITY, *noun* ability, affinity, aptitude, aptness, art, attraction, bent, bias, capacity, deftness, dexterity, disposition, facility, fancy, favor, felicity, fondness, forte, genius, gift, inclination, knack, leaning, liking, mind, partiality, passion, penchant, ply, predilection, predisposition, preference, *proclivitas,* proclivity, proneness, *pronus,* propenseness, propension, *propensus,* qualification, readiness, relish, sharpness, skill, talent, taste, tendency, warp, weakness
ASSOCIATED CONCEPTS: propensity to commit a crime, viscous propensities

PROPER, *adjective* acceptable, accurate, adapted, apposite, appropriate, apt, *aptus,* becoming, befitting, condign, conventional, correct, decorous, ethical, fitting, formal, free of error, honest, *idoneus,* legitimate, moral, opportune, orthodox, particular, precise, *rectus,* relevant, respectable, right, righteous, seasonable, seemly, suitable, suited, tasteful, true, unmistaken, virtuous, well-bred
ASSOCIATED CONCEPTS: proper party
FOREIGN PHRASES: *Non solum quid licet, sed quid est conveniens, est considerandum; quia nihil quod est inconveniens est licitum.* Not only that which is lawful, but that which is convenient is to be considered, because nothing which is inconvenient is lawful.

PROPERTY *(Distinctive attribute), noun* aspect, attitude, attribute, character, characteristic, disposition, distinction, distinguishing quality, distinguishing trait, earmark, feature, individuality, mark, marked feature, marked quality, particularity, peculiarity, personality, point, *proprietas,* quality, singularity, specific quality, style, temperament, tone, trait

PROPERTY *(Land), noun* acreage, acres, demesne, domain, dominions, estate, freehold, ground, grounds, holding, homestead, household, land, landed interests, landed property, leasehold, lot, parcel, plot, premises, real estate, real property, realty, territory, tract
ASSOCIATED CONCEPTS: abandoned property, absolute property, accretions to property, acquisition of property, after-acquired property, assessable property, assessed valuation of taxable property, base property, commercial property, community property, corporate property, damage to property, devising property, distributable property, encumbrance on property, estate, execution against property, freehold, homestead, individual property, joint property, lien on property, market value, property tax, public property, purchase of property, separate and distinct properties, similar property, special property, specific property, suit affecting property, suit concerning property, taking of property for private purposes, taking of property for public use without just compensation, taxable property, title to real property, transfer of interest in property, transfer of property intended to take effect at death, unplatted land, urban property, value of the property
FOREIGN PHRASES: *Transit terra cum onere.* Land passes subject to any encumbrances affecting it. *Jus descendit, et non terra.* The right descends, not the land. *Regulariter non valet pactum de re mea non alienanda.* It is a rule that an agreement not to alienate my property is not binding. *Cujus est solum, ejus est usque ad coelum et ad inferos.* He who owns the soil owns also up to the sky above it, and to the center of the earth beneath it.

PROPERTY *(Possessions), noun* accessories, appointments, assets, available means, belongings, *bona,* chattels, effects, estate, financial resources, funds, goods, hereditaments, holdings, immovables, investments, material assets, movables, ownership, pecuniary resources, personal effects, personal resources, possessions, resources, substance, tangible assets, tangibles, valuables
ASSOCIATED CONCEPTS: appurtenance, articles of personalty, bequeathing property, fixtures, intangibles, moveables, proceeds of property, receiving stolen property, tangible property, trust property
FOREIGN PHRASES: *Nemo cogitur rem suam vendere, etiam justo pretio.* No one is compelled to sell his own property, even for a just price. *Quae ab hostibus capiuntur, statim capientium fiunt.* Things taken from enemies immediately become the property of the captors. *Duorum in solidum dominium vel possessio esse non potest.* Sole ownership of possessions cannot be in two persons. *Jus triplex est,-propietatis, possessionis, et possibilitatis.* Right is

threefold,-of property, of possession, and of possibility. **Nemo alienae rei, sine satisdatione, defensor idoneus intelligitur.** No one is considered a competent defender of another's property, without security. **Nul charter, nul vente, ne nul done vault perpetualment, si le donor n'est seise al temps de contracts de deux droits, sc. del droit de possession et del droit de propertie.** No grant, no sale, no gift, is valid forever, unless the donor, at the time of the contract, has two rights, namely, the right of possession, and the right of property. **Prohibetur ne quis faciat in suo quod nocere possit alieno.** It is forbidden for any one to do on his own property what may injure another's. **Proprietas verborum est salus proprietatum.** Propriety of words is the salvation of property. **In re communi neminem dominorum jure facere quicquam, invito altero posse.** One of the owners of common property may not exercise any authority over it against the will of another of them. **Expedit reipublicae ne sua re quis male utatur.** It is for the interest of the state no one should make ill use of his property. **Mobilia non habent situm.** Movables have no situs or local habitation. **Catalla juste possessa amitti non possunt.** Chattels cannot be deprived of when they are lawfully possessed. **Interest reipublicae ne sua quis male utatur.** It concerns the state that people do not misuse their property. **Rerum suarum quilibet est moderator et arbiter.** Every one is the manager and master of his own affairs or his property. **In re pari potiorem causam esse prohibentis constat.** Where a thing is owned in common, it is clear that the cause of the party prohibiting its use is the stronger. **In re communi potior est conditio prohibentis.** In relation to property held in common, the position of the one who prohibits is the more favorable.

PROPHETIC, adjective alarming, augural, bodeful, clairvoyant, divinatory, *divinus,* farseeing, farsighted, fateful, fatidic, fatidical, *fatidicus,* fatiloquent, foreboding, forecasting, foreknowing, foreseeing, foresighted, foretelling, forewarning, haruspical, indicative, mantic, menacing, minacious, minatorial, minatory, monitorial, monitory, ominous, oracular, portentous, precognitive, precursive, predictive, predictory, prefigurative, preindicative, premonitory, presageful, presaging, prescient, presentient, prognostic, prognosticative, prophetical, pythonic, sibylic, sibylline, vatic, vaticinal

PROPHYLACTIC, adjective preservative, preventative, preventive, protective, safeguarding, salutary
ASSOCIATED CONCEPTS: prophylactic rule

PROPINQUITY (Kinship), **noun** affiliation, affinity, agnation, alliance, association, bond, close association, cognation, common ancestry, connection, consanguinity, family connection, filiation, kindred, link, nearness of blood, nearness of relation, relationship, tie

PROPINQUITY (Proximity), **noun** adjacency, apposition, closeness, contiguity, juxtaposition, nearness, vicinage

PROPINQUITY (Similarity), **noun** accord, affinity, affinity of nature, alikeness, comparison, compatibility, concert, concord, congeniality, correspondence, equivalence, harmony, homogeneity, likeness, parallelism, proximity, resemblance, semblance, similitude, synonymity, unity

PROPITIATE, verb accommodate, appeal to, appease, beguile, calm, conciliate, content, disarm, gain the favor of, humor, ingratiate, make amends, make favorably inclined, make peace, mollify, offer sacrifice, pacificate, pacify, placare, placate, please, *propitiare,* reconcile, satisfy, soften, soothe, tranquilize, win over

PROPITIOUS, adjective accommodating, advantageous, approving, auspicious, beneficial, benevolent, benign, benignant, cheering, clear, clement, cloudless, conducive, disposed to bestow favors, encouraging, expedient, favorable, favorably inclined, felicitous, fortunate, friendly, full of promise, generous, golden, gracious, happy, heartening, heaven sent, helpful, helping, hopeful, indulgent, inspiriting, kind, kindhearted, kindly, lucky, merciful, obliging, opportune, presenting favorable conditions, promising, *propitius,* providential, reassuring, roseate, seasonable, supporting, sympathetic, timely, unhostile, well-disposed, well-intentioned, well-meaning

PROPONENT, noun abettor, advocate, ally, apologist, backer, benefactor, champion, defender, endorser, enthusiast, espouser, exponent, friend, justifier, partisan, patron, pleader, protector, seconder, spokesman, sponsor, subscriber, supporter, sympathizer, upholder, vindicator, votary, wellwisher
ASSOCIATED CONCEPTS: proponent of a will

PROPORTION, noun allotment, apportionment, commensuration, comparative size, comparison, concinnity, correlation, distribution, eurhythmy, factional part, fraction, grace, harmony, interrelation, measure, *pars,* part, percent, percentage, portion, quantum, quotum, ratio, relation, relationship, relative estimate, relativity, share, symmetry

PROPORTIONATE, adjective agreeing, analogous, balanced, commeasurable, commensurate, comparable, comparative, compatible, consistent, correlative, corresponding, distributional, equivalent, even, harmonious, proportionable, proportional, relative, scaled, uniform, well-balanced
ASSOCIATED CONCEPTS: per capita, per stirpes, pro rata

PROPOSAL (Report), **noun** analysis, appraisal, commentary, critical analysis, examination, in-depth analysis, plan, summary, writing

PROPOSAL (Suggestion), **noun** design, draft, exhortation, idea, measure, motion, offer, overture, plan, possibility, presentation, proffer, proposition, recommendation, scheme, submission, suggestion, tender, thought

PROPOSE, verb advance, advise, advocate, contend, counsel, declare, introduce, lay before, make a motion, make a suggestion, move, nominate, offer, plan, *ponere,* pose, postulate, present, proffer, propound, put forward, recommend, set forth, submit, suggest, tender, voice

PROPOSITION, noun approach, arrangement, assertion, assumption, bid, *condicio,* conjecture, course of action, declaration, declared intention, design, formulated intention, hypothesis, idea, offer, overture, plan, position, postulate, premise, presentation, program of action, project, proposal, *propositio,* prospectus, provisional hypothesis, recommendation, resolution, *rogatio,* scheme, strategy, submission, suggestion, supposition, tender, tentative approach, tentative statement, terms proposed, theory, thesis

PROPOUND, verb advance, advocate, allege, argue, aver, contend, exhibit, hypothesize, introduce, lay before, maintain, make a motion, moot, move, offer, pose, posit, postulate, predicate, present, proffer, project, propose, put forth, put forward, recommend, set forth, submit, suggest, tender, throw out, voice
ASSOCIATED CONCEPTS: propound the law

PROPRIETARY, adjective entailed, exclusive, holding property, landed, pertaining to ownership, pertaining to property, praedial, restrictive
ASSOCIATED CONCEPTS: proprietary function, proprietary interest, proprietary lease, proprietary right

PROPRIETOR, noun dominus, householder, landlord, landowner, manager, master, owner, possessor, proprietary

PROPRIETY (Appropriateness), **noun** accordance, adaptation, admissibility, advisability, agreeableness, applicability, aptitude, aptness, becomingness, compatibility, conformity, congruity, consonance, correspondence, dueness, equity, expedience, expediency, felicity, fitness, harmony, justness, pertinence, properness, reasonableness, relevance, right, rightness, seemliness, suitability, suitableness, utility

PROPRIETY (Correctness), **noun** convention, conventional conduct, conventionalities, correctitude, correctness, courteousness, courtesy, decency, decorousness, decorum, delicacy, demureness, dignity, discrimination, elegance, ethicality, etiquette, good behavior, good breeding, good manners, grace, manners, modesty, morality, politeness, proper formality, properness, rectitude, refinement, respectability, restraint, ritual, taste, tradition
FOREIGN PHRASES: Proprietates verborum observandae sunt. The proper meanings of words are to be observed.

PRORATE, verb allocate, allot, apportion, apportion pro rata, assess pro rata, assess proportionally, distribute, distribute proportionally, divide, divide proportionally, dole, mete out, parcel out, portion, split up
ASSOCIATED CONCEPTS: prorate taxes

PROSAIC, adjective boresome, boring, colorless, common, commonplace, dry, dull, everyday, flat, frigidus, hackneyed, humdrum, ieiunus, jejune, matter of fact, mediocre, monotone, monotonous, mundane, ordinary, pedestrian, plain, platitudinous, prolix, prosaical, prosy, spiritless, stale, stock, tame, tedious, tiresome, trite, unentertaining, unimaginative, unimpassioned, uninspiring, uninteresting, unoriginal, unpoetic, unpoetical, unvaried, usual, vapid, wearisome

PROSCRIBE (Denounce), **verb** accuse, anathematize, banish, blame, castigate, censure, charge, condemn, criticize, curse, damn, denunciate, execrate, incriminate, ostracize, outlaw, reject

PROSCRIBE (Prohibit), **verb** abrogate, ban, bar, circumscribe, disallow, embargo, enjoin, exclude, forbid, halt, oppose, outlaw, prevent, proscribere, refuse, refuse permission, repudiate, restrain, restrict, revoke, taboo

PROSCRIPTION, noun ban, banishment, boycott, censure, condemnation, countermand, denial, denunciation, disallowance, disfavor, elimination, embargo, eviction, exclusion, forbiddance, inhibition, injunction, interdict, interdiction, intolerance, prohibition, proscriptio, rejection, relegation

PROSECUTE (Carry forward), **verb** advance, be resolute in, be steadfast, bring about, bring to pass, carry on, carry out, conduct, continue, follow up, go after, maintain, persequi, persevere in, persist, proceed with, pursue, put through
ASSOCIATED CONCEPTS: dismissal for want of prosecution, failure to prosecute, prosecute a claim, prosecute an action

PROSECUTE (Charge), **verb** accusare, arraign, bring action against, bring before a court, bring suit, bring to justice, file a charge, file a claim, prefer a claim, prefer charges, proceed against civilly, proceed against criminally, sue, summon, take one to court
ASSOCIATED CONCEPTS: prosecute for a criminal offense, prosecuting attorney

PROSECUTING ATTORNEY, noun attorney general, district attorney, government attorney, people's attorney, prosecution, prosecutor, public prosecutor, state's attorney, U.S. attorney
ASSOCIATED CONCEPTS: criminal law

PROSECUTION (Criminal trial), **noun** action, bringing to trial, legal action, legal process, legal trial, litigation, pursuit by a law enforcement agency, suit, trial, undertaking
ASSOCIATED CONCEPTS: criminal prosecution, lawful prosecution, pending prosecution, want of prosecution

PROSECUTION (Government agency), **noun** the government, the people, the prosecuting attorney, the state, state's attorney
ASSOCIATED CONCEPTS: the prosecution

PROSECUTOR, noun accusator, attorney general, criminal trial lawyer for the people, district attorney, government attorney, prosecuting attorney, prosecution, public prosecutor, state's attorney
ASSOCIATED CONCEPTS: public prosecutor, special prosecutor

PROSPECT (Outlook), **noun** ambition, anticipation, assurance, calculation, certainty, chance, coming events, confidence, contemplation, destiny, expectance, expectancy, expectation, fair chance, faith, fate, forecast, fortune, futurity, good chance, hope, intention, likelihood, likeliness, plan, possibility, prediction, presumption, probability, promise, reasonable chance, reliance, speculation, time ahead, trust, well-grounded hope

PROSPECT (Prospective patron), **noun** applicant, candidate, interested party, likely client, likely customer, likely patron, likely person, possibility, possible client, possible customer, possible patron, prospective client, prospective customer, recruit

PROSPECTIVE, adjective abeyant, about to be, anticipated, approaching, arranged, awaited, close at hand, coming, conceivable, considered, destined, earmarked, eventual, expectant, expected, foreseen, forthcoming, future, futurus, hoped for, imaginable, immediate, imminent, impending, in prospect, in store, in view, intended, likely, looked for, looming, on the horizon, planned, possible, potential, preparing, projected, promised, scheduled, soon to be, soon to happen, subsequent, to be, to come, ultimate, upcoming
ASSOCIATED CONCEPTS: prospective contract, prospective liabilities, prospective relief, prospective rights
FOREIGN PHRASES: Nova constitutio futuris formam imponere debet non praeteritis. A new law ought to affect the future, not what is past. **Lex prospicit, non respicit.** The law looks forward, not backward.

PROSPECTUS, noun analysis, announcement, blueprint, bulletin, catalogue, description, outline, plan, platform, program, scheme, sketch, statement, summary, syllabus, synopsis

PROSPERITY, noun abundance, achievement, affluence, blessings, boom, booming economy, comfort, comfortable circumstances, ease, expansion, felicity, fortunate condition, full purse, good fortune, good luck, good times, heyday, luck, luxury, opulence, palmy days, plenty, profit, *prosperitas,* prosperousness, *res secundae,* riches, richness, run of luck, success, successfulness, thriving condition, weal, wealth, well being

PROSPEROUS, *adjective*   abounding in riches, affluent, ascendant, blooming, booming, comfortable, established, *florens,* flourishing, flush, fortunate, happy, in clover, in easy circumstances, lucky, moneyed, palmy, pecunious, profiting, *prosperus,* providential, rich, rising, *secundus,* successful, thriving, unbeaten, undefeated, wealthy, well off, wellsituated, well to do

PROSTRATION, *noun*   abasement, bow, breakdown, cataclysm, collapse, consumption, debility, decay, decrepitude, defeat, dejection, demolition, depression, desolation, despair, despondency, destruction, distress, downfall, downthrow, enervation, exhaustion, extinction, extremity, faint, fall, fatigue, feebleness, genuflection, helplessness, horizontality, illness, impotence, kneeling, lassitude, loss of power, lowliness, misery, obeisance, overset, overthrow, overturn, ravage, recumbency, repose, rout, ruin, ruination, sickness, stupor, subjection, submission, suffering, surrender, swoon, tiredness, undoing, upset, vanquishment, waste, weakness, weariness, wrack, wreck, wretchedness

PROTAGONIST, *noun*   agent, champion, hero, lead, leader, leading character, main character, most important character, mouthpiece, prime mover, principal, principal character

PROTEAN, *adjective*   alterable, assuming different forms, changeable, changeful, everchanging, fluid, kaleidoscopic, metamorphic, mobile, modifiable, movable, multiform, multiphase, mutable, nonuniform, omniform, permutable, polymorphic, polymorphous, proteiform, transformable, unsettled, variable, varying, versatile

PROTECT, *verb*   arm, armor, attend, barricade, bulwark, care for, champion, chaperone, cherish, conduct, conserve, convoy, cover, cushion, *custodire,* defend, *defendere,* ensure, escort, fight for, flank, fortify, foster, garrison, guard, harbor, haven, house, immunize, inoculate, insulate, keep, look after, maintain, mount guard, nurse, patrol, patronize, preserve, safeguard, save, screen, seclude, secure, sentinel, shade, sheathe, shelter, shepherd, shield, shroud, shutter, sponsor, support, sustain, take care of, treasure, *tutari,* veil, ward, watch over
ASSOCIATED CONCEPTS: self-defense

PROTECTION, *noun*   aegis, armor, asylum, barricade, buckler, bulwark, citadel, conservation, covering, covert, coverture, custody, defense, fortification, freedom from danger, guarantee, guard, guardianship, haven, hedge, immunity, invulnerability, oversight, palladium, panoply, patronage, *praesidium,* preservation, preserve, refuge, safe conduct, safeguard, safekeeping, safety, salvation, sanctuary, security, shelter, shield, strength, stronghold, supervision, support, *tutela,* tutelage, wardship, wing
FOREIGN PHRASES: *Inde datae leges ne fortior omnia posset.* Laws were make lest the stronger might become all-powerful.

PROTECTIVE, *adjective*   armored, conservational, conservative, conservatory, covering, custodial, defensive, fortified, guardian, heedful, preservative, preventive, prophylactic, safeguarding, screening, sheltering, shielding, solicitous, strengthened, tutelary, vigilant, watchful
ASSOCIATED CONCEPTS: protective custody, protective order

PROTECTIVE ORDER, *noun*   defense, guard against danger, order of protection, order to ensure safety, protection, protection against a danger, refuge, safeguard, safekeeping, safety, sanctuary, security, shelter, shield, temporary restraining order
ASSOCIATED CONCEPTS: family law and domestic violence protective orders, restraining order

PROTÉGÉ, *noun*   adherent, apprentice, charge, dependent, disciple, follower, initiate, learner, novice, pensioner, pupil, student, trainee, trust, ward

PROTEST, *noun*   challenge, clamor, complaint, counteraction, criticism, declaration of disapproval, declaration of dissent, declaration of opposition, defiance, demonstration, disapproval, dissent, dissidence, formal criticism, formal declaration, formal declaration of dissent, hostile demonstration, opposition, outcry, *recusatio,* remonstrance, remonstration, repudiation, resistance
ASSOCIATED CONCEPTS: file a protest

PROTEST, *verb*   announce, attack, challenge, complain, contradict, contravene, cry out against, dehort, demur, denounce, deny, disaffirm, disagree, disapprove, disclaim, discountenance, dispute, dissent, exclaim against, exhort against, express opposition, go contrary to, impugn, *intercedere,* inveigh, negate, oppose, raise objections, *recusare,* refuse, remonstrate, reprehend, repudiate, revolt, speak against, take exception, traverse, veto, vote against
ASSOCIATED CONCEPTS: payment under protest, protest a will, protest an election, written notice of protest

PROTOCOL (Agreement), ***noun***   arrangement, charter, compact, concord, concordat, contract, covenant, diplomatic agreement, pact, stipulation, treaty, understanding

PROTOCOL (Etiquette), ***noun***   behavior, ceremony, code, code of behavior, conventional practice, conventionalities, correct behavior, correctitude, correctness, courtesy, customs, decorum, dictates, diplomatic code, form, formalities, good behavior, good form, good manners, manners, politeness, practice, prevailing form, proper behavior, proprieties, punctilio, regulations, rules, set of rules, set of standards, system of rules

PROTOTYPE, *noun*   archetype, example, exemplar, *exemplum,* first, guide, ideal, model, mold, original, paradigm, paragon, pattern, precedent, protoplast, sample, source, standard

PROTRACT (Prolong), ***verb***   delay, drag out, filibuster, gain time, hold up, procrastinate, retard

PROTRACT (Stall), ***verb***   continue, elongate, extend, lengthen out, shelve, string out

PROTRACTED, *adjective*   continuing, dragged out, drawn out, elongated, extended, lengthened, lengthy, lingering, long, long-continued, long-drawn, meandering, never-ending, ongoing, prolix, prolonged, unending

PROUD (Conceited), ***adjective***   affected, aloof, arrogant, assuming, boastful, braggart, condescending, contemptuous, defiant, disdainful, egoistic, egoistical, flaunting, haughty, imperious, insolent, lordly, obstinate, orgulous, overweening, overbearing, patronizing, pompous, presumptuous, prideful, puffed up, self-applauding, self-important, self-satisfied, supercilious, swollen, turgescent, turgid, uppish, uppity, vain, vainglorious, without modesty

PROUD (Self-respecting), **adjective**   content, contented, delighted, dignified, grand, gratified, happy, honored, imposing, impressive, lofty, magnificent, majestic, noble, pleased, satisfied, splendid, stately, thrilled, well-pleased, well-satisfied

PROVABLE, adjective   ascertainable, capable of being demonstrated, capable of being proven, capable of being shown, capable of positive proof, capable of proof, confirmable, deducible, demonstrable, determinable, discoverable, establishable, incontestable, indisputable, inferable, irrefutable, supportable, susceptible of proof, sustainable, unimpeachable, verifiable, verificatory, well-founded, well-grounded
ASSOCIATED CONCEPTS: provable claim

PROVE, verb   ascertain, ascertain as truth, authenticate, confirm, corroborate, *declarare,* demonstrate, establish, establish as truth, establish the genuineness of, establish the validity of, evince, manifest, ostendere, *probare,* put to the proof, put to the test, show, show clearly, substantiate, support, uphold, validate, verify
FOREIGN PHRASES: *In rebus manifestis, errat qui auctoritates legum allegat; quia perspicua vera non sunt probanda.* In clear cases, he makes mistakes who cites legal authorities; for obvious truths are not to be proved.

PROVERBIAL, adjective   acknowledged, aphoristic, axiomatic, common, commonly known, commonplace, epigrammatic, familiar, general, known, legendary, notorious, oft repeated, popular, prevalent, recognized, sententious, succinct, traditional, universal, unquestioned, well-known, widely known

PROVIDE (Arrange for), **verb**   anticipate needs, appoint, care for, *consulere,* contract, direct, engage, get ready, look after, make allowance for, make preparations, make provision, make ready, manage, organize, pave the way, plan, prepare, *providere,* ready, serve, take into account, take measures, take steps

PROVIDE (Supply), **verb**   accommodate, accord, administer, afford, allow, award, bestow, confer, contribute, deliver, donate, endow, equip, feed, fund, furnish, give, grant, impart, maintain, *ornare, praebere,* present, produce, purvey, replenish, stock, *suppeditare,* sustain

PROVIDED, adverb   assuming that, on condition that, provisionally, subject to, with the understanding, with the stipulation, with this proviso
ASSOCIATED CONCEPTS: as provided by law

PROVIDENT (Frugal), **adjective**   careful, economical, money conscious, parsimonious, penurious, prudent, saving, sparing, stingy, thrifty, unlavish

PROVIDENT (Showing foresight), **adjective**   alert, anticipating, calculating, careful, cautious, chary, circumspect, discerning, discreet, equipped, farseeing, forecasting, forehanded, foreseeing, heedful, judicious, on guard, politic, precautionary, precautious, predictive, prepared, prognostic, prudent, prudential, ready, thoughtful, vigilant, wary, watchful

PROVINCE, noun   appointment, area, assigned task, assignment, business, canton, capacity, charge, circuit, colony, compass, county, demesne, department, district, division, domain, dominion, duty, field, function, job, jurisdiction, occupation, office, orbit, part, precinct, *provincia,* realm, region, scope, section, specialty, sphere, subdivision, territory, tract

PROVINCIAL, adjective   annexed, backwood, boorish, bucolic, churlish, closed-minded, colonial, divisional, dogmatic, fanatical, gauche, gawky, hayseed, ill-mannered, illiberal, inflexible, ingrown, insular, intolerant, inurbane, local, loutish, narrow, narrow-minded, oafish, outlying, parochial, petty, regional, rigid, rough, rude, sectional, small-minded, strait-laced, unbroadened, uncourtly, uncouth, ungraceful, unpolished, unrefined, unsophisticated, untraveled

PROVISION (Act of supplying), **noun**   accommodation, arrangement, catering, donation, endowment, furnishing, preparation, procurement, providence, purveyance, servicing, serving

PROVISION (Clause), **noun**   article of agreement, *condicio,* condition, limitation, obligation, proviso, qualification, requirement, reservation, restriction, specification, stipulation, term
ASSOCIATED CONCEPTS: damages provision, express provision, forfeiture provision, mandatory provision, penal provision, procedural provision, restrictive provision, self-executing provision, statutory provision, substantive provision, technical provision
FOREIGN PHRASES: *Quando abest provisio partis, adest provisio legis.* When a provision of the party is lacking, the provision of the law supplies it.

PROVISION (Something provided), **noun**   cache, cumulation, fund, hoard, maintenance, ration, reserve, resources, staples, stock, stockpile, store, supply

PROVISIONAL, adjective   alterable, conditional, contingent, dependent on circumstances, equivocal, for a time, in a state of uncertainty, *in tempus,* indefinite, indeterminate, interim, limited, makeshift, modifiable, nonpermanent, of short duration, passing, provisory, subject to change, subject to terms, substitute, temporarily established, temporary, tentative, transient, transitional, transitory, unascertained, unassured, unconfirmed, undecided, undetermined, unsettled
ASSOCIATED CONCEPTS: provisional appointment, provisional court, provisional employee, provisional government, provisional receiver, provisional remedy

PROVOCATION, noun   abuse, actuation, affront, aggression, agitation, angering, annoyance, causation, cause, defiance, exasperation, excitation, excitement, fomentation, goad, grievance, impulsion, incentive, incitement, inducement, inflammation, inspiration, instigation, insult, invitation, irritation, motivation, motive, offense, pressure, prick, prodding, prompting, provocative, spur, stimulant, stimulation, stimulus, taunt, temptation, urge, vexation
ASSOCIATED CONCEPTS: defense of provocation, extreme provocation, just provocation, legal provocation

PROVOCATIVE, adjective   aggravating, alluring, annoying, arousing, attractive, bellicose, captivating, challenging, defiant, desirable, electric, electrifying, enchanting, entrancing, exasperating, exciting, galling, galvanic, galvanical, grating, inciting, inflaming, inflammatory, influential, inspirational, interesting, intoxicating, intriguing, invidious, inviting, irksome, irresistible, irritating, motivating, persuasive, piquant, provoking, ravishing, seductive, stimulating, stimulative, stirring, suggestive, tantalizing, tempting, thrilling, titillating, urgent, vexatious, vexing

PROVOKE, verb actuate, affront, aggravate, agitate, anger, animate, annoy, antagonize, arouse, awaken, badger, bait, begin, beset, bother, bring about, call forth, cause, challenge, defy, discompose, displease, disquiet, distress, drive, effect, egg on, elicit, enkindle, enrage, envenom, evoke, exacerbate, exasperate, excite, fire, fret, gall, generate, give offense, give origin, give rise, grate, harass, heckle, hector, hound, impel, incense, incite, induce, inflame, infuriate, instigate, insult, irk, irritate, kindle, madden, motivate, move, move to anger, nettle, occasion, offend, originate, persecute, perturb, pique, plague, promote, prompt, propel, push, put out, put out of humor, rally, roil, rouse, spur, stimulate, sting, stir, stir up, taunt, tease, torment, try one's patience, vex, work into a passion, work up, wound

PROWESS (Ability), **noun** adeptness, adroitness, cleverness, competence, competency, craft, deftness, dexterity, excellence, expertise, expertness, facility, finesse, know-how, mastership, mastery, proficiency, skill, skillfulness, virtuosity, wizardry

PROWESS (Bravery), **noun** absence of fear, backbone, boldness, braveness, constancy, contempt of danger, courage, courageous deeds, courageousness, daring, dauntlessness, defiance of danger, derringdo, doggedness, doughtiness, fearlessness, fiber, firmness, gallant acts, gallantness, gallantry, grit, hardihood, hardiness, heroic achievement, heroism, intrepidity, lustiness, manliness, mettle, might, nerve, perseverence, pluck, resoluteness, sinew, spirit, stability, stamina, stout heart, strength, sturdiness, valiancy, valor, valorousness, vigor, *virtus,* vitality

PROWL, verb be stealthy, creep, cruise, drift, gad, go about stealthily, gumshoe, hover, lie in ambush, lie in wait, loiter, lurk, meander, move secretly, move under cover, peragrare, peregrinate, ramble, range, roam, rove, scavenge, skulk, slink, sneak, stay incognito, steal, stray, stroll, tramp, *vagari,* wander about

PROXIMATE, adjective about to happen, abutting, adjacent, adjoining, approaching, at hand, attached, bordering, bordering upon, close, close at hand, close by, closest, connected, connecting, contactual, conterminal, conterminous, contiguous, edging, expected, following, forthcoming, fringing, immediate, imminent, impendent, impending, in close proximity, juxtaposed, near, nearest, neighboring, next, nigh, prospective, proximal, *proximus,* sequent, subsequent, succeeding, tangent, tangential, touching, upcoming, verging, vicinal
ASSOCIATED CONCEPTS: proximate cause

PROXIMATE CAUSE, noun causation, derivation, immediate legal basis, immediate legal cause, immediate legal genesis, proper cause, proximate causation, sufficient legal basis, sufficient legal causation, sufficient legal cause, sufficient legal factor, sufficient legal genesis, sufficient legal inducement, sufficient legal source
ASSOCIATED CONCEPTS: contribution-efficient cause, contributory negligence, immediate cause, intervening cause, negligence, proximate consequence, proximate result, torts

PROXY, noun agency, agent, authority to act for another, broker, delegate, deputy, dummy, emissary, envoy, lieutenant, messenger, *procurator,* representation, representative, substitute, substitution, surrogate, *vicarius,* written authorization
ASSOCIATED CONCEPTS: proxy statement, solicitation of proxy

PRUDENCE, noun attention, calculation, care, careful budgeting, carefulness, *cautio,* caution, *circumspectio,* circumspection, close watch, common sense, concern, conservation, conservatism, considerateness, consideration, cunning, deliberation, discretion, discrimination, economy, forethought, foresight, frugality, heed, heedfulness, husbandry, judgment, judiciousness, precaution, preparedness, presence of mind, providence, *prudentia,* regard, sense, shrewdness, tact, temperance, thrift, vigilance, watchfulness

PRUDENT, adjective advertent, calculating, canny, careful, cautious, *cautus,* chary, circumspect, *circumspectus,* considerate, discreet, discriminating, economical, farsighted, forearmed, foreseeing, foresighted, frugal, guarded, heedful, judicious, levelheaded, mindful, politic, precautionary, precautious, prepared, provident, *prudens,* prudential, regardful, sagacious, sage, sapient, saving, sensible, shrewd, sober, sparing, thoughtful, thrifty, wary, well-advised, wise
ASSOCIATED CONCEPTS: prudent person, reasonable man
FOREIGN PHRASES: **Prudenter agit qui praecepto legis obtemperat.** He acts prudently who obeys the precept of the law. **Sapiens omnia agit cum consilio.** A wise man does everything deliberately.

PRURIENT, adjective bawdy, carnal, coarse, concupiscent, cyprian, debauched, dirty, dissipated, dissolute, erotic, fleshly, foul, immodest, impure, indecent, lascivious, lecherous, lewd, *libidinosus,* libidinous, licentious, lickerish, lubricious, lustful, obscene, pornographic, ribald, salacious, satyric, shameless, smutty, suggestive, unchaste, unclean, unvirtuous, wanton
ASSOCIATED CONCEPTS: pornography, prurient interests

PUBLIC (Affecting people), **adjective** civic, civil, collective, common, communal, country-wide, federal, general, government, governmental, municipal, national, nationwide, social, societal, state
ASSOCIATED CONCEPTS: public authorities, public benefit, public benefit corporation, public business, public charge, public charity, public convenience, public corporation, public document, public function, public funds, public good, public improvements, public interest, public necessity, public notice, public nuisance, public office, public policy, public purpose, public safety, public sector, public service commission, public use, public utilities, public welfare, public works
FOREIGN PHRASES: **Pacta privata juri publico derogare non possunt.** Private contracts cannot derogate from public right. **Necessitas publica major est quam privata.** Public necessity is greater than private. **Jura publica anteferenda privatis.** Public rights are to be preferred to private parts. **Privatum commodum publico cedit.** Private good yields to public good. **Privatum incommodum publico bono pensatur.** Private inconvenience is compensated for by public benefit. **Lex citius tolerare vult privatum damnum quam publicum malum.** The law would rather tolerate a private loss than a public evil.

PUBLIC (Known), **adjective** acknowledged, aired, announced, apparent, broadcast, bruited about, circulated, commonly known, disclosed, disseminated, divulged, encyclic, encyclical, evident, exoteric, familiar, manifest, notorious, obvious, overt, popular, proclaimed, promulgated, propagated, *publicus,* published, recognized, released, renowned, reported, revealed, spread abroad, ventilated, well-known, widely known

PUBLIC *(Open),* **adjective**   accessible, approachable, attainable, available, community, free to all, not private, permitted, reachable, unbarred, unprohibited, unreserved, unrestricted
ASSOCIATED CONCEPTS: public accommodations, public documents, public domain, public hearing, public institutions, public place, public property, public records, public sale

PUBLIC, *noun*   body politic, citizenry, commonalty, commonwealth, community, folk, general public, *homines,* laymen, nation, persons, polity, populace, population, *populus,* social group, society
ASSOCIATED CONCEPTS: public good, public use, public utility, public welfare

PUBLIC DOMAIN, *noun*   available for use by the public, creative work freely usable, dominion to use, free to all, freely used by the community, invention freely usable, logo freely usable, not private, open for the community, permitted, publicly accessible, publicly obtainable, publicly usable, unreserved, unrestricted, within the province of the public
ASSOCIATED CONCEPTS: copyrights, patents, promietary rights

PUBLICATION *(Disclosure),* **noun**   advertisement, announcement, broadcast, circulation, communication, currency, dissemination, enlightenment, *expositio,* issuance, notice, notification, *praedicatio,* presentation to the public, proclamation, promulgation, pronouncement, *pronuntiatio,* propagation, public announcement, release, report, revealment, revelation, statement, transmission
ASSOCIATED CONCEPTS: defamation, libel, slander

PUBLICATION *(Printed matter),* **noun**   book, *editio libri,* edition, folio, issue, literary magazine, literature, magazine, organ, periodical, printing, reading matter, tome, volume, work, writing, written discourse

PUBLICITY, *noun*   advertisement, advertising, airing, announcement, billing, broadcast, bulletin, common knowledge, disclosure, dissemination, divulgation, divulgement, divulgence, enunciation, evulgation, exposure, fame, famousness, information, issuance, limelight, news, notice, notification, notoriety, presentation, press agentry, press notice, proclamation, promotion, promulgation, propagation, public distribution, public notice, public relations, publication, release, report, revealment, revelation, spotlight, utterance, ventilation, write-up

PUBLISH, *verb*   advertise, air, announce, blazon, bring before the public, bring out, broadcast, call public attention to, circulate, communicate, cover, declare, deliver, diffuse, disclose, disseminate, distribute, *divulgare,* divulge, emit, expose, express, give out, give public notice of, go to press, have printed, herald, impart, inform, issue, issue a statement, issue for distribution, issue for public sale, lay before the public, make known, make public, praedicare, print, proclaim, *proferre,* publicize, put forth, put into circulation, put out, put to press, report, reveal, run off, spread, state, tell, trumpet, utter, ventilate
ASSOCIATED CONCEPTS: publish libel, publish slander

PUERILE, *adjective*   asinine, callow, childish, childishly foolish, fatuous, foolish, green, immature, inadequate, inane, infantile, infantine, injudicious, jejune, juvenile, kiddish,

naive, nonsensical, petty, piddling, *puerilis,* raw, senseless, shallow, silly, simple, unwise, unworthy of serious consideration

PUERILITY, *noun*   babyishness, boyishness, childishness, childlike, girlishness, infantilism

PUGNACIOUS, *adjective*   aggressive, antagonistic, argumentative, bellicose, belligerent, bickering, combative, contentious, defiant, disposed to fight, disputatious, dissentious, factious, fighting, fractious, given to fighting, hostile, inimical, militant, militaristic, offensive, quarrelsome, rebellious, rowdy, stubborn, threatening, unfriendly, unpacific, unpeaceful, warlike

PUISSANCE, *noun*   authoritativeness, brawn, dint, dominance, energy, force, lustiness, masterfulness, might, mightiness, potence, potency, power, predominance, robustness, stamina, stoutness, strength, vigor, vitality

PULLULATE, *verb*   be fruitful, be productive, bloom, blossom, breed, bud, burgeon, burst forth, come forth, develop, flourish, flower, generate, germinate, increase, luxuriate, multiply, open, procreate, produce, proliferate, pul*lalare,* put forth, reproduce, rise, shoot forth, spring up, sprout, teem, vegetate, wax

PUNCTILIOUS, *adjective*   accurate, attentive, careful, ceremonious, conscientious, correct, *diligens,* dutiful, exact, exacting, faithful, fastidious, finical, finicking, finicky, formal, fussy, methodical, meticulous, minutely correct, observant of decorum, particular, precise, refined, rigid, rigorous, scrupulous, starched, stiff, strict, systematic, thorough, uncompromising

PUNCTUAL, *adjective*   accurate, ad *tempus advenire,* attentive, conscientious, dependable, diligent, early, exact, exacting, expeditious, fussy, meticulous, minutely correct, never late, on schedule, on time, precise, prompt, properly timed, ready, regular, scrupulous, seasonable, steady, strict, systematic, timed, timely, well-timed

PUNISH, *verb*   amerce, bring to retribution, call to account, *castigare,* castigate, chasten, chastise, condemn, correct, discipline, exact retribution, flog, inflict penalty, lash, penalize, reprimand, retaliate, scourge, sentence, slate, smite, subject to penalty, take to task, take vengeance on, teach a lesson to, torture, trounce, *ulcisci,* whip
ASSOCIATED CONCEPTS: cruel and excessive punishment, cruel and inhuman punishment, cruel and unusual punishment, excessive punishment
FOREIGN PHRASES: *In quo quis delinquit, in eo de jure est puniendus.* In whatever the offense, he is to be punished by the law.

PUNISHMENT, *noun*   amercement, avengement, *castigatio,* castigation, censure, chastening, chastisement, compulsory payment, correction, damages, deprivation, disciplinary action, discipline, forfeiture, infliction, mulct, nemesis, penal retribution, penalization, penalty, penalty imposed on an offender, penance, *poena,* punition, reprimand, retribution, retributive justice, talion, vengeance
ASSOCIATED CONCEPTS: capital punishment, corporal punishment, cruel and inhuman punishment, excessive punishment
FOREIGN PHRASES: *Nulla curia quae recordum non habet potest imponere finem neque aliquem mandare carceri; quia ista spectant tantummodo ad curias de recordo.* No court which has not a record can impose a fine nor commit

any person to prison; because those powers belong only to courts of record. ***Poena ad paucos, metus ad omnes perveniat.*** If punishment is inflicted on a few, a fear comes to all. ***Nemo prudens punit ut praeterita revocentur, sed ut futura praeveniantur.*** No wise man punishes in order that past things may be revoked, but that future wrongs may be prevented. ***Ubi damna dantur, victus victori in expensis condemnari debet.*** Where damages are given, the losing party ought to be condemned to pay costs to the victor. ***Interest reipublicae ne maleficia remaneant impunita.*** It concerns the state that crimes do not go unpunished. ***Tutius semper est errare acquietando, quam in puniendo, ex parte misericordiae quam ex parte justitiae.*** It is always safer to err in acquitting than in punishing, on the side of mercy rather than on the side of justice. ***In omnibus poenalis judiciis, et aetati et imprudentiae succurritur.*** In all penal judgments, allowance is made for youth and lack of prudence. ***Qui peccat ebrius luat sobrius.*** He who offends when drunk shall be punished when sober. ***Melior est justitia vere praeveniens quam severe puniens.*** Truly preventative justice is better than severe punishment. ***Justitia est duplex, viz., severe puniens et vere praeveniens.*** Justice is double, that is to say punishing severely, and truly preventing. ***Qui parcit nocentibus innocentes punit.*** He who spares those who are guilty punishes those who are innocent. ***Reus laesae majestatis punitur ut pereat unus ne pereant omnes.*** A traitor is punished that one may die lest all perish. ***Poena non potest, culpa perennis erit.*** Punishment cannot be everlasting but error or sin will be. ***Judex damnatur cum nocens absolvitur.*** The judge is condemned when a guilty person is acquitted. ***Lubricum linguae non facile trahendum est in poenam.*** A slip of the tongue ought not readily be subjected to punishment. ***In atrocioribus delictis punitur affectus licet non sequatur effectus.*** In the more atrocious crimes the intent is punished, although an effect does not follow. ***Judex non potest injuriam sibi datam punire.*** A judge cannot punish a wrong done to himself. ***Nemo bis punitur pro eodem delicto.*** No one can be punished twice for the same offense. ***Transgressione multiplicata, crescat poenae inflictio.*** Upon the multiplication of transgression, let the infliction of punishment be increased. ***Poena suos tenere debet actores et non alios.*** Punishment belongs to the guilty, and not others. ***Nemo cogitationis poenam patitur.*** No one suffers punishment on account of his thoughts. ***Receditur a placitis juris, potius quam injuriae et delicta maneant impunita.*** In order that crimes not go unpunished, the law will be departed from.

PUNITIVE, *adjective*   avenging, castigatory, disciplinary, mulctuary, penal, penalizing, punishing, punitory, retaliatory, retributive, talionic, vindictive
ASSOCIATED CONCEPTS: punitive action, punitive damages

PUNITIVE DAMAGES, *noun*   award for wrongdoing, award to deter similar conduct, award to punish the defendant, compensation for wrongdoing, penalty for wrongdoing, recovery for highly offensive conduct, recovery for improper action, retributive damages
ASSOCIATED CONCEPTS: compensatory damages restitution, due process, Fifth Amendment, Fourth Amendment, irreparable damages, malicious conduct, nominal damages, reckless disregard, restitution, statutory damages

PURCHASE, *verb*   acquire, acquire ownership of, assume ownership, buy, buy up, collect, gain, invest in, make payment for, obtain, order, pay for, pick up, procure, procure title to, redeem, secure, secure for a consideration
ASSOCIATED CONCEPTS: words of purchase

PURE, *adjective*   absolute, chaste, clean, clear, complete, disinfected, entire, expurgated, faultless, flawless, guileless, guiltless, homogeneous, honorable, immaculate, incorrupt, innocent, *integer,* perfect, positive, *purus,* real, righteous, sheer, simple, sincere, sinless, spotless, stainless, sterilized, taintless, total, true, unadulterated, unblemished, unclouded, uncontaminated, uncorrupt, uncorrupted, undefiled, unmarred, unmingled, unmitigated, unmixed, unpolluted, unspotted, unstained, unsullied, untainted, untarnished, untouched, upright, utter, virtuous, whole
ASSOCIATED CONCEPTS: pure comparative negligence

PURELY *(Positively),* *adverb*   absolutely, decidedly, downright, entirely, essentially, fundamentally, in all respects, in truth, perfectly, really, seriously, thoroughly, totally, unconditionally, unequivocally, utterly
ASSOCIATED CONCEPTS: purely charitable institution, purely charitable purpose, purely manufacturing purposes, purely public charity

PURELY *(Simply),* *adverb*   barely, essentially, merely, mostly, plainly

PURGE *(Purify),* *verb*   clarify, clean, cleanse, clear, depurate, deterge, discharge, edulcorate, eliminate, elutriate, empty, eradicate, evacuate, excrete, expel, expurgate, filter, free from impurity, get rid of, rectify, refine, rout out, sanctify, scour, separate, strain, sublimate, sweep out, wash away

PURGE *(Wipe out by atonement),* *verb*   absolve, acquit, clear, exculpate, excuse, exempt, forgive, grant absolution, pardon, reclaim, redeem, shrive
ASSOCIATED CONCEPTS: purge of contempt

PURLOIN, *verb*   appropriate dishonestly, appropriate fraudulently, *avertere,* burglarize, cheat, commit larceny, defalcate, defraud, embezzle, filch, *furari,* misapply, misappropriate, misuse, peculate, pilfer, poach, rob, seize, snatch, spirit away, steal, *surripere,* swindle, take, take by fraud, take dishonestly, take feloniously, take wrongfully, thieve, unlawfully deprive

PURPORT, *verb*   allege, allude, claim, connote, convey, declare, declare with positiveness, denote, express, imply, *indicare,* indicate, infer, insinuate, intend, intimate, mean, pose as, pretend, profess, represent, say, show, *significare,* signify, state, suggest

PURPORTED, *adjective*   alleged, assumed, avowedly, claimed, in name only, ostensible, pretended, pretexed, professed, specious, so-called

PURPOSE, *noun*   aim, ambition, application, aspiration, avail, basis, constancy, deliberation, design, desire, desired result, destination, determination, direction, doggedness, drive, eagerness, end, expectation, final cause, firmness, force, function, goal, guiding principle, hope, idea, *institutum,* intended result, intent, intention, *mens,* mission, motivating idea, motive, object, objective, perseverance, persistence, plan, point, *propositum,* resolution, resolve, service, significance, singleness, target, tenacity, use, volition, voluntariness, will, wish, zeal
ASSOCIATED CONCEPTS: business purpose, charitable purpose, intent, malice, unlawful purpose
FOREIGN PHRASES: ***Lex neminem cogit ad vana seu inutilia peragenda.*** The law compels no one to do futile or useless things. ***Lex nil facit frustra, nil jubet frustra.*** The law does not do anything nor commands anyone to do anything which would

be futile. ***Impunitas continuum affectum tribuit delinquendi.*** Impunity confirms the disposition of a delinquent. ***Benigne faciendae sunt interpretationes, propter simplicitatem laicorum, ut res magis valeat quam pereat; et verba intentioni, non e contra, debent inservire.*** Interpretations should be liberal, because of the lack of training of laymen, so that the subject matter should be valid rather than void, and words should be subject to the intention, not the intention to the words. ***Frustra fit per plura, quod fieri potest per pauciora.*** That is needlessly done by many which can be done by fewer. ***Potentia inutilis frustra est. Useless power is vain.***

PURPOSEFUL, *adjective*   advantageous, beneficial, bound, calculated, contributory, decided, dedicated, deliberate, designed, determined, devoted, dogged, earnest, firm, helpful, inexorable, intended, intense, intent, intentional, intransigent, meant, obstinate, persevering, persistent, pertinacious, planned, practical, productive, purposive, resolute, resolved, sedulous, serious, single-minded, stalwart, staunch, steadfast, steady, strong-minded, strongwilled, stubborn, studied, telic, tenacious, uncompromising, undeviating, unfaltering, unflagging, unflinching, unhesitating, unshrinking, unswerving, unwavering, useable, useful, utilitarian, valuable, willful, worthwhile, zealous

PURPOSELY, *adverb*   according to plan, by choice, by design, by will, calculatedly, consciously, deliberately, designedly, expressly, intentionally, knowingly, on purpose, pointedly, purposefully, studiously, volitionally, voluntarily, willfully, willingly, with forethought, with free will, with intent, with premeditation, wittingly
ASSOCIATED CONCEPTS: intent, malice

PURSUANT TO, *preposition*   according to, agreeable to, agreeing to, commensurate with, compatible to, conforming to, consistent with, consonant with, in accord with, in accordance with, in harmony with
ASSOCIATED CONCEPTS: pursuant to the law

PURSUE *(Carry on)*, *verb*   adhere to, cling to, conduct, continue, cultivate, enact, engage, execute, follow, go in for, keep on, keep up, maintain, perform, *permanere*, persevere, persist, *persistere*, practice, proceed, prosecute, stick to

PURSUE *(Chase)*, *verb*   *consectari*, ferret out, follow, follow a trail, go after, go in pursuit of, hunt, *prosequi*, prowl, quest, run after, run down, search, seek, *sequi*, trace, track, trail

PURSUE *(Strive to gain)*, *verb*   aim, aspire to, attempt, be bent upon, be determined to get, be intent upon, bid for, *consectari*, contrive to gain, court, covet, desire, endeavor to gain, exert oneself for, intend, labor for, progress, push toward, seek, seek to attain, *sequi*, set as a goal, solicit, steer for, strive for, struggle for, try for, try one's best, try to obtain, work for

PURSUIT *(Chase)*, *noun*   chase, *consectatio*, effort to secure, hunt, inquest, inquiry, inquisition, investigation, probe, prosecution, quest, search, stalk, *studium*
ASSOCIATED CONCEPTS: hot pursuit doctrine

PURSUIT *(Effort to secure)*, *noun*   attempt, campaign, consectatio, effort, endeavor, exertion, hunt, investigation, laborious application, probe, quest, search, strenuous effort, struggle, sustained trial, try, undertaking, venture
ASSOCIATED CONCEPTS: hot pursuit doctrine

PURSUIT *(Goal)*, *noun*   aim, ambition, destination, end, object, objective, purpose, target

PURSUIT *(Occupation)*, *noun*   activity, appointment, artificium, avocation, business, calling, capacity, career, chosen work, concern, craft, department, employment, endeavor, engagement, enterprise, field, function, job, lifework, line, living, means of livelihood, metier, *negotium*, occupatio, office, position, post, practice, profession, project, province, regular employment, situation, specialization, specialty, sphere, task, trade, undertaking, venture, vocation, work

PURVIEW, *noun*   ambit, area, arena, borderline, boundary, bounds, breadth, circumscription, compass, concern, confine, contemplation, delimitation, department, design, extent, latitude, *latitudo*, limit, limitation, limits, *locus*, magnitude, meaning, orbit, perimeter, plan, province, purpose, range, reach, scope, span, sphere, stretch, term, territory, view, zone
ASSOCIATED CONCEPTS: purview of a statute

PUSH, *noun*   acceleration, assault, attack, boost, foray, impact, impetus, impulse, impulsion, incursion, main force, pressure, propulsion, shove, stimulus, thrust

PUSH, *verb*   advocate, animate, back, be resolute, boost, carry to a conclusion, coerce, constrain, dispatch, drive, drive on, endeavor, endure, exert one's self, exhort, expedite, facilitate, follow up, foray, force, forge ahead, get behind, give impetus to, goad, grind, impact, impel, importune, incite, induce, instigate, jostle, launch, motivate, nudge, persevere, persist, plod, plug away, press, press forward, press on, pressure, prod, project, promote, provoke, quicken, see it through, set in motion, shove, speed, spur, stimulate, strive, struggle, struggle on, support, thrust, urge, urge to action

PUT *(Place)*, *verb*   apply, assign a place, attach, base, deposit, dispense, fix, give, imbed, implant, infuse, inject, install, instill, introduce, lodge, park, place, plant, position, raise, repose, seat, set, site, situate, station, submit, tender
ASSOCIATED CONCEPTS: constructive bailment, involuntary bailment

PUT *(Phrase)*, *verb*   ascribe, attribute, cast, describe, express, impute, pose, posit, postulate, present, propound, say, set forth, state, throw

PUT FORTH, *verb*   advance, advise, air, argue, communicate, display, emit, employ, exert, exhibit, extend, go forth, issue, make a suggestion, move, offer, parade, pass, plead, posit, postulate, present, profess, proffer, propose, proposition, propound, publish, pullulate, put forward, raise, reach forth, set forth, start, start out, submit, use, venture to say
ASSOCIATED CONCEPTS: examine a witness, introduce into evidence, proffer into evidence, put allegations in a complaint, put forth pleadings

PUTATIVE, *adjective*   acknowledged, alleged, assumed, attributed, avowed, believed, claimed, commonly considered, conjectured, deemed, *falsus*, ostensible, presumed, presumptive, professed, purported, recognized, reported, reputed, speculative, supposed
ASSOCIATED CONCEPTS: putative father, putative parent

Q

QUAGMIRE, *noun* complication, crisis, critical situation, dead end, deadlock, difficulty, dilemma, distress, emergency, entanglement, exigency, imbroglio, impasse, involvement, mess, misfortune, muddle, nonplus, perplexity, pinch, plight, predicament, problem, quandary, scrape, spot, state, strait, tight situation, trial, tribulation, trouble

QUALIFICATION *(Condition), noun* condicio, exceptio, exception, exemption, limitation, modification, provision, proviso, requirement, requisite, reservation, restriction, specification, stipulation, term

QUALIFICATION *(Fitness), noun* ability, acceptability, admissibility, applicability, appositeness, appropriateness, aptitude, aptness, capability, capacity, compatibility, competency, correctness, desirability, efficiency, eligibility, endowment, entitlement, expedience, fittingness, occasion, pertinence, preparation, preparedness, propriety, readiness, relevance, right, rightness, skill, suitability, suitableness, suitedness, worthiness

QUALIFIED *(Competent), adjective* able, acceptable, accomplished, adapted, adept, adequate, apt, capable, deft, efficacious, eligible, entitled, equal to, equipped, experienced, expert, fit, knowing, licensed, practiced, proficient, skilled, skillful, suitable, trained, versed, well-suited, worthy, worthy of choice
ASSOCIATED CONCEPTS: qualified applicant, qualified elector

QUALIFIED *(Conditioned), adjective* accommodatus, checked, circumscribed, circumstanced, conditional, contingent upon, controlled, curbed, decreased, defined, delimited, dependent, diminished, idoneus, limitary, limited, moderated, modified, not absolute, prerequisite, prescribed, provisional, provisionary, provisory, restricted, stipulatory, subject to terms
ASSOCIATED CONCEPTS: qualified acceptance, qualified endorsement, qualified privilege, qualified right

QUALIFY *(Condition), verb* alter, attemper, bound, circumscribere, confine, control, correct, extenuare, govern, introduce changes, introduce new conditions, keep within limits, limit, modify, narrow, regulate, restrict, revise, specify, temper
ASSOCIATED CONCEPTS: qualified acceptance, qualified fee, qualified gift, qualified endorsement, qualified privilege

QUALIFY *(Meet standards), verb* accredit, allow, *aptum,* authorize, certify, confer a right, empower, enable, endorse, entitle, give a permit, give a warrant, have the qualifications, have the requisites, license, make capable, make competent, make suitable, measure up, meet the demands, meet the specifications, permit, practice, prepare, sanction
ASSOCIATED CONCEPTS: failure to qualify, qualify for appointment

QUALITY *(Attribute), noun* characteristic, endowment, feature, idiocrasy, idiosyncrasy, individualism, nature, particularity, peculiarity, property, singularity, trait

QUALITY *(Excellence), noun* ability, ableness, aptness, caliber, character, class, competency, fineness, goodness, grade, merit, might, potency, potentiality, power, puissance, rank, soundness, standing, status, superiority, validity, value, worth

QUALITY *(Grade), noun* ability, ableness, aptness, character, condition, distinction, earmark, endowment, feature, merit, nature, particularity, property, standing, tendency, worth
ASSOCIATED CONCEPTS: inferior quality, warranty as to quality

QUALM, *noun* anxiety, apprehension, apprehensiveness, compunction, concern, diffidence, disquiet, distrust, doubt, doubtfulness, dubiety, dubiousness, equivocalness, feeling of uncertainty, foreboding, hesitance, hesitancy, hesitation, incertitude, lack of certainty, lack of confidence, lack of conviction, misgiving, mistrust, nervousness, pause, question, scruple, skepticism, suspicion, twinge of conscience, uncertainty, undecidedness, uneasiness, want of confidence, worry

QUANDARY, *noun* bafflement, bewilderment, confoundment, confusedness, confusion, difficulty, dilemma, disconcertion, doubt, doubtfulness, dubiety, dubiosity, dubiousness, dubitation, incertitude, indecision, indetermination, irresolution, nonplus, perplexity, perturbation, plight, predicament, puzzlement, quagmire, state of doubt, uncertainness, uncertainty

QUANTITY, *noun* abundance, aggregate, allotment, amount, amplitude, apportionment, batch, bulk, bunch, crowd, fullness, heap, host, large number, legion, lot, mass, measure, measurement, mess, muchness, multiplicity, multitude, multitudinousness, myriads, number, *numerus,* pack, plenty, portion, profusion, *quantitas,* quantum, store, sum, sum total, supply, totality, volume

QUANTUM MERUIT, noun compensation for value received, contractual obligation to pay for value received, indemnification for value received, payment, payment for as much as deserved, payment for benefit received, payment for value obtained, payment for value provided, payment for value received, recompense, recovery, redress, remuneration for value received

QUARANTINE, noun confinement, custody, detachment, medical segregation, period of detention, period of isolation, restraint of movement, sanitary cordon, seclusion, segregation, separation, strict isolation

QUASH, verb abate, abolish, annul, cancel, countermand, declare null and void, destroy, disannul, discard, disestablish, dismiss, dispel, dissolve, end, eradicate, extinguish, extirpate, infirmare, iritum facere, invalidate, make void, nullify, obliterate, overrule, overthrow, overturn, overwelm, put an end to, put down, quell, quench, repeal, repress, rescind, *rescindere,* reverse, squelch, stop, subdue, suppress, terminate, vacate, withdraw
ASSOCIATED CONCEPTS: motion to quash, quash a subpoena

QUASI, adjective almost, imitation, mock, mostly, near, not entirely, pseudo, pseudonymous
ASSOCIATED CONCEPTS: quasi civil action, quasi contract, quasi corporation, quasi crime, quasi criminal, quasi criminal proceeding, quasi derelict, quasi easement, quasi estoppel, quasi fee, quasi guardian, quasi in rem, quasi individual, quasi judicial officer, quasi jurisdictional facts, quasi legislative agency, quasi lien, quasi municipal corporation, quasi partnership, quasi party, quasi powers, quasi proceedings, quasi public corporation, quasi remainder, quasi trustee

QUASI, adverb almost as, apparently, as if, as though, as though it were, in a certain sense, in a manner, in name only, just as, seemingly but not actually, to a certain extent

QUERULOUS, adjective bewailing, canting, captious, carping, censorious, clamorous, complaining, contentious, cross, difficult, difficult to please, discontented, disputatious, dissatisfied, exceptious, faultfinding, fractious, fretful, grouchy, grumbling, hard to please, hypercritical, hypersensitive, irritable, lamentative, lamenting, maledicent, mournful, nagging, overcritical, peevish, pettish, petulant, plaintful, plaintive, pugnacious, puling, quarrelsome, *queribundus,* querimonious, *querulus,* shrewish, splenetic, tearful, testy, touchy, vixenish, wailful, waspish, whimpering, whining, whiny

QUEST, noun chase, crusade, expedition, exploration, hunt, inquiry, journey, perquisition, pursuit, research, search, searching, seeking

QUESTION (Inquiry), noun asking, essay, examination, exploration, inquisition, interpellation, interrogation, interrogatory, investigation, probe, *quaestio,* query, *rogatio,* scrutiny, search, subject of inquiry, survey, test, theme of inquiry
ASSOCIATED CONCEPTS: leading question
FOREIGN PHRASES: *Rogationes, quaestiones, et positiones debent esse simplices.* Demands, questions, and claims ought to be simple. ***Multiplex et indistinctum parit confusionem; et quaestiones quo simpliciores, eo lucidiores.*** Multiplicity and indistinctness produce confusion; and the more simple the questions, the more lucid they are.

QUESTION (Issue), noun bone of contention, case, enigma, mystery, point in dispute, problem, proposition, puzzle, subject, theme, topic
ASSOCIATED CONCEPTS: mixed question of law and fact, political question, question of fact, question of law

QUESTION THE VERACITY OF, verb be doubtful, be dubious, be skeptical, be suspicious, be uncertain, challenge, disbelieve, discredit, dispute, distrust, doubt, doubt the truth of, entertain doubts, find hard to believe, give no credence to, greet with skepticism, harbor certain doubts, harbor suspicions, have misgivings about, have one's doubts, have questions over, have reservations, hesitate to accept as true, impugn, lack confidence in, misbelieve, mistrust, question, suspect, withhold reliance
ASSOCIATED CONCEPTS: cross examination, examination of a witness, interrogation, question under oath

QUESTION UNDER OATH, verb ask, conduct questioning, cross-examine, examine, examine judicially, examine on direct, examine while on trial, grill, inquire, interrogate, investigate, probe, put to the question, question, request, rest, subject to intense cross-examination, subject to questioning

QUESTIONABLE (Dubious), adjective ambiguous, arguable, at issue, contestable, controversial, controvertible, debatable, disputable, doubtable, doubtful, dubious, dubitable, enigmatical, equivocal, experimental, fallible, hard to believe, hardly possible, improbable, inconceivable, incredible, indefinite, indeterminate, in dispute, in question, moot, more than doubtful, not axiomatic, objectionable, open to doubt, open to question, perplexing, puzzling, speculative, suspect, suspicious, tentative, unauthentic, uncertain, unconvincing, undecided, undetermined, unlikely, unreliable, unsettled, unsound, unsure, unsustainable, untenable, untrustworthy, vague

QUESTIONABLE (Unethical), adjective corrupt, dishonest, dishonorable, disreputable, ill-gotten, immoral, perfidious, shady, unconscionable, underhanded, unprincipled, unscrupulous, untrustworthy

QUESTIONNAIRE, noun blank, canvas, census, examination, examination paper, form, form to be completed, form to be filled in, inquiry, poll, public opinion poll, question list, request for information, statement, study, survey
ASSOCIATED CONCEPTS: questionable testimony

QUEUE, noun assemblage, chain, file, lineup, order, progression, range, rank, retinue, row of people, sequence, series, single file, string, succession, tier, train

QUIBBLE, verb bicker, cavil, contend with, differ, disagree, dispute, dissent, equivocate, fence, haggle, join issue, oppose, palter, quarrel, tergiversate, wrangle

QUICK (Discerning), adjective acute, adept, adroit, agile, aggressive, astute, brainy, bright, brilliant, clever, deft, dexterous, discerning, educable, educatable, fiery, instructable, intelligent, irascible, irritable, keen, nimble-fingered, of ready intelligence, peppery, sagacious, schoolable, sharp, skillful, snappish, teachable, trainable

QUICK (Fleeting), **adjective**   active, artful, born, brief, caducous, cursory, deft, elusive, ephemeral, evanescent, expeditious, express, facile, fast, fleet, fleeting, frisky, hasty, hurried, immediate, impermanent, impulsive, instant, instantaneous, meteoric, momentary, nimble, passing, perfunctory, perishable, perspicacious, precipitate, proficient, prompt, rapid, ready, short-lived, speedy, spirited, sudden, summary, swift, temporary, transient, transitory, vivacious, volatile, wide-awake

QUID PRO QUO, noun   agreement, counterbalance, counterpoise, equipoise, exchange, express agreement, give and take, interchange, measure for measure, mutual agreement, mutual consideration, mutual understanding, one thing in return for another, reciprocality, reciprocation, reciprocity, something equivalent, something for something, substitute, understanding

QUIESCENCE, noun   abeyance, calm, calmness, cessation, composure, dead calm, dead stop, dormancy, dying down, hush, immobility, inaction, inactivity, inertia, inertness, intermission, latency, lethargy, lull, motionlessness, passivity, pause, peace, peacefulness, placidity, quiet, quietness, quietude, remission, repose, rest, restfulness, serenity, silence, sleep, stagnation, standstill, stillness, subsidence, suspense, tranquility

QUIET (Low key), **adjective**   at rest, collected, contented, cool, cool-headed, decent, demure, diffident, dispassionate, dormant, easy-going, gentle, humble, imperturbable, inconspicuous, inexcitable, laconic, lifeless, meek, mild, moderate, modest, orderly, patient, peaceable, placid, private, resting, restrained, retiring, sedate, serene, sober, solemn, stagnant, static, subdued, taciturn, unassuming, undemonstrative, unemphatic, unobtrusive, unostentatious, unperturbed, unpresumptuous, unpretentious, unresisting, vegetating

QUIET (Soundless), **adjective**   calm, glassy, halcyon, hushed, inarticulate, latent, lethargic, mum, mute, noiseless, passive, peaceful, quiescent, reserved, reticent, speechless, silent, still, tranquil, uncommunicative, unmoved, voiceless
ASSOCIATED CONCEPTS: covenant of quiet enjoyment, quieting title

QUIET, noun   calm, calmness, cessation, composure, dormancy, ease, freedom from disturbance, gentleness, hush, immobility, intermission, latency, lull, moderation, muteness, noiselessness, passivity, patience, pause, peace, peacefulness, placidity, quiescence, quietness, quietude, relaxation, repose, reserve, rest, restfulness, reticence, serenity, silence, soundlessness, stagnation, still, stillness, tranquility, uncommunicativeness

QUIET, verb   alleviate, appease, assuage, blunt, calm, close, comfort, compose, conclude, cut short, decrease, dulcify, dull, lull, mitigate, moderate, mollify, mute, pacify, palliate, placate, put a stop to, quell, relieve, remit, repress, silence, sober, soften, soothe, stifle, strangle, subdue, subside, temper, terminate, tranquilize, wind-up

QUINTESSENCE, noun   acme, acme of perfection, center, character, characteristic, consequence, consummation, content, core, cornerstone, corpus, culmination, distilled essence, elixir, essence, essentialness, essential part, gist, heart, height, kernel, lifeblood, main point, marrow, ne plus ultra, optimum, prime, quiddity, soul, spirit, substance, summit, superlative, ultimate

QUIRK (Accident), **noun**   accidental occurrence, casualty, chance, circumstance, fate, fortuitous event, fortuity, freak, hap, inadvertence, luck, misadventure, mischance, mishap, nonintentional occurrence, turn, twist, undesigned occurrence, unforeseen event, unforeseen occurrence, unintentionality, unplanned happening, unpremeditation

QUIRK (Idiosyncrasy), **noun**   aberration, abnormality, abnormity, anomaly, bizarreness, defiance of custom, departure, deviation, divergence, eccentricity, exception, fancy, habit, idiocrasy, individuality, infringement of custom, irregularity, kink, mannerism, nonconformity, oddity, outlandishness, particularity, peculiarity, queerness, singularity, strange behavior, strange occurrence, strangeness, twist, unconformity, unconventionality, unorthodoxy, unusualness, vagary

QUIT (Discontinue), **verb**   abandon, abdicate, abjure, abort, acknowledge defeat, admit defeat, apostatize, arrest, back out, become inactive, break off, bring to an end, call a halt, capitulate, cause a stoppage, cause to halt, cease, cease progress, cease to use, cease work, check, come to a standstill, cut out, desist from, drop, finish, forgo, forsake, forswear, give up, go into retirement, go out of business, halt, have done with, intermit, lay aside, leave off, leave unfinished, make an end of, nol-pros, put a stop to, put an end to, relinquish, renounce, resign, retire, secede, stand aside, step down, stop, succumb, suffer defeat, surcease, surrender, suspend, tergiversate, terminate, withdraw, yield

QUIT (Evacuate), **verb**   abandon, abscond, beat a retreat, decamp, defect, depart from, desert, disappear, egress, emigrate, escape, exit, flee, forsake, get out, go, go away, go forth, go out, hurry away, leave, make a departure, make an exit, move away, part, pull out, remove oneself, retire, retreat, run away, separate from, set forth, set out, take flight, take leave, take leave of, take oneself away, turn one's back on, vacate, vanish, walk away, walk out, withdraw
ASSOCIATED CONCEPTS: notice to quit, quit

QUIT (Free of), **verb**   absolve, acquit, clear, deliver, discharge, disembroil, disencumber, disengage, disentangle, emancipate, exonerate, extricate, grant amnesty to, liberate, lift controls, manumit, pardon, release, render free, rescue, set at liberty, set free

QUIT (Repay), **verb**   balance accounts, be even with, clear a debt, clear accounts, compensate, discharge a debt, indemnify, make compensation, make payment, make reparation, make restitution, pay a debt, pay an indemnity, pay back, pay in full, pay off, pay old debts, recompense, refund, reimburse, remunerate, restore, return, settle a debt, settle an account

QUITCLAIM, noun   acquittance, deed exculpating the transferor, deed of release, quittance, receipt, waiver
ASSOCIATED CONCEPTS: quitclaim and convey, quitclaim deed, quitclaim sales

QUIXOTIC, adjective   chimerical, dreamy, fanciful, idealistic, illusory, impracticable, impractical, mad, notional, quixotical, romantic, unrealistic, utopian, visionary

QUIZ, noun   catechism, examination, inquest, inquiry, inquisition, investigation, interrogation, quest, questioning, quizzing, request, review, test

QUIZ, verb   ask, catechize, check, cross-examine, cross-question, examine, grill, inquire, interrogate, investigate, probe, query, question, question under oath, test

QUORUM, *noun* abundance, adequacy, adequateness, ampleness, completeness, enough, full measure, legal minimum, plentifulness, plenty, plenum, quota, sufficience, sufficiency, sufficient number, sufficient quantity
ASSOCIATED CONCEPTS: absence of quorum, full quorum

QUOTA, *noun* allocation, allotment, allowance, apportionment, appropriation, assignment, check, circumscription, constraint, containment, contingent, control, curb, dispensation, extent, inhibition, limit, limitation, measure, number, percentage, portion, proportion, quantity, quantum, ratio, ra-

tion, regulation, restraint, restriction, share, suppression
ASSOCIATED CONCEPTS: quota system, racial quota

QUOTE, *verb* adduce, *adferre,* circumstantiate, cite, cite a holding of a case, corroborate, detail, document, duplicate, establish, excerpt, extract, give word for word, go into detail, instance, make reference, paraphrase, point out, produce an instance, *proferre,* recapitulate, recite, recount, refer, reiterate, repeat, rephrase, report, reproduce, restate, retell, reword, specify, substantiate, support, validate, verify

RACE, *noun* ancestry, birth, breed, class, cultural group, culture, descent, ethnic group, ethnic stock, extraction, family, folk, genealogy, genus, group, kind, line, parentage, people, phylum, stem, stirps, stock, strain
ASSOCIATED CONCEPTS: discrimination, race, creed, and color

RACE, *verb* accelerate, bolt, chase, compete, dart, dash, engage in a contest of speed, enter a competition, fly, gallop, hasten, hie, hurry, hustle, move at an accelerated rate of speed, plunge ahead, pursue, run, run a race, run swiftly, rush, scamper, scramble, scud, speed, sprint, spurt, tear, whiz
ASSOCIATED CONCEPTS: assumption of risk, race to the recording office, racing commission

RACKET, *noun* conspiracy, corruption, criminal activity, criminality, dishonesty, fraud, fraudulence, illegitimate undertaking, illicit business, illicit scheme, improbity, lawbreaking, lawlessness, misdealing, organized illegal activity, scheme, thievery, trick, underworld activity

RACKETEER, *noun* contrabandist, criminal, dealer in illicit goods, extorter, gangleader, gangster, illicit dealer, malefactor, member of organized crime, miscreant, mobster, offender, underworld character, underworld gangster

RADIATE, *verb* beam, branch out, coruscate, diffuse, disperse, emanate in rays, emit heat, emit rays, exude, *fulgere,* irradiate, issue rays, overspread, *radiare,* ramify, reflect, scatter, send, send forth, shed, splay, spread, throw off heat, throw out, transmit

RADICAL *(Extreme), **adjective*** absolute, altogether, complete, comprehensive, entire, exhaustive, intensive, maximal, plenary, sweeping, thorough, thoroughgoing, total, whole

RADICAL *(Favoring drastic change), **adjective*** advocating change, fanatical, freethinking, iconoclastic, insurgent,

insurrectionary, militant, mutinous, progressive, rebellious, recusant, revolutionary, ultraist, uncompromising

RAINMAKER, *noun* activity to develop business, bringing in a case flow, bringing in cases, bringing in new business, bringing in new clients, bringing in new files, bringing in new matters, bringing in work, client development, producing business, producing new clients, producing new work
ASSOCIATED CONCEPTS: business development, client development, marketing

RAISE *(Advance), **verb*** aggrandize, augment, boost, bring up, dignify, elevate, enhance, enlarge, ennoble, exalt, further, glorify, heighten, honor, increase, lift, move up, prize, promote, propose, *provehere,* put, suggest, uplift, upraise
ASSOCIATED CONCEPTS: raise an objection

RAISON D'ETRE, *noun* animus, arterial blood, basic, basic nutrition, driving force, essence of life, essential ingredient, force of life, foundation, fundamental, inspiration, inspiriting force, inspiriting power, life essence, lifeblood, moving force, spirit, vital energy, vital flame, vital fluid, vital force, vital principle, vital spark, vital spirit

RAISE *(Collect), **verb*** accumulate, assemble, bring together, *conligere,* gather together, get, levy, muster, obtain, procure

RAMPANT, *adjective* dominant, everywhere, excessive, extravagant, exuberant, *ferox,* flourishing, growing, irrepressible, overabundant, prevalent, prolific, rife, spreading, *superbire,* unchecked, uncontrolled, unrestrained, unstopped, widespread, wild

RANCOR, *noun* acerbity, acrimony, animosity, antagonism, antipathy, aversion, bitter feelings, bitterness, enmity, grudge, harshness, hate, hatred, hostility, ill feeling, ill will, *invidia,* malevolence, malice, malignity, *odium,* resentment, revenge, revengefulness, ruthlessness, spite, spitefulness, uncharitableness, unfriendliness, vendetta, vengeance, vengefulness, venom, venomousness, vindictiveness, virulence

RANDOM, *adjective* accidental, aimless, blind, casual, chance, cursory, designless, desultory, done without reason, fortuitous, haphazard, immethodical, incidental, indiscriminate, irregular, orderless, promiscuous, purposeless, stray, unaimed, unarranged, uncoordinated, undesigned, undirected, unguided, unorganized, unpremeditated

RANGE, *noun* ambit, area, arena, boundaries, bounds, breadth, compass, distance, earshot, extent, field, gamut, *genus,* hearing, limit, line, perimeter, power, reach, scope, space, span, sphere, stretch, sweep

RANSOM, *noun* cost of reclamation, cost of recovery, deliverance, extrication, *pretium,* price of redemption, price of retaking, price of retrieval, redemption, rescue

RAPACIOUS, *adjective* avaricious, *avidus,* cormorant, depredatory, devouring, grasping, greedy, insatiable, insatiate, living on prey, lupine, marauding, pillaging, piratical, plundering, predacious, predatory, preying, *rapax,* ravening, ravenous, voracious, vulturine, vulturous, wolfish

RAPE, *noun* abuse, assault, constupration, defilement, defloration, depredation, despoliation, forcible violation, pillage, plunder, plunderage, *rapere,* rapine, ravage, ravishment, seduction, sexual assault, spoliation, stupration, violation
ASSOCIATED CONCEPTS: criminal assault, statutory rape

RAPID, *adjective* accelerated, active, bustling, expeditious, express, fast, feverish, fleet, galloping, hasty, hurried, instant, light-footed, lively, nimble, posthaste, quick, *rapidus,* rushing, smart, speedy, swift, *velox,* winged

RAPPORT, *noun* accord, accordance, affinity, agreement, alliance, closeness, compatibility, concord, concordance, concurrence, congruity, consonance, empathy, harmonious relation, harmony, intimacy, mutual appreciation, mutuality, relationship, understanding

RAPPROCHEMENT, *noun* accord, accordance, agreement, alliance, amiability, amicability, amity, concord, concordance, cordial relations, cordiality, fellow feeling, fellowship, fraternization, friendliness, friendship, harmony, improved relations, mutual friendliness, mutuality, neighborliness, rapport, reciprocity, reconcilement, reconciliation, reunion, unanimity, understanding, unison, unity

RARE, *adjective* choice, curious, different, excellent, exceptional, exquisite, extraordinary, fine, incomparable, inconceivable, infrequent, *inusitatus,* matchless, noteworthy, out of circulation, out of the ordinary, peerless, precious, priceless, *rarus,* scarce, seldom seen, select, singular, *singularis,* special, strange, superlative, uncommon, uncustomary, unequaled, unexampled, unfamiliar, unique, unparalleled, unusual

RATE, *noun* amount, assessment, charge, cost, expense, fare, fee, hire, *magno,* obligation, pace, *parvo emere,* payment, price, quotation, standard, tempo, valuation, value, velocity, worth
ASSOCIATED CONCEPTS: legal rate of interest, rate of exchange

RATE, *verb* *aestimare,* appraise, apprize, assess, calculate, class, classify, compute, determine, esteem, estimate,

evaluate, figure, fix the price of, gauge, grade, judge, measure, merit, price, quantify, rank, reckon, set a value on, tag, value, weigh

RATIFICATION, *noun* acceptance, acknowledgment, approbation, approval, assent, certification, confirmation, consent, corroboration, endorsement, *sanctio,* sanction, stamp of approval, substantiation, validation
ASSOCIATED CONCEPTS: implied ratification, ratification of a contract, ratification of unauthorized acts
FOREIGN PHRASES: *Ratihabitio mandato aequiparatur.* Ratification is equivalent to an express command. ***Omnis ratihabitio retrotrahitur et mandato priori aequiparatur.*** Every ratification relates back and is taken to be the equal of prior authority. ***In maleficio, ratihabitio mandato comparatur.*** In tort, a ratification is regarded as a command.

RATIFY, *verb* accept, accredit, acknowledge, affirm, agree to, approve, assent, assure, attest, authenticate, back, bear out, buttress, certify, circumstantiate, concur, confirm, consent, corroborate, countenance, countersign, embrace, endorse, establish, guarantee, indorse, insure, make valid, pass, sanction, seal, sign, subscribe, substantiate, support, sustain, uphold, validate, verify, warrant
ASSOCIATED CONCEPTS: estoppel, express ratification, principal and agent

RATING, *noun* analysis, appraisal, assessment, classification, determination, estate, estimation, evaluation, grade, grading, grouping, measurement, placement, quantification, rank, ranking, status, valorization, valuation

RATIO, *noun* amount, balance, correlation, degree, differential, fixed relation, measure, percentage, perspective, proportion, proportional relation, proportionality, quota, range, relative estimate, relative quantity, scale, share, standard

RATIOCINATION, *noun* analysis, argumentation, cerebration, cogitation, deduction, dialectics, intellection, intellectualization, logic, *ratiocinatio,* rationality, rationalization, reasoning, thinking, thought

RATION, *noun* allotment, allowance, apportionment, appropriation, assignment, *demensum,* dispensation, distribution, division, dole, helping, measure, parcel, part, percentage, piece, pittance, portion, proportion, provision, quantity, quota, serving, share, slice

RATIONAL, *adjective* agreeable to reason, analytical, balanced, cerebral, clearheaded, cognitive, *consentaneus,* discerning, discriminating, endowed with reason, enlightened, exercising reason, intelligent, judicious, justifiable, knowing, legitimate, levelheaded, logical, lucid, objective, plausible, ratiocinative, *ratione praeditus,* reasonable, reasoning, reflective, sagacious, sage, sane, sensible, sober, sound, stable, thinking, thoughtful, understanding, well-grounded, wise
ASSOCIATED CONCEPTS: rational basis

RATIONALE, *noun* account, basis, cause, elucidation, explanation, explication, exposition, fundamental reason, ground, logical reasoning, motivation, motive, presumption, proposition, reason, reasoning, speculation, surmise, theory

RATIONALIZE, *verb* account for, adduce, analyze, cogitate, construe, excogitate, excuse, explain, explain away, justify, make acceptable, make allowances, make excuses, reason, reconcile, reflect, theorize, think, think logically, vindicate

REACH, verb accomplish, achieve, amount to, approach, arrive, attain, catch up, come to, communicate with, contact, equal, extend to, gain, get, get at, get in touch with, get through to, impress, influence, keep pace with, meet, move, obtain, overtake, strike, succeed, touch, triumph
ASSOCIATED CONCEPTS: overreaching

REACTION (Opposition), **noun** backfire, backlash, challenge, clash, conflict, contradiction, contrariety, countertendency, differences, disagreement, disapprobation, discountenance, expression of disapproval, objection, offset, polarity, protest, rebound, rebuff, recalcitration, renitence, renitency, reprisal, resistance, retaliation, retroaction

REACTION (Response), **noun** answer, attitude, effect, emotion, feeling, impact, impression, perception, reciprocal action, rejoinder, repercussion, reply, return, reverberation, sensation, sense, sentiment, view
ASSOCIATED CONCEPTS: allergic reaction

READ, verb apprehend, collect, con, conclude, consider probable, decipher, deduce, derive, digest, discern, draw a conclusion, gather, glean, grasp, guess, infer, interpret, know, leaf through, make out, perceive, peruse, pore over, presume, reason, scan, skim, study, thumb through, understand

READILY, adverb eagerly, easily, effortlessly, enthusiastically, freely, gladly, graciously, heartily, lief, *prompte,* promptly, quickly, smoothly, voluntarily, willingly

READY (Prepared), **adjective** able, accessible, armed, arranged, at hand, available, equipped, expectant, fit, groomed, in harness, in order, in position, in readiness, in working order, loaded, mature, mobilized, on call, *paratus,* primed, prompt, *promptus,* quick, ripe, set, speedy, standing by, swift, waiting

READY (Willing), **adjective** acquiescent, agreeable, alacritous, alert, animated, anxious, ardent, assenting, available, avid, cheerful, compliant, consenting, delighted, disposed, eager, enthusiastic, expeditious, favorably minded, fervent, given, glad, happy, inclined, keen, predisposed, prone, propense, zealous, zestful

REAFFIRM, verb accent, accentuate, buttress, confirm, emphasize, fortify, go over, insist, iterate, punctuate, reassert, reiterate, repeat, restate, retell, stress, sustain, underline

REAFFIRMATION, noun absolute assertion, acknowledgment, affirmance, approval, authentication, certification, confirmation, declaration, formal declaration in support or against, pronouncement, ratification, statement, substantiation, swearing, validation, verification
ASSOCIATED CONCEPTS: bankruptcy, reaffirmation agreement

REAL, adjective accurate, actual, ascertained, authentic, bonafide, conformable to fact, correct, dependable, factual, genuine, *germanus,* inartificial, incontestable, indisputable, irrefutable, legitimate, natural, right, scientific, *sincerus,* sure, true, trustworthy, truthful, undeniable, undoubtable, unerroneous, unfallacious, unfeigned, unimagined, unimpeachable, unmistaken, unquestionable, unsimulated, unspurious, unsynthetic, valid, veracious, veritable, verus
ASSOCIATED CONCEPTS: real estate, real party interest, real property, real servitude

REAL ESTATE, noun acreage, block, chattels real, domain, estate, fee, freehold, ground, hereditament, land, landed estate, lot, parcel, plot, property, real property, realty

REALISTIC, adjective actual, authentic, depictive, exact, faithful, genuine, graphic, lifelike, natural, naturalistic, practical, pragmatic, real, representational, representative, truthful, undisguised, undistorted, unidealistic, unromantic, veracious

REALITY, noun actual existence, actuality, authenticity, being, existence, factualness, genuineness, legitimacy, realness, substance, substantiality, substantialness, truth, veracity, *veritas,* verity

REALIZATION, noun accomplishment, achievement, acquirement, acquisition, actualization, apperception, appreciation, apprehension, attainment, awareness, cognition, cognizance, completion, comprehension, consciousness, consummation, discernment, discovery, effectuation, *effectus,* execution, fruition, fulfilment, illumination, implementation, ken, knowledge, materialization, mindfulness, perception, performance, production, profit, receipt, recognition, sensibility, substantiation, understanding

REALIZE (Make real), **verb** accomplish, achieve, actualize, bring about, bring to pass, carry into effect, carry out, carry through, complete, consummate, do, effect, effectuate, *efficere,* engineer, *facere,* implement, materialize, perform, produce, substantiate

REALIZE (Obtain as a profit), **verb** achieve, acquire, attain, benefit, clear, come by, earn, enjoy, gain, get, make, net, obtain, obtain a return, *pecuniam redigere,* procure, produce, profit, reap, receive, turn into cash, turn into money

REALIZE (Understand), **verb** absorb, appreciate, apprehend, assimilate, become aware, become conscious, cognize, comprehend, *comprehendere,* digest, discern, fathom, grasp, *intellegere,* know, learn, make out, perceive, recognize, see, take in

REALM, noun area, authority, bailiwick, country, demesne, department, domain, dominion, empire, field, jurisdiction, kingdom, land, monarchy, orbit, perimeters, power, province, region, *respublica,* sphere, territory

REALTY, noun acres, estate, grounds, holdings, land, land owned, property, real estate, real property
ASSOCIATED CONCEPTS: conveyance of realty, description of realty, interest in realty, sale of realty, title to realty

REAP, verb achieve, acquire, attain, be rewarded, benefit, clear, collect, cull, cut, *demetere,* derive, draw, earn, gain, gather, get, glean, harvest, obtain, pick, pick up, procure, profit, realize, receive, recover, retrieve, secure, take, take in, take the yield, win

REAPPORTION, verb allot again, apportion anew, deal out anew, dispense, distribute again, distribute anew, dole out, parcel, portion out, ration, reallocate, reallot, reappoint, rearrange, reassign, reassort, reclassify, redisperse, redistribute, redistrict, redivide, remeasure, repartition, rezone, split again
ASSOCIATED CONCEPTS: reapportion a legislature

REARREST, verb catch again, constrain again, legally restrain again, make captive again, place in custody again, recapture, recommit, reconfine, redetain, reimprison, rejail, seize again, take prisoner again

REASON *(Basis)*, **noun**   account, actuation, aim, argument, *causa,* causation, cause, consideration, defense, derivation, design, end, excuse, explanation, extenuation, foundation, genesis, goal, ground, impetus, incentive, incitation, inducement, inspiration, instigation, intent, intention, mainspring, motivation, motive, object, origin, prime mover, principle, provocation, purpose, *ratio,* rationale, root, sake, source, spring, stimulation, vindication, wherefore
ASSOCIATED CONCEPTS: reason for classification
FOREIGN PHRASES: *Causa patet.* The reason is apparent. *Eadem est ratio, eadem est lex.* The reason being the same, the law is the same. *Vitium est quod fugi debet, ne, si rationem non invenias, mox legem sine ratione esse clames.* It is a fault which ought to be avoided, that if you cannot discover the reason you presently exclaim that the law is without reason. *Ratio potest allegari deficiente lege; sed vera et legalis et non apparens.* Where the law is deficient, the reason can be alleged, but it must be true and lawful and not merely apparent.

REASON *(Sound judgment)*, **noun**   ability to know, acumen, apperception, awareness, clearheadedness, cognition, cognizance, common sense, comprehension, *consilium,* discernment, discretion, discrimination, good sense, insight, intellect, intelligence, judiciousness, knowledge, logic, logicalness, lucidity, *mens,* mental capacity, mind, perception, percipiency, rationality, recognition, sagacity, sanity, sense, sensibility, sensibleness, sobriety, thinking, thought, understanding, wisdom
ASSOCIATED CONCEPTS: business reason, rule of reason
FOREIGN PHRASES: *Quaere de dubiis, quia per rationes pervenitur ad legitimam rationem.* Inquire into doubtful matters, because by reasoning we arrive at legal reason. *Lex est dictamen rationis.* Law is the dictate of reason. *Lex est ratio summa, quae jubet quae sunt utilia et necessaria, et contraria prohibet.* That which is law is the consummation of reason, which commands those things useful and necessary, while prohibiting the contrary. *Nihil quod est contra rationem est licitum.* Nothing is lawful which is contrary to reason. *Lex plus laudatur quando ratione probatur.* The law is most praiseworthy when it is consistent with reason. *Ratio non clauditur loco.* Reason is not confined to any place. *Ratio et auctoritas duo clarissima mundi lumina.* Reason and authority are the two brightest lights in the world. *Ratio legis est anima legis.* The reason of the law is the spirit of the law. *Ratio in jure aequitas integra.* Reason in law is impartial equity. *Ratio est formalis causa consuetudinis.* Reason is the source and cause of custom. *Lex semper intendit quod convenit rationi.* The law always intends what is agreeable to reason. *Quod naturalis ratio inter omnes homines constituit, vocatur jus gentium.* The rule which natural reason has established among all men is called the law of nations. *Ratio est legis anima; mutata legis ratione mutatur et lex.* Reason is the soul of law; the reason of law being changed, the law is also changed.

REASON *(Conclude)*, **verb**   analyze, cerebrate, cogitate, conclude, consider, contemplate, deduce, deliberate, derive, draw inferences, examine, excogitate, figure out, gather, hypothesize, infer, intellectualize, judge, make deductions, philosophize, ponder, *ratiocinari,* ratiocinate, rationalize, reflect, resolve, study, suppose, theorize, think, think through, try conclusions, turn over in the mind, weigh

REASON *(Persuade)*, **verb**   advise, argue, bring to reason, coax, contend, convince, debate, demonstrate, discuss, dissuade, establish, explain, expostulate, expound, join issue, justify, move, persuade, plead, point out, prevail upon, prove, remonstrate, set forth, speak logically, talk over, urge, ventilate a question, win over

REASONABLE *(Fair)*, **adjective**   *aequus,* conscionable, equitable, fit, fitting, judicious, just, *modicus,* not excessive, not extreme, proper, *rationi consentaneus,* restrained, suitable, temperate, tempered, tolerable, unextravagant, unextreme
ASSOCIATED CONCEPTS: reasonable agreement, reasonable allowance, reasonable attorney's fees, reasonable market value, reasonable notice, reasonable opportunity to cure, reasonable restraint, reasonable return, reasonable time, reasonable value
FOREIGN PHRASES: *Quam rationabilis debet esse finis, non definitur, sed omnibus circumstantiis inspectis pendet ex justiciariorum discretione.* What a reasonable fine ought to be is not defined, but is left to the discretion of the judges, all the circumstances being considered. *Quam longum debet esse rationabile tempus non definitur in lege, sed pendet ex discretione justiciariorum.* How long a reasonable time ought to be is not defined by law, but is left to the discretion of the judges.

REASONABLE *(Rational)*, **adjective**   amenable to reason, broad-minded, capable of reason, clearheaded, cognitive, credible, discerning, fit, intelligent, judicious, justifiable, logical, lucid, perceiving, percipient, persuable, plausible, probable, proper, *prudens,* ratiocinative, rational, *rationis particeps,* realistic, right, sagacious, sapient, sensible, sound, tenable, understandable, unjaundiced, unprejudiced, valid, warrantable, well-advised, well-founded, wise
ASSOCIATED CONCEPTS: reasonable care, reasonable cause, reasonable certainty, reasonable degree of care, reason-able diligence, reasonable doubt, reasonable excuse, reasonable ground, reasonable inference, reasonable injury, reasonable interpretation, reasonable judgment, reasonable notice, reasonable person, reasonable probability, reasonable use

REASSESS, verb   reappraise, reappreciate, reapprise, recalculate, recharge, reclass, reestimate, reevaluate, regauge, rejudge, relevy, remeasure, rerank, retax, revalue
ASSOCIATED CONCEPTS: reassessed tax

REASSIGN, verb   assign again, change, commit again, consign again, deal again, portion out again, reallocate, reallot, reappoint, reappropriate, recommission, redistribute, redivide, reengage, reinstall, rezone, transfer
ASSOCIATED CONCEPTS: reassign a case

REASSURE, verb   affirm, approve, assure again, bolster up, buoy up, certify, cheer, comfort, confirm, *confirmare,* convince, dismiss doubt, ease, embolden, encourage, enhearten, give confidence, give hope, guarantee, hearten, help, hold out hope, infuse courage, inspire, inspirit, nerve, rally, *recreare,* refresh, remove doubt, remove fear, restore courage to, restore to assurance, restore to confidence, sanction, satisfy, solace, strengthen, support, sustain, uphold, uplift, warrant

REBATE, noun   allowance, cut, decrease, deduction, diminution, discount, lessening of price, markdown, reduction, refund, reimbursement, repayment

REBATE, verb   allow, allow as a discount, cut, deduct, diminish, discount, give back, lessen, make allowance, mark down, offer a discount, pare, pay back, reduce, refund, reimburse, render, repay, replace, restore, return, slash, strike off, subtract, take off

REBEL, verb arise, be disloyal, be insubordinate, be treasonable, betray, break with, *concitare,* defy, denounce, dethrone, disobey, insurrect, mutiny, oppose, overthrow, recalcitrate, refuse to conform, refuse to support, renounce, resist, resist lawful authority, revolt, revolutionize, riot, rise, rise in arms, *seditionem,* strike, take up arms, tergiversate, turn against, undermine

REBELLION, noun breach of orders, contumacy, defiance, disobedience, indiscipline, insubordination, insurgence, insurgency, insurrection, lack of discipline, lese majesty, *motus,* mutiny, opposition, outbreak, overthrow, overturn, resistance, resistance movement, revolt, revolution, riot, rising, *seditio,* sedition, strike, subversion, treason, upheaval, uprising, upset, violation

REBUFF, noun admonition, censure, check, chiding, cold shoulder, condemnation, counteraction, criticism, defeat, defiance, disapproval, discouragement, discourtesy, disregard, flat refusal, insult, opposition, peremptory refusal, rebuke, recoil, refusal, rejection, renouncement, renunciation, reprimand, reproach, reproof, repudiation, *repulsa,* repulse, resistance, rudeness, scolding, slight, snub, spurn

REBUFF, verb affront, brush aside, cast aside, check, chide, decline, despise, disallow, discard, disdain, dismiss, disown, disregard, drive back, ignore, insult, jilt, keep at a distance, neglect, rebuke, refuse, *reicere,* reject, renounce, repel, *repellere,* reprobate, reprove, repudiate, repulse, resist, scorn, send away, set aside, slight, snub, spurn, turn away

REBUKE, verb accuse, admonish, animadvert on, berate, blame, bring to book, call down, call to account, call to task, castigate, censure, charge, chastise, chide, correct, criminate, criticize, disapprove, exprobrate, find fault with, judge, lecture, objurgate, rate, remonstrate with, reprehend, *reprehendere,* reprimand, reproach, reprove, revile, scold, slate, take to task, tax, upbraid, *vituperare, vituperate*

REBUT, verb answer, argue, argue against, conflict, confute, contradict, contravene, controvert, countercharge, counterclaim, deny, disagree, disprove, dispute, explode, join issue, negate, negative, oppose, parry, prove false, rebuff, *redarguere,* refute, rejoin, *repellere,* reply, repudiate, respond, retaliate, retort, surrebut, surrejoin, take a stand against
ASSOCIATED CONCEPTS: rebut a presumption, rebut an argument

REBUTTAL, noun answer, arguments against the opposition, arguments in opposition, countercharges, defense, denials, pleading, refutation, reply, repudiation, reputation, response, retort, statement made in response
ASSOCIATED CONCEPTS: rebuttal evidence, rebuttal witness, rebutter, surrebuttal

RECALCITRANT, adjective balky, callous, contrary, contumacious, defiant, disobedient, fractious, hardened, headstrong, immovable, insubordinate, intractable, mulish, mutinous, noncooperative, obstinate, obstreperous, opposing, oppugnant, pervicacious, rebellious, recusant, refractory, relentless, renitent, resistant, resistive, restive, stubborn, uncompliant, uncomplying, uncontrollable, uncooperative, ungovernable, unmanageable, unrelenting, unsubmissive, unwilling, unyielding, willful
ASSOCIATED CONCEPTS: recalcitrant witness

RECALL *(Call back),* **verb** abolish, abrogate, annul, cancel, disannul, dismiss, disqualify, invalidate, nullify, reanimate, reassemble, reconvene, repudiate, rescind, resuscitate, revive, revivify, *revocare,* revoke, summon back, take back, unsay, void, withdraw

RECALL *(Remember),* **verb** be reminded of, call up, commemorate, conjure up, dwell upon, evoke, fix in the mind, have memories of, keep in mind, know again, know by heart, look back upon, memorialize, memorize, place, recognize, recollect, *recordari,* recover knowledge of, refresh one's memory, relive, reminisce, retain, retrace, retrospect, review, revive, see in retrospect, summon up, think back to

RECANT, verb abjure, abrogate, annul, cancel, contradict, countermand, disaffirm, disannul, disavow, disclaim, disenact, disown, negate, nullify, recall, *recantare,* renounce, repudiate, rescind, retract, *retractare,* reverse, revoke, take back, tergiversate, unsay, vacate, void, withdraw
ASSOCIATED CONCEPTS: recant a confession, recant prior testimony

RECAPITULATE, verb *commemorare,* enumerate, give a summary of, go over, ingeminate, paraphrase, recite, recount, *referre,* reiterate, relate, repeat, rephrase, restate, retell, retrospect, reutter, review, reword, run over, say again, sum up, summarize, tell again

RECEIPT *(Act of receiving),* **noun** acceptance, *acceptio,* accession, acquirement, acquisition, admittance, assumption, attainment, gain, income, intake, obtainment, possession, reception, recipience
ASSOCIATED CONCEPTS: receipt of dividend, receipt of letters
FOREIGN PHRASES: **Quicquid recipitur, recipitur secundum modum recipientis.** Whatever is received is received in accordance with the intention of the recipient.

RECEIPT *(Proof of receiving),* **noun** acknowledgment of payment, acquittance, *apocha,* certificate of deposit, discharge, proof of delivery, proof of payment, quittance, release, signed notice, slip, stub, voucher
ASSOCIATED CONCEPTS: receipt in full, receipt of goods, receipt of letters, receipt of message, receipt of payment, rent receipt, warehouse receipt

RECEIPT *(Voucher),* **noun** assumption, bill, payment, reimbursement

RECEIVABLE, adjective due, due to be paid, in arrears, mature, outstanding, owed, owing, payable, redeemable, unpaid

RECEIVE *(Acquire),* **verb** accept, *accipere,* assume, be given, *capere,* catch, collect, come by, derive, draw, earn, gain, gather, get, inherit, make, obtain, pick up, pocket, procure, realize, reap, secure, seize, take, take in, take possession, win
ASSOCIATED CONCEPTS: contructively received, receive process, receive stolen property

RECEIVE *(Permit to enter),* **verb** absorb, accept, admit, adopt, allow, allow entrance, approve, embrace, entertain, give entrance, grant asylum, include, induct, initiate, install, let in, let through, permit, shelter, show in, take in, tolerate, usher in
ASSOCIATED CONCEPTS: receive into evidence, receive into the record

RECEIVER, *noun*   accepter, assignee, benefactor, beneficiary, collector, consignee, depositary, fence, grantee, holder, receptacle, *receptor,* recipient, trustee
ASSOCIATED CONCEPTS: ancillary receiver, appointment of a receiver, equitable receiver, general receiver, joint receivers, legal receiver, principal receiver, provisional receiver, receiver in bankruptcy, receiver of stolen property, receivership, statutory receiver, temporary receiver

RECENT, *adjective*   fresh, lately, new, newly arrived, not long past, novel, of recent occurrence, up-to-date
ASSOCIATED CONCEPTS: in recent memory, recent possession, recently

RECEPTIVE, *adjective*   accessible, admissive, admitting, affectible, alert, amenable, aware, broad-minded, cognitive, compassionate, comprehending, conscious, cordial, disposed, favorable, flexible, friendly, gracious, hospitable, impartial, impressible, impressionable, inclined, influenceable, interested, keen, movable, observant, open, open-minded, open to suggestion, perceptive, persuadable, reasonable, receiving, recipient, responsive, sensitive, susceptible, sympathetic, tolerant, tractable, unbiased, understanding, unjaundiced, unprejudiced, unswayed, welcoming, willing

RECESS, *noun*   break, cessation, halt, hiatus, interim, interlude, intermission, interruption, interval, intervening period, lull, pause, repose, respite, rest, spell, stop, stoppage, time out, vacation, withdrawal

RECESS, *verb*   adjourn, break, break up, dissolve, halt, hesitate, intermit, interrupt, lay off, pause, postpone, prorogue, relax, rest, retire, stop, suspend, take a recess, take a rest, take time out, vacation, withdraw
ASSOCIATED CONCEPTS: recess the court

RECIDIVATE, *verb*   backslide, degenerate, deteriorate, relapse, regress, retrograde, slip back

RECIDIVISM, *noun*   backsliding, degeneration, deterioration, habitual relapse into crime, recreancy, regression, relapse, repeated relapse into crime, retrogradation, retrogression, reversion

RECIDIVIST, *noun*   convict, criminal, delinquent, guilty person, habitual criminal, hardened offender, lawbreaker, malefactor, malfeasant, malfeasor, offender, outlaw, repeat offender, reprobate, transgressor, wrongdoer

RECIPIENT, *noun*   accepter, assignee, beneficiary, consignee, devisee, donee, grantee, heir, holder, inheritor, legatee, liquidator, object, payee, receiver, repository, transferee

RECIPROCAL, *adjective*   alternating, bilateral, common, commutual, complemental, complementary, contingent, correlative, corresponding, give and take, interchangeable, interconnected, interdependent, interrelated, mutual, *mutuus,* parallel, reciprocative, requited, responded to, retaliative, retaliatory, retributive, returned, two-sided
ASSOCIATED CONCEPTS: reciprocal agreements, reciprocal promises, reciprocal wills

RECIPROCATE, *verb*   act interchangeably, alternate, cooperate, exchange, follow successively, give and take, give in return, *inter se dare,* interchange, pay back, perform by turns, perform responsively, recompense, refund, reimburse, repay, requite, respond, retaliate, return, share, switch, take a turn, trade

RECIPROCITY, *noun*   concord, cooperation, correspondence, exchange, give and take, interchange, interplay, mutuality, reciprocality, reciprocalness, reciprocation, return, *vicissitudo*
ASSOCIATED CONCEPTS: reciprocity of enforcement of laws between states

RECITAL, *noun*   account, depiction, description, detailed statement, discourse, dissertation, *enumeratio,* explanation, exposition, graphic account, iteration, lecture, *narratio,* narration, narrative, oration, reaffirmation, reassertion, recapitulation, recitation, recountal, recounting, reiteration, relation, rendition, report, representation, restatement, retelling, review, statement, story, summary, summing up, telling
ASSOCIATED CONCEPTS: recital in a deed, recital of consideration

RECITE, *verb*   address, articulate, chant, communicate, declaim, delineate, deliver, detail, *dicere,* discourse, divulge, dramatize, enact, *enumerare,* enumerate, *exponere,* express, give a verbal account, give expression, hold forth, interpret, lecture, list, make a speech, mouth, narrate, orate, parrot, perform, portray, preach, prelect, present, pronounce, quote, recapitulate, recount, reel off, rehearse, reiterate, relate, render, repeat, repeat by rote, repeat from memory, report, retell, say by heart, set forth, soliloquize, speak, spout, state, talk, tell, utter, voice

RECKLESS, *adjective*   careless, disregardful, foolhardy, foolish, hasty, heedless, impetuous, improvident, imprudent, impulsive, inattentive, incautious, *incautus,* inconsiderate, *inconsideratus,* indifferent, indiscreet, *injudicious,* insensible, irrational, irresponsible, mindless, neglectful, *neglegens,* negligent, overconfident, overhasty, precipitate, temerous, thoughtless, unaware, uncircumspect, unconcerned, unheeding, unmindful, unobservant, unthinking, unwary, unwatchful, unwise, wanton, wild, without caution, without prudence
ASSOCIATED CONCEPTS: reckless abandon, reckless conduct, reckless disregard, reckless driving, reckless endangerment, reckless indifference

RECLAIM, *verb*   appropriate, develop, get back, reacquire, rebuild, recall, recover, redeem, reestablish, regain, regenerate, reinstate, reoccupy, replevin, replevy, repossess, retake, retrieve
ASSOCIATED CONCEPTS: reclaim land

RECLASSIFICATION, *noun*   change, changed ordering of priorities, changed priorities, reallocation, reallotment, reanalysis, reapportionment, rearrangement, reassignment, reassorting, reassortment, reconstitution, redistributing, redistribution, reestablishment, regradation, regrouping, reordering, reorganization, retabulating
ASSOCIATED CONCEPTS: reclassification of job titles

RECOGNITION, *noun*   acceptance, acknowledgment, admission, apperception, appreciation, approval, attention, audition, avowal, award, awareness, citation, cognition, cognizance, commemoration, comprehension, consciousness, consideration, detection, diagnosis, discovery, distinguishment, divination, espial, finding, floor, gratitude, identification, insight, insite, knowledge, memory, nod, notice, perception, prize, realization, recall, recollection, regard, remembrance, reward, thanks, tribute
ASSOCIATED CONCEPTS: identification of a defendent

RECOGNIZANCE, *noun*   acknowledgment, assurance, avowal, bond, commitment, guaranty, obligation, promise, security, *sponsio,* surety, warranty

RECOGNIZE *(Acknowledge),* **verb**   accept, admit, allow, appreciate, avow, cite, commemorate, concede, confess, consent, defer to, dignify, exalt, give the floor to, give the nod to, grant, greet, honor, *noscere,* own, permit, realize, salute, suffer, tolerate, yield to

RECOGNIZE *(Perceive),* **verb**   *agnoscere,* apprehend, ascertain, be aware of, be familiar with, call to mind, catch sight of, *cognoscere,* comprehend, conceive, descry, diagnose, discern, discover, distinguish, espy, identify, know, make out, mark, *noscitare,* notice, place, recall, recollect, recover knowledge, reidentify, remember, retain the impression of, see, sight, spy, understand, verify, view

RECOLLECT, **verb**   be reminded of, bring to mind, call to mind, *commeminisse,* conjure up, go back, know again, look back upon, place, recall, *recognize, recordari,* relive, remember, reminisce, *reminisci,* renew, retrospect, review, revive, summon up, think of

RECOLLECTION, *noun*   afterthought, consciousness, contemplation of the past, memoir, *memoria,* memory, mental image, mental picture, mindfulness, recall, recognition, *recordatio,* remembrance, reminiscence, retrospection
ASSOCIATED CONCEPTS: past recollection recorded, present recollection revived

RECOMMEND, **verb**   acclaim, advance, advise, advocate, applaud, approbate, approve, back, be satisfied with, celebrate, commend, *commendare,* compliment, counsel, countenance, direct, endorse, esteem, exalt, exhort, extol, favor, give credit, glorify, guarantee, guide, instruct, laud, lend approval, lend support, make desirable, make preferable, move, persuade, praise, prescribe, present as worthy, prize, *probare,* promote, prompt, propose, ratify, sanction, second, speak highly of, speak well of, stand by, suggest, support, think highly of, uphold, urge, value, vouch for

RECOMMENDATION, *noun*   admonition, advice, advocacy, advocation, approbation, approval, boost, celebration, certificate, *commendatio,* commendation, counsel, credential, encouragement, endorsement, esteem, exhortation, good opinion, guidance, injunction, instruction, judgment, *laudatio,* laudation, motion, opinion, praise, precept, prescription, proposal, proposition, reference, sanction, suggestion, support, testimonial, tip, tribute
FOREIGN PHRASES: Simplex commendatio non obligat. A mere recommendation is not binding. **Liberum est cuique apud se explorare an expediat sibi consilium.** Everyone is free to determine for himself whether a recommendation is advantageous to his interests.

RECOMMIT, **verb**   call back, commit again, commit anew, give back, order back, refer back, remand, remit, return, send back

RECOMPENSE, *noun*   amends, compensation, consideration, damages, defrayment, deserts, earnings, emolument, fee, gratuity, guerdon, income, indemnification, indemnity, meed, *merces,* payment, *praemium,* price, quittance, recoupment, recovery, redress, reimbursement, *remuneratio,* remuneration, reparation, repayment, requital, requitement, restitution, return, reward, salary, satisfaction, settlement, solatium, substitution, wage

RECONCILE, **verb**   accustom, adapt, adjust, appease, arbitrate, bring into harmony, bring to acquiescence, bring to terms, bring together, conciliate, dictate peace, harmonize, heal the breach, intercede, make compatible, make consistent, make contented, make peace, make up, mediate, mend, mollify, negotiate, pacify, placate, propitiate, render concordant, resign, restore harmony, restore to friendship, reunite, settle, unite, win over

RECONCILIATION, *noun*   accord, adjustment, agreement, amnesty, appeasement, arbitration, conciliation, concord, concordance, forgiveness, harmony, improved relations, mediation, mollification, mutual forgiveness, pacification, peace, peacemaking, propitiation, rapprochement, reconcilement, restoration of harmony, reunion, settlement, understanding, union
ASSOCIATED CONCEPTS: reconciliation of contradictory clauses

RECONDITE, *adjective*   abstract, abstruse, arcane, cabalistic, complex, complicated, concealed, convoluted, covert, crabbed, cryptic, cryptical, dark, deep, difficult, elusive, enigmatic, esoteric, *exquisitus,* hidden, impenetrable, imperspicuous, intricate, involved, knotty, little-known, mysterious, mystic, mystical, nebulous, obscure, occult, orphic, perdu, perplexing, profound, puzzling, *reconditus,* secret, subtle, tangled, transcendental, unfamiliar, unintelligible

RECONFIRM, **verb**   make certain, make sure again, reacknowledge, reaffirm, reapprove, reauthenticate, recertify, recheck, reendorse, reenforce, reestablish, resanction, resubstantiate, revalidate, verify again

RECONSIDER, **verb**   amend, consider again, consult again, *denuo,* go over, have second thoughts, redeliberate, reevaluate, reexamine, reflect again, rehear, rejudge, reponder, *reputare,* rethink, retry, review, revise one's thoughts, reweigh, rework, think better of, think over
ASSOCIATED CONCEPTS: reconsider a judicial decision

RECONSTITUTE, **verb**   bring back, make over, put back, reactivate, rebuild, recondition, reconstruct, reconvert, redo, reestablish, reform, regenerate, reintegrate, remake, remodel, remold, renew, renovate, reorganize, replace, restore

RECONSTRUCT, **verb**   duplicate, make over, modernize, rearrange, rebuild, recast, reclaim, recompose, recondition, reconstitute, recreate, redo, reestablish, refashion, *reficere,* reform, refresh, refurbish, regenerate, rehabilitate, remake, remodel, remold, renew, renovate, reorganize, *restituere,* restore, revamp, rework
ASSOCIATED CONCEPTS: reconstruct the scene of a crime

RECONVERSION, *noun*   change, change over, demilitarization, disarmament, palingenesis, passage, readjustment, rebirth, redintegration, reestablishment, regenerateness, regeneration, regenesis, rehabilitation, renaissance, reorganization, restoration, retrogression, retroversion, return, reversal, reversion, shift, transformation, transit, transition

RECORD, *noun*   account, affidavit, annal, archive, attestation, catalogue, certificate, chronicle, contract, *diurna,* docket, documentation, dossier, entry, evidence, file, history, journal, list, log, memorandum, minute, note, proceedings, recording, register, roll, roster, transcript, transcription, *urbana,* written material
ASSOCIATED CONCEPTS: courts of record, judicial record, liens of record, matter of record, public record, record of convictions, record of encumbrances, Recording Acts

RECORD, **verb**   book, calendar, catalogue, chronicle, copy, docket, document, enroll, enter, file, formalize, historify,

historize, *in tabulas referre,* index, inscribe, insert, jot down, journalize, keep accounts, list, log, make a memorandum, make a note, make an entry, mark, note, *perscribere,* post, preserve, put in writing, put on paper, put on record, register, report, set down, tabulate, take down, take minutes, tally, write, write down
ASSOCIATED CONCEPTS: record a deed, record a lien, record a mortgage

RECORDATION, *noun* documentation instrument, filing, filing with copyright office
ASSOCIATED CONCEPTS: registration

RECOUNT, *verb* articulate, *commemorare,* communicate, convey, delineate, depict, describe, detail, divulge, *enarrare,* give an account, give the facts, give the particulars, hold forth, impart, iterate, narrate, particularize, picture, portray, recapitulate, recite, *referre,* reiterate, relate, render, repeat, report, retail, retell, reword, set forth, state, summarize, talk, tell, tell in detail, unfold

RECOUP *(Regain),* ***verb*** gain anew, get back, reacquire, reassume, recapture, reclaim, recover, redeem, reobtain, replace, replevin, replevy, repossess, retake, retrieve, take back, win back

RECOUP *(Reimburse),* ***verb*** compensate, give back, indemnify, make amends, make good, make reparations, make restitution, make up for, pay, pay back, quit, recompense, refund, remunerate, repay, replace, requite, restitute, restore, return, satisfy, settle

RECOURSE, *noun* avail, benefit, *confugere,* corrective device, corrective measure, device, disposal, legal redress, means, redress, remedy, resource, *se applicare, se conferre*
FOREIGN PHRASES: *Electa una via, non datur recursus ad alteram.* He who has chosen one course cannot have recourse to another.

RECOVER, *verb* achieve, acquire, attain, carry back, confer again, devolve again, *emergere,* gain anew, gain possession, get back, get by judgment, grant again, obtain, obtain by course of law, pass on again, procure, reacquire, realize, reassign, recapture, rechannel, reclaim, recoup, recuperare, redeem, regain, reobtain, *reparare,* replevy, repossess, resell, retake, retransmit, retrieve, salvage, secure, transfer again, transfer back, transport back, win back

RECOVERY *(Award),* ***noun*** compensation, damages, defrayal, discharge, financial remuneration, indemnification, indemnity, reckoning, reclamation, recompense, recoupment, redress, remittal, remuneration, reparation, repayment, restitution, satisfaction
ASSOCIATED CONCEPTS: primary recovery, recovery from an adversary
FOREIGN PHRASES: *Frustra agit qui judicium prosequi nequit cum effectu.* He sues vainly who cannot prosecute his judgment with effect. ***Qui melius probat melius habet.*** He who proves most recovers most.

RECOVERY *(Repossession),* ***noun*** acquisition, *evictio,* obtainment, procuration, procurement, recapture, reclamation, recouping, redemption, regaining, regainment, replevin, replevy, rescue, restoration, retrieval, return, reversion, revindication, salvage, trover
ASSOCIATED CONCEPTS: recovery of chattels

RECREANT, *adjective* afraid, apostate, apostatic, apostatical, base, betraying, caitiff, conniving, corrupt, cowardly, cowering, craven, dastardly, deceitful, derelict, designing, disaffected, disgraceful, dishonest, dishonorable, disloyal, dissembling, double-dealing, fainthearted, faithless, false, falsehearted, fearful, frightened, guileful, hesitant, inglorious, insidious, knavish, lilylivered, perfidious, pigeonhearted, poltroon, pusillanimous, renegade, reprobate, scheming, sham, skulking, sneaking, spiritless, timid, timorous, traitorous, treacherous, treasonable, two-faced, unconscienced, uncourageous, undependable, unfaithful, unmanly, unreliable, unscrupulous, untrue, untrustworthy, villainous, without honor, yellow

RECREATE, *verb* create anew, duplicate, fascimile, heal, invigorate, make over, mend, reanimate, rebuild, recast, reconstruct, redo, reestablish, refashion, refocillate, reform, refresh, regenerate, rehabilitate, rejuvenate, remake, remodel, renew, *renovare,* renovate, reorganize, reproduce, restore, revamp, revive

RECRIMINATE, *verb* accuse, bring a countercharge, come back at, countercharge, get even with, give in kind, have revenge, hit back, lash back, match, pay back, requite, retaliate, retort, retort a charge, return an accusation, return the charge, shift the blame, strike back, turn on, turn the tables on

RECRUDESCENCE, *noun* backsliding, eruption, fresh outbreak, lapse, new outbreak, reactivation, reanimation, reappearance, recidivation, recrudescency, recurrence, regression, reinfection, relapse, renewal, resumption, resurgence, return, reversal, reverse, reversion, revival, revivification, reviviscence, reviviscency

RECRUIT, *verb* add, augment, call up, collect, *conscribere,* conscript, draft, employ, enlarge, enlist, enroll, find manpower, gain, gather, increase, induct, muster, obtain, provide, raise, raise troops, reinvigorate, replenish, select, sign up, strengthen, supply, swell the ranks, take in

RECTIFY, *verb* adjust, alter, ameliorate, amend, better, correct, *corrigere,* cure, emend, *emendare,* emendate, improve, make corrections, make right, meliorate, mend, perfect, put to rights, redress, reform, rehabilitate, remedy, renovate, repair, restore, revise, right, set right, set to rights, straighten, untangle

RECTITUDE, *noun* character, conscientiousness, correctness, equity, fairness, faithfulness, faultlessness, fidelity, goodness, honesty, honor, honorableness, impartiality, impeccability, *integritas,* integrity, justice, justness, loyalty, merit, morality, principle, *probitas,* probity, propriety, purity, reputability, responsibility, right, righteousness, scrupulousness, straight course, straightforwardness, straightness, trustworthiness, uncorruptibility, uprightness, upstandingness, veracity, virtue, worthiness

RECUR, *verb* be persistent, come again, come back, continue, crop up again, happen again, haunt, intermit, keep on, occur again, persevere, persist, reappear, recrudesce, renew, reoccur, repeat, resume, return, revert

RECUSANT, *adjective* abjuratory, antagonistic, apostate, contrary, contumacious, differing, disagreeing, discordant, disobedient, dissentient, dissenting, dissident, heretic, heterodox, hostile, iconoclastic, impenitent, inflexible, inimical, insubordinate, negative, nonconformist, nonjuring, nonobservant, obdurate, obstinate, oppugnant, protestant, rebellious, recalcitrant, resistant, restive, schismatic, uncompliant, unconformable, unconforming, unconsenting, unfriendly, unrepentant, unresigned, unsubmissive, unwilling

REDACT, verb blot out, censor, cut out, delete, edit, edit out, erase, excise, expunge, extirpate, make deletions, redraft, revamp, rework, rewrite, strike out, work over
ASSOCIATED CONCEPTS: censorship, redact testimony

REDEEM (Repurchase), **verb** buy back, deliver, emancipate, get back, liberate, obtain, ransom, recall, recapture, reclaim, recoup, recover, regain, release, replevin, replevy, repossess, rescue, retrieve
ASSOCIATED CONCEPTS: right to redeem

REDEEM (Satisfy debts), **verb** absolve, atone, compensate, do penance, expiate, give satisfaction, make amends, make up for, offset bad debts, propitiate, reform, satisfy, set straight, shrive, turn from sin

REDEMPTION, noun deliverance, indemnification, reclamation, recovery, release, reparation, replevin, repossession, repurchase, rescue, restoration, retrieval, return, salvation
ASSOCIATED CONCEPTS: right of redemption

REDIRECT, verb change course, change direction, direct again, forward, mail again, post on, readdress, remail, reship, send forward, send on, transmit

REDISTRIBUTE, verb allot again, deal out again, dole out again, give out again, hand out again, parcel out again, readminister, reallot, reapportion, rearrange, reassign, reassort, reclass, reclassify, redivide, regroup, reissue, repartition, replace

REDOUND, verb accrue, arise, cause, conduce, contribute, effect, ensue, flow from, follow, germinate from, influence, lead, proceed, *redundare*, result, spring, sprout from, yield

REDRESS, verb adjust, aid, allay, alleviate, appease, atone, change, *compensare*, compensate, correct, cure, ease, expiate, fix, heal, help, improve, make amends, make good, make reparation, make up for, mend, pacify, palliate, propitiate, put right, readjust, rectify, relieve, remedy, repair, *restituere*, restore, right, satisfy, set right
ASSOCIATED CONCEPTS: legal redress

REDUCE, verb abate, abbreviate, abridge, attenuate, bring low, compact, compress, condense, contract, curtail, cut down, decimate, decrease, demean, diminish, disgrace, downgrade, humble, *imminuere*, lessen, lower, make less, make smaller, minimize, narrow, shorten, shrink, thin
ASSOCIATED CONCEPTS: reduce a sentence, reduce damages

REDUCED, adjective attenuated, brief, contracted, cut, decreased, deficient, depressed, diluted, diminished, inferior, less, lesser, lowered, minimal, minor, nominal, shorter, slashed, smaller, thinned
ASSOCIATED CONCEPTS: reduced charge, reduced sentence

REDUNDANCY, noun duplication, excess, excessiveness, immoderation, inordinacy, inordinate amount, needlessness, nimiety, overplus, oversupply, pleonasm, recurrence, redundance, *redundantia*, reiteration, repetition, restatement, retelling, superabundance, superfluity, surplus, tautology

REDUNDANT, adjective excessive, inordinate, needless, otiose, overmuch, periphrastic, pleonastic, repetitive, repititious, superabundant, superfluous, supernumerary, *supervacaneus*, surplus, tautologic, tautological, uncalled-for, undue, unnecessary, unrequired, useless, verbose, wordy

REEXAMINE, verb check upon again, cross-examine, cross-question, go back over, reanalyze, recheck, reconsider, reinquire, reinvestigate, reprobe, requestion, rescrutinize, restudy, retrace, review

REFER (Direct attention), **verb** adduce, allude, appertain, apply, assign, bear upon, cite, concern, connect, connote, denote, hint at, indicate, mention, perstringere, pertain, point, quote, relate, signify, suggest, touch on

REFER (Send for action), **verb** ask help of, assign, call in, call on, consign, consult, deliver, entrust, recommend, *referre*, seek advice, send, submit, transfer

REFEREE, noun adjudicator, arbiter, arbitrator, compromiser, conciliator, interceder, intercessor, intermediary, intermediate, intermediator, internuncio, intervener, judge, judicator, mediator, moderator, peacemaker, propitiator, reconciler, settler, umpire
ASSOCIATED CONCEPTS: appointment of referee, referee in bankruptcy, referee's findings, special referee, trial before referee

REFERENCE (Allusion), **noun** attribution, clue, connotation, cue, hint, implication, implied indication, imputation, incidental mention, indication, indirect implication, inference, inkling, innuendo, insinuation, intimation, mention, ratio, referment, subtle communication, suggestion

REFERENCE (Citation), **noun** ascription, assignation, assignment, authority, citing, connecting, credit, data, derivation from, designation, documentation, enumeration, indicating, mention, mentioning, pointing out, quotation, quoted passage, quoting, recitation, referment, referral, relating, source, source material, substantiation
ASSOCIATED CONCEPTS: incorporation by reference
FOREIGN PHRASES: *Verba relata hoc maxime operantur per referentiam, ut in eis inesse videntur.* Words incorporated by reference have as great an effect through reference, as they are deemed to be inserted.

REFERENCE (Recommendation), **noun** affirmation, assurance, attestation, attesting declaration, authenticated confirmation, averment, avouchment, avowal, avowance, certificate of character, certification, commendation, confirmation, declaration, endorsement, laudation, letter in support, letter of introduction, letter of recommendation, substantiation, testification, testimony, validification, verification, voucher, vouching, witnessing

REFERENDUM, noun ballot, decision, determination, discretion, election, expression of choice, mandate, plebiscite, poll, popular choice, popular decision, popular vote, preference, say, selection, voice, vote

REFERRAL, noun allusion, implication, inference, innuendo, insinuation, making reference, mention, reference, referment

REFINANCE, verb back again, contribute to again, finance again, fund again, invest in again, lend to again, loan to again, provide capital again, provide funds for again, reinvest, sponsor again, subsidize again, support again, underwrite again

REFINE, *verb* advance, amend, better, clarify, cleanse, clear, correct, cultivate, develop, edit, elaborate, elevate, emend, enhance, filter, filtrate, improve, improve upon, make improvements, meliorate, modify, perfect, polish, purify, rectify, sanitize, sensitize, sharpen, soften, strain, temper, uplift

REFLECT *(Mirror), verb* bounce back, cast back, copy, ditto, emulate, give back, give forth, imitate, *ostendere,* rebound, repeat, reproduce, send back, show an image, simulate, throw back

REFLECT *(Ponder), verb* analyze, brood over, cerebrate, *cogitare,* cogitate, commune with oneself, conceive, concentrate, consider, *considerare,* contemplate, deduce, deliberate, dream, dwell upon, excogitate, give thought to, meditate, mull over, muse, pore over, puzzle over, reason, revolve in the mind, ruminate, speculate, study, theorize, think, turn over, weigh, wonder

REFLECTION *(Image), noun* counterpart, double, duplicate, echo, *imago,* impression, likeness, semblance, specter

REFLECTION *(Thought), noun* absorption, analysis, cerebration, *cogitatio,* cogitation, concentration, *consideratio,* consideration, contemplation, deliberation, excogitation, exercise of the intellect, intellection, meditation, mentation, musing, pondering, *ratio,* reasoning, reverie, rumination, self-communing, self-counsel, speculation, study, thinking, weighing
FOREIGN PHRASES: ***Nemo cogitationis poenam patitur.*** No one suffers punishment on account of his thoughts.

REFLECTIVE, *adjective* abstruse, astute, complicated, deep, erudite, esoteric, intellectual, intellectually profound, penetrating, perceptive, philosophical, profound, recondite, sagacious, sage, scholarly, thoughtful, wise
ASSOCIATED CONCEPTS: deep constituted interpretation

REFORM, *noun* advancement, alteration, amelioration, amendment, betterment, change, *correctio,* correction, development, elevation, *emendatio,* enhancement, enrichment, improvement, innovation, melioration, progress, progression, progressivism, recast, reclamation, reconstitution, reconstruction, recovery, recreation, rectification, refinement, reformation, regeneration, remaking, renewal, renovation, repair, revision

REFORM, *verb* ameliorate, amend, better, change, convert, correct, *corrigere,* cure, emend, enhance, fix, form anew, improve, make better, make over, meliorate, mend, modify, rearrange, recast, reclaim, reconstitute, reconstruct, rectify, redeem, redo, redress, reestablish, refashion, refine, regenerate, rehabilitate, remake, remedy, remodel, renew, renovate, reorganize, repair, repent, reshape, restore, revise, revolutionize, rework, set straight, uplift
ASSOCIATED CONCEPTS: reform a contract, reform a deed, reform a lease, reform a will, reform an instrument

REFORMATORY, *noun* bridewell, correction facility, house of correction, house of detention, jail, penal institution, penitentiary, prison, reform school

REFRAIN, *verb* abstain, avoid, be temperate, break off, cease, check, contain oneself, curb oneself, decline, desist, discontinue, dispense with, do without, eschew, evade, exercise self-control, forbear, forestall, forgo, forsake, halt, have nothing to do with, hold back, keep from, leave off, refuse, renounce, *se abstinere, se continere,* shun, stop, swear off, take no part in, waive, withdraw, withhold

REFUGE, *noun* ark, asylum, citadel, covert, coverture, harbor, haven, hiding place, lee, *perfugium,* place of protection, place of safety, protection, *receptaculum, refugium,* resort, retreat, safe place, safety, sanctuary, security, shelter, stronghold
ASSOCIATED CONCEPTS: flight
FOREIGN PHRASES: ***Domus sua cuique est tutissimum refugium.*** Everyone's home is his safest refuge. ***Debet sua cuique domus esse perfugium tut issimum.*** Everyman's home should be a perfectly safe refuge.

REFUND, *noun* compensation, cut, discount, indemnification, money back, payment for expenses, rebate, recompense, recoupment, reduction, refundment, reimbursement, repayment, replacement, restitution, return, satisfaction, settlement

REFUND, *verb* adjust, compensate, *dissolvere,* give back, honor a claim, indemnify, make amends, make compensation, make good, make restitution, pay back, rebate, recompense, *reddere,* redeem, reimburse, repay, replace, requite, restore, return, satisfy, settle, square

REFUSAL, *noun* abjuration, abnegation, ban, debarment, declination, declinature, defiance, denial, disallowance, disapprobation, disapproval, disavowal, disclaimer, discountenance, enjoinment, exclusion, incompliance, interdiction, negation, negative answer, nonacceptance, noncompliance, nonconsent, prohibition, proscription, rebuff, *recusatio,* regrets, rejection, renouncement, renunciation, repudiation, repulse, resistance, unwillingness, veto
ASSOCIATED CONCEPTS: refusal to answer, refusal to bargain, refusal to proceed, refusal to testify, right of first refusal
FOREIGN PHRASES: ***Reprobata pecunia liberat solventem.*** Money refused releases the debtor.

REFUSE, *verb* abjure, abnegate, abstain, balk, bar, be obstinate, be unwilling, beg to be excused, cast aside, debar, decline, demur, deny, disaccord with, disallow, disapprove, disavow, disclaim, discountenance, discredit, dismiss, disown, dispense with, dissent, exclude, forswear, grudge, hesitate, hold back, negative, object to, oppose, pass up, prohibit, protest, rebuff, recoil, regret, reject, renege, renounce, repel, repudiate, resist, revoke, scruple, send regrets, shirk, shun, shy at, spurn, stick at, stickle, traverse, turn down, turn from, veto, withdraw, withhold consent

REFUTE, *verb* abnegate, belie, cancel, confute, contend, contradict, contravene, controvert, crush, debate, defeat, demolish, deny, destroy, disaffirm, disclaim, discredit, dispose of, disprove, explode, falsify, gainsay, impugn, invalidate, negate, oppose, oppugn, overthrow, parry, prove false, quash, rebut, *redarguere, refellere,* repel, repudiate, retort, squelch, tear down, traverse

REGARD *(Attention), noun* advertence, advertency, alertness, application, attentiveness, care, concentration, concern, consideration, examination, heed, heedfulness, intentness, interest, mindfulness, notice, observation, scrutiny, vigilance, watch, watchfulness

REGARD *(Esteem), noun* admiration, affection, appreciation, approbation, approval, attachment, awe, celebrity, consideration, credit, deference, devotion, distinction, eminence, estimation, fame, famousness, favor, fondness, good name, honor, interest, judgment, liking, loyalty, note, opinion, reputability, reputation, repute, respect, *respectus,* reverence, *studium,* valuation, value, veneration

REGARD *(Hold in esteem)*, **verb**   admire, adore, appreciate, approve, be fond of, be impressed, be in awe, care for, cherish, defer to, esteem, exalt, extol, glorify, have a liking for, have regard for, hold a high opinion of, hold dear, hold in affection, hold in regard, honor, idolize, look up to, pay homage to, pay tribute, praise, prize, respect, respicere, revere, reverence, think highly of, think well of, treasure, value, venerate, worship

REGARD *(Pay attention)*, **verb**   advert to, attend, be attentive, be aware of, be conscious of, be mindful, bear in mind, behold, consider, contemplate, deem, *ducere*, gaze, give heed to, heed, keep in sight, look, look at, look upon, mark, mind, note, notice, *observare*, observe, perceive, peruse, scan, scrutinize, see, survey, take cognizance of, take notice, think about, view, watch, witness
ASSOCIATED CONCEPTS: due regard

REGARDLESS, **adverb**   albeit, all the same, although, anyhow, anyway, anywise, at any rate, by any means, despite, even though, however, in any case, in any event, in spite of, *incuriosus*, irrespective of, *neglegens*, nevertheless, nonetheless, notwithstanding, still, though, without regard to, without respect to

REGIME, **noun**   administration, authority, command, directorship, dominion, governance, government, incumbency, management, political system, power, primacy, regency, regimen, reign, rule, sovereignty, supervision, supremacy

REGION, **noun**   area, circle, circuit, clime, compass, confines, country, county, demesne, diocese, district, division, domain, environs, field, land, latitude, limited area, locale, locality, location, *locus*, neighborhood, part, place, portion, precinct, province, purlieus, quarter, range, realm, *regio*, scene, scope, section, sector, situation, space, sphere, spot, terrain, territory, *tractus*, vicinage, vicinity, ward, zone

REGIONAL, **adjective**   circumscribed, district, divisional, geographical, insular, local, localized, native, neighborhood, parochial, provincial, restricted, sectional, specific, subdivisional, territorial, vernacular, zonal

REGISTER, **noun**   agenda, *album*, almanac, archive, arrangement, balance sheet, calendar, catalogue, chronicle, chronology, day book, diary, docket, ephemeris, file, invoice, journal, ledger, *liber*, list, log, log book, memorandum, minutes, notes, proceedings, record, registration book, roll, roster, schedule, *tabulae*, written record
ASSOCIATED CONCEPTS: register a complaint, register to vote

REGISTER, **verb**   book, calendar, catalogue, check in, chronicle, engage, enlist, enroll, enter, file, *in album*, index, inscribe, join, matriculate, note down, order, *perscribere*, post, program, record, reserve, schedule, sign in, sign up, subscribe, *tabulas referre*, tabulate
ASSOCIATED CONCEPTS: register to vote

REGISTRATION, **noun**   booking, bookkeeping, cataloguing, certification, chronicling, enlistment, enrolling, enrollment, filing, inscribing, installing, listing, matriculation, noting down, record keeping, recording, registry, reservation, signing up, tabulation

REGRESS, **verb**   backslide, fall again into, fall back, fall behind, go back, move backward, pass back, recede, relapse, retrocede, retrograde, retrogress, return, reverse, revert, turn back

REGRESSIVE, **adjective**   atavistic, backsliding, backward, decadent, degenerate, ill-advised, lapsing, on the decline, receding, recessive, recidivistic, recidivous, refluent, relapsing, retrocedent, retrograde, retrogressive, reverse, reversed, reversional, reversionary, tergiversating, withering
ASSOCIATED CONCEPTS: regressive tax

REGRET, **verb**   apologize, be disturbed over, be penitent, be remorseful, be sorry for, bemoan, bewail, blame oneself, cry over, deplore, disapprove of, feel conscience stricken, feel uneasy about, fret, grieve at, have a bad conscience, have qualms about, lament, mourn for, repent, repine, reproach oneself, rue, sorrow for, weep over

REGRETTABLE, **adjective**   adverse, calamitous, catastrophic, deplorable, dire, disadvantageous, disastrous, dreadful, grievous, ill-boding, ill-fated, ill-omened, inauspicious, inopportune, lamentable, *paenitendus*, regretted, ruinous, sad, scandalous, terrible, unfavorable, unfortunate, unhappy, unlucky, unpropitious, unsuccessful, untimely, untoward, woeful

REGULAR *(Conventional)*, **adjective**   according to rule, accustomed, average, classic, common, commonplace, conformable, consuetudinal, consuetudinary, conventional, customary, everyday, expected, familiar, general, habitual, *iustus*, natural, normal, *ordinarius*, ordinary, popular, predictable, prevailing, prevalent, routine, run of the mill, standard, stock, traditional, typical, unchanged, undeviating, unexceptional, usual, wonted, workaday
ASSOCIATED CONCEPTS: regular employment, regular interest

REGULAR *(Orderly)*, **adjective**   balanced, *certus*, *constans*, controlled, cyclic, established, even, fixed, invariable, measured, methodical, patterned, periodic, periodical, recurring, regulated, rhythmic, seasonal, stable, steady, successive, symmetrical, systematic, uniform, unvarying, well-regulated
ASSOCIATED CONCEPTS: presumption of regularity, regular course of business, regular election

REGULARITY, **noun**   balance, clockwork precision, conformity, congruity, consistency, *constantia*, even tenor, evenness, exactness, harmony, homogeneity, invariability, levelness, method, methodicalness, order, orderliness, *ordo*, periodicity, precision, proportion, punctuality, recurrence, regular recurrence, regular return, regularness, rhythm, sameness, steadiness, symmetry, uniformity
ASSOCIATED CONCEPTS: presumption of regularity

REGULATE *(Adjust)*, **verb**   administrare, allocate, arrange, balance, coordinate, correct, dispose, level, make right, make uniform, methodize, moderate, modulate, normalize, order, organize, put in order, rectify, reduce to method, regularize, remedy, render accordant, restore equilibrium, set right, square, standardize, straighten out, systematize, temper

REGULATE *(Manage)*, **verb**   administer, conduct, control, determine, direct, discipline, govern, guide, handle, have authority over, have charge of, head, lead, order, oversee, police, preside over, rule, steer, superintend, supervise
ASSOCIATED CONCEPTS: regulate commerce, regulated by law

REGULATION *(Management)*, **noun**   adjustment, *administratio*, administration, arrangement, conduct, coordination, disposal, disposition, economy, government, guidance, handling, lawmaking, moderation, organization, regimentation, steerage, superintendence, supervision, systematization

REGULATION *(Rule),* **noun** act, bylaw, canon, code, command, commandment, decree, dictate, direction, directive, discipline, edict, enactment, injunction, instruction, *iussum,* law, legislation, mandate, measure, order, ordinance, *praeceptum,* precept, prescript, prescription, regimen, statute
ASSOCIATED CONCEPTS: municipal regulation, reasonable regulation, zoning regulation

REGULATIONS, *noun* code, codification, dictates, directives, instructions, ordinances, provisions of the regulations, rules, section of the regulations
ASSOCIATED CONCEPTS: promulgation of administrative rules, promulgation of regulations

REHABILITATE, *verb* ameliorate, amend, bring back, fix, furbish, improve, make over, meliorate, mend, readjust, rebuild, reclaim, recondition, reconstitute, reconstruct, reconvert, rectify, redeem, redintegrate, reestablish, refashion, refit, refurbish, reintegrate, reinvigorate, remake, renew, renovate, repair, reproduce, *restituere,* restore, revamp, revive, revivify, salvage
ASSOCIATED CONCEPTS: rehabilitate an offender, rehabilitate an insurance company

REHABILITATION, *noun* adjustment, alteration, amelioration, development, improvement, instauration, melioration, readjustment, rebuilding, reclamation, reconstitution, reconstruction, recreation, recuperation, redemption, redintegration, reeducation, reestablishment, reformation, regeneration, reindoctrination, reinstatement, reinvigoration, remaking, remodeling, renewal, renovation, reorganization, repair, reparation, restitution, restoration, resurrection, resuscitation, return, revival, revivement, revivification, salvation
ASSOCIATED CONCEPTS: company rehabilitation

REHEARING, *noun* new hearing, reassessment, reexamination, reinquiry, retrial

REIGN, *noun* administration, authority, command, control, dominance, domination, dominion, government, hold, influence, jurisdiction, mastery, might, power, predominance, prerogative, privilege, regency, right, rule, sovereignty, supreme power, suzerainty, sway

REIGN, *verb* administer, command, dominate, exercise authority, govern, influence, master, predominate, preside, prevail, regulate, rule

REIMBURSE, *verb* compensate, indemnify, make good, make reparation, make restitution, pay back, rebate, recompense, *reddere,* redress, refund, remit, remunerate, repay, replace, requite, restore, satisfy, settle

REIMBURSEMENT, *noun* compensation, damages, defrayal, disbursement, giving back, indemnification, indemnity, paying back, payment, rebate, recompense, recoupment, redress, refund, remuneration, reparation, repayment, replacement, restitution, restoration
FOREIGN PHRASES: *Frustra petis quod statim alteri reddere cogeris.* You ask in vain that which you will immediately be compelled to restore to another.

REINFORCE, *verb* augment, bolster, boost, brace, buttress, *confirmare,* energize, fortify, intensify, reconstitute,

redouble, reestablish, refurbish, reinvigorate, reorganize, replenish, strengthen, supplement, support

REINFORCEMENT, *noun* addition, additional strength, aid, assistance, augmentation, auxiliary, backing, boost, buttress, fresh supply, furtherance, help, helping hand, increase, prop, protection, relief, replenishment, strengthener, supplement, *supplementum,* support

REINSTATE, *verb* bring back, place in a former state, put back, put back into service, reappoint, reconstitute, reestablish, rehabilitate, rehire, reinaugurate, reinstall, reinvest, remit, replace, reseat, *restituere,* restore, restore to office, restore to power, return, revest, revive
ASSOCIATED CONCEPTS: reinstate to a job

REITERATE, *verb* duplicate, echo, go over, harp upon, ingeminate, *iterare,* iterate, reaffirm, reassert, recapitulate, redouble, repeat, rephrase, reproduce, restate, retell, reutter, review, reword, say again, say repeatedly, state again

REITERATION, *noun* battology, duplication, echo, encore, iteration, reassertion, recapitulation, recital, recount, recounting, recurrence, redundancy, re-echoing, rehash, repetition, repetitiveness, reproduction, restatement, retelling, review, summary, tautology

REJECT, *verb* abandon, abhor, abjure, abnegate, banish, blackball, boycott, brush aside, cashier, cast aside, cast away, cast off, challenge, contravene, controvert, decline, demur, deny, despise, detest, disaffirm, disallow, disapprove, disavow, disbelieve, discard, disclaim, discount, discredit, disdain, disinherit, dismiss, disown, dispute, disregard, dissent, dodge, eject, eliminate, eradicate, excise, exclude, expel, extirpate, extract, forbid, forswear, gainsay, get rid of, hold in contempt, ignore, impugn, jeer, jettison, jilt, keep out, lay aside, leave out, neglect, object, oppose, ostracize, oust, overrule, pass by, pass over, preclude, prohibit, proscribe, protest, rebuff, refuse, refuse to accept, refuse to consider, *reicere,* remove, renounce, repel, reprobate, *repudiare,* repudiate, repulse, revolt, scoff at, scout, scrap, screen out, set aside, shun, slight, snub, spurn, take exception to, throw aside, throw out, traverse, uproot, veto, vote against, waive, weed out

REJECTION, *noun* abandonment, abhorrence, abjuration, abnegation, averseness, ban, banishment, cashiering, contempt, contravention, debarment, declension, declination, declinature, defeat, denial, deportation, deposal, disaffirmation, disagreement, disallowance, disapprobation, disapproval, disbelief, discardure, discharge, discrediting, disdain, disfavor, disinheritance, dislike, dislodgment, dismissal, disownment, dissent, distrust, dubiety, dubiousness, elimination, eradication, erasure, eviction, excision, exclusion, excommunication, exile, exilement, expatriation, expulsion, extirpation, firing, gainsaying, hatred, intolerance, intoleration, mistrust, negation, neglect, nonacceptance, noninclusion, objection, omission, opposition, ostracism, ouster, overruling, prohibition, proscription, rebuff, recantation, refusal, *reiectio,* relegation, removal, renunciation, reprobation, *repudiatio,* repudiation, repulse, revilement, revolt, riddance, scorn, slight, snub, spurning, uprooting, veto, waiver
ASSOCIATED CONCEPTS: rejection of claim

REJOIN *(Congregate),* **verb** assemble, associate, cluster, collect, concentrate, convocate, forgather, meet with, muster, reassemble, reconcentrate, regroup, rendezvous with, reunite

507

REJOIN (*Retort*), **verb**   acknowledge, answer, confute, counter, countercharge, rebut, refute, reply, respond, return and answer, riposte
ASSOCIATED CONCEPTS: pleadings, rejoinder

REJOINDER, noun   answer, counteraccusation, counterargument, countercharge, counterstatement, defense, plea in rebuttal, reply, response, retort

RELAPSE, noun   backsliding, declension, declination, decline, degeneration, deterioration, escheat, fall, lapse, *recidere*, recidivation, recidivism, recrudescence, recrudescency, recurrence, regress, regression, reoccurrence, repetition, retrocession, retrogradation, retrogression, retroversion, return, reversal, reverse, reversion, setback, sinking, weakening

RELAPSE, verb   backslide, decline, degenerate, deteriorate, fall, fall back, *recidere*, recidivate, recrudesce, regress, *relabi*, renew, retrocede, retrograde, retrogress, retrovert, return, reverse, revert, sink back, slide back, slip back, start again, start fresh, suffer a relapse, wane, weaken

RELATE (*Establish a connection*), **verb**   affect, affiliate, ally, appertain to, apply, associate, bear upon, bracket, concern, connect, consociate, correlate, draw a parallel, filiate, group, have a bearing on, identify, integrate, interconnect, interrelate, link, parallel, pertain, *pertinere,* tie, unite

RELATE (*Tell*), **verb**   acquaint, advise, air, announce, apprise, broadcast, communicate, convey, declare, describe, detail, disclose, divulge, elucidate, *enarrare,* express, give a report, give an account, impart, inform, make known, mention, narrate, notify, observe, particularize, phrase, portray, put into words, recite, recount, repeat, report, represent in words, retell, reveal, say, set forth, speak, state, utter, vent, ventilate, verbalize

RELATED, adjective   affiliated, affined, affinitive, agnate, akin, allied, analogous, applicable, apposite, appropriate, appurtenant, associated, cognate, *cognatus,* collateral, commutual, complementary, congeneric, congenerical, congenerous, connate, connatural, connected, consanguine, consanguineous, consociate, contingent, correlated, correlative, correspondent, dependent, enmeshed, germane, implicated, interconnected, interdependent, interrelated, intertwined, interwoven, kindred, knit, like, linked, mutual, pertinent, *propinquus, proximus,* reciprocal, relative, relevant, tied

RELATION (*Connection*), **noun**   affiliation, affinity, alliance, analogy, applicability, appositeness, apposition, association, bearing, bond, closeness, cognation, comparableness, connation, connaturalness, *connexion,* correlation, correspondence, homology, indentification, interconnection, interrelationship, liaison, likeness, link, mutuality, nearness, nexus, pertinence, propinquity, reference, relationship, relative position, relevance, resemblance, similarity, similitude, tie, tie-in

RELATION (*Kinship*), **noun**   blood relative, blood tie, *cognatus,* common ancestry, common descent, common lineage, common stock, consanguinity, family connection, family tie, kin, kindred, kinsman, *propinquus,* relationship, relative

RELATIONSHIP (*Connection*), **noun**   alignment, amalgamation, analogy, appositeness, association, bearing, bond, coaction, coalition, *cognatio,* cognation, combination,

confederacy, *coniunctio,* connecting link, consociation, correlation, interconnection, interdependence, interrelation, interrelationship, involvement, likeness, link, linkage, mutuality, nearness, pertinence, rapport, reciprocity, relation, relevance, relevancy, tie, unification, union, unity
ASSOCIATED CONCEPTS: privity

RELATIONSHIP (*Family tie*), **noun**   affinity, blood relation, blood ties, consanguinity, extraction, family connection, filiation, kindredship, kinship, lineage, *propinquitas,* relation
ASSOCIATED CONCEPTS: blood relationship, intestate succession, paternity proceeding
FOREIGN PHRASES: *Affinis mei affinis non est mihi affinis.* One who is a relative of my relative by marriage is not my relative.

RELATIVE (*Comparative*), **adjective**   analogous, commensurable, commensurate, *comparare,* compared, contrastive, correlative, correspondent, corresponding, proportional, proportionate
ASSOCIATED CONCEPTS: dependent relative revocation, relative fault

RELATIVE (*Relevant*), **adjective**   affinitive, allied, applicable, apposite, appositional, appropriate, appurtenant, apropos, apt, associated, bearing on, cognate, collateral, compatible, concerning, connected, connective, correlated, fit, fitting, germane, interconnected, kindred, material, pertaining, pertinent, referring, related, relating, relational, respecting, suitable

RELATIVE, noun   blood relation, clansman, cognate, *cognatus,* connection, family, kin, kindred, kinsman, kith, member of the family, *propinquus,* relation, sib

RELAX, verb   abate, allay, assuage, be lenient, bend, diminish, ease, give, lenify, lessen, milden, mitigate, moderate, modify, modulate, reduce, relent, remit, show clemency, show pity, slacken, soften, temper, weaken, yield
ASSOCIATED CONCEPTS: relax a restriction

RELAXATION OF LAW, noun   absolution, acquittal, assuagement, discharge, dismissal, dispensation, exculpation, exemption, exoneration, grace, grant, immunity, indulgence, license, mollification, pardon, privilege, reduction, release from liability, release from obligation, relief, reprieve, special privilege, tolerance, toleration, vindication

RELEASE, noun   abandonment, absolution, acquittal, acquittance, amnesty, casting away, cession, clearance, compurgation, deliverance, disbanding, discarding, discharge, disculpation, disengagement, disentanglement, disenthrallment, dismissal, dispensation, disposal, emancipation, exculpation, excusal, excuse, exemption, exoneration, extrication, forgiveness, freeing, immunity, laying aside, *liberatio,* liberation, manumission, *missio,* pardon, pardonment, quietus, relinquishment, salvation, setting free, sparing, unchaining, unfettering, unharnessing, untying, waiver, yielding
ASSOCIATED CONCEPTS: binding release
FOREIGN PHRASES: *Eodem modo quo oritur, eodem modo dissolvitur.* It is discharged in the same manner in which it was created. *Quodque dissolvitur eodem modo quo ligatur.* A thing is unbound in the same manner that it is made binding.

RELEASE, verb   clear, deliver, discharge, disengage, disenthrall, dismiss, emancipate, enfranchise, exculpate, excuse, exempt, exonerate, *exsolvere,* extricate, forgive, free, give clearance, give up, *laxare,* let go, let out, *liberare,* liberate, manumit, relieve, relinquish, remit, reprieve, save, set at large, set at liberty, set free, set loose, spare, unburden, unfetter, yield

ASSOCIATED CONCEPTS: release a claim, release a lien

RELEASE FROM PRISON, *verb* deliver, demobilize, discharge, dismiss, free, let go, let go free, let loose, let off, let out, let out on bail, pardon, parole, release from custody, unbridle, unchain, unfetter, unharness, unlatch, unleash, unlock, unshackle

ASSOCIATED CONCEPTS: appeal, habeas corpus

RELEGATE, *verb* allocate, assign, ban, banish, bar, cast out, consign, convey, delegate, deport, depute, discard, dislodge, dismiss, dispatch, displace, elide, eliminate, entrust, eradicate, exclude, excommunicate, exile, expatriate, expel, isolate, omit, ostracize, oust, outlaw, proscribe, push aside, refer, reject, remand, remove, segregate, send away, separate, set apart, shut out, throw out, transfer, transport, turn over to

RELENT, *verb* abate severity, accede, acquiesce, be assuaged, be compassionate, be compliant, be forgiving, be merciful, be mollified, be placated, be pliant, be submissive, be tolerant, bend, defer to, feel compassion, feel for, forgive, give, give in, give quarter, give way, grow lenient, grow less severe, have mercy, have sympathy, *iram remittere, molliri,* pity, relax, remit, resign, show mercy, soften, spare, succumb, sympathize, unbend, yield

RELENTLESS, *adjective* assiduous, bowelless, brutish, cold, cold-blooded, cold-hearted, continuous, cruel, determined, dictatorial, endless, hard, hard of heart, hardhearted, harsh, heedless, *immisericors,* impenitent, imperious, implacable, inclement, indefatigable, *inexorabilis,* inexorable, inflexible, insensitive, insistent, intolerant, intransigent, iron, merciless, obdurate, obstinate, perseverant, persevering, persistent, pertinacious, pitiless, pressing, rancorous, remorseless, resolute, rigid, ruthless, sedulous, severe, steadfast, stern, stony-hearted, stringent, stubborn, tenacious, truculent, tyrannical, unappeasable, unbending, uncompassionate, uncompromising, undaunted, undeviating, unfaltering, unfeeling, unflinching, unforgiving, unintermitting, unmerciful, unmitigable, unmoved by pity, unpitying, unrelenting, unremitting, unshrinking, unsparing, unswerving, unsympathetic, unyielding, vindictive, without regrets

RELEVANCE, *noun* affinity, applicability, application, appositeness, appropriateness, aptness, association, bearing, compatibility, concern, congruence, congruency, congruity, connection, correlation, correspondence, importance, materiality, pertinence, reference, relation, relationship, significance, suitability, suitableness, tie-in

ASSOCIATED CONCEPTS: objection as to relevance

RELEVANCY, *noun* accord, affinity, applicability, application, appositeness, appropriateness, aptness, association, bearing, comparability, compatibility, congruence, congruency, congruity, connection, correlation, correspondence, fitness, harmoniousness, importance, materiality, pertinence, propriety, reference, relation, relationship, scope, significance, suitability, suitableness, tie-in

ASSOCIATED CONCEPTS: legal relevancy, logical relevancy, relevancy of evidence

RELEVANT, *adjective* *ad rem spectare,* admissible, affinitive, allied, applicable, apposite, appropriate, appurtenant,

apropos, apt, associated, cognate, compatible, concerning, conformant, conforming, congruent, congruous, connected, consentaneous, consistent, consonant, correlated, correspondent, felicitous, fit, fitting, germane, important, material, pertaining to, pertinent, proper, referring to, related, relative, seasonable, suitable, tied in with, to the point, to the purpose

ASSOCIATED CONCEPTS: relevant evidence, relevant question

RELIABILITY *(Authoritativeness), **noun*** candor, certainty, certification, credibility, honor, loyalty, trustworthiness

RELIABILITY *(Predictability), **noun*** constancy, dependability, firmness, punctuality, responsibility, secureness, solidity, soundness, stability, substantiality

RELIABLE, *adjective* accurate, assured, authentic, believable, certain, competent, conclusive, conscientious, constant, credible, definite, dependable, devoted, evidential, exact, faithful, genuine, guaranteed, honest, honorable, incontestable, incontrovertible, indisputable, indubitable, inerrable, inerrant, infallible, irrefutable, legitimate, loyal, proved, real, reputable, respectable, responsible, safe, scrupulous, secure, sincere, sound, stable, stanch, steadfast, steady, strong, sure, tried, true, trustworthy, trusty, truthful, undeniable, unequivocal, unerring, unfailing, unhazardous, unperilous, unquestionable, upright, veracious, veridical, worthy of trust

ASSOCIATED CONCEPTS: reliable evidence, reliable testimony, reliable witness

RELIANCE, *noun* acceptance, affiance, assurance, assuredness, belief, certainty, certitude, confidence, conviction, credence, credulity, dependability, dependence, expectation, faith, *fides, fiducia,* security, support, sureness, troth, trust

RELIEF *(Aid), **noun*** accommodation, assistance, attention, *auxilium,* avail, backing, care, cooperation, encouragement, help, ministration, ministry, promotion, reinforcement, rescue, respite, salvation, *subsidium,* succor, support, sustenance, treatment

RELIEF *(Legal redress), **noun*** award, compensation, correction, decision, indemnification, judgment, payment, recompense, rectification, remedy, reparation, restitution, restoration, retribution, satisfaction

ASSOCIATED CONCEPTS: affirmative relief, bill of discovery and relief, complete relief, declaratory relief, further relief, primary relief, supplemental relief

FOREIGN PHRASES: *Judex non reddit plus quam quod petens ipse requirit.* A judge should not render judgments for a larger sum than the plaintiff demands.

RELIEF *(Release), **noun*** abatement, alleviation, amelioration, assuagement, deliverance, diminishment, diminution, discharge, disencumbrance, easement, liberation, mitigation, palliation, reduction, *remedium,* remission, reprieve, respite, rest, *sublevatio*

RELIEVE *(Free from burden), **verb*** abate, allay, assuage, deliver, disburden, disencumber, disengage, emancipate, exempt, extricate, free, liberate, lighten, manumit, mitigate, moderate, relax, release, rid, set free, unburden, unload

RELIEVE *(Give aid), **verb*** aid, alleviate, ameliorate, assist, better, calm, comfort, cure, ease, give help, give relief, heal, help, improve, medicate, meliorate, minister to, palliate, reenforce, remedy, render assistance, salve, soothe, succor, treat

RELINQUISH, verb abandon, abdicate, abjure, cast off, cease, cede, deliver, demit, desert, disclaim, discontinue, dismiss, do without, drop, eliminate, forgo, forsake, forswear, give over, give up, give up claim to, go without, hand over, jettison, lay aside, leave, let go, part with, pull out, quit, reject, release, *relinquere,* renounce, resign, rid, sacrifice, secede from, sign away, spare, surrender, throw away, turn one's back on, vacate, waive, withdraw, yield
ASSOCIATED CONCEPTS: relinquish a claim

RELINQUISHMENT, noun abandonment, abdication, abjuration, cessation, demission, discontinuance, dismissal, elimination, forswearance, rejection, release, renouncement, renunciation, resignation, succession, surrender, vacation, waiver, withdrawal
ASSOCIATED CONCEPTS: custody relinquishment, relinquishment of rights

RELISH, verb appreciate, bask in, be fond of, be pleased with, delight in, derive pleasure from, enjoy, fancy, feel gratification, feel joy, feel pleasure, gloat over, like, luxuriate in, prefer, rejoice in, revel in, savor, take pleasure in

RELOCATE, verb reassign, reestablish, replace, reposition, rereside, resettle, resite, restation

RELUCTANCE, noun antipathy, averseness, aversion, coactus, deprecation, diffidence, disaffection, disapproval, disfavor, disinclination, dislike, dissent, distaste, doubt, hesitance, hesitancy, hesitation, indisposedness, indisposition, indocility, *invitus,* misgiving, nolition, objection, obstinacy, qualms, recoiling, renitence, renitency, repugnance, reservations, resistance, scruples, shyness, skepticism, squeamishness, uncertainty, unwillingness

RELUCTANT, adjective adverse, averse, avoiding, begrudging, diffident, discontented, disinclined, dissenting, dissentious, evasive, grudging, hesitant, hesitating, hesitative, inacquiescent, indisposed, involuntary, irreconcilable, not disposed, not inclined, opposed, protestant, querulous, recalcitrant, refusing, rejective, renitent, shrinking, shunning, squeamish, uncertain, uncomplaisant, uncomplying, unconsenting, uncooperated, uninclined, unwilling
ASSOCIATED CONCEPTS: reluctant witness

RELY, verb bank on, be confident, be dependent on, believe in, confide, *confidere,* count upon, depend, entrust, feel sure, have confidence in, have faith in, lean on, look to, place trust in, put confidence in, put faith in, rely on, trust

REMAIN (Continue), **verb** adhere, be constant, be permanent, be steadfast, be tenacious, carry on, continue, endure, exist, extend, go on, hang on, hold out, keep, keep going, keep on, last, linger, maintain, outlast, outlive, perdure, perpetuate, persevere, persist, prevail, proceed, progress, prolong, pursue, stand fast, stand firm, stay, subsist, survive, sustain

REMAIN (Occupy), **verb** be present, dwell, enjoy, have, have possession, hold, hold possession, inhabit, live in, lodge, maintain, own, possess, reside, retain

REMAIN (Stay), **verb** adhere, await, be anchored, be dormant, be immobile, be immovable, be inert, be motionless, be sedentary, be stationary, be transfixed, come to stay, delay, *durare,* hold, last, linger, lodge, pause, *remanere,* repose, rest, set in, stand, stand fast, wait

ASSOCIATED CONCEPTS: remain in possession after the expiration of a lease, remain on premises

REMAINDER (Estate in property), **noun** estate, excess, expectancy, interest, property, residual estate, reversionary estate, surplus
ASSOCIATED CONCEPTS: contingent remainder, vested remainder

REMAINDER (Remaining part), **noun** balance, carryover, excess, leftover, overplus, *quod restat, reliquum,* remaining portion, remains, residuals, residue, *residuum,* rest, reversion, superfluity, surplus

REMAND, verb command back, commit, commit to an institution, consign, delegate, entrust, imprison again, order back, reassign, recommit, reincarcerate, reinstitutionalize, relegate, remit, *remittere,* replace, restore, return, return to prison, send, send back, transfer
ASSOCIATED CONCEPTS: general remand, reversed and remanded

REMARK, noun animadversion, assertion, averment, comment, commentary, declaration, *dictum,* exclamation, expression, interjection, mention, note, observation, point, pronouncement, recitation, reflection, saying, speech, statement, thought, utterance, word

REMARK, verb affirm, animadvert, articulate, assert, asseverate, aver, come out with, comment, communicate, convey, dare say, declare, deliver, *dicere,* discuss, emit, expound, express, give utterance, let fall, make mention, make note of, mention, note, observe, present, recite, relate, respond, say, speak, state, suggest, talk about, tell, utter, verbalize, vocalize, voice

REMARKABLE, adjective amazing, astonishing, astounding, celebrated, consequential, conspicuous, *conspicuus,* curious, distinct, distinctive, distinguished, egregious, exceptional, extraordinary, eye-catching, fabulous, flagrant, great, important, imposing, impressive, incredible, lofty, marked, marvelous, memorable, miraculous, momentous, monumental, notable, noteworthy, outstanding, overwhelming, peculiar, predominent, prominent, rare, salient, signal, significant, singular, *singularis,* special, strange, striking, stupendous, surprising, unbelievable, uncommon, unforgettable, unique, unparalleled, unspeakable, unusual, visible, wonderful, wondrous, worthy of note

REMEDIAL, adjective alleviating, alleviative, alterative, amendatory, analeptic, anodyne, antidotal, assuasive, balmy, beneficial, benign, bracing, calmative, cleansing, compensatory, corrective, counteracting, curative, curing, easing, emollient, healing, health-giving, healthful, invigorating, lenitive, medical, medicative, medicinal, palliative, prophylactic, purifying, recuperative, reformative, reparative, reparatory, restitutive, restorative, revivifying, roborant, salubrious, *salutaris,* salutary, salutiferous, sanative, sanatory, sanitary, soothing, stimulating, strengthening, therapeutic, tonic, wholesome
ASSOCIATED CONCEPTS: remedial act, remedial laws

REMEDIAL STATUTE, noun correction, corrective measure, cure, legislative cure, legislative redress, rectification, relief, remedial measure, remedy
ASSOCIATED CONCEPTS: remedial act, remedial action, remedial cases, remedial legislation, remedial right, remedial statute, remedial writ

REMEDY *(Legal means of redress),* **noun** aid, alleviation, amelioration, assistance, compensation, corrective measure, counteraction, effective help, help, recompense, rectification, rehabilitation, relief, remedial measure, reparation, reparative measure, restitution, solution

ASSOCIATED CONCEPTS: adequate remedy at law, ancillary relief, appropriate relief, equitable remedy, exclusive remedy, exhaustion of administrative remedies, extraordinary remedy, inadequate remedy, legal remedy, mutuality of remedy, provisional remedy, statutory remedy

REMEDY *(That which corrects),* **noun** aid, antidote, assistance, correction, corrective measure, cure, help, medicina, palliative, relief, remedial measure, remedium, restorative

REMEDY, *verb* adjust, aid, alleviate, ameliorate, amend, assist, assuage, attend, calm, change, correct, cure, ease, fix, heal, help, improve, indemnify, make amends, make better, make sound, *medicamentum,* medicate, *medicina,* meliorate, mend, minister to, mitigate, mollify, neutralize, overhaul, palliate, put into condition, put into shape, readjust, rectify, redress, reinvigorate, relieve, *remedium,* renew, repair, restore, resuscitate, retrieve, revise, revive, revivify, right, satisfy, save, set straight, solve, soothe, succor, treat, work a cure

REMEMBER, *verb* be reminded of, bear in memory, bear in mind, bring to mind, call to mind, call up, commemorate, conjure up, fix in the mind, keep in mind, know again, know by heart, look back, master, memorialize, memorize, not forget, place, preserve a memory, recall, recognize, recollect, *recordari,* recover knowledge of, reidentify, relive, remind oneself, reminisce, *reminisci,* retain, review, summon up, think back

REMEMBRANCE *(Commemoration),* **noun** acclaim, aggrandizement, celebration, ceremony, commendation, consecration, dignification, elevation, enshrinement, exaltation, glorification, holiday, homage, honoring, immortalization, keepsake, memento, memorial, memorialization, monument, observance, perpetuation, praise, ritual, salutation, solemnization, souvenir, testimonial, token, tribute

REMEMBRANCE *(Recollection),* **noun** *memoria,* memory, mental image, recall, recognition, recognizance, reconstruction, reidentification, reminiscence, retention, retrospect, retrospection, revival in the mind

REMIND, *verb* *admonere,* advise, awaken memories, bring back, bring to recollection, bring up, cause to recollect, cause to remember, *commonere,* cue, drop a hint, give notice, haunt, hint, jog the memory, make an allusion to, note, point out, prod, prompt, refresh the memory, renew memories, state, stress, suggest, tell, warn

REMINDER, *noun* allusion, commemoration, cue, hint, jog, keepsake, memento, memo, memorandum, memorial, mnemonic, mnemonic device, notation, note, phylactery, prod, prompt, reference, relic, remembrance, shrine, souvenir, suggestion, testimonial

REMISE, *verb* cede, give back, give up, grant, quit, quitclaim, release, relinquish, remit, resign, surrender

REMISS, *adjective* careless, delinquent, derelict, dilatory, disregardant, disregardful, dutiless, forgetful, heedless, idle, improvident, imprudent, inattentive, inconsiderate, indifferent, indolent, injudicious, lackadaisical, late, lax, lazy, loafing, neglectful, *neglegens,* negligent, omissive, procrastinative, reckless, shiftless, slack, slothful, tardy, temerarious, thoughtless, uncircumspect, unconcerned, unheeding, unmindful, unsolicitous, unthinking, unwatchful, unwilling

REMISSION, *noun* abatement, absolution, acquittal, acquittance, allayment, alleviation, amnesty, assuagement, break, cancellation, cessation, check, clearance, condonation, decrease, diminution, discharge, discontinuance, exculpation, exemption, exoneration, forbearance, forgiveness, grace, halt, indulgence, intermission, interruption, interval, lapse, lessening, letup, liberation, lull, mitigation, moderation, modulation, pardon, pause, quietus, quittance, recess, reduction, relaxation, release, relief, relinquishment, *remissio,* reprieve, respite, rest, standstill, stay, stop, stoppage, subsidence, suspense, suspension, tranquilization, *venia*

REMIT *(Relax),* *verb* abate, alleviate, assuage, attemper, brake, calm, check, *condonare,* decrease, diminish, ease, give up, halt, hold up, lenify, lessen, let slacken, let up, loosen, make less violent, minimize, mitigate, moderate, palliate, quell, quiet, reduce, relinquish, *remittere,* soften, soothe, stall, stop, suspend, tranquilize, weaken

REMIT *(Release from penalty),* *verb* absolve, acquit, amnesty, assoil, cancel, clear, condone, discharge, dismiss, disregard, drop charges, exculpate, excuse, exempt, exonerate, forgive, free, give amnesty, let go, let out, liberate, overlook, pardon, pass over, reinstate, release, reprieve, respite, show clemency, show mercy, spare, vindicate, waive

REMIT *(Send payment),* *verb* compensate, defray, disburse, discharge, forward payment, make payment, *mittere,* pay, recompense, remunerate, render, repay, requite, satisfy, send money, send payment, settle, tender, transmit payment

REMIT *(Submit for consideration),* *verb* advance, commit, consign, forward, offer, present, proffer, propose, refer, relegate, remand, send, tender, transmit

REMITTANCE, *noun* acquittal, defrayal, defrayment, disbursement, expenditure, money sent, payment, *pecunia,* quittance, recompense, reimbursement, remuneration, reparation, transmittal

REMONSTRANCE, *noun* admonishment, *admonitio,* admonition, animadversion, argument, castigation, censure, challenge, chastisement, correction, criticism, dehortation, demur, determent, discouragement, dissuasion, exception, exhortation, expostulation, exprobration, gainsaying, objection, objurgation, opposition, protest, protestation, rebuke, *reclamatio,* reprimand, reproach, reprobation, reproof, reproval, warning

REMONSTRATE, *verb* admonish, advise, advise against, altercate, animadvert, argue against, berate, castigate, censure, challenge, chastise, correct, counsel, counsel against, criticize, cry out against, decry, demur, deprecate, deter, disapprove, discourage, disparage, dispute, dissuade, exhort, expostulate, express disapproval, exprobate, find fault, find flaws, frown upon, make objections, object, objurgate, oppose, protest, raise objections, rebuke, reclamare, reprehend, reproach, reprove, scold, stickle, take exception, upbraid, urge against, warn

REMONSTRATIVE, *adjective* admonitive, admonitory, argumentative, censorious, contentious, corrective, critical, dehortative, dehortatory, demurring, deprecative, deprecatory, discouraging, disputatious, dissuasive, enjoining, expostulatory, exprobrative, exprobratory, objecting, objurgatory, protesting, rebuking, remonstrant, reprimanding, reproachful, reprobative, reprobatory, reproving, warning

REMORSE, noun anguish, chagrin, compunction, concern, conscience, *conscientia mala,* contriteness, contrition, disquiet, feelings of guilt, grief, pangs of conscience, penitence, regret, regretfulness, remorsefulness, repentance, rue, self-accusation, self-condemnation, self-conviction, self-criticism, self-reproach, self-reproof, sorriness, sorrow

REMORSEFUL, adjective apologetic, compunctious, conscience-smitten, conscience-stricken, contrite, full of regret, lamenting, penitent, penitential, regretful, repentant, repenting, rueful, sad, self-accusatory, self-condemnatory, self-reproaching, sorrowful, sorry

REMORSELESS, adjective cruel, dispiteous, hardened, heartless, *immisericors,* impenitent, implacable, indurate, indurated, insensitive, intolerant, lacking remorse, merciless, obdurate, pitiless, relentless, ruthless, shameless, unappeasable, uncompassionate, unforgiving, unmerciful, unpitying, unregenerate, unrelenting, unremorseful, unrepentant

REMOTE (Not proximate), **adjective** at a great distance, distant, far, far-off, far removed, indirect, not immediate, *remotus,* removed
ASSOCIATED CONCEPTS: remote cause, remote damages
FOREIGN PHRASES: **Id quod est magis remotum, non trahit ad se quod est magis junctum, sed e contrario in omni casu.** That which is more remote does not draw to itself that which is more proximate but the contrary in every case.

REMOTE (Secluded), **adjective** alone, apart, curtained, detached, disassociated, distant, far, far-off, faraway, hidden, inaccessible, insular, isolated, not close, not near, not nearby, out of the way, private, remote, removed, seclusive, segregated, separated, sequestered, shut away, solitary, unapproachable, unassociated, unconnected, unfrequented

REMOTE (Small), **adjective** diminutive, faint, in small amount, inappreciable, inconsequential, inconsiderable, insignificant, insubstantial, little, minimal, minute, scant, slight, slim, small, superficial, tiny, trivial, unessential, unimportant

REMOTE CAUSE, noun auxiliary cause, distant basis, distant cause, distant reason, far cause, far-off cause, far-removed cause, immaterial cause, indirect cause, insufficient legal basis, insufficient legal cause, insufficient legal factor, insufficient legal genesis, insufficient legal inducement, insufficient legal source, no imediate legal cause, nonimmediate legal basis, not immediate cause, not immediate legal genesis, removed cause
ASSOCIATED CONCEPTS: intervening cause, liability, negligence, proximate cause

REMOVAL, noun abatement, abolition, *amotio,* amotion, banishment, cashiering, change of place, conveyance, debarment, deduction, demission, demotion, departure, deportation, deposal, deposition, deprivation of office, detachment, discard, discharge, disemployment, dislocation, dislodgment, dismissal, displacement, divestment, ejection, elimination, eradication, erasure, evacuation, evulsion, exception, excision, exclusion, exile, expulsion, extermination, extirpation, extraction, extrication, isolation, layoff, noninclusion, obliteration, omission, ousting,

purge, reallocation, rejection, relegation, remotion, retirement, retreat, riddance, segregation, separation, sequestration, shift, sublation, subtraction, suppression, taking away, transfer, transference, transhipment, translocation, transplacement, transplantation, transportation, unseating, withdrawal
ASSOCIATED CONCEPTS: removal from office, removal of cloud from title, removal to federal court

REMOVE (Dismiss from office), **verb** cashier, depose, disassociate, disbar, discharge, dismiss, displace, dissociate, divest, eject, expel, fire, get rid of, impeach, oust, put out, relieve, replace, suspend, turn out
ASSOCIATED CONCEPTS: removal proceeding, remove from office

REMOVE (Eliminate), **verb** abolish, annihilate, bar, cancel, clear, confiscate, debar, deduct, delete, delocalize, detach, deterge, detruncate, disassociate, disconnect, disjoin, dislocate, dislodge, displace, disroot, dissociate, disturb, divest, drain, eliminate, eradicate, except, exclude, exhume, export, expunge, exterminate, extirpate, extract, extricate, isolate, kill, liquidate, obliterate, obviate, omit, part, purge, reject, segregate, separate, sequester, sequestrate, set apart, strip, subtract, take away, take out, truncate, unattach, unbind, unfasten, unload, untie, uproot, withdraw
ASSOCIATED CONCEPTS: remove a cloud on title, remove disabilities, remove obstructions

REMOVE (Transfer), **verb** amovere, change address, change place, change venue, convey to, deliver to, forward, move, relocate, *removere,* send, send forth, shift, switch, transmit
ASSOCIATED CONCEPTS: removal from the state, remove a case to federal court, remove a cause of action

REMUNERATE, verb acquit, award, compensate, defray, disburse, discharge, give payment, indemnify, make payment, make up for, pay, recompense, reimburse, remit, *remunerari,* repay, requite, reward, satisfy, settle
ASSOCIATED CONCEPTS: legal fees

REMUNERATION, noun award, compensation, defrayal, defrayment, indemnification, indemnity, money, pay, payment, *praemium,* quittance, recompense, reimbursement, *remuneratio,* requital, restitution, return, reward, satisfaction, settlement

REMUNERATIVE, adjective advantageous, beneficial, compensative, compensatory, gainful, fruitful, lucrative, maintaining, productive, profitable, reimbursing, rewardful, rewarding, salutary, satisfying, supporting, valuable, well-paying, worthwhile

RENASCENT, adjective awakened, overhauled, reanimated, reappearing, reborn, reclaimed, reconditioned, reconstituted, reconstructed, recreated, redintegrated, redivivus, reestablished, refashioned, reformed, refreshed, regenerated, rehabilitated, rejuvenated, remade, renewed, renovated, repaired, reproduced, restored, resurgent, resurrected, resuscitated, revived, revivified, salvaged

REND, verb break, burst, cleave, crack, cut, dilacerate, discerp, *disscindere,* dissect, dissever, disunite, divide, fracture, lacerate, lancinate, rip, rive, rupture, sever, shatter, shiver, slash, slice, snap, splinter, split, sunder, tear, tear asunder

RENDER (Administer), **verb** accomplish, accord, administrate, bring about, conduct, contribute, dispense, execute, furnish, give, mete out, perform, preside over, provide, provide with, put into effect

RENDER *(Deliver)*, **verb** communicate, confer, convey, execute, give, give back, hand down, hand over, impart, pass down, present, *reddere, referre,* set down, submit, surrender, *tribuere*

ASSOCIATED CONCEPTS: render a judgment, render a verdict, render an accounting

RENDER *(Depict)*, **verb** characterize, construe, define, delineate, describe, detail, elucidate, illustrate, interpret, outline, picture, portray, record, represent, reproduce, set forth, show, sketch, translate

RENDER A JUDGMENT, verb adjudge, adjudicate, authorize, award, constitute, decide, decree, deliver judgment, enact, establish by law, hand down a judgment, impose, institute, legalize, pass, pass judgment, pass upon, sanction

ASSOCIATED CONCEPTS: render a verdict

RENDER IMPOSSIBLE, verb ban, block, check, debar, disallow, enjoin, exclude, forbid, foreclose, halt, hinder, impede, interdict, obstruct, oppose, preclude, prevent, prohibit, proscribe, refuse permission, restrain, restrict, stop, thwart, veto

RENDER NULL AND VOID, verb abolish, abrogate, annul, cancel, countermand, deprive of legal force, disown, dissolve, frustrate, invalidate, make useless, make valueless, negate, neutralize, nullify, obliterate, offset, override, overrule, overturn, renege, renounce, repeal, rescind, reverse, revoke, suspend, vacate, vitiate, void

RENDEZVOUS, noun appointment, assembly, assignation, concourse, confluence, congregation, congress, date, encounter, engagement, gathering, gathering place, get-together, ingathering, meeting, meeting place, muster, place of assignation, place of meeting, tryst

RENDEZVOUS, verb assemble, be closeted with, become acquainted, come together, congregate, convene, encounter, forgather, gather, keep a date, keep an appointment, meet, muster

RENDITION *(Explication)*, **noun** account, construction, definition, delineation, explanation, interpretation, reading, rendering, report, representation, rewording, statement, translation

RENDITION *(Restoration)*, **noun** compensation, indemnification, recommitment, rehabilitation, reparation, restitution, return, submission, surrender

RENEGE, verb abandon, abolish, abrogate, annul, back out, bolt, break a promise, call back, contradict, counterorder, countermand, desert, disannul, dissolve, go back on a commitment, go back on a promise, invalidate, nullify, pull out, quit, recall, refuse to honor a commitment, refuse to honor a promise, repeal, rescind, retract, retreat, reverse, revoke, secede, vacate, withdraw

RENEW *(Begin again)*, **verb** continue, *iterare*, launch again, progress, put back, readmit, recommence, *redintegrare*, reembark, reenter, regenerate, reinstall, reinstate, reinstitute, reintroduce, reopen, reorganize, repeat, *repetere*, resume, return to, revive, set going again, start again, stimulate, transform

ASSOCIATED CONCEPTS: leave to renew, renew a motion, renew an objection

RENEW *(Refurbish)*, **verb** ameliorate, amend, bring up to date, cure, enhance, fix, freshen, give new life to, improve, invigorate, make over, make perfect, make sound, make well, make whole, meliorate, mend, modernize, overhaul, patch up, perfect, put into shape, reanimate, reawaken, rebuild, reclaim, *reconcinnare*, recondition, reconstitute, reconstruct, reconvert, recover, recreate, rectify, redesign, redintegrate, redo, redress, refashion, *reficere*, refinish, refit, refresh, refurbish, regenerate, rehabilitate, reintegrate, reinvigorate, rejuvenate, rekindle, remake, remodel, *renovare*, renovate, repair, replace, replenish, reproduce, restore, resurge, resurrect, resuscitate, retouch, revamp, revise, revitalize, revive, rework, salvage, save

RENEWAL, noun amelioration, comeback, continuance, enhancement, fixing, improvement, instauration, making over, melioration, mending, modernization, new start, readjustment, reanimation, rearrangement, rebirth, recharging, reclamation, recommencement, reconstitution, reconstruction, recrudescence, recrudescency, recurrence, redoubling, reestablishment, refitting, reformation, refreshment, regeneration, rehabilitation, reinstatement, reinvigoration, reissue, rejuvenation, relapse, renaissance, renascence, *renovatio*, renovation, reopening, repair, repetition, replenishment, reproduction, restoration, resumption, resurrection, resuscitation, return, revamping, revision, revival, revivification, salvage

ASSOCIATED CONCEPTS: motion to renew, renewal of a claim, renewal of a license, renewal of a motion

RENITENT, adjective adverse, antagonistic, antipathetic, antipathetical, conflicting, counteracting, counteractive, demurring, disapproving, disgusted, disinclined, dissenting, firm, indisposed, indocile, insurrectional, intractable, intransigent, loath, mutinous, opposed, opposing, reactionary, recalcitrant, reluctant, resistant, resisting, rigid, stiff, unsubmissive, unwilling

RENOUNCE, verb abandon, abdicate, abhor, abjure, abnegate, banish, break with, cast aside, cast off, cease, decline, demit, deny, deprive oneself, desert, desist from, despise, detest, disagree, disapprove, disavow, discard, disclaim, discountenance, disdain, dismiss, disown, dissent, divorce oneself from, drop, eliminate, exclude, forbear, forbid, forgo, forsake, forswear, give away, give up, give up claim to, go without, interdict, lay aside, leave, let go, oppose, ostracize, part with, proscribe, protest, quit, rebuff, recant, refuse, reject, relinquish, renege, repel, repudiate, repulse, resign, rid oneself of, scorn, spurn, surrender, swear off, take exception to, turn from, waive

ASSOCIATED CONCEPTS: renounce a will

FOREIGN PHRASES: *Cuilibet licet juri pro se introducto renunciare.* Anyone may renounce the benefit of a legal right that exists only for his protection.

RENOVATE, verb ameliorate, amend, convert, fix, improve, make better, make new, make over, make sound, make whole, meliorate, mend, modernize, perfect, readjust, reanimate, rebuild, recondition, reconstitute, reconstruct, reconvert, recreate, redeem, redintegrate, reestablish, refashion, *reficere*, refit, refresh, refurbish, regenerate, rehabilitate, reinvigorate, rejuvenate, remake, remodel, renew, renovize, reorganize, repair, replace, restore, resurrect, revamp, revive, revivify, salvage

RENOWNED, adjective acclaimed, applauded, celebrated, *clarus*, consequential, conspicuous, distinguished, eminent, exalted, extraordinary, famed, famous, far-famed, foremost, great, honored, illustrious, important, *inlustris,* known, leading, matchless, much touted, notable, noted, noteworthy, notorious, outstanding, popular, preeminent, prominent, recognized, remarkable, reputable, singular, talked about, top-flight, unexampled, unique, unparalled, unprecedented, well-known

RENT, noun assessment, compensation, cost, fee, income, income from real estate, land revenue, *merces,* payment, proceeds, *reditus,* remuneration, rental, return, revenue
ASSOCIATED CONCEPTS: action for rent, assignment of rent, ejectment, fair rent, fair rental value, holdover, month-to-month rental, prepayment of rent, reasonable rent, rent strike, rents and proceeds, security, suit for rent, tenancy by will, unaccrued rent

RENT, verb allow residency, allow the use of, charter, *conducere,* contract, demise, enjoy the use of premises, engage, give occupation, grant a lease, hire out, lease, lend, let, let out, *locare,* make available, sublease, sublet, subrent, take a lease, underlease, underlet, use premises
ASSOCIATED CONCEPTS: option to rent

RENUNCIATION, noun abandonment, abdicatio, abdication, abjuration, abnegation, cancellation, cession, declination, demission, denial, disaffirmation, disallowance, disapprobation, disapproval, disavowal, disavowment, discard, disclaimer, discontinuance, disinheritance, dismissal, disownment, elimination, exclusion, forswearing, giving up, negation, omission, proscription, rebuff, recantation, refusal, *reiectio,* rejection, relinquishment, renouncement, reprobation, *repudiatio,* repudiation, repulsion, resignation, retraction, sacrifice, shutting out, spurning, swearing off, veto, waiver, withdrawal, yielding
ASSOCIATED CONCEPTS: renunciation of a contract, renunciation of a will

REOPEN, verb *aperire,* begin again, carry on, come back to, commence again, continue, *iterum,* open again, proceed, recommence, reembark, reestablish, reinstitute, renew, repeat, resume, return to, revive, start over
ASSOCIATED CONCEPTS: motion to reopen, reopen a case, reopen a hearing, reopen an investigation

REORGANIZATION, noun alteration, amelioration, betterment, change, conversion, improvement, melioration, overhauling, readjustment, rearrangement, rebuilding, recasting, reconstitution, reconstruction, rectification, reestablishment, reformation, rehabilitation, remaking, remodeling, restoration, restructuring, revising, revision, transformation
ASSOCIATED CONCEPTS: bankruptcy, corporate reorganization

REPAIR, noun adjustment, alteration, amelioration, betterment, correction, cure, fixing, improvement, melioration, mending, overhaul, patching, reanimation, reassembling, reconditioning, reconstruction, recovery, rectification, redintegration, refitting, reform, reformation, rehabilitation, remedy, remodeling, renewal, renovation, reorganization, reparation, restoration, resurrection, retouching, revival
ASSOCIATED CONCEPTS: duty to repair, failure to keep in repair, opportunity to make repairs

REPAIR, verb adjust, ameliorate, amend, brush up, condition, correct, cure, darn, fix, improve, make better, make good, make improvements, meliorate, mend, overhaul, patch, piece, put in order, put into shape, put right, readjust, rebuild, recondition, reconstruct, rectify, redress,

reficere, refit, reform, refresh, refurbish, rehabilitate, rejuvenate, remedy, render better, renew, *reparare,* reshape, restore, resurrect, retouch, retread, revamp, revive, right, salvage, service, tinker, touch up, vamp
ASSOCIATED CONCEPTS: duty to repair

REPARATION *(Indemnification),* **noun** adjustment, amends, atonement, compensation, conscience money, correction, damages, expiation, financial remuneration, indemnity, payment, peace offering, penalty, quittance, recompense, redress, reimbursement, relief, remedy, repayment, restitution, restoration, return, *satisfactio,* satisfaction, settlement, wergild

REPARATION *(Keeping in repair),* **noun** correction, instauration, overhaul, readjustment, rebuilding, reconditioning, reconstruction, rectification, refurbishment, rehabilitation, rejuvenation, remedy, renewal, renovation, repair, replacement, restoral, restoration, revamping, salvage, service

REPAY, verb avenge, compensate, get even, give back, give in exchange, indemnify, make amends, make payment, make reparation, make requital, make restitution, pay back, pay in kind, punish, rebate, reciprocate, recompense, *reddere,* refund, reimburse, remunerate, replace, *reponere,* requite, restore, retaliate, return, revenge, reward, satisfy, square accounts

REPEAL, verb abolish, *abrogare,* abrogate, annul, avoid, cancel, countermand, declare null and void, delete, eliminate, formally withdraw, invalidate, make void, negate, nullify, obliterate, officially withdraw, override, overrule, quash, recall, render invalid, rescind, *rescindere,* retract, reverse, revoke, set aside, vacate, void, withdraw
ASSOCIATED CONCEPTS: repeal a bylaw, repeal a law, repeal a statute, repeal by implication
FOREIGN PHRASES: *Leges posteriores priores contrarias abrogant.* Subsequent laws repeal prior laws that are repugnant to them. *Jura eodem modo destituuntur quo constituuntur.* Laws are abrogated by the same means by which they are enacted.

REPEAT *(Do again),* **verb** backslide, copy, do over, duplicate, give an encore, imitate, ingeminate, *iterare,* persist, reconstruct, recreate, recur, redo, reduplicate, reenact, regenerate, reinstitute, relapse, remake, renew, replicate, reproduce, resume, retrace, return, revert

REPEAT *(State again),* **verb** chant, drum, dwell on, echo, emphasize, harp on, insist upon, iterate, paraphrase, parrot, quote, read back, reaffirm, reassert, recapitulate, recite, recount, rehash, reiterate, relate, rephrase, report, restate, retell, review, reword, run over, say again, say over, sum up, summarize, tell again, tell over, utter again

REPEATED, adjective common, commonplace, consuetudinal, consuetudinary, copied, customary, done again, done over, duplicated, echoed, everyday, frequent, habitual, imitated, incessant, monotonous, multiple, paraphrased, periodic, persistent, recited, recurrent, recurring, redone, redoubled, redundant, reduplicated, reduplicative, regular, rehearsed, reiterated, renewed, repetitional, repetitionary, repetitious, repetitive, reproduced, restated, retold, reuttered, reworded, said again, standard, stock, successive, twice-told, uniform
ASSOCIATED CONCEPTS: repeated wrongdoing

REPEL *(Disgust),* **verb** alienate, appall, be unpalatable, cause aversion, cause dislike, displease, excite dislike, fill with loathing, frighten, give offense, grate, horrify, incense, irritate, make one shudder, make one sick, make unwelcome, nauseate, offend, repulse, revolt, scandalize, shock, sicken, vex

REPEL *(Drive back),* **verb** avert, beat back, cast aside, challenge, chase away, check, checkmate, confound, confront, deflect, dispel, disperse, divert, drive away, drive back, fend off, fight off, foil, forbid, force back, forestall, frustrate, *fugare,* keep at bay, make a stand against, oppose, parry, prevent, prohibit, push back, put to flight, rebuff, renounce, *repellere,* repercuss, repudiate, repulse, resist, retrude, rout, scatter, spurn, stave off, strive against, throw off, thrust back, traverse, ward off, withstand

REPENT, *verb* apologize, atone for, be conscience striken, be penitent, be sorry for, beg pardon, bemoan, bewail, cry over, deplore, do penance, expiate, feel contrition, feel regret, feel remorse, grieve, have a guilty conscience, have qualms, humble oneself, lament, make amends, make up for, mourn, pay the penalty, plead guilty, recant, redress, reform, regret, remember with sorrow, rue, show regret for, think better of, weep over

REPENTANT, *adjective* apologetic, atoning, compunctious, confessing, conscience-smitten, conscience-stricken, contrite, full of regrets, humble, lamenting, *paenitens,* penitent, penitential, reclaimed, reformative, reformatory, reformed, regretful, regretting, remorseful, rueful, self-abasing, self-accusatory, self-condemnatory, self-convicted, self-denouncing, self-reproachful, self-reproving, sorrowful, sorry, weeping

REPERCUSSION, *noun* backfire, backlash, blast, counteraction, echo, explosion, force, impact, reaction, rebound, reciprocal action, recoil, reflection, reflex, report, response, retroaction, reverberation, ricochet, shock

REPETITIOUS, *adjective* duplicative, echoic, echoing, harping, incessant, invariable, monotonous, pleonastic, pleonastical, recapitulatory, recurrent, recurring, redundant, reduplicative, reechoed, reiterant, reiterative, repeated, repeating, repetitional, repetitionary, repetitive, stale, tedious

REPLACE, *verb* act for, alternate, change, commute, compensate, cover for, depute, deputize, duplicate, exchange, fill in for, interchange, make amends, pay back, put back, refund, reimburse, reinstall, reinstate, repay, *reponere,* represent, restitute, stand for, subrogate, *substituere,* substitute, succeed, supersede, supplant, supply an equivalent, surrogate, swap, switch, symbolize, understudy, vary

REPLACEMENT, *noun* alternate, alternative, change, commutation, compensation, counterfeit, delegate, deputy, dislocation, displacement, envoy, equivalent, exchange, fill in, interchange, makeshift, proxy, reclamation, reconstitution, reconstruction, recovery, refund, reinstatement, relief, removal, renewal, renovation, reorganization, reparation, representative, reproduction, restitution, restoration, second, secondary, shift, stand in, subrogation, substitute, substitution, successor, supersedure, supersession, supplantation, supplanter, surrogate, surrogation, swap, switch, temporary expedient, transfer, transposition, understudy
ASSOCIATED CONCEPTS: replacement cost

REPLENISH, *verb* build up, complete, contribute, deposit, enrich, fill, fill in, fill up, furnish, give, make complete, make full, make up, make up a lack, make whole, present,

provender, provide, provision, purvey, recharge, refill, refresh, refuel, reload, renew, replace, *replere,* restock, resupply, saturate, stock, store, supplement, *supplere,* supply, supply deficiencies

REPLETE, *adjective* abounding, abundant, affluent, ample, bounteous, bountiful, brimfull, brimming, chockfull, closely packed, cloyed, complete, completely full, copious, crammed, crammed solid, filled, filled to repletion, flush, fraught, full, fully supplied, gorged, jam-packed, jammed, laden, lavish, loaded, luxurious, overflowing, packed, plenitudinous, plenteous, plentiful, plethoric, pregnant, profuse, refilled, replenished, rife, satiated, satisfied, saturated, stocked, stuffed, surfeited, teeming, well-provided, well-stocked

REPLEVIN, *noun* acquisition, action to recover personal chattels, action to recover personal property, action to regain possessions, action to regain property, action to revert ownership, articles of commerce, assets, backslide, belongings, chattels, delivery back, reclamation, recoupment, recovery, recovery of property, redelivery, redemption, repossession, retaking, retrieval, salvage, writ of replevin
ASSOCIATED CONCEPTS: bailment, conversion, detinue, *ex delicto, in specie,* personal replevin, replenish bond, replevin bond, trover

REPLY, *noun* answer, counterstatement, reaction, rebuttal, reciprocation, rejoinder, remonstrance, replication, response, *responsio, responsum,* retort, return, surrebuttal
ASSOCIATED CONCEPTS: reply brief, sham reply, surreply
FOREIGN PHRASES: ***Ambigua responsio contra proferentem est accipienda.*** An ambiguous answer is to be taken against him who offers it.

REPLY, *verb* acknowledge, answer, come back at, confute, counter, make rejoinder, parry, react, rebut, refute, rejoin, respond, *respondere,* retort, return, riposte, surrebut, surrejoin
ASSOCIATED CONCEPTS: reply to a counterclaim, reply to new matter contained in an answer, surreply

REPORT *(Detailed account),* **noun** account, address, article, brief, broadcast, bulletin, chronicle, communication, criticism, description, digest, disclosure, dissemination, exposition, history, information, intelligence, manifesto, message, minute, narration, news, news story, note, notice, notification, proclamation, propagation, recapitulation, recital, recitation, record, recounting, *relatio,* relation, release, *renuntiatio,* revelation, review, saga, specification, statement, summary, talk, tidings, ventilation
ASSOCIATED CONCEPTS: accident report, grand jury report

REPORT *(Rumor),* **noun** bruit, *fama,* gossip, grapevine, hearsay, hint, intimation, scuttlebutt, talk, tattle, unconfirmed report, unverified news, whisper

REPORT *(Disclose),* **verb** acquaint, *adferre,* advise, air, announce, annunciate, apprise, broadcast, bruit, circulate publicly, communicate, declare, deliver information, describe, detail, disseminate, divulgate, divulge, enlighten, expose, expound, express, give an account of, give the facts, herald, impart, inform, make an announcement, make known, mention, notify, outline, proclaim, promulgate, publish, recite, recount, *referre, renuntiare,* report, reveal, set forth, speak about, specify, state, tell, testify to, unmask, voice, write up

REPORT *(Present oneself),* **verb** announce one's presence, answer, answer a summons, appear, appear for duty, arrive, attend, be at hand, be in attendance, check in, come, *comparere,* fulfill an engagement, meet, present oneself, put in an appearance, reveal oneself, show oneself

REPOSE *(Place),* **verb**   deposit, establish, fix, invest, lodge, plant, put, reposit, set, settle, store, vest in

REPOSE *(Rest),* **verb**   be calm, be serene, be tranquil, compose oneself, lie down, recline, relax, rest, settle, sleep, slumber

REPOSITORY, *noun*   arsenal, bank, bursary, cache, chest, coffer, conservatory, container, depository, depot, garner, promptuary, receptacle, *receptaculum,* reservatory, reservoir, safe, storehouse, storeroom, treasurehouse, treasury, warehouse

REPOSSESS, *verb*   capture, foreclose, obtain again, reacquire, recall, recapture, reclaim, recoup, recover, redeem, regain, replevy, retrieve, secure, seize, take back, take possession of
ASSOCIATED CONCEPTS: attachment, security interest

REPREHEND, *verb*   accuse, admonish, animadvert, berate, betongue, blame, bring to book, call down, call to account, cast blame upon, castigate, censure, charge, chastise, chide, condemn, correct, criticize, decry, denounce, disapprove, dress down, expostulate, exprobate, find fault with, impeach, impugn, increpate, lash, lay blame upon, lecture, object, objurgate, protest, punish, rate, rebuke, recriminate, *reprehendere,* reprimand, reproach, reprobate, reprove, run down, scold, slate, take exception, take to task, trounce, upbraid, voice disapproval

REPREHENSIBLE, *adjective*   accusable, bad, base, blamable, blameful, blameworthy, censurable, chargeable, condemnable, convictable, criminal, *culpa dignus,* culpable, delinquent, deserving censure, deserving reproof, discreditable, disgraceful, disgusting, dishonorable, disreputable, evil, exceptionable, flagitious, flagrant, foul, guilty, hateful, heinous, horrendous, ignoble, illaudable, immoral, impeachable, incorrigible, indefensible, inexcusable, inexpiable, infamous, iniquitous, monstrous, naughty, nefarious, objectionable, obnoxious, odious, offensive, open to criticism, opprobrious, peccable, peccant, rebukable, recreant, *reprehendendus,* reproachable, reprobate, reprovable, shameful, shocking, sinful, uncommendable, unjustifiable, unpardonable, unprincipled, unrighteous, unworthy, vicious, villainous, wicked, wrong

REPRESENT *(Portray),* **verb**   adumbrate, characterize, connote, delineate, denote, depict, designate, evoke, exemplify, *exprimere,* illustrate, image, indicate, mean, outline, picture, show, signify, stand for, symbolize, typify

REPRESENT *(Substitute),* **verb**   act, act as broker, act as delegate, act for, act in place of, act on behalf of, act vicariously, appear for, be ambassador for, be an agent for, be attorney for, be deputy for, be proxy for, be spokesman for, factor, replace, speak for, stand in the place of, take the part of
ASSOCIATED CONCEPTS: agency, represent a client's interests, represent a defendant, represent a principal

REPRESENTATION *(Acting for others),* **noun**   acting as attorney for, advocacy, agency, agentship, body of delegates, body of deputies, deputation, rendering legal advice, rendering legal assistance, speaking for another, substitution, supplying another's place

REPRESENTATION *(Statement),* **noun**   account, assertion of facts, asseveration, declaration, depiction, description, *effigies,* explanation, illustration, *imago,* indication, narration, narrative, portraiture, portrayal, presentation, relation, report, setting forth
ASSOCIATED CONCEPTS: false representation, material representation, misrepresentation, public representation

REPRESENTATIVE, *adjective*   acting, adumbrative, agential, characteristic, connotative, delegated, denotative, depictive, deputative, deputed, distinctive, emblematic, exemplary, faithful, figurative, graphic, graphical, illustrational, illustrative, indicative, indicatory, representational, sample, standard, symbolic, symbolical, typical, typifying
ASSOCIATED CONCEPTS: representative action, representative capacity, representative suit

REPRESENTATIVE *(Example),* **noun**   exemplar, model, paragon, sample, specimen, symbol, typical example, typical instance

REPRESENTATIVE *(Proxy),* **noun**   agent, barrister, broker, counsel, delegate, deputy, emissary, envoy, go-between, lawyer, messenger, middle man, solicitor, spokesman, substitute, substitution, trustee, *vicarius*
ASSOCIATED CONCEPTS: lawful representative, legal representative

REPRESS, *verb*   allay, bottle up, bridle, censor, check, choke, *comprimere,* control, cork, crush, curb, damp, dampen, deaden, domineer, dull, enchain, gag, hinder, hobble, hold back, hold in, hush, inhibit, keep down, keep in, keep in check, keep under control, kill, leash, limit, master, muffle, mute, muzzle, *opprimere,* overbear, overcome, overmaster, overpower, pen up, press back, prohibit, put down, quell, quench, quiet, reduce to subjection, rein in, restrain, restrict, seal up, shackle, silence, smother, squash, stay, stifle, still, strangle, subdue, subjugate, suffocate, suppress, trammel, vanquish, withhold

REPRIEVE, *noun*   day of grace, deferment, delay, delay in execution, delay in punishment, dispensation, interval of ease, moratorium, pause, postponement, postponement of penalty, quittance, respite, respite from impending punishment, stay, stay of execution, stop, suspension of execution, suspension of punishment, temporary escape, temporary relief, temporary suspension of the execution of a sentence, withdrawal of a sentence
ASSOCIATED CONCEPTS: executive reprieve, judicial reprieve, pardon

REPRIMAND, *noun*   admonishment, admonition, animadversion, blame, castigation, censure, chiding, condemnation, correction, criticism, denunciation, derogation, disapprobation, disapproval, displeasure, dispraise, dressing down, exception, exprobration, improbation, increpation, jobation, lecture, objection, objurgation, rating, rebuke, remonstrance, *reprehensio,* reprehension, reproach, reprobation, reproof, reproval, revilement, scolding, sermon, sharp censure, sharp words, stricture, trimming, upbraiding, *vituperatio,* warning
ASSOCIATED CONCEPTS: reprimand issued by the grievance committee of the bar association

REPRIMAND, *verb*   accuse, admonish, animadvert on, asperse, berate, blame, call to account, call to task, castigate, censure formally, chastise, chide, condemn, correct, criminate, decry, denounce, deprecate, disapprove, discommend, disparage, dispraise, dress down, execrate, exprobrate, find fault, flay, fulminate against, impeach, impugn, inveigh against, lash, lecture, objurgate, rail at, rant, rebuke, recriminate, remonstrate, reprehend, *reprehendere,* reproach, reprobate, reprove, revile, run down, scold, thunder against, trounce, upbraid, vilify, vilipend, *vituperare,* vituperate, warn

ASSOCIATED CONCEPTS: reprimand by the grievance committee

REPRISAL, *noun* avengement, counterattack, counterblast, counterplot, counterstroke, desert, disciplinary action, discipline, due, due punishment, getting even, measure for measure, nemesis, penalty, punishment, punition, punitive action, reaction, reciprocation, repayment, requital, retaliation, retribution, retributive justice, return, revenge, revengefulness, talion, vendetta, vengeance, vengefulness, vindictiveness

REPROACH, *noun* accusation, animadversion, blame, castigation, censure, chastisement, chiding, complaint, condemnation, contempt, *contumelia,* contumely, correction, degradation, denouncement, denunciation, derogation, disapprobation, disapproval, discredit, disgrace, dishonor, disparagement, disrepute, dressing down, exprobration, *exprobratio,* impeachment, increpation, incrimination, inculpation, indignity, jobation, objection, objurgation, obloquy, opprobrium, *probrum,* rating, rebuke, reprehension, reprimand, reprobation, reproof, revilement, scolding, shame, sharp criticism, slur, stigma, taint, tarnish, upbraiding, vilification

REPROACH, *verb* abuse, accuse, admonish, animadvert, asperse, berate, blame, brand, call to account, castigate, censure, chide, complain, condemn, criminate, criticize, decry, defame, denounce, denunciate, deprecate, disapprove, discredit, disgrace, dishonor, disparage, excoriate, express displeasure, exprobrate, find fault with, flay, frown upon, increpate, *increpitare,* incriminate, inculpate, *incusare,* inveigh against, lecture, malign, objurgate, protest against, put to shame, rail at, rant at, rebuke, reprehend, reprimand, reprobate, reprove, revile, scold, slate, speak ill of, take to task, tax, tongue lash, traduce, upbraid, vilify, vilipend, vituperate

REPROBATE, *adjective* accusable, bad, base, blameworthy, corrupt, criminal, culpable, degenerate, depraved, disgusting, disreputable, dissolute, evil-minded, facinorous, felonious, flagitious, flagrant, hardened, heinous, immoral, incorrigible, infamous, iniquitous, irreclaimable, irredeemable, irreverent, knavish, lost, morally abandoned, naughty, nefarious, obdurate, peccant, *perditus,* profligate, *profligatus,* rascally, recidivous, recreant, roguish, shameless, sinful, unconscionable, unprincipled, unregenerate, unrighteous, vicious, vile, vitiated, wicked, worthless

REPRODUCE, *verb* beget, breed, bring forth, conceive, copy, create, do again, double, duplicate, engender, father, fecundate, fructify, generate, give birth to, imitate, make again, manifold, mirror, multiply, parallel, portray, procreate, progenerate, proliferate, propagate, rebuild, reconstitute, reconstruct, recreate, redo, reduplicate, refashion, reform, *regignere,* remake, renew, repeat, replicate, sire, spawn

ASSOCIATED CONCEPTS: copyright, reproduce a record on appeal

REPROOF, *noun* admonishment, admonition, animadversion, aspersion, berating, blame, castigation, censure, charge, condemnation, contempt, criticism, denunciation, depreciation, derogation, diatribe, disapprobation, discipline, disparagement, execration, expostulation, exprobration, impeachment, objection, objurgation, obloquy, rebuff, rebuke, reprehension, reprimand, reproach, reprobation, reproval, revilement, scolding, upbraiding

REPUDIATE, *verb* abandon, abdicate, abjure, abnegate, abolish, abrogate, cancel, change sides, contradict, contravene, countermand, declare null and void, decline, default, demur, deny, disallow, disannul, disavow, disbar, discard, disclaim, dishonor, dissent, dissolve, exclude, forswear, negate, neglect, nullify, override, overrule, proscribe, protest, recant, refuse to accept, refuse to acknowledge, *reicere,* reject, renounce, repeal, *repudiare,* retract, reverse, revoke, set aside, spurn, withdraw

ASSOCIATED CONCEPTS: repudiate a cause of action, repudiate a contract

REPUDIATION, *noun* abjuration, abolition, abrogation, annulment, breach, cancellation, confutation, contradiction, counterorder, countermand, declination, defeasance, defection, denial, deposition, disaffirmation, disagreement, disallowance, disapproval, disavowal, disclaimer, disclamation, disproof, disproval, dissent, dissociation, exclusion, forswearing, negation, nonobservance, nullification, recantation, refusal, refutation, rejection, renouncement, renunciation, repeal, repellence, *repudiatio,* rescission, retractation, retraction, reversal, revocation, setting aside, veto, voidance, withdrawal

ASSOCIATED CONCEPTS: repudiation of a contract

REPUGNANT (*Exciting aversion*), ***adjective*** abhorrent, abominable, detestable, disagreeable, disgustful, disgusting, disliked, displeasing, distasteful, *diversus,* forbidding, fulsome, hateful, inedible, insufferable, loathsome, nauseating, noisome, objectionable, obnoxious, odious, offending, offensive, out of favor, painful, repellent, repelling, *repugnans,* repulsive, revolting, unacceptable, unappetizing, undesirable, unpalatable, unpleasant, unpopular, unsavory

REPUGNANT (*Incompatible*), ***adjective*** adverse, alien, antagonistic, at odds, at variance, clashing, conflicting, contradictory, contrary, different, disagreeing, discordant, hostile, inaccordant, incongruous, inconsistent, inharmonious, inimical, irreconcilable, jarring, opposed, opposing, unconformable

ASSOCIATED CONCEPTS: repugnant to the Constitution

REPULSE, *verb* beat back, beat off, chase, check, counteract, countervail, defeat, dispel, drive away, drive back, eschew, fend off, frustrate, gainsay, grapple with, hinder, impede, keep at bay, make a stand, obstruct, oppose, oppugn, overthrow, *propulsare,* push back, put to flight, rebuff, reject, repel, *repellere,* repercuss, repudiate, resist, retrude, rout, scorn, send away, shun, snub, spurn, stem, throw back, thwart, turn away, ward off, withstand

REPULSIVE, *adjective* abhorrent, abominable, appalling, arousing aversion, beastly, contemptible, despicable, detestable, dirty, disagreeable, disgusting, disliked, displeasing, distasteful, dreadful, execrable, fearful, feculent, filthy, *foedus,* forbidding, foul, frightful, ghastly, grim, grisly, gross, hateful, hideous, horrible, horrid, horrifying, insufferable, loathsome, misshapen, monstrous, nasty, nauseating, nauseous, noisome, noxious, objectionable, obnoxious, obscene, *odiosus,* odious, offensive, rank, repellent, repelling, repugnant, revolting, rotten, shocking, sickening, sloppy, squalid, ugly, unbearable, unclean, uninviting, unpalatable, unpleasant, unprepossessing, unsavory, unsightly, vile

REPUTABLE, adjective acclaimed, celebrated, conscientious, creditable, dependable, dignified, distinguished, eminent, esteemed, estimable, ethical, faithful, famed, held in esteem, held in good repute, high-principled, honest, hon*estus*, honorable, honored, illustrious, incorruptible, known, meritorious, moral, noble, notable, principled, prominent, reliable, renowned, respectable, respected, revered, reverenced, righteous, scrupulous, trustworthy, uncorrupt, unimpeachable, upright, venerated, virtuous, well-known, well thought of, worthy

REPUTATION, noun acclaim, celebration, celebrity, consequence, credit, distinction, eminence, esteem, estimation, *fama,* fame, famousness, glory, good name, illustriousness, importance, luster, mark, name, notability, note, notoriety, *opinio,* popular favor, position, position in society, precedence, preeminence, prestige, prominence, rank, regard, renown, report, repute, respect, respectability, standing, station, status
ASSOCIATED CONCEPTS: character witness, reputation evidence

REPUTED, adjective accepted by general opinion, accepted by public opinion, asserted, assumed, concluded, considered, declared, deduced, deemed, held out as, imagined to be, implied, inferred, insinuated, judged to be, known to be, maintained as, perceived as, presumed as, presupposed to be, proposed to be, propounded to be, purported, putative, regarded as, supposed, understood to be
ASSOCIATED CONCEPTS: reputed owner

REPUTEDLY, adverb according to general belief, according to reputation, allegedly, assumedly, assumptively, presumably, reportedly, rumored, seemingly, supposedly

REQUEST, noun appeal, application, asking, begging, behest, beseechment, bid, call, claim, demand, desideratum, entreaty, exaction, expressed desire, impetration, imploration, importunity, insistence, invitation, invocation, motion, obsecration, order, petition, plea, *postulatio,* postulation, prayer, *preces,* proposal, requirement, requisition, *rogatio,* solicitation, suggestion, supplication, wish

REQUEST, verb adjure, appeal, apply for, ask for, beckon, beg for, beseech, bid, cadge, call for, canvass, claim, clamor for, command, cry for, demand, desire, dun, enjoin, entreat, exact, impetrate, *implorare,* implore, importune, invite, make application, mendicate, nag, *obsecrare,* obtest, order, petition, petition for, plead for, pray, put in for, require, requisition, *rogare,* seek, send for, solicit, sue for, summon, supplicate, urge, want

REQUIRE (Compel), verb assess, call for, cause, coerce, command, constrain, decree, demand, dictate, direct, draft, drive, enact, enforce, enjoin, entail, exact, *exigere,* force, impose, insist on, issue a command, levy, make, necessitate, obligate, oblige, ordain, order, *poscere,* postulate, prescribe, requisition, subject, summon, tax
ASSOCIATED CONCEPTS: required by law

REQUIRE (Need), verb crave, demand, *desiderare,* desire, *egere,* fall short, feel the necessity for, have an insufficiency, lack, miss, necessitate, request, *requirere,* stand in need of, want

REQUIREMENT, noun adjuration, behest, bidding, call, claim, command, commandment, compulsion, conscription, constraint, decree, decretal, demand, dictate, direction, directive, edict, enforcement, enjoinment, essential, essential desideratum, exaction, exigency, extremity, fiat, imperative, imposition, indispensable item, injunction, mandate, matter of necessity, must, necessitation, necessity, need, obligation, obsession, onus, order, precondition, prerequisite, prescript, prescription, pressing concern, pressure, proviso, regulation, request, requisite, requisition, rescript, responsibility, ruling, specification, ukase, ultimatum, urgency, vital part, want, warrant
ASSOCIATED CONCEPTS: requirement contract

REQUISITE, adjective basic, binding, called for, compulsory, crying, demanded, entailed, essential, exigent, expedient, imperative, important, in demand, incumbent on, indispensable, ineluctable, inevasible, instant, mandatory, must, *necessarius,* necessary, necessitated, needed, needful, obligatory, postulated, prerequisite, pressing, required, requisitory, urgent, vital, wanted

REQUISITION, noun application, behest, bidding, call, claim, compulsory acquisition, demand, direction, exaction, forcible demand, formal request, indent, injunction, levy, mandate, necessitation, necessity, need, order, petition, *postulatio,* request, requirement, requisite, want

REQUITEMENT, noun compensation, consideration, indemnification, indemnity, payment, quittance, recompense, redress, remuneration, reparation, repayment, requital, restitution, restoration, satisfaction

REQUITAL, noun acknowledgment, *compensare,* compensation, consideration, desert, emolument, guerdon, indemnification, indemnity, meed, pay, payment, quittance, recompense, redress, remuneration, reparation, repayment, reprisal, requitement, restitution, retaliation, return, reward, satisfaction

RES IPSA LOQUITUR, noun automatic lack of due diligence, automatic negligence, automatic responsibility, breach of duty, certain dereliction, definite carelessness, doctrine of *res ipsa loquitur,* imprudence, irresponsibility, lack of attention, liability imposed for obvious responsibility, liability for sole and exclusive control, obvious and certain negligence, the thing speaks for itself
ASSOCIATED CONCEPTS: negligence

RES JUDICATA, noun accommodated, adjudication, adjusted, agreed, arranged, brought to termination, came to determination, concluded, decided, decision, decree, determination, judgment, negotiated, resolved

RESCIND, verb abolish, *abrogare,* abrogate, annul, call back, cancel, countermand, counterorder, cut off, cut short, declare null and void, disannul, discard, disestablish, dismiss, dissolve, do away with, end, erase, invalidate, negate, nullify, obliterate, override, overrule, quash, recall, recant, remove, render invalid, renege, renounce, repeal, repudiate, *rescindere,* retract, reverse, revoke, set aside, sweep aside, take back, vacate, void, wipe out, withdraw
ASSOCIATED CONCEPTS: rescind a contract, rescind an offer

RESCISION, noun abandonment, abjuration, abnegation, abolishment, abolition, abrogation, annulment, cancellation, change of mind, countermand, counterorder, defeasance, deletion, destruction, disannulment, disavowal, disclaimer, dissolution, eradication, invalidation, negation, nullification, overruling, overthrow, quashing, recall, recantation, renunciation, repeal, repudiation, rescindment,

retraction, reversal, revocation, revokement, suspension, termination, vitiation, voidance, withdrawal
ASSOCIATED CONCEPTS: rescision and restriction

RESCUE, verb aid, deliver, disenthrall, disimprison, emancipate, *exsolvere,* extricate, free, free from confinement, free from danger, let escape, let out, *liberare,* liberate, manumit, preserve, ransom, recapture, reclaim, recover, redeem, release, retake, retrieve, safeguard, salvage, save, set free, set loose, take to safety, unbind, unchain, unfetter, unloose, unshackle, untrammel
ASSOCIATED CONCEPTS: Good Samaritan laws, rescue doctrine

RESEARCH, noun analysis, careful search, close inquiry, *eruditio,* examination, experimentation, exploration, factfinding, indagation, inquest, inquiry, inquisition, inspection, investigation, observation, probe, pursuit, quest, questioning, reconnaissance, scrutiny, search, study, survey, testing program

RESEARCH, verb analyze, burrow, chase after, check on, delve into, dissect, examine, experiment, explore, go in quest of, hunt, indagate, inquire, inspect, investigate, look into, probe into, pry, pursue, pursue an inquiry, quest, read up on, scan, scrutinize, search, seek, sleuth, study, test, trace, track, unearth

RESEMBLANCE, noun affinity, agreement, alikeness, analogy, approximation, closeness, conformance, conformity, correspondence, counterpart, ditto, double, duplication, effigy, equality, fascimile, fellow, homogeneity, identicalness, identity, image, imitation, kinship, likeness, match, mate, mold, parallel, parity, reflection, replica, representation, reproduction, sameness, selfsameness, semblance, similarity, similitude, *similitudo,* type, uniformity

RESENT, verb be angry, be indignant, be insulted, be offended, be piqued, be provoked, be revengeful, be vengeful, be vexed, bear malice, bridle, bristle, chafe, dislike, express annoyance, express ill will, feel annoyance, feel displeasure, feel hurt, feel ill will, feel resentment, find intolerable, harbor a grudge, hate, *moleste ferre,* show indignation, take amiss, take exception to, take offense, take poorly, take umbrage, view with dissatisfaction

RESENTFUL, adjective acrimonious, angry, bitter, bristling, choleric, churlish, discontented, displeased, distrustful, embittered, envious, furious, galled, grouchy, grudging, grumpy, huffy, hurt, ill-disposed, implacable, in a huff, in high dudgeon, indignant, infuriated, *iracundus,* jealous, malevolent, malicious, malignant, miffed, mistrustful, moody, offended, outraged, pained, peevish, piqued, querulous, resentive, revengeful, sore, spiteful, splenetic, sulky, sullen, surly, suspicious, touchy, umbrageous, unforgiving, up in arms, vengeful, venomous, vindictive, waspish

RESENTMENT, noun acrimony, affront, anger, animosity, animus, antagonism, bile, bitterness, choler, dander, disaffection, discontent, displeasure, dissatisfaction, dudgeon, enmity, envy, fury, gall, grudge, hatred, huff, ill will, indignation, *ira,* ire, jealousy, malice, malignity, offense, pique, rankling, resentfulness, soreness, spite, spleen, stomachus, umbrage, vengefulness, venom, vindictiveness, wounded pride, wrath

RESERVATION (Condition), **noun** condition, *exceptio,* exception, exemption, limitation, provision, proviso, qualification, requisite, restriction, salvo, saving clause, specification, stipulation

ASSOCIATED CONCEPTS: conditional contracts, reservation contained in acceptance, reservation contained in grant, reservation in deed, reservation in insurance policy

RESERVATION (Engagement), **noun** booking, preengagement, promise to set aside, registration, retaining, retainment, retention, saving, withholding
ASSOCIATED CONCEPTS: reservation of interest, reservation of life estate, reservation of rights, reservation of title
FOREIGN PHRASES: *Quod sub certa forma concessum vel reservatum est non trahitur ad valorem vel compensationem.* That which is granted or reserved under a certain form, cannot be twisted into a valuation or compensation.

RESERVE, noun assets, cache, conservation, *copia,* depository, fund, means, provision, resource, resources, savings, stock, store, storehouse, supply
ASSOCIATED CONCEPTS: accumulated reserve, held in reserve, insurance reserve, legal reserve, minimum reserves, premium reserve, reserve funds, reserve valve, reserved powers

RESERVE, verb accumulate, amass, bank, bespeak, cache, create a fund, deposit, earmark, except, garner, hide, hoard, hold, hold back, keep, keep back, keep in reserve, keep on hand, lay away, maintain, preselect, preserve, put aside, *reponere,* retain, save, set apart, set aside, shelve, stock pile, store, store away, store up, withhold
ASSOCIATED CONCEPTS: reserve an interest, reserve one's rights

RESIDE, verb abide, be located, be quartered, be situated, become a citizen, bide, be domicile, domiciliate, dwell, establish oneself, *habitare,* have an address, *incolere,* indwell, inhabit, *inhabitare,* live, live at, lodge, occupy, remain, settle, sojourn, squat, stay, take up abode, take up residence, tarry, tenant

RESIDENCE, noun abode, accommodations, address, billet, commorance, commorancy, domicile, domiciliation, *domicilium, domus,* dwelling, habitancy, habitat, habitation, home, housing, inhabitancy, inhabitation, living place, living quarters, lodgings, lodgment, place, place of residence, quarters, residency, sedes
ASSOCIATED CONCEPTS: domicile, legal residence, residency requirement

RESIDENT, noun addressee, boarder, burgess, denizen, dweller, habitant, *habitator,* indweller, inhabitant, inhabiter, inmate, lodger, native, occupant, occupier, oppidan, residentiary, resider, settler, sojourner, tenant, townsman, villager

RESIDENTIAL, adjective domestic, domiciliary, fit for habitation, home, household, inhabited, living, not commercial, not public, occupied, private
ASSOCIATED CONCEPTS: residential area, residential property, residential purposes, residential use

RESIDUAL, noun balance, excess, leftover, remainder, remains, residuary, residue, residuum, surplus

RESIDUARY, adjective excess, excessive, left over, outstanding, remaining, residual, resultant, spare, surplus, unspent
ASSOCIATED CONCEPTS: residuary bequest, residuary clause, residuary devise, residuary estate, residuary fund, residuary interest, residuary legacy, residuary legatee

RESIGN, verb abandon, abdicate, *abire,* abjure, capitulate, cease work, cede, *cedere,* demit, depart, *deponere,* desist from, disclaim, divest oneself of, drop out, forego, forsake, give notice, give up, leave, quit, reject, relinquish, renounce, repudiate, retreat, stand aside, step down, surrender, tender one's resignation, vacate, withdraw, yield

RESIGNATION *(Passive acceptance)*, **noun**   acquiescence, *animus submissus,* capitulation, deference, docility, endurance, fatalism, forbearance, fortitude, lack of complaint, lack of resistance, longanimity, meekness, nonresistance, obedience, passiveness, passivity, patience, stoicism, submission, submissiveness, sufferance, surrender, tolerance, toleration, yeilding

RESIGNATION *(Relinquishment)*, **noun**   abandonment, *abdicatio,* abdication, abjuration, abjurement, cession, demission, departure, evacuation, forsaking, giving up, leaving, quitting, renouncement, renunciation, retirement, secession, surrender, termination, vacation, withdrawal, yielding
FOREIGN PHRASES: *Resignatio est juris proprii spontanea refutatio.* Resignation is a spontaneous relinquishment of one's own right.

RESIGNED, *adjective*   adapted, adjusted, agreeable, biddable, defeatist, easily managed, enduring, forbearant, forbearing, long-suffering, manageable, meek, nonresistant, passive, patient, reconciled, resistless, stoic, stoical, submissive, surrendered, tame, tolerant, tractable, unassertive, uncomplaining, unrepining, unresisting, willing, yielding

RESILIENT, *adjective*   able to endure, adaptable, adaptive, adjustable, bendable, bouncing, buoyant, durable, elastic, flexible, flexile, jaunty, malleable, *mollis,* pliable, pliant, recoiling, responsive, responsive to change, rubbery, sequacious, spongy, sprightly, springy, strong, tractable, wiry, yielding

RESIST *(Oppose)*, **verb**   assail, assault, bar, beat back, block, breast, check, combat, confront, contradict, contravene, counter, counteract, cross, defy, dissent, fight, hinder, impugn, make a stand against, obstruct, offer resistance, oppugn, parry, prevent, protest, rebel, rebuff, recalcitrate, refuse to yield, reluctate, repel, repulse, retaliate, rival, stem, stop, strike, strike back, strive against, thwart
FOREIGN PHRASES: *Error qui non resistitur approbatur.* An error which is not resisted or opposed is waived.

RESIST *(Withstand)*, **verb**   be immune, be strong, be unsusceptible, bear, bear up, challenge, continue, cope with, disregard, endure, fend off, hold off, hold out, hold up, last, maintain, persevere, persist, prevail against, refuse to submit, remain, stand, stand fast, stand firm, stand up to, stay, tolerate, weather
ASSOCIATED CONCEPTS: resisting arrest

RESISTANCE, *noun*   antagonism, assault, attack, battle, blocking, check, combat, confrontation, contention, contrariety, contrariness, contravention, contumacy, counteraction, defiance, disobedience, fight, hindrance, immunity, imperviousness, insubordination, insurgence, insurrection, interference, mutiny, noncompliance, nonconformance, obstinacy, obstruction, oppugnance, oppugnation, protest, rebellion, rebuff, recalcitrance, recusancy, refusal, reluctance, renitence, repugnance, repulsion, revolt, revolution, sedition, stand, strife, strike, struggle, unalterableness, unsusceptibility, unwillingness, unyieldingness, uprising, withstanding

RESOLUTE, *adjective*   adamant, bent, *constans,* constant, decided, determined, diligent, dogged, earnest, faithful, firm, *firmus,* fixed, *fortis,* immutable, indefatigable,

indomitable, industrious, inexorable, inflexible, intent upon, intransigent, obdurate, obstinate, persevering, persistent, pertinacious, purposeful, relentless, resolved, sedulous, serious, set, settled, stanch, steadfast, steady, strong-willed, stubborn, tenacious, unalterable, unbending, unchanging, uncompromising, undaunted, undeviating, unfaltering, unflinching, unrelenting, unshaken, unswerving, untiring, unwavering, unyielding, vigorous, zealous

RESOLUTION *(Decision)*, **noun**   application, constancy, decretum, determination, earnestness, firmness, indefatigability, intention, obduracy, obstinacy, perseverance, persistence, purpose, resoluteness, resolve, *scitum, sententia,* spunk, staying power, steadfastness, steadiness, tenacity, will, will power, zealotry

RESOLUTION *(Formal statement)*, **noun**   declaration, deliverance, formal expression, plan, presentation, pronouncement, proposal, proposition, statement, written announcement

RESOLVE *(Decide)*, **verb**   arrive at a conclusion, arrive at a decision, ascertain, be firm, be settled in opinion, come to a determination, *constituere, decernere,* determine, devote oneself to, fix in purpose, make a choice, make a decision, make up one's mind, plan, propose, purpose, settle on by deliberate will, settle upon, statuere, take a stand, will

RESOLVE *(Solve)*, **verb**   clarify, clear up, decipher, disentangle, dispel misunderstanding, elucidate, enucleate, figure out, find a solution, find the answer, hit upon a solution, illuminate, interpret, make clear, make plain, provide the answer, remove misunderstanding, reveal, reveal the answer, shed light upon, throw light upon, understand, unravel, unscramble, untangle

RESORT, *verb*   administer, adopt, apply, avail oneself of, bring into play, call forth, employ, enlist, exercise, fall back upon, have recourse, look to, make use of, practice, press into service, put to use, try, turn to for help, turn to for support, use, utilize

RESOUNDING, *adjective*   absolute, booming, certain, clear, decided, definite, echoing, emphatic, explicit, forceful, incontestable, incontrovertible, intensive, loud, marked, overwhelming, pealing, positive, rebounding, repercussive, reverberant, reverberating, reverberatory, rich, ringing, sonorous, sounding, strong, thunderous, undisputed, vigorous

RESOURCE, *noun*   accumulation, asset, available means, capital, contrivance, dependence, device, essential, estate, expedient, *facultates,* fund, income, instrument, material, means, property, provision, reserve, reserve fund, resort, revenue, source, stock, stock in trade, store, supply, support, tool, wealth, wherewithal

RESOURCEFUL, *adjective*   able, able to meet situations, accomplished, adroit, apt, artful, bright, *callidus,* capable, clever, competent, conversant, crafty, creative, cunning, deft, dexterous, efficient, endowed, enterprising, experienced, facile, felicitous, fertile, gifted, habile, handy, imaginative, *ingeniosus,* ingenious, inventive, original, practiced, prepared, proficient, sagacious, sharp, shrewd, skillful, smart, *sollers,* talented, trained, venturesome, versatile

RESPECT, *noun*   admiration, adoration, appreciation, approbation, approval, attention, awe, civility, commendation, consideration, courtesy, courtliness, credit, deference, devoirs, dignity, esteem, estimation, etiquette, favor, good manners, good will, homage, honor, humbleness, humility, idolization, laudation, note, obeisance, *observantia,* ovation, polite regard, politeness, praise, prestige, recognition, regard, repute, reverence, testimonial, tribute, veneration, worship, worth

RESPECTFULLY, *adverb* compliantly, courteously, decorously, deferentially, dutifully, humbly, obediently, politely, regardfully, *reverenter,* reverently, submissively, *summisse,* unassumingly, *verecunde,* with all respect, with compliance, with deference, with due deference, with due respect, with the highest respect
ASSOCIATED CONCEPTS: respectfully submitted to the court

RESPECTIVELY, *adverb* apiece, each, each in turn, in turn, independently, individually, one at a time, one by one, separately, severally, singly

RESPITE *(Interval of rest),* **noun** abeyance, break, breathing spell, breathing time, cessation, halt, interim, interlude, intermediate time, intermission, interruption, lapse, letup, lull, pause, recess, relaxation, rest, spell, stay, stop, suspension, temporary stoppage, wait

RESPITE *(Reprieve),* **noun** acquittal, amnesty, clearance, deliverance, discharge, exemption, grace, immunity, pardon, release, stay of execution

RESPOND, *verb* acknowledge, answer, counterclaim, debate, discuss, exchange opinions, explain, give an answer, join issue, make a rejoinder, parry, plead, provide an answer, react, rebut, rejoin, reply, retort, return an answer

RESPONDENT, *noun* answerer, appellant, co-respondent, defendant, party answering a summons or bill, replier, responder

RESPONSE, *noun* acknowledgment, answer, antiphon, countercharge, counterstatement, explanation, plea, reaction, rebuttal, rejoinder, replication, reply, respondence, responsal, retort, return, riposte, surrebutter, surrejoinder

RESPONSIBILITY *(Accountability),* **noun** accountableness, amenability, answerability, bounden duty, boundness, burden, chargeability, commitment, compulsion, culpability, duty, encumbrance, engagement, imperative duty, liability, obligation, obligatoriness, pledge, promise, *rationem rei,* subjection to, that which is owing
ASSOCIATED CONCEPTS: diminished responsibility

RESPONSIBILITY *(Conscience),* **noun** claims of conscience, compunction, conscientiousness, dependability, ethical judgment, faithfulness, feeling of obligation, incorruptibility, inviolability, inward monitor, moral consciousness, moral faculty, moral obligation, moral sense, morality, scruples, scrupulousness, sense of duty, sense of obligation, sense of right and wrong, stability, trustworthiness, unperfidiousness, untreacherousness, uprightness

RESPONSIBLE *(Dependable),* **adjective** accountable, answerable, assailable, at fault, blamable, blameworthy, chargeable, culpable, guilty, indebted, negligent, obligated, obliged, reckless
ASSOCIATED CONCEPTS: duty, responsible cause, responsible party

RESPONSIBLE *(Liable),* **adjective** accountable, answerable, dependable, dutiful, legally accountable, legally obligated, legitimate, liable, obligated, trustworthy

RESPONSIVE, *adjective* accessible, active, acute, admissive, alert, alive, answering, communicative, discerning, keen, perceptive, prudent, reacting, reactive, receptive, reciprocative, rejoining, replying, respondent, sensible, sensitive, sentient, sharp, susceptible
ASSOCIATED CONCEPTS: responsive answers, responsive pleading

REST *(Be supported by),* **verb** couch, lay, lean, lie, lounge, perch, prop, recline, squat

REST *(Cease from action),* **verb** abstain, be at ease, be peaceful, be quiet, be still, be tranquil, calm down, cease, come to a standstill, desist, discontinue, end, halt, idle, keep quiet, lounge, pause, recess, relax, repose, retire, settle, stand still, stay, stop, stop work, take a break, take time out, terminate

REST *(End a legal case),* **verb** cease to litigate, complete prosecution, conclude proceeding, end the introduction of evidence, end the presentation of evidence, finish litigation, submit the case, terminate a trial
ASSOCIATED CONCEPTS: rest a case

RESTATE, *verb* construe, copy, duplicate, echo, elucidate, explain, go over, go over the same ground, iterate, paraphrase, parrot, plagiarize, reaffirm, reassert, recapitulate, recite, recount, rehash, reiterate, repeat, rephrase, restate, retell, review, reword, run over, say over again, summarize, sum up, tautologize

RESTATEMENT, *noun* abridgment, abstract, brief, compendium, condensation, *conlectio,* conspectus, digest, *enumeratio,* epitome, explanation, going over, iteration, paraphrase, reaffirmation, reassertion, recapitulation, recital, recountal, recounting, rehash, reiteration, repetition, rephrasing, replay, retelling, review, rewording, summary, synopsis, translation

RESTITUTION, *noun* adjustment, amends, atonement, compensation, damages, emolument, expiation, giving back, indemnification, paying back, payment, quittance, rebate, reclamation, recompense, recoupment, recovery, reddition, redemption, redress, refund, reimbursement, reinstatement, remitter, remuneration, reparation, repayment, replacement, requital, requitement, restoration, retrieval, return, reversion, satisfaction, settlement
ASSOCIATED CONCEPTS: order of restitution, partial restitution, *quantum meruit,* writ of restitution
FOREIGN PHRASES: *In restitutionibus benignissima interpretatio facienda est.* The most favorable construction is to be adopted in restitutions.

RESTIVE, *adjective* averse, balking, balky, cantankerous, contumacious, crossgrained, crotchety, deaf to reason, demurring, difficult, discontented, disinclined, disobedient, exceptious, excitable, excited, fidgety, fractious, fretful, grumpy, headstrong, humorsome, ill at ease, impatient, incorrigible, inflexible, insubordinate, insurgent, intractable, intransigent, irreconcilable, lawless, loath, moody, mulish, mutinous, obdurate, obstinate, on edge, out-of-sorts, peevish, perverse, pervicacious, rebellious, recalcitrant, recusant, refractory, reluctant, renitent, resentful, resisting control, restiff, restless, revolutionary, seditious, skittish, splenetic, stickling, stubborn, sulky, sullen, unaccommodating, uncomplaisant, uncompliant, uncomplying, unconsenting, uncontrollable, uneasy, ungovernable, unmanageable, unquiet, unrestful, unruly, unsettled, unsubmissive, unwilling, unyielding, wayward, willful

RESTORE *(Renew),* **verb**   ameliorate, amend, correct, cure, doctor up, energize, fix, heal, improve, make better, make whole, meliorate, mend, patch, patch up, put in order, put in repair, put right, reanimate, rearrange, rebuild, recondition, reconstitute, reconstruct, recreate, rectify, redintegrate, redo, refashion, refit, reform, refresh, regenerate, rehabilitate, reinvigorate, rejuvenate, remake, remedy, remodel, renovate, reorganize, repair, restitute, resuscitate, retouch, revive, revivify

RESTORE *(Return),* **verb**   atone, bring back, give back, hand back, indemnify, make amends, make good, make reparation, make restitution, put back, recompense, recoup, *reddere,* redeem, redress, reestablish, *referre,* refund, reimburse, reinstall, reinstate, reinvest with, remit, render up, repay, replace, revest, satisfy, send back
ASSOCIATED CONCEPTS: restore to one's former position, restored to possession
FOREIGN PHRASES: ***Reddere, nil aliud est quam acceptum restituere; seu, reddere est quasi retro dare, et redditur dicitur a redeundo, quia retro it.*** To render is nothing more than to restore that which has been received; or, to render is as it were to give back, and it is called "rendering" from "returning", because it goes back again.

RESTRAIN, verb   arrest, bar, bind, blockade, bridle, call a halt, check, confine, constrain, contain, control, cramp, curb, curtail, debar, delimit, deprive of liberty, detain, deter, disallow, discountenance, enchain, enclose, enjoin, fasten, fetter, forbid, govern, hamper, handcuff, handicap, harness, hinder, hold, hold back, hold in check, hold in custody, immure, impound, imprison, incarcerate, inhibit, interdict, jail, keep, keep under control, keep within bounds, limit, lock up, manacle, moderate, obstruct, oppose, prevent, prohibit, proscribe, quell, repress, *reprimere,* restrict, *retinere,* shackle, stifle, stop, subdue, subjugate, suppress, take into custody, take prisoner, *tenere,* tie, trammel, vanquish, wall in, withhold
ASSOCIATED CONCEPTS: restraining order, restraining statute
FOREIGN PHRASES: ***Exempla illustrant non restrigunt legem.*** Examples illustrate, but do not restrain, the law.

RESTRAINT, noun   arrest, ban, bar, barricade, blockade, bondage, brake, bridle, captivity, caution, censure, check, circumscription, confinement, constraint, containment, control, curb, custody, damper, deprivation of liberty, detention, determent, deterrence, deterrent, disallowance, discipline, dissuasion, durance, embargo, forbearance, forbiddance, guardianship, hamper, hindrance, holdback, impediment, *impedimentum,* imprisonment, incarceration, inhibition, injunction, interception, interference, limitation, *moderatio,* moderation, obstacle, obstruction, opposition, prevention, prohibition, proscription, repression, reserve, restriction, retardation, self-control, self-denial, servitude, shackle, slavery, stay, stop, stoppage, suppression, taboo, temperance, veto
ASSOCIATED CONCEPTS: combination in restraint of trade, conspiracy in restraint of trade, prior restraint, restraint on alienation

RESTRICT, verb   astrict, bar, bind, bound, bridle, cage, censor, chain, check, circumscribe, *circumscribere,* cloister, *coercere,* confine, constrain, control, coop, cramp, curb, debar, define, delimit, delimitate, demarcate, diminish, disallow, enchain, encumber, entrammel, exclude, fetter, forbid, frustrate, hamper, handcuff, handicap, hedge in, hem in, hobble, hold back, immure, inhibit, interdict, keep within limits, limit, localize, manacle, modify, muzzle, narrow, obstruct, pen, pin down, pinion, preclude, prevent, prohibit, proscribe, put under restraint, qualify, reduce, repress, restrain, restringe, secure, shackle, shut out, specialize, stifle, stop, suppress, taboo, tether, tie up, trammel, veto, wall in
ASSOCIATED CONCEPTS: restricted allotment, restricted assets

RESTRICTED *(Confidential),* **adjective**   close, confined, exclusive, intimate, inviolate, irrevealable, personal, private, privy, reserved, secret

RESTRICTED *(Limited),* **adjective**   burdensome, conditional, confining, contingent, cumbrous, defining, definite, definitive, dependent, exact, exceptional, exclusive, hindering, impeditive, inhibitive, interdictive, limitative, local, narrow, onerous, partial, precise, prohibitive, prohibitory, proscriptive, provisional, qualified, qualifying, regional, repressive, restrictive, restringent, specific, suppressive
ASSOCIATED CONCEPTS: restricted covenant, restricted endorsement, restrictive condition

RESTRICTION, noun   *angustiae,* bonds, boundary, bounds, check, circumscription, condition, confinement, constraint, constriction, containment, curb, demarcation, distinction, *finis,* impediment, interdiction, limitation, *modus,* obligation, prohibition, qualification, regulation, reservation, restraint
ASSOCIATED CONCEPTS: restriction on alienation

RESTRICTIVE, adjective   circumscriptive, clannish, cliquish, conditional, contingent, defining, deterrent, exclusive, hindering, impeditive, inflexible, interdictive, interdictory, limitary, limitative, limiting, modificatory, modifying, narrow, preclusive, preventative, preventive, prohibitionary, prohibitive, prohibitory, proscriptive, provisional, provisory, qualifying, repressive, restraining, select, selective, stiff, straitlaced, suppressive
ASSOCIATED CONCEPTS: restrictive covenant, restrictive endorsement, restrictive interpretation, restrictive provisions, restrictive title

RESULT, noun   aftermath, conclusion, consequence, *consequentia,* decision, denouement, determination, development, effect, end, eventuality, *exitus,* finding, *fructus,* fruit, fruition, harvest, judgment, outcome, outgrowth, output, product, resolution, resultant, termination, turnout, upshot, verdict, yield

RESULT, verb   accrue, arise, be due to, be the effect, be the outcome, come forth, come from, conclude, *consequi,* derive from, develop, emanate, emerge, end, ensue, *evenire,* eventuate, *fieri,* flow, follow, issue, originate, proceed, proceed from, redound, rise, spring, terminate, turn out
ASSOCIATED CONCEPTS: causation, direct result, necessary result, probable result, proximate result, result in damages suffered

RESUME, verb   advance, begin again, carry on, continue, follow, forge ahead, get a fresh start, go on, move ahead, proceed, progress, pursue, *recolere,* recommence, renew, *repetere,* return to, start afresh, start again, start forward again, take up again

RESUMPTION, noun   continuance, fresh start, new beginning, recommencement, recrudescence, reentry, reinstatement, renewal, reopening, reprise, resurgence, resurrection, return to normal, revival

RESURGENCE, *noun* come back, fresh spurt, new energy, reanimation, reappearance, rebirth, recovery, recuperation, recurrence, reestablishment, regeneration, regenesis, rejuvenation, renaissance, renascence, renewal, restoration, resumption, resurgence, resurrection, resuscitation, reversion, revival, revivification

RESURRECT, *verb* bring back, bring to, call back, reanimate, rebuild, recall to life, recondition, regenerate, reincarnate, rejuvenate, rekindle, renew, reorganize, restore, resuscitate, revitalize, revive, revivify

RESUSCITATE, *verb* breath fresh life into, bring back to life, cure, improve, reanimate, recreate, recuperate, reestablish, refresh, regenerate, rehabilitate, reinvigorate, rekindle, remedy, renew, restore, restore to life, resurrect, revivify, renovate, revitalize, revive

RETAIL, *adjective* by the piece, commercial, engaged in commerce, marketing, mercantile, singly

RETAIN *(Employ),* ***verb*** book, commission, contract for, engage, enlist, give a job, hire, keep, keep in pay, maintain, put to work, recruit, reserve, secure

RETAIN *(Keep in possession),* ***verb*** bear in mind, call up, cause to be remembered, cling to, clutch, *conservare,* continue to hold, detain, grasp, have, hold, hold fast, hold in possession, impress upon the memory, keep, keep hold of, keep in mind, maintain, possess, preserve, put away, recall, recollect, remember, reserve, save, secure, sustain, *tenere,* withhold

RETAINER, *noun* *arrhabo,* compensation, employment fee, engaging fee, fee contingent on future legal services, fee paid to secure legal services, income, payment, professional fee, recompense, remuneration, retaining fee
ASSOCIATED CONCEPTS: attorney's retainer

RETALIATE, *verb* answer back, avenge, counter, exchange blows, get back, get even, give measure for measure, match, pay back, rebut, reciprocate, repay, repay in kind, requite, return, revenge, strike back, take retribution, take revenge, take vengeance, *ulcisci*

RETARD *(Delay),* ***verb*** check, countercheck, defer, detain, ease off, hamper, hinder, hold up, impede, inhibit, interfere, procrastinate, stall, stem

RETARD *(Obstruct),* ***verb*** arrest, bar, block, check, clog, condemn, constrict, control, cramp, curb, debar, diminish, disadvantage, discontinue, encumber, entrammel, hamper, hinder, hold up, impede, inhibit, intercept, interfere, interpose, interrupt, occlude, preclude, prevent, thwart, trammel, withstand

RETARD *(Slow up),* ***verb*** brake, check, crawl, dawdle, decelerate, hamper, hinder, inhibit, interfere, linger, move slowly, slow down

RETENTION, *noun* *conservatio,* constraint, control, custodianship, grasp, hold, holding action, holding power, keeping, memory, *possessio,* reservation, restraint, retainment, *retentio,* tenacity
ASSOCIATED CONCEPTS: retention of benefits

RETICENT, *adjective* cautious, concise, confidential, constrained, detached, distant, evasive, guarded, laconic, mute, noncommittal, recondite, remote, reserved, restrained, retiring, secretive, sparing of words, standoffish, succinct, taciturn, uncommunicative, unobtrusive, unresponsive, withdrawn

RETIRE *(Conclude a career),* ***verb*** abdicate, demit, drop out, give notice, give up office, give up work, leave, quit, relinquish, resign, stand aside, take leave, tender one's resignation, vacate

RETIRE *(Retreat),* ***verb*** abandon, *abire, concedere,* decamp, depart, discharge, fall back, go back, leave, part, recede, *recedere,* remove, retrocede, seclude oneself, separate oneself, shelve, take leave, turn in, vacate, withdraw

RETORT, *verb* answer, answer back, come back, counter, countercharge, counterclaim, make a rebuttal, parry, rebut, rejoin, replicate, reply, requite, respond, *respondere,* return, riposte, say in reply, snap back, surrebut, surrejoin

RETRACE, *verb* copy, go over again, recall, reexamine, regress, reminisce, repeat, return, revert, review, think back upon, trace back, turn back

RETRACTION, *noun* abjuration, abolishment, annulment, cancellation, contradiction, countermand, counterorder, disannulment, disavowal, gainsaying, negation, nullification, palinode, recall, recantation, recision, renunciation, repeal, repudiation, rescindment, retractation, reversal, revocation, taking back, unsaying, voidance, withdrawal
ASSOCIATED CONCEPTS: retraction of erroneous or defamatory statements

RETREAT, *verb* abandon, back away, back out, backtrack, bolt, decamp, depart, desert, disengage, draw back, ebb, escape, evacuate, fall back, fall to the rear, flee, *fugere,* give way, go away, go back, leave, lose ground, make oneself scarce, move back, *pedem referre,* pull back, quit, recede, recoil, regrade, remove oneself, retire, retrocede, reverse, run away, rusticate, *se recipere,* seclude oneself, shrink, slip away, take flight, turn tail, vacate, withdraw

RETRENCH, *verb* abridge, be economical, be frugal, *circumcidere,* clip, confine, *contrahere,* curtail, cut, cut down, cut short, decrease, deduct, delete, diminish, economize, lessen, limit, lop, pare, pinch, practice economy, prune, reduce, reduce expenses, remove, shorten, subduct, subtract, *sumptus minuere*

RETRIBUTION, *noun* amends, atonement, avengement, compensation, counterstroke, desert, due, indemnification, justice, measure for measure, nemesis, payment, penalty, *poena,* punishment, punitive action, reciprocation, reparation, repayment, reprisal, requital, requitement, retaliation, retributive justice, return, revenge, reward, satisfaction, vengeance, vengefulness, vindictiveness

RETROACTIVE, *adjective* affecting the past, beginning before, commencing before, effective before, having prior application, having prior effect, operational before, starting before, taking effect before
ASSOCIATED CONCEPTS: ex post facto, retroactive effect

RETROSPECT, *noun* afterthought, contemplation of the past, hindsight, looking back, memory, recall, recapitulation, recollection, reconsideration, reexamination, remembrance, rememoration, reminiscence, *respectus,* retentive memory, review, survey, thoughts of the past
ASSOCIATED CONCEPTS: ex post facto

RETURN (Go back), **verb**   backslide, come again, come back, double back, reappear, rebound, recidivate, *redire*, reenter, reestablish, relapse, resume, retrace one's steps, retreat, retrograde, reverse direction, revert, *reverti*, revisit

RETURN (Refund), **verb**   compensate, give back, indemnify, make compensation, make good, make reparation, make restitution, pay back, *reddere*, reimburse, repay, restore, satisfy, settle

RETURN (Respond), **verb**   acknowledge, answer, answer back, counter, countercharge, exchange, field questions, give an answer, interchange, make a rebuttal, make a rejoinder, make acknowledgment, react, rebut, reciprocate, recriminate, rejoin, reply, *respondere*, retaliate, retort, riposte, say in reply, surrebut, surrejoin

REVEAL, **verb**   acknowledge, admit, advise, affirm, announce, apprise, bare, blazon, blurt out, break the news, bring to light, bruit, circulate, communicate, concede, confess, confide, confirm, debunk, declare, describe, disabuse, disclose, display, disseminate, divulgate, divulge, enlighten, evince, *evulgare*, evulgate, explain, expose, give inside information, give out, grant, impart, indicate, inform, make known, make public, make publicly known, manifest, mention, notify, open, *patefacere*, promulgate, publish, set right, tell, uncloak, uncover, uncurtain, undeceive, unearth, unfold, unmask, unseal, unshroud, unveil, utter, vent, verify, voice
ASSOCIATED CONCEPTS: disclosure of grand jury secrets, disclosure of secret, scientific information

REVENGE, **noun**   avengement, counterblast, counterstroke, desert, feud, implacability, nemesis, punishment, punitive action, quittance, reciprocation, repayment, reprisal, requital, retaliation, retaliatory punishment, retribution, retributive punishment, revengefulness, satisfaction, *ultio*, vendetta, vengeance, vengefulness, *vindicta*, vindictiveness

REVENUE, **noun**   compensation, dividends, earnings, emolument, gain, hire, income, intake, interest, livelihood, pay, payment, perquisites, proceeds, profit, receipts, recompense, *reditus*, remuneration, return, reward, salary, *vectigal*, wages, yield
ASSOCIATED CONCEPTS: appropriation law, internal revenue, revenue bills, revenue law, revenue-producing income, revenue tax

REVERSAL, **noun**   abolishment, abolition, about-face, abrogation, annulment, backslide, cancellation, change, change of mind, check, countermandment, counterorder, disavowal, invalidation, inversion, nonapproval, nullification, overriding, overruling, overthrowing, rebuff, rebuke, recantation, rejection, renouncement, renunciation, repeal, repudiation, rescission, retraction, reversion, revocation, revokement, tergiversation, turnabout, undoing, voidance, voiding
ASSOCIATED CONCEPTS: reversal of a lower court's decision

REVERSION (Act of returning), **noun**   about-face, backslide, recidivism, regress, regression, relapse, retroaction, retrocession, retrogradation, retrogression, retroversion, return, reversal, reverse, reverting, throwback, turnabout, turnaround

REVERSION (Remainder of an estate), **noun**   future interest, future possession, *hereditas*, remainder over, residue, right of future enjoyment, right of future possession, right of succession

ASSOCIATED CONCEPTS: equitable reversion, life estate, partial reversion, reversionary interest, right of reversion

REVERSION RIGHTS, **noun**   automatic reversionary rights, retroaction, retroversion, reversal of rights, reversionary interest, reverting

REVERT, **verb**   backslide, change back, lapse, recede, recoil, regress, retreat, retrograde, retrogress, retrovert, return, reverse, turn back

REVIEW (Critical evaluation), **noun**   account, analysis, appraisal, comment, commentary, critical article, critical discussion, criticism, critique, editorial, essay, exposition, report
ASSOCIATED CONCEPTS: law review

REVIEW (Official reexamination), **noun**   investigation, judicial reconsideration, recapitulation, reconsideration, reinquiry, scrutiny, second examination, study, survey
ASSOCIATED CONCEPTS: administrative review, judicial review, scope of review

REVIEW, **verb**   abstract, analyze, brood over, check thoroughly, comment upon, *contemplari*, criticize, critique, deliberate, describe, digest, epitomize, examine, explain, go over, inspect, *inspicere*, interpret, investigate, look over, make corrections, make improvements, mull over, notice critically, overlook, recapitulate, recheck, reconsider, reexamine, rehearse, reiterate, remember, restate briefly, retell, retrace, revise, reword, run over, scrutinize, skim, study, sum up, summarize, survey, view retrospectively, weigh

REVILEMENT, **noun**   abuse, affront, animadversion, aspersion, berating, billingsgate, bitter words, castigation, censure, condemnation, contumely, criticism, cursing, denunciation, depreciation, detraction, diatribe, discommendation, disparagement, execration, exprobration, increpation, insult, invective, *maledictio*, malediction, objurgation, obloquy, opprobrium, philippic, reprehension, reproach, reprobation, reproof, stricture, tirade, traducement, upbraiding, verbal abuse, vilification, vituperation

REVISE, **verb**   alter, amend, bring up to date, change, correct, develop, doctor, edit, examine, exchange, improve, modify, overhaul, polish, recast, reconsider, reconstruct, rectify, redact, reexamine, remold, *retractare*, revamp, review, rework, rewrite, touch up, work over
ASSOCIATED CONCEPTS: revise a statute

REVISION (Corrected version), **noun**   corrected edition, current edition, *emendatio*, improved version, improvement, new edition, rescript, revised edition, rewrite, updated version

REVISION (Process of correcting), **noun**   alteration, change, correcting, editing, elaboration, overhauling, rectification, refining, reform, removal of errors, restyling, review, revisal, rewriting
ASSOCIATED CONCEPTS: law revision commission, revision of a statute

REVIVAL, **noun**   awakening, comeback, convalescence, freshening, improvement, invigoration, new version, palingenesis, phoenix, quickening, reanimation, reappearance, reawakening, rebirth, reclamation, recovery, recreation, recuperation, recurrence, redintegration, reestablishment, refreshment, regeneracy, regeneration, regenesis, reincarnation, rejuvenation, rejuvenescence, renaissance, renascence, renewal, reproduction, restoration, resumption, resurgence, resurrection, resuscitation, return, revivification, reviviscence, vivification

ASSOCIATED CONCEPTS: abatement and revival, revival of a cause of action

REVOCATION, *noun* abolishment, abolition, *abrogatio,* abrogation, annulment, cancellation, cancelling, countermand, counterorder, defeasance, disavowal, disownment, invalidation, negation, nullification, recall, recantation, recission, renouncement, repeal, repudiation, rescindment, retractation, retraction, reversal, *revocatio,* revokement, revoking, vacatur, withdrawal

ASSOCIATED CONCEPTS: dependent relative revocation, express revocation, implied revocation, power of revocation, presumption of revocation, revocation of a contract, revocation of a license, revocation of a will

FOREIGN PHRASES: *Non refert verbis an factis fit revocatio.* It matters not whether a revocation is made by words or by acts. *Quod inconsulto fecimus, consultius revocemus.* That which we have done without due consideration, we should revoke upon further consideration.

REVOKE, *verb* abjure, abolish, *abrogare,* abrogate, annul, cancel, countermand, counterorder, declare null and void, disannul, discard, disclaim, dismiss, dissolve, expunge, invalidate, make void, negate, nullify, override, prohibit, quash, recall, recant, remove, renege, renounce, *renuntiare,* repeal, repudiate, rescind, *rescindere,* retract, reverse, revert, suppress, suspend, vacate, vitiate, void, wipe out, withdraw

ASSOCIATED CONCEPTS: dependent relative revocation, revoke a license, revoke a will

REVOLT, *noun* agitation, apostasy, change of sides, contrariety, counteraction, defection, *defectio,* defiance, desertion, disobedience, dissension, faithlessness, inconstancy, insubordination, insurgency, insurrection, *motus,* mutiny, noncompliance, opposition, outbreak, overthrow, overturn, political upheaval, rebellion, recalcitrance, resistance, revolution, rising, secession, *seditio,* sedition, strife, strike, subversion, tergiversation, *tumultus,* uprising

REVOLUTION, *noun* anarchy, *débâcle,* general uprising, insurrection, lawlessness, outbreak, overthrow, overthrow of authority, overturn of authority, overturn of government, political upheaval, public uprising, rebellion, resistance to government, revolt, sweeping change, tumult, turbulence, upheaval, uprising, violent change

REWARD, *noun* acknowledgment, award, benefit, bonus, booty, bounty, compensation, consideration, donation, emolument, fee, gift, grant, gratuity, guerdon, honorarium, incentive, indemnification, indemnity, meed, pay, payment, perquisite, *praemium proponere,* premium, presentation, prize, purse, quittance, recognition, recompense, remembrance, remuneration, requital, requitement, return, solatium, tip, tribute

REWRITE, *verb* amend, bring up-to-date, change, copy, correct, edit, emend, improve, improve upon, make corrections, make improvements, modify, overhaul, recast, recreate, rectify, redraft, refine, reform, remold, revamp, revise, rework

RHETORIC *(Insincere language), noun* affectation, artificial eloquence, bombastic speech, declamation, euphuism, grandiloquence, grandiosity, inflated language, loftiness, magniloquence, pomposity, pompous speech, pompousness, pretension, pretentiousness

RHETORIC *(Skilled speech), noun* address, allocution, appeal, *ars dicendi,* art of composition, art of discourse, art of prose, command of words, compositional skill, delivery, diction, discourse, elocution, eloquence, exhortation, expression, flowery language, forensic oratory, language, oratory, parlance, phraseology, phrasing, public speaking, recitation, *rhetorica,* science of oratory, speech-making, wording

RICH *(Affluent), adjective* comfortable, moneyed, opulent, pecunious, prosperous, successful, wealthy, well-off, well provided for, well-to-do

RICH *(Plentiful), adjective* abundant, ample, bounteous, bountiful, copious, elaborate, eloquent, fecund, fertile, fruitful, full, generous, lavish, lush, luxuriant, magnificent, plenteous, prodigal, productive, profuse, prolific, replete, resounding, savory, strong, well-provided

RIDER, *noun* accompaniment, addendum, additament, addition, additional clause, adjunct, affix, amendment, appendage, appendant, appendix, appurtenance, attachment, augmentation, complement, continuation, endorsement, extension, insertion, postscript, subjunction, subscript, supplement

ASSOCIATED CONCEPTS: codicil, rider to a contract

RIDICULE, *noun* buffoonery, burlesque, caricature, chaff, contempt, derision, derisiveness, disdain, disparagement, disrespect, game, gibe, jeer, lampoonery, ludicrous representation, mimicry, mockery, pasquinade, raillery, *ridiculum,* sarcasm, satire, scorn, scornful imitation, sneer, sniggering, sport, squib, taunt, travesty

RIFE, *adjective* abundant, accustomed, bristling, catholic, common, considerable, crowded, current, customary, dense, dominant, endless, epidemic, extensive, far-reaching, galore, general, manifold, many, multitudinous, numerous, pandemic, plenteous, plentiful, popular, populous, predominant, prevailing, prevalent, profuse, rampant, regnant, reigning, replete, swarming, teeming, thick, unending, universal, usual, well-supplied, widespread, worldwide

RIFT *(Disagreement), noun* argument, break, clash, contention, controversy, difference, disceptation, dispute, estrangement, fight, misunderstanding, parting, split, variance

RIFT *(Gap), noun* aperture, breach, break, chasm, chink, cleft, crack, cranny, crevice, disjunction, fault, fissure, fracture, gash, hiatus, interstice, opening, parting, rent, rima, rupture, scissure, separation, split

RIGHT *(Correct), adjective* aboveboard, accurate, equitable, ethical, fair, honest, honorable, in accordance with duty, in accordance with justice, in accordance with morality, in accordance with truth, legitimate, reasonable, righteous, rightful, scrupulous, truthful, unswerving, upright, upstanding, valid, veracious, virtuous

RIGHT *(Direct), adjective* absolute, exact, immediate, straight, straightaway, straightforward, undeviating, unswerving

RIGHT *(Suitable), adjective* accepted, admissible, allowable, appropriate, apt, conventional, customary, fit, fitting, orderly, perfect, proper, reasonable, recognized, satisfactory, seemly, suitable, valid, virtuous, well-done, well-performed, well-regulated

RIGHT *(Entitlement),* **noun** authority, authorization, due, fair claim, heritage, inalienable interest, *ius, iusta,* just claim, justification, legal claim, legal power, legal title, ownership, power, prerogative, privilege, sanction, stake, title, vested interest, warrant

ASSOCIATED CONCEPTS: absolute right, accrued rights, Bill of Rights, claim of right, color of right, Constitutional right, contingent right, established right, exclusive right, future right, inchoate right, incorporeal right, inherent right, marital rights, material rights, mineral rights, natural rights, permissive right, preemptive right, preferential right, prescriptive right, prima facie right, proprietary right, prospective right, reciprocal rights, right of action, right of entry, right of privacy, right of redemption, right of way, right to bear arms, right to counsel, right to jury trial, right to vote, right-to-work laws, riparian rights, substantive right, vested rights

FOREIGN PHRASES: *Assignatus utitur jure auctoris.* An assignee is clothed with the right of his principal. *Nul charter, nul vente, ne nul done vault perpetualment, si le donor n'est seise al temps de contracts de deux droits, sc. del droit de possession et del droit de propertie.* No grant, no sale, no gift, is valid forever, unless the donor, at the time of contract, has two rights, namely, the right of possession, and the right of property. *Non videtur vim facere, qui jure suo utitur et ordinaria actione experitur.* He is not considered to use force who exercises his own right, and proceeds by ordinary action. *Nemo plus juris ad alienum transferre potest quam ipse habet.* No one can transfer to another any greater right than he himself has. *Cui jus est donandi, eidem et vendendi et concedendi jus est.* He who has the right to give has also the right to sell and to grant. *L'ou le ley done chose, la ceo done remedie a vener a ceo.* Where the law gives a right, it gives a remedy to recover. *Ubi jus, ibi remedium.* Where there is a right, there is a remedy. *Non debeo melioris conditionis esse, quam auctor meus a quo jus in me transit.* I ought not to be in better condition than he to whose rights I succeed. *Nemo potest plus juris ad alium transferre quam ipse habet.* No one can transfer a greater right to another than he himself has. *Jus publicum privatorum pactis mutari non potest.* A public right cannot be changed by agreement of private persons. *Nullus jus alienum forisfacere potest.* No man can forfeit the right of another. *Neminem laedit qui jure suo utitur.* He who stands on his own rights injures no one. *Cujus est instituere, ejus est abrogare.* Whose right it is to institute anything, may also abrogate it. *Qui jure suo utitur, nemini facit injuriam.* One who exercises his legal rights, injures no one. *Ignorantia juris sui non praejudicat juri.* Ignorance of one's right does not prejudice the right. *Jus triplex est,-propietatis, possessionis, et possibilitatis.* Right is threefold—of property, of possession, and of possibility. *Nullus videtur dolo facere qui suo jure utitur.* No one is considered to have committed a wrong who exercises his legal rights. *Cuilibet licet juri pro se introducto renunciare.* Any one may wave the benefit of a legal right that exists only for his protection. *Qui prior est tempore potior est jure.* He who is first in time is first in right.

RIGHT *(Righteousness),* **noun** correctness, due, duty, equitableness, equity, evenhanded justice, excellence, fair treatment, fairness, good actions, good behavior, goodness, honor, integrity, justice, justness, merit, morality, morals, nobleness, principle, probity, propriety, rectitude, *rectus,* straight course, truth, uprightness, *verus,* virtue, worthiness

FOREIGN PHRASES: *Fiat justitia, ruat coelum.* Let right be done, though the heavens fall. *Ipsae leges cupiunt ut jure regantur.* The laws themselves are desirous of being governed by

what is right. *Jus et fraus nunquam cohabitant.* Right and fraud never dwell together. *Jus naturale est quod apud homines eandem habet potentiam.* Natural right is that which has the same force among all mankind. *Pacta privata juri publico derogare non possunt.* Private compacts cannot derogate from public right. *Jus est norma recti; et quicquid estcontra normam recti est injuria.* Law is the rule of right; and whatever is contrary to the rule of right is an injury. *Lex est norma recti.* Law is the rule of right. *Quid sit jus, et in quo consistit injuria, legis est definire.* What constitutes right, and what injury, it is the business of the law to define. *Jus ex injuria non oritur.* A right does not arise from a wrong.

RIGHT TO CONTROL, noun authority, control, discretion, final determination, final say, force, power, prerogative, right to determine, right to determine one's course, right to settle issues

RIGHT TO COUNSEL, noun assistance of counsel, guaranty to be represented, right of representation, right to consult an attorney, right to legal assistance, Sixth Amendment

RIGHT TO DIE, noun choosing time of one's death, choosing to die, denial of life support, refusal of extraordinary means to prolong life, right to reject medical treatment to prolong life
Generally: choice to die, prerogative to die
ASSOCIATED CONCEPTS: living will

RIGHT TO LIFE, noun advocate, against abortion, antiabortion, diametrically opposed to abortion, in favor of life, in opposition to abortion, pro-life advocate
ASSOCIATED CONCEPTS: abortion, capital punishment, euthanasia, partial birth abortion

RIGHT TO PRIVACY, noun constitutional right to privacy, inalienable right to secretiveness, prerogative in favor of privacy, privilege in favor of privacy, right to privacy, right to solitude
ASSOCIATED CONCEPTS: civil liberties, genetic privacy, internet privacy, medical privacy, political privacy, privacy from governmental interference

RIGHT TO REMAIN SILENT, noun Fifth Amendment, privilege against self-incrimination, protection against self-incrimination, right to refrain from testifying against one's self
ASSOCIATED CONCEPTS: Miranda warnings

RIGHTFUL, adjective according to law, allowable, allowed, appropriate, authentic, authorized, becoming, befitting, chartered, constitutional, correct, deserved, due, enfranchised, equitable, fair, fitting, genuine, honest, inalienable, *iustus,* just, justifiable, lawful, legal, legalized, legitimate, licit, meet, merited, ordained, permitted, prescriptive, privileged, proper, real, reasonable, right, sanctioned, seemly, square, statutory, suitable, true, valid, warranted, within the law

RIGID, adjective austere, dour, *durus,* exact, exacting, firm, firmly set, fixed, flinty, formal, hard, harsh, hidebound, indurate, indurated, indurative, inelastic, inexorable, inflexible, intractable, motionless, obdurate, obstinate, orthodox, precise, punctilious, puritanical, relentless, renitent, resistant, *rigidus,* rigorous, set, severe, *severus,* starched, starchy, static, steely, stern, stiff, stony, straitlaced, strict, stringent, stubborn, taut, tense, tough, unadaptable, unalterable, unbending, uncompromising, unconformable, undeviating, unmalleable, unmitigated, unmoving, unpliant, unrelaxed, unrelenting, unyielding, wooden

RIGOR, *noun* accuracy, asperity, austerity, care, carefulness, conscientiousness, discipline, *duritia,* exactitude, exactness, firmness, force, freedom from deviation, intensity, keenness, meticulousness, preciseness, precision, relentlessness, rigidity, rigidness, rigorousness, scrupulousness, *severitas,* sharpness, sternness, strictness, stringency, tenacity, uncompromisingness, unyieldingness

RIOT, *noun* affray, bedlam, brawl, breach of the peace, broil, commotion, confusion, disorder, disorderliness, disturbance, ferment, fracas, fray, furor, hubbub, insurgence, insurrection, lawlessness, melee, outbreak, outburst, pandemonium, rebellion, revolt, row, rumpus, shindy, tumult, *tumultus, turba,* turmoil, unruliness, uprising, uproar, wild confusion
ASSOCIATED CONCEPTS: disturbing the peace, inciting a riot

RIPE, *adjective* adult, advanced, brought to perfection, complete, consummate, filled out, finished, fit, full, full-blown, full-grown, fully developed, fully grown, grown, ideal, mature, *maturus,* mellow, perfect, prepared, prime, primed, ready, seasoned, *tempestivus,* usable, well-developed
ASSOCIATED CONCEPTS: ripe for adjudication

RISE *(Appreciation), **noun*** accession, acclivity, accretion, accrual, accumulation, addition, advance, advancement, amplification, appearance, appreciation, ascension, ascent, augmentation, boom, climb, derivation, elevation, enhancement, enlargement, expansion, extension, gain, grade, gradient, growth, inception, increment, inflation, hill, increase, lift, progress, progression, promotion, propagation, reaction, slope, uprising

RISE *(Origin), **noun*** beginning, cause, commencement, debut, derivation, development, fountainhead, genesis, germ, growth, inception, incipience, introduction, nascency, onset, origin, origination, outset, overture, preamble, preface, prelude, prologue, source, spring, start, starting point, uprising, upswing

RISE *(Originate), **verb*** arise, begin, come into existence, come to be, emanate, emerge, happen, inaugurate, increase, initiate, issue, occur, spring up

RISE *(Prosper), **verb*** appreciate, arise, bear fruit, benefit, be successful, blossom, build, excel, flourish, improve, incept from, originate from, progress, spring from, strive, succeed

RISE *(Soar), **verb*** arise, ascend, bear fruit, blossom, build, climb, elevate, emerge, erect, escalate, extend directly upward, flourish, go further, go higher, grow, heighten, hover, improve, inaugurate, inflate, initiate, levitate, mount, pullulate, raise, rear, rebel, rise up, scale, surmount, tower, transcend, uprise, wax

RISK, *noun* *alea,* bet, chance, danger, *discrimen,* endangerment, exposure, exposure to harm, gamble, gaming, hazard, imperilment, insecurity, instability, jeopardy, *periculum,* peril, plunge, possibility, possibility of injury, possibility of loss, precariousness, speculation, stake, uncertainty, venture, vulnerability, wager
ASSOCIATED CONCEPTS: acceptance of risk, assumption of risk, extraordinary risk, forseeable risk, incurred risk, insurance risk, limitation of risk, mutuality of risk, risk of loss, shifting of risk, unreasonable risk
FOREIGN PHRASES: *Periculum rei venditae, nondum traditae, est emptoris.* The risk of a thing sold, but not yet delivered,

is the purchaser's. *Ubi periculum, ibi et lucrum collocatur.* He who risks a thing, should receive the profits arising from it. *Cujus est dominium ejus est periculum.* He who has the ownership should bear the risk.

RIVAL, *noun* adversary, *aemulus,* antagonist, aspirant, bidder, candidate, challenger, combatant, competition, competitor, contender, contestant, corrival, disputant, enemy, entrant, foe, litigant, opponent, opposition

ROB, *verb* appropriate illegally, burglarize, commit robbery, *despoliare, exspoliare,* hold up, loot, misappropriate, peculate, pilfer, pillage, plunder, purloin, seize, steal, take by force, take unlawful possession

ROBBERY, *noun* depredation, felonious taking, felonious taking of the property of another, holdup, larceny by force, *latrocinium,* piracy, plundering, *rapina, spoliatio,* stealing, theft, thievery

RODOMONTADE, *noun* bluster, boastfulness, boasting, brag, braggadocio, braggartism, bragging, bunkum, embroidery, empty talk, exaggeration, extravagance, fanfaronade, gasconade, hyperbole, inflation, jactitation, ostentation, pretense, pretension, pretentious talk, puffery, rant, swagger, swashbuckling, tall talk, turgescence, vainglorious boasting, vainglory, vaporing

ROLE, *noun* act, assignment, billet, capacity, character, characterization, department, false show, function, guise, impersonation, job, mission, part, *partes,* performance, place, pose, position, post, posture, presentation, pretense, province, representation, sham, task, undertaking, work

ROLL, *noun* account, *album,* catalogue, census, chronicle, directory, docket, document, enumeration, index, inventory, ledger, list, membership, muster, record, register, registry, roster, schedule, *tabula*

ROLL-OVER CLAUSE, *noun* automatic renewal, automatic renewal terms, automatic restoration, automatic resumption
Generally: continuance, means to obtain the status quo

ROUTINE, *adjective* accustomed, automatic, common, commonplace, conventional, customary, established, everyday, expected, familiar, fixed, frequent, general, habitual, ingrained, mechanical, normal, popular, prevalent, recurrent, recurring, regular, repeated, ritual, set, standard, stereotyped, stock, uniform, usual, *usus,* well-trodden

RUBRIC *(Authoritative rule), **noun*** act, bylaw, canon, code, convention, dictate, enactment, institution, law, legislation, measure, ordinance, precept, prescription, regulation, rule, ruling, statute

RUBRIC *(Title), **noun*** caption, classification, denomination, designation, division, genus, grouping, head, heading, headline, label, superscription

RUDIMENTARY, *adjective* abecedarian, basal, basic, beginning, crude, elemental, elementary, embryonic, essential, formative, fundamental, germinal, germinative, immature, inceptive, inchoate, *incohatus,* incomplete, initial, initiative, initiatory, original, originative, primal, primary, primitive, primordial, protomorphic, rudimental, simple, starting, uncompleted, underlying, undeveloped, unfinished

RULE (Guide), **noun**   code, course, criterion, custom, direction, formula, habit, matter of course, method, model, norm, *norma,* order, pattern, policy, practice, procedure, protocol, prototype, *regula,* routine, standard, standing order, system

RULE (Legal dictate), **noun**   act, bylaw, canon, charge, code, command, commandment, decree, dictate, direction, doctrine, dogma, edict, enactment, formula, formulary, formulation, law, legislation, maxim, order, ordinance, *praeceptum, praescriptum,* precept, prescription, principle, regulation, standing order, statute, tenet

ASSOCIATED CONCEPTS: administrative rule, court rule, cy-pres rule, discriminatory rule, home rule, parol evidence rule, rule against perpetuities, Rule in Shelley's Case, rules of construction, rules of evidence, rules of procedure

FOREIGN PHRASES: *Ubi non est condendi auctoritas, ibi non est parendi necessitas.* Where there is no authority for establishing a rule, there is no need of obeying it. *Exceptio probat regulam de rebus non exceptis.* The exception proves the rule in matters not excepted. *Exceptio firmat regulam in contrarium.* An exception affirms the rule to be the contrary. *Non est certandum de regulis juris.* There is no disputing about rules of the law. *Regula est, juris quidem ignorantiam cuique nocere, facti vero ignorantiam non nocere.* The rule is that a person's ignorance of the law may prejudice him, but that his ignorance of fact will not. *Non jus ex regula, sed regula ex jure.* The law does not arise from the rule but the rule comes from the law. *Omnis regula suas patitur exceptiones.* Every rule is subject to its own exceptions. *Exceptio firmat regulam in casibus non exceptis.* An exception confirms the rule in cases not excepted.

RULE (Decide), **verb**   adjudge, adjudicate, ascertain, come to a conclusion, come to a determination, conclude, decide by judicial sentence, declare, declare authoritatively, decree, deliver judgment, determine, draw a conclusion, establish, exercise judgment, find, fix conclusively, give an opinion, give judgment, hold, make a decision, make a resolution, pass judgment, pass sentence, pass upon, pronounce, pronounce judgment, reach an official decision, resolve, settle, settle by decree, umpire

ASSOCIATED CONCEPTS: rule from the bench

RULE (Govern), **verb**   administer, be in power, command, compel, conduct, control, decree, dictate, direct, dispose, domineer, enact, enforce obedience, exercise authority, exert authority, give orders, guide, have authority, have control, have jurisdiction over, have predominating influence, have responsibility, hold authority, hold dominion, hold office, keep in order, manage, manipulate, master, officiate, order, oversee, police, possess authority, predominate, prescribe, preside over, *regnare,* regulate, reign, restrain, run, serve the people, superintend, supervise

RULING, **noun**   adjudication, award, command, conclusion, court's finding, decision, decree, determination, edict, finding, findings of fact and conclusions of law, holding, judgment, judicial determination, judicial proclamation, judicial pronouncement, opinion of the court, order, order of the court, pronouncement, resolution, rule, sentence, verdict

ASSOCIATED CONCEPTS: judicial ruling, ruling from the bench

RUMINATION, **noun**   analyzing, close study, cogitation, concentrating, consideration, contemplation, deliberation, dialectic, excogitation, hindsight, meditation, musing, pondering, reflection, retrospection, speculation, thinking

RUN (Contend), **verb**   announce a candidacy, aspire to political office, be a candidate, be designated a candidate, become an office seeker, campaign, campaign for office, campaign for public office, canvass, challenge an incumbent, compete, run for office, seek election, seek re-election, seek to become a public official, solicit votes, stand for election, strive, vie

RUN (Flee), **verb**   abscond, break away, dash, decamp, depart, disengage, escape, fly, hasten, hurry, leave, move swiftly, quit, race, retreat, rush, scamper, take flight

RUN (Flow), **verb**   advance, continue, drain out, elapse, extend, flood, go on, pass, proceed, pour, team, surge, trickle

ASSOCIATED CONCEPTS: conditions and deeds running with the land, covenants running with the land, running at large, running of the statute of limitations

RUN (Manage), **verb**   carry on, conduct, direct, drive, function, govern, guide, handle, influence, maintain, operate, oversee, perform, regulate, steer, superintend, supervise, work

RUSE, **noun**   art, artifice, bait, blind, camouflage, cheat, chicane, chicanery, chouse, circumvention, craft, crafty device, deceit, deception, decoy, delusion, design, disguise, dodge, *dolus,* duplicity, evasion, feint, fetch, finesse, flimflam, fraud, guile, hoax, humbug, imposture, jugglery, machination, maneuver, mask, masquerade, plot, pretext, scheme, sham, sharp practice, shift, snare, stratagem, strategy, subterfuge, trick, trickery, wile

RUSH, **noun**   acceleration, bustle, celerity, crush, dash, deluge, expeditiousness, flood, flurry, haste, hurried activity, hurry, no time to lose, onrush, precipitance, press of work, promptitude, rampage, run, scamper, scramble, scurry, sprint, spurt, stampede, torrent, urgency, velocity, whirlwind

ASSOCIATED CONCEPTS: time of the essence, date certain

RUSH, **verb**   accelerate, bustle, charge, expedite, hasten, hustle, lose no time, make haste, precipitate, quicken, rush to and fro, scramble, scurry, speed, spout, spur, spurt, surge, work under pressure

RUTHLESS, **adjective**   atrocious, barbarous, bloodthirsty, brutal, brutish, callous, cold, cold-blooded, coldhearted, cruel, deadly, demoniac, devilish, diabolical, dispiteous, fell, feral, ferine, ferocious, fiendish, grim, hard, hardhearted, harsh, heartless, *immisericors,* implacable, inclement, *inexorabilis,* inexorable, inflexible, inhuman, inhumane, *inhumanus,* insensitive, lethal, maleficent, malevolent, malign, malignant, marble-hearted, merciless, murderous, obdurate, pitiless, poisonous, rancorous, relentless, remorseless, retaliative, revengeful, sadistic, sanguinary, savage, stony-hearted, treacherous, truculent, uncompassionate, unfeeling, unforgiving, unkind, unmerciful, unpitying, unrelenting, unsparing, unsympathetic, vengeful, venomous, vicious, vindictive, virulent, without pity

S

SABOTEURS, *noun* cell, enemy combatants, enemy group, extremist group, extremists, incendiaries, insurgents, rebel organization, revolutionaries, subversives, underground extremists

ASSOCIATED CONCEPTS: justice courts, military tribunals, Patriot Act, prison cells, sleeper cells, terrorism, terrorist cells

SACRIFICE *(Forfeiture), **noun*** abandonment, capitulation, cessation, cost, deprivation, destruction, dispensation, expense, giving up, loss, oblation, release, relinquishment, renunciation, resignation, yielding

SACRIFICE *(Victim), **noun*** dupe, immolation, martyr, oblation, offering, peace offering, prey

SACRIFICE, *verb* cede, dispose of, drop, forbear, forfeit, forgo, forswear, give up, incur loss, let go, part with, release, relinquish, sell at a loss, spare, suffer loss, surrender, undercharge, underrate, waive, yield

SACROSANCT, *adjective* anointed, awesome, blessed, ceremonial, consecrated, dedicated, devotional, divine, elevated, enshrined, godly, hallowed, heavenly, holy, ineffable, inviolable, inviolate, mystical, purified, religious, revered, reverend, sacramental, sacred, sainted, sanctified, set apart, solemn, spiritual, theistic, theologic, theological, transcedent, venerable, venerated, worshiped

SAFE, *adjective* armed, armored, benign, cared for, certain, covered, defended, dependable, ensconced, entrenched, *fidus,* foolproof, free from danger, free from harm, free from hurt, free from injury, free from risk, guaranteed, guarded, harmless, impervious, impregnable, insured, intact, invulnerable, looked after, maintained, on guard, out of danger, panoplied, preserved, proof, protected, prudent, regulated, reliable, safeguarded, salubrious, scatheless, screened, screened from danger, secure, *securus,* sheltered, shielded, sound, sure, sustained, tested, trustworthy, *tutus,* unadventurous, unassailable, unattackable, unbroken, undamaged, undaring, under cover, unendangered, unexposed, unharmed, unhazarded, unhurt, unimpaired, uninjured, unmolested, unscathed, unshakable, unthreatened, whole, without risk

SAFE HAVEN, *noun* area free from danger, area free from harm, area of protection, area out of danger, area screened from danger, asylum, confined area, guaranteed safe area, harbor, place of safety, port, protected area, refuge, retreat, safe area, safe harbor, safeguarded area, sanctuary, secure area, shelter, sheltered area, shielded area, untreatened area

ASSOCIATED CONCEPTS: safe haven in contracts, safe haven in statutes

SAFE WORKPLACE, *noun* harmonious workplace, protected workplace, safe-guarded place, secure place of work, unhazardous workplace

ASSOCIATED CONCEPTS: Labor Law, OSHA standards, recalcitrant worker doctrine, safe standards, sanctity of the workplace

SAFEGUARD, *noun* armor, assurance, buffer, bulwark, cover, defense, fortification, insurance, *munimentum,* palladium, precaution, preventive measure, propugnaculum, protection, provision, screen, security, shield, surety

SAFEKEEPING, *noun* aegis, auspices, care, charge, conservation, custody, defense, guard, guardianship, keeping, lee, patronage, preservation, protection, protective custody, salvation, security, shelter, superintendence, supervision, support, tutelage, upkeep, wardship, watch

ASSOCIATED CONCEPTS: bailment

SAFETY, *noun* asylum, cover, custody, immunity, inviolability, preservation, protection, refuge, safeguard, safekeeping, safeness, sanctuary, security, shelter

ASSOCIATED CONCEPTS: safety devices

SAFETY VALVE, *noun* alternative, aperture, boundary condition, choice, circumstance, clause condition, contingency, contrivance, definition, device, escalator clause, esca clause, escape valve, escape way, evasion, exception, excuse, exit strategy, expedient, frame of reference, given, grounds, hole to creep out of, limitation, limiting condition, loophole, means of escape, mechanism for evasion, obligation, opening, out, outlet, parameter, prerequisite, pretext, provision, proviso, requisite, saving clause, specification, stipulation, technicality, terms, ultimatum, uncommunicativeness, vehicle of escape, way of escape, way out, whereas

ASSOCIATED CONCEPTS: safety valve consideration, safety valve function, stop valve

SAFETY VALVE PROVISIONS, *noun*   certain solution in statutes, escape hatch in statutes, impregnable solution in statutes, insured solution in statutes, invulnerable solution in statutes, means of resolution in statutes, method of preservation in statutes, safeguards in statutes, secure methodology in statutes, solution in statutes, sound solution in statutes, sure solution in statutes, unassailable solution in statutes

SAGA, *noun*   account, adventure, chronicle, epic, epos, heroic story, history, legend, myth, mythology, report, story, tale, yarn

SAGACIOUS, *adjective*   astute, circumspect, clever, cognizant, diplomatic, discerning, discreet, discriminating, enlightened, far-sighted, intelligent, judicial, judicious, keen-sighted, knowing, learned, lucid, omniscient, penetrating, perceptive, perspicacious, politic, prescient, profound, prudent, quick, rational, reasonable, resourceful, sage, sapient, sensible, sharp, shrewd, smart, solid, subtle, understanding, wise

SAGACITY, *noun*   acuity, acumen, acuteness, apperception, arguteness, astuteness, awareness, brilliance, clear thinking, clear thought, cleverness, comprehension, discernment, discrimination, excellent judgment, farsightedness, foresight, genius, good judgment, incisiveness, insight, intelligence, intuition, judgment, keenness, keen-sightedness, levelheadedness, mentality, penetration, perception, percipience, perspicaciousness, *perspicacitas,* perspicacity, profundity, prudence, *prudentia,* quickness, rationality, reason, reasoning power, sagaciousness, *sagacitas,* sapience, sapiency, sense, sharpness, shrewdness, smartness, sobriety, understanding, vision, wisdom

SAID, *adjective*   above-mentioned, aforegoing, aforenamed, aforesaid, already indicated, before mentioned, earlier, exact, foregoing, forementioned, named, preceding, prevenient, previous, previously mentioned, previously named, previously referred to, prior, specific

SALACIOUS, *adjective*   bawdy, carnal, coarse, concupiscent, corrupt, debauched, depraved, dirty, dissolute, erotic, Fescennine, filthy, foul, free, goatish, gross, immoral, impure, incontinent, indecent, lascivious, lecherous, lewd, libertine, libidinous, licentious, lickerish, lickerous, loose, lurid, lustful, obscene, offensive, Paphian, polluted, pornographic, profligate, provocative, prurient, ribald, risque, ruttish, satyric, satyrical, scabrous, scarlet, scrofulous, scurrile, scurrilous, sensual, sexy, shameful, shameless, sinful, smutty, spicy, suggestive, titillating, unblushing, unbowdlerized, unchaste, unclean, unexpurgated, unprintable, unvirtuous, virtueless, wanton

SALE, *noun*   disposal, exchange, trade, transaction, transfer, vendition
ASSOCIATED CONCEPTS: sales and exchange, sale and return, sale at auction, sale by commercial broker, sale by sample, sale confirmed, sale for payment, sale of debt, sale of office, sale on credit, sale on return, sale on trial

SALIENT, *adjective*   bold, capital, cardinal, chief, clear, commanding, conspicuous, distinct, distinguished, dominant, dominating, eminent, evident, exalted, explicit, extraordinary, flagrant, foremost, glaring, illustrious, important, imposing, indubitable, leading, main, marked, memorable, notable, noticeable, obvious, outstanding, overt, paramount, plain, *praecipuus,* predominant, primary, prime, principal, prominent, pronounced, protrudent, protruding, protrusive, protuberant, recognized, remarkable, showing, significant, standing out, striking, towering, unconcealed, unmistakable, visible, well-known, worthy of notice, worthy of remark

SALIENT POINT, *noun*   basis, cardinal point, central point, core, cornerstone, elixir, essence, essential part, feature, focal point, gist, gravamen, highlight, implication, import, important point, kernel, keystone, main issue, main point, marrow, material point, nucleus, pith, prominent part, quintessence, significance, significant fundamental, substance, sum and substance

SALUBRIOUS, *adjective*   advantageous, analeptic, beneficial, corrective, corroborant, curative, favorable to health, healing, health-promoting, healthful, healthy, invigorating, life-giving, medicinal, nourishing, nutritious, nutritive, recuperative, remedial, reparative, restorative, reviviscent, roborant, salutary, salutiferous, sanatory, stimulating, sustentative, therapeutic, therapeutical, tonic, wholesome

SALUTARY, *adjective*   advantageous, aidant, analeptic, beneficial, benign, bracing, constitutional, corrective, corroborant, curative, edifying, favorable, good, harmless, healing, health-giving, health-preserving, healthful, healthy, helpful, hurtless, hygienic, innocuous, innoxious, invigorating, medicinal, nourishing, nutritious, nutritive, palliative, preventive, profitable, promoting health, prophylactic, protective, remedial, reparative, reparatory, restorative, roborant, safe, salubrious, *salutaris,* salutiferous, sanative, sanatory, sanitary, sustaining, sustentative, therapeutic, tonic, uninjurious, useful, *utilis,* wholesome

SALVAGE, *noun*   conservation, deliverance, extrication, property saved, recapture, reclaimed materials, reclamation, recoupment, recovery, redemption, remains, reoccupation, repossession, rescue, retrieval, return, salvation, scrap
ASSOCIATED CONCEPTS: equitable salvage, net salvage, salvage charges, salvage loss, salvage service

SALVO, *noun*   condition, defense, escape clause, evasion, exception, exemption, explosion, fusillade, general discharge, proviso, qualification, quibbling excuse, reservation, restriction, salute, saving clause, simultaneous discharge of shots, volley

SAMARITAN, *noun*   aid, aider, altruist, assister, befriender, benefactor, champion, defender, friend, good neighbor, help, helper, helping hand, kind person, ministering angel, ministrant, patron, philanthropist, protector, savior, succorer, sympathizer, well-wisher
ASSOCIATED CONCEPTS: Good Samaritan laws, rescue doctrine

SAME, *adjective*   alike, cognate, duplicate, equal, equivalent, exactly like, identical, one and the same, parallel, similar, synonymous, twin, uniform, without difference
ASSOCIATED CONCEPTS: same act or transaction, same as, same cause, same cause of action, same character of work, same class of subject, same compensation, same condition(s), same descriptive properties, same direction, same extent, same fees, same fund, same general business, same grade of employment, same grantor, same manner, same offense, same parties, same punishment, same rate of interest, same right

SAME, *noun*   consistency, counterpart, double, equal, equivalent, idem, identical, match, mate, reciprocal, resemblance, similarity, synonym

SAMPLE, *noun*   archetype, case in point, cross section, *documentum,* ensample, example, exemplar, exemplification, *exemplum,* guide, illustration, instance, model, original, paradigm, prototype, representation, representative, representative selection, showpiece, *specimen,* standard of comparison, swatch, typical example

SANCTION *(Permission),* **noun** acceptance, acquiescence, affirmance, affirmation, agreement, allowance, approbation, approval, assent, *auctoritas,* authorization, charter, *confirmatio,* consent, cooperation, countenance, empowerment, encouragement, endorsement, favor, grant, homologation, immunity, indulgence, legality, license, permission, permit, ratification, seal, stamp of approval, subscription, sufferance, support, tolerance, toleration, validation, vouchsafement, willingness

FOREIGN PHRASES: *Multa conceduntur per obliquum quae non conceduntur de directo.* Many things are allowed indirectly which are not allowed directly.

SANCTION *(Punishment),* **noun** condemnation, denunciation, deprivation, disciplinary action, discipline, imposition, infliction, penal retribution, penalty, retributive action, suffering

SANCTION, *verb* accede, accept, acquiesce, agree to, allow, approbate, approve, assent to, authenticate, authorize, charter, confer a privilege, confer a right, *confirmare,* consent to, countenance, empower, enable, endorse, entitle, foster, give approval, give permission, go along with, grant, gratify, homologate, indulge, legitimate, legitimatize, legitimize, license, permit, privilege, promote, ratify, *ratum facere, sancire,* stand behind, subscribe to, suffer, support, tolerate, uphold, validate, vouchsafe

ASSOCIATED CONCEPTS: civil sanctions, criminal sanctions, penal sanctions

SANE, *adjective* *animi,* balanced, clearheaded, competent, coolheaded, judicious, legitimate, levelheaded, logical, lucid, mentally sound, *mentis compos,* normal, rational, realistic, reasonable, responsible, *sanus,* sensible, sober, sober-minded, sound, understanding, undisturbed

SANGUINE, *adjective* anticipative, assured, bright, buoyant, cheerful, confident, encouraged, enthusiastic, expectant, full of hope, hopeful, in good spirits, inspirited, optimistic, reassured, sanguineous, trustful, trusting, undespairing, undoubting

SANITY, *noun* balance, clear thinking, clearmindedness, comprehension, health of mind, healthy mind, levelheadedness, lucidity, mental balance, mental equilibrium, mental health, normalcy, normality, rationality, reason, reasonableness, saneness, sense, sensibleness, sound understanding, soundmindedness, soundness, understanding

ASSOCIATED CONCEPTS: competency hearing, presumption of sanity

SAPID, *adjective* acceptable, affecting, agreeable, alluring, ambrosial, amusing, appealing, appetizing, arresting, attractive, bewitching, captivating, challenging, charming, delectable, delicious, delightful, dulcet, enchanting, engaging, entertaining, enthralling, enticing, entrancing, exciting, fascinating, fine, flavorful, flavorous, flavorsome, flavory, full-bodied, full-flavored, good, good-tasting, gratifying, gustable, gustful, impressive, inspiring, interesting, intriguing, inviting, likable, lovely, luscious, nectareous, palatable, piquant, pleasant, pleasing, pleasurable, popular, prepossessing, provocative, provoking, refreshing, relishable, saporous, satisfying, savory, scrumptious, seasoned, stirring, succulent,

sweet, tantalizing, tasty, tempting, thought-provoking, titallative, titillating, welcome, winning, winsome

SAPIENT, *adjective* acute, astute, bright, clear-headed, clever, deep, discerning, discriminating, farsighted, intellectual, intelligent, judicious, keen, knowing, learned, perceptive, perspicacious, profound, quick of apprehension, quick-witted, rational, sagacious, sage, *sapiens,* sensible, sharp, shrewd, thinking, wise

SATISFACTION *(Discharge of debt),* **noun** acquitment, acquittal, acquittance, amortizement, clearance, compensation, damages, defrayal, defrayment, discharge, guerdon, indemnification, indemnity, payment, quittance, receipted payment, recompense, recoupment, redress, reimbursement, release from debt, remuneration, reparation, repayment, requital, requitement, restitution, return, settlement, solatium

ASSOCIATED CONCEPTS: accord and satisfaction, ademption, reasonable satisfaction, satisfaction of lien, satisfaction piece

SATISFACTION *(Fulfilment),* **noun** accomplishment, achievement, appeasement, attainment, consummation, content, contentedness, contentment, enjoyment, *expletio,* fruition, gratification, pleasure, realization, reparation, success, sufficiency

ASSOCIATED CONCEPTS: satisfaction of judgment

SATISFY *(Discharge),* **verb** arrange a settlement, carry into execution, carry out, clear, compensate, fulfill an obligation, make compensation, make good, make payment, meet an obligation, pay, pay in full, pay off, pay up, recompense, reimburse, remit, remunerate, render, repay, requite, settle, settle accounts, tender

ASSOCIATED CONCEPTS: satisfy a debt, satisfy a judgment

SATISFY *(Fulfill),* **verb** answer the purpose, appease, avail, be agreeable, be sufficient, carry out, comply with, conform to, content, fill, fit, gratify, meet requirements, please, prove acceptable, qualify, quench, sate, satiate, serve the purpose, set at ease, slake, suffice, suit, surfeit

ASSOCIATED CONCEPTS: satisfy to a moral certainty

SAVE, *conjunction* bar, barring, besides, but for, deducting, excepting, lacking, leaving out, not including, short of, without

SAVE, *preposition* but, except, exclusive of, less, minus, omitting

SAVE *(Conserve),* **verb** hold, keep safe, preserve, redeem, salvage

SAVE *(Hold back),* **verb** economize, hoard, keep, reserve, retain

SAVE *(Rescue),* **verb** avert, defend, fend off, give salvation, help, liberate, protect, safeguard, shield

SAVORY, *adjective* agreeable, ambrosiac, ambrosial, ambrosian, appetizing, *conditus,* delectable, delicious, delightful, flavor, flavored, flavorous, flavorsome, full-bodied, full-flavored, good, good-tasting, gustable, gustative, likable, luscious, nectarean, nectareous, palatable, piquant, pleasant, pleasing, rich, sapid, sweet, tasty, tempting

SAY-SO, *noun* acceptance, accord, affirmance, affirmation, agreement, approval, assent, authorization, compliance, confirmation, consent, endorsement, go-ahead, green

531

light, imprimatur, leave, liberty, license, nod, okay, permission, ratification, sanction, sign-off, special permission, validation, willingness

SCANDAL, noun aspersion, attaint, bad name, bad reputation, bad repute, baseness, brand, censure, damaging report, dedecoration, defamation, degradation, disapprobation, disapproval, discredit, disesteem, disgrace, dishonor, disrepute, humiliation, ignominy, ill repute, imputation, infamy, ingloriousness, loss of honor, loss of reputation, malicious gossip, notoriety, obloquy, odium, opprobrium, reproach, shame, slur, stain, stigma, taint, talk, tarnish, tarnished honor, vilification
ASSOCIATED CONCEPTS: defamatory reports, deformatory rumors

SCANDALOUS, adjective arrant, atrocious, base, black, condemnatory, corrupt, damnatory, dastardly, defamatory, denunciatory, deplorable, despicable, discreditable, disgraceful, dishonorable, disreputable, disrespectable, execrable, facinorous, flagitious, flagrant, fulsome, heinous, horrifying, ignoble, ignominious, illaudable, immodest, immoral, indecent, infamous, inglorious, iniquitous, lewd, licentious, low, mean, nefarious, notorious, objurgatory, odious, offensive, opprobrious, outrageous, probrosus, profligate, reprehensible, scurrilous, shameful, shocking, thersitical, turpis, ugly, uncommendable, unworthy, wicked
ASSOCIATED CONCEPTS: motion to strike scandalous matter, scandalous allegations, scandalous pleading

SCARCE, adjective at a premium, dear, deficient, few, inadequate, incomplete, inconsiderable, insufficient, limited, little, low, meager, minute, not abundant, not plentiful, out of the way, paltry, rare, rarus, scant, seldom met with, short, skimpy, sparing, sparse, thinly scattered, unavailable, uncommon, unique, unobtainable, unplentiful, unusual, wanting

SCATHING, adjective acerbus, acrimonious, aculeatus, biting, brutal, burning, cruel, cutting, damaging, envenomed, excoriating, harmful, harsh, hurtful, insulting, maleficent, malevolent, malicious, malignant, mordacious, mordax, rancorous, scatheful, searing, severe, sharp, spiteful, stinging, trenchant, unbenevolent, uncharitable, uncompromising, ungentle, unkind, venemous, virulent, vitriolic, withering

SCENARIO, noun abstract, analysis, brief, capsule, compression, condensation, contents, digest, essence, narrative, outline, plot, recap, recapitulation, report, review, script, sketch, story, sum and substance, summary, synopsis, text

SCENE, noun act, arena, background, display, episode, eyereach, eyeshot, field, landscape, locale, locality, location, locus, panorama, place, range, scaena, scope, setting, sight, site, spectacle, sphere, stage, stage setting, surroundings, theater, view, vista, whereabouts
ASSOCIATED CONCEPTS: scene of an accident

SCHEDULE, noun agenda, calendar, check list, docket, enumeration, index, inventory, libellus, list, outline, plan, program, roll, tabula, timetable
ASSOCIATED CONCEPTS: payment schedule, schedule of assets

SCHEME, noun arrangement, cabal, consilium, contrivance, course of action, delineation, design, device, enterprise, machination, maneuver, method, operation, order, organization, plan, plot, policy, procedure, program of action, project, ratio, schedule, stratagem, strategy, subterfuge, system, tactics
ASSOCIATED CONCEPTS: conspiracy

SCHEME, verb arrange, be cunning, cabal, calculate, chart, collude, complot, compose, concoct, connive, conspire, contrive, design, devise, diagram, engineer, excogitate, fabricate, fashion, frame, hatch, have designs, improvise, intrigue, invent, lay a plan, machinate, make arrangements, maneuver, manipulate, map, map out, organize, outline, plan, plot, predesign, predetermine, premeditate, prepare, project, ratio, think ahead, think out, weave a plot, work out, work up
ASSOCIATED CONCEPTS: collude, conspire

SCHISM, noun breach, break, cabal, desertion, difference, disassociation, disconnection, discord, dissension, dissent, disunion, division, faction, falling out, nonconformity, partition, recusancy, rent, rift, rupture, schisma, secession, sectarianism, sectarism, separation, severance, split, withdrawal

SCIENCE (Study), **noun** body of fact, branch of knowledge, data, discipline, facts, information, knowledge, learning, organized knowledge, scientia, system of knowledge

SCIENCE (Technique), **noun** ability, adroitness, aptitude, aptness, capacity, competence, competency, dexterity, expertness, facility, finesse, genius, highly developed skill, know-how, mastery, method, proficiency, skill, skillfulness

SCIENTER, noun appreciation, apprehension, awareness, cognition, cognizance, comprehension, consciousness, discernment, familiarity, intent, intention, knowledge, perception, recognition, understanding

SCIENTIAL, adjective able, accomplished, adapted, adept, adequate, capable, competent, deft, educated, efficacious, fitted, gifted, intelligent, knowing, knowledgeable, learned, proficient, qualified, schooled, skillful, suitable, suited, trained, up to, well-suited

SCINTILLA, noun bit, corpuscle, grain, insignificant amount, iota, minim, modicum, particle, small amount, small quantity, spark, tittle, trace, trifle, whit
ASSOCIATED CONCEPTS: scintilla of evidence

SCOPE, noun ambit, amplitude, area, boundary, bounds, circle, circuit, compass, confines, demesne, expanse, extent, field, latitude, limit, locus, margin, orbit, purview, range, reach, realm, region, room, space, span, sphere, spread, stretch, sweep, territory, zone
ASSOCIATED CONCEPTS: scope of a patent, scope of authority, scope of employment, scope of jurisdiction, scope of review

SCREEN (Guard), **verb** camouflage, cloak, conceal, cover, defend, disguise, fence, harbor, haven, hide, mask, protect, safeguard, shade, shelter, shield, shroud, veil

SCREEN (Select), **verb** choose, class, classify, discard, discriminate, eliminate, evaluate, exclude, filter, grade, group, keep out, pick, prefer, segregate, separate, sieve, sift, single out, sort, strain, weed, winnow
ASSOCIATED CONCEPTS: screen prospective jurors

SCRIPT, noun book, calligraphy, characters, cursive hand, dialogue, handwriting, jottings, libretto, lines, longhand, manuscript, penmanship, penscript, playbook, printing, scrawl, scription, text, writing, written characters, written matter

SCRUPLE, noun anxiety, apprehension, apprehensiveness, compunction, concern, *cunctatio,* doubt, doubtfulness, drawback, dubiety, dubiousness, *dubitatio,* fear, fearfulness, *haesitatio,* hesitancy, hesitation, misgiving, objection, qualm, question, reluctance, uncertainty, unease, uneasiness, unwillingness

SCRUPULOUS, adjective aboveboard, *accuratus,* admirable, careful, choosy, *diligens,* discriminating, discriminative, equitable, ethical, fair, forthright, honest, honorable, laudable, legitimate, moral, noble, principled, reliable, religiosus, reputable, sincere, sound, thorough, trustworthy, truthful, upright, worthy

SCRUTABLE, adjective apprehensible, beholdable, cognizable, comprehensible, conspicuous, discoverable, easily observed, easily seen, easily understood, evident, explicable, explicit, fathomable, intelligible, knowable, manifest, noticeable, observable, obvious, open, overt, penetrable, perceptible, plain, seeable, unconcealed, understandable, unhidden, unmasked, unveiled

SCRUTINIZE, verb analyze, anatomize, audit, canvass, check, contemplate, delve into, dissect, examine, explore, eye, give close attention, inquire into, inspect, *inspicere, investigare,* investigate, keep under surveillance, look at closely, look into, look over, observe, overhaul, peer into, *perscrutari,* peruse, probe, pry into, question, regard carefully, research, review, scan, search, search into, sift, stare, study, survey, view, watch

SCRUTINY, noun analysis, attention, careful examination, close investigation, close look, close search, consideration, critical examination, examination, exploration, indagation, inquest, inquiry, inquisition, inspection, investigation, minute attention, observance, observation, *perscrutatio,* perusal, probe, research, review, scrutation, search, study, surveillance, survey

SCURRILOUS, adjective abusive, coarse, *contumeliosus,* disgusting, disrespectful, foul, gross, indecent, indelicate, insulting, lascivious, lewd, libidinous, licentious, low, mean, obscene, offensive, opprobrious, *probrosus,* ribald, risque, salacious, scabrous, scurrile, *scurrilis,* shameless, vile, vulgar

SEAL *(Close),* **verb** bar, block off, bolt, close up, cover, keep from public view, keep in confidence, keep in secrecy, lock, occlude, secret, secure
ASSOCIATED CONCEPTS: sealed case, sealed grand jury report, sealed indictment, sealed instrument, sealed verdict

SEAL *(Solemnize),* **verb** accept, accredit, approve, attest, authenticate, authorize, bear witness, certify, confirm, endorse, enstamp, impress with mark, imprint, inscribe, legalize, license, ratify, sanction, sign, stamp, substantiate, support, undersign, validate, verify, vouch

SEALED RECORD, noun classified record, concealed record, confidential record, private record, record which cannot be disclosed, record which cannot be revealed, restricted record, secret record
ASSOCIATED CONCEPTS: open records policy, sealed instrument, sealed verdict

SEARCH, verb chase after, closely examine, comb, delve, examine, examine by inspection, explore, ferret, follow the trail of, go through, hunt, indagate, inquire into, inspect, investigate, look into, look over, look through, probe, pry into, pursue, scan, scour, scout, scrutinize, seek, trace, track, track down, trail
ASSOCIATED CONCEPTS: illegal search by law enforcement officers, searching premises, unlawful search, unreasonable search and seizure

SEARCH WARRANT, noun authority to search, bench warrant, court order, judicial order to search, judicial process, legal document to search, legal order, legal process, order authorizing a search, process, writ
ASSOCIATED CONCEPTS: illegal search warrant, probable cause to issue search warrant

SEASONABLE, adjective acceptable, apposite, appropriate, auspicious, befitting, convenient, due, expedient, favorable, fit, opportune, *opportunus,* proper, properly timed, propitious, seemly, suitable, *tempestivus,* timeful, timely, towardly, well-timed

SEAT, noun base, berth, capital, center, *domicilium,* headquarters, home, locale, locality, location, perch, place, position, post, region, residence, *sedes,* site, spot, station, vital center
ASSOCIATED CONCEPTS: county seat

SECEDE, verb abandon, *abire,* apostatize, break away, decedere, depart, desert, disaffiliate, dissent, evacuate, insurrect, leave, mutiny, pull out, quit, rebel, refuse to support, relinquish, remove oneself, repudiate, resign, retire, retract, revolt, separate, sever one's connections, tergiversate, vacate, walk out, withdraw

SECERN, verb differentiate, discern, discriminate, distinguish, note the distinctions, perceive differences

SECLUDE, verb banish, blockade, bury, conceal, confine, cover, cut off, deport, disassociate, dissociate, embargo, exclude, excommunicate, exile, expatriate, hide, imprison, insulate, isolate, keep apart, keep in detention, keep in private, keep out, maroon, ostracize, outlaw, quarantine, relegate, remove, *removere,* retire, retire from sight, retreat, rope off, screen out, *secludere, segregare,* segregate, separate, sequester, set apart, set aside, shut out, withdraw

SECOND *(Backer),* **noun** advocate, aide, angel, backer, champion, co-signer, endorser, patron, promoter, supporter

SECOND *(Moment),* **noun** before you know it, brief period of time, flash, flash of an eyelid, instant

SECOND, verb approve, assist, authorize, back, back up, confirm, endorse, favor, pass, ratify, receipt, recommend, sanction, stand behind, subscribe, support, undersign, validate, vote for, warrant
ASSOCIATED CONCEPTS: second lien

SECONDARY, adjective accessory, alternative, ancillary, auxiliary, collateral, contingency, derived, following, indirect, inferior, junior, less important, lesser, minor, *secundarius,* subaltern, subordinate, subsequent, subsidiary, substitute, unessential, unimportant, vicarious
ASSOCIATED CONCEPTS: secondary boycott, secondary evidence, secondary liability

SECONDARY RIGHTS, noun ancillary rights, contingent rights, indirect rights, subordinated rights, subsequent rights

SECRET, adjective abstruse, acroamatic, acroamatical, arcane, *arcanus,* clandestine, close, concealed, confidential, covert, cryptic, dark, esoteric, furtive, hidden, latent,

mysterious, not public, obscure, occult, *occultus,* private, privy, recondite, secluded, secretus, shrouded, sly, surreptitious, undisclosed, undivulged, unknown, unpublished, unrevealed, unseen, untold, veiled
ASSOCIATED CONCEPTS: secret lien, undisclosed principal

SECRET, *noun*   abstruse knowledge, *arcana,* cabal, classified information, concealed knowledge, confidence, confidential communication, confidential matter, enigma, hidden knowledge, inside information, intimacy, intrigue, mystery, obscure information, personal matter, private affair, private communication, private matter, privileged communication, privileged information, puzzle, recondite knowledge, *res arcana, res occulta,* unknown information, veiled information

SECTION *(Division),* *noun*   category, class, compartment, component, department, detachment, fraction, fragment, group, grouping, part, segment, separate part, separation, subdivision, subgroup

SECTION *(Vicinity),* *noun*   area, block, clime, demesne, environs, field, locale, locality, location, *locus,* milieu, neighborhood, parcel of land, part, plot, plot of ground, plot of land, province, purlieus, *regio,* region, surroundings, territory, tract, vicinage, *vicinitas*
ASSOCIATED CONCEPTS: block, plot, and section

SECURE *(Confident),* *adjective*   assured, carefree, certain, convinced, not nervous, not scared, positive, reassured, sure, unafraid, unanxious, unconcerned, undisturbed, unfrightened, unhesitating, unshaken, unsuspecting

SECURE *(Free from danger),* *adjective*   armored, defended, dependable, guaranteed, guarded, impregnable, in safety, insured, inviolable, invulnerable, protected, safe, sheltered, stable, unassailable, unattackable, unharmable, unimperiled, unthreatened
ASSOCIATED CONCEPTS: secured transactions

SECURE *(Sound),* *adjective*   dependable, fast, fastened, firm, fixed, immovable, infallible, reliable, solid, sound, stable, strong, substantial, trustworthy, trusty, unerring, unfailing, unimpeachable

SECURITIES, *noun*   assets, bonds, capital, evidences of debts, evidences of obligations, holdings, invested property, investment, negotiables, property, shares, stocks
ASSOCIATED CONCEPTS: corporate securities, investment securities, sale of securities

SECURITY *(Pledge),* *noun*   bail, bond, collateral, debenture, deposit, earnest, gage, guarantee, indemnity, insurance, lien, pawn, pignoration, promise, promissory note, stipulation, surety, token, vadium, voucher, warranty
ASSOCIATED CONCEPTS: collateral security, investment securities, issuing securities, public securities, real security, sale of securities, security agreement, security deposit, security interest, treasury securities, valuable securities

SECURITY *(Safety),* *noun*   anchor, assurance, asylum, bastion, bulwark, certainty, defense, dependability, faith, freedom from danger, freedom from harm, guard, immovability, immunity, impregnability, *incolumitas,* invulnerability, maintenance, palladium, preservation, protection, rampart, reliance, safe conduct, safeguard, safeness, *salus,* salvation, sanctuary, secureness, shelter, stability, support, trust, unassailability, unattackability
ASSOCIATED CONCEPTS: national security

SECURITY *(Stock),* *noun*   assets, bill of exchange, capital, cautio, certificate of debt, certificate of indebtedness, coupon, funds, indenture, invested property, investment, money invested, negotiable instrument, negotiable paper, obligation, *pignus,* secured debenture

SEDITION, *noun*   apostasy, defection, defiance, desertion, disloyalty, disobedience, dissidence, infidelity, infraction, insubordination, insurgence, insurrection, *motus,* mutiny, noncompliance, overthrow, rebellion, recreance, recreancy, recusancy, resistance to authority, revolt, revolution, riot, rising, *seditio,* seditiousness, subversion, tergiversation, treachery, treason, underground activity, uprising, violation
ASSOCIATED CONCEPTS: alien and sedition acts, seditious libel

SEDUCTION, *noun*   allure, allurement, attraction, bait, bewitchment, blandishment, cajolery, captivation, coaxing, *corruptela,* corruption, defilement, enchantment, enticement, fascination, inducement, inveiglement, invitation, lure, persuasion, seducement, solicitation, *stuprum,* tantalization, temptation

SEDULOUS, *adjective*   active, *adsiduus,* alert, ardent, assiduous, attentive, avid, brisk, busily engaged, busy, conscientious, constant, diligent, dogged, eager, energetic, firm, hardworking, indefatigable, industrious, keen, laborious, painstaking, patient, perseverant, persevering, persistent, pertinacious, relentless, resolute, resolved, *sedulus,* stalwart, steadfast, tenacious, uncompromising, undeviating, unfaltering, unflagging, unrelenting, unremitting, unswerving, untiring, unwearying, unyielding, zealous

SEE, *verb*   call to mind, call up, conceive, conjure up, conjure up an image, contemplate in the imagination, envisage, envision, have a picture of, perceive, realize, view, visualize

SEGMENT, *noun*   bit, branch, cantle, cantlet, chapter, chunk, component, constituent, detached part, detail, division, element, fraction, fractional part, fragment, *fragmentum,* ingredient, installment, measure, moiety, *pars,* part, piece, portion, section, sector, *segmentum,* share, slice, small part, subdivision

SEGREGATION *(Isolation by races),* *noun*   apartheid, discrimination, division by races, ostracism, prejudice, racial prejudice, racialism, racism, separation by races
ASSOCIATED CONCEPTS: equal protection clause

SEGREGATION *(Separation),* *noun*   classification, detachment, differentiation, disassociation, disconnection, disengagement, dissociation, distinguishment, disunion, division, grouping, isolation, partition, *seiunctio,* setting apart
ASSOCIATED CONCEPTS: segregation of trust funds

SEISIN, *noun*   control, hold, mastery, occupancy, occupation, ownership, possession, possessorship, tenancy, tenure, title
ASSOCIATED CONCEPTS: actual seisin, constructive seisin, covenant of seisin, equitable seisin, seisin in deed, seisin in fact, seisin in law

SEIZE *(Apprehend),* *verb*   apprehendere, arrest, arrest with authority, capture, catch, *comprehendere,* detain by criminal process, imprison, incarcerate, jail, put in duress, rapere, take, take in, take into custody, take prisoner

SEIZE *(Confiscate),* **verb**   annex, appropriate, arrogate, assume, capture, cause to be forfeited, commandeer, deprive of, dispossess, disseise, distrain, expropriate, grasp, impound, impress, mulct, pillage, pirate, pounce upon, put in possession, sequester, sequestrate, take, take possession of, usurp, wrest

ASSOCIATED CONCEPTS: attachment, execution on property, garnishment, seize property

SELECT, *adjective*   accepted, adopted, appointed, best, capital, choice, chosen, culled, designated, elected, *electus,* elite, embraced, excellent, exceptional, exclusive, *exquisitus,* first-rate, good, handpicked, matchless, named, picked, popular, preferable, preferred, prime, quality, rare, selected, superior, top-notch, unequaled, unexcelled

ASSOCIATED CONCEPTS: select committee

SELECT, *verb*   abstract, adopt, appoint, assign, be jaundiced, be prejudiced, champion, choose, collect, cull, decide, designate, determine, differentiate, discriminate, distinguish between, draft, elect, *eligere,* eliminate, excerpt, exclude, extract, fix upon, glean, have a bias, isolate, lay aside, lean, *legere,* make a choice, make a distinction, make a selection, mark, name, nominate, pick, point out, prefer, prize, put aside, reject, segregate, seperate, set apart, shut out, sift, single out, sort out, specialize, specify, stipulate, take out, weed out, winnow

ASSOCIATED CONCEPTS: select a jury

SELECTION *(Choice),* **noun**   adoption, appointment, appropriation, assignment, compilation, cooptation, decision, *delectus,* denomination, designation, determination, *electio,* election, extraction, indication, naming, nomination, ordainment, ordination, preference, reservation, segregation, separation, specification, stipulation

ASSOCIATED CONCEPTS: jury selection

SELECTION *(Collection),* **noun**   accumulation, aggregation, anthology, arrangement, array, assemblage, assembly, assortment, batch, bunch, cluster, collectanea, combination, compilation, conglomeration, cumulation, examples, gathering, group, hoard, mass, pile, quantity, samples, treasury, variety

SELFSAMENESS, *noun*   analogousness, close resemblance, cognate, comparability, complement, correspondence, corresponding, counterpart, equality, equivalence, exactness, general resemblance, identicalness, indistinguishability, likeness, oneness, parallelism, resemblance, sameness, semblance, similarity, similitude, synonymity, synonymy, the like

SELL, *verb*   auction, barter, bring to market, deal in, dispense, dispose of for profit, *divendere,* drive a trade, effect a sale, exchange, furnish, give title to, handle, hawk, huckster, make a sale, market, merchandise, offer for sale, peddle, provide, put on sale, put up for sale, trade in, traffic in, transfer for a consideration, vend, *vendere*

SEMBLANCE, *noun*   air, appearance, aspect, bearing, closeness, copy, counterpart, effect, example, exterior, guise, identity, illusion, image, *imago,* likeness, look, mien, outward form, replica, representation, resemblance, sameness, show, similarity, similitude, simulacrum, *species,* uniformity, visage

SEMI, *adjective*   fractional, fragmentary, half, half finished, not whole, partial, unfinished

ASSOCIATED CONCEPTS: semiannually

SEND, *verb*   *ablegare,* advance, broadcast, cast, circulate, convey, direct, discharge, dismiss, dispatch, displace, drive, ejaculate, eject, emit, *emittere,* export, fling, forward, freight, give, give forth, hurl, impel, issue, jaculate, launch, mail, *mittere,* post, project, propel, relay, route, send forth, send out, ship, shoot, throw, toss, transfer, transmit

SENIOR *(Higher in priority),* **noun**   chief, first, foremost, key major, most important, most significant, paramount, takes precedence, uppermost

ASSOCIATED CONCEPTS: bankruptcy, seniority

SENIOR *(Older),* **noun**   adult, advanced in years, ancestor, ancient, antiquated, antique, archaic, early, elderly, matured, older, older man, older woman, one of the older generation, original, senior citizen, superannuated, veteran, vintage

ASSOCIATED CONCEPTS: elder law

SENSE *(Feeling),* **noun**   apperception, apprehension, awareness, consciousness, discernment, idea, impression, instinct, mental image, mindfulness, notion, opinion, perception, realization, sensation, *sensus,* speculation, understanding

SENSE *(Intelligence),* **noun**   acumen, astuteness, awareness, brightness, brilliance, cleverness, cognition, cognitive faculties, cognitive powers, comprehension, depth, enlightenment, foresight, genius, good judgment, grasp, insight, intellect, intellectual ability, intellectuality, *iudicium,* judgment, judiciousness, mentality, observation, perception, perspicacity, prudence, *prudentia,* rational faculty, rationality, reason, recognition, sagaciousness, sagacity, sapience, shrewdness, smartness, talent, understanding, wisdom, wiseness

SENSIBILITY, *noun*   acuteness, affectibility, alertness, appreciation, attentiveness, awareness, comprehension, consciousness, delicacy, delicacy of feeling, discernment, discrimination, emotion, feeling, fineness, impressibility, judgment, keenness, mindfulness, perception, perceptivity, response, responsiveness, sensation, sensitiveness, sensitivity, sharpness, susceptibility, sympathy, taste

ASSOCIATED CONCEPTS: peculiar sensibilities

SENSIBLE, *adjective*   advisable, apprised, astute, conscious, cool-headed, discerning, discreet, discriminating, enlightened, farsighted, informed, intelligent, judicious, justifiable, knowing, knowledgeable, levelheaded, logical, observant, palpable, perceptive, politic, *prudens,* prudent, ratiocinative, rational, reasonable, sagacious, sage, sane, sapient, sapiential, shrewd, sober, sound, thinking, thoughtful, understanding, well-advised, wise

SENSITIVE *(Discerning),* **adjective**   aesthetic, alert, alive to, apperceptive, appercipient, astute, attentive, awake to, aware, cognizant, conscious, critical, discriminating, discriminative, fastidious, heedful, keen, mindful, observant, penetrating, perceptive, percipient, perspicacious, quick of apprehension, responsive, *sensilis,* sentient, understanding

SENSITIVE *(Easily affected),* **adjective**   easily excited, easily offended, emotive, feeling, high-strung, hypercritical, impassionable, impressible, impressionable, irritable, merciful, *mollis,* moving, overemotional, peevish, perceptive, quick-tempered, reactive, sentimental, softhearted, susceptible, susceptive, sympathetic, temperamental, tenderhearted, touchy, uncontrolled

SENTENCE, noun adjudication, award of punishment, censure, conviction, decision, declaration of penalty, decree of punishment, *decretum,* determination, determined punishment, doom, edict, formally pronounced judgment, *iudicium,* order of penalty, order of the court, penalty, prescribed punishment, pronouncement, punishment, ruling, verdict
ASSOCIATED CONCEPTS: concurrent sentences, consecutive sentences, cumulative sentences, excessive sentence, indeterminative sentence, life sentence, presentence hearing, suspended sentence

SENTENCE, verb adjudge, bring in a verdict, commit, condemn, *condemnare,* convict, *damnare,* decide, declare guilty of an offense, decree, determine, find, find guilty, hold, immure, impose penalty, imprison, inflict penalty, *multare,* order, pass judgment upon, prescribe punishment, pronounce guilty, pronounce judgment, proscribe, reprobate
ASSOCIATED CONCEPTS: presentence report

SENTENTIOUS, adjective abridged, aphoristic, apothegmatic, blunt, commatic, compact, compressed, concise, condensed, direct, economical of words, epigrammatic, epigrammatical, expressive, full of meaning, gnomic, laconic, meaningful, meaty, packed with meaning, pithy, pointed, precise, *sententiosus,* sparing of words, succinct, summarized, telegraphic, terse, to the point

SEPARABLE, adjective breakable, cleavable, detachable, divisible, partible, severable
ASSOCIATED CONCEPTS: joint and separable liability, separability of arbitration, separable controversy, separable interest, separate provision

SEPARATE, adjective alone, apart, asunder, departing, detached, different, disassociated, disconnected, *disiunctus,* disjoined, disjointed, disjunct, disparate, disrelated, dissimilar, dissociated, distinct, disunited, divergent, diverse, divided, divorced, independent, individual, insular, isolated, lone, loose, parted, removed, secluded, *secretus,* segregated, separated, *separatus,* set apart, severed, solitary, split, sundered, unaccompanied, unaffiliated, unallied, unassociated, unattached, unattended, unconnected
ASSOCIATED CONCEPTS: separate action, separate cause of action, separate maintenance

SEPARATE, verb alienate, break, break off, break up, cleave, come apart, come between, cut adrift, cut off, detach, disassociate, disband, disconnect, disengage, *disiungere,* disjoin, dismember, dispart, disperse, dissever, dissociate, dissolve, disunite, divide, exclude, fractionize, hold apart, intersect, keep apart, part, part company, part ways, rend, rive, rupture, section, sectionalize, segment, segregate, *separare,* set apart, sever, splinter, split, split up, sunder, tear, unbind, uncouple, unloose, unmarry, unravel, untie, unyoke, winnow
ASSOCIATED CONCEPTS: annul, divorce

SEPARATION, noun alienation, breach, break, cleavage, detachment, disassociation, *disiunctio,* disseverance, dissociation, dissolution, dissolution of marriage, disunion, division, divorce, divorcement, estrangement, legal dissolution of marriage, parting, rending, rupture, *separatio,* severance, split, sundering, tearing, termination of marital cohabitation, uncoupling
ASSOCIATED CONCEPTS: judgment of separation, judicial separation, just cause for separation, legal separation, separation agreement, separation by consent, separation decree, separation of powers, separation order, voluntary separation

SEQUACIOUS, adjective accommodating, acquiescent, adaptable, amenable, bendable, bending, compliant, deferential, dependent, docile, ductile, easily influenced, easily led, easily taught, easygoing, elastic, facile, fictile, flexible, flexile, giving, governable, impressible, impressionable, lacking individuality, malleable, manageable, meek, moldable, obedient, obeisant, obliging, obsequious, passive, plastic, pliable, pliant, reverential, servile, slavish, submissive, subordinate, sycophantic, teachable, toadying, tractable, unassertive, undeviating, unimaginative, without originality, yielding

SEQUENCE, noun alternation, arrangement, array, catenation, chain, classification, concatenation, consecution, continuum, cycle, flow, gradation, group, list, logical order, nexus, order, *ordo,* procession, progression, rotation, serialization, *series,* string, succession

SEQUESTER *(Seclude),* **verb** cloister, closet, conceal, confine, exclude, isolate, quarantine, remove, retire, secret, segregate, separate, withdraw
ASSOCIATED CONCEPTS: sequester a jury, sequester a witness

SEQUESTER *(Seize property),* **verb** annex, appropriate, arrogate, attach, confiscate, dispossess, distrain, impound, impress, levy, preempt, replevy, separate, sequestrate, set apart, set aside, take, take hold of, wrest
ASSOCIATED CONCEPTS: sequester assets

SEQUESTRATION, noun annexation, appropriation, attachment, confiscation, deprivation, displacement, distraint, distress, divestment, execution, garnishment, impoundage, impoundment, impressment, levy, seizure, take-over

SERIAL, noun consecution, fascicle, issue, periodical, procession, progression, series, successive portion

SERIOUS *(Devoted),* **adjective** ardent, assiduous, decided, dedicated, determined, devout, dogged, dutiful, eager, earnest, faithful, fervent, firm, fixed, intent, loyal, passionate, purposeful, relentless, resolute, resolved, settled, sincere, steadfast, steady, tenacious, true, uncompromising, unfaltering, unswerving, unyielding, zealous
ASSOCIATED CONCEPTS: serious crime, serious wrongdoing

SERIOUS *(Grave),* **adjective** *austerus,* consequential, critical, crucial, dangerous, dire, dreadful, fatal, *gravis,* great, grim, highly serious, important, intense, momentous, pensive, pressing, *serius,* severe, *severus,* sober, solemn, stern, weighty
ASSOCIATED CONCEPTS: serious and willful misconduct, serious bodily injury, serious crime, serious harm, serious wrongdoing

SERVE *(Assist),* **verb** accommodate, administer to, advance, afford aid, aid, assist, attend, be of use, care for, come to the aid of, *commodare,* comply, confer a benefit, contribute to, cooperate, *deservire,* discharge one's duty, do a service, do one's bidding, fill an office, forward, furnish aid, furnish assistance, give help, help, lend aid, minister to, promote, render help, *servire,* submit, succor, supply aid, take care of, tend, wait on, work for

SERVE *(Deliver a legal instrument),* **verb** afford notice, deliver, deliver a summons and complaint, deliver over, forward, give notice to, hand over, issue, make delivery of legal process, present, subpoena, summon, turn over
ASSOCIATED CONCEPTS: serve with process

SERVICE *(Assistance),* **noun** abetment, accommodation, advice, aid, attendance, backing, benefit, care, cooperation, favor, guidance, help, helping hand, *ministerium,* ministration, *opera,* relief, succor, support, useful office, usefulness

ASSOCIATED CONCEPTS: essential service, professional service, public service, service contract, service mark

SERVICE *(Delivery of legal process),* **noun** commencement of an action, delivery of a writ, delivery of process, handing over legal papers, institution of proceedings, notification of legal action

ASSOCIATED CONCEPTS: actual service of process, constructive service of process, personal service, service by mail, service by publication, service of notice, service of subpoena, service of summons, service rendered, special service, substituted service of process

SERVILE, *adjective* abiectus, abject, compliant, deferential, downtrodden, fawning, groveling, harnessed, humble, *humilis,* ingratiating, low, mean, meek, menial, obedient, obeisant, obsequious, passive, prostrate, respectful, *servilis,* slavish, subject, submissive, subordinate, supple, sycophantic, tractable, truckling, unassertive, unresisting, vernile

SERVITUDE, *noun* bonds, burden, captivity, charge, compulsion, enslavement, enthrallment, fetters, helotism, helotry, indenture, obedience, oppression, restraint, service, *servitium, servitus,* slavery, subjection, subjugation, submission, subordination, subservience, suppression, thrall, thralldom

ASSOCIATED CONCEPTS: involuntary servitude, penal servitude, real servitude

SESQUIPEDALIAN, *adjective* grandiloquent, lengthy, long, magniloquent, multisyllabic, pedantic, sonorous

SESSION, *noun* assembly, audience, caucus, conclave, conference, congregation, congress, consultation, convention, *conventus,* convocation, council, diet, forgathering, forum, gathering, hearing, meeting, parley, plenum, rendezvous, round table, sitting, synod, term, union

ASSOCIATED CONCEPTS: general sessions, joint session, regular session, session laws, special sessions

SET ASIDE *(Annul),* **verb** abandon, abjure, abnegate, abrogate, accumulate, amass, cast off, discard, dispense with, dispose of, disuse, drop, omit, reject, relegate, relinquish, renounce, repudiate, shunt, spurn

ASSOCIATED CONCEPTS: set aside a verdict

SET ASIDE *(Reserve),* **verb** keep in reserve, lay aside, pigeonhole, pile up, put aside, put away, save up, set apart, shelve, store up

SET DOWN, *verb* book, calender, chronicle, commit to writing, docket, enter, jot down, line up, list, note, place, plan, post, program, put on record, record, register, schedule, slate

ASSOCIATED CONCEPTS: set down for trial

SET FORTH, *verb* allege, argue, articulate, assert, characterize, cite, commence, communicate, contend, convey, declare, delineate, demonstrate, depict, describe, detail, develop, disclose, display, divulge, enunciate, evince, expound, express, illustrate, issue, manifest, plead, portray, posit, present, proclaim, profess, proffer,

promulgate, propose, propound, reason, recite, recount, relate, render, report, represent, show, signify, state, trace, unfold

ASSOCIATED CONCEPTS: set forth the allegations of a crime

SETOFF, *noun* allowance, balance, compensation, counter, counter demand, counterbalance, credit, equalization, equivalent, offset, opposite, outstanding indebtedness, satisfaction

ASSOCIATED CONCEPTS: affirmative defense, counterclaim

SETTLE, *verb* settle order on notice, accommodate, adjust, agree, agree upon, approve, arrange, arrange matters, arrange matters in dispute, ascertain, bring to terms, bring together, clear up, come to a determination, come to an agreement, come to an understanding, come to terms, compromise, conclude, *conficere, constituere,* decide, determine, determine once for all, dispose of, end, even the score, harmonize, make a compact, mend, negotiate, put in order, reach a compromise, reconcile, rectify, resolve, restore harmony, set at rest, set in place, settle, solve, stabilize, straighten out, strike a bargain, work out

ASSOCIATED CONCEPTS: settle a bill of exceptions, settle a claim, settle a judgment, settle an account, settle an estate, settle an order, settle issues, settle property, settled account

SETTLED METHOD, *noun* accordance, common practice, compliance, conformity, conventionalism, conventionality, custom, established mode, formality, mere form, observance of form, prescription, propriety, protocol, *punctilio,* rigidity, rule of procedure, usual custom

SETTLEMENT, *noun* accommodation, adjustment, agreement, arrangement, arrangement of difficulties, bargain, *compositio,* composure of differences, composure of doubts, compromise, conciliation, concordat, *constitutio,* contract, determination by agreement, discharge, disposition, final terms, negotiation, pact, *pactum,* payment, reconciliation, release, satisfaction, set of terms, terms, understanding

ASSOCIATED CONCEPTS: deed of settlement, final settlement, settlement of a case, voluntary settlement

SEVER, *verb* break apart, break off, cleave, cut, cut adrift, detach, *dirimere,* disband, disconnect, disengage, disjoin, dismember, dispair, dispart, dissever, dissociate, dissolve, disunite, divide, *dividere,* divorce, fissure, isolate, keep apart, lacerate, lop off, part, partition, rend, rend asunder, rive, rupture, segment, segregate, *separare,* separate, set apart, slit, splinter, split, subdivide, sunder, tear, unbind, uncouple, unfasten, untie, wrench

ASSOCIATED CONCEPTS: sever a claim, sever a party, sever an action, severable cause of action, severable contract

SEVERABLE, *adjective* apportionable, cleavable, detachable, dissoluable, dividual, *dividuus,* divisible, fissile, fissionable, fractional, partible, scissile, *separabilis,* separable

ASSOCIATED CONCEPTS: severable contract, severable statute

SEVERAL *(Plural),* **adjective** assorted, certain, diverse, few, more than one, some, sundry

SEVERAL *(Separate),* **adjective** appropriate, certain, chosen, definite, different, distinctive, distinguishable, exclusive, fixed, independent, marked, peculiar, personal, private, proper, representative, singular, unique

ASSOCIATED CONCEPTS: several defendants, several liability, several ownership, several tracts, several trusts, several transactions, severally

SEVERANCE, noun bifurcation, cleavage, demarcation, detachment, differentiation, disassociation, discrimination, distinction, distinguishment, division, divorce, fission, isolation, scission, segregation, separation, sunderance, withdrawal

ASSOCIATED CONCEPTS: severance damage, severance of statute, severance pay, severance tax

SEVERE, adjective acrimonious, afflictive, agonizing, astringent, austere, *austerus,* bearish, brutal, censorious, churlish, coercive, cold, condemnatory, critical, cruel, despotic, difficult, domineering, dour, drastic, *durus,* exacting, excruciating, exigent, faultfinding, fierce, firm, forbidding, furious, grievous, grim, gruff, hard, hard to endure, harsh, hypercritical, ill-natured, ill-tempered, immovable, implacable, inclement, inexorable, inflexible, insufferable, intense, intractable, ironclad, ironhanded, mordant, nasty, obdurate, oppressive, overbearing, overpowering, painful, peremptory, pitiless, punitive, puritanic, puritanical, raging, relentless, rigid, rigorous, rough, rugged, ruthless, savage, *severus,* sharp, sour, stark, stern, stiff, stinging, stony, stony-hearted, stormy, strait-laced, strict, stringent, stubborn, tempestuous, tough, trying, tyrannical, unbending, uncompromising, unfeeling, ungentle, ungracious, unjust, unkind, unmerciful, unmitigated, unrelenting, unsparing, unyielding, vicious, vindictive, violent

ASSOCIATED CONCEPTS: severe penalties

SEVERITY, noun *acerbitas,* acerbity, acrimony, asperity, austerity, causticity, cruel treatment, cruelty, ferity, ferociousness, ferocity, fierceness, force, fury, *gravitas,* gravity, grimness, harshness, inclemency, inexorability, inflexibility, inhumanity, intensity, might, relentlessness, rigor, rigorousness, ruthlessness, savagery, seriousness, *severitas,* sharpness, sternness, strictness, stringency, turbulence, tyranny, unkindness, venom, violence, virulence

SEXUAL ASSAULT, noun crime, criminal action, criminal activity, criminal offense, felony, illegal action, illegality, offense against the state, serious offense against law, sexual abuse, sexual attack, sexual force, sexual injury

SEXUAL HARASSMENT, noun actionable annoyance at place of employment, actionable conduct, gender harassment in the workplace, offensive verbal abuse in the workplace, plan of physical harassment by superiors, policy of verbal harassment by superiors, unsolicited physical behavior in the workplace, unsolicited verbal abuse in the workplace, unwarranted advances, unwelcome sexual advances, verbal abuse at work

ASSOCIATED CONCEPTS: hostile workplace

SHALL, verb as required will, by compulsion will, by imperative will, mandatorily will, obligatorily will

ASSOCIATED CONCEPTS: shall be lawful, shall be legal, shall become, shall give, shall have, shall not, shall perform, shall work

SHAM, noun chicanery, counterfeit, deception, delusion, *dolus,* fabrication, fake, *fallacia,* false show, feint, forgery, *fraud,* fraus, guise, imitation, impersonation, impostor, imposture, masquerade, misrepresentation, mock, pretense, reproduction, simulacrum, simulation, trick, trickery

ASSOCIATED CONCEPTS: sham defense, sham pleading

SHAMBLES, noun cataclysm, chaos, confusion, destruction, disorder, disorganization, disruption, havoc, holocaust, jumble, *laniena,* madhouse, maelstrom, mayhem, mess, pandemonium, scene of destruction, scene of disorder, state of violence, turmoil, upheaval, uproar, welter

SHAME, noun abasement, abjectness, abuse, aspersion, attaint, bad name, baseness, blot, contempt, debasement, defamation, defilement, degradation, discredit, disesteem, disfavor, disgrace, dishonor, disrepute, disrespect, humiliation, *ignominia,* ignominy, ill repute, *infamia,* infamy, loss of honor, loss of reputation, obloquy, odium, opprobrium, reproach, scandal, scorn, smirch, stain, stigma, taint, tarnish, tarnished honor, turpitude, vileness

SHAPE, noun appearance, build, cast, color, complexion, condition, configuration, contour, criterion, cut, delineation, fashion, feature, features, figure, form, guise, image, impression, likeness, look, manner, mien, mode, mold, motif, organization, outline, pattern, physique, posture, presence, profile, seeming, semblance, state, structure, style, turn

SHAPE, verb adapt, carve, compose, conform, create, delineate, design, devise, fashion, figure, form, formalize, formulate, frame, influence, make, manufacture, model, mold, pattern, produce, sculpture, style, tailor

ASSOCIATED CONCEPTS: shaping of a claim, shaping of a defense

SHARE (Interest), **noun** allocation, allotment, apportioned lot, commission, dole, measure, *pars,* part, percent, percentage, portio, portion, proportion, quotum, ratio, ration, right, section, segment, slice

ASSOCIATED CONCEPTS: distributive share, equal share, share and share alike, share of capital, similiar share

SHARE (Stock), **noun** asset, capital, corporate interest, holding, invested property, investment, property, security, stockholding

ASSOCIATED CONCEPTS: bank shares, corporate shares, share of corporate stock, shareholder, treasury shares

SHAREHOLDER, noun investor, owner, property owner, stockholder, stockholder of record, stockowner

ASSOCIATED CONCEPTS: shareholder action, shareholder's derivative suit

SHED LIGHT ON, verb account for, clarify, clear the air, clear up, decipher, demonstrate, demystify, elucidate, enlighten, explain, explain away, explain oneself, explain the meaning of, expound on, get to the bottom of, get to the heart of, illuminate, illustrate, interpret, make sense of, provide insight, provide reason for, provide the meaning of, show, solve, spell out, unfold, unlock, unravel

SHELTER (Protection), **noun** aid, *asylum,* care, cover, covering, coverture, defense, habitation, harbor, haven, home, house, lodging, place of refuge, preservation, *receptaculum,* refuge, retreat, roof, safety, sanctuary, screen, security, shield, stronghold, support

SHELTER (Tax benefit), **noun** advantage, gain, hedge, refuge, security, tax haven, tax sanctuary

ASSOCIATED CONCEPTS: tax shelter

SHIELD, noun aegis, buckler, buffer, bulwark, *clipeus,* cover, covert, coverture, defense, guard, protection, protector, rampart, refuge, safeguard, sanctuary, screen, *scutum,* security, shelter

SHIFTING, adjective alternating, changeable, changing, deviating, digressive, discursive, drifting, fluctuating, inconstant, interim, roaming, roving, straying, transient, transitory, uncertain, vacillating, varying, wandering, wavering

ASSOCIATED CONCEPTS: shifting risk, shifting the burden of proof, shifting trust, shifting use

SHIRK, verb abstain, avoid, cheat, *detrectare,* dodge, duck, elude, escape from, evade, funk, ignore, keep away from, leave undone, malinger, neglect, quit, refuse, run from, shrink, shun, slink away, stay away, steer clear

SHORT (Brief), **adjective** abbreviated, abridged, compact, compressed, concise, condensed, crisp, cursory, curtailed, deficient, delinquent, devoid, fleet, fleeting, fugacious, hasty, laconic, meager, minimal, momentary, perfunctory, petulant, poor, quick, scarce, short-lived, shy, skimpy, sparse, succinct, temporary, terse, transient, unelevated
ASSOCIATED CONCEPTS: short clause, short form decision of the court, short notice

SHORT (Caustic), **adjective** abrupt, acetous, acrimonious, blunt, brusque, curt, discourteous, froward, grouchy, gruff, impolite, irascible, peevish, sharp, sour, sullen, surly, terse, touchy, testy, trenchant, ungraceful, volatile

SHORT (Imperfect), **adjective** defective, inadequate, incommensurate, incomplete, insufficient, lacking, low, meager, needing, sparse, unenduring, wanting

SHOW (Display), **noun** affectation, amusement, appearance, array, ceremony, chance, color, deceptive appearance, delusion, demonstration, distortion, exhibit, exhibition, expression, façade, flashiness, flourish, frills, front, illusion, impression, manifestation, materialization, occasion, outward show, parade, phenomenon, pomp, pomposity, pompousness, pose, presence, pretense, pretext, revelation, scene, semblance, show, showiness, sight, simulation, specious appearance, splash, trick, veneer, window-dressing
ASSOCIATED CONCEPTS: show cause

SHOW (Production), **noun** entertainment, exhibition, exposition, performance, presentation, spectacle

SHOW (Come into view), **verb** be seen, be visible, bring under notice, make one see, materialize, present one's self

SHOW (Detail), **verb** adduce, attest, bare, be visible, bear, cite, clarify, demean, demonstrate, denote, depict, designate, detail, disclose, display, document, edify, educate, establish, evidence, evince, exemplify, exhibit, explain, expose, express, furnish evidence, illustrate, indicate, inform, instruct, lay bare, make known, manifest, point out, point the way, portray, present, present one's self, produce, prove, render, represent, reveal, set forth, set straight, signify, specify, tell, testify, unveil, unfold, unmask

SHOW CAUSE, verb present a case, present argument, present cause, present reason, show grounds for
ASSOCIATED CONCEPTS: order to show cause

SHROUD, verb adumbrate, becloud, befog, blanket, bury, cloak, closet, conceal, cover, curtain, darken, eclipse, encase, ensconce, envelop, enwrap, hide, mask, muffle, obscure, overshadow, protect, render invisible, screen, seclude, sheathe, shelter, suppress, *tegere,* veil, *velare,* wrap

SHUN, verb abhor, abstain, avoid, back away, boycott, bypass, circumvent, cold-shoulder, *defugere,* deliberately avoid, disregard, dodge, draw back, elude, escape, eschew, evade, give a wide berth to, have no part of, have

nothing to do with, hide from, ignore, keep away from, keep clear of, keep one's distance, leave, let alone, malinger, neglect, rebuff, recoil from, refrain, shirk, shrink from, shy away from, snub, spurn, stay away from, steer clear of, turn aside, turn away from, *vitare,* ward off

SHUT, verb bar, barricade, block, block off, block up, blockade, bound, bung, button, cease, choke off, clasp, *claudere,* cloister, close, close down, *coercere,* cork, corral, cover, dam, discontinue, encase, enclose, end, envelop, enwrap, fasten, fence in, finish, halt, hem in, *includere,* intern, latch, lock, obstruct, occlude, plug, prevent passage, retard flow, seal, secure, shut down, stop, stop up, stopper, terminate, throttle, turn off

SIDE, noun affiliation, angle, aspect, body of partisans, cause, coalition, conception, direction, facet, faction, outlook, *pars,* party, point of view, position, sect, slant, standpoint, surface, verge, view, viewpoint

SIDE, verb advocate, aid, assist, back up, befriend, bolster, brace, buttress, champion, defend, encourage, endorse, favor, further, help, plead for, promote, protect, rally around, reinforce, second, stand behind, stand by, stick up for, strengthen, support, sustain, take the part of, unite with, uphold, vote for, vouch for

SIGHT (Appearance), **noun** apparency, curiosity, display, effect, exposure, figure, front, glance, guise, impression, inspection, ken, mien, object, panorama, perception, perspective, phenomenon, prospect, regard, respect, scene, scrutiny, show, spectacle, view, vision, vista

SIGHT (Condition), **noun** complexion, eyesore, fright, look, mess

SIGHT (Eyesight), **noun** eyeshot, field of view, line of sight, range or scope of vision, visualization

SIGHT, verb behold, contemplate, descry, detect, discern, distinguish, espy, gape, gaze, glimpse, look, look on or upon, notice, observe, peek, peer, perceive, recognize, regard, scan, scrutinize, see, set one's sights, set or lay eyes on, spot, spy, study, survey, view, take in, witness

SIGN, verb accept, accredit, acknowledge, affix a signature, affix one's name, affix one's signature to, agree to, approve, authenticate, authorize, autograph, certify, confirm, *consignare,* covenant, enter into a contract, execute, indorse, initial, inscribe one's name, inscribe one's signature, license, paraph, ratify, sanction, seal, set one's name to, subscribe, *subscribere,* undersign, underwrite, validate
ASSOCIATED CONCEPTS: countersign

SIGNIFICANCE, noun bearing, concern, concernment, consequence, distinction, eminence, essentiality, excellence, force, gist, gravity, greatness, import, importance, interest, mark, materiality, materialness, matter, meaning, merit, moment, momentousness, notability, note, paramountcy, pith, portent, precedence, preeminence, primacy, priority, prominence, relevance, salience, salient point, seriousness, *significatio,* signification, substance, substantiality, supremacy, value, *vis,* weight, weightiness, worth

SIGNIFICATION, noun acceptation, aim, connotation, designation, drift, effect, essence, explanation, force, gist, impact, implication, import, importance, indication, inference, intent, intention, interpretation, meaning, meat, moral, object, pith, point, purport, purpose, sense, significance, *significatio*, substance, tenor, value, vis, worth

SIGNIFY (Denote), *verb* betoken, connotate, connote, delineate, demonstrate, depict, evidence, evince, exemplify, hint, illustrate, imply, indicate, insinuates, intimate, manifest, mark, mean, point out, portray, purport, represent, reveal, show, stand for, suggest, symbolize, tell of, typify

SIGNIFY (Inform), *verb* acquaint, advance, advise, air, announce, apprise, assert, bruit, caution, communicate, convey, convey knowledge, declare, demonstrate, designate, direct the attention to, disclose, disseminate, divulge, enlighten, enumerate, express, give notice, give sign, impart, instruct, issue, make known, make obvious, make plain, make public, mention, notify, proclaim, promulgate, publish, report, reveal, set forth, specify, state, stipulate, tell, vent, voice

SILENCE, *noun* absolute quiet, hush, lack of sound, noiselessness, quiescence, quiescency, quiet, quietness, quietude, *silentium,* soundlessness, speechlessness, stillness, suppression of sound, *taciturnitas,* wordlessness
ASSOCIATED CONCEPTS: estopped by silence, silence as an admission
FOREIGN PHRASES: *Qui tacet, consentire videtur.* He who is silent is deemed to consent. ***Qui tacet consentire videtur, ubi tractatur de ejus commodo.*** He who is silent is deemed to consent, when his interest is at stake.

SIMILAR, *adjective* agreeing, allied, analogous, approximate, close, cognate, collateral, companion, comparable, conformable, congeneric, congenerical, congruent, connatural, consimilar, consubstantial, correspondent, corresponding, equivalent, homogeneous, identical, indistinguishable, kindred, like, matching, par, parallel, related, resembling, same, similis, synonymous, twin, uniform
FOREIGN PHRASES: *Ubi eadem ratio, ibi idem jus; et de similibus idem est judicium.* Where there is the same reason, there is the same law; and where there are similar situations, the judgment is the same.

SIMPLE, *adjective* artless, bare, basal, basic, clear, crude, downright, elemental, elementary, frank, free of duplicity, fundamental, guileless, homespun, homogeneous, inartificial, incomplex, *inconditus*, ingenuous, inornate, intelligible, irreducible, mere, natural, open, plain, primary, pure, rudimentary, rustic, simple-minded, *simplex*, simplified, sincere, *sincerus*, single, straightforward, unadorned, unadulterated, unaffected, unalloyed, unblended, uncombined, uncomplicated, uncompounded, unconstrained, undecorated, understandable, undesigning, unembellished, uninvolved, unmingled, unmixed, unpretentious, unsophisticated, unstudied, unvarnished, without confusion
ASSOCIATED CONCEPTS: simple assault, simple battery, simple contract, simple larceny, simple will

SIMPLIFY (Clarify), *verb* clear up, elucidate, explain, make clear, make plain, unfold, untwist

SIMPLIFY (Make easier), *verb* disentangle, make plain, streamline, uncomplicate, unravel

SIMULATE, *verb* act, copy, counterfeit, fabricate, feign, imitate, make believe, mock, play-act, pretend, represent
ASSOCIATED CONCEPTS: simulated conveyance, simulated sale, simulation

SIMULTANEOUS, *adjective* accompanying, at the same time, coetaneous, coeval, coexistent, coexisting, coincident, coinstantaneous, concomitant, concurrent, contemporaneous, contemporary, cotemporary, *eodem tempore,* in concert, *simul,* synchronal, synchronic, synchronical, synchronistic, synchronistical, synchronous
ASSOCIATED CONCEPTS: simultaneous death

SINCERE, *adjective* aboveboard, bona fide, candid, deceitless, direct, earnest, faithful, fervent, forthright, frank, genuine, guileless, honest, open, pure, real, reliable, scrupulous, serious, straight, straightforward, true, trustworthy, truthful, undeceitful, veracious, wholehearted

SINE DIE, *adverb* at no period, at no time, never, never again, on no occasion, without date

SINE QUA NON, *noun* absolute condition, absolute prerequisite, antecedent, condition, contingency, essential clause, essential condition, essential matter, essential part, essential qualification, indispensable condition, indispensable item, necessity, precondition, prerequisite, prime constituent, prime ingredient, qualification, requirement, vital concern

SINECURE, *noun* easily managed job, easy chore, easy employment, easy job, easy labor, effortless assignment, effortless employment, effortless undertaking, effortless work, light labor, light work, simple job, soft job, undemanding chore, undemanding job, undemanding task

SINEW, *noun* brawn, brawniness, effectiveness, endurance, energy, force, forcefulness, grit, lustiness, might, muscle, *nervus,* potence, potency, power, powerfulness, robustness, stamina, staying power, strength, thews, vigor, vigorousness

SINGULAR, *adjective* different, distinct, eccentric, *egregius,* eminent, especial, exceptional, exclusive, extraordinary, individual, isolated, lone, matchless, nonpareil, odd, out of the ordinary, particular, peculiar, peerless, queer, rare, remarkable, separate, single, *singularis,* sole, special, unaccompanied, uncommon, uncustomary, unequaled, unexampled, *unicus,* unique, unparalleled, unprecedented, unusual

SINISTER, *adjective* alarming, baleful, baneful, blameworthy, censurable, cold-blooded, comminatory, conscienceless, contemptible, corrupt, creepy, cruel, culpable, dangerous, demoniac, demoniacal, deserving of condemnation, designing, despiteful, destructive, detrimental, diabolic, diabolical, dishonest, disingenuous, dismaying, disquieting, disreputable, disturbing, dreadful, eerie, envenomed, evil, exceptionable, facinorous, fear-inspiring, fearsome, fiendish, flagitious, flawed, frightening, ghoulish, harmful, heartless, heinous, horrible, horrid, hurtful, ignoble, ill-disposed, illaudable, immeritorious, immoral, impious, inauspicious, infamous, injurious, inquitous, insidious, intimidating, lawless, malefic, maleficent, maleficial, malevolent, malicious, malign, malignant, menacing, minatory, mischievous, miscreant, murderous, nefarious, nocuous, noisome, noxious, obliquitous, peccable, peccant, pernicious, perverse, portending evil, *pravus,* presageful, rascally, remorseless, reprehensible, satanic, scatheful, scheming, scoundrelly, sinful, spiteful, tainted, terrible, threatening, treacherous, truculent, unbenevolent, uncommendable, unfair, unfavorable, unjustifiable, unprincipled, unpromising, unpropitious, unrighteous, untrustworthy, unwholesome, venomous, villainous, virulent, wicked, worthy of blame, wrong

SINUOUS, adjective ambagious, ambagitory, anfractuous, circuitous, coiled, complex, complicated, convolute, convoluted, convolutional, crooked, curved, curvilinear, deviating, deviative, devious, entangled, flexuous, indirect, intricate, involute, involuted, involutional, involutionary, involved, labyrinthian, labyrinthine, mazy, meandering, meandrous, oblique, plexiform, rambling, reticular, roundabout, serpentine, sinuate, *sinuosus,* snaky, spiral, tangled, tortile, tortuous, turning, twisted, twisting, volute, winding, zigzag

SITE, noun address, base, environs, habitat, locale, locality, location, neighborhood, place, position, setting, situation, situs, stead, territory, vicinity

SITE, verb arrange, assign, base, center, localize, locate, place, position, situate

SITUATED, adjective anchored, bestead, *conlocatus,* embedded, ensconced, established, fixed, found, housed, implanted, installed, laid, located, lodged, occupying, placed, planted, posited, positioned, positus, posted, proximate to, put, quartered, rooted, seated, set, settled, *situs,* stationed
ASSOCIATED CONCEPTS: similarly situated

SITUATION, noun arrangement, case, circumstance, circumstances, condition, crisis, environment, exigency, happening, incidence, instance, juncture, lot, mishap, occurrence, plight, position, post, posture, predicament, *situs,* standing, state, station, status

SITUS, noun locale, locality, location, locus, place, placement, point, position, site, situation
ASSOCIATED CONCEPTS: situs of a crime

SIZE *(Frequency),* **noun** area, bigness, body, cubic content, expanse, extent, girth, intensity, quantity, scope, tonnage, volume

SIZE *(Physical magnitude),* **noun** amplitude, bulk, caliber, capacity, dimensions, extent, frequency, greatness, largeness, magnitude, mass, measurement, proportions
ASSOCIATED CONCEPTS: size of a market share, size of jury pool

SKEPTICAL, adjective agnostic, cynical, disbelieving, distrustful, distrusting, doubting, dubious, faithless, freethinking, heretical, heterodox, iconoclastic, incredulous, questioning, quizzical, scoffing, suspecting, suspicious, unbelieving, uncertain, unorthodox, unsure, untrusting, wary

SKILL, noun ability, adeptness, adroitness, aptitude, aptness, art, artistry, cleverness, command, competence, craft, cunning, deftness, dexterity, ease, endowment, excellence, experience, expertness, facility, felicity, finesse, fluency, gift, handiness, ingeniousness, ingenuity, knack, knowledge, mastery, *peritia,* proficiency, prowess, quickness, *scientia,* sollertia, talent

SLANDER, noun abusive language, accusation, aspersion, *calumnia,* calumniation, calumny, censure, character assassination, *criminatio,* damaging report, defamation, defamatory words, denigration, denunciation, disparagement, execration, false report, imprecation, insinuation, invective, libel, *maledictio,* malicious report, obloquy, opprobrium, reproach, revilement, scandal, scurrility, slur, smear, stricture, traducement, vilification
ASSOCIATED CONCEPTS: malice, publication, slander of title, slander per quod, slander per se

SLANT, verb angle, bias, color, distort, doctor, embroider, exaggerate, falsify, incline, interpret falsely, misapply, miscolor, misconstrue, misdirect, misinterpret, misquote, misrender, misrepresent, misstate, overstate, pervert, predispose, prejudice, prepossess, stretch, turn, twist, varnish, veer, warp, wrest

SLAPP SUIT, noun action against public, action to deter protests, harassment through legal means, infliction of punishment for protesting, judicial process as a means to discourage protests, lawsuit to deter opposition, litigation to deter opposition, participation suit, retaliation for protests, retribution for protesting, retributive justice, scare tactics, strategic lawsuit, vengeance
ASSOCIATED CONCEPTS: antislapp suit

SLAY, verb annihilate, assassinate, deprive of life, destroy, dispatch, dispose of, execute, exterminate, *interficere, interimere,* kill, liquidate, massacre, murder, *occidere,* put to death, slaughter, take a life, terminate, victimize
ASSOCIATED CONCEPTS: homicide

SLIGHT, adjective ancillary, auxiliary, diminutive, exiguous, *exiguus,* immaterial, inappreciable, inconsequential, inconsiderable, inferior, insignificant, *levis,* light, limited, little, meager, mean, minor, minute, modest, negligible, niggardly, nonessential, nugatory, of small account, of small importance, paltry, petty, scant, secondary, slender, slim, small, stinted, subaltern, subordinate, subsidiary, *tenuis,* tenuous, thin, trifling, trivial, unessential, unimportant, unsubstantial
ASSOCIATED CONCEPTS: slight care, slight evidence, slight fault, slight negligence

SLIP AND FALL CASE, noun accident, action, calamity, casualty claim, cause of action, claim, general liability claim, injurious occurrence, injury, liability claim, litigation, misfortune, mishap, negligence case, personal injury case, trip and fall
ASSOCIATED CONCEPTS: insurance, mitigating slip and fall liability, trial lawyers

SLIPSHOD, adjective careless, disordered, disorderly, disorganized, haphazard, heedless, imprecise, improper, inaccurate, indifferent, inexact, lackadaisical, lax, negligent, offhand, orderless, poor, remiss, shabby, sloppy, slovenly, thoughtless, uncareful, uncaring, uncoordinated, unmeticulous, unneat, unorganized, unseemly, untidy

SLOTH, noun acedia, apathy, *desidia,* disinclination to action, disinclination to labor, dullness, faineance, idleness, *ignavia,* inaction, inactivity, indifference, indolence, inertia, inertness, inexertion, languidness, laxness, laziness, leadenness, lethargy, listlessness, lumpishness, neglectfulness, otiosity, passivity, phlegm, *segnitia,* shiftlessness, slackness, sluggishness, stupor, supineness, torpescence, torpidity, torpor, unconcern

SLY, adjective arch, artful, astute, *astutus,* calculating, clandestine, conniving, covert, covinous, crafty, crooked, cunning, deceitful, deceiving, deceptious, deceptive, delusive, designing, devious, dishonest, dishonorable, disingenuous, double-dealing, evasive, feline, foxy, furtive, guileful, hidden, insidious, intriguing, keen, obreptitious, plotting, scheming, secret, secretive, sharp, shifty, shrewd, skulking, slippery, sneaking, sneaky, stealthy, *subdolus,* subtle, surreptitious, treacherous, tricky, uncandid, undercover, underhand, underhanded, unscrupulous, vafer, vulpine, wily

SMEAR, verb   asperse, attack, attaint, belittle, besmear, besmirch, besmut, blacken, blemish, brand, calumniate, cast a slur, contaminate, decry, defame, defile, degrade, denigrate, denounce, depreciate, derogate, destroy one's reputation, detract, discredit, dishonor, disparage, disrate, expose to infamy, hold up to shame, humiliate, *inlinere,* libel, make scandal, malign, mar, mark, *oblinere,* pillory, pollute, render unclean, ridicule, slander, slur, smirch, soil, speak evil of, stain, stigmatize, sully, taint, tarnish, traduce, undermine, vilify, vilipend
ASSOCIATED CONCEPTS: defamation

SNARL, noun   complexus, complication, confusion, disarray, disorder, entanglement, *gannitus,* imbroglio, involute, kink, knot, labyrinth, mat, maze, mess, ravel, snag, tangle, twist

SOBRIQUET, noun   byname, cognomen, fanciful name, fictitious, nickname, nom de plume, pseudonym

SOCIAL SECURITY, noun   insurance coverage for aged Americans, retirement benefits, retirement coverage, retirement insurance, retirement protection
Generally: economic assistance, social insurance, support for the disabled, support of the retired

SOCIETY, noun   alliance, aristocracy, association, bloc, body, brethren, brotherhood, circle, citizenry, civilization, class, clique, club, coalition, colleagueship, combine, commonwealth, community, companionship, comradeship, confederacy, confederation, confraternity, consociation, culture, denomination, faction, federation, fellowship, fold, folk, fraternal order, fraternity, fraternization, gentility, group, guild, higher class, *homines,* institute, league, order, organization, organized group, patriciate, peerage, polity, population, privileged class, religious order, sect, set, sodality, tribe, union, upper class

SODALITY, noun   alignment, alliance, amity, association, bond, brotherhood, brotherliness, camaraderie, clique, club, colleagueship, combination, communion, community, community of interest, companionship, compatibility, comradeship, concord, confederacy, confederation, confraternity, consolidation, copartnership, faction, federation, fellowship, fraternity, fraternization, friendliness, friendly relations, friendship, group, guild, intercourse, league, order, organization, partnership, social group, society, sorosis, unification, union

SODOMY, noun   buggery, degeneration, depravity, deviation, indecency, pederasty, perversion, sexual deviation, unlawful sexual intercourse, unnatural carnal intercourse, unnatural sexual intercourse, vice

SOLACE, noun   abatement, allayment, alleviation, amelioration, cheer, comfort, commiseration, condolence, *consolatio,* consolation, ease, easement, encouragement, help, kindliness, melioration, mitigation, palliation, reassurance, refreshment, relief, *solatium,* sympathy, tranquility

SOLE, adjective   individual, insular, isolated, lone, one, only, separate, single, singular, solitary, solus, unaccompanied, unattended, *unicus,* unique, *unus*
ASSOCIATED CONCEPTS: sole actor, sole and exclusive cause, sole and unconditional owner, sole proprietor, sole surviving heir

SOLELY (Purely), adverb   barely, merely, plainly, purely, simply

SOLELY (Singly), adverb   alone, entirely, exclusively, only, wholly

SOLEMN, adjective   august, awe-inspiring, awesome, ceremonial, ceremonious, devotional, devout, earnest, formal, funereal, gloomy, grave, *gravis,* grim, hallowed, holy, imposing, impressive, majestic, meditative, mirthless, mournful, pensive, quiet, reflective, religious, reverential, ritual, sacramental, sacred, sanctified, sedate, serious, *severus,* sober, somber, spiritual, staid, stately, stern, stirring, subdued, *tristis,* venerable, worshipful

SOLEMNITY, noun   awesomeness, ceremoniousness, ceremony, dignity, graveness, *gravitas,* gravity, impressiveness, pomp, seriousness, *severitas,* soberness, sobriety, solemn feeling, stateliness, tradition, *tristitia*

SOLICIT, verb   appeal for, appeal to, apply, ask, ask earnestly, beseech, call for, canvass, *captare,* clamor for, coax, demand, entreat, *flagitare,* implore, importune, induce, make a request, obsecrate, obtest, *petere,* petition, plead, press, request, supplicate, urge

SOLICITATION, noun   appeal for, appeal to, application, asking, asking earnestly, beseechment, calling for, canvassing, clamor for, coaxing, entreatment, imploration, importuning, importunity, inducement, inquiry, making a request, obtestation, petition, pleading, press, reuest, supplication, urging, writing for contributions
ASSOCIATED CONCEPTS: criminal solicitation, peddlers and solicitors

SOLICITOUS, adjective   ambitious, anxious, *anxius,* apprehensive, aspiring, bent on, beseeching, caring, concerned, craving, desirous, eager, hopeful, inclined, intent on, keen, optative, petitionary, *sollicitus,* supplicatory, wanting, willing, yearning

SOLID (Compact), adjective   bunched, close, coagulated, compressed, concentrated, condensed, congealed, consolidated, dense, firm, grumose, hard, hardened, impenetrable, impermeable, incompressible, indiscerptible, indivisible, inflexible, insecable, inseparable, massed, massive, monolithical, nonporous, ossified, packed, packed together, pressed together, rigid, serried, solidified, stiff, thick, tight, undissolved, united, unyielding

SOLID (Sound), adjective   able to pay, assured, considered, convincing, dependable, durable, enduring, established, faithworthy, fast, firm, *firmus,* guaranteed, incontestable, incontrovertible, irrefutable, judicious, just, lasting, logical, politic, precautional, precautionary, precautious, prudent, prudential, rational, reasonable, reliable, responsible, rugged, safe, sagacious, sage, sapient, secure, sensible, *solidus,* solvent, *stabilis,* stable, stanch, steadfast, steady, strong, sturdy, substantial, substantive, true, trustworthy, trusty, unconfutable, unerring, unfailing, unimpeachable, unquestionable, unrefutable, valid, weighty, well-built, well-constructed, well-established, well-founded, well-grounded, well-made, wise

SOLITARY, adjective   abandoned, aloof, anchoretic, anchoretical, avoiding the society of others, celibate, cloistered, companionless, deserted, desolate, detached, disjoined, disjunct, enisled, eremetical, eremitic, eremitish, estranged, fellowless, forsaken, friendless, hermitic, hermitical, homeless, insular, isolated, kithless, lone, lonely, lonesome, orphaned, private, reclusive, remote, removed, rootless, secluded, separate, separated, single, sole, solo, *solus,*

unabetted, unaccompanied, unaided, unassisted, unattended, unconnected, unescorted, uninhabited, unmatched, unoccupied, unpaired, unseconded, unshared, unsupported, unvisited, without companions, without company
ASSOCIATED CONCEPTS: solitary confinement

SOLUTION (Answer), **noun**   clarification, decipherment, determination, elucidation, explanation, *explicatio,* explication, exposition, finding, illumination, interpretation, key, reason, resolution, right answer, *solutio*
ASSOCIATED CONCEPTS: equitable solution

SOLUTION (Substance), **noun**   admixture, amalgam, blend, combination, commixture, composite, composition, compound, *dilutum,* emulsion, intermixture, mix, mixture, solvent, suspension

SOLVABLE, adjective   ascertainable, cognizable, decipherable, decodable, determinable, discoverable, exegetical, explainable, explicative, explicatory, expository, fathomable, intelligible, recognizable, resolvable, scrutable, soluble, workable

SOLVE, verb   account for, answer, arrive at the truth, ascertain, bring out, clear up, crack, decipher, decode, deduce, discover, disentangle, disinter, *dissolvere,* educe, elucidate, *enodare,* enucleate, *expedire,* explain, fathom, ferret out, figure out, find out, find the cause, find the key, find the solution, guess correctly, guess right, interpret, learn the answer, make out, make plain, penetrate, piece together, puzzle out, realize, reason out, render intelligible, resolve, root out, shed light upon, think out, throw light upon, trace, understand, unearth, unfold, unlock, unravel, unriddle, unscramble, untangle, work out
ASSOCIATED CONCEPTS: solve a crime

SOLVENT, adjective   able to pay, clear of encumbrance, creditworthy, financially sound, in good financial condition, moneyed, not owing, out of debt, owing nothing, pecunious, unindebted, with funds, with good credit
ASSOCIATED CONCEPTS: solvent debt
FOREIGN PHRASES: Id solum nostrum quod debitis deductis nostrum est. That only is ours which remains to us after deduction of our debts.

SOOTHE, verb   allay, alleviate, ameliorate, appease, assuage, attemper, balm, becalm, blunt, calm, comfort, compose, deaden, dulcify, dull, ease, free from anxiety, free from pain, give relief, humor, hush, lenify, *lenire,* lessen, lull, mitigate, moderate, mollify, *mulcere,* obtund, pacificate, pacify, palliate, *placare,* placate, propitiate, quell, quench, quiet, relax, relieve, relieve pressure, render less painful, salve, slake, smooth, soften, still, succor, tame, temper, tranquilize

SOPHISTIC, adjective   *captiosus,* captious, casuistic, casuistical, contrary to reason, erroneous, fallacious, false, faulty in logic, groundless, ill-reasoned, illogical, inconsequent, inconsistent, incorrect, invalid, irrational, misleading, paralogical, sophistical, specious, tricky, unfounded, ungrounded, unreasonable, unsound, untenable, unwarranted, wrong

SOPHISTICATED, adjective   advanced, avant garde, complex, contemporary, forward looking, innovative, knowledgeable, modern, new, progressive, ultramodern, up to date, up to the minute, urbane

SOPHISTRY, noun   casuistry, cavil, chicanery, deception, distortion, equivocation, evasion, evasive reasoning, fallacious reasoning, false logic, misrepresentation, specious reasoning

SORDID, adjective   *abiectus,* abject, abominable, base, corrupt, debased, decayed, defiled, degraded, deteriorated, dilapidated, disgusting, foul, fouled, fulsome, fusty, grimy, gruesome, *inliberalis,* mucky, odious, repellent, slatternly, slovenly, *sordidus,* squalid, undesirable

SORT, verb   allocate, allot, apportion, arrange, array, assign places to, assort, catalogue, categorize, class, classify, collocate, deal, *digerere,* disentangle, distribute, divide, file, grade, graduate, group, methodize, order, organize, parcel out, place in order, put in order, range, rank, reduce to order, screen, segregate, separate, sieve, sift, size, split, subdivide, systematize, tabulate

SOUND, adjective   accurate, acknowledged, admitted, cogent, compelling, convincing, correct, credible, effective, effectual, efficacious, factual, forceful, incontrovertible, irrefutable, justified, legitimate, persuasive, potent, powerful, proven, right, rightful, scientific, solid, strong, substantial, true, truthful, unanswerable, unchallengeable, unconfutable, undisputable, undistorted, unexaggerated, unimagined, unimpeachable, veracious, veritable, weighty, well-founded, well-grounded
ASSOCIATED CONCEPTS: sound discretion, sound value

SOUND REASONING, noun   accurate assessment, cogent reasoning, compelling reasoning, convincing logic, correct assessment, effective analysis, forceful reasoning, incontrovertible logic, irrefutable conclusions, judicious analysis, justified analysis, legitimate analysis, methodical analysis, persuasive reasoning, plausible reasoning, potent logic, powerful conclusions, proven reasoning, reasonable analysis, solid reasoning, sound rationale, strong reasoning, unchallengeable reasoning, undisputable reasoning, unimpeachable reasoning, well-founded logic, well-grounded logic, well-reasoned opinion
ASSOCIATED CONCEPTS: judicial opinions

SOURCE, noun   ancestry, authority, basis, beginning, *caput,* cause, cradle, derivation, *fons,* font, foundation, fount, fountain, fountainhead, generator, genesis, germ, headspring, incunabula, informant, inspiration, lineage, motive, origin, original, origination, *origo,* parent, parentage, place, provenance, provenience, root, spring, springhead, stem, well, wellhead, wellspring
ASSOCIATED CONCEPTS: source of income, source of information

SOVEREIGN (Absolute), **adjective**   authoritative, chief, commanding, controlling, dominant, governing, hegemonic, hegemonical, imperial, influential, leading, master, most powerful, paramount, potent, powerful, predominant, prepollent, prepotent, regent, regnant, reigning, royal, ruling, supreme

SOVEREIGN (Independent), **adjective**   at liberty, autonomous, enjoying liberty, enjoying political independence, exempt from external authority, free, liberated, politically independent, removed from bondage, self-determined, self-directing, self-governed, self-ruling, *sui iuris,* unattached, unbound, unconquered, uncontrolled, unenslaved, unrestricted, unsubjected, unvanquished
ASSOCIATED CONCEPTS: sovereign right, sovereign states

SPACE, noun   accommodation, acreage, area, capaciousness, capacity, compass, distance, expanse, extent, field, footage, gap, interstice, interval, latitude, *locus,* margin, mileage, range, room, scope, size, spaciousness, span, *spatium,* stretch, sweep, territory, vastness, yardage

SPACE HATCH, noun   avenue to explore, channel to pursue, door, egress, excuse, exit, harbor, loophole, means, opening, out, port, pretext, safety valve, shelter, vehicle, vent, way out

SPARTAN, adjective   aggressive, *audax,* bellicose, bold, brave, courageous, daring, dauntless, determined, disciplined, doughty, fearless, fierce, firm, formidable, *fortis,* hardy, hero-like, heroic, highly disciplined, indomitable, intrepid, iron-hearted, lionhearted, manly, martial, mighty, militant, plucky, pugnacious, resisting, resolute, resolved, self-reliant, severe, soldier-like, soldierly, stalwart, stoic, stoical, stout, stout-hearted, *strenuus,* strong, unafraid, unapprehensive, unblenching, unconquerable, undaunted, unflinching, unshrinking, valiant, valorous, virile, warlike, well-disciplined

SPATE, noun   abundance, cataract, deluge, flood, outburst, profusion, rush, torrent

SPEAK, verb   address, air, announce, annunciate, apprise, articulate, aver, badinage, bandy words, bear witness, break silence, carry on a conversation, colloque, communicate with, converse, declaim, declare, deliver, deliver an address, denote, *dicere,* disclose, discourse, divulge, engage in a conversation, engage in a dialogue, enunciate, exchange opinions, explain, expound, express, give a talk, give expression, give indication of, give voice, give words to, have a dialogue, hold a conversation, hold a discussion, indicate, inform, issue a statement, join in a conversation, make a speech, make a statement, make mention, make oral communication, make oral mention, make solemn affirmation, make solemn declaration, murmur, mutter, palaver, parley, phrase, pour forth, proclaim, pronounce, publish, put into words, recite, remark, render an account of, repeat, report, reveal, say, sermonize, state, state emphatically, state one's case, state with conviction, talk, tell, utter, utter forth, utter with conviction, utter words

FOREIGN PHRASES: ***Idem est nihil dicere et insufficienter dicere.*** It is the same thing to say nothing, and to say a thing insufficiently.

SPECIAL, adjective   amazing, astonishing, astounding, atypical, awe-inspiring, awesome, certain, conspicuous, different, distinctive, distinguished, *egregius,* endemic, esoteric, especial, exceptional, *eximius,* extraordinary, fabulous, fantastic, gala, important, imposing, incredible, individualistic, infrequent, marked, marvelous, memorable, miraculous, notable, noteworthy, outstanding, particular, *praecipuus,* prodigious, rare, remarkable, significant, singular, specific, striking, stupendous, superior, unaccustomed, uncommon, uncustomary, unexampled, unfamiliar, unforgettable, unimitative, unique, unparalleled, unprecedented, unusual, wonderful

ASSOCIATED CONCEPTS: special act, special appearance, special assessment, special benefits, special case, special circumstances, special damages, special election, special interest, special law, special legislation, special proceeding, special remedy, special tax, special verdict

FOREIGN PHRASES: ***Statutum generaliter est intelligendum quando verba statuti sunt specialia, ratio autem generalis.*** When the words of a statute are special, but the reason general, the statute is to be understood generally. ***Generalia praecedunt, specialia sequuntur.*** General matters precede, special matters follow.

SPECIAL INTEREST, noun   advocate, appealer, aspirant, influencer, instigator, lobby, lobbyist, mover, petitioner, pressure group, prompter, seeker, solicitor, suggester, suitor, suppliant

SPECIALIST, noun   authority, connoisseur, consultant, degreeholder, devotee, experienced person, expert, homo *peritus,* knowing person, learned person, master, practiced hand, practitioner, professional, professor, proficient, proficient person, qualified person, savant, scholar, skilled hand, skilled person, skilled practitioner, skilled worker, specializer, technician, trained person, veteran, virtuoso

SPECIALITY, noun   badge, character, distinction, distinctive characteristic, distinctive mark, distinctive quality, distinctiveness, feature, identification, individual characteristic, individual trait, individuality, mark, oddity, particularity, peculiarity, quality, quirk, singularity, specialness, stamp

SPECIALIZE, verb   address oneself to, apply oneself, bound, concentrate on, concern oneself with, dedicate oneself to, devote oneself to, focus attention on, give attention to, limit, narrow, practice exclusively, pursue, qualify, restrict, select, take up, train

SPECIALTY (Contract), **noun**   agreement, arrangement, bargain under seal, bond, commitment, compact, concordat, contractual obligation, contractual statement, covenant, covenant of indemnity, debenture, engagement, guaranty, hypothecation, indenture, legal agreement, obligation, pact, pledge, pledged word, promise under seal, recognizance, security, stipulation, understanding, undertaking, warranty

ASSOCIATED CONCEPTS: specialty debts, suit upon a specialty

SPECIALTY (Distinctive mark), **noun**   attribute, badge, brand, character, characteristic, definiteness, disconformity, dissimilarity, distinction, distinctive feature, distinctiveness, distinctness, dominant characteristic, earmark, eccentricity, feature, idiosyncrasy, impress, inconsistency, individualism, mannerism, mark, oddity, particular characteristic, particular item, particular matter, particular point, particularity, peculiar idiom, peculiar temperament, peculiarity, personal characteristic, point of difference, property, quality, quirk, rarity, singularity, special characteristic, special item, special matter, special point, specific quality, specificness, stamp, token, trait, uniqueness, unlikeness

SPECIALTY (Special aptitude), **noun**   ability, accomplishment, adeptness, aptness, artistry, calling, capability, career, competence, craft, dexterity, endowment, expertise, expertness, faculty, forte, function, genius, handicraft, inborn aptitude, ingenuity, innate ability, knowledge, main interest, mastership, mastery, natural ability, object of study, occupation, particular object of pursuit, professionalism, proficiency, pursuit, qualification, skill, skillfulness, special line of work, special project, special skill, special study, specialization, strong point, talent, task, technique, virtuosity, vocation

SPECIFIC, adjective   appropriate, categorical, certain, characteristic, definite, denominational, determinate, determined, different, *disertus,* distinctive, divisional, endemic, endemical, esoteric, especial, exact, exceptional, exclusive, explicit, express, idiomatic, idiosyncratic, idiosyncratical, indigenous, individual, individualistic, limited, marked, narrow, out of the ordinary, particular, peculiar, *peculiaris,*

precise, precisely formulated, *proprius,* respective, restricted, sectarian, select, special, uncommon, unique, unusual
ASSOCIATED CONCEPTS: specific bequest, specific denial, specific devise, specific legacy, specific performance

SPECIFICATION, *noun* assignment, condition, definition, delimitation, description, designation, detail, detailed statement, determination, distinction, enumeration, item, itemization, minute account, nicety, particular, particularization, proviso, recital, special point, statement of particulars, stipulation, written requirement

SPECIFY, *verb* advert to, circumscribe, cite, clearly define, demarcate, *denotare,* designate, detail, differentiate, disclose, *enumerare,* enumerate, explain, express, give full particulars, go into detail, indicate, instance, itemize, list, mark out, mention, name, particularize, point out, refer to, represent, select, show, state in detail, state precisely, stipulate

SPECIMEN, *noun* case in point, *documentum,* ensample, example, *exemplum,* exponent, guide, illustration, instance, model, paradigm, pattern, representative, representative selection, sample

SPECIOUS, *adjective* affected, apparent, appearing, artificial, assumed, believable, bogus, casuistic, casuistical, colorable, colored, convincing, counterfeit, credible, deceiving, deceptive, deluding, delusive, delusory, erroneous, exterior, external, fake, fallacious, false, hypocritical, illusional, illusive, illusory, misleading, ostensible, outward, persuasive, phony, plausible, posed, pretend, pretended, professed, purported, put on, resembling truth, seeming, simulated, so-called, sophistic, sophistical, *speciosus,* spurious, unfounded, would-be
ASSOCIATED CONCEPTS: specious argument, specious defense

SPECTER, *noun* apparition, appearance, eidolon, form, illusion, presence, revenant, shadow, shape, spirit, sprite

SPECULATE *(Chance),* ***verb*** assume a risk, bet, chance, dare, deal in futures, gamble, hazard, invest, lay money on, play the market, plunge, risk, stake, take a chance, try one's luck, venture, wager

SPECULATE *(Conjecture),* ***verb*** assume, *cogitare,* consider, dare say, debate, deliberate, guess, have a theory, hypothesize, judge, muse, philosophize, ponder, puzzle over, *quaerere,* reckon, ruminate, suppose, surmise, theorize, think, turn over in the mind, venture, weigh, wonder about
ASSOCIATED CONCEPTS: speculative damages

SPECULATION *(Conjecture),* ***noun*** assumption, *coniectura,* contemplation, deliberation, guesswork, hypothesis, inference, presumption, reasoning, rumination, supposition, surmise, suspicion, theorization, theory
ASSOCIATED CONCEPTS: speculative damages, speculative testimony

SPECULATION *(Risk),* ***noun*** bet, calculated risk, chance, fortuity, fortune, gamble, gambling, gaming, hazard, uncertainty, venture, wager

SPECULATIVE, *adjective* abstract, academic, aleatory, assumptive, chancy, cogitative, *coniecturalis,* conjectural, contemplative, contestable, controvertible, debatable, deliberative, doubtful, dubious, experimental, hazardous, hypothetical, imaginary, impractical, indefinite, indistinct, insecure, irresolute, meditative, presumptive, projected, provisional, questionable, risky, speculatory, suppositional, tentative, theoretical, uncertain, unconfirmed, undemonstrated, undetermined, unproven, unsafe, unsettled
ASSOCIATED CONCEPTS: speculative testimony

SPECULATOR, *noun* adventurer, backer, bettor, entrepreneur, experimenter, gambler, hazarder, prospector, risk taker, trader, venturer, wagerer

SPEECH, *noun* address, allocution, articulation, audible expression, colloquy, confabulation, conversation, declamation, declaration, delivery, dialect, diction, discourse, enunciation, expression, idiom, interlocution, language, lecture, lingo, locution, oral communication, oral expression, *oratio,* oration, oratory, palaver, parlance, phonation, phraseology, prattle, pronouncement, pronunciation, recital, recitation, rhetoric, say, sermon, spoken language, spoken word, statement, talk, tongue, utterance, verbal expression, verbal intercourse, vocalization, words
ASSOCIATED CONCEPTS: First Amendment, freedom of speech
FOREIGN PHRASES: *Lubricum linguae non facile trahendum est in poenam.* A slip of the tongue ought not readily be subjected to punishment.

SPEECHLESS, *adjective* agape, aghast, amazed, aphonic, astonished, awe-struck, bewildered, dumb, dumb-struck, *elinguis,* gagged, inarticulate, incapable of utterance, indisposed to words, mum, mute, *mutus,* noiseless, open-mouthed, quiet, silent, soundless, stunned, stupefied, *tacere,* thunderstruck, tongue-tied, unable to speak, unvocal, voiceless, wordless

SPEEDY TRIAL, *noun* criminal trial held diligently, criminal trial held promptly, criminal trial held punctually, criminal trial held within allowed time, criminal trial held within designated periods of time, criminal trial held within imposed time frames, criminal trial held within prescribed deadlines, criminal trial held within required time frame, speedy trial period
ASSOCIATED CONCEPTS: Sixth Amendment, the right to a speedy and public trial, waiver

SPEND, *verb* apply, bestow, consume, *consumere,* contribute, deplete, devote, disburse, dispense, dispose of, donate, drain, employ, empty, exhaust, expend, give, go through, impoverish, incur expense, *insumere,* invest, lay out money, make expenditure, outlay, part with, pay, run through, splurge, use, use up, wear away, wear out
ASSOCIATED CONCEPTS: spendthrift

SPHERE, *noun* ambit, arena, ball, bounds, capacity, circle, circuit, demesne, department, domain, field, field of activity, field of operation, function, globe, globoid, globular mass, influence, office, orb, orbit, pale, province, *provincia,* range, realm, region, round body, scope, *sphaera,* spheroid

SPIRIT, *noun* angel, *anima,* animation, apparition, ardor, boldness, bravery, character, characteristic quality, cheer, cheerfulness, complexion, courage, daring, dash, disposition, earnestness, energy, enterprise, enthusiasm, essence, essential part, fire, firmness, force, fortitude, frame of mind, gist, humor, hypostasis, immaterial substance, immortal part, *ingenium,* intent, life, liveliness, meaning, mettle, mood, nature, passion, psyche, purport, quintessence, resoluteness, resolution, sense, sentiment, significance, soul, sparkle, specter, spice, substance, supernatural being, temper, temperament, tenor, turn of mind, verve, vigor, vim, vital essence, vitality, vivacity, zeal
ASSOCIATED CONCEPTS: spirit of the law

SPIRIT, verb   actuate, animate, arouse, encourage, enliven, *excitare,* excite, exhilarate, exhort, impassion, impel, *incitare,* incite, inspire, inspirit, instigate, kindle, motivate, move, press, prod, prompt, propel, provoke, push, rouse, spur, *stimulare,* stimulate, stir up, urge on

SPIRITED, adjective   active, adventurous, alive, animated, avid, bold, brisk, buoyant, dashing, dynamic, eager, ebullient, effervescent, energetic, enthusiastic, exuberant, fervent, fiery, full of life, full of pep, hearty, intense, intrepid, irrepressible, keen, lively, mettlesome, passionate, peppy, sparkling, sprightly, spry, stalwart, undaunted, unrestrained, vehement, venturesome, vibrant, vigorous, vivacious, zealous, zestful

SPITE, noun   acrimoniousness, acrimony, animosity, animus, antagonism, bitterness, cattiness, contempt, defiance, despite, enmity, gall, grudge, harsh feeling, hate, hatred, hostility, ill feeling, ill nature, ill will, inimicality, intolerance, *livor,* malevolence, *malevolentia,* malice, maliciousness, malignance, malignancy, malignitas, malignity, rancor, resentment, revengefulness, spitefulness, vengeance, venom, viciousness, vindictiveness, virulence, virulency

SPITEFUL, adjective   acrimonious, antagonistic, antipathetic, belligerent, caustic, contrary, despiteful, envenomed, evil-minded, froward, harsh, hateful, hostile, ill-disposed, ill-intentioned, ill-natured, inimical, invidious, *lividus,* malevolent, *malevolus,* malicious, malign, malignant, *malignus,* mean, rancorous, resentful, revengeful, testy, venemous, vicious, vindictive, viperous, virulent

SPLIT, noun   aperture, bifurcation, bisection, breach, break, chasm, chink, cleavage, cleft, crack, crater, crevice, cut, detachment, dichotomy, difference, dilaceration, dimidiation, diremption, disagreement, disassociation, discerption, disconnection, disengagement, disjunction, dismemberment, disruption, dissection, dissension, disseverance, disunion, divarication, divergence, division, divorce, divulsion, faction, *fissura,* fissure, fork, fracture, furrow, gap, gash, gulf, hiatus, incision, interruption, lacuna, partage, partition, perforation, quarrel, rent, rift, *rima,* rip, scission, *scissura,* scissure, sect, segmentation, segregation, separation, severance, slit, slot, subdivision, sunderance, variance
ASSOCIATED CONCEPTS: split among the Circuit Courts, split in authority, split sentence, splitting a cause of action

SPLIT, verb   abscind, allocate, allot, apportion, assign, bisect, break, break with, carve, chop, cleave, crack, cut, deal, detach, dichotomize, *diffindere,* disconnect, disjoin, dispense, dissect, dissever, distribute, disunite, divide, dole, fissure, fracture, give way, hack, halve, hew, incise, intersect, isolate, lance, mete, open, parcel out, part, part company, partition, rend, rift, rip, rive, rupture, *scindere,* section, segment, segregate, separate, sever, share, shiver, slash, slice, slit, snap, splinter, subdivide, sunder, tear, unbind, untie
ASSOCIATED CONCEPTS: split a cause of action

SPOIL *(Impair),* **verb**   addle, blemish, blight, botch, break, bungle, butcher, *corrumpere,* corrupt, damage, damage irreparably, debase, decay, decompose, deface, defile, deform, demolish, destroy, deteriorate, dilapidate, disable, disfigure, go bad, harm, hurt, impair, injure, lay waste, mangle, mar, mess up, mutilate, *perdere,* putrefy, rot, ruin, ruinate, sabotage, smash, sour, turn, vitiate, wreck

SPOIL *(Pillage),* **verb**   despoil, forage, foray, loot, maraud, pirate, plunder, raid, ransack, ravage, rob, *spoliare,* spoliate, steal, waste

SPOILAGE, noun   blight, corrosion, corruption, decay, decomposition, decrement, deterioration, dilapidation, disintegration, dissolution, erosion, putrefaction, putrescence, rot, wastage, waste

SPOILS, noun   booty, gains, grab, graft, haul, ill-gotten gains, loot, pelf, pickings, pillage, plunder, plunderage, prize, ravin, *spolia,* stolen goods, swag, take, takings, winnings

SPOKESMAN, noun   advocate, agent, ambassador, attorney, *auctor,* broker, delegate, deputy, emissary, envoy, go-between, interlocutor, mediary, mediator, messenger, mouthpiece, negotiator, *patronus,* plenipotentiary, prolocutor, representative, speaker, speechmaker, suasor, vicar, voice

SPOLIATION, noun   attack, brigandage, buccaneer-ing, depredation, deprivation, desolation, despoliation, destruction, devastation, *direptio,* direption, *expilatio,* foray, looting, marauding, pilfering, pillage, pillaging, piracy, plunder, plunderage, plundering, raid, ransack, rapine, robbery, sack, theft, thievery

SPONSOR, noun   advocate, *auctor,* backer, benefactor, champion, favorer, guarantor, guardian, insurer, patron, promoter, protector, succorer, surety, sympathizer
ASSOCIATED CONCEPTS: sponsor of legislation

SPONSOR, verb   accept responsibility for, act as surety for, answer for, assure, back, be responsible for, befriend, certify, champion, defend, endorse, ensure, favor, finance, financier, guarantee, insure, patronize, pay for, promote, protect, provide for, put up the money, secure, stand behind, subscribe to, support, sustain, sympathize, take responsibility for, underwrite, uphold, vouch for, warrant
ASSOCIATED CONCEPTS: sponsor a bill

SPONTANEOUS, adjective   discretional, discretionary, elective, extemporal, extemporaneous, extemporary, extempore, free, free-willed, impetuous, impromptu, improvisatorial, improvised, impulsive, indeliberate, independent, natural, optional, rash, self-acting, self-determined, snap, *spontaneus,* sudden, unbidden, uncompelled, unconstrained, uncontrived, uncontrolled, unforced, unintentional, unplanned, unpremeditated, unprepared, unprompted, unrehearsed, unstudied, untaught, unthinking, volitient, volitional, volitive, *voluntarius,* voluntary, willful
ASSOCIATED CONCEPTS: res gestae, spontaneous declaration

SPORADIC, adjective   appearing at intervals, casual, changeable, desultory, disconnected, discontinuous, disjunct, dispersed, erratic, fitful, fluctuating, immethodical, inconstant, indefinite, infrequent, intermittent, intermitting, *inusitatus,* irregular, isolated, nonuniform, now and then, occasional, periodic, periodical, rare, *rarus,* recurrent, recurring, remittent, scattered, scrappy, separate, shifting, single, sparse, spasmodic, sporadical, spotty, stray, uncertain, uneven, unsteady, unsuccessive, unsystematic, variable, wavering

SPOUSAL SUPPORT, noun   alimony, allotment, allowance, dispensation, maintenance, provision, support *Generally:* emolument, subsidization, subsidy, subsistence, sustenance, upkeep

SPOUSE, *noun* *coniunx,* consort, espouse, helpmate, helpmeet, husband, marital partner, marriage partner, mate, wife

SPREAD, *verb* advertise, bestrew, bloat, branch, broadcast, broaden, bruit, circulate, cover, deploy, diffuse, dilate, disperse, disseminate, distribute, divaricate, *divulgare,* divulge, emanate, expand, *explicare,* extend, fan, fill out, flow, fork, inflate, irradiate, lengthen, make known, make public, mantle, open, outspread, overrun, overspread, penetrate, permeate, pervade, promulgate, propagate, publicize, publish, radiate, ramify, roll out, rumor, scatter, smear, sow, *spargere,* splay, sprawl, sprinkle, straggle, stretch, stretch out, strew, suffuse, swell, uncoil, unfold, unfurl, unravel, unroll, unwind, vent, widen

SPURIOUS, *adjective* apocryphal, artificial, bogus, counterfeit, deceitful, deceptive, delusive, ersatz, fabricated, fake, faked, false, feigned, fictitious, forged, fraudulent, illegitimate, imitation, misrepresented, mock, pinchbeck, pretend, pseudo, quasi, sham, simulated, synthetic, unauthentic, ungenuine, unreal, untrue
ASSOCIATED CONCEPTS: spurious claim

SPURN, *verb* *aspernari,* belittle, boot, brush aside, cast aside, cast out, censure, contemn, decline, depreciate, despise, disapprove, discard, disdain, disparage, disregard, drive away, drive back, elude, evade, *fastidire,* flout, frown upon, have nothing to do with, hold in contempt, ignore, jilt, kick, laugh at, look down upon, neglect, ostracize, rebuff, refuse, refuse to accept, reject, renounce, repel, reprobate, repudiate, repulse, scorn, scout, set at nought, shun, slight, slur, sneer, snub, trample, tread on, treat with disdain, turn down

SPY, *noun* agent, detective, *emissarius, explorator,* informant, informer, intelligence agent, intelligencer, investigator, lookout, observer, reconnoiterer, reporter, scout, secret agent, sleuth, snoop, snooper, source, *speculator,* undercover agent, undercover man, watcher
ASSOCIATED CONCEPTS: espionage

SPY, *verb* behold, catch sight of, descry, detect, discern, discover, discover by artifice, distinguish, eavesdrop, espy, examine secretely, *explorare,* follow, glimpse, inspect secretely, look at, look for, make a reconnaissance, make out, make secret observations, observe, peep, peer, perceive, pry, recognize, reconnoiter, scrutinize, search out, see, shadow, sight, snoop, *speculari,* spy upon, take note, trail, view, watch, watch secretely

STABILIZE, *verb* balance, clinch, counterbalance, establish, firm up, round, secure, set, settle, steady

STABLE, *adjective* abiding, anchored, chronic, constans, constant, continuing, deep-rooted, diligent, durable, endless, enduring, established, everlasting, faithful, fast, fastened, firm, *firmus,* fixed, grounded, immovable, immutable, indissoluble, indomitable, industrious, inert, inexorable, intact, invariable, inveterate, irremovable, irreversible, irrevocable, lasting, long-lasting, long-lived, long-standing, moored, motionless, perdurable, permanent, perpetual, persistent, plodding, relentless, reliable, riveted, rooted, secure, sedulous, settled, solid, sound, stabile, *stabilis,* stalwart, stanch, stationary, steadfast, steady, strong, sturdy, substantial, sure, tenacious, unalterable, unchangeable, unchanging, uncompromising, undeviating, unfailing, unfaltering, unflagging, unflinching, unhesitating, unremitting, unshakeable, unshaken, unswerving, untiring, unwavering, unyielding, well-built, well-grounded

STAFF, *noun* *adiutores,* aides, assistants, associates, body of employees, cadre, clerical staff, complement, corps, council, crew, deputies, employees, faculty, force, help, *legatio,* management, personnel, professional force, professional staff, servants, staff members, workers

STAGNANT, *adjective* apathetic, dormant, dull, hebetudinous, idle, immobile, inactive, indolent, inert, lacking activity, lazy, *lentus,* lethargic, lifeless, listless, lumpish, motionless, otiose, passive, phlegmatic, phlegmatical, *piger,* quiescent, sluggish, *stagnans,* stagnating, standing, static, stationary, still, supine, torpid, torporific, unflowing, unmoving, unstirring, without current, without motion

STAIN, *verb* attaint, bedaub, befoul, besmear, besmirch, blacken, blemish, blot, blotch, bring reproach upon, color, contaminate, corrupt, damage, daub, debase, defame, defile, detract from, dirty, discolor, discredit, disgrace, dishonor, dye, grime, impair, *inquinare, maculare,* maculate, malign, mar, mark, *polluere,* pollute, ruin, smear, smirch, smudge, soil, spatter, splotch, spoil, spot, stigmatize, sully, taint, tarnish, tinge, tint

STAKE *(Award),* *noun* ante, bet, pot, prize, purse, spoils, wager, winnings

STAKE *(Interest),* *noun* claim, equity, holding, ownership, right, share, title
ASSOCIATED CONCEPTS: interpleader stake deposited in court

STALE, *adjective* banal, boring, common, commonplace, decayed, declining, dull, effete, faded, fetid, flat, flavorless, fusty, hackneyed, humdrum, insipid, jejune, mildewed, moldy, monotonous, musty, *obsoletus,* off, old, pedestrian, prosaic, prosy, rancid, rotten, savorless, shopworn, sour, soured, spoiled, tasteless, timeworn, trite, unimaginative, uninteresting, unvaried, vapid, *vetus,* vitiated, wasted, wilted, withered, without novelty, worn out
ASSOCIATED CONCEPTS: stale cause of action, stale check

STALL, *verb* arrest, avert, bar, block, bog, break down, bring to a standstill, check, dally, dawdle, defer, delay, detain, dillydally, disable, filibuster, halt, hamper, hinder, hold up, impede, incapacitate, inhibit, interrupt, keep back, lag, linger, obstruct, paralyze, postpone, procrastinate, put off, render powerless, retard, *stabulare,* stalemate, still, stop, take time, temporize, ward off
ASSOCIATED CONCEPTS: dilatory motions

STAMP, *noun* attestation, authentication, brand, cast, certification, die, endorsement, engraving, form, hallmark, identification, impress, impression, imprint, intaglio, mark, *nota,* pattern, print, ratification, seal, sigil, signit, *signum,* validation
ASSOCIATED CONCEPTS: tax stamps

STAND *(Position),* *noun* attitude, belief, bent, bias, consistere, inclination, leaning, opinion, outlook, point of view, position, slant, standpoint, vantage point, view, viewpoint

STAND *(Witness' place in court),* *noun* booth, box, corner, place, platform, position, post, stall, station, witness box, witness stand

STANDARD, *noun* archetype, basis of comparison, canon, comparison, criterion, example, exemplar, frame of reference, gauge, grade of excellence, guide, ideal, level of excellence, measure, model, norm, *norma,* paradigm, paragon, pattern, precedent, prototype, *regula,* touchstone

ASSOCIATED CONCEPTS: standard established by law, standard of care, standard of conduct, standard of proof

STANDARD PROCEDURE, *noun*   approach, avenue, behavior, common practice, conduct, consuetude, course of conduct, custom, customary course, fashion, line of conduct, manner, manner of operating, matter of course, means, method, mode, mode of operation, mode of procedure, *modus operandi,* pattern, practice, prescribed form, procedure, process, routine, tactics, technique, way of doing things

STANDING, *adjective*   constant, continued, continuing, conventional, enduring, established, fixed, lasting, permanent, perpetual, perpetuated, settled, stationary, still, traditional, unceasing, unchanging
ASSOCIATED CONCEPTS: standing committee

STANDPOINT, *noun*   angle, aspect, attitude, belief, bent, conviction, direction, disposition, inclination, judgment, leaning, location, observation post, opinion, orientation, outlook, perspective, persuasion, point, point of view, position, post, predilection, proclivity, propensity, seat, *sententia,* situation, spot, station, tendency, vantage point, view, viewpoint, vision

STARE DECISIS, *noun*   authoritative example, basis, foundation, precedent, principle of law, rule, standard
ASSOCIATED CONCEPTS: *stare decisis et non quieta movere, stare in judicio*

STARK, *adjective*   absolute, bald, bare, complete, conspicuous, decided, downright, entire, glaring, gross, obvious, outright, plain, positive, pure, *rigidus,* sheer, simple, staring, total, unmitigated, unqualified, utter, very

START, *noun*   beginning, birth, commencement, dawn, derivation, embarkation, emergence, evolution, exordium, first step, foundation, genesis, inauguration, inception, inchoation, incipience, incipiency, infancy, initiation, *initium,* onset, opening, origin, origination, outbreak, outset, *profectio,* rise, scare, source, threshold

START, *verb*   begin, commence, create, embark on, emerge, evolve, file, give birth to, inaugurate, incept, initiate, insinuate, install, introduce, invent, open, originate, set off, take the first step, take the initiative
ASSOCIATED CONCEPTS: commence an action, start proceedings

STATE *(Condition),* **noun**   appearance, aspect, circumstance, class, complexion, disposition, grade, mien, mood, plight, position, posture, predicament, shape, situation, standing, station, *status,* way
ASSOCIATED CONCEPTS: state of mind

STATE *(Political unit),* **noun**   body politic, civil community, *civitas,* commonwealth, governmental unit, mandated territory, nation, political division, polity, sovereign unit
ASSOCIATED CONCEPTS: state's evidence, state's rights
FOREIGN PHRASES: *Privilegium non valet contra rempublicam.* A privilege is of no avail against the state.

STATED, *adjective*   aforementioned, aforesaid, arranged, ascertained, decided, defined, detailed, determined, established, expressed, fixed, prearranged, predetermined, prescribed, reported, said, set forth, settled, specified, stipulated, told, uttered, voiced
ASSOCIATED CONCEPTS: stated capital, stated term

STATEMENT, *noun*   account, affidavit, affirmation, announcement, assertion, asseveration, averment, avowal, claim, comment, declaration, deposition, detailed account, dictum, enumeration, exclamation, explanation, exposition, manifesto, narrative, observation, prepared announcement, prepared text, pronouncement, recapitulation, recital, recitation, remark, report, story, summary, testimony, utterance
ASSOCIATED CONCEPTS: statement of claim, statement of defense, statement of particulars

STATEMENT OF FACTS, *noun*   affirmation, allegation of facts, allegations, assertion, asseveration, attestation, averment, avouchment, declaration, description, enumeration, one's position, one's stand, review, summary
ASSOCIATED CONCEPTS: brief, memorandum of law

STATIC, *adjective*   changeless, dormant, fixed, immobile, *immobilis, immotus,* inactive, inert, motionless, passive, permanent, quiescent, quiet, resting, rigid, stable, stagnant, standing, statical, stationary, still, suspended, torpid, unmoving, unprogressive

STATUS, *noun*   caliber, caste, circumstance, class, condition, dignity, elevation, eminence, esteem, footing, grade, importance, notability, place, position, posture, prestige, prominence, quality, rank, rating, situation, standing, state, station, superiority
ASSOCIATED CONCEPTS: proof of status, status of purchaser, status of trustee

STATUS QUO, *noun*   absence of change, conservation of the same situation, equilibrium, existing conditions, existing state, maintenance of regularity, preservation of the same conditions, same conditions, stable state, static condition, things as they are

STATUTE, *noun*   act, canon, code, codified law, commandment, decree, dictate, edict, enactment, *ius,* law, legislation, legislative enactment, *lex,* mandate, measure, order, ordinance, provision of the law, regulation, rubric, rule, written law
ASSOCIATED CONCEPTS: affirmative statute, criminal statute, declaratory statute, enabling statute, penal statute, private statute, remedial statute, statute of frauds, statute of limitations
FOREIGN PHRASES: *Quae communi lege derogant stricte interpretantur.* Statutes which derogate from the common law are to be strictly construed. *Optima statuti interpretatrix est ipsum statutum.* The best interpreter of a statute is the statute itself. *Ex malis moribus bonae leges natae sunt.* Good laws arise from evil morals. *Casus omissus et oblivioni datus dispositioni communis juris relinquitur.* A case omitted and forgotten is left to the disposal of the common law. *Statutum generaliter est intelligendum quando verba statuti sunt specialia ratio autem generalis.* When the words of a statute are special, but the reason general, the statute is to be understood generally. *Constructio legis non facit injuriam.* The interpretation of the law works no injury. *Ad ea quae frequentius accidunt jura adaptantur.* Laws are adapted to those cases which occur. *Jus constitui oportet in his quae ut plurimum accidunt non quae ex inopinato.* Laws ought to be made with a view to those cases which occur most frequently, and not to those which are of rare or accidental occurrence. *Nova constitutio futuris formam imponere debet non praeteritis.* A new law ought to affect the future, not what is past. *A verbis legis non est recendendum.* From the words of a statute there must be no

departure. **Lex posterior derogat priori.** A later law takes away the effect of a prior one. **Leges posteriores priores contrarias abrogant.** Subsequent laws repeal prior laws that are repugnant to them. **Non est novum ut priores leges ad posteriores trahantur.** It is not novel that prior statutes should give way to later ones. **In rebus quae sunt favorabilia animae, quamvis sunt damnosa rebus, fiat aliquando extensio statuti.** In matters that are favorable to the spirit, though injurious to things, an extension of a statute should sometimes be made. **Est ipsorum legislatorum tanquam viva vox; rebus et non verbis legem imponimus.** The voice of the lawmakers is like the living voice; we impose law upon things and not upon words. **Statutum speciale statuto speciali non derogat.** One special statute does not derogate from another special statute. **Statutum affirmativum non derogat communi legi.** An affirmative statute does not derogate from the common law.

STATUTORY, adjective according to law, authorized, established, fixed, lawful, legal, legalized, legislative, legislatorial, licit, sanctioned, within the law
ASSOCIATED CONCEPTS: statutory crime

STAUNCH, adjective certus, constant, dependable, devoted, faithful, fast, fidus, firm, firmus, inflexible, iron, loyal, reliable, resolute, solid, sound, stable, stalwart, steadfast, steady, strong, substantial, sure, tried, true, trustworthy, trusty, unfailing, unfaltering, unshakeable, unwavering, unyielding

STAVE, verb avert, avoid, beat off, block, check, deflect, drive away, fend off, fugare, hamper, hinder, hold off, impede, inhibit, intercept, keep at bay, keep off, obstruct, prevent, propulsare, push away, put off, repel, repellere, shun, turn aside, ward off

STAY, noun abeyance, abeyancy, bar, cessation, check, curb, delay, desistance, discontinuance, halt, hindrance, interruption, mansio, obstacle, obstruction, prevention, reprieve, respite, restraint, stop, stoppage, suspension, wait
ASSOCIATED CONCEPTS: judicial stay, stay of enforcement, stay of execution, stay of proceedings, stay pending appeal

STAY (Halt), **verb** arrest, bar, block, check, cohibere, constrain, curb, delay, demorari, desist, detain, deter, detinere, discontinue, forbid, foreclose, forestall, frustrate, hamper, hinder, hold, impede, intercept, interrupt, obstruct, obviate, preclude, prevent, prohibit, put an end to, quell, reprieve, respite, restrain, stem, stop, stymie, suppress, thwart
ASSOCIATED CONCEPTS: permanent injunction, stay enforcement, stay of execution, stay order, stay proceedings, temporary injunction, temporary restraining order

STAY (Continue), **verb** endure, extend, keep on, last, persevere, persist, prolong, remain, subsist
ASSOCIATED CONCEPTS: stay in occupancy

STAY (Rest), **verb** await, be anchored, be dormant, be fixed, be immobile, be inert, be inmovable, be motionless, be riveted, be sedentary, be stationary, be transfixed, halt, lodge, park, pause, remain, repose, stand, stop, wait

STEADFAST, adjective abiding, anchored, assiduous, constans, constant, decided, dedicated, dependable, determined, devoted, diligent, enduring, established, faithful, fast, firm, firmly established, firmus, fixed, gritty, indissoluble, indomitable, industrious, inexorable, inflexible, intransigent, lasting, long-lasting, loyal, obstinate, patient,

perseverant, persevering, persistent, pertinacious, plodding, relentless, reliable, resolute, resolved, riveted, rooted, secure, sedulous, serious, settled, single-minded, stabilis, stable, stationary, staunch, steady, strong, strong-willed, tenacious, tried, true, trustworthy, unalterable, unchanging, uncompromising, undaunted, undeviating, undistracted, unfailing, unfaltering, unflagging, unflinching, unhesitating, unmoved, unshaken, unswerving, untiring, unvarying, unwavering, unyielding, zealous

STEAL, verb abscond with, abstract, burglarize, depredate, despoil, embezzle, filch, fleece, furari, hold up, lift, mulct, nim, peculate, pilfer, pillage, pirate, plagiarize, plunder, poach, pocket, prig, purloin, rifle, rob, shoplift, snatch, subducere, surripere, take unlawfully, thieve, usurp

STEALTHY, adjective arcane, artful, catlike, clandestine, clandestinus, cloaked, concealed, covert, crafty, elusive, evasive, feline, furtive, furtivus, hidden, masked, obreptitious, obscure, occultus, privy, prowling, secret, secretive, shrouded, silent, skulking, sly, sneaking, sneaky, stealthful, surreptitious, thievish, undercover, underhand, undisclosed, unrevealed, unseen, veiled

STELLAR, adjective astral, capital, celebrated, celestial, chief, crowning, distinguished, dominant, eminent, eventful, extraordinary, famous, first, foremost, grand, heavenly, impressive, leading, main, marked, memorable, momentous, noteworthy, outstanding, paramount, predominant, primary, principal, prominent, sidereal, starlike, starry, uranic

STEM (Check), **verb** arrest, balk, bear up against, block, bung, checkmate, choke, clog, coercere, cohibere, cork, counteract, curb, dam up, deadlock, deter, foil, frustrate, halt, hamper, hinder, hold back, impede, intercept, interrupt, keep at bay, keep in, obstruct, oppose, plug, prevent, quell, rein in, repel, repulse, resist, restrain, retard, scotch, stall, stanch, stay, stop, suppress, thwart, veto

STEM (Originate), **verb** arise, begin, branch off, come, commence, derive, descend, emanate, ensue, flow, follow, germinate, grow, issue, originate, proceed, result, rise, spring, sprout, start, trail

STEP, noun achievement, act, action, advance, advancement, deed, degree, expedient, footpace, footstep, gait, gradation, grade, maneuver, milestone, move, pace, procedure, proceeding, process, progression, rundle, rung, stride, tramp, tread

STEP-BY-STEP, adjective by degrees, continuous, creeping, gradational, gradual, graduated, in steps, leisurely, measured, methodical, orderly, paced, part of a process, progressive, regular, slow, slow-paced, snail-like, systematic, unhurried

STERLING, adjective authentic, bona fide, bonus, consummate, costly, creditable, excellent, exceptional, exemplary, extraordinary, genuine, good, high-grade, high-quality, honest, honorable, matchless, meritorious, noble, peerless, precious, prime, pure, quality, real, splendid, superb, superior, superlative, true, unadulterated, unalloyed, unmingled, unsynthetic, upright, valuable, verus, virtuous, worthy

STIFLE, verb annihilate, arrest, balk, bar, block, check, choke, conceal, constrain, contain, control, crush, damp, deaden, destroy, drown, dull, extinguish, frustrate, gag, hush, inhibit, kill, mask, muffle, mute, muzzle, obstruct, opprimere, prevent, put down, quell, quench, repress, reprimere, restrain, silence, smother, snuff out, squash, squelch, still, stop, strangle, strangulate, stymie, subdue, suffocate, suppress, throttle, withhold

STIGMA, noun   badge of infamy, blemish, blot, brand, defect, disgrace, dishonor, disrepute, flaw, imputation, infamousness, infamy, mark of disgrace, mark of shame, nota, notoriety, notoriousness, reproach, *scandalum magnatum,* scar, shame, slur, smear, smirch, spot, stain, taint, tarnish

STIMULATE, verb   activate, actuate, animate, arouse, awaken, brace, drive, egg on, encourage, energize, enkindle, enliven, *excitare,* excite, fan, fillip, fire, foment, goad, impel, *incitare,* incite, inflame, initiate, *inritare,* inspire, inspirit, instigate, invigorate, jog, kindle, motivate, move, move to action, pique, prod, prompt, propel, provoke, rally, rouse, spur, stir up, vitalize, vivify, whet, work up

STIMULUS, noun   activator, animator, arouser, *calcar,* catalyst, catalytic agent, cause, drive, encouragement, excitant, fillip, goad, impetus, impulse, incentive, *incitamentum,* incitement, inducement, influence, *inritamentum,* motivating force, motive, needle, prod, provocation, push, reason, shock, spur, stimulant, stimulation, stimulative, stimulator, sting, urge, whet

STIPULATE, verb   adjust, agree, arrange, assent, bargain, become bound, clarify, condition, contract, covenant, decide, denominate, designate, determine, engage, guarantee, include in an agreement, insist upon, lay down, make a condition, make a point of, make clear, make definition, mention, name, negotiate, pledge, postulate, predicate, promise, provide, set, settle, settle terms, signify, specify, state, *stipulari*
ASSOCIATED CONCEPTS: stipulated damages, stipulated fact, stipulation of a bill of particulars, stipulation of an adjournment, stipulation of appeal, stipulation of guilt, stipulation of judgment, stipulation of matters of law, stipulation of proof, stipulation of the record

STIPULATION, noun   agreement, arrangement, article of agreement, bargain, bond, compact, concordat, condicio, condition, contract, convention, covenant, deal, engagement, pact, *pactum,* promise, provise, specification, *stipulatio,* treaty, understanding
ASSOCIATED CONCEPTS: stipulated facts, stipulation of settlement

STOCK (Shares), **noun**   assets, capital, fund, holdings, invested property, investment, negotiables, property, security
ASSOCIATED CONCEPTS: bank stock, bonus stock, capital stock, common stock, debenture stock, ordinary stock, original stock, outstanding stock, preferred stock, prepaid stock, sale of stock, shares of stock, special stock, stock certificate, subscription to stock, treasury stock, value of stock, watered stock

STOCK (Store), **noun**   accumulation, *copia,* effects, hoard, inventory, provision, reserve, reservoir, supply, vis

STOCK IN TRADE, noun   articles of commerce, available assets, contents, equipment, goods, line, merchandise, products, provisions, resources, staple, stock, store, supply, supply on hand, vendibles, wares

STOICAL, adjective   apathetic, ascetic, controlled, dispassionate, impassive, imperturbable, indifferent, longsuffering, passionless, passive, patient, philosophic, placid, repressing emotion, resigned, self-controlled, self-disciplined, spartan, tolerant, undemonstrative, undisturbed,

unimpassioned, unimpressible, unmoved, unresisting, unruffled

STOP, verb   abandon, abolish, arrest, bar, barricade, block, block up, blockade, brake, break off, bring to a close, bring to a standstill, bring to naught, cease, check, checkmate, choke, clog, close, come to a standstill, conclude, counteract, countermand, crush, cut short, dam up, delay, desist, detain, deter, die away, disallow, discontinue, drop, end, expire, finish, foil, forbear, forbid, forestall, freeze, halt, hamper, hinder, hold, hold back, impede, *inhibere,* intercept, interrupt, lapse, lay an embargo on, leave off, obstruct, occlude, pause, plug, preclude, prevent, *prohibere,* prohibit, put an end to, quell, quit, refrain, render impassable, repress, rest, restrain, silence, sojourn, stall, stanch, stay, stem, stifle, stopper, stopple, stymie, suppress, suspend, tarry, terminate, thwart, ward off, wipe out, withdraw from
ASSOCIATED CONCEPTS: stop and frisk

STOPGAP, noun   alternate, alternative, auxiliary, expedient, impermanent fixture, makeshift, means, measure, provisional measure, replacement, reserve, resort, substitute, substitution, succedaneum, temporary arrangement, temporary expedient, temporary substitute

STORE (Business), **noun**   booth, business house, concern, emporium, establishment, exchange, market, market place, mart, outlet, shop, stall

STORE (Depository), **noun**   abundance, *abundantia,* accumulation, amassment, assets, backlog, cache, collection, conservatory, *copia,* deposit, depository, fund, great quantity, hoard, inventory, nest egg, plenty, profusion, provisions, reserve, reservoir, savings, stack, stock, stockpile, storehouse, sufficiency, supplies, supply, treasure, treasury, wealth

STORE, verb   accumulate, acquire, amass, assemble, bank, cache, collect, conserve, *copia,* cumulate, deposit, garner, gather, hoard, hold, husband, keep, lay away, maintain, mass, pile up, put by, reposit, reserve, retain, save, stock, stockpile, stow away, treasure, warehouse

STORM (Barrage), **noun**   assault, attack, battle, besiegement, blast, blitz, blitzkrieg, blizzard, bombardment, clash, combat, commotion, conflict, confusion, disquiet, disruption, embroilment, eruption, excitement, explosion, fight, flare-up, imbroglio, melee, mutiny, outbreak, outburst, rebellion, revolt, revolution, skirmish, stir, struggle, tempest, tumult, turbulence, turmoil, unrest, upheaval, uprising
ASSOCIATED CONCEPTS: damage, flood damage, hurricanes

STORM (Rain), **noun**   blizzard, cloudburst, cyclone, deluge, downpour, endless rain, gale, hailstorm, heavy showers, heavy winds, hurricane, moisture, precipitation, rainstorm, sheets of rain, snowstorm, storming, stormy winds, tempest, thundershower, thunderstorm, tornado, torrent, tropical rains, tropical storm, turbulence, twister, typhoon, whirlwind
ASSOCIATED CONCEPTS: cyber storm, storm models, storm predicting, storm victims, storm water

STORY (Falsehood), **noun**   canard, concoction, deceit, deception, deliberate falsification, dissemblance, dissimulation, distortion, duplicity, evasion, fabrication, faithlessness, false statement, falsification, falsity, fantasy, fib, fiction, figment, inaccuracy, incorrectness, insincerity, intentional misstatement, intentional untruth, invention, inveracity, lie, *mendacium,* misrepresentation, misstatement, myth, perversion of truth, pretense, prevarication, suppression of truth, untrue statement, untruth, want of fidelity

STORY *(Narrative),* **noun** account, adventures, article, chronicle, conte, description, dispatch, epic, *fabula,* historiette, history, legend, memoir, *narratio,* narration, news, news article, news item, newspaper report, particulars, piece, portrayal, press notice, publicity, recapitulation, recital, recitation, record, recountal, relation, report, saga, sketch, summary of facts, tale, tidings

STRAIGHTFORWARD, *adjective* aboveboard, *apertus,* artless, candid, direct, forthright, frank, guileless, honest, honorable, ingenuous, legitimate, open, outspoken, plain-spoken, scrupulous, *simplex,* sincere, straight, truth-speaking, truthful, unaffected, uncontrived, uncorrupt, undesigning, undeviating, undissembling, undistorted, unfeigned, unperjured, unswerving, unturned, unwavering, upright, veracious, veridical

STRAIGHT-OUT, *adjective* aboveboard, blunt, candid, clear, clear-cut, crystal clear, decent, direct, distinct, evident, explicit, express, forthright, frank, honest, ingenuous, manifest, obvious, on the up and up, open, open and aboveboard, open and genuine, open and sincere, sincere, straight, straightforward, unequivocal, unreserved, upfront
ASSOCIATED CONCEPTS: franking privilege

STRANGER, **noun** *advena,* alien, foreign person, foreigner, *hospes,* newcomer, outsider, strange person, tramontane, unknown person

STRANGLE, *verb* arrest, block, check, choke off, crush, extinguish, hush, inhibit, keep back, keep down, mask, muzzle, put a stop to, quell, quiet, repress, reserve, restrain, silence, smother, snuff out, squelch, still, stop, *strangulare,* subdue, suppress, withhold

STRATAGEM, **noun** *ars,* artful contrivance, artifice, blind, cheat, chicane, contrivance, crafty device, cunning, deceit, deception, device, dodge, *dolus,* evasion, excuse, expedient, feint, finesse, gimmick, intrigue, machination, maneuver, manipulation, plan, plot, ploy, pretext, ruse, scheme, shift, strategy, subterfuge, tactic, trap, trick, wile

STRATEGIC, *adjective* calculated, clever, consequential, contrived, critical, crucial, decisive, designed, diplomatic, diplomatical, important, key, momentous, planned, politic, pregnant, significant, strategical, tactical, telling, tricky, turning, vital, well thought out

STRATEGY, **noun** approach, arrangement, art of war, artifice, battle maneuver, campaign, careful methods, careful plans, *consilium,* contrivance, course, course of action, cunning, design, devices, engineering, forethought, intrigue, intriguery, invention, machination, management, maneuvering, maneuvers, manipulation, method, military evolutions, military science, mode of operation, plan, plan of action, plan of attack, planned campaign, platform, policy, procedure, proceedings, program, proposal, proposed action, proposition, *propositum,* rules of war, scheme, schemery, set of maneuvers, skillful management, soldiership, system, tactics, technique
ASSOCIATED CONCEPTS: trial strategy

STRENGTH, **noun** brawn, cogency, concentration, durability, efficacy, emphasis, endurance, energy, fervor, firmness, force, hardiness, health, impregnability, intensity, main, mainstay, might, mightiness, muscle, opes, potency, power, proof, puissance, *robur,* robustness, solidity, soundness, stalwartness, stamina, stoutness, sturdiness, substantiality, substantialness, superiority, tenaciousness,

tenacity, toughness, validity, vigor, *vires,* virility, vitality, vividness, willpower

STRENUOUS, *adjective* active, arduous, burdensome, demanding, difficult, exacting, exhausting, grueling, hard, Herculean, intense, intensive, laborious, onerous, operose, oppressive, painstaking, rigorous, strenuous, toilsome, vigorous, wearisome
ASSOCIATED CONCEPTS: strenuous law enforcement

STRESS *(Accent),* **noun** accentuation, attention, beat, distinction, emphasis, force, import, importance, inflection, insistence, intonation, paramountcy, primacy, prominence, pronunciation, significance, superiority, tone, urgency, weight

STRESS *(Strain),* **noun** adversity, affliction, agony, alarm, anxiety, apprehension, apprehensiveness, burden, coercion, compulsion, cross, demand, disquiet, disquietude, distention, dread, duress, exertion, exigency, extension, fear, fearfulness, ferment, fluster, force, fright, load, misgiving, *momentum,* need, nervousness, overexertion, pinch, pondus, pressure, pull, stretch, tautness, tenseness, tension, tensity, tightness, traction, trepidation, trial, urgency

STRICT, *adjective* absolute, accurate, austere, authoritarian, authoritative, autocratic, careful, close, conscientious, despotic, dictatorial, *diligens,* disciplined, exact, exacting, extreme, faithful, fastidious, formal, hard, harsh, high-principled, imperious, inexorable, inflexible, limited, literal, meticulous, obdurate, obligatory, orthodox, particular, positive, precise, principled, punctilious, puritanical, rigid, *rigidus,* rigorous, scrupulous, severe, *severus,* stern, stiff, straitlaced, stringent, tyrannical, unbending, uncompromising, unconditional, unerring, unyielding, veracious
ASSOCIATED CONCEPTS: strict construction, strict interpretation, strict necessity

STRICT CONSTRUCTION, **noun** absolutely by the snidest interpretation, according to the letter, by chapter and verse, by the rules, conservative interpretation, exactly as written, in a conservative interpretation, in an orthodox interpretation, literally as written, plainly within the language, precisely as written, specific interpretation, strictly read, with a strict interpretation, with fastidious rigidity, with hard and fast interpretation, with inflexible interpretation, with literal interpretation, with meticulous rigidity, with narrow interpretation, with punctilious rigidity, with rigid interpretation, with unyielding interpretation
ASSOCIATED CONCEPTS: constitutional interpretation, literal construction, loose construction

STRICT MEANING, **noun** accurate meaning, correct meaning, defined meaning, definition, distinct meaning, exact meaning, explanation, explicit meaning, express meaning, faithful meaning, inflexible meaning, literal meaning, methodical meaning, meticulous meaning, narrow meaning, not subject to interpretation, ordinary meaning, plain meaning, precise meaning, prescribed meaning, rigid meaning, rigorous meaning, sharply defined meaning, significance, specific meaning, unbending meaning, uncompromising meaning, unequivocal meaning
ASSOCIATED CONCEPTS: construction, literal contract, literal proof, plain meaning rule, rules of statutory, soft plain meaning rule, textualism

STRICTURE, **noun** accusation, adverse comment, adverse criticism, *animadversio,* animadversion, aspersion, blame, castigation, censure, critical remark, criticism, denunciation, deprecation, depreciation, diatribe, disapprobation, disapproval, exception, faultfinding, objection, objurgation, obloquy, philippic, rebuke, reprehensio, reprehension, reproach, reprobation, reproof, tirade, unfavorable remark, vituperation

STRIFE, *noun*   agitation, altercation, animosity, battle, belligerency, broil, *certamen, certatio,* clash, combat, competition, conflict, contention, contest, contestation, contrariety, controversy, counteraction, disaccord, disaggreement, discord, disputation, dispute, disquiet, dissension, dissent, dissidence, encounter, engagement, eruption, faction, factionalism, fight, fighting, fray, friction, imbroglio, incompatibility, match, opposition, outbreak, outburst, polemics, quarrel, race, rift, rivalry, row, squabble, struggle, trouble, unrest, upheaval, variance, violence, war, warfare, wrangle

STRIKE, *noun*   boycott, collective refusal to work, concerted refusal to work, group refusal to work, job action, labor dispute, organized refusal to work, shutdown, stoppage, suspension of work, walkout, work stoppage
ASSOCIATED CONCEPTS: lockout, mass strike, picketing, secondary strike

STRIKE *(Assault),* *verb*   afflict, aggress, assail, attack, bat, batter, beat, besiege, damage, deal a blow, fall upon, harm, hit, hurt, inflict harm, inflict injury, lunge at, pound, slap, smash, smite, storm

STRIKE *(Collide),* *verb*   butt, come in contact, come into collision, come together, *conlidere,* crash, encounter, hit, hit against, jar, jolt, knock into, meet, smash

STRIKE *(Refuse to work),* *verb*   blockade, boycott, cease work, discontinue work, halt work, interrupt work, leave the job, obstruct work, quit work, rebel, refrain from working, revolt, stop work, suspend work, terminate work, walk out
ASSOCIATED CONCEPTS: economic strike, general strike, wildcat strike

STRINGENT, *adjective*   authoritative, binding, compelling, compulsory, despotic, dictatorial, draconian, exact, exacting, exigent, forceful, hard, harsh, inescapable, inflexible, ironhanded, precise, puritanical, rigid, rigorous, rough, stern, stiff, strait-laced, strict, tyrannical, uncompromising, unyielding

STRIVE, *verb*   aim, aspire, attempt, bestir oneself, bid for, carry into execution, compete, *conari,* contend, *contendere,* contest, do all one can, do one's best, do one's utmost, drive at, drudge, employ one's time, employ oneself, endeavor, endeavor to accomplish, endeavor to effect, *eniti,* exert one's energies, exert oneself, fight, go after, labor for, make a bid, make an attempt, make an effort, point at, pursue, put forth an effort, seek, strain, struggle, tackle, take action, take pains, take steps, take trouble, tax one's energies, toil, travail, trouble oneself, try, try for, try one's best, undertake, venture, vie, work, work hard

STRONG, *adjective*   able, brawny, burly, clear, compelling, concentrated, crushing, determined, durable, effective, enduring, energetic, firm, forceful, forcible, formidable, *fortis,* hard, hardy, harsh, healthy, Herculean, husky, inflexible, intense, lasting, lusty, manly, mighty, omnipotent, overpowering, overwhelming, perseverant, persevering, persistent, persuasive, potent, powerful, puissant, reinforced, reliable, resolute, rich, robust, *robustus,* rugged, secure, solid, sound, stable, stalwart, staunch, steadfast, steady, stiff, stout, strapping,

strengthful, sturdy, tenacious, titanic, tough, unflimsy, unmixed, unpliant, unremitting, unyielding, *valens,* vibrant, vigorous, violent, virile, vivid, well-built, well-made, wiry
ASSOCIATED CONCEPTS: strong case, strong evidence, strong probability

STRUCTURE *(Composition),* *noun*   arrangement, configuration, constitution, design, disposition, essence, fabric, form, formation, layout, make up, organization, pattern, plan, set up, shape, style, substance

STRUCTURE *(Edifice),* *noun*   building, establishment, erection, location, premises
ASSOCIATED CONCEPTS: corporate structure

STRUGGLE, *noun*   affray, agitation, attempt, battle, broil, *certamen,* clash, combat, competition, conflict, confrontation, contention, contestation, controversy, disagreement, dissension, effort, encounter, endeavor, engagement, essay, exertion, feud, fight, force, fracas, grind, haul, labor, *luctatio,* opposition, pains, pursuit, push, quarrel, rencounter, resistance, scrimmage, scuffle, strain, striving, tussle, work

STUDY, *verb*   acquire knowledge, analyze, apply the mind, attend, audit, cerebrate, consider, contemplate, devote oneself to, dissect, do research, educate oneself, examine, excogitate, explore, eye, *incumbere,* inquire into, inspect, intellectualize, investigate, learn, meditate, mull over, muse, note, observe, peruse, ponder, pore over, probe, pursue, read, reconnoiter, reflect upon, research, review, revolve in the mind, ruminate, scan, school oneself, scrutinize, search into, sift, specialize, *studere,* survey, think about, train in, view, weigh

STYLE, *noun*   appearance, artistry, aspect, cast, character, class, custom, denomination, description, expression, fashion, form, genre, *genus,* guise, habit, individual method, kind, make, manner, manner of presentation, method, mode, model, *modus,* pattern, presentation, rage, *ratio,* school, shape, taste, technique, tone, trend, type, vogue, way

STYMIE, *verb*   block, circumscribe, counteract, curb, deadlock, debar, delay, disadvantage, encumber, estop, forestall, frustrate, hamper, handicap, hinder, impede, inconvenience, inhibit, obstruct, parry, preclude, prevent, put an end to, stall, stand in the way, stay, stifle, stop, thwart, stump, suppress

SUA SPONTE, *noun*   elective, offered, on one's own accord, on the court's own initiative, on the court's own volition, on the court's own will, optional and freely initiated, self-initiated, self-willed, uncompelled, volitional, voluntary, willful

SUASIBLE, *adjective*   accessible, amenable, convincible, docile, easily convinced, easily persuaded, easygoing, facile, flexible, inducible, influenceable, movable, open, open-minded, persuadable, persuasible, pervious, pliable, pliant, receptive, responsive, swayable, tractable

SUBALTERN, *adjective*   baser, humble, inferior, junior, less, lesser, low, lower, lower in rank, lowly, minor, of lower rank, secondary, servile, subalternate, *subcenturio,* subordinate, subsidiary, under

SUBDIVIDE, *verb*   apportion, bisect, break down, categorize, classify, cleave, cut, dissect, dissever, distribute, divide, divide into parcels, divide up, graduate, group, parcel, partition, portion, redistribute, redivide, separate, sever, share, split, sunder

SUBDIVISION, *noun* bisection, categorization, category, class, classification, compartment, component, division, fraction, fragment, group, grouping, *pars,* part, partition, section, sector, segment, separation, subcategory, subclass, subgroup, subheading
ASSOCIATED CONCEPTS: political subdivision, subdivision of a statute

SUBDUE, *verb* abate, allay, beat, beat down, bend, best, break, bring under rule, calm, captivate, capture, choke, conquer, control, crush, curb, deaden, defeat, discipline, discomfit, *domare,* dominate, dull, enthrall, foil, get the better of, harness, humble, inhibit, lessen, lower, make docile, make submissive, make tractable, master, moderate, mollify, muffle, mute, obtund, oppress, overbear, overcome, overpower, overwhelm, put down, quell, quiet, reduce, rein, repress, restrain, silence, slacken, smash, smother, soften, *subiungere,* subject, subjugate, suppress, tame, temper, tone down, tranquilize, triumph over, vanquish, worst
ASSOCIATED CONCEPTS: subdue an assailant

SUBHEADING, *noun* article, categorization, chapter, classification, clause, division, heading, paragraph, section, segment, subdivision, subgroup, subsection, title

SUBJECT *(Conditional),* *adjective* contingent, dependent, dependent on circumstances, depending upon, incident to, incidental, provisional, relying upon, *subiectus,* subordinate, uncertain
ASSOCIATED CONCEPTS: subject to approval, subject to defeasance, subject to review

SUBJECT *(Exposed),* *adjective* accountable, answerable, at the mercy of, chargeable, liable, open, prone, susceptible, unexempt from, vulnerable

SUBJECT *(Object),* *noun* case, experimentee, liegeman, recipient, testee, victim
ASSOCIATED CONCEPTS: subject of an investigation

SUBJECT *(Topic),* *noun* affair, *argumentum,* content, course, gist, issue, material, matter, motif, pith, point, point at issue, *quaestio,* study, text, theme, thesis
ASSOCIATED CONCEPTS: interest in subject matter, subject of agreement, subject of bailment, subject of commerce, subject of statute, subject of tax

SUBJECT, *verb* bring under domination, bring under rule, cause to undergo, conquer, control, crush, defeat, disfranchise, dominate, enslave, enthrall, expose, get the better of, govern, hold down, hold in bondage, hold in subjection, humble, keep down, make liable, make submissive, make subordinate, make subservient, master, *obnoxium reddere,* oppress, overcome, overmaster, overthrow, quell, repress, rule, subdue, *subicere,* subjugate, subordinate, suppress, tame, triumph over, vanquish, worst

SUBJECT MATTER, *noun* content, contents, context, framework, import, material, matter, scope, study, substance, sum and substance, text, writing
ASSOCIATED CONCEPTS: subject matter jurisdiction

SUBJECTION, *noun* bondage, captivity, conquest, control, disenfranchisement, disfranchisement, duress, enslavement, enthrallment, force, helotry, inferior rank, involuntary servitude, loss of freedom, *officium,* servitude, *servitus,* slavery, subdual, subjugation, submission, subordination, subserviency, thrall, yielding, yoke

SUBJECTIVE, *adjective* biased, colored by bias, emotional, individual, individualized, internal, introspective, nonobjective, personal, personalized, prejudiced, unrealistic

SUBJUGATE, *verb* beat, bring to terms, command, conquer, control, crush, defeat, dominate, enslave, enthrall, govern, hold captive, hold in bondage, hold sway over, humble, master, overbear, overcome, overpower, overrule, overthrow, overwhelm, put down, quash, quell, reduce, restrain, rob of freedom, rout, rule over, sell into slavery, subdue, subject, suppress, tame, trample, triumph over, vanquish

SUBLEASE, *verb* allow the use of, demise, grant a demise, grant a lease, hire, let out, make available for rent, rent, rent out, sublet, subrent, underlet

SUBLET, *verb* allow the use of, contract to lease, lease, let out, relet, rent, rent out, sublease, subrent, underlet
ASSOCIATED CONCEPTS: assignment, covenant against subletting, restriction against subletting

SUBMIT *(Give),* *verb* advance, commit, extend, hold out, introduce, make a motion, make a suggestion, present, propose, propound, put, put forth, put forward, refer, *referre,* suggest, tender
ASSOCIATED CONCEPTS: submit to arbitration, submit to the court, submit to the jury

SUBMIT *(Yield),* *verb* accede, accept, acknowledge defeat, acquiesce, admit defeat, bear with, bend, bow to, capitulate, cease resistance, comply, endure, give in, give up, give way to, heed, listen to, make the best of, mind, obey, put up with, reconcile oneself to, relent, resign, succumb, surrender, tolerate
ASSOCIATED CONCEPTS: submit to the jurisdiction of the court

SUBORDINATE, *adjective* subordinate position, accessory, ancillary, auxiliary, collateral, humble, inferior, junior, less important, less significant, lesser, low-level, lower, lower in rank, lowly, minor, secondary, subaltern, subject, subjected, submissive, subservient, subsidiary
ASSOCIATED CONCEPTS: subordinate interest, subordinate lien

SUBORN, *verb* bribe, bribe to take a false oath, buy off, corrupt, fraudulently induce, induce, induce another to commit perjury, induce by illegal gratuity, instigate, offer an inducement, procure another to commit perjury, procure indirectly, seduce, *subornare,* tamper with
ASSOCIATED CONCEPTS: suborn perjury

SUBPOENA, *noun* call, citation, command, command to appear, demand, denuntiatio *testimonii,* directive, imperative, instruction, invocation, judicial imperative, legal mandate, legal process, mandate, notification, order, order to appear, order to appear in court, process, request, requirement to attend, summons, writ
ASSOCIATED CONCEPTS: information subpoena, judicial subpoena, subpoena ad testificandum, subpoena duces tecum

SUBPOENA, *verb* beckon, call for the presence of, call forth, call out, call to witness, call with authority, command to appear, compel attendance, demand, *denuntiatio*

testimonii, direct, direct the attendance of, issue a command, issue a court directive, issue a writ, issue process, notify to appear, order, order to appear, require compliance, require to attend, send for, summon, summon to court
ASSOCIATED CONCEPTS: subpoena a witness, subpoena before a jury, subpoena records, subpoena to a Grand Jury

SUBPOENA DUCES TECUM, *noun* judicial command, judicial demand for an accounting, judicial demand for archive, judicial demand for documentation, judicial demand for documents, judicial demand for files, judicial directive to produce documents, judicial mandate to produce documents, judicial order to produce documents
ASSOCIATED CONCEPTS: subpoena ad testificandum

SUBREPTION, *noun* deception, deliberate misrepresentation, fabrication, false swearing, falsehood, falsification, guile, invention, lying, mendacity, misrepresentation, perjury, prevarication, untruth

SUBROGATION, *noun* change, commutation, displacement, exchange, interchange, replacement, replacing, substitution, succession, supersedure, supersession, supplantation, supplanting, surrogation, switch, transfer, transference
ASSOCIATED CONCEPTS: conventional subrogation, legal subrogation, rights of subrogation

SUBSCRIBE (Promise), ***verb*** advocate, agree, assent, consent, donate to, enroll, guarantee, patronize, pledge, promise to contribute, register, support, warrant

SUBSCRIBE (Sign), ***verb*** acknowledge, affix one's signature, approve, attest, certify, confirm, endorse, inscribe, mark, ratify, seal, set a name to, sign a name to, undersign, underwrite, witness, write

SUBSCRIPTION, *noun* acceptance, affirmation, agreement, approval, assent, authentication, certification, confirmation, consent, endorsement, enrollment, ratification, registration, sanction, signature, validation

SUBSEQUENT, *adjective* coming, ensuing, eventual, following, future, *insequens*, later, latter, next, *posterior*, sequent, sequential, succeeding, trailing
ASSOCIATED CONCEPTS: subsequent condition, subsequent creditor

SUBSERVIENT, *adjective* abject, accessory, adjuvant, aidful, aiding, ancillary, auxiliary, base, contributory, cringing, deferential, dependent, enslaved, fawning, helpful, inferior, ingratiating, junior, lesser, lower, menial, ministrant, obedient, obeisant, *obsequens*, obsequious, prostrate, secondary, serviceable, servile, slavish, subaltern, subject, submissive, subordinate, subsidiary, sycophantic, toadying, tractable, truckling, unassertive, unctious, useful, utilitarian, valuable

SUBSIDE, *verb* abate, become less active, calm, *considere*, decline, decrease, descend, die away, diminish, dip, drop, dwindle, ebb, fall, fall away, fall off, grow less, lapse, lessen, let up, lull, melt away, mitigate, moderate, peter out, quiet, recede, relax, remit, *residere*, settle, shrink, sink, slack off, slacken, taper off, wane

SUBSIDIARY, *noun* adjuvant, aiding, assistant, auxiliary, cooperating, helping, secondary, subordinate, subservient, subsidiarius, supplemental, supplementary
ASSOCIATED CONCEPTS: subsidiary corporation

SUBSIDIZE, *verb* abet, *adiuvare*, advance, afford aid, afford support, aid, assist, back, befriend, bestow, bolster, contribute, endow, finance, foster, furnish aid, furnish support, further, give, give a grant to, give aid, give support to, help, help with money, keep, lend one's aid, lend support, maintain, patronize, pay, pay for, pay towards, promote, provide capital for, provide financing, provide for, provide funds for, provide money for, render assistance, stand behind, stand by, subscribe, subserve, subventionize, supply aid, supply support, support, sustain, underwrite, uphold

SUBSIDY, *noun* allotment, allowance, backing, bounty, contribution, gift, grant, grant-in-aid, stipend, subsistence, subvention
ASSOCIATED CONCEPTS: government subsidy

SUBSIST, *verb* abide, be, be nurtured, be supported, be sustained, *constare*, continue, endure, esse, exist, go on, hold on, last, live, maintain, outlast, outlive, perdure, persist, prevail, remain, remain alive, stand fast, stay, stay alive, survive

SUBSTANCE (Essential nature), ***noun*** actuality, backbone, basis, body, content, core, drift, essence, essential part, force, gist, heart, hypostasis, idea, import, marrow, material, meaning, pith, principle, purport, reality, res, sense, significance, signification, soul, sum, tenor, vital part

SUBSTANCE (Material possessions), ***noun*** assets, capital, command of money, *corpus*, estate, fortune, income, means, money, ownership, property, resources, revenue, riches, treasure, wealth, wherewithal

SUBSTANTIAL, *adjective* abundant, ample, concrete, consequential, considerable, established, existent, existing, *firmus*, flush, genuine, *gravis*, great, important, large, plentiful, real, significant, sizable, strong, substantive, valid
ASSOCIATED CONCEPTS: substantial breach, substantial claim, substantial compliance, substantial controversy, substantial damages, substantial error, substantial evidence, substantial factor, substantial impairment, substantial injury, substantial interest, substantial issue, substantial justice, substantial performance, substantial question, substantial right, substantial use

SUBSTANTIAL CAUSE SHOWN, *noun* good cause shown, legitimate basis proven, proper cause demonstrated, reasonable basis shown, substantial factors proven, sufficient foundation, sufficient grounds
ASSOCIATED CONCEPTS: temporary restraining orders

SUBSTANTIATE, *verb* actualize, affirm, attest, authenticate, bear out, bear witness, certify, circumstantiate, confirm, corroborate, demonstrate, embody, establish by proof, evidence, make good, materialize, objectify, prove, ratify, realize, reify, substantialize, support, uphold, validate, verify, vindicate
ASSOCIATED CONCEPTS: substantiate a claim, substantiate charges

SUBSTANTIATION, *noun* authenticating evidence, confirmation, confirming evidence, corroborating evidence, evidence which bears out the truth, evidence which proves a supposition, evidence which ratifies a position, evidence which validates a supposition, supporting evidence, verification
ASSOCIATED CONCEPTS: substantiation of charges

SUBSTANTIVE, *adjective* actual, appreciable, basic, concrete, considerable, constituent, elemental, essential, existent, existing, fundamental, important, independent, main, material, not subordinate, objective, palpable, positive, primary, principal, real, requisite, separate, solid, substantial, tangible, underlying, vital

ASSOCIATED CONCEPTS: substantive law, substantive right, substantive statute of limitations

SUBSTANTIVE ISSUE, *noun* benchmark, bookmark, critical point, crucial point, crux, essence, essential matter, fundamental part, gist, gravamen, heart, key point, linchpin, main point, material point, milestone, pivotal point, prime issue, salient point, substance, substantive point, turning point

SUBSTITUTE, *noun* agent, alternate, alternative, auxiliary, delegate, deputy, double, emissary, envoy, factor, lieutenant, pinch hitter, plenipotentiary, proxy, regent, relief, replacement, representation, representative, stand-in, steward, stopgap, substitution, supplanter, surrogate, symbol, temporary expedient, trustee, understudy

SUBSTITUTION OF COUNSEL, *noun* appointment of new counsel, change of counsel, hiring a new attorney, replacement of the current attorney, replacing the current counsel, retaining a new attorney-at-law, retaining a new barrister, retention of new counsel, substituting for the current lawyer

ASSOCIATED CONCEPTS: ineffective assistance of counsel, right to counsel

SUBTERFUGE, *noun* artifice, camouflage, chicane, chicanery, concealment, counterfeit, deception, *deverticulum,* device, dodge, duplicity, elusion, evasion, excuse, fabrication, falsehood, fib, fiction, finesse, forgery, guise, imposture, jugglery, *latebra,* lie, loophole, machination, maneuver, mask, plan, pretense, pretext, prevarication, ruse, sham, shift, smoke screen, sophistry, stratagem, subtlety, trick, untruth

SUBTLE (*Insidious*), *adjective* canny, contriving, crafty, cunning, deceitful, deceptive, designing, feline, guileful, illusive, implied, indistinct, inferred, insinuated, intriguing, serpentine, shifty, shrewd, sly, sophistical, stealthy, tricky, underhand, vulpine, wily

SUBTLE (*Refined*), *adjective* accomplished, airy, apt, artful, artistic, astute, clever, deft, delicate, diplomatic, discerning, discreet, discriminating, exact, expert, keen, light, masterly, meticulous, perceptive, politic, precise, sagacious, sharp, skillful, slender, sophisticated, strategic, subtile, superfine, tactful

SUBTRACTION, *noun* abstraction, ademption, curtailment, decrease, decrement, deduction, diminution, discount, exception, lessening, reduction, removal, retrenchment, shortening, shrinkage, subduction, withdrawal

SUBVERSION, *noun* abolition, annihilation, breakup, debacle, defeat, demolition, destruction, devastation, disestablishment, disruption, *eversio,* extinction, extirpation, incendiarism, inversion, overset, overthrow, overturn, perdition, rebellion, revolt, revolution, ruin, ruination, sabotage, sedition, subversive activities, upheaval, uprising, upset

SUBVERSIVES, *noun* cell, enemy combatant, enemy group, extremist group, extremists, incendiaries, insurgents, rebel organization, revolutionaries, saboteurs, underground extremists

ASSOCIATED CONCEPTS: justice courts, military tribunals, Patriot Act, prison cells, sleeper cell, terrorism, terrorist cell

SUBVERT, *verb* annihilate, confound, corrupt, defeat, demolish, demoralize, despoil, destroy, devastate, disestablish, dismantle, disrupt, *evertere,* extinguish, extirpate, impair, injure, lay waste, level, overset, overthrow, overturn, pervert, pull down, put an end to, ruin, spy against, *subvertere,* throw down, topple, tumble, turn over, undermine, undo, upset, vitiate

ASSOCIATED CONCEPTS: subvert the laws

SUCCEDANEUM, *noun* change, ersatz, exchange, replacement, secondary, substitute, substitution

SUCCEED (*Attain*), *verb* accomplish, achieve, acquire, advance, be victorious, bear fruit, bloom, capture, come through, conquer, do well, earn, fare well, flourish, fulfill, gain, gain a victory, make a hit, manage, master, meet with success, obtain, prevail, profit, progress, prosper, reach, realize, reap, *rem bene,* score a success, secure, surmount obstacles, thrive, triumph, vanquish, win, wrest

SUCCEED (*Follow*), *verb* arise, be subsequent, come after, come subsequently, derive, develop, displace, ensue, *excipere,* follow after, follow in order, give place to, go after, go next, outmode, postdate, relieve, remove, replace, serve as a substitute, set aside, subrogate, substitute for, *succedere,* supersede, supervene, supplant, take over, take the place of

SUCCESSFUL, *adjective* affluent, auspicious, blooming, blossoming, booming, champion, comfortable, effective, efficacious, felicitous, *felix,* flourishing, fortunate, *fortunatus,* fruitful, gainful, prevailing, profitable, prospering, prosperous, rich, satisfied, thriving, triumphant, unbeaten, undefeated, unvanquished, victorious, wealthy, well-off, well-situated, well-to-do, winning

SUCCESSION, *noun* chain, concatenation, consecution, consecutive order, *continuatio,* cycle, descent, devolution, family, issue, lineage, offspring, order, posterity, procession, progeny, progression, sequence, series, successorship, train

ASSOCIATED CONCEPTS: hereditary succession, intestate succession, legal succession, line of succession, natural succession, successor employer, successor interest, testamentary succession

FOREIGN PHRASES: *Haereditas est successio in universum jus quod defunctus habuerit.* Inheritance is the succession to every right which the deceased had possessed. ***Haereditas nihil aliud est, quam successio in universum jus, quod defunctus habuerit.*** An inheritance is nothing other than the succession to all the rights which the deceased had. ***Qui in jus dominiumve alterius succedit jure ejus uti debet.*** One who succeeds to the ownership rights of another, should enjoy the rights of the other. ***Non debeo melioris conditionis esse, quam auctor meus a quo jus in me transit.*** I ought not to be in better condition than he to whose rights I succeed.

SUCCESSIVE, *adjective* after, consecutive, ensuing, following, later, subsequent, succeeding, sequent, sequential

ASSOCIATED CONCEPTS: successive application, successive continuance, successive proceeding, successive term of imprisonment, successive writ

SUCCESSOR, *noun* beneficiary, descendant, follower, grantee, newcomer, next in line, replacement, scion

ASSOCIATED CONCEPTS: successor in estate, successor in interest, successor in office, successor in trust

SUCCINCT, *adjective* abbreviated, *brevis,* brief, compact, compendious, concise, condensed, curt, epigrammatic, expressed in few words, irreducible, laconic, pauciloquent, pithy, sententious, short, summary, synoptic, terse, to the point, trenchant

SUCCUMB, *verb* accede, acquiesce, be defeated, bend, bow, break down, capitulate, cave in, cease, collapse, come to naught, come to terms, comply, concede, die, droop, drop, end, expire, fail, fall, flag, give in, give way, go down, go under, knuckle under, lose, perish, relent, resign, stoop, submit, *succumbere,* surrender, tire, yield

SUE, *verb* appeal to the law, apply for, ask for relief, beseech, bring a legal action, bring an action, bring to justice, bring to the bar, claim, commence a suit, contest, entreat, file a legal claim, file suit, implore, initiate a civil action, institute a legal proceeding, institute process, legally pursue, litigate against, make appeal to, *orare,* petition, plead, prefer a claim, press a claim, pursue a claim, put on trial, *rogare,* seek by request, supplicate, take to court
ASSOCIATED CONCEPTS: power to sue, right to sue, standing to sue
FOREIGN PHRASES: *Nemo alieno nomine lege agere potest.* No one can sue in the name of another.

SUFFER (Permit), *verb* abide, accede, accept, acquiesce, allow, assent, authorize, be reconciled, be resigned, bear with, brook, comply, concede, consent, empower, give consent, give leave, give permission, grant, grant permission, indulge, let, license, oblige, *pati, permittere,* put up with, *sinere,* tolerate

SUFFER (Sustain loss), *verb* agonize, ail, anguish, be afflicted, be impaired, be injured, be racked, be stricken, be subjected to, be wounded, bear, endure, experience loss, feel pain, hurt, incur loss, languish, lose, *minui,* sacrifice, sustain damage
ASSOCIATED CONCEPTS: suffer harm, suffer loss

SUFFERANCE, *noun* allowance, authorization, calmness, capacity to endure, composure, concession, control, countenance, forbearance, fortitude, imperturbation, indulgence, leave, license, longanimity, patience, patient endurance, *patientia,* permission, resignation, sanction, self-control, self-possession, self-restraint, stoicism, submission, suffering, tolerance, *toleratio,* toleration

SUFFICIENCY, *noun* abundance, accumulation, adequacy, adequate resources, affluence, ample stock, ampleness, amplitude, cache, capacity, competence, competency, copiousness, cornucopia, enough, fill, full measure, fullness, fund, glut, hoard, large amount, plenitude, plenty, plethora, profuseness, profusion, *quod satis est,* redundance, repletion, reservoir, satiety, satisfactoriness, saturation, shower, store, sufficientness, superabundance, supply, surfeit, treasure, wealth, wherewithal
ASSOCIATED CONCEPTS: legal sufficiency, sufficiency of the evidence

SUFFICIENT, *adjective* adequate, ample, capable, comfortable, commensurate, commensurate with, competent, enough, equal to, fair, in fair condition, in good condition, just, meritorious, operative, plentiful, plenty, qualified, replete, satisfactory, satisfying, suitable

ASSOCIATED CONCEPTS: sufficient cause, sufficient evidence, sufficient facts

SUFFICIENT FOUNDATION, *noun* good cause shown, legitimate basis proven, proper cause demonstrated, reasonable basis shown, substantial cause shown, substantial factors proven, sufficient grounds
ASSOCIATED CONCEPTS: temporary restraining orders

SUFFICIENT PROOF, *noun* adequate evidence, adequate proof legally presented at trial, burden of going forward, burden of proof, legal responsibility, obligation of going forward, sufficient corroboration, sufficient evidence in a case, sufficient evidence to establish a case, sufficient proof of facts, validation of proof of a case, verification of proof of a case
ASSOCIATED CONCEPTS: cause of action of claim, evidence, evidential burden, failure to sustain, preponderance of the evidence, *prima facie* case, rebuttal, weight of evidence
FOREIGN PHRASES: *Onus Probani.* Burden of proof.

SUFFRAGE, *noun* affranchisement, autonomy, choice, emancipation, enfranchisement, exemption from control, exemption from restraint, franchise, freedom, freedom of choice, liberation, liberty, license, manumission, option, popular decision, prerogative, right to vote, say, self-determination, self-government, *suffragium,* voice, vote
ASSOCIATED CONCEPTS: election law, voters' rights

SUGGEST, *verb* advise, advocate, allude, argue, charge, coax, connote, convey, counsel, denote, evidence, exhort, hint, implicate, imply, indicate, insinuate, instruct, mention, nominate, offer, persuade, pose, postulate, prescribe, present, proffer, promise, prompt, propose, propound, purport, put forth, put forward, recommend, refer, remark, remind, signify, submit, urge
ASSOCIATED CONCEPTS: suggestive terms, suggestive interrogatories

SUGGESTION, *noun* *admonitio,* advancement, advice, allusion, breath, clue, *consilium,* counsel, cue, exhortation, glimmer, hint, idea, implication, indication, inference, inkling, innuendo, insinuation, intimation, lead, motion, outline, overtone, pointer, possibility, prompting, prompture, proposal, proposition, recommendation, reminder, representation, resolution, scheme, slight trace, statement, suggested plan, suspicion, symbol, tentative statement, thought, tip, touch, trace, whisper
ASSOCIATED CONCEPTS: suggestion of error, suggestive interrogation

SUGGESTIVE (Evocative), *adjective* allusive, commemorative, commemoratory, connotative, demonstrative, expressive, graphic, graphical, implicative, indicant, indicative, indicatory, inferential, insinuative, insinuatory, intriguing, lifelike, meaningful, ominous, pictorial, provocative, recollective, redolent, referential, remindful, reminiscent, reminiscential, symbolic, thought-provoking, vivid
ASSOCIATED CONCEPTS: suggestive lineup

SUGGESTIVE (Risqué), *adjective* bawdy, carnal, coarse, erotic, improper, indecent, indelicate, lascivious, lecherous, lewd, libidinous, lickerish, loose, lurid, lustful, obscene, off-color, pornographic, provocative, racy, ribald, salacious, seductive, sexy, shameless, smutty, spicy, titillating, wanton

SUI GENERIS, *noun* in its own category, in its own group, of its own character, of its own class, of its own classification, of its own denomination, of its own designation, of its own genre, of its own kind, of its own nature, of its own type, of its own variety, peculiar, special, the only one of its kind, unique

SUIT, *noun*   actio, action, action at law, action to serve justice, case, *causa,* cause, cause in court, judicial contest, lawsuit, legal action, legal proceeding, legal remedy, *lis,* litigation, petition, proceeding, suit in law, trial
ASSOCIATED CONCEPTS: class suits, nonsuit, suit against state
FOREIGN PHRASES: *Secta est pugna civilis; sicut actores armantur actionibus, et, quasi, accinguntur gladiis, ita rei muniuntur exceptionibus, et defenduntur, quasi, clypeis.* A suit is a civil battle; for as the plaintiffs are armed with actions, and, as it were, girded with swords, so the defendants are fortified with pleas, and are defended, as it were, with shields. *Frustra agit qui judicium prosequi nequit cum effectu.* He sues vainly who cannot prosecute his judgment with effect. *Nemo alieno nomine lege agere potest.* No one can sue in the name of another.

SUITABLE, *adjective*   acceptable, accommodating, accordant, adapted, adequate, admissible, advantageous, advisable, applicable, apposite, appropriate, apropos, apt, *aptus,* becoming, befitting, commensurate, commodious, compatible, condign, conformable, congenial, congruent, congruous, *consentaneous,* consentaneus, consistent, consonant, convenient, correct, correspondent, decent, decorous, deserved, desirable, due, eligible, expedient, favorable, feasible, felicitous, fit, fitting, germane, harmonious, idoneous, *idoneus,* just, likely, meet, merited, opportune, pat, pertinent, practicable, proper, proportionate, qualified, reasonable, reconcilable, relevant, right, rightful, satisfactory, seasonable, seemly, sufficient, suited, timely, valid, worthy
ASSOCIATED CONCEPTS: suitable for a particular purpose

SUITOR, *noun*   appellant, applicant, claimant, litigant, litigator, party to a suit, petitioner, plaintiff, pleader, seeker, solicitor, suppliant, supplicant

SULLY, *verb*   asperse, attaint, bedim, begrime, belittle, bemire, besmear, blacken, blemish, blot, blur, brand, contaminate, corrupt, daub, debase, decry, deface, defame, defile, degrade, denigrate, denounce, deprecate, depreciate, dirty, discredit, disgrace, dishonor, disparage, dispraise, drabble, dull, foul, gibbet, impeach, impugn, injure, *inquinare,* knock, *maculare,* make unclean, malign, mar, pollute, put to shame, run down, shame, slur, smear, smirch, smudge, soil, spatter, speak ill of, splash, spoil, spot, stain, stigmatize, taint, tarnish, traduce, vilify, vilipend, vitiate

SUM *(tally),* *noun*   compendium, essence, figure, gist, idea conveyed, meaning, score, substance, summary

SUM *(total),* *noun*   aggregate amount, all, entirety, everything, gross amount, sum total, the whole, totality, wholeness
ASSOCIATED CONCEPTS: sum paid, sum and substance, sum in controversy, sum certain, sum demanded, sum in question

SUM, *verb*   add, compute, count up, figure up, reckon up, summate, total

SUMMARIZATION, *noun*   abbreviation, abridgment, analysis, brief, compendium, compilation, conclusion, condensation, core, digest, overview, recap, recapitulation, report, restatement, review, skeleton, summary, syllabus, synopsis
ASSOCIATED CONCEPTS: summarization presented to the jury

SUMMARY, *adjective*   brevis, concise, direct, done without delay, expeditious, hasty, hurried, immediate, instantaneous, prompt, quick, quickly executed, quickly performed, rapid, speedy, sudden, swift
ASSOCIATED CONCEPTS: summary action, summary contempt, summary conviction, summary hearing, summary judgment, summary proceeding, summary process, summary punishment

SUMMARY, *noun*   abbreviation, abridgment, abstract, analysis, brief, compend, compendium, compilation, compressed statement, conspectus, core, digest, *epitoma,* epitome, minute, note, outline, pandect, recap, recapitulation, report, restatement, review, short version, skeleton, *summarium,* syllabus, synopsis

SUMMON, *verb*   advocare, appellare, beckon, bid, call for, call for the presence of, call forth, call into action, call to witness, call with authority, charge, cite, command, command to appear, compel attendance, demand, give orders, issue a command, issue a court directive, issue process, notify to appear, order, order to appear, require compliance, require to attend, send for, subpoena
ASSOCIATED CONCEPTS: summon to appear in court

SUMMONS, *noun*   authoritative citation to appear before a court, authoritative command, bid, calling to court, citation, command to appear, commandment, direction, invocation, legal process, mandate, notification to appear, official call, official court order, official notice, official order, order to appear, request to appear, writ, written notification to appear in court

SUNSET LAW, *noun*   a law which will be discontinued, a law which will be eliminated, a statute which automatically ends, a statute which automatically terminates, a statute which expires, a statute which will cease, ending law, expiring law, statute with a fixed lifespan, terminating law

SUNSHINE LAWS, *noun*   availability of government documents, availability of government information, availability of governmental records, freedom of information laws, freely available government information, open access to government information laws, open government laws
ASSOCIATED CONCEPTS: Freedom of Information Act

SUPERANNUATE, *verb*   antiquate, cancel, dismiss, make extinct, make obsolete, make outdated, remove, replace, retire, shelve, withdraw

SUPERCILIOUS, *adjective*   arrogant, assumptive, bumptious, cavalier, condescending, contemptuous, contumelious, derisive, dictatorial, disdainful, disrespectful, domineering, egotistic, *fastidiosus,* haughty, imperious, inso-lent, intolerant, irreverent, lofty, lordly, magisterial, overbearing, overweening, patronizing, peremptory, pompous, presumptuous, prideful, proud, puffed up, scornful, *superbus,* swollen, toplofty, uppish, uppity, vainglorious, withering

SUPERFICIAL, *adjective*   careless, cursory, depthless, desultory, empty, exterior, external, frivolous, hasty, hurried, inane, insubstantial, *lax, levis,* outward, perfunctory, sciolistic, shallow, shoal, silly, skin-deep, slapdash, slight, surface, trifling, trivial, unthinking

SUPERFLUOUS, *adjective*   additional, adscititious, dispensable, duplicate, excess, excrescent, expendable, extra, extravagant, inessential, inordinate, lavish, luxuriant,

luxurious, more than enough, more than sufficient, needless, overflowing, overmuch, prodigal, profuse, redundant, remaining, remanent, residual, residuary, spare, superabundant, supererogative, supererogatory, supernumerary, supervacaneous, *supervacaneus, supervacuus,* supplemental, surplus, uncalled-for, unessential, unnecessary, useless, wasteful
ASSOCIATED CONCEPTS: superfluous lands

SUPERFUND, *noun*   environmental clean-up, Federal program to restore environmentally unsound sites, fund to reclaim the environment, mechanism to fund the environment, reserve for environment contingencies
Generally: fund for repairs, reserves for removing wastes

SUPERINTEND, *verb*   administer, *administrare,* administrate, boss, caretake, command, control, direct, exercise charge over, exercise supervision over, govern, guide, handle, have charge of, head, instruct, keep in order, lead, look after, manage, overlook, oversee, pilot, praeesse, *procurare,* regulate, rule, see to, steer, supervise, watch

SUPERINTENDENT, *noun*   administrator, agent, captain, caretaker, chief, controller, curator, custodian, director, foreman, governor, guardian, intendant, leader, manager, master, monitor, overseer, *praefectus,* proctor, steward, supervisor, taskmaster, warden

SUPERIOR (Excellent), *adjective*   above average, above par, better, choice, deluxe, distinguished, exceptional, finer, first-rate, foremost, greater, high-class, high-grade, high-quality, illustrious, incomparable, matchless, *melior,* noble, nonpareil, peerless, *praestantior,* preferable, preferred, second to none, superexcellent, superlative, supreme, topping, transcendent, unequaled, unexcelled, unparalleled, unrivalled, unsurpassed

SUPERIOR (Higher), *adjective*   chief, greater, more elevated, of greater influence, of higher rank, paramount, senior
ASSOCIATED CONCEPTS: respondeat superior, superior court, superior force

SUPERLATIVE, *adjective*   best, champion, chief, consummate, crowning, excellent, excessive, *eximius,* extreme, first-rate, foremost, greatest, highest, immoderate, incomparable, inflated, inimitable, matchless, most eminent, nonpareil, *optimus,* paramount, peerless, prime, principal, second to none, sovereign, super, superexcellent, superfine, superior, supreme, surpassing, tiptop, transcendent, unequaled, unexcelled, unmatched, unparalleled, unrivaled, unsurpassed, utmost, without parallel

SUPERSEDE, *verb*   abolish, annul, discard, displace, make obsolete, make void, nullify, obviate, oust, override, overrule, preclude, put in the place of, remove, repeal, replace, set aside, stand in stead of, subrogate, substitute, *succedere,* succeed, supplant, take the place of, void
ASSOCIATED CONCEPTS: superseding cause

SUPERSEDING CAUSE, *noun*   annulment, break, displacement, immediate legal basis, immediate legal cause, immediate legal genesis, interceding break, nullification, obviation, ousting, overriding cause, overruling cause, preclusion, put in the place of, removal, replacement, substitution, succession, sufficient legal basis, sufficient legal cause, sufficient legal factor, sufficient legal genesis, sufficient legel inducements, sufficient legal source, supplanting legal cause, voidance
ASSOCIATED CONCEPTS: intervening clause

SUPERVENE, *verb*   arise, be subsequent, bechance, befall, come to pass, *crop* up, ensue, eventuate, follow, happen, issue, occur, result, spring up, succeed, *supervenire,* take place

SUPERVISE, *verb*   administer, care, caretake, check, command, conduct, control, direct, discipline, govern, guide, handle, have charge of, lead, look after, manage, moderate, officiate, operate, oversee, pilot, preside, preside over, regulate, rule, steer, watch over
ASSOCIATED CONCEPTS: employer/employee, principal and agent

SUPERVISION, *noun*   administration, care, charge, command, control, direction, government, gubernation, guidance, inspection, jurisdiction, management, oversight, *procuratio,* proctorage, regulation, steerage, stewardship, superintendence, surveillance
ASSOCIATED CONCEPTS: direct supervision, general supervision, person in need of supervision, personal supervision, right of supervision, supervision and control, supervisory powers

SUPPLANT, *verb*   abolish, act for, bring low, cashier, cause the downfall of, depose, deracinate, dethrone, discharge, dismiss, displace, drive away, drive out, eject, eradicate, expel, extirpate, fire, force out, oust, overthrow, overpower, remove, replace, retire, subrogate, substitute, subvert, succeed, supersede, take over, take the place of, transfer, turn out, undermine, unseat, uproot, upset, usurp

SUPPLEMENT, *verb*   add, add to, amend, amplify, augment, bolster, broaden, buttress, complement, contribute to, enhance, enlarge, enrich, expand, fortify, improve, increase, lengthen, magnify, reinforce, strengthen, subsidize, superadd, widen

SUPPLEMENTAL, *adjective*   accompanying, additional, additive, adjunct, adventitious, ancillary, appurtenant, attendant, augmentative, auxiliary, collateral, concomitant, contributory, extra, extrinsic, incidental, nonessential, pendent, spare, submitted at a later time, subordinate, subsidiary, superfluous, supernumerary, supervenient, supplementary, unessential, unnecessary
ASSOCIATED CONCEPTS: supplemental affidavit, supplemental answer, supplemental claim, supplemental complaint, supplemental condition, supplemental findings, supplemental insurance, supplemental policy, supplemental procedure, supplemental questions

SUPPLEMENTARY, *adjective*   accessory, additional, additive, adjunct, adscititious, ancillary, attendant, augmentative, auxiliary, collateral, concomitant, extra, incidental, nonessential, secondary, spare, subordinate, subsidiary, supervenient, supplemental, suppletive, suppletory, unessential
ASSOCIATED CONCEPTS: supplementary proceedings

SUPPLIER, *noun*   caterer, chandler, commissary, contractor, furnisher, giver, merchant, provider, provisioner, purveyor, seller, steward, trader, victualer

SUPPLY, *verb*   accommodate with, accouter, administer, afford, bestow, cater, contribute, deal out, deliver, distribute, endow, endue, equip, feed, fill up, fit out, furnish, give, grant, invest, lavish, maintain, minister, *ministrare,* oblige, outfit, present, provide, provision, purvey, recruit, refill, render, replenish, satisfy, serve, stock, *suppeditare,* suppeditate, sustain, victual, yield

SUPPORT (Assistance), **noun**   accommodation, *adiumentum,* aid, assist, assistance, *auxilium,* backing, comfort, contribution, cooperation, defense, encouragement, endowment, help, helping hand, lift, livelihood, mainstay, maintenance, patronage, preservation, promotion, protection, relief, subsistence, succor, *subsidium,* sustenance, upkeep

ASSOCIATED CONCEPTS: alimony, child support, failure to provide support, inadequate support, maintenance

SUPPORT (Corroboration), **noun**   affirmation, approval, attestation, authentication, backing, certification, circumstantiation, confirmation, documentation, endorsement, fortification, justification, ratification, strengthening, substantiation, validation, verification, vindication

SUPPORT (Assist), **verb**   accommodate, *adesse,* aid, back, bolster, champion, come to the defense of, come to the help of, contribute, cooperate with, defend, endorse, facilitate, feed, finance, furnish funds, further, help, lend money to, maintain, minister to, nourish, patronize, promote, protect, provide for, reinforce, second, subsidize, *suffragari,* supply the necessities of, sustain, take care of, take the part of, uphold

FOREIGN PHRASES: *Parentum est liberos alere atiam nothos.* It is the duty of parents to support their children even when illegitimate.

SUPPORT (Corroborate), **verb**   accredit, affirm, attest, authenticate, back up, bear out, buttress, certify, circumstantiate, confirm, establish, make absolute, make good, make more certain, prove, ratify, reinforce, strengthen, substantiate, sustain, uphold in evidence, validate, verify, vindicate, vouch for

SUPPORT (Justify), **verb**   account for, approve, defend, defend successfully, explain, give grounds for, make defense for, make legitimate, provide justification, say in defense, stand up for, vindicate

SUPPORTING EVIDENCE, noun   authenticating evidence, certification, confirmation, confirming documentation, confirming documents, confirming evidence, confirming means of proof, corroboration, evidence which bears out the truth, evidence which buttresses a case, evidence which strengthens a case, reinforcing evidence, substantiating proof, substantiation, validation, verification

ASSOCIATED CONCEPTS: circumstantial evidence

SUPPOSE, verb   allude to, anticipate, assume, believe, be of the opinion, calculate, conceive, conclude, conjecture, consider, deduce, deduct, deem, estimate, expect, feel, gather, gauge, generalize, guess, hint, hypothesize, imagine, imply, infer, insinuate, intimate, judge, opine, posit, predicate, presume, presuppose, propose, propound, reason, regard, speculate, surmise, suspect, take for granted, theorize, understand, view

SUPPOSITION, noun   assumption, belief, conception, *coniectura,* conjecture, guess, hypothesis, likelihood, likeliness, *opinio,* opinion, position, postulate, premise, presumption, probability, speculation, supposal, surmise, suspicion, theorem, theory, thesis

FOREIGN PHRASES: In claris non est locus conjecturis. In matters which are obvious there is no room for conjecture.

SUPPRESS, verb   arrest, ban, burke, bury, cancel, censor, check, choke, choke back, cloak, conceal, cover up, crush, delete, end, *exstinguere,* extinguish, gag, hush up, inhibit, keep back, keep down, keep out of sight, keep secret, mask, muffle, obstruct, overcome, overpower, overthrow, overwhelm, prevent, prohibit, quash, quell, quench, repress, *reprimere,* restrain, screen, shroud, silence, smother, stifle, still, stop, strangle, subdue, *supprimere,* vanquish, veil

ASSOCIATED CONCEPTS: motion to suppress evidence

SUPPRESSION OF EVIDENCE, verb   extinguishment, judicial ban of evidence, prevention of the introduction of evidence, prohibition of the use of evidence, quashing evidence, repressing evidence, restraining the use of evidence, substantiation, that which furnishes proof, that which tends to prove, validation, vanquish veil, verification

ASSOCIATED CONCEPTS: exclusionary rule, Fifth Amendment, Fourteenth Amendment, illegal search and seizure

SUPREMACY, noun   ascendancy, authority, championship, chieftaincy, command, control, direction, *dominatio,* domination, dominion, governance, headship, highest position, importance, influence, leadership, lordship, management, masterdom, mastership, mastery, omnipotence, paramountcy, power, precedence, predominance, predominancy, predomination, preeminence, primacy, *principatus,* regulation, rule, scepter, sovereignty, superintendence, superiority, supervision, supreme authority, supremeness, sway, transcendence, transcendency, triumph, upperhand, victory

ASSOCIATED CONCEPTS: Supremacy Clause

SURCHARGE, noun   added charge, additional charge, excessive burden, excessive charge, extra charge, extra fee, overassessment, overburden, overcharge, overload, penalty

ASSOCIATED CONCEPTS: identifiable surcharge, surcharge for services

SURETY (Certainty), **noun**   absolute confidence, absoluteness, affirmance, affirmation, aplomb, ascertainment, asseveration, assurance, assuredness, averment, avowal, avowance, certain knowledge, certification, certitude, complete conviction, confirmation, contract, conviction, convincement, declaration, definiteness, determination, earnest averment, earnest avowal, earnest declaration, firmness, guaranty, hardihood, persuasion, positiveness, pronouncement, reassurance, reliance on, self-assurance, self-conviction, solemn averment, solemn avowal, solemn declaration, sureness, unequivocalness, unmistakableness, unquestionableness, vow, warrant

SURETY (Guarantor), **noun**   attester, backer, certifier, confirmer, consignee, endorser, financer, indemnitor, insurer, promisor, ratifier, signatory, signer, sponsor, subscriber, supporter, underwriter, voucher, warrantor

ASSOCIATED CONCEPTS: surety bond, surety company, surety insurance, surety of the peace

FOREIGN PHRASES: *In veram quantitatem fidejussor teneatur, nisi pro certa quantitate accessit.* A surety should be held for the true quantity, unless he agreed for a certain quantity. *Natura fide jussionis sit strictissimi juris et non durat vel extendatur de re ad rem, de persona ad personam, de tempore ad tempus.* The nature of a suretyship is one of strictest law and cannot endure or be extended from one thing to another, from one person to another, or from one time to another.

SURFEIT, noun   avalanche, deluge, excess, excessive amount, fullness, glut, inundation, nimiety, overabundance, overdose, overflow, overfullness, overload, oversupply, plenty, profuseness, profusion, redundance, repletion, satiation, *satietas,* satiety, satisfaction, saturation, superabundance, superfluity, supersaturation, surplus, surplusage

SURMISE, verb apprehend, assume, *augurari,* be of the opinion, believe, conceive, conclude, conjecture, count, deduce, deem, divine, esteem, fancy, feel, gather, guess, have an idea, hazard a guess, hypothesize, imagine, infer, judge, opine, posit, predicate, presume, presuppose, regard, speculate, suppose, suspect, *suspicari,* theorize, think, trow, understand, view, ween

SURMOUNT, verb beat, clear, climb, command, conquer, crest, crown, defeat, dominate, exceed, excel, exsuperare, get the better of, go beyond, master, outdo, outmaneuver, outrival, overcome, overpass, overpower, overthrow, overturn, pass, prevail over, rise above, rout, scale, subdue, subjugate, surpass, top, transcend, transcendere, triumph over, upset, vanquish, vault

SURPASS, verb antecellere, be greater, be superior, beat, better, break the record, cap, come first, distance, eclipse, exceed, excel, *excellere,* get ahead, go beyond, go one better, have the upper hand, improve upon, leave behind, outmaneuver, outclass, outdo, outmatch, outnumber, outplay, outrank, outrival, outrun, outshine, outstrip, outvie, outweigh, overshadow, pass, predominate, prevail, rank first, reach a new high, rise above, rival, supererogate, take precedence, top, tower over, transcend, triumph over

SURPLUS, noun balance, bonus, excess, expletive, glut, leavings, margin, nimiety, overabundance, overage, overflow, overmeasure, overplus, overrun, oversupply, redundance, redundancy, remainder, residue, *residuum,* spare, superabundance, superfluity, surplus, supersaturation, surfeit, surplusage
ASSOCIATED CONCEPTS: accumulated surplus, distribution of surplus, surplus after sale, surplus goods, surplus income, surplus of proceeds, transfer to surplus

SURPLUSAGE, noun balance, continuing, extra, left, leftover, over, spare, staying
ASSOCIATED CONCEPTS: no child left behind, remainder

SURPRISE, noun admiratio, amazement, astonishment, astoundment, bafflement, bewilderment, consternation, lack of warning, *miratio,* shock, unexpected event, unexpected occurrence, unforeseen contingency, unforeseen event, unforeseen occurrence, unsuspected event, unusual occurrence, wonder, wonderment
ASSOCIATED CONCEPTS: take an opposing party by surprise

SURRENDER (Give back), **verb** abdicate, abjure, abnegate, cede, disclaim, disown, forego, forfeit, forsake, forswear, hand over, let go, part with, reinstate, relinquish, render up, renounce, resign, restore, return, waive

SURRENDER (Yield), **verb** acquiesce, agree to, back down, be submissive, capitulate, concede, *dedere,* give in, obey, relent, submit, succumb, *tradere*

SURREPTITIOUS, adjective artful, clandestine, *clandestinus,* concealed, conniving, covert, crafty, cunning, deceitful, deceptive, delitescent, disguised, done by stealth, evasive, faked, fraudulently introduced, furtive, *furtivus,* guileful, hidden, indirect, insidious, lurking, mysterious, obreptitious, private, secret, secretive, sneaky, stealthy, subdolous, subtle, tricky, uncommunicative, undercover, underground, underhand, undisclosed, unknown, unseen, unspied, unsuspected, veiled, vulpine, wily

SURROGATE, adjective acting, alternate, delegated, deputy, foster, imitation, makeshift, provisional, proxy, pseudo, representative, simulated, stand-in, substitute, substitutional, vicarial, vicarious, *vicarius*

SURVEILLANCE, noun care, charge, circumspection, examination, guard, heed, inspection, lookout, observation, oversight, protection, scrutiny, stewardship, superintendence, supervision, vigil, vigilance, watch, watchfulness

SURVEY (Examine), **verb** analyze, appraise, consider, *considerare, contemplari,* evaluate, inspect, keep an eye upon, keep watch, look at, observe, overlook, oversee, peruse, reconnoiter, review, scan, scrutinize, search, *spectare,* study, view, watch, weigh

SURVEY (Poll), **verb** canvass, compute, count, count ballots, count votes, enroll, enumerate, estimate, list, register, review, tabulate, take stock, test, total

SURVIVAL, noun being, continuance, continuation, continuation of life, durability, duration, endurance, existence, extension, life, maintenance, permanence, prolongation

SURVIVE, verb abide, be left, be spared, continue, endure, exist, last, live longer, live on, make a comeback, outlast, outlive, persevere, persist, remain, result, subsist, sustain, weather the storm
ASSOCIATED CONCEPTS: survival of a debt, survival of an action, survive a contract, surviving party, survivor statutes, survivorship

SUSCEPTIBILITY, noun affectability, aptitude, bent, capability of being affected, capacity for emotion, capacity for receiving impressions, empathy, impressibility, impressionability, inclination, leaning, penchant, proclivity, propensity, sensibility, sensitive feelings, sensitiveness, sensitivity, tendency, tendency to be emotionally affected

SUSCEPTIBLE (Responsive), **adjective** compassionate, easily affected, flexible, impressible, impressionable, influenceable, *mollis,* movable, persuadable, pliant, reactive, readily impressed, receptive, sensitive, susceptive, swayable, sympathetic

SUSCEPTIBLE (Unresistent), **adjective** exposed, helpless, in danger, liable, nonresistant, open, predisposed, resistless, sensitive, undefended, unprotected, unsafe, vulnerable, yielding

SUSPECT, noun accused, accused person, alleged malfeasor, alleged offender, alleged transgressor, alleged wrongdoer, individual under suspicion, one suspected of a crime, person accused of crime, presumed wrongdoer, suspected criminal
ASSOCIATED CONCEPTS: defendant

SUSPECT (Distrust), **verb** be doubtful, be dubious, be skeptical, be suspicious, disbelieve, doubt, feel distrust, harbor suspicious, have no confidence in, lack confidence in, misdoubt, misgive, mistrust, question, without reliance in
ASSOCIATED CONCEPTS: suspect of wrongdoing

SUSPECT (Think), **verb** assume, be of the opinion, believe, conclude, conjecture, consider, deduce, deem, divine, fancy, gather, guess, have the idea, hold, hypothesize, imagine, infer, judge, opine, posit, presume, presuppose, reckon, speculate, suppose, surmise, *suspicari, suspicionem habere,* take for granted, theorize, understand, view

SUSPEND, verb arrest, break off, bring to a standstill, bring to a stop, cease, check, defer, delay, desist, *differre*, discharge, discontinue, halt, hinder, hold in abeyance, interfere with, intermit, *intermittere*, interrupt, lay aside, lay off, leave off, postpone, put off, remit, remove, shelve, stall, stay, stop, table, temporize
ASSOCIATED CONCEPTS: suspend a license, suspend a sentence, suspend an employee, suspend payment, suspend the power of alienation, suspend the writ of habeas corpus

SUSPICION (Mistrust), **noun** apprehension, cynicism, disbelief, distrust, doubt, doubtfulness, dubiety, dubiousness, fear, fearfulness, incredulity, lack of faith, lack of trust, misdoubt, misgiving, qualm, skepticism, suspicio, suspiciousness, trepidation, unbelief
ASSOCIATED CONCEPTS: suspicious circumstances, suspicious origin
FOREIGN PHRASES: **Dona clandestina sunt semper suspiciosa.** Clandestine gifts are always open to suspicion.

SUSPICION (Uncertainty), **noun** chance, conjecture, doubtfulness, guess, hint, impression, incertitude, inconclusiveness, inference, inkling, insecurity, intimation, notion, postulate, postulation, question, speculation, suggestion, supposition, surmise, trace, unsureness

SUSPICIOUS (Distrustful), **adjective** apprehensive, cautious, concerned, disposed to doubt, doubting, dubious, fearful, hard to convince, hesitant, inconvincible, jealous, leery, mistrustful, nervous, quizzical, skeptical, suspecting, *suspiciosus*, untrustful, untrusting, untrustworthy, wary, watchful

SUSPICIOUS (Questionable), **adjective** abnormal, cryptic, doubtful, dubious, enigmatic, equivocal, farfetched, hard to believe, irregular, open to doubt, open to question, peculiar, strange, suspect, unbelievable, uncertain, unconvincing, unplausible, unworthy of belief
ASSOCIATED CONCEPTS: suspicious circumstances, suspicious origin

SUSTAIN (Confirm), **verb** affirm, approve, assent to, attest, authenticate, bear out, buttress, certify, circumstantiate, consent to, corroborate, defend, document, endorse, establish, evidence, justify, make firm, prove, ratify, reinforce, sanction, settle, strenghten, substantiate, support, uphold, uphold in evidence, validate, verify, vindicate
ASSOCIATED CONCEPTS: sustain a lower court's decision

SUSTAIN (Prolong), **verb** attentuate, bolster, conserve, continue, contribute to, elongate, extend, fortify, guard, keep going, keep up, lengthen, maintain, nourish, perpetuate, preserve, promote, protect, protract, reinforce, save, spare, strengthen, stretch, *sustentare, sustinere*, uphold

SUSTENANCE, noun aliment, alimentation, *alimentum*, food, keep, living, maintenance, means of sustaining life, necessities, nourishment, nutriment, nutrition, provisions, subsistence, supplies, support, sustentation, upkeep, victuals, *victus*

SWAY, noun authority, command, control, domain, dominance, domination, dominion, force, governance, influence, jurisdiction, leadership, power, predominance, prestige, primacy, reign, rule, supremacy

SWAY (Persuade), **verb** actuate, coax, control, convert, convince, dominate, encourage, force, goad, govern, incline, induce, influence, inspire, inveigle, manage, motivate, move, predispose, predominate, prejudice, preside, pressure, prevail, prevail upon, prod, prompt, spur, stimulate, urge

SWAY (Vacillate), **verb** falter, flounder, fluctuate, hesitate, lean, oscillate, pulsate, seesaw, shift, shuffle, swing, undulate, veer, waffle, waver

SWEAR, verb adjure, affirm, allege under oath, assert as true, assure, authenticate, aver, avow, bear witness, bind oneself by oath, certify, confirm, declare, declare solemnly, declare true, give a promise, give evidence, give one's word, guarantee, *iurare, iureiurando adfirmare*, maintain under oath, promise, put one's trust in, state, state under oath, utter an oath, vouch, vow
ASSOCIATED CONCEPTS: false swearing, public swearing
FOREIGN PHRASES: **In judicio non creditur nisi juratis.** In a court of justice no one is given credence who is not sworn.

SWORN, verb adjured, affirmed, alleged under oath, asserted as true under oath, assured under oath, authenticated under oath, averred, avowed, certified under oath, confirmed under oath, declared solemnly, declared true under oath, declared under oath, given evidence under oath, maintained under oath, stated under oath, vowed, witnessed
ASSOCIATED CONCEPTS: sworn enemy, sworn statements

SWORN DECLARANT, noun affiant, author, compiler, composer, declarant, drafter, party, scriptor, undersigned, writer
ASSOCIATED CONCEPTS: accommodation endorser, accommodation maker, dying declaration

SYMBOL, noun abbreviation, badge, clue, connotation, cue, delineation, depiction, emblem, enactment, ensign, exponent, gesture, image, index, indication, manifestation, mark, model, notation, note, picture, portrayal, representation, seal, sign, signal, signification, *signum, symbolum*, symptom, token, trademark, visible sign
ASSOCIATED CONCEPTS: trademark

SYMPATHIZE, verb be compassionate, be moved, be sorry for, be touched, be understanding, comfort, commiserate, condole, *congruere*, console, *eadem sentire*, empathize, express sympathy, feel for, grieve with, have pity, identify with, lament with, *misereri*, mourn with, pity, share grief, share sorrow, show mercy, show tenderness, solace, soothe, understand

SYMPTOM, noun alarm, augury, characteristic, clue, danger signal, diagnostic, evidence, evincement, feature, forewarning, guide, index, indicant, indication, indicator, indice, *indicium*, intimation, manifestation, mark, means of recognition, monition, monitor, nota, notice, preindication, premonitor, premonitory sign, prognostic, sign, signal, token, trait, warning, warning sign

SYNCHRONISM, noun accompaniment, accord, *aequalitas temporum*, agreement, attunement, coexistence, coincidence, compatibility, concord, concurrence, conformity, consistency, harmony, simultaneity, simultaneousness, unison

SYNDICATE, noun alliance, association, cartel, coalition, combine, company, consortium, council, federation, guild, league, machine, merger, organization, partnership, pool, ring, *societas*, union

SYNERGETIC, adjective coacting, coactive, collaborative, concurrent, concurring, co-operant, cooperative, coworking, in agreement, in concord

SYNERGY, noun coaction, coincidence, collaboration, combined action, combined effect, combined operation, concert, concurrence, cooperation, cooperative action, joint effect, synergism, united action

SYNOPSIS, noun abridgment, abstract, brief, compend, compendium, condensation, conspectus, digest, *epitome*, minute, outline, recapitulation, review, *summarium*, summary, summation

SYNTHETIC, adjective artificial, counterfeit, ersatz, factitious, illegitimate, man-made, manufactured, mock, not genuine, not natural, pretended, pseudo, quasi, spurious, unnatural

SYSTEM, noun arrangement, *artificium*, classification, design, *formula*, logical process, manner, means, method, mode of management, operation, order, orderliness, orderly combination, organization, pattern, plan, policy, practice, procedure, process, program, recipe, regime, regimen, regularity, routine, scheme, settled procedure, state of order, strategy, technique, way

ASSOCIATED CONCEPTS: commercial system, governmental system, judicial system, legal system, retirement system

SYSTEMATIC, adjective according to rule, *accuratus*, arranged, businesslike, classified, disciplined, exact, habitual, in order, methodical, ordered, orderly, organized, precise, regular, regulated, routine, standardized, systematical, thorough, thoroughgoing, under control, uniform, well-ordered, well-organized, well-regulated

TABULATE, noun alphabetize, allocate, arrange, assign places to, catalogue, chart, chronicle, codify, coordinate, docket, enumerate, file, grade, graduate, group, index, inventory, itemize, list, marshal, methodize, organize, rank, register, sort, systematize

TACIT, adjective allusive, assumed, connoted, implicit, implied, indicated, inferential, inferred, not openly expressed, silent, suggested, symbolized, *tacitus*, taken for granted, undeclared, understood, unexpressed, unmentioned, unpronounced, unsaid, unspoken, unstated, untold, unvoiced, wordless

ASSOCIATED CONCEPTS: tacit approval, tacit consent

TACITURN, adjective brusque, close, closemouthed, curt, dumb, guarded, habitually silent, inarticulate, laconic, mum, mute, pauciloquent, quiet, reserved, restrained, reticent, secretive, silent, sparing of words, speechless, *taciturnus*, uncommunicative, ungarrulous, unloquacious, unsociable, untalkative, unvocal, withdrawn

TACTICAL, adjective aimed, artful, *astutus*, blueprinted, calculated, *cautus*, considered, contrived, crafty, cunning, deliberate, designed, devised, diplomatic, diplomatical, engineered, intended, intriguing, knowing, maneuvering, organized, planned, plotted, politic, prepared, *prudens*, purposed, purposeful, skillful, strategic, strategical, studied, systematized, weighed, well-planned, well-thought-out

TACTICS, noun artifice, contrivance, course of action, devices, direction, evolution, expedients, intrigue, machination, maneuvering, manipulation, manner, mode of procedure, *modus operandi*, policy, politics, practice, procedure, process, scheme, stratagem, strategy, temporizing

TAINT (Contaminate), verb adulterate, alloy, befoul, besmirch, blemish, blight, *contaminare*, decay, defile, degrade, dirty, disease, envenom, foul, *imbuere*, infect, make noxious, make putrid, poison, pollute, putrefy, render impure, rot, soil, spoil, sully

ASSOCIATED CONCEPTS: tainted evidence

TAINT (Corrupt), verb cause to be dishonest, debase, debauch, defile, degenerate, demoralize, deprave, despoil, destroy the integrity of, lower morally, misuse, pervert, suborn, tarnish, violate, vitiate

TAINTED (Contaminated), adjective adulterated, befouled, blighted, defiled, dirtied, dirty, diseased, envenomed, foul, impaired, impure, infected, noxious, poisoned, polluted, putrefied, putrid, rancid, rotten, smirched, soiled, spoiled, stained, sullied, unclean

ASSOCIATED CONCEPTS: Fruit of the Poisonous Tree Doctrine, tainted evidence

TAINTED (Corrupted), adjective abandoned, criminal, debased, debauched, degenerate, degraded, demoralized, depraved, dishonest, dissolute, evil, immoral, low, perverted, profligate, reprobate, rotten, shameless, vicious, vitiated, warped, wicked

TAKE (Acquire), verb adopt, attach, carry, derive, endure, excise, gain, get, impound, impress, obtain, preempt, procure, profit, reap, secure, sequester

ASSOCIATED CONCEPTS: take effect, take over

TAKE (Deceive), verb betray, cheat, cozen, defraud, dupe, fool, gull, lead astray, mislead, victimize

TAKE (Seize), verb apprehend, appropriate, arrogate, capture, confiscate, embezzle, extort, grab, hijack, impound, loot, pilfer, plunder, purloin, usurp

ASSOCIATED CONCEPTS: burglary, grand larceny, grand theft, larceny, take a case from the jury, trespassing

TAKE *(Understand)*, *verb* adopt, catch on, estimate, get the meaning of, grasp the meaning, hold as, set down as account as, take for, view as

TAKE ISSUE WITH, *verb* be against, be antagonistic to, be antipathetic to, be at odds with, be contra to, be contrary to, be different to, be hostile to, be inimical to, be opposed to, be repugnant to, challenge, clash, conflict with, contradict, oppose, render inopportune
ASSOCIATED CONCEPTS: take issue with the opportunity

TAKE POSSESSION OF, *verb* accumulate, achieve, acquire, appropriate, attain, capture, collect, earn, elicit, gain, gain possession of, gather, get, harvest, obtain, possess, procure, realize, receive, recover, secure, seize, take, take over
ASSOCIATED CONCEPTS: devices and bequests under a will, laws of intestacy

TAKE THE NECESSARY MEASURE, *verb* accomplish, achieve, act, attain, be instrumental, bring to fruition, conclude, decide, determine, discharge, effectuate, enforce, execute, find a method, find the means, find the way, follow through, fulfill, gain, gain results, get, obtain, perform, produce, realize
ASSOCIATED CONCEPTS: attach, contempt, execution, filing a judgment, filing an appeal, order of the court

TAKEOVER, *noun* acquirement of a corporation, acquisition, acquisition of a company, appropriation, assumption of control over management, assumption of ownership, impropriation, obtainment, procurement, procurement of a business, purchase, transference
Generally: acquirement, assumption, attainment, obtainment, possession, procuration, securement
ASSOCIATED CONCEPTS: corporate raider, corporate takeover, friendly takeover, hostile takeover, tender offer, white knight

TAKEOVER, *verb* arrogate, assume, command, seize, take command, take charge, take possession, usurp

TAKING, *noun* abduction, *acceptio,* acquisition, ademption, appropriation, capture, confiscation, deprivation, dispossession, distraint, divestment, expropriation, foreclosure, impoundage, impoundment, *occupatio,* preemption, seizure, sequestration
ASSOCIATED CONCEPTS: attachment, eminent domain

TALENT, *noun* ability, adequacy, caliber, capability, capacity, competence, competency, creative thought, creativity, efficacy, efficiency, endowment, facility, faculty, fitness, flair, forte, genius, gift, high caliber, inspiration, long suit, proficiency, qualification, strength, strong point, strong suit, sufficiency, susceptibility

TALK, *verb* advise, answer, articulate, carry on a conversation, comment on, communicate with, confer with, consult with, debate, discuss, dissertate, exchange ideas, exchange views, express, have dialogue, have verbal intercourse with, impart thoughts, inform, interview, make a speech, make a statement, parley, recite, recount, relate, relate ideas, relay ideas, say, speak with, state, utter
ASSOCIATED CONCEPTS: freedom of speech, wiretaps

TAMPER, *verb* alter, change, convert, corrupt, debase, hinder, interfere, intermeddle, intervene, manipulate, meddle
ASSOCIATED CONCEPTS: tamper with a jury, tamper with evidence

TANGENTIAL, *adjective* akin, associated, attendant, connected, correlated, dependent on, digressive, excursive, extraneous, germane, incidental, interrelated, nonessential, pertinent, related, subordinate, tangent, touching

TANGIBLE, *adjective* actual, certain, clear-cut, concrete, corporal, corporeal, definite, discernible by touch, embodied, evident, manifest, material, not elusive, not vague, obvious, palpable, perceivable, perceptible, physical, plain, positive, real, solid, somatic, substantial, substantive, tactile, tactual, touchable, *tractabilis,* verifiable, visible, well-defined
ASSOCIATED CONCEPTS: tangible object, tangible property, tangible value

TANTAMOUNT, *adjective* analogous, comparable, corresponding to, ditto, equal, equivalent, identical, parallel, similar, synonymous

TARGET, *noun* aim, ambition, aspiration, butt, center, contemplation, design, desired object, destination, end, goal, hope, intention, mark, motive, object, objective, plan, point

TARIFF *(Bill)*, *noun* account, itemized account, list, list of items, money's worth, quoted price, price list, scale of prices, table of charges

TARIFF *(Duties)*, *noun* assessment, duty, excise, impost, levy, schedule of duties, tax

TARNISH, *verb* asperse, befoul, blacken, blemish, blot, brand, cloud, contaminate, corrode, darken, deface, defame, degrade, denigrate, desecrate, dim, dirty, discolor, discredit, disgrace, dishonor, dull, fade, foul, *inquinare,* lose luster, maculate, pollute, shame, slander, slur, smear, smirch, smudge, soil, spot, stain, stigmatize, sully, taint, vilify
ASSOCIATED CONCEPTS: defamation

TARTUFFISH, *adjective* affected, dissembling, false, feigned, hypocritical, insincere, pious, pretended, puritanical, sanctimonious, two-faced

TASK, *noun* act, activity, assigned work, assignment, burden, charge, chore, concern, duty, employment, endeavor, engagement, enterprise, function, job, labor, mission, obligation, operation, practice, project, pursuit, role, specialty, trade, undertaking, venture, work

TAUTOLOGY, *noun* battology, duplication, loquacity, pleonasm, profuseness, redundancy, repetition, superfluousness, surfeit, verbiage, verbosity

TAWDRY, *adjective* baroque, bedizened, blatant, brummagem, catchpenny, cheap, common, crass, crude, flashy, garish, gaudy, glaring, glittering, inelegant, loud, meretricious, ostentatious, pretentious, shoddy, showy, sleazy, tasteless, tinsel, vulgar

TAX, *noun* assessment, capitation, charge, dues, duty, exaction, exactment, excise, imposition, impost, levy, pollage, *portorium,* scot, tariff, taxation, tithe, toll, tribute, *vectigal*
ASSOCIATED CONCEPTS: action for taxes, *ad valorem tax,* apportionment of taxes, back taxes, collection of taxes, current tax, delinquent tax, direct tax, discriminatory tax, double taxation, estate tax, evasion of taxation, excess profits tax, excessive tax, excise tax, federal estate tax, federal taxes, franchise tax, general tax, graduated tax, income tax, indirect tax, inheritance tax, land tax, levy a tax, personal

tax, power of taxation, power to tax, progressive tax, property tax, proportional tax, regulatory tax, retroactive tax, sales tax, tax anticipation note, tax assessor, tax deed, tax district, tax lien, tax roll, tax sale, tax title, tax warrants, taxpayer, transfer tax, withholding taxes

TAX *(Levy)*, *verb*   assess, collect, exact, lay a duty, require

TAX *(Overwork)*, *verb*   burden, cumber, debilitate, deplete, deprive of strength, disable, drain, encumber, enervate, exact, fatigue, load, make excessive demands, oppress, overexercise, overexert, overfatigue, overload, overstrain, overtire, overuse, push too far, require, saddle with, strain, task, tire out, tyrannize, use hard, weaken, wear down, wear out, weary, weigh down

TEACH, *verb*   advise, apprise, brief, catechize, communicate, convey, counsel, demonstrate, direct, disabuse, disseminate, edify, educate, elucidate, enlarge the mind, enlighten, explain, expound, give lessons to, guide, imbue, impart, impart knowledge, implant, inculcate, indoctrinate, inform, instill, instruct, lecture, moralize, nurture, persuade, preach, school, sermonize, show, tell, train, tutor

TECHNICAL, *adjective*   abstruse, difficult to understand, highly specialized, highly specific, industrial, mechanical, occupational, professional, scientific, special, specialized, specific, trained, vocational

TECHNICALITY, *noun*   aspect, detail, distinctive feature, fact, feature, fine point, inessentiality, item, method, minor point, minutiae, nuance, particular, particularity, peculiarity, petty detail, point, precept, rule, singularity, special point, speciality, specific, specification, subtlety, technical term, term, trifle, triviality

TECHNIQUE *(Method)*, *noun*   aptitude, art, deftness, dexterity, endowment, execution, felicity, finesse, flair, form, forte, genius for, gift, ingenuity, knack, know-how, mastery, proficiency, science, skillfulness, touch

TECHNIQUE *(Technical skill)*, *noun*   artistry, avenue, bravura, discretion, expedient, facility, skill, technology, virtuosity

TECHNOLOGY, *noun*   best technical knowledge, know-how, latest scientific knowledge, scientific advancement, state of the art, state of the industry, updated scientific knowledge *Generally:* application, development, latest products, modern science, science

TELL, *verb*   acquaint, advise, annunciate, apprise, betray, blurt out, come out with, communicate, confess, constrain, convey, declare, depict, detail, direct, disclose, distinguish, divulge, enumerate, enunciate, express, give an account of, give vent to, have a strong effect, impart, influence, inform, instruct, let on, make known, mention, narrate, notify, order, proclaim, profess, pronounce, publish, recite, record, recount, register, relate, remark, report, reveal, signify, speak, talk, tell a story
ASSOCIATED CONCEPTS: Fifth Amendment Rights, informant

TEMERITY, *noun*   audacity, boldness, carelessness, daring, effrontery, foolhardiness, foolishness, gall, hastiness, heedlessness, impetuosity, improvidence, imprudence, impudence, incautiousness, inconsiderateness, indiscretion, injudiciousness, nerve, overconfidence, presumptuousness, procacity, rashness, recklessness, rudeness,

shamelessness, *temeritas,* thoughtlessness, unthoughtfulness, venturesomeness, want of caution

TEMPERAMENT, *noun*   aptitude, attitude, carriage, character, composition, constitution, demeanor, disposition, ethos, makeup, mentality, nature, patience, personality, qualities, structure, style, tendency, tenor, way

TEMPERANCE, *noun*   abnegation, abstemiousness, abstention, abstinence, calmness, control, forbearance, frugality, indulgence, moderateness, *moderatio,* moderation, patience, prohibition, prudence, restraint, self-control, self-denial, self-restraint, soberness, sobriety, sparing use, teetotalism, *temperantia,* temperateness, tolerance, toleration, unexcessiveness

TEMPERED, *adjective*   adapted, adjusted, altered, changed, corrected, indurate, indurated, moderated, modified, recast, reconstructed, remolded, reshaped, revised, transformed, treated

TEMPESTUOUS, *adjective*   angry, disgusted, enraged, frantic, frenzied, fuming, furious, hostile, inflamed, infuriated, ireful, livid, offended, offensive, outraged, raging, storming, tumultuous, turbulent

TEMPORARY, *adjective*   acting, *ad tempus,* brief, changeable, deciduous, elusive, ephemeral, evanescent, fleeting, fugacious, fugitive, impermanent, interim, limited, makeshift, momentary, monohemerous, nondurable, passing, perishable, provisional, shifting, short-lived, stopgap, temporal, transient, transitional, transitive, transitory, unenduring, unstable, volatile
ASSOCIATED CONCEPTS: temporary restraining order

TENABLE, *adjective*   acceptable, befitting, believable, capable of being maintained, defendable, defensible, dependable, deserving, fitting, immune, imperdible, impregnable, inviolable, invulnerable, justifiable, legitimate, logical, maintainable, plausible, proper, rational, reasonable, reliable, strong, supportable, trustworthy, unassailable, unattackable, unchallengeable, unquestionable, vindicable, warrantable, well-founded, well-grounded

TENACITY, *noun*   ability to pursue, adhesiveness, backbone, cohesiveness, constancy, courage, determination, diligence, doggedness, endurance, firmness, grip, grit, immovability, indefatigability, intransigence, iron will, obduracy, obstinacy, perseverance, persistence, persistency, *pertinacia,* pertinaciousness, pertinacity, recalcitrance, re*soluteness,* resolution, stamina, steadfastness, strength, stubbornness, tenaciousness, *tenacitas,* toughness, unyieldingness, will

TENANCY, *noun*   holding, holding by title, leasing, occupancy, occupation, ownership, possession, possessorship, proprietorship, renting, residency, temporary possession, tenure
ASSOCIATED CONCEPTS: joint tenancy, month to month tenancy, tenancy at sufferance, tenancy at will, tenancy by the entirety, tenancy for years, tenancy in common

TENANT, *noun*   border, *conductor,* dweller, holder, householder, *incola,* inhabitant, *inquilinus,* landholder, landowner, leaseholder, lessee, lodger, occupant, occupier, one holding land of another, one occupying another's land, one occupying real property, one using real property, owner, paying guest, possessor, proprietor, rent payer, renter, resident

ASSOCIATED CONCEPTS: disorderly tenant, eviction, holdover tenant, joint tenant, life tenant, objectionable tenant, subtenant, tenant at sufferance, tenant at will, tenant by the entirety, tenant for a fixed term, tenant from month to month, tenant in common, tenant per autre vie

TENDENCY, *noun* aptitude, aptness, bearing, bent, bias, character, direction, disposition, facility, gift, gravitation, idiosyncrasy, *inclinatio,* inclination, instinct, leaning, natural disposition, nature, partiality, penchant, predisposition, prejudice, *proclivitas,* proclivity, proneness, propensity, slant, susceptibility, temperament, trend, turn, twist, warp

TENDER, *verb* advance, *deferre,* deliver, extend, furnish, give, grant, hold out, issue, lay before, offer, pay, present, present for payment, proffer, propose, put forward, render, submit, urge upon, volunteer
ASSOCIATED CONCEPTS: tender payment, tender performance
FOREIGN PHRASES: *Reprobata pecunia liberat solventem.* Money refused releases the debtor.

TENDER OFFER, *noun* broad offer, broad request to purchase, broad solicitation, collective offer, offer to purchase a large number of shares, offer to purchase a large number of stock shares, offer to purchase a significant number of securities in a corporation, public offer, public offer to buy stock, takeover bid

TENOR, *noun* cast, character, content, course, cut, direction, drift, *exemplum,* feeling, form, gist, idea, import, manner, meaning, mode, mood, nature, purport, sense, *sententia,* significance, signification, spirit, stamp, subject matter, tendency, tone, trend, vein

TENTATIVE, *adjective* cautious, conditional, contingent, dependent, experimental, exploratory, groping, interim, probationary, probative, proposed, provisional, provisory, questionable, speculative, temporary, trial, undecided, unsettled
ASSOCIATED CONCEPTS: tentative agreement

TENUOUS, *adjective* airy, attenuated, delicate, diminutive, fine, flimsy, illusory, inconsequential, infinitesimal, insignificant, little, miniature, minute, narrow, paltry, petty, scant, slender, slight, small, thin, tiny, trifling, trivial, unimportant, unsubstantial

TENURE, *noun* duration, holding, occupancy, occupation, period, *possessio, possidere,* regime, term
ASSOCIATED CONCEPTS: tenure in office
FOREIGN PHRASES: *Tenura est pactio contra communem feudi naturam ac rationem, in contractu interposita.* Tenure is a compact contrary to the common nature and reason of the fee, put into a contract.

TERGIVERSATE, *verb* apostatize, avoid, be uncertain, be unsure, change one's mind, change sides, desert, dodge, equivocate, evade, hedge, quibble, recant, renege, renounce, shift, straddle, turn renegade, use evasions, use subterfuge, vacillate

TERM (*Duration*), *noun* age, course, era, incumbency, interval, lifetime, period, reign, season, session, span, *spatium temporis,* spell, stage, tenancy, tenure, time
ASSOCIATED CONCEPTS: term for years, term insurance, term of a lease, term of confinement, term of court, term of office
FOREIGN PHRASES: *Terminus annorum certus debet esse et determinatus.* A term of years ought to be certain and determinate.

TERM (*Expression*), *noun* appellation, appellative, cognomen, denomination, designation, epithet, heading, idiom, locution, name, phrase, title, verbalism, *verbum,* vocable, *vocabulum,* word
ASSOCIATED CONCEPTS: definition of terms

TERM (*Provision*), *noun* agreement, arrangement, article of agreement, bargain, clause, *condicio,* condition, covenant, item, *lex,* limitation, particular, point, proviso, qualification, specification, stipulation, understanding
ASSOCIATED CONCEPTS: terms and conditions of a contract, terms of a policy, terms of payment, terms of sale

TERMINABLE, *adjective* capable of being bounded, capable of being completed, capable of being concluded, capable of being conditioned, capable of being ended, capable of being fixed, capable of being limited, capable of being made definite, conditional, defeasible, finite, limitable
ASSOCIATED CONCEPTS: terminable at will, terminable fee, terminable interest, terminable trust, terminable upon a condition subsequent

TERMINALLY ILL, *adjective* incurable, *in extremis,* in final stages, *in terminus,* near an end, seriously ill, terminally diseased

TERMINATE, *verb* abolish, annul, bring to an end, bring to completion, cancel, cease, close, come to an end, complete, conclude, culminate, die, discontinue, drop, eliminate, end, expire, finish, fire from employment, halt, let go, put an end to, release, run out, stop, wind up
ASSOCIATED CONCEPTS: notice to terminate, terminate a contract, terminate a lease, terminate an action, terminate an agreement, terminate employment

TERMINATION, *noun* abatement, adjournment, cancellation, climax, close, completion, conclusion, confine, consequence, consummation, culmination, denouement, destination, discharge, discontinuance, effect, end, ending, end of the matter, end result, epilogue, expiration, extremity, finale, finality, finish, lapse, limit, outcome, pay-off, result, sequel, stoppage, terminal, upshot, windup
ASSOCIATED CONCEPTS: termination of a contract, termination of employment, termination of parental rights

TERRIBLE, *adjective* abhorrent, abominable, appalling, atrocious, contemptible, deplorable, despicable, detestable, dreadful, foul, frightening, frightful, ghastly, grisly, gruesome, heinous, hideous, horrendous, horrid, horrifying, macabre, monstrous, obnoxious, odious, offensive, outrageous, pathetic, pitiful, regrettable, repellent, reprehensible, repulsive, revolting, serious, severe, shameful, shocking, terrifying, vile

TERRIFIC, *adjective* celebrated, colossal, commanding, distinguished, enormous, esteemed, exalted, excellent, exceptional, expert, extraordinary, far-reaching, first-rate, gigantic, glorious, grand, great, high-minded, illustrious, immense, incredible, incredible performances, incredible results, leading, lofty, major, marvelous, massive, momentous, monstrous, notable, noted, outrageous, outstanding, paramount, perfect, potent, powerful, preeminent, prime, profound, remarkable, renowned, skillful, solid, splendid, strong, superior, supreme, vast, widely remarkable results, wonderful

TERRORISM, *noun* acts by subversives, acts of annihilation, criminal act, demolition, destruction, extermination, fanaticism, revolution, terrorist act, tyranny

TERRORIST, noun abductor, active combatant in the foreign theater of conflict, anarchist, assailant, assassin, attacker, combatant, demoniac force, destroyer, enemy alien, enemy combatant, enemy force, enemy operation, faction at war, fanatic, foreign assailant, foreign force, hostile force, insurgent, killer, mercenary, militant, murderer, opponent, radical, rebel, revolutionary, revolutionist, revolutionizer, savage, subversive force

ASSOCIATED CONCEPTS: Department of Homeland Security, enemy combatant, military tribunals, terrorist attacks, terrorist demands, terrorist groups, terrorist incidents, terrorist networks, terrorist organizations

TERRORIST ACTIVITY, verb anarchist's act, assassin's plot, criminal act, destroyer's action, enemy deed, enemy pursuits, enemy undertakings, fanatical act, fanatical action, foreign combatant's efforts, insurgent's acts, insurgent's plans, operations of combatants, radical efforts, rebel cell's plot, revolutionary plot, subversive plans

ASSOCIATED CONCEPTS: enemy combatants, military tribunals, terrorist cells, U.S. Patriot Act, weapons of mass destruction

TERRITORY, noun *ager,* area, beat, circuit, clime, demesne, district, division, domain, dominion, environs, expanse, field, land, latitude, locale, place, precinct, property, province, quarter, realm, *regio,* region, scene, section, terrain, tract, zone

TEST, noun analysis, audit, check, checkup, effort, endeavor, examination, experience, experiment, exploration, inquest, inquiry, inquisition, inspection, interrogation, investigation, observation, questioning, quiz, research, review, scrutiny, search, study, survey, trial, try, tryout

ASSOCIATED CONCEPTS: blood test, clear and present danger test, compelling state interest test, prudent man test, right from wrong test, substantial evidence test

TESTAMENT, noun agreement, binding agreement, contract, covenant, engagement, expression of conviction, formal declaration, legal will, promise, solemn agreement, solemn promise, testamentary declaration, testamentary decree, *testamentum,* will, writing

ASSOCIATED CONCEPTS: codicil, last will and testament, testamentary capacity, testamentary devise, testamentary trust

FOREIGN PHRASES: *Omne testamentum morte consummatum est.* Every will or testament is consummated by death.

TESTAMENTARY, adjective by way of a will, bequeathed by will, contained in a will, devised by will, distributed by will, given by testament, hereditary, patrimonial, set forth in a will, transferred by a legacy, transferred by bequest, transferred by devise

ASSOCIATED CONCEPTS: letters testamentary, testamentary assets, testamentary capacity, testamentary condition, testamentary devise, testamentary disposition, testamentary gifts, testamentary guardian, testamentary guardianship, testamentary instrument, testamentary intent, testamentary inventory, testamentary power, testamentary succession, testamentary trust, testamentary trustee

TESTATE, adjective having left a will, having written a testament, relating to a will, with a valid will, with an executed will

ASSOCIATED CONCEPTS: intestate succession

TESTIFY, verb acknowledge openly, affirm, affirm under oath, allege, assert, asseverate, attest, aver, avow, be sworn, bear witness, declare, depone, depose, establish, express, give evidence, give one's word, indicate, make solemn declaration, profess, prove, show, state, state a fact, state a truth, swear, take one's oath, take the stand, *testari, testificari,* verify

ASSOCIATED CONCEPTS: compulsion to testify, privilege against self-incrimination, testify in one's own defense, testify under oath

TESTIMONY, noun affidavit, affirmation, assertion, asseveration, attestation, averment, avowal, declaration, declaration of facts, deposition, disclosure, evidence, evidence by a competent witness, evidence in support of, expression, profession, proof, proof by a witness, revelation, statement, statement of facts, *testimonium*

ASSOCIATED CONCEPTS: circumstantial testimony, compelled testimony, corroborative testimony, cross-examination, deposition, direct examination, expert testimony, impeachment of testimony, incompetent testimony, involuntary testimony, oral testimony, perjured testimony, preservation of testimony, testimony under oath

THEFT, noun burglary, embezzlement, felonious taking, filchery, fraudulent taking, *furtum,* larceny, looting, misappropriation, peculation, pilferage, pilfering, purloining, purloinment, robbery, stealing, swindling, thievery, wrongful taking

ASSOCIATED CONCEPTS: theft of services

FOREIGN PHRASES: *Contrectatio rei alienae animo furando, est furtum.* The touching or removing of another's property, with an intention of stealing, is theft.

THEORETICAL, adjective abstract, academic, assumed, conjectural, *doctrina,* doctrinaire, hypothetical, ideational, ideative, ideological, impractical, open to proof, philosophical, postulated, postulatory, presumed, presumptive, pure, *ratio,* speculative, speculatory, stated as a premise, supposable, suppositional, suppositive, unapplied, unproved, unproven, unsubstantiated, visionary

THEORY, noun assumption, belief, conjecture, *doctrina,* doctrine, dogma, guesswork, hypothesis, ideology, opinion, philosophy, postulate, presupposition, proposition, *ratio,* speculation, supposition, surmise, thesis, thought, untested opinion, view

ASSOCIATED CONCEPTS: conflicts of law theory, contract theory, inconsistent theories, rescue theory, theory of the case

THERE, adverb at a distance, at that established place, at that location, at that place, at that point, beyond, exactly at that place, exactly at that spot, in that place, in that respect, in that spot, in the distance, into that place, just there, not here, over there, precisely at that place, precisely at that point, precisely at that spot, to or toward that point

THEREBY, adverb by means of, by use of, by virtue of, in consequence of, per, through, through the medium of, whereby, with the aid of

THEREAFTER, adverb after, afterwards, at a later period, from that time, later, next, since, subsequently

THERETOFORE, adverb before, earlier, formerly, heretofore, previous to, prior to

THESIS, noun affirmation, argument, belief, claim, conjecture, debatable issue, debatable point, doctrine, dogma, hypothesis, issue, moot point, position, postulate, postulation, premise, principle, problem, proposition, question, speculation, stand, subject, supposition, tenet, theme, theory, topic, tract

THIEF, noun bandit, contrabandist, criminal, defalcator, defaulter, defrauder, depredator, embezzler, lawbreaker, lifter, marauder, outlaw, peculator, pilferer, pillager, pirate, purloiner, robber, stealer, swindler
ASSOCIATED CONCEPTS: burglary, larceny, robbery

THINK, verb anticipate, apprehend, believe, be of the opinion, cerebrate, cogitate, compass, conceive, conclude, consider, contemplate, contrive, deduce, deduct, deem, deliberate, determine, digest, dwell intently upon, envisage, envision, exercise the mind, expect, form ideas, guess, have the idea, hypothesize, ideate, imagine, intellectualize, judge, mean, meditate, mentalize, mull over, opine, philosophize, picture, plan, plot, ponder, presume, presuppose, propose, rationalize, reason, recall, reckon, recollect, reflect, reminisce, ruminate, speculate, surmise, theorize

THOROUGH, adjective absolute, accurate, all-inclusive, assiduous, careful, complete, comprehensive, consummate, definitive, detailed, diligent, downright, entire, exhaustive, extensive, full, fully executed, inclusive, intensive, meticulous, painstaking, perfect, plenary, sheer, sound, sweeping, systematic, thoroughgoing, total, trustworthy, unabridged, uncompromising, unmitigated, unqualified, utter, zealous

THOUGHT (Concept), noun belief, conception, credo, creed, hint, idea, insight, notion, opinion, perspective, point, proposal, rationale, suggestion, tenet, view

THOUGHT (Concern), noun attentiveness, care, impression, philosophy, reaction, regard, sentiment, solicitousness, thoughtfulness

THOUGHT (Thinking), noun absorption, abstraction, application, apprehension, association of ideas, belief, brainwork, cerebration, cogitation, concept, conception, consciousness, consideration, contemplation, deliberation, fancy, introversion, meditation, mental process, perception, perspective, ratiocination, reason, recollection, reflection, remark, retrospection, reverie, rumination, self-communing, speculation, study, suggestion, theory, view

THOUGHTLESS, adjective absent-minded, abstracted, blank, blockish, careless, casual, dazed, disregardful, distracted, distrait, dull, flighty, foolhardy, giddy, harebrained, headlong, heedless, ill-advised, improvident, *imprudens,* imprudent, impulsive, inadvertent, inane, inattentive, incogitant, inconsiderate, *inconsultus,* indelicate, indifferent, indiscreet, insensate, irrational, irresponsible, neglectful, *neglegens,* negligent, precipitate, rash, reckless, regardless, remiss, scatterbrained, selfish, stupid, tactless, unaccommodating, unconcerned, unmindful, unobliging, unobservant, unreasoning, unreflecting, unreflective, unthinking, unthoughtful, unwatchful, vacant, vacuous, without consideration

THRALL, noun bondage, captivity, confinement, custody, durance, enslavement, enthrallment, helotry, oppression, servitude, *servitus,* slavery, subjection, subjugation, submission, thralldom, tyranny, vassalage, yoke

THREAT, noun alarm, augury, auspice, commination, danger, *denuntiatio,* foreboding, fulmination, hazard, imminence, impendence, impendency, insecurity, intimidation, jeopardy, menace, *minae,* omen, peril, portent, presage, risk, sign, warning
ASSOCIATED CONCEPTS: coercion

FOREIGN PHRASES: ***Non videtur consensum retinuisse si quis ex praescripto minantis aliquid immutavit.*** He does not appear to have retained consent, who has changed anything at the command of a threatening party.

THREATEN, verb admonish, augur, be near at hand, blackmail, bode, browbeat, coerce, *comminari,* comminate, forebode, foreshadow, forewarn, frighten, fulminate, hector, intimidate, menace, portend, presage, terrorize, use threats

THRESHOLD (Commencement), noun beginning, foreword, inception, onset, outbreak, overture, preamble, prelude, prologue, start

THRESHOLD (Entrance), noun door, entrance way, entry, gateway, sill

THRESHOLD (Verge), noun brink, edge
ASSOCIATED CONCEPTS: monetary threshold

THROUGH, adjective completed, concluded, decided, done, done with, ended, finished, set at rest, settled, terminated

THROUGH (By means of), adverb by means of, by the hand of, by way of, using, using the help of

THROUGH (From beginning to end), adverb all along, all the way, by way of, via

THROUGH (Until now), adverb to this day

THROUGHOUT (All over), adverb all over, every bit, extensively, from beginning to end, from first to last, from the ground up, from the word go, inside and out, over all, to the end

THROUGHOUT (During), adverb for the duration, for the period of, in the course of, until the conclusion of

THWART, verb avert, baffle, balk, bar, blight, bring to naught, check, contravene, counteract, countermine, counterwork, cripple, cross, damp, debar, defeat, foil, forestall, frustrate, hamper, hinder, impede, inhibit, intercept, interfere, interrupt, nip, obstruct, oppose, outmaneuver, override, preclude, prevent, restrain, retard, ruin, spoil, stave off, stifle, stop, stultify, stymie, traverse, turn aside, undermine, ward off

TIDE TURNING, verb about-face, adoption, afterthoughts, backsliding, change like a chameleon, change of heart, change of mind, conversion, defection, divergence, diversion, dramatically opposed stance, flip-flop, 180-degree about-face, qualification, realignment, regression, restructuring, reversal, reversion, temporizer, tergiversation, turnabout
ASSOCIATED CONCEPTS: flip-flop on a political stance

TIES, noun adherences, adhesions, attachments, bands, bonds, chains, commitments, connections, engagements, interconnections, knots, liaisons, links, pledges, unions, vincula

TIME, noun age, chronology, duration, end of the matter, era, extent, interlude, interim, interval, period, tenancy, tenure, term
ASSOCIATED CONCEPTS: time being of the essence, time certificate, time deposit, time fixed by agreement, time of absence, time of adjudication, time of bankruptcy, time of injury, time of memory, time option, time policy, time studies, timetables

TIMELINESS, *noun* appropriateness, aptness, auspiciousness, climacteric, compliance, convenient time, felicitousness, fitness, matureness, opportuneness, proper time, seasonableness, suitability, suitable time, time, within appropriate time provided
ASSOCIATED CONCEPTS: laches, notice, statute of limitations

TIP *(Clue), **noun*** advice, aviso, communication, confidential information, cue, enlightenment, forewarning, guidance, head, hint, indication, inside information, insinuation, instruction, intimation, key, lead, mention, point, pointer, prenotification, recommendation, report, suggestion, warning, whisper

TIP *(Gratuity), **noun*** award, benefaction, bestowment, bonus, compensation, consideration, contribution, donation, donative, gift, guerdon, meed, offering, payment, perquisite, reward
ASSOCIATED CONCEPTS: unreported income

TITLE *(Designation), **noun*** appellation, caption, denomination, heading, inscription, label, name, rubric, sign, signification, superscription, tag
ASSOCIATED CONCEPTS: title of statute

TITLE *(Division), **noun*** article, branch, chapter, clause, item, paragraph, part, portion, provision, section, statement, term

TITLE *(Position), **noun*** employment, office, post, rank, situation, station, status

TITLE *(Right), **noun*** authority, authorization, claim, deed, domain, droit, entitlement, equity, interest, legal title, ownership, permission, possession, power, prerogative, prescription, proprietorship, right, sanction, stake, tenure, vested interest
ASSOCIATED CONCEPTS: absolute title, abstract of title, acquisition of title, apparent title, chain of title, claim of title, clear title, cloud on title, color of title, defeasible title, disparagement of title, documents of title, equitable title, failure of title, good title, imperfect title, marketable title, merchantable title, nominal title, paramount title, perfection of title, prima facie title, quieting title, reservation of title, superior title, title by adverse possession, title by deeds, title by prescription, title insurance, title search, title to property, unmarketable title, warranty of title, worthier title
FOREIGN PHRASES: *Praescriptio est titulus ex usu et tempore substantiam capiens ab auctoritate legis.* Prescription is a title by authority of law, deriving its force from use and time. ***A piratis et latronibus capta dominum non mutant.*** Things captured by pirates and robbers do not change title.

TOKEN, *noun* augury, auspice, chip, device, emblem, evidence, expression, favor, figurehead, indicant, indicator, keepsake, manifestation, memento, omen, portent, proof, relic, remembrance, sign, souvenir, symbol

TOLERANCE, *noun* abiding, ability to bear, ability to endure, ability to tolerate, ability to withstand, allowance, bravery, broad-mindedness, capacity to endure, capacity to stand suffering, capacity to take pain, charter, compassion, constancy, courage, durability, endurance, fortitude, franchise, freedom, freedom from bigotry, freedom from prejudice, good will, humanity, immunity, immunization, impunity, indulgence, *indulgentia*, lack of bias, liberality, license, patience, perseverance, persistence, resignation, stamina, stoicism, strength, submission, sufferance, sustainment, sympathy, *tolerantia*, toleration, understanding

TOLERATE, *verb* abide, accept, acquiesce, allow, be lenient, bear, bear with, brook, carry on, consent, endure, forbear, indulge, make the best of, oblige, permit, put up with, receive, sanction, stand, stomach, submit to, suffer, swallow, take patiently, *tolerare*, undergo

TOLL *(Effect), **noun*** casualties, consequence, cost, damage, distress, effect, exaction, forfeit, grievous price, loss, payment, result, ruinous price, setback, suffering

TOLL *(Tax), **noun*** assessment, charge, exaction, excise, fare, fee, impost, levy, payment, *portorium*, tithe, vectigal
ASSOCIATED CONCEPTS: collection of tolls, toll bridges, toll roads

TOLL *(Exact payment), **verb*** collect payment, exact tribute, extort, levy, raise taxes, tax

TOLL *(Stop), **verb*** arrest, block, check, cut off, embar, estop, frustrate, halt, hinder, hold back, impede, inhibit, interrupt, limit, obstruct, put a stop to, restrain, restrict, stay, suspend, thwart
ASSOCIATED CONCEPTS: toll a statute of limitations

TOOL, *noun* agent, apparatus, channel, contrivance, device, implement, instrument, machine, means, mechanism, medium, recourse, resource, utensil, vehicle

TOP-NOTCH, *adjective* altissimo, apical, best, capital, chief, critical, crowning, crucial, crying, deep, desperate, earnest, essential, far-reaching, forcible, gravest, head, heavy, highest, intense, intensified, maximal, maximum, momentous, most, of great force, of great number, overmost, paramount, potent, preeminent, pressing, principal, serious, sharp, strong, superlative, supreme, telling, tiptop, top, topmost, urgent, vigorous, violent, vital, weighty, zenithal
ASSOCIATED CONCEPTS: highest degree of care, highest proved value

TORMENT, *noun* abomination, acute distress, affliction, agony, angst, anguish, annoyance, bane, constant anxiety, convulsion, despair, distress, extreme pain, harassment, infliction, misery, oppression, pain, pique, scourge, torture, vexation

TORMENT, *verb* abuse, anguish, annoy, badger, bait, beset, besiege, chafe, crucify, discompose, distress, endanger, excruciate, harass, harrow, harry, haze, hector, ill use, inflict, irritate, lacerate, maltreat, mistreat, molest, needle, nettle, obsess, persecute, pester, plague, press, provoke, rile, taunt, tease, treat maliciously, trouble, vex

TORPID, *adjective* apathetic, benumbed, comatose, dead, disinterested, dormant, drowsy, dull, heavy, idle, impervious, inactive, inanimate, indifferent, indolent, *iners*, inert, inexcitable, insensate, insensible, languid, languorous, lazy, leaden, *lentus*, lethargic, lifeless, listless, motionless, numb, otiose, passive, phlegmatic, sedentary, sleepy, slow, sluggish, somnolent, spiritless, stagnant, static, stupefied, stuperous, stupid, supine, torpescent, torporific, unconcerned, unconscious, unfeeling

TORT, *noun* breach of legal duty, civil wrong, dereliction of duty, error, fault, invasion of a legal right, legal wrong, malfeasance, misdeed, misdoing, misfeasance, negligent act, personal wrong, private wrong, transgression, violation of a legal duty, wrong, wrongdoing, wrongful act

ASSOCIATED CONCEPTS: action founded in tort, comparative negligence, continuing tort, contributory negligence, foreseeable consequences, intentional tort, prima facie tort, proximate cause, standard of care, strict liability in tort, successive torts, tort feasor, tortious act, tortious conduct

TORTIOUS ACT, noun actionable act, criminal act, felonious act, illegitimate act, improper act, incorrect act, nefarious act, punishable act, triable act, unlawful act, wrongful act

TORTIOUS INTERFERENCE, noun encouraging a breach, infringing on another's agreement, interceding, interfering with contract, interfering with contractual commitments, interfering with contractual obligation, interfering with contractual rights, intermeddling, intermeddling with business activities, obstruction, work against anothers contractual relationship, wrongful interference with business relationships, wrongful interference with contractual relationships
ASSOCIATED CONCEPTS: employment law

TORTUOUS (Bending), **adjective** anfractuous, circuitous, complicated, conniving, contorted, convoluted, curved, curvilinear, indirect, involved, irregular, labyrinthine, mazy, meandering, roundabout, serpentine, sinuate, sinuated, sinuous, snakelike, torsional, tortile, turning, twisted, twisting, undulatory, vermicular, vermiculate, vermiculated, winding, wreathed, zigzag

TORTUOUS (Corrupt), **adjective** crafty, crooked, deceitful, devious, dishonest, dishonorable, disingenuous, fraudulent, immoral, knavish, perfidious, treacherous, unscrupulous

TOTAL, adjective absolute, aggregate, all, complete, downright, entire, full, global, gross, inclusive, integral, omnis, outright, radical, thorough, thoroughgoing, totus, undivided, universal, universus, unqualified, utter, whole, with no exception, without omission

TOTALITY, noun aggregate, aggregation, allness, collectivity, completeness, comprehensiveness, entireness, entirety, entity, everything, gross, integration, lump, mass, sum, totalness, unity, whole
ASSOCIATED CONCEPTS: totality of the circumstances

TOUGH (Difficult), **adjective** arduous, bothersome, burdensome, complex, complicated, convoluted, difficult, enigmatic, entangled, grueling, hard, hard to deal with, hard to manage, hard to understand, impenetrable, incomprehensible, insoluble, insurmountable, intractable, involved, involving obstacles, labored, laborious, mettlesome, painstaking, perplexing, problematic, puzzling, troublesome, unachievable, unapproachable

TOUGH (Durable), **adjective** built to last, enduring, fortified, lasting, long-lasting, reinforced, rugged, solid, sound, stable, steady, strong, sturdy, well-built, well-constructed, well-established, well-made

TOUGH (Strong), **adjective** firm, hard, hard to deal with, hard to manage, impenetrable, intractable, intransigent, obdurate, obstinate, perplexing, resolute, rugged, strenuous, tenacious, too hard, troublesome
ASSOCIATED CONCEPTS: tough laws

TOXIC, adjective damaging, deadly, deleterious, fatal, festering, harmful, injurious, insalubrious, lethal, malign, noxious, pestilent, pernicious, poisonous, purulent, risky, unsafe, venomous, virulent

ASSOCIATED CONCEPTS: toxic chemicals, toxic dementia, toxic ingredients, toxic psychosis, toxic torts

TOXIC TORT, noun
Generally: lethal wrongdoing, noxious injury, poison
Specifically: asbestos poisoning, environmental poisoning
ASSOCIATED CONCEPTS: asbestos, electromagnetic fields, lead paint, lead poisoning, radon

TRACE (Delineate), **verb** copy, define, describe, designare, detail, draw, duplicate, explain, go over, mark out, reproduce, set forth, sketch

TRACE (Follow), **verb** chase, detect, ensue, ferret out, hound, hunt out, inquire, investigare, investigate, odorari, probe, pursue, scent, search, seek, shadow, track, track down, trail, unearth

TRACTABLE, adjective acquiescent, adaptable, amenable, bendable, compliant, conformable, controllable, docile, docilis, ductile, easily lead, easily managed, easily taught, easygoing, elastic, facile, facilis, flexible, flexile, formable, governable, guidable, impressionable, leadable, malleable, manageable, obedient, plastic, pliable, pliant, readily wrought, submissive, teachable, tractabilis, tractile, willing, yielding

TRADE (Commerce), **noun** barter, business, business affairs, business intercourse, buying and selling, commercial enterprise, deal, exchange, exchange of commodities, interchange, marketing, mercantile business, mercantile relations, mercatus, merchandising, merchantry, negotiation, nundination, open market, patronage, purchase, sale, sales, swap, traffic, transaction, truck
ASSOCIATED CONCEPTS: combination in restraint of trade, hazardous trade, in the ordinary course of trade or business, restraint of trade, stock in trade, unfair trade

TRADE (Occupation), **noun** ars, assignment, avocation, berth, business, calling, concern, craft, duty, employment, engagement, function, handicraft, job, line, line of work, livelihood, living, metier, office, position, post, practice, profession, pursuit, situation, specialty, task, vocation

TRADE, verb bargain, barter, buy, buy and sell, carry on commerce, chaffer, commercari, deal, do business, drive a bargain, exchange, huckster, interchange, mercaturam, merchandise, negotiate, purchase, scorse, sell, shop, traffic, transact
ASSOCIATED CONCEPTS: combination in restraint of trade, trade acceptance, trade in interstate commerce

TRADE SECRET, noun knowledge which provides superiority, protected design used by a business, protected formula used by a business, protected information used by a business, protected instrument used by a business, protected knowledge which provides an edge, protected pattern used by a business, protected practice used by a business, protected special knowledge, protected unique knowledge
ASSOCIATED CONCEPTS: database rights, fair use, mask work, plant breeders' rights

TRADEMARK, noun badge, brand, countermark, countersign, hallmark, identification, imprint, label, mark, signet, symbol, ticket, trade sign

TRADITIONAL, adjective accepted, acknowledged, ancestral, classic, classical, common, confirmed, conformable, consuetudinal, consuetudinary, conventional, customary, established, fixed, habitual, handed down, historic, historical, ingrained, inherited, inveterate, long-established, long-standing, old, orthodox, prescribed, prescriptive, regular, rooted, sanctioned, time-honored, traditionary, traditive

ASSOCIATED CONCEPTS: custom and usage, past practices, prior conduct between the parties

TRAGEDY, *noun*   accident, adversity, affliction, bale, blow, calamity, casualty, cataclysm, catastrophe, disaster, doom, dreadful event, fatal affair, hardship, misadventure, misfortune, mishap, reverse, sorrow, *tragoedia,* woe

TRAIT, *noun*   attribute, characteristic, detail, differentia, distinguished quality, feature, habit, idiosyncrasy, individualism, item, lineament, manner, mannerism, mark, nature, nota, oddity, particularity, peculiarity, property, proprietas, quality, singularity, specialty, temperament

TRAMMEL, *verb*   bind, bridle, check, clog, confine, constrain, control, cramp, cumber, curb, debar, discommode, enchain, encumber, entangle, entrammel, fasten, fetter, frustrate, hamper, handicap, hinder, hobble, hold back, impede, incommode, inconvenience, keep within bounds, manacle, obstruct, oppose, pinion, put in irons, repress, restrain, restrict, retard, shackle, suppress, tether, thwart, tie, tie up

TRANSACT, *verb*   accomplish, achieve, carry on, carry on business, carry out, conduct, consummate, deal, deal with, discharge, do business, execute, fulfill, *gerere,* make terms, manage, negotiate, operate, perform, proceed with, put into practice, render, *transigere*

ASSOCIATED CONCEPTS: transact business

TRANSACTION, *noun*   accomplishment, achievement, act, action, activity, administration, adventure, affair, business, commission, completion, consummation, deal, dealing, deed, direction, effectuation, enactment, enterprise, execution, exercise, exploit, management, measure, negotiation, *negotium,* operation, performance, proceeding, process, purchase, sale, undertaking

ASSOCIATED CONCEPTS: arms length transaction, transacting business, transactional immunity

FOREIGN PHRASES: *Res inter alios judicatae nullum aliis praejudicium faciunt.* Transactions between strangers ought not to injure those who are not parties to them.

TRANSCEND, *verb*   be better, be superior, best, better, eclipse, exceed, excel, *excellere, exsuperare,* go beyond, outdistance, outdo, outrank, outrival, outshine, outstrip, outvie, outweigh, overpass, overshadow, overstep, overtop, pass, predominate, prevail, rise above, rival, surmount, surpass, take precedence, top, tower above

TRANSCRIPT, *noun*   apograph, copy, *exemplar, exemplum,* facsimile, minutes, record, recording, reprint, reproduction, rescript, stenographic copy, transcription, written copy

ASSOCIATED CONCEPTS: stenographic transcript, transcript of proceedings, transcript on appeal, trial transcript

TRANSFER, *verb*   assign, bequeath, bestow, carry, confer, consign, deed, deliver, deliver over, demise, devolve, forward, grant, hand on, pass, pass on, remove, send, shift, *traducere, transferre,* transmit, *transmittere,* transport

ASSOCIATED CONCEPTS: transfer an interest

TRANSFEREE, *noun*   acceptor, allottee, assignee, beneficiary, consignee, devisee, donee, grantee, heir, inheritor, legatee, licensee, payee, recipient, successor, trustee

TRANSFEROR, *noun*   allotter, assignor, consignor, devisor, donor, grantor, lessor, licensor, payor

TRANSFORM, *verb*   adjust, alter, change, commute, convert, denature, do over, make over, metamorphose, modify, mutate, recast, recondition, reconstruct, reconvert, redo, reform, regenerate, remake, remodel, remold, render different, renovate, reorganize, restyle, revamp, revise, revolutionize, shift, substitute, switch, tailor, transfigure, translate, transmogrify, transmute, transshape, transubstantiate, turn, vary

TRANSGRESSION, *noun*   abuse, breach, contravention, crime, *delictum,* delinquency, dereliction, disobedience, encroachment, error, fault, guilty act, illegal action, illegality, infraction, infringement, iniquity, misbehavior, misconduct, misdeed, misdoing, misfeasance, noncompliance, nonobservance, offense, *peccatum,* sin, slip, transcursion, trespass, violation, wrong, wrongdoing

FOREIGN PHRASES: *Frustra legis auxilium quaerit qui in legem committit.* He vainly seeks the aid of the law who transgresses the law.

TRANSGRESSOR, *noun*   criminal, degenerate, delinquent, lawbreaker, malefactor, malfeasant, miscreant, offender, profligate, recreant, reprobate, violator, wrongdoer

ASSOCIATED CONCEPTS: target of an investigation

TRANSIENT, *adjective*   *brevis,* brief, caducous, deciduous, elusive, ephemeral, ephemerous, evanescent, fading, fleeting, *fluxus,* fugacious, *fugax,* fugitive, hasty, impermanent, inconstant, interim, meteoric, migratory, momentary, passing, perishable, provisional, provisory, roaming, roving, short, short-lived, temporal, temporary, transitory, unenduring, unstable, vanishing, volatile

TRANSITION, *noun*   alteration, break, change, changeover, conversion, development, flux, graduation, growth, jump, leap, metastasis, modification, motion, movement, passage, passing, phase, progress, realignment, shift, transference, transformation, transit, *transitio,* transmigration, transmutation, turn

TRANSITORY, *adjective*   brief, cursory, ephemeral, evanescent, fleeting, flitting, fugacious, impermanent, momentary, not permanent, passing away, provisional, short lived, temporal, temporary, transient, unenduring, unstable, volatile

ASSOCIATED CONCEPTS: transitory actions, transitory causes of action, transitory possession of property, transitory seizen, transitory trade name, transitory use and occupation, transitory work

TRANSMIT, *verb*   bear, carry, cede, communicate, conduct, consign, convey, deliver, dispatch, forward, give, hand on, hand over, impart, issue, pass, pass on, provide, radiate, remit, send, send a message, send on, ship, transfer, *transmittere,* transport

TRANSMITTAL, *noun*   circulation, communication, conveyance, deliverance, delivery, direction, dispatch, forwarding, impartation, letter, movement, note, passage, propagation, remittance, sending, transfer, transference, translocation, transmission, transmittance, transplantation, transportation

TRANSPARENT, *adjective* apparent, candid, clear, clear as crystal, clear-cut, direct, distinct, evident, explicit, frank, honest, innocent, intelligible, lucent, lucid, manifest, obvious, open, palpable, patent, pellucid, perceivable, perceptible, perspicuous, pervious, plain, plain-speaking, porous, revealing, self-evident, simple, translucent, translucid, unambiguous, undisguised, unequivocal, unmistakable, visible

TRANSPORT, *verb* banish, bear, bring, carry, cart, conduct, consign, convey, deliver, deport, dispatch, drive out, exile, expel, extradite, fetch, imprison, move, ostracize, remove, send, ship, take, transfer, transmit, *transmittere,* transplant, *transportare*
ASSOCIATED CONCEPTS: transport across state lines, transport contraband, transport illegal goods, transport in interstate commerce

TRAP, *noun* ambush, artifice, bait, catch, catch-all, lure, maneuver, net, pitfall, snare, stratagem

TRAP, *verb* bait, catch, ensnare, entangle, entrap, hook, inveigle, snare, snatch

TRAVEL, *noun* flying, get to, go, go abroad, go by air, go by airplane, go by car, go by jet, go by plane, go by sea, go to, ride to a spot, sail to a place, see the sights, see the world, sojourn, take a trip, take a vacation, tour on vacation, touring, traverse, visit during a vacation
ASSOCIATED CONCEPTS: emigration, immigration, travel law, travel rights

TRAVERSE, *verb* course, crisscross, cross, cross in opposition, cross in traveling, cut across, ford, go across, intersect, march, over pass, pass, pass from point to point, pass through, patrol, probe, survey carefully, tramp, travel over, trek

TRAVESTY, *noun* burlesque, burlesque translation, caricature, crude presentation, distortion, exaggeration, farce, imitation, lampoon, low comedy, ludicrous presentation, mimicry, mockery, parody, perversion, ridicule, take-off

TREASON, *noun* betrayal, betrayal of a trust, breach of allegiance, breach of faith, disloyalty, infidelity, insurgence, insurrection, *maiestas,* mutiny, *perfidia,* perfidy, rebellion, rebellion against the government, revolt, revolution, sedition, subversion, treachery, violation of allegiance
FOREIGN PHRASES: *Felonia implicatur in qualibet proditione.* Felony is implied in every treason. *Reus laesae majestatis punitur ut pereat unus ne pereant omnes.* A traitor is punished that one may die lest all perish. *Crimen laesae majestatis omnia alia crimina excedit quoad poenam.* The crime of high treason exceeds all other crimes in its punishment. *In alta proditione nullus potest esse accessorius sed principalis solummodo.* In high treason each one is a principal. *Qui molitur insidias in patriam id facit quod insanus nauta perforans navem in qua vehitur.* He who betrays his country is like the insane sailor who bores a hole in the ship which carries him.

TREASURY, *noun* accumulation, *aerarium,* bank, bursary, cache, capital, central money office, *coffer,* conservatory, deposit, depository, depot, exchequer, *fiscus,* fund, place of deposit, purse, receptacle, repertory, repository, reservatory, reserve, reserve fund, safe, store, storehouse, strongbox, thesaurus, till, treasure house, vault

TREAT, *noun* amusement, delight, diversion, festival, pleasure, refreshment, repast, revelry

TREAT (Process), ***verb*** act on, analyze, attend, bargain with, behave towards, comment upon, confer, correct, deal with, debate, deliberate, discuss, edit, entertain, examine, handle, heal, investigate, modify, negotiate, parley, reason, reason about, revise, use, work on, write about

TREAT (Remedy), ***verb*** ameliorate, better, cure, improve

TREATMENT, *noun* adjustment, analysis, arrangement, consideration, cure, design, examination, execution, handling, investigation, management, modification, process, processing, study, technique, therapy, transaction, way
ASSOCIATED CONCEPTS: inhuman treatment, medical treatment

TREATY, *noun* accord, agreement, agreement between nations, alliance, armistice, arrangement, bargain, bond, cartel, charter, compact, concordance, concordat, contract, *conventio,* convention, covenant, deal, entente, formal contract, international compact, negotiation, pact, *pactio,* protocol, settlement, truce, understanding
ASSOCIATED CONCEPTS: insurance treaty

TRENCHANT, *adjective* acrimonious, acute, biting, brisk, caustic, clear-cut, cutting, distinct, dynamic, energetic, explicit, forceful, incisive, intense, keen, mordant, penetrating, penetrative, piercing, pointed, powerful, pungent, sarcastic, scathing, severe, sharp, spirited, stinging, telling, thoroughgoing, unsparing, vigorous

TREPIDATION, *noun* affright, agitation, alarm, apprehension, awe, consternation, disconcertion, dismay, disquiet, disquietude, dread, fear, flutter, fret, fright, funk, horror, jitteriness, jumpiness, nervousness, oscillation, panic, perturbation, quaking, quivering, restlessness, scare, shaking, terror, trembling, tremor, tremulousness, *trepidatio,* trepidity, uneasiness, unrest

TRESPASS, *verb* advance upon, breach, break in, break the law, contravene, deviate from rectitude, disobey, disobey the law, disregard, encroach, enter unlawfully, exceed, go astray, ignore limits, *in alienum fundum ingredi,* infringe, intrude, invade, offend, overrun, overstep, sin, transgress, usurp, violate
ASSOCIATED CONCEPTS: action of trespass, constructive trespass, continuing trespass, forcible trespass, innocent trespass, malicious trespass, technical trespass, willful and deliberate trespass
FOREIGN PHRASES: *Aedificare in tuo proprio solo non licet quod alteri noceat.* It is not lawful to build upon one's own land what may injure another. *Prohibetur ne quis faciat in suo quod nocere possit alieno.* It is forbidden for anyone to do on his own property what may injure another's.

TRIABLE, *adjective* actionable, cognizable, justiciable, legally enforceable

TRIAL (Experiment), ***noun*** analysis, attempt, check, endeavor, evaluation, examination, experimental method, *experimentum,* exploration, in-depth analysis, inquiry, inspection, probe, review, scrutiny, study, test, testing
ASSOCIATED CONCEPTS: trial period

TRIAL (Legal proceeding), ***noun*** action, action at law, case, cause, contest, court action, examination, formal examination by a court of law, formal examination of facts by a court, hearing, *iudicium,* inquest, inquiry, inquisition, judicial contest, lawsuit, legal dispute, litigation, proceeding, *quaestio,* suit, suit at law

ASSOCIATED CONCEPTS: appeal from a trial, close of a trial, examination before trial, fair trial, former trial, impartial trial, joint trial, jury trial, mistrial, new trial, order of trial, post-trial evidence, pretrial evidence, proceed to trial, public trial, retrial, separate trial, speedy trial, trial by jury, trial by the court, trial court, trial de novo, trial judge

FOREIGN PHRASES: *Triatio ibi semper debet fieri, ubi juratores meliorem possunt habere notitiam.* Trial ought always to be had where the jurors can have the best information.

TRIAL BALLOON, *noun* attempt, dry run, effort, endeavor, experiment, experimental method, exploration, first attempt, inquiry, inspection, investigation, probe, rehearsal, research, search, stab, straw man, test, trial, trial run, try, undertaking, venture

TRIBUNAL, *noun* bench, chancery, court, court of justice, court of law, forum, *iudicium,* judges, judgment seat, judiciary, law court, panel of judges

ASSOCIATED CONCEPTS: administrative tribunal, appellate tribunal, fair tribunal, inferior tribunal, tribunal of limited jurisdiction

TRICK, *noun* antic, artifice, bunko, canard, caper, caprice, contrivance, deception, decoy, delusion, device, dodge, escapade, evasion, expedient, fake, false pretense, feint, fraud, gimmick, hoax, illusion, imposture, instinct, intrigue, knavery, legerdemain, machination, maneuver, peculiarity, plot, ploy, prank, prestidigitation, pretense, pretext, quirk, racket, ruse, scheme, sham, sleight, sophistry, stratagem, subterfuge, wile

ASSOCIATED CONCEPTS: false pretenses

TRICK, *verb* bait, bamboozle, beguile, betray, cheat, circumvent, cozen, deceive, decoy, defraud, delude, dupe, ensnare, evade, hoax, hoodwink, illude, inveigle, mislead, misrepresent, pettifog, swindle, take in, trap, victimize

TRIP AND FALL CASE, *noun* accident case, action, action for an injury, calamity, casualty claim, cause of action, claim of negligence, general liability claim, injurious occurrence, liability claim, litigation, misfortune, mishap, negligence case, personal injury, slip and fall

ASSOCIATED CONCEPTS: liability insurance, plaintiff law firms, trials bar

TRITE, *adjective* banal, boring, bromidic, common, commonplace, conventional, dull, familiar, hackneyed, known, much used, oft repeated, old, ordinary, overused, *pervulgatus,* platitudinous, prosaic, proverbial, routine, run of the mill, shopworn, stale, stereotyped, stock, tedious, threadbare, too familiar, *tritus,* uncreative, unexciting, unimaginative, unoriginal, used, wearisome, well-known, widely known, worn, worn out

TRIVIAL, *adjective* cursory, empty, foolish, frivolous, inane, inappreciable, inconsiderable, indifferent, idle, immaterial, inconsequential, inferior, insignificant, *levis,* light, little, meager, meaningless, mediocre, minute, negligible, nominal, nonessential, nugatory, of little consequence, petty, picayune, scanty, shallow, slight, slim, small, superficial, trashy, trifling, unimportant, useless, worthless

ASSOCIATED CONCEPTS: trivial defect rule, trivial matter

TROUBLE, *noun* ado, adversity, affliction, ailment, annoyance, bane, blow, bother, burden, calamity, catastrophe, cause of distress, commotion, difficulty, discomfort, discontent, discord, dissatisfaction, distress, disturbance, fuss, grievance, hardship, hindrance, ill, inconvenience, misfortune, obstruction, ordeal, pitfall, plague, problem, reverse, row, setback, snag, *sollicitudo,* suffering, torment, trial, tribulation

TROVER, *noun* atonement, award, compensation, damages, fine, forfeiture, indemnification, indemnity, mulct, payment, penalty, quittance, recompense, recoupment, recovery, redress, reparation, requital, requitement, restitution, retrieval, retrievement, return, satisfaction, solatium

TRUANT, *adjective* absent, apathetic, dilatory, errant, flown, fugitive, idle, inattentive, indifferent, indolent, laggard, lazy, loitering, missing, neglectful, nonattendant, remiss, shiftless, shirking, slack, slothful, straying, unconcerned, unemployed, unpersevering, wandering

TRUCKLE, *verb* crawl, cringe, fawn, grovel, toady, yield to the wishes of others

TRUE (Authentic), *adjective* according to the facts, accurate, actual, as represented, authenticated, certain, correct, creditable, dependable, exact, factual, *fidelis, fidus,* founded on fact, genuine, honest, legitimate, literal, not false, not faulty, not fictitious, original, precise, pure, real, realistic, reliable, right, rightful, sound, trustworthy, truthful, unadulterated, unaffected, uncolored, undisguised, undisputed, undistorted, unexaggerated, unfabricated, unfallacious, unfeigned, unfictitious, unimagined, unimpeachable, unmistaken, unperjured, unpretended, unquestionable, unspurious, unvarnished, valid, veracious, veridical, verifiable, veritable, *verus,* well-based, well-founded

ASSOCIATED CONCEPTS: true bill, true copy, true value, true verdict

TRUE (Loyal), *adjective* ardent, assiduous, compliant, complying, conscientious, constant, dedicated, dependable, devoted, duteous, dutiful, earnest, faithful, fervent, firm in adherence, firm in allegiance, incorruptible, obedient, reliable, resolute, responsible, sincere, stanch, steadfast, steady, sure, tried, truehearted, trustworthy, trusty, unbetraying, unfailing, unfalse, unperfidious, unswerving, untreacherous, unwavering, zealous

TRUST (Combination of businesses), *noun* association, cartel, combination of companies, combine, consortium, corporation, merger, monopolistic organization, monopoly, pool, syndicate

ASSOCIATED CONCEPTS: antitrust laws, combination in restraint of trade

TRUST (Confidence), *noun* assurance, belief, certainty, confident expectation, conviction, credence, credulity, dependence, faith, *fides, fiducia,* reassurance, reliance, sureness, trustworthiness

ASSOCIATED CONCEPTS: breach of trust, office of trust, public trust

TRUST (Custody), *noun* care, charge, control, duty, guardianship, holding, keeping, management, obligation, possession and control, power over, protection, responsibility, safety

ASSOCIATED CONCEPTS: beneficiary of trust, business trust, *cestui que trust,* charitable trust, constructive trust, continuing trust, corpus of trust, de facto trust, declaration of trust, discretionary trust, dormant trust, dry trust, execution of trust, executory trust, express trust, implied trust, parol trust, presumptive trust, principal of a trust, private trust, residuary trust, resultant trust, revocable trust, shifting trust, special trust, spendthrift trust, totten trust, trust agreement, trust certificate, trust company, trust deed, trust estate, trust funds, trust mortgage, trust receipts

FOREIGN PHRASES: *Fides est obligatio conscientiae alicujus ad intentionem alterius.* A trust is an obligation of conscience of one to the wishes of another.

TRUST, verb   accept, accredit, assume, be confident, confide, *confidere,* count upon, *credere,* credit, depend upon, expect, feel sure, give credence to, give credit to, have faith in, have no doubt, have no reservations, hope, lean on, *mandare,* place reliance in, presume, put confidence in, rely on, swear by, take, take for granted

TRUSTEE, noun   administrator, agent, appointee, caretaker, curator, custodian, *custos,* depositary, fiduciary, financier, functionary, guardian, holder of the legal estate, one to whom something is entrusted, person appointed to administer affairs, recipient

ASSOCIATED CONCEPTS: acting trustee, appointment of trustee, bare trustee, change of trustee, corporate trustee, cotrustees, de facto trustee, designation of trustee, disinterested trustee, duty of trustee, fiduciary responsibility, interested trustee, involuntary trustee, liability of trustee, nominal trustee, public trustee, qualification of trustees, quasi trustee, removal of trustee, successor trustee, testamentary trustee, trustee by deed, trustee of an estate, trustee ex maleficio, trustee in bankruptcy

TRUSTWORTHINESS, noun   dependability, faithfulness, honesty, integrity, loyalty, probity, rectitude, reliability, uprightness

TRUTH, noun   accuracy, actuality, authenticity, candor, conformity to fact, correctness, exactness, fact, genuineness, honesty, integrity, precision, probity, realism, reality, right, sincerity, veracity, *veritas,* verity

ASSOCIATED CONCEPTS: credibility of a witness, reputation for truth, truth in lending laws

FOREIGN PHRASES: *Error fucatus nuda veritate in multis, est probabilior; et saepenumero rationibus vincit veritatem error.* Error artfully disguised is, in many instances, more probable than naked truth; and frequently error overwhelms truth by argumentation. *Veritas nimium altercando amittitur.* Truth is lost by too much altercation. *Sacramentum habet in se tres comites,-veritatem, justitiam, et judicium; veritus habenda est in jurato; justitia et justicium in judice.* An oath has in it three components,-truth, justice, and judgment; truth in the party swearing; justice and judgment in the judge administering the oath. *Fictio cedit veritati. fictio juris non est ubi veritas.* Fiction yields to truth. where truth is, fiction of law does not exist. *Qui non libere veritatem pronunciat proditor est veritatis.* He who does not freely speak the truth is a betrayer of the truth. *Veritas, quae minime defensatur opprimitur; et qui non improbat, approbat.* Truth which is not sufficiently defended is overpowered; and he who does not disapprove, approves. *Veritas nihil veretur nisi abscondi.* Truth fears nothing but concealment.

TRUTHFUL, adjective   aboveboard, accurate, actual, believable, credible, exact, fact, factual, faithful, honest, honorable, legitimate, right-minded, truth-loving, truth-speaking, truth-telling, upright, veracious

ASSOCIATED CONCEPTS: impeachment, the veracity of a witness, truthful testimony

TRY (Attempt), verb   aim, aspire, *conari,* endeavor, exert oneself, make an effort, put forth effort, seek, strain, strive, tackle, take a chance, *temptare,* test, undertake, venture

TRY (Conduct a trial), verb   adjudge, adjudicate, cognoscere, consider, decide, deliberate, examine, examine judicially, hear a case, hear a cause, *iudicare,* judge, legally determine, pronounce, rule, sit in judgment

ASSOCIATED CONCEPTS: try a case before a judge, try a case before a jury

TUMULTUOUS, adjective   angry, disgusted, enraged, frantic, frenzied, fuming, furious, hostile, inflamed, infuriated, ireful, livid, offended, offensive, outraged, raging, storming, tempestuous, turbulent

TURGID, adjective   bombastic, circumlocutory, declamatory, diffuse, digressive, euphuistic, flowery, fustian, grandiloquent, high-flown, inflated, long-winded, magniloquent, orotund, periphrastic, pleonastic, plethoric, pompous, prolix, puffed up, redundant, rhetorical, sesquipedalian, stilted, swelled, swollen, tumid, turgent, wordy

TURMOIL, noun   activity, ado, agitation, bedlam, bustle, chaos, commotion, confusion, convulsion, discord, disorder, disquiet, distraction, disturbance, excitement, ferment, fracas, fuss, havoc, huddle, imbroglio, jumble, melee, muddle, pandemonium, perturbation, pother, row, rumpus, stir, storm, tempest, trouble, tumult, *turba,* turbulence, turbulency, unrest, upheaval, uproar, welter

TURN (Change), noun   bend, change of direction, curve, detour, deviation, diversion, particular interpretation, twist, vicissitude

ASSOCIATED CONCEPTS: turnover order

TURN (Rotation), noun   circuit, cycle, gyration, perambulation, revolution, shift, span stretch, stint

TURN (Change), verb   alter, avert, bend, change, change opinion, coil, contort, convert, curdle, curl, deviate, digress, ferment, form, induce, influence, metamorphose, mold, persuade, prevail upon, recast, reconstruct, reorganize, shift, sinuate, slue, sway, swerve, transform, transmute, transpose, veer, wind, win over

TURN (Deflect), verb   alter belief, argue, avert, change course, convince, gainsay, maneuver, outmaneuver, revolutionize, transform, vary

ASSOCIATED CONCEPTS: turn state's evidence

TURN (Rotate), verb   change, gyrate, jibe, move, move clockwise, move counterclockwise, pivot, pull, push, revolve, spin, swivel, whirl

TURNS ON, verb   arises from, centers on, emanates from, ensues from, exists because of, hinges on, is decided on, issues from, springs from, the conclusion originates from, the critical point is, the crowning point is, the crucial moment is, the crux of the matter is, the culmination is, the determination is, the juncture is, the outcome is derived from, the pivotal moment is, the result is, the watershed event is

TURPITUDE, noun   bad character, bad name, baseness, character, corruption, decadence, degeneracy, degradation, depravity, disrepute, ill repute, immorality, infamy, obscenity, perfidy, shady reputation, vileness, wickedness, wrongdoing

TWEAKING, noun accommodation, adjustment, advance, advancement, alteration, amelioration, amendment, bettering, betterment, breakthrough, change, change for the better, changeover, constructive change, deviation, difference, divergence, enhancement, enrichment, improvement, increase, lift, melioration, modification, progress, progression, progressive change, redesign, reform, reformation, reshaping, restoration, restructuring, transition, upgrade
ASSOCIATED CONCEPTS: punitive damages

TWO-PART TRIAL, noun bifurcated trial, bisection of a case, segmentation in a case, segregation in a case, separate liability and damage phases, separate quilt and insanity defense phases, separation in a case, severance in a case, split in a case, split trial, two or more hearings held
ASSOCIATED CONCEPTS: financial betterment, improvement in real estate value

FOREIGN PHRASES: *Nul ne doit s'enrichir aux despens des autres.* No man should enrich himself at the expense of others.

TYPICAL, adjective according to custom, according to routine, accustomed, average, characteristic, common, commonplace, conformable, conformable to rule, consistent, conventional, current, customary, everyday, exemplifying a class, familiar, habitual, illustrative, in character, indicative, indicatory, model, normal, of everyday occurrence, of frequent occurrence, oft-repeated, ordinary, orthodox, popular, prevailing, prevalent, *proprius,* prosaic, recurrent, regular, representative, *solitus,* standard, standardized, stereotyped, stock, traditional, true to type, *typicus,* unexceptional, usual

TYRANNOUS, adjective arbitrary, brutal, despotic, domineering, grinding, hard, harsh, high-handed, imperious, lordly, masterful, oppressive, overbearing, peremptory, severe, strict, tyrannical, uncompromising, unjustly severe

UBIQUITOUS, adjective ever-present, omnipresent, permeative, pervading, pervasive, ubiquitary, universal, worldwide

ULTERIOR, adjective concealed, hidden, not manifest, obscure, secret, unadvertised, unavowed, undisclosed, undivulged, unevident, unexpressed, unknown, unmentioned, unobvious, unperceived, unrevealed, unseen
ASSOCIATED CONCEPTS: ulterior motive

ULTIMATE, adjective basic, conclusive, conclusory, crowning, elemental, elementary, end, ending, essential, eventual, extreme, extremus, farthest, final, fundamental, furthermost, furthest, greatest possible, last, maximum, most distant, most remote, primary, rudimental, rudimentary, supreme, terminal, terminative, *ultimus*
ASSOCIATED CONCEPTS: ultimate facts

ULTIMATUM, noun condition, demand, exaction, *extrema condicio,* final condition, final offer, final proposal, final proposition, last offer, notice, proposition, provision, proviso, requirement, requisite, specification, stipulation, threat, warning

ULTRA VIRES, adjective illegitimate, unallowed, unauthorized, unchartered, unlicensed, unsanctioned, unwarranted
ASSOCIATED CONCEPTS: *ultra vires* act, *ultra vires* doctrine

UMBRAGE, noun acrimony, alienation, anger, animosity, annoyance, bad blood, bile, bitterness, choler, disaffection, discord, dislike, displeasure, dissatisfaction, dudgeon, enmity, estrangement, grudge, hatred, hostility, ill humor, ill will, indignation, irritation, offense, pique, rancor, resentment, soreness, spleen, wrath

UMPIRE, noun adjudicator, arbiter, arbitrator, compromiser, *disceptator,* go-between, interagent, intercessor, intermediary, intermediator, intermedium, intervenor, judge, mediator, moderator, peacemaker, reconciler, referee

UNABASHED, adjective aweless, barefaced, bold, brazen, forward, hardened, immodest, *impudens,* not ashamed, not disconcerted, shameless, unafraid, unapprehensive, unashamed, unawed, unblushing, unconcerned, uncringing, undaunted, undismayed, unembarrassed, unfearing, unflinching, unshaken, unshrinking, without shame

UNABLE, adjective defenseless, disabled, feckless, forceless, helpless, impotent, inadequate, incapable, incompetent, ineffective, inefficient, inept, inoperative, insufficient, lame, not able, powerless, unfit, unqualified, useless, worthless

UNACCEPTABLE, adjective displeasing, distasteful, exceptionable, impossible, inadmissible, inappropriate, *ingratus, iniucundus,* intolerable, not fitting, objectionable, offensive, repugnant, unappealing, unattractive, undesirable, undesired, uninviting, unpleasant, unpleasing, unpopular, unsatisfactory, unsuitable, unwanted, unwelcome

UNACCOUNTABLE, adjective anything goes, defiant, devolving on, disobedient, insubordinate, irresponsible, licentious, not accountable, mutinous, not properly accounted for, not responsible, not traceable, rebellious, riotous, seditious, unchecked, uncontrolled, uncurbed, undisciplined, ungoverned, unrestrained

UNACCUSTOMED, adjective a stranger to, aberrant, abnormal, amazing, anomalous, astonishing, bizarre, curious, different, disaccustomed, eccentric, exceptional, exotic, extraordinary, first time experiencing, first time for, foreign, freakish, green, ignorant, inexperienced, *insolitus, insuetus,* inusitate, irregular, naive, new, new to, not accustomed to, not common, not conversant with, not familiar with, not in the habit of, not usual, not used to, novel, odd, out of the habit of, out of the ordinary, outlandish, peculiar, queer, rare, raw, remarkable, rusty, shaky, singular, strange, surprising, unacquainted, unacquainted with, unaware of, uncommon, unconventional, unconversant, uncustomary, unfamiliar, unfamiliar with, unhabituated, uninitiated, uninured, unique, unnatural, unordinary, unpracticed, unseasoned, unskilled, untrained, untried, unusual, unversed

UNACQUAINTED, adjective *ignarus,* ignorant, inexperienced, *inscius,* new, strange, unaccustomed, unapprized, unaware, unconversant, unenlightened, unfamiliar, uninformed, unknowing, unversed

UNADULTERATED, adjective genuine, *integer, merus,* neat, pure, simple, *sincerus,* straight, true, unalloyed, uncombined, uncompounded, uncontaminated, uncorrupted, undebased, undefiled, undiluted, undistorted, unmingled, unmixed, unsophisticated, untouched, unvarnished, virgin

UNAFFECTED (Sincere), **adjective** aboveboard, artless, candid, *candidus,* childlike, direct, downright, forthright, frank, free from affectation, guileless, honest, inartificial, ingenuous, innocent, modest, naive, natural, open, outspoken, plain, plainspoken, simple, *simplex,* spontaneous, straightforward, truthful, unassuming, uncounterfeited, undeceptive, undesigning, unfeigning, unpretending, unpretentious, unreserved, unsimulated, unsophisticated, unsynthetic, upright, wholesome

UNAFFECTED (Uninfluenced), **adjective** aweless, callous, calm, *constans,* disdainful, frigid, hardhearted, heartless, icy, *immotus,* impassive, impervious, implacable, indifferent, inflexible, insensitive, insentient, inured, obdurate, obtuse, pitiless, remorseless, steely, stoic, stoical, stony, unaltered, uncaring, unchanged, uncompassionate, unconcerned, unexcited, unfeeling, unimpressed, uninspired, unmoved, unresponsive, unstirred, unstruck, unswayed, unsympathetic, untouched, unyielding

UNALIENABLE, adjective absolute, actual, certain, conclusive, definite, fixed, imprescriptible, inalienable, incapable of being surrendered, indefeasible, inviolable, lawful, prescriptive, privileged, rightful, unalterable, unchallengeable, unimpeachable, untransferable
ASSOCIATED CONCEPTS: unalienable rights

UNALTERABLE, adjective adamant, changeless, constant, definite, determined, fated, firm, fixed, *immutabilis,* immutable, inalterable, incommutable, inevitable, inflexible, invariable, irreversible, obdurate, permanent, relentless, resolute, rigid, settled, stable, unbending, unchangeable, undeviating, unmodifiable, unpliant, unwavering, unyielding

UNAMBIGUOUS, adjective *apertus,* articulate, certain, *clarus,* clear, clear-cut, clearly defined, comprehensible, defined, definite, *definitus,* distinct, distinguishable, evident, exact, explicit, express, intelligible, lucid, not vague, obvious, perspicuous, plain, precise, recognizable, sure, transparent, unconfused, understandable, unequivocal, univocal, unmistakable, well-defined
ASSOCIATED CONCEPTS: plain language

UNANTICIPATED, adjective abrupt, *improvisus, inexspectatus, insperatus,* startling, sudden, surprising, uncontemplated, unexpected, unforeseen, unlooked for, unthought of

UNAPPROACHABLE, adjective aloof, austere, beyond reach, distant, far-off, faraway, forbidding, formidable, impregnable, inaccessible, inaffable, incomparable, inimitable, matchless, nongregarious, out of reach, out-of-the-way, peerless, *rari aditus,* remote, removed, reserved, secluded, separated, standoffish, stern, superior, superlative, supreme, unattainable, unequaled, unexcelled, unique, unobtainable, unparalleled, unreachable, unsociable, unsurpassed, withdrawn

UNASSAILABLE, adjective as strong as a fortress, completely defensible, impenetrable, impossible to disprove, impossible to dispute, impregnable, not attackable, not capable of being, not subject to attack, not vulnerable, strong, undeniable

UNATTAINABLE, adjective impossible, impracticable, impractical, inaccessible, infeasible, insuperable, insurmountable, out of reach, out of the question, unachievable, unacquirable, unapproachable, unavailable, unfeasible, ungettable, unobtainable, unperformable, unprocurable, unreachable, unsecurable

UNATTENDED, adjective abandoned, all by one's lonesome, alone, disregarded, forgotten, helpless, ignored, insular, isolated, left alone, lone, lonesome, neglected, not associated with, not cared for, on one's own, removed, separate, separated, unaccompanied, unaided, unassisted, unescorted, unguarded, unheeded, unprotected, unsheltered, unshielded, unsupported, unsuspecting, untended, unwarned, unwatched, withdrawn
ASSOCIATED CONCEPTS: attractive nuisance, negligence

UNAUTHORIZED, adjective disallowed, forbidden, inappropriate, incorrect, illegal, illegitimate, improper, prohibited, proscribed, unaccredited, unaffirmed, unapproved, uncertified, unchartered, uncommanded, uncommissioned, unconstitutional, undue, unempowered, unendorsed, unentitled, unjustified, unlawful, unlicensed, unpermitted, unratified, unsanctioned, unsuitable, unsupported, unwarranted, wrongful
ASSOCIATED CONCEPTS: unauthorized conduct, unauthorized use

UNAVAILABILITY, noun inaccessibility, unacquirability, unapproachability, unattainability, unobtainability

UNAVAILING, adjective abortive, barren, bootless, empty, fruitless, futile, *futilis,* idle, impotent, inadequate, incompetent, ineffective, ineffectual, inefficacious, inefficient, inoperative, *inritus,* inutile, invalid, nugatory, of no avail, pointless, profitless, purposeless, successless, to no end, to no purpose, uneventful, unproductive, unprofitable, unserviceable, unsuccessful, useless, vain, valueless, *vanus,* wasted, wasteful, worthless

UNAVOIDABLE (Inevitable), **adjective** avoidless, certain, coercive, compelling, compulsory, fated, fixed, impending, imperative, inavertible, ineluctable, ineludible, inescapable, inevasible, *inevitabilis,* inexorable, involuntary, irresistible, irrevocable, mandatory, *necessarius,* necessary, obligatory, resistless, sure, uncontrollable, unpreventable

ASSOCIATED CONCEPTS: unavoidable accident, unavoidable casualty, unavoidable cause, unavoidable consequences, unavoidable dangers

UNAVOIDABLE *(Not voidable),* **adjective** binding, fixed, indefeasible, *inrevocabilis,* irrebuttable, irrefutable, irrevocable, mandatory, settled, unable to be annulled, unchangeable

UNAWARE, *adjective* blinded, heedless, *ignarus,* ignorant, inattentive, incognizant, inexpectant, *inscius,* insensible, mindless, nescient, *nescius,* oblivious, off guard, surprised, unacquainted, unadvised, unapprised, unconscious, undiscerning, unenlightened, unfamiliar with, unforewarned, unguarded, unheeding, uninformed, unknowing, unmindful, unobservant, unprepared, unrealizing, unsuspecting, unversed, unwarned, unwary, without notice

UNBEARABLE, *adjective* enough to drive one mad, indefensible, inequitable, inexcusable, insufferable, insupportable, intolerable, not capable of being endured, too much, unconscionable, unendurable, unjustifiable, unwarranted

ASSOCIATED CONCEPTS: unbearable loss, unbearable suffering

UNBEATABLE, *adjective* beyond comparison, championship, first, in a class all by itself, incomparable, inimitable, matchless, never-to-be-equaled, peerless, top, unapproachable, unequaled, unexampled, unexcelled, unique, unmatchable, unmatched, unparalleled, unrivaled, unsurpassable, unsurpassed, without equal

UNBECOMING, *adjective* awkward, degrading, dishonorable, disreputable, graceless, improper, in bad taste, inapposite, inappropriate, incongruous, incorrect, indecent, indecorous, *indecorus,* indelicate, *indignus,* infelicitous, offensive, out of keeping, out of place, unapt, unbefitting, unbeseeming, uncomely, undignified, unfit, unfitted, ungenteel, unhandsome, unladylike, unmeet, unpraiseworthy, unseemly, unsuitable, unsuited, untasteful, vulgar

UNBELIEVABLE, *adjective* absurd, difficult to accept, difficult to believe, disbelieved, distrusted, doubtful, dubious, farfetched, hard to believe, implausible, improbable, inconceivable, incredible, open to doubt, open to suspicion, palpably false, questionable, staggering, suspect, suspicious, unconvincing, unimaginable, unlikely, untenable, unthinkable

UNBENDING, *adjective* adamant, *durus,* firm, fixed, hard, immobile, immovable, implacable, inflexible, intractable, intransigent, narrow-minded, obdurate, obstinate, relentless, renitent, resistant, resolute, rigid, *rigidus,* stern, stiff, straight, straitlaced, strict, strong-minded, stubborn, unchangeable, uncompromising, unpliant, unrelenting, unyielding, willful

UNBIASED, *adjective* broad-minded, detached, disinterested, dispassionate, equitable, fair, fair-minded, impartial, impersonal, independent, indifferent, just, liberal, neutral, nonpartisan, objective, open, open-minded, tolerant, unbigoted, uncolored, uninfluenced, unjaundiced, unprejudiced, unslanted, unswayed, unwarped

UNBLEMISHED *(Clean),* **adjective** above suspicion, acquitted, blameless, bright, clean-handed, clear, decent, faultless, free from criminal record, free from guilt, guiltless, honest, honorable, immaculate, impeccable, in the clear, incorrupt, incorruptible, innocent, irreproachable, law-abiding, lawful, pure, righteous, right-minded, scrupulous, soil-free, spotless, squeaky clean, stainless, strictly honest, unimpeachable, unobjectionable, unoffending, unsoiled, unstained, untainted, untarnished, veracious, virtuous, without a stain, without reproach

ASSOCIATED CONCEPTS: a clean criminal record

UNBLEMISHED *(Honest),* **adjective** above suspicion, absolute, acquitted, angelic, beyond all praise, beyond reproach, blameless, bloodless, chaste, clean, clean-handed, clean-minded, creditable, decent, defectless, entirely defensible, estimable, ethical, fair, faultless, flawless, free from impurities, full of integrity, good, guileless, high-minded, high-principled, highly respectable, honorable, ideal, immaculate, impeccable, incorrupt, incorruptible, indefectible, indefective, infallible, innocent, inviolable, inviolate, irreprehensible, irreproachable, irreprovable, just, just right, law-abiding, lawful, law-loving, law-revering, matchless, moral, noble, not guilty, not responsible, not to be improved, number-one, peedess, perfect, principled, pure, pure in heart, reputable, respectable, right, righteous, right-minded, scrupulous, sinless, spotless, squeaky-clean, stainless, sterling, straight, strictly honest, taintless, true-dealing, true-devoted, true-disposing, truehearted, true-souled, true-spirited, unadulterated, unblamable, unbribed, uncontaminated, uncorrupt, uncorrupted, unculpable, unerring, unexceptionable, unfaultable, unflawed, unguilty, unimpeachable, uninvolved, unmixed, unmuddied, unobjectionable, unoffending, unstained, unsullied, untainted, untarnished, unviolated, uprighteous, upstanding, veracious, virtuous, without reproach, world-class, worthy

ASSOCIATED CONCEPTS: unblemished record

UNBOUND, *adjective* disunited, exempt, free, liberated, limitless, manumitted, paroled, released, set free, uncaught, unchained, unchecked, unconfined, unconstrained, uncontrolled, unencumbered, unfastened, unfettered, unfixed, unhindered, unlimited, unobstructed, unprevented, unrestrained, unrestricted, untied, untrammeled

UNBRIDLED AUTHORITY, *noun* absolute discretion, authority, blank check, carte blanche, complete liberty, discretion, every option, free hand, freedom, full authority, full delegated authority, full power, full range, latitude, leeway, maneuvering space, total discretion, unbridled discretion, unhampered authority

UNCANNY, *adjective* astonishing, exceptional, inconceivable, incredible, intuitional, magical, mysterious, mystifying, noteworthy, odd, peculiar, preternatural, rare, remarkable, secret, singular, strange, supernatural, unaccountable, unbelievable, uncommon, unearthly, unfamiliar, unheard of, unnatural, weird

UNCERTAIN *(Ambiguous),* **adjective** amphibolic, cryptic, enigmatical, inconclusive, indeterminate, indistinct, mistakable, mysterious, mystifying, nebulous, not certain, not clear, not plain, obscure, occult, open to various interpretations, perplexing, puzzling, unclear, unintelligible, vague

FOREIGN PHRASES: *Ubi jus incertum, ibi jus nullum.* Where the law is uncertain, there is no law. *Res est misera ubi jus est vagum et incertum.* It is a sorry state of affairs when law is vague and mutable. *Incerta pro nullis habentur.* Uncertain things are regarded as nothing.

UNCERTAIN *(Questionable),* **adjective** arguable, conjectural, contestable, contingent, controvertible, debatable, disputable, doubtful, dubious, equivocal, insecure, liable to question, not sure, open to discussion, open to question, precarious, problematic, problematical, provisional, suspect, suspicious, tentative, unconfirmed, undecided, undetermined, unreliable, unsettled, unsure, untrustworthy

UNCERTAINTY, *noun* ambiguity, ambivalence, chance, confusion, contingency, darkness, desultoriness, dilemma, dimness, doubt, doubtfulness, dubiousness, equivocation, faintness, feebleness, gamble, hazard, hesitancy, hesitation, improbability, incertitude, inconstancy, incredulity, indecision, indefiniteness, indetermination, insecurity, instability, irresolution, jeopardy, misgiving, obscurity, peril, perplexity, possibility, precariousness, qualm, quandary, reluctance, risk, shadowiness, speculation, suspense, undependability, unevenness, unpredictability, unreliability, unsteadiness, unsureness, vacillation, vagueness, wavering, weakness

UNCHECKED, *adjective* allowed, allowed freely, easy, lax, out of control, out of hand, permitted, rampant, riotous, tolerated, unbridled, unconditional, unconstrained, uncontrolled, uncurbed, ungoverned, unhampered, uninhibited, unregulated, unrepressed, unreserved, unrestrained, unruly
ASSOCIATED CONCEPTS: unchecked presidential power

UNCLAIMED, *adjective* forgotten, unallocated, unapplied, unappropriated, unasked for, uncalled-for, undemanded, unexacted, unpossessed, unrequisitioned, unsought, untaken
ASSOCIATED CONCEPTS: last property, unclaimed property

UNCLEAN HANDS, *noun* a blemished record, a record of proven fault, equitable defense, improper history, personal deficiencies, personal problems, problems in the past, tainted past

UNCLEAR, *adjective* ambiguous, blurred, blurry, clouded, cloudy, confused, difficult to comprehend, difficult to understand, dim, equivocal, faint, foggy, fuzzy, hazy, ill-defined, illegible, imperspicuous, incomprehensible, inconspicuous, indistinct, indistinguishable, misty, muddy, murky, obscure, out of focus, poorly defined, poorly seen, shadowy, sketchy, turbid, uncertain, undefined, unevident, unexplicit, unintelligible, unobvious, unplain, unreadable, unrecognizable, vague

UNCOMMON, *adjective* aberrant, abnormal, anomalous, bizarre, curious, different, distinctive, eccentric, exceptional, exotic, extraordinary, infrequent, *insolitus,* inusitate, *inusitatus,* marked, noteworthy, novel, occasional, odd, out of the way, outstanding, peculiar, rare, *rarus,* remarkable, scarce, seldom met with, singular, special, startling, strange, surprising, unaccustomed, unconventional, uncustomary, unexampled, unfamiliar, unheard of, unimitated, unique, unorthodox, unparalleled, unprecedented, unusual

UNCOMPROMISING, *adjective* adamant, austere, conservative, determined, difficult, exacting, exigent, fanatic, fanatical, firm, hard, immovable, implacable, incorruptible, inexorable, inflexible, intransigent, irreconcilable, narrow, obdurate, obstinate, orthodox, puritanic, puritanical, relentless, resolute, resolved, rigid, ruthless, severe, steadfast, strict, stringent, unbending, unchangeable, unrelenting, unremitting, unyielding

UNCONCERNED, *adjective* aloof, apathetic, careless, casual, cold, cold-blooded, contemptuous, cool, cruel, derelict, disinterested, dispassionate, distant, free from anxiety, frigid, hard-hearted, heartless, heedless, icy, impartial, inaccessible, incurious, indifferent, insensitive, insouciant, lax, listless, negligent, neutral, nonchalant, obdurate, passionless, perfunctory, phlegmatic, remiss, serene, sluggish, stoical, stolid, stony, supercilious, thick-skinned, thoughtless, torpid, truant, unabashed, unaffected, unalarmed, unapprehensive, uncaring, unconcerned, undaunted, undismayed, unemotional, unfeeling, uninquisitive, uninterested, uninvolved, unmindful, unmoved, unperturbed, unresponsive, unshrinking, unsolicitous, unsusceptible, unsympathetic, untroubled
ASSOCIATED CONCEPTS: failure to cooperate, recalcitrant witness

UNCONDITIONAL, *adjective* absolute, categorical, complete, not limited by conditions, *purus, simplex,* unbounded, unchecked, unconfined, unqualified, unrestricted, utter, without conditions, without reservations
ASSOCIATED CONCEPTS: unconditional claim, unconditional guaranty, unconditional pardon, unconditional payment, unconditional promise, unconditional refusal

UNCONDITIONAL AUTHORITY, *noun* alternatives, artistic license, authority, blanket permission, carte blanche, civil liberty, decontrols, deregulation, discretion, emancipation, franchise, free choice, free will, freedom of choice, lack of censorship, *laissez-faire,* latitude, liberation, liberty, license, noninterference, nonintervention, openness, permission, prerogative, privilege, right of selection, self-determination, self-direction, unbridled discretion, unconstraint, unrestraint, unrestricted use

UNCONFIRMED, *adjective* inconclusive, indecisive, unascertained, unattested, unauthenticated, uncertain, uncertified, unchecked, uncorroborated, undemonstrated, unestablished, unproved, unproven, unratified, unsettled, unshown, unsubstantiated, unsupported, untried, unvalidated, unverified, unwitnessed

UNCONFORMABLE, *adjective* discordant, discrepant, disparate, disproportionate, dissident, dissimilar, eccentric, inadjustable, inapplicable, inappropriate, incommensurate, incompatible, incongruent, incongruous, inconsistent, inconsonant, irreconcilable, irreducible, irregular, lawless, nonconforming, original, peculiar, repugnant, rigid, unique, unorthodox, unrelated

UNCONNECTED, *adjective* absonant, alien, apart, broken, collateral, desultory, detached, disconnected, discontinued, discontinuous, disengaged, disjoined, disjunctive, disparate, distinct, disunited, divided, foreign, gratuitous, inapposite, incongruous, inconsequential, inconsistent, independent, individual, insular, irrelative, irrelevant, isolated, loose, obscure, parted, remote, removed, segregate, separate, separated, solitary, sundered, unaffiliated, unallied, unassociated, unattached, unrelated, without context
ASSOCIATED CONCEPTS: unconnected subjects in a bill

UNCONSCIONABLE, *adjective* atrocious, blackguard, completely unreasonable, conniving, conscienceless, corrupt, criminal, designing, dishonest, dishonorable, disingenuous, excessive, exorbitant, extreme, grievous, grossly unjust, immoderate, impermissible, incomprehensible, indefensible, inequitable, inexcusable, inexpiable, inordinate, intemperate, intriguing, knavish, monstrous, outrageous, preposterous, rascally, reprehensible, scheming, tricky, unbalanced, unconscienced, undue, unequal, unethical, unfair, unforgivable, unjust, unjustifiable, unpardonable, unprincipled, unreasonable, unscrupulous, unwarrantable, wrong

ASSOCIATED CONCEPTS: unconscionable bargain, unconscionable conduct, unconscionable contract

UNCONSCIONABILITY, *noun* amoral action, evil action, immoral action, inconceivableness, indefensibleness, inexcusableness, inexpiableness, shameless action, unethical actoin, unfair action, unfounded action, unprincipled action, unreasonable action, unreasonableness, unscrupulous action, unwarranted action, wicked action

ASSOCIATED CONCEPTS: contract of adhesion, enforcement of contracts, integration clause, unconscionable bargain, unconscionable conduct

UNCONTESTED, *adjective* accepted, admitted, axiomatic, believed, incontestable, incontrovertible, indubitable, irrefragable, irrefutable, not argued over, not challenged, not disputed, *sine certamine,* unchallengeable, unchallenged, uncontradicted, uncontroversial, uncontroverted, undeniable, undisputed, undoubted, unquestionable, unquestioned

ASSOCIATED CONCEPTS: uncontested action, uncontested divorce, uncontested election

UNCONTROLLABLE, *adjective* bullheaded, carried away, disobedient, disorderly, fractious, frenzied, headstrong, hysterical, impetuous, *impotens,* incorrigible, indocile, indomitable, insuppressible, insurgent, intractable, irrepressible, irresistable, lawless, mulish, obdurate, obstinate, obstreperous, opinionated, out of control, rampageous, rampant, recalcitrant, refractory, restive, riotous, rowdy, stubborn, troublesome, unappeasable, ungovernable, unmalleable, unmanageable, unrestrainable, unruly, unsubmissive, untoward, violent, wild, willful

ASSOCIATED CONCEPTS: uncontrollable impulse

UNCONTROVERTED, *adjective* beyond doubt, doubtless, indubious, past dispute, unchallenged, uncontested, uncontradicted, undisputed, undoubted, unquestioned

ASSOCIATED CONCEPTS: uncontroverted fact, uncontroverted truth

UNCORROBORATED, *adjective* unattested, unauthenticated, unauthorative, unconfirmed, undemonstrated, unofficial, unproven, unratified, unsubstantiated, unsupported, unvalidated, unverified

ASSOCIATED CONCEPTS: uncorroborated evidence, uncorroborated fact

UNCOUTH, *adjective* *agrestis,* awkward, barbaric, barbarous, boorish, brutish, callow, churlish, clownish, clumsy, coarse, crass, crude, discourteous, doltish, gawky, graceless, gross, heavy-handed, ill-bred, ill-mannered, impolite, *incultus,* indelicate, inelegant, loutish, plebeian, rough, rude, *rudis,* rustic, strange, uncivil, uncourteous, uncourtly, uncultivated, uncultured, ungainly, ungentlemanly, unmannerly, unpolished, unrefined, unseemly, vulgar

UNCURBED, *adjective* abandoned, *effrenatus, effusus,* incontinent, *infrenatus,* irresponsible, lawless, lax, licentious, out of control, out of hand, reinless, unaccountable, unanswerable, unbound, unbridled, unchained, unchecked, unconfined, unconstrained, uncontrolled, undisciplined, ungoverned, unhindered, unimpeded, uninhibited, unmuzzled, unobstructed, unprevented, unreined, unrepressed, unrestrained, unruly, unshackled, unsuppressed

UNDAUNTED, *adjective* bold, brave, courageous, daring, dauntless, doughty, dreadless, fearless, firm, gallant, gritty, heroic, *impavidus,* indefatigable, indomitable, *interritus,* intrepid, *intrepidus,* mettlesome, perseverant, persevering, persistent, persisting, resolute, stalwart, steady, stouthearted, tireless, unafraid, unalarmed, unapprehensive, unblenched, unconcerned, undiscouraged, undismayed, unfaltering, unfearing, unflinching, unfrightened, unrelenting, unshaken, unshrinking, unsubdued, unterrified, untimid, valiant, valorous

UNDECIDED, *adjective* ambiguous, *ambiguus,* changeful, contestable, debatable, disputable, doubtful, doubting, drawn, dubious, *dubius,* hesitant, *incertus,* indecisive, indefinite, irresolute, moot, open, pending, problematical, questionable, speculative, tentative, unascertained, uncertain, unconvinced, undetermined, unfixed, unresolved, unsettled, unsure, vacillating, vacillatory, vague, wavering

UNDEFINABLE, *adjective* esoteric, indefinable, indescribable, indeterminate, indistinct, ineffable, inexplicable, inexpressible, unexplainable, untranslatable, vague

UNDENIABLE, *adjective* axiomatic, axiomatical, beyond a doubt, beyond all question, beyond dispute, certain, clear, compelling, conclusive, convincing, demonstrable, established, *evidens,* evident, firm, *haud dubius,* inappealable, incontestable, incontrovertible, indisputable, indubitable, inescapable, infallible, irrefragable, irrefutable, obvious, past dispute, proven, sound, unanswerable, unavoidable, unimpeachable, unquestionable

UNDEPENDABLE, *adjective* capricious, careless, changeable, deceitful, dishonest, double-dealing, erratic, fickle, fluctuating, frivolous, inconstant, irresponsible, mercurial, open to error, perfidious, shifty, slippery, tergiversating, timeserving, treacherous, two-faced, uncertain, unpredictable, unreliable, unstable, unsteadfast, unsteady, unsure, untrustworthy, vacillating, variable, wavering

UNDER ARREST, *noun* captured, caught, collared, committed, confined, constrained, detained, held, held in custody, immurred, imprisoned, incarcerated, interned, jailed, kept in custody, legally restrained, made captive, made prisoner, remanded, remanded into custody, restrained, seized, sent to prison, taken, taken by force by the authorities, taken into custody

UNDER OATH, *adjective* adjure, affirm, allege under oath, assert as true, assure under oath, authenticate under oath, aver, avow, bear witness under oath, bind by oath, certify under oath, confirm under oath, declare under oath, declare solemnly, declare as true under oath, maintain under oath, promise under oath, provide evidence under oath, put one's trust in state, state under oath, vouch, vow under oath

UNDERESTIMATE, *verb* belittle, deprecate, depreciate, detract from, discredit, disesteem, disparage, do scant justice to, make light of, minimize, *minoris aestimare, minoris facere,* misjudge, misprize, rate below the true value, rate too low, run down, set at naught, set little store by, slight, think too little of, underprice, underprize, underrate, underreckon, undervalue

UNDERHANDED, *adjective* against the rules, backroom, bad, below-the-belt, calculating, clandestine, cloak-and dagger, corrupt, covert, criminal, crooked, cunning, deceitful, designing, dishonest, dishonorable, double-dealing, felonious, furtive, guileful, illegal, illicit, immoral, insidious, malfeasant, perfidious, plotting, scheming, secret, shady, slippery, sly, sneaking, stealthy, surreptitious, treacherous, unauthorized, unconscionable, undercover, underground, underhand, under-the-counter, under-the-table, unfair, unlawful, unobtrusive, unscrupulous, wily, wrong, wrongful

UNDERLYING, adjective based on, basic, built on, deep-rooted, elemental, elementary, essential, fundamental, latent, not evident, obscure, original, primal, primary, rudimentary, supporting, undermost, unseen
ASSOCIATED CONCEPTS: underlying contract, underlying fact, underlying obligation

UNDERMINE, verb deaden, debilitate, devitalize, dull, enervate, enfeeble, eviscerate, extenuate, harm, impair, incapacitate, injure, mitigate, negate, rattle, reduce, ruin, sabotage, sap the foundation out of, sap the strength out of, subvert, unnerve, unstrengthen, weaken
ASSOCIATED CONCEPTS: undermine credibility

UNDERSIGNED, noun attestant, attester, author, covenanter, endorser, petitioner, ratifier, signatory, signer, subscriber, supporter

UNDERSTAND, verb absorb, apperceive, appreciate, apprehend, assimilate, be apprised, be informed, cognize, comprehend, conceive, conclude, conjecture, deduce, digest, discern, fathom, gather, glean, grasp, infer, *intellegere*, internalize, know, learn, master, perceive, retain, take to mean
ASSOCIATED CONCEPTS: express understanding, want of understanding

UNDERSTANDABLE, adjective comprehensible, knowable

UNDERSTANDING (Agreement), noun accord, accordance, alliance, arrangement, common view, compact, compliance, concord, concordance, congruence, consentaneity, contract, cooperation, covenant, harmony, likemindedness, meeting of minds, mutual pledge, pact, rapport, unanimity
ASSOCIATED CONCEPTS: express understanding, understanding of the parties
FOREIGN PHRASES: Conventio facit legem. An agreement creates the law, i.e. the parties to a binding contract will be held to their promises.

UNDERSTANDING (Comprehension), noun apperception, apprehension, assimilation, awareness, conception, discernment, grasp, *ingenium,* insight, intelligence, knowledge, *mens,* mental ability, perception, power to understand, prehension, realization, reason, recognition, sense, wisdom
ASSOCIATED CONCEPTS: intent, want of understanding
FOREIGN PHRASES: Sermones semper accipiendi sunt secundum subjectam materiam, et conditionem personarum. Language is always to be understood according to its subject matter and the condition of the person. **Probationes debent esse evidentes, id est, perspicuae et faciles intelligi.** Proofs ought to be evident, that is, clear and easily understood. **Quod tacite intelligitur deesse non videtur.** What is tacitly understood does not appear to be wanting.

UNDERSTANDING (Tolerance), noun acceptance, altruism, benevolence, charitableness, compassion, condonation, consideration, empathy, good will, humanity, indulgence, kindliness, lack of prejudice, mercy, patience, sensitivity, sufferance, sympathy, toleration

UNDERSTATEMENT, noun conservative estimate, grossly inadequate representation, minimization, misrepresentation, underestimation, undervaluation

UNDERTAKE, verb accept, address oneself to, agree, answer for, apply oneself to, assume, attempt, be answerable for, begin, carry on, carry out, commence, commit, commit oneself to, contract, covenant, devote oneself to, embark upon, endeavor, engage in, enter into, enter upon, execute, go in for, guarantee, *in se recipere,* incur a duty, indent, indenture, initiate, launch, make an effort, obligate oneself, pledge, pledge one's word, promise, pursue, set about, set in motion, start, strive, *suscipere,* tackle, take in hand, take up, take upon oneself, try, venture, vow
ASSOCIATED CONCEPTS: overt act

UNDERTAKING (Attempt), noun design, effort, plan, purpose, quest, search, task undertaken, trial

UNDERTAKING (Bond), noun pledge, security

UNDERTAKING (Business), noun engagement, enterprise, project, pursuit, task, transaction, venture

UNDERTAKING (Commitment), noun agreement, contract, obligation, pledge

UNDERTAKING (Enterprise), noun adventure, affair, attempt, business, *coeptum,* concern, effort, emprise, endeavor, engagement, essay, exercise, *inceptum,* job, move, occupation, operation, plan, program, project, pursuit, quest, search, task, trial, venture
ASSOCIATED CONCEPTS: joint undertaking

UNDERTAKING (Pledge), noun agreement, assurance, avowal, commitment, compact, contract, covenant, engagement, guarantee, insurance, oath, obligation, parole, pledged word, promise, security, stipulation, troth, vow, warrant, word
ASSOCIATED CONCEPTS: bail undertaking, insufficiency of undertaking, statutory undertaking, undertaking

UNDERWRITE, verb agree to support, assume a risk, assure, back, consent to support, countersign, endorse, finance, fund, guarantee, guaranty, insure, pledge, promise, secure, shoulder, sponsor, support, take responsibility, undertake, uphold, vouch for

UNDESIRABLE, adjective abominable, annoying, bothersome, defective, disadvantageous, disagreeable, disliked, displeasing, distasteful, dreaded, exceptionable, improper, inadvisable, inappropriate, incommodious, inconvenient, ineligible, inexpedient, insufferable, intolerable, loathed, loathsome, objectionable, obnoxious, out of character, out of keeping, outcast, rejected, repellent, repulsive, scorned, shunned, thankless, troublesome, unacceptable, unalluring, unappealing, unapprovable, unattractive, unbecoming, unbefitting, unfit, uninviting, unlikable, unmeet, unpalatable, unpleasant, unpleasing, unpopular, unsatisfactory, unseemly, unsought, unsuitable, unwanted, unwelcome, unwished, unworthy

UNDIMINISHED, adjective in full force, *indelibatus, inlibatus,* intact, *integer,* not decreased, not lessened, unabated, unallayed, unceasing, uncut, undamaged, undivided, unfaded, unimpaired, unincreased, unlessened, unreduced, unretarded, unsevered, unweakened, unworn, whole, without loss

UNDISCLOSED, adjective concealed, covert, hidden, invisible, latent, mysterious, occult, sealed, secret, suppressed, tacit, ulterior, unaired, unannounced, unapparent, unbreathed, uncommunicated, unconveyed, undeclared, undetected, undivulged, unexplained, unexposed, unexpressed, unheralded, unimparted, unknown, unmentioned, unproclaimed, unpronounced, unpublicized, unpublished, unrevealed, unsaid, unseen, untalked of, untold, unvoiced
ASSOCIATED CONCEPTS: undisclosed interest, undisclosed principal

UNDISPUTED, adjective absolute, accepted, acknowledged, assured, axiomatic, believed, beyond doubt, beyond question, certain, *certus,* conclusive, doubtless, *haud dubius,* incontestable, incontrovertible, indisputable, indubitable, irrefragable, irrefutable, past dispute, positive, questionless, trusted, unanswerable, unchallengeable, unchallenged, uncontroversial, undebatable, undeniable, undoubted, unquestioned, without doubt, without question
ASSOCIATED CONCEPTS: undisputed fact

UNDISTORTED, adjective authentic, direct, exact, faithful, genuine, natural, original, right, scrupulous, straight, true, true to nature, truthful, unbiased, undeviating, undisguised, unembroidered, unexaggerated, unfaked, unfictitious, unjaundiced, unperverted, unprejudiced, unswerving, unwarped, veracious

UNDO, verb abolish, abrogate, annul, answer, cancel, counteract, counterbalance, countermand, debug, decode, decrypt, defeat, destroy, disestablish, declare null and void, dispense with, eliminate, impeach, invalidate, neutralize, nullify, obviate, offset, put an end to, quash, ravel, remove, repeal, rescind, resolve, retract, reverse, revoke, ruin, terminate, thwart, unravel, untangle, untwist, unweave, vacate, vitiate, worst
ASSOCIATED CONCEPTS: undo charges, undo the law

UNDUE (Excessive), **adjective** disproportionate, exceeding propriety, excessive, exorbitant, extravagant, extreme, ill-advised, immoderate, *immodicus,* improper, inappropriate, indecorous, inordinate, needless, *nimius,* objectionable, out of bounds, outrageous, overmuch, profuse, superfluous, unbecoming, unbefitting, uncalled-for, undeserved, unfit, unjustified, unmerited, unnecessary, unneeded, unreasonable, unseemly, unsuitable, unwarranted
ASSOCIATED CONCEPTS: undue influence

UNDUE (Not owing), **adjective** not mature, not yet due, not yet payable, premature, unowed, unseasonable, untimely

UNDUE DELAY, noun culpability, default, delay, dereliction, dilatoriness, disregard, dutilessness, impropriety, inattention, indifference, laches, laxity, neglect, neglectfulness, negligence, noncompliance, non-observance, nonperformance, peccadillo, procrastination, tardiness
ASSOCIATED CONCEPTS: undue delay as cause for a dismissal

UNDUE INFLUENCE, noun absolutism, arbitrary power, coercion, compulsion, conscription, constraint, despotism, dominance, domination, duress, enforcement, high pressure methods, impelling, impressment, inducement, insistence, necessitation, predominance, pressure, repression, subjugation
ASSOCIATED CONCEPTS: exertion of undue influence, invalidation of a will

UNDULY, adverb excessively, exorbitantly, extremely, immoderately, inordinately, intemperately, overly
ASSOCIATED CONCEPTS: unduly harsh criminal sanctions

UNDYING, adjective abiding, ceaseless, constant, continuing, continuous, deathless, endless, eternal, fadeless, immortal, imperishable, impregnable, incessant, indefatigable, indelible, indestructible, indivisible, ineffaceable, ineradicable, inerasable, inexpugnable, inextinguishable, invulnerable, lasting, never-dying, never-ending, never-fading, nonperishable, permanent, perpetual, persistent, protracted, sustained, unceasing, undiminished, undying, unending, unfading, unremitting, untiring, unwavering

UNEMOTIONAL, adjective aloof, anesthetized, apathetic, arctic, callous, calm, catatonic, chilly, cold, cold-blooded, cold-hearted, composed, cool, demure, dispassionate, distant, emotionless, formal, frigid, frosted, frosty, frozen, hardened, heartless, impassive, imperturbable, impervious, indifferent, languid, neutral, nonchalant, obdurate, passionless, reserved, restrained, reticent, sedate, self-absorbed, self-centered, self-controlled, sober, soulless, spiritless, staid, stiff, stoical, thick-skinned, unaffectionate, unexcitable, unfeeling, unimpassioned, unimpressionable, unmoved, unperturbed, unresponsive, unruffled, unstirred, unsusceptible, unsympathetic

UNEMPLOYED, adjective disengaged, disused, doing nothing, idle, inactive, jobless, leisured, not employed, not working, *otiosus,* out of employment, out of work, unengaged, unoccupied, unused, *vacuus,* without employment, workless
ASSOCIATED CONCEPTS: unemployment insurance

UNEMPLOYMENT INSURANCE, noun coverage for the unemployed, insurance coverage for the unemployed, promise to pay benefits for the unemployed, unemployment benefits, unemployment compensation

UNENCUMBERED, adjective clear, disembarrassed, free, no encumbrances, no liens, unburdened, unhampered, unhindered, unimpeded, unobstructed
ASSOCIATED CONCEPTS: title

UNENDURABLE, adjective displeasing, excessive, extreme, impalatable, impossible, insufferable, intolerable, objectionable, obnoxious, offensive, past bearing, past enduring, unacceptable, unbearable, undesirable, unpalatable, unpleasant, unsavory

UNEQUAL (Unequivalent), **adjective** different, differing, *dispar,* disparate, disproportionate, dissimilar, *impar, inaequalis,* irregular, unbalanced, uneven, unlike, unmatched
ASSOCIATED CONCEPTS: unequal bargaining powers

UNEQUAL (Unjust), **adjective** biased, inequitable, influenced, jaundiced, one-sided, partial, prejudiced, prepossessed, unfair, unjustifiable

UNEQUIVOCAL, adjective absolute, categorical, certain, clear, clear-cut, decided, defined, definite, downright, evident, explicit, forthright, inappealable, incontestable, incontrovertible, indisputable, indubitable, irrefragable, irrefutable, outright, peremptory, plain, positive, straightforward, sure, unambiguous, unanswerable, unchallenged, undeniable, undisputed, unmistakable, unqualified, unquestionable, utter

UNERRING, adjective accurate, actual, authentic, certain, correct, errorless, exact, factual, faultless, flawless, inerrable, inerrant, not liable to err, on target, on the beam, perfect, positive, precise, real, right, sound, sure, true, unfailing, valid, veracious

UNESSENTIAL, _adjective_   _adventicius,_ dispensable, extraneous, extrinsic, immaterial, inapposite, incidental, inconsequential, inconsiderable, insignificant, irrelevant, meaningless, minor, needless, negligible, nonessential, of no account, of no consequence, secondary, superfluous, trifling, trivial, uncalled-for, unimportant, unnecessary, unneeded
ASSOCIATED CONCEPTS: _minimis_

UNETHICAL, _adjective_   corrupt, corruptible, dishonest, dishonorable, disreputable, ignoble, immoral, inglorious, questionable, shady, uncommendable, unconscionable, underhanded, unfair, unprincipled, unprofessional, unscrupulous, unworthy, wrong

UNEXPECTED, _adjective_   abrupt, accidental, astonishing, chance, extemperaneous, extempore, fortuitous, impetuous, impromptu, impulsive, _inexpectatus, insperatus,_ instantaneous, precipitate, shocking, startling, subitaneous, sudden, surprising, unannounced, unanticipated, unawaited, uncontemplated, undesigned, unforeseen, unheralded, unintended, unintentional, unlooked for, unpredicted, unpremeditated, unprepared for, unthought of, untimely, unusual

UNEXPIRED TERM, _noun_   remaining period, remaining time, residual time, surplus time, unelapsed period

UNFAIR, _adjective_   biased, fraudulent, inequitable, iniquitous, jaundiced, not equitable, one-sided, prejudiced, unequal, uneven, unjust, unprincipled, unreasonable, unsporting, weighted
ASSOCIATED CONCEPTS: unfair advantage, unfair claim practices, unfair competition, unfair labor practices, unfair proceedings, unfair trade

UNFAVORABLE, _adjective_   adverse, adversus, antagonistic, bad, calamitous, contrary, damaging, derogatory, deterrent, disadvantageous, disapprobatory, discouraging, disparaging, foul, hopeless, hostile, ill-boding, ill-disposed, ill-omened, impedimental, impedimentary, impedimentive, inadvisable, inappropriate, inauspicious, inclement, inconvenient, indisposed, inexpedient, infelicitous, inhibitive, inimical, _iniquus,_ inopportune, malapropos, malign, misfortunate, noxious, ominous, opposed, poor, prejudicial, repugnant, sinister, unfortunate, unfriendly, unlucky, unpromising, unpropitious, unsatisfactory, unsuited, untimely, untoward

UNFIT, _adjective_   badly qualified, foolish, ill-adapted, ill-advised, impertinent, improper, inadequate, inadvisable, inapplicable, inapposite, inappropriate, inapt, incapable, _incommodus,_ incompetent, incongruous, inconvenient, _indignus,_ ineligible, inept, inexpedient, inexpert, injudicious, inopportune, inutile, _inutilis,_ irrelevant, maladjusted, malapropos, objectionable, out of keeping, out of place, unable, unadapted, unbecoming, unbefitting, undesirable, undue, unequipped, unfitting, unlikely, unprepared, unpromising, unqualified, unseemly, unsuitable, unsuited, unusable, unwise, unworthy, useless, valueless, wrong
ASSOCIATED CONCEPTS: unfit for consumption, unfit for occupancy, unfit parent

UNFLAGGING, _adjective_   ardent, assiduous, continuing, decided, determined, diligent, earnest, enduring, energetic, faithful, fervent, firm, fixed, gritty, hard, hardworking, immutable, inalterable, indefatigable, indomitable, insistent, intent, invincible, laborious, lasting, loyal, never idle,

never-tiring, perseverant, persevering, persistent, persisting, pertinacious, plugging, purposeful, relentless, resolute, resolved, sedulous, single-minded, staunch, steadfast, steady, strenuous, stubborn, tenacious, tireless, undaunted, undeviating, undiscouraged, unfailing, unfaltering, unflinching, unhesitating, uninterrupted, unrelenting, unremitting, unsleeping, unswerving, untiring, unwavering, unwearied, unyielding, vehement, zealous

UNFORESEEABLE, _adjective_   contrary to expectations, improbable, startling, subitaneous, sudden, surprise, unaccountable, unanticipated, uncertain, unexpected, unintended, unlooked for, unplanned, unprecedented, unpredictable, unpredicted, unprepared for, unthought of, unusual, unwonted
ASSOCIATED CONCEPTS: unforseeable consequences, unforseeable events

UNFORESEEN, _adjective_   accidental, sudden, surprise, unanticipated, undesigned, unexpected, unheralded, unintended, unpredicted, unthought of
ASSOCIATED CONCEPTS: unforeseen cause, unforeseen difficulties, unforeseen event, unforeseen peril

UNFORESEEN CIRCUMSTANCES, _adjective_   atypical, different, exceptional, extraordinary, first, first ever, improbable, incomparable, matchless, never before encountered, new, not to be expected, novel, of its own kind, off the beaten track, offbeat, original, out of the ordinary, out of the pale, out-of-the-way, rare, remarkable, sensational, singular, strange, surprising, unaccustomed, uncommon, uncustomary, unequaled, unexampled, unexpected, unfamiliar, unheard of, unique, unmatched, unparalleled, unprecedented, unthought-of, unusual

UNFORTUNATE, _adjective_   bad, bad timing, counterproductive, dire, discommodious, down on one's luck, failed, failing, fatal, fortuneless, fruitless, futile, hapless, hopeless, ill-considered, ill-timed, impolitic, impracticable, impractical, inadvisable, inappropriate, inapt, inauspicious, inconvenient, ineffectual, inefficacious, inexpedient, infelicitous, inopportune, intrusive, jinxed, luckless, malfunctioning, miscarried, miscarrying, mistimed, off-base, ominous, out of luck, pathetic, pitiable, poor, sad, too late, unbefitting, under adverse circumstances, underprivileged, undesirable, unfavorable, unlucky, unprofitable, unpropitious, unseasonable, unseemly, unsuccessful, unsuitable, untimely, unworkable, useless
ASSOCIATED CONCEPTS: Medicaid, welfare

UNFOUNDED, _adjective_   baseless, empty, erroneous, fabricated, fallacious, false, fictitious, _fictus,_ fraudulent, groundless, idle, illogical, insubstantial, invented, spurious, suppositional, supposititious, trumped up, unattested, unauthenticated, unestablished, ungrounded, unproven, unsubstantial, unsupportable, unsupported, untenable, untrue, unwarranted, _vanus,_ without basis, without foundation, without reality, without substance

UNGUARDED _(Direct),_ **_adjective_**   aboveboard, brash, candid, frank, genuine, honest, indiscreet, open, open and aboveboard, open and sincere, straightforward, up front

UNGUARDED _(Without Protection),_ **_adjective_**   careless, defenseless, derelict, foolish, heedless, helpless, ill-advised, ill-considered, imprudent, inadvertent, inattentive, incautious, inconsiderate, indiscreet, injudicious, insecure, irresponsible, lax, mindless, neglectful, neglecting, negligent, nonobservant, nonrestrictive, permissive,

pregnable, relaxed, remiss, slack, unattended, undefended, unfortified, unheeding, unmindful, unobservant, unprotected, unscreened, unsheltered, unshielded, unsuspecting, unthinking, unvigilant, unwarned, unwary, unwatched, unwatchful, unwise, vulnerable, weaponless
ASSOCIATED CONCEPTS: abandonment

UNHEARD OF, *adjective* atypical, different, exceptional, exemplary, extraordinary, first, first ever, improbable, incomparable, matchless, never before encountered, new, not to be expected, novel, of its own kind, original, out of the ordinary, out of the pale, out of the way, rare, remarkable, sensational, singular, strange, surprising, tremendous, unaccustomed, uncommon, uncustomary, unequaled, unexampled, unexpected, unfamiliar, unheard of, unique, unknown, unmatched, unparalleled, unprecedented, unthought of, unusual

UNIFORM, *adjective* *aequabilis,* alike, compatible, conformable, consistent, consonant, *constans,* constant, conventional, correspondent, equable, equal, even, harmonious, homogeneous, identical, invariable, matched, orderly, orthodox, regular, same, similar, standard, steady, systematic, unaltered, unchanging, undeviating, undiversified, universal, unswerving, unvaried, unvarying, well-matched
ASSOCIATED CONCEPTS: uniform accounting system, uniform act, uniform commercial code, uniform fiduciary act, uniform laws, uniformity of laws, uniform operation of laws, uniform rate of taxation, uniform rates, uniform rule of taxation, uniform sales, uniform taxation

UNIFORMITY, *noun* absence of diversity, absence of variation, conformity, consistency, constancy, continuity, equability, evenness, homogeneity, levelness, order, persistence, regularity, singleness, smoothness, stability, standardization, symmetry, unity

UNILATERAL, *adjective* independent, lone, not reciprocal, one-sided, single, singular, unaided
ASSOCIATED CONCEPTS: unilateral action, unilateral contract, unilateral mistake

UNIMPEACHABLE, *adjective* above reproach, approved, believable, beyond reproach, blameless, commendable, credible, creditable, excellent, faultless, guiltless, ideal, impeccable, incontestable, incontrovertible, inculpable, indefeasible, innocent, irrefragable, irrefutable, irreprehensible, irreproachable, laudable, *locuples,* meritorious, noncontroversial, perfect, questionless, reputable, *sanctus,* sinless, spotless, stainless, unable to be discredited, unassailable, unblamable, unblameworthy, unblemished, uncensurable, unchallengeable, unconfutable, undeniable, undisputed, undoubted, unexceptionable, unmarred, unobjectionable, unquestionable, unrefutable, untainted, upright, worthy

UNINTENTIONAL, *adjective* accidental, adventitious, casual, chance, fortuitous, inadvertent, *insciens,* involuntary, purposeless, spontaneous, uncalculated, unconscious, undeliberate, undesigned, unexpected, unforeseen, unintended, unknowing, unmeant, unpremeditated, unpurposeful, unthinking, unwitting
ASSOCIATED CONCEPTS: unintentional act

UNION (Labor organization), *noun* affiliation, alliance of workers, amalgamation, association, brotherhood, confederacy, consociation, council, federation, fellowship, fraternity, guild, league, organization, organized labor, sodality, trade association

ASSOCIATED CONCEPTS: anti-union animus, craft union, international union, labor union, local union, trade union, union membership, union shop

UNION (Unity), *noun* accord, accordance, agreement, coalition, coherence, combination, concert, concord, concurrence, *congregatio,* connection, consensus, *consociatio,* consolidation, cooperation, coupling, fusion, harmony, homogeneity, joining, junction, oneness, unification, uniformity, unison

UNIQUE, *adjective* anomalous, atypical, beyond comparison, bizarre, curious, different, dissimilar, exceptional, extraordinary, incomparable, individual, matchless, nonpareil, nonuniform, novel, odd, original, peculiar, peerless, rare, single, singular, *singularis,* sole, special, uncommon, unconformable, unequaled, unexampled, *unicus,* unimitated, unmatched, unparalleled, unprecedented, unrepeated, unrivaled, unusual

UNIT (Department), *noun* branch, division, group, staff

UNIT (Item), *noun* ace, component, constituent, element, formation, integral, measure, monad, one, part, piece, quantity

UNITE, *verb* act in concert, add, affiliate, agglomerate, agree, ally, amalgamate, amass, assemble, assimilate, associate, be one, become one, blend, bring together, cement, centralize, cluster, coact, coalesce, collect, combine, come together, commingle, concur, confederate, conglomerate, congregate, *coniungere,* conjoin, connect, consolidate, consubstantiate, converge, cooperate, coordinate, *copulare,* couple, cowork, entwine, fall in with, form a league, form a single unit, form an alliance, fuse, gather together, group, grow together, harmonize, incorporate, interfuse, join, join forces, league, link, marry, mass, meet, meld, merge, mingle, *miscere,* mix, pool, pull together, reconcile, side with, solidify, syncretize, unify, wed
ASSOCIATED CONCEPTS: join in an action, united in interest

UNITED, *adjective* affiliated, allied, amalgamated, associated, attached, banded together, blended, bonded, cemented, coadunate, coexistent, coherent, cohesive, collective, combined, compatible, composite, compound, concerted, concordant, concurrent, conglomerate, conjoint, conjunctive, connected, consolidated, coupled, fused, harmonious, incorporated, indivisible, infrangible, inseparable, interrelated, joined, joint, linked, merged, mutual, one, solid, undivided
ASSOCIATED CONCEPTS: unitary trial, unity of interest, unity of possession, unity of title

UNITY, *noun* accordance, affinity, agreement, assent, closeness, coherence, cohesion, community of interests, comradeship, concert, concord, concurrence, congeniality, congruence, congruity, congruousness, consensus, consentaneity, consentaneousness, equivalence, feeling of identity, fellowship, fraternity, friendship, fusion, good feeling, good vibrations, good will, harmony, identity, inseparability, integrality, integration, integrity, kinship, likeness, mutual supportiveness, mutuality, one voice, oneness, rapport, reciprocity, resemblance, sameness, selfsameness, sharing, similarity, similitude, simplicity, singleness, singularity, solidarity, solidification, solidity, team spirit, togetherness, unanimity, understanding, unification, uniformity, union, unison, uniting
ASSOCIATED CONCEPTS: unity of interest, unity of possession, unity of title

UNIVERSAL, *adjective*   absolute, across-the-board, all-comprehensive, all-embracing, all-encompassing, all-including, all-inclusive, all-pervading, blanket, boundless, broad-based, complete, comprehensive, downright, encyclopedic, endless, every aspect, every facet, exhaustive, general, global, infinite, intensive, international, measureless, omnibus, outright, overall, panoramic, sweeping, the entire gamut, the entire universe, thorough, total, unlimited, unqualified, unrestricted, whole, wholesale, widespread, without exception
ASSOCIATED CONCEPTS: *ius cogens,* universal agar, universal causation, universal representation

UNJUST, *adjective*   biased, crooked, dishonorable, heinous, immoral, improper, inequitable, influenced, iniquitous, *iniquus, iniurius, iniustus,* interested, jaundiced, partial, prejudiced, prepossessed, undeserved, unequal, unfair, unjustifiable, unmerited, unprincipled, unreasonable, unwarranted, venal, warped, wicked, wrong, wrongful
ASSOCIATED CONCEPTS: unjust decision, unjust enrichment, unjust penalty, unjust sentence

UNJUST ENRICHMENT, *noun*   improper benefit, improper gain, inequitable benefit, inequitable gain, undeserved gain, unfair betterment, unfair gain, unfair profit, unjustifiable gain, unmerited benefit, wrongful benefit

UNJUSTIFIABLE, *adjective*   accusable, blameworthy, censurable, chargeable, culpable, discreditable, dishonorable, groundless, impeachable, indefensible, inexcusable, *iniquus, iniurius, iniustus,* irremissible, objectionable, reprehensible, unallowable, unforgivable, unjust, unjustified, unpardonable, unreasonable, vicious, wicked, without excuse, wrong
ASSOCIATED CONCEPTS: unjustifiable cause, unjustifiable claim, unjustifiable deviation

UNKNOWINGLY, *adverb*   adventitiously, fortuitously, ignorantly, inadvertently, innocently, insensibly, unawares, unconsciously, unintentionally, unmindfully, unsuspectingly, unwittingly, witlessly

UNKNOWN, *adjective*   alien, anonymous, concealed, cryptic, esoteric, foreign, hidden, incognito, indeterminate, inscrutable, insoluble, insolvable, mysterious, nameless, never experienced before, new, no credit to, novel, obscure, secret, strange, to be announced, unaccounted for, unascertained, undesignated, undetermined, undiscovered, undistinguished, unfamiliar, unfixed, unheard-of, unidentified, uninvestigated, unlabeled, unmeasured, unnamed, unnoted, unnoticed, unpopular, unrenowned, unrevealed, unseen, unset, unsettled, unspecified, unstudied, untold, untraced, untracked, withheld, without a name

UNLAWFUL, *adjective*   actionable, against the law, contraband, criminal, forbidden, illegal, illegitimate, illicit, *inlicitus,* lawless, *non legitimus,* not allowed by law, outlawed, prohibited, transgressive, unallowed, unauthorized, unconstitutional, unlicensed, unsanctioned, unwarranted, *vetitus,* wrongful, wrongous
ASSOCIATED CONCEPTS: unlawful accumulation, unlawful act, unlawful assembly, unlawful combination, unlawful contract, unlawful detainer, unlawful detention, unlawful enrichment, unlawful entrapment, unlawful entry, unlawful flight, unlawful force, unlawful picketing
FOREIGN PHRASES: *Ex pacto illicito non oritur actio.* From an unlawful agreement, no action will lie.

UNLESS, *preposition*   except, excepting, however, precluding, save, without

UNLIKE, *adjective*   alien, contrary, deviative, different, differing, discordant, discrepant, disparate, dissimilar, distinct, distinctive, divergent, diverse, heterogeneous, ill-matched, incongruous, irreconcilable, irrelative, not comparable, opposite, peculiar, unalike, unequal, unidentical, unrelated, unresembling, unsimilar, variant, varied

UNLIMITED, *adjective*   boundless, endless, free, immeasurable, *immensus,* incalculable, indefinite, inexhaustible, infinite, *infinitus,* interminable, limitless, measureless, perpetual, termless, unbounded, unchecked, unconditional, unconfined, uncontrolled, unending, unfathomable, universal, unrestrained, unrestricted, untold, vast, without number
ASSOCIATED CONCEPTS: unlimited liability

UNMANAGEABLE (Cumbersome), *adjective*   awkward, beyond control, bulky, difficult, impractical, incommodious, inconvenient, not disciplined, out of hand, uncomfortable, ungainly, unhandy, unruly

UNMANAGEABLE (Defiant), *adjective*   incorrigible, indocile, indomitable, insuppressible, irascible, irrepressible, obstreperous, out of hand, rebellious, recalcitrant, refractory, resistant, resisting, uncontrollable, uncooperative, ungovernable, unreconstructed, untamable, unyielding

UNMARKETABLE, *adjective*   not readily salable, nonsalable, unsalable, unvendible
ASSOCIATED CONCEPTS: unmarketable title

UNMISTAKABLE, *adjective*   apparent, autoptic, autoptical, bald, certain, clear, conclusive, conspicuous, decided, defined, distinct, distinguishable, evident, explicit, express, glaring, identifiable, indubitable, intelligible, known, lucid, manifest, notorious, obvious, open, overt, palpable, patent, perspicuous, plain, positive, pronounced, recognizable, sure, unambiguous, unconcealed, unconfusing, uncontestable, undeniable, undisguised, undoubted, unequivocal, unquestionable, visible, well-defined

UNMITIGATED, *adjective*   absolute, complete, consummate, downright, exhaustive, full, intensive, plenary, rank, rigid, severe, sheer, stark, thorough, unbounded, unconditional, unqualified, unsoftened, unsuppressed, untamed, untempered, unyielding, utter

UNNECESSARY, *adjective*   auxiliary, avoidable, dispensable, excess, excessive, expendable, expletive, extra, extraneous, extrinsic, gratuitous, inessential, irrelevant, needless, *non necessarius,* noncompulsory, optional, overmuch, redundant, spare, supererogative, supererogatory, superfluous, *supervacaneus, supervacuus,* supplemental, supplementary, surplus, uncalled-for, uncritical, unessential, unimportant, unneeded, unrequired
ASSOCIATED CONCEPTS: unnecessary force

UNOBJECTIONABLE, *adjective*   acceptable, adequate, admissible, allowable, condonable, defensible, harmless, inoffensive, irreprehensible, irreproachable, irreprovable, passable, satisfactory, tolerable, unblameworthy, uncensurable, unexceptionable, unimpeachable, vindicable

UNOBTRUSIVE, *adjective*   clandestine, covert, humble, meek, modest, natural, passive, quiet, reserved, restrained, reticent, retiring, self-effacing, shrinking, simple, subdued, surreptitious, unassuming, unconspicuous, undercover, underground, unimposing, unostentatious, unseen

UNOFFICIAL, *adjective* casual, informal, not to be quoted, off the record, personal, unauthoritative, unauthorized, unendorsed, without authority, without ceremony
ASSOCIATED CONCEPTS: unofficial ruling

UNORTHODOX, *adjective* *a ceteris dissentire,* aberrant, anomalous, deviative, different, divergent, eccentric, heretical, heterodox, irregular, lawless, out of step, unaccepted, unapproved, uncanonical, uncommon, unconformable, unconventional, unfashionable, unobservant, unusual

UNPAID, *adjective* due, free, given, gratis, gratuitous, in arrears, outstanding, owing, payable, uncollected, uncompensated, undischarged, unrecompensed, unremunerated, unrequited, unrewarded, unsalaried, unsettled, volunteer

UNPALATABLE, *adjective* abrasive, bitter, disagreeable, dislikable, displeasing, distasteful, foul-tasting, hostile, ill-flavored, inedible, noisome, objectionable, obnoxious, offensive, rancid, repellent, repelling, repugnant, repulsive, revolting, savorless, sour, unappealing, unappetizing, undesirable, unfriendly, uninviting, unlikable, unpleasant, unpleasing, unsavory, unwelcome

UNPARALLELED, *adjective* best, beyond compare, beyond comparison, cardinal, exceptional, extraordinary, incomparable, inestimable, inimitable, invaluable, isolated, leading, major, marvelous, matchless, nonconforming, nonpareil, outstanding, paramount, peerless, phenomenal, premium, prime, prodigious, rare, remarkable, singular, special, stupendous, superior, superlative, unapproachable, uncommon, unequaled, unexampled, unexcelled, unheard of, unique, unmatched, unparagoned, unprecedented, unrivaled, unsurpassed, unusual, without parallel, wonderful

UNPOLITIC, *adjective* careless, clumsy, foolish, harebrained, hasty, heedless, ill-advised, ill-judged, impolitic, improvident, imprudent, incautious, inconsiderate, indiscreet, inexpedient, injudicious, rash, reckless, senseless, stupid, tactless, temerarious, undiplomatic, unsagacious, unshrewd, untactful, unwary, unwise

UNPRECEDENTED, *adjective* anomalous, exceptional, extraordinary, first, *inauditus,* incomparable, initial, miraculous, modern, new, newfangled, novel, *novus,* original, rare, singular, uncustomary, unequaled, unexampled, unexpected, unfamiliar, unheard of, unique, unknown, unmatched, unparalleled, unrivaled, untraditional, unusual

UNPREDICTABLE, *adjective* aberrant, arbitrary, capricious, causeless, changeable, changeful, deviative, eccentric, erratic, fanciful, fickle, fitful, incalculable, inconstant, irregular, mercurial, mutable, random, spasmodic, speculative, unaccountable, uncertain, undependable, uneven, unexpected, unforeseeable, unmethodical, unreliable, unstable, unsteadfast, unsteady, unsure, unsystematic, variable, vicissitudinous, wavering

UNPREJUDICED, *adjective* broadminded, detached, disinterested, dispassionate, equitable, even-handed, fair, fairminded, impartial, independent, *integer,* judicial, just, neutral, nonpartisan, objective, open, openminded, proper, reasonable, tolerant, unbiased, unbigoted, uncolored, uninfluenced, unjaundiced, unprepossessed, unslanted, unswayed, unwarped
ASSOCIATED CONCEPTS: right to fair trial

UNPREMEDITATED, *adjective* extemporaneous, extempore, hasty, impromptu, improvisate, improvised, impulsive, indeliberate, not intended, offhand, rash, snap, spontaneous, thoughtless, uncalculated, unconsidered, undesigned, unintended, unintentional, unmeant, unplanned, unprepared, unpurposeful, unrehearsed, unstudied, unthinking
ASSOCIATED CONCEPTS: manslaughter, unpremeditated murder

UNPRETENTIOUS, *adjective* artless, humble, *inadfectatus,* informal, matter of fact, meek, modest, *modicus,* natural, plain, quiet, retiring, simple, *simplex,* unaffected, unassuming, undistinguished, unelaborate, unobtrusive, unostentatious, without airs

UNPRODUCTIVE, *adjective* abortive, arid, barren, doomed, dry, effete, exhausted, fallow, fruitless, futile, impotent, ineffectual, inefficacious, inefficient, infecund, *infecundus,* infertile, inoperative, issueless, jejune, nugatory, otiose, profitless, sterile, *sterilis,* unavailing, unfruitful, unprofitable, unprolific, unremunerative, unrewarding, unsuccessful, unyielding, useless, wasteful, without results, worthless

UNPROFESSIONAL, *adjective* amateurish, contrary to professional ethics, improper, imprudent, inappropriate, indiscreet, injudicious, nonexpert, not of high standards, unbefitting, unbusinesslike, undignified, unethical, unfitting, unscholarly, unseemly, unsuitable
ASSOCIATED CONCEPTS: Code of Professional Responsibility, disbarment, grievance committee, unprofessional conduct

UNPROPITIOUS, *adjective* adverse, hopeless, ill-disposed, ill-omened, ill-timed, inauspicious, minatory, ominous, sinister, threatening, unfavorable, unfortunate, unpromising, untoward

UNQUALIFIED *(Not competent),* ***adjective*** deficient, disqualified, ill-qualified, inadequate, incapable, incompetent, ineffective, inefficient, ineligible, inept, inexperienced, inexpert, unable, unadapted, uneffective, unequipped, unfit, unprepared, unready, unsuited
ASSOCIATED CONCEPTS: unqualified opinion

UNQUALIFIED *(Unlimited),* ***adjective*** absolute, all-encompassing, boundless, complete, consummate, downright, full, illimitable, immoderate, limitless, measureless, not modified, outright, plenary, *summus,* sweeping, total, unbound, unchecked, unconditional, unconstrained, uncontrolled, unmitigated, unmodified, unreserved, unrestrained, unrestricted, unsparing, unstinted, utter
ASSOCIATED CONCEPTS: unqualified acceptance, unqualified ownership

UNQUESTIONABLE, *adjective* above criticism, above reproach, absolute, authoritative, believable, beyond all question, certain, clear, conclusive, decided, definite, definitive, doubtless, evident, ideal, incontrovertible, indisputable, indubitable, irrefutable, irreprehensible, irreproachable, irresponsible to question, manifest, obvious, patent, plausible, real, realistic, reliable, self-evident, sure, unassailable, unchallenged, uncontestable, undeniable, undisputed, undoubted, unimpeachable, unmistakable
ASSOCIATED CONCEPTS: that cannot be impeached, unquestionable integrity

UNREASONABLE, *adjective* absurd, asinine, capricious, contorted, contrary, exaggerated, excessive, exorbitant, extravagant, extreme, foolish, groundless, ill-advised,

ill-judged, illogical, immoderate, *iniquus,* indefensible, injudicious, inordinate, intemperate, irrational, ludicrous, nonsensical, pervicacious, pointless, preposterous, recalcitrant, ridiculous, senseless, twisted, undue, unfair, unjust, unjustifiable, unsensible, unsound, untenable, unwarranted, unwise
ASSOCIATED CONCEPTS: arbitrary and capricious action, unreasonable delay, unreasonable force, unreasonable rate of interest, unreasonable restraint, unreasonable restraint on alienation, unreasonable search, unreasonable use

UNREFUTABLE, *adjective* accurate, certain, demonstrated, doubtless, factual, inappealable, incontestable, incontrovertible, indisputable, indubitable, irrefragable, irrefutable, positive, proved, proven, sure, true, unanswerable, unconfutable, uncontroversial, undeniable, unequivocal, unimpeachable, unquestionable, valid, veracious, veritable

UNRELATED, *adjective* alien, different, differing, discrepant, disparate, dissimilar, diverse, extraneous, foreign, heterogeneous, incomparable, incompatible, incongruous, independent, irrelative, irrelevant, mismatched, separate, strange, unaffiliated, unallied, unassociated, unattached, unconformable, unconnected, ungermane, unlike, unmatched
ASSOCIATED CONCEPTS: unrelated claims

UNRELENTING, *adjective* adamant, austere, ceaseless, constant, continual, continuous, cruel, determined, diligent, endless, enduring, hard, *immitis,* implacable, incessant, inclement, indefatigable, *inexorabilis,* inexorable, inflexible, merciless, obdurate, perseverant, persevering, persistent, pertinacious, pitiless, relentless, remorseless, resolved, rigid, rigorous, ruthless, sedulous, severe, steadfast, stern, stubborn, tenacious, unappeasable, unbending, uncompassionate, uncompromising, undeviating, unforgiving, unmerciful, unpitying, unsoftening, unsparing, unsympathetic, unwavering, unyielding

UNRELIABLE, *adjective* capricious, changeful, deceitful, faithless, fallible, false, fickle, inconstant, insecure, irresponsible, perfidious, precarious, shifty, tergiversating, treacherous, two-faced, undependable, unpredictable, unsound, unstable, unsteady, untrue, untrustworthy, vacillating, wavering
ASSOCIATED CONCEPTS: unreliable evidence, unreliable testimony, unreliable witness

UNREMITTING, *adjective* *adsiduus,* assiduous, ceaseless, constant, continual, continuous, *continuus,* diligent, durable, enduring, incessant, indefatigable, perennial, perpetual, perseverant, persevering, persistent, pertinacious, sedulous, tenacious, unabated, unbroken, unceasing, unchanging, unfailing, unintermittent, uninterrupted, unshifting, unswerving, untiring, unvarying, unwearied

UNREQUITED, *adjective* thankless, unacknowledged, unanswered, uncompensated, unrecompensed, unremunerated, unrepaid, unreturned, unrewarded

UNRESPONSIVE, *adjective* aloof, cold, cool, dispassionate, elusive, emotionless, evasive, impassive, inattentive, indifferent, insensitive, irresponsive, laconic, mum, mute, pitiless, reserved, reticent, secretive, taciturn, unanswering, uncommunicative, uncompassionate, unconcerned, unconversable, uncooperative, unemotional, unfeeling, unimpressible, unimpressionable, uninfluenceable, uninterested, unmoved, unreacting, unreplying, unresponding, unsociable, unsympathetic
ASSOCIATED CONCEPTS: evasive contempt, unresponsive answer, unresponsive testimony

UNRESTRAINED *(Not in custody),* **adjective** free, independent, unbounded, unbridled, unchecked, unconfined, unconstrained, uncurbed, unencumbered, unfettered, unhampered, unhindered, unimpeded, unlimited, unobstructed, unprevented, unshackled, unsuppressed, untrammeled

UNRESTRAINED *(Not repressed),* **adjective** dissolute, effusive, excessive, extravagant, immoderate, incontinent, intemperate, lawless, lewd, libertine, licentious, loose, prodigal, rampant, spirited, unbridled, unchecked, unconstrained, uncontrolled, uncurbed, undisciplined, unfettered, ungoverned, unhampered, unhindered, unlimited, unreined, unrepressed, unreserved, unsuppressed, wanton, wild

UNRESTRICTED, *adjective* boundless, *effrenatus,* free, immoderate, independent, limitless, open, permitted, unbound, unbounded, unbridled, unchecked, unconditional, unconfined, unconstrained, uncontained, uncontrolled, unfettered, unforbidden, unlimited, unobstructed, unqualified, unrestrained, unshackled, untrammeled, without strings
ASSOCIATED CONCEPTS: unrestricted use

UNRULY, *adjective* chaotic, contrary, contumacious, disobedient, disorderly, *effrenatus, ferox,* fractious, froward, hard to control, headstrong, incorrigible, indocile, insubordinate, intractable, irrepressible, lawless, mutinous, obstinate, obstreperous, out of control, perverse, rampant, rebellious, recalcitrant, refractory, resistive, restive, riotous, rowdy, stormy, stubborn, troublesome, turbulent, unbridled, uncompliant, uncomplying, uncontrollable, uncurbed, ungovernable, unmanageable, unrestrained, unsubmissive, untoward, unyielding, wanton, wayward, wild, willful

UNSATISFACTORY, *adjective* deficient, disagreeable, disappointing, disapproved, displeasing, disquieting, distressing, disturbing, faulty, feeble, imperfect, inadequate, inappropriate, inapt, inept, inexpedient, inferior, insufficient, intolerable, lame, *non idoneus,* not up to par, objectionable, offensive, poor, rejected, unacceptable, unapt, unbefitting, undesirable, unfavorable, unfit, ungratifying, unpleasant, unsatisfying, unseemly, unsuitable, untoward, unwelcome, unworthy, upsetting, useless, vexing, wanting, weak
ASSOCIATED CONCEPTS: unsatisfactory testimony

UNSATISFIED *(Delinquent),* **adjective** due, due and owing, in arrears, outstanding, payable, uncollected, unfilled, unpaid
ASSOCIATED CONCEPTS: unsatisfied judgment funds, unsatisfied judgments

UNSATISFIED *(Disappointed),* **adjective** despondent, discontented, disgruntled, displeased, dissatisfied, frustrated, greedy, insatiable, insatiate, malcontented, quenchless, thwarted, ungratified, unhappy, unquenchable, unslaked

UNSAVORY, *adjective* disagreeable, disgusting, disliked, distasteful, intolerable, loathsome, mawkish, nasty, nauseating, nauseous, objectionable, obnoxious, offensive, repelling, repugnant, revolting, sickening, unalluring, unappetizing, unattractive, undelectable, undesirable, uninviting, unpalatable, unpleasant, unpleasing

UNSCRUPULOUS, *adjective* base, conscienceless, corrupt, crooked, deceitful, dishonest, dishonorable, disingenuous, faithless, false, fraudulent, immoral, inequitable, iniquitous, lawless, perfidious, profligate, questionable, roguish, ruthless, shifty, sly, treacherous, two-faced, underhand, unethical, unfair, unjust, unlawful, unprincipled, unrestrained, vicious, villainous, wanton, wicked, without integrity, without scruples, wrongful

UNSEEMLY, adjective base, boorish, coarse, crude, discreditable, disreputable, distasteful, gross, ignoble, improper, in bad taste, inappropriate, incongruous, incorrect, indecent, indecorous, *indecorus,* indelicate, inelegant, offensive, out of character, out of place, preposterous, reprehensible, rude, shameful, unapt, unbecoming, unbefitting, undignified, undue, unfit, unfitting, ungenteel, unhandsome, unmanly, unmeet, unpraiseworthy, unpresentable, unrefined, unsightly, unsuitable, untasteful, vulgar, wrong

UNSETTLED, adjective adrift, afloat, agitated, capricious, changeable, changing, conjectural, deranged, desolate, disarranged, disputable, disturbed, doubtful, dubious, due, fickle, *incertus, inconstans,* inconstant, migratory, mutable, nervous, new, open, outstanding, owing, pending, perturbed, restless, speculative, tentative, transient, troubled, unadjusted, unattached, unbalanced, uncertain, unchartered, uncollected, undecided, undetermined, uneasy, unessayed, unexplored, unfixed, uninhabited, unnerved, unoccupied, unpaid, unresolved, unrooted, unstable, unstaid, unsteady, untried, untrodden, unventured, upset, vacillating, *varius,* wandering, wavering

UNSOLICITED, adjective complimentary, free, gratuitous, offered, proffered, unasked, unbidden, uncalled-for, undesired, uninvited, unrequested, unsought, unwanted, unwelcome, unwished, voluntary, volunteered
ASSOCIATED CONCEPTS: unsolicited response, unsolicited sale

UNSOUND *(Fallacious),* **adjective** absurd, defective, disputable, erroneous, false, faulty, groundless, ill-founded, illogical, improbable, incongruous, incorrect, insubstantial, invalid, irrational, mistaken, questionable, senseless, sophistical, speculative, unauthentic, ungrounded, unreal, unreasonable, unreasoned, unsubstantial, untenable, untrue, unwarranted, worthless, wrong

UNSOUND *(Not strong),* **adjective** below par, broken, decayed, decrepit, defective, deficient, deranged, deteriorated, diseased, disturbed, exhausted, faulty, feeble, ill, impaired, imperfect, infirm, insecure, insolvent, precarious, sickly, tainted, unbacked, unhealthy, unreliable, unsafe, unsettled, unstable, unsteady, unsubstantial, untrustworthy, unwell, warped, wasted, weak, worn

UNSPECIFIED, adjective anonymous, general, generic, indefinable, indefinite, indeterminate, indistinct, non specific, obscure, unacknowledged, unclear, undefined, undesignated, unfixed, unnamed, unsettled, vague

UNSUITABLE, adjective absurd, *alienus,* amiss, awkward, conflicting, contrary, discordant, discrepant, disparate, dissonant, disturbing, divergent, ill-adapted, impertinent, improper, imprudent, in bad taste, inadequate, inadmissible, inadvisable, inapplicable, inapposite, inappropriate, inapt, incommodious, *incommodus,* incompatible, incongruous, inconvenient, indecorous, inexpedient, infelicitous, inharmonious, inopportune, intolerable, irrelevant, malapropos, mismatched, objectionable, out of character, out of keeping, out of place, poorly adapted, unacceptable, unapt, unbecoming, unbeseeming, uncongenial, undesirable, unfavorable, unfit, unfitting, unfortunate, unsatisfactory, unsatisfying, unseasonable, unseemly, unsuited, untimely, untoward
ASSOCIATED CONCEPTS: unsuitable for consumption

UNSUPPORTED, adjective based on conjecture, baseless, groundless, not authenticated, not established, not substantiated, suppositional, supposititious, unabetted, unaided, unassisted, unattested, unauthenticated, unbacked, uncertified, uncollaborated, unconfirmed, uncorroborated, undemonstrated, unfounded, unproved, unproven, unseconded, unsubstantiated, unsustained, untenable, unvalidated, unverified, without basis, without foundation
ASSOCIATED CONCEPTS: unsupported by a preponderance of the evidence

UNSURE, adjective ambiguous, ambivalent, between, betwixt, chancy, changeable, constrained, dicey, doubtful, doubting, dubious, equivocal, fickle, hesitant, hesitating, holding back, indecisive, indemonstrable, irresolute, not certain, not decided, not definitive, not resolved, not sure, of two minds, on the fence, precarious, provisional, shaky, skeptical, suspicious, tentative, unaccountable, uncountable, undecided, unpredictable, unsteady, unsubstantial, up in the air, wavering
ASSOCIATED CONCEPTS: unsure of guilt

UNSURPASSED, adjective absolute, best, beyond comparison, beyond praise, cardinal, consummate, dazzling, dominant, excellent, exceptional, incomparable, infallible, inimitable, leading, matchless, *ne plus ultra,* paramount, peerless, premium, primary, prime, second to none, superior, superlative, supreme, the acme, transcendent, unapproachable, unequaled, unexampled, unexcelled, unique, unmatched, unparagoned, unparalleled, unrivaled, without equal, without parallel

UNSUSPECTING, adjective believing, credulous, easily deceived, gullible, *incautus,* innocent, *minime* suspicax, naive, off guard, simple, trustful, trusting, unaware, unconscious, undoubting, unexpectant, unguarded, unquestioning, unsuspecting, unsuspicious, unwarned, without suspicion

UNSUSTAINABLE, adjective baseless, controvertible, doubtful, erroneous, false, groundless, incorrect, insupportable, questionable, unauthentic, unconfirmable, undemonstrable, unmaintainable, unprovable, untenable, untrue, untrustworthy, unverifiable, wrong

UNTENABLE, adjective accessible, baseless, controvertible, defenseless, erroneous, exposed, fallacious, false, faulty, groundless, hollow, illogical, implausible, incapable of being defended, incapable of being held, incapable of being maintained, incorrect, indefensible, insupportable, invalid, irrational, powerless, pregnable, questionable, refutable, ridiculous, specious, undefended, undemonstrable, unfortified, unguarded, unjustifiable, unmaintainable, unprotected, unreasonable, unsound, unsustainable, unwarrantable, vincible, vulnerable, weak, wrong

UNTIL, adverb as far as, by the time that, down to, pending, til, to, to the time when, up to, up to the time of

UNTIMELY, adjective anachronic, anachronistic, anachronous, badly timed, erroneous in date, ill-advised, ill-considered, ill-timed, *immaturus,* improper, imprudent, inapposite, inappropriate, inappropriately timed, inauspicious, inconvenient, infelicitous, inopportune, *intempestivus,* malapropos, misjudged, mistimed, out of keeping, out of place, poorly timed, unfavorable, unpromising, unpropitious, unpunctual, unseasonable, unsuitably timed

UNTROUBLED, *adjective* balanced, calm, collected, composed, controlled, cool, dispassionate, easygoing, even-tempered, impassive, imperturbable, in control, laid-back, level-headed, mellow, peaceful, placid, poised, rational, reasonable, relaxed, self-controlled, sensible, steady, unbothered, undisturbed, unemotional, unexcited, unflappable, unflustered, unimpassioned, unmoved, unperturbed, unruffled, unstirred

UNTRUE, *adjective* all wrong, amiss, apocryphal, awry, bogus, contradictory, contrary to fact, counterfeit, deceitful, deceiving, deceptive, defective, delusive, devoid of truth, dishonest, disingenuous, disloyal, disobedient, duplicitous, errant, erring, erroneous, faithless, fake, faked, fallacious, false, false-principled, *falsus,* faulty, fictitious, flawed, forged, fraudulent, groundless, guileful, hypocritical, in error, inaccurate, inconstant, incorrect, incredulous, insidious, insincere, invalid, invented, lying, mendacious, miscalculated, misleading, misrepresentative, mistaken, mock, not true, off base, perfidious, perverse, perverted, prevaricating, recreant, scheming, sham, shifty, spurious, traitorous, treacherous, treasonable, trumped up, truthless, two-faced, uncandid, underhanded, undutiful, unfaithful, unfounded, ungrounded, unorthodox, unproved, unreal, unsound, unsubstantial, untrustworthy, unveracious, wrong
ASSOCIATED CONCEPTS: liable, slander

UNTRUSTWORTHY, *adjective* capricious, changeable, conniving, deceitful, deceptive, dishonest, dishonorable, disloyal, double-dealing, faithless, fallible, false, fickle, fly-by-night, fraudulent, frivolous, illusive, inconstant, insecure, insidious, irresponsible, mercurial, perfidious, precarious, questionable, shifty, slippery, tergiversating, treacherous, two-faced, unauthenticated, uncertain, undependable, unfaithful, unreliable, unsafe, unsound, unstable, unsteadfast, untrue, unworthy of confidence, unworthy of trust, variable, wavering

UNUSUAL, *adjective* aberrant, abnormal, alien, amazing, anomalous, astonishing, astounding, atypical, bizarre, choice, conspicuous, curious, different, distinctive, distinguished, exceptional, extraordinary, extreme, fantastic, fresh, important, incomparable, inconceivable, inconsistent, incredible, indescribable, individual, infrequent, inusitate, irregular, little-known, marked, marvelous, matchless, memorable, modern, new, newfangled, nonpareil, notable, noteworthy, novel, occasional, odd, offbeat, original, out of the ordinary, outlandish, outstanding, particular, peculiar, peerless, phenomenal, portentous, prodigious, prominent, radical, rare, refreshing, remarkable, scarce, significant, singular, special, startling, strange, striking, supernormal, surprising, unaccustomed, unclassifiable, uncommon, unconventional, uncustomary, unequaled, unexpected, unfamiliar, unhabitual, unheard of, unique, unmatched, unnatural, unorthodox, unparalleled, unprecedented, unprevalent, unrivaled, unroutine, untraditional, untypical, unwonted
ASSOCIATED CONCEPTS: cruel and unusual punishment

UNVEIL, *verb* *aperire,* bare, begin, bring to light, demonstrate, denude, *detegere,* disclose, display, divest, divulge, exhibit, expose, extract, lay open, make known, make plain, make visible, manifest, open up, originate, present, reveal, show, start, strip, uncase, uncloak, unconceal, uncover, uncurtain, undrape, undress, unfold, unmask, unrobe, unseal, unwrap

UNVERSED, *adjective* ignorant, illiterate, *imperitus,* inexperienced, inexpert, raw, *rudis,* unacquainted, unclever,

unconversant, undisciplined, undrilled, uneducated, unexcercised, unfamiliar, unindoctrinated, uninformed, uninitiated, unknowing, unknowledgeable, unlearned, unlettered, unpracticed, unprepared, unproficient, unqualified, unread, unschooled, unskilled, unstudied, untaught

UNWARRANTED, *adjective* arbitrary, baseless, excessive, fulsome, groundless, immoderate, improper, indefensible, inexcusable, inordinate, needless, objectionable, outrageous, overmuch, superabundant, superfluous, supernumerary, unauthorized, uncalled-for, unconscionable, undue, unentitled, unfair, unfounded, unjust, unjustifiable, unjustified, unlawful, unnecessary, unreasonable, unsanctioned, unwarrantable, wrongful

UNWILLING, *adjective* adverse, against, diametrically opposed, disagreeing, disinclined, disobedient, dissenting, forced, independent of one's will, indisposed, involuntary, loathe, not opposed, reluctant, renitent, resistant, unconscious, unintentional, unthinking, unwilled, unwitting, willingly
ASSOCIATED CONCEPTS: contumacious witness, hostile witness, unwilling witness

UNWILLINGLY, *adverb* adversely, demurringly, indisposedly, involuntarily, recalcitrantly, reluctantly, unconsentingly, without assent, without consent
ASSOCIATED CONCEPTS: unknowingly

UNWISE, *adjective* detrimental, disadvantageous, fatuous, foolish, ill-advised, ill-considered, ill-contrived, ill-devised, ill-judged, ill-managed, illogical, impolitic, imprudent, inadvisable, inane, inappropriate, inapt, incongruous, inept, inexpedient, injudicious, insensate, irrational, misadvised, reckless, senseless, short-sighted, stupid, thoughtless, unfit, unintelligent, unpolite, unreasonable, unreasoning, unsound, unthinking

UNWITTING, *adjective* accidental, adventitious, aimless, blind, chance, fortuitous, ignorant, inadvertent, *insciens, inscius,* involuntary, purposeless, thoughtless, unapprized, unaware, unconscious, undesigned, unexpected, uninformed, unintended, unintentional, unknowing, unmeant, unmindful, unpremeditated, unpurposed, unsuspecting, unthinking

UNWORKABLE, *adjective* effort-wasting, impossible, impracticable, impractical, inadequate, incapable of being done, inconceivable, ineffective, ineffectual, inefficacious, infeasible, inoperable, insurmountable, otiose, out of the question, useless, unachievable, unattainable, undoable, unfeasible, unnegotiable, unobtainable, unperformable, unrealizable, unviable

UNWORTHY, *adjective* base, contemptible, inferior, lacking worth, meager, meritless, not fit, undeserving, unfit, unqualified, worthless

UNYIELDING, *adjective* adamant, adamantine, constant, decided, dedicated, determined, devoted, enduring, faithful, firm, fixed, hard, headstrong, immobile, immovable, impliant, indomitable, inductile, inexorable, inflexible, intractable, intransigent, invariable, obdurate, obstinate, opinionated, perseverant, persevering, persistent, pertinacious, perverse, pervicacious, recalcitrant, refractory, relentless, renitent, resisting, resolute, resolved, rigid, sedulous, set, settled, solid, stable, stanch, steadfast, steady, stern, stiff, strong, stubborn, tenacious, tough, true, unbending, unchangeable, uncompromising, uncontrollable,

587

undeviating, ungovernable, unimpressible, uninfluenceable, unmanageable, unpliable, unwavering, wayward, willful, zealous

UPBRAID, verb   admonish, berate, blame, blast, call on the carpet, call to account, castigate, censure, chastise, chew out, chide, condemn, correct, criticize, curse, decry, denounce, denunciate, fulminate against, give a piece of one's mind, give a tongue-lashing, have harsh words with, indict, inveigh against, lash, lay out in lavender, lecture, objurgate, rail against, rake over the coals, rap on the knuckles, read the riot act, rebuke, remonstrate, reprehend, reprimand, reproach, reprobate, reprove, revile, scold, set straight, straighten out, take a hard line with, take to task, tell off, vilify, vilipend

UPHEAVAL, noun   blowup, break, chaos, collapse, convulsion, disorder, disquiet, disruption, eruption, explosion, furor, hurricane, insurrection, irruption, quake, rebellion, revolt, revolution, sudden change, tempest, tornado, tumult, unrest
ASSOCIATED CONCEPTS: terrorism

UPHOLD, verb   accept, acknowledge, advocate, affirm, agree with, aid, approve, assert, assist, authenticate, back, back up, bear up, bolster, brace, buttress, carry, champion, confirm, corroborate, countenance, decide in favor of, defend, elevate, encourage, endorse, espouse, favor, guard, help, hold up, justify, keep, maintain, perpetuate, preserve, prop, protect, raise, sanction, second, speak for, stand by, stand up for, stay, *substantiate,* support, sustain, *sustentare,* sustinere, upraise, vindicate, warrant
ASSOCIATED CONCEPTS: uphold a decision, uphold the law

UPKEEP, noun   aid, backing, care, care-giving, caring, economic support, endowment, fosterage, life support, maintenance, nourishment, nurturance, operating costs, preservation, provision, relief, safekeeping, subsidization, subsidy, subsistence, support, support services, sustenance, sustentation, total support, welfare
ASSOCIATED CONCEPTS: maintenance

UPRIGHT, adjective   aboveboard, candid, circumspect, conscientious, erect, estimable, ethical, fair, forthright, good, guileless, highly principled, honest, *honestus,* honorable, incorruptible, *integer,* just, laudable, legitimate, moral, *probus,* pure, reasonable, reputable, respectable, righteous, scrupulous, square, straightforward, trustworthy, truthful, uncorrupt, unimpeachable, upstanding, veracious, virtuous, worthy

UPRISING, noun   anarchy, chaos, civil disorder, coup d'etat, fighting in the streets, general uprising, insurgence, insurgency, insurrection, mass confusion, mutiny, outbreak, overthrow, rebellion, resistance, revolt, revolution, riot, rise, upheaval

UPROAR, noun   ado, affray, agitation, bedlam, blowup, bluster, boiling, brawl, brouhaha, chaos, clamor, commotion, conflict, disorder, disruption, disturbance, embroilment, fracas, furor, hullabaloo, pandemonium, ruckus, scuffle, struggle, tumult, turbulence, turmoil

UPSET, verb   agitate, beat, bother, capsize, confuse, conquer, crush, defeat, demolish, derange, destroy, disarrange, discomfit, discompose, disconcert, disorganize, displace, disquiet, distress, disturb, embarrass, enrage, *evertere,* fluster, invert, overpower, overthrow, overturn, overwhelm, perturb, put out of order, quash, reverse, ruin, shock, startle, subvert, *subvertere,* supersede, tip over,

topple, tumble, turn upside down, undo, unnerve, unsettle, upend, vanquish, worst
ASSOCIATED CONCEPTS: upset a lower court's ruling

URGE, verb   activate, adjure, advance, advise, advocate, appeal to, beg, beseech, coax, drive, encourage, entreat, evoke, exhort, expostulate, goad, hurry, impel, *impellere,* implore, importune, *incitare,* incite, insist, instigate, invite, motivate, move, persuade, prescribe, press, prevail upon, prod, promote, prompt, propel, provoke, push, recommend, request, rouse, solicit, spur, stimulate, *urgere*

URGENCY, noun   crisis, critical situation, crucial situation, dire necessity, emergency, exigency, expeditious need, hurried need, immediate need, importance, instant need, matter of life and death, necessity, pressing need, urgent need
ASSOCIATED CONCEPTS: good samaritan laws, *in extremis,* stay of execution, statute of limitations, temporary restraining order

URGENT, adjective   clamant, compelling, compulsory, critical, crucial, crying, demanding, earnest, essential, exigent, grave, *gravis,* impelling, imperative, important, importunate, indispensable, insistent, instant, *necessarius,* necessary, necessitous, pressing, required, serious, vital, weighty

USABLE, adjective   appliable, applicable, appropriateness, compliant, effective, effectual, employable, exploitable, fitting, operable, practical, recyclable, reusable, serviceable, utilizable
ASSOCIATED CONCEPTS: fit for the intended purpose

USAGE, noun   application, conduct, consuetude, *consuetudo,* convention, custom, customary use, disposition, employment, established custom, established practice, fashion, fixed procedure, form, formula, habit, habitual use, habitude, management, manner, method, mode, *mos,* operation, practice, prescription, prevalence, routine, service, style, system, tradition, treatment, use, utilization, vogue, wear, wont
ASSOCIATED CONCEPTS: common usage, custom and usage, general usage
FOREIGN PHRASES: *Consuetudo ex certa causa rationabili usitata privat communem legem.* A custom, based on a certain and reasonable cause, supersedes the common law. *Optimus interpres rerum usus.* Usage is the best interpreter of things. *In contractibus, tacite insunt quae sunt moris et consuetudinis.* In contracts, matters of custom and usage are tacitly implied. *Non ex opinionibus singulorum, sed ex communi usu, nomina exaudiri debent.* The names of things ought to be understood, not according to individual opinions, but according to common usage. *Obtemperandum est consuetudini rationabili tanquam legi.* A reasonable custom is to be obeyed like law. *Quae praeter consuetudinem et morem majorum fiunt neque placent neque recta videntur.* Things which are done contrary to the custom and manner of our ancestors neither please nor appear right.

USE, noun   adhibition, adoption, application, avail, benefit, convenience, disposal, disposition, employment, enjoyment, exercitation, exploitation, function, means, practice, purpose, service, serviceability, suitability, usage, usefulness, *usus, utilitas,* utility, utilization
ASSOCIATED CONCEPTS: actual use, apparent use, beneficial use, best and highest use, business use, charitable use, common use, contingent use, convenient use, corporate use, customary use, declared use, domestic use, dominent use, exclusive use, existing use, forseeable use, hostile use, lawful use, mutual use, nonconforming use, nonpublic use,

normal use, offensive use, official use, ordinary use, permissive use, personal use, primary use, principal use, private use, reasonable use, resulting use, secondary use, shifting use, Statute of Uses, suitable use, unfit for use, use and derivate use

USEFUL, *adjective* advantageous, advisable, applicable, appropriate, availing, befitting, beneficial, commodious, conducive, congruous, constructive, contributing, contributory, convenient, decent, desirable, doable, effective, effectual, efficacious, employable, expedient, favorable, feasible, fit, fitting, functional, good, handy, instrumental, of use, operative, opportune, positive, practical, pragmatic, productive, profitable, proper, remedial, rewarding, right, salutary, seemly, suitable, usable, valuable, wise, worthwhile
ASSOCIATED CONCEPTS: usefulness

USELESS, *adjective* aimless, barren, counterproductive, effete, empty, failed fatuitous, fatuous, feckless, for naught, frivolous, fruitless, functionless, futile, idle, impotent, impracticable, inadequate, inane, incapable, incompetent, inconsequential, ineffective, ineffectual, inefficacious, inefficient, inept, inessential, inoperative, inutile, invalid, meaningless, needless, no go, no good, not serving any purpose, nugatory, null and void, of no avail, of no force, of no purpose, of no use, otiose, pointless, powerless, profitless, purposeless, redundant, superfluous, to no avail, to no purpose, trivial, unavailing, unfit, unhelpful, unimportant, unnecessary, unproductive, unprofitable, unsatisfactory, unserviceable, unsuccessful, unusable, vain, valueless, void, worthless

USUAL, *adjective* abundant, accepted, accustomed, acknowledged, average, banal, casual, characteristic, characterless, colorless, common, commonplace, conformable, conforming, consistent, consuetudinal, consuetudinary, conventional, current, customary, daily, established, everyday, expected, familiar, frequent, general, habitual, humdrum, inconspicuous, indifferent, insignificant, known, mediocre, middling, moderate, monotonous, natural, nondescript, normal, ordinary, orthodox, pat, pedestrian, plain, plentiful, popular, prevailing, prevalent, prosaic, prosy, recurrent, regular, repeated, representative, rife, routine, set, stale, standard, stereotyped, stock, tedious, traditional, trivial, typical, undistinctive, undistinguished, unexceptional, unimaginitive, unimpressive, uninteresting, universal, unmarked, unmemorable, unoriginal, unremarkable, unsophisticated, unsurprising, unvaried, vernacular, well-known, well-trodden, wonted, workaday
ASSOCIATED CONCEPTS: usual conduct, usual course of conduct, usual place of abode, usual terms

USURIOUS, *adjective* criminal interest, excessive, exorbitant, extortionate, illegal, immoderate, improper rate of interest, inordinate, unconscionable, undue, unreasonable

USURP, *verb* accroach, appropriate unlawfully, arrogate, assume, assume command, assume without authority, commandeer, encroach, help oneself to, hold by force, lay hold of, seize, seize power, *sibi adsumere,* squat, steal, take, take charge, take possession, wrest

USURY, *noun* criminal rate of interest, excessive interest, excessive rate, exorbitant interest, exploitation, *faeneratio,* high interest, illegal interest, overcharge, unconscionable rate of interest

UTILITY *(Public service),* ***noun*** public business, public company, public corporation, public industry

UTILITY *(Usefulness),* ***noun*** adequacy, advantage, advantageousness, applicability, avail, benefit, convenience, efficacy, employability, fruitfulness, function, helpfulness, practicality, productiveness, productivity, profit, profitability, service, serviceability, suitability, usability, use, value
FOREIGN PHRASES: ***Omne magnum exemplum habet aliquid ex iniquo, quod publica utilitate compensatur.*** Every great example has some unfairness, which is compensated by the public utility.

UTILIZATION, *noun* applicability, employability, practicality, serviceability, usability, usefulness

UTILIZE, *verb* adopt, apply, avail, benefit, employ, enjoy, exploit, incorporate, practice, purpose, service, use

UTMOST, *adjective* extreme, furthest, greatest, highest, maximal, maximum, most, superlative, supreme
ASSOCIATED CONCEPTS: utmost care

UTMOST, *noun* best, degree, extreme limit, extremity, farthest reach, furthest point, greatest amount, greatest degree, highest, maximum, optimum, the most possible

UTTER, *verb* air, announce, articulate, assert, asseverate, aver, breathe, broach, circulate, come out with, communicate, declaim, declare, deliver, *dicere,* disclose, divulge, emit, enunciate, express, give expression to, give forth, impart, issue, make known, mouth, proclaim, pronounce, propound, publicize, publish, recite, reveal, sound, speak, spread, state, talk, tell, vent, voice

UTTERANCE, *noun* account, affirmation, announcement, assertion, asseveration, averment, avowal, comment, declaration, deposition, detailed account, enumeration, exclamation, explanation, exposition, observation, pronouncement, recapitulation, recital, recitation, remark, report, statement, story, summary, testimony

VACANT, *adjective* bare, blank, clear, depleted, deserted, devoid, disengaged, empty, exhausted, free, hollow, idle, not in use, not occupied, open, unemployed, unfilled, uninhabited, unoccupied, unpossessed, untenanted, unused, unutilized, vacuous, *vacuus,* void

VACATE *(Leave),* ***verb*** abandon, cease, depart, depart from, desert, empty, evacuate, exit, forgo, go away, move, move out, quit, relinquish, remove, retreat, surrender, *vacuefacere,* withdraw
ASSOCIATED CONCEPTS: vacate premises

VACATE *(Void),* ***verb*** abandon, abdicate, abolish, abrogate, annul, cancel, countermand, deprive of force, disannul, do away with, eliminate, evacuate, invalidate, make void, negate, nullify, overrule, quash, recant, relinquish, render inoperative, repeal, rescind, retract, reverse, revoke, set aside
ASSOCIATED CONCEPTS: vacate a default, vacate a judgment, vacate an award, vacate an order, vacate occupancy, vacate office

VACATION, *noun* absence, break, breather, cruise, day off, escape, excursion, holiday, interval, jaunt, leave of absence, paid vacation, respite, rest, rest and recuperation, sabbatical, time off, tour, trip, voyage, week off

VACATUR, *noun* abolishment, abrogation, annulment, canceling, cancellation, cessation, defeasance, deprivation, dissolution, invalidation, neutralization, nullification, rescission, revocation, undoing, vacation, vitiation
ASSOCIATED CONCEPTS: vacating a judgment

VACILLATE, *verb* alternate, be capricious, be inconstant, be irresolute, be uncertain, be unsettled, be unsteady, be unsure, change, debate, demur, equivocate, falter, feel uncertain, fluctuate, hesitate, hover, librate, move to and fro, oscillate, rock, seesaw, shift, show indecision, stagger, sway, swing, totter, undulate, *vacillare,* vibrate, waver

VACUOUS, *adjective* absent, barren, blank, depleted, devoid, drained, dull, empty, empty-headed, exhausted, expressionless, fatuous, foolish, hollow, idle, inadequate, inane, incogitative, insufficient, lacking content, missing, null, purposeless, senseless, silly, stupid, thoughtless, unfilled, unintelligent, unoccupied, unreasoning, unthinking, vacant, void, wanting

VAGRANCY, *noun* evagation, hoboism, indolence, itinerancy, pererration, roaming, roving, shiftlessness, vagabondage, vagabondism, wandering, wayfaring
ASSOCIATED CONCEPTS: common-law vagrancy, loitering

VAGUE, *adjective* ambiguous, *ambiguus,* amorphous, blurred, blurry, broad, cloudy, confused, cryptic, dim, doubtful, dubious, *dubius,* enigmatic, equivocal, evasive, faint, general, ill-defined, impalpable, imprecise, *incertus,* incomprehensible, indecisive, indefinite, indeterminate, indistinct, indistinguishable, inexplicit, intangible, misunderstood, mysterious, nebulous, obscure, perplexing, poorly defined, problematical, questionable, shadowy, uncertain, unclear, undefined, undetermined, unsettled, unspecified, unsure
ASSOCIATED CONCEPTS: void for vagueness
FOREIGN PHRASES: ***Res est misera ubi jus est vagum et incertum.*** It is a sorry state of affairs when law is vague and mutable.

VAIN ATTEMPT, *noun* aborted mission, all talk and no action, barren, efforts to no avail, efforts to no purpose, empty effort, fruitless effort, futile effort, hallow efforts, idle efforts, impotent efforts, inadequate efforts, inane efforts, ineffective efforts, ineffectual efforts, inefficacious efforts, interrupted mission, meaningless attempt, unavailing efforts, unsuccessful efforts, useless attempt, worthless effort

VALIANT, *adjective* adventurous, bold, bold-spirited, brave, chivalric, chivalrous, courageous, daring, dashing, dauntless, fearless, gallant, gutsy, hero-like, heroic, intrepid, knightly, lionhearted, nervy, reckless, self-assured, self-reliant, soldierly, stalwart-like, stout, stouthearted, unafraid, unalarmed, undaunted, valorous, virile

VALID, *adjective* accurate, attested, authentic, authoritative, authorized, binding, bona fide, canonic, canonical, conclusive, confirmed, constitutional, correct, credible, effective, effectual, enforceable, executed with proper formalities, factual, *firmus,* forcible, good, *gravis,* having legal force, having legal strength, *iustus,* lawful, legal, legalized, legally binding, legitimate, licit, logical, official, potent, powerful, proved, sanctioned, scientific, solid, sound, statutory, strong, substantial, supportable by law, sustainable in law, true, truthful, veritable, warranted, well-grounded

ASSOCIATED CONCEPTS: valid argument, valid case, valid claim, valid commitment, valid consideration, valid contract, valid delivery, valid existing marriage, valid gift, valid judgment, valid obligation, valid reasoning, valid reasons, valid statute

VALIDATE, *verb* accept, affirm, approve, attest, authorize, certify, circumstantiate, confirm, corroborate, declare legal, declare valid, endorse, give legal force, legalize, legitimatize, legitimize, make binding, make legal, make valid, prove, qualify, ratify, sanction, seal, stamp, substantiate, verify, warrant
ASSOCIATED CONCEPTS: validate a sale, validate records

VALIDATION, *noun* affirmation, approval, authentication, authorization, backing, certification, confirmation, documentation, endorsement, fortification, justification, ratification, strengthening, substantiation, verification, vindication

VALIDITY, *noun* authenticity, authority, correctness, force, forcefulness, genuineness, *gravitas,* lawfulness, legal force, legality, legitimacy, legitimateness, meritoriousness, *pondus,* potency, power, puissance, reality, realness, significance, soundness, strength, trueness, truth, veracity, verity
ASSOCIATED CONCEPTS: validity of a statute
FOREIGN PHRASES: *Quod in minori valet valebit in majori; et quod in majori non valet nec valebit in minori.* That which is valid in the greater shall be valid in the less; and that which is not valid in the greater shall neither be valid in the less. *Nul charter, nul vente, ne nul done vault perpetualment, si le donor n'est seise al temps de contracts de deux droits, sc. del droit de possession et del droit de propertie.* No grant, no sale, no gift, is valid forever, unless the donor, at the time of the contract, has two rights, namely, the right of possession, and the right of property. *Quae ab initio non valent, ex post facto convalescere non possunt.* Things invalid from the beginning cannot be made valid by a subsequent act. *Semper praesumitur pro matrimonio.* The presumption is always in favor of the validity of a marriage. *Quod initio vitiosum est non potest tractu temporis convalescere.* That which is void from the beginning cannot become valid by lapse of time. *Pacta conventa quae neque contra leges neque dolo malo inita sunt omni modo observanda sunt.* Agreements which are not contrary to the laws nor entered into with a fraudulent design must be observed in all respects. *Quod initio non valet, tractu temporis non valet.* That which is void at the beginning does not become valid by lapse of time.

VALOROUS, *adjective* adventurous, audacious, bold, bold as a lion, bold-spirited, brave, chivalric, chivalrous, courageous, daring, dauntless, fearless, foolhardy, gallant, heroic, hero-like, high-spirited, intrepid, knightly, lion-hearted, rash, reckless, soldierly, stalwart, stout, stout-hearted, unafraid, unalarmed, undaunted, valiant, virile

VALUABLE, *adjective* above par, advantageous, beneficial, choice, commanding a good price, costly, dear, desirable, edifying, effective, effectual, efficacious, esteemed, estimable, excellent, expensive, favorable, fine, gainful, good, helpful, important, in demand, inestimable, invaluable, marketable, operative, precious, *pretiosus,* prizable, profitable, rare, relevant, remunerative, rewarding, salable, select, serviceable, significant, suitable, superior, treasured, useful, utilitarian, worthy
ASSOCIATED CONCEPTS: valuable consideration

VALUATION, *noun* assessment, calculation, computation, determination, estimate, estimated value, estimation,

evaluation, examination, fixing a price, measurement, quantification, reckoning, setting a price, setting the value, summary, survey
ASSOCIATED CONCEPTS: property

VALUE, *noun* advantage, *aestimatio,* amount, appraisal, assessment, benefit, caliber, consequence, cost, desirability, effect, equivalent, esteem, estimate, estimation, excellence, expense, force, impact, importance, merit, price, purport, quality, quotation, significance, substance, superiority, use, usefulness, utility, valuation, worth, worthiness
ASSOCIATED CONCEPTS: acquisition value, actual cash value, actual market value, appraised value, assessed value, book value, cash market value, cash surrender value, current market value, face value, fair and reasonable value, fair market value, fair value, full cash value, good faith purchaser for value, gross value, highest market value, holder for value, instrument of value, insurable value, intrinsic value, market value, negotiable instrument, nominal value, nuisance value, par value, pecuniary value, present value, probative value, prospective value, purchaser for value, real value, reasonable value, relative value, rental value, reserve value, residual value, retention value, substantial value, sufficient value, surrender value, tangible value, taxable value, transfer for value, true value, value received
FOREIGN PHRASES: *Libertas non recipit aestimationem.* Freedom does not admit a valuation. *Tantum bona valent, quantum vendipossunt.* Goods are worth as much as they are sold for. *Res per pecuniam aestimatur, et non pecunia per rem.* The value of a thing is estimated according to its worth in money, but the value of money is not estimated by reference to property. *Sapientia legis nummario pretio non est aestimanda.* The wisdom of the law cannot be computed in money value.

VANDAL, *noun* criminal, defacer, demolisher, destroyer, evildoer, lawbreaker, pillager, plunderer, raider, ravager, reprobate, robber, ruiner, spoiler, transgressor, wrecker

VANQUISH, *adjective* baffle, bar, beat, best, block, break, bring down, check, checkmate, circumvent, confound, conquer, crush, defeat, destroy, discomfit, dispel, dissipate, end, floor, foil, get the better of, humble, master, outmaneuver, outwit, overcome, overpower, override, overrun, overthrow, overwhelm, prevail over, prevent, put a stop to, put an end to, quash, quell, rout, smash, stop, subdue, suppress, surmount, surpass, terminate, thwart, trample, triumph over, trounce

VANWARD, *adverb* forward, frontward, headward, in advance, in front, in the lead, onward

VARIABLE, *adjective* aberrant, alterable, capricious, changeable, changeful, erratic, faithless, fanciful, fast and loose, fickle, fitful, fluctuating, inconstant, irregular, irresponsible, mercurial, modifiable, oscillating, protean, shifting, spasmodic, uneven, unreliable, unsettled, unstable, unsteadfast, unsteady, vagrant, variant, volatile, wavering, wayward

VARIANCE *(Disagreement),* **noun** alienation, altercation, breach, contention, contrariety, controversy, difference, disaccord, discongruity, discord, *discordia,* discrepancy, disharmony, disparity, dispute, *dissensio,* dissension, dissent, dissidence, disunity, divergence, diversity, division, incompatibility, nonagreement, odds, opposition, quarrel, rupture, split, strife, unconformity

VARIANCE *(Exemption),* **noun** anomaly, deviation, divergence, exception, leave, special dispensation

591

VARIATION, noun adaptation, adjustment, adverseness, alteration, antipathy, antithesis, array, change, choice, contrast, departure, deviation, difference, differentiation, disaccord, disagreement, discontinuity, discord, discordance, discrepancy, disharmony, disjunction, disparity, dissemblance, dissension, dissimilarity, dissimilitude, dissonance, distinctness, distortion, divergence, divergency, diverseness, exchange, fluctuation, incongruence, incongruity, incongruousness, inconsistency, inconsonance, inconstancy, inharmoniousness, metamorphosis, modification, modulation, mutual exclusiveness, nonconformity, oppositeness, opposition, reformation, reforming, remake, revision, revolutionize, separateness, substitution, switch, transfiguration, transformation, uniqueness, unlikeness, variance, variety

VARIED, adjective assorted, complex, composite, compound, conglomerate, different, differing, disparate, dissimilar, distinct, diverse, diversified, indiscriminate, intricate, jumbled, medley, mixed, multifarious, multifold, multiform, multiple, scrambled, separate, thrown together, variant, variegated, varying

VARY, verb alter, alternate, assort, be inconstant, be unlike, change, contrast, depart, deviate, differ, diverge, diversify, exchange, fluctuate, give variety, innovate, interchange, make a change, make different, modify, *mutare,* mutate, reorganize, rotate, shift, show variety, transfigure, transform, transmute, turn into, vacillate, *variare,* variegate, veer, waver
ASSOCIATED CONCEPTS: vary the terms of an agreement

VARYING, verb altering, bearing no resemblance, being at variance, being contrary, being dissimilar, being distinctly different, being distinguished from, being inharmonious, being opposite, unique, being unlike, contrasting, departing from, differing, digressing, disagreeing, diverging from, having a dissimilar opinion, lacking resemblance, not comparing with, not conforming, showing contrasting, showing variety

VEHEMENT, adjective agitated, angry, ardent, boisterous, burning, clamorous, demonstrative, eager, earnest, emphatic, enthusiastic, excited, explosive, fanatical, *fervens,* fervent, fervid, fierce, fiery, forceful, forcible, frenzied, furious, glowing, headstrong, heated, hot, impassioned, impetuous, impulsive, *incitatus,* inflamed, insistent, intense, lusty, mighty, passionate, perfervid, powerful, rabid, rampant, strong, tempestuous, turbulent, unequivocal, urgent, violent, volcanic, wild, zealous

VEHICLE (Car), **noun** automobile, carriage, means of carriage, means of transportation, means to an end, medium of transportation, method of transportation, motor vehicle, transportation

VEHICLE (Means), **noun** access, agency, agent, channel, conduit, contrivance, conveyor, course, device, expediter, facilitator, intermediate, means to an end, mechanism, medium, method, path

VEIL, noun camouflage, cloak, cloud, concealment, cover, covering, curtain, guise, *involucrum, integumentum,* mantle, mask, pall, protection, screen, shade, shelter, shield, shroud, visor, vizard
ASSOCIATED CONCEPTS: pierce the corporate veil

VENAL, adjective avaricious, bribable, corrupt, corruptible, dishonorable, extortionate, grasping, greedy, mercenary, *nummarius,* purchasable, self-seeking, *venalis*

VEND, verb auction, deal in, dispense, make a sale, market, offer for sale, peddle, put up for sale, retail, sell, trade, unload
ASSOCIATED CONCEPTS: vendee, vendor, vendor's lien

VENDOR, noun businessman, chapman, dealer, hawker, huckster, merchant, monger, peddler, retailer, salesman, seller, trader, tradesman
ASSOCIATED CONCEPTS: good faith vendor, vendor's liability, vendor's lien, vendor's title

VENERABLE, adjective advanced in life, ageless, at an advanced age, august, creditable, dateless, eminent, esteemed, estimable, hallowed, held in esteem, highly regarded, highly reputed, highly respectable, honorable, honored, illustrious, immemorial, in favor, in high favor, noble, of repute, patriarchal, prestigious, reputable, respectable, respected, revered, time-honored, timeless, venerated, well-thought-of, worthy

VENGEANCE, noun avengement, enmity, implacability, malevolence, nemesis, punishment, rancor, repayment, reprisal, retaliation, retribution, retributive punishment, revenge, revengefulness, *ultio,* vendetta, vengefulness, *vindicta,* vindictiveness

VENGEFULNESS, noun acrimony, anger, avengement, danger, dangerousness, feud, getting even, hostility, implacableness, inexorableness, intractableness punitiveness, recrimination, reprisal, retaliation, retribution, revenge, spitefulness, unappeasableness, unforgivingness, vendetta, vengeance, vindictiveness, wrath, wrathfulness

VENIRE, noun authoritative citation to appear before a court, command to appear, notification to appear, required to attend, subpoena, summons

VENTURE, noun adventure, alea, attempt, business, campaign, chance, crusade, danger, dangerous undertaking, endeavor, enterprise, essay, experiment, *facinus,* gamble, hazard, investment, jeopardy, move, *periculum,* peril, plunge, project, quest, risk, risky undertaking, speculation, step, task, test, trial, uncertainty, wager
ASSOCIATED CONCEPTS: business venture, joint venture, private venture

VENUE, noun county, jurisdiction, locale, locality, location, neighborhood, place of jurisdiction, political subdivision, position, seat, site, station, territory
ASSOCIATED CONCEPTS: *forum non conveniens*
FOREIGN PHRASES: **Triatio ibi semper debet fieri, ubi juratores meliorem possunt habere notitiam.** Trial ought always to be had where the jurors can have the best information.

VERACIOUS, adjective aboveboard, accurate, believable, accurate, candid, credible, ethical, factual, frank, honest, honorable, ingenuous, legitimate, noble, precise, principled, sincere, straightforward, straight-talking, truthful, truth-telling, upstanding, with certitude, with verity
ASSOCIATED CONCEPTS: veracious witness

VERACITY, noun accuracy, actuality, artlessness, authenticity, candidness, candor, conformity to fact, correctness, credibility, exactitude, exactness, factualness, faithfulness, frankness, genuiness, guilelessness, honesty, ingenuousness, integrity, precision, principle, probity, rectitude, sincerity, trustworthiness, truth, truthfulness, veraciousness, veridicality, *veritas,* verity, virtue

ASSOCIATED CONCEPTS: reputation for veracity, veracity of a witness

VERBAL, *adjective*   audible, expressed, nuncupative, oral, parole, pronounced, recited, spoken, stated, unwritten, uttered, *verbum,* voiced, *vox*
ASSOCIATED CONCEPTS: Statute of Frauds, verbal acts, verbal agreements, verbal contracts, verbal gift, verbal no fault threshold

VERBATIM, *adjective*   exact, following the letter, literal, precise, true to the letter, word for word

VERBATIM, *adverb*   chapter and verse, in the same words, literally, literatim, strictly to the letter, to the letter, word for word

VERBOSE, *adjective*   conversational, expressive, inconcise, superfluous, talkative, verbal, wordy

VERDICT, *noun*   adjudication, answer, assessment, award, conclusion, decision, decision of a jury, declaration of a jury, decree of a jury, definitive answer, determination, finding, *iudicium,* judgment, opinion of the jury, pronouncement of a jury, resolution by a jury, ruling, sentence, *sententia*
ASSOCIATED CONCEPTS: adverse verdict, arbitrary verdict, compromise verdict, directed verdict, estoppel by verdict, excessive verdict, final verdict, general verdict, incongruous verdict, informal verdict, judgment notwithstanding verdict, open verdict, partial verdict, quotient verdict, recorded verdict, rendering of a verdict, special verdict, unanimous verdict, void verdict
FOREIGN PHRASES: *Veredictum, quasi dictum veritatis; ut judicium, quasi juris dictum.* A verdict is, as it were, the expression of the truth; as a judgment is, as it were, the expression of the law. *Non obstante veredicto.* Notwithstanding the verdict.

VERIDICAL, *adjective*   authentic, bona fide, genuine, honest, inartificial, legitimate, natural, real, sincere, true, truth-telling, truthful, uncounterfeited, unfaked, unfictitious, unperjured, unpretending, unsynthetic, veracious, verifiable

VERIFICATION, *verb*   acceptance, accord, acknowledgment, affidavit, affirmance, affirmation, approval, assent, assurance, attestation, authentication, authorization, averment, avouchment, certification, check, confirmation of authority, confirmation of truth, declaration, formal assertion, legal pledge, oath, solemn averment, solemn avowal, solemn declaration, substantiation, swearing, validation, warrant

VERIFY (Prove), ***verb***   accredit, acknowledge, agree to, agree with, approve, assent, assure, attest, authenticate, authorize, avow, bear out, certify, charter, check, circumstantiate, commend, concur, confirm, *confirmare,* consent, corroborate, document, endorse, establish, establish the truth of fortify, give evidence, guarantee, license, make certain, make sure, pass, permit, *probare,* produce evidence, prove, prove the accuracy, prove the truth, review and approve, sanction, seal, second, substantiate, support, sustain, uphold, validate

VERIFY (Swear), ***verb***   affirm, asseverate, attest, avouch, avow, declare, evidence, guarantee, state, testify, vouch for, vow, warrant, witness
ASSOCIATED CONCEPTS: verify pleadings

VERSATILE, *adjective*   able, adaptable, all-around, all-purpose, capable, changeable, gifted, handy, inconstant, many-sided, multifaceted, multipurpose, resourceful, talented

VEST, *verb*   authorize, bestow upon, clothe, confer, consign, empower, enable, endow, entrust, establish, furnish, give authority, give control, invest, place authority, place control, put in possession, sanction
ASSOCIATED CONCEPTS: contingently vested, estate vested subject to being divested, indefeasibly vested, vested estate, vested future estate, vested gift, vested in possession, vested interest, vested legacy, vested property right, vested remainder, vested remainder subject to open, vested right, vesting of title

VEST IN, *verb*   authorize, become effective, confer, consign, empower, enable, endow, entrust, establish, furnish, give, give authority, give control, grant a right in, invest, place authority, place control, sanction, start effectively

VESTED, *adjective*   bestowed, earned, empowered, endowed, established, owned, vouchsafed
ASSOCIATED CONCEPTS: pension rights

VETERAN, *adjective*   adept, adroit, apt, capable, deft, dexterous, disciplined, experienced, expert, facile, finished, knowing, practiced, proficient, qualified, seasoned, skilled, sophisticated, talented, trained, tried, world-wise

VETERAN, *noun*   dean, expert, knowing person, old campaigner, old soldier, person of experience, practiced hand, senior statesman, sophisticate

VETO, *noun*   ban, bar, denial, disallowance, embargo, forbiddance, inhibition, injunction, *intercessio,* interdict, interdiction, interference, negative, prevention, prohibition, proscription, refusal of approval, refusal to sanction, rejection, restraint, restriction, taboo

VEX, *verb*   acerbate, aggravate, anger, annoy, badger, bedevil, beleaguer, beset, bother, chafe, chivy, concern, distress, disturb, envenom, gall, harass, harry, incense, infuriate, irk, irritate, miff, offend, pester, provoke, rankle, roil

VEXATIOUS, *adjective*   aggravating, annoying, bothersome, disturbing, exasperating, galling, harassing, irksome, irritating, maddening, pestering, provocative, provoking, syncophantic, tiresome, troublesome, trying, wearisome

VIABLE, *adjective*   acceptable, actable, alive, appropriate, apt, capable of development, capable of growth, conceivable, doable, effective, effectual, efficacious, encouraging, expedient, favorable, feasible, functional, imaginable, legitimate, likely, living, logical, operative, performable, plausible, possible, potential, practicable, practical, promising, propitious, reasonable, sensible, sound, suitable, thinkable, usable, useful, valid, vital, workable

VIATICAL SETTLEMENT, *noun*   life insurance agreement, life insurance payment, life insurance settlement, reformation of a life insurance policy, revision of a life insurance agreement

VICARIOUS (Delegated), ***adjective***   acting, acting as a substitute, commissioned, deputed, empathic, intermediary, mental, perceptive, procuratory, sympathetic, sympathizing, taking the place of another, understanding

VICARIOUS *(Substitutional),* **adjective** alternate, alternative, equivalent, ersatz, makeshift, provisional, representational, temporary, tentative
ASSOCIATED CONCEPTS: vicarious liability

VICE, noun atrocity, bad habit, blemish, corruption, debauchery, defect, deficiency, degeneracy, delinquency, depravation, depravity, dereliction, dissipation, dissoluteness, evil, excess, failing, failure, fault, flaw, foible, fraility, immoral habit, immorality, imperfection, impurity, inadequacy, incontinence, indecency, indulgence, infamy, infirmity, iniquity, lack, lewdness, libertinism, licentiousness, looseness, mar, maleficence, malignance, misconduct, misdeed, obliquity, outrage, perversion, profligacy, shortcoming, sin, sinfulness, transgression, turpitude, unchastity, vileness, wantonness, weak point, weakness, wickedness, wrong, wrongdoing

VICINITY, noun area, confines, environs, neighborhood, outskirts, precincts, propinquity, proximity, purlieu, region, scene, setting, suburbs, surroundings, territory, zone

VICIOUS, adjective abandoned, acrimonious, atrocious, barbarous, beastly, blameworthy, brutal, censurable, contrary, corrupt, criminal, cruel, dangerous, debased, degenerate, demoralized, depraved, devilish, diabolical, disgraceful, evil, evil-minded, ferocious, fierce, flawed, foul, frightful, given to vice, guilty, hateful, heinous, horrid, ill-disposed, ill-natured, immoral, imperfect, improper, impure, incorrigible, inhuman, inimical, iniquitous, malevolent, malicious, malign, malignant, mean, merciless, mischievous, nasty, offensive, pernicious, perverse, profligate, recalcitrant, refractory, reprehensible, reprobate, savage, scandalous, shameless, spiteful, steeped in vice, treacherous, *turpis,* uncivilized, unfriendly, unprincipled, unrighteous, unruly, untamed, venomous, vile, villainous, virulent, *vitiosus,* wicked, wrong
ASSOCIATED CONCEPTS: vicious propensity

VICISSITUDES, noun alteration, alternating conditions, alternation, changes, fluctuations, interchanges, modifications, successions, successive phases, transformations, ups and downs, variations

VICTIM, noun casualty, complainant, complaining witness, *hostia,* injured, prey, quarry, sufferer, target, unfortunate person, unlucky person, *victima*

VICTIMIZE, verb beguile, betray, cheat, con, damage, deceive, defraud, delude, do out of, dupe, exploit, fast-talk, finagle, fleece, flimflam, fool, hoodwink, injure, mislead, obtain under false pretenses, prey on, snooker, subject to a swindle, subject to fraud, swindle, take advantage of, to subject to fraud, trick, use

VIEW *(Opinion),* **noun** advice, apprehension, aspect, assumption, attitude, belief, concept, conception, conclusion, conviction, credence, creed, discernment, doctrine, estimate, estimation, idea, impression, intent, judgment, notion, perception, perspective, platform, position, posture, regard, representation, respect, sentiment, slant, stand, standpoint, supposition, theory, thought

VIEW *(Sight),* **noun** appearance, aspect, complexion, conspectus, contemplation, coverage, design, gaze, glimpse, ken, lookout, object, observation, outlook, panorama, posture, preview, prospect, purpose, purview, reaction, scene, scenery, scrutiny, show, side, spectacle, vision, vista

ASSOCIATED CONCEPTS: demand of a view, inspection of the scene of an accident, view of an inquest

VIEW, verb apprehend, attend, behold, consider, contemplate, detect, discern, envisage, examine, explore, glance at, have in sight, inspect, look at, look on, notice, observe, opine, perceive, pierce, recognize, reconnoiter, reflect upon, regard, scan, scrutinize, see, study, surmise, survey, take stock of, think about, watch, witness
ASSOCIATED CONCEPTS: view the crime scene

VIEWPOINT, noun angle, attitude, basis, conception, feeling, frame of reference, framework, impression, inclination, mental view, opinion, orientation, outlook, perspective, point of observation, point of vantage, point of view, position, posture, reference, respect, sentiment, slant, stance, stand, standpoint, vantage point, view

VIGILANT, adjective alert, apprehensive, attentive, canny, careful, cautious, circumspect, guarded, heedful, *intentus,* judicious, keenly aware, observant, on guard, precautious, prescient, provident, *providus,* prudent, regardful, scrupulous, searching, sharp, suspicious, unsleeping, unslumbering, *vigilans,* wakeful, wary, watchful, wide awake

VIGOROUS, adjective active, acute, aggressive, all-out, animated, brisk, dynamic, energetic, enthusiastic, feisty, forceful, forcible, full of life, go-getting, go-go, hardy, healthy, intense, keen, lively, lusty, proactive, robust, spirited, strenuous, strong, strong and healthy, vibrant, vivacious, vivid, wholehearted, zestful, zesty

VILE, adjective bawdy, debauched, foul, immoral, impure, indecent, indelicate, lewd, lurid, offensive, offensive to decency, offensive to modesty, offensive to morality, patently offensive, profane, profligate, ribald, salacious, shameful, shameless, vulgar, wanton

VILIFICATION, noun abuse, abusive language, blackening, calumniation, calumny, contemptuous language, contumely, defamation, denigration, denunciation, detraction, impugnment, invective, malediction, opprobrium, revilement, scorn, slander, smear, traducement, verbal attack, vituperation

VILLAINOUS, adjective abhorrent, abominable, accursed, arrant, atrocious, baleful, baneful, base, criminal, cursed, damnable, deceiving, delinquent, depraved, despicable, detestable, devilish, diabolic, disgraceful, dishonorable, dissipated, dissolute, evil, evildoing, evil-minded, execrable, facinorous, faithless, fell, felon, felonious, flagitious, foul, hateful, heinous, horrible, ignoble, ill-intentioned, immoral, incorrigible, infamous, iniquitous, knavish, lawless, loathsome, malefic, maleficent, malevolent, malicious, malignant, mean, menacing, misfeasant, monstrous, nefarious, nefast, notorious, obnoxious, odious, offensive, opprobrious, perfidious, pernicious, profligate, rancorous, rascally, repellent, reprehensible, reprobate, repugnant, repulsive, revolting, roguish, ruffianly, satanic, shameful, unregenerate, unrepentant, unscrupulous, venomous, vile, virulent, wicked

VINDICATE, verb absolve, account for, acquit, clear, declare innocent, discharge, dismiss, exculpate, excuse, exonerate, give good reasons for, justify, pardon, *probare,* pronounce not guilty, *purgare,* release, relieve of burden, reprieve, set free

VINDICTIVE, adjective angry, avenging, grudgeful, implacable, inclined to vengeance, malevolent, malicious, malignant, punitive, punitory, rancorous, resentful, retaliative, retaliatory, retributive, revengeful, spiteful, *ulciscendi cupidus,* unforgiving, unrelenting, vengeful, vindicatory

VIOLATE, *verb* act illegally, break, constuprate, contravene, defy, desecrate, dishonor, disobey, disregard, disrespect, do violence to, encroach upon, fail to keep, fail to observe, infringe, injure, invade, offend against the law, *rumpere,* trample on, transgress, treat improperly, treat without reverence, trespass, *violare*
ASSOCIATED CONCEPTS: violate the law

VIOLATION, *noun* abuse, breach, *contra leges,* dereliction, desecration, disturbance, encroachment, illegality, impiety, infraction, infringement, interruption, invasion, irreverence, lawbreaking, misbehavior, mistreatment, misuse, nonobservance, offense, recusancy, transgression, trespass, wrong
ASSOCIATED CONCEPTS: crime, felony, misdemeanor
FOREIGN PHRASES: *Mulcta damnum famae non irrogat.* A fine does not impose a loss of reputation.

VIOLENCE, *noun* assault, attack, brutality, clash, convulsion, disorder, eruption, explosion, ferocity, force, fracas, furiousness, fury, inclemency, *manus,* onslaught, outburst, rage, rampage, ruthlessness, savagery, severity, unlawful force, vehemence, *violentia,* wildness
FOREIGN PHRASES: *Insanus est qui, abjecta ratione, omnia cum impetu et furore facit.* A person is insane who, deprived of reason, does everything with violence and rage. *Paci sunt maxime contraria vis et injuria.* Violence and injury are especially hostile to peace. *Est autem vis legem simulans.* Violence may also be masquerading as the law.

VIOLENT, *adjective* acrimonious, afire, aflame, astir, astringent, blown-up, brutal, brutish, caustic, clamorous, crazed, cruel, damaging, destructive, disorderly, excited, explosive, ferocious, feverish, forceful, frantic, frenetic, frenzied, furious, in a furious rage, in a furor, in rage, inflamed, raging, raised to a fever pitch, ruthless, seething, severe, sharp, uncontrollable, ungovernable, vicious

VIRTUAL, *adjective* basic, capable, constructive, deep down, deep rooted, deep seated, equivalent, essential, fundamental, implicit, indirect, inherent, intrinsic, material, potent, potential, powerful, practical, substantive, tantamount to, underlying, viable
ASSOCIATED CONCEPTS: virtual adoption, virtual representation

VIRULENT, *adjective* *acerbus,* acrid, acrimonious, antagonistic, baleful, baneful, bitter, deadly, deleterious, despiteful, destructive, envenomed, *gravis,* harmful, hateful, hostile, hurtful, injurious, lethal, malevolent, malicious, malign, malignant, mordacious, noxious, pernicious, poison, poisonous, rancorous, spiteful, toxic, treacherous, unfriendly, venomous, violent

VISIBLE (In full view), ***adjective*** clear, distinct, in focus, in full view, in plain sight, in sight, in view, manifest, perceptible, plain, seeable, showing, viewable, well defined

VISIBLE (Noticeable), ***adjective*** apparent, conspicuous, detectable, discernible, observable, perceivable, recognizable
ASSOCIATED CONCEPTS: visible easements, visible mark, visible means of support, visible possession, visible property, visible risk, visible sign of injury

VISION (Dream), ***noun*** abstraction, apparition, appearance, concept, conception, discernment, fantasy, form, glance, glimpse, illusion, image, look, perception, perspective, phenomenon, picture, presence, revelation, shape, spectacle, specter

VISION (Sight), ***noun*** field of view, vista

VITAL, *adjective* basic, cardinal, chief, critical, essential, extremely important, fundamental, important, indispensable, irreplaceable, life-supporting, main, necessary to life, needed, paramount, pressing, primary, principal, radical, required, requisite, urgent, vitalic, *vitalis*

VITIATE, *verb* abolish, abrogate, annul, blight, cancel, counteract, damage, *depravare,* destroy, disannul, impair, injure, invalidate, make faulty, make imperfect, make impure, make ineffective, make void, mar, negate, negative, neutralize, nullify, overturn, pervert, poison, pollute, quash, render defective, render inefficacious, rescind, reverse, spoil, sully, tamper with, undo, *vitiare,* weaken
FOREIGN PHRASES: *Crimen omnia ex se nata vitiat.* Crime vitiates all that is born of it.

VIVID, *adjective* bright, clear, colorful, demonstrative, direct, distinct, emphatic, evident, exact, explicit, express, expressive, graphic, identifiable, in bold relief, in evidence, in strong relief, manifest, observable, outspoken, overt, patent, pellucid, perceivable, perceptible, perspicuous, plain, prominent, pronounced, salient, self-evident, showing, shown, straightforward, striking, transparent, unblurred, unclouded, uncovered, unequivocal, unmistakable, visible, well-defined, well-marked, well-seen

VOICE, *verb* announce authoritatively, announce officially, assert, avow, break silence, clarify, communicate, declare, deliver, emphasize, enounce, enunciate, express, form, frame, observe, phrase, present, proclaim, pronounce, recite, recount, remark, say, sound, speak, state, stress, tell, utter, verbalize, vocalize

VOID (Empty), ***adjective*** abandoned, bare, barren, blank, deserted, desolate, destitute, devoid, forsaken, free, hollow, *inanis,* lacking, unfilled, unfurnished, uninhabited, unoccupied, unsupplied, untenanted, vacant, vacuous, vacuus, wanting, without contents

VOID (Invalid), ***adjective*** cancelled, ineffective, ineffectual, inoperative, *irritus,* insubstantial, meaningless, not binding, not in force, nugatory, null, null and void, unenforceable, useless, *vanus,* without legal force
ASSOCIATED CONCEPTS: void act, void contract, void in part, void in toto, void judgment, void marriage, void on its face, void process, voidable
FOREIGN PHRASES: *Quae ab initio non valent, ex post facto convalescere non possunt.* Things invalid from the beginning cannot be made valid by a subsequent act. *Judicium a non suo judice datum nullius est momenti.* A judgment rendered by one who is not the proper judge is of no force. *Quod initio non valet, tractu temporis non valet.* That which is void at the beginning does not become valid by lapse of time. *Quod initio vitiosum est non potest tractu temporis convalescere.* That which is void from the beginning cannot become valid by lapse of time.

VOIDABLE, *adjective* capable of being adjudged invalid, capable of being adjudged void, capable of being annulled, capable of being declared ineffectual, capable of being declared void, defeasible, liable to be annulled, nullifiable, revocable, subject to being revoked, subject to cancellation

ASSOCIATED CONCEPTS: voidable contract, voidable judgment, voidable marriage, voidable preference

VOIR DIRE, *noun* examination for qualification for jury service, hearing before the court, hearing without jury's presence, inquiry, judicial examination

VOLATILE, *adjective* active, animated, brief, brisk, buoyant, capricious, changeable, cometary, deciduous, desultory, effervescent, elastic, elusive, ephemeral, erratic, evanescent, evaporable, excitable, explosive, fickle, fleeting, flighty, full of spirit, giddy, humorsome, inconstant, instable, irresolute, *levis,* lively, mercurial, *mobilis,* momentary, passing, precarious, quick, shallow, short-lived, spirited, sprightly, transient, transitory, unstable, unsteady, vacillating, vaporable, vaporizable, vaporous, *volaticus,* wavering

VOLITION, *noun* accord, choice, decision, desire, determination, discretion, election, elective preference, exercise of will, free agency, free will, intent, option, pick, power of choice, preference, purpose, resolution, selection, *voluntas,* will, willingness, wish

VOLUBLE, *adjective* copious, declamatory, discursive, eloquent, effusive, expansive, fluent, garrulous, glib, long-winded, loquacious, multiloquent, profuse, rambling, ready-tongued, rhetorical, talkative, verbose, wordy

VOLUNTARY, *adjective* conative, deliberate, designed, discretionary, effected by choice, elective, facultative, free, intended, intentional, offered, optional, purposeful, self-willed, unaccidental, unbidden, uncoerced, uncompelled, unconstrained, unforced, unprompted, unrestrained, volens, volitient, volitional, volitionary, *voluntarius,* willful, without compulsion, without constraint
ASSOCIATED CONCEPTS: voluntary abandonment, voluntary acceptance, voluntary act, voluntary agreement, voluntary appearance, voluntary assignment, voluntary confession, voluntary conveyance, voluntary discontinuance, voluntary dismissal, voluntary exposure, voluntary gift, voluntary grant, voluntary homicide, voluntary manslaughter, voluntary partition, voluntary payment, voluntary petition in bankruptcy, voluntary retirement, voluntary separation, voluntary statement, voluntary suspension, voluntary testimony, voluntary trust, voluntary waste

VOLUNTEER, *noun* amateur, enlisted man, enlisted person, enlistee, freewill worker, gratuitous worker, non-professional, recruit, taker, unpaid worker, voluntary worker
ASSOCIATED CONCEPTS: Good Samaritan

VOTE, *noun* ballot, chirotony, choice, choosing, decision, determination, election, formal expression of choice, judgment, option, pick, poll, predilection, preference, *punctum,* selection, *sententia, suffragium*

VOTE, *verb* approve, ballot, be counted, cast a ballot, cast a vote, choose, elect, exercise the right of suffrage, judge, poll, *suffragium ferre*

VOUCH, *verb* acknowledge, *adseverare,* affirm, assererate, assure, attest, authenticate, aver, avouch, back, bear witness, certify, confirm, corroborate, declare, depone, depose, endorse, give assurance, give evidence, give one's word, guarantee, maintain by affirmation, pledge, promise, *rem praestare,* secure, support, sustain, swear to, testify, underwrite, uphold, warrant, witness

VOUCHSAFE, *verb* accord, acquiesce, admit, allow, assent, bear with, bestow, comply with, concede, *concedere,* condescend, condescend to grant, consent, deign to give, deign to grant, favor with, give in, grant, grant by favor, gratify, humor, indulge, let, permit, satisfy, show favor, stoop, suffer, tolerate, yield

VOW, *noun* affirmation, asseveration, assurance, aver, avow, covenant, *devotio,* endorsement, *fides,* formal guaranty, oath, pledge, promise, *promissum,* solemn assertion, solemn declaration, solemn promise, subscription, undertaking, vouch, warrant, word, word of honor, written assurance

VULGAR, *adjective* bawdy, broad, debauched, disgusting, foul, immodest, immoral, impure, indecent, indelicate, lascivious, lecherous, lewd, licentious, lubricous, lurid, lustful, obscene, offensive, offensive to decency, offensive to modesty, offensive to the senses, patently offensive, pornographic, profane, profligate, prurient, ribald, salacious, scabrous, sensual, sexy, shameful, shameless, vile, wanton

VULNERABLE, *adjective* accessible, approachable, assailable, attainable, beatable, capable of receiving injuries, defenseless, exposed, fallible, guardless, indefensible, insecure, liable to attack, obtainable, open, penetrable, precarious, pregnable, *qui vulnerari potest,* reachable, risky, susceptible, unguarded, unprepared, unprotected, unsafe, unshielded, untenable, vincible, weak, woundable

WAGE, *noun* allowance, compensation, earnings, emolument, fee, hire, income, meed, *merces,* pay, payment, quittance, rate of pay, recompense, remuneration, revenue, reward for service, salary, stipend
ASSOCIATED CONCEPTS: minimum wage, wage rate

WAIT, *verb* abide, await, be patient, bear with composure, bide, continue, defer, delay, discontinue, extend, forbear, halt, hesitate, linger, loiter, mark time, pause, postpone, procrastinate, prorogate, protract, put off, remain, remand, reserve, retard, shelve, stall, stay, suspend, table, tarry, waive

WAIT, noun adjournment, cessation, deferment, delay, dilatoriness, halt, hindrance, moratorium, obstacle, pause, postponement, procrastination, prorogation, remand, reprieve, respite, retardation, stay, stop, suspension

WAIVE, verb cast off, cease, *de re decedere,* desist from, disclaim, dismiss, disown, dispense with, forgo, give up, give up claim to, not retain, not use, put aside, refrain from, refuse, reject, relinquish, *rem concedere,* renounce, repudiate, sacrifice, set aside, surrender, yield
ASSOCIATED CONCEPTS: election of remedy, waive a jury trial, waive jurisdictional requirements, waive objections, waive rights, waive rights to payment under a contract

WAIVER, noun abandonment, abandonment of a known right, abdication, abrogation, absolution, acquittal, act of relinquishing a right, clearance, deed of release, discharge, excusal, forgoing, giving up, intentional relinquishment, loss of right, release, relinquishment, renunciation, surrender, voluntary relinquishment
ASSOCIATED CONCEPTS: express waiver, implied waiver, waiver of immunity
FOREIGN PHRASES: *Omnis consensus tollit errorem.* Every consent removes error. ***Potest quis renunciare pro se et suis juri quod pro se introductum est.*** One may relinquish for himself and his successors a right which was introduced for his own benefit. ***Cuilibet licet juri pro se introducto renunciare.*** Anyone may waive a legal right which is for his protection. ***Ab assuetis non fit injuria.*** No legal injury is done by things long acquiesced in. ***Omnes licentiam habere his quae pro se indulta sunt, renunciare.*** All are free to renounce those privileges which have been allowed for their benefit.

WALL noun blockage, divider, dividing wall, division, impediment, impenetrable obstacle, insurmountable task, isolated part, lone part, obstacle, obstruction, occlusion, overwhelming obstacle, separation
ASSOCIATED CONCEPTS: Chinese wall, common wall, party wall

WANT, noun absence, *conatus,* dearth, default, defect, deficiency, deficit, desideratum, desire, destitution, distress, exigency, impoverishment, insufficiency, lack, meagerness, necessitude, necessity, need, needfulness, neediness, paucity, pauperism, pennilessness, privation, request, requirement, requisition, scarcity, shortness, shortage
ASSOCIATED CONCEPTS: want of capacity, want of consideration, want of jurisdiction, want of knowledge

WANT, verb be deficient in, be desirous, be destitute of, be found wanting, be without, covet, crave, desiderate, desire, fancy, feel the lack of, have occasion for, hope for, lack, like, long for, miss, need, request, require, stand in need of, will, wish

WANT OF CAPACITY *(Mental deficiency),* **noun** amentia, defectiveness, dementedness, dementia, feeblemindedness, imbecility, moronity, retardment
ASSOCIATED CONCEPTS: insanity defense

WANT OF CAPACITY *(Underage),* **noun** callowness, defectiveness, immaturity, inexperience, juvenile, lack of development, minor, undevelopment, unfledged

WANT OF JURISDICTION, adverb beyond the jurisdiction of the court, improper jurisdiction, not legitimate, want of authority, without judicial authority

WANT OF KNOWLEDGE, noun denseness, ignorance, illiteracy, incomprehension, ineruditon, inexperience, lack of education, lack of knowledge, lack of learning, unenlightenment, unfamiliarity, unintellectuality, unintelligence, unknowingness, unlearnedness, untaught state
ASSOCIATED CONCEPTS: ignorance of the law

WANTON, adjective careless, dissolute, froward, groundless, heedless, immoral, *impudicus,* intemperate, *lascivus,* lewd, libidinous, licentious, lustful, luxuriant, reckless, unjustifiable, unmanageable, unprovoked
ASSOCIATED CONCEPTS: wanton act, wanton disregard, wanton indifference, wanton injury, wanton misconduct, wanton negligence

WARD, noun care, charge, custody, defense, guard, guardianship, keeping, preservation, protection, safeguard, safekeeping, security, trusteeship, tutelage, vigilance, watch, watchfulness
ASSOCIATED CONCEPTS: ward of the state

WARDEN, noun chaperon, claviger, custodian, *custos,* gatekeeper, guard, guardian, jailer, overseer, patrolman, protector, sentry, superintendent, supervisor, supervisory official, turnkey, warder, watchman

WARN, verb admonish, advise, alert, apprise, caution, caution against danger, communicate to, counsel, deter, discourage, dissuade, exhort, expostulate, forebode, forewarn, give warning, herald, inform, make aware, notice, notify, portend, predict, premonish, presage, put on one's guard, remind, remonstrate, reprimand, signal, sound the alarm, urge to take heed
ASSOCIATED CONCEPTS: warning order, warning regarding product liability, warn of a danger, warn of known and obvious defects

WARNING, noun *admonitio,* admonition, alarm, alert, augury, caution, caveat, commination, contraindication, foreboding, foreshadow, monition, *monitus,* notice of danger, omen, portent, presage, prognostic, symptom, threat, ultimatum
ASSOCIATED CONCEPTS: adequate warning, ample warning, duty to warn, failure to warn, proper warning, sufficient warning, timely warning, warning attached to a products label

WARRANT *(Authorization),* **noun** *auctoritas,* authority, brevet, charter, commission, credentials, license, *mandatum,* permission, permit, *potestas,* power, sanction, voucher
ASSOCIATED CONCEPTS: warrant of attorney

WARRANT *(Guaranty),* **noun** agreement, assurance, authentication, covenant, pledge, promise, security, surety, warranty

WARRANT *(Judicial writ),* **noun** certificate, decree, edict, judicial authorization, judicial order, legal process, mandate of a court, order, process, subpoena, summons
ASSOCIATED CONCEPTS: arrest warrant, bench warrant, dispossess warrant, fugitive warrant, search warrant, tax warrant, warrant of attachment, warrant of commitment

WARRANTY, noun assurance, certificate, contractual assurance, contractual promise, contractual representation, covenant, guarantee, guaranty, pledge, promise, *satisdatio,* voucher
ASSOCIATED CONCEPTS: affirmative warranty, breach of warranty, disclaimer of warranty, express warranty, implied warranty, limited warranty, material warranty, prospective warranty, warranty deed, warranty of fitness, warranty of merchantability, warranty of title

FOREIGN PHRASES: *Ea quae, commendandi causa, in venditionibus dicuntur, si palam appareant, venditorem non obligant.* Those things which are said as praise of the things sold, if they are openly apparent do not bind the seller.

WASTE, *noun* careless loss, consumption, depletion, diminution, *dispendium,* dispersion, dissipation, *effusio,* excessive use, exhaustion, expenditure, extravagance, illusage, improvidence, intemperance, lavishness, misapplication, misemployment, misusage, misuse, prodigality, profusion, ruination, squandering, *sumptus,* unnecessary loss, unthriftiness, useless consumption, wanton destruction, wastage, wastefulness, wasting
ASSOCIATED CONCEPTS: economic waste, permissive waste, voluntary waste, waste of public property, wasting assets

WATCH, *noun* advertency, alertness, attention, charge, concern, custody, guard, heed, inspection, lookout, observance, observation, oversight, precaution, regard, safeguard, safekeeping, sentinel, sentry, shift, spell of work, superintendence, supervision, surveillance, view, vigil, vigilance, ward, watchfulness

WATCH, *verb* attend, be a spectator, be careful, be cautious of, be closely observant, be on guard, be on the alert, be on the lookout, behold, contemplate, espy, eye, gaze at, guard, heed, inspect, keep under observation, look after, look at, mark, mind, monitor, not lose sight of, note, notice, observe, oversee, pay attention to, peer, perceive, police, preserve, regard, safeguard, scan, scrutinize, stare at, superintend, survey, take care, take care of, tend, view, witness

WAVERING, *adjective* between changing, debating, delaying, deliberating, demurring, dubitating, equivocating, faltering, feeling unsure, fluctuating, having difficulty deciding, having qualms, having reservations, hesitating, holding off, in a quandary, in between, irresolute, judgmental, pausing, pondering, pushing aside, putting off a decision, puzzled, puzzling over, scrupling, stopping to consider, tabling, thinking it over, uncertain, undecided, undermined, vacillating, withholding

WAY (Channel), *noun* alley, artery, avenue, custom, direction, lane, mode, path, pathway, plan, road, roadway, route, throughway

WAY (Manner), *noun* behavior, fashion, habit, means, progression, ritual
ASSOCIATED CONCEPTS: way appurtenant, way by dedication, way of necessity, way reserved, wayfarer, waylay

WEAK (Decrepit), *adjective* ailing, atonic, brittle, debilitated, delicate, dilapidated, dim, enervated, enfeebled, faint, feeble, flaccid, fragile, impotent, infirm, passive, spent, timorous, unfortified, unhealthy, vulnerable, wasted

WEAK (Deficient), *adjective* confused, defective, fallible, flimsy, helpless, illogical, imperfect, inadequate, incapable, ineffective, ineffectual, insubstantial, insufficient, invalid, jejune, languid, marginal, not thought out, obscure, poor, powerless, tenuous, thin, uncertain, unsound, unsteady, untenable, vague

WEAKENED, *adjective* debilitating, defective, deficient, fallible, flimsy, helpless, imperfect, improper, inadequate, incapable, ineffective, ineffectual, inferior, insubstantial, insufficient, invalid, languid, marginal, poor, unsound, untenable, weak

WEALTH, *noun* abundance, achievement, affluence, assessed valuation, assets, assets and liabilities, blessings, bottom line, circumstances, comfort, condition, current assets, dividends, earnings, ease, fixed assets, fortune, funds, gain, gains, good fortune, good luck, good times, gross profit, handsome fortune, high income, intangible assets, intangibles, interest, liquid assets, material assets, material wealth, means, money, money to burn, net assets, net worth, opulence, possessions, proceeds, profit, profits, property, prosperity, prosperousness, resources, riches, richness, spoils, success, successfulness, tangible assets, tangibles, thriving condition, total assets, total resources, treasure, wealthiness, well-being, what one is worth, winnings, worth

WEALTHY, *adjective* abundantly affluent, affluent, established and affluent, extraordinarily affluent, fabulously rich, incredibly affluent, loaded (slang), made of money (slang), moneyed, of extreme means, of great achievement, of great means, of substantial means, old money, rich, rich and powerful, well-endowed, well-established, well-heeled, well-off, well-to-do, worth substantial funds
ASSOCIATED CONCEPTS: fat cats, maximum campaign contributions, millionaire

WELFARE, *noun* accommodation, advantage, assistance, benefaction, comfort, convenience, enjoyment, expediency, gain, good, gratification, improvement, pleasure, profit, relief, return, safety, satisfaction, security, solace, success, succor, utility, utilization, well-being, worth

WEAPONS, *noun* armaments, *armorum,* arms, deadly devices, deadly weapons, instruments of combat, lethal instruments, lethal weapons, munitions
ASSOCIATED CONCEPTS: concealed weapons, deadly weapons, possession of a weapon
FOREIGN PHRASES: *Arma in armatos sumere jura sinunt.* The laws permit the use of arms against those who are armed.

WEAR AND TEAR, *noun* corrosion, damage, decay, depletion, depreciation, deterioration, dissolution, dilapidation, diminution, erosion, exhaustion, impairment, ravage, ruination, wastage
ASSOCIATED CONCEPTS: award with wear and tear excepted

WEIGH, *verb* balance, bear heavily, burden, cogitate, consider, *considerare,* contemplate, cumber, deliberate, determine the heaviness of, encumber, estimate, evaluate, examine, find the weight of, gauge, load down, measure according to weight, meditate upon, mull over, ponder, press, put on the scale, reflect upon, *reputare,* ruminate, study
ASSOCIATED CONCEPTS: weigh the evidence

WEIGHT (Burden), *noun* care, cumbrance, duty, encumbrance, incubus, liability, load, mass, obligation, onus, oppression, ponderousness, pressure, responsibility

WEIGHT (Credibility), *noun* belief, certainty, confidence, credence, credibleness, credit, faith, impressiveness, likelihood, positiveness, reliance, trustworthiness, validity

WEIGHT (Importance), *noun* authority, consequence, degree of importance, effect, efficacy, eminence, emphasis, enormity, force, import, impressiveness, influence, interest, magnitude, merit, moment, potency, power, prominence, quality, seriousness, significance, value
ASSOCIATED CONCEPTS: weight of the evidence

FOREIGN PHRASES: *Ponderantur testes, non numerantur.* Witnesses are weighed, not counted. *Testimonia ponderanda sunt, non numeranda.* Evidence is to be weighed, not counted.

WEIGHT OF EVIDENCE, *noun* adequate evidence, adequate proof legally presented at trial, burden of going forward, legal responsibility, obligation of going forward, sufficient corroboration, sufficient evidence in a case, sufficient evidence to establish a case, sufficient proof, sufficient proof of facts, validation of proof of a case, verification of proof of a case
ASSOCIATED CONCEPTS: cause of action or claim, evidence, evidential burden, failure to sustain, preponderance of the evidence, prima facie case, rebuttal
FOREIGN PHRASES: *Onus probani.* Burden of proof.

WELFARE, *noun* advantage, affluence, assistance, benefit, *commodis consulere,* fortune, good, haleness, happiness, health, *hominis,* interest, luck, prosperity, prosperousness, soundness, success, weal, well-being
ASSOCIATED CONCEPTS: public welfare

WELL-BEING, *noun* abounding in riches, affluent, blooming, booming, comfortable, established, flourishing, fortunate, lucky, moneyed, profiting, providential, rich, safety, security, successful, thriving, wealthy, well-off, well-situated well-to-do

WELL-FOUNDED, *adjective* according to law, age-old, allowed, appropriate, authorized, correct, enacted, established, genuine, in accord with the law, in accord with legal provisions, in accord with statutory law, justification, law-abiding, lawful, legal, legalized, licensed, mandated, official, permitted, proper, recognized by law, real, sanctioned, sanctioned by law, sanctioned by legal authority, sound, statutory, suitable, valid, well-grounded, within the law

WELL-GROUNDED, *adjective* firm, legitimate, positive, solid, sound, steady, strong, well-based, well-founded

WELL-KNOWN, *adjective* acclaimed, celebrated, established, esteemed, famed, famous, glorified, illustrious, important, notable, noted, notorious, popular, preeminent, prominent, respected, universally known, well-established, well-positioned, widely known, with a distinct name, with a luster, with celebrity status, with distinction, with eminence, with prestige, with regard, with renown, with standing, with star quality, with station, with status
ASSOCIATED CONCEPTS: judicial notice

WELL-OFF, *adjective* booming, doing quite well, flourishing, fortuitous, fortunate, halcyon, happy, moneyed, of adequate means, on top of the world, prosperous, successful, thriving, triumphant, wealthy, well-heard

WHATEVER, *adverb* at all, of any description, of any kind or sort, whatsoever, whichever

WHATSOEVER, *adjective* all without specification, any, anything, every, everything, some, whatever
ASSOCIATED CONCEPTS: plain language

WHATSOEVER, *adverb* any kind, any sort, at all, of any description, whatever

WHENEVER, *adverb* at whatever time, at which time, no matter when, once, when

WHEREABOUTS, *noun* abode, address, area, coordinates, direction, district, emplacement, environment, habitat, latitude and longitude, locale, locality, location, neighborhood, pinpointed location, place, placement, point of location, position, region, setting, site, situation, *situs,* spot, venue, the very point of location, the very spot of location, vicinage, vicinity
ASSOCIATED CONCEPTS: plain language

WHEREBY, *conjunction* as a result of which, by which, in accordance with which, through which
ASSOCIATED CONCEPTS: plain language

WHEREIN, *adverb* concerning, during which, herein, in regard to which, in the course of which, in what, in which, inwardly, of which, regarding, respecting, therein touching, whereon, whereupon, within
ASSOCIATED CONCEPTS: plain language

WHILE, *conjunction* although, at the same time that, concurrently with, contemporaneously, currently, during, during the time that, even though, in the time that, simultaneously with, though, throughout the time that

WHOEVER, *noun* any individual, any person, anybody, anyone, no matter who, whomever, whomsoever, whosoever

WHOLE *(Undamaged),* ***adjective*** aggregate, all, complete, entire, gross, intact, solid, total, undiminished, unhurt, unimpaired, unreduced, without loss
ASSOCIATED CONCEPTS: whole capital, whole estate, whole quantity, whole truth

WHOLE *(Unified),* ***adjective*** holistic, indivisible, one, single, total, undivisible, universal

WHOLE, *noun* aggregate, all, allness, assemblage, collectiveness, collectivity, completeness, entirety, everything, gross amount, indivisibility, intactness, integer, integrity, sum total, totality, undividedness, universality, wholeness

WHOLLY, *adverb* altogether, as a whole, collectively, completely, entirely, fully, in all respects, in the aggregate, in the main, in the mass, in toto, outright, roundly, throughout, totally, utterly
ASSOCIATED CONCEPTS: wholly dependant, wholly liable

WHOLLY INADEQUATE, *adjective* abhorrent, abominable, atrocious, awful, beneath contempt, contemptible, deplorable, despicable, detestable, dreadful, drive, foul, frightening, frightful, ghastly, ghoulish, gruesome, harrowing, hateful, heinous, horrendous, horrid, horrifying, indefensible, loathsome, macabre, obnoxious, odious, offensive, outrageous, pathetic, pitiful, repellent, reprehensible, repulsive, revolting, shameful, shocking, terrible, terrifying, unspeakable, vile, villainous
ASSOCIATED CONCEPTS: deplorable conditions

WICKED, *adjective* abhorrent, abominable, arrant, atrocious, bad, baleful, baneful, base, criminal, crude, damnable, dastardly, debased, despicable, detestable, dishonorable, dissolute, dreadful, evil, evildoing, evil-minded, hateful, heinous, hideous, horrible, horrid, ignoble, ignominious, incorrigible, infamous, iniquitous, invidious, knavish, loathsome, malefic, maleficent, malevolent, malicious, malignant, monstrous, noxious, obnoxious, opprobrious, pernicious, perverse, perverted, reprehensible, repulsive, revolting, satanic, scurrilous, unseemly, unspeakable, untoward, vicious, vile, villainous, vulgar, wanton
ASSOCIATED CONCEPTS: moral turpitude

WIDESPREAD, adjective ample, broad, capacious, collective, common, comprehensive, current, diffuse, epidemic, extensive, familiar, far-flung, far-reaching, general, global, indiscriminate, large-scale, omnibus, ordinary, predominant, prevailing, prevalent, rampant, rife, spacious, sparse, sporadic, spreading, substantial, sweeping, wide-open, wideranging

WIELD, verb avail oneself of, brandish, carry, command, control, direct, employ, exercise, exert, govern, handle, make use of, manage, manipulate, operate, ply, rule, sway, swing, *tractare,* use, utilize, work

WILL *(Desire),* **noun** *animus,* aspiration, backbone, choice, command, decision, desideration, determination, disposition, grit, hankering, hope, inclination, intent, longing, mind, pleasure, power of choosing, power of determination, preference, purpose, resoluteness, resolution, self-control, self-discipline, velleity, volition, *voluntas,* want, wish, yearning

FOREIGN PHRASES: *Voluntas donatoris in charta doni sui manifeste expressa observetur.* The will of the donor which is clearly expressed in his deed of gift should be observed. ***Furiosi nulla voluntas est.*** A madman has no will.

WILL *(Testamentary instrument),* **noun** bequeathal, bestowal, document, dispensation, disposition, instrument, legacy, testament, *testamentum*

ASSOCIATED CONCEPTS: absolute will, alienation, alteration, ambulatory will, appointment of an administrator, attempt to defeat will, bequest, cancellation, challenge to a will, codicil, commercial will, conditional will, conjoint will, contested will, contractual wills, counter wills, devise, election, execute a will, executor named in a will, existence of a will, forgery of a will, gift inter vivos, holographic will, incorporation by reference, instructions, joint wills, mutual wills, nuncupative will, precatory words, probate, property which passes by will, pursuant to terms of will, reciprocal wills, revocation of a will, suit for construction of a will, suit to annul or suspend a will, unconditional will, validity of a will, voidable will, witness to a will, written instrument

FOREIGN PHRASES: *Da tua dum tua sunt, post mortem tunc tua non sunt.* Give that which is yours while it is yours; after death it is not yours. ***Haereditas est successio in universum jus quod defunctus habuerit.*** Inheritance is the succession to every right which the deceased had possessed. ***Sola ac per se senectus donationem testamentum aut transactionem non vitiat.*** Old age does not alone and of itself vitiate a will, gift, or transaction. ***Haereditas nihil aliud est, quam successio in universum jus, quod defunctus habuerit.*** An inheritance is nothing other than the succession to all the rights which the deceased had. ***In testamentis plenius testatoris intentionem scrutamur.*** In wills, the intentions of the testators should be fully regarded. ***In testamentis ratio tacita non debet considerari, sed verba solum spectari debent; adeo per divinationem mentis a verbis recedere durum est.*** In wills an unexpressed intention ought not to be considered, but the words alone ought to be regarded; for it is difficult to recede from the words by guessing at their intention. ***In dubiis, non praesumitur pro testamento.*** In doubtful cases, there is no presumption in favor of the will. ***Interest reipublicae suprema hominum testamenta rata haberi.*** It concerns the state that men's last wills be held valid. ***Quae in testamento ita sunt scripta ut intelligi non possint, perinde sunt ac si scripta non essent.*** Things which are so written in a will that they cannot be understood, are the same as if they had not been written at all. ***Testatoris ultima voluntas est perimplenda secundum veram intentionem suam.*** The last will of a testator is to be thoroughly fulfilled according to his true intention. ***Non aliter***

a significatione verborum recedi oportet quam cum manifestum est, aliud sensisse testatorem. The ordinary meaning of the words ought not to be departed from unless it is evident that the testator intended otherwise. ***Ubi pugnantia inter se in testamento juberentur, neutrum ratum est.*** When two directions conflicting with each other are given in a will, neither is held valid. ***Cum in testamento ambigue aut etiam perperam scriptum est benigne interpretari et secundum id quod credibile est cogitatum credendum est.*** When an ambiguous, or even an incorrectly written, expression is found in a will, it should be interpreted liberally and according to what is the probable intention of the testator. ***Omne testamentum morte consummatum est.*** Every will or testament is consummated by death. ***Nemo plus commodi haeredi suo relinquit quam ipse habuit.*** No one leaves a greater advantage for his heir than he himself had. ***Ambulatoria est voluntas defunctiusque ad vitae supremum exitum.*** The will of a deceased person is revocable until the last moment of life. ***Relatio semper fiat ut valeat dispositio.*** Reference should always be made that a testamentary disposition may be effective. ***Cum duo inter se pugnantia reperiuntur in testamento, ultimum ratum est.*** When two repugnant matters are found in a will, the last one will be confirmed. ***Voluntas facit quod in testamento scriptum valeat.*** The will of the testator gives validity to what is written in the will. ***Opinio quae favet testamento est tenenda.*** An opinion which favors a will is to be followed.

WILLFUL, adjective conscious, contemplated, contumax, deliberate, designed, inflexible, intended, intentional, intractable, intransigent, obdurate, obstinate, *obstinatus, pertinax,* planned, premeditated, purposed, purposeful, restive, retractory, studied, tenacious, uncompromising, unconstrained, unyielding, volitional, volitive, voluntary

ASSOCIATED CONCEPTS: willful acts

WILLING *(Desirous),* **adjective** assenting, disposed, eager, earnest, enthusiastic, partial to, ready, volitional, zealous

WILLING *(Not averse),* **adjective** acquiescent, agreeable, amenable, compliant, content, consenting, fain, favorably inclined, favorable, genial, receptive, responsive, susceptible, tractable, unreluctant, voluntary, yielding

WILLING *(Uncompelled),* **adjective** gratuitous, unbidden, unforced

WILLINGNESS, noun acceptableness, accommodation, accordance, acquiescence, amiability, appropriateness, complaisance, compliance, concordance, conformableness, congeniality, congruousness, consent, cordiality, courteousness, delightfulness, enjoyableness, flexibleness, friendliness, geniality, pliancy, suitability

WISDOM, noun acumen, astuteness, caliber, clear thinking, cognition, common sense, comprehension, discernment, discretion, edification, enlightenment, erudition, experience, good judgment, information, insight, intellectuality, intelligence, knowledge, learning, lore, perspicuity, prescience, profound thought, profundity, rationality, reason, sagacity, sapience, savvy, scholarship, sense, shrewdness, sound understanding, understanding, wiseness, worldly wisdom

ASSOCIATED CONCEPTS: expert witness, in the wisdom of the court

WITHDRAW, verb abandon, abdicate, abjure, abolish, abscond, absent oneself, abstract, back out, backtrack, cease, deduct, depart, desert, disappear, disassociate, disavow, disengage, disestablish, dissociate, draw out, evacuate, extract, invalidate, keep apart, leave, nullify, overrule, pull back, quash, quit, recall, recant, recede, relinquish, remove, renege, repeal, rescind, resign, retire, retract, retreat, reverse, revoke, secede, separate, sequester, sequestrate, subduce, subduct, subtract, surrender, take away, take back, unsheathe, vacate, wean

WITHDRAWAL, *noun*   abandonment, abdication, abjuration, abolition, abrogation, absence, annulment, cancellation, clearance, cloture, defeasance, denial, departure, desertion, disavowal, discontinuance, disengagement, dissociation, eradication, evacuation, evulsion, exit, exodus, extraction, hegira, invalidation, leave-taking, nullification, parting, recall, recantation, recess, relinquishment, removal, renunciation, repudiation, rescindment, rescission, resignation, retirement, retraction, retreat, revocation, riddance, secession

ASSOCIATED CONCEPTS: error cured by withdrawal, withdrawal from the commission of a crime, withdrawal of a case, withdrawal of a default, withdrawal of a judgment, withdrawal of a partner from a partnership, withdrawal of an action, withdrawal of charges, withdrawal of pleadings

WITHHOLD, *verb*   abstain, begrudge, block, censor, check, *comprimere,* conceal, constrain, curb, debar, deny, disallow, forbear, forbid, hide, hinder, hold, hold back, hold in, hold out, hush up, inhibit, keep, keep back, keep in, keep secret, muzzle, prohibit, refrain, refuse, refuse to disclose, rein in, repress, reserve, restrain, restrict, *retinere,* smother, stifle, suppress, *supprimere*

WITHOUT A SHRED OF EVIDENCE, *noun*   absence of confirmation, basis for belief, corroboration, documentation, grounds to believe, indicia of evidence, modicum of evidence, modicum of proof, some evidence, some grounds, some means of proof, some persuasive evidence, some proof, some proof of facts, substantiation, validation, verification

ASSOCIATED CONCEPTS: circumstantial evidence, direct evidence, relevant evidence

WITHOUT RECOURSE, *adverb*   conditional endorsement, qualified endorsement, restricted, subject to terms
ASSOCIATED CONCEPTS: endorsement without recourse

WITHOUT RESTRAINT, *adjective*   all-encompassing, all-inclusive, all-out, broad, complete, comprehensive, entire, every possible combination, extensive, full-fledged, liberal, maximum, thorough, total, unabridged, unbridled, unrestrained, vast, voluminous, whole, without abridgment, without limitation, without reduction

WITHSTAND, *verb*   block, breast, challenge, check, confront, contravene, cope with, counteract, countercheck, countervail, defy, endure, face, face danger, face up to, fight, foil, hamper, hinder, hold out, impede, inhibit, interrupt, last, *obsistere, obstare,* obstruct, offer resistance, oppose, preclude, prevail against, prevent, refuse to submit, repel, repulse, resist, *resistere,* retard, stand fast, stand firm, stand up to, stave off, stay, stem, stop, thwart, weather

ASSOCIATED CONCEPTS: withstand a challenge on appeal

WITNESS, *noun*   attestant, attestor, beholder, bystander, compurgator, corroborator, deponent, informant, informer, looker, looker-on, observer, one who gives testimony, onlooker, person affording evidence, reporter, swearer, testifier, *testis*

ASSOCIATED CONCEPTS: adverse witness, attestation, attesting witness, available witness, call as a witness, compel the attendance of witnesses, competent disinterested witness, competent witness, confronting a witness, credible witness, cross-examination, discredited witness, disinterested witness, expert witness, eyewitness, hostile witness, impeachment of a witness, material witness, nonexpert witness, prosecution witness, res gestae witness, skilled witness, specially qualified witness, state witness, subscribing witness, tampering with a witness, voluntary witness

FOREIGN PHRASES: *Habemus optimum testem, confitentem reum.* We have the best witness, a confessing defendant. *Nemo allegans suam turpitudinem audien dus est.* No one should be permitted to testify as a witness to his own baseness or wickedness. *Nullus idoneus testis in re sua intelligitur.* No person is deemed to be a competent witness in his own behalf. *Judex non potest esse testis in propria causa.* A judge cannot be a witness in his own case. *Jurato creditur in judicio.* He who makes an oath is to be believed in a judicial proceeding. *Quod constat curiae opere testium non indiget.* That which is clear to the court needs not the help of witnesses. *Nemo tenetur edere instrumenta contra se.* No one is bound to produce writings against himself. *Nemo tenetur jurare in suam turpitudinem.* No one is bound to testify to his own turpitude. *Nemo tenetur prodere seipsum.* No one is bound to betray himself. *Testis nemo in sua causa esse potest.* No one can be a witness in his own cause. *Testis de visu praeponderat aliis.* An eyewitness is preferred to others. *Nemo in propria causa testis esse debet.* No one ought to be a witness in his own cause.

WITNESS (Attest to), *verb*   acknowledge, affirm, authenticate, bear out, bear witness, certify, confirm, corroborate, cosign, countersign, endorse, give evidence, give testimony, say under oath, sign, substantiate, sustain, swear, take one's oath, testari, *testificari,* testify to, *testimonium dicere,* undersign, uphold, validate, verify, vouch for, warrant
ASSOCIATED CONCEPTS: witness a crime, witness a document, witness a will

WITNESS (Have direct knowledge of), *verb*   be a spectator, be present and note, behold, mark, note, notice, observe, recognize, see, sight, *spectare,* spot, take cognizance of, *videre,* view, watch

WORD (News), *noun*   account, advice, bulletin, communication, dispatch, information, intelligence, mention, message, report, statement

WORD (Promise), *noun*   affirmation, agreement, assurance, averment, avouchment, avowal, declaration, pledge, profession, solemn declaration, statement, undertaking, vow, warrant

WORD (Term), *noun*   adage, antonym, argument, articulation, coined word, colloquy, command, contention, conversation, dialogue, discourse, expression, homonym, maxim, mot, motto, observation, palaver, parlay, part of speech, phrase, proverb, remark, saying, statement, synonym, utterance, verbalism
ASSOCIATED CONCEPTS: actionable words, words of art, words of limitation

WORK (Effort), *noun*   application, attempt, campaign, chore, diligence, drudgery, endeavor, enterprise, essay, exercise, exertion, grind, industry, labor, opus, strain, stress, strife, struggle, toil, undertaking

WORK *(Employment),* **noun**   assignment, avocation, business, calling, charge, craft, duty, engagement, function, incumbency, industry, job, line, metier, occupation, office, position, post, profession, pursuit, specialty, task, trade, vocation

WORK FOR HIRE, noun   appointed sub-author, delegated author, sub-author, under-author

WORLDWIDE, adjective   all-embracing, all-inclusive, complete, comprehensive, extensive, far-reaching, global, international, nonsectarian, omnipresent, overall, pandemic, prevailing, prevalent, total, universal, widespread

WORRY, noun   affliction, annoyance, anxiety, apprehension, apprehensiveness, care, concern, consternation, difficulty, discomfort, discomposure, dismay, disquiet, distress, distress one's self, dread, fear, fearfulness, grief, malaise, mental agitation, misgiving, nuisance, pain, perplexity, perturbation, premonition, qualm, restiveness, solicitude, torment, trepidation, trouble, troubles, unease, uneasiness, vexation

WORRY, verb   agitate, agonize, annoy, badger, be anxious, be apprehensive, be troubled, bedevil, beset, bother, brood over, despair, discommode, discompose, displease, disquiet, distress, disturb, dread, embarrass, feel uneasy, fret, grieve over, harass, harry, hector, hound, incommode, irritate, mistreat, oppress, pain, perplex, persecute, perturb, pique, plague, press, trouble, upset, vex

WORTH, noun   account, advantage, *aestimatio,* appraisal, appraisement, avail, benefit, caliber, charge, cost, credit, desert, esteem, estimation, excellence, expense, importance, merit, par, *pretium,* price, profit, profitableness, quality, quotation, rate, regard, respect, service, serviceableness, use, utility, valuation, value, *virtus,* worthiness
FOREIGN PHRASES: *Tantum bona valent, quantum vendi possunt.* Goods are worth as much as they are sold for.

WRIT, noun   bid, bidding, command, commandment, decree, decretal, dictate, direction, directive, fiat, mandate, order, ordinance, precept, regulation, requirement
ASSOCIATED CONCEPTS: concurrent writ, judicial writ, original writ, preemptory writ, prerogative writ, writ of attachment, writ of certiorari, writ of covenant, writ of detinue, writ of error, writ of error coram nobis, writ of execution, writ of habeas corpus, writ of inquiry, writ of mandemus, writ of prohibition, writ of protection, writ of quo warranto, writ of replevin, writ of right

WRITE OFF, verb   abandon, abdicate, abjure, abstain, avoid, cease, cede, deny oneself, desist from, dispense with, disposed of, do without, drop, eschew, fast, forbear, forfeit, forego, forgo, forswear, give up, give up on, go without, hold back, hold off, lay down, leave off, let alone, make do without, not use, pass up, refrain, release, relinquish, renounce, reserve, resign, sacrifice, shun, surrender, waive, withhold, yield, yield up
ASSOCIATED CONCEPTS: forego interest owed, forego opportunity

WRONG, noun   abomination, abuse, atrocity, crime, delinquency, dereliction, evil, grievance, harm, illegality, immorality, improbity, infraction, iniquity, *iniuria,* injury, injustice, lawlessness, malfeasance, malpractice, miscreancy, misdeed, misdoing, mistake, mistreatment, obliquity, offense, outrage, sin, transgression, trespass, turpitude, unfairness, unrighteousness, vice, villainy, violation, violation of right, wickedness

FOREIGN PHRASES: *Scienti et volenti non fit injuria.* A wrong is not done to a person who understands and consents. ***Peccatum peccato addit qui culpae quam facit patrocinium defensionis adjungit.*** He adds one offense to another who connects a wrong which he has committed with his defense. ***Nemo ex suo delicto meliorem suam conditionem facere potest.*** No one can improve his condition by his own misdeed. ***Nemo ex proprio dolo consequitur actionem.*** No one acquires a right of action from his own fraud. ***Un ne doit prise advantage de son tort demesne.*** One ought not to take advantage of his own wrong. ***Nemo damnum facit, nisi qui id fecit quod facere jus non habet.*** No one is considered as doing damage, except he who does that which he has no right to do. ***Jus ex injuria non oritur.*** A right does not arise from a wrong. ***Injuria non excusat injuriam.*** One wrong does not excuse another. ***Ubi et dantis et accipientis turpitudo versatur, non posse repeti dicimus; quotiens autem accipientis turpitudo versatur, repeti posse.*** Where there is turpitude by both giver and receiver, we say it cannot be recovered back; but whenever the turpitude is in the receiver only, it can be recovered. ***Ubicunque est injuria, ibi damnum sequitur.*** Wherever there is a wrong, there damage follows. ***Nullum iniquum est praesumendum in jure.*** Nothing iniquitous is to be presumed in law. ***Nullus videtur dolo facere qui suo jure utitur.*** No one is considered to have committed a wrong who exercises his legal rights. ***Aliquid conceditur ne injuria remaneat impunita, quod alias non concederetur.*** Something is conceded, lest a wrong remain unredressed, which otherwise would not be conceded.

WRONGDOER, noun   criminal, debauchee, delinquent, evildoer, homo *maleficus,* lawbreaker, malefactor, malfeasant, miscreant, misdemeanant, misdoer, offender, outlaw, profligate, reprobate, scoundrel, sinner, transgressor, villain
FOREIGN PHRASES: *In pari delicto potior est conditio possidentis, defendentis.* Where the parties are equally guilty of wrongdoing, the defendant holds the stronger position. ***Nullus videtur dolo facere qui suo jure utitur.*** No one is considered to have committed a wrong who exercises his legal rights.

WRONGFUL, adjective   against the law, bad, criminal, felonious, illegal, illegitimate, illicit, improper, incorrect, iniquitous, *iniuriosus, iniustus,* lawless, malicious, mischievous, unauthorized, undue, unfair, unjust, unlawful, unseemly, unsuitable, wrong
ASSOCIATED CONCEPTS: wrongful act, wrongful conversion, wrongful death, wrongful detention, wrongful discharge, wrongful interference
FOREIGN PHRASES: *Fictio legis inique operatur alieni damnum vel injuriam.* Fiction of law is wrongful if it works loss or harm to anyone.

WRONGFUL ACT, noun   breach, breach of legal duty, civil wrong, contravention, delinquency, dereliction, dereliction of duty, guilty act, illegality, impropriety, injustice, malefaction, malpractice, misbehavior, misconduct, misdeed, misdoing, misfeasance, offense, offense against the law, tort, transgression, trespass, violation, willful wrongdoing, wrong, wrongful conduct
ASSOCIATED CONCEPTS: criminal act, illegality, perjury, tortuous act, wrongful attachment, wrongful conviction, wrongful death, wrongful execution, wrongful foreclosure, wrongful injunction, wrongful institution of an action, wrongful levy, wrongful testimony

WRONGFUL CONDUCT, *noun* bad conduct, breach, contravention, corruption, crime, delinquency, dereliction, deviation from rectitude, ill conduct, illegal action, illegality, impropriety, infringement, injurious action, injustice, malfeasance, malpractice, misbehavior, misdeed, misdoing, transgression, violation, wrongful action

WRONGFUL USE, *noun* abuse, corrupt use, deformation, distortion, errancy, incorrect usage, malapropism, misapplication, misappropriation, misconstruction, misdirection, misemployment, mishandling, mismanagement, misusage, misuse, wrong application, wrong use
ASSOCIATED CONCEPTS: product liability, warnings

YARDSTICK, *noun* aspect, benchmark, borderline indication, boundary, confinement, dictate, dimension, direction, formula, gauge, general guideline, guide, guideline, idea, instruction, key, limitation, margin, marker, measure, outer limits, parameter, perimeter, restraint, restriction, rule, specific, standard

YIELD *(Produce a return)*, ***verb*** accord, accrue, afford, bear, bestow, bring, bring about, bring forth, bring in, fetch, furnish, generate, give, provide, render, return, supply

YIELD *(Submit)*, ***verb*** abandon, abdicate, accede, accept, acquiesce, admit, agree to, allow, assent, back down, be submissive, bend, bow, capitulate, cede, comply, concede, *concedere,* consent, *dedere,* forgo, give in, give up, give way, grant, leave, let go, make way, obey, pay homage to, permit, quit, relent, relinquish, renounce, resign, sacrifice, succumb, suffer defeat, surrender, waive

YIELDING, *adjective* accommodating, acquiescent, alterable, amenable, complaisant, compliant, docile, easy, easygoing, elastic, facile, *facilis,* flexible, impressible, impressionable, malleable, manageable, obedient, obliging, *obsequens,* obsequious, passive, pliable, pliant, soft, submissive, supple, tractable, unresistant, unresisting
ASSOCIATED CONCEPTS: confessions

YOUR HONOR, *noun* adjudicator, administrator of justice, her honor, his honor, honorable justice, interpreter, judge, jurist, justice, magistrate, member of the judiciary, one who dispenses justice, the court

ZEALOUS, *adjective* active, ardent, assiduous, attentive, bent upon, dedicated, desirous, devoted, devout, eager, earnest, enthusiastic, fanatical, fervent, fervid, fiery, hearty, impassioned, impetuous, industrious, infatuated, keen, loving, passionate, perfervid, perseverant, persistent, pious, rabid, raving, ready, sedulous, solicitous, *studiosus,* willing
ASSOCIATED CONCEPTS: overly zealous representation of a client

ZONE, *noun* accommodation, address, area, arena, bailiwick, band, belt, circumference, compartment, confines, corridor, department, district, division, domain, environs, hemisphere, land, latitude, locale, locality, location, neighborhood, orb, orbit, permieter, periphery, place, precinct, premises, province, region, section, sector, sphere, terrain, territory, turf, vicinage, vicinity
ASSOCIATED CONCEPTS: economic zone, free trade zone, zone of employment, zoning ordinances

ZONING LAWS, *noun* building laws, building restrictions, construction laws, limitations on commercial buildings, by area, limitations on private residences by area, restrictions by area, restrictions set by zones, statutory provisions of the zoning law, zoning ordinances
ASSOCIATED CONCEPTS: variances permitted under the law

Index

A

a ceteris dissentire unorthodox
a commanding portion bulk
a fortiori discursive *(analytical)*. SEE MAIN ENTRY
a good deal of considerable
a posteriori discursive *(analytical)*
a priori axiomatic. SEE MAIN ENTRY
a priori discursive *(analytical)*
à propos admissible, applicable
a savoir SEE MAIN ENTRY
a.k.a. alias
ab initio SEE MAIN ENTRY
ab origine ab initio
ab ovo ab initio
ab re desistere abandon *(withdraw)*
ab re discrepare contradict
abalienare alienate *(estrange)*, alienate *(transfer title)*, estrange
abalienate alienate *(transfer title)*, assign *(transfer ownership)*, cede, consign, convey *(transfer)*.
abalienatio alienation *(transfer of title)*, pass *(advance)*
abalienation alienation *(transfer of title)*, assignment *(transfer of ownership)*, cession, demise *(conveyance)*, estrangement. SEE MAIN ENTRY
abandon betray *(lead astray)*, cede, disclaim, disinherit, disown *(refuse to acknowledge)*, fail *(neglect)*, flee, forfeit, forgo, forswear, leave *(depart)*, pretermit, quit *(discontinue)*, quit *(evacuate)*, reject, relinquish, renege, renounce, repudiate, resign, retire *(retreat)*, retreat, secede, set aside *(annul)*, stop, vacate *(leave)*, vacate *(void)*, withdraw, yield *(submit)*. SEE MAIN ENTRY
abandon allegiance defect
abandon nationality expatriate
abandoned dissolute, helpless *(defenseless)*, licentious, obsolete, solitary, tainted *(corrupted)*, uncurbed, vicious, void *(empty)*. SEE MAIN ENTRY
abandoned child orphan
abandoned infant orphan
abandoned to vice profligate *(corrupt)*
abandoning cancellation
abandonment abdication, abjuration, absence *(nonattendance)*, cancellation, capitulation, cessation *(termination)*, cloture, dereliction, desertion, desuetude, disclaimer, disuse, estrangement, expense *(sacrifice)*, halt, neglect, negligence, rejection, release, renunciation, rescision, resignation *(relinquishment)*, waiver. SEE MAIN ENTRY
abandonment of a known right waiver
abandonment of a trademark SEE MAIN ENTRY
abandonment of allegiance desertion, infidelity
abase adulterate, betray *(lead astray)*, damage, debase, demean *(make lower)*, demote, denigrate, depress, derogate, disgrace, dishonor *(deprive of honor)*, humiliate. SEE MAIN ENTRY
abasement attaint, bad repute, degradation, deterioration, disgrace, dishonor *(shame)*, disrepute, ignominy, infamy, obloquy, opprobrium, perversion, prostration, shame
abash browbeat, confound, confuse *(bewilder)*, disconcert, disgrace, disorient, dissuade, embarrass, humiliate, intimidate, perturb

abashed diffident
abashment embarrassment
abasing contemptuous
abate abolish, allay, alleviate, assuage, cease, check *(restrain)*, commute, curtail, decrease, deduct *(reduce)*, diminish, discount *(minimize)*, discount *(reduce)*, ease, enjoin, give *(yield)*, lapse *(cease)*, lessen, mitigate, moderate *(temper)*, modify *(moderate)*, mollify, obtund, quash, reduce, relax, relieve *(free from burden)*, remit *(relax)*, subdue, subside. SEE MAIN ENTRY
abate in intensity mitigate
abate severity relent
abatement abridgment *(disentitlement)*, curtailment, decline, decrease, decrement, deduction *(diminution)*, diminution, discount, lull, mitigation, mollification, outflow, relief *(release)*, remission, removal, solace. SEE MAIN ENTRY
abatement of differences adjustment, arrangement *(understanding)*, collective bargaining, compromise, conciliation
abating mitigating
abbreviate abridge *(shorten)*, abstract *(summarize)*, commute, condense, constrict *(compress)*, curtail, decrease, digest *(summarize)*, dilute, diminish, discount *(minimize)*, lessen, minimize, reduce
abbreviated brief, compact *(pithy)*, concise, laconic, minimal, succinct
abbreviation abridgment *(condensation)*, abstract, capsule, compendium, curtailment, decrease, digest, diminution, outline *(synopsis)*, summary, symbol
abbreviatory compact *(pithy)*
abbreviature abridgment *(condensation)*, abstract, curtailment
abdere hide
abdicate abandon *(withdraw)*, cede, defect, demit, forfeit, leave *(depart)*, quit *(discontinue)*, relinquish, renounce, repudiate, resign, retire *(conclude a career)*, surrender *(give back)*, vacate *(void)*, withdraw, yield *(submit)*. SEE MAIN ENTRY
abdicatio abdication, renunciation, resignation *(relinquishment)*
abdication abandonment *(discontinuance)*, renunciation, resignation *(relinquishment)*, waiver. SEE MAIN ENTRY
abditus latent
abduce carry away
abduct carry away, hijack, kidnap. SEE MAIN ENTRY
abduction taking. SEE MAIN ENTRY
abecedarian elementary, neophyte, rudimentary
aberemurder SEE MAIN ENTRY
aberrance deviation, error, indirection *(indirect action)*, irregularity, perversion. SEE MAIN ENTRY
aberrancy deviation, digression, error, indirection *(indirect action)*, irregularity, perversion. SEE MAIN ENTRY
aberrant anomalous, astray, atypical, deviant, devious, disordered, disorderly, disparate, dissimilar, divergent, eccentric, errant, erroneous, faulty, irregular *(not usual)*, licentious, nonconforming, peccant *(culpable)*, peculiar *(curious)*, unaccustomed, uncommon, unorthodox, unpredictable, unusual, variable. SEE MAIN ENTRY
aberrare detour, deviate, digress
aberration deviation, digression, discrepancy, error, fault *(mistake)*, insanity, irregularity, nonconformity, perversion, quirk *(idiosyncrasy)*. SEE MAIN ENTRY

aberration of mind insanity
abet aid, assist, bear *(support)*, conduce, conspire, contribute *(assist)*, countenance, enable, espouse, foment, foster, help, maintain *(sustain)*, promote *(organize)*, subsidize. SEE MAIN ENTRY
abetment aid *(help)*, auspices, collusion, conspiracy, contribution *(participation)*, favor *(sanction)*, help, service *(assistance)*. SEE MAIN ENTRY
abetting ancillary *(auxiliary)*, concerted, concurrent *(united)*, promotion *(encouragement)*. SEE MAIN ENTRY
abettor accessory, accomplice, advocate *(espouser)*, assistant, backer, benefactor, catalyst, coactor, coadjutant, coconspirator, cohort, colleague, confederate, consociate, conspirator, conspirer, contributor *(contributor)*, copartner *(coconspirator)*, participant, partner, proponent. SEE MAIN ENTRY
abeyance cessation *(interlude)*, check *(bar)*, cloture, desuetude, discontinuance *(act of discontinuing)*, extension *(postponement)*, halt, hiatus, inaction, interruption, interval, moratorium, nonuse, pause, pendency, respite *(interval of rest)*, stay. SEE MAIN ENTRY
abeyancy stay
abeyant dormant, inactive, prospective
abhor blame, condemn *(ban)*, contemn, disdain, forswear, reject, renounce, shun
abhorrence alienation *(estrangement)*, contempt *(disdain)*, disapprobation, disapproval, disdain, hatred, odium, phobia, rejection
abhorrent antipathetic *(distasteful)*, bad *(offensive)*, contemptible, heinous, loathsome, objectionable, obnoxious, offensive *(offending)*, repugnant *(exciting aversion)*, repulsive
abide adhere *(persist)*, allow *(endure)*, bear *(tolerate)*, continue *(persevere)*, dwell *(reside)*, endure *(last)*, inhabit, lodge *(reside)*, occupy *(take possession)*, persist, reside, subsist, suffer *(permit)*, tolerate. SEE MAIN ENTRY
abide by accede *(concede)*, adhere *(maintain loyalty)*, comply, concede, conform, defer *(yield in judgment)*, fulfill, keep *(fulfill)*, obey, observe *(obey)*, perform *(adhere to)*
abide together cohabit
abider habitant, inhabitant
abiding constant, continuance, durable, habitation *(act of inhabiting)*, indestructible, lasting, live *(existing)*, noncancellable, permanent, persistent, stable, steadfast, tolerance. SEE MAIN ENTRY
abiding place building *(structure)*, domicile, habitation *(dwelling place)*
abiding together cohabitation *(living together)*
abiectus contemptible, servile, sordid
ability aptitude, caliber *(mental capacity)*, capacity *(aptitude)*, efficiency, facility *(easiness)*, force *(strength)*, gift *(flair)*, performance *(workmanship)*, potential, proclivity, propensity, qualification *(fitness)*, quality *(excellence)*, quality *(grade)*, science *(technique)*, skill, specialty *(special aptitude)*. SEE MAIN ENTRY
ability to bear tolerance
ability to distinguish judgment *(discernment)*
ability to endure tolerance
ability to get along with others discretion *(quality of being discreet)*

ability to know comprehension, reason (*sound judgment*)
ability to make distinctions perception
ability to perceive intellect
ability to pursue tenacity
ability to reason intellect
ability to tolerate tolerance
ability to understand insight, intellect
ability to withstand tolerance
abire disappear, resign, retire (*retreat*), secede
abject base (*inferior*), blameful, blameworthy, caitiff, contemptible, contemptuous, ignoble, loathsome, odious, servile, sordid, subservient. SEE MAIN ENTRY
abject fear phobia
abject slavery bondage
abjection bad faith, bad repute, degradation, dishonor (*shame*), ignominy. SEE MAIN ENTRY
abjectness bad faith, bad repute, disgrace, dishonor (*shame*), disrepute, ignominy, shame. SEE MAIN ENTRY
abjudge hold (*decide*). SEE MAIN ENTRY
abjudicate hold (*decide*)
abjuration abdication, denial, desertion, disclaimer, disdain, negation, refusal, rejection, renunciation, repudiation, rescision, resignation (*relinquishment*), retraction. SEE MAIN ENTRY
abjuratory contradictory, recusant
abjure abandon (*relinquish*), abrogate (*annul*), cede, controvert, disaffirm, disallow, disown (*deny the validity*), disown (*refuse to acknowledge*), forfeit, forgo, forswear, leave (*depart*), quit (*discontinue*), recant, refuse, reject, relinquish, renounce, repudiate, resign, revoke, set aside (*annul*), surrender (*give back*), withdraw. SEE MAIN ENTRY
abjurement confutation, disclaimer, resignation (*relinquishment*)
able adequate, artful, capable, competent, deft, effective (*efficient*), efficient, expert, fit, omnipotent, potent, powerful, practiced, professional (*trained*), proficient, qualified (*competent*), ready (*prepared*), resourceful, sciential, strong. SEE MAIN ENTRY
able to be altered ambulatory
able to be confirmed deductible (*provable*)
able to be felt palpable
able to be handled palpable
able to be pierced penetrable
able to be seen apparent (*perceptible*), ostensible
able to be shown deductible (*provable*)
able to be subducted deductible (*capable of being deducted from taxes*)
able to be subtracted for tax purposes deductible (*capable of being deducted from taxes*)
able to be touched palpable
able to contain a great deal capacious
able to endure resilient
able to improve corrigible
able to meet situations resourceful
able to pay solid (*sound*), solvent
able to recognize conscious (*awake*)
able to withstand insusceptible (*resistant*)
able-bodied powerful
ablegare send
ableness ability, caliber (*mental capacity*), capacity (*aptitude*), dint, efficiency, faculty (*ability*), force (*strength*), quality (*excellence*), quality (*grade*). SEE MAIN ENTRY
ablude conflict, disaccord

abnegate abrogate (*annul*), adeem, annul, condemn (*ban*), controvert, countercharge, decline (*reject*), deny (*refuse to grant*), disaffirm, disallow, disapprove (*reject*), disavow, disclaim, disown (*deny the validity*), forgo, forswear, negate, refuse, refute, reject, renounce, repudiate, set aside (*annul*), surrender (*give back*). SEE MAIN ENTRY
abnegation abandonment (*repudiation*), ademption, declination, denial, disdain, negation, refusal, rejection, renunciation, rescision, temperance. SEE MAIN ENTRY
abnegative contrary
abnormal anomalous, atypical, deviant, disordered, irregular (*not usual*), non compos mentis, peculiar (*curious*), prodigious (*amazing*), suspicious (*questionable*), unaccustomed, uncommon, unusual. SEE MAIN ENTRY
abnormality deviation, incongruity, insanity, irregularity, nonconformity, perversion, quirk (*idiosyncrasy*). SEE MAIN ENTRY
abnormity irregularity, nonconformity, quirk (*idiosyncrasy*). SEE MAIN ENTRY
abnormous peculiar (*curious*)
abode address, base (*place*), building (*structure*), domicile, dwelling, habitation (*dwelling place*), home (*domicile*), house, inhabitation (*place of dwelling*), lodging, residence. SEE MAIN ENTRY
abolere abolish, annul, obliterate
abolish abate (*extinguish*), abrogate (*annul*), abrogate (*rescind*), adeem, annul, cancel, destroy (*void*), disaffirm, discharge (*release from obligation*), discontinue (*abandon*), eliminate (*eradicate*), eradicate, extinguish, extirpate, invalidate, kill (*defeat*), negate, nullify, obliterate, overthrow, overturn, quash, recall (*call back*), remove (*eliminate*), renege, repeal, repudiate, rescind, revoke, stop, supersede, supplant, terminate, vacate (*void*), vitiate, withdraw. SEE MAIN ENTRY
abolish the organization of disorganize
abolished inactive, null (*invalid*), null and void
abolishing cancellation
abolishment abolition, ademption, annulment, cancellation, countermand, defeasance, discharge (*annulment*), discontinuance (*act of discontinuing*), dissolution (*termination*), disuse, negation, rescission, retraction, reversal, revocation. SEE MAIN ENTRY
abolition abatement (*extinguishment*), ademption, annulment, cancellation, censorship, countermand, defeasance, destruction, discharge (*annulment*), discharge (*release from obligation*), discontinuance (*act of discontinuing*), dissolution (*termination*), disuse, negation, obviation, removal, repudiation, rescission, reversal, revocation, subversion. SEE MAIN ENTRY
abominable bad (*offensive*), contemptible, contemptuous, depraved, disgraceful, disreputable, heinous, invidious, loathsome, nefarious, objectionable, obnoxious, odious, offensive (*offending*), outrageous, repugnant (*exciting aversion*), repulsive, sordid, undesirable
abominableness disrepute
abominari deprecate
abominate contemn
abomination alienation (*estrangement*), atrocity, bad repute, contaminate, contempt (*disdain*), defilement, disgrace, hatred, misdeed, perversion, wrong

aboriginal incipient, native (*domestic*), prime (*original*), primordial
abort cancel, conclude (*complete*), destroy (*efface*), discontinue (*abandon*), dissolve (*terminate*), extinguish, frustrate, invalidate, negate, quit (*discontinue*)
aborted attempt failure (*lack of success*)
aborticide abortion (*feticide*)
abortio abortion (*feticide*)
abortion miscarriage. SEE MAIN ENTRY
abortive futile, imperfect, ineffective, ineffectual, otiose, unavailing, unproductive
abortive attempt frustration, miscarriage
abortive effort miscarriage
abound increase, proliferate
abounding ample, copious, full, profuse, replete
abounding in error fallacious, false (*inaccurate*)
abounding in riches opulent, prosperous
about to be imminent, prospective
about to happen forthcoming, immediate (*imminent*), imminent, inevitable, pending (*imminent*), proximate
about-face reversal, reversion (*act of returning*)
aboutir abut
above before mentioned, last (*preceding*)
above all a fortiori, particularly
above all price inestimable
above all value inestimable
above appraisal inestimable
above average extraordinary, superior (*excellent*)
above meanness magnanimous
above par meritorious, notable, noteworthy, preferable, superior (*excellent*), valuable
above pettiness magnanimous
above reproach blameless, unimpeachable
above suspicion blameless, clean, incorruptible, inculpable, irreprehensible, not guilty. SEE MAIN ENTRY
above the average best
above-cited before mentioned, last (*preceding*), previous
above-mentioned aforesaid, before mentioned, last (*preceding*), previous, said. SEE MAIN ENTRY
above-named before mentioned, last (*preceding*), previous. SEE MAIN ENTRY
above-stated before mentioned, last (*preceding*)
aboveboard bona fide, candid, direct (*forthright*), ethical, honest, ingenuous, irreprehensible, moral, right (*correct*), scrupulous, straightforward, unaffected (*sincere*), upright
abrade diminish, erode, expunge
abrasion deterioration, erosion
abrasive caustic
abreaction catharsis
abreast equal, informed (*having information*)
abrégé capsule
abri cache (*hiding place*)
abridge abstract (*summarize*), commute, condense, constrict (*compress*), curtail, decrease, digest (*summarize*), diminish, discount (*minimize*), expurgate, extract, lessen, minimize, reduce, retrench. SEE MAIN ENTRY
abridged brief, compact (*pithy*), concise, laconic, minimal, partial (*relating to a part*), sententious. SEE MAIN ENTRY
abridgment abstract, brief, capsule, censorship, compendium, curtailment, decrease, decrement, deduction (*diminution*), denial, deterrence, digest, mitigation, outline

(synopsis), paraphrase, restatement, summary, synopsis. SEE MAIN ENTRY

abrogare abrogate *(annul)*, annul, discredit, repeal, rescind, revoke

abrogate abate *(extinguish)*, abolish, adeem, annul, ban, bear false witness, cancel, cease, condemn *(ban)*, contradict, controvert, countervail, debar, disallow, discharge *(release from obligation)*, disclaim, discontinue *(abandon)*, disinherit, dissolve *(terminate)*, invalidate, kill *(defeat)*, negate, nullify, overrule, proscribe *(prohibit)*, recall *(call back)*, recant, renege, repeal, repudiate, rescind, revoke, set aside *(annul)*, vacate *(void)*, vitiate. SEE MAIN ENTRY

abrogated defunct, inactive, invalid, lifeless *(dead)*, null *(invalid)*, null and void, powerless. SEE MAIN ENTRY

abrogatio revocation

abrogation abandonment *(desertion)*, abandonment *(discontinuance)*, abatement *(extinguishment)*, abolition, ademption, annulment, avoidance *(cancellation)*, cancellation, condemnation *(seizure)*, countermand, default, defeasance, desuetude, discharge *(annulment)*, discharge *(release from obligation)*, dissolution *(termination)*, inaction, mistrial, negation, nollo prosequi, obviation, repudiation, rescision, reversal, revocation, waiver. SEE MAIN ENTRY

abrupt caustic, impulsive *(rash)*, instantaneous, precipitate, unanticipated, unexpected

abruption impasse

abruptness disrespect

abscind break *(violate)*, excise *(cut away)*, split. SEE MAIN ENTRY

abscission cancellation

abscond abandon *(physically leave)*, defect, depart, disappear, elude, escape, evacuate, flee, leave *(depart)*, move *(alter position)*, quit *(evacuate)*, withdraw. SEE MAIN ENTRY

abscond with hold up *(rob)*, jostle *(pickpocket)*, loot, pilfer, steal

abscondence bad faith

absconder fugitive

abscondere hide

absconding flight

absconditus hidden, latent

absence blank *(emptiness)*, dearth, deficiency, deficit, desuetude, furlough, insufficiency, need *(deprivation)*, nonresidence, nonuse, paucity, poverty, privation. SEE MAIN ENTRY

absence of authority anarchy
absence of ceremony informality
absence of change status quo
absence of diversity uniformity
absence of doubt certainty
absence of fear prowess *(bravery)*
absence of feeling insentience
absence of foreign rule liberty
absence of guilt innocence
absence of meaning incoherence, platitude
absence of restraint latitude, liberty
absence of sensation insentience
absence of servitude liberty
absence of variation uniformity
absence without leave desertion, nonappearance

absent lost *(taken away)*, oblivious, truant, vacuous

absent oneself abandon *(physically leave)*, abscond, depart, evacuate, flee, withdraw

absent-minded perfunctory, thoughtless
absentation leave *(absence)*, nonappearance
absenteeism nonappearance
absentia absence *(nonattendance)*
absentminded lax, oblivious
absentmindedness neglect
absinthal bitter *(acrid tasting)*
absinthian bitter *(acrid tasting)*
absolute actual, affirmative, arbitrary and capricious, axiomatic, cardinal *(outstanding)*, categorical, certain *(fixed)*, certain *(positive)*, clear *(certain)*, compelling, complete *(all-embracing)*, conclusive *(determinative)*, convincing, decisive, definite, definitive, demonstrable, dogmatic, explicit, gross *(flagrant)*, implicit, inappealable, incontrovertible, indubious, outright, plenary, positive *(incontestable)*, pure, radical *(extreme)*, resounding, right *(direct)*, stark, strict, thorough, total, unalienable, unconditional, undisputed, unequivocal, unmitigated, unqualified *(unlimited)*. SEE MAIN ENTRY
absolute assertion affirmance *(legal affirmation)*, affirmation
absolute certainty certification *(certainness)*, certitude, fact
absolute condition sine qua non
absolute confidence certainty, certification *(certainness)*, surety *(certainty)*
absolute difference antipode, antithesis
absolute inheritance fee *(estate)*
absolute interest in realty fee *(estate)*
absolute leader dictator
absolute prerequisite sine qua non
absolute quiet silence
absolute reality fact
absolute requisite necessity
absolute right birthright
absolute ruler dictator
absolutely de facto, fairly *(clearly)*, faithfully, in toto, ipso facto, purely *(positively)*
absolutely clear incontestable
absoluteness belief *(state of mind)*, certainty, certitude, surety *(certainty)*
absolutio acquittal
absolution acquittal, amnesty, clemency, compurgation, condonation, discharge *(liberation)*, discharge *(release from obligation)*, dispensation *(exception)*, exoneration, grace, immunity, impunity, liberation, pardon, release, remission, waiver. SEE MAIN ENTRY
absolution of a charge exoneration
absolutistic dictatorial
absolutus absolute *(complete)*
absolve acquit, clear, condone, discharge *(liberate)*, discharge *(release from obligation)*, exculpate, excuse, exonerate, extenuate, forgive, free, justify, palliate *(excuse)*, purge *(wipe out by atonement)*, quit *(free of)*, redeem *(satisfy debts)*, remit *(release from penalty)*, vindicate. SEE MAIN ENTRY
absolve of a charge exonerate
absolve of fault exculpate
absolve of wrongdoing exculpate
absolved blameless, clear, free from criminal charges, exempt, free *(relieved from a burden)*, immune. SEE MAIN ENTRY
absolvere absolve, acquit, dispatch *(dispose of)*, perfect
absonant contradictory, opposite
absorb comprehend *(understand)*, conceive *(comprehend)*, concern *(involve)*, digest *(comprehend)*, engage *(involve)*, immerse *(engross)*, impress *(affect deeply)*, include, incorporate *(include)*, interest, merge, monopolize, occupy *(engage)*,

penetrate, realize *(understand)*, receive *(permit to enter)*, understand
absorb the attention occupy *(engage)*
absorb the mind occupy *(engage)*
absorb the thoughts occupy *(engage)*
absorbed internal, oblivious, pensive
absorbed interest preoccupation
absorbent penetrable
absorbing moving *(evoking emotion)*
absorption centralization, contemplation, interest *(concern)*, merger, notice *(heed)*, obsession, osmosis, preoccupation, reflection *(thought)*
absorption of mind diligence *(care)*
abstain abandon *(relinquish)*, decline *(reject)*, defer *(yield in judgment)*, desist, discontinue *(abandon)*, eschew, forbear, refrain, refuse, rest *(cease from action)*, shirk, shun, withhold. SEE MAIN ENTRY
abstain from avoid *(evade)*, cease, forgo
abstain from inserting omit
abstain from recognizing ignore
abstainment abstention, continence
abstemious frugal
abstemiousness abstention, austerity, moderation, temperance
abstention absence *(nonattendance)*, continence, desuetude, temperance. SEE MAIN ENTRY
abstention from buying boycott
abstention from using boycott
absterge decontaminate
absterrere deter
abstinence abstention, continence, disuse, moderation, nonuse, temperance
abstinence from action abstention, inaction, laissez faire
abstract abridgment *(condensation)*, capsule, compendium, condense, delineation, digest, digest *(summarize)*, extract, hold up *(rob)*, intangible, lessen, moot, note *(brief comment)*, outline *(synopsis)*, recondite, restatement, review, scenario, select, speculative, steal, summary, synopsis, theoretical, withdraw. SEE MAIN ENTRY
abstract idea concept
abstract on the law hornbook
abstracted compact *(pithy)*, concise, disconnected, oblivious, pensive, perfunctory, thoughtless
abstraction concept, generality *(vague statement)*, idea, impalpability, larceny, notion, preoccupation, vision *(dream)*
abstruse ambiguous, complex, elusive, esoteric, hidden, inapprehensible, incomprehensible, indefinable, inexplicable, mysterious, nebulous, private *(confidential)*, profound *(esoteric)*, recondite, secret, technical. SEE MAIN ENTRY
abstruse knowledge secret
abstruseness ambiguity, mystery
absumere consume, exhaust *(deplete)*
absurd egregious, fatuous, impossible, incredible, inept *(inappropriate)*, infeasible, irrational, ludicrous, lunatic, outrageous, unbelievable, unreasonable, unsound *(fallacious)*, unsuitable
absurd story myth
absurdity incongruity
absurdly foolish fatuous
absurdness incongruity
absurdus illogical, irrational
abundance boom *(prosperity)*, bulk, plethora, prosperity, quantity, quorum, spate, store *(depository)*, sufficiency
abundant ample, considerable, copious, full, liberal *(generous)*, multiple, predominant,

prevailing *(current)*, prevalent, profuse, prolific, replete, rife, substantial, usual

abundantia store *(depository)*

abuse aspersion, atrocity, attack, badger, beat *(strike)*, contumely, criticism, damage, debauch, defamation, diatribe, dissipate *(expend foolishly)*, endanger, exploit *(take advantage of)*, harm, ill use, imprecation, infliction, injury, injustice, malign, maltreat, misapplication, misappropriation, misemploy, mishandle *(maltreat)*, mishandle *(mismanage)*, mistreat, misusage, misuse, molest *(subject to indecent advances)*, molestation, obloquy, offend *(insult)*, oppression, persecute, perversion, pervert, provocation, rape, reproach, revilement, shame, transgression, vilification, violation, wrong. SEE MAIN ENTRY

abuse a privilege infringe

abuse of privilege infringement

abuse of public trust corruption

abuse one's rights infringe

abused aggrieved *(harmed)*. SEE MAIN ENTRY

abusive calumnious, contemptuous, hostile, impertinent *(insolent)*, insolent, libelous, offensive *(offending)*, outrageous, pejorative, scurrilous. SEE MAIN ENTRY

abusive harangue diatribe

abusive language diatribe, obloquy, phillipic, slander, vilification

abusive speech harangue, malediction

abusiveness oppression

abut contact *(touch)*, juxtapose. SEE MAIN ENTRY

abut on adjoin

abut upon border *(approach)*, border *(bound)*

abuti abuse *(misuse)*, ill use, misemploy

abutment bulwark, contact *(touching)*. SEE MAIN ENTRY

abuttal connection *(abutment)*, contact *(touching)*

abutting adjacent, coalescence, contiguous, immediate *(not distant)*, proximate

abysmal profound *(intense)*

abyss pitfall

academic didactic, disciplinary *(educational)*, moot, speculative, theoretical

academic honor degree *(academic title)*

academician pedagogue

academy institute

accede acknowledge *(respond)*, admit *(concede)*, agree *(comply)*, allow *(endure)*, assent, cede, coincide *(concur)*, concede, confirm, conform, consent, defer *(yield in judgment)*, grant *(concede)*, obey, relent, sanction, submit *(yield)*, succumb, suffer *(permit)*, yield *(submit)*. SEE MAIN ENTRY

accede to accept *(admit as sufficient)*, accept *(assent)*, approve, bear *(tolerate)*, certify *(approve)*, comply, concur *(agree)*, countenance, inherit, pass *(approve)*

accedence acceptance, acquiescence, compliance, consent

accedere approach

accedere ad approximate

accelerare hasten, precipitate *(hasten)*

accelerate expedite, facilitate, hasten, precipitate *(hasten)*, race

accelerated expeditious, rapid

accelerated decision accelerated judgment

accelerated judgment SEE MAIN ENTRY

accelerating cumulative *(intensifying)*

acceleration boom *(increase)*, haste. SEE MAIN ENTRY

acceleration lane causeway

accendere incense

accent consequence *(significance)*, dwell *(linger over)*, emphasis, enunciate, inflection, insist, pronounce *(speak)*, reaffirm

accentuate dwell *(linger over)*, insist, pronounce *(speak)*, reaffirm. SEE MAIN ENTRY

accentuation emphasis, inflection, intonation, stress *(accent)*

accept abide, accede *(concede)*, accommodate, accredit, acquire *(receive)*, admit *(concede)*, adopt, agree *(comply)*, allow *(endure)*, approve, assent, assume *(undertake)*, bear *(tolerate)*, certify *(approve)*, coincide *(concur)*, collect *(recover money)*, comply, concede, conceive *(comprehend)*, concur *(agree)*, condone, conform, consent, defer *(yield in judgment)*, espouse, gain, grant *(concede)*, obey, partake, pass *(approve)*, receive *(acquire)*, receive *(permit to enter)*, recognize *(acknowledge)*, sanction, seal *(solemnize)*, sign, submit *(yield)*, suffer *(permit)*, tolerate, trust, undertake, uphold, validate, yield *(submit)*. SEE MAIN ENTRY

accept a liability promise *(vow)*

accept advice hear *(give attention to)*

accept an obligation assume *(undertake)*, promise *(vow)*

accept an offer close *(agree)*, contract

accept as a citizen naturalize *(make a citizen)*

accept as a member enroll

accept responsibility promise *(vow)*

accept responsibility for sponsor

accept the loan of borrow

acceptability admissibility, expedience, mediocrity, qualification *(fitness)*

acceptable adequate, admissible, allowable, allowed, applicable, commensurate, convenient, conventional, desirable *(qualified)*, eligible, fair *(satisfactory)*, fit, justifiable, mediocre, meritorious, palatable, passable, proper, qualified *(competent)*, sapid, seasonable, suitable, tenable, unobjectionable, viable. SEE MAIN ENTRY

acceptable evidence admissible evidence

acceptably fairly *(moderately)*

acceptance acquiescence, acquisition, affirmance *(judicial sanction)*, approval, assent, assumption *(adoption)*, charter *(sanction)*, compliance, concession *(compromise)*, confirmation, consent, credence, faith, indorsement, lenience, ratification, receipt *(act of receiving)*, recognition, reliance, sanction *(permission)*, subscription, understanding *(tolerance)*. SEE MAIN ENTRY

acceptance bill draft

acceptance of penalty nollo contendere

acceptation acquisition, meaning, signification

accepted allowable, allowed, assumed *(inferred)*, boiler plate, common *(customary)*, conventional, customary, familiar *(customary)*, formal, general, ordinary, plausible, popular, prescriptive, prevailing *(current)*, prevalent, right *(suitable)*, select, traditional, uncontested, undisputed, usual

accepted belief principle *(axiom)*

accepted fact common knowledge

accepted language plain language

accepted meaning content *(meaning)*

acceptedly admittedly

accepter disciple, receiver, recipient

accepting orthodox

acceptio acceptance, receipt *(act of receiving)*, taking

acceptor bearer, customer, devisee, donee, feoffee, grantee, heir, payee, transferee

access admission *(entry)*, admittance *(means of approach)*, entrance, entry *(entrance)*, ingress, outlet, portal. SEE MAIN ENTRY

access road causeway

accesses approaches

accessibility access *(opening)*

accessible amenable, available, convenient, destructible, indefensible, obvious, open-minded, passable, penetrable, potential, present *(attendant)*, public *(open)*, ready *(prepared)*, receptive, responsive, suasible, untenable, vulnerable. SEE MAIN ENTRY

accessible to all competitive *(open)*

accessible to bribery mercenary

accessibleness amenability

accessio accession *(annexation)*, addition, appendix *(supplement)*, augmentation

accession acceptance, acknowledgment *(acceptance)*, acquiescence, addition, appurtenance, arrogation, collection *(accumulation)*, cumulation, receipt *(act of receiving)*. SEE MAIN ENTRY

accessories paraphernalia *(apparatus)*, paraphernalia *(personal belongings)*, property *(possessions)*

accessory abettor, accomplice, addition, additional, adjunct, ancillary *(auxiliary)*, appendix *(accession)*, appliance, appurtenance, appurtenant, assistant, attachment *(thing affixed)*, augmentation, circumstantial, clerical, coactor, coadjutant, coconspirator, codicil, cohort, collateral *(accompanying)*, colleague, confederate, consociate, conspirer, contributor *(contributor)*, contributory, copartner *(coconspirator)*, expendable, extrinsic, incident, incidental, inferior *(lower in position)*, minor, nonessential, participant, partner, secondary, subordinate, subservient, supplementary. SEE MAIN ENTRY

accessory after the fact accomplice, coactor, coconspirator, conspirer, copartner *(coconspirator)*

accessory before the fact accomplice, coactor, coconspirator, conspirer, copartner *(coconspirator)*

accessus access *(right of way)*

accident act of god, casualty, catastrophe, contingency, emergency, happenstance, misfortune, tragedy. SEE MAIN ENTRY

accidental coincidental, fortuitous, haphazard, inadvertent, incidental, random, unexpected, unforeseen, unintentional, unwitting. SEE MAIN ENTRY

accidental death fatality

accidental homocide manslaughter

accidental occurrence happenstance, quirk *(accident)*

accipere accept *(take)*, construe *(comprehend)*, enfranchise, hear *(give attention to)*, receive *(acquire)*

accipient assignee

acclaim honor *(outward respect)*, honor, mention *(tribute)*, recommend, remembrance *(commemoration)*, reputation

acclaimed famous, illustrious, notable, renowned, reputable

acclamation consensus, mention *(tribute)*

acclamatory favorable *(expressing approval)*

acclimate inure *(accustom)*

acclimated accustomed *(familiarized)*

acclimation compatibility, habituation

acclimatization habituation

acclimatize adapt, attune, conform, inure (accustom)

acclimatized accustomed (familiarized)

accolade prize

accommodare accommodate, adjust (regulate)

accommodate adjust (regulate), agree (comply), assist, attune, comply, compromise (settle by mutual agreement), conform, contribute (assist), fund, furnish, help, loan, naturalize (acclimate), negotiate, obey, pacify, propitiate, provide (supply), serve (assist), settle, support (assist). SEE MAIN ENTRY

accommodate oneself adapt, condescend (deign)

accommodate with lend, supply

accommodated fit, res judicata

accommodating benevolent, charitable (lenient), civil (polite), consenting, malleable, philanthropic, pliable, pliant, propitious, sequacious, suitable, yielding. SEE MAIN ENTRY

accommodatio adjustment

accommodation accord, accordance (compact), accordance (understanding), adjustment, advance (allowance), advancement (loan), advantage, aid (help), amenity, arrangement (understanding), assistance, benefit (betterment), comity, compatibility, compliance, conciliation, condonation, conformity (agreement), consideration (recompense), consideration (sympathetic regard), consortium (marriage companionship), coverage (scope), dispensation (act of dispensing), favor (act of kindness), help, latitude, loan, lodging, provision (act of supplying), relief (aid), service (assistance), settlement, space, support (assistance). SEE MAIN ENTRY

accommodations domicile, habitation (dwelling place), house, residence

accommodative concordant, nonmilitant

accommodativeness amenability

accommodatus adequate, appropriate, convenient, qualified (conditioned)

accompanied composite

accompanier colleague, consort, copartner (coconspirator)

accompaniment appurtenance, attendance, codicil, rider, synchronism

accompaniments paraphernalia (apparatus)

accompany coincide (correspond), concur (coexist). SEE MAIN ENTRY

accompanying coincidental, concomitant, concurrent (at the same time), incidental, simultaneous. SEE MAIN ENTRY

accompanying events circumstances

accomplice abettor, accessory, assistant, coactor, coadjutant, coconspirator, cohort, colleague, confederate, consociate, conspirer, contributor (contributor), copartner (coconspirator), participant, partner. SEE MAIN ENTRY

accomplice in crime abettor, accessory, coactor, conspirer, copartner (coconspirator)

accomplish attain, avail (bring about), carry (succeed), commit (perpetrate), complete, compose, consummate, culminate, discharge (perform), dispatch (dispose of), effectuate, evoke, finish, fulfill, gain, implement, make, operate, pass (satisfy requirements), perfect, perform (execute), perpetrate, procure, produce (manufacture), reach, realize (make real), render (administer), succeed (attain), transact

accomplish promptly expedite

accomplished capable, cognizant, competent, complete (ended), deft, expert,

facile, familiar (informed), informed (educated), learned, literate, practiced, proficient, qualified (competent), resourceful, sciential, subtle (refined)

accomplished efficiently expeditious

accomplished fact fait accompli, performance (execution)

accomplished practitioner professional

accomplishment act (undertaking), action (performance), boom (prosperity), commission (act), development (outgrowth), discharge (performance), effect, end (termination), fait accompli, finality, fruition, output, performance (execution), performance (workmanship), product, progress, realization, satisfaction (fulfilment), specialty (special aptitude), transaction

accomplishments civilization, education

accord accede (concede), accordance (compact), adjust (resolve), adjustment, administer (tender), agree (comply), agreement (concurrence), allow (endure), approval, arbitrate (conciliate), arrangement (understanding), ascribe, assent (noun), assent (verb), attune, authorize, bargain, bestow, cartel, certify (approve), cohere (be logically consistent), coincide (concur), comity, compatibility, compliance, concert, concession (compromise), conciliation, concordance, concur (agree), condescend (deign), confer (give), confirm, confirmation, conform, conformity (agreement), consensus, consent (noun), consent (verb), contact (association), contract, contribute (supply), correspondence (similarity), defer (yield in judgment), delegate, endue, give (grant), grant (concede), impart, indorsement, league, leave (give), mutual understanding, peace, present (make a gift), propinquity (similarity), provide (supply), rapport, rapprochement, reconciliation, render (administer), synchronism, treaty, understanding (agreement), union (unity), volition, vouchsafe, yield (produce a return). SEE MAIN ENTRY

accord one's approval certify (approve), notarize, permit

accord recognition to accept (recognize)

accord superiority to defer (yield in judgment)

accord with comport (agree with)

accordance acceptance, accommodation (adjustment), accord, acquiescence, adjustment, arrangement (understanding), assent, bargain, capacity (authority), cartel, coalescence, compatibility, compliance, concert, conciliation, concordance, confirmation, conformity (agreement), contract, indulgence, leave (permission), license, propriety (appropriateness), rapport, rapprochement, understanding (agreement), union (unity). SEE MAIN ENTRY

accordance with law legality

accordant agreed (harmonized), apposite, appropriate, commensurate, concerted, concordant, concurrent (united), congruous, consensual, consenting, consistent, consonant, contractual, correlative, felicitous, germane, harmonious, suitable

accordant with the facts authentic

according to pursuant to

according to contract as agreed upon

according to custom orthodox, typical

according to desires arbitrary

according to edict licit

according to established form formal

according to fiat lawful

according to general belief reputedly

according to habit habitual

according to law choate lien, de jure, due (regular), jural, juridical, just, law-abiding, lawful, legitimate (rightful), licit, permissible, rightful, statutory. SEE MAIN ENTRY

according to plan purposely

according to regulation orthodox

according to reputation reputedly

according to routine typical

according to rule normal (regular), orthodox, regular (conventional), systematic

according to the agreement as agreed upon

according to the bargain as agreed upon

according to the book orthodox

according to the contract as agreed upon

according to the facts authentic, true (authentic)

according to the law legal

according to usage customary

according to value ad valorem

accordingly a fortiori, a priori, consequently. SEE MAIN ENTRY

accost approach, assail, assault, confront (encounter). SEE MAIN ENTRY

accost bellicosely assault

accoster assailant

account amount (sum), behalf, bill (invoice), brief, calculate, census, computation, deem, delineation, description, distinction (reputation), entry (record), intelligence (news), invoice (bill), narration, rationale, reason (basis), recital, record, rendition (explication), report (detailed account), representation (statement), review (critical evaluation), roll, statement, story (narrative), tariff (bill), worth. SEE MAIN ENTRY

account book ledger

account debtor debtor

account for enlighten, explain, exposit, justify, rationalize, solve, support (justify), vindicate

account of goods shipped invoice (itemized list)

account of merchandise invoice (itemized list)

account of transactions ledger

account outstanding debt

account owing debt

account rendered invoice (bill)

accountability blame (responsibility), burden, charge (lien), charge (responsibility), commitment (responsibility), duty (obligation), fault (responsibility), liability, obligation (liability). SEE MAIN ENTRY

accountable actionable, bound, cognizable, determinable (ascertainable), liable, subject (exposed). SEE MAIN ENTRY

accountableness charge (responsibility), commitment (responsibility), liability, responsibility (accountability)

accountancy budget, computation

accountant comptroller. SEE MAIN ENTRY

accounted detailed

accounted for present (attendant)

accounting attribution, computation. SEE MAIN ENTRY

accounts budget, finance, ledger

accounts collectable due

accounts outstanding due

accounts payable bill (invoice)

accouple cement, join (bring together)

accouplement marriage (intimate relationship)

accouter clothe, furnish, supply

accouterment equipment

accouterments paraphernalia (apparatus)

accredit allow *(authorize)*, ascribe, authorize, bestow, certify *(approve)*, concur *(agree)*, confirm, cosign, countenance, delegate, empower, honor, indorse, notarize, qualify *(meet standards)*, seal *(solemnize)*, sign, support *(corroborate)*, trust, verify *(confirm)*. SEE MAIN ENTRY

accredit with attribute

accreditation jurat

accredited authentic, documentary, official, popular

accreted coherent *(joined)*

accretion accession *(enlargement)*, boom *(increase)*, collection *(accumulation)*, compilation, cumulation, development *(progression)*, increment. SEE MAIN ENTRY

accretive coherent *(joined)*

accroach annex *(arrogate)*, assume *(seize)*, condemn *(seize)*, impropriate, obtrude, overreach, overstep, usurp. SEE MAIN ENTRY

accroachment appropriation *(taking)*

accrual accession *(enlargement)*, additive, appreciation *(increased value)*, augmentation, boom *(increase)*, interest *(profit)*

accruance profit

accrue accumulate *(enlarge)*, arise *(originate)*, bear *(yield)*, compound, develop, hoard, increase, mature, redound, result, yield *(produce a return)*. SEE MAIN ENTRY

accrued SEE MAIN ENTRY

accruement appreciation *(increased value)*, augmentation, boom *(increase)*, cumulation

accruing cumulative *(increasing)*

accumulare accumulate *(amass)*

accumulate accrue *(increase)*, aggregate, codify, collect *(gather)*, compile, concentrate *(consolidate)*, congregate, conjoin, consolidate *(unite)*, convene, crystallize, cull, expand, fund, garner, glean, hoard, increase, inure *(benefit)*, join *(bring together)*, keep *(shelter)*, obtain, procure, raise *(collect)*, reserve, set aside *(annul)*, store. SEE MAIN ENTRY

accumulated accrued, collective, conglomerate

accumulation accession *(enlargement)*, agglomeration, appreciation *(increased value)*, arsenal, assemblage, augmentation, boom *(increase)*, bounty *(prosperity)*, bulk, compilation, conglomeration, cumulation, deposit, development *(progression)*, entirety, fund, growth *(increase)*, hoard, plethora, profit, resource, selection *(collection)*, stock *(store)*, store *(depository)*, sufficiency, treasury. SEE MAIN ENTRY

accumulative collective, cumulative *(increasing)*, lucrative

accuracy honesty, rigor, truth, veracity

accurate absolute *(conclusive)*, actual, appropriate, authentic, bona fide, definite, definitive, detailed, documentary, exact, explicit, factual, faithful *(true to fact)*, genuine, honest, literal, particular *(exacting)*, precise, proper, punctilious, punctual, real, reliable, right *(correct)*, sound, strict, thorough, true *(authentic)*, unrefutable, valid. SEE MAIN ENTRY

accurately duly, faithfully

accuratus careful, circumstantial, scrupulous, systematic

accursed arrant *(onerous)*, diabolic, iniquitous, loathsome, odious, peccant *(culpable)*

accusable bad *(offensive)*, blameful, blameworthy, culpable, delinquent *(guilty of a misdeed)*, illicit, peccant *(culpable)*, reprehensible, reprobate, unjustifiable

accusal accusation, blame *(culpability)*, complaint, denunciation, impeachment, incrimination, indictment, information *(charge)*

accusant accuser, claimant, complainant

accusare accuse, arraign, charge *(accuse)*, complain *(charge)*, fault, impeach, indict, prosecute *(charge)*

accusatio accusation, charge *(accusation)*, denunciation, impeachment, indictment

accusation arraignment, blame *(culpability)*, claim *(legal demand)*, complaint, condemnation *(blame)*, count, criticism, denunciation, diatribe, disparagement, impeachment, incrimination, inculpation, indictment, information *(charge)*, innuendo, libel, objurgation, obloquy, onus *(blame)*, outcry, pleading, presentment, reproach, slander, stricture. SEE MAIN ENTRY

accusation in court arraignment

accusative inculpatory

accusator prosecutor

accusatory contemptuous, incriminatory, **inculpatory**. SEE MAIN ENTRY

accusatrix accuser

accuse arraign, blame, book, complain *(charge)*, complain *(criticize)*, condemn *(blame)*, contemn, defame, denigrate, denounce *(inform against)*, fault, impeach, implicate, incriminate, indict, inform *(betray)*, involve *(implicate)*, lodge *(bring a complaint)*, pillory, present *(prefer charges)*, proscribe *(denounce)*, rebuke, recriminate, reprehend, reprimand, reproach. SEE MAIN ENTRY

accuse falsely defame, frame *(charge falsely)*, libel

accuse in writing libel

accuse of maladministration impeach

accuse of misconduct impeach

accuse of wrong arraign

accuse unfairly frame *(charge falsely)*

accuse unjustly frame *(charge falsely)*

accused convict, suspect. SEE MAIN ENTRY

accused litigant defendant

accused party defendant

accused person convict, suspect

accuser claimant, complainant, district attorney, informant, informer *(one providing criminal information)*, plaintiff. SEE MAIN ENTRY

accusing critical *(faultfinding)*, incriminatory, inculpatory

accustom discipline *(train)*, inure *(accustom)*, naturalize *(acclimate)*, reconcile

accustom oneself to endure *(suffer)*

accustomary habitual, mundane, ordinary, prevailing *(current)*, prevalent

accustomed addicted, conventional, customary, daily, familiar *(customary)*, frequent, habitual, household *(familiar)*, inveterate, ordinary, orthodox, prevailing *(current)*, prevalent, regular *(conventional)*, rife, routine, typical, usual. SEE MAIN ENTRY

accustoming habituation

ace unit *(item)*

acedia sloth

acer acute, intense

acerb harsh

acerbate aggravate *(annoy)*, annoy, bitter *(acrid tasting)*

acerbic bitter *(acrid tasting)*, harsh, mordacious

acerbitas intolerance, severity

acerbity ill will, rancor, severity

acerbus bitter *(acrid tasting)*, caustic, scathing, virulent

acervation assemblage, collection *(accumulation)*, cumulation

acervus collection *(accumulation)*, hoard

ache pain

achievability feasibility, possibility

achievable passable, possible, potential, practicable

achieve accomplish, acquire *(receive)*, attain, build *(construct)*, carry *(succeed)*, commit *(perpetrate)*, complete, compose, consummate, discharge *(perform)*, dispatch *(dispose of)*, earn, effectuate, evoke, execute *(accomplish)*, finish, fulfill, function, gain, implement, make, obtain, operate, pass *(satisfy requirements)*, perform *(adhere to)*, perform *(execute)*, perpetrate, procure, produce *(manufacture)*, reach, realize *(make real)*, realize *(obtain as a profit)*, reap, recover, succeed *(attain)*, transact. SEE MAIN ENTRY

achieve by continued effort earn

achieve liberty escape

achieved complete *(ended)*

achievement act *(undertaking)*, action *(performance)*, boom *(prosperity)*, commission *(act)*, development *(outgrowth)*, discharge *(performance)*, effect, end *(termination)*, endeavor, fait accompli, finality, fruition, monument, objective, outcome, output, performance *(execution)*, performance *(workmanship)*, progress, prosperity, realization, satisfaction *(fulfilment)*, step, transaction

achievement of liberty liberation

aching painful

acid astringent, bitter *(acrid tasting)*, harsh, mordacious

acidulous bitter *(acrid tasting)*

acidus bitter *(acrid tasting)*

acknowledge abide, accede *(concede)*, accept *(recognize)*, admit *(concede)*, agree *(comply)*, allow *(authorize)*, answer *(reply)*, appreciate *(comprehend)*, assent, avouch *(avow)*, avow, bear *(adduce)*, betray *(disclose)*, certify *(approve)*, certify *(attest)*, comply, concede, concur *(agree)*, confess, confirm, correspond *(communicate)*, corroborate, defer *(yield in judgment)*, disclose, grant *(concede)*, hear *(give attention to)*, keep *(fulfill)*, note *(notice)*, notice *(observe)*, posit, prescriptive, profess *(avow)*, reply, respond, return *(respond)*, reveal, sign, subscribe *(sign)*, uphold, vouch, witness *(attest to)*. SEE MAIN ENTRY

acknowledge defeat quit *(discontinue)*, submit *(yield)*

acknowledge one's guilt confess

acknowledge openly bear *(adduce)*, testify

acknowledge through possession prescriptive

acknowledge through use prescriptive

acknowledged alleged, allowed, customary, familiar *(customary)*, nunc pro tunc, orthodox, proverbial, public *(known)*, putative, sound, traditional, undisputed, usual. SEE MAIN ENTRY

acknowledged elsewhere as alias

acknowledged judgment cognovit

acknowledgment acceptance, acquiescence, admission *(disclosure)*, adoption *(acceptance)*, affirmance *(authentication)*, affirmation, answer *(reply)*, approval, assent, asseveration, attribution, avouchment, avowal, charter *(sanction)*, common knowledge, concession *(compromise)*, confession, confirmation, consensus, consent, corroboration, disclosure *(something disclosed)*, expiation, grant, honorarium, ratification, recognition, recognizance, requital, response, reward. SEE MAIN ENTRY

acknowledgment of guilt confession
acknowledgment of payment receipt
(*proof of receiving*)
acme ceiling, culmination, pinnacle
acme of perfection paragon
acolyte coactor
acquaint apprise, communicate, convey
(*communicate*), disabuse, disclose, divulge,
enlighten, impart, inform (*notify*), instruct
(*teach*), inure (*accustom*), mention, notify,
relate (*tell*), report (*disclose*), signify (*inform*)
acquaintance cognition, experience (background), knowledge (*awareness*)
acquaintanceship contact (*association*)
acquainted accustomed (*familiarized*),
cognizant, expert, familiar (*informed*), informed (*having information*), knowing. SEE
MAIN ENTRY
acquainted with conscious (*aware*),
learned, privy
acquainting informatory
acquest demesne
acquiesce abide, accede (*concede*), accept
(*admit as sufficient*), accept (*assent*), admit
(*concede*), agree (*comply*), allow (*endure*),
assent, bear (*tolerate*), coincide (*concur*), concede, concur (*agree*), confirm, consent, defer
(*yield in judgment*), grant (*concede*), obey,
observe (*obey*), pass (*approve*), relent,
sanction, submit (*yield*), succumb, suffer (*permit*), surrender (*yield*), tolerate, vouchsafe,
yield (*submit*). SEE MAIN ENTRY
acquiesce in approve, authorize, comply,
countenance, indorse
acquiesced in consensual
acquiescence acceptance, acknowledgment (*acceptance*), affirmance (*judicial sanction*), affirmation, amenability, approval,
assent, capitulation, charter (*sanction*), compliance, concession (*compromise*), confession, confirmation, conformity (*agreement*),
consent, deference, discipline (*obedience*),
dispensation (*exception*), indorsement, indulgence, leave (*permission*), permission,
resignation (*passive acceptance*), sanction
(*permission*). SEE MAIN ENTRY
acquiescent amenable, charitable (*lenient*),
concurrent (*united*), congruous, consensual,
consenting, favorable (*expressing approval*),
harmonious, inclined, law-abiding, malleable, obedient, open (*persuasible*), passive, patient, permissive, pliable, pliant,
ready (*willing*), sequacious, tractable, willing (*not averse*), yielding
acquiescently faithfully
acquiescing consenting
acquire accept (*take*), accrue (*arise*), accrue (*increase*), aggregate, appropriate, attain, collect (*gather*), collect (*recover
money*), condemn (*seize*), derive (*receive*),
gain, garner, hoard, impress (*procure by
force*), incur, inherit, obtain, occupy (*take
possession*), possess, procure, profit, purchase, realize (*obtain as a profit*), reap, recover, store, succeed (*attain*). SEE MAIN ENTRY
acquire beforehand preempt
acquire by purchase buy
acquire by service earn
acquire currency circulate
acquire from ancestors inherit
acquire information ascertain
acquire information about find (*discover*)
acquire intelligence about ascertain
acquire knowledge study
acquire ownership of buy, purchase
acquire the habit practice (*train by repetition*)

acquired facts information (*knowledge*),
intelligence (*news*)
acquired knowledge civilization, information (*knowledge*)
acquired mode of behavior habit
acquired right option (*contractual provision*)
acquirement acquisition, distress (*seizure*),
edification, realization, receipt (*act of receiving*)
acquirements education
acquisition accession (*enlargement*), adverse possession, appropriation (*taking*),
assumption (*adoption*), boom (*prosperity*),
collection (*accumulation*), cumulation, distress (*seizure*), profit, realization, receipt (*act
of receiving*), recovery (*repossession*), replevin, takeover, taking. SEE MAIN ENTRY
acquisition by right of eminent domain
condemnation (*seizure*)
acquisition of knowledge discovery, education
acquisitive confiscatory, insatiable, mercenary, parsimonious
acquisitiveness greed
acquit absolve, clear, comport (*behave*),
demean (*deport oneself*), deport (*conduct
oneself*), discharge (*liberate*), exculpate, excuse, exonerate, extenuate, forgive, free,
liberate, palliate (*excuse*), pardon, pay,
purge (*wipe out by atonement*), quit (*free
of*), remit (*release from penalty*), remunerate, vindicate. SEE MAIN ENTRY
acquitment acquittal, discharge (*payment*), satisfaction (*discharge of debt*)
acquittal absolution, compurgation, condonation, discharge (*liberation*), discharge
(*payment*), discharge (*release from obligation*), emancipation, exoneration, immunity, impunity, liberation, pardon, payment
(*act of paying*), release, remission, remittance, respite (*reprieve*), satisfaction (*discharge of debt*), waiver. SEE MAIN ENTRY
acquittance acquittal, amnesty, collection
(*payment*), compurgation, discharge (*payment*), exoneration, liberation, payment (*act
of paying*), quitclaim, receipt (*proof of receiving*), release, remission, satisfaction
(*discharge of debt*)
acquitted blameless, clean, clear (*free
from criminal charges*), free (*relieved from a
burden*). SEE MAIN ENTRY
acreage homestead, parcel, plot (*land*),
property (*land*), real estate, space
acres estate (*property*), freehold, homestead, property (*land*), realty
acrid astringent, bitter (*acrid tasting*),
caustic, harsh, mordacious, virulent
acrimonious astringent, bitter (*penetrating*), bitter (*reproachful*), caustic, cruel, cynical, harsh, hostile, libelous, malevolent,
malicious, mordacious, negative, outrageous, pejorative, petulant, resentful, scathing, severe, spiteful, trenchant, vicious,
virulent. SEE MAIN ENTRY
acrimoniousness spite
acrimony alienation (*estrangement*), malice, philippic, rancor, resentment, severity,
spite, umbrage
acroamatic esoteric, inapprehensible, incomprehensible, inexplicable, profound
(*esoteric*), secret
acroamatical esoteric, inapprehensible,
incomprehensible, inexplicable, profound
(*esoteric*), secret
acroatic esoteric, inapprehensible, incomprehensible, inexplicable, learned, profound
(*esoteric*)

act amendment (*legislation*), canon, codification, commit (*perpetrate*), comport (*behave*), constitution, course, demean (*deport
oneself*), deport (*conduct oneself*), dictate,
enactment, execute (*accomplish*), exercise
(*discharge a function*), fake, false pretense,
function, law, measure, mock (*imitate*), officiate, operate, operation, palter, performance (*execution*), portray, prescription
(*directive*), pretend, procedure, proceed
(*go forward*), regulation (*rule*), represent
(*substitute*), role, rubric, rubric (*authoritative rule*),
rule (*legal dictate*), scene, simulate, statute,
step, transaction. SEE MAIN ENTRY
act a part impersonate
act against counter, gainsay
act against with equal force compensate (*counterbalance*), countervail
act as assume (*simulate*), pose (*impersonate*)
act as agent intercede. SEE MAIN ENTRY
act as assistant to assist
act as broker represent (*substitute*)
act as chairman moderate (*preside
over*), preside
act as delegate represent (*substitute*)
act as go-between intercede
act as mediator intercede
act as moderator moderate (*preside over*)
act as one combine (*act in concert*)
act as president moderate (*preside over*),
preside
act as surety for sponsor
act committed in violation of law misdemeanor
act contrary disoblige
act demanded by social custom decorum
act despite override
act dishonestly cheat
act effectively function
act falsely fake
act foolishly mismanage
act for displace (*replace*), replace, represent (*substitute*), supplant
act illegally disobey, violate. SEE MAIN
ENTRY
act improperly mismanage
act in accordance with orders obey
act in advance forestall
act in collusion plot
act in combination conspire
act in concert concur (*agree*), connive, conspire, cooperate, federalize (*associate*), federate, involve (*participate*), join (*associate
oneself with*), participate, unite. SEE MAIN ENTRY
act in harmony conspire
act in opposition fight (*battle*)
act in opposition to antagonize, confront
(*oppose*), counter, counteract, cross (*disagree with*), fight (*counteract*), oppose
act in place of represent (*substitute*)
act in response to answer (*reply*)
act in support adhere (*maintain loyalty*)
act insincerely palter
act interchangeably alternate (*take turns*),
reciprocate
act jointly combine (*act in concert*), cooperate
act of bearing witness attestation
act of believing credence
act of berating diatribe, disparagement
act of bribing corruption
act of bringing in introduction
act of coming together chain (*nexus*)
act of compassing coverage (*scope*)
act of comprehending coverage (*scope*)
act of containing coverage (*scope*)

611

act of copying counterfeit
act of coupling chain *(nexus)*
act of crumbling decline
act of despising disdain
act of discrediting disdain, impeachment
act of dissembling color *(deceptive appearance)*
act of driving out eviction
act of dwelling together cohabitation *(living together)*
act of dwindling decline
act of embracing coverage *(scope)*
act of encircling coverage *(scope)*
act of encompassing coverage *(scope)*
act of engrossing coverage *(scope)*
act of facing confrontation *(act of setting face to face)*
act of falling away decline
act of ferocity atrocity
act of forestalling constraint *(restriction)*
act of forsaking desertion
act of generosity favor *(act of kindness)*
act of giving one's word pledge *(binding promise)*
act of God calamity. SEE MAIN ENTRY
act of grace amnesty, favor (act of kindness)
act of hampering constraint *(restriction)*
act of hardening congealment
act of holding harmless indemnity
act of hostility assault
act of indemnity exoneration
act of inhumanity brutality
act of joining chain *(nexus)*
act of judgment adjudication, award, choice *(decision)*, holding *(ruling of a court)*
act of keeping in constraint *(imprisonment)*
act of killing dispatch *(act of putting to death)*, murder
act of lawbreaking misdemeanor
act of lessening decline
act of living together as husband and wife cohabitation *(married state)*
act of loathing disdain
act of looking backward hindsight
act of losing ground decline
act of maneuvering connivance
act of mercy amnesty
act of oath-breaking perjury
act of pairing cohabitation *(married state)*
act of profiteering corruption
act of promise-making coverage *(insurance)*
act of protecting custody *(supervision)*
act of pursuing course
act of quelling constraint *(restriction)*
act of relinquishing a right waiver
act of reverting escheatment
act of running down disparagement
act of scheming connivance
act of scorning disdain
act of setting forth delineation
act of shrinking decline
act of shunning disdain
act of slaying dispatch *(act of putting to death)*, murder
act of slipping back decline
act of spanning coverage *(scope)*
act of spurning disdain
act of stifling constraint *(restriction)*
act of strangling constraint *(restriction)*
act of subsuming coverage *(scope)*
act of surrounding coverage *(scope)*
act of taking life murder
act of taunting disdain
act of throwing out eviction
act of thwarting constraint *(restriction)*

act of uniting chain *(nexus)*
act of wasting away decline
act of weakening decline
act of working together collusion
act of worsening decline
act on affect, award, commit *(perpetrate)*, discharge *(perform)*, militate, obey, treat *(process)*
act on *(complete)*. SEE MAIN ENTRY
act on *(rule)*. SEE MAIN ENTRY
act on behalf of represent *(substitute)*
act on one's own authority choose
act out impersonate
act prohibited by law crime
act the part of displace *(replace)*, exemplify, impersonate, pose *(impersonate)*
act together cooperate, participate
act upon execute *(accomplish)*, operate
act vicariously represent *(substitute)*
acta diurna journal
actable viable
acte act *(enactment)*
acting histrionics, operative, representative, surrogate, temporary, vicarious *(delegated)*. SEE MAIN ENTRY
acting as a substitute vicarious *(delegated)*
acting as attorney for representation *(acting for others)*
acting in conjunction concurrent *(united)*
acting out catharsis
acting with force drastic
acting without due consideration ill-judged
actio action *(proceeding)*, delivery, proceeding, suit
action act *(undertaking)*, award, campaign, case *(lawsuit)*, cause *(lawsuit)*, cause of action, contest *(dispute)*, controversy *(lawsuit)*, course, day in court, fight *(battle)*, happening, hearing, holding *(ruling of a court)*, lawsuit, matter *(case)*, operation, overt act, performance *(execution)*, performance (workmanship), ploy, procedure, proceeding, process *(course)*, prosecution *(criminal trial)*, step, suit, transaction, trial *(legal proceeding)*. SEE MAIN ENTRY
action at law action *(proceeding)*, cause of action, lawsuit, proceeding, suit, trial *(legal proceeding)*
action in court cause *(lawsuit)*
action to defeat plaintiff's demand counterclaim
action to serve justice suit
actionable illegal, illicit, impermissible, justiciable, litigable, litigious, moot, triable, unlawful. SEE MAIN ENTRY
actionable act tortious act
actions behavior, conduct, dealings, deportment, manner *(behavior)*. SEE MAIN ENTRY
activate empower, launch *(initiate)*, maintain *(commence)*, motivate, originate, prompt, stimulate, urge. SEE MAIN ENTRY
activating impulsive *(impelling)*
activator catalyst, stimulus
active alert *(vigilant)*, conscious *(awake)*, effective *(operative)*, expeditious, fervent, industrious, moving *(in motion)*, operative, potent, rapid, responsive, sedulous, volatile, zealous. SEE MAIN ENTRY
active application diligence *(care)*
active attention diligence *(care)*
active discouragement deterrence
active element catalyst
active espousal advocacy
active giving charity
active ill will malice
active partisan catalyst

active partisans lobby
active reformer catalyst
active reformers lobby
active study diligence *(care)*, examination *(study)*
active supporters lobby
active thought diligence *(care)*
actively opposed hostile, malevolent
actively represent lobby
activeness life *(vitality)*
activism campaign
activists lobby
activities affairs, dealings. SEE MAIN ENTRY
activity agency *(legal relationship)*, business *(affair)*, business *(occupation)*, calling, campaign, career, course, employment, enterprise *(undertaking)*, life *(vitality)*, occupation *(vocation)*, project, pursuit *(occupation)*, transaction, turmoil. SEE MAIN ENTRY
actor actor. SEE MAIN ENTRY
acts conduct, dealings, legislation *(enactments)*, manner *(behavior)*. SEE MAIN ENTRY
actual absolute *(conclusive)*, accurate, authentic, bona fide, certain *(positive)*, clear *(certain)*, corporeal, de facto, definite, documentary, factual, genuine, honest, material *(physical)*, objective, peremptory *(absolute)*, physical, real, realistic, substantive, tangible, true *(authentic)*, unalienable. SEE MAIN ENTRY
actual existence reality
actual occurrence fact
actual possession occupancy
actual reality fact
actuality entity, fact, fait accompli, reality, substance *(essential nature)*, truth, veracity
actualization commission *(act)*, embodiment, fait accompli, realization
actualize compose, consummate, embody, exemplify, forge *(produce)*, implement, make, realize *(make real)*, substantiate
actually de facto
actuary SEE MAIN ENTRY
actuate agitate *(activate)*, bait *(lure)*, constrain *(compel)*, impel, induce, influence, inspire, lobby, motivate, persuade, prevail *(persuade)*, prompt, provoke, spirit, stimulate
actuating impulsive *(impelling)*, persuasive
actuation commission *(act)*, impetus, impulse, incentive, instigation, persuasion, provocation, reason *(basis)*
actuator abettor, catalyst
actus reus SEE MAIN ENTRY
acuity insight, perception, sagacity
aculeatus scathing
acumen caliber *(mental capacity)*, common sense, discrimination *(good judgment)*, insight, intelligence *(intellect)*, judgment *(discernment)*, perception, reason *(sound judgment)*, sagacity, sense *(intelligence)*. SEE MAIN ENTRY
acuminate acute
acute artful, caustic, conscious *(awake)*, critical *(crucial)*, crucial, exigent, important *(urgent)*, incisive, insufferable, intense, intensive, knowing, mordacious, perceptive, politic, profound *(intense)*, responsive, sapient, trenchant. SEE MAIN ENTRY
acute alcoholism dipsomania
acute dissatisfaction ill will
acuteness caliber *(mental capacity)*, discretion *(quality of being discreet)*, discrimination *(good judgment)*, insight, judgment *(discernment)*, perception, sagacity, sensibility
acutus acute, perspicacious
ad administrationem pertimens clerical
ad aerarium pertinens financial

ad captandum colorable *(plausible)*

ad damnum clause SEE MAIN ENTRY

ad hoc SEE MAIN ENTRY

ad hominem confugere apply *(request)*

ad infinitum SEE MAIN ENTRY

ad inritum redigere frustrate, nullify

ad interim SEE MAIN ENTRY

ad persuadendum accommodatus convincing

ad pugnam provocare challenge

ad rem apposite

ad rem spectare relevant

ad sententiam adopt

ad tempus temporary

ad tempus advenire punctual

ad vadimonium non venire default *(noun)*, default *(verb)*

ad valorem SEE MAIN ENTRY

ad vanum frustrate

adage catchword, maxim, phrase, principle *(axiom)*

adamant callous, immutable, implacable, inexorable, inflexible, intractable, irreconcilable, persistent, pertinacious, resolute, unalterable, unbending, uncompromising, unrelenting, unyielding. SEE MAIN ENTRY

adamantine callous, unyielding

adapertus open *(unclosed)*

adapt accommodate, adjust *(regulate)*, agree *(comply)*, alter, apply *(put in practice)*, arrange *(methodize)*, attune, change, conform, modify *(alter)*, naturalize *(acclimate)*, orchestrate, reconcile. SEE MAIN ENTRY

adapt to correspond *(be equivalent)*

adaptability ability, amenability, compliance, conciliation

adaptable applicable, corrigible, disposable, flexible, malleable, pliable, pliant, practical, resilient, sequacious, tractable. SEE MAIN ENTRY

adaptable to change liberal *(broadminded)*

adaptation accommodation *(adjustment)*, adjustment, compromise, habituation, innovation, modification, propriety *(appropriateness)*

adapted accustomed *(familiarized)*, agreed *(harmonized)*, apposite, congruous, consonant, correlative, effective *(efficient)*, felicitous, fit, fitting, harmonious, pertinent, proper, qualified *(competent)*, resigned, sciential, suitable, tempered. SEE MAIN ENTRY

adapted to applicable, appropriate

adapted to argumentation forensic

adapted to teach didactic

adapted to the understanding coherent *(clear)*

adaption arrangement *(ordering)*

adaptive pliable, resilient

add affix, append, attach *(join)*, conjoin, contribute *(supply)*, extend *(enlarge)*, heighten *(augment)*, interject, recruit, sum, supplement, unite. SEE MAIN ENTRY

add as a third party implead

add as an accessory attach *(join)*

add details embellish

add on accrue *(increase)*, increase

add strength to confirm

add to accumulate *(enlarge)*, aggravate *(exacerbate)*, amend, amplify, build *(augment)*, collect *(gather)*, compound, conjoin, consolidate *(strengthen)*, elaborate, enhance, enlarge, expand, increase, intensify, magnify, supplement

add to the payroll employ *(engage services)*, hire

add together aggregate

add up to consist

add water dilute

add weight to aggravate *(exacerbate)*

added additional, ancillary *(auxiliary)*, attached *(annexed)*, expendable, extrinsic, incidental, nonessential

added charge surcharge

added monetary worth appreciation *(increased value)*

added protection buffer zone

added time extension *(postponement)*

added to accrued

added together cumulative *(increasing)*

addend addition

addendum addition, additive, adjunct, allonge

addendum appendix *(supplement)*

addendum appurtenance, attachment *(thing affixed)*, codicil, insertion, rider. SEE MAIN ENTRY

addere append, appendix *(supplement)*

addicere adjudge, allot, award

addict SEE MAIN ENTRY

addicted accustomed *(familiarized)*, inveterate. SEE MAIN ENTRY

addicted to lewdness lecherous

addictedness dipsomania

addiction dipsomania

adding augmentation, computation

additament addendum, addition, adjunct, allonge, appendix *(accession)*, appurtenance, boom *(increase)*, codicil, insertion, rider

addition accession *(annexation)*, accession *(enlargement)*, accretion, addendum, additive, adjunct, allonge, appendix *(supplement)*, appreciation *(increased value)*, appurtenance, boom *(increase)*, codicil, collection *(accumulation)*, continuation *(prolongation)*, corollary, cumulation, exaggeration, expletive, extension *(expansion)*, growth *(increase)*, increment, insertion, offshoot, reinforcement, rider. SEE MAIN ENTRY

addition to adjoiner

addition to a will codicil

addition to realty fixture

additional ancillary *(auxiliary)*, circumstantial, collateral *(accompanying)*, contributory, cumulative *(increasing)*, expendable, extraneous, extrinsic, gratuitous *(unwarranted)*, incidental, nonessential, pendent, superfluous, supplementary. SEE MAIN ENTRY

additional charge surcharge

additional clause rider

additional strength reinforcement

additional time extension *(postponement)*

additionally also, further.

additive addition, additional, bonus, codicil, cumulative *(increasing)*, factor *(ingredient)*, supplementary. SEE MAIN ENTRY

additory boom *(increase)*, cumulative *(increasing)*

additum attachment *(thing affixed)*, codicil

additur SEE MAIN ENTRY

additus additional

addle confuse *(bewilder)*, decay, discompose, muddle, obfuscate, spoil *(impair)*

addlebrained opaque

addled fatuous

addleheaded opaque

addlepated opaque

address abode, accost, bestow, building *(structure)*, call *(appeal)*, conduct, converse, declaim, declamation, deportment, discourse *(noun)*, discourse *(verb)*, dispatch *(send off)*, domicile, habitation *(dwelling place)*, locality, lodging, manner

(behavior), parlance, peroration, recite, report *(detailed account)*, residence, rhetoric *(skilled speech)*, site, speak, speech. SEE MAIN ENTRY

address a petition call *(appeal to)*

address a request call *(appeal to)*, plead *(implore)*, pray

address a warning to admonish *(warn)*, notice *(give formal warning)*

address oneself to call *(appeal to)*, endeavor, occupy *(engage)*, specialize, undertake

address to dedicate

address to the jury charge *(statement to the jury)*

addressee inhabitant, lodger, occupant, resident

addriri assault

adduce allege, depose *(testify)*, mention, proffer, quote, rationalize, refer *(direct attention)*. SEE MAIN ENTRY

adduce evidence corroborate

adduced alleged. SEE MAIN ENTRY

adducere adduce, induce

adeem assume *(seize)*, attach *(seize)*, confiscate. SEE MAIN ENTRY

adeemed attached *(seized)*

ademption taking. SEE MAIN ENTRY

adept artful, capable, competent, deft, diplomatic, expert, practiced, professional *(trained)*, proficient, qualified *(competent)*, sciential, veteran. SEE MAIN ENTRY

adept practitioner professional

adeptness ability, efficiency, facility *(easiness)*, gift *(flair)*, prowess *(ability)*, skill, specialty *(special aptitude)*

adequacy ability, caliber *(mental capacity)*, competence *(ability)*, quorum, sufficiency, utility *(usefulness)*. SEE MAIN ENTRY

adequate ample, capable, commensurate, competent, effective *(efficient)*, fair *(satisfactory)*, fit, functional, habitable, mediocre, operative, prima facie *(legally sufficient)*, proficient, qualified *(competent)*, sciential, suitable, unobjectionable. SEE MAIN ENTRY

adequate notice SEE MAIN ENTRY

adequate proof SEE MAIN ENTRY

adequate resources sufficiency

adequately fairly *(moderately)*

adequately perceive appreciate *(value)*

adequateness admissibility, mediocrity, quorum

adesse appear *(attend court proceedings)*, support *(assist)*

adeundi copiam admit *(give access)*

adferre entail, quote, report *(disclose)*

adficere affect

adfigere affix, attach *(join)*

adfinis germane

adfirmare affirm *(uphold)*, assert, contend *(maintain)*, maintain *(carry on)*

adfirmatio affirmation, allegation, assertion, indorsement, possess

adfligere overthrow

adgredi assail, assault, attack

adherance concrescence

adhere abide, affix, attach *(join)*, cement, confirm, join *(bring together)*, maintain *(sustain)*, persevere, remain *(continue)*, remain *(stay)*. SEE MAIN ENTRY

adhere to bear *(tolerate)*, comply, conform, fulfill, keep *(fulfill)*, obey, observe *(obey)*, pursue *(carry on)*. SEE MAIN ENTRY

adherence accession *(annexation)*, adhesion *(affixing)*, adhesion *(loyalty)*, allegiance, coalescence, coherence, compliance, conformity (*obedience*), continuation (*prolongation*), loyalty. SEE MAIN ENTRY

adherence to duty adhesion (*loyalty*), allegiance

adherences ties

adherency loyalty

adherent addict, advocate (*espouser*), backer, coadunate, coherent (*joined*), cohesive (*sticking*), consociate, disciple, partisan, protégé. SEE MAIN ENTRY

adhering coadunate, coherent (*joined*), cohesive (*sticking*), inextricable

adhering to a purpose pertinacious

adhering to an original faithful (*true to fact*)

adhesion accession (*annexation*), coalescence, coherence, contact (*touching*). SEE MAIN ENTRY

adhesions ties

adhesive coadunate, coherent (*joined*), cohesive (*sticking*)

adhesiveness adhesion (*affixing*), coherence, tenacity. SEE MAIN ENTRY

adhibition use

adhortari exhort

adiacere adjoin, border (*bound*)

adiectio addition

adiectus additional

adipisci acquire (*receive*), obtain

adit access (*right of way*), entrance, entry (*entrance*)

aditus access (*right of way*), entrance

adiudicare adjudge, award

adiumentum assistance, support (*assistance*)

adiungere append, appendix (*accession*)

adiutor assistant, promoter

adiutores staff

adiutrix assistant

adiuvare abet, contribute (*assist*), cooperate, subsidize

adjacency conjunction, contact (*touching*), propinquity (*proximity*)

adjacent close (*near*), contiguous, immediate (*not distant*), local, present (*attendant*), proximate. SEE MAIN ENTRY

adjective procedural

adjective law procedure. SEE MAIN ENTRY

adjoin abut, affix, attach (*join*), border (*approach*), border (*bound*), contact (*touch*), juxtapose, overlap. SEE MAIN ENTRY

adjoiner SEE MAIN ENTRY

adjoining accession (*annexation*), adjacent, close (*near*), contiguous, immediate (*not distant*), local, proximate

adjourn cease, conclude (*complete*), defer (*put off*), delay, discontinue (*break continuity*), halt, hold up (*delay*), postpone, procrastinate, recess. SEE MAIN ENTRY

adjournal adjournment, cloture

adjourned arrested (*checked*)

adjournment cessation (*interlude*), close (*conclusion*), cloture, deferment, discontinuance (*act of discontinuing*), end (*termination*), extension (*postponement*), hiatus, pendency. SEE MAIN ENTRY

adjournment of a cause continuance

adjournment of a proceeding continuance

adjudge adjudicate, ascertain, award, condemn (*punish*), confer (*give*), criticize (*evaluate*), decide, decree, deem, determine, find (*determine*), gauge, judge, opine, pronounce (*pass judgment*), rule (*decide*), sentence, try (*conduct a trial*). SEE MAIN ENTRY

adjudge innocent absolve, palliate (*excuse*)

adjudge the validity of a will probate

adjudge to be due award

adjudged juridical

adjudger judge, juror

adjudgment adjudication, arbitration, award, conviction (*finding of guilt*), decree, determination, judgment (*formal court decree*)

adjudgment body jury

adjudicate adjudge, arbitrate (*adjudge*), award, decide, decree, determine, find (*determine*), hear (*give a legal hearing*), judge, pronounce (*pass judgment*), rule (*decide*), try (*conduct a trial*). SEE MAIN ENTRY

adjudicate the validity of a will probate

adjudication award, cognovit, conclusion (*determination*), conviction (*finding of guilt*), decree, determination, direction (*order*), holding (*ruling of a court*), judgment (*formal court decree*), opinion (*judicial decision*), res judicata, ruling, sentence, verdict. SEE MAIN ENTRY

adjudicator arbiter, arbitrator, judge, juror, referee, umpire

adjudicators jury

adjunct addendum, addition, additive, allonge, ancillary (*auxiliary*), appendix (*supplement*), appliance, appurtenance, appurtenant, associate, attachment (*thing affixed*), backer, coactor, codicil, colleague, confederate, consociate, copartner (*coconspirator*), corollary, pendent, rider, supplementary. SEE MAIN ENTRY

adjunct in crime coconspirator

adjunction addition, attachment (*act of affixing*)

adjuration affirmance (*legal affirmation*), asseveration, assurance, attestation, averment, avouchment, call (*appeal*), charge (*statement to the jury*), claim (*legal demand*), entreaty, oath, petition, requirement. SEE MAIN ENTRY

adjure attest, bear (*adduce*), call (*appeal to*), command, direct (*order*), exhort, importune, motivate, order, petition, pray, press (*beseech*), pressure, promise (*vow*), request, swear, urge. SEE MAIN ENTRY

adjurement affirmation, averment, avowal

adjust accommodate, adapt, alter, amend, apply (*put in practice*), arrange (*methodize*), attune, change, check (*restrain*), compromise (*settle by mutual agreement*), conform, coordinate, decide, defray, discharge (*pay a debt*), discharge (*perform*), emend, fix (*arrange*), fix (*repair*), inure (*accustom*), liquidate (*determine liability*), mediate, mitigate, modify (*alter*), naturalize (*acclimate*), orchestrate, organize (*arrange*), pay, reconcile, rectify, redress, refund, remedy, repair, settle, stipulate, transform. SEE MAIN ENTRY

adjust differences agree (*comply*), agree (*contract*), arbitrate (*conciliate*), dicker

adjust difficulties mediate

adjust oneself to countenance

adjustable flexible, malleable, pliable, resilient

adjusted accustomed (*familiarized*), fit, harmonious, res judicata, resigned, tempered

adjuster SEE MAIN ENTRY

adjustment accord, accordance (*compact*), accordance (*understanding*), amendment (*correction*), arbitration, arrangement (*understanding*), collection (*payment*), collective bargaining, compatibility, compromise, conciliation, conformity (*agreement*), correction (*change*), disposition (*determination*), disposition (*final arrangement*), expiation,

habituation, justification, mediation, mitigation, modification, order (*arrangement*), reconciliation, regulation (*management*), rehabilitation, repair, reparation (*indemnification*), restitution, settlement, treatment. SEE MAIN ENTRY

adjustment by agreement arrangement (*understanding*)

adjustment of differences peace

adjustment of difficulties mediation

adjutant abettor, acting, assistant, backer, coactor, coadjutant, colleague, confederate, consociate, conspirer, copartner (*coconspirator*), partner

adjutant in crime coconspirator

adjutor partner

adjuvancy assistance

adjuvant ancillary (*auxiliary*), assistant, backer, coactor, coadjutant, colleague, confederate, copartner (*business associate*), copartner (*coconspirator*), participant, partner, subservient, subsidiary. SEE MAIN ENTRY

adjuvant in crime coconspirator

adlevare alleviate

adlicere lure

adligare affix, attach (*join*), connect (*join together*)

admeasure distribute, divide (*distribute*), dole, measure, mete. SEE MAIN ENTRY

admeasurement estimate (*approximate cost*), estimation (*calculation*), measurement

administer allocate, allot, apportion, bestow, commit (*perpetrate*), conduct, confer (*give*), contribute (*supply*), control (*regulate*), direct (*supervise*), disburse (*distribute*), discharge (*perform*), discipline (*control*), dispense, disperse (*disseminate*), distribute, divide (*distribute*), dominate, drug, exercise (*discharge a function*), govern, handle (*manage*), manage, mete, moderate (*preside over*), officiate, operate, overlook (*superintend*), oversee, parcel, predominate (*command*), prescribe, preside, provide (*supply*), regulate (*manage*), resort, rule (*govern*), superintend, supply. SEE MAIN ENTRY

administer a penalty inflict

administer a rebuke admonish (*warn*), blame, censure

administer badly misgovern

administer correction condemn (*punish*), discipline (*punish*)

administer improperly misgovern, mishandle (*mismanage*), mismanage

administer inefficiently mismanage

administer poorly misgovern, mismanage

administer punishment inflict

administer to accommodate, assist, bequeath, care (*regard*), concern (*care*), serve (*assist*)

administrare conduct, direct (*supervise*), manage, regulate (*adjust*), superintend. SEE MAIN ENTRY

administrate administer (*conduct*), conduct, control (*regulate*), direct (*supervise*), govern, manage, operate, preside, render (*administer*), superintend

administrating clerical

administratio administration, government (*administration*), management (*supervision*), regulation (*management*)

administration act (*enactment*), action (*performance*), agency (*commission*), apportionment, authorities, bureau, bureaucracy, charge (*custody*), control (*supervision*), custody (*supervision*), direction (*guidance*), dispensation (*act of* dispensing), disposition *(final arrangement)*, economy *(economic system)*, enforcement, generalship, government *(political administration)*, management (directorate), management *(supervision)*, regime, regulation *(management)*, supervision, transaction. SEE MAIN ENTRY

administration of economics economy *(economic system)*

administration of justice judicature, judiciary

administration of resources economy *(economic system)*

administrative clerical, executive, ministerial, political. SEE MAIN ENTRY

administrative head administrator, official

administrative unit bureau

administrator caretaker *(one fulfilling the function of office)*, director, employer, executive, executor, functionary, liaison, official, procurator, superintendent, trustee. SEE MAIN ENTRY

administrator of a will executor

administrator of justice judge

administrator of the decedent's estate executor

administrators hierarchy *(persons in authority)*, management *(directorate)*, management *(supervision)*

administratorship generalship

administratrix executor

adminster enforce, give *(grant)*

admirable high-minded, laudable, meritorious, professional *(stellar)*, scrupulous

admiratio surprise

admiration affection, estimation *(esteem)*, honor *(outward respect)*, interest *(concern)*, regard *(esteem)*, respect

admire regard *(hold in esteem)*

admired popular

admirer disciple

admiring favorable *(expressing approval)*

admiscere implicate

admissibility propriety *(appropriateness)*, qualification *(fitness)*. SEE MAIN ENTRY

admissible allowable, allowed, appropriate, justifiable, licit, pardonable, passable, permissible, relevant, right *(suitable)*, suitable, unobjectionable. SEE MAIN ENTRY

admissible evidence SEE MAIN ENTRY

admission access *(right of way)*, acknowledgment *(avowal)*, admittance *(acceptance)*, admittance *(means of approach)*, adoption *(acceptance)*, charter *(sanction)*, concession *(compromise)*, confession, confirmation, consent, declaration, disclosure *(act of disclosing)*, disclosure *(something disclosed)*, entrance, entry *(entrance)*, ingress, installation, recognition. SEE MAIN ENTRY

admission of fault confession

admission of foreigners immigration

admission of guilt confession. SEE MAIN ENTRY

admission of postponement continuance

admission of the facts nollo contendere

admissive receptive, responsive

admit accede *(concede)*, acknowledge *(declare)*, acknowledge *(verify)*, adopt, authorize, avow, bare, bear *(adduce)*, betray *(disclose)*, certify *(approve)*, confess, disclose, grant *(concede)*, induct, initiate, instate, profess *(avow)*, receive *(permit to enter)*, recognize *(acknowledge)*, reveal, vouchsafe, yield *(submit)*. SEE MAIN ENTRY

admit a right acknowledge *(verify)*

admit as satisfactory accept *(admit as sufficient)*

admit citizenship naturalize *(make a citizen)*

admit defeat quit *(discontinue)*, submit *(yield)*

admit frankly avow

admit guilt confess

admit the charge acknowledge *(verify)*

admit to citizenship enfranchise

admittance access *(right of way)*, acknowledgment *(acceptance)*, admission *(entry)*, ingress, introduction, receipt *(act of receiving)*. SEE MAIN ENTRY

admitted allowed, prescriptive, sound, uncontested. SEE MAIN ENTRY

admitted judgment cognovit

admitted maxim principle *(axiom)*

admitted testimony evidence

admittedly SEE MAIN ENTRY

admittere admit *(give access)*

admitting concession *(compromise)*, receptive

admitting of decision determinable *(ascertainable)*

admitting of doubt debatable, disputable

admitting of no deviation exact

admix amalgamate, combine *(join together)*, commingle, desegregate

admixed composite, miscellaneous

admixture coalescence, integration *(amalgamation)*, melange, solution *(substance)*. SEE MAIN ENTRY

admonere admonish *(advise)*, remind

admonish blame, castigate, caution, censure, charge *(instruct on the law)*, complain *(criticize)*, decry, disabuse, disapprove *(condemn)*, exhort, expostulate, fault, impeach, lash *(attack verbally)*, rebuke, remonstrate, reprehend, reprimand, reproach, threaten. SEE MAIN ENTRY

admonish beforehand forewarn

admonishment admonition, caveat, deterrent, disapprobation, disparagement, monition *(warning)*, notice *(warning)*, objurgation, remonstrance, reprimand

admonitio remonstrance, suggestion, warning

admonition caution *(warning)*, caveat, charge *(statement to the jury)*, criticism, deterrence, deterrent, diatribe, direction *(guidance)*, guidance, impeachment, monition *(warning)*, notice *(warning)*, objurgation, rebuff, recommendation, remonstrance, reprimand, warning. SEE MAIN ENTRY

admonitive remonstrative

admonitor monitor

admonitory hortative, informatory, remonstrative

admovere apply *(put in practice)*

adnectere affix

adnotare note *(record)*

adnotatio note *(brief comment)*

adnuere assent

ado furor, noise, trouble, turmoil

adolescence nonage. SEE MAIN ENTRY

adolescent child, jejune *(lacking maturity)*, juvenile, minor. SEE MAIN ENTRY

adolescere develop

adopt accept *(embrace)*, acquire *(receive)*, agree *(comply)*, apply *(put in practice)*, appropriate, approve, assume *(seize)*, choose, copy, embrace *(accept)*, espouse, gain, impropriate, naturalize *(make a citizen)*, pass *(approve)*, prefer, receive *(permit to enter)*, resort, select. SEE MAIN ENTRY

adopt a measure enact

adopt an opinion deem

adopt and pass off as one's own pirate *(reproduce without authorization)*

adopt as a citizen naturalize *(make a citizen)*

adopt as one's own plagiarize

adopt into a nation naturalize *(make a citizen)*

adoptare adopt

adopted assumed *(feigned)*, preferred *(favored)*, select

adoptio adoption *(affiliation)*

adoption acceptance, appropriation *(taking)*, approval, arrogation, consent, distress *(seizure)*, selection *(choice)*, use. SEE MAIN ENTRY

adoptive SEE MAIN ENTRY

adoptivus adoptive

adorable attractive

adoration affection, respect

adore regard *(hold in esteem)*

adoriri accost, assail, attack

adorn embellish, meliorate

adorned pretentious *(ostentatious)*

adornment motif

adquirere acquire *(secure)*

adrift astray, derelict *(abandoned)*, disconnected, insecure, lost *(disoriented)*, unsettled

adrogans impervious, presumptuous

adrogantia intolerance

adroit artful, capable, competent, deft, efficient, expert, practiced, proficient, resourceful, veteran

adroit practitioner professional

adroitness competence *(ability)*, efficiency, experience *(background)*, facility *(easiness)*, faculty *(ability)*, gift *(flair)*, prowess *(ability)*, science *(technique)*, skill

adsciscere enfranchise

adscititious circumstantial, nonessential, pendent, superfluous, supplementary

adscribere encompass *(include)*, enroll, include

adsecula parasite

adsensio assent

adsensus acquiescence, assent

adsentari assent

adsentire consent

adsequi attain

adseverare vouch

adsiduitas continuance, continuation *(prolongation)*, diligence *(care)*, industry *(activity)*

adsiduus continual *(perpetual)*, incessant, industrious, perpetual, sedulous, unremitting

adsignare allot, apportion, ascribe, attribute, impute

adsignatio allotment

adstrictorius astringent

adstrictus laconic

adstringere bind *(obligate)*

adsuefacere inure *(accustom)*

adsuetus accustomed *(customary)*

adsumere assume *(seize)*

adulate overestimate. SEE MAIN ENTRY

adulation doxology, honor *(outward respect)*, mention *(tribute)*. SEE MAIN ENTRY

adulescentia adolescence

adult ripe. SEE MAIN ENTRY

adulterare adulterate

adulterate contaminate, corrupt, debase, denature, deteriorate, fake, falsify, harm, impair, infect, lessen, pollute, taint *(contaminate)*. SEE MAIN ENTRY

adulterated inferior *(lower in quality)*, tainted *(contaminated)*. SEE MAIN ENTRY

adulteration contaminate, defilement, detriment, dissolution (disintegration). SEE MAIN ENTRY

adultered bad (inferior)

adulterine artificial, bastard, illegitimate (born out of wedlock)

adulterium adultery

adultery SEE MAIN ENTRY

adulthood maturity

adultus adult

adumbrare delineate

adumbrate blind (obscure), camouflage, hint, obfuscate, obnubilate, obscure, portend, portray, predict, presage, represent (portray), shroud

adumbratio delineation, outline (synopsis)

adumbration hint, obscuration. SEE MAIN ENTRY

adumbrative representative. SEE MAIN ENTRY

advance abet, accession (enlargement), accretion, accrue (increase), adduce, advancement (loan), aid (help), aid, allege, ameliorate, appreciate (increase), approach, argue, assert, augmentation, bid, boom (increase), boom (prosperity), capitalize (provide capital), certify (attest), cite (state), compound, conduce, contend (maintain), contribute (assist), course, credit (delayed payment), cultivate, declare, develop, development (progression), elevate, evolve, expand, expedite, extend (offer), facilitate, favor, finance, foster, further, gain, hasten, headway, heighten (augment), help, honor, installment, inure (benefit), invest (fund), invitation, lend, loan (noun), loan (verb), lobby, meliorate, nurture, offer (tender), onset (assault), overture, plead (allege in a legal action), pose (propound), posit, postulate, precipitate (hasten), precursory, preface, prefer, proceed (go forward), proffer, profit, progress (noun), progress (verb), promotion (advancement), propose, propound, prosecute (carry forward), recommend, remit (submit for consideration), resume, send, serve (assist), signify (inform), step, submit (give), subsidize, succeed (attain), tender, urge. SEE MAIN ENTRY

advance against assail

advance beyond proper limits overstep

advance guard precursor

advance in rank promote (advance)

advance in successive gradation develop

advance in value enhance

advance in worth appreciation (increased value)

advance near to approximate

advance notice admonition, caveat

advance planning forethought, premeditation

advance stealthily infringe

advance toward perfection mature

advance upon assail, attack, impinge, trespass

advanced alleged, liberal (broad minded), proficient, progressive (advocating change), ripe, sophisticated. SEE MAIN ENTRY

advanced in years elderly, old

advancement advocacy, application, augmentation, boom (increase), boom (prosperity), civilization, development (progression), edification, elevation, favor (sanction), growth (evolution), growth (increase), incursion, loan, longevity, preference (priority), profit, progress, reform, step, suggestion. SEE MAIN ENTRY

advancement of knowledge civilization

advancing cumulative (increasing), forthcoming, future, progressive (going forward)

advantage behalf, benefit (betterment), chance (fortuity), dividend, edification, help, interest (profit), inure (benefit), leverage, patronage (power to appoint jobs), precedence, preference (priority), prerogative, priority, privilege, prize, profit, shelter (tax benefit), utility (usefulness), value, welfare, worth. SEE MAIN ENTRY

advantage in land easement

advantage in votes cast plurality

advantageous ancillary (auxiliary), beneficial, constructive (creative), convenient, disposable, effective (efficient), fit, functional, gainful, instrumental, lucrative, operative, opportune, practical, preferential, productive, profitable, propitious, purposeful, salubrious, salutary, suitable, valuable

advantageous position edge (advantage)

advantageousness expedience, feasibility, utility (usefulness)

advena alien, stranger

advent occasion

adventare approach

adventicius foreign, unessential

adventitious fortuitous, haphazard, unintentional, unwitting. SEE MAIN ENTRY

adventitiously unknowingly

adventitiousness accident (chance occurrence)

adventure bet, enterprise (undertaking), event, experience (encounter), transaction, undertaking (enterprise), venture. SEE MAIN ENTRY

adventurer pioneer, speculator

adventures story (narrative)

adventurous aleatory (perilous), imprudent, impulsive (rash)

adventus appearance (emergence), immigration

adversarius adversary, foe, opponent, opposite

adversary contender, contestant, disputant, foe, litigant, opponent, party (litigant), plaintiff, rival. SEE MAIN ENTRY

adversative contradictory, contrary

adverse antipathetic (oppositional), averse, competitive (antagonistic), contradictory, contrary, deleterious, detrimental, disadvantageous, discordant, disinclined, hostile, inadvisable, inauspicious, inimical, malevolent, noxious, ominous, opposite, pernicious, regrettable, reluctant, renitent, repugnant (incompatible), unfavorable, unpropitious. SEE MAIN ENTRY

adverse argument objection

adverse charge objection

adverse circumstance disadvantage, plight. SEE MAIN ENTRY

adverse circumstances adversity, predicament

adverse comment criticism, diatribe, disapprobation, disapproval, impugnation, objection, stricture

adverse criticism disparagement, exception (objection), impugnation, stricture

adverse event misfortune. SEE MAIN ENTRY

adverse fortune adversity, calamity, misfortune

adverse lot misfortune

adverse luck misfortune

adverse party adversary, contender, contestant, disputant, foe, litigant, opponent

adverse possession SEE MAIN ENTRY

adverse reason objection

adverse to contra (adverb), contra (preposition), deviant. SEE MAIN ENTRY

adversely unwillingly

adversely affected aggrieved (victimized). SEE MAIN ENTRY

adverseness antipode, antithesis, conflict, contradiction, difference, ill will

adversity accident (misfortune), burden, calamity, casualty, catastrophe, damage, debacle, detriment, disadvantage, disaster, hardship, injury, misfortune, pain, plight, predicament, stress (strain), tragedy, trouble. SEE MAIN ENTRY

adversus adverse (opposite), antipode, contrary, unfavorable

advert allude, hear (give attention to), hint, imply. SEE MAIN ENTRY

advert to consider, indicate, mention, note (notice), regard (pay attention), specify

advertence diligence (care), notice (heed), observation, regard (attention). SEE MAIN ENTRY

advertency consideration (contemplation), diligence (care), notice (heed), observation, regard (attention)

advertent prudent

advertise communicate, divulge, expose, herald, inform (notify), notify, post, proclaim, proffer, promote (organize), propagate (spread), publish, spread. SEE MAIN ENTRY

advertisement publication (disclosure), publicity

advertising promotion (encouragement), publicity

advice admonition, advocacy, charge (statement to the jury), direction (guidance), guidance, help, instruction (direction), monition (warning), recommendation, service (assistance), suggestion, tip (clue). SEE MAIN ENTRY

advice of counsel SEE MAIN ENTRY

advisability propriety (appropriateness)

advisable favorable (advantageous), fit, profitable, sensible, suitable. SEE MAIN ENTRY

advise advocate, alert, annunciate, apprise, charge (instruct on the law), communicate, confer (consult), contribute (assist), converse, convey (communicate), counsel, disabuse, disclose, exhort, forewarn, help, impart, incite, inform (notify), instruct (direct), motivate, notice (give formal warning), notify, persuade, predict, presage, prognosticate, prompt, propose, reason (persuade), recommend, relate (tell), remind, remonstrate, report (disclose), reveal, signify (inform), urge. SEE MAIN ENTRY

advise against admonish (warn), caution, discourage, dissuade, expostulate, forewarn, remonstrate

advise beforehand forewarn

advise together deliberate

advise with consult (ask advice of), deliberate

advised acquainted, deliberate, express, familiar (informed), informed (having information)

advisedly knowingly

advisement advice, caveat, consideration (contemplation), deliberation, disclosure (act of disclosing), guidance

adviser accessory, accomplice, advocate (counselor), arbiter, counsel, counselor, esquire, informant, informer (a person who provides information), pedagogue, procurator

advisers management (directorate)

advising hortative, informatory, juridical

advisory hortative, informative, informatory, juridical, precatory. SEE MAIN ENTRY

advisory board council (assembly)

advisory body congress, panel (discussion group)

advisory group commission (agency), committee

advisory limitation guideline

advocacy advice, aid (help), assistance, behalf, direction (guidance), favor (sanction), guidance, persuasion, recommendation, representation (acting for others). SEE MAIN ENTRY

advocare call (summon), summon

advocate abet, abettor, adhere (maintain loyalty), admonish (advise), advise, amicus curiae, apologist, approve, assistant, attorney, authorize, backer, barrister, benefactor, certify (attest), claim (maintain), coactor, colleague, conduit (intermediary), corroborate, council (consultant), counsel (noun), counsel (verb), counselor, countenance, defend, disciple, embrace (accept), espouse, esquire, exhort, favor, foster, incite, indorse, instruct (direct), jurist, lawyer, maintain (sustain), partisan, pass (approve), patron (influential supporter), petition, plead (argue a case), plenipotentiary, posit, prescribe, pressure, proctor, profess (avow), promote (advance), promote (organize), promoter, proponent, propose, propound, recommend, side, special interest, spokesman, sponsor, subscribe (promise), uphold, urge. SEE MAIN ENTRY

advocated alleged

advocates bar (body of lawyers), lobby

advocating change radical (favoring drastic change)

advocation labor (work), recommendation

adynamic languid, nonsubstantial (not sturdy), powerless

adynamy incapacity

aedes house

aedificatio building (business of assembling)

aedificium building (structure), premises (buildings)

aeger patient

aegis auspices, custody (supervision), favor (sanction), protection, safekeeping, shield. SEE MAIN ENTRY

aegrotus patient

aemulus contestant, rival

aenigma enigma

aeonian constant, durable

aequabilis impartial, uniform

aequalis coequal, equal, par (equality)

aequalitas temporum synchronism

aeque fairly (impartially)

aequiperare compare

aequitas equity (justice), fairness, justice, objectivity

aequo animo nonchalant

aequum equity (justice)

aequus admissible, equal, equitable, fair (just), impartial, just, par (equality), reasonable (fair)

aequus animus composure

aerarium finance, treasury

aerial intangible

aes money

aes alienum debt

aes alienum contrahere overdraw

Aesculapian medicinal

aesthetic elegant, sensitive (discerning). SEE MAIN ENTRY

aesthetic judgment discretion (quality of being discreet)

aestimare appreciate (value), assess (appraise), estimate, rate

aestimatio assessment (estimation), estimate (approximate cost), value, worth

aetas age, lifetime

aetate provectus elderly

aevum lifetime

affability comity, courtesy, informality

affable amicable, benevolent, civil (polite), obeisant

affair event, happening, incident, occasion, occurrence, subject (topic), transaction, undertaking (enterprise). SEE MAIN ENTRY

affairs case (set of circumstances), dealings. SEE MAIN ENTRY

affect appertain, apply (pertain), concern (involve), dispose (incline), emotion, fake, feign, interest, militate, modify (alter), motivate, prejudice (influence), pretend, prevail upon, profess (pretend), relate (establish a connection). SEE MAIN ENTRY

affect detrimentally prejudice (injure)

affect dishonorably disgrace

affect entirely pervade

affect injuriously impair

affectation bombast, color (deceptive appearance), false pretense, fustian, histrionics, pretense (ostentation), pretext, pride, rhetoric (insincere language)

affected bogus, formal, grandiose, histrionic, inclined, interested, orgulous, orotund, pretentious (pompous), proud (conceited), specious, tartuffish

affected manner pride

affectedness false pretense, histrionics, pretense (ostentation), pride

affecter pedant

affectibility sensibility

affectible receptive

affecting moving (evoking emotion), potent, sapid. SEE MAIN ENTRY

affecting a previous act ex post facto

affecting the nation as a whole national

affecting the past retroactive

affection affinity (regard), benevolence (disposition to do good), predilection, predisposition, regard (esteem). SEE MAIN ENTRY

affiance confidence (faith), reliance

affiant declarant, deponent. SEE MAIN ENTRY

affidavit certificate, confirmation, record, statement, testimony. SEE MAIN ENTRY

affiliate adopt, ascribe, chapter (branch), connect (relate), consolidate (unite), corporate (associate), correlate, correlative, embrace (accept), federalize (associate), federate, incorporate (form a corporation), join (associate oneself with), member (individual in a group), organ, organize (unionize), relate (establish a connection), unite. SEE MAIN ENTRY

affiliate with combine (act in concert), participate, pool

affiliated akin (germane), akin (related by blood), allied, apposite, associated, cognate, collateral (accompanying), conjoint, consanguineous, correlative, incident, interested, interrelated, related. SEE MAIN ENTRY

affiliates constituency

affiliation affinity (family ties), ancestry, association (alliance), bloodline, cartel, chain (nexus), coalescence, coalition, combination, compatibility, confederacy (compact), connection (relation), consolidation, consortium (marriage companionship), contact (association), corporation, degree (kinship), federation, filiation, integration (amalgamation), kinship, league, merger, nexus, organization (association), privity, propinquity (kinship), relation (connection), side, union (labor organization). SEE MAIN ENTRY

affined cognate, correlative, related

affinitive allied, apposite, correlative, germane, interrelated, pendent, pertinent, related, relative (relevant), relevant

affinity analogy, blood, chain (nexus), conformity (agreement), consortium (marriage companionship), inclination, instinct, kinship, partiality, penchant, predilection, propensity, propinquity (kinship), propinquity (similarity), rapport, relation (connection), relationship (family tie), relevance, resemblance. SEE MAIN ENTRY

affinity of nature propinquity (similarity)

affirm accept (assent), accredit, acknowledge (declare), admit (concede), allege, annunciate, approve, argue, assert, assure (insure), attest, authorize, avouch (avow), avow, bear (adduce), certify (attest), claim (maintain), concede, concur (agree), consent, contend (maintain), convey (communicate), corroborate, countenance, declare, depose (testify), enunciate, express, indorse, mention, notarize, pass (approve), plead (allege in a legal action), posit, profess (avow), promise (vow), reassure, remark, reveal, substantiate, support (corroborate), sustain (confirm), swear, testify, uphold, validate, verify (swear), vouch, witness (attest to). SEE MAIN ENTRY

affirm explicitly certify (attest), plead (allege in a legal action)

affirm in an official capacity certify (attest)

affirm positively promise (vow)

affirm the contrary bear false witness, contradict, disown (deny the validity)

affirm under oath depose (testify), testify

affirm with confidence avouch (avow)

affirmance affirmation, approval, assent, asseveration, averment, avouchment, avowal, certification (certification of proficiency), confirmation, consensus, consent, indorsement, sanction (permission), surety (certainty). SEE MAIN ENTRY

affirmant declarant. SEE MAIN ENTRY

affirmation acknowledgment (avowal), adjuration, approval, assent, assertion, asseveration, assurance, attestation, attribution, averment, avouchment, avowal, certification (attested copy), claim (assertion), confirmation, consensus, consent, corroboration, declaration, declaratory judgment, disclosure (something disclosed), jurat, legalization, oath, parole, permit, profession (declaration), promise, pronouncement, reference (recommendation), sanction (permission), statement, subscription, support (corroboration), surety (certainty), testimony, thesis, vow. SEE MAIN ENTRY

affirmation of truth oath

affirmation of truth of a statement oath

affirmation under oath affidavit. SEE MAIN ENTRY

affirmations premises (hypotheses)

affirmative SEE MAIN ENTRY

affirmative action SEE MAIN ENTRY

affirmatory affirmative

affirmed agreed (promised), alleged, alleged

affirmer affirmant

affix addendum, allonge, annex (add), append, attach (join), cement, cohere (adhere), combine (join together), levy, rider. SEE MAIN ENTRY

affix a date to date

affix a legal signature notarize

affix a signature sign

affix an earlier date antedate

affix an impost assess (tax)

affix one's name sign

affix one's signature subscribe (sign)

affix one's signature to notarize, sign

affixation accession (annexation), attachment (act of affixing), codicil

affixed attached (annexed), conjoint

affixed property immovable

affixed to realty fixture

affixture attachment (thing affixed), codicil

afflicting pernicious

afflict affront, badger, bait (harass), beat (strike), discommode, discompose, distress, harass, harm, ill use, mistreat, persecute, plague, strike (assault). SEE MAIN ENTRY

afflicted aggrieved (harmed), deplorable, disconsolate

afflicting detrimental, harmful, peccant (unhealthy)

affliction accident (misfortune), adversity, burden, calamity, casualty, catastrophe, damage, detriment, disability (physical inability), disaster, disease, disorder (abnormal condition), grievance, handicap, hardship, misfortune, nuisance, onus (burden), pain, stress (strain), tragedy, trouble. SEE MAIN ENTRY

afflictive adverse (negative), bitter (penetrating), oppressive, painful, severe

affluence boom (prosperity), money, prosperity, sufficiency, welfare

affluent full, opulent, profuse, prosperous, replete, successful

afford administer (tender), allow (endure), bear (yield), bequeath, bestow, contribute (supply), fund, furnish, give (grant), lend, provide (supply), supply, yield (produce a return)

afford advantages favor

afford aid abet, assist, capitalize (provide capital), contribute (assist), serve (assist), subsidize

afford notice serve (deliver a legal instrument)

afford proof of bear (adduce)

afford sanctuary harbor, lodge (house)

afford support capitalize (provide capital), subsidize

affording no undue advantage fair (just), just

affording proof demonstrative (illustrative)

affranchise enfranchise, free, let (permit), liberate

affranchisement freedom, liberation, liberty, privilege, suffrage

affray altercation, belligerency, collision (dispute), commotion, conflict, confrontation (altercation), disaccord, disturbance, embroilment, fight (battle), fracas, fray, outbreak, outburst, pandemonium, riot, struggle. SEE MAIN ENTRY

affreightment carriage

affright consternation, discourage, fear, fright, frighten, intimidate, menace, panic, trepidation

affront accost, annoy, aspersion, bait (harass), challenge, contumely, defiance, defy, discommode, disoblige, disparage, disregard (lack of respect), disrespect, flout, humiliate, irritate, offend (insult), pique,

provocation, provoke, rebuff, resentment, revilement. SEE MAIN ENTRY

affront hostilely assault

affronting outrageous

afield astray

afloat unsettled

aforecited aforesaid

aforedescribed aforesaid. SEE MAIN ENTRY

aforegiven aforesaid

aforegoing aforesaid, last (preceding), said. SEE MAIN ENTRY

aforehand before mentioned. SEE MAIN ENTRY

aforementioned aforesaid, last (preceding), preliminary, previous, stated. SEE MAIN ENTRY

aforenamed aforesaid, before mentioned, said

aforesaid before mentioned, last (preceding), previous, said, stated

aforestated aforesaid, before mentioned. SEE MAIN ENTRY

aforethought express, premeditated, premeditation. SEE MAIN ENTRY

afraid caitiff, leery, recreant. SEE MAIN ENTRY

afresh anew, de novo

after ensuing, ex post facto, successive, thereafter

after death posthumous

after the act is committed ex post facto

after the fact ex post facto

after the same pattern boiler plate

after time dilatory, late (tardy)

after-comer heir

after-generations heir

aftereffect consequence (conclusion), outcome, outgrowth

aftergrowth consequence (conclusion), development (outgrowth)

aftermath consequence (conclusion), development (outgrowth), effect, outcome, outgrowth, result. SEE MAIN ENTRY

aftermost last (final)

afterthought hindsight, recollection, retrospect

afterward ex post facto

afterwards hereafter (henceforth), thereafter

agacerie catalyst

again anew, de novo

against contiguous, contra (adverb), contra (preposition), disinclined

against fair trade antitrust act

against free commerce antitrust act

against free mercantilism antitrust act

against free trade antitrust act

against one's will compulsory, involuntary. SEE MAIN ENTRY

against open business antitrust act

against open markets antitrust act

against reason ill-judged

against the admonition of law felonious

against the law felonious, illegal, illegitimate (illegal), illicit, impermissible, lawless, unlawful, wrongful

against the rules deviant, felonious, irregular (improper)

agape open (unclosed), penetrable, speechless

age annum, cycle, duration, lifetime, longevity, mature, period, phase (period), term (duration), time. SEE MAIN ENTRY

age of discretion majority (adulthood). SEE MAIN ENTRY

age of majority majority (adulthood)

age of responsibility majority (adulthood)

aged elderly

ageless durable, immutable, permanent

agellus plot (land)

agency bureau, bureaucracy, committee, conduit (channel), delegation (assignment), department, expedient, facility (institution), facility (instrumentality), forum (medium), instrument (tool), medium, organ, proxy, representation (acting for others). SEE MAIN ENTRY

agency of the state government (political administration)

agenda calendar (list of cases), calendar (record of yearly periods), docket, outline (synopsis), plan, program, register, schedule. SEE MAIN ENTRY

agent assistant, broker, cause (reason), conduit (intermediary), dealer, deputy, detective, determinant, employee, factor (commission merchant), factor (ingredient), fiduciary, forum (medium), go-between, instrument (tool), interagent, intermediary, liaison, medium, plenipotentiary, proctor, procurator, protagonist, proxy, representative (proxy), spokesman, spy, substitute, superintendent, tool, trustee. SEE MAIN ENTRY

agent provocateur catalyst

agent provocateur conspirer

agential ministerial, representative

agents deputation (delegation)

agentship delegation (assignment), representation (acting for others)

ager district, estate (property), territory

agger causeway

agglomerate accumulate (amass), agglomeration, aggregate (noun), aggregate (verb), cement, coadunate, cohere (adhere), compile, composite, concentrate (consolidate), conglomerate, corporation, cumulation, desegregate, hoard, unite

agglomeration adhesion (affixing), arsenal, assemblage, coalescence, collection (accumulation), compilation, conglomeration, cumulation. SEE MAIN ENTRY

agglutinate adhere (fasten), affix, attach (join), cement, cohere (adhere), coherent (joined), cohesive (sticking), combine (join together)

agglutinated attached (annexed)

agglutination adhesion (affixing), agglomeration, coalescence

agglutinative coherent (joined), cohesive (sticking)

aggrandize accrue (increase), accumulate (enlarge), bear (yield), build (augment), compound, elevate, empower, enhance, enlarge, expand, extend (enlarge), honor, increase, inflate, magnify, overestimate, promote (advance), raise (advance)

aggrandized extreme (exaggerated), inflated (overestimated)

aggrandizement accession (enlargement), advancement (improvement), augmentation, boom (prosperity), elevation, eminence, exaggeration, extension (expansion), growth (increase), honor (outward respect), hyperbole, inflation (increase), overstatement, remembrance (commemoration). SEE MAIN ENTRY

aggravate alienate (estrange), annoy, badger, bait (harass), compound, deteriorate, discommode, discompose, distress, exacerbate, expand, harm, heighten (augment), incense, intensify, irritate, plague, press (goad), provoke. SEE MAIN ENTRY

aggravated gross (flagrant)

aggravating provocative, vexatious

aggravation complication, damage, detriment, harm, molestation, nuisance, pain. SEE MAIN ENTRY

aggravative cumulative *(intensifying)*

aggregate accumulate *(amass)*, agglomeration, amount *(quantity)*, coadunate, collect *(gather)*, collection *(accumulation)*, collective, combination, compile, complex *(development)*, composite, compound, comprise, concentrate *(consolidate)*, conglomerate, conglomeration, congregate, congregation, corpus, cumulation, entirety, garner, glean, gross *(total)*, hoard, in solido, join *(bring together)*, mass *(body of persons)*, multiple, quantity, total, totality, whole *(undamaged)*, whole. SEE MAIN ENTRY

aggregate amount sum *(total)*

aggregated coadunate, collective, composite, compound, miscellaneous

aggregation adhesion *(affixing)*, affiliation *(amalgamation)*, agglomeration, aggregate, assemblage, assembly, body *(collection)*, centralization, chamber *(body)*, collection *(accumulation)*, collection *(assembly)*, combination, company *(assemblage)*, compilation, complex *(development)*, conglomeration, congregation, consolidation, corpus, cumulation, hoard, incorporation *(blend)*, organization *(association)*, selection *(collection)*, totality. SEE MAIN ENTRY

aggress antagonize, assail, assault, attack, impinge, infringe, invade, oppugn, strike *(assault)*

aggression assault, belligerency, foray, incursion, infringement, intrusion, invasion, offense, onset *(assault)*, outbreak, provocation. SEE MAIN ENTRY

aggressive contentious, disorderly, forcible, hostile, hot-blooded, industrious, litigious, malevolent, obtrusive, offensive *(taking the initiative)*, pugnacious, spartan

aggressive action assault

aggressive argument dispute

aggressiveness belligerency, main force

aggressor assailant, offender. SEE MAIN ENTRY

aggrieve affront, aggravate *(annoy)*, badger, bait *(harass)*, distress, harrow, harry *(harass)*, mistreat, persecute, plague

aggrieved despondent. SEE MAIN ENTRY

aggrieved party actor, appellant, complainant

aggroup aggregate, congregate, convene, hoard, join *(bring together)*

aghast speechless

agile deft

agilis movable

agio brokerage

agitare discuss

agitari oscillate

agitate bait *(harass)*, bicker, debate, discommode, discompose, disconcert, dislocate, disorganize, disrupt, distress, disturb, foment, harass, harrow, impel, incense, incite, inflict, irritate, militate, obsess, oscillate, perturb, pique, provoke, upset. SEE MAIN ENTRY

agitate against counter, counteract, countervail

agitated disordered, disorderly, unsettled, vehement

agitating moving *(evoking emotion)*

agitatio commotion

agitation affray, aggravation *(exacerbation)*, apprehension *(fear)*, commotion, consternation, distress *(anguish)*, disturbance, embroilment, emotion, entanglement *(confusion)*, fright, furor, instigation, outbreak, outburst, pandemonium, panic, passion, provocation, revolt, strife, struggle, trepidation, turmoil

agitational offensive *(taking the initiative)*

agitative incendiary

agitator catalyst, demagogue, hoodlum, insurgent, malcontent

agitators lobby

agnate associated, cognate, consanguineous, correlate, correlative, interrelated, related

agnation affiliation *(bloodline)*, blood, propinquity *(kinship)*

agnomen call *(title)*

agnoscere recognize *(perceive)*

agnostic skeptical

agonize bait *(harass)*, brood, distress, harass, inflict, persecute, press *(goad)*, suffer *(sustain loss)*

agonizing cruel, insufferable, painful, severe

agony distress *(anguish)*, pain, plaint, stress *(strain)*

agora market *(business)*, market place

agree abide, accommodate, acknowledge *(respond)*, admit *(concede)*, allow *(endure)*, assent, bond *(secure a debt)*, certify *(approve)*, cohere *(be logically consistent)*, coincide *(concur)*, compromise *(settle by mutual agreement)*, concede, conform, consent, conspire, contract, correspond *(be equivalent)*, decide, defer *(yield in judgment)*, fix *(settle)*, grant *(concede)*, obey, promise *(vow)*, settle, stipulate, subscribe *(promise)*, undertake, unite. SEE MAIN ENTRY

agree beforehand predetermine

agree in principle concede

agree to accede *(concede)*, accept *(admit as sufficient)*, accept *(assent)*, approve, authorize, certify *(approve)*, confirm, countenance, embrace *(accept)*, pass *(approve)*, permit, sanction, sign, surrender *(yield)*, yield *(submit)*. SEE MAIN ENTRY

agree to beforehand prearrange

agree to indemnify for loss assure *(insure)*

agree to support underwrite

agree upon settle

agree with comply, confirm, uphold

agreeability compliance

agreeable amenable, attractive, benevolent, concordant, congruous, consensual, consenting, convenient, favorable *(expressing approval)*, harmonious, inclined, malleable, nonmilitant, palatable, patient, peaceable, pliant, prone, ready *(willing)*, resigned, sapid, savory, willing *(not averse)*. SEE MAIN ENTRY

agreeable manner amenity

agreeable to pursuant to

agreeable to reason rational

agreeable way amenity

agreeableness amenability, amenity, benevolence *(disposition to do good)*, comity, propriety *(appropriateness)*

agreed concerted, congruous, conjoint, contractual, res judicata. SEE MAIN ENTRY

agreed to contractual

agreed upon consensual

agreeing coequal, coextensive, commensurate, concerted, concordant, concurrent *(united)*, consenting, consistent, consonant, correlative, felicitous, harmonious, proportionate, similar

agreeing to pursuant to

agreement acceptance, accommodation *(adjustment)*, accord, accordance *(compact)*, accordance *(understanding)*, acknowledgment *(acceptance)*, acquiescence, adjustment, analogy, approval, arrangement *(understanding)*, assent, attornment, bargain, cartel, coherence, collusion, commitment *(responsibility)*, compact, compatibility, compliance, composition *(agreement in bankruptcy)*, compromise, concert, concession *(compromise)*, conciliation, concordance, conformity *(agreement)*, conjunction, consensus, consent, contract, correspondence *(similarity)*, covenant, deal, identity *(similarity)*, indenture, indorsement, integration *(assimilation)*, league, lease, leave *(permission)*, mutual understanding, obligation *(duty)*, option *(contractual provision)*, pact, peace, pledge *(binding promise)*, policy *(contract)*, promise, quid pro quo, rapport, rapprochement, reconciliation, resemblance, sanction *(permission)*, settlement, specialty *(contract)*, stipulation, subscription, synchronism, term *(provision)*, testament, treaty, undertaking *(commitment)*, undertaking *(pledge)*, union *(unity)*, warrant *(guaranty)*. SEE MAIN ENTRY

agreement as to time and place of meeting appointment *(meeting)*

agreement before marriage antenuptial agreement

agreement between nations treaty

agreement between parties compact. SEE MAIN ENTRY

agreement for fraud collusion

agreement to accomplish an unlawful end conspiracy

agreement to commit a crime conspiracy

agreement to pay insurance

agreement to work indenture

agressive eager

agrestis uncouth

agrorum possessor landlord, landowner

ahead of time premature

aid abet, accommodate, accomplice, advantage, advocacy, assist, assistance, associate, avail *(be of use)*, bear *(support)*, behalf, benefactor, benefit *(conferment)*, bolster, capitalize *(provide capital)*, charity, coactor, coadjutant, conduce, confederate, conspire, conspirer, contribute *(assist)*, contribution *(participation)*, copartner *(coconspirator)*, countenance, enable, endow, endowment, espouse, expedite, facilitate, factor *(ingredient)*, favor *(sanction)*, favor, finance, foment, foster, harbor, help *(noun)*, help *(verb)*, instrument *(tool)*, inure *(benefit)*, largess *(generosity)*, lend, loan, maintain *(sustain)*, maintenance *(support of spouse)*, nurture, participant, participate, partner, patronage *(support)*, promotion *(encouragement)*, redress, reinforcement, relieve *(give aid)*, remedy *(legal means of redress)*, remedy *(that which corrects)*, remedy, rescue, samaritan, serve *(assist)*, service *(assistance)*, shelter *(protection)*, side, subsidize, support *(assistance)*, support *(assist)*, uphold

aid a judge clerk

aid in organizing promote *(organize)*

aid with a subsidy capitalize *(provide capital)*

aidance aid *(help)*, behalf

aidant salutary

aide abettor, assistant, coadjutant, consociate, contributor *(contributor)*, good samaritan. SEE MAIN ENTRY

aide in crime coconspirator

aide in wrongdoing coconspirator

aide-de-camp assistant
aide-de-camp associate, coactor, copartner (coconspirator)
aide-mémoire memorandum
aider abettor, accessory, accomplice, assistant, backer, benefactor, coactor, coadjutant, confederate, conspirer, donor, good samaritan, partner, promoter, samaritan
aider and abettor accomplice, coactor, cohort, colleague, conspirer, copartner (coconspirator)
aider in wrongdoing coconspirator
aides staff
aidful ancillary (auxiliary), beneficial, subservient
aiding ancillary (auxiliary), beneficial, concurrent (united), contributory, donative, instrumental, practical, profitable, subservient, subsidiary
aiding and abetting concerted
aidless helpless (defenseless)
ail languish, suffer (sustain loss)
ailment disability (physical inability), disease, disorder (abnormal condition), pain, trouble
aim cause (reason), contemplation, content (meaning), desideratum, design (intent), destination, direction (course), end (intent), endeavor (noun), endeavor (verb), forethought, goal, idea, intend, intent, intention, mission, motive, object, objective, plan, point (purpose), predetermination, project, purpose, pursue (strive to gain), pursuit (goal), reason (basis), signification, strive, target, try (attempt)
aim at attempt
aimed deliberate, direct (straight), tactical
aiming for effect flagrant, histrionic
aiming to destroy deadly
aiming to kill deadly
aimless casual, discursive (digressive), disjointed, random, unwitting
air appearance (look), atmosphere, bare, behavior, betray (disclose), conduct, deportment, disabuse, disclose, discuss, divulge, expose, express, flaunt, herald, issue (publish), manifest, manner (behavior), posture (attitude), presence (poise), proclaim, produce (offer to view), promulgate, propagate (spread), publish, relate (tell), report (disclose), semblance, signify (inform), speak, utter
air pollution SEE MAIN ENTRY
aired public (known)
airfreight carriage
airing publicity
airs disdain, histrionics, pretense (ostentation), pride
airspace atmosphere
airtight impervious
airy insubstantial, intangible, subtle (refined), tenuous
airy spirit phantom
ajar open (unclosed), penetrable
akin allied, analogous, associated, cognate, comparable (capable of comparison), congruous, consanguineous, correlative, interrelated, related, tangential. SEE MAIN ENTRY
alacritas life (vitality)
alacritious expeditious
alacritous eager, ready (willing)
alacrity dispatch (promptness), haste, industry (activity). SEE MAIN ENTRY
alarm admonition, agitate (perturb), alert, apprehension (fear), caution (warning), consternation, disconcert, disturb, fear, forewarn, fright, frighten, harrow, intimidate,

menace, monition (warning), panic, perturb, phobia, stress (strain), symptom, threat, trepidation, warning
alarming dangerous, formidable, imminent, ominous, portentous (ominous), precarious, prophetic, sinister
albeit regardless
album register, roll
alcohol SEE MAIN ENTRY
alcoholic addiction dipsomania
alcoholic beverage alcohol
alcoholism dipsomania, inebriation
alcove chamber (compartment)
alderman lawmaker
alderwoman lawmaker
alea risk, venture
alea ludere gamble
aleatory speculative
alere develop, foster
alert acute, admonish (advise), advise, apprise, careful, caution (warning), caveat, circumspect, cognizant, conscious (awake), forewarn, guarded, meticulous, monition (warning), notify, perspicacious, preventive, prompt, provident (showing foresight), ready (willing), receptive, responsive, sedulous, sensitive (discerning), vigilant, warning. SEE MAIN ENTRY
alert to danger forewarn
alertness comprehension, diligence (care), life (vitality), notice (heed), precaution, regard (attention), sensibility
alexipharmic medicinal
alias call (title). SEE MAIN ENTRY
alias dictus alias
alibi compurgation, excuse, pretext. SEE MAIN ENTRY
alien antipathetic (oppositional), apart, different, extraneous, extrinsic, foreign, impertinent (irrelevant), inapplicable, inapposite, inappropriate, incongruous, irrelative, irrelevant, nonconforming, novel, obscure (remote), peculiar (curious), repugnant (incompatible), stranger, unrelated, unusual. SEE MAIN ENTRY
alienable heritable, negotiable
alienate antagonize, assign (transfer ownership), cede, convey (transfer), disaffect, disown (refuse to acknowledge), estrange, repel (disgust), separate. SEE MAIN ENTRY
alienate by breach of condition forfeit
alienated antipathetic (oppositional), hostile, inimical, irreconcilable
alienatio alienation (estrangement), estrangement
alienation assignment (transfer of ownership), conveyance, demise (conveyance), disposition (transfer of property), estrangement, feud, ill will, insanity, odium, separation, umbrage, variance (disagreement). SEE MAIN ENTRY
alienation of affection estrangement
alienation of mind insanity
alienation of property conveyance
alienigena alien
alienus averse, extraneous, incongruous, irrelevant, unsuitable
alight SEE MAIN ENTRY
align conform, convert (persuade), file (arrange), fix (arrange), join (associate oneself with), juxtapose, organize (arrange), persuade. SEE MAIN ENTRY
align convergently border (approach)
aligned coextensive, concerted, concomitant, concordant
alignment affiliation (connectedness), confederacy (compact), league, persuasion, relationship (connection), sodality

alike akin (germane), analogous, approximate, cognate, comparable (capable of comparison), consistent, consonant, equal, equivalent, identical, same, uniform. SEE MAIN ENTRY
alikeness comparison, identity (similarity), parity, propinquity (similarity), resemblance
aliment sustenance
alimentation sustenance
alimentum sustenance
alimony maintenance (support of spouse). SEE MAIN ENTRY
alius different, diverse
alive alert (agile), alert (vigilant), conscious (awake), extant, responsive, viable
alive to sensitive (discerning)
all complete (all-embracing), entirety, sum (total), total, whole (undamaged), whole. SEE MAIN ENTRY
all along through (from beginning to end)
all gone defunct
all in all in toto
all over throughout (all over)
all over with defunct
all right mediocre
all the more a fortiori
all the same notwithstanding, regardless
all the time always (forever)
all the way through (from beginning to end)
all the while always (forever)
all together en banc, en masse
all-comprehending complete (all-embracing)
all-comprehensive complete (all-embracing), nonsectarian
all-covering complete (all-embracing), comprehensive
all-destroying disastrous
all-embracing composite, comprehensive, inclusive, nonsectarian, omnibus, prevailing (current), prevalent
all-encompassing unqualified (unlimited)
all-important necessary (required)
all-including nonsectarian
all-inclusive complete (all-embracing), comprehensive, detailed, gross (total), nonsectarian, omnibus, thorough
all-knowing expert, omniscient
all-out outright
all-pervading complete (all-embracing), comprehensive
all-powerful cardinal (outstanding), invincible, omnipotent, predominant
all-purpose practical
all-searching interrogative
all-seeing omniscient
all-sufficing complete (all-embracing)
all-wise omniscient
allay alleviate, ameliorate, assuage, commute, decrease, discount (minimize), lessen, lull, mitigate, moderate (temper), modify (moderate), mollify, obtund, palliate (abate), placate, redress, relax, relieve (free from burden), repress, soothe, subdue. SEE MAIN ENTRY
allay fears disarm (set at ease)
allay mistrust disarm (set at ease)
allaying palliative (abating)
allayment mollification, remission, solace
allegation accusation, assertion, attestation, bad repute, charge (accusation), claim (assertion), color (deceptive appearance), complaint, contention (argument), count, indictment, information (charge), mention (reference), plea, pleading. SEE MAIN ENTRY

allegation of criminal wrongdoing arraignment

allegation of facts bill *(formal declaration)*, pleading

allege adduce, argue, avouch *(avow)*, bear *(adduce)*, certify *(attest)*, cite *(accuse)*, claim *(maintain)*, comment, express, plead *(allege in a legal action)*, posit, propound, purport, testify. SEE MAIN ENTRY

allege as a fact avouch *(avow)*, avow

allege in support advocate, assert, defend, justify

allege in vindication justify

allege to be guilty implicate

allege to belong ascribe

allege under oath swear. SEE MAIN ENTRY

alleged colorable *(plausible)*, purported, putative. SEE MAIN ENTRY

alleged malfeasor suspect

alleged motive color *(deceptive appearance)*

alleged offender suspect

alleged purpose pretext

alleged reason cover *(pretext)*, gist *(ground for a suit)*, pretext

alleged transgressor suspect

alleged wrongdoer suspect

allegedly reputedly

allegiance adherence *(devotion)*, adhesion *(loyalty)*, charge *(responsibility)*, commitment *(responsibility)*, duty *(obligation)*, faith, fealty, fidelity, homage, loyalty, nationality. SEE MAIN ENTRY

allegiant loyal

allegorical demonstrative *(illustrative)*

alleviate abate *(lessen)*, allay, assuage, commute, diminish, disencumber, ease, help, lessen, lull, mitigate, moderate *(temper)*, mollify, obtund, pacify, palliate *(abate)*, redress, relieve *(give aid)*, remedy, remit *(relax)*, soothe. SEE MAIN ENTRY

alleviating mitigating, palliative *(abating)*, remedial

alleviating circumstances extenuating circumstances

alleviation abatement *(reduction)*, decrease, mitigation, moderation, mollification, relief *(release)*, remedy *(legal means of redress)*, remission, solace

alleviative corrigible, medicinal, narcotic, palliative *(abating)*, remedial

alleviator narcotic

alley way *(channel)*

alliance adhesion *(loyalty)*, affiliation *(amalgamation)*, agreement *(contract)*, band, cartel, centralization, chain *(nexus)*, coaction, coalescence, coalition, cohabitation *(living together)*, collusion, committee, concert, confederacy *(compact)*, conformity *(agreement)*, conjunction, connection *(relation)*, connivance, consortium *(marriage companionship)*, contact *(association)*, contribution *(participation)*, cooperative, corporation, federation, integration *(amalgamation)*, integration *(assimilation)*, league, marriage *(intimate relationship)*, matrimony, merger, mutual understanding, nexus, organization *(association)*, pact, partnership, peace, pool, propinquity *(kinship)*, rapport, rapprochement, relation *(connection)*, society, sodality, syndicate, treaty, understanding *(agreement)*. SEE MAIN ENTRY

alliance of workers union *(labor organization)*

allied affiliated, akin *(germane)*, analogous, apposite, associated, close *(intimate)*, coadunate, cognate, coherent *(joined)*, concomitant, concordant, concurrent *(united)*, conjoint, consanguineous, corporate *(associate)*, correlative, federal, germane, harmonious, incident, incidental, interrelated, intimate, joint, nuptial, related, relative *(relevant)*, relevant, similar. SEE MAIN ENTRY

allied to pendent

allness totality, whole

allocate allot, apportion, arrange *(methodize)*, assign *(allot)*, classify, delegate, demarcate, detail *(assign)*, disburse *(distribute)*, dispense, disperse *(disseminate)*, distribute, divide *(distribute)*, dole, expend *(disburse)*, marshal, mete, parcel, partition, pigeonhole, prorate, regulate *(adjust)*, relegate, sort, split, tabulate. SEE MAIN ENTRY

allocated per capita

allocation allotment, appointment *(act of designating)*, apportionment, appropriation *(allotment)*, assignment *(allotment)*, budget, circulation, classification, consignment, coupon, dispensation *(act of dispensing)*, distribution *(apportionment)*, division *(act of dividing)*, order *(arrangement)*, part *(portion)*, quota, share *(interest)*

allocute converse

allocution declamation, discourse, parlance, rhetoric *(skilled speech)*, speech

allot allocate, apportion, attorn, bear *(yield)*, bestow, classify, commit *(entrust)*, contribute *(supply)*, delegate, delimit, demarcate, devise *(give)*, devote, disburse *(distribute)*, dispense, distribute, divide *(distribute)*, dole, endow, endue, expend *(disburse)*, fund, give *(grant)*, leave *(give)*, marshal, mete, parcel, partition, pigeonhole, present *(make a gift)*, prorate, sort, split. SEE MAIN ENTRY

allot again reapportion, redistribute

allot the parts orchestrate

alloted pro rata

alloting disbursement *(act of disbursing)*

allotment alimony, annuity, appointment *(act of designating)*, apportionment, budget, circulation, classification, commission *(fee)*, consignment, disbursement *(act of disbursing)*, dispensation *(act of dispensing)*, distribution *(apportionment)*, dividend, division *(act of dividing)*, dower, endowment, equity *(share of ownership)*, grant, installment, loan, moiety, order *(arrangement)*, payment *(remittance)*, pension, proportion, quantity, quota, ration, share *(interest)*, subsidy. SEE MAIN ENTRY

allotment by chance lottery

allottee assignee, heir, transferee

allotter transferor

allow accept *(admit as sufficient)*, accept *(assent)*, accept *(recognize)*, agree *(comply)*, approve, assent, authorize, bear *(tolerate)*, bequeath, bestow, certify *(approve)*, concede, concur *(agree)*, condone, consent, countenance, deign, dole, empower, enable, endow, endue, enfranchise, grant *(concede)*, indorse, let *(permit)*, loan, pass *(approve)*, permit, provide *(supply)*, qualify *(meet standards)*, rebate, receive *(permit to enter)*, recognize *(acknowledge)*, sanction, suffer *(permit)*, tolerate, vouchsafe, yield *(submit)*. SEE MAIN ENTRY

allow a margin discount *(reduce)*

allow as a discount rebate

allow credit lend

allow entrance admit *(give access)*, receive *(permit to enter)*

allow for compensate *(counterbalance)*, compensate *(remunerate)*, excuse, extenuate, palliate *(excuse)*

allow residency rent

allow the use of lease, let *(lease)*, rent, sublease, sublet

allow with condescension deign

allowable admissible, allowed, deductible *(capable of being deducted from taxes)*, due *(regular)*, justifiable, lawful, legal, licit, open *(accessible)*, pardonable, passable, permissible, potential, right *(suitable)*, rightful, unobjectionable. SEE MAIN ENTRY

allowableness admissibility, legality

allowance acceptance, acquiescence, advancement *(loan)*, alimony, annuity, apportionment, appropriation *(allotment)*, approval, assignment *(allotment)*, budget, capacity *(authority)*, cession, charter *(sanction)*, commission *(fee)*, concession *(authorization)*, concession *(compromise)*, condonation, consent, disbursement *(funds paid out)*, discount, dispensation *(exception)*, dower, endowment, excuse, exemption, franchise *(license)*, gift *(present)*, grant, indulgence, justification, leave *(permission)*, license, maintenance *(support of spouse)*, offset, option *(contractual provision)*, part *(portion)*, pay, payment *(remittance)*, payroll, pension, permission, perquisite, privilege, quota, ration, rebate, sanction *(permission)*, subsidy, sufferance, tolerance, wage

allowed admissible, choate lien, definite, entitled, lawful, legal, legitimate *(rightful)*, licit, open *(accessible)*, permissible, potential, privileged, rightful. SEE MAIN ENTRY

allowedly admittedly

allowing consenting, lenient, permissive

allowing no departure from the standard exact

alloy commingle, incorporate *(include)*, join *(bring together)*, pollute, taint *(contaminate)*

alloyed composite, promiscuous

allude adduce, hint, purport, refer *(direct attention)*. SEE MAIN ENTRY

allude to appertain, bear *(adduce)*, connote, disclose, imply, indicate, mention

alluded to implied

allure amenity, bait *(lure)*, cajole, coax, convince, decoy, ensnare, entice, entrap, incentive, inveigle, lure, motivate, seduction

allurement bribery, cause *(reason)*, decoy, incentive, inducement, invitation, seduction

alluring attractive, provocative, sapid

allusion attribution, connotation, hint, implication *(inference)*, indication, inference, innuendo, insinuation, intimation, mention *(reference)*, referral, reminder, suggestion

allusive implicit, implied, indirect, suggestive *(evocative)*, tacit. SEE MAIN ENTRY

allusory allusive

alluvion cataclysm. SEE MAIN ENTRY

ally affiliate, backer, bear *(support)*, benefactor, coactor, coadjutant, cohort, colleague, combine *(act in concert)*, confederate, confirm, conjoin, connect *(relate)*, consociate, consolidate *(unite)*, contributor *(contributor)*, cooperate, correlate, disciple, espouse, federalize *(associate)*, federate, involve *(implicate)*, join *(associate oneself with)*, merge, participant, partisan, partner, pool, proponent, relate *(establish a connection)*, unite

ally in crime coconspirator

ally in wrongdoing coconspirator

almanac calendar (record of yearly periods), register

almightiness predominance

almighty omnipotent, predominant

almoner contributor (giver)

almost approximate, quasi. SEE MAIN ENTRY

almost as quasi

almost certainly high probability

alms contribution (donation), donation, largess (gift)

almsgiver contributor (giver), donor

almsgiving charitable (benevolent), charity, largess (generosity), liberal (generous), philanthropic, philanthropy

alodium domain (land owned)

alone apart, insular, only, remote (secluded), separate, solely (singly). SEE MAIN ENTRY

along SEE MAIN ENTRY

along in years elderly

along the river banks fluvial

along the way en route

alonge SEE MAIN ENTRY

alongside adjacent

aloof cold-blooded, controlled (restrained), disdainful, dispassionate, insusceptible (uncaring), orgulous, phlegmatic, proud (conceited), solitary, unapproachable, unresponsive

aloofness disinterest (lack of interest), disregard (lack of respect), indifference, neutrality

alphabetize tabulate

already indicated previous, said

already mentioned aforesaid

already said aforesaid

also alias. SEE MAIN ENTRY

also acknowledged as alias

also acknowledging the name of alias

also answering to alias

also called alias

also known as alias. SEE MAIN ENTRY

also known by alias

also known under the name of alias

also recognized as alias

alter adapt, amend, change, commute, convert (change use), countervail, denature, edit, emend, falsify, fix (repair), fluctuate, qualify (condition), rectify, revise, tamper, transform, vary. SEE MAIN ENTRY

alter course deviate, digress

alter ego counterpart (complement). SEE MAIN ENTRY

alter fraudulently falsify

alter one's course detour

alter the appearance of camouflage, disguise

alter the position move (alter position)

alter with intent to deceive fake

alterable aleatory (uncertain), conditional, indefinite, mutable, pliable, protean, provisional, variable, yielding

alterant drug

alteration conversion (change), correction (change), deviation, digression, diversification, innovation, modification, reform, rehabilitation, reorganization, repair, revision (process of correcting), transition, vicissitudes. SEE MAIN ENTRY

alterative ambulatory, corrigible, remedial

altercari dispute (contest)

altercate bicker, brawl, collide (clash), contend (dispute), contest, debate, disaccord, dispute (contest), fight (battle), litigate, remonstrate

altercatio altercation, controversy (argument), dispute

altercation affray, argument (contention), belligerency, brawl, collision (dispute), commotion, conflict, contest (dispute), controversy (argument), disagreement, dispute, feud, fight (argument), fracas, strife, variance (disagreement). SEE MAIN ENTRY

altered different, tempered

altered for the worse dilapidated

alternare alternate (take turns)

alternate agent, alter ego, attorney in fact, beat (pulsate), cover (substitute), deputy, disjunctive (alternative), fluctuate, intermittent, oscillate, reciprocate, replace, replacement, stopgap, substitute, surrogate, vacillate, vary, vicarious (substitutional). SEE MAIN ENTRY

alternate choice alternative (option), option (choice)

alternate route detour

alternating reciprocal, shifting

alternating conditions vicissitudes

alternation cycle, interchange, sequence, vicissitudes

alternative call (option), cover (substitute), elective (selective), expedient, loophole, option (choice), plan, replacement, secondary, stopgap, substitute, vicarious (substitutional). SEE MAIN ENTRY

alternative dispute resolution SEE MAIN ENTRY

alterner alternate (take turns)

although notwithstanding, regardless

altiloquence fustian

altiloquent inflated (bombastic)

altior heighten (elevate)

altisonant inflated (bombastic)

altitude ceiling, elevation

altogether in toto, outright, radical (extreme), wholly

altruism benevolence (disposition to do good), charity, goodwill, humanity (humaneness), largess (generosity), philanthropy, understanding (tolerance)

altruist benefactor, contributor (giver), donor, good samaritan, samaritan

altruistic benevolent, charitable (benevolent), humane, liberal (generous), magnanimous, nonprofit, philanthropic

always invariably. SEE MAIN ENTRY

amalgam melange, solution (substance)

amalgamate cement, collect (gather), combine (join together), commingle, connect (join together), consolidate (unite), cooperate, crystallize, desegregate, federalize (associate), federate, hoard, join (bring together), merge, organize (unionize), pool, unite. SEE MAIN ENTRY

amalgamated collective, composite, compound, concerted, concurrent (united), conglomerate, conjoint, correlative, joint, miscellaneous, promiscuous

amalgamating concrescence

amalgamation association (alliance), building (business of assembling), cartel, centralization, coalescence, coalition, combination, consolidation, federation, incorporation (blend), merger, pool, relationship (connection), union (labor organization)

amalgamative coadunate, coherent (joined)

amanuensis SEE MAIN ENTRY

amaranthine durable, perpetual

amass accrue (increase), aggregate, collect (gather), compile, concentrate (consolidate), congregate, conjoin, consolidate (strengthen), consolidate (unite), convene, cull, fund, garner, glean, hoard, join (bring together), keep (shelter), meet, reserve, set aside (annul), store, unite

amassed collective, composite, conglomerate. SEE MAIN ENTRY

amassing centralization

amassment agglomeration, assemblage, collection (accumulation), conglomeration, congregation, corpus, cumulation, hoard, store (depository)

amateur inexperienced, layman, neophyte, novice, volunteer. SEE MAIN ENTRY

amateurish incompetent, unprofessional

amaze impress (affect deeply)

amazed speechless

amazement incredulity, phenomenon (unusual occurrence), surprise

amazing extraordinary, ineffable, noteworthy, portentous (eliciting amazement), remarkable, special, unaccustomed, unusual

amazing thing phenomenon (unusual occurrence)

ambages enigma, evasion

ambagious circuitous, devious, indirect, labyrinthine, sinuous

ambagitory labyrinthine, sinuous

ambassador deputy, plenipotentiary, spokesman

ambassadorial function embassy

ambassadorial office embassy

ambassadorial residence embassy

ambience atmosphere

ambigere dispute (debate)

ambiguitas ambiguity

ambiguity doubt (indecision), incertitude. SEE MAIN ENTRY

ambiguous aleatory (uncertain), allusive, debatable, disputable, dubious, enigmatic, equivocal, inapprehensible, incomprehensible, indefinite, indeterminate, indistinct, inexact, inscrutable, nebulous, opaque, problematic, unclear, undecided, vague. SEE MAIN ENTRY

ambiguous saying enigma

ambiguus ambiguous, equivocal, evasive, indefinite, undecided, vague

ambire canvass

ambit border, capacity (sphere), circuit, contour (outline), coverage (scope), frontier, limit, outline (boundary), periphery, purview, range, scope, sphere. SEE MAIN ENTRY

ambition desideratum, design (intent), desire, end (intent), goal, intention, objective, plan, project, prospect (outlook), purpose, pursuit (goal), target

ambitious eager, solicitous

ambivalence SEE MAIN ENTRY

ambivalent ambiguous, equivocal, evasive, oblique (evasive)

amble perambulate

ambrosiac savory

ambrosial palatable, sapid, savory

ambrosian palatable, savory

ambulant itinerant, moving (in motion)

ambulative moving (in motion)

ambulator pedestrian

ambulatory itinerant, moving (in motion). SEE MAIN ENTRY

ambuscade cache (hiding place), ensnare, lurk

ambush accost, decoy, ensnare, trap. SEE MAIN ENTRY

ambushed hidden

ameliorable corrigible

ameliorate amend, commute, cure, ease, emend, fix (repair), help, meliorate, mitigate, modify (alter), mollify, progress, rectify, reform, rehabilitate, relieve (give aid), remedy, renew *(refurbish)*, renovate, repair, restore *(renew)*, soothe, treat *(remedy)*. SEE MAIN ENTRY

amelioration amendment *(correction)*, boom *(prosperity)*, correction *(change)*, development *(progression)*, improvement, mollification, progress, promotion *(advancement)*, reform, rehabilitation, relief *(release)*, remedy *(legal means of redress)*, renewal, reorganization, repair, solace

ameliorative mitigating

amenability decorum, liability, responsibility *(accountability)*. SEE MAIN ENTRY

amenable actionable, corrigible, facile, inclined, liable, malleable, obedient, open *(persuasible)*, open-minded, palatable, passive, pliable, receptive, sequacious, suasible, tractable, willing *(not averse)*, yielding. SEE MAIN ENTRY

amenable to law justiciable, permissible
amenable to measurement determinable *(ascertainable)*

amenable to reason reasonable *(rational)*
amenableness decorum, liability

amend adjust *(resolve)*, alter, convert *(change use)*, edit, emend, fix *(repair)*, meliorate, modify *(alter)*, reconsider, rectify, reform, rehabilitate, remedy, renew *(refurbish)*, renovate, repair, restore *(renew)*, revise, supplement. SEE MAIN ENTRY

amend by removing expurgate
amendable ambulatory, corrigible
amendatory ambulatory, remedial
amending correction *(change)*
amendment correction *(change)*, reform, rider. SEE MAIN ENTRY

amends collection *(payment)*, compensation, damages, expiation, indemnification, indemnity, recompense, reparation *(indemnification)*, restitution, retribution

amenities decorum. SEE MAIN ENTRY
amenity comity, courtesy. SEE MAIN ENTRY
amentia insanity
amerce fine, mulct *(fine)*, penalize, punish
amercement correction *(punishment)*, cost *(penalty)*, discipline *(punishment)*, fine, forfeiture *(thing forfeited)*, penalty, punishment. SEE MAIN ENTRY

amercing disciplinary *(punitory)*
amiability benevolence *(disposition to do good)*, comity, courtesy, rapprochement
amiable amenable, amicable, benevolent, civil *(polite)*, malleable, obeisant, peaceable
amicability rapprochement
amicable benevolent, harmonious, nonmilitant, peaceable. SEE MAIN ENTRY
amicableness benevolence *(disposition to do good)*

amicire clothe
amicus curiae SEE MAIN ENTRY
amid among
amidst among
amiss astray, defective, disordered, errant, erroneous, faulty, improper, inaccurate, inappropriate, incorrect, unsuitable
amittere lose *(be deprived of)*
amity accordance *(understanding)*, agreement *(concurrence)*, comity, compatibility, concordance, goodwill, mutual understanding, peace, rapprochement, sodality
ammassment arsenal
ammount accrued cumulation
ammunition bomb. SEE MAIN ENTRY
amnesty absolution, acquittal, clear, clemency, condonation, dispensation *(exception)*, exoneration, impunity, pardon, reconciliation, release, remission, remit

(release from penalty), respite *(reprieve)*. SEE MAIN ENTRY
amoenitas amenity
among SEE MAIN ENTRY
amoral bad *(offensive)*, diabolic, immoral, peccant *(culpable)*
amoralism bad repute
amoralistic diabolic
amorality bad repute, laxity
amorous hot-blooded
amorousness affection
amorphic indefinite
amorphous indefinite, intangible, vague
amortization discharge *(payment)*, payment *(act of paying)*. SEE MAIN ENTRY
amortize discharge *(pay a debt)*
amortizement discharge *(payment)*, payment *(act of paying)*, satisfaction *(discharge of debt)*
amotio removal
amotion removal
amount aggregate, bulk, caliber *(measurement)*, compound, degree *(magnitude)*, entirety, expenditure, expense *(cost)*, extent, measurement, par *(face amount)*, part *(portion)*, payment *(remittance)*, price, quantity, rate, value. SEE MAIN ENTRY
amount accrued collection *(accumulation)*
amount assessed as payable assessment *(levy)*
amount computed computation
amount deducted discount
amount due bill *(invoice)*, debit, debt, obligation *(liability)*
amount expended outlay
amount for which anything is insured coverage *(insurance)*
amount of surface area *(surface)*
amount over par premium *(excess value)*
amount owing debt
amount paid periodically premium *(insurance payment)*
amount payable debit
amount produced output
amount reserved margin *(spare amount)*
amount to aggregate, comprise, consist, reach
amovere avert, remove *(transfer)*
amphibolic uncertain *(ambiguous)*
amphibological equivocal
amphibolous equivocal
amphigory parody
ample adequate, broad, capacious, considerable, copious, extensive, liberal *(generous)*, multiple, operative, profuse, replete, substantial. SEE MAIN ENTRY
ample notice adequate notice
ample stock sufficiency
ampleness capacity *(maximum)*, maximum *(amplitude)*, quorum, sufficiency
ampliare adjourn, compound
ampliation development *(progression)*, discontinuance *(interruption of a legal action)*
amplificare compound, enhance, enlarge, heighten *(augment)*, increase, intensify, magnify
amplificatio augmentation, promotion *(encouragement)*
amplification accession *(enlargement)*, advance *(increase)*, advancement *(improvement)*, aggravation *(exacerbation)*, augmentation, boom *(increase)*, clarification, development *(progression)*, explanation, extension *(expansion)*, growth *(increase)*, hyperbole, inflation *(increase)*, overstatement. SEE MAIN ENTRY

amplified extreme *(exaggerated)*, inflated *(enlarged)*, inflated *(overestimated)*
amplify accrue *(increase)*, accumulate *(enlarge)*, aggravate *(exacerbate)*, build *(augment)*, detail *(particularize)*, develop, elaborate, enhance, enlarge, expand, extend *(enlarge)*, heighten *(augment)*, increase, inflate, magnify, supplement. SEE MAIN ENTRY
amplifying cumulative *(intensifying)*
amplissimus gradus eminence
amplitude boom *(increase)*, boom *(prosperity)*, caliber *(measurement)*, capacity *(maximum)*, degree *(magnitude)*, latitude, magnitude, mass *(weight)*, plethora, quantity, scope, sufficiency
amplitudinous broad
amplitudo bulk, magnitude
amplus broad, extensive, illustrious
amputate mutilate
amuse occupy *(engage)*
amusement enjoyment *(pleasure)*, treat
amusing jocular, ludicrous, sapid
an equal percentage per capita
anabasis development *(progression)*
anachronic untimely
anachronistic obsolete, outdated, outmoded, untimely. SEE MAIN ENTRY
anachronize antedate
anachronous obsolete, outdated, outmoded, untimely
anacoluthon non sequitur. SEE MAIN ENTRY
analagous coextensive, commensurable, commensurate, comparable *(capable of comparison)*
analagous to comparative
analagousness balance *(equality)*
analect abstract
analeptic curative, medicinal, remedial, salubrious, salutary
analgesic drug
analogical analogous, cognate, commensurable, comparable *(capable of comparison)*, congruous
analogical procedure collation, comparison
analogize compare
analogous akin *(germane)*, coequal, cognate, congruous, correlative, interrelated, proportionate, related, relative *(comparative)*, similar, tantamount. SEE MAIN ENTRY
analogue correlate, counterpart *(complement)*
analogy collation, comparison, connection *(relation)*, correspondence *(similarity)*, parity, relation *(connection)*, relationship *(connection)*, resemblance. SEE MAIN ENTRY
analysis capsule, choice *(decision)*, classification, criticism, deliberation, diagnosis, digest, discretion *(power of choice)*, discrimination *(differentiation)*, examination *(study)*, hornbook, indagation, judgment *(discernment)*, measurement, pandect *(treatise)*, probe, proposal *(report)*, prospectus, rating, ratiocination, reflection *(thought)*, research, review *(critical evaluation)*, scenario, scrutiny, summary, test, treatment, trial *(experiment)*. SEE MAIN ENTRY
analytic deductive, discursive *(analytical)*, logical
analytical clinical, deductive, demonstrative *(illustrative)*, empirical, logical, rational. SEE MAIN ENTRY
analyzation hornbook, inquiry *(systematic investigation)*
analyze canvass, classify, consider, construe *(comprehend)*, construe *(translate)*, deliberate, detail *(particularize)*, diagnose,

digest *(comprehend)*, discuss, examine *(study)*, identify, investigate, peruse, ponder, rationalize, reason *(conclude)*, reflect *(ponder)*, research, review, scrutinize, study, survey *(examine)*, treat *(process)*. SEE MAIN ENTRY

anamorphosis distortion

anarchic disorderly, lawless

anarchical disordered, disorderly, lawless

anarchism disorder *(lack of order)*, misrule

anarchist insurgent, malcontent

anarchistic contumacious, disorderly, incendiary

anarchy confusion *(turmoil)*, disorder *(lack of order)*, havoc, insurrection, lynch law, misrule, pandemonium, revolution. SEE MAIN ENTRY

anathema denunciation, expletive, imprecation, malediction

anathematize blame, condemn *(blame)*, defame, denounce *(condemn)*, malign, proscribe *(denounce)*

anatomical organic

anatomize analyze, examine *(study)*, scrutinize

anatomy body *(person)*, configuration *(form)*, content *(structure)*

anceps critical *(crucial)*, dubious, equivocal, indeterminate

ancestor ascendant, derivation, forerunner, kindred, parents, precursor, predecessor, primogenitor, progenitor. SEE MAIN ENTRY

ancestorial hereditary

ancestors lineage

ancestral consanguineous, hereditary, paternal, traditional

ancestral descent origin *(ancestry)*

ancestral relation kindred, primogenitor

ancestral relative primogenitor

ancestry affiliation *(bloodline)*, affinity *(family ties)*, birth *(lineage)*, birthright, blood, bloodline, derivation, descent *(lineage)*, family *(common ancestry)*, heritage, lineage, origination, parentage, paternity, race, source. SEE MAIN ENTRY

anchor adhere *(fasten)*, mainstay, security *(safety)*

anchorage haven

anchored firm, fixed *(securely placed)*, situated, stable, steadfast

anchoretic solitary

anchoretical solitary

ancient antique, hereditary, obsolete, old, outdated, outmoded

ancillary appurtenant, collateral *(accompanying)*, dependent, pendent, secondary, slight, subordinate, subservient, supplementary. SEE MAIN ENTRY

ancillary relief. SEE MAIN ENTRY

and all et al.

and everyone et al.

and more of the same et al.

and other parties et al.

and other things et al.

and others et al.

and the rest et al.

anecdotal narrative

anemic languid

anent correlative

anesthetic drug, narcotic *(adjective)*, narcotic *(noun)*

anesthetic agent drug

anesthetize drug, obtund

anew de novo. SEE MAIN ENTRY

anfractuous circuitous, sinuous, tortuous *(bending)*

angel spirit

angelic clean

anger bait *(harass)*, harass, incense, irritate, molest *(annoy)*, offend *(insult)*, passion, pique, provoke, resentment, umbrage

angering provocation

angle outlook, phase *(aspect)*, side, slant, standpoint

angle of vision perspective

angle off deviate

angled oblique *(slanted)*

angry resentful, vehement, vindictive

angry disagreement dissension

angry dispute altercation

anguilliform circuitous

anguine circuitous

anguish pain, plaint, remorse, suffer *(sustain loss)*. SEE MAIN ENTRY

anguished aggrieved *(harmed)*, disconsolate

anguishing painful

angustiae predicament, restriction

angustus limited

anility incapacity

anima life *(period of existence)*, spirit

animadversio correction *(punishment)*, notice *(heed)*, stricture

animadversion admonition, bad repute, comment, condemnation *(blame)*, correction *(punishment)*, criticism, diatribe, disapprobation, disapproval, discredit, impeachment, impugnation, obloquy, remark, remonstrance, reprimand, reproach, revilement, stricture. SEE MAIN ENTRY

animadvert blame, comment, complain *(criticize)*, condemn *(blame)*, criticize *(find fault with)*, denounce *(condemn)*, disapprove *(condemn)*, fault, impeach, remark, remonstrate, reprehend, reproach

animadvert on rebuke, reprimand

animadvert upon censure, expostulate, lash *(attack verbally)*

animadvertere notice *(observe)*, observe *(watch)*

animal SEE MAIN ENTRY

animalism bestiality

animam edere expire

animans animal

animate conscious *(awake)*, exhort, generate, incite, inspire, live *(conscious)*, motivate, prompt, provoke, spirit, stimulate

animated alert *(agile)*, born *(alive)*, fervent, live *(conscious)*, ready *(willing)*, volatile

animating impulsive *(impelling)*, moving *(evoking emotion)*

animation birth *(beginning)*, instigation, life *(vitality)*, spirit

animator catalyst, stimulus

animi sane

animi motus emotion, impression

animosity alienation *(estrangement)*, belligerency, conflict, contempt *(disdain)*, disaccord, discord, feud, hatred, ill will, incompatibility *(difference)*, malice, odium, rancor, resentment, spite, strife, umbrage

animum attendere concentrate *(pay attention)*

animum frangere discourage

animus character *(personal quality)*

animus design *(intent)*, feud

animus frame *(mood)*

animus hatred, ill will, malice, odium, resentment, spite

animus will *(desire)*. SEE MAIN ENTRY

animus ingratus ingratitude

animus submissus resignation *(passive acceptance)*

annal record

annals calendar *(record of yearly periods)*, documentation

annex accrue *(increase)*, acquire *(secure)*, addendum, addition, adopt, affix, append, appropriate, appurtenance, assume *(seize)*, attach *(join)*, attach *(seize)*, attachment *(thing affixed)*, cement, codicil, combine *(join together)*, compound, confiscate, conjoin, connect *(join together)*, contact *(touch)*, distrain, enlarge, impropriate, increase, join *(bring together)*, juxtapose, occupy *(take possession)*, offshoot, organ, preempt, seize *(confiscate)*, sequester *(seize property)*. SEE MAIN ENTRY

annex for public use eminent domain

annexation accretion, addendum, addition, appendix *(accession)*, appropriation *(taking)*, appurtenance, assumption *(seizure)*, attachment *(act of affixing)*, attachment *(seizure)*, boom *(increase)*, coalescence, codicil, distraint, distress *(seizure)*, garnishment, sequestration

annexe addendum, appurtenance

annexed accrued, appurtenant, attached *(seized)*, provincial

annexing accession *(annexation)*, coalescence

annexion attachment *(act of affixing)*

annihilate abolish, annul, cancel, consume, destroy *(efface)*, eliminate *(eradicate)*, eradicate, extinguish, extirpate, negate, obliterate, overturn, remove *(eliminate)*, slay, stifle, subvert. SEE MAIN ENTRY

annihilated lifeless *(dead)*, lost *(taken away)*

annihilating deadly, destructive

annihilation abolition, assassination, demise *(death)*, destruction, dissolution *(termination)*, homicide, killing, subversion

annihilative dire, disastrous, fatal, lethal

annotate comment, describe, edit, elucidate, explain, interpret, note *(record)*

annotated detailed

annotated text hornbook

annotation caption, comment, explanation, memorandum, notation, note *(brief comment)*, observation

annotative demonstrative *(illustrative)*, interpretive

announce allege, annunciate, apprise, assert, bare, circulate, communicate, convey *(communicate)*, declare, disabuse, disclose, disseminate, enunciate, herald, inform *(betray)*, inform *(notify)*, issue *(publish)*, mention, notify, observe *(remark)*, pass *(determine)*, portend, posit, proclaim, profess *(avow)*, promulgate, pronounce *(speak)*, protest, publish, relate *(tell)*, report *(disclose)*, reveal, signify *(inform)*, speak, utter. SEE MAIN ENTRY

announce a conclusion find *(determine)*

announce authoritatively pronounce *(pass judgment)*, pronounce *(speak)*

announce in advance anticipate *(prognosticate)*, predict, presage

announce officially pronounce *(speak)*

announce one's presence report *(present oneself)*

announce publicly post

announced alleged, oral, public *(known)*

announcement assertion, averment, caveat, charter *(declaration of rights)*, common knowledge, communication *(statement)*, declaration, declaratory judgment, dictum, disclosure *(act of disclosing)*, disclosure *(something disclosed)*, issuance, judgment *(formal court decree)*, notification, proclamation, profession (declaration), pronouncement, prospectus, publication (disclosure), publicity, statement

announcer harbinger, informant, informer (a person who provides information), precursor

annoy aggravate (annoy), badger, bait (harass), discommode, discompose, disconcert, disrupt, distress, disturb, embarrass, harass, harrow, harry (harass), hinder, inconvenience, irritate, mistreat, obsess, offend (insult), persecute, perturb, pique, plague, press (goad), provoke. SEE MAIN ENTRY

annoy excessively badger

annoyance dissatisfaction, disturbance, grievance, hindrance, mischief, molestation, nuisance, provocation, trouble, umbrage

annoyed petulant

annoying irksome, loathsome, objectionable, obnoxious, odious, offensive (offending), provocative, undesirable, vexatious

annua pension

annua pecunia annuity

annual allowance annuity, pension

annual commitment premium (insurance payment)

annual encumbrance premium (insurance payment)

annual fee premium (insurance payment)

annual installment premium (insurance payment)

annual liability premium (insurance payment)

annual obligation premium (insurance payment)

annual payment premium (insurance payment)

annual rate of insurance premium (insurance payment)

annual remittance premium (insurance payment)

annually per annum

annuciative declaratory

annuity allotment, pension, perquisite. SEE MAIN ENTRY

annul abate (extinguish), abolish, abrogate (rescind), adeem, avoid (cancel), cancel, cease, contradict, counteract, destroy (void), disable, discharge (release from obligation), disclaim, discontinue (abandon), disinherit, disown (deny the validity), divorce, eradicate, expunge, extinguish, extirpate, frustrate, impede, invalidate, kill (defeat), negate, neutralize, nullify, obliterate, overreach, override, overrule, quash, recall (call back), recant, renege, repeal, rescind, revoke, supersede, terminate, vacate (void), vitiate. SEE MAIN ENTRY

annul a marriage divorce

annulled defunct, lifeless (dead), null (invalid), null and void

annulling avoidance (cancellation), cancellation

annulment abatement (extinguishment), abolition, ademption, avoidance (cancellation), cancellation, countermand, defeasance, disclaimer, dismissal (termination of a proceeding), dissolution (termination), invalidity, mistrial, negation, repudiation, rescision, retraction, reversal, revocation. SEE MAIN ENTRY

annulment of debt discharge (payment)

annulment of marriage divorce

annum SEE MAIN ENTRY

annunciate allege, assert, convey (communicate), disseminate, enunciate, inform

(notify), mention, notify, proclaim, promulgate, report (disclose), speak. SEE MAIN ENTRY

annunciation common knowledge, communication (statement), declaration, notification, proclamation, pronouncement

annunciator harbinger, informant, informer (a person who provides information)

annunciatory declaratory

annus annum

anodyne beneficial, drug, medicinal, narcotic (adjective), narcotic (noun), remedial

anodynous narcotic

anoint drug

anointed sacrosanct

anomalistic anomalous, irregular (not usual), peculiar (curious)

anomalistical peculiar (curious)

anomalous atypical, disordered, eccentric, irregular (not usual), noteworthy, novel, peculiar (curious), prodigious (amazing), unaccustomed, uncommon, unique, unorthodox, unprecedented, unusual. SEE MAIN ENTRY

anomalousness deviation, nonconformity

anomaly deviation, discrepancy, irregularity, nonconformity, quirk (idiosyncrasy), variance (exemption). SEE MAIN ENTRY

anon instantly

anonymous unspecified. SEE MAIN ENTRY

another additional

another addressee cotenant

another denizen cotenant

another dweller cotenant

another inhabitant cotenant

another inhabiter cotenant

another leaseholder cotenant

another lessee cotenant

another lodger cotenant

another occupant cotenant

another occupier cotenant

another paying guest cotenant

another possessor cotenant

another renter cotenant

another resident cotenant

another residentiary cotenant

another time anew, de novo

answer acknowledge (respond), acknowledgment (acceptance), appear (attend court proceedings), appearance (coming into court), controvert, converse, counterargument, countercharge, disclosure (something disclosed), find (discover), fulfill, key (solution), outcome, panacea, plea, pleading, reaction (response), rebut, rejoinder, reply (noun), reply (verb), report (present oneself), respond, response, retort, return (respond), solve, verdict. SEE MAIN ENTRY

answer a purpose function

answer a summons report (present oneself)

answer back contradict, countercharge, retaliate, retort, return (respond)

answer conclusively controvert

answer for assure (insure), cosign, displace (replace), guarantee, indemnify, justify, sponsor, undertake. SEE MAIN ENTRY

answer the purpose correspond (be equivalent), satisfy (fulfill)

answer to obey

answerability duty (obligation), fault (responsibility), liability, responsibility (accountability)

answerable accountable (responsible), actionable, ascertainable, blameworthy, bound, consonant, liable, subject (exposed)

answerer respondent

answering contrary, responsive

antagonism alienation (estrangement), argument (contention), bad repute, belligerency, collision (dispute), conflict, contention (opposition), contest (dispute), contradistinction, contraposition, contravention, controversy (argument), disaccord, discord, feud, hatred, ill will, impugnation, incompatibility (difference), malice, rancor, resentment, resistance, spite

antagonist adversary, aggressor, assailant, contender, contestant, disputant, foe, rival

antagonistic adverse (hostile), antipathetic (oppositional), averse, contradictory, different, discordant, disinclined, dissident, hostile, inimical, litigious, malevolent, malicious, negative, offensive (taking the initiative), opposite, pugnacious, recusant, renitent, repugnant (incompatible), spiteful, unfavorable, virulent

antagonistic to contrary

antagonistical adverse (hostile)

antagonize affront, alienate (estrange), collide (clash), counter, counteract, disaffect, disoblige, incense, provoke. SEE MAIN ENTRY

antagonized irreconcilable

antagonizing obnoxious

ante bet, parlay (bet), stake (award)

ante nuptial agreement SEE MAIN ENTRY

ante up bet

antecede precede. SEE MAIN ENTRY

antecedence precedence, priority

antecedens antecedent, last (preceding)

antecedent aforesaid, ascendant, before mentioned, derivation, forerunner, former, last (preceding), original (initial), precursor, precursory, predecessor, preexisting, preliminary, previous, primogenitor, prior, progenitor, sine qua non. SEE MAIN ENTRY

antecedents family (common ancestry), lineage, parentage

antecedere precede

antecellere surpass

antecessor forerunner, predecessor, progenitor

antechamber chamber (compartment)

antecursor harbinger

antedate antecede, precede. SEE MAIN ENTRY

antedeluvian antique

antediluvian obsolete, outdated, outmoded

antegredi precede

anteire precede

anteponere prefer

anterior aforesaid, antecedent, before mentioned, last (preceding), preexisting, preliminary, previous, prior

anteroom chamber (compartment), entrance

antetype model, pattern

antevertere anticipate (expect), forestall

anthologize compile

anthology compilation, digest, selection (collection)

antibiotic drug

anticipatable foreseeable

anticipate forestall, precede, preconceive, predict, presage, presume. SEE MAIN ENTRY

anticipate danger fear

anticipate injury fear

anticipate needs provide (arrange for)

anticipated foreseeable, forseen, forthcoming, future, immediate (imminent), pending (imminent), possible, potential, presumptive, prospective

anticipated loan advance (allowance)

anticipating provident (showing foresight)

anticipation advancement (loan), expectation, forethought, likelihood, possibility, precaution, preconception, preparation, presumption, probability, prospect (*outlook*). SEE MAIN ENTRY

anticipation of adversity apprehension (*fear*)

anticipative sanguine

anticipatory premature, preparatory

antidotal medicinal, preventive, remedial

antidote cure, remedy (*that which corrects*)

antifebrile medicinal

antilogy contrary, inconsistency, paradox

antimony antipode

antinomy inconsistency, opposition, paradox

antipathetic averse, bitter (*reproachful*), contrary, disinclined, hostile, inimical, malevolent, negative, objectionable, obnoxious, offensive (*offending*), renitent, spiteful. SEE MAIN ENTRY

antipathetical discordant, disinclined, inimical, malevolent, negative, renitent

antipathy alienation (*estrangement*), antipode, conflict, contradiction, deviation, difference, hatred, ill will, incompatibility (*difference*), malice, odium, phobia, rancor, reluctance. SEE MAIN ENTRY

antiphon response

antipodal adverse (*opposite*), hostile, inverse, opposite

antipode antithesis, contra, contrary. SEE MAIN ENTRY

antipodean adverse (*opposite*), antipathetic (*oppositional*), inverse, opposite

antipodes antipode

antipoison cure

antipole antipode

antipollution project ecology

antiquate superannuate

antiquated obsolete, old, outdated, outmoded. SEE MAIN ENTRY

antique obsolete, old, outdated, outmoded. SEE MAIN ENTRY

antiseptic preventive

antisepticize decontaminate

antithesis antipode, contra, contradiction, contradistinction, contraposition, contrary, deviation, difference, distinction (*difference*), incompatibility (*inconsistency*). SEE MAIN ENTRY

antithetic antipathetic (*oppositional*), contrary, different, hostile, opposite

antithetical adverse (*opposite*), antipathetic (*oppositional*), contradictory, contrary, discordant, hostile, inverse, opposite

antitheticalness difference

antitoxin cure

antitrust act SEE MAIN ENTRY

antonomasia call (*title*)

antonym contra

antonymous adverse (*opposite*), discordant, hostile

anxietude disturbance, misgiving

anxiety apprehension (*fear*), burden, concern (*interest*), consternation, distress (*anguish*), disturbance, doubt (*indecision*), fear, fright, interest (*concern*), misgiving, nuisance, panic, phobia, pressure, problem, qualm, scruple, stress (*strain*)

anxious eager, ready (*willing*), solicitous

anxious concern consternation, misgiving

anxiousness consternation, distress (*anguish*), disturbance, misgiving, pressure

anxius solicitous

any individual whoever

any person whoever

anybody whoever

anyhow regardless

anyone whoever

anyway regardless

anywise regardless

apart alone (*solitary*), bipartite, disconnected, discrete, extrinsic, insular, irrelative, only, partial (*part*), private (*secluded*), remote (*secluded*), separate. SEE MAIN ENTRY

apartheid exclusion, segregation (*isolation by races*)

apartment chamber (*compartment*), home (*domicile*), lodging. SEE MAIN ENTRY

apartness exception (*exclusion*)

apathetic casual, cursory, inactive, indolent, inexpressive, insensible, insusceptible (*uncaring*), languid, lax, lifeless (*dull*), nonchalant, otiose, passive, perfunctory, phlegmatic, stagnant, stoical, torpid, truant. SEE MAIN ENTRY

apathetical languid

apathy disinterest (*lack of interest*), indifference, inertia, languor, laxity, sloth

ape copy, impersonate, mock (*imitate*), pose (*impersonate*)

aperçu abridgment (*condensation*)

aperire betray (*disclose*), disclose, manifest, reopen, unveil

aperte fairly (*clearly*)

aperture loophole, outlet, portal, rift (*gap*), split

apertus evident, explicit, ingenuous, manifest, obvious, open (*in sight*), open (*persuasible*), overt, patent, straightforward, unambiguous

apertus sincerus candid

apery caricature, parody

apex ceiling, culmination, pinnacle

aphonic speechless

aphorism maxim, phrase

aphoristic axiomatic, brief, compact (*pithy*), proverbial, sententious

aphoristic expression maxim

aphoristical compact (*pithy*)

apical cardinal (*basic*)

apiece respectively

aplomb composure, confidence (*faith*)

aplomb indestructibility

aplomb surety (*certainty*). SEE MAIN ENTRY

apocha receipt (*proof of receiving*)

apocryphal assumed (*feigned*), disputable, fictitious, ill-founded, spurious, untrue

apodictic axiomatic, categorical, incontrovertible

apodosis denouement

apogee ceiling, culmination, pinnacle

apograph transcript

apologetic contrite, palliative (*excusing*), penitent, remorseful, repentant

apologist advocate (*counselor*), advocate (*espouser*), proponent. SEE MAIN ENTRY

apologize regret, repent

apology expiation

apostasize abandon (*relinquish*), defect, discontinue (*abandon*)

apostasy abandonment (*desertion*), bad faith, blasphemy, desertion, disloyalty, dissent (*difference of opinion*), infidelity, nonconformity, revolt, sedition

apostate heretic, recreant, recusant

apostatic recreant

apostatical recreant

apostatize bear false witness, quit (*discontinue*), secede, tergiversate

apostatizing disobedient, faithless, false (*disloyal*)

apostil clarification

apostle disciple, partisan

apotheca depository

apothegm phrase

apothegmatic compact (*pithy*), sententious

apothegmatical compact (*pithy*)

apotheosis exemplar

appall discompose, disconcert, harrow, repel (*disgust*)

appalling deplorable, dire, disastrous, egregious, formidable, loathsome, lurid, repulsive

appalling SEE MAIN ENTRY

appanage addendum, adjunct, appurtenance, codicil, dower, grant, inheritance

apparatus appliance, device (*mechanism*), equipment, expedient, facility (*instrumentality*), instrument (*tool*), paraphernalia (*apparatus*), tool

apparatus belli ammunition

apparent axiomatic, blatant (*conspicuous*), candid, circumstantial, coherent (*clear*), colorable (*plausible*), conclusive (*determinative*), conspicuous, constructive (*inferential*), demonstrable, discernible, distinct (*clear*), elementary, evident, flagrant, lucid, manifest, naked (*perceptible*), obvious, open (*in sight*), ostensible, overt, palpable, patent, pellucid, perceivable, perceptible, plausible, presumptive, probable, prominent, public (*known*), specious, unmistakable, visible (*noticeable*). SEE MAIN ENTRY

apparent character color (*complexion*), complexion

apparent right color (*deceptive appearance*)

apparent state complexion

apparentation affiliation (*bloodline*)

apparently prima facie (*self-evident*), quasi

apparently right colorable (*plausible*)

apparere appear (*materialize*)

apparition phantom, phenomenon (*manifestation*), specter, spirit, vision (*dream*)

appeal address (*petition*), amenity, call (*appeal to*), challenge, coax, entreaty, habeas corpus, importune, incentive, invitation, motivate, press (*beseech*), request (*noun*), request (*verb*), rhetoric (*skilled speech*). SEE MAIN ENTRY

appeal against expostulate

appeal for petition, solicit

appeal to bait (*lure*), pray, propitiate, solicit, urge

appeal to a higher court certiorari

appeal to arms fight (*battle*), fight (*battle*)

appeal to the law litigate, sue

appealable litigable

appealer appellant, special interest

appealing attractive, precatory, sapid

appealing conclusively cogent

appealing forcibly cogent

appealing to reason disputable

appear bare, comport (*behave*), demean (*deport oneself*), emerge, report (*present oneself*). SEE MAIN ENTRY

appear for represent (*substitute*)

appear for duty report (*present oneself*)

appearance aspect, color (*deceptive appearance*), complexion, condition (*state*), configuration (*form*), demeanor, deportment, expression (*manifestation*), face value (*first blush*), first appearance, manifestation, manner (*behavior*), phantom, phenomenon (*manifestation*), presence (*poise*), pretense (*pretext*), semblance, specter, state (*condition*), style, vision (*dream*). SEE MAIN ENTRY

appearance of truth   credibility, probability
appearing   apparent *(presumptive)*, colorable *(specious)*, evident, ostensible, perceivable, specious
appearing at intervals   sporadic
appeasable   nonmilitant, placable
appease   allay, assuage, disarm *(set at ease)*, mitigate, moderate *(temper)*, mollify, pacify, palliate *(abate)*, placate, propitiate, reconcile, redress, satisfy *(fulfill)*, soothe
appeased   agreed *(harmonized)*
appeasement   conciliation, mollification, reconciliation, satisfaction *(fulfilment)*. SEE MAIN ENTRY
appeaser   go-between
appelare   appeal
appelation   cognomen
appellant   claimant, contender, contestant, litigant, party *(litigant)*, respondent, suitor. SEE MAIN ENTRY
appellare   summon
appellate court   SEE MAIN ENTRY
appellate review   appeal
appellatio   appeal
appellation   call *(title)*, denomination, designation *(naming)*, identification, term *(expression)*, title *(designation)*. SEE MAIN ENTRY
appellative   call *(title)*, cognomen, term *(expression)*
appellator   appellant
appellee   litigant, party *(litigant)*
append   affix, annex *(add)*, attach *(join)*, combine *(join together)*, compound, connect *(join together)*, join *(bring together)*. SEE MAIN ENTRY
appendage   accession *(annexation)*, addendum, adjoiner, adjunct, allonge, appendix *(accession)*, appendix *(supplement)*, appurtenance, attachment *(thing affixed)*, codicil, organ, rider
appendant   appurtenance, attached *(annexed)*, rider
appended   additional, appurtenant, attached *(annexed)*
appendix   addendum, allonge, appurtenance, attachment *(thing affixed)*, codicil, insertion, rider. SEE MAIN ENTRY
apperceive   note *(notice)*, perceive, understand
apperception   appreciation *(perception)*, cognition, insight, judgment *(discernment)*, knowledge *(awareness)*, perception, realization, reason *(sound judgment)*, recognition, sagacity, sense *(feeling)*, understanding *(comprehension)*. SEE MAIN ENTRY
apperceptive   cognizant, conscious *(aware)*, judicious, knowing, omniscient, perceptive, perspicacious, sensitive *(discerning)*
appercipient   sensitive *(discerning)*
appertain   correspond *(be equivalent)*, pertain, refer *(direct attention)*. SEE MAIN ENTRY
appertain to   concern *(involve)*, connect *(relate)*, relate *(establish a connection)*
appertaining   akin *(germane)*, applicable, appurtenant, cognate, collateral *(accompanying)*, pertinent
appertaining to   incident
appetence   predilection, predisposition, proclivity
appetency   desire, greed, predilection, predisposition, proclivity
appetent   eager
appetere   assault
appetite   desire, penchant, predilection, predisposition

appetitio   desire
appetitus   instinct
appetizing   palatable, sapid, savory
applaud   honor, recommend
applauded   famous, illustrious, renowned
applause   mention *(tribute)*
appliable   applicable
appliance   device *(mechanism)*, expedient, facility *(instrumentality)*, instrument *(tool)*. SEE MAIN ENTRY
appliances   paraphernalia *(apparatus)*
applicability   admissibility, aptitude, connection *(relation)*, propriety *(appropriateness)*, qualification *(fitness)*, relation *(connection)*, relevance, utility *(usefulness)*, utilization. SEE MAIN ENTRY
applicable   admissible, akin *(germane)*, apposite, appropriate, congruous, constructive *(creative)*, convenient, correlative, felicitous, fit, functional, germane, operative, pertinent, practical, related, relative *(relevant)*, relevant, suitable. SEE MAIN ENTRY
applicable to a class   generic
applicant   candidate, claimant, contender, petitioner, prospect *(prospective patron)*, suitor. SEE MAIN ENTRY
application   arrogation, assignation, call *(appeal)*, call *(title)*, connection *(relation)*, connotation, diligence *(care)*, diligence *(perseverance)*, endeavor, industry *(activity)*, infliction, interest *(concern)*, means *(opportunity)*, motion, obsession, petition, prayer, purpose, regard *(attention)*, relevance, request, requisition, resolution *(decision)*, usage, use, work *(effort)*. SEE MAIN ENTRY
application for a ruling   motion
application for an order   motion
application for discharge   habeas corpus
application for liberty   habeas corpus
application for proposed relief   motion
application for relief   prayer
application for retrial   appeal, certiorari
application for review by a higher tribunal   appeal
application of force   compulsion *(coercion)*
applied   functional
applied energy   effort
applied from without   extrinsic
applied logic   dialectic
apply   ascribe, concern *(involve)*, devote, employ *(make use of)*, exercise *(use)*, exert, expend *(consume)*, exploit *(make use of)*, impute, inflict, manipulate *(utilize skillfully)*, move *(judicially request)*, refer *(direct attention)*, relate *(establish a connection)*, resort, solicit, spend. SEE MAIN ENTRY
apply a closure   complete
apply a remedy   cure, drug, help
apply dishonestly   convert *(misappropriate)*
apply for   desire, petition, request, sue
apply for a loan   borrow
apply for a reexamination of a case   appeal
apply for a retrial   appeal
apply for a review of a case to a higher tribunal   appeal
apply one's self to   practice *(train by repetition)*
apply oneself   labor, persevere, specialize
apply oneself to   address *(direct attention to)*, commit *(perpetrate)*, endeavor, occupy *(engage)*, undertake
apply pressure   coerce, constrain *(compel)*, foist, force *(coerce)*
apply reason   deduce, deduct *(conclude by reasoning)*

apply the attention to   occupy *(engage)*
apply the closure   close *(terminate)*
apply the mind   concentrate *(pay attention)*, ponder, study
apply the mind to   occupy *(engage)*
apply to   appertain, call *(appeal to)*, importune, petition, pray
apply to one's own uses   impropriate, plagiarize
applying to   apposite, germane
appoint   allocate, allot, assign *(designate)*, authorize, bestow, charge *(empower)*, choose, clothe, delegate, designate, detail *(assign)*, dispense, employ *(engage services)*, empower, engage *(hire)*, entrust, furnish, hire, induct, instate, invest *(vest)*, nominate, parcel, provide *(arrange for)*, select. SEE MAIN ENTRY
appoint as agent   delegate
appoint as representative   delegate
appoint beforehand   preordain
appoint by act   enact
appoint by vote   elect *(select by a vote)*
appoint in advance   preordain
appoint the time of   date
appointed   select
appointed counsel   SEE MAIN ENTRY
appointed group   commission *(agency)*, committee
appointee   agent, deputy, licensee, nominee *(delegate)*, proctor, procurator, trustee
appointer   licensor
appointing   deputation *(selection of delegates)*
appointive   adoptive, elective *(voluntary)*
appointment   agency *(legal relationship)*, allotment, assignment *(designation)*, charge *(responsibility)*, delegation *(assignment)*, deputation *(selection of delegates)*, designation *(naming)*, dispensation *(act of dispensing)*, election *(choice)*, employment, equipment, mission, nomination, office, position *(business status)*, post, province, pursuit *(occupation)*, rendezvous, selection *(choice)*. SEE MAIN ENTRY
appointment by vote   election *(selection by vote)*
appointments   paraphernalia *(personal belongings)*, property *(possessions)*
apportion   allocate, allot, arrange *(methodize)*, assign *(allot)*, bestow, classify, demarcate, devote, dichotomize, disburse *(distribute)*, dispense, disperse *(disseminate)*, divide *(distribute)*, dole, endue, expend *(disburse)*, fund, furnish, leave *(give)*, marshal, mete, parcel, partition, prorate, sort, split, subdivide. SEE MAIN ENTRY
apportion anew   reapportion
apportion by measure   mete
apportion pro rata   prorate
apportionable   divisible, severable
apportioned   pro rata. SEE MAIN ENTRY
apportioned lot   share *(interest)*
apportioning   disbursement *(act of disbursing)*
apportionment   allotment, appropriation *(allotment)*, arbitration, assignment *(allotment)*, classification, decentralization, disbursement *(act of disbursing)*, dispensation *(act of dispensing)*, division *(act of dividing)*, equity *(share of ownership)*, order *(arrangement)*, proportion, quantity, quota, ration. SEE MAIN ENTRY
appose   adjoin, border *(bound)*, contrast, juxtapose
apposite   appropriate, congruous, correlative, felicitous, fit, germane, harmonious,

pertinent, proper, related, relative *(relevant)*, relevant, seasonable, suitable. SEE MAIN ENTRY

appositeness admissibility, affiliation *(connectedness)*, collation, qualification *(fitness)*, relation *(connection)*, relationship *(connection)*, relevance

apposition affiliation *(connectedness)*, propinquity *(proximity)*, relation *(connection)*. SEE MAIN ENTRY

appositional relative *(relevant)*

appraisable appreciable, determinable *(ascertainable)*

appraisal account *(evaluation)*, appreciation *(perception)*, arbitration, assessment *(estimation)*, choice *(decision)*, computation, concept, cost *(price)*, determination, discretion *(power of choice)*, discrimination *(differentiation)*, estimate *(approximate cost)*, estimation *(calculation)*, expense *(cost)*, generalization, idea, inspection, judgment *(discernment)*, measurement, par *(face amount)*, perception, price, proposal *(report)*, rating, review *(critical evaluation)*, value, worth. SEE MAIN ENTRY

appraise calculate, charge *(assess)*, consider, criticize *(evaluate)*, diagnose, estimate, evaluate, excise *(levy a tax)*, gauge, judge, measure, opine, ponder, rate, survey *(examine)*. SEE MAIN ENTRY

appraised ad valorem

appraisement ad valorem, appraisal, assessment *(estimation)*, determination, estimate *(approximate cost)*, estimation *(calculation)*, expense *(cost)*, measurement, par *(face amount)*, price, worth

appraiser juror

appraising discriminating *(judicious)*

appraisment appreciation *(perception)*

appreciable corporeal, determinable *(ascertainable)*, perceivable, ponderable, substantive. SEE MAIN ENTRY

appreciate accrue *(increase)*, apprehend *(perceive)*, comprehend *(understand)*, conceive *(comprehend)*, digest *(comprehend)*, discern *(detect with the senses)*, enhance, gauge, increase, note *(notice)*, notice *(observe)*, perceive, pierce *(discern)*, realize *(understand)*, recognize *(acknowledge)*, regard *(hold in esteem)*, relish, understand. SEE MAIN ENTRY

appreciation accession *(enlargement)*, augmentation, boom *(increase)*, cognition, comprehension, computation, concept, determination, discretion *(quality of being discreet)*, discrimination *(differentiation)*, estimation *(esteem)*, honor *(outward respect)*, knowledge *(awareness)*, mention *(tribute)*, perception, realization, recognition, regard *(esteem)*, respect, scienter, sensibility. SEE MAIN ENTRY

appreciation of differences diagnosis

appreciative conscious *(aware)*

appreciativeness discretion *(quality of being discreet)*, knowledge *(awareness)*

apprehend appreciate *(comprehend)*, capture, comprehend *(understand)*, conceive *(comprehend)*, construe *(comprehend)*, detain *(hold in custody)*, discern *(detect with the senses)*, ensnare, expect *(consider probable)*, fear, find *(discover)*, jail, mistrust, perceive, pierce *(discern)*, presume, read, realize *(understand)*, recognize *(perceive)*, surmise, understand. SEE MAIN ENTRY

apprehend clearly discern *(detect with the senses)*

apprehend danger fear

apprehend harm fear

apprehend punishment fear

apprehendere seize *(apprehend)*

apprehending attachment *(seizure)*, conscious *(aware)*, knowing

apprehensibility coherence

apprehensible cognizable, coherent *(clear)*, comprehensible, perceivable, perceptible, scrutable. SEE MAIN ENTRY

apprehension appropriation *(taking)*, arrest, cloud *(suspicion)*, cognition, comprehension, concept, consternation, constraint *(imprisonment)*, detection, dialectic, doubt *(indecision)*, doubt *(suspicion)*, fear, fright, idea, impression, misgiving, notion, perception, phobia, position *(point of view)*, qualm, realization, scienter, scruple, sense *(feeling)*, stress *(strain)*, suspicion *(mistrust)*, trepidation, understanding *(comprehension)*. SEE MAIN ENTRY

apprehension and transfer extradition

apprehension of danger fear

apprehension of harm fear

apprehension of injury fear

apprehension of punishment fear

apprehensive cognizant, leery, perceptive, solicitous, suspicious *(distrustful)*, vigilant. SEE MAIN ENTRY

apprehensiveness apprehension *(fear)*, cloud *(suspicion)*, consternation, doubt *(indecision)*, fear, misgiving, qualm, scruple, stress *(strain)*

apprentice amateur, assistant, coadjutant, disciple, employee, neophyte, novice, probationer *(one being tested)*, protégé. SEE MAIN ENTRY

apprenticed indentured

apprenticeship experience *(background)*, preparation

apprenticeship agreement indenture

apprisal disclosure *(act of disclosing)*

apprise advise, annunciate, caution, communicate, convey *(communicate)*, disabuse, disclose, disseminate, divulge, enlighten, enunciate, herald, impart, inform *(notify)*, mention, notice *(give formal warning)*, notify, relate *(tell)*, report *(disclose)*, reveal, signify *(inform)*, speak. SEE MAIN ENTRY

apprised acquainted, cognizant, conscious *(aware)*, familiar *(informed)*, knowing, literate, sensible

apprised of learned

apprisement determination

appriser informant

apprize assess *(appraise)*, rate

apprized informed *(having information)*

apprizement determination

apprizer affirmant, bystander, deponent

approach access *(right of way)*, accost, address *(direct attention to)*, admittance *(means of approach)*, approximate, avenue *(means of attainment)*, avenue *(route)*, bid, confrontation *(act of setting face to face)*, converge, correspond *(be equivalent)*, course, design *(intent)*, direction *(course)*, entrance, gravitate, impend, inflow, ingress, invitation, maneuver *(tactic)*, manner *(behavior)*, modus operandi, overture, policy *(plan of action)*, portal, practice *(procedure)*, progress, proposition, reach, strategy. SEE MAIN ENTRY

approach closely approximate

approach in amount approximate

approach of danger peril

approach one another converge

approach road causeway

approachability access *(opening)*

approachable available, open *(accessible)*, passable, public *(open)*, vulnerable

approaches SEE MAIN ENTRY

approaching approximate, close *(near)*, forthcoming, future, immediate *(imminent)*, imminent, inevitable, instant, pending *(imminent)*, prospective, proximate

approaching an end determinable *(liable to be terminated)*

approaching death in extremis

approaching the finish determinable *(liable to be terminated)*

approbare approve, countenance, pass *(satisfy requirements)*

approbate approve, concur *(agree)*, countenance, pass *(approve)*, recommend, sanction. SEE MAIN ENTRY

approbatio approval

approbation acceptance, adoption *(acceptance)*, advocacy, approval, assent, consent, estimation *(esteem)*, favor *(sanction)*, honor *(outward respect)*, indorsement, leave *(permission)*, license, mention *(tribute)*, permit, ratification, recommendation, regard *(esteem)*, respect, sanction *(permission)*. SEE MAIN ENTRY

approbative favorable *(expressing approval)*

appropinquare approach

appropriate accroach, acquire *(secure)*, admissible, adopt, allocate, annex *(arrogate)*, applicable, apposite, ascribe, assign *(allot)*, assume *(seize)*, attach *(seize)*, certain *(specific)*, collect *(recover money)*, commensurate, condemn *(seize)*, condign, confiscate, congruous, consonant, convenient, correlative, devote, dispense, distrain, distribute, divide *(distribute)*, dole, due *(regular)*, eligible, fair *(just)*, favorable *(advantageous)*, felicitous, fit, fitting, garnish, germane, hijack, hold up *(rob)*, impound, impress *(procure by force)*, impropriate, loot, mete, monopolize, obtain, occupy *(take possession)*, opportune, parcel, pertinent, pirate *(reproduce without authorization)*, plagiarize, poach, preempt, procure, proper, reclaim, related, relative *(relevant)*, relevant, right *(suitable)*, rightful, seasonable, seize *(confiscate)*, sequester *(seize property)*, several *(separate)*, specific, suitable, viable. SEE MAIN ENTRY

appropriate activity function

appropriate behavior decorum

appropriate criminally peculate

appropriate dishonestly peculate, purloin

appropriate for federal use nationalize

appropriate for government use nationalize

appropriate for residence habitable

appropriate for use preempt

appropriate fraudulently bilk, embezzle, purloin

appropriate illegally peculate, pilfer, rob

appropriate to one's own use defalcate, embezzle

appropriate to public use confiscate

appropriate unlawfully usurp

appropriate wrongfully convert *(misappropriate)*, peculate

appropriated attached *(seized)*

appropriately pro rata

appropriateness admissibility, decorum, expedience, fairness, qualification *(fitness)*, relevance, timeliness

appropriating confiscatory

appropriation acquisition, adverse possession, allotment, arrogation, assignment *(allotment)*, assumption *(seizure)*, budget, condemnation *(seizure)*, consignment, conversion *(misappropriation)*, distraint, distress *(seizure)*, distribution *(apportionment)*, embezzlement, endowment, garnishment, housebreaking, larceny, pillage, plagiarism, preemption, quota, ration, selection *(choice)*, sequestration, taking. SEE MAIN ENTRY

appropriation for a dishonest use misappropriation

appropriation for a wrongful use misappropriation

appropriation of a literary composition plagiarism

approvable admissible, allowable, allowed, laudable, meritorious, permissible

approval acceptance, adoption *(acceptance)*, advantage, advocacy, affirmation, assent, charter *(sanction)*, confirmation, consent, designation *(naming)*, dispensation *(exception)*, estimation *(esteem)*, favor *(partiality)*, favor *(sanction)*, honor *(outward respect)*, indorsement, indulgence, leave *(permission)*, legalization, license, mention *(tribute)*, option *(contractual provision)*, permission, permit, ratification, recognition, recommendation, regard *(esteem)*, respect, sanction *(permission)*, subscription, support *(corroboration)*. SEE MAIN ENTRY

approve accede *(concede)*, accredit, advocate, affirm *(uphold)*, agree *(comply)*, allow *(authorize)*, allow *(endure)*, appoint, assent, authorize, bear *(tolerate)*, coincide *(concur)*, concur *(agree)*, confirm, conform, consent, cosign, countenance, enable, endorse, favor, grant *(concede)*, legalize, legitimate, let *(permit)*, notarize, permit, prefer, reassure, receive *(permit to enter)*, recommend, regard *(hold in esteem)*, sanction, seal *(solemnize)*, settle, sign, subscribe *(sign)*, support *(justify)*, sustain *(confirm)*, uphold, validate, vote. SEE MAIN ENTRY

approve of countenance, permit

approved agreed *(promised)*, allowable, allowed, conventional, eligible, formal, legal, meritorious, official, orthodox, permissible, preferred *(favored)*, unimpeachable. SEE MAIN ENTRY

approving consensual, consenting, ecstatic, favorable *(expressing approval)*, propitious

approximate border *(approach)*, close *(near)*, comparable *(capable of comparison)*, copy, correspond *(be equivalent)*, inaccurate, inexact, similar. SEE MAIN ENTRY

approximate calculation estimate *(approximate cost)*, estimation *(calculation)*

approximate judgment of value estimate *(approximate cost)*, estimation *(calculation)*

approximate value estimate *(approximate cost)*

approximately almost, on or about

approximation estimate *(approximate cost)*, estimation *(calculation)*, parity, resemblance. SEE MAIN ENTRY

approximative inexact

appulsion meeting *(encounter)*

appurtenance additive, appliance, attachment *(thing affixed)*, augmentation, boom *(increase)*, corollary, droit, rider. SEE MAIN ENTRY

appurtenances goods

appurtenant apposite, cognate, germane, pendent, pertinent, related, relative *(relevant)*, relevant. SEE MAIN ENTRY

apriorism prolepsis

apropos akin *(germane)*, apposite, appropriate, felicitous, fit, germane, incident,

pertinent, relative *(relevant)*, relevant, suitable. SEE MAIN ENTRY

apt acute, applicable, apposite, appropriate, artful, consonant, deft, expert, felicitous, fit, germane, harmonious, inclined, opportune, pertinent, possible, practiced, probable, prone, proper, qualified *(competent)*, relative *(relevant)*, relevant, resourceful, right *(suitable)*, subtle *(refined)*, suitable, veteran, viable. SEE MAIN ENTRY

apt to change suddenly capricious

apt to distrust cynical

apt to flee elusive

apt to quarrel fractious

aptare adapt, adjust *(regulate)*

aptitude ability, caliber *(mental capacity)*, chance *(possibility)*, competence *(ability)*, disposition *(inclination)*, faculty *(ability)*, gift *(flair)*, inclination, instinct, intelligence *(intellect)*, performance *(workmanship)*, potential, predisposition, proclivity, propensity, propriety *(appropriateness)*, qualification *(fitness)*, science *(technique)*, skill, temperament, tendency. SEE MAIN ENTRY

aptness ability, admissibility, capacity *(aptitude)*, expedience, inclination, instinct, liability, performance *(workmanship)*, predisposition, proclivity, propensity, propriety *(appropriateness)*, qualification *(fitness)*, quality *(excellence)*, quality *(grade)*, relevance, science *(technique)*, skill, specialty *(special aptitude)*, tendency, timeliness

aptum qualify *(meet standards)*

aptus adequate, appropriate, attached *(annexed)*, capable, fit, proper, suitable

aqua et igni interdicere outlaw

arable fertile

arbiter arbitrator, eyewitness, go-between, intermediary, judge, juror, referee, umpire. SEE MAIN ENTRY

arbiters jury

arbitrage adjudication, arbitration, collective bargaining, intercession

arbitrament adjudication, collective bargaining, conclusion *(determination)*, judgment *(formal court decree)*, negotiation

arbitrari opine

arbitrarily invented fictitious

arbitrary contemptuous, dictatorial, disobedient, haphazard, irresponsible, tyrannous, unpredictable, unwarranted. SEE MAIN ENTRY

arbitrary and capricious SEE MAIN ENTRY

arbitrary power force *(compulsion)*

arbitrate adjudge, adjudicate, decide, intercede, judge, mediate, negotiate, reconcile. SEE MAIN ENTRY

arbitrate terms dicker

arbitrated agreed *(harmonized)*

arbitrater adjuster

arbitration adjudication, collective bargaining, intercession, mediation, negotiation, reconciliation. SEE MAIN ENTRY

arbitrator arbiter, go-between, intermediary, judge, magistrate, referee, umpire. SEE MAIN ENTRY

arbitrators jury

arbitrium arbitration, determination, freedom

arca coffer

arcana secret

arcane clandestine, confidential, esoteric, hidden, latent, mysterious, private *(confidential)*, privy, recondite, secret, stealthy. SEE MAIN ENTRY

arcanum enigma, mystery

arcanus confidential, mysterious, private *(confidential)*, secret

arch jocular, machiavellian, master, paramount, project *(extend beyond)*, sly

archaic antique, obsolete, old, outdated, outmoded. SEE MAIN ENTRY

archaism desuetude, disuse

archaistic obsolete

archetypal primordial

archetype example, exemplar, model, paradigm, pattern, precedent, prototype, sample, standard

architect author *(originator)*, contractor. SEE MAIN ENTRY

architectural monument edifice

architecture building *(business of assembling)*

architectus architect

archive dossier, file, record, register

archives depository

archivist caretaker *(one caring for property)*, clerk

ardency ardor, passion

ardens fervent, intense

ardent eager, fanatical, fervent, industrious, intense, intensive, ready *(willing)*, sedulous, serious *(devoted)*, true *(loyal)*, vehement, zealous. SEE MAIN ENTRY

ardent admirer addict

ardent champion of change malcontent

ardent impulse desire

ardor adhesion *(loyalty)*, affection

ardor ardor

ardor compulsion *(obsession)*, desire, diligence *(perseverance)*, emotion, industry *(activity)*, life *(vitality)*, passion, penchant, predisposition, spirit. SEE MAIN ENTRY

arduous difficult, formidable, onerous, operose, oppressive, painful. SEE MAIN ENTRY

arduousness effort

area area *(province)*

area bailiwick, caliber *(measurement)*, capacity *(sphere)*, circuit, department, dimension, district, division *(administra-tive unit)*, extent, locality, location, parcel, part *(place)*, province, purview, range, realm, region, scope, section *(vicinity)*, space, territory, vicinity, zone. SEE MAIN ENTRY

area of disagreement contention *(argument)*

area of education discipline *(field of study)*

area of learning discipline *(field of study)*

arena area *(province)*, bailiwick, capacity *(sphere)*, enclosure, focus, purview, range, scene, sphere

argot jargon *(technical language)*, phraseology

arguable controversial, debatable, disputable, doubtful, dubious, forensic, justiciable, litigable, moot, plausible, uncertain *(questionable)*. SEE MAIN ENTRY

argue bear *(adduce)*, bespeak, bicker, challenge, collide *(clash)*, conflict, contend *(dispute)*, contend *(maintain)*, contest, contradict, controvert, cross *(disagree with)*, debate, differ *(vary)*, disaccord, disagree, dispute *(debate)*, dissent *(differ in opinion)*, expostulate, haggle, insist, posit, propound, reason *(persuade)*, rebut. SEE MAIN ENTRY

argue a case dispute *(debate)*

argue a point dispute *(debate)*

argue against confront *(oppose)*, discourage, dispute *(contest)*, dissuade, oppose, rebut, remonstrate

argue at the bar plead *(argue a case)*

argue for adhere *(maintain loyalty)*, advocate, assert, defend, espouse, justify

629

argue for and against   discuss
argue in opposition   dispute *(debate)*
argue into   convince, prevail *(persuade)*
argue price   dicker
argue pros and cons   debate
argue the case   controvert, discuss
argue the point   controvert, discuss, plead *(argue a case)*
argue to no purpose   bicker
argue vehemently   dispute *(contest)*
argued   alleged
arguendo   SEE MAIN ENTRY
arguer   contender
arguer in defense   apologist
arguere   accuse, charge *(accuse)*
argufy   dispute *(debate)*
arguing   disputable, dissenting, hostile, litigious
argument   altercation, brief, conflict, confrontation *(altercation)*, contest *(dispute)*, contravention, disaccord, disagreement, discourse, disparity, dispute, dissent *(difference of opinion)*, dissidence, persuasion, pleading, point *(item)*, reason *(basis)*, remonstrance, rift *(disagreement)*, thesis. SEE MAIN ENTRY
argument at the bar   argument *(pleading)*
argumental   litigious, polemic
argumentari   argue
argumentation   conflict, contention *(argument)*, controversy *(argument)*, dialectic, disaccord, disagreement, discord, discourse, dissension, ratiocination. SEE MAIN ENTRY
argumentative   contentious, discursive *(analytical)*, disputable, dissenting, forensic, hostile, insistent, litigable, litigious, negative, petulant, polemic, pugnacious, remonstrative. SEE MAIN ENTRY
argumentative person   disputant
arguments at the bar   plea
argumentum   context, proof, subject *(topic)*
argus   guardian
argute   perspicacious
arguteness   caliber *(mental capacity)*, sagacity
arid   barren, lifeless *(dull)*, otiose, pedestrian, unproductive
arise   appear *(materialize)*, commence, disobey, emerge, ensue, occur *(happen)*, proceed *(go forward)*, rebel, redound, result, stem *(originate)*, succeed *(follow)*, supervene. SEE MAIN ENTRY
arise from   develop, emanate, evolve
aristocracy   elite, society
ark   refuge
arm   affiliate, clothe, cudgel, empower, enable, endue, furnish, organ, protect
arm of the law   judiciary, marshal, peace officer, police, posse
arma homini adimere   disarm *(divest of arms)*
armament   ammunition, bomb, gun
armaments   weapons
armature   ammunition, panoply
armatus   armed
armed   defensible, ready *(prepared)*, safe. SEE MAIN ENTRY
armed action   fight *(battle)*
armed attack   foray
armed band   posse
armed enemy   foe
armiger   esquire
armipotent   powerful
armistice   cessation *(interlude)*, halt, interruption, lull, pause, peace, treaty
armor   panoply, protect, protection, safeguard

armored   immune, protective, safe, secure *(free from danger)*
armored protection   panoply
armorum   weapons
arms   ammunition, gun, weapons
army   band
arouse   abet, agitate *(activate)*, alert, bait *(harass)*, discommode, disturb, elicit, evoke, exacerbate, exhort, foment, harass, impel, impress *(affect deeply)*, incense, incite, influence, inspire, interest, lobby, molest *(annoy)*, originate, perturb, prompt, provoke, spirit, stimulate
arouse desire   motivate
arouse ire   incense
arouse notice   interest
arouse one's enthusiasm   interest
arouse resentment   incense, pique
arouse to action   incite
arouser   cannabis, stimulus
arousing   moving *(evoking emotion)*, persuasive, provocative
arousing aversion   repulsive
arraign   blame, charge *(accuse)*, complain *(charge)*, denounce *(inform against)*, prosecute *(charge)*. SEE MAIN ENTRY
arraigned   accused *(charged)*
arraignment   charge *(accusation)*, impeachment, presentment. SEE MAIN ENTRY
arrange   accommodate, adapt, adjust *(resolve)*, allocate, arbitrate *(adjudge)*, arbitrate *(conciliate)*, classify, codify, compile, compose, contrive, coordinate, devise *(invent)*, disentangle, dispose *(incline)*, distribute, edit, fix *(settle)*, form, formulate, frame *(formulate)*, frame *(prearrange)*, maneuver, marshal, orchestrate, pigeonhole, plan, plot, program, regulate *(adjust)*, scheme, settle, site, sort, stipulate, tabulate. SEE MAIN ENTRY
arrange a settlement   satisfy *(discharge)*
arrange beforehand   prearrange
arrange by mutual concession   compromise *(settle by mutual agreement)*
arrange differences   mediate
arrange for   negotiate
arrange for the services of   engage *(hire)*
arrange for the use of   engage *(hire)*
arrange in advance   prearrange
arrange in succession   continue *(prolong)*
arrange itself   crystallize
arrange materials for publication   compile
arrange matters   settle
arrange matters in dispute   settle
arrange methodically   file *(arrange)*
arrange side by side   juxtapose
arrange terms   dicker
arranged   agreed *(harmonized)*, agreed *(promised)*, consonant, contractual, fixed *(settled)*, harmonious, prospective, ready *(prepared)*, res judicata, stated, systematic. SEE MAIN ENTRY
arranged within a small space   compact *(dense)*
arrangement   accommodation *(adjustment)*, accord, accordance *(compact)*, adjustment, agreement *(concurrence)*, agreement *(contract)*, allotment, array *(order)*, attornment, bargain, building *(business of assembling)*, case *(set of circumstances)*, classification, combination, compact, compilation, composition *(agreement in bankruptcy)*, composition *(makeup)*, conciliation, configuration *(form)*, contract, covenant, creation, deal, digest, disposition *(final arrangement)*, expedient, formation, hierarchy

(arrangement in a series), honorarium, indenture, lineup, method, motif, organization *(structure)*, pact, plan, policy *(contract)*, practice *(procedure)*, preparation, program, proposition, protocol *(agreement)*, provision *(act of supplying)*, register, regulation *(management)*, scheme, selection *(collection)*, sequence, settlement, situation, specialty *(contract)*, stipulation, strategy, structure *(composition)*, system, term *(provision)*, treatment, treaty, understanding *(agreement)*. SEE MAIN ENTRY
arrangement for disposal   disposition *(transfer of property)*
arrangement of difficulties   settlement
arrangement of laws   codification
arrangement of parts   content *(structure)*
arrangement of rules   codification
arrangement of statutes   code, codification
arrangements   dealings
arrangment   course
arrant   bad *(offensive)*, blameworthy, disreputable, egregious, flagrant, heinous, immoral, lawless, nefarious, notorious, outrageous, scandalous. SEE MAIN ENTRY
array   assemblage, band, chain *(series)*, clothe, composition *(makeup)*, conglomeration, disposition *(final arrangement)*, distribute, embellish, file *(arrange)*, fix *(arrange)*, form *(arrangement)*, formation, jury, marshal, order *(arrangement)*, selection *(collection)*, sequence, sort. SEE MAIN ENTRY
arraying   arrangement *(ordering)*
arrear   default
arrearage   arrears, debt, delinquency *(shortage)*
arrears   debit, debt, deficit, delinquency *(shortage)*, due. SEE MAIN ENTRY
arrest   abeyance, apprehension *(act of arresting)*, avert, block, bondage, book, capture, cease, cessation *(interlude)*, check *(bar)*, check *(restrain)*, clog, cloture, commit *(institutionalize)*, confine, constrain *(imprison)*, constraint *(imprisonment)*, constrict *(inhibit)*, contain *(restrain)*, control *(restrain)*, curb, custody *(incarceration)*, debar, defer *(put off)*, delay, desist, desuetude, detain *(hold in custody)*, detain *(restrain)*, detention, discontinue *(abandon)*, discontinue *(break continuity)*, durance, forestall, halt *(noun)*, halt *(verb)*, hamper, hinder, hindrance, hold up *(delay)*, impede, incarceration, inhibit, interdict, interfere, interrupt, interruption, keep *(restrain)*, kill *(defeat)*, lock, obstacle, occlude, palliate *(abate)*, prevent, quit *(discontinue)*, restrain, restraint, seize *(apprehend)*, stall, stay *(halt)*, stem *(check)*, stifle, stop, strangle, suppress, suspend, toll *(stop)*. SEE MAIN ENTRY
arrest temporarily   continue *(adjourn)*, delay, hold up *(delay)*, postpone
arrest the attention   occupy *(engage)*
arrest with authority   seize *(apprehend)*
arrested   SEE MAIN ENTRY
arresting   moving *(evoking emotion)*, obviation, preventive, sapid
arrestment   custody *(incarceration)*
arrêt   arrest *(apprehend)*
arrhabo   retainer
arrière pensée   propaganda
arrival   birth *(beginning)*, birth *(emergence of young)*, inflow
arrival into view   appearance *(emergence)*
arrive   emerge, enter *(go in)*, reach, report *(present oneself)*. SEE MAIN ENTRY
arrive at   attain, obtain

arrive at a conclusion arbitrate *(adjudge)*, ascertain, deduce, deduct *(conclude by reasoning)*, determine, find *(determine)*, fix *(settle)*, gauge, resolve *(decide)*

arrive at a decision resolve *(decide)*

arrive at a judgment decide

arrive at a price dicker

arrive at a settlement agree *(contract)*

arrive at a verdict find *(determine)*

arrive at an agreement close *(agree)*, coincide *(concur)*, concede, fix *(settle)*

arrive at an understanding coincide *(concur)*

arrive at terms coincide *(concur)*, conform

arrive at the end of finish

arrive at the truth solve

arriving future

arrogance contempt *(disdain)*, contumely, disdain, disrespect

arrogant brazen, contemptuous, cynical, dictatorial, disdainful, dogmatic, impertinent *(insolent)*, inflated *(vain)*, insolent, orgulous, presumptuous, pretentious *(pompous)*, proud *(conceited)*, supercilious

arrogate accroach, adopt, appropriate, assume *(seize)*, attach *(seize)*, collect *(recover money)*, condemn *(seize)*, demand, deprive, harass, hijack, impress *(procure by force)*, impropriate, infringe, invade, seize *(confiscate)*, sequester *(seize property)*, takeover, usurp. SEE MAIN ENTRY

arrogate to oneself preempt

arrogated attached *(seized)*

arrogation assignation, assumption *(seizure)*, condemnation *(seizure)*, disseisin, distress *(seizure)*, infringement, misappropriation. SEE MAIN ENTRY

arrondissement circuit

ars performance *(workmanship)*, stratagem, trade *(occupation)*

ars dicendi rhetoric *(skilled speech)*

ars ludicra histrionics

arsenal repository. SEE MAIN ENTRY

arson SEE MAIN ENTRY

arsonist lawbreaker

art performance *(workmanship)*, propensity, ruse, skill

art of composition rhetoric *(skilled speech)*

art of discourse rhetoric *(skilled speech)*

art of monetary relations finance

art of negotiating discretion *(quality of being discreet)*

art of prose rhetoric *(skilled speech)*

art of speaking declamation

art of war strategy

arterial causeway

arterial highway causeway

artery causeway, conduit *(channel)*, way *(channel)*

artful collusive, colorable *(specious)*, competent, delusive, devious, diplomatic, disingenuous, evasive, expert, insidious, machiavellian, mendacious, original *(creative)*, perspicacious, politic, practiced, resourceful, sly, stealthy, subtle *(refined)*, surreptitious, tactical. SEE MAIN ENTRY

artful contrivance artifice, stratagem

artful dodge evasion, machination, maneuver *(trick)*

artful management discretion *(quality of being discreet)*

artfully contrived politic

artfulness artifice, discretion *(quality of being discreet)*, fraud, hypocrisy, improbity, knavery, performance *(workmanship)*, pettifoggery

article chapter *(division)*, clause, condition *(contingent provision)*, instrument *(tool)*, item, law, member *(constituent part)*, pandect *(treatise)*, particular, product, report *(detailed account)*, story *(narrative)*, subheading, title *(division)*. SEE MAIN ENTRY

article of agreement provision *(clause)*, stipulation, term *(provision)*

article of belief principle *(axiom)*

article of commerce freight

article of faith dogma, principle *(axiom)*

article of merchandise product

article of trade product

articled indentured

articles commodities, merchandise, paraphernalia *(apparatus)*

articles of agreement contract

articles of commerce commodities, goods, merchandise, stock in trade

articles of merchandise commodities

articles of trade commodities

articulate avow, clarify, coherent *(clear)*, communicate, comprehensible, converse, convey *(communicate)*, eloquent, enunciate, express, lucid, observe *(remark)*, phrase, pronounce *(speak)*, recite, recount, remark, speak, unambiguous, utter. SEE MAIN ENTRY

articulated nuncupative, oral

articulation conversation, expression *(comment)*, speech

artifex artisan

artifice bad faith, contrivance, deception, device *(contrivance)*, disguise, duplicity, evasion, expedient, false pretense, fraud, hoax, knavery, machination, maneuver *(trick)*, pettifoggery, ploy, ruse, stratagem, strategy, subterfuge, trap. SEE MAIN ENTRY

artificer architect, artisan, contractor, materialman, practitioner

artificial bogus, deceptive, disingenuous, false *(not genuine)*, fictitious, histrionic, imitation, inflated *(bombastic)*, meretricious, orotund, pretentious *(ostentatious)*, specious, spurious, synthetic. SEE MAIN ENTRY

artificial behavior for effect histrionics

artificial eloquence rhetoric *(insincere language)*

artificial entity corporation

artificial person corporation

artificiality artifice, false pretense, pretense *(ostentation)*

artificiosus artificial

artificium maneuver *(trick)*, performance *(workmanship)*, pursuit *(occupation)*, system

artillery fire barrage

artisan practitioner. SEE MAIN ENTRY

artist practitioner

artistic aesthetic, artful, subtle *(refined)*

artistic effort creation

artistic judgment discretion *(quality of being discreet)*

artistry skill, specialty *(special aptitude)*, style

artless honest, inadept, inexperienced, ingenuous, natural, simple, straightforward, unaffected *(sincere)*, unpretentious

artless person philistine

artlessness honesty, veracity

as a body en masse

as a consequence a priori, consequently. SEE MAIN ENTRY

as a favor gratis

as a group en masse

as a matter of course as a rule, consequently

as a matter of fact de facto

as a matter of form pro forma

as a matter of right SEE MAIN ENTRY

as a result consequently

as a result of a priori

as a rule generally, invariably. SEE MAIN ENTRY

as a start ab initio

as a substitute for in lieu of

as a substitute for a parent loco parentis

as a unit en banc

as a whole en banc, en masse, in toto, wholly

as agreed upon SEE MAIN ENTRY

as an alternative in lieu of

as an alternative for a parent loco parentis

as arranged by the agreement as agreed upon

as contained as so defined

as contained in the statutes as provided by law

as contracted for as agreed upon

as delineated as so defined

as explained as so defined

as far as until

as good as equivalent

as great as another coequal

as if quasi

as is a priori. SEE MAIN ENTRY

as it is as is

as it stands as is

as matters stand consequently

as near as may be cy pres

as near as possible cy pres

as near as practicable cy pres

as negotiated for as agreed upon

as offered as is

as one en masse

as pledged as agreed upon

as presented as is

as promised as agreed upon

as provided by law SEE MAIN ENTRY

as proxy for in lieu of

as represented actual, as is, authentic, bona fide, honest, true *(authentic)*

as required duly

as required will shall

as seen as is

as set forth as so defined

as set forth by law as provided by law

as settled upon as agreed upon

as shown as is

as so defined SEE MAIN ENTRY

as soon as can be reasonably expected forthwith

as soon as feasible SEE MAIN ENTRY

as soon as possible as soon as feasible

as soon as reasonably possible as soon as feasible

as specified as so defined

as specified in the law as provided by law

as the case may be consequently

as things are as is

as though quasi

as though it were quasi

as well also

ascend expand, progress

ascendance dominance, hegemony, influence, prestige. SEE MAIN ENTRY

ascendancy advantage, dominance, dominion *(supreme authority)*, force *(strength)*, hegemony, influence, occupation *(possession)*, primacy, supremacy

ascendant ancestor, dominant, predominant, prevailing *(having superior force)*, prevalent, primogenitor, prosperous. SEE MAIN ENTRY

ascendants ancestry

ascendency predominance, prestige

ascent headway

ascertain assess *(appraise)*, bear *(adduce)*, decide, deduce, deduct *(conclude by reasoning)*, determine, discern *(detect with the senses)*, discover, distinguish, elucidate, ensure, establish *(show)*, find *(determine)*, find *(discover)*, fix *(settle)*, gauge, hold *(decide)*, judge, notice *(observe)*, prove, recognize *(perceive)*, resolve *(decide)*, rule *(decide)*, settle, solve. SEE MAIN ENTRY

ascertain a position locate

ascertain after reasoning arbitrate *(adjudge)*

ascertain and declare find *(determine)*

ascertain as truth prove

ascertain by judicial inquiry find *(determine)*

ascertain dimensions measure

ascertain liability liquidate *(determine liability)*

ascertain mathematically calculate

ascertain size measure

ascertain the amount of evaluate

ascertain the amount of indebtedness liquidate *(determine liability)*

ascertain the balance due liquidate *(determine liability)*

ascertain the meaning of construe *(comprehend)*

ascertain the time of date

ascertainable appreciable, cognizable, comprehensible, deductible *(provable)*, perceptible, ponderable, provable, solvable. SEE MAIN ENTRY

ascertained actual, axiomatic, certain *(positive)*, certain *(specific)*, clear *(certain)*, cognizable, common *(customary)*, conclusive *(determinative)*, conclusive *(settled)*, definite, definitive, factual, genuine, incontrovertible, indubious, positive *(incontestable)*, real, stated. SEE MAIN ENTRY

ascertained fact certification *(certainness)*, certitude

ascertained principle conviction *(persuasion)*

ascertainment analysis, certification *(certainness)*, collation, conclusion *(determination)*, detection, determination, discovery, finding, holding *(ruling of a court)*, identification, inspection, observation, opinion *(judicial decision)*, perception, surety *(certainty)*

ascetic dispassionate, harsh, stoical

asceticism continence

ascribable derivative

ascribe acknowledge *(declare)*, assign *(designate)*, attribute, impute. SEE MAIN ENTRY

ascribe blame incriminate

ascribe personal qualities to personify

ascribe to blame

ascribere ascribe, impute, inscribe

ascription accusation, arrogation, assignation, attribution, blame *(responsibility)*, citation *(attribution)*, condemnation *(blame)*, reference *(citation)*. SEE MAIN ENTRY

aseptic preventive

aside innuendo

aside from the point extraneous, inapposite, irrelevant

asinine fatuous, ludicrous, obtuse, opaque, puerile, unreasonable

asininity opacity

ask apply *(request)*, call *(appeal to)*, canvass, consult *(ask advice of)*, demand, desire, inquire, investigate, pose *(propound)*, solicit

ask advice consult *(ask advice of)*

ask an opinion consult *(ask advice of)*

ask earnestly canvass, pray, press *(beseech)*, solicit

ask for call *(appeal to)*, claim *(demand)*, delve, desire, exact, move *(judicially request)*, petition, request

ask for credit borrow

ask for recommendations consult *(ask advice of)*

ask for relief sue

ask for suggestions consult (ask ad-vice of)

ask for with authority call *(demand)*, demand

ask help of refer *(send for action)*

ask questions cross-examine

ask solemnly for invoke

ask to come call *(summon)*

ask urgently importune

asked for popular

asker petitioner

askew disordered, oblique *(slanted)*

asking inquiry *(systematic investigation)*, precatory, question *(inquiry)*, request

asking for what is due demand

asking price cost *(price)*

asking questions cross-examination

aslant oblique *(slanted)*

asleep dormant

asomatous incorporeal, intangible

aspect appearance *(look)*, characteristic, complexion, component, condition *(state)*, conduct, demeanor, deportment, detail, factor *(ingredient)*, feature *(appearance)*, feature *(characteristic)*, ingredient, manner *(behavior)*, outlook, particular, posture *(attitude)*, presence *(poise)*, property *(distinctive attribute)*, semblance, side, standpoint, state *(condition)*, style, technicality. SEE MAIN ENTRY

aspects character *(personal quality)*, color *(complexion)*. SEE MAIN ENTRY

aspectus appearance *(look)*, aspect

asper bitter *(acrid tasting)*

asperity rigor, severity

aspernari disdain, spurn

asperse brand *(stigmatize)*, complain *(criticize)*, condemn *(blame)*, contemn, defame, denigrate, denounce *(condemn)*, deprecate, derogate, discommend, discredit, dishonor *(deprive of honor)*, disparage, libel, malign, pillory, reprimand, reproach, smear, sully, tarnish

aspersion bad repute, contempt *(disdain)*, contumely, conviction *(finding of guilt)*, criticism, defamation, denunciation, disapprobation, discredit, dishonor *(shame)*, disparagement, imprecation, infamy, innuendo, insinuation, libel, obloquy, phillipic, revilement, scandal, shame, slander, stricture. SEE MAIN ENTRY

aspersive libelous

aspirant amateur, applicant *(candidate)*, candidate, contender, novice, rival, special interest

aspiration desideratum, design *(intent)*, desire, destination, end *(intent)*, goal, objective, purpose, target, will *(desire)*

aspire desire, endeavor, strive, try *(attempt)*

aspire to intend, pursue *(strive to gain)*

aspirer candidate

aspiring eager, solicitous

assail accost, ambush, assault, attack, badger, censure, complain *(criticize)*, confront *(oppose)*, defame, denounce *(condemn)*, despoil, engage *(involve)*, fight *(battle)*, harass, harrow, harry *(plunder)*, impugn, invade, lash *(attack verbally)*, maltreat, mishandle *(maltreat)*, mistreat, persecute, resist *(oppose)*, strike *(assault)*. SEE MAIN ENTRY

assail by argument impugn

assail with censure condemn *(blame)*, denounce *(condemn)*

assailability danger

assailable dangerous, destructible, inadequate, indefensible, penetrable, vulnerable. SEE MAIN ENTRY

assailant aggressor, disputant, foe, offender, offensive *(taking the initiative)*. SEE MAIN ENTRY

assailer aggressor, assailant

assailing offensive *(taking the initiative)*

assailment assault, onset *(assault)*

assassinate dispatch *(put to death)*, extinguish, kill *(murder)*, slay

assassination aberemurder, dispatch *(act of putting to death)*, homicide, killing, murder. SEE MAIN ENTRY

assault accost, ambush, assail, attack, barrage, battery, belligerency, denounce *(condemn)*, fight *(battle)*, fight *(battle)*, incursion, invade, invasion, mishandle *(maltreat)*, mistreat, molest *(subject to indecent advances)*, offense, oppugn, outbreak, rape, resist *(oppose)*, resistance, violence. SEE MAIN ENTRY

assault belligerently accost, assail, assault

assaulter aggressor, assailant

assaulting hostile

assay analysis, attempt, diagnosis, endeavor, experiment, inquiry *(systematic investigation)*. SEE MAIN ENTRY

assemblage agglomeration, aggregate

assemblage assemblage. SEE MAIN ENTRY

assemblage assembly, body *(collection)*, caucus, coalescence, collection *(assembly)*, combination, compilation, congregation, congress, consolidation, corpus, cumulation, distribution *(arrangement)*, entirety, joinder, manufacture, mass *(body of persons)*, selection *(collection)*, whole

assemble accumulate *(amass)*, aggregate, attach *(join)*, build *(construct)*, call *(summon)*, codify, collect *(gather)*, commingle, compile, concentrate *(consolidate)*, congregate, conjoin, connect *(join together)*, convene, converge, federate, form, garner, glean, join *(bring together)*, make, manufacture, meet, orchestrate, produce *(manufacture)*, raise *(collect)*, rendezvous, store, unite

assemble and apportion assets liquidate *(determine liability)*

assemble by summons call *(summon)*

assemble parts fabricate *(construct)*

assemble the facts document

assembled coadunate, collective, composite, conglomerate

assembled body company *(assemblage)*

assemblée caucus, chamber *(body)*, company *(assemblage)*

assembling building *(business of assembling)*, centralization

assembly aggregate, assemblage, caucus, chamber *(body)*, company *(assemblage)*, conference, conglomeration, congregation, congress, cumulation, legislature, manufacture, meeting *(conference)*, parley, rendezvous, selection *(collection)*, session. SEE MAIN ENTRY

assembly of persons congregation

assemblyman lawmaker

assemblywoman lawmaker

assent abide, accede (concede), acceptance, accordance (understanding), acknowledgment (acceptance), acquiescence, admit (concede), affirmance (judicial sanction), agree (comply), agreement (concurrence), allow (endure), approval, bear (adduce), capitulation, certify (approve), charter (sanction), coincide (concur), compliance, concede, concession (compromise), concordance, confirm, confirmation, conformity (agreement), consent (noun), consent (verb), corroborate, defer (yield in judgment), deference, franchise (license), grant (concede), indorsement, leave (permission), let (permit), obey, pass (approve), permission, permit, ratification, sanction (permission), stipulate, subscribe (promise), subscription, suffer (permit), vouchsafe, yield (submit). SEE MAIN ENTRY

assent to approve, authorize, certify (approve), comply, concur (agree), countenance, indorse, sanction, sustain (confirm)

assented consensual

assentient consenting

assenting concerted, concordant, concurrent (united), congruous, consenting, favorable (expressing approval), harmonious, inclined, pliable, ready (willing), willing (desirous)

assentive concordant, consenting

assererate vouch

assert acknowledge (declare), adduce, advocate, affirm (claim), allege, annunciate, argue, attest, avouch (avow), avow, bear (adduce), cast (register), certify (attest), claim (maintain), comment, communicate, contend (maintain), convey (communicate), declare, enunciate, express, mention, observe (remark), plead (allege in a legal action), pose (propound), posit, proclaim, profess (avow), promise (vow), pronounce (speak), remark, signify (inform), testify, uphold, utter. SEE MAIN ENTRY

assert a right to call (demand), demand

assert absolutely bear (adduce)

assert an oath promise (vow)

assert as one's own claim (demand)

assert as one's right claim (demand)

assert as true swear

assert formally certify (attest), issue (publish), plead (allege in a legal action)

assert in court litigate

assert incorrectly misrepresent

assert on oath avow

assert one's rights demand

assert oneself certify (attest), constrain (compel)

assert peremptorily avouch (avow), avow

assert positively avouch (avow), certify (attest), plead (allege in a legal action), promise (vow)

assert solemnly pledge (promise the performance of), promise (vow)

assert the contrary contradict

assert the opposite contradict

assert under oath avouch (avow), avow, certify (attest), promise (vow)

assertative declaratory

asserted alleged

asserted formally alleged

asserter claimant

asserting the contrary contradictory

asserting the opposite contradictory

assertion accusation, acknowledgment (avowal), admission (disclosure), affirmance (authentication), affirmation, allegation, as-

severation, attestation, averment, avouchment, avowal, comment, confession, confirmation, count, declaration, dictum, disclosure (act of disclosing), disclosure (something disclosed), expression (comment), hypothesis, mention (reference), observation, plea, postulate, principle (axiom), profession (declaration), pronouncement, proposition, remark, statement, testimony. SEE MAIN ENTRY

assertion against the plaintiff counterclaim

assertion of facts representation (statement)

assertion of legal right demand

assertion of the contrary contradiction

assertion of the opposite contradiction

assertions premises (hypotheses)

assertive certain (positive), compelling, declaratory, dogmatic, insistent, peremptory (imperative). SEE MAIN ENTRY

assertment averment

assertory dogmatic

assertory oath affidavit, affirmance (legal affirmation), affirmation, averment

assess arbitrate (adjudge), calculate, consider, criticize (evaluate), encumber (financially obligate), evaluate, exact, excise (levy a tax), gauge, judge, levy, measure, mete, notice (observe), rate, require (compel), tax (levy). SEE MAIN ENTRY

assess a tax upon charge (assess)

assess pro rata charge (assess), prorate

assess proportionally prorate

assessable ad valorem, appreciable, determinable (ascertainable)

assessment account (evaluation), ad valorem, appraisal, appreciation (perception), arbitration, charge (cost), choice (decision), computation, concept, conclusion (determination), cost (price), determination, discretion (power of choice), discrimination (differentiation), duty (tax), estimate (approximate cost), estimation (calculation), excise, expense (cost), idea, inspection, judgment (discernment), judgment (formal court decree), levy, measurement, opinion (judicial decision), perception, rate, rating, rent, tariff (duties), tax, toll (tax), value, verdict. SEE MAIN ENTRY

assessment of damages additur

assessor judge, juror, magistrate. SEE MAIN ENTRY

assessor of liability and damages juror

assessors jury

asset advantage, chattel, holding (property owned), item, possession (property), resource, share (stock)

assets capital, commodities, effects, estate (property), fund, goods, interest (ownership), means (funds), merchandise, money, paraphernalia (personal belongings), personalty, possessions, principal (capital sum), property (possessions), reserve, securities, security (stock), stock (shares), store (depository), substance (material possessions). SEE MAIN ENTRY

assets and liabilities estate (property)

assets in hand principal (capital sum)

assever assert

asseverate acknowledge (declare), affirm (claim), affirm (declare solemnly), allege, assert, assure (insure), avouch (avow), avow, bear (adduce), certify (attest), claim (maintain), contend (maintain), declare, depose (testify), enunciate, express, posit, proclaim, profess (avow), promise (vow), remark, testify, utter, verify (swear)

asseverated alleged

asseveration acknowledgment (avowal), affirmance (legal affirmation), affirmation, assertion, attestation, averment, avouchment, avowal, claim (assertion), expression (comment), jurat, oath, promise, pronouncement, representation (statement), statement, surety (certainty), testimony, vow. SEE MAIN ENTRY

assidous pertinacious

assiduity diligence (perseverance), effort, endeavor, industry (activity), interest (concern)

assiduous active, circumspect, close (rigorous), conscientious, diligent, eager, earnest, faithful (diligent), industrious, meticulous, painstaking, patient, persistent, relentless, sedulous, serious (devoted), steadfast, thorough, true (loyal), unremitting, zealous

assiduousness diligence (perseverance), effort, industry (activity)

assign abalienate, adduce, alienate (transfer title), allocate, allot, appoint, apportion, ascribe, attorn, attribute, authorize, bear (yield), cede, charge (assess), charge (empower), commit (entrust), contribute (supply), convey (transfer), delegate, demarcate, designate, devise (give), devote, direct (supervise), disburse (distribute), dispense, disperse (disseminate), distribute, divide (distribute), dole, employ (engage services), empower, endue, entrust, expend (disburse), give (grant), grant (transfer formally), impute, induct, leave (give), marshal, mete, nominate, parcel, refer (direct attention), refer (send for action), relegate, select, site, split, transfer. SEE MAIN ENTRY

assign a duty delegate

assign a meaning to construe (translate), explain

assign a time to date

assign again reassign

assign dower bequeath

assign one's share to charge (assess)

assign places to distribute, file (arrange), fix (arrange), sort, tabulate

assign power of attorney to delegate

assign the care of entrust

assign the parts orchestrate

assign to blame, consign

assign to a place locate

assign to a position delegate, hire

assign to an earlier date antedate

assign to battle stations deploy

assign to lodgings lodge (house)

assign to positions deploy

assignable heritable, negotiable. SEE MAIN ENTRY

assignable rights of action intangible

assignation alienation (transfer of title), arrogation, assignment (allotment), assignment (transfer of ownership), attribution, blame (responsibility), consignment, conveyance, incrimination, reference (citation), rendezvous. SEE MAIN ENTRY

assignation of title feoffment

assigned certain (specific), positive (prescribed)

assigned task office, province

assigned time date

assignee deputy, feoffee, licensee, payee, receiver, recipient, transferee. SEE MAIN ENTRY

assignee in fact licensee

assigning designation (naming)

assigning by lot disbursement (act of disbursing)

assignment activity, agency (legal relationship), alienation (transfer of title), allotment, appointment (act of designating), apportionment, arrogation, assignation, attribution, blame (responsibility), burden, capacity (job), cession, charge (responsibility), citation (attribution), classification, commitment (responsibility), consignment, conveyance, deed, department, deputation (selection of delegates), designation (naming), devolution, dispensation (act of dispensing), disposition (transfer of property), distribution (apportionment), duty (obligation), employment, function, job, labor (work), mission, nomination, position (business status), project, province, quota, ration, reference (citation), role, selection (choice), specification, trade (occupation), work (employment). SEE MAIN ENTRY

assignment by share allotment

assignment in proportion apportionment

assignment of cause hypothesis

assignment of paternity filiation

assignor contributor (giver), donor, feoffor, grantor, licensor, transferer

assimilate adopt, comprehend (understand), conceive (comprehend), conform, construe (comprehend), coordinate, desegregate, digest (comprehend), naturalize (acclimate), naturalize (make a citizen), realize (understand), understand, unite

assimilated compound, conjoint

assimilation adoption (acceptance), conformity (obedience), incorporation (blend), merger, osmosis, understanding (comprehension)

assist abet, accommodate, aid, avail (be of use), bear (support), conduce, contribute (assist), countenance, enable, espouse, expedite, facilitate, favor, finance, foster, help (noun), help (verb), indorse, inure (benefit), lend, maintain (sustain), nurture, pander, profit, promote (organize), relieve (give aid), remedy, serve (assist), side, subsidize, support (assistance), uphold. SEE MAIN ENTRY

assist a judge clerk

assist in accomplishing a purpose avail (be of use)

assist substantially contribute (assist)

assist the progress facilitate

assistance accommodation (backing), advantage, advocacy, aid (help), auspices, behalf, benefit (betterment), benevolence (act of kindness), charity, consortium (marriage companionship), contribution (donation), contribution (participation), endowment, favor (sanction), help, largess (generosity), largess (gift), loan, maintenance (support of spouse), panacea, patronage (power to appoint jobs), patronage (support), promotion (encouragement), reinforcement, relief (aid), remedy (legal means of redress), remedy (that which corrects), support (assistance). SEE MAIN ENTRY

assistant abettor, accessory, accomplice, affiliate, agent, ancillary (auxiliary), associate, clerical, coactor, coadjutant, coconspirator, cohort, colleague, confederate, consociate, conspirer, contributor (contributor), copartner (coconspirator), employee, good samaritan, participant, partner, plenipotentiary, procurator, subsidiary. SEE MAIN ENTRY

assistants personnel, staff

assister backer, benefactor, good samaritan, samaritan

assisting clerical, contributory, instrumental, practical, profitable

assize bar (court), forum (court)

associate abettor, accomplice, affiliate (noun), affiliate (verb), appertain, assistant, chapter (branch), coactor, coadjutant, cohort, colleague, combine (act in concert), commingle, confederate, connect (relate), consociate, consort, conspire, conspirer, constituent (member), contributor (contributor), cooperate, copartner (business associate), copartner (coconspirator), corporation, correlate, desegregate, engage (involve), federalize (associate), federate, implicate, involve (implicate), involve (participate), join (associate oneself with), meet, member (individual in a group), merge, organ, organize (unionize), participant, participate, partner, peer, pool, relate (establish a connection), unite. SEE MAIN ENTRY

associate in crime accomplice, coconspirator

associate in guilt accomplice, coconspirator

associate with accompany, espouse

associated affiliated, akin (germane), allied, analogous, apposite, coadunate, cognate, collateral (accompanying), collective, comparable (capable of comparison), compound, concomitant, concurrent (at the same time), conjoint, corporate (joint), correlative, federal, germane, incident, incidental, interested, interrelated, joint, pertinent, related, relative (relevant), relevant, tangential. SEE MAIN ENTRY

associated concepts SEE MAIN ENTRY

associated with intimate

associates constituency, staff

associating concurrent (united)

association adhesion (loyalty), affiliation (amalgamation), affiliation (connectedness), assemblage, attribution, band, cartel, centralization, chain (nexus), coaction, coalescence, coalition, collection (assembly), collusion, committee, company (enterprise), comparison, complex (development), confederacy (compact), conformity (obedience), congregation, conjunction, connection (relation), connivance, consolidation, consortium (business cartel), consortium (marriage companionship), contribution (participation), cooperative, corporation, denomination, federation, firm, foundation (organization), incorporation (formation of a business entity), institute, integration (amalgamation), integration (assimilation), kinship, league, merger, nexus, partnership, party (political organization), profession (vocation), propinquity (kinship), relation (connection), relationship (connection), relevance, society, sodality, syndicate, trust (combination of businesses), union (labor organization). SEE MAIN ENTRY

associative apposite, correlative, pertinent

assoil condone, palliate (excuse), remit (release from penalty)

assonance accordance (understanding), consensus

assonant concurrent (united)

assort allocate, apportion, classify, codify, distribute, fix (arrange), organize (arrange), pigeonhole, sort, vary

assorted composite, diverse, heterogeneous, manifold, miscellaneous, multiple, several (plural)

assortment class, classification, conglomeration, diversification, diversity, melange, selection (collection)

assuage allay, alleviate, diminish, disarm (set at ease), lessen, lull, meliorate, mitigate, moderate (temper), modify (moderate), mollify, obtund, pacify, palliate (abate), placate, relax, relieve (free from burden), remedy, remit (relax), soothe. SEE MAIN ENTRY

assuagement mitigation, moderation, mollification, relief (release), remission

assuager cure

assuaging mitigating, narcotic, palliative (abating)

assuasive medicinal, narcotic, palliative (abating), remedial

assuasive drug narcotic

assumable constructive (inferential), ostensible

assume accede (succeed), accroach, acquire (secure), adopt, annex (arrogate), anticipate (expect), appropriate, collect (recover money), condemn (seize), confiscate, copy, deduce, deduct (conclude by reasoning), deem, embrace (accept), endeavor, expect (consider probable), forejudge, gain, generalize, guess, impropriate, incur, occupy (take possession), opine, posit, postulate, preconceive, preempt, presume, presuppose, pretend, receive (acquire), seize (confiscate), speculate (conjecture), surmise, suspect (think), takeover, trust, undertake, usurp. SEE MAIN ENTRY

assume a character impersonate

assume a fighting attitude defy

assume a lofty bearing patronize (condescend toward)

assume a mask camouflage

assume a patronizing air condescend (patronize)

assume a pattern crystallize

assume a risk speculate (chance), underwrite

assume authority federalize (place under federal control), hold (possess)

assume command govern, hijack, hold (possess), preside, usurp

assume definite characteristics crystallize

assume for public use eminent domain

assume ownership acquire (secure), annex (arrogate), appropriate, condemn (seize), distrain, impropriate, occupy (take possession), possess, purchase

assume responsibility conduct, guarantee, operate

assume responsibility for avouch (guarantee)

assume the appearance of mock (imitate)

assume the character of pose (impersonate)

assume the offensive attack, fight (battle)

assume the role of pose (impersonate)

assume unlawful rights of ownership convert (misappropriate)

assume without authority usurp

assumed artificial, false (not genuine), hypothetical, implied, ostensible, presumptive, purported, putative, specious, tacit, theoretical. SEE MAIN ENTRY

assumed position platform

assumed positions premises (hypotheses)

assumed truth postulate

assumedly reputedly

assuming brazen, impertinent (insolent), insolent, obtrusive, orgulous, presumptuous, proud (conceited)

assuming different forms protean

assuming ownership disseisin

assuming that provided

assumption acquisition, adoption *(acceptance)*, adverse possession, appropriation *(taking)*, arrogation, basis, concept, condemnation *(seizure)*, conjecture, conviction *(persuasion)*, deduction *(conclusion)*, distress *(seizure)*, estimate *(idea)*, estimation *(calculation)*, generalization, ground, hypothesis, inference, opinion *(belief)*, postulate, preconception, presumption, prolepsis, proposition, receipt *(act of receiving)*, receipt *(voucher)*, speculation *(conjecture)*, supposition, theory. SEE MAIN ENTRY

assumptive apparent *(presumptive)*, presumptive, speculative, supercilious

assumptively reputedly

assurance acceptance, accommodation *(backing)*, affirmance *(authentication)*, approval, avouchment, bail, belief *(state of mind)*, binder, bond, certainty, certification *(attested copy)*, certification *(certainness)*, certitude, commitment *(responsibility)*, confidence *(faith)*, confirmation, consent, contract, conviction *(persuasion)*, corroboration, coverage *(insurance)*, credence, expectation, faith, guaranty, license, mainstay, pact, pledge *(binding promise)*, principle *(axiom)*, profession *(declaration)*, promise, proof, prospect *(outlook)*, recognizance, reference *(recommendation)*, reliance, safeguard, security *(safety)*, surety *(certainty)*, trust *(confidence)*, undertaking *(pledge)*, vow, warrant *(guaranty)*, warranty. SEE MAIN ENTRY

assurance against loss indemnity, insurance

assurance of secrecy confidence *(relation of trust)*

assure avouch *(guarantee)*, bear *(adduce)*, bond *(secure a debt)*, certify *(attest)*, contend *(maintain)*, convince, corroborate, cosign, declare, disarm *(set at ease)*, ensure, guarantee, pledge *(promise the performance of)*, profess *(avow)*, promise *(vow)*, sponsor, swear, underwrite, verify *(confirm)*, vouch. SEE MAIN ENTRY

assure again reassure

assure oneself ascertain

assured agreed *(promised)*, alleged, axiomatic, categorical, certain *(fixed)*, certain *(positive)*, conclusive *(determinative)*, convincing, credible, decisive, definite, demonstrable, dependable, dogmatic, incontrovertible, indubious, inevitable, infallible, official, positive *(confident)*, reliable, sanguine, secure *(confident)*, solid *(sound)*, undisputed

assured belief conviction *(persuasion)*

assured expectation faith

assuredly admittedly

assuredness assurance, belief *(state of mind)*, certainty, certification *(certainness)*, certitude, reliance, surety *(certainty)*

assurer insurer

assuring convincing

assymetrical disproportionate

asthenic languid, nonsubstantial *(not sturdy)*, powerless

astir conscious *(awake)*

astonish confound, confuse *(bewilder)*, overcome *(overwhelm)*, overwhelm

astonished speechless

astonishing moving *(evoking emotion)*, notable, noteworthy, peculiar *(curious)*, portentous *(eliciting amazement)*, prodigious *(amazing)*, remarkable, special,

unaccustomed, uncanny, unexpected, unusual

astonishing thing phenomenon *(unusual occurrence)*

astonishment bombshell, phenomenon *(unusual occurrence)*, surprise

astound confound, discommode, discompose, disconcert, impress *(affect deeply)*

astounding ineffable, noteworthy, prodigious *(amazing)*, remarkable, special, unusual

astoundment surprise

astral stellar

astray errant, lost *(disoriented)*, peccant *(culpable)*. SEE MAIN ENTRY

astrict clog, constrict *(inhibit)*, debar, disadvantage, restrict

astriction constraint *(restriction)*

astringe constrict *(compress)*

astringent bitter *(penetrating)*, caustic, harsh, particular *(exacting)*, severe. SEE MAIN ENTRY

astronomical prodigious *(enormous)*

astute acute, artful, circumspect, cognizant, discreet, discriminating *(judicious)*, judicious, knowing, perceptive, perspicacious, politic, profound *(esoteric)*, sapient, sensible, sensitive *(discerning)*, sly, subtle *(refined)*

astuteness common sense, insight, intelligence *(intellect)*, judgment *(discernment)*, perception, sagacity, sense *(intelligence)*

astutus artful, politic, sly, tactical

asunder apart, disconnected, discrete, disperse *(scatter)*, separate

asylum bulwark, haven, lodging, protection, refuge, security *(safety)*. SEE MAIN ENTRY

asylum shelter *(protection)*

asymmetric irregular *(not usual)*

asymmetrical dissimilar, irregular *(not usual)*

asymmetry difference, discrepancy, disparity, inequality, irregularity

at a fixed interval per annum

at a fixed time hereafter *(eventually)*

at a great distance remote *(not proximate)*

at a later period ex post facto, thereafter

at a later time ex post facto

at a premium scarce

at a subsequent period ex post facto

at a succeeding time ex post facto

at all whatever

at all times always *(forever)*

at an end complete *(ended)*

at any rate regardless

at close quarters contiguous, present *(attendant)*

at cross purposes contra, contrary, discordant

at cross-purposes antipathetic *(oppositional)*, dissenting

at ease complacent

at fault blameful, blameworthy, culpable, delinquent *(guilty of a misdeed)*, errant, guilty. SEE MAIN ENTRY

at first ab initio

at first glance prima facie *(self-evident)*

at first sight prima facie *(self-evident)*

at first view prima facie *(self-evident)*

at hand available, close *(near)*, forthcoming, immediate *(imminent)*, immediate *(not distant)*, imminent, inevitable, pending *(imminent)*, present *(attendant)*, present *(current)*, proximate, ready *(prepared)*

at home household *(domestic)*

at issue arguable, competitive *(antagonistic)*, contestable, contrary, controversial,

debatable, disputable, dissenting, doubtful. SEE MAIN ENTRY

at large free *(not restricted)*

at least only

at liberty autonomous *(self governing)*, clear *(free from criminal charges)*, exempt, free *(not restricted)*, sovereign *(independent)*

at loggerheads dissenting

at no period sine die

at no time sine die

at odds contradictory, controversial, disproportionate, dissenting, hostile, incongruous, repugnant *(incompatible)*

at odds with dissident, negative, nonconforming

at once forthwith, instant, instantly

at one concordant, consonant

at one with consensual

at one's disposal available

at one's end in extremis

at one's own risk caveat emptor

at other times known as alias

at peace placid

at peril at risk

at rest dead, dormant, lifeless *(dead)*

at risk SEE MAIN ENTRY

at sight prima facie *(self-evident)*

at the beginning ab initio

at the conclusion of life in extremis

at the edge extreme *(last)*

at the first opportunity as soon as feasible

at the first possible moment as soon as feasible

at the last stage in extremis

at the mercy of subject *(exposed)*

at the point of death in extremis

at the present time instant

at the same instant concurrent *(at the same time)*

at the same time ad interim, coincidental, en masse, simultaneous

at the start ab initio

at the termination of life in extremis

at the utmost point extreme *(last)*

at the very least only

at the wrong time inopportune

at this moment instant, present *(current)*

at this time present *(current)*

at variance adverse *(opposite)*, competitive *(antagonistic)*, contradictory, contrary, controversial, discordant, disproportionate, dissenting, hostile, inapplicable, inapposite, inapt, incommensurate, incongruous, inconsistent, inept *(inappropriate)*, inimical, irreconcilable, litigious, repugnant *(incompatible)*

at variance with dissident, nonconforming

at variance with the facts ludicrous

at war with inimical

at whatever time whenever

at which time whenever

at will employment. SEE MAIN ENTRY

at work active, effective *(operative)*, operative

atavistic genetic, regressive

athirst eager, hot-blooded

athwart contra

atmosphere climate, environment. SEE MAIN ENTRY

atomization dissolution *(disintegration)*

atomize dissolve *(disperse)*

atone compensate *(counterbalance)*, redeem *(satisfy debts)*, redress, restore *(return)*

atone for repent

atonement compensation, expiation, reparation *(indemnification)*, restitution, retribution, trover

atoning compensatory, penitent, repentant
atrabilious deplorable, disconsolate
atrocious arrant *(onerous)*, bad *(offensive)*, brutal, contemptible, cruel, deplorable, disgraceful, gross *(flagrant)*, heinous, inexcusable, iniquitous, loathsome, malignant, outrageous, ruthless, scandalous, vicious
atrocious crime atrocity
atrocitas atrocity
atrocity abuse *(physical misuse)*, cruelty, delinquency *(misconduct)*, misdeed, vice, wrong. SEE MAIN ENTRY
atrophy decay, decline, degenerate, depreciate, deteriorate, deterioration, detriment, dissolution *(disintegration)*
attach abridge *(divest)*, abut, adhere *(fasten)*, affiliate, affix, annex *(add)*, append, ascribe, bond *(hold together)*, border *(bound)*, cement, cohere *(adhere)*, combine *(join together)*, condemn *(seize)*, confiscate, conjoin, connect *(join together)*, contact *(touch)*, deprive, distrain, divest, fix *(make firm)*, garnish, impound, impress *(procure by force)*, impute, join *(bring together)*, levy, lock, sequester *(seize property)*. SEE MAIN ENTRY
attach a legal signature notarize
attach little importance to minimize
attach oneself to adopt
attach too much importance to overestimate
attache employee
attached addicted, appurtenant, cohesive *(sticking)*, conjoint, inextricable, inseparable, proximate. SEE MAIN ENTRY
attached to another jurisdiction foreign
attaching attachment *(act of affixing)*, confiscating
attachment accession *(annexation)*, addendum, addition, additive, adherence *(adhesion)*, adherence *(devotion)*, adhesion *(affixing)*, adhesion *(loyalty)*, adjoiner, affection, affinity *(regard)*, allegiance, allonge, appendix *(accession)*, appendix *(supplement)*, appliance, appurtenance, arrogation, boom *(increase)*, chain *(nexus)*, coalescence, codicil, coherence, connection *(fastening)*, consortium *(marriage companionship)*, disseisin, distraint, distress *(seizure)*, expropriation *(divestiture)*, favor *(partiality)*, favoritism, levy, loyalty, nexus, partiality, penchant, predilection, predisposition, privation, privity, regard *(esteem)*, rider, sequestration. SEE MAIN ENTRY
attachment to adoption *(acceptance)*
attachment to realty fixture
attachments paraphernalia *(apparatus)*, ties
attack accost, accuse, ambush, assail, assault *(noun)*, assault *(verb)*, bait *(harass)*, barrage, battery, beat *(strike)*, belligerency, cavil, censure, charge *(accusation)*, charge *(accuse)*, condemn *(blame)*, condemnation *(blame)*, controvert, course, denigrate, denounce *(condemn)*, despoil, discommend, disease, engage *(involve)*, fault, fight *(battle)*, fight *(battle)*, foray, grapple, harm, harry *(plunder)*, impeach, impeachment, impinge, impugn, impugnation, incursion, intrusion, invade, invasion, inveigh, malign, mistreat *(subject to indecent advances)*, object, offense, onset *(assault)*, oppugn, outbreak, outburst, persecute, protest, resistance, smear, spoliation, strike *(assault)*, violence. SEE MAIN ENTRY
attack by words impugn
attack from a concealed position ambush

attack on rights invasion
attack physically assault
attack the reputation of malign
attackable penetrable
attacked accused *(attacked)*
attacker aggressor, assailant, foe
attacking negative, offensive *(taking the initiative)*
attain accede *(succeed)*, accomplish, acquire *(secure)*, carry *(succeed)*, consummate, discharge *(perform)*, dispatch *(dispose of)*, earn, effectuate, execute *(accomplish)*, gain, make, obtain, operate, pass *(satisfy requirements)*, procure, reach, realize *(obtain as a profit)*, reap, recover. SEE MAIN ENTRY
attain by effort find *(discover)*
attain majority mature
attain maturity mature
attain the goal consummate
attainability chance *(possibility)*, feasibility, possibility
attainable available, facile, open *(accessible)*, possible, potential, practicable, public *(open)*, vulnerable
attainment accession *(enlargement)*, acquisition, adverse possession, boom *(prosperity)*, caliber *(mental capacity)*, commission *(act)*, development *(outgrowth)*, discharge *(performance)*, edification, end *(termination)*, fait accompli, fruition, outcome, performance *(execution)*, performance *(workmanship)*, realization, receipt *(act of receiving)*, satisfaction *(fulfilment)*
attaint bad repute, brand *(stigmatize)*, convict, denigrate, discredit, disgrace *(noun)*, disgrace *(verb)*, dishonor *(shame)*, dishonor *(deprive of honor)*, ignominy, impeach, notoriety, opprobrium, pillory, scandal, shame, smear, stain, sully. SEE MAIN ENTRY
attemper adjust *(regulate)*, assuage, attune, check *(restrain)*, denature, extenuate, moderate *(temper)*, mollify, palliate *(abate)*, qualify *(condition)*, remit *(relax)*, soothe
attempt assume *(undertake)*, conatus, effort, endeavor *(noun)*, endeavor *(verb)*, enterprise *(undertaking)*, experiment, project, pursue *(strive to gain)*, pursuit *(effort to secure)*, strive, struggle, trial *(experiment)*, undertake, undertaking *(enterprise)*, venture, work *(effort)*. SEE MAIN ENTRY
attempt strenuously endeavor
attempt to disprove debate
attempt to divert dissuade, expostulate
attempt to equal competition
attempt to obstruct legislation filibuster
attempt to prevent dissuade
attempt violence to assault
attend care *(regard)*, concentrate *(pay attention)*, concern *(care)*, devote, focus, immerse *(engross)*, maintain *(sustain)*, monitor, note *(notice)*, observe *(obey)*, observe *(watch)*, overhear, pander, patrol, protect, regard *(pay attention)*, remedy, report *(present oneself)*, serve *(assist)*, study, treat *(process)*. SEE MAIN ENTRY
attend *(To be present at)*. SEE MAIN ENTRY
attend as consequence ensue
attend minutely concentrate *(pay attention)*, focus
attend to assume *(undertake)*, care *(regard)*, concern *(care)*, hear *(give attention to)*, heed, notice *(observe)*, obey, oversee, preserve
attend to business labor
attend to instructions conform

attend to orders comply, obey
attendance service *(assistance)*. SEE MAIN ENTRY
attendant ancillary *(auxiliary)*, caretaker *(one caring for property)*, clerical, coactor, coadjutant, cohort, collateral *(accompanying)*, colleague, concomitant, concurrent *(at the same time)*, consociate, copartner *(coconspirator)*, guardian, incidental, ministerial, participant, party *(participant)*, present *(current)*, supplementary, tangential
attendant conditions circumstances
attended by obstacles difficult
attended with death deadly
attended with risk dangerous
attending circumspect, clerical, concomitant, concurrent *(at the same time)*, ministerial
attention adhesion *(loyalty)*, caution *(vigilance)*, concern *(interest)*, consideration *(contemplation)*, contemplation, diligence *(care)*, discretion *(quality of being discreet)*, emphasis, homage, industry *(activity)*, interest *(concern)*, notice *(heed)*, observation, perception, precaution, prudence, recognition, relief *(aid)*, respect, scrutiny, stress *(accent)*
attention to detail diligence *(care)*, interest *(concern)*
attentive alert *(vigilant)*, careful, circumspect, close *(rigorous)*, conscientious, conscious *(aware)*, deliberate, diligent, faithful *(diligent)*, guarded, meticulous, obedient, painstaking, particular *(exacting)*, pensive, punctilious, punctual, sedulous, sensitive *(discerning)*, vigilant, zealous
attentive to detail particular *(exacting)*
attentiveness caution *(vigilance)*, comprehension, consideration *(contemplation)*, consideration *(sympathetic regard)*, notice *(heed)*, observation, preoccupation, regard *(attention)*, sensibility
attentuate deduct *(reduce)*, sustain *(prolong)*
attentus careful, economical, intent
attenuare attenuate
attenuate alleviate, decrease, depreciate, dilute, disarm *(divest of arms)*, discount *(minimize)*, extenuate, lessen, minimize, reduce. SEE MAIN ENTRY
attenuated deficient, impalpable, narrow, nonsubstantial *(not sturdy)*, tenuous
attenuation decrease, deduction *(diminution)*, mitigation
attest affirm *(declare solemnly)*, affirmation, allege, assert, assure *(insure)*, attestation, averment, avouch *(avow)*, avouchment, avow, bear *(adduce)*, bespeak, certify *(attest)*, cite *(state)*, claim *(maintain)*, confirm, contend *(maintain)*, corroborate, depose *(testify)*, endorse, establish *(show)*, evidence, manifest, posit, profess *(avow)*, promise *(vow)*, seal *(solemnize)*, subscribe *(sign)*, substantiate, support *(corroborate)*, sustain *(confirm)*, testify, validate, verify *(confirm)*, verify *(swear)*, vouch. SEE MAIN ENTRY
attest to acknowledge *(declare)*, converse, notarize, plead *(allege in a legal action)*
attestable convincing
attestant affiant, affirmant, bystander, deponent, eyewitness, indicator, undersigned, witness
attestation adjuration, admission *(disclosure)*, affirmance *(authentication)*, affirmance *(legal affirmation)*, affirmation, assertion, asseveration, assurance, averment, avouchment, avowal, certificate,

certification (*attested copy*), certitude, confirmation, corroboration, declaration, jurat, oath, pledge (*binding promise*), profession (*declaration*), proof, record, reference (*recommendation*), stamp, support (*corroboration*), testimony. SEE MAIN ENTRY

attestator affirmant, deponent

attested agreed (*promised*), authentic, certain (*fixed*), certain (*positive*), definite, documentary, factual, indubious, official, valid

attested statement affidavit

attester affiant, affirmant, bystander, deponent, eyewitness, indicator, surety (*guarantor*), undersigned

attesting declaration attestation, certification (*attested copy*), reference (*recommendation*)

attesting statement jurat

attestor deponent, witness

attestor of documents notary public

attinere concern (*involve*)

attingere adjoin, allude, border (*bound*)

attire oneself clothe

attitude conduct, conviction (*persuasion*), demeanor, deportment, frame (*mood*), generalization, habit, manner (*behavior*), opinion (*belief*), outlook, perspective, platform, position (*point of view*), property (*distinctive attribute*), reaction (*response*), stand (*position*), standpoint, temperament

attollere elevate

attonement consensus

attorn SEE MAIN ENTRY

attorney advocate (*counselor*), barrister, counsel, counselor, esquire, jurist, lawyer, practitioner, spokesman. SEE MAIN ENTRY

attorney for the people district attorney

attorney general prosecutor

attorney in fact SEE MAIN ENTRY

attorney representing the state's interest district attorney

attorney-at-law advocate (*counselor*), attorney, barrister, counsel, counselor, esquire, jurist, lawyer

attorney-client-privilege SEE MAIN ENTRY

attorneys bar (*body of lawyers*)

attorneys-at-law bar (*body of lawyers*)

attornment SEE MAIN ENTRY

attract bait (*lure*), coax, interest, inveigle, lure, motivate

attract notice interest

attract the attention occupy (*engage*)

attract the mind occupy (*engage*)

attract the thoughts occupy (*engage*)

attracting attractive

attraction affinity (*regard*), chain (*nexus*), decoy, desire, favor (*partiality*), incentive, inducement, invitation, obsession, partiality, penchant, predisposition, propensity, seduction

attractive popular, provocative, sapid. SEE MAIN ENTRY

attractive feature amenity

attractive nuisance. SEE MAIN ENTRY

attractive quality amenity

attractiveness amenity, draw (*attraction*)

attrahent attractive

attribuere ascribe, assign (*allot*), bestow, impute

attributable derivative

attribute ascribe, assign (*designate*), caliber (*quality*), character (*personal quality*), characteristic, color (*complexion*), differential, feature (*characteristic*), impute, property (*distinctive attribute*), specialty (*distinctive mark*), trait. SEE MAIN ENTRY

attribute to blame

attribute vicariously impute

attributed putative

attributed to contingent

attributes personality

attribution accusation, arrogation, assignation, blame (*responsibility*), incrimination, reference (*allusion*). SEE MAIN ENTRY

attrition erosion. SEE MAIN ENTRY

attroupement caucus, company (*assemblage*), cumulation

attune accommodate, comport (*agree with*), conform. SEE MAIN ENTRY

attuned consonant

attuned to acquainted, consensual

attunement adjustment, compatibility, synchronism

atypical anomalous, deviant, different, disordered, disparate, dissimilar, infrequent, irregular (*not usual*), notable, noteworthy, peculiar (*distinctive*), special, unique, unusual. SEE MAIN ENTRY

atypicality difference

auctio auction

auction handle (*trade*), sell, vend. SEE MAIN ENTRY

auctione vendere auction

auctor advocate (*espouser*), author (*originator*), informant, informer (*one providing criminal information*), promoter, spokesman, sponsor

auctor esse authorize

auctor generis ancestor

auctor gentis ancestor

auctorem esse advise

auctoritas authority (*power*), consequence (*significance*), credibility, patronage (*power to appoint jobs*), sanction (*permission*), warrant (*authorization*)

auctus development (*progression*), growth (*increase*)

audacia audacity

audacious brazen, bumptious, disdainful, flagrant, impertinent (*insolent*), insolent, presumptuous

audaciousness audacity

audacity contempt (*disobedience to the court*), disrespect, temerity. SEE MAIN ENTRY

audax lawless, spartan

audi alteram partem counterargument

audible coherent (*clear*), oral, verbal

audible expression speech

audience assemblage, bystander, collection (*assembly*), confrontation (*act of setting face to face*), congregation, interview, session

audiendi inquisitive

audio rights SEE MAIN ENTRY

audit analysis, analyze, bill (*invoice*), canvass, check (*inspect*), computation, examination (*study*), examine (*study*), indagation, monitor, scrutinize, study, test. SEE MAIN ENTRY

auditing accounting

auditio hearsay

audition hear (*give attention to*), interview, recognition

auditor comptroller

auditor disciple

augere compound, enhance, enlarge, extend (*enlarge*), heighten (*augment*), increase, intensify, magnify

augeri develop

augment accrue (*increase*), accumulate (*enlarge*), aggravate (*exacerbate*), aid, amplify, append, bear (*yield*), boom (*increase*), conduce, develop, elaborate, enhance, enlarge,

exacerbate, expand, extend (*enlarge*), hoard, increase, intensify, magnify, raise (*advance*), recruit, reinforce, supplement

augmentation accession (*enlargement*), accretion, addition, additive, adjunct, advance (*increase*), aggravation (*exacerbation*), boom (*increase*), boom (*prosperity*), codicil, continuation (*prolongation*), cumulation, exaggeration, extension (*expansion*), growth (*increase*), increment, profit, progress, reinforcement, rider. SEE MAIN ENTRY

augmentative cumulative (*intensifying*), supplementary

augmented inflated (*enlarged*)

augur anticipate (*prognosticate*), forewarn, harbinger, herald, indicate, portend, predict, presage, prognosticate, threaten

augur well promise (*raise expectations*)

augural portentous (*ominous*), presageful, prophetic

augurari guess, presage, surmise

augurate portend, presage, prognosticate

augurial ominous, presageful

augurous portentous (*ominous*)

augury caution (*warning*), caveat, harbinger, indicant, indication, indicator, precursor, premonition, symptom, threat, token, warning

august meritorious, outstanding (*prominent*), solemn

aura atmosphere, climate, environment, prestige

aura popularis distinction (*reputation*)

auribus hear (*perceive by ear*)

auricular confidential, privy

aurora onset (*commencement*)

ausculate hear (*give attention to*)

auspicate anticipate (*prognosticate*), commence, embark, portend, predict, presage, prognosticate

auspice forerunner, harbinger, indicant, indication, indicator, premonition, threat, token

auspices advocacy, aid (*help*), behalf, charge (*custody*), control (*supervision*), custody (*supervision*), direction (*guidance*), favor (*sanction*), power, safekeeping. SEE MAIN ENTRY

auspicial ominous, presageful

auspicious favorable (*advantageous*), fitting, opportune, propitious, seasonable, successful. SEE MAIN ENTRY

auspiciousness boom (*prosperity*), opportunity, timeliness

auspicium auspices

austere astringent, bitter (*penetrating*), bleak (*severely simple*), caustic, draconian, harsh, rigid, severe, strict, unapproachable, uncompromising, unrelenting

austeritas austerity

austerity cruelty, rigor, severity. SEE MAIN ENTRY

austerus serious (*grave*), severe

autarch dictator

autarchic autonomous (*self-governing*)

autarkic independent

authentic accurate, actual, convincing, de facto, definitive, documentary, factual, genuine, honest, literal, natural, original (*initial*), positive (*incontestable*), prime (*original*), real, realistic, reliable, rightful, sterling, undistorted, valid, veridical. SEE MAIN ENTRY

authentically admittedly

authenticate accredit, affirm (*uphold*), approve, attest, avouch (*guarantee*), avow, bear (*adduce*), certify (*attest*), cite *(state)*, confirm, corroborate, demonstrate *(establish)*, document, endorse, establish *(show)*, evidence, indorse, notarize, prove, sanction, seal *(solemnize)*, sign, substantiate, support *(corroborate)*, sustain *(confirm)*, swear, uphold, vouch, witness *(attest to)*

authenticate a will probate

authenticated actual, definitive, fully executed *(signed)*, genuine, official, true *(authentic)*

authenticated confirmation certification *(attested copy)*, reference *(recommendation)*

authenticated incident fact

authentication acknowledgment *(avowal)*, affirmation, approval, attestation, avowal, certificate, confirmation, consent, corroboration, deed, documentation, jurat, stamp, subscription, support *(corroboration)*, warrant *(guaranty)*

authentication of a will probate

authentication proceeding probate

authenticity honesty, reality, truth, validity, veracity

authentification certification *(attested copy)*

author architect, compose, derivation, elicit, engender, generate, invent *(produce for the first time)*, make, maker, originate, undersigned. SEE MAIN ENTRY

authoritarian dictatorial, dogmatic, ex officio, strict

authoritative arbitrary and capricious, assertive, authentic, categorical, certain *(positive)*, clear *(certain)*, cogent, compelling, compulsory, consequential *(substantial)*, decisive, definite, definitive, determinative, dictatorial, documentary, dogmatic, dominant, factual, forcible, incontrovertible, influential, juridical, master, official, peremptory *(imperative)*, persuasive, powerful, predominant, prevailing *(having superior force)*, sovereign *(absolute)*, strict, stringent, valid

authoritative assertion dictum

authoritative attestation certification *(attested copy)*

authoritative citation to appear monition *(legal summons)*

authoritative citation to appear before a court process *(summons)*, summons, venire

authoritative command edict, mandate, monition *(legal summons)*, order *(judicial directive)*, process *(summons)*, summons

authoritative decision adjudication, award, decree

authoritative estimate determination

authoritative example authority *(documentation)*, precedent, stare decisis

authoritative law codification

authoritative opinion conclusion *(determination)*, determination

authoritative order fiat, mandate

authoritative power clout

authoritative request demand

authoritative rule ordinance, precedent

authoritative rule for future similar cases authority *(documentation)*

authoritative statement instruction *(direction)*, opinion *(judicial decision)*, pronouncement

authoritative stoppage of trade embargo

authoritative suggestion dictate

authoritatively admittedly

authoritativeness authority *(power)*, certainty, certification *(certainness)*, force *(strength)*, puissance

authorities bureaucracy, hierarchy *(persons in authority)*. SEE MAIN ENTRY

authority advantage, agency *(commission)*, agency *(legal relationship)*, auspices, bailiwick, basis, bureau, certification *(certification of proficiency)*, charter *(license)*, charter *(sanction)*, clout, concession *(authorization)*, consent, control *(supervision)*, copyright, derivation, determinant, dint, documentation, dominance, dominion *(supreme authority)*, droit, eminence, expert, force *(compulsion)*, generalship, government *(political administration)*, hegemony, influence, judicature, jurisdiction, license, management *(directorate)*, management *(supervision)*, mastermind, occupation *(possession)*, patronage *(power to appoint jobs)*, permission, permit, possession *(ownership)*, power, precedence, precedent, predominance, prerogative, prescription *(claim of title)*, prescription *(directive)*, prestige, primacy, privilege, professional, realm, reference *(citation)*, regime, right *(entitlement)*, source, specialist, supremacy, title *(right)*, validity, warrant *(authorization)*, weight *(importance)*. SEE MAIN ENTRY

authority *(Legal expert)*. SEE MAIN ENTRY

authority to act for another proxy

authority to hear and decide a case jurisdiction

authority to search search warrant

authorization appointment *(act of designating)*, approval, assent, assignment *(designation)*, brevet, capacity *(authority)*, certificate, certification *(certification of proficiency)*, charter *(sanction)*, concession *(authorization)*, confirmation, consent, copyright, credentials, delegation *(assignment)*, deputation *(selection of delegates)*, designation *(naming)*, dispensation *(exception)*, droit, fiat, franchise *(license)*, government *(administration)*, indorsement, leave *(permission)*, legality, legalization, legitimacy, license, mittimus, nomination, option *(contractual provision)*, permission, permit, prerogative, privilege, right *(entitlement)*, sanction *(permission)*, sufferance, title *(right)*

authorize accept *(assent)*, accredit, appoint, approve, assent, assign *(designate)*, bestow, certify *(approve)*, charge *(empower)*, command, commit *(entrust)*, confirm, consent, consign, cosign, delegate, designate, detail *(assign)*, employ *(engage services)*, empower, enable, enfranchise, entrust, grant *(concede)*, hire, indorse, invest *(vest)*, legalize, legislate, legitimate, let *(permit)*, notarize, pass *(approve)*, permit, qualify *(meet standards)*, sanction, seal *(solemnize)*, sign, suffer *(permit)*, validate, vest. SEE MAIN ENTRY

authorize formally charge *(empower)*, delegate

authorize to represent delegate

authorized admissible, allowable, allowed, de jure, due *(regular)*, entitled, fully executed *(signed)*, juridical, legal, legitimate *(rightful)*, licit, permissible, privileged, rightful, statutory, valid

authorized by law de jure, lawful, legal

authorized might force *(legal efficacy)*

authorizing deputation *(selection of delegates)*

authorless anonymous

authors press

authorship creation

authortative decision precedent

authortative principle of law precedent

autochthonal native *(domestic)*

autochthonic native *(domestic)*

autochthonous native *(domestic)*

autocrat dictator

autocratic dictatorial, powerful, strict

autocratic master dictator

autocratical powerful

autograph brand *(mark)*, inscription, sign

autography handwriting

automated industrial

automatic habitual, routine

automatic lack of due diligence res ipsa loquitur

automatic negligence res ipsa loquitur

automatic reaction instinct

autonomic autonomous *(self-governing)*, free *(enjoying civil liberty)*

autonomical free *(enjoying civil liberty)*

autonomous free *(enjoying civil liberty)*, independent, nonpartisan, sovereign *(independent)*. SEE MAIN ENTRY

autonomous being individual, person

autonomy freedom, home rule, latitude, liberty, suffrage

autoptic unmistakable

autoptical unmistakable

auxiliari assist

auxiliary abettor, additional, adjunct, affiliate, appurtenance, appurtenant, associate, backer, clerical, coactor, coadjutant, cohort, collateral *(accompanying)*, colleague, confederate, consociate, contributor *(contributor)*, contributory, copartner *(business associate)*, expedient, expendable, inferior *(lower in position)*, instrumental, ministerial, nonessential, participant, pendent, reinforcement, secondary, slight, stopgap, subordinate, subservient, subsidiary, substitute, supplementary, unnecessary

auxiliary in crime coconspirator

auxilium assistance, help, relief *(aid)*, support *(assistance)*

avail advantage, aid, behalf, benefit *(betterment)*, edification, enjoyment *(use)*, function, gain, help *(noun)*, help *(verb)*, inure *(benefit)*, output, profit, promote *(organize)*, purpose, recourse, relief *(aid)*, satisfy *(fulfill)*, use, utility *(usefulness)*, worth. SEE MAIN ENTRY

avail against countervail

avail oneself of adopt, capitalize *(seize the chance)*, employ *(make use of)*, exercise *(use)*, expend *(consume)*, exploit *(make use of)*, impropriate, plagiarize, resort, wield

availability access *(opening)*, possibility

available amenable, convenient, disposable, open *(accessible)*, present *(attendant)*, present *(current)*, public *(open)*, ready *(prepared)*, ready *(willing)*. SEE MAIN ENTRY

available assets stock in trade

available facts information *(knowledge)*

available means assets, capital, cash, personalty, property *(possessions)*, resource

availing adequate, beneficial

avails boom *(prosperity)*, proceeds, profit

avalanche cataclysm, overage, surfeit

avant garde sophisticated

avant-courier precursor

avarice greed

avaricious illiberal, insatiable, mercenary, parsimonious, rapacious, venal

avariciousness greed

avaritia greed

avarus illiberal

avenge penalize, repay, retaliate

avengement conviction *(finding of guilt)*, punishment, reprisal, retribution, revenge, vengeance

avenging punitive, vindictive

avenue admission *(entry)*, admittance *(means of approach)*, causeway, conduit *(channel)*, outlet, way *(channel)*. SEE MAIN ENTRY

avenues approaches

aver adduce, affirm *(claim)*, affirm *(declare solemnly)*, allege, annunciate, assert, assure *(insure)*, attest, avouch *(avow)*, avow, bear *(adduce)*, certify *(attest)*, claim *(maintain)*, contend *(maintain)*, convey *(communicate)*, corroborate, declare, depose *(testify)*, enunciate, express, observe *(remark)*, posit, profess *(avow)*, promise *(vow)*, propound, remark, speak, swear, testify, utter, vouch, vow

average cross section, customary, general, imperfect, intermediate, marginal, mediocre, mediocrity, mundane, nondescript, norm, normal *(regular)*, ordinary, regular *(conventional)*, typical, usual. SEE MAIN ENTRY

average out calculate

averageness mediocrity

averment adjuration, affidavit, affirmance *(legal affirmation)*, affirmation, allegation, assertion, asseveration, assurance, attestation, avouchment, avowal, claim *(assertion)*, comment, confirmation, corroboration, count, disclosure *(something disclosed)*, profession *(declaration)*, pronouncement, proof, reference *(recommendation)*, remark, statement, surety *(certainty)*, testimony. SEE MAIN ENTRY

averred alleged

averse antipathetic *(oppositional)*, contrary, disinclined, disobedient, hesitant, involuntary, negative, reluctant, restive. SEE MAIN ENTRY

averseness disincentive, rejection, reluctance

aversion alienation *(estrangement)*, consternation, contempt *(disdain)*, hatred, ill will, intolerance, malice, odium, phobia, rancor, reluctance

aversus averse, disinclined

avert arrest *(stop)*, avoid *(evade)*, balk, bar *(hinder)*, block, counter, deter, discourage, estop, forestall, parry, prevent, repel *(drive back)*, save *(rescue)*, stall, stave, thwart. SEE MAIN ENTRY

avertere alienate *(estrange)*, avert, divert, embezzle, purloin

averting preventive

aveu avowal

avid eager, fervent, hot-blooded, ready *(willing)*, sedulous

aviditas greed

avidity desire, greed, passion

avidus eager, rapacious

aviso dispatch *(message)*, intelligence *(news)*, notification, tip *(clue)*

avocare disengage

avocat lawyer

avocation business *(occupation)*, career, employment, job, occupation *(vocation)*, position *(business status)*, practice *(professional business)*, profession *(vocation)*, pursuit *(occupation)*, trade *(occupation)*, work *(employment)*

avoid abscond, adeem, annul, avert, cancel, default, deter, detour, discriminate *(treat differently)*, disdain, disfavor, elude, escape, eschew, estrange, evade *(deceive)*, evade *(elude)*, exclude, fail *(neglect)*, forestall, forgo, forswear, parry, picket, pretermit, prevent, refrain, repeal, shirk, shun, stave, tergiversate. SEE MAIN ENTRY

avoid a straight answer equivocate

avoid arrest escape

avoid capture escape

avoid doing circumvent

avoid peril escape

avoid using conserve

avoidable needless, nonessential, unnecessary

avoidance absence *(nonattendance)*, abstention, boycott, default, evasion, exclusion, flight, nonperformance, odium, ostracism. SEE MAIN ENTRY

avoidance of extremes moderation

avoidance of waste economy *(frugality)*

avoided derelict *(abandoned)*

avoider fugitive

avoiding evasive, reluctant

avoiding extravagance economical

avoiding the society of others solitary

avoidless certain *(positive)*, necessary *(inescapable)*, unavoidable *(inevitable)*

avouch affirm *(declare solemnly)*, allege, assert, assure *(insure)*, avow, bear *(adduce)*, certify *(attest)*, claim *(maintain)*, corroborate, depose *(testify)*, evidence, posit, profess *(avow)*, promise *(vow)*, verify *(swear)*, vouch. SEE MAIN ENTRY

avouched alleged

avouchment adjuration, affidavit, affirmance *(legal affirmation)*, affirmation, assertion, asseveration, attestation, averment, avowal, certification *(attested copy)*, claim *(assertion)*, confirmation, contract, corroboration, jurat, oath, reference *(recommendation)*. SEE MAIN ENTRY

avow acknowledge *(declare)*, affirm *(declare solemnly)*, agree *(comply)*, assert, assurance, assure *(insure)*, bear *(adduce)*, betray *(disclose)*, certify *(attest)*, claim *(maintain)*, confirm, contend *(maintain)*, convey *(communicate)*, declare, depose *(testify)*, pledge *(promise the performance of)*, posit, promise *(vow)*, recognize *(acknowledge)*, swear, testify, verify *(swear)*, vow. SEE MAIN ENTRY

avowal adjuration, admission *(disclosure)*, affidavit, affirmance *(legal affirmation)*, affirmation, assertion, asseveration, assurance, attestation, averment, avouchment, claim *(assertion)*, contract, conviction *(persuasion)*, covenant, disclosure *(something disclosed)*, jurat, oath, pledge *(binding promise)*, profession *(declaration)*, promise, recognition, recognizance, reference *(recommendation)*, statement, surety *(certainty)*, testimony, undertaking *(pledge)*. SEE MAIN ENTRY

avowal of guilt confession

avowance acknowledgment *(avowal)*, adjuration, affidavit, assurance, avouchment, avowal, common knowledge, oath, pledge *(binding promise)*, reference *(recommendation)*, surety *(certainty)*

avowed agreed *(promised)*, alleged, manifest, ostensible, putative

avowedly admittedly, purported

avulsion evulsion. SEE MAIN ENTRY

await expect *(anticipate)*, forestall, remain *(stay)*, stay *(rest)*

awaited forseen, forthcoming, prospective

awaiting expectation

awake guarded

awake a suspicion doubt *(distrust)*

awake to discern *(detect with the senses)*, discover, sensitive *(discerning)*

awaken disabuse, elicit, foment, incite, inspire, originate, perceive, provoke, stimulate

awaken memories remind

awakened acquainted, penitent, renascent

awakening moving *(evoking emotion)*, revival

award adjudge, adjudicate, adjudication, apportion, benefit *(conferment)*, bestow, bounty, cession, confer *(give)*, contribute *(supply)*, contribution *(donation)*, convey *(transfer)*, decide, decree *(noun)*, decree *(verb)*, dedicate, degree *(academic title)*, delegate, demise, determination, determine, dole, dower, endow, endowment, endue, finding, gift *(present)*, give *(grant)*, grant, grant *(transfer formally)*, gratuity *(present)*, largess *(gift)*, leave *(give)*, parcel, pass *(advance)*, pay *(noun)*, pay *(verb)*, present *(make a gift)*, prize, provide *(supply)*, recognition, relief *(legal redress)*, remunerate, remuneration, reward, ruling, tip *(gratuity)*, trover, verdict. SEE MAIN ENTRY

award assent permit

award judgment adjudicate

award of punishment sentence

awarding donative

aware acute, artful, cognizant, guarded, knowing, learned, literate, perceptive, receptive, sensitive *(discerning)*

aware of acquainted, familiar *(informed)*

awareness appreciation *(perception)*, cognition, comprehension, insight, judgment *(discernment)*, perception, realization, reason *(sound judgment)*, recognition, sagacity, scienter, sense *(feeling)*, sense *(intelligence)*, sensibility, understanding *(comprehension)*

awareness of comprehension

away SEE MAIN ENTRY

awe fear, impress *(affect deeply)*, interest *(concern)*, panic, phobia, regard *(esteem)*, respect, trepidation

awe-inspiring formidable, ineffable, notable, solemn, special

awe-strike overcome *(overwhelm)*

awe-struck speechless

aweless brazen, unabashed, unaffected *(uninfluenced)*

awesome formidable, ineffable, notable, sacrosanct, solemn, special

awesomeness solemnity

awestricken diffident

awestruck diffident

awful dire, heinous, lamentable. SEE MAIN ENTRY

awkward difficult, improper, inadept, incompetent, inelegant, inept *(incompetent)*, ponderous, unbecoming, uncouth, unsuitable

awkward predicament dilemma

awkward situation dilemma, embarrassment, plight

awkwardness embarrassment

AWOL desertion

awry anomalous, astray, defective, disordered, errant, faulty, incorrect, oblique *(slanted)*

axiom dogma, maxim, postulate, precept, prescription *(directive)*

axiomatic absolute *(conclusive)*, certain *(positive)*, definite, evident, irrefutable, obvious, peremptory *(absolute)*, positive *(incontestable)*, proverbial, uncontested, undeniable, undisputed. SEE MAIN ENTRY

axiomatical evident, irrefutable, obvious, positive *(incontestable)*, undeniable
axioms premises *(hypotheses)*
axis center *(central position)*, league
ayslum inhabitation *(place of dwelling)*

B

babble jargon *(unintelligible language)*, prattle
babbling loquacious
babel imbroglio
babies children
baby infant, minor. SEE MAIN ENTRY
babyish jejune *(lacking maturity)*
babyishness puerility
bacchanalia debauchery
bacchanalianism inebriation
back abet, adhere *(maintain loyalty)*, advocate, assist, avouch *(guarantee)*, bear *(support)*, bolster, capitalize *(provide capital)*, cosign, countenance, delinquent *(overdue)*, document, encourage, endorse, espouse, favor, finance, guarantee, help, invest *(fund)*, justify, nurture, parlay *(bet)*, promote *(organize)*, recommend, sponsor, subsidize, support *(assist)*, underwrite, uphold, vouch. SEE MAIN ENTRY
back again refinance
back away retreat, shun
back away from eschew
back down abandon *(withdraw)*, accede *(concede)*, disavow, surrender *(yield)*, yield *(submit)*
back off abandon *(withdraw)*
back out abandon *(physically leave)*, abandon *(withdraw)*, defect, disavow, quit *(discontinue)*, renege, retreat, withdraw
back payments arrears
back up bear *(support)*, capitalize *(provide capital)*, encourage, side, support *(corroborate)*, uphold
back-up data
backbiting denunciation, diatribe
backbone cornerstone, gist *(substance)*, ground, main point, mainstay, prowess *(bravery)*, substance *(essential nature)*, tenacity, will *(desire)*. SEE MAIN ENTRY
backbreaking onerous, operose
backed-up fully secured
backer abettor, advocate *(espouser)*, assistant, benefactor, colleague, creditor, disciple, donor, mainstay, partisan, patron *(influential supporter)*, promoter, proponent, speculator, sponsor, surety *(guarantor)*. SEE MAIN ENTRY
backfire reaction *(opposition)*, repercussion
background atmosphere, basis, case *(set of circumstances)*, context, determinant, preparation, scene
backhanded indirect, oblique *(evasive)*
backing advocacy, aid *(help)*, auspices, charity, coverage *(insurance)*, favor *(sanction)*, guaranty, guidance, help, indorsement, investment, loan, patronage *(power to appoint jobs)*, patronage *(support)*, promotion *(encouragement)*, reinforcement, relief *(aid)*, service *(assistance)*, subsidy, support *(assistance)*, support *(corroboration)*. SEE MAIN ENTRY
backlash reaction *(opposition)*, repercussion
backlog store *(depository)*
backroom cache *(hiding place)*
backset casualty, damper *(depressant)*, misfortune

backslide recidivate, regress, relapse, repeat *(do again)*, return *(go back)*, reversal, reversion *(act of returning)*, revert
backsliding recidivism, recrudescence, regressive, relapse. SEE MAIN ENTRY
backstair furtive
backtrack retreat, withdraw
backward back *(in reverse)*, regressive. SEE MAIN ENTRY
backward step decline
backwood provincial
baculum cudgel
bad deleterious, delinquent *(guilty of a misdeed)*, deplorable, depraved, detrimental, disastrous, disreputable, harmful, heinous, immoral, imperfect, iniquitous, nefarious, noxious, peccable, peccant *(culpable)*, perverse, poor *(inferior in quality)*, profane, reprehensible, reprobate, unfavorable, wrongful. SEE MAIN ENTRY
bad behavior miscarriage, misdeed
bad blood umbrage
bad character bad repute, disgrace, dishonor *(shame)*, disrepute, turpitude. SEE MAIN ENTRY
bad check SEE MAIN ENTRY
bad conduct malfeasance, misconduct
bad debt nonpayment. SEE MAIN ENTRY
bad example convict
bad faith dishonesty, infidelity. SEE MAIN ENTRY
bad favor dishonor *(shame)*
bad feeling odium
bad fortune calamity, casualty, misfortune, privation
bad habit vice
bad idea miscue
bad influence bad repute
bad intent ill will, malice
bad intention malice
bad job maladministration
bad judgment misestimation, misjudgment. SEE MAIN ENTRY
bad language expletive
bad light opprobrium
bad logic non sequitur
bad luck misfortune, privation
bad management misconduct
bad manners disregard *(lack of respect)*
bad match misjoinder
bad name attaint, bad character, bad repute, disgrace, dishonor *(shame)*, ignominy, ill repute, infamy, opprobrium, scandal, shame, turpitude
bad report disgrace, notoriety
bad reporting misstatement
bad reputation attaint, bad character, disgrace, dishonor *(shame)*, disrepute, ignominy, infamy, notoriety, scandal
bad repute attaint, bad character, disgrace, dishonor *(shame)*, disrepute, ignominy, ill repute, notoriety, scandal
bad review disparagement
bad taste impropriety
bad treatment abuse *(physical misuse)*, misusage
bad turn disservice
bad wishes imprecation
bad-hearted diabolic
bad-natured perverse
bad-tempered fractious, perverse, petulant
badge brand, designation *(symbol)*, indicant, indication, indicator, manifestation, onus *(stigma)*, speciality, specialty *(distinctive mark)*, symbol, trademark
badge of infamy disgrace, dishonor *(shame)*, ignominy, stigma

badge of office device *(distinguishing mark)*
badger annoy, bait *(harass)*, browbeat, discommode, discompose, disturb, harass, harrow, harry *(harass)*, hector, importune, intimidate, irritate, mistreat, molest *(annoy)*, persecute, perturb, plague, press *(goad)*, provoke. SEE MAIN ENTRY
badinage speak
badly advised misadvised
badly calculated inopportune
badly made inferior *(lower in quality)*, poor *(inferior in quality)*
badly needed exigent
badly qualified unfit
badly timed inopportune, untimely
badness delinquency *(misconduct)*, misdoing
baffle balk, confound, confuse *(bewilder)*, dilemma, disadvantage, disorient, elude, embarrass, foil, frustrate, muddle, obfuscate, perplex, perturb, prevent, thwart. SEE MAIN ENTRY
baffled lost *(disoriented)*
bafflement ambiguity, complication, confusion *(ambiguity)*, dilemma, embarrassment, problem, quandary, surprise
baffling debatable, elusive, enigmatic, inexplicable, inscrutable, labyrinthine, mysterious
bag gain, procure
baggage cargo
baggy full
bail security *(pledge)*. SEE MAIN ENTRY
bail out discharge *(liberate)*, disenthrall, liberate
bailiff marshal
bailiwick domain *(sphere of influence)*, realm. SEE MAIN ENTRY
bailment SEE MAIN ENTRY
bait badger, bilk, cajole, coax, decoy, ensnare, entice, entrap, harry *(harass)*, hector, incentive, inveigle, lure, mislead, pique, plague, provoke, ruse, seduction, trap *(noun)*, trap *(verb)*. SEE MAIN ENTRY
bait a trap ambush
baiting bribery
balance adjust *(regulate)*, collation, comparison, compatibility, compensate *(counterbalance)*, composure, coordinate, countervail, earnings, equipoise, fairness, moderation, neutralize, offset, overage, par *(equality)*, parity, proceeds, regularity, regulate *(adjust)*, remainder *(remaining part)*, residual, sanity, stabilize, surplus, weigh. SEE MAIN ENTRY
balance accounts check *(inspect)*, quit *(repay)*
balance against compare
balance due arrears, bill *(invoice)*, nonpayment
balance owed debt
balance sheet budget, ledger, register
balance statement budget
balance to pay debt, deficit, due
balanced agreed *(harmonized)*, coextensive, consonant, equal, fair *(just)*, firm, proportionate, rational, regular *(orderly)*, sane. SEE MAIN ENTRY
balanced contrast antithesis
balanced judgment common sense
balances capital
balancing compensatory, equivalent
bald evident, honest, manifest, obvious, stark, unmistakable. SEE MAIN ENTRY
baldness honesty
bale adversity, assemblage, disaster, misfortune, tragedy

baleful bad *(offensive)*, dangerous, deadly, deleterious, destructive, dire, disadvantageous, harmful, heinous, insalubrious, lethal, malevolent, malignant, noxious, ominous, pernicious, pestilent, portentous *(ominous)*, sinister, virulent. SEE MAIN ENTRY

balefulness harm

balk bar *(obstruction)*, contravene, disadvantage, discontinue *(break continuity)*, disoblige, foil, frustrate, halt, hamper, hesitate, hold out *(resist)*, interrupt, obstacle, obstruction, oppose, prevent, refuse, stem *(check)*, stifle, thwart. SEE MAIN ENTRY

balk at avoid *(evade)*

balking disinclined, hesitant, restive

balky hesitant, intractable, recalcitrant, restive

ball sphere

ballistics ammunition

balloon expand, inflate, magnify

ballooned inflated *(enlarged)*

ballot cast *(register)*, franchise *(right to vote)*, plebiscite, poll *(casting of votes)*, poll, primary, referendum, vote

balloter constituent *(part)*

balloting election *(selection by vote)*

balm cure, panacea, soothe

balmy medicinal, placid, remedial

bamboozle bait *(lure)*, betray *(lead astray)*, bilk, ensnare, inveigle

bamboozlement bunko, pettifoggery

ban bar *(obstruction)*, bar *(exclude)*, block, boycott, censor, constrain *(restrain)*, countermand, debar, deter, disapprobation, eliminate *(exclude)*, embargo, enjoin, estop, estoppel, exclude, exclusion, expulsion, forbid, inhibit, injunction, obstruction, ostracism, preclude, prohibit, prohibition, proscribe *(prohibit)*, proscription, refusal, rejection, relegate, restraint, suppress, veto. SEE MAIN ENTRY

banal insipid, lifeless *(dull)*, mediocre, mundane, ordinary, pedestrian, stale, trite, usual. SEE MAIN ENTRY

banality platitude

band assemblage, cabal, commingle, connect *(join together)*, consolidate *(unite)*, denomination, desegregate, federate, join *(bring together)*, league, lock, posse, zone. SEE MAIN ENTRY

band in a federation federalize *(associate)*

band of armed men posse

band of employees personnel

band of men armed with legal authority posse

band of union affiliation *(connectedness)*

band together adhere *(fasten)*, combine *(act in concert)*, concur *(agree)*, connect *(join together)*, federalize *(associate)*, join *(associate oneself with)*, meet, merge, organize *(unionize)*, pool

banded corporate *(associate)*, federal

banded together concordant, concurrent *(united)*, conjoint

bandit burglar, criminal, hoodlum, malefactor, outlaw, thief

bands ties

bandy circulate, debate

bandy with fight *(battle)*

bandy words bicker, communicate, discuss, dispute *(debate)*, speak

bane detriment, disaster, injury, trouble

baneful bad *(offensive)*, dangerous, deleterious, disadvantageous, disastrous, harmful, heinous, hostile, insalubrious, lethal, malevolent, malignant, noxious, pernicious, pestilent, sinister, virulent. SEE MAIN ENTRY

bang impinge

bang into jostle *(bump into)*

banish ban, condemn *(ban)*, dislodge, dispel, displace *(remove)*, eliminate *(exclude)*, exclude, expatriate, expel, isolate, oust, outlaw, prohibit, proscribe *(denounce)*, reject, relegate, renounce, seclude, transport. SEE MAIN ENTRY

banishment deportation, disqualification *(rejection)*, expulsion, layoff, ostracism, prohibition, proscription, rejection, removal. SEE MAIN ENTRY

bank coffer, deposit *(submit to a bank)*, edge *(border)*, fund, garner, hoard, keep *(shelter)*, margin *(outside limit)*, pool, repository, reserve, store, treasury. SEE MAIN ENTRY

bank annuities capital

bank check draft

bank note draft, money

bank notes currency

bank on rely

bank paper check *(instrument)*, draft

bank robber burglar

bankbook ledger

banker comptroller

banknote check *(instrument)*

bankroll money

bankrupt destitute, impecunious, insolvent, poor *(underprivileged)*. SEE MAIN ENTRY

bankruptcy default, privation. SEE MAIN ENTRY

banned barred, illegal, illegitimate *(illegal)*, illicit, impermissible, inadmissible

banned goods contraband

banner caption, heading

banner head caption

banner line caption

banning boycott

banshee phantom

bantling bastard

baptism call *(title)*

bar abrogate *(rescind)*, balk, ban, barrier, bench, block, blockade *(barrier)*, censor, censorship, clog, condemn *(ban)*, constrain *(restrain)*, constraint *(restriction)*, court, cudgel, damper *(stopper)*, debar, deport *(banish)*, deter, disable, disapprobation, disqualify, eliminate *(exclude)*, embargo, enjoin, estop, estoppel, exclude, exclusion, forbid, halt, hamper, impasse, impediment, inhibit, interdict, interfere, interruption, judiciary, keep *(restrain)*, key *(passport)*, lock, obstruct, obstruction, obviation, occlude, outlaw, preclude, prevent, prohibit, prohibition, proscribe *(prohibit)*, refuse, relegate, remove *(eliminate)*, resist *(oppose)*, restrain, restraint, restrict, save, seal *(close)*, shut, stall, stay, stay *(halt)*, stifle, stop, thwart, veto. SEE MAIN ENTRY

bar from access preclude

bar of justice bench, court, judicatory

bad sinister SEE MAIN ENTRY

bar someone's way halt

bar to an allegation estoppel

barbaric disorderly, uncouth

barbarity atrocity, bestiality, brutality, cruelty

barbarize brutalize

barbarous brutal, cold-blooded, cruel, disorderly, hot-blooded, malevolent, malignant, ruthless, uncouth, vicious

barbarousness bestiality, cruelty

barbiturate narcotic

bare barren, betray *(disclose)*, bleak *(exposed and barren)*, brief, clarify, confess, convey *(communicate)*, denude, devoid,

disclose, disinter, divulge, expose, find *(discover)*, manifest *(adjective)*, manifest *(verb)*, marginal, mere, naked *(lacking embellishment)*, only *(no more than)*, open *(in sight)*, reveal, simple, stark, unveil, vacant, void *(empty)*. SEE MAIN ENTRY

bare possibility chance *(possibility)*, improbability

bare subsistence austerity, indigence, paucity, poverty

barefaced brazen, outrageous, unabashed

barely purely *(simply)*, solely *(purely)*

barely acceptable marginal

barely adequate marginal

barely passable poor *(inferior in quality)*

barely possible ludicrous

barely seen impalpable, inconspicuous, indefinite

bargain adjustment, agree *(contract)*, agreement *(contract)*, barter, close *(agree)*, compact, compromise, compromise *(settle by mutual agreement)*, contract, deal *(noun)*, deal *(verb)*, dicker, discount, exchange, haggle, negotiate, pact, settlement, stipulate, stipulation, term *(provision)*, trade, treaty. SEE MAIN ENTRY

bargain for buy, expect *(anticipate)*, incur. SEE MAIN ENTRY

bargain under seal specialty *(contract)*

bargain with treat *(process)*

bargainer customer

bargaining collective bargaining, commerce, negotiation

bargaining agent broker

barge in impinge, interrupt

barnacle parasite

barometer criterion. SEE MAIN ENTRY

baroque elaborate, tawdry

barrage onset *(assault)*. SEE MAIN ENTRY

barratry disloyalty

barred blind *(impassable)*, inadmissible. SEE MAIN ENTRY

barren bleak *(exposed and barren)*, deficient, devoid, futile, ineffective, ineffectual, lifeless *(dull)*, otiose, pedestrian, unavailing, unproductive, vacuous, void *(empty)*. SEE MAIN ENTRY

barrenness blank *(emptiness)*

barricade bar *(obstruction)*, bar *(hinder)*, barrier, block, blockade *(barrier)*, bulwark, check *(bar)*, clog, confine, constrict *(inhibit)*, contain *(restrain)*, damper *(stopper)*, debar, deter, enjoin, estop, halt, hamper, hinder, impede, lock, obstacle, obstruct, obstruction, occlude, protect, protection, restraint, shut, stop. SEE MAIN ENTRY

barricaded blind *(impassable)*

barrier bar *(obstruction)*, bulwark, check *(bar)*, complication, damper *(stopper)*, deterrence, deterrent, enclosure, estoppel, handicap, hindrance, impediment, limitation, mete, obstacle, obstruction, panoply, predicament, prohibition. SEE MAIN ENTRY

barring deterrent, estoppel, save

barring out lockout

barrister advocate *(counselor)*, attorney, counsel, counselor, esquire, jurist, lawyer, representative *(proxy)*. SEE MAIN ENTRY

barrister-at-law advocate *(counselor)*, counsel, counselor, lawyer

barristerial forensic

barristers bar *(body of lawyers)*

barter alienate *(transfer title)*, business *(commerce)*, commerce, deal, dealings, dicker, exchange, handle *(trade)*, interchange, sell, trade *(commerce)*, trade. SEE MAIN ENTRY

bartering commerce

basal cardinal *(basic)*, central *(essential)*, elementary, essential *(inherent)*, fundamental, naked *(lacking embellishment)*, organic, original *(initial)*, primary, prime *(original)*, primordial, rudimentary, simple

base arrant *(onerous)*, bad *(inferior)*, bad *(offensive)*, basis, caitiff, cause *(reason)*, center *(essence)*, consequence *(significance)*, contemptible, contemptuous, cornerstone, depraved, derivation, determinant, disgraceful, disreputable, felonious, foundation *(basis)*, gist *(ground for a suit)*, ground, headquarters, heinous, ignoble, immoral, inelegant, inexpiable, inferior *(lower in quality)*, iniquitous, loathsome, machiavellian, nefarious, objectionable, obnoxious, odious, outrageous, peccant *(culpable)*, perfidious, perverse, plant *(place firmly)*, poor *(inferior in quality)*, profligate *(corrupt)*, recreant, reprehensible, reprobate, scandalous, seat, site *(noun)*, site *(verb)*, sordid, subservient, unscrupulous, unseemly, unworthy. SEE MAIN ENTRY

base camp headquarters

base conduct bad faith

base of authority headquarters

base of operations headquarters

base-minded depraved, dissolute

baseborn caitiff, ignoble, illegitimate *(born out of wedlock)*

based on underlying. SEE MAIN ENTRY

based on conjecture unsupported

based on evidence deductible *(provable)*

based on evidence of the senses empirical

based on observation empirical

based on proof deductible *(provable)*

baseless arbitrary and capricious, gratuitous *(unwarranted)*, ill-founded, immaterial, insubstantial, invalid, unfounded, unsupported, unsustainable, untenable, unwarranted. SEE MAIN ENTRY

baseless charge frame up

baseness abuse *(corrupt practice)*, bad character, corruption, degradation, delinquency *(misconduct)*, discredit, disgrace, dishonor *(shame)*, disrepute, ill repute, infamy, mediocrity, perversion, scandal, shame, turpitude

baser subaltern

bases circumstances, premises *(hypotheses)*

bashful diffident

basic central *(essential)*, elementary, essential *(inherent)*, essential *(required)*, fundamental, implicit, indispensable, initial, innate, integral, material *(important)*, naked *(lacking embellishment)*, native *(inborn)*, necessary *(required)*, organic, original *(initial)*, primary, prime *(original)*, primordial, requisite, rudimentary, simple, substantive, ultimate, underlying, virtual, vital. SEE MAIN ENTRY

basic doctrine principle *(axiom)*

basic facts SEE MAIN ENTRY

basic ingredient necessity

basic law principle *(axiom)*

basic part essence

basic rule principle *(axiom)*

basic substance component

basic truth principle *(axiom)*

basilar essential *(inherent)*, fundamental, original *(initial)*

basilary essential *(inherent)*, fundamental

basilica court

basis assumption *(supposition)*, base *(foundation)*, cause *(reason)*, center *(essence)*, consequence *(significance)*, content *(meaning)*, criterion, derivation, determinant, documentation, gist *(ground for a suit)*, gist *(substance)*, ground, main point, pattern, precedent, preparation, purpose, rationale, source, stare decisis, substance *(essential nature)*. SEE MAIN ENTRY

basis for development embryo

basis for relief cause of action

basis of argument gist *(ground for a suit)*

basis of comparison standard

basis of litigation gist *(ground for a suit)*

bask in relish

bastard illegitimate *(born out of wedlock)*. SEE MAIN ENTRY

bastardism bar sinister

bastardization bar sinister

bastardize debase

bastardy bar sinister

baste beat *(strike)*

bastille prison

bastinado beat *(strike)*, cudgel, lash *(strike)*

bastion bulwark, mainstay, security *(safety)*. SEE MAIN ENTRY

bat cudgel, strike *(assault)*

batch assemblage, body *(collection)*, bulk, congregation, quantity, selection *(collection)*

batch together glean, hoard

bate abridge *(shorten)*, attenuate, check *(restrain)*, commute, decrease, deduct *(reduce)*, dilute, diminish, ease, lessen, palliate *(abate)*

bathe imbue, immerse *(plunge into)*, permeate, pervade

baton bar sinister

batter beat *(strike)*, force *(break)*, lash *(strike)*, mishandle *(maltreat)*, mutilate, strike *(assault)*

battering ram cudgel

battery SEE MAIN ENTRY

battle affray, bicker, collision *(dispute)*, compete, conflict, confrontation *(altercation)*, contend *(dispute)*, contest *(dispute)*, contest, defy, disagree, engage *(involve)*, fracas, fray, grapple, oppose, resistance, strife, struggle. SEE MAIN ENTRY

battle maneuver strategy

battle verbally debate

battlement bulwark

battler contestant

battling belligerency, hostile, offensive *(taking the initiative)*

battology tautology

batture alluvion

bawdiness obscenity, pornography

bawdy lascivious, lecherous, lewd, licentious, obscene, prurient, salacious, suggestive *(risqué)*

bazaar exchange, market *(business)*

be exist, subsist

be a benefactor fund

be a candidate compete

be a coward fear

be a customer of patronize *(trade with)*

be a drag on impede

be a drunkard carouse

be a factor concern *(involve)*

be a feature constitute *(compose)*

be a good investment pay

be a name for denote

be a part of involve *(participate)*

be a participator in commit *(perpetrate)*

be a party to commit *(perpetrate)*, connive, contribute *(assist)*, cooperate, involve *(participate)*, partake, participate

be a reproach to disgrace

be a sign of denote, indicate

be a sound argument cohere *(be logically consistent)*

be a spectator observe *(watch)*, witness *(have direct knowledge of)*

be a suppliant call *(appeal to)*

be a token of indicate

be a winner prevail *(triumph)*

be a witness observe *(watch)*

be absorbed in devote

be abstracted muse

be accepted pass *(satisfy requirements)*

be accordant agree *(comply)*, cohere *(be logically consistent)*, coincide *(concur)*, comport *(agree with)*, correspond *(be equivalent)*

be accorded hold *(possess)*

be accountable answer *(be responsible)*

be acquainted comprehend *(understand)*

be acquainted with apprehend *(perceive)*, perceive, pierce *(discern)*

be active with occupy *(engage)*

be adjacent to abut, adjoin, border *(bound)*

be afflicted suffer *(sustain loss)*

be afraid fear

be after desire

be against confront *(oppose)*, disapprove *(reject)*

be agreeable satisfy *(fulfill)*

be ahead of precede

be akin appertain, correspond *(be equivalent)*

be alarmed fear

be alive exist

be all over cease

be allowable lie *(be sustainable)*

be ambassador for represent *(substitute)*

be ambiguous equivocate

be an accomplice commit *(perpetrate)*

be an agent for represent *(substitute)*

be an impediment constrict *(inhibit)*, hinder

be an indication of denote

be an obstacle constrict *(inhibit)*, hinder, interfere

be an obstacle to impede, interpose

be an omen portend

be anchored remain *(stay)*, stay *(rest)*

be angry resent

be annihilated perish

be answerable allow *(endure)*, answer *(be responsible)*

be answerable for avouch *(guarantee)*, justify, pledge *(promise the performance of)*, promise *(vow)*, undertake

be antagonistic collide *(clash)*

be anxious fear, mistrust

be apologist for justify

be applicable appertain, apply *(pertain)*, comport *(agree with)*

be applicable to concern *(involve)*

be apposite comport *(agree with)*

be apprehensive doubt *(distrust)*, fear, misdoubt, mistrust

be apprised understand

be apprized comprehend *(understand)*

be apprized of apprehend *(perceive)*, perceive, pierce *(discern)*

be appropriate comport *(agree with)*, lie *(be sustainable)*, pertain

be apt comport *(agree with)*

be armed forestall

be associated with attend *(accompany)*, pertain

be assuaged relent

be at an end cease

be at cross purposes conflict, counter, counteract, differ *(vary)*, dispute *(contest)*, oppose

be at cross-purposes collide *(clash)*, confront *(oppose)*, fight *(counteract)*
be at ease rest *(cease from action)*
be at fault lapse *(fall into error)*
be at hand impend, report *(present oneself)*
be at loggerheads bicker
be at one with agree *(comply)*, coincide *(concur)*, conform
be at the head of moderate *(preside over)*, preside
be at the helm overlook *(superintend)*, oversee
be at variance bicker, collide *(clash)*, conflict, demurrer, deviate, differ *(vary)*, disaccord, disagree, dispute *(contest)*, dissent *(differ in opinion)*, except *(object)*, object
be at work attempt
be at work on occupy *(engage)*
be attendant on attend *(take care of)*
be attentive consider, devote, hear *(give attention to)*, heed, immerse *(engross)*, note *(notice)*, notice *(observe)*, observe *(watch)*, regard *(pay attention)*
be attentive to attend *(heed)*, perceive
be attorney for represent *(substitute)*
be attracted gravitate
be augmented compound, expand
be auxiliary to aid
be available lie *(be sustainable)*
be averse object
be aware comprehend *(understand)*, heed, observe *(watch)*
be aware of appreciate *(comprehend)*, apprehend *(perceive)*, construe *(comprehend)*, perceive, pierce *(discern)*, recognize *(perceive)*, regard *(pay attention)*
be banded together conspire
be beholden owe
be benevolent help
be bent upon desire, pursue *(strive to gain)*
be bereft of lack
be better transcend
be better for gain, profit
be bewildered misjudge
be biased favor, preconceive, predetermine, presuppose
be blind to ignore
be born arise *(originate)*
be bound answer *(be responsible)*, avow, owe
be calm repose *(rest)*
be capable of holding accommodate
be capricious vacillate
be careful beware, hedge, heed
be careless neglect
be careless with endanger
be caused by ensue
be cautious beware, care *(be cautious)*, hedge, heed, mistrust
be censorious denounce *(condemn)*
be certain expect *(anticipate)*
be changeful fluctuate
be characteristic of appertain
be chargeable answer *(be responsible)*
be chary beware
be circumjacent encompass *(surround)*
be circumjacent to border *(bound)*
be circumspect beware
be clear cohere *(be logically consistent)*
be closeted with rendezvous
be cognizant comprehend *(understand)*
be cognizant of appreciate *(comprehend)*, apprehend *(perceive)*, perceive
be coherent cohere *(be logically consistent)*
be compassionate relent, sympathize

be compelled answer *(be responsible)*
be complemental correspond *(be equivalent)*
be compliant relent
be composed of comprehend *(include)*, comprise, consist, contain *(comprise)*, include
be compounded of contain *(comprise)*
be comprised of comprehend *(include)*, consist
be concealed camouflage, elude
be concerned care *(be cautious)*, care *(regard)*, fear
be concerned for care *(regard)*
be concerned with appertain, apply *(pertain)*, occupy *(engage)*, pertain
be concomitant coincide *(correspond)*
be concomittant concur *(coexist)*
be confident expect *(anticipate)*, rely, trust
be confounded lose *(undergo defeat)*
be confused misconstrue, misunderstand
be congruent appertain, coincide *(correspond)*, correspond *(be equivalent)*
be congruous cohere *(be logically consistent)*
be connected to pertain
be connected with appertain, apply *(pertain)*, attend *(accompany)*
be conscience striken repent
be conscious comprehend *(understand)*, observe *(watch)*
be conscious of appreciate *(comprehend)*, apprehend *(perceive)*, detect, heed, notice *(observe)*, perceive, pierce *(discern)*, regard *(pay attention)*
be consistent comport *(agree with)*
be consonant comport *(agree with)*
be conspicuous flaunt
be constant adhere *(persist)*, endure *(last)*, keep *(continue)*, persevere, remain *(continue)*
be constituted of contain *(comprise)*
be consumed decrease
be contained in consist
be contemporaneous coincide *(correspond)*, concur *(coexist)*
be contemporary concur *(coexist)*
be contemptuous condescend *(patronize)*
be contemptuous of contemn, disdain, flout, misprize
be conterminous border *(bound)*
be contiguous abut, border *(bound)*, contact *(touch)*
be continguous to adjoin
be contrary collide *(clash)*, conflict, counter, counteract, countervail, differ *(vary)*, disagree, disapprove *(reject)*, dispute *(debate)*, dissent *(differ in opinion)*, fight *(counteract)*, gainsay, oppugn
be contrary to contravene, oppose
be conversant with comprehend *(understand)*
be converted change
be convinced opine
be convivial carouse
be counted vote
be courteous condescend *(deign)*
be cowardly fear
be critical complain *(criticize)*
be cunning cheat, circumvent, delude, illude, scheme
be daunted fear
be debited with overdraw
be deceitful bear false witness, fake, palter, pretend
be deceived err, misapprehend, misconceive, misread, mistake
be deceptive misstate, palter

be defeated fail *(lose)*, lose *(undergo defeat)*, succumb
be deficient default, lack
be dejected brood
be delinquent default
be demoted fail *(lose)*
be dense cohere *(adhere)*
be dependent on rely
be dependent upon appertain
be deprived of forfeit, lack, lose *(be deprived of)*
be deputy for represent *(substitute)*
be derelict break *(violate)*, default, disobey
be derived accrue *(arise)*, arise *(originate)*
be derogatory derogate
be deserving earn
be desirous lack
be destitute lack
be destroyed degenerate, lose *(undergo defeat)*, perish
be determined persevere, persist
be determined to intend
be determined to get pursue *(strive to gain)*
be devoid of truth bear false witness
be devoted adhere *(maintain loyalty)*, adhere *(persist)*
be devoted to obey
be different conflict, deviate
be diffuse digress
be dilatory defer *(put off)*, delay, hesitate, hold up *(delay)*, procrastinate
be diligent labor
be disappointed lose *(undergo defeat)*
be disclosed bare
be discordant bicker, collide *(clash)*, conflict, contend *(dispute)*, differ *(disagree)*, disagree
be discourteous offend *(insult)*
be dishonest bear false witness, betray *(lead astray)*, cheat, hoodwink, lie *(falsify)*, mislead, palter, prevaricate
be disjoined estrange
be disloyal defect, disobey, rebel
be disposed to choose
be disrespectful flout
be dissatisfied complain *(criticize)*
be dissimilar differ *(vary)*
be distended expand
be distinct differ *(vary)*
be distinguished from deviate, differ *(vary)*
be distracted muse
be disturbed over regret
be disunited disagree
be dormant remain *(stay)*, stay *(rest)*
be doubtful disbelieve, doubt *(distrust)*, misdoubt, mistrust, oscillate, suspect *(distrust)*
be drunk carouse
be dubious doubt *(distrust)*, hesitate, mistrust, pause, suspect *(distrust)*
be due owe
be due to ensue, result
be durable continue *(persevere)*, endure *(last)*
be eager desire
be economical retrench
be effaced disappear
be effective function, prevail *(triumph)*
be efficacious prevail *(triumph)*
be effusive outpour
be employed labor, occupy *(engage)*, practice *(engage in)*
be engaged in commit *(perpetrate)*
be engrossed in commit *(perpetrate)*, concentrate *(pay attention)*, devote

be entitled to as a matter of right, earn
be equivalent compensate *(counterbalance)*
be eradicated perish
be erased disappear
be erroneous bear false witness, err, miscalculate, misread, misstate, mistake
be established lie *(be sustainable)*
be established in inhabit
be evasive evade *(deceive)*, palter, prevaricate
be even with quit *(repay)*
be evidence of manifest
be evident lie *(be sustainable)*
be extinguished perish
be extravagant dissipate *(expend foolishly)*
be faithful adhere *(maintain loyalty)*
be faithful to comply, fulfill, keep *(fulfill)*, obey, observe *(obey)*, perform *(adhere to)*
be faithless bear false witness, default
be fallacious bear false witness
be false bear false witness, equivocate, misrepresent, palter, perjure
be false to betray *(lead astray)*
be familiar with recognize *(perceive)*
be favorable to authorize, bestow, favor
be fearful fear
be firm endure *(last)*, maintain *(sustain)*, resolve *(decide)*
be firmly fixed maintain *(sustain)*
be fitting lie *(be sustainable)*
be fixed stay *(rest)*
be foiled lose *(undergo defeat)*
be fond of prefer, regard *(hold in esteem)*, relish
be forewarned beware, forestall
be forfeited back escheat
be forgiving relent
be formed of comprise, consist, contain *(comprise)*, include
be forsworn bear false witness
be forthcoming impend
be fraudulent bear false witness, palter
be frightened fear
be frugal retrench
be fruitful proliferate, propagate *(increase)*, pullulate
be frustrated lose *(undergo defeat)*
be given acquire *(receive)*, collect *(recover money)*, receive *(acquire)*
be given to understand construe *(comprehend)*
be gluttonous overindulge
be gone abandon *(physically leave)*, depart, part *(leave)*
be good to avail *(be of use)*
be governed by obey
be gracious condescend *(deign)*
be graduated pass *(satisfy requirements)*
be granted a legacy inherit
be greater surpass
be greater in value outbalance
be greater in weight outbalance
be greedy overindulge
be guarded beware
be guided by hear *(give attention to)*, heed, obey, observe *(obey)*
be guilty of perpetrate
be guilty of infraction break *(violate)*
be handed down to devolve
be handed over devolve
be harbinger portend
be harmonious attune
be hateful alienate *(estrange)*
be heir to hold *(possess)*
be helpful contribute *(assist)*
be horrified fear

be humbled lose *(undergo defeat)*
be hurtful ill use, mistreat
be hypocritical palter, pretend
be identical coincide *(correspond)*
be idle loiter, procrastinate
be ignorant misunderstand
be imminent impend
be immobile remain *(stay)*, stay *(rest)*
be immoderate carouse, dissipate *(expend foolishly)*
be immovable remain *(stay)*
be immune resist *(withstand)*
be impaired suffer *(sustain loss)*
be impolite offend *(insult)*
be impoverished lose *(be deprived of)*
be impressed regard *(hold in esteem)*
be improved by gain, profit
be in a quandary doubt *(hesitate)*
be in a reverie muse
be in accordance with comport *(agree with)*
be in action attempt
be in antagonism collide *(clash)*
be in arrears default
be in attendance appear *(attend court proceedings)*, report *(present oneself)*
be in authority moderate *(preside over)*, preside
be in awe fear, regard *(hold in esteem)*
be in charge preside
be in collusion maneuver, plot
be in collusion with connive
be in conflict with contravene
be in conjunction with border *(bound)*
be in contact with border *(bound)*
be in control prevail *(triumph)*
be in debt default, overdraw, owe
be in effect exist
be in error misapprehend, miscalculate, misconstrue
be in favor of approve, authorize, consent, countenance, embrace *(accept)*, pass *(approve)*, permit
be in general use prevail *(be in force)*, prevail *(triumph)*
be in harmony conform
be in harmony with agree *(comply)*
be in keeping comport *(agree with)*, conform
be in league with involve *(participate)*, participate
be in need lack
be in operation function
be in opposition disagree
be in possession of hold *(possess)*, own, possess
be in possession of the facts comprehend *(understand)*
be in power govern, manage, rule *(govern)*
be in present force exist
be in proximity approach
be in receipt of obtain, own, possess
be in sight appear *(materialize)*
be in sight of approach
be in store impend
be in the ascendant prevail *(triumph)*
be in the chair preside
be in the majority predominate *(outnumber)*
be in the neighborhood of approach
be in the running compete
be in the vicinity of approach, approximate, border *(approach)*
be in the way impede
be in the wrong err, mistake, misunderstand

be in tune with comport *(agree with)*
be in unison agree *(comply)*
be in want lack
be inadequate lack
be inattentive ignore, muse, neglect
be inattentive to overlook *(superintend)*
be incident to appertain
be inclined to think assume *(suppose)*, deem, presuppose
be incompatible collide *(clash)*
be incongruent differ *(disagree)*
be inconsistent conflict
be inconstant change, palter, vacillate, vary
be incredulous disbelieve, doubt *(distrust)*
be incurious disregard
be indebted owe
be indecisive oscillate
be indifferent disregard
be indifferent to discount *(disbelieve)*
be indignant resent
be indiscreet impart
be indulgent of allow *(endure)*, permit
be indulgent toward favor
be industrious labor
be inert procrastinate, remain *(stay)*, stay *(rest)*
be inferior lack
be influenced predetermine
be influential prevail upon
be informed comprehend *(understand)*, pierce *(discern)*, understand
be informed of perceive
be inharmonious conflict, differ *(disagree)*, differ *(vary)*
be inherent constitute *(compose)*
be inimical collide *(clash)*, counter
be injured suffer *(sustain loss)*
be inmovable stay *(rest)*
be insensitive disregard
be insincere bear false witness, palter
be insolent disparage
be instrumental pander
be insubordinate disobey, rebel
be insufficient lack
be insulted resent
be intelligible cohere *(be logically consistent)*
be intemperate carouse, debauch, dissipate *(expend foolishly)*, overindulge
be intent upon pursue *(strive to gain)*
be interdependent with concern *(involve)*
be intermittent fluctuate
be intimate cohabit
be intimidated fear
be intolerant persecute
be intrinsic appertain
be involved concern *(involve)*, participate
be irresolute change, doubt *(hesitate)*, hesitate, misdoubt, oscillate, pause, vacillate
be jaundiced preconceive, predetermine, presuppose, select
be joined conjoin
be joined to adjoin
be juxtaposed border *(bound)*
be lax neglect
be left behind lose *(undergo defeat)*
be lenient bear *(tolerate)*, condone, palliate *(excuse)*, relax, tolerate
be liable answer *(be responsible)*, owe
be loath disfavor, mistrust
be located dwell *(reside)*, reside
be logical cohere *(be logically consistent)*
be long-lived last
be lost to view disappear
be loyal adhere *(maintain loyalty)*
be loyal to obey
be lucid cohere *(be logically consistent)*

be made of   comprise, consist
be made up of   comprehend (include), consist, include
be malevolent   bait (harass), endanger, harass, harm, ill use, mistreat, persecute
be malicious   persecute
be manifest   appear (attend court proceedings), appear (materialize)
be master   direct (supervise)
be master of   handle (manage), hold (possess), own
be mendacious   bear false witness, palter
be merciful   condone, relent
be mindful   concern (care), regard (pay attention)
be misguided   err, miscalculate, misconceive, mistake, misunderstand
be misinformed   misconceive
be misled   err, misapprehend, miscalculate, misconceive, misconstrue, misinterpret, mistake, misunderstand
be mistaken   err, misapprehend, miscalculate, misconceive, misread, mistake, misunderstand
be mixed   desegregate
be mollified   relent
be more specific   elaborate
be motionless   remain (stay), stay (rest)
be moved   sympathize
be mutinous   disobey
be mutually opposed   collide (clash)
be near   approach, approximate, border (approach), impend
be near at hand   impend, threaten
be needy   lack
be neglectful   default, procrastinate
be negligent   default, disobey
be nervous   doubt (distrust), fear, misdoubt, mistrust
be no more   die
be noisy   brawl
be null and void   perish
be numerous   compound, proliferate
be nurtured   subsist
be obedient   obey
be obligated   answer (be responsible), owe
be obliged   answer (be responsible)
be oblique   deviate
be obstinate   adhere (persist), insist, persevere, persist, refuse
be obstructive   balk, clog, counter, fight (counteract), foil, frustrate, inconvenience
be occupied in concentration   muse
be occupied in study   muse
be occupied with   address (direct attention to)
be of contrary sentiment   dissent (differ in opinion)
be of different opinions   disagree
be of greater significance   outweigh
be of help   assist
be of service   aid, avail (be of use), contribute (assist), pander
be of the opinion   assume (suppose), deem, guess, surmise, suspect (think)
be of the same mind   coincide (concur)
be of use   assist, help, inure (benefit), profit, serve (assist)
be of value   avail (be of use)
be off   abandon (physically leave), leave (depart)
be offended   resent
be offensive   affront, bait (harass), harry (harass), mistreat, persecute
be offered   hold (possess)
be on one's guard   beware
be on the alert   beware, patrol

be on the lookout   beware, patrol
be on the watch   beware, patrol
be one   unite
be one of   concern (involve)
be one with   coincide (concur), merge
be opposed   conflict, disagree
be opposed to   conflict, cross (disagree with), disapprove (reject)
be opposite   confront (oppose), differ (vary)
be ostentatious   flaunt
be outdistanced   lose (undergo defeat)
be outvoted   lose (undergo defeat)
be overawed   fear
be overbearing   condescend (patronize)
be overthrown   lose (undergo defeat)
be paid   collect (recover money)
be parallel   concur (coexist)
be part of   appertain, constitute (compose)
be partial   discriminate (treat differently)
be partial to   favor, prefer
be partisan   adhere (maintain loyalty)
be patent   appear (seem to be)
be patient   bear (tolerate), forbear
be peaceful   rest (cease from action)
be penitent   regret, repent
be peremptory   insist
be perfidious   bear false witness, disobey, palter
be periodic   alternate (fluctuate), fluctuate
be perjured   bear false witness
be permanent   continue (persevere), endure (last), remain (continue)
be permissible   lie (be sustainable)
be permitted   lie (be sustainable)
be perplexed   misjudge
be persistent   recur
be persuaded   concede, grant (concede), opine
be pertinent   appertain, apply (pertain)
be pertinent to   concern (involve)
be petrified   fear
be piqued   resent
be pitiless   brutalize, mistreat
be placated   relent
be pleased with   relish
be plentiful   proliferate
be pliant   relent
be poor   lack
be possessed of   hold (possess), occupy (take possession), own
be possible   lie (be sustainable)
be precise   detail (particularize)
be predisposed   discriminate (treat differently)
be prejudiced   favor, forejudge, preconceive, predetermine, presuppose, select
be prepared   beware, expect (anticipate)
be prepossessed   predetermine
be present   appear (attend court proceedings), dwell (reside), remain (occupy)
be present and note   witness (have direct knowledge of)
be present to answer   appear (attend court proceedings)
be preserved   endure (last)
be prevalent   prevail (triumph)
be prewarned   beware
be prodigal   bestow, dissipate (expend foolishly), overdraw
be productive   pullulate
be proffered   hold (possess)
be profitable   avail (be of use), inure (benefit), pay
be prolix   outpour
be prolonged   endure (last)
be promoted   pass (satisfy requirements)

be prone to   gravitate
be proper   lie (be sustainable)
be proper to   apply (pertain)
be protracted   endure (last)
be provoked   resent
be proxy for   represent (substitute)
be prudent   beware
be public   bare, circulate
be published   circulate
be puzzled   doubt (hesitate)
be quartered   reside
be quiescent   desist
be quiet   rest (cease from action)
be racked   suffer (sustain loss)
be rash   forejudge
be rationally connected   cohere (be logically consistent)
be ready for   anticipate (expect)
be reasonable   cohere (be logically consistent)
be recalcitrant   disobey
be reconciled   condone, suffer (permit)
be recusant   disobey
be reduced in worth   decay, degenerate
be regulated by   conform, obey, observe (obey)
be related   correspond (be equivalent)
be related to   concern (involve)
be relevant   apply (pertain), concern (involve)
be reminded of   recall (remember), recollect, remember
be remiss   default
be remorseful   regret
be resident in   inhabit
be resigned   suffer (permit)
be resolute   choose, endeavor, insist, persevere, persist
be resolute in   prosecute (carry forward)
be respondent   countercharge
be responsible   cause, compose, create, induce
be responsible for   guarantee, sponsor
be responsive   acknowledge (respond), answer (reply), countercharge
be revengeful   resent
be rewarded   reap
be rife   pervade, predominate (outnumber)
be riveted   stay (rest)
be rude   affront, disparage, harry (harass), ignore, mistreat
be ruined   lose (undergo defeat), perish
be ruled by   obey
be ruthless   persecute
be satisfied   opine
be satisfied with   approve, recommend
be scared   fear
be scornful   flout
be sedentary   remain (stay), stay (rest)
be seized of   possess
be selfish   overindulge
be sensitive to   perceive
be serene   repose (rest)
be servile   pander
be settled   dwell (reside)
be settled in opinion   resolve (decide)
be severe   castigate
be severed   part (separate)
be showy   flaunt
be silent   cease
be simultaneous   coincide (correspond)
be situated   dwell (reside), reside
be skeptical   disbelieve, doubt (distrust), impugn, misdoubt, mistrust, suspect (distrust)
be sly   circumvent
be so good as to   deign
be so minded   choose

be solid crystallize

be sorry for deplore, regret, repent, sympathize

be sovereign predominate *(command)*

be specific describe, designate, enumerate, itemize, pinpoint

be spokesman for represent *(substitute)*

be spurious bear false witness

be stable last

be startled fear

be stationary remain *(stay)*, stay *(rest)*

be stationed dwell *(reside)*

be steadfast adhere *(maintain loyalty)*, adhere *(persist)*, keep *(continue)*, persevere, persist, prolong, prosecute *(carry forward)*, remain *(continue)*

be steady adhere *(persist)*, persevere, persist

be stealthy conspire, lurk, prowl

be still rest *(cease from action)*

be stricken suffer *(sustain loss)*

be strong resist *(withstand)*

be stubborn persevere

be subject answer *(be responsible)*, obey

be subjected to bear *(tolerate)*, endure *(suffer)*, suffer *(sustain loss)*

be submissive relent, surrender *(yield)*, yield *(submit)*

be submissive to observe *(obey)*

be subsequent ensue, succeed *(follow)*, supervene

be subservient pander

be successful attain, earn, pass *(satisfy requirements)*, prevail *(triumph)*

be sufficient fulfill, satisfy *(fulfill)*

be suitable comport *(agree with)*, lie *(be sustainable)*, pertain

be suited lie *(be sustainable)*

be sundered part *(separate)*

be superior beat *(defeat)*, outbalance, surpass, transcend

be superior in number predominate *(outnumber)*

be supportable lie *(be sustainable)*

be supported subsist

be supreme beat *(defeat)*, predominate *(command)*

be surety answer *(be responsible)*

be surety for avouch *(guarantee)*, cosign

be suspicious doubt *(distrust)*, suspect *(distrust)*

be sustained subsist

be swallowed up merge

be swayed predetermine

be sworn certify *(attest)*, testify

be tacked together cohere *(adhere)*

be taken for exemplify

be temperate forbear, refrain

be tenacious persevere, persist, remain *(continue)*

be tentative hesitate

be terrified fear

be the agent compose, create

be the author create

be the author of cause

be the cause generate

be the cause of compose, create, engender, evoke

be the chairman preside

be the effect result

be the effect of ensue

be the embodiment personify

be the equivalent of exemplify

be the guiding force oversee

be the heir of inherit

be the outcome result

be the reason compose, create

be the victor prevail *(triumph)*

be thorough follow-up

be thwarted lose *(undergo defeat)*

be timeless endure *(last)*, last

be timid fear

be tolerant condone, forbear, relent

be touched sympathize

be tranquil repose *(rest)*, rest *(cease from action)*

be transferred devolve

be transfixed remain *(stay)*, stay *(rest)*

be treasonable rebel

be treasonous disobey

be triumphant prevail *(triumph)*

be true adhere *(maintain loyalty)*

be true to keep *(fulfill)*

be unable to respect decry, disgrace

be unaccommodating disoblige

be uncandid palter

be uncertain confound, doubt *(distrust)*, doubt *(hesitate)*, hesitate, misdoubt, mistrust, oscillate, pause, tergiversate, vacillate

be unclear equivocate

be unconsumed last

be unconvinced disbelieve

be uncooperative inconvenience

be undecided doubt *(hesitate)*, oscillate

be under legal obligation answer *(be responsible)*

be under obligation owe

be under the impression apprehend *(perceive)*, deem

be understandable cohere *(be logically consistent)*

be understanding sympathize

be undetermined doubt *(hesitate)*, misdoubt, oscillate

be undisciplined disobey

be unexhausted last

be unfaithful default

be unfriendly alienate *(estrange)*

be unique differ *(vary)*

be united join *(associate oneself with)*

be unlike differ *(vary)*, vary

be unpalatable repel *(disgust)*

be unresolved oscillate

be unruly disobey

be unseen lurk

be unsettled alternate *(fluctuate)*, vacillate

be unsteady fluctuate, oscillate, vacillate

be unsuccessful fail *(lose)*, lose *(undergo defeat)*

be unsure oscillate, tergiversate, vacillate

be unsusceptible resist *(withstand)*

be untruthful bear false witness, equivocate, fabricate *(make up)*, lie *(falsify)*, palter, perjure, prevaricate

be unwilling conflict, disoblige, dissent *(withhold assent)*, hold out *(resist)*, refuse

be unyielding adhere *(persist)*, persevere, persist

be uppermost in the mind occur *(come to mind)*

be useful avail *(be of use)*, function, pander

be vagrant loiter

be vague equivocate

be vengeful resent

be vexed resent

be vicious to brutalize

be victorious carry *(succeed)*, pass *(satisfy requirements)*, prevail *(triumph)*, succeed *(attain)*

be victorious over beat *(defeat)*, overthrow

be vigilant caution, concern *(care)*, observe *(watch)*

be violent fight *(battle)*, mistreat

be voracious overindulge

be vouchsafed hold *(possess)*

be wanting lack

be warned beware

be warranted lie *(be sustainable)*

be wary beware

be watchful concern *(care)*

be wicked to brutalize

be willing agree *(comply)*, comply, consent

be willing to bear assume *(undertake)*

be without lack, lose *(be deprived of)*

be worse degenerate

be worthy earn

be wounded suffer *(sustain loss)*

be wrong miscalculate, misconstrue

beach littoral

beachfront littoral

beacon indicant, indicator

beam emit, radiate

bear allow *(endure)*, carry *(transport)*, demean *(deport oneself)*, endure *(suffer)*, engender, produce *(manufacture)*, propagate *(increase)*, resist *(withstand)*, suffer *(sustain loss)*, tolerate, transmit, transport, yield *(produce a return)*. SEE MAIN ENTRY

bear a grudge against discriminate *(treat differently)*

bear a part contribute *(assist)*

bear away distrain, hijack, impropriate

bear down coerce, pressure

bear down against compel

bear down on press *(constrain)*

bear down upon attack

bear false witness frame *(charge falsely)*, lie *(falsify)*, misrepresent, palter, perjure, prevaricate. SEE MAIN ENTRY

bear fruit avail *(bring about)*, succeed *(attain)*

bear hard upon compel

bear heavily weigh

bear in memory remember

bear in mind care *(be cautious)*, regard *(pay attention)*, remember, retain *(keep in possession)*

bear malice alienate *(estrange)*, discriminate *(treat differently)*, mistreat, resent

bear no malice forgive

bear no resemblance deviate, differ *(vary)*

bear off deviate, kidnap

bear on appertain

bear oneself deport *(conduct oneself)*

bear out attest, certify *(attest)*, corroborate, document, evidence, justify, substantiate, support *(corroborate)*, sustain *(confirm)*, verify *(confirm)*, witness *(attest to)*

bear pain endure *(suffer)*

bear resemblance correspond *(be equivalent)*

bear the cost bear the expense, defray, pay

bear the cost of disburse *(pay out)*, expend *(disburse)*

bear the expense defray. SEE MAIN ENTRY

bear the expense of disburse *(pay out)*, expend *(disburse)*

bear the responsibility of hold *(possess)*

bear up resist *(withstand)*, uphold

bear up against maintain *(sustain)*, stem *(check)*

bear up under endure *(suffer)*

bear upon affect, apply *(pertain)*, based on, pertain, prejudice *(influence)*, refer *(direct attention)*, relate *(establish a connection)*. SEE MAIN ENTRY

bear with condone, excuse, forbear, submit *(yield)*, suffer *(permit)*, tolerate, vouchsafe

bear without resistance endure *(suffer)*

bear witness acknowledge *(declare)*, avouch *(avow)*, avow, certify *(attest)*, corroborate, notarize, promise *(vow)*, seal *(solemnize)*, speak, substantiate, swear, testify, vouch, witness *(attest to)*. SEE MAIN ENTRY

bear witness against betray *(disclose)*, denounce *(inform against)*, inform *(betray)*

bear witness to attest, certify *(attest)*, depose *(testify)*, evidence

bearable fair *(satisfactory)*, passable

beard defy

beardless inexperienced

bearer SEE MAIN ENTRY

bearing behavior, color *(complexion)*, conduct, connection *(relation)*, connotation, content *(meaning)*, demeanor, deportment, direction *(course)*, magnitude, manner *(behavior)*, position *(point of view)*, posture *(attitude)*, presence *(poise)*, relation *(connection)*, relationship *(connection)*, relevance, semblance, significance, tendency

bearing good will benevolent

bearing no name anonymous

bearing offspring freely fertile

bearing on relative *(relevant)*

bearing on the question pertinent

bearing out corroboration

bearing revenue lucrative

bearing the cost collection *(payment)*

bearing upon apposite, cognate, germane, incident

bearings locality

bearish brutal, fractious, petulant, severe

beast animal

beast of burden animal

beast of the field animal

beastliness bestiality, disrepute

beastly brutal, disreputable, heinous, obnoxious, odious, repulsive, vicious

beat attack, defeat, kill *(defeat)*, lash *(strike)*, oscillate, outweigh, overcome *(surmount)*, overwhelm, stress *(accent)*, strike *(assault)*, subdue, subjugate, surmount, surpass, territory, upset. SEE MAIN ENTRY

beat a retreat quit *(evacuate)*

beat back repel *(drive back)*, repulse, resist *(oppose)*

beat down browbeat, haggle, subdue

beat off parry, repulse, stave

beatable vulnerable

beaten despondent, passable

beatific ecstatic

beatify elevate

beating battery, defeat, failure *(lack of success)*

beauteous attractive

beautification motif

beautified elaborate

beautiful attractive, elegant

beautify embellish, meliorate

becalm pacify, soothe

becalmed dormant

because consequently

because of this a priori

bechance supervene

beckon call *(summon)*, entrap, request, subpoena, summon

beckoning attractive

becloud blind *(obscure)*, camouflage, confound, cover *(conceal)*, disguise, muddle, obfuscate, obnubilate, obscure, shroud

become arise *(originate)*, comport *(agree with)*, convert *(change use)*, develop, evolve, germinate. SEE MAIN ENTRY

become a citizen reside

become a component incorporate *(include)*

become a fact occur *(happen)*

become a member join *(associate oneself with)*

become a participator espouse

become a partisan espouse

become a party to an action intervene

become a reality crystallize

become acquainted rendezvous

become acquainted with ascertain, discern *(detect with the senses)*, find *(discover)*

become added accrue *(increase)*

become an ingredient incorporate *(include)*

become apparent develop, emerge

become apprised of find *(discover)*

become apprized discern *(detect with the senses)*

become aware note *(notice)*, occur *(come to mind)*, realize *(understand)*

become aware of apprehend *(perceive)*, detect, discern *(detect with the senses)*, hear *(perceive by ear)*, notice *(observe)*, overhear, perceive

become bankrupt fail *(lose)*, overdraw

become better progress

become bound promise *(vow)*, stipulate

become bound to pledge *(promise the performance of)*

become broad expand

become connected with join *(associate oneself with)*

become conscious note *(notice)*, realize *(understand)*

become conscious of hear *(perceive by ear)*, notice *(observe)*, perceive

become definite crystallize

become delineated crystallize

become depraved degenerate

become detached disengage

become deteriorated degenerate, depreciate

become disheartened languish

become due accrue *(arise)*, mature

become enfeebled decay, degenerate

become enforceable accrue *(arise)*

become extinct disappear, perish

become familiar with practice *(train by repetition)*

become firm crystallize

become flexible give *(yield)*

become forfeit lapse *(cease)*

become free escape

become fully developed mature

become greater accrue *(increase)*, appreciate *(increase)*, compound, expand, increase

become habituated naturalize *(acclimate)*

become heir to accede *(succeed)*

become ill languish

become impaired degenerate

become imperceptible disappear

become inactive quit *(discontinue)*

become informed discern *(detect with the senses)*, discover, find *(discover)*

become insolvent fail *(lose)*, overdraw

become involved care *(regard)*, engage *(involve)*

become involved with participate

become known convey *(communicate)*, occur *(happen)*

become larger accrue *(increase)*, compound, expand, increase

become less active subside

become less rigid give *(yield)*

become liable guarantee

become liable for incur

become like conform

become lower in quality decay, degenerate

become manifest arise *(appear)*, emerge

become more numerous appreciate *(increase)*

become notably worse degenerate

become noticeable arise *(appear)*

become of greater value appreciate *(increase)*

become of less worth depreciate

become one consolidate *(unite)*, unite

become operative arise *(occur)*

become payable mature

become perfected mature

become perverted degenerate

become plain emerge

become pliant give *(yield)*

become poorer by lose *(be deprived of)*

become present accrue *(arise)*

become prime mature

become public circulate

become putrescent decay

become responsible for assume *(undertake)*, incur

become ripe mature

become settled crystallize

become similar conform

become smaller decrease, diminish

become solid cohere *(adhere)*, crystallize

become surety for guarantee

become tainted degenerate

become unable to meet obligations default

become visible appear *(materialize)*, arise *(appear)*, crystallize, emerge, occur *(come to mind)*

become void cease, expire, lapse *(cease)*

become weak languish

become worse degenerate, deteriorate

becoming attractive, consonant, favorable *(advantageous)*, felicitous, fit, fitting, harmonious, palatable, proper, rightful, suitable

becoming greater cumulative *(increasing)*

becoming larger cumulative *(increasing)*

becoming more intense cumulative *(intensifying)*

becomingness propriety *(appropriateness)*

becripple disable

becurtain blind *(obscure)*, camouflage

bed lodge *(house)*, plant *(place firmly)*

bedaub stain

bedazzle discompose, disconcert

bedeck clothe, embellish

bedecked elaborate

bedevil annoy, discompose, disconcert, disorganize, distress, disturb, embarrass, harass, harrow, obsess, perplex, persecute, pique, plague

bedevilment detriment, harm, nuisance

bedim blind *(obscure)*, camouflage, obfuscate, obnubilate, obscure, sully

bedizen embellish

bedizened meretricious, tawdry

bedlam imbroglio, pandemonium, riot, turmoil

bedraggled disordered

bedrape clothe

bedridden disabled *(made incapable)*

bedrock center *(essence)*, foundation *(basis)*

bedwarf minimize

befall supervene

befalling accident *(chance occurrence)*, chance *(fortuity)*, contingency, experience *(encounter)*

befit applicable, comport *(agree with)*, pertain

befitting applicable, apposite, appropriate, condign, convenient, due *(regular)*, eligible, favorable *(advantageous)*,

647

felicitous, fit, just, opportune, proper, rightful, seasonable, suitable, tenable

befog blind (obscure), camouflage, confuse (bewilder), cover (conceal), disorganize, muddle, obscure, shroud

befogged lost (disoriented)

befool bait (lure), betray (lead astray), bilk, cheat, deceive, defraud, delude, dupe, entrap, hoodwink, humiliate, illude, inveigle, misguide, mislead

before theretofore

before further examination prima facie (self-evident)

before mentioned last (preceding), said

before now heretofore

before one's eyes perceivable

before time premature

before-mentioned aforesaid. SEE MAIN ENTRY

beforehand aforethought. SEE MAIN ENTRY

beforesaid aforesaid

befoul contaminate, corrupt, debase, infect, pillory, pollute, stain, taint (contaminate), tarnish

befouled tainted (contaminated)

befoulment contaminate

befriend favor, foster, promote (organize), side, sponsor, subsidize

befriender good samaritan, samaritan

befuddle confuse (bewilder), discompose, disorganize, disorient, disturb, muddle, obfuscate

befuddled lost (disoriented)

befuddlement confusion (ambiguity)

beg exhort, importune, press (beseech), pressure, urge

beg a favor call (appeal to), desire

beg for invoke, request

beg leave call (appeal to)

beg pardon repent

beg the question prevaricate

beg to be excused refuse

beg to differ demur

beget create, elicit, engender, generate, make, originate, produce (manufacture), propagate (increase), reproduce

begetter architect, author (originator), derivation, parents

begettor progenitor

beggar deplete, parasite

beggared impecunious, poor (underprivileged)

beggarliness poverty

beggarly destitute, ignoble, impecunious, petty, poor (inferior in quality)

beggary poverty, privation

begging request

begin arise (originate), assume (undertake), commence, conceive (invent), embark, establish (launch), generate, initiate, launch (initiate), maintain (commence), originate, preface, provoke, stem (originate), undertake, unveil. SEE MAIN ENTRY

begin a corporation incorporate (form a corporation)

begin again continue (resume), proceed (continue), reopen, resume

begin from develop

begin hostilities against attack

begin over continue (resume)

begin where one left off proceed (continue)

beginner amateur, apprentice, neophyte, novice, probationer (one being tested)

beginning causative, creation, derivation, elementary, embryo, foundation (basis), genesis, inception, inchoate, incipient, initial, nascency, onset (commencement), origin

(source), original (initial), origination, outset, overture, preamble, precursory, preface, preliminary, prelude, preparatory, prime (original), primordial, rudimentary, source, start, threshold (commencement). SEE MAIN ENTRY

beginning before retroactive

beginnings overt act

begird circumscribe (surround by boundary), embrace (encircle), encompass (surround), include

begloom obfuscate, obscure

begotten born (alive)

begrime deface, pollute, sully

begrudge withhold

begrudging jealous, reluctant

beguile bait (lure), betray (lead astray), bilk, cheat, circumvent, cloak, deceive, defraud, delude, disarm (set at ease), dupe, ensnare, entrap, evade (deceive), fabricate (make up), fake, feign, foist, hoodwink, illude, interest, inveigle, lure, misguide, mislead, misrepresent, palter, pettifog, pretend, propitiate

beguilement artifice, deceit, deception, falsification, fraud, hoax, knavery, pretense (pretext)

beguiling attractive, collusive, deceptive, delusive, dishonest, evasive, fallacious, false (not genuine), fraudulent, insidious

begun but not completed inchoate

behalf SEE MAIN ENTRY

behave demean (deport oneself), deport (conduct oneself), obey

behave towards treat (process)

behaved obedient

behavior conduct, demeanor, deportment, modus operandi, practice (custom), presence (poise), procedure, protocol (etiquette), way (manner). SEE MAIN ENTRY

behavior pattern conduct, manner (behavior)

behaviorism casuistry

behest canon, demand, dictate, directive, mandate, order (judicial directive), process (summons), request, requirement, requisition

behind back (in arrears), delinquent (overdue)

behind bars in custody

behind the age outdated, outmoded

behind the scenes clandestine, latent

behind the times outdated, outmoded

behind time back (in arrears), dilatory, late (tardy), overdue

behindhand delinquent (overdue)

behold detect, discern (detect with the senses), discover, notice (observe), observe (watch), pierce (discern), regard (pay attention), spy, witness (have direct knowledge of). SEE MAIN ENTRY

beholdable discernible, manifest, open (in sight), perceivable, perceptible, scrutable

beholden accountable (responsible), bound, indebted, loyal

beholder bystander, witness

behoof advantage, behalf, benefit (betterment)

behoove pertain

being character (an individual), entity, identity (individuality), individual, person, personality, presence (attendance), reality, survival. SEE MAIN ENTRY

being analyzed at issue

being done current

being in ill repute disreputable

being in two corresponding parts bipartite

being of no importance collateral (immaterial)

bejewel embellish

belated back (in arrears), dilatory, late (tardy), overdue

belaud honor. SEE MAIN ENTRY

belay handcuff

beleaguer attack, contain (enclose), envelop, harry (harass)

belie bear false witness, cloak, deceive, disguise, disprove, fake, falsify, feign, lie (falsify), misrepresent, prevaricate, refute

belief assumption (supposition), concept, conjecture, credence, credulity, doctrine, dogma, estimate (idea), faith, idea, impression, notion, presumption, principle (axiom), reliance, stand (position), standpoint, supposition, theory, thesis, trust (confidence), weight (credibility). SEE MAIN ENTRY

beliefs behavior

believability credibility, probability

believable convincing, credible, defensible, ostensible, plausible, possible, presumptive, probable, reliable, specious, tenable, unimpeachable. SEE MAIN ENTRY

believableness credibility

believe deem, expect (consider probable), guess, opine, presume, presuppose, surmise, suspect (think). SEE MAIN ENTRY

believe in confide (trust), rely

believe on consideration deem

believed convincing, putative, uncontested, undisputed

believer addict, disciple, partisan

believing convincing, credulous, naive, orthodox, positive (confident), unsuspecting

belittle cavil, condescend (patronize), contemn, decry, defame, demean (make lower), demote, denigrate, denounce (condemn), deprecate, depreciate, derogate, dilute, diminish, disapprove (condemn), discommend, discount (disbelieve), disdain, disparage, lessen, minimize, misprize, pillory, smear, spurn, sully, underestimate

belittlement disparagement, disregard (lack of respect)

belittling derogatory, disparagement, pejorative

bellicose contentious, disorderly, impertinent (insolent), inimical, insolent, litigious, malevolent, offensive (taking the initiative), perverse, provocative, pugnacious, spartan

bellicosity belligerency

belligerence belligerency

belligerent inimical

belligerency argument (contention), conflict, ill will, strife. SEE MAIN ENTRY

belligerent aggressor, argumentative, contentious, contestant, disputant, foe, litigious, malevolent, negative, perverse, pugnacious, spiteful

bellowing blatant (obtrusive)

belong comport (agree with), constitute (compose), correspond (be equivalent), pertain

belong as a part appertain

belong as an attribute appertain

belong intrinsically constitute (compose)

belong to affiliate, apply (pertain), join (associate oneself with)

belonger member (individual in a group)

belonging applicable, appurtenant, chattel, cognate, collateral (accompanying), correlative, holding (property owned), incident, pertinent, possession (property)

belonging equally to common (shared)

belonging to apposite, germane

belonging to all common (shared)

belonging to another country foreign
belonging to courts of justice forensic
belonging to debate forensic
belonging to many common *(shared)*
belonging to the house domestic *(household)*
belonging to the time current
belongings assets, capital, effects, estate *(property)*, goods, interest *(ownership)*, merchandise, personalty, possessions, property *(possessions)*
beloved popular
below a savoir
below contempt loathsome
below par defective, deficient, faulty, ignoble, imperfect, inferior *(lower in quality)*, marginal, nonsubstantial *(not sturdy)*, paltry, peccable, perfunctory, poor *(inferior in quality)*, unsound *(not strong)*
below standard poor *(inferior in quality)*
below standards defective
below the mark minimal
below the surface latent
belt circumscribe *(surround by boundary)*, contain *(enclose)*, embrace *(encircle)*, encompass *(surround)*
bemask blind *(obscure)*, camouflage, disguise, pretend
bemingle denature
bemire pollute, sully
bemist obfuscate
bemoan deplore, regret, repent
bemock disparage, jape
bemuddle confuse *(bewilder)*
bemuddled disordered, lost *(disoriented)*
bemuse perplex
ben trovato colorable *(plausible)*
bench bar *(court)*, chamber *(body)*, court, judicatory, judicature, judiciary, tribunal. SEE MAIN ENTRY
bench of judges chamber *(body)*
bench warrant search warrant
bencher jurist
benchmark SEE MAIN ENTRY
bend conform, contort, dispose *(incline)*, distort, relax, relent, subdue, submit *(yield)*, succumb, yield *(submit)*
bend out of shape contort
bend to obey
bend to one's will persuade, prejudice *(influence)*
bendable flexible, malleable, pliable, pliant, resilient, sequacious, tractable
bending flexible, malleable, sequacious
bene moratus law-abiding, moral
beneath consideration inappreciable
beneath contempt blameworthy, loathsome, offensive *(offending)*, paltry. SEE MAIN ENTRY
beneath notice inappreciable, inconsiderable, negligible, null *(insignificant)*, paltry
beneath one's dignity disgraceful
beneath standards defective
benediction laudation
benefaction aid *(subsistence)*, appropriation *(donation)*, behalf, benefit *(betterment)*, benefit *(conferment)*, benevolence *(act of kindness)*, boom *(prosperity)*, bounty, charity, clemency, contribution *(donation)*, donation, endowment, favor *(act of kindness)*, favor *(sanction)*, gift *(present)*, goodwill, grant, gratuity *(present)*, help, inheritance, largess *(generosity)*, largess *(gift)*, perquisite, profit, tip *(gratuity)*
benefactor backer, contributor *(giver)*, donor, good samaritan, patron *(influential*

supporter), promoter, proponent, receiver, samaritan, sponsor. SEE MAIN ENTRY
benefactress donor
beneficence benevolence *(act of kindness)*, benevolence *(disposition to do good)*, clemency, consideration *(sympathetic regard)*, goodwill, humanity *(humaneness)*, largess *(generosity)*, philanthropy
beneficent beneficial, charitable *(benevolent)*, charitable *(lenient)*, donative, humane, liberal *(generous)*, magnanimous, nonprofit, philanthropic
beneficent friend benefactor
beneficentia charity
bénéficiaire heir
beneficial ancillary *(auxiliary)*, contributory, convenient, corrigible, favorable *(advantageous)*, gainful, instrumental, lucrative, medicinal, operative, palliative *(abating)*, practical, profitable, propitious, purposeful, remedial, salubrious, salutary, valuable. SEE MAIN ENTRY
beneficial interest claim *(right)*
bénéfficiare beneficiary
beneficiary devisee, donee, grantee, heir, legatee, receiver, recipient, successor, transferee. SEE MAIN ENTRY
beneficience benefit *(conferment)*
beneficient benevolent
beneficium favor *(act of kindness)*, privilege
beneficus charitable *(benevolent)*
benefit accommodate, advantage, aid *(help)*, aid *(subsistence)*, aid, assistance, avail *(be of use)*, behalf, bonus, capitalize *(seize the chance)*, contribution *(donation)*, dividend, edge *(advantage)*, edification, endowment, favor *(act of kindness)*, favor, function, gain, grant, help *(noun)*, help *(verb)*, largess *(gift)*, output, preference *(priority)*, prerogative, privilege, proceeds, profit *(noun)*, profit *(verb)*, promote *(organize)*, promotion *(encouragement)*, realize *(obtain as a profit)*, reap, recourse, reward, service *(assistance)*, use, utility *(usefulness)*, value, welfare, worth. SEE MAIN ENTRY
benefit of doubt compurgation
benefiter benefactor
benefits consideration *(recompense)*
benevolence assistance, behalf, benefit *(conferment)*, bounty, charity, clemency, comity, consideration *(sympathetic regard)*, favor *(act of kindness)*, goodwill, help, humanity *(humaneness)*, indulgence, lenience, philanthropy, understanding *(tolerance)*. SEE MAIN ENTRY
benevolentia benevolence *(act of kindness)*, philanthropy
benevolently fairly *(impartially)*
benevolentness charity
benevolus benevolent
benight blind *(obscure)*, obscure
benighted blind *(not discerning)*, incognizant, opaque
benightedness ignorance
benign beneficial, benevolent, charitable *(lenient)*, favorable *(expressing approval)*, harmless, humane, nontoxic, paternal, philanthropic, propitious, remedial, safe, salutary
benign favor auspices

benignancy benevolence *(disposition to do good)*, humanity *(humaneness)*, largess *(generosity)*, philanthropy
benignant beneficial, charitable *(lenient)*, philanthropic, propitious
benignitas indulgence
benignity clemency, consideration *(sympathetic regard)*, favor *(act of kindness)*, humanity *(humaneness)*, largess *(generosity)*, philanthropy
benignus charitable *(benevolent)*
bent animus, aptitude, character *(personal quality)*, design *(intent)*, desire, direction *(course)*, disposition *(inclination)*, favor *(partiality)*, frame *(mood)*, inclination, inclined, instinct, partiality, penchant, pertinacious, position *(point of view)*, posture *(attitude)*, preconception, predilection, predisposition, prejudice *(preconception)*, proclivity, prone, propensity, resolute, stand *(position)*, standpoint, tendency
bent on solicitous
bent upon eager, earnest, insistent, zealous
benumb drug, obtund
benumbed insensible, torpid
benumbing chilling effect, lifeless *(dull)*
bepraise honor
bequeath abalienate, bestow, cede, contribute *(supply)*, convey *(transfer)*, demise, descend, devise *(give)*, devolve, endow, give *(grant)*, grant *(transfer formally)*, leave *(give)*, pass *(advance)*, present *(make a gift)*, transfer. SEE MAIN ENTRY
bequeathable heritable
bequeathal bequest, demise *(conveyance)*, devolution, endowment, grant, legacy, will *(testamentary instrument)*
bequeathed by will testamentary
bequeather donor, feoffor, grantor
bequest benefit *(conferment)*, contribute *(supply)*, contribution *(donation)*, devolution, donation, dower, endowment, estate *(hereditament)*, grant, hereditament, heritage, inheritance, legacy. SEE MAIN ENTRY
berate blame, castigate, censure, complain *(criticize)*, condemn *(blame)*, criticize *(find fault with)*, decry, defame, denounce *(condemn)*, deprecate, disapprove *(condemn)*, fault, lash *(attack verbally)*, mistreat, pillory, rebuke, remonstrate, reprehend, reprimand, reproach
berating contumely, objurgation, obloquy, revilement
bereave deprive, despoil
bereaved disconsolate
bereaved child orphan
bereavement cost *(penalty)*, privation
bereft bankrupt, destitute
bereft of devoid, insufficient
bereft of funds poor *(underprivileged)*
bereft of life dead, deceased, lifeless *(dead)*
bereft of reason deranged, lunatic, non compos mentis
beribbon embellish
berserk frenetic
berth employment, lodge *(house)*, lodging, office, post, seat, trade *(occupation)*
beseech call *(appeal to)*, exhort, importune, petition, plead *(implore)*, pray, pressure, prevail upon, request, solicit, sue, urge
beseeching precatory, solicitous
beseechment call *(appeal)*, entreaty, prayer, request
beseige dun, envelop

beset accost, assail, attack, badger, bait (*harass*), discommode, dun, embarrass, envelop, harass, harrow, harry (*harass*), hector, importune, inflict, obsess, perplex, persecute, pique, plague, press (*goad*), provoke

beset with danger dangerous

beset with difficulties painful

beset with difficulty difficult

beset with perils aleatory (*perilous*)

besetting hostile

besetting idea compulsion (*obsession*)

beside adjacent, contiguous

beside oneself ecstatic

beside the mark impertinent (*irrelevant*), inapposite, irrelevant

beside the point immaterial, impertinent (*irrelevant*), inapposite, irrelevant, needless, nonessential, peripheral

beside the question immaterial, impertinent (*irrelevant*), irrelevant, nonessential

besides also, further, save

besiege assault, attack, bait (*harass*), harass, harrow, importune, obsess, overwhelm, strike (*assault*)

besiegement assault

besieger aggressor

besmear brand (*stigmatize*), defame, denigrate, denounce (*condemn*), disgrace, dishonor (*deprive of honor*), disparage, pillory, smear, stain, sully

besmirch brand (*stigmatize*), contemn, defame, denigrate, denounce (*condemn*), derogate, discredit, dishonor (*deprive of honor*), infect, libel, malign, pillory, pollute, smear, stain, taint (*contaminate*)

besmirched blemished

besmirching defilement

besmut smear

bespangle embellish

bespangled pretentious (*ostentatious*)

bespatter brand (*stigmatize*), defame, denigrate, derogate, disparage, humiliate, pillory, pollute

bespeak call (*appeal to*), denote, evince, indicate, manifest, reserve. SEE MAIN ENTRY

bespread diffuse

besprinkle diffuse

best absolute (*ideal*), cardinal (*outstanding*), premium, prime (*most valuable*), select, subdue, superlative, transcend, utmost. SEE MAIN ENTRY

best behavior decorum

best of taste decorum

best part elite

best people elite

bestead avail (*be of use*), promote (*organize*), situated

bestial brutal

bestiality brutality. SEE MAIN ENTRY

bestir oneself endeavor, strive

bestow bear (*yield*), confer (*give*), contribute (*supply*), dedicate, delegate, descend, devise (*give*), dispel, dispense, dole, endow, endue, fund, furnish, give (*grant*), grant (*transfer formally*), impart, leave (*give*), mete, parcel, post, present (*make a gift*), provide (*supply*), spend, subsidize, supply, transfer, vouchsafe, yield (*produce a return*). SEE MAIN ENTRY

bestow by judicial decree award

bestow by will demise

bestow in shares disperse (*disseminate*)

bestow on administer (*tender*)

bestow thought upon muse

bestow upon bequeath, dispense, vest

bestow voluntarily grant (*transfer formally*)

bestowable heritable

bestowal appropriation (*donation*), benefit (*conferment*), cession, charity, concession (*authorization*), contribution (*donation*), conveyance, dedication, dispensation (*act of dispensing*), dower, endowment, grant, legacy, will (*testamentary instrument*)

bestowed gratuitous (*given without recompense*)

bestowed by ballot elective (*selective*)

bestower contributor (*giver*), donor, feoffor, grantor, obligee

bestowing donative

bestowment conveyance, dispensation (*act of dispensing*), donation, dower, endowment, gift (*present*), largess (*gift*), tip (*gratuity*)

bestowment of a share contribution (*donation*)

bestrew cast (*throw*), diffuse, dispel, disperse (*disseminate*), dissipate (*spread out*), spread

bet gamble, lottery, risk, speculate (*chance*), speculation (*risk*), stake (*award*). SEE MAIN ENTRY

bet on parlay (*bet*)

betoken anticipate (*prognosticate*), denote, evince, exemplify, herald, indicate, label, manifest, portend, predict, presage, prognosticate, promise (*raise expectations*), signify (*denote*)

betokening success auspicious

betongue lash (*attack verbally*), reprehend

betray bear false witness, bilk, cheat, defect, disobey, misrepresent, palter, rebel. SEE MAIN ENTRY

betray the secret inform (*betray*)

betrayal bad faith, bad repute, disloyalty, infidelity, treason

betrayal of a trust treason

betrayal of oath infidelity

betrayal of trust disloyalty, infidelity

betraying perfidious, recreant

betrayment bad faith

betrothed conjugal, nuptial

better ameliorate, amend, bettor, embellish, emend, enhance, help, meliorate, meritorious, outbalance, outweigh, preferable, preferential, promote (*advance*), rectify, reform, relieve (*give aid*), superior (*excellent*), surpass, transcend, treat (*remedy*)

better part generality (*bulk*), majority (*greater part*)

betterment advancement (*improvement*), amendment (*correction*), behalf, correction (*change*), development (*progression*), edification, headway, improvement, progress, promotion (*advancement*), reform, reorganization, repair

betterment SEE MAIN ENTRY

bettor betterment speculator. SEE MAIN ENTRY

between among, intermediate

bevy assemblage, band

bewail deplore, regret, repent

bewailing querulous

beware care (*be cautious*). SEE MAIN ENTRY

bewilder confound, discompose, disorganize, disorient, disturb, embarrass, misguide, muddle, obfuscate, overcome (*overwhelm*), overwhelm, perplex, perturb

bewildered insensible, lost (*disoriented*), speechless

bewildering complex, enigmatic, equivocal, labyrinthine, opaque

bewilderment ambiguity, bombshell, confusion (*ambiguity*), enigma, ignorance, incertitude, quandary, surprise

bewitch lure, obsess

bewitching attractive, sapid

bewitchment seduction

beyond further

beyond a doubt definitive, undeniable

beyond a question demonstrable

beyond a shadow of a doubt clear (*certain*), incontrovertible

beyond a shadow of doubt categorical, certain (*positive*)

beyond all dispute certain (*positive*), clear (*certain*), decisive, definite, definitive, inappealable

beyond all doubt demonstrable

beyond all praise prime (*most valuable*)

beyond all question axiomatic, categorical, certain (*positive*), decisive, definite, inappealable, incontestable, positive (*incontestable*), undeniable

beyond belief implausible, incredible, ludicrous

beyond compare absolute (*ideal*), best, leading (*ranking first*), paramount, prime (*most valuable*)

beyond comparison paramount, unique

beyond comprehension inapprehensible, incomprehensible

beyond contradiction incontrovertible

beyond control impracticable, insuperable, intractable

beyond correction irremediable

beyond cure irremediable

beyond dispute axiomatic, conclusive (*settled*), undeniable

beyond doubt absolute (*conclusive*), explicit, irrefutable, positive (*incontestable*), uncontroverted, undisputed

beyond expression indefinable, ineffable

beyond help incorrigible

beyond hope irremediable

beyond one's power insurmountable

beyond one's reach difficult, insurmountable

beyond price inestimable, invaluable, priceless

beyond question inappealable, undisputed

beyond reach inaccessible, unapproachable

beyond recall irrecoverable, irremediable, irrevocable

beyond redress irremediable

beyond reform incorrigible

beyond remedy irredeemable, irremediable, irreversible

beyond reproach unimpeachable

beyond the bounds of possibility insurmountable

beyond the jurisdiction of the court want of jurisdiction

beyond the limit extreme (*exaggerated*)

beyond the ordinary extraordinary

beyond understanding inapprehensible

bhang cannabis

bi-facial bilateral

bias bait (*lure*), discrimination (*bigotry*), dispose (*incline*), disposition (*inclination*), favor (*partiality*), favoritism, inclination, inequality, inequity, injustice, intolerance, nepotism, partiality, penchant, position (*point of view*), preconception, predetermination, predilection, predisposition, preference (*choice*), prejudice (*preconception*), prejudice (*influence*), proclivity, propensity, slant, stand (*position*), tendency. SEE MAIN ENTRY

biased disadvantageous, ex parte, exclusive (*limited*), illiberal, interested, one-sided, parochial, partisan, preferential, prejudicial, prone, subjective, unequal *(unjust)*, unfair, unjust

biased judgment inequity, partiality

bibacity dipsomania

bibliophilic learned

bibulosity inebriation

bibulousness inebriation

bicameral bipartite. SEE MAIN ENTRY

bicker brawl, contend *(dispute)*, dicker, differ *(disagree)*, disaccord, disagree, dispute *(debate)*, dissent *(differ in opinion)*. SEE MAIN ENTRY

bickering altercation, argument *(contention)*, contest *(dispute)*, discord, dispute, dissension, dissidence, fight *(argument)*, fracas, fractious, negative, pugnacious

bid appeal *(noun)*, appeal *(verb)*, application, call *(appeal)*, command, detail *(assign)*, dictate, direct *(order)*, endeavor *(noun)*, endeavor *(verb)*, enjoin, impose *(enforce)*, insist, instruct *(direct)*, invitation, invoke, mandate, offer *(propose)*, overture, petition *(noun)*, petition *(verb)*, pray, prescribe, proffer, proposition, request *(noun)*, request *(verb)*, summon, summons, writ. SEE MAIN ENTRY

bid against counter, counteract

bid come call *(summon)*

bid defiance to challenge

bid fair promise *(raise expectations)*

bid farewell leave *(depart)*

bid for attempt, dicker, haggle, negotiate, pursue *(strive to gain)*, strive

bid-rigging SEE MAIN ENTRY

biddable loyal, obedient, pliable, resigned

bid-rigging SEE MAIN ENTRY

bidder applicant *(candidate)*, customer, rival

bidding demand, directive, guidance, injunction, instruction *(direction)*, invitation, monition *(legal summons)*, process *(summons)*, requirement, requisition, writ

bide continue *(persevere)*, defer *(put off)*, endure *(suffer)*, last, persist, reside

bide time pause

bienséance decorum

bifurcate dichotomize, divergent, part *(separate)*. SEE MAIN ENTRY

bifurcated bicameral, bipartite, divergent

bifurcated trial SEE MAIN ENTRY

bifurcation dichotomy, severance, split

bifurcous bipartite

big capacious, extensive, gross *(flagrant)*, important *(significant)*, major, momentous, ponderous, prodigious *(enormous)*

big-hearted benevolent

biggest part generality *(bulk)*

biggest share majority *(greater part)*

bighearted philanthropic

bigness mass *(weight)*

bigot SEE MAIN ENTRY

bigoted exclusive *(limited)*, illiberal, narrow, partial *(biased)*

bigotry bias, inequity, intolerance

bilateral mutual *(reciprocal)*, reciprocal. SEE MAIN ENTRY

bilateral contract mutual understanding

bile resentment, umbrage

bileful bilious

bilious bitter *(penetrating)*, dyseptic, malevolent. SEE MAIN ENTRY

bilk defraud, dupe, ensnare, peculate, pilfer. SEE MAIN ENTRY

bilked aggrieved *(harmed)*

bill act *(enactment)*, amendment *(legislation)*, cash, charge *(assess)*, check *(instrument)*, codification, debt, draft, enactment, instrument *(document)*, measure, receipt *(voucher)*. SEE MAIN ENTRY

bill drafter lawmaker

bill of accounts dun

bill of complaint allegation, claim *(legal demand)*

bill of costs dun

bill of exchange check *(instrument)*, draft, security *(stock)*

bill of indemnity exoneration

bill of indictment accusation, complaint

bill of lading invoice *(itemized list)*

billet domicile, dwell *(reside)*, employment, job, lodging, note *(brief comment)*, office, post, residence, role

billing publicity

billingsgate profanity, revilement

bills currency, debit, legislation *(enactments)*

billy cudgel

bind affix, amalgamate, annex *(add)*, attach *(join)*, cement, combine *(join together)*, confine, connect *(join together)*, consolidate *(strengthen)*, constrain *(imprison)*, constrict *(compress)*, contain *(enclose)*, contain *(restrain)*, detain *(restrain)*, engage *(hire)*, estop, fetter, hamper, handcuff, impose *(enforce)*, join *(bring together)*, limit, pledge *(promise the performance of)*, press *(constrain)*, promise *(vow)*, restrain, restrict, trammel. SEE MAIN ENTRY

bind by a pledge promise *(vow)*

bind oneself pledge *(promise the performance of)*, promise *(vow)*

bind oneself by oath promise *(vow)*, swear

bind together commingle

binder connection *(fastening)*. SEE MAIN ENTRY

binding accession *(annexation)*, attachment *(act of affixing)*, choate lien, coalescence, coalition, compelling, compulsory, concurrent *(united)*, contractual, decretal, essential *(required)*, forcible, fully executed *(signed)*, indefeasible, irrevocable, mandatory, necessary *(required)*, obligatory, positive *(prescribed)*, prescriptive, requisite, stringent, unavoidable *(not voidable)*, valid. SEE MAIN ENTRY

binding agreement adjustment, contract, covenant, testament

binding promise agreement *(contract)*

bioecology ecology

bioethic SEE MAIN ENTRY

bioethics SEE MAIN ENTRY

biographical record journal

bionomics ecology

bipartisanship conciliation, consensus

bipartite bicameral. SEE MAIN ENTRY

bipartition dichotomy

birch lash *(strike)*

birdbrained opaque

birth bloodline, creation, derivation, descent *(lineage)*, family *(common ancestry)*, genesis, inception, nascency, nationality, onset *(commencement)*, origin *(ancestry)*, origin *(source)*, origination, outset, parentage, race, start. SEE MAIN ENTRY

birth out of wedlock bar sinister

birthplace derivation, home *(place of origin)*, origin *(source)*

birthright bequest, descent *(lineage)*, droit, estate *(hereditament)*, heritage. SEE MAIN ENTRY

bisect bifurcate, cross *(intersect)*, dichotomize, divide *(separate)*, split, subdivide

bisectable divisible

bisected bicameral, bipartite, divisive

bisection dichotomy, split, subdivision

bit iota, minimum, part *(portion)*, scintilla, segment

biting bitter *(acrid tasting)*, bitter *(penetrating)*, bitter *(reproachful)*, caustic, harsh,

incisive, mordacious, offensive *(offending)*, scathing, trenchant

bitter antipathetic *(distasteful)*, astringent, dyseptic, harsh, hostile, malevolent, malignant, mordacious, resentful, virulent. SEE MAIN ENTRY

bitter animosity malice

bitter enemy foe

bitter feelings ill will, rancor

bitter harangue diatribe

bitter language philippic

bitter words diatribe, phillipic, revilement

bitterness alienation *(estrangement)*, feud, ill will, rancor, resentment, spite, umbrage

bivium intersection

bizarre eccentric, egregious, inept *(inappropriate)*, irrational, ludicrous, noteworthy, novel, peculiar *(curious)*, prodigious *(amazing)*, unaccustomed, uncommon, unique, unusual

bizarreness nonconformity, quirk *(idiosyncrasy)*

blabber jargon *(unintelligible language)*

blabbing loquacious

black deplorable, heinous, iniquitous, outrageous, portentous *(ominous)*, scandalous

black marketeer bootlegger

black out eradicate, expunge

black-listing boycott

black-market impermissible

blackball condemn *(ban)*, denounce *(condemn)*, exclusion, humiliate, ostracism, picket, reject

blackballing boycott

blacken brand *(stigmatize)*, deface, defame, denigrate, denounce *(condemn)*, derogate, disgrace, disparage, humiliate, obfuscate, obnubilate, obscure, pillory, smear, stain, sully, tarnish

blacken one's good name denigrate

blackening calumnious, defilement, pejorative, vilification

blackguard criminal, hoodlum, lash *(attack verbally)*, unconscionable

blackhearted malignant

blackjack cudgel

blacklist bar *(exclude)*, denounce *(condemn)*, isolate, ostracism

blackmail coercion, compel, extort, extortion, graft, hush money, threaten. SEE MAIN ENTRY

blackmailer extortionist

blackout censorship, insentience, obscuration

blamable blameful, blameworthy, culpable, delinquent *(guilty of a misdeed)*, guilty, peccable, reprehensible

blame accuse, arraign, assignation, censure, charge *(accusation)*, charge *(accuse)*, cite *(accuse)*, complain *(charge)*, complain *(criticize)*, conviction *(finding of guilt)*, criticism, criticize *(find fault with)*, culpability, denounce *(inform against)*, denunciation, diatribe, disparagement, fault *(responsibility)*, fault, guilt, impeach, impeachability, impeachment, impute, incriminate, incrimination, inculpation, indict, involve *(implicate)*, obloquy, odium, ostracism, outcry, present *(prefer charges)*, proscribe *(denounce)*, rebuke, reprehend, reprimand *(noun)*, reprimand *(verb)*, reproach *(noun)*, reproach *(verb)*, stricture. SEE MAIN ENTRY

blame falsely frame *(charge falsely)*

blame oneself regret

blame unfairly frame *(charge falsely)*

blame unjustly frame (*charge falsely*)
blameful blameworthy, delinquent (*guilty of a misdeed*), peccant (*culpable*), reprehensible. SEE MAIN ENTRY
blameless clean, incorruptible, inculpable, innocent, irreprehensible, not guilty, pardonable, unimpeachable. SEE MAIN ENTRY
blamelessness innocence
blameworthiness blame (*culpability*), culpability, guilt, impeachability, onus (*blame*)
blameworthy blameful, contemptible, culpable, delinquent (*guilty of a misdeed*), disgraceful, guilty, inexcusable, inexpiable, loathsome, notorious, obnoxious, odious, peccable, peccant (*culpable*), reprehensible, reprobate, sinister, unjustifiable, vicious. SEE MAIN ENTRY
blameworthy conduct criminality
blaming critical (*faultfinding*), incriminatory, inculpatory
blandish coax, inveigle, persuade, pressure
blandishment bribery, inducement, mention (*tribute*), persuasion, seduction
blank bleak (*exposed and barren*), devoid, form (*document*), inexpressive, inscrutable, nonentity, oblivious, thoughtless, vacant, vacuous, void (*empty*). SEE MAIN ENTRY
blanked blind (*impassable*)
blanket absolute (*complete*), blind (*obscure*), broad, camouflage, complete (*all-embracing*), cover (*protection*), ensconce, enshroud, envelop, generic, indiscriminate, omnibus, shroud
blankness indifference, insentience, nullity
blare barrage, noise, proclaim
blase casual
blasé dispassionate
blase nonchalant
blaspheme malign
blaspheming expletive
blasphemous offensive (*offending*), profane
blasphemy imprecation, profanity. SEE MAIN ENTRY
blast barrage, destroy (*efface*), discharge (*shot*), discharge (*shoot*), extirpate, inveigh, outburst, repercussion
blasting blasphemy, discharge (*shot*)
blatancy noise, pretense (*ostentation*)
blatant brazen, flagrant, manifest, open (*in sight*), tawdry. SEE MAIN ENTRY
blatant violation of law lynch law
blather jargon (*unintelligible language*), prattle (*noun*), prattle (*verb*)
blaze brand (*mark*), burn, conflagration, deflagrate, outburst, promulgate, propagate (*spread*)
blaze abroad proclaim
blazon disclose, embellish, herald, inform (*notify*), promulgate, propagate (*spread*), publish, reveal
bleak devoid, jejune (*dull*). SEE MAIN ENTRY
bleakness damper (*depressant*)
blear blind (*obscure*)
bleared nebulous
bleed deplete, exude
blemish damage, deface, defacement, defame, defect, denigrate, detriment, disgrace, dishonor (*shame*), flaw, foible, frailty, handicap, mutilate, onus (*stigma*), smear, spoil (*impair*), stain, stigma, sully, taint (*contaminate*), tarnish, vice
blemished defective, deficient, faulty, imperfect, inferior (*lower in quality*), marred. SEE MAIN ENTRY
blend amalgamate, attune, bond (*hold together*), combine (*join together*), commingle,

conjoin, connect (*join together*), consolidate (*strengthen*), converge, denature, desegregate, integration (*amalgamation*), join (*bring together*), melange, merge, pool, solution (*substance*), unite
blended composite, compound, concerted, concurrent (*united*), conglomerate, conjoint, harmonious, inseparable, miscellaneous, promiscuous
blending coherence, concordant, concrescence, integration (*amalgamation*)
blessed sacrosanct
blessing laudation, permission
blessings prosperity
blight calamity, casualty, damage, decay, destroy (*efface*), disaster, distress (*anguish*), impair, infect, pain, spoil (*impair*), spoilage, taint (*contaminate*), thwart, vitiate
blight one's optical powers blind (*deprive of sight*)
blighted marred, tainted (*contaminated*)
blighted hope pessimism
blighting disastrous
blind camouflage, cloak, deceive, deception, decoy, heedless, hidden, hoodwink, ill-judged, inadvertent, incognizant, injudicious, insensible, insusceptible (*uncaring*), obfuscate, obnubilate, obscure, opaque, random, ruse, stratagem, unwitting. SEE MAIN ENTRY
blind chance accident (*chance occurrence*)
blind faith credulity
blind to impervious
blind zeal discrimination (*bigotry*)
blinded unaware
blindfold hoodwink
blindness ignorance, nescience
bliss enjoyment (*pleasure*)
blissful ecstatic
blister burn
blistered blemished
blitz barrage
blitzkrieg onset (*assault*)
bloat inflate, spread
bloated inflated (*enlarged*)
bloatedness inflation (*increase*)
bloc cartel, league, organization (*association*), society
block arrest (*stop*), balk, ban, bar (*obstruction*), bar (*hinder*), bind (*restrain*), blockade (*barrier*), bulk, censorship, check (*bar*), check (*restrain*), clog, condemn (*ban*), constrain (*restrain*), constrict (*inhibit*), contain (*restrain*), damper (*stopper*), deadlock, debar, defeat, delay, deter, deterrence, deterrent, disadvantage, disqualify, encumber (*hinder*), enjoin, exclude, forbid, halt (*noun*), halt (*verb*), hamper, hinder, hold up (*delay*), impasse, impede, impediment, interdict, interfere, interpose, interruption, keep (*restrain*), kill (*defeat*), limitation, lock, obstacle, obstruct, obstruction, obturate, occlude, oppose, parcel, parry, plot (*land*), preclude, prevent, procrastinate, prohibit, prohibition, real estate, resist (*oppose*), section (*vicinity*), shut, stall, stave, stay (*halt*), stem (*check*), stifle, stop, strangle, toll (*stop*), withhold, withstand. SEE MAIN ENTRY
block off seal (*close*), shut
block out delineate, frame (*construct*), plan, program
block the way estop
block up clog, encumber (*hinder*), estop, shut, stop
blockade bar (*hinder*), block, contain (*enclose*), control (*restriction*), deterrence,

disadvantage, eliminate (*exclude*), enclose, enclosure, enjoin, estop, exclude, halt, hindrance, impasse, impede, impediment, lock, obstruction, occlude, ostracism, picket, restrain, restraint, seclude, shut, stop, strike (*refuse to work*). SEE MAIN ENTRY
blockaded blind (*impassable*)
blockage bar (*obstruction*), blockade (*barrier*), censorship, check (*bar*), damper (*stopper*), deadlock, disadvantage, estoppel, filibuster, impasse, impediment, obstruction, obviation
blockbuster bomb
blocked arrested (*checked*), blind (*impassable*), impervious
blocking preventive, resistance
blockish obtuse, opaque, thoughtless
blockishness opacity
blood ancestry, bloodline, descent (*lineage*). SEE MAIN ENTRY
blood connection family (*common ancestry*)
blood kindred next of kin
blood money hush money
blood related consanguineous
blood relation affiliation (*bloodline*), degree (*kinship*), next of kin, relationship (*family tie*), relative
blood relations kindred
blood relationship affiliation (*bloodline*), ancestry, degree (*kinship*), filiation
blood relative affinity (*family ties*), next of kin, relation (*kinship*)
blood relatives kindred, lineage
blood tie ancestry, relation (*kinship*)
blood ties relationship (*family tie*)
blood-thirsty cruel
bloodless clean, insipid, peaceable, phlegmatic
bloodline ancestry, birth (*lineage*), descent (*lineage*), lineage, origin (*ancestry*), parentage, posterity, progeny. SEE MAIN ENTRY
bloodshed dispatch (*act of putting to death*), fight (*battle*), outbreak
bloodsucker parasite
bloodthirstiness bestiality, cruelty
bloodthirsty malevolent, malignant, predatory, ruthless
bloody brutal
bloody murder killing
bloom pullulate, succeed (*attain*)
blooming prosperous, successful
blossom proliferate, pullulate
blossoming successful
blot brand (*stigmatize*), deface, defacement, defect, derogate, disgrace (*noun*), disgrace (*verb*), dishonor (*shame*), dishonor (*deprive of honor*), disparage, flaw, ignominy, infamy, onus (*stigma*), opprobrium, pillory, shame, stain, stigma, sully, tarnish
blot out censor, condone, deface, delete, destroy (*efface*), eliminate (*eradicate*), eradicate, expunge, extinguish, extirpate, obliterate, redact
blotch deface, defacement, onus (*stigma*), stain
blotting out defacement
blow bombshell, debacle, detriment, infliction, misfortune, tragedy, trouble
blow up expand, inflate, outbreak
blowing up inflation (*increase*)
blown up inflated (*enlarged*)
blowout outburst
blows fracas
blowup outburst
bludgeon coerce, cudgel, harass

bludgeon man assailant
blue ribbon prize
blue sky law SEE MAIN ENTRY
blue-pencil expurgate
blue-penciling censorship
blueprint agenda, arrange *(plan)*, delineate, delineation, design *(construction plan)*, direction *(course)*, method, program, prospectus. SEE MAIN ENTRY
blueprinted tactical
bluff betray *(lead astray)*, bilk, brazen, cloak, deception, delude, ensnare, fake, palter, pettifog, pretend, pretense *(pretext)*
bluffer pedant
bluffing lying
blunder abortion *(fiasco)*, disaster, err, fault *(mistake)*, indiscretion, maladministration, misapprehend, miscalculate, misconceive, misconstrue, miscue, misdeed, misdoing, misinterpret, misjudge, mismanage, misread, misstatement, mistake, misunderstand, oversight *(carelessness)*
blundering erroneous, inaccurate, inept *(incompetent)*
blunt allay, alleviate, assuage, candid, clear *(apparent)*, decrease, deter, direct *(forthright)*, harmless, honest, impair, ingenuous, moderate *(temper)*, modify *(moderate)*, mollify, obtund, obtuse, sententious, soothe
blunt-witted obtuse
bluntness candor *(straightforwardness)*, disrespect, honesty
blur blind *(obscure)*, deface, indistinctness, obfuscate, obnubilate, obscuration, obscure, sully
blur the outline blind *(obscure)*
blurred inconspicuous, indefinite, indistinct, nebulous, obscure *(faint)*, unclear, vague
blurriness indistinctness
blurry indefinite, indistinct, nebulous, obscure *(faint)*, unclear, vague
blurt interject
blurt out divulge, reveal
blushful diffident
blushing diffident
bluster hector, outburst, rodomontade. SEE MAIN ENTRY
blustering disorderly, orgulous, orotund
blustery disorderly
board bench, bureau, chamber *(body)*, commission *(agency)*, committee, council *(assembly)*, enter *(go in)*, inhabit, lodge *(reside)*, management *(directorate)*. SEE MAIN ENTRY
board of directors management *(directorate)*, management *(supervision)*
board of inquiry commission *(agency)*
boarder habitant, inhabitant, lessee, lodger, resident
boardinghouse building *(structure)*
boast bluster *(speech)*, exaggeration, flaunt, include, jactation
boastful grandiose, inflated *(vain)*, orgulous, pretentious *(pompous)*, proud *(conceited)*
boastfulness bombast, jactation, pride, rodomontade
boasting bombast, orgulous, overstatement, pretentious *(pompous)*, rodomontade
boatload cargo
bode portend, predict, presage, prognosticate, threaten
bodeful ominous, portentous *(ominous)*, prophetic
bodement caveat
bodiless immaterial, incorporeal, insubstantial, intangible

bodilessness impalpability
bodiliness materiality *(physical existence)*
bodily concrete, corporal, corporeal, in person, material *(physical)*, mundane, physical. SEE MAIN ENTRY
bodily deviation from health disease
bodily existence materiality *(physical existence)*
bodily presentation embodiment
bodily representation embodiment
boding consternation, inauspicious, portentous *(ominous)*, premonition
body aggregate, assemblage, assembly, band, character *(an individual)*, committee, community, confederacy *(compact)*, configuration *(form)*, content *(structure)*, cornerstone, corporation, corpse, corpus, entity, generality *(bulk)*, individual, majority *(greater part)*, mass *(body of persons)*, mass *(weight)*, materiality *(physical existence)*, party *(political organization)*, society, substance *(essential nature)*. SEE MAIN ENTRY
body corporate cartel, company *(enterprise)*, corporation
body of commissioners commission *(agency)*
body of consultants committee
body of delegates commission *(agency)*, delegation *(envoy)*, deputation *(delegation)*, representation *(acting for others)*
body of deputies commission *(agency)*, representation *(acting for others)*
body of employees personnel, staff
body of fact science *(study)*
body of facts on which belief is based evidence
body of judges chamber *(body)*, judiciary
body of jurors array *(jury)*, jury, panel *(jurors)*
body of knowledge education
body of law constitution, pandect *(code of laws)*
body of laws code, jurisprudence
body of laws enacted legislation *(enactments)*
body of members constituency
body of men armed with legal process posse
body of men summoned by a sheriff posse
body of office holders government *(political administration)*
body of partisans caucus, side
body of persons summoned as jurors panel *(jurors)*
body of persons sworn to render a verdict panel *(jurors)*
body of persons who formulate laws legislature
body of principles platform
body of professors faculty *(teaching staff)*
body of representatives delegation *(envoy)*, deputation *(delegation)*
body of rules law
body of rules of government constitution
body politic community, nationality, polity, populace, population, public, state *(political unit)*
bodyguard guardian
boeotian opaque
bog stall
boggle mismanage
bogus assumed *(feigned)*, counterfeit, deceptive, delusive, dishonest, false *(not genuine)*, fraudulent, imitation, specious, spurious. SEE MAIN ENTRY

Bohemian nonconforming
Bohemianism nonconformity
boil down abridge *(shorten)*, distill, lessen
boiler plate SEE MAIN ENTRY
boisterous blatant *(obtrusive)*, disorderly, vehement
boisterousness bluster *(commotion)*
bold brazen, flagrant, heroic, hot-blooded, impertinent *(insolent)*, impulsive *(rash)*, indomitable, insolent, obtrusive, palpable, perceivable, presumptuous, prominent, salient, spartan, unabashed, undaunted
bold front audacity
boldfaced brazen
boldness audacity, confidence *(faith)*, prowess *(bravery)*, spirit, temerity
bolster bear *(support)*, favor, inure *(benefit)*, justify, maintain *(sustain)*, nurture, preserve, promote *(organize)*, reinforce, side, subsidize, supplement, support *(assist)*, sustain *(prolong)*, uphold. SEE MAIN ENTRY
bolster up corroborate, reassure
bolt abscond, assemblage, bar *(hinder)*, escape, impede, lock, race, renege, retreat, seal *(close)*
bomb SEE MAIN ENTRY
bombard attack
bombardment barrage, discharge *(shot)*, onset *(assault)*
bombast fustian, harangue, peroration. SEE MAIN ENTRY
bombastic flatulent, fustian, grandiose, orotund, pretentious *(pompous)*, prolix, turgid
bombastic language fustian
bombastic speech rhetoric *(insincere language)*
bombastical flatulent
bombastry fustian
bombings barrage
bombshell bomb. SEE MAIN ENTRY
bona assets, effects, possession *(property)*, property *(possessions)*
bona fide accurate
bona fide actual, adherence *(devotion)*, adhesion *(loyalty)*
bona fide authentic, convincing. SEE MAIN ENTRY
bona fide corporeal, de facto
bona fide genuine, good faith, in good faith, sterling, valid, veridical
bonafide real
bonanza bounty
bond adherence *(adhesion)*, adherence *(devotion)*, adhesion *(loyalty)*, affiliation *(connectedness)*, agreement *(contract)*, association *(connection)*, attachment *(act of affixing)*, bail, chain *(nexus)*, charge *(lien)*, coalescence, coalition, connection *(fastening)*, contact *(association)*, contract, coverage *(insurance)*, debenture, fetter, guaranty, handcuff, hostage, kinship, liaison, loyalty, marriage *(intimate relationship)*, nexus, note *(written promise to pay)*, pact, pawn, pledge *(deposit)*, promise, propinquity *(kinship)*, recognizance, relation *(connection)*, relationship *(connection)*, security *(pledge)*, sodality, specialty *(contract)*, stipulation, treaty. SEE MAIN ENTRY
bond against risk insurance
bond of matrimony cohabitation *(married state)*, marriage *(wedlock)*
bond of slavery bondage
bond of union chain *(nexus)*
bondage captivity, coercion, constraint *(imprisonment)*, custody *(incarceration)*,

durance, duress, incarceration, restraint, subjection, thrall. SEE MAIN ENTRY
bonded allied, concerted, concordant, concurrent (united), fully secured, harmonious
bondman captive
bonds bondage, constraint (imprisonment), durance, restriction, securities, servitude, ties
bondsman captive
bone of contention problem, question (issue)
bonfire conflagration
boni bonus
bonorum possessions
bonus benefit (conferment), bounty, commission (fee), contribution (donation), gratuity (present), largess (gift), perquisite, premium (excess value), prize, reward
bonus sterling
bonus surplus, tip (gratuity). SEE MAIN ENTRY
bony ossified
book document, engage (hire), enroll, file (place among official records), program, publication (printed matter), record, register, retain (employ), script, set down. SEE MAIN ENTRY
book learning information (knowledge)
book of accounts ledger
book of records ledger
booking registration, reservation (engagement)
bookish learned
bookkeeper accountant, comptroller
bookkeeping accounting, computation, registration
bookkeeping expert comptroller
books ledger
boom barrage, prosperity. SEE MAIN ENTRY
booming prosperous, resounding, successful
booming economy boom (prosperity), prosperity
boon behalf, benefit (conferment), benevolence (act of kindness), bonus, bounty, contribution (donation), endowment, favor (act of kindness), grant, help, largess (gift)
boorish ignoble, inelegant, perverse, provincial, uncouth, unseemly
boost boom (increase), elevate, encourage, enhance, favor, help, impetus, increase, increment, intensify, magnify, parlay (exploit successfully), raise (advance), recommendation, reinforce, reinforcement
boost in prices inflation (decrease in value of currency)
boosting cumulative (intensifying), promotion (encouragement)
boot spurn
booth stand (witness' place in court), store (business)
bootlegged commerce contraband
bootlegged goods contraband
bootlegged trade contraband
bootlegged traffic contraband
bootlegger SEE MAIN ENTRY
bootless futile, otiose, unavailing
booty pillage, plunder, prize, reward, spoils
border ambit, boundary, circumscribe (define), circumscribe (surround by boundary), connection (abutment), contact (touch), contain (enclose), demarcate, enclosure, encompass (surround), end (termination), extremity (furthest point), frontier, hedge, juxtapose, limit, margin (outside limit), mete, outline (boundary), periphery, tenant. SEE MAIN ENTRY

border on abut, adjoin, approximate, contact (touch), correspond (be equivalent)
bordering adjacent, close (near), contiguous, immediate (not distant), proximate
bordering upon proximate
borderland border, frontier, mete, periphery
borderline boundary, end (termination), extremity (furthest point), insecure, marginal, mete, purview
borders configuration (confines), confines, extent
bore enter (penetrate), penetrate, pierce (lance)
boredom disinterest (lack of interest)
boresome irksome, jejune (dull), pedestrian, prolix, prosaic
boring insipid, irksome, jejune (dull), lifeless (dull), nondescript, ordinary, pedestrian, ponderous, prolix, prosaic, stale, trite
born native (inborn). SEE MAIN ENTRY
born in wedlock legitimate (lawfully conceived). SEE MAIN ENTRY
born of parents legally married legitimate (lawfully conceived)
borough community
borrow adopt, appropriate, copy. SEE MAIN ENTRY
borrow dishonestly pirate (reproduce without authorization), plagiarize
borrower debtor, obligor, parasite
borrowing limit. SEE MAIN ENTRY
bosom close (intimate)
boss chief, direct (supervise), director, employer, manage, principal (director), superintend
botch fail (lose), failure (lack of success), miscue, mismanage, muddle, spoil (impair)
botchery maladministration
bother aggravate (annoy), annoy, badger, bait (harass), burden, care (regard), discommode, disorganize, distress, disturb, embarrass, harass, harrow, harry (harass), hector, hinder, hindrance, impede, importune, inconvenience, irritate, mistreat, molest (annoy), molestation, nuisance, perplex, persecute, perturb, pique, plague, press (goad), provoke, trouble, upset
botheration burden
bothering enigmatic
bothersome difficult, irksome, operose, undesirable, vexatious
bottle up repress
bottleneck blockade (barrier)
bottomless baseless, profound (intense)
boulevard avenue (route)
bounce oscillate
bounce back reflect (mirror)
bouncing resilient
bound abut, accountable (responsible), actionable, attached (annexed), barrier, boundary, circumscribe (surround by boundary), confine, definite, delimit, demarcate, detain (restrain), diminish, en route, enclose, encompass (surround), end (termination), frontier, hedge, include, indebted, inextricable, limit, loyal, mete, palliate (abate), periphery, purposeful, qualify (condition), restrict, shut, specialize. SEE MAIN ENTRY
bound by agreement indentured
bound by contract indentured
bound by convention orthodox
bound by duty moral
bound in equity liable
bound in law liable
bound to liable
bound to respond liable

bound together conjoint
boundaries capacity (sphere), confines, dimension, range
boundary ambit, barrier, border, configuration (confines), edge (border), enclosure, end (termination), extremity (furthest point), frontier, guideline, limit, margin (outside limit), mete, purview, restriction, scope. SEE MAIN ENTRY
boundary line ambit, frontier, limit, mete, periphery
boundary lines confines
boundary mark mete
boundary marker landmark (conspicuous object)
bounded certain (specific), limited
bounded with precision definite
bounden indebted, loyal, mandatory, necessary (required)
bounden duty allegiance, burden, liability, responsibility (accountability)
bounding contiguous, immediate (not distant)
boundless continual (perpetual), far reaching, indefinite, indeterminate, infinite, innumerable, myriad, open-ended, profuse, unlimited, unqualified (unlimited), unrestricted
boundlessly ad infinitum
boundlessness perpetuity
boundness responsibility (accountability)
bounds ambit, area (province), border, capacity (sphere), circuit, configuration (confines), confines, constraint (imprisonment), contour (outline), coverage (scope), custody (incarceration), edge (border), extent, margin (outside limit), mete, outline (boundary), premises (buildings), purview, range, restriction, scope, sphere
bounteous benevolent, charitable (benevolent), humane, liberal (generous), philanthropic, profuse, replete
bounteousness charity, largess (generosity), philanthropy
bountiful ample, benevolent, copious, donative, liberal (generous), philanthropic, profuse, replete
bountifulness benevolence (disposition to do good), boom (prosperity), charity, largess (generosity), philanthropy
bounty bonus, consideration (recompense), contribution (donation), donation, endowment, favor (act of kindness), grant, largess (generosity), largess (gift), philanthropy, premium (excess value), prize, reward, subsidy. SEE MAIN ENTRY
bourgeois ordinary, prevailing (current)
bourn destination, end (intent), outline (boundary)
bourse exchange, market (business)
bout competition, confrontation (altercation), contest (competition), fight (battle), period
bout of sickness disease
bovine phlegmatic
bow prostration, succumb, yield (submit)
bow to obey, observe (obey), submit (yield)
bowdlerization censorship
bowdlerize censor, expurgate. SEE MAIN ENTRY
bowelless relentless
bowing compliance
bowl over overcome (overwhelm)
box chamber (compartment), envelop, stand (witness' place in court)
box number address
boy child

boycott condemn *(ban)*, disapprove *(reject)*, eschew, exclude, exclusion, ignore, picket, proscription, reject, shun, strike, strike *(refuse to work)*. SEE MAIN ENTRY

boyishness puerility

brabble affray, bicker, disaccord, fray

brace bear *(support)*, mainstay, reinforce, side, stimulate, uphold

bracing remedial, salutary

bracket class, connect *(relate)*, enclose, enclosure, include, pigeonhole, relate *(establish a connection)*

brag exaggeration, jactation, rodomontade

braggadocio jactation, pride, rodomontade

braggardism jactation

braggardly pretentious *(pompous)*

braggart inflated *(vain)*, pretentious *(pompous)*, proud *(conceited)*

braggartism pride, rodomontade

braggery bombast

bragging bluster *(speech)*, orgulous, rodomontade

braid cross *(intersect)*, intertwine

brain intellect

brain child invention

brain damage insanity

brainless fatuous, irrational, opaque

brains intelligence *(intellect)*

braintwister enigma

brainwash convert *(persuade)*, influence

brainwashing propaganda

brainwork dialectic

brake control *(restriction)*, curb, hamper, hold up *(delay)*, impede, impediment, obstruct, remit *(relax)*, restraint, stop

branch adjunct, affiliate, bifurcate, bureau, class, denomination, department, dichotomize, division *(administrative unit)*, member *(constituent part)*, offshoot, organ, segment, spread, title *(division)*, unit *(department)*

branch member chapter *(branch)*

branch of instruction discipline *(field of study)*

branch of knowledge discipline *(field of study)*, science *(study)*

branch off bifurcate, stem *(originate)*

branch office chapter *(branch)*, organ

branch organization affiliate

branch out accrue *(increase)*, bifurcate, compound, deploy, deviate, digress, expand, increase, radiate

branching divergent, extensive

branching off deviation

branching out circulation, decentralization

brand arraign, attaint, burn, class, classify, defame, denigrate, denounce *(condemn)*, derogate, disapprove *(condemn)*, discredit, disgrace *(noun)*, disgrace *(verb)*, dishonor *(shame)*, dishonor *(deprive of honor)*, disparagement, disrepute, earmark, humiliate, ignominy, implicate, indicant, indication, infamy, involve *(implicate)*, label *(noun)*, label *(verb)*, manner *(kind)*, onus *(stigma)*, opprobrium, pillory, reproach, scandal, smear, specialty *(distinctive mark)*, stamp, stigma, sully, tarnish, trademark. SEE MAIN ENTRY

brand incorrectly mislabel

brand with reproach arraign

brandish display, flaunt, wield. SEE MAIN ENTRY

brangle bicker, brawl *(noun)*, brawl *(verb)*, disaccord

brash brazen, caustic, impertinent *(insolent)*, improvident, imprudent, obtrusive, presumptuous

brashness disrespect

brassy pretentious *(ostentatious)*

bravado audacity, pretense *(ostentation)*

brave bear *(tolerate)*, confront *(encounter)*, defy, endure *(suffer)*, heroic, indomitable, spartan, undaunted. SEE MAIN ENTRY

brave SEE MAIN ENTRY

brave face audacity

braveness prowess *(bravery)*

bravery spirit, tolerance

bravura audacity

brawl affray, bicker, bluster *(commotion)*, commotion, confrontation *(altercation)*, contend *(dispute)*, contest *(dispute)*, controversy *(argument)*, disaccord, embroilment, fight *(battle)*, fracas, fray, outbreak, outcry, riot. SEE MAIN ENTRY

brawler malcontent

brawn force *(strength)*, puissance, sinew, strength

brawniness sinew

brawny powerful, strong

braying blatant *(obtrusive)*

braze cement

brazen contemptuous, flagrant, impertinent *(insolent)*, insolent, obtrusive, outrageous, presumptuous, unabashed. SEE MAIN ENTRY

brazenness disrespect

breach alienation *(estrangement)*, argument *(contention)*, break *(violate)*, conflict, default, delinquency *(failure of duty)*, dereliction, difference, disassociation, disloyalty, embroilment, encroach, encroachment, estrangement, feud, flaw, force *(break)*, incursion, infraction, infringe, infringement, invasion, irregularity, neglect, offense, omission, outbreak, repudiation, rift *(gap)*, schism, separation, split, transgression, trespass, variance *(disagreement)*, violation. SEE MAIN ENTRY

breach of a promise delinquency *(failure of duty)*

breach of allegiance treason

breach of duty negligence, res ipsa loquitur

breach of faith bad faith, bribery, corruption, dishonor *(nonpayment)*, disloyalty, infidelity, infraction, treason

breach of law crime, guilt, infraction, misdemeanor, misfeasance

breach of legal duty tort

breach of orders default, disregard *(omission)*, infraction, rebellion

breach of peace disorder *(lack of order)*

breach of practice deviation, exception *(exclusion)*, malpractice

breach of privilege infraction

breach of profession malpractice

breach of promise dishonor *(nonpayment)*, disloyalty, infidelity, infraction, nonperformance

breach of the law delinquency *(misconduct)*, offense

breach of the peace brawl, fracas, infraction, outbreak, outburst, riot

breach of trust abuse *(corrupt practice)*, corruption, disloyalty, embezzlement, improbity, infidelity, infraction, misappropriation

breach the agreement default

breadth caliber *(measurement)*, capacity *(maximum)*, extent, gamut, purview, range

break adjournment, alienation *(estrangement)*, breach, cessation, cloture, controversy *(argument)*, damage, digression, disable, disassociation, discontinue *(abandon)*, discontinue *(break continuity)*,

estrangement, extension *(postponement)*, halt *(noun)*, halt *(verb)*, hiatus, infringe, interrupt, interruption, interval, leave *(absence)*, lull, luxate, moratorium, part *(separate)*, pause *(noun)*, pause *(verb)*, pendency, recess *(noun)*, recess *(verb)*, remission, rend, respite *(interval of rest)*, rift *(disagreement)*, rift *(gap)*, schism, separate, separation, split *(noun)*, split *(verb)*, spoil *(impair)*, subdue, transition, violate. SEE MAIN ENTRY

break a law disobey, offend *(violate the law)*

break a promise renege

break a rule disobey

break apart disband, disjoint, disrupt, dissolve *(separate)*, sever

break away defect, elude, leave *(depart)*, part *(leave)*, secede

break bounds accroach, deviate, impinge, infringe

break camp evacuate, move *(alter position)*

break down classify, codify, damage, decay, erode, overcome *(overwhelm)*, pigeonhole, stall, subdivide, succumb

break faith bear false witness, cheat, inform, misrepresent, palter

break faith with betray *(lead astray)*

break fealty defect

break forth issue *(send forth)*

break from prison escape

break ground initiate, originate

break in discipline *(train)*, interfere, interrupt, intervene, invade, obtrude, trespass

break in on impinge

break in upon infringe, overstep

break into infringe, interpose, loot, penetrate

break loose elude, escape

break news divulge

break off alienate *(estrange)*, close *(terminate)*, conclude *(complete)*, detach, discontinue *(abandon)*, discontinue *(break continuity)*, forbear, forswear, halt, quit *(discontinue)*, refrain, separate, sever, stop, suspend

break one's oath perjure

break one's promise betray *(lead astray)*, fail *(neglect)*

break one's promise to disappoint

break one's trust default

break one's word fail *(neglect)*, perjure

break out escape

break silence pronounce *(speak)*, speak

break the association of disband

break the connection with disengage

break the contract default

break the law disobey, offend *(violate the law)*, trespass

break the news notify, reveal

break the pattern deviate

break the peace brawl, fight *(battle)*

break the record surpass

break through emerge, lancinate

break to pieces destroy *(efface)*

break trust inform *(betray)*

break up decay, degenerate, destroy *(void)*, diffuse, disband, disintegrate, disjoint, dispel, dissipate *(spread out)*, dissociate, dissolve *(separate)*, dissolve *(terminate)*, overthrow, partition, recess, separate

break up into opposing factions polarize

break with defect, disaccord, disagree, estrange, rebel, renounce, split

breakability frailty

breakable destructible, divisible, nonsubstantial (not sturdy), separable

breakage injury

breakdown debacle, decentralization, defeat, diagnosis, disassociation, disaster, disease, erosion, failure (lack of success), miscarriage, prostration

breakdown of administration anarchy, lynch law, misrule

breaking division (act of dividing), infraction

breaking an obligation contravention

breaking and entering burglary, housebreaking

breaking down decadent, destruction

breaking of precedent innovation

breaking of the law offense

breaking off discontinuance (act of discontinuing)

breaking up dissolution (disintegration), dissolution (termination)

breaking with tradition anomalous, peculiar (curious)

breakneck dangerous, impulsive (rash), precipitate

breakup defeasance, division (act of dividing), subversion

breast confront (encounter), defy, resist (oppose), withstand

breath suggestion

breathe communicate, divulge, exist, express, pause, utter

breathe one's last die

breather lull, pause

breathing born (alive), conscious (awake), live (conscious)

breathing spell halt, lull, pause, respite (interval of rest)

breathing time lull, respite (interval of rest)

breathless dead, lifeless (dead)

breathtaking moving (evoking emotion), noteworthy, portentous (eliciting amazement)

breed bear (yield), blood, cause, class, descent (lineage), engender, foster, generate, kind, occasion, originate, produce (manufacture), proliferate, propagate (increase), pullulate, race, reproduce

breeding conduct, deportment

breedy prolific

breeziness life (vitality)

brethren affinity (family ties), blood, kindred, society

brevet warrant (authorization). SEE MAIN ENTRY

breviary compendium

brevis ephemeral, laconic, limited, succinct, summary, transient

brew maneuver

brewing imminent, inevitable

bribable mercenary, venal

bribe coax, corrupt, hush money, lure, suborn. SEE MAIN ENTRY

bribe to take a false oath suborn

bribery corruption, graft. SEE MAIN ENTRY

bribing bribery

bridal conjugal, nuptial

bridewell reformatory

bridge chain (nexus), connect (join together), connect (relate), connection (fastening), contact (touch), join (bring together), nexus

bridle bar (hinder), block, clog, constrain (imprison), constrain (restrain), contain (restrain), damper (stopper), disadvantage, discipline (control), fetter, hamper, handcuff (noun), handcuff (verb), handicap, inhibit,

limit, obstacle, obstruct, obstruction, repress, resent, restrain, restraint, restrict, trammel

bridled arrested (checked)

brief abridgment (condensation), abstract, account (report), apprise, capsule, compact (pithy), compendium, concise, cursory, digest, disabuse, dossier, edify, educate, ephemeral, impart, indicate, inform (notify), instruct (direct), laconic, memorandum, minimal, note (brief comment), notify, outline (synopsis), paraphrase, pithy, report (detailed account), restatement, scenario, succinct, summary, synopsis, temporary, transient, transitory, volatile. SEE MAIN ENTRY

brief silence lull

briefed acquainted, familiar (informed), informed (having information)

briefing guidance

briefly pro tempore

brigand hoodlum, malefactor, outlaw

brigandage foray, larceny, pillage, spoliation

brigandine panoply

brigandish larcenous

bright illustrious, obvious, perspicacious, resourceful, sanguine, sapient

brighten enhance

brightness sense (intelligence)

brilliance distinction (reputation), intellect, intelligence (intellect), sagacity, sense (intelligence)

brilliant illustrious, politic, prominent

brim border, edge (border), margin (outside limit)

brimful full, replete

brimming replete

brimming over full

bring carry (transport), cause, commence, procure, transport, yield (produce a return)

bring a case lodge (bring a complaint)

bring a charge accuse, cite (accuse), impeach

bring a countercharge recriminate

bring a formal accusation against indict

bring a legal action sue

bring a person to his senses persuade

bring a suit complain (charge), lodge (bring a complaint)

bring about accomplish, attain, bear (yield), cause, commit (perpetrate), compose, conduce, constitute (establish), create, discharge (perform), dispatch (dispose of), elicit, engender, establish (launch), evoke, execute (accomplish), fulfill, generate, implement, incite, induce, inflict, inspire, make, occasion, operate, originate, perpetrate, produce (manufacture), prosecute (carry forward), provoke, realize (make real), render (administer), yield (produce a return)

bring about by force constrain (compel)

bring about by legislation constitute (establish)

bring about change militate

bring accusation accuse, arraign, charge (accuse), denounce (inform against), incriminate, involve (implicate), lodge (bring a complaint)

bring action against litigate, prosecute (charge)

bring aid capitalize (provide capital), contribute (assist)

bring an action cite (accuse), complain (charge), litigate, sue

bring an action against lodge (bring a complaint)

bring around convert (persuade), disarm (set at ease), persuade, prevail (persuade)

bring back reconstitute, rehabilitate, reinstate, remind, restore (return), resurrect

bring before a court arraign, prosecute (charge)

bring before the public circulate, publish

bring charges complain (charge), denounce (inform against), impeach, involve (implicate)

bring charges against incriminate, lodge (bring a complaint)

bring discredit on decry

bring disgrace upon discredit

bring disrepute upon defame

bring down cause, demean (make lower), demote, depress, derogate, disgrace, dispatch (put to death), overthrow

bring forth avail (bring about), bear (yield), develop, educe, elicit, engender, evoke, extract, generate, make, manifest, produce (manufacture), reproduce, yield (produce a return)

bring forward bear (adduce), certify (attest), cite (state), elicit, exhibit, manifest, offer (propose), plead (allege in a legal action), posit, prefer, produce (offer to view), proffer

bring from obscurity into view disinter

bring in induct, introduce, yield (produce a return)

bring in a supply bear (yield)

bring in a true bill accuse

bring in a verdict award, determine, sentence

bring in as a third party implead

bring in contact join (bring together)

bring in contact with commingle, connect (join together)

bring in question canvass, dispute (contest)

bring into a small compass concentrate (consolidate)

bring into accord attune

bring into agreement arbitrate (conciliate), attune

bring into being compose, conceive (invent), create, develop, engender, establish (launch), fabricate (construct), forge (produce), generate, invent (produce for the first time), make, produce (manufacture), propagate (increase)

bring into close connection affiliate

bring into close relation affiliate

bring into comparison compare, contrast, measure

bring into concord agree (contract)

bring into conflict engage (involve)

bring into conformity with law legalize

bring into connection with implicate

bring into consistency accommodate

bring into court plead (argue a case)

bring into custody imprison

bring into danger compromise (endanger)

bring into discredit brand (stigmatize), censure, condemn (blame), denounce (condemn), derogate, discommend, disgrace, dishonor (deprive of honor), fault, impeach, malign

bring into disfavor discredit

bring into disorder confound, discompose, perturb

bring into disrepute decry, demean (make lower)

bring into effect compose

bring into existence cause, compose, conceive (invent), engender, establish (launch), fabricate (construct), forge (produce), generate, make, originate, produce (manufacture)

bring into focus converge, focus
bring into harmony arbitrate *(conciliate)*, intercede, reconcile
bring into meaningful relation with compare
bring into operation exert, perform *(execute)*
bring into order arrange *(methodize)*, codify, file *(arrange)*, fix *(arrange)*, orchestrate
bring into peril endanger
bring into play exercise *(use)*, exert, exploit *(make use of)*, resort
bring into question audit
bring into relation compare
bring into relation with correspond *(be equivalent)*
bring into the open betray *(disclose)*, disclose, find *(discover)*, issue *(publish)*, manifest, promulgate
bring into use initiate
bring into view bare, disclose, evince, produce *(offer to view)*
bring low demean *(make lower)*, demote, depress, derogate, reduce, supplant
bring near converge, juxtapose
bring new evidence appeal
bring off dispatch *(dispose of)*, implement
bring off successfully attain
bring on cause, conduce, create, incite, incur, induce, originate, precipitate *(hasten)*
bring out circulate, comment, create, disclose, disinter, educe, elicit, evoke, manifest, produce *(offer to view)*, publish, solve
bring out in evidence bare
bring out more clearly elucidate
bring over disarm *(set at ease)*, persuade, prevail upon
bring pressure to bear coerce, influence, lobby, prejudice *(influence)*, press *(constrain)*
bring pressure to bear upon compel, constrain *(compel)*
bring proceedings against complain *(charge)*, incriminate, lodge *(bring a complaint)*
bring reproach upon discredit, disgrace, disparage, stain
bring shame upon derogate, disgrace, dishonor *(deprive of honor)*, humiliate, pillory
bring suit litigate, prosecute *(charge)*
bring the mind to bear upon focus
bring to resurrect
bring to a close complete, conclude *(complete)*, consummate, discontinue *(abandon)*, finish, stop
bring to a common center collect *(gather)*
bring to a complete condition develop
bring to a conclusion dispatch *(dispose of)*, perfect
bring to a more advanced state develop
bring to a point of union collect *(gather)*
bring to a standstill arrest *(stop)*, check *(restrain)*, delay, discontinue *(break continuity)*, enjoin, forestall, halt, hold up *(delay)*, impede, obstruct, palliate *(abate)*, stall, stop, suspend
bring to a state of obedience discipline *(control)*
bring to a stop arrest *(stop)*, estop, suspend
bring to account condemn *(punish)*, denounce *(condemn)*, impeach, penalize
bring to acquiescence reconcile
bring to agreement adjust *(resolve)*
bring to an end cease, close *(terminate)*, complete, conclude *(complete)*, determine, discontinue *(abandon)*, dispatch *(dispose of)*, dissolve *(terminate)*, extinguish, finish, perfect, quit *(discontinue)*, terminate

bring to an understanding intercede, mediate
bring to attention address *(direct attention to)*
bring to bear avail *(be of use)*, exercise *(use)*, exert
bring to book rebuke, reprehend
bring to completion finish, fulfill, perfect, terminate
bring to conclusion complete, dissolve *(terminate)*
bring to effect consummate, create, make
bring to full development mature
bring to fullness perfect
bring to its peak mature
bring to justice convict, determine, impeach, lodge *(bring a complaint)*, prosecute *(charge)*, sue
bring to light bare, bear *(adduce)*, betray *(disclose)*, clarify, denude, detect, disclose, discover, display, divulge, educe, evidence, exhibit, expose, ferret, locate, manifest, produce *(offer to view)*, reveal, unveil. SEE MAIN ENTRY
bring to light by degrees develop
bring to market handle *(trade)*, sell
bring to maturity complete, effectuate, mature, nurture
bring to mind allude, recollect, remember
bring to naught destroy *(void)*, foil, stop, thwart
bring to nothing obliterate
bring to notice address *(direct attention to)*, exhibit, manifest
bring to nought frustrate
bring to order marshal
bring to pass attain, carry *(succeed)*, cause, commit *(perpetrate)*, create, discharge *(perform)*, dispatch *(dispose of)*, effectuate, enforce, evoke, execute *(accomplish)*, fulfill, implement, induce, make, originate, perform *(execute)*, perpetrate, produce *(manufacture)*, prosecute *(carry forward)*, realize *(make real)*
bring to perfection complete, mature
bring to reason convince, persuade, prevail upon, reason *(persuade)*
bring to recollection remind
bring to rest conclude *(complete)*
bring to retribution discipline *(punish)*, punish
bring to ruin destroy *(efface)*, extirpate, pillage
bring to terms accommodate, arbitrate *(conciliate)*, arrange *(methodize)*, beat *(defeat)*, intercede, mediate, negotiate, pacify, placate, reconcile, settle, subjugate
bring to the bar litigate, lodge *(bring a complaint)*, sue
bring to the fore adduce, produce *(offer to view)*
bring to the front manifest, produce *(offer to view)*
bring to trial arraign, litigate, lodge *(bring a complaint)*
bring to view evidence, exhibit, manifest
bring together accumulate *(amass)*, aggregate, annex *(add)*, arbitrate *(conciliate)*, collect *(gather)*, compile, congregate, conjoin, consolidate *(strengthen)*, consolidate *(unite)*, convene, converge, crystallize, focus, garner, glean, hoard, incorporate *(include)*, intercede, juxtapose, mediate, orchestrate, raise *(collect)*, reconcile, settle, unite
bring together in a crowd congregate

bring toward a central point concentrate *(consolidate)*
bring unawares into danger entrap
bring unawares into evil entrap
bring under domination subject
bring under rule impose *(subject)*, subdue, subject
bring under subjection discipline *(control)*
bring up bear *(adduce)*, discipline *(train)*, educate, foster, nurture, raise *(advance)*, remind
bring up for investigation arraign, impeach
bring up on charges arraign, complain *(charge)*, incriminate, lodge *(bring a complaint)*
bring up to date renew *(refurbish)*, revise
bring upon inflict
bring upon oneself incur
bring word communicate, mention, notify
bringing forth creation
bringing to trial prosecution *(criminal trial)*
bringing together centralization, combination, cumulation, joinder
brink border, edge *(border)*, extremity *(furthest point)*, margin *(outside limit)*, outline *(boundary)*, penumbra, threshold *(verge)*
brisk brief, expeditious, incisive, sedulous, trenchant, volatile
briskness dispatch *(promptness)*, haste, life *(vitality)*
bristle resent
bristling hostile, resentful, rife
bristling with arms armed
brittle nonsubstantial *(not sturdy)*
brittleness frailty
broach assume *(undertake)*, commence, initiate, mention, pose *(propound)*, proclaim, utter
broad capacious, collective, comprehensive, extensive, general, generic, inaccurate, inclusive, indefinite, indiscriminate, inexact, liberal *(not literal)*, nonsectarian, obscene, omnibus, passable, vague. SEE MAIN ENTRY
broad enough ample
broad guage caliber *(measurement)*
broad meaning connotation, gist *(substance)*, implication *(inference)*
broad statement generality *(vague statement)*, generalization
broad-based complete *(all-embracing)*, extensive, nonsectarian
broad-minded impartial, nonpartisan, objective, open-minded, permissive, reasonable *(rational)*, receptive, unbiased, unprejudiced
broad-mindedness disinterest *(lack of prejudice)*, objectivity, tolerance
broadcast circulate, communicate, convey *(communicate)*, diffuse, dispel, disseminate, divulge, issuance, issue *(publish)*, proclaim, promulgate, propagate *(spread)*, public *(known)*, publication *(disclosure)*, publicity, publish, relate *(tell)*, report *(detailed account)*, report *(disclose)*, send, spread
broaden accrue *(increase)*, accumulate *(enlarge)*, deploy, develop, enlarge, expand, extend *(enlarge)*, increase, inflate, magnify, parlay *(exploit successfully)*, spread, supplement
broadening accession *(enlargement)*, augmentation, boom *(increase)*, cumulative *(increasing)*, extension *(expansion)*
broadness caliber *(measurement)*
broadside barrage

broil altercation, brawl *(noun)*, brawl *(verb)*, controversy *(argument)*, disaccord, embroilment, fight *(argument)*, fracas, fray, furor, imbroglio, riot, strife, struggle

broke bankrupt, impecunious, insolvent

broken bankrupt, defective, desultory, disconnected, disjunctive *(tending to disjoin)*, imperfect, intermittent, unsound *(not strong)*. SEE MAIN ENTRY

broken faith bad faith, infidelity

broken in spirit contrite

broken marriage divorce

broken off disconnected

broken promise bad faith, disloyalty

broken silence outcry

broken thread anacoluthon

broken word infidelity

brokenhearted disconsolate

broker dealer, deputy, factor *(commission merchant)*, interagent, medium, plenipotentiary, proctor, procurator, proxy, representative *(proxy)*, spokesman. SEE MAIN ENTRY

brokerage SEE MAIN ENTRY

bromidic ordinary, trite

brood blood, children, deliberate, family *(household)*, muse, offspring, progeny. SEE MAIN ENTRY

brood over deplore, dwell *(linger over)*, ponder, reflect *(ponder)*, review

brooding contemplation, deliberation

brook allow *(endure)*, endure *(suffer)*, suffer *(permit)*, tolerate

brook no denial insist

brother colleague, counterpart *(complement)*

brotherhood denomination, goodwill, kinship, peace, philanthropy, society, sodality, union *(labor organization)*

brotherliness benevolence *(disposition to do good)*, philanthropy, sodality

brotherly close *(intimate)*, humane, intimate, philanthropic

brotherly love philanthropy

brought about by force forcible

brought charges accused *(charged)*

brought to a conclusion complete *(ended)*

brought to fruition choate lien

brought to light naked *(perceptible)*

brought to perfection best, ripe

brought to termination res judicata

brought together collective, conglomerate

brouillerie dissension

browbeat bait *(harass)*, discompose, frighten, harass, harrow, harry *(harass)*, hector, intimidate, persecute, plague, press *(goad)*, threaten. SEE MAIN ENTRY

browse peruse

bruise beat *(strike)*, damage, harm, ill use, lash *(strike)*, mistreat, mutilate

bruised blemished, defective, marred

bruit declare, disseminate, notoriety, outcry, proclaim, promulgate, report *(rumor)*, report *(disclose)*, reveal, signify *(inform)*, spread

bruit abroad circulate

bruited about public *(known)*

brummagem meretricious, tawdry

brunt burden, pressure

brush affray, confrontation *(altercation)*

brush aside discount *(disbelieve)*, disdain, dismiss *(put out of consideration)*, ignore, rebuff, reject, spurn

brush off parry

brush up repair

brusque harsh, laconic, taciturn

brusqueness disrespect

brutal bitter *(penetrating)*, callous, cold-blooded, cruel, diabolic, disorderly, harsh,

hot-blooded, inexcusable, malevolent, malicious, malignant, noxious, pernicious, ruthless, scathing, severe, tyrannous, vicious. SEE MAIN ENTRY

brutality bestiality, cruelty, oppression, violence. SEE MAIN ENTRY

brutalize SEE MAIN ENTRY

brutalized diabolic

brutalness brutality, cruelty

brute animal

brute creation animal

brute force coercion, main force, oppression, pressure

brute-like brutal

brutify brutalize

brutilization brutality

brutish brutal, caitiff, cold-blooded, malignant, relentless, ruthless, uncouth

brutishness bestiality, brutality, cruelty

brutum fulmen disaster

buccaneer criminal, plunder

buccaneering spoliation

buck defy, oppose, oppugn

buckler protection, shield

bucolic provincial

bud embryo, germinate, proliferate, pullulate

budding inchoate, incipient

budget appropriation *(allotment)*, estimate, finance, overhead, program. SEE MAIN ENTRY

budgetary financial, fiscal, pecuniary

budgeted items expense *(cost)*, outlay

budgeting appropriation *(allotment)*

buffer bulwark, intermediary, panoply, safeguard, shield

buffer zone SEE MAIN ENTRY

buffered impervious

buffet beat *(strike)*, ill use, jostle *(bump into)*

buffoonery parody, ridicule

buggery sodomy

build accrue *(increase)*, compose, create, enlarge, establish *(launch)*, fabricate *(construct)*, forge *(produce)*, form, frame *(structure)*, frame *(construct)*, increase, invent *(produce for the first time)*, make, manufacture, organization *(structure)*, produce *(manufacture)*. SEE MAIN ENTRY

build up accrue *(increase)*, accumulate *(enlarge)*, aggregate, compound, consolidate *(strengthen)*, cumulation, develop, elevate, enlarge, expand, extend *(enlarge)*, heighten *(augment)*, heighten *(elevate)*, hoard, magnify, parlay *(exploit successfully)*, promote *(organize)*, replenish

build-up augmentation

builder architect, contractor, developer, materialman

building creation, edifice, frame *(structure)*, preparation, structure *(edifice)*. SEE MAIN ENTRY

building entrepeneur developer

building of imposing appearance edifice

built on based on, underlying

bulge project *(extend beyond)*

bulk amount *(quantity)*, assemblage, cargo, corpus, cumulation, majority *(greater part)*, mass *(weight)*, measurement, plurality, quantity. SEE MAIN ENTRY

bulk transfer SEE MAIN ENTRY

bulkhead buffer zone, bulwark

bulky ponderous

bulletin declaration, dispatch *(message)*, entry *(record)*, issuance, notice *(announcement)*, notification, prospectus, publicity, report *(detailed account)*

bullheaded pertinacious, uncontrollable

bully badger, browbeat, brutalize, endanger, frighten, harrow, harry *(harass)*, hector, intimidate, irritate, mistreat, persecute, pique

bullyrag frighten, pique, plague

bulwark barrier, bear *(support)*, buffer zone, mainstay, protect, protection, safeguard, security *(safety)*, shield. SEE MAIN ENTRY

bump collide *(crash against)*, impinge, jostle *(bump into)*

bump against jostle *(bump into)*

bump into collide *(crash against)*

bumper crop. SEE MAIN ENTRY

bumptious contemptuous, disdainful, inflated *(vain)*, insolent, perverse, supercilious. SEE MAIN ENTRY

bunch assemblage, compile, congregate, hoard, quantity, selection *(collection)*

bunch together compile

bunched compact *(dense)*, solid *(compact)*

bundle assemblage

bung shut, stem *(check)*

bungle fail *(lose)*, miscue, misdoing, mismanage, mistake, muddle, spoil *(impair)*

bungling fault *(mistake)*, incompetent, inept *(incompetent)*, maladministration, neglect, negligent

bunk dwell *(reside)*

bunker depository

bunko SEE MAIN ENTRY

bunkum rodomontade

buoy up assure *(give confidence to)*, bear *(support)*, bolster, reassure

buoyant resilient, sanguine, volatile

burden bind *(obligate)*, charge *(lien)*, charge *(responsibility)*, clog, cloud *(incumbrance)*, commitment *(responsibility)*, compel, constrain *(compel)*, disadvantage *(noun)*, disadvantage *(verb)*, duty *(obligation)*, duty *(tax)*, embarrass, encumber *(financially obligate)*, encumber *(hinder)*, encumbrance, grievance, hamper, handicap, harass, impede, impediment, impose *(enforce)*, inflict, interfere, liability, load, mistreat, nuisance, obligation *(duty)*, overcome *(overwhelm)*, overload, parasite, part *(role)*, pressure, responsibility *(accountability)*, servitude, stress *(strain)*, tax *(overwork)*, trouble, weigh. SEE MAIN ENTRY

burden of going forward. SEE MAIN ENTRY

burden of proof SEE MAIN ENTRY

burdened disadvantaged, disconsolate

burdensome difficult, onerous, operose, oppressive, ponderous

burdensome requirement onus *(burden)*

bureau agency *(commission)*, board, chapter *(branch)*, commission *(agency)*, committee, department, facility *(institution)*, firm, management *(directorate)*, office, organ. SEE MAIN ENTRY

bureaucracy hierarchy *(persons in authority)*, management *(directorate)*. SEE MAIN ENTRY

bureaucrat functionary, incumbent, official

bureaucratic ministerial, political

burgeon compound, expand, germinate, increase, proliferate, pullulate

burgeoning accession *(enlargement)*, boom *(increase)*, boom *(prosperity)*

burgess resident

burgher denizen

burglar criminal, hoodlum. SEE MAIN ENTRY

burglarious larcenous

burglarize loot, pillage, purloin, rob, steal

burglarizing housebreaking

burglary housebreaking, theft. SEE MAIN ENTRY

buried blind (concealed), dead, hidden, personal (private), privy

burke suppress

burlesque imitation, jape, mock (imitate), parody, ridicule, travesty

burlesque translation travesty

burly strong

burn deflagrate, destroy (efface), expend (consume). SEE MAIN ENTRY

burn fiercely deflagrate

burn to a cinder burn

burn up consume, deflagrate, dissipate (expend foolishly)

burning bitter (penetrating), caustic, fanatical, harsh, hot-blooded, perfervid, scathing, vehement

burrow delve, hunt, research

bursal financial, fiscal

bursar comptroller

bursary bank, repository, treasury

burst barrage, break (fracture), discharge (shot), discharge (shoot), outbreak, outburst, rend

burst forth emerge, issue (send forth), pullulate

burst in obtrude

burst in upon penetrate

burst into flame burn, deflagrate

burst of sound outcry

bury camouflage, cloak, cover (conceal), embed, hide, immerse (engross), inundate, overwhelm, plant (covertly place), seclude, shroud, suppress

busily employed active

busily engaged active, industrious, sedulous

busily intent diligent

business agenda, assignment (task), calling, career, commerce, commercial, company (enterprise), concern (business establishment), corporation, dealings, employment, enterprise (economic organization), firm, function, job, livelihood, mercantile, mission, occupation (vocation), office, position (business status), post, practice (professional business), profession (vocation), province, pursuit (occupation), trade (commerce), trade (occupation), transaction, undertaking (enterprise), venture, work (employment). SEE MAIN ENTRY

business affairs agenda, commerce, trade (commerce)

business agreement consortium (business cartel)

business association corporation

business combine consortium (business cartel)

business contact client, customer, patron (regular customer)

business deals commerce

business entente consortium (business cartel)

business establishment company (enterprise), corporation, enterprise (economic organization), firm, house

business expense cost (expenses)

business expenses overhead

business firm house

business house firm, store (business)

business intercourse commerce, dealings, exchange, trade (commerce)

business manager comptroller

business on hand agenda, matter (subject)

business owner lessor

business profits income

business representative procurator

business science finance

business transaction deal, dealings

business transactions commerce

businesslike commercial, diligent, formal, professional (stellar), prompt, systematic

businessman dealer, vendor

businessperson dealer, merchant

bustle dispatch (promptness), industry (activity), turmoil

bustling rapid

busy active, diligent, engage (involve), industrious, sedulous

busy oneself with occupy (engage), ply

busyness industry (activity)

but only, save

but for save

but for the fact that only

butcher extinguish, mutilate, spoil (impair)

butchery homicide

butt abut, border (bound), jostle (bump into), object, strike (collide), target

butt against collide (crash against), contact (touch), impinge

butt in interrupt, obtrude

button shut

buttress bear (support), bulwark, corroborate, document, mainstay, maintain (sustain), reaffirm, reinforce, reinforcement, side, supplement, support (corroborate), sustain (confirm), uphold

buy procure, purchase, trade. SEE MAIN ENTRY

buy and sell barter, deal, trade

buy back redeem (repurchase)

buy from patronize (trade with)

buy into invest (fund)

buy off suborn

buy stock invest (fund)

buy up purchase

buyer consumer, customer, patron (regular customer)

buyer of labor client, consumer, customer

buyer of stolen goods fence

buyer of stolen property fence

buying and selling business (commerce), commerce, dealings, exchange, trade (commerce)

buying power money

buying price expense (cost)

by a stronger reason a fortiori

by all appearances prima facie (self-evident)

by and large as a rule

by and large each and every time always (without exception)

by any means regardless

by choice purposely

by circumstance coincidental

by compulsion will shall

by course of conduct pro forma

by custom pro forma

by degrees piecemeal

by design intentional, purposely

by divine right ex officio

by habit pro forma

by imperative will shall

by inference a fortiori, circumstantial

by law de jure, ex officio. SEE MAIN ENTRY

by means of hereby, thereby, through (by means of)

by one party ex parte

by order de jure

by past practice pro forma

by proxy in lieu of

by reason of a priori, consequently

by right as a matter of right, ex officio

by right of law de jure

by statute de jure

by the act itself ipso facto

by the aid of hereby

by the fact itself ipso facto

by the hand of through (by means of)

by the mere fact ipso facto

by the piece retail

by the same sign consequently

by the same token consequently

by the time that until

by the very fact ipso facto

by trade and usage pro forma

by usage pro forma

by use of thereby

by virtue of hereby, thereby

by vote elective (selective)

by way of through (by means of), through (from beginning to end)

by way of a will testamentary

by way of gift gratuitous (given without recompense)

by will purposely

by word of mouth oral

by-passage causeway, detour

by-product development (outgrowth), follow-up

bygone antique, former, obsolete, outdated, outmoded

bylaw code, regulation (rule), rubric (authoritative rule), rule (legal dictate)

bylaws codification

byname cognomen, sobriquet

bypass avoidance (evasion), circumvent, detour, eschew, forgo, ignore, omit, pretermit, shun

byproduct offshoot

bystander eyewitness, witness. SEE MAIN ENTRY

byword call (title), catchword, cognomen, maxim, phrase

C

cabal band, collusion, confederacy (conspiracy), conspire, cooperate, faction, frame up, machination, maneuver, plan (noun), plan (verb), plot (secret plan), plot, scheme (noun), scheme (verb), schism, secret. SEE MAIN ENTRY

cabala mystery

cabalism mystery

cabalistic esoteric, mysterious, recondite

cabalistical esoteric

cabinet bench, board, chamber (body), commission (agency), committee

cache depository, fund, garner, harbor, hide, hoard (noun), hoard (verb), keep (shelter), plant (covertly place), provision (something provided), repository, reserve (noun), reserve (verb), store (depository), store, sufficiency, treasury. SEE MAIN ENTRY

cachet earmark, label

cacoethes dipsomania

cacophonous discordant

cacophony noise

cadaver body (person). SEE MAIN ENTRY

cadaver corpse

cadaveric lifeless (dead)

cadaverous dead, lifeless (dead)

cadeau bounty

cadence inflection, intonation

cadenced periodic

cadent periodic

cadere abate (extinguish), fail (lose), miscarriage

cadet offspring

cadge request

cadger parasite

cadre division *(administrative unit)*, staff

caducity deterioration, impuissance, incapacity. SEE MAIN ENTRY

caducous ephemeral, transient

caducus ephemeral

caecus blind *(sightless)*

caedere beat *(strike)*

caedes assassination, homicide, murder

caelum climate

caerimonia ceremony

cage cell, confine, contain *(restrain)*, envelop, keep *(restrain)*, lock, restrict

cagey machiavellian

cairn landmark *(conspicuous object)*, monument

caitiff recreant. SEE MAIN ENTRY

cajole coax, entice, importune, influence, inveigle, lure, persuade, pressure, prevail *(persuade)*. SEE MAIN ENTRY

cajolement bribery, persuasion

cajolery bribery, instigation, persuasion, seduction

cajoling persuasion

calamitas adversity, calamity, catastrophe, disaster, misfortune

calamitosus disastrous

calamitous adverse *(negative)*, deadly, deplorable, dire, disastrous, fatal, harmful, hostile, insalubrious, pernicious, regrettable, unfavorable

calamity accident *(misfortune)*, adversity, casualty, catastrophe, debacle, disaster, fatality, loss, misfortune, pain, tragedy, trouble. SEE MAIN ENTRY

calcar stimulus

calcified ossified

calculable appreciable, foreseeable

calculate arrange *(plan)*, assess *(appraise)*, conspire, deduce, deduct *(conclude by reasoning)*, devise *(invent)*, evaluate, find *(determine)*, gauge, intend, measure, plan, rate, scheme. SEE MAIN ENTRY

calculate approximately estimate

calculate on anticipate *(expect)*

calculate upon expect *(anticipate)*

calculate wrongly miscalculate

calculated aforethought, cold-blooded, deliberate, express, intentional, premeditated, purposeful, strategic, tactical

calculated risk speculation *(risk)*

calculated to give a false impression deceptive

calculated to provoke resentment invidious

calculated to stir eloquent

calculatedly purposely

calculating artful, cold-blooded, collusive, discreet, judicious, machiavellian, pensive, politic, provident *(showing foresight)*, prudent, sly

calculation appraisal, assessment *(estimation)*, census, computation, contemplation, deduction *(conclusion)*, deliberation, estimate *(approximate cost)*, expectation, forethought, idea, ledger, measurement, prospect *(outlook)*, prudence

calculator accountant

calculator of insurance risks actuary

calendar agenda, date, docket, empanel, file *(place among official records)*, note *(record)*, program *(noun)*, program *(verb)*, record, register *(noun)*, register *(verb)*, schedule. SEE MAIN ENTRY

calender set down

caliber degree *(magnitude)*, materiality *(consequence)*, performance *(workmanship)*, quality *(excellence)*, status, value, worth. SEE MAIN ENTRY

calibrate adjust *(regulate)*, assess *(appraise)*, gauge, measure

caliginosus lurid

call bespeak, charge *(command)*, contact *(communicate)*, convene, deem, demand, denominate, detail *(assign)*, entreaty, identify, impetus, invitation, label, market *(demand)*, monition *(legal summons)*, nominate, phrase, prayer, request, requirement, requisition, subpoena. SEE MAIN ENTRY

call a halt check *(restrain)*, close *(terminate)*, condemn *(ban)*, halt, hold up *(delay)*, quit *(discontinue)*, restrain

call attention to address *(direct attention to)*, admonish *(advise)*, indicate, notice *(observe)*, notify

call back annul, disavow, recommit, renege, rescind, resurrect

call before a court arraign

call by a distinctive title label

call by name denominate

call down rebuke, reprehend

call for command, demand, desire, entail, exact, market *(demand)*, necessitate, request, require *(compel)*, solicit, summon

call for aid call *(appeal to)*, petition

call for help call *(appeal to)*

call for the presence of subpoena, summon

call forth educe, elicit, engender, evoke, foment, incite, induce, order, provoke, resort, subpoena, summon

call in consult *(ask advice of)*, refer *(send for action)*

call in question disown *(deny the validity)*, dispute *(contest)*, except *(object)*, impeach, impugn, object, oppugn

call into action summon

call into being compose, engender, fabricate *(construct)*, generate, make

call into existence compose, generate, make

call names defame, denigrate

call of duty allegiance, burden, commitment *(responsibility)*

call off desist, discontinue *(abandon)*, dissolve *(terminate)*, hold up *(delay)*

call on refer *(send for action)*

call on for a blessing invoke

call on for help invoke

call out challenge, proclaim, subpoena

call public attention to issue *(publish)*, post, publish

call the roll poll

call to account arraign, blame, castigate, cite *(accuse)*, condemn *(blame)*, convict, denounce *(condemn)*, disapprove *(condemn)*, discipline *(punish)*, impeach, indict, lodge *(bring a complaint)*, penalize, punish, rebuke, reprehend, reprimand, reproach

call to answer challenge, contest

call to mind bear *(adduce)*, conjure, recognize *(perceive)*, recollect, remember

call to notice address *(direct attention to)*

call to task rebuke, reprimand

call to witness corroborate, subpoena, summon

call together convene

call up convene, evoke, induct, invoke, recall *(remember)*, recruit, remember, retain *(keep in possession)*

call upon address *(petition)*, call *(appeal to)*, command, delegate, direct *(order)*,

importune, instruct *(direct)*, order, petition, plead *(implore)*, pray, press *(beseech)*

call with authority subpoena, summon

called by duty bound

called for essential *(required)*, important *(urgent)*, indispensable, mandatory, requisite

callidus artful, expert, resourceful

calligraphy handwriting, script

calling business *(occupation)*, career, designation *(naming)*, employment, job, labor *(work)*, livelihood, mission, occupation *(vocation)*, position *(business status)*, practice *(professional business)*, profession *(vocation)*, pursuit *(occupation)*, specialty *(special aptitude)*, trade *(occupation)*, work *(employment)*. SEE MAIN ENTRY

calling to account incrimination

calling to court summons

callosus callous

callous cold-blooded, diabolic, impervious, insensible, insusceptible *(uncaring)*, obdurate, obtuse, phlegmatic, recalcitrant, ruthless, unaffected *(uninfluenced)*. SEE MAIN ENTRY

calloused ossified

callousness disinterest *(lack of interest)*, disregard *(lack of respect)*

callow inexperienced, jejune *(lacking maturity)*, juvenile, naive, puerile, uncouth

calm allay, alleviate, composure, controlled *(restrained)*, dispassionate, ease, lull *(noun)*, lull *(verb)*, moderate *(temper)*, mollify, nonchalant, obtund, pacify, passive, patient, peace, peaceable, phlegmatic, placate, placid, propitiate, relieve *(give aid)*, remedy, remit *(relax)*, soothe, subdue, subside, unaffected *(uninfluenced)*

calm before a storm crossroad *(turning point)*

calm down rest *(cease from action)*

calmant narcotic

calmative mitigating, narcotic *(adjective)*, narcotic *(noun)*, palliative *(abating)*, placid, remedial

calme dispassionate

calmness common sense, composure, lull, moderation, mollification, peace, sufferance, temperance

calumnia aspersion, slander

calumniari cavil, defame, misrepresent

calumniate contemn, defame, denigrate, denounce *(condemn)*, derogate, disparage, lessen, libel, malign, pillory, smear

calumniating contemptuous

calumniation aspersion, bad repute, defamation, slander, vilification

calumniatory calumnious, contemptuous, derogatory

calumnious contemptuous, derogatory, libelous, pejorative. SEE MAIN ENTRY

calumny aspersion, bad repute, defamation, denunciation, dishonor *(shame)*, libel, lie, slander, vilification

camarade copartner *(coconspirator)*

camaraderie comity, contact *(association)*, sodality

camarilla cabal, faction

came to determination res judicata

camera chamber *(compartment)*

camouflage blind *(obscure)*, cloak, conceal, concealment, cover *(pretext)*, cover *(conceal)*, deceit, deception, decoy, disguise *(noun)*, disguise *(verb)*, distort, distortion, ensconce, enshroud, evasion, falsify, hide, misrepresent, plant *(covertly place)*, pretense *(pretext)*, pretext, ruse, screen *(guard)*, subterfuge, veil. SEE MAIN ENTRY

camouflaged   blind *(concealed)*, clandestine, deceptive, hidden, indiscernible, latent
camp   dwelling, lodge *(reside)*
campaign   activity, course, endeavor, enterprise *(undertaking)*, expedient, fight *(battle)*, operation, plan, program, promotion *(encouragement)*, pursuit *(effort to secure)*, strategy, venture, work *(effort)*. SEE MAIN ENTRY
campaign promises   platform
campaigner   contender, politician
campaigning   politics
canaille   populace
canard   falsehood, fiction, figment, hoax, story *(falsehood)*. SEE MAIN ENTRY
canation   license
cancel   abate *(extinguish)*, abolish, abrogate *(annul)*, abrogate *(rescind)*, adeem, annul, cease, censor, condemn *(ban)*, countervail, debar, delete, disable, discharge *(release from obligation)*, disclaim, discontinue *(abandon)*, dissolve *(terminate)*, eliminate *(eradicate)*, expunge, expurgate, extinguish, extirpate, forestall, forgive, frustrate, invalidate, kill *(defeat)*, negate, neutralize, nullify, obliterate, override, overrule, quash, recall *(call back)*, recant, refute, remit *(release from penalty)*, remove *(eliminate)*, repeal, repudiate, rescind, revoke, superannuate, suppress, terminate, vacate *(void)*, vitiate. SEE MAIN ENTRY
cancel a punishment   pardon
cancel an offense   pardon
cancel debts   liquidate *(determine liability)*
cancel out   annul, counteract, countervail, neutralize
canceled   inactive, invalid, lifeless *(dead)*, null *(invalid)*, null and void, powerless
canceling   defeasance, discharge *(annulment)*
cancellation   abandonment *(repudiation)*, abatement *(extinguishment)*, abolition, ademption, annulment, censorship, condonation, countermand, defeasance, desuetude, discharge *(annulment)*, discharge *(release from obligation)*, discontinuance *(act of discontinuing)*, dismissal *(termination of a proceeding)*, dissolution *(termination)*, invalidity, mistrial, negation, nollo prosequi, obviation, remission, renunciation, repudiation, rescision, retraction, reversal, revocation. SEE MAIN ENTRY
cancellation of a legacy   ademption
cancelled   defunct, void *(invalid)*
cancelling   avoidance *(cancellation)*, discontinuance *(act of discontinuing)*, dissolution *(termination)*, revocation
cancerous   malignant
candid   bona fide, direct *(forthright)*, honest, ingenuous, objective, straightforward, unaffected *(sincere)*, upright. SEE MAIN ENTRY
candidate   contender, contestant, politician, probationer *(one being tested)*, prospect *(prospective patron)*, rival. SEE MAIN ENTRY
candidate under consideration   applicant *(candidate)*
candidatus   candidate
candidness   candor *(straightforwardness)*, honesty, probity, veracity
candidus   candid, open *(persuasible)*, unaffected *(sincere)*
candied   nectarious
candor   disinterest *(lack of prejudice)*, honesty, probity, truth, veracity. SEE MAIN ENTRY
cane   cudgel
canker   decay, degenerate, infect, pervert
cankered   decadent, marred

cannabis   SEE MAIN ENTRY
cannabis sativa   cannabis
cannonade   barrage
canny   artful, deft, machiavellian, perspicacious, politic, practiced, prudent, subtle *(insidious)*, vigilant
canon   article *(precept)*, belief *(something believed)*, bylaw, code, codification, constitution, direction *(order)*, doctrine, dogma, edict, law, legislation *(enactments)*, mandate, maxim, ordinance, pandect *(code of laws)*, precept, prescription *(directive)*, principle *(axiom)*, regulation *(rule)*, rubric *(authoritative rule)*, rule *(legal dictate)*, standard, statute. SEE MAIN ENTRY
canon of laws   pandect *(code of laws)*
canonic   valid
canonical   dogmatic, orthodox, valid
canonization   elevation
canonize   elevate, honor
canons   legislation *(enactments)*
canons regarding securities   blue sky law
canorus   harmonious
cant   jargon *(technical language)*, palter, phraseology
cantankerous   contentious, fractious, froward, hostile, inflexible, negative, perverse, petulant, restive
canting   querulous
cantle   element, segment
cantlet   segment
canton   division *(administrative unit)*, province
canvass   analyze, check *(inspect)*, debate, examine *(study)*, poll, request, scrutinize, solicit, survey *(poll)*. SEE MAIN ENTRY
canvassing   analysis, inquiry *(systematic investigation)*
cap   culminate, culmination, finish, pinnacle, surpass. SEE MAIN ENTRY
capability   ability, caliber *(mental capacity)*, caliber *(quality)*, capacity *(aptitude)*, competence *(ability)*, competence *(sanity)*, comprehension, efficiency, facility *(easiness)*, faculty *(ability)*, force *(strength)*, gift *(flair)*, performance *(workmanship)*, potential, qualification *(fitness)*, specialty *(special aptitude)*
capable   adequate, artful, competent, deft, effective *(efficient)*, efficient, eligible, expert, familiar *(informed)*, fit, omnipotent, operative, possible, potent, practiced, proficient, qualified *(competent)*, resourceful, sciential, veteran, virtual. SEE MAIN ENTRY
capable of being adjudged invalid   voidable
capable of being adjudged void   voidable
capable of being annulled   voidable
capable of being appeased   placable
capable of being bounded   terminable
capable of being completed   terminable
capable of being concluded   terminable
capable of being conditioned   terminable
capable of being conquered   indefensible
capable of being debated   debatable, forensic, litigable
capable of being decided by a court   justiciable
capable of being declared ineffectual   voidable
capable of being declared void   voidable
capable of being deducted   deductible *(capable of being deducted from taxes)*
capable of being demonstrated   provable
capable of being divided   divisible

capable of being done   practicable
capable of being ended   terminable
capable of being examined   cognizable
capable of being exchanged   convertible
capable of being figured out   deductible *(provable)*
capable of being fixed   terminable
capable of being inhabited   habitable
capable of being limited   terminable
capable of being made definite   terminable
capable of being maintained   tenable
capable of being overcome   indefensible
capable of being pacified   placable
capable of being perceived   appreciable
capable of being proved   deductible *(provable)*
capable of being proven   provable
capable of being rebated   deductible *(capable of being deducted from taxes)*
capable of being shown   provable
capable of being transferred   negotiable
capable of being tried in the court   cognizable
capable of conforming to new situations   flexible
capable of decision   determinable *(ascertainable)*
capable of development   viable
capable of growth   viable
capable of holding much   capacious
capable of loss   at risk
capable of passing   passable
capable of positive proof   provable
capable of proof   certain *(positive)*, incontrovertible, provable
capable of reason   reasonable *(rational)*
capable of receiving injuries   vulnerable
capable of resisting   insusceptible *(resistant)*, insusceptible *(uncaring)*
capable of responding to changing situations   flexible
capable of withstanding   insusceptible *(uncaring)*
capableness   caliber *(mental capacity)*, capacity *(aptitude)*, efficiency
capacious   ample, complete *(all-embracing)*, comprehensive, extensive. SEE MAIN ENTRY
capaciousness   measurement, space
capacitate   empower, enable
capacity   ability, appointment *(position)*, caliber *(mental capacity)*, cargo, competence *(ability)*, coverage *(scope)*, employment, faculty *(ability)*, gift *(flair)*, maximum *(amplitude)*, means *(opportunity)*, measurement, occupation *(vocation)*, office, penchant, performance *(workmanship)*, post, potential, propensity, province, pursuit *(occupation)*, qualification *(fitness)*, role, science *(technique)*, space, sphere, sufficiency. SEE MAIN ENTRY
capacity to decide the matter in issue   jurisdiction
capacity to endure   sufferance, tolerance
capacity to hear the controversy   jurisdiction
capacity to stand suffering   tolerance
capacity to take pain   tolerance
capacity to understand   comprehension
capere   capture, contain *(comprise)*, ensnare, entrap, gain, occupy *(take possession)*, receive *(acquire)*
capital   assets, cardinal *(basic)*, cash, central *(essential)*, deadly, fund, important *(significant)*, leading *(ranking first)*, master, material *(important)*, monetary, money,

possessions, premium, prime *(most valuable)*, principal *(capital sum)*, resource, salient, seat, securities, security *(stock)*, select, share *(stock)*, stellar, stock *(shares)*, substance *(material possessions)*, treasury. SEE MAIN ENTRY

capital crime   felony, homicide
capital gains   boom *(prosperity)*
capital goods   merchandise
capital invested   investment
capital murder   homicide
capital outlay   investment
capital punishment   SEE MAIN ENTRY
capitalize   finance. SEE MAIN ENTRY
capitalize on   exploit *(make use of)*
capitalize upon   employ *(make use of)*
capitation   assessment *(levy)*, duty *(tax)*, excise, poll *(canvass)*, tax
capitulary   code, codification
capitulate   accede *(concede)*, defer *(yield in judgment)*, forfeit, quit *(discontinue)*, resign, submit *(yield)*, succumb, surrender *(yield)*, yield *(submit)*
capitulation   capsule, concession *(compromise)*, hornbook, resignation *(passive acceptance)*. SEE MAIN ENTRY
caprice   notion
capricious   aleatory *(uncertain)*, arbitrary, disordered, haphazard, inconsistent, irresolute, irresponsible, lawless, mutable, undependable, unpredictable, unreasonable, unreliable, unsettled, untrustworthy, variable, volatile. SEE MAIN ENTRY
capriciousness   inconsistency
capsize   upset
capsule   abridgment *(condensation)*, abstract, brief, compendium, concise, digest, hornbook, scenario. SEE MAIN ENTRY
capsulize   abridge *(shorten)*, abstract *(summarize)*, condense, constrict *(compress)*, digest *(summarize)*
capsulized   concise
captain   chief, superintendent
captainship   generalship
captare   solicit
captio   fallacy
caption   apprehension *(act of arresting)*, call *(title)*, denomination, heading, inscription, phrase, rubric *(title)*, title *(designation)*. SEE MAIN ENTRY
captiosus   sophistic
captious   contentious, contrary, critical *(faultfinding)*, fractious, froward, perverse, petulant, querulous, sophistic
captivate   coax, lure, motivate, occupy *(engage)*, subdue
captivating   attractive, moving *(evoking emotion)*, provocative, sapid
captivation   seduction
captive   convict, hostage, in custody, inmate, prisoner. SEE MAIN ENTRY
captivitas   captivity
captivity   bondage, constraint *(imprisonment)*, custody *(incarceration)*, detention, durance, duress, incarceration, restraint, servitude, subjection, thrall. SEE MAIN ENTRY
captivus   captive
capture   apprehend *(arrest)*, apprehension *(act of arresting)*, appropriate, appropriation *(taking)*, arrest, arrest *(apprehend)*, carry away, confine, deprive, detain *(hold in custody)*, disseisin, distraint, distress *(seizure)*, enclose, ensnare, gain, hijack, jail, kidnap, obtain, occupy *(take possession)*, preempt, prize, procure, repossess, seize *(apprehend)*, seize *(confiscate)*, subdue, succeed *(attain)*, taking. SEE MAIN ENTRY

capture and deportation   extradition
captured   arrested *(apprehended)*
captured goods   contraband
captured person   captive
capturing   confiscatory
captus   captive, inmate
caput   article *(precept)*, capital, chapter *(division)*, chief, clause, main point, person, point *(item)*, principal *(capital sum)*, source
carbine   gun
carbon   counterpart *(parallel)*, duplicate
carbon copy   counterpart *(parallel)*, duplicate
carcass   body *(person)*, cadaver, corpse
carcer   custody *(supervision)*, incarceration, jail, prison
card   coupon, form *(document)*
card index   file
cardholder   member *(individual in a group)*
cardinal   central *(essential)*, considerable, dominant, fundamental, indispensable, integral, leading *(ranking first)*, material *(important)*, paramount, prime *(most valuable)*, principal, salient, vital. SEE MAIN ENTRY
cardinal feature   main point
cardinal point   center *(essence)*, content *(meaning)*, cornerstone, gist *(ground for a suit)*, gravamen, landmark *(significant change)*, main point
care   administration, agency *(legal relationship)*, alimony, apprehension *(fear)*, auspices, burden, caution *(vigilance)*, charge *(custody)*, concern *(interest)*, consideration *(sympathetic regard)*, constraint *(imprisonment)*, control *(supervision)*, custody *(supervision)*, direction *(guidance)*, discretion *(quality of being discreet)*, generalship, help, interest *(concern)*, maintenance *(upkeep)*, management *(supervision)*, notice *(heed)*, particularity, patronage *(support)*, precaution, preservation, problem, prudence, regard *(attention)*, relief *(aid)*, rigor, safekeeping, service *(assistance)*, shelter *(protection)*, supervision, surveillance, trust *(custody)*, ward, weight *(burden)*. SEE MAIN ENTRY
care for   attend *(take care of)*, cover *(guard)*, foster, harbor, hold *(possess)*, keep *(shelter)*, maintain *(sustain)*, manage, nurture, police, preserve, protect, provide *(arrange for)*, regard *(hold in esteem)*, serve *(assist)*
care nothing for   condescend *(patronize)*, disdain, flout
cared for   safe
career   business *(occupation)*, calling, employment, livelihood, occupation *(vocation)*, position *(business status)*, post, practice *(professional business)*, profession *(vocation)*, professional *(trained)*, pursuit *(occupation)*, specialty *(special aptitude)*. SEE MAIN ENTRY
carefree   complacent, convenient, nonchalant, secure *(confident)*
careful   accurate, circumspect, close *(rigorous)*, conscientious, deliberate, discreet, economical, exact, faithful *(diligent)*, frugal, guarded, judicious, leery, literal, meticulous, noncommittal, painstaking, particular *(exacting)*, politic, precise, preventive, provident *(frugal)*, provident *(showing foresight)*, prudent, punctilious, scrupulous, strict, thorough, vigilant. SEE MAIN ENTRY
careful appreciation   diagnosis
careful attention   notice *(heed)*
careful budgeting   prudence
careful consideration   deliberation
careful examination   scrutiny
careful management   economy *(frugality)*

careful methods   strategy
careful noting of details   examination *(study)*
careful plans   strategy
careful scrutiny   inspection
careful search   indagation, investigation, probe, research
careful study   indagation, investigation
carefully considered   deliberate
carefully weighed   deliberate
carefulness   caution *(vigilance)*, deliberation, diligence *(care)*, discretion *(quality of being discreet)*, economy *(frugality)*, notice *(heed)*, particularity, precaution, prudence, rigor
carefulness in outlay   economy *(frugality)*
careless   blind *(not discerning)*, cursory, derelict *(negligent)*, disorderly, heedless, hot-blooded, ill-judged, impolitic, improvident, imprudent, impulsive *(rash)*, inaccurate, inadvertent, inexact, lax, negligent, oblivious, perfunctory, prodigal, reckless, remiss, slipshod, superficial, thoughtless, undependable, unpolitic, wanton. SEE MAIN ENTRY
careless abandon   neglect
careless loss   waste
careless mistake   oversight *(carelessness)*
careless omission   oversight *(carelessness)*
carelessness   delinquency *(failure of duty)*, dereliction, disinterest *(lack of interest)*, disregard *(unconcern)*, inconsideration, indiscretion, laxity, malpractice, neglect, negligence, omission, temerity
caretake   operate, superintend
caretaker   custodian *(warden)*, fiduciary, guardian, proctor, procurator, superintendent, trustee. SEE MAIN ENTRY
caretakers   management *(directorate)*
careworn   disconsolate
carfare   fare
cargo   freight, merchandise. SEE MAIN ENTRY
caricature   copy, disguise, distort, distortion, exaggeration, jape, mock *(imitate)*, parody, ridicule, travesty. SEE MAIN ENTRY
caring   solicitous
caritas   dearth
carload   cargo, freight
carmen famosum   libel
carnage   aberemurder, havoc, homicide
carnal   bodily, dissolute, lascivious, lewd, mundane, physical, promiscuous, prurient, salacious, suggestive *(risqué)*
carnivorous   predatory
carouse   SEE MAIN ENTRY
carp   blame, cavil, complain *(criticize)*
carp at   discompose, persecute, press *(goad)*
carpenter   build *(construct)*, frame *(construct)*
carpere   cavil, cull
carping   critical *(faultfinding)*, criticism, denunciation, diatribe, fractious, petulant, querulous
carriage   behavior, complexion, conduct, demeanor, deportment, manner *(behavior)*, presence *(poise)*, temperament. SEE MAIN ENTRY
carried   consensual
carried away   ecstatic, uncontrollable
carried through   complete *(ended)*
carrier   bearer. SEE MAIN ENTRY
carrion   body *(person)*, corpse
carry   bear *(support)*, convey *(transfer)*, deliver, demean *(deport oneself)*, handle *(trade)*, move *(alter position)*, pass *(approve)*, transfer, transmit, transport, uphold, wield. SEE MAIN ENTRY

carry a report   disseminate

carry a suggestion   connote, imply

carry authority   dominate, prevail *(triumph)*

carry away   abduct, capture, displace *(remove)*, distrain, hijack, hold up *(rob)*, impropriate. SEE MAIN ENTRY

carry back   recover

carry beyond the limit   extend *(enlarge)*

carry conviction   convince

carry forward   keep *(continue)*, perpetuate

carry further   extend *(enlarge)*

carry into effect   comply, consummate, discharge *(perform)*, effectuate, enforce, execute *(accomplish)*, fulfill, implement, make, realize *(make real)*

carry into execution   abide, commit *(perpetrate)*, comply, compose, discharge *(perform)*, effectuate, enforce, execute *(accomplish)*, exercise *(discharge a function)*, implement, make, operate, perform *(adhere to)*, perform *(execute)*, perpetrate, satisfy *(discharge)*, strive

carry off   carry away, dislodge, distrain, hijack, hold up *(rob)*, kidnap, loot, perpetrate, plunder, poach

carry on   adhere *(persist)*, attempt, bear *(tolerate)*, commit *(perpetrate)*, conduct, continue *(resume)*, endure *(last)*, exercise *(discharge a function)*, function, keep *(continue)*, last, manage, militate, operate, oversee, perpetrate, perpetuate, persevere, persist, ply, proceed *(continue)*, promote *(organize)*, prosecute *(carry forward)*, remain *(continue)*, reopen, resume, tolerate, transact, undertake

carry on a conversation   converse, discuss, speak

carry on a lawsuit   litigate

carry on a trade   handle *(trade)*

carry on an argument   contend *(dispute)*, dispute *(debate)*

carry on an inquiry   canvass

carry on business   handle *(trade)*, practice *(engage in)*, transact

carry on commerce   handle *(trade)*, trade

carry on hostilities   engage *(involve)*

carry on intensive research   delve

carry on negotiations   deal, handle *(trade)*

carry on under   allow *(endure)*

carry on war   fight *(battle)*

carry oneself   deport *(conduct oneself)*

carry out   administer *(conduct)*, apply *(put in practice)*, commit *(perpetrate)*, complete, comply, conduct, consummate, discharge *(perform)*, dispatch *(dispose of)*, enforce, execute *(accomplish)*, exercise *(discharge a function)*, finish, function, implement, keep *(fulfill)*, obey, observe *(obey)*, officiate, operate, perfect, perform *(adhere to)*, perpetrate, prosecute *(carry forward)*, realize *(make real)*, satisfy *(discharge)*, satisfy *(fulfill)*, transact, undertake

carry out a sentence   condemn *(punish)*, discipline *(punish)*, penalize

carry over   continue *(resume)*, holdover

carry tales   inform *(notify)*

carry through   attain, commit *(perpetrate)*, complete, consummate, discharge *(perform)*, dispatch *(dispose of)*, effectuate, enforce, finish, follow-up, implement, perpetrate, realize *(make real)*

carry to completion   complete, conclude *(complete)*, consummate, dispatch *(dispose of)*, exhaust *(try all possibilities)*

carry to excess   carouse, overindulge

carry too far   overindulge

carry weight   influence, motivate, predominate *(command)*, prejudice *(influence)*

carry weight with   prevail *(persuade)*, prevail upon

carry-over   balance *(amount in excess)*, remainder *(remaining part)*

carrying   carriage

carrying charge   cost *(price)*, maintenance *(upkeep)*

carrying into effect   enforcement, performance *(execution)*

carrying on   continuation *(resumption)*

carrying out   action *(performance)*, commission *(act)*, enforcement

carrying through   discharge *(performance)*, fait accompli, performance *(execution)*

cart   carry *(transport)*, deliver, transport

cart away   dislodge, displace *(remove)*

cartage   carriage

carte blanche   dispensation *(exception)*

carte blanche   latitude

carte blanche   permit

cartel   business *(commercial enterprise)*, coalition, compact, confederacy *(compact)*, consortium *(business cartel)*, league, pool, syndicate, treaty, trust *(combination of businesses)*. SEE MAIN ENTRY

cartload   cargo

cartoon   caricature, copy, parody

cartridges   ammunition

carve   create, disjoint, divide *(distribute)*, parcel, part *(separate)*, partition, split

carve up   apportion

cascade   outpour

case   action *(proceeding)*, cause *(lawsuit)*, check *(inspect)*, complaint, controversy *(lawsuit)*, day in court, enshroud, example, incident, instance, lawsuit, matter *(subject)*, particular, patient, plight, predicament, proceeding, question *(issue)*, situation, subject *(object)*, suit, trial *(legal proceeding)*. SEE MAIN ENTRY

case at law   controversy *(lawsuit)*, hearing

case for decision   lawsuit

case for the prosecution   complaint, count

case history   dossier

case in point   example, illustration, instance, sample, specimen

case in question   matter *(subject)*

case of conscience   allegiance

cases ready for argument   calendar *(list of cases)*

cash   currency, money. SEE MAIN ENTRY

cash box   bank

cash in   liquidate *(convert into cash)*

cash in on   gain, profit

cash paid   expenditure

cash payment   advance *(allowance)*, collection *(payment)*

cash supplies   capital

cashbook   journal, ledger

casher   bearer

cashier   comptroller, demote, discharge *(dismiss)*, dislodge, dismiss *(discharge)*, eliminate *(exclude)*, reject, remove *(dismiss from office)*, supplant

cashier's check   draft

cashiering   dismissal *(discharge)*, layoff, rejection, removal

cassation   cancellation, defeasance, negation

cast   allocate, build *(construct)*, characteristic, configuration *(form)*, copy, discharge *(dismiss)*, disposition *(inclination)*, fabricate *(construct)*, frame *(formulate)*, inclination,

launch *(project)*, make, nuance, personnel, posture *(attitude)*, predisposition, project *(impel forward)*, send, stamp, style, tenor. SEE MAIN ENTRY

cast a ballot   vote

cast a reproach   censure

cast a shadow   obnubilate, obscure

cast a slur   smear

cast a slur on   blame, dishonor *(deprive of honor)*, involve *(implicate)*

cast a slur upon   brand *(stigmatize)*, censure, denounce *(condemn)*, derogate, disgrace, fault, humiliate, malign, pillory

cast a vote   vote

cast accounts   calculate

cast adrift   dispel

cast an imputation upon   impeach

cast anchor   pause

cast aside   abandon *(relinquish)*, condemn *(ban)*, derelict *(abandoned)*, forgo, forswear, nullify, omit, pretermit, rebuff, refuse, reject, renounce, repel *(drive back)*, spurn

cast aspersions   complain *(criticize)*, contemn, denigrate, denounce *(condemn)*, deprecate, derogate, dishonor *(deprive of honor)*, malign

cast aspersions at   brand *(stigmatize)*

cast aspersions on   defame, disapprove *(condemn)*, discredit, pillory

cast away   abandon *(relinquish)*, depose *(remove)*, disown *(refuse to acknowledge)*, forswear, reject

cast back   reflect *(mirror)*

cast blame upon   censure, condemn *(blame)*, convict, disapprove *(condemn)*, fault, impeach, incriminate, lodge *(bring a complaint)*, reprehend

cast dishonor upon   disgrace

cast doubt   impugn

cast doubt upon   debunk

cast down   disconsolate, discourage, humiliate, overthrow

cast eyes on   discern *(detect with the senses)*

cast forth   diffuse, disperse *(disseminate)*, dissipate *(spread out)*, eject *(expel)*, outpour

cast into prison   arrest *(apprehend)*, immure, imprison, jail

cast light upon   elucidate. SEE MAIN ENTRY

cast loose   discharge *(dismiss)*, free *(not restricted)*, parole

cast lots   bet

cast off   abandon *(physically leave)*, abandon *(relinquish)*, defect, derelict *(abandoned)*, disencumber, disown *(refuse to acknowledge)*, dispel, disperse *(disseminate)*, forgo, forswear, reject, relinquish, renounce, set aside *(annul)*, waive

cast out   condemn *(ban)*, deport *(banish)*, depose *(remove)*, disinherit, dislocate, dislodge, dismiss *(discharge)*, dispel, displace *(remove)*, eject *(evict)*, eject *(expel)*, eliminate *(exclude)*, emit, exclude, expatriate, expose, ineligible, oust, relegate, spurn

cast overboard   jettison

cast reflection upon   censure, denounce *(condemn)*, impugn

cast reproach upon   denounce *(condemn)*, disgrace, dishonor *(deprive of honor)*, expostulate, lash *(attack verbally)*

cast shame upon   discredit

cast the majority of ballots for   elect *(select by a vote)*

castaway   derelict *(abandoned)*, discard, orphan, pariah

caste   bloodline, class, status

castigare   castigate, punish

663

castigate blame, censure, complain (criticize), condemn (blame), criticize (find fault with), denounce (condemn), disapprove (condemn), discipline (punish), expostulate, fault, ill use, impeach, lash (attack verbally), penalize, proscribe (denounce), punish, rebuke, remonstrate, reprehend, reprimand, reproach. SEE MAIN ENTRY

castigating critical (faultfinding)

castigatio correction (punishment), punishment

castigation bad repute, blame (culpability), charge (accusation), condemnation (blame), contumely, correction (punishment), denunciation, diatribe, discipline (punishment), discredit, disparagement, impeachment, indictment, infliction, objurgation, obloquy, outcry, penalty, phillipic, punishment, remonstrance, reprimand, reproach, revilement, stricture

castigatory calumnious, disciplinary (punitory), pejorative, penal, punitive

casting away release

casting of ballots poll (casting of votes)

casting out deportation

castoff discard

casual careless, coincidental, cursory, fortuitous, haphazard, informal, lax, nonchalant, perfunctory, promiscuous, random, sporadic, thoughtless, unintentional, unofficial, usual. SEE MAIN ENTRY

casualness informality

casualties toll (effect)

casualty accident (misfortune), corpse, damage, disaster, expense (sacrifice), fatality, happenstance, misfortune, quirk (accident), tragedy, victim. SEE MAIN ENTRY

casuistic artificial, illusory, sophistic, specious

casuistical illusory, sophistic, specious

casuistry duplicity, ethics, sophistry. SEE MAIN ENTRY

casus accident (chance occurrence), chance (fortuity), contingency, emergency, fatality, happening, hazard, incident, occurrence

casus foederis counteroffer

catachresis SEE MAIN ENTRY

cataclysm calamity, catastrophe, debacle, disaster, fatality, havoc, misfortune, outbreak, prostration, shambles, tragedy. SEE MAIN ENTRY

cataclysmal disastrous

cataclysmic deadly, dire, disastrous, harmful

catalog codify, docket, enumerate, impanel, index (relate), itemize

catalogue classify, detail (particularize), digest (summarize), directory, enroll, enter (record), file, file (arrange), fix (arrange), identify, inventory, note (record), order (arrangement), organize (arrange), pigeonhole, program, prospectus, record (noun), record (verb), register (noun), register (verb), roll, sort, tabulate

catalogue of persons poll (canvass)

cataloguing classification, registration

catalyst stimulus. SEE MAIN ENTRY

catalytic agent catalyst, stimulus

catapult cast (throw), impel, launch (project), precipitate (throw down violently)

cataract spate

catastrophe adversity, calamity, casualty, debacle, disaster, fatality, loss, misfortune, tragedy, trouble. SEE MAIN ENTRY

catastrophic adverse (negative), deplorable, dire, disastrous, fatal, harmful, pernicious, regrettable

catastrophical dire

catch apprehend (arrest), apprehension (act of arresting), arrest (apprehend), capture, connection (fastening), ensnare, entrap, lock, obstacle, obstruction, overhear, pitfall, preempt, prize, receive (acquire), seize (apprehend), trap (noun), trap (verb)

catch a glimpse of find (discover)

catch again rearrest

catch by artifice entrap

catch by perfidy ambush

catch fire burn

catch phrase catchword

catch sight of discern (detect with the senses), recognize (perceive), spy

catch the attention occupy (engage)

catch the eye interest

catch unprepared ensnare

catch up reach

catch-all reach

catchall depository. SEE MAIN ENTRY

catching attractive, contagious

catchpenny tawdry

catchword SEE MAIN ENTRY

catchy attractive

catechization interrogation

catechize cross-examine, examine (interrogate), inquire

catechumen neophyte, novice

categorical absolute (conclusive), actual, affirmative, axiomatic, certain (specific), clear (certain), compelling, conclusive (determinative), convincing, decisive, definite, dogmatic, explicit, express, positive (incontestable), specific, unconditional, unequivocal. SEE MAIN ENTRY

categorical imperative conscience, instruction (direction)

categorically true actual, candid

categorization classification, denomination, department, designation (naming), diagnosis, distribution (arrangement), hierarchy (arrangement in a series), manner (kind), order (arrangement), subdivision, subheading

categorization of laws codification

categorize classify, codify, file (arrange), index (docket), organize (arrange), pigeonhole, sort, subdivide

category class, classification, denomination, department, diagnosis, division (administrative unit), kind, manner (kind), member (constituent part), section (division), subdivision

catena chain (series), fetter

catenas fetter

catenation chain (series), connection (fastening), sequence

cater bestow, pander, supply

cater to excessively overindulge

caterer supplier

catering provision (act of supplying)

catharsis SEE MAIN ENTRY

catholic general, omnibus, prevailing (current), prevalent, rife

catholicity disinterest (lack of prejudice)

catholicon cure, panacea

catlike furtive, stealthy

cattiness spite

caucas company (assemblage)

caucus assemblage, assembly, chamber (body), meeting (conference), panel (discussion group), party (political organization), session. SEE MAIN ENTRY

caught arrested (apprehended)

causa cause (reason), cause, ground, inducement, issue (matter in dispute), matter (case), motive, reason (basis), suit

causal causative. SEE MAIN ENTRY

causality derivation, incentive

causam hear (give a legal hearing)

causam agere plead (argue a case)

causation building (business of assembling), cause (reason), creation, derivation, incentive, instigation, motive, origination, provocation, reason (basis)

causative causal, constructive (creative), productive. SEE MAIN ENTRY

cause action (proceeding), activity, answer (solution), avail (bring about), base (foundation), basis, bear (yield), campaign, case (lawsuit), catalyst, cause of action, compel, compose, conduce, contention (argument), contrive, controversy (lawsuit), create, derivation, effectuate, elicit, endeavor, engender, enterprise (undertaking), evoke, factor (ingredient), forge (produce), generate, gist (ground for a suit), ground, impel, incentive, incite, induce, inducement, inflict, inspire, issue (matter in dispute), make, matter (case), motivate, occasion, operate, origin (source), originate, origination, proceeding, procure, prompt, provocation, provoke, rationale, reason (basis), redound, require (compel), side, source, stimulus, suit, trial (legal proceeding). SEE MAIN ENTRY

cause a discontinuance discontinue (abandon)

cause a fuss perturb

cause a mistake misguide

cause a rift disaffect

cause a scandal pillory

cause a stoppage check (restrain), close (terminate), hold up (delay), quit (discontinue)

cause against an opposing party counterclaim

cause agitation perturb

cause alarm menace, perturb

cause aversion repel (disgust)

cause chaos disrupt

cause confusion disrupt, embarrass, perturb

cause damage to prejudice (injure)

cause detriment damage, prejudice (injure)

cause discomfort embarrass

cause discontent disappoint, disconcert, discourage

cause dislike affront, alienate (estrange), antagonize, disaffect, discourage, incense, repel (disgust)

cause disorder perturb

cause displeasure disoblige

cause doubt discourage, dissuade

cause error delude, err, misguide, mislead

cause evil ill use, mistreat

cause for alarm hazard

cause for blame fault (responsibility)

cause for complaint ground

cause for concern problem

cause for protest ground

cause growth magnify

cause hostility disaffect

cause illness infect

cause in court action (proceeding), lawsuit, matter (case), suit

cause-in-fact. SEE MAIN ENTRY

cause injury damage

cause loathing alienate (estrange), incense

cause mischief damage

cause of action claim (legal demand), gist (ground for a suit), incentive. SEE MAIN ENTRY

cause of action in favor of defendants counterclaim. SEE MAIN ENTRY

cause of distress   nuisance, trouble
cause of reproach   disgrace
cause of shame   disgrace
cause of sorrow   grievance
cause offense   affront, antagonize
cause pain   aggravate (annoy), harm, mistreat, prejudice (injure)
cause problems   disadvantage
cause resentment   bait (harass), incense, pique
cause scission   disrupt
cause suffering   distress
cause the downfall of   supplant
cause to   constrain (compel)
cause to alter   affect
cause to arrive late   hold up (delay)
cause to be   compose, fabricate (construct), generate
cause to be continued   perpetuate
cause to be dishonest   corrupt, taint (corrupt)
cause to be forfeited   confiscate, seize (confiscate)
cause to be nugatory   foil
cause to be remembered   retain (keep in possession)
cause to be smaller   diminish
cause to be still   allay
cause to be understood   explain
cause to bend   divert
cause to bulge   inflate
cause to cease   eradicate, interrupt
cause to contract   constrict (compress)
cause to curve   divert
cause to delay   impede, interrupt
cause to descend   demote
cause to deviate   divert
cause to diminish   decrease
cause to disappear   expunge
cause to endure   establish (entrench), keep (shelter), perpetuate
cause to exist   compose, create, engender, fabricate (construct), make
cause to expand   develop
cause to feel certain   assure (give confidence to)
cause to feel ill at ease   embarrass
cause to forfeit   dispossess
cause to grow   develop, extend (enlarge)
cause to halt   cease, enjoin, quit (discontinue)
cause to happen   carry (succeed), effectuate, evoke
cause to last   keep (shelter), perpetuate
cause to move with undue slowness   hold up (delay)
cause to pass to another   devolve
cause to put off to a later time   hold up (delay)
cause to recollect   remind
cause to relax   lull
cause to remember   remind
cause to rise   elevate
cause to sink   demote, depress
cause to subside   allay
cause to suffer   inflict
cause to taper   diminish
cause to turn from   divert
cause to undergo   subject
cause to vary   affect
cause to yield   force (coerce)
cause umbrage   antagonize
cause upset   perturb
caused   causative, derivative
causeless   casual, gratuitous (unwarranted), needless, unpredictable
causer   author (originator)

causerie   conversation
causeway   SEE MAIN ENTRY
causey   causeway
causidical   actionable
causing danger   dangerous, noxious
causing death   fatal
causing destruction   fatal
causing disagreement   divisive
causing disassociation   divisive
causing disjunction   divisive
causing pleasure   palatable
causing separation   divisive
caustic   astringent, bitter (acrid tasting), bitter (reproachful), calumnious, critical (faultfinding), cynical, harsh, incisive, malignant, mordacious, spiteful, trenchant. SEE MAIN ENTRY
causticity   severity
cautel   notice (heed)
cauterize   burn
cautio   caution (vigilance), prudence, security (stock)
caution   admonish (warn), admonition, advise, alert, castigate, caveat, charge (instruct on the law), counsel, deliberation, deter, deterrent, diligence (care), discourage, discretion (quality of being discreet), dissuade, exhort, expostulate, forewarn, hesitation, indicant, monition (warning), notice (heed), notice (warning), notification, notify, portend, precaution, premonition, prudence, restraint, signify (inform), warning. SEE MAIN ENTRY
caution against danger   forewarn
caution beforehand   forewarn
caution in advance   forewarn
caution money   bail, binder
cautionary   advisory, portentous (ominous)
cautious   careful, circumspect, deliberate, diffident, discreet, frugal, guarded, hesitant, judicious, leery, noncommittal, politic, preventive, provident (showing foresight), prudent, suspicious (distrustful), tentative, vigilant
cautious in dealing   diplomatic
cautiousness   deliberation, discretion (quality of being discreet), notice (heed)
cautus   circumspect, discreet, guarded, prudent, tactical
cavalier   cynical, disdainful, impertinent (insolent), presumptuous, supercilious
cavalierness   disrespect
cave in   break (fracture), succumb
caveat   admonition
caveat   caution (warning), deterrence, deterrent, instruction (direction), measure, monition (warning), notice (warning), warning. SEE MAIN ENTRY
caveat emptor   SEE MAIN ENTRY
cavil   bicker, blame, complain (criticize), denounce (condemn), differ (disagree), disagree, disapprove (condemn), disparage, pettifog, sophistry. SEE MAIN ENTRY
caviler   disputant, malcontent
caviling   contentious, critical (faultfinding), criticism, disaccord, disapprobation, dissension, dissent (difference of opinion), dissenting, fractious
cavillari   flout, jeer
cavilling   petulant
cease   abandon (relinquish), close (terminate), cloture, conclude (complete), desist, discontinue (abandon), dissipate (spread out), dissolve (terminate), expire, finish, forbear, forgo, halt, interrupt, leave (allow to remain), palliate (abate), pause, perish, quit (discontinue), refrain, relinquish, renounce,

rest (cease from action), shut, stop, succumb, suspend, terminate, vacate (leave), waive, withdraw. SEE MAIN ENTRY
cease existing   decease
cease living   decease, die, perish
cease progress   quit (discontinue)
cease resistance   comply, submit (yield)
cease to be   decease, dissipate (spread out), expire, perish
cease to exist   decease, die, perish
cease to litigate   rest (end a legal case)
cease to live   decease, perish
cease to use   quit (discontinue)
cease using   discontinue (abandon)
cease work   quit (discontinue), resign, strike (refuse to work)
ceaseless   chronic, continual (perpetual), continuous, durable, incessant, infinite, open-ended, permanent, perpetual, unrelenting, unremitting
ceaselessness   indestructibility, perpetuity
ceasing   cessation (interlude)
cede   abandon (relinquish), attorn, bequeath, bestow, confer (give), contribute (supply), convey (transfer), defer (yield in judgment), devolve, disown (refuse to acknowledge), forfeit, give (grant), grant (concede), grant (transfer formally), offer (tender), pass (advance), relinquish, remise, resign, surrender (give back), transmit, yield (submit). SEE MAIN ENTRY
cede back   escheat
cedere   resign
ceiling   cap, pinnacle. SEE MAIN ENTRY
celare   hide
celeber   famous, populous
celebrare   honor
celebrate   carouse, honor, keep (fulfill), recommend
celebrated   blatant (conspicuous), famous, household (familiar), illustrious, notable, noteworthy, notorious, outstanding (prominent), popular, prominent, remarkable, renowned, reputable, stellar
celebrated in public   famous
celebration   ceremony, dedication, holiday, memory (commemoration), mention (tribute), recommendation, remembrance (commemoration), reputation
celebrity   character (reputation), distinction (reputation), eminence, notoriety, prestige, regard (esteem), reputation
celer   expeditious
celerity   dispatch (promptness), haste
celestial   stellar
celibate   solitary
cell   chamber (compartment), jail, penitentiary, prison. SEE MAIN ENTRY
cella   cell
cement   adhere (fasten), bond (hold together), cohere (adhere), conjoin, connect (join together), crystallize, lock, merge, unite. SEE MAIN ENTRY
cement a union   affiliate, organize (unionize)
cementation   accession (annexation), adherence (adhesion), adhesion (affixing)
cemented   concordant, concurrent (united), conjoint, inseparable
cementitious   cohesive (sticking)
cenotaph   monument
censeo   comment
censere   comment, estimate, judge
censor   assessor
censor   ban, bowdlerize. SEE MAIN ENTRY
censor   censor

665

censor condemn *(ban)*, constrain *(re-strain)*, delete, eliminate *(exclude)*, exclude, expunge, expurgate, forestall, redact, repress, restrict, suppress, withhold
censored illicit
censorious blameful, calumnious, critical *(faultfinding)*, cynical, derogatory, dictatorial, pejorative, petulant, querulous, remonstrative, severe
censorious writing libel
censoriousness bad repute
censorship SEE MAIN ENTRY
censurability blame *(culpability)*, guilt, impeachability
censurable blameful, blameworthy, contemptible, culpable, delinquent *(guilty of a misdeed)*, disgraceful, guilty, inexpiable, obnoxious, peccable, peccant *(culpable)*, reprehensible, sinister, unjustifiable, vicious
censurableness blame *(culpability)*, culpability
censure admonish *(warn)*, admonition, aspersion, bad repute, blame *(culpability)*, blame, charge *(accusation)*, charge *(accuse)*, cite *(accuse)*, complain *(charge)*, complain *(criticize)*, condemnation *(blame)*, contemn, convict, conviction *(finding of guilt)*, correction *(punishment)*, criticism, criticize *(find fault with)*, decry, defame, denounce *(condemn)*, denunciation, depreciate, diatribe, disapprobation, disapproval, disapprove *(condemn)*, discommend, discredit, disparage, fault, impeach, impeachment, impugnation, incrimination, judgment *(formal court decree)*, lessen, libel, notoriety, obloquy, odium, onus *(stigma)*, ostracism, outcry, phillipic, proscribe *(denounce)*, proscription, punishment, rebuff, rebuke, remonstrance, remonstrate, reprehend, reprimand, reproach *(noun)*, reproach *(verb)*, restraint, revilement, scandal, sentence, slander, spurn, stricture. SEE MAIN ENTRY
censure as faulty decry
censure bitterly castigate
censure formally reprimand
censure frivolously cavil
censured blameful
censurer malcontent
censuring critical *(faultfinding)*
census assessment *(levy)*, census
census poll *(canvass)*, roll. SEE MAIN ENTRY
census report poll *(canvass)*
census return poll *(canvass)*
center average *(midmost)*, base *(place)*, central *(situated near center)*, concentrate *(consolidate)*, focus *(noun)*, focus *(verb)*, gravamen, headquarters, interior, seat, site, target. SEE MAIN ENTRY
center around meet
center of activity focus
center of attention focus. SEE MAIN ENTRY
center of attraction focus
center of authority headquarters
center of consciousness focus
center of focus. SEE MAIN ENTRY
center of gravity center *(central position)*
center of interest focus
center of operations headquarters
center upon converge
centering centralization
centermost average *(midmost)*, central *(situated near center)*
cento melange
central cardinal *(basic)*, cardinal *(outstanding)*, federal, fundamental, indispensable, integral, intermediate, leading *(ranking*

first), master, material *(important)*, primary. SEE MAIN ENTRY
central element necessity
central headquarters base *(place)*
central idea main point
central money office treasury
central nature center *(essence)*
central office management *(directorate)*
central point center *(central position)*, focus, gravamen, highlight
central station headquarters
centralism centralization
centrality focus
centralization affiliation *(amalgamation)*, coalescence, consolidation, federation, incorporation *(blend)*, merger. SEE MAIN ENTRY
centralize amalgamate, concentrate *(consolidate)*, consolidate *(unite)*, converge, federalize *(associate)*, focus, incorporate *(include)*, organize *(unionize)*, unite
centralized coadunate, concurrent *(united)*
centric central *(situated near center)*
centrical central *(situated near center)*
cerebral rational
cerebrate consider, deliberate, muse, ponder, reason *(conclude)*, reflect *(ponder)*, study
cerebration contemplation, deliberation, dialectic, intellect, ratiocination, reflection *(thought)*
ceremonial formal, sacrosanct, solemn
ceremonial rite formality
ceremonious formal, official, punctilious, solemn
ceremoniously pro forma
ceremoniousness formality, solemnity
ceremony custom, form *(arrangement)*, formality, protocol *(etiquette)*, remembrance *(commemoration)*, solemnity. SEE MAIN ENTRY
ceremony of induction into an office installation
certain absolute *(conclusive)*, actual, affirmative, axiomatic, conclusive *(determinative)*, concrete, constant, convincing, corporeal, de facto, decisive, definite, dependable, dogmatic, explicit, express, incontrovertible, indubious, inevitable, irrefutable, lucid, necessary *(inescapable)*, official, palpable, peremptory *(absolute)*, pertinacious, positive *(confident)*, positive *(incontestable)*, reliable, resounding, safe, secure *(confident)*, several *(plural)*, several *(separate)*, special, specific, tangible, true *(authentic)*, unalienable, unambiguous, unavoidable *(inevitable)*, undeniable, undisputed, unequivocal, unmistakable, unrefutable. SEE MAIN ENTRY
certain dereliction res ipsa loquitur
certain knowledge certification *(certainness)*, surety *(certainty)*
certainly a fortiori, admittedly, fairly *(clearly)*
certainness certitude
certainty belief *(state of mind)*, certification *(certainness)*, certitude, confidence *(faith)*, constant, conviction *(persuasion)*, credence, fact, fait accompli, faith, proof, prospect *(outlook)*, reliance, security *(safety)*, trust *(confidence)*, weight *(credibility)*. SEE MAIN ENTRY
certainty of meaning certitude
certamen contest *(competition)*, fight *(argument)*, strife, struggle
certare compete
certatio contest *(competition)*, strife
certifiable ascertainable, determinable *(ascertainable)*
certificate charter *(license)*, check *(instrument)*, coupon, deed, degree *(academic*

title), document, instrument *(document)*, permit, recommendation, record, warrant *(judicial writ)*, warranty. SEE MAIN ENTRY
certificate of character reference *(recommendation)*
certificate of debt bond, security *(stock)*
certificate of deposit receipt *(proof of receiving)*
certificate of exemption dispensation *(exception)*
certificate of indebtedness bond, security *(stock)*
certificate of invention copyright, patent
certificate of permission charter *(license)*
certificates credentials
certification acknowledgment *(avowal)*, affirmance *(authentication)*, affirmation, appointment *(act of designating)*, asseveration, attestation, capacity *(authority)*, certainty, certificate, confirmation, consent, copyright, corroboration, credentials, documentation, droit, guaranty, indorsement, jurat, leave *(permission)*, license, proof, ratification, reference *(recommendation)*, registration, stamp, subscription, support *(corroboration)*, surety *(certainty)*. SEE MAIN ENTRY
certified alleged, allowed, certain *(fixed)*, certain *(positive)*, definite, documentary, familiar *(informed)*, fully secured, official
certified public accountant accountant
certifier comaker, surety *(guarantor)*
certify accredit, acknowledge *(declare)*, affirm *(uphold)*, allow *(authorize)*, approve, ascertain, assert, assure *(insure)*, attest, audit, authorize, avouch *(avow)*, avouch *(guarantee)*, avow, bear *(adduce)*, bond *(secure a debt)*, cite *(state)*, claim *(maintain)*, corroborate, cosign, countersign, depose *(testify)*, endorse, ensure, establish *(show)*, evidence, guarantee, indorse, legitimate, let *(permit)*, manifest, notarize, posit, promise *(vow)*, qualify *(meet standards)*, reassure, seal *(solemnize)*, sign, sponsor, subscribe *(sign)*, substantiate, support *(corroborate)*, sustain *(confirm)*, swear, validate, verify *(confirm)*, vouch, witness *(attest to)*. SEE MAIN ENTRY
certify a will probate
certiorari SEE MAIN ENTRY
certitude belief *(state of mind)*, certainty, certification *(certainness)*, confidence *(faith)*, conviction *(persuasion)*, faith, reliance, surety *(certainty)*. SEE MAIN ENTRY
certus authentic, certain *(particular)*, certain *(positive)*, certainty, conclusive *(settled)*, definite, fixed *(securely placed)*, infallible, irrefutable, positive *(confident)*, regular *(orderly)*, staunch, undisputed
cess assessment *(levy)*
cessare loiter
cessatio delay, inaction
cessation abandonment *(discontinuance)*, abeyance, avoidance *(cancellation)*, check *(bar)*, close *(conclusion)*, cloture, conclusion *(outcome)*, defeasance, desuetude, discharge *(annulment)*, discontinuance *(act of discontinuing)*, discontinuance *(interruption of a legal action)*, dissolution *(termination)*, end *(termination)*, expiration, finality, halt, hiatus, impasse, inaction, interruption, layoff, lull, moratorium, pause, pendency, recess, remission, respite *(interval of rest)*, stay. SEE MAIN ENTRY
cessation of activity lull
cessation of being extremity *(death)*
cessation of employment lockout

cessation of existence extremity *(death)*
cessation of life death, demise *(death)*, extremity *(death)*
cessation of sound lull
cessation of the furnishing of work lockout
cessation of use disuse
cession abandonment *(desertion)*, alienation *(transfer of title)*, assignment *(transfer of ownership)*, consignment, demise *(conveyance)*, expense *(sacrifice)*, release, renunciation, resignation *(relinquishment)*. SEE MAIN ENTRY
cession of a fee feoffment
chafe affront, aggravate *(annoy)*, annoy, badger, bait *(harass)*, discommode, discompose, harrow, incense, irritate, resent
chaff jape, mock *(deride)*, ridicule
chaffer haggle, handle *(trade)*, trade
chaffering commerce
chagrin disconcert, dissatisfaction, distress, embarrass, embarrassment, harrow, ignominy, ill will, offend *(insult)*, remorse
chain constrain *(imprison)*, constrain *(restrain)*, contain *(restrain)*, detain *(restrain)*, fetter *(noun)*, fetter *(verb)*, handcuff *(noun)*, handcuff *(verb)*, hierarchy *(arrangement in a series)*, restrict, sequence, succession. SEE MAIN ENTRY
chain of custody. SEE MAIN ENTRY
chain of evidence. SEE MAIN ENTRY
chain of reasoning dialectic
chains bondage, ties
chair chairman, management *(directorate)*, moderate *(preside over)*, preside
chairman chief. SEE MAIN ENTRY
chairmen management *(directorate)*
chairperson chief
chalk out compose
challenge argue, charge *(accuse)*, cite *(accuse)*, claim *(legal demand)*, compete, competition, complain *(charge)*, conflict, confront *(oppose)*, confutation, contend *(dispute)*, contention *(opposition)*, contest *(competition)*, contest *(dispute)*, contest, contradict, counter, counterargument, cross-examination, cross-examine, defiance, defy, demonstrate *(protest)*, demur, demurrer, denial, denounce *(condemn)*, disaccord, disaffirm, disagree, disagreement, disbelieve, disown *(deny the validity)*, dispute, dispute *(contest)*, dissent *(difference of opinion)*, dissent *(withhold assent)*, doubt *(distrust)*, examine *(interrogate)*, except *(object)*, exception *(objection)*, fight *(battle)*, impeach, impeachment, impugnation, indagation, invitation, misdoubt, motivate, object, objection, oppose, opposition, oppugn, protest *(noun)*, protest *(verb)*, provoke, reaction *(opposition)*, reject, remonstrance, remonstrate, repel *(drive back)*, resist *(withstand)*, withstand. SEE MAIN ENTRY
challenge as false impugn
challenge the credibility of impeach
challenge to the sufficiency of the pleading demurrer
challenger accuser, candidate, complainant, contender, contestant, opponent, party *(litigant)*, rival
challenging competitive *(antagonistic)*, contemptuous, dissident, hostile, provocative, sapid
chamber bench, cell. SEE MAIN ENTRY
chambers lodging
chambre chamber *(compartment)*
champain bar sinister

champion absolute *(ideal)*, adhere *(maintain loyalty)*, advocate *(counselor)*, advocate *(espouser)*, advocate, amicus curiae, apologist, assistant, backer, bear *(support)*, benefactor, colleague, custodian *(protector)*, defend, espouse, favor, guardian, justify, mainstay, maintain *(sustain)*, paragon, paramount, partisan, patron *(influential supporter)*, preserve, prime *(most valuable)*, promote *(organize)*, proponent, protagonist, protect, samaritan, select, side, sponsor *(noun)*, sponsor *(verb)*, successful, superlative, support *(assist)*, uphold
championing accommodation *(backing)*
championship advocacy, assistance, favor *(sanction)*, indorsement, supremacy
chance access *(opening)*, bet, coincidental, contingency, fortuitous, gamble, haphazard, happenstance, hazard, likelihood, lottery, occasion, opportunity, possibility, potential, privilege, probability, prospect *(outlook)*, quirk *(accident)*, random, risk, speculate *(chance)*, speculation *(risk)*, suspicion *(uncertainty)*, unexpected, unintentional, unwitting, venture. SEE MAIN ENTRY
chance event happening
chance happening happenstance. SEE MAIN ENTRY
chance occurrence act of god
chance the odds bet
chance to borrow money on time credit *(delayed payment)*
chance upon discover, find *(discover)*
chancellor judge, plenipotentiary
chancery equity *(justice)*, tribunal
chancy dubious, precarious, speculative
chandler dealer, merchant, supplier
change adapt, adjust *(resolve)*, affect, alter, alternative *(substitute)*, amend, amendment *(correction)*, commute, conflict, convert *(change use)*, denature, development *(progression)*, difference, digression, diversification, emend, exchange, fluctuate, innovation, interchange, modification, modify *(alter)*, money, nonconformity, pass *(advance)*, progress, reassign, reclassification, reconversion, redress, reform *(noun)*, reform *(verb)*, remedy, reorganization, replace, replacement, reversal, revise, revision *(process of correcting)*, subrogation, succedaneum, tamper, transform, transition, vacillate, vary. SEE MAIN ENTRY
change address remove *(transfer)*
change an abode move *(alter position)*
change back revert
change by alternation alternate *(take turns)*
change continuously fluctuate
change course redirect
change direction detour, deviate, digress, redirect
change for displace *(replace)*
change for the better ameliorate, improvement
change for the worse adulterate
change from higher to lower descent *(declination)*
change from one to another devolve
change hands bequeath, circulate
change in method innovation
change into convert *(change use)*, develop, evolve
change into cash liquidate *(convert into cash)*
change into money liquidate *(convert into cash)*
change national allegiance expatriate

change of direction deviation
change of hands devolution
change of mind rescision, reversal
change of national location immigration
change of place extradition, removal
change of position deviation
change of sides revolt
change one's mind tergiversate
change out of recognition distort
change over convert *(change use)*, reconversion
change ownership devolve, grant *(transfer formally)*, pass *(advance)*
change penalties commute
change place move *(alter position)*, remove *(transfer)*
change places circulate
change residence move *(alter position)*
change sides defect, repudiate, tergiversate
change the appearance of disguise
change the bearing detour
change the course of avert, divert
change the face of camouflage, disguise, distort
change the guise of disguise
change the place of displace *(remove)*
change venue remove *(transfer)*
change-over devolution, transition
changeable aleatory *(uncertain)*, ambulatory, capricious, conditional, convertible, debatable, disordered, faithless, inconsistent, indefinite, insecure, irresolute, irresponsible, mutable, noncommittal, pliable, precarious, protean, shifting, sporadic, temporary, undependable, unpredictable, unsettled, untrustworthy, variable, volatile
changeableness incertitude, inconsistency, indecision, irregularity
changed different, tempered
changed ordering of priorities reclassification
changed priorities reclassification
changeful aleatory *(uncertain)*, capricious, disordered, insecure, irresolute, mutable, protean, undecided, unpredictable, unreliable, variable
changeless certain *(fixed)*, certain *(positive)*, constant, durable, fixed *(settled)*, indelible, inflexible, irrevocable, permanent, static, unalterable
changelessly invariably
changelessness indestructibility
changer dealer
changes circumstances, vicissitudes
changing capricious, moving *(in motion)*, open-ended, shifting, unsettled
channel avenue *(route)*, facility *(instrumentality)*, forum *(medium)*, instrument *(tool)*, instrumentality, medium, outlet, tool. SEE MAIN ENTRY
channels approaches
chant recite, repeat *(state again)*
chaos anarchy, confusion *(turmoil)*, disorder *(lack of order)*, embroilment, entanglement *(confusion)*, havoc, imbroglio, incoherence, misrule, pandemonium, shambles, turmoil. SEE MAIN ENTRY
chaotic complex, disordered, haphazard, labyrinthine, promiscuous, unruly. SEE MAIN ENTRY
chaotic state havoc
chap person
chaperon guardian, warden
chaperonage charge *(custody)*
chaperone protect
chapman vendor

chapter affiliate, article *(distinct section of a writing)*, constituency, department, division *(administrative unit)*, organ, segment, subheading, title *(division)*. SEE MAIN ENTRY
chapter and verse verbatim
char burn
character animus, behavior, caliber *(quality)*, color *(complexion)*, complexion, condition *(state)*, configuration *(form)*, disposition *(inclination)*, entity, frame *(mood)*, honor *(good reputation)*, individual, integrity, kind, merit, part *(role)*, person, personality, predisposition, principle *(virtue)*, property *(distinctive attribute)*, quality *(excellence)*, quality *(grade)*, rectitude, role, speciality, specialty *(distinctive mark)*, spirit, style, temperament, tendency, tenor, turpitude. SEE MAIN ENTRY
character assassination slander
characteristic certain *(specific)*, customary, demonstrative *(illustrative)*, differential, disposition *(inclination)*, distinct *(distinguished from others)*, distinctive, general, identity *(individuality)*, indicant, natural, nondescript, ordinary, particular *(individual)*, particular *(specific)*, particularity, peculiar *(distinctive)*, personal *(individual)*, prevailing *(current)*, prevalent, property *(distinctive attribute)*, quality *(attribute)*, representative, specialty *(distinctive mark)*, specific, symptom, trait, typical, usual. SEE MAIN ENTRY
characteristic behavior habit
characteristic difference distinction *(difference)*
characteristic feature necessity
characteristic marks indicia
characteristic mood character *(personal quality)*, disposition *(inclination)*
characteristic part epitome
characteristic quality particularity, spirit
characteristic way custom
characteristically repeated action habit
characteristics color *(complexion)*, indicia, personality
characterization caption, caricature, cross section, denomination, description, role
characterize call *(title)*, construe *(translate)*, define, depict, describe, designate, differentiate, discriminate *(distinguish)*, distinguish, interpret, label, personify, portray, render *(depict)*, represent *(portray)*. SEE MAIN ENTRY
characterize precisely construe *(translate)*, define
characterized by argument argumentative
characterized by art artful
characterized by decision decisive
characterized by excess excessive
characterized by reflection deliberate
characterizing descriptive
characterless arrant *(onerous)*, disreputable, inexpressive, lifeless *(dull)*, pedestrian, usual
characters script
charade pretext
charge accusation, ad valorem, admonish *(advise)*, agency *(commission)*, agency *(legal relationship)*, allegation, allege, ammunition, appoint, arraign, assessment *(levy)*, assign *(designate)*, assignation, assignment *(task)*, attack, auspices, authorize, bad repute, bind *(obligate)*, blame *(responsibility)*, blame, bomb, brevet, brokerage, burden, cargo, cite *(accuse)*, claim *(maintain)*, cloud *(incumbrance)*, command,

commit *(entrust)*, commitment *(responsibility)*, complaint, condemn *(blame)*, condemnation *(blame)*, consign, constrain *(compel)*, constraint *(imprisonment)*, control *(supervision)*, conviction *(finding of guilt)*, cost *(expenses)*, cost *(price)*, count, criticism, custody *(supervision)*, decree, defame, delegate, delegation *(assignment)*, denigrate, denounce *(inform against)*, denunciation, dependent, deprecate, detail *(assign)*, dictate *(noun)*, dictate *(verb)*, direct *(order)*, direction *(guidance)*, direction *(order)*, directive, due, duty *(obligation)*, duty *(tax)*, encumber *(financially obligate)*, encumber *(hinder)*, encumbrance, enjoin, estimate *(approximate cost)*, exact, exception *(objection)*, excise, excise *(levy a tax)*, exhort, expenditure, expense *(cost)*, fare, fault, generality, grievance, impeach, impeachment, implicate, impose *(enforce)*, imposition *(tax)*, incriminate, incrimination, indict, indictment, inform *(betray)*, information *(charge)*, innuendo, instruct *(direct)*, instruction *(direction)*, invest *(vest)*, involve *(implicate)*, levy, lien, management *(supervision)*, mandamus, mandate, mechanics lien, mission, mortgage, motivate, obligation *(duty)*, obligation *(liability)*, occupation *(possession)*, office, onset *(assault)*, onus *(blame)*, onus *(burden)*, outcry, outlay, part *(role)*, payment *(remittance)*, plead *(implore)*, post, precept, prescribe, prescription *(directive)*, present *(prefer charges)*, presentment, price, proscribe *(denounce)*, protégé, province, rate, rebuke, reprehend, rule *(legal dictate)*, safekeeping, servitude, summon, supervision, surveillance, tax, toll *(tax)*, trust *(custody)*, ward, work *(employment)*, worth. SEE MAIN ENTRY
charge beyond normal premium *(excess value)*
charge duty excise *(levy a tax)*
charge falsely frame *(prearrange)*
charge for carriage of passengers fare
charge for conveyance of a person fare
charge for services fee *(charge)*
charge imposed on specific property lien, mechanics lien
charge levied assessment *(levy)*
charge to impeach, impute
charge to excess premium *(excess value)*
charge unfairly frame *(charge falsely)*
charge unjustly frame *(charge falsely)*
charge upon impute
charge with accuse, ascribe, attribute, commit *(entrust)*, complain *(charge)*, impeach, lodge *(bring a complaint)*
charge with a duty entrust
charge with a trust entrust
charge with an errand delegate
charge with an offense incriminate
charge with offense indict
charge with one's share assess *(tax)*
charge with the commission of a crime indict
chargeability blame *(culpability)*, impeachability, responsibility *(accountability)*
chargeable accountable *(responsible)*, actionable, ad valorem, blameful, blameworthy, bound, culpable, delinquent *(overdue)*, due *(owed)*, guilty, liable, peccant *(culpable)*, reprehensible, subject *(exposed)*, unjustifiable
chargeableness culpability
charged accused *(charged)*, ad valorem, full
charged party defendant

chargeless gratuitous *(given without recompense)*
charger assessor, complainant, contender, party *(litigant)*
charges bill *(invoice)*, brokerage, overhead
chargeship appointment *(position)*
charging with fault inculpation
charging with guilt incriminatory, inculpation, inculpatory
chariness austerity, discretion *(quality of being discreet)*, doubt *(suspicion)*, economy *(frugality)*
charismatic leader demagogue
charitable benevolent, donative, gratuitous *(given without recompense)*, humane, lenient, liberal *(generous)*, magnanimous, meritorious, nonprofit, philanthropic, placable. SEE MAIN ENTRY
charitable effort benevolence *(act of kindness)*
charitable institution foundation *(organization)*
charitableness benevolence *(disposition to do good)*, humanity *(humaneness)*, largess *(generosity)*, philanthropy, understanding *(tolerance)*
charity aid *(subsistence)*, benefit *(conferment)*, benevolence *(act of kindness)*, benevolence *(disposition to do good)*, clemency, condonation, contribution *(donation)*, donation, favor *(act of kindness)*, foundation *(organization)*, goodwill, gratuity *(present)*, help, largess *(generosity)*, largess *(gift)*, lenience, philanthropy. SEE MAIN ENTRY
charivari noise
charlatan fake
charlatanism fraud, hypocrisy
charlatanry artifice, deception, fraud, hypocrisy
charm lure
charming attractive, moving *(evoking emotion)*, sapid
chart delineation, design *(construction plan)*, scheme, tabulate
charter allow *(authorize)*, appoint, appointment *(act of designating)*, authorize, bestow, brevet, bylaw, capacity *(authority)*, certificate, certify *(approve)*, code, confirm, constitute *(establish)*, constitution, contract, countenance, deed, delegate, enactment, engage *(hire)*, establish *(launch)*, franchise *(license)*, immunity, incorporate *(form a corporation)*, instrument *(document)*, invest *(vest)*, law, lease, let *(lease)*, license, ordinance, pact, pandect *(code of laws)*, permit, prerogative, privilege, protocol *(agreement)*, rent, sanction *(permission)*, sanction, tolerance, treaty, warrant *(authorization)*. SEE MAIN ENTRY
chartered allowed, licit, privileged, rightful
chartered accountant accountant, comptroller
chartering incorporation *(formation of a business entity)*
chary circumspect, discreet, frugal, guarded, leery, parsimonious, penurious, provident *(showing foresight)*, prudent
chary of expense economical
chase embellish, hunt, pursuit *(chase)*, quest, race, repulse, trace *(follow)*. SEE MAIN ENTRY
chase after hunt, research, search
chase away parry, repel *(drive back)*
chase off parry
chase out oust
chasm hiatus, pitfall, rift *(gap)*, split
chassis frame *(structure)*

chaste pure

chasten assuage, castigate, discipline (punish), moderate (temper), punish

chastened contrite, penitent

chastening condemnation (blame), correction (punishment), disciplinary (punitory), discipline (punishment), punishment

chastise blame, castigate, censure, complain (criticize), denounce (condemn), disapprove (condemn), discipline (punish), expostulate, fault, lash (attack verbally), penalize, punish, rebuke, remonstrate, reprehend, reprimand

chastisement condemnation (blame), correction (punishment), discipline (punishment), obloquy, phillipic, punishment, remonstrance, reproach

chastity continence

chat conversation

chattel holding (property owned), merchandise, possession (property). SEE MAIN ENTRY

chattel property effects

chattels assets, commodities, effects, estate (property), goods, paraphernalia (personal belongings), personalty, possessions, property (possessions)

chattels personal movable

chattels real demesne, estate (property), real estate

chatter bombast, prattle

chattering loquacious

chatty informatory, loquacious

chauvinism intolerance

cheap base (inferior), disreputable, economical, frugal, inferior (lower in quality), meretricious, nominal, paltry, parsimonious, penurious, poor (inferior in quality), tawdry

cheapen damage, debase, deduct (reduce), demean (make lower), denature, depreciate, depress, dilute, diminish, disparage, minimize

cheapening decline

cheapness of operation economy (frugality)

cheat betray (lead astray), bilk, copy, deceive, deception, defalcate, defraud, delude, dupe, ensnare, fake, feign, hoax, hoodwink, illude, imposture, inveigle, knavery, maneuver, mislead, mulct (defraud), overreach, palter, peculate, pretend, pretense (pretext), purloin, ruse, shirk, stratagem. SEE MAIN ENTRY

cheat out of money defraud

cheated aggrieved (victimized)

cheater embezzler

cheating artifice, bunko, deceit, deceptive, dishonest, dishonesty, embezzlement, fraud, fraudulent, insidious, knavery, machiavellian, perfidious, pettifoggery

check abeyance, allay, alleviate, arrest (stop), assuage, audit, avert, balk, ban, barrier, bill (invoice), bind (restrain), block, cease, cloture, collation, concern (care), condemn (ban), constrain (restrain), constrict (inhibit), contain (restrain), control (restriction), control (regulate), countervail, coupon, cross-examine, curb, damper (stopper), deadlock, debar, desist, detain (restrain), deter, deterrence, disadvantage (noun), disadvantage (verb), discipline (control), discontinue (abandon), discontinue (break continuity), disincentive, disqualify, draft, ensure, examination (study), examine (study), fetter (noun), fetter (verb), foil, forbid, forestall, frisk, frustrate, halt (noun), halt (verb), hamper, heed, hinder,

hindrance, hold up (delay), impasse, impede, impediment, indagation, inhibit, interdict, interfere, interrupt, interruption, keep (restrain), kill (defeat), lessen, limit, lock, mitigate, moderate (temper), modify (moderate), mollification, mollify, monitor, note (written promise to pay), observation, obstacle, obstruct, obstruction, obviation, occlude, palliate (abate), peruse, police, preclude, prevent, prohibit, prohibition, quit (discontinue), quota, rebuff (noun), rebuff (verb), refrain, remission, remit (relax), repel (drive back), repress, repulse, resist (oppose), resistance, restrain, restraint, restrict, restriction, reversal, scrutinize, stall, stave, stay, stay (halt), stifle, stop, strangle, suppress, suspend, test, thwart, toll (stop), trammel, trial (experiment), verify (confirm), withhold, withstand. SEE MAIN ENTRY

check a reference consult (seek information from)

check a source consult (seek information from)

check holder bearer

check in enter (record), register, report (present oneself)

check list invoice (itemized list), schedule

check on audit, research

check over probe

check thoroughly review

check up check (inspect)

check upon again reexamine

check-up diligence (care)

checked broken (interrupted), limited, qualified (conditioned)

checking collation, cross-examination, discovery, limiting, preventive

checklist inventory

checkmate beat (defeat), check (bar), clog, deadlock, defeat, frustrate, prevent, repel (drive back), stem (check), stop

checkup test

cheer assure (give confidence to), honor, promise (raise expectations), reassure, solace, spirit

cheerful ready (willing), sanguine

cheerful consent goodwill

cheerful giver donor

cheerful willingness goodwill

cheerfulness spirit

cheering propitious

cheerless bleak (severely simple), disconsolate, grave (solemn), lugubrious, pessimistic

cheerlessness damper (depressant), pessimism

chemical substance drug

cheque coupon

cherish foster, keep (shelter), nurture, preserve, protect, regard (hold in esteem)

cherish a belief credit

cherish doubts misdoubt, mistrust

cherishing preservation

chest repository

chevy persecute

chic elegant

chicane deceive, deception, dishonesty, evasion, false pretense, fraud, imposture, pettifoggery, plot (secret plan), ruse, stratagem, subterfuge

chicanery artifice, bunko, collusion, connivance, deception, dishonesty, duplicity, evasion, false pretense, fraud, hoax, knavery, maneuver (trick), pettifoggery, ruse, sham, sophistry, subterfuge

chide blame, browbeat, castigate, censure, complain (criticize), condemn (blame),

criticize (find fault with), denounce (condemn), disapprove (condemn), expostulate, fault, lash (attack verbally), rebuff, rebuke, reprehend, reprimand, reproach

chiding condemnation (blame), critical (faultfinding), criticism, denunciation, diatribe, disapprobation, objurgation, obloquy, outcry, rebuff, reprimand, reproach

chief best, cardinal (basic), cardinal (outstanding), central (essential), critical (crucial), director, dominant, employer, essential (required), grave (important), important (significant), leading (ranking first), major, master, necessary (required), outstanding (prominent), paramount, prevailing (having superior force), prevalent, primary, prime (most valuable), principal, principal (director), salient, sovereign (absolute), stellar, superintendent, superior (higher), superlative, vital. SEE MAIN ENTRY

chief accounting officer comptroller

chief actor principal (director)

chief authority principal (director)

chief constituent content (meaning)

chief controller chief

chief executive administrator, principal (director)

chief feature main point

chief issue main point

chief office headquarters

chief part bulk, center (essence), content (meaning), corpus, main point

chief party principal (director)

chief point main point

chief reliance mainstay

chiefly a fortiori, ab initio, as a rule, generally, particularly

chieftain chief, principal (director)

chieftaincy supremacy

child dependent, descendant, infant, issue (progeny), juvenile, minor, offspring. SEE MAIN ENTRY

child born before marriage bastard

child born out of wedlock bastard

child without parents orphan

child-stealing abduction

childbirth birth (emergence of young)

childhood minority (infancy), nonage

childish frivolous, jejune (lacking maturity), juvenile, naive, puerile

childishly foolish puerile

childishness puerility

childless barren

childlike ingenuous, juvenile, naive, puerility, unaffected (sincere)

children blood, issue (progeny), offspring, posterity, progeny. SEE MAIN ENTRY

chill damper (depressant), deter

chilling effect SEE MAIN ENTRY

chime in interrupt

chime in with comport (agree with)

chimera figment, phantom

chimerical delusive, fictitious, illusory, immaterial, insubstantial, nonexistent, quixotic

chinese wall. SEE MAIN ENTRY

chink rift (gap), split

chip part (portion), token

chipped blemished

chirographum bond, handwriting

chirography handwriting

chirotony vote

chisel bilk, create

chivalric civil (polite), meritorious

chivalrous civil (polite), magnanimous, meritorious

chivalry consideration (sympathetic regard), courtesy

choate lien   SEE MAIN ENTRY
chock-full   full, replete
choice   adoption *(acceptance)*, advantage, alternative *(option)*, appointment *(act of designating)*, best, call *(option)*, certain *(specific)*, conatus, decision *(judgment)*, discretion *(power of choice)*, exclusive *(limited)*, franchise *(right to vote)*, inestimable, intent, latitude, liberty, meritorious, nomination, noteworthy, option *(choice)*, patronage *(power to appoint jobs)*, plebiscite, poll *(casting of votes)*, predilection, preferable, preferential, preferred *(favored)*, premium, primary, prime *(most valuable)*, professional *(stellar)*, rare, select, suffrage, superior *(excellent)*, unusual, valuable, volition, vote, will *(desire)*. SEE MAIN ENTRY
choice between alternatives   election *(choice)*
choice group   elite
choice of language   phraseology
choice of words   parlance, phraseology
choiceless   necessary *(inescapable)*
choke   bar *(hinder)*, block, clog, constrict *(inhibit)*, extinguish, hamper, inhibit, obstruct, overload, preclude, repress, stem *(check)*, stifle, stop, subdue, suppress
choke back   suppress
choke off   bar *(hinder)*, occlude, shut, strangle
choler   resentment, umbrage
choleric   bilious, bitter *(penetrating)*, critical *(faultfinding)*, dyseptic, fractious, petulant, resentful
choose   adopt, appoint, conclude *(decide)*, cull, decide, delegate, designate, determine, edit, espouse, extract, nominate, prefer, screen *(select)*, select, vote. SEE MAIN ENTRY
choose a course of action   decide
choose an alternative   decide
choose an option   decide
choose for office   elect *(select by a vote)*
choosing   adoptive, decision *(election)*, designation *(naming)*, elective *(selective)*, nomination, vote
choosing by vote   election *(selection by vote)*
choosy   particular *(exacting)*, scrupulous
chop   split
chore   assignment *(task)*, burden, duty *(obligation)*, function, job, part *(role)*, work *(effort)*
chorus   outcry
chose in action   estate *(property)*, intangible
chosen   particular *(specific)*, preferable, preferred *(favored)*, select, several *(separate)*
chosen career   practice *(professional business)*
chosen few   elite
chosen field   practice *(professional business)*
chosen profession   practice *(professional business)*
chosen representative   nominee *(candidate)*
chosen work   calling, career, occupation *(vocation)*, profession *(vocation)*, pursuit *(occupation)*
chouse   bait *(lure)*, illude, inveigle, ruse
christen   call *(title)*, denominate
chronic   constant, durable, habitual, incorrigible, inveterate, permanent, perpetual, persistent, stable. SEE MAIN ENTRY
chronic alcoholism   dipsomania
chronic disability   disease

chronical   inveterate
chronicle   book, calendar *(record of yearly periods)*, detail *(particularize)*, enter *(record)*, entry *(record)*, file *(place among official records)*, journal, memorandum, narration, notation, note *(record)*, record *(noun)*, record *(verb)*, register *(noun)*, register *(verb)*, report *(detailed account)*, roll, set down, story *(narrative)*, tabulate
chronicled   documentary
chronicler   clerk
chronicling   registration
chronological   consecutive
chronologize   date
chronology   calendar *(record of yearly periods)*, journal, order *(arrangement)*, register, time
chuck   precipitate *(throw down violently)*
chunk   part *(portion)*, segment
churlish   brutal, caitiff, disorderly, fractious, illiberal, impertinent *(insolent)*, inelegant, malevolent, penurious, perverse, petulant, provincial, resentful, severe, uncouth
churn   disturb, perturb. SEE MAIN ENTRY
chute   outlet
cibarious   palatable
cinch   lock
cincture   border *(bound)*, embrace *(encircle)*, enclosure, encompass *(surround)*
cingere   enclose, encompass *(surround)*
cipher   blank *(emptiness)*, calculate, designation *(symbol)*, indicant, nonentity
ciphering   census
circle   bailiwick, contour *(outline)*, cycle, enclosure, encompass *(surround)*, hedge, perambulate, region, scope, society, sphere
circonvenir   circumvent
circuit   bench, circulate, circumscribe *(surround by boundary)*, contour *(outline)*, cycle, detour, district, encompass *(surround)*, extent, gamut, outline *(boundary)*, periphery, province, region, scope, sphere, territory. SEE MAIN ENTRY
circuitous   astray, complex, devious, discursive *(digressive)*, indirect, labyrinthine, oblique *(evasive)*, sinuous, tortuous *(bending)*. SEE MAIN ENTRY
circuitous action   indirection *(indirect action)*
circuitous route   detour, indirection *(indirect action)*
circuitousness   indirection *(indirect action)*
circuitus   circuit
circuity   digression, indirection *(indirect action)*
circular   dispatch *(message)*, notice *(announcement)*
circular reasoning   non sequitur
circularize   circulate
circulate   diffuse, disburse *(distribute)*, disclose, disperse *(disseminate)*, disseminate, herald, issue *(publish)*, post, proclaim, promulgate, propagate *(spread)*, publish, reveal, send, spread, utter. SEE MAIN ENTRY
circulate publicly   report *(disclose)*
circulated   public *(known)*
circulating capital   principal *(capital sum)*
circulating medium   currency
circulation   coverage *(scope)*, publication *(disclosure)*, transmittal. SEE MAIN ENTRY
circulus   circuit, cycle
circumagere   circulate, circulation
circumambience   atmosphere
circumambiency   climate, periphery
circumambulate   detour, perambulate
circumambulating   circuitous, indirect
circumcidere   abridge *(shorten)*, retrench

circumcludere   encompass *(surround)*
circumduction   cancellation
circumference   ambit, border, contour *(outline)*, margin *(outside limit)*, outline *(boundary)*, periphery, zone
circumferential   peripheral
circumflexion   indirection *(indirect action)*
circumfluent   circuitous
circumfluous   circuitous
circumfundere   envelop
circumfuse   diffuse
circumire   patrol
circumjacence   blockade *(enclosure)*, border, enclosure
circumjacencies   frontier
circumlocution   indirection *(indirect action)*
circumlocutory   circuitous, indirect, oblique *(evasive)*, prolix, turgid
circumplecti   encompass *(surround)*
circumpose   border *(bound)*
circumscribe   bar *(exclude)*, comprehend *(include)*, confine, constrain *(imprison)*, delimit, delineate, demarcate, detain *(restrain)*, deter, disadvantage, embrace *(encircle)*, enclose, encompass *(surround)*, envelop, hedge, impede, imprison, include, limit, obstruct, palliate *(abate)*, prohibit, proscribe *(prohibit)*, restrict, specify. SEE MAIN ENTRY
circumscribed   arrested *(checked)*, certain *(specific)*, limited, narrow, qualified *(conditioned)*, regional
circumscribere   circumscribe *(define)*, circumvent, define, defraud, limit, overreach, qualify *(condition)*, restrict
circumscribing   limiting
circumscriptio   fraud, limit, limitation
circumscription   bar *(obstruction)*, blockade *(enclosure)*, boundary, configuration *(confines)*, constraint *(restriction)*, contour *(outline)*, coverage *(scope)*, custody *(incarceration)*, delineation, detention, enclosure, limit, limitation, mete, outline *(boundary)*, periphery, prohibition, purview, quota, restraint, restriction
circumscriptive   limited, restrictive
circumspect   careful, discreet, guarded, irreprehensible, leery, meticulous, politic, provident *(showing foresight)*, prudent, upright, vigilant. SEE MAIN ENTRY
circumspectio   prudence
circumspection   caution *(vigilance)*, deliberation, diligence *(care)*, discretion *(quality of being discreet)*, discrimination *(good judgment)*, forethought, judgment *(discernment)*, notice *(heed)*, precaution, prudence, surveillance
circumspective   circumspect
circumspectness   discretion *(quality of being discreet)*
circumspectus   guarded, prudent
circumstance   accident *(chance occurrence)*, case *(set of circumstances)*, chance *(fortuity)*, condition *(state)*, context, contingency, detail, experience *(encounter)*, happenstance, occurrence, particular, plight, posture *(situation)*, predicament, quirk *(accident)*, situation, state *(condition)*, status
circumstanced   qualified *(conditioned)*
circumstances   environment, position *(situation)*, situation. SEE MAIN ENTRY
circumstances in a case   evidence
circumstantial   coincidental, descriptive, fortuitous, incident, presumptive. SEE MAIN ENTRY
circumstantial event   contingency
circumstantiality   detail, particularity

circumstantiate bear *(adduce)*, cite *(state)*, corroborate, demonstrate *(establish)*, detail *(particularize)*, document, establish *(show)*, evidence, itemize, quote, substantiate, support *(corroborate)*, sustain *(confirm)*, validate, verify *(confirm)*

circumstantiation corroboration, documentation, support *(corroboration)*

circumvalate border *(bound)*

circumvallate circumscribe *(surround by boundary)*, enclose

circumvallation blockade *(enclosure)*, enclosure

circumvenire circumvent, overreach

circumvent betray *(lead astray)*, bilk, border *(bound)*, deceive, dupe, escape, evade *(deceive)*, illude, overreach, pettifog, prevent, shun. SEE MAIN ENTRY

circumvention artifice, deception, device *(contrivance)*, evasion, false pretense, hoax, knavery, maneuver *(trick)*, pettifoggery, ruse

circumvention of truth false pretense

cista coffer

citadel bulwark, haven, protection, refuge

citare accuse, arraign

citation accusation, canon, certification *(certification of proficiency)*, charge *(accusation)*, complaint, count, direction *(order)*, excerpt, mention *(tribute)*, monition *(legal summons)*, paraphrase, presentment, process *(summons)*, recognition, subpoena, summons. SEE MAIN ENTRY

cite accuse, allege, allude, arraign, bear *(adduce)*, blame, charge *(accuse)*, complain *(charge)*, denounce *(condemn)*, exemplify, extract, honor, illustrate, mention, order, posit, present *(prefer charges)*, quote, recognize *(acknowledge)*, refer *(direct attention)*, specify, summon. SEE MAIN ENTRY

cite a holding of a case quote

cite evidence establish *(show)*

cited alleged

citing reference *(citation)*

citizen denizen, domiciliary, inhabitant. SEE MAIN ENTRY

citizenize naturalize *(make a citizen)*

citizenry community, nationality, populace, population, public, society

citizens population

city community. SEE MAIN ENTRY

civic civil *(public)*, local, political, public *(affecting people)*. SEE MAIN ENTRY

civic-minded philanthropic

civicus civic

civil civic, obeisant, public *(affecting people)*. SEE MAIN ENTRY

civil code code

civil community state *(political unit)*

civil constitution polity

civil law constitution

civil liberty freedom

civil liberties. SEE MAIN ENTRY

civil officer peace officer

civil wrong misfeasance, tort

civilian civil *(public)*, layman

civilian police posse

civilis civic, political

civilis ratio politics

civility amenity, comity, consideration *(sympathetic regard)*, courtesy, decorum, respect

civilization community, society. SEE MAIN ENTRY

civilize educate

civilized civil *(polite)*

civilized behavior decorum

civilized life civilization

civilized society civilization

civis citizen

civitas community, state *(political unit)*

civitatis constitution

civium population

clades calamity, disaster

claim adduce, allegation, allege, appeal, appropriate, argue, assert, bear *(adduce)*, bill *(formal declaration)*, call *(demand)*, case *(lawsuit)*, cause of action, certify *(attest)*, cloud *(incumbrance)*, contend *(maintain)*, count, cover *(pretext)*, declare, demand *(noun)*, demand *(verb)*, dominion *(absolute ownership)*, droit, due, dun, encumbrance, equity *(share of ownership)*, exact, excise *(levy a tax)*, impropriate, interest *(ownership)*, lawsuit, lien, matter *(case)*, matter *(subject)*, motion, need, occupy *(take possession)*, own, ownership, plea, pleading, posit, prayer, prerogative, prescription *(claim of title)*, pretense *(pretext)*, pretext, profess *(pretend)*, profession *(declaration)*, purport, request *(noun)*, request *(verb)*, requirement, requisition, stake *(interest)*, statement, sue, thesis, title *(right)*. SEE MAIN ENTRY

claim a victory beat *(defeat)*

claim advanced by defendant counterclaim

claim as a right call *(demand)*

claim as one's due demand

claim falsely fake, pretend

claim for damages ad damnum clause

claim for relief cause of action

claim for relief by defendant counterclaim

claim on property charge *(lien)*, cloud *(incumbrance)*, lien, mechanics lien

claim one's thoughts occupy *(engage)*

claim presented by defendant counterclaim

claim to know contend *(maintain)*

claim unduly impropriate

claimable due *(owed)*

claimant applicant *(petitioner)*, complainant, contender, contestant, litigant, party *(litigant)*, plaintiff, suitor. SEE MAIN ENTRY

claimed alleged, ostensible, purported, putative

claimer claimant

claims of conscience responsibility *(conscience)*

clairvoyance precognition

clairvoyant prophetic

clamant exigent, important *(urgent)*, urgent

clamare call *(appeal to)*

clamor barrage, brawl, commotion, confusion *(turmoil)*, demonstrate *(protest)*, exception *(objection)*, furor, noise, outburst, outcry, pandemonium, protest

clamor against decry, discommend

clamor for call *(demand)*, desire, exact, importune, necessitate, need, petition, plead *(implore)*, pray, request, solicit

clamor for payment dun

clamorous blatant *(obtrusive)*, important *(urgent)*, insistent, querulous, vehement

clamorousness noise, outcry

clamp adhere *(fasten)*

clan affinity *(family ties)*, blood, descent *(lineage)*, family *(common ancestry)*, house, kindred, lineage

clandestine allusive, collusive, covert, evasive, furtive, hidden, mysterious, personal

(private), private *(confidential)*, privy, secret, sly, stealthy, surreptitious, unobtrusive. SEE MAIN ENTRY

clandestinus clandestine, stealthy, surreptitious

clangor noise

clannish exclusive *(limited)*, partisan, restrictive

clansman relative

clansmen kindred

clap together conjoin

claque assemblage

clare fairly *(clearly)*

clarification clarification, comment, construction, definition, explanation, illustration, instance, solution *(answer)*. SEE MAIN ENTRY

clarified clear *(apparent)*

clarify adjust *(resolve)*, comment, construe *(translate)*, define, demonstrate *(establish)*, describe, detail *(particularize)*, distill, elucidate, enlighten, explain, explicate, exposit, expound, illustrate, interpret, purge *(purify)*, resolve *(solve)*, stipulate. SEE MAIN ENTRY

clarifying demonstrative *(illustrative)*, informatory, interpretive

clarifying statement justification

clarus conspicuous, distinct *(clear)*, open *(in sight)*, patent, renowned, unambiguous

clash affray, bicker, collision *(dispute)*, commotion, compete, conflict *(noun)*, conflict *(verb)*, confrontation *(altercation)*, contend *(dispute)*, contest *(competition)*, contest *(dispute)*, contradict, contravene, contravention, counter, counteract, deviate, differ *(disagree)*, disaccord, disagree, discrepancy, dispute *(contest)*, dissent *(difference of opinion)*, dissent *(differ in opinion)*, embroilment, feud, fight *(argument)*, fracas, fray, incompatibility *(difference)*, incompatibility *(inconsistency)*, meeting *(encounter)*, oppugn, reaction *(opposition)*, rift *(disagreement)*, strife, struggle, violence

clash of arms conflict, fight *(battle)*

clash of opinions dispute

clash of temperament difference

clash with deviate

clashing argument *(contention)*, belligerency, competitive *(antagonistic)*, contention *(opposition)*, contradictory, contradistinction, controversy *(argument)*, deviant, difference, different, disaccord, discord, discordant, disparate, dissension, dissenting, dissidence, dissident, dissimilar, hostile, inapplicable, inapposite, inappropriate, inapt, incongruous, inept *(inappropriate)*, negative, opposite, repugnant *(incompatible)*

clasp adhere *(fasten)*, cohere *(adhere)*, grapple, lock, shut

clasp together conjoin

class allocate, classification, classify, denomination, department, distribute, division *(administrative unit)*, evaluate, file *(arrange)*, fix *(arrange)*, form *(arrangement)*, gauge, index *(relate)*, kind, manner *(kind)*, organize *(arrange)*, pigeonhole, quality *(excellence)*, race, rate, screen *(select)*, section *(division)*, society, sort, state *(condition)*, status, style, subdivision. SEE MAIN ENTRY

class action law suit SEE MAIN ENTRY

class prejudice discrimination *(bigotry)*

classic regular *(conventional)*, traditional

classical conventional, traditional

classification array *(order)*, chain *(series)*, class, compilation, degree *(station)*, denomination, department, diagnosis, distribution (arrangement), division (administrative unit), form (arrangement), hierarchy (arrangement in a series), identification, kind, label, manner (kind), method, order (arrangement), organization (structure), rating, rubric (title), segregation (separation), sequence, subdivision, subheading, system. SEE MAIN ENTRY

classificatory descriptive
classificatory description diagnosis
classified confidential, systematic
classified communication confidence (relation of trust)
classified index file
classified information secret
classify allocate, apportion, call (title), characterize, codify, denominate, diagnose, differentiate, digest (summarize), discriminate (distinguish), distinguish, distribute, file (arrange), fix (arrange), identify, include, index (relate), label, organize (arrange), rate, screen (select), sort, subdivide. SEE MAIN ENTRY
classify as classify, constitute (compose)
classify incorrectly mislabel
classis class
classmaster pedagogue
clatter noise
claudere close (terminate), shut
clause amendment (legislation), article (distinct section of a writing), caption, chapter (division), condition (contingent provision), limitation, phrase, subheading, term (provision), title (division). SEE MAIN ENTRY
claviger warden
clean blameless, decontaminate, honest, meticulous, pure, purge (purify). SEE MAIN ENTRY
clean up expurgate
clean-cut precise
clean-handed clean, not guilty
cleaned out impecunious
cleanminded clean
cleanse decontaminate, expurgate, purge (purify)
cleansing medicinal, remedial
clear absolute (conclusive), absolve, acquit, apparent (perceptible), arrant (definite), blameless, blatant (conspicuous), certain (positive), clean, cognizable, comment, comprehensible, conclusive (settled), condone, conspicuous, decisive, definite, demonstrable, descriptive, direct (forthright), discharge (liberate), discharge (pay a debt), disencumber, disentangle, earn, evident, exculpate, excuse, exonerate, explicit, express, extenuate, extricate, facilitate, flagrant, forgive, free (relieved from a burden), free, gain, immune, inappealable, incontestable, lucid, manifest, naked (perceptible), net, obvious, open (in sight), orotund, ostensible, overt, palliate (excuse), palpable, passable, patent, pay, pellucid, perceivable, perceptible, positive (incontestable), profit, propitious, pure, purge (purify), purge (wipe out by atonement), quit (free of), realize (obtain as a profit), reap, release, remit (release from penalty), remove (eliminate), resounding, salient, satisfy (discharge), simple, strong, surmount, unambiguous, unblemished, undeniable, unequivocal, unmistakable, vacant, vindicate, visible (in full view). SEE MAIN ENTRY
clear a debt quit (repay)
clear accounts quit (repay)
clear away disencumber, displace (remove)
clear cut exact
clear demonstration proof

clear from free (not restricted)
clear from a charge exculpate
clear from alleged guilt exculpate
clear from imputation of fault exculpate
clear from obscurity ascertain
clear indication proof
clear language plain language
clear of an imputation of guilt exonerate
clear of doubt ascertain
clear of encumbrance solvent
clear of obscurity ascertain, elucidate, explain, expound
clear out eliminate (eradicate), evacuate, flee
clear perception appreciation (perception)
clear sight perception
clear the mind disabuse
clear the way expedite, facilitate
clear thinking common sense, sagacity, sanity
clear thought sagacity
clear to the mind distinct (clear)
clear to the senses distinct (clear)
clear up clarify, construe (translate), elucidate, explain, exposit, expound, interpret, resolve (solve), settle, simplify (clarify), solve. SEE MAIN ENTRY
clear-cut accurate, categorical, certain (positive), certain (specific), clear (apparent), coherent (clear), comprehensible, conspicuous, definite, demonstrable, distinct (clear), incontrovertible, lucid, manifest, palpable, pellucid, precise, tangible, trenchant, unambiguous, unequivocal
clear-headed sapient
clear-minded lucid
clear-sighted acute, cognizant, discriminating (judicious), perspicacious
clear-thinking lucid, pragmatic
clear-witted lucid
clearance absolution, acquittal, amortization, collection (payment), composition (agreement in bankruptcy), compurgation, concession (authorization), condonation, discharge (liberation), discharge (payment), dispensation (exception), exoneration, indulgence, justification, liberty, license, margin (spare amount), pardon, payment (act of paying), profit, release, remission, respite (reprieve), satisfaction (discharge of debt), waiver
cleared acquitted, clear (free from criminal charges), exempt, free (relieved from a burden). SEE MAIN ENTRY
clearheaded lucid, perspicacious, rational, reasonable (rational), sane
clearheadedness reason (sound judgment)
clearing exoneration
clearly define specify
clearly defined absolute (conclusive), certain (specific), decisive, distinct (clear), explicit, perceptible, unambiguous. SEE MAIN ENTRY
clearly expressed explicit
clearly formulated explicit
clearly indicated express
clearly known certain (positive)
clearly marked perceptible
clearly stated certain (specific), explicit, express
clearmindedness competence (sanity), sanity
cleavable divisible, divisive, separable, severable
cleavage coherence, disaccord, division (act of dividing), estrangement, separation, severance, split

cleave bifurcate, break (separate), cohere (adhere), detach, disjoint, divide (separate), lancinate, rend, separate, sever, split, subdivide
cleave in two dichotomize
cleaving coherent (joined), cohesive (sticking)
cleaving together coherent (joined)
cleft rift (gap), split
clemency benevolence (disposition to do good), charity, condonation, consideration (sympathetic regard), grace, humanity (humaneness), indulgence, lenience, pardon. SEE MAIN ENTRY
clemens humane, lenient
clement charitable (lenient), humane, lenient, placable, propitious
clementia clemency, humanity (humaneness)
clementness clemency
clench constrict (compress)
clerical SEE MAIN ENTRY
clerical staff personnel, staff
clerk accountant, amanuensis, assistant. SEE MAIN ENTRY
clerk of the court notary public
clever artful, deft, expert, machiavellian, original (creative), perspicacious, politic, practiced, proficient, resourceful, sapient, strategic, subtle (refined)
clever in deception mendacious
cleverness artifice, discretion (quality of being discreet), faculty (ability), gift (flair), insight, intelligence (intellect), perception, prowess (ability), sagacity, sense (intelligence), skill
clew catchword
cliché catchword
cliche expression (comment), platitude
cliched familiar (customary)
click comport (agree with)
cliens client
client consumer, customer, patron (regular customer). SEE MAIN ENTRY
clientele consumer
climacteric critical (crucial), crossroad (turning point), crucial, emergency, timeliness
climactic critical (crucial), last (final)
climactical last (final)
climate atmosphere. SEE MAIN ENTRY
climatic condition atmosphere
climax ceiling, cessation (termination), conclude (complete), consequence (conclusion), crossroad (turning point), culminate, culmination, denouement, pinnacle
climb headway, progress, surmount
climb down alight
clime climate, region, section (vicinity), territory
clinch complete, ensure, grapple, stabilize
clinch an argument convince
cling cohere (adhere), persevere
cling tenaciously adhere (persist), persevere
cling to adhere (fasten), hold (possess), keep (shelter), observe (obey), perform (adhere to), persist, prefer, pursue (carry on), retain (keep in possession)
clinging adhesion (affixing), coadunate, coherent (joined), cohesive (sticking)
clinical SEE MAIN ENTRY
clip curtail, excise (cut away), minimize, retrench
clipeus shield
clipping excerpt
clique cabal, denomination, faction, society, sodality

cliquish exclusive *(limited)*, partisan, restrictive

cloak blind *(obscure)*, camouflage, circumvent, clothe, color *(deceptive appearance)*, conceal, cover *(conceal)*, disguise *(noun)*, disguise *(verb)*, ensconce, enshroud, envelop, harbor, hide, obfuscate, obnubilate, obscure, plant *(covertly place)*, pretense *(pretext)*, screen *(guard)*, shroud, suppress, veil. SEE MAIN ENTRY

cloaked clandestine, covert, furtive, hidden, mysterious, oblique *(evasive)*, stealthy

clockwork precision regularity

cloddish inelegant, opaque

clog block, damper *(stopper)*, hamper, hinder, impediment, interfere, interrupt, interruption, obstruction, obturate, stem *(check)*, stop, trammel. SEE MAIN ENTRY

cloister circumscribe *(surround by boundary)*, envelop, restrict, sequester *(seclude)*, shut

cloistered private *(secluded)*, solitary

clone. SEE MAIN ENTRY

cloning SEE MAIN ENTRY

close approximate, block, brief, cease, cessation *(termination)*, clog, cognate, coherent *(joined)*, cohesive *(compact)*, compact *(dense)*, comparable *(capable of comparison)*, complete, conclude *(complete)*, conclusion *(outcome)*, constrict *(inhibit)*, contestable, contiguous, culminate, defeasance, denouement, discontinue *(abandon)*, dispatch *(dispose of)*, dissolution *(termination)*, end *(termination)*, exact, expiration, expire, extremity *(death)*, faithful *(true to fact)*, finality, finish, future, grapple, halt, hidden, illiberal, immediate *(imminent)*, immediate *(not distant)*, inarticulate, indivisible, inseparable, instant, intense, intimate, literal, local, lock, moratorium, noncommittal, obturate, occlude, outcome, parsimonious, pendent, pending *(imminent)*, penurious, populous, precise, present *(attendant)*, proximate, secret, shut, similar, solid *(compact)*, stop, strict, taciturn, terminate. SEE MAIN ENTRY

close application diligence *(care)*

close around circumscribe *(surround by boundary)*

close association propinquity *(kinship)*

close at hand close *(near)*, forthcoming, future, immediate *(imminent)*, immediate *(not distant)*, instant, pending *(imminent)*, present *(attendant)*, prospective, proximate

close attention deliberation, diligence *(care)*, interest *(concern)*

close by close *(near)*, present *(attendant)*, proximate

close contact adhesion *(affixing)*

close correspondence parity

close down shut

close fast lock

close identification adhesion *(loyalty)*

close in border *(bound)*, circumscribe *(surround by boundary)*, contain *(enclose)*, enclose, envelop, include

close in upon converge

close inquiry analysis, cross-questioning, examination *(study)*, hearing, indagation, investigation, research

close investigation scrutiny

close look scrutiny

close observance conformity *(obedience)*

close observation examination *(study)*, judgment *(discernment)*

close off clog

close on border *(approach)*

close relation analogy

close relationship marriage *(intimate relationship)*

close relative next of kin

close resemblance analogy

close search scrutiny

close study deliberation, diligence *(care)*

close the curtain camouflage

close thought diligence *(care)*

close to almost

close together compact *(dense)*

close union contact *(association)*

close up seal *(close)*

close watch prudence

close with fight *(battle)*, grapple

close-fisted penurious

close-fitting limiting

close-handed penurious

close-knit compact *(dense)*

close-lipped mute

close-out lockout

close-set compact *(dense)*

closed blind *(impassable)*, complete *(ended)*, fixed *(settled)*, impervious, personal *(private)*, private *(not public)*

closed purse austerity

closed-minded provincial

closed-minded person pedant

closed-mindedness predetermination

closefisted illiberal, parsimonious

closely faithfully

closely acquainted familiar *(informed)*, intimate

closely allied affiliated, associated, cognate, consanguineous

closely associated intimate

closely connected pendent

closely examine search

closely packed populous, replete

closely related affiliated, akin *(germane)*, associated, cognate, collateral *(accompanying)*, consanguineous

closely resemble approximate

closely united compact *(dense)*

closemouthed laconic, mute, taciturn

closeness affection, affinity *(regard)*, coalescence, consortium *(marriage companionship)*, density, identity *(similarity)*, kinship, marriage *(intimate relationship)*, propinquity *(proximity)*, rapport, relation *(connection)*, resemblance, semblance

closest proximate

closet chamber *(compartment)*, hide, private *(confidential)*, sequester *(seclude)*, shroud

closing cessation *(termination)*, close *(conclusion)*, cloture, conclusive *(settled)*, definitive, denouement, dissolution *(termination)*, expiration, final, halt, last *(final)* closing arguments SEE MAIN ENTRY

closing in imminent

closing piece end *(termination)*

closure cessation *(termination)*, close *(conclusion)*, cloture, conclusion *(outcome)*, denouement, end *(termination)*, expiration, finality, obstruction, payoff *(result)*

clot cohere *(adhere)*

clothe vest. SEE MAIN ENTRY

clothe in words phrase

cloture cessation *(interlude)*. SEE MAIN ENTRY

cloud blind *(obscure)*, camouflage, cloak, damper *(depressant)*, ensconce, enshroud, hide, muddle, obfuscate, obnubilate, obscuration, obscure, tarnish, veil. SEE MAIN ENTRY

cloud over obnubilate

clouded hidden, nebulous, opaque, unclear

cloudless propitious

cloudy equivocal, indefinite, inscrutable, nebulous, opaque, unclear, vague

clout SEE MAIN ENTRY

clownish uncouth

cloyed full, replete

cloying nectarious

club beat *(strike)*, cudgel, league, organization *(association)*, party *(political organization)*, society, sodality

clue catchword, hint *(noun)*, hint *(verb)*, indicant, indication, indicator, insinuation, reference *(allusion)*, suggestion, symbol, symptom. SEE MAIN ENTRY

clueless incognizant, insensible

clump aggregate, assemblage, bulk

clumsiness abortion *(fiasco)*

clumsy incompetent, inept *(incompetent)*, ponderous, uncouth, unpolitic

clumsy performance miscue

cluster agglomeration, aggregate, assemblage, bulk, compile, concentrate *(consolidate)*, congregate, hoard, mass *(body of persons)*, meet, selection *(collection)*, unite

clustered compact *(dense)*, composite

clutch grapple, retain *(keep in possession)*

clutter complex *(entanglement)*, confuse *(create disorder)*, confusion *(turmoil)*, disorganize

co-existent contemporary

co-obligor comaker

co-operant synergetic

co-opt adopt, choose

co-optation adoption *(acceptance)*

co-respondent respondent

coacervare accumulate *(amass)*, hoard

coach advise, counsel, direct *(supervise)*, discipline *(train)*, edify, educate, foster, instruct *(direct)*, nurture, oversee

coaching direction *(guidance)*, discipline *(training)*, education, guidance

coact combine *(act in concert)*, consolidate *(unite)*, conspire, cooperate, join *(bring together)*, unite

coacting concerted, concurrent *(at the same time)*, concurrent *(united)*, synergetic

coaction affiliation *(connectedness)*, concert, concordance, contribution *(participation)*, duress, enforcement, force *(compulsion)*, relationship *(connection)*, synergy. SEE MAIN ENTRY

coactive associated, compulsory, concerted, concurrent *(at the same time)*, concurrent *(united)*, insistent, obligatory, synergetic

coactor accomplice, confederate, conspirer. SEE MAIN ENTRY

coactor in crime coconspirator

coactus involuntary, reluctance

coaddressee cotenant

coadjument concert

coadjutant associate, backer, coactor, colleague, concerted, confederate, conspirer, copartner *(business associate)*, copartner *(coconspirator)*, mutual *(collective)*, partner. SEE MAIN ENTRY

coadjutive mutual *(collective)*

coadjutor abettor, assistant, associate, backer, coactor, coadjutant, coconspirator, cohort, colleague, confederate, consociate, conspirer, contributor *(contributor)*, copartner *(coconspirator)*, participant, partner

coadjutorship combination

coadjutress colleague, copartner *(coconspirator)*

673

coadjutrix colleague

coadjuvancy affiliation *(connectedness)*, aid *(help)*, association *(connection)*, cartel, collusion, concert

coadjuvant ancillary *(auxiliary)*, associate, backer, colleague, concerted, mutual *(collective)*

coadjuvate consolidate *(unite)*

coadunate amalgamate, associated, coherent *(joined)*, joint, mutual *(collective)*. SEE MAIN ENTRY

coadunation adhesion *(affixing)*, coalescence, consolidation, integration *(amalgamation)*

coagency collusion, concert, connivance

coagent plenipotentiary

coagulate bond *(hold together)*, cement, cohere *(adhere)*, coherent *(joined)*, crystallize

coagulated coadunate, coherent *(joined)*, solid *(compact)*

coagulation adhesion *(affixing)*, agglomeration, coalescence, congealment

coagulative coadunate

coaid assistant, colleague, copartner *(coconspirator)*

coaider in crime coconspirator

coalesce adhere *(fasten)*, amalgamate, bond *(hold together)*, cement, cohere *(adhere)*, combine *(join together)*, concentrate *(consolidate)*, conjoin, connect *(join together)*, consolidate *(strengthen)*, consolidate *(unite)*, converge, desegregate, incorporate *(include)*, unite

coalesced coadunate

coalescence centralization, combination, concrescence, conspiracy, incorporation *(blend)*, joinder, merger. SEE MAIN ENTRY

coalescent coadunate, coherent *(joined)*, concerted, conjoint

coalescing centralization

coalition affiliation *(amalgamation)*, affiliation *(connectedness)*, association *(alliance)*, association *(connection)*, band, cabal, cartel, centralization, coaction, coalescence, combination, company *(assemblage)*, concert, confederacy *(compact)*, connection *(relation)*, consortium *(business cartel)*, conspiracy, contact *(association)*, contribution *(participation)*, corporation, federation, incorporation *(formation of a business entity)*, institute, integration *(amalgamation)*, integration *(assimilation)*, league, merger, organization *(association)*, pact, partnership, party *(political organization)*, pool, relationship *(connection)*, side, society, syndicate, union *(unity)*. SEE MAIN ENTRY

coalitional concurrent *(united)*, conjoint, joint, mutual *(collective)*

coapplicant comaker

coaptation adjustment

coarct constrict *(compress)*

coarctate decrease

coarctation bondage

coarguere expose

coarse blatant *(obtrusive)*, brutal, disreputable, impertinent *(insolent)*, inelegant, lascivious, lurid, odious, offensive *(offending)*, poor *(inferior in quality)*, profane, prurient, salacious, scurrilous, suggestive *(risqué)*, uncouth, unseemly

coarsen debase

coarseness obscenity

coartare curtail

coastal littoral

coastland littoral

coating cover *(protection)*

coax agitate *(activate)*, cajole, entice, exhort, importune, inveigle, lure, persuade, pressure, prevail *(persuade)*, prevail upon, reason *(persuade)*, solicit, urge. SEE MAIN ENTRY

coaxing instigation, persuasion, persuasive, seduction

coborrower comaker

cockiness pride

cocksureness confidence *(faith)*

coconspirator accessory, accomplice. SEE MAIN ENTRY

coddle excessively overindulge

code act *(enactment)*, bylaw, canon, conduct, criterion, digest, ethics, jargon *(technical language)*, law, ordinance, pandect *(code of laws)*, precept, protocol *(etiquette)*, regulation *(rule)*, rubric *(authoritative rule)*, rule *(guide)*, rule *(legal dictate)*, statute. SEE MAIN ENTRY

code of behavior protocol *(etiquette)*

code of duty conscience

code of honor conscience

code of laws constitution

code of morals ethics

code of right and wrong ethics

code of what is fitting decorum

coded mysterious

codefendant accomplice

codenizen cotenant

codes legislation *(enactments)*

codex accepti et expensi ledger

codicil addendum, appendix *(supplement)*. SEE MAIN ENTRY

codicilli note *(brief comment)*

codification classification, code, compilation, constitution, enactment, legalization, pandect *(code of laws)*. SEE MAIN ENTRY

codification of laws legislation *(lawmaking)*

codified law code, constitution, pandect *(code of laws)*, statute

codify classify, constitute *(establish)*, digest *(summarize)*, enact, file *(arrange)*, fix *(arrange)*, index *(docket)*, legislate, tabulate. SEE MAIN ENTRY

codirector accessory, accomplice, colleague

codweller cotenant

coefficiency concert

coemptor consumer

coeptum undertaking *(enterprise)*

coequal analogous, coextensive, commensurable, commensurate, comparable *(equivalent)*, counterpart *(complement)*, equal, equivalent, identical, peer. SEE MAIN ENTRY

coequality identity *(similarity)*, mutuality, parity

coerce compel, constrain *(compel)*, enforce, exact, extort, foist, harass, impose *(enforce)*, impose *(subject)*, inflict, intimidate, necessitate, press *(constrain)*, pressure, require *(compel)*, threaten. SEE MAIN ENTRY

coercere coerce, confine, control *(regulate)*, govern, restrict, shut, stem *(check)*

coercion constraint *(restriction)*, duress, extortion, force *(compulsion)*, oppression, pressure, stress *(strain)*. SEE MAIN ENTRY

coercitio coercion

coercive binding, compelling, compulsory, forcible, insistent, involuntary, mandatory, necessary *(required)*, obligatory, severe, unavoidable *(inevitable)*

coercive refusal to furnish work lockout

coetaneous concurrent *(at the same time)*, simultaneous

coetus company *(enterprise)*, congregation

coeval concerted, concurrent *(at the same time)*, contemporaneous, simultaneous

coexist accompany, coincide *(correspond)*

coexistence compatibility, integration *(amalgamation)*, integration *(assimilation)*, peace, synchronism

coexistent coincidental, concerted, concordant, concurrent *(at the same time)*, congruous, contemporaneous, harmonious, simultaneous

coexisting coincidental, concerted, concordant, concurrent *(at the same time)*, congruous, contemporaneous, harmonious, simultaneous

coextending coextensive

coextensive coequal, commensurable, commensurate, equal. SEE MAIN ENTRY

coffer bank, depository, repository, treasury. SEE MAIN ENTRY

cofunction cooperate

cog deceive

cogency force *(strength)*, strength

cogent clear *(certain)*, coherent *(clear)*, convincing, important *(urgent)*, influential, irresistible, logical, persuasive, potent, powerful, predominant, sound. SEE MAIN ENTRY

cogere compel, constrain *(compel)*, necessitate

cogitable plausible, possible

cogitare intend, reflect *(ponder)*, speculate *(conjecture)*

cogitate brood, consider, deliberate, muse, ponder, rationalize, reason *(conclude)*, reflect *(ponder)*, weigh

cogitatio idea, reflection *(thought)*

cogitation consideration *(contemplation)*, contemplation, deliberation, dialectic, ratiocination, reflection *(thought)*

cogitative deliberate, speculative. SEE MAIN ENTRY

cogitatus deliberate, intentional

cognate analogous, apposite, comparable *(capable of comparison)*, consanguineous, correlate, correlative, germane, interrelated, pendent, related, relative *(relevant)*, relative, relevant, same, similar. SEE MAIN ENTRY

cognati kindred

cognatio affinity *(family ties)*, relationship *(connection)*

cognation affinity *(family ties)*, ancestry, blood, degree *(kinship)*, filiation, kinship, propinquity *(kinship)*, relation *(connection)*, relationship *(connection)*

cognatus related, relation *(kinship)*, relative

cognitio cognition, hearing, inquiry *(systematic investigation)*, insight, knowledge *(learning)*

cognition appreciation *(perception)*, apprehension *(perception)*, comprehension, insight, intellect, intelligence *(intellect)*, knowledge *(awareness)*, observation, perception, realization, reason *(sound judgment)*, recognition, scienter, sense *(intelligence)*. SEE MAIN ENTRY

cognitive cognizant, familiar *(informed)*, knowing, perceptive, rational, reasonable *(rational)*, receptive

cognitive faculties judgment *(discernment)*, sense *(intelligence)*

cognitive faculty intellect, intelligence *(intellect)*

cognitive powers judgment *(discernment)*, sense *(intelligence)*

cognitive process cognition

cognitus acquainted

cognizable appreciable, ascertainable, coherent *(clear)*, comprehensible, concrete, determinable *(ascertainable)*, discernible, justiciable, naked *(perceptible)*, perceivable, perceptible, ponderable, scrutable, solvable, triable. SEE MAIN ENTRY

cognizable in courts of law legal

cognizance appreciation *(perception)*, apprehension *(perception)*, cognition, comprehension, experience *(background)*, identification, insight, knowledge *(awareness)*, notice *(heed)*, observation, perception, realization, reason *(sound judgment)*, recognition, scienter

cognizant certain *(positive)*, circumspect, conscious *(aware)*, expert, familiar *(informed)*, knowing, learned, perceptive, sensitive *(discerning)*. SEE MAIN ENTRY

cognizant of acquainted, privy

cognize apprehend *(perceive)*, comprehend *(understand)*, construe *(comprehend)*, digest *(comprehend)*, discern *(detect with the senses)*, note *(notice)*, notice *(observe)*, perceive, pierce *(discern)*, realize *(understand)*, understand

cognized household *(familiar)*

cognomen call *(title)*, sobriquet, term *(expression)*. SEE MAIN ENTRY

cognomination call *(title)*

cognoscere ascertain, discover, find *(discover)*, hear *(give a legal hearing)*, hear *(give attention to)*, investigate, perceive, recognize *(perceive)*, try *(conduct a trial)*

cognoscible comprehensible

cognovit SEE MAIN ENTRY

cohabit SEE MAIN ENTRY

cohabitant inhabitant

cohabitation marriage *(intimate relationship)*, marriage *(wedlock)*, matrimony. SEE MAIN ENTRY

cohaerens coherent *(clear)*, coherent *(joined)*

cohaerere cohere *(adhere)*, cohere *(be logically consistent)*

cohelper associate, coactor, cohort, colleague, consociate, conspirer, contributor *(contributor)*, copartner *(business associate)*, copartner *(coconspirator)*, partner

cohere adhere *(fasten)*, adjoin, affix, attach *(join)*, bond *(hold together)*, cement, combine *(join together)*, comport *(agree with)*, conjoin, connect *(join together)*, connect *(relate)*, consolidate *(strengthen)*, conspire, contact *(touch)*, correspond *(be equivalent)*, crystallize. SEE MAIN ENTRY

coherence adherence *(adhesion)*, adhesion *(affixing)*, coalescence, competence *(sanity)*, connection *(relation)*, contact *(touching)*, continuity, union *(unity)*. SEE MAIN ENTRY

coherency coherence, connection *(relation)*

coherent agreed *(harmonized)*, cohesive *(sticking)*, commensurable, consensual, consistent, consonant, convincing, logical. SEE MAIN ENTRY

cohering coadunate, coherent *(joined)*, cohesive *(sticking)*, consistent

cohesion accession *(annexation)*, adherence *(adhesion)*, adhesion *(affixing)*, attachment *(act of affixing)*, coaction, coalescence, coherence, congealment, connection *(fastening)*

cohesive coadunate, coherent *(joined)*, compact *(dense)*, concerted, concurrent *(united)*, conjoint, inextricable, infrangible. SEE MAIN ENTRY

cohesiveness adherence *(adhesion)*, adhesion *(affixing)*, coalescence, coherence, tenacity

cohibere confine, keep *(restrain)*, stay *(halt)*, stem *(check)*

cohibit block

cohors cohort

cohort associate, consociate, copartner *(coconspirator)*. SEE MAIN ENTRY

cohouseholder cotenant

coiled sinuous

coin cash, conceive *(invent)*, currency, denominate, frame *(construct)*, invent *(produce for the first time)*, make, money, originate, produce *(manufacture)*

coin of the realm cash

coinage cash, formation, invention, money, origination

coincide agree *(comply)*, certify *(approve)*, comport *(agree with)*, concur *(coexist)*, correspond *(be equivalent)*. SEE MAIN ENTRY

coincidence concordance, conformity *(agreement)*, connivance, contingency, happenstance, synchronism, synergy

coincident coequal, coincidental, concerted, concomitant, concurrent *(at the same time)*, congruous, consonant, contemporaneous, corporate *(joint)*, simultaneous

coincident with consensual

coincidental contingent, fortuitous. SEE MAIN ENTRY

coinciding coincidental, concerted, concordant, congruous, contemporaneous, correlative

coined words jargon *(technical language)*

coinhabitant cotenant

coinhabiter cotenant

coinstantaneous coincidental, concurrent *(at the same time)*, contemporaneous, simultaneous

coire converge

cojugate conjugal

cold bleak *(exposed and barren)*, bleak *(severely simple)*, callous, cold-blooded, cruel, disdainful, dispassionate, inexpressive, insusceptible *(uncaring)*, malevolent, obdurate, pedestrian, phlegmatic, relentless, ruthless, severe, unresponsive

cold of heart callous

cold shoulder rebuff

cold-blooded callous, cruel, dispassionate, malevolent, malignant, phlegmatic, relentless, ruthless, sinister. SEE MAIN ENTRY

cold-hearted cold-blooded, cruel, dispassionate, relentless

cold-shoulder shun

coldhearted callous, malignant, ruthless

coldness indifference

coleaseholder cotenant

colere cultivate, honor

colessee cotenant

collaborate aid, combine *(act in concert)*, cooperate, federalize *(associate)*, federate, involve *(participate)*, organize *(unionize)*, participate, pool

collaborated mutual *(collective)*

collaborating concerted, consensual

collaboration bad faith, coaction, collusion, concert, conformity *(agreement)*, connivance, contribution *(participation)*, league, pool, synergy

collaborationist coactor, conspirer

collaborative concurrent *(united)*, joint, mutual *(collective)*, synergetic

collaborator abettor, accessory, accomplice, assistant, associate, coactor, coadjutant,

coconspirator, cohort, colleague, confederate, consociate, conspirer, contributor *(contributor)*, copartner *(business associate)*, copartner *(coconspirator)*, participant, partner

collapse catastrophe, debacle, decline, defeat, destruction, deteriorate, detriment, disaster, disease, disrepair, fail *(lose)*, failure *(lack of success)*, give *(yield)*, languish, miscarriage, mistrial, prostration, succumb

collar handcuff

collared arrested *(apprehended)*

collateral additional, akin *(germane)*, ancillary *(auxiliary)*, bail, binder, circumstantial, coextensive, concurrent *(at the same time)*, consanguineous, correlative, deposit, downpayment, extrinsic, hostage, hypothecation, incident, pendent, peripheral, pledge *(security)*, related, relative *(relevant)*, secondary, security *(pledge)*, similar, subordinate, supplementary. SEE MAIN ENTRY

collateral relative next of kin

collateral review of detention habeas corpus

collateral security binder, deposit, mortgage

collaterial review habeas corpus

collation SEE MAIN ENTRY

colleague affiliate, assistant, associate, coactor, coadjutant, cohort, confederate, consociate, consort, conspirer, contributor *(contributor)*, copartner *(business associate)*, participant. SEE MAIN ENTRY

colleague in crime coconspirator

colleagueship affiliation *(connectedness)*, association *(connection)*, cartel, coaction, society, sodality

collect accrue *(increase)*, accumulate *(amass)*, aggregate, codify, compile, concentrate *(consolidate)*, congregate, conjoin, convene, cull, excise *(levy a tax)*, extract, fund, gain, garner, glean, hoard, hold *(possess)*, join *(bring together)*, levy, meet, obtain, purchase, read, reap, receive *(acquire)*, recruit, select, store, tax *(levy)*, unite. SEE MAIN ENTRY

collect evidence document

collect facts investigate

collect into a focus congregate

collect into a mass accumulate *(amass)*, aggregate

collect knowledge discover

collect payment collect *(recover money)*, toll *(exact payment)*

collect the vote poll

collect together accumulate *(amass)*

collectable due *(owed)*, payable

collectanea selection *(collection)*

collected composite, conglomerate, dispassionate, miscellaneous, nonchalant, placid

collected writings information *(knowledge)*

collection agglomeration, aggregate, assemblage, assembly, band, code, combination, compilation, conglomeration, congregation, corpus, cumulation, depository, digest, hoard, levy, store *(depository)*. SEE MAIN ENTRY

collection of facts investigation

collection of laws code, constitution, pandect *(code of laws)*

collection of statutes code, codification

collective broad, common *(shared)*, composite, conjoint, cooperative, generic, joint, nonsectarian, omnibus, pool, public *(affecting people)*. SEE MAIN ENTRY

collective action coaction
collective agreement bargain, contract, covenant
collective assets estate *(property)*
collective bargaining SEE MAIN ENTRY
collective members constituency
collective refusal to work strike
collectively en banc, en masse, in toto, wholly. SEE MAIN ENTRY
collectively agreed contractual
collectiveness entirety, whole
collectivism pool
collectivity complex *(development)*, corpus, entirety, totality, whole
collectivized conglomerate
collector assessor, caretaker *(one fulfilling the function of office)*, receiver
college institute
collegiate distinction degree *(academic title)*
collide conflict, counter, counteract, cross *(disagree with)*, disagree, dispute *(contest)*, dissent *(differ in opinion)*, impinge, jostle *(bump into)*, meet, oppose. SEE MAIN ENTRY
collide with contact *(touch)*
colliding competitive *(antagonistic)*, discordant
colligate accumulate *(amass)*, aggregate
combine *(join together)*, join *(bring together)*
colligation assemblage, body *(collection)*, collection *(assembly)*, compilation, corpus
collision antipode, conflict, confrontation *(altercation)*, meeting *(encounter)*. SEE MAIN ENTRY
collocate allocate, arrange *(methodize)*, classify, file *(arrange)*, fix *(arrange)*, join *(bring together)*, marshal, pigeonhole, sort
collocation arrangement *(ordering)*, array *(order)*, building *(business of assembling)*, chamber *(body)*, collection *(assembly)*, compilation, distribution *(arrangement)*, hierarchy *(arrangement in a series)*
collocution communication *(discourse)*, conversation, parley
collop part *(portion)*
colloque speak
colloquial ordinary, prevailing *(current)*, prevalent
colloquial discourse conversation
colloquialism catchword
colloquy communication *(discourse)*, conference, confrontation *(act of setting face to face)*, conversation, interview, meeting *(conference)*, parley, speech
collude combine *(act in concert)*, connive, conspire, contrive, cooperate, involve *(participate)*, maneuver, plan, plot, scheme. SEE MAIN ENTRY
colluder coactor, coconspirator, confederate, conspirator, conspirer, copartner *(coconspirator)*, partner
colluding concerted
collusion bad faith, bribery, cabal, coaction, confederacy *(conspiracy)*, connivance, conspiracy, contribution *(participation)*, contrivance, deceit, fraud, machination, plot *(secret plan)*. SEE MAIN ENTRY
collusive clandestine, deceptive, machiavellian, mendacious. SEE MAIN ENTRY
collusory machiavellian
colonial provincial
colonies possessions
colonist migrant, pioneer
colonization immigration
colonize inhabit, occupy *(take possession)*
colonizer pioneer

colony province
colophon brand
color camouflage
color complexion
color falsify, misrepresent, prejudice *(influence)*, pretense *(pretext)*, slant, stain. SEE MAIN ENTRY
colorable ostensible, plausible, specious. SEE MAIN ENTRY
colored one-sided, prejudicial, specious
colored by bias subjective
coloring connotation, context, implication *(inference)*, overstatement
colorless insipid, jejune *(dull)*, lifeless *(dull)*, mediocre, pedestrian, prosaic, usual
colossal capacious, gross *(flagrant)*, prodigious *(enormous)*
colporteur dealer
column chapter *(division)*
columnists press
comaker SEE MAIN ENTRY
comate accomplice, associate, cohort, colleague, confederate, consociate, consort, copartner *(business associate)*, copartner *(coconspirator)*, participant, partner
comatose inactive, insensible, phlegmatic, torpid
comb search
combat affray, attack, belligerency, collision *(dispute)*, compete, competition, conflict *(noun)*, conflict *(verb)*, confrontation *(altercation)*, contend *(dispute)*, contention *(opposition)*, contest *(dispute)*, contest, dispute *(contest)*, embroilment, engage *(involve)*, fight *(battle)*, fight *(battle)*, fray, grapple, oppose, oppugn, resist *(oppose)*, resistance, strife, struggle
combat an opinion challenge
combatant aggressor, competitive *(antagonistic)*, contender, contestant, disputant, foe, rival
combative argumentative, competitive *(antagonistic)*, contentious, hostile, litigious, offensive *(taking the initiative)*, pugnacious
combativeness belligerency
combatting competitive *(antagonistic)*
combination accession *(annexation)*, affiliation *(amalgamation)*, affiliation *(connectedness)*, assemblage, association *(alliance)*, association *(connection)*, band, cabal, cartel, centralization, coalescence, coalition, company *(enterprise)*, compilation, composition *(makeup)*, concert, confederacy *(compact)*, connection *(fastening)*, consolidation, consortium *(business cartel)*, conspiracy, contact *(association)*, content *(structure)*, contribution *(participation)*, corporation, federation, incorporation *(blend)*, integration *(amalgamation)*, integration *(assimilation)*, joinder, league, melange, merger, organization *(association)*, partnership, pool, relationship *(connection)*, selection *(collection)*, sodality, solution *(substance)*, union *(unity)*. SEE MAIN ENTRY
combination for fraud collusion
combination of companies trust *(combination of businesses)*
combination of financial institutions consortium *(business cartel)*
combination of funds pool
combinative concordant, concurrent *(united)*
combine accumulate *(amass)*, affix, amalgamate, annex *(add)*, association *(alliance)*, attach *(join)*, bond *(hold together)*, business *(commercial enterprise)*, cartel, cement, coalition, cohere *(adhere)*, commingle, compile,

concentrate *(consolidate)*, confederacy *(compact)*, conjoin, connect *(join together)*, connive, consolidate *(strengthen)*, consolidate *(unite)*, conspire, cooperate, coordinate, corporation, crystallize, federalize *(associate)*, federate, federation, include, incorporate *(include)*, join *(associate oneself with)*, join *(bring together)*, league, merge, organize *(arrange)*, organize *(unionize)*, party *(political organization)*, pool *(noun)*, pool *(verb)*, society, syndicate, trust *(combination of businesses)*, unite. SEE MAIN ENTRY
combine for some evil design conspire
combine forces cooperate
combine operations conspire
combine racially desegregate
combine with desegregate
combine with water dilute
combined associated, coadunate, coherent *(joined)*, collective, composite, compound, concerted, concurrent *(united)*, conglomerate, conjoint, federal, harmonious, inextricable, inseparable, joint, miscellaneous, mutual *(collective)*
combined action concert, synergy
combined effect synergy
combined effort coaction, concert
combined operation collusion, conformity *(agreement)*, connivance, conspiracy, synergy
combining accession *(annexation)*, concerted, concrescence, congruous
come accrue *(arise)*, report *(present oneself)*, stem *(originate)*
come about arise *(occur)*, occur *(happen)*
come across confront *(encounter)*
come after accede *(succeed)*, ensue, succeed *(follow)*
come afterward ensue
come again recur, return *(go back)*
come and go beat *(pulsate)*
come apart separate
come at call obey
come away move *(alter position)*
come back recur, resurgence, retort, return *(go back)*
come back at recriminate, reply
come back to reopen
come before precede
come between alienate *(estrange)*, disaffect, interpose, interrupt, intervene, separate
come by attain, gain, procure, realize *(obtain as a profit)*, receive *(acquire)*
come clean betray *(disclose)*
come close border *(approach)*
come close in estimation approximate
come close to approximate
come closer converge
come down decline *(fall)*, degenerate
come down by transmission descend
come down lineally descend
come face to face meet
come face to face with confront *(encounter)*
come first outweigh, precede, surpass
come formally before a tribunal appear *(attend court proceedings)*
come forth arise *(appear)*, confess, emanate, emerge, pullulate, result
come forward approach, emerge, issue *(send forth)*
come from arise *(originate)*, emanate, evolve, result
come gradually into existence develop
come in enter *(go in)*

come in conflict with confront *(oppose)*, contradict, counter, counteract, disap-prove *(reject)*, except *(object)*, grapple, oppose

come in contact collide *(crash against)*, confront *(encounter)*, congregate, strike *(collide)*

come in last lose *(undergo defeat)*

come in sight arise *(appear)*

come in view arise *(appear)*

come into gain

come into action arise *(originate)*

come into being arise *(originate)*, occur *(happen)*

come into collision collide *(crash against)*, conflict, impinge, strike *(collide)*

come into court appear *(attend court proceedings)*

come into existence arise *(originate)*, commence, exist, occur *(happen)*

come into notice emerge

come into possession derive *(receive)*, obtain

come into possession as an heir inherit

come into possession of acquire *(receive)*, possess

come into sight appear *(materialize)*

come into the world commence

come into view appear *(materialize)*, emerge, occur *(come to mind)*

come near approach, approximate

come near in position approximate

come next accede *(succeed)*, ensue

come of age mature

come onto the horizon issue *(send forth)*

come out circulate, declare, emerge, issue *(send forth)*

come out in the open issue *(send forth)*

come out of hiding emerge

come out with phrase, remark, utter

come round conform

come short fail *(lose)*

come subsequently succeed *(follow)*

come through succeed *(attain)*

come to attain, reach

come to a close cease, expire, finish

come to a conclusion ascertain, decide, deduce, deduct *(conclude by reasoning)*, determine, find *(determine)*, hold *(decide)*, rule *(decide)*

come to a decision determine

come to a determination conclude *(decide)*, determine, fix *(settle)*, resolve *(decide)*, rule *(decide)*, settle

come to a focus converge

come to a hasty conclusion presume

come to a point border *(approach)*, converge, focus

come to a resolution fix *(settle)*

come to a standstill cease, pause, quit *(discontinue)*, rest *(cease from action)*, stop

come to a stop cease *(terminate)*, halt

come to an agreement agree *(contract)*, arrange *(methodize)*, coincide *(concur)*, compromise *(settle by mutual agreement)*, concur *(agree)*, decide, fix *(settle)*, settle

come to an arrangement close *(agree)*

come to an end cease, close *(terminate)*, decease, expire, finish, lapse *(cease)*, perish, terminate

come to an understanding agree *(comply)*, agree *(contract)*, close *(agree)*, coincide *(concur)*, compromise *(settle by mutual agreement)*, concur *(agree)*, settle

come to be arise *(originate)*, develop, evolve

come to blows fight *(battle)*

come to know apprehend *(perceive)*, ascertain, discover, perceive

come to light appear *(materialize)*, arise *(appear)*, emerge

come to maturity develop

come to naught fail *(lose)*, perish, succumb

come to nothing fail *(lose)*

come to notice arise *(appear)*

come to pass arise *(occur)*, occur *(happen)*, supervene

come to pieces disorganize

come to ruin perish

come to stay remain *(stay)*

come to terms agree *(comply)*, agree *(contract)*, arrange *(methodize)*, close *(agree)*, coincide *(concur)*, compromise *(settle by mutual agreement)*, concede, concur *(agree)*, consent, decide, dicker, negotiate, settle, succumb

come to the aid of assist, help, promote *(organize)*, serve *(assist)*

come to the defense of maintain *(sustain)*, support *(assist)*

come to the help of support *(assist)*

come to the rescue free

come to understand comprehend *(understand)*

come together cohere *(adhere)*, collide *(crash against)*, concur *(agree)*, congregate, contact *(touch)*, converge, crystallize, meet, rendezvous, strike *(collide)*, unite

come uninvited intrude

come up to the standard pass *(satisfy requirements)*

come upon discover, find *(discover)*, invent *(produce for the first time)*, locate

comeback renewal, revival

comedown descent *(declination)*, disgrace, misfortune

comely attractive

comes consort, count

comestible palatable

cometary brief, volatile

comfort accommodate, assuage, assure *(give confidence to)*, benefit *(betterment)*, consortium *(marriage companionship)*, ease, prosperity, reassure, relieve *(give aid)*, solace, soothe, support *(assistance)*, sympathize

comfortable habitable, opulent, prosperous, successful

comfortable circumstances prosperity

comforting mitigation

comfortless bleak *(severely simple)*, disconsolate, lamentable

comic jocular

comical ludicrous

comical representation parody

coming appearance *(emergence)*, close *(near)*, forthcoming, future, immediate *(imminent)*, imminent, onset *(commencement)*, pending *(imminent)*, prospective, subsequent

coming after consecutive

coming before preliminary

coming between mesne

coming down descent *(declination)*

coming events prospect *(outlook)*

coming from derivative

coming from another land alien *(foreign)*

coming from without extraneous

coming in inflow

coming soon forthcoming

coming to an end determinable *(liable to be terminated)*

coming together coalition, confrontation *(act of setting face to face)*

comissari carouse

comitas courtesy

comity compatibility, courtesy. SEE MAIN ENTRY

command agency *(commission)*, agency *(legal relationship)*, call *(demand)*, canon, claim *(legal demand)*, coerce, coercion, compel, conduct, constrain *(compel)*, control *(supervision)*, control *(regulate)*, decree *(noun)*, decree *(verb)*, demand *(noun)*, demand *(verb)*, detail *(assign)*, dictate *(noun)*, dictate *(verb)*, direct *(order)*, direct *(supervise)*, direction *(order)*, directive, discipline *(control)*, dominate, dominion *(supreme authority)*, edict, efficiency, enact, enjoin, exhort, fiat, force *(compulsion)*, force *(strength)*, force *(coerce)*, generalship, govern, government *(administration)*, handle *(manage)*, hegemony, hold *(possess)*, impose *(enforce)*, influence, injunction, insist, instruct *(direct)*, instruction *(direction)*, jurisdiction, knowledge *(learning)*, law, manage, management *(directorate)*, management *(supervision)*, mandamus, mandate, manipulate *(utilize skillfully)*, mittimus, moderate *(preside over)*, monition *(legal summons)*, motivate, occupation *(possession)*, occupy *(take possession)*, officiate, operate, order *(judicial directive)*, order, ordinance, overcome *(surmount)*, overlook *(superintend)*, oversee, own, possess, power, precept, predominance, predominate *(command)*, prescribe, prescription *(directive)*, preside, press *(constrain)*, pressure, prevail *(triumph)*, primacy, process *(summons)*, regime, regulation *(rule)*, request, require *(compel)*, requirement, rule *(legal dictate)*, rule *(govern)*, ruling, skill, subjugate, subpoena, summon, superintend, supervision, supremacy, surmount, takeover, wield, will *(desire)*, writ. SEE MAIN ENTRY

command a view observe *(watch)*

command a view of discern *(detect with the senses)*, overlook *(superintend)*

command back remand

command by the court mandate

command influence constrain *(compel)*

command not to do forbid

command of idiom parlance, phraseology

command of language parlance, phraseology

command of money substance *(material possessions)*

command of one's faculties composure

command of temper composure

command of thought comprehension

command of words parlance, rhetoric *(skilled speech)*

command to appear call *(summon)*, citation *(charge)*, subpoena *(noun)*, subpoena *(verb)*, summon, summons, venire

command to incarcerate mittimus

command to undo wrong injunction

commandant chief, principal *(director)*

commanded compulsory, decretal, mandatory, obligatory, positive *(prescribed)*

commanded by long use prescriptive

commandeer assume *(seize)*, carry away, deprive, garnish, hijack, procure, seize *(confiscate)*, usurp

commandeering condemnation *(seizure)*, confiscatory, disseisin

commander chief, principal *(director)*

commanders authorities, hierarchy *(persons in authority)*

commanding cardinal *(outstanding)*, cogent, compelling, considerable, convincing, critical *(crucial)*, decisive, decretal, dictatorial, dominant, forcible, important *(significant)*, influential, insistent, mandatory, master, noteworthy, peremptory *(imperative)*, potent, powerful, predominant, prescriptive, prevailing *(having superior force)*, salient, sovereign *(absolute)*

commanding a good price valuable

commanding a high price priceless

commanding belief credible, fiduciary, plausible

commanding confidence credible, fiduciary

commanding position priority

commandment canon, charge *(command)*, codification, decree, dictate, direction *(order)*, directive, instruction *(direction)*, mandate, monition *(legal summons)*, order *(judicial directive)*, precept, regulation *(rule)*, requirement, rule *(legal dictate)*, statute, summons, writ

commatic sententious

commeasurable commensurate, proportionate

commeatus furlough, leave *(absence)*

commeminisse recollect

commemorare recapitulate, recount

commemorate honor, keep *(fulfill)*, recall *(remember)*, recognize *(acknowledge)*, remember

commemoratio mention *(reference)*

commemoration ceremony, recognition, reminder

commemorative honorary, suggestive *(evocative)*

commemoratory suggestive *(evocative)*

commence embark, initiate, originate, preface, stem *(originate)*, undertake. SEE MAIN ENTRY

commence a suit sue

commence again reopen

commence proceedings against a third party implead

commencement birth *(beginning)*, derivation, embryo, genesis, inception, nascency, origin *(source)*, origination, outset, overt act, preface, prelude, start

commencement of an action service *(delivery of legal process)*

commencing incipient, initial, original *(initial)*

commencing before retroactive

commend advocate, confirm, counsel, countenance, endorse, honor, indorse, recommend

commendable congruous, laudable, meritorious, moral, professional *(stellar)*, unimpeachable

commendableness expedience

commendare recommend

commendatio recommendation

commendation consent, credit *(recognition)*, estimation *(esteem)*, honor *(outward respect)*, mention *(tribute)*, patronage *(support)*, recommendation, reference *(recommendation)*, remembrance *(commemoration)*, respect

commendatory honorary, meritorious

commending favorable *(expressing approval)*

commensurability balance *(equality)*

commensurable commensurate, comparable *(capable of comparison)*, correlative, relative *(comparative)*. SEE MAIN ENTRY

commensurate adequate, coequal, cognate, commensurable, comparable *(equivalent)*, congruous, consonant, correlative,

proportionate, relative *(comparative)*, suitable. SEE MAIN ENTRY

commensurate notice adequate notice

commensurate with pursuant to

commensuration proportion

comment construction, convey *(communicate)*, discourse, discuss, express, interject, mention *(reference)*, muse, notation, note *(brief comment)*, notice *(observe)*, observation, observe *(remark)*, phrase, pronouncement, remark *(noun)*, remark *(verb)*, review *(critical evaluation)*, statement. SEE MAIN ENTRY

comment on converse, edit

comment upon clarify, discuss, elucidate, expound, instruct *(teach)*, mention, review, treat *(process)*

commentary clarification, comment, construction, criticism, discourse, explanation, hornbook, marginalia, notation, note *(brief comment)*, observation, pandect *(treatise)*, proposal *(report)*, remark, review *(critical evaluation)*. SEE MAIN ENTRY

commentate elucidate, expound

commentators press

commenticius fictitious

commentum falsehood, fiction

commercari trade

commerce contact *(association)*, deal, dealings, exchange. SEE MAIN ENTRY

commerce with communicate

commercial industrial, marketable, mercantile, retail. SEE MAIN ENTRY

commercial advantage goodwill

commercial agent factor *(commission merchant)*

commercial backing patronage *(support)*

commercial building development *(building)*

commercial enterprise company *(enterprise)*, corporation, dealings, firm, trade *(commerce)*

commercial establishment enterprise *(economic organization)*, house

commercial failure failure *(bankruptcy)*

commercial house firm

commercial instrument check *(instrument)*

commercial intercourse business *(commerce)*, commerce, dealings

commercial paper check *(instrument)*, draft

commercial profits income

commercial rights SEE MAIN ENTRY

commercial theory finance

commercial transaction deal

commercialize deal

commercium commerce, commercial

comminari threaten

comminate denounce *(condemn)*, menace, threaten

commination denunciation, disapprobation, imprecation, menace, notice *(warning)*, phillipic, threat, warning

comminatory calumnious, critical *(faultfinding)*, sinister

commingle accompany, amalgamate, combine *(join together)*, desegregate, diffuse, join *(bring together)*, unite. SEE MAIN ENTRY

commingled miscellaneous, promiscuous

comminisci invent *(falsify)*

comminute break *(fracture)*

commiscere commingle

commiserate sympathize

commiseration pity, solace

commissaries deputation *(delegation)*

commissary deputy, functionary, supplier

commission act *(undertaking)*, agency *(legal relationship)*, allow *(authorize)*, appoint, assign *(designate)*, assignment *(designation)*, assignment *(task)*, authorize, bestow, board, brokerage, bureau, charge *(command)*, charge *(empower)*, commit *(entrust)*, committee, constitute *(establish)*, delegate, delegation *(assignment)*, delegation *(envoy)*, deputation *(delegation)*, deputation *(selection of delegates)*, designate, detail *(assign)*, dictate, discharge *(performance)*, duty *(obligation)*, earnings, embassy, employ *(engage services)*, employment, empower, engage *(hire)*, hire, induct, infliction, instruction *(direction)*, invest *(vest)*, let *(permit)*, mission, nominate, performance *(execution)*, post, retain *(employ)*, share *(interest)*, transaction, warrant *(authorization)*. SEE MAIN ENTRY

commission agent broker, dealer

commission man dealer

commission merchant broker

commissioned allowed, vicarious *(delegated)*

commissioner caretaker *(one fulfilling the function of office)*, deputy, functionary, incumbent

commissioner of oaths notary public

commissioning delegation *(assignment)*, designation *(naming)*

commit apprehend *(arrest)*, arrest *(apprehend)*, confide *(trust)*, confine, consign, constrain *(imprison)*, contribute *(supply)*, delegate, deliver, deposit *(submit to a bank)*, detain *(hold in custody)*, entrust, execute *(accomplish)*, give *(grant)*, inflict, perpetrate, remand, remit *(submit for consideration)*, sentence, submit *(give)*, undertake. SEE MAIN ENTRY

commit a breach infringe

commit a breach of the law offend *(violate the law)*

commit a crime disobey, offend *(violate the law)*

commit a debauch carouse

commit a fault offend *(violate the law)*

commit again reassign, recommit

commit an error err, lapse *(fall into error)*, miscalculate, mistake, misunderstand

commit an infraction encroach, offend *(violate the law)*

commit anew recommit

commit breach of trust cheat, defraud

commit forgery forge *(counterfeit)*

commit hostilities attack, fight *(battle)*

commit larceny embezzle, pilfer, purloin

commit murder dispatch *(put to death)*

commit offense offend *(violate the law)*

commit oneself assume *(undertake)*, avow, cast *(register)*, decide, guarantee, pledge *(promise the performance of)*, promise *(vow)*

commit oneself to undertake

commit oneself to a course choose

commit perjury lie *(falsify)*

commit piracy pirate *(take by violence)*

commit powers to another assign *(designate)*, delegate

commit robbery hold up *(rob)*, pirate *(take by violence)*, rob

commit sin offend *(violate the law)*

commit to an institution arrest *(apprehend)*, constrain *(imprison)*, immure, imprison, jail, remand

commit to another's trust assign *(transfer ownership)*, consign

commit to prison   arrest *(apprehend)*, confine, constrain *(imprison)*, contain *(restrain)*, immure, imprison, jail
commit to the hands of   delegate
commit to writing   inscribe, note *(record)*, set down. SEE MAIN ENTRY
commit violence   prey
commitment   adhesion *(loyalty)*, agreement *(contract)*, allegiance, assurance, attornment, captivity, charge *(lien)*, charge *(responsibility)*, cloud *(incumbrance)*, compact, constraint *(imprisonment)*, contract, covenant, custody *(incarceration)*, debit, detention, durance, duty *(obligation)*, guaranty, incarceration, incumbrance *(lien)*, indenture, infliction, obligation *(duty)*, pledge *(binding promise)*, promise, recognizance, responsibility *(accountability)*, specialty *(contract)*, undertaking *(pledge)*. SEE MAIN ENTRY
commitments   ties
committal   captivity, commitment *(confinement)*, detention
committed   agreed *(promised)*, arrested *(apprehended)*, bound, contractual, loyal
committed to payment   promissory
committee   agency *(commission)*, assemblage, bureau, caucus, chamber *(body)*, council *(assembly)*, delegation *(envoy)*, deputation *(delegation)*, management *(directorate)*. SEE MAIN ENTRY
committeeperson   member *(individual in a group)*
committere   consign, delegate, entrust, perpetrate
commix   amalgamate, combine *(join together)*, commingle, desegregate
commixed   composite, compound, concerted, miscellaneous
commixtion   incorporation *(blend)*
commixture   coalescence, melange, solution *(substance)*
commodare   lend, loan, serve *(assist)*
commodious   ample, capacious, convenient, extensive, practical, suitable
commodis consulere   welfare
commodities   cargo, goods, merchandise. SEE MAIN ENTRY
commodity   appliance, chattel, item, object, product
commodus   favorable *(advantageous)*, fit, opportune
common   accustomed *(customary)*, average *(standard)*, base *(inferior)*, blatant *(obtrusive)*, boiler plate, civic, cognate, competitive *(open)*, concurrent *(united)*, conjoint, conventional, customary, daily, familiar *(customary)*, frequent, general, generic, habitual, household *(familiar)*, ignoble, inelegant, informal, jejune *(dull)*, joint, mediocre, mundane, mutual *(collective)*, national, nondescript, normal *(regular)*, orthodox, poor *(inferior in quality)*, predominant, prevailing *(current)*, prevalent, pro forma, profane, prosaic, proverbial, public *(affecting people)*, reciprocal, regular *(conventional)*, repeated, rife, routine, stale, tawdry, traditional, trite, typical, usual. SEE MAIN ENTRY
common agreement   mutual understanding
common ancestry   affinity *(family ties)*, blood, propinquity *(kinship)*, relation *(kinship)*
common assent   agreement *(concurrence)*, concordance
common consent   agreement *(concurrence)*, cartel, consensus

common course   practice *(custom)*
common denominator   connection *(relation)*
common derivation   affiliation *(bloodline)*
common descent   relation *(kinship)*
common effort   coaction
common extraction   family *(common ancestry)*
common feature   analogy
common folk   populace
common forebears   family *(common ancestry)*
common fund   pool
common knowledge   publicity. SEE MAIN ENTRY
common lineage   family *(common ancestry)*, relation *(kinship)*
common lot   mediocrity
common occurrence   frequency
common ownership   pool
common parentage   family *(common ancestry)*
common people   populace
common practice   habit, matter of course, procedure
common reference   connection *(relation)*
common run   generality *(bulk)*, matter of course
common saying   catchword
common sense   prudence, reason *(sound judgment)*. SEE MAIN ENTRY
common state of affairs   matter of course
common stock   relation *(kinship)*
common to many   general
common understanding   mutual understanding
common usage   custom
common view   accordance *(understanding)*, agreement *(concurrence)*, compatibility, understanding *(agreement)*
commonage   populace
commonality   mutuality
commonalty   community, populace, population, public
commonere   admonish *(warn)*, remind
commoners   populace
commonition   admonition
commonly   as a rule, generally, invariably
commonly considered   putative
commonly known   household *(familiar)*, proverbial, public *(known)*
commonly observed   customary
commonly practiced   customary
commonness   frequency, mediocrity
commonplace   accustomed *(customary)*, average *(standard)*, boiler plate, common *(customary)*, customary, familiar *(customary)*, habitual, household *(familiar)*, jejune *(dull)*, lifeless *(dull)*, mediocre, mundane, nondescript, normal *(regular)*, ordinary, orthodox, pedestrian, prevailing *(current)*, prevalent, prosaic, proverbial, regular *(conventional)*, repeated, routine, stale, trite, typical, usual
commonplace expression   platitude
commonplace idea   platitude
commonplace phrase   platitude
commonplaceness   mediocrity
commonwealth   community, nationality, polity, public, society, state *(political unit)*
commorance   residence
commorancy   residence
commotion   affray, altercation, brawl, confusion *(turmoil)*, disorder *(lack of order)*, disturbance, embroilment, entanglement *(confusion)*, fracas, fray, furor, imbroglio, outbreak, outburst, pandemonium, riot, trouble, turmoil. SEE MAIN ENTRY

commovere   affect, disturb, move *(alter position)*
communal   civic, civil *(public)*, common *(shared)*, concurrent *(united)*, joint, mutual *(collective)*, public *(affecting people)*
communal business establishment   cooperative
communal society   cooperative
communalistic   mutual *(collective)*
commune   communicate, community, cooperative
commune with   converse, discourse
commune with oneself   muse, ponder, reflect *(ponder)*
communicable   contagious
communicant   deponent, informant, informer *(a person who provides information)*
communicare   communicate, impart
communicate   advise, annunciate, apprise, bestow, circulate, connote, declare, deliver, depict, disabuse, disclose, disseminate, divulge, express, herald, impart, inform *(betray)*, inform *(notify)*, issue *(publish)*, mention, notice *(give formal warning)*, notify, observe *(remark)*, pass *(advance)*, phrase, post, proclaim, promulgate, pronounce *(speak)*, publish, recite, recount, relate *(tell)*, remark, render *(deliver)*, report *(disclose)*, reveal, signify *(inform)*, transmit, utter. SEE MAIN ENTRY
communicate effectively.   SEE MAIN ENTRY
communicate orally   discourse
communicate to   caution
communicate with   converse, reach, speak
communicated   oral
communicatio   communication *(discourse)*
communication   admission *(disclosure)*, caveat, contact *(association)*, conversation, correspondence *(communication by letters)*, disclosure *(act of disclosing)*, disclosure *(something disclosed)*, dispatch *(message)*, expression *(comment)*, information *(knowledge)*, intelligence *(news)*, issuance, language, mention *(reference)*, note *(brief comment)*, notice *(announcement)*, notice *(warning)*, notification, parley, publication *(disclosure)*, report *(detailed account)*, tip *(clue)*, transmittal. SEE MAIN ENTRY
communication of knowledge   advice, declaration
communicative   declaratory, demonstrative *(expressive of emotion)*, eloquent, informative, informatory, loquacious, narrative, responsive
communicator   deponent, informant, informer *(a person who provides information)*
communicatory   advisory, informative
communion   accordance *(understanding)*, concordance, mutual understanding, sodality
communiqué   communication *(discourse)*, declaration, dispatch *(message)*
communique   information *(facts)*, information *(knowledge)*, intelligence *(news)*, issuance, notice *(announcement)*, notification
communis   common *(shared)*, general, joint, ordinary
community   body *(collection)*, civic, coalition, constituency, contact *(association)*, denomination, joint, organization *(association)*, populace, population, public *(open)*, public, society, sodality. SEE MAIN ENTRY
community of interest   cartel, sodality
community of interests   agreement *(concurrence)*, peace
community of possession   pool
commutability   mutuality
commutable   convertible, mutable

commutare alter, modify *(alter)*

commutation clemency, compensation, compromise, exchange, immunity, mutuality, replacement, subrogation

commutative convertible, mutual *(reciprocal)*

commute alter, convert *(change use)*, replace, transform. SEE MAIN ENTRY

commutual common *(shared)*, concurrent *(united)*, conjoint, correlative, mutual *(collective)*, reciprocal, related

compact abstract *(summarize)*, adjustment, agreement *(contract)*, arrangement *(understanding)*, attornment, bargain, brief, cartel, coadunate, composition *(agreement in bankruptcy)*, concentrate *(consolidate)*, conciliation, concise, concordance, conjoint, consensus, consolidate *(strengthen)*, consolidation, consortium *(marriage companionship)*, conspiracy, constrict *(compress)*, contract, corporate *(joint)*, covenant, crystallize, decrease, indenture, league, mutual understanding, pact, pithy, pledge *(binding promise)*, populous, promise, protocol *(agreement)*, reduce, sententious, specialty *(contract)*, stipulation, succinct, treaty, understanding *(agreement)*, undertaking *(pledge)*. SEE MAIN ENTRY

compact to govern constitution

compacted compact *(dense)*, concise

compacting centralization

compactness congealment, density

compages complex *(development)*, corpus

compages frame *(structure)*

companion associate, cohort, colleague, complement, confederate, consociate, consort, copartner *(business associate)*, copartner *(coconspirator)*, correlate, participant, partner, peer, similar

companion in crime coconspirator

companionless solitary

companionship compatibility, consortium *(marriage companionship)*, contact *(association)*, society, sodality

company assemblage, assembly, association *(alliance)*, body *(collection)*, business *(commercial enterprise)*, collection *(assembly)*, concern *(business establishment)*, corporation, enterprise *(economic organization)*, firm, house, organization *(association)*, personnel, syndicate. SEE MAIN ENTRY

comparabilis comparable *(capable of comparison)*

comparability analogy, balance *(equality)*, collation, correspondence *(similarity)*, identity *(similarity)*, parity

comparable analogous, apposite, approximate, coequal, coextensive, cognate, commensurable, commensurate, comparative, correlative, equivalent, identical, proportionate, similar, tantamount. SEE MAIN ENTRY

comparableness balance *(equality)*, relation *(connection)*

comparare compare, contrast, procure, relative *(comparative)*

comparatio comparison

comparative cognate, correlative, proportionate. SEE MAIN ENTRY

comparative estimate collation, comparison

comparative size proportion

comparativeness balance *(equality)*

comparativus comparative

compare correspond *(be equivalent)*, discriminate *(distinguish)*, measure. SEE MAIN ENTRY

compare by observing differences contrast

compare critically diagnose

compare opinions confer *(consult)*

compare to contrast

compare with approximate, contrast

compared cognate, relative *(comparative)*

comparere appear *(attend court proceedings)*, report *(present oneself)*

comparison analogy, collation, correlate, identification, parity, propinquity *(similarity)*, proportion, standard. SEE MAIN ENTRY

compartment cell, section *(division)*, subdivision, zone

compartmentalize insulate, part *(separate)*, partition

compass blockade *(enclosure)*, boundary, caliber *(measurement)*, capacity *(maximum)*, circumscribe *(surround by boundary)*, comprehend *(include)*, demarcate, embrace *(encircle)*, enclose, encompass *(surround)*, envelop, extent, frontier, gamut, hedge, include, outline *(boundary)*, periphery, province, purview, range, region, scope, space

compassion benevolence *(disposition to do good)*, clemency, condonation, consideration *(sympathetic regard)*, humanity *(humaneness)*, indulgence, lenience, pity, tolerance, understanding *(tolerance)*

compassionate lenient, placable, receptive, susceptible *(responsive)*

compatibility accordance *(understanding)*, concert, conformity *(agreement)*, consensus, propinquity *(similarity)*, propriety *(appropriateness)*, qualification *(fitness)*, rapport, relevance, sodality, synchronism. SEE MAIN ENTRY

compatible apposite, concordant, concurrent *(united)*, congruous, conjoint, consensual, consistent, consonant, correlative, fit, harmonious, proportionate, relative *(relevant)*, relevant, suitable, uniform

compatible to pursuant to

compeer associate, colleague, consort, contributor *(contributor)*, copartner *(business associate)*, partner, peer

compel bait *(harass)*, bait *(lure)*, bind *(obligate)*, bind *(restrain)*, cause, coerce, command, constrain *(compel)*, convince, detail *(assign)*, dictate, dominate, enforce, exact, extort, foist, force *(coerce)*, impose *(enforce)*, impose *(subject)*, instruct *(direct)*, make, motivate, necessitate, obsess, order, persuade, press *(constrain)*, pressure, rule *(govern)*. SEE MAIN ENTRY

compel attendance summon

compel attendence subpoena

compel belief convince

compel by intimidation extort

compel by threat extort

compel obedience enforce

compel payment excise *(levy a tax)*

compel to accept foist

compellare accost

compellation call *(title)*

compelled bound

compeller extortionist

compellere compel, constrain *(compel)*

compelling binding, causal, cogent, compulsory, considerable, convincing, decisive, dictatorial, eloquent, exigent, forcible, important *(urgent)*, impulsive *(impelling)*, insistent, irresistible, material *(important)*, necessary *(inescapable)*, necessary *(required)*, obligatory, persuasive, potent, powerful, sound, stringent, strong, unavoidable *(inevitable)*, undeniable, urgent. SEE MAIN ENTRY

compelling quality necessity

compend capsule, compendium, outline *(synopsis)*, summary, synopsis

compendious brief, compact *(pithy)*, comprehensive, concise, laconic, omnibus, pithy, succinct

compendium abridgment *(condensation)*, abstract, brief, capsule, codification, digest, hornbook, outline *(synopsis)*, pandect *(treatise)*, restatement, sum *(tally)*, summary, synopsis. SEE MAIN ENTRY

compensare compensate *(counterbalance)*, redress, requital

compensate bear the expense, contribute *(indemnify)*, defray, disburse *(pay out)*, indemnify, outbalance, pay, quit *(repay)*, recoup *(reimburse)*, redeem *(satisfy debts)*, redress, refund, reimburse, remit *(send payment)*, remunerate, repay, replace, return *(refund)*, satisfy *(discharge)*. SEE MAIN ENTRY

compensate for cover *(provide for)*

compensate for injury indemnify

compensate for loss indemnify

compensate for loss sustained indemnify

compensating compensatory, disbursement *(act of disbursing)*, lucrative

compensatio collection *(payment)*, compensation

compensation advance *(allowance)*, aid *(subsistence)*, benefit *(conferment)*, brokerage, collection *(payment)*, commission *(fee)*, consideration *(recompense)*, contribution *(indemnification)*, damages, disbursement *(funds paid out)*, discharge *(payment)*, earnings, expiation, fee *(charge)*, honorarium, income, indemnification, indemnity, offset, out of pocket, pay, payment *(act of paying)*, payment *(remittance)*, payroll, pension, perquisite, price, profit, recompense, recovery *(award)*, refund, reimbursement, relief *(legal redress)*, remedy *(legal means of redress)*, remuneration, rendition *(restoration)*, rent, reparation *(indemnification)*, replacement, requital, restitution, retainer, retribution, revenue, reward, satisfaction *(discharge of debt)*, tip *(gratuity)*, trover, wage. SEE MAIN ENTRY

compensation for delay demurrage

compensation for injury insurance

compensation for labor fee *(charge)*

compensation for loss insurance

compensation for professional service fee *(charge)*

compensation owed due

compensative compensatory

compensator insurer

compensatory equivalent, lucrative, remedial. SEE MAIN ENTRY

comperire ascertain, discover

compes fetter

compete contend *(dispute)*, dispute *(contest)*, engage *(involve)*, participate, race, strive. SEE MAIN ENTRY

compete for endeavor

compete with antagonize, counter, fight *(battle)*, grapple

competence ability, caliber *(mental capacity)*, capacity *(aptitude)*, discretion *(quality of being discreet)*, efficiency, experience *(background)*, facility *(easiness)*, faculty *(ability)*, force *(strength)*, gift *(flair)*, penchant, performance *(workmanship)*, potential, power, prowess *(ability)*, science (technique), skill, specialty (special aptitude), sufficiency. SEE MAIN ENTRY

competency ability, capacity (aptitude), efficiency, experience (background), faculty (ability), performance (workmanship), prowess (ability), qualification (fitness), quality (excellence), science (technique), sufficiency. SEE MAIN ENTRY

competent adequate, capable, deft, effective (efficient), efficient, expert, familiar (informed), fit, operative, practiced, professional (trained), proficient, reliable, resourceful, sane, sciential. SEE MAIN ENTRY

competent practitioner professional

competere competent

competing competitive (antagonistic), contestable

competition conflict, contention (opposition), rival, strife, struggle. SEE MAIN ENTRY

competitive contentious, hostile, jealous. SEE MAIN ENTRY

competitiveness contention (opposition)

competitor adversary, candidate, contender, foe, peer, rival

competitory competitive (antagonistic)

compilare hold up (rob), plunder

compilation abstract, assemblage, body (collection), building (business of assembling), centralization, code, codification, collection (accumulation), composition (makeup), conglomeration, corpus, cumulation, digest, selection (choice), selection (collection), summary. SEE MAIN ENTRY

compilation of law code, constitution

compilation of laws code

compilations information (knowledge)

compile accumulate (amass), aggregate, build (construct), codify, collect (gather), compose, congregate, garner. SEE MAIN ENTRY

compiled collective

compiler author (writer)

compiler of tables of mortality actuary

complacence composure

complacent benevolent. SEE MAIN ENTRY

complain cite (accuse), criticize (find fault with), deplore, object, protest, reproach. SEE MAIN ENTRY

complain against accuse, arraign, blame, charge (accuse), denounce (inform against), impeach, incriminate

complain frivolously cavil

complain publicly demonstrate (protest)

complainant accuser, actor, claimant, contender, contestant, declarant, informer (one providing criminal information), litigant, malcontent, party (litigant), plaintiff, victim. SEE MAIN ENTRY

complained of accused (charged)

complainer malcontent

complaining criticism, diatribe, disapproval, fractious, querulous

complaining party complainant

complaining witness victim

complaint allegation, charge (accusation), claim (legal demand), condemnation (blame), criticism, denunciation, disapprobation, disapproval, disorder (abnormal condition), disparagement, dissatisfaction, exception (objection), grievance, ground, impeachment, incrimination, indictment, outcry, plaint, pleading, protest, reproach. SEE MAIN ENTRY

complaint to a higher court habeas corpus

complaint to a superior court appeal

complaisance consideration (sympathetic regard), courtesy, deference

complaisant complacent, obedient, obeisant, permissive, yielding

complecti embrace (encircle), encompass (include), include

complement addendum, addition, adjunct, allonge, appendix (accession), boom (increase), codicil, component, content (structure), corollary, correlate, correspond (be equivalent), rider, staff, supplement. SEE MAIN ENTRY

complemental concomitant, correlative, mutual (reciprocal), reciprocal

complemental term correlate

complementary cognate, concordant, concurrent (united), convertible, correlative, mutual (reciprocal), pendent, reciprocal, related

complementing ancillary (subsidiary)

complementum complement

complete accomplish, adjust (resolve), arrant (definite), attain, cap, carry (succeed), categorical, close (terminate), commit (perpetrate), comply, comprehensive, conclusive (settled), consummate, culminate, definitive, detailed, discharge (perform), discontinue (abandon), dispatch (dispose of), effectuate, execute (accomplish), exhaust (try all possibilities), fabricate (construct), finish, follow-up, fulfill, full, gross (total), implement, intact, inviolate, keep (fulfill), lapse (cease), make, omnibus, outright, peremptory (absolute), perfect, perform (adhere to), perform (execute), plenary, pure, radical (extreme), realize (make real), replenish, replete, ripe, stark, terminate, thorough, total, unconditional, unmitigated, unqualified (unlimited), whole (undamaged). SEE MAIN ENTRY

complete a purchase buy

complete body of laws pandect (code of laws)

complete conviction certainty, certification (certainness), surety (certainty)

complete digest pandect (treatise)

complete lawsuit day in court

complete prosecution rest (end a legal case)

complete report accounting

complete sequence gamut

complete series gamut

complete standstill impasse

complete substitution novation

complete trust credence

completed complete (ended), conclusive (settled), definitive, fully executed (consummated), fully executed (signed), through

completely fairly (clearly), in toto, wholly

completely end destroy (void)

completely full replete

completeness conclusion (outcome), entirety, fait accompli, finality, quorum, totality, whole

completing ancillary (auxiliary), conclusive (settled), final

completion cessation (termination), close (conclusion), commission (act), complement, conclusion (outcome), consequence (conclusion), course, denouement, discharge (performance), dissolution (termination), end (termination), entirety, expiration, extremity (death), fait accompli, finality, follow-up, maturity, outcome, performance (execution), realization, transaction. SEE MAIN ENTRY

completive complete (ended), comprehensive, conclusive (settled), last (final)

completory last (final)

complex composite, compound, conglomerate, difficult, elaborate, inextricable, intricate, labyrinthine, obscure (abstruse), problematic, recondite, sinuous, sophisticated. SEE MAIN ENTRY

complexion appearance (look), condition (state), spirit, state (condition). SEE MAIN ENTRY

complexity complication, confusion (turmoil), enigma, entanglement (confusion), imbroglio, impasse, involution, problem

complexness complication

complexus complex (entanglement)

complexus complication

complexus corpus, snarl

compliable complacent, consenting, consistent, facile, obedient, obsequious, passive, pliant

compliance acceptance, accordance (understanding), acknowledgment (acceptance), acquiescence, adherence (devotion), amenability, assent, capitulation, comity, compatibility, conciliation, conduct, conformity (obedience), conjunction, consent, consortium (marriage companionship), conspiracy, deference, discipline (obedience), fealty, homage, indorsement, loyalty, timeliness, understanding (agreement). SEE MAIN ENTRY

compliancy amenability, compliance

compliant amenable, charitable (lenient), complacent, concordant, consensual, consenting, facile, favorable (expressing approval), loyal, malleable, obedient, obeisant, obsequious, orthodox, passive, patient, pliable, pliant, prone, ready (willing), sequacious, servile, tractable, true (loyal), willing (not averse), yielding. SEE MAIN ENTRY

compliantly faithfully, respectfully

complicate aggravate (exacerbate), confound, dislocate, disorganize, muddle, obfuscate, perplex, perturb. SEE MAIN ENTRY

complicated circuitous, complex, compound, difficult, elaborate, inextricable, intricate, labyrinthine, problematic, profound (esoteric), recondite, sinuous, tortuous (bending)

complicated misunderstanding imbroglio

complicated state complication

complication aggravation (annoyance), complex (entanglement), confusion (ambiguity), embroilment, entanglement (confusion), hindrance, imbroglio, involution, predicament, problem, quagmire, snarl. SEE MAIN ENTRY

complicity bad faith, bribery, cabal, coaction, collusion, concert, confederacy (conspiracy), connivance, conspiracy, contribution (participation), contrivance, corruption, implication (incriminating involvement), league, plot (secret plan). SEE MAIN ENTRY

compliment belaud, doxology, honor, mention (tribute), recommend

complimentary free (at no charge), gratis, gratuitous (given without recompense), unsolicited

complot cabal, collusion, confederacy (conspiracy), connivance, connive, maneuver, plan (noun), plan (verb), plot (secret plan), scheme

complotter conspirator

comply abide, accede (concede), accept (admit as sufficient), accept (assent), adhere (maintain loyalty), assent, concur (agree), conform, consent, defer (yield in judgment), discharge (perform), hear (give *attention to),* heed, obey, serve *(assist),* submit *(yield),* succumb, suffer *(permit),* yield *(submit).* SEE MAIN ENTRY

comply with adapt, agree *(comply),* concede, correspond *(be equivalent),* fulfill, keep *(fulfill),* observe *(obey),* perform *(adhere to),* satisfy *(fulfill),* vouchsafe

complying law-abiding, obedient, passive, true *(loyal)*

component adjunct, affiliate, chapter *(branch),* chapter *(division),* color *(complexion),* constituent *(part),* detail, element, factor *(ingredient),* feature *(characteristic),* ingredient, integral, item, member *(constituent part),* organ, part *(portion),* section *(division),* segment, subdivision, unit *(item).* SEE MAIN ENTRY

component part component, constituent *(part),* detail, element, ingredient

components contents

componere agree *(comply),* arrange *(methodize),* compare, compile, compose, constitute *(compose),* frame *(formulate),* organize *(arrange),* pacify

comport demean *(deport oneself).* SEE MAIN ENTRY

comport oneself deport *(conduct oneself)*

comport with cohere *(be logically consistent),* correspond *(be equivalent)*

comportment behavior, conduct, demeanor, deportment, manner *(behavior),* presence *(poise)*

compose accommodate, allay, alleviate, assuage, build *(construct),* compile, conceive *(invent),* contrive, create, devise *(invent),* fabricate *(construct),* forge *(produce),* form, formulate, frame *(construct),* invent *(produce for the first time),* lull, make, manufacture, marshal, mollify, orchestrate, originate, produce *(manufacture),* scheme, soothe. SEE MAIN ENTRY

compose differences intercede

compose oneself repose *(rest)*

composed complacent, dispassionate, nonchalant, patient, peaceable, placid

composed of several elements multiple

composer architect, author *(originator)*

composer of a literary work author *(writer)*

composite coherent *(joined),* collective, complex *(development),* compound, concerted, conglomerate, conjoint, content *(structure),* miscellaneous, omnibus, promiscuous, solution *(substance).* SEE MAIN ENTRY

composite representation cross section

compositio accommodation *(adjustment),* arrangement *(ordering),* composition *(makeup),* settlement

composition adjustment, arrangement *(ordering),* array *(order),* building *(business of assembling),* combination, compromise, configuration *(form),* conspiracy, content *(structure),* coverage *(scope),* creation, formation, invention, language, manufacture, melange, motif, order *(arrangement),* organization *(structure),* origination, performance *(workmanship),* phraseology, solution *(substance),* temperament. SEE MAIN ENTRY

composition of differences accommodation *(adjustment)*

compositional skill rhetoric *(skilled speech)*

compositus composite, compound

composure common sense, longanimity, moderation, sufferance. SEE MAIN ENTRY

composure of differences settlement

composure of doubts settlement

compound adhere *(fasten),* close *(enclosed area),* coalescence, collective, combination, combine *(join together),* commingle, complex *(development),* composite, confines, conglomerate, conjoin, consolidate *(strengthen),* consolidate *(unite),* desegregate, incorporate *(include),* incorporation *(blend),* join *(bring together),* make, melange, merge, solution *(substance).* SEE MAIN ENTRY

compounded composite, conglomerate, inextricable. SEE MAIN ENTRY

compounding building *(business of assembling),* composition *(makeup)*

comprehend apprehend *(perceive),* discern *(detect with the senses),* include, perceive, pierce *(discern),* realize *(understand),* recognize *(perceive),* understand. SEE MAIN ENTRY

comprehendable comprehensible

comprehended from accompanying words noscitur a sociis

comprehendere apprehend *(arrest),* apprehend *(perceive),* arrest *(apprehend),* capture, comprehend *(understand),* contain *(comprise),* embrace *(encircle),* include, realize *(understand),* seize *(apprehend)*

comprehending cognizant, conscious *(aware),* knowing, lucid, omniscient, perceptive, receptive

comprehensibility coherence

comprehensible cognizable, coherent *(clear),* explicit, lucid, obvious, pellucid, perceptible, ponderable, scrutable, unambiguous. SEE MAIN ENTRY

comprehensio comprehension

comprehension appreciation *(perception),* apprehension *(perception),* caliber *(mental capacity),* cognition, connotation, coverage *(scope),* discrimination *(differentiation),* information *(knowledge),* insight, intellect, intelligence *(intellect),* judgment *(discernment),* knowledge *(awareness),* perception, realization, reason *(sound judgment),* recognition, sagacity, sanity, scienter, sense *(intelligence),* sensibility. SEE MAIN ENTRY

comprehensive absolute *(complete),* ample, broad, capacious, collective, competitive *(open),* complete *(all-embracing),* detailed, extensive, far reaching, full, generic, gross *(total),* inclusive, indiscriminate, major, nonsectarian, omnibus, outright, plenary, prevailing *(current),* radical *(extreme),* thorough. SEE MAIN ENTRY

comprehensive digest pandect *(treatise)*

comprehensively in toto

comprehensiveness capacity *(maximum),* corpus, coverage *(scope),* entirety, extent, totality. SEE MAIN ENTRY

compress abridge *(shorten),* abstract *(summarize),* cohere *(adhere),* concentrate *(consolidate),* condense, consolidate *(strengthen),* consolidate *(unite),* crystallize, decrease, diminish, impact, lessen, reduce

compressed brief, coherent *(joined),* cohesive *(compact),* compact *(dense),* concise, laconic, narrow, pithy, sententious, solid *(compact)*

compressed statement summary

compression abridgment *(condensation),* abstract, blockade *(limitation),* capsule, centralization, curtailment, outline *(synopsis),* scenario

comprimere repress, withhold

comprisal composition *(makeup),* coverage *(scope)*

comprise comprehend *(include),* consist, constitute *(compose),* encompass *(include).* SEE MAIN ENTRY

comprising comprehensive, inclusive

comprobare approve, confirm, corroborate

comprobatio acceptance, approval, indorsement

compromisable convertible

compromise accommodation *(adjustment),* accord, adjustment, agree *(contract),* arrangement *(understanding),* bargain, collective bargaining, compact, conciliation, contract, deal, denigrate, endanger, find *(determine),* give *(yield),* mediate, negotiation, pact, settle, settlement. SEE MAIN ENTRY

compromise agreement composition *(agreement in bankruptcy)*

compromised agreed *(harmonized)*

compromiser referee, umpire

compromising calumnious, contemptuous, disgraceful, intermediate

compromittere compromise *(settle by mutual agreement)*

compte rendu account *(evaluation)*

comptroller SEE MAIN ENTRY

compulsatory obligatory

compulsion coercion, constraint *(restriction),* deterrence, dipsomania, duress, enforcement, extortion, force *(compulsion),* main force, motive, need *(requirement),* obligation *(duty),* obsession, oppression, pressure, requirement, responsibility *(accountability),* servitude, stress *(strain).* SEE MAIN ENTRY

compulsive compelling, obligatory

compulsorily acquire condemn *(seize),* confiscate, distrain

compulsory binding, choate lien, compelling, essential *(required),* exigent, forcible, imperative, indispensable, involuntary, mandatory, necessary *(required),* obligatory, peremptory *(imperative),* positive *(prescribed),* prescriptive, requisite, stringent, unavoidable *(inevitable),* urgent. SEE MAIN ENTRY

compulsory acquisition condemnation *(seizure),* disseisin, requisition

compulsory detail necessity, need *(requirement)*

compulsory execution enforcement

compulsory payment fine, penalty, punishment

compulsory purchase expropriation *(right of eminent domain)*

compulsory service bondage

compunction conscience, qualm, remorse, responsibility *(conscience),* scruple

compunctious blameful, contrite, penitent, remorseful, repentant

compurgate acquit, confess

compurgation acquittal, deposition, justification, pardon, release. SEE MAIN ENTRY

compurgator deponent, eyewitness, witness

computable appreciable, determinable *(ascertainable)*

computare calculate

computation accounting, appraisal, census, estimate *(approximate cost),* estimation *(calculation),* ledger, measurement. SEE MAIN ENTRY

compute assess *(appraise),* calculate, charge *(assess),* gauge, measure, poll, rate, sum, survey *(poll)*

comrade cohort, colleague, confederate, consociate, consort, contributor *(contributor),* copartner *(coconspirator),* member (*individual in a group*), participant, partisan, peer

comrade in crime coconspirator

comrade in wrongdoing coconspirator

comradeship consortium (*marriage companionship*), contribution (*participation*), society, sodality

con contra, deception, peruse, read

con game bunko

conari attempt, endeavor, strive, try (*attempt*)

conation conatus

conative discretionary, voluntary

conative will conatus

conatus effort, endeavor. SEE MAIN ENTRY

concatenate combine (*join together*), consolidate (*strengthen*), join (*bring together*)

concatenation chain (*series*), conjunction, connection (*fastening*), joinder, sequence, succession

conceal blind (*obscure*), camouflage, circumvent, cloak, clothe, disguise, distort, ensconce, enshroud, envelop, expurgate, harbor, hedge, hide, misguide, misinform, obfuscate, obliterate, obnubilate, obscure, screen (*guard*), seclude, sequester (*seclude*), shroud, stifle, suppress, withhold. SEE MAIN ENTRY

conceal from knowledge hide

conceal from sight blind (*obscure*), hide

conceal oneself lurk

conceal the truth cloak, prevaricate

concealed clandestine, confidential, covert, esoteric, evasive, furtive, hidden, impalpable, incomprehensible, inconspicuous, indiscernible, inexplicable, inscrutable, latent, mysterious, oblique (*evasive*), obscure (*faint*), opaque, personal (*private*), potential, private (*confidential*), privy, recondite, secret, stealthy, surreptitious, ulterior, undisclosed. SEE MAIN ENTRY

concealed knowledge secret

concealment artifice, color (*deceptive appearance*), confidence (*relation of trust*), disguise, evasion, mystery, nonappearance, obscuration, privacy, subterfuge, veil. SEE MAIN ENTRY

concealment of truth indirection (*deceitfulness*)

concede abandon (*relinquish*), acknowledge (*verify*), agree (*comply*), allow (*endure*), assent, authorize, bear (*tolerate*), bestow, cede, compromise (*settle by mutual agreement*), confess, confirm, conform, forfeit, give (*grant*), give (*yield*), let (*permit*), recognize (*acknowledge*), reveal, succumb, suffer (*permit*), surrender (*yield*), vouchsafe, yield (*submit*). SEE MAIN ENTRY

conceded agreed (*harmonized*), allowed, consensual

conceded judgment cognovit

concededly admittedly

concedere admit (*concede*), cede, comply, concede, grant (*concede*), grant (*transfer formally*), let (*permit*), retire (*retreat*), vouchsafe, yield (*submit*)

conceit idea, jactation

conceited inflated (*vain*), orgulous, presumptuous, pretentious (*pompous*)

conceivability chance (*possibility*), likelihood, possibility, probability

conceivable believable, colorable (*plausible*), comprehensible, constructive (*inferential*), plausible, possible, potential, presumptive, probable, prospective, viable

conceivableness chance (*possibility*), likelihood, possibility

conceive appreciate (*comprehend*), compose, comprehend (*understand*), conjure, contrive, create, deem, devise (*invent*), frame (*formulate*), initiate, invent (*produce for the first time*), originate, presume, produce (*manufacture*), recognize (*perceive*), reflect (*ponder*), reproduce, surmise, understand. SEE MAIN ENTRY

conceive of apprehend (*perceive*), construe (*comprehend*)

conceived of parents legally married legitimate (*lawfully conceived*)

concent consensus

concenter concentrate (*consolidate*), converge, focus

centralization centralization

concentralize converge

concentrate accumulate (*amass*), border (*approach*), collect (*gather*), congregate, consolidate (*strengthen*), consolidate (*unite*), constrict (*compress*), converge, decrease, devote, distill, draw (*extract*), intensify, muse, reflect (*ponder*). SEE MAIN ENTRY

concentrate on focus, occupy (*engage*), specialize

concentrate the mind focus

concentrate the thoughts focus

concentrate upon ponder

concentrated cohesive (*compact*), collective, compact (*dense*), intense, intensive, solid (*compact*), strong

concentrating cumulative (*intensifying*), earnest, pensive

concentration assemblage, barrage, centralization, collection (*accumulation*), contemplation, corpus, cumulation, density, emphasis, interest (*concern*), observation, preoccupation, reflection (*thought*), regard (*attention*), strength. SEE MAIN ENTRY

concentric coextensive

concentus consensus

concept conviction (*persuasion*), idea, impression, notion, vision (*dream*). SEE MAIN ENTRY

conception apprehension (*perception*), arrangement (*plan*), cognition, comprehension, concept, conviction (*persuasion*), design (*construction plan*), idea, impression, notion, perspective, presumption, side, supposition, understanding (*comprehension*), vision (*dream*)

conceptualize conceive (*comprehend*), conjure

concern affinity (*regard*), agitate (*perturb*), appertain, apply (*pertain*), apprehension (*fear*), business (*affair*), business (*commercial enterprise*), calling, caution (*vigilance*), charge (*custody*), company (*enterprise*), consideration (*sympathetic regard*), corporation, devote, diligence (*care*), discretion (*quality of being discreet*), enterprise (*economic organization*), fear, firm, house, importance, institute, interest, magnitude, market (*business*), matter (*subject*), misgiving, mission, object, part (*role*), pertain, position (*business status*), profession (*vocation*), prudence, pursuit (*occupation*), purview, qualm, refer (*direct attention*), regard (*attention*), relate (*establish a connection*), relevance, remorse, scruple, significance, store (*business*), trade (*occupation*), undertaking (*enterprise*). SEE MAIN ENTRY

concern oneself with address (*direct attention to*), discharge (*perform*), occupy (*engage*), specialize

concerned careful, interested, solicitous, suspicious (*distrustful*)

concerning correlative, germane, pertinent, relative (*relevant*), relevant, wherein

concerning the law forensic, juridical

concernment concern (*interest*), importance, significance

concerns affairs

concert affiliation (*connectedness*), cartel, coherence, collusion, combine (*act in concert*), conciliation, concordance, conformity (*agreement*), conjunction, connivance, connive, consensus, consolidate (*unite*), conspiracy, conspire, contribution (*participation*), cooperate, federate, federation, orchestrate, propinquity (*similarity*), synergy, union (*unity*). SEE MAIN ENTRY

concert of action coaction

concertare dispute (*contest*)

concerted associated, coadunate, collective, concurrent (*at the same time*), concurrent (*united*), conjoint, consonant, joint. SEE MAIN ENTRY

concerted refusal to work strike

concessio admission (*disclosure*), concession (*authorization*)

concession accord, acknowledgment (*acceptance*), acquiescence, admission (*disclosure*), advancement (*loan*), appropriation (*allotment*), cession, compliance, compromise, conciliation, consent, consignment, copyright, disclosure (*act of disclosing*), disclosure (*something disclosed*), expense (*sacrifice*), franchise (*license*), grace, grace period, grant, sufferance. SEE MAIN ENTRY

concessive obsequious, passive, pliant

concidere fail (*lose*)

concierge caretaker (*one caring for property*)

conciliable nonmilitant

conciliate arbitrate (*adjudge*), compromise (*settle by mutual agreement*), disarm (*set at ease*), intercede, mediate, mollify, pacify, placate, propitiate, reconcile

conciliated agreed (*harmonized*)

conciliatio conciliation

conciliation accordance (*compact*), amnesty, arbitration, collective bargaining, condonation, intercession, mediation, mollification, peace, reconciliation, settlement. SEE MAIN ENTRY

conciliative nonmilitant

conciliator go-between, intermediary

conciliator referee

conciliatory nonmilitant, obeisant, penitent, placable. SEE MAIN ENTRY

concinere agree (*comply*)

concinnity accordance (*understanding*), conformity (*agreement*), consensus, proportion

concinnous felicitous, harmonious

concipere conceive (*invent*), frame (*formulate*)

concise brief, coherent (*clear*), cohesive (*compact*), compact (*pithy*), laconic, pithy, sententious, succinct, summary. SEE MAIN ENTRY

concise treatment compendium

concitare rebel

conclave assemblage, assembly, caucus, company (*assemblage*), conference, congregation, council (*assembly*), meeting (*conference*), parley, session

conclude adjudge, adjudicate, adjust (*resolve*), ascertain, assume (*suppose*), award, cap, cease, close (*terminate*), complete, construe (*comprehend*), consummate, culminate, decide, deduce, deduct (*conclude by reasoning*), deem, derive (*deduce*), determine, discharge (*perform*), discontinue (*abandon*), dispatch (*dispose of*), dissolve (*terminate*), expect (*consider probable*), expire, find (*determine*), finish, fix (*settle*), generalize, hold (*decide*), infer, judge, lapse (*cease*), liquidate (*convert into cash*), opine, perfect, perform (*adhere to*), presume, pronounce (*pass judgment*), read, reason (*conclude*), result, rule (*decide*), settle, stop, surmise, suspect (*think*), terminate, understand. SEE MAIN ENTRY

conclude from evidence construe (*comprehend*), infer

conclude proceeding rest (*end a legal case*)

concluded complete (*ended*), res judicata, through. SEE MAIN ENTRY

concludere conclude (*decide*), infer, lock

concluding dialectic, extreme (*last*), final, last (*final*)

concluding part end (*termination*)

conclusible deductible (*provable*)

conclusio close (*conclusion*), conclusion (*determination*), conclusion (*outcome*), inference

conclusion adjudication, alternative (*option*), amount (*result*), belief (*something believed*), belief (*state of mind*), cessation (*termination*), choice (*decision*), concept, consequence (*conclusion*), conviction (*persuasion*), defeasance, denouement, destination, determination, development (*outgrowth*), diagnosis, discharge (*performance*), disposition (*determination*), dissolution (*termination*), divorce, end (*termination*), expiration, extremity (*death*), finality, finding, generalization, holding (*ruling of a court*), inference, judgment (*discernment*), judgment (*formal court decree*), observation, opinion (*belief*), opinion (*judicial decision*), payoff (*result*), position (*point of view*), result, ruling, verdict. SEE MAIN ENTRY

conclusion beforehand predetermination

conclusion drawn from accepted truths hypothesis

conclusion in advance predetermination

conclusion of a proceeding dismissal (*termination of a proceeding*)

conclusion of an action dismissal (*termination of a proceeding*)

conclusion of the matter holding (*ruling of a court*), opinion (*judicial decision*)

conclusive categorical, certain (*fixed*), certain (*positive*), clear (*certain*), cogent, complete (*ended*), convincing, crucial, decisive, definite, definitive, demonstrable, determinative, extreme (*last*), final, inappealable, incontestable, incontrovertible, last (*final*), official, positive (*incontestable*), reliable, ultimate, unalienable, undeniable, undisputed, unmistakable, valid. SEE MAIN ENTRY

conclusive evidence corroboration

conclusive proof certification (*certainness*), corroboration

conclusiveness certainty, certification (*certainness*), certitude, proof. SEE MAIN ENTRY

conclusory conclusive (*settled*), decisive, definitive, final, last (*final*), ultimate

concoct conceive (*invent*), contrive, create, feign, forge (*produce*), frame (*construct*), frame (*formulate*), invent (*produce*

for the first time*), lie (*falsify*), make, maneuver, originate, palter, plan, prearrange, prevaricate, produce (*manufacture*), profess (*pretend*), scheme

concoct a plot conspire

concocted artificial, false (*inaccurate*), fictitious, mendacious

concoction arrangement (*plan*), composition (*makeup*), creation, fiction, figment, formation, invention, myth, story (*falsehood*)

concomitance conjunction

concomitant addendum, appurtenance, coincidental, collateral (*accompanying*), concurrent (*at the same time*), conjoint, consensual, contemporaneous, simultaneous, supplementary. SEE MAIN ENTRY

concord accord, accordance (*compact*), affirmance (*judicial sanction*), agree (*comply*), agreement (*concurrence*), arrangement (*understanding*), assent, bargain, cartel, collusion, comity, compact, compatibility, compliance, concert, conciliation, concordance, condonation, conformity (*agreement*), conjunction, connivance, consensus, consent, cooperate, league, pact, partnership, peace, propinquity (*similarity*), protocol (*agreement*), rapport, rapprochement, reciprocity, reconciliation, sodality, synchronism, understanding (*agreement*), union (*unity*)

concord before marriage antenuptial agreement

concordance acceptance, accord, accordance (*compact*), acquiescence, affirmance (*judicial sanction*), agreement (*concurrence*), approval, assent, bargain, cartel, compatibility, concert, consensus, consent, consortium (*marriage companionship*), mutual understanding, pact, peace, rapport, rapprochement, reconciliation, treaty, understanding (*agreement*). SEE MAIN ENTRY

concordancy peace

concordant agreed (*harmonized*), appropriate, commensurable, commensurate, concerted, concurrent (*united*), congruous, consensual, consenting, consistent, consonant, correlative, felicitous, fit, harmonious, joint, nonmilitant. SEE MAIN ENTRY

concordat agreement (*contract*), bargain, cartel, compact, contract, covenant, league, pact, protocol (*agreement*), settlement, specialty (*contract*), stipulation, treaty

concordia agreement (*contract*), peace

concors concordant, harmonious

concours meeting (*encounter*)

concourse assemblage, assembly, caucus, causeway, coaction, intersection, rendezvous

concredere entrust

concrescence coalescence. SEE MAIN ENTRY

concrete actual, appreciable, cement, certain (*positive*), certain (*specific*), cohesive (*compact*), corporeal, distinct (*clear*), material (*physical*), objective, physical, substantial, substantive, tangible. SEE MAIN ENTRY

concrete expression embodiment

concrete results action (*performance*)

concreteness congealment, materiality (*physical existence*)

concretion adherence (*adhesion*), adhesion (*affixing*), congealment, corpus, density

concupiscence desire

concupiscent dissolute, lascivious, lecherous, lewd, licentious, prurient, salacious

concur abide, accede (*concede*), acknowledge (*respond*), admit (*concede*), agree (*comply*), assent, certify (*approve*), comply, comport (*agree with*), confirm, conform,

consent, conspire, cooperate, correspond (*be equivalent*), grant (*concede*), meet, unite. SEE MAIN ENTRY

concur in approve, certify (*approve*), countenance, embrace (*accept*), indorse

concurred in consensual

concurrence accordance (*compact*), accordance (*understanding*), acknowledgment (*acceptance*), acquiescence, adjustment, approval, assent, cartel, charter (*sanction*), coaction, coalescence, coalition, collusion, compatibility, compliance, concert, concession (*compromise*), conciliation, concordance, confederacy (*compact*), conformity (*agreement*), conjunction, connivance, consensus, consent, indorsement, league, leave (*permission*), mutual understanding, permission, rapport, synchronism, synergy, union (*unity*)

concurrence in opinions concordance

concurrency concert

concurrent coextensive, cognate, coincidental, collateral (*accompanying*), collective, commensurable, concerted, concomitant, concordant, congruous, conjoint, consensual, consonant, contemporaneous, corporate (*joint*), correlative, current, joint, mutual (*reciprocal*), simultaneous, synergetic. SEE MAIN ENTRY

concurrent cause. SEE MAIN ENTRY

concurrent effort cooperative

concurrent opinion conformity (*agreement*), conjunction, connivance

concurrere coincide (*correspond*), meet

concurring concerted, concordant, concurrent (*united*), contemporaneous, synergetic

concursio collision (*dispute*)

concursus collision (*dispute*), meeting (*conference*)

concuss beat (*strike*), necessitate

concussion collision (*accident*)

condemn blame, cavil, censure, charge (*accuse*), complain (*criticize*), confiscate, convict, criticize (*find fault with*), decry, defame, denigrate, discommend, disparage, execute (*sentence to death*), fault, impeach, incriminate, judge, libel, proscribe (*denounce*), punish, reprehend, reprimand, reproach, sentence. SEE MAIN ENTRY

condemn after judicial investigation convict

condemn as worthless decry

condemn beforehand prejudge

condemn openly denounce (*condemn*)

condemn to death execute (*sentence to death*)

condemn to public use confiscate

condemnable blameful, blameworthy, contemptible, culpable, delinquent (*guilty of a misdeed*), felonious, guilty, inexcusable, inexpiable, irregular (*improper*), reprehensible

condemnare condemn (*blame*), disapprove (*reject*), sentence

condemnatio condemnation (*blame*)

condemnation aspersion, bad repute, blame (*culpability*), charge (*accusation*), confutation, contempt (*disdain*), conviction (*finding of guilt*), correction (*punishment*), count, criticism, denunciation, diatribe, disapprobation, disapproval, discredit, disparagement, expropriation (*right of eminent domain*), ignominy, impeachment, impugnation, inculpation, judgment (*formal court decree*), onus (*stigma*), ostracism, outcry, proscription, rebuff, reprimand, reproach, revilement, sanction (*punishment*). SEE MAIN ENTRY

condemnation for public use expropriation *(right of eminent domain)*
condemnatory blameworthy, calumnious, contemptible, critical *(faultfinding)*, cynical, derogatory, incriminatory, inculpatory, libelous, scandalous, severe
condemned blameful, blameworthy, dilapidated
condemned person convict
condemned prisoner convict
condemning critical *(faultfinding)*, incriminatory, inculpatory
condensation abstract, adhesion *(affixing)*, brief, capsule, centralization, compendium, congealment, curtailment, digest, hornbook, outline *(synopsis)*, paraphrase, restatement, scenario, synopsis
condense abridge *(shorten)*, abstract *(summarize)*, concentrate *(consolidate)*, consolidate *(strengthen)*, constrict *(compress)*, crystallize, decrease, digest *(summarize)*, discount *(minimize)*, distill, draw *(extract)*, lessen, reduce. SEE MAIN ENTRY
condensed brief, compact *(dense)*, compact *(pithy)*, concise, laconic, pithy, sententious, solid *(compact)*, succinct
condere garner, keep *(shelter)*
condescend deign, vouchsafe. SEE MAIN ENTRY
condescend to grant vouchsafe
condescending disdainful, inflated *(vain)*, orgulous, proud *(conceited)*, supercilious
condescension disrespect, pride
condicio article *(precept)*, condition *(contingent provision)*, condition *(state)*, contract, overture, posture *(situation)*, proposition, provision *(clause)*, qualification *(condition)*, stipulation, term *(provision)*
condicio mortalis mortality
condign appropriate, due *(owed)*, just, proper, suitable. SEE MAIN ENTRY
condire preserve
condisciple disciple
condition aspect, attornment, case *(set of circumstances)*, clause, climate, discipline *(train)*, disease, disorder *(abnormal condition)*, frame *(mood)*, health, inure *(accustom)*, limitation, modify *(moderate)*, plight, position *(situation)*, posture *(situation)*, practice *(train by repetition)*, predicament, prerequisite, provision *(clause)*, quality *(grade)*, repair, reservation *(condition)*, restriction, salvo, sine qua non, situation, specification, status, stipulation, term *(provision)*, ultimatum. SEE MAIN ENTRY
condition of a married woman coverture
condition of infamy disgrace
condition of insufficiency emergency
conditional circumstantial, dependent, doubtful, dubious, provisional, qualified *(conditioned)*, restrictive, tentative, terminable. SEE MAIN ENTRY
conditional conveyance of land mortgage
conditional deed held in trust escrow
conditional deliverance parole
conditional discharge parole
conditional disenthrallment parole
conditional disimprisonment parole
conditional emancipation parole
conditional endorsement without recourse
conditional event contingency
conditional freedom parole
conditional freedom from confinement parole
conditional independence parole

conditional instrument escrow
conditional liberation parole
conditional liberty parole
conditional property transfer mortgage
conditional release parole
conditional reprieve parole
conditional suspension of sentence probation
conditionally release parole
conditionally release from imprisonment parole
conditioned accustomed *(familiarized)*, conditional, contingent, controlled *(restrained)*, *dependent*
conditioning discipline *(training)*, habituation, propaganda
conditions circumstances
conditiosine qua non clause
conditus savory
condole sympathize
condolement pity
condolence pity, solace
condolent benevolent
condonable blameless, defensible, justifiable, palliative *(excusing)*, pardonable, unobjectionable
condonare forgive, overlook *(superintend)*, remit *(relax)*
condonation amnesty, impunity, lenience, remission, understanding *(tolerance)*. SEE MAIN ENTRY
condone bear *(tolerate)*, concur *(agree)*, excuse, extenuate, forgive, justify, overlook *(excuse)*, palliate *(excuse)*, pardon, remit *(release from penalty)*. SEE MAIN ENTRY
condoned clear *(free from criminal charges)*
condoning charitable *(lenient)*, lenient, palliative *(excusing)*
conduce affect, avail *(bring about)*, contribute *(assist)*, generate, induce, redound. SEE MAIN ENTRY
conduce to cause
conducere conduce, engage *(hire)*, hire, rent
conducive ancillary *(auxiliary)*, beneficial, contributory, convenient, favorable *(advantageous)*, instrumental, practical, propitious
conduct administration, agency *(legal relationship)*, behavior, comport *(behave)*, control *(regulate)*, course, decorum, demean *(deport oneself)*, demeanor, deportment, direct *(show)*, direct *(supervise)*, direction *(guidance)*, discipline *(training)*, ethics, exercise *(discharge a function)*, govern, handle *(manage)*, manage, management *(judicious use)*, manipulate *(utilize skillfully)*, manner *(behavior)*, modus operandi, officiate, operate, orchestrate, overlook *(superintend)*, oversee, practice *(procedure)*, prescribe, presence *(poise)*, procedure, process *(course)*, prosecute *(carry forward)*, protect, pursue *(carry on)*, regulate *(manage)*, regulation *(management)*, render *(administer)*, rule *(govern)*, transact, transmit, transport, usage. SEE MAIN ENTRY
conduct a search frisk, hunt
conduct a trial hear *(give a legal hearing)*
conduct an inquiry analyze, audit, canvass, delve, investigate, monitor, probe
conduct business handle *(trade)*
conduct dishonestly mishandle *(mismanage)*
conduct involving graft corruption
conduct of a lawsuit proceeding
conduct of affairs agency *(legal relationship)*

conduct research inquire
conduct research on examine *(study)*, peruse, poll, probe
conduct without efficiency mishandle *(mismanage)*
conduct without honesty mishandle *(mismanage)*
conductio contract, lease
conductive causal
conductor chairman, guardian
conductor lessee
conductor procurator
conductor tenant
conductus mercenary
conduit dealer, outlet. SEE MAIN ENTRY
conectere join *(bring together)*
confabulate communicate, converse, discourse, discuss
confabulation conference, conversation, speech
confectio consumption
confederacy affiliation *(amalgamation)*, association *(alliance)*, cabal, chamber *(body)*, coaction, coalescence, collusion, committee, company *(enterprise)*, connivance, consortium *(business cartel)*, conspiracy, corporation, federation, league, partnership, pool, relationship *(connection)*, society, sodality, union *(labor organization)*. SEE MAIN ENTRY
confederate abettor, accessory, accomplice, affiliate, allied, assistant, associate, coactor, coadjutant, coconspirator, cohort, colleague, collective, combine *(act in concert)*, conjoint, consociate, consolidate *(unite)*, conspirator, conspire, conspirer, contributor *(contributor)*, cooperate, copartner *(coconspirator)*, desegregate, federal, federalize *(associate)*, federate, involve *(participate)*, join *(associate oneself with)*, joint, member *(individual in a group)*, organize *(unionize)*, participant, participate, partisan, partner, pool, unite. SEE MAIN ENTRY
confederate for an unlawful purpose conspire
confederated affiliated, associated, concurrent *(united)*, conjoint, mutual *(collective)*
confederation affiliation *(amalgamation)*, association *(alliance)*, band, cartel, chamber *(body)*, coalescence, committee, concert, confederacy *(compact)*, consolidation, contribution *(participation)*, federation, integration *(amalgamation)*, integration *(assimilation)*, league, merger, partnership, party *(political organization)*, pool, society, sodality
confer administer *(tender)*, attorn, bear *(yield)*, bestow, cede, consider, consult *(ask advice of)*, contribute *(supply)*, counsel, dedicate, devise *(give)*, discourse, discuss, dispense, enable, endue, give *(grant)*, grant *(transfer formally)*, impart, leave *(give)*, present *(make a gift)*, provide *(supply)*, render *(deliver)*, transfer, treat *(process)*, vest. SEE MAIN ENTRY
confer a benefit serve *(assist)*
confer a benefit on avail *(be of use)*, profit
confer a corporate franchise upon incorporate *(form a corporation)*
confer a privilege authorize, bestow, grant *(concede)*, permit, sanction
confer a right authorize, qualify *(meet standards)*, sanction
confer a trust commit *(entrust)*
confer again recover
confer an honor elevate

confer by will demise

confer corporate status upon incorporate *(form a corporation)*

confer distinction bestow

confer distinction on honor

confer formally deliberate, grant *(transfer formally)*

confer honor on dedicate

confer on price dicker

confer ownership attorn, devolve, grant *(transfer formally)*, pass *(advance)*

confer ownership on oneself impropriate

confer power invest *(vest)*

confer power on charge *(empower)*, delegate, empower

confer privileges of a native citizen naturalize *(make a citizen)*

confer rights of citizenship naturalize *(make a citizen)*

confer with advise, converse, debate, discuss

conference assembly, caucus, collective bargaining, communication *(discourse)*, company *(assemblage)*, confrontation *(act of setting face to face)*, congregation, council *(assembly)*, discourse, inquiry *(systematic investigation)*, interview, negotiation, panel *(discussion group)*, parlance, parley, session. SEE MAIN ENTRY

conferment alienation *(transfer of title)*, assignment *(transfer of ownership)*, bounty, concession *(authorization)*, contribution *(donation)*, conveyance, demise *(conveyance)*, deputation *(selection of delegates)*, dispensation *(act of dispensing)*, legacy

conferment between the living inter vivos

conferral alienation *(transfer of title)*, assignment *(transfer of ownership)*, concession *(authorization)*, demise *(conveyance)*, dispensation *(act of dispensing)*

conferral of a fee feoffment

conferre bestow, collect *(gather)*, compare, confer *(give)*, contribution *(donation)*, converse

conferrer donor, grantor

conferring donative

conferrment of title feoffment

confess acknowledge *(verify)*, admit *(concede)*, avow, bare, betray *(disclose)*, certify *(attest)*, disclose, inform *(betray)*, recognize *(acknowledge)*, reveal. SEE MAIN ENTRY

confessed judgment cognovit

confessedly admittedly

confessing repentant

confessio acknowledgment *(avowal)*, avowal

confession acknowledgment *(avowal)*, admission *(disclosure)*, avowal, disclosure *(act of disclosing)*, disclosure *(something disclosed)*, profession *(declaration)*. SEE MAIN ENTRY

confessor penitent

conficere conclude *(complete)*, consummate, dispatch *(dispose of)*, exhaust *(deplete)*, finish, kill *(defeat)*, kill *(murder)*, settle

confidant confederate, consociate

confidante associate

confide commit *(entrust)*, convey *(communicate)*, delegate, divulge, impart, inform *(notify)*, notify, rely, reveal, trust. SEE MAIN ENTRY

confide for care delegate

confide for use delegate

confide in confer *(consult)*

confide to mention

confidence assurance, belief *(state of mind)*, certification *(certainness)*, certitude, credence, credit *(delayed payment)*, faith, prospect *(outlook)*, reliance, secret, weight *(credibility)*. SEE MAIN ENTRY

confidence in one's powers audacity

confidence trick bunko

confident assertive, categorical, certain *(fixed)*, certain *(positive)*, definite, dogmatic, indubious, sanguine

confident expectation likelihood, trust *(confidence)*

confidential clandestine, close *(intimate)*, collusive, esoteric, fiduciary, intimate, personal *(private)*, privy, secret. SEE MAIN ENTRY

confidential communication confidence *(relation of trust)*, secret. SEE MAIN ENTRY

confidential information tip *(clue)*

confidential matter confidence *(relation of trust)*, secret

confidentiality privacy. SEE MAIN ENTRY

confidentialness privacy

confidentness assurance, certainty, certitude, confidence *(faith)*

confidere rely, trust

confiding intimate

configuration boundary, construction, content *(structure)*, contour *(outline)*, contour *(shape)*, delineation, formation, organization *(structure)*, structure *(composition)*. SEE MAIN ENTRY

configurattion dimension

confine apprehend *(arrest)*, arrest *(apprehend)*, bind *(restrain)*, border, border *(bound)*, boundary, capture, circumscribe *(surround by boundary)*, close *(enclosed area)*, commit *(institutionalize)*, conceal, constrain *(imprison)*, contain *(enclose)*, contain *(restrain)*, control *(restrain)*, debar, delimit, demarcate, detain *(hold in custody)*, detain *(restrain)*, enclose, enclosure, envelop, fetter, hamper, immure, impede, imprison, isolate, jail, keep *(restrain)*, limit, lock, mete, outline *(boundary)*, periphery, purview, qualify *(condition)*, restrain, restrict, retrench, seclude, sequester *(seclude)*, trammel. SEE MAIN ENTRY

confine forcibly constrain *(imprison)*

confined arrested *(apprehended)*, in custody, insular, limited, narrow, partial *(part)*, private *(not public)*

confined individual prisoner

confined room cell

confined to a select circle esoteric

confinement apprehension *(act of arresting)*, arrest, blockade *(limitation)*, bondage, boundary, cache *(hiding place)*, captivity, cell, concealment, constraint *(imprisonment)*, custody *(incarceration)*, detention, durance, duress, enclosure, fetter, incarceration, quarantine, restraint, restriction, thrall

confinement by public authority incarceration

confinement in a jail incarceration

confinement in a penitentiary incarceration

confinement under legal process incarceration

confinements confines

confines area *(province)*, barrier, circuit, edge *(border)*, region, scope, vicinity. SEE MAIN ENTRY

confining binding, commitment *(confinement)*, limited, limiting, oppressive

confinis contiguous

confinium frontier

confirm accept *(admit as sufficient)*, accept *(assent)*, accredit, acknowledge *(verify)*, admit *(concede)*, affirm *(uphold)*, agree *(comply)*, appoint, approve, ascertain, assent, assure *(insure)*, attest, authorize, avouch *(avow)*, avow, bind *(obligate)*, bond *(secure a debt)*, certify *(approve)*, certify *(attest)*, corroborate, cosign, countenance, countersign, demonstrate *(establish)*, determine, document, endorse, ensure, establish *(show)*, evidence, fix *(make firm)*, indorse, legalize, notarize, pass *(approve)*, prove, reaffirm, reassure, reveal, seal *(solemnize)*, sign, subscribe *(sign)*, substantiate, support *(corroborate)*, swear, uphold, validate, vouch, witness *(attest to)*. SEE MAIN ENTRY

confirm as correct certify *(attest)*

confirm by law legalize

confirm by oath avouch *(avow)*

confirm in conviction assure *(give confidence to)*

confirm officially authorize, certify *(approve)*, indorse, notarize

confirm the validity of a will probate

confirmable ascertainable, convincing, provable

confirmare affirm *(uphold)*, assert, certify *(attest)*, contend *(maintain)*, enforce, establish *(entrench)*, instate, maintain *(carry on)*, reassure, reinforce, sanction, verify *(confirm)*

confirmatio assurance, indorsement, sanction *(permission)*

confirmation acknowledgment *(avowal)*, admittance *(acceptance)*, affirmance *(authentication)*, affirmation, approval, assent, asseveration, averment, avowal, certification *(attested copy)*, certification *(certification of proficiency)*, charter *(sanction)*, collation, confession, consent, contract, corroboration, disclosure *(something disclosed)*, document, documentation, evidence, indorsement, jurat, legalization, license, permit, proof, ratification, reference *(recommendation)*, subscription, support *(corroboration)*, surety *(certainty)*. SEE MAIN ENTRY

confirmation under oath affidavit

confirmative affirmative, definitive, demonstrative *(illustrative)*

confirmatory affirmative, convincing, demonstrative *(illustrative)*

confirmed accustomed *(customary)*, agreed *(promised)*, arrant *(definite)*, certain *(fixed)*, chronic, customary, firm, formal, habitual, immutable, indefeasible, ingrained, inveterate, permanent, traditional, valid

confirmed habit habituation, practice *(custom)*

confirmed judgment cognovit

confirmed opposition dissent *(difference of opinion)*

confirmed way habit

confirmer surety *(guarantor)*

confirming conclusive *(settled)*, consensual, convincing, demonstrative *(illustrative)*

confirmist affirmant

confiscate annex *(arrogate)*, assume *(seize)*, attach *(seize)*, condemn *(seize)*, deprive, distrain, divest, garnish, impound, levy, penalize, remove *(eliminate)*, sequester *(seize property)*. SEE MAIN ENTRY

confiscated attached *(seized)*, lost *(taken away)*

confiscated goods contraband

confiscated property contraband

confiscation appropriation *(taking)*, attachment *(seizure)*, condemnation *(seizure)*, disseisin, distraint, distress *(seizure)*, escheatment, expropriation *(divestiture)*, foreclosure, forfeiture *(act of forfeiting)*, garnishment, levy, privation, sequestration, taking

confiscatory SEE MAIN ENTRY

confiteri avow, confess

confixation attachment *(act of affixing)*

conflagrate burn, deflagrate

conflagration SEE MAIN ENTRY

conflate amalgamate

conflation merger. SEE MAIN ENTRY

conflict affray, altercation, antipode, antithesis, argument *(contention)*, belligerency, bicker, collision *(dispute)*, commotion, competition, confrontation *(altercation)*, contend *(dispute)*, contention *(argument)*, contention *(opposition)*, contest, contradict, contradiction, contrary, contravention, controversy *(argument)*, disaccord *(noun)*, disaccord *(verb)*, disagree, disagreement, discord, discrepancy, dispute, dispute *(contest)*, dissension, dissent *(difference of opinion)*, dissent *(differ in opinion)*, dissidence, embroilment, estrangement, feud, fight *(argument)*, fracas, ill will, impugnation, incompatibility *(difference)*, incompatibility *(inconsistency)*, opposition, oppugn, outbreak, reaction *(opposition)*, rebut, strife, struggle. SEE MAIN ENTRY

conflict of interest disagreement

conflict of opinion conflict, controversy *(argument)*, difference, disaccord, disagreement, disparity, dispute, dissension, dissent *(difference of opinion)*

conflict with antagonize, collide *(clash)*, contravene, counter, counteract, countervail, cross *(disagree with)*, defy, deviate, differ *(disagree)*, disaffirm, gainsay

conflicting adverse *(opposite)*, antipathetic *(oppositional)*, competitive *(antagonistic)*, contradictory, contrary, discordant, disparate, disproportionate, dissenting, hostile, incongruous, inconsistent, litigious, negative, opposite, polemic, renitent, repugnant *(incompatible)*, unsuitable

conflicting evidence contradiction

conflictive adverse *(opposite)*, dissenting

conflictory discordant, dissenting

confligere collide *(crash against)*

confluence assemblage, coalescence, coalition, company *(assemblage)*, corpus, crossroad *(intersection)*, rendezvous

confluent coadunate

confluere meet

conflux assemblage, chamber *(body)*, collection *(assembly)*, company *(assemblage)*

confodere pierce *(lance)*

conform abide, accede *(concede)*, adapt, adhere *(maintain loyalty)*, adjust *(resolve)*, cohere *(be logically consistent)*, comport *(agree with)*, copy, correspond *(be equivalent)*, obey, observe *(obey)*. SEE MAIN ENTRY

conform to adopt, assent, coincide *(concur)*, coincide *(correspond)*, comply, defer *(yield in judgment)*, keep *(fulfill)*, pass *(satisfy requirements)*, satisfy *(fulfill)*

conform with concur *(agree)*

conformability amenability, compliance, conciliation, identity *(similarity)*

conformable appropriate, commensurable, concerted, concordant, congruous, consistent, consonant, conventional, correlative, faithful *(true to fact)*, felicitous, fit, malleable, obedient, orthodox, passive, pliable,

pliant, prevailing *(current)*, prevalent, regular *(conventional)*, similar, suitable, tractable, traditional, typical, uniform, usual

conformable to fact real

conformable to law lawful

conformable to rule typical

conformable with the law juridical, lawful

conformance accordance *(understanding)*, adjustment, agreement *(concurrence)*, compliance, concordance, conduct, conformity *(agreement)*, conformity *(obedience)*, consensus, resemblance

conformant relevant

conformare form

conformatio formation

conformation adjustment, arrangement *(ordering)*, building *(business of assembling)*, composition *(makeup)*, configuration *(form)*, conformity *(agreement)*, conformity *(obedience)*, consensus, construction, content *(structure)*, contour *(shape)*, dimension, formation, organization *(structure)*

conforming agreed *(harmonized)*, concerted, concordant, concurrent *(united)*, congruous, consonant, conventional, harmonious, law-abiding, malleable, normal *(regular)*, obedient, orthodox, pliable, pliant, relevant, usual

conforming to consensual, pursuant to

conforming to accepted standards conventional

conforming to moral standards ethical

conforming to professional conduct ethical

conformist philistine

conformity accordance *(understanding)*, adjustment, compatibility, compliance, conciliation, concordance, conjunction, consensus, constant, correspondence *(similarity)*, decorum, propriety *(appropriateness)*, regularity, resemblance, synchronism, uniformity. SEE MAIN ENTRY

conformity to fact truth, veracity

conformity to law legality, legitimacy

conformity with the law legality

confound confuse *(bewilder)*, defeat, discompose, disconcert, dislocate, disorganize, disorient, disturb, fight *(counteract)*, foil, frustrate, harass, misdirect, mismanage, muddle, negate, obfuscate, overcome *(overwhelm)*, overwhelm, perplex, perturb, repel *(drive back)*, subvert. SEE MAIN ENTRY

confounded heinous, nefarious, odious

confounded meaning ambiguity

confounding enigmatic, labyrinthine

confoundment confusion *(ambiguity)*, dilemma, quandary

confraternity confederacy *(compact)*, society, sodality

confrère accessory, accomplice, assistant

confrere associate

confrère colleague

confrere confederate, consociate

confrère consort

confrere contributor *(contributor)*

confrère copartner *(business associate)*, copartner *(coconspirator)*

confront accost, approach, challenge, collide *(clash)*, contrast, cross *(disagree with)*, defy, fight *(battle)*, grapple, oppose, oppugn, repel *(drive back)*, resist *(oppose)*, withstand. SEE MAIN ENTRY

confrontation contraposition, contravention, disaccord, experience *(encounter)*, fight *(argument)*, impugnation, meeting *(encounter)*, resistance, struggle. SEE MAIN ENTRY

confrontment confrontation *(altercation)*, contraposition

confugere recourse

confundere confound, confuse *(bewilder)*, disorganize, muddle

confuse circumvent, confound, discompose, disconcert, dislocate, disorganize, disrupt, disturb, embarrass, misapprehend, misconstrue, misdirect, misinterpret, misread, mistake, misunderstand, muddle, obfuscate, overwhelm, perplex, perturb, upset. SEE MAIN ENTRY

confused ambiguous, complex, deranged, disjointed, disordered, disorderly, haphazard, inextricable, lost *(disoriented)*, nebulous, opaque, promiscuous, unclear, vague

confused language jargon *(unintelligible language)*

confused mass melange

confused meaning ambiguity

confused talk jargon *(unintelligible language)*

confusedness confusion *(ambiguity)*, entanglement *(confusion)*, pandemonium, panic, quandary

confusing dubious, enigmatic, equivocal, indefinable, labyrinthine, opaque

confusing situation imbroglio

confusing statement enigma

confusio confusion *(turmoil)*

confusion ambiguity, anarchy, commotion, complex *(entanglement)*, complication, dilemma, disorder *(lack of order)*, disturbance, doubt *(indecision)*, embarrassment, embroilment, enigma, havoc, imbroglio, involution, irregularity, jargon *(unintelligible language)*, misrule, opacity, pandemonium, panic, quandary, riot, shambles, snarl, turmoil. SEE MAIN ENTRY

confutable contestable, controversial, debatable, defeasible, disputable, dubious, litigable

confutation answer *(judicial response)*, bad repute, contradiction, counterargument, defeat, defense, demurrer, denial, disparagement, negation, opposition, repudiation. SEE MAIN ENTRY

confutative contradictory, contrary, negative

confute answer *(reply)*, argue, challenge, contradict, controvert, counter, counteract, countercharge, countervail, cross *(disagree with)*, debate, disagree, disapprove *(reject)*, disown *(deny the validity)*, disprove, dispute *(contest)*, dispute *(debate)*, dissent *(differ in opinion)*, fight *(counteract)*, impeach, impugn, invalidate, negate, oppose, parry, rebut, refute, reply. SEE MAIN ENTRY

confuting contradictory, contrary

congé dispensation *(exception)*

congeal cement, cohere *(adhere)*, consolidate *(strengthen)*, consolidate *(unite)*

congealed coherent *(joined)*, ossified, solid *(compact)*

congealment SEE MAIN ENTRY

congelation adhesion *(affixing)*, congealment

congener complement, correlate, counterpart *(complement)*

congeneric apposite, cognate, comparable *(capable of comparison)*, correlative, identical, pendent, related, similar

congenerical pendent, related, similar

congenerous apposite, cognate, consanguineous, correlative, identical, pendent, related

congenial apposite, cognate, consonant, harmonious, informal, palatable, suitable

congeniality compatibility, concordance, conformity *(agreement)*, propinquity *(similarity)*

congenital born *(innate)*, genetic, hereditary, innate, native *(inborn)*

congerere collect *(gather)*

congeries agglomeration, assemblage, body *(collection)*, entirety

congest concentrate *(consolidate)*, obstruct, overload

congestion confusion *(turmoil)*, obstruction, plethora

congestus collection *(accumulation)*

congiarium largess *(generosity)*

conglomerate agglomeration, aggregate, assemblage, coadunate, coalition, coherent *(joined)*, collect *(gather)*, collection *(accumulation)*, combine *(join together)*, commingle, compile, complex *(development)*, composite, compound, concentrate *(consolidate)*, congregate, consolidate *(unite)*, corporation, corpus, crystallize, cumulation, desegregate, join *(bring together)*, merge, unite. SEE MAIN ENTRY

conglomeratic coadunate, coherent *(joined)*

conglomeration adhesion *(affixing)*, agglomeration, aggregate, arsenal, assemblage, body *(collection)*, centralization, coalescence, collection *(accumulation)*, compilation, complex *(development)*, cumulation, melange, selection *(collection)*. SEE MAIN ENTRY

conglutemate bond *(hold together)*. SEE MAIN ENTRY

conglutinare cement

conglutinate cement, combine *(join together)*, join *(bring together)*

conglutination adherence *(adhesion)*, adhesion *(affixing)*, coalescence

conglutinative cohesive *(sticking)*

congratulate honor

congregari congregate

congregate collective, concentrate *(consolidate)*, conglomerate, convene, converge, meet, rendezvous, unite. SEE MAIN ENTRY

congregated coadunate, compound, conglomerate

congregated body congregation

congregatio union *(unity)*

congregation assemblage, assembly, band, centralization, collection *(assembly)*, combination, committee, company *(assemblage)*, cumulation, mass *(body of persons)*, rendezvous, session. SEE MAIN ENTRY

congregational collective

congregative collective

congress assemblage, chamber *(body)*, coalition, company *(assemblage)*, government *(political administration)*, legislature, parley, rendezvous, session. SEE MAIN ENTRY

congressio interview, meeting *(conference)*

congressional legislative

congressman lawmaker, legislator

congresswoman lawmaker

congruence adjustment, agreement *(concurrence)*, coherence, concordance, conformity *(agreement)*, consensus, correspondence *(similarity)*, relevance, understanding *(agreement)*. SEE MAIN ENTRY

congruency agreement *(concurrence)*, concordance, conformity *(agreement)*, relevance

congruens appropriate, coherent *(clear)*, coherent *(joined)*, consonant, harmonious

congruent coequal, coextensive, commensurate, concerted, concordant, congruous, conjoint, consensual, consonant, correlative, germane, harmonious, relevant, similar, suitable

congruent with consistent

congruentia correspondence *(similarity)*

congruere agree *(comply)*, coincide *(correspond)*, correspond *(be equivalent)*, sympathize

congruity adjustment, agreement *(concurrency)*, analogy, coherence, compatibility, conformity *(agreement)*, consortium *(marriage companionship)*, correspondence *(similarity)*, propriety *(appropriateness)*, rapport, regularity, relevance

congruous appropriate, commensurable, commensurate, concerted, concordant, consistent, consonant, correlative, felicitous, fit, germane, harmonious, relevant, suitable. SEE MAIN ENTRY

congruousness compatibility, consortium *(marriage companionship)*

conicere cast *(throw)*, interpret

coniectio discharge *(shot)*

coniectura hypothesis, inference, presumption, speculation *(conjecture)*, supposition

coniecturalis speculative

coniectus discharge *(shot)*

coniugalis conjugal

coniugium marriage *(wedlock)*

coniunctio affinity *(family ties)*, combination, incorporation *(formation of a business entity)*, relationship *(connection)*

coniunctus intimate

coniungere combine *(join together)*, join *(bring together)*, unite

coniunx spouse

coniurare conspire, plot

coniuratio confederacy *(conspiracy)*, conspiracy, plot *(secret plan)*

coniuratus conspirator

conjacent cohesive *(compact)*

conjecturable colorable *(plausible)*, debatable, ostensible, plausible, presumptive, probable

conjectural apparent *(presumptive)*, circumstantial, debatable, disputable, doubtful, enigmatic, hypothetical, presumptive, speculative, theoretical, uncertain *(questionable)*, unsettled. SEE MAIN ENTRY

conjecture anticipate *(prognosticate)*, assume *(suppose)*, assumption *(supposition)*, concept, deduce, deduct *(conclude by reasoning)*, estimate *(idea)*, estimate, estimation *(calculation)*, expect *(consider probable)*, guess, hypothesis, idea, infer, inference, opine, opinion *(belief)*, postulate *(noun)*, postulate *(verb)*, presume, presumption, presuppose, prognosis, prognosticate, proposition, supposition, surmise, suspect *(think)*, suspicion *(uncertainty)*, theory, thesis, understand. SEE MAIN ENTRY

conjectured assumed *(inferred)*, presumptive, putative

conjoin abut, adjoin, affix, annex *(add)*, append, attach *(join)*, border *(bound)*, cohere *(adhere)*, combine *(join together)*, commingle, concentrate *(consolidate)*, connect *(join together)*, consolidate *(strengthen)*, consolidate *(unite)*, conspire, contact *(touch)*, cooperate, correspond *(be equivalent)*, desegregate, federate, join *(bring together)*, merge, pool, unite. SEE MAIN ENTRY

conjoined attached *(annexed)*, coadunate, coherent *(joined)*, collateral *(accompanying)*, concerted, concordant, concurrent *(united)*, promiscuous

conjoiner adjoiner

conjoining accession *(annexation)*, coalition, conjunction, contiguous, immediate *(not distant)*

conjoint associated, coadunate, common *(shared)*, composite, compound, concerted, concomitant, consolidate *(strengthen)*, corporate *(joint)*, correlative, joint, mutual *(collective)*. SEE MAIN ENTRY

conjugal nuptial. SEE MAIN ENTRY

conjugal bliss cohabitation *(married state)*

conjugal partner consort

conjugal union marriage *(wedlock)*

conjugality cohabitation *(married state)*, coverture, marriage *(wedlock)*, matrimony

conjugate coadunate, cohabit, compound, interrelated, joint

conjugation coalescence, combination, joinder

conjunct associated, coadunate, coherent *(joined)*, cohesive *(compact)*, composite, compound, concerted, conjoint, consensual, contiguous, corporate *(joint)*, correlative, inextricable, joint. SEE MAIN ENTRY

conjunctio coalition

conjunction adhesion *(affixing)*, affiliation *(connectedness)*, association *(connection)*, attachment *(act of affixing)*, building *(business of assembling)*, cartel, chain *(nexus)*, coalescence, coalition, coherence, collusion, combination, concert, concordance, conformity *(agreement)*, connection *(fastening)*, connivance, consolidation, contact *(association)*, intersection, joinder, league, partnership. SEE MAIN ENTRY

conjunctional coincidental, concomitant, concordant

conjunctive composite, concomitant, concurrent *(at the same time)*, conjoint, correlative

conjuncture case *(set of circumstances)*, coalition, consolidation, crossroad *(intersection)*, crossroad *(turning point)*, occasion, point *(period of time)*, posture *(situation)*, predicament

conjure invoke. SEE MAIN ENTRY

conjure up conceive *(comprehend)*, occur *(come to mind)*, recall *(remember)*, recollect, remember. SEE MAIN ENTRY

conjuring illusory, prestidigitation

conlatio collation, comparison

conlectio restatement

conlega colleague

conlegium association *(alliance)*, association *(connection)*, board, corporation, facility *(institution)*, foundation *(organization)*, institute

conlidere strike *(collide)*

conligere argue, concentrate *(consolidate)*, conclude *(decide)*, hoard, infer, raise *(collect)*

conlocatio arrangement *(ordering)*, disposition *(final arrangement)*

conlocatus situated

conlocutio discourse

conloqui discourse, parley

conloquium conversation, discourse, interview, negotiation

conlusio collusion

connatal hereditary

connate akin *(related by blood)*, associated, born *(innate)*, correlative, hereditary, inherent, native *(inborn)*, natural, related

connation degree *(kinship)*, relation *(connection)*

connatural apposite, born *(innate)*, consanguineous, correlative, interrelated, native *(inborn)*, pendent, related, similar

connaturalness relation *(connection)*

connect abut, adjoin, affiliate, affix, annex *(add)*, append, attach *(join)*, bond *(hold together)*, border *(bound)*, cement, combine *(join together)*, commingle, conjoin, consolidate *(strengthen)*, consolidate *(unite)*, contact *(touch)*, desegregate, engage *(involve)*, implicate, involve *(implicate)*, involve *(participate)*, join *(bring together)*, juxtapose, lock, pool, refer *(direct attention)*, relate *(establish a connection)*, unite. SEE MAIN ENTRY

connect with ascribe, attribute

connect with a crime incriminate

connected affiliated, akin *(germane)*, allied, apposite, appurtenant, associated, attached *(annexed)*, coadunate, cognate, coherent *(joined)*, cohesive *(sticking)*, collateral *(accompanying)*, composite, compound, concurrent *(united)*, conjoint, consecutive, contiguous, correlative, direct *(uninterrupted)*, germane, incident, inextricable, interested, interrelated, pertinent, proximate, related, relative *(relevant)*, relevant, tangential. SEE MAIN ENTRY

connected series chain *(series)*

connected with comparative

connectedness adherence *(adhesion)*, association *(connection)*, chain *(nexus)*, coherence, continuity

connectere connect *(join together)*

connecting proximate, reference *(citation)*

connecting link chain *(nexus)*, go-between, intermediary, nexus, relation-ship *(connection)*

connecting medium chain *(nexus)*, privity

connection adhesion *(affixing)*, adjoiner, affiliation *(connectedness)*, affinity *(family ties)*, ancestry, attachment *(act of affixing)*, attribution, chain *(nexus)*, coalescence, coalition, coherence, conjunction, contact *(association)*, contact *(touching)*, context, continuity, degree *(kinship)*, go-between, implication *(incriminating involvement)*, intermediary, intersection, joinder, kinship, liaison, nexus, partnership, privity, propinquity *(kinship)*, relative, relevance, union *(unity)*. SEE MAIN ENTRY

connections ties

connective concerted, contact *(touching)*, correlative, interlocking, nexus, relative *(relevant)*

connexion relation *(connection)*

connivance artifice, bad faith, bribery, cabal, collusion, confederacy *(conspiracy)*, conspiracy, contrivance. SEE MAIN ENTRY

connivant collusive

connive conspire, contrive, cooperate, maneuver, pettifog, plan, plot, scheme. SEE MAIN ENTRY

conniver conspirator

conniving collusive, concerted, dishonest, fraudulent, insidious, machiavellian, perfidious, recreant, sly, surreptitious, tortuous *(bending)*, unconscionable, untrustworthy

connoisseur expert, specialist

connotate signify *(denote)*

connotation context, gist *(substance)*, hint, implication *(inference)*, import, indication, innuendo, meaning, reference *(allusion)*, signification, symbol. SEE MAIN ENTRY

connotative allusive, demonstrative *(illustrative)*, representative, suggestive *(evocative)*

connote allude, bespeak, construe *(translate)*, depict, exemplify, hint, imply, indicate, purport, refer *(direct attention)*, represent *(portray)*, signify *(denote)*. SEE MAIN ENTRY

connoted assumed *(inferred)*, constructive *(inferential)*, implied, tacit

connubial conjugal, nuptial

connubiality cohabitation *(married state)*, marriage *(wedlock)*, matrimony

comprehensible ascertainable

conquer beat *(defeat)*, defeat, demean *(make lower)*, occupy *(take possession)*, overcome *(surmount)*, overthrow, overturn, overwhelm, pass *(satisfy requirements)*, prevail *(triumph)*, subdue, subject, subjugate, succeed *(attain)*, surmount, upset

conquerable facile, helpless *(defenseless)*, indefensible, penetrable

conqueri de rem complain *(criticize)*

conquering confiscatory, prevailing *(having superior force)*

conquest subjection

conquirere hoard

consanguine akin *(related by blood)*, cognate, consanguineous, related

consanguineal relations next of kin

consanguinean akin *(related by blood)*

consanguinei kindred

consanguineous akin *(related by blood)*, cognate, interrelated, related. SEE MAIN ENTRY

consanguineus akin *(related by blood)*

consanguinitas affinity *(family ties)*

consanguinity affiliation *(bloodline)*, affinity *(family ties)*, ancestry, blood, connection *(relation)*, contact *(association)*, degree *(kinship)*, family *(common ancestry)*, kinship, propinquity *(kinship)*, relation *(kinship)*, relationship *(family tie)*

conscendere embark

conscendere commitment *(responsibility)*, probity, remorse. SEE MAIN ENTRY

conscience money reparation *(indemnification)*

conscience-smitten contrite, penitent, remorseful, repentant

conscience-smitten person penitent

conscience-stricken contrite, penitent, remorseful, repentant

conscience-stricken person penitent

conscienceless brazen, delinquent *(guilty of a misdeed)*, diabolic, dishonest, disingenuous, disreputable, immoral, machiavellian, sinister, unconscionable, unscrupulous

conscientia conscience

conscientia mala remorse

conscientious accurate, circumspect, close *(rigorous)*, dependable, diligent, earnest, faithful *(diligent)*, high-minded, honest, loyal, meritorious, meticulous, moral, painstaking, particular *(exacting)*, punctilious, punctual, reliable, reputable, sedulous, strict, true *(loyal)*, upright. SEE MAIN ENTRY

conscientiously faithfully

conscientiousness adhesion *(loyalty)*, caution *(vigilance)*, conscience, fidelity, honesty, interest *(concern)*, particularity, rectitude, responsibility *(conscience)*, rigor

conscionable reasonable *(fair)*

conscious circumspect, cognizant, deliberate, express, familiar *(informed)*, intentional, knowing, perceptive, premeditated, receptive, sensible, sensitive *(discerning)*, willful. SEE MAIN ENTRY

conscious of acquainted

conscious purpose deliberation

conscious violation of law malice

consciously purposely

consciousness appreciation *(perception)*, cognition, comprehension, impression, insight, knowledge *(awareness)*, perception, realization, recognition, recollection, scienter, sense *(feeling)*, sensibility

conscius accessory, accomplice, cognizant, conscious *(aware)*

conscribere recruit

conscript bind *(obligate)*, coerce, impose *(enforce)*, induct, levy, recruit

conscription requirement

consecrare dedicate, devote

consecrate dedicate, devote, elevate, honor

consecrated inviolate, sacrosanct

consecration adhesion *(loyalty)*, dedication, elevation, remembrance *(commemoration)*

consectari hunt, pursue *(chase)*, pursue *(strive to gain)*

consectatio pursuit *(chase)*, pursuit *(effort to secure)*

consecutio consequence *(conclusion)*, effect

consecution chain *(series)*, continuity, cycle, sequence, serial, succession

consecutive continuous, direct *(uninterrupted)*, progressive *(going forward)*, successive. SEE MAIN ENTRY

consecutive order succession

consecutiveness continuity

consensual concerted, concordant, congruous, contractual. SEE MAIN ENTRY

consensus accordance *(understanding)*, concordance, conformity *(agreement)*. SEE MAIN ENTRY

consensus consent

consensus poll *(casting of votes)*, union *(unity)*

consensus omnium compatibility

consent accede *(concede)*, acceptance, acquiescence, advocate, agree *(comply)*, agree *(contract)*, agreement *(concurrence)*, allow *(endure)*, approval, assent *(noun)*, assent *(verb)*, bestow, capacity *(authority)*, capitulation, certify *(approve)*, charter *(sanction)*, close *(agree)*, coincide *(concur)*, compatibility, compliance, concede, concordance, concur *(agree)*, confirm, conformity *(agreement)*, conformity *(obedience)*, contribution *(participation)*, defer *(yield in judgment)*, dispensation *(exception)*, enable, franchise *(license)*, grant *(concede)*, indorsement, leave *(permission)*, let *(permit)*, license, obey, option *(contractual provision)*, pass *(approve)*, permission, permit, promise, promise *(vow)*, ratification, recognize *(acknowledge)*, sanction *(permission)*, subscribe *(promise)*, subscription, suffer *(permit)*, tolerate, vouchsafe, yield *(submit)*. SEE MAIN ENTRY

consent decree SEE MAIN ENTRY

consent order SEE MAIN ETNRY

consent to approve, authorize, comply, countenance, embrace *(accept)*, indorse, sanction, sustain *(confirm)*

consent to support underwrite

consentaneity agreement *(concurrence)*, assent, compatibility, concert, concordance, consensus, pact, peace, understanding *(agreement)*

consentaneous concerted, concordant, concurrent *(united)*, congruous, consensual, consenting, consonant, correlative, harmonious, relevant, suitable

consentaneousness agreement (concurrence), concordance, consensus, peace

consentaneus consonant, rational, suitable

consented allowed

consentience accordance (understanding), agreement (concurrence), consensus

consentient concerted, congruous, consensual, consenting, consonant, contractual, harmonious

consenting concerted, concordant, inclined, ready (willing), willing (not averse). SEE MAIN ENTRY

consentire agree (contract), consent, plot

consensus cartel

consequence amount (result), clout, concern (interest), conclusion (outcome), degree (magnitude), development (outgrowth), effect, eminence, emphasis, follow-up, force (strength), import, importance, influence, interest (concern), magnitude, outcome, prestige, primacy, reputation, result, significance, toll (effect), value, weight (importance). SEE MAIN ENTRY

consequent conclusion (outcome), consecutive, consonant, derivative, development (outgrowth)

consequentia result

consequential considerable, contingent, crucial, decisive, derivative, grave (important), important (significant), influential, major, material (important), momentous, outstanding (prominent), powerful, prominent, remarkable, renowned, serious (grave), strategic, substantial. SEE MAIN ENTRY

consequently a fortiori, a priori. SEE MAIN ENTRY

consequi attain, gain, obtain, result

conservare conserve, observe (obey), preserve, retain (keep in possession)

conservatio maintenance (upkeep), preservation, retention

conservation ecology, maintenance (upkeep), preservation, protection, prudence, reserve, safekeeping, salvage. SEE MAIN ENTRY

conservation of the same situation status quo

conservational protective

conservatism continence, moderation, prudence

conservative frugal, guarded, illiberal, orthodox, protective, uncompromising

conservative estimate understatement

conservative reading. SEE MAIN ETNRY

conservator guardian

conservatory protective, repository, store (depository), treasury

conserve fund, hold (possess), keep (shelter), maintain (sustain), preserve, protect, store, sustain (prolong). SEE MAIN ENTRY

consider analyze, assess (appraise), assume (suppose), brood, calculate, care (be cautious), concern (care), contrive, criticize (evaluate), debate, deem, deliberate, digest (comprehend), discuss, gauge, heed, investigate, judge, muse, opine, pause, peruse, ponder, postulate, reason (conclude), reflect (ponder), regard (pay attention), speculate (conjecture), study, survey (examine), suspect (think), try (conduct a trial), weigh. SEE MAIN ENTRY

consider again reconsider

consider again with a view to a change or action appeal

consider as belonging to attribute

consider as true accept (embrace), presume

consider attentively deliberate, probe

consider beforehand prearrange

consider beneath notice condescend (patronize), disdain

consider beneath oneself disdain

consider carefully deliberate

consider closely concentrate (pay attention)

consider implausible disbelieve

consider in advance anticipate (expect)

consider likely expect (consider probable)

consider not to be true disbelieve

consider pro and con deliberate

consider probable deduce, deduct (conclude by reasoning), infer, presume, read

consider unproven disbelieve

consider untrue disbelieve

consider unworthy of regard disdain

considerable appreciable, consequential (substantial), copious, critical (crucial), extensive, far reaching, gross (flagrant), important (significant), major, manifold, material (important), multiple, noteworthy, ponderable, rife, substantial, substantive. SEE MAIN ENTRY

considerare consider, deliberate, ponder, reflect (ponder), survey (examine), weigh

considerate benevolent, charitable (lenient), circumspect, humane, judicial, judicious, lenient, philanthropic, politic, prudent

considerateness charity, comity, consideration (sympathetic regard), discretion (quality of being discreet), philanthropy, prudence

consideratio consideration (contemplation), reflection (thought)

consideration advancement (loan), analysis, benevolence (disposition to do good), cause (reason), caution (vigilance), charity, clemency, comity, commission (fee), compensation, concept, concern (interest), conclusion (determination), contemplation, conviction (persuasion), cost (price), courtesy, credit (recognition), decorum, deference, deliberation, determinant, determination, dialectic, diligence (care), discretion (power of choice), discretion (quality of being discreet), discrimination (differentiation), emphasis, estimate (idea), examination (study), expense (cost), extenuating circumstances, fee (charge), forethought, hindsight, homage, honor (outward respect), honorarium, impression, incentive, inducement, interest (concern), judgment (discernment), judgment (formal court decree), lenience, magnitude, motive, notice (heed), observation, opinion (belief), opinion (judicial decision), pay, payment (remittance), perquisite, phase (aspect), philanthropy, point (item), prudence, reason (basis), recognition, recompense, reflection (thought), regard (attention), regard (esteem), requital, respect, reward, scrutiny, tip (gratuity), treatment, understanding (tolerance). SEE MAIN ENTRY

consideration in advance forethought

consideratus deliberate, discreet, intentional

considere subside

considered deliberate, intentional, judicious, meticulous, premeditated, prospective, solid (sound), tactical

considered decision choice (decision)

considered guess estimate (approximate cost), estimation (calculation)

considered opinion determination, holding (ruling of a court)

considered together collective

considered true assumed (inferred)

consign alienate (transfer title), allocate, assign (transfer ownership), attorn, authorize, cede, commit (entrust), commit (institutionalize), confide (trust), contribute (supply), convey (transfer), delegate, detail (assign), disperse (disseminate), divide (distribute), entrust, give (grant), grant (transfer formally), leave (give), mete, refer (send for action), relegate, remand, remit (submit for consideration), transfer, transmit, transport, vest. SEE MAIN ENTRY

consign again reassign

consignable assignable, heritable, negotiable

consignare indorse, inscribe, sign

consignation alienation (transfer of title), assignment (transfer of ownership), consignment, conveyance

consignee heir, licensee, nominee (delegate), payee, receiver, recipient, surety (guarantor), transferee

consigner dealer, merchant

consignify construe (comprehend)

consigning delegation (assignment)

consignment alienation (transfer of title), apportionment, assignment (transfer of ownership), cargo, delegation (assignment), freight. SEE MAIN ENTRY

consignor donor, licensor, transferor

consiliari advise

consilium advice, assembly, committee, counsel, design (intent), determination, direction (guidance), end (intent), expedient, facility (instrumentality), guidance, intention, judgment (discernment), object, panel (discussion group), policy (plan of action), project, reason (sound judgment), scheme, strategy, suggestion

consilium dare advise

consimilar identical, similar

consimilarity identity (similarity)

consimilitude identity (similarity)

consimility identity (similarity)

consist SEE MAIN ENTRY

consist of comprehend (include), comprise, constitute (compose), contain (comprise), encompass (include), include

consistence congealment

consistency adjustment, coherence, compatibility, concordance, conformity (obedience), consensus, constant, continuity, method, regularity, same, synchronism, uniformity

consistent apposite, appropriate, certain (positive), cohesive (sticking), commensurable, commensurate, concordant, consonant, constant, fit, harmonious, logical, natural, proportionate, relevant, suitable, typical, uniform, usual. SEE MAIN ENTRY

consistent with concerted, congruous, consensual, pursuant to

consistent with the agreement as agreed upon

consistently faithfully

consistere consist, halt, stand (position)

consisting of inclusive

consisting of a guarantee promissory

consisting of a pledge promissory

consistory board, meeting (conference)

consociare combine (join together)

consociate accessory, accomplice, affiliate, coactor, coadjutant, cohort, colleague, confederate, connect (relate), conspirer, contact *(communicate)*, copartner *(business associate)*, copartner *(coconspirator)*, correlative, federalize *(associate)*, federate, interrelated, involve *(implicate)*, join *(associate oneself with)*, partner, relate *(establish a connection)*, related. SEE MAIN ENTRY

consociate in crime coconspirator
consociated intimate
consociatio union *(unity)*
consociation affiliation *(connectedness)*, association *(connection)*, cartel, coalescence, coalition, company *(enterprise)*, connection *(relation)*, consortium *(marriage companionship)*, contact *(association)*, corporation, integration *(assimilation)*, partnership, relationship *(connection)*, society, union *(labor organization)*
consolatio solace
consolation pity, solace
consolatory palliative *(abating)*
console alleviate, assure *(give confidence to)*, ease, sympathize
consolidate amalgamate, annex *(add)*, attach *(join together)*, bond *(hold together)*, cement, cohere *(adhere)*, collect *(gather)*, combine *(join together)*, commingle, condense, conjoin, connect *(join together)*, constrict *(compress)*, convene, converge, crystallize, desegregate, federalize *(associate)*, fix *(make firm)*, include, incorporate *(include)*, join *(bring together)*, merge, organize *(unionize)*, pool, unite. SEE MAIN ENTRY
consolidated coadunate, coherent *(joined)*, cohesive *(compact)*, collective, compact *(dense)*, concerted, concurrent *(united)*, conjoint, inseparable, joint, solid *(compact)*
consolidation abridgment *(condensation)*, abstract, accession *(annexation)*, adhesion *(affixing)*, agglomeration, centralization, coalescence, coalition, coherence, combination, compilation, concrescence, confederacy *(compact)*, congealment, conglomeration, connection *(fastening)*, consortium *(business cartel)*, corporation, digest, incorporation *(blend)*, integration *(amalgamation)*, merger, pool, sodality, union *(unity)*. SEE MAIN ENTRY
consonance accordance *(compact)*, accordance *(understanding)*, agreement *(concurrence)*, assent, coherence, compatibility, compliance, concert, conciliation, concordance, conformity *(agreement)*, consensus, propriety *(appropriateness)*, rapport. SEE MAIN ENTRY
consonancy accordance *(understanding)*, cartel, compliance
consonant apposite, appropriate, boiler plate, commensurable, concerted, concordant, concurrent *(united)*, congruous, consistent, correlative, felicitous, fit, harmonious, relevant, suitable, uniform. SEE MAIN ENTRY
consonant with pursuant to
consort accompany, cartel, coactor, colleague, consociate, contributor *(contributor)*, copartner *(business associate)*, join *(associate oneself with)*, spouse. SEE MAIN ENTRY
consort with commingle
consortem participate
consortio partnership
consortium affiliation *(amalgamation)*, cartel, coalition, consolidation, contact *(association)*, matrimony, pact, partnership, pool, syndicate, trust *(combination of businesses)*. SEE MAIN ENTRY
consortship consortium *(marriage companionship)*
conspecific correlative

conspectus abridgment *(condensation)*, abstract, brief, capsule, compendium, digest, outline *(synopsis)*, pandect *(treatise)*, restatement, summary, synopsis
conspici appear *(materialize)*
conspicuous apparent *(perceptible)*, appreciable, arrant *(definite)*, conclusive *(determinative)*, distinct *(clear)*, distinctive, evident, famous, flagrant, illustrious, manifest, naked *(perceptible)*, notable, noteworthy, notorious, obvious, open *(in sight)*, outrageous, outstanding *(prominent)*, palpable, patent, pretentious *(ostentatious)*, prominent, remarkable, renowned, salient, scrutable, special, stark, unmistakable, unusual, visible *(noticeable)*. SEE MAIN ENTRY
conspicuously fairly *(clearly)*
conspicuousness notoriety
conspicuus conspicuous, remarkable
conspiracy cabal, collusion, connivance, faction, frame up, machination, plan, plot *(secret plan)*, racket. SEE MAIN ENTRY
conspirare conspire, plot
conspiratio coalition, plot *(secret plan)*
conspirational collusive
conspirative collusive
conspirator abettor, coactor, confederate, conspirer. SEE MAIN ENTRY
conspiratorial collusive, malevolent
conspire combine *(act in concert)*, connive, contrive, cooperate, maneuver, plan, plot, scheme. SEE MAIN ENTRY
conspire against frame *(charge falsely)*, frame *(prearrange)*
conspirer coactor, confederate, copartner *(coconspirator)*. SEE MAIN ENTRY
conspiring clandestine, collusive
constable peace officer
constabulary police
constancy adherence *(devotion)*, adhesion *(loyalty)*, allegiance, constant, continuity, diligence *(perseverance)*, discipline *(obedience)*, faith, fealty, fidelity, homage, indestructibility, industry *(activity)*, loyalty, perpetuity, prowess *(bravery)*, purpose, resolution *(decision)*, tenacity, tolerance, uniformity. SEE MAIN ENTRY
constans consistent, constant *(adjective)*, constant *(noun)*, immutable, regular *(orderly)*, resolute, stable, steadfast, unaffected *(uninfluenced)*, uniform
constant chronic, continual *(connected)*, continuous, dependable, diligent, durable, faithful *(diligent)*, faithful *(loyal)*, habitual, immutable, incessant, loyal, patient, permanent, perpetual, reliable, resolute, sedulous, stable, standing, staunch, steadfast, true *(loyal)*, unalterable, uniform, unrelenting, unremitting, unyielding. SEE MAIN ENTRY
constant flow chain *(series)*
constant progression perpetuity
constantia fidelity, regularity
constantly faithfully, in good faith, invariably
constantly recurring continual *(connected)*
constantly together inseparable
constare persevere, subsist
consternation apprehension *(fear)*, bombshell, cloud *(suspicion)*, confusion *(ambiguity)*, doubt *(suspicion)*, fear, fright, panic, surprise, trepidation. SEE MAIN ENTRY
constituency chamber *(body)*, constituent *(member)*, district. SEE MAIN ENTRY
constituent component, element, factor *(ingredient)*, feature *(characteristic)*, ingredient, integral, item, member *(individual in a group)*, part *(portion)*, segment, substantive, unit *(item)*. SEE MAIN ENTRY

constituent part component, ingredient
constituents constituency, contents
constituere adopt, agree *(contract)*, appoint, arrange *(methodize)*, constitute *(establish)*, decide, determine, establish *(launch)*, fix *(arrange)*, fix *(settle)*, instate, legislate, resolve *(decide)*, settle
constitute comprehend *(include)*, comprise, consist, create, embody, establish *(launch)*, frame *(construct)*, make, nominate. SEE MAIN ENTRY
constituting creation
constituting a difference differential
constitutio settlement
constitution building *(business of assembling)*, character *(personal quality)*, characteristic, charter *(declaration of rights)*, code, color *(complexion)*, composition *(makeup)*, configuration *(form)*, construction, content *(structure)*, disposition *(inclination)*, frame *(mood)*, organization *(structure)*, polity, structure *(composition)*, temperament. SEE MAIN ENTRY
constitutional fundamental, hereditary, innate, lawful, legal, legitimate *(rightful)*, licit, organic, permissible, rightful, salutary, valid
constitutionality legality
constitutionally opposed antipathetic *(oppositional)*
constitutive causal, causative, primary
constitutive element determinant, factor *(ingredient)*
constitutive principle center *(essence)*
constitutus definite
constrain allay, apprehend *(arrest)*, arrest *(apprehend)*, bind *(obligate)*, bind *(restrain)*, check *(restrain)*, coerce, command, commit *(institutionalize)*, compel, confine, constrict *(inhibit)*, contain *(restrain)*, control *(restrain)*, debar, detain *(restrain)*, disadvantage, enjoin, exact, foist, force *(coerce)*, hinder, immure, impose *(enforce)*, impose *(subject)*, imprison, inhibit, jail, keep *(restrain)*, limit, make, moderate *(temper)*, pressure, require *(compel)*, restrain, restrict, stay *(halt)*, stifle, trammel, withhold. SEE MAIN ENTRY
constrain again rearrest
constrain by force extort
constrained arrested *(apprehended)*, bound, controlled *(restrained)*, obligatory
constraining binding, compelling, compulsory, necessary *(inescapable)*
constraining force pressure
constraining power force *(compulsion)*
constraint bar *(obstruction)*, bondage, captivity, coercion, commitment *(confinement)*, composure, compulsion *(coercion)*, control *(restriction)*, custody *(incarceration)*, detention, deterrence, deterrent, discipline *(obedience)*, disincentive, duress, embarrassment, enforcement, fetter, force *(compulsion)*, incarceration, limitation, moderation, obstacle, obstruction, pressure, prohibition, quota, requirement, restraint, restriction, retention. SEE MAIN ENTRY
constraint by force bondage, coercion
constraint to obedience compulsion *(coercion)*
constrict attenuate, block, clog, concentrate *(consolidate)*, decrease, deter, limit. SEE MAIN ENTRY
constricted compact *(dense)*, limited
constricting limiting
constriction compulsion *(coercion)*, constraint *(restriction)*, curtailment, decrease, deterrence, deterrent, force *(compulsion)*, hindrance, obstruction, restriction

constringe attenuate, constrict (*compress*), decrease

constringed compact (*dense*)

constringent bitter (*penetrating*)

construability construction

construable accountable (*explainable*), circumstantial, determinable (*ascertainable*)

construal construction

construct build (*construct*), compose, create, devise (*invent*), establish (*launch*), forge (*produce*), form, generate, invent (*produce for the first time*), make, manufacture, orchestrate, produce (*manufacture*)

construct a figure delineate

construction building (*business of assembling*), building (*structure*), composition (*makeup*), configuration (*form*), connotation, content (*structure*), creation, development (*building*), edifice, formation, frame (*structure*), manufacture, motif, organization (*structure*), performance (*workmanship*), rendition (*explication*). SEE MAIN ENTRY

constructional constructive (*inferential*)

constructive beneficial, causative, interpretive, productive, virtual. SEE MAIN ENTRY

constructive criticism advocacy

constructor architect, contractor, materialman

construe characterize, clarify, deduce, deduct (*conclude by reasoning*), define, derive (*deduce*), elucidate, expound, infer, interpret, rationalize, render (*depict*). SEE MAIN ENTRY

construe falsely cloak

construe wrongly misconstrue

constuprate violate

constupration rape

consubstantial congruous, identical, similar

consubstantiate unite

consuescere cohabit

consuetude behavior, custom, habit, manner (*behavior*), practice (*custom*), usage

consuetudinal accustomed (*customary*), frequent, regular (*conventional*), repeated, traditional, usual

consuetudinary accustomed (*customary*), customary, familiar (*customary*), frequent, habitual, ordinary, regular (*conventional*), repeated, traditional, usual

consuetudo habit, practice (*procedure*), usage

consul plenipotentiary

consulate deputation (*delegation*), embassy

consulere provide (*arrange for*)

consult consider, counsel, deliberate, discuss, refer (*send for action*). SEE MAIN ENTRY

consult again reconsider

consult with advise, confer (*consult*), converse, debate

consultant specialist

consultants commission (*agency*)

consultare confer (*consult*), consult (*ask advice of*), deliberate

consultatio deliberation

consultation caucus, conference, confrontation (*act of setting face to face*), conversation, guidance, interview, meeting (*conference*), negotiation, parley, session

consultation meeting conference

consultative hortative

consultative body board

consulting advisory

consultive body congress

consulto design (*intent*)

consultor client, patron (*regular customer*)

consultum edict

consumable disposable

consume burn, decay, deflagrate, degenerate, deplete, despoil, destroy (*efface*), diminish, dissipate (*expend foolishly*), eliminate (*eradicate*), erode, exhaust (*deplete*), exploit (*make use of*), extirpate, obliterate, prey, spend. SEE MAIN ENTRY

consume completely exhaust (*deplete*)

consume one's substance dissipate (*expend foolishly*)

consumed irredeemable

consumer client, customer, patron (*regular customer*). SEE MAIN ENTRY

consumer demand market (*demand*)

consumer durables goods, merchandise

consumer goods merchandise

consumere consume, exhaust (*deplete*), spend

consuming deadly, deleterious, harmful, malignant

consummare consummate, finish

consummate absolute (*ideal*), accomplish, arrant (*definite*), attain, cease, close (*terminate*), commit (*perpetrate*), complete (*all-embracing*), complete, comprehensive, conclude (*complete*), culminate, definitive, discharge (*perform*), discontinue (*abandon*), dispatch (*dispose of*), finish, fulfill, implement, mature, outright, perfect, perform (*adhere to*), realize (*make real*), ripe, sterling, superlative, thorough, transact, unmitigated, unqualified (*unlimited*). SEE MAIN ENTRY

consummated choate lien, complete (*ended*)

consummation action (*performance*), cessation (*termination*), close (*conclusion*), commission (*act*), conclusion (*outcome*), consequence (*conclusion*), denouement, destination, discharge (*performance*), end (*termination*), expiration, fait accompli, finality, fruition, maturity, outcome, payoff (*result*), performance (*execution*), pinnacle, realization, satisfaction (*fulfilment*), transaction

consumptio consumption

consumption decline, destruction, deterioration, erosion, expense (*sacrifice*), prostration, waste. SEE MAIN ENTRY

consumptive fatal, harmful

contact coalescence, collision (*accident*), connection (*abutment*), convey (*communicate*), correspond (*communicate*), impinge, liaison, meeting (*encounter*), notify, reach. SEE MAIN ENTRY

contactual proximate

contactus contact (*touching*), contact (*communicate*)

contagion contaminate, disease

contagious pestilent. SEE MAIN ENTRY

contain accommodate, border (*bound*), circumscribe (*surround by boundary*), comprehend (*include*), comprise, confine, consist, constitute (*compose*), detain (*hold in custody*), detain (*restrain*), embrace (*encircle*), enclose, encompass (*include*), hold up (*delay*), include, incorporate (*include*), keep (*restrain*), limit, own, restrain, stifle. SEE MAIN ENTRY

contain oneself refrain

contained arrested (*checked*)

contained in a will testamentary

container catchall, coffer, depository, enclosure, repository

containing comprehensive, inclusive, limiting

containing a penalty penal

containing a pledge promissory

containing an assurance promissory

containing error erroneous

containing power capacity (*maximum*)

containing stipulations conditional

containment blockade (*enclosure*), constraint (*imprisonment*), enclosure, quota, restraint, restriction

contaminare infect, taint (*contaminate*)

contaminate adulterate, corrupt, damage, debase, impair, infect, pervert, pollute, smear, stain, sully, tarnish. SEE MAIN ENTRY

contaminated marred, noxious, peccant (*unhealthy*)

contaminating contagious

contamination air pollution, defilement, detriment, perversion

contankerous contumacious

conte story (*narrative*)

contemn condescend (*patronize*), decry, denounce (*condemn*), depreciate, discommend, disdain, dishonor (*deprive of honor*), disparage, flout, humiliate, misprize, spurn. SEE MAIN ENTRY

contemned blameworthy, contemptible

contemnendus contemptible

contemplari review, survey (*examine*)

contemplate anticipate (*expect*), brood, concentrate (*pay attention*), conjure, consider, deliberate, devote, digest (*comprehend*), examine (*study*), muse, peruse, ponder, presume, reason (*conclude*), reflect (*ponder*), regard (*pay attention*), scrutinize, study, weigh

contemplated apparent (*presumptive*), deliberate, foreseeable, intentional, willful

contemplatio contemplation

contemplation deliberation, design (*intent*), dialectic, diligence (*care*), discretion (*power of choice*), discrimination (*differentiation*), expectation, forethought, hindsight, intent, introspection, judgment (*discernment*), prospect (*outlook*), purview, reflection (*thought*), speculation (*conjecture*), target. SEE MAIN ENTRY

contemplation of past events hindsight

contemplation of the past hindsight, recollection, retrospect

contemplative circumspect, cogitative, deliberate, pensive, politic, speculative

contemplativeness deliberation

contemporaneous coincidental, concomitant, concurrent (*at the same time*), current, present (*current*), simultaneous. SEE MAIN ENTRY

contemporary concomitant, concurrent (*at the same time*), contemporaneous, current, peer, present (*current*), prevailing (*current*), simultaneous, sophisticated. SEE MAIN ENTRY

contemporary account journal

contempt contumely, disdain, disgrace, dishonor (*shame*), disparagement, disregard (*lack of respect*), disrespect, ignominy, impertinent (*insolent*), infamy, malice, misprision, obloquy, odium, opprobrium, rejection, reproach, ridicule, shame, spite. SEE MAIN ENTRY

contempt of danger prowess (*bravery*)

contemptibility bad repute, disrepute, ignominy, ill repute

contemptible bad (*offensive*), base (*bad*), blameful, blameworthy, contemptuous, depraved, disgraceful, disreputable, heinous, ignoble, inferior (*lower in quality*), loathsome, nefarious, notorious, obnoxious, odious, offensive (*offending*), outrageous, paltry, perverse, petty, poor (*inferior in quality*), repulsive, sinister, unworthy. SEE MAIN ENTRY

contemptibleness ignominy, ill repute

contemptio disdain

contemptousness disregard (*lack of respect*)

contemptuous blameful, blameworthy, calumnious, contumacious, cynical, disdainful, impertinent (*insolent*), inflated (*vain*), insolent, libelous, orgulous, proud (*conceited*), supercilious. SEE MAIN ENTRY

contemptuous language vilification

contemptuous resistance contempt (*disobedience to the court*)

contemptuous treatment contumely

contemptuousness contempt (*disdain*), contumely, disdain, disrespect

contemptus contempt (*disdain*), contemptible

contend allege, answer (*reply*), argue, assert, avouch (*avow*), avow, bear (*adduce*), bicker, claim (*maintain*), collide (*clash*), compete, conflict, contest, counter, counteract, cross (*disagree with*), debate, declare, dicker, differ (*disagree*), disaccord, dispute (*contest*), engage (*involve*), insist, litigate, oppose, oppugn, plead (*allege in a legal action*), posit, postulate, profess (*avow*), propose, propound, reason (*persuade*), refute, strive. SEE MAIN ENTRY

contend against antagonize, confront (*oppose*)

contend against in discussion controvert

contend for advocate, dispute (*contest*), justify, plead (*argue a case*)

contend in argument argue, dispute (*debate*)

contend in words discuss

contend with confront (*oppose*)

contended alleged

contender adversary, aggressor, appellant, candidate, contestant, disputant, foe, litigant, opponent, party (*litigant*), peer, rival. SEE MAIN ENTRY

contendere contend (*dispute*), contend (*maintain*), contest, endeavor, exert, hasten, labor, maintain (*carry on*), strive

contending competitive (*antagonistic*)

content complacent, component, composure, disarm (*set at ease*), element, factor (*ingredient*), inclined, ingredient, meaning, propitiate, proud (*self-respecting*), satisfaction (*fulfilment*), satisfy (*fulfill*), subject (*topic*), substance (*essential nature*), tenor, willing (*not averse*). SEE MAIN ENTRY

contented complacent, peaceable, proud (*self-respecting*)

contentedness satisfaction (*fulfilment*)

contentio antithesis, competition, effort, endeavor

contention avowal, case (*lawsuit*), collision (*dispute*), conflict, confrontation (*altercation*), contest (*dispute*), contravention, controversy (*argument*), disaccord, disagreement, discord, dispute, dissension, embroilment, feud, fracas, fray, lawsuit, opposition, resistance, rift (*disagreement*), strife, struggle, variance (*disagreement*). SEE MAIN ENTRY

contentious argumentative, competitive (*antagonistic*), debatable, dissenting, forensic, fractious, hostile, litigious, moot, negative, offensive (*taking the initiative*), petulant, polemic, pugnacious, querulous, remonstrative. SEE MAIN ENTRY

contentious group faction

contentiousness argument (*contention*), belligerency, conflict, contention (*opposition*)

contentment composure, satisfaction (*fulfilment*)

contents capsule, cargo, composition (*makeup*), effects, inventory, merchandise, outline (*synopsis*), scenario, stock in trade. SEE MAIN ENTRY

conterminal proximate

conterminous adjacent, contiguous, immediate (*not distant*), proximate

contest answer (*reply*), answer (*respond legally*), appeal, argue, bicker, compete, competition, conflict (*noun*), conflict (*verb*), contend (*dispute*), contention (*argument*), contention (*opposition*), contravene, contravention, controversy (*argument*), controversy (*lawsuit*), controvert, cross (*disagree with*), debate, disagree, discuss, disown (*deny the validity*), embroilment, engage (*involve*), fight (*argument*), fight (*battle*), fight (*battle*), fray, gainsay, grapple, hearing, impugn, lawsuit, oppose, prevent, primary, strife, strive, sue, trial (*legal proceeding*). SEE MAIN ENTRY

contest a case by asking for review appeal

contest in court litigate

contest in law litigate

contestability cloud (*suspicion*)

contestable arguable, controversial, debatable, disputable, doubtful, dubious, dubitative, forensic, litigable, moot, polemic, problematic, speculative, uncertain (*questionable*), undecided. SEE MAIN ENTRY

contestant adversary, candidate, contender, disputant, foe, litigant, party (*litigant*), rival. SEE MAIN ENTRY

contestation affray, altercation, belligerency, confrontation (*altercation*), contention (*opposition*), controversy (*argument*), primary, strife, struggle

contested litigious, moot

contester adversary, contender, contestant

contesting hostile, negative

context case (*set of circumstances*), connotation, environment, posture (*situation*). SEE MAIN ENTRY

contextual incident

contexture content (*structure*)

contextus coherence, coherent (*joined*)

contiguity border, contact (*touching*), propinquity (*proximity*)

contiguous adjacent, close (*near*), immediate (*not distant*), proximate. SEE MAIN ENTRY

contiguousness connection (*abutment*), contact (*touching*)

contiguus adjacent

continence moderation. SEE MAIN ENTRY

continens consecutive, contiguous

continentia continence, moderation

continere contain (*enclose*), control (*restrain*), encompass (*include*), involve (*implicate*)

contingence contact (*touching*), contingency

contingency chance (*possibility*), incident, occurrence, secondary, sine qua non. SEE MAIN ENTRY

contingent circumstantial, contingency, correlative, dependent, dubious, executory, extrinsic, incident, provisional, quota, reciprocal, related, restrictive, subject (*conditional*), tentative, uncertain (*questionable*). SEE MAIN ENTRY

contingent deed held in trust escrow

contingent event contingency

contingent interest claim (*right*)

contingent on conditional

contingent upon based on, qualified (*conditioned*)

continual chronic, consecutive, constant, continuous, direct (*uninterrupted*), durable, habitual, immutable, incessant, periodic, unrelenting, unremitting. SEE MAIN ENTRY

continually increasing cumulative (*increasing*)

continually recurring constant

continualness continuity, perpetuity

continuance continuation (*prolongation*), continuation (*resumption*), continuity, diligence (*perseverance*), duration, extension (*postponement*), habitation (*act of inhabiting*), indestructibility, life (*period of existence*), longevity, pendency, period, perpetuity, phase (*period*), renewal, survival. SEE MAIN ENTRY

continuance in time duration

continuatio continuance, continuation (*prolongation*), continuity, succession

continuation adjournment, appendix (*supplement*), continuance, continuity, extension (*postponement*), longevity, perpetuity, rider, survival. SEE MAIN ENTRY

continuation in time duration

continuation of life survival

continue adhere (*persist*), adjourn, bear (*tolerate*), dwell (*linger over*), endure (*last*), exist, extend (*enlarge*), last, maintain (*carry on*), pass (*advance*), persevere, persist, preserve, prolong, propagate (*increase*), prosecute (*carry forward*), protract (*stall*), pursue (*carry on*), recur, remain (*continue*), renew (*begin again*), reopen, resist (*withstand*), resume, subsist, sustain (*prolong*). SEE MAIN ENTRY

continue onward progress

continue to be endure (*last*), exist

continue to exist endure (*last*)

continue to hold retain (*keep in possession*)

continue to live exist

continue under pain endure (*suffer*)

continued continual (*connected*), live (*existing*), open-ended, permanent, persistent, standing

continued existence perpetuity

continued movement process (*course*)

continuing chronic, consecutive, constant, continual (*connected*), continuous, durable, infallible, lasting, live (*existing*), open-ended, patient, permanent, persistent, pertinacious, protracted, stable, standing

continuing after death posthumous

continuing development process (*course*)

continuing for a short time ephemeral

continuing offer option (*contractual provision*)

continuing offer to buy option (*contractual provision*)

continuity chain (*series*), coherence, frequency, indestructibility, uniformity. SEE MAIN ENTRY

continuous adjacent, chronic, consecutive, constant, continual (*perpetual*), direct (*uninterrupted*), immutable, incessant, perpetual, persistent, progressive (*going forward*), relentless, unrelenting, unremitting. SEE MAIN ENTRY

continuous time perpetuity

continuousness continuity, perpetuity

continuum continuity, sequence

continuum of days annum
continuus continual *(connected)*, incessant, unremitting
contio assembly, harangue
contorquere launch *(project)*
contort distort, misrepresent. SEE MAIN ENTRY
contorted circuitous, tortuous *(bending)*, unreasonable
contortion distortion
contour ambit, boundary, circumscribe *(surround by boundary)*, complexion, configuration *(confines)*, configuration *(form)*, delineate, delineation, outline *(boundary)*, periphery. SEE MAIN ENTRY
contra SEE MAIN ENTRY
contra dicere recusare object
contra leges violation
contra rem facere militate
contraband impermissible, unlawful. SEE MAIN ENTRY
contrabandist bootlegger, racketeer, thief
contract abridge *(shorten)*, abstract *(summarize)*, accordance *(compact)*, adjustment, arrangement *(understanding)*, assume *(undertake)*, attenuate, bargain, bond *(secure a debt)*, buy, cartel, clause, commitment *(responsibility)*, compact, composition *(agreement in bankruptcy)*, condense, consolidate *(strengthen)*, constrict *(compress)*, covenant, deal, decrease, diminish, employ *(engage services)*, incur, indenture, lease, lessen, let *(lease)*, mutual understanding, obligation *(duty)*, pact, pledge *(binding promise)*, promise, promise *(vow)*, protocol *(agreement)*, provide *(arrange for)*, record, reduce, rent, settlement, stipulate, stipulation, surety *(certainty)*, testament, treaty, understanding *(agreement)*, undertake, undertaking *(commitment)*, undertaking *(pledge)*. SEE MAIN ENTRY
contract a debt owe
contract against future loss insurance
contract against unknown contingencies insurance
contract an obligation pledge *(promise the performance of)*, promise *(vow)*
contract before marriage antenuptial agreement
contract for assume *(undertake)*, engage *(hire)*, hire, retain *(employ)*
contract for exclusive possession lease
contract for exclusive possession of lands lease
contract for possession and profits lease
contract for possession of land lease
contract for use and occupation lease
contract obligation liability. SEE MAIN ENTRY
contract of mortgage hypothecation
contract of pledge hypothecation
contract payment installment, premium *(insurance payment)*
contract talks negotiation
contract to lease sublet
contract to work indenture
contracted agreed *(promised)*, brief, compact *(dense)*, compact *(pithy)*, concise, indentured, laconic, narrow
contracting party privy
contraction abridgment *(condensation)*, abstract, blockade *(limitation)*, compendium, curtailment, decline, decrease, decrement, digest, diminution, outline *(synopsis)*
contractor materialman, supplier. SEE MAIN ENTRY
contracts dealings
contractual SEE MAIN ENTRY

contractual assurance warranty. SEE MAIN ENTRY
contractual bond privity
contractual clause article *(distinct section of a writing)*
contractual obligation bill *(formal declaration)*, compact, covenant, indenture, mortgage, policy *(contract)*, specialty *(contract)*
contractual promise warranty
contractual representation warranty
contractual statement agreement *(contract)*, compact, covenant, indenture, policy *(contract)*, specialty *(contract)*
contractual terms condition *(contingent provision)*, counteroffer
contractus narrow
contradicere contradict
contradict abrogate *(annul)*, annul, answer *(reply)*, bear false witness, challenge, collide *(clash)*, conflict, confront *(oppose)*, contend *(dispute)*, contest, contravene, controvert, counter, counteract, countercharge, countervail, cross *(disagree with)*, demur, differ *(disagree)*, disaccord, disagree, disallow, disapprove *(reject)*, disown *(deny the validity)*, dispute *(contest)*, dispute *(debate)*, dissent *(differ in opinion)*, except *(object)*, fight *(counteract)*, gainsay, impugn, negate, oppose, oppugn, protest, rebut, recant, refute, renege, repudiate, resist *(oppose)*. SEE MAIN ENTRY
contradict absolutely controvert
contradicting contradictory, contrary, dissenting
contradictio objection
contradiction antipode, antithesis, collision *(dispute)*, conflict, confutation, contradistinction, contraposition, contrary, contravention, counterargument, denial, difference, disaccord, disagreement, disapproval, discrepancy, disparity, dissidence, exception *(objection)*, impugnation, incongruity, inconsistency, negation, paradox, reaction *(opposition)*, repudiation, retraction. SEE MAIN ENTRY
contradiction of terms non sequitur
contradictive opposite
contradictoriness contradistinction, incompatibility *(difference)*, incongruity, inconsistency
contradictory adverse *(opposite)*, antipathetic *(oppositional)*, contrary, different, discordant, disparate, hostile, illogical, incongruous, inconsistent, negative, opposite, polemic, repugnant *(incompatible)*. SEE MAIN ENTRY
contradictory evidence answer *(judicial response)*
contradistinct adverse *(opposite)*, antipathetic *(oppositional)*, contradictory, contrary, different, discordant, discriminating *(distinguishing)*
contradistinction antipode, antithesis, contradiction, contraposition, contrary, difference, disparity. SEE MAIN ENTRY
contradistinctive different
contradistinguish demarcate, distinguish
contrahere abridge *(shorten)*, concentrate *(consolidate)*, contract, retrench
contraindicate discourage
contraindicating contradictory, contrary
contraindication admonition, antipode, contradiction, deterrence, deterrent, warning
contrapose confront *(oppose)*, polarize
contraposition antipode, antithesis, conflict, contradiction, difference, disagreement,

disparity, dissent *(difference of opinion)*. SEE MAIN ENTRY
contrapositive adverse *(opposite)*, antipathetic *(oppositional)*, contradictory, contrary
contraption invention
contraremonstrance counterargument, counterclaim
contrariae irreconcilable
contrariant adverse *(opposite)*, hostile
contraries contradiction
contrariety admonition, antipode, antithesis, collision *(dispute)*, conflict, confutation, contention *(opposition)*, contradiction, contradistinction, contraposition, difference, disaccord, disagreement, dissent *(nonconcurrence)*, dissidence, distinction *(difference)*, exception *(exclusion)*, ill will, impugnation, incompatibility *(difference)*, incongruity, inconsistency, opposition, paradox, reaction *(opposition)*, resistance, revolt, strife, variance *(disagreement)*
contrarily contra
contrariness antipode, conflict, contradiction, difference, disaccord, disagreement, impugnation, incongruity, resistance
contrarious adverse *(opposite)*, contradictory, discordant, hostile, lawless
contrarium antithesis
contrarius adverse *(opposite)*, contradictory, contrary, inconsistent, opposite
contrariwise contra *(adverb)*, contra *(preposition)*
contrary adverse *(opposite)*, antipathetic *(oppositional)*, antipode, antithesis, competitive *(antagonistic)*, contentious, contra, contradictory, deviant, different, discordant, disinclined, disobedient, dissident, dissimilar, eccentric, fractious, froward, hostile, incongruous, inconsistent, inimical, intractable, inverse, litigious, negative, nonconforming, opposite, perverse, recalcitrant, recusant, repugnant *(incompatible)*, spiteful, unfavorable, unreasonable, unruly, unsuitable, vicious. SEE MAIN ENTRY
contrary action opposition
contrary advice admonition
contrary assertion confutation, contradiction, denial
contrary to common sense ludicrous
contrary to decency improper
contrary to expectations unforeseeable
contrary to experience implausible
contrary to fact dishonest, fallacious, false *(inaccurate)*, fraudulent, untrue. SEE MAIN ENTRY
contrary to good business antitrust act
contrary to good taste improper
contrary to law felonious, illegal, illegally, illegitimate *(illegal)*, illicit, impermissible. SEE MAIN ENTRY
contrary to professional ethics unprofessional
contrary to reason arbitrary, contradictory, disproportionate, illogical, impossible, irrational, ludicrous, sophistic
contrary to the rules of logic illogical
contrast antipode, antithesis, collation, compare, comparison, conflict *(noun)*, conflict *(verb)*, contradict, contradiction, contradistinction, contraposition, contrary, deviate, deviation, differ *(vary)*, difference, differentiate, discrepancy, discriminate *(distinguish)*, disparity, distinction *(difference)*, diversification, incompatibility *(difference)*, incompatibility *(inconsistency)*, inequality, nonconformity, offset, polarize, vary. SEE MAIN ENTRY

contrast with collide (clash), confront (oppose)

contrastable adverse (opposite)

contrasted antipathetic (oppositional), contradictory, contrary, dissimilar, distinct (distinguished from others), negative, opposite, peculiar (distinctive)

contrasting contrary, different, discriminating (distinguishing), discrimination (differentiation), disparate, dissimilar, distinct (distinguished from others), distinctive, negative, opposite, peculiar (distinctive)

contrasting quality differential

contrastive comparative, different, diverse, peculiar (distinctive), relative (comparative)

contravene abrogate (annul), annul, answer (reply), circumvent, collide (clash), complain (criticize), confront (oppose), contest, contradict, controvert, counter, countervail, cross (disagree with), defeat, demonstrate (protest), demur, deny (contradict), disaccord, disaffirm, disagree, disallow, disapprove (reject), discommode, disobey, disown (deny the validity), disprove, dispute (contest), except (object), gainsay, negate, object, offend (violate the law), oppose, oppugn, protest, rebut, refute, reject, repudiate, resist (oppose), thwart, trespass, violate, withstand. SEE MAIN ENTRY

contravened broken (unfulfilled)

contravening contradictory, negative

contravention ademption, annulment, breach, conflict, confutation, contention (opposition), contradiction, counterargument, crime, criticism, denial, disagreement, disapproval, exception (objection), impugnation, infraction, infringement, negation, opposition, rejection, resistance, transgression. SEE MAIN ENTRY

contraway contrary

contrawise contra

contretemps accident (misfortune), adversity

contretemps casualty, catastrophe, debacle

contretemps deterrence, disaster

contribuere contribution (donation)

contribute abet, bear (yield), bequeath, bestow, capitalize (provide capital), convey (transfer), cooperate, create, defray, dole, endow, fund, furnish, give (grant), help, inure (benefit), involve (participate), participate, pay, present (make a gift), profit, provide (supply), redound, render (administer), replenish, spend, subsidize, supply, support (assist). SEE MAIN ENTRY

contribute to bear (support), cause, compound, espouse, further, promote (organize), serve (assist), supplement, sustain (prolong)

contribute to again refinance

contribute toward conduce, conspire

contributing concerted, concurrent (united), contributory, donative

contributing force determinant, expedient, factor (ingredient), instrument (tool)

contribution appropriation (donation), behalf, benefit (conferment), charity, collection (payment), donation, endowment, gift (present), gratuity (present), help, largess (gift), subsidy, support (assistance), tip (gratuity). SEE MAIN ENTRY

contributive beneficial, constructive (creative), lucrative

contributor benefactor, determinant, donor, grantor. SEE MAIN ENTRY

contributors press

contributory ancillary (auxiliary), beneficial, donative, gratuitous (given without recompense), instrumental, purposeful, subservient. SEE MAIN ENTRY

contrite penitent, remorseful, repentant. SEE MAIN ENTRY

contrite person penitent

contriteness remorse

contrition remorse

contrivance appliance, arrangement (plan), artifice, collusion, conduit (channel), connivance, conspiracy, expedient, facility (instrumentality), instrument (tool), invention, loophole, machination, ploy, project, resource, scheme, stratagem, strategy, tool. SEE MAIN ENTRY

contrivances paraphernalia (apparatus)

contrive arrange (plan), build (construct), cause, circumvent, compose, conceive (invent), conspire, create, devise (invent), forge (produce), form, frame (construct), frame (formulate), frame (prearrange), generate, invent (produce for the first time), make, maneuver, manufacture, militate, originate, plan, produce (manufacture), scheme. SEE MAIN ENTRY

contrive a result frame (prearrange), predetermine

contrive to gain pursue (strive to gain)

contrived aforethought, assumed (feigned), controlled (automatic), strategic, tactical

contrived in advance aforethought

contriver accomplice, architect, author (originator), coactor, conspirer

contriving artful, building (business of assembling), collusion, creation, machiavellian, subtle (insidious)

control administer (conduct), administration, agency (commission), agency (legal relationship), allay, authority (power), capacity (authority), censor, censorship, charge (custody), check (bar), check (restrain), coercion, compel, composure, conduct, confine, constrain (restrain), constraint (imprisonment), constrict (inhibit), contain (restrain), curb, custody (supervision), damper (stopper), detain (hold in custody), detain (restrain), detention, deterrence, dint, direct (supervise), discipline (obedience), disposition (final arrangement), dominance, dominate, dominion (absolute ownership), dominion (supreme authority), duress, fetter, force (compulsion), force (strength), force (coerce), govern, government (administration), handle (manage), hegemony, hold (possess), hold up (delay), impose (subject), influence, inhibit, jurisdiction, keep (restrain), longanimity, manage, management (supervision), manipulate (utilize skillfully), militate, mitigate, moderate (preside over), moderation, monitor, monopolize, monopoly, obsess, occupancy, occupation (possession), occupy (take possession), operate, overlook (superintend), oversee, own, ownership, patronage (power to appoint jobs), police, possess, power, preclude, predominance, prescribe, preside, prestige, prevail (be in force), prevail (triumph), primacy, prohibit, qualify (condition), quota, regulate (manage), repress, restrain, restraint, restrict, retention, rule (govern), seisin, stifle, subdue, subject, subjection, subjugate, sufferance, superintend, supervision, supremacy, temperance, trammel, trust (custody), wield. SEE MAIN ENTRY

control market supply monopolize

control of the market monopoly

control of trade embargo, monopoly

control prices monopolize

control the flow of news censor

control trade monopolize

controllable corrigible, malleable, obedient, pliable, tractable

controlled arrested (checked), deliberate, dispassionate, limited, patient, qualified (conditioned), regular (orderly), stoical. SEE MAIN ENTRY

controlled by dependent

controller caretaker (one fulfilling the function of office), employer, principal (director), superintendent

controllers hierarchy (persons in authority), management (directorate), management (supervision)

controlling cardinal (basic), cardinal (outstanding), dictatorial, dominant, forcible, influential, leading (guiding), master, powerful, predominant, prevailing (having superior force), principal, sovereign (absolute)

controlling factors circumstances

controlling force main force

controlling influence predominance

controlling power clout, main force, patronage (power to appoint jobs), pressure

controlment power

controversia controversy (argument), dispute, lawsuit

controversial arguable, contestable, debatable, disputable, dubious, dubitative, equivocal, forensic, litigable, litigious, moot, polemic, problematic. SEE MAIN ENTRY

controversialist contender, disputant, litigant, party (litigant)

controversion contest (dispute), contradiction, contravention, counterargument

controversus controversial

controversy altercation, argument (contention), belligerency, case (lawsuit), conflict, contention (argument), contention (opposition), contest (dispute), contradiction, difference, disaccord, disagreement, discord, disparity, dispute, dissension, dissidence, feud, fight (argument), incompatibility (difference), lawsuit, rift (disagreement), strife, struggle, variance (disagreement). SEE MAIN ENTRY

controversy before a court lawsuit

controvert answer (reply), answer (respond legally), argue, bicker, challenge, collide (clash), conflict, confront (oppose), contest, contradict, cross (disagree with), debate, demonstrate (protest), demur, deny (contradict), disaccord, disaffirm, disagree, disallow, disapprove (reject), disown (deny the validity), disprove, dispute (contest), dispute (debate), gainsay, impugn, negate, object, oppose, oppugn, rebut, refute, reject. SEE MAIN ENTRY

controvertibility cloud (suspicion)

controvertible actionable, arguable, contestable, controversial, debatable, disputable, doubtful, dubious, dubitative, forensic, indefinite, litigable, litigious, moot, problematic, speculative, uncertain (questionable), unsustainable, untenable

controverting dissenting

controvertist disputant

contumacious contentious, disobedient, disorderly, froward, impertinent (insolent), inflexible, insolent, insubordinate, intractable, lawless, perverse, recalcitrant, recusant, restive, unruly. SEE MAIN ENTRY

695

contumaciousness contempt *(disobedience to the court)*, dissidence

contumacy contempt *(disobedience to the court)*, defiance, disloyalty, disrespect, rebellion, resistance

contumax contumacious, froward, insolent, willful

contumelia contumely, reproach

contumeliosus outrageous, scurrilous

contumelious blameworthy, bumptious, calumnious, contemptible, contemptuous, cynical, derogatory, disdainful, impertinent *(insolent)*, insolent, offensive *(offending)*, outrageous, perverse, presumptuous, supercilious

contumeliousness disdain

contumely aspersion, bad repute, contempt *(disdain)*, contempt *(disobedience to the court)*, denunciation, disapprobation, discredit, dishonor *(shame)*, disregard *(lack of respect)*, disrespect, phillipic, reproach, revilement, vilification. SEE MAIN ENTRY

contund beat *(strike)*

conturbare disturb, embarrass

contuse beat *(strike)*

convalesce progress

convalescence revival

convalescent patient

convalescent case patient

convenance decorum

convenant certify *(attest)*

convene call *(summon)*, collect *(gather)*, congregate, converge, join *(bring together)*, meet, rendezvous. SEE MAIN ENTRY

convenience accommodate, advantage, appliance, benefit *(betterment)*, easement, expedience, expedient, opportunity, use, utility *(usefulness)*

conveniences paraphernalia *(apparatus)*

conveniens consistent, consonant

convenient available, beneficial, constructive *(creative)*, effective *(efficient)*, favorable *(advantageous)*, fitting, functional, opportune, practical, present *(attendant)*, seasonable, suitable. SEE MAIN ENTRY

convenient time timeliness

convenientia coherence, conformity *(agreement)*

convenire coincide *(correspond)*

conventicle collection *(assembly)*

conventio contract, covenant, treaty

convention agreement *(contract)*, assemblage, assembly, bargain, caucus, collection *(assembly)*, compact, company *(assemblage)*, conference, conformity *(agreement)*, congregation, constant, covenant, custom, decorum, formality, habit, meeting *(conference)*, mode, pact, parley, prescription *(custom)*, propriety *(correctness)*, rubric *(authoritative rule)*, session, stipulation, treaty, usage

conventional accustomed *(customary)*, average *(standard)*, boiler plate, common *(customary)*, customary, familiar *(customary)*, formal, household *(familiar)*, mundane, nondescript, normal *(regular)*, ordinary, orthodox, popular, prevailing *(current)*, prevalent, proper, regular *(conventional)*, right *(suitable)*, routine, standing, traditional, trite, typical, uniform, usual. SEE MAIN ENTRY

conventional conduct propriety *(correctness)*

conventional language plain language

conventional practice protocol *(etiquette)*

conventional usage prescription *(custom)*

conventionalism custom

conventionalist philistine

conventionalities propriety *(correctness)*, protocol *(etiquette)*

conventionality ceremony, conformity *(obedience)*, custom, decorum, formality, habit, practice *(custom)*

conventionalize conform, formalize

conventionally invariably

conventions decorum

conventions of society decorum

conventus assembly, collection *(assembly)*, compact, congregation, meeting *(conference)*, session

converge adjoin, border *(approach)*, collide *(crash against)*, concentrate *(consolidate)*, congregate, contact *(touch)*, convene, meet, unite. SEE MAIN ENTRY

converge upon approach

convergence adjoiner, caucus, center *(central position)*, centralization, coalescence, coalition, collection *(accumulation)*, collision *(accident)*, company *(assemblage)*, congregation, contact *(touching)*, focus, meeting *(encounter)*

convergency meeting *(encounter)*

convergent adjacent, concurrent *(at the same time)*, contiguous

converging centralization, coalescence, concerted, concurrent *(at the same time)*

converging point center *(central position)*, focus

conversance competence *(ability)*

conversant cognizant, competent, expert, familiar *(informed)*, learned, literate, practiced, proficient, resourceful

conversant with acquainted, informed *(educated)*

conversation communication *(discourse)*, discourse, interview, parlance, parley, speech. SEE MAIN ENTRY

conversational nuncupative

conversations conference

converse adverse *(opposite)*, antipathetic *(oppositional)*, antipode, antithesis, communicate, contra, contradictory, contraposition, contrary *(adjective)*, contrary *(noun)*, discourse, discuss, inverse, negative, opposite, speak. SEE MAIN ENTRY

conversely contra

conversing conversation

conversion appropriation *(taking)*, exchange, misappropriation, persuasion, propaganda, reorganization, transition. SEE MAIN ENTRY

conversion to the government escheatment

conversus inverse

convert adapt, alter, annex *(arrogate)*, change, convince, denature, deprive, impropriate, modify *(alter)*, persuade, pilfer, prevail *(persuade)*, reform, renovate, tamper, transform. SEE MAIN ENTRY

convert to use apply *(put in practice)*, capitalize *(seize the chance)*

convertere convert *(change use)*

convertere in change

convertible SEE MAIN ENTRY

convertible terms call *(title)*

convey abalienate, advise, alienate *(transfer title)*, allude, annunciate, assign *(transfer ownership)*, attorn, bear *(yield)*, bespeak, bestow, carry *(transport)*, cede, circulate, commit *(entrust)*, communicate, confer *(give)*, connote, consign, construe *(translate)*, contribute *(supply)*, dedicate, delegate, deliver, demise, depict, devise *(give)*, devolve, disabuse, disperse *(disseminate)*,

displace *(remove)*, disseminate, express, grant *(transfer formally)*, impart, indicate, let *(lease)*, move *(alter position)*, notify, pass *(advance)*, phrase, post, present *(make a gift)*, purport, recount, relate *(tell)*, relegate, remark, render *(deliver)*, send, signify *(inform)*, transmit, transport. SEE MAIN ENTRY

convey a meaning denote

convey a verbal image portray

convey an impression exemplify, portray

convey an impression of delineate

convey away abduct, carry away, hijack, jostle *(pickpocket)*, kidnap

convey by deed grant *(transfer formally)*

convey for a designated period lease

convey information instruct *(teach)*, mention

convey knowledge apprise, mention, signify *(inform)*

convey knowledge to notice *(give formal warning)*

convey real property for a specified period lease

convey the impression appear *(seem to be)*, demean *(deport oneself)*

convey the meaning of interpret

convey to remove *(transfer)*

conveyable assignable, contagious, heritable, moving *(in motion)*, negotiable

conveyance alienation *(transfer of title)*, assignment *(transfer of ownership)*, cargo, carriage, cession, consignment, deed, delivery, devolution, disposition *(transfer of property)*, removal, transmittal. SEE MAIN ENTRY

conveyance between the living inter vivos

conveyance in consideration of recompense lease

conveyance of interest in real property lease

conveyance of land for a designated period lease

conveyance of realty feoffment

conveyancing alienation *(transfer of title)*, assignment *(transfer of ownership)*, consignment, delivery, demise *(conveyance)*, disposition *(transfer of property)*, feoffment

conveyed orally nuncupative

conveying donative

conveying title feoffment

conveyor carrier

convicium outcry

convict captive, condemn *(punish)*, criminal, felon, hoodlum, inmate, lawbreaker, malefactor, outlaw, prisoner, recidivist, sentence. SEE MAIN ENTRY

convictable culpable, reprehensible

convicted blameworthy, guilty

convicting incriminatory, inculpatory

conviction belief *(something believed)*, belief *(state of mind)*, certainty, certification *(certainness)*, certitude, condemnation *(punishment)*, confidence *(faith)*, credence, determination, dogma, faith, idea, notion, opinion *(belief)*, principle *(axiom)*, principle *(virtue)*, reliance, sentence, standpoint, surety *(certainty)*, trust *(confidence)*. SEE MAIN ENTRY

convictive convincing, persuasive. SEE MAIN ENTRY

convince assure *(give confidence to)*, coax, convert *(persuade)*, inculcate, induce, influence, inspire, motivate, persuade, prejudice *(influence)*, prevail *(persuade)*, prevail upon, reason *(persuade)*, reassure. SEE MAIN ENTRY

convince to the contrary discourage, dissuade, expostulate

convinced affirmative, categorical, certain (*positive*), definite, indubious, inexorable, positive (*confident*), secure (*confident*)

convincement surety (*certainty*)

convincible suasible

convincing believable, categorical, cogent, colorable (*plausible*), credible, determinative, eloquent, forcible, influential, persuasive, plausible, potent, solid (*sound*), sound, specious, undeniable. SEE MAIN ENTRY

convocare call (*summon*), collect (*gather*), convene

convocate call (*summon*), congregate, converge

convocation assemblage, assembly, caucus, chamber (*body*), commission (*agency*), company (*assemblage*), conference, congregation, meeting (*conference*), session

convoke call (*summon*), convene, meet

convolute sinuous

convoluted circuitous, complex, compound, difficult, inextricable, recondite, sinuous, tortuous (*bending*)

convolution complex (*entanglement*), digression, distortion, involution

convolutional circuitous, sinuous

convoy accompany, caretaker (*one caring for property*), carry (*transport*), protect

convulse agitate (*shake up*), beat (*pulsate*), churn, discompose, harass

convulsion cataclysm, commotion, outbreak, outburst, pandemonium, turmoil, violence

cooccupant cotenant

cooccupier cotenant

cool controlled (*restrained*), inimical, insusceptible (*uncaring*), moderate (*temper*), mollify, nonchalant, phlegmatic, placid, unresponsive

cool-headed dispassionate, sensible, sane

coolness disinterest (*lack of interest*), ill will, indifference, moderation

coop restrict

cooperancy coaction

cooperant associated, mutual (*collective*)

cooperate abide, agree (*comply*), agree (*contract*), combine (*act in concert*), concur (*agree*), conduce, connive, consolidate (*unite*), conspire, contribute (*assist*), espouse, federalize (*associate*), help, involve (*participate*), join (*associate oneself with*), observe (*obey*), participate, promote (*organize*), reciprocate, serve (*assist*), unite. SEE MAIN ENTRY

cooperate with abet, aid, assist, comply, support (*assist*)

cooperate with secretly connive

cooperating concerted, consonant, subsidiary

cooperation accommodation (*backing*), agreement (*concurrence*), aid (*help*), assistance, cartel, coaction, coalition, collusion, compatibility, compliance, concert, conciliation, concordance, conformity (*agreement*), conjunction, connivance, consensus, contact (*association*), contact (*association*), contribution (*participation*), favor (*sanction*), federation, help, integration (*assimilation*), league, pact, partnership, peace, pool, reciprocity, relief (*aid*), sanction (*permission*), service (*assistance*), support (*assistance*), synergy, understanding (*agreement*), union (*unity*)

cooperation for fraud collusion

cooperative ancillary (*auxiliary*), associated, beneficial, benevolent, coadunate, common (*shared*), concerted, concurrent (*united*), consensual, constructive (*creative*),

favorable (*expressing approval*), harmonious, joint, mutual (*collective*), synergetic. SEE MAIN ENTRY

cooperative action synergy

cooperative society partnership

cooperativeness coaction

cooperator abettor, accessory, accomplice, assistant, associate, coactor, coadjutant, cohort, colleague, confederate, consociate, conspirer, contributor (*contributor*), copartner (*business associate*), copartner (*coconspirator*), member (*individual in a group*), participant, partner, party (*participant*)

cooperator in crime coconspirator

cooptatio incorporation (*formation of a business entity*)

cooptation election (*choice*), selection (*choice*)

cooptive elective (*selective*)

coordinate adjust (*regulate*), arrange (*methodize*), centralization, classify, codify, coequal, coextensive, cognate, combine (*act in concert*), commensurable, complement, concordant, conform, correlate, correlative, correspond (*be equivalent*), counterpart (*complement*), equal, file (*arrange*), fix (*arrange*), juxtapose, marshal, orchestrate, pool, regulate (*adjust*), tabulate, unite. SEE MAIN ENTRY

coordinated harmonious, joint

coordination adjustment, compatibility, contribution (*participation*), regulation (*management*)

coowner partner

copartner accessory, assistant, associate, coactor, consociate, consort, contributor (*contributor*), member (*individual in a group*), participant, partisan, partner. SEE MAIN ENTRY

copartner in crime coconspirator, copartner (*coconspirator*)

copartnership affiliation (*connectedness*), association (*connection*), company (*enterprise*), league, partnership, pool, sodality

cope with manage, resist (*withstand*), withstand

copia fund, hoard, license, opportunity, permission, reserve, stock (*store*), store (*depository*), store

copied false (*not genuine*), imitation, repeated

copiosus copious

copious ample, comprehensive, liberal (*generous*), profuse, prolific, prolix, replete, voluble. SEE MAIN ENTRY

copious in speech loquacious

copiousness boom (*prosperity*), sufficiency

copossessor cotenant

copula connection (*fastening*)

copulare join (*bring together*), unite

copulate cohabit

copy certification (*certification of proficiency*), correspond (*be equivalent*), counterfeit, counterpart (*parallel*), duplicate, facsimile, fake, forgery, form (*document*), impersonate, mock (*imitate*), model, personify, pirate (*reproduce without authorization*), pose (*impersonate*), record, reflect (*mirror*), repeat (*do again*), reproduce, semblance, simulate, trace (*delineate*), transcript. SEE MAIN ENTRY

copy fraudulently forge (*counterfeit*)

copy from plagiarize

copy in miniature model

copying plagiarism

copyist clerk

copyright SEE MAIN ENTRY

copyright infringement plagiarism

copyright label brand

coquere mature

coratifier comaker

cordial amicable, benevolent, civil (*polite*), receptive

cordial assistance patronage (*support*)

cordial relations rapprochement

cordiality benevolence (*disposition to do good*), comity, consideration (*sympathetic regard*), courtesy, goodwill, rapprochement

cordon blockade (*barrier*), chain (*series*), prize

core body (*main part*), center (*central position*), center (*essence*), consequence (*significance*), content (*structure*), cornerstone, corpus, epitome, essence, gist (*substance*), gravamen, interior, main point, outline (*synopsis*), point (*purpose*), substance (*essential nature*), summary. SEE MAIN ENTRY

corenter cotenant

coresident cotenant

coresidentiary cotenant

corival adversary

cork damper (*stopper*), obstruction, obturate, occlude, repress, shut, stem (*check*)

cormorant rapacious

corner edge (*border*), monopolize, perplex, plight, predicament, stand (*witness' place in court*)

corner the market monopolize

cornerstone corpus, foundation (*basis*), gravamen, mainstay. SEE MAIN ENTRY

cornucopia boom (*prosperity*), sufficiency

corollary adjunct. SEE MAIN ENTRY

coronation elevation

corporal bodily, corporeal, physical, tangible. SEE MAIN ENTRY

corporal hereditament fee (*estate*)

corporal punishment. SEE MAIN ENTRY

corporality body (*person*), corpus, materiality (*physical existence*)

corporalness body (*person*)

corporate collective, conjoint, joint. SEE MAIN ENTRY

corporate body company (*enterprise*), corporation, enterprise (*economic organization*)

corporate interest share (*stock*)

corporate governance. SEE MAIN ENTRY

corporation affiliation (*amalgamation*), association (*alliance*), business (*commercial enterprise*), company (*enterprise*), concern (*business establishment*), enterprise (*economic organization*), league, trust (*combination of businesses*)

corporeal bodily, corporal, material (*physical*), mundane, objective, physical, tangible. SEE MAIN ENTRY

corporeal body object

corporeality body (*person*)

corporealize embody

corporeity corpus, embodiment, materiality (*physical existence*)

corporeous bodily, physical

corporeus bodily, material (*physical*)

corps assemblage, band, organization (*association*), staff

corps of employees personnel

corpse body (*person*), cadaver, dead. SEE MAIN ENTRY

corpulent ponderous

corpus body (*main part*), body (*person*). SEE MAIN ENTRY

corpus bulk, cornerstone, corpse, entity

corpus substance (*material possessions*)

corpus delecti cadaver
corpus juris code
corpus juris jurisprudence
corpuscle scintilla
corral border (*bound*), encompass (*surround*), envelop, shut
correal corporate (*joint*), joint
correct accurate, actual, adjust (*resolve*), admonish (*advise*), ameliorate, amend, appropriate, certain (*positive*), cure, definite, disabuse, discipline (*punish*), documentary, due (*regular*), edit, emend, exact, expostulate, factual, faithful (*true to fact*), fitting, fix (*repair*), help, honest, literal, meliorate, meticulous, modify (*alter*), moral, official, orthodox, penalize, perfect, precise, proper, punctilious, punish, qualify (*condition*), real, rebuke, rectify, redress, reform, regulate (*adjust*), remedy, remonstrate, repair, reprehend, reprimand, restore (*renew*), revise, rightful, sound, suitable, treat (*process*), true (*authentic*), valid. SEE MAIN ENTRY
correct behavior protocol (*etiquette*)
correct English plain language
correct valuation appreciation (*perception*)
correctable corrigible
corrected tempered
corrected edition revision (*corrected version*)
correcting revision (*process of correcting*)
correctio amendment (*correction*), correction (*change*), reform
correction adjustment, discipline (*punishment*), modification, panacea, punishment, reform, relief (*legal redress*), remedial statute, remedy (*that which corrects*), remonstrance, repair, reparation (*indemnification*), reparation (*keeping in repair*), reprimand, reproach. SEE MAIN ENTRY
correction facility reformatory
correctitude propriety (*correctness*), protocol (*etiquette*)
corrective curative, cure, disciplinary (*punitory*), medicinal, palliative (*abating*), panacea, penal, progressive (*advocating change*), remedial, remonstrative, salubrious, salutary. SEE MAIN ENTRY
corrective device recourse
corrective measure correction (*punishment*), recourse, remedial statute, remedy (*legal means of redress*), remedy (*that which corrects*)
correctly as a matter of right, duly
correctness conduct, decorum, formality, propriety (*correctness*), protocol (*etiquette*), qualification (*fitness*), rectitude, right (*righteousness*), truth, validity, veracity
correlate adapt, classify, compare, complement, conform, connect (*relate*), correspond (*be equivalent*), counterpart (*complement*), measure, organize (*arrange*), relate (*establish a connection*). SEE MAIN ENTRY
correlated apposite, cognate, collateral (*accompanying*), concordant, germane, interrelated, related, relative (*relevant*), relevant, tangential
correlation analogy, chain (*nexus*), collation, comparison, connection (*relation*), corollary, correspondence (*similarity*), counterpart (*complement*), mutuality, parity, proportion, relation (*connection*), relationship (*connection*), relevance. SEE MAIN ENTRY
correlative agreed (*harmonized*), akin (*germane*), analogous, apposite, coequal, coextensive, cognate, comparable (*capable of comparison*), comparative, concomitant,

concordant, congruous, convertible, counterpart (*complement*), harmonious, incident, interlocking, interrelated, mutual (*reciprocal*), proportionate, reciprocal, related, relative (*comparative*). SEE MAIN ENTRY
correlative agreement mutual understanding
correlativeness mutuality
correlativity mutuality
correspond agree (*comply*), cohere (*be logically consistent*), coincide (*concur*), communicate, compensate (*counterbalance*), comport (*agree with*), conform, contact (*communicate*). SEE MAIN ENTRY
correspondence analogy, balance (*equality*), coherence, communication (*discourse*), concordance, conformity (*agreement*), consensus, consortium (*marriage companionship*), corollary, dispatch (*message*), mutuality, parity, propinquity (*similarity*), propriety (*appropriateness*), reciprocity, relation (*connection*), relevance, resemblance. SEE MAIN ENTRY
correspondency coherence
correspondent agreed (*harmonized*), akin (*germane*), analogous, apposite, appropriate, coequal, coextensive, cognate, collateral (*accompanying*), commensurable, complement, concomitant, concordant, congruous, consistent, consonant, contemporaneous, correlate, correlative, counterpart (*complement*), fit, germane, harmonious, litigant, mutual (*reciprocal*), pendent, related, relative (*comparative*), relevant, similar, suitable, uniform. SEE MAIN ENTRY
correspondents press
corresponding akin (*germane*), analogous, apposite, coequal, coextensive, cognate, coincidental, collateral (*accompanying*), commensurate, concerted, concomitant, concordant, congruous, consonant, contemporaneous, correlative, faithful (*true to fact*), harmonious, mutual (*reciprocal*), pendent, proportionate, reciprocal, relative (*comparative*), similar. SEE MAIN ENTRY
corresponding part complement, counterpart (*parallel*)
corresponding to comparative, tantamount
corresponding to the contract as agreed upon
corridor avenue (*route*), portal
corrigendum error, miscue
corrigere ameliorate, amend, emend, rectify, reform
corrigible SEE MAIN ENTRY
corrival contender, contestant, opponent, peer, rival
corrivalry competition, conflict, contest (*competition*)
corroborant salubrious, salutary
corroborate attest, bear (*adduce*), certify (*attest*), confirm, countenance, countersign, demonstrate (*establish*), document, ensure, establish (*show*), prove, quote, substantiate, sustain (*confirm*), uphold, validate, verify (*confirm*), vouch, witness (*attest to*). SEE MAIN ENTRY
corroborating convincing, demonstrative (*illustrative*)
corroboration avowal, certainty, certification (*attested copy*), confirmation, consent, documentation, evidence, ratification. SEE MAIN ENTRY
corroborative convincing, deductible (*provable*). SEE MAIN ENTRY
corroborative excuse alibi

corroborative statement confirmation
corroborator bystander, eyewitness, witness
corrode corrupt, decay, depreciate, destroy (*efface*), deteriorate, harm, tarnish
corroding caustic, deleterious, peccant (*unhealthy*)
corrosion decline, deterioration, detriment, disrepair, dissolution (*disintegration*), spoilage, wear and tear
corrosive adverse (*negative*), bitter (*penetrating*), caustic, decadent, deleterious, disadvantageous, harmful, harsh, malignant, mordacious, peccant (*unhealthy*), pernicious
corrumpere adulterate, corrupt, debase, debauch, deteriorate, falsification, falsify, pervert, spoil (*impair*)
corrupt adulterate, bad (*offensive*), betray (*lead astray*), blameful, blameworthy, brand (*stigmatize*), brutalize, contaminate, contemptible, damage, debase, debauch, decadent, decay, degenerate, delinquent (*guilty of a misdeed*), denature, depraved, deteriorate, disgrace, dishonest, disreputable, dissolute, distort, faithless, false (*disloyal*), fraudulent, harm, ignoble, immoral, imperfect, infect, iniquitous, lascivious, lawless, lecherous, lewd, machiavellian, mercenary, misemploy, misguide, mislead, nefarious, odious, outrageous, perfidious, perverse, pervert, pollute, recreant, reprobate, salacious, scandalous, sinister, sordid, spoil (*impair*), stain, suborn, subvert, sully, tamper, unconscionable, unethical, unscrupulous, venal, vicious. SEE MAIN ENTRY
corrupt agreement connivance, conspiracy
corrupt collusion connivance
corrupt consent connivance
corrupt consenting connivance
corrupt cooperation connivance
corrupt demander extortionist
corrupt demanding extortion
corrupt inducement bribery, corruption
corrupt money bribe, hush money
corrupt offering bribe
corrupt payment bribery
corrupt person degenerate
corrupt use misapplication
corrupted dissolute, marred, perverse, profligate (*corrupt*)
corruptela corruption, seduction
corruptibility bribery, corruption, nepotism
corruptible dishonest, faithless, mercenary, unethical, venal
corrupting detrimental, noxious
corrupting gift gratuity (*bribe*)
corruptio corruption, perversion
corruption bad repute, bribery, crime, decline, defilement, delict, delinquency (*misconduct*), deterioration, detriment, dishonesty, dissolution (*disintegration*), graft, gratuity (*bribe*), guilt, improbity, knavery, malfeasance, misusage, nepotism, perversion, pettifoggery, racket, seduction, spoilage, turpitude, vice. SEE MAIN ENTRY
corruption of purity defilement
corruptness criminality, dishonesty, illegality
coruscate radiate
cosh cudgel
cosharer member (*individual in a group*)
cosharing pool
cosign indorse, witness (*attest to*). SEE MAIN ENTRY

cosignatory comaker

cosigner comaker

cosmopolitanism experience (background)

cost bill (invoice), detriment, expenditure, fee (charge), forfeiture (thing forfeited), loss, maintenance (upkeep), outlay, overhead, penalty, price, rate, rent, toll (effect), value, worth. SEE MAIN ENTRY

cost effective economic

cost incurred expenditure, expense (cost), overhead

cost of commutation fare

cost of conveyance fare

cost of living overhead

cost of reclamation ransom

cost of recovery ransom

cost of transportation fare

cost reducing economic

cost-reducing economical

costing nothing free (at no charge)

costless free (at no charge), gratis, gratuitous (given without recompense)

costliness expense (cost), expense (sacrifice)

costly harmful, inestimable, invaluable, priceless, sterling, valuable

costs damages, disbursement (funds paid out), out of pocket. SEE MAIN ENTRY

costume clothe

cotemporary simultaneous

cotenant SEE MAIN ENTRY

coterie association (alliance), band, confederacy (compact), denomination, organization (association)

cottage home (domicile)

couch camouflage, cloak, phrase, rest (be supported by)

couch in terms express, observe (remark)

council bench, board, cabal, caucus, chamber (body), commission (agency), committee, congress, panel (discussion group), parley, session, staff, syndicate, union (labor organization). SEE MAIN ENTRY

council meeting caucus

councilman lawmaker

councilwoman lawmaker

counsel admonish (advise), admonition, advice, advise, advocate, apprise, attorney, bar (body of lawyers), barrister, caution, charge (instruct on the law), confer (consult), counselor, deliberation, direction (guidance), esquire, exhort, forewarn, guidance, incite, instruct (direct), jurist, lawyer, notice (warning), notify, persuade, prognosticate, propose, recommend, recommendation, remonstrate, representative (proxy), suggestion. SEE MAIN ENTRY

counsel against admonish (warn), remonstrate

counsel learned in the law advocate (counselor)

counseled familiar (informed)

counselling advisory

counselor attorney, barrister, council (consultant), counsel, esquire, jurist, lawyer, practitioner. SEE MAIN ENTRY

counselor-at-law advocate (counselor), attorney, barrister, counsel, counselor, esquire, jurist, lawyer

counselors bar (body of lawyers)

counselors-at-law bar (body of lawyers)

count amount (quantity), amount (sum), assess (appraise), calculate, canvass, census, charge (accusation), complaint, computation, enumerate, item, itemize, poll (canvass), poll, surmise, survey (poll). SEE MAIN ENTRY

count against confront (oppose)

count ballots survey (poll)

count for displace (replace)

count on anticipate (expect), expect (anticipate)

count out eliminate (exclude), except (exclude), exclude, omit

count up sum

count upon presume, presuppose, rely, trust

count votes survey (poll)

countable appreciable, determinable (ascertainable)

counted upon foreseeable

countenance advocacy, aid (help), allow (endure), approval, approve, auspices, authorize, behalf, certify (approve), charter (sanction), concur (agree), condone, consent, demeanor, embrace (accept), endure (suffer), favor (sanction), favor, feature (appearance), foster, goodwill, indorse, justify, leave (permission), maintain (sustain), patronage (support), permission, recommend, sanction (permission), sanction, sufferance, uphold. SEE MAIN ENTRY

countenancer advocate (espouser)

counter adverse (opposite), answer (reply), antipathetic (oppositional), balk, collide (clash), condemn (ban), contest, contra (adverb), contra (noun), contra (preposition), contradict, contradictory, contrary, controvert, counteract, countercharge, countervail, demonstrate (protest), discordant, disinclined, fight (counteract), foil, frustrate, gainsay, negate, offset, oppose, opposite, oppugn, parry, prevent, reply, resist (oppose), retaliate, retort, return (respond), setoff. SEE MAIN ENTRY

counter order nollo prosequi

counter to deviant

counteraccusation contradiction, counterargument, rejoinder

counteract antagonize, avert, balk, circumvent, collide (clash), compensate (counterbalance), conflict, confront (oppose), contradict, contravene, counter, countervail, demonstrate (protest), discommode, disprove, disqualify, foil, forestall, frustrate, halt, hamper, interfere, kill (defeat), negate, nullify, oppose, outbalance, override, prevent, prohibit, repulse, resist (oppose), stem (check), stop, thwart, vitiate, withstand. SEE MAIN ENTRY

counteractant contradictory, cure, disadvantageous, offset, preventive

counteracting contrary, hostile, preventive, remedial, renitent

counteraction antipode, collision (dispute), conflict, contention (opposition), contradiction, contravention, counterattack, counterclaim, deterrent, impediment, impugnation, opposition, protest, rebuff, remedy (legal means of redress), repercussion, resistance, revolt, strife

counteractive adverse (opposite), competitive (antagonistic), hostile, negative, renitent

counteragent offset

counterapplication counterclaim

counterargument contradiction, defense, objection, rejoinder. SEE MAIN ENTRY

counterassault counterattack

counterattack confront (oppose), oppose, opposition, reprisal. SEE MAIN ENTRY

counterbalance counteract, cover (provide for), equipoise, neutralize, offset, oppose, outbalance, quid pro quo, setoff, stabilize

counterbalanced agreed (harmonized)

counterbid counteroffer

counterblast answer (respond legally), counterattack, offset, reprisal, revenge

counterblow counterattack

counterchangeable convertible

countercharge answer (judicial response), answer (respond legally), charge (accusation), confutation, contradiction, count, counterargument, counterclaim, diatribe, impeachment, objection, rebut, recriminate, rejoinder, response, retort, return (respond). SEE MAIN ENTRY

countercheck arrest (stop), balk, check (restrain), counter, prevent, withstand

counterclaim answer (judicial response), answer (reply), answer (respond legally), claim (legal demand), counterargument, rebut, respond, retort. SEE MAIN ENTRY

counterclause counteroffer

counterconditions counteroffer

counterdebt setoff

counterdeclaration counterclaim

counterdemand counterclaim, setoff

counterevidence answer (judicial response), confutation, contradiction

counterexception counteroffer

counterfeit assume (simulate), assumed (feigned), bogus, copy, deception, deceptive, disguise (noun), disguise (verb), dishonest, disingenuous, dupe, erroneous, fabricate (make up), fake, false (not genuine), falsification, feign, fictitious, forgery, hoax, illusory, imitation, imposture, invent (falsify), lie (falsify), mendacious, meretricious, mislead, mock (imitate), palter, pirate (reproduce without authorization), plagiarize, pose (impersonate), pretend, prevaricate, profess (pretend), replacement, sham, simulate, specious, spurious, subterfuge, synthetic, untrue. SEE MAIN ENTRY

counterfeit copy fake

counterfeit evidence frame up

counterfeited artificial, fraudulent

counterfeiting forgery

countering negative

counterintelligence. SEE MAIN ENTRY

counterlimitation counteroffer

countermand abrogate (rescind), annul, cancel, cancellation, counter, counteract, debar, disown (deny the validity), negate, nollo prosequi, nullify, override, overrule, proscription, quash, recant, renege, repeal, repudiate, repudiation, rescind, rescision, retraction, revocation, revoke, stop, vacate (void). SEE MAIN ENTRY

countermandment reversal

countermark trademark

countermeaning antipode

countermeasure counterattack, counter offer

countermine connive, conspiracy, conspire, counteract, fight (counteract), foil, maneuver, oppose, thwart

countermotion counterclaim

countermovement counterattack

counteroath contradiction

counteroffensive counterattack

counteroffer SEE MAIN ENTRY

counterorder annul, cancel, cancellation, countermand, prohibition, renege, repudiation, rescind, rescision, retraction, reversal, revocation, revoke

counterpart alter ego, antipode, antithesis, complement, conspirer, contraposition, copy, correlate, reflection (image), resemblance, same, semblance. SEE MAIN ENTRY

counterpetition counterclaim

699

counterplan counteroffer

counterplot collusion, connive, conspiracy, conspire, contrive, counterattack, maneuver, opposition, plan, plot *(secret plan)*, reprisal

counterpoint contradistinction, difference

counterpoise cancel, compensate *(counterbalance)*, counteract, countervail, equipoise, negate, neutralize, offset, oppose, outbalance, quid pro quo, setoff

counterpole antipode, antithesis

counterpose fight *(counteract)*

counterpostulation counterclaim

counterpresentation counteroffer

counterpressure deterrent

counterproposal counterclaim, counter offer

counterproposition counteroffer

counterprotest counterargument

counterprovision counteroffer

counterpush counterattack

counterqualification counteroffer

counterreclamation counterclaim

counterrecommendation counteroffer

counterreply answer *(judicial response)*, counterargument

counterrequest counterclaim, counteroffer

counterreservation counteroffer

countersign certify *(attest)*, confirm, corroborate, cosign, indorse, trademark, underwrite, witness *(attest to)*. SEE MAIN ENTRY

countersignature affirmance *(authentication)*, affirmance *(judicial sanction)*

counterstatement answer *(judicial response)*, argument *(pleading)*, confutation, contradiction, counterargument, plea, pleading, rejoinder, reply, response

counterstipulation counteroffer

counterstrike counterattack

counterstroke counterattack, reprisal, retribution, revenge

countersuggestion counteroffer

countersuit counterclaim

countertendency reaction *(opposition)*

counterterrorism. SEE MAIN ENTRY

counterthrust counterattack

countervail collide *(clash)*, compensate *(counterbalance)*, contradict, contravention, counter, counteract, disprove, interfere, neutralize, obstruct, oppose, oppugn, outbalance, repulse, withstand. SEE MAIN ENTRY

countervailing contradictory, contrary

counterweigh compensate *(counterbalance)*, oppose, outbalance

counterweight equipoise, offset, setoff

counterwork circumvent, collide *(clash)*, confront *(oppose)*, contradict, counteract, fight *(counteract)*, impugnation, oppose, oppugn, thwart

counterworking contradictory, opposition

counting census, computation

countless copious, infinite, innumerable, myriad, profuse

country home *(place of origin)*, nationality, polity, realm, region

country house homestead

country of origin home *(place of origin)*

country-wide national, public *(affecting people)*

county province, region, venue

county officer marshal

coup de bec denunciation, diatribe

coup de grâce dispatch *(put to death)*

couple affix, attach *(join)*, bond *(hold together)*, cement, cohabit, combine *(join together)*, commingle, connect *(join together)*, connection *(fastening)*, consolidate *(unite)*, incorporate *(include)*, join *(bring together)*, lock, unite

coupled affiliated, associated, coherent *(joined)*, composite, concomitant, concurrent *(at the same time)*, concurrent *(united)*, conjoint, conjugal, contiguous, nuptial

coupled with along, collateral *(accompanying)*

couplement marriage *(intimate relationship)*

coupling accession *(annexation)*, coalescence, joinder, marriage *(intimate relationship)*, nexus, union *(unity)*

coupon security *(stock)*. SEE MAIN ENTRY

courage confidence *(faith)*, prowess *(bravery)*, spirit, tenacity, tolerance

courageous heroic, indomitable, spartan, undaunted

courageous deeds prowess *(bravery)*

courageousness prowess *(bravery)*

courier harbinger, informer *(a person who provides information)*

course access *(right of way)*, act *(undertaking)*, admission *(entry)*, admittance *(means of approach)*, array *(order)*, avenue *(means of attainment)*, avenue *(route)*, behavior, conduit *(channel)*, cycle, discipline *(field of study)*, duration, expedient, method, mode, modus operandi, perambulate, period, platform, policy *(plan of action)*, polity, practice *(procedure)*, procedure, program, rule *(guide)*, strategy, subject *(topic)*, tenor, term *(duration)*, traverse. SEE MAIN ENTRY

course of action arrangement *(plan)*, avenue *(means of attainment)*, campaign, design *(intent)*, direction *(course)*, manner *(behavior)*, method, operation, plan, platform, policy *(plan of action)*, practice *(custom)*, practice *(procedure)*, procedure, proposition, scheme, strategy

course of an action at law proceeding

course of behavior conduct

course of business custom

course of conduct action *(performance)*, behavior, campaign, habit, maneuver *(tactic)*, manner *(behavior)*, modus operandi, policy *(plan of action)*, practice *(custom)*, practice *(procedure)*

course of events case *(set of circumstances)*, circumstances, happening

course of law certiorari

course of life behavior

course of proceeding campaign

course of reasoning argument *(pleading)*

coursing fluvial

court bench, board, chamber *(body)*, chamber *(compartment)*, close *(enclosed area)*, courtroom, curtilage, homage, judicatory, judicature, lure, pursue *(strive to gain)*, tribunal. SEE MAIN ENTRY

court action case *(lawsuit)*, lawsuit, matter *(case)*, trial *(legal proceeding)*

court commandment order *(judicial directive)*

court decision determination

court employee clerk

court favor pander

court instruction order *(judicial directive)*

court of appellate jurisdiction appellate court

court of justice bar *(court)*, bench, forum *(court)*, judicatory, tribunal

court of law bar *(court)*, bench, forum *(court)*, judicatory, judicature, tribunal

court of review appellate court

court officer marshal

court official clerk

court order search warrant

court order of imprisonment mittimus

court proceeding action *(proceeding)*

court rule authority *(documentation)*

court scribe clerk

court's finding ruling

court's jurisdiction judicature

court's log calendar *(list of cases)*

courteous civil *(polite)*, obeisant

courteous conduct courtesy

courteously respectfully

courteousness consideration *(sympathetic regard)*, courtesy, propriety *(correctness)*

courtesy benefit *(conferment)*, benevolence *(disposition to do good)*, comity, consideration *(sympathetic regard)*, decorum, deference, favor *(act of kindness)*, honor *(outward respect)*, propriety *(correctness)*, protocol *(etiquette)*, respect. SEE MAIN ENTRY

courtliness consideration *(sympathetic regard)*, courtesy, respect

courtly civil *(polite)*

courtly politeness comity

courtroom forum *(court)*. SEE MAIN ENTRY

courts judiciary

courts of justice judiciary

courtyard close *(enclosed area)*, curtilage

cove haven

coven assemblage

covenant adjustment, agree *(contract)*, agreement *(contract)*, assurance, bargain, bond *(secure a debt)*, cartel, certificate, clause, commitment *(responsibility)*, compact, contract *(noun)*, contract *(verb)*, coverage *(insurance)*, deed, indenture, league, obligation *(duty)*, pact, pledge *(binding promise)*, pledge *(promise the performance of)*, promise, promise *(vow)*, protocol *(agreement)*, sign, specialty *(contract)*, stipulate, stipulation, term *(provision)*, testament, treaty, understanding *(agreement)*, undertake, undertaking *(pledge)*, vow, warrant *(guaranty)*, warranty. SEE MAIN ENTRY

covenant of indemnity specialty *(contract)*

covenanted agreed *(promised)*

covenanter undersigned

coventry ostracism

cover artifice, blind *(obscure)*, camouflage, circumvent, cloak, clothe, comprehend *(include)*, conceal, concealment, consist, disguise *(noun)*, disguise *(verb)*, embrace *(encircle)*, encompass *(include)*, ensconce, enshroud, envelop, harbor, hedge, hide, include, incorporate *(include)*, maintain *(sustain)*, obfuscate, obliterate, obnubilate, obscure, occlude, outbalance, overlap, patrol, penumbra, perambulate, pretense *(pretext)*, pretext, protect, publish, safeguard, screen *(guard)*, seal *(close)*, seclude, shelter *(protection)*, shield, shroud, shut, spread, veil. SEE MAIN ENTRY

cover a beat patrol

cover against loss insure

cover for replace

cover up blind *(obscure)*, camouflage, cloak, clothe, conceal, deface, ensconce, fake, hide, obliterate, obnubilate, obscure, plant *(covertly place)*, suppress

cover with water immerse *(plunge into)*

coverage extent. SEE MAIN ENTRY

covered blind *(concealed)*, covert, fully secured, hidden, impalpable, ironclad, latent, safe

covering cover *(protection)*, disguise, panoply, protection, protective, shelter *(protection)*, veil

covering a wide area extensive

covering all cases broad
covering fire barrage
covering up evasion
coverless open (unclosed)
covert allusive, asylum (hiding place), blind (concealed), clandestine, esoteric, evasive, furtive, hidden, impalpable, inconspicuous, indirect, latent, mysterious, personal (private), potential, private (confidential), privy, protection, recondite, refuge, secret, shield, sly, stealthy, surreptitious, undisclosed, unobtrusive. SEE MAIN ENTRY
covert allusion hint
coverture cohabitation (married state), cover (protection), protection, refuge, shelter (protection), shield. SEE MAIN ENTRY
covet desire, pursue (strive to gain)
coveted popular
covetous eager, illiberal, insatiable, jealous, mercenary
covetousness desire, greed
covey band
covin collusion, fraud, machination
covinous collusive, deceptive, evasive, insidious, lying, machiavellian, mendacious, sly
cow browbeat, deter, frighten, hector, humiliate, intimidate
cowardice fear, fright, panic
cowardliness fear
cowardly base (bad), ignoble, recreant
cower fear
cowering recreant
cowork consolidate (unite), conspire, cooperate, unite
coworker accessory, accomplice, assistant, associate, coactor, coadjutant, cohort, colleague, confederate, consociate, contributor (contributor), copartner (business associate), participant, partisan, partner
coworker in crime coconspirator
coworkers personnel
coworking affiliation (connectedness), associated, association (connection), coaction, concerted, concurrent (united), conjoint, synergetic
coxcombry pride
cozen bait (lure), betray (lead astray), bilk, cheat, deceive, defraud, delude, dupe, ensnare, fake, hoodwink, illude, inveigle, mislead, palter, peculate, pretend
cozenage artifice, bad faith, deceit, deception, dishonesty, false pretense, fraud, hoax, indirection (deceitfulness), knavery, maneuver (trick), pettifoggery
crabbed perverse, petulant, recondite
crabby fractious, petulant
crack break (separate), deface, defacement, flaw, force (break), rend, rift (gap), solve, split (noun), split (verb)
cradle bear (support), genesis, lull, origin (source), origination, source
craft business (occupation), calling, career, contrivance, deception, device (contrivance), discretion (quality of being discreet), employment, imposture, indirection (deceitfulness), knavery, labor (work), livelihood, occupation (vocation), performance (workmanship), pettifoggery, profession (vocation), prowess (ability), pursuit (occupation), ruse, skill, specialty (special aptitude), trade (occupation), work (employment)
craftiness artifice, deceit, deception, evasion, fraud, improbity, indirection (deceitfulness), knavery, pettifoggery
craftsman artisan, practitioner
craftsmanship building (business of assembling), performance (workmanship)

craftworker artisan
crafty artful, colorable (specious), deceptive, delusive, devious, disingenuous, evasive, fraudulent, furtive, insidious, machiavellian, perspicacious, politic, practiced, resourceful, sly, stealthy, subtle (insidious), surreptitious, tactical, tortuous (corrupt)
crafty design machination
crafty device artifice, machination, maneuver (trick), ruse, stratagem
crafty plan machination
cram constrict (compress), impact, load, overload
crammed compact (dense), full, inordinate, populous, replete
crammed solid replete
cramp block, constrict (compress), deter, disadvantage, encumber (hinder), hamper, hinder, impede, interfere, obstruct, preclude, restrain, restrict, trammel
cramped limited, narrow
cranky fractious, perverse, petulant
cranny rift (gap)
crapulence dipsomania, greed
crapulent gluttonous
crapulous gluttonous
crash cataclysm, collision (accident), debacle, discharge (shot), fail (lose), intrude, strike (collide)
crash into collide (crash against), jostle (bump into)
crash together collide (crash against)
crasis condition (state)
crass blatant (obtrusive), disreputable, inelegant, tawdry, uncouth
crater split
crave desire, lack, need, require (need)
craven caitiff, ignoble, recreant
cravenness fear
craving desire, eager, insatiable, solicitous
craving for drink dipsomania
crawl truckle
crawling obsequious
crawling with people populous
craze compulsion (obsession), furor, mode, obsess, obsession, passion
crazed frenetic, lunatic, non compos mentis
craziness insanity, lunacy
crazy frenetic, irrational, ludicrous, lunatic, non compos mentis
cream main point
cream of society elite
creare appoint, create, elect (choose), make
create appoint, bear (yield), build (construct), cause, conceive (invent), conjure, constitute (compose), constitute (establish), devise (invent), engender, establish (launch), fabricate (construct), find (discover), forge (produce), form, frame (construct), frame (formulate), generate, induce, invent (produce for the first time), make, manufacture, occasion, organize (unionize), originate, produce (manufacture), propagate (increase), reproduce. SEE MAIN ENTRY
create a corporation incorporate (form a corporation)
create a disturbance brawl, disrupt
create a false appearance feign
create a false impression delude, dupe, misdirect, misguide, misinform, mislead, profess (pretend)
create a fund reserve
create a need necessitate
create a riot brawl
create a stoppage estop
create an opening admit (give access), capitalize (seize the chance)

create anew recreate
create by law constitute (establish), legislate
create disorder disrupt
create havoc harry (plunder), mistreat
create strife disagree
create the impression appear (seem to be), demean (deport oneself)
created being animal
creating building (business of assembling)
creating dissension divisive
creating disunity divisive
creating hostility divisive
creation birth (beginning), composition (makeup), formation, genesis, invention, manufacture, nascency, origin (source), origination, outcome, output, performance (workmanship), product. SEE MAIN ENTRY
creation of a lien hypothecation
creation of housing project development (building)
creation of the imagination phantom
creation of the mind figment, phantom
creational productive
creative causal, causative, fertile, primordial, productive, prolific, resourceful
creative effort invention
creative fabrication invention
creative genius mastermind
creative worker practitioner
creator architect, author (originator), derivation, developer, mastermind, parents
creature animal, entity
creature of habit addict
creber frequent
crebritas frequency
credal convincing
credence belief (state of mind), confidence (faith), conviction (persuasion), faith, reliance, trust (confidence), weight (credibility). SEE MAIN ENTRY
credendum doctrine, dogma
credential believable, certification (certification of proficiency), recommendation
credentials certificate, certification (certification of proficiency), degree (academic title), warrant (authorization). SEE MAIN ENTRY
credere delegate, presume, trust
credibilis credible
credibility probability, veracity. SEE MAIN ENTRY
credible authentic, believable, colorable (plausible), competent, convincing, defensible, ostensible, persuasive, plausible, possible, presumptive, probable, reasonable (rational), reliable, sound, specious, unimpeachable, valid. SEE MAIN ENTRY
credible evidence. SEE MAIN ENTRY
credibleness credibility, probability, weight (credibility)
credit advance (allowance), authorize, character (reputation), citation (attribution), coupon, credence, degree (academic title), distinction (reputation), estimation (esteem), honor (outward respect), impute, loan, mention (tribute), merit, prestige, reference (citation), regard (esteem), reputation, respect, trust, weight (credibility), worth. SEE MAIN ENTRY
credit account letter of credit
credit check coupon
credit note letter of credit
credit with ascribe
credit-worthy meritorious
creditable believable, convincing, honest, laudable, meritorious, moral, reputable, sterling, true (authentic), unimpeachable

creditable evidence admissible evidence
credited prominent
creditor SEE MAIN ENTRY
credits capital
creditworthy candid, credible, solvent
credo belief *(something believed)*, doctrine, dogma, principle *(axiom)*
credulitas credulity
credulity belief *(state of mind)*, confidence *(faith)*, reliance, trust *(confidence)*. SEE MAIN ENTRY
credulous certain *(positive)*, naive, unsuspecting. SEE MAIN ENTRY
credulousness credulity
credulus credulous
creed belief *(something believed)*, conviction *(persuasion)*, doctrine, dogma
creedal dogmatic
creep prowl
creepy sinister
cremate burn, deflagrate
crescere develop, increase
crest culmination, pinnacle, surmount
crestfallen disappointed, disconsolate, lugubrious
crevice rift *(gap)*, split
crew band, personnel, staff
crib pirate *(reproduce without authorization)*
crier harbinger, informer *(a person who provides information)*
crime bribery, burglary, corruption, delict, delinquency *(misconduct)*, guilt, homicide, infraction, misdeed, misdoing, offense, transgression, wrong. SEE MAIN ENTRY
crime committed misdemeanor
crime graver than a misdemeanor felony
crimen accusation, charge *(accusation)*, indictment
criminal aggressor, assailant, blameful, blameworthy, burglar, convict, culpable, delinquent *(guilty of a misdeed)*, delinquent, embezzler, felon, felonious, guilty, hoodlum, illegal, illegitimate *(illegal)*, illicit, immoral, impermissible, iniquitous, irregular *(improper)*, larcenous, lawbreaker, lawless, malefactor, nefarious, offender, outlaw, peccant *(culpable)*, prisoner, racketeer, recidivist, reprehensible, reprobate, tainted *(corrupted)*, thief, unconscionable, unlawful, vandal, vicious, wrongdoer, wrongful. SEE MAIN ENTRY
criminal ablation asportation
criminal accusal information *(charge)*
criminal act misdemeanor, offense, overt act, tortious act
criminal activity crime, felony, guilt, misdemeanor, racket
criminal agreement confederacy *(conspiracy)*
criminal attitude criminality
criminal conduct criminality
criminal deed guilt, offense
criminal design mens rea
criminal guilt mens rea
criminal imitation counterfeit
criminal information supplier informer *(one providing criminal information)*
criminal intent mens rea
criminal interest usurious
criminal offense crime, felony, guilt, misdemeanor
criminal proceeding impeachment
criminal purpose mens rea
criminal rate of interest usury
criminal released at large probationer *(released offender)*

criminal remotion asportation
criminal removement asportation
criminal setting of fires arson
criminal transmission asportation
criminal trial lawyer for the people prosecutor
criminal unchastity adultery
criminal under suspension of sentence probationer *(released offender)*
criminality bad repute, bribery, conviction *(finding of guilt)*, corruption, culpability, delinquency *(misconduct)*, guilt, illegality, knavery, mens rea, mischief, offense, racket. SEE MAIN ENTRY
criminally illegally
criminate accuse, arraign, blame, charge *(accuse)*, complain *(charge)*, denounce *(condemn)*, implicate, incriminate, involve *(implicate)*, present *(prefer charges)*, rebuke, reprimand, reproach
criminate falsely frame *(charge falsely)*
criminate unfairly frame *(charge falsely)*
criminate unjustly frame *(charge falsely)*
criminatio accusation, slander
crimination accusation, allegation, bad repute, blame *(culpability)*, charge *(accusation)*, complaint, count, impeachment, implication *(incriminating involvement)*, incrimination, inculpation
crimination through law enforcement arraignment
criminative critical *(faultfinding)*, incriminatory, inculpatory
criminatory calumnious, critical *(faultfinding)*, incriminatory, inculpatory
criminologist detective
criminosus calumnious
criminous blameful, blameworthy, culpable, felonious, guilty, irregular *(improper)*, peccant *(culpable)*. SEE MAIN ENTRY
criminousness guilt
cringe truckle
cringing obsequious, subservient
cripple damage, debilitate, disable, disarm *(divest of arms)*, foil, frustrate, harm, hinder, impair, interfere, maim, mutilate, obstruct, preclude, thwart
crippled defective, disabled *(made incapable)*, helpless *(powerless)*, imperfect, incapable, marred, powerless
crippling detriment, detrimental, disabling, harmful, pernicious
crisis crossroad *(turning point)*, danger, emergency, exigency, jeopardy, peril, plight, predicament, pressure, problem, quagmire, situation
crisp compact *(pithy)*
crisscross cross *(intersect)*, intertwine, traverse
criterion canon, pattern, precedent, rule *(guide)*, standard. SEE MAIN ENTRY
critic malcontent
critical acute, crucial, cynical, decisive, discriminating *(judicious)*, essential *(required)*, exigent, grave *(important)*, imperative, important *(urgent)*, indispensable, key, material *(important)*, momentous, necessary *(required)*, nonconsenting, particular *(exacting)*, pejorative, precarious, precise, remonstrative, sensitive *(discerning)*, serious *(grave)*, severe, strategic, urgent, vital. SEE MAIN ENTRY
critical analysis proposal *(report)*
critical appraisal diagnosis
critical article review *(critical evaluation)*
critical attitude doubt *(suspicion)*, misgiving

critical discussion review *(critical evaluation)*
critical examination analysis, criticism, inspection, probe, scrutiny
critical faculty judgment *(discernment)*
critical feature main point
critical happening landmark *(significant change)*
critical juncture landmark *(significant change)*
critical moment crossroad *(turning point)*
critical occasion landmark *(significant change)*
critical period crossroad *(turning point)*
critical point cornerstone, crossroad *(turning point)*, emergency, main point. SEE MAIN ENTRY
critical remark stricture
critical remarks criticism
critical scrutiny diagnosis
critical situation exigency, plight, predicament, quagmire
critical spirit judgment *(discernment)*
critical viewing inspection
criticalness judgment *(discernment)*, particularity
criticism bad repute, blame *(culpability)*, complaint, condemnation *(blame)*, denunciation, diatribe, disapprobation, disapproval, discredit, disparagement, exception *(objection)*, grievance, ground, guidance, impeachment, impugnation, objection, obloquy, odium, ostracism, outcry, protest, rebuff, remonstrance, report *(detailed account)*, reprimand, review *(critical evaluation)*, revilement, stricture. SEE MAIN ENTRY
criticize blame, comment, condemn *(blame)*, contemn, decry, defame, denigrate, denounce *(condemn)*, disapprove *(condemn)*, discommend, disparage, evaluate, fault, impeach, impugn, judge, minimize, object, proscribe *(denounce)*, rebuke, remonstrate, reprehend, reproach, review. SEE MAIN ENTRY
criticize adversely oppugn
criticize frivolously cavil
criticize severely castigate, denounce *(condemn)*
criticize severly lash *(attack verbally)*
criticized blameful, blameworthy
criticizing severely critical *(faultfinding)*
critique analysis, criticism, diagnosis, inspection, judgment *(discernment)*, review *(critical evaluation)*, review
cromlech monument
crook convict, embezzler
crooked circuitous, devious, fraudulent, indirect, labyrinthine, machiavellian, sinuous, sly, tortuous *(corrupt)*, unjust, unscrupulous
crookedness criminality, fraud, improbity, indirection *(indirect action)*, irregularity
crop output, product
crop up emerge, occur *(come to mind)*, supervene
crop up again recur
cross annoy, antagonize, bitter *(reproachful)*, conflict, confront *(oppose)*, contentious, contravene, counter, counteract, countervail, discompose, disobey, fight *(counteract)*, fractious, froward, harrow, inimical, interfere, intertwine, oppugn, pass *(advance)*, perambulate, perverse, petulant, plague, querulous, resist *(oppose)*, stress *(strain)*, thwart, traverse. SEE MAIN ENTRY
cross dimension caliber *(measurement)*
cross fire barrage, counterattack
cross in opposition traverse

cross in traveling   traverse
cross interrogate   cross-examine
cross interrogation   cross-examination
cross measurement   caliber *(measurement)*
cross off   delete, expunge
cross one's mind   occur *(come to mind)*
cross out   deface, delete, edit, expunge, expurgate
cross purposes   contention *(opposition)*
cross question   cross-examine
cross section   sample
cross the threshold   enter *(go in)*
cross with   commingle
cross-action   counterclaim
cross-bill   counterclaim
cross-check   collation
cross-examination   cross-questioning, interrogation. SEE MAIN ENTRY
cross-examine   inquire, reexamine. SEE MAIN ENTRY
cross-grained   fractious
cross-interrogation   cross-questioning
cross-purposes   argument *(contention)*, disaccord. SEE MAIN ENTRY
cross-questioning   SEE MAIN ENTRY
cross-tempered   petulant
cross-way   crossroad *(intersection)*
crossable   passable
crossbred   promiscuous
crosscut   cross *(intersect)*
crossed   promiscuous
crossgrained   restive
crossing   crossroad *(intersection)*, intersection
crossing point   intersection
crosspoint   intersection
crossroad   causeway, intersection. SEE MAIN ENTRY
crosswalk   intersection
crossways   crossroad *(intersection)*, crossroad *(turning point)*
crotchet   obsession
crotchety   restive
crouch   lurk
crouching   obsequious
crowd   assembly, collection *(assembly)*, company *(assemblage)*, congregation, constrict *(compress)*, impact, jostle *(bump into)*, mass *(body of persons)*, overload, populace, quantity
crowd together   concentrate *(consolidate)*, congregate
crowded   compact *(dense)*, populous, profuse, rife
crown   culminate, culmination, honor, maximum *(pinnacle)*, pinnacle, surmount
crowning   absolute *(ideal)*, best, cardinal *(outstanding)*, definitive, final, last *(final)*, master, paramount, prime *(most valuable)*, stellar, superlative, ultimate. SEE MAIN ENTRY
crowning point   crossroad *(turning point)*, pinnacle
crowning touch   culmination
crucial   acute, central *(essential)*, decisive, essential *(required)*, exigent, imperative, important *(significant)*, important *(urgent)*, indispensable, key, major, mandatory, material *(important)*, momentous, necessary *(required)*, peremptory *(imperative)*, serious *(grave)*, strategic, urgent. SEE MAIN ENTRY
crucial feature   main point
crucial moment   crossroad *(turning point)*
crucial part   necessity, need *(requirement)*
crucial period   emergency
crucial point   cornerstone, landmark *(significant change)*, main point. SEE MAIN ENTRY

cruciare   harry *(harass)*
cruciation   intersection
crucify   persecute
crude   blatant *(obtrusive)*, elementary, harsh, imperfect, inelegant, inexact, inferior *(lower in quality)*, natural, poor *(inferior in quality)*, rudimentary, simple, tawdry, uncouth, unseemly
crude presentation   travesty
crudelis   cruel
crudelitas   cruelty
cruel   bad *(offensive)*, brutal, caustic, cold-blooded, diabolic, harmful, harsh, inexcusable, malevolent, malicious, malignant, oppressive, outrageous, pernicious, relentless, remorseless, ruthless, scathing, severe, sinister, unrelenting, vicious. SEE MAIN ENTRY
cruel act   cruelty, misdeed, misdoing
cruel conduct   cruelty
cruel hearted   cold-blooded
cruel treatment   severity
cruelness   brutality
cruelty   bestiality, brutality, inconsideration, mischief, oppression, severity. SEE MAIN ENTRY
cruise   prowl
crumb   iota
crumble   decay, degenerate, disintegrate, ebb, give *(yield)*, impair, perish
crumbled   broken *(fractured)*
crumbling   decadent, dissolution *(disintegration)*, erosion, old, precarious
crusade   activity, campaign, operation, quest, venture
crusader   malcontent
crush   beat *(defeat)*, constrict *(compress)*, damage, defeat, demean *(make lower)*, disable, extinguish, foil, humiliate, kill *(defeat)*, overcome *(overwhelm)*, override, overturn, refute, repress, stifle, stop, strangle, subdue, subject, subjugate, suppress, upset
crushed   disconsolate, pessimistic
crushed spirits   damper *(depressant)*
crushing   disastrous, harmful, insufferable, onerous, operose, oppressive, strong
crushing reverse   disaster
crusty   fractious, froward, perverse, petulant
crutch   mainstay
crux   cornerstone, gravamen, main point
cry   call *(appeal)*, call *(appeal to)*, entreaty, herald, noise, outcry, plaint, proclaim
cry down   decry, denounce *(condemn)*
cry for   call *(demand)*, exact, need, request
cry for help   pray
cry out against   challenge, decry, demonstrate *(protest)*, denounce *(condemn)*, except *(object)*, inveigh, protest, remonstrate
cry out for   desire
cry over   deplore, regret, repent
cry to   call *(appeal to)*, importune
crying   blatant *(obtrusive)*, exigent, important *(urgent)*, insistent, manifest, requisite, urgent
cryptic   covert, debatable, disputable, enigmatic, esoteric, hidden, indefinable, indefinite, indeterminate, indistinct, mysterious, obscure *(abstruse)*, opaque, oracular, personal *(private)*, private *(confidential)*, privy, problematic, recondite, secret, suspicious *(questionable)*, uncertain *(ambiguous)*, vague
cryptical   covert, obscure *(abstruse)*, private *(confidential)*, privy, problematic, recondite
crystal clear   distinct *(clear)*, manifest, palpable

crystal-clear   explicit
crystalline   lucid, pellucid
crystallization   congealment
crystallize   cement, consolidate *(strengthen)*. SEE MAIN ENTRY
crystallized   ossified
cubicle   cell, chamber *(compartment)*
cubiculum   cell, chamber *(compartment)*
cuckoldry   adultery, infidelity
cudgel   beat *(strike)*, lash *(strike)*. SEE MAIN ENTRY
cue   frame *(mood)*, guidance, hint *(noun)*, hint *(verb)*, indicant, indication, indicator, reference *(allusion)*, remind, reminder, suggestion, symbol, tip *(clue)*
cue word   catchword
cuff   beat *(strike)*
cuirass   panoply
cul-de-sac   impasse
cull   choose, compile, extract, glean, reap, select. SEE MAIN ENTRY
culled   select
cully   bilk, delude, dupe, mislead
culminate   carry *(succeed)*, cease, conclude *(complete)*, discharge *(perform)*, mature, perfect, terminate. SEE MAIN ENTRY
culminated   complete *(ended)*
culminating   conclusive *(settled)*, decisive
culmination   ceiling, conclusion *(outcome)*, consequence *(conclusion)*, crossroad *(turning point)*, discharge *(performance)*, end *(termination)*, issuance, maturity, maximum *(pinnacle)*, outcome, performance *(execution)*, pinnacle. SEE MAIN ENTRY
culpa   blame *(culpability)*
culpa   dereliction
culpa   fault *(responsibility)*, guilt
culpa   negligence
culpa dignus   reprehensible
culpa vacuus   innocent
culpability   conviction *(finding of guilt)*, criminality, delinquency *(misconduct)*, fault *(responsibility)*, guilt, ignominy, impeachability, implication *(incriminating involvement)*, mens rea, misdoing, onus *(blame)*, opprobrium, responsibility *(accountability)*. SEE MAIN ENTRY
culpable   at fault, blameful, blameworthy, contemptible, delinquent *(guilty of a misdeed)*, disobedient, felonious, guilty, iniquitous, peccable, reprehensible, reprobate, sinister, unjustifiable. SEE MAIN ENTRY
culpable conduct   criminality
culpable omission   misdeed
culpable professional neglect   malpractice
culpable recklessness   malice
culpableness   blame *(culpability)*, ignominy
culpae socius   accessory, accomplice
culpandus   culpable
culpare   blame, condemn *(blame)*, criticize *(find fault with)*, fault
culprit   convict, delinquent, embezzler, felon, malefactor
cultivate   ameliorate, cause, develop, discipline *(train)*, educate, enhance, foster, meliorate, nurture, promote *(organize)*, pursue *(carry on)*. SEE MAIN ENTRY
cultivate a habit   naturalize *(acclimate)*, practice *(train by repetition)*
cultivated   civil *(polite)*, literate
cultivated taste   decorum
cultivation   civilization, development *(progression)*, discipline *(training)*, education, promotion *(encouragement)*
cultural   disciplinary *(educational)*
cultural group   race

culture civilization, education, race, society
cultured aesthetic, informed (educated), literate
cultus homage
cum homine contendere compete
cumber clog, deter, disadvantage, encumber (hinder), hold up (delay), impede, load, overload, tax (overwork), trammel, weigh
cumbersome onerous, oppressive, ponderous
cumbrance burden, weight (burden)
cumbrous oppressive, ponderous
cumulare perfect
cumulate accumulate (amass), aggregate, compile, glean, hoard, store
cumulated conglomerate
cumulation agglomeration, assemblage, collection (accumulation), conglomeration, corpus, hoard, provision (something provided), selection (collection). SEE MAIN ENTRY
cumulative collective, consecutive. SEE MAIN ENTRY
cumulative effect augmentation
cumulativeness augmentation
cunctari hesitate
cunctatio delay, hesitation, scruple
cunctation deferment, delay, filibuster
cunctative indolent
cunning artful, artifice, clandestine, collusive, color (deceptive appearance), deceit, deception, deceptive, deft, delusive, devious, diplomatic, dishonest, disingenuous, faculty (ability), fraud, fraudulent, furtive, gift (flair), imposture, indirection (deceitfulness), insidious, knavery, lying, machiavellian, mendacious, perspicacious, pettifoggery, politic, proficient, prudence, resourceful, skill, sly, stratagem, strategy, subtle (insidious), surreptitious, tactical
cunning contrivance maneuver (trick)
cunning practice management (judicious use)
cunningness artifice, evasion, knavery
cup prize
cupere desire
cupiditas desire, greed
cupidity desire, greed
cupidus inquisitive, partial (biased)
cura caution (vigilance), management (supervision)
curable corrigible
curare care (be cautious), care (regard), charge (custody), concern (care), heed
curative correction (change), medicinal, palliative (abating), panacea, remedial, salubrious, salutary. SEE MAIN ENTRY
curative preparation drug
curator administrator, caretaker (one caring for property), custodian (protector), director, guardian
curator procurator
curator superintendent, trustee
curb adjust (resolve), allay, arrest (stop), assuage, balk, bar (obstruction), bar (hinder), block, blockade (barrier), censorship, check (bar), check (restrain), constrain (restrain), constraint (restriction), constrict (inhibit), contain (restrain), control (restriction), damper (stopper), debar, delay, detain (restrain), deterrence, deterrent, diminish, disadvantage (noun), disadvantage (verb), discipline (obedience), discipline (control), disincentive, encumbrance, enjoin, fetter (noun), fetter (verb), halt, hamper, hinder, hold up (delay), impede, inhibit, interfere, keep (restrain), lessen, limit, limitation, lock, margin (outside limit), mitigate, moderate

(temper), modify (moderate), mollification, mollify, obstacle, obstruct, obstruction, palliate (abate), preclude, prohibit, prohibition, quota, repress, restrain, restraint, restrict, restriction, stay, stay (halt), stem (check), subdue, trammel, withhold. SEE MAIN ENTRY
curb oneself refrain
curbed arrested (checked), limited, qualified (conditioned)
curbing limiting
curbs confines
cure correction (change), drug, help (noun), help (verb), meliorate, panacea, preserve, rectify, redress, reform, relieve (give aid), remedial statute, remedy (that which corrects), remedy, renew (refurbish), repair (noun), repair (verb), restore (renew), treat (remedy), treatment. SEE MAIN ENTRY
cure for all ills panacea
cure-all panacea
cureless incorrigible, inoperable (incurable), irredeemable, irremediable, irreversible
curia bar (court), board
curing preservation, remedial
curiosa pornography
curiosity interest (concern), phenomenon (unusual occurrence)
curiosus inquisitive
curious eccentric, extraordinary, inquisitive, noteworthy, prodigious (amazing), rare, remarkable, unaccustomed, uncommon, unique, unusual
curiousness interest (concern)
curmudgeonly parsimonious, petulant
currency cash, money, publication (disclosure). SEE MAIN ENTRY
currency devaluation inflation (decrease in value of currency)
current common (customary), extant, familiar (customary), instant, outflow, popular, present (current), prevailing (current), prevalent, rife, typical, usual. SEE MAIN ENTRY
current edition revision (corrected version)
current expenses overhead
currently existing extant
currently perceived common (customary)
curricular didactic
curriculum career
curriculum discipline (field of study), plan, program. SEE MAIN ENTRY
currish caitiff
curse expletive, imprecation, malediction, malign, proscribe (denounce)
cursed diabolic, odious
cursing blasphemy, profanity, revilement
cursive holographic
cursive hand script
cursive writing handwriting
cursory brief, careless, casual, informal, minor, perfunctory, random, superficial, transitory, trivial. SEE MAIN ENTRY
cursus career, direction (course)
curt caustic, compact (pithy), laconic, succinct, taciturn
curtail abate (lessen), abridge (shorten), allay, arrest (stop), attenuate, bowdlerize, commute, condense, decrease, diminish, discount (minimize), lessen, minimize, palliate (abate), reduce, restrain, retrench. SEE MAIN ENTRY
curtailed brief, concise
curtailment abatement (reduction), abridgment (condensation), abridgment (disentitlement), decrease, decrement. SEE MAIN ENTRY
curtain blind (obscure), camouflage, cessation (termination), cloak, conceal, cover

(conceal), disguise, end (termination), ensconce, enshroud, envelop, hide, obfuscate, obnubilate, obscure, shroud, veil
curtained remote (secluded)
curtate concise
curtilage SEE MAIN ENTRY
curtilages confines
curtness disrespect
curved circuitous, sinuous, tortuous (bending)
curvilinear sinuous, tortuous (bending)
cushion bear (support), ease, mitigate, modify (moderate), protect
custodia charge (custody), custody (supervision), detention, incarceration
custodial protective. SEE MAIN ENTRY
custodial detention arrest
custodian administrator, caretaker (one caring for property), executor, fiduciary, guardian, superintendent, trustee, warden. SEE MAIN ENTRY
custodian of the law peace officer
custodians management (directorate)
custodians of the law police, posse
custodianship bondage, constraint (imprisonment), custody (supervision), detention, incarceration, retention. SEE MAIN ENTRY
custodire protect
custody adoption (affiliation), auspices, bondage, captivity, constraint (imprisonment), control (supervision), detention, durance, enclosure, incarceration, possession (ownership), preservation, protection, quarantine, restraint, safekeeping, thrall, ward. SEE MAIN ENTRY
custom criterion, decorum, excise, form (arrangement), formality, habit, manner (behavior), method, mode, procedure, rule (guide), style, usage, way (channel). SEE MAIN ENTRY
customarily as a rule, generally, invariably
customariness habituation
customary boiler plate, conventional, current, formal, frequent, general, habitual, household (familiar), inveterate, mundane, normal (regular), ordinary, orthodox, popular, prescriptive, prevailing (current), prevalent, pro forma, regular (conventional), repeated, rife, right (suitable), routine, traditional, typical, usual. SEE MAIN ENTRY
customary action habit
customary conduct habit
customary course practice (custom)
customary manner of procedure course
customary procedure manner (behavior), matter of course
customary use usage
customary way avenue (means of attainment)
customer client, consumer, patron (regular customer). SEE MAIN ENTRY
customer approval goodwill
customer encouragement goodwill
customers' man broker
customs protocol (etiquette)
customs documents bill (formal declaration)
custos guardian, trustee, warden
cut bowdlerize, break (fracture), censor, commute, curtail, decrease (noun), decrease (verb), decrement, deduct (reduce), deduction (diminution), delete, depreciate, discontinue (break continuity), discount (reduce), divide (separate), division (act of dividing), edit, excise (cut away), expurgate, ignore, interrupt, lancinate, lessen,

minimal, mutilate, reap, rebate *(noun)*, rebate *(verb)*, refund, rend, retrench, sever, split *(noun)*, split *(verb)*, subdivide, tenor

cut across   cross *(intersect)*, traverse

cut adrift   dissociate, separate, sever

cut apart   disconnected

cut back   decrease, diminish

cut down   abridge *(shorten)*, curtail, decrease, deduct *(reduce)*, digest *(summarize)*, diminish, dispatch *(put to death)*, extirpate, lessen, minimize, reduce, retrench

cut down to size   minimize

cut in halves   dichotomize

cut in two   bifurcate, dichotomize, disconnected, part *(separate)*

cut into   enter *(penetrate)*, lancinate

cut loose   disengage, extricate

cut off   border *(bound)*, check *(restrain)*, decrease, disband, discrete, disengage, disinherit, disown *(refuse to acknowledge)*, dissociate, estop, estrange, insulate, isolate, lock, preclude, prevent, rescind, seclude, separate, toll *(stop)*

cut off from inheritance   disinherit

cut out   bowdlerize, delete, eliminate *(eradicate)*, eviscerate, excise *(cut away)*, expel, expurgate, extinguish, omit, quit *(discontinue)*, redact

cut out of one's will   disinherit, disown *(refuse to acknowledge)*

cut short   brief, condense, curtail, decrease, discontinue *(break continuity)*, halt, minimize, rescind, retrench, stop

cut through   enter *(penetrate)*, penetrate, pierce *(lance)*

cut up   disjoint, partition

cut-back   curtailment

cut-rate   nominal

cutback   decrease

cutting   acute, bitter *(acrid tasting)*, bitter *(penetrating)*, caustic, division *(act of dividing)*, incisive, mordacious, part *(portion)*, scathing, trenchant

cutting down   curtailment

cutting off   curtailment

cutting words   diatribe

cy press   SEE MAIN ENTRY

cyber crime.   SEE MAIN ENTRY

cycle   annum, frequency, life *(period of existence)*, sequence, succession. SEE MAIN ENTRY

cyclic   intermittent, periodic, regular *(orderly)*

cyclical   chronic, intermittent, periodic

cyclopean   prodigious *(enormous)*

cynical   critical *(faultfinding)*, disdainful, inconvincible, ironic, pejorative, pessimistic, skeptical. SEE MAIN ENTRY

cynicism   irony, pessimism, suspicion *(mistrust)*

cynosure   highlight, landmark *(conspicuous object)*

cyprian   prurient

D

dab   iota

daedal   elaborate

daft   lunatic

daftness   insanity

daily   habitual, ordinary, usual. SEE MAIN ENTRY

daily paper   journal

daily register   journal

dalliance   deferment, delay

dally   hesitate, pause, procrastinate, stall

dallying   hesitant, otiose

dam   block, clog, constrict *(inhibit)*, halt, lock, obstacle, obstruction, shut

dam up   discontinue *(break continuity)*, impede, occlude, stem *(check)*, stop

damage   abuse *(physical misuse)*, cost *(penalty)*, countervail, decrement, deface, defacement, defect, detriment, disable, disadvantage *(noun)*, disadvantage *(verb)*, disrepair, disservice, drawback, endanger, eviscerate, expense *(sacrifice)*, harm *(noun)*, harm *(verb)*, ill use, impair, injury, maim, mischief, mutilate, persecute, pillage, prejudice *(injury)*, prejudice *(injure)*, spoil *(impair)*, stain, strike *(assault)*, toll *(effect)*, vitiate, wear and tear. SEE MAIN ENTRY

damage a reputation   pillory

damage irreparably   spoil *(impair)*

damage one's reputation   defame

damaged   aggrieved *(victimized)*, blemished, broken *(fractured)*, defective, dilapidated, faulty, imperfect, inferior *(lower in quality)*, marred

damages   amercement, compensation, cost *(penalty)*, expiation, out of pocket, punishment, recompense, recovery *(award)*, reimbursement, reparation *(indemnification)*, restitution, satisfaction *(discharge of debt)*, trover. SEE MAIN ENTRY

damaging   calumnious, chilling effect, contemptuous, deleterious, destructive, detrimental, disabling, disadvantageous, disastrous, disgraceful, harmful, incriminatory, inculpatory, insalubrious, libelous, malevolent, malignant, noxious, pejorative, pernicious, pestilent, prejudicial, scathing, toxic, unfavorable. SEE MAIN ENTRY

damaging report   scandal, slander

damn   proscribe *(denounce)*

damnable   contemptible, heinous, odious

damnare   condemn *(punish)*, sentence

damnatio   conviction *(finding of guilt)*

damnation   blame *(culpability)*, conviction *(finding of guilt)*, denunciation, disapprobation, disparagement, imprecation, malediction

damnatory   blameful, blameworthy, calumnious, critical *(faultfinding)*, incriminatory, inculpatory, libelous, profane, scandalous

damnified   aggrieved *(harmed)*

damning   incriminatory, inculpatory

damnosus   prejudicial

damnum   detriment, harm, injury, loss, mischief

damnum restituere   indemnify

damnum sarcire   indemnify

damp   repress, stifle, thwart

damp down   diminish

dampen   alleviate, decrease, depress, deter, diminish, discourage, moderate *(temper)*, repress. SEE MAIN ENTRY

damper   check *(bar)*, deterrent, disincentive, impediment, restraint. SEE MAIN ENTRY

dander   resentment

dandify   embellish

dandyism   pride

danger   hazard, jeopardy, menace, mischief, peril, pitfall, predicament, risk, threat, venture. SEE MAIN ENTRY

danger signal   symptom

danger-loving   hot-blooded

dangerous   aleatory *(perilous)*, deadly, formidable, harmful, insalubrious, insecure, lethal, malignant, noxious, ominous, peccant *(unhealthy)*, pestilent, precarious, serious *(grave)*, sinister, vicious. SEE MAIN ENTRY

dangerous condition   predicament

dangerous course   hazard

dangerous person   delinquent

dangerous situation   hazard, jeopardy, menace, peril

dangerous spot   pitfall

dangerous to life   deadly

dangerous undertaking   venture

dangerousness   jeopardy

dangle before the eyes   brandish

dare   defiance, defy, endanger

dare   grant *(concede)*

dare   speculate *(chance)*

dare not   fear

dare say   opine, presume, remark, speculate *(conjecture)*

daredevil   hot-blooded

daring   audacity, brazen, defiance, flagrant, heroic, hot-blooded, impulsive *(rash)*, original *(creative)*, presumptuous, prowess *(bravery)*, spartan, spirit, temerity, undaunted. SEE MAIN ENTRY

dark   bleak *(not favorable)*, covert, hidden, incomprehensible, lugubrious, mysterious, ominous, opaque, portentous *(ominous)*, private *(confidential)*, privy, recondite, secret

dark *(devoid of light)*. SEE MAIN ENTRY

dark *(dismal)*. SEE MAIN ENTRY

darken   depress, obfuscate, obnubilate, obscure, shroud, tarnish

dark *(evil)*. SEE MAIN ENTRY

darkening   obscuration

darkle   obscure

darkness   ignorance, nescience, obscuration, opacity

darn   repair

dart   race

dash   beat *(defeat)*, dispatch *(promptness)*, foil, haste, hasten, iota, minimum, race, spirit

dash against   impinge

dash one's expectation   disappoint

dash one's hopes   foil

dashed   disappointed

dashed hopes   pessimism

dastardly   caitiff, recreant, scandalous

data   clue, documentation, dossier, ground, information *(facts)*, intelligence *(news)*, proof, reference *(citation)*, science *(study)*. SEE MAIN ENTRY

data paper   pandect *(treatise)*

data sheet   blank *(form)*, form *(document)*

database   SEE MAIN ENTRY

date   age, appointment *(meeting)*, rendezvous. SEE MAIN ENTRY

date back   antedate

date before the true date   antedate

date before the true time   antedate

date earlier than the fact   antedate

date rape.   SEE MAIN ENTRY

dated   obsolete, outdated, outmoded

dated *(antiquated)*. SEE MAIN ENTRY

dated *(date-stamped)*. SEE MAIN ENTRY

dateless   permanent

daub   stain, sully

daughter   child

daunt   browbeat, discourage, dissuade, frighten, intimidate

dauntless   heroic, indomitable, spartan, undaunted

dauntlessness   prowess *(bravery)*

dawdle   pause, procrastinate, stall

dawn   emerge, genesis, inception, onset *(commencement)*, origin *(source)*, origination, outset, start

dawning   prime *(original)*

day   date

day *(24 hours)*. SEE MAIN ENTRY

day *(morning)*. SEE MAIN ENTRY

day book register
day in court SEE MAIN ENTRY
day of festivities holiday
day of grace reprieve
day of the week date
day off holiday
daybook calendar *(record of yearly periods)*, journal, ledger
daydream muse
daydreaming preoccupation
daze confuse *(bewilder)*, discompose, disorganize, muddle, obfuscate, overcome *(overwhelm)*, overwhelm
dazed insensible, thoughtless
dazzle delude, discompose, prestige
dazzling meritorious
de facto actual
de facto bodily. SEE MAIN ENTRY
de facto material *(physical)*
de jure ex officio. SEE MAIN ENTRY
de jure jural
de minimus SEE MAIN ENTRY
de novo SEE MAIN ENTRY
de re decedere waive
de re disserere argue
de rigueur binding
déabacle disaster
deactivate counteract, disable, disarm *(divest of arms)*, disband, disorganize, neutralize, palliate *(abate)*. SEE MAIN ENTRY
deactivated dormant, lifeless *(dull)*
deactivation deterrent
dead deceased, defunct, late *(defunct)*, null *(invalid)*, obsolete, pedestrian, torpid. SEE MAIN ENTRY
dead body cadaver, corpse
dead certainty certitude
dead end deadlock, impasse, quagmire
dead heat deadlock, draw *(tie)*
dead man decedent
dead person corpse, decedent
dead set. SEE MAIN ENTRY
dead stop impasse
dead-end blind *(impassable)*
deaden allay, drug, extinguish, mollify, neutralize, obtund, repress, soothe, stifle, subdue
deadened lifeless *(dull)*
deadening abatement *(extinguishment)*, mollification, narcotic
deadliness fatality, harm
deadlock abeyance, check *(bar)*, clog, draw *(tie)*, halt *(noun)*, halt *(verb)*, impasse, impede, interruption, quagmire, stem *(check)*. SEE MAIN ENTRY
deadly dangerous, deleterious, diabolic, dire, disastrous, fatal, irremediable, lethal, malevolent, malignant, peccant *(unhealthy)*, pedestrian, pernicious, pestilent, ruthless, toxic, virulent. SEE MAIN ENTRY
deadly accident fatality
deadly device cudgel
deadly devices weapons
deadly weapon cudgel
deadly weapons weapons
deadpan inexpressive, inscrutable
deadstop check *(bar)*
deadweight incumbrance *(burden)*
deaf heedless, incognizant, insensible, insusceptible *(uncaring)*
deaf to impervious
deaf to reason restive
deafening powerful
deafening row brawl
deal agreement *(contract)*, allocate, allot, attornment, barter, bestow, compact, compromise, contract, dicker, dispense,

disperse *(disseminate)*, distribute, dole, exchange, give *(grant)*, haggle, inflict, league, pact, project, sort, split, stipulation, trade *(commerce)*, trade, transact, transaction, treaty. SEE MAIN ENTRY
deal a blow assault, oppugn, strike *(assault)*
deal a blow to lash *(strike)*
deal a death blow dispatch *(put to death)*
deal a stroke lash *(strike)*
deal again reassign
deal crookedly palter
deal destruction destroy *(efface)*, eradicate, extinguish, extirpate
deal hard measure to ill use
deal in handle *(trade)*, sell, vend
deal in futures invest *(fund)*, speculate *(chance)*
deal in generalities generalize
deal out administer *(tender)*, allocate, apportion, assign *(allot)*, diffuse, disburse *(distribute)*, dispel, disperse *(disseminate)*, dispose *(apportion)*, disseminate, marshal, mete, parcel, supply
deal out again redistribute
deal out anew reapportion
deal retributive justice castigate, condemn *(punish)*, discipline *(punish)*
deal secretly plot
deal to dispense
deal with appertain, apply *(pertain)*, communicate, concern *(involve)*, conduct, correspond *(be equivalent)*, handle *(manage)*, militate, operate, patronize *(trade with)*, transact, treat *(process)*
deal with definitely dispatch *(dispose of)*
deal with gently favor
dealer broker, go-between, merchant, vendor. SEE MAIN ENTRY
dealer in illicit goods racketeer
dealing act *(undertaking)*, commerce, management *(judicious use)*, transaction
dealing death aberemurder, capital punishment
dealing out disbursement *(act of disbursing)*, distribution *(apportionment)*
dealings business *(commerce)*, conduct, contact *(association)*, overt act. SEE MAIN ENTRY
deals dealings
dean veteran
dear close *(intimate)*, exorbitant, priceless, scarce, valuable
dearth deficiency, deficit, delinquency *(shortage)*, indigence, insufficiency, need *(deprivation)*, paucity, poverty, privation. SEE MAIN ENTRY
dearth of ideas platitude
death capital punishment, dissolution *(termination)*, end *(termination)*, expiration, fatality, mortality. SEE MAIN ENTRY
death by accident fatality
death by violence dispatch *(act of putting to death)*
death sentence capital punishment
death-bringing deadly, lethal, malignant, pernicious
death-dealing deadly, fatal, lethal, malignant, pernicious, pestilent
death penalty SEE MAIN ENTRY
death sentence SEE MAIN ENTRY
deathblow dispatch *(act of putting to death)*
deathful deadly, pernicious
deathless perpetual
deathly deadly, fatal, lethal, malignant, pernicious, pestilent
débâcle casualty

debacle cataclysm
débâcle catastrophe
debacle failure *(lack of success)*
débâcle revolution
debacle subversion. SEE MAIN ENTRY
debar bar *(exclude)*, block, condemn *(ban)*, constrain *(restrain)*, disable, disqualify, eliminate *(exclude)*, exclude, fight *(counteract)*, forbid, halt, hamper, inhibit, interdict, obstruct, occlude, preclude, prevent, prohibit, refuse, remove *(eliminate)*, restrain, restrict, thwart, trammel, withhold. SEE MAIN ENTRY
debarkation point destination
debarment embargo, exclusion, expulsion, prohibition, refusal, rejection, removal
debarred barred
debarring blockade *(limitation)*, boycott
debase adulterate, brand *(stigmatize)*, contaminate, contemn, corrupt, damage, debauch, degenerate, demean *(make lower)*, demote, depreciate, derogate, deteriorate, disapprove *(condemn)*, discredit, disgrace, dishonor *(deprive of honor)*, disoblige, disparage, harm, humiliate, infect, libel, mistreat, pillory, pollute, spoil *(impair)*, stain, sully, taint *(corrupt)*, tamper. SEE MAIN ENTRY
debase in quality degenerate
debased depraved, dissolute, ignoble, sordid, tainted *(corrupted)*, vicious
debased person degenerate
debasement abuse *(physical misuse)*, attaint, bad faith, bad repute, contempt *(disdain)*, corruption, defilement, degradation, depression, deterioration, discredit, disgrace, dishonor *(shame)*, disrepute, ignominy, misusage, obloquy, odium, opprobrium, perversion, shame
debatable arguable, contestable, controversial, disputable, doubtful, dubious, equivocal, indefinite, litigious, moot, polemic, problematic, speculative, uncertain *(questionable)*, undecided. SEE MAIN ENTRY
debatable issue issue *(matter in dispute)*
debatable point issue *(matter in dispute)*, matter *(subject)*, thesis
debate answer *(reply)*, argue, argument *(contention)*, challenge, conflict *(noun)*, conflict *(verb)*, consider, contention *(argument)*, contention *(opposition)*, contest *(dispute)*, contest, contravention, controversy *(argument)*, controvert, converse, cross *(disagree with)*, deliberate, deliberation, disaccord *(noun)*, disaccord *(verb)*, disagree, disagreement, discourse, discuss, dispute, doubt *(hesitate)*, fight *(argument)*, muse, oppose, oscillate, parley, ponder, reason *(persuade)*, refute, respond, speculate *(conjecture)*, treat *(process)*, vacillate. SEE MAIN ENTRY
debater contender
debating dissenting, hesitant
debauch abuse *(violate)*, betray *(lead astray)*, carouse, contemn, corrupt, debase, degenerate, deteriorate, dishonor *(deprive of honor)*, pervert, pollute, taint *(corrupt)*. SEE MAIN ENTRY
débauche delineation
debauched bad *(offensive)*, decadent, depraved, dissolute, gluttonous, immoral, lascivious, lecherous, licentious, obscene, peccant *(culpable)*, perverse, profligate *(corrupt)*, promiscuous, prurient, salacious, tainted *(corrupted)*
debauchee degenerate, wrongdoer
debauchery perversion, vice. SEE MAIN ENTRY

debauchment debauchery, defilement. SEE MAIN ENTRY

debenture bond, charge *(lien)*, check *(instrument)*, draft, note *(written promise to pay)*, security *(pledge)*, specialty *(contract)*. SEE MAIN ENTRY

debere owe

deberi due

debilitare disable, impair

debilitate adulterate, attenuate, depreciate, deteriorate, disable, disarm *(divest of arms)*, eviscerate, exhaust *(deplete)*, extenuate, impair, mutilate, tax *(overwork)*. SEE MAIN ENTRY

debilitated disabled *(made incapable)*, helpless *(powerless)*, lifeless *(dull)*, powerless

debilitating disabling

debilitation disability *(physical inability)*, impotence

debility disability *(physical inability)*, fault *(weakness)*, frailty, impotence, impuissance, languor, prostration

debit arrears, charge *(cost)*, debt, due, expense *(cost)*, liability, obligation *(liability)*. SEE MAIN ENTRY

debitus condign, due *(owed)*, overdue

debouch emanate

debouchment issuance

debrief. SEE MAIN ENTRY

debris discard

debt arrears, cloud *(incumbrance)*, debit, delinquency *(shortage)*, due, duty *(obligation)*, liability, lien, obligation *(duty)*, obligation *(liability)*. SEE MAIN ENTRY

debt limit. SEE MAIN ENTRY

debt owed setoff

debt service. SEE MAIN ENTRY

debt unpaid though due arrears

debtee creditor

debtor obligor. SEE MAIN ENTRY

debunk disabuse, disapprove *(reject)*, disgrace, reveal. SEE MAIN ENTRY

debut birth *(beginning)*, first appearance, inception, nascency

debutant neophyte

decadence caducity, degradation, delinquency *(misconduct)*, deterioration, detriment, disrepair, turpitude

decadency decline, degradation, disrepair

decadent dissolute, old, regressive. SEE MAIN ENTRY

decadent person degenerate

decamp abandon *(physically leave)*, abduct, abscond, depart, disappear, escape, evacuate, flee, leave *(depart)*, quit *(evacuate)*, retire *(retreat)*, retreat

decampment abandonment *(desertion)*, flight

decant outpour

decay caducity, consumption, corrupt, decline, decline *(fall)*, degenerate, depreciate, deteriorate, deterioration, detriment, disintegrate, disrepair, dissolution *(disintegration)*, disuse, ebb, erode, erosion, languish, prostration, spoil *(impair)*, spoilage, taint *(contaminate)*, wear and tear. SEE MAIN ENTRY

decayed old, sordid, stale, unsound *(not strong)*

decaying bad *(inferior)*, decadent

decease death, demise *(death)*, die, end *(termination)*, expire. SEE MAIN ENTRY

deceased corpse, dead, decedent, defunct, late *(defunct)*, lifeless *(dead)*. SEE MAIN ENTRY

deceased person decedent

decedent dead. SEE MAIN ENTRY

decedere secede

deceit artifice, bad faith, canard, collusion, color *(deceptive appearance)*, deception, dishonesty, evasion, false pretense, falsification, fraud, hoax, hypocrisy, imposture, improbity, indirection *(deceitfulness)*, knavery, lie, misstatement, pettifoggery, pretense *(pretext)*, ruse, story *(falsehood)*, stratagem. SEE MAIN ENTRY

deceitful collusive, colorable *(specious)*, deceptive, delusive, devious, dishonest, disingenuous, evasive, faithless, fallacious, false *(disloyal)*, false *(not genuine)*, fraudulent, furtive, insidious, lying, machiavellian, mendacious, meretricious, perfidious, politic, recreant, sly, spurious, subtle *(insidious)*, surreptitious, tortuous *(corrupt)*, undependable, unreliable, unscrupulous, untrue, untrustworthy

deceitful agreement collusion

deceitful compact collusion

deceitful practice fraud

deceitfulness bad faith, collusion, concealment, deceit, dishonesty, duplicity, evasion, false pretense, falsification, fraud, hypocrisy, improbity, infidelity, knavery, misrepresentation

deceivability credulity

deceivable credulous, naive

deceive bait *(lure)*, betray *(lead astray)*, bilk, camouflage, cheat, circumvent, cloak, defraud, delude, disguise, dupe, ensnare, entrap, equivocate, fabricate *(make up)*, fake, feign, foist, hide, hoodwink, illude, inveigle, lie *(falsify)*, misguide, misinform, mislabel, mislead, misrepresent, misstate, mulct *(defraud)*, overreach, palter, peculate, pettifog, pretend, prevaricate. SEE MAIN ENTRY

deceive by treachery betray *(lead astray)*

deceive oneself miscalculate, misconceive

deceiver conspirator

deceiving colorable *(specious)*, deceptive, delusive, dishonest, disingenuous, evasive, fallacious, false *(inaccurate)*, fictitious, fraudulent, illusory, insidious, machiavellian, mendacious, ostensible, perfidious, sly, specious

decelerate decrease, diminish, hold up *(delay)*, impede, moderate *(temper)*, palliate *(abate)*

deceleration decrease, delay

decencies decorum

decency clemency, decorum, propriety *(correctness)*

decent benevolent, clean, ethical, fair *(satisfactory)*, honest, humane, mediocre, meritorious, moral, suitable

decently fairly *(moderately)*

decentralization SEE MAIN ENTRY

decentralize diffuse, disperse *(scatter)*, dissolve *(separate)*, distribute

deception artifice, bad faith, canard, collusion, color *(deceptive appearance)*, contrivance, corruption, counterfeit, decoy, disguise, dishonesty, distortion, duplicity, evasion, fallacy, falsehood, falsification, figment, forgery, fraud, hoax, hypocrisy, imposture, indirection *(deceitfulness)*, knavery, lie, maneuver *(trick)*, misrepresentation, misstatement, pettifoggery, plot *(secret plan)*, pretense *(pretext)*, pretext, ruse, sham, sophistry, story *(falsehood)*, stratagem, subreption, subterfuge. SEE MAIN ENTRY

deceptious sly

deceptive artificial, assumed *(feigned)*, collusive, colorable *(specious)*, delusive, dishonest, disingenuous, equivocal, evasive, fallacious, false *(inaccurate)*, false *(not genuine)*, fraudulent, illusory, imitation, insidious, lying, machiavellian, meretricious, ostensible, sly, specious, spurious, subtle *(insidious)*, surreptitious, untrue, untrustworthy. SEE MAIN ENTRY

deceptive belief fallacy

deceptive check bad check

deceptive covering color *(deceptive appearance)*, disguise

deceptive representation of fact false pretense

deceptive statement misrepresentation

deceptiveness deceit, fraud, misrepresentation

decernere contend *(dispute)*, decide, determine, resolve *(decide)*

decerpere cull

decessio discount, discount *(disbelieve)*

decide adjudge, adjudicate, arbitrate *(adjudge)*, ascertain, award, choose, deem, determine, dispose *(incline)*, elect *(choose)*, find *(determine)*, fix *(settle)*, gauge, hear *(give a legal hearing)*, judge, pass *(determine)*, prescribe, pronounce *(pass judgment)*, select, sentence, settle, stipulate, try *(conduct a trial)*. SEE MAIN ENTRY

decide a question of fact find *(determine)*

decide against overrule

decide beforehand predetermine, presuppose

decide between opposing parties arbitrate *(adjudge)*

decide by judicial sentence rule *(decide)*

decide in advance forejudge, predetermine, preordain, presuppose

decide in favor of uphold

decide legally hold *(decide)*

decide upon conclude *(decide)*, determine, find *(determine)*

decided absolute *(conclusive)*, actual, affirmative, axiomatic, categorical, certain *(fixed)*, certain *(positive)*, complete *(ended)*, conclusive *(settled)*, definite, definitive, demonstrable, dogmatic, explicit, express, fixed *(settled)*, inappealable, inevitable, inexorable, inflexible, intentional, necessary *(inescapable)*, obdurate, official, patient, peremptory *(absolute)*, pertinacious, positive *(confident)*, positive *(incontestable)*, purposeful, res judicata, resolute, resounding, serious *(devoted)*, stark, stated, steadfast, through, unequivocal, unmistakable, unyielding. SEE MAIN ENTRY

decided by competition vying competitive *(antagonistic)*

decided upon preferred *(favored)*

decidedly fairly *(clearly)*, purely *(positively)*

decidedly different distinct *(distinguished from others)*

deciding critical *(crucial)*, crucial, determinative

deciduous ephemeral, temporary, transient, volatile

decimate destroy *(efface)*, diminish, disarm *(divest of arms)*, eliminate *(eradicate)*, lessen, minimize, reduce

decimation aberemurder, catastrophe, destruction, killing

decipere mislead

decipher ascertain, clarify, construe *(comprehend)*, construe *(translate)*, detect, elucidate,

decipherable

explain, find *(discover),* interpret, read, resolve *(solve),* solve

decipherable ascertainable, cognizable, coherent *(clear),* comprehensible, determinable *(ascertainable),* solvable

deciphering clarification, explanation

decipherment definition, solution *(answer)*

decision adjudication, alternative *(option),* animus, arbitration, authority *(documentation),* award, call *(option),* cognovit, conclusion *(determination),* consequence *(conclusion),* conviction *(finding of guilt),* decree, determination, dilemma, discretion *(power of choice),* disposition *(determination),* election *(choice),* finding, holding *(ruling of a court),* judgment *(discernment),* judgment *(formal court decree),* opinion *(judicial decision),* outcome, poll *(casting of votes),* pronouncement, referendum, relief *(legal redress),* res judicata, result, ruling, selection *(choice),* sentence, verdict, volition, vote, will *(desire).* SEE MAIN ENTRY

decision beforehand predetermination

decision in advance predetermination

decision making government *(administration)*

decision of a jury verdict

decision-making body management *(directorate)*

decision-making power over the case jurisdiction

decisive absolute *(conclusive),* axiomatic, categorical, certain *(fixed),* certain *(positive),* compelling, conclusive *(settled),* convincing, critical *(crucial),* crucial, definite, definitive, determinative, final, inappealable, key, last *(final),* major, material *(important),* peremptory *(absolute),* peremptory *(imperative),* positive *(confident),* strategic. SEE MAIN ENTRY

decisive factor determinant

decisive moment crossroad *(turning point)*

decisive turn landmark *(significant change)*

decisively fairly *(clearly)*

decivilize brutalize

deck embellish

declaim enunciate, recite, speak, utter. SEE MAIN ENTRY

declaim against censure, complain *(charge),* condemn *(blame),* decry, denounce *(condemn),* disapprove *(condemn),* expostulate, fault, impeach

declaimer demagogue

declamatio bluster *(speech),* declamation

declamation bombast, charge *(statement to the jury),* discourse, fustian, harangue, peroration, rhetoric *(insincere language),* speech. SEE MAIN ENTRY

declamatory flatulent, fustian, inflated *(bombastic),* orotund, turgid, voluble

declamatory speech harangue

declarant SEE MAIN ENTRY

declarare declare, express, manifest, proclaim, prove

declaratio declaration, manifestation

declaration acknowledgment *(avowal),* adjudication, adjuration, admission *(disclosure),* affirmance *(authentication),* affirmation, alibi, allegation, assertion, asseveration, assurance, attestation, averment, avouchment, avowal, brevet, certificate, certification *(attested copy),* certification *(certification of proficiency),* claim *(assertion),* claim *(legal demand),* cognovit, common knowledge, communication *(statement),* conclusion *(determination),* confession, confirmation, count, declaratory

judgment, decree, determination, dictum, directive, disclosure *(act of disclosing),* disclosure *(something disclosed),* discovery, edict, expression *(comment),* judgment *(formal court decree),* measure, notice *(announcement),* notification, observation, opinion *(judicial decision),* order *(judicial directive),* parole, platform, proclamation, promise, pronouncement, proposition, reference *(recommendation),* remark, representation *(statement),* resolution *(formal statement),* speech, statement, surety *(certainty),* testimony. SEE MAIN ENTRY

declaration of a jury verdict

declaration of disapproval protest

declaration of dissent protest

declaration of facts testimony

declaration of faith conviction *(persuasion),* dogma, principle *(axiom),* profession *(declaration)*

declaration of opposition protest

declaration of penalty sentence

declaration of policy platform

declaration of war outbreak

declaration under oath affidavit, deposition

declarative declaratory, demonstrative *(illustrative),* narrative

declaratory narrative. SEE MAIN ENTRY

declaratory judgment SEE MAIN ENTRY

declare adduce, admit *(concede),* allege, annunciate, assert, attest, avouch *(avow),* avow, bare, bear *(adduce),* betray *(disclose),* claim *(maintain),* comment, communicate, conclude *(decide),* confess, contend *(maintain),* convey *(communicate),* designate, determine, disclose, enact, enunciate, express, inform *(betray),* issue *(publish),* manifest, notify, observe *(remark),* pass *(determine),* phrase, pose *(propound),* posit, proclaim, profess *(avow),* promise *(vow),* promulgate, pronounce *(speak),* propose, publish, purport, relate *(tell),* remark, report *(disclose),* reveal, rule *(decide),* signify *(inform),* speak, swear, testify, utter, verify *(swear),* vouch. SEE MAIN ENTRY

declare a verdict find *(determine)*

declare authoritatively rule *(decide)*

declare blameless exonerate

declare forfeit dispossess

declare guiltless exculpate, justify, palliate *(excuse)*

declare guilty of an offense convict, sentence

declare illegal ban, forbid, interdict, outlaw

declare incidentally mention

declare innocent acquit, exonerate, vindicate

declare invalid cancel, negate

declare lawful authorize, constitute *(establish),* legitimate, pass *(approve)*

declare legal validate

declare not guilty exculpate, exonerate

declare not to be true disavow

declare null and void abolish, abrogate *(annul),* abrogate *(rescind),* adeem, cancel, discharge *(release from obligation),* disclaim, negate, nullify, quash, repeal, repudiate, rescind, revoke

declare one's right claim *(demand)*

declare openly avouch *(avow),* avow

declare opposition demonstrate *(protest)*

declare positively avow

declare solemnly affirm *(declare solemnly),* swear

declare the truth of attest, avow, certify *(attest)*

declare to be pronounce *(pass judgment)*

declare to be fact affirm *(claim),* bear *(adduce)*

declare to be false deny *(contradict)*

declare to be forfeited condemn *(seize)*

declare to be genuine evidence

declare to be true certify *(attest),* evidence

declare to be untrue deny *(contradict)*

declare true swear

declare under oath depose *(testify)*

declare unlawful outlaw

declare valid validate

declare war fight *(battle)*

declare with positiveness avouch *(avow),* purport

declared agreed *(promised),* alleged, nuncupative, ostensible

declared insane non compos mentis

declared intention proposition

declarer. SEE MAIN ENTRY

déclassé discard

declension curtailment, decrease, decrement, degradation, deterioration, rejection, relapse

declinare deviate

declinatio deviation

declination abandonment *(repudiation),* abatement *(reduction),* damage, decrease, degradation, deterioration, disdain, dishonor *(nonpayment),* negation, refusal, rejection, relapse, renunciation, repudiation. SEE MAIN ENTRY

declinatory nonconsenting

declinature negation, refusal, rejection

decline abate *(lessen),* abatement *(reduction),* avoid *(evade),* caducity, curtailment, damage, decay, decrease *(noun),* decrease *(verb),* deduction *(diminution),* degenerate, degradation, depreciate, depress, depression, deteriorate, disavow, disdain, dismiss *(put out of consideration),* disoblige, dissent *(withhold assent),* ebb, end *(termination),* expense *(sacrifice),* fail *(lose),* forbear, forgo, forswear, languish, lapse *(expiration),* lessen, loss, rebuff, refrain, refuse, reject, relapse *(noun),* relapse *(verb),* renounce, repudiate, spurn, subside. SEE MAIN ENTRY

decline and fall decrease

decline to agree dissent *(withhold assent)*

decline to pay dishonor *(refuse to pay)*

decline to redeem dishonor *(refuse to pay)*

decline to sanction disapprove *(reject)*

declining decadent, old, stale

declining to agree dissenting

decoct distill

decoctor bankrupt

decodable solvable

decode construe *(comprehend),* construe *(translate),* elucidate, find *(discover),* interpret, solve

decoding definition

decommission. SEE MAIN ENTRY

decompose decay, degenerate, deteriorate, disintegrate, disorganize, dissolve *(disperse),* spoil *(impair)*

decomposed dilapidated

decomposing decadent

decomposition consumption, destruction, deterioration, dissolution *(disintegration),* spoilage

decompound decay

decontaminate SEE MAIN ENTRY

decontrol disengage, freedom

decorare embellish, garnish, honor

decorate embellish, honor

decorated elaborate, pretentious *(ostentatious)*

decoration mention *(tribute)*, motif, prize

decorous formal, obeisant, proper, suitable

decorously respectfully

decorousness decorum, propriety *(correctness)*

decorum behavior, conduct. SEE MAIN ENTRY

decorum decorum

decorum deportment, formality, manner *(behavior)*, presence *(poise)*, propriety *(correctness)*, protocol *(etiquette)*

decoy bait *(lure)*, betray *(lead astray)*, cloak, deceive, deception, delude, ensnare, entice, entrap, fake, illude, inveigle, lure, maneuver *(trick)*, mislead, ruse. SEE MAIN ENTRY

decrease abate *(lessen)*, abatement *(reduction)*, abridge *(shorten)*, allay, attenuate, attrition, curtail, curtailment, decline, decrement, deduct *(reduce)*, deduction *(diminution)*, deplete, depreciate, depress, deteriorate, diminish, diminution, discount, discount *(reduce)*, ebb, erode, erosion, lessen, minimize, mitigate, mitigation, moderate *(temper)*, modify *(moderate)*, mollification, mollify, palliate *(abate)*, rebate, reduce, remission, remit *(relax)*, retrench, subside. SEE MAIN ENTRY

decrease a punishment commute

decrease in excellence impair

decrease in importance demote

decrease in purchasing power inflation *(decrease in value of currency)*

decreased qualified *(conditioned)*

decree adjudge, adjudicate, adjudication, appointment *(act of designating)*, arbitrate *(adjudge)*, arbitration, award *(noun)*, award *(verb)*, brevet, canon, charter *(declaration of rights)*, citation *(charge)*, codification, cognovit, command, compel, conclude *(decide)*, conclusion *(determination)*, constitute *(establish)*, constrain *(compel)*, conviction *(finding of guilt)*, decide, decision *(judgment)*, declaration, detail *(assign)*, determination, determine, dictate *(noun)*, dictate *(verb)*, direct *(order)*, direction *(order)*, directive, edict, enact, enactment, enjoin, fiat, finding, hold *(decide)*, holding *(ruling of a court)*, impose *(enforce)*, instruct *(direct)*, instruction *(direction)*, issuance, judge, judgment *(formal court decree)*, law, legislate, mandamus, mandate, measure, mittimus, monition *(legal summons)*, necessitate, notice *(announcement)*, opinion *(judicial decision)*, order *(judicial directive)*, order, ordinance, pass *(approve)*, pass *(determine)*, precept, prescribe, prescription *(directive)*, press *(constrain)*, proclamation, pronounce *(pass judgment)*, pronouncement, regulation *(rule)*, require *(compel)*, requirement, res judicata, rule *(legal dictate)*, rule *(decide)*, rule *(govern)*, ruling, sentence, statute, warrant *(judicial writ)*, writ. SEE MAIN ENTRY

decree absolute law

decree authoritatively arbitrate *(adjudge)*

decree beforehand preordain

decree by deliberate judgment award

decree by judicial authority conclude *(decide)*, determine

decree by law legalize

decree having the force of law fiat

decree of a jury verdict

decree of nullity annulment, divorce

decree of punishment sentence

decree to be merited award

decreed decretal, legal, mandatory, necessary *(inescapable)*, positive *(prescribed)*

decreeing legislative

decreement declaration, opinion *(judicial decision)*

decrement abatement *(reduction)*, consumption, damage, decline, decrease, deduction *(diminution)*, discount, erosion, loss, spoilage. SEE MAIN ENTRY

decremental drawback

decrepit decadent, dilapidated, disabled *(made incapable)*, imperfect, old, powerless, unsound *(not strong)*

decrepitude decline, deterioration, disrepair, impuissance, prostration

decreptitude caducity

decrescence curtailment, decrease, decrement, deduction *(diminution)*

decrescere abate *(lessen)*

decretal declaratory, determinative, directive, mandate, mittimus, prescriptive, proclamation, requirement, writ. SEE MAIN ENTRY

decretive compulsory, declaratory, decretal

decretory declaratory, decretal

decretum decree, edict, holding *(ruling of a court)*, ordinance, principle *(axiom)*, resolution *(decision)*, sentence

decrial bad repute, blame *(culpability)*, conviction *(finding of guilt)*, denunciation, disapprobation, dishonor *(shame)*, disparagement, impugnation, incrimination, ostracism

decried blameful

decry brand *(stigmatize)*, cavil, censure, complain *(criticize)*, condemn *(blame)*, contemn, criticize *(find fault with)*, debunk, defame, denigrate, denounce *(condemn)*, deprecate, depreciate, derogate, disapprove *(condemn)*, discommend, discredit, disdain, disparage, except *(object)*, fault, impeach, lash *(attack verbally)*, lessen, libel, malign, minimize, remonstrate, reprehend, reprimand, reproach, smear, sully. SEE MAIN ENTRY

decrying calumnious, contemptuous, cynical, pejorative

decurrence decline

decursio maneuver *(tactic)*

decursus maneuver *(tactic)*

decussatio intersection

decussation intersection

dedecorare disgrace, dishonor *(deprive of honor)*

dedecorate demote

dedecoration ignominy, notoriety, scandal

dedecori esse disgrace

dedecus degradation, discredit, opprobrium

dedere deliver, devote, surrender *(yield)*, yield *(submit)*

dedicare dedicate

dedicate devote. SEE MAIN ENTRY

dedicate oneself to specialize

dedicated industrious, loyal, obedient, purposeful, sacrosanct, serious *(devoted)*, steadfast, true *(loyal)*, unyielding, zealous

dedication adherence *(devotion)*, inscription, loyalty. SEE MAIN ENTRY

dedicatory honorary

deditum esse adhere *(maintain loyalty)*

deduce ascertain, assume *(suppose)*, conclude *(decide)*, comprehend *(comprehend)*, deduct *(conclude by reasoning)*, detect, determine, discover, educe, extract, find *(determine)*, gauge, infer, interpret, judge, presume, presuppose, read, reason *(conclude)*, reflect *(ponder)*, solve, surmise, suspect *(think)*, understand. SEE MAIN ENTRY

deduce by interpretation construe *(comprehend)*

deduce the meaning of construe *(comprehend)*

deduced circumstantial

deducere derive *(deduce)*, divert

deducible accountable *(explainable)*, convincing, deductible *(provable)*, deductive, determinable *(ascertainable)*, provable

deducibly a priori

deducing dialectic

deduct construe *(comprehend)*, decrease, deduce, depreciate, diminish, except *(exclude)*, excise *(cut away)*, lessen, minimize, rebate, remove *(eliminate)*, retrench, withdraw. SEE MAIN ENTRY

deduct from discount *(reduce)*

deductible SEE MAIN ENTRY

deducting save

deductio deduction *(diminution)*, discount, discount *(disbelieve)*

deduction computation, concept, conclusion *(determination)*, consequence *(conclusion)*, construction, corollary, decrease, decrement, dialectic, diminution, discount, estimate *(idea)*, estimation *(calculation)*, holding *(ruling of a court)*, hypothesis, inference, perception, presumption, ratiocination, rebate, removal. SEE MAIN ENTRY

deductive discursive *(analytical)*, logical. SEE MAIN ENTRY

deductively a priori

deed act *(enactment)*, act *(undertaking)*, alienate *(transfer title)*, cede, contribute *(supply)*, convey *(transfer)*, descend, dominion *(absolute ownership)*, endeavor, give *(grant)*, grant *(transfer formally)*, instrument *(document)*, overt act, performance *(execution)*, present *(make a gift)*, step, title *(right)*, transaction, transfer. SEE MAIN ENTRY

deed done fait accompli

deed exculpating the transferor quitclaim

deed of agreement indenture

deed of release quitclaim, waiver

deed of savagery atrocity

deeding alienation *(transfer of title)*, demise *(conveyance)*

deeds conduct, dealings

deem adjudge, adjudicate, conclude *(decide)*, deduce, deduct *(conclude by reasoning)*, guess, judge, opine, presume, presuppose, regard *(pay attention)*, surmise, suspect *(think)*. SEE MAIN ENTRY

deem true assume *(suppose)*

deem unbecoming disdain

deem unsuitable disdain

deemed putative

deemphasize. SEE MAIN ENTRY

deep broad, capacious, esoteric, extensive, incomprehensible, ingrained, intense, obscure *(abstruse)*, profound *(intense)*, recondite, sapient

deep application diligence *(care)*

deep attention diligence *(care)*

deep down virtual

deep pockets. SEE MAIN ENTRY

deep rooted virtual. SEE MAIN ENTRY

deep-rooted chronic, inherent, inveterate, organic, stable, underlying

deep-rooted belief faith

deep seated intrinsic *(deep down)*, virtual. SEE MAIN ENTRY

deep-seated chronic, ingrained, permanent

deep study diligence *(care)*, preoccupation, probe

deep thought diligence *(care)*

deepen aggravate *(exacerbate)*, enhance, expand, extend *(enlarge)*, intensify, magnify

deepening aggravation (exacerbation), boom (increase), cumulative (intensifying)
deeply felt profound (intense)
deescalate disarm (divest of arms)
deface damage, destroy (efface), harm, maim, mutilate, spoil (impair), sully, tarnish. SEE MAIN ENTRY
defaced blemished, marred
defacement flaw. SEE MAIN ENTRY
defacer vandal
defalcate cheat, embezzle, loot, purloin. SEE MAIN ENTRY
defalcation bad faith, embezzlement, misappropriation
defalcator embezzler, thief
defamation aspersion, denunciation, dishonor (shame), hatred, infamy, libel, malediction, obloquy, opprobrium, phillipic, scandal, shame, slander, vilification. SEE MAIN ENTRY
defamatory calumnious, contemptuous, critical (faultfinding), cynical, derogatory, incriminatory, libelous, pejorative, scandalous
defamatory words slander
defamatory writing libel
defame brand (stigmatize), denigrate, denounce (condemn), depreciate, derogate, disgrace, dishonor (deprive of honor), disparage, expose, humiliate, lessen, libel, malign, pillory, reproach, smear, stain, sully, tarnish. SEE MAIN ENTRY
defame by a published writing libel
defamed accused (attacked)
default arrears, breach, defeat, defect, deficit, delinquency (failure of duty), delinquency (shortage), dereliction, dishonor (nonpayment), disregard (omission), failure (bankruptcy), forfeit, infraction, lapse (expiration), maladministration, miscarriage, neglect, nonappearance, nonpayment, nonperformance, omission, repudiate. SEE MAIN ENTRY
default in performance omission
defaultant delinquent (overdue)
defaulter convict, fugitive, thief
defaulting bankrupt, bankruptcy, delinquent (overdue), insolvent
defeasance abolition, countermand, discharge (annulment), discharge (release from obligation), discontinuance (act of discontinuing), dissolution (termination), repudiation, rescision, revocation. SEE MAIN ENTRY
defeasible terminable, voidable. SEE MAIN ENTRY
defeat abate (extinguish), abatement (extinguishment), answer (reply), avoid (cancel), balk, circumvent, contravene, controvert, counteract, debacle, failure (lack of success), foil, frustrate, frustration, halt, miscarriage, negate, nonsuit, obliterate, overcome (surmount), override, overthrow, overturn, overwhelm, preclude, prevent, prostration, rebuff, refute, rejection, repulse, subdue, subject, subjugate, subversion, subvert, surmount, thwart, upset. SEE MAIN ENTRY
defeat of the prosecution compurgation
defeat one's own purpose overreach
defeat oneself by overdoing matters overreach
defeated despondent, disappointed, null (invalid), null and void
defeating prevailing (having superior force)
defeatism pessimism
defeatist cynical, despondent, pessimistic, resigned
defect abandon (physically leave), defacement, deficiency, disadvantage, disease,

disqualification (factor that disqualifies), drawback, fault (weakness), flaw, foible, frailty, handicap, leave (depart), part (leave), quit (evacuate), stigma, vice. SEE MAIN ENTRY
defect-free accurate
defectio failure (falling short), revolt
defection abandonment (desertion), abjuration, absence (nonattendance), bad faith, dereliction, desertion, disloyalty, infidelity, repudiation, revolt, sedition
defective bad (inferior), blemished, broken (fractured), deficient, faulty, imperfect, inferior (lower in quality), insufficient, marred, non compos mentis, nonsubstantial (not sturdy), peccable, poor (inferior in quality), undesirable, unsound (fallacious), unsound (not strong). SEE MAIN ENTRY
defective check bad check
defectiveness failure (falling short), frailty
defectless absolute (ideal), infallible
defend adhere (maintain loyalty), advocate, answer (reply), answer (respond legally), corroborate, countercharge, cover (guard), espouse, harbor, justify, lobby, maintain (sustain), palliate (excuse), preserve, protect, save (rescue), screen (guard), side, sponsor, support (assist), support (justify), sustain (confirm), uphold. SEE MAIN ENTRY
defend a case plead (argue a case)
defend as conformable to law justify
defend as conformable to right justify
defend successfully support (justify)
defendable defensible, justifiable, tenable
defendant convict, litigant, party (litigant), respondent. SEE MAIN ENTRY
defendant's answer to charges plea, pleading
defended guarded, insusceptible (resistant), ironclad, safe, secure (free from danger)
defender advocate (counselor), advocate (espouser), apologist, backer, benefactor, custodian (protector), guardian, partisan, patron (influential supporter), proponent, samaritan
defendere parry, protect
defense advocacy, alibi, ammunition, answer (judicial response), argument (pleading), behalf, bulwark, compurgation, counterargument, excuse, explanation, justification, panoply, plea, pleading, preservation, pretext, protection, reason (basis), rejoinder, safeguard, safekeeping, salvo, security (safety), shelter (protection), shield, support (assistance), ward. SEE MAIN ENTRY
defenseless disabled (made incapable), indefensible, insecure, open (accessible), powerless, precarious, unable, untenable, vulnerable
defenselessness danger, impotence
defensible inexpugnable, justifiable, pardonable, plausible, tenable, unobjectionable. SEE MAIN ENTRY
defensio assertion
defensive preventive, protective
defensive arms panoply
defensive clothing panoply
defensive equipment panoply
defensive evidence alibi
defensive plea alibi
defensor apologist, guardian
defer accommodate, adjourn, continue (adjourn), delay, discontinue (break continuity), hold up (delay), postpone, procrastinate, stall, suspend. SEE MAIN ENTRY
defer to acknowledge (verify), comply, concur (agree), hear (give attention to),

honor, obey, recognize (acknowledge), regard (hold in esteem), relent
deference allegiance, character (reputation), comity, consideration (sympathetic regard), courtesy, discipline (obedience), estimation (esteem), fealty, homage, honor (outward respect), regard (esteem), resignation (passive acceptance), respect. SEE MAIN ENTRY
deferential civil (polite), malleable, obedient, obeisant, obsequious, pliant, sequacious, servile, subservient
deferentially respectfully
deferment adjournment, delay, extension (postponement), pause, reprieve. SEE MAIN ENTRY
deferral deferment, extension (postponement), moratorium
deferre devolve, invest (vest), tender
deferred arrested (checked), back (in arrears), late (tardy)
deferred payment arrears, bill (invoice), debit, debt, nonpayment
deferring dilatory, obeisant
defiance conflict, contradiction, disrespect, impugnation, infraction, insurrection, mutiny, negation, noncompliance (nonobservance), nonconformity, protest, provocation, rebellion, rebuff, refusal, resistance, revolt, sedition, spite. SEE MAIN ENTRY
defiance of custom deviation, exception (exclusion), quirk (idiosyncrasy)
defiance of danger audacity, prowess (bravery)
defiance of orders contempt (disobedience to the court), infraction
defiance of precedent creation
defiant brazen, contemptuous, contumacious, disobedient, disorderly, impertinent (insolent), indomitable, insolent, insubordinate, intractable, nonconforming, nonconsenting, proud (conceited), provocative, pugnacious, recalcitrant
deficere fail (lose)
deficiency absence (omission), dearth, defect, deficit, delinquency (shortage), disadvantage, failure (falling short), fault (weakness), flaw, foible, frailty, handicap, insufficiency, mediocrity, need (deprivation), paucity, poverty, vice. SEE MAIN ENTRY
deficient defective, delinquent (overdue), devoid, fallible, faulty, imperfect, inadequate, incompetent, inferior (lower in quality), insufficient, minimal, nonsubstantial (not sturdy), nonsubstantial (not sufficient), paltry, partial (relating to a part), perfunctory, poor (inferior in quality), scarce, unqualified (not competent), unsatisfactory, unsound (not strong). SEE MAIN ENTRY
deficient in reason fatuous
deficient work noncompliance (improper completion)
deficit arrears, debt, decrement, deficiency, delinquency (shortage), due, insufficiency, need (deprivation), poverty. SEE MAIN ENTRY
defile abuse (violate), adulterate, betray (lead astray), brand (stigmatize), contaminate, contemn, damage, debase, deteriorate, disgrace, dishonor (deprive of honor), infect, malign, misemploy, mishandle (maltreat), molest (subject to indecent advances), pillory, pollute, smear, spoil (impair), stain, sully, taint (contaminate), taint (corrupt)
defiled sordid, tainted (contaminated)

defilement abuse *(physical misuse)*, air pollution, attaint, bad repute, contaminate, contempt *(disdain)*, debauchment, disgrace, dishonor *(shame)*, misusage, perversion, rape, seduction, shame. SEE MAIN ENTRY
definability construction
definable accountable *(explainable)*, ascertainable, determinable *(ascertainable)*
define border *(bound)*, call *(title)*, clarify, comment, construe *(translate)*, delimit, delineate, demarcate, describe, designate, distinguish, elucidate, explain, explicate, expound, illustrate, interpret, label, render *(depict)*, restrict, trace *(delineate)*. SEE MAIN ENTRY
define limits locate
define location locate
defined actual, coherent *(clear)*, comprehensible, exact, express, manifest, narrow, perceptible, precise, qualified *(conditioned)*, stated, unambiguous, unequivocal, unmistakable. SEE MAIN ENTRY
defined meaning. SEE MAIN ENTRY
defining restrictive
definire circumscribe *(define)*, define, fix *(settle)*
definite absolute *(conclusive)*, actual, apparent *(perceptible)*, axiomatic, categorical, certain *(fixed)*, certain *(positive)*, certain *(specific)*, clear *(certain)*, cogent, cognizable, coherent *(clear)*, conclusive *(determinative)*, concrete, conspicuous, corporeal, decisive, definitive, demonstrable, distinct *(clear)*, dogmatic, explicit, express, factual, fixed *(settled)*, inappealable, incontrovertible, indubious, inevitable, irrevocable, limited, official, overt, palpable, particular *(individual)*, peremptory *(absolute)*, positive *(confident)*, positive *(incontestable)*, precise, reliable, resounding, several *(separate)*, specific, tangible, unalienable, unalterable, unambiguous, unequivocal. SEE MAIN ENTRY
definite carelessness res ipsa loquitur
definite form embodiment
definite procedure avenue *(means of attainment)*, modus operandi
definitely fairly *(clearly)*
definiteness belief *(state of mind)*, certainty, certitude, specialty *(distinctive mark)*, surety *(certainty)*
definition clarification, construction, description, explanation, identification, meaning, rendition *(explication)*, specification. SEE MAIN ENTRY
definitional descriptive
definitions on the law charge *(statement to the jury)*
definitive absolute *(conclusive)*, categorical, clear *(certain)*, cogent, complete *(ended)*, conclusive *(settled)*, crucial, decisive, descriptive, determinative, dogmatic, extreme *(last)*, factual, final, inappealable, interpretive, last *(final)*, thorough. SEE MAIN ENTRY
definitive answer verdict
definitiveness finality
definitus categorical, definite, explicit, unambiguous
deflagrate burn. SEE MAIN ENTRY
deflagration conflagration
deflate attenuate, browbeat, debunk, decrease, deduct *(reduce)*, demean *(make lower)*, demote, denounce *(condemn)*, depreciate, depress, diminish, disable, discount *(minimize)*, disgrace, disparage, exhaust *(deplete)*, humiliate, lessen, minimize

deflated disgraceful
deflation decline, decrease, depression, diminution, disgrace
deflect avert, counter, deter, detour, deviate, discourage, divert, parry, prevent, repel *(drive back)*, stave
deflection alienation *(estrangement)*, detour
deflere deplore
defloration debauchment, rape
deflower dishonor *(deprive of honor)*
deflowering debauchment, defilement
defluxion outflow
defoliate denude
deform camouflage, contort, damage, deface, denature, disorganize, distort, mutilate, spoil *(impair)*
deform one's character brutalize
deformare deface
deformation defacement, detriment, distortion
deformed blemished, defective, marred
deformity defacement, defect, distortion, flaw
defraud betray *(lead astray)*, bilk, cheat, circumvent, corrupt, deceive, defalcate, delude, dupe, embezzle, ensnare, evade *(deceive)*, fake, hoodwink, illude, inveigle, mislabel, mislead, misrepresent, overreach, palter, peculate, prevaricate, purloin. SEE MAIN ENTRY
defraudare defraud
defraudation bunko, conversion *(misappropriation)*, deception, hoax, knavery, misappropriation
defrauded aggrieved *(victimized)*
defrauder criminal, embezzler, lawbreaker, thief
defrauding collusive
defraudment deception
defray bear the expense, compensate *(remunerate)*, disburse *(pay out)*, pay, remit *(send payment)*, remunerate. SEE MAIN ENTRY
defray expenses bear the expense
defray in advance prepay
defray the cost bear the expense, disburse *(pay out)*
defrayal amortization, collection *(payment)*, compensation, disbursement *(funds paid out)*, discharge *(payment)*, expenditure, expense *(cost)*, pay, payment *(act of paying)*, recovery *(award)*, reimbursement, remittance, remuneration, satisfaction *(discharge of debt)*. SEE MAIN ENTRY
defrayment advance *(allowance)*, amortization, collection *(payment)*, commission *(fee)*, compensation, consideration *(recompense)*, disbursement *(funds paid out)*, discharge *(payment)*, expenditure, expense *(cost)*, pay, payment *(act of paying)*, recompense, remittance, remuneration, satisfaction *(discharge of debt)*
defrock disgrace
deft artful, capable, competent, diplomatic, efficient, expert, facile, familiar *(informed)*, practiced, proficient, qualified *(competent)*, resourceful, sciential, subtle *(refined)*, veteran. SEE MAIN ENTRY
deftness discretion *(quality of being discreet)*, efficiency, facility *(easiness)*, faculty *(ability)*, gift *(flair)*, propensity, prowess *(ability)*, skill
defugere shun
defunct dead, deceased, lifeless *(dead)*, null *(invalid)*, null and void, outdated. SEE MAIN ENTRY

defy break *(violate)*, challenge, complain *(criticize)*, conflict, confront *(oppose)*, contest, contravene, counter, counteract, cross *(disagree with)*, disaffirm, disagree, disobey, dissent *(withhold assent)*, fight *(counteract)*, flout, oppose, oppugn, provoke, rebel, resist *(oppose)*, violate, withstand. SEE MAIN ENTRY
defying contemptuous
defying lawful authority contumacious
degeneracy bad repute, caducity, decline, delinquency *(misconduct)*, turpitude, vice
degenerare degenerate
degenerate bad *(offensive)*, contaminate, corrupt, debauch, decadent, decay, decline *(fall)*, depraved, depreciate, deteriorate, dissolute, ebb, ignoble, immoral, lawless, lessen, nefarious, perverse, pervert, profligate *(corrupt)*, recidivate, regressive, relapse, reprobate, taint *(corrupt)*, tainted *(corrupted)*, vicious. SEE MAIN ENTRY
degenerateness decline
degeneratess degradation
degenerating decadent
degeneration decline, degradation, detriment, disrepair, recidivism, relapse, sodomy
degenerative bad *(inferior)*
degradation attaint, bad repute, defilement, deterioration, discredit, disgrace, dishonor *(shame)*, disrepute, ignominy, ill repute, infamy, libel, misusage, misuse, notoriety, obloquy, odium, onus *(stigma)*, opprobrium, perversion, reproach, scandal, shame, turpitude. SEE MAIN ENTRY
degrade abuse *(violate)*, adulterate, contaminate, damage, debase, debauch, decry, defame, degenerate, demean *(make lower)*, demote, denigrate, denounce *(condemn)*, depreciate, deteriorate, discredit, disgrace, dishonor *(deprive of honor)*, disoblige, disparage, humiliate, libel, minimize, pillory, pollute, smear, sully, taint *(contaminate)*, tarnish
degraded bad *(inferior)*, bad *(offensive)*, depraved, disreputable, dissolute, ignoble, notorious, sordid, tainted *(corrupted)*
degraded person degenerate
degrading disgraceful, unbecoming
degredi deviate
degree caliber *(measurement)*, extent, magnitude, nuance, prestige, step, utmost. SEE MAIN ENTRY
degree of importance weight *(importance)*
degreeholder specialist
dehiscent open *(unclosed)*, penetrable
dehonestare disgrace, dishonor *(deprive of honor)*
dehort admonish *(warn)*, discourage, expostulate, protest
dehortari dissuade
dehortation admonition, monition *(warning)*, notice *(warning)*, remonstrance
dehortative remonstrative
dehortatory remonstrative
dehumanize brutalize, debase
dehumanized diabolic
deicere disappoint, dislodge, eject *(evict)*, overthrow, precipitate *(throw down violently)*
deific omniscient
deifical omniscient
deification elevation
deify elevate
deign accede *(concede)*, bestow, patronize *(condescend toward)*. SEE MAIN ENTRY
deign to give vouchsafe

711

deign to grant   vouchsafe
deject   depress, discourage
dejected   despondent, disappointed, disconsolate, lugubrious, pessimistic
dejectedness   pessimism
dejection   depression, dissatisfaction, pessimism, prostration
delate   complain (charge), denigrate, implicate, involve (implicate)
delatio   denunciation
delation   accusation, blame (culpability), charge (accusation), count, denunciation, indictment
delation by criminal charges   arraignment
delator   accuser, appellant, complainant, informant
delator   informer (a person who provides information)
delay   abeyance, adjourn, arrest (stop), balk, block, cessation (interlude), check (bar), check (restrain), constrict (inhibit), continue (adjourn), curb, damper (stopper), defer (put off), deferment, detain (restrain), discontinue (break continuity), doubt (hesitate), extension (postponement), filibuster, halt, hamper, hesitate, hesitation, hiatus, impede, inhibit, interrupt, interruption, keep (restrain), laches, moratorium, obstacle, obstruct, pause (noun), pause (verb), postpone, prevent, procrastinate, protract (prolong), remain (stay), reprieve, stall, stay, stay (halt), stop, suspend. SEE MAIN ENTRY
delay attended by change of position   laches
delay enforcing rights   forbear
delay in execution   reprieve
delay in legislation   filibuster
delay in punishment   reprieve
delay that results in disadvantage   laches
delayed   arrested (checked), back (in arrears), dilatory, late (tardy), overdue. SEE MAIN ENTRY
delaying   dilatory
dele   delete, edit
delectable   nectarious, palatable, sapid, savory
delectare   interest
delectation   enjoyment (pleasure)
delectus   choice (alternatives offered), choice (decision), selection (choice)
delegare   delegate
delegate   agent, appoint, assign (designate), charge (empower), commit (entrust), conduit (intermediary), deliver, deputy, detail (assign), employ (engage services), empower, entrust, executor, factor (commission merchant), functionary, hire, induct, intermediary, invest (vest), liaison, medium, plenipotentiary, proctor, procurator, proxy, relegate, remand, replacement, representative (proxy), spokesman, substitute. SEE MAIN ENTRY
delegate authority to   charge (empower)
delegate to   authorize
delegate upon another   devolve
delegated   representative, surrogate
delegated authority   bureaucracy
delegates   delegation (envoy), deputation (delegation), government (political administration)
delegating   delegation (assignment), designation (naming)
delegation   agency (commission), agency (legal relationship), appointment (act of designating), assignment (designation),

charter (sanction), commission (agency), committee, constituency, decentralization, deputation (delegation), deputation (selection of delegates), designation (naming), devolution, embassy, mission, nomination. SEE MAIN ENTRY
delegation of duties   devolution
delere   abolish, cancel, expunge, obliterate
delete   abolish, bowdlerize, censor, deface, diminish, edit, eliminate (eradicate), eradicate, except (exclude), excise (cut away), expunge, expurgate, obliterate, omit, redact, remove (eliminate), repeal, retrench, suppress. SEE MAIN ENTRY
deleted   null (invalid)
deleterious   adverse (negative), bad (inferior), detrimental, disadvantageous, disastrous, fatal, harmful, inadvisable, insalubrious, malevolent, malignant, noxious, peccant (unhealthy), pernicious, pestilent, prejudicial, toxic, virulent. SEE MAIN ENTRY
deletion   annulment, cancellation, rescision
deliberare   deliberate. SEE MAIN ENTRY
deliberate   aforethought, circumspect, cogitative, cold-blooded, confer (consult), consider, consult (ask advice of), debate, discreet, doubt (hesitate), express, hesitant, intentional, judicious, knowing, muse, oscillate, pause, ponder, premeditated, purposeful, reason (conclude), reflect (ponder), review, speculate (conjecture), tactical, treat (process), try (conduct a trial), voluntary, weigh, willful. SEE MAIN ENTRY
deliberate application   diligence (care)
deliberate attention   diligence (care)
deliberate burning of property   arson
deliberate choice   election (choice)
deliberate determination   adjudication
deliberate falsification   story (falsehood)
deliberate intent   premeditation
deliberate intention   forethought, premeditation
deliberate malice   cruelty, ill will
deliberate misrepresentation   subreption
deliberate omission   dispensation (exception). SEE MAIN ENTRY
deliberate over   brood
deliberate study   diligence (care)
deliberate thought   diligence (care)
deliberate upon   discuss, investigate
deliberately   knowingly, purposely
deliberately avoid   shun
deliberately intended   premeditated
deliberately slow   dilatory
deliberateness   animus, contemplation, moderation
deliberatio   deliberation
deliberation   conference, contemplation, conversation, council (consultant), dialectic, discretion (quality of being discreet), examination (study), forethought, hindsight, negotiation, parley, prudence, purpose, reflection (thought), speculation (conjecture). SEE MAIN ENTRY
deliberative   circumspect, cogitative, deliberate, pensive, speculative
deliberative body   panel (discussion group)
deliberative group   commission (agency)
delicacy   consideration (sympathetic regard), decorum, discretion (quality of being discreet), fault (weakness), frailty, nuance, propriety (correctness), sensibility
delicacy of feeling   sensibility
delicate   destructible, impalpable, intricate, nonsubstantial (not sturdy), palatable, precarious, subtle (refined), tenuous

delicate distinction   differential
delicatus   particular (exacting)
delicious   nectarious, palatable, sapid, savory
delict   crime, guilt, misdeed, offense. SEE MAIN ENTRY
delictum   crime, delict, delinquency (misconduct), fault (responsibility), misconduct, misdeed, misdemeanor, offense, transgression
deligere   choose, elect (choose)
delight   enjoyment (pleasure), treat
delight in   relish
delighted   ecstatic, inclined, proud (self-respecting), ready (willing)
delightful   attractive, palatable, sapid, savory
delightfulness   amenity
delimit   allot, apportion, border (bound), circumscribe (define), demarcate, determine, hedge, restrain, restrict. SEE MAIN ENTRY
delimitate   border (bound), demarcate, hedge, restrict
delimitation   boundary, definition, periphery, purview, specification
delimited   qualified (conditioned)
delineate   amplify, analyze, border (bound), characterize, circumscribe (define), circumscribe (surround by boundary), clarify, construe (translate), define, depict, describe, detail (particularize), draw (depict), exemplify, expound, hedge, identify, interpret, locate, portray, recite, recount, render (depict), represent (portray), signify (denote). SEE MAIN ENTRY
delineated   detailed
delineation   analysis, boundary, clarification, configuration (confines), construction, contour (outline), definition, description, design (construction plan), explanation, identification, narration, rendition (explication), scheme, symbol. SEE MAIN ENTRY
delineation lines   ambit
delineative   descriptive
delineatory   demonstrative (illustrative)
delinquence   default
delinquency   arrears, bad repute, blame (culpability), breach, crime, culpability, default, dereliction, dishonor (nonpayment), disregard (omission), failure (falling short), fault (responsibility), guilt, lapse (expiration), misconduct, misdeed, misdoing, misprision, neglect, negligence, nonfeasance, nonpayment, nonperformance, offense, omission, transgression, vice, wrong. SEE MAIN ENTRY
delinquent   blameful, blameworthy, broken (unfulfilled), convict, culpable, derelict (negligent), disobedient, due (owed), felon, guilty, lawbreaker, malefactor, negligent, offender, outlaw, outstanding (unpaid), overdue, recidivist, remiss, reprehensible, wrongdoer. SEE MAIN ENTRY
deliquare   clarify
deliquesce   lessen
delirious (incoherent). SEE MAIN ENTRY
delirious (wildly happy). SEE MAIN ENTRY
delirious with joy   ecstatic
delirium   insanity
delitescence   indistinctness, privacy
delitescency   indistinctness
delitescent   covert, hidden, indiscernible, indistinct, latent, surreptitious
delitescere   abscond, lurk
deliver   assign (transfer ownership), attorn, bear (yield), bestow, cede, clear, confer (give), consign, contribute (supply), convey

(transfer), delegate, devolve, discharge (liberate), disengage, disenthrall, dole, extricate, free, give (grant), grant (transfer formally), impart, liberate, pardon, parole, pass (determine), phrase, post, present (make a gift), pronounce (speak), provide (supply), publish, quit (free of), recite, redeem (repurchase), refer (send for action), release, relieve (free from burden), relinquish, remark, rescue, serve (deliver a legal instrument), speak, supply, tender, transfer, transmit, transport, utter. SEE MAIN ENTRY

deliver a charge   discharge (shoot)

deliver a judgment   pass (determine)

deliver a speech   discourse

deliver a summons and complaint   serve (deliver a legal instrument)

deliver a talk   address (talk to), discourse

deliver an address   discourse, pronounce (speak), speak

deliver an instrument   file (place among official records)

deliver as one's act and deed   certify (attest)

deliver formally   consign, pronounce (speak)

deliver from a hindrance   disencumber

deliver from bondage   disenthrall, free

deliver from uncertainty   assure (give confidence to)

deliver in trust   delegate

deliver information   report (disclose)

deliver into custody   commit (institutionalize)

deliver judgment   adjudge, adjudicate, award, conclude (decide), decree, determine, find (determine), pronounce (pass judgment), rule (decide)

deliver oratorically   declaim

deliver over   alienate (transfer title), consign, convey (transfer), delegate, demise, pass (advance), serve (deliver a legal instrument), transfer

deliver over to a successor   devolve

deliver to   bequeath, remove (transfer)

deliver to the care of   confide (trust)

deliver up   betray (lead astray), forfeit

deliverable   assignable

deliverance   absolution, alienation (transfer of title), catharsis, delivery, demise (conveyance), devolution, discharge (liberation), discharge (release from obligation), disposition (transfer of property), emancipation, freedom, help, holding (ruling of a court), liberation, liberty, mainstay, parole, pronouncement, ransom, redemption, release, relief (release), resolution (formal statement), respite (reprieve), salvage, transmittal

deliverance from bondage   emancipation

delivered   clear (free from criminal charges), free (relieved from a burden)

deliverer   donor, good samaritan

delivering to   consignment

delivery   alienation (transfer of title), assignment (transfer of ownership), birth (emergence of young), cession, conveyance, course, demise (conveyance), devolution, discharge (release from obligation), disposition (transfer of property), intonation, issuance, liberation, parlance, rhetoric (skilled speech), speech, transmittal. SEE MAIN ENTRY

delivery back   replevin

delivery of a writ   service (delivery of legal process)

delivery of process   service (delivery of legal process)

delivery of title   feoffment

delocalization   asportation

delocalize   dislodge, displace (remove), remove (eliminate)

deludable   naive

delude   bait (lure), betray (lead astray), bilk, circumvent, deceive, defraud, dupe, ensnare, evade (deceive), fabricate (make up), fake, feign, hoodwink, illude, inveigle, lie (falsify), misguide, misinform, mislead, misrepresent, misstate, palter, pretend, prevaricate. SEE MAIN ENTRY

delude oneself   err, misconceive, misunderstand

deluded   blind (not discerning)

deludere   delude

deluding   delusive, illusory, ostensible, prestidigitation, specious

deluge   cataclysm, immerse (plunge into), inundate, overage, overcome (overwhelm), overload, overwhelm, plethora, spate, surfeit

delusion   artifice, bad faith, deception, error, fallacy, false pretense, figment, hoax, insanity, lunacy, phantom, ruse, sham

delusional   ostensible

delusional insanity   paranoia

delusions   paranoia

delusive   assumed (feigned), colorable (specious), deceptive, dishonest, disingenuous, evasive, fallacious, false (inaccurate), fictitious, fraudulent, illusory, lying, machiavellian, meretricious, ostensible, sly, specious, spurious, untrue. SEE MAIN ENTRY

delusiveness   bad faith, deceit, fraud

delusory   colorable (specious), deceptive, delusive, dishonest, disingenuous, fallacious, false (not genuine), fraudulent, lying, ostensible, specious

deluxe   elaborate, elegant, superior (excellent)

delve   search. SEE MAIN ENTRY

delve for   hunt

delve into   analyze, canvass, examine (study), inquire, investigate, peruse, probe, research, scrutinize

delving into evidence   inquiry (systematic investigation)

demagnetize   neutralize

demagogue   insurgent. SEE MAIN ENTRY

demand   call (demand), canon, cause of action, coerce, command, compel, compulsion (coercion), constrain (compel), detail (assign), dictate (noun), dictate (verb), direct (order), direction (order), directive, dun (noun), dun (verb), entail, exact, excise, excise (levy a tax), force (compulsion), force (coerce), importune, impose (enforce), insist, instruct (direct), levy, motion, necessitate, need (deprivation), need (requirement), need, order, outlet, petition, prerequisite, prescribe, press (constrain), request (noun), request (verb), require (compel), require (need), requirement, requisition, solicit, stress (strain), subpoena (noun), subpoena (verb), summon, ultimatum. SEE MAIN ENTRY

demand a payment   assess (tax)

demand and obtain payment   collect (recover money)

demand for payment   bill (invoice)

demand made on a stock holder   call (option)

demand payment   charge (assess), dun, exact, excise (levy a tax)

demand toll   assess (tax), exact, excise (levy a tax)

demand with threats   dun

demanded   compulsory, decretal, essential (required), mandatory, necessary (required), popular, positive (prescribed), requisite

demanded damages   ad damnum clause

demander   extortionist

demanding   exigent, imperative, insistent, operose, particular (exacting), peremptory (imperative), urgent

demanding attention   important (urgent)

demanding belief   plausible

demands   interrogatories

demarcate   allot, apportion, border (bound), circumscribe (define), delimit, differentiate, distinguish, divide (separate), hedge, label, locate, restrict, specify. SEE MAIN ENTRY

demarcation   definition, discrimination (differentiation), limitation, outline (boundary), periphery, restriction, severance

demarcation line   edge (border), frontier

demark   circumscribe (define), demarcate

dematerialize   disappear, dissipate (spread out)

demean   comport (behave), demote, deprecate, derogate, disgrace, humiliate, reduce. SEE MAIN ENTRY

demeaning   disgraceful

demeanor   appearance (look), behavior, complexion, conduct, decorum, deportment, manner (behavior), posture (attitude), presence (poise), temperament. SEE MAIN ENTRY

démêlé   dispute

demens   deranged

demensum   ration

dement   discompose, disorient, obsess

dementate   lunatic

demented   deranged, lunatic, non compos mentis

dementedness   insanity

dementia   insanity

dementia   lunacy

demergere   overwhelm

demerit   defect, flaw, foible, frailty

demesne   area (province), domain (land owned), dominion (absolute ownership), locality, location, possession (ownership), property (land), province, realm, region, scope, section (vicinity), sphere, territory. SEE MAIN ENTRY

demetere   reap

demetiri   measure

demilitarization   reconversion

demilitarize   disarm (divest of arms)

deminuere   decrease, diminish, lessen

deminutio   abatement (reduction), decline, decrease, deduction (diminution)

demise   abalienate, alienate (transfer title), alienation (transfer of title), assignment (transfer of ownership), attorn, bequeath, bequest, contribute (supply), convey (transfer), conveyance, death, decease, descend, devolution, die, dissolution (termination), end (termination), extremity (death), grant (transfer formally), lease, leave (give), let (lease), rent, sublease, transfer. SEE MAIN ENTRY

demised   dead, deceased, decedent, defunct, late (defunct), lifeless (dead)

demission   abandonment (desertion), abdication, deterioration, removal, renunciation, resignation (relinquishment)

demit   abandon (relinquish), defect, discontinue (abandon), forfeit, relinquish, renounce, resign, retire (conclude a career). SEE MAIN ENTRY

demiurgic   original (creative), productive

demiurgical   original (creative), productive

demobilize disarm *(divest of arms)*, disband, dismiss *(discharge)*, disorganize, dissociate, dissolve *(separate)*. SEE MAIN ENTRY

democratic equal, free *(enjoying civil liberty)*

demode outdated

demoded outmoded

demography census

demolish consume, damage, defeat, destroy *(efface)*, devastate, eliminate *(eradicate)*, eradicate, extinguish, extirpate, harm, impair, obliterate, overturn, prejudice *(injure)*, refute, spoil *(impair)*, subvert, upset

demolisher vandal

demolishing dire, disastrous, fatal

demolishment debacle, destruction, detriment

demolition debacle, destruction, dissolution *(disintegration)*, prostration, subversion

demoniac cold-blooded, diabolic, malevolent, malicious, ruthless, sinister

demoniacal cruel, malevolent, malicious, malignant, sinister

demonial malevolent

demonic diabolic

demonstrability corroboration

demonstrable actual, ascertainable, certain *(positive)*, cogent, concrete, convincing, corporeal, de facto, deductible *(provable)*, definite, genuine, incontrovertible, indubious, irrefutable, provable, undeniable. SEE MAIN ENTRY

demonstrate bear *(adduce)*, clarify, communicate, construe *(translate)*, disagree, display, document, elucidate, establish *(show)*, evidence, evince, exemplify, exhibit, explain, illustrate, manifest, picket, present *(introduce)*, produce *(offer to view)*, prove, reason *(persuade)*, signify *(denote)*, signify *(inform)*, substantiate, unveil. SEE MAIN ENTRY

demonstrate against picket

demonstrate protest picket

demonstrated actual, authentic, certain *(positive)*, conclusive *(determinative)*, indubious, unrefutable

demonstrating cogent

demonstratio manifestation

demonstration argument *(pleading)*, case *(example)*, clarification, corroboration, example, explanation, expression *(manifestation)*, instance, manifestation, pretense *(ostentation)*, proof, protest

demonstrative clear *(apparent)*, declaratory, probative, suggestive *(evocative)*, vehement. SEE MAIN ENTRY

demonstrator malcontent

demoralization bad repute, confusion *(turmoil)*, defilement, perversion

demoralize brutalize, debase, deteriorate, discompose, discourage, disgrace, pervert, subvert, taint *(corrupt)*

demoralized bad *(offensive)*, tainted *(corrupted)*, vicious

demoralizing deplorable, disgraceful, disreputable

demorari stay *(halt)*

demortuus late *(defunct)*

demote depose *(remove)*, derogate, dislodge, humiliate, minimize. SEE MAIN ENTRY

demotion degradation, ignominy, removal

demulcent medicinal

demur demonstrate *(protest)*, disaffirm, disagree, disapprove *(reject)*, disoblige, disown *(deny the validity)*, dissent *(difference of opinion)*, dissent *(withhold assent)*, doubt *(hesitate)*, except *(object)*, hesitate,

negate, object, oppose, pause *(noun)*, pause *(verb)*, protest, refuse, reject, remonstrance, remonstrate, repudiate, vacillate. SEE MAIN ENTRY

demure diffident

demureness propriety *(correctness)*

demurrage SEE MAIN ENTRY

demurral delay, disagreement, pause

demurrer disapproval, exception *(objection)*. SEE MAIN ENTRY

demurring disapproval, disinclined, dissenting, hesitant, negative, remonstrative, renitent, restive

demurringly unwillingly

den chamber *(compartment)*

denaturalize contaminate, denature, pollute

denature adulterate, convert *(change use)*, debilitate, deteriorate, transform. SEE MAIN ENTRY

deniability cloud *(suspicion)*

deniable contestable, debatable, disputable, dubitative

denial abandonment *(repudiation)*, abjuration, answer *(judicial response)*, answer *(reply)*, contravention, counterargument, declination, disapproval, disclaimer, disdain, embargo, exclusion, incredulity, injunction, negation, opposition, pleading, prohibition, proscription, refusal, rejection, renunciation, repudiation, veto. SEE MAIN ENTRY

denial of entry exclusion

denial of justice injustice

denial of the allegations demurrer

denial of the pleading demurrer

denial of the statements demurrer

denigrate cavil, censure, condemn *(blame)*, contemn, decry, defame, denounce *(condemn)*, deprecate, depreciate, derogate, discommend, discredit, dishonor *(deprive of honor)*, disoblige, disparage, fault, impeach, libel, malign, pillory, smear, sully, tarnish. SEE MAIN ENTRY

denigrating pejorative

denigration aspersion, bad repute, condemnation *(blame)*, contempt *(disdain)*, defamation, defilement, denunciation, disparagement, impeachment, libel, slander, vilification

denigratory calumnious, contemptuous

dénigrement disparagement

denizen citizen, domiciliary, dwell *(reside)*, habitant, inhabitant, lodger, occupant, occupy *(take possession)*, resident. SEE MAIN ENTRY

denizenize adopt, naturalize *(make a citizen)*

denominare denominate

denominate call *(title)*, define, denote, designate, identify, label, mention, nominate, phrase. SEE MAIN ENTRY

denomination class, classification, cognomen, color *(complexion)*, designation *(naming)*, identification, kind, manner *(kind)*, nomination, rubric *(title)*, selection *(choice)*, society, style, term *(expression)*, title *(designation)*. SEE MAIN ENTRY

denominational partisan, specific

denotare specify

denotate denote

denotation connotation, content *(meaning)*, designation *(naming)*, meaning

denotative representative

denote bear *(adduce)*, bespeak, connote, construe *(translate)*, denominate, designate, evidence, evince, exemplify, express, identify, imply, label, manifest, purport, refer

(direct attention), represent *(portray)*, speak. SEE MAIN ENTRY

dénouement cessation *(termination)*

dénouement conclusion *(outcome)*, consequence *(conclusion)*. SEE MAIN ENTRY

dénouement denouement

denouement end *(termination)*, finality, outcome, result

denounce accuse, arraign, blame, cavil, censure, challenge, charge *(accuse)*, cite *(accuse)*, complain *(charge)*, complain *(criticize)*, condemn *(blame)*, contemn, convict, decry, defame, demonstrate *(protest)*, denigrate, deprecate, depreciate, disapprove *(condemn)*, discommend, dishonor *(deprive of honor)*, disoblige, except *(object)*, expose, fault, impeach, implicate, impugn, incriminate, inform *(betray)*, inveigh, involve *(implicate)*, libel, malign, oppugn, pillory, protest, rebel, reprehend, reprimand, reproach, smear, sully. SEE MAIN ENTRY

denounce falsely frame *(charge falsely)*

denounce unfairly frame *(charge falsely)*

denounce unjustly frame *(charge falsely)*

denouncement blame *(culpability)*, charge *(accusation)*, complaint, conviction *(finding of guilt)*, denunciation, disapprobation, disapproval, disparagement, impeachment, incrimination, reproach

denouncer accuser, complainant, contender

denouncing inculpatory

dense cohesive *(compact)*, impervious, obtuse, opaque, ossified, ponderous, populous, rife, solid *(compact)*

denseness ignorance, opacity

densified compact *(dense)*

densify concentrate *(consolidate)*, consolidate *(strengthen)*

density mass *(weight)*, opacity. SEE MAIN ENTRY

dented blemished

denudate denude

denude abduct, bare, deprive, despoil, expose, unveil. SEE MAIN ENTRY

denuded of devoid, insufficient

denunciate arraign, censure, charge *(accuse)*, complain *(charge)*, convict, denounce *(condemn)*, disapprove *(condemn)*, impeach, proscribe *(denounce)*, reproach

denunciation allegation, aspersion, bad repute, blame *(culpability)*, charge *(accusation)*, complaint, condemnation *(blame)*, contempt *(disdain)*, contradiction, conviction *(finding of guilt)*, count, criticism, diatribe, disapprobation, disapproval, discredit, disparagement, expletive, ignominy, impeachment, imprecation, inculpation, indictment, libel, malediction, notoriety, objection, objurgation, obloquy, onus *(stigma)*, outcry, phillipic, profanity, proscription, reprimand, reproach, revilement, sanction *(punishment)*, slander, stricture, vilification. SEE MAIN ENTRY

denunciatory calumnious, contemptuous, critical *(faultfinding)*, cynical, derogatory, incriminatory, inculpatory, libelous, pejorative, scandalous

denuntiatio innuendo, intimation, notice *(announcement)*, notice *(warning)*, notice *(give formal warning)*, notification, threat

denuntiatio testimonii subpoena *(noun)*, subpoena *(verb)*

denuo reconsider

deny adeem, annul, answer *(reply)*, ban, bar *(exclude)*, bear false witness, cancel, condemn *(ban)*, confront *(oppose)*, constrain *(restrain)*, contradict, contravene, controvert, demur, disaccord, disaffirm, disagree, disallow, disapprove *(reject)*, disavow, disclaim, dismiss *(put out of consideration)*, disown *(deny the validity)*, disprove, dispute *(contest)*, disqualify, forbid, forswear, gainsay, interdict, negate, oppose, prohibit, protest, rebut, refuse, refute, reject, renounce, repudiate, withhold. SEE MAIN ENTRY

deny absolutely   disavow, disown *(deny the validity)*, dispute *(contest)*

deny access   deter

deny any knowledge of   disclaim

deny connection with   disavow

deny emphatically   disavow, dispute *(contest)*

deny entirely   disavow, dispute *(contest)*

deny entry   exclude

deny flatly   dispute *(contest)*

deny oneself   eschew, forbear

deny oneself nothing   dissipate *(expend foolishly)*

deny peremptorily   disavow, disown *(deny the validity)*, dispute *(contest)*

deny permission   forbid

deny respect   decry, disfavor, disgrace

deny responsibility for   disavow

deny the genuineness of   dispute *(contest)*

deny the possibility   disown *(deny the validity)*

deny wholly   disavow, disown *(deny the validity)*

denying   contradictory, contrary, dissenting, negative

deobstruct   extricate, facilitate

deontology   casuistry

depart   abscond, alight, decease, defect, die, digress, disagree, disperse *(scatter)*, evacuate, expire, move *(alter position)*, part *(leave)*, perish, resign, retire *(retreat)*, retreat, secede, vacate *(leave)*, vary, withdraw. SEE MAIN ENTRY

depart custody   escape

depart from   abandon *(physically leave)*, avoid *(evade)*, conflict, detour, deviate, differ *(vary)*, quit *(evacuate)*, vacate *(leave)*

depart from life   decease

depart from one's course   detour, deviate

depart unlawfully   escape

departed   corpse, dead, deceased, decedent, defunct, late *(defunct)*, lifeless *(dead)*

departed this life   dead

departing   divergent, flight, separate

departing from   deviant, disparate, distinct *(distinguished from others)*

departing from the usual course   eccentric

department   agency *(commission)*, bailiwick, board, bureau, chapter *(branch)*, district, division *(administrative unit)*, domain *(sphere of influence)*, member *(constituent part)*, organ, post, province, pursuit *(occupation)*, purview, realm, role, section *(division)*, sphere. SEE MAIN ENTRY

department of justice   judiciary

department store   market *(business)*

departmentalization   bureaucracy, division *(act of dividing)*

departure   abandonment *(desertion)*, abdication, demise *(death)*, desertion, detour, deviation, difference, digression, discrepancy, egress, end *(termination)*, extremity *(death)*, flight, indirection *(indirect action)*, innovation, leave *(absence)*, nonconformity, quirk *(idiosyncrasy)*, removal, resignation *(relinquishment)*

departure from   contradistinction, difference

departure from life   death

departure from usage   deviation

departure from usual   exception *(exclusion)*

dépêche   dispatch *(promptness)*

depellere   dislodge, evict

depend   rely

depend upon   appertain, trust

dependability   adhesion *(loyalty)*, certification *(certainness)*, loyalty, probity, reliance, responsibility *(conscience)*, security *(safety)*, trustworthiness

dependable   accurate, authentic, believable, certain *(positive)*, constant, credible, demonstrable, diligent, factual, faithful *(loyal)*, incorruptible, infallible, loyal, official, punctual, real, reliable, reputable, safe, secure *(free from danger)*, secure *(sound)*, solid *(sound)*, staunch, steadfast, tenable, true *(authentic)*, true *(loyal)*. SEE MAIN ENTRY

dependence   faith, mainstay, mutuality, reliance, resource, trust *(confidence)*

dependence on   credence

dependency   appurtenance

dependent   ancillary *(subsidiary)*, contingent, correlative, dubious, helpless *(powerless)*, insecure, minor, protégé, qualified *(conditioned)*, related, sequacious, subject *(conditional)*, subservient, tentative. SEE MAIN ENTRY

dependent event   contingency

dependent on   appurtenant, based on, conditional, contingent, incident, tangential

dependent on circumstances   contingent, provisional, subject *(conditional)*

depending   aleatory *(uncertain)*, contingent

depending on   conditional

depending on a future event   conditional

depending upon   subject *(conditional)*

depict   characterize, construe *(translate)*, copy, delineate, denote, describe, detail *(particularize)*, exemplify, interpret, portray, recount, represent *(portray)*, signify *(denote)*. SEE MAIN ENTRY

depict the essential qualities of   define

depiction   brief, caricature, delineation, description, design *(construction plan)*, illustration, narration, recital, representation *(statement)*, symbol

depiction of essential features   delineation

depictive   demonstrative *(illustrative)*, realistic, representative

depictment   illustration, narration

depicture   denote, portray

depingere   delineate, depict, describe, portray

depletable   destructible

deplete   deduct *(reduce)*, dissipate *(expend foolishly)*, expend *(consume)*, impair, lessen, overdraw, spend, tax *(overwork)*. SEE MAIN ENTRY

depleted   deficient, destitute, inadequate, lost *(taken away)*, nonsubstantial *(not sufficient)*, poor *(underprivileged)*, vacant, vacuous

depletion   consumption, decrement, delinquency *(shortage)*, insufficiency, poverty, waste, wear and tear

deplorable   arrant *(onerous)*, bad *(inferior)*, bad *(offensive)*, blameful, blameworthy, contemptible, disgraceful, disreputable, gross *(flagrant)*, heinous, lamentable, loathsome, nefarious, notorious, objectionable, obnoxious, outrageous, regrettable, scandalous. SEE MAIN ENTRY

deplorare   deplore

deplore   blame, deprecate, except *(object)*, regret, repent. SEE MAIN ENTRY

deplored   blameful

deploy   maneuver, spread. SEE MAIN ENTRY

deplume   despoil, plunder

depone   acknowledge *(declare)*, affirm *(declare solemnly)*, attest, bear *(adduce)*, certify *(attest)*, depose *(testify)*, testify, vouch

deponent   affiant, affirmant, witness. SEE MAIN ENTRY

deponere   deposit *(place)*, give *(yield)*, resign

depopulate   devastate, diminish, pillage

deport   comport *(behave)*, dislodge, displace *(remove)*, eliminate *(exclude)*, exclude, expatriate, expel, relegate, seclude, transport. SEE MAIN ENTRY

deportation   banishment, exclusion, expulsion, extradition, ostracism, rejection, removal. SEE MAIN ENTRY

deportee   pariah

deportment   behavior, conduct, demeanor, manner *(behavior)*, presence *(poise)*. SEE MAIN ENTRY

deposal   abolition, disqualification *(rejection)*, rejection, removal

deposcere   call *(demand)*

depose   acknowledge *(declare)*, affirm *(declare solemnly)*, assert, attest, avouch *(avow)*, avow, bear *(adduce)*, certify *(attest)*, demote, discharge *(dismiss)*, dislodge, dismiss *(discharge)*, dispossess, divest, oust, remove *(dismiss from office)*, supplant, testify, vouch. SEE MAIN ENTRY

deposed   powerless

deposit   alluvion, binder, downpayment, embed, fund, garner, handsel, hoard, installment, keep *(shelter)*, leave *(allow to remain)*, locate, pawn, pay, plant *(place firmly)*, pledge *(security)*, replenish, repose *(place)*, reserve, security *(pledge)*, store *(depository)*, store, treasury. SEE MAIN ENTRY

deposit among records of the court   file *(place among official records)*

deposit as collateral   pawn

deposit as security   pawn

deposit formally   cast *(register)*

deposit with   consign, delegate

depositary   comptroller, receiver, trustee

deposition   abdication, affirmation, alluvion, confirmation, disclosure *(something disclosed)*, dismissal *(discharge)*, entry *(record)*, removal, repudiation, statement, testimony. SEE MAIN ENTRY

depository   arsenal, bank, cache *(storage place)*, catchall, coffer, repository, reserve, store *(depository)*, treasury. SEE MAIN ENTRY

depositum   deposit

depot   depository, repository, treasury

depravare   contort, corrupt, debauch, deteriorate, misrepresent, pervert, vitiate

depravatio   corruption, perversion

depravation   damage, defilement, perversion, vice

deprave   corrupt, debase, debauch, degenerate, pervert, pollute, taint *(corrupt)*

depraved   bad *(offensive)*, blameworthy, contemptible, decadent, dissolute, ignoble, immoral, iniquitous, lascivious, lecherous, lewd, nefarious, perverse, profligate *(corrupt)*, reprobate, salacious, tainted *(corrupted)*, vicious. SEE MAIN ENTRY

depraved person   degenerate

depravity bad repute, delinquency *(misconduct)*, dishonor *(shame)*, perversion, sodomy, turpitude, vice

deprecari intercede

deprecate admonish *(warn)*, blame, cavil, censure, complain *(criticize)*, condemn *(blame)*, criticize *(find fault with)*, decry, denounce *(condemn)*, disapprove *(condemn)*, disapprove *(reject)*, discommend, discourage, discredit, disoblige, fault, jeer, malign, misprize, remonstrate, reprimand, reproach, sully, underestimate. SEE MAIN ENTRY

deprecating diffident, disdainful

deprecatio intercession

deprecation admonition, bad repute, condemnation *(blame)*, contempt *(disdain)*, contempt *(disobedience to the court)*, criticism, denunciation, diatribe, disapprobation, disapproval, disparagement, reluctance, stricture

deprecative diffident, remonstrative

deprecator intermediary

deprecatory adverse *(hostile)*, calumnious, derogatory, remonstrative

depreciate adulterate, blame, censure, contemn, criticize *(find fault with)*, debase, decay, decrease, decry, deduct *(reduce)*, defame, demean *(make lower)*, demote, denigrate, denounce *(condemn)*, depress, derogate, deteriorate, dilute, diminish, discommend, discount *(disbelieve)*, discount *(reduce)*, discredit, disparage, fault, humiliate, jeer, lessen, minimize, misprize, smear, spurn, sully, underestimate. SEE MAIN ENTRY

depreciate publicly decry

depreciating contemptuous

depreciation contempt *(disdain)*, criticism, damage, decline, decrease, denunciation, depression, deterioration, diatribe, disapprobation, disparagement, disregard *(lack of respect)*, disrespect, revilement, stricture, wear and tear

depreciative calumnious, contemptuous, derogatory, pejorative

depreciatory calumnious, derogatory, pejorative

depredate despoil, devastate, hold up *(rob)*, loot, pillage, plunder, prey, steal

depredation foray, havoc, pillage, plunder, rape, robbery, spoliation. SEE MAIN ENTRY

depredator thief

depredatory predatory, rapacious

deprehendere arrest *(apprehend)*

depress debase, decrease, depreciate, derogate, diminish, discourage, disgrace. SEE MAIN ENTRY

depressant narcotic *(adjective)*, narcotic *(noun)*

depressed despondent, disconsolate, pessimistic

depressing bleak *(not favorable)*, bleak *(severely simple)*, deplorable, lamentable, lugubrious, ominous, oppressive

depressing influence damper *(depressant)*

depression curtailment, decrease, distress *(anguish)*, pessimism, prostration. SEE MAIN ENTRY

depressive deplorable, lamentable

deprival expense *(sacrifice)*

deprival of honor degradation

deprivation abridgment *(disentitlement)*, absence *(omission)*, attachment *(seizure)*, censorship, condemnation *(seizure)*, constraint *(restriction)*, conversion *(misappropriation)*, curtailment, defeasance, deficiency, detriment, discipline

(punishment), disqualification *(rejection)*, disseisin, distress *(seizure)*, escheatment, expense *(sacrifice)*, expropriation *(divestiture)*, expulsion, foreclosure, forfeiture *(act of forfeiting)*, injury, loss, ouster, paucity, penalty, pillage, privation, punishment, sanction *(punishment)*, sequestration, spoliation, taking

deprivation of a right forfeiture *(act of forfeiting)*

deprivation of liberty restraint

deprivation of office removal

deprivation of possession disseisin, eviction

deprivative confiscatory

deprive abduct, condemn *(ban)*, confiscate, demote, derogate, despoil, diminish, disfranchise, disinherit, dispossess, divest, exclude, forbid, impress *(procure by force)*, keep *(restrain)*, mulct *(fine)*. SEE MAIN ENTRY

deprive dishonestly defraud

deprive illegally pilfer

deprive of abridge *(divest)*, adeem, confiscate, distrain, impound, seize *(confiscate)*

deprive of advantage disadvantage

deprive of an important part mutilate

deprive of arms disarm *(divest of arms)*

deprive of corporal possession condemn *(seize)*

deprive of courage discourage

deprive of credit discredit

deprive of dishonestly cheat

deprive of efficacy nullify

deprive of essential parts eviscerate

deprive of force abolish, cancel, dismiss *(discharge)*, eviscerate, negate, vacate *(void)*

deprive of form deface

deprive of freedom of movement imprison

deprive of hereditary succession disinherit, disown *(refuse to acknowledge)*

deprive of legal effect invalidate

deprive of legal force nullify

deprive of liberty arrest *(apprehend)*, imprison, restrain

deprive of life dispatch *(put to death)*, execute *(sentence to death)*, kill *(murder)*, slay

deprive of means of defense disarm *(divest of arms)*

deprive of occupancy dispossess

deprive of office discharge *(dismiss)*, oust

deprive of organization disorganize

deprive of ownership condemn *(seize)*

deprive of possession evict

deprive of power abrogate *(rescind)*, disable, disarm *(divest of arms)*, disqualify, impair

deprive of protection expose

deprive of rank depose *(remove)*

deprive of strength debilitate, disable, disarm *(divest of arms)*, exhaust *(deplete)*, extenuate, tax *(overwork)*

deprive of the right to inherit disown *(refuse to acknowledge)*

deprive of vital parts eviscerate

deprive of weapons disarm *(divest of arms)*

deprive oneself renounce

deprived destitute, disadvantaged, nonsubstantial *(not sufficient)*, poor *(underprivileged)*

deprived of devoid

deprived of legal rights aggrieved *(harmed)*

deprived of life dead, deceased

deprived of one's wits non compos mentis

deprived of sensation insensible

deprived of sight blind *(sightless)*

deprived of strength disabled *(made incapable)*

deprivement abridgment *(disentitlement)*, attachment *(seizure)*, denial, distress *(seizure)*, privation

depriving confiscatory

depth caliber *(mental capacity)*, sense *(intelligence)*

depth of thought preoccupation

depthless superficial

depurate decontaminate, expurgate, purge *(purify)*

depurative medicinal

deputation agency *(legal relationship)*, appointment *(act of designating)*, assignment *(designation)*, delegation *(assignment)*, designation *(naming)*, embassy, representation *(acting for others)*. SEE MAIN ENTRY

deputative acting, representative

depute appoint, assign *(designate)*, authorize, delegate, detail *(assign)*, empower, entrust, hire, invest *(vest)*, relegate, replace

deputed representative, vicarious *(delegated)*

deputies delegation *(envoy)*, staff

deputization delegation *(assignment)*, deputation *(selection of delegates)*, nomination

deputize charge *(empower)*, empower, entrust, replace

deputy acting, assistant, broker, coadjutant, conduit *(intermediary)*, factor *(commission merchant)*, liaison, medium, plenipotentiary, proctor, procurator, proxy, replacement, representative *(proxy)*, spokesman, substitute, surrogate. SEE MAIN ENTRY

dequantitate lessen

deracinate disinter, dislodge, eliminate *(eradicate)*, eradicate, extinguish, extirpate, obliterate, supplant

deracination evulsion

derail dislocate

derange confuse *(create disorder)*, degenerate, discompose, dislocate, disorganize, disorient, disrupt, disturb, mismanage, muddle, obsess, perturb, upset

deranged anomalous, broken *(interrupted)*, disjointed, disorderly, frenetic, lunatic, non compos mentis, unsettled, unsound *(not strong)*. SEE MAIN ENTRY

deranged intellect insanity

derangement complex *(entanglement)*, disorder *(lack of order)*, embroilment, entanglement *(confusion)*, havoc, insanity, lunacy, pandemonium

derelict broken *(unfulfilled)*, degenerate, delinquent *(guilty of a misdeed)*, discard, disobedient, faithless, lax, negligent, pariah, recreant, remiss. SEE MAIN ENTRY

derelictio abandonment *(discontinuance)*, desertion

dereliction abandonment *(desertion)*, abortion *(fiasco)*, bad faith, blame *(culpability)*, breach, contempt *(disobedience to the court)*, crime, culpability, default, delinquency *(misconduct)*, failure *(falling short)*, fault *(responsibility)*, laches, lapse *(expiration)*, laxity, malfeasance, misconduct, misdeed, misdemeanor, misfeasance, neglect, negligence, nonfeasance, omission, transgression, vice, violation, wrong. SEE MAIN ENTRY

dereliction of allegiance disloyalty

dereliction of duty bad faith, default, delict, delinquency (failure of duty), disregard (omission), laches, maladministration, malpractice, nonperformance, tort

deride bait (harass), brand (stigmatize), cavil, contemn, decry, denigrate, depreciate, discommend, disdain, disgrace, dishonor (deprive of honor), disparage, flout, harry (harass), humiliate, illude, jeer, lessen

deridere jeer, mock (deride)

derisible ludicrous

derision aspersion, bad repute, contempt (disdain), contumely, disdain, disrespect, ignominy, infamy, obloquy, odium, ridicule

derisive calumnious, caustic, contemptuous, cynical, disdainful, impertinent (insolent), insolent, pejorative, supercilious

derisive language profanity

derisiveness disrespect, ridicule

derisory caustic, contemptuous

derivable deductible (provable)

derivare divert

derivate derivative

derivation ancestry, birth (lineage), blood, bloodline, cause (reason), citation (attribution), connotation, consequence (conclusion), corollary, descent (lineage), development (outgrowth), genesis, inception, origin (ancestry), origin (source), origination, parentage, paternity, reason (basis), source, start. SEE MAIN ENTRY

derivation from reference (citation)

derivational ancillary (subsidiary), derivative

derivative ancillary (subsidiary), consequence (conclusion), consequential (deducible), dependent, offshoot. SEE MAIN ENTRY

derivative authority agency (legal relationship)

derivative interest privity

derivative work SEE MAIN ENTRY

derivatively a priori

derive acquire (receive), ascertain, deduce, deduct (conclude by reasoning), draw (extract), educe, ensue, extract, gain, infer, judge, presume, read, reap, reason (conclude), receive (acquire), stem (originate), succeed (follow). SEE MAIN ENTRY

derive by reasoning construe (comprehend), infer

derive from ascribe, develop, emanate, evolve, infer, result

derive pleasure from relish

derived derivative, secondary

derived from dependent

derived from experience empirical

derived from within innate, organic

derived from without extraneous, extrinsic

derived principle conclusion (determination), corollary

deriving derivative, dialectic

derogare derogate, discredit

derogate brand (stigmatize), condemn (blame), contemn, debunk, decry, demean (make lower), denounce (condemn), deprecate, diminish, discommend, disgrace, disparage, humiliate, lessen, libel, malign, minimize, smear. SEE MAIN ENTRY

derogate from depreciate, discredit

derogation attaint, bad repute, condemnation (blame), contempt (disdain), criticism, defamation, denunciation, disapprobation, discredit, disgrace, dishonor (shame), disparagement, ignominy, obloquy, opprobrium, reprimand, reproach

derogation of religion blasphemy

derogative contemptuous, cynical, pejorative

derogatory bad (offensive), calumnious, contemptuous, critical (faultfinding), cynical, disgraceful, libelous, pejorative, unfavorable. SEE MAIN ENTRY

derogatory criticism aspersion

derring-do audacity

derringdo prowess (bravery)

descant censure, comment, converse, declaim

descend alight, condescend (deign), deign, demean (make lower), stem (originate), subside. SEE MAIN ENTRY

descend by inheritance devolve

descend from develop, emanate, evolve

descend on attack

descend to particulars characterize

descend upon devolve, oppugn

descendant derivative, heir, kindred, offshoot, successor. SEE MAIN ENTRY

descendants children, issue (progeny), offspring, posterity, progeny

descended derivative

descendere alight, condescend (deign), descend

descension decline

descent affiliation (bloodline), ancestry, birth (lineage), blood, bloodline, decline, derivation, family (common ancestry), heritage, lineage, origin (ancestry), parentage, paternity, posterity, race, succession. SEE MAIN ENTRY

descent by forfeiture escheatment

descrial discovery

describable accountable (explainable)

describe apprise, characterize, construe (translate), convey (communicate), define, delineate, depict, detail (particularize), disclose, draw (depict), elucidate, explain, explicate, express, identify, inform (notify), interpret, label, phrase, portray, recount, relate (tell), render (depict), report (disclose), reveal, review, trace (delineate). SEE MAIN ENTRY

describe incorrectly mislabel

describe the properties of define

described detailed, documentary

describere delineate, depict, describe

descriptio delineation, description, design (construction plan), organization (structure)

description account (report), brief, call (title), caption, character (personal quality), clarification, color (complexion), construction, definition, delineation, denomination, designation (naming), explanation, label, manner (kind), narration, paraphrase, prospectus, recital, report (detailed account), representation (statement), specification, story (narrative), style. SEE MAIN ENTRY

descriptive demonstrative (illustrative), detailed, informatory, narrative. SEE MAIN ENTRY

descriptive account narration

descry ascertain, comprehend (understand), detect, discern (detect with the senses), discover, expose, identify, observe (watch), pierce (discern), recognize (perceive), spy

desecrate contaminate, contemn, debase, dishonor (deprive of honor), impair, misemploy, mistreat, pollute, tarnish, violate

desecration blasphemy, defilement, misusage, profanity, violation

desegrate SEE MAIN ENTRY

desensitize drug, obtund

deserere neglect

desert abandon (physically leave), abandon (relinquish), abscond, default, defect, depart, disclaim, escape, fail (neglect), flee, forswear, leave (depart), merit, quit (evacuate), relinquish, renege, renounce, reprisal, requital, retreat, retribution, revenge, secede, tergiversate, vacate (leave), withdraw, worth

deserted bleak (exposed and barren), derelict (abandoned), devoid, helpless (defenseless), solitary, vacant, void (empty)

deserter fugitive

desertion absence (nonattendance), dereliction, disloyalty, flight, infidelity, revolt, schism, sedition. SEE MAIN ENTRY

deserts recompense

deserve earn

deserved condign, due (owed), entitled, equitable, fair (just), just, rightful, suitable

deservedly duly

deservedness merit

deserving entitled, laudable, meritorious, moral, tenable

deserving belief credible, fiduciary, plausible

deserving blame culpable

deserving censure culpable, reprehensible

deserving of blame guilty

deserving of commendation meritorious

deserving of compliment meritorious

deserving of condemnation sinister

deserving of confidence credible

deserving of praise meritorious

deserving of preference preferable

deserving of punishment guilty

deserving of reward meritorious

deserving reproach disgraceful

deserving reproof guilty, reprehensible

deservingness probity

deservire serve (assist)

deses indolent

desiderare desire, require (need)

desiderate desire, lack

desideration desideratum, end (intent), need (requirement), will (desire)

desideratum condition (contingent provision), end (intent), need (requirement), request. SEE MAIN ENTRY

desiderium desire

desidia sloth

design animus, arrange (plan), array (order), artifice, blueprint, building (business of assembling), cabal, calculate, campaign, cause (reason), composition (makeup), conceive (invent), configuration (form), conspire, contemplation, content (meaning), content (structure), contrivance, contrive, course, criterion, delineation, device (contrivance), device (distinguishing mark), devise (invent), direction (course), direction (guidance), end (intent), expedient, forethought, form (arrangement), form, frame (construct), frame (formulate), function, goal, intend, intent, intention, invent (produce for the first time), machination, maneuver (trick), maneuver, mission, mode, model, motif, motive, object, objective, order (arrangement), organization (structure), pattern, plan (noun), plan (verb), plot (secret plan), point (purpose), premeditation, program (noun), program (verb), project, proposal (suggestion), proposition, purpose, purview, reason (basis), ruse, scheme (noun), scheme (verb), strategy, structure (composition), system, target, treatment, undertaking (attempt). SEE MAIN ENTRY

designare allude, characterize, constitute (establish), denote, designate, nominate, trace (delineate)

designate allocate, allot, appoint, call (title), connote, define, delegate, denominate, denote, detail (assign), direct (show), discriminate (distinguish), enumerate, future, identify, instate, itemize, label, manifest, nominate, phrase, prescribe, represent (portray), select, signify (inform), specify, stipulate. SEE MAIN ENTRY

designate a place locate

designate for appointment nominate

designate for election nominate

designate for office by vote elect (select by a vote)

designate incorrectly mislabel

designate to a post delegate, hire

designated certain (specific), necessary (inescapable), select

designated ground point (item)

designating descriptive

designatio designation (naming), nomination

designation admittance (acceptance), allotment, call (title), caption, choice (decision), citation (attribution), class, classification, cognomen, color (complexion), delegation (assignment), denomination, department, deputation (selection of delegates), device (distinguishing mark), diagnosis, discretion (power of choice), earmark, election (choice), identification, kind, manner (kind), nomination, reference (citation), rubric (title), selection (choice), signification, specification, term (expression). SEE MAIN ENTRY

designation of use appropriation (allotment)

designation to office appointment (act of designating)

designed aforethought, deliberate, intentional, knowing, purposeful, strategic, tactical, voluntary, willful

designed for the initiated esoteric

designed misrepresentation false pretense

designed to deceive false (not genuine)

designedly knowingly, purposely

designee candidate

designer architect, contractor, developer, materialman

designing collusive, creation, deceptive, devious, dishonest, disingenuous, fraudulent, insidious, machiavellian, perfidious, recreant, sinister, sly, subtle (insidious), unconscionable

designing power contrivance

designless casual, fortuitous, haphazard, indiscriminate, random

desinere cease, desist

desirability qualification (fitness), value

desirable attractive, constructive (creative), convenient, eligible, entitled, favorable (advantageous), felicitous, fitting, meritorious, popular, premium, profitable, provocative, suitable, valuable. SEE MAIN ENTRY

desirable feature amenity

desire choose, conatus, desideratum, design (intent), end (intent), intend, intention, lack, market (demand), need, notion, objective, passion, predilection, predisposition, purpose, pursue (strive to gain), request, require (need), volition. SEE MAIN ENTRY

desire the presence of call (summon)

desire to buy market (demand)

desire to hoard wealth greed

desire to know interest (concern)

desire to obtain market (demand)

desired objective, popular, preferential

desired object objective, target

desired result end (intent), purpose

desirer candidate

desiring jealous

desirous eager, hot-blooded, inclined, jealous, lecherous, solicitous, zealous

desirous of forgiveness contrite

desist abandon (relinquish), cease, discontinue (abandon), dissolve (terminate), halt, interrupt, leave (allow to remain), palliate (abate), pause, refrain, rest (cease from action), stay (halt), stop, suspend. SEE MAIN ENTRY

desist from discontinue (abandon), forbear, forgo, quit (discontinue), renounce, resign, waive

desistance abandonment (discontinuance), abeyance, cessation (interlude), closure, desuetude, discontinuance (act of discontinuing), discontinuance (interruption of a legal action), halt, impasse, layoff, lull, moratorium, stay

desistere cease, desist

desk book hornbook

desolate barren, bleak (exposed and barren), derelict (abandoned), despoil, despondent, destroy (efface), devastate, devoid, disconsolate, eliminate (eradicate), extirpate, obliterate, pillage, plunder, solitary, unsettled, void (empty)

desolating disastrous

desolation catastrophe, consumption, distress (anguish), havoc, prostration, spoliation

despair brood, consternation, distress (anguish), languish, panic, pessimism, prostration

despairing despondent, disconsolate, pessimistic

despatch delegate

desperado convict, malefactor

desperate drastic, hot-blooded, pessimistic

desperate criminal convict

desperate situation peril

desperation pessimism

despicability bad repute, disrepute

despicable bad (offensive), base (bad), blameful, blameworthy, caitiff, contemptible, deplorable, disgraceful, disreputable, heinous, ignoble, loathsome, nefarious, objectionable, obnoxious, odious, outrageous, paltry, repulsive, scandalous

despicableness bad repute, disrepute

despicere disdain

despise contemn, decry, disdain, disfavor, dishonor (deprive of honor), flout, misprize, rebuff, reject, renounce, spurn. SEE MAIN ENTRY

despised base (bad), contemptible, disreputable, notorious

despisedness ignominy

despising cynical, disdainful

despite contumely, irrespective, notwithstanding, odium, regardless, spite

despiteful bitter (reproachful), harsh, malevolent, malignant, outrageous, sinister, spiteful, virulent

despiteful treatment contumely

despoil debauch, deface, deprive, devastate, divest, harry (plunder), hold up (rob), loot, pillage, pirate (take by violence),

plunder, prey, spoil (pillage), steal, subvert, taint (corrupt). SEE MAIN ENTRY

despoiled marred

despoiler burglar

despoilment defilement, pillage

despoliare rob

despoliation pillage, rape, spoliation

despond brood, languish

despondence depression, pessimism

despondency depression, distress (anguish), pessimism, prostration

despondent disappointed, disconsolate, lugubrious, pessimistic. SEE MAIN ENTRY

despot dictator

despotic brutal, dictatorial, peremptory (imperative), severe, strict, stringent, tyrannous

despotic commander dictator

despotic master dictator

despotism oppression

destillare distill

destinare appoint

destinate predetermine

destination design (intent), end (intent), end (termination), goal, intention, object, objective, purpose, pursuit (goal), target. SEE MAIN ENTRY

destine allocate, predetermine, preordain

destined bound, forthcoming, future, imminent, inevitable, necessary (inescapable), prospective

destined lot predetermination

destiny destination, end (termination), predetermination, prospect (outlook)

destituere abandon (physically leave)

destitute bankrupt, impecunious, insolvent, poor (underprivileged), void (empty). SEE MAIN ENTRY

destitute of devoid, insufficient

destitute of good faith dishonest, fraudulent

destitute of integrity dishonest, fraudulent

destitute of life dead, deceased, lifeless (dead)

destitute of reason fatuous

destituteness bankruptcy

destitution bankruptcy, dearth, deficiency, indigence, paucity, poverty, privation

destroy abate (extinguish), abolish, abrogate (rescind), annul, break (fracture), consume, countervail, damage, deface, denounce (condemn), devastate, discontinue (abandon), dispatch (put to death), dissolve (terminate), eliminate (eradicate), eradicate, expunge, extinguish, extirpate, kill (defeat), kill (murder), mistreat, negate, obliterate, overcome (surmount), overturn, overwhelm, pillage, pollute, prejudice (injure), prey, quash, refute, slay, spoil (impair), stifle, subvert, upset, vitiate. SEE MAIN ENTRY

destroy a reputation pillory

destroy confidence discourage

destroy form deface

destroy good will antagonize

destroy goodwill alienate (estrange)

destroy one's perception blind (deprive of sight)

destroy one's reputation defame, smear

destroy the affection of disaffect

destroy the effect of counteract, neutralize

destroy the efficacy of avoid (cancel)

destroy the form of disorganize

destroy the integrity of taint (corrupt)

destroy thoroughly eradicate

destroyable destructible

destroyed broken (fractured), inactive, lost (taken away)

destroyer vandal

destroying deadly, destructive, dire, disastrous, fatal

destruct destroy *(efface)*

destructibility frailty

destructible nonsubstantial *(not sturdy)*. SEE MAIN ENTRY

destruction abatement *(extinguishment)*, abolition, assassination, calamity, catastrophe, consumption, damage, debacle, defacement, defeat, deterioration, detriment, dispatch *(act of putting to death)*, dissolution *(termination)*, fatality, havoc, killing, misfortune, mortality, murder, pillage, prostration, rescision, shambles, spoliation, subversion. SEE MAIN ENTRY

destruction of a right forfeiture *(act of forfeiting)*

destruction of human life murder

destruction of life aberemurder, homicide, murder

destruction of property by fire arson

destructive adverse *(negative)*, bad *(offensive)*, dangerous, deadly, detrimental, dire, disadvantageous, disastrous, disorderly, fatal, harmful, hostile, insalubrious, lethal, malicious, malignant, noxious, pernicious, pestilent, prejudicial, sinister, virulent. SEE MAIN ENTRY

destructive agency parasite

destructive criticism disparagement

destructive fire conflagration

destructiveness murder

destruere destroy *(efface)*

desuete outmoded

desuetude abolition, disuse, nonuse. SEE MAIN ENTRY

desuetudo desuetude

desultoriness irregularity

desultory broken *(interrupted)*, casual, cursory, deviant, discursive *(digressive)*, disjointed, disjunctive *(tending to disjoin)*, haphazard, indirect, intermittent, random, sporadic, superficial, volatile. SEE MAIN ENTRY

detach abstract *(separate)*, alienate *(estrange)*, break *(separate)*, dichotomize, disband, disengage, disentangle, disjoint, displace *(remove)*, dissociate, dissolve *(separate)*, divide *(separate)*, divorce, extricate, insulate, isolate, luxate, part *(separate)*, remove *(eliminate)*, separate, sever, split. SEE MAIN ENTRY

detachable divisible, moving *(in motion)*, separable, severable

detachable part of a certificate coupon

detachable portion coupon

detached alien *(unrelated)*, alone *(solitary)*, apart, autonomous *(independent)*, bipartite, clinical, controlled *(restrained)*, disconnected, discrete, disjunctive *(tending to disjoin)*, dispassionate, equitable, evenhanded, fair *(just)*, foreign, impartial, impervious, independent, individual, insular, insusceptible *(uncaring)*, irrelative, just, nonpartisan, objective, open-minded, phlegmatic, remote *(secluded)*, separate, solitary, unbiased, unprejudiced

detached part segment

detachment candor *(impartiality)*, disassociation, disinterest *(lack of interest)*, disinterest *(lack of prejudice)*, division *(act of dividing)*, estrangement, exception *(exclusion)*, fairness, indifference, neutrality, objectivity, part *(portion)*, quarantine, removal, section *(division)*, segregation *(separation)*, separation, severance, split

detachment of police posse

detail allocate, assign *(designate)*, band, characterize, convey *(communicate)*, delegate, delineate, depict, describe, designate, develop, dispatch *(send off)*, dispense, elaborate, element, elucidate, enumerate, explicate, feature *(characteristic)*, inform *(notify)*, item, itemize, motif, part *(portion)*, particular, particularity, point *(item)*, portray, posse, quote, recite, recount, relate *(tell)*, render *(depict)*, report *(disclose)*, segment, specification, specify, technicality, trace *(delineate)*, trait. SEE MAIN ENTRY

detail the law charge *(instruct on the law)*

detailed descriptive, elaborate, exact, full, narrative, precise, stated, thorough. SEE MAIN ENTRY

detailed account statement

detailed examination investigation

detailed plan blueprint

detailed statement instruction *(teaching)*, recital, specification

details circumstances, contents, description, intelligence *(news)*. SEE MAIN ENTRY

details now to be provided a savoir

details on the law charge *(statement to the jury)*

detain apprehend *(arrest)*, arrest *(apprehend)*, arrest *(stop)*, balk, check *(restrain)*, clog, confine, constrain *(imprison)*, constrict *(inhibit)*, contain *(restrain)*, curb, debar, defer *(put off)*, delay, hinder, hold up *(delay)*, immure, impede, imprison, jail, keep *(restrain)*, preclude, prevent, restrain, retain *(keep in possession)*, stall, stay *(halt)*, stop. SEE MAIN ENTRY

detain by criminal process arrest *(apprehend)*, seize *(apprehend)*

detain by legal process apprehend *(arrest)*

detain in custody imprison

detained arrested *(apprehended)*, back *(in arrears)*, in custody, late *(tardy)*

detainee prisoner

detainer SEE MAIN ENTRY

detainment check *(bar)*, constraint *(imprisonment)*, constraint *(restriction)*, delay, detainer, detention, deterrence, disadvantage, obstacle

detect apprehend *(perceive)*, comprehend *(understand)*, discern *(detect with the senses)*, discover, disinter, expose, find *(discover)*, hear *(perceive by ear)*, identify, locate, notice *(observe)*, overhear, perceive, pierce *(discern)*, spy, trace *(follow)*. SEE MAIN ENTRY

detect differences discern *(discriminate)*

detectable apparent *(perceptible)*, appreciable, discernible, palpable, perceivable, perceptible, visible *(noticeable)*

detectible determinable *(ascertainable)*

detection discovery, observation, perception, recognition. SEE MAIN ENTRY

detective peace officer, spy. SEE MAIN ENTRY

detective force police

detegere betray *(disclose)*, disclose, expose, unveil

detention apprehension *(act of arresting)*, bondage, captivity, check *(bar)*, commitment *(confinement)*, constraint *(imprisonment)*, custody *(incarceration)*, delay, durance, fetter, halt, hindrance, incarceration, restraint. SEE MAIN ENTRY

detention camp penitentiary

detention cell jail

detention center jail, penitentiary

detention of ships embargo

detention station jail

deter arrest *(stop)*, avert, check *(restrain)*, constrict *(inhibit)*, debar, discourage, divert, expostulate, forbid, forestall, forewarn, frighten, halt, hamper, hold up *(delay)*, impede, interdict, interfere, keep *(restrain)*, limit, occlude, preclude, prevent, remonstrate, restrain, stay *(halt)*, stem *(check)*, stop. SEE MAIN ENTRY

deter from one's purpose dissuade

deterge decontaminate, purge *(purify)*, remove *(eliminate)*

deterimental inadvisable

deterior inferior *(lower in position)*

deterior condicio deterioration

deteriorate adulterate, aggravate *(exacerbate)*, debase, decay, decline *(fall)*, degenerate, depreciate, depress, disorganize, ebb, erode, exacerbate, fail *(lose)*, languish, lessen, recidivate, relapse, spoil *(impair)*. SEE MAIN ENTRY

deteriorated bad *(inferior)*, blemished, decadent, depraved, imperfect, old, sordid, unsound *(not strong)*

deteriorating decadent

deterioration caducity, damage, decline, decrease, degradation, detriment, disability *(physical inability)*, disease, disrepair, dissolution *(disintegration)*, erosion, expense *(sacrifice)*, recidivism, relapse, spoilage, wear and tear. SEE MAIN ENTRY

determent constraint *(restriction)*, damper *(stopper)*, deterrent, disadvantage, disincentive, prohibition, remonstrance, restraint

determinable accountable *(explainable)*, appreciable, ascertainable, provable, solvable. SEE MAIN ENTRY

determinant causal, causative, decisive, derivation, factor *(ingredient)*. SEE MAIN ENTRY

determinate absolute *(conclusive)*, actual, axiomatic, certain *(fixed)*, certain *(specific)*, concrete, de facto, definite, definitive, demonstrable, explicit, express, peremptory *(absolute)*, positive *(incontestable)*, precise, specific

determinatio limitation

determination adjudication, alternative *(option)*, animus, appraisal, assessment *(estimation)*, award, cessation *(termination)*, choice *(decision)*, cognovit, collation, conatus, consequence *(conclusion)*, contemplation, conviction *(finding of guilt)*, decision *(judgment)*, denouement, design *(intent)*, diligence *(perseverance)*, discretion *(power of choice)*, election *(choice)*, end *(termination)*, estimate *(idea)*, finality, finding, goal, holding *(ruling of a court)*, industry *(activity)*, intent, intention, judgment *(formal court decree)*, motive, opinion *(belief)*, opinion *(judicial decision)*, payoff *(result)*, perception, poll *(casting of votes)*, project, purpose, rating, referendum, res judicata, resolution *(decision)*, result, ruling, selection *(choice)*, sentence, solution *(answer)*, specification, surety *(certainty)*, tenacity, verdict, volition, vote, will *(desire)*. SEE MAIN ENTRY

determination by agreement settlement

determination of a child's paternity filiation

determination of damages inquest. SEE MAIN ENTRY

determination of issues adjudication

determination prepense deliberation

determinative causal, cause *(reason)*, cogent, decisive, definitive, extreme *(last)*, final, influential, last *(final)*. SEE MAIN ENTRY

determine adjudge, adjudicate, arbitrate *(adjudge)*, arrange *(methodize)*, ascertain, assess *(appraise)*, award, calculate, call *(title)*, choose, circumscribe *(define)*, complete, conclude *(decide)*, constitute *(establish)*, construe *(comprehend)*, decide, deduce, deduct *(conclude by reasoning)*, deem, delimit, delineate, demarcate, designate, detect, discover, dispose *(incline)*, elucidate, fix *(settle)*, gauge, hold *(decide)*, identify, judge, opine, pass *(determine)*, postulate, predominate *(command)*, program, pronounce *(pass judgment)*, rate, regulate *(manage)*, resolve *(decide)*, rule *(decide)*, select, sentence, settle. SEE MAIN ENTRY

determine a controversy arbitrate *(adjudge)*, find *(determine)*

determine a point at issue arbitrate *(adjudge)*

determine after judicial inquiry find *(determine)*

determine an issue find *(determine)*

determine beforehand predetermine, preordain, presuppose

determine boundaries circumscribe *(surround by boundary)*, demarcate

determine exactly construe *(comprehend)*

determine finally adjudicate

determine in advance forejudge, predetermine, presuppose

determine in favor of elect *(choose)*

determine once for all settle

determine size measure

determine the amount of indebtedness liquidate *(determine liability)*

determine the essential qualities of define

determine the essentials discriminate *(distinguish)*

determine the heaviness of weigh

determine the worth of evaluate

determine upon choose, intend, plan

determine value measure

determine with precision define

determined certain *(fixed)*, definite, deliberate, earnest, fixed *(settled)*, indomitable, industrious, inevitable, inexorable, inflexible, intentional, obdurate, patient, peremptory *(absolute)*, persistent, pertinacious, positive *(confident)*, prescriptive, purposeful, relentless, resolute, serious *(devoted)*, spartan, specific, stated, steadfast, strong, unalterable, uncompromising, unrelenting, unyielding. SEE MAIN ENTRY

determined by conditional

determined by chance haphazard

determined by no principle arbitrary

determined punishment sentence

determiner arbiter, arbitrator

determiners jury

determining conclusive *(settled)*, contributory, critical *(crucial)*, crucial, decisive, definitive, prevailing *(having superior force)*, primary. SEE MAIN ENTRY

determining circumstance determinant

determining element determinant

determining influence determinant

determining of a controversy arbitration

deterred arrested *(checked)*

deterrence control *(restriction)*, deterrent, disadvantage, disincentive, fetter, impasse, prohibition, restraint. SEE MAIN ENTRY

deterrent ammunition, control *(restriction)*, cudgel, damper *(stopper)*, deterrence, disadvantage, disincentive, fetter, halt, hindrance, impediment, obviation,

panoply, preventive, prohibition, prohibitive *(restrictive)*, restraint, restrictive, unfavorable. SEE MAIN ENTRY

deterrere deter, discourage, dissuade, intimidate

deterring chilling effect, formidable, preventive

detersion catharsis

detest contemn, disdain, reject, renounce

detestabilis heinous

detestable contemptible, contemptuous, disgraceful, disreputable, heinous, loathsome, nefarious, objectionable, obnoxious, odious, offensive *(offending)*, repugnant *(exciting aversion)*, repulsive

detestableness infamy

detestation contempt *(disdain)*, disdain, disgrace, hatred, ill will, malice, odium, phobia

dethrone demote, depose *(remove)*, dislodge, overthrow, rebel, supplant

dethronement abdication, disqualification *(rejection)*

detinere delay, hold up *(delay)*, stay *(halt)*

detineri employ *(engage services)*

detonate discharge *(shoot)*

detonation discharge *(shot)*, noise, outburst

detonator bomb

detorquere contort

detour avoidance *(evasion)*, deter, deviation, digress, digression. SEE MAIN ENTRY

detract bait *(harass)*, blame, debunk, decry, denounce *(condemn)*, deprecate, derogate, diminish, discommend, discount *(minimize)*, discount *(reduce)*, disparage, lessen, minimize, smear. SEE MAIN ENTRY

detract from decrease, decry, demean *(make lower)*, depreciate, dilute, diminish, stain, underestimate

detracting abusive, contemptuous, derogatory, harmful, libelous, pejorative

detraction aspersion, bad repute, contempt *(disdain)*, criticism, defamation, denunciation, detriment, disapprobation, disapproval, disdain, dishonor *(shame)*, disparagement, disrespect, phillipic, revilement, vilification

detractive libelous

detractor foe, malcontent

detractory calumnious, derogatory

detrahere derogate

detrectare depreciate, disparage, shirk

detriment damage, disadvantage, disservice, expense *(sacrifice)*, handicap, harm, hindrance, impairment *(damage)*, impairment *(drawback)*, injury, mischief, prejudice *(injury)*. SEE MAIN ENTRY

detrimental adverse *(negative)*, bad *(inferior)*, bad *(offensive)*, destructive, disadvantageous, disastrous, harmful, insalubrious, malignant, noxious, oppressive, peccant *(unhealthy)*, pernicious, prejudicial, sinister. SEE MAIN ENTRY

detrimentum detriment, disservice, harm, injury, loss, prejudice *(injury)*

detrition erosion

detritus discard

detrude dislodge, eject *(expel)*, outpour

detrudere evict

detruncate condense, excise *(cut away)*, remove *(eliminate)*

detrusion expulsion

deturbare dispossess, evict

deuterogamy digamy

devaluate deduct *(reduce)*, depreciate, depress, lessen

devaluation decline, decrease

devalue adulterate, corrupt, damage, denature, depreciate, depress, deteriorate, disable, impair. SEE MAIN ENTRY

devastate damage, despoil, destroy *(efface)*, extinguish, extirpate, harm, obliterate, pillage, prejudice *(injure)*, subvert. SEE MAIN ENTRY

devastating dire, disastrous, fatal

devastation catastrophe, conflagration, consumption, debacle, defilement, destruction, disaster, havoc, plunder, spoliation, subversion. SEE MAIN ENTRY

develop accrue *(arise)*, ameliorate, amplify, bear *(yield)*, build *(augment)*, cause, compose, compound, conceive *(invent)*, constitute *(establish)*, convert *(change use)*, create, crystallize, cultivate, elaborate, engender, enhance, enlarge, ensue, establish *(launch)*, evolve, expand, explicate, expound, extend *(enlarge)*, forge *(produce)*, generate, germinate, increase, make, mature, nurture, occur *(happen)*, parlay *(exploit successfully)*, progress, promote *(organize)*, pullulate, reclaim, result, revise, succeed *(follow)*. SEE MAIN ENTRY

develop a course contrive

develop in greater detail expand

develop too fast overextend

develop too much overextend

developed complete *(all-embracing)*

developed minutely elaborate

developer SEE MAIN ENTRY

development accession *(enlargement)*, advancement *(improvement)*, augmentation, boom *(increase)*, boom *(prosperity)*, building *(business of assembling)*, complication, consequence *(conclusion)*, creation, denouement, discipline *(training)*, effect, event, growth *(evolution)*, happening, headway, manufacture, nascency, offshoot, outcome, outgrowth, preparation, progress, reform, rehabilitation, result, transition. SEE MAIN ENTRY

development of industrial sites development *(building)*

developmental constructive *(creative)*, corrigible

deversari lodge *(reside)*

deversor lodger

deversorium lodging

devertere lodge *(reside)*

deverticulum lodging, subterfuge

devestation pillage

deviant eccentric, errant. SEE MAIN ENTRY

deviate alter, change, conflict, depart, detour, digress, disaccord, disagree, disobey, divert, miscalculate, palter, prevaricate, vary. SEE MAIN ENTRY

deviate from differ *(vary)*

deviate from a direct course detour

deviate from rectitude trespass

deviate from the proper path lapse *(fall into error)*

deviate from the truth bear false witness, lie *(falsify)*, perjure, prevaricate. SEE MAIN ENTRY

deviate from virtue lapse *(fall into error)*

deviating astray, circuitous, desultory, deviant, devious, different, discursive *(digressive)*, disordered, disparate, dissimilar, divergent, eccentric, errant, indirect, individual, irrelevant, labyrinthine, nonconforming, peculiar *(distinctive)*, perverse, shifting, sinuous. SEE MAIN ENTRY

deviating from the common rule anomalous

deviating from the general rule irregular *(not usual)*

deviating from the norm irregular *(not usual)*. SEE MAIN ENTRY

deviating from the standard irregular *(not usual)*

deviation avoidance *(evasion)*, defect, detour, difference, digression, discrepancy, disparity, diversification, error, exception *(exclusion)*, incongruity, inconsistency, indirection *(indirect action)*, inequality, irregularity, miscue, nonconformity, quirk *(idiosyncrasy)*, sodomy, variance *(exemption)*. SEE MAIN ENTRY

deviation from a direct course detour

deviation from probity dishonesty

deviation from rectitude abuse *(corrupt practice)*, attaint, bad faith, bad repute, blame *(culpability)*, corruption, crime, disgrace, dishonor *(shame)*, guilt, malfeasance, misconduct, misdoing, misfeasance, misprision. SEE MAIN ENTRY

deviation from truth fallacy, misstatement

deviation from virtue bad repute

deviative anomalous, devious, discursive *(digressive)*, divergent, diverse, eccentric, irregular *(not usual)*, sinuous, unorthodox, unpredictable

deviatory circuitous, divergent, errant, indirect

device appliance, artifice, color *(deceptive appearance)*, conduit *(channel)*, contrivance, deception, evasion, expedient, facility *(instrumentality)*, false pretense, hoax, instrument *(tool)*, instrumentality, loophole, maneuver *(tactic)*, maneuver *(trick)*, ploy, project, recourse, resource, scheme, stratagem, subterfuge, token, tool. SEE MAIN ENTRY

devices means *(opportunity)*, strategy

devil plague

devil-like diabolic

devilish cold-blooded, cruel, diabolic, heinous, malevolent, malignant, nefarious, ruthless, vicious

devilishness delinquency *(misconduct)*

devilment mischief, nuisance

deviltry cruelty, mischief

devious artful, blameworthy, circuitous, discursive *(digressive)*, disingenuous, disreputable, indirect, insidious, machiavellian, oblique *(evasive)*, sinuous, sly, tortuous *(corrupt)*. SEE MAIN ENTRY

deviousness bad faith, bad repute, corruption, improbity, indirection *(deceitfulness)*, indirection *(indirect action)*, knavery

devisable assignable, heritable

devisal bequest

devise arrange *(methodize)*, arrange *(plan)*, attorn, benefit *(conferment)*, bequeath, bequest, build *(construct)*, calculate, circumvent, compose, conceive *(invent)*, conjure, conspire, constitute *(establish)*, contrive, conveyance, create, demise, devolution, estate *(hereditament)*, fabricate *(construct)*, forge *(produce)*, form, formulate, frame *(construct)*, frame *(formulate)*, give *(grant)*, grant, grant *(transfer formally)*, hereditament, inheritance, invent *(produce for the first time)*, leave *(give)*, make, maneuver, manufacture, originate, plan, plot, produce *(manufacture)*, program, scheme. SEE MAIN ENTRY

devise falsely fabricate *(make up)*

devise treachery conspire

devised controlled *(automatic)*, tactical

devised by will testamentary

devisee donee, feoffee, grantee, heir, legatee, payee, recipient, transferee. SEE MAIN ENTRY

deviser architect, author *(originator)*, coactor, contractor, materialman

devising building *(business of assembling)*, creation

devisor donor, feoffor, grantor, maker, transferor

devitalization fault *(weakness)*

devitalize adulterate, attenuate, debilitate, disable, disarm *(divest of arms)*, eviscerate, exhaust *(deplete)*, kill *(defeat)*

devitalized disabled *(made incapable)*

devius devious, indirect

devoid deficient, vacant, vacuous, void *(empty)*. SEE MAIN ENTRY

devoid of insufficient

devoid of consideration naked *(lacking embellishment)*

devoid of dissimulation ingenuous

devoid of expression inexpressive

devoid of feeling insusceptible *(uncaring)*

devoid of life dead, deceased, defunct, lifeless *(dead)*

devoid of truth dishonest, erroneous, fallacious, false *(inaccurate)*, fraudulent, lying, mendacious. SEE MAIN ENTRY

devoir burden

devoir commitment *(responsibility)*

devoirs respect

devolution conveyance, delegation *(assignment)*, deputation *(selection of delegates)*, succession. SEE MAIN ENTRY

devolve alienate *(transfer title)*, cede, convey *(transfer)*, detail *(assign)*, entrust, pass *(advance)*, transfer. SEE MAIN ENTRY

devolve again recover

devolve on delegate

devolve upon assign *(transfer ownership)*, attorn, bequeath, demise, grant *(transfer formally)*, hold *(possess)*, possess

devolvement assignment *(transfer of ownership)*

devolving on accountable *(responsible)*

devote contribute *(supply)*, dedicate, give *(grant)*, occupy *(engage)*, spend. SEE MAIN ENTRY

devote attention to consider, observe *(watch)*

devote oneself adhere *(maintain loyalty)*

devote oneself to address *(direct attention to)*, concern *(care)*, discharge *(perform)*, labor, peruse, ply, practice *(engage in)*, resolve *(decide)*, specialize, study, undertake

devote thought to ponder

devoted close *(intimate)*, dependable, earnest, faithful *(loyal)*, fanatical, fervent, indebted, industrious, inseparable, loyal, obedient, partisan, purposeful, reliable, staunch, steadfast, true *(loyal)*, unyielding, zealous. SEE MAIN ENTRY

devoted to convention orthodox

devoted to others philanthropic

devotedly faithfully, in good faith

devotedness adherence *(devotion)*, adhesion *(loyalty)*, allegiance, diligence *(perseverance)*, fidelity, homage, industry *(activity)*, loyalty

devotee addict, disciple, partisan, specialist

devotio vow

devotion adhesion *(loyalty)*, affection, affinity *(regard)*, allegiance, dedication, diligence *(perseverance)*, discipline *(obedience)*, fealty, fidelity, homage, honor

(outward respect), industry *(activity)*, loyalty, preoccupation, regard *(esteem)*. SEE MAIN ENTRY

devotion to others philanthropy

devotional sacrosanct, solemn

devour consume, despoil, destroy *(efface)*, eliminate *(eradicate)*, expend *(consume)*, extirpate, obliterate, prey

devouring harmful, oppressive, pernicious, predatory, rapacious

devouring element conflagration

devout faithful *(loyal)*, serious *(devoted)*, solemn, zealous

devoutness adhesion *(loyalty)*

devovere devote

dexterity competence *(ability)*, efficiency, facility *(easiness)*, faculty *(ability)*, gift *(flair)*, performance *(workmanship)*, propensity, prowess *(ability)*, science *(technique)*, skill, specialty *(special aptitude)*

dexterous artful, competent, deft, diplomatic, efficient, expert, facile, familiar *(informed)*, proficient, resourceful, veteran

dexterousness efficiency

dextrous practiced

dextrousness gift *(flair)*

diabolic bad *(offensive)*, cold-blooded, heinous, malevolent, malicious, odious, pernicious, sinister. SEE MAIN ENTRY

diabolical cruel, malevolent, malicious, malignant, nefarious, ruthless, sinister, vicious

diacritical discriminating *(distinguishing)*, distinctive

diagnose decide, detect, discover, interpret, opine, recognize *(perceive)*. SEE MAIN ENTRY

diagnosis construction, determination, judgment *(discernment)*, recognition. SEE MAIN ENTRY

diagnostic empirical, indicant, interrogative, symptom

diagnosticate detect

diagonal oblique *(slanted)*

diagram blueprint, characterize, contour *(outline)*, delineate, delineation, depict, design *(construction plan)*, scheme

dialect language, phraseology, speech. SEE MAIN ENTRY

dialectic controversial, discursive *(analytical)*, logical, polemic

dialectical argumentative, logical, polemic

dialectics ratiocination

dialogize discuss

dialogue communication *(discourse)*, conference, confrontation *(act of setting face to face)*, conversation, discourse, interview, parley, script. SEE MAIN ENTRY

diameter caliber *(measurement)*

diameter of a cylindrical body caliber *(measurement)*

diametric different

diametrically opposed opposite

diametrically opposite adverse *(opposite)*, antipathetic *(oppositional)*, contradictory, contrary, inverse

diaphanous lucid, pellucid

diary calendar *(record of yearly periods)*, journal, ledger, register

diatribe bombast, denunciation, disapprobation, harangue, obloquy, outcry, phillipic, revilement, stricture. SEE MAIN ENTRY

dicendi genus phraseology

dicere appoint, assert, call *(title)*, nominate, pronounce *(speak)*, recite, remark, speak, utter

dichotomize bifurcate, split. SEE MAIN ENTRY

721

dichotomous   bipartite

dichotomy   disassociation, split. SEE MAIN ENTRY

dicio   dominion *(supreme authority)*

dicker   barter, haggle, negotiate. SEE MAIN ENTRY

dickering   negotiation

dictate   act *(enactment)*, canon, charge *(command)*, citation *(charge)*, coerce, compel, constitution, decree *(noun)*, decree *(verb)*, detail *(assign)*, direct *(order)*, direction *(order)*, directive, dominate, edict, enact, enactment, enforce, enjoin, fiat, govern, holding *(ruling of a court)*, impose *(enforce)*, insist, instruct *(direct)*, legislate, manage, mandamus, mandate, measure, monition *(legal summons)*, necessitate, order *(judicial directive)*, order, oversee, pass *(approve)*, precept, prescribe, prescription *(directive)*, prevail *(be in force)*, regulation *(rule)*, require *(compel)*, requirement, rubric *(authoritative rule)*, rule *(legal dictate)*, rule *(govern)*, statute, writ. SEE MAIN ENTRY

dictate of conscience   duty *(obligation)*

dictate peace   reconcile

dictated   boiler plate, indispensable, necessary *(required)*, nuncupative, obligatory, positive *(prescribed)*, prescriptive

dictated term   article *(precept)*

dictates   legislation *(enactments)*, protocol *(etiquette)*

dictates of society   custom, decorum

dictating   master

dictation   canon, coercion, compulsion *(coercion)*, enforcement, force *(compulsion)*, mandate

dictator   SEE MAIN ENTRY

dictatorial   arbitrary and capricious, dogmatic, peremptory *(imperative)*, presumptuous, relentless, strict, stringent, supercilious. SEE MAIN ENTRY

dictatorial mogul   dictator

dictatorius   dictatorial

dictators   hierarchy *(persons in authority)*

dictatorship   oppression

dictio   delivery

diction   parlance, phraseology, rhetoric *(skilled speech)*, speech

dicto audiens   obedient

dicto oboediens   amenable

dictum   canon, comment

dictum   declaration

dictum   dogma, law

dictum   observation

dictum   phrase, pronouncement. SEE MAIN ENTRY

dictum   remark

dictum   statement

didactic   disciplinary *(educational)*, hortative, informative. SEE MAIN ENTRY

didactical   disciplinary *(educational)*

die   decease, expire, pattern, perish, stamp, succumb, terminate. SEE MAIN ENTRY

die away   expire, lessen, perish, stop, subside

die down   decrease

die out   expire, perish

die-hard   bigot

diehard   malcontent

dies   date

dies festus   holiday

diet   session

differ   bicker, challenge, collide *(clash)*, complain *(criticize)*, conflict, contend *(dispute)*, contradict, contrast, demur, depart, deviate, disaccord, disaffirm, disagree,

dispute *(contest)*, dispute *(debate)*, dissent *(differ in opinion)*, except *(object)*, vary. SEE MAIN ENTRY

differ in opinion   collide *(clash)*, conflict, disaccord, disagree

differ in sentiment   dissent *(differ in opinion)*

differ violently   collide *(clash)*

difference   conflict, contention *(opposition)*, contradistinction, deviation, disaccord, disagreement, disapproval, discord, discrepancy, disparity, dispute, dissidence, diversification, estrangement, feud, fight *(argument)*, identity *(individuality)*, impugnation, incongruity, inconsistency, inequality, nonconformity, nuance, objection, rift *(disagreement)*, schism, split, variance *(disagreement)*. SEE MAIN ENTRY

difference of degree   differential

difference of opinion   argument *(contention)*, contest *(dispute)*, contradiction, controversy *(argument)*, disagreement, disapproval, dispute, dissension, embroilment

differences   dissension, reaction *(opposition)*

different   alien *(unrelated)*, contrary, discrete, disparate, dissimilar, distinct *(distinguished from others)*, distinctive, divergent, diverse, eccentric, extraordinary, foreign, heterogeneous, inconsistent, individual, multifarious, multiple, nonconforming, noteworthy, novel, original *(creative)*, peculiar *(distinctive)*, rare, repugnant *(incompatible)*, separate, several *(separate)*, singular, special, specific, unaccustomed, uncommon, unequal *(unequivalent)*, unique, unorthodox, unrelated, unusual. SEE MAIN ENTRY

differentia   characteristic, distinction *(difference)*, trait

differential   characteristic, discrepancy, distinction *(difference)*, particular *(specific)*. SEE MAIN ENTRY

differentiate   call *(title)*, characterize, compare, contrast, define, demarcate, discern *(discriminate)*, discriminate *(distinguish)*, distinguish, enumerate, except *(exclude)*, label, secern, select, specify. SEE MAIN ENTRY

differentiated   disparate, individual, particular *(specific)*, peculiar *(distinctive)*

differentiating   discriminating *(distinguishing)*, distinctive, personal *(individual)*

differentiating trait   differential

differentiation   collation, denomination, diagnosis, difference, discrepancy, distinction *(difference)*, diversification, nuance, segregation *(separation)*, severance. SEE MAIN ENTRY

differentiative   discriminating *(distinguishing)*, distinctive

differing   discordant, discriminating *(distinguishing)*, disparate, dissenting, dissident, dissimilar, distinct *(distinguished from others)*, distinctive, divergent, diverse, eccentric, nonconforming, peculiar *(distinctive)*, recusant, unequal *(unequivalent)*, unrelated. SEE MAIN ENTRY

differre   defer *(put off)*, postpone, procrastinate, suspend

difficile   difficult

difficilis   difficult, fractious, froward, intractable

difficult   complex, elusive, formidable, fractious, froward, impracticable, insuperable, intricate, labyrinthine, lawless, obscure *(abstruse)*, onerous, opaque, operose,

oppressive, painful, perverse, petulant, problematic, querulous, recondite, restive, severe, uncompromising. SEE MAIN ENTRY

difficult choice   dilemma

difficult situation   imbroglio, nuisance

difficult to accept   unbelievable

difficult to alter   ironclad

difficult to appraise   intangible

difficult to bear   oppressive

difficult to believe   unbelievable

difficult to break   ironclad

difficult to catch   elusive

difficult to change   ironclad

difficult to classify   nondescript

difficult to comprehend   ambiguous, elusive, esoteric, incomprehensible, opaque, unclear

difficult to describe   nondescript

difficult to endure   painful

difficult to explain   indefinable

difficult to feel   impalpable

difficult to perceive   impalpable

difficult to please   particular *(exacting)*, querulous

difficult to see   impalpable

difficult to translate   indefinable

difficult to understand   elusive, indefinable, obscure *(abstruse)*, opaque, technical, unclear

difficultas   predicament

difficulty   adversity, aggravation *(annoyance)*, bar *(obstruction)*, burden, complex *(entanglement)*, complication, confusion *(ambiguity)*, confusion *(turmoil)*, damper *(stopper)*, dilemma, disadvantage, distress *(anguish)*, emergency, encumbrance, enigma, exigency, handicap, hindrance, imbroglio, impasse, impediment, impossibility, nuisance, obstacle, obstruction, plight, poverty, predicament, problem, quagmire, quandary, trouble

diffidence   fear, hesitation, qualm, reluctance

diffidens   diffident

diffident   hesitant, reluctant. SEE MAIN ENTRY

diffindere   split

diffiteri   disavow

diffluent   fluvial

diffundere   diffuse

diffundi   diffuse

diffuse   broad, circulate, deploy, desultory, disburse *(distribute)*, disintegrate, dispel, disperse *(scatter)*, disseminate, dissipate *(spread out)*, dissolve *(disperse)*, extensive, intersperse, pedestrian, permeate, pervade, prevailing *(current)*, profuse, prolix, propagate *(spread)*, publish, radiate, spread, turgid. SEE MAIN ENTRY

diffusion   circulation, decentralization, osmosis

diffusive   extensive

dig down into   delve

dig into   canvass, delve, investigate, probe

dig out   disinter, eviscerate, extract, ferret

dig up   disinter, expose, procure

dig up out of the earth   disinter

digerere   arrange *(methodize)*, codify, sort

digest   abridgment *(condensation)*, abstract, brief, capsule, code, compendium, conceive *(comprehend)*, condense, consider, muse, outline *(synopsis)*, pandect *(code of laws)*, pandect *(treatise)*, ponder, read, realize *(understand)*, report *(detailed account)*, restatement, review, scenario, summary, synopsis, understand. SEE MAIN ENTRY

digest of law   pandect *(code of laws)*

digest of the law hornbook
digested compact *(pithy)*
digestion osmosis
dignification degree *(academic title)*, elevation, remembrance *(commemoration)*
dignified civil *(polite)*, elegant, important *(significant)*, meritorious, prominent, proud *(self-respecting)*, reputable
dignify bestow, elevate, prefer, promote *(advance)*, raise *(advance)*, recognize *(acknowledge)*
dignitary functionary, incumbent
dignitas distinction *(reputation)*, honor *(good reputation)*, merit
dignity decorum, deportment, distinction *(reputation)*, eminence, prestige, propriety *(correctness)*, respect, solemnity, status
dignus eligible
digredi detour, digress
digress depart, detour, deviate, differ *(vary)*. SEE MAIN ENTRY
digressing indirect
digressio deviation, digression
digression detour, indirection *(indirect action)*, innovation. SEE MAIN ENTRY
digressive alien *(unrelated)*, circuitous, desultory, disparate, indirect, labyrinthine, shifting, tangential, turgid
diiudicare decide, discriminate *(distinguish)*
dijudicare arbitrate *(adjudge)*
dilacerate rend
dilaceration damage, split
dilapidate decay, degenerate, deteriorate, impair, spoil *(impair)*
dilapidated base *(inferior)*, decadent, old, sordid. SEE MAIN ENTRY
dilapidation decline, deterioration, detriment, disrepair, dissolution *(disintegration)*, spoilage, wear and tear
dilatare compound, deploy, enlarge, expand, increase
dilatation extension *(expansion)*
dilate compound, declaim, discourse, enlarge, expand, extend *(enlarge)*, increase, inflate, spread
dilate upon comment
dilated inflated *(enlarged)*
dilatio adjournment
dilation extension *(expansion)*, inflation *(increase)*
dilatoriness deferment, delay
dilatory indolent, otiose, remiss, truant. SEE MAIN ENTRY
dilatory obstruction filibuster
dilemma complication, confusion *(ambiguity)*, deadlock, emergency, entanglement *(involvement)*, imbroglio, impasse, incertitude, indecision, plight, predicament, problem, quagmire, quandary. SEE MAIN ENTRY
diligence caution *(vigilance)*
diligence dispatch *(promptness)*
diligence industry *(activity)*, tenacity, work *(effort)*. SEE MAIN ENTRY
diligens careful, diligent, economical, exact, meticulous, precise, punctilious, scrupulous, strict
diligent circumspect, close *(rigorous)*, conscientious, eager, earnest, industrious, intense, meticulous, painstaking, patient, persistent, pertinacious, punctual, resolute, sedulous, stable, steadfast, thorough, unrelenting, unremitting. SEE MAIN ENTRY
diligent application diligence *(care)*
diligent attention diligence *(care)*, examination *(study)*, interest *(concern)*
diligent exercise discipline *(training)*

diligent practice discipline *(training)*
diligent study diligence *(care)*
diligent thought diligence *(care)*
diligentia diligence *(care)*, industry *(activity)*
diligently faithfully
dilly dally procrastinate
dillydally stall
diluere dilute
dilute commute, deduct *(reduce)*, denature, depreciate, diminish, disarm *(divest of arms)*, extenuate, lessen. SEE MAIN ENTRY
diluted insipid
dilutum solution *(substance)*
dim blind *(concealed)*, blind *(obscure)*, equivocal, incomprehensible, inconspicuous, indefinite, indistinct, inexpressive, intangible, nebulous, obfuscate, obnubilate, obscure *(faint)*, obscure, opaque, tarnish, unclear, vague
dim-sighted blind *(sightless)*
dim-witted non compos mentis
dimension degree *(magnitude)*, magnitude, mass *(weight)*. SEE MAIN ENTRY
dimensions area *(surface)*, caliber *(measurement)*, configuration *(confines)*, extent, measurement
dimidiate bifurcate
dimidiation split
diminish abate *(lessen)*, abridge *(shorten)*, allay, alleviate, assuage, attenuate, check *(restrain)*, commute, curtail, damage, decrease, deduct *(reduce)*, demean *(make lower)*, demote, depress, derogate, discount *(minimize)*, disgrace, erode, excise *(cut away)*, extenuate, impair, lessen, minimize, mitigate, moderate *(temper)*, mollify, palliate *(abate)*, rebate, reduce, relax, remit *(relax)*, restrict, retrench, subside. SEE MAIN ENTRY
diminish in effect attenuate
diminish in quality impair
diminish the price of depreciate
diminish the value of depreciate
diminished minimal, qualified *(conditioned)*
diminishing abatement *(reduction)*, decline, mitigating
diminishment consumption, curtailment, decrease, decrement, diminution, erosion, mitigation, mollification, relief *(release)*
diminution abatement *(reduction)*, consumption, curtailment, damage, decrease, decrement, discount, erosion, mitigation, moderation, mollification, rebate, relief *(release)*, remission, waste, wear and tear. SEE MAIN ENTRY
diminutive immaterial, minimal, paltry, petty, remote *(small)*, slight, tenuous
dimissio discharge *(dismissal)*, dismissal *(discharge)*
dimittere disband, discharge *(dismiss)*, dispense, forgo
dimming obscuration
dimness indistinctness, obscuration, opacity
dimwitted opaque
din brawl, noise, outcry, pandemonium
dint puissance. SEE MAIN ENTRY
diocese region
dioristic perspicacious
dip immerse *(plunge into)*, subside
diploma degree *(academic title)*, document
diplomacy consideration *(sympathetic regard)*, discretion *(quality of being discreet)*, intercession, negotiation, parley
diplomat go-between, intermediary, plenipotentiary

diplomatic civil *(polite)*, discreet, judicious, politic, strategic, subtle *(refined)*, tactical. SEE MAIN ENTRY
diplomatic agent plenipotentiary
diplomatic agreement protocol *(agreement)*
diplomatic code protocol *(etiquette)*
diplomatic corps embassy
diplomatical strategic, tactical
diplomatis patent
dipsomania inebriation. SEE MAIN ENTRY
dirae malediction
dire adverse *(negative)*, bad *(offensive)*, deplorable, disastrous, drastic, fatal, gross *(flagrant)*, harmful, heinous, ominous, outrageous, pernicious, portentous *(ominous)*, regrettable, serious *(grave)*. SEE MAIN ENTRY
direct accurate, administer *(conduct)*, advise, appoint, arrange *(methodize)*, candid, cause, charge *(instruct on the law)*, clear *(apparent)*, coherent *(clear)*, command, compact *(pithy)*, conduct, control *(regulate)*, counsel, decree, demand, determine, dictate, discipline *(control)*, discipline *(train)*, dispatch *(send off)*, edify, educate, enjoin, explicit, express, govern, handle *(manage)*, hold *(possess)*, impose *(enforce)*, inculcate, indicate, influence, initiate, instill, manage, mandamus, manipulate *(utilize skillfully)*, militate, moderate *(preside over)*, motivate, nurture, officiate, operate, order, overlook *(superintend)*, oversee, predominate *(command)*, prescribe, preside, prevail *(be in force)*, program, provide *(arrange for)*, recommend, regulate *(manage)*, require *(compel)*, rule *(govern)*, send, sententious, straightforward, subpoena, summary, superintend, unaffected *(sincere)*, undistorted, wield. SEE MAIN ENTRY
direct a threat against menace
direct affairs conduct
direct again redirect
direct approach access *(right of way)*
direct attention devote
direct attention to indicate, note *(notice)*, notice *(give formal warning)*
direct cause. SEE MAIN ENTRY
direct imperatively command
direct one's attention instruct *(teach)*
direct one's thoughts to focus
direct opposite antipode, antithesis, contradiction
direct the attendance of subpoena
direct the attention to concern *(care)*, convey *(communicate)*, disabuse, mention, occupy *(engage)*, signify *(inform)*
direct the eyes to observe *(watch)*
direct the mind to occupy *(engage)*
direct the mind upon concentrate *(pay attention)*
direct to address *(direct attention to)*
direct toward one object focus
directed against prejudicial
directed verdict nonsuit
directing advisory, determinative, executive, leading *(guiding)*, prevailing *(having superior force)*
directing agency patronage *(power to appoint jobs)*
directing head chief, principal *(director)*
directing power clout
direction administration, advice, agency *(legal relationship)*, canon, caveat, charge *(command)*, charge *(statement to the jury)*, conatus, control *(supervision)*, course, custody *(supervision)*, decree, design *(intent)*, dictate, directive, disposition *(final*

arrangement), edification, education, fiat, forethought, generalship, government *(administration),* guidance, inclination, intention, management *(supervision),* mandate, monition *(legal summons),* occupation *(possession),* order *(judicial directive),* ordinance, penchant, precept, prescription *(directive),* process *(summons),* purpose, regulation *(rule),* requirement, requisition, rule *(guide),* rule *(legal dictate),* side, standpoint, summons, supervision, supremacy, tendency, tenor, transaction, transmittal, way *(channel),* writ. SEE MAIN ENTRY

direction post landmark *(conspicuous object)*

direction to imprison mittimus

directive causative, decretal, direction *(order),* fiat, guidance, mandate, order *(judicial directive),* procedural, regulation *(rule),* requirement, subpoena, writ. SEE MAIN ENTRY

directly instantly

directly affected by the outcome of a controversy interested

directly after ex post facto

directness candor *(straightforwardness)*

director administrator, caretaker *(one fulfilling the function of office),* chairman, chief, employer, principal *(director),* procurator, superintendent. SEE MAIN ENTRY

directorate board, generalship, management *(supervision)*

directorial administrative

directors authorities, hierarchy *(persons in authority),* management *(directorate),* management *(supervision).* SEE MAIN ENTRY

directorship board, direction *(guidance),* generalship, hegemony, management *(directorate),* management *(supervision),* regime

directory roll. SEE MAIN ENTRY

direful dire, ominous, portentous *(ominous)*

diremption split

direptio pillage, spoliation

direption spoliation

dirge plaint

dirigere direct *(supervise)*

dirimere sever

dirtied tainted *(contaminated)*

dirtiness defilement, obscenity

dirty base *(inferior),* brand *(stigmatize),* infect, machiavellian, odious, pollute, profane, prurient, repulsive, salacious, stain, sully, taint *(contaminate),* tainted *(contaminated),* tarnish

diruere destroy *(efface),* overthrow

disability detriment, disadvantage, disease, disorder *(abnormal condition),* disqualification *(factor that disqualifies),* handicap, impediment, impuissance, inability, incapacity, inefficacy, pain. SEE MAIN ENTRY

disable damage, disarm *(divest of arms),* disqualify, foil, impede, maim, mutilate, neutralize, obstruct, spoil *(impair),* stall, tax *(overwork).* SEE MAIN ENTRY

disabled helpless *(powerless),* inactive, inadequate, incapable, ineffective, marred, powerless, unable. SEE MAIN ENTRY

disablement abortion *(fiasco),* detriment, disability *(legal disqualification),* disability *(physical inability),* disadvantage, disqualification *(factor that disqualifies),* harm, impuissance, inability, incapacity, inefficacy

disabling SEE MAIN ENTRY

disabuse debunk, inform *(notify),* reveal. SEE MAIN ENTRY

disaccommodate disadvantage, discommode, disoblige

disaccord altercation, argument *(contention),* bicker, collide *(clash),* conflict *(noun),* conflict *(verb),* contend *(dispute),* contention *(opposition),* contest *(dispute),* contradiction, controversy *(argument),* deviation, differ *(vary),* difference, disagreement, discord, discrepancy, disparity, dispute, dissension, dissent *(difference of opinion),* dissidence, distinction *(difference),* division *(act of dividing),* faction, feud, incompatibility *(difference),* inconsistency, inequality, strife, variance *(disagreement).* SEE MAIN ENTRY

disaccord with differ *(vary),* disapprove *(reject),* refuse

disaccordance deviation, discord

disaccordant discordant, disproportionate, dissenting, incongruous, negative

disaccustom forswear

disadvantage damper *(stopper),* detriment, discommode, drawback, encumber *(hinder),* encumbrance, expense *(sacrifice),* fetter, handicap, harm, hindrance, impairment *(drawback),* inconvenience, incumbrance *(burden),* inexpedience, liability, misfortune, penalty, prejudice *(injury),* prejudice *(injure).* SEE MAIN ENTRY

disadvantaged SEE MAIN ENTRY

disadvantageous adverse *(negative),* deleterious, detrimental, harmful, illadvised, inadvisable, inauspicious, injudicious, insalubrious, noxious, peccant *(unhealthy),* pernicious, prejudicial, regrettable, undesirable, unfavorable. SEE MAIN ENTRY

disadvantageousness inexpedience

disaffect alienate *(estrange),* antagonize, discourage, disfavor, estrange. SEE MAIN ENTRY

disaffected faithless, false *(disloyal),* hostile, inimical, malevolent, recreant

disaffection abandonment *(desertion),* alienation *(estrangement),* bad faith, contempt *(disobedience to the court),* desertion, disaccord, dissatisfaction, dissension, estrangement, ill will, infidelity, malice, odium, reluctance, resentment, umbrage. SEE MAIN ENTRY

disaffiliate disaffirm, disown *(refuse to acknowledge),* secede

disaffirm contest, controvert, deny *(contradict),* disaccord, disallow, disavow, disclaim, disinherit, disown *(deny the validity),* gainsay, negate, oppose, protest, recant, refute, reject. SEE MAIN ENTRY

disaffirmation abjuration, denial, disclaimer, negation, rejection, renunciation, repudiation. SEE MAIN ENTRY

disaffirming contrary

disaggreement strife

disagree argue, bicker, challenge, collide *(clash),* complain *(criticize),* conflict, contend *(dispute),* contest, contradict, contravene, debate, demur, deny *(contradict),* deviate, differ *(vary),* disaccord, disaffirm, disallow, disown *(deny the validity),* dispute *(debate),* dissent *(differ in opinion),* gainsay, object, oppose, oppugn, protest, rebut, renounce. SEE MAIN ENTRY

disagree in opinion dissent *(differ in opinion)*

disagree with confront *(oppose),* controvert, disapprove *(reject),* dispute *(contest)*

disagreeable adverse *(hostile),* antipathetic *(distasteful),* bitter *(acrid tasting),* deplorable, disorderly, invidious, loathsome, objectionable, obnoxious, odious, offensive *(offending),* petulant, repugnant *(exciting aversion),* repulsive, undesirable, unsatisfactory, unsavory

disagreeing contradictory, contrary, discordant, disparate, dissenting, dissident, dissimilar, diverse, hostile, inapplicable, inapposite, inappropriate, incongruous, inconsistent, litigious, nonconforming, opposite, peculiar *(distinctive),* recusant, repugnant *(incompatible)*

disagreeing party faction

disagreement antipode, antithesis, argument *(contention),* belligerency, collision *(dispute),* conflict, confrontation *(altercation),* contention *(opposition),* contest *(dispute),* contradiction, contraposition, contravention, controversy *(argument),* deviation, difference, disaccord, disapprobation, disapproval, discord, discrepancy, disparity, dispute, dissatisfaction, dissension, dissent *(difference of opinion),* dissent *(nonconcurrence),* dissidence, distinction *(difference),* division *(act of dividing),* estrangement, feud, fight *(argument),* fracas, fray, imbroglio, impugnation, incompatibility *(difference),* incompatibility *(inconsistency),* incongruity, inconsistency, inequality, negation, nonconformity, objection, opposition, paradox, reaction *(opposition),* rejection, repudiation, split, struggle. SEE MAIN ENTRY

disallow ban, bar *(exclude),* censor, condemn *(ban),* constrain *(restrain),* controvert, debar, deny *(contradict),* disaffirm, disapprove *(reject),* dismiss *(put out of consideration),* disown *(deny the validity),* disown *(refuse to acknowledge),* dissent *(withhold assent),* eliminate *(exclude),* enjoin, exclude, forbid, forestall, gainsay, halt, inhibit, interdict, interfere, negate, prohibit, proscribe *(prohibit),* rebuff, refuse, reject, repudiate, restrain, restrict, stop, withhold. SEE MAIN ENTRY

disallow payment dishonor *(refuse to pay)*

disallowance abjuration, constraint *(restriction),* control *(restriction),* countermand, defeasance, denial, disapproval, disclaimer, estoppel, limitation, obstacle, obstruction, prohibition, proscription, refusal, rejection, renunciation, repudiation, restraint, veto. SEE MAIN ENTRY

disallowance of trade embargo

disallowed barred, impermissible, inadmissible, ineligible, unauthorized

disallowing prohibitive *(restrictive)*

disannul abolish, abrogate *(annul),* abrogate *(rescind),* disclaim, disown *(deny the validity),* invalidate, nullify, quash, recall *(call back),* recant, renege, repudiate, rescind, revoke, vacate *(void),* vitiate. SEE MAIN ENTRY

disannulled null *(invalid),* null and void

disannulment mistrial, rescision, retraction

disappear abandon *(physically leave),* abscond, consume, depart, dissipate *(spread out),* escape, evacuate, expire, flee, leave *(depart),* perish, quit *(evacuate),* withdraw. SEE MAIN ENTRY

disappearance absence *(omission),* concealment, erosion, flight, obscuration. SEE MAIN ENTRY

disappearing ephemeral

disappoint fail *(lose),* foil, frustrate. SEE MAIN ENTRY

disappointed SEE MAIN ENTRY

disappointing deficient, inadequate, nonsubstantial *(not sufficient)*, unsatisfactory

disappointment defeat, dissatisfaction, failure *(lack of success)*, miscarriage, misfortune

disapprobation abandonment *(repudiation)*, attaint, bad repute, charge *(accusation)*, condemnation *(blame)*, conflict, constraint *(restriction)*, contempt *(disdain)*, denunciation, disapproval, discredit, disdain, disgrace, dishonor *(shame)*, disparagement, disqualification *(rejection)*, dissatisfaction, exception *(objection)*, ignominy, impugnation, infamy, negation, notoriety, objection, obloquy, opposition, opprobrium, outcry, reaction *(opposition)*, refusal, rejection, renunciation, reprimand, reproach, scandal, stricture. SEE MAIN ENTRY

disapprobatory derogatory, unfavorable

disapproval abandonment *(repudiation)*, blame *(culpability)*, condemnation *(blame)*, contempt *(disdain)*, criticism, denunciation, disapprobation, discredit, disdain, disgrace, disparagement, dissatisfaction, dissent *(nonconcurrence)*, exception *(objection)*, ignominy, ill repute, impeachment, impugnation, infamy, negation, objection, odium, opposition, outcry, protest, rebuff, refusal, rejection, reluctance, renunciation, reprimand, reproach, repudiation, scandal, stricture. SEE MAIN ENTRY

disapprove abrogate *(annul)*, blame, cavil, censor, censure, challenge, complain *(criticize)*, condemn *(ban)*, condemn *(blame)*, conflict, confront *(oppose)*, contemn, counter, criticize *(find fault with)*, decry, demur, denounce *(condemn)*, deprecate, disaccord, disagree, disallow, discommend, disfavor, dissent *(withhold assent)*, enjoin, except *(object)*, expostulate, fault, fight *(counteract)*, forbid, impeach, object, oppose, protest, rebuke, refuse, reject, remonstrate, renounce, reprehend, reprimand, reproach, spurn. SEE MAIN ENTRY

disapprove of decry, discriminate *(treat differently)*, regret

disapproved blameful, disadvantageous, impermissible, inadmissible, inadvisable, ineligible, nonconforming, outmoded, unsatisfactory

disapproving calumnious, contemptuous, critical *(faultfinding)*, cynical, derogatory, disdainful, dissenting, nonconsenting, pejorative, renitent

disarm disable, disqualify, placate, propitiate. SEE MAIN ENTRY

disarmament reconversion

disarmed disabled *(made incapable)*

disarrange agitate *(shake up)*, confuse *(create disorder)*, discompose, dislocate, disorganize, disorient, disrupt, disturb, mismanage, muddle, perturb, upset. SEE MAIN ENTRY

disarranged anomalous, broken *(interrupted)*, deranged, desultory, disjointed, disordered, disorderly, unsettled

disarrangement complex *(entanglement)*, confusion *(turmoil)*, disorder *(lack of order)*, disturbance, embroilment, entanglement *(confusion)*, irregularity, pandemonium

disarray complex *(entanglement)*, confuse *(create disorder)*, confusion *(turmoil)*, disorder *(lack of order)*, pandemonium, snarl

disarry entanglement *(confusion)*

disarticulate disjoint

disarticulated disjunctive *(tending to disjoin)*

disassemble disable, disjoint

disassembly dissolution *(disintegration)*

disassociate depart, disjoint, dissociate, part *(separate)*, remove *(dismiss from office)*, remove *(eliminate)*, seclude, separate, withdraw. SEE MAIN ENTRY

disassociated disconnected, discrete, disjointed, distinct *(distinguished from others)*, remote *(secluded)*, separate. SEE MAIN ENTRY

disassociation division *(act of dividing)*, estrangement, inconsequence, privacy, schism, segregation *(separation)*, separation, severance, split. SEE MAIN ENTRY

disaster abortion *(fiasco)*, accident *(misfortune)*, adversity, calamity, casualty, cataclysm, catastrophe, debacle, fatality, loss, misfortune, tragedy. SEE MAIN ENTRY

disastrous adverse *(negative)*, bad *(offensive)*, dangerous, deadly, deplorable, detrimental, dire, fatal, harmful, hostile, insalubrious, ominous, pernicious, pestilent, regrettable. SEE MAIN ENTRY

disavow controvert, defect, demur, deny *(contradict)*, disaccord, disaffirm, disallow, disapprove *(reject)*, disclaim, disdain, dismiss *(put out of consideration)*, disown *(deny the validity)*, gainsay, negate, recant, refuse, reject, renounce, repudiate, withdraw. SEE MAIN ENTRY

disavowal abandonment *(desertion)*, abandonment *(repudiation)*, abjuration, bad faith, confutation, declination, denial, disclaimer, disdain, dissent *(nonconcurrence)*, negation, refusal, renunciation, repudiation, rescision, retraction, reversal, revocation

disavowing contrary, negative

disavowment renunciation

disband break *(separate)*, degenerate, diffuse, disintegrate, disjoint, disorganize, disperse *(scatter)*, dissociate, dissolve *(separate)*, dissolve *(terminate)*, estrange, separate, sever. SEE MAIN ENTRY

disbanding dissolution *(disintegration)*, release

disbandment decentralization, division *(act of dividing)*

disbar discharge *(dismiss)*, disgrace, dislodge, eliminate *(exclude)*, exclude, remove *(dismiss from office)*, repudiate. SEE MAIN ENTRY

disbarment disqualification *(rejection)*, exclusion, expulsion, ostracism

disbelief cloud *(suspicion)*, discredit, doubt *(suspicion)*, incredulity, rejection, suspicion *(mistrust)*

disbelieve disavow, disclaim, disown *(deny the validity)*, doubt *(distrust)*, impugn, misdoubt, reject, suspect *(distrust)*. SEE MAIN ENTRY

disbelieved unbelievable

disbelieving doubtful, inconvincible, skeptical

disbench disbar

disburden alleviate, clear, disencumber, disentangle, ease, extricate, facilitate, free, relieve *(free from burden)*

disburden one's conscience confess

disburdened clear *(free from criminal charges)*, clear *(unencumbered)*, free *(relieved from a burden)*

disburse administer *(tender)*, defray, manage, pay, remit *(send payment)*, remunerate, spend. SEE MAIN ENTRY

disbursement advance *(allowance)*, amortization, appropriation *(donation)*, charge *(cost)*, collection *(payment)*, commission *(fee)*, consideration *(recompense)*, cost *(expenses)*, expenditure, fee *(charge)*, installment, maintenance *(upkeep)*, outlay, overhead, payment *(act of paying)*, price, reimbursement, remittance. SEE MAIN ENTRY

disbursement of salary payroll

discard abandon *(relinquish)*, cancel, delete, depose *(remove)*, disavow, discharge *(dismiss)*, disclaim, discontinue *(abandon)*, disdain, disinherit, displace *(remove)*, eject *(expel)*, eliminate *(exclude)*, exclusion, expel, forgo, forswear, ignore, jettison, leave *(allow to remain)*, omit, override, quash, rebuff, reject, relegate, removal, renounce, renunciation, repudiate, rescind, revoke, screen *(select)*, set aside *(annul)*, spurn, supersede. SEE MAIN ENTRY

discarded derelict *(abandoned)*, obsolete, outdated, outmoded

discarding desuetude, layoff, release

discardure rejection

discarnate intangible

discedere depart, leave *(depart)*

discept contend *(dispute)*, debate, differ *(vary)*, disaccord, dispute *(debate)*

disceptare arbitrate *(conciliate)*, discuss, dispute *(debate)*, parley

disceptatio controversy *(argument)*, dispute

disceptation contest *(dispute)*, controversy *(argument)*, rift *(disagreement)*

disceptator arbiter, arbitrator, umpire

discern appreciate *(comprehend)*, apprehend *(perceive)*, comprehend *(understand)*, conceive *(comprehend)*, construe *(comprehend)*, detect, diagnose, discover, distinguish, find *(discover)*, judge, locate, note *(notice)*, notice *(observe)*, perceive, read, realize *(understand)*, recognize *(perceive)*, secern, spy, understand. SEE MAIN ENTRY

discern between differentiate

discern something audible hear *(perceive by ear)*

discernere discriminate *(distinguish)*

discernible apparent *(perceptible)*, appreciable, ascertainable, blatant *(conspicuous)*, cognizable, coherent *(clear)*, conspicuous, determinable *(ascertainable)*, evident, manifest, naked *(perceptible)*, obvious, open *(in sight)*, ostensible, palpable, perceivable, perceptible, ponderable, prominent, visible *(noticeable)*. SEE MAIN ENTRY

discernible by touch tangible

discernibly fairly *(clearly)*

discerning acute, circumspect, cognizant, conscious *(aware)*, discreet, discriminating *(judicious)*, incisive, judicious, juridical, lucid, omniscient, perceptive, perspicacious, provident *(showing foresight)*, rational, reasonable *(rational)*, responsive, sapient, sensible, subtle *(refined)*. SEE MAIN ENTRY

discernment alternative *(option)*, appreciation *(perception)*, apprehension *(perception)*, caliber *(mental capacity)*, cognition, comprehension, conclusion *(determination)*, diagnosis, discovery, discretion *(quality of being discreet)*, discrimination *(good judgment)*, insight, knowledge *(awareness)*, notice *(heed)*, perception, realization, reason *(sound judgment)*, sagacity, scienter, sense *(feeling)*, sensibility, understanding *(comprehension)*, vision *(dream)*. SEE MAIN ENTRY

discerp lancinate, rend
discerpted disjointed
discerption disassociation, split
discharge absolution, absolve, accomplish, acquit, acquittal, action *(performance)*, amnesty, amortization, banishment, bear the expense, clear, collection *(payment)*, commission *(act)*, commit *(perpetrate)*, complete, composition *(agreement in bankruptcy)*, conclude *(complete)*, condonation, conduct, defeasance, defray, depose *(remove)*, disband, disburse *(distribute)*, disclaim, disenthrall, dislodge, dispel, displace *(remove)*, disqualification *(rejection)*, divest, egress, eject *(expel)*, emancipation, emit, excuse, execute *(accomplish)*, exemption, exonerate, exoneration, expel, expenditure, expulsion, extricate, exude, free, freedom, fulfill, immunity, implement, issuance, keep *(fulfill)*, layoff, liberate, liberation, liquidate *(determine liability)*, observe *(obey)*, operate, outburst, outflow, outpour, output, palliate *(excuse)*, pardon *(noun)*, pardon *(verb)*, parole *(noun)*, parole *(verb)*, payoff *(payment in full)*, perform *(execute)*, precipitate *(throw down violently)*, project *(impel forward)*, purge *(purify)*, quit *(free of)*, receipt *(proof of receiving)*, recovery *(award)*, rejection, release *(noun)*, release *(verb)*, relief *(release)*, remission, remit *(release from penalty)*, remit *(send payment)*, removal, remove *(dismiss from office)*, remunerate, respite *(reprieve)*, retire *(retreat)*, satisfaction *(discharge of debt)*, send, settlement, supplant, suspend, transact, vindicate, waiver. SEE MAIN ENTRY
discharge a debt compensate *(remunerate)*, pay, quit *(repay)*
discharge a duty perform *(execute)*
discharge a function officiate
discharge a liability liquidate *(determine liability)*
discharge debts liquidate *(determine liability)*
discharge from accusation acquit
discharge from employment dismissal *(discharge)*
discharge from office depose *(remove)*
discharge in advance prepay
discharge of a debt expense *(cost)*, payment *(act of paying)*
discharge of emotions catharsis
discharge of responsibility exonerate
discharge one's duty serve *(assist)*
discharge the duties of commit *(perpetrate)*
discharged clear *(free from criminal charges)*, exempt, free *(relieved from a burden)*, fully executed *(consummated)*
discidium divorce, estrangement
disciple addict, amateur, novice, partisan, protégé. SEE MAIN ENTRY
disciplina discipline *(obedience)*
disciplinarian dictator
disciplinary penal, punitive. SEE MAIN ENTRY
disciplinary action condemnation *(punishment)*, correction *(punishment)*, penalty, punishment, reprisal, sanction *(punishment)*
discipline castigate, comport *(behave)*, condemn *(punish)*, control *(supervision)*, correction *(punishment)*, criterion, edify, educate, force *(compulsion)*, inculcate, labor *(exertion)*, method, moderate *(preside over)*, penalize, practice *(train by repetition)*, punish, punishment, regulate *(manage)*, regulation *(rule)*, reprisal, restraint,

rigor, sanction *(punishment)*, science *(study)*, subdue. SEE MAIN ENTRY
disciplined controlled *(restrained)*, literate, spartan, strict, systematic, veteran
discipulus disciple
disclaim answer *(reply)*, cancel, contradict, controvert, deny *(contradict)*, deprecate, disaccord, disaffirm, disallow, disapprove *(reject)*, disavow, disdain, disinherit, disown *(deny the validity)*, disown *(refuse to acknowledge)*, forswear, gainsay, ignore, negate, protest, recant, refuse, refute, reject, relinquish, renounce, repudiate, resign, revoke, surrender *(give back)*, waive. SEE MAIN ENTRY
disclaim the responsibility for disown *(refuse to acknowledge)*
disclaimer abjuration, declination, denial, dissent *(nonconcurrence)*, negation, refusal, renunciation, repudiation, rescision. SEE MAIN ENTRY
disclaiming contradictory
disclamation abjuration, ademption, denial, disclaimer, disdain, repudiation
disclose acknowledge *(declare)*, adduce, admit *(concede)*, apprise, bare, communicate, confess, confide *(divulge)*, construe *(translate)*, convey *(communicate)*, declare, denude, disabuse, display, divulge, enlighten, evidence, exhibit, expose, express, find *(discover)*, impart, inform *(betray)*, inform *(notify)*, issue *(publish)*, manifest, mention, notice *(give formal warning)*, notify, present *(introduce)*, produce *(offer to view)*, profess *(avow)*, promulgate, publish, relate *(tell)*, reveal, signify *(inform)*, speak, specify, unveil, utter. SEE MAIN ENTRY
disclose intentionally inform *(betray)*
disclose secrets inform *(betray)*
disclose something secret confide *(divulge)*
disclosed comprehensible, evident, manifest, naked *(perceptible)*, overt, palpable, patent, pellucid, perceivable, perceptible, public *(known)*
disclosed judgment cognovit
disclosing disclosure *(act of disclosing)*, informative, informatory
disclosure assertion, common knowledge, communication *(statement)*, confession, denouement, deposition, detection, discovery, divulgation, exhibit, expression *(manifestation)*, identification, manifestation, notice *(announcement)*, notification, profession *(declaration)*, publicity, report *(detailed account)*, testimony. SEE MAIN ENTRY
disclosure of fault confession
disclosure proceedings discovery
discolor stain, tarnish
discoloration defacement
discolored blemished, marred
discomfit beat *(defeat)*, discompose, disconcert, disturb, embarrass, overcome *(overwhelm)*, overwhelm, perturb, subdue, upset
discomfiture confusion *(ambiguity)*, disturbance, embarrassment
discomfort agitate *(perturb)*, badger, discompose, disconcert, disease, dissatisfaction, distress *(anguish)*, embarrass, embarrassment, nuisance, pain, trouble
discomforting painful
discommend blame, denounce *(condemn)*, deprecate, disapprove *(condemn)*, fault, lessen, reprimand. SEE MAIN ENTRY
discommendable blameful

discommendation bad repute, criticism, defamation, denunciation, diatribe, disapprobation, disapproval, exception *(objection)*, ignominy, impeachment, revilement
discommode annoy, badger, bait *(harass)*, condemn *(ban)*, deter, disadvantage, discompose, disoblige, encumber *(hinder)*, hinder, inconvenience, molest *(annoy)*, plague, trammel. SEE MAIN ENTRY
discommodious detrimental
discommodity disadvantage, handicap
discompose annoy, badger, confuse *(bewilder)*, disconcert, disorganize, disorient, disrupt, distress, disturb, embarrass, harass, harrow, harry *(harass)*, incense, irritate, muddle, obsess, perplex, perturb, pique, plague, provoke, upset. SEE MAIN ENTRY
discomposed disordered, disorderly
discomposure disorder *(lack of order)*, distress *(anguish)*, disturbance, embarrassment, pandemonium, panic
disconcert affront, agitate *(perturb)*, badger, confuse *(bewilder)*, counteract, discommode, discompose, disorganize, disorient, disturb, embarrass, frustrate, harrow, harry *(harass)*, menace, muddle, obfuscate, obsess, perplex, perturb, upset. SEE MAIN ENTRY
disconcerted deranged
disconcerting enigmatic
disconcertion ambiguity, confusion *(ambiguity)*, disturbance, quandary, trepidation
disconformity exception *(exclusion)*, incompatibility *(inconsistency)*, nonconformity, specialty *(distinctive mark)*
discongruity controversy *(argument)*, deviation, difference, disaccord, discord, discrepancy, dissidence, distinction *(difference)*, diversity, incompatibility *(inconsistency)*, variance *(disagreement)*
disconnect break *(separate)*, detach, dichotomize, disband, discontinue *(abandon)*, discontinue *(break continuity)*, disengage, disentangle, disjoint, dislocate, dissociate, dissolve *(separate)*, divide *(separate)*, estrange, interrupt, isolate, luxate, part *(separate)*, remove *(eliminate)*, separate, sever, split
disconnectable divisible
disconnected alien *(unrelated)*, apart, bipartite, broken *(interrupted)*, desultory, discrete, discursive *(digressive)*, disjunctive *(tending to disjoin)*, foreign, impertinent *(irrelevant)*, independent, separate, sporadic. SEE MAIN ENTRY
disconnectedness anacoluthon, non sequitur
disconnection difference, disassociation, division *(act of dividing)*, estrangement, hiatus, incoherence, inconsequence, interruption, pause, schism, segregation *(separation)*, split
disconsolate despondent, lugubrious, pessimistic. SEE MAIN ENTRY
disconsolation pessimism
discontent disapprobation, disparagement, dissatisfaction, dissent *(nonconcurrence)*, exception *(objection)*, grievance, ill will, outcry, plaint, resentment, trouble
discontented disappointed, dissident, insatiable, jealous, nonconsenting, querulous, reluctant, resentful, restive
discontentedness dissatisfaction
discontenting deficient
discontentment dissatisfaction

discontinu discrete

discontinuance abatement *(extinguishment)*, abeyance, abolition, ademption, annulment, cancellation, cessation *(interlude)*, close *(conclusion)*, cloture, defeasance, desuetude, discharge *(annulment)*, dismissal *(termination of a proceeding)*, dissolution *(termination)*, disuse, expiration, extremity *(death)*, halt, impasse, interruption, layoff, lull, moratorium, remission, renunciation, stay. SEE MAIN ENTRY

discontinuance of activity impasse

discontinuance of business failure *(bankruptcy)*

discontinuation abandonment *(discontinuance)*, abeyance, adjournment, avoidance *(cancellation)*, cessation *(interlude)*, close *(conclusion)*, cloture, disassociation, discontinuance *(act of discontinuing)*, discontinuance *(interruption of a legal action)*, disuse, expiration, extremity *(death)*, halt, impasse, layoff, lull

discontinue abandon *(relinquish)*, abate *(extinguish)*, abolish, annul, cancel, cease, close *(terminate)*, conclude *(complete)*, continue *(adjourn)*, defer *(put off)*, desist, discharge *(release from obligation)*, disrupt, dissolve *(terminate)*, expire, finish, forgo, forswear, halt, interrupt, lapse *(cease)*, negate, palliate *(abate)*, pause, refrain, relinquish, rest *(cease from action)*, shut, stay *(halt)*, stop, suspend, terminate. SEE MAIN ENTRY

discontinue work strike *(refuse to work)*

discontinued obsolete, old

discontinuity anacoluthon, deviation, difference, disturbance, hiatus, incoherence, irregularity, non sequitur, pendency

discontinuous broken *(interrupted)*, desultory, disconnected, discrete, disordered, disorderly, infrequent, intermittent, sporadic

discord anarchy, argument *(contention)*, belligerency, collision *(dispute)*, conflict, confrontation *(altercation)*, confusion *(turmoil)*, contend *(dispute)*, contention *(argument)*, contention *(opposition)*, contest *(dispute)*, contradiction, contravention, controversy *(argument)*, deviation, difference, disaccord, disagree, disagreement, discrepancy, disparity, dispute, dissension, dissent *(difference of opinion)*, dissidence, division *(act of dividing)*, estrangement, faction, feud, fight *(argument)*, fracas, impugnation, incompatibility *(difference)*, incompatibility *(inconsistency)*, inconsistency, noise, schism, strife, trouble, turmoil, umbrage, variance *(disagreement)*. SEE MAIN ENTRY

discordance conflict, controversy *(argument)*, difference, disaccord, disagreement, disapproval, discord, discrepancy, disparity, dissension, dissent *(difference of opinion)*, dissidence, incompatibility *(difference)*, incompatibility *(inconsistency)*, incongruity, inconsistency

discordancy disaccord, disagreement, dissidence, incompatibility *(inconsistency)*, incongruity, inconsistency

discordant adverse *(hostile)*, argumentative, competitive *(antagonistic)*, contentious, contradictory, contrary, deviant, different, disjointed, disparate, disproportionate, dissenting, dissident, dissimilar, divisive, harsh, hostile, improper, inapplicable, inapposite, inappropriate, inapt, incommensurate, incongruous, inconsistent, inept *(inappropriate)*, litigious, negative,

nonconforming, opposite, peculiar *(distinctive)*, polemic, recusant, repugnant *(incompatible)*, unsuitable. SEE MAIN ENTRY

discordia discord, dissension, variance *(disagreement)*

discors discordant

discount brokerage, deduct *(reduce)*, deduction *(diminution)*, depreciate, discredit, disparage, drawback, except *(exclude)*, exclude, lessen, minimize, rebate *(noun)*, rebate *(verb)*, refund, reject. SEE MAIN ENTRY

discountable deductible *(capable of being deducted from taxes)*

discountenance bad repute, blame, censor, condemn *(ban)*, condemn *(blame)*, condemnation *(blame)*, denounce *(condemn)*, denunciation, deter, disapprobation, disapproval, disapprove *(condemn)*, disclaim, disconcert, discount *(disbelieve)*, discourage, disfavor, dismiss *(put out of consideration)*, enjoin, except *(object)*, fault, forbid, forswear, protest, reaction *(opposition)*, refusal, refuse, renounce, restrain

discountenancing disdain

discounting mitigating

discourage browbeat, check *(restrain)*, debar, depress, deter, disappoint, dissuade, expostulate, forbid, forewarn, frustrate, hinder, preclude, prevent, remonstrate. SEE MAIN ENTRY

discouraged arrested *(checked)*, disappointed, disconsolate, lugubrious, pessimistic

discouragement damper *(depressant)*, damper *(stopper)*, deterrence, deterrent, disadvantage, disincentive, dissatisfaction, hindrance, impediment, pessimism, prohibition, rebuff, remonstrance

discouraging chilling effect, remonstrative, unfavorable

discourse address *(talk to)*, charge *(statement to the jury)*, conversation, converse, declaim, declamation, discuss, instruction *(teaching)*, narration, pandect *(treatise)*, parlance, peroration, recital, recite, rhetoric *(skilled speech)*, speak, speech. SEE MAIN ENTRY

discourse about deliberate, discuss

discourse at length outpour

discourse designed to convince argument *(pleading)*

discourse on the law hornbook

discourse upon comment

discourse with communicate

discourteous contemptuous, disdainful, disorderly, impertinent *(insolent)*, insolent, offensive *(offending)*, pejorative, perverse, presumptuous, uncouth

discourteousness disrespect

discourtesy contumely, disparagement, disregard *(lack of respect)*, disrespect, rebuff

discover ascertain, detect, discern *(detect with the senses)*, disinter, educe, expose, ferret, initiate, invent *(produce for the first time)*, locate, manifest, note *(notice)*, notice *(observe)*, perceive, pierce *(discern)*, recognize *(perceive)*, solve, spy. SEE MAIN ENTRY

discover by artifice spy

discover by observation apprehend *(perceive)*

discover by search locate

discover by survey locate

discover the location of locate

discover the place of locate

discoverable appreciable, ascertainable, cognizable, conspicuous, determinable *(ascertainable)*, naked *(perceptible)*, obvious, open *(in sight)*, palpable, patent, perceivable, perceptible, ponderable, provable, scrutable, solvable

discoverer author *(originator)*, pioneer

discovery detection, disclosure *(something disclosed)*, invention, manifestation, observation, origination, perception, realization, recognition. SEE MAIN ENTRY

discredit attaint, bad character, bad repute, brand *(stigmatize)*, cavil, cite *(accuse)*, condemnation *(blame)*, contemn, debase, decry, defame, degradation, demean *(make lower)*, denounce *(condemn)*, deprecate, depreciate, derogate, disaccord, disallow, disapprove *(condemn)*, disavow, disbelieve, discommend, discount *(disbelieve)*, disfavor, disgrace *(noun)*, disgrace *(verb)*, dishonor *(shame)*, dishonor *(deprive of honor)*, disparage, disprove, doubt *(suspicion)*, doubt *(distrust)*, humiliate, ignominy, impeach, impeachability, impugn, incredulity, infamy, lessen, libel, negate, notoriety, obloquy, onus *(stigma)*, opprobrium, pillory, refuse, refute, reject, reproach *(noun)*, reproach *(verb)*, scandal, shame, smear, stain, sully, tarnish, underestimate. SEE MAIN ENTRY

discredit in writing libel

discreditable arrant *(onerous)*, blameful, blameworthy, calumnious, contemptible, culpable, disgraceful, dishonest, disreputable, fraudulent, ignoble, libelous, nefarious, notorious, reprehensible, scandalous, unjustifiable, unseemly

discreditableness bad character, disrepute, ignominy

discredited blameful, blameworthy, blemished, disreputable

discrediting derogatory, libelous, rejection

discreet careful, circumspect, diplomatic, guarded, judicious, noncommittal, politic, provident *(showing foresight)*, prudent, sensible, subtle *(refined)*. SEE MAIN ENTRY

discreetness discretion *(quality of being discreet)*, discrimination *(good judgment)*

discrepance inequality

discrepancy conflict, deviation, difference, disaccord, disagreement, discord, disparity, distinction *(difference)*, incompatibility *(inconsistency)*, incongruity, inconsistency, inequality, paradox, variance *(disagreement)*. SEE MAIN ENTRY

discrepans different, discordant

discrepant contradictory, deviant, different, discordant, disparate, disproportionate, dissenting, dissident, dissimilar, distinct *(distinguished from others)*, divergent, diverse, divisive, improper, inapplicable, inapposite, inappropriate, inapt, incommensurate, incongruous, inconsistent, inept *(inappropriate)*, peculiar *(distinctive)*, polemic, unrelated, unsuitable. SEE MAIN ENTRY

discrepantia contradiction, difference, disagreement, diversity

discrepare conflict, contrast, differ *(vary)*, disagree

discrete disconnected, disjunctive *(tending to disjoin)*, distinct *(distinguished from others)*, individual, insular. SEE MAIN ENTRY

discretion alternative *(option)*, call *(option)*, choice *(alternatives offered)*, diagnosis, discrimination *(good judgment)*, franchise *(right to vote)*, latitude, option *(choice)*, preference *(choice)*, prudence, reason *(sound judgment)*, referendum, volition. SEE MAIN ENTRY

discretional adoptive, discreet, discretionary, disjunctive *(alternative)*, permissive, spontaneous

discretionary circumspect, discreet, disjunctive *(alternative)*, elective *(voluntary)*, judicious, juridical, spontaneous, voluntary. SEE MAIN ENTRY

discretionary order call *(option)*

discretive discrete

discrimen danger, discrimination *(differentiation)*, distinction *(difference)*, emergency, risk

discriminate call *(title)*, choose, contrast, demarcate, designate, differentiate, discreet, discriminating *(distinguishing)*, distinct *(distinguished from others)*, distinguish, except *(exclude)*, identify, perceive, screen *(select)*, secern, select. SEE MAIN ENTRY

discriminate between choose, compare

discriminating circumspect, cognizant, discreet, distinctive, judicious, juridical, lucid, particular *(exacting)*, perceptive, perspicacious, preferential, prudent, rational, sapient, scrupulous, sensible, sensitive *(discerning)*, subtle *(refined)*. SEE MAIN ENTRY

discriminating judgment diagnosis, perception

discriminating taste discretion *(quality of being discreet)*

discriminatingness particularity

discrimination alternative *(option)*, caliber *(mental capacity)*, choice *(alternatives offered)*, decorum, diagnosis, difference *(difference)*, discretion *(power of choice)*, discretion *(quality of being discreet)*, distinction *(difference)*, expedience, favoritism, inequity, insight, intolerance, judgment *(discernment)*, nuance, partiality, particularity, perception, prejudice *(preconception)*, propriety *(correctness)*, prudence, reason *(sound judgment)*, sagacity, segregation *(isolation by races)*, sensibility, severance. SEE MAIN ENTRY

discriminative aesthetic, circumspect, discreet, discretionary, juridical, particular *(exacting)*, perceptive, personal *(individual)*, perspicacious, preferential, scrupulous, sensitive *(discerning)*

discriminatory inequitable, one-sided, partial *(biased)*. SEE MAIN ENTRY

discriminatory powers discretion *(quality of being discreet)*

discrown demote

disculpate palliate *(excuse)*

disculpated clear *(free from criminal charges)*

disculpation amnesty, release

discursive circuitous, comprehensive, desultory, forensic, profuse, prolix, shifting, voluble. SEE MAIN ENTRY

discursive faculties judgment *(discernment)*

discursive reasoning dialectic

discuss address *(talk to)*, canvass, comment, confer *(consult)*, consult *(ask advice of)*, controvert, converse, counsel, debate, deliberate, discourse, investigate, mention, reason *(persuade)*, remark, respond, treat *(process)*. SEE MAIN ENTRY

discuss in the abstract generalize

discuss private affairs confide *(divulge)*

discussant disputant

discussion caucus, conference, confrontation *(act of setting face to face)*, conversation,

deliberation, discourse, interview, meeting *(conference)*, negotiation, pandect *(treatise)*, parley

discutere breach, dispel

disdain affront, condemn *(blame)*, condemnation *(blame)*, condescend *(patronize)*, contemn, contumely, criticism, debunk, decry, deprecate, disapprobation, disapproval, disavow, discount *(disbelieve)*, disfavor, disinterest *(lack of interest)*, disoblige, disown *(refuse to acknowledge)*, disregard *(lack of respect)*, disrespect, eliminate *(exclude)*, exclude, flout, forswear, ignore, misprize, neglect, rebuff, reject, rejection, renounce, ridicule, spurn. SEE MAIN ENTRY

disdainful blameworthy, contemptuous, cynical, derogatory, hostile, impertinent *(insolent)*, inflated *(vain)*, insolent, offensive *(offending)*, orgulous, pejorative, presumptuous, proud *(conceited)*, supercilious, unaffected *(uninfluenced)*. SEE MAIN ENTRY

disdainfulness contempt *(disdain)*, contumely

disease contaminate, disorder *(abnormal condition)*, pain, taint *(contaminate)*. SEE MAIN ENTRY

disease-ridden pestilent

diseased peccant *(unhealthy)*, pestilent, tainted *(contaminated)*, unsound *(not strong)*

diseased in mind non compos mentis

diseased mind insanity, paranoia

disembark alight

disembarrass extricate

disembarrassed free *(relieved from a burden)*

disembodied disconnected, intangible

disembodied spirit phantom

disembody disband

disembogue exude, outpour

disemboguement outflow

disembowel eviscerate

disembroil clear, disencumber, disengage, disentangle, extricate, free, liberate, quit *(free of)*

disembroiling liberation

disemploy depose *(remove)*, discharge *(dismiss)*, dislodge, dismiss *(discharge)*

disemployment dismissal *(discharge)*, layoff, removal

disenable disable, disarm *(divest of arms)*, disqualify, neutralize

disenabled disabled *(deprived of legal right)*, disabled *(made incapable)*

disenablement incapacity

disenact recant

disenchant debunk, deter, disaffect, disappoint, discourage, dissuade

disenchanted disappointed

disencourage deter

disencumber clear, disengage, disentangle, dissociate, ease, extricate, facilitate, free, quit *(free of)*, relieve *(free from burden)*. SEE MAIN ENTRY

disencumberance relief *(release)*

disencumbered clear *(unencumbered)*, free *(relieved from a burden)*

disendow deprive, disinherit, disown *(refuse to acknowledge)*, dispossess, divest. SEE MAIN ENTRY

disendowment defeasance, disseisin

disenfranchise disable

disenfranchisement forfeiture *(act of forfeiting)*, subjection

disengage abstract *(separate)*, break *(separate)*, depart, detach, disband, discontinue

(break continuity), disencumber, disentangle, disenthrall, disjoint, dissociate, dissolve *(separate)*, divide *(separate)*, extricate, free, isolate, liberate, luxate, part *(separate)*, quit *(free of)*, release, relieve *(free from burden)*, retreat, separate, sever, withdraw. SEE MAIN ENTRY

disengaged apart, bipartite, controlled *(restrained)*, discrete, dispassionate, free *(not restricted)*, free *(relieved from a burden)*, idle, neutral, nonpartisan, otiose, unemployed, vacant

disengagement disassociation, division *(act of dividing)*, estrangement, evulsion, exemption, freedom, liberation, release, segregation *(separation)*, split

disengaging divisive

disentail disencumber

disentangle ascertain, break *(separate)*, clarify, clear, construe *(comprehend)*, detach, disencumber, disengage, elucidate, explain, extricate, facilitate, find *(discover)*, free, part *(separate)*, quit *(free of)*, resolve *(solve)*, simplify *(make easier)*, solve, sort. SEE MAIN ENTRY

disentangled free *(relieved from a burden)*

disentanglement denouement, release

disenthrall disengage, enfranchise, extricate, free, liberate, release, rescue. SEE MAIN ENTRY

disenthrallment discharge *(liberation)*, freedom, liberation, release

disenthrone dislodge

disentitle condemn *(seize)*, confiscate, depose *(remove)*, deprive, disinherit, dispossess, disqualify, divest, impress *(procure by force)*

disentitled ineligible

disentitlement denial, disqualification *(rejection)*, foreclosure, forfeiture *(act of forfeiting)*

disentomb disinter

disequalization discrimination *(differentiation)*

disequilibrium difference, disparity

disertus eloquent, specific

disestablish abolish, annul, cancel, depose *(remove)*, dislodge, quash, rescind, subvert, withdraw

disestablished null *(invalid)*, null and void

disestablishment annulment, defeasance, subversion

disesteem attaint, bad character, bad repute, contemn, contempt *(disdain)*, decry, depreciate, disapprobation, disapproval, discount *(disbelieve)*, discredit, disdain *(noun)*, disdain *(verb)*, disgrace, dishonor *(shame)*, disparage, disparagement, disregard *(lack of respect)*, disrepute, disrespect, dissatisfaction, ignominy, ill repute, infamy, malign, misprize, notoriety, obloquy, odium, opprobrium, scandal, shame, underestimate

disfavor alienation *(estrangement)*, bad character, bad repute, condemn *(ban)*, condemnation *(blame)*, contempt *(disdain)*, deprecate, disaffect, disapprobation, disapproval, disapprove *(condemn)*, discommend, discredit, discriminate *(treat differently)*, disdain, disgrace, dishonor *(shame)*, disparage, disparagement, disqualification *(rejection)*, disregard *(lack of respect)*, dissatisfaction, estrangement, ignominy, ill repute, impugnation, infamy, notoriety, obloquy, odium, proscription, rejection, reluctance, shame. SEE MAIN ENTRY

disfiguration defacement
disfigure damage, deface, harm, mutilate, spoil *(impair)*
disfigured blemished, imperfect, marred
disfigurement defacement, flaw
disfranchise disable, disqualify, subject. SEE MAIN ENTRY
disfranchisement disqualification *(rejection)*, infringement, subjection
disfurnish denude
disgorge eject *(expel)*, forfeit, outpour
disgorgement expulsion, outburst
disgrace attaint, bad character, bad repute, brand, brand *(stigmatize)*, corruption, debase, defame, defilement, degradation, demean *(make lower)*, depreciate, derogate, discredit *(noun)*, discredit *(verb)*, dishonor *(shame)*, dishonor *(deprive of honor)*, disparage, humiliate, ignominy, ill repute, infamy, notoriety, obloquy, odium, onus *(stigma)*, opprobrium, pillory, reduce, reproach *(noun)*, reproach *(verb)*, scandal, shame, stain, stigma, sully, tarnish. SEE MAIN ENTRY
disgraced bad *(offensive)*, blemished, disreputable
disgraceful arrant *(onerous)*, contemptible, disorderly, disreputable, heinous, ignoble, inexcusable, inexpiable, nefarious, notorious, odious, outrageous, profligate *(corrupt)*, recreant, reprehensible, scandalous, vicious. SEE MAIN ENTRY
disgracefulness bad repute, disrepute
disgracing libelous
disgruntle disappoint, discourage
disgruntled disappointed
disgruntlement dissatisfaction
disguise artifice, camouflage, cloak, clothe, conceal, concealment, cover *(pretext)*, cover *(conceal)*, deception, decoy, denature, distort, distortion, ensconce, enshroud, equivocate, fake, false pretense, falsification, feign, hide, misrepresent, obnubilate, obscure, palter, plant *(covertly place)*, pretend, pretense *(pretext)*, pretext, profess *(pretend)*, ruse, screen *(guard)*. SEE MAIN ENTRY
disguised assumed *(feigned)*, blind *(concealed)*, clandestine, covert, deceptive, hidden, indiscernible, mysterious, surreptitious
disguisement concealment
disgust contempt *(disdain)*, dissatisfaction, distress, odium, pique
disgusted renitent
disgustful repugnant *(exciting aversion)*
disgusting antipathetic *(distasteful)*, bad *(offensive)*, contemptible, gross *(flagrant)*, heinous, loathsome, lurid, objectionable, obnoxious, odious, offensive *(offending)*, reprehensible, reprobate, repugnant *(exciting aversion)*, repulsive, scurrilous, sordid, unsavory
disharmonious dissenting, divergent, incongruous
disharmonize disaccord
disharmony conflict, contention *(opposition)*, contest *(dispute)*, controversy *(argument)*, deviation, difference, disaccord, disagreement, discord, discrepancy, disorder *(lack of order)*, disparity, dissension, dissent *(difference of opinion)*, dissidence, distinction *(difference)*, division *(act of dividing)*, estrangement, incompatibility *(inconsistency)*, incongruity, pandemonium, variance *(disagreement)*
dishearten deter, disappoint, discommode, discourage, dissuade

disheartened disconsolate, lugubrious, pessimistic
disheartener damper *(depressant)*
disheartening bleak *(not favorable)*, deplorable, disastrous, lamentable
disheartenment depression, pessimism
disherit deprive, disinherit
dishevel agitate *(shake up)*, discompose, disorganize, disrupt, disturb
disheveled disordered, disorderly
dishevelment disorder *(lack of order)*, disturbance
dishonest culpable, deceptive, delinquent *(guilty of a misdeed)*, disgraceful, disingenuous, disreputable, faithless, false *(disloyal)*, felonious, fraudulent, ignoble, immoral, iniquitous, insidious, irregular *(improper)*, larcenous, lying, machiavellian, mendacious, peccant *(culpable)*, perfidious, recreant, sinister, sly, tainted *(corrupted)*, tortuous *(corrupt)*, unconscionable, undependable, unethical, unscrupulous, untrue, untrustworthy. SEE MAIN ENTRY
dishonest application misapplication
dishonest management misconduct
dishonest use misapplication
dishonesty abuse *(corrupt practice)*, bad faith, corruption, deception, false pretense, fraud, guilt, hypocrisy, improbity, indirection *(deceitfulness)*, knavery, misdoing, pettifoggery, racket. SEE MAIN ENTRY
dishonor abuse *(physical misuse)*, abuse *(violate)*, aspersion, attaint, bad character, bad faith, bad repute, brand *(stigmatize)*, browbeat, contemn, contumely, corruption, debase, defame, default, defilement, degradation, demean *(make lower)*, denigrate, denounce *(condemn)*, derogate, discredit *(noun)*, discredit *(verb)*, disfavor, disgrace *(noun)*, disgrace *(verb)*, dishonesty, disoblige, disparage, disparagement, disregard *(lack of respect)*, disrepute, disrespect, fail *(lose)*, humiliate, ignominy, ill repute, impeachability, infamy, infidelity, malign, nonpayment, notoriety, obloquy, odium, onus *(stigma)*, opprobrium, pillory, pollute, reproach *(noun)*, reproach *(verb)*, repudiate, scandal, shame, smear, stain, stigma, sully, tarnish, violate. SEE MAIN ENTRY
dishonor by false reports malign
dishonorable bad *(offensive)*, blameful, blameworthy, contemptible, contemptuous, disgraceful, dishonest, disreputable, faithless, false *(disloyal)*, fraudulent, ignoble, immoral, libelous, machiavellian, nefarious, notorious, outrageous, perfidious, recreant, reprehensible, scandalous, sly, tortuous *(corrupt)*, unbecoming, unconscionable, unethical, unjust, unjustifiable, unscrupulous, untrustworthy, venal
dishonorableness bad character, bad repute, disrepute, ignominy
dishonored blemished
dishonored bill bad debt, nonpayment
dishonoring abuse *(physical misuse)*, contemptuous, default, derogatory, libelous
disillusion debunk, disabuse, disaffect, disappoint, discourage, dissuade
disillusioned cynical, disappointed
disillusionize disappoint
disillusionment disparagement
disimprison liberate, parole, rescue
disimprisonment freedom, liberation
disincentive deterrence, deterrent. SEE MAIN ENTRY
disinclination bias, disincentive, reluctance

disinclination to action sloth
disinclination to labor sloth
disincline deter, discourage, expostulate
disinclined adverse *(hostile)*, averse, dissident, reluctant, renitent, restive. SEE MAIN ENTRY
disinfect decontaminate
disinfectant preventive
disinfected pure
disingenuity improbity, indirection *(deceitfulness)*
disingenuous deceptive, dishonest, fraudulent, lying, machiavellian, oblique *(evasive)*, sinister, tortuous *(corrupt)*, unconscionable, unscrupulous, untrue. SEE MAIN ENTRY
disingenuousness bad faith, color *(deceptive appearance)*, dishonesty, evasion, improbity, indirection *(deceitfulness)*
disingeuous sly
disinherit adeem, confiscate, deprive, disown *(refuse to acknowledge)*, reject. SEE MAIN ENTRY
disinheritance rejection, renunciation
disinhume disinter
disintegrate break *(separate)*, decay, degenerate, destroy *(efface)*, diffuse, disorganize, dispel, disperse *(scatter)*, dissipate *(spread out)*, dissolve *(disperse)*, erode, obliterate. SEE MAIN ENTRY
disintegrated broken *(fractured)*, old
disintegrating decadent
disintegration attrition, decentralization, deterioration, detriment, erosion, spoilage
disinter detect, ferret, find *(discover)*, solve. SEE MAIN ENTRY
disinterest discourage, disregard *(unconcern)*, neutrality, objectivity. SEE MAIN ENTRY
disinterested dispassionate, equitable, evenhanded, factual, impartial, judicial, just, neutral, objective, open-minded, perfunctory, phlegmatic, torpid, unbiased, unprejudiced
disinterestedly fairly *(impartially)*
disinterestedness candor *(impartiality)*, disinterest *(lack of interest)*, disregard *(unconcern)*, fairness, indifference, neutrality, objectivity
disinterestness candor *(impartiality)*
disinvigorate disarm *(divest of arms)*
disinvolve disentangle. SEE MAIN ENTRY
disiunctio separation
disiunctus separate
disiungere detach, divide *(separate)*, separate
disjoin abstract *(separate)*, break *(separate)*, depart, detach, dichotomize, disband, discontinue *(abandon)*, discontinue *(break continuity)*, disencumber, disengage, disentangle, disjoint, dislocate, disorganize, disperse *(scatter)*, disrupt, dissociate, dissolve *(separate)*, divide *(separate)*, divorce, excise *(cut away)*, extricate, interrupt, isolate, luxate, part *(separate)*, remove *(eliminate)*, separate, sever, split. SEE MAIN ENTRY
disjoined alien *(unrelated)*, apart, bipartite, desultory, disconnected, discrete, disjunctive *(tending to disjoin)*, divisive, individual, separate, solitary
disjoining decentralization
disjoint apart, disband, discrete, disjunctive *(tending to disjoin)*, dislocate, force *(break)*, luxate. SEE MAIN ENTRY
disjointed apart, bipartite, deranged, disconnected, disjunctive *(tending to disjoin)*, disorderly, separate. SEE MAIN ENTRY
disjointure disassociation

disjunct anomalous, apart, bipartite, broken *(interrupted)*, desultory, disconnected, discrete, disordered, individual, separate, solitary, sporadic

disjunction abandonment *(discontinuance)*, decentralization, difference, disassociation, division *(act of dividing)*, estrangement, hiatus, incoherence, inconsequence, interruption, rift *(gap)*, split

disjunctive disconnected, disjointed, divisive, elective *(selective)*. SEE MAIN ENTRY

disjuncture division *(act of dividing)*

dislikable contemptuous, objectionable

dislike conflict *(noun)*, conflict *(verb)*, contempt *(disdain)*, deprecate, disapprobation, disapproval, disapprove *(condemn)*, disdain, disfavor, disparagement, dissatisfaction, exception *(objection)*, hatred, ignominy, ill repute, ill will, incompatibility *(difference)*, intolerance, malice, odium, outcry, phobia, rejection, reluctance, resent, umbrage. SEE MAIN ENTRY

disliked disreputable, invidious, loathsome, repugnant *(exciting aversion)*, repulsive, undesirable, unsavory

disliking averse

dislocate break *(separate)*, contort, disband, discompose, disjoint, dislodge, disorient, displace *(remove)*, disturb, isolate, luxate, remove *(eliminate)*. SEE MAIN ENTRY

dislocated anomalous, deranged, disordered

dislocation deportation, disturbance, removal, replacement

dislodge deport *(banish)*, depose *(remove)*, disengage, dislocate, disorient, displace *(remove)*, dispossess, disturb, divest, eject *(evict)*, evict, expel, extricate, liberate, oust, relegate, remove *(eliminate)*. SEE MAIN ENTRY

dislodgment dismissal *(discharge)*, disqualification *(rejection)*, eviction, exclusion, expropriation *(divestiture)*, expulsion, foreclosure, liberation, ostracism, ouster, rejection, removal

disloyal broken *(unfulfilled)*, disobedient, faithless, hostile, insidious, insubordinate, irresponsible, perfidious, recreant, untrue, untrustworthy

disloyalty bad faith, corruption, desertion, estrangement, infidelity, mutiny, noncompliance *(nonobservance)*, sedition, treason. SEE MAIN ENTRY

dismal bleak *(not favorable)*, bleak *(severely simple)*, deplorable, despondent, dire, disconsolate, lamentable, lifeless *(dull)*, lugubrious. SEE MAIN ENTRY

dismantle break *(separate)*, destroy *(void)*, disable, disjoint, disorganize, dissolve *(separate)*, eviscerate, extinguish, mutilate, subvert

dismantlement dissolution *(disintegration)*

dismask disclose

dismay aggravate *(annoy)*, agitate *(perturb)*, consternation, deter, discompose, disconcert, discourage, disturb, doubt *(suspicion)*, fear, fright, harrow, intimidate, perturb, pique, trepidation. SEE MAIN ENTRY

dismayed pessimistic

dismaying ominous, sinister

dismember disband, disjoint, divide *(separate)*, mutilate, part *(separate)*, separate, sever

dismembered broken *(fractured)*, disjunctive *(tending to disjoin)*

dismemberment disassociation, division *(act of dividing)*, split

dismiss cancel, cede, clear, condone, controvert, decry, deport *(banish)*, depose *(remove)*, disband, discharge *(release from obligation)*, discontinue *(abandon)*, dislodge, dispel, displace *(remove)*, disregard, eject *(expel)*, eliminate *(exclude)*, except *(exclude)*, exclude, exculpate, expel, forgo, free, liberate, oust, override, quash, rebuff, recall *(call back)*, refuse, reject, release, relegate, relinquish, remit *(release from penalty)*, remove *(dismiss from office)*, renounce, rescind, revoke, send, superannuate, supplant, vindicate, waive. SEE MAIN ENTRY

dismiss all doubt assure *(give confidence to)*

dismiss charges palliate *(excuse)*. SEE MAIN ENTRY

dismiss doubt ensure, reassure

dismiss from favor demote, disgrace

dismiss from service disband

dismiss from the bar disbar

dismiss from the legal profession disbar

dismissal abandonment *(repudiation)*, absolution, acquittal, avoidance *(cancellation)*, banishment, cancellation, compurgation, condonation, deportation, discharge *(release from obligation)*, discontinuance *(act of discontinuing)*, discontinuance *(interruption of a legal action)*, disqualification *(rejection)*, dissolution *(termination)*, exclusion, expulsion, layoff, liberation, ostracism, pardon, rejection, release, removal, renunciation. SEE MAIN ENTRY

dismissal from office degradation

dismissal of an accusation absolution

dismissal of charges exoneration

dismissed clear *(free from criminal charges)*, free *(relieved from a burden)*, obsolete. SEE MAIN ENTRY

dismissible defeasible

dismount alight

disobedience anarchy, bad faith, breach, contempt *(disobedience to the court)*, defiance, disloyalty, disregard *(lack of respect)*, disrespect, infraction, infringement, insurrection, invasion, mutiny, nonconformity, offense, rebellion, resistance, revolt, sedition, transgression

disobedient adverse *(hostile)*, broken *(unfulfilled)*, contumacious, disorderly, dissident, froward, insolent, insubordinate, intractable, irresponsible, lawless, nonconforming, nonconsenting, perfidious, perverse, recalcitrant, recusant, restive, uncontrollable, unruly, untrue. SEE MAIN ENTRY

disobey break *(violate)*, defect, defy, rebel, trespass, violate. SEE MAIN ENTRY

disobey the law offend *(violate the law)*, trespass

disobeyed lawless

disobeying lawless

disoblige affront, disaffect, discommode, mistreat. SEE MAIN ENTRY

disobliging insolent, invidious, malevolent, negative, outrageous

disorder agitate *(shake up)*, anarchy, commotion, complex *(entanglement)*, confuse *(create disorder)*, confusion *(turmoil)*, degenerate, detriment, disability *(physical inability)*, discompose, disease, dislocate, disorganize, disorient, disrupt, disturb, disturbance, embroilment, entanglement *(confusion)*, havoc, imbroglio, incoherence, insurrection, irregularity, misrule, muddle, pandemonium, panic, perturb, riot, shambles, snarl, turmoil, violence. SEE MAIN ENTRY

disordered anomalous, broken *(interrupted)*, deranged, disjointed, haphazard, lunatic, slipshod. SEE MAIN ENTRY

disordered intellect insanity

disordered mind insanity, lunacy

disordered reason insanity, paranoia

disorderliness anarchy, commotion, confusion *(turmoil)*, irregularity, lynch law, riot

disorderly culpable, disjointed, disobedient, haphazard, lawless, licentious, perverse, slipshod, uncontrollable, unruly. SEE MAIN ENTRY

disorderly conduct disorder *(lack of order)*, misconduct, misdoing

disorganization anarchy, commotion, complex *(entanglement)*, confusion *(turmoil)*, disorder *(lack of order)*, dissolution *(disintegration)*, disturbance, entanglement *(confusion)*, havoc, misrule, pandemonium, shambles

disorganize confuse *(create disorder)*, disband, discompose, dislocate, disorient, disrupt, disturb, muddle, upset. SEE MAIN ENTRY

disorganized anomalous, deranged, disjointed, disordered, disorderly, lax, slipshod

disorient dislocate, perplex. SEE MAIN ENTRY

disorientate disorganize, disturb

disorientation insanity

disoriented non compos mentis

disown condemn *(ban)*, defect, deny *(contradict)*, deprive, disaffirm, disallow, disavow, disclaim, disdain, disinherit, exclude, expel, rebuff, recant, refuse, reject, renounce, surrender *(give back)*, waive. SEE MAIN ENTRY

disowned blameful, derelict *(abandoned)*

disownment abandonment *(repudiation)*, abjuration, ademption, attachment *(seizure)*, disclaimer, disdain, exclusion, rejection, renunciation, revocation

dispair sever

dispar dissimilar, diverse, unequal *(unequivalent)*

disparage blame, brand *(stigmatize)*, censure, complain *(criticize)*, condemn *(blame)*, condescend *(patronize)*, contemn, criticize *(find fault with)*, damage, debunk, decry, defame, demean *(make lower)*, denounce *(condemn)*, deprecate, depreciate, derogate, disapprove *(condemn)*, discommend, discount *(disbelieve)*, discredit, disdain, dishonor *(deprive of honor)*, disoblige, fault, humiliate, impeach, jeer, lessen, libel, malign, minimize, misprize, mock *(deride)*, pillory, remonstrate, reprimand, reproach, smear, spurn, sully, underestimate. SEE MAIN ENTRY

disparage frivolously cavil

disparagement aspersion, bad repute, blame *(culpability)*, condemnation *(blame)*, contempt *(disdain)*, criticism, defamation, denunciation, diatribe, disapprobation, disapproval, discredit, disgrace, dishonor *(shame)*, disrepute, disrespect, exception *(objection)*, ignominy, libel, notoriety, obloquy, phillipic, profanity, reproach, revilement, ridicule, slander. SEE MAIN ENTRY

disparaging calumnious, contemptuous, cynical, derogatory, incriminatory, inculpatory, libelous, nonconsenting, pejorative, unfavorable. SEE MAIN ENTRY

disparate different, disconnected, disproportionate, dissimilar, divergent, diverse, heterogeneous, miscellaneous, multifarious, peculiar *(distinctive)*, separate, unequal *(unequivalent)*, unrelated, unsuitable. SEE MAIN ENTRY

disparity contradistinction, contraposition, deviation, difference, disaccord, discord, discrepancy, dissent *(difference of opinion)*, distinction *(difference)*, distortion, incompatibility *(inconsistency)*, incongruity, inconsistency, inequality, nonconformity, variance *(disagreement)*. SEE MAIN ENTRY

dispart break *(separate)*, detach, disengage, disjoint, disperse *(scatter)*, dissociate, dissolve *(separate)*, divide *(separate)*, estrange, luxate, separate, sever

dispassion disinterest *(lack of prejudice)*, objectivity

dispassionate clinical, cold-blooded, deliberate, discriminating *(judicious)*, equitable, evenhanded, fair *(just)*, impartial, just, neutral, nonchalant, objective, open-minded, perfunctory, phlegmatic, stoical, unbiased, unprejudiced, unresponsive. SEE MAIN ENTRY

dispassionately fairly *(impartially)*

dispassionateness candor *(impartiality)*, disinterest *(lack of prejudice)*, fairness, moderation, neutrality, objectivity

dispatch acceleration, accomplish, close *(terminate)*, commission *(act)*, complete, conduct, delegate, discharge *(performance)*, discharge *(perform)*, dismiss *(discharge)*, displace *(remove)*, eliminate *(eradicate)*, execute *(sentence to death)*, expedite, haste, hasten, intelligence *(news)*, issuance, kill *(defeat)*, kill *(murder)*, note *(brief comment)*, notice *(announcement)*, notification, relegate, send, slay, story *(narrative)*, transmit, transmittal, transport. SEE MAIN ENTRY

dispatch news annunciate, disseminate

dispatcher carrier, informant

dispatches correspondence *(communication by letters)*

dispatching assassination

dispatchment consignment

dispel disband, disorganize, disperse *(scatter)*, disprove, dissolve *(disperse)*, extinguish, obliterate, quash, repel *(drive back)*, repulse. SEE MAIN ENTRY

dispel misunderstanding resolve *(solve)*

dispellere dispel, disperse *(scatter)*

dispendium expense *(cost)*, waste

dispensable disposable, expendable, extraneous, gratuitous *(unwarranted)*, inconsequential, minor, needless, negligible, nonessential, null *(insignificant)*, otiose, petty, superfluous, unessential, unnecessary. SEE MAIN ENTRY

dispensation administration, alimony, allotment, appointment *(act of designating)*, appropriation *(allotment)*, assignment *(allotment)*, benefit *(conferment)*, capacity *(authority)*, charter *(license)*, circulation, contribution *(donation)*, discharge *(release from obligation)*, disposition *(final arrangement)*, disposition *(transfer of property)*, distribution *(apportionment)*, donation, excuse, exoneration, franchise *(license)*, gift *(present)*, grant, gratuity *(present)*, impunity, inheritance, leave *(permission)*, legacy, pardon, privilege, quota, ration, release, reprieve, will *(testamentary instrument)*. SEE MAIN ENTRY

dispense adjudge, administer *(tender)*, allocate, allot, apportion, assign *(allot)*, bear *(yield)*, bequeath, bestow, confer

(give), contribute *(supply)*, convey *(transfer)*, disburse *(distribute)*, dispense, disperse *(disseminate)*, disseminate, distribute, divide *(distribute)*, dole, endue, fund, give *(grant)*, impart, issue *(publish)*, mete, parcel, present *(make a gift)*, reapportion, render *(administer)*, sell, spend, split, vend. SEE MAIN ENTRY

dispense judgment adjudge

dispense with abandon *(relinquish)*, abolish, censor, disavow, disclaim, dismiss *(discharge)*, disown *(refuse to acknowledge)*, extinguish, forbear, forgo, forswear, jettison, refrain, refuse, set aside *(annul)*, waive. SEE MAIN ENTRY

dispensed with derelict *(abandoned)*

dispensing circulation, donative

dispergere circulate, circulation, disperse *(scatter)*, disseminate

dispersal circulation, decentralization, disbursement *(act of disbursing)*, dispensation *(act of dispensing)*, dissolution *(disintegration)*, division *(act of dividing)*

disperse administer *(tender)*, allocate, allot, break *(separate)*, circulate, diffuse, disband, disintegrate, disorganize, dispel, dispense, displace *(remove)*, disseminate, dissipate *(spread out)*, dissociate, divide *(distribute)*, issue *(publish)*, move *(alter position)*, radiate, repel *(drive back)*, separate, spread. SEE MAIN ENTRY

disperse completely dispel

dispersed desultory, sporadic

dispersion circulation, decentralization, dispensation *(act of dispensing)*, division *(act of dividing)*, havoc, waste. SEE MAIN ENTRY

dispertire apportion, distribute

dispirit depress, discourage, dissuade, harass, intimidate

dispirited despondent, disconsolate, lugubrious, pessimistic

dispiritedness depression, pessimism

dispiriting ominous

dispiteous remorseless, ruthless

displace accede *(succeed)*, change, confuse *(create disorder)*, deport *(banish)*, depose *(remove)*, discharge *(dismiss)*, discompose, disjoint, dislocate, dislodge, dismiss *(discharge)*, dispossess, dissociate, disturb, divest, eject *(evict)*, eradicate, evict, exclude, inconvenience, luxate, oust, relegate, remove *(dismiss from office)*, remove *(eliminate)*, send, succeed *(follow)*, supersede, supplant, upset. SEE MAIN ENTRY

displaced deranged

displaced person derelict

displacement banishment, deportation, discharge *(dismissal)*, dismissal *(discharge)*, disqualification *(rejection)*, disturbance, evulsion, exclusion, expulsion, layoff, ostracism, preemption, removal, replacement, sequestration, subrogation

displacement of rightful owner disseisin

displacency bad repute

displant disengage, dislodge, disturb

display bare, bear *(adduce)*, brandish, color *(deceptive appearance)*, complexion, demonstrate *(establish)*, disinter, evidence, evince, exemplify, exhibit *(noun)*, exhibit *(verb)*, expose, expression *(manifestation)*, flaunt, histrionics, illustrate, illustration *(manifestation)*, manifest, manifestation, phenomenon *(manifestation)*, present *(introduce)*, pretense *(ostentation)*, produce *(offer to view)*, reveal, scene, unveil. SEE MAIN ENTRY

display line caption

display oneself boldly flaunt

display with effrontery flaunt

displease agitate *(perturb)*, annoy, antagonize, bait *(harass)*, disappoint, discommode, disturb, harrow, harry *(harass)*, irritate, offend *(insult)*, pique, plague, provoke, repel *(disgust)*. SEE MAIN ENTRY

displeased disappointed, resentful

displeasing antipathetic *(distasteful)*, deplorable, inadequate, inferior *(lower in quality)*, objectionable, obnoxious, odious, offensive *(offending)*, repugnant *(exciting aversion)*, repulsive, unacceptable, undesirable, unendurable, unsatisfactory

displeasure disapprobation, disapproval, disparagement, dissatisfaction, exception *(objection)*, nuisance, odium, pain, plaint, reprimand, resentment, umbrage

displume plunder

disponere marshal

disposable assignable, expendable. SEE MAIN ENTRY

disposal administration, allotment, cession, conveyance, disbursement *(act of disbursing)*, dismissal *(termination of a proceeding)*, dispatch *(act of putting to death)*, dispensation *(act of dispensing)*, disposition *(determination)*, disposition *(final arrangement)*, disposition *(transfer of property)*, distribution *(apportionment)*, enjoyment *(use)*, expense *(sacrifice)*, management *(judicious use)*, order *(arrangement)*, recourse, regulation *(management)*, release, sale, use

dispose abolish, allocate, allot, bait *(lure)*, classify, convince, disperse *(disseminate)*, divide *(distribute)*, prompt, regulate *(adjust)*, rule *(govern)*. SEE MAIN ENTRY

dispose of abandon *(relinquish)*, administer *(conduct)*, assign *(transfer ownership)*, attorn, bequeath, bestow, close *(terminate)*, complete, conclude *(complete)*, contribute *(supply)*, debar, decide, discharge *(perform)*, dispatch *(put to death)*, dispense, dissolve *(terminate)*, eliminate *(eradicate)*, eradicate, expel, expunge, forgo, give *(grant)*, jettison, liquidate *(determine liability)*, parcel, post, refute, set aside *(annul)*, settle, slay, spend

dispose of for profit sell

disposed eager, inclined, prone, ready *(willing)*, receptive, willing *(desirous)*

disposed of complete *(ended)*

disposed to believe credulous

disposed to bestow favors propitious

disposed to cavil fractious

disposed to cheat dishonest

disposed to controversy litigious

disposed to doubt cynical, inconvincible, incredulous, suspicious *(distrustful)*

disposed to envy jealous

disposed to fight pugnacious

disposed to good benevolent

disposed to insist insistent

disposed to mercy placable

disposed to peace peaceable

disposed to question debatable, doubtful

disposed to talk freely loquacious

disposed to yield flexible

disposer of stolen goods fence

dispositio disposition *(final arrangement)*

disposition adjudication, adjustment, administration, allotment, animus, apportionment, array *(order)*, assignment *(transfer of ownership)*, bias, cession, character *(personal quality)*, choice *(decision)*, classification,

731

complexion, conatus, dispensation (act of dispensing), distribution (arrangement), favor (partiality), frame (mood), habit, legacy, penchant, personality, posture (attitude), predilection, predisposition, preference (choice), proclivity, propensity, property (distinctive attribute), regulation (management), settlement, spirit, standpoint, state (condition), structure (composition), temperament, tendency, usage, use, will (desire), will (testamentary instrument). SEE MAIN ENTRY.

disposition of mind   posture (attitude)

disposition of personalty   legacy

disposition to believe   credulity

disposition to deceive   dishonesty

disposition to defraud   dishonesty

disposition to inquire   interest (concern)

disposition to lie   dishonesty

disposition to mercy   clemency, lenience

disposition to pardon   clemency, condonation

disposition to please   comity

disposition to resist   contempt (disobedience to the court)

dispositioned   inclined

dispossess   assume (seize), condemn (seize), confiscate, demote, depose (remove), deprive, despoil, dislodge, dismiss (discharge), disown (refuse to acknowledge), displace (remove), divest, eject (evict), evict, expel, hijack, oust, seize (confiscate), sequester (seize property). SEE MAIN ENTRY.

dispossess of   abridge (divest)

dispossess of hereditary right   disinherit, disown (refuse to acknowledge)

dispossess of right   disqualify

dispossess oneself of   abandon (relinquish)

dispossessed   poor (underprivileged)

dispossession   abridgment (disentitlement), appropriation (taking), assumption (seizure), attachment (seizure), condemnation (seizure), disqualification (rejection), disseisin, distraint, distress (seizure), eviction, expropriation (divestiture), expulsion, foreclosure, forfeiture (act of forfeiting), garnishment, infringement, ouster, privation, taking. SEE MAIN ENTRY.

disposure   array (order), distribution (arrangement)

dispraise   blame (culpability), blame, censure, condemn (blame), condemnation (blame), contempt (disdain), criticism, criticize (find fault with), decry, defame, denounce (condemn), denunciation, deprecate, depreciate, derogate, diatribe, disapprobation, disapprove (condemn), discommend, discredit, exception (objection), fault, ignominy, inveigh, lessen, malediction, malign, onus (stigma), reprimand (noun), reprimand (verb), sully. SEE MAIN ENTRY.

dispraised   blameful

dispread   diffuse

disprison   extricate

disprize   contemn, decry, derogate, minimize, misprize

disproof   confutation, contradiction, counterargument, negation, repudiation

disproportion   difference, distort, distortion, exaggeration, inequality, inequity

disproportionate   disparate, excessive, inapposite, inappropriate, inapt, incommensurate, incongruous, inept (inappropriate), undue (excessive), unequal (unequivalent). SEE MAIN ENTRY.

disproportionateness   inequality

disprovable   defeasible

disproval   repudiation

disprove   answer (reply), contradict, controvert, disown (deny the validity), impugn, invalidate, negate, rebut, refute. SEE MAIN ENTRY.

disputability   cloud (suspicion)

disputable   actionable, arguable, contestable, controversial, debatable, doubtful, dubious, dubitative, equivocal, forensic, justiciable, litigable, litigious, moot, problematic, uncertain (questionable), undecided, unsettled, unsound (fallacious). SEE MAIN ENTRY.

disputant   adversary, apologist, contender, contestant, foe, litigant, opponent, party (litigant), rival. SEE MAIN ENTRY.

disputare   discuss, dispute (debate)

disputatio   argument (contention), contention (argument)

disputation   altercation, argument (contention), argument (pleading), belligerency, collision (dispute), contention (argument), contention (opposition), contest (dispute), controversy (argument), disaccord, disagreement, fight (argument), impugnation, strife

disputatious   argumentative, competitive (antagonistic), contentious, debatable, disputable, dissenting, fractious, hostile, litigious, moot, petulant, polemic, pugnacious, querulous, remonstrative. SEE MAIN ENTRY.

disputative   dissenting, forensic, litigious

dispute   altercation, answer (reply), argue, argument (contention), bicker, brawl, challenge, collide (clash), conflict (noun), conflict (verb), confront (oppose), confrontation (altercation), contention (argument), contention (opposition), contest (dispute), contest, contradict, contradiction, contravene, controversy (argument), controvert, cross (disagree with), debate, deny (contradict), differ (disagree), disaccord (noun), disaccord (verb), disaffirm, disagree, disallow, disapprove (reject), disbelieve, discord, dissension, dissent (differ in opinion), doubt (distrust), except (object), exception (objection), feud, fight (argument), fight (battle), fracas, fray, gainsay, haggle, impeach, impugn, impugnation, incompatibility (difference), lawsuit, matter (case), matter (subject), negate, nonconformity, object, oppose, oppugn, proceeding, protest, rebut, reject, remonstrate, rift (disagreement), strife, variance (disagreement). SEE MAIN ENTRY.

dispute angrily.   brawl

dispute resolution.   SEE MAIN ENTRY.

disputed   moot

disputed point   conflict, contention (argument), controversy (argument), discrepancy

disputed point of law   issue (matter in dispute). SEE MAIN ENTRY.

disputed question   controversy (argument), issue (matter in dispute)

disputer   malcontent

disputing   dissenting, negative

disqualification   disability (physical inability), expulsion, inability, incapacity, invalidity, prohibition. SEE MAIN ENTRY.

disqualified   disabled (deprived of legal right), incompetent, ineligible, inept (incompetent), powerless, unqualified (not competent)

disqualify   ban, censor, condemn (ban), disable, eliminate (exclude), exclude, invalidate, prohibit, recall (call back). SEE MAIN ENTRY.

disqualify as an attorney   disbar

disqualifying   prohibitive (restrictive)

disquiet   affront, agitate (perturb), annoy, badger, commotion, confusion (turmoil), consternation, discommode, discompose, disconcert, disrupt, dissatisfaction, distress (anguish), distress, disturb, disturbance, embarrass, embroilment, frighten, harass, harrow, ill will, incense, inflict, intimidate, menace, misgiving, molest (annoy), outburst, perplex, perturb, pique, plague, press (goad), provoke, qualm, remorse, stress (strain), strife, trepidation, turmoil, upset

disquieting   ominous, sinister, unsatisfactory

disquietude   commotion, concern (interest), confusion (turmoil), consternation, distress (anguish), disturbance, fear, fright, outburst, pandemonium, panic, stress (strain), trepidation

disquisition   charge (statement to the jury), discourse, harangue, inquiry (systematic investigation), narration, pandect (treatise)

disquisitional   discursive (analytical), narrative

disrank   humiliate

disrate   contemn, demote, derogate, humiliate, smear

disregard   anarchy, breach, break (violate), condonation, condone, contemn, contempt (disdain), contravene, default, defiance, defy, dereliction, disaffirm, discount (disbelieve), disdain (noun), disdain (verb), disfavor, dishonor (nonpayment), dishonor (refuse to pay), disinterest (lack of interest), dismiss (put out of consideration), disobey, disoblige, disown (deny the validity), disparage, disrespect, disuse, eliminate (exclude), except (exclude), exclude, flout, ignore, inconsideration, indifference, jeer, laxity, misprize, muse, negate, neglect (noun), neglect (verb), negligence, nonfeasance, nonperformance, omission, overlook (excuse), override, pretermit, rebuff (noun), rebuff (verb), reject, remit (release from penalty), resist (withstand), shun, spurn, trespass, violate. SEE MAIN ENTRY.

disregard of duty   nonfeasance

disregard of orders   contempt (disobedience to the court), defiance, noncompliance (nonobservance)

disregard one's duty   default

disregard one's obligations   default

disregard prestige   condescend (deign)

disregard the law   offend (violate the law)

disregardant   negligent, remiss

disregarded   broken (unfulfilled), inappreciable, null (insignificant)

disregardful   broken (unfulfilled), careless, contemptuous, derelict (negligent), heedless, inadvertent, insolent, negligent, perfunctory, reckless, remiss, thoughtless

disregardfulness   disregard (lack of respect), disregard (omission), disregard (unconcern)

disregarding   disobedient, lax

disrelated   alien (unrelated), apart, separate

disrepair   damage, deterioration, impairment (damage). SEE MAIN ENTRY.

disreputability   attaint, bad character, bad repute, discredit, disgrace, dishonor (shame), disrepute, ignominy, ill repute, notoriety

disreputable arrant *(onerous)*, bad *(offensive)*, base *(bad)*, blameful, blameworthy, contemptible, delinquent *(guilty of a misdeed)*, depraved, disgraceful, dishonest, fraudulent, ignoble, immoral, iniquitous, lawless, notorious, profligate *(corrupt)*, reprehensible, reprobate, scandalous, sinister, unbecoming, unethical, unseemly. SEE MAIN ENTRY

disreputable person degenerate

disreputableness bad repute, disrepute, ignominy, notoriety

disreputation ignominy, ill repute

disrepute attaint, bad character, bad faith, bad repute, contempt *(disdain)*, corruption, defamation, degradation, discredit, disgrace, dishonor *(shame)*, disparagement, ignominy, impeachability, infamy, notoriety, obloquy, odium, opprobrium, reproach, scandal, shame, stigma, turpitude. SEE MAIN ENTRY

disreputed blameful

disrespect attaint, blasphemy, condescend *(patronize)*, contemn, contempt *(disobedience to the court)*, contumely, decry, disapprobation, disdain, disfavor, disgrace *(noun)*, disgrace *(verb)*, dishonor *(shame)*, disparage, disparagement, disregard *(lack of respect)*, disrepute, inconsideration, infamy, jeer, notoriety, obloquy, opprobrium, profanity, ridicule, shame, violate. SEE MAIN ENTRY

disrespectability bad repute, ill repute
disrespectable blameworthy, disreputable, notorious, scandalous
disrespectful brazen, calumnious, contemptuous, disdainful, disobedient, harsh, impertinent *(insolent)*, insolent, offensive *(offending)*, outrageous, pejorative, presumptuous, profane, scurrilous, supercilious
disrespectfulness bad repute, contempt *(disobedience to the court)*, disparagement, disrespect, inconsideration

disrobe denude, divest
disroot remove *(eliminate)*
disrupt circumvent, counteract, damage, disconcert, discontinue *(break continuity)*, disorganize, foil, overthrow, subvert. SEE MAIN ENTRY
disrupter insurgent
disruption abandonment *(discontinuance)*, alienation *(estrangement)*, check *(bar)*, debacle, disaccord, disassociation, discontinuance *(act of discontinuing)*, dissolution *(disintegration)*, estrangement, exception *(exclusion)*, furor, havoc, outbreak, outburst, pandemonium, shambles, split, subversion
disruptive offensive *(taking the initiative)*
dissatisfaction disapprobation, disapproval, dissent *(nonconcurrence)*, distress *(anguish)*, exception *(objection)*, ill will, objection, outcry, plaint, resentment, trouble, umbrage. SEE MAIN ENTRY
dissatisfactory loathsome
dissatisfied disappointed, dissident, jealous, querulous
dissatisfiedness dissatisfaction
dissatisfy disaffect, disappoint
disscindere rend
dissect analyze, canvass, dichotomize, disjoint, examine *(study)*, investigate, partition, probe, rend, research, scrutinize, split, study, subdivide
dissectible divisible
dissection analysis, dichotomy, hornbook, indagation, split

disseise abridge *(divest)*, adeem, annex *(arrogate)*, attach *(seize)*, condemn *(seize)*, confiscate, dispossess, impress *(procure by force)*, impropriate, levy, seize *(confiscate)*
disseised attached *(seized)*
disseisin appropriation *(taking)*, distress *(seizure)*, expropriation *(divestiture)*. SEE MAIN ENTRY
disseize deprive, dispossess, divest
disseizing confiscatory
dissemblance color *(deceptive appearance)*, difference, distortion, false pretense, story *(falsehood)*
dissemble assume *(simulate)*, camouflage, cheat, cloak, deceive, delude, disguise, distort, equivocate, evade *(deceive)*, fabricate *(make up)*, fake, falsify, feign, hide, misguide, mislead, misrepresent, misstate, palter, pretend, prevaricate, profess *(pretend)*
dissembling deceit, fraud, hypocrisy, lying, perfidious, recreant, tartuffish
disseminare disseminate
disseminate annunciate, apportion, cast *(throw)*, circulate, convey *(communicate)*, correspond *(communicate)*, diffuse, disburse *(distribute)*, disclose, dispel, dispense, dissipate *(spread out)*, distribute, herald, intersperse, issue *(publish)*, notify, proclaim, promulgate, propagate *(spread)*, publish, report *(disclose)*, reveal, signify *(inform)*, spread. SEE MAIN ENTRY
disseminated pervade, public *(known)*
disseminating disbursement *(act of disbursing)*
dissemination circulation, common knowledge, communication *(statement)*, disbursement *(act of disbursing)*, disclosure *(act of disclosing)*, dispensation *(act of dispensing)*, distribution *(apportionment)*, division *(act of dividing)*, divulgation, notification, publication *(disclosure)*, publicity, report *(detailed account)*
dissensio conflict, disagreement, discord, dissent *(difference of opinion)*, variance *(disagreement)*
dissension argument *(contention)*, belligerency, breach, case *(lawsuit)*, conflict, contempt *(disobedience to the court)*, contention *(opposition)*, contest *(dispute)*, contradiction, controversy *(argument)*, difference, disaccord, disagreement, discord, dispute, dissent *(difference of opinion)*, dissent *(nonconcurrence)*, dissidence, distinction *(difference)*, division *(act of dividing)*, embroilment, faction, feud, fight *(argument)*, fracas, fray, incompatibility *(difference)*, opposition, revolt, schism, split, strife, struggle, variance *(disagreement)*. SEE MAIN ENTRY
dissent argument *(contention)*, bicker, challenge, collide *(clash)*, conflict *(noun)*, conflict *(verb)*, contend *(dispute)*, contention *(opposition)*, contest *(dispute)*, contradict, contradiction, contravention, demonstrate *(protest)*, demur, denial, deny *(contradict)*, differ *(vary)*, disaccord *(noun)*, disaccord *(verb)*, disaffirm, disagree, disagreement, disallow, disapprobation, disapproval, disavow, discord, disown *(deny the validity)*, dispute *(debate)*, dissatisfaction, dissension, dissidence, except *(object)*, exception *(objection)*, faction, gainsay, impugnation, incompatibility *(difference)*, negation, nonconformity, object, objection, oppugn, outcry, protest *(noun)*, protest *(verb)*, refuse, reject, rejection,

reluctance, renounce, repudiate, repudiation, resist *(oppose)*, schism, secede, strife, variance *(disagreement)*. SEE MAIN ENTRY
dissent from dispute *(contest)*
dissenter disputant, heretic, malcontent
dissentience breach, disapproval, discord, dispute, dissension, dissent *(difference of opinion)*, embroilment
dissentient adversary, argumentative, contradictory, discordant, dissenting, dissident, divisive, heretic, hostile, malcontent, negative, nonconforming, nonconsenting, polemic, recusant
dissentient voice dissent *(nonconcurrence)*
dissenting contradictory, discordant, disinclined, dissident, hostile, nonconforming, nonconsenting, recusant, reluctant, renitent. SEE MAIN ENTRY
dissentious contentious, dissenting, dissident, hostile, litigious, pugnacious, reluctant
dissentire conflict, differ *(vary)*, disagree, dissent *(differ in opinion)*
disserere discuss
dissertate converse, declaim, discourse, discuss
dissertation communication *(discourse)*, conversation, discourse, pandect *(treatise)*, recital
dissertation on the law hornbook
disserve damage, harm
disservice grievance, harm, injury, mischief, prejudice *(injure)*. SEE MAIN ENTRY
disserviceable adverse *(negative)*, deleterious, disadvantageous, harmful, peccant *(unhealthy)*, pernicious, prejudicial
dissever detach, dichotomize, disband, discontinue *(abandon)*, discontinue *(break continuity)*, disengage, disjoint, dissociate, dissolve *(separate)*, divide *(separate)*, estrange, excise *(cut away)*, interrupt, isolate, luxate, part *(separate)*, rend, separate, sever, split, subdivide
disseverable divisible
disseverance division *(act of dividing)*, separation, split
disseverence disassociation
dissevering estrangement
dissidence argument *(contention)*, conflict, contention *(opposition)*, contravention, controversy *(argument)*, deviation, disaccord, disagreement, disapprobation, disapproval, discord, dispute, dissension, dissent *(difference of opinion)*, incompatibility *(difference)*, nonconformity, protest, sedition, strife, variance *(disagreement)*. SEE MAIN ENTRY
dissident competitive *(antagonistic)*, deviant, discordant, dissenting, divisive, heretic, hostile, insubordinate, malcontent, negative, nonconforming, nonconsenting, recusant. SEE MAIN ENTRY
dissidere differ *(vary)*, disagree, dissent *(differ in opinion)*
dissidium disagreement, discord
dissimilar atypical, different, discordant, disparate, distinct *(distinguished from others)*, divergent, diverse, heterogeneous, multifarious, nonconforming, peculiar *(distinctive)*, separate, unequal *(unequivalent)*, unique, unrelated. SEE MAIN ENTRY
dissimilarity contradistinction, contraposition, deviation, difference, discord, discrepancy, distortion, diversity, identity *(individuality)*, incompatibility *(inconsistency)*, incongruity, inconsistency, inequality, nonconformity, specialty *(distinctive mark)*

dissimilis dissimilar, heterogeneous

dissimilitude difference, disagreement, discrepancy, disparity, distortion, diversity, incompatibility *(inconsistency)*, incongruity, inconsistency, inequality

dissimilitudo disparity, inequality

dissimulare cloak, pretend

dissimulate assume *(simulate)*, cloak, deceive, disguise, equivocate, fabricate *(make up)*, fake, feign, lie *(falsify)*, misrepresent, palter, pretend, prevaricate, profess *(pretend)*

dissimulatio hypocrisy, irony

dissimulation color *(deceptive appearance)*, deceit, deception, disguise, duplicity, false pretense, falsehood, falsification, fraud, indirection *(deceitfulness)*, story *(falsehood)*

dissipare dispel, disperse *(scatter)*, dissipate *(spread out)*

dissipate carouse, debauch, deplete, diffuse, disappear, disorganize, dispel, disperse *(scatter)*, dissolve *(disperse)*, exhaust *(deplete)*, expend *(consume)*, impair, misemploy, obliterate, overdraw. SEE MAIN ENTRY

dissipated depraved, dissolute, immoral, improvident, irredeemable, irretrievable, lascivious, lecherous, licentious, lost *(taken away)*, prodigal, profligate *(corrupt)*, prurient

dissipation consumption, debauchery, decentralization, decrease, decrement, dissolution *(disintegration)*, division *(act of dividing)*, expense *(sacrifice)*, privation, vice, waste

dissipative prodigal, profligate *(corrupt)*

dissociability ostracism

dissociate abstract *(separate)*, break *(separate)*, depart, detach, disband, disengage, disjoint, disrupt, dissolve *(separate)*, divide *(separate)*, divorce, estrange, isolate, luxate, part *(separate)*, remove *(dismiss from office)*, remove *(eliminate)*, seclude, separate, sever, withdraw. SEE MAIN ENTRY

dissociate oneself disagree, disavow, disown *(refuse to acknowledge)*

dissociated alien *(unrelated)*, apart, discrete, foreign, independent, separate

dissociation disassociation, disclaimer, division *(act of dividing)*, estrangement, inconsequence, privacy, repudiation, segregation *(separation)*, separation

dissoluable severable

dissoluble defeasible

dissolute culpable, depraved, disorderly, disreputable, felonious, immoral, iniquitous, lascivious, lecherous, lewd, licentious, nefarious, profligate *(corrupt)*, promiscuous, prurient, reprobate, salacious, tainted *(corrupted)*, unrestrained *(not repressed)*, wanton. SEE MAIN ENTRY

dissoluteness debauchery, delinquency *(misconduct)*, vice

dissolutio abolition, dissolution *(termination)*

dissolution abatement *(extinguishment)*, abolition, ademption, annulment, cancellation, cessation *(termination)*, debacle, decentralization, decline, defeasance, denouement, destruction, disassociation, discharge *(annulment)*, end *(termination)*, erosion, expense *(sacrifice)*, expiration, extremity *(death)*, interruption, rescision, separation, spoilage, wear and tear. SEE MAIN ENTRY

dissolution of marriage divorce, separation

dissolution of the marriage bond divorce

dissolutus dissolute, lax, licentious

dissolvable destructible

dissolve abate *(extinguish)*, abolish, abrogate *(annul)*, cancel, degenerate, destroy *(efface)*, disappear, discharge *(release from obligation)*, discontinue *(abandon)*, discontinue *(break continuity)*, disintegrate, disorganize, dispel, disperse *(scatter)*, dissipate *(spread out)*, eliminate *(eradicate)*, eradicate, erode, extirpate, interrupt, nullify, obliterate, part *(separate)*, quash, recess, renege, repudiate, rescind, revoke, separate, sever. SEE MAIN ENTRY

dissolve by dismissal disband

dissolve of the bonds of matrimony divorce

dissolve the marriage of divorce

dissolved irretrievable

dissolvere disburse *(pay out)*, dissolve *(disperse)*, refund, solve

dissolving cancellation

dissonance conflict, contention *(opposition)*, contest *(dispute)*, controversy *(argument)*, deviation, difference, disaccord, disagreement, discord, discrepancy, disparity, dissension, dissent *(difference of opinion)*, dissidence, distinction *(difference)*, division *(act of dividing)*, estrangement, incompatibility *(inconsistency)*, incongruity, inconsistency, inequality, paradox

dissonant deranged, deviant, different, discordant, dissenting, divisive, inapposite, inappropriate, inapt, incongruous, inconsistent, inept *(inappropriate)*, peculiar *(distinctive)*, polemic, unsuitable

dissonus discordant

dissuade caution, check *(restrain)*, counsel, debar, deter, discourage, expostulate, forewarn, reason *(persuade)*, remonstrate. SEE MAIN ENTRY

dissuade from entering picket

dissuadere dissuade

dissuasion admonition, deterrence, deterrent, disincentive, persuasion, remonstrance, restraint

dissuasive adverse *(hostile)*, remonstrative

distance extent, ostracism, perspective, range, space, surpass

distant controlled *(restrained)*, disdainful, distinct *(distinguished from others)*, foreign, inaccessible, insusceptible *(uncaring)*, obscure *(remote)*, phlegmatic, remote *(not proximate)*, remote *(secluded)*, unapproachable

distant *(detached)*. SEE MAIN ENTRY

distant *(far)*. SEE MAIN ENTRY

distantly related consanguineous

distare apart

distaste dissatisfaction, odium, phobia, reluctance

distasteful bitter *(acrid tasting)*, deplorable, heinous, loathsome, objectionable, offensive *(offending)*, repugnant *(exciting aversion)*, repulsive, unacceptable, undesirable, unsavory, unseemly

distemper discompose, disease, disorder *(abnormal condition)*, disturb, pique

distend compound, enlarge, expand, extend *(enlarge)*, inflate, overextend

distended inflated *(enlarged)*

distension boom *(increase)*, inflation *(increase)*

distention extension *(expansion)*, growth *(increase)*, stress *(strain)*

distill extract. SEE MAIN ENTRY

distillation corpus

distinct apparent *(perceptible)*, categorical, certain *(particular)*, certain *(positive)*, certain *(specific)*, clear *(apparent)*, cognizable, coherent *(clear)*, concrete, conspicuous, definite, different, discrete, disjunctive *(tending to disjoin)*, disparate, distinctive, diverse, evident, exclusive *(singular)*, explicit, express, individual, insular, lucid, manifest, naked *(perceptible)*, nonconforming, obvious, open *(in sight)*, overt, palpable, particular *(individual)*, particular *(specific)*, peculiar *(distinctive)*, perceivable, perceptible, personal *(individual)*, precise, prominent, remarkable, salient, separate, singular, trenchant, unambiguous, unmistakable, visible *(in full view)*. SEE MAIN ENTRY

distinct indivisible entity individual

distinct intention deliberation

distinct meaning. SEE MAIN ENTRY

distinct purpose forethought, premeditation

distinct statement count

distincte fairly *(clearly)*

distinctio discrimination *(differentiation)*, distinction *(difference)*

distinction alternative *(option)*, character *(reputation)*, characteristic, color *(complexion)*, consequence *(significance)*, contradistinction, credit *(recognition)*, degree *(academic title)*, denomination, difference, differential, discretion *(power of choice)*, discretion *(quality of being discreet)*, discrimination *(differentiation)*, eminence, emphasis, feature *(characteristic)*, honor *(outward respect)*, identity *(individuality)*, importance, inequality, materiality *(consequence)*, merit, notoriety, nuance, personality, prestige, prize, property *(distinctive attribute)*, quality *(grade)*, regard *(esteem)*, reputation, restriction, severance, significance, speciality, specialty *(distinctive mark)*, specification, stress *(accent)*. SEE MAIN ENTRY

distinctive different, discriminating *(distinguishing)*, distinct *(distinguished from others)*, individual, meritorious, noteworthy, novel, outstanding *(prominent)*, particular *(individual)*, particular *(specific)*, prominent, remarkable, representative, several *(separate)*, special, specific, uncommon, unusual. SEE MAIN ENTRY

distinctive characteristic speciality

distinctive feature characteristic, differential, highlight, identity *(individuality)*, particularity, specialty *(distinctive mark)*, technicality

distinctive mark speciality

distinctive quality speciality

distinctive social attitude manner *(behavior)*

distinctive trait feature *(characteristic)*

distinctively fairly *(clearly)*

distinctiveness caliber *(quality)*, identity *(individuality)*, personality, speciality, specialty *(distinctive mark)*

distinctly fairly *(clearly)*, particularly

distinctly expressed explicit

distinctly indicated express

distinctly stated explicit, express

distinctness contradistinction, deviation, difference, emphasis, identity *(individuality)*, nonconformity, specialty *(distinctive mark)*

distinctus distinct *(clear)*, distinct *(distinguished from others)*

distinguere discriminate *(distinguish)*, distinguish

distinguish call *(title)*, characterize, circumscribe *(define)*, classify, contrast, demarcate, detect, diagnose, differentiate, discern *(discriminate)*, elevate, honor, identify, notice *(observe)*, perceive, pierce *(discern)*, recognize *(perceive)*, secern, spy. SEE MAIN ENTRY

distinguish between compare, contrast, select

distinguish by a mark label

distinguish by mark brand *(mark)*

distinguish by name denominate

distinguish by special selection elect *(choose)*

distinguishable appreciable, ascertainable, cognizable, conspicuous, determinable *(ascertainable)*, distinct *(clear)*, diverse, individual, naked *(perceptible)*, obvious, particular *(specific)*, peculiar *(distinctive)*, perceivable, perceptible, ponderable, several *(separate)*, unambiguous, unmistakable SEE MAIN ENTRY.

distinguishably fairly *(clearly)*

distinguished best, certain *(specific)*, conspicuous, discrete, disparate, elegant, famous, illustrious, important *(significant)*, influential, major, meritorious, nonconforming, notable, noteworthy, outstanding *(prominent)*, paramount, particular *(individual)*, particular *(specific)*, peculiar *(distinctive)*, preferential, prominent, remarkable, renowned, reputable, salient, special, stellar, superior *(excellent)*, unusual

distinguished by nature distinct *(distinguished from others)*

distinguished by station distinct *(distinguished from others)*

distinguished quality trait

distinguishing discovery, discreet, distinctive, personal *(individual)*

distinguishing characteristic distinction *(difference)*, identity *(individuality)*

distinguishing feature differential

distinguishing mark designation *(symbol)*, earmark

distinguishing quality distinction *(difference)*, identity *(individuality)*, property *(distinctive attribute)*

distinguishing trait characteristic, property *(distinctive attribute)*

distinguishment discrimination *(differentiation)*, recognition, segregation *(separation)*, severance

distorquere contort, distort

distort bear false witness, camouflage, cloak, contort, corrupt, deface, denature, disguise, fabricate *(make up)*, fake, falsify, invent *(falsify)*, misapprehend, misconstrue, misemploy, misguide, misinform, misinterpret, mislead, misread, misrepresent, misstate, misunderstand, mutilate, palter, prejudice *(influence)*, prevaricate, slant. SEE MAIN ENTRY

distort intentionally misrepresent

distort the meaning misconceive. SEE MAIN ENTRY

distort the truth feign

distorted defective, fallacious, false *(inaccurate)*, faulty, mendacious

distorted conception error

distorted idea misestimation

distorted impression misestimation

distortio distortion

distortion abuse *(corrupt practice)*, artifice, catachresis, color *(deceptive appearance)*, defacement, difference, error, evasion, exaggeration, fallacy, falsehood, falsification, irregularity, lie, misapplication, misrepresentation, misstatement, misusage,

overstatement, parody, propaganda, sophistry, story *(falsehood)*, travesty. SEE MAIN ENTRY

distortion of the truth perjury. SEE MAIN ENTRY

distortion of truth falsehood

distract bait *(harass)*, confuse *(bewilder)*, disorganize, disorient, disrupt, disturb, divert, interrupt, perturb

distracted oblivious, thoughtless

distraction confusion *(ambiguity)*, confusion *(turmoil)*, preoccupation, turmoil

distrahere perplex

distrain annex *(arrogate)*, assume *(seize)*, attach *(seize)*, compel, condemn *(seize)*, confiscate, deprive, divest, garnish, impound, levy, mulct *(fine)*, seize *(confiscate)*, sequester *(seize property)*. SEE MAIN ENTRY

distrained attached *(seized)*

distrainer attachment *(seizure)*

distraining confiscatory

distraint attachment *(seizure)*, condemnation *(seizure)*, disseisin, distress *(seizure)*, expropriation *(divestiture)*, foreclosure, garnishment, sequestration, taking. SEE MAIN ENTRY

distrait thoughtless

distraught deranged, non compos mentis

distress adversity, affront, aggravation *(annoyance)*, annoy, attach *(seize)*, attachment *(seizure)*, badger, bait *(harass)*, condemnation *(seizure)*, discommode, disseisin, distraint, disturb, embarrass, expropriation *(divestiture)*, foreclosure, garnishment, harass, harry *(harass)*, hector, inflict, mistreat, obsess, offend *(insult)*, pain, persecute, perturb, plague, plaint, poverty, privation, prostration, provoke, quagmire, sequestration, toll *(effect)*, trouble, upset. SEE MAIN ENTRY

distressed aggrieved *(harmed)*, destitute, disappointed, disconsolate, impecunious, poor *(underprivileged)*

distressful lamentable, painful

distressing bleak *(not favorable)*, cruel, deplorable, detrimental, disastrous, insufferable, irksome, lamentable, loathsome, oppressive, painful, pernicious, unsatisfactory

distribuere allot, apportion, dispense, distribute, divide *(distribute)*, parcel

distribute administer *(tender)*, allocate, allot, apportion, assign *(allot)*, bequeath, bestow, cast *(throw)*, circulate, classify, deploy, detail *(assign)*, diffuse, dispense, disperse *(disseminate)*, dispose *(apportion)*, disseminate, dole, expend *(disburse)*, file *(arrange)*, fix *(arrange)*, give *(grant)*, intersperse, issue *(publish)*, marshal, mete, parcel, partition, post, prorate, publish, sort, split, spread, subdivide, supply. SEE MAIN ENTRY

distribute again reapportion

distribute anew reapportion

distribute assets liquidate *(convert into cash)*

distribute proportionally prorate

distribute proportionately apportion

distributed pro rata

distributed by will testamentary

distributee legatee

distributer merchant

distributing center headquarters

distributing justice equitable

distribution administration, allotment, appointment *(act of designating)*, apportionment, appropriation *(allotment)*, assignment

(allotment), assignment *(transfer of ownership)*, budget, circulation, classification, consignment, decentralization, dispensation *(act of dispensing)*, disposition *(final arrangement)*, disposition *(transfer of property)*, division *(act of dividing)*, form *(arrangement)*, hierarchy *(arrangement in a series)*, order *(arrangement)*, proportion, ration. SEE MAIN ENTRY

distribution by lot allotment

distribution of earnings dividend

distribution of profits dividend

distributional proportionate

distributor merchant

distributor of largess donor

district bailiwick, circuit, constituency, department, division *(administrative unit)*, local, locality, location, parcel, province, region, regional, territory. SEE MAIN ENTRY

district attorney prosecutor. SEE MAIN ENTRY

district officer caretaker *(one fulfilling the function of office)*

distrust apprehension *(fear)*, cloud *(suspicion)*, disbelieve, discount *(disbelieve)*, discredit, doubt *(suspicion)*, incredulity, misdoubt, misgiving, mistrust, qualm, rejection, suspicion *(mistrust)*

distrusted unbelievable

distrustful cynical, doubtful, inconvincible, incredulous, jealous, leery, pessimistic, resentful, skeptical

distrustfulness cloud *(suspicion)*, doubt *(suspicion)*, incredulity

distrusting skeptical

distrusting the motives of others cynical

disturb affront, aggravate *(annoy)*, agitate *(perturb)*, annoy, badger, bait *(harass)*, confuse *(create disorder)*, discommode, discompose, disconcert, discontinue *(break continuity)*, dislocate, dislodge, disorganize, disorient, displace *(remove)*, disrupt, distress, embarrass, evict, harass, harrow, harry *(harass)*, hector, impair, inconvenience, interfere, interrupt, irritate, menace, mistreat, molest *(annoy)*, muddle, obfuscate, offend *(insult)*, perplex, persecute, perturb, pique, plague, remove *(eliminate)*, upset. SEE MAIN ENTRY

disturb keenly badger

disturb the composure of discompose

disturbance affray, altercation, belligerency, bluster *(commotion)*, brawl, cataclysm, commotion, confusion *(turmoil)*, consternation, detriment, disorder *(lack of order)*, dispute, embarrassment, embroilment, fracas, fray, furor, imbroglio, insurrection, molestation, nuisance, outbreak, outburst, outcry, pandemonium, panic, phobia, riot, trouble, turmoil, violation. SEE MAIN ENTRY

disturbed disorderly, unsettled, unsound *(not strong)*

disturbing detrimental, formidable, ominous, painful, sinister, unsatisfactory, unsuitable, vexatious

disunion anarchy, argument *(contention)*, conflict, contravention, controversy *(argument)*, disaccord, disagreement, disassociation, discord, dissension, dissidence, division *(act of dividing)*, divorce, estrangement, hiatus, incompatibility *(difference)*, interruption, schism, segregation *(separation)*, separation, split

disunite abstract *(separate)*, alienate *(estrange)*, bicker, break *(separate)*, demarcate, detach, dichotomize, disaccord, disaffect, disband, discontinue *(abandon)*, discontinue (break continuity), disengage, disintegrate, disjoint, dislocate, disperse (scatter), dissociate, dissolve (separate), divide (separate), divorce, estrange, interrupt, isolate, luxate, part (separate), rend, separate, sever, split

disunited apart, bipartite, disconnected, discrete, disjunctive (tending to disjoin), dissenting, separate, unbound

disuniting division (act of dividing)

disunity argument (contention), conflict, contravention, controversy (argument), disaccord, disagreement, discord, disparity, dispute, dissension, dissent (nonconcurrence), dissidence, division (act of dividing), estrangement, incompatibility (difference), variance (disagreement)

disusage abolition, desuetude, disuse, nonuse

disuse abandon (relinquish), abolition, cancellation, desuetude, discontinuance (act of discontinuing), dissolution (termination), leave (allow to remain), nonuse, set aside (annul). SEE MAIN ENTRY

disused barren, obsolete, otiose, outdated, outmoded, unemployed

disvaluation contempt (disdain), criticism, ignominy

disvalue denounce (condemn), deprecate, discommend, lessen

dithyrambic ecstatic

ditto copy, duplicate, reflect (mirror), resemblance, tantamount

diurna record

diurnal daily

diuturnity period

divagate digress

divagation deviation, digression, indirection (indirect action)

divaricate bifurcate, bipartite, break (separate), conflict, deviate, dichotomize, digress, disaccord, disagree, disjoint, spread

divaricate from differ (vary)

divaricating disparate, divergent

divarication dichotomy, digression, disassociation, split

divendere sell

diverge bifurcate, change, depart, deploy, detour, deviate, dichotomize, digress, disaccord, disagree, dissipate (spread out), vary

diverge from conflict, differ (vary)

divergence antithesis, circulation, conflict, contention (opposition), contradiction, contradistinction, controversy (argument), deviation, difference, digression, disaccord, disassociation, discrepancy, disparity, dispute, dissension, dissent (difference of opinion), dissidence, incompatibility (difference), incompatibility (inconsistency), inconsistency, inequality, innovation, irregularity, nonconformity, quirk (idiosyncrasy), split, variance (disagreement), variance (exemption)

divergent anomalous, deviant, different, disconnected, discordant, disordered, disparate, disproportionate, dissenting, dissident, dissimilar, distinct (distinguished from others), diverse, eccentric, inapplicable, inappropriate, incongruous, inconsistent, irregular (not usual), multiple, peculiar (distinctive), separate, unorthodox, unsuitable. SEE MAIN ENTRY

divergent opinion contradiction

divergent opinions conflict, controversy (argument), disagreement, discord, dispute, dissension

diverging divergent, divisive

divers dissimilar, diverse, manifold

diverse atypical, different, discordant, disordered, dissimilar, distinct (distinguished from others), divergent, heterogeneous, manifold, miscellaneous, multifarious, multiple, promiscuous, separate, several (plural), unrelated. SEE MAIN ENTRY

diverseness deviation, difference, distinction (difference), diversity, nonconformity

diversification innovation. SEE MAIN ENTRY

diversified composite, dissimilar, divergent, diverse, heterogeneous, manifold, miscellaneous, multifarious, multifold, multiple, nonconforming

diversiform different, diverse, heterogeneous, miscellaneous, multifold

diversify convert (change use), differ (vary), differentiate, vary

diversion decoy, detour, deviation, digression, enjoyment (pleasure), misappropriation, misusage, treat

diversitas difference, diversity

diversity difference, discord, disparity, inconsistency, inequality, nonconformity, variance (disagreement). SEE MAIN ENTRY

diversity of opinion disaccord, disagreement, dissension, dissent (difference of opinion)

diversus apart, contradictory, different, diverse, heterogeneous, miscellaneous, repugnant (exciting aversion)

divert alleviate, avert, cloak, deter, detour, digress, discourage, entice, hold up (rob), misemploy, peculate, pervert, repel (drive back). SEE MAIN ENTRY

divert by appeal dissuade, expostulate

divert by persuasion expostulate

divert from deter, dissuade

divert from its course detour, deviate

divert from original use estrange

divert from the original possessor estrange

divert funds defalcate

divert one's attention interest

divert to one's own use embezzle

diverting jocular

divest adeem, confiscate, demote, denude, depose (remove), deprive, despoil, diminish, disinherit, disown (refuse to acknowledge), dispossess, distrain, eject (evict), excise (cut away), expose, levy, plunder, remove (dismiss from office), remove (eliminate), unveil. SEE MAIN ENTRY

divest of abridge (divest)

divest of legal office disbar

divest of office dislodge, oust

divest of property condemn (seize)

divest of right disqualify

divest of suspicion disarm (set at ease)

divest oneself forswear

divest oneself of abandon (relinquish), disclaim, resign

divesting confiscatory

divestiture abridgment (disentitlement), garnishment

divestiture of property forfeiture (act of forfeiting)

divestment appropriation (taking), attachment (seizure), condemnation (seizure), curtailment, denial, disseisin, distraint, distress (seizure), eviction, expropriation (divestiture), foreclosure, forfeiture (act of forfeiting), privation, removal, sequestration, taking

dividable divisible

divide alienate (estrange), allocate, allot,

apportion, classify, codify, cross (intersect), demarcate, detach, dichotomize, disaccord, disaffect, disagree, disburse (distribute), discontinue (break continuity), discriminate (distinguish), disjoint, disperse (disseminate), disperse (scatter), dissociate, dissolve (separate), distinguish, distribute, dole, estrange, fix (arrange), hedge, interrupt, lancinate, mete, parcel, part (separate), partition, pigeonhole, prorate, rend, separate, sever, sort, split, subdivide. SEE MAIN ENTRY

divide according to rule apportion

divide and bestow in shares allocate

divide in portions assign (allot), dispense

divide into distinct portions partition

divide into parcels subdivide

divide into portions partition

divide into shares apportion, parcel, partition

divide into two bifurcate

divide on differ (disagree), dispute (debate)

divide proportionally prorate

divide proportionately apportion, partition

divide up apportion, partition, subdivide

divided bicameral, bipartite, broken (fractured), broken (interrupted), discrete, disjunctive (tending to disjoin), dissident, hostile, partial (part), partial (relating to a part), polemic, separate

divided on dissenting

dividend bonus, commission (fee), coupon, installment, interest (profit), profit. SEE MAIN ENTRY

dividends revenue

dividere distribute, divide (distribute), divide (separate), parcel, part (separate), sever

dividing disbursement (act of disbursing), divisive

dividing line edge (border)

dividing point crossroad (turning point)

dividual divisible, severable

dividuus severable

divinare guess

divination deduction (conclusion), premonition, recognition

divinatory ominous, oracular, portentous (ominous), prophetic

divine anticipate (prognosticate), assume (suppose), construe (comprehend), deduce, deduct (conclude by reasoning), detect, discover, expect (consider probable), find (discover), guess, portend, predict, presage, presume, presuppose, prognosticate, sacrosanct, surmise, suspect (think)

divinus prophetic

divisible divisive, partial (part), partial (relating to a part), separable, severable. SEE MAIN ENTRY

divisio division (act of dividing)

division affiliate, alienation (estrangement), apportionment, argument (contention), article (distinct section of a writing), assignment (allotment), bureau, capacity (sphere), chamber (compartment), chapter (branch), class, classification, component, conflict, constituency, constituent (part), decentralization, denomination, de-partment, detail, dichotomy, disaccord, disassociation, discord, discrimination (differentiation), dispensation (act of dispensing), dissension, distribution (apportionment), equity (share of ownership), estrangement, faction, incompatibility *(difference)*, installment, kind, manner *(kind)*, member *(constituent part)*, moiety, offshoot, organ, part *(place)*, part *(portion)*, plot *(land)*, province, ration, region, rubric *(title)*, schism, segment, segregation *(separation)*, separation, severance, split, subdivision, subheading, territory, unit *(department)*, variance *(disagreement)*. SEE MAIN ENTRY

division by races segregation *(isolation by races)*

division in proportion apportionment

division line boundary, mete

division lines confines

divisional local, provincial, regional, specific

divisive SEE MAIN ENTRY

divisiveness argument *(contention)*, contravention, discord

divorce depart, detach, disassociation, disband, disengage, disjoint, disown *(refuse to acknowledge)*, dissociate, dissolve *(separate)*, divide *(separate)*, division *(act of dividing)*, estrangement, separation, sever, severance, split. SEE MAIN ENTRY

divorce oneself from renounce

divorced disconnected, disjunctive *(tending to disjoin)*, distinct *(distinguished from others)*, separate

divorcement disassociation, estrangement, separation

divortium divorce

divulgare circulate, circulation, publish, spread

divulgate bare, circulate, confide *(divulge)*, convey *(communicate)*, divulge, report *(disclose)*, reveal

divulgation disclosure *(act of disclosing)*, notification, publicity. SEE MAIN ENTRY

divulge adduce, admit *(concede)*, apprise, bare, bear *(adduce)*, betray *(disclose)*, circulate, communicate, confess, convey *(communicate)*, declare, denounce *(inform against)*, disabuse, disclose, display, enlighten, expose, find *(discover)*, inform *(betray)*, inform *(notify)*, issue *(publish)*, manifest, mention, notice *(give formal warning)*, notify, proclaim, produce *(offer to view)*, profess *(avow)*, promulgate, publish, recite, recount, relate *(tell)*, report *(disclose)*, reveal, signify *(inform)*, speak, spread, unveil, utter. SEE MAIN ENTRY

divulged alleged, public *(known)*

divulgement communication *(statement)*, confession, disclosure *(act of disclosing)*, divulgation, publicity

divulgence admission *(disclosure)*, confession, disclosure *(act of disclosing)*, disclosure *(something disclosed)*, discovery, divulgation, manifestation, publicity

divulger informant, informer *(a person who provides information)*

divulsion avulsion, split

dizen embellish

DNA. SEE MAIN ENTRY

do conduct, discharge *(perform)*, execute *(accomplish)*, fulfill, generate, implement, operate, perform *(execute)*, perpetrate, realize *(make real)*

do a favor for accommodate

do a job labor

do a service assist, help, serve *(assist)*

do a service for accommodate

do again reproduce

do all one can endeavor, strive

do an injustice to exploit *(take advantage of)*, ill use, mistreat, persecute

do away with delete, destroy *(efface)*, dispatch *(put to death)*, dispel, dispense,

eliminate *(eradicate)*, eliminate *(exclude)*, eradicate, expunge, extinguish, extirpate, override, rescind, vacate *(void)*

do away with completely eradicate

do battle with grapple

do business deal, handle *(trade)*, trade, transact

do business with deal, patronize *(trade with)*

do disservice to damage

do duty exercise *(discharge a function)*, officiate

do evil harm, ill use

do harm persecute

do harm to ill use

do honor dedicate

do honor to defer *(yield in judgment)*

do like copy

do likewise mock *(imitate)*

do mischief harm, persecute

do nothing procrastinate

do of one's own accord choose

do one's best attempt, endeavor, strive

do one's bidding serve *(assist)*

do one's utmost endeavor, strive

do over emend, repeat *(do again)*, transform

do penance redeem *(satisfy debts)*, repent

do repairs fix *(repair)*

do repeatedly practice *(train by repetition)*

do research study

do scant justice to underestimate

do service avail *(be of use)*, pander

do subtraction diminish

do the deed dispatch *(dispose of)*

do the needful attempt

do the will of obey, observe *(obey)*

do thoroughly consummate

do violence harm, ill use, persecute

do violence to damage, mistreat, violate

do well pass *(satisfy requirements)*, succeed *(attain)*

do without dispense, eschew, forbear, forgo, forswear, refrain, relinquish

do work labor

do work with ply

do wrong ill use, lapse *(fall into error)*, mistreat

do wrong to persecute

doable potential, practicable, viable

docere edify, inform *(notify)*, instruct *(teach)*

docile facile, malleable, obedient, obsequious, passive, patient, pliable, pliant, sequacious, suasible, tractable, yielding

docilis tractable

docility amenability, capitulation, resignation *(passive acceptance)*

dock diminish, lessen

docket agenda, book, calendar *(list of cases)*, calendar *(record of yearly periods)*, empanel, enroll, file, file *(place among official records)*, label *(noun)*, label *(verb)*, note *(record)*, pigeonhole, program *(noun)*, program *(verb)*, record *(noun)*, record *(verb)*, register, roll, schedule, set down, tabulate. SEE MAIN ENTRY

docket incorrectly mislabel

doctor cure, denature, falsify, meliorate, palter, revise, slant

doctor assisted suicide SEE MAIN ENTRY

doctor up restore *(renew)*

doctrina instruction *(teaching)*, knowledge *(learning)*, theoretical, theory

doctrinaire bigot, dogmatic, theoretical

doctrinaire opinion dogma

doctrinal disciplinary *(educational)*, dogmatic, informatory, orthodox

doctrinal statement belief *(something believed)*

doctrine belief *(something believed)*, codification, concept, conviction *(persuasion)*, discipline *(field of study)*, dogma, idea, platform, policy *(plan of action)*, precept, prescription *(directive)*, principle *(axiom)*, rule *(legal dictate)*, theory, thesis. SEE MAIN ENTRY

doctrines of lawmaking jurisprudence

doctus learned

document bear *(adduce)*, blank *(form)*, certify *(attest)*, cite *(state)*, confirm, corroborate, deed, dossier, establish *(show)*, evidence, file *(place among official records)*, index *(relate)*, itemize, note *(record)*, quote, record, roll, sustain *(confirm)*, verify *(confirm)*, will *(testamentary instrument)*. SEE MAIN ENTRY

document granting permission permit

document produced as evidence exhibit

document which passes a present interest deed

documentable deductible *(provable)*

documental documentary

documentary convincing, informatory. SEE MAIN ENTRY

documentary evidence certification *(attested copy)*

documentation certification *(attested copy)*, certification *(certification of proficiency)*, confirmation, corroboration, deposition, dossier, evidence, jurat, proof, record, reference *(citation)*, support *(corroboration)*. SEE MAIN ENTRY

documented authentic, convincing, documentary

documented event fact

documents credentials, data, evidence. SEE MAIN ENTRY

documentum example, sample, specimen

dodge abscond, avoid *(evade)*, avoidance *(evasion)*, contrivance, deception, default, elude, equivocate, evade *(deceive)*, evade *(elude)*, evasion, hedge, ignore, imposture, machination, maneuver *(trick)*, omit, palter, parry, pettifog, prevaricate, reject, ruse, shirk, shun, stratagem, subterfuge, tergiversate

dodgery artifice, pettifoggery

dodging disingenuous

doff denude

dogged diligent, faithful *(diligent)*, inexorable, inflexible, intractable, obdurate, patient, persistent, pertinacious, purposeful, resolute, sedulous, serious *(devoted)*

doggedness diligence *(perseverance)*, prowess *(bravery)*, purpose, tenacity

dogma article *(precept)*, belief *(something believed)*, conviction *(persuasion)*, doctrine. SEE MAIN ENTRY

dogma dogma

dogma idea, precept, principle *(axiom)*, rule *(legal dictate)*, theory, thesis

dogmatic arbitrary and capricious, assertive, categorical, dictatorial, fanatical, illiberal, insistent, narrow, obdurate, parochial, provincial. SEE MAIN ENTRY

dogmatic theorist bigot

dogmatical obdurate

dogmatist bigot, pedant

dogmatizer bigot

doing act *(undertaking)*, action *(performance)*, commission *(act)*

doing away with dispatch *(act of putting to death)*

doing good   benevolent

doing nothing   unemployed

doings   dealings, overt act

dole   allot, allotment, bestow, disperse (*disseminate*), distribute, distribution (*apportionment*), divide (*distribute*), fund, gratuity (*present*), largess (*gift*), loan, prorate, ration, share (*interest*), split. SEE MAIN ENTRY

dole out   administer (*tender*), allocate, apportion, assign (*allot*), contribute (*supply*), disburse (*distribute*), dispense, disperse (*disseminate*), dispose (*apportion*), divide (*distribute*), mete, parcel, partition, present (*make a gift*), reapportion

dole out again   redistribute

doleful   deplorable, disconsolate, lamentable, lugubrious

dolefulness   depression, pessimism

doling out   apportionment

dollar currency   cash

dolmen   monument

dolor   pain

dolorous   deplorable, despondent, disconsolate, grave (*solemn*), lugubrious

dolosus   fraudulent, insidious

doltish   obtuse, opaque, uncouth

doltishness   opacity

dolus   deceit, machination, maneuver (*trick*), ruse, sham, stratagem

domain   ambit, area (*province*), bailiwick, capacity (*sphere*), circuit, coverage (*scope*), demesne, department, district, dominion (*absolute ownership*), freehold, holding (*property owned*), jurisdiction, locality, possessions, property (*land*), province, real estate, realm, region, sphere, territory, title (*right*). SEE MAIN ENTRY

domare   subdue

domestic   internal, local, national, native (*domestic*), residential. SEE MAIN ENTRY

domestic circle   family (*household*), household

domestic domicile   household

domestic establishment   family (*household*), household

domesticate   inure (*accustom*)

domestication   cohabitation (*married state*)

domesticus   household (*domestic*), internal

domicile   abode, address, building (*structure*), dwell (*reside*), dwelling, habitation (*dwelling place*), house, inhabit, inhabitation (*place of dwelling*), lodge (*house*), lodge (*reside*), lodging, reside, residence. SEE MAIN ENTRY

domiciled   household (*domestic*)

domiciles   premises (*buildings*)

domiciliary   domestic (*household*), habitant, household (*domestic*), residential. SEE MAIN ENTRY

domiciliate   dwell (*reside*), reside

domiciliated   household (*domestic*)

domiciliation   residence

domicilium   domicile, dwell (*reside*), dwelling, habitation (*dwelling place*), home (*domicile*), house, inhabitation (*place of dwelling*), residence, seat

dominance   advantage, authority (*power*), control (*supervision*), dominion (*supreme authority*), duress, hegemony, influence, patronage (*power to appoint jobs*), power, predominance, preponderance, puissance. SEE MAIN ENTRY

dominancy   clout, dominance, dominion (*supreme authority*)

dominant   cardinal (*outstanding*), causative, central (*essential*), compelling, considerable, forcible, influential, leading (*ranking first*), master, omnipotent, potent, powerful, predominant, prevailing (*current*), prevailing (*having superior force*), prevalent, primary, prime (*most valuable*), principal, rampant, rife, salient, sovereign (*absolute*), stellar. SEE MAIN ENTRY

dominant characteristic   specialty (*distinctive mark*)

dominant quality   character (*personal quality*)

dominant strength   main force

dominant theme   motif

dominate   coerce, constrain (*compel*), control (*regulate*), direct (*supervise*), discipline (*control*), govern, handle (*manage*), hold (*possess*), manage, manipulate (*control unfairly*), monopolize, obsess, occupy (*take possession*), outbalance, outweigh, overcome (*surmount*), override, oversee, own, predominate (*command*), prevail (*be in force*), prevail (*triumph*), subdue, subject, subjugate, surmount. SEE MAIN ENTRY

dominating   leading (*ranking first*), omnipotent, powerful, predominant, prevailing (*having superior force*), salient

dominating action   obsession

dominatio   supremacy

domination   authority (*power*), compulsion (*coercion*), control (*supervision*), dominance, dominion (*supreme authority*), force (*strength*), hegemony, influence, jurisdiction, monopoly, occupation (*possession*), oppression, patronage (*power to appoint jobs*), possession (*ownership*), power, predominance, preponderance, primacy, supremacy. SEE MAIN ENTRY

domineer   browbeat, dominate, impose (*subject*), prevail (*be in force*), repress, rule (*govern*)

domineering   brutal, dictatorial, dogmatic, influential, peremptory (*imperative*), presumptuous, severe, supercilious, tyrannous

dominion   agency (*legal relationship*), ambit, bailiwick, circuit, clout, control (*supervision*), coverage (*scope*), demesne, domain (*sphere of influence*), dominance, force (*strength*), government (*administration*), hegemony, influence, interest (*ownership*), jurisdiction, occupancy, occupation (*possession*), ownership, possession (*ownership*), power, predominance, primacy, province, realm, regime, supremacy, territory. SEE MAIN ENTRY

dominions   possessions, property (*land*)

dominium   ownership

dominus   proprietor

domus   abode, building (*structure*), domicile, dwelling, habitation (*dwelling place*), home (*domicile*), house, household, premises (*buildings*), residence

don   assume (*simulate*), pedagogue

donare   impart, present (*make a gift*)

donate   bequeath, bestow, cede, contribute (*supply*), convey (*transfer*), dedicate, dispense, endow, endue, fund, give (*grant*), leave (*give*), present (*make a gift*), proffer, provide (*supply*), spend

donate to   subscribe (*promise*)

donated   gratuitous (*given without recompense*)

donation   benefit (*conferment*), bonus, cession, charity, endowment, gift (*present*), grant, largess (*gift*), perquisite, provision

(*act of supplying*), reward, tip (*gratuity*). SEE MAIN ENTRY

donative   gift (*present*), gratuity (*present*), largess (*gift*), tip (*gratuity*). SEE MAIN ENTRY

donator   contributor (*giver*), donor, grantor

done   complete (*ended*), through

done again   repeated

done at pleasure   arbitrary

done by force   forcible

done by one person   ex parte

done by stealth   surreptitious

done for effect   flagrant

done on purpose   deliberate

done over   repeated

done quickly   expeditious

done reciprocally   mutual (*reciprocal*)

done with   through

done with expedition   expeditious

done with intent to commit crime   felonious

done with skill   artful

done with thoroughness   elaborate

done without delay   summary

done without reason   random

donee   assignee, beneficiary, devisee, feoffee, grantee, heir, legatee, licensee, payee, recipient, transferee. SEE MAIN ENTRY

donee of a corporeal hereditament   feoffee

donor   benefactor, contributor (*giver*), feoffor, good samaritan, maker, transferor. SEE MAIN ENTRY

donum   donation, gift (*present*), grant

doom   condemn (*punish*), convict, predetermine, sentence, tragedy

doomed   unproductive

doomful   portentous (*ominous*)

door   entrance, outlet, portal, threshold (*entrance*)

doorway   egress, portal

dope   narcotic

doppelganger   counterpart (*complement*)

dormancy   abeyance, cessation (*interlude*), desuetude, inaction, inertia

dormant   dead, inactive, insensible, lifeless (*dull*), otiose, passive, potential, stagnant, static, torpid. SEE MAIN ENTRY

dormant energy   potential

dormitory   dwelling, home (*domicile*), lodging

dos   dower

dose   drug

dossier   blank (*form*), file, record. SEE MAIN ENTRY

dotage   caducity, incapacity

dotation   charity, donation, dower, largess (*gift*), legacy

doted on   popular

double   alter ego, copy, correlate, counterpart (*parallel*), duplicate, reflection (*image*), reproduce, resemblance, same, substitute

double back   return (*go back*)

double dealing   deceptive

double for   displace (*replace*), impersonate, pose (*impersonate*)

double jeopardy   SEE MAIN ENTRY

double prosecution   double jeopardy

double punishment   double jeopardy

double talk   jargon (*unintelligible language*)

double-cross   betray (*disclose*), mislead

double-crossing   machiavellian, perfidious

double-dealing   bad faith, bunko, collusion, deceit, deception, dishonest, duplicity, faithless, false (*disloyal*), fraud, fraudulent, hypocrisy, infidelity, knavery, lying, machiavellian, perfidious, recreant, sly, undependable, untrustworthy

double-edged bitter *(penetrating)*

double-tongued false *(disloyal)*, machiavellian

doubling boom *(increase)*

doubt cloud *(suspicion)*, confusion *(ambiguity)*, disbelieve, discount *(disbelieve)*, dispute *(contest)*, hesitate, hesitation, improbability, incertitude, incredulity, indecision, misdoubt, misgiving, mistrust, qualm, quandary, reluctance, scruple, suspect *(distrust)*, suspicion *(mistrust)*. SEE MAIN ENTRY

doubt the truth of impugn

doubtable debatable, disputable, doubtful, dubitative, impalpable, implausible, ludicrous

doubtful ambiguous, controversial, cynical, debatable, disputable, dubious, dubitative, equivocal, hesitant, implausible, inconclusive, inconvincible, incredible, incredulous, indefinite, irresolute, leery, moot, precarious, problematic, speculative, suspicious *(questionable)*, unbelievable, uncertain *(questionable)*, undecided, unsettled, unsustainable, vague. SEE MAIN ENTRY

doubtful event contingency

doubtful meaning ambiguity

doubtful narrative myth

doubtfulness ambiguity, confusion *(ambiguity)*, doubt *(suspicion)*, improbability, incertitude, incredulity, indecision, misgiving, qualm, quandary, scruple, suspicion *(mistrust)*, suspicion *(uncertainty)*

doubting cynical, disputable, doubtful, hesitant, inconvincible, incredulous, irresolute, jealous, leery, skeptical, suspicious *(distrustful)*, undecided. SEE MAIN ENTRY

doubtless axiomatic, categorical, certain *(positive)*, clear *(certain)*, definite, demonstrable, indubious, uncontroverted, undisputed, unrefutable

doubtlessly a priori, admittedly, fairly *(clearly)*

douceur grant

doughtiness prowess *(bravery)*

doughty heroic, indomitable, spartan, undaunted

dour astringent, bleak *(severely simple)*, rigid, severe

douse immerse *(plunge into)*

dovetail correspond *(be equivalent)*

dower SEE MAIN ENTRY

down *(dejected)*. SEE MAIN ENTRY

down *(lowest point)*. SEE MAIN ENTRY

down payment deposit, handsel, installment. SEE MAIN ENTRY

down to until

downcast despondent, disconsolate, lugubrious, pessimistic

downcastness pessimism

downfall catastrophe, debacle, decline, defeat, disaster, failure *(lack of success)*, fatality, miscarriage, prostration. SEE MAIN ENTRY

downgrade debase, decline, deduct *(reduce)*, demote, deteriorate, discredit, disgrace, disparage, humiliate, reduce. SEE MAIN ENTRY

downhearted disconsolate, pessimistic

downheartedness damper *(depressant)*, pessimism

downhill decline

downright absolute *(complete)*, clear *(apparent)*, honest, ingenuous, outright, purely *(positively)*, simple, stark, thorough,

total, unaffected *(sincere)*, unequivocal, unmitigated, unqualified *(unlimited)*

downrush descent *(declination)*

downthrow prostration

downtrend decline, decrease

downtrodden servile

downturn decline, decrease

downward inclination decline

downward incline decline

downward trend decline, decrease

dowry endowment

doxology laudation. SEE MAIN ENTRY

doxy dogma

drab ordinary, pedestrian

drabble sully

draconian harsh, stringent. SEE MAIN ENTRY

draft bill *(proposed act)*, blueprint, check *(instrument)*, coerce, compose, conceive *(invent)*, contrive, delineate, design *(construction plan)*, direction *(course)*, enroll, formulate, frame *(construct)*, frame *(formulate)*, instrument *(document)*, invent *(produce for the first time)*, make, nominate, note *(written promise to pay)*, originate, pattern, plan, program *(noun)*, program *(verb)*, proposal *(suggestion)*, recruit, require *(compel)*, select. SEE MAIN ENTRY

draft a brief. SEE MAIN ENTRY

rdraft a document. SEE MAIN ENTRY

draft a will. SEE MAIN ENTRY

draft holder bearer

drafter author *(writer)*

draftsman architect

drag impede

drag away carry away

drag on persist

drag out continue *(prolong)*, prolong, protract *(prolong)*

dragged out protracted

dragonnade onset *(assault)*

dragoon bait *(harass)*, coerce, persecute

drain consume, decrease, decrement, deplete, diminish, dissipate *(expend foolishly)*, exhaust *(deplete)*, expense *(sacrifice)*, exude, outflow, outpour, remove *(eliminate)*, spend, tax *(overwork)*

drain of resources deplete

drain on resources expense *(cost)*, expense *(sacrifice)*, maintenance *(upkeep)*, overhead

drainage outflow

drained insufficient, nonsubstantial *(not sufficient)*, poor *(underprivileged)*, vacuous

dramatic histrionic, moving *(evoking emotion)*, potent

dramatic art histrionics

dramatic representation histrionics

dramatic rights SEE MAIN ENTRY

dramatically opposed. SEE MAIN ENTRY

dramatize produce *(offer to view)*, recite

dramaturgy histrionics

drape clothe

drastic extreme *(exaggerated)*, forcible, harsh, outrageous, severe. SEE MAIN ENTRY

draw bait *(lure)*, bet, characterize, choose, copy, deadlock, delineate, depict, detail *(particularize)*, educe, exhaust *(deplete)*, extract, gain, inveigle, lottery, motivate, portray, reap, receive *(acquire)*, trace *(delineate)*. SEE MAIN ENTRY

draw a comparison contrast

draw a conclusion ascertain, deduce, deduct *(conclude by reasoning)*, derive *(deduce)*, determine, find *(determine)*, infer, judge, read, rule *(decide)*

draw a distinction distinguish

draw a parallel compare, connect *(relate)*, correspond *(be equivalent)*, relate *(establish a connection)*

draw a picture delineate

draw an inference construe *(comprehend)*, derive *(deduce)*, gauge, infer, presuppose

draw apart estrange

draw as an implication construe *(comprehend)*

draw as by a lure entrap

draw aside divert

draw away divert

draw back retreat, shun. SEE MAIN ENTRY

draw by artful inducements entrap

draw forth disinter, distill, educe, elicit, evoke, extract

draw from derive *(receive)*, exact

draw gradually together converge

draw in converge, engage *(involve)*, entrap, implicate, incriminate, involve *(implicate)*

draw inferences generalize, reason *(conclude)*

draw lots bet

draw near accost, approach, approximate, border *(approach)*, gravitate, impend

draw off disengage

draw on exercise *(use)*, lure

draw one's sword brandish

draw out compose, continue *(prolong)*, disinter, distill, educe, elicit, evoke, exhaust *(deplete)*, extend *(enlarge)*, extract, prolong, withdraw

draw out by compulsion extort

draw out by force extort

draw out the essence distill

draw profit from profit

draw rein check *(restrain)*

draw the inference assume *(suppose)*

draw the line delimit, differentiate, discriminate *(distinguish)*. SEE MAIN ENTRY

draw the veil camouflage

draw to a close cease, complete, dissolve *(terminate)*, expire

draw together collect *(gather)*, compile, consolidate *(unite)*, constrict *(compress)*, convene, glean, hoard

draw toward gravitate

draw up compile, compose, devise *(invent)*, formulate, frame *(construct)*, frame *(formulate)*, make, produce *(manufacture)*

drawback burden, check *(bar)*, defect, disadvantage, encumbrance, fault *(weakness)*, handicap, hindrance, impediment, liability, obstacle, onus *(burden)*, scruple

drawee debtor, obligor

drawer payee

drawing attractive, design *(construction plan)*, lottery

drawing conclusions dialectic

drawing near forthcoming, immediate *(imminent)*, imminent

drawing out evulsion

drawing to a close determinable *(liable to be terminated)*

drawn undecided

drawn battle deadlock

drawn game deadlock

drawn out chronic, protracted

drayage carriage

dread consternation, fear *(noun)*, fear *(verb)*, fright, mistrust, panic, phobia, portentous *(ominous)*, stress *(strain)*, trepidation

dreaded dire, undesirable

dreadful adverse *(negative)*, bad *(inferior)*, deplorable, detrimental, dire, disastrous, disreputable, formidable, gross *(flagrant)*, heinous, hostile, insufferable, lamentable, loathsome, nefarious, portentous *(ominous)*, regrettable, repulsive, serious *(grave)*, sinister

dreadful event tragedy

dreadless undaunted

dream end *(intent)*, objective, phantom, reflect *(ponder)*

dream up conceive *(invent)*, conjure, invent *(produce for the first time)*

dreaminess preoccupation

dreaming pensive

dreamy delusive, oblivious, pensive, quixotic

drear bleak *(severely simple)*

drearisome jejune *(dull)*, lifeless *(dull)*, pedestrian, ponderous, prolix

dreary bleak *(severely simple)*, deplorable, despondent, insipid, jejune *(dull)*, lifeless *(dull)*, lugubrious, pedestrian, ponderous, portentous *(ominous)*

drench imbue, immerse *(plunge into)*, inundate, overload, permeate, pervade

dress clothe

dress as impersonate

dress down browbeat, denounce *(condemn)*, disapprove *(condemn)*, fault, reprehend, reprimand

dress to conceal disguise

dress up camouflage, cloak, disguise, embellish

dressing down diatribe, obloquy, reprimand, reproach

dried up otiose

drift conatus, connotation, content *(meaning)*, contents, detour, deviate, digress, digression, direction *(course)*, gist *(substance)*, import, main point, meaning, prowl, signification, substance *(essential nature)*, tenor

drifter derelict, itinerant

drifting discursive *(digressive)*, moving *(in motion)*, shifting

drill discipline *(training)*, educate, enter *(penetrate)*, practice *(train by repetition)*

drilling discipline *(training)*

drink carouse

drink to excess carouse

drinkable palatable

drip exude

drive activity, ardor, bind *(obligate)*, browbeat, campaign, causeway, coerce, compel, compulsion *(obsession)*, constrain *(compel)*, enforce, foray, force *(compulsion)*, impact, impetus, impose *(enforce)*, impulse, incite, inducement, industry *(activity)*, life *(vitality)*, manipulate *(utilize skillfully)*, obsess, operate, press *(constrain)*, press *(goad)*, pressure *(noun)*, pressure *(verb)*, project *(impel forward)*, provoke, purpose, require *(compel)*, send, stimulate, stimulus, urge

drive a bargain dicker, haggle, handle *(trade)*, trade

drive a trade deal, sell

drive against collide *(crash against)*

drive apart estrange

drive at attempt, intend, strive

drive away deport *(banish)*, dispel, parry, repel *(drive back)*, repulse, spurn, stave, supplant

drive away by scattering dispel

drive back parry, rebuff, repel *(drive back)*, repulse, spurn

drive firmly in impact

drive forward hasten, impel

drive from one's native land expatriate

drive in inject

drive into collide *(crash against)*, pierce *(lance)*

drive off in various directions dispel

drive on expedite

drive onward impel

drive out deport *(banish)*, depose *(remove)*, divest, expel, oust, supplant, transport

driveway causeway

driving compelling, important *(urgent)*, impulsive *(impelling)*, insistent

driving force determinant, incentive, motive

driving out deportation, expulsion

droit birthright, capacity *(authority)*, due, franchise *(license)*, interest *(ownership)*, prerogative, title *(right)*. SEE MAIN ENTRY

droning ponderous

dronish lifeless *(dull)*, obtuse

droop descent *(declination)*, languish, succumb

drooping languid, powerless

droopy powerless

drop abandon *(relinquish)*, cancel, cease, decline, decline *(fall)*, decrease *(noun)*, decrease *(verb)*, delete, demote, depose *(remove)*, depreciate, depress, descent *(declination)*, discharge *(dismiss)*, discontinue *(abandon)*, distill, ebb, exude, forswear, iota, languish, leave *(allow to remain)*, minimum, omit, precipitate *(throw down violently)*, quit *(discontinue)*, relinquish, renounce, set aside *(annul)*, stop, subside, succumb, terminate

drop a case. SEE MAIN ENTRY

drop a hint imply, remind

drop by drop piecemeal

drop charges remit *(release from penalty)*

drop in strength decline *(fall)*

drop off diminish, ebb, lessen

drop out leave *(depart)*, resign, retire *(conclude a career)*

drought paucity

drove assemblage, mass *(body of persons)*

drown immerse *(plunge into)*, overcome *(overwhelm)*, stifle

drown out extinguish

drowsiness languor

drowsy torpid

drub defeat, lash *(strike)*, overcome *(surmount)*

drubbing failure *(lack of success)*

drudge labor, palliative *(abating)*, strive

drudgery work *(effort)*

drug cannabis, narcotic. SEE MAIN ENTRY

drugged insensible

drum repeat *(state again)*

drum out of the legal profession disbar

drunk SEE MAIN ENTRY

drunkenness dipsomania, inebriation

dry jejune *(dull)*, languid, lifeless *(dull)*, pedestrian, prosaic, unproductive

dry run experiment

dry up deplete

dual bilateral

dual chambered bicameral

duality duplicity

dub denominate, phrase

dubiety ambiguity, ambivalence, confusion *(ambiguity)*, doubt *(suspicion)*, hesitation, incertitude, incredulity, indecision, misgiving, qualm, quandary, rejection, scruple, suspicion *(mistrust)*

dubiosity incertitude, quandary

dubious aleatory *(uncertain)*, ambiguous, controversial, cynical, debatable, disputable, doubtful, dubitative, equivocal, inconvincible, incredulous, indefinite, leery, moot, poor *(inferior in quality)*, precarious, problematic, skeptical, speculative, suspicious *(distrustful)*, suspicious *(questionable)*, unbelievable, uncertain *(questionable)*, undecided, unsettled, vague. SEE MAIN ENTRY

dubiousness ambiguity, confusion *(ambiguity)*, doubt *(suspicion)*, incertitude, incredulity, indecision, qualm, quandary, rejection, scruple, suspicion *(mistrust)*

dubitable controversial, debatable, disputable, doubtful, dubitative, impalpable, implausible, ludicrous

dubitancy ambivalence, incertitude, indecision

dubitare hesitate

dubitate doubt *(hesitate)*

dubitatio doubt *(indecision)*, hesitation, indecision, scruple

dubitation confusion *(ambiguity)*, doubt *(suspicion)*, hesitation, incertitude, indecision, quandary

dubitative debatable, disputable, dubious. SEE MAIN ENTRY

dubito doubt *(indecision)*

dubius critical *(crucial)*, doubtful, dubious, equivocal, indefinite, indeterminate, irresolute, precarious, problematic, undecided, vague

ducere regard *(pay attention)*

duck immerse *(plunge into)*, shirk

ductile flexible, malleable, obedient, pliable, pliant, sequacious, tractable

ductilis malleable

ductility amenability

ductus generalship, guidance

dudgeon estrangement, odium, resentment, umbrage

due birthright, charge *(cost)*, claim *(right)*, condign, delinquent *(overdue)*, droit, entitled, expense *(cost)*, forthcoming, just, liability, opportune, outstanding *(unpaid)*, overdue, payable, prerogative, price, receivable, reprisal, retribution, right *(entitlement)*, right *(righteousness)*, rightful, seasonable, suitable, unpaid, unsettled. SEE MAIN ENTRY

due date maturity

due order array *(order)*

due process SEE MAIN ENTRY

due punishment reprisal

due to contingent, dependent

due to be paid receivable

duel compete, fight *(battle)*

dueness droit, propriety *(appropriateness)*

dues charge *(cost)*, fee *(charge)*, tax

dulce domum building *(structure)*

dulcet nectareous, palatable, sapid

dulcification mollification

dulcify alleviate, lull, mollify, pacify, placate, soothe

dulcis palatable

dull allay, alleviate, bleak *(severely simple)*, diminish, drug, impair, inexpressive, insensible, insipid, languid, lessen, moderate *(temper)*, mollify, nondescript, obfuscate, obnubilate, obscure, obtund, obtuse, opaque, pedestrian, phlegmatic, ponderous, prosaic, repress, soothe, stagnant, stale, stifle, subdue, sully, tarnish, thoughtless, torpid, trite, vacuous

dull comment platitude

dull-witted non compos mentis, obtuse, opaque

dull-wittedness opacity
dulling narcotic
dullness indistinctness, inertia, languor, opacity, sloth
duly as a matter of right, ex officio. SEE MAIN ENTRY
dumb fatuous, mute, speechless, taciturn
dumb-struck speechless
dumbfound confound
dumbfounding prodigious (amazing)
dummy imitation, proxy
dump deposit (place)
dun charge (assess), claim (demand), exact, importune, request. SEE MAIN ENTRY
duncelike opaque
duncical opaque
dunk immerse (plunge into)
dupable naive
dupe bait (lure), betray (lead astray), bilk, cheat, cloak, deceive, defraud, delude, ensnare, entrap, fake, hoodwink, illude, mislead, misrepresent, overreach, palter, pettifog, pretend, prevaricate. SEE MAIN ENTRY
dupery bunko, deception, false pretense, falsification, fraud, hoax, knavery
duplexity duplicity
duplexity in meaning ambiguity
duplicate copy (noun), copy (verb), correlate, counterpart (parallel), expendable, facsimile, identical, mock (imitate), plagiarize, quote, reconstruct, recreate, reflection (image), reiterate, repeat (do again), replace, reproduce, same, superfluous, trace (delineate). SEE MAIN ENTRY
duplicated repeated
duplication boom (increase), copy, counterpart (parallel), identity (similarity), plagiarism, redundancy, resemblance, tautology
duplicative iterative, repetitious
duplicitous agreement conspiracy
duplicity artifice, bad faith, collusion, concealment, deceit, deception, dishonesty, false pretense, falsification, fraud, hoax, hypocrisy, imposture, improbity, indirection (deceitfulness), knavery, misstatement, pettifoggery, pretense (pretext), ruse, story (falsehood), subterfuge. SEE MAIN ENTRY
durability indestructibility, longevity, strength, survival, tolerance
durable constant, firm, immutable, indelible, indestructible, infrangible, noncancellable, permanent, persistent, resilient, solid (sound), stable, strong, unremitting. SEE MAIN ENTRY
durableness indestructibility, longevity
durables goods
durance bondage, captivity, commitment (confinement), custody (incarceration), restraint, thrall. SEE MAIN ENTRY
durance vile detention
durare continue (prolong), endure (last), last, remain (stay)
duration life (period of existence), longevity, period, phase (period), survival, tenure, time. SEE MAIN ENTRY
duration of existence age
duration of life lifetime
duress captivity, coercion, compulsion (coercion), constraint (restriction), force (compulsion), intimidate, main force, pressure, stress (strain), subjection. SEE MAIN ENTRY
during the interval ad interim. SEE MAIN ENTRY
during the journey en route
during the last moments of life in extremis

during travel en route
duritia rigor
durus callous, rigid, severe, unbending
dusk obscure
dusky indistinct, nebulous
duteous conscientious, faithful (loyal), loyal, meritorious, moral, obedient, obeisant, passive, true (loyal)
duteously faithfully
duteousness allegiance, fealty
dutiable ad valorem
dutiful conscientious, faithful (loyal), law-abiding, loyal, meritorious, moral, obedient, obeisant, passive, patient, punctilious, serious (devoted), true (loyal)
dutiful adherence fidelity
dutifully faithfully, respectfully
dutifulness adhesion (loyalty), allegiance, compliance, conformity (obedience), discipline (obedience), fidelity
dutiless broken (unfulfilled), derelict (negligent), irresponsible, remiss
dutilessness dereliction, infidelity, misdeed, misdoing, nonperformance
duty ad valorem, agency (legal relationship), assignment (task), burden, business (affair), business (occupation), charge (lien), commitment (responsibility), compulsion (coercion), employment, excise, fealty, function, imposition (tax), job, labor (work), levy, liability, loyalty, mission, office, position (business status), province, responsibility (accountability), right (righteousness), tariff (duties), tax, trade (occupation), trust (custody), weight (burden), work (employment). SEE MAIN ENTRY
duty owed obligation (duty)
duty to pay liability
duty to pay money obligation (liability)
duty unfulfilled delict
dux chief, marshal
dwarf lessen, minimize. SEE MAIN ENTRY
dwell lodge (reside), occupy (take possession), pause, remain (occupy), reside. SEE MAIN ENTRY
dwell in inhabit, occupy (take possession)
dwell on repeat (state again)
dwell permanently inhabit
dwell together cohabit
dwell upon brood, recall (remember), reflect (ponder)
dweller citizen, denizen, domiciliary, habitant, inhabitant, inmate, lodger, occupant, resident, tenant
dwellers population
dwelling abode, address, building (structure), domicile, habitation (act of inhabiting), habitation (dwelling place), home (domicile), house, inhabitation (act of dwelling in), inhabitation (place of dwelling), lodging, residence. SEE MAIN ENTRY
dwelling place abode, address, building (structure), home (domicile), house, inhabitation (place of dwelling), lodging
dwellings premises (buildings)
dwindle consume, decrease, deduct (reduce), depreciate, diminish, ebb, lessen, subside
dwindling attrition, decrease, deduction (diminution)
dye stain
dying death, expiration, in extremis
dynamic impulsive (impelling), intense, potent, powerful, progressive (going forward), trenchant
dynamic quality life (vitality)
dynamical impulsive (impelling)

dynamism industry (activity), life (vitality)
dynamite bomb
dynamite charge. SEE MAIN ENTRY
dynasty bloodline, descent (lineage), family (common ancestry), origin (ancestry)
dyspeptic bilious, bitter (penetrating). SEE MAIN ENTRY

E

each respectively. SEE MAIN ENTRY
each and every collective, in solido
each in turn respectively
each to each per capita, pro rata
eadem sentire sympathize
eager earnest, fervent, hot-blooded, inclined, industrious, prompt, prone, ready (willing), sedulous, serious (devoted), solicitous, vehement, willing (desirous), zealous. SEE MAIN ENTRY
eager for knowledge inquisitive
eager to please obeisant
eagerly readily
eagerness ardor, desire, emotion, greed, industry (activity), interest (concern), life (vitality), passion, penchant, purpose
eagerness to act quickly haste
earlier antecedent, back (in arrears), before mentioned, former, heretofore, last (preceding), precursory, preexisting, previous, prior, said, theretofore
earliest original (initial), primary, prime (original)
earliest stage embryo
early initial, instant, obsolete, old, preliminary, preparatory, previous, prime (original), prompt, punctual. SEE MAIN ENTRY
early stage nonage
earmark allocate, allot, brand, brand (mark), designate, designation (symbol), device (distinguishing mark), distinction (difference), index (catalog), label, property (distinctive attribute), quality (grade), reserve, specialty (distinctive mark). SEE MAIN ENTRY
earmarked prospective
earn attain, bear (yield), gain, obtain, pass (satisfy requirements), procure, realize (obtain as a profit), reap, receive (acquire), succeed (attain). see main entry
earn out SEE MAIN ENTRY
earned condign, due (owed), entitled
earned income earnings
earnest bail, binder, close (rigorous), eager, fervent, honest, industrious, intense, painstaking, pertinacious, pledge (security), purposeful, resolute, security (pledge), serious (devoted), solemn, true (loyal), urgent, vehement, willing (desirous), zealous. SEE MAIN ENTRY
earnest averment surety (certainty)
earnest avowal surety (certainty)
earnest declaration assurance, surety (certainty)
earnest entreaty prayer
earnest money handsel. SEE MAIN ENTRY
earnest payment pledge (security)
earnest pledge deposit
earnest request call (appeal), entreaty, petition, prayer
earnest seeking market (demand)
earnestly faithfully
earnestness adhesion (loyalty), compulsion (obsession), diligence (care), diligence (perseverance), goodwill, industry (activity), intention, resolution (decision), spirit

earnings annuity, boom (*prosperity*), commission (*fee*), compensation, honorarium, income, interest (*profit*), output, pay, payment (*remittance*), possessions, proceeds, profit, recompense, revenue, wage. SEE MAIN ENTRY

earshot range

earthly material (*physical*), mundane, physical

earthly possessions estate (*property*)

earthquake cataclysm

earthshaking momentous

earthy inelegant

earwitness bystander

ease alleviate, ameliorate, assuage, commute, disencumber, disentangle, expedite, facilitate, facility (*easiness*), favor, give (*yield*), help, informality, lessen, lull, mitigate, moderate (*temper*), modify (*moderate*), mollify, obtund, pacify, palliate (*abate*), prosperity, reassure, redress, relax, relieve (*give aid*), remedy, remit (*relax*), skill, solace, soothe. SEE MAIN ENTRY

ease of movement latitude

ease the burden alleviate, disencumber, ease

easeful palliative (*abating*), placid

easement advantage, droit, instigation, mollification, relief (*release*), solace. SEE MAIN ENTRY

easily readily

easily (*by far*). SEE MAIN ENTRY

easily (*without trouble*). SEE MAIN ENTRY

easily accessible convenient

easily affected perceptive, susceptible (*responsive*)

easily bent flexible, malleable, pliable, pliant

easily convinced credulous, suasible

easily deceived credulous, unsuspecting

easily done convenient, facile

easily duped credulous

easily excited sensitive (*easily affected*)

easily influenced facile, malleable, pliable, sequacious

easily lead tractable

easily led sequacious

easily managed flexible, resigned, tractable

easily managed job sinecure

easily observed scrutable

easily offended sensitive (*easily affected*)

easily perceived distinct (*clear*), palpable

easily persuaded facile, malleable, pliable, pliant, prone, suasible

easily seen apparent (*perceptible*), evident, gross (*flagrant*), overt, palpable, scrutable

easily taken in credulous

easily taught sequacious, tractable

easily understood coherent (*clear*), comprehensible, distinct (*clear*), scrutable

easiness informality

easiness of belief credulity

easing mitigating, mitigation, mollification, remedial

easy convenient, elementary, facile, lenient, malleable, passable, promiscuous, yielding

easy (*effortless*). SEE MAIN ENTRY

easy (*lenient*). SEE MAIN ENTRY

easy (*obvious*). SEE MAIN ENTRY

easy chore sinecure

easy employment sinecure

easy job sinecure

easy labor sinecure

easy to be seen patent, perceptible

easy to believe presumptive

easy to grasp coherent (*clear*)

easy to perceive evident

easy to see evident, manifest, naked (*perceptible*), perceivable

easy to understand coherent (*clear*), comprehensible, elementary, explicit, pellucid

easy-mannered civil (*polite*)

easygoing facile, lenient, malleable, nonchalant, patient, peaceable, placid, pliable, sequacious, suasible, tractable, yielding

easygoingness informality

eat consume, prey

eat away diminish

eat excessively overindulge

eatable palatable

eavesdrop monitor, overhear, spy. SEE MAIN ENTRY

ebb decline, decline (*fall*), decrease (*noun*), decrease (*verb*), degenerate, depreciate, depress, deteriorate, diminish, languish, lessen, outflow, retreat, subside. SEE MAIN ENTRY

ebb and flow beat (*pulsate*)

ebb of life death

eblandiri elicit

ebrietas inebriation

ebriosity dipsomania

ebrius drunk

ebullient. SEE MAIN ENTRY

ebullition bluster (*speech*), commotion, emotion, outbreak, outburst

eccentric anomalous, deviant, divergent, irregular (*not usual*), ludicrous, nonconforming, novel, original (*creative*), particular (*specific*), peculiar (*curious*), singular, unaccustomed, uncommon, unorthodox, unpredictable. SEE MAIN ENTRY

eccentricity irregularity, nonconformity, quirk (*idiosyncrasy*), specialty (*distinctive mark*)

echelon class, degree (*station*), position (*business status*)

echo concur (*agree*), copy, mock (*imitate*), reflection (*image*), reiterate, repeat (*state again*), repercussion. SEE MAIN ENTRY

echoed repeated

echoic repetitious

echoing iterative, repetitious, resounding

eclat notoriety

éclat prestige

eclat prestige

eclectic miscellaneous

eclipse blind (*obscure*), cloak, conceal, ensconce, enshroud, obfuscate, obnubilate, obscure, outbalance, outweigh, overcome (*surmount*), predominate (*outnumber*), shroud, surpass, transcend. SEE MAIN ENTRY

eclipsed allusive, hidden

ecology SEE MAIN ENTRY

economic commercial, fiscal, mercantile, pecuniary. SEE MAIN ENTRY

economic decline depression

economic downfall failure (*bankruptcy*)

economic prosperity boom (*prosperity*)

economic resources capital, principal (*capital sum*)

economic science economy (*economic system*)

economic use management (*judicious use*)

economical economic, frugal, parsimonious, pecuniary, provident (*frugal*), prudent. SEE MAIN ENTRY

economical of space compact (*dense*)

economical of words laconic, sententious

economically imprudent profligate (*extravagant*)

economicalness austerity, economy (*frugality*)

economics finance

economize diminish, preserve, retrench, save (*hold back*)

economizing economical

economy austerity, conservation, moderation, prudence, regulation (*management*). SEE MAIN ENTRY

economy-minded frugal

ecphonesis expletive

ecstasy enjoyment (*pleasure*), passion

ecstatic SEE MAIN ENTRY

ectype copy, duplicate

ecumenical general, nonsectarian

edacious gluttonous

edacity greed

eddying fluvial

edere issue (*publish*)

edge advantage, border, border (*bound*), boundary, circumscribe (*surround by boundary*), delimit, enclosure, encompass (*surround*), end (*termination*), envelop, extremity (*furthest point*), frontier, hedge, margin (*outside limit*), outline (*boundary*), penumbra, periphery, threshold (*verge*). SEE MAIN ENTRY

edge close to approach

edges configuration (*confines*), confines

edging border, contiguous, edge (*border*), outline (*boundary*), proximate

edible palatable

edicere enunciate, order

edico direction (*order*)

edict act (*enactment*), adjudication, award, brevet, canon, constitution, declaration, decree, dictate, direction (*order*), directive, enactment, fiat, mandate, measure, mittimus, monition (*legal summons*), order (*judicial directive*), ordinance, precept, prescription (*directive*), proclamation, pronouncement, regulation (*rule*), requirement, rule (*legal dictate*), ruling, sentence, statute, warrant (*judicial writ*). SEE MAIN ENTRY

edictum declaration, decree, edict, order (*judicial directive*), ordinance, proclamation

edification education, guidance, instruction (*direction*), instruction (*teaching*). SEE MAIN ENTRY

edifice building (*structure*), dwelling, inhabitation (*place of dwelling*). SEE MAIN ENTRY

edifices premises (*buildings*)

edify disabuse, educate, enlighten, instruct (*teach*), profit. SEE MAIN ENTRY

edifying beneficial, didactic, informative, meritorious, profitable, salutary, valuable

edit amend, digest (*summarize*), redact, revise, treat (*process*). SEE MAIN ENTRY

edit out bowdlerize, delete, expunge, redact

editing revision (*process of correcting*)

editio libri publication (*printed matter*)

edition publication (*printed matter*)

editorial review (*critical evaluation*). SEE MAIN ENTRY

editorialize. SEE MAIN ENTRY

editors press

educare develop, educate

educate convey (*communicate*), direct (*supervise*), disabuse, discipline (*train*), edify, enlighten, impart, inculcate, inform (*notify*), instill, instruct (*teach*), nurture. SEE MAIN ENTRY

educate oneself study

educated cognizant, familiar (*informed*), knowing, learned, literate, sciential

educated guess estimate *(approximate cost)*, estimation *(calculation)*

educating didactic

education direction *(guidance)*, discipline *(field of study)*, edification, experience *(background)*, guidance, information *(knowledge)*, instruction *(teaching)*, knowledge *(learning)*, preparation. SEE MAIN ENTRY

educational didactic, informative, informatory

educational clarification edification

educational institution institute

educational knowledge edification

educative didactic, disciplinary *(educational)*, informative

educator pedagogue

educe deduce, deduct *(conclude by reasoning)*, detect, disinter, elicit, evoke, extract, solve. SEE MAIN ENTRY

edulcorate purge *(purify)*

eel-shaped circuitous

eellike circuitous

eerie sinister

efface annul, deface, delete, dissolve *(terminate)*, eliminate *(eradicate)*, eradicate, expunge, expurgate, extinguish, extirpate, obliterate. SEE MAIN ENTRY

effaced lost *(taken away)*

effacement annulment, defacement, dissolution *(termination)*

effect accomplish, administer *(conduct)*, amount *(result)*, article *(commodity)*, attain, avail *(bring about)*, carry *(succeed)*, cast *(register)*, cause, chattel, chilling effect, commit *(perpetrate)*, compose, conclusion *(outcome)*, conduce, consequence *(conclusion)*, consequence *(significance)*, constitute *(establish)*, consummate, contrive, create, culminate, development *(outgrowth)*, discharge *(perform)*, dispatch *(dispose of)*, effectuate, elicit, enforce, engender, evoke, execute *(accomplish)*, fulfill, generate, holding *(property owned)*, implement, impose *(subject)*, impression, induce, influence, inspire, item, legislate, lobby, magnitude, make, occasion, operate, originate, outcome, outgrowth, perform *(execute)*, perpetrate, possession *(property)*, proceeds, procure, produce *(manufacture)*, product, provoke, reaction *(response)*, realize *(make real)*, redound, result, semblance, signification, toll *(effect)*, value, weight *(importance)*. SEE MAIN ENTRY

effect a change modify *(alter)*

effect a cure cure

effect a dissolution dissolve *(terminate)*

effect a sale handle *(trade)*, sell

effect an agreement mediate

effect an entrance enter *(go in)*

effect by legislation constitute *(establish)*

effected complete *(ended)*

effected by choice voluntary

effecter author *(originator)*

effectible practicable

effecting commission *(act)*

effectio operation

effective active, capable, causal, cogent, competent, constructive *(creative)*, efficient, eloquent, expert, felicitous, functional, incisive, influential, material *(important)*, omnipotent, operative, persuasive, politic, potent, powerful, practical, predominant, prevailing *(having superior force)*, proficient, sound, strong, successful, valid, valuable, viable. SEE MAIN ENTRY

effective before retroactive

effective help remedy *(legal means of redress)*

effective rejoinder confutation

effectiveness competence *(ability)*, dint, efficiency, force *(strength)*, influence, sinew

effectless null *(invalid)*, null and void

effects assets, dower, estate *(property)*, goods, merchandise, movable, paraphernalia *(personal belongings)*, personalty, possessions, property *(possessions)*, stock *(store)*. SEE MAIN ENTRY

effectual active, adequate, capable, causal, cogent, competent, constructive *(creative)*, decisive, effective *(efficient)*, effective *(operative)*, efficient, functional, influential, ministerial, omnipotent, operative, potent, powerful, practical, prevailing *(having superior force)*, sound, valid, valuable, viable. SEE MAIN ENTRY

effectuality capacity *(aptitude)*, competence *(ability)*, dint, force *(strength)*, influence

effectuate administer *(conduct)*, attain, avail *(bring about)*, bear *(yield)*, carry *(succeed)*, cause, constitute *(establish)*, consummate, discharge *(perform)*, dispatch *(dispose of)*, elicit, enforce, engender, evoke, execute *(accomplish)*, fulfill, function, generate, implement, induce, inspire, make, operate, perfect, perform *(execute)*, perpetrate, produce *(manufacture)*, realize *(make real)*. SEE MAIN ENTRY

effectuated complete *(ended)*

effectuation act *(undertaking)*, action *(performance)*, building *(business of assembling)*, commission *(act)*, conclusion *(outcome)*, course, development *(progression)*, discharge *(performance)*, effect, enforcement, fait accompli, fruition, output, realization, transaction

effectus effect, realization

effervescence life *(vitality)*

effervescent volatile

effete decadent, ineffective, ineffectual, otiose, powerless, stale, unproductive

efficacious active, beneficial, cogent, competent, effective *(efficient)*, functional, influential, politic, potent, powerful, practical, predominant, prevailing *(having superior force)*, proficient, qualified *(competent)*, sciential, sound, successful, valuable, viable

efficacy caliber *(mental capacity)*, competence *(ability)*, dint, efficiency, force *(strength)*, strength, utility *(usefulness)*, weight *(importance)*

efficax effective *(efficient)*, operative

efficere compose, constitute *(compose)*, execute *(accomplish)*, exercise *(discharge a function)*, fulfill, realize *(make real)*

efficiency caliber *(mental capacity)*, qualification *(fitness)*. SEE MAIN ENTRY

efficient active, competent, constructive *(creative)*, deft, economical, expeditious, expert, functional, operative, potent, practical, practiced, productive, proficient, prompt, resourceful. SEE MAIN ENTRY

efficientia efficiency

effigies counterpart *(parallel)*, embodiment, imitation, representation *(statement)*

effigy counterpart *(parallel)*, resemblance

effingere depict

efflagitare insist

effluence issuance, outflow

effluency issuance

efflux outflow

effodere disinter

efform compose, forge *(produce)*, formulate, make

efformation building *(business of assembling)*, composition *(makeup)*, form *(arrangement)*, formation

effort campaign, course, endeavor, enterprise *(undertaking)*, industry *(activity)*, labor *(exertion)*, main force, performance *(workmanship)*, pursuit *(effort to secure)*, struggle, test, undertaking *(attempt)*, undertaking *(enterprise)*. SEE MAIN ENTRY

effort to secure pursuit *(chase)*

effortful operose

effortless convenient, facile, practiced

effortless *(accomplished)*. SEE MAIN ENTRY

effortless *(easy)*. SEE MAIN ENTRY

effortless assignment sinecure

effortless employment sinecure

effortless undertaking sinecure

effortless work sinecure

effortlessly readily

effortlessness facility *(easiness)*

effractura burglary

effrenatus lawless, uncurbed, unrestricted, unruly

effrontery contumely, disrespect, temerity

effugere flee

effugium flight

effulgent lucid

effundi emanate

effuse diffuse, emanate, exude, outpour. SEE MAIN ENTRY

effusio waste

effusion expulsion, harangue, issuance, outflow, prolixity

effusive demonstrative *(expressive of emotion)*, loquacious, unrestrained *(not repressed)*, voluble. SEE MAIN ENTRY

effusiveness ardor

effusus profuse, uncurbed

egens poor *(underprivileged)*

egere require *(need)*

egestas indigence, necessity, privation

egg on provoke, stimulate

ego SEE MAIN ENTRY

egocentric inflated *(vain)*, orgulous

egohood personality

egoism pride

egoistic inflated *(vain)*, orgulous, presumptuous, proud *(conceited)*

egoistical inflated *(vain)*, orgulous, proud *(conceited)*

egotism pride

egotistic inflated *(vain)*, orgulous, presumptuous, supercilious

egotistical inflated *(vain)*, orgulous, presumptuous

egredi issue *(send forth)*

egregious contemptible, gross *(flagrant)*, heinous, noteworthy, notorious, outrageous, remarkable. SEE MAIN ENTRY

egregius singular, special

egress alight, avenue *(route)*, issuance, issue *(send forth)*, outlet, quit *(evacuate)*. SEE MAIN ENTRY

egression egress, issuance, outflow

egressus egress, outlet

eicere eject *(expel)*, expel

eidetic distinct *(clear)*

eidolon phantom, specter

either. SEE MAIN ENTRY

eiuratio abdication

ejaculate precipitate *(throw down violently)*, send

ejaculation outburst

eject cast *(throw)*, censor, deport *(banish)*, depose *(remove)*, discharge *(dismiss)*, dislocate, dislodge, dismiss *(discharge),* dispel, displace *(remove),* eliminate *(exclude),* emanate, emit, eradicate, evict, exclude, expatriate, expel, jettison, launch *(project),* luxate, oust, outpour, project *(impel forward),* reject, remove *(dismiss from office),* send, supplant. SEE MAIN ENTRY

eject from possession dispossess

ejection banishment, deportation, discharge *(dismissal),* dismissal *(discharge),* disqualification *(rejection),* eviction, evulsion, exclusion, expropriation *(divestiture),* expulsion, layoff, ostracism, ouster, removal

ejectment deportation, eviction, expulsion, layoff

elabi escape

elaborare elaborate

elaborate amplify, compound *(adjective),* compound *(verb),* develop, embellish, enhance, enlarge, expand, intricate, meliorate, painstaking. SEE MAIN ENTRY

elaborated complex, detailed

elaboration accession *(enlargement),* advance *(increase),* advancement *(improvement),* amendment *(correction),* development *(progression),* overstatement, revision *(process of correcting)*

elaboratus elaborate

élan ardor

elapse expire. SEE MAIN ENTRY

elapsed back *(in arrears)*

elastic flexible, malleable, pliable, pliant, resilient, sequacious, tractable, volatile, yielding

elated ecstatic. SEE MAIN ENTRY

elatio elevation

elbow jostle *(bump into)*

elbowroom margin *(spare amount)*

elder adult, predecessor, primogenitor. SEE MAIN ENTRY

elderliness longevity

elderly old. SEE MAIN ENTRY

elect adopt, choose, decide, entrust, intend, prefer, premium, select, vote. SEE MAIN ENTRY

elected preferred *(favored),* select

elected representative officer

electio election *(choice),* selection *(choice)*

election adoption *(acceptance),* alternative *(option),* choice *(alternatives offered),* choice *(decision),* discretion *(power of choice),* nomination, option *(choice),* plebiscite, poll *(casting of votes),* preference *(choice),* primary, referendum, selection *(choice),* volition, vote. SEE MAIN ENTRY

election contest primary

electioneering politics

elective adoptive, discretionary, disjunctive *(alternative),* spontaneous, voluntary. SEE MAIN ENTRY

elective preference volition

elective privilege poll *(casting of votes)*

electorate constituency. SEE MAIN ENTRY

electors constituency

electric incisive, provocative

electrify agitate *(activate),* impress *(affect deeply)*

electrifying moving *(evoking emotion),* provocative

electronic rights SEE MAIN ENTRY

electus select

electrocution. SEE MAIN ENTRY

eleemosynary benevolent, charitable *(benevolent),* donative, nonprofit, philanthropic

eleemosynary corporation foundation *(organization)*

elegance propriety *(correctness)*

elegance of manners courtesy

elegans critical *(faultfinding),* elegant, particular *(exacting),* precise

elegant attractive. SEE MAIN ENTRY

elegiac disconsolate, lugubrious

element aspect, atmosphere, component, constituent *(part),* detail, determinant, factor *(ingredient),* feature *(characteristic),* ingredient, item, member *(constituent part),* segment, unit *(item).* SEE MAIN ENTRY

elemental cardinal *(basic),* central *(essential),* elementary, essential *(inherent),* fundamental, inchoate, incipient, integral, organic, original *(initial),* primary, prime *(original),* primordial, rudimentary, simple, substantive, ultimate, underlying. SEE MAIN ENTRY

elementary cardinal *(basic),* fundamental, inchoate, incipient, initial, naked *(lacking embellishment),* original *(initial),* primary, prime *(original),* primordial, rudimentary, simple, ultimate, underlying. SEE MAIN ENTRY

elementary detail necessity

elementary unit component, factor *(ingredient)*

elementum constituent *(part),* element

elephantine ponderous, prodigious *(enormous)*

elevare disparage

elevate ameliorate, build *(augment),* build *(construct),* cultivate, enhance, expand, honor, meliorate, parlay *(exploit successfully),* prefer, promote *(advance),* raise *(advance),* uphold. SEE MAIN ENTRY

elevated ecstatic, famous, magnanimous, meritorious, outstanding *(prominent),* prominent, sacrosanct

elevated place elevation

elevated rank eminence

elevation advance *(progression),* advancement *(improvement),* building *(structure),* eminence, inflation *(increase),* precedence, promotion *(advancement),* reform, remembrance *(commemoration),* status. SEE MAIN ENTRY

elevation in rank promotion *(advancement)*

élève disciple

eleventh hour crossroad *(turning point),* dilatory

elicere elicit, evoke

elicit cause, compel, discover, disinter, educe, evoke, exact, extract, ferret, find *(discover),* generate, inspire, originate, provoke. SEE MAIN ENTRY

elicit by threat coerce, extort

elicitation evulsion

elide delete, eliminate *(exclude),* relegate. SEE MAIN ENTRY

eligere elect *(choose),* select

eligibility admissibility, competence *(ability),* droit, qualification *(fitness)*

eligible admissible, allowed, convenient, desirable *(qualified),* entitled, fit, qualified *(competent),* suitable. SEE MAIN ENTRY

eliminate abate *(extinguish),* abolish, abrogate *(annul),* abrogate *(rescind),* censor, close *(terminate),* debar, delete, deplete, destroy *(efface),* dislodge, eject *(expel),* eradicate, except *(exclude),* exclude, expel, expurgate, extirpate, exude, forgo, jettison, obliterate, palliate *(abate),* purge *(purify),* reject, relegate, relinquish, remove *(eliminate),* renounce, repeal, screen *(select),* select, terminate, vacate *(void).* SEE MAIN ENTRY

eliminate racial segregation desegregate

eliminate the alternatives choose, elect *(choose)*

eliminated ineligible, lost *(taken away)*

elimination abatement *(extinguishment),* aberemurder, abolition, cancellation, censorship, curtailment, deduction *(diminution),* deportation, discharge *(dismissal),* dismissal *(discharge),* disqualification *(rejection),* dissolution *(termination),* end *(termination),* evulsion, expulsion, homicide, killing, layoff, murder, obviation, ostracism, ouster, prohibition, proscription, rejection, removal, renunciation. SEE MAIN ENTRY

elimination of ambiguousness clarification

elimination of complexity clarification

elimination of complication clarification

elinguis speechless

elite preferential, select. SEE MAIN ENTRY

elixir cure, main point

elliptical brief

elocutio delivery

elocution declamation, parlance, rhetoric *(skilled speech)*

elocutionary orotund

elongate extend *(enlarge),* protract *(stall),* sustain *(prolong)*

elongated protracted

elongation SEE MAN ENTRY

eloquence parlance, rhetoric *(skilled speech)*

eloquens eloquent

eloquent descriptive, persuasive, voluble. SEE MAIN ENTRY

else further

elsewhere. SEE MAIN ENTRY

elsewhere known as alias

elucidate argue, bear *(adduce),* characterize, clarify, comment, construe *(translate),* convey *(communicate),* define, demonstrate *(establish),* describe, detail *(particularize),* enlighten, exemplify, explain, explicate, exposit, expound, illustrate, instruct *(teach),* notice *(observe),* relate *(tell),* render *(depict),* resolve *(solve),* simplify *(clarify),* solve. SEE MAIN ENTRY

elucidating declaratory

elucidation answer *(solution),* clarification, comment, definition, discourse, education, explanation, illustration, instance, paraphrase, rationale

elucidative demonstrative *(illustrative),* interpretive

elucidatory informatory

elude abscond, avoid *(evade),* bilk, circumvent, default, equivocate, escape, eschew, ignore, parry, prevaricate, shirk, shun, spurn. SEE MAIN ENTRY

eludere balk, elude, foil

eludication solution *(answer)*

eluding evasive

eluding clear perception elusive

elusion abstention, avoidance *(evasion),* flight, subterfuge

elusive delusive, ephemeral, evasive, inaccessible, oblique *(evasive),* recondite, stealthy, temporary, transient, unresponsive, volatile. SEE MAIN ENTRY

elusiveness evasion

elusory elusive, evasive, oblique *(evasive).* SEE MAIN ENTRY

elutriate purge *(purify)*

emaciate decrease

emaciation deterioration

emanare emanate

emanate accrue *(arise),* arise *(originate),* develop, emerge, issue *(send forth),* proceed (*go forward*), result, spread, stem (*originate*). SEE MAIN ENTRY

emanate in rays   radiate

emanation   circulation, consequence (*conclusion*), development (*outgrowth*), discharge (*shot*), face value (*first blush*), issuance, outflow, output, product

emancipate   discharge (*liberate*), disencumber, disengage, disenthrall, enable, enfranchise, free, liberate, pardon, parole, quit (*free of*), redeem (*repurchase*), release, relieve (*free from burden*), rescue

emancipated   free (*enjoying civil liberty*), liberal (*broad minded*)

emancipation   discharge (*liberation*), discharge (*release from obligation*), freedom, liberation, liberty, parole, release, suffrage. SEE MAIN ENTRY

emasculate   bowdlerize, debilitate, disable, inadequate

emasculated   ineffective, ineffectual, powerless

emasculating   operose

emasculation   fault (*weakness*), languor. SEE MAIN ENTRY

embankment   bulwark

embar   bar (*hinder*), obstruct, toll (*stop*)

embargo   attachment (*seizure*)

embargo   ban, bar (*obstruction*), boycott, check (*bar*), condemn (*ban*), debar, enjoin, hindrance, interdict, obstacle, obstruction, prohibit, prohibition, proscribe (*prohibit*), proscription, restraint, seclude, veto. SEE MAIN ENTRY

embargoed goods   contraband

embark   launch (*initiate*), leave (*depart*). SEE MAIN ENTRY

embark on   commence

embark upon   assume (*undertake*), maintain (*commence*), undertake

embarkation   birth (*beginning*), inception, onset (*commencement*), outset, start

embarrass   confuse (*bewilder*), disgrace, humiliate, impede, offend (*insult*), perplex, perturb, upset. SEE MAIN ENTRY

embarrassed   diffident, impecunious, poor (*underprivileged*)

embarrassed circumstances   poverty

embarrassing position   plight, predicament

embarrassing situation   imbroglio, plight

embarrassment   confusion (*ambiguity*), disadvantage, disgrace, ignominy, indigence, obstruction, predicament. SEE MAIN ENTRY

embassage   embassy

embassy   commission (*agency*), delegation (*envoy*), mission. SEE MAIN ENTRY

embed   fix (*make firm*), inseminate, plant (*place firmly*). SEE MAIN ENTRY

embedded   ingrained, situated

embellish   camouflage, cloak, falsify, meliorate. SEE MAIN ENTRY

embellished   elaborate, inflated (*overestimated*), pretentious (*ostentatious*)

embellishment   bombast, exaggeration, expletive, motif

embezzle   bilk, cheat, convert (*misappropriate*), defalcate, defraud, impropriate, loot, mulct (*defraud*), peculate, pilfer, purloin, steal. SEE MAIN ENTRY

embezzlement   conversion (*misappropriation*), larceny, misappropriation, theft. SEE MAIN ENTRY

embezzler   hoodlum, thief. SEE MAIN ENTRY

embitter   affront, alienate (*estrange*), antagonize, bait (*harass*), discompose, incense

embittered   bitter (*reproachful*), dyseptic, hostile, malevolent, resentful

embittering   operose

emblaze   brand (*mark*)

emblazon   embellish

emblem   brand, designation (*symbol*), device (*distinguishing mark*), earmark, indicant, indication, indicator, label, manifestation, symbol, token. SEE MAIN ENTRY

emblematic   representative. SEE MAIN ENTRY

embodied   bodily, compound, concrete, corporeal, physical, tangible

embodied terms   contract

embodiment   affiliation (*amalgamation*), appearance (*look*), body (*person*), composition (*makeup*), corpus, coverage (*scope*), cross section, entity, epitome, essence, instance, materiality (*physical existence*). SEE MAIN ENTRY

embody   attach (*join*), commingle, comprehend (*include*), comprise, concern (*involve*), consist, constitute (*compose*), contain (*comprise*), depict, exemplify, form, include, incorporate (*include*), personify, substantiate. SEE MAIN ENTRY

embodying   inclusive

embolden   abet, assure (*give confidence to*), encourage, promise (*raise expectations*), reassure. SEE MAIN ENTRY

embolium   cessation (*interlude*)

emboss   brand (*mark*), embellish

embowel   eviscerate

embox   contain (*enclose*), envelop

embrace   accept (*embrace*), adopt, affiliate, attach (*join*), border (*bound*), choose, circumscribe (*surround by boundary*), collect (*gather*), comprehend (*include*), comprise, concern (*involve*), constitute (*compose*), contact (*touch*), contain (*comprise*), contain (*enclose*), coverage (*scope*), enclose, enclosure, encompass (*include*), envelop, espouse, include, incorporate (*include*), keep (*shelter*), personify, prefer, receive (*permit to enter*). SEE MAIN ENTRY

embrace an offer   assent

embrace an opinion   deem

embraced   select

embracement   adoption (*acceptance*), alternative (*option*)

embracing   inclusive

embracing a large area   extensive

embrangle   confound, disorganize, muddle

embrangled   inextricable

embranglement   brawl, disaccord, dispute, embroil, imbroglio

embroider   camouflage, cloak, clothe, embellish, falsify, invent (*falsify*), misrepresent, slant

embroidered   histrionic, mendacious

embroidery   distortion, exaggeration, overstatement, rodomontade

embroil   bicker, collide (*clash*), confound, confuse (*create disorder*), disrupt, implicate, incense

embroilment   affray, belligerency, bluster (*commotion*), brawl, collision (*dispute*), commotion, conflict, contest (*dispute*), controversy (*argument*), disaccord, dispute, disturbance, entanglement (*confusion*), fight (*argument*), imbroglio, involution, pandemonium. SEE MAIN ENTRY

embryo   SEE MAIN ENTRY

embryonic   inchoate, incipient, initial, original (*initial*), premature, prime (*original*), rudimentary

emend   amend, convert (*change use*), edit, fix (*repair*), meliorate, modify (*alter*),

rectify, reform. SEE MAIN ENTRY

emendable   ambulatory, corrigible

emendare   amend, emend, rectify

emendate   adjust (*resolve*), amend, edit, emend, modify (*alter*), rectify

emendatio   amendment (*correction*), correction (*change*), reform, revision (*corrected version*)

emendation   advancement (*improvement*), amendment (*correction*), correction (*change*), progress

emendatory   ambulatory, curative, progressive (*advocating change*)

emerge   appear (*materialize*), arise (*appear*), develop, emanate, evolve, germinate, issue (*send forth*), occur (*come to mind*), occur (*happen*), result. SEE MAIN ENTRY

emergence   egress, expression (*manifestation*), issuance, manifestation, nascency, origination, outflow, start. SEE MAIN ENTRY

emergency   casualty, catastrophe, debacle, disaster, peril, plight, predicament, quagmire. SEE MAIN ENTRY

emergere   emerge, recover

emersion   egress, outflow

emigrant   alien

emigrate   abandon (*physically leave*), abscond, depart, leave (*depart*), move (*alter position*), quit (*evacuate*)

emigration   egress, outflow

eminence   advantage, caliber (*quality*), character (*reputation*), clout, distinction (*reputation*), dominance, elevation, emphasis, importance, influence, magnitude, materiality (*consequence*), notoriety, power, prestige, primacy, regard (*esteem*), reputation, significance, status, weight (*importance*). SEE MAIN ENTRY

eminency   elevation

eminent   consequential (*substantial*), dominant, famous, illustrious, influential, master, meritorious, notable, noteworthy, outstanding (*prominent*), prime (*most valuable*), prominent, renowned, reputable, salient, singular, stellar

eminent domain   dominion (*supreme authority*). SEE MAIN ENTRY

eminent person   paragon

eminently   particularly

emissaries   deputation (*delegation*)

emissarium   outlet

emissarius   spy

emissary   agent, conduit (*intermediary*), deputy, intermediary, liaison, medium, plenipotentiary, procurator, proxy, representative (*proxy*), spokesman, substitute

emissio   discharge (*shot*)

emission   issuance, outburst

emit   bear (*yield*), cast (*throw*), discharge (*shot*), emanate, enunciate, expel, exude, outpour, project (*impel forward*), promulgate, pronounce (*speak*), publish, remark, send, utter. SEE MAIN ENTRY

emit heat   radiate

emit rays   radiate

emittere   emit, send

emmission   discharge (*shot*)

emollient   cure, medicinal, remedial

emolument   advance (*allowance*), alimony, bounty, brokerage, commission (*fee*), compensation, consideration (*recompense*), disbursement (*funds paid out*), earnings, fee (*charge*), honorarium, pay, payment (*remittance*), pension, perquisite, profit, recompense, requital, restitution, revenue, reward, wage. SEE MAIN ENTRY

emolumental profitable

emotion ardor, passion, reaction (response), sensibility. SEE MAIN ENTRY

emotional demonstrative (expressive of emotion), ecstatic, impulsive (rash), intense, subjective

emotional display for effect histrionics

emotional release catharsis

emotional tone outlook

emotionless insensible, unresponsive

emotive demonstrative (expressive of emotion), sensitive (easily affected)

empanel SEE MAIN ENTRY

empathetic benevolent, charitable (lenient)

empathic vicarious (delegated). SEE MAIN ENTRY

empathize sympathize. SEE MAIN ENTRY

empathy rapport, understanding (tolerance)

emper charge (empower)

empery dominion (supreme authority)

emphasis content (meaning)

emphasis emphasis

emphasis importance, inflection, strength, stress (accent), weight (importance). SEE MAIN ENTRY

emphasize argue, assert, bear (adduce), contend (maintain), dwell (linger over), enhance, insist, intensify, magnify, plead (allege in a legal action), pronounce (speak), reaffirm, repeat (state again). SEE MAIN ENTRY

emphatic categorical, clear (apparent), compelling, dogmatic, express, forcible, insistent, resounding, vehement. SEE MAIN ENTRY

emphatic assertion asseveration

emphatic inquiry demand

empierce enter (penetrate), lancinate, penetrate, pierce (lance)

empire demesne, realm

empiric probative

empirical probative. SEE MAIN ENTRY

empiricism casuistry, experience (background)

employ agency (legal relationship), apply (put in practice), appoint, capitalize (seize the chance), commit (entrust), delegate, employment, engage (hire), exercise (use), exert, expend (consume), exploit (make use of), exploitation, hire, impropriate, induct, labor (work), manipulate (utilize skillfully), ply, practice (engage in), recruit, resort, spend, wield. SEE MAIN ENTRY

employ capital invest (fund)

employ force compel, enforce

employ improperly misemploy

employ one's professional skill practice (engage in)

employ one's time strive

employ oneself attempt, commit (perpetrate), perform (execute), strive

employ oneself in practice (engage in)

employ stratagem compete

employability utility (usefulness), utilization

employable disposable, eligible, functional, practical

employed operative

employee assistant. SEE MAIN ENTRY

employees personnel, staff

employees' earnings payroll

employees' salaries payroll

employer chief, executive, principal (director). SEE MAIN ENTRY

employer of legal advice client

employer work stoppage lockout

employment agency (legal relationship), appointment (position), business (occupation), calling, career, course, enjoyment (use), function, industry (activity), job, labor (work), livelihood, management (judicious use), means (opportunity), occupation (vocation), office, position (business status), post, practice (professional business), profession (vocation), project, pursuit (occupation), title (position), trade (occupation), usage, use. SEE MAIN ENTRY

employment discrimination SEE MAIN ENTRY

employment fee retainer

employment of capital investment

employment of force compulsion (coercion)

empoison infect

emporium market (business), market place, store (business)

empower allow (authorize), appoint, assign (designate), authorize, bestow, certify (approve), clothe, commit (entrust), constitute (establish), countenance, delegate, detail (assign), employ (engage services), enable, endue, enfranchise, entrust, grant (concede), invest (vest), let (permit), permit, qualify (meet standards), sanction, suffer (permit), vest. SEE MAIN ENTRY

empower to act for another delegate

empowered allowed, entitled, ex officio, influential, permissible, powerful, privileged

empowering consent, deputation (selection of delegates)

empowerment charter (sanction), droit, force (strength), freedom, license, sanction (permission)

emprise campaign, endeavor, undertaking (enterprise)

emptiness insufficiency

emptor consumer

emptor customer, patron (regular customer)

empty barren, baseless, consume, deficient, deplete, devoid, diminish, dissipate (expend foolishly), evacuate, exhaust (deplete), ill-founded, inexpressive, languid, lifeless (dull), null (insignificant), outpour, purge (purify), spend, superficial, trivial, unavailing, unfounded, vacant, vacate (leave), vacuous. SEE MAIN ENTRY

empty (noting left). SEE MAIN ENTRY

empty (without substance). SEE MAIN ENTRY

empty of devoid

empty out deplete

empty show pretense (ostentation)

empty talk bombast, fustian, jargon (unintelligible language), rodomontade

empty words pretense (pretext)

empty-handed poor (underprivileged)

empty-headed vacuous

emulate copy, mock (imitate), pose (impersonate), reflect (mirror)

emulation contest (competition), fake

emulative competitive (antagonistic)

emulous. SEE MAIN ENTRY

emulsion solution (substance)

en attendant ad interim

en banc SEE MAIN ENTRY

en bloc en banc, en masse

en masse en banc. SEE MAIN ENTRY

en rapport concurrent (united), conjoint

en route SEE MAIN ENTRY

enable allow (authorize), authorize, charge (empower), clothe, delegate, empower, endue, facilitate, furnish, grant (concede), invest (vest), let (permit), permit, qualify (meet standards), sanction, vest. SEE MAIN ENTRY

enable to comprehend enlighten

enable to see enlighten

enablement ability, capacity (authority), competence (ability), faculty (ability), force (strength)

enabling legislation. SEE MAIN ENTRY

enact accomplish, command, conduct, constitute (establish), effectuate, execute (accomplish), govern, impersonate, implement, impose (enforce), instruct (direct), legislate, make, pass (approve), perform (adhere to), perform (execute), pursue (carry on), recite, require (compel), rule (govern). SEE MAIN ENTRY

enact beforehand preordain

enact by law legalize

enact laws legislate

enacted legitimate (rightful), positive (prescribed)

enacting legislative

enacting laws legislation (lawmaking)

enacting punishment penal

enactment code, codification, commission (act), constitution, dictate, direction (order), edict, fiat, law, mandate, measure, ordinance, pandect (code of laws), performance (execution), prescription (directive), regulation (rule), rubric (authoritative rule), rule (legal dictate), statute, symbol, transaction. SEE MAIN ENTRY

enactment of rules code

enarrare recount, relate (tell)

enarratio description

encage immure

encamp lodge (reside)

encapsulate comprise, contain (enclose), envelop

encase border (bound), clothe, contain (enclose), enclose, encompass (surround), ensconce, enshroud, envelop, shroud, shut

encasement enclosure

enchain confine, contain (restrain), fetter, handcuff, repress, restrain, restrict, trammel

enchanted ecstatic

enchanting attractive, moving (evoking emotion), provocative, sapid

enchantment affection, compulsion (obsession), seduction

enchase border (bound)

enchorial native (domestic)

enchoric native (domestic)

encincture blockade (enclosure), constraint (imprisonment), contain (enclose), embrace (encircle), enclose, encompass (surround)

encircle border (bound), circumscribe (surround by boundary), comprehend (include), contain (enclose), delimit, detour, enclose, encompass (surround), envelop, hedge, include, incorporate (include), lock

encirclement blockade (enclosure), enclosure

encircling comprehensive, inclusive

enclasp concern (involve), contain (enclose)

enclave bailiwick, parcel

enclose affix, border (bound), circumscribe (surround by boundary), confine, constrain (imprison), delimit, demarcate, embrace (encircle), encompass (surround), ensconce, enshroud, envelop, fetter, hedge, immure, imprison, keep (restrain), limit, lock, restrain, shut. SEE MAIN ENTRY

enclose on all sides encompass (surround)

enclose within bounds border (bound)

enclose within walls immure

enclosed internal, limited

enclosed cage cell

enclosed space enclosure

enclosing blockade *(enclosure)*, inclusive

enclosure barrier, boundary, chamber *(compartment)*, close *(enclosed area)*, constraint *(imprisonment)*, coverage *(scope)*, curtilage, parcel. SEE MAIN ENTRY

enclosures confines

encloud obscure

encomiastic favorable *(expressing approval)*

encomium laudation

encompass border *(bound)*, circumscribe *(surround by boundary)*, comprehend *(include)*, comprise, consist, constitute *(compose)*, contain *(enclose)*, delimit, demarcate, embrace *(encircle)*, enclose, envelop, hedge, include, incorporate *(include)*. SEE MAIN ENTRY

encompass with gloom obnubilate

encompassed with difficulties difficult

encompassing a wide area extensive

encompassment blockade *(enclosure)*, coverage *(scope)*, enclosure

encore de novo

encounter affray, affront, assail, assault, belligerency, collide *(clash)*, collision *(accident)*, collision *(dispute)*, commotion, compete, competition, conflict, confrontation *(act of setting face to face)*, contact *(touch)*, contend *(dispute)*, contest *(competition)*, contest *(dispute)*, discover, embroilment, endure *(suffer)*, engage *(involve)*, fight *(battle)*, find *(discover)*, grapple, meet, meeting *(conference)*, onset *(assault)*, oppose, rendezvous *(noun)*, rendezvous *(verb)*, strife, strike *(collide)*, struggle

encounter the risk bet

encounter with a shock collide *(crash against)*

encourage abet, assure *(give confidence to)*, coax, conduce, contribute *(assist)*, counsel, exhort, expedite, facilitate, favor, foment, foster, help, impel, incite, indorse, inspire, lobby, motivate, nurture, prevail upon, promise *(raise expectations)*, promote *(advance)*, promote *(organize)*, prompt, reassure, side, spirit, stimulate, uphold, urge. SEE MAIN ENTRY

encourage repose lull

encouraged sanguine

encouragement advocacy, approval, auspices, catalyst, contribution *(participation)*, favor *(sanction)*, guidance, help, impetus, impulse, incentive, indorsement, inducement, influence, instigation, invitation, motive, patronage *(support)*, persuasion, recommendation, relief *(aid)*, sanction *(permission)*, solace, stimulus, support *(assistance)*

encourager abettor, accessory, accomplice, advocate *(espouser)*, catalyst, partisan, promoter

encouraging auspicious, favorable *(advantageous)*, favorable *(expressing approval)*, moving *(evoking emotion)*, propitious, viable

encroach accroach, border *(approach)*, impinge, impose *(intrude)*, interfere, intervene, intrude, invade, obtrude, overlap, overreach, overstep, trespass, usurp. SEE MAIN ENTRY

encroach upon violate

encroached upon broken *(unfulfilled)*

encroaching culpable, obtrusive

encroachment assumption *(seizure)*, breach, contempt *(disobedience to the court)*, crime, imposition *(excessive burden)*, incursion, infraction, injustice, intrusion, invasion, offense, transgression, violation. SEE MAIN ENTRY

encrust embellish

encumber bind *(obligate)*, bind *(restrain)*, block, check *(restrain)*, contain *(restrain)*, detain *(restrain)*, disadvantage, embarrass, estop, hamper, hinder, hold up *(delay)*, impede, impose *(enforce)*, inconvenience, interfere, obstruct, overcome *(overwhelm)*, overload, perplex, preclude, restrict, tax *(overwork)*, trammel, weigh. SEE MAIN ENTRY

encumbered arrested *(checked)*, disconsolate, indebted

encumbrance barrier, burden, charge *(lien)*, constraint *(restriction)*, damper *(stopper)*, debt, disadvantage, fetter, handicap, hindrance, impediment, imposition *(excessive burden)*, liability, mortgage, onus *(burden)*, pressure, responsibility *(accountability)*, weight *(burden)*. SEE MAIN ENTRY

encyclic public *(known)*

encyclical public *(known)*

encyclopedia hornbook

encyclopedic broad, collective, complete *(all-embracing)*, comprehensive, expert, omnibus, omniscient

encyclopedical omnibus

end annul, arrest *(stop)*, border, cancel, cap, cause *(reason)*, cease, cessation *(termination)*, close *(conclusion)*, close *(terminate)*, complete, conclude *(complete)*, conclusion *(outcome)*, consummate, culminate, decide, defeasance, denouement, design *(intent)*, desist, destination, discontinue *(abandon)*, dispatch *(put to death)*, dissolution *(termination)*, dissolve *(terminate)*, eliminate *(eradicate)*, expiration, expire, extinguish, extirpate, extremity *(death)*, extremity *(furthest point)*, final, finality, finish, goal, halt *(noun)*, halt *(verb)*, impasse, intent, lapse *(cease)*, last *(final)*, mete, moratorium, motive, object, objective, outcome, output, payoff *(result)*, perform *(adhere to)*, periphery, point *(purpose)*, project, purpose, pursuit *(goal)*, quash, reason *(basis)*, rescind, rest *(cease from action)*, result *(noun)*, result *(verb)*, settle, shut, stop, succumb, suppress, target, terminate, ultimate. SEE MAIN ENTRY

end at abut

end by a decision arbitrate *(adjudge)*, conclude *(decide)*, determine

end in view design *(intent)*, intention

end intended intention

end life dispatch *(put to death)*, execute *(sentence to death)*

end of hostilities peace

end of life death, demise *(death)*, extremity *(death)*

end of the matter defeasance, time

end one's life decease, die

end product conclusion *(outcome)*, effect, outcome, output

end result amount *(result)*, conclusion *(outcome)*, destination, effect, outgrowth, proceeds, product

end the introduction of evidence rest *(end a legal case)*

end the presentation of evidence rest *(end a legal case)*

end to end contiguous

endamage disable, harm, persecute

endanger expose, jeopardize. SEE MAIN ENTRY

endangered aleatory *(perilous)*, insecure

endangerment hazard, jeopardy, peril, risk

endearment affection

endeavor activity, attempt, business *(occupation)*, calling, campaign, conatus, course, creation, effort, enterprise *(undertaking)*, experiment, industry *(activity)*, intend, labor *(exertion)*, labor, profession *(vocation)*, project, pursuit *(effort to secure)*, pursuit *(occupation)*, strive, struggle, test, trial *(experiment)*, try *(attempt)*, undertake, undertaking *(enterprise)*, venture, work *(effort)*. SEE MAIN ENTRY

endeavor to accomplish strive

endeavor to effect strive

endeavor to gain pursue *(strive to gain)*

endeavor to overtake chase

ended dead, defunct, lifeless *(dead)*, through

endemic domestic *(indigenous)*, native *(domestic)*, special, specific

endemical native *(domestic)*, specific

endenizen adopt

ending cessation *(termination)*, close *(conclusion)*, conclusion *(outcome)*, defeasance, denouement, destination, development *(outgrowth)*, dissolution *(termination)*, end *(termination)*, expiration, extreme *(last)*, final, finality, halt, last *(final)*, moratorium, outcome, ultimate

ending of a proceeding dismissal *(termination of a proceeding)*

ending of an action dismissal *(termination of a proceeding)*

endless chronic, constant, continual *(perpetual)*, continuous, durable, far reaching, incessant, indestructible, indeterminate, infinite, innumerable, myriad, permanent, perpetual, profuse, progressive *(going forward)*, relentless, rife, stable, unlimited, unrelenting. SEE MAIN ENTRY

endless duration perpetuity

endless time perpetuity

endlessly ad infinitum

endlessness indestructibility, perpetuity

endmost extreme *(last)*, last *(final)*

endorse abet, accept *(assent)*, accredit, acknowledge *(declare)*, advocate, affirm *(uphold)*, allow *(authorize)*, approve, assent, assist, assure *(insure)*, attest, authorize, avouch *(guarantee)*, bear *(adduce)*, bond *(secure a debt)*, brand *(mark)*, certify *(approve)*, certify *(attest)*, close *(agree)*, coincide *(concur)*, concede, concur *(agree)*, confirm, consent, constitute *(establish)*, corroborate, cosign, countenance, countersign, embrace *(accept)*, encourage, ensure, espouse, favor, justify, let *(permit)*, pass *(approve)*, qualify *(meet standards)*, recommend, sanction, seal *(solemnize)*, side, sponsor, subscribe *(sign)*, support *(assist)*, sustain *(confirm)*, underwrite, uphold, validate, vouch, witness *(attest to)*. SEE MAIN ENTRY

endorse over assign *(transfer ownership)*

endorsed agreed *(promised)*, allowed, consensual, official, preferred *(favored)*

endorsee holder, payee

endorsement acceptance, accommodation *(backing)*, acknowledgment *(acceptance)*, advocacy, affirmance *(authentication)*, affirmance *(judicial sanction)*, affirmation, aid *(help)*, approval, assent, attestation, avowal, certificate, certification *(attested copy)*, charter *(sanction)*, confirmation, consent, corroboration, favor *(sanction)*, guaranty, jurat, leave *(permission)*, license, ratification, recommendation, reference *(recommen-dation)*, rider, sanction *(permission)*, stamp, subscription, support *(corroboration)*, vow. SEE MAIN ENTRY

endorsement *(signature)*. SEE MAIN ENTRY

endorser backer, comaker, patron *(influential supporter)*, proponent, surety *(guarantor)*, undersigned

endow authorize, bear *(yield)*, bestow, charge *(empower)*, clothe, confer *(give)*, contribute *(supply)*, convey *(transfer)*, dedicate, demise, descend, devise *(give)*, divide *(distribute)*, empower, enable, endue, fund, furnish, give *(grant)*, impart, instate, leave *(give)*, pass *(advance)*, present *(make a gift)*, provide *(supply)*, subsidize, supply, vest. SEE MAIN ENTRY

endow the power charge *(empower)*

endow with bequeath

endow with authority invest *(vest)*

endow with political privilege enfranchise

endow with power authorize

endow with rights of citizenship naturalize *(make a citizen)*

endowed resourceful

endowed institution foundation *(organization)*

endowed with consciousness cognizant

endowed with life conscious *(awake)*, live *(conscious)*

endowed with reason cognizant, rational

endowing donative

endowment aid *(subsistence)*, appropriation *(donation)*, aptitude, behalf, benefit *(conferment)*, bequest, caliber *(mental capacity)*, charity, color *(complexion)*, competence *(ability)*, concession *(authorization)*, contribution *(donation)*, dedication, donation, dower, faculty *(ability)*, foundation *(organization)*, fund, gift *(flair)*, gift *(present)*, grant, inheritance, investment, largess *(gift)*, legacy, pension, performance *(workmanship)*, perquisite, potential, provision *(act of supplying)*, qualification *(fitness)*, quality *(attribute)*, quality *(grade)*, skill, specialty *(special aptitude)*, support *(assistance)*. SEE MAIN ENTRY

ends confines

endue clothe, endow, fund, furnish, supply. SEE MAIN ENTRY

endurance continuance, diligence *(perseverance)*, force *(strength)*, indestructibility, industry *(activity)*, lenience, life *(period of existence)*, longanimity, longevity, resignation *(passive acceptance)*, sinew, strength, survival, tenacity, tolerance

endure abide, adhere *(persist)*, bear *(tolerate)*, concede, exist, forbear, keep *(continue)*, last, persevere, persist, remain *(continue)*, resist *(withstand)*, stay *(continue)*, submit *(yield)*, subsist, suffer *(sustain loss)*, tolerate, withstand. SEE MAIN ENTRY

endure the cost of disburse *(pay out)*

enduring chronic, constant, diligent, durable, indelible, indestructible, infallible, infinite, lasting, lenient, live *(existing)*, passive, patient, permanent, perpetual, persistent, pertinacious, resigned, solid *(sound)*, stable, standing, steadfast, strong, unrelenting, unremitting, unyielding

enduring only a very short time ephemeral

enemy adversary, foe, rival. SEE MAIN ENTRY

enemy alien. SEE MAIN ENTRY

enemy combatant. SEE MAIN ENTRY

energetic active, forcible, indomitable, industrious, intense, painstaking, potent, sedulous, strong, trenchant. SEE MAIN ENTRY

energize agitate *(activate)*, empower, incite, reinforce, restore *(renew)*, stimulate. SEE MAIN ENTRY

energizing impulsive *(impelling)*

energumen bigot

energy ardor, force *(strength)*, impetus, industry *(activity)*, labor *(exertion)*, life *(vitality)*, main force, puissance, sinew, spirit, strength. SEE MAIN ENTRY

enervare disable

enervate debilitate, depreciate, disable, disarm *(divest of arms)*, eviscerate, exhaust *(deplete)*, extenuate, impair, tax *(overwork)*. SEE MAIN ENTRY

enervate oneself carouse

enervated helpless *(powerless)*, nonsubstantial *(not sturdy)*

enervating operose

enervation frailty, languor, prostration

enfeeble debilitate, depreciate, disable, disarm *(divest of arms)*, eviscerate, exhaust *(deplete)*, extenuate, impair

enfeebled disabled *(made incapable)*, old

enfeeblement decline

enfeebling disabling

enfeoff alienate *(transfer title)*, bequeath, convey *(transfer)*

enfeoffment alienation *(transfer of title)*

enflame bait *(harass)*

enfold clothe, consist, contain *(comprise)*, embrace *(encircle)*, enclose, envelop

enfoldment enclosure

enforce administer *(conduct)*, compel, constrain *(compel)*, discharge *(perform)*, effectuate, exact, force *(coerce)*, implement, inflict, insist, make, operate, perform *(adhere to)*, press *(constrain)*, require *(compel)*. SEE MAIN ENTRY

enforce censorship censor, expurgate

enforce obedience constrain *(compel)*, force *(coerce)*, rule *(govern)*

enforce payment excise *(levy a tax)*

enforceable choate lien, valid

enforceable claim cause of action

enforceable in a court of law legal

enforced compulsory, forcible, obligatory

enforced abstention prohibition

enforced withdrawal expulsion

enforcement action *(performance)*, commission *(act)*, compulsion *(coercion)*, discharge *(performance)*, duress, force *(compulsion)*, requirement. SEE MAIN ENTRY

enforcement of judgment collection *(payment)*

enforcement of mortgage foreclosure

enforcing compelling

enframe frame *(construct)*

enframement border

enfranchise allow *(authorize)*, authorize, bestow, disenthrall, free, let *(permit)*, liberate, release. SEE MAIN ENTRY

enfranchised allowed, autonomous *(self governing)*, free *(enjoying civil liberty)*, rightful

enfranchisement charter *(sanction)*, copyright, emancipation, franchise *(right to vote)*, freedom, home rule, liberation, liberty, license, privilege, suffrage

engage agree *(contract)*, appoint, assume *(undertake)*, book, charge *(empower)*, coax, commit *(entrust)*, contend *(dispute)*, contract, delegate, employ *(engage services)*, fight *(battle)*, hire, immerse *(engross)*, implicate, induct, lease, monopolize, nominate, participate, promise *(vow)*, provide *(arrange for)*, pursue *(carry on)*, register, rent, retain *(employ)*, stipulate. SEE MAIN ENTRY

engage in commence, endeavor, exercise *(discharge a function)*, labor, operate, participate, ply, practice *(engage in)*, undertake. SEE MAIN ENTRY

engage in a contest compete

engage in a contest of speed race

engage in a conversation communicate, discuss, speak

engage in a dialogue speak

engage in an enterprise embark

engage in conflict with confront *(oppose)*

engage in conversation discuss

engage in hostilities attack

engage in oral controversy debate, discuss

engage in solemn manner promise *(vow)*

engage premises for a designated period lease

engage solemnly pledge *(promise the performance of)*

engage the attention interest, occupy *(engage)*

engage the mind interest, occupy *(engage)*

engage the thoughts interest, occupy *(engage)*

engage to give pledge *(promise the performance of)*

engage with grapple

engaged bound, indentured

engaged in business industrial

engaged in commerce commercial, retail

engaged in traffic industrial

engagement agreement *(contract)*, appointment *(meeting)*, assurance, burden, charge *(responsibility)*, commitment *(responsibility)*, competition, conflict, confrontation *(act of setting face to face)*, confrontation *(altercation)*, contest *(competition)*, contract, covenant, duty *(obligation)*, embroilment, employment, enterprise *(undertaking)*, fight *(battle)*, meeting *(encounter)*, mortgage, profession *(vocation)*, project, promise, pursuit *(occupation)*, rendezvous, responsibility *(accountability)*, specialty *(contract)*, stipulation, strife, struggle, testament, trade *(occupation)*, undertaking *(business)*, undertaking *(enterprise)*, undertaking *(pledge)*, work *(employment)*. SEE MAIN ENTRY

engagements ties

engager of services principal *(director)*

engaging attractive, sapid

engaging fee retainer

engaging in bigamy polygamous

engaging in unlawful marriage polygamous

engender avail *(bring about)*, bear *(yield)*, cause, constitute *(establish)*, create, foment, generate, make, originate, produce *(manufacture)*, propagate *(increase)*, reproduce. SEE MAIN ENTRY

engenderment creation

engine. SEE MAIN ENTRY

engineer administer *(conduct)*, arrange *(plan)*, build *(construct)*, cause, compose, connive, contractor, control *(regulate)*, create, devise *(invent)*, direct *(supervise)*, manage, maneuver, manipulate *(utilize skillfully)*, manufacture, materialman, militate, operate, originate, oversee, plan, plot, program, realize *(make real)*, scheme. SEE MAIN ENTRY

engineered tactical

engineering building *(business of assembling)*, contrivance, strategy

engird circumscribe *(surround by boundary)*, contain *(enclose)*, embrace *(encircle)*, encompass *(surround)*, include

engorgement plethora

engraft embed, plant (place firmly)
engrafted ingrained, permanent
engrave brand (mark), delineate, inscribe
engraving inscription, stamp
engross engage (involve), interest, monopolize, occupy (engage). SEE MAIN ENTRY
engross the mind interest, occupy (engage)
engross the thoughts interest, occupy (engage)
engrossed pensive
engrossment compulsion (obsession), contemplation, notice (heed), obsession, preoccupation
engulf immerse (plunge into), inundate, overcome (overwhelm). SEE MAIN ENTRY
engulfing oppressive
engulfment osmosis
enhance ameliorate, amend, build (augment), compound, embellish, enlarge, expand, heighten (augment), intensify, inure (benefit), magnify, meliorate, progress, raise (advance), reform, renew (refurbish), supplement. SEE MAIN ENTRY
enhance the degree of appreciate (increase)
enhancement accession (enlargement), additive, advance (increase), amendment (correction), augmentation, boom (increase), development (progression), hyperbole, progress, reform, renewal. SEE MAIN ENTRY
enhancing cumulative (intensifying)
enhearten assure (give confidence to), promise (raise expectations), reassure
enigma confusion (ambiguity), mystery, paradox, problem, question (issue), secret. SEE MAIN ENTRY
enigmatic complex, debatable, difficult, disputable, elusive, equivocal, esoteric, inapprehensible, incomprehensible, indefinable, indefinite, indistinct, inexplicable, inexpressive, inscrutable, mysterious, obscure (abstruse), opaque, oracular, problematic, recondite, suspicious (questionable), vague. SEE MAIN ENTRY
enigmatical equivocal, esoteric, hidden, inapprehensible, incomprehensible, indefinable, indefinite, indistinct, inexplicable, inexpressive, mysterious, obscure (abstruse), problematic, uncertain (ambiguous)
enisle isolate
enisled insular, solitary
eniti endeavor, strive
enixus earnest
enjoin admonish (advise), arrest (stop), ban, bar (hinder), coerce, condemn (ban), debar, demand, detail (assign), dictate, direct (order), enact, exact, exhort, expostulate, forbid, force (coerce), forestall, impose (enforce), inhibit, insist, interdict, necessitate, prescribe, press (beseech), prohibit, proscribe (prohibit), request, require (compel), restrain. SEE MAIN ENTRY
enjoin from contain (restrain)
enjoinder injunction
enjoined positive (prescribed)
enjoining bar (obstruction), obstacle, obstruction, prohibition, remonstrative
enjoinment directive, refusal, requirement
enjoy own, possess, realize (obtain as a profit), relish, remain (occupy)
enjoy the use of premises rent
enjoyable desirable (pleasing), palatable, preferable
enjoyed popular
enjoying liberty free (enjoying civil liberty), sovereign (independent)

enjoying political independence sovereign (independent)
enjoyment benefit (betterment), occupancy, satisfaction (fulfilment), use. SEE MAIN ENTRY
enkindle burn, foment, incense, inspire, provoke, stimulate
enlace intertwine
enlarge accrue (increase), amplify, bear (yield), build (augment), compound, develop, enhance, expand, extricate, heighten (augment), increase, inflate, magnify, overestimate, raise (advance), recruit, supplement. SEE MAIN ENTRY
enlarge in size accumulate (enlarge)
enlarge on expand
enlarge the mind disabuse, edify
enlarge the scope of extend (enlarge)
enlarge upon develop, elaborate, outpour
enlarged extreme (exaggerated), inflated (overestimated), liberal (not literal)
enlarged by swelling inflated (enlarged)
enlargement accretion, addition, advance (increase), advancement (improvement), aggravation (exacerbation), augmentation, bombast, boom (increase), distortion, exaggeration, extension (expansion), growth (increase), hyperbole, increment, inflation (increase), overstatement. SEE MAIN ENTRY
enlarging augmentation, cumulative (increasing)
enlighten admit (concede), advise, apprise, clarify, comment, communicate, construe (translate), convey (communicate), disabuse, discipline (train), disclose, divulge, edify, educate, elucidate, explain, explicate, exposit, herald, illustrate, impart, inform (notify), initiate, instruct (teach), mention, notify, report (disclose), reveal, signify (inform). SEE MAIN ENTRY
enlightened acquainted, cognizant, familiar (informed), informed (educated), informed (having information), judicious, juridical, learned, literate, politic, rational, sensible
enlightener bystander, deponent, informant
enlightening advisory, demonstrative (illustrative), didactic, informative, informatory, interpretive
enlightenment admission (disclosure), civilization, clarification, cognition, comprehension, direction (guidance), disclosure (act of disclosing), dispatch (message), edification, education, experience (background), guidance, information (knowledge), insight, intelligence (news), knowledge (awareness), knowledge (learning), mention (reference), monition (warning), notice (announcement), notification, publication (disclosure), sense (intelligence), tip (clue). SEE MAIN ENTRY
enlist appoint, bait (lure), coax, convert (persuade), convince, employ (engage services), engage (hire), enroll, hire, instate, join (associate oneself with), levy, lobby, persuade, prevail (persuade), prevail upon, procure, recruit, register, resort, retain (employ)
enlist employees in a labor union organize (unionize)
enlist in a labor union organize (unionize)
enlist in one's service engage (hire)
enlist jurors empanel
enlist with combine (act in concert)
enlisted man volunteer
enlisted person volunteer
enlistee member (individual in a group), volunteer

enlistment persuasion, registration
enliven inspire, spirit, stimulate
enlivened born (alive), conscious (awake)
enmesh bait (lure), betray (lead astray), engage (involve), ensnare, entrap, implicate, incriminate, intertwine
enmeshed interrelated, related
enmeshment complex (entanglement), entanglement (confusion), implication (incriminating involvement)
enmity alienation (estrangement), belligerency, breach, conflict, contention (opposition), cruelty, disaccord, discord, estrangement, feud, hatred, ill will, malice, odium, opposition, rancor, resentment, spite, umbrage, vengeance
ennoble honor, raise (advance). SEE MAIN ENTRY
enodare explicate, solve
enormity degree (magnitude), magnitude, weight (importance). SEE MAIN ENTRY
enormous exorbitant, far reaching, flagrant, grandiose, gross (flagrant), major, outrageous, ponderous. SEE MAIN ENTRY
enough adequate, quorum, sufficiency. SEE MAIN ENTRY
enounce declare, enunciate, proclaim, promulgate, pronounce (speak)
enquiry cross-examination
enrage aggravate (annoy), alienate (estrange), annoy, bait (harass), discompose, disturb, exacerbate, harass, incense, irritate, offend (insult), persecute, pique, provoke, upset. SEE MAIN ENTRY
enraptured ecstatic
enregister note (record)
enrich amend, bestow, compound, contribute (supply), cultivate, elaborate, embellish, endow, endue, enhance, impart, inure (benefit), meliorate, nurture, progress, replenish, supplement
enriched literate
enriching didactic, informative
enrichment advance (increase), development (progression), endowment, progress, reform. SEE MAIN ENTRY
enring encompass (surround)
enrobe clothe
enroll empanel, employ (engage services), enter (record), enumerate, file (place among official records), inscribe, instate, join (associate oneself with), record, recruit, register, subscribe (promise), survey (poll). SEE MAIN ENTRY
enrolled person member (individual in a group)
enrolling registration
enrollment constituency, registration, subscription
ensample instance, sample, specimen
ensconce blind (obscure), camouflage, cloak, enshroud, harbor, hide, instate, plant (place firmly), preserve, shroud. SEE MAIN ENTRY
ensconce oneself lurk
ensconced clandestine, safe, situated. SEE MAIN ENTRY
enscroll inscribe
ensemble assemblage, corpus, en masse, entirety
enshield ensconce
enshrine dedicate
enshrined sacrosanct
enshrinement dedication, remembrance (commemoration)
enshrining honorary
enshroud blind (obscure), camouflage, cloak, conceal, cover (conceal), ensconce,

envelop, obnubilate, obscure. SEE MAIN ENTRY

enshrouded hidden

ensign device *(distinguishing mark)*, indicant, indicator, symbol

enslave force *(coerce)*, impose *(subject)*, subject, subjugate

enslaved indentured, obsequious, subservient

enslavement bondage, captivity, oppression, servitude, subjection, thrall

enslaving dictatorial

ensnare abduct, ambush, bait *(lure)*, betray *(lead astray)*, bilk, coax, deceive, dupe, entrap, hunt, illude, inveigle, kidnap, mislead, pettifog, trap. SEE MAIN ENTRY

ensnarement bunko

ensnaring insidious

ensphere border *(bound)*, circumscribe *(surround by boundary)*, contain *(enclose)*, encompass *(surround)*, envelop, hedge

enstamp seal *(solemnize)*

ensual consequence *(conclusion)*, development *(outgrowth)*

ensue accrue *(arise)*, arise *(originate)*, proceed *(go forward)*, redound, result, stem *(originate)*, succeed *(follow)*, supervene, trace *(follow)*. SEE MAIN ENTRY

ensue from emanate

ensuing ancillary *(subsidiary)*, consecutive, derivative, forthcoming, future, subsequent, successive. SEE MAIN ENTRY

ensure avouch *(guarantee)*, bond *(secure a debt)*, certify *(attest)*, cover *(guard)*, guarantee, preserve, protect, sponsor. SEE MAIN ENTRY

ensure a result frame *(prearrange)*, prearrange

ensured certain *(positive)*, definite

ensurer backer

entail bequest, concern *(involve)*, consist, require *(compel)*. SEE MAIN ENTRY

entailed proprietary, requisite

entangle bait *(lure)*, bicker, bilk, collide *(clash)*, confound, confuse *(create disorder)*, disorganize, encumber *(hinder)*, engage *(involve)*, ensnare, entrap, implicate, incriminate, interest, intertwine, inveigle, involve *(implicate)*, muddle, perplex, perturb, trammel, trap

entangled complex, compound, disordered, inextricable, labyrinthine, sinuous

entangled by difficulties difficult

entanglement commotion, complication, confusion *(turmoil)*, embroilment, imbroglio, implication *(incriminating involvement)*, involution, pandemonium, predicament, quagmire, snarl. SEE MAIN ENTRY

entente arrangement *(understanding)*, bargain, compact

entente compatibility

entente conciliation

entente contract

entente mutual understanding, pact, treaty

entente cordiale accordance *(compact)*, compact

enter book, compete, embark, enroll, file *(place among official records)*, impanel, inscribe, introduce, join *(associate oneself with)*, note *(record)*, penetrate, pervade, record, register, set down. SEE MAIN ENTRY

enter a competition race

enter a demurrer demur, object

enter a plea address *(petition)*

enter a protest challenge, object

enter a suit for address *(petition)*

enter an appearance appear *(attend court proceedings)*

enter by stealth encroach

enter competition compete

enter hostilely invade

enter into contract, contribute *(assist)*, engage *(involve)*, espouse, incur, involve *(participate)*, participate, undertake

enter into a contract sign

enter into a contractual obligation close *(agree)*

enter into a league organize *(unionize)*

enter into an account deposit *(submit to a bank)*

enter into collision collide *(crash against)*

enter into conflict with engage *(involve)*

enter into detail designate, develop, expand, itemize

enter into partnership with combine *(act in concert)*, pool

enter into possession obtain, possess

enter on a list enroll

enter on a record enroll

enter on a register enroll

enter the mind occur *(come to mind)*

enter the picture emerge, occur *(come to mind)*

enter those names designated as jurors empanel

enter uninvited intrude

enter unlawfully impose *(intrude)*, intrude, trespass

enter upon assume *(undertake)*, commence, embark, initiate, undertake

enter upon the domain of another encroach

enter wrongfully encroach

enterprise act *(undertaking)*, activity, calling, campaign, corporation, employment, endeavor, firm, industry *(activity)*, industry *(business)*, labor *(exertion)*, livelihood, occupation *(vocation)*, operation, project, pursuit *(occupation)*, scheme, spirit, transaction, undertaking *(business)*, venture, work *(effort)*

enterpriser architect, developer, promoter

enterprising active, competent, progressive *(advocating change)*, resourceful

entertain engage *(involve)*, interest, occupy *(engage)*, receive *(permit to enter)*, treat *(process)*

entertain doubts doubt *(distrust)*, misdoubt, mistrust

entertain suspicions doubt *(distrust)*, misdoubt, mistrust

entertaining sapid

entertaining suspicion leery

entertainment enjoyment *(pleasure)*. SEE MAIN ENTRY

entêté contumacious

enthrall coerce, commit *(institutionalize)*, confine, constrain *(imprison)*, detain *(hold in custody)*, force *(coerce)*, immerse *(engross)*, interest, lock, monopolize, obsess, occupy *(engage)*, subdue, subject, subjugate

enthralling attractive, sapid

enthrallment constraint *(imprisonment)*, constraint *(restriction)*, custody *(incarceration)*, preoccupation, servitude, subjection, thrall

enthuse incite

enthusiasm ardor, compulsion *(obsession)*, emotion, industry *(activity)*, interest *(concern)*, life *(vitality)*, penchant, spirit. SEE MAIN ENTRY

enthusiast addict, partisan, proponent. SEE MAIN ENTRY

enthusiastic eager, earnest, ecstatic, fanatical, fervent, industrious, ready *(willing)*, sanguine, vehement, willing *(desirous)*, zealous. SEE MAIN ENTRY

enthusiastically readily

entice bait *(lure)*, betray *(lead astray)*, cajole, coax, ensnare, entrap, interest, inveigle, lure, prevail upon. SEE MAIN ENTRY

enticement bribery, cause *(reason)*, decoy, draw *(attraction)*, hush money, incentive, inducement, invitation, persuasion, seduction. SEE MAIN ENTRY

enticing attractive, sapid

entire absolute *(complete)*, collective, complete *(all-embracing)*, full, gross *(total)*, intact, outright, plenary, pure, radical *(extreme)*, stark, thorough, total, whole *(undamaged)*. SEE MAIN ENTRY

entire amount entirety

entire number aggregate

entire quantity aggregate

entirely en banc, in toto, purely *(positively)*, solely *(singly)*, wholly

entirely defensible blameless, clean, inculpable

entirely occupied full

entireness entirety, finality, totality

entirety aggregate, finality, sum *(total)*, totality, whole. SEE MAIN ENTRY

entitle allow *(authorize)*, authorize, bestow, call *(title)*, certify *(approve)*, delegate, denominate, designate, label, let *(permit)*, nominate, permit, phrase, qualify *(meet standards)*, sanction

entitled desirable *(qualified)*, meritorious, privileged, qualified *(competent)*. SEE MAIN ENTRY

entitled to acceptance and belief authentic

entitlement birthright, certification *(certification of proficiency)*, charter *(sanction)*, consent, droit, due, freedom, license, privilege, qualification *(fitness)*, title *(right)*

entitlement for a term of years copyright

entity body *(collection)*, body *(person)*, item, materiality *(physical existence)*, totality. SEE MAIN ENTRY

entomb conceal, constrain *(imprison)*, immure, imprison

entombment bondage, captivity

entrammel arrest *(apprehend)*, encumber *(hinder)*, fetter, handcuff, interfere, restrict, trammel

entrance access *(right of way)*, admission *(entry)*, admittance *(acceptance)*, admittance *(means of approach)*, avenue *(route)*, entry *(entrance)*, incursion, inflow, ingress, nascency, occupy *(engage)*, onset *(commencement)*, outset, portal. SEE MAIN ENTRY

entrance by stealth encroachment

entrance in a case appearance *(coming into court)*

entrance into a lawsuit intervention *(imposition into a lawsuit)*

entrance of a third party intervention *(imposition into a lawsuit)*

entrance upon domain of another infringement

entrance upon the domain of another encroachment

entrance way access *(right of way)*, threshold *(entrance)*

entranced ecstatic

entrances approaches

entranceway portal

entranceways approaches

entrancing attractive, provocative, sapid
entrant amateur, applicant *(candidate)*, candidate, contender, neophyte, novice, probationer *(one being tested)*, rival
entrap ambush, bait *(lure)*, betray *(lead astray)*, deceive, dupe, ensnare, inveigle, mislead, trap. SEE MAIN ENTRY
entrapment entanglement *(involvement)*
entreat bait *(lure)*, call *(appeal to)*, desire, exhort, invoke, petition, plead *(implore)*, pray, press *(beseech)*, pressure, prevail upon, request, solicit, sue, urge
entreat against except *(object)*
entreat earnestly petition
entreat persistently importune, pray
entreating precatory
entreaty bait *(lure)*, call *(appeal)*, dun, petition, prayer, request. SEE MAIN ENTRY
entree admittance *(acceptance)*
entrench embed, fix *(make firm)*, impose *(intrude)*, overstep. SEE MAIN ENTRY
entrench on impinge
entrenched chronic, constant, fixed *(settled)*, indefeasible, ingrained, inveterate, irreversible, permanent, safe
entrepreneur merchant, speculator. SEE MAIN ENTRY
entries ledger
entrust appoint, assign *(designate)*, assign *(transfer ownership)*, authorize, charge *(empower)*, confide *(trust)*, consign, delegate, deliver, deposit *(submit to a bank)*, descend, detail *(assign)*, empower, endue, give *(grant)*, instate, invest *(vest)*, leave *(give)*, lend, let *(permit)*, refer *(send for action)*, relegate, rely, remand, vest. SEE MAIN ENTRY
entrust to the care of another delegate
entrust with a task employ *(engage services)*
entrust with information notice *(give formal warning)*
entrust with management employ *(engage services)*
entrust with private information confide *(divulge)*
entrusted cause charge *(custody)*
entrusted object charge *(custody)*
entrusting delegation *(assignment)*
entrustment delegation *(assignment)*, deputation *(selection of delegates)*, escrow, loan
entry access *(right of way)*, admittance *(acceptance)*, admittance *(means of approach)*, avenue *(route)*, entrance, file, inflow, ingress, inscription, insertion, item, marginalia, nascency, notation, note *(brief comment)*, portal, record, threshold *(entrance)*. SEE MAIN ENTRY
entry book docket
entry of aliens immigration
entry under paramount title eviction
entryway admission *(entry)*, admittance *(means of approach)*, entrance
entryways approaches
entwine combine *(join together)*, commingle, conjoin, connect *(join together)*, intertwine, join *(bring together)*, lock, merge, unite
entwined cognate, collateral *(accompanying)*
enucleate comment, elucidate, enlighten, exemplify, explain, explicate, exposit, expound, resolve *(solve)*, solve
enucleation comment, explanation, illustration, paraphrase
enumerare enumerate, recite, specify
enumerate book, calculate, define, detail

(particularize), express, impanel, index *(relate)*, itemize, mention, pinpoint, poll, recapitulate, recite, signify *(inform)*, specify, survey *(poll)*, tabulate. SEE MAIN ENTRY
enumerated detailed
enumeratio recital, restatement
enumeration account *(evaluation)*, census, computation, disclosure *(act of disclosing)*, docket, index *(catalog)*, inventory, invoice *(itemized list)*, poll *(canvass)*, reference *(citation)*, roll, schedule, specification, statement
enumeration of causes arranged for trial calendar *(list of cases)*
enumeration of the essential qualities delineation
enunciate affirm *(claim)*, allege, annunciate, argue, assert, avow, cite *(state)*, communicate, construe *(translate)*, declare, depict, express, herald, issue *(publish)*, notify, pass *(determine)*, phrase, plead *(allege in a legal action)*, posit, pronounce *(speak)*, propagate *(spread)*, speak, utter. SEE MAIN ENTRY
enunciated alleged, nuncupative, oral
enunciation assertion, declaratory judgment, disclosure *(something disclosed)*, notice *(announcement)*, notification, profession *(declaration)*, pronouncement, publicity, speech
enunciative declaratory
enunciatory declaratory
enuntiare pronounce *(speak)*
envelop blind *(obscure)*, border *(bound)*, camouflage, circumscribe *(surround by boundary)*, cloak, clothe, comprehend *(include)*, conceal, consist, contain *(comprise)*, contain *(enclose)*, embrace *(encircle)*, enclose, encompass *(surround)*, ensconce, enshroud, hide, include, shroud, shut. SEE MAIN ENTRY
envelopment blockade *(enclosure)*, coverage *(scope)*, enclosure, panoply. SEE MAIN ENTRY
envenom aggravate *(annoy)*, alienate *(estrange)*, antagonize, bait *(harass)*, disaffect, discompose, incense, infect, provoke, taint *(contaminate)*
envenomed bitter *(reproachful)*, caustic, deadly, deleterious, malevolent, malignant, peccant *(unhealthy)*, pernicious, scathing, sinister, spiteful, tainted *(contaminated)*, virulent
envenomed tongue aspersion
enviable meritorious
envious jealous, resentful
environ border *(bound)*, enclose, envelop
environing influence atmosphere
environment atmosphere, climate, locality, location, situation. SEE MAIN ENTRY
environmental conditions climate
environmental conservation SEE MAIN ENTRY
environmental science ecology
environmental studies ecology
environs confines, environment, locality, region, section *(vicinity)*, site, territory, vicinity
envisage compose, conceive *(comprehend)*, conjure, invent *(produce for the first time)*
envisagement contemplation
envision conceive *(comprehend)*, expect *(consider probable)*, predict, presage
envisioning original *(creative)*
envisionment contemplation
envoy agent, conduit *(intermediary)*, deputy, factor *(commission merchant)*,

informant, informer *(a person who provides information)*, liaison, medium, plenipotentiary, procurator, proxy, replacement, representative *(proxy)*, spokesman, substitute
envoys deputation *(delegation)*
envy resentment
enwrap clothe, contain *(enclose)*, encompass *(surround)*, ensconce, enshroud, envelop, shroud, shut
eodem tempore simultaneous
eon age, cycle, period
epagogic discursive *(analytical)*
epexegesis clarification
ephemeral brief, insubstantial, nonsubstantial *(not sturdy)*, temporary, transient, transitory, volatile. SEE MAIN ENTRY
ephemerally. SEE MAIN ENTRY
ephemeris journal
ephemeris register
ephemerous ephemeral, transient
epic narrative, story *(narrative)*. SEE MAIN ENTRY
epicenter center *(central position)*
epicurean palatable, particular *(exacting)*
epidemic contagious, disease, far reaching, general, pestilent, predominant, prevailing *(current)*, prevalent, rife. SEE MAIN ENTRY
epigrammatic brief, compact *(pithy)*, concise, laconic, pithy, proverbial, sententious, succinct
epigrammatical sententious
epilogue codicil, denouement
epilogus peroration
epiphany. SEE MAIN ENTRY
episode event, experience *(encounter)*, happening, incident, occasion, occurrence, scene. SEE MAIN ENTRY
epistle dispatch *(message)*
epistolize correspond *(communicate)*
epistula dispatch *(message)*, note *(brief comment)*
epistulae correspondence *(communication by letters)*
epithet blasphemy, call *(title)*, term *(expression)*
epitoma abstract, compendium, summary
epitome abridgment *(condensation)*, abstract, capsule, compendium, cross section, digest, outline *(synopsis)*, restatement, summary. SEE MAIN ENTRY
epitome synopsis
epitomization abridgment *(condensation)*
epitomize abridge *(shorten)*, abstract *(summarize)*, condense, extract, review
epitomized brief, compact *(pithy)*, concise
epoch age, cycle, duration, lifetime, period, phase *(period)*
eponym call *(title)*
equability composure, parity, uniformity
equable agreed *(harmonized)*, coextensive, comparable *(equivalent)*, consistent, consonant, equal, harmonious, just, peaceable, placid, uniform
equably fairly *(impartially)*
equal agreed *(harmonized)*, coequal, coextensive, cognate, commensurable, competitive *(open)*, congruous, consistent, consonant, correlate, correspond *(be equivalent)*, counterpart *(parallel)*, equitable, equivalent, evenhanded, fair *(just)*, identical, peer, reach, same *(adjective)*, same *(noun)*, tantamount, uniform. SEE MAIN ENTRY
equal distribution of weight equipoise
equal footing par *(equality)*
equal in effect equivalent
equal in extent commensurate
equal in force equivalent

equal in measure   commensurate
equal in power   equivalent
equal in scope   coextensive
equal in significance   equivalent
equal in space   coextensive
equal in time   coextensive
equal in value   comparable *(equivalent)*, equivalent
equal part   moiety
equal share   moiety
equal to   capable, commensurate, effective *(efficient)*, proficient, qualified *(competent)*
equal to the need   adequate
equal value   par *(equality)*
equal worth   par *(equality)*
equality   fairness, identity *(similarity)*, par *(equality)*, parity, resemblance
equality of force   equipoise
equality of weight   equipoise
equalization   balance *(equality)*, offset
equalize   compensate *(counterbalance)*, conform, coordinate, counteract, neutralize, outbalance
equalized   agreed *(harmonized)*, coextensive, equal, equivalent
equally   fairly *(impartially)*
equally divided   equal
equalness   par *(equality)*
equanimity   compatibility, composure, moderation
equate   compare, compensate *(counterbalance)*. SEE MAIN ENTRY
equation   balance *(equality)*, comparison, parity
equibalanced   coequal
equidistance   center *(central position)*
equidistant   central *(situated near center)*, coextensive, equal, intermediate
equilateral   coextensive, equal
equilibrate   compensate *(counterbalance)*
equilibration   balance *(equality)*, equipoise
equilibrium   balance *(equality)*, composure, equipoise, parity, status quo
equip   bear *(yield)*, bestow, clothe, contribute *(supply)*, fund, furnish, give *(grant)*, provide *(supply)*, supply
equipage   paraphernalia *(apparatus)*
equipment   appliance, chattel, competence *(ability)*, device *(mechanism)*, expedient, faculty *(ability)*, instrument *(tool)*, instrumentality, paraphernalia *(apparatus)*, preparation, stock in trade. SEE MAIN ENTRY
equipoise   balance *(equality)*, parity, quid pro quo. SEE MAIN ENTRY
equipollence   balance *(equality)*, identity *(similarity)*, par *(equality)*
equipollency   identity *(similarity)*
equipollent   analogous, coequal, coextensive, comparable *(equivalent)*, equal, equivalent
equiponderance   balance *(equality)*, equipoise
equiponderant   coequal, coextensive
equiponderate   counteract, countervail, outbalance
equipondious   coextensive
equipped   practiced, provident *(showing foresight)*, qualified *(competent)*, ready *(prepared)*
equipped with arms   armed
equitable   equal, evenhanded, fair *(just)*, honest, impartial, judicial, juridical, just, neutral, nonpartisan, objective, open-minded, reasonable *(fair)*, right *(correct)*, rightful, scrupulous, unbiased, unprejudiced. SEE MAIN ENTRY
equitable interest   claim *(right)*

equitable treatment   fairness
equitableness   candor *(impartiality)*, disinterest *(lack of prejudice)*, fairness, justice, objectivity, probity, right *(righteousness)*
equitably   fairly *(impartially)*
equity   candor *(impartiality)*, disinterest *(lack of prejudice)*, estate *(property)*, fairness, justice, objectivity, possessions, probity, propriety *(appropriateness)*, rectitude, right *(righteousness)*, stake *(interest)*, title *(right)*. SEE MAIN ENTRY
equivalence   analogy, balance *(equality)*, correspondence *(similarity)*, identity *(similarity)*, par *(equality)*, parity, propinquity *(similarity)*
equivalency   parity
equivalent   agreed *(harmonized)*, analogous, coequal, coextensive, cognate, commensurable, commensurate, compensatory, congruous, correlate, correlative, counterpart *(parallel)*, disjunctive *(alternative)*, faithful *(true to fact)*, identical, mutual *(reciprocal)*, offset, peer, pendent, proportionate, replacement, same *(adjective)*, same *(noun)*, similar, tantamount, value, vicarious *(substitutional)*, virtual. SEE MAIN ENTRY
equivalent claim   setoff
equivalent given for injury   compensation
equivalent given for loss sustained   compensation
equivalent item   cover *(substitute)*
equivalent meaning   definition, paraphrase
equivalently   pro rata
equivocal   aleatory *(uncertain)*, ambiguous, conditional, disputable, doubtful, dubious, elusive, hesitant, impalpable, indefinite, indeterminate, oblique *(evasive)*, precarious, problematic, provisional, suspicious *(questionable)*, uncertain *(questionable)*, unclear, vague. SEE MAIN ENTRY
equivocalness   ambiguity, ambivalence, color *(deceptive appearance)*, indecision, qualm
equivocate   bicker, doubt *(hesitate)*, evade *(deceive)*, lie *(falsify)*, misrepresent, palter, prevaricate, tergiversate, vacillate. SEE MAIN ENTRY
equivocating   equivocal, evasive, lying, oblique *(evasive)*
equivocation   ambiguity, color *(deceptive appearance)*, deceit, deception, duplicity, evasion, falsehood, hesitation, pettifoggery, sophistry
equivocatory   equivocal
era   age, cycle, duration, lifetime, period, phase *(period)*, term *(duration)*, time
eradere   eradicate
eradicable   destructible
eradicare   extirpate
eradicate   abolish, cancel, censor, consume, delete, destroy *(efface)*, excise *(cut away)*, exclude, expunge, extinguish, extirpate, overthrow, purge *(purify)*, quash, reject, relegate, remove *(eliminate)*, supplant. SEE MAIN ENTRY
eradicated   lost *(taken away)*
eradication   abolition, cancellation, catastrophe, destruction, dissolution *(termination)*, evulsion, prohibition, rejection, removal, rescision
eradicative   dire, disastrous, fatal
erase   censor, deface, delete, destroy *(efface)*, dissolve *(terminate)*, edit, eliminate *(eradicate)*, eradicate, expunge, expurgate, extinguish, extirpate, invalidate, obliterate, redact, rescind. SEE MAIN ENTRY

erasure   cancellation, defacement, dissolution *(termination)*, rejection, removal
erasure of ambiguity   clarification
eratic   disjunctive *(tending to disjoin)*
erect   build *(construct)*, create, devise *(invent)*, elevate, fabricate *(construct)*, frame *(construct)*, honest, make, produce *(manufacture)*, upright
erect a barrier   bar *(hinder)*, impede
erection   building *(structure)*, development *(building)*, elevation, structure *(edifice)*
erectus   intent
eremetical   solitary
eremitic   solitary
eremitish   solitary
ergo   a fortiori, a priori, consequently
eripere   disabuse, hold up *(rob)*
eristic   argumentative, controversial, debatable, disputable, litigious, polemic
eristical   argumentative, litigious, polemic
ernest   decisive
erode   degenerate, depreciate, diminish, impair, lessen. SEE MAIN ENTRY
erogare   expend *(disburse)*
erosion   attrition, decline, decrement, deterioration, detriment, dissolution *(disintegration)*, expense *(sacrifice)*, spoilage, wear and tear. SEE MAIN ENTRY
erosive   caustic
erotic   lascivious, lecherous, prurient, salacious, suggestive *(risqué)*
erotica   pornography
erotical   lecherous
err   deviate, fail *(lose)*, lapse *(fall into error)*, misapprehend, miscalculate, misconceive, misinterpret, misjudge, misread, mistake, misunderstand, offend *(violate the law)*. SEE MAIN ENTRY
err in judgment   misjudge
errable   fallible
errancy   misapplication
errand   burden, mission
errant   astray, blameful, blameworthy, deviant, devious, discursive *(digressive)*, fallible, faulty, truant. SEE MAIN ENTRY
errare   err, lapse *(fall into error)*, miscalculate
erratic   anomalous, astray, broken *(interrupted)*, capricious, desultory, disjointed, eccentric, inconsistent, infrequent, irregular *(not usual)*, irresolute, periodic, sporadic, undependable, unpredictable, variable, volatile. SEE MAIN ENTRY
erratum   error
erratum   fault *(mistake)*, miscue, misstatement
erratum   oversight *(carelessness)*
erring   at fault, blameworthy, delinquent *(guilty of a misdeed)*, errant, erroneous, fallible, guilty, inaccurate, incorrect, peccable
erroneous   baseless, errant, fallacious, false *(inaccurate)*, faulty, fictitious, ill-founded, improper, inaccurate, incorrect, inexact, peccant *(culpable)*, sophistic, specious, unfounded, unsound *(fallacious)*, unsustainable, untenable, untrue. SEE MAIN ENTRY
erroneous in date   untimely
erroneous reasoning   fallacy
erroneous statement   error
erroneous trial   mistrial
erroneous use   abuse *(corrupt practice)*, misuse
erroneousness   fallacy, invalidity, misestimation
error   delinquency *(failure of duty)*
error   error
error   failure *(lack of success)*, fallacy, fault *(mistake)*, flaw, indiscretion

error lapse *(expiration)*

error lapse *(expiration)*, misapplication, misconduct, miscue, misdoing, misestimation, misjudgment, misstatement, onus *(blame)*, oversight *(carelessness)*, tort, transgression. SEE MAIN ENTRY

error in naming misnomer

error of judgment fault *(mistake)*

error of the court injustice

errori obnoxius fallible

errorless accurate, factual, infallible

ersatz artificial, counterfeit, imitation, spurious, succedaneum, synthetic, vicarious *(substitutional)*

erstwhile former, late *(defunct)*, previous

eruct eject *(expel)*, outpour

eructate eject *(expel)*, emit, outpour

erudire educate, instruct *(teach)*

erudite cognizant, didactic, familiar *(informed)*, informed *(educated)*, learned, literate, profound *(esoteric)*

eruditio instruction *(teaching)*, research

erudition comprehension, education, information *(knowledge)*, knowledge *(learning)*

eruditus learned

eruere disinter

erumpere issue *(send forth)*

erupt emit, penetrate

eruption bluster *(commotion)*, cataclysm, commotion, disturbance, expulsion, furor, outbreak, outburst, outflow, passion, recrudescence, strife, violence

escalate accrue *(increase)*, enhance, enlarge, expand, increase, inflate, intensify, parlay *(exploit successfully)*

escalating cumulative *(intensifying)*

escalation boom *(increase)*, boom *(prosperity)*, growth *(increase)*, inflation *(increase)*

escapade experience *(encounter)*

escape abscond, avoid *(evade)*, circumvent, disappear, egress, elude, evacuate, evade *(elude)*, exude, flee, impunity, issuance, leave *(depart)*, outflow, parry, part *(leave)*, quit *(evacuate)*, retreat, shun. SEE MAIN ENTRY

escape by artifice elude

escape by cleverness evasion

escape by trickery evasion

escape clause loophole, salvo. SEE MAIN ENTRY

escape detection elude, lurk

escape from shirk

escape hatch loophole. SEE MAIN ENTRY

escape notice elude, evade *(elude)*, lurk

escape observation lurk

escape recognition lurk

escape valve loophole

escape-clause dispensation *(exception)*

escaped prisoner fugitive

escapee convict, fugitive

escaper fugitive

escaping elusive, flight

escheat forfeit, relapse. SEE MAIN ENTRY

escheatment SEE MAIN ENTRY

eschew abscond, avoid *(evade)*, decline *(reject)*, forgo, forswear, refrain, repulse, shun. SEE MAIN ENTRY

eschewal abstention, continence

eschewment avoidance *(evasion)*

escort consort, guardian, protect

escrow binder. SEE MAIN ENTRY

esculent palatable

esoteric certain *(specific)*, enigmatic, exclusive *(limited)*, hidden, incomprehensible, inexplicable, mysterious, obscure *(abstruse)*, private *(confidential)*,

profound *(esoteric)*, recondite, secret, special, specific, undefinable. SEE MAIN ENTRY

esoterical esoteric, private *(confidential)*

especial certain *(particular)*, certain *(specific)*, exclusive *(singular)*, extraordinary, noteworthy, outstanding *(prominent)*, particular *(individual)*, particular *(specific)*, singular, special, specific

especially a fortiori, particularly

especially liked preferred *(favored)*

especially prepared express

espial discovery, espionage, observation, perception, recognition

espieglerie artifice

espier detective

espionage observation. SEE MAIN ENTRY

espousal adoption *(acceptance)*, aid *(help)*, alternative *(option)*, defense, favor *(sanction)*, marriage *(wedlock)*, matrimony

espouse adhere *(maintain loyalty)*, adopt, advocate, assert, assure *(insure)*, defend, embrace *(accept)*, justify, lobby, prefer, spouse, uphold. SEE MAIN ENTRY

espouse the cause of justify, maintain *(sustain)*

espoused conjugal, nuptial

espousement marriage *(wedlock)*, matrimony

espouser proponent

espy detect, discern *(detect with the senses)*, identify, observe *(watch)*, perceive, recognize *(perceive)*, spy

esquire SEE MAIN ENTRY

essay attempt, effort, endeavor *(noun)*, endeavor *(verb)*, experiment, pandect *(treatise)*, project, question *(inquiry)*, review *(critical evaluation)*, struggle, undertaking *(enterprise)*, venture, work *(effort)*

essayist author *(writer)*

esse exist, subsist

esse participem participate

essence basis, capsule, character *(personal quality)*, characteristic, compendium, connotation, consequence *(significance)*, content *(meaning)*, contents, cornerstone, corpus, digest, epitome, gist *(substance)*, gravamen, import, interior, main point, necessary, outline *(synopsis)*, point *(purpose)*, scenario, signification, spirit, structure *(composition)*, substance *(essential nature)*, sum *(tally)*. SEE MAIN ENTRY

essence of a grievance gravamen

essential actual, cardinal *(basic)*, critical *(crucial)*, crucial, exigent, fundamental, grave *(important)*, imperative, important *(urgent)*, indispensable, ingrained, inherent, innate, integral, major, mandatory, material *(important)*, native *(inborn)*, necessary *(required)*, necessary, necessity, obligatory, peremptory *(imperative)*, primary, principal, requirement, requisite, resource, rudimentary, substantive, ultimate, underlying, urgent, virtual, vital. SEE MAIN ENTRY

essential clause sine qua non

essential condition sine qua non

essential desideratum prerequisite, requirement

essential element necessity, need *(requirement)*

essential ground gist *(ground for a suit)*

essential matter content *(meaning)*, cornerstone, gist *(ground for a suit)*, main point, sine qua non

essential meaning connotation, content *(meaning)*, gist *(substance)*

essential nature materiality *(physical existence)*

essential object of desire desideratum

essential part body *(main part)*, center *(essence)*, character *(personal quality)*, characteristic, content *(meaning)*, element, essence, gist *(ground for a suit)*, gist *(substance)*, gravamen, ingredient, main point, sine qua non, spirit, substance *(essential nature)*

essential point gravamen, main point

essential provision condition *(contingent provision)*

essential qualification sine qua non

essential quality consequence *(significance)*

essential quality of one's nature character *(personal quality)*

essential status priority

essential to completeness integral

essentiality importance, magnitude, market *(demand)*, necessary, need *(requirement)*, significance

essentially ipso facto, purely *(positively)*, purely *(simply)*

essentially different disparate

essentialness character *(personal quality)*, main point, need *(requirement)*

essentials basic facts

establish affirm *(claim)*, affirm *(uphold)*, appoint, argue, ascertain, authorize, award, bear *(adduce)*, build *(construct)*, cast *(register)*, certify *(approve)*, circumscribe *(define)*, cite *(state)*, confirm, create, decide, decree, define, document, enact, evidence, fabricate *(construct)*, fix *(arrange)*, fix *(make firm)*, fix *(settle)*, form, instate, launch *(initiate)*, legislate, locate, make, organize *(unionize)*, originate, pass *(approve)*, plant *(place firmly)*, prove, quote, reason *(persuade)*, repose *(place)*, rule *(decide)*, stabilize, support *(corroborate)*, sustain *(confirm)*, testify, verify *(confirm)*, vest. SEE MAIN ENTRY

establish a corporation incorporate *(form a corporation)*

establish as facts find *(determine)*

establish as truth prove

establish beforehand preordain

establish boundaries demarcate

establish by agreement close *(agree)*

establish by law enact, legislate, pass *(approve)*

establish by proof substantiate

establish connection contact *(communicate)*, contact *(touch)*

establish equilibrium adjust *(regulate)*

establish guide lines organize *(arrange)*

establish guidelines for plan

establish in an office instate

establish oneself lodge *(reside)*, reside

establish parameters organize *(arrange)*

establish the authenticity of a will probate

establish the genuineness of prove

establish the genuineness of a will probate

establish the truth of verify *(confirm)*

establish the validity of prove

establish the validity of a will probate

establish with certainty ascertain

establishable convincing, provable

established accustomed *(customary)*, certain *(positive)*, chronic, common *(customary)*, conventional, convincing, customary, daily, definite, demonstrable, durable, familiar *(customary)*, firm, fixed *(settled)*, habitual, inappealable, incontrovertible, indefeasible, ingrained, inveterate, lawful, normal *(regular)*, official, ordinary, orthodox, permanent, positive *(prescribed)*, prescriptive, prevailing *(current)*, prevalent, professional *(trained)*, prosperous, regular *(orderly)*, routine, situated, solid *(sound)*, stable, standing, stated, statutory, steadfast, substantial, traditional, undeniable, usual

established by custom customary

established by general consent conventional

established by law legal

established by the federal government national

established custom usage

established division of time calendar *(record of yearly periods)*

established law code

established matter fact

established method procedure

established mode formality

established order code, method, policy *(plan of action)*, practice *(custom)*, practice *(procedure)*

established patronage goodwill

established phenomenon fact

established popularity goodwill

established practice conduct, form *(arrangement)*, usage

established principle canon, maxim

established reputation goodwill

established rule law, principle *(axiom)*

established way of doing things custom

establisher developer, pioneer

establishing guilt incriminatory, inculpatory

establishment affirmance *(authentication)*, affirmation, birth *(beginning)*, building *(business of assembling)*, building *(structure)*, business *(commercial enterprise)*, company *(enterprise)*, composition *(makeup)*, concern *(business establishment)*, corporation, corroboration, creation, enactment, facility *(institution)*, firm, formation, foundation *(organization)*, household, industry *(business)*, inhabitation *(place of dwelling)*, installation, institute, market *(business)*, onset *(commencement)*, organization *(association)*, preparation, proof, store *(business)*, structure *(edifice)*

establishment of a firm incorporation *(formation of a business entity)*

establishment of an ambassador embassy

establishment of foreign residence immigration

establishment of proof corroboration

estate assets, demesne, domain *(land owned)*, dower, effects, freehold, holding *(property owned)*, homestead, paraphernalia *(personal belongings)*, parcel, possessions, property *(land)*, property *(possessions)*, rating, real estate, realty, remainder *(estate in property)*, resource, substance *(material possessions)*. SEE MAIN ENTRY

estate for a fixed term leasehold

estate for a fixed term of years leasehold

estate for life freehold

estate in fee freehold

estate in realty leasehold

estate owner landholder, landowner

estate planning SEE MAIN ENTRY

esteem appreciate *(value)*, character *(reputation)*, consideration *(sympathetic regard)*, credit *(recognition)*, deem, defer *(yield in judgment)*, deference, eminence, homage, honor *(outward respect)*, honor, indorse-

ment, interest *(concern)*, mention *(tribute)*, opine, prestige, rate, recommend, recommendation, regard *(hold in esteem)*, reputation, respect, status, surmise, value, worth

esteem of no account disdain

esteem of small account disdain

esteem slightly flout

esteemed famous, important *(significant)*, influential, outstanding *(prominent)*, popular, reputable, valuable

estimable appreciable, considerable, determinable *(ascertainable)*, high-minded, honest, laudable, meritorious, moral, popular, premium, reputable, upright, valuable

estimableness honesty, integrity

estimate appraisal, assess *(appraise)*, assessment *(estimation)*, bid, calculate, charge *(assess)*, computation, concept, determine, diagnose, estimation *(calculation)*, evaluate, gauge, generalization, guess, idea, judge, judgment *(discernment)*, measure, measurement, opine, opinion *(belief)*, perception, presume, presuppose, price, prognosis, rate, survey *(poll)*, value, weigh. SEE MAIN ENTRY

estimate incorrectly miscalculate, misconceive, misjudge

estimate relatively compare

estimate too highly overestimate

estimated approximate, inexact

estimated by comparison comparative

estimated expenditures budget

estimated value appraisal

estimation appraisal, appreciation *(perception)*, character *(reputation)*, computation, conclusion *(determination)*, consideration *(sympathetic regard)*, diagnosis, discrimination *(differentiation)*, estimate *(approximate cost)*, generalization, homage, honor *(outward respect)*, idea, judgment *(discernment)*, measurement, notion, observation, opinion *(belief)*, prestige, price, rating, regard *(esteem)*, reputation, respect, value, worth

estimator juror

estop balk, ban, bar *(hinder)*, block, check *(restrain)*, constrict *(inhibit)*, debar, forestall, halt, hamper, impede, inhibit, obstruct, preclude, prevent, toll *(stop)*. SEE MAIN ENTRY

estoppage end *(termination)*, halt

estoppel bar *(obstruction)*, check *(bar)*, halt, impediment, obstacle, prohibition. SEE MAIN ENTRY

estrange antagonize, disaffect. SEE MAIN ENTRY

estranged hostile, inimical, irreconcilable, solitary

estrangement feud, fight *(argument)*, rift *(disagreement)*, separation, umbrage. SEE MAIN ENTRY

et al. SEE MAIN ENTRY

etch delineate

eternal constant, continual *(perpetual)*, durable, immutable, incessant, infinite, permanent, perpetual

eternally ad infinitum

eternalness indestructibility, perpetuity

eternity perpetuity

eternization preservation

eternize perpetuate

ethereal immaterial, incorporeal, intangible

ethical high-minded, honest, incorruptible, just, law-abiding, meritorious, moral, proper, reputable, right *(correct)*, scrupulous, upright. SEE MAIN ENTRY

ethical judgment conscience, responsibil-

ity *(conscience)*

ethical philosophy casuistry, conscience

ethical self conscience

ethicality propriety *(correctness)*

ethics conduct, conscience, principle *(virtue)*. SEE MAIN ENTRY

ethnic group blood, family *(common ancestry)*, race

ethnic stock race

ethnicity family *(common ancestry)*

ethology casuistry

ethos character *(personal quality)*, temperament

etiquette conduct, courtesy, custom, decorum, formality, manner *(behavior)*, propriety *(correctness)*, respect

étranger alien

etymology origination

eulogistic favorable *(expressing approval)*

eulogistic speech mention *(tribute)*

eulogistical favorable *(expressing approval)*

eulogize belaud, honor

eulogy laudation, mention *(tribute)*

euphemism bombast

euphuism fustian, rhetoric *(insincere language)*

euphuistic turgid

eurhythmy proportion

euthauasis. SEE MAIN ENTRY

evacuate abandon *(physically leave)*, alight, depart, deplete, dislocate, dislodge, eliminate *(eradicate)*, eliminate *(exclude)*, flee, leave *(depart)*, outpour, part *(leave)*, purge *(purify)*, retreat, secede, vacate *(leave)*, vacate *(void)*, withdraw. SEE MAIN ENTRY

evacuation abandonment *(desertion)*, egress, flight, outflow, removal, resignation *(relinquishment)*

évacué discard

evade abscond, bilk, circumvent, default, dishonor *(refuse to pay)*, elude, equivocate, escape, eschew, fail *(neglect)*, flee, hedge, ignore, palter, parry, pettifog, prevaricate, refrain, shirk, shun, spurn, tergiversate. SEE MAIN ENTRY

evade the truth palter, prevaricate

evader fugitive

evadere escape

evagari maneuver

evagation vagrancy

evaluate assess *(appraise)*, calculate, consider, estimate, gauge, measure, ponder, rate, screen *(select)*, survey *(examine)*, weigh. SEE MAIN ENTRY

evaluated ad valorem

evaluation appraisal, census, computation, concept, conclusion *(determination)*, determination, discretion *(power of choice)*, discrimination *(differentiation)*, estimate *(approximate cost)*, estimation *(calculation)*, idea, inspection, judgment *(discernment)*, judgment *(formal court decree)*, opinion *(belief)*, par *(face amount)*, perception, poll *(canvass)*, rating, trial *(experiment)*

evaluator juror

evanesce disappear, dissipate *(spread out)*, dissolve *(disperse)*, perish

evanescence mortality

evanescent elusive, ephemeral, indiscernible, temporary, transient, transitory, volatile

evanescere disappear

evaporable volatile

evaporate consume, disappear, lessen, perish

evasion abstention, artifice, avoidance (evasion), color (deceptive appearance), concealment, dereliction, duplicity, falsehood, flight, loophole, nonpayment, nonperformance, pettifoggery, pretext, privacy, ruse, salvo, sophistry, story (falsehood), stratagem, subterfuge. SEE MAIN ENTRY

evasion of duty default, infidelity, infraction, maladministration, nonperformance

evasion of truth false pretense

evasive allusive, clandestine, disingenuous, elusive, furtive, indefinite, machiavellian, noncommittal, reluctant, sly, stealthy, surreptitious, unresponsive, vague. SEE MAIN ENTRY

evasive action avoidance (evasion)

evasive reasoning sophistry

evasiveness privacy

evellere eradicate, extract

even adjust (regulate), coequal, coextensive, commensurable, comparable (equivalent), compensate (counterbalance), equal, equivalent, impartial, notwithstanding, placid, precise, proportionate, regular (orderly), uniform

even balance equipoise

even more a fortiori

even tenor regularity

even the score settle

even though regardless

even-handed dispassionate, unprejudiced. SEE MAIN ENTRY

even-handedness candor (impartiality)

even-sided coextensive

even-tempered dispassionate

evenhanded equal, equitable, fair (just), honest, impartial, just, law-abiding, nonpartisan, open-minded

evenhanded justice fairness, right (righteousness)

evenhandedly fairly (impartially)

evenhandedness disinterest (lack of prejudice), equity (justice), fairness

evenire result

evenly fairly (impartially)

evenly balanced impartial

evenness candor (impartiality), composure, equipoise, par (equality), regularity, uniformity

event chance (fortuity), development (outgrowth), experience (encounter), fact, happening, incident, landmark (significant change), occasion, occurrence, particular. SEE MAIN ENTRY

eventful cardinal (outstanding), critical (crucial), stellar

events circumstances

eventual forthcoming, future, pending (imminent), prospective, subsequent, ultimate

eventuality conclusion (outcome), consequence (conclusion), development (outgrowth), occurrence, outcome, outgrowth, result

eventually in due course

eventuate accrue (arise), arise (occur), arise (originate), crystallize, ensue, result, supervene

eventuation denouement, development (outgrowth), effect, outcome, outgrowth

eventus effect, event

ever-abiding perpetual

ever-present chronic, ubiquitous

ever-victorious invincible

ever-widening cumulative (increasing)

everchanging capricious, protean

everlasting chronic, continual (perpetual), durable, incessant, indestructible,

infallible, infinite, infrangible, permanent, perpetual, perpetuity, persistent, stable

everlastingness indestructibility

evermore now and forever

eversio subversion

evertere overturn, subvert, upset

every collective

every bit throughout (all over)

everyday common (customary), conventional, customary, familiar (customary), household (familiar), mediocre, mundane, nondescript, normal (regular), prevailing (current), prevalent, prosaic, regular (conventional), repeated, routine, typical, usual

everything entirety, sum (total), totality, whole

everywhere rampant

evict deport (banish), depose (remove), dislocate, dislodge, displace (remove), dispossess, divest, eliminate (exclude), expel. SEE MAIN ENTRY

evictio eviction, recovery (repossession)

eviction banishment, deportation, discharge (dismissal), disqualification (rejection), expropriation (divestiture), expulsion, foreclosure, forfeiture (act of forfeiting), ostracism, ouster, proscription, rejection. SEE MAIN ENTRY

evidence adduce, bear (adduce), certification (attested copy), certify (attest), cite (state), clue, connote, corroboration, data, disclose, display, document (noun), document (verb), documentation, evince, exemplify, exhibit (noun), exhibit (verb), expression (manifestation), ground, indicate, indication, indicia, manifest, manifestation, notarize, produce (offer to view), proof, record, signify (denote), substantiate, sustain (confirm), symptom, testimony, token, verify (swear). SEE MAIN ENTRY

evidence against confutation

evidence by a competent witness testimony

evidence from impersonal knowledge hearsay

evidence in support of testimony

evidence of a debt bond

evidence on oath affidavit, affirmance (legal affirmation)

evidence on the other side confutation

evidence-seeking cross-examination

evidenced solely by speech parol

evidences of debts securities

evidences of obligations securities

evidens evident, manifest, palpable, undeniable

evident apparent (perceptible), appreciable, certain (positive). SEE MAIN ENTRY

évident clear (apparent)

evident clear (apparent), coherent (clear), comprehensible, conclusive (determinative), conspicuous, convincing, definite, demonstrable, discernible, distinct (clear), explicit, gross (flagrant), lucid, manifest, naked (perceptible), obvious, open (in sight), ostensible, overt, palpable, patent, perceivable, perceptible, positive (incontestable), prominent, public (known), salient, scrutable, tangible, unambiguous, undeniable, unequivocal, unmistakable

evident demonstration proof

evidential apparent (presumptive), categorical, certain (positive), cogent, conclusive (settled), deductive, definite, documentary, presumptive, probative, reliable

evidential record documentation

evidential writing instrument (document)

evidentiary probative. SEE MAIN ENTRY

evidentiary record document, documentation

evidently fairly (clearly)

evil arrant (onerous), bad (offensive), contemptible, delinquency (misconduct), delinquent (guilty of a misdeed), depraved, detriment, diabolic, harm, harmful, heinous, immoral, inexpiable, iniquitous, lethal, malevolent, malicious, malignant, mischief, nefarious, objectionable, odious, peccant (culpable), pernicious, perverse, pestilent, profane, profligate (corrupt), reprehensible, sinister, tainted (corrupted), vice, vicious, wrong

evil adumbration premonition

evil behavior delinquency (misconduct), offense, perversion

evil conduct mischief

evil deed misdeed, offense

evil disposition malice

evil fame infamy

evil fortune calamity, misfortune

evil intent malice

evil lot calamity

evil luck calamity

evil-doing delinquent (guilty of a misdeed), diabolic

evil-minded cruel, delinquent (guilty of a misdeed), diabolic, dissolute, malevolent, malicious, malignant, perverse, profligate (corrupt), reprobate, spiteful, vicious

evil-speaking calumnious, malediction

evildoer convict, criminal, delinquent, embezzler, felon, hoodlum, malefactor, offender, outlaw, vandal, wrongdoer

evildoing felonious, misdoing

evince adduce, allude, attest, bare, bear (adduce), certify (attest), cite (state), convey (communicate), demonstrate (establish), depict, disclose, disinter, display, divulge, evidence, exemplify, exhibit, expose, indicate, manifest, produce (offer to view), prove, reveal, signify (denote). SEE MAIN ENTRY

evincement appearance (emergence), expression (manifestation), indication, manifestation, symptom

evincible ascertainable, convincing

evincive explicit

eviscerate bowdlerize, debilitate, extract. SEE MAIN ENTRY

evitare elude

evocare elicit, evoke

evocative moving (evoking emotion)

evoke bait (lure), cause, coax, depict, disinter, educe, elicit, extract, generate, inspire, originate, provoke, recall (remember), represent (portray), urge. SEE MAIN ENTRY

evolution civilization, course, development (progression), maturity, nascency, preparation, start

evolve arise (originate), avail (bring about), bear (yield), build (construct), change, convert (change use), develop, devise (invent), educe, forge (produce), germinate, make, manufacture, mature. SEE MAIN ENTRY

evolved derivative

evolved from dependent

evolvement development (progression), growth (evolution), nascency

evolvere evolve

evulgate reveal

evulgate bare, propagate (spread), reveal

evulgation divulgation, notification, publicity

evulse disinter

evulsion avulsion, removal. SEE MAIN ENTRY

ex concesso a priori

ex officio clerical. SEE MAIN ENTRY

ex parte determinative. SEE MAIN ENTRY

ex post facto SEE MAIN ENTRY

exacerbare exacerbate

exacerbate compound, distress, expand, harm, heighten (augment), incense, intensify, irritate, prejudice (injure), provoke. SEE MAIN ENTRY

exacerbation damage

exact absolute (conclusive), accurate, acquire (secure), actual, appropriate, attach (seize), bind (obligate), brief, call (demand), certain (particular), certain (specific), charge (assess), clear (apparent), close (rigorous), coerce, coherent (clear), command, compel, constrain (compel), decree, definite, definitive, demand, detailed, diligent, dun, enforce, enjoin, excise (levy a tax), explicit, express, extort, factual, faithful (true to fact), genuine, honest, identical, impose (enforce), insist, instruct (direct), laconic, levy, literal, meticulous, narrow, necessitate, need, precise, prescribe, press (constrain), punctilious, punctual, realistic, reliable, request, require (compel), right (direct), rigid, said, specific, strict, stringent, subtle (refined), systematic, tax (levy), tax (overwork), true (authentic), unambiguous, undistorted, verbatim. SEE MAIN ENTRY

exact a charge assess (tax)

exact a fine mulct (fine)

exact a penalty condemn (punish), discipline (punish), fine, penalize

exact a toll assess (tax)

exact amount face amount

exact as due claim (demand)

exact by force extort

exact copy facsimile

exact data information (facts)

exact meaning definition

exact moment point (period of time)

exact payment collect (recover money)

exact retribution condemn (punish), discipline (punish), fine, penalize, punish

exact statement definition

exact tribute toll (exact payment)

exacted positive (prescribed)

exacter extortionist

exacting circumspect, confiscatory, conscientious, critical (faultfinding), dictatorial, draconian, faithful (diligent), ironclad, mercenary, meticulous, onerous, operose, oppressive, painstaking, punctilious, punctual, rigid, severe, strict, stringent, uncompromising

exactingness particularity

exactio expulsion

exaction assessment (levy), assumption (seizure), blackmail, charge (cost), claim (legal demand), coercion, dun, duress, duty (tax), enforcement, excise, expense (cost), extortion, force (compulsion), forfeiture (act of forfeiting), levy, price, request, requirement, requisition, tax, toll (effect), toll (tax), ultimatum

exaction by oppression extortion

exaction of penalty condemnation (punishment), conviction (finding of guilt)

exactitude caution (vigilance), diligence (care), honesty, particularity, rigor, veracity

exactly faithfully

exactly alike identical

exactly like same

exactly the same identical

exactment assessment (levy), charge (cost), duty (tax), excise, expense (cost), fee (charge), levy, tax

exactness caution (vigilance), diligence (care), particularity, regularity, rigor, truth, veracity

exactus exact

exaggerare accumulate (enlarge), heighten (augment), magnify

exaggerate cloak, compound, distort, enhance, enlarge, expand, falsify, inflate, intensify, invent (falsify), magnify, misinform, misrepresent, overestimate, slant

exaggerated excessive, histrionic, inflated (overestimated), inordinate, lurid, outrageous, unreasonable

exaggerated likeness caricature

exaggerated statement overstatement

exaggerating cumulative (intensifying)

exaggeration bombast, caricature, catachresis, color (deceptive appearance), distortion, falsification, histrionics, hyperbole, inflation (increase), misrepresentation, overstatement, parody, rodomontade, travesty. SEE MAIN ENTRY

exaggerative inflated (overestimated)

exagitare harass, plague

exalt belaud, compound, elevate, honor, magnify, overestimate, parlay (exploit successfully), promote (advance), raise (advance), recognize (acknowledge), recommend, regard (hold in esteem)

exaltation distinction (reputation), elevation, eminence, homage, honor (outward respect), laudation, mention (tribute), precedence, prestige, promotion (advancement), remembrance (commemoration)

exalted famous, irreprehensible, magnanimous, outstanding (prominent), prominent, renowned, salient

examinant detective

examination analysis, appraisal, collation, consideration (contemplation), contemplation, cross-examination, deliberation, discretion (power of choice), discrimination (differentiation), experiment, habeas corpus, hearing, indagation, inquest, inquiry (request for information), inquiry (systematic investigation), inspection, interrogation, investigation, judgment (discernment), observation, probe, proposal (report), question (inquiry), regard (attention), research, scrutiny, surveillance, test, treatment, trial (experiment), trial (legal proceeding). SEE MAIN ENTRY

examination for qualification for jury service voir dire

examination for the purpose of ascertaining facts discovery

examination into facts or principles inquiry (request for information)

examine analyze, audit, canvass, check (inspect), consider, criticize (evaluate), cross-examine, deliberate, delve, discern (detect with the senses), frisk, inquire, investigate, judge, monitor, muse, observe (watch), overlook (superintend), oversee, peruse, ponder, probe, reason (conclude), research, review, revise, scrutinize, search, study, treat (process), try (conduct a trial), weigh. SEE MAIN ENTRY

examine a question debate

examine a source consult (seek information from)

examine by argument debate

examine by inspection search

examine carefully deliberate

examine closely concentrate (pay attention), focus, frisk, notice (observe)

examine critically analyze, diagnose

examine financial accounts audit

examine in detail investigate

examine intently concern (care), frisk, notice (observe)

examine judicially hear (give a legal hearing), try (conduct a trial)

examine searchingly canvass

examine secretely spy

examine the accounts officially audit

examine the particulars investigate

examine the witnesses hear (give a legal hearing)

examine with care and accuracy investigate

examinee contender

examiner detective, juror

examiner of business accounts comptroller

example comment, criterion, cross section, exemplar, illustration, indicant, instance, model, paradigm, paragon, pattern, precedent, prototype, sample, semblance, specimen, standard. SEE MAIN ENTRY

examples selection (collection)

exanimate dead, deceased, defunct, insensible, languid, lifeless (dead)

exanimis dead

exanimus dead, lifeless (dead)

exasperate aggravate (annoy), annoy, badger, bait (harass), discommode, discompose, disturb, incense, irritate, perturb, pique, plague, provoke

exasperating provocative, vexatious

exasperation provocation

exauctorare disband

exaudire overhear

excavate disinter, extract

excavation evulsion

excedere leave (depart)

exceed carouse, outbalance, outweigh, overestimate, overlap, overreach, overstep, predominate (outnumber), prevail (triumph), surmount, surpass, transcend, trespass

exceed in importance outweigh

exceed in value outweigh

exceeding drastic, excessive, extreme (exaggerated), inordinate, intemperate

exceeding propriety undue (excessive)

exceeding the bounds of moderation extreme (exaggerated)

exceeding the law illegal, illicit

exceeding the usual extraordinary

exceeding what is usual excessive

exceedingly ardent perfervid

excel beat (defeat), outweigh, prevail (triumph), surmount, surpass, transcend

excellence caliber (quality), efficiency, merit, prowess (ability), right (righteousness), significance, skill, value, worth

excellence of behavior courtesy

excellency primacy

excellent cardinal (outstanding), competent, exemplary, felicitous, illustrious, laudable, meritorious, noteworthy, outstanding (prominent), preferable, premium, professional (stellar), proficient, rare, select, sterling, superlative, unimpeachable, valuable

excellent judgment sagacity

excellent prospect likelihood

exceller paragon

excellere surpass, transcend

excelling absolute (*ideal*), outstanding (*prominent*), preferable, prime (*most valuable*)

except bar (*exclude*), eliminate (*exclude*), exclude, object, remove (*eliminate*), reserve, save, unless. SEE MAIN ENTRY

excepted barred, inadmissible, privileged

excepting palliative (*excusing*), save, unless

excepting that only

exceptio exception (*exclusion*), plea, qualification (*condition*), reservation (*condition*)

exception clause, condition (*contingent provision*), criticism, demurrer, disagreement, disapproval, discharge (*release from obligation*), disparagement, dispensation (*exception*), exemption, extenuating circumstances, immunity, irregularity, license, loophole, modification, nonconformity, objection, phenomenon (*unusual occurrence*), qualification (*condition*), quirk (*idiosyncrasy*), remonstrance, removal, reprimand, reservation (*condition*), salvo, stricture, variance (*exemption*). SEE MAIN ENTRY

exception in favor of dispensation (*exception*)

exception to a pleading demurrer

exceptionable blameful, objectionable, peccable, reprehensible, sinister, unacceptable, undesirable

exceptional atypical, best, extraordinary, individual, infrequent, irregular (*not usual*), notable, noteworthy, novel, original (*creative*), outstanding (*prominent*), particular (*specific*), peculiar (*distinctive*), portentous (*eliciting amazement*), preferential, prime (*most valuable*), prodigious (*amazing*), rare, remarkable, select, singular, special, specific, sterling, superior (*excellent*), unaccustomed, uncanny, uncommon, unique, unprecedented, unusual

exceptionality nonconformity

exceptionem facere demur

exceptious fractious, litigious, querulous, restive

excerpere extract

excerpt choose, digest (*summarize*), extract, part (*portion*), quote, select. SEE MAIN ENTRY

excerption excerpt

excess balance (*amount in excess*), boom (*prosperity*), debauchery, exaggeration, expendable, greed, needless, nonessential, overage, plethora, redundancy, remainder (*estate in property*), remainder (*remaining part*), residual, residuary, superfluous, surfeit, surplus, unnecessary, vice. SEE MAIN ENTRY

excessive brutal, disproportionate, drastic, egregious, excess, exorbitant, expendable, extreme (*exaggerated*), fanatical, gluttonous, gratuitous (*unwarranted*), harsh, hot-blooded, inflated (*overestimated*), inordinate, intemperate, needless, onerous, outrageous, prodigal, profuse, rampant, redundant, residuary, superlative, unconscionable, undue (*excessive*), unendurable, unnecessary, unreasonable, unrestrained (*not repressed*), unwarranted, usurious. SEE MAIN ENTRY

excessive amount surfeit

excessive burden surcharge

excessive charge premium (*excess value*), surcharge

excessive demand imposition (*excessive burden*)

excessive drinking dipsomania

excessive interest usury

excessive rate usury

excessive use abuse (*corrupt practice*), waste

excessively unduly

excessively bold presumptuous

excessively confident presumptuous

excessively critical particular (*exacting*)

excessively frugal parsimonious

excessiveness debauchery, dipsomania, exaggeration, redundancy

exchange barter, business (*commerce*), change, commerce, communication (*discourse*), commute, conference, contact (*association*), conversation, convert (*change use*), cover (*substitute*), deal (*noun*), deal (*verb*), dealings, displace (*replace*), finance, handle (*trade*), interchange, market (*business*), market place, mercantile, mutuality, novation, quid pro quo, reciprocate, reciprocity, replace, replacement, return (*respond*), revise, sale, sell, store (*business*), subrogation, succedaneum, trade (*commerce*), trade, vary. SEE MAIN ENTRY

exchange blows fight (*battle*), retaliate

exchange fisticuffs fight (*battle*)

exchange for money liquidate (*convert into cash*)

exchange ideas converse

exchange in commerce handle (*trade*)

exchange letters correspond (*communicate*)

exchange observations confer (*consult*), consult (*ask advice of*), counsel, discourse, discuss

exchange of blows fight (*battle*)

exchange of commodities trade (*commerce*)

exchange of letters correspondence (*communication by letters*)

exchange of obligations innovation

exchange of views conversation, discourse, interview, meeting (*conference*), negotiation, panel (*discussion group*), parley

exchange opinions discuss, respond, speak

exchange penalties commute

exchange value price

exchange views converse

exchangeable assignable, convertible, correlative, heritable, marketable, negotiable

exchequer treasury

excidere eradicate, extirpate

excipere disqualify, except (*exclude*), overhear, succeed (*follow*)

excisable ad valorem

excise assess (*tax*), bowdlerize, cancel, delete, diminish, duty (*tax*), expunge, imposition (*tax*), levy, redact, reject, tariff (*duties*), tax, toll (*tax*). SEE MAIN ENTRY

exciseman assessor

excision cancellation, expulsion, rejection, removal

excitability passion

excitable demonstrative (*expressive of emotion*), fractious, hot-blooded, restive, volatile

excitant catalyst, stimulus

excitare evoke, inspire, spirit, stimulate

excitation aggravation (*exacerbation*), dispatch (*promptness*), instigation, provocation

excitation of feeling affection

excitation of feelings ardor

excite aggravate (*annoy*), agitate (*activate*), bait (*harass*), bait (*lure*), discompose, engender, evoke, exacerbate, foment, harass, incense, incite, interest, perturb, prompt, provoke, spirit, stimulate

excite anger irritate

excite disapprobation brand (*stigmatize*), denounce (*condemn*)

excite dislike repel (*disgust*)

excite expectation promise (*raise expectations*)

excite hate antagonize

excite hatred incense

excite impatience irritate

excite indignation bait (*harass*), incense

excite the attention occupy (*engage*)

excited eager, ecstatic, fervent, frenetic, restive, vehement

excitement ardor, commotion, furor, interest (*concern*), passion, provocation, turmoil

exciter catalyst, demagogue

exciting moving (*evoking emotion*), offensive (*taking the initiative*), provocative, sapid

exciting fear formidable

excitive moving (*evoking emotion*)

exclaim interject, observe (*remark*), proclaim

exclaim against censure, denounce (*condemn*), disapprove (*condemn*), expostulate, inveigh, protest

exclamation confession, proclamation, remark, statement

exclude abrogate (*rescind*), ban, block, censor, clog, condemn (*ban*), debar, deport (*banish*), discharge (*dismiss*), dislodge, displace (*remove*), disqualify, eject (*expel*), eliminate (*exclude*), estrange, expatriate, expel, forbid, isolate, omit, outlaw, preclude, preempt, prohibit, proscribe (*prohibit*), refuse, reject, relegate, remove (*eliminate*), renounce, repudiate, restrict, screen (*select*), seclude, select, separate, sequester (*seclude*). SEE MAIN ENTRY

exclude from inheritance disinherit

exclude from the profession of law disbar

excluded barred, derelict (*abandoned*), exempt, inadmissible, ineligible, privileged

excludere debar, exclude

excluding omission

exclusio exclusion

exclusion bar (*obstruction*), blockade (*limitation*), boycott, control (*restriction*), deportation, disapprobation, dismissal (*discharge*), dispensation (*exception*), disqualification (*rejection*), disregard (*unconcern*), expulsion, omission, ostracism, ouster, preemption, prohibition, proscription, refusal, rejection, removal, renunciation, repudiation. SEE MAIN ENTRY

exclusion from commerce embargo

exclusion from favor disgrace

exclusion of entitled owner disseisin

exclusion of workers lockout

exclusionary exclusive (*limited*)

exclusive certain (*particular*), certain (*specific*), distinctive, only (*sole*), particular (*individual*), preferential, private (*not public*), privy, prohibitive (*restrictive*), proprietary, restrictive, select, several (*separate*), singular, specific. SEE MAIN ENTRY

exclusive application diligence (*care*)

exclusive area circuit

exclusive attention diligence (*care*), obsession

exclusive competition primary

exclusive contest primary

exclusive control monopoly

exclusive election primary

757

exclusive license   patent
exclusive of   save
exclusive political competition   primary
exclusive political contest   primary
exclusive possession   holding (property owned), monopoly
exclusive privilege   patent, prerogative
exclusive privilege of publication   copyright
exclusive privilege of publication and sale   copyright
exclusive privilege to carry on a traffic   monopoly
exclusive right   monopoly, patent, possession (ownership), prerogative
exclusive right of production   copyright
exclusive study   diligence (care)
exclusive thought   diligence (care)
exclusive title   patent
exclusively   only, solely (singly)
exclusory   exclusive (limited), prohibitive (restrictive)
excogitare   conjure, contrive, devise (invent), invent (produce for the first time), program
excogitate   conceive (invent), conjure, deliberate, frame (formulate), invent (produce for the first time), ponder, rationalize, reason (conclude), reflect (ponder), scheme, study
excogitatio   contrivance
excogitation   contemplation, deliberation, idea, reflection (thought)
excogitative   deliberate
excolere   develop
excommunicate   condemn (ban), debar, eliminate (exclude), exclude, expel, isolate, relegate, seclude
excommunication   banishment, expulsion, ostracism, rejection
excorciating   caustic
excoriate   castigate, censure, denounce (condemn), deprecate, disapprove (condemn), lash (attack verbally), reproach
excoriating   scathing
excoriation   bad repute, blame (culpability), denunciation, disapprobation
excrescence   outgrowth
excrescent   superfluous
excrete   exude, purge (purify)
excruciare   harrow
excruciate   badger, harass
excruciating   caustic, insufferable, painful, severe
exculpable   blameless, inculpable, not guilty, palliative (excusing)
exculpate   absolve, acquit, clear, discharge (liberate), excuse, exonerate, extenuate, forgive, free, justify, liberate, palliate (excuse), purge (wipe out by atonement), release, remit (release from penalty), vindicate. SEE MAIN ENTRY
exculpated   acquitted, blameless, clear (free from criminal charges)
exculpating   palliative (excusing)
exculpation   absolution, acquittal, amnesty, compurgation, discharge (liberation), discharge (release from obligation), dispensation (exception), excuse, exoneration, immunity, innocence, justification, liberation, release, remission
exculpatory   defensible, mitigating. SEE MAIN ENTRY
exculpatory clause.   SEE MAIN ENTRY
exculpatory excuse   alibi
excurse   detour
excursion   detour

excursive   circuitous, devious, indirect, labyrinthine, tangential
excursus   appendix (supplement), digression, discourse, hornbook, pandect (treatise)
excusabilis   pardonable
excusable   allowable, defensible, justifiable, pardonable
excusal   condonation, release, waiver
excusare   exculpate, excuse, justify
excusatio   excuse, justification, plea
excusatory   palliative (excusing)
excuse   absolve, acquit, alibi, clear, clemency, compurgation, condone, cover (pretext), discharge (release from obligation), discharge (liberate), discharge (release from obligation), dispensation (exception), exclude, exculpate, exonerate, exoneration, extenuate, forgive, free, grace, justification, justify, loophole, overlook (excuse), pardon, pretense (pretext), pretext, purge (wipe out by atonement), rationalize, reason (basis), release (noun), release (verb), remit (release from penalty), stratagem, subterfuge, vindicate. SEE MAIN ENTRY
excuse oneself   decline (reject)
excused   clear (free from criminal charges), exempt, free (relieved from a burden), immune, privileged
excuser   apologist
excusing   mitigating
execrable   arrant (onerous), bad (offensive), blameful, blameworthy, contemptible, contemptuous, depraved, diabolic, heinous, loathsome, malignant, nefarious, objectionable, obnoxious, odious, offensive (offending), outrageous, peccant (culpable), repulsive, scandalous
execrableness   disrepute
execrate   blame, castigate, censure, condemn (blame), contemn, denounce (condemn), proscribe (denounce), reprimand
execration   alienation (estrangement), aspersion, blasphemy, condemnation (blame), condemnation (punishment), denunciation, disapprobation, expletive, imprecation, malediction, obloquy, odium, outcry, phillipic, profanity, revilement, slander
execrative   profane
execute   abide, accomplish, apply (put in practice), certify (attest), close (agree), collect (recover money), commit (perpetrate), compose, conclude (complete), conduct, consummate, countersign, culminate, discharge (perform), dispatch (dispose of), dispatch (put to death), effectuate, enforce, engender, exercise (discharge a function), fabricate (construct), fulfill, function, garnish, generate, handle (manage), implement, impose (enforce), kill (murder), levy, make, manage, obey, observe (obey), officiate, operate, oversee, perfect, perform (adhere to), perpetrate, produce (manufacture), pursue (carry on), render (administer), render (deliver), sign, slay, transact, undertake. SEE MAIN ENTRY
execute a sentence   condemn (punish), discipline (punish), penalize
execute judgment   discipline (punish), penalize
execute justice   condemn (punish), discipline (punish)
executed   complete (ended), fully executed (signed)
executed and delivered writing   instrument (document)
executed with care   accurate
executed with exactness   elaborate

executed with proper formalities   valid
execution   act (undertaking), action (performance), administration, assassination, attachment (seizure), capital punishment, commission (act), consequence (conclusion), course, discharge (performance), dispatch (act of putting to death), distraint, enforcement, fait accompli, finality, fruition, garnishment, infliction, killing, manufacture, operation, realization, sequestration, transaction, treatment
execution of sentence   conviction (finding of guilt)
executions   dealings
executive   administrator, director, employer, official, principal (director). SEE MAIN ENTRY
executive arm   management (supervision)
executive charge   administration
executive committee   commission (agency), management (directorate)
executive office   management (directorate)
executive officer   official, principal (director)
executive privilege   SEE MAIN ENTRY
executives   authorities, management (directorate), management (supervision)
executor   director, fiduciary, procurator. SEE MAIN ENTRY
executory   SEE MAIN ENTRY
exegesis   comment, construction, content (meaning), explanation, note (brief comment)
exegetic   demonstrative (illustrative), narrative
exegetical   demonstrative (illustrative), narrative, solvable
exemplar   representative (example), sample, standard. SEE MAIN ENTRY
exemplary   absolute (ideal), best, laudable, meritorious, moral, prime (most valuable), professional (stellar), representative, sterling. SEE MAIN ENTRY
exempli gratia   cross section
exemplification   case (example), clarification, comment, construction, corroboration, cross section, epitome, example, explanation, illustration, instance, sample
exemplify   bear (adduce), characterize, cite (state), clarify, comment, define, demonstrate (establish), depict, elucidate, evidence, explain, illustrate, personify, represent (portray), signify (denote). SEE MAIN ENTRY
exemplifying a class   typical
exemplum   cross section, duplicate, example, exemplar, illustration, instance, model, pattern, precedent, prototype, sample, specimen, tenor, transcript
exempt   acquit, clear (unencumbered), clear, condone, discharge (release from obligation), eliminate (exclude), except (exclude), exclude, excuse, forgive, free, immune, palliate (excuse), privileged, purge (wipe out by atonement), release, relieve (free from burden), remit (release from penalty), unbound. SEE MAIN ENTRY
exempt from external authority   free (enjoying civil liberty), sovereign (independent)
exempted   clear (free from criminal charges), exempt, free (relieved from a burden), privileged
exemptible   justifiable
exempting   palliative (excusing)
exemption   clause, clemency, condonation, discharge (liberation), discharge (release from obligation), dispensation

(exception), exception (exclusion), exclusion, excuse, franchise (license), freedom, grace period, immunity, impunity, leave (permission), privilege, probation, qualification (condition), release, remission, reservation (condition), respite (reprieve), salvo. SEE MAIN ENTRY

exemption from control   latitude, liberty, suffrage

exemption from external control   freedom, liberty

exemption from judgment   impunity

exemption from law   dispensation (exception)

exemption from penalty   impunity

exemption from punishment   immunity, impunity, pardon

exemption from restraint   freedom, liberty, suffrage

exenterate   eviscerate

exercere   discipline (control), exercise (discharge a function), plague, ply, practice (engage in)

exercise   apply (put in practice), campaign, commission (act), discipline (training), employ (make use of), endeavor, exert, exploit (make use of), labor, officiate, operate, ply, practice (train by repetition), problem, resort, transaction, undertaking (enterprise), wield, work (effort). SEE MAIN ENTRY

exercise an option   elect (choose)

exercise authority   command, dictate, direct (supervise), govern, handle (manage), manage, police, prescribe, rule (govern)

exercise charge over   superintend

exercise critical judgment   compare

exercise direction over   discipline (control), handle (manage), hold (possess)

exercise discretion   discern (discriminate), distinguish, elect (choose)

exercise discrimination   differentiate, distinguish

exercise exclusive rights   monopolize

exercise federal authority over   federalize (place under federal control)

exercise influence   lobby, persuade

exercise influence over   induce, prejudice (influence), prevail upon

exercise influence upon   prejudice (influence), prevail upon

exercise influence with   prevail upon

exercise judgment   adjudge, gauge, rule (decide)

exercise judicial authority   adjudicate

exercise of the intellect   reflection (thought)

exercise of will   volition

exercise one's choice   cast (register), choose

exercise one's discretion   choose

exercise one's option   adopt, choose

exercise one's options   cast (register)

exercise one's preference   choose

exercise power over   force (coerce), govern, handle (manage), operate

exercise self-control   refrain

exercise supervision   direct (supervise), preside

exercise supervision over   superintend

exercise the function of legislation   legislate

exercise the judgment   determine

exercise the right of suffrage   vote

exercise the will   choose

exercising   commission (act)

exercising reason   rational

exercitatio   practice (procedure)

exercitation   course, use

exert   apply (put in practice), expend (consume), operate, wield. SEE MAIN ENTRY

exert authority   federalize (place under federal control), govern, handle (manage), police, rule (govern)

exert effort   endeavor

exert energy   labor

exert federal control   federalize (place under federal control)

exert influence   affect, constrain (compel), convince, incite, inspire, lobby, motivate, persuade, prejudice (influence)

exert one's energies   strive

exert oneself   attempt, endeavor, labor, persevere, strive, try (attempt)

exert oneself for   pursue (strive to gain)

exert pressure   bait (lure), coax, incite, insist, lobby

exert pressure on   browbeat

exertion   campaign, effort, endeavor, industry (activity), pressure, pursuit (effort to secure), stress (strain), struggle, work (effort)

exhale   emit

exhaurire   exhaust (try all possibilities)

exhaust   conclude (complete), consume, debilitate, deplete, disable, dissipate (expend foolishly), emit, expend (consume), outlet, outpour, overdraw, spend. SEE MAIN ENTRY

exhausted   inadequate, languid, lost (taken away), otiose, powerless, unproductive, unsound (not strong), vacant, vacuous

exhaustible   destructible

exhausting   operose, oppressive

exhaustion   consumption, decrement, impuissance, insufficiency, privation, prostration, waste, wear and tear

exhaustive   absolute (complete), complete (all-embracing), comprehensive, definitive, detailed, full, gross (total), inclusive, intensive, omnibus, outright, plenary, radical (extreme), thorough, unmitigated

exhaustive inquiry   analysis, examination (study), hearing, indagation, judgment (discernment)

exhaustive study   indagation, investigation, probe

exhaustive tract   pandect (treatise)

exhaustiveness   entirety

exhaustless   infallible, infinite, innumerable

exheredare   disinherit

exhibere   exhibit

exhibit   bare, bear (adduce), brandish, cite (state), demonstrate (establish), denude, depict, disclose, disinter, display, document, documentation, evidence, evince, exemplify, expose, expression (manifestation), flaunt, illustrate, manifest, manifestation, present (introduce), produce (offer to view), propound, unveil. SEE MAIN ENTRY

exhibit boastfully   flaunt

exhibit hostile intentions   menace

exhibit in visible form   embody

exhibit the differences between   contrast

exhibited   palpable

exhibiting equity   equitable

exhibiting lust   lewd

exhibiting pros and cons   controversial

exhibiting purpose   pertinacious

exhibition   exhibit, expression (manifestation), manifestation, performance (workmanship)

exhibitionistic   histrionic

exhibits   evidence

exhibits submitted to jury   evidence

exhilarate   spirit

exhilaration   ardor, enjoyment (pleasure)

exhort   admonish (advise), admonish (warn), advocate, agitate (activate), bait (harass), bait (lure), caution, charge (instruct on the law), coax, coerce, confer (consult), enjoin, forewarn, incite, insist, motivate, notify, persuade, press (beseech), pressure, prevail upon, prompt, recommend, remonstrate, spirit, urge. SEE MAIN ENTRY

exhort against   dissuade, expostulate, protest

exhort to take heed   caution

exhortation   admonition, caution (warning), charge (statement to the jury), direction (guidance), discourse, guidance, harangue, inducement, instigation, monition (warning), persuasion, pressure, proposal (suggestion), recommendation, remonstrance, rhetoric (skilled speech), suggestion

exhortative   hortative

exhortatory   hortative

exhume   disinter, remove (eliminate)

exigence   exigency

exigency   coercion, cornerstone, demand, desideratum, emergency, necessity, need (deprivation), paucity, poverty, predicament, prerequisite, pressure, priority, quagmire, requirement, situation, stress (strain). SEE MAIN ENTRY

exigent   astringent, compulsory, critical (crucial), crucial, essential (required), grave (important), imperative, important (urgent), indispensable, insistent, mandatory, necessary (required), obligatory, particular (exacting), peremptory (imperative), requisite, severe, stringent, uncompromising, urgent. SEE MAIN ENTRY

exigere   expel, require (compel)

exiguitas   insignificance

exiguity   dearth, insufficiency, paucity

exiguous   minimal, slight

exiguousness   dearth, insufficiency

exiguus   inconsiderable, slight

exile   asylum (hiding place), banishment, bar (exclude), deport (banish), deportation, depose (remove), derelict, dislodge, displace (remove), eliminate (exclude), exclude, exclusion, expatriate, expel, expulsion, isolate, ostracism, pariah, rejection, relegate, removal, seclude, transport

exilement   banishment, deportation, ostracism, rejection

eximere   except (exclude), exclude, free

eximious   illustrious, outstanding (prominent)

eximius   special, superlative

exire   issue (send forth)

exist   continue (persevere), endure (last), last, lie (be sustainable), remain (continue), subsist. SEE MAIN ENTRY

exist together   coincide (correspond), concur (coexist)

exist uninterruptedly   endure (last)

exist widely   prevail (be in force)

exist without break   endure (last)

existence   entity, life (period of existence), materiality (physical existence), reality, survival

existenceless   nonentity

existent   actual, bodily, concrete, conscious (awake), corporeal, current, de facto, extant, instant, live (conscious), live (existing), present (current), substantial, substantive

existent thing   fact

759

existimatio character *(reputation)*, honor *(good reputation)*

existing actual, bodily, certain *(positive)*, concrete, conscious *(awake)*, current, de facto, definite, extant, live *(conscious)*, present *(current)*, substantial, substantive

existing as an independent entity autonomous *(independent)*

existing conditions status quo

existing for a short time ephemeral

existing from birth innate

existing in equity equitable

existing in fact de facto

existing state case *(set of circumstances)*, posture *(situation)*, status quo

exit alight, depart, disappear, egress, emerge, evacuate, issuance, issue *(send forth)*, leave *(depart)*, move *(alter position)*, outlet, quit *(evacuate)*, vacate *(leave)*

exitialis deadly, fatal, lethal

exitiosus pernicious

exitus egress, end *(termination)*, event, outlet, result

exodus egress, flight, outflow

exomologesis confession

exonerate absolve, acquit, clear, condone, discharge *(liberate)*, discharge *(release from obligation)*, disencumber, exculpate, excuse, extenuate, extricate, forgive, free, justify, liberate, palliate *(excuse)*, pardon, quit *(free of)*, release, remit *(release from penalty)*, vindicate. SEE MAIN ENTRY

exonerated acquitted, blameless, clear *(free from criminal charges)*, free *(relieved from a burden)*

exonerating circumstance justification

exonerating fact justification

exoneration absolution, acquittal, amnesty, compurgation, condonation, discharge *(liberation)*, discharge *(release from obligation)*, dispensation *(exception)*, excuse, innocence, justification, liberation, pardon, release, remission. SEE MAIN ENTRY

exorabilis placable

exorable charitable *(lenient)*, lenient, placable

exorare prevail upon

exorbitance boom *(prosperity)*, exaggeration, plethora

exorbitancy boom *(prosperity)*, exaggeration, plethora

exorbitant excess, excessive, extreme *(exaggerated)*, grandiose, inordinate, intemperate, needless, outrageous, profuse, prohibitive *(costly)*, unconscionable, undue *(excessive)*, unreasonable, usurious. SEE MAIN ENTRY

exorbitant interest usury

exorbitantly unduly

exordial preliminary

exordium birth *(beginning)*

exordium genesis, inception, onset *(commencement)*, origination, outset, overture

exordium preamble

exordium preface, prelude, start

exornare embellish, garnish

exoteric coherent *(clear)*, comprehensible, obvious, pellucid, perceivable, public *(known)*

exoterical coherent *(clear)*, obvious

exotic nonconforming, unaccustomed, uncommon

expand accrue *(increase)*, accumulate *(enlarge)*, amplify, build *(augment)*, compound, declaim, deploy, develop, elaborate, enhance, extend *(enlarge)*, heighten *(augment)*, increase, inflate, magnify, overestimate, parlay *(exploit successfully)*, progress, spread, supplement. SEE MAIN ENTRY

expand on comment

expand upon develop

expanded capacious, extensive, inflated *(enlarged)*

expanding cumulative *(increasing)*

expange deface

expanse area *(province)*, area *(surface)*, caliber *(measurement)*, coverage *(scope)*, degree *(magnitude)*, extent, latitude, scope, space, territory

expansion accession *(enlargement)*, advance *(increase)*, advancement *(improvement)*, area *(surface)*, augmentation, bombast, boom *(increase)*, boom *(prosperity)*, development *(progression)*, distortion, exaggeration, growth *(evolution)*, growth *(increase)*, increment, inflation *(increase)*, latitude, overstatement, prosperity

expansive ample, broad, capacious, complete *(all-embracing)*, comprehensive, extensive, omnibus, open-ended, voluble

exparte one-sided

expatiate declaim, digress, discourse, enlarge

expatiate on expand

expatiation harangue

expatriate alien, deport *(banish)*, dislodge, displace *(remove)*, eliminate *(exclude)*, exclude, expel, pariah, relegate, seclude. SEE MAIN ENTRY

expatriate oneself abscond, depart

expatriation banishment, deportation, exclusion, expulsion, immigration, ostracism, rejection

expect intend, plan, presume, presuppose, trust. SEE MAIN ENTRY

expectable deductible *(provable)*

expectance contemplation, expectation, likelihood, possibility, prospect *(outlook)*

expectancy claim *(right)*, expectation, likelihood, possibility, prospect *(outlook)*, remainder *(estate in property)*

expectant pending *(imminent)*, preparatory, prospective, ready *(prepared)*, sanguine

expectare expect *(anticipate)*

expectation belief *(something believed)*, belief *(state of mind)*, contemplation, design *(intent)*, end *(intent)*, likelihood, objective, possibility, probability, prospect *(outlook)*, purpose, reliance. SEE MAIN ENTRY

expectations heritage

expected apparent *(presumptive)*, customary, foreseeable, forseen, forthcoming, future, habitual, immediate *(imminent)*, imminent, necessary *(inescapable)*, ordinary, potential, prospective, proximate, regular *(conventional)*, routine, usual

expedience advantage, behalf, feasibility, pragmatism, propriety *(appropriateness)*, qualification *(fitness)*. SEE MAIN ENTRY

expediency artifice, benefit *(betterment)*, boom *(prosperity)*, expedience, feasibility, pragmatism, propriety *(appropriateness)*

expedient appropriate, convenient, due *(regular)*, effective *(efficient)*, efficient, favorable *(advantageous)*, fitting, functional, help, instrumentality, loophole, medium, necessary *(required)*, opportune, plan, politic, practical, pragmatic, profitable, propitious, requisite, resource, seasonable, step, stopgap, stratagem, suitable, viable. SEE MAIN ENTRY

expediential practical

expediousness dispatch *(promptness)*

expedire disengage, disentangle, expedite, explain, extricate, facilitate, solve

expedite conduce, dispatch *(send off)*, ease, facilitate, hasten, help, precipitate *(hasten)*. SEE MAIN ENTRY

expedited determination accelerated judgment

expedited judgment accelerated judgment

expedition acceleration, advance *(progression)*, campaign

expédition dispatch *(promptness)*

expedition haste, quest

expeditious alert *(agile)*, efficient, instantaneous, prompt, punctual, rapid, ready *(willing)*, summary. SEE MAIN ENTRY

expeditious performance acceleration, dispatch *(promptness)*

expeditiously as soon as feasible, instantly

expeditiousness haste

expel condemn *(ban)*, delete, deport *(banish)*, depose *(remove)*, discharge *(dismiss)*, discharge *(shoot)*, dislocate, dislodge, dismiss *(discharge)*, dispel, displace *(remove)*, dispossess, distill, divest, eject *(evict)*, eliminate *(exclude)*, emit, evict, exclude, expatriate, jettison, luxate, oust, outlaw, outpour, precipitate *(throw down violently)*, project *(impel forward)*, purge *(purify)*, reject, relegate, remove *(dismiss from office)*, supplant, transport. SEE MAIN ENTRY

expel from the bar disbar

expel from the legal profession disbar

expelled ineligible

expellere dislodge, eject *(expel)*, expel

expelling expulsion

expend bear the expense, consume, defray, deplete, disburse *(pay out)*, dissipate *(expend foolishly)*, emit, exert, exhaust *(deplete)*, pay, spend. SEE MAIN ENTRY

expend gradually conserve

expend slowly conserve

expendable disposable, minor, needless, negligible, nonessential, null *(insignificant)*, otiose, petty, superfluous, unnecessary. SEE MAIN ENTRY

expended irredeemable

expendere consider, expend *(disburse)*

expenditure advance *(allowance)*, charge *(cost)*, collection *(payment)*, consumption, cost *(expenses)*, decrement, disbursement *(funds paid out)*, expense *(cost)*, fee *(charge)*, finance, maintenance *(upkeep)*, outflow, outlay, payment *(act of paying)*, payment *(remittance)*, price, remittance, waste. SEE MAIN ENTRY

expenditure of energy effort

expenditures bill *(invoice)*, overhead

expense charge *(cost)*, disbursement *(funds paid out)*, expenditure, fare, fee *(charge)*, maintenance *(upkeep)*, outflow, outlay, overhead, payment *(remittance)*, price, rate, value, worth. SEE MAIN ENTRY

expense of transportation fare

expense outlay binder

expenseless free *(at no charge)*, gratis, gratuitous *(given without recompense)*

expenses bill *(invoice)*, damages, expenditure, out of pocket

expensive exorbitant, invaluable, priceless, prohibitive *(costly)*, valuable

expensiveness cost *(price)*

expensum debit

experience bear *(tolerate)*, common knowledge, common sense, competence *(ability)*, discern *(detect with the senses)*, endure *(suffer)*, event, fact, happening, incident, information *(knowledge)*, occasion, occurrence, partake, particular, perceive, phenomenon *(unusual occurrence)*, skill, test. SEE MAIN ENTRY

experience a loss lose *(be deprived of)*

experience loss suffer *(sustain loss)*

experience unpleasantly endure *(suffer)*

experienced artful, competent, expert, familiar *(informed)*, learned, practiced, professional *(trained)*, proficient, qualified *(competent)*, resourceful, veteran

experienced hand expert

experienced person expert, professional, specialist

experienced personnel expert

experienced view common sense

experientia experience *(background)*

experiment check *(inspect)*, endeavor *(noun)*, endeavor *(verb)*, research, test, venture. SEE MAIN ENTRY

experimental probative, speculative, tentative

experimental method trial *(experiment)*

experimentation research

experimentee subject *(object)*

experimenter speculator

experimentum experiment, trial *(experiment)*

expers corporis immaterial

expert capable, cognizant, competent, deft, efficient, familiar *(informed)*, informed *(educated)*, learned, mastermind, practiced, professional *(trained)*, professional, proficient, qualified *(competent)*, specialist, subtle *(refined)*, veteran *(adjective)*, veteran *(noun)*. SEE MAIN ENTRY

expertise comprehension, experience *(background)*, facility *(easiness)*, faculty *(ability)*, gift *(flair)*, knowledge *(learning)*, prowess *(ability)*, specialty *(special aptitude)*

expertness discretion *(quality of being discreet)*, efficiency, experience *(background)*, facility *(easiness)*, faculty *(ability)*, gift *(flair)*, performance *(workmanship)*, prowess *(ability)*, science *(technique)*, skill, specialty *(special aptitude)*

expetere desire

expiable justifiable, pardonable

expiate redeem *(satisfy debts)*, redress, repent

expiating compensatory, palliative *(excusing)*

expiatio expiation

expiation condonation, damages, reparation *(indemnification)*, restitution. SEE MAIN ENTRY

expiatory compensatory, penitent

expilare hold up *(rob)*, plunder

expilatio pillage, spoliation

expiration cessation *(termination)*, close *(conclusion)*, death, defeasance, demise *(death)*, dissolution *(termination)*, end *(termination)*, extremity *(death)*, finality. SEE MAIN ENTRY

expire cease, close *(terminate)*, decease, die, discontinue *(abandon)*, dissolve *(terminate)*, lapse *(cease)*, perish, stop, succumb, terminate. SEE MAIN ENTRY

expired back *(in arrears)*, dead, defunct, lifeless *(dead)*, obsolete, outdated, outmoded

expiring in extremis

expiry end *(termination)*, expiration, finality, lapse *(expiration)*

explain annunciate, argue, clarify, comment, construe *(comprehend)*, construe *(translate)*, convey *(communicate)*, define, depict, describe, detail *(particularize)*, discourse, discuss, educate, elucidate, enlighten, enunciate, explicate, exposit, expound, illustrate, inform *(notify)*, instruct *(teach)*, interject, interpret, justify, manifest, rationalize, reason *(persuade)*, respond, reveal, review, simplify *(clarify)*, solve, speak, specify, support *(justify)*, trace *(delineate)*. SEE MAIN ENTRY

explain away negate, rationalize

explain incorrectly misinterpret

explain the meaning interpret

explain the nature of define

explain wrongly misrepresent

explainable ascertainable, determinable *(ascertainable)*, solvable

explained coherent *(clear)*

explanare elucidate, explain, interpret

explanatio explanation

explanation alibi, answer *(solution)*, clarification, comment, construction, content *(meaning)*, definition, description, disclosure *(something disclosed)*, education, illustration, instruction *(teaching)*, justification, meaning, pandect *(treatise)*, paraphrase, rationale, reason *(basis)*, recital, rendition *(explication)*, representation *(statement)*, response, restatement, signification, solution *(answer)*, statement. SEE MAIN ENTRY

explanation for some delinquency excuse

explanatory coherent *(clear)*, declaratory, demonstrative *(illustrative)*, descriptive, explicit, informative, informatory, interpretive, narrative. SEE MAIN ENTRY

explanatory comment note *(brief comment)*

explanatory note comment

explanatory remark note *(brief comment)*

explere fulfill

expletio satisfaction *(fulfilment)*

expletive blasphemy, expendable, imprecation, needless, surplus, unnecessary. SEE MAIN ENTRY

explicability construction

explicable accountable *(explainable)*, cognizable, coherent *(clear)*, comprehensible, determinable *(ascertainable)*, scrutable. SEE MAIN ENTRY

explicare clear, deploy, describe, disentangle, evolve, explicate, spread

explicate clarify, comment, construe *(translate)*, depict, elucidate, enlighten, exemplify, explain, exposit, expound, interpret. SEE MAIN ENTRY

explicatio analysis, development *(progression)*, explanation, solution *(answer)*

explication clarification, comment, construction, content *(meaning)*, definition, explanation, illustration, paraphrase, rationale, solution *(answer)*

explicative demonstrative *(illustrative)*, informative, informatory, interpretive, narrative, solvable

explicators of the law judiciary

explicatory coherent *(clear)*, demonstrative *(illustrative)*, descriptive, informative, informatory, narrative, solvable. SEE MAIN ENTRY

explicit absolute *(conclusive)*, accurate, apparent *(perceptible)*, candid, certain *(specific)*, clear *(apparent)*, cognizable, coherent *(clear)*, comprehensible, concrete, demonstrative *(illustrative)*, detailed, direct *(forthright)*, distinct *(clear)*, evident, exact, express, informative, lucid, manifest, naked *(perceptible)*, obvious, ostensible, overt, palpable, pellucid, perceivable, perceptible, positive *(incontestable)*, precise, resounding, salient, scrutable, specific, trenchant, unambiguous, unequivocal, unmistakable. SEE MAIN ENTRY

explicit utterance declaration

explicitly fairly *(clearly)*

explode discharge *(shoot)*, rebut, refute

exploit bilk, capitalize *(seize the chance)*, employ *(make use of)*, endeavor, manipulate *(control unfairly)*, operation, ply, transaction. SEE MAIN ENTRY

exploitable disposable, naive

exploitation abuse *(corrupt practice)*, function, graft, misusage, use, usury. SEE MAIN ENTRY

exploitative immoral, mercenary

explorare ascertain, spy

exploration analysis, cross-examination, cross-questioning, discovery, examination *(study)*, indagation, inquiry *(request for information)*, inquiry *(systematic investigation)*, inspection, interrogation, investigation, probe, quest, question *(inquiry)*, research, scrutiny, test, trial *(experiment)*

explorator spy

exploratory interrogative, precursory, probative, tentative

exploratory examination indagation, probe

explore analyze, canvass, check *(inspect)*, delve, examine *(study)*, find *(discover)*, frisk, hunt, inquire, investigate, peruse, probe, research, scrutinize, search, study

explorer pioneer

explosion discharge *(shot)*, outbreak, outburst, outcry, passion, repercussion, salvo, violence

explosions barrage

explosive ammunition, bomb, dangerous, disorderly, vehement, volatile

explosive device bomb

exponent abettor, advocate *(espouser)*, amicus curiae, apologist, backer, example, exemplar, illustration, indicant, indication, proponent, specimen, symbol. SEE MAIN ENTRY

exponere elucidate, exhibit, explain, expose, recite

export displace *(remove)*, outflow, remove *(eliminate)*, send

export and import deal

exportation outflow

exporter dealer

exposcere dun, insist

expose accuse, admit *(concede)*, bare, bear *(adduce)*, betray *(disclose)*, clarify

exposé common knowledge

expose confess, contemn, convey *(communicate)*, debunk, denigrate, denude

exposé denunciation

expose detect, disabuse, disclose. SEE MAIN ENTRY

exposé disclosure *(something disclosed)*

expose discover, dishonor *(deprive of honor)*, disinter, divulge, emerge, endanger, evidence, exhibit, find *(discover)*, impeach, implicate, incriminate, inform *(betray)*, issue *(publish)*, locate, manifest, manifestation, pillory, produce *(offer to view)*, publish, report *(disclose)*, reveal, subject, unveil. SEE MAIN ENTRY

expose onself to incur

expose to danger compromise *(endanger)*, endanger, jeopardize

expose to infamy humiliate, pillory, smear
expose to injury endanger
expose to loss endanger
expose to public contempt libel
expose to view bare, disinter, manifest, present (introduce)
exposed aleatory (perilous), apparent (perceptible), blatant (conspicuous), bleak (exposed and barren), conspicuous, evident, helpless (defenseless), indefensible, insecure, manifest, naked (perceptible), obvious, open (in sight), overt, patent, perceivable, perceptible, precarious, susceptible (unresistent), untenable, vulnerable
exposed to liable
exposed to penalty liable
exposed to risk aleatory (perilous), dangerous, insecure
exposed to view conspicuous, distinct (clear), open (in sight), patent, perceivable, perceptible
exposit clarify, construe (translate), elucidate, expound. SEE MAIN ENTRY
exposit on comment
expositer apologist
expositio description, narration, publication (disclosure)
exposition body (main part), clarification, comment, construction, content (meaning), declaration, disclosure (act of disclosing), disclosure (something disclosed), discourse, discovery, exhibit, explanation, expression (manifestation), hornbook, illustration, instruction (teaching), justification, manifestation, market place, narration, pandect (treatise), rationale, recital, report (detailed account), review (critical evaluation), solution (answer), statement
expositive descriptive, informative, informatory, narrative
expository declaratory, demonstrative (illustrative), descriptive, didactic, informative, informatory, narrative, solvable. SEE MAIN ENTRY
expostulate admonish (warn), argue, blame, castigate, censure, charge (accuse), counsel, demonstrate (protest), discourage, forewarn, reason (persuade), remonstrate, reprehend, urge. SEE MAIN ENTRY
expostulation admonition, blame (culpability), complaint, condemnation (blame), criticism, disapprobation, dissent (difference of opinion), guidance, objection, objurgation, remonstrance. SEE MAIN ENTRY
expostulative hortative
expostulatory hortative, remonstrative
exposure admission (disclosure), bad repute, detection, disclosure (act of disclosing), discovery, expression (manifestation), impeachment, manifestation, publicity, risk. SEE MAIN ENTRY
exposure to danger peril, pitfall
exposure to destruction peril
exposure to harm danger, peril, pitfall, risk
exposure to injury peril
exposure to loss peril
expound clarify, comment, construe (translate), declaim, define, describe, discourse, elucidate, enlighten, explain, explicate, exposit, illustrate, instruct (teach), interpret, reason (persuade), remark, report (disclose), speak. SEE MAIN ENTRY
expounder advocate (espouser), apologist, pedagogue
expounding comment, construction, explanation

express absolute (conclusive), acknowledge (declare), advise, affirm (claim), allege, annunciate, apparent (perceptible), argue, assert, avow, bear (adduce), bespeak, candid, causeway, certain (specific), cite (state), clear (apparent), coherent (clear), comment, communicate, compose, comprehensible, connote, construe (translate), contend (maintain), convey (communicate), declaratory, definite, denote, depict, designate, display, distinct (clear), enunciate, evident, exact, exemplify, exhibit, expeditious, explicit, frame (formulate), interject, lucid, manifest (adjective), manifest (verb), mention, naked (perceptible), observe (remark), ostensible, overt, particular (specific), pellucid, perceivable, perceptible, peremptory (absolute), phrase, portray, posit, precise, pronounce (speak), publish, purport, rapid, recite, relate (tell), remark, report (disclose), signify (inform), speak, specific, specify, testify, unambiguous, unmistakable, utter. SEE MAIN ENTRY
express a wish to obtain desire
express agreement quid pro quo
express an objection object
express an opinion evaluate, opine
express annoyance resent
express briefly indicate
express concurrence assent, grant (concede)
express deep grief for deplore
express disagreement demonstrate (protest)
express disapproval demonstrate (protest), except (object), object, remonstrate
express displeasure reproach
express dissatisfaction criticize (find fault with), demonstrate (protest)
express generally indicate
express highway causeway
express ill will resent
express in a formula formulate
express in a systematic way formulate
express in concrete form embody
express in fuller form expand
express in precise form formulate
express opposition protest
express permission charter (license)
express precisely characterize
express shipper carrier
express sympathy sympathize
expressage consignment
expressed certain (specific), oral, parol, stated, verbal
expressed command law
expressed concisely compact (pithy)
expressed desire request
expressed in few words succinct
expressed in words nuncupative, oral
expressed in writing in writing
expressed indirectly implied
expressed meaning definition
expressed opinion expression (comment)
expressed outright explicit
expressed solely by speech parol
expressing disdain contemptuous
expressing entreaty precatory
expression admission (disclosure), assertion, call (title), comment, connotation, creation, declaration, demeanor, disclosure (something disclosed), inflection, language, manifestation, maxim, mention (reference), parlance, phraseology, pronouncement, remark, rhetoric (skilled speech), speech, style, testimony, token. SEE MAIN ENTRY
expression of choice referendum

expression of contrary opinions fight (argument)
expression of conviction testament
expression of disapproval reaction (opposition)
expression of discontent plaint
expression of grief plaint
expression of ideas phraseology
expression of merit mention (tribute)
expression of opinion observation
expression of opinion for or against argument (pleading)
expression of pain plaint
expression of satisfaction approval
expression of views discourse
expression of will poll (casting of votes)
expressionless inexpressive, inscrutable, vacuous
expressions indicia
expressive clear (apparent), coherent (clear), declaratory, demonstrative (expressive of emotion), demonstrative (illustrative), eloquent, informative, moving (evoking emotion), sententious, suggestive (evocative). SEE MAIN ENTRY
expressive of opinion advisory
expressly faithfully, particularly, purposely
expressway causeway
exprimere express, extort, force (coerce), represent (portray)
exprobate contemn, deprecate, remonstrate, reprehend
exprobation blame (culpability)
exprobrate lash (attack verbally), rebuke, reprimand, reproach
exprobratio reproach
exprobration obloquy, remonstrance, reprimand, reproach, revilement
exprobrative remonstrative
exprobratory remonstrative
expropriate abridge (divest), annex (arrogate), assume (seize), attach (seize), carry away, condemn (seize), confiscate, convert (misappropriate), deprive, dislodge, displace (remove), dispossess, divest, hijack, impress (procure by force), occupy (take possession), plagiarize, seize (confiscate). SEE MAIN ENTRY
expropriated attached (seized)
expropriation appropriation (taking), assumption (seizure), attachment (seizure), condemnation (seizure), disseisin, distraint, distress (seizure), foreclosure, forfeiture (act of forfeiting), garnishment, taking. SEE MAIN ENTRY
expropriatory confiscatory
expugnable helpless (defenseless)
expulsio expulsion
expulsion banishment, deportation, discharge (dismissal), dismissal (discharge), disqualification (rejection), eviction, exception (exclusion), exclusion, expropriation (divestiture), foreclosure, layoff, ostracism, outburst, outflow, rejection, removal. SEE MAIN ENTRY
expulsion of a fetus abortion (feticide)
expunction cancellation, dissolution (termination)
expunge annul, bowdlerize, cancel, censor, delete, destroy (efface), edit, eliminate (eradicate), eradicate, excise (cut away), expurgate, extinguish, obliterate, redact, remove (eliminate), revoke. SEE MAIN ENTRY
expunge the record of pardon
expurgare excuse, expurgate
expurgate bowdlerize, censor, censure, diminish, eliminate (eradicate), eradicate,

excise *(cut away)*, purge *(purify)*. SEE MAIN ENTRY

expurgated pure. SEE MAIN ENTRY

expurgation censorship

exquisite attractive, elegant, prime *(most valuable)*, rare

exquisitus recondite, select

exsanguis lifeless *(dull)*

exsecratio imprecation, malediction

exsect eviscerate

exsection evulsion

exsequi enforce

exsistere appear *(materialize)*, exist

exsolvere disburse *(pay out)*, disentangle, extricate, pay, release, rescue

exspectatio expectation

exspirare expire

exspiratio expiration

exspoliare rob

exstare exist, extant

exstinguere abolish, suppress

exstirpare eradicate, extirpate

exsuperare surmount, transcend

extant conscious *(awake)*, live *(existing)*, present *(current)*. SEE MAIN ENTRY

extemperaneous unexpected

extemplo instantly

extemporal spontaneous

extemporaneous ad hoc, impulsive *(rash)*, informal, spontaneous, unpremeditated

extemporaneousness informality

extemporary impulsive *(rash)*, spontaneous

extempore informal, spontaneous, unexpected, unpremeditated

extend accrue *(increase)*, accumulate *(enlarge)*, administer *(tender)*, amplify, append, bestow, build *(augment)*, compound, continue *(prolong)*, defer *(put off)*, deploy, develop, dwell *(linger over)*, endure *(last)*, enhance, enlarge, expand, increase, inflate, keep *(continue)*, lie *(be sustainable)*, magnify, offer *(tender)*, postpone, present *(make a gift)*, proceed *(go forward)*, proffer, prolong, protract *(stall)*, remain *(continue)*, spread, stay *(continue)*, submit *(give)*, sustain *(prolong)*, tender. SEE MAIN ENTRY

extend beyond overlap, overreach

extend citizenship to an alien naturalize *(make a citizen)*

extend credit capitalize *(provide capital)*, lend, loan

extend in duration continue *(prolong)*

extend over overreach

extend through pervade

extend to abut, border *(bound)*, reach

extended broad, capacious, chronic, comprehensive, continuous, extensive, far reaching, inflated *(enlarged)*, liberal *(not literal)*, prolix, prominent, protracted

extended meaning context

extendere expand, extend *(enlarge)*, prolong

extending broad, cumulative *(intensifying)*, extensive

extension accession *(enlargement)*, accretion, addition, additive, adjournment, adjunct, advance *(increase)*, appendix *(accession)*, appurtenance, augmentation, boom *(increase)*, continuance, continuation *(prolongation)*, deferment, development *(progression)*, growth *(increase)*, increment, inflation *(increase)*, insertion, latitude, magnitude, offshoot, organ, rider, stress *(strain)*, survival. SEE MAIN ENTRY

extension in time duration

extension of credit loan

extension of time deferment

extensive ample, broad, capacious, complete *(all-embracing)*, comprehensive, far reaching, general, inclusive, major, material *(important)*, omnibus, predominant, prevailing *(current)*, prevalent, rife, thorough. SEE MAIN ENTRY

extensive flood cataclysm

extensively generally, throughout *(all over)*

extent amount *(quantity)*, caliber *(measurement)*, capacity *(maximum)*, capacity *(sphere)*, circuit, configuration *(confines)*, degree *(magnitude)*, duration, gamut, magnitude, mass *(weight)*, measurement, purview, quota, range, scope, space, time. SEE MAIN ENTRY

extent of authority jurisdiction

extent of surface area *(surface)*

extent of the court's authority judicature

extent of view coverage *(scope)*

extents confines

extenuare attenuate, decrease, disparage, qualify *(condition)*

extenuate alleviate, attenuate, dilute, diminish, ease, excuse, lessen, modify *(moderate)*, palliate *(excuse)*. SEE MAIN ENTRY

extenuating mitigating, palliative *(excusing)*

extenuating circumstances SEE MAIN ENTRY

extenuation clemency, condonation, excuse, extenuating circumstances, justification, reason *(basis)*

extenuative palliative *(excusing)*

exterior extrinsic, peripheral, periphery, semblance, specious, superficial

exterminate abate *(extinguish)*, abolish, annul, cancel, destroy *(efface)*, dispatch *(put to death)*, eliminate *(eradicate)*, eradicate, extinguish, extirpate, kill *(murder)*, obliterate, overthrow, remove *(eliminate)*, slay

exterminated lost *(taken away)*

extermination abatement *(extinguishment)*, aberemurder, abolition, dispatch *(act of putting to death)*, homicide, killing, removal

exterminative dire, disastrous, fatal

exterminatory disastrous

external alien *(foreign)*, extrinsic, peripheral, physical, specious, superficial

external appearance color *(deceptive appearance)*, complexion, feature *(appearance)*

external aspect appearance *(look)*

external form configuration *(form)*, outline *(boundary)*

externalize perceive

externus foreign

exterrere frighten

extinct dead, defunct, lifeless *(dead)*, null *(invalid)*, null and void, obsolete, outdated, outmoded

extinction aberemurder, abolition, ademption, cancellation, catastrophe, death, demise *(death)*, destruction, dissolution *(termination)*, end *(termination)*, extremity *(death)*, mortality, prostration, subversion

extinction of a debt amortization

extinguere extinguish

extinguish abolish, annul, cancel, cease, destroy *(efface)*, destroy *(void)*, disappear, eradicate, expunge, extirpate, inhibit, kill *(defeat)*, obliterate, quash, stifle, strangle, subvert, suppress. SEE MAIN ENTRY

extinguish indebtedness liquidate *(determine liability)*

extinguish visual discernment blind *(deprive of sight)*

extinguishable destructible

extinguished dead, lost *(taken away)*, null *(invalid)*, null and void

extinguishment abolition, death, demise *(death)*, deterrence, dissolution *(termination)*, end *(termination)*, extremity *(death)*

extinguishment of claim amortization

extirpate abolish, bowdlerize, delete, destroy *(efface)*, eliminate *(eradicate)*, eradicate, expunge, extinguish, obliterate, overthrow, quash, redact, reject, remove *(eliminate)*, subvert, supplant. SEE MAIN ENTRY

extirpated lost *(taken away)*

extirpation abolition, destruction, dissolution *(termination)*, evulsion, rejection, removal, subversion

extirpative detrimental, dire, disastrous, fatal, pernicious

extirpatory dire

extol belaud, honor, overestimate, recommend, regard *(hold in esteem)*

extorquere extort, force *(coerce)*

extort acquire *(secure)*, coerce, deprive, exact, force *(coerce)*, impose *(enforce)*, press *(constrain)*, prey, toll *(exact payment)*. SEE MAIN ENTRY

extort belief convince

extorter racketeer

extortion blackmail, coercion. SEE MAIN ENTRY

extortionary confiscatory

extortionate exorbitant, inordinate, prohibitive *(costly)*, usurious, venal

extortionist criminal. SEE MAIN ENTRY

extra additional, also, ancillary *(auxiliary)*, balance *(amount in excess)*, bonus, excess, excessive, expendable, extraneous, extrinsic, further, gratuity *(present)*, needless, nonessential, overage, premium *(excess value)*, superfluous, supplementary, unnecessary

extra amount for contingencies margin *(spare amount)*

extra amount for emergencies margin *(spare amount)*

extra charge surcharge

extra compensation commission *(fee)*

extra fee surcharge

extra time extension *(postponement)*

extract abridgment *(condensation)*, abstract, acquire *(secure)*, brief, compendium, deduce, deduct *(conclude by reasoning)*, derive *(deduce)*, derive *(receive)*, detect, digest, disencumber, disinter, dislodge, distill, educe, elicit, eradicate, eviscerate, evoke, except *(exclude)*, excerpt, excise *(cut away)*, gain, glean, infer, liberate, quote, reject, remove *(eliminate)*, select, unveil, withdraw. SEE MAIN ENTRY

extract from other works compile

extracted individual

extraction birth *(lineage)*, blood, bloodline, degree *(kinship)*, derivation, descent *(lineage)*, evulsion, family *(common ancestry)*, lineage, origin *(ancestry)*, parentage, race, relationship *(family tie)*, removal, selection *(choice)*

extradite deport *(banish)*, transport

extradition banishment, deportation, expulsion. SEE MAIN ENTRY

extrahere extract

extrajudicial opinion dictum

extralegal felonious

extramarital promiscuity adultery

extramarital relations adultery

763

extraneous circumstantial, collateral *(immaterial)*, expendable, extrinsic, foreign, gratuitous *(unwarranted)*, immaterial, impertinent *(irrelevant)*, inapposite, irrelevant, needless, nonessential, peripheral, tangential, unessential, unnecessary, unrelated. SEE MAIN ENTRY

extraneus extraneous

extraordinally particularly

extraordinarily burdensome requirement imposition *(excessive burden)*

extraordinarius extraordinary

extraordinary best, eccentric, individual, infrequent, inordinate, irregular *(not usual)*, major, meritorious, notable, noteworthy, novel, outstanding *(prominent)*, paramount, particular *(specific)*, peculiar *(distinctive)*, portentous *(eliciting amazement)*, preferential, priceless, prodigious *(amazing)*, rare, remarkable, renowned, salient, singular, special, stellar, sterling, unaccustomed, uncommon, unique, unprecedented, unusual. SEE MAIN ENTRY

extraordinary remedy habeas corpus

extraordinary writ habeas corpus

extravagance exaggeration, hyperbole, misapplication, overstatement, rodomontade, waste

extravagancy overstatement

extravagant copious, egregious, excess, excessive, exorbitant, improvident, inordinate, intemperate, pretentious *(pompous)*, prodigal, profuse, prohibitive *(costly)*, rampant, superfluous, undue *(excessive)*, unreasonable, unrestrained *(not repressed)*

extravagant statement exaggeration

extravasate outpour

extravasation outflow

extrema condicio ultimatum

extrema lineamenta outline *(boundary)*

extreme brutal, ceiling, conclusive *(settled)*, contra, dire, draconian, drastic, end *(termination)*, excess, excessive, exorbitant, fanatical, final, gross *(flagrant)*, harsh, hot-blooded, inordinate, insufferable, intemperate, intense, last *(final)*, lurid, noteworthy, outrageous, strict, superlative, ultimate, unconscionable, undue *(excessive)*, unendurable, unreasonable, unusual, utmost. SEE MAIN ENTRY

extreme boundary limit

extreme edge periphery

extreme fear fright

extreme limit extremity *(furthest point)*, utmost

extreme penalty capital punishment

extreme point end *(termination)*

extremely unduly

extremely important vital

extremes exaggeration

extremist bigot, malcontent

extremitas extremity *(furthest point)*

extremities confines

extremity border, boundary, ceiling, disaster, edge *(border)*, emergency, end *(termination)*, finality, need *(deprivation)*, outline *(boundary)*, pinnacle, prostration, requirement, utmost. SEE MAIN ENTRY

extremus extreme *(last)*, final, ultimate

extricable corrigible

extricate clear, discharge *(liberate)*, disencumber, disengage, disentangle, disenthrall, disinter, educe, free, quit *(free of)*, release, relieve *(free from burden)*, remove *(eliminate)*, rescue. SEE MAIN ENTRY

extrication condonation, discharge *(liberation)*, discharge *(release from obligation)*,

emancipation, evulsion, freedom, ransom, release, removal, salvage

extrinsic alien *(foreign)*, extraneous, foreign, incidental, nonessential, unessential, unnecessary. SEE MAIN ENTRY

extrinsical extraneous, extrinsic, nonessential

extrude expel

extrudere eject *(expel)*

extrusion deportation, eviction, expulsion, ostracism, outflow

exuberance life *(vitality)*

exuberant copious, loquacious, profuse, rampant

exudation outflow

exude emanate, emit, issue *(send forth)*, radiate. SEE MAIN ENTRY

exultant ecstatic

eye center *(central position)*, observe *(watch)*, scrutinize, study

eye opener bombshell

eye-catching manifest, open *(in sight)*, remarkable

eyeless blind *(sightless)*

eyereach perspective, scene

eyeshot scene

eyewitness bystander. SEE MAIN ENTRY

F

faber artisan

fable fiction, lie *(falsify)*, myth

fabled famous, fictitious

fabric building *(structure)*, frame *(structure)*, structure *(composition)*

fabrica manufacture

fabricari fabricate *(construct)*, form, make, manufacture

fabricate build *(construct)*, conceive *(invent)*, conjure, contrive, create, devise *(invent)*, fake, falsify, feign, forge *(produce)*, form, formulate, frame *(construct)*, generate, invent *(falsify)*, invent *(produce for the first time)*, lie *(falsify)*, make, manufacture, misrepresent, originate, palter, plagiarize, prevaricate, produce *(manufacture)*, profess *(pretend)*, scheme, simulate. SEE MAIN ENTRY

fabricate evidence frame *(charge falsely)*

fabricated assumed *(feigned)*, fictitious, illusory, mendacious, spurious, unfounded

fabricating lying

fabrication artifice, building *(business of assembling)*, canard, composition *(makeup)*, counterfeit, creation, deceit, deception, evasion, fake, false pretense, falsehood, falsification, fiction, figment, formation, fraud, hoax, invention, lie, manufacture, misrepresentation, myth, origination, pretense *(pretext)*, pretext, sham, story *(falsehood)*, subreption, subterfuge

fabricative constructive *(creative)*

fabricator author *(originator)*

fabula fiction, myth, story *(narrative)*

fabulous exorbitant, remarkable, special

facade disguise, false pretense

face appearance *(look)*, confront *(encounter)*, endure *(suffer)*, withstand

face amount SEE MAIN ENTRY

face danger fight *(battle)*, withstand

face to face direct *(forthright)*

face up to withstand

face value cost *(price)*, par *(face amount)*. SEE MAIN ENTRY

facere appoint, exercise *(discharge a function)*, glean, make, practice *(engage in)*, realize *(make real)*

facet aspect, complexion, phase *(aspect)*, side

facetious jocular

facies form *(arrangement)*

facile artful, capable, deft, expert, pliable, practiced, proficient, resourceful, sequacious, suasible, tractable, veteran, yielding. SEE MAIN ENTRY

facility instrument *(tool)*

facilis facile, flexible, tractable, yielding

facilitas facility *(easiness)*

facilitate abet, aid, bestow, ease, enable, expedite, favor, further, hasten, help, permit, promote *(organize)*, support *(assist)*. SEE MAIN ENTRY

facilitated decision accelerated judgment

facilitation advance *(progression)*, aid *(help)*, help. SEE MAIN ENTRY

facility appliance, competence *(ability)*, device *(mechanism)*, discretion *(quality of being discreet)*, gift *(flair)*, power, prison, proclivity, propensity, prowess *(ability)*, science *(technique)*, skill, tendency. SEE MAIN ENTRY

facing opposite

facinorous heinous, inexpiable, iniquitous, reprobate, scandalous, sinister

facinus crime, venture

facsimile copy, delineation, duplicate, fake, model. SEE MAIN ENTRY

fact fait accompli, ground, particular, technicality, truth. SEE MAIN ENTRY

fact of comprehending coverage *(scope)*

fact put in controversy by the pleadings issue *(matter in dispute)*. SEE MAIN ENTRY

fact-finding interrogative. SEE MAIN ENTRY

factfinding research

factio cabal, faction

faction cabal, conflict, constituency, contention *(opposition)*, denomination, disaccord, disagreement, discord, dissidence, disturbance, division *(act of dividing)*, feud, incompatibility *(difference)*, organization *(association)*, party *(political organization)*, schism, side, society, sodality, split, strife. SEE MAIN ENTRY

factional divergent, partial *(part)*, partisan

factional part proportion

factionalism strife

factionary demagogue, partisan

factioneer demagogue

factious argumentative, contentious, controversial, contumacious, dissenting, dissident, divergent, divisive, hostile, negative, polemic, pugnacious. SEE MAIN ENTRY

factious leader demagogue

factiousness contention *(opposition)*

factitare practice *(engage in)*

factitious assumed *(feigned)*, colorable *(specious)*, false *(not genuine)*, imitation, synthetic. SEE MAIN ENTRY

factor aspect, broker, cause *(reason)*, component, constituent *(part)*, dealer, deputy, determinant, element, feature *(characteristic)*, ingredient, member *(constituent part)*, part *(portion)*, plenipotentiary, procurator, represent *(substitute)*, substitute. SEE MAIN ENTRY

factorage brokerage

factors case *(set of circumstances)*, circumstances, deputation *(delegation)*

factory-made industrial

factotum employee

factotums personnel

facts circumstances, data, dossier, evidence, proof, science *(study)*

facts admitted at trial   evidence
facts judicially noted   evidence
facts which bear on the point in question
evidence
facts which establish the point in issue
evidence
factual   accurate, actual, authentic, certain
(positive), de facto, documentary, genuine,
honest, incontrovertible, indubious, literal,
objective, real, sound, true *(authentic)*,
unrefutable, valid. SEE MAIN ENTRY
factual basis   documentation
factual matter   evidence
factual statement   affirmation
factualness   honesty, reality, veracity
factum   action *(performance)*, event, fact
facultas   ability, facility *(instrumentality)*,
permission, possibility
facultate   bestow
facultatem facere   enable
facultates   resource
facultative   voluntary
faculty   ability, aptitude, caliber *(mental
capacity)*, capacity *(aptitude)*, color *(complexion)*, competence *(ability)*, droit, gift
(flair), performance *(workmanship)*, specialty
(special aptitude), staff. SEE MAIN ENTRY
faculty member   pedagogue
faculty of speech   language
fad   mode
fade   decay, depart, disappear, dissipate
(spread out), languish, perish, tarnish. SEE
MAIN ENTRY
fade away   diminish, disappear, dissipate
(spread out), ebb, expire, perish
fade out   perish
faded   blemished, indistinct, stale
faded reputation   ignominy
fadeless   indelible, indestructible
fading   attrition, brief, transient
faeneratio   usury
faenus   interest *(profit)*
fagging   operose
fail   decay, default, disappoint, ebb, languish, lapse *(fall into error)*, lose *(undergo
defeat)*, mismanage, neglect, perish, succumb. SEE MAIN ENTRY
fail in duty   default
fail in health   languish
fail to accommodate   disoblige
fail to act   default
fail to answer   default
fail to appear   default
fail to appreciate   decry, overlook *(disregard)*
fail to comply   disobey
fail to comply with   disoblige
fail to do   omit
fail to exact a penalty   pardon
fail to find   lose *(be deprived of)*
fail to include   omit
fail to insert   omit
fail to keep   forfeit, lose *(be deprived of)*,
violate
fail to meet financial engagements   default
fail to mention   omit
fail to notice   disregard
fail to observe   disregard, overlook *(disregard)*, violate
fail to pay   default
fail to perform   default
fail to recognize   misjudge
fail to retain   forfeit
fail to see   overlook *(disregard)*
fail to understand   misapprehend, misconceive, misconstrue, misinterpret, misunderstand

fail to win   lose *(undergo defeat)*
failed   bankrupt, insolvent
failing   decadent, decline, defect, deficiency, disadvantage, fault *(mistake)*, fault
(weakness), flaw, foible, frailty, imperfect,
insufficient, misconduct, perfunctory, vice.
SEE MAIN ENTRY
failing in duty   delinquent *(overdue)*,
derelict *(negligent)*
failure   abortion *(fiasco)*, bankruptcy,
breach, debacle, defeat, delinquency *(failure
of duty)*, disaster, dishonor *(nonpayment)*,
disqualification *(factor that disqualifies)*, flaw,
foible, frailty, frustration, impossibility, impotence, impuissance, inability, incapacity,
inefficacy, infraction, lapse *(expiration)*, loss,
miscarriage, misconduct, mistrial, neglect,
negligence, nonfeasance, nonpayment,
offense, omission, oversight *(carelessness)*,
vice. SEE MAIN ENTRY
failure in duty   culpability, dereliction
failure of credit   default
failure of duty   default, infraction, laches,
maladministration
failure of obligation   delinquency *(failure
of duty)*
failure of strength   frailty
failure of vital functions   death
failure to act   delinquency *(failure of duty)*,
inaction
failure to agree   conflict, contest *(dispute)*,
controversy *(argument)*, difference, disaccord, disagreement, discord, disparity, dispute, dissent *(difference of opinion)*
failure to answer   default
failure to appear   default, nonappearance
failure to carry out   disregard *(omission)*
failure to comply   deficiency. SEE MAIN
ENTRY
failure to correspond   discrepancy
failure to establish a cause of action
nonsuit
failure to litigate within reasonable period
laches
failure to maintain solvency   failure *(bankruptcy)*
failure to make a case   nonsuit
failure to meet one's obligations   default
failure to meet the burden of proof   nonsuit
failure to notice   oversight *(carelessness)*
failure to pay   default, nonpayment
failure to perform   nonperformance, omission
failure to present sufficient evidence
nonsuit
failure to use   desuetude, disuse
fain   willing *(not averse)*
fainaigue   deceive
faineance   sloth
faineant   otiose
faint   inconspicuous, indefinite, indistinct,
insufficient, languid, nebulous, powerless,
prostration, remote *(small)*, unclear, vague
faint hope   pessimism
faint outline   hint
faint suggestion   hint
faint-hearted   caitiff
fainthearted   diffident, recreant
faintheartedness   fear
faintish   powerless
faintness   indistinctness, obscuration
fair   adequate, attractive, average *(standard)*, clean, dispassionate, equal, equitable, evenhanded, high-minded, honest,
impartial, imperfect, judicial, juridical, just,
marginal, market *(business)*, mediocre,

neutral, nonpartisan, objective, open-
minded, passable, right *(correct)*, rightful,
scrupulous, unbiased, unprejudiced,
upright. SEE MAIN ENTRY
fair chance   likelihood, opportunity, probability, prospect *(outlook)*
fair claim   right *(entitlement)*
fair expectation   probability
fair notice   adequate notice
fair play   disinterest *(lack of prejudice)*, fairness, justice, objectivity, probity
fair prospect   likelihood
fair sample   cross section
fair sharing   dispensation *(act of dispensing)*
fair trade agreement   SEE MAIN ENTRY
fair treatment   candor *(impartiality)*, disinterest *(lack of prejudice)*, equity *(justice)*, fairness, justice, right *(righteousness)*
fair value   expense *(cost)*
fair-dealing   honest
fair-haired   popular
fair-minded   equal, equitable, evenhanded, fair *(just)*, impartial, just, liberal
(broad minded), neutral, nonpartisan, objective, open-minded, unbiased
fair-mindedness   equity *(justice)*, fairness,
justice, objectivity
fairish   mediocre
fairly   duly, in good faith. SEE MAIN ENTRY
fairminded   unprejudiced
fairness   candor *(impartiality)*, disinterest
(lack of prejudice), equity *(justice)*, honesty,
integrity, justice, mediocrity, moderation,
objectivity, probity, rectitude, right *(righteousness)*. SEE MAIN ENTRY
fait accompli   denouement. SEE MAIN
ENTRY
faith   allegiance, conviction *(persuasion)*,
credence, fealty, fidelity, probity, prospect
(outlook), reliance, security *(safety)*, trust
(confidence), weight *(credibility)*. SEE MAIN
ENTRY
faithful   accurate, actual, authentic, bona
fide, close *(intimate)*, conscientious, constant, credible, dependable, diligent, exact,
factual, identical, infallible, intimate, literal,
loyal, meticulous, obedient, persistent, pertinacious, precise, punctilious, realistic, reliable, representative, reputable, resolute,
serious *(devoted)*, stable, staunch, steadfast,
strict, true *(loyal)*, undistorted, unyielding.
SEE MAIN ENTRY
faithful companion   cohort
faithfully   in good faith, invariably. SEE MAIN
ENTRY
faithfulness   adherence *(devotion)*, adhesion *(loyalty)*, allegiance, commitment
(responsibility), conformity *(obedience)*,
credibility, discipline *(obedience)*, fealty,
fidelity, homage, integrity, loyalty, rectitude,
responsibility *(conscience)*, trustworthiness,
veracity. SEE MAIN ENTRY
faithless   derelict *(negligent)*, dishonest,
false *(disloyal)*, lying, machiavellian, malevolent, perfidious, profane, recreant, skeptical, unreliable, unscrupulous, untrue,
untrustworthy, variable. SEE MAIN ENTRY
faithlessness   dereliction, dishonesty, disloyalty, doubt *(suspicion)*, incredulity, infidelity, revolt, story *(falsehood)*
faithworthy   credible, solid *(sound)*
fake   assumed *(feigned)*, camouflage,
cloak, copy, counterfeit, deceive, deception,
disguise, dishonest, fabricate *(make up)*,
false *(not genuine)*, false pretense, falsification, falsify, fictitious, forge *(counterfeit)*, forgery, frame *(prearrange)*, fraudulent, hoax,

765

imposture, invent *(falsify)*, meretricious, misrepresent, mock *(imitate)*, palter, pretend, sham, specious, spurious, untrue. SEE MAIN ENTRY

fake charges against   frame *(charge falsely)*
fake the evidence   frame *(prearrange)*
faked   artificial, dishonest, fictitious, fraudulent, imitation, lying, spurious, surreptitious
faked charge   frame up
fakery   false pretense
faking   disguise
fall   debacle, decline, decline *(fall)*, decrease *(noun)*, decrease *(verb)*, depreciate, ebb, failure *(lack of success)*, prostration, relapse *(noun)*, relapse *(verb)*, subside, succumb
fall again into   regress
fall against   impinge
fall apart   decay, degenerate
fall away   degenerate, diminish, ebb, subside
fall back   regress, relapse, retire *(retreat)*, retreat
fall back on   exploit *(make use of)*
fall back upon   resort
fall behind   decrease, regress
fall below   decrease
fall by inheritance   devolve
fall by succession   devolve
fall due   accrue *(arise)*, mature
fall exactly together   coincide *(correspond)*
fall foul of   bicker
fall from grace   lapse *(fall into error)*
fall from repute   degradation
fall heir to   inherit
fall ill   languish
fall in   conform
fall in with   comply, comport *(agree with)*, defer *(yield in judgment)*, obey, unite
fall into   incur
fall into decay   degenerate
fall into error   deviate, err, miscalculate, misconceive, misread, mistake, misunderstand
fall into line   conform, crystallize
fall off   decrease, degenerate, ebb, subside
fall out   alienate *(estrange)*, bicker, disaccord, emanate, estrange. SEE MAIN ENTRY
fall short   fail *(lose)*, lack, require *(need)*
fall sick   languish
fall to pieces   decay, degenerate, disintegrate
fall to the rear   retreat
fall upon   accost, assail, attack, oppugn, strike *(assault)*
fallabity   frailty
fallacia   deceit, fraud, imposture, sham
fallacious   deceptive, delusive, dishonest, errant, erroneous, false *(inaccurate)*, faulty, fraudulent, ill-founded, illogical, illusory, inaccurate, incorrect, invalid, ludicrous, nonsubstantial *(not sturdy)*, sophistic, specious, unfounded, untenable, untrue. SEE MAIN ENTRY
fallacious argument   fallacy, non sequitur
fallacious reasoning   non sequitur, sophistry
fallaciousness   bad faith, deceit, fraud, invalidity, misestimation. SEE MAIN ENTRY
fallacy   invalidity, misjudgment, non sequitur. SEE MAIN ENTRY
fallax   delusive, fallacious, insidious
fallen   peccable, profligate *(corrupt)*
fallen into desuetude   obsolete, outdated, outmoded

fallen into disuse   obsolete, outdated, outmoded
fallen into ruin   dilapidated
fallere   hoodwink, mislead
falli   err, miscalculate
fallible   disputable, dubious, peccable, unreliable, untrustworthy, vulnerable. SEE MAIN ENTRY
falling   decadent, descent *(declination)*
falling away   decline
falling due   maturity
falling into ruin   decadent
falling off   attrition
falling out   disaccord, schism
falling short   defective, deficiency, deficient, insufficiency
falling-off   decline, decrease
fallow   barren, idle, otiose, unproductive
falsa docere   misinform
false   artificial, assumed *(feigned)*, baseless, bogus, colorable *(specious)*, deceptive, delusive, dishonest, disingenuous, erroneous, faithless, fallacious, faulty, fictitious, fraudulent, ill-founded, illusory, imitation, immoral, improper, inaccurate, incorrect, insidious, lying, mendacious, meretricious, perfidious, recreant, sophistic, specious, spurious, tartuffish, unfounded, unreliable, unscrupulous, unsound *(fallacious)*, unsustainable, untenable, untrue, untrustworthy. SEE MAIN ENTRY
false accusation   defamation, libel
false alarm   hoax
false and injurious   libelous
false appearance   color *(deceptive appearance)*, deception, disguise, fallacy, pretense *(ostentation)*, pretense *(pretext)*, pretext
false assertion   falsehood
false charge   frame up
false claim   artifice
false coloring   catachresis, distortion
false colors   disguise
false conception   error
false conduct   duplicity, fraud, imposture
false construction   catachresis, distortion, misapplication
false copy   counterfeit, disguise, distortion
false duplication   counterfeit
false evidence   frame up
false fabrication   forgery
false front   deception, disguise
false ground   pretext
false hearted   disingenuous, false *(disloyal)*
false idea   misestimation
false impression   error, misestimation
false information   frame up
false logic   sophistry
false motive   pretext
false plea   pretense *(pretext)*
false pretense   pretext. SEE MAIN ENTRY
false pretenses   bad faith
false pretension   bad faith
false pretensions   artifice
false profession   hypocrisy
false publication   defamation, libel
false reading   catachresis, distortion
false reason   pretext
false reasoning   non sequitur
false report   canard, defamation, hoax, slander
false representation   counterfeit, fake, fraud, misrepresentation
false representation of fact   false pretense
false reproduction   counterfeit
false rumor   canard

false show   histrionics, pretense *(ostentation)*, pretense *(pretext)*, pretext, role, sham
false statement   canard, falsehood, fiction, libel, lie, misrepresentation, misstatement, perjury, story *(falsehood)*
false step   fault *(mistake)*
false story   myth
false swearing   bad faith, dishonesty, perjury, subreption
false teaching   propaganda
false-hearted   dishonest
falsehearted   faithless, insidious, machiavellian, perfidious, recreant
falseheartedness   bad faith, deceit, dishonesty, duplicity, infidelity
falsehood   canard, counterfeit, deceit, deception, dishonesty, fake, false pretense, fiction, figment, improbity, indirection *(deceitfulness)*, libel, lie, misrepresentation, misstatement, myth, perjury, pretense *(pretext)*, subreption, subterfuge. SEE MAIN ENTRY
falsely call to account   frame *(charge falsely)*
falsely characterize   mislabel
falsely testify   bear false witness
falseness   bad faith, color *(deceptive appearance)*, counterfeit, deceit, deception, dishonesty, disloyalty, duplicity, fallacy, false pretense, fraud, improbity, indirection *(deceitfulness)*, invalidity, libel, perjury, pretense *(pretext)*
falsification   artifice, canard, color *(deceptive appearance)*, counterfeit, deceit, deception, dishonesty, distortion, fake, false pretense, falsehood, fiction, figment, forgery, fraud, hoax, hypocrisy, libel, lie, misrepresentation, misstatement, overstatement, perjury, pretense *(pretext)*, pretext, story *(falsehood)*, subreption. SEE MAIN ENTRY
falsified   dishonest, fraudulent, mendacious
falsify   bear false witness, cloak, copy, deceive, defame, delude, disguise, distort, evade *(deceive)*, fabricate *(make up)*, fake, feign, forge *(counterfeit)*, invent *(falsify)*, lie *(falsify)*, malign, misguide, misinform, mislead, misrepresent, misstate, negate, palter, perjure, pervert, plagiarize, pretend, prevaricate, refute, slant. SEE MAIN ENTRY
falsify accounts   defalcate
falsify testimony   perjure
falsity   counterfeit, deceit, dishonesty, disloyalty, fallacy, false pretense, falsehood, fraud, improbity, infidelity, invalidity, lie, misrepresentation, story *(falsehood)*
falsum   falsehood, lie
falsus   counterfeit, delusive, erroneous, false pretense, illusory, inaccurate, incorrect, putative, untrue
falter   beat *(pulsate)*, doubt *(hesitate)*, hesitate, oscillate, vacillate
faltering   diffident, disinclined, doubt *(indecision)*, hesitant, hesitation, irresolute, noncommittal
fama   character *(reputation)*, honor *(good reputation)*, notoriety, prestige, report *(rumor)*, reputation
fame   character *(reputation)*, credit *(recognition)*, distinction *(reputation)*, eminence, importance, notoriety, prestige, publicity, regard *(esteem)*, reputation
famed   famous, illustrious, notable, notorious, outstanding *(prominent)*, renowned, reputable
familia   family *(household)*, household
familiar   accustomed *(familiarized)*,

brazen, close *(intimate)*, cognizable, cognizant, common *(customary)*, conventional, customary, frequent, habitual, informal, informed *(having information)*, intimate, learned, mundane, nondescript, ordinary, presumptuous, prevailing *(current)*, prevalent, proverbial, public *(known)*, regular *(conventional)*, routine, trite, typical, usual. SEE MAIN ENTRY

familiar discourse   conversation
familiar object   landmark *(conspicuous object)*
familiar through use   accustomed *(familiarized)*
familiar way   custom
familiaris   familiar *(customary)*, intimate
familiarity   cognition, common knowledge, comprehension, consortium *(marriage companionship)*, experience *(background)*, information *(knowledge)*, knowledge *(awareness)*, knowledge *(learning)*, scienter
familiarization   habituation, knowledge *(learning)*
familiarize   advise, apprise, communicate, educate, inform *(notify)*, initiate, instruct *(teach)*, inure *(accustom)*, naturalize *(acclimate)*
familiarize oneself   perceive
familiarize with   instill, practice *(train by repetition)*
familiarized   informed *(having information)*
family   affiliation *(bloodline)*, affinity *(family ties)*, ancestry, bloodline, derivation, descendant, domestic *(household)*, house, household *(domestic)*, household, issue *(progeny)*, kindred, kinship, lineage, next of kin, offspring, origin *(ancestry)*, parentage, paternal, posterity, progeny, race, relative, succession. SEE MAIN ENTRY
family abode   household
family circle   household
family connection   affiliation *(bloodline)*, affinity *(family ties)*, ancestry, blood, degree *(kinship)*, filiation, kinship, next of kin, parentage, propinquity *(kinship)*, relation *(kinship)*, relationship *(family tie)*
family dwelling place   household
family patronage   nepotism
family related   consanguineous
family relationship   blood, degree *(kinship)*
family tie   affiliation *(bloodline)*, blood, degree *(kinship)*, next of kin, relation *(kinship)*
family tree   ancestry, blood, bloodline, descent *(lineage)*, parentage
family unit   family *(household)*
famine   paucity, poverty, privation
famous   blatant *(conspicuous)*, household *(familiar)*, illustrious, important *(significant)*, notable, noteworthy, notorious, outstanding *(prominent)*, popular, prominent, renowned, stellar. SEE MAIN ENTRY
famousness   notoriety, prestige, publicity, regard *(esteem)*, reputation
fan   addict, spread, stimulate
fan out   deploy, expand
fanatic   addict, addicted, bigot, demagogue, dictatorial, drastic, eager, fanatical, malcontent, outrageous, partisan, uncompromising
fanatical   demonstrative *(expressive of emotion)*, dogmatic, draconian, drastic, eager, excessive, extreme *(exaggerated)*, illiberal, inordinate, narrow, outrageous,

parochial, provincial, radical *(favoring drastic change)*, uncompromising, vehement, zealous. SEE MAIN ENTRY
fanaticism   ardor, compulsion *(obsession)*, obsession, passion
fanaticus   fanatical
fancied   delusive, fictitious, illusory, nonexistent, preferred *(favored)*
fancier   addict
fanciful   arbitrary, arbitrary and capricious, capricious, delusive, fictitious, ill-founded, illusory, insubstantial, original *(creative)*, quixotic, unpredictable, variable
fanciful name   sobriquet
fancy   affection, compulsion *(obsession)*, conatus, concept, conjure, desire, elaborate, expect *(consider probable)*, favor, fiction, figment, idea, notion, obsession, opine, opinion *(belief)*, penchant, predilection, predisposition, prefer, preference *(choice)*, propensity, quirk *(idiosyncrasy)*, relish, surmise, suspect *(think)*
fanfare   noise
fanfaronade   histrionics, jactation, pretense *(ostentation)*, rodomontade
fanfaronading   orgulous
fantasied   capricious
fantastic   delusive, ludicrous, nonexistent, noteworthy, prodigious *(amazing)*, special, unusual. SEE MAIN ENTRY
fantastical   capricious, delusive, ludicrous, nonexistent
fantasy   fiction, figment, myth, story *(falsehood)*, vision *(dream)*
far   inaccessible, obscure *(remote)*, remote *(not proximate)*, remote *(secluded)*. SEE MAIN ENTRY
far away   inaccessible
far from the point   irrelevant
far off   inaccessible
far removed   remote *(not proximate)*
far-famed   outstanding *(prominent)*, renowned
far-fetched   inapposite. SEE MAIN ENTRY
far-flung   broad, extensive, far reaching
far-gone   dilapidated
far-off   remote *(not proximate)*, remote *(secluded)*, unapproachable
far-ranging   extensive, far reaching
far-reaching   broad, comprehensive, critical *(crucial)*, extensive, important *(significant)*, major, material *(important)*, momentous, rife. SEE MAIN ENTRY
far-spread   broad
faraway   oblivious, remote *(secluded)*, unapproachable
farce   caricature, parody, travesty. SEE MAIN ENTRY
farcical   ludicrous
fare   fee *(charge)*, price, rate, toll *(tax)*. SEE MAIN ENTRY
fare well   succeed *(attain)*
farfetched   suspicious *(questionable)*, unbelievable
farm   cultivate, homestead
farm land   homestead
farmplace   homestead
farmstead   homestead
farrago   confusion *(turmoil)*, melange
farseeing   omniscient, perspicacious, prophetic, provident *(showing foresight)*
farsighted   perspicacious, politic, prophetic, prudent, sapient, sensible
farsightedness   sagacity
farthest   extreme *(last)*, last *(final)*, peripheral, ultimate
farthest end   extremity *(furthest point)*

farthest point   ceiling, extremity *(furthest point)*
farthest reach   extremity *(furthest point)*, utmost
farthest removed   extreme *(last)*
fascicle   serial
fascimile   recreate, resemblance, transcript
fascinate   immerse *(engross)*, interest, occupy *(engage)*. SEE MAIN ENTRY
fascinating   attractive, sapid
fascination   compulsion *(obsession)*, obsession, preoccupation, seduction
fascist   dictatorial
fashion   adapt, build *(construct)*, complexion, compose, conduct, contrive, create, crystallize, custom, devise *(invent)*, fabricate *(construct)*, forge *(produce)*, form *(arrangement)*, form, formulate, frame *(construct)*, frame *(formulate)*, habit, invent *(produce for the first time)*, make, manner *(behavior)*, manner *(kind)*, manufacture, means *(opportunity)*, mode, parlance, prescription *(custom)*, produce *(manufacture)*, scheme, style, usage, way *(manner)*
fashionable   customary, elegant, popular
fashionable society   elite
fashionableness   custom
fashioning   building *(business of assembling)*, creation, manufacture, onset *(commencement)*
fast   close *(intimate)*, expeditious, firm, fixed *(securely placed)*, indelible, inextricable, inseparable, instantly, loyal, permanent, rapid, secure *(sound)*, solid *(sound)*, stable, staunch, steadfast
fast and loose   variable
fast rate   dispatch *(promptness)*
fasten   affix, annex *(add)*, append, attach *(join)*, bar *(hinder)*, cement, cohere *(adhere)*, combine *(join together)*, commingle, handcuff, lock, occlude, restrain, shut, trammel
fasten in position securely   fix *(make firm)*
fasten oneself upon   hunt
fasten securely   fix *(make firm)*
fasten together   attach *(join)*, connect *(join together)*
fasten upon   grapple
fastened   attached *(annexed)*, firm, fixed *(securely placed)*, secure *(sound)*, stable
fastened together   conjoint
fastener   connection *(fastening)*, handcuff
fastening   accession *(annexation)*, attachment *(act of affixing)*
fastidiosus   disdainful, supercilious
fastidious   conscientious, diligent, discriminating *(judicious)*, meticulous, particular *(exacting)*, precise, punctilious, sensitive *(discerning)*, strict
fastidiousness   decorum, diligence *(care)*, particularity
fastidire   disdain, spurn
fastidium   contempt *(disdain)*, disdain
fastigium   eminence
fastness   dispatch *(promptness)*
fat cat   SEE MAIN ENTRY
fatal   deadly, deleterious, dire, lethal, malignant, noxious, pernicious, pestilent, serious *(grave)*, toxic. SEE MAIN ENTRY
fatal accident   fatality
fatal affair   tragedy
fatal casualty   dead, fatality
fatal mishap   fatality
fatalism   resignation *(passive acceptance)*
fatality   dead, death, mortality. SEE MAIN ENTRY

fate end *(termination)*, happenstance, predetermination, predetermine, prospect *(outlook)*, quirk *(accident)*. SEE MAIN ENTRY

fated forthcoming, future, inevitable, necessary *(inescapable)*, unalterable, unavoidable *(inevitable)*. SEE MAIN ENTRY

fateful critical *(crucial)*, fatal, key, major, momentous, necessary *(inescapable)*, portentous *(ominous)*, prophetic

fateri admit *(concede)*, avow, confess

father generate, originate, parents, primogenitor, propagate *(increase)*, reproduce

fatherhood filiation, paternity

fatherland home *(place of origin)*, nationality

fatherlike paternal

fatherly paternal

fathership filiation, paternity

fathom apprehend *(perceive)*, ascertain, comprehend *(understand)*, conceive *(comprehend)*, construe *(comprehend)*, delve, digest *(comprehend)*, discern *(detect with the senses)*, find *(discover)*, gauge, measure, pierce *(discern)*, realize *(understand)*, solve, understand

fathomable appreciable, cognizable, coherent *(clear)*, comprehensible, determinable *(ascertainable)*, scrutable, solvable

fathomless incomprehensible, profound *(intense)*

fatidic ominous, oracular, prophetic

fatidical ominous, oracular, prophetic

fatidicus prophetic

fatigare importune

fatigue exhaust *(deplete)*, languor, prostration, tax *(overwork)*

fatigued languid

fatiguing difficult, onerous, operose, oppressive

fatiloquent portentous *(ominous)*, prophetic

fatten enlarge, expand, inflate

fatten upon prey

fatuitous fatuous, illusory, opaque

fatuity opacity

fatuous ludicrous, misadvised, nugatory, opaque, puerile, vacuous. SEE MAIN ENTRY

fatuus fatuous

faubourg frontier

fault blame *(culpability)*, blame, culpability, decry, defacement, defect, deficiency, delinquency *(misconduct)*, deprecate, depreciate, disadvantage, discommend, drawback, error, flaw, foible, frailty, guilt, impeach, mischief, misconduct, misdeed, misdoing, onus *(blame)*, rift *(gap)*, tort, transgression, vice. SEE MAIN ENTRY

fault finding cynical

fault of the court injustice

fault-finding criticism, dissatisfaction

faultfind cavil, complain *(criticize)*

faultfinder malcontent

faultfinding denunciation, derogatory, diatribe, disapproval, disparagement, fractious, impugnation, inculpation, nonconsenting, obloquy, particular *(exacting)*, pejorative, querulous, severe, stricture

faultful defective, errant, fallacious, peccant *(culpable)*

faultiness defect, deficiency, fallacy, handicap

faultless absolute *(ideal)*, accurate, best, blameless, clean, faithful *(true to fact)*, incorruptible, inculpable, infallible, innocent, intact, irreprehensible, literal, not guilty, pardonable, precise, pure, unblemished, unimpeachable. SEE MAIN ENTRY

faultlessness rectitude

faulty bad *(inferior)*, blameful, blemished, defective, deficient, derelict *(negligent)*, errant, erroneous, fallacious, fallible, false *(inaccurate)*, illogical, imperfect, inaccurate, incorrect, inexact, inferior *(lower in quality)*, invalid, marred, obnoxious, peccable, poor *(inferior in quality)*, unsatisfactory, unsound *(fallacious)*, unsound *(not strong)*, untenable. SEE MAIN ENTRY

faulty in logic fallacious, sophistic

faulty reasoning fallacy

faulty work noncompliance *(improper completion)*

fautor backer

fautor partisan, promoter

favere favor, patronize *(trade with)*

favor accommodate, advantage, advocate, approval, approve, assent, auspices, behalf, benefit *(conferment)*, benevolence *(act of kindness)*, bounty, capitalize *(provide capital)*, complexion, concur *(agree)*, conduce, countenance, deign, discriminate *(treat differently)*, embrace *(accept)*, espouse, estimation *(esteem)*, foster, franchise *(license)*, further, gift *(present)*, goodwill, grace, grant, grant *(concede)*, gratuity *(present)*, help, honor *(outward respect)*, indorsement, indulgence, inequity, largess *(gift)*, leave *(permission)*, lenience, let *(permit)*, nepotism, option *(contractual provision)*, partiality, pass *(approve)*. SEE MAIN ENTRY

favor patronage *(power to appoint jobs)*

favor patronage *(support)*, patronize *(condescend toward)*, predilection, predisposition, prefer, preserve, prestige, privilege, promote *(advance)*, propensity, recommend, regard *(esteem)*, respect, sanction *(permission)*, service *(assistance)*, side, sponsor, token, uphold

favor excessively overindulge

favor owed due

favor with bestow, impart, vouchsafe

favor with one's patronage patronize *(trade with)*

favorable auspicious, beneficial, constructive *(creative)*, fitting, inclined, profitable, prone, propitious, receptive, salutary, seasonable, suitable, valuable, viable, willing *(not averse)*. SEE MAIN ENTRY

favorable chance likelihood, opportunity, probability

favorable decision SEE MAIN ENTRY

favorable disposition goodwill

favorable opinion credit *(recognition)*, estimation *(esteem)*

favorable opportunity advantage, possibility

favorable position edge *(advantage)*. SEE MAIN ENTRY

favorable prospect chance *(possibility)*, high probability, likelihood, possibility

favorable reception adoption *(acceptance)*

favorable recognition estimation *(esteem)*

favorable regard goodwill

favorable repute estimation *(esteem)*

favorable time chance *(fortuity)*, opportunity

favorable to health salubrious

favorable trade balance boom *(prosperity)*

favorable verdict acquittal

favorable verdict to the defendant compurgation

favorableness expedience

favorably disposed partial *(biased)*

favorably inclined consenting, propitious, willing *(not averse)*

favorably minded ready *(willing)*

favorably prejudiced favorable *(expressing approval)*

favored exempt, popular, preferential, privileged

favored by fortune auspicious

favored treatment preference *(priority)*

favorer abettor, advocate *(espouser)*, apologist, benefactor, disciple, partisan, patron *(influential supporter)*, sponsor

favoring auspicious, favorable *(expressing approval)*, inequitable, lenient

favoring circumstance advantage

favoring influence auspices

favorite best, popular, preferable, preference *(choice)*, preferred *(favored)*

favoritism bias, discrimination *(bigotry)*, favor *(partiality)*, inequity, injustice, nepotism, partiality, predisposition, prejudice *(preconception)*. SEE MAIN ENTRY

fawn truckle

fawning obsequious, servile, subservient

fealty adherence *(devotion)*, adhesion *(loyalty)*, allegiance, fidelity, loyalty. SEE MAIN ENTRY

fear cloud *(suspicion)*, consternation, fright, misgiving, mistrust, panic, phobia, scruple, stress *(strain)*, suspicion *(mistrust)*, trepidation. SEE MAIN ENTRY

fear of danger fright

fear-inspiring formidable, ominous, sinister

fear-stricken caitiff

fearful dire, formidable, ineffable, ominous, pending *(imminent)*, portentous, recreant, repulsive, suspicious *(distrustful)*

fearfulness consternation, fear, misgiving, panic, scruple, stress *(strain)*, suspicion *(mistrust)*. SEE MAIN ENTRY

fearless heroic, indomitable, spartan, undaunted. SEE MAIN ENTRY

fearlessness confidence *(faith)*, prowess *(bravery)*

fearsome dangerous, sinister

feasibility expedience, possibility, potential. SEE MAIN ENTRY

feasible colorable *(plausible)*, plausible, possible, potential, practicable, pragmatic, presumptive, probable, suitable, viable

feasibleness feasibility

feast carouse

feast upon prey

feat act *(undertaking)*, endeavor

featherbrained opaque

feature aspect, characteristic, complexion, component, constituent *(part)*, contour *(shape)*, detail, differential, element, exhibit, expose, factor *(ingredient)*, ingredient, item, member *(constituent part)*, particular, particularity, phase *(aspect)*, phenomenon *(manifestation)*, point *(item)*, property *(distinctive attribute)*, quality *(attribute)*, quality *(grade)*, speciality, specialty *(distinctive mark)*, symptom, technicality, trait. SEE MAIN ENTRY

featured attraction feature *(special attraction)*

featureless indeterminate

features character *(personal quality)*, circumstances, color *(complexion)*, configuration *(form)*, indicia

febrifugal medicinal

febrile hot-blooded

feckless futile, inadept, inadequate, ineffective, ineffectual, lax, otiose, unable

feculent   repulsive

fecund   fertile, original *(creative)*, productive, prolific

fecundate   proliferate, propagate *(increase)*, reproduce

fecundify   proliferate

fecundus   fertile

federal   mutual *(collective)*, national, public *(affecting people)*. SEE MAIN ENTRY

federal officer   marshal

federal union   federation

federalization   integration *(amalgamation)*

federalize   affiliate, join *(bring together)*. SEE MAIN ENTRY

federate   affiliate, allied, associated, combine *(act in concert)*, consolidate *(unite)*, cooperate, federal, federalize *(associate)*, intimate, join *(bring together)*, mutual *(collective)*, organize *(unionize)*, pool. SEE MAIN ENTRY

federated   affiliated, associated, conjoint, mutual *(collective)*

federation   affiliation *(amalgamation)*, association *(alliance)*, cartel, chamber *(body)*, coaction, coalescence, coalition, committee, company *(enterprise)*, confederacy *(compact)*, consolidation, contact *(association)*, contribution *(participation)*, cooperative, corporation, integration *(assimilation)*, league, merger, organization *(association)*, partnership, pool, society, sodality, syndicate, union *(labor organization)*. SEE MAIN ENTRY

federative   collective, conjoint, corporate *(associate)*, federal, mutual *(collective)*

fee   advance *(allowance)*, brokerage, charge *(cost)*, compensation, due, excise, expense *(cost)*, fare, honorarium, pay, payment *(remittance)*, pension, perquisite, price, rate, real estate, recompense, rent, reward, toll *(tax)*, wage. SEE MAIN ENTRY

fee contingent on future legal services   retainer

fee-for-service   SEE MAIN ENTRY

fee paid to secure legal services   retainer

fee simple   freehold. SEE MAIN ENTRY

feeble   decadent, helpless *(powerless)*, imperfect, inadept, inadequate, incapable, inconspicuous, ineffective, ineffectual, insipid, insubstantial, insufficient, languid, lifeless *(dull)*, nonsubstantial *(not sturdy)*, passive, powerless, unsatisfactory, unsound *(not strong)*

feeble-eyed   blind *(sightless)*

feeble-minded   non compos mentis

feebleness   caducity, disability *(physical inability)*, fault *(weakness)*, frailty, impotence, impuissance, incapacity, inefficacy, languor, prostration

feed   maintain *(sustain)*, nurture, provide *(supply)*, supply, support *(assist)*

feed upon   prey

feedback   SEE MAIN ENTRY

feel   deem, detect, endure *(suffer)*, opine, perceive, surmise. SEE MAIN ENTRY

feel a dearth   lack

feel annoyance   resent

feel compassion   relent

feel conscience stricken   regret

feel contempt for   contemn, disdain, flout, misprize

feel contrition   repent

feel disapproval   except *(object)*

feel displeasure   resent

feel distrust   doubt *(distrust)*, suspect *(distrust)*

feel for   relent, sympathize

feel gratification   relish

feel hurt   resent

feel ill will   resent

feel joy   relish

feel no concern   disregard

feel out   peruse

feel pain   suffer *(sustain loss)*

feel pleasure   relish

feel regret   repent

feel remorse   repent

feel resentment   resent

feel sure   rely, trust

feel sure of   confide *(trust)*

feel terror   fear

feel the necessity for   need, require *(need)*

feel the want of   need

feel uncertain   vacillate

feel uneasy about   regret

feel unsure   doubt *(hesitate)*

feel utter contempt for   decry, disdain

feeling   affection, climate, concept, fervent, humanity *(humaneness)*, impression, notion, opinion *(belief)*, passion, perceptive, perspective, pity, position *(point of view)*, posture *(attitude)*, premonition, reaction *(response)*, sensibility, sensitive *(easily affected)*, tenor. SEE MAIN ENTRY

feeling of dejection   damper *(depressant)*

feeling of depression   damper *(depressant)*

feeling of obligation   responsibility *(conscience)*

feeling of uncertainty   doubt *(indecision)*, qualm

feelingless   cold-blooded

feelings of guilt   remorse

fees   consideration *(recompense)*, disbursement *(funds paid out)*

feign   assume *(simulate)*, cloak, disguise, fabricate *(make up)*, fake, falsify, forge *(counterfeit)*, invent *(falsify)*, misrepresent, mock *(imitate)*, palter, perjure, pretend, prevaricate, profess *(pretend)*, simulate. SEE MAIN ENTRY

feigned   artificial, colorable *(specious)*, deceptive, delusive, dishonest, disingenuous, evasive, false *(not genuine)*, fictitious, fraudulent, illusory, imitation, lying, mendacious, spurious, tartuffish. SEE MAIN ENTRY

feigned copy   fake

feigned story   fiction, figment

feint   artifice, color *(deceptive appearance)*, deception, false pretense, maneuver *(trick)*, pretense *(pretext)*, pretext, ruse, sham, stratagem. SEE MAIN ENTRY

felicitous   auspicious, ecstatic, favorable *(advantageous)*, propitious, relevant, resourceful, successful, suitable. SEE MAIN ENTRY

felicitousness   expedience, timeliness

felicity   gift *(flair)*, propensity, propriety *(appropriateness)*, prosperity, skill

feline   furtive, machiavellian, politic, sly, stealthy, subtle *(insidious)*

felix   auspicious, successful

fell   brutal, dire, disastrous, fatal, harmful, lethal, malignant, overthrow, pernicious, precipitate *(throw down violently)*, ruthless

fell stroke   disaster

fellow   cohort, colleague, confederate, consort, contributor *(contributor)*, copartner *(business associate)*, correlate, correlative, member *(individual in a group)*, participant, peer, person, resemblance. SEE MAIN ENTRY

fellow companion   colleague, consociate, consort

fellow conspirator   accessory, accomplice, coactor, coconspirator, cohort, colleague, consociate, conspirer

fellow feeling   comity, philanthropy, pity, rapprochement

fellow machinator   coconspirator

fellow plotter   coconspirator

fellow schemer   coconspirator

fellow strategist   coconspirator

fellow suffering   pity

fellow traiter   coconspirator

fellow worker   associate, coadjutant, colleague, consociate, copartner *(business associate)*, participant, partisan, partner

fellow workers   personnel

fellowless   solitary

fellowship   coaction, coalition, committee, confederacy *(compact)*, contact *(association)*, contribution *(participation)*, informality, integration *(assimilation)*, league, merger, partnership, peace, rapprochement, society, sodality, union *(labor organization)*

fellowship in sorrow   pity

felon   assailant, captive, convict, criminal, hoodlum, lawbreaker, malefactor, offender, outlaw, prisoner. SEE MAIN ENTRY

felonious   culpable, illegal, illicit, impermissible, iniquitous, larcenous, lawless, nefarious, reprobate, wrongful. SEE MAIN ENTRY

felonious abreption   asportation

felonious act   tortious act

felonious conduct   criminality, guilt

felonious removal   asportation

felonious stealing   larceny

felonious taking   robbery, theft

felonious taking of the property of another   robbery

felonious transference   asportation

felonious translocation   asportation

feloniously   illegally

feloniousness   corruption, criminality

felony   burglary, crime, delict, homicide, housebreaking, misdeed, offense. SEE MAIN ENTRY

felony murder   homicide

female   SEE MAIN ENTRY

fence   bar *(hinder)*, barrier, bicker, enclosure, equivocate, hedge, obstacle, obstruction, palter, parry, pettifog, prevaricate, receiver, screen *(guard)*. SEE MAIN ENTRY

fence in   circumscribe *(surround by boundary)*, confine, contain *(enclose)*, enclose, encompass *(surround)*, envelop, shut

fence off   demarcate

fenced   curtilage, guarded

fenced in area   enclosure

fend   counter, deter

fend off   avert, block, deter, estop, parry, prevent, repel *(drive back)*, repulse, resist *(withstand)*, save *(rescue)*, stave

fender   panoply

feod   fee *(estate)*

feoffee   legatee. SEE MAIN ENTRY

feoffment   SEE MAIN ENTRY

feoffor   SEE MAIN ENTRY

feracious   fertile, prolific

feral   deadly, destructive, fatal, harsh, lethal, malicious, malignant, pestilent, ruthless

ferax   fertile, productive

fergiversate   prevaricate

feriae   holiday

ferine   harsh, ruthless

ferire   beat *(strike)*

ferity atrocity, cruelty, severity

ferment agitate (activate), catalyst, commotion, confusion (turmoil), decompose, discompose, disturb, disturbance, embroilment, emotion, entanglement (confusion), foment, furor, pandemonium, passion, perturb, riot, stress (strain), turmoil. SEE MAIN ENTRY

fermentation commotion

ferocious brutal, cruel, harsh, malevolent, malicious, malignant, outrageous, ruthless, vicious

ferociousness bestiality, cruelty, severity

ferocity atrocity, bestiality, cruelty, furor, outbreak, severity, violence. SEE MAIN ENTRY

ferox rampant, unruly

ferre bear (support), legalize

ferret hunt, search. SEE MAIN ENTRY

ferret out ascertain, cross-examine, delve, detect, discover, disinter, educe, find (discover), locate, pursue (chase), solve, trace (follow)

ferrier carrier

fertile beneficial, gainful, lucrative, original (creative), productive, prolific, resourceful. SEE MAIN ENTRY

fertilis fertile

fertility maternity

ferule cudgel

ferus brutal

fervency affection, ardor, compulsion (obsession), furor, passion

fervens fervent, vehement

fervent demonstrative (expressive of emotion), eager, earnest, fanatical, hot-blooded, intense, intensive, ready (willing), serious (devoted), true (loyal), vehement, zealous. SEE MAIN ENTRY

fervid fervent, hot-blooded, vehement, zealous. SEE MAIN ENTRY

fervidness ardor

fervidus eager, fervent

fervor affection

fervor ardor

fervor emotion, passion, strength

Fescennine salacious

fester annoy

festering toxic

festinatio dispatch (promptness), haste

festival holiday, treat

festive occasion ceremony

festivity ceremony

festooned elaborate

fetch procure, ruse, transport, yield (produce a return)

fetching attractive

fete holiday

fetid stale

fetish compulsion (obsession), obsession

fetter apprehend (arrest), bind (restrain), constraint (imprisonment), constraint (restriction), constrict (inhibit), contain (restrain), custody (incarceration), detain (restrain), detention, deter, hamper, handcuff (noun), handcuff (verb), hinder, impede, impediment, interfere, restrain, restrict, trammel. SEE MAIN ENTRY

fetters bondage, servitude

fettle color (complexion)

fetus embryo

feud altercation, argument (contention), belligerency, brawl, collide (clash), contention (opposition), contest (dispute), controversy (argument), disaccord, disagreement, dispute, fee (estate), freehold, revenge, struggle. SEE MAIN ENTRY

feuder contender

feuding malevolent

fever furor SEE MAIN ENTRY

fever pitch SEE MAIN ENTRY

feverish demonstrative (expressive of emotion), frenetic, hot-blooded, rapid

feverish haste dispatch (promptness)

feverishness ardor

few deficient, infrequent, scarce, several (plural). SEE MAIN ENTRY

few and far between SEE MAIN ENTRY

fewness insufficiency, paucity

fiasco debacle, disaster, failure (lack of success), miscarriage

fiat brevet, canon, declaration, decree, dictate, direction (order), directive, edict, enactment, law, license, mandate, monition (legal summons), order (judicial directive), ordinance, permit, precept, proclamation, pronouncement, requirement, writ. SEE MAIN ENTRY

fib invent (falsify), lie (falsify), mislead, prevaricate, story (falsehood), subterfuge

fibbing falsification

fiber character (personal quality), frame (mood), prowess (bravery)

fickle capricious, faithless, false (disloyal), inconsistent, irresolute, mutable, undependable, unpredictable, unreliable, unsettled, untrustworthy, variable, volatile

fickleness disloyalty, indecision, infidelity

fictile pliable, sequacious

fiction canard, falsehood, figment, lie, misstatement, myth, phantom, story (falsehood), subterfuge. SEE MAIN ENTRY

fiction of the mind figment

fictional fictitious

fictionalize fabricate (make up), invent (falsify)

fictitious artificial, assumed (feigned), erroneous, evasive, false (inaccurate), illusory, lying, mendacious, sobriquet, spurious, unfounded, untrue. SEE MAIN ENTRY

fictitious story myth

fictive evasive, fictitious, original (creative)

fictive creation phantom

fictus apparent (perceptible), false (not genuine), false pretense, fictitious, ostensible, unfounded

fidelis faithful (diligent), loyal, true (authentic)

fidelitas fidelity, loyalty

fideliter faithfully

fidelity adherence (devotion), adhesion (loyalty), allegiance, conformity (obedience), discipline (obedience), faith, fealty, homage, honesty, integrity, loyalty, rectitude. SEE MAIN ENTRY

fides allegiance, confidence (faith), credibility, duty (obligation), faith, fidelity, guarantee, honesty, loyalty, promise, reliance, trust (confidence), vow

fidgety restive

fiducia assurance, confidence (faith), reliance, trust (confidence)

fiducial fiduciary, pecuniary

fiduciary executor, pecuniary, trustee. SEE MAIN ENTRY

fiduciary currency check (instrument)

fidus confidential, faithful (diligent), loyal, safe, staunch, true (authentic)

fief fee (estate), freehold

field area (province), bailiwick, calling, capacity (sphere), career, circuit, coverage (scope), department, employment, latitude, occupation (vocation), parcel, plot (land), post, profession (vocation), province, pursuit (occupation), range, realm, region, scene, scope, section (vicinity), space, sphere, territory

field of activity department, sphere

field of inquiry issue (matter in dispute), matter (subject)

field of interest discipline (field of study)

field of learning discipline (field of study)

field of operation sphere

field of view outlook, perspective, vision (sight)

field of vision perception, perspective

field questions return (respond)

fiend (addict). SEE MAIN ENTRY

fiend (enthusiast). SEE MAIN ENTRY

fiendish cold-blooded, cruel, diabolic, harmful, malevolent, malignant, peccant (culpable), pernicious, ruthless, sinister

fiendishness atrocity, bestiality

fiendlike diabolic, malignant

fierce brutal, cruel, demonstrative (expressive of emotion), fervent, formidable, intense, severe, spartan, vehement, vicious. SEE MAIN ENTRY

fierceness bestiality, cruelty, passion, severity

fieri occur (happen), result

fieriness life (vitality)

fiery demonstrative (expressive of emotion), fervent, hot-blooded, intense, vehement, zealous

Fifth Amendment SEE MAIN ENTRY

fifty percent moiety

fifty-two weeks annum

fight affray, altercation, beat (strike), bicker, brawl (noun), brawl (verb), collision (dispute), commotion, conflict, confrontation (altercation), contend (dispute), contention (opposition), contest (dispute), contest, disagree, fracas, fray, grapple, incompatibility (difference), oppose, oppugn, resist (oppose), resistance, rift (disagreement), strife, strive, struggle, withstand. SEE MAIN ENTRY

fight against counter, counteract

fight for protect

fight off counter, parry, repel (drive back)

fight offensively attack

fight with engage (involve)

fighter aggressor, contender, foe, malcontent

fighting belligerency, conflict, litigious, offensive (taking the initiative), pugnacious, strife

figment fiction, myth, phantom, story (falsehood). SEE MAIN ENTRY

figment of the imagination phantom

figmental fictitious

figura contour (shape), form (arrangement)

figurare form

figuration configuration (form), contour (outline), contour (shape), formation, motif, organization (structure)

figurative representative. SEE MAIN ENTRY

figure bill (invoice), body (main part), build (construct), calculate, character (an individual), color (complexion), complexion, configuration (form), contour (outline), contour (shape), delineate, estimate, indicant, motif, organization (structure), phenomenon (manifestation), plan, price, rate, sum (tally). SEE MAIN ENTRY

figure costs estimate, evaluate

figure of speech phrase

figure out ascertain, calculate, conceive (comprehend), construe (comprehend), find (discover), interpret, reason (conclude), resolve (solve), solve

figure up sum

figure work computation

figure-work census

figurehead ineffective, ineffectual, nonentity, powerless, token

figures census, information *(facts)*

figuring census, computation

filch embezzle, pilfer, poach, purloin, steal

filcher burglar, criminal

filchery theft

filching burglary, housebreaking

file book, classify, defer *(put off)*, distribute, dossier, enroll, enter *(record)*, entry *(record)*, erode, fix *(arrange)*, index *(docket)*, ledger, lineup, organize *(arrange)*, pigeonhole, record *(noun)*, record *(verb)*, register *(noun)*, register *(verb)*, sort, tabulate. SEE MAIN ENTRY

file a charge complain *(charge)*, prosecute *(charge)*

file a claim charge *(accuse)*, complain *(charge)*, impeach, lodge *(bring a complaint)*, prosecute *(charge)*

file a legal claim sue

file a suit complain *(charge)*, lodge *(bring a complaint)*

file for petition

file suit sue

filed charges accused *(charged)*

filed notice lis pendens

filia child

filial loyal

filiality affiliation *(bloodline)*

filiate ascribe, relate *(establish a connection)*

filiation affiliation *(bloodline)*, affinity *(family ties)*, ancestry, blood, degree *(kinship)*, descent *(lineage)*, family *(common ancestry)*, origin *(ancestry)*, parentage, propinquity *(kinship)*, relationship *(family tie)*. SEE MAIN ENTRY

filibuster detain *(restrain)*, forestall, hold up *(delay)*, procrastinate, protract *(prolong)*, stall. SEE MAIN ENTRY

filing registration

filing of charges accusation

filius child

filius familias minor

fill fulfill, imbue, impact, load, penetrate, permeate, pervade, replenish, satisfy *(fulfill)*, sufficiency. SEE MAIN ENTRY

fill a position employ *(engage services)*, engage *(hire)*, hire

fill a post hold *(possess)*

fill a vacancy employ *(engage services)*, hire

fill an office officiate, serve *(assist)*

fill an opening employ *(engage services)*

fill another's position displace *(replace)*

fill identical times coincide *(correspond)*

fill in compound, develop, replacement, replenish

fill in for displace *(replace)*, replace

fill one's time engage *(involve)*

fill out compound, develop, enlarge, expand, inflate, spread

fill to capacity impact

fill to superfluity inundate

fill up load, replenish, supply

fill with air inflate

fill with doubt perplex

fill with enthusiasm inspire

fill with information disabuse, instruct *(teach)*

fill with loathing repel *(disgust)*

fill with longing motivate

fill with shame humiliate

filled copious, full, inflated *(enlarged)*, replete

filled out ripe

filled to repletion replete

filled to utmost capacity full

filled with pride disdainful

fillip inducement, stimulate, stimulus

filminess indistinctness

filmy indistinct

filter distill, purge *(purify)*, screen *(select)*. SEE MAIN ENTRY

filter in penetrate

filter through pervade

filth pornography

filthify pollute

filthiness defilement

filthy objectionable, repulsive, salacious

filtrate distill

fimbriae edge *(border)*

finagling fraudulent

final absolute *(complete)*, absolute *(conclusive)*, binding, categorical, certain *(positive)*, complete *(ended)*, conclusive *(determinative)*, conclusive *(settled)*, crucial, decisive, definitive, determinative, extreme *(last)*, inappealable, irrevocable, last *(final)*, peremptory *(absolute)*, positive *(incontestable)*, ultimate. SEE MAIN ENTRY

final appeal SEE MAIN ENTRY

final assessment determination

final authority arbiter

final cause object, purpose

final condemnation conviction *(finding of guilt)*

final condition ultimatum

final demand dun

final determination adjudication

final event end *(termination)*

final happening denouement

final judgment adjudication, conclusion *(determination)*, decree, holding *(ruling of a court)*, opinion *(judicial decision)*

final notice dun

final offer ultimatum

final outcome product

final point extremity *(furthest point)*, limit, objective

final proposal ultimatum

final proposition ultimatum

final result conclusion *(outcome)*, consequence *(conclusion)*, effect, issuance

final settlement of a matter disposition *(determination)*

final state end *(termination)*

final statement denouement

final terms condition *(contingent provision)*, settlement

final touch denouement

finale cessation *(termination)*, close *(conclusion)*, conclusion *(outcome)*, consequence *(conclusion)*

finale denouement

finale end *(termination)*, payoff *(result)*

finality divorce, end *(termination)*. SEE MAIN ENTRY

finalization denouement

finalize close *(agree)*, complete, conclude *(complete)*, consummate, decide, finish. SEE MAIN ENTRY

finalize an agreement close *(agree)*

finally consequently. SEE MAIN ENTRY

finally settled inappealable

finalty conclusion *(outcome)*

finance bear *(support)*, bestow, capitalize *(provide capital)*, fund, invest *(fund)*, lend,

maintain *(sustain)*, pay, sponsor, subsidize, support *(assist)*, underwrite. SEE MAIN ENTRY

finance again refinance

financer patron *(influential supporter)*, surety *(guarantor)*

finances capital, cash, means *(funds)*, money

financial commercial, fiscal, mercantile, monetary, pecuniary. SEE MAIN ENTRY

financial affairs finance

financial assistance consideration *(recompense)*

financial backer promoter

financial backing investment, maintenance *(support of spouse)*

financial center market *(business)*, market place

financial disaster bankruptcy, default, failure *(bankruptcy)*

financial failure bankruptcy

financial loss failure *(bankruptcy)*

financial officer comptroller

financial provision capital

financial remuneration compensation, honorarium, income, pension, perquisite, recovery *(award)*, reparation *(indemnification)*

financial resources capital, finance, income, property *(possessions)*

financial reward perquisite, profit

financial ruin bankruptcy, failure *(bankruptcy)*

financial shortage deficit

financial statement account *(evaluation)*

financial straits privation

financially prudent economical

financially sound solvent

financier obligee, promoter, sponsor, trustee

financing investment, loan, maintenance *(support of spouse)*

find acquisition, adjudge, adjudicate, ascertain, award, conclude *(decide)*, decide, decree, detect, determine, disinter, ferret, hold *(decide)*, invent *(produce for the first time)*, judge, locate, prize, procure, pronounce *(pass judgment)*, rule *(decide)*, sentence. SEE MAIN ENTRY

find a clue elucidate

find a middle ground compromise *(settle by mutual agreement)*

find a place for lodge *(house)*

find a remedy counteract

find a solution resolve *(solve)*

find a way devise *(invent)*

find against convict

find an indictment against impeach

find cause to blame criticize *(find fault with)*

find fault blame, complain *(criticize)*, decry, deprecate, discommend, except *(object)*, object, remonstrate, reprimand

find fault with cavil, censure, complain *(criticize)*, denounce *(condemn)*, depreciate, disapprove *(condemn)*, disparage, expostulate, impugn, incriminate, rebuke, reprehend, reproach

find flaws remonstrate

find freedom escape

find guilty condemn *(blame)*, convict, sentence

find hard to believe doubt *(distrust)*

find help employ *(engage services)*

find indispensable need

find intolerable resent

find liable convict

find manpower recruit

find necessary need
find not guilty absolve, acquit, clear
find nothing to praise decry
find one's advantage in capitalize (seize the chance)
find out ascertain, detect, discover, disinter, overhear, solve
find out exactly ascertain
find out the meaning of construe (comprehend)
find outlet exude
find passage exude
find probable assume (suppose)
find room for lodge (house)
find the answer ascertain, resolve (solve)
find the cause solve
find the key solve
find the solution ascertain, solve
find the value of evaluate
find the weight of weigh
find unfounded disprove
find useful exploit (make use of)
find vent exude
find words for express
find words to express communicate, phrase
finding adjudication, answer (solution), arbitration, award, choice (decision), clue, cognovit, comment, conclusion (determination), consequence (conclusion), conviction (finding of guilt), decree, detection, determination, dictum, disposition (determination), holding (ruling of a court), invention, judgment (formal court decree), observation, opinion (judicial decision), outcome, perception, recognition, result, ruling, solution (answer), verdict. SEE MAIN ENTRY
finding a middle course mediation
finding another mate digamy
finding another spouse digamy
finding of guilt condemnation (punishment). SEE MAIN ENTRY
finding out discovery
findings of fact and conclusions of law ruling
fine acute, amercement, appropriate, cost (penalty), damages, forfeiture (thing forfeited), impalpable, meritorious, narrow, penalize, penalty, premium, rare, sapid, tenuous, trover, valuable. SEE MAIN ENTRY
fine-mannered civil (polite)
fine point technicality
fine print SEE MAIN ENTRY
fineness quality (excellence), sensibility
finer superior (excellent)
finesse artifice, discretion (quality of being discreet), management (judicious use), performance (workmanship), prowess (ability), ruse, science (technique), skill, stratagem, subterfuge. SEE MAIN ENTRY
finest cardinal (outstanding), leading (ranking first), premium, prime (most valuable)
fingere conjure, create, feign, pretend
fingerprints SEE MAIN ENTRY
finical meticulous, particular (exacting), precise, punctilious
finicality particularity
finicalness particularity
finicking meticulous, punctilious
finicky meticulous, particular (exacting), precise, punctilious
finire conclude (complete), limit
finis boundary, cessation (termination), close (conclusion), conclusion (outcome)
finis denouement, dissolution (termination)

finis end (termination), frontier, limit, object, restriction
finish accomplish, attain, cap, cease, cessation (termination), close (conclusion), close (terminate), commit (perpetrate), complete, conclude (complete), conclusion (outcome), consequence (conclusion), consummate, culminate, defeasance, denouement, deplete, desist, destination, discontinue (abandon), dispatch (dispose of), dissolution (termination), dissolve (terminate), end (termination), exhaust (try all possibilities), expend (consume), expiration, expire, extremity (death), finality, fulfill, liquidate (convert into cash), mature, outcome, pass (satisfy requirements), payoff (result), perfect, perform (adhere to), quit (discontinue), shut, stop, terminate. SEE MAIN ENTRY
finish litigation rest (end a legal case)
finish off cap, extinguish
finish up close (terminate)
finished absolute (complete), choate lien, complete (ended), conclusive (settled), defunct, expert, irredeemable, ripe, through, veteran. SEE MAIN ENTRY
finished product fait accompli, performance (execution)
finishing conclusive (settled), extreme (last), final, last (final)
finishing stroke denouement
finite terminable
finite quantity paucity
finitimus adjacent
fire ardor, barrage, burn, conflagration, deflagrate, depose (remove), discharge (dismiss), discharge (shoot), dismiss (discharge), foment, life (vitality), passion, provoke, remove (dismiss from office), spirit, stimulate, supplant. SEE MAIN ENTRY
fire at discharge (shoot)
fire from employment terminate
fire up motivate
fire-raising arson
firearm gun
firearms ammunition
fireball bomb
firebrand demagogue, hoodlum
fireside home (domicile)
firing arson, discharge (dismissal), discharge (shot), dismissal (discharge), layoff, rejection
firing a charge discharge (shot)
firm business (commercial enterprise), certain (fixed), cohesive (compact), compact (dense), company (enterprise), concern (business establishment), concrete, constant, corporation, corporeal, definite, durable, earnest, enterprise (economic organization), faithful (loyal), fixed (securely placed), house, immutable, indomitable, inexorable, inflexible, infrangible, inseparable, institute, intractable, ironclad, irreconcilable, irrevocable, loyal, obdurate, ossified, partnership, patient, peremptory (imperative), pertinacious, purposeful, renitent, resolute, rigid, secure (sound), sedulous, serious (devoted), severe, solid (compact), solid (sound), spartan, stable, staunch, steadfast, strong, unalterable, unbending, uncompromising, undaunted, undeniable, unyielding, well-grounded. SEE MAIN ENTRY
firm advice instruction (direction)
firm attachment affection
firm belief confidence (faith), conviction (persuasion), credence, faith

firm hold coherence
firm in adherence true (loyal)
firm in allegiance true (loyal)
firm in principle high-minded
firm opposition conflict
firm principle code, law
firm up stabilize
firmly faithfully
firmly established fixed (securely placed), ingrained, inveterate, steadfast
firmly fixed ingrained
firmly implanted fixed (securely placed)
firmly seated fixed (securely placed)
firmly set fixed (securely placed), rigid
firmly united compact (dense)
firmness adherence (adhesion), adhesion (loyalty), certainty, constant, force (strength), inertia, prowess (bravery), purpose, resolution (decision), rigor, spirit, strength, surety (certainty), tenacity. SEE MAIN ENTRY
firmness of belief certainty
firmness of purpose diligence (perseverance)
firmus constant (adjective), constant (noun), durable, firm, irrefutable, resolute, solid (sound), stable, staunch, steadfast, substantial, valid
first ab initio, cardinal (basic), central (essential), dominant, important (significant), initial, leading (ranking first), original (initial), paramount, precursory, preferred (given priority), previous, primary, prime (original), primordial, principal, prior, prototype, stellar, unprecedented. SEE MAIN ENTRY
First Amendment SEE MAIN ENTRY
first and foremost ab initio
first and last only (sole)
first appearance nascency, onset (commencement). SEE MAIN ENTRY
first attempt experiment
first cause derivation
first charge first offense
first competition primary
first contest primary
first crime first offense
first criminal violation first offense
first election primary
first impression SEE MAIN ENTRY
first in quality prime (most valuable)
first installment handsel
first move onset (commencement), outset
first occasion derivation
first of all ab initio
first offender convict
first offense SEE MAIN ENTRY
first payment handsel
first place primacy, priority, prize
first pleading complaint
first political competition primary
first political contest primary
first position SEE MAIN ENTRY
first receipts handsel
first sight discovery
first stage embryo, nascency
first step nascency, onset (commencement), outset, start. SEE MAIN ENTRY
first violation first offense
first-class best, premium, prime (most valuable)
firsthand SEE MAIN ENTRY
first-rate best, meritorious, preferential, premium, prime (most valuable), select, superior (excellent), superlative
firstly ab initio
fiscal commercial, financial, mercantile, monetary, pecuniary. SEE MAIN ENTRY
fiscal exchange commerce

fiscalis fiscal
fiscus finance, treasury
fish out ferret
fishing expedition SEE MAIN ENTRY
fissile divisible, severable
fission severance
fissionable divisible, severable
fissura split
fissure break (fracture), force (break), part (separate), rift (gap), sever, split (noun), split (verb)
fisticuffs affray, brawl
fit accommodate, adapt, adequate, agree (comply), applicable, apposite, appropriate, available, capable, competent, comply, comport (agree with), condign, conform, congruous, consonant, due (regular), effective (efficient), eligible, entitled, familiar (informed), favorable (advantageous), felicitous, just, normal (sane), opportune, outbreak, outburst, pertinent, qualified (competent), ready (prepared), reasonable (fair), reasonable (rational), relative (relevant), relevant, right (suitable), ripe, satisfy (fulfill), seasonable, suitable. SEE MAIN ENTRY
fit exactly coincide (correspond)
fit for a purpose attune
fit for appointment eligible
fit for dwelling habitable
fit for election eligible
fit for habitation habitable, residential
fit for sale marketable
fit for selection eligible
fit for travel open (accessible), passable
fit for use disposable, effective (operative), functional
fit in comport (agree with), conform
fit out clothe, furnish, supply
fit the pattern naturalize (acclimate)
fit time opportunity
fit to be chosen eligible
fit to be occupied habitable
fit to live in habitable
fit together comport (agree with), frame (construct), join (bring together)
fitful broken (interrupted), disjunctive (tending to disjoin), disorderly, haphazard, inconsistent, intermittent, sporadic, unpredictable, variable
fitfulness inconsistency, irregularity
fitness ability, admissibility, aptitude, competence (ability), expedience, faculty (ability), health, instinct, propriety (appropriateness), timeliness. SEE MAIN ENTRY
fitted capable, commensurate, convenient, familiar (informed), fit, sciential
fitted for legal argumentation forensic
fitted for public argumentation forensic
fitted to teach didactic
fittedness ability
fitting applicable, apposite, appropriate, as a matter of right, condign, congruous, consonant, convenient, conventional, correlative, eligible, fair (just), favorable (advantageous), felicitous, fit, germane, just, opportune, permissible, pertinent, practical, proper, reasonable (fair), relative (relevant), relevant, right (suitable), rightful, suitable, tenable. SEE MAIN ENTRY
fitting occasion opportunity
fitting time opportunity
fittingness decorum, expedience, qualification (fitness)
fix adjust (resolve), affix, allocate, annex (add), arrange (methodize), award, bind (restrain), bond (hold together), cement, decide, define, delimit, designate, dispose

(apportion), embed, emend, entanglement (involvement), help, hold (decide), marshal, plant (place firmly), predicament, redress, reform, rehabilitate, remedy, renew (refurbish), renovate, repair, repose (place), restore (renew). SEE MAIN ENTRY
fix a charge charge (assess)
fix a valuation assess (tax)
fix attention on note (notice)
fix beforehand preordain
fix blame accuse
fix bounds circumscribe (surround by boundary)
fix by agreement close (agree)
fix conclusively arbitrate (adjudge), rule (decide)
fix deeply establish (entrench)
fix firmly embed
fix in pinpoint
fix in purpose resolve (decide)
fix in the mind recall (remember), remember
fix limits circumscribe (surround by boundary), demarcate
fix on focus
fix one's attention concentrate (pay attention)
fix permanently establish (entrench)
fix the blame for lodge (bring a complaint)
fix the burden of impute
fix the date date
fix the meaning define
fix the mind upon intend
fix the order arrange (methodize), file (arrange)
fix the position locate
fix the price at charge (assess)
fix the price of rate
fix the responsibility present (prefer charges)
fix the responsibility for impute
fix the thoughts upon focus
fix the time date
fix the value assess (appraise)
fix together cement
fix up embellish
fix upon determine, impute, prefer, select
fix with precision define
fixable ascertainable, corrigible, determinable (ascertainable)
fixation compulsion (obsession), constant, location, obsession, preoccupation. SEE MAIN ENTRY
fixed absolute (conclusive), accustomed (customary), attached (annexed), certain (specific), constant, conventional, customary, definite, definitive, deliberate, durable, express, firm, formal, habitual, immutable, inappealable, indelible, inevitable, inextricable, inflexible, ingrained, inherent, inveterate, irrevocable, limited, necessary (inescapable), ordinary, permanent, perpetual, positive (prescribed), prescriptive, regular (orderly), resolute, rigid, routine, secure (sound), serious (devoted), several (separate), situated, stable, standing, stated, static, statutory, steadfast, traditional, unalienable, unalterable, unavoidable (inevitable), unavoidable (not voidable), unbending, unyielding. SEE MAIN ENTRY
fixed amount of damages ad damnum clause
fixed assets immovable
fixed belief credence
fixed capital principal (capital sum)

fixed charge fee (charge)
fixed chattel immovable
fixed conviction compulsion (obsession)
fixed direction intention
fixed future predetermination
fixed idea compulsion (obsession), obsession, preconception, preoccupation
fixed intention project
fixed opinion conviction (persuasion)
fixed order array (order), method
fixed procedure usage
fixed property immovable
fixed purpose animus, design (intent), forethought, goal, intention, objective
fixed residence abode, home (domicile)
fixed ways practice (custom)
fixedly invariably
fixedness adherence (adhesion)
fixing attachment (act of affixing), designation (naming), renewal, repair
fixing a bid SEE MAIN ENTRY
fixing a price appraisal
fixity of purpose diligence (perseverance)
fixture attachment (thing affixed), device (mechanism), immovable. SEE MAIN ENTRY
flaccid powerless
flag indicant, indicator, languish, succumb
flag bearer nominee (candidate)
flagellare lash (strike)
flagellate beat (strike), ill use, lash (strike)
flagging languid
flagitare call (demand), dun, solicit
flagitiosus disgraceful
flagitious bad (offensive), blameworthy, depraved, disgraceful, flagrant, heinous, immoral, inexcusable, inexpiable, iniquitous, nefarious, outrageous, profligate (corrupt), reprehensible, reprobate, scandalous, sinister. SEE MAIN ENTRY
flagitious villainy atrocity
flagitiousness atrocity, bad repute, crime
flagitous blameful
flagrancy atrocity, bad repute, notoriety, pretense (ostentation)
flagrant arrant (onerous), bad (offensive), blameworthy, brazen, conspicuous, delinquent (guilty of a misdeed), disgraceful, egregious, extreme (exaggerated), heinous, manifest, nefarious, notorious, outrageous, outright, prominent, remarkable, reprehensible, reprobate, salient, scandalous. SEE MAIN ENTRY
flagrant abuse of the law lynch law
flagrante delicto blameworthy, delinquency (misconduct)
flagrantly bad arrant (onerous)
flail beat (strike)
flair aptitude, competence (ability), faculty (ability). SEE MAIN ENTRY
flam falsehood
flamboyant elaborate, grandiose, pretentious (ostentatious). SEE MAIN ENTRY
flame deflagrate
flame up burn, deflagrate
flaming hot-blooded, intense
flaming into notice flagrant
flange border
flank border (bound), hedge, protect
flap brandish, oscillate
flare burn, deflagrate, discharge (shot)
flare up deflagrate, outburst
flare-up bluster (commotion), furor, outbreak
flaring blatant (obtrusive)
flash deflagrate, discharge (shot), flaunt, immediate (at once)

flashiness pretense *(ostentation)*

flashy elaborate, flagrant, grandiose, pretentious *(ostentatious)*, tawdry

flat impecunious, insipid, jejune *(dull)*, lifeless *(dull)*, pedestrian, prosaic, stale

flat broke impecunious

flat refusal rebuff

flat saying platitude

flatten depress

flatter overestimate

flattering obsequious

flattery mention *(tribute)*

flatulence bombast

flatulent fustian, inflated *(bombastic)*, loquacious, orotund. SEE MAIN ENTRY

flaunt brandish, display. SEE MAIN ENTRY

flaunting blatant *(obtrusive)*, brazen, flagrant, grandiose, orgulous, proud *(conceited)*

flavor color *(complexion)*, savory. SEE MAIN ENTRY

flavored savory

flavorful palatable, sapid

flavorless insipid, jejune *(dull)*, stale

flavorous palatable, sapid, savory

flavorsome palatable, sapid, savory

flavory sapid

flaw deface, defacement, defect, deficiency, drawback, error, fault *(mistake)*, fault *(weakness)*, foible, frailty, miscue, onus *(blame)*, stigma, vice. SEE MAIN ENTRY

flaw in reasoning fallacy

flaw in the argument non sequitur

flawed blemished, defective, deficient, fallible, faulty, imperfect, incorrect, inexact, marred, peccable, sinister, vicious. SEE MAIN ENTRY

flawless absolute *(ideal)*, best, infallible, intact, precise, pure, unblemished. SEE MAIN ENTRY

flay denude, lash *(attack verbally)*, lash *(strike)*, plunder, reprimand, reproach

flebilis deplorable, lamentable, lugubrious

fledging amateur

fledgling juvenile, neophyte, novice

flee abscond, depart, disappear, elude, escape, evacuate, evade *(elude)*, leave *(depart)*, move *(alter position)*, quit *(evacuate)*, retreat. SEE MAIN ENTRY

flee from avoid *(evade)*, eschew

fleece betray *(lead astray)*, defraud, deprive, dupe, prey, steal

fleeced aggrieved *(victimized)*

fleeing flight

fleer flout, fugitive, mock *(deride)*

fleet expeditious, rapid

fleeting brief, elusive, ephemeral, temporary, transient, transitory, volatile

flesh and blood physical

fleshly corporeal, lascivious, lecherous, mundane, physical, prurient

fleshy corporal

flexibilis flexible, pliable

flexibility amenability, facility *(easiness)*, informality, lenience

flexible amenable, deft, facile, liberal *(broad minded)*, malleable, open *(persuasible)*, passive, pliable, pliant, receptive, resilient, sequacious, suasible, susceptible *(responsive)*, tractable, yielding. SEE MAIN ENTRY

flexibleness amenability

flexile flexible, malleable, pliable, resilient, sequacious, tractable

flexuous circuitous, complex, laby-rinthine, sinuous

flicker beat *(pulsate)*

flickering intermittent

flier notice *(announcement)*

flight abandonment *(desertion)*, desertion, evasion. SEE MAIN ENTRY

flight of fancy figment

flightiness inconsistency

flighty capricious, frivolous, inconsistent, irresponsible, thoughtless, volatile

flimflam bunko, falsification, ruse. SEE MAIN ENTRY

flimsiness frailty, impalpability

flimsy frivolous, inconclusive, inconsequential, inferior *(lower in quality)*, insubstantial, nonsubstantial *(not sturdy)*, poor *(inferior in quality)*, tenuous

fling cast *(throw)*, dispatch *(send off)*, impel, launch *(project)*, precipitate *(throw down violently)*, project *(impel forward)*, send

fling dishonor upon disgrace

fling downward precipitate *(throw down violently)*

fling off dispel

flint-hearted brutal, malignant

flinty rigid

flip a coin bet

flipflop SEE MAIN ENTRY

flippancy disrespect

flippant brazen, frivolous, impertinent *(insolent)*, insolent, presumptuous

flitter beat *(pulsate)*

flitting transitory

float finance. SEE MAIN ENTRY

flock assemblage, mass *(body of persons)*, meet

flog beat *(strike)*, lash *(strike)*, punish

flood assemblage, cataclysm, immerse *(plunge into)*, inundate, load, outflow, overcome *(overwhelm)*, overload, plethora, spate. SEE MAIN ENTRY

floodgate crossroad *(turning point)*, outlet. SEE MAIN ENTRY

floor recognition. SEE MAIN ENTRY

florens prosperous

floridness bombast

flounder mismanage

floundering incompetent

flourish brandish, display, flaunt, gain, germinate, increase, pretense *(ostentation)*, proliferate, pullulate, succeed *(attain)*

flourishing cumulative *(increasing)*, opulent, prosperous, rampant, successful

flourishing condition boom *(prosperity)*

flout contemn, defy, disdain, disrespect, jape, mock *(deride)*, override, spurn. SEE MAIN ENTRY

flouting contemptuous, disdainful

flow accrue *(arise)*, arise *(originate)*, circulate, circulation, cycle, ensue, issue *(send forth)*, pass *(advance)*, proceed *(go forward)*, progress, result, sequence, spread, stem *(originate)*. SEE MAIN ENTRY

flow forth emanate

flow from redound

flow in penetrate

flow into pervade

flow of language parlance

flow of words parlance

flow out exude, issue *(send forth)*

flow over inundate

flower proliferate, pullulate

flowering fertile, fruition, growth *(evolution)*

flowery turgid

flowery language rhetoric *(skilled speech)*

flowing circulation, copious, eloquent, facile, fluvial, full

flown truant

fluctuant indeterminate

fluctuare fluctuate

fluctuate beat *(pulsate)*, change, doubt *(hesitate)*, oscillate, vacillate, vary. SEE MAIN ENTRY

fluctuating capricious, disorderly, faithless, hesitant, intermittent, irresolute, irresponsible, mutable, periodic, shifting, sporadic, undependable, variable

fluctuation hesitation, indecision

fluctuations vicissitudes

fluency facility *(easiness)*, parlance, skill

fluent eloquent, facile, fluvial, loquacious, voluble

fluere emanate

fluff SEE MAIN ENTRY

fluid fluvial, indeterminate, protean. SEE MAIN ENTRY

fluidic fluvial

fluke SEE MAIN ENTRY

flunk fail *(lose)*

flurry confuse *(bewilder)*, dispatch *(promptness)*, haste, outburst, perturb

flush full, opulent, profuse, prosperous, replete, substantial

fluster agitate *(perturb)*, confuse *(bewilder)*, confusion *(ambiguity)*, discompose, disconcert, disorient, disrupt, disturb, embarrass, embarrassment, harry *(harass)*, muddle, obfuscate, perturb, stress *(strain)*, upset

flutter beat *(pulsate)*, oscillate, panic, trepidation

fluvial SEE MAIN ENTRY

fluviatic fluvial

fluviatile fluvial

fluvicoline fluvial

flux circulation, outflow, transition

fluxus transient

fly flee, leave *(depart)*, race

fly at attack

fly in the face of override

fly off at a tangent deviate, digress

fly-by-night untrustworthy

fob off on foist

focal central *(situated near center)*

focal point center *(central position)*, focus, gravamen, highlight. SEE MAIN ENTRY

focal point of the complaint gist *(ground for a suit)*

focalization centralization

focalize concentrate *(consolidate)*, converge

focus center *(central position)*, concentrate *(consolidate)*, concentrate *(pay attention)*, converge, devote, gravamen, pinpoint. SEE MAIN ENTRY

focus attention on concentrate *(pay attention)*, specialize

focus of attention center *(central position)*

fodere delve

fodicare jostle *(bump into)*

foe adversary, aggressor, contender, contestant, rival. SEE MAIN ENTRY

foedare deface

foederatus federal

foedere sociatus federal

foedus confederacy *(compact)*, league, loathsome, pact, repulsive

foeman foe

fog confuse *(bewilder)*, discompose, ignorance, incertitude, indistinctness, muddle, obfuscate, obnubilate, obscure, perplex

fogginess indistinctness, obscuration

foggy indistinct, nebulous, opaque, unclear

foible defect, deficiency, fault *(weakness)*, flaw, frailty, vice. SEE MAIN ENTRY

foil arrest *(stop)*, balk, check *(bar)*, circumvent, constrict *(inhibit)*, contravene, counter, counteract, defeat, deter, disadvantage, discontinue *(break continuity)*, enjoin, fight *(counteract)*, frustrate, frustration, halt, hamper, interfere, interrupt, keep *(restrain)*, oppugn, overturn, parry, preclude, prevent, repel *(drive back)*, stem *(check)*, stop, subdue, thwart, withstand. SEE MAIN ENTRY.

foiled disappointed

foist coerce. SEE MAIN ENTRY.

foist off fake

foist oneself intrude

foist upon bilk

fold fail *(lose)*, society

folder file

folio publication *(printed matter)*

folk family *(common ancestry)*, kindred, lineage, populace, population, public, race, society

folk speech language

folklore myth

folks populace

folktale myth

follow abide, accrue *(arise)*, adhere *(maintain loyalty)*, adopt, arise *(originate)*, chase, conform, copy, ensue, evolve, fulfill, heed, hunt, keep *(fulfill)*, mock *(imitate)*, obey, observe *(obey)*, observe *(watch)*, proceed *(go forward)*, pursue *(carry on)*, pursue *(chase)*, redound, result, resume, spy, stem *(originate)*, supervene. SEE MAIN ENTRY.

follow a calling practice *(engage in)*

follow a course proceed *(go forward)*

follow a profession practice *(engage in)*

follow a trail pursue *(chase)*

follow after succeed *(follow)*

follow as a consequence ensue

follow as a model plagiarize

follow as an occupation practice *(engage in)*

follow close upon hunt

follow from emanate

follow in a train of events ensue

follow in order accede *(succeed)*, succeed *(follow)*

follow one another interchangeably alternate *(take turns)*

follow one another reciprocally alternate *(take turns)*

follow one's vocation labor

follow orders obey

follow precedent conform

follow routine conform

follow successively reciprocate

follow suit copy, mock *(imitate)*

follow the example of copy, mock *(imitate)*

follow the trail delve, hunt

follow the trail of search

follow through complete, consummate, exhaust *(try all possibilities)*, follow-up, perpetrate. SEE MAIN ENTRY.

follow to a conclusion perfect

follow up maintain *(carry on)*, persevere, probe, prosecute *(carry forward)*. SEE MAIN ENTRY.

follow up an inquiry canvass

follower addict, coadjutant, cohort, consociate, disciple, member *(individual in a group)*, parasite, partisan, protégé, successor

following ancillary *(subsidiary)*, business *(occupation)*, consequential *(deducible)*, continuous, deductible *(provable)*, deductive, derivative, ensuing, forthcoming, future, immediate *(imminent)*, imminent, inevitable, malleable, proximate, secondary, subsequent, successive. SEE MAIN ENTRY.

following death posthumous

following established custom formal

following established form formal

following established rules formal

following in a series consecutive

following in time ex post facto

following the letter verbatim

following upon incident

folly abortion *(fiasco)*, inexpedience, lunacy. SEE MAIN ENTRY.

foment abet, agitate *(activate)*, cause, conduce, incite, outbreak, outburst, stimulate. SEE MAIN ENTRY.

fomentation aggravation *(exacerbation)*, commotion, disturbance, instigation, origination, outbreak, outburst, provocation

fomenter demagogue

fomentor abettor, determinant

fond of home household *(domestic)*

fond of investigation inquisitive

fondness affection, affinity *(regard)*, desire, estimation *(esteem)*, favor *(partiality)*, favoritism, inclination, partiality, penchant, predilection, predisposition, propensity, regard *(esteem)*

fons origin *(source)*, source

font origin *(source)*, origination, source

food sustenance

fool bilk, deceive, defraud, delude, dupe, ensnare, entrap, evade *(deceive)*, illude, inveigle, jape, lie *(falsify)*, misguide, mislead, misrepresent, overreach, palter, pretend

foolable naive

foolhardiness inconsideration, temerity

foolhardy hot-blooded, imprudent, impulsive *(rash)*, precipitate, presumptuous, reckless, thoughtless

foolish fatuous, ill-advised, impolitic, imprudent, inept *(incompetent)*, irrational, ludicrous, lunatic, puerile, reckless, trivial, unfit, unpolitic, unreasonable, vacuous. SEE MAIN ENTRY.

foolishness credulity, ignorance, inexpedience, jargon *(unintelligible language)*, lunacy, temerity

foolproof indubious, infallible, safe

foot pay

foot passenger pedestrian

foot the bill defray

foot traveler pedestrian

footage space

footing ground, plight, position *(situation)*, posture *(situation)*, status

footnote comment, marginalia, notation, note *(brief comment)*

footpace step

footstep step

foppishness pride

for in furtherance, in lieu of. SEE MAIN ENTRY.

for a beginning ab initio

for a certainty a fortiori

for a select few esoteric

for a still stronger reason a fortiori

for a time ad interim, pro tempore, provisional

for all history always *(forever)*

for all to see distinct *(clear)*

for cause SEE MAIN ENTRY.

for each and every day per diem

for each day per diem

for ever and ever now and forever

for every day per diem

for just reason for cause

for legitimate reason for cause

for mere discussion only arguendo

for nothing free *(at no charge)*, gratis, gratuitous *(given without recompense)*

for one party ex parte

for one's good beneficial

for one's interest beneficial

for reasons given consequently

for that cause consequently

for that reason a priori, consequently

for the duration throughout *(during)*

for the moment pro tempore

for the most part as a rule, generally

for the period of throughout *(during)*

for the present occasion pro tempore

for the sake of ad hoc, in furtherance

for the sake of appearances pro forma

for the sake of argument arguendo

for the sake of form pro forma

for the time being ad interim, pro tempore

for the use of all common *(shared)*

for this case alone ad hoc

for this reason a priori, consequently

for which reason a priori, consequently

forage despoil, harry *(plunder)*, hunt, loot, prey, spoil *(pillage)*

foramen loophole

foraminated penetrable

foraminous penetrable

foray depredation, despoil, harry *(plunder)*, impinge, incursion, invasion, onset *(assault)*, pillage, plunder, prey, spoil *(pillage)*, spoliation. SEE MAIN ENTRY.

forbear abandon *(relinquish)*, allow *(endure)*, avoid *(evade)*, bear *(tolerate)*, cease, condone, defer *(put off)*, desist, endure *(suffer)*, eschew, forgo, leave *(allow to remain)*, palliate *(excuse)*, pause, refrain, renounce, stop, tolerate, withhold. SEE MAIN ENTRY.

forbearance abstention, benevolence *(disposition to do good)*, clemency, composure, continence, grace, lenience, longanimity, moderation, remission, resignation *(passive acceptance)*, restraint, sufferance, temperance

forbearant passive, placable, resigned

forbearing charitable *(lenient)*, lenient, patient, placable, resigned

forbid ban, bar *(exclude)*, bar *(hinder)*, block, censor, clog, condemn *(ban)*, constrain *(restrain)*, debar, deny *(refuse to grant)*, deter, enjoin, estop, forestall, forewarn, gainsay, halt, inhibit, interdict, interfere, obstruct, preclude, prevent, prohibit, proscribe *(prohibit)*, reject, renounce, repel *(drive back)*, restrain, restrict, stay *(halt)*, stop, withhold. SEE MAIN ENTRY.

forbid by law enjoin, outlaw

forbiddance bar *(obstruction)*, constraint *(restriction)*, embargo, estoppel, obstacle, obstruction, prohibition, proscription, restraint, veto

forbidden illegal, illegitimate *(illegal)*, illicit, impermissible, improper, unauthorized, unlawful

forbidden by law illicit

forbidding bleak *(not favorable)*, censorship, loathsome, lugubrious, odious, ominous, portentous *(ominous)*, repugnant *(exciting aversion)*, repulsive, severe, unapproachable

forbodement misgiving

forboding ominous

force ardor, attack, authority *(power)*, band, bind *(obligate)*, cast *(throw)*, catalyst, clout, coerce, coercion, command, compel, compulsion *(coercion)*, connotation, consequence *(significance)*, constrain *(compel)*, constraint *(restriction)*, content *(meaning)*, context, dint, dominance, draw *(attraction)*, duress, emphasis, enforce, enforcement, entail, exact, extort, foist, hijack, impact, impetus, impose *(subject)*, inflict, infliction, infringement, leverage, levy, main point, make, mistreat, misusage, necessitate, obtrude, oppression, overload, potential, power, press *(constrain)*, pressure *(noun)*, pressure *(verb)*, prestige, puissance, purpose, repercussion, require *(compel)*, rigor, severity, significance, signification, sinew, spirit, staff, strength, stress *(accent)*, stress *(strain)*, struggle, subjection, substance *(essential nature)*, validity, value, violence, weight *(importance)*. SEE MAIN ENTRY

force a passage penetrate, pervade
force an entrance impose *(intrude)*
force apart break *(separate)*
force armed with legal authority posse
force away expel
force back parry, repel *(drive back)*
force from acquire *(secure)*, preempt, procure
force in inject, interject, interpose
force of argument dialectic
force of circumstances predetermination
force of expression emphasis
force of voice emphasis
force oneself intrude
force oneself in impinge, impose *(intrude)*
force open break *(separate)*
force out deport *(banish)*, dislodge, eject *(expel)*, exclude, expel, oust, supplant
force payment exact, excise *(levy a tax)*
force together impact
force upon foist, impose *(enforce)*, inflict, insist
forced bound, compulsory, inappropriate, involuntary, obligatory, ponderous
forced confinement bondage, durance
forced departure deportation
forced entrance intrusion, onset *(assault)*
forced entry incursion
forced into smaller space compact *(dense)*
forced labor bondage
forced leave taking deportation
forced sale condemnation *(seizure)*
forceful categorical, cogent, convincing, decisive, dogmatic, drastic, eloquent, forcible, indomitable, insistent, intensive, irresistible, orotund, persuasive, potent, powerful, predominant, prevailing *(having superior force)*, resounding, sound, stringent, strong, trenchant, vehement
forceful persuasion advocacy
forcefulness ardor, dint, force *(strength)*, influence, main force, sinew, validity
forceless null *(invalid)*, null and void, powerless, unable
forcelessness impotence, inefficacy
forces of law and order police
forces of nature climate
forcible cogent, compelling, compulsory, indomitable, irresistible, obligatory, potent, powerful, strong, valid, vehement. SEE MAIN ENTRY
forcible demand dun, requisition
forcible detention durance
forcible entry burglary, housebreaking
forcible expulsion from property eviction
forcible extraction avulsion
forcible inducement compulsion *(coercion)*

forcible restraint of liberty bondage
forcible seizure condemnation *(seizure)*, disseisin, distraint, expropriation *(divestiture)*, forfeiture *(act of forfeiting)*
forcible urging compulsion *(coercion)*, enforcement
forcible violation rape
forcing coercion, compulsion *(coercion)*
ford traverse
fordable passable
fore antecedent, back *(in arrears)*, last *(preceding)*, previous
forearm anticipate *(expect)*, caution, prearrange
forearmed prudent
forearming precaution
forebear ancestor, ascendant, forerunner, parents, primogenitor, progenitor
forebearance nonuse
forebearer precursor, predecessor
forebears ancestry, lineage, parentage
forebode admonish *(warn)*, anticipate *(prognosticate)*, forewarn, portend, predict, presage, prognosticate, promise *(raise expectations)*, threaten
foreboding admonition, apprehension *(fear)*, caution *(warning)*, expectation, fear, misgiving, pessimistic, portentous *(ominous)*, precognition, premonition, presageful, prognosis, prophetic, qualm, threat, warning. SEE MAIN ENTRY
forecast anticipate *(prognosticate)*, contrive, expect *(consider probable)*, forseen, forewarn, herald, portend, predetermine, predict, presage, prognosis, prognosticate, promise *(raise expectations)*, prospect *(outlook)*. SEE MAIN ENTRY
forecasted foreseeable, imminent
forecasting prophetic, provident *(showing foresight)*
foreclose arrest *(stop)*, ban, bar *(hinder)*, block, clog, condemn *(seize)*, confiscate, deprive, deter, dispossess, impede, preclude, prevent, prohibit, repossess, stay *(halt)*. SEE MAIN ENTRY
foreclosed attached *(seized)*
foreclosing confiscatory
foreclosure attachment *(seizure)*, bar *(obstruction)*, condemnation *(seizure)*, disseisin, expropriation *(divestiture)*, forfeiture *(act of forfeiting)*, taking. SEE MAIN ENTRY
foredate antedate
foredoom predetermination, preordain
forefather ancestor, ascendant, precursor, predecessor, primogenitor, progenitor
forefathers ancestry, lineage, parentage
forefeeling expectation, premonition
forefeiture penalty
forefend balk
foregathering caucus
forego abandon *(relinquish)*, disclaim, forswear, resign, surrender *(give back)*. SEE MAIN ENTRY
foregoer ancestor, precursor, predecessor, progenitor
foregoing aforesaid, antecedent, before mentioned, former, last *(preceding)*, precursory, preliminary, previous, prior, said. SEE MAIN ENTRY
foregone previous
foregone conclusion bias, inequity, preconception, predetermination, predisposition. SEE MAIN ENTRY
forehanded economical, provident *(showing foresight)*
forehandedness economy *(frugality)*

foreign apart, different, extraneous, extrinsic, inapplicable, inapposite, irrelevant, novel, obscure *(remote)*, peculiar *(curious)*, unaccustomed, unrelated. SEE MAIN ENTRY
foreign influx immigration
foreign language rights SEE MAIN ENTRY
foreign person stranger
foreign-born alien *(foreign)*
foreigner alien, stranger
forejudge guess, preconceive, predetermine, prejudge, preordain, presume, presuppose. SEE MAIN ENTRY
forejudgment foregone conclusion, preconception, predetermination, prejudice *(preconception)*
foreknow anticipate *(prognosticate)*, predict, presage
foreknowable foreseeable
foreknowing oracular, prophetic
foreknowledge expectation, precognition, prognosis
forelay bait *(lure)*
foreman chief, director, superintendent. SEE MAIN ENTRY
forementioned before mentioned, previous, said
foremost best, cardinal *(basic)*, cardinal *(outstanding)*, central *(essential)*, critical *(crucial)*, dominant, famous, important *(significant)*, influential, leading *(ranking first)*, master, notable, noteworthy, outstanding *(prominent)*, paramount, predominant, prime *(most valuable)*, principal, professional *(stellar)*, prominent, renowned, salient, stellar, superior *(excellent)*, superlative. SEE MAIN ENTRY
forenamed aforesaid, before mentioned
forensic juridical. SEE MAIN ENTRY
forensic oratory rhetoric *(skilled speech)*
forensis forensic, judicial
foreordain prearrange, predetermine
foreordained inevitable, necessary *(inescapable)*, premeditated
foreordainment predetermination
foreordinate predetermine
foreordination foregone conclusion
foreparent predecessor
foreparents parentage
foreperson chief, principal *(director)*
forerun antecede, herald, precede
forerunner ancestor, ascendant, harbinger, pioneer, precursor, predecessor, primogenitor, progenitor. SEE MAIN ENTRY
forerunning antecedent, precursory, previous
foresee expect *(consider probable)*, preconceive, predict, presage, prognosticate. SEE MAIN ENTRY
foresee the future prognosticate
foreseeable forthcoming, future, probable. SEE MAIN ENTRY
foreseeing acute, omniscient, prophetic, provident *(showing foresight)*, prudent
foreseen foreseeable, immediate *(imminent)*, pending *(imminent)*, prospective. SEE MAIN ENTRY
foreshadow forewarn, portend, predict, preordain, presage, prognosticate, promise *(raise expectations)*, threaten, warning. SEE MAIN ENTRY
foreshadowing hint, indicator, pending *(imminent)*, precursory, premonition
foreshorten abridge *(shorten)*, condense
foreshow anticipate *(prognosticate)*, caution, forewarn, herald, portend, predict, presage, prognosticate, promise *(raise expectations)*

foresight diligence *(care)*, expectation, precaution, precognition, preparation, prognosis, prudence, sagacity, sense *(intelligence)*. SEE MAIN ENTRY

foresighted careful, perspicacious, prophetic, prudent

forespeak anticipate *(prognosticate)*, predict

forestall arrest *(stop)*, avert, balk, clog, condemn *(ban)*, debar, defer *(put off)*, detain *(restrain)*, deter, discourage, enjoin, estop, frustrate, prevent, refrain, repel *(drive back)*, stay *(halt)*, stop, thwart. SEE MAIN ENTRY

forestalling bar *(obstruction)*, deterrence, deterrent, obviation, preventive

foretell herald, portend, predict, presage, prognosticate, promise *(raise expectations)*

foretellable foreseeable

foretelling caution *(warning)*, oracular, portentous *(ominous)*, prognosis, prophetic

forethought caution *(vigilance)*, consideration *(contemplation)*, contemplation, deliberation, design *(intent)*, plan, precaution, precognition, predetermination, premeditation, preparation, prudence, strategy. SEE MAIN ENTRY

forethoughtful discreet, perspicacious

foretoken caveat, harbinger, herald, indicant, indicate, indication, portend, predict, premonition, presage, prognosticate

foretold forseen

forever chronic, now and forever, perpetuity

forevermore now and forever

forewarn admonish *(warn)*, advise, caution, counsel, notice *(give formal warning)*, notify, portend, predict, presage, promise *(raise expectations)*, threaten. SEE MAIN ENTRY

forewarned informed *(having information)*

forewarning admonition, caution *(warning)*, caveat, harbinger, monition *(warning)*, notice *(warning)*, portentous *(ominous)*, precursory, premonition, prophetic, symptom, tip *(clue)*

foreword overture, preamble, preface, prelude, threshold *(commencement)*

forfeit amercement, confiscate, deposit, detriment, discontinue *(abandon)*, disfranchise, disinherit, divest, expense *(sacrifice)*, fine, lose *(be deprived of)*, lose *(undergo defeat)*, loss, penalize, penalty, surrender *(give back)*, toll *(effect)*. SEE MAIN ENTRY

forfeited attached *(seized)*, irretrievable, lost *(taken away)*

forfeiting confiscatory

forfeiture amercement, cost *(penalty)*, detriment, disqualification *(rejection)*, escheatment, expense *(sacrifice)*, fine, foreclosure, loss, punishment, trover. SEE MAIN ENTRY

forfend ban, contain *(restrain)*, deter, forbid, forestall, prevent, prohibit

forgather meet, rendezvous

forgathering collection *(assembly)*, conglomeration, congregation, session

forge copy, create, fake, form, formulate, frame *(construct)*, frame *(formulate)*, invent *(produce for the first time)*, make, manufacture, originate, plagiarize. SEE MAIN ENTRY

forge ahead continue *(persevere)*, endure *(last)*, keep *(continue)*, progress, resume

forged artificial, false *(not genuine)*, fictitious, spurious, untrue

forged check bad check

forged copy counterfeit

forged duplicate fake

forgery artifice, copy, counterfeit, deceit, deception, fake, false pretense, falsification, imposture, plagiarism, pretense *(pretext)*, sham, subterfuge. SEE MAIN ENTRY

forget condone, forgive, leave *(allow to remain)*, lose *(be deprived of)*, neglect, overlook *(disregard)*, pretermit

forgetful careless, lax, oblivious, remiss

forgetfulness inconsideration

forging manufacture, onset *(commencement)*

forgivable justifiable, pardonable

forgive absolve, clear, condone, discharge *(liberate)*, discharge *(release from obligation)*, excuse, exonerate, extenuate, free, justify, overlook *(excuse)*, palliate *(excuse)*, pardon, purge *(wipe out by atonement)*, release, relent, remit *(release from penalty)*. SEE MAIN ENTRY

forgiven clear *(free from criminal charges)*

forgiveness absolution, amnesty, clemency, condonation, dispensation *(exception)*, exoneration, grace, indulgence, lenience, longanimity, pardon, reconciliation, release, remission

forgiveness of sins absolution

forgiving charitable *(lenient)*, lenient, magnanimous, nonmilitant, palliative *(excusing)*, patient, peaceable, placable

forgivingness clemency, lenience, longanimity

forgo forbear, forfeit, quit *(discontinue)*, refrain, relinquish, renounce, vacate *(leave)*, waive, yield *(submit)*. SEE MAIN ENTRY

forgoing waiver

forgotten back *(in arrears)*, derelict *(abandoned)*, outdated, outmoded, unclaimed

fork bifurcate, split, spread

forking divergent

forlorn derelict *(abandoned)*, disappointed, disconsolate, lugubrious, pessimistic

forlorn hope pessimism

form appearance *(look)*, body *(main part)*, build *(construct)*, color *(complexion)*, complexion, compose, consist, constant, constitute *(compose)*, construction, content *(structure)*, contour *(outline)*, contour *(shape)*, contrive, create, criterion, crystallize, decorum, delineation, devise *(invent)*, discipline *(train)*, embodiment, embody, establish *(launch)*, fabricate *(construct)*, feature *(appearance)*, fix *(arrange)*, forge *(produce)*, formalize, formulate, frame *(construct)*, frame *(formulate)*, generate, influence, invent *(produce for the first time)*, kind, make, manner *(kind)*, manufacture, means *(opportunity)*, mode, motif, order *(arrangement)*, organization *(structure)*, organize *(unionize)*, originate, pattern, phenomenon *(manifestation)*, practice *(procedure)*, principle *(axiom)*, produce *(manufacture)*, pronounce *(speak)*, protocol *(etiquette)*, specter, stamp, structure *(composition)*, style, tenor, usage, vision *(dream)*. SEE MAIN ENTRY

form a cartel federalize *(associate)*

form a circle round circumscribe *(surround by boundary)*, encompass *(surround)*

form a coalition conspire

form a company incorporate *(form a corporation)*

form a conception conceive *(comprehend)*

form a connection affiliate

form a core crystallize

form a fork bifurcate

form a judgment conclude *(decide)*, deem, determine

form a labor union organize *(unionize)*

form a league unite

form a network intertwine

form a plan plot, program

form a plot maneuver

form a resolution conclude *(decide)*, decide, determine

form a single unit unite

form a union combine *(act in concert)*, combine *(join together)*, federalize *(associate)*

form an alliance unite

form an estimate calculate, gauge, measure

form an estimation guess

form an image conjure

form an opinion conclude *(decide)*, construe *(comprehend)*, decide, deem, estimate, evaluate, gauge, measure, presume

form anew reform

form into a body organize *(unionize)*

form into classes classify, organize *(arrange)*, partition, pigeonhole

form into ranks marshal

form of expression language

form of government polity

form plots conspire

forma aspect, contour *(shape)*, design *(construction plan)*, form *(arrangement)*, formation, kind

formable flexible, malleable, pliable, pliant, tractable

formal official, orthodox, perfunctory, proper, punctilious, rigid, solemn, strict. SEE MAIN ENTRY

formal accusal arraignment

formal accusation indictment, information *(charge)*

formal allegation complaint

formal assertion declaration, pleading

formal averment allegation, information *(charge)*, pleading

formal charge accusation, information *(charge)*

formal complaint charge *(accusation)*

formal consent permission

formal contract treaty

formal criminal charge information *(charge)*

formal criminal complaint information *(charge)*

formal criticism protest

formal declaration acknowledgment *(avowal)*, affirmation, protest, testament

formal declaration of dissent protest

formal discourse pandect *(treatise)*

formal discussion discourse

formal essay pandect *(treatise)*

formal examination by a court of law trial *(legal proceeding)*

formal examination of facts by a court trial *(legal proceeding)*

formal expression resolution *(formal statement)*

formal expression of choice poll *(casting of votes)*, vote

formal guaranty vow

formal notice declaration

formal occasion ceremony

formal permission license

formal petition bill *(formal declaration)*

formal presentation introduction

formal proceeding hearing

formal prosecution action *(proceeding)*

formal questioning hearing, interrogation

777

formal request requisition
formal scrutiny investigation
formal speech peroration
formal statement opinion *(judicial decision)*, pronouncement
formal writing instrument *(document)*
formal writing embodying a request petition
formal written plea petition
formal written request petition
formalis formal
formalistic draconian, formal
formalities decorum, protocol *(etiquette)*
formality ceremony, custom, decorum, form *(arrangement)*. SEE MAIN ENTRY
formalization of laws codification
formalize authorize, characterize, codify, define, frame *(formulate)*, record. SEE MAIN ENTRY
formally pro forma
formally accuse arraign
formally advise notice *(give formal warning)*
formally charge arraign, indict
formally charge with a crime indict
formally criminate arraign
formally incriminate arraign
formally pronounced judgment sentence
formally sanction authorize
formally urge petition
formally withdraw repeal
formalness formality
format configuration *(form)*, content *(structure)*, form *(arrangement)*, formation, motif. SEE MAIN ENTRY
formation arrangement *(ordering)*, building *(business of assembling)*, composition *(makeup)*, configuration *(form)*, content *(structure)*, contour *(shape)*, coverage *(scope)*, creation, distribution *(arrangement)*, embodiment, form *(arrangement)*, genesis, invention, lineup, manufacture, nascency, order *(arrangement)*, organization *(structure)*, performance *(workmanship)*, structure *(composition)*, unit *(item)*. SEE MAIN ENTRY
formation of a company incorporation *(formation of a business entity)*
formation of a corporation incorporation *(formation of a business entity)*
formation of an organization incorporation *(formation of a business entity)*
formative causal, causative, constructive *(creative)*, original *(initial)*, pliable, primary, prime *(original)*, productive, rudimentary
formative notion concept
former aforesaid, antecedent, back *(in arrears)*, before mentioned, deceased, last *(preceding)*, late *(defunct)*, outdated, outmoded, preliminary, previous, prior. SEE MAIN ENTRY
former generations ancestry, parentage
former incumbent predecessor
former officeholder predecessor
formerly heretofore, theretofore
formidable important *(significant)*, indomitable, inexpugnable, insuperable, insurmountable, irresistible, onerous, operose, oppressive, potent, spartan, strong, unapproachable. SEE MAIN ENTRY
formidolosus formidable
forming creation, manufacture, onset *(commencement)*
formless indefinite, indeterminate
formula avenue *(means of attainment)*, criterion, expedient, expression *(com-*

ment), form *(arrangement)*, method, mode, phrase, prescription *(directive)*, principle *(axiom)*, rule *(guide)*, rule *(legal dictate)*. SEE MAIN ENTRY
formula system
formula usage
formularize formulate
formulary boiler plate, code, form *(arrangement)*, prescription *(directive)*, rule *(legal dictate)*
formulate arrange *(plan)*, avow, bear *(adduce)*, codify, compose, conceive *(invent)*, conjure, constitute *(establish)*, create, crystallize, define, designate, devise *(invent)*, express, forge *(produce)*, form, frame *(construct)*, generate, legislate, make, manufacture, organize *(unionize)*, originate, phrase, produce *(manufacture)*. SEE MAIN ENTRY
formulate by law constitute *(establish)*
formulated belief doctrine, principle *(axiom)*
formulated intention objective, proposition
formulating questions cross-examination
formulating rules for the future legislation *(lawmaking)*
formulation averment, avouchment, building *(business of assembling)*, code, composition *(makeup)*, construction, creation, definition, description, expression *(comment)*, language, parlance, phraseology, rule *(legal dictate)*. SEE MAIN ENTRY
formulation of a mental image creation
formulation of a principle creation
formulation of an idea creation
formulation of laws codification
formulator of laws lawmaker
formulize formulate
fors hazard
forsake abandon *(physically leave)*, abandon *(relinquish)*, abandon *(withdraw)*, avoid *(evade)*, default, defect, depart, disclaim, discontinue *(abandon)*, disinherit, disown *(refuse to acknowledge)*, fail *(neglect)*, forgo, forswear, leave *(depart)*, quit *(discontinue)*, quit *(evacuate)*, refrain, relinquish, renounce, resign, surrender *(give back)*
forsaken derelict *(abandoned)*, helpless *(defenseless)*, solitary, void *(empty)*
forsaking desertion, resignation *(relinquishment)*
forswear abandon *(relinquish)*, answer *(reply)*, bear false witness, betray *(lead astray)*, cloak, deceive, deny *(contradict)*, disaffirm, disavow, disclaim, disown *(deny the validity)*, eschew, exclude, fabricate *(make up)*, forfeit, forgo, lie *(falsify)*, palter, perjure, prevaricate, quit *(discontinue)*, refuse, reject, relinquish, renounce, repudiate, surrender *(give back)*. SEE MAIN ENTRY
forswearing abjuration, bad faith, desertion, falsification, negation, renunciation, repudiation
forsworn fraudulent, lying
fort bulwark
forte competence *(ability)*, gift *(flair)*, performance *(workmanship)*, propensity, specialty *(special aptitude)*
forte oblatus fortuitous, incidental
forthcoming close *(near)*, future, immediate *(imminent)*, imminent, inevitable, instant, pending *(imminent)*, portentous *(ominous)*, prospective, proximate. SEE MAIN ENTRY
forthright bona fide, candid, coherent *(clear)*, direct *(forthright)*, explicit, genuine,

honest, ingenuous, scrupulous, straightforward, unaffected *(sincere)*, unequivocal, upright. SEE MAIN ENTRY
forthrightness candor *(straightforwardness)*
forthwith as soon as feasible, instant, instantly. SEE MAIN ENTRY
fortification barrier, bulwark, corroboration, panoply, protection, safeguard, support *(corroboration)*
fortified armed, insusceptible *(resistant)*, protective
fortify bear *(support)*, certify *(attest)*, compound, confirm, consolidate *(strengthen)*, corroborate, document, endue, help, nurture, protect, reaffirm, reinforce, supplement, sustain *(prolong)*. SEE MAIN ENTRY
fortis heroic, resolute, spartan, strong
fortis et invictus heroic
fortitude composure, longanimity, resignation *(passive acceptance)*, spirit, sufferance, tolerance
fortress bear *(support)*, bulwark
fortuitous casual, coincidental, random, unexpected, unintentional, unwitting. SEE MAIN ENTRY
fortuitous event accident *(chance occurrence)*, quirk *(accident)*
fortuitously unknowingly
fortuitousness act of god, chance *(fortuity)*, happenstance
fortuitus coincidental, fortuitous
fortuity accident *(chance occurrence)*, act of god, happenstance, occurrence, opportunity, quirk *(accident)*, speculation *(risk)*. SEE MAIN ENTRY
fortuna adversa misfortune
fortunate auspicious, favorable *(advantageous)*, felicitous, propitious, prosperous, successful. SEE MAIN ENTRY
fortunate condition prosperity
fortunatus successful
fortune chattel, contingency, money, possessions, predetermination, prospect *(outlook)*, speculation *(risk)*, substance *(material possessions)*, welfare
fortuneless poor *(underprivileged)*
forum bar *(court)*
forum bench, chamber *(body)*, conference, council *(assembly)*. SEE MAIN ENTRY
forum forum *(court)*
forum judicatory, judicature
forum market place
forum meeting *(conference)*, panel *(discussion group)*, session, tribunal
forum for adjusting disputes court
forum non conveniens SEE MAIN ENTRY
forum of justice bench, court, judiciary
forward along, ameliorate, brazen, bumptious, contemptuous, countenance, cultivate, deliver, dispatch *(send off)*, eager, expedite, facilitate, foster, further, hasten, help, impertinent *(insolent)*, inure *(benefit)*, meliorate, nurture, obtrusive, precipitate *(hasten)*, presumptuous, progressive *(going forward)*, promote *(advance)*, redirect, remit *(submit for consideration)*, remove *(transfer)*, send, serve *(assist)*, serve *(deliver a legal instrument)*, transfer, transmit, unabashed, vanward. SEE MAIN ENTRY
forward looking progressive *(advocating change)*, sophisticated
forward motion advance *(progression)*, headway
forward movement advance *(progression)*

forward moving progressive *(going forward)*

forward payment remit *(send payment)*

forwarding advance *(progression)*, promotion *(advancement)*, transmittal

fossil prime *(original)*

fossilized ossified

foster abet, adopt, assist, bear *(support)*, bestow, care *(regard)*, concern *(care)*, conduce, cultivate, discipline *(train)*, expedite, facilitate, foment, further, keep *(shelter)*, nurture, preserve, promote *(organize)*, protect, sanction, subsidize, surrogate. SEE MAIN ENTRY

foster child child

foster hope promise *(raise expectations)*

fosterage adoption *(affiliation)*, auspices, favor *(sanction)*, guidance, help

fostering conservation, promotion *(encouragement)*

foul arrant *(onerous)*, bad *(inferior)*, contemptible, debase, deface, deleterious, depraved, disgraceful, disreputable, harmful, heinous, infect, iniquitous, irregular *(improper)*, loathsome, malignant, nefarious, objectionable, obnoxious, obscene, odious, offensive *(offending)*, outrageous, peccant *(culpable)*, pestilent, pollute, profligate *(corrupt)*, prurient, reprehensible, repulsive, salacious, scurrilous, sordid, sully, taint *(contaminate)*, tainted *(contaminated)*, tarnish, unfavorable, vicious

foul invective expletive

foul language expletive, imprecation, malediction, profanity. SEE MAIN ENTRY

foul play collusion, frame up, grievance, inequity, knavery, machination, mischief, misdoing, pettifoggery. SEE MAIN ENTRY

foul talk profanity

foul-spoken profane

fouled marred, sordid

foulmouthed profane

foulness defilement, delinquency *(misconduct)*, perversion

found build *(construct)*, create, establish *(launch)*, generate, initiate, instate, launch *(initiate)*, originate, situated. SEE MAIN ENTRY

found guilty blameful, blameworthy

found wanting blameful, devoid, faulty

foundation assumption *(supposition)*, basis, building *(business of assembling)*, cause *(reason)*, cornerstone, corporation, creation, criterion, derivation, facility *(institution)*, formation, fund, genesis, ground, institute, mainstay, nascency, onset *(commencement)*, organization *(association)*, origin *(source)*, origination, outset, postulate, preamble, precedent, preparation, principle *(axiom)*, reason *(basis)*, source, stare decisis, start. SEE MAIN ENTRY

foundation of a suit gist *(ground for a suit)*

foundational central *(essential)*, elementary, incipient, original *(initial)*, precursory, preparatory

foundationless baseless

foundations premises *(hypotheses)*

founded in confidence fiduciary

founded in law jural

founded on based on

founded on circumstances circumstantial

founded on fact authentic, documentary, true *(authentic)*

founded on fiction fictitious

founder architect, author *(originator)*, pioneer, predecessor, promoter

founder of the family parents, primogenitor

founding nascency

founding father pioneer

foundling discard, orphan

fount derivation, fund, source

fountain origination, source

fountainhead derivation, origin *(source)*, origination, source

four corners crossroad *(intersection)*

Fourteenth Amendment SEE MAIN ENTRY

fovea pitfall

fovere foment

foxy devious, insidious, machiavellian, politic, sly

foyer entrance

fracas affray, altercation, belligerency, bluster *(commotion)*, brawl, collision *(dispute)*, commotion, confrontation *(altercation)*, contest *(dispute)*, disaccord, disorder *(lack of order)*, disturbance, embroilment, fight *(battle)*, fray, furor, imbroglio, noise, outbreak, outcry, pandemonium, riot, struggle, turmoil, violence. SEE MAIN ENTRY

fraction constituent *(part)*, element, installment, member *(constituent part)*, modicum, moiety, part *(portion)*, paucity, proportion, section *(division)*, segment, subdivision

fractional broken *(fractured)*, partial *(relating to a part)*, semi, severable

fractional part detail, segment

fractionalize lancinate

fractionize divide *(separate)*, separate

fractious adverse *(hostile)*, contumacious, disobedient, froward, insubordinate, negative, perverse, petulant, pugnacious, querulous, recalcitrant, restive, uncontrollable, unruly. SEE MAIN ENTRY

fractiousness contempt *(disobedience to the court)*

fracture hiatus, rend, rift *(gap)*, split *(noun)*, split *(verb)*

fradulent copy counterfeit

fragile insecure, insubstantial, nonsubstantial *(not sturdy)*, powerless

fragilitas frailty

fragility frailty

fragment break *(fracture)*, chapter *(division)*, component, constituent *(part)*, detail, dichotomize, disintegrate, divide *(separate)*, element, ingredient, iota, lancinate, minimum, modicum, moiety, part *(portion)*, section *(division)*, segment, subdivision

fragmentable divisive

fragmentary broken *(fractured)*, imperfect, inchoate, minimal, partial *(part)*, partial *(relating to a part)*, semi

fragmentation decentralization

fragmentum segment

frail imperfect, insecure, insubstantial, nonsubstantial *(not sturdy)*, powerless

fraility vice

frailty defect, disability *(physical inability)*, disadvantage, fault *(weakness)*, flaw, foible, impuissance. SEE MAIN ENTRY

frailty of character foible

frame arrange *(plan)*, border, border *(bound)*, build *(construct)*, building *(structure)*, circumscribe *(surround by boundary)*, compose, conceive *(invent)*, configuration *(form)*, conjure, conspire, construction, contain *(enclose)*, contour *(outline)*, contour *(shape)*, contrive, create, delineate, devise *(invent)*, edge *(border)*, envelop, forge *(produce)*, form, formulate, foundation *(basis)*, frame up, generate, make, maneuver, margin *(outside limit)*, originate,

outline *(boundary)*, plan, plot, program, pronounce *(speak)*, scheme. SEE MAIN ENTRY

frame of mind character *(personal quality)*, disposition *(inclination)*, outlook, position *(point of view)*, spirit

frame of reference cornerstone, criterion, exemplar, instance, outlook, precedent, standard

frame up SEE MAIN ENTRY

framer architect

framework building *(structure)*, configuration *(confines)*, configuration *(form)*, construction, content *(structure)*, contour *(outline)*, delineation, foundation *(basis)*, frame *(structure)*, organization *(structure)*, perspective

framing blockade *(enclosure)*, building *(business of assembling)*, creation

franchise charter *(sanction)*, droit, empower, enfranchise, free, freedom, home rule, immunity, let *(permit)*, liberate, liberty, license, prerogative, privilege, suffrage, tolerance. SEE MAIN ENTRY

franchised free *(enjoying civil liberty)*, permissible, privileged

franchisement freedom, liberation

frangere impair, infringe

frangible nonsubstantial *(not sturdy)*

frank candid, clear *(apparent)*, credible, direct *(forthright)*, genuine, honest, ingenuous, simple, straightforward, unaffected *(sincere)*. SEE MAIN ENTRY

frankhearted candid

frankness candor *(straightforwardness)*, honesty, probity, veracity

frantic frenetic, hot-blooded

fraternal akin *(related by blood)*, close *(intimate)*, consanguineous, harmonious, humane, interrelated, intimate

fraternal order society

fraternalism peace

fraternity coaction, concordance, society, sodality, union *(labor organization)*

fraternization rapprochement, society, sodality

fraternize cooperate, join *(associate oneself with)*

fraud bad faith, bad repute, betray *(lead astray)*, bilk, canard, collusion, conversion *(misappropriation)*, deceit, deception, duplicity, embezzlement, fake, false pretense, falsehood, falsification, forgery, hoax, hypocrisy, imposture, improbity, indirection *(deceitfulness)*, knavery, lie, maneuver *(trick)*, misappropriation, misrepresentation, pettifoggery, pretense *(pretext)*, pretext, racket, ruse, sham. SEE MAIN ENTRY

fraudare cheat

fraudulence artifice, bad repute, collusion, corruption, criminality, deceit, deception, dishonesty, false pretense, falsehood, forgery, fraud, hoax, hypocrisy, imposture, improbity, knavery, pettifoggery, pretense *(pretext)*, racket

fraudulency abuse *(corrupt practice)*, bad faith, corruption, deception, dishonesty, false pretense, hoax, improbity, indirection *(deceitfulness)*, pettifoggery

fraudulent assumed *(feigned)*, collusive, colorable *(specious)*, deceptive, delusive, dishonest, disingenuous, fallacious, false *(not genuine)*, felonious, insidious, larcenous, lying, machiavellian, mendacious, meretricious, perfidious, spurious, tortuous *(corrupt)*, unfair, unfounded, unscrupulous, untrue, untrustworthy. SEE MAIN ENTRY

fraudulent application   misapplication
fraudulent appropriation   embezzlement
fraudulent appropriation of money   embezzlement
fraudulent check   bad check
fraudulent conversion   embezzlement, misappropriation
fraudulent document   forgery
fraudulent expedient   maneuver *(trick)*
fraudulent imitation   counterfeit
fraudulent income   graft
fraudulent practice   pettifoggery
fraudulent replica   fake
fraudulent taking   larceny, theft
fraudulently induce   suborn
fraudulently introduced   surreptitious
fraudulentus   dishonest, fraudulent
fraught   full, replete
fraught with danger   aleatory *(perilous)*, dangerous, insalubrious, insecure, noxious, precarious
fraught with evil   pernicious
fraught with harm   disastrous, pernicious
fraught with peril   dangerous
fraus   deceit, dishonesty, fraud, hypocrisy, imposture, knavery, sham
fray   affray, brawl, collision *(dispute)*, commotion, confrontation *(altercation)*, contest *(dispute)*, embroilment, fight *(battle)*, fracas, furor, outbreak, outburst, riot, strife. SEE MAIN ENTRY
frayed   dilapidated
freak   quirk *(accident)*
freak occurrence   phenomenon *(unusual occurrence)*
freakish   irregular *(not usual)*, prodigious *(amazing)*, unaccustomed
free   absolve, alleviate, autonomous *(independent)*, autonomous *(self governing)*, clear *(unencumbered)*, clear, competitive *(open)*, condone, discharge *(liberate)*, disencumber, disengage, disentangle, disenthrall, dissociate, enfranchise, exculpate, excuse, exempt, extricate, gratis, gratuitous *(given without recompense)*, immune, independent, liberal *(generous)*, liberate, licentious, parole, passable, philanthropic, promiscuous, release, relieve *(free from burden)*, remit *(release from penalty)*, rescue, salacious, sovereign *(independent)*, spontaneous, unbound, unlimited, unpaid, unrestrained *(not in custody)*, unrestricted, unsolicited, vacant, void *(empty)*, voluntary. SEE MAIN ENTRY
free agency   volition
free course   latitude
free decision   discretion *(power of choice)*, latitude, option *(choice)*
free enterprise   SEE MAIN ENTRY
free fight   affray
free for use   disposable
free from a mistaken belief   disabuse
free from accusation   exonerate
free from affectation   natural, unaffected *(sincere)*
free from ambiguity   clarify
free from anxiety   ease, soothe
free from bias   impartial
free from blame   exculpate, exonerate
free from bondage   disenthrall
free from burden   clear *(unencumbered)*
free from confinement   rescue
free from confusion   clarify
free from danger   rescue, safe
free from desecration   inviolate
free from difficulty   facilitate
free from doubt   assure *(give confidence to)*, clear *(certain)*

free from encumbrance   clear *(unencumbered)*, disencumber
free from engagement   disengage
free from error   disabuse
free from extraneous matter   distill
free from fault   inculpable, irreprehensible
free from fraud   honest
free from guilt   blameless, clean, inculpable, innocent, not guilty
free from harm   safe
free from hindrance   clear *(unencumbered)*, facilitate
free from hurt   safe
free from ignorance   enlighten
free from impairment   inviolate
free from impediment   clear *(unencumbered)*, facilitate
free from imperfection   infallible, intact, unblemished
free from impurities   clean
free from impurity   purge *(purify)*
free from injury   safe
free from limitation   clear *(unencumbered)*
free from mistake   infallible
free from narrowness   liberal *(not literal)*
free from objectionable content   expurgate
free from obstruction   clear *(unencumbered)*, facilitate
free from pain   soothe
free from pledge   disengage
free from political disabilities   enfranchise
free from prejudice   enlighten, fairly *(impartially)*
free from reserve   ingenuous
free from risk   safe
free from sin   clean
free from superstition   enlighten
free from thralldom   disenthrall
free from uncertainty   assure *(give confidence to)*
free from vindictiveness   charitable *(lenient)*, lenient
free from vow   disengage
free from war   peaceable
free from waste   economical
free from wrong   blameless
free giver   benefactor, donor
free giving   largess *(generosity)*, philanthropy
free hand   latitude. SEE MAIN ENTRY
free in expression   demonstrative *(expressive of emotion)*
free of   privileged
free of access   open *(accessible)*
free of binding obligation   exempt
free of charge   gratis
free of cost   gratis, gratuitous *(given without recompense)*
free of duplicity   simple
free of error   accurate, proper
free of expense   gratis, gratuitous *(given without recompense)*
free of guilt   irreprehensible
free of pettiness   magnanimous
free play   latitude
free selection   alternative *(option)*, option *(choice)*
free thought   latitude
free to all   competitive *(open)*, open *(accessible)*, patent, public *(open)*
free to choose   autonomous *(independent)*, impartial
free trade   SEE MAIN ENTRY
free translation   paraphrase

free will   discretion *(power of choice)*, latitude, liberty, option *(choice)*, volition
free wording   paraphrase
free-handedness   philanthropy
free-living   dissolute
free-willed   spontaneous
freed   clear *(free from criminal charges)*, free *(enjoying civil liberty)*
freed from   exempt
freed of wrongdoing   acquitted
freedom   dispensation *(exception)*, emancipation, exemption, exoneration, immunity, impunity, informality, latitude, liberation, liberty, license, option *(choice)*, parole, prerogative, privilege, probation, suffrage, tolerance. SEE MAIN ENTRY
freedom from accusation   exoneration
freedom from affectation   informality
freedom from ailment   health
freedom from bias   disinterest *(lack of prejudice)*, justice
freedom from bigotry   tolerance
freedom from blame   innocence
freedom from captivity   liberty
freedom from danger   asylum *(protection)*, preservation, protection, security *(safety)*
freedom from deviation   rigor
freedom from difficulty   facility *(easiness)*
freedom from disease   health
freedom from domination   home rule
freedom from doubt   faith
freedom from duty   exemption, leave *(absence)*
freedom from error   certification *(certainness)*, certitude
freedom from exemption   immunity
freedom from extravagance   economy *(frugality)*
freedom from guilt   exoneration, innocence
freedom from harm   security *(safety)*
freedom from illegality   innocence
freedom from interference   home rule
freedom from judgment   impunity
freedom from liability   exemption
freedom from obligation   exemption, immunity
freedom from penalty   impunity
freedom from prejudice   disinterest *(lack of prejudice)*, tolerance
freedom from prosecution   immunity
freedom from punishment   impunity
freedom from requirements   exemption
freedom from self-interest   disinterest *(lack of prejudice)*
freedom from service   exemption
freedom from vindictiveness   lenience
freedom from war   peace
freedom of action   home rule, latitude, liberty
freedom of association   SEE MAIN ENTRY
freedom of choice   call *(option)*, discretion *(power of choice)*, franchise *(right to vote)*, home rule, liberty, option *(choice)*, suffrage. SEE MAIN ENTRY
freedom of information request   SEE MAIN ENTRY
freedom of press   SEE MAIN ENTRY
freedom to discharge   SEE MAIN ENTRY
freehanded   benevolent, charitable *(bene-volent)*, donative, philanthropic
freehandedness   largess *(generosity)*
freehold   demesne, domain *(land owned)*, dominion *(absolute ownership)*, estate *(property)*, fee *(estate)*, leasehold, property *(land)*, real estate. SEE MAIN ENTRY

freeholder landholder, landowner, occupant

freeing liberation, release

freeing from blame exoneration

freeing from prison parole

freelance independent

freely readily

freely giving liberal *(generous)*

freeness largess *(generosity)*

freethinking liberal *(broad minded)*, licentious, radical *(favoring drastic change)*, skeptical

freeway causeway

freewill worker volunteer

freeze check *(restrain)*, desist, embargo, stop

freight cargo, load, merchandise, send. SEE MAIN ENTRY

freightage cargo, freight

frenetic deranged, lunatic. SEE MAIN ENTRY

frenzied deranged, frenetic, lunatic, uncontrollable, vehement

frenzy bluster *(commotion)*, confusion *(turmoil)*, furor, haste, insanity, lunacy, outburst, pandemonium, panic, passion

frequence draw *(attendance)*, frequency

frequency SEE MAIN ENTRY

frequens frequent, populous

frequent attend *(be present at)*, chronic, common *(customary)*, customary, familiar *(customary)*, habitual, incessant, innumerable, inveterate, mundane, ordinary, patronize *(trade with)*, periodic, prevailing *(current)*, prevalent, repeated, routine, usual. SEE MAIN ENTRY

frequent as a customer patronize *(trade with)*

frequent repetition practice *(custom)*

frequenter addict, patron *(regular customer)*

frequentia frequency

frequently invariably

frequently met prevalent

frequently repeated act habit

fresh impertinent *(insolent)*, insolent, novel, original *(creative)*, recent, unusual

fresh outbreak recrudescence

fresh spurt resurgence

fresh start continuation *(resumption)*

fresh supply reinforcement

freshen fix *(repair)*, renew *(refurbish)*

freshen up fix *(repair)*

freshening revival

freshest last *(preceding)*

freshly de novo

freshman amateur, neophyte, novice

fret agitate *(perturb)*, annoy, badger, brood, discompose, fear, harrow, harry *(harass)*, hector, irritate, languish, oscillate, perturb, pique, plague, provoke, regret, trepidation

fret over deplore

fretful fractious, petulant, querulous, restive

fretter malcontent

friable dilapidated

fribble petty

friction collision *(dispute)*, conflict, contention *(opposition)*, contravention, controversy *(argument)*, disaccord, discord, dissension, dissent *(difference of opinion)*, strife. SEE MAIN ENTRY

frictional hostile

frictionless harmonious

friend associate, benefactor, cohort, confederate, partisan, patron *(influential supporter)*, proponent, samaritan. SEE MAIN ENTRY

friend at court advocate *(counselor)*

friend in court advocate *(counselor)*, amicus curiae

friendless derelict *(abandoned)*, helpless *(defenseless)*, solitary

friendliness affinity *(regard)*, benevolence *(disposition to do good)*, comity, consideration *(sympathetic regard)*, courtesy, informality, peace, rapprochement, sodality

friendly amicable, benevolent, close *(intimate)*, harmonious, intimate, peaceable, propitious, receptive. SEE MAIN ENTRY

friendly agreement accommodation *(adjustment)*

friendly association affiliation *(connectedness)*

friendly disposition goodwill

friendly interest patronage *(support)*

friendly relations sodality

friendly turn favor *(act of kindness)*

friendship affinity *(regard)*, benevolence *(disposition to do good)*, concordance, consortium *(marriage companionship)*, patronage *(support)*, peace, rapprochement, sodality

fright consternation, fear, frighten, panic, phobia, stress *(strain)*, trepidation. SEE MAIN ENTRY

frighten browbeat, intimidate, menace, repel *(disgust)*, threaten. SEE MAIN ENTRY

frighten away discourage, dissuade

frightened leery, recreant

frightening dire, formidable, odious, portentous *(ominous)*, sinister

frightful deplorable, disastrous, formidable, insufferable, loathsome, ominous, portentous *(ominous)*, repulsive, vicious. SEE MAIN ENTRY

frigid cold-blooded, insensible, insusceptible *(uncaring)*, phlegmatic, unaffected *(uninfluenced)*

frigidus insipid, lifeless *(dull)*, prosaic

frill embellish

fringe border, edge *(border)*, extremity *(furthest point)*, frontier, limit, margin *(outside limit)*, penumbra, peripheral, periphery. SEE MAIN ENTRY

fringement crime

fringes confines, outline *(boundary)*

fringing contiguous, proximate

frisk SEE MAIN ENTRY

frisky jocular

frivolous capricious, inconsequential, irresolute, irresponsible, jocular, nonessential, nugatory, petty, superficial, trivial, undependable, untrustworthy. SEE MAIN ENTRY

frock clothe

frolic carouse. SEE MAIN ENTRY

frolicsome jocular

frolicsomeness mischief

from a general law to a particular instance a priori

from abroad alien *(foreign)*

from beginning to end throughout *(all over)*

from cause to effect a priori

from competent sources authentic

from first to last throughout *(all over)*

from here on hereafter *(henceforth)*

from its birth ab initio

from now on hereafter *(henceforth)*

from nowhere alien *(unrelated)*

from that cause a priori, consequently

from that time thereafter

from the beginning ab initio, de novo

from the ground up throughout *(all over)*

from the original data authentic

from the river fluvial

from the start heretofore

from the word go throughout *(all over)*

from this cause a priori

from this time on hereafter *(henceforth)*

fronder censure

front defy, hypocrisy, prime *(most valuable)*. SEE MAIN ENTRY

front office management *(directorate)*

front position preference *(priority)*

frontage SEE MAIN ENTRY

frontier border, edge *(border)*, extremity *(furthest point)*, limit, outline *(boundary)*, periphery. SEE MAIN ENTRY

frontiers configuration *(confines)*

frontiersman pioneer

frontward vanward

frothy nugatory

froward disobedient, disorderly, insolent, insubordinate, intractable, perverse, petulant, spiteful, unruly, wanton. SEE MAIN ENTRY

frown on disfavor

frown upon denounce *(condemn)*, disparage, remonstrate, reproach, spurn

frowning grave *(solemn)*

fructiferous fertile, productive

fructify ameliorate, bear *(yield)*, reproduce. SEE MAIN ENTRY

fructuosus profitable

fructuous fertile, productive

fructus enjoyment *(pleasure)*, fruition, profit, result

frugal economical, parsimonious, penurious, prudent. SEE MAIN ENTRY

frugality austerity, management *(judicious use)*, moderation, prudence, temperance. SEE MAIN ENTRY

frugalness austerity, economy *(frugality)*

frugi economical, frugal

frugifer profitable

fruit effect, issuance, outcome, outgrowth, output, product, progeny, result

fruit of labor earnings

fruitbearing prolific

fruitful fertile, gainful, lucrative, operative, productive, profitable, prolific, successful

fruitfulness utility *(usefulness)*

fruition commission *(act)*, consequence *(conclusion)*, creation, denouement, discharge *(performance)*, effect, fait accompli, growth *(evolution)*, outcome, realization, result, satisfaction *(fulfilment)*. SEE MAIN ENTRY

fruitless barren, futile, idle, ineffective, ineffectual, needless, otiose, unavailing, unproductive

fruitless effort failure *(lack of success)*

fruitless trial mistrial

fruits profit

frustrari balk, disappoint

frustrari frustrate

frustrate arrest *(stop)*, balk, bar *(hinder)*, block, check *(restrain)*, clog, condemn *(ban)*, constrict *(inhibit)*, contravene, counteract, defeat, deter, disadvantage, discontinue *(break continuity)*, encumber *(hinder)*, enjoin, fight *(counteract)*, foil, forestall, halt, hamper, impede, inhibit, interrupt, keep *(restrain)*, obstruct, perturb, preclude, prevent, repel *(drive back)*, repulse, restrict, stay *(halt)*, stem *(check)*, stifle, thwart, toll *(stop)*, trammel. SEE MAIN ENTRY

frustrate by contrary action counter, counteract

frustrated disappointed

frustration abortion *(fiasco)*, aggravation *(annoyance)*, check *(bar)*, deadlock, deterrence, failure *(lack of success)*, impediment, miscarriage. SEE MAIN ENTRY

fuddle confusion *(ambiguity)*, muddle

fudge mulct *(defraud)*

fuga flight, lapse *(break)*

fugacious ephemeral, temporary, transient, transitory

fugaciousness mortality

fugacity mortality

fugam petere flee

fugare repel *(drive back)*, stave

fugax transient

fugere escape, retreat

fugitive convict, criminal, derelict, elusive, ephemeral, moving *(in motion)*, outlaw, pariah, temporary, transient, truant. SEE MAIN ENTRY

fugitive from the law outlaw

fugitivus fugitive

fulcrum basis, center *(central position)*

fulfill accomplish, close *(terminate)*, commit *(perpetrate)*, complete, comply, conclude *(complete)*, consummate, discharge *(perform)*, dispatch *(dispose of)*, effectuate, execute *(accomplish)*, implement, obey, observe *(obey)*, operate, pass *(satisfy requirements)*, perform *(adhere to)*, perpetrate, succeed *(attain)*, transact. SEE MAIN ENTRY

fulfill an engagement report *(present oneself)*

fulfill an obligation satisfy *(discharge)*

fulfill the commands of obey

fulfilled complacent, fully executed *(consummated)*

fulfillment cessation *(termination)*, conclusion *(outcome)*, discharge *(performance)*, end *(termination)*, fait accompli, finality, fruition, maturity, outcome

fulfilment collection *(payment)*, commission *(act)*, performance *(execution)*, realization

fulgent pretentious *(ostentatious)*

fulgere radiate

fulgid lucid, pretentious *(ostentatious)*

fulguration discharge *(shot)*

full absolute *(complete)*, broad, complete *(all-embracing)*, comprehensive, copious, gross *(total)*, inclusive, intact, orotund, outright, plenary, populous, profuse, replete, ripe, thorough, total, unmitigated, unqualified *(unlimited)*. SEE MAIN ENTRY

full age majority *(adulthood)*, maturity

full appraisal appreciation *(perception)*

full array panoply

full assurance credence

full authority permission

full belief credence

full chance day in court

full complement capacity *(maximum)*

full development maturity

full effect amount *(result)*

full extent capacity *(maximum)*

full force main force

full growth maturity

full legal age majority *(adulthood)*

full measure plethora, quorum, sufficiency

full observance conformity *(obedience)*

full of affectation pretentious *(pompous)*

full of contempt disdainful

full of curves labyrinthine

full of details detailed

full of enterprise eager

full of enthusiasm eager

full of exhortation hortative

full of faults faulty

full of feeling ecstatic, eloquent

full of fun jocular

full of good will benevolent

full of hate hostile, malevolent

full of hope sanguine

full of initiative eager

full of life live *(conscious)*

full of malice hostile, malevolent

full of meaning eloquent, pithy, sententious

full of mischief peccant *(culpable)*

full of power forcible

full of promise favorable *(advantageous)*, probable, propitious

full of regret remorseful

full of regrets contrite, penitent, repentant

full of remorse contrite

full of revenge malevolent

full of risk aleatory *(perilous)*, dangerous, precarious

full of sin diabolic

full of spirit volatile

full of spite malevolent

full of strength forcible

full of substance eloquent

full of thought deliberate, pensive

full of turns labyrinthine

full of urgency hortative

full of verbiage prolix

full pardon condonation

full particulars circumstances

full play latitude

full purse prosperity

full report accounting

full round of the seasons annum

full satisfaction collection *(payment)*, discharge *(payment)*, expiation, indemnity

full size caliber *(measurement)*

full stop check *(bar)*

full throttle SEE MAIN ENTRY

full volume capacity *(maximum)*

full-blown plenary, ripe

full-bodied sapid, savory

full-charged plenary

full-flavored sapid, savory

full-fledged outright. SEE MAIN ENTRY

full-grown ripe

fullness capacity *(maximum)*, corpus, entirety, finality, mass *(weight)*, maximum *(amplitude)*, plethora, quantity, sufficiency, surfeit

fullness of heart affection

fully fairly *(clearly)*, in toto, wholly

fully constituted plenary

fully convinced certain *(positive)*, definite, positive *(confident)*

fully detailed analysis accounting

fully developed ripe

fully developed person adult

fully executed thorough. SEE MAIN ENTRY

fully furnished plenary

fully grown ripe

fully grown person adult

fully realized comprehensive

fully secured SEE MAIN ENTRY

fully sufficient adequate

fully supplied replete

fulminate defame, discharge *(shoot)*, inveigh, threaten. SEE MAIN ENTRY

fulminate against censure, condemn *(blame)*, denounce *(condemn)*, disapprove *(condemn)*, lash *(attack verbally)*, malign, reprimand

fulmination denunciation, discharge *(shot)*, imprecation, malediction, threat

fulsome arrant *(onerous)*, bad *(inferior)*, bad *(offensive)*, contemptible, detrimental, excessive, gross *(flagrant)*, heinous, loathsome, lurid, objectionable, obnoxious, odious, outrageous, repugnant *(exciting aversion)*, scandalous, sordid, unwarranted

fumble miscue, mismanage

fumigate decontaminate

function activity, agency *(legal relationship)*, appointment *(position)*, assignment *(task)*, business *(occupation)*, calling, capacity *(job)*, charge *(responsibility)*, demean *(deport oneself)*, duty *(obligation)*, employment, job, office, officiate, operate, operation, part *(role)*, perform *(execute)*, position *(business status)*, post, province, purpose, pursuit *(occupation)*, role, specialty *(special aptitude)*, sphere, trade *(occupation)*, use, utility *(usefulness)*, work *(employment)*. SEE MAIN ENTRY

functional beneficial, corrigible, effective *(efficient)*, efficient, ministerial, operative, practical, procedural, viable. SEE MAIN ENTRY

functionary agent, conduit *(intermediary)*, incumbent, notary public, officer, official, proctor, trustee. SEE MAIN ENTRY

functioning acting, active, in full force, operative

functionless barren, expendable

functus officio defeasible

fund bear *(yield)*, bestow, capitalize *(provide capital)*, endow, endowment, finance, garner, hoard, principal *(capital sum)*, provide *(supply)*, provision *(something provided)*, reserve, resource, stock *(shares)*, store *(depository)*, sufficiency, treasury, underwrite. SEE MAIN ENTRY

fund again refinance

fund invested for a charitable purpose foundation *(organization)*

fundamenta foundation *(basis)*

fundamental born *(innate)*, cardinal *(basic)*, central *(essential)*, cornerstone, elementary, essential *(inherent)*, essential *(required)*, gravamen, inchoate, incipient, indispensable, initial, innate, integral, material *(important)*, naked *(lacking embellishment)*, native *(inborn)*, natural, necessary *(required)*, necessity, need *(requirement)*, organic, original *(initial)*, prerequisite, primary, prime *(original)*, primordial, rudimentary, simple, substantive, ultimate, underlying, virtual, vital. SEE MAIN ENTRY

fundamental doctrine principle *(axiom)*

fundamental feature main point

fundamental law constitution, principle *(axiom)*

fundamental part component, essence, ingredient, main point

fundamental point main point

fundamental principle canon, foundation *(basis)*, necessity

fundamental principles policy *(plan of action)*

fundamental principles of government polity

fundamental reason rationale

fundamental research inquiry *(systematic investigation)*

fundamental rule principle *(axiom)*

fundamental unit necessity

fundamentally purely *(positively)*

fundamentals basis, gist *(substance)*

fundemental part element

funding appropriation *(donation)*, endowment, loan
funds assets, capital, cash, finance, money, personalty, possessions, principal *(capital sum)*, property *(possessions)*, security *(stock)*. SEE MAIN ENTRY
funds for investment capital
funds in hand capital
funds paid out expenditure
fundus basis
funereal disconsolate, lugubrious, solemn
funestus disastrous, fatal, lethal
funk shirk, trepidation
funny jocular, ludicrous
furari pilfer, purloin, steal
furbish rehabilitate
furcate bifurcate, bipartite, dichotomize, divergent
furcated divergent
furcular bipartite
furens frenetic
furibund frenetic
furious demonstrative *(expressive of emotion)*, resentful, severe, vehement
furiousness violence
furlough holiday, leave *(absence)*. SEE MAIN ENTRY
furnish accommodate, adduce, bear *(yield)*, bequeath, bestow, clothe, contribute *(supply)*, dole, endow, endue, engender, fund, give *(grant)*, lend, pander, present *(make a gift)*, produce *(manufacture)*, provide *(supply)*, render *(administer)*, replenish, sell, supply, tender, vest, yield *(produce a return)*. SEE MAIN ENTRY
furnish aid abet, assist, capitalize *(provide capital)*, contribute *(assist)*, inure *(benefit)*, serve *(assist)*, subsidize
furnish an equivalent compensate *(counterbalance)*
furnish an estimate calculate
furnish an example illustrate
furnish assistance bear *(support)*, help, serve *(assist)*
furnish credit lend
furnish evidence bear *(adduce)*, evince
furnish foundations capitalize *(provide capital)*
furnish funds loan, support *(assist)*
furnish occupation for employ *(engage services)*, hire
furnish room for lodge *(house)*
furnish support bear *(support)*, capitalize *(provide capital)*, subsidize
furnish sustenance bear *(support)*
furnish with a date date
furnish with quarters lodge *(house)*
furnish with rank invest *(vest)*
furnished with weapons armed
furnisher supplier
furnishing donative, provision *(act of supplying)*
furnishings cargo
furor ardor, commotion, emotion, outburst, outcry, passion, riot. SEE MAIN ENTRY
furrow split
further accrue *(increase)*, additional, aggravate *(exacerbate)*, aid, assist, compound, countenance, cultivate, develop, expand, expedite, facilitate, favor, foster, help, inure *(benefit)*, nurture, parlay *(exploit successfully)*, precipitate *(hasten)*, prefer, promote *(advance)*, promote *(organize)*, raise *(advance)*, side, subsidize, support *(assist)*. SEE MAIN ENTRY
further time extension *(postponement)*

furtherance advancement *(improvement)*, advocacy, aid *(help)*, assistance, behalf, course, development *(progression)*, favor *(sanction)*, headway, help, longevity, progress, promotion *(encouragement)*, reinforcement. SEE MAIN ENTRY
furthermore also, further. SEE MAIN ENTRY
furthermost ultimate
furthermost part end *(termination)*
furthest extreme *(last)*, last *(final)*, ultimate, utmost
furthest extent ambit
furthest point ambit, limit, utmost
furtim feras intercipere poach
furtive clandestine, collusive, covert, evasive, fraudulent, insidious, mysterious, oblique *(evasive)*, privy, secret, sly, stealthy, surreptitious. SEE MAIN ENTRY
furtive removal asportation
furtiveness bad faith, concealment, deceit, dishonesty, fraud, improbity
furtivus clandestine, furtive, stealthy, surreptitious
furtum burglary, larceny, theft
fury furor, outbreak, outburst, passion, resentment, severity, violence
fuscus dun
fuse adhere *(fasten)*, amalgamate, bond *(hold together)*, cement, combine *(join together)*, commingle, conjoin, connect *(join together)*, consolidate *(strengthen)*, consolidate *(unite)*, desegregate, incorporate *(include)*, join *(bring together)*, lock, merge, unite. SEE MAIN ENTRY
fused coadunate, coherent *(joined)*, composite, compound, concerted, concurrent *(united)*, conjoint, inseparable, promiscuous
fusing coalescence, coalition, concordant
fusion accession *(annexation)*, adhesion *(affixing)*, affiliation *(amalgamation)*, cartel, centralization, coaction, coalescence, coalition, coherence, combination, concrescence, confederacy *(compact)*, consolidation, incorporation *(blend)*, integration *(amalgamation)*, league, meeting *(encounter)*, merger, union *(unity)*
fusion of interests coalition, concert
fuss disturbance, fracas, furor, outburst, pretense *(ostentation)*, trouble, turmoil
fussiness particularity
fussy meticulous, particular *(exacting)*, precise, punctilious, punctual
fustian bombast, flatulent, grandiose, inflated *(bombastic)*, orotund, turgid. SEE MAIN ENTRY
fustigate beat *(strike)*, lash *(strike)*
fustis cudgel
fusty sordid, stale
futile expendable, idle, ineffective, ineffectual, invalid, minor, needless, nugatory, otiose, powerless, unavailing, unproductive. SEE MAIN ENTRY
futile effort frustration, miscarriage
futilis futile, unavailing
futility impossibility
future forthcoming, imminent, potential, prospective, subsequent. SEE MAIN ENTRY
future generation descendant
future interest reversion *(remainder of an estate)*
future payment credit *(delayed payment)*
future possession heritage, reversion *(remainder of an estate)*
future relatives posterity
futures portfolio

futurity prospect *(outlook)*
futurus future, prospective
fuzziness indistinctness, obscuration
fuzzy unclear

G

gab prattle
gabble prattle
gabby loquacious
gad prowl
gadget device *(mechanism)*, item
gag inhibit, repress, stifle, suppress
gag rule SEE MAIN ENTRY
gage bail, binder, defiance, deposit, guaranty, security *(pledge)*
gagged speechless
gaiety enjoyment *(pleasure)*
gain accession *(enlargement)*, accretion, accrue *(increase)*, accumulate *(enlarge)*, acquire *(receive)*, acquire *(secure)*, acquisition, advancement *(improvement)*, advantage, appreciation *(increased value)*, attain, augmentation, bear *(yield)*, benefit *(betterment)*, boom *(increase)*, boom *(prosperity)*, carry *(succeed)*, collect *(gather)*, collect *(recover money)*, development *(progression)*, dividend, earn, edification, expand, headway, increase, increment, inherit, interest *(profit)*, inure *(benefit)*, obtain, output, perquisite, possess, prize, proceeds, procure, profit *(noun)*, profit *(verb)*, progress *(noun)*, progress *(verb)*, purchase, reach, realize *(obtain as a profit)*, reap, receipt *(act of receiving)*, receive *(acquire)*, recruit, revenue, shelter *(tax benefit)*, succeed *(attain)*. SEE MAIN ENTRY
gain a victory prevail *(triumph)*, succeed *(attain)*
gain admittance enter *(go in)*
gain advantage profit
gain anew recoup *(regain)*, recover
gain by labor earn
gain by service earn
gain by wrongful methods extort
gain control over defeat
gain derived from capital income
gain derived from labor income
gain entry enter *(go in)*
gain for oneself possess
gain ground compound, increase, proceed *(go forward)*, progress
gain in worth appreciate *(increase)*, appreciation *(increased value)*
gain indemnity against loss insure
gain insight comprehend *(understand)*
gain insight into perceive
gain knowledge detect
gain liberty escape
gain more time postpone
gain one's end attain
gain over disarm *(set at ease)*, prejudice *(influence)*
gain possession obtain, preempt, recover
gain strength compound, expand
gain the advantage prevail *(triumph)*
gain the ascendancy outbalance
gain the confidence of convince, disarm *(set at ease)*, persuade, prevail *(persuade)*
gain the favor of propitiate
gain the upper hand predominate *(command)*, prevail *(triumph)*
gain time defer *(put off)*, hold up *(delay)*, procrastinate, protract *(prolong)*
gain wrongfully extort
gainful beneficial, functional, lucrative,

productive, profitable, successful, valuable. SEE MAIN ENTRY

gaingiving misgiving

gainless disadvantageous, futile, ineffective, ineffectual

gains earnings, income, spoils

gainsay contend (dispute), contest, contravene, cross (disagree with), debar, deny (contradict), disaccord, disaffirm, disagree, disapprove (reject), dispute (contest), except (object), expostulate, negation, oppugn, prohibit, refute, reject, repulse.

gainsaying contravention, counterargument, denial, diatribe, disagreement, disapprobation, negation, negative, rejection, remonstrance, retraction

gait step

gala holiday, special

galbe configuration (form)

gall affront, annoy, irritate, offend (insult), perturb, pique, plague, provoke, resentment, spite, temerity

gallant heroic, magnanimous, undaunted

gallant acts prowess (bravery)

gallantness prowess (bravery)

gallantry consideration (sympathetic regard), courtesy, prowess (bravery)

galled resentful

gallimaufry melange

galling malevolent, oppressive, outrageous, provocative, vexatious

gallop race

galloping rapid

galore rife

galvanic incisive, provocative

galvanical provocative

galvanize foment, impress (affect deeply). SEE MAIN ENTRY

gambit first appearance

gamble bet, hazard, invest (fund), lottery, parlay (bet), possibility, risk, speculate (chance), speculation (risk), venture. SEE MAIN ENTRY

gambler bettor, speculator

gambling speculation (risk)

game bet, contest (competition), ridicule

game of chance lottery

gamesome jocular

gamester bettor

gaming risk, speculation (risk)

gammon bait (lure), betray (lead astray), palter

gamut range. SEE MAIN ENTRY

gang assemblage, band, cabal, league

gangleader racketeer

gangster burglar, criminal, malefactor, racketeer

gangway entrance

gannitus snarl

gap flaw, hiatus, interruption, interval, pause, space, split

gaping open (unclosed), penetrable

garb clothe

garble cloak, falsify, misconstrue, misinterpret, misread. SEE MAIN ENTRY

garbled imperfect, inaccurate, marred

garbling catachresis

garden cultivate, curtilage

gargantuan prodigious (enormous)

garish meretricious, pretentious (ostentatious), tawdry. SEE MAIN ENTRY

garishness pretense (ostentation)

garner accumulate (amass), collect (gather), compile, fund, glean, hoard, repository, reserve, store. SEE MAIN ENTRY

garner up hoard

garnering arsenal

garnish attach (seize), distrain, embellish, impress (procure by force), levy. SEE MAIN ENTRY

garnished elaborate

garnisheed attached (seized)

garnishing bombast, confiscatory

garnishment attachment (seizure), distraint, motif, sequestration. SEE MAIN ENTRY

garrison bear (support), lodge (house), protect

garrulous flatulent, loquacious, profuse, voluble. SEE MAIN ENTRY

garrulus loquacious

gasconade exaggeration, jactation, rodomontade

gasconading orgulous

gash lancinate, mutilate, rift (gap), split

gate egress, entrance, immure, outlet, portal

gatekeeper guardian, warden

gates approaches

gateway easement, egress, entrance, outlet, portal, threshold (entrance)

gather accrue (increase), accumulate (amass), aggregate, assume (suppose), call (summon), compile, concentrate (consolidate), congregate, conjoin, connect (join together), construe (comprehend), convene, converge, cull, deduce, deduct (conclude by reasoning), expect (consider probable), extract, gain, garner, glean, guess, hold (possess), infer, join (bring together), levy, obtain, presume, presuppose, procure, read, reap, reason (conclude), receive (acquire), recruit, rendezvous, store, surmise, suspect (think), understand. SEE MAIN ENTRY

gather for oneself hoard

gather in hoard

gather into a mass accumulate (amass)

gather knowledge find (discover)

gather together accumulate (amass), aggregate, collect (gather), compile, consolidate (unite), convene, meet, raise (collect), unite

gather up accumulate (amass), hoard

gathered collective, composite

gathered into a round mass conglomerate

gathered into a whole composite

gathering assemblage, assembly, body (collection), caucus, chamber (body), collection (assembly), company (assemblage), compilation, conference, congregation, levy, mass (body of persons), meeting (conference), rendezvous, selection (collection), session. SEE MAIN ENTRY

gathering place focus, rendezvous

gathering together centralization

gauche incompetent, provincial

gaudiness pretense (ostentation)

gaudium enjoyment (pleasure)

gaudy blatant (obtrusive), meretricious, pretentious (ostentatious), tawdry

gauge assess (appraise), calculate, consider, criterion, criticize (evaluate), estimate (approximate cost), estimate, estimation (calculation), evaluate, extent, magnitude, mass (weight), measure, measurement, model, rate, standard, weigh. SEE MAIN ENTRY

gaugeable appreciable, determinable (ascertainable)

gausape fustian (adjective), fustian (noun)

gavel SEE MAIN ENTRY

gawky incompetent, provincial, uncouth

gay jocular. SEE MAIN ENTRY

gay marriage SEE MAIN ENTRY

gaze regard (pay attention)

gaze at observe (watch)

gazette herald, journal, proclaim

gear clothe, device (mechanism), furnish, paraphernalia (apparatus)

gear with engage (involve)

geared to fitting

gelatinization congealment

gelling congealment

gemination duplicate

gemmate germinate

gender SEE MAIN ENTRY

gender bias SEE MAIN ENTRY

gender discrimination SEE MAIN ENTRY

genealogical hereditary

genealogical tree blood, origin (ancestry), parentage

genealogy ancestry, blood, bloodline, descent (lineage), family (common ancestry), lineage, origin (ancestry), parentage, race

genera class

general broad, chief, collective, competitive (open), conventional, customary, familiar (customary), generic, habitual, inaccurate, inclusive, inexact, liberal (not literal), mutual (collective), national, nonsectarian, omnibus, ordinary, predominant, prevailing (current), prevalent, proverbial, public (affecting people), regular (conventional), rife, routine, unspecified, usual, vague. SEE MAIN ENTRY

general agreement consensus. SEE MAIN ENTRY

general course practice (custom)

general denial demurrer

general discharge salvo

general expenses overhead

general fire conflagration

general guidelines policy (plan of action), practice (procedure)

general information common knowledge, education

general law generality (vague statement)

general meaning connotation, content (meaning), gist (substance). SEE MAIN ENTRY

general notion impression

general pardon amnesty

general performance norm

general principle generality (vague statement)

general principles policy (plan of action). SEE MAIN ENTRY

general public populace, population, public

general reciprocity comity

general rule canon, generality (vague statement)

general run matter of course

general statement generality (vague statement), generalization

general store market (business)

general uprising revolution

generalis general

generality generalization, majority (greater part), norm. SEE MAIN ENTRY

generalization generality (vague statement). SEE MAIN ENTRY

generalize SEE MAIN ENTRY

generalized broad, inaccurate

generally as a rule, invariably. SEE MAIN ENTRY

generally accepted prevailing (current), prevalent

generally known common (customary), notorious

generally practiced ordinary

generally seen familiar (customary)

generally speaking as a rule
generals management *(directorate)*
generalship management *(supervision)*. SEE MAIN ENTRY
generare engender, generate
generate avail *(bring about)*, bear *(yield)*, cause, compose, conceive *(invent)*, create, elicit, engender, evoke, fabricate *(construct)*, germinate, induce, inspire, launch *(initiate)*, make, manufacture, occasion, originate, produce *(manufacture)*, propagate *(increase)*, provoke, pullulate, reproduce, yield *(produce a return)*. SEE MAIN ENTRY
generatim generalize
generating causal
generation formation, lifetime
generations of man humanity *(mankind)*
generative causal, causative, constructive *(creative)*, potent, prime *(original)*, prolific
generator architect, author *(originator)*, cause *(reason)*, derivation, determinant, source
generic broad, omnibus, unspecified. SEE MAIN ENTRY
generic class kind
generical omnibus
generis kind
generosity benevolence *(disposition to do good)*, charity, clemency, consideration *(sympathetic regard)*, contribution *(donation)*, indulgence, largess *(generosity)*, philanthropy
generous ample, benevolent, capacious, charitable *(benevolent)*, copious, donative, favorable *(expressing approval)*, humane, lenient, liberal *(generous)*, magnanimous, meritorious, multiple, philanthropic, placable, profuse, propitious. SEE MAIN ENTRY
generous giver donor
generous giving charity
generousness clemency, indulgence, largess *(generosity)*, lenience
genesis ancestry, birth *(beginning)*, cause *(reason)*, derivation, determinant, embryo, formation, inception, nascency, onset *(commencement)*, origin *(source)*, origination, outset, parentage, reason *(basis)*, source, start. SEE MAIN ENTRY
genetic born *(innate)*, hereditary, native *(inborn)*. SEE MAIN ENTRY
genetic engineering SEE MAIN ENTRY
genial amicable, benevolent, civil *(polite)*, willing *(not averse)*
genialis nuptial
geniality consideration *(sympathetic regard)*, courtesy, goodwill
genitor ancestor, ascendant, parents, progenitor
genius caliber *(mental capacity)*, expert, gift *(flair)*, intellect, intelligence *(intellect)*, mastermind, propensity, sagacity, science *(technique)*, sense *(intelligence)*, specialty *(special aptitude)*. SEE MAIN ENTRY
genocide murder. SEE MAIN ENTRY
genre class, denomination, kind, style. SEE MAIN ENTRY
gens lineage
gens humana humanity *(mankind)*
genteel civil *(polite)*
gentility blood, comity, courtesy, decorum, presence *(poise)*, society
gentle harmless, lenient, nonmilitant, peaceable, placid
gentleman of fortune bettor
gentlemanlike civil *(polite)*
gentlemanliness decorum
gentlemanly civil *(polite)*

gentleness clemency, consideration *(sympathetic regard)*, humanity *(humaneness)*, lenience, moderation
gentry elite
genuflection prostration
genuine accurate, actual, authentic, bona fide, convincing, de facto, direct *(forthright)*, documentary, factual, faithful *(true to fact)*, honest, ingenuous, legitimate *(rightful)*, natural, prime *(original)*, real, realistic, reliable, rightful, sterling, substantial, true *(authentic)*, unadulterated, undistorted, veridical. SEE MAIN ENTRY
genuine in origin authentic
genuinely admittedly
genuineness candor *(straightforwardness)*, honesty, legitimacy, reality, truth, validity
genuiness veracity
genus ancestry, blood, class
genus kind
genus lineage, parentage
genus race
genus range
genus rubric *(title)*
genus style
geographical regional
gerere conduct, transact
germ consequence *(significance)*, embryo, source
germane applicable, apposite, appropriate, cognate, congruous, correlative, felicitous, interrelated, pertinent, related, relative *(relevant)*, relevant, suitable, tangential. SEE MAIN ENTRY
germanus genuine, real
germicidal preventive
germinal original *(initial)*, prime *(original)*, rudimentary
germinare germinate
germinate develop, pullulate, stem *(originate)*. SEE MAIN ENTRY
germinate from redound
germination development *(progression)*, growth *(evolution)*
germinative rudimentary
gerrymander illude
gestare bear *(support)*
gesture brandish, symbol
get acquire *(secure)*, attain, derive *(receive)*, gain, incur, obtain, possess, procure, raise *(collect)*, reach, realize *(obtain as a profit)*, reap, receive *(acquire)*. SEE MAIN ENTRY
get a fresh start resume
get a glimpse of discover
get a profit earn
get abroad circulate
get across annunciate, convey *(communicate)*. SEE MAIN ENTRY
get ahead compound, proceed *(go forward)*, progress, surpass
get ahead of outbalance, outweigh
get as one's own possess
get at reach
get away elude
get away from evade *(elude)*, part *(leave)*
get away with *(let off)* SEE MAIN ENTRY
get away with *(put over on)*. SEE MAIN ENTRY
get back collect *(recover money)*, reclaim, recoup *(regain)*, recover, redeem *(repurchase)*, retaliate
get back to work proceed *(continue)*
get by pass *(satisfy requirements)*
get by effort attain, earn
get by judgment recover
get control hold *(possess)*

get done attain, cap
get down alight
get even repay, retaliate
get even with discipline *(punish)*, recriminate. SEE MAIN ENTRY
get free break *(separate)*
get going originate
get hold of grapple, obtain
get in exchange buy
get in formation organize *(arrange)*
get in the act participate
get in the way disrupt, hinder, interrupt
get in the way of foil
get in touch convey *(communicate)*
get in touch with reach
get loose break *(separate)*
get money collect *(recover money)*
get near approach
get off alight
get off the subject deviate
get on proceed *(continue)*, proceed *(go forward)*
get on credit borrow
get on the nerves of annoy
get out quit *(evacuate)*
get possession of attain, collect *(recover money)*, gain, hold *(possess)*, obtain
get ready provide *(arrange for)*
get rid of delete, discharge *(dismiss)*, disown *(refuse to acknowledge)*, dispel, eject *(evict)*, eliminate *(eradicate)*, expel, extirpate, jettison, purge *(purify)*, reject, remove *(dismiss from office)*
get temporary use of borrow
get the best of beat *(defeat)*
get the better of beat *(defeat)*, overcome *(surmount)*, overreach, subdue, subject, surmount
get the start on anticipate *(expect)*
get the upper hand overcome *(overwhelm)*, overcome *(surmount)*, prevail *(triumph)*
get through annunciate, cease, pass *(satisfy requirements)*
get through to contact *(communicate)*, reach
get through with cap
get to contact *(communicate)*
get to safety escape
get to the bottom of find *(discover)*
get together congregate, hoard, meet
get under way arise *(occur)*, dispatch *(send off)*, embark
get up originate
get used to inure *(accustom)*, naturalize *(acclimate)*
get worse degenerate, depreciate
get wrong misconstrue, mistake
get-together rendezvous
getting even reprisal
getting less decrease
getting together congregation
ghastly deplorable, heinous, loathsome, lurid, repulsive
ghost phantom
ghostly nonsubstantial *(not sturdy)*
ghostly form phantom
ghoulish sinister
giant prodigious *(enormous)*
gibberish jargon *(unintelligible language)*
gibbet defame, denigrate, denounce *(condemn)*, pillory, sully
gibe disdain, disparage, flout, hector, jeer, mock *(deride)*, plague, ridicule
gibe at jape
giddy capricious, frivolous, thoughtless, volatile

gift appropriation *(donation)*, aptitude, behalf, benefit *(conferment)*, bequest, bonus, bounty, caliber *(mental capacity)*, cession, charity, competence *(ability)*, contribution *(donation)*, donation, endowment, faculty *(ability)*, grant, gratuity *(present)*, inheritance, perquisite, proclivity, propensity, reward, skill, subsidy, tendency, tip *(gratuity)*. SEE MAIN ENTRY
gift by succession estate *(hereditament)*
gift by will legacy
gift of a freehold interest feoffment
gift of property by will legacy
gifted artful, capable, deft, original *(creative)*, practiced, resourceful, sciential
giftedness capacity *(aptitude)*
gigantic capacious, copious, gross *(flagrant)*, prodigious *(enormous)*
gignere engender, generate, propagate *(increase)*
gild camouflage, embellish
gimcrack poor *(inferior in quality)*
gimmick device *(contrivance)*, stratagem. SEE MAIN ENTRY
gingerly meticulous
gird border *(bound)*, circumscribe *(surround by boundary)*, embrace *(encircle)*, enclose, encompass *(surround)*
girdle circumscribe *(surround by boundary)*, embrace *(encircle)*, enclose, enclosure, encompass *(surround)*, hedge, include
girdling blockade *(enclosure)*
girl child
girlishness puerility
girth caliber *(measurement)*, measurement
gist center *(essence)*, connotation, content *(meaning)*, contents, context, essence, gravamen, import, main point, significance, signification, spirit, subject *(topic)*, substance *(essential nature)*, sum *(tally)*, tenor. SEE MAIN ENTRY
gist of a charge gravamen
gite abode
givable heritable
give adduce, administer *(tender)*, allow *(authorize)*, ascribe, attorn, bear *(yield)*, bequeath, bestow, cede, confer *(give)*, contribute *(supply)*, convey *(transfer)*, dedicate, delegate, descend, devise *(give)*, devolve, disburse *(distribute)*, dole, endow, endue, extend *(offer)*, fund, furnish, grant *(concede)*, grant *(transfer formally)*, lend, loan, pander, present *(make a gift)*, proffer, provide *(supply)*, relax, relent, render *(administer)*, render *(deliver)*, replenish, send, spend, subsidize, supply, tender, transmit, yield *(produce a return)*. SEE MAIN ENTRY
give a bad name defame, denigrate, pillory
give a beating lash *(strike)*
give a blow beat *(strike)*
give a color to camouflage
give a detailed explanation explicate
give a directive direct *(order)*, instruct *(direct)*, prescribe
give a false appearance camouflage, pretend
give a false coloring camouflage, cloak, disguise, misrepresent
give a false idea delude, distort, mislead
give a false impression delude, distort, misdirect, misinform, mislead, misstate, profess *(pretend)*
give a false representation misrepresent
give a favorable verdict acquit
give a final notice charge *(assess)*

give a formal hearing to hear *(give a legal hearing)*
give a formal speech declaim
give a grant to subsidize
give a guarantee certify *(attest)*, pledge *(promise the performance of)*
give a guilty verdict convict
give a hand assist
give a hint imply, mention
give a job retain *(employ)*
give a job to employ *(engage services)*, engage *(hire)*, hire
give a judicial hearing to hear *(give a legal hearing)*
give a lesson exposit
give a mandate appoint, delegate, entrust, instruct *(direct)*, invest *(vest)*, prescribe
give a name call *(title)*
give a name to denominate, identify
give a new form to modify *(alter)*
give a performance produce *(offer to view)*
give a permit qualify *(meet standards)*
give a position to employ *(engage services)*
give a post to employ *(engage services)*
give a present bestow
give a prize dedicate
give a promise swear
give a recommendation counsel
give a report inform *(notify)*, relate *(tell)*
give a reprieve clear, condone, free
give a responsibility to delegate, entrust
give a right authorize
give a ruling conclude *(decide)*, determine, pronounce *(pass judgment)*
give a sense to comment
give a signal indicate
give a situation to engage *(hire)*
give a solemn declaration depose *(testify)*
give a speech address *(talk to)*, discourse
give a start expedite
give a strained meaning distort
give a summary of recapitulate
give a talk discourse, speak
give a thrashing beat *(strike)*, lash *(strike)*
give a turn distort
give a verbal account recite
give a vote cast *(register)*
give a warrant qualify *(meet standards)*
give a wide berth eschew
give a wide berth to shun
give a wrong idea misstate
give ability empower, enable
give absolution clear, condone, exonerate, forgive, free, pardon
give absolution to exculpate, excuse
give additional information elaborate
give admittance to instate
give advice admonish *(advise)*, advise, advocate, caution, charge *(instruct on the law)*, confer *(consult)*, counsel, incite
give advice against expostulate
give aid aid, assist, capitalize *(provide capital)*, contribute *(assist)*, nurture, subsidize
give allegiance to obey
give amnesty condone, palliate *(excuse)*, remit *(release from penalty)*
give an account communicate, convey *(communicate)*, depict, describe, detail *(particularize)*, inform *(notify)*, recount, relate *(tell)*
give an account of characterize, depose *(testify)*, report *(disclose)*
give an address discourse

give an answer respond, return *(respond)*
give an appellation to identify
give an approximate value estimate
give an encore copy, repeat *(do again)*
give an estimate evaluate
give an example exemplify
give an explanation elucidate
give an impetus impel, inspire
give an inclination prejudice *(influence)*
give an inkling hint
give an instance exemplify, illustrate
give an interpretation elucidate
give an introduction present *(introduce)*
give an official hearing to hear *(give a legal hearing)*
give an opinion adjudge, advise, conclude *(decide)*, determine, evaluate, find *(determine)*, pass *(determine)*, pronounce *(pass judgment)*, rule *(decide)*
give an order direct *(order)*, instruct *(direct)*, prescribe
give and bequeath devise *(give)*
give and take barter, interchange, quid pro quo, reciprocal, reciprocate, reciprocity. SEE MAIN ENTRY
give approval bestow, consent, pass *(approve)*, sanction
give as a gift present *(make a gift)*
give as a guarantee pledge *(deposit)*
give as an excuse justify
give as example cite *(state)*
give as security pawn
give as security for a debt pledge *(deposit)*
give as security for an obligation pledge *(deposit)*
give as surety pledge *(deposit)*
give assent accede *(concede)*, agree *(comply)*, bestow, certify *(approve)*, coincide *(concur)*, defer *(yield in judgment)*
give assurance agree *(contract)*, avouch *(guarantee)*, close *(agree)*, cosign, guarantee, pledge *(promise the performance of)*, promise *(vow)*, vouch
give attention concern *(care)*, devote, focus
give attention to concentrate *(pay attention)*, note *(notice)*, observe *(watch)*, perceive, specialize
give audience hear *(give attention to)*
give authoritative instructions to instruct *(direct)*
give authority allow *(authorize)*, authorize, empower, enable, grant *(concede)*, invest *(vest)*, vest
give authority to charge *(empower)*, delegate
give away abandon *(relinquish)*, bestow, betray *(disclose)*, cede, contribute *(supply)*, devise *(give)*, disburse *(distribute)*, disperse *(disseminate)*, dole, expose, forfeit, grant *(transfer formally)*, parcel, post, renounce
give away at death bequeath
give back bestow, contribute *(indemnify)*, indemnify, rebate, recommit, recoup *(reimburse)*, reflect *(mirror)*, refund, remise, render *(deliver)*, repay, restore *(return)*, return *(refund)*
give base bear *(support)*
give being to develop
give birth propagate *(increase)*
give birth to conceive *(invent)*, create, make, originate, produce *(manufacture)*, reproduce
give by way of information instruct *(teach)*
give by will bequeath, demise, descend, devise *(give)*, leave *(give)*

give cause for occasion
give cause for alarm disconcert, frighten, perturb
give chase hunt
give clearance bestow, certify *(approve)*, facilitate, grant *(concede)*, permit, release
give close attention scrutinize
give color to disguise
give compensation for defray
give compensation for in advance prepay
give concrete form to embody, exemplify
give confidence reassure
give consent agree *(comply)*, assent, bestow, certify *(approve)*, consent, defer *(yield in judgment)*, grant *(concede)*, permit, suffer *(permit)*
give consent to comply
give control vest
give counsel admonish *(advise)*, advise
give credence to trust
give credit concur *(agree)*, lend, recommend
give credit to trust
give currency promulgate
give currency to circulate
give definite form to embody
give denial to contradict, controvert, dispute *(contest)*
give details detail *(particularize)*
give directions command, direct *(order)*, discipline *(train)*, prescribe
give dispensation bestow, excuse, palliate *(excuse)*
give earnestly dedicate
give employment delegate, employ *(engage services)*
give employment to engage *(hire)*, hire
give entrance receive *(permit to enter)*
give entrance to induct, initiate, instate, penetrate
give equal value compensate *(remunerate)*
give evidence bear *(adduce)*, confess, depose *(testify)*, swear, testify, verify *(confirm)*, vouch, witness *(attest to)*
give expectation promise *(raise expectations)*
give explanation to construe *(translate)*
give expression communicate, enunciate, recite, speak
give expression to depict, express, observe *(remark)*, phrase, utter
give fair warning caution, forewarn, notice *(give formal warning)*
give final notice dun
give force to implement
give form to formalize, formulate
give formal approval to formalize
give formal status to formalize
give forth circulate, develop, emit, post, reflect *(mirror)*, send, utter
give foundation bear *(support)*
give freedom liberate
give freely bestow
give full particulars specify
give good reasons for vindicate
give ground bear *(support)*
give grounds for support *(justify)*
give heed concentrate *(pay attention)*
give heed to attend *(heed)*, care *(be cautious)*, notice *(observe)*, observe *(watch)*, regard *(pay attention)*
give help relieve *(give aid)*, serve *(assist)*
give honor dedicate
give hope assure *(give confidence to)*, promise *(raise expectations)*, reassure

give impetus incite
give impulse to originate
give in accede *(concede)*, concede, defer *(yield in judgment)*, relent, submit *(yield)*, succumb, surrender *(yield)*, vouchsafe, yield *(submit)*
give in charge delegate
give in custody arrest *(apprehend)*
give in earnest pawn
give in exchange barter, change, repay
give in kind recriminate
give in return reciprocate
give in trust confide *(trust)*, consign, delegate
give increase bear *(yield)*
give indication evidence, speak
give indirect information connote, imply
give information advise, apprise, bear *(adduce)*, notice *(give formal warning)*
give inside information reveal
give instructions direct *(order)*, discipline *(train)*
give intimation of impending evil caution, forewarn
give into another's keeping deliver
give judgment adjudicate, arbitrate *(adjudge)*, conclude *(decide)*, decree, determine, find *(determine)*, pronounce *(pass judgment)*, rule *(decide)*
give leave allow *(authorize)*, authorize, bestow, grant *(concede)*, let *(permit)*, permit, suffer *(permit)*
give legal force validate
give legal form to constitute *(establish)*
give legislative sanction enact
give legislative sanction to pass *(approve)*
give lessons educate
give lessons in discipline *(train)*, instruct *(teach)*
give liberty to disenthrall, enfranchise, liberate
give life to generate
give means enable
give measure for measure retaliate
give money bear the expense, disburse *(pay out)*, expend *(disburse)*, fund
give money over lend
give new life to renew *(refurbish)*
give no credence to disbelieve, doubt *(distrust)*, misdoubt
give no credit to disbelieve, misdoubt, mistrust
give no heed disregard
give notice admonish *(advise)*, advise, alert, annunciate, apprise, caution, communicate, convey *(communicate)*, demand, discharge *(dismiss)*, forewarn, inform *(notify)*, mention, notify, predict, remind, resign, retire *(conclude a career)*, signify *(inform)*
give notice of proclaim, promulgate
give notice to serve *(deliver a legal instrument)*
give notification communicate
give occasion for cause
give occupation rent
give off emit, exude
give offense irritate, pique, provoke, repel *(disgust)*
give offense to affront, bait *(harass)*, disoblige, humiliate
give one a talking to browbeat
give one an idea of interpret
give one an impression of interpret
give one his deserts discipline *(punish)*
give one pause discourage

give one to understand advise, communicate
give one's attention concern *(care)*
give one's blessing countenance
give one's hand to bestow
give one's honor promise *(vow)*
give one's signature cosign, pledge *(deposit)*
give one's word bear *(adduce)*, certify *(attest)*, guarantee, pledge *(promise the performance of)*, promise *(vow)*, swear, testify, vouch
give one's word for confirm
give one's word of honor promise *(vow)*
give opportunity for permit
give oral evidence affirm *(declare solemnly)*
give orders command, decree, dictate, direct *(order)*, enjoin, govern, rule *(govern)*, summon
give origin provoke
give origin to avail *(bring about)*, cause, create, make, originate
give out allocate, assign *(allot)*, bestow, circulate, deliver, disburse *(distribute)*, dispense, distribute, divide *(distribute)*, dole, emit, issue *(publish)*, mete, parcel, post, proclaim, publish, reveal
give out again redistribute
give out among a number disperse *(disseminate)*
give out in payment disburse *(pay out)*
give out in shares bestow
give out information inform *(notify)*
give over abandon *(relinquish)*, cease, present *(make a gift)*, relinquish
give over to grant *(transfer formally)*
give over to the foe betray *(lead astray)*, inform *(betray)*
give pain aggravate *(annoy)*, harrow, inflict, mistreat
give payment pay, remunerate
give permission allow *(authorize)*, authorize, bestow, certify *(approve)*, consent, empower, enable, grant *(concede)*, let *(permit)*, permit, sanction, suffer *(permit)*
give place to succeed *(follow)*
give play to the imagination conjure
give political privileges to enfranchise
give power authorize, bestow, delegate, empower, enable, invest *(vest)*, permit
give power of attorney delegate
give power to charge *(empower)*
give precise meaning to characterize
give previous notice to forewarn
give previous warning to forewarn
give proof depose *(testify)*
give proof by a witness depose *(testify)*
give public notice of issue *(publish)*, post, publish
give publicity to promulgate
give quarter relent
give reason for enlighten, explain, exposit
give references document
give refuge harbor
give relief mitigate, mollify, relieve *(give aid)*, soothe
give repose ease
give rest ease
give right empower
give right of entry to admit *(give access)*
give rise provoke
give rise to avail *(bring about)*, cause, compose, create, develop, engender, establish *(launch)*, evoke, generate, make, originate, produce *(manufacture)*

give salvation save *(rescue)*
give satisfaction indemnify, redeem *(satisfy debts)*
give satisfaction for damage compensate *(remunerate)*
give satisfaction for injury compensate *(remunerate)*
give security assure *(insure)*, bond *(secure a debt)*, confirm, ensure, pledge *(deposit)*, promise *(vow)*
give sense to construe *(translate)*
give shape to form
give sign signify *(inform)*
give strength to compound
give suggestions advise
give suggestions to charge *(instruct on the law)*, counsel
give support adhere *(maintain loyalty)*, aid, assist, bear *(support)*, capitalize *(provide capital)*, preserve
give support to subsidize
give surety ensure
give sworn evidence affirm *(declare solemnly)*
give sworn testimony depose *(testify)*
give tangible form to embody
give terms dicker
give testimony witness *(attest to)*
give the cold shoulder ignore
give the death blow dispatch *(put to death)*
give the details of characterize, delineate
give the effect appear *(seem to be)*
give the facts communicate, inform *(notify)*, notify, recount, report *(disclose)*
give the floor to recognize *(acknowledge)*
give the impression appear *(seem to be)*
give the meaning define
give the mind to focus
give the nod to recognize *(acknowledge)*
give the particulars recount
give the right to vote enfranchise
give the signal instruct *(direct)*
give the sum and substance abridge *(shorten)*
give the word instruct *(direct)*
give the word of command instruct *(direct)*
give thought to ponder, reflect *(ponder)*
give tidings herald, inform *(notify)*
give title to denominate, sell
give to delegate
give to the world circulate
give to understand disabuse, instruct *(teach)*, notify
give token portend
give tongue communicate
give tongue to observe *(remark)*, phrase
give trouble balk, inconvenience
give twist distort
give umbrage pique
give umbrage to bait *(harass)*
give up abandon *(relinquish)*, bestow, cede, demit, disclaim, discontinue *(abandon)*, disown *(refuse to acknowledge)*, forfeit, forgo, forswear, leave *(allow to remain)*, quit *(discontinue)*, release, relinquish, remise, remit *(relax)*, renounce, resign, submit *(yield)*, waive, yield *(submit)*
give up claim to abandon *(relinquish)*, cede, forfeit, forgo, relinquish, renounce, waive
give up office retire *(conclude a career)*
give up the argument forfeit
give up the point forfeit
give up the right to forgo

give up treacherously betray *(lead astray)*
give up work retire *(conclude a career)*
give utterance communicate, enunciate, mention, phrase, remark
give utterance to betray *(disclose)*, disclose, observe *(remark)*
give validity to implement
give variety vary
give vent to express
give verbal evidence affirm *(declare solemnly)*
give voice communicate, speak
give voice to express, observe *(remark)*, phrase
give warning admonish *(warn)*, advise, caution, notice *(give formal warning)*, notify
give warning of possible harm caution, forewarn
give way defer *(yield in judgment)*, hear *(give attention to)*, obey, relent, retreat, split, succumb, yield *(submit)*
give way to submit *(yield)*
give witness bear *(adduce)*
give word for word quote
give words to phrase, portray, speak
give work to employ *(engage services)*, hire
given assumed *(inferred)*, free *(at no charge)*, gratuitous *(given without recompense)*, prone, ready *(willing)*, unpaid
given away donative, free *(at no charge)*, gratuitous *(given without recompense)*
given by testament testamentary
given due consideration deliberate
given name call *(title)*
given over addicted
given preference preferred *(given priority)*
given to accustomed *(familiarized)*
given to controversy argumentative
given to deceit false *(not genuine)*
given to disputation litigious
given to fighting pugnacious
given to joking jocular
given to lying mendacious
given to research inquisitive
given to suspicion inconvincible
given to thought pensive
given to vice vicious
given up derelict *(abandoned)*, irretrievable
giver benefactor, donor, feoffor, good samaritan, grantor, supplier
giver of evidence eyewitness
giving charitable *(benevolent)*, concession *(authorization)*, dedication, disposition *(transfer of property)*, donative, philanthropic, sequacious
giving back reimbursement, restitution
giving beforehand advance *(allowance)*
giving each his due equitable
giving in concession *(compromise)*
giving over delegation *(assignment)*
giving up bailment, cession, renunciation, resignation *(relinquishment)*, waiver
giving up claim to cession
giving way capitulation
glad ecstatic, inclined, ready *(willing)*
gladly readily
glamor prestige
glamorize embellish
glamorous attractive
glance vision *(dream)*. SEE MAIN ENTRY
glance at notice *(observe)*
glance off deviate
glance over peruse

glare pretense *(ostentation)*
glaring blatant *(obtrusive)*, clear *(apparent)*, distinct *(clear)*, egregious, evident, flagrant, gross *(flagrant)*, manifest, notorious, obvious, open *(in sight)*, outrageous, overt, palpable, patent, perceivable, perceptible, prominent, salient, stark, tawdry, unmistakable. SEE MAIN ENTRY
glaringly bad arrant *(onerous)*
glaringly vivid lurid
glean acquire *(receive)*, compile, construe *(comprehend)*, cull, derive *(receive)*, extract, gain, infer, procure, read, reap, select, understand. SEE MAIN ENTRY
glean information peruse
glean knowledge of overhear
gleaning acquisition
gleeful jocular
gleesome jocular
glib loquacious, voluble
glimmer suggestion
glimpse find *(discover)*, pierce *(discern)*, spy, vision *(dream)*
gliscere increase
glitter pretense *(ostentation)*
glittering tawdry
gloat over relish
global complete *(all-embracing)*, nonsectarian, prevailing *(current)*, prevalent, total. SEE MAIN ENTRY
globe sphere
globoid sphere
globular mass sphere
glomerate composite, conglomerate
glomeration agglomeration, conglomeration, cumulation
gloom damper *(depressant)*, depression, indistinctness, obscuration, pessimism. SEE MAIN ENTRY
gloominess obscuration, pessimism
gloomy bleak *(not favorable)*, bleak *(severely simple)*, despondent, disconsolate, lugubrious, ominous, pessimistic, portentous *(ominous)*, solemn
gloomy outlook pessimism
gloria prestige
glorification doxology, homage, honor *(outward respect)*, laudation, mention *(tribute)*, remembrance *(commemoration)*
glorified famous
glorify belaud, compound, elevate, honor, magnify, overestimate, raise *(advance)*, recommend, regard *(hold in esteem)*. SEE MAIN ENTRY
gloriosus pretentious *(pompous)*
glorious famous, illustrious, meritorious. SEE MAIN ENTRY
glory eminence, honor *(outward respect)*, prestige, reputation
gloss color *(deceptive appearance)*, comment *(noun)*, comment *(verb)*, distortion, note *(brief comment)*
gloss over cloak, discount *(disbelieve)*, neglect, pretermit, prevaricate
glow passion
glowing moving *(evoking emotion)*, vehement
glue adhere *(fasten)*, bond *(hold together)*, cement, combine *(join together)*, join *(bring together)*, lock
glued inseparable
glum disconsolate, lugubrious, pessimistic
glumness damper *(depressant)*, pessimism
glut inundate, overage, overcome *(overwhelm)*, overload, plethora, sufficiency, surfeit, surplus

glutinosity   adhesion *(affixing)*
glutinous   cohesive *(sticking)*
glutted   full
gluttonous   inordinate, insatiable, lecherous. SEE MAIN ENTRY
gluttonous appetite   greed
gluttony   greed
gnarus   familiar *(informed)*
gnaw   obsess, pique
gnomic   compact *(pithy)*, pithy, sententious
gnomic saying   maxim
gnomical   compact *(pithy)*
gnostic   profound *(esoteric)*
go   expire, leave *(depart)*, move *(alter position)*, part *(leave)*, pass *(advance)*, perish, proceed *(go forward)*, quit *(evacuate)*. SEE MAIN ENTRY
go about   discharge *(perform)*, occupy *(engage)*
go about stealthily   prowl
go across   cross *(intersect)*, traverse
go adrift   deviate
go after   attempt, chase, hunt, prosecute *(carry forward)*, pursue *(chase)*, strive, succeed *(follow)*
go against   antagonize, confront *(oppose)*, contradict, contravene, counter, counteract, disapprove *(reject)*, oppose, oppugn
go ahead   proceed *(go forward)*, progress. SEE MAIN ENTRY
go ahead of   precede
go all out for   attempt
go along with   attend *(accompany)*, authorize, coincide *(concur)*, comply, concur *(agree)*, conform, cooperate, countenance, defer *(yield in judgment)*, participate, sanction. SEE MAIN ENTRY
go amiss   deviate, err, miscalculate, mistake
go apart   disband
go around   detour, envelop, perambulate
go astray   deviate, digress, err, lapse *(fall into error)*, miscalculate, mistake, trespass
go away   leave *(depart)*, move *(alter position)*, part *(leave)*, quit *(evacuate)*, retreat, vacate *(leave)*
go awry   deviate, lapse *(fall into error)*, miscalculate
go back   escheat, recollect, regress, retire *(retreat)*, retreat
go back on   abandon *(relinquish)*
go back on a commitment   renege
go back on a promise   renege
go back on one's word   bear false witness
go back over   reexamine
go back to   continue *(resume)*
go bad   degenerate, spoil *(impair)*
go before   antecede, precede
go between   SEE MAIN ENTRY
go beyond   outweigh, overlap, overstep, predominate *(outnumber)*, surmount, surpass, transcend
go by   pass *(advance)*
go contrary to   collide *(clash)*, conflict, contradict, counter, except *(object)*, oppose, protest
go counter to   contradict, countervail, disobey
go deep into   delve
go different ways   disband, disperse *(scatter)*
go down   succumb
go down in defeat   lose *(undergo defeat)*
go downhill   decrease
go for a walk   perambulate

go forth   circulate, leave *(depart)*, move *(alter position)*, part *(leave)*, proceed *(go forward)*, quit *(evacuate)*
go forward   persevere, persist, progress
go from home   move *(alter position)*
go in advance   precede
go in different directions   diffuse, disperse *(scatter)*
go in for   pursue *(carry on)*, undertake
go in front of   precede
go in many directions   diffuse
go in opposition to   collide *(clash)*, conflict, contradict, counter, counteract
go in pursuit of   chase, delve, hunt, pursue *(chase)*
go in quest of   chase, research
go in search of   delve, hunt
go into   deliberate, embark, enter *(go in)*, investigate
go into a decline   languish
go into detail   develop, elaborate, expand, quote, specify
go into litigation   litigate
go into partnership   cooperate, federalize *(associate)*
go into retirement   demit, quit *(discontinue)*
go into the particulars   detail *(particularize)*
go near   approach
go next   succeed *(follow)*
go off on a tangent   deviate
go on   continue *(persevere)*, endure *(last)*, exist, keep *(continue)*, maintain *(carry on)*, move *(alter position)*, pass *(advance)*, persevere, persist, progress, remain *(continue)*, resume, subsist
go on a spree   carouse
go on an outing   perambulate
go on foot   perambulate
go one better   surpass
go one's way   move *(alter position)*
go out   quit *(evacuate)*
go out of   emanate
go out of business   fail *(lose)*, quit *(discontinue)*
go out of one's way   detour, deviate
go out of the path   detour
go out of the way   detour
go over   check *(inspect)*, examine *(study)*, overstep, peruse, reaffirm, recapitulate, reconsider, reiterate, review, trace *(delineate)*
go past   pass *(advance)*
go round about   detour, deviate
go separate ways   disband, disperse *(scatter)*
go the rounds   patrol
go through   bear *(tolerate)*, delve, endure *(suffer)*, penetrate, permeate, pervade, search, spend
go through phases   change
go through the books   audit
go through the motions   fake
go through with   commit *(perpetrate)*, discharge *(perform)*, follow-up
go to   attend *(be present at)*
go to any lengths   adhere *(persist)*
go to contract   close *(agree)*. SEE MAIN ENTRY
go to pieces   degenerate
go to press   publish
go to the limit   adhere *(persist)*
go to the polls   cast *(register)*
go to war   fight *(battle)*
go too far   overextend, overstep
go under   fail *(lose)*, succumb
go undercover   cloak

go up against   SEE MAIN ENTRY
go with   coincide *(correspond)*
go without   relinquish, renounce
go wrong   deviate, err, mistake
go-between   agent, broker, conduit *(intermediary)*, interagent, intermediary, liaison, medium, procurator, representative *(proxy)*, spokesman, umpire
goad   abet, agitate *(activate)*, badger, bait *(harass)*, bait *(lure)*, browbeat, catalyst, constrain *(compel)*, discompose, exhort, foment, harass, hector, impetus, incentive, incite, inducement, motivate, pique, pressure, prompt, provocation, stimulate, stimulus, urge. SEE MAIN ENTRY
goading   instigation
goal   cause *(reason)*, contemplation, desideratum, design *(intent)*, destination, end *(intent)*, focus, intention, mission, motive, object, objective, point *(purpose)*, predetermination, project, purpose, reason *(basis)*, target. SEE MAIN ENTRY
goatish   lascivious, lecherous, salacious
god-forsaken   diabolic
godless   profane
godlike   omnipotent, omniscient
godly   sacrosanct
going before in time   antecedent
going contrary to   dissenting
going down   descent *(declination)*
going on   open-ended, present *(current)*
going over   restatement
going to the utmost lengths   extreme *(exaggerated)*
going too far   extreme *(exaggerated)*
golden   propitious
gone   defunct, irredeemable, irretrievable, lifeless *(dead)*, lost *(taken away)*, null *(invalid)*. SEE MAIN ENTRY
gone by   outdated
gone out   outdated, outmoded
gone out of existence   defunct
gone to waste   irredeemable, lost *(taken away)*
good   advantage, appropriate, auspicious, behalf, benefit *(betterment)*, clean, competent, ethical, favorable *(advantageous)*, item, meritorious, moral, palatable, preferable, proficient, salutary, sapid, savory, select, sterling, upright, valid, valuable, welfare. SEE MAIN ENTRY
good actions   merit, right *(righteousness)*
good and effectual in law   legal
good at   deft
good behavior   courtesy, merit, propriety *(correctness)*, protocol *(etiquette)*, right *(righteousness)*
good breeding   courtesy, propriety *(correctness)*
good cause shown   SEE MAIN ENTRY
good chance   likelihood, opportunity, prospect *(outlook)*
good conduct   ethics
good deed   benevolence *(act of kindness)*, favor *(act of kindness)*
good disposition   benevolence *(disposition to do good)*
good enough   fair *(satisfactory)*, mediocre
good example   exemplar, paragon
good excuse   justification
good faith   fidelity, integrity, loyalty, probity. SEE MAIN ENTRY
good for nothing   ineffective, ineffectual
good for one's advantage   beneficial
good form   decorum, protocol *(etiquette)*
good fortune   boom *(prosperity)*, chance *(fortuity)*, opportunity, prosperity

good intention benevolence *(disposition to do good)*

good judgment caliber *(mental capacity)*, common sense, sagacity, sense *(intelligence)*

good luck prosperity

good management austerity, economy *(frugality)*

good manners consideration *(sympathetic regard)*, courtesy, decorum, propriety *(correctness)*, protocol *(etiquette)*, respect

good men and true array *(jury)*

good name credit *(recognition)*, goodwill, honor *(good reputation)*, regard *(esteem)*, reputation

good nature benevolence *(disposition to do good)*, goodwill, philanthropy

good neighbor samaritan

good notice adequate notice

good offices patronage *(power to appoint jobs)*

good opinion estimation *(esteem)*, favor *(sanction)*, honor *(good reputation)*, recommendation

good order array *(order)*

good prospect likelihood

good reputation estimation *(esteem)*, goodwill

good repute prestige

Good Samaritan benefactor, donor. SEE MAIN ENTRY

good sense common sense, discretion *(quality of being discreet)*, discrimination *(good judgment)*, reason *(sound judgment)*

good service favor *(act of kindness)*

good standing estimation *(esteem)*. SEE MAIN ENTRY

good taste decorum

good times prosperity

good to eat palatable

good treatment benevolence *(act of kindness)*

good turn benefit *(conferment)*, benevolence *(act of kindness)*, favor *(act of kindness)*, help

good understanding agreement *(concurrence)*

good will affinity *(regard)*, benevolence *(disposition to do good)*, charity, clemency, comity, humanity *(humaneness)*, peace, philanthropy, respect, tolerance, understanding *(tolerance)*. SEE MAIN ENTRY

good works philanthropy

good-fellowship comity

good-hearted philanthropic

good-heartedness philanthropy

good-humored benevolent, obeisant

good-natured benevolent, obeisant, philanthropic

good-quality meritorious

good-tasting palatable, sapid, savory

good-tempered peaceable

goodly major

goodness benevolence *(disposition to do good)*, decorum, ethics, good faith, honor *(good reputation)*, integrity, merit, principle *(virtue)*, probity, quality *(excellence)*, rectitude, right *(righteousness)*

goodness and mercy benevolence *(disposition to do good)*

goods assets, cargo, commodities, effects, estate *(property)*, freight, merchandise, movable, paraphernalia *(personal belongings)*, possession *(property)*, possessions, property *(possessions)*, stock in trade. SEE MAIN ENTRY

goods exported illegally contraband

goods for sale merchandise

goods imported illegally contraband

goods shipped consignment

goods subject to confiscation contraband

goods subject to seizure contraband

gore enter *(penetrate)*, lancinate, penetrate, pierce *(lance)*

gorge overload

gorged full, replete

gorgeous elegant

gospel doctrine, principle *(axiom)*

gossip hearsay, report *(rumor)*

gossipy informatory

govern administer *(conduct)*, command, control *(regulate)*, curb, direct *(order)*, direct *(supervise)*, discipline *(control)*, dominate, handle *(manage)*, inhibit, manage, manipulate *(utilize skillfully)*, moderate *(preside over)*, officiate, operate, overlook *(superintend)*, predominate *(command)*, preside, prevail *(be in force)*, qualify *(condition)*, regulate *(manage)*, restrain, subject, subjugate, superintend, wield. SEE MAIN ENTRY

govern badly misgovern

govern strictly discipline *(control)*

governable corrigible, malleable, obedient, pliable, sequacious, tractable

governance agency *(legal relationship)*, authority *(power)*, bureaucracy, dominance, government *(administration)*, hegemony, influence, management *(supervision)*, politics, regime, supremacy. SEE MAIN ENTRY

governed arrested *(checked)*

governed by inferior *(lower in position)*

governed by law legal

governing dominant, influential, master, predominant, prevailing *(having superior force)*, sovereign *(absolute)*

governing body board, management *(directorate)*

governing course of action policy *(plan of action)*, practice *(procedure)*

governing factors circumstances

governing plan policy *(plan of action)*, practice *(procedure)*

governing principle policy *(plan of action)*. SEE MAIN ENTRY

government authorities, bureaucracy, civic, control *(supervision)*, dominion *(supreme authority)*, hierarchy *(persons in authority)*, management *(directorate)*, national, politics, public *(affecting people)*, regime, regulation *(management)*, supervision. SEE MAIN ENTRY

government appropriation of private land expropriation *(right of eminent domain)*

government attorney prosecutor

government by bureaus bureaucracy

government notes currency

government office bureaucracy

government officers police

government paper bond

government servant caretaker *(one fulfilling the function of office)*

government-owned national

governmental civic, civil *(public)*, federal, national, political, public *(affecting people)*

governmental body congress

governmental control censorship

governmental grant patent

governmental leader politician

governmental order of prohibition embargo

governmental procedure bureaucracy

governmental system for decision-making bureaucracy

governmental unit state *(political unit)*

governor caretaker *(one caring for property)*, director, pedagogue, principal *(director)*, superintendent. SEE MAIN ENTRY

governorship direction *(guidance)*

grab obtain, prey, spoils

grace absolution, amenity, amnesty, charity, clemency, condonation, consent, decorum, dispensation *(exception)*, embellish, facility *(easiness)*, favor *(act of kindness)*, franchise *(license)*, leave *(permission)*, lenience, permission, proportion, propriety *(correctness)*, remission, respite *(reprieve)*. SEE MAIN ENTRY

grace period SEE MAIN ENTRY

graceful diplomatic, elegant, eloquent

gracefulness facility *(easiness)*

graceless dissolute, immoral, inelegant, pedestrian, unbecoming, uncouth

gracious benevolent, charitable *(benevolent)*, charitable *(lenient)*, civil *(polite)*, favorable *(expressing approval)*, meritorious, obeisant, philanthropic, placable, propitious, receptive

graciously readily

graciousness benevolence *(disposition to do good)*, comity, consideration *(sympathetic regard)*, courtesy, largess *(generosity)*, philanthropy

gradation array *(order)*, chain *(series)*, class, classification, degree *(station)*, differential, distribution *(arrangement)*, hierarchy *(arrangement in a series)*, order *(arrangement)*, sequence, step. SEE MAIN ENTRY

grade caliber *(measurement)*, caliber *(quality)*, class, classify, condition *(state)*, degree *(station)*, differential, file *(arrange)*, fix *(arrange)*, measure, organize *(arrange)*, pigeonhole, quality *(excellence)*, rate, rating, screen *(select)*, sort, state *(condition)*, status, step, tabulate. SEE MAIN ENTRY

grade A premium

grade of excellence standard

grading rating

gradual deliberate. SEE MAIN ENTRY

gradual crumbling decline

gradual decline deterioration

gradual eating away erosion

gradual evolution development *(progression)*

gradual impairment decline, deterioration

gradual wearing away erosion

gradually piecemeal

gradually eat away erode

graduate file *(arrange)*, fix *(arrange)*, measure, prefer, promote *(advance)*, sort, subdivide, tabulate

graduation differential, distribution *(arrangement)*, promotion *(advancement)*, transition

graduation certificate degree *(academic title)*

gradus degree *(station)*

gradus amplior advancement *(improvement)*

graft bribe, connect *(join together)*, corruption, crime, gratuity *(bribe)*, hush money, improbity, spoils. SEE MAIN ENTRY

grafter criminal

grain character *(personal quality)*, disposition *(inclination)*, frame *(mood)*, iota, modicum, scintilla

grand elegant, illustrious, important *(significant)*, momentous, orgulous, paramount, prodigious *(enormous)*, proud *(self-respecting)*, stellar. SEE MAIN ENTRY

grand jury's accusation indictment
grand larceny SEE MAIN ENTRY
grand total corpus
grand vizier caretaker *(one fulfilling the function of office)*
grandchild child
grandeur character *(reputation)*, distinction *(reputation)*, eminence, importance, prestige
grandiloquence bombast, declamation, peroration, rhetoric *(insincere language)*. SEE MAIN ENTRY
grandiloquent flatulent, fustian, grandiose, inflated *(bombastic)*, orotund, pretentious *(pompous)*, sesquipedalian, turgid
grandiose elaborate, fustian, inflated *(vain)*, orgulous, orotund, pretentious *(pompous)*. SEE MAIN ENTRY
grandiosity bombast, pretense *(ostentation)*, rhetoric *(insincere language)*
grandsire ancestor, primogenitor
grant abalienate, accede *(concede)*, acquiescence, admit *(concede)*, alimony, allocate, allow *(authorize)*, appropriation *(donation)*, assign *(transfer ownership)*, assignment *(transfer of ownership)*, attorn, authorize, award, bear *(yield)*, bequeath, bestow, bounty, brevet, cede, cession, charge *(empower)*, charity, charter *(license)*, charter *(sanction)*, concede, concession *(authorization)*, concession *(compromise)*, condescend *(deign)*, confer *(give)*, consent *(noun)*, consent *(verb)*, contribute *(supply)*, contribution *(donation)*, convey *(transfer)*, copyright, deign, descend, devise *(give)*, devolve, dispensation *(exception)*, dispense, dole, donation, empower, enable, endow, endowment, endue, enfranchise, franchise *(license)*, fund, furnish, gift *(present)*, gratuity *(present)*, indulgence, largess *(gift)*, lease, leave *(permission)*, leave *(give)*, legacy, lend, let *(lease)*, let *(permit)*, liberty, license, loan, option *(contractual provision)*, parcel, patent, patronize *(condescend toward)*, pay, pension, permit, prerogative, present *(make a gift)*, privilege, provide *(supply)*, recognize *(acknowledge)*, remise, reveal, reward, sanction *(permission)*, sanction, subsidy, suffer *(permit)*, supply, tender, transfer, vouchsafe, yield *(submit)*. SEE MAIN ENTRY
grant a boon bestow
grant a demise sublease
grant a lease rent, sublease
grant a reprieve clear, exonerate, free
grant a request bestow
grant absolution palliate *(excuse)*, purge *(wipe out by atonement)*
grant again recover
grant amnesty clear, condone, exonerate, forgive, free, palliate *(excuse)*, pardon
grant amnesty to excuse, quit *(free of)*
grant asylum harbor, receive *(permit to enter)*
grant authority empower, invest *(vest)*
grant authority to commit *(entrust)*. SEE MAIN ENTRY
grant by favor vouchsafe
grant by will demise
grant claims authorize
grant clemency pardon
grant exclusive possession for a designated period lease
grant exemption palliate *(excuse)*
grant favors to favor, prefer
grant for support pension
grant forgiveness pardon
grant immunity condone, palliate *(excuse)*

grant in aid pension
grant monetary compensation indemnify
grant of a share contribution *(donation)*
grant of authority patent
grant of realty lease
grant of rights SEE MAIN ENTRY
grant of use and possession lease
grant pardon forgive, free
grant permission allow *(authorize)*, authorize, bestow, permit, suffer *(permit)*
grant power empower, invest *(vest)*
grant remission acquit, clear, pardon
grant the occupancy of let *(lease)*
grant use and possession lease
grant-in-aid subsidy
grantable assignable, plausible, possible
granted allowable, allowed, assumed *(inferred)*, consensual, definite, permissible
granted amnesty immune
granted on certain terms conditional, dependent
grantee assignee, bearer, beneficiary, devisee, donee, feoffee, legatee, payee, receiver, recipient, successor, transferee. SEE MAIN ENTRY
granter contributor *(giver)*
granting concession *(compromise)*, donative, permissive
granting freedom parole
grantor contributor *(giver)*, donor, feoffor, obligee, transferor. SEE MAIN ENTRY
grapevine report *(rumor)*
graph delineation, design *(construction plan)*, measure
graphic clear *(apparent)*, coherent *(clear)*, comprehensible, demonstrative *(illustrative)*, descriptive, detailed, distinct *(clear)*, holographic, lurid, narrative, realistic, representative, suggestive *(evocative)*. SEE MAIN ENTRY
graphic account recital
graphic treatment caricature
graphical comprehensible, representative, suggestive *(evocative)*
grapple lock. SEE MAIN ENTRY
grapple with contest, fight *(battle)*, repulse
grasp apprehension *(perception)*, cognition, cohere *(adhere)*, competence *(ability)*, comprehend *(understand)*, comprehension, conceive *(comprehend)*, coverage *(scope)*, digest *(comprehend)*, gain, grapple, hold *(possess)*, information *(knowledge)*, judgment *(discernment)*, jurisdiction, knowledge *(awareness)*, perception, pierce *(discern)*, read, realize *(understand)*, retain *(keep in possession)*, retention, seize *(confiscate)*, sense *(intelligence)*, understand, understanding *(comprehension)*. SEE MAIN ENTRY
grasp mentally construe *(comprehend)*
grasping illiberal, insatiable, mercenary, parsimonious, rapacious, venal
grass cannabis
grass-roots SEE MAIN ENTRY
grate annoy, badger, bait *(harass)*, irritate, plague, provoke, repel *(disgust)*
gratia patronage *(power to appoint jobs)*
gratification benefit *(betterment)*, bounty, enjoyment *(pleasure)*, fruition, indulgence, satisfaction *(fulfilment)*. SEE MAIN ENTRY
gratification of desire indulgence
gratified complacent, proud *(self-respecting)*
gratify accommodate, bestow, consent, favor, grant *(concede)*, pander, sanction, satisfy *(fulfill)*, vouchsafe

gratify to excess overindulge
gratifying desirable *(pleasing)*, palatable, sapid
gratiis gratis
grating harsh, provocative
gratis free *(at no charge)*, gratuitous *(given without recompense)*, unpaid. SEE MAIN ENTRY
gratitude recognition SEE MAIN ENTRY
gratuito gratis
gratuitous baseless, donative, elective *(voluntary)*, expendable, free *(at no charge)*, impertinent *(irrelevant)*, inappropriate, irrelevant, needless, nonessential, unnecessary, unpaid, unsolicited, willing *(uncompelled)*. SEE MAIN ENTRY
gratuitous remark dictum
gratuitous worker volunteer
gratuitus free *(at no charge)*, gratuitous *(unwarranted)*
gratuity benefit *(conferment)*, bonus, bounty, consideration *(recompense)*, contribution *(donation)*, dedication, donation, gift *(present)*, grant, honorarium, hush money, largess *(gift)*, payment *(remittance)*, perquisite, recompense, reward. SEE MAIN ENTRY
gravamen center *(essence)*, content *(meaning)*, cornerstone, gist *(ground for a suit)*, impugnation, main point. SEE MAIN ENTRY
gravamen of a charge complaint, gist *(ground for a suit)*
gravamen of the complaint gist *(ground for a suit)*
grave bleak *(not favorable)*, critical *(crucial)*, crucial, deadly, dire, earnest, exigent, gross *(flagrant)*, important *(significant)*, lamentable, major, momentous, solemn, urgent. SEE MAIN ENTRY
grave consequence SEE MAIN ENTRY
grave culpability impeachability
grave injustice ground, misjudgment
graveness solemnity
gravis compelling, considerable, earnest, grave *(important)*, important *(significant)*, influential, insalubrious, irksome, offensive *(offending)*, onerous, peccant *(unhealthy)*, ponderous, serious *(grave)*, solemn, substantial, urgent, valid, virulent
gravitas severity, solemnity, validity
gravitate SEE MAIN ENTRY
gravitate toward border *(approach)*
gravitation penchant, proclivity, tendency
gravity draw *(attraction)*, import, importance, interest *(concern)*, magnitude, materiality *(consequence)*, severity, significance, solemnity. SEE MAIN ENTRY
gray area SEE MAIN ENTRY
grayness indistinctness
graze contact *(touch)*
graze against jostle *(bump into)*
great capacious, compelling, consequential *(substantial)*, considerable, copious, extensive, far reaching, gross *(flagrant)*, illustrious, ineffable, inordinate, magnanimous, major, master, meritorious, momentous, outstanding *(prominent)*, paramount, portentous *(eliciting amazement)*, powerful, prodigious *(enormous)*, profound *(intense)*, remarkable, renowned, serious *(grave)*, substantial. SEE MAIN ENTRY
great fear panic
great feeling emotion
great misfortune catastrophe, disaster
great mishap disaster

great number plurality
great person paragon
great point gist *(ground for a suit)*
great quantity boom *(prosperity)*, plethora, store *(depository)*
great span of life longevity
great station eminence
greaten accrue *(increase)*, accumulate *(enlarge)*, compound, expand, heighten *(augment)*, increase
greater best, superior *(excellent)*, superior *(higher)*
greater number majority *(greater part)*
greater part body *(main part)*, generality *(bulk)*
greatest cardinal *(outstanding)*, leading *(ranking first)*, maximum *(amplitude)*, paramount, primary, prime *(most valuable)*, superlative, utmost
greatest amount cap, capacity *(maximum)*, utmost
greatest degree utmost
greatest extent capacity *(maximum)*
greatest number generality *(bulk)*
greatest part bulk
greatest possible cardinal *(outstanding)*, ultimate
greatest size capacity *(maximum)*
greathearted charitable *(benevolent)*, meritorious
greatness degree *(magnitude)*, dint, distinction *(reputation)*, eminence, importance, mass *(weight)*, materiality *(consequence)*, measurement, merit, prestige, primacy, significance
greed SEE MAIN ENTRY
greediness greed
greedy exorbitant, gluttonous, illiberal, insatiable, jealous, mercenary, penurious, predatory, rapacious, venal
green credulous, inexperienced, naive, premature, puerile, unaccustomed
greenback money
greenness ignorance, nescience
greet recognize *(acknowledge)*
greet with skepticism doubt *(distrust)*
grenade bomb
grew accrued
grex band, company *(enterprise)*
grief pain, plaint, remorse. SEE MAIN ENTRY
grief-stricken disconsolate
grievance aggravation *(annoyance)*, complaint, criticism, damage, dissatisfaction, exception *(objection)*, gravamen, impugnation, nuisance, objection, outcry, provocation, trouble, wrong. SEE MAIN ENTRY
grieve affront, annoy, brood, discommode, distress, harass, languish, perturb, repent. SEE MAIN ENTRY
grieve at regret
grieve for deplore
grieve with sympathize
grieved aggrieved *(harmed)*, disconsolate, pessimistic
grieving disconsolate, lugubrious, plaint
grievous arrant *(onerous)*, deplorable, detrimental, dire, disastrous, gross *(flagrant)*, lamentable, oppressive, painful, regrettable, severe. SEE MAIN ENTRY
grievous harm calamity
grievous price toll *(effect)*
grievous trouble pain
grill cross-examine
grilling cross-examination, interrogation
grim bleak *(not favorable)*, bleak *(severely simple)*, brutal, dire, disastrous, grave *(solemn)*, harsh, malevolent, ominous,

portentous *(ominous)*, repulsive, ruthless, serious *(grave)*, severe, solemn
grime pollute, stain
grimness severity
grimy sordid
grind erode, ill use, struggle, work *(effort)*
grinding erosion, onerous, operose, oppressive, tyrannous
grip dominion *(supreme authority)*, grapple, immerse *(engross)*, interest, monopolize, tenacity
gripe discompose
griper malcontent
gripping moving *(evoking emotion)*
grisly repulsive
grit prowess *(bravery)*, sinew, tenacity, will *(desire)*
gritty steadfast, undaunted
groan deplore, plaint
groom discipline *(train)*
groomed ready *(prepared)*
grooming discipline *(training)*
grope for hunt
groping blind *(sightless)*, hesitant, tentative
gross aggregate, blatant *(obtrusive)*, brutal, depraved, entirety, excessive, exorbitant, extreme *(exaggerated)*, flagrant, heinous, improper, inelegant, iniquitous, lurid, manifest, nefarious, objectionable, obnoxious, outrageous, repulsive, salacious, scurrilous, stark, total, totality, uncouth, unseemly, whole *(undamaged)*. SEE MAIN ENTRY
gross amount aggregate, corpus, entirety, principal *(capital sum)*, sum *(total)*, whole
gross injustice misjudgment
gross offense atrocity, felony
gross offense against law crime
gross profit proceeds
gross return income
gross revenues SEE MAIN ENTRY
gross wrong ground
grossly inadequate representation understatement
grossly offensive outrageous
grossness bestiality, brutality, debauchery
grotesque odious, prodigious *(amazing)*
grotesque portrayal caricature
grotesque rendition caricature
grouchy fractious, petulant, querulous, resentful
ground assumption *(supposition)*, basis, cause *(reason)*, cause of action, contention *(argument)*, derivation, fix *(make firm)*, gist *(ground for a suit)*, instill, parcel, plant *(place firmly)*, plot *(land)*, point *(item)*, position *(situation)*, property *(land)*, rationale, real estate, reason *(basis)*. SEE MAIN ENTRY
ground for believing presumption
ground for excusing justification
ground gained headway
ground of argument discrepancy
ground of proof evidence
ground oneself alight
ground plan arrangement *(plan)*, blueprint
ground rules criterion
grounded stable
grounded on based on
groundless arbitrary and capricious, baseless, erroneous, fallacious, false *(inaccurate)*, gratuitous *(unwarranted)*, ill-founded, illogical, immaterial, inaccurate, insubstantial, needless, sophistic, unfounded, unjustifiable, unreasonable, unsound *(falla-*

cious), unsupported, unsustainable, untenable, untrue, unwarranted, wanton. SEE MAIN ENTRY
groundless rumor hearsay
groundless story canard
grounds case *(set of circumstances)*, circumstances, close *(enclosed area)*, data, documentation, estate *(property)*, homestead, premises *(buildings)*, premises *(hypotheses)*, property *(land)*, realty. SEE MAIN ENTRY
grounds for belief documentation, evidence
grounds for complaint grievance
groundwork basis, cornerstone, foundation *(basis)*, frame *(structure)*, preparation, prerequisite
group aggregate, allocate, arrange *(methodize)*, assemblage, assembly, band, call *(summon)*, cartel, chamber *(body)*, class, classification, classify, coalition, codify, collect *(gather)*, collection *(accumulation)*, collection *(assembly)*, combine *(join together)*, community, company *(assemblage)*, compile, complex *(development)*, conglomeration, congregate, connect *(relate)*, constituency, convene, denomination, division *(administrative unit)*, file *(arrange)*, fix *(arrange)*, garner, hoard, index *(relate)*, join *(bring together)*, kind, league, marshal, meet, organization *(association)*, organize *(arrange)*, partition, party *(political organization)*, pigeonhole, race, relate *(establish a connection)*, screen *(select)*, section *(division)*, selec-tion *(collection)*, sequence, society, sodality, sort, subdivide, subdivision, tabulate, unit *(department)*, unite. SEE MAIN ENTRY
group feeling loyalty
group of delegates committee
group of deputies posse
group of jurors panel *(jurors)*
group of persons organized with legal authorization posse
group refusal to work strike
group together compile
grouped collective
grouping building *(business of assembling)*, centralization, class, classification, corpus, denomination, disposition *(final arrangement)*, distribution *(arrangement)*, division *(administrative unit)*, form *(arrangement)*, hierarchy *(arrangement in a series)*, lineup, manner *(kind)*, order *(arrangement)*, organization *(structure)*, rating, rubric *(title)*, section *(division)*, segregation *(separation)*, subdivision
grovel truckle
groveling obsequious, servile
grow accrue *(increase)*, accumulate *(enlarge)*, build *(augment)*, develop, enlarge, expand, germinate, increase, inflate, progress, proliferate, stem *(originate)*. SEE MAIN ENTRY
grow aware comprehend *(understand)*, construe *(comprehend)*
grow better develop, progress
grow from develop, emanate, evolve
grow in number proliferate
grow in value appreciate *(increase)*
grow larger accumulate *(enlarge)*, compound, expand
grow lenient relent
grow less decrease, depreciate, diminish, subside
grow less severe relent

grow out of arise (*originate*), emanate, ensue

grow together cohere (*adhere*), unite

grow too fast overextend

grow too much overextend

grow up mature, progress

grow weak degenerate, languish

grow worse decay, degenerate, depreciate

growing cumulative (*increasing*), live (*conscious*), progressive (*going forward*), rampant

growing by successive additions cumulative (*increasing*)

growling petulant

grown ripe

grown old outdated, outmoded

grown-up person adult

growth accession (*enlargement*), accretion, advancement (*improvement*), appreciation (*increased value*), augmentation, boom (*increase*), boom (*prosperity*), development (*progression*), extension (*expansion*), headway, increment, inflation (*increase*), profit, progress, transition. SEE MAIN ENTRY

growth by addition collection (*accumulation*), cumulation

growth in value appreciation (*increased value*)

grudge dissatisfaction, feud, rancor, refuse, resentment, spite, umbrage

grudgeful malevolent, vindictive

grudging disinclined, illiberal, jealous, malevolent, parsimonious, penurious, reluctant, resentful

grueling difficult, harsh, onerous, operose, painful. SEE MAIN ENTRY

gruesome lurid, sordid

gruff brutal, harsh, severe

grumbler malcontent

grumbling criticism, petulant, querulous

grumbly petulant

grumose solid (*compact*)

grumpy petulant, resentful, restive

guage caliber (*measurement*)

guarantee accommodation (*backing*), assure (*insure*), bear (*adduce*), bond, bond (*secure a debt*), certificate, certify (*attest*), charge (*lien*), close (*agree*), confirm, consent, contract, corroborate, cosign, covenant, coverage (*insurance*), deposit, ensure, hostage, hypothecation, indemnify, indorse, insurer, oath, pact, pawn, pledge (*binding promise*), pledge (*security*), pledge (*deposit*), pledge (*promise the performance of*), precaution, promise, promise (*vow*), protection, reassure, recommend, security (*pledge*), sponsor, stipulate, subscribe (*promise*), swear, undertake, undertaking (*pledge*), verify (*swear*), vouch, warranty. SEE MAIN ENTRY

guarantee against loss insurance, insure

guaranteed agreed (*promised*), certain (*fixed*), certain (*positive*), conclusive (*determinative*), definite, dependable, fully secured, indubious, inevitable, official, promissory, reliable, safe, secure (*free from danger*), solid (*sound*). SEE MAIN ENTRY

guarantor backer, insurer, sponsor. SEE MAIN ENTRY

guaranty assurance, bail, binder, bond, certify (*attest*), charge (*lien*), coverage (*insurance*), letter of credit, option (*contractual provision*), recognizance, specialty (*contract*), surety (*certainty*), underwrite, warranty. SEE MAIN ENTRY

guard attend (*take care of*), bulwark, care (*be cautious*), caretaker (*one caring for property*), conserve, control (*restrain*), cover (*protection*), defend, detain (*hold in custody*), diligence (*care*), ensconce, enshroud, guarantee, guaranty, guardian, harbor, hedge, keep (*shelter*), maintain (*sustain*), monitor, notice (*heed*), panoply, patrol, peace officer, preserve, protect, protection, safekeeping, security (*safety*), shield, surveillance, sustain (*prolong*), uphold, ward, warden. SEE MAIN ENTRY

guard against anticipate (*expect*). SEE MAIN ENTRY

guarded alert (*vigilant*), careful, circumspect, controlled (*restrained*), discreet, inarticulate, intimate, leery, noncommittal, politic, preventive, prudent, safe, secure (*free from danger*), taciturn, vigilant. SEE MAIN ENTRY

guardedness caution (*vigilance*), discretion (*quality of being discreet*), precaution

guardian administrator, caretaker (*one caring for property*), custodian (*protector*), fiduciary, patron (*influential supporter*), protective, sponsor, superintendent, trustee, warden. SEE MAIN ENTRY

guardian of the peace peace officer

guardianship administration, adoption (*affiliation*), auspices, bondage, charge (*custody*), control (*supervision*), custody (*supervision*), detention, patronage (*support*), preservation, protection, restraint, safekeeping, trust (*custody*), ward. SEE MAIN ENTRY

guarding bondage, conservation, preservation, preventive

guardless helpless (*defenseless*), precarious, vulnerable

gubernare overrule

gubernatio direction (*guidance*), government (*administration*)

gubernation supervision

guerdon appropriation (*donation*), bounty, collection (*payment*), compensation, consideration (*recompense*), contribution (*indemnification*), expiation, honorarium, payment (*remittance*), prize, recompense, requital, reward, satisfaction (*discharge of debt*), tip (*gratuity*)

guess concept, conjecture, deduce, deduct (*conclude by reasoning*), estimate (*idea*), estimate, estimation (*calculation*), expect (*consider probable*), hypothesis, idea, infer, inference, opine, opinion (*belief*), postulate, presume, presuppose, prognosis, read, speculate (*conjecture*), supposition, surmise, suspect (*think*), suspicion (*uncertainty*). SEE MAIN ENTRY

guess correctly solve

guess right solve

guess wrong misconceive

guessed inexact

guesswork conjecture, estimate (*idea*), estimation (*calculation*), inference, speculation (*conjecture*), theory

guest SEE MAIN ENTRY

guidable tractable

guidance administration, advice, advocacy, aid (*help*), auspices, charge (*custody*), charge (*statement to the jury*), control (*supervision*), custody (*supervision*), discipline (*training*), edification, education, generalship, government (*administration*), help, instruction (*direction*), instruction (*teaching*), management (*supervision*), patronage (*support*), recommendation, regulation (*management*),

service (*assistance*), supervision, tip (*clue*). SEE MAIN ENTRY

guide administer (*conduct*), advise, charge (*instruct on the law*), clue, code, conduct, control (*regulate*), counsel, criterion, direct (*show*), direct (*supervise*), director, discipline (*train*), edify, educate, example, exemplar, generalization, govern, guideline, handle (*manage*), inculcate, index (*gauge*), indicate, indication, influence, instill, instruct (*direct*), instruct (*teach*), manage, manipulate (*utilize skillfully*), marshal, model, motivate, officiate, overlook (*superintend*), oversee, paradigm, pattern, pedagogue, precedent, precept, precursor, predominate (*command*), prescribe, preside, prevail (*be in force*), prevail (*persuade*), prototype, recommend, regulate (*manage*), rule (*govern*), sample, specimen, standard, superintend, symptom. SEE MAIN ENTRY

guide astray mislead

guide into error mislead

guide the studies of instruct (*teach*)

guide wrongly mislead

guidebook directory

guided direct (*straight*)

guided by experiment empirical

guideline code. SEE MAIN ENTRY

guidepost landmark (*conspicuous object*)

guiding administrative, advisory

guiding conception impression

guiding principle end (*intent*), purpose

guild association (*alliance*), company (*enterprise*), confederacy (*compact*), cooperative, institute, league, partnership, society, sodality, syndicate, union (*labor organization*)

guildsman member (*individual in a group*)

guile artifice, bad faith, collusion, color (*deceptive appearance*), deception, duplicity, evasion, fraud, hoax, hypocrisy, imposture, improbity, indirection (*deceitfulness*), knavery, pettifoggery, ruse, subreption

guileful collusive, delusive, dishonest, evasive, fallacious, fraudulent, insidious, machiavellian, perfidious, recreant, sly, subtle (*insidious*), surreptitious

guileless clean, direct (*forthright*), genuine, honest, ingenuous, pure, simple, straightforward, unaffected (*sincere*), upright

guilelessness candor (*straightforwardness*), honesty, probity, veracity

guilt blame (*culpability*), criminality, culpability. SEE MAIN ENTRY

guilt-free blameless, not guilty

guiltiness blame (*culpability*), culpability, impeachability, onus (*blame*)

guiltless blameless, clean, clear (*free from criminal charges*), incorruptible, inculpable, innocent, irreprehensible, meritorious, not guilty, pardonable, pure, unblemished, unimpeachable

guiltlessness innocence

guilty arrant (*onerous*), at fault, blameful, blameworthy, contrite, culpable, delinquent (*guilty of a misdeed*), diabolic, illicit, peccable, peccant (*culpable*), reprehensible, vicious. SEE MAIN ENTRY

guilty act crime, misconduct, misdeed, misdemeanor, misdoing, transgression

guilty man convict, delinquent

guilty of transgression peccant (*culpable*)

guilty person convict, criminal, felon, lawbreaker, recidivist

guilty plea   SEE MAIN ENTRY

guilty verdict   condemnation *(punishment)*

guise   appearance *(look)*, color *(deceptive appearance)*, complexion, conduct, cover *(pretext)*, demeanor, deportment, disguise, false pretense, manner *(behavior)*, means *(opportunity)*, mode, presence *(poise)*, pretense *(pretext)*, pretext, role, semblance, sham, style, subterfuge, veil

gulf   hiatus, split

gull   deceive, delude, dupe, ensnare, foist, illude, inveigle

gullibility   credulity

gullible   credulous, naive, unsuspecting

gullibleness   credulity

gulosity   greed

gumminess   adhesion *(affixing)*

gummosity   adhesion *(affixing)*

gumshoe   prowl

gun   SEE MAIN ENTRY

gun control   SEE MAIN ENTRY

gun for   hunt

gunfire   barrage

gunman   criminal, hoodlum

gunnery   ammunition

gunpowder   ammunition, bomb

gunrunner   bootlegger

gush   emit, exude, issuance, outburst, outflow

gushy   loquacious

gustable   sapid, savory

gustative   savory

gustful   sapid

gusto   enjoyment *(pleasure)*, passion

gut   burn, destroy *(efface)*, devastate, eviscerate, extirpate, obliterate, prey

gyp   bunko

gypsy   migrant

gyve   detain *(restrain)*, fetter *(noun)*, fetter *(verb)*, handcuff

H

habere   dwell *(reside)*, hold *(possess)*, own, possess

habeus corpus   SEE MAIN ENTRY

habile   resourceful

habilis   convenient, efficient

habilitated   proficient

habit   custom, manner *(behavior)*, method, mode, norm, practice *(custom)*, prescription *(custom)*, procedure, quirk *(idiosyncrasy)*, rule *(guide)*, style, trait, usage, way *(manner)*. SEE MAIN ENTRY

habit of a majority   custom

habitabilis   habitable

habitable   SEE MAIN ENTRY

habitance   domicile

habitancy   abode, domicile, habitation *(act of inhabiting)*, inhabitation *(act of dwelling in)*, nationality, population, residence

habitant   citizen, denizen, domiciliary, inhabitant, inmate, lodger, occupant, resident. SEE MAIN ENTRY

habitants   populace, population

habitare   dwell *(reside)*, inhabit, reside

habitat   abode, building *(structure)*, domicile, habitation *(dwelling place)*, home *(domicile)*, locality, lodging, residence, site

habitation   abode, address, building *(structure)*, domicile, dwelling, enjoyment *(use)*, home *(domicile)*, house, household, inhabitation *(act of dwelling in)*, lodging, occupancy, residence, shelter *(protection)*. SEE MAIN ENTRY

habitator   habitant, inhabitant, resident

habits   behavior, conduct

habitual   accustomed *(customary)*, boiler plate, chronic, constant, conventional, customary, daily, familiar *(customary)*, frequent, general, household *(familiar)*, ingrained, inveterate, normal *(regular)*, ordinary, orthodox, periodic, prevailing *(current)*, prevalent, regular *(conventional)*, repeated, routine, systematic, traditional, typical, usual. SEE MAIN ENTRY

habitual activity   custom

habitual course   practice *(custom)*

habitual criminal   outlaw, recidivist

habitual devotion   diligence *(perseverance)*

habitual offender   outlaw

habitual practice   custom, manner *(behavior)*

habitual relapse into crime   recidivism

habitual use   usage

habitually   generally, invariably

habitually silent   taciturn

habituate   discipline *(train)*, inure *(accustom)*, naturalize *(acclimate)*

habituated   accustomed *(familiarized)*, addicted, inveterate, practiced

habituation   behavior, custom, practice *(custom)*. SEE MAIN ENTRY

habitude   behavior, condition *(state)*, custom, practice *(custom)*, usage

habitus   deportment, habit

hack   split

hacking into   SEE MAIN ENTRY

hackneyed   familiar *(customary)*, mundane, nondescript, ordinary, pedestrian, prosaic, stale, trite

hackneyed expression   platitude

hackneyed idea   platitude

hackneyed phrase   platitude

hackneyed saying   platitude

hactenus   extent

haerere   hesitate

haereticus   heretic

haesitatio   hesitation, indecision, scruple

haggle   barter, cavil, dicker, negotiate. SEE MAIN ENTRY

haggling   negotiation

hail   honor

hairsplitting   particular *(exacting)*

halcyon   harmonious, nonmilitant, peaceable, placid

halcyonian   peaceable, placid

haleness   health, welfare

half   moiety, semi

half believe   doubt *(distrust)*

half distance   center *(central position)*

half finished   semi

half-begun   inchoate

half-done   inchoate

half-seen   indistinct

halfhearted   hesitant, insipid, lax, perfunctory, phlegmatic

halfway   center *(central position)*, central *(situated near center)*, intermediate

hall   chamber *(compartment)*

hallmark   brand, designation *(symbol)*, device *(distinguishing mark)*, label, stamp, trademark. SEE MAIN ENTRY

hallow   dedicate

hallowed   infrangible, inviolate, laudable, sacrosanct, solemn. SEE MAIN ENTRY

hallowing   honorary

hallucination   figment, insanity, phantom

hallucinative   delusive

hallucinatory   delusive, insubstantial, nonexistent

halt   abeyance, balk, block, cease, cessation *(interlude)*, check *(bar)*, check *(restrain)*, close *(terminate)*, cloture, conclude *(complete)*, condemn *(ban)*, constrict *(inhibit)*, curtail, debar, defeat, desist, desuetude, detain *(restrain)*, deterrence, discontinue *(abandon)*, dissolve *(terminate)*, embargo, end *(termination)*, estop, finality, finish, forestall, hiatus, hinder, hold up *(delay)*, impasse, interdict, interruption, interval, keep *(restrain)*, layoff, lull, moratorium, obstruct, pause *(noun)*, pause *(verb)*, pendency, prevent, prohibit, proscribe *(prohibit)*, quit *(discontinue)*, recess *(noun)*, recess *(verb)*, refrain, remission, remit *(relax)*, respite *(interval of rest)*, rest *(cease from action)*, shut, stall, stay, stay *(rest)*, stem *(check)*, stop, suspend, terminate, toll *(stop)*. SEE MAIN ENTRY

halt work   strike *(refuse to work)*

halting   broken *(interrupted)*

halve   bifurcate, cross *(intersect)*, dichotomize, divide *(separate)*, part *(separate)*, split

halved   bipartite

halving   dichotomy

hammer in   impact

hammer out   forge *(produce)*, formulate, make

hammer together   frame *(construct)*

hamper   balk, bar *(hinder)*, bind *(restrain)*, block, clog, condemn *(ban)*, constrain *(restrain)*, constrict *(inhibit)*, control *(restrain)*, damper *(stopper)*, debar, delay, detain *(restrain)*, deter, disadvantage *(noun)*, disadvantage *(verb)*, encumber *(hinder)*, enjoin, estop, fetter *(noun)*, fetter *(verb)*, foil, halt, handcuff, hinder, hindrance, hold up *(delay)*, impede, impediment, inconvenience, interfere, keep *(restrain)*, limit, lock, obstacle, obstruct, obstruction, occlude, overcome *(overwhelm)*, prevent, prohibit, restrain, restraint, restrict, stall, stave, stay *(halt)*, stem *(check)*, stop, thwart, trammel, withstand. SEE MAIN ENTRY

hampered   arrested *(checked)*, limited

hampering   binding, deterrent, encumbrance, limiting

hamstring   deter, hinder, obstruct

hamstrung   marred

hand   deliver, employee, handwriting, help, present *(make a gift)*

hand back   restore *(return)*

hand down   abalienate, bequeath, confer *(give)*, convey *(transfer)*, deliver, demise, descend, endow, leave *(give)*, render *(deliver)*

hand grenade   bomb

hand in one's resignation   demit

hand on   bequeath, descend, transfer, transmit

hand out   allocate, bestow, convey *(transfer)*, disburse *(distribute)*, dispense, dole, endow, endue, fund, mete

hand out again   redistribute

hand over   abalienate, bestow, consign, contribute *(supply)*, delegate, discharge *(pay a debt)*, dole, endow, pay, present *(make a gift)*, relinquish, render *(deliver)*, serve *(deliver a legal instrument)*, surrender *(give back)*, transmit

hand over to   bequeath

hand-to-hand fight   affray

handbook   directory, pandect *(treatise)*

handcuff   fetter, restrain, restrict. SEE MAIN ENTRY

handed down   traditional

handicap burden, clog, constrict (inhibit), detriment, disability (physical inability), disadvantage (noun), disadvantage (verb), disease, disorder (abnormal condition), disqualification (factor that disqualifies), estop, fetter (noun), fetter (verb), hamper, hinder, hindrance, impede, impediment, incumbrance (burden), interfere, liability, nuisance, obstacle, obstruct, onus (burden), penalty, preclude, prevent, restrain, restrict, trammel. SEE MAIN ENTRY

handicapped disabled (made incapable), disadvantaged

handicraft business (occupation), performance (workmanship), specialty (special aptitude), trade (occupation)

handicraftsman artisan

handiness efficiency, faculty (ability), gift (flair), means (opportunity), performance (workmanship), skill

handing out disbursement (act of disbursing), distribution (apportionment)

handing over cession

handing over into custody commitment (confinement)

handing over legal papers service (delivery of legal process)

handiwork building (business of assembling), invention, performance (workmanship), product

handle administer (conduct), conduct, control (regulate), deal, manage, manipulate (utilize skillfully), militate, operate, oversee, ply, regulate (manage), sell, superintend, treat (process), wield. SEE MAIN ENTRY

handle badly mishandle (maltreat), mishandle (mismanage)

handler merchant

handling administration, agency (legal relationship), course, management (judicious use), operation, process (course), regulation (management), treatment. SEE MAIN ENTRY

handout donation, gratuity (present), largess (gift)

handpicked preferred (favored), select

hands-off policy laissez faire

handsel binder, bounty, grant, largess (gift), launch (initiate), originate. SEE MAIN ENTRY

handsome elegant, liberal (generous), magnanimous

handwriting script. SEE MAIN ENTRY

handwritten holographic

handy available, close (near), deft, effective (efficient), expert, functional, immediate (not distant), practical, practiced, present (attendant), proficient, resourceful

hang SEE MAIN ENTRY

hang around loiter

hang back pause, procrastinate

hang on cohere (adhere), endure (last), grapple, last, persevere, remain (continue)

hang on to hoard

hang over project (extend beyond)

hang together cohere (be logically consistent)

hangdog furtive

hanger on partisan

hanger-on disciple

hankering desire, will (desire)

hap contingency, event, opportunity, quirk (accident)

haphazard casual, fortuitous, indiscriminate, random, slipshod. SEE MAIN ENTRY

hapless ominous

happen arise (occur), supervene. SEE MAIN ENTRY

happen again recur

happen at the same time concur (coexist)

happen simultaneously concur (coexist)

happen together coincide (correspond), concur (coexist)

happen upon find (discover)

happening accident (chance occurrence), chance (fortuity), contingency, event, experience (encounter), incident, occasion, occurrence, situation. SEE MAIN ENTRY

happening by chance fortuitous

happenings circumstances

happenstance occurrence. SEE MAIN ENTRY

happiness welfare

happy ecstatic, felicitous, inclined, propitious, prosperous, proud (self-respecting), ready (willing). SEE MAIN ENTRY

happy medium compromise

happy-go-lucky improvident

harangue address (talk to), bombast, declaim, declamation, diatribe, outpour, phillipic. SEE MAIN ENTRY

haranguer demagogue

harass annoy, badger, browbeat, discompose, distress, harrow, hector, importune, incense, inflict, intimidate, irritate, mistreat, molest (annoy), persecute, perturb, pique, prey, provoke. SEE MAIN ENTRY

harassing vexatious

harassment aggravation (annoyance), infliction, nuisance, oppression. SEE MAIN ENTRY

harbinger anticipate (prognosticate), forerunner, herald, indicator, informant, informer (a person who provides information), precede, precursor. SEE MAIN ENTRY

harbor conceal, cover (guard), foster, haven, hide, lodge (house), lodging, nurture, preserve, protect, refuge, screen (guard), shelter (protection)

harbor a design intend, plan

harbor a grudge harass, resent

harbor doubts disbelieve, doubt (distrust), mistrust

harbor suspicions disbelieve, discount (disbelieve), doubt (distrust), misdoubt, mistrust. SEE MAIN ENTRY

harbor suspicious suspect (distrust)

harboring conservation

harborless insecure

hard callous, close (rigorous), cohesive (compact), cold-blooded, compact (dense), cruel, difficult, durable, impervious, inflexible, insusceptible (uncaring), obdurate, onerous, operose, oppressive, ossified, powerful, relentless, rigid, ruthless, severe, solid (compact), strict, stringent, strong, tyrannous, unbending, uncompromising, unrelenting, unyielding

hard bargaining counteroffer

hard blow disaster

hard cash currency, money

hard core SEE MAIN ENTRY

hard feelings argument (contention), ill will, malice

hard money cash

hard of heart callous, malignant, relentless

hard task campaign

hard to believe debatable, disputable, implausible, incredible, ludicrous, suspicious (questionable), unbelievable

hard to comprehend opaque

hard to control unruly

hard to convince impervious, inconvincible, incredulous, suspicious (distrustful)

hard to cope with operose

hard to deal with difficult, impracticable, perverse

hard to define elusive

hard to endure painful, severe

hard to explain indefinable

hard to express elusive

hard to get rid of pertinacious

hard to grasp elusive

hard to lift ponderous

hard to maintain elusive

hard to manage difficult, perverse

hard to overcome formidable

hard to please particular (exacting), querulous

hard to see obscure (faint)

hard to translate indefinable

hard to understand difficult, elusive, enigmatic, equivocal, incomprehensible, indefinable, inexplicable, opaque

hard up impecunious, poor (underprivileged)

hard upon critical (faultfinding)

hard work effort, industry (activity)

hard working industrious, patient

hard-bitten obdurate

harden cement, cohere (adhere), consolidate (strengthen), fix (make firm), inure (accustom)

harden the heart alienate (estrange)

hardened callous, cold-blooded, impervious, incorrigible, inexpressive, inflexible, insusceptible (uncaring), inveterate, obdurate, ossified, recalcitrant, remorseless, reprobate, solid (compact), unabashed. SEE MAIN ENTRY

hardened criminal malefactor, outlaw

hardened offender criminal, recidivist

hardheaded perspicacious

hardhearted brutal, callous, cold-blooded, cruel, malevolent, obdurate, relentless, ruthless, unaffected (uninfluenced)

hardheartedness malice

hardhitting critical (faultfinding)

hardihood audacity, prowess (bravery), surety (certainty)

hardiness force (strength), health, prowess (bravery), strength

hardly SEE MAIN ENTRY

hardly begun inchoate

hardly credible incredible

hardly possible implausible, insurmountable

hardly worth mention nominal

hardness brutality, congealment

hardness of heart brutality

hardship adversity, burden, calamity, casualty, catastrophe, damage, detriment, grievance, misfortune, nuisance, plight, pressure, privation, tragedy, trouble. SEE MAIN ENTRY

hardworking diligent, painstaking, sedulous

hardy durable, indestructible, indomitable, inexpugnable, spartan, strong

harebrained impolitic, precipitate, thoughtless, unpolitic

hark heed

harm abuse (violate), annoy, assault, cost (penalty), damage (noun), damage (verb), detriment, disable, disadvantage (noun), disadvantage (verb), disaster, disservice, drawback, endanger, eviscerate, expense (sacrifice), harrow, ill use, impair, impairment (damage), infect, inflict, injury, mischief, mistreat, molest (annoy), penalize, prejudice *(injury)*, prejudice *(injure)*, spoil *(impair)*, strike *(assault)*, wrong. SEE MAIN ENTRY

harmed imperfect, marred

harmful adverse *(negative)*, dangerous, deleterious, destructive, detrimental, disadvantageous, disastrous, fatal, hostile, inadvisable, incendiary, inimical, insalubrious, invidious, lethal, malevolent, malicious, malignant, noxious, oppressive, outrageous, painful, peccant *(unhealthy)*, pernicious, pestilent, prejudicial, scathing, sinister, toxic, virulent. SEE MAIN ENTRY

harmful act injury

harmful action mischief

harmful desire malice

harmful physical contact battery

harming disabling, incriminatory

harmless innocuous, nontoxic, powerless, safe, salutary, unobjectionable. SEE MAIN ENTRY

harmonious amicable, appropriate, concerted, concordant, congruous, consensual, consistent, consonant, felicitous, fit, joint, proportionate, suitable, uniform. SEE MAIN ENTRY

harmonious relation rapport

harmoniousness peace

harmonization accommodation *(adjustment)*, accordance *(understanding)*, arrangement *(understanding)*

harmonize accommodate, arbitrate *(conciliate)*, attune, cohere *(be logically consistent)*, coincide *(concur)*, combine *(act in concert)*, commingle, comport *(agree with)*, compromise *(settle by mutual agreement)*, concur *(agree)*, coordinate, correspond *(be equivalent)*, merge, naturalize *(acclimate)*, orchestrate, reconcile, settle, unite

harmonize with comply

harmonized concerted, congruous, consensual

harmonizing concurrent *(united)*

harmony accordance *(understanding)*, adjustment, agreement *(concurrence)*, coherence, comity, compatibility, compliance, composure, concert, conciliation, concordance, conformity *(agreement)*, conjunction, consensus, consent, contribution *(participation)*, correspondence *(similarity)*, peace, propinquity *(similarity)*, proportion, propriety *(appropriateness)*, rapport, rapprochement, reconciliation, regularity, synchronism, understanding *(agreement)*, union *(unity)*

harness confine, constrain *(imprison)*, constrain *(restrain)*, curb, discipline *(control)*, handcuff, inhibit, join *(bring together)*, restrain, subdue. SEE MAIN ENTRY

harness together connect *(join together)*

harnessed servile

harp SEE MAIN ENTRY

harp on repeat *(state again)*

harp upon dwell *(linger over)*, reiterate

harping insistent, iterative, repetitious

harrassed aggrieved *(victimized)*

harried aggrieved *(victimized)*

harrow badger, distress, harass, hector, mistreat, prey. SEE MAIN ENTRY

harrowing disastrous, insufferable, onerous, painful

harry annoy, badger, bait *(harass)*, discommode, discompose, distress, harass, harrow, hector, loot, mistreat, molest *(annoy)*, perturb, pique, plague, press *(goad)*. SEE MAIN ENTRY

harsh astringent, bitter *(penetrating)*, bla-

tant *(obtrusive)*, brutal, caustic, close *(rigorous)*, contemptuous, cruel, draconian, drastic, hostile, incisive, insufferable, lurid, malevolent, mordacious, obdurate, offensive *(offending)*, onerous, oppressive, pejorative, relentless, rigid, ruthless, scathing, severe, spiteful, strict, stringent, strong, tyrannous. SEE MAIN ENTRY

harsh feeling spite

harsh sound noise

harshness brutality, cruelty, oppression, rancor, severity

haruspical prophetic

harvest gain, glean, output, product, profit *(noun)*, profit *(verb)*, reap, result

has as a component consist

hash cannabis, melange

hashish cannabis

haste dispatch *(promptness)*. SEE MAIN ENTRY

hasten dispatch *(send off)*, evoke, expedite, facilitate, induce, race. SEE MAIN ENTRY

hasten away flee

hasten on dispatch *(send off)*

hasten one's end dispatch *(put to death)*

hastening acceleration

hastily instantly

hastiness dispatch *(promptness)*, inconsideration, temerity

hasty brief, careless, cursory, expeditious, heedless, hot-blooded, ill-advised, ill-judged, impolitic, improvident, imprudent, impulsive *(rash)*, injudicious, instantaneous, perfunctory, precipitate, premature, rapid, reckless, summary, superficial, transient, unpolitic, unpremeditated

hasty departure abandonment *(desertion)*, flight

hatch conceive *(invent)*, engender, frame *(formulate)*, make, outlet, produce *(manufacture)*, scheme

hatch a plot conspire

hatch a plot against frame *(charge falsely)*

hatched illusory

hate malice, odium, rancor, resent, spite. SEE MAIN ENTRY

hate crime SEE MAIN ENTRY

hateful antipathetic *(distasteful)*, contemptible, contemptuous, disreputable, heinous, invidious, loathsome, malevolent, malicious, malignant, nefarious, objectionable, obnoxious, odious, offensive *(offending)*, outrageous, reprehensible, repugnant *(exciting aversion)*, repulsive, spiteful, vicious, virulent

hatred conflict, incompatibility *(difference)*, intolerance, malice, odium, rancor, rejection, resentment, spite, umbrage. SEE MAIN ENTRY

haud accuratus inexact

haud dubius infallible, undeniable, undisputed

haud sufficiens insufficient

haughtiness contumely, disdain, pride

haughty cynical, disdainful, impertinent *(insolent)*, inflated *(vain)*, insolent, orgulous, presumptuous, pretentious *(pompous)*, proud *(conceited)*, supercilious

haughty contempt disdain

haughty indifference disdain

haul cargo, carry *(transport)*, deliver, plunder, spoils, struggle

haunt bailiwick, harass, obsess, plague, recur, remind

haunting ominous, portentous *(ominous)*

hauteur disdain

have accommodate, hold *(possess)*, keep *(shelter)*, own, possess, remain *(occupy)*, retain *(keep in possession)*

have a bad conscience regret

have a bearing on concern *(involve)*, relate *(establish a connection)*

have a bias forejudge, preconceive, presuppose, select

have a care beware

have a certain semblance appear *(seem to be)*

have a common origin evolve

have a comparison correspond *(be equivalent)*

have a conference on discuss

have a connection concern *(involve)*, correspond *(be equivalent)*

have a connection to apply *(pertain)*

have a deed for own, possess

have a dialogue speak

have a dissimilar opinion differ *(vary)*

have a fancy for prefer

have a feud with dispute *(contest)*

have a firm grip on hold *(possess)*

have a good influence meliorate

have a guilty conscience repent

have a habitation dwell *(reside)*

have a hand in involve *(participate)*, partake, participate

have a hunch expect *(consider probable)*, guess, opine

have a impulse desire

have a liking for regard *(hold in esteem)*

have a loan owe

have a part in participate

have a part of participate

have a policy plan

have a portion of partake

have a prejudice forejudge

have a prepossession forejudge

have a presentiment anticipate *(prognosticate)*, expect *(consider probable)*, presage

have a proclivity desire

have a proclivity for gravitate

have a propensity for gravitate

have a reference concern *(involve)*

have a relation concern *(involve)*, correspond *(be equivalent)*

have a right claim *(demand)*

have a right to earn

have a row brawl

have a share of partake, participate

have a strong effect impress *(affect deeply)*

have a theory speculate *(conjecture)*

have a title to hold *(possess)*, own, possess

have a verbal controversy over dispute *(debate)*

have a vision conjure

have a wrong impression misjudge

have a yearning desire

have absolute disposal of hold *(possess)*, possess

have all to oneself monopolize

have an address reside

have an affection for discriminate *(treat differently)*

have an altercation bicker, contend *(dispute)*, dispute *(contest)*

have an appetite desire

have an effect upon affect

have an exchange contact *(communicate)*

have an idea conceive *(comprehend)*, devise *(invent)*, opine, surmise

have an idea that assume *(suppose)*
have an impression apprehend *(perceive)*
have an incorrect impression misconstrue
have an insufficiency require *(need)*
have an obligation owe
have an opinion deem, opine
have an understanding of apprehend *(perceive)*
have an urge for need
have anxiety mistrust
have as its foundation consist
have as property hold *(possess)*, possess
have at one's command possess
have at one's disposal possess
have authority govern, handle *(manage)*, police, rule *(govern)*
have authority over oversee, preside, prevail *(be in force)*, regulate *(manage)*
have bearing on apply *(pertain)*
have being exist
have business relations deal
have by inheritance hold *(possess)*
have by tenure hold *(possess)*
have capacity for accommodate
have charge of control *(regulate)*, handle *(manage)*, moderate *(preside over)*, operate, overlook *(superintend)*, oversee, police, prevail *(be in force)*, regulate *(manage)*, superintend
have charges against accused *(charged)*
have claim upon hold *(possess)*, own
have cognizance of apprehend *(perceive)*, perceive
have commerce deal, handle *(trade)*
have confidence in confide *(trust)*, rely
have control command, conduct, manage, preside, rule *(govern)*
have conveyed consign, dispatch *(send off)*
have currency circulate
have dealings dicker
have dealings with contact *(communicate)*, deal, patronize *(trade with)*
have designs plot, scheme
have designs on desire
have dialogue converse
have differences conflict, disaccord, dispute *(contest)*
have dissension disagree
have dominion over prevail *(be in force)*
have done with discontinue *(abandon)*, quit *(discontinue)*
have doubts disbelieve, doubt *(distrust)*, mistrust
have doubts about misdoubt
have duration endure *(last)*
have effect function, prevail *(persuade)*
have effect on militate
have efficacy avail *(be of use)*
have every indication appear *(seem to be)*
have evidence bear *(adduce)*
have executed enforce
have executive charge of administer *(conduct)*, govern
have existence exist
have faith opine
have faith in confide *(trust)*, rely, trust
have fears doubt *(distrust)*, misdoubt, mistrust
have for one's own possess
have for sale handle *(trade)*
have force avail *(bring about)*, prevail *(be in force)*

have foreknowledge preconceive
have hold of own
have ill feelings toward discriminate *(treat differently)*
have implications for pertain
have in hand hold *(possess)*, own, possess
have in mind intend
have in one's charge control *(regulate)*
have in one's possession hold *(possess)*
have in production make
have in prospect anticipate *(expect)*, expect *(anticipate)*
have in sight discern *(detect with the senses)*, observe *(watch)*, pierce *(discern)*
have in store hoard
have in view intend
have influence affect, constrain *(compel)*, predominate *(command)*
have influence on militate
have influence over prejudice *(influence)*, prevail upon
have influence upon prejudice *(influence)*, prevail upon
have influence with prevail upon
have inherited hold *(possess)*
have insight diagnose, discern *(discriminate)*
have intercourse communicate
have interrelationship with concern *(involve)*, pertain
have it out bicker
have jurisdiction over govern, rule *(govern)*
have knowledge of apprehend *(perceive)*, perceive, pierce *(discern)*
have life exist
have mastery prevail *(triumph)*
have memories of recall *(remember)*
have mercy relent
have misgivings doubt *(distrust)*, mistrust
have need for need
have no concern with dissociate
have no confidence in misdoubt, suspect *(distrust)*
have no doubt opine, trust
have no end endure *(last)*
have no faith in misdoubt, mistrust
have no objection authorize, consent, grant *(concede)*, let *(permit)*, permit
have no part of shun
have no regard for decry, disfavor, jeer
have no reservations trust
have no respect for decry, disfavor, disgrace
have no trust in mistrust
have no use for decry, disdain, disfavor
have nothing to do with avoid *(evade)*, disown *(refuse to acknowledge)*, eschew, exclude, refrain, shun, spurn
have occasion for need
have offspring proliferate
have one's address at dwell *(reside)*
have one's heart set on desire
have one's plans backfire overreach
have origin arise *(originate)*
have pity sympathize
have possession remain *(occupy)*
have possession of occupy *(take possession)*
have power dominate
have precedence antecede
have predominating influence rule *(govern)*
have printed publish
have progeny proliferate

have qualms disbelieve, doubt *(hesitate)*, fear, mistrust, repent
have qualms about regret
have quarters inhabit
have questions doubt *(distrust)*, misdoubt
have recourse resort
have recourse to employ *(make use of)*
have reference appertain, apply *(pertain)*
have reference to pertain
have regard care *(be cautious)*
have regard for regard *(hold in esteem)*
have relation appertain, apply *(pertain)*
have relation to pertain
have relevance pertain
have reservations disbelieve, doubt *(hesitate)*, hesitate, misdoubt, mistrust
have responsibility rule *(govern)*
have revenge recriminate
have rights to hold *(possess)*, occupy *(take possession)*, own, possess
have run its course close *(terminate)*
have second thoughts reconsider
have significance for pertain
have succession as an heir inherit
have superiority prevail *(triumph)*
have superiority over prevail *(be in force)*
have suspicions doubt *(distrust)*, misdoubt, mistrust
have sway predominate *(command)*
have sympathy relent
have tenacity adhere *(persist)*
have the advantage beat *(defeat)*, outbalance
have the care of handle *(manage)*, hold *(possess)*
have the charge of hold *(possess)*
have the direction of control *(regulate)*, handle *(manage)*, hold *(possess)*, oversee
have the edge on outbalance
have the idea suspect *(think)*
have the impression deem
have the mien demean *(deport oneself)*
have the qualifications qualify *(meet standards)*
have the requisites qualify *(meet standards)*
have the upper hand predominate *(command)*, surpass
have the wrong impression misapprehend, miscalculate
have title to hold *(possess)*, occupy *(take possession)*
have to do with deal
have to one's name own
have under command manage
have under control control *(regulate)*, handle *(manage)*, hold *(possess)*
have underwritten insure
have use of need
have verbal intercourse converse
have volition choose
have words bicker
have words with brawl, contend *(dispute)*, disaccord, dispute *(contest)*, fight *(battle)*
haven asylum *(hiding place)*, bulwark, harbor, home *(domicile)*, preserve, protect, protection, refuge, screen *(guard)*, shelter *(protection)*. SEE MAIN ENTRY
having a bad reputation disreputable
having a common measure commensurate
having a double meaning ambiguous
having a natural contrariety antipathetic *(oppositional)*
having a significant impact far reaching

having a strong effect forcible
having direct bearing pertinent
having fixed limits definite
having force forcible
having formal education literate
having great strength forcible
having home interests household (domestic)
having immunity insusceptible (resistant)
having independent qualities apart
having integrity incorruptible
having investments in interested
having left a will testate
having legal force effective (operative), valid
having legal strength valid
having multiple husbands polygamous
having multiple wives polygamous
having no acknowledged name anonymous
having no alternative bound
having no force invalid
having no foundation baseless. SEE MAIN ENTRY
having no limit comprehensive, perpetual
having plurality of wives or husbands polygamous
having prior application retroactive
having prior effect retroactive
having priority preferred (given priority)
having resistance insusceptible (resistant)
having seniority preferred (given priority)
having substance corporeal
having suffered invasion of legal rights aggrieved (harmed)
having the possibility of termination determinable (liable to be terminated)
having the privilege to choose disjunctive (alternative)
having the right entitled
having to do with pertinent
having unique features apart
having unique qualities apart
having violated the law culpable
having written a testament testate
havoc catastrophe, confusion (turmoil), debacle, depredation, disturb, pillage, shambles, turmoil. SEE MAIN ENTRY
hawk handle (trade), hunt, sell
hawk about proclaim, promulgate, propagate (spread)
hawker dealer, merchant, vendor
hayseed provincial
hazard accident (chance occurrence), bet, compromise (endanger), danger, endanger, expose, jeopardy, menace, parlay (bet), peril, pitfall, risk, speculate (chance), speculation (risk), threat, venture. SEE MAIN ENTRY
hazard a guess presume, surmise
hazard a supposition postulate
hazard an opinion deem
hazarder bettor, speculator
hazardous aleatory (perilous), dangerous, imprudent, insalubrious, insecure, noxious, precarious, speculative. SEE MAIN ENTRY
haze bait (harass), harry (harass), ignorance, incertitude, obnubilate, obscure
haziness confusion (ambiguity), indistinctness
hazy dubious, equivocal, indeterminate, indistinct, inexact, nebulous, opaque, unclear
he who has passed away decedent

head call (title), caption, chairman, chapter (division), chief, culmination, derivation, direct (supervise), employer, govern, heading, manage, master, moderate (preside over), officiate, oversee, paramount, pinnacle, preface, preside, prime (most valuable), principal (director), regulate (manage), rubric (title), superintend, tip (clue). SEE MAIN ENTRY
head of affairs administrator
head of government official
head of the household parents
head off avert, check (restrain)
head-on SEE MAIN ENTRY
head start advantage, edge (advantage)
head toward gravitate
heading caption, chapter (division), denomination, direction (course), prevailing (having superior force), rubric (title), subheading, term (expression), title (designation). SEE MAIN ENTRY
headline caption, heading, rubric (title)
headlong blind (not discerning), impolitic, improvident, precipitate, thoughtless
headman chairman, chief
headmaster pedagogue
headmen management (directorate)
headnote caption
headperson chief, principal (director)
headquarters address, base (place), building (structure), habitation (dwelling place), management (directorate), seat. SEE MAIN ENTRY
heads authorities, hierarchy (persons in authority)
headship direction (guidance), generalship, hegemony, primacy, supremacy
headspring source
headstrong contumacious, disobedient, froward, hot-blooded, ill-judged, inexorable, inflexible, intractable, obdurate, pertinacious, perverse, precipitate, recalcitrant, restive, uncontrollable, unruly, unyielding, vehement. SEE MAIN ENTRY
headward vanward
headway advance (progression), margin (spare amount), progress, promotion (advancement). SEE MAIN ENTRY
heady precipitate
heal cure, drug, fix (repair), help, recreate, redress, relieve (give aid), remedy, restore (renew), treat (process). SEE MAIN ENTRY
heal the breach placate, reconcile
healing curative, medicinal, remedial, salubrious, salutary
healing agent cure, panacea
health strength, welfare. SEE MAIN ENTRY
health care SEE MAIN ENTRY
health maintenance organization SEE MAIN ENTRY
health of mind sanity
health-giving medicinal, remedial, salutary
health-preserving salutary
health-promoting salubrious
healthful remedial, salubrious, salutary
healthy salubrious, salutary, strong
healthy mind sanity
healthy mindedness competence (sanity)
heap assemblage, bulk, collection (accumulation), hoard (noun), hoard (verb), plethora, quantity
heap upon bestow
hear adjudicate, heed, notice (observe), overhear. SEE MAIN ENTRY

hear a case try (conduct a trial)
hear a cause try (conduct a trial)
hear the case adjudicate
hearer juror
hearing action (proceeding), day in court, inquest, inquiry (request for information), inquiry (systematic investigation), interview, parley, proceeding, range, session, trial (legal proceeding). SEE MAIN ENTRY
hearing before the court voir dire
hearing of evidence inquiry (systematic investigation)
hearing officer SEE MAIN ENTRY
hearing on the merits action (proceeding)
hearing without jury's presence voir dire
hearken concentrate (pay attention), defer (yield in judgment), eavesdrop
hearken to heed, note (notice)
hearsay report (rumor). SEE MAIN ENTRY
heart center (essence), confidence (faith), consequence (significance), cornerstone, essence, focus, frame (mood), main point, substance (essential nature). SEE MAIN ENTRY
heart of stone brutality
heart-stirring profound (intense)
heartbreaking disastrous
heartbroken disconsolate
hearten assure (give confidence to), encourage, reassure
heartening propitious. SEE MAIN ENTRY
heartfelt ecstatic, profound (intense)
heartily readily
heartiness health
heartless callous, cold-blooded, cruel, dispassionate, insusceptible (uncaring), obdurate, remorseless, ruthless, sinister, unaffected (uninfluenced). SEE MAIN ENTRY
heartlessness brutality, cruelty
heartsick disconsolate
hearty fervent, powerful, zealous
heat passion
heated hot-blooded, vehement
heated debate altercation
heave impel, launch (project), precipitate (throw down violently)
heave up elevate
heaven SEE MAIN ENTRY
heaven sent propitious
heavenly sacrosanct, stellar
heaviness damper (depressant), languor, pressure
heaviness of heart pessimism
heaviness of spirit damper (depressant), pessimism
heavy grave (solemn), onerous, oppressive, pedestrian, ponderous, profound (intense), torpid. SEE MAIN ENTRY
heavy demand market (demand)
heavy-handed uncouth. SEE MAIN ENTRY
heavy-hearted lugubrious
heavy-laden disconsolate
heavyhearted pessimistic
hebes obtuse
hebetude languor, opacity
hebetudinous languid, lifeless (dull), phlegmatic, stagnant
heckle annoy, badger, bait (harass), discompose, harass, harry (harass), hector, mistreat, mock (deride), pique, plague, press (goad), provoke
hector annoy, badger, bait (harass), intimidate, irritate, plague, press (goad), provoke, threaten. SEE MAIN ENTRY
hectoring insolent
hedge equivocate, evade (deceive), offset, outbalance, parry, prevaricate,

protection, shelter *(tax benefit),* tergiversate. SEE MAIN ENTRY

hedge in circumscribe *(surround by boundary),* envelop, occlude, restrict

hedging evasive, noncommittal

heed abide, care *(be cautious),* caution *(vigilance),* consider, consideration *(contemplation),* deliberation, devote, diligence *(care),* discretion *(quality of being discreet),* fulfill, hear *(give attention to),* interest *(concern),* keep *(fulfill),* note *(notice),* notice *(observe),* obey, observation, observe *(obey),* observe *(watch),* precaution, prudence, regard *(attention),* regard *(pay attention),* submit *(yield),* surveillance. SEE MAIN ENTRY

heedful careful, circumspect, conscientious, conscious *(aware),* diligent, guarded, judicious, knowing, leery, meticulous, noncommittal, painstaking, particular *(exacting),* politic, protective, provident *(showing foresight),* prudent, sensitive *(discerning),* vigilant

heedfulness caution *(vigilance),* deliberation, diligence *(care),* discretion *(quality of being discreet),* interest *(concern),* notice *(heed),* observation, precaution, prudence, regard *(attention)*

heedless blind *(not discerning),* careless, cursory, derelict *(negligent),* hot-blooded, ill-judged, impolitic, improvident, imprudent, impulsive *(rash),* inadvertent, incognizant, injudicious, insensible, intractable, irrational, lawless, lax, negligent, oblivious, passive, perfunctory, prodigal, reckless, relentless, remiss, slipshod, thoughtless, unaware, unpolitic, wanton. SEE MAIN ENTRY

heedlessness dereliction, disinterest *(lack of interest),* disregard *(lack of respect),* disregard *(unconcern),* inconsideration, ingratitude, laxity, neglect, negligence, oversight *(carelessness),* temerity

heft elevate

hegemonic influential, master, paramount, powerful, prevailing *(having superior force),* principal, sovereign *(absolute)*

hegemonical dominant, influential, master, paramount, powerful, prevailing *(having superior force),* principal, sovereign *(absolute)*

hegemony clout, dominion *(supreme authority),* influence, primacy. SEE MAIN ENTRY

hegira flight

height ceiling, culmination, elevation, eminence, pinnacle, primacy. SEE MAIN ENTRY

height of one's ambition objective

height of perfection paragon

heighten accrue *(increase),* aggravate *(exacerbate),* build *(augment),* compound, elevate, enhance, exacerbate, expand, intensify, magnify, raise *(advance).* SEE MAIN ENTRY

heightened inflated *(overestimated),* intense

heightening aggravation *(exacerbation),* boom *(increase),* cumulative *(intensifying),* growth *(increase)*

heinous arrant *(onerous),* bad *(offensive),* base *(bad),* blameful, contemptible, depraved, diabolic, disgraceful, disorderly, disreputable, gross *(flagrant),* immoral, inexcusable, inexpiable, iniquitous, loathsome, malevolent, malignant, nefarious, objectionable, obnoxious, odious, offensive *(offending),* outrageous, peccant *(culpable),* profligate *(corrupt),* reprehensible, reprobate, scandalous, sinister, unjust, vicious. SEE MAIN ENTRY

heinous conduct criminality

heinous crime felony

heinous misconduct felony

heinousness atrocity, delinquency *(misconduct),* disrepute

heir beneficiary, descendant, devisee, offspring, recipient, transferee. SEE MAIN ENTRY

heir apparent legatee

heir at law legatee

heirdom bequest

heiress beneficiary, legatee

heirloom bequest, hereditament

heirs children, issue *(progeny),* posterity, progeny

held arrested *(apprehended),* in custody

held back arrested *(checked)*

held in contempt blameful, disreputable, notorious

held in custody arrested *(apprehended)*

held in esteem reputable

held in good repute reputable

held in high esteem famous

held in pledge bailment, in trust

held in trust in trust

held responsible accused *(charged)*

held up late *(tardy)*

helical circuitous

helicoid circuitous

helicoidal circuitous

hellbent precipitate

hellish cruel, diabolic, heinous, loathsome, malevolent, malignant, obnoxious

helm SEE MAIN ENTRY

helot captive

helotism servitude

helotry bondage, servitude, subjection, thrall

help abet, accommodate, advantage, advocacy, aid *(help),* aid, ameliorate, assist, assistance, avail *(be of use),* behalf, benefactor, capitalize *(provide capital),* charity, coadjutant, consortium *(marriage companionship),* contribute *(assist),* contribution *(participation),* countenance, emend, employee, enable, endow, espouse, expedite, facilitate, favor *(sanction),* favor, foster, guidance, inure *(benefit),* largess *(generosity),* largess *(gift),* mainstay, nurture, pander, patronage *(support),* personnel, profit, promote *(advance),* promote *(organize),* promotion *(encouragement),* reassure, redress, reinforcement, relief *(aid),* relieve *(give aid),* remedy *(legal means of redress),* remedy *(that which corrects),* remedy, samaritan, save *(rescue),* serve *(assist),* service *(assistance),* side, solace, staff, subsidize, support *(assistance),* support *(assist),* uphold. SEE MAIN ENTRY

help a judge clerk

help along assist, ease, hasten

help oneself to assume *(seize),* hijack, impropriate, occupy *(take possession),* pirate *(reproduce without authorization),* procure, usurp

help to bestow

help with money subsidize

helper abettor, accessory, accomplice, assistant, backer, benefactor, coactor, coadjutant, cohort, colleague, confederate, consociate, conspirer, contributor *(contributor),* copartner *(business associate),* copartner *(coconspirator),* donor, employee, good samaritan, participant, partner, patron *(influential supporter),* samaritan

helpful ancillary *(auxiliary),* beneficial, benevolent, charitable *(lenient),* constructive *(creative),* contributory, convenient,

disposable, effective *(efficient),* favorable *(advantageous),* favorable *(expressing approval),* functional, humane, instrumental, medicinal, ministerial, obeisant, operative, palliative *(abating),* philanthropic, practical, profitable, propitious, purposeful, salutary, subservient, valuable

helpfulness aid *(help),* assistance, benevolence *(act of kindness),* benevolence *(disposition to do good),* consideration *(sympathetic regard),* efficiency, goodwill, help, instigation, largess *(generosity),* philanthropy, utility *(usefulness)*

helping beneficial, clerical, contributory, ministerial, part *(portion),* propitious, ration, subsidiary

helping hand good samaritan, reinforcement, samaritan, service *(assistance),* support *(assistance)*

helpless dependent, derelict *(abandoned),* disabled *(deprived of legal right),* disabled *(made incapable),* inadequate, indefensible, insecure, powerless, susceptible *(unresistent),* unable. SEE MAIN ENTRY

helpless person dependent

helplessness danger, disability *(physical inability),* impotence, impuissance, inability, incapacity, inefficacy, languor, peril, prostration

helpmate accessory, accomplice, assistant, confederate, consociate, consort, conspirer, contributor *(contributor),* copartner *(coconspirator),* spouse

helpmeet spouse

hem border, margin *(outside limit)*

hem in border *(bound),* circumscribe *(surround by boundary),* enclose, encompass *(surround),* envelop, limit, occlude, restrict, shut

hemisphere circuit, zone

hemp cannabis

hence a savoir, consequently. SEE MAIN ENTRY

henceforth SEE MAIN ENTRY

henchman abettor, coactor, coadjutant. SEE MAIN ENTRY

her honor judge

herald anticipate *(prognosticate),* declare, forerunner, harbinger, indicator, inform *(notify),* informant, informer *(a person who provides information),* notify, portend, precede, precursor, predict, preface, proclaim, prognosticate, promulgate, propagate *(spread),* publish, report *(disclose).* SEE MAIN ENTRY

heralding portentous *(ominous)*

Herculean omnipotent, onerous, operose, powerful, prodigious *(enormous),* strong

herd together congregate

here present *(current).* SEE MAIN ENTRY

hereabouts SEE MAIN ENTRY

hereafter SEE MAIN ENTRY

hereby SEE MAIN ENTRY

hereditable hereditary, heritable

hereditament bequest, demesne, domain *(land owned),* estate *(property),* fee *(estate),* freehold, heritage, real estate. SEE MAIN ENTRY

hereditaments property *(possessions)*

hereditarius hereditary

hereditary born *(innate),* consanguineous, derivative, genetic, heritable, native *(inborn),* testamentary. SEE MAIN ENTRY

hereditary enmity feud

hereditas heritage, inheritance, reversion *(remainder of an estate)*

hereditas caduca escheat

heredity affiliation *(bloodline)*, ancestry, birth *(lineage)*, blood, bloodline, descent *(lineage)*
heredium heritage
herein wherein. SEE MAIN ENTRY
hereinafter SEE MAIN ENTRY
hereof SEE MAIN ENTRY
heresy blasphemy, nonconformity
heretic malcontent, pariah, recusant. SEE MAIN ENTRY
heretical deviant, nonconforming, skeptical, unorthodox
heretofore theretofore. SEE MAIN ENTRY
hereunder a savoir
hereupon a savoir
herewith SEE MAIN ENTRY
heriditary innate
heritable bequest, hereditament, hereditary. SEE MAIN ENTRY
heritage affinity *(family ties)*, bequest, birth *(lineage)*, birthright, blood, claim *(right)*, descent *(lineage)*, estate *(hereditament)*, hereditament, inheritance, origin *(ancestry)*, right *(entitlement)*. SEE MAIN ENTRY
heritance birthright, estate *(hereditament)*, hereditament, heritage, legacy
hermetic impervious
hermitic solitary
hermitical solitary
hero paragon, protagonist. SEE MAIN ENTRY
hero worship doxology
hero-like spartan
heroic illustrious, meritorious, spartan, undaunted. SEE MAIN ENTRY
heroic achievement prowess *(bravery)*
heroism prowess *(bravery)*
herolike heroic
hesitance pause, qualm, reluctance
hesitancy doubt *(indecision)*, hesitation, incertitude, indecision, pause, qualm, reluctance, scruple
hesitant disinclined, irresolute, leery, noncommittal, recreant, reluctant, suspicious *(distrustful)*, undecided. SEE MAIN ENTRY
hesitate defer *(put off)*, discontinue *(break continuity)*, misdoubt, mistrust, oscillate, pause, procrastinate, recess, refuse, vacillate. SEE MAIN ENTRY
hesitating diffident, disinclined, hesitant, irresolute, leery, noncommittal, reluctant
hesitation ambivalence, cloud *(suspicion)*, doubt *(suspicion)*, halt, incertitude, indecision, misgiving, pause, qualm, reluctance, scruple. SEE MAIN ENTRY
hesitative hesitant, reluctant
hest directive, fiat
heteroclite irregular *(not usual)*
heterodox recusant, skeptical, unorthodox
heterodoxy disaccord, nonconformity
heterogeneity difference, diversification, diversity, nonconformity
heterogeneous composite, different, disordered, dissimilar, diverse, miscellaneous, multifarious, promiscuous, unrelated. SEE MAIN ENTRY
hew break *(fracture)*, split
heyday prosperity
hiatus absence *(omission)*, blank *(emptiness)*, cessation *(interlude)*. SEE MAIN ENTRY
hiatus hiatus
hiatus interruption, interval, lapse *(break)*, pendency, recess, rift *(gap)*, split
hibernating dormant
hic current
hidden blind *(concealed)*, clandestine, confidential, covert, enigmatic, esoteric, furtive, impalpable, inapprehensible,

incomprehensible, inconspicuous, indirect, indiscernible, inexplicable, inscrutable, lost *(taken away)*, mysterious, obscure *(abstruse)*, obscure *(faint)*, personal *(private)*, private *(confidential)*, private *(secluded)*, privy, recondite, remote *(secluded)*, secret, sly, stealthy, surreptitious, ulterior, undisclosed. SEE MAIN ENTRY
hidden from view latent
hidden knowledge secret
hidden meaning implication *(inference)*, mystery, nuance
hide abscond, blind *(obscure)*, camouflage, cloak, conceal, cover *(conceal)*, disguise, elude, ensconce, enshroud, envelop, flee, harbor, hedge, hoard, lurk, obfuscate, obnubilate, obscure, reserve, screen *(guard)*, seclude, shroud, withhold. SEE MAIN ENTRY
hide away blind *(obscure)*, camouflage, cloak, ensconce, hoard, plant *(covertly place)*
hide from evade *(elude)*, shun
hide from view ensconce
hide one's identity camouflage, disguise
hide securely ensconce
hide the identity of blind *(obscure)*
hide the truth perjure
hide under a mask pretend
hide underground blind *(obscure)*
hideaway cache *(hiding place)*
hidebound illiberal, parochial, rigid
hideous loathsome, odious, offensive *(offending)*, repulsive. SEE MAIN ENTRY
hideout haven
hiding concealment, disguise, nonappearance
hiding place refuge
hie race
hierarchy class
hieroglyphic hidden
higgle haggle
high disdainful, priceless
high character honesty, integrity
high coloring bombast
high explosive bomb
high honor prestige
high ideals conscience
high interest usury
high land elevation
high level executive
high official caretaker *(one fulfilling the function of office)*
high opinion estimation *(esteem)*, mention *(tribute)*
high point landmark *(significant change)*
high position eminence, primacy
high powered in full force
high pressure duress
high pressure methods compulsion *(coercion)*
high prices inflation *(decrease in value of currency)*
high principles honesty, probity
high priority exigent
high probability SEE MAIN ENTRY
high rank eminence
high regard credit *(recognition)*, estimation *(esteem)*, homage, honor *(good reputation)*, honor *(outward respect)*
high repute prestige
high reward character *(reputation)*
high society elite
high spot highlight
high standards conscience
high station eminence
high structure edifice

high worth cost *(price)*
high-class superior *(excellent)*
high-flown flatulent, fustian, inflated *(bombastic)*, orotund, turgid
high-grade preferential, premium, sterling, superior *(excellent)*
high-handed tyrannous
high-level important *(significant)*, major
high-minded clean, law-abiding, magnanimous, meritorious, moral. SEE MAIN ENTRY
high-mindedness honesty, integrity
high-paying lucrative
high-potency powerful
high-powered SEE MAIN ENTRY
high-pressure intense
high-priced exorbitant, priceless, prohibitive *(costly)*
high-principled clean, high-minded, incorruptible, law-abiding, meritorious, moral, reputable, strict
high-priority important *(urgent)*, indispensable
high-quality premium, sterling, superior *(excellent)*
high-sounding fustian, grandiose, inflated *(bombastic)*
high-sounding words bombast, fustian
high-spirited hot-blooded
high-strung hot-blooded, sensitive *(easily affected)*
high-technology SEE MAIN ENTRY
higher class society
higher court appellate court
highest absolute *(ideal)*, best, cardinal *(outstanding)*, paramount, primary, prime *(most valuable)*, principal, superlative, utmost *(adjective)*, utmost *(noun)*. SEE MAIN ENTRY
highest degree ceiling, pinnacle
highest point ceiling, culmination, pinnacle
highest position supremacy
highest quality professional *(stellar)*
highest ranking person chief
highhanded dictatorial
highlight cornerstone, emphasis, feature *(special attraction)*, indicate. SEE MAIN ENTRY
highly SEE MAIN ENTRY
highly developed skill science *(technique)*
highly disciplined spartan
highly important central *(essential)*
highly important detail necessity, need *(requirement)*
highly principled upright
highly reputed famous
highly serious serious *(grave)*
highly specialized technical
highly specific technical
highly thought of popular
highly wrought elaborate
highness elevation
highroad causeway
highway causeway
highways approaches
hijack SEE MAIN ENTRY
hike boom *(increase)*, perambulate
hike in prices inflation *(decrease in value of currency)*
hilarious jocular
hinder arrest *(stop)*, balk, bind *(restrain)*, block, check *(restrain)*, clog, conflict, constrain *(restrain)*, constrict *(inhibit)*, contain *(restrain)*, control *(restrain)*, counter, counteract, countervail, curb, debar, defer *(put off)*, delay, detain *(restrain)*, deter, disable, disadvantage, disappoint, discommode,

discontinue (break continuity), discourage, disrupt, enjoin, estop, fetter, fight (counteract), foil, forbid, forestall, frustrate, halt, hamper, hold up (delay), impair, impede, inconvenience, inhibit, interdict, interfere, interpose, interrupt, keep (restrain), limit, lock, obstruct, obturate, occlude, oppugn, preclude, prevent, prohibit, repress, repulse, resist (oppose), restrain, stall, stave, stay (halt), stem (check), stop, suspend, tamper, thwart, toll (stop), trammel, withhold, withstand. SEE MAIN ENTRY

hinder movement encumber (hinder)
hindered arrested (checked), broken (interrupted)
hinderer deterrent
hindering binding, detrimental, disadvantageous, encumbrance, intrusive, limiting, preventive, prohibitive (restrictive), restrictive
hindermost back (in reverse), extreme (last), last (final)
hindmost back (in reverse), extreme (last), last (final)
hindrance admonition, bar (obstruction), barrier, burden, censorship, check (bar), complication, constraint (restriction), damper (stopper), deterrence, deterrent, disadvantage, disincentive, disturbance, encumbrance, estoppel, fetter, filibuster, frustration, handicap, impediment, imposition (excessive burden), interruption, liability, nuisance, obstacle, obstruction, onus (burden), pressure, prohibition, resistance, restraint, stay, trouble. SEE MAIN ENTRY
hindsight retrospect. SEE MAIN ENTRY
hindward back (in reverse)
hinge crossroad (turning point). SEE MAIN ENTRY
hint allude, clue, connotation, connote, guidance, implication (inference), indicant, indicate, indication, indicator, infer, inference, innuendo, insinuation, intimation, mention (reference), monition (warning), prompt, reference (allusion), remind, reminder, report (rumor), signify (denote), suggestion, suspicion (uncertainty), tip (clue). SEE MAIN ENTRY
hint at imply, mention, refer (direct attention)
hints indicia
hire delegate, employ (engage services), fare, let (lease), pay, procure, rate, retain (employ), revenue, sublease, wage. SEE MAIN ENTRY
hire out let (lease), rent
hired mercenary
hired hand employee
hireling employee, mercenary
hirer client
his honor judge
historic traditional
historical honest, traditional
historical record journal
historically speaking heretofore
historiette story (narrative)
historify record
historize record
history account (report), ancestry, bloodline, calendar (record of yearly periods), common knowledge, record, report (detailed account), story (narrative). SEE MAIN ENTRY
histrionic demonstrative (expressive of emotion), orotund. SEE MAIN ENTRY
histrionics exaggeration, pretense (ostentation). SEE MAIN ENTRY

hit attack, beat (strike), collide (crash against), contact (touch), impinge, impress (affect deeply), lash (strike), strike (assault), strike (collide). SEE MAIN ENTRY
hit against jostle (bump into), strike (collide)
hit and run SEE MAIN ENTRY
hit back recriminate
hit upon find (discover)
hit upon a solution resolve (solve)
hitch connection (fastening), damper (stopper), encumbrance, obstruction, period
hive hoard
hoard accumulate (amass), collection (accumulation), fund (noun), fund (verb), garner, preserve, provision (something provided), reserve, save (hold back), selection (collection), stock (store), store (depository), store, sufficiency. SEE MAIN ENTRY
hoary elderly, old
hoax artifice, betray (lead astray), bilk, bunko, canard, circumvent, collusion, deceive, deception, defraud, delude, dupe, ensnare, evade (deceive), fake (noun), fake (verb), false pretense, falsification, frame up, hoodwink, illude, imposture, knavery, maneuver (trick), misrepresent, palter, pretense (pretext), ruse. SEE MAIN ENTRY
hobble block, maim, repress, restrict, trammel
hoboism vagrancy
hodgepodge melange
hoggish insatiable
hoist elevate. SEE MAIN ENTRY
hold accommodate, adjudge, advantage, apprehend (arrest), arrest (apprehend), arrest (stop), chamber (compartment), claim (maintain), comprise, conclude (decide), confine, consist, constrain (imprison), contain (comprise), contend (maintain), decide, deem, delay, depository, desist, detain (hold in custody), determine, dominance, dominion (supreme authority), embrace (encircle), encompass (include), find (determine), grapple, halt, handcuff, immerse (engross), immure, include, influence, judge, keep (restrain), keep (shelter), lock, moratorium, obtain, occupy (take possession), opine, own, possess, power, primacy, remain (occupy), remain (stay), reserve, restrain, retain (keep in possession), retention, rule (decide), save (conserve), seisin, sentence, stay (halt), stop, store, suspect (think), withhold. SEE MAIN ENTRY
hold a brief for bear (support)
hold a conference confer (consult), discourse
hold a consultation confer (consult), deliberate
hold a conversation speak
hold a convocation meet
hold a discussion speak
hold a high opinion of regard (hold in esteem)
hold a meeting convene, meet
hold a position of authority preside
hold a session convene, meet
hold accountable denounce (inform against), incriminate. SEE MAIN ENTRY
hold aloft elevate
hold an argument dispute (debate)
hold an inquiry analyze, audit, canvass, delve, investigate
hold an office officiate
hold an opinion deem
hold apart separate

hold as a hostage confine
hold as hostage constrain (imprison)
hold at bay counter, parry
hold at fault impeach
hold authority govern, handle (manage), preside, rule (govern)
hold back arrest (stop), avoid (evade), balk, clog, confine, constrain (restrain), constrict (inhibit), contain (restrain), control (restrain), curb, debar, decline (reject), defer (put off), delay, detain (restrain), deter, disadvantage, forbear, forestall, hamper, hesitate, hinder, hoard, impede, inhibit, keep (restrain), limit, mistrust, parry, pause, prevent, procrastinate, refrain, refuse, repress, reserve, restrain, restrict, stem (check), stop, toll (stop), trammel, withhold
hold back action encumber (hinder)
hold back by force constrain (imprison), constrain (imprison)
hold by force usurp
hold captive capture, confine, constrain (imprison), detain (hold in custody), immure, imprison, jail, obsess, subjugate
hold cheap decry, disdain, disfavor, misprize
hold conclave deliberate, discuss
hold conference converse, discuss
hold conversations discuss
hold court adjudicate, hear (give a legal hearing)
hold dear foster, regard (hold in esteem)
hold different views differ (disagree)
hold dominion predominate (command), rule (govern)
hold down constrain (restrain), dominate, extinguish, subject
hold fast adhere (fasten), cohere (adhere), grapple, hold (possess), hold out (resist), persevere, persist, retain (keep in possession)
hold firmly adhere (fasten)
hold for ransom kidnap
hold forth declaim, exposit, offer (propose), recite, recount
hold in constrain (restrain), inhibit, keep (restrain), repress, withhold
hold in abeyance adjourn, defer (put off), delay, discontinue (break continuity), forbear, hold up (delay), suspend. SEE MAIN ENTRY
hold in affection regard (hold in esteem)
hold in belief deem
hold in bondage subject, subjugate
hold in captivity capture, confine, immure, imprison, jail
hold in check balk, check (restrain), clog, confine, constrain (restrain), contain (restrain), control (restrain), curb, detain (hold in custody), disadvantage, enjoin, immure, impede, moderate (preside over), restrain
hold in constraint commit (institutionalize)
hold in contempt condescend (patronize), contemn, decry, disdain, flout, ignore, misprize, reject, spurn
hold in custody contain (restrain), jail, restrain
hold in derision flout, humiliate, jeer, mock (deride)
hold in despite contemn
hold in disrespect condescend (patronize), flout, humiliate
hold in esteem defer (yield in judgment), honor
hold in leash discipline (control)
hold in legal custody impound

hold in line   discipline *(control)*
hold in one's grasp   hold *(possess)*
hold in possession   retain *(keep in possession)*
hold in preventive custody   detain *(hold in custody)*
hold in regard   regard *(hold in esteem)*
hold in restraint   commit *(institutionalize)*, constrain *(imprison)*, imprison
hold in subjection   subject
hold in thrall   confine, detain *(hold in custody)*
hold in view   anticipate *(expect)*, observe *(watch)*
hold intercourse   discuss
hold liable   convict, encumber *(financially obligate)*
hold no brief for   blame, disown *(deny the validity)*
hold not to be true   disbelieve
hold off   cease, counter, defer *(put off)*, doubt *(hesitate)*, forbear, parry, pause, postpone, resist *(withstand)*, stave. SEE MAIN ENTRY
hold office   govern, predominate *(command)*, rule *(govern)*
hold on   adhere *(persist)*, cohere *(adhere)*, last, persevere, persist, subsist
hold on property   charge *(lien)*, cloud *(incumbrance)*, lien, mechanics lien
hold one's ground   endure *(last)*
hold ones own   hold out *(resist)*
hold opposite views   collide *(clash)*, conflict, discaccord, disagree
hold out   endure *(last)*, extend *(offer)*, last, offer *(propose)*, persevere, persist, profess *(avow)*, proffer, remain *(continue)*, resist *(withstand)*, submit *(give)*, tender, withhold, withstand. SEE MAIN ENTRY
hold out against   counter, oppugn
hold out allurement   bait *(lure)*, entrap, lure
hold out hope   reassure
hold out temptation   entrap, lure
hold over   adjourn, continue *(adjourn)*, delay, prolong
hold possession   remain *(occupy)*
hold prisoner   confine
hold questionable   misdoubt
hold responsible   blame, charge *(accuse)*, convict, delegate, denounce *(inform against)*, implicate
hold responsible for   confide *(trust)*. SEE MAIN ENTRY
hold spellbound   immerse *(engross)*, monopolize
hold sway   govern, preside
hold sway over   moderate *(preside over)*, subjugate
hold the advantage   beat *(defeat)*
hold the attention   interest
hold the chair   moderate *(preside over)*, preside
hold the interest of   engage *(involve)*, monopolize
hold the opinion   assume *(suppose)*, contend *(maintain)*
hold the reins   overlook *(superintend)*
hold tight   adhere *(persist)*
hold to blame   fault
hold together   annex *(add)*, cement, cohere *(adhere)*, cohere *(be logically consistent)*, conjoin, conspire
hold under duress   detain *(hold in custody)*
hold up   bear *(support)*, clog, cohere *(adhere)*, curb, defer *(put off)*, delay, detain

(restrain), deter, elevate, encumber *(hinder)*, heighten *(elevate)*, impede, keep *(restrain)*, last, maintain *(sustain)*, manifest, procrastinate, promote *(organize)*, protract *(prolong)*, remit *(relax)*, resist *(withstand)*, rob, stall, steal, uphold. SEE MAIN ENTRY
hold up one's hand   cast *(register)*
hold up to execration   censure, disapprove *(condemn)*
hold up to public ridicule   expose
hold up to reprobation   blame, censure, disapprove *(condemn)*
hold up to ridicule   mock *(deride)*, pillory
hold up to scorn   flout. SEE MAIN ENTRY
hold up to shame   brand *(stigmatize)*, discredit, disgrace, pillory, smear
hold up to view   manifest, produce *(offer to view)*
hold upon the property of another   lien
hold with   concur *(agree)*, countenance
hold within bounds   immure
hold-over   adjournment
holdback   disadvantage, hindrance, impediment, restraint. SEE MAIN ENTRY
holder   bearer, catchall, coffer, depository, receiver, recipient, tenant. SEE MAIN ENTRY
holder of an estate by virtue of a lease   lessee
holder of an office   incumbent
holder of legal title   landholder, landowner
holder of the legal estate   trustee
holdfast   connection *(fastening)*
holding   chattel, custody *(incarceration)*, demesne, domain *(land owned)*, dominion *(absolute ownership)*, fee *(estate)*, interest *(ownership)*, occupancy, ownership, possession *(property)*, property *(land)*, ruling, share *(stock)*, stake *(interest)*, tenancy, tenure, trust *(custody)*. SEE MAIN ENTRY
holding a low opinion of mankind   cynical
holding ability   capacity *(maximum)*
holding action   retention
holding back   hesitation
holding by title   tenancy
holding company   corporation, firm
holding in constraint   commitment *(confinement)*
holding in custody   apprehension *(act of arresting)*
holding in restraint   commitment *(confinement)*
holding legal rights conferred by another   acting
holding off   abstention
holding power   retention
holding property   proprietary
holding public interest   famous
holding to a purpose   pertinacious
holding together   adherence *(adhesion)*, coherence, coherent *(joined)*, cohesive *(sticking)*
holding up well   durable
holdings   assets, capital, commodities, effects, estate *(property)*, paraphernalia *(personal belongings)*, personalty, portfolio, possessions, principal *(capital sum)*, property *(possessions)*, realty, securities, stock *(shares)*
holdover   SEE MAIN ENTRY
holdup   robbery
holdup man   burglar, hoodlum
hole   outlet, predicament. SEE MAIN ENTRY
holiday   furlough, leave *(absence)*, remembrance *(commemoration)*. SEE MAIN ENTRY
holistic   whole *(unified)*

hollow   chamber *(compartment)*, deficient, jejune *(dull)*, perfunctory, untenable, vacant, vacuous, void *(empty)*. SEE MAIN ENTRY
hollow place   chamber *(compartment)*
hollow pretense   hypocrisy, imposture
hollowness   blank *(emptiness)*
holocaust   atrocity, cataclysm, catastrophe, disaster, havoc, shambles
holographic   SEE MAIN ENTRY
holy   infrangible, sacrosanct, solemn
homage   adherence *(devotion)*, adhesion *(loyalty)*, allegiance, estimation *(esteem)*, fealty, fidelity, honor *(outward respect)*, mention *(tribute)*, remembrance *(commemoration)*, respect. SEE MAIN ENTRY
home   abode, address, apartment, building *(structure)*, domestic *(household)*, domestic *(indigenous)*, domicile, habitation *(dwelling place)*, homestead, house, household *(domestic)*, household, inhabitation *(place of dwelling)*, lodging, residence, residential, seat, shelter *(protection)*. SEE MAIN ENTRY
home base   headquarters
home circle   family *(household)*
home invasion   SEE MAIN ENTRY
home office   headquarters
home rule   SEE MAIN ENTRY
home-grown   native *(domestic)*
home-loving   household *(domestic)*
home-owning   household *(domestic)*
homeland   home *(domicile)*, home *(place of origin)*, nationality
homeless   derelict *(abandoned)*, solitary
homeless child   orphan
homely   familiar *(customary)*, inelegant, nondescript, ordinary
homemade   domestic *(indigenous)*. SEE MAIN ENTRY
homemaking   domestic *(household)*, household *(domestic)*
homeostasis   balance *(equality)*
homes   premises *(buildings)*
homespun   inelegant, mundane, ordinary, simple
homestead   abode, building *(structure)*, dwelling, habitation *(dwelling place)*, home *(domicile)*, house, household, property *(land)*. SEE MAIN ENTRY
homicidal   deadly
homicide   aberemurder, assassination, dispatch *(act of putting to death)*, killing, manslaughter, murder. SEE MAIN ENTRY
homicidium   manslaughter
homiletic   informative
homiletical   informative
homily   peroration
hominem   endow
hominem adire   apply *(request)*
hominem adloqui   address *(talk to)*
hominem armis exuere   disarm *(divest of arms)*
hominem deserere   abandon *(physically leave)*
hominem imitari   impersonate
hominem iubere facere   command
hominem permulcere   coax
homines   public, society
homini blandiri   coax
homini civitatem dare   naturalize *(make a citizen)*
homini gratiam debere   obligation *(duty)*
homini imperare   command
homini obsistere   cross *(disagree with)*
homini placere   appeal
homini praecipere ut faciat   command
homini rei   empower, enable

homini suadere advise

homini viam monstrare direct *(show)*

hominis welfare

hominis bona vendere distrain

hominis caedes manslaughter

hominis nomen deferre inform *(betray)*

hominum generis humanity *(mankind)*

homo inhabitant, person

homo maleficus delinquent *(guilty of a misdeed)*, delinquent, malefactor, wrong-doer

homo peritus specialist

homo rerum novarum cupidus malcontent

homo sapiens humanity *(mankind)*

homo sceleratus malefactor

homo studiosus partisan

homo trium literarum burglar

homogeneity identity *(similarity)*, propinquity *(similarity)*, regularity, resemblance, uniformity, union *(unity)*

homogeneous boiler plate, cognate, comparable *(capable of comparison)*, identical, pure, similar, simple, uniform

homologate agree *(comply)*, assent, authorize, concur *(agree)*, confirm, correspond *(be equivalent)*, countenance, sanction

homologation sanction *(permission)*

homological correlative

homologize coordinate, correspond *(be equivalent)*

homologous analogous, coequal, coextensive, cognate, comparable *(capable of comparison)*, equal

homologue counterpart *(complement)*

homology analogy, relation *(connection)*

homosexual SEE MAIN ENTRY

honest actual, authentic, bona fide, candid, clean, conscientious, credible, direct *(forthright)*, equitable, ethical, factual, fair *(just)*, faithful *(true to fact)*, genuine, high-minded, impartial, incorruptible, ingenuous, irreprehensible, just, law-abiding, meritorious, moral, proper, reliable, reputable, right *(correct)*, rightful, scrupulous, sterling, straightforward, true *(authentic)*, unaffected *(sincere)*, upright, veridical. SEE MAIN ENTRY

honest effort good faith

honestly fairly *(impartially)*, faithfully, in good faith

honestus moral, reputable, upright

honesty candor *(straightforwardness)*, conscience, equity *(justice)*, ethics, fairness, integrity, principle *(virtue)*, probity, rectitude, trustworthiness, truth, veracity. SEE MAIN ENTRY

honeyed nectarious

honor accept *(recognize)*, character *(reputation)*, compensate *(remunerate)*, conscience, credit *(recognition)*, dedicate, defer *(yield in judgment)*, deference, discharge *(pay a debt)*, distinction *(reputation)*, elevate, eminence, estimation *(esteem)*, ethics, homage, integrity, keep *(fulfill)*, laudation, mention *(tribute)*, merit, observe *(obey)*, pay, prestige, principle *(virtue)*, privilege, prize, probity, raise *(advance)*, recognize *(acknowledge)*, rectitude, regard *(esteem)*, regard *(hold in esteem)*, respect, right *(righteousness)*. SEE MAIN ENTRY

honor a bill defray

honor a claim refund

honor with bestow

honorable bona fide, clean, conscientious, equitable, ethical, exemplary, fair *(just)*, high-minded, honest, impartial, incorruptible, ingenuous, just, law-abiding, loyal, magnanimous, meritorious, moral, obeisant, outstanding *(prominent)*, pure, reliable, reputable, right *(correct)*, scrupulous, sterling, straightforward, upright. SEE MAIN ENTRY

honorable justice judge

honorableness honesty, integrity, principle *(virtue)*, probity, rectitude

honorably fairly *(impartially)*, faithfully

honorarium bonus, bounty, contribution *(donation)*, payment *(remittance)*, reward. SEE MAIN ENTRY

honorary nominal. SEE MAIN ENTRY

honored famous, illustrious, influential, outstanding *(prominent)*, prominent, proud *(self-respecting)*, renowned, reputable. SEE MAIN ENTRY

honorific honorary

honorifical honorary

honoring dedication, obedient, remembrance *(commemoration)*

hood enshroud

hoodlum lawbreaker, malefactor. SEE MAIN ENTRY

hoodwink betray *(lead astray)*, bilk, deceive, delude, ensnare, fake, pretend, prevaricate. SEE MAIN ENTRY

hook connect *(join together)*, ensnare, trap

hooligan malefactor

hoot mock *(deride)*

hope chance *(possibility)*, design *(intent)*, end *(intent)*, expectation, faith, goal, objective, plan, possibility, prospect *(outlook)*, purpose, target, trust, will *(desire)*. SEE MAIN ENTRY

hope for desire

hoped for prospective

hopeful apparent *(presumptive)*, auspicious, candidate, novice, propitious, sanguine, solicitous

hopeless despondent, diabolic, disconsolate, futile, impossible, impracticable, incorrigible, inoperable *(incurable)*, irredeemable, irremediable, irreversible, ominous, pessimistic, unfavorable, unpropitious

hopeless failure miscarriage

hopelessly lost irretrievable

hopelessness impasse, impossibility, peril, pessimism

horde assemblage, band, congregation

horizon SEE MAIN ENTRY

horizontality prostration

horn in intrude

hornbook SEE MAIN ENTRY

horrendous contemptible, depraved, disastrous, disreputable, heinous, reprehensible. SEE MAIN ENTRY

horrible contemptible, deplorable, diabolic, dire, disastrous, disgraceful, formidable, gross *(flagrant)*, heinous, lamentable, loathsome, lurid, nefarious, obnoxious, odious, offensive *(offending)*, repulsive, sinister. SEE MAIN ENTRY

horrid deplorable, dire, disastrous, disreputable, heinous, lamentable, loathsome, objectionable, obnoxious, odious, offensive *(offending)*, repulsive, sinister, vicious

horrific deplorable

horrify frighten, offend *(insult)*, repel *(disgust)*. SEE MAIN ENTRY

horrifying deplorable, dire, formidable, lurid, outrageous, repulsive, scandalous

horror consternation, fear, fright, odium, panic, phobia, trepidation. SEE MAIN ENTRY

hors de combat disabled *(made incapable)*

hortans hortative

hortation instigation

hortative informative, informatory, persuasive. SEE MAIN ENTRY

hortatory hortative, informative, informatory, persuasive

hospes stranger

hospitable benevolent, humane, liberal *(generous)*, philanthropic, receptive

hospitableness largess *(generosity)*, philanthropy

hospital case patient

hospitality charity, largess *(generosity)*, philanthropy

hospitalized person patient

hospitio excipere lodge *(house)*

host body *(collection)*, mass *(body of persons)*, plurality, quantity. SEE MAIN ENTRY

hostage captive, prisoner. SEE MAIN ENTRY

hostel lodge *(house)*

hostia victim

hostile averse, bitter *(reproachful)*, discordant, disobedient, impertinent *(insolent)*, inimical, irreconcilable, litigious, malevolent, malicious, malignant, negative, nonconsenting, offensive *(taking the initiative)*, opposite, prejudicial, pugnacious, recusant, repugnant *(incompatible)*, spiteful, unfavorable, virulent. SEE MAIN ENTRY

hostile attack diatribe, impugnation

hostile contest confrontation *(altercation)*

hostile criticism diatribe, disparagement, impeachment

hostile demonstration protest

hostile eloquence diatribe

hostile encounter confrontation *(altercation)*, fight *(battle)*

hostile entrance incursion

hostile entry invasion

hostile invasion foray

hostile person foe

hostile verdict conviction *(finding of guilt)*, nonsuit

hostile witness SEE MAIN ENTRY

hostilities conflict

hostility alienation *(estrangement)*, argument *(contention)*, belligerency, collision *(dispute)*, conflict, contention *(opposition)*, discord, estrangement, feud, hatred, ill will, impugnation, incompatibility *(difference)*, malice, odium, ostracism, rancor, spite, umbrage

hostis foe

hot vehement

hot-blooded SEE MAIN ENTRY

hot-headed hot-blooded, imprudent, outrageous, petulant, precipitate

hot-tempered fractious, hot-blooded, petulant

hotheaded impulsive *(rash)*

hound badger, bait *(harass)*, harry *(harass)*, hector, hunt, importune, molest *(annoy)*, obsess, press *(goad)*, prompt, provoke, trace *(follow)*

hour point *(period of time)*

hour of decision crossroad *(turning point)*

house abode, building *(structure)*, concern *(business establishment)*, domicile, dwelling, enterprise *(economic organization)*, family *(common ancestry)*, firm, habitation *(dwelling place)*, home *(domicile)*, homestead, inhabitation *(place of dwelling)*, institute, locate, market *(business)*, parentage, preserve, protect, shelter *(protection)*. SEE MAIN ENTRY

house arrest SEE MAIN ENTRY

house of correction jail, penitentiary, prison, reformatory

house of detention jail, penitentiary, prison, reformatory

house of reform prison

house of representatives legislature

house with the grounds belonging to it premises (buildings)

house-building program development (building)

housebreaker burglar

housebreaking burglary. SEE MAIN ENTRY

housed situated

household domestic (household), familiar (customary), home (domicile), homestead, house, ordinary, prevalent, property (land), residential. SEE MAIN ENTRY

householder inhabitant, occupant, proprietor, tenant

housekeeping domestic (household), household (domestic)

housing development (building), habitation (dwelling place), lodging, residence

hover prowl, vacillate

however notwithstanding, regardless, unless

howl outcry

hub body (main part), focus

hubbub bluster (commotion), brawl, noise, riot

hubris pride

huckster dealer, merchant, sell, trade, vendor

huddle meet, turmoil

hue color (complexion)

huff resentment

huffy petulant, resentful

huge capacious, exorbitant, far reaching, formidable, grandiose, gross (flagrant), prodigious (enormous)

hulking ponderous

hullabaloo noise, outcry

human bodily, character (an individual), person, physical. SEE MAIN ENTRY

human being body (person), character (an individual), individual, person

human beings humanity (mankind)

human creature person

human environment ecology

human race mortality

human weakness foible, frailty

humane benevolent, charitable (lenient), lenient, liberal (generous), philanthropic. SEE MAIN ENTRY

humaneness benevolence (disposition to do good), charity, clemency, philanthropy

humanism benevolence (disposition to do good)

humanitarian benefactor, benevolent, charitable (lenient), donor, good samaritan, humane, liberal (generous), nonprofit, philanthropic

humanitarianism aid (subsistence), charity, help, philanthropy

humanitas civilization, humanity (humaneness), philanthropy

humanity benevolence (disposition to do good), charity, clemency, consideration (sympathetic regard), goodwill, lenience, mortality, populace, population, tolerance, understanding (tolerance). SEE MAIN ENTRY

humanize personify

humankind humanity (mankind)

humanness mortality

humanum genus humanity (mankind)

humanus humane, philanthropic

humble browbeat, contrite, debase, demean (make lower), demote, derogate, diffident, familiar (customary), humiliate, ignoble, marginal, obeisant, obsequious, paltry, penitent, reduce, repentant, servile, subaltern, subdue, subject, subjugate, subordinate, unobtrusive, unpretentious

humble entreaty prayer

humble oneself condescend (deign), repent

humble oneself to obey

humble service fealty

humbled contrite, diffident

humbled pride disgrace

humbleness poverty, respect

humbling disgrace

humbly respectfully

humbug bilk, deceive, invent (falsify), pettifoggery, ruse

humbuggery deception, knavery

humdrum ordinary, prosaic, stale, usual

humiliate browbeat, debase, demean (make lower), denigrate, disgrace, disparage, smear. SEE MAIN ENTRY

humiliating disgraceful, libelous

humiliating rudeness contumely

humiliation attaint, contumely, degradation, disgrace, dishonor (shame), embarrassment, ignominy, infamy, obloquy, odium, opprobrium, scandal, shame. SEE MAIN ENTRY

humiliative disgraceful

humilis ignoble, servile

humility homage, respect

humor characteristic, disposition (inclination), notion, pander, placate, propitiate, soothe, spirit, vouchsafe

humor excessively overindulge

humoring indulgence, lenient

humorless grave (solemn), pedestrian

humorous jocular, ludicrous

humorsome restive, volatile

hunch premonition

hunger desire, passion

hunger for lack, need

hunt chase, ferret, frisk, prey, pursue (chase), pursuit (chase), pursuit (effort to secure), quest, research, search. SEE MAIN ENTRY

hunt down expose

hunt for delve

hunt out trace (follow)

hunt through delve, frisk

hunted person fugitive

hurdle bar (obstruction), barrier, deterrence, deterrent, encumbrance, handicap, negotiate, obstacle, obstruction. SEE MAIN ENTRY

hurl cast (throw), emit, impel, launch (project), project (impel forward), send

hurl defiance at challenge

hurl headlong precipitate (throw down violently)

hurricane SEE MAIN ENTRY

hurried brief, careless, cursory, ephemeral, impulsive (rash), instantaneous, perfunctory, precipitate, rapid, summary, superficial

hurriedly instantly

hurriedness haste

hurry dispatch (promptness), dispatch (send off), expedite, haste, hasten, precipitate (hasten), race, urge. SEE MAIN ENTRY

hurry along dispatch (send off), hasten

hurry away quit (evacuate)

hurry off with distrain

hurry on dispatch (send off)

hurrying acceleration

hurt abuse (physical misuse), aggravate (annoy), aggrieved (harmed), brutalize, damage (noun), damage (verb), deface, detriment, disable, disconsolate, distress, drawback, endanger, expense (sacrifice), harm (noun), harm (verb), harrow, ill use, impair, impairment (damage), imperfect, inflict, injury, maim, marred, mischief, mistreat, molest (annoy), offend (insult), pain, penalize, pique, prejudice (injury), prejudice (injure), resentful, spoil (impair), strike (assault), suffer (sustain loss)

hurt the feelings affront, discompose

hurtful adverse (negative), bitter (reproachful), caustic, dangerous, detrimental, disadvantageous, disastrous, fatal, harmful, inadvisable, inimical, insalubrious, insufferable, invidious, lethal, malevolent, malignant, noxious, oppressive, painful, pernicious, pestilent, prejudicial, scathing, sinister, virulent

hurtfulness harm

hurting disabling, painful

hurtle against collide (crash against)

hurtless harmless, innocuous, nontoxic, salutary

husband consort, hoard, keep (shelter), preserve, spouse, store

husband one's resources hoard

husbanding of resources economy (frugality)

husbandry austerity, prudence

hush allay, lull (noun), lull (verb), moderate (temper), mollify, peace, placate, repress, silence, soothe, stifle, strangle

hush money blackmail, bribe, graft, gratuity (bribe). SEE MAIN ENTRY

hush up hide, suppress, withhold

hushed mute

husky strong

hustle haste, hasten, jostle (bump into), race

hyaline pellucid

hybridize commingle

hybridized compound

hygienic preventive, salutary

hygienize decontaminate

hyperbole bombast, caricature, distortion, exaggeration, overstatement, rodomontade. SEE MAIN ENTRY

hyperbolic extreme (exaggerated), inflated (overestimated). SEE MAIN ENTRY

hyperbolical outrageous

hyperbolism overstatement

hypercritical critical (faultfinding), particular (exacting), querulous, sensitive (easily affected), severe

hypercriticism diatribe, disparagement

hypersensitive querulous

hyphenate connect (join together)

hypnotic narcotic (adjective), narcotic (noun)

hypocrisy bad faith, duplicity, indirection (deceitfulness), pretense (pretext). SEE MAIN ENTRY

hypocritical dishonest, disingenuous, evasive, faithless, false (disloyal), insidious, machiavellian, perfidious, specious, tartuffish, untrue

hypostasis center (essence), essence, spirit, substance (essential nature)

hypothecate bond (secure a debt), guarantee, pawn, pledge (deposit), promise (vow)

hypothecated fully secured

hypothecation charge *(lien)*, cloud *(incumbrance)*, guaranty, specialty *(contract)*. SEE MAIN ENTRY
hypothesis assumption *(supposition)*, basis, conjecture, deduction *(conclusion)*, generalization, idea, inference, opinion *(belief)*, postulate, presumption, prolepsis, proposition, speculation *(conjecture)*, supposition, theory, thesis. SEE MAIN ENTRY
hypothesization assumption *(supposition)*
hypothesize generalize, guess, opine, posit, postulate, presume, presuppose, propound, reason *(conclude)*, speculate *(conjecture)*, surmise, suspect *(think)*
hypothesized assumed *(inferred)*, presumptive
hypothetic hypothetical
hypothetical conditional, debatable, disputable, moot, nonexistent, speculative, theoretical. SEE MAIN ENTRY
hypothetically arguendo
hysteria furor, outburst, panic
hysterical frenetic, uncontrollable
hysterical state outburst
hystericalness panic
hysterics outburst

I

iacere dormant
iactans pretentious *(ostentatious)*, pretentious *(pompous)*
iactare cast *(throw)*, flaunt
iactura loss
iconoclasm blasphemy
iconoclast heretic
iconoclastic radical *(favoring drastic change)*, recusant, skeptical
icy disdainful, unaffected *(uninfluenced)*
icy aloofness disdain
idea apprehension *(perception)*, clue, concept, connotation, end *(intent)*, hint, import, intimation, meaning, notion, objective, opinion *(belief)*, perception, project, proposal *(suggestion)*, proposition, purpose, sense *(feeling)*, substance *(essential nature)*, suggestion, tenor. SEE MAIN ENTRY
idea conveyed gist *(substance)*, sum *(tally)*
ideal criterion, example, exemplar, exemplary, felicitous, model, nonexistent, paradigm, paragon, pattern, prototype, ripe, standard, unimpeachable. SEE MAIN ENTRY
ideal justice equity *(justice)*
idealism casuistry
idealistic ethical, meritorious, moral, quixotic
idealize magnify
ideals conscience, ethics
ideate conceive *(comprehend)*, create
ideational theoretical
ideative cogitative, theoretical
idée fixe preoccupation
idem identical
idem same
identical comparable *(equivalent)*, equivalent, same *(adjective)*, same *(noun)*, similar, tantamount, uniform. SEE MAIN ENTRY
identical in amount equal
identical in quantity equal
identical in size commensurable, equal, equivalent
identical in value coequal, equal, equivalent
identical value parity

identicalness identity *(similarity)*, par *(equality)*, parity, resemblance
identifiable apparent *(perceptible)*, arrant *(definite)*, clear *(apparent)*, manifest, palpable, unmistakable
identification classification, connection *(relation)*, credentials, definition, denomination, designation *(naming)*, discovery, earmark, fingerprints, label, recognition, speciality, stamp, trademark. SEE MAIN ENTRY
identification mark brand, designation *(symbol)*, device *(distinguishing mark)*
identification records fingerprints
identification tag brand, label
identified with congruous
identifier eyewitness
identify brand *(mark)*, call *(title)*, characterize, classify, define, describe, detect, diagnose, discover, find *(discover)*, label, recognize *(perceive)*, relate *(establish a connection)*. SEE MAIN ENTRY
identify by name call *(title)*
identify incorrectly mislabel, mistake
identify with compare, sympathize. SEE MAIN ENTRY
identifying descriptive
identity par *(equality)*, personality, resemblance, semblance. SEE MAIN ENTRY
identity classification identification
identity comparison identification
identity theft SEE MAIN ENTRY
identity verification identification
ideological theoretical
ideology theory
idiocrasy characteristic, quality *(attribute)*, quirk *(idiosyncrasy)*
idiom expression *(comment)*, language, parlance, phrase, phraseology, speech, term *(expression)*
idiomatic distinctive, specific
idiosyncrasy characteristic, disposition *(inclination)*, feature *(characteristic)*, identity *(individuality)*, irregularity, nonconformity, quality *(attribute)*, specialty *(distinctive mark)*, tendency, trait
idiosyncratic different, distinct *(distinguished from others)*, distinctive, eccentric, noteworthy, particular *(specific)*, peculiar *(distinctive)*, personal *(individual)*, specific
idiosyncratical specific
idiotic fatuous, ludicrous, non compos mentis, obtuse
idle barren, baseless, inactive, indolent, ineffectual, lax, loiter, otiose, procrastinate, remiss, rest *(cease from action)*, stagnant, torpid, trivial, truant, unavailing, unemployed, unfounded, vacant, vacuous. SEE MAIN ENTRY
idle expenditure misapplication
idle fancy figment
idle speech fustian
idle speeches bombast
idle threat SEE MAIN ENTRY
idleness desuetude, inaction, languor, lull, neglect, nonperformance, sloth
idling layoff
idolatory doxology
idolatry laudation
idolization respect
idolize honor, regard *(hold in esteem)*
idoneous suitable
idoneus adequate, capable, convenient, eligible, fit, opportune, proper, qualified *(conditioned)*, suitable
ieiunus prosaic
if it were not that only

igitur consequently
ignarus inexperienced, unacquainted, unaware
ignavia sloth
ignavus idle, inactive, indolent
ignis conflagration
ignite burn, deflagrate, discharge *(shoot)*
igniting discharge *(shot)*
ignobility bad character, bad repute, dishonor *(shame)*, disrepute, ignominy, infamy, odium, opprobrium
ignoble bad *(offensive)*, caitiff, calumnious, disgraceful, disreputable, immoral, machiavellian, nefarious, notorious, odious, offensive *(offending)*, outrageous, reprehensible, scandalous, sinister, unethical, unseemly. SEE MAIN ENTRY
ignominia degradation, discredit, disgrace, dishonor *(shame)*, ignominy, infamy, shame
ignominious blameful, blameworthy, caitiff, calumnious, contemptible, contem-ptuous, disgraceful, disreputable, ignoble, libelous, notorious, odious, scandalous
ignominiousness bad repute, disrepute, infamy, opprobrium
ignominy attaint, bad character, bad faith, bad repute, degradation, discredit, disgrace, dishonor *(shame)*, disrepute, infamy, notoriety, obloquy, odium, opprobrium, scandal, shame. SEE MAIN ENTRY
ignomy ignominy, notoriety
ignorance nescience. SEE MAIN ENTRY
ignorance of law SEE MAIN ENTRY
ignorant incognizant, incompetent, inept *(incompetent)*, inexperienced, insensible, obtuse, opaque, unacquainted, unaware, unversed, unwitting SEE MAIN ENTRY
ignorantly unknowingly
ignorare mistake
ignoration nescience
ignore discount *(disbelieve)*, disdain, dismiss *(put out of consideration)*, disobey, disoblige, disregard, exclude, fail *(neglect)*, neglect, overlook *(superintend)*, override, pretermit, rebuff, reject, shirk, shun, spurn. SEE MAIN ENTRY
ignore distinctions generalize, muddle
ignore ethics cheat
ignore limits trespass
ignore one's obligations default
ignored derelict *(abandoned)*
ignorement disuse
ignoscere amnesty, forgive, overlook *(superintend)*
ii qui reipublicae praesunt government *(political administration)*
ilk class, kind, manner *(kind)*
ill pain, trouble, unsound *(not strong)*. SEE MAIN ENTRY
ill at ease restive
ill conduct guilt, malfeasance
ill consequence mischief
ill disposition ill will
ill fame attaint, opprobrium
ill favor attaint, bad character, ignominy, obloquy
ill feeling argument *(contention)*, discord, hatred, malice, rancor, spite
ill fortune calamity, casualty, expense *(sacrifice)*, loss, misfortune
ill hap casualty
ill health disease
ill humor umbrage
ill individual patient
ill judgment indiscretion

ill luck loss, misfortune

ill management misconduct

ill nature spite

ill repute attaint, bad character, bad repute, ignominy, infamy, notoriety, obloquy, opprobrium, scandal, shame, turpitude

ill treat misemploy, mishandle *(maltreat)*, mistreat, persecute

ill treatment abuse *(physical misuse)*, injury, misusage, misuse, molestation, oppression

ill turn disservice

ill usage abuse *(corrupt practice)*, abuse *(physical misuse)*, misusage, misuse, molestation

ill use abuse *(corrupt practice)*, abuse *(physical misuse)*, misemploy, mishandle *(maltreat)*, mistreat, misuse, persecute

ill will argument *(contention)*, discord, estrangement, feud, hatred, malice, odium, rancor, resentment, spite, umbrage

ill wishes imprecation, malediction

ill-adapted disproportionate, improper, inapplicable, inapposite, inapt, inept *(inappropriate)*, unfit, unsuitable

ill-advised detrimental, fatuous, ill-judged, impolitic, imprudent, inadvisable, inept *(inappropriate)*, injudicious, irrational, misadvised, regressive, thoughtless, undue *(excessive)*, unfit, unpolitic, unreasonable, untimely. SEE MAIN ENTRY

ill-behaved blatant *(obtrusive)*, disobedient, perverse

ill-boding dire, ominous, portentous *(ominous)*, regrettable, unfavorable

ill-bred blatant *(obtrusive)*, inelegant, offensive *(offending)*, presumptuous, uncouth

ill-chosen ill-judged, inopportune

ill-conceived SEE MAIN ENTRY

ill-consequence harm

ill-considered ill-advised, ill-judged, impolitic, imprudent, impulsive *(rash)*, inadvisable, irrational, misadvised, negligent, premature, untimely. SEE MAIN ENTRY

ill-contrived detrimental, ill-judged. SEE MAIN ENTRY

ill-defined inconspicuous, indefinite, indeterminate, indistinct, nebulous, opaque, unclear, vague

ill-disciplined lawless

ill-disposed hostile, malevolent, malicious, resentful, sinister, spiteful, unfavorable, unpropitious, vicious. SEE MAIN ENTRY

ill-done perfunctory

ill-fame dishonor *(shame)*, disrepute

ill-fated ominous, portentous *(ominous)*, regrettable

ill-favor disgrace, dishonor *(shame)*, disrepute

ill-feeling ill will

ill-founded baseless, improper, unsound *(fallacious)*. SEE MAIN ENTRY

ill-furnished devoid

ill-gotten gains spoils

ill-gotten goods plunder

ill-humored petulant

ill-intent ill will

ill-intentioned cruel, harmful, malevolent, malignant, spiteful

ill-judged ill-advised, impolitic, imprudent, inadvisable, injudicious, irrational, misadvised, unpolitic, unreasonable. SEE MAIN ENTRY

ill-manage mismanage

ill-mannered blatant *(obtrusive)*, disorderly, impertinent *(insolent)*, inelegant, presumptuous, provincial, uncouth

ill-matched disparate, disproportionate, incongruous

ill-nature cruelty

ill-natured cruel, harsh, malevolent, malicious, perverse, severe, spiteful, vicious. SEE MAIN ENTRY

ill-omened dire, disastrous, ominous, regrettable, unfavorable, unpropitious

ill-proportioned disproportionate

ill-provided devoid

ill-provided for poor *(underprivileged)*

ill-qualified inept *(incompetent)*, inexperienced, unqualified *(not competent)*

ill-reasoned sophistic

ill-repute disgrace, dishonor *(shame)*, disrepute. SEE MAIN ENTRY

ill-seasoned inopportune

ill-sorted disproportionate

ill-starred ominous, portentous *(ominous)*

ill-stored devoid

ill-suited disproportionate, inapt, inept *(inappropriate)*

ill-tempered fractious, perverse, petulant, severe

ill-timed improper, inapposite, inapt, inauspicious, inept *(inappropriate)*, inopportune, premature, unpropitious, untimely

ill-treat affront, exploit *(take advantage of)*, harass, harm, harrow, ill use, maltreat

ill-treated aggrieved *(harmed)*

ill-treatment harm. SEE MAIN ENTRY

ill-usage cruelty, waste

ill-use abuse *(misuse)*, abuse *(violate)*, exploit *(take advantage of)*, harass, harm, harrow, maltreat. SEE MAIN ENTRY

ill-used aggrieved *(victimized)*

ill-will cruelty. SEE MAIN ENTRY

ill-willed cruel, hostile, libelous, negative

ill-wishing malevolent

illapse entrance

illaqueate inveigle

illation consequence *(conclusion)*, deduction *(conclusion)*, generalization, inference

illative deductible *(provable)*

illaudable blameful, blameworthy, immoral, objectionable, peccable, reprehensible, scandalous, sinister

illegal felonious, illicit, immoral, impermissible, irregular *(improper)*, lawless, peccant *(culpable)*, unauthorized, unlawful, usurious, wrongful. SEE MAIN ENTRY

illegal act offense

illegal action malfeasance, transgression

illegal agreement confederacy *(conspiracy)*

illegal amotion asportation

illegal application misapplication

illegal carriage asportation

illegal compact confederacy *(conspiracy)*

illegal compulsion blackmail, coercion, extortion

illegal conduct offense

illegal custody detainer

illegal detention detainer

illegal donation bribe

illegal evasion breach

illegal exacter extortionist

illegal gain gratuity *(bribe)*

illegal incentive bribe

illegal incitation bribe, bribery

illegal inducement bribe, bribery

illegal infliction of punishment lynch law

illegal interest usury

illegal intrusion encroachment

illegal lure bribe

illegal offer bribe

illegal offering bribe

illegal pact collusion

illegal present bribe

illegal profit graft

illegal property contraband

illegal restraint detainer

illegal reward bribe

illegal subduction asportation

illegal taker extortionist

illegal traffic contraband

illegal transmittance asportation

illegal transplantation asportation

illegal transshipment asportation

illegal use of property misappropriation

illegal withholding detainer

illegality burglary, corruption, crime, criminality, felony, infringement, injustice, irregularity, misconduct, misdeed, misdemeanor, misdoing, offense, prohibition, transgression, violation, wrong. SEE MAIN ENTRY

illegalize disfranchise

illegally SEE MAIN ENTRY

illegally exported goods contraband

illegally imported goods contraband

illegibility incoherence

illegible indistinct, unclear

illegitimacy bar sinister, illegality, incompetence, prohibition

illegitimate felonious, illegal, illicit, impermissible, irregular *(improper)*, spurious, synthetic, ultra vires, unauthorized, unlawful, wrongful. SEE MAIN ENTRY

illegitimate act tortious act

illegitimate child bastard

illegitimate undertaking racket

illegitimately illegally

illegitimateness bar sinister

illegitimation bar sinister

illiberal bigot, exclusive *(limited)*, narrow, parochial, parsimonious, penurious, provincial. SEE MAIN ENTRY

illiberality discrimination *(bigotry)*, intolerance

illicit illegal, illegitimate *(illegal)*, immoral, impermissible, improper, irregular *(improper)*, unlawful, wrongful. SEE MAIN ENTRY

illicit business racket

illicit dealer bootlegger, racketeer

illicit gains contraband, plunder

illicit intercourse adultery

illicit love adultery

illicit procreation bar sinister

illicit profit graft

illicit revenue graft

illicit scheme racket

illicit sexual intercourse adultery

illicitly illegally

illicitly covert collusive

illicitness breach, criminality

illimitable infinite, myriad, omnipotent, open-ended, profuse, unqualified *(unlimited)*

illimitably ad infinitum

illimited open-ended

illiteracy ignorance. SEE MAIN ENTRY

illiterate unversed

illiterateness ignorance

illness disability *(physical inability)*, disease, disorder *(abnormal condition)*, prostration. SEE MAIN ENTRY

illogical arbitrary, baseless, disordered, disproportionate, erroneous, fatuous, ill-judged, improper, inapposite, incongruous, inconsistent, inept *(inappropriate)*, irrational, misadvised, nonsubstantial *(not sturdy)*, sophistic, unfounded, unreasonable, unsound *(fallacious)*, untenable. SEE MAIN ENTRY

illogical conclusion   non sequitur
illogical deduction   non sequitur
illogical result   non sequitur
illude   delude. SEE MAIN ENTRY
illuminate   clarify, comment, construe *(translate)*, delineate, demonstrate *(establish)*, depict, describe, detail *(particularize)*, elucidate, embellish, enlighten, exemplify, explain, explicate, exposit, illustrate, interpret, manifest, resolve *(solve)*. SEE MAIN ENTRY
illuminated   coherent *(clear)*, lucid
illuminating   demonstrative *(illustrative)*, descriptive, informative, informatory, interpretive, narrative
illumination   civilization, clarification, cognition, comment, construction, definition, explanation, illustration, motif, realization, solution *(answer)*. SEE MAIN ENTRY
illuminative   demonstrative *(illustrative)*, descriptive, narrative
illumine   disabuse, enlighten, instruct *(teach)*
illumined   lucid
illusion   artifice, deception, distortion, fallacy, figment, phantom, prestidigitation, semblance, specter, vision *(dream)*. SEE MAIN ENTRY
illusional   ostensible, specious
illusionary   delusive, ostensible
illusive   deceptive, delusive, fallacious, fictitious, illusory, insubstantial, ostensible, specious, subtle *(insidious)*, untrustworthy
illusory   artificial, deceptive, delusive, fallacious, fictitious, insubstantial, nonexistent, ostensible, quixotic, specious, tenuous. SEE MAIN ENTRY
illustrate   bear *(adduce)*, characterize, cite *(state)*, clarify, comment, construe *(translate)*, define, delineate, demonstrate *(establish)*, depict, describe, detail *(particularize)*, display, elucidate, embellish, enlighten, evidence, evince, exemplify, exhibit, explain, explicate, expound, interpret, manifest, portray, render *(depict)*, represent *(portray)*, signify *(denote)*. SEE MAIN ENTRY
illustration   case *(example)*, clarification, comment, example, explanation, expression *(manifestation)*, instance, representation *(statement)*, sample, specimen. SEE MAIN ENTRY
illustrational   representative
illustrative   descriptive, exemplary, general, narrative, representative, typical. SEE MAIN ENTRY
illustrative statement   dictum
illustrious   famous, important *(significant)*, influential, magnanimous, notable, noteworthy, outstanding *(prominent)*, professional *(stellar)*, prominent, renowned, reputable, salient, superior *(excellent)*. SEE MAIN ENTRY
illustriousness   distinction *(reputation)*, prestige, reputation
image   apprehension *(perception)*, color *(complexion)*, complexion, conceive *(comprehend)*, concept, copy, counterpart *(parallel)*, impression, model, perception, phantom, phenomenon *(manifestation)*, presence *(poise)*, represent *(portray)*, resemblance, semblance, symbol, vision *(dream)*. SEE MAIN ENTRY
image in the mind   impression
imaginability   chance *(possibility)*
imaginable   plausible, possible, potential, prospective, viable
imaginal   original *(creative)*

imaginary   artificial, delusive, fictitious, hypothetical, illusory, insubstantial, nonexistent, speculative
imagination   comprehension, creation. SEE MAIN ENTRY
imaginative   artful, fertile, original *(creative)*, productive, resourceful. SEE MAIN ENTRY
imagine   compose, conceive *(comprehend)*, conjure, contrive, deem, devise *(invent)*, expect *(consider probable)*, feign, gauge, guess, invent *(produce for the first time)*, opine, presuppose, pretend, profess *(pretend)*, surmise, suspect *(think)*. SEE MAIN ENTRY
imagined   artificial, delusive, fictitious, illusory, insubstantial, nonexistent, presumptive
imagined thought   figment
imago   phantom, reflection *(image)*, representation *(statement)*, semblance
imbalance   difference, disparity, distortion, inequality. SEE MAIN ENTRY
imbecilic   fatuous, obtuse, opaque
imbecillitas   impotence
imbed   inject
imbibe   carouse
imbricate   overlap
imbroglio   brawl, commotion, complex *(entanglement)*, complication, confusion *(turmoil)*, dilemma, disaccord, dispute, embroilment, entanglement *(confusion)*, fight *(argument)*, involution, pandemonium, plight, predicament, quagmire, snarl, strife, turmoil. SEE MAIN ENTRY
imbrue   infuse, penetrate, pervade
imbruement   infusion
imbue   inculcate, infuse, inject, inspire, permeate, pervade. SEE MAIN ENTRY
imbued   full
imbued with   addicted
imbued with life   conscious *(awake)*, live *(conscious)*
imbuement   infusion
imbuere   imbue, initiate, taint *(contaminate)*
imitari   copy
imitate   adopt, copy, fake, forge *(counterfeit)*, impersonate, plagiarize, pose *(impersonate)*, pretend, reflect *(mirror)*, repeat *(do again)*, reproduce, simulate. SEE MAIN ENTRY
imitate deceptively   feign
imitate falsely   forge *(counterfeit)*
imitate fraudulently   forge *(counterfeit)*
imitate insultingly   disparage, jape
imitated   imitation, repeated
imitation   artificial, caricature, copy, counterfeit, decoy, disguise, duplicate, fake, false *(not genuine)*, forgery, imposture, meretricious, model, parody, plagiarism, pretense *(pretext)*, quasi, resemblance, sham, spurious, surrogate, travesty. SEE MAIN ENTRY
imitation of an original   plagiarism
imitative   artificial, derivative, imitation
imitator   disciple
immaculate   absolute *(ideal)*, blameless, clean, pure, unblemished. SEE MAIN ENTRY
immanence   characteristic
immanent   born *(innate)*, essential *(inherent)*, inherent, innate
immanis   brutal, outrageous, prodigious *(enormous)*
immanitas   brutality
immaterial   frivolous, impertinent *(irrelevant)*, imponderable, inapposite, inconsequential, inconsiderable, incorporeal,

insubstantial, intangible, irrelevant, minor, negligible, nugatory, null *(insignificant)*, slight, trivial, unessential. SEE MAIN ENTRY
immaterial substance   spirit
immateriality   impalpability, inconsequence, insignificance. SEE MAIN ENTRY
immaterialness   impalpability
immateriate   impalpable, imponderable, incorporeal
immature   inchoate, incipient, inexperienced, jejune *(lacking maturity)*, juvenile, naive, puerile, rudimentary. SEE MAIN ENTRY
immature person   juvenile
immature stage   embryo
immaturity   adolescence, minority *(infancy)*, nonage
immaturus   premature, untimely
immeasurable   far reaching, indeterminate, inestimable, infinite, innumerable, profuse, unlimited. SEE MAIN ENTRY
immeasurably   ad infinitum
immediacy   SEE MAIN ENTRY
immediate   current, direct *(straight)*, expeditious, instantaneous, pending *(imminent)*, precipitate, present *(current)*, prompt, prospective, proximate, right *(direct)*, summary. SEE MAIN ENTRY
immediate forebear   parents
immediately   forthwith, instantly. SEE MAIN ENTRY
immediateness   dispatch *(promptness)*
immedicable   chronic, inoperable *(incurable)*, irremediable
immemor   oblivious
immense   broad, capacious, exorbitant, far reaching, grandiose, gross *(flagrant)*, innumerable, myriad, outrageous, prodigious *(enormous)*. SEE MAIN ENTRY
immensity   magnitude, mass *(weight)*
immensurable   inestimable
immensus   unlimited
immeritorious   arrant *(onerous)*, blameful, depraved, sinister
immerse   concern *(involve)*, inundate, occupy *(engage)*, overcome *(overwhelm)*, overwhelm. SEE MAIN ENTRY
immersion   obsession, preoccupation
immethodical   cursory, disordered, disorderly, haphazard, indiscriminate, random, sporadic
immigrant   alien *(foreign)*, alien. SEE MAIN ENTRY
immigration   entry *(entrance)*, inflow. SEE MAIN ENTRY
imminence   threat
imminent   close *(near)*, forthcoming, future, inevitable, instant, necessary *(inescapable)*, prospective, proximate. SEE MAIN ENTRY
imminent danger   menace, pitfall
imminere   command, imminent, impend, overlap
imminuere   decrease, impair, lessen, reduce
imminui   abate *(lessen)*
imminutio   decrease
immiscere   intersperse
immisericors   relentless, remorseless, ruthless
immitigable   irredeemable, irremediable, irrevocable
immitis   unrelenting
immittere   launch *(project)*
immix   combine *(join together)*, commingle
immixture   coalescence
immobile   firm, inflexible, stagnant, static, unbending, unyielding

immobilis immovable, static

immobility abeyance, inaction, inertia, insentience, languor

immobilization inertia

immobilize bind (restrain), fetter, lock. SEE MAIN ENTRY

immoderacy exaggeration

immoderate disorderly, dissolute, drastic, egregious, excess, excessive, exorbitant, extreme (exaggerated), fanatical, gluttonous, hot-blooded, incendiary, inordinate, intemperate, outrageous, prodigal, profligate (extravagant), profuse, prohibitive (costly), superlative, unconscionable, undue (excessive), unqualified (unlimited), unreasonable, unrestrained (not repressed), unrestricted, unwarranted, usurious. SEE MAIN ENTRY

immoderately unduly

immoderateness exaggeration

immoderation debauchery, exaggeration, redundancy

immoderatus excessive, inordinate, outrageous

immodest brazen, flagrant, improper, inflated (vain), lascivious, lewd, obscene, orgulous, pretentious (pompous), promiscuous, prurient, scandalous, unabashed

immodesty obscenity, pride

immodicus excessive, exorbitant, inordinate, undue (excessive)

immoral bad (offensive), base (bad), brazen, decadent, delinquent (guilty of a misdeed), depraved, diabolic, dishonest, disreputable, dissolute, felonious, illicit, improper, inexcusable, iniquitous, irregular (improper), lascivious, lawless, lecherous, lewd, licentious, machiavellian, nefarious, obscene, peccant (culpable), profligate (corrupt), promiscuous, reprehensible, reprobate, salacious, scandalous, sinister, tainted (corrupted), tortuous (corrupt), unethical, unjust, unscrupulous, vicious, wanton. SEE MAIN ENTRY

immoral habit vice

immoral person degenerate

immorality bad repute, delinquency (misconduct), guilt, misdoing, obscenity, perversion, turpitude, vice, wrong. SEE MAIN ENTRY

immortal constant, durable, permanent, perpetual. SEE MAIN ENTRY

immortal part spirit

immortality distinction (reputation), indestructibility. SEE MAIN ENTRY

immortalization dedication, preservation, remembrance (commemoration)

immortalize dedicate, perpetuate

immotile firm

immotus immovable, static, unaffected (uninfluenced)

immovability inertia, objectivity, security (safety), tenacity

immovable dispassionate, durable, firm, fixed (securely placed), immutable, implacable, indelible, inexorable, inextricable, inflexible, irreconcilable, irrevocable, obdurate, pertinacious, recalcitrant, secure (sound), severe, stable, unbending, uncompromising, unyielding. SEE MAIN ENTRY

immovables property (possessions)

immune clear (free from criminal charges), exempt. SEE MAIN ENTRY

immune freehold

immune inexpugnable, insusceptible (resistant), privileged, tenable

immune from restriction free (not restricted)

immunis exempt, free (relieved from a burden), immune, privileged

immunitas exemption, immunity, privilege

immunitio infraction, infringement

immunity dispensation (exception), exclusion, exemption, franchise (license), impunity, privilege, protection, release, resistance, respite (reprieve), sanction (permission), security (safety), tolerance. SEE MAIN ENTRY

immunity from assault inviolability

immunization tolerance

immunize protect. SEE MAIN ENTRY

immunized immune, insusceptible (resistant), privileged

immuration bondage, captivity, constraint (imprisonment), custody (incarceration), detention

immure arrest (apprehend), capture, commit (institutionalize), confine, constrain (imprison), contain (enclose), detain (hold in custody), enclose, encompass (surround), imprison, jail, lock, restrain, restrict, sentence. SEE MAIN ENTRY

immurement bondage, captivity, constraint (imprisonment), custody (incarceration), detention, durance, enclosure, incarceration

immuring commitment (confinement)

immurred arrested (apprehended)

immutabilis immutable, unalterable

immutability constant, indestructibility

immutable conclusive (determinative), constant, definite, durable, indefeasible, indelible, inexorable, inflexible, ironclad, irreconcilable, irreversible, irrevocable, obdurate, permanent, pertinacious, resolute, stable, unalterable. SEE MAIN ENTRY

immutably invariably

immutare alter, change

impact collision (accident), connotation, contact (touching), content (meaning), effect, force (strength), impression, reaction (response), repercussion, signification, value. SEE MAIN ENTRY

impacted inextricable

impair abrogate (annul), adulterate, aggravate (exacerbate), check (restrain), contaminate, damage, debase, debilitate, deface, denature, disable, disadvantage, disorient, endanger, eviscerate, harm, hinder, impede, infect, maim, mistreat, mutilate, pollute, prejudice (injure), spoil (impair), stain, subvert, vitiate. SEE MAIN ENTRY

impair in worth debase

impair one's reputation libel

impair the force of obtund

impair the legibility of deface

impair the looks of deface

impair the reputation of discredit

impaired defective, deficient, dilapidated, disabled (made incapable), faulty, imperfect, inadequate, marred, tainted (contaminated), unsound (not strong)

impaired condition disrepair. SEE MAIN ENTRY

impaired reputation bad repute, discredit

impairing disabling, noxious

impairment abuse (physical misuse), cost (penalty), damage, defacement, defect, deficiency, defilement, deterioration, detriment, disability (legal disqualification), disability (physical inability), disrepair, expense (sacrifice), fault (weakness), handicap, harm,

injury, prejudice (injury), wear and tear. SEE MAIN ENTRY

impairment of mental faculties lunacy

impairment of reputation libel

impalatable objectionable, obnoxious, unendurable

impale enter (penetrate), lancinate, penetrate, pierce (lance)

impalpability SEE MAIN ENTRY

impalpable elusive, imponderable, inappreciable, incorporeal, indiscernible, insubstantial, intangible, minimal, obscure (abstruse), obscure (faint), vague. SEE MAIN ENTRY

impanel SEE MAIN ENTRY

impar disproportionate, inadequate, insufficient, one-sided, unequal (unequivalent)

imparity difference, inequality

impart administer (tender), advise, annunciate, attorn, bear (yield), bestow, betray (disclose), cast (throw), communicate, concede, confer (give), contribute (supply), convey (communicate), convey (transfer), deliver, disabuse, disclose, disseminate, divulge, enlighten, express, give (grant), grant (transfer formally), inform (betray), inform (notify), instill, instruct (teach), leave (give), manifest, mention, notify, observe (remark), pass (determine), phrase, post, present (make a gift), produce (offer to view), provide (supply), publish, recount, relate (tell), render (deliver), report (disclose), reveal, signify (inform), transmit, utter. SEE MAIN ENTRY

impart gradually instill

impart knowledge apprise

impart knowledge of notice (give formal warning)

impart momentum impel, incite

impart motion dispatch (send off), impel

impart motion to agitate (shake up)

impart power to empower

impart thoughts converse

impart to notice (give formal warning)

impartation dispensation (act of dispensing), donation, transmittal

imparted alleged

imparted in secret confidential

impartial discriminating (judicious), dispassionate, equal, equitable, evenhanded, fair (just), honest, judicial, juridical, just, liberal (broad minded), neutral, nonpartisan, objective, open-minded, receptive, unbiased, unprejudiced. SEE MAIN ENTRY

impartial justice equity (justice)

impartiality disinterest (lack of prejudice), fairness, honesty, justice, neutrality, objectivity, probity, rectitude

impartialness disinterest (lack of prejudice)

impartible contagious, indivisible, inseparable

imparting donative

imparting of skill education

imparting of thoughts conversation

impartment concession (authorization), delivery, dispensation (act of dispensing), donation, legacy

impassable difficult, impervious, impossible, impracticable, insurmountable

impasse deadlock, dilemma, draw (tie), halt, imbroglio, predicament, quagmire. SEE MAIN ENTRY

impassible insuperable

impassion foment, incite, inspire, spirit. SEE MAIN ENTRY

impassionable sensitive (easily affected)
impassioned eager, earnest, eloquent, fanatical, fervent, intense, perfervid, vehement, zealous
impassionedness ardor, life (vitality)
impassive callous, controlled (restrained), dispassionate, impervious, inexpressive, inscrutable, insusceptible (uncaring), nonchalant, phlegmatic, stoical, unaffected (uninfluenced), unresponsive
impassiveness indifference
impatience SEE MAIN ENTRY
impatient eager, fractious, hot-blooded, ill-judged, petulant, restive
impavidus undaunted
impeach accuse, blame, cite (accuse), condemn (blame), defame, denounce (inform against), depose (remove), disapprove (condemn), discharge (dismiss), except (object), fault, impugn, inform (betray), remove (dismiss from office), reprehend, reprimand, sully. SEE MAIN ENTRY
impeach falsely frame (charge falsely)
impeach unfairly frame (charge falsely)
impeach unjustly frame (charge falsely)
impeachability guilt. SEE MAIN ENTRY
impeachable blameful, blameworthy, reprehensible, unjustifiable
impeached accused (charged)
impeacher accuser, complainant, informer (one providing criminal information)
impeachment charge (accusation), condemnation (blame), disparagement, incrimination, reproach. SEE MAIN ENTRY
impeachment of virtue libel
impeccability rectitude
impeccable absolute (ideal), best, blameless, clean, honest, incorruptible, inculpable, irreprehensible, meritorious, not guilty, unblemished, unimpeachable. SEE MAIN ENTRY
impecuniosity bankruptcy, indigence, poverty, privation
impecunious bankrupt, destitute, insolvent, poor (underprivileged). SEE MAIN ENTRY
impecuniousness poverty, privation
impedance deterrent, offset
impede arrest (stop), balk, bar (hinder), bind (restrain), block, check (restrain), clog, condemn (ban), constrain (restrain), constrict (inhibit), contain (restrain), control (restrain), counter, curb, debar, defer (put off), delay, detain (restrain), deter, disadvantage, discommode, disrupt, encumber (hinder), enjoin, estop, fetter, fight (counteract), foil, forbid, forestall, halt, hamper, hinder, hold up (delay), inconvenience, inhibit, interdict, interfere, interpose, keep (restrain), limit, lock, obstruct, occlude, preclude, prevent, prohibit, repulse, stall, stave, stay (halt), stem (check), stop, thwart, toll (stop), trammel, withstand. SEE MAIN ENTRY
impede the progress of delay, hold up (delay)
impeded arrested (checked), disadvantaged, limited
impeder deterrent
impediment bar (obstruction), barrier, blockade (barrier), burden, censorship, check (bar), complication, constraint (restriction), damper (stopper), delay, deterrence, disadvantage, drawback, encumbrance, estoppel, fetter, filibuster, frustration, halt, handicap, hindrance, impasse, imposition (excessive burden),

incumbrance (burden), interruption, obstacle, obstruction, onus (burden), predicament, prohibition, restraint, restriction. SEE MAIN ENTRY
impedimenta cargo, paraphernalia (apparatus)
impedimental preventive, unfavorable
impedimentary unfavorable
impedimentive unfavorable
impedimentum check (bar), encumbrance, handicap, hindrance, impediment, obstacle, obstruction, restraint
impeding limiting, preventive, prohibitive (restrictive)
impedire clog, embarrass, encumber (financially obligate), fetter, hamper, hinder, impede, incriminate, prevent
impedite balk, check (restrain), clog, disadvantage, hamper, obstruct
impedition bar (obstruction), check (bar), damper (stopper), deterrence, obstruction
impeditive preventive, restrictive. SEE MAIN ENTRY
impeditus difficult, impervious, labyrinthine
impel agitate (activate), bait (harass), bait (lure), cast (throw), coax, coerce, compel, constrain (compel), convince, dispatch (send off), enforce, entail, exact, exhort, further, impose (enforce), influence, inspire, motivate, necessitate, operate, persuade, press (constrain), prevail (persuade), prevail upon, prompt, provoke, send, spirit, stimulate, urge. SEE MAIN ENTRY
impel forward launch (project)
impelled bound
impellent impetus, impulsive (impelling)
impeller abettor, catalyst
impellere induce, influence, urge
impelling causative, coercion, compelling, decisive, force (compulsion), forcible, important (urgent), insistent, moving (evoking emotion), persuasive, potent, powerful, urgent
impelling force impetus, impulse
impelling power motive
impend menace, presage. SEE MAIN ENTRY
impendence threat
impendency threat
impendent immediate (imminent), imminent, proximate
impendere expend (disburse), imminent, impend, overlap
impending close (near), forthcoming, future, immediate (imminent), imminent, inevitable, instant, necessary (inescapable), pending (imminent), prospective, proximate, unavoidable (inevitable). SEE MAIN ENTRY
impendium expense (cost)
impenetrabilis impervious
impenetrability congealment, inviolability, opacity
impenetrable callous, cohesive (compact), complex, difficult, impervious, inapprehensible, incomprehensible, indefinable, inexplicable, inexpressive, inexpugnable, inscrutable, insurmountable, mysterious, opaque, recondite, solid (compact). SEE MAIN ENTRY
impenitent callous, incorrigible, recusant, relentless, remorseless
impensa cost (price), expense (cost), outlay
imperare order
imperative binding, canon, charge (command), compelling, compulsory, critical

(crucial), crucial, decisive, decree, dictate, dictatorial, direction (order), directive, exigent, grave (important), important (urgent), indispensable, injunction, insistent, mandate, mandatory, necessary (required), necessity, obligatory, order (judicial directive), ordinance, positive (prescribed), pronouncement, requirement, requisite, subpoena, unavoidable (inevitable), urgent. SEE MAIN ENTRY
imperative duty allegiance, charge (responsibility), responsibility (accountability)
imperative request demand
imperativeness exigency, pressure
imperceptibility impalpability, indistinctness, nonappearance, opacity
imperceptible blind (concealed), impalpable, inappreciable, inconspicuous, indiscernible, indistinct, intangible, latent, negligible, obscure (faint). SEE MAIN ENTRY
imperceptive insensible, obtuse, opaque
impercipient insensible, lifeless (dead), obtuse
imperdible inexpugnable, tenable
imperfect bad (inferior), blemished, defective, deficient, dilapidated, errant, fallible, faulty, inchoate, incorrect, inexact, inferior (lower in quality), insufficient, marred, partial (relating to a part), peccable, perfunctory, poor (inferior in quality), unsatisfactory, unsound (not strong), vicious. SEE MAIN ENTRY
imperfection defect, deficiency, disadvantage, fault (weakness), flaw, foible, frailty, handicap, irregularity, vice. SEE MAIN ENTRY
imperfectness disadvantage, flaw, frailty
imperfectus defective, executory, imperfect
imperforate impervious
imperial sovereign (absolute). SEE MAIN ENTRY
imperil compromise (endanger), endanger, expose, jeopardize. SEE MAIN ENTRY
imperiled aleatory (perilous)
imperilment danger, hazard, jeopardy, menace, peril, risk
imperiosus dictatorial, impervious
imperious dictatorial, disdainful, dogmatic, influential, insolent, oppressive, orgulous, peremptory (absolute), peremptory (imperative), powerful, presumptuous, proud (conceited), relentless, strict, supercilious, tyrannous. SEE MAIN ENTRY
imperious commandant dictator
imperious direction dictate
imperishability indestructibility
imperishable constant, durable, indefeasible, indelible, indestructible, infallible, infinite, permanent, perpetual
imperitus inexperienced, unversed
imperium direction (order), dominion (supreme authority), fiat, injunction
imperium predominance
impermanence mortality
impermanent acting, ephemeral, interim, precarious, temporary, transient, transitory
impermanent fixture stopgap
impermeability congealment
impermeable cohesive (compact), impervious, solid (compact). SEE MAIN ENTRY
impermissible illegal, illegitimate (illegal), illicit. SEE MAIN ENTRY
impermissibly illegally
impero imperative
impersonal clinical, dispassionate, impartial, neutral, objective, unbiased. SEE MAIN ENTRY

impersonality disinterest *(lack of prejudice)*, objectivity

impersonally fairly *(impartially)*. SEE MAIN ENTRY

impersonate assume *(simulate)*, copy, feign, mock *(imitate)*, pretend. SEE MAIN ENTRY

impersonation artifice, part *(role)*, role, sham

imperspicuity incoherence

imperspicuous allusive, equivocal, indefinite, nebulous, opaque, problematic, recondite, unclear

impersuadable impervious

impersuadible inflexible

impersuasible impervious, inflexible

impertinence contempt *(disobedience to the court)*, disrespect, inconsequence

impertinency inconsequence

impertinent brazen, collateral *(immaterial)*, contemptuous, extraneous, immaterial, inapplicable, inapposite, inappropriate, inconsequential, insolent, irrelative, irrelevant, obtrusive, offensive *(offending)*, peripheral, presumptuous, unfit, unsuitable. SEE MAIN ENTRY

impertire bestow, impart

imperturable placid

imperturbability composure, indifference

imperturbable callous, clinical, cold-blooded, controlled *(restrained)*, dispassionate, impervious, inexpressive, nonchalant, patient, peaceable, phlegmatic, stoical. SEE MAIN ENTRY

imperturbation composure, longanimity, sufferance

imperviable impervious

impervious callous, cold-blooded. SEE MAIN ENTRY

impervious impervious

impervious inexpressive, insuperable, insusceptible *(uncaring)*, obdurate, opaque, safe, torpid, unaffected *(uninfluenced)*

impervious to change durable

imperviousness resistance

impetrate call *(appeal to)*, importune, pray, press *(beseech)*, request

impetration call *(appeal)*, dun, entreaty, request

impetuosity dispatch *(promptness)*, inconsideration, outburst, passion, temerity

impetuous arbitrary and capricious, careless, disordered, impulsive *(rash)*, precipitate, reckless, spontaneous, uncontrollable, unexpected, vehement, zealous. SEE MAIN ENTRY

impetus assault

impetus boom *(prosperity)*, catalyst, determinant. SEE MAIN ENTRY

impetus force *(strength)*, impulse

impetus incentive, instigation, reason *(basis)*, stimulus

impietas profanity

impiety blasphemy, violation. SEE MAIN ENTRY

impiger active

impignorate guarantee, pawn, pledge *(deposit)*

impinge border *(bound)*, collide *(crash against)*, contact *(touch)*, encroach, infringe, invade, overlap, overstep. SEE MAIN ENTRY

impingement collision *(accident)*, encroachment

impingi impinge

impious diabolic, nefarious, offensive *(offending)*, peccant *(culpable)*, profane, sinister. SEE MAIN ENTRY

impious utterance blasphemy

impiousness blasphemy

impishness mischief

impius profane

implacabilis implacable, irreconcilable

implacability alienation *(estrangement)*, revenge, vengeance

implacable callous, cruel, immutable, inexorable, irreconcilable, malevolent, pertinacious, relentless, remorseless, resentful, ruthless, severe, unaffected *(uninfluenced)*, unbending, uncompromising, unrelenting, vindictive. SEE MAIN ENTRY

implacably opposed irreconcilable

implant educate, embed, enter *(insert)*, fix *(make firm)*, imbue, inculcate, infuse, initiate, inject, inseminate, instill, instruct *(teach)*, interject, pervade, plant *(place firmly)*

implant firmly establish *(entrench)*

implantation infusion, propaganda

implanted ingrained, internal, organic, situated. SEE MAIN ENTRY

implausibility improbability

implausible doubtful, incredible, ludicrous, unbelievable, untenable. SEE MAIN ENTRY

implead SEE MAIN ENTRY

implement appliance, consummate, device *(mechanism)*, discharge *(perform)*, dispatch *(dispose of)*, empower, enable, enforce, expedient, exploit *(make use of)*, facility *(instrumentality)*, instrument *(tool)*, instrumentality, operate, perpetrate, realize *(make real)*, tool. SEE MAIN ENTRY

implemental effective *(efficient)*, ministerial, practical

implementation act *(undertaking)*, action *(performance)*, building *(business of assembling)*, campaign, commission *(act)*, course, discharge *(performance)*, enforcement, fait accompli, finality, fruition, performance *(execution)*, realization. SEE MAIN ENTRY

implements paraphernalia *(apparatus)*

implere fulfill

impletion plethora

impliant unyielding

implicare hamper, implicate, incriminate

implicate accuse, arraign, blame, cite *(accuse)*, complain *(charge)*, condemn *(blame)*, denigrate, denounce *(inform against)*, impeach, incriminate, indict, inform *(betray)*, present *(prefer charges)*. SEE MAIN ENTRY

implicate falsely frame *(charge falsely)*

implicate oneself acknowledge *(declare)*

implicate unfairly frame *(charge falsely)*

implicate unjustly frame *(charge falsely)*

implicated complex, incident, related

implicating incriminatory, inculpatory

implicatio complication, embarrassment, entanglement *(involvement)*, involution

implication affiliation *(connectedness)*, attribution, blame *(responsibility)*, caveat, condemnation *(blame)*, connotation, content *(meaning)*, context, deduction *(conclusion)*, entanglement *(involvement)*, gist *(substance)*, hint, incrimination, inculpation, indicant, indication, inference, innuendo, insinuation, intimation, main point, mention *(reference)*, nuance, reference *(allusion)*, referral, signification, suggestion. SEE MAIN ENTRY

implicational allusive, circumstantial, leading *(guiding)*

implicative allusive, circumstantial, constructive *(inferential)*, incriminatory, inculpatory, leading *(guiding)*, suggestive *(evocative)*. SEE MAIN ENTRY

implicatory circumstantial, constructive *(inferential)*, incriminatory, inculpatory, leading *(guiding)*

implicit assumed *(inferred)*, constructive *(inferential)*, essential *(inherent)*, implied, indirect, inherent, intrinsic *(belonging)*, peremptory *(absolute)*, tacit, virtual. SEE MAIN ENTRY

implicit belief credence, faith

implicit confidence faith

implied constructive *(inferential)*, implicit, subtle *(insidious)*, tacit. SEE MAIN ENTRY

implied assent connivance

implied consent acquiescence

implied in law constructive *(inferential)*

implied indication innuendo, reference *(allusion)*

implied rather than expressly stated implicit

implode SEE MAIN ENTRY

implorare invoke, petition, request

imploratio prayer

imploration call *(appeal)*, entreaty, prayer, request

imploratory precatory

implore call *(appeal to)*, exhort, importune, invoke, petition, pray, press *(beseech)*, pressure, request, solicit, sue, urge. SEE MAIN ENTRY

imploring precatory

imply allude, bear *(adduce)*, bespeak, connote, denote, evidence, hint, indicate, infer, purport, signify *(denote)*. SEE MAIN ENTRY

impolicy misrule

impolite disorderly, impertinent *(insolent)*, insolent, perverse, presumptuous, uncouth

impoliteness disregard *(lack of respect)*, disrespect

impolitic detrimental, disadvantageous, ill-advised, imprudent, inadvisable, inappropriate, inapt, inept *(inappropriate)*, injudicious, misadvised, unpolitic. SEE MAIN ENTRY

impolitical injudicious

impoliticness indiscretion

imponderable intangible. SEE MAIN ENTRY

imponderous imponderable

imponere impose *(enforce)*, inflict

imporous impervious

import allude, amount *(result)*, bespeak, connotation, consequence *(significance)*, content *(meaning)*, context, corpus, degree *(magnitude)*, gist *(substance)*, implication *(inference)*, importance, interest *(concern)*, magnitude, main point, materiality *(consequence)*, meaning, point *(purpose)*, prestige, significance, signification, stress *(accent)*, substance *(essential nature)*, tenor, weight *(importance)*. SEE MAIN ENTRY

importance authority *(power)*, caliber *(quality)*, clout, concern *(interest)*, consequence *(significance)*, corpus, degree *(magnitude)*, distinction *(reputation)*, dominance, eminence, emphasis, force *(strength)*, hegemony, import, influence, interest *(concern)*, magnitude, materiality *(consequence)*, power, precedence, prestige, primacy, priority, relevance, reputation, significance, signification, status, stress *(accent)*, supremacy, value, worth. SEE MAIN ENTRY

important consequential *(substantial)*, considerable, constructive *(creative)*, critical *(crucial)*, crucial, decisive, determinative, essential (required), exigent, famous, germane, illustrious, indispensable, influential, key, major, momentous, necessary (required), notable, noteworthy, outstanding (prominent), peremptory (imperative), potent, powerful, predominant, primary, prime (most valuable), prominent, relevant, remarkable, renowned, requisite, salient, serious (grave), special, strategic, substantial, substantive, unusual, urgent, valuable, vital. SEE MAIN ENTRY

important event highlight

important feature main point

important part center (essence), main point

important point gist (ground for a suit), main point

important station eminence

importation inflow

imported alien (foreign)

importunate important (urgent), insistent, obligatory, precatory, urgent

importunateness pressure

importune annoy, badger, bait (harass), bait (lure), cajole, call (appeal to), dun, exhort, harry (harass), insist, inveigle, persuade, plead (implore), pray, press (beseech), prevail upon, request, solicit, urge. SEE MAIN ENTRY

importunitas intrusion

importunity call (appeal), dun, entreaty, prayer, request

impose bind (obligate), charge (assess), coerce, command, compel, constrain (compel), decree, demand, detail (assign), encumber (hinder), enforce, enjoin, exact, foist, force (coerce), impinge, impose (intrude), inflict, infringe, insist, intrude, levy, necessitate, obtrude, order, perpetrate, prescribe, press (constrain), require (compel). SEE MAIN ENTRY

impose a ban censor, enjoin, exclude

impose a charge assess (tax), encumber (financially obligate)

impose a duty compel, constrain (compel), delegate, enjoin, exact, instruct (direct), order

impose a duty on excise (levy a tax)

impose a fine mulct (fine)

impose a forfeiture fine

impose a levy assess (tax)

impose a lien encumber (financially obligate)

impose a mulct fine

impose a penalty condemn (punish), demote, discipline (punish), fine, penalize. SEE MAIN ENTRY

impose a penalty on convict

impose a task enjoin, instruct (direct), order

impose a tax exact

impose an order dictate

impose by fraud foist

impose difficulties discourage

impose hardship inconvenience

impose payment for misconduct fine

impose pecuniary punishment fine

impose penalty condemn (punish), sentence

impose punishment inflict

impose restraint fetter

impose restrictions coerce, constrain (restrain)

impose upon accroach, discommode, mishandle (maltreat)

impose with authority enjoin

imposed indispensable, necessary (required), obligatory, positive (prescribed)

imposed upon aggrieved (victimized)

imposing critical (crucial), important (significant), major, moving (evoking emotion), outstanding (prominent), prominent, proud (self-respecting), remarkable, salient, solemn, special

imposing a condition conditional, dependent

imposing building edifice

imposition ad valorem, assessment (levy), burden, canon, charge (command), compulsion (coercion), conviction (finding of guilt), deception, demand, disadvantage, duty (tax), encroachment, encumbrance, enforcement, excise, fiat, force (compulsion), forgery, hoax, incumbrance (lien), infliction, injustice, intrusion, misjudgment, nuisance, requirement, sanction (punishment), tax. SEE MAIN ENTRY

imposition of veil of secrecy censorship

impossibility impasse, improbability. SEE MAIN ENTRY

impossible impracticable, incredible, infeasible, insufferable, insuperable, insurmountable, intolerable, ludicrous, prohibitive (restrictive), unacceptable, unattainable, unendurable. SEE MAIN ENTRY

impossible task impasse

impossible to alter ironclad

impossible to better irremediable

impossible to break ironclad

impossible to calculate imponderable

impossible to change ironclad, irreversible, irrevocable

impossible to defeat invincible

impossible to describe ineffable

impossible to explain indefinable

impossible to express ineffable

impossible to influence obdurate

impossible to measure imponderable

impossible to overcome irresistible

impossible to reach inaccessible

impossible to resist irresistible

impossible to reverse irreversible

impossible to stop perpetual

impossible to translate indefinable

impossible to understand inapprehensible, incomprehensible, indefinable, inscrutable

impossible to vanquish invincible

impossible to weigh imponderable

impossible to withstand irresistible

impossibleness impossibility

impost assessment (levy), duty (tax), excise, excise (levy a tax), levy, tariff (duties), tax, toll (tax)

imposter fake

impostor sham

impostrous deceptive

imposture artifice, deception, false pretense, falsification, forgery, hoax, hypocrisy, ruse, sham, subterfuge. SEE MAIN ENTRY

impotence desuetude, detriment, disability (physical inability), fault (weakness), frailty, impuissance, inability, inaction, incapacity, inefficacy, languor, prostration. SEE MAIN ENTRY

impotency defect, disability (physical inability), impotence

impotens powerless, uncontrollable

impotent barren, devoid, disabled (deprived of legal right), disabled (made incapable), expendable, harmless, helpless (powerless), inadept, inadequate, ineffective, ineffectual, inept (incompetent), insipid, languid, null (invalid), null and void,

otiose, powerless, unable, unavailing, unproductive. SEE MAIN ENTRY

impound annex (arrogate), attach (seize), commit (institutionalize), condemn (seize), confine, confiscate, constrain (imprison), contain (restrain), deprive, detain (hold in custody), distrain, enclose, garnish, immure, impress (procure by force), jail, lock, restrain, seize (confiscate), sequester (seize property). SEE MAIN ENTRY

impoundage attachment (seizure), distraint, distress (seizure), sequestration, taking

impounded attached (seized)

impounding condemnation (seizure), confiscatory

impoundment appropriation (taking), attachment (seizure), bondage, captivity, commitment (confinement), constraint (imprisonment), custody (incarceration), detention, distraint, distress (seizure), enclosure, garnishment, incarceration, sequestration, taking

impoverish deplete, depreciate, deprive, despoil, plunder, spend

impoverished bankrupt, deficient, destitute, impecunious, insolvent, penurious, poor (underprivileged)

impoverishment dearth, indigence, poverty

impower delegate

impracticability impossibility

impracticable impossible, infeasible, insuperable, insurmountable, otiose, quixotic, unattainable. SEE MAIN ENTRY

impractical hot-blooded, impracticable, otiose, quixotic, speculative, theoretical, unattainable

impracticality impossibility

imprecation contempt (disdain), expletive, malediction, slander. SEE MAIN ENTRY

imprecation of evil blasphemy

imprecative calumnious, profane

imprecatory calumnious, profane

imprecise approximate, equivocal, faulty, inaccurate, incorrect, indefinite, inexact, lax, liberal (not literal), slipshod, vague

imprecise statement generalization

imprecision generality (vague statement), laxity, misstatement

impregnability incontestability, inviolability, security (safety), strength

impregnable defensible, immune, inappealable, incontestable, indomitable, inexpugnable, insuperable, insurmountable, powerful, safe, secure (free from danger), tenable, unapproachable

impregnate infuse, inject, inseminate, penetrate, permeate, pervade, plant (place firmly)

impregnation infusion

imprescriptible indefeasible, unalienable

impress abduct, affect, attach (seize), brand, brand (mark), capture, coerce, confiscate, convince, copy, distrain, distress (seizure), dwell (linger over), embed, hijack, hold up (rob), inculcate, induct, influence, kidnap, overwhelm, persuade, reach, seize (confiscate), sequester (seize property), specialty (distinctive mark), stamp. SEE MAIN ENTRY

impress by repeated statement inculcate

impress on insist

impress upon the memory instruct (teach), retain (keep in possession)

impress upon the mind discipline (train), imbue, inculcate, instill, instruct (teach)

impress with mark   seal *(solemnize)*
impressed with oneself   inflated *(vain)*
impressibility   credulity, sensibility
impressible   open *(persuasible)*, perceptive, pliant, receptive, sensitive *(easily affected)*, sequacious, susceptible *(responsive)*, yielding
impression   apprehension *(perception)*, assumption *(supposition)*, color *(deceptive appearance)*, complexion, concept, conviction *(persuasion)*, copy, estimate *(idea)*, fingerprints, idea, inference, notion, opinion *(belief)*, pattern, perception, perspective, reaction *(response)*, reflection *(image)*, sense *(feeling)*, stamp, suspicion *(uncertainty)*. SEE MAIN ENTRY
impression of fingers   fingerprints
impressionable   amenable, facile, malleable, open *(persuasible)*, perceptive, pliable, pliant, receptive, sensitive *(easily affected)*, sequacious, susceptible *(responsive)*, tractable, yielding
impressive   considerable, eloquent, forcible, important *(significant)*, influential, major, momentous, moving *(evoking emotion)*, notable, noteworthy, outstanding *(prominent)*, persuasive, potent, prodigious *(amazing)*, profound *(intense)*, proud *(self-respecting)*, remarkable, sapid, solemn, stellar. SEE MAIN ENTRY
impressive effect   pretense *(ostentation)*
impressiveness   emphasis, solemnity, weight *(credibility)*, weight *(importance)*
impressment   abduction, attachment *(seizure)*, compulsion *(coercion)*, distress *(seizure)*, duress, force *(compulsion)*, levy, sequestration
imprest   loan
imprimatur   charter *(license)*, leave *(permission)*, license
imprint   brand, brand *(mark)*, caption, copy, embed, fingerprints, impression, inculcate, inscribe, label, seal *(solemnize)*, stamp, trademark
imprison   arrest *(apprehend)*, capture, commit *(institutionalize)*, confine, contain *(restrain)*, detain *(hold in custody)*, enclose, immure, jail, lock, restrain, seclude, seize *(apprehend)*, sentence, transport. SEE MAIN ENTRY
imprison again   remand
imprisoned   arrested *(apprehended)*, in custody
imprisoned person   captive
imprisonment   apprehension *(act of arresting)*, arrest, bondage, captivity, commitment *(confinement)*, custody *(incarceration)*, detention, enclosure, fetter, incarceration, restraint. SEE MAIN ENTRY
improbability   doubt *(indecision)*, doubt *(suspicion)*. SEE MAIN ENTRY
improbable   disputable, doubtful, implausible, impossible, incredible, unbelievable, unforeseeable, unsound *(fallacious)*. SEE MAIN ENTRY
improbare   impugn
improbatio   disapproval
improbation   bad repute, exception *(objection)*, reprimand
improbitas   dishonesty
improbity   attaint, bad faith, bad repute, bribery, contempt *(disobedience to the court)*, corruption, culpability, delinquency *(misconduct)*, dishonesty, dishonor *(nonpayment)*, dishonor *(shame)*, disloyalty, fraud, guilt, hypocrisy, indirection *(deceitfulness)*,

injustice, misdemeanor, misdoing, racket, wrong. SEE MAIN ENTRY
improbus   bad *(offensive)*, dishonest, incorrect, iniquitous
improficient   incompetent, libelous
impromptu   impulsive *(rash)*, spontaneous, unexpected, unpremeditated. SEE MAIN ENTRY
improper   bad *(offensive)*, blatant *(obtrusive)*, culpable, delinquent *(guilty of a misdeed)*, disgraceful, disorderly, disreputable, drastic, false *(inaccurate)*, faulty, illegal, illegitimate *(illegal)*, illicit, immoral, impertinent *(insolent)*, inaccurate, inadmissible, inapplicable, inapposite, inappropriate, inapt, incongruous, incorrect, inelegant, ineligible, inept *(inappropriate)*, iniquitous, lascivious, nefarious, objectionable, perverse, profane, slipshod, suggestive *(risqué)*, unauthorized, unbecoming, undesirable, undue *(excessive)*, unfit, unjust, unprofessional, unseemly, unsuitable, untimely, unwarranted, vicious, wrongful. SEE MAIN ENTRY
improper act   tortious act
improper action   impropriety, misfeasance
improper behavior   impropriety, misdeed
improper conduct   guilt, misconduct
improper jurisdiction   want of jurisdiction
improper performance   misfeasance
improper professional action   malpractice
improper professional conduct   malpractice
improper rate of interest   usurious
improper usage   abuse *(corrupt practice)*, misusage, misuse
improper use   abuse *(corrupt practice)*, misapplication, misusage, misuse
improper venue   SEE MAIN ENTRY
improperly   illegally
improperly proportioned   disproportionate
improperness   ill repute, irregularity
impropriate   condemn *(seize)*, hold *(possess)*, impress *(procure by force)*, preempt. SEE MAIN ENTRY
impropriation   appropriation *(taking)*, arrogation, assignment *(transfer of ownership)*, assumption *(seizure)*, condemnation *(seizure)*, disseisin, distress *(seizure)*
impropriety   bad repute, breach, delinquency *(misconduct)*, fault *(mistake)*, ill repute, illegality, incongruity, indecency, misapplication, misconduct, miscue, misdeed, misdemeanor, misdoing, misusage, obscenity, offense. SEE MAIN ENTRY
improvable   corrigible
improve   accrue *(increase)*, ameliorate, amend, appreciate *(increase)*, cultivate, cure, develop, edify, edit, elevate, embellish, emend, enhance, fix *(repair)*, gain, heighten *(augment)*, help, inure *(benefit)*, meliorate, modify *(alter)*, mollify, nurture, profit, progress, rectify, redress, reform, rehabilitate, relieve *(give aid)*, remedy, renew *(refurbish)*, renovate, repair, restore *(renew)*, revise, supplement, treat *(remedy)*. SEE MAIN ENTRY
improve upon   elaborate, fix *(repair)*, modify *(alter)*, surpass
improved relations   rapprochement, reconciliation
improved version   correction *(change)*, revision *(corrected version)*
improvement   advance *(increase)*, advan-

tage, amendment *(correction)*, augmentation, behalf, benefit *(betterment)*, boom *(increase)*, boom *(prosperity)*, correction *(change)*, development *(progression)*, edification, growth *(evolution)*, headway, panacea, profit, progress, promotion *(advancement)*, reform, rehabilitation, renewal, reorganization, repair, revision *(corrected version)*, revival. SEE MAIN ENTRY
improvement of the mind   education
improvement-minded   progressive *(advocating change)*
improvidence   disregard *(unconcern)*, inconsideration, laches, laxity, neglect, negligence, temerity, waste
improvident   careless, derelict *(negligent)*, heedless, imprudent, injudicious, lax, negligent, prodigal, profligate *(extravagant)*, profuse, reckless, remiss, thoughtless, unpolitic. SEE MAIN ENTRY
improvidus   improvident
improving   beneficial, constructive *(creative)*
improvisate   unpremeditated
improvisation   invention
improvisatorial   spontaneous
improvise   compose, conjure, contrive, create, devise *(invent)*, invent *(produce for the first time)*, make, originate, scheme. SEE MAIN ENTRY
improvised   ad hoc, impulsive *(rash)*, spontaneous, unpremeditated
improvisus   unanticipated
imprudence   disregard *(unconcern)*, impropriety, inconsideration, indiscretion, inexpedience, neglect, negligence, res ipsa loquitur, temerity. SEE MAIN ENTRY
imprudens   impolitic, improvident, inadvertent, thoughtless
imprudent   careless, heedless, hotblooded, ill-advised, ill-judged, impolitic, improvident, impulsive *(rash)*, inadvisable, inept *(inappropriate)*, injudicious, irrational, lax, misadvised, negligent, precipitate, prodigal, reckless, remiss, thoughtless, unpolitic, unprofessional, unsuitable, untimely. SEE MAIN ENTRY
imprudentia   ignorance
impudence   contempt *(disobedience to the court)*, defiance, disregard *(lack of respect)*, disrespect, temerity. SEE MAIN ENTRY
impudency   defiance
impudens   brazen, flagrant, insolent, unabashed
impudent   brazen, contemptuous, impertinent *(insolent)*, insolent, offensive *(offending)*, perverse, presumptuous
impudentia   indiscretion
impudicity   debauchery
impudicus   lewd, licentious, wanton
impugn   answer *(reply)*, attack, bear false witness, blame, brand *(stigmatize)*, censure, condemn *(blame)*, contend *(dispute)*, contest, contradict, contravene, criticize *(find fault with)*, demonstrate *(protest)*, denounce *(condemn)*, deprecate, disaccord, disaffirm, disallow, disapprove *(condemn)*, disown *(deny the validity)*, dispute *(contest)*, doubt *(distrust)*, except *(object)*, fault, gainsay, impeach, inveigh, lash *(attack verbally)*, malign, negate, protest, refute, reject, reprehend, reprimand, resist *(oppose)*, sully. SEE MAIN ENTRY
impugn a witness   SEE MAIN ENTRY
impugnare   impugn
impugnation   bad repute, belligerency, contest *(dispute)*, controversy *(argument)*,

disparagement, dispute, exception *(objection)*, opposition. SEE MAIN ENTRY

impugning negative

impugnment belligerency, contest *(dispute)*, impugnation, opposition, vilification

impuissance fault *(weakness)*, impotence, inability, incapacity. SEE MAIN ENTRY

impuissant incapable, null *(insignificant)*, powerless

impulse catalyst, cause *(reason)*, desire, impetus, incentive, motive, passion, stimulus. SEE MAIN ENTRY

impulsio impulse

impulsion impetus, impulse, incentive, instigation, provocation

impulsive careless, heedless, improvident, imprudent, precipitate, reckless, spontaneous, thoughtless, unexpected, unpremeditated, vehement. SEE MAIN ENTRY

impulsiveness inconsideration

impulsus impulse

impunitas impunity

impunity condonation, tolerance. SEE MAIN ENTRY

impure bad *(inferior)*, blemished, disreputable, dissolute, immoral, lewd, licentious, marred, obscene, profane, prurient, salacious, tainted *(contaminated)*, vicious. SEE MAIN ENTRY

impure air air pollution

impurity vice

impurus lascivious, lewd

imputable blameful, guilty

imputation accusation, allegation, aspersion, assignation, attaint, attribution, blame *(responsibility)*, charge *(accusation)*, condemnation *(blame)*, conjecture, count, criticism, defamation, disapprobation, discredit, disgrace, dishonor *(shame)*, disparagement, ignominy, incrimination, inculpation, innuendo, notoriety, onus *(stigma)*, opprobrium, presentment, reference *(allusion)*, scandal, stigma. SEE MAIN ENTRY

imputation from criminal proceeding arraignment

imputation of blame accusation

imputation of dereliction impeachment

imputation of fault impeachment

imputation of wrongdoing incrimination

imputative calumnious, incriminatory, inculpatory

impute ascribe, attribute, charge *(accuse)*, cite *(accuse)*, complain *(charge)*, denounce *(inform against)*, fault, implicate, present *(prefer charges)*. SEE MAIN ENTRY

impute fault to impeach

impute guilt to incriminate

impute shame to discredit, disgrace, pillory

impute to blame

imputed accused *(attacked)*, alleged

imputing blame incriminatory, inculpatory

in herein

in a body en banc

in a certain sense quasi

in a different class peculiar *(distinctive)*

in a dilemma doubtful

in a fair manner fairly *(impartially)*

in a huff resentful

in a line consecutive

in a manner quasi

in a mass en banc

in a quandary doubtful

in a row consecutive

in a state of action active

in a state of uncertainty contingent,

indeterminate, pending *(unresolved)*, provisional

in abeyance back *(in arrears)*, dormant, pending *(unresolved)*

in accord commensurate, concerted, concordant, concurrent *(united)*, congruous, consenting, consonant, contractual

in accord with pursuant to

in accord with ethics ethical

in accordance therefore consequently

in accordance with apposite, concerted, congruous, contractual, in strict conformity, pursuant to. SEE MAIN ENTRY

in accordance with conventional requirements formal

in accordance with duty right *(correct)*

in accordance with justice right *(correct)*

in accordance with law de jure, legitimate *(rightful)*

in accordance with legal provisions legitimate *(rightful)*

in accordance with morality right *(correct)*

in accordance with the contract as agreed upon

in accordance with the law juridical, lawful, licit

in accordance with the ordinance de jure

in accordance with the rules for right conduct ethical

in accordance with the standards of a profession ethical

in accordance with the statute de jure

in accordance with truth right *(correct)*

in action effective *(operative)*, functional, operative

in actual process active

in addition also, ancillary *(auxiliary)*, further. SEE MAIN ENTRY

in advance vanward

in agreement commensurate, concerted, concordant, concurrent *(united)*, consensual, consenting, consonant, synergetic. SEE MAIN ENTRY

in album register

in alienum fundum ingredi trespass

in all in toto

in all cases invariably

in all likelihood high probability. SEE MAIN ENTRY

in all respects in toto, purely *(positively)*, wholly. SEE MAIN ENTRY

in alliance concerted, conjoint, consensual

in any case notwithstanding, regardless

in any event notwithstanding, regardless

in arms armed

in arrears deficient, delinquent *(overdue)*, due *(owed)*, indebted, insolvent, outstanding *(unpaid)*, overdue, past due, receivable, unpaid

in assembly en masse

in attendance present *(attendant)*

in authority ex officio

in bad taste inappropriate, inelegant, unbecoming, unseemly, unsuitable

in behalf of one party ex parte

in being extant

in between SEE MAIN ENTRY

in black and white holographic, in writing

in bold relief clear *(apparent)*, conspicuous, manifest, perceptible

in camera SEE MAIN ENTRY

in carcerem imprison, jail

in chaos disordered

in character typical

in charge ex officio

in check controlled *(restrained)*

in chief a fortiori

in close proximity close *(near)*, contiguous, proximate

in clover prosperous

in cogitatione defixus pensive

in common conjoint, mutual *(collective)*

in common boundaries with contiguous

in common with cognate

in company with along

in compensation compensatory

in competition competitive *(antagonistic)*

in concert concordant, simultaneous

in conclusion consequently. SEE MAIN ENTRY

in concord consonant, synergetic

in conflict dissenting

in conflict with contra *(adverb)*, contra *(preposition)*

in conformity contractual

in conformity to the law juridical, lawful

in conformity with law legal

in conjunction concordant, conjoint

in conjunction with along, apposite

in connection with comparative, incident

in consequence a priori

in consequence of thereby

in consideration of ad hoc

in consonance pari materia

in conspiracy with SEE MAIN ENTRY

in contact contiguous

in contemplation at issue

in contrast to contra

in control ex officio

in correspondence with the contract as agreed upon

in current use extant

in custodiam imprison, jail

in custodiam dare arrest *(apprehend)*

in custody guarded. SEE MAIN ENTRY

in danger helpless *(defenseless)*, liable, susceptible *(unresistent)*

in darkness blind *(sightless)*

in debt indebted, past due

in decadence decadent

in decline decadent

in default insufficient, past due

in default of devoid

in defiance of the law lawless

in demand important *(urgent)*, popular, requisite, valuable

in despair despondent, disconsolate

in disagreement different, discordant, dissenting

in disarray disjointed, disordered

in discrimen endanger

in disgrace disreputable

in disguise evasive

in disorder anomalous, deranged, disjointed

in dispute arguable, at issue, controversial, debatable, disputable, doubtful, dubious, litigable, moot

in distress penurious, poor *(underprivileged)*

in doubt disputable, doubtful, dubious, dubitative, indefinite, indeterminate, leery

in dubio esse abeyance

in due course SEE MAIN ENTRY

in due form pro forma

in easy circumstances prosperous

in effect constructive *(inferential)*, effective *(operative)*, operative

in embarrassed circumstances poor *(underprivileged)*

in equal shares   pro rata
in equilibrium   coextensive
in error   at fault, culpable, delinquent *(guilty of a misdeed)*, fallacioadmit *(give access)*, cause, commence, constitute *(establish)*, create, embark, establish *(launch)*, generate, induct, initiate, instate, invest *(vest)*, launch *(initiate)*, originate, preface
in every respect   faithfully
in evidence   clear *(apparent)*, coherent *(clear)*, conspicuous, evident, manifest, obvious, palpable, perceivable, perceptible
in exact agreement   commensurate
in existence   conscious *(awake)*, corporeal, de facto, extant
in extremis   SEE MAIN ENTRY
in fact   actual, de facto
in fashion   current
in fault   blameworthy, delinquent *(guilty of a misdeed)*
in favor   popular
in favor of   in furtherance
in focus   manifest, visible *(in full view)*
in force   effective *(operative)*, operative
in front   vanward
in full   in toto
in full effect   in full force
in full force   undiminished. SEE MAIN ENTRY
in full gear   SEE MAIN ENTRY
in full view   distinct *(clear)*, evident, manifest, open *(in sight)*, overt, patent, perceivable, perceptible, visible *(in full view)*
in furtherance   SEE MAIN ENTRY
in genera describere   classify
in general   as a rule, generally. SEE MAIN ENTRY
in good faith   bona fide, faithfully. SEE MAIN ENTRY
in good financial condition   solvent
in good order   intact
in good spirits   sanguine
in good taste   elegant
in good time   in due course
in harmony   concordant, consonant, pari material. SEE MAIN ENTRY
in harmony with   congruous, consenting, pursuant to. SEE MAIN ENTRY
in harness   operative, ready *(prepared)*
in heavy spirits   disconsolate
in high dudgeon   resentful
in high esteem   popular
in high favor   popular
in hysterics   disordered
in installments   in part, piecemeal
in issue   debatable, disputable, moot
in its entirety   in toto
in its infancy   ab initio, inchoate
in its present condition   as is
in its present form   as is
in its present state   as is
in iudicium venire   appear *(attend court proceedings)*
in ius vocare   implead
in keeping   fit
in keeping with   in strict conformity
in league   conjoint
in lieu of   SEE MAIN ENTRY
in light of   SEE MAIN ENTRY
in line with   in strict conformity
in loco   apposite
in longhand   holographic
in margine positus   marginal
in margine scriptus   marginal
in mass   en masse
in memory of   honorary
in most cases   as a rule, generally
in most instances   high probability

in name only   nominal, purported, quasi
in narrow circumstances   poor *(underprivileged)*
in nature is   consist
in need   impecunious, penurious, poor *(underprivileged)*
in obedience to the agreement   as agreed upon
in obedience with   in strict conformity
in office   ex officio
in one piece   intact
in one's last moments   in extremis
in one's own person   in person
in operation   active, effective *(operative)*, functional, operative
in opposition   hostile
in opposition to   contra *(adverb)*, contra *(preposition)*, contrary
in order   consecutive, functional, ready *(prepared)*, systematic
in part   SEE MAIN ENTRY
in partnership   common *(shared)*
in passage   en route
in penury   poor *(underprivileged)*
in perfect condition   intact
in periculum   endanger, jeopardize
in perpetuum ratus   indefeasible
in person   SEE MAIN ENTRY
in pinched circumstances   poor *(underprivileged)*
in place   felicitous, fit
in place of   in lieu of
in place of a parent   loco parentis
in plain sight   conspicuous, overt, perceivable, perceptible, visible *(in full view)*
in plain view   naked *(perceptible)*
in play   operative
in point   congruous, exemplary
in point of fact   de facto
in position   ready *(prepared)*
in posse   colorable *(plausible)*
in practice   active, constructive *(inferential)*
in print   holographic
in prison   in custody
in process   instant
in profusion   copious
in progress   en route
in proportion   pro rata
in proportion to   comparative
in prospect   prospective
in question   aleatory *(uncertain)*, arguable, at issue, controversial, debatable, disputable, doubtful, dubious, moot, pending *(unresolved)*
in rapport   concordant, congruous, consonant
in re commorari   dwell *(linger over)*
in re connivere   connive
in re stare   adhere *(persist)*
in re versari   occupy *(engage)*
in readiness   ready *(prepared)*
in reality   de facto
in receivership   bankrupt
in reduced circumstances   poor *(underprivileged)*
in regard to which   wherein
in regular order   consecutive
in relation to   comparative, incident
in relation with   apposite, comparative
in residence   household *(domestic)*
in respect to   comparative
in safety   secure *(free from danger)*
in se recipere   undertake
in sequence   consecutive
in set form   pro forma
in sight   apparent *(perceptible)*, discernible, evident, manifest, perceivable,

perceptible, visible *(in full view)*
in small amount   remote *(small)*
in small doses   piecemeal
in small quantities   piecemeal
in solido   SEE MAIN ENTRY
in solitude   alone *(solitary)*
in some measure   in part
in spite of   irrespective, notwithstanding, regardless
in store   forthcoming, imminent, inevitable, prospective
in straitened circumstances   impecunious, poor *(underprivileged)*
in strict compliance with   in strict conformity
in strict conformity   SEE MAIN ENTRY
in strong relief   clear *(apparent)*
in style   current
in substance is   consist
in sum   en banc
in suspense   dormant, doubtful, outstanding *(unresolved)*
in tabulas referre   record
in tempus   provisional
in terrorem   SEE MAIN ENTRY
in that case   consequently
in that event   consequently
in the absence of   devoid
in the aggregate   en masse, in toto, wholly
in the area   close *(near)*
in the background   clandestine
in the beginning   ab initio
in the blood   born *(innate)*
in the clear   clean
in the company of   present *(attendant)*
in the course of   ad interim, throughout *(during)*
in the eyes of the law   de jure
in the fad   current
in the field of public debate   forensic
in the final moments of life   in extremis
in the first place   ab initio
in the foreground   conspicuous, manifest
in the general time frame   on or about
in the habit   addicted
in the habit of   accustomed *(familiarized)*
in the hands of receivers   bankrupt
in the heat of   SEE MAIN ENTRY
in the immediate vicinity of   on or about
in the interest of one party   ex parte
in the interim   ad interim
in the intervening time   ad interim
in the jaws of death   in extremis
in the lead   vanward
in the limelight   famous
in the long run   in due course
in the main   a fortiori, as a rule, generally, wholly
in the market   commercial
in the mass   wholly
in the meantime   ad interim
in the meanwhile   ad interim
in the middle of   among
in the name of   in furtherance
in the neighborhood   close *(near)*
in the neighborhood of   on or about
in the offing   immediate *(imminent)*, imminent, inevitable
in the opposite scale   contradictory
in the past   heretofore
in the power of   inferior *(lower in position)*
in the presence of   present *(attendant)*
in the public eye   famous
in the red   impecunious
in the same category   cognate, comparative

in the same way   as is
in the same words   verbatim
in the service of   in furtherance
in the spotlight   famous
in the usual course of things   as a rule, generally
in the vicinity   close *(near)*, present *(attendant)*
in the vicinity of   approximate
in the whole   in toto
in the wind   imminent
in the wrong   blameful, blameworthy, culpable, delinquent *(guilty of a misdeed)*, guilty
in the wrong place   anomalous
in time   in due course
in toto   en banc
in toto   wholly.   SEE MAIN ENTRY
in transit   en route
in tribute   honorary
in trust   SEE MAIN ENTRY
in truth   purely *(positively)*
in turn   consecutive, respectively
in two   bipartite
in unbroken sequence   consecutive
in uninterrupted succession   consecutive
in unison   concerted, concordant, concurrent *(united)*, consonant
in unison with   congruous
in unum vergere   converge
in view   apparent *(perceptible)*, conspicuous, evident, immediate *(imminent)*, imminent, manifest, obvious, patent, perceivable, perceptible, present *(attendant)*, present *(current)*, prospective, visible *(in full view)*
in violation of   deviant
in violation of law   felonious, illegally
in vogue   current, popular, prevailing *(current)*
in want   impecunious, penurious, poor *(underprivileged)*
in want of   devoid
in which case   consequently
in whole   in solido
in working order   ready *(prepared)*
in writing   documentary, holographic. SEE MAIN ENTRY
in-depth analysis   proposal *(report)*, trial *(experiment)*
inability   abortion *(fiasco)*, disability *(physical inability)*, disqualification *(factor that disqualifies)*, failing *(falling short)*, impairment *(drawback)*, impotence, impuissance, incapacity, inefficacy. SEE MAIN ENTRY
inability of performance   frustration
inability to accept   incredulity
inability to act   inertia, insentience
inability to be completed   frustration
inability to believe   incredulity
inability to decide   doubt *(indecision)*, indecision
inability to doubt   certainty
inability to maintain solvency   failure *(bankruptcy)*
inability to meet financial obligations   failure *(bankruptcy)*
inability to pay   bankruptcy, delinquency *(shortage)*, dishonor *(nonpayment)*
inability to perceive   insentience
inability to wait   dispatch *(promptness)*, haste
inability to work   disability *(physical inability)*
inabstinence   indulgence
inabstinent   gluttonous, inordinate, intemperate

inaccessibility   impossibility, unavailability
inaccessible   immune, impervious, impossible, infeasible, insuperable, insurmountable, private *(secluded)*, remote *(secluded)*, unapproachable, unattainable. SEE MAIN ENTRY
inaccessus   inaccessible
inaccordance   controversy *(argument)*, difference, discrepancy
inaccordant   discordant, dissident, inapposite, inapt, incommensurate, incongruous, inept *(inappropriate)*, repugnant *(incompatible)*
inaccuracy   error, exaggeration, fallacy, falsehood, fault *(mistake)*, figment, laxity, misestimation, misjudgment, misrepresentation, misstatement, story *(falsehood)*. SEE MAIN ENTRY
inaccurate   erroneous, fallacious, faulty, ill-founded, improper, incorrect, inexact, lax, slipshod, untrue. SEE MAIN ENTRY
inaccurateness   misestimation, misjudgment
inacquiescent   dissident, hostile, nonconsenting, reluctant
inaction   abeyance, abstention, cessation *(interlude)*, desuetude, inertia, insentience, languor, neglect, sloth. SEE MAIN ENTRY
inactivate   disable
inactive   barren, dead, defunct, dormant, idle, indolent, insipid, languid, lifeless *(dull)*, otiose, powerless, stagnant, static, torpid, unemployed. SEE MAIN ENTRY
inactivity   abeyance, cessation *(interlude)*, desuetude, halt, inertia, insentience, languor, leave *(absence)*, lull, nonperformance, sloth
inadept   inept *(incompetent)*. SEE MAIN ENTRY
inadequacy   absence *(omission)*, dearth, defect, deficiency, deficit, delinquency *(shortage)*, detriment, disability *(physical inability)*, disadvantage, disqualification *(factor that disqualifies)*, fault *(weakness)*, frailty, impotence, inability, incapacity, incompetence, inefficacy, insufficiency, invalidity, need *(deprivation)*, paucity, vice
inadequate   defective, deficient, faulty, imperfect, incapable, incompetent, ineffective, ineffectual, inept *(incompetent)*, inferior *(lower in quality)*, insubstantial, insufficient, invalid, nonsubstantial *(not sturdy)*, nonsubstantial *(not sufficient)*, nugatory, paltry, peccable, perfunctory, poor *(inferior in quality)*, powerless, puerile, scarce, unable, unavailing, unfit, unqualified *(not competent)*, unsatisfactory, unsound, vacuous. SEE MAIN ENTRY
inadequate final work   noncompliance *(improper completion)*
inadequateness   dearth, deficiency, insufficiency
inadfectatus   unpretentious
inadmissable   unacceptable. SEE MAIN ENTRY
inadmissibility   disqualification *(rejection)*. SEE MAIN ENTRY
inadmissible   impertinent *(irrelevant)*, improper, inapplicable, inapposite, inappropriate, inapt, ineligible, inept *(inappropriate)*, unsuitable
inadvertence   contingency, inconsideration, laxity, miscue, neglect, negligence, omission, quirk *(accident)*
inadvertency   inconsideration, laxity, miscue, negligence, oversight *(carelessness)*. SEE MAIN ENTRY

inadvertent   blind *(not discerning)*, careless, lax, negligent, thoughtless, unintentional, unwitting. SEE MAIN ENTRY
inadvertently   unknowingly
inadvisability   detriment, inexpedience
inadvisable   disadvantageous, ill-advised, impolitic, imprudent, inapt, inauspicious, inept *(inappropriate)*, inopportune, misadvised, objectionable, undesirable, unfavorable, unfit, unsuitable. SEE MAIN ENTRY
inaequabilis   irregular *(not usual)*
inaequalis   disproportionate, one-sided, unequal *(unequivalent)*
inaequalitas   inequality
inaestimabilis   inestimable, invaluable, priceless
inaffable   offensive *(offending)*, perverse, unapproachable. SEE MAIN ENTRY
inalienable   absolute *(conclusive)*, indefeasible, rightful, unalienable. SEE MAIN ENTRY
inalienable interest   right *(entitlement)*
inalienable right   prerogative, prescription *(claim of title)*
inalterable   certain *(positive)*, constant, unalterable
inane   barren, fatuous, ludicrous, nugatory, puerile, superficial, thoughtless, trivial, vacuous. SEE MAIN ENTRY
inanimate   inactive, insensible, lifeless *(dead)*, torpid
inanimateness   insentience
inanimation   desuetude, insentience
inanis   frivolous, futile, void *(empty)*
inanitas   nullity
inanity   bombast, jargon *(unintelligible language)*, platitude
inappealable   certain *(positive)*, definite, incontestable, incontrovertible, irrefutable, positive *(incontestable)*, undeniable, unequivocal, unrefutable. SEE MAIN ENTRY
inappetance   disinterest *(lack of interest)*
inappetancy   disinterest *(lack of interest)*
inapplicability   incongruity, inconsequence, inconsistency
inapplicable   collateral *(immaterial)*, disproportionate, expendable, extraneous, immaterial, impertinent *(irrelevant)*, impracticable, improper, inadmissible, inapposite, inappropriate, inapt, incongruous, inconsequential, inept *(inappropriate)*, irrelative, irrelevant, unfit, unsuitable. SEE MAIN ENTRY
inapposite   disproportionate, extraneous, gratuitous *(unwarranted)*, impertinent *(irrelevant)*, improper, inadmissible, inapplicable, inappropriate, inapt, incongruous, inept *(inappropriate)*, irrelative, irrelevant, unbecoming, unessential, unfit, unsuitable, untimely. SEE MAIN ENTRY
inappositeness   inconsequence
inappreciability   impalpability
inappreciable   immaterial, impalpable, inconsequential, inconsiderable, intangible, marginal, minimal, minor, negligible, null *(insignificant)*, petty, remote *(small)*, slight, trivial. SEE MAIN ENTRY
inappreciation   disregard *(lack of respect)*, ingratitude
inapprehensibility   incoherence, opacity
inapprehensible   impalpable, incomprehensible, inexplicable, inscrutable. SEE MAIN ENTRY
inapproachable   inaccessible
inappropos   irrelevant
inappropriate   alien *(unrelated)*, collateral *(immaterial)*, detrimental, disproportionate, gratuitous *(unwarranted)*, ill-advised, immaterial, impertinent *(irrelevant)*, improper,

inadmissible, inadvisable, inapplicable, inapposite, inapt, incongruous, inconsequential, incorrect, ineligible, injudicious, inopportune, irrelevant, objectionable, unacceptable, unauthorized, unbecoming, undesirable, undue *(excessive)*, unfavorable, unfit, unprofessional, unsatisfactory, unseemly, unsuitable, untimely. SEE MAIN ENTRY

inappropriate behavior impropriety
inappropriately timed untimely
inappropriateness impropriety, incongruity, inconsistency, inexpedience
inapropos impertinent *(irrelevant)*
inapt improper, inapplicable, inapposite, inappropriate, ineligible, inept *(inappropriate)*, inept *(incompetent)*, inexperienced, irrelevant, nugatory, powerless, unfit, unsatisfactory, unsuitable. SEE MAIN ENTRY
inaptitude disadvantage, disqualification *(factor that disqualifies)*, impuissance, incapacity
inarticulate mute, speechless, taciturn. SEE MAIN ENTRY
inarticulated indeterminate
inartificial authentic, genuine, honest, ingenuous, real, simple, unaffected *(sincere)*, veridical
inartificiality honesty
inartistic poor *(inferior in quality)*
inattention dishonor *(nonpayment)*, disinterest *(lack of interest)*, disregard *(unconcern)*, disuse, inconsideration, indifference, laches, laxity, neglect, negligence, nonfeasance, oversight *(carelessness)*
inattention to consequences inconsideration
inattentive blind *(not discerning)*, careless, casual, cursory, derelict *(negligent)*, heedless, hot-blooded, inadvertent, lax, negligent, oblivious, perfunctory, reckless, remiss, thoughtless, truant, unaware, unresponsive. SEE MAIN ENTRY
inattentiveness disinterest *(lack of interest)*, disregard *(lack of respect)*, disregard *(unconcern)*, laxity, neglect, negligence
inaudibility indistinctness
inaudible inarticulate, indistinct. SEE MAIN ENTRY
inauditus unprecedented
inaugural initial, original *(initial)*, precursory, preliminary, preparatory, primary, prime *(original)*, prior. SEE MAIN ENTRY
inaugural competition primary
inaugural contest primary
inaugural election primary
inaugural political competition primary
inaugural political contest primary
inaugurare induct, instate
inaugurate admit *(give access)*, cause, commence, constitute *(establish)*, create, embark, establish *(launch)*, generate, induct, initiate, instate, invest *(vest)*, launch *(initiate)*, originate, preface
inauguration birth *(beginning)*, first appearance, inception, installation, nascency, onset *(commencement)*, origination, outset, prelude, start
inaugurator author *(originator)*
inauguratory original *(initial)*, precursory
inauspicious adverse *(hostile)*, bleak *(not favorable)*, dire, inopportune, ominous, portentous *(ominous)*, regrettable, sinister, unfavorable, unpropitious, untimely. SEE MAIN ENTRY
invertible unavoidable *(inevitable)*
inborn born *(innate)*, hereditary, ingrained, inherent, innate, natural, organic

inborn ability penchant
inborn aptitude gift *(flair)*, specialty *(special aptitude)*
inborn proclivity instinct
inbred born *(innate)*, hereditary, ingrained, inherent, innate, native *(inborn)*, natural, organic. SEE MAIN ENTRY
incalculable aleatory *(uncertain)*, imponderable, incomprehensible, indeterminate, inestimable, infinite, innumerable, invaluable, myriad, priceless, profuse, unlimited, unpredictable. SEE MAIN ENTRY
incalculably ad infinitum
incandesce burn, deflagrate
incapabable of being done impossible
incapability disability *(physical inability)*, disqualification *(factor that disqualifies)*, impotence, impuissance, inability, incapacity, incompetence, inefficacy
incapable helpless *(powerless)*, inadept, inadequate, incompetent, inept *(incompetent)*, insufficient, powerless, unable, unfit, unqualified *(not competent)*. SEE MAIN ENTRY
incapable of being accomplished impracticable
incapable of being affected impervious
incapable of being appraised invaluable
incapable of being bought back irredeemable
incapable of being conveyed inalienable
incapable of being counted innumerable
incapable of being defeated indefeasible
incapable of being defended untenable
incapable of being deleted indelible
incapable of being divided indivisible
incapable of being done insurmountable
incapable of being evaluated imponderable
incapable of being explained inexplicable
incapable of being held untenable
incapable of being impaired impervious
incapable of being influenced impervious
incapable of being injured impervious
incapable of being justified inexcusable
incapable of being maintained untenable
incapable of being overcome insuperable, insurmountable, invincible
incapable of being parted inseparable
incapable of being perceived impalpable
incapable of being reviewed inappealable
incapable of being revoked indefeasible
incapable of being satisfied insatiable
incapable of being separated indivisible
incapable of being sold inalienable
incapable of being subdued indomitable
incapable of being surmounted insuperable
incapable of being surrendered unalienable
incapable of being transferred inalienable
incapable of caring insusceptible *(uncaring)*
incapable of correction incorrigible
incapable of deceit honest
incapable of discharging liabilities bankrupt
incapable of error infallible
incapable of existing impossible
incapable of feeling insensible
incapable of happening impossible
incapable of knowing right from wrong SEE MAIN ENTRY

incapable of managing one's own affairs fatuous
incapable of perceiving insensible
incapable of revocation irrevocable
incapable of speech mute
incapable of success insurmountable
incapable of utterance speechless
incapacious narrow
incapacitate damage, debilitate, disable, disarm *(divest of arms)*, disqualify, harm, maim, mutilate, neutralize, stall
incapacitated disabled *(deprived of legal right)*, disabled *(made incapable)*, incompetent, powerless
incapacitating disabling
incapacitation disability *(physical inability)*, disqualification *(factor that disqualifies)*, impotence, inability, incapacity, inefficacy
incapacity abortion *(fiasco)*, disability *(physical inability)*, disqualification *(factor that disqualifies)*, fault *(weakness)*, frustration, ignorance, impotence, impuissance, inability, incompetence, inefficacy. SEE MAIN ENTRY
incapacity to endure intolerance
incarcerate arrest *(apprehend)*, capture, commit *(institutionalize)*, confine, constrain *(imprison)*, contain *(restrain)*, detain *(hold in custody)*, enclose, immure, imprison, jail, lock, restrain, seize *(apprehend)*. SEE MAIN ENTRY
incarcerated arrested *(apprehended)*, in custody
incarcerated person captive, prisoner
incarcerating commitment *(confinement)*
incarceration apprehension *(act of arresting)*, arrest, bondage, captivity, cell, commitment *(confinement)*, constraint *(imprisonment)*, detention, durance, enclosure, fetter, restraint. SEE MAIN ENTRY
incarceration facility prison
incarnate bodily, born *(innate)*, corporal, corporeal, embody, genetic, live *(conscious)*, personify, physical
incarnation embodiment
incase contain *(enclose)*
incaution disregard *(unconcern)*, inconsideration, indiscretion
incautious careless, cursory, heedless, hot-blooded, impolitic, improvident, imprudent, impulsive *(rash)*, injudicious, lax, misadvised, negligent, perfunctory, reckless, unpolitic
incautiousness inconsideration, indiscretion, negligence, temerity
incautus heedless, improvident, reckless, unsuspecting
incendere incense, inspire
incendiarism arson, conflagration, subversion
incendiarize burn
incendiary disorderly. SEE MAIN ENTRY
incendium conflagration
incense aggravate *(annoy)*, alienate *(estrange)*, bait *(harass)*, disaffect, discompose, exacerbate, harass, irritate, molest *(annoy)*, offend *(insult)*, pique, provoke, repel *(disgust)*. SEE MAIN ENTRY
incensurable blameless
incentive bonus, catalyst, consideration *(recompense)*, impetus, impulse, instigation, motive, premium *(excess value)*, profit, provocation, reason *(basis)*, reward, stimulus. SEE MAIN ENTRY
incentor demagogue
incept commence
inception birth *(beginning)*, causal, derivation, genesis, nascency, onset *(com-*

mencement), origin (source), origination, outset, prelude, start, threshold (commencement). SEE MAIN ENTRY.

inceptive causative, elementary, inchoate, incipient, initial, preparatory, prime (original), rudimentary

inceptum enterprise (undertaking), inception, project, undertaking (enterprise)

incertitude ambiguity, ambivalence, confusion (ambiguity), doubt (indecision), hesitation, indecision, qualm, quandary, suspicion (uncertainty). SEE MAIN ENTRY

incertus dubious, indefinite, indeterminate, insecure, irresolute, precarious, problematic, undecided, unsettled, vague

incessancy continuity, perpetuity

incessant chronic, constant, continual (perpetual), continuous, durable, insistent, perpetual, repeated, repetitious, unrelenting, unremitting. SEE MAIN ENTRY

incessere inveigh

incest SEE MAIN ENTRY

incestuous SEE MAIN ENTRY

incestus lewd

inch by inch piecemeal

inchoate conceive (invent), establish (launch), incipient, initial, initiate, original (initial), premature, rudimentary. SEE MAIN ENTRY

inchoation embryo, genesis, inception, nascency, onset (commencement), origination, outset, start

inchoative fundamental, incipient, original (initial)

incidence situation. SEE MAIN ENTRY

incident accident (chance occurrence), appurtenant, casualty, contingency, event, experience (encounter), happening, occasion, occurrence, particular. SEE MAIN ENTRY

incident to contingent, dependent, subject (conditional)

incidental appurtenance, casual, circumstantial, collateral (immaterial), extraneous, extrinsic, impertinent (irrelevant), inapposite, nonessential, particular, random, subject (conditional), supplementary, tangential, unessential. SEE MAIN ENTRY

incidental mention reference (allusion)

incidental opinion dictum

incidental profits perquisite

incidentals circumstances

incidere impinge, occur (happen)

incinerate burn, deflagrate, destroy (efface). SEE MAIN ENTRY

incipere commence, engage (involve), initiate

incipience birth (beginning), embryo, genesis, inception, nascency, onset (commencement), origination, outset, start

incipiency birth (beginning), genesis, inception, nascency, origination, outset, start

incipient inchoate, initial, original (initial), preliminary, preparatory, prime (original). SEE MAIN ENTRY

incipient organism embryo

incircumspection inconsideration, indiscretion, negligence

incise break (separate), lancinate, split

incision split

incisive bitter (penetrating), compelling, eloquent, harsh, mordacious, pithy, trenchant. SEE MAIN ENTRY

incisiveness judgment (discernment), sagacity

incitamentum incentive, inducement, stimulus

incitare impel, incite, inspire, spirit, stimulate, urge

incitation catalyst, inducement, influence, instigation, persuasion, reason (basis)

incitatus vehement

incite abet, agitate (activate), bait (harass), bait (lure), cause, coax, engender, evoke, exacerbate, exhort, foment, hasten, impel, induce, influence, inspire, motivate, pique, press (goad), prevail (persuade), prompt, provoke, spirit, stimulate, urge. SEE MAIN ENTRY

incite to action impel

incitement catalyst, cause (reason), incentive, inducement, influence, instigation, invitation, persuasion, provocation, stimulus

inciter demagogue

inciting incendiary, moving (evoking emotion), offensive (taking the initiative), provocative

incitive incendiary

incivility contempt (disdain), disregard (lack of respect), disrespect. SEE MAIN ENTRY

inclemency severity, violence

inclement callous, harsh, relentless, ruthless, severe, unfavorable, unrelenting. SEE MAIN ENTRY

inclinatio bias, inclination, penchant, predisposition, tendency

inclination affection, affinity (regard), amenability, animus, aptitude, bias, character (personal quality), characteristic, color (complexion), conatus, conviction (persuasion), design (intent), desire, direction (course), disposition (inclination), favor (partiality), habit, instinct, notion, partiality, penchant, perspective, position (point of view), posture (attitude), preconception, predilection, predisposition, preference (choice), prejudice (preconception), proclivity, propensity, stand (position), standpoint, tendency, will (desire). SEE MAIN ENTRY

inclination downward descent (declination)

inclination to ask questions interest (concern)

incline convince, desire, dispose (incline), gravitate, lobby, motivate, preconceive, prompt, slant

incline to conduce

incline toward discriminate (treat differently)

incline toward each other converge

inclined eager, oblique (slanted), partial (biased), pliable, prone, ready (willing), receptive, solicitous. SEE MAIN ENTRY

inclined to anger fractious

inclined to assent consenting

inclined to delay dilatory

inclined to judge with severity critical (faultfinding)

inclined to lewdness lecherous

inclined to suspect inconvincible

inclined to vengeance vindictive

inclining oblique (slanted)

inclose contain (enclose)

inclosure jail

include append, circumscribe (surround by boundary), comprise, consist, constitute (compose), contain (comprise), embrace (encircle), implicate, interject, receive (permit to enter). SEE MAIN ENTRY

include as a necessary consequence entail

include by implication imply

include in an agreement stipulate

included additional, constituent (part)

includere confine, embody, enclose, immure, imprison, shut

including also

inclusion accession (annexation), addendum, admittance (acceptance), affiliation (connectedness), appendix (accession), composition (makeup), coverage (scope), insertion. SEE MAIN ENTRY

inclusive broad, complete (all-embracing), comprehensive, detailed, extensive, general, gross (total), omnibus, thorough, total. SEE MAIN ENTRY

inclusiveness corpus, coverage (scope), entirety

inclusivity coverage (scope)

inclusory inclusive, omnibus

incogitant thoughtless

incogitative vacuous

incognito anonymous, concealment. SEE MAIN ENTRY

incognizable inapprehensible, inscrutable

incognizance ignorance, insentience, nescience

incognizant blind (not discerning), unaware. SEE MAIN ENTRY

incognoscible incomprehensible

incohatus inchoate, rudimentary

incoherence jargon (unintelligible language). SEE MAIN ENTRY

incoherent disconnected, disjointed, disordered, incomprehensible. SEE MAIN ENTRY

incoherent discourse jargon (unintelligible language)

incola denizen, habitant, inhabitant, tenant

incolarum numerus population

incolere inhabit, reside

incolumitas security (safety)

income alimony, annuity, capital, earnings, finance, honorarium, money, pay, proceeds, profit, receipt (act of receiving), recompense, rent, resource, retainer, revenue, substance (material possessions), wage. SEE MAIN ENTRY

income from real estate rent

incoming inflow, ingress. SEE MAIN ENTRY

incoming population immigration

incommensurability difference, disparity

incommensurable different, disparate, disproportionate, inapplicable, incommensurate. SEE MAIN ENTRY

incommensurate disproportionate, insufficient. SEE MAIN ENTRY

incommode annoy, badger, bait (harass), deter, disadvantage, discommode, disoblige, disturb, embarrass, encumber (hinder), harass, hinder, hold up (delay), impede, inconvenience, molest (annoy), pique, plague, trammel

incommoded aggrieved (harmed)

incommodious undesirable, unsuitable

incommodum detriment, disadvantage (noun), disadvantage (verb), disservice, infliction, injury, mischief, misfortune

incommodus disadvantageous, unfit, unsuitable

incommunicable ineffable. SEE MAIN ENTRY

incommunicative inarticulate, mute, noncommittal

incommutable certain (positive), conclusive (determinative), definite, irreversible, irrevocable, permanent, unalterable

incomparable absolute (ideal), best, cardinal (outstanding), different, diverse, master, outstanding (prominent), paramount, premium, priceless, professional

817

(stellar), rare, superior *(excellent),* superlative, unapproachable, unique, unprecedented, unrelated, unusual. SEE MAIN ENTRY

incompatability   feud

incompatibility   antithesis, conflict, contraposition, contrary, disaccord, disagreement, discord, discrepancy, disparity, estrangement, ill will, incongruity, inconsistency, inequality, paradox, strife, variance *(disagreement).* SEE MAIN ENTRY

incompatible   different, discordant, disproportionate, dissident, divergent, hostile, inapplicable, inapposite, inappropriate, inapt, incongruous, inconsistent, inept *(inappropriate),* negative, opposite, unrelated, unsuitable. SEE MAIN ENTRY

incompetence   abortion *(fiasco),* disability *(physical inability),* disqualification *(factor that disqualifies),* impotence, impuissance, inability, incapacity, inefficacy, insufficiency, invalidity. SEE MAIN ENTRY

incompetency   abortion *(fiasco),* disability *(physical inability),* disqualification *(factor that disqualifies),* impotence, inability, incapacity, inefficacy, maladministration

incompetent   deficient, deranged, disabled *(made incapable),* helpless *(powerless),* inadept, inadequate, inadmissible, incapable, ineffective, ineffectual, inept *(incompetent),* insufficient, nugatory, powerless, unable, unavailing, unfit, unqualified *(not competent).* SEE MAIN ENTRY

incomplete   broken *(interrupted),* defective, deficient, devoid, imperfect, inadequate, inchoate, insufficient, nonsubstantial *(not sufficient),* outstanding *(unresolved),* paltry, partial *(part),* partial *(relating to a part),* perfunctory, rudimentary, scarce. SEE MAIN ENTRY

incompletely   in part

incompleteness   dearth, defect, deficiency, deficit, hiatus, insufficiency, need *(deprivation)*

incompletion   defect, deficiency, delinquency *(failure of duty)*

incomplex   simple

incompliance   refusal

incompositus   disjointed

incomprehensibility   complication, incoherence, opacity

incomprehensible   difficult, inapprehensible, inarticulate, indefinable, indistinct, inexplicable, inexpressive, innumerable, inscrutable, mysterious, obscure *(abstruse),* opaque, unclear, vague. SEE MAIN ENTRY

incomprehensibly   ad infinitum

incomprehensive   SEE MAIN ENTRY

incomprehension   ignorance, incapacity, insentience

incompressibility   congealment

incompressible   solid *(compact)*

incomputable   imponderable, innumerable

inconceivability   impossibility

inconceivable   debatable, doubtful, implausible, impossible, impracticable, incomprehensible, incredible, ineffable, infeasible, portentous *(eliciting amazement),* prodigious *(amazing),* rare, unbelievable, uncanny, unusual. SEE MAIN ENTRY

inconclusive   circumstantial, indeterminate, uncertain *(ambiguous),* unconfirmed. SEE MAIN ENTRY

inconclusiveness   suspicion *(uncertainty)*

incondite   defective

inconditus   simple

inconformable   disproportionate, incongruous, peculiar *(distinctive)*

inconformity   diversity

incongruence   conflict, controversy *(argument),* difference, disaccord, discord, discrepancy, disparity, dissidence

incongruency   discrepancy

incongruens   incongruous

incongruent   discordant, disjointed, disparate, disproportionate, dissimilar, distinct *(distinguished from others),* inapplicable, inapposite, inappropriate, inapt, incongruous, inept *(inappropriate),* peculiar *(distinctive).* SEE MAIN ENTRY

incongruity   conflict, contradiction, deviation, difference, disaccord, discord, discrepancy, disparity, dissidence, incompatibility *(inconsistency),* inconsistency, inequality, misjoinder, nonconformity, paradox. SEE MAIN ENTRY

incongruous   different, discordant, disjointed, disparate, disproportionate, dissenting, distinct *(distinguished from others),* heterogeneous, impertinent *(irrelevant),* improper, inapplicable, inapposite, inappropriate, inapt, inconsistent, inept *(inappropriate),* irrelevant, ludicrous, nonconforming, peculiar *(distinctive),* repugnant *(incompatible),* unbecoming, unfit, unrelated, unseemly, unsound *(fallacious),* unsuitable. SEE MAIN ENTRY

incongruousness   difference, impropriety, incongruity, inconsistency, inequality

inconsequence   immateriality, insignificance, non sequitur. SEE MAIN ENTRY

inconsequent   disproportionate, extraneous, impertinent *(irrelevant),* inapposite, incongruous, inconsequential, irrelevant, sophistic

inconsequential   collateral *(immaterial),* de minimus, expendable, extraneous, immaterial, inapposite, inappreciable, inconsiderable, insubstantial, irrelevant, mediocre, minor, negligible, nonessential, nugatory, null *(insignificant),* paltry, peripheral, petty, remote *(small),* slight, tenuous, trivial, unessential. SEE MAIN ENTRY

inconsequentiality   inconsequence, insignificance

inconsiderable   inappreciable, inconsequential, insubstantial, insufficient, minimal, minor, negligible, nominal, null *(insignificant),* paltry, petty, remote *(small),* scarce, slight, trivial, unessential. SEE MAIN ENTRY

inconsiderableness   inconsequence, mediocrity

inconsiderate   blind *(not discerning),* careless, derelict *(negligent),* ill-advised, ill-judged, impolitic, imprudent, injudicious, oblivious, reckless, remiss, thoughtless, unpolitic. SEE MAIN ENTRY

inconsiderateness   disregard *(lack of respect),* inconsideration, ingratitude, temerity

inconsideration   disinterest *(lack of interest),* disregard *(lack of respect),* disregard *(unconcern),* indifference, ingratitude, negligence. SEE MAIN ENTRY

inconsideratus   injudicious, reckless

inconsistence   inconsequence

inconsistency   antipode, conflict, contradiction, contrary, controversy *(argument),* deviation, difference, disaccord, discrepancy, exception *(exclusion),* incongruity, inconsequence, inequality, irregularity, nonconformity, paradox, specialty *(distinctive mark).* SEE MAIN ENTRY

inconsistent   anomalous, contradictory, deranged, desultory, disconnected, discor-

dant, discriminating *(distinguishing),* disjunctive *(tending to disjoin),* disordered, disparate, disproportionate, dissenting, divergent, illogical, inapplicable, inapposite, inappropriate, inapt, incommensurate, incongruous, inept *(inappropriate),* ludicrous, miscellaneous, opposite, repugnant *(incompatible),* sophistic, unusual. SEE MAIN ENTRY

inconsistent with   dissident, hostile

inconsolable   despondent, disconsolate

inconsonance   deviation, difference, disaccord, disagreement, incompatibility *(inconsistency),* incongruity, inconsistency, inequality, paradox

inconsonant   discordant, disparate, disproportionate, incongruous, inconsistent

inconspicuous   blind *(concealed),* impalpable, indiscernible, intangible, obscure *(faint),* unclear, usual. SEE MAIN ENTRY

inconspicuousness   concealment

inconstancy   disloyalty, inconsistency, infidelity, lapse *(expiration),* revolt

inconstans   capricious, desultory, inconsistent, mutable, unsettled

inconstant   broken *(interrupted),* capricious, desultory, faithless, false *(disloyal),* inconsistent, infrequent, insidious, irresponsible, mutable, noncommittal, perfidious, shifting, sporadic, transient, undependable, unpredictable, unreliable, unsettled, untrue, untrustworthy, variable, volatile

inconstantia   inconsistency, indecision

inconsultus   ill-advised, impolitic, imprudent, injudicious, precipitate, thoughtless

incontestability   certainty, certification *(certainness),* certitude. SEE MAIN ENTRY

incontestable   axiomatic, believable, categorical, certain *(fixed),* certain *(positive),* clear *(certain),* cogent, conclusive *(determinative),* decisive, definite, definitive, demonstrable, factual, inappealable, incontrovertible, indefeasible, indubious, infallible, irrebuttable, irrefutable, positive *(incontestable),* provable, real, reliable, resounding, solid *(sound),* uncontested, undeniable, undisputed, unequivocal, unimpeachable, unrefutable. SEE MAIN ENTRY

incontestably   admittedly. SEE MAIN ENTRY

incontinence   debauchery, greed, vice

incontinent   dissolute, gluttonous, promiscuous, salacious, uncurbed, unrestrained *(not repressed)*

incontrollable   disordered

incontrovertibility   certainty, certification *(certainness),* certitude, incontestability

incontrovertible   axiomatic, believable, categorical, certain *(fixed),* certain *(positive),* clear *(certain),* cogent, conclusive *(determinative),* definitive, factual, immutable, inappealable, incontestable, indefeasible, infallible, irrefutable, peremptory *(absolute),* positive *(incontestable),* reliable, resounding, solid *(sound),* sound, uncontested, undeniable, undisputed, unequivocal, unimpeachable, unrefutable. SEE MAIN ENTRY

incontrovertible incident   fact

incontrovertibly   admittedly

inconvenience   aggravation *(annoyance),* annoy, bait *(harass),* detriment, disadvantage *(noun),* disadvantage *(verb),* discommode, drawback, encumber *(hinder),* encumbrance, handicap, hinder, hindrance, hold up *(delay),* impede, impediment, molest *(annoy),* molestation, nuisance, obstacle, trammel, trouble. SEE MAIN ENTRY

inconvenient ill-advised, inopportune, undesirable, unfavorable, unfit, unsuitable, untimely. SEE MAIN ENTRY
inconversable inarticulate
inconvertible certain (positive), constant, irredeemable
inconvertible bill bad debt
inconvincability incredulity
inconvincible cynical, doubtful, suspicious (distrustful). SEE MAIN ENTRY
incorporal incorporeal, intangible
incorporality impalpability
incorporate affix, annex (add), attach (join), cement, collect (gather), commingle, comprehend (include), comprise, conjoin, consist, consolidate (unite), constitute (compose), contain (comprise), corporate (associate), desegregate, digest (comprehend), embody, embrace (encircle), encompass (include), federalize (associate), include, intangible, interject, join (bring together), merge, organize (unionize), unite. SEE MAIN ENTRY
incorporated affiliated, associated, coadunate, coherent (joined), composite, compound, conjoint
incorporation accession (annexation), building (business of assembling), centralization, coalescence, combination, compilation, consolidation, coverage (scope), integration (amalgamation), merger. SEE MAIN ENTRY
incorporeal immaterial, impalpable, insubstantial, intangible. SEE MAIN ENTRY
incorporeal being phantom
incorporeal entity intangible
incorporeal hereditament heritage
incorporealism impalpability
incorporeality immateriality, impalpability
incorporeity impalpability
incorrect defective, errant, erroneous, fallacious, false (inaccurate), faulty, ill-founded, improper, inaccurate, inexact, mendacious, sophistic, unauthorized, unbecoming, unseemly, unsound (fallacious), unsustainable, untenable, untrue, wrongful. SEE MAIN ENTRY
incorrect act tortious act
incorrect application misapplication
incorrect appraisal misestimation
incorrect assertion misrepresentation
incorrect belief error
incorrect evaluation misestimation
incorrect statement misstatement
incorrect usage catachresis, misapplication, misuse
incorrect use misapplication, misuse
incorrect valuation misestimation
incorrectness impropriety, misdoing, story (falsehood)
incorrigible delinquent (guilty of a misdeed), disobedient, disorderly, dissolute, inexcusable, iniquitous, intractable, irrecoverable, irredeemable, lawless, obdurate, peccant (culpable), perverse, reprehensible, reprobate, restive, uncontrollable, unruly, vicious. SEE MAIN ENTRY
incorrupt blameless, clean, dependable, equitable, high-minded, honest, impartial, law-abiding, loyal, meritorious, moral, not guilty, pure
incorruptibility adhesion (loyalty), honesty, honor (good reputation), integrity, inviolability, loyalty, principle (virtue), probity, responsibility (conscience)
incorruptible clean, conscientious, credible, equitable, faithful (loyal), high-minded, honest, irreprehensible, just, law-abiding,

loyal, meritorious, moral, reputable, true (loyal), uncompromising, upright. SEE MAIN ENTRY
incorruptibly faithfully
incorruption innocence
incorruptus impartial, incorruptible
incrassate ossified
incrassated ossified
increase accession (enlargement), accumulate (enlarge), addition, advance (increase), advancement (improvement), aggravate (exacerbate), aggravation (exacerbation), amplify, appreciation (increased value), augmentation, build (augment), compound, enlarge, exacerbate, expand, extend (enlarge), extension (expansion), heighten (augment), increment, inflate, inflation (increase), intensify, magnify, profit, progress (noun), progress (verb), prolong, promotion (advancement), pullulate, raise (advance), recruit, reinforcement, supplement. SEE MAIN ENTRY
increase clarity explain
increase dimensions inflate
increase in amount of wealth income
increase in bulk expand
increase in extent expand
increase in size development (progression)
increase of clarity clarification
increase of clearness clarification
increase of damages additur
increase of intelligibility clarification
increase of jury award additur
increase of size extension (expansion)
increase of speed acceleration
increase the capacity of expand
increase the chances conduce
increase the length of extend (enlarge)
increase the market price of appreciate (increase)
increase the number of proliferate
increase the numbers compound
increase the size of magnify
increase the strength of develop
increase the value of enhance
increased accrued
increased price appreciation (increased value)
increased value premium (excess value)
increasement boom (increase)
increasing augmentation, boom (increase)
incredibilis gross (total), incredible, ineffable
incredibility doubt (suspicion). SEE MAIN ENTRY
incredible debatable, disputable, doubtful, implausible, impossible, ludicrous, noteworthy, portentous (eliciting amazement), prodigious (amazing), remarkable, special, unbelievable, uncanny, unusual. SEE MAIN ENTRY
incredulity cloud (suspicion), discredit, doubt (suspicion), suspicion (mistrust). SEE MAIN ENTRY
incredulous inconvincible, skeptical. SEE MAIN ENTRY
incredulousness cloud (suspicion), doubt (suspicion), incredulity
incredulus incredulous
increment accretion, addition, additive, advance (increase), appreciation (increased value), augmentation, behalf, boom (increase), boom (prosperity), commission (fee), dividend, extension (expansion), growth (increase), interest (profit), profit, progress. SEE MAIN ENTRY

incremental cumulative (increasing)
incrementum growth (increase), increment
increpare inveigh
increpate lash (attack verbally), reprehend, reproach
increpation admonition, bad repute, reprimand, reproach, revilement
increpitare reproach
incriminate accuse, arraign, blame, charge (accuse), cite (accuse), complain (charge), condemn (blame), denigrate, denounce (inform against), implicate, indict, inform (betray), involve (implicate), libel, lodge (bring a complaint), present (prefer charges), proscribe (denounce), reproach. SEE MAIN ENTRY
incriminate unjustly frame (charge falsely), frame (prearrange)
incriminated guilty
incriminating inculpatory
incriminating statement confession
incrimination accusation, arraignment, attribution, blame (culpability), charge (accusation), complaint, condemnation (blame), denunciation, entanglement (involvement), inculpation, innuendo, reproach. SEE MAIN ENTRY
incriminator accuser, complainant
incriminatory inculpatory. SEE MAIN ENTRY
incubare brood
incubate SEE MAIN ENTRY
incubus weight (burden)
inculcare inculcate, obtrude
inculcate discipline (train), educate, imbue, infuse, instill, instruct (teach). SEE MAIN ENTRY
inculcation discipline (training), education, guidance, infusion, instruction (teaching), propaganda
inculcator pedagogue
inculculate initiate
inculpable blameless, incorruptible, irreprehensible, justifiable, not guilty, unimpeachable. SEE MAIN ENTRY
inculpate accuse, arraign, blame, charge (accuse), complain (charge), confess, denigrate, denounce (condemn), denounce (inform against), deprecate, impeach, implicate, incriminate, indict, inform (betray), involve (implicate), lodge (bring a complaint), reproach. SEE MAIN ENTRY
inculpate falsely frame (charge falsely)
inculpate unfairly frame (charge falsely)
inculpate unjustly frame (charge falsely)
inculpating inculpatory
inculpation accusation, allegation, bad repute, blame (culpability), charge (accusation), condemnation (blame), count, denunciation, diatribe, entanglement (involvement), implication (incriminating involvement), incrimination, reproach. SEE MAIN ENTRY
inculpation by prosecution arraignment
inculpatory incriminatory. SEE MAIN ENTRY
inculpatory statement confession
incultus uncouth
incumbency appointment (position), commitment (responsibility), employment, office, position (business status), post, regime, term (duration), work (employment)
incumbent binding, forcible, necessary (required). SEE MAIN ENTRY
incumbent on mandatory, obligatory, requisite

incumbent upon compulsory, essential *(required)*
incumbere study
incumbrance lien. SEE MAIN ENTRY
incunabula birth *(beginning)*, genesis, nascency, onset *(commencement)*, origination, source
incunabular incipient, original *(initial)*
incur SEE MAIN ENTRY
incur a debt charge *(assess)*, overdraw, owe
incur a duty assume *(undertake)*, promise *(vow)*, undertake
incur a loss forfeit, lose *(be deprived of)*
incur an expense expend *(disburse)*
incur blame denounce *(inform against)*, humiliate, impeach
incur costs bear the expense, disburse *(pay out)*, expend *(disburse)*. SEE MAIN ENTRY
incur disapproval disoblige
incur disgrace derogate
incur expense spend
incur expenses bear the expense, disburse *(pay out)*. SEE MAIN ENTRY
incur loss suffer *(sustain loss)*
incur the hostility of antagonize
incur the risk bet
incurable deadly, incorrigible, irredeemable, irremediable, irreparable, irreversible. SEE MAIN ENTRY
incuria neglect, negligence, oversight *(carelessness)*
incuriosity disinterest *(lack of interest)*
incuriosus regardless
incuriousness disinterest *(lack of interest)*
incurrere incur, invade
incursio incursion, invasion
incursion assault, encroachment, foray, inflow, infringement, ingress, intrusion, invasion, onset *(assault)*. SEE MAIN ENTRY
incursionem invade
incursive offensive *(taking the initiative)*
incursus assault
incusare reproach
incutere infuse, intimidate
indagate probe, research, search
indagatio investigation
indagation probe, research, scrutiny. SEE MAIN ENTRY
indagator detective
indebted insolvent, loyal. SEE MAIN ENTRY
indebtedness arrears, charge *(lien)*, cloud *(incumbrance)*, debit, debt, due, duty *(obligation)*, liability, lien, mortgage, obligation *(liability)*
indebtment arrears, cloud *(incumbrance)*, delinquency *(shortage)*, lien
indecency impropriety, obscenity, pornography, sodomy, vice. SEE MAIN ENTRY
indecent bad *(offensive)*, brazen, depraved, disgraceful, disreputable, dissolute, ignoble, immoral, improper, lascivious, lewd, licentious, nefarious, obscene, offensive *(offending)*, profligate *(corrupt)*, prurient, salacious, scandalous, scurrilous, suggestive *(risqué)*, unbecoming, unseemly. SEE MAIN ENTRY
indecent assault abuse *(physical misuse)*
indeciduous constant, durable
indecipherable SEE MAIN ENTRY
indecision ambivalence, dilemma, hesitation, incertitude, inertia, quandary. SEE MAIN ENTRY
indecisive circumstantial, debatable, doubtful, equivocal, hesitant, inconclusive, indefinite, ineffective, ineffectual, irresolute,

noncommittal, open-ended, pliant, unconfirmed, undecided, vague. SEE MAIN ENTRY
indecisiveness ambivalence, confusion *(ambiguity)*
indecorous blatant *(obtrusive)*, brazen, disorderly, disreputable, improper, inappropriate, inelegant, inept *(inappropriate)*, unbecoming, undue *(excessive)*, unseemly, unsuitable
indecorousness impropriety, indecency
indecorum bad repute, disrespect, impropriety, obscenity
indecorus improper, unbecoming, unseemly
indeed SEE MAIN ENTRY
indefatigability diligence *(perseverance)*, industry *(activity)*, resolution *(decision)*, tenacity
indefatigable diligent, faithful *(diligent)*, incessant, indomitable, industrious, infallible, patient, permanent, persistent, pertinacious, potent, relentless, resolute, sedulous, undaunted, unrelenting, unremitting
indefeasable unimpeachable
indefeasibility incontestability, indestructibility
indefeasible certain *(positive)*, clear *(certain)*, compulsory, conclusive *(determinative)*, definite, incontestable, indelible, indestructible, irreversible, irrevocable, permanent, unalienable, unavoidable *(not voidable)*. SEE MAIN ENTRY
indefeasible right birthright
indefectible infallible
indefective infallible
indefensible blameful, blameworthy, illogical, inadequate, inexcusable, inexpiable, powerless, reprehensible, unjustifiable, unreasonable, untenable, unwarranted, vulnerable. SEE MAIN ENTRY
indefinable ineffable, inexplicable, undefinable, unspecified. SEE MAIN ENTRY
indefinite aleatory *(uncertain)*, ambiguous, broad, conditional, debatable, disputable, equivocal, impalpable, incomprehensible, inconspicuous, indeterminate, intangible, obscure *(faint)*, open-ended, outstanding *(unresolved)*, pending *(unresolved)*, provisional, speculative, sporadic, undecided, unlimited, unspecified, vague. SEE MAIN ENTRY
indefinite meaning ambiguity
indefinite portion moiety
indefinite share moiety
indefinitely ad infinitum
indefiniteness ambiguity, confusion *(ambiguity)*, doubt *(indecision)*, indistinctness, perpetuity
indelibatus undiminished
indeliberate impulsive *(rash)*, spontaneous, unpremeditated
indelibilis indelible
indelibility indestructibility
indelible constant, durable, indestructible, ingrained, irrevocable, noncancellable, permanent, perpetual, profound *(intense)*. SEE MAIN ENTRY
indelicacy impropriety, indecency, obscenity
indelicate blatant *(obtrusive)*, disreputable, gross *(flagrant)*, improper, inelegant, lewd, licentious, lurid, obscene, profane, scurrilous, suggestive *(risqué)*, thoughtless, unbecoming, uncouth, unseemly
indemnification collection *(payment)*, compensation, consideration *(recompense)*, damages, expiation, indemnity, insurance,

payment *(remittance)*, recompense, recovery *(award)*, redemption, refund, reimbursement, relief *(legal redress)*, remuneration, rendition *(restoration)*, requital, restitution, retribution, reward, satisfaction *(discharge of debt)*, trover. SEE MAIN ENTRY
indemnificatory compensatory
indemnifier insurer
indemnify bear the expense, compensate *(remunerate)*, defray, outbalance, pay, quit *(repay)*, recoup *(reimburse)*, refund, reimburse, remedy, remunerate, repay, restore *(return)*, return *(refund)*. SEE MAIN ENTRY
indemnify against loss ensure
indemnitor insurer, surety *(guarantor)*
indemnity bail, binder, clemency, collection *(payment)*, compensation, condonation, consideration *(recompense)*, contribute *(indemnify)*, contribution *(indemnification)*, coverage *(insurance)*, damages, expiation, guaranty, honorarium, indemnification, pay, payment *(remittance)*, recompense, recovery *(award)*, reimbursement, remuneration, reparation *(indemnification)*, requital, reward, satisfaction *(discharge of debt)*, security *(pledge)*, trover. SEE MAIN ENTRY
indemnity against loss insurance
indemonstrable SEE MAIN ENTRY
indent bind *(obligate)*, depress, requisition, undertake
identification relation *(connection)*
indenture bind *(obligate)*, bond, bond *(secure a debt)*, compact, obligation *(liability)*, pact, security *(stock)*, servitude, specialty *(contract)*, undertake. SEE MAIN ENTRY
indentured SEE MAIN ENTRY
independence freedom, home rule, latitude, liberty, nonconformity. SEE MAIN ENTRY
independent alien *(unrelated)*, apart, disparate, eccentric, foreign, free *(enjoying civil liberty)*, free *(not restricted)*, impartial, impertinent *(irrelevant)*, individual, irrelative, neutral, nonconforming, nonpartisan, open-minded, peremptory *(absolute)*, separate, several *(separate)*, spontaneous, substantive, unbiased, unilateral, unprejudiced, unrelated, unrestrained *(not in custody)*, unrestricted. SEE MAIN ENTRY
independent of law arbitrary
independent of rule arbitrary
independent of volition involuntary
independently alone *(solitary)*, respectively
indescribable indefinable, ineffable, nondescript, portentous *(eliciting amazement)*, prodigious *(amazing)*, undefinable, unusual. SEE MAIN ENTRY
indestructibility inviolability. SEE MAIN ENTRY
indestructible certain *(positive)*, constant, immutable, indefeasible, indelible, infinite, infrangible, invincible, irrevocable, permanent, perpetual. SEE MAIN ENTRY
indeterminable conditional, open-ended
indeterminableness confusion *(ambiguity)*
indeterminacy ambiguity, ambivalence, chance *(possibility)*
indeterminate broad, casual, conditional, debatable, disputable, equivocal, generic, indefinite, nebulous, oblique *(evasive)*, pending *(unresolved)*, provisional, uncertain *(ambiguous)*, undefinable, unspecified, vague. SEE MAIN ENTRY
indeterminately ad infinitum
indeterminateness chance *(possibility)*, confusion *(ambiguity)*, doubt *(indecision)*

indetermination ambivalence, doubt *(indecision)*, incertitude, indecision, quandary. SEE MAIN ENTRY

index book, classify, clue, codify, directory, enumerate, fix *(arrange)*. SEE MAIN ENTRY

index gist *(substance)*

index indicant, indicate, indication, indicator

index inscription, inventory

index itemize, ledger, marshal, pigeonhole, record, register, roll, schedule, symbol, symptom, tabulate

indicant device *(distinguishing mark)*, index *(catalog)*, indication, suggestive *(evocative)*, symptom, token. SEE MAIN ENTRY

indicare denote, disclose, enunciate, imply, indicate, purport

indicate adduce, allot, allude, bear *(adduce)*, bespeak, cite *(state)*, connote, construe *(translate)*, convey *(communicate)*, demonstrate *(establish)*, denote, depict, designate, direct *(show)*, disabuse, disclose, display, evidence, evince, exemplify, exhibit, express, hint, imply, infer, label, manifest, mention, notify, portend, predict, purport, refer *(direct attention)*, represent *(portray)*, reveal, signify *(denote)*, speak, specify, testify. SEE MAIN ENTRY

indicate beforehand portend, predict, presage, prognosticate

indicate in advance presage, prognosticate

indicate willingness consent

indicated assumed *(inferred)*, constructive *(inferential)*, implied, tacit

indicating reference *(citation)*

indicating difference distinctive

indication admonition, attribution, call *(title)*, caveat, clue, designation *(naming)*, earmark, expression *(comment)*, expression *(manifestation)*, guideline, hint, implication *(inference)*, indicant, innuendo, manifestation, mention *(reference)*, monition *(warning)*, reference *(allusion)*, representation *(statement)*, selection *(choice)*, signification, suggestion, symbol, symptom, tip *(clue)*. SEE MAIN ENTRY

indication of contents caption

indications indicia

indicative allusive, circumstantial, distinctive, portentous *(ominous)*, prophetic, representative, suggestive *(evocative)*, typical

indicator bystander, clue, deponent, designation *(symbol)*, index *(catalog)*, indicant, indication, symptom, token. SEE MAIN ENTRY

indicatory circumstantial, representative, suggestive *(evocative)*, typical

indice symptom

indicia SEE MAIN ENTRY

indicium designation *(symbol)*

indicium disclosure *(something disclosed)*, evidence *(noun)*, evidence *(verb)*, indication, manifestation, proof, symptom

indict accuse, blame, charge *(accuse)*, condemn *(blame)*, defame, denounce *(inform against)*, impeach, incriminate. SEE MAIN ENTRY

indict for maladministration impeach

indictable blameful, blameworthy, culpable, guilty

indictable offense crime, felony

indicted accused *(charged)*

indicter complainant, informer *(one providing criminal information)*

indictment accusation, bill *(formal declaration)*, charge *(accusation)*, complaint, count, criticism, denunciation, diatribe,

disapprobation, impeachment, incrimination, presentment. SEE MAIN ENTRY

indictor accuser, complainant

indifference dereliction, disinterest *(lack of interest)*, disregard *(lack of respect)*, disregard *(unconcern)*, insentience, languor, laxity, neglect, negligence, neutrality, nonfeasance, sloth. SEE MAIN ENTRY

indifference to act delinquency *(failure of duty)*

indifferent blind *(not discerning)*, callous, careless, casual, cold-blooded, collateral *(immaterial)*, cursory, derelict *(negligent)*, disdainful, dispassionate, evenhanded, faithless, impartial, imperfect, impervious, inactive, indolent, inferior *(lower in quality)*, insusceptible *(uncaring)*, jejune *(dull)*, languid, lax, marginal, mediocre, negligent, neutral, nonchalant, obdurate, oblivious, open-minded, passive, perfunctory, phlegmatic, poor *(inferior in quality)*, reckless, remiss, slipshod, stoical, thoughtless, torpid, trivial, truant, unaffected *(uninfluenced)*, unbiased, unresponsive, usual. SEE MAIN ENTRY

indifferent to suffering cruel

indigen citizen

indigence bankruptcy, dearth, need *(deprivation)*, poverty, privation. SEE MAIN ENTRY

indigene citizen

indigenous born *(innate)*, hereditary, innate, native *(domestic)*, native *(inborn)*, natural, organic, specific

indigent bankrupt, destitute, impecunious, penurious, poor *(underprivileged)*

indignant bitter *(reproachful)*, contemptuous, disdainful, resentful

indignant aversion contempt *(disdain)*, disdain

indignation disparagement, resentment, umbrage. SEE MAIN ENTRY

indignity contumely, defilement, disgrace, dishonor *(shame)*, notoriety, opprobrium, reproach

indignus improper, unbecoming, unfit

indiligence neglect

indiligens inaccurate, negligent

indiligentia neglect, negligence

indirect allusive, astray, circuitous, circumstantial, collusive, constructive *(inferential)*, deceptive, devious, discursive *(digressive)*, furtive, insidious, labyrinthine, oblique *(evasive)*, remote *(not proximate)*, secondary, sinuous, surreptitious, tortuous *(bending)*, virtual. SEE MAIN ENTRY

indirect allusion innuendo, insinuation

indirect comment insinuation

indirect evidence hearsay

indirect hint mention *(reference)*

indirect implication insinuation, reference *(allusion)*

indirect influence impression

indirect path detour

indirect quotation paraphrase

indirect suggestion hint

indirection corruption, deceit, deception, falsification, improbity, pettifoggery. SEE MAIN ENTRY

indirectly meant constructive *(inferential)*

indirectly state imply

indirectness deception

indiscernable hidden

indiscernibility nonappearance, opacity

indiscernible blind *(concealed)*, inconspicuous, inscrutable, intangible, latent, obscure *(faint)*. SEE MAIN ENTRY

indiscerptibility entirety

indiscerptible indivisible, infrangible, inseparable, solid *(compact)*

indiscerptibleness entirety

indiscipline anarchy, contempt *(disobedience to the court)*, latitude, rebellion

indiscreet careless, culpable, impolitic, improvident, imprudent, misadvised, precipitate, reckless, thoughtless, unpolitic, unprofessional. SEE MAIN ENTRY

indiscrete injudicious

indiscretion bad faith, delinquency *(misconduct)*, impropriety, inconsideration, misconduct, misdemeanor, misdoing, temerity. SEE MAIN ENTRY

indiscriminate blind *(not discerning)*, broad, casual, conglomerate, disjointed, haphazard, miscellaneous, omnibus, promiscuous, random. SEE MAIN ENTRY

indiscriminating blind *(not discerning)*

indiscrimination disinterest *(lack of prejudice)*

indiscriminative promiscuous

indispensability market *(demand)*, need *(requirement)*

indispensable cardinal *(basic)*, central *(essential)*, compulsory, essential *(required)*, exigent, fundamental, grave *(important)*, imperative, important *(urgent)*, instrumental, integral, mandatory, material *(important)*, necessary *(required)*, necessity, obligatory, requisite, urgent, vital. SEE MAIN ENTRY

indispensable condition sine qua non

indispensable item prerequisite, requirement, sine qua non

indispensable party SEE MAIN ENTRY

indispensable person key man

indispensable provision necessity, need *(requirement)*

indispensable thing necessary

indispose deter, disable, discourage

indisposed adverse *(hostile)*, averse, disabled *(made incapable)*, disinclined, disobedient, reluctant, renitent, unfavorable. SEE MAIN ENTRY

indisposed to action indolent

indisposed to believe cynical, inconvincible, incredulous

indisposed to mercy callous

indisposed to talk mute

indisposed to words speechless

indisposedly unwillingly

indisposedness reluctance

indisposition disability *(physical inability)*, disease, disincentive, disorder *(abnormal condition)*, reluctance

indisposition to admit incredulity

indisposition to believe incredulity

indisposition to move inertia

indisputability certainty, certification *(certainness)*, certitude, incontestability

indisputable absolute *(conclusive)*, believable, categorical, certain *(fixed)*, certain *(positive)*, clear *(certain)*, conclusive *(determinative)*, credible, definite, definitive, demonstrable, evident, explicit, inappealable, incontestable, incontrovertible, irrebuttable, irrefutable, lucid, manifest, obvious, official, palpable, positive *(incontestable)*, provable, real, reliable, undeniable, undisputed, unequivocal, unrefutable. SEE MAIN ENTRY

indisputable event fact

indisputably admittedly

indissolubility indestructibility

indissoluble constant, firm, indefeasible, indestructible, inextricable, infrangible, inseparable, irreversible, irrevocable, stable, steadfast

indissoluble entity aggregate

indissolvable infrangible, irreversible, irrevocable

indistinct ambiguous, impalpable, inapprehensible, inarticulate, inconspicuous, indefinite, indeterminate, nebulous, obscure *(faint)*, opaque, speculative, subtle *(insidious)*, uncertain *(ambiguous)*, unclear, undefinable, unspecified, vague. SEE MAIN ENTRY

indistinct in character or meaning doubtful

indistinctness confusion *(ambiguity)*, obscuration, opacity. SEE MAIN ENTRY

indistinguishability indistinctness, opacity

indistinguishable identical, inarticulate, indefinite, indiscernible, indistinct, promiscuous, similar, unclear, vague. SEE MAIN ENTRY

indisturbance composure

indite formulate

individual certain *(particular)*, certain *(specific)*, corpse, different, discrete, disjunctive *(tending to disjoin)*, distinct *(distinguished from others)*, eccentric, entity, noteworthy, only *(sole)*, original *(creative)*, particular *(specific)*, patent, peculiar *(distinctive)*, person, private *(not public)*, separate, singular, sole, specific, subjective, unique, unusual. SEE MAIN ENTRY

individual admitted to the bar counselor

individual characteristic speciality

individual held in custody prisoner

individual in possession holder

individual jailed prisoner

individual method style

individual part detail

individual rights SEE MAIN ENTRY

individual selected for jury service juror

individual trait speciality

individual under age minor

individual under guardianship dependent

individual under suspicion suspect

individual under the age of majority minor

individual who brings a lawsuit plaintiff

individual who stays on holdover

individual's nearest relative next of kin

individualism character *(personal quality)*, disposition *(inclination)*, home rule, identity *(individuality)*, personality, quality *(attribute)*, specialty *(distinctive mark)*, trait. SEE MAIN ENTRY

individualistic distinctive, noteworthy, special, specific

individuality character *(personal quality)*, characteristic, difference, distinction *(difference)*, feature *(characteristic)*, individual, nonconformity, particularity, personality, property *(distinctive attribute)*, quirk *(idiosyncrasy)*, speciality. SEE MAIN ENTRY

individualization discrimination *(differentiation)*

individualize call *(title)*, characterize, define, detail *(particularize)*, discriminate *(distinguish)*, distinguish

individualized individual, private *(not public)*, subjective

individualizing discriminating *(distinguishing)*, distinctive

individually in person, particularly, respectively

individuals populace

individuate characterize, define

individuus indivisible

indivisibility congealment, whole

indivisible coherent *(joined)*, cohesive *(compact)*, conjoint, inextricable, infrangible, inseparable, solid *(compact)*, whole *(unified)*. SEE MAIN ENTRY

indivisible entity aggregate

indocile contumacious, fractious, froward, indomitable, inflexible, insubordinate, intractable, petulant, renitent, uncontrollable, unruly

indocilis intractable

indocility contempt *(disobedience to the court)*, reluctance

indoctrinate convince, discipline *(train)*, educate, imbue, inculcate, initiate, instill, instruct *(teach)*, persuade, prevail *(persuade)*. SEE MAIN ENTRY

indoctrination discipline *(training)*, education, guidance, instruction *(teaching)*, propaganda

indolen truant

indolence inaction, inertia, languor, laxity, sloth, vagrancy

indolent dilatory, idle, inactive, lax, lifeless *(dull)*, otiose, passive, remiss, stagnant, torpid. SEE MAIN ENTRY

indoles disposition *(inclination)*

indomitable contumacious, formidable, inexorable, inexpugnable, infallible, inflexible, insuperable, insurmountable, intractable, invincible, irresistible, pertinacious, potent, powerful, resolute, spartan, stable, steadfast, uncontrollable, undaunted, unyielding. SEE MAIN ENTRY

indomitus indomitable

indorse certify *(approve)*, cosign, pledge *(deposit)*, sign. SEE MAIN ENTRY

indorsement certification *(certification of proficiency)*, leave *(permission)*. SEE MAIN ENTRY

indorser notary public

indubious axiomatic, decisive, definite, incontestable, incontrovertible, irrefutable, uncontroverted. SEE MAIN ENTRY

indubitability certainty, certification *(certainness)*, certitude

indubitable absolute *(conclusive)*, apparent *(perceptible)*, axiomatic, believable, categorical, certain *(fixed)*, certain *(positive)*, clear *(certain)*, cogent, conclusive *(determinative)*, credible, definite, definitive, demonstrable, distinct *(clear)*, evident, incontestable, incontrovertible, indefeasible, irrebuttable, irrefutable, manifest, ostensible, palpable, perceptible, positive *(incontestable)*, probable, reliable, salient, uncontested, undeniable, undisputed, unequivocal, unmistakable, unrefutable

indubitable fact certification *(certainness)*, certitude

indubitableness certainty, certitude, incontestability

indubitably admittedly, fairly *(clearly)*

induce affect, agitate *(activate)*, bait *(lure)*, cause, coax, coerce, constrain *(compel)*, contrive, convert *(persuade)*, convince, create, dispose *(incline)*, engender, entice, evoke, exhort, generate, impel, incite, influence, inspire, inveigle, launch *(initiate)*, lobby, lure, motivate, occasion, originate, persuade, pressure, prevail *(persuade)*, prevail upon, prompt, provoke, solicit, suborn. SEE MAIN ENTRY

induce another to commit perjury suborn

induce by illegal gratuity suborn

induce forgetfulness lull

induce pain mistreat

induced causative

inducement bribery, catalyst, cause *(reason)*, coercion, consideration *(recompense)*, decoy, determinant, force *(compulsion)*, hush money, incentive, instigation, invitation, motive, persuasion, prize, provocation, reason *(basis)*, seduction, stimulus. SEE MAIN ENTRY

inducer abettor

inducere cancel, expunge, induce, introduce

inducible open *(persuasible)*, suasible

inducing causal, causative

inducive advisory, cogent, compelling

induct admit *(give access)*, enroll, hire, initiate, instate, introduce, invest *(vest)*, receive *(permit to enter)*, recruit. SEE MAIN ENTRY

inductile unyielding

inductio introduction

induction admittance *(acceptance)*, consequence *(conclusion)*, dialectic, inflow, installation, introduction, nascency, outset, prelude

inductional logical

inductive causative, discursive *(analytical)*, logical, persuasive

induere sibi vestem clothe

indulge bestow, enable, foster, furnish, give *(grant)*, grant *(concede)*, let *(permit)*, pander, patronize *(condescend toward)*, sanction, suffer *(permit)*, tolerate, vouchsafe

indulge in argument discuss, dispute *(debate)*

indulge in dissipation carouse

indulge in extravagance dissipate *(expend foolishly)*

indulge one's fancy prefer

indulge oneself carouse, dissipate *(expend foolishly)*

indulgence benevolence *(disposition to do good)*, clemency, condonation, consent, dispensation *(exception)*, favor *(act of kindness)*, franchise *(license)*, grace, grant, greed, largess *(generosity)*, leave *(permission)*, lenience, longanimity, philanthropy, privilege, remission, sanction *(permission)*, sufferance, temperance, tolerance, understanding *(tolerance)*, vice. SEE MAIN ENTRY

indulgent addicted, benevolent, dissolute, gluttonous, intemperate, lenient, patient, permissive, philanthropic, placable, pliant, propitious

indulgentia connivance, indulgence, patronage *(power to appoint jobs)*, tolerance

indulging lenient

indurate callous, cold-blooded, impervious, insusceptible *(uncaring)*, obdurate, remorseless, rigid, tempered. SEE MAIN ENTRY

indurated callous, cold-blooded, impervious, insusceptible *(uncaring)*, obdurate, ossified, remorseless, rigid, tempered

indurative rigid

industria diligence *(care)*, industry *(activity)*

industrial commercial, mercantile, productive, technical. SEE MAIN ENTRY

industrial area development *(building)*

industrial building development *(building)*

industrialist executive

industrialized industrial

industrious active, diligent, eager, faithful *(diligent)*, meticulous, painstaking, pertinacious, resolute, sedulous, stable, steadfast, zealous. SEE MAIN ENTRY

industriousness diligence *(perseverance)*
industrius active, diligent, industrious
industry building *(business of assembling)*, business *(commerce)*, business *(commercial enterprise)*, calling, commerce, corporation, effort, employment, enterprise *(economic organization)*, firm, labor *(exertion)*, occupation *(vocation)*, work *(effort)*, work *(employment)*. SEE MAIN ENTRY
industry and trade commerce
indwell dwell *(reside)*, occupy *(take possession)*, reside
indweller citizen, denizen, domiciliary, habitant, inhabitant, lodger, resident
indwelling ingrained
inebriant alcohol
inebriated drunk
inebriation dipsomania. SEE MAIN ENTRY
inebriety dipsomania, inebriation
inedible repugnant *(exciting aversion)*
ineducation illiteracy
ineffable mysterious, sacrosanct, undefinable. SEE MAIN ENTRY
ineffaceable indelible, indestructible, ingrained, inherent, noncancellable
ineffective disabled *(made incapable)*, futile, inadept, inadequate, incapable, incompetent, inconclusive, ineffectual, inept *(incompetent)*, insipid, invalid, languid, nugatory, null *(invalid)*, null and void, otiose, powerless, unable, unavailing, unqualified *(not competent)*, void *(invalid)*. SEE MAIN ENTRY
ineffective trial mistrial
ineffectiveness disability *(physical inability)*, impotence, inefficacy, invalidity, miscarriage
ineffectual disabled *(deprived of legal right)*, expendable, futile, inadept, inadequate, incapable, incompetent, ineffective, inept *(incompetent)*, invalid, minor, nugatory, null *(invalid)*, null and void, otiose, powerless, unavailing, unproductive, void *(invalid)*. SEE MAIN ENTRY
ineffectual attempt miscarriage
ineffectuality abortion *(fiasco)*, disability *(physical inability)*, impotence, inefficacy
ineffectualness detriment, disability *(physical inability)*, failure *(lack of success)*, impotence, inability, inefficacy
inefficacious defunct, disabled *(made incapable)*, futile, inadept, inadequate, ineffective, ineffectual, inept *(incompetent)*, invalid, nugatory, null *(invalid)*, null and void, otiose, powerless, unavailing, unproductive. SEE MAIN ENTRY
inefficaciousness impotence, inefficacy
inefficacy abortion *(fiasco)*, disability *(physical inability)*, impotence, impuissance, inability, incapacity, nullity. SEE MAIN ENTRY
inefficiency detriment, disability *(physical inability)*, impotence, impuissance, inability, incapacity, incompetence, inefficacy, maladministration
inefficient inadept, incompetent, inept *(incompetent)*, otiose, unable, unavailing, unproductive, unqualified *(not competent)*
inefficient management maladministration
inelastic inflexible, rigid
inelegance impropriety
inelegans inelegant
inelegant disreputable, imperfect, inferior *(lower in quality)*, pedestrian, tawdry, uncouth, unseemly. SEE MAIN ENTRY
ineligibility disqualification *(rejection)*

ineligible inadmissible, inappropriate, undesirable, unfit, unqualified *(not competent)*. SEE MAIN ENTRY
ineluctable inevitable, irrevocable, necessary *(inescapable)*, requisite, unavoidable *(inevitable)*
ineludible inevitable, necessary *(inescapable)*, unavoidable *(inevitable)*
inept amateur, disabled *(made incapable)*, fatuous, ill-judged, improper, inadept, inadequate, inapposite, incapable, incompetent, ineffective, ineffectual, inexperienced, nugatory, powerless, unable, unfit, unqualified *(not competent)*, unsatisfactory. SEE MAIN ENTRY
ineptitude abortion *(fiasco)*, disqualification *(factor that disqualifies)*, ignorance, impotence, impuissance, inability, incapacity. SEE MAIN ENTRY
ineptness inability
ineptus fatuous, inept *(incompetent)*, insipid
inequality difference, discrepancy, disparity, favoritism, incompatibility *(inconsistency)*, inconsistency, injustice. SEE MAIN ENTRY
inequitable iniquitous, unequal *(unjust)*, unfair, unjust, unscrupulous. SEE MAIN ENTRY
inequitable action injustice
inequitableness inequity, misjudgment, nepotism
inequity favoritism, ground, injustice, misjudgment, nepotism. SEE MAIN ENTRY
ineradicable durable, indefeasible, indelible, invincible, irreversible, irrevocable, permanent, perpetual
ineradicableness indestructibility
inerasable durable, indelible, indestructible
inerasableness indestructibility
inermis helpless *(defenseless)*
inerrability certainty, certitude
inerrable infallible, reliable
inerrancy certainty, certification *(certainness)*, certitude
inerrant accurate, certain *(positive)*, infallible, reliable
iners inactive, indolent, torpid
inert dead, dormant, idle, inactive, languid, lifeless *(dull)*, otiose, phlegmatic, stable, stagnant, static, torpid
inertia desuetude. SEE MAIN ENTRY
inertia insentience
inertia sloth
inertion abeyance
inertness abeyance, inaction, inertia, insentience, languor, sloth
inerudition ignorance, illiteracy
inescapable certain *(fixed)*, certain *(positive)*, compulsory, definite, exigent, forthcoming, important *(urgent)*, inevitable, irrevocable, obligatory, positive *(incontestable)*, stringent, unavoidable *(inevitable)*, undeniable. SEE MAIN ENTRY
inescapable duty allegiance, charge *(responsibility)*, onus *(burden)*
inessential circumstantial, expendable, gratuitous *(unwarranted)*, immaterial, inapposite, inappropriate, inconsequential, irrelevant, minor, nonessential, null *(insignificant)*, peripheral, superfluous, unnecessary
inessentiality immateriality, insignificance, technicality
inestimable imponderable, invaluable, priceless, valuable. SEE MAIN ENTRY
inevasible definite, inevitable, irrevocable, requisite, unavoidable *(inevitable)*

inevitabilis inevitable, unavoidable *(inevitable)*
inevitability predetermination
inevitable categorical, certain *(fixed)*, certain *(positive)*, definite, forthcoming, future, irremediable, irrevocable, necessary *(inescapable)*, necessity, unalterable. SEE MAIN ENTRY
inevitable occurrence accident *(chance occurrence)*
inevitable result foregone conclusion
inevitableness certification *(certainness)*, certitude, predetermination
inexact ambiguous, approximate, erroneous, generic, ill-judged, imperfect, improper, inaccurate, incorrect, indefinite, lax, liberal *(not literal)*, oblique *(evasive)*, open-ended, partial *(relating to a part)*, perfunctory, slipshod. SEE MAIN ENTRY
inexact statement generalization
inexactitude exaggeration, generality *(vague statement)*, informality, laxity, misestimation, misjudgment, misstatement
inexactness confusion *(ambiguity)*, error, exaggeration, generality *(vague statement)*, informality, laxity, misestimation, misjudgment, misstatement
inexcitability composure, inertia, languor, longanimity
inexcitable callous, dispassionate, insensible, lifeless *(dull)*, torpid
inexcusability misdoing
inexcusable blameful, indefensible, inexpiable, peccant *(culpable)*, reprehensible, unjustifiable, unwarranted. SEE MAIN ENTRY
inexcusable delay laches. SEE MAIN ENTRY
inexcusable delay in assertion of rights laches
inexcusable neglect SEE MAIN ENTRY
inexecution neglect, nonperformance
inexertion neglect, sloth
inexhaustible copious, durable, infallible, infinite, innumerable, myriad, perpetual, profuse, unlimited
inexistence blank *(emptiness)*, nonappearance, nonentity, nullity
inexistent nonexistent
inexorabilis implacable, inexorable, irreconcilable, relentless, ruthless, unrelenting
inexorability certainty, certitude, severity
inexorable brutal, callous, certain *(positive)*, definite, dictatorial, immutable, implacable, inflexible, ironclad, irreconcilable, necessary *(inescapable)*, obdurate, peremptory *(imperative)*, pertinacious, purposeful, relentless, resolute, rigid, ruthless, severe, stable, steadfast, strict, unavoidable *(inevitable)*, uncompromising, unrelenting, unyielding. SEE MAIN ENTRY
inexorable fate predetermination
inexpectant unaware
inexpectation bombshell, happenstance, improbability
inexpectatus unexpected
inexpedience detriment, disadvantage, hindrance, impropriety
inexpediency detriment, impropriety, inexpedience. SEE MAIN ENTRY
inexpedient harmful, ill-advised, ill-judged, impolitic, imprudent, inadvisable, inappropriate, inapt, inauspicious, inept *(inappropriate)*, injudicious, inopportune, misadvised, objectionable, undesirable, unfavorable, unfit, unpolitic, unsatisfactory, unsuitable
inexpensive economical, nominal

inexperience ignorance, minority (infancy), nescience

inexperienced incompetent, jejune (lacking maturity), juvenile, naive, unaccustomed, unacquainted, unqualified (not competent), unversed. SEE MAIN ENTRY

inexperienced person amateur, juvenile, novice

inexpert inadept, incompetent, inept (incompetent), inexperienced, unfit, unqualified (not competent), unversed

inexpertness abortion (fiasco), disqualification (factor that disqualifies), incompetence

inexpiable implacable, indefensible, inexcusable, irreconcilable, irremediable, peccant (culpable), reprehensible. SEE MAIN ENTRY

inexplebilis insatiable

inexplicabilis inexpiable, inexplicable, inextricable

inexplicable enigmatic, inapprehensible, incomprehensible, indefinable, inexpressive, inscrutable, mysterious, peculiar (curious), undefinable. SEE MAIN ENTRY

inexplicable statement enigma

inexplicableness mystery

inexplicit indefinite, vague

inexpressible inapprehensible, indefinable, ineffable, undefinable

inexpressive SEE MAIN ENTRY

inexpugnabilis inexpugnable

inexpugnability inviolability

inexpugnable immune, insurmountable, invincible. SEE MAIN ENTRY

inexpungeable durable

inexspectatus unanticipated

inexsuperabilis invincible

inextinguishable certain (positive), constant, indefeasible, indelible, indestructible, indomitable, inexpungable, invincible, irreversible, irrevocable, permanent

inextinguished chronic

inextricabilis inextricable, labyrinthine

inextricability complication, constant, impasse

inextricable complex, inseparable. SEE MAIN ENTRY

infallibilism certitude

infallibility certainty, certification (certainness), certitude

infallible certain (fixed), certain (positive), conclusive (determinative), factual, positive (incontestable), reliable, secure (sound), undeniable. SEE MAIN ENTRY

infallibleness certitude

infamia discredit, disgrace, dishonor (shame), disrepute, ignominy, infamy, notoriety, shame

infamis disputable, disreputable

infamous arrant (onerous), bad (offensive), contemptible, contemptuous, disgraceful, disreputable, flagrant, heinous, ignoble, illicit, inexpiable, iniquitous, machiavellian, malevolent, nefarious, notorious, odious, outrageous, peccant (culpable), profligate (corrupt), reprehensible, reprobate, scandalous, sinister. SEE MAIN ENTRY

infamous conduct criminality, misconduct, misdeed, misdemeanor, misdoing

infamous misbehavior criminality

infamousness bad repute, disrepute, infamy, notoriety, opprobrium, stigma

infamy atrocity, attaint, bad character, bad repute, contempt (disdain), defamation, discredit, disgrace, dishonor (shame), disrepute, ignominy, ill repute, notoriety,

obloquy, odium, onus (stigma), opprobrium, scandal, shame, stigma, turpitude, vice. SEE MAIN ENTRY

infancy birth (beginning), nascency, nonage, onset (commencement), origination, outset, start

infandus ineffable

infans child, infant

infant child, inchoate, incipient, minor, original (initial). SEE MAIN ENTRY

infant status minority (infancy)

infantile jejune (lacking maturity), puerile

infantilism puerility

infantine jejune (lacking maturity), juvenile, puerile

infants children

infarction bar (obstruction)

infatuate bigot, obsess

infatuated zealous

infatuation affection, compulsion (obsession), obsession, passion, predilection

infeasibility impossibility

infeasible impossible, unattainable. SEE MAIN ENTRY

infect adulterate, contaminate, foment, harm, motivate, pervert, pollute, taint (contaminate). SEE MAIN ENTRY

infected marred, tainted (contaminated)

infection contaminate, disease

infectious contagious, harmful, pestilent

infective contagious

infectus executory

infecund barren, unproductive

infecundus unproductive

infelicitous disconsolate, disproportionate, ill-advised, improper, inadvisable, inapplicable, inapposite, inappropriate, inapt, inept (inappropriate), misadvised, unbecoming, unfavorable, unsuitable, untimely

infelicity distress (anguish), inexpedience, misfortune

infelix inauspicious

infensus adverse (hostile), hostile

infer allude, assume (suppose), conclude (decide), connote, construe (comprehend), deduce, deduct (conclude by reasoning), derive (deduce), determine, educe, evidence, expect (consider probable), guess, hint, implicate, imply, judge, opine, postulate, presume, presuppose, purport, read, reason (conclude), surmise, suspect (think), understand. SEE MAIN ENTRY

inferable constructive (inferential), deductible (provable), deductive, presumptive, provable

inferable harm SEE MAIN ENTRY

inference conclusion (determination), conjecture, connotation, construction, generalization, hint, hypothesis, idea, innuendo, insinuation, intimation, mention (reference), presumption, reference (allusion), referral, signification, speculation (conjecture), suggestion, suspicion (uncertainty). SEE MAIN ENTRY

inferential accountable (explainable), allusive, circumstantial, consequential (deducible), deductible (provable), deductive, discursive (analytical), implied, leading (guiding), suggestive (evocative), tacit

inferentially a priori

inferior deficient, faulty, ignoble, imperfect, inadequate, mediocre, minor, null (insignificant), pedestrian, poor (inferior in quality), secondary, slight, subaltern, subordinate, subservient, trivial, unsatisfactory, unworthy. SEE MAIN ENTRY

inferior rank subjection

inferiority disadvantage, flaw, handicap, mediocrity

inferiorness mediocrity

infernal blameworthy, diabolic, heinous, malevolent, malignant, nefarious, odious

infernal machine bomb

inferre entail, inflict

inferred allusive, constructive (inferential), implied, presumptive, subtle (insidious), tacit

inferred in law constructive (inferential). SEE MAIN ENTRY

inferring dialectic

infertile barren, otiose, unproductive

infest annoy, harass

infestus hostile

inficere imbue

infidel heretic

infidelis faithless

infidelitas disloyalty, infidelity

infidelity adultery, bad faith, bad repute, breach, dishonesty, disloyalty, sedition, treason. SEE MAIN ENTRY

infiltrate encroach, enter (penetrate), interject, interpose, penetrate, permeate, pervade

infiltration encroachment, entrance, incursion, inflow, infusion, intrusion, invasion, osmosis

infinite continual (perpetual), far reaching, incessant, indeterminate, inestimable, innumerable, myriad, open-ended, permanent, perpetual, profuse, unlimited. SEE MAIN ENTRY

infinite duration perpetuity

infinitely powerful omnipotent

infinitely wise omniscient

infiniteness perpetuity

infinitesimal impalpable, inappreciable, intangible, minimal, tenuous

infinitus arbitrary, infinite, unlimited

infinity perpetuity. SEE MAIN ENTRY

infirm defective, imperfect, insecure, insubstantial, nonsubstantial (not sturdy), powerless, precarious, unsound (not strong). SEE MAIN ENTRY

infirm of purpose irresolute, irresponsible, noncommittal

infirmare quash

infirmitas frailty, impotence, inability

infirmity defect, deficiency, disability (physical inability), disadvantage, disease, disorder (abnormal condition), fault (weakness), flaw, frailty, impuissance, inability, incapacity, vice

infirmity of old age caducity

infirmity of purpose doubt (indecision), indecision

infirmus invalid, powerless

infitiari disavow, disown (deny the validity), disown (refuse to acknowledge)

infitias ire deny (contradict), disavow

infitiatio negation

infix embed, fix (make firm), inculcate, inject, instill, plant (place firmly)

infixed ingrained, innate, internal

inflame aggravate (annoy), agitate (activate), bait (harass), burn, deflagrate, discompose, exacerbate, foment, incense, intensify, irritate, molest (annoy), motivate, offend (insult), perturb, pique, provoke, stimulate. SEE MAIN ENTRY

inflame with wrath incense

inflamed hot-blooded, painful, vehement

inflamer demagogue

inflaming moving (evoking emotion), provocative

inflammable fractious

inflammation aggravation *(exacerbation)*, provocation

inflammatory disorderly, hot-blooded, incendiary, offensive *(taking the initiative)*, provocative. SEE MAIN ENTRY

inflare inflate

inflate compound, distort, enlarge, expand, extend *(enlarge)*, increase, magnify, overestimate, spread. SEE MAIN ENTRY

inflated flatulent, fustian, grandiose, orgulous, orotund, pretentious *(pompous)*, superlative, turgid. SEE MAIN ENTRY

inflated language fustian, rhetoric *(insincere language)*

inflated speech fustian

inflated statement overstatement

inflated style fustian

inflatio inflation *(increase)*

inflation bombast, boom *(prosperity)*, exaggeration, growth *(increase)*, overstatement, pretense *(ostentation)*, rodomontade. SEE MAIN ENTRY

inflatus inflated *(bombastic)*, inflated *(enlarged)*, pretentious *(pompous)*

inflection intonation, stress *(accent)*. SEE MAIN ENTRY

inflexibility severity

inflexible callous, certain *(positive)*, constant, decisive, definite, draconian, firm, formal, immutable, implacable, inexorable, insusceptible *(uncaring)*, intractable, ironclad, irreconcilable, irrevocable, obdurate, orthodox, particular *(exacting)*, peremptory *(imperative)*, pertinacious, precise, provincial, recusant, relentless, resolute, restive, restrictive, rigid, ruthless, severe, solid *(compact)*, staunch, steadfast, strict, stringent, strong, unaffected *(uninfluenced)*, unalterable, unbending, uncompromising, unrelenting, unyielding, willful. SEE MAIN ENTRY

inflexible routine bureaucracy

inflict bait *(harass)*, beat *(strike)*, commit *(perpetrate)*, compel, encumber *(hinder)*, foist, levy, perpetrate. SEE MAIN ENTRY

inflict a penalty penalize

inflict a penalty on convict

inflict a penalty upon fine

inflict capital punishment execute *(sentence to death)*

inflict evil mistreat, persecute

inflict harm strike *(assault)*

inflict injury harm, prejudice *(injure)*, strike *(assault)*

inflict pain harrow, mistreat

inflict pain on plague

inflict penalty condemn *(punish)*, discipline *(punish)*, punish, sentence

inflict penance upon discipline *(punish)*

inflict punishment condemn *(punish)*, convict, penalize

inflicting commission *(act)*

infliction casualty, catastrophe, commission *(act)*, condemnation *(punishment)*, correction *(punishment)*, damage, discipline *(punishment)*, encumbrance, ground, imposition *(excessive burden)*, mischief, nuisance, pain, penalty, punishment, sanction *(punishment)*. SEE MAIN ENTRY

infliction of pain cruelty

inflictive disciplinary *(punitory)*, penal

infligere inflict

inflow penetrate. SEE MAIN ENTRY

influence advantage, affect, agitate *(activate)*, authority *(power)*, bait *(lure)*, cause *(reason)*, cause, clout, coax, concern

(involve), conduce, consequence *(significance)*, convert *(persuade)*, convince, dint, dispose *(incline)*, dominance, dominate, draw *(attraction)*, eminence, exhort, force *(strength)*, hegemony, imbue, impetus, importance, impress *(affect deeply)*, impression, incentive, incite, induce, inducement, inspire, instigation, inveigle, leverage, lobby, manipulate *(control unfairly)*, militate, motivate, motive, occupation *(possession)*, patronage *(power to appoint jobs)*, patronage *(support)*, persuade, persuasion, power, predominance, predominate *(command)*, pressure *(noun)*, pressure *(verb)*, prestige, prevail *(persuade)*, prevail upon, primacy, prompt, reach, redound, sphere, stimulus, supremacy, weight *(importance)*. SEE MAIN ENTRY

influence against prejudice *(influence)*

influence by a gift gratuity *(bribe)*

influence of liquor inebriation

influenceability amenability

influenceable amenable, open *(persuasible)*, pliant, receptive, suasible, susceptible *(responsive)*

influenced interested, one-sided, partial *(biased)*, partisan, passive, unequal *(unjust)*, unjust. SEE MAIN ENTRY

influencer special interest

influencers lobby

influences climate

influencing moving *(evoking emotion)*

influential assertive, causal, causative, cogent, compelling, consequential *(substantial)*, considerable, contributory, convincing, crucial, decisive, dominant, forcible, important *(significant)*, key, master, material *(important)*, outstanding *(prominent)*, persuasive, potent, powerful, predominant, prevailing *(having superior force)*, prominent, provocative, sovereign *(absolute)*. SEE MAIN ENTRY

influential persons lobby

influential sponsor patron *(influential supporter)*

influentiality clout, force *(strength)*, patronage *(power to appoint jobs)*, pressure, prestige

influx entrance, incursion, inflow

infold contain *(enclose)*

inform admonish *(advise)*, advise, annunciate, apprise, bear *(adduce)*, betray *(disclose)*, caution, charge *(instruct on the law)*, communicate, construe *(translate)*, contact *(communicate)*, converse, convey *(communicate)*, declare, denounce *(inform against)*, disabuse, disclose, disseminate, divulge, edify, educate, enlighten, enunciate, forewarn, herald, impart, initiate, instill, instruct *(teach)*, issue *(publish)*, mention, notice *(give formal warning)*, notify, posit, proclaim, publish, relate *(tell)*, report *(disclose)*, reveal, speak. SEE MAIN ENTRY

inform against betray *(disclose)*, cite *(accuse)*, complain *(charge)*, implicate, incriminate

inform on betray *(disclose)*, denounce *(inform against)*, expose

informal casual, unofficial, unpretentious. SEE MAIN ENTRY

informality SEE MAIN ENTRY

informalness informality

informant bystander, deponent, eyewitness, indicator, informer *(one providing criminal information)*, source, spy, witness. SEE MAIN ENTRY

information accusation, advice, charge *(accusation)*, clue, communication *(statement)*, complaint, comprehension, connotation, data, direction *(guidance)*, disclosure *(something disclosed)*, dispatch *(message)*, edification, file, guidance, intelligence *(news)*, knowledge *(awareness)*, knowledge *(learning)*, monition *(warning)*, notice *(announcement)*, notification, presentment, publicity, report *(detailed account)*, science *(study)*. SEE MAIN ENTRY

information against complaint

information blank form *(document)*

information giver informant

information preserved in writing entry *(record)*

information supplier informer *(one providing criminal information)*

informational didactic, disciplinary *(educational)*, informatory, narrative. SEE MAIN ENTRY

informative demonstrative *(illustrative)*, didactic, disciplinary *(educational)*, eloquent, informatory, loquacious, narrative. SEE MAIN ENTRY

informed acquainted, cognizant, conscious *(aware)*, knowing, learned, literate, omniscient, perspicacious, practiced, sensible. SEE MAIN ENTRY

informer accuser, bystander, deponent, eyewitness, harbinger, indicator, informant, spy, witness. SEE MAIN ENTRY

informing demonstrative *(illustrative)*, disclosure *(act of disclosing)*

informing against denunciation

infract infringe

infraction bad faith, breach, delinquency *(misconduct)*, disregard *(omission)*, encroachment, illegality, infringement, invasion, misdeed, offense, perversion, sedition, transgression, violation, wrong. SEE MAIN ENTRY

infraction of rule exception *(exclusion)*

infraction of the law delinquency *(misconduct)*

infrangible callous, inseparable. SEE MAIN ENTRY

infrenatus uncurbed

infrequency improbability, paucity

infrequent extraordinary, intermittent, noteworthy, rare, special, sporadic, uncommon, unusual. SEE MAIN ENTRY

infringe accroach, break *(violate)*, contravene, disobey, disrupt, encroach, impinge, impose *(intrude)*, interfere, interpose, intervene, intrude, invade, obtrude, offend *(violate the law)*, overlap, overstep, plagiarize, trespass, violate. SEE MAIN ENTRY

infringe a law deviate, offend *(violate the law)*

infringe copyright copy

infringe custom deviate

infringed broken *(unfulfilled)*

infringement assumption *(seizure)*, breach, conflict, contempt *(disobedience to the court)*, contravention, crime, delinquency *(misconduct)*, disregard *(omission)*, encroachment, illegality, imposition *(excessive burden)*, incursion, infraction, injustice, intrusion, invasion, irregularity, malfeasance, misdeed, misfeasance, nuisance, offense, plagiarism, transgression, violation. SEE MAIN ENTRY

infringement of custom quirk *(idiosyncrasy)*

infringing broken *(unfulfilled)*, intrusive

infundere infuse, inject

infuriate aggravate *(annoy)*, bait *(harass)*, discompose, exacerbate, harass, incense, irritate, offend *(insult)*, perturb, pique, provoke

infuriated resentful

infuriating outrageous

infuse denature, develop, discipline *(train)*, enter *(insert)*, imbue, inculcate, inject, instill, permeate, pervade. SEE MAIN ENTRY

infuse courage reassure

infuse funds invest *(fund)*

infuse life into foment

infused compound

infusio infusion

infusion incorporation *(blend)*. SEE MAIN ENTRY

ingather congregate

ingathering assemblage, caucus, chamber *(body)*, collection *(assembly)*, company *(assemblage)*, conglomeration, congregation, rendezvous

ingeminate recapitulate, reiterate, repeat *(do again)*

ingenerate hereditary, native *(inborn)*, natural

ingeniosus resourceful

ingenious artful, competent, deft, expert, fertile, original *(creative)*, politic, proficient, resourceful

ingeniousness gift *(flair)*, skill

ingenit native *(inborn)*

ingenium ability, character *(personal quality)*, disposition *(inclination)*, personality, spirit, understanding *(comprehension)*

ingens prodigious *(enormous)*

ingenue child

ingenuity artifice, gift *(flair)*, performance *(workmanship)*, skill, specialty *(special aptitude)*

ingenuous bona fide, candid, credible, direct *(forthright)*, honest, simple, straightforward, unaffected *(sincere)*. SEE MAIN ENTRY

ingenuousness candor *(straightforwardness)*, honesty, informality, probity, veracity

ingerere obtrude

inglorious blameworthy, contemptible, disgraceful, disreputable, ignoble, mediocre, notorious, recreant, scandalous, unethical

ingloriousness attaint, degradation, discredit, disgrace, dishonor *(shame)*, dispute, ignominy, infamy, notoriety, obloquy, opprobrium, scandal

ingoing inflow, ingress

ingraft fix *(make firm)*

ingrain embed, establish *(entrench)*, fix *(make firm)*, infuse. SEE MAIN ENTRY

ingrained born *(innate)*, genetic, habitual, indelible, inherent, innate, internal, inveterate, native *(inborn)*, natural, organic, permanent, routine, traditional. SEE MAIN ENTRY

ingrained with accustomed *(familiarized)*

ingratiate propitiate

ingratiate oneself pander

ingratiating obsequious, servile, subservient

ingratitude SEE MAIN ENTRY

ingratus unacceptable

ingredient component, constituent *(part)*, detail, element, feature *(characteristic)*, inherent, item, member *(constituent part)*, part *(portion)*, segment. SEE MAIN ENTRY

ingress access *(right of way)*, admission *(entry)*, admittance *(means of approach)*, avenue *(route)*, entrance, entry *(entrance)*, immigration, incursion, inflow, osmosis, portal. SEE MAIN ENTRY

ingress wrongfully encroach

ingresses approaches

ingression entry *(entrance)*, incursion, inflow, ingress

ingressus ingress

ingrown ingrained, provincial

inhabilis incapable, incompetent

inhabit dwell *(reside)*, lodge *(reside)*, occupy *(take possession)*, remain *(occupy)*, reside. SEE MAIN ENTRY

inhabitable habitable

inhabitance domicile, habitation *(act of inhabiting)*, lodging

inhabitancy abode, address, domicile, habitation *(act of inhabiting)*, inhabitation *(act of dwelling in)*, lodging, nationality, occupancy, residence

inhabitant citizen, denizen, domiciliary, habitant, inmate, lodger, occupant, resident, tenant. SEE MAIN ENTRY

inhabitants community, populace, population

inhabitare reside

inhabitation abode, habitation *(act of inhabiting)*, nationality, occupation *(possession)*, residence. SEE MAIN ENTRY

inhabited populous, residential

inhabiter citizen, domiciliary, habitant, inhabitant, lodger, resident

inhabitual infrequent

inhaerere adhere *(fasten)*

inharmonious different, discordant, disproportionate, dissenting, divisive, harsh, improper, inapposite, inapt, incongruous, inept *(inappropriate)*, offensive *(offending)*, opposite, polemic, repugnant *(incompatible)*, unsuitable. SEE MAIN ENTRY

inharmoniousness conflict, controversy *(argument)*, deviation, difference, disaccord, disagreement, disparity, dissidence, incompatibility *(inconsistency)*, incongruity

inharmony contest *(dispute)*, controversy *(argument)*, difference, disaccord, incompatibility *(inconsistency)*, inconsistency

inhere appertain, exist

inhere in constitute *(compose)*

inherence characteristic

inherent implicit, ingrained, innate, interior, intrinsic *(belonging)*, native *(inborn)*, organic, virtual. SEE MAIN ENTRY

inherent ability proclivity

inherent in incident

inherit accede *(succeed)*, hold *(possess)*, receive *(acquire)*. SEE MAIN ENTRY

inheritable heritable

inheritable property hereditament

inheritance bequest, birth *(lineage)*, birthright, dower, estate *(hereditament)*, hereditament, heritage, legacy. SEE MAIN ENTRY

inherited born *(innate)*, genetic, hereditary, innate, native *(inborn)*, traditional

inherited characteristics character *(personal quality)*

inherited lot heritage

inherited portion heritage

inherited property inheritance

inherited rights birthright

inheritor beneficiary, devisee, heir, legatee, recipient, transferee

inheritrix heir

inhersion characteristic

inhibere stop

inhibit arrest *(stop)*, bar *(hinder)*, bind *(restrain)*, censor, check *(restrain)*, constrain *(restrain)*, contain *(restrain)*, control *(restrain)*, counter, counteract, countervail,

curb, debar, detain *(restrain)*, deter, disadvantage, disqualify, encumber *(hinder)*, enjoin, estop, fight *(counteract)*, forbid, forestall, halt, hamper, hinder, hold up *(delay)*, impede, interdict, interfere, interrupt, keep *(restrain)*, lock, obstruct, occlude, prevent, prohibit, repress, restrain, restrict, stall, stave, stifle, strangle, subdue, suppress, thwart, toll *(stop)*, withhold, withstand. SEE MAIN ENTRY

inhibit motion fetter

inhibit movement fetter

inhibited arrested *(checked)*, controlled *(restrained)*

inhibiting binding

inhibition censorship, constraint *(restriction)*, control *(restriction)*, damper *(stopper)*, deterrence, deterrent, disadvantage, estoppel, fetter, hindrance, impediment, obstacle, prohibition, proscription, quota, restraint, veto

inhibitive preventive, prohibitive *(restrictive)*, unfavorable

inhibitor deterrent

inhibitory preventive, prohibitive *(restrictive)*

inhonestus disgraceful, ignoble

inhospitable illiberal

inhospitality ostracism

inhuman brutal, cruel, diabolic, harsh, malignant, oppressive, ruthless, vicious

inhumane cold-blooded, cruel, harsh, ruthless

inhumanity atrocity, bestiality, brutality, cruelty, oppression, severity

inhumanus brutal, ruthless

inicere infuse, intimidate

inimical adverse *(hostile)*, antipathetic *(oppositional)*, averse, contentious, detrimental, discordant, hostile, irreconcilable, litigious, negative, opposite, pernicious, perverse, prejudicial, pugnacious, recusant, repugnant *(incompatible)*, spiteful, unfavorable, vicious. SEE MAIN ENTRY

inimical descent foray

inimicality belligerency, conflict, contention *(opposition)*, feud, ill will, incompatibility *(difference)*, spite

inimicalness odium

inimicitia feud

inimicus foe, hostile, inimical

inimitable best, cardinal *(outstanding)*, inestimable, original *(creative)*, paramount, premium, superlative, unapproachable

iniquitas disadvantage, partiality

iniquitous bad *(offensive)*, blameful, blameworthy, delinquent *(guilty of a misdeed)*, depraved, diabolic, disgraceful, dishonest, disreputable, dissolute, fraudulent, heinous, illicit, immoral, impermissible, malevolent, malignant, nefarious, outrageous, peccable, peccant *(culpable)*, profligate *(corrupt)*, reprehensible, reprobate, scandalous, unfair, unjust, unscrupulous, vicious, wrongful. SEE MAIN ENTRY

iniquity atrocity, delinquency *(misconduct)*, grievance, ground, guilt, injustice, misdeed, transgression, vice, wrong

iniquus detrimental, iniquitous, one-sided, oppressive, partial *(biased)*, unfavorable, unjust, unjustifiable, unreasonable

inire enter *(go in)*

initial designation *(symbol)*, first appearance, inchoate, incipient, indorse, original *(initial)*, preliminary, preparatory, previous, primary, prime *(original)*, rudimentary, sign, unprecedented. SEE MAIN ENTRY

initially ab initio

initiare initiate, instate

initiate admit *(give access)*, amateur, arise *(originate)*, cause, commence, conceive *(invent)*, create, educate, elicit, embark, enroll, establish *(launch)*, evoke, form, generate, incite, induct, instate, invent *(produce for the first time)*, maintain *(commence)*, make, novice, originate, preface, probationer *(one being tested)*, prompt, protégé, receive *(permit to enter)*, stimulate, undertake. SEE MAIN ENTRY

initiate a civil action sue

initiate a corporation incorporate *(form a corporation)*

initiated practiced

initiation admittance *(acceptance)*, discipline *(training)*, genesis, inception, inflow, installation, instigation, nascency, onset *(commencement)*, origin *(source)*, origination, outset, prelude, preparation, propaganda, start

initiative initial, original *(initial)*, overture, preparatory, rudimentary

initiative seizer aggressor

initiator author *(originator)*, maker

initiatory elementary, incipient, initial, original *(initial)*, precursory, preliminary, preparatory, previous, rudimentary

initium creation, inception, outset, start

iniucundus unacceptable

iniungere impose *(enforce)*

iniuria encroachment, grievance, injustice, oppression, wrong

iniuriosus wrongful

iniurius unjust, unjustifiable

iniustitia injustice

iniustus iniquitous, unjust, unjustifiable, wrongful

inject drug, enter *(insert)*, imbue, impact, infuse, inseminate, instill, interject, interpose, introduce, penetrate, permeate, pervade, plant *(place firmly)*. SEE MAIN ENTRY

injection expletive, infusion

injudicial illicit

injudicious arbitrary, careless, ill-advised, ill-judged, impolitic, improvident, imprudent, impulsive *(rash)*, inadvisable, inept *(inappropriate)*, irrational, misadvised, negligent, precipitate, puerile, reckless, remiss, unfit, unpolitic, unprofessional, unreasonable. SEE MAIN ENTRY

injudicious treatment malpractice

injudiciousness inconsideration, indiscretion, inexpedience, temerity

injunction bar *(obstruction)*, charge *(command)*, check *(bar)*, dictate, direction *(guidance)*, direction *(order)*, fiat, obstacle, obstruction, precept, prescription *(directive)*, prohibition, proscription, recommendation, regulation *(rule)*, requirement, requisition, restraint, veto. SEE MAIN ENTRY

injunctive prohibitive *(restrictive)*

injure abuse *(misuse)*, abuse *(victimize)*, aggravate *(annoy)*, brutalize, damage, debase, debilitate, deface, disable, disadvantage, endanger, eviscerate, harm, harrow, ill use, impair, inflict, maim, mishandle *(maltreat)*, mistreat, molest *(annoy)*, mutilate, offend *(insult)*, persecute, spoil *(impair)*, subvert, sully, violate, vitiate. SEE MAIN ENTRY

injure another's reputation libel

injure by a published writing libel

injure fatally kill *(murder)*

injure one's reputation libel

injure persistently harass

injure the credit of discredit

injure the good name of defame

injure the good reputation of defame

injured aggrieved *(harmed)*, aggrieved *(victimized)*, blemished, broken *(fractured)*, defective, faulty, imperfect, marred, victim

injuring contemptuous, disabling, inculpatory

injurious adverse *(negative)*, bad *(inferior)*, bad *(offensive)*, blameworthy, calumnious, contemptuous, dangerous, derogatory, destructive, detrimental, disadvantageous, disastrous, fatal, harmful, inadvisable, insalubrious, invidious, lethal, libelous, malevolent, malignant, noxious, outrageous, peccant *(unhealthy)*, pejorative, pernicious, pestilent, prejudicial, sinister, toxic, virulent. SEE MAIN ENTRY

injurious act delict

injurious action malfeasance

injurious conduct mischief

injurious exercise of authority misfeasance

injurious exercise of lawful authority misfeasance

injurious force battery

injurious interference nuisance

injurious occurrence accident *(misfortune)*

injurious to health deleterious

injurious treatment by a professional malpractice

injuriousness adversity, detriment, mischief

injury abuse *(physical misuse)*, adversity, assault, casualty, cost *(penalty)*, damage, damages, defacement, delict, detriment, disadvantage, disservice, drawback, expense *(sacrifice)*, flaw, grievance, ground, harm, impairment *(damage)*, infliction, mischief, misdeed, offense, pain, wrong. SEE MAIN ENTRY

injury to character libel

injury to one's reputation libel

injury to outward appearance defacement

injustice corruption, disservice, error, grievance, ground, inequality, inequity, infringement, mischief, misdeed, misdoing, misjudgment, nepotism, oppression, partiality, prejudice *(injury)*, wrong. SEE MAIN ENTRY

inkling clue, hint, inference, intimation, notion, perception, reference *(allusion)*, suggestion, suspicion *(uncertainty)*

inland interior

inlay plant *(place firmly)*

inlecebra inducement

inlet access *(right of way)*, admission *(entry)*, admittance *(means of approach)*, entrance, ingress, portal

inlets approaches

inlex decoy

inlibatus undiminished

inliberalis ignoble, illiberal, sordid

inlicere ensnare, entrap, lure

inlicitus felonious, illegal, illicit, inadmissible, unlawful

inligare implicate

inlinere smear

inludere hoodwink

inluminare enlighten

inlustrare enlighten, illustrate

inlustris famous, illustrious, renowned

inmate captive, citizen, convict, denizen, habitant, inhabitant, lodger, occupant, patient, prisoner, resident. SEE MAIN ENTRY

inmost central *(situated near center)*, internal, intimate, privy

inmost nature center *(essence)*, essence

inmost recesses cache *(hiding place)*

inmost substance center *(essence)*

innate genetic, hereditary, implicit, ingrained, inherent, interior, internal, native *(inborn)*, natural, organic. SEE MAIN ENTRY

innate ability aptitude, gift *(flair)*, penchant, specialty *(special aptitude)*

innate disposition proclivity

innate inclination instinct

innate proclivity instinct

innate quality gift *(flair)*

innate sense proclivity

innatus inherent, innate, natural

innavigable impossible, insuperable

innectere intertwine

inner central *(situated near center)*, interior, internal, intrinsic *(deep down)*

inner being essence

inner drive motive

inner nature character *(personal quality)*

inner part interior

inner reality center *(essence)*

inner voice conscience

innermost interior, internal, intimate

innermost thoughts introspection

innocence compurgation, credulity, ignorance. SEE MAIN ENTRY

innocency innocence

innocens harmless, inculpable, innocent, irreprehensible

innocent blameless, clean, harmless, honest, inculpable, inexperienced, infant, ingenuous, innocuous, irreprehensible, moral, naive, nontoxic, not guilty, pardonable, pure, unaffected *(sincere)*, unblemished, unimpeachable, unsuspecting. SEE MAIN ENTRY

innocent bystander SEE MAIN ENTRY

innocentia innocence, integrity

innocently unknowingly

innocents children

innocuous blameless, harmless, nontoxic, salutary. SEE MAIN ENTRY

innocuousness moderation

innocuus harmless, innocuous

innominate anonymous

innovate alter, change, conceive *(invent)*, vary

innovater author *(originator)*

innovation invention, reform. SEE MAIN ENTRY

innovative novel, sophisticated

innovator pioneer

innoxious harmless, innocuous, irreprehensible, nontoxic, salutary

innoxius harmless

innuendo connotation, implication *(inference)*, indication, insinuation, intimation, reference *(allusion)*, referral, suggestion. SEE MAIN ENTRY

innumerabilis innumerable

innumerable copious, infinite, manifold, multiple, myriad, profuse. SEE MAIN ENTRY

innumerably ad infinitum

innumerous myriad

innumerus innumerable

inobservance breach, contempt *(disobedience to the court)*, delinquency *(failure of duty)*, dishonor *(nonpayment)*, disregard *(unconcern)*, informality, infraction, laches, laxity, negligence, offense

inobservant broken *(unfulfilled)*, negligent

inoccupation inaction

inoculate inject, protect
inoculation propaganda
inoffensive blameless, harmless, innocuous, irreprehensible, nontoxic, pardonable,
peaceable, unobjectionable
inoperability impossibility
inoperable impracticable. SEE MAIN ENTRY
inoperative defective, defunct, disabled
(deprived of legal right), dormant, expendable, inactive, inadequate, ineffective, ineffectual, invalid, nugatory, null *(invalid)*, null
and void, otiose, powerless, unable,
unavailing, unproductive, void *(invalid)*
inopia dearth, inability, indigence, insufficiency, privation
inopportune detrimental, disadvantageous, ill-advised, improper, imprudent,
inadvisable, inapposite, inappropriate,
inapt, inauspicious, inept *(inappropriate)*,
injudicious, premature, regrettable, unfavorable, unfit, unsuitable, untimely. SEE MAIN
ENTRY
inopportuneness impropriety, inexpedience
inopportunus ineligible, inopportune
inops deficient, destitute, helpless
(defenseless), poor *(underprivileged)*
inordinacy exaggeration, redundancy
inordinate disproportionate, drastic,
egregious, excess, excessive, exorbitant,
extreme *(exaggerated)*, fanatical, gluttonous, intemperate, needless, outrageous,
profuse, prohibitive *(costly)*, redundant,
superfluous, unconscionable, undue *(excessive)*, unreasonable, unwarranted, usurious.
SEE MAIN ENTRY
inordinate amount redundancy
inordinate desire greed
inordinate desire to gain greed
inordinately particularly, unduly
inordinateness exaggeration
inornate simple
inosculate amalgamate, combine *(join
together)*, contact *(touch)*, intertwine, join
(bring together)
inosculated associated
inpermeable invincible
inpour inflow
inpouring inflow
input *(data)* SEE MAIN ENTRY
input *(thinking)* SEE MAIN ENTRY
inquest cross-examination, examination
(study), hearing, indagation, inquiry *(systematic investigation)*, inspection, interrogation, pursuit *(chase)*, research, scrutiny,
test, trial *(legal proceeding)*. SEE MAIN ENTRY
inquietude commotion, consternation,
dissatisfaction, distress *(anguish)*, disturbance, misgiving, pandemonium, panic
inquilinus lodger, tenant
inquinare stain, sully, tarnish
inquinatus obscene
inquire canvass, examine *(interrogate)*,
research, trace *(follow)*. SEE MAIN ENTRY
inquire for delve, hunt
inquire into analyze, canvass, check
(inspect), delve, examine *(study)*, hear *(give
a legal hearing)*, investigate, monitor,
peruse, probe, scrutinize, search, study. SEE
MAIN ENTRY
inquire into systematically investigate
inquire of consult *(seek information
from)*, cross-examine
inquire to ascertain facts investigation
inquirer applicant *(candidate)*, detective
inquirere examine *(interrogate)*
inquiries interrogatories

inquiring inquisitive
inquiry analysis, conversation, cross-
examination, cross-questioning, deliberation, discovery, hearing, indagation, inquest, inspection, interrogation, investigation, judgment *(discernment)*, market
(demand), matter *(case)*, poll *(canvass)*,
probe, pursuit *(chase)*, quest, research,
scrutiny, test, trial *(experiment)*, trial
(legal proceeding), voir dire. SEE MAIN
ENTRY
inquiry agent detective
inquisitio examination *(study)*, inquiry
(systematic investigation), investigation
inquisition cross-examination, examination *(study)*, hearing, indagation, inquiry
(request for information), inquiry *(systematic investigation)*, interrogation, pursuit
(chase), question *(inquiry)*, research,
scrutiny, test, trial *(legal proceeding)*. SEE
MAIN ENTRY
inquisitional interrogative
inquisitive interrogative. SEE MAIN ENTRY
inquisitive attention diligence *(care)*
inquisitor detective, dictator
inquisitorial dictatorial, interrogative
inquitous sinister
inreparabilis irretrievable
inretire ensnare, entrap
inrevocabilis irrevocable, unavoidable
(not voidable)
inridere jeer, mock *(deride)*
inritamentum incentive, stimulus
inritare irritate, stimulate
inritum facere invalidate, quash
inritus invalid, null *(invalid)*, unavailing,
void *(invalid)*
inroad encroachment, entrance, foray,
incursion, inflow, ingress, invasion. SEE MAIN
ENTRY
inrumpere force *(break)*
inruptio invasion
inrush inflow
insagacious inept *(inappropriate)*
insalubrious adverse *(negative)*, blameful, blameworthy, deleterious, detrimental,
disadvantageous, harmful, inadvisable,
malignant, noxious, peccant *(unhealthy)*,
pernicious, pestilent, toxic. SEE MAIN ENTRY
insalubriousness disadvantage
insalubris insalubrious, peccant
(unhealthy)
insalubrity disease
insane deranged, lunatic, non compos
mentis. SEE MAIN ENTRY
insanely deluded non compos mentis
insaneness lunacy
insania insanity
insanity lunacy, paranoia. SEE MAIN ENTRY
insanus deranged, frenetic
insatiabilis insatiable
insatiability greed
insatiable gluttonous, rapacious. SEE MAIN
ENTRY
insatiableness greed
insatiate rapacious
insciens unintentional, unwitting
inscientia ignorance
inscitia ignorance, incapacity
inscitus incompetent
inscius unacquainted, unaware, unwitting
inscribe book, brand *(mark)*, dedicate,
enroll, enter *(record)*, file *(place among official records)*, record, register, seal *(solemnize)*, subscribe *(sign)*. SEE MAIN ENTRY
inscribe one's name sign
inscribe one's signature indorse, sign

inscribed holographic
inscribere inscribe
inscribing registration
inscriptio address, device *(distinguishing
mark)*, inscription
inscription caption, dedication, entry
(record), marginalia, notation, phrase, title
(designation). SEE MAIN ENTRY
inscriptional holographic
inscroll enter *(record)*
inscrutability complication, mystery,
opacity
inscrutable complex, dispassionate, inapprehensible, incomprehensible, indefinable,
inexplicable, inexpressive, mysterious,
opaque. SEE MAIN ENTRY
inscrutable person enigma
inscrutableness mystery
insecable solid *(compact)*
insectari inveigh
insecure dubious, open *(accessible)*, precarious, speculative, uncertain *(questionable)*, unreliable, unsound *(not strong)*,
untrustworthy, vulnerable. SEE MAIN ENTRY
insecurity doubt *(indecision)*, hazard,
incertitude, jeopardy, peril, risk, suspicion
(uncertainty), threat. SEE MAIN ENTRY
inseminate SEE MAIN ENTRY
insensate callous, deranged, impervious,
insensible, insusceptible *(uncaring)*, irrational, lifeless *(dead)*, lunatic, thoughtless,
torpid
insensateness insentience
insensibility ignorance, ingratitude, insentience
insensible blind *(not discerning)*, callous,
incognizant, insusceptible *(uncaring)*, intangible, lifeless *(dull)*, oblivious, phlegmatic,
reckless, torpid, unaware. SEE MAIN ENTRY
insensibleness insentience
insensibly unknowingly
insensient lifeless *(dead)*
insensitive blind *(not discerning)*, callous, cold-blooded, cruel, draconian,
impervious, insensible, insusceptible *(uncaring)*, obdurate, obtuse, relentless,
remorseless, ruthless, unaffected *(uninfluenced)*, unresponsive. SEE MAIN ENTRY
insensitivity disinterest *(lack of interest)*,
disregard *(lack of respect)*, insentience
insentience SEE MAIN ENTRY
insentient callous, inactive, insensible,
unaffected *(uninfluenced)*
inseparability adhesion *(affixing)*
inseparable close *(intimate)*, coherent
(joined), cohesive *(compact)*, compound,
conglomerate, conjoint, indivisible, inextricable, infrangible, joint, solid *(compact)*. SEE
MAIN ENTRY
inseparable intermixture confusion *(turmoil)*
inseparableness adhesion *(affixing)*
insequens subsequent
inserere graft, incorporate *(form a corporation)*
insert affix, append, attach *(join)*, book,
embed, immerse *(plunge into)*, impact,
infuse, inject, inscribe, inseminate, interject,
interpose, introduce, penetrate, pierce
(lance), plant *(place firmly)*, record. SEE MAIN
ENTRY
insert in a wrapper enclose
insert in an envelope enclose
insert names on a register empanel
insert surreptitiously foist
inserted intermediate
insertion addendum, appendix *(accession)*,

attachment (act of affixing), codicil, enclosure, entrance, expletive, inflow, infusion, intervention (imposition into a lawsuit), rider. SEE MAIN ENTRY

inset insertion, plant (place firmly)

inseverable indivisible, inextricable, inseparable. SEE MAIN ENTRY

inside herein, interior, internal

inside and out throughout (all over)

inside information disclosure (something disclosed), secret, tip (clue)

insider bystander, member (individual in a group)

insider trading SEE MAIN ENTRY

insidiosus insidious

insidious bad (offensive), collusive, contemptible, covert, deceptive, detrimental, devious, dishonest, disingenuous, fraudulent, furtive, harmful, illusory, lawless, machiavellian, perfidious, pernicious, recreant, sinister, sly, surreptitious, untrue, untrustworthy. SEE MAIN ENTRY

insidiousness artifice, bad faith, deceit, fraud, improbity

insight cognition, comprehension, discretion (quality of being discreet), discrimination (good judgment), intelligence (intellect), judgment (discernment), perception, reason (sound judgment), recognition, sagacity, sense (intelligence), understanding (comprehension). SEE MAIN ENTRY

insignia brand, designation (symbol), device (distinguishing mark), label

insignificance immateriality, inconsequence, mediocrity, nonentity, nullity. SEE MAIN ENTRY

insignificancy nonentity

insignificant collateral (immaterial), de minimus, expendable, frivolous, futile, ignoble, immaterial, inapposite, inappreciable, inconsequential, inconsiderable, inferior (lower in position), insubstantial, irrelevant, mediocre, minor, negligible, nominal, nonessential, nonsubstantial (not sufficient), nugatory, paltry, petty, remote (small), slight, tenuous, trivial, unessential, usual. SEE MAIN ENTRY

insignificant amount modicum, scintilla

insignificant number minority (outnumbered group)

insincere deceptive, dishonest, disingenuous, disreputable, faithless, false (disloyal), histrionic, machiavellian, mendacious, tartuffish, untrue. SEE MAIN ENTRY

insincerity bad faith, deceit, deception, dishonesty, disloyalty, duplicity, falsification, hypocrisy, improbity, indirection (deceitfulness), knavery, misstatement, pretense (ostentation), pretext, story (falsehood)

insinuate allude, connote, hint, imply, impose (intrude), incriminate, indicate, infer, mention, purport. SEE MAIN ENTRY

insinuated assumed (inferred), constructive (inferential), implied, subtle (insidious)

insinuates signifies (denotes)

insinuating calumnious, contemptuous, leading (guiding)

insinuation attribution, charge (accusation), clue, connotation, criticism, defamation, disparagement, hint, implication (inference), indication, innuendo, intimation, mention (reference), reference (allusion), referral, slander, suggestion, tip (clue). SEE MAIN ENTRY

insinuative leading (guiding), suggestive (evocative)

insinuatory circumstantial, suggestive (evocative)

insipid inferior (lower in quality), jejune (dull), lifeless (dull), nondescript, ordinary, pedestrian, stale. SEE MAIN ENTRY

insipid remark platitude

insist certify (attest), claim (maintain), coax, coerce, compel, constrain (compel), contend (maintain), demand, dun, dwell (linger over), force (coerce), importune, persist, posit, press (constrain), pressure, reaffirm, urge. SEE MAIN ENTRY

insist on call (demand), constrain (compel), enforce, enjoin, order, require (compel)

insist upon assert, claim (demand), enforce, exact, impose (enforce), necessitate, repeat (state again)

insistance instigation

insisted alleged

insistence assertion, coercion, diligence (perseverance), dun, enforcement, force (compulsion), instigation, persuasion, pressure, request, stress (accent)

insistence on a claim assertion

insistence on a right assertion

insistence upon enforcement

insistent dogmatic, exigent, persistent, pertinacious, positive (confident), relentless, urgent, vehement. SEE MAIN ENTRY

insistent demand call (appeal), dun

insisting on notice insistent

insite recognition

insitus ingrained, inherent, innate

insobriety dipsomania, inebriation

insolence bad repute, contempt (disdain), contempt (disobedience to the court), contumely, defiance, disdain, disregard (lack of respect), disrespect

insolens impertinent (insolent), insolent

insolent brazen, calumnious, contemptuous, contumacious, disdainful, disorderly, lawless, obtrusive, offensive (offending), orgulous, outrageous, presumptuous, proud (conceited), supercilious. SEE MAIN ENTRY

insolentia disrespect

insolently disobedient contumacious

insolicitous insusceptible (uncaring)

insolitus unaccustomed, uncommon

insoluble difficult, incomprehensible, inexplicable, inextricable, infrangible, inscrutable, inseparable, insurmountable, problematic

insoluble difference deadlock, impasse

insolvable incomprehensible, inexplicable

insolvency bankruptcy, default, dishonor (nonpayment), failure (bankruptcy), indigence, poverty

insolvent bankrupt, destitute, impecunious, poor (underprivileged), unsound (not strong). SEE MAIN ENTRY

insolvent debtor delinquent

insons innocent

insouciance disinterest (lack of interest), disregard (unconcern), indifference

insouciant careless, casual, heedless, insusceptible (uncaring), nonchalant

inspect audit, canvass, consider, discern (detect with the senses), examine (study), frisk, investigate, monitor, notice (observe), observe (watch), overlook (superintend), patrol, peruse, probe, research, review, scrutinize, search, study, survey (examine)

inspect accounts officially audit

inspect secretely spy

inspection contemplation, cross-questioning, deliberation, diligence (care), discovery, examination (study), indagation, interrogation, judgment (discernment), observation, probe, research, scrutiny, supervision, surveillance, test, trial (experiment). SEE MAIN ENTRY

inspector detective, director

inspector of accounts comptroller

insperatus unanticipated, unexpected

inspicere examine (interrogate), review, scrutinize

inspiration catalyst, incentive, inducement, influence, instigation, motive, provocation, reason (basis), source

inspirational provocative

inspire agitate (activate), assure (give confidence to), cause, coax, convince, encourage, evoke, exhort, imbue, impress (affect deeply), incite, inculcate, influence, infuse, interest, motivate, originate, prevail (persuade), prompt, reassure, spirit, stimulate. SEE MAIN ENTRY

inspire fear discourage, menace

inspire hope assure (give confidence to)

inspired causative, felicitous, original (creative)

inspirer abettor, catalyst

inspiring persuasive, potent, sapid

inspirit agitate (activate), exhort, foment, incite, infuse, lobby, motivate, promise (raise expectations), reassure, spirit, stimulate

inspirited conscious (awake), sanguine

inspiriting auspicious, moving (evoking emotion), potent, propitious

instabilis insecure

instability doubt (indecision), fault (weakness), frailty, inconsistency, indecision, jeopardy, risk

instability of mental powers lunacy

instable volatile

install admit (give access), bestow, commence, constitute (establish), deposit (place), hire, induct, initiate, instate, invest (vest), locate, lodge (house), nominate, plant (place firmly), receive (permit to enter). SEE MAIN ENTRY

installation appointment (act of designating), building (business of assembling), deputation (selection of delegates), designation (naming). SEE MAIN ENTRY

installed situated

installing registration

installment advance (allowance), binder, collection (payment), component, constituent (part), deposit, downpayment, handsel, honorarium, installation, pledge (security), segment

installment buying credit (delayed payment)

instance call (appeal), case (example), detail, evidence, example, exemplify, expression (manifestation), illustrate, illustration, occasion, occurrence, particular, quote, sample, situation, specify, specimen. SEE MAIN ENTRY

instances circumstances

instant crucial, current, expeditious, immediate (at once), imminent, important (urgent), insistent, instantaneous, pending (imminent), point (period of time), present (current), prompt, rapid, requisite, urgent. SEE MAIN ENTRY

instantaneity dispatch (promptness)

instantaneous immediate (at once), prompt, summary, unexpected. SEE MAIN ENTRY

instantaneously forthwith, instantly

instantly forthwith. SEE MAIN ENTRY

instar omnium pendent

instare insist

instate delegate, induct, invest *(vest)*. SEE MAIN ENTRY

instatement installation

instauration rehabilitation, renewal, reparation *(keeping in repair)*

instead of in lieu of

instead of a parent loco parentis

instigare incite, press *(goad)*

instigate abet, agitate *(activate)*, bait *(harass)*, evoke, exhort, foment, impel, incite, induce, inspire, lobby, motivate, pique, press *(goad)*, prompt, provoke, spirit, stimulate, suborn, urge. SEE MAIN ENTRY

instigating moving *(evoking emotion)*, offensive *(taking the initiative)*

instigation cause *(reason)*, determinant, impetus, incentive, inducement, influence, origination, provocation, reason *(basis)*. SEE MAIN ENTRY

instigative incendiary, offensive *(taking the initiative)*

instigator abettor, catalyst, demagogue, malcontent, special interest

instill communicate, discipline *(train)*, imbue, inculcate, infuse, initiate, inject, instruct *(teach)*, pervade, plant *(place firmly)*. SEE MAIN ENTRY

instillare instill

instillation infusion

instinct caliber *(mental capacity)*, gift *(flair)*, proclivity, sense *(feeling)*, tendency. SEE MAIN ENTRY

instinctive born *(innate)*, hereditary, inherent, innate, native *(inborn)*, natural, organic

instinctive belief credence

instinctual born *(innate)*, hereditary, native *(inborn)*, natural

instituere discipline *(train)*, educate, establish *(launch)*, instate, instruct *(teach)*

institute admit *(give access)*, building *(structure)*, cause, chamber *(body)*, commence, company *(enterprise)*, constitute *(establish)*, corporation, create, embark, establish *(launch)*, facility *(institution)*, foundation *(organization)*, generate, initiate, invest *(vest)*, launch *(initiate)*, legislate, maintain *(commence)*, make, organization *(association)*, organize *(unionize)*, originate, pass *(approve)*, preface, produce *(manufacture)*, society. SEE MAIN ENTRY

institute a comparison contrast

institute a lawsuit complain *(charge)*. SEE MAIN ENTRY

institute a legal proceeding sue

institute an action against a third party implead

institute an inquiry analyze, canvass, delve, probe

institute by law enact, pass *(approve)*

institute commingling of races desegregate

institute legal proceedings litigate

institute process sue

instituted positive *(prescribed)*

institutio instruction *(teaching)*

institution building *(business of assembling)*, concern *(business establishment)*, corporation, custom, firm, formation, foundation *(organization)*, installation, institute, organization *(association)*, prescription *(custom)*, rubric *(authoritative rule)*. SEE MAIN ENTRY

institution of commercial sites development *(building)*

institution of learning institute

institution of proceedings service *(delivery of legal process)*

institution where justice is rendered judicatory

institutionalize confine, constrain *(imprison)*, jail

institutive causal, causative, prime *(original)*

institutor author *(originator)*

institutum determination, intention, matter *(subject)*, principle *(axiom)*, purpose

instruct admonish *(advise)*, apprise, charge *(instruct on the law)*, command, communicate, control *(regulate)*, convey *(communicate)*, counsel, decree, demonstrate *(establish)*, dictate, direct *(order)*, direct *(show)*, disabuse, discipline *(train)*, edify, educate, enjoin, enlighten, exhort, impart, inculcate, inform *(notify)*, initiate, instill, notice *(give formal warning)*, notify, nurture, order, oversee, prescribe, recommend, signify *(inform)*, superintend. SEE MAIN ENTRY

instruct badly misdirect

instructed acquainted, familiar *(informed)*, informed *(educated)*, knowing, learned

instructing advisory

instruction admonition, advice, canon, caveat, charge *(command)*, dictate, direction *(guidance)*, directive, discipline *(training)*, dispatch *(message)*, edification, education, experience *(background)*, fiat, guidance, law, mandate, order *(judicial directive)*, precept, preparation, prescription *(directive)*, principle *(axiom)*, recommendation, regulation *(rule)*, subpoena, tip *(clue)*. SEE MAIN ENTRY

instruction to appear process *(summons)*

instructional didactic, disciplinary *(educational)*, informative, leading *(guiding)*

instructional corps faculty *(teaching staff)*

instructional personnel faculty *(teaching staff)*

instructions charge *(statement to the jury)*, direction *(order)*

instructive decretal, didactic, disciplinary *(educational)*, informative, informatory, leading *(guiding)*

instructor counselor, pedagogue

instructors faculty *(teaching staff)*

instruere endow, furnish, garnish, marshal

instrument appliance, blank *(form)*, certificate, charter *(license)*, conduit *(channel)*, deed, device *(mechanism)*, document, expedient, form *(instrumentality)*, form *(document)*, forum *(medium)*, indenture, instrumentality, interagent, lease, medium, organ, proctor, resource, tool, will *(testamentary instrument)*. SEE MAIN ENTRY

instrument evidencing an agreement contract

instrument for use in combat cudgel

instrument granting possession of premises lease

instrument held until the performance of a condition escrow

instrument in proof affidavit, averment

instrument of proof certification *(attested copy)*, evidence

instrument of war cudgel

instrument of warfare bomb

instrument which transfers title to realty deed

instrumental causal, clerical, constructive *(creative)*, contributory, effective *(efficient)*, functional, intermediate, ministerial, operative, practical. SEE MAIN ENTRY

instrumentality agency *(legal relationship)*, intercession, medium, organ. SEE MAIN ENTRY

instruments paraphernalia *(apparatus)*

instruments of combat weapons

instrumentum appliance, document, instrument *(tool)*

insubmission contempt *(disobedience to the court)*, defiance

insubmissive froward, insubordinate

insubordinate broken *(unfulfilled)*, contumacious, disobedient, froward, impertinent *(insolent)*, insurgent, intractable, lawless, malcontent, nonconsenting, perverse, recalcitrant, recusant, restive, unruly. SEE MAIN ENTRY

insubordination anarchy, contempt *(disobedience to the court)*, defiance, disloyalty, disrespect, insurrection, mutiny, rebellion, resistance, revolt, sedition

insubstantial circumstantial, collateral *(immaterial)*, deficient, delusive, ill-founded, illusory, immaterial, inadequate, inappreciable, inconsiderable, insipid, intangible, minor, negligible, nonsubstantial *(not sufficient)*, nugatory, null *(insignificant)*, perfunctory, remote *(small)*, superficial, unfounded, unsound *(fallacious)*, void *(invalid)*. SEE MAIN ENTRY

insubstantiality artifice, blank *(emptiness)*, immateriality, impalpability, insignificance, nonentity

insuetus unaccustomed

insufferable contemptible, deplorable, intolerable, loathsome, objectionable, obnoxious, odious, painful, repugnant *(exciting aversion)*, repulsive, severe, undesirable, unendurable. SEE MAIN ENTRY

insufferable harm SEE MAIN ENTRY

insufficiency abortion *(fiasco)*, dearth, defect, deficiency, deficit, delinquency *(shortage)*, detriment, disability *(physical inability)*, disadvantage, disqualification *(factor that disqualifies)*, failure *(falling short)*, fault *(weakness)*, handicap, immateriality, impotence, inability, incompetence, indigence, inefficacy, market *(demand)*, need *(deprivation)*, paucity, privation. SEE MAIN ENTRY

insufficiency as a matter of law nonsuit

insufficiency of funds failure *(bankruptcy)*

insufficiency of service emergency

insufficient barren, defective, deficient, devoid, imperfect, inadept, inadequate, incapable, incompetent, ineffective, ineffectual, inferior *(lower in quality)*, minimal, null *(insignificant)*, partial *(relating to a part)*, scarce, unable, unsatisfactory, vacuous. SEE MAIN ENTRY

insufficient evidence nonsuit. SEE MAIN ENTRY

insufficient funds default

insufficient income indigence

insufficiently considered injudicious

insular alien *(unrelated)*, alone *(solitary)*, disjunctive *(tending to disjoin)*, limited, parochial, private *(secluded)*, provincial, regional, remote *(secluded)*, separate, sole, solitary. SEE MAIN ENTRY

insulate isolate, protect, seclude. SEE MAIN ENTRY

insulation buffer zone, bulwark
insulator bulwark
insulse lifeless *(dull)*
insulsus insipid
insult affront, aspersion, bait *(harass)*, contumely, defamation, defilement, denigrate, diatribe, disoblige, disparage, disregard *(lack of respect)*, disrespect, flout, hector, humiliate, jeer, mock *(deride)*, pique, provocation, provoke, rebuff *(noun)*, rebuff *(verb)*, revilement. SEE MAIN ENTRY
insulting abusive, calumnious, caustic, contemptuous, disdainful, impertinent *(insolent)*, insolent, libelous, offensive *(offending)*, outrageous, pejorative, perverse, presumptuous, scathing, scurrilous
insumere spend
insuperabilis irresistible
insuperability impasse, impossibility
insuperable impossible, impracticable, indomitable, inexpugnable, insurmountable, invincible, unattainable. SEE MAIN ENTRY
insuperable obstacle deterrent, impasse
insuperableness impossibility
insupportable indefensible, insufferable, intolerable, unsustainable, untenable
insuppressible hot-blooded, intractable, manifest, uncontrollable
insurable interest SEE MAIN ENTRY
insurance guaranty, safeguard, security *(pledge)*, undertaking *(pledge)*. SEE MAIN ENTRY
insurance adviser actuary
insurance company insurer
insurance contract policy *(contract)*
insure avouch *(guarantee)*, bond *(secure a debt)*, certify *(attest)*, cosign, cover *(guard)*, cover *(provide for)*, ensure, guarantee, harbor, indemnify, pledge *(deposit)*, preserve, promise *(vow)*, sponsor, underwrite. SEE MAIN ENTRY
insured agreed *(promised)*, definite, fully secured, official, safe, secure *(free from danger)*
insurer sponsor, surety *(guarantor)*. SEE MAIN ENTRY
insurgence anarchy, commotion, defiance, insurrection, mutiny, outbreak, outburst, rebellion, resistance, riot, sedition, treason
insurgency defiance, disloyalty, insurrection, mutiny, rebellion, revolt. SEE MAIN ENTRY
insurgent disobedient, insubordinate, malcontent, radical *(favoring drastic change)*, restive, uncontrollable. SEE MAIN ENTRY
insurmountability impossibility
insurmountable cardinal *(outstanding)*, difficult, impossible, impracticable, indomitable, inexpugnable, insuperable, invincible, unattainable. SEE MAIN ENTRY
insurrect disobey, rebel, secede
insurrection anarchy, commotion, defiance, disloyalty, mutiny, outbreak, outburst, rebellion, resistance, revolt, revolution, riot, sedition, treason. SEE MAIN ENTRY
insurrectional disobedient, renitent
insurrectionary disorderly, insubordinate, insurgent, radical *(favoring drastic change)*
insurrectionist insurgent, malcontent
insusceptibility to change indestructibility
insusceptible indestructible. SEE MAIN ENTRY
insusceptible of change indefeasible
insusceptible to change permanent

insusceptire insusceptible *(uncaring)*
intact gross *(total)*, inviolate, live *(existing)*, safe, stable, unblemished, undiminished, whole *(undamaged)*. SEE MAIN ENTRY
intactile intangible
intactilis intangible *(adjective)*, intangible *(noun)*
intactness entirety, whole
intactus intact, inviolate
intaglio stamp
intake receipt *(act of receiving)*, revenue
intakes approaches
intaking acquisition
intangibility immateriality, impalpability
intangible elusive, immaterial, impalpable, imponderable, inappreciable, incorporeal, nonsubstantial *(not sturdy)*, vague. SEE MAIN ENTRY
intangible assets estate *(property)*
integer full, impartial, incorruptible, inculpable
integer individual
integer intact, inviolate, pure, unadulterated, unblemished, undiminished, unprejudiced, upright
integer whole
integral essential *(inherent)*, indispensable, inherent, necessary *(required)*, total, unit *(item)*. SEE MAIN ENTRY
integral part component, constituent *(part)*, detail, element, factor *(ingredient)*, ingredient, member *(constituent part)*, necessity, need *(requirement)*
integrality corpus
integrant constituent *(part)*, detail, integral
integrant part constituent *(part)*
integrate aggregate, connect *(relate)*, coordinate, desegregate, embody, embrace *(encircle)*, relate *(establish a connection)*. SEE MAIN ENTRY
integrated coadunate, collective, composite, compound, conjoint, inseparable
integration affiliation *(amalgamation)*, coalition, consolidation, corpus, federation, merger, totality. SEE MAIN ENTRY
integrative collective
integritas innocence, integrity, principle *(virtue)*, rectitude
integrity adhesion *(loyalty)*, conscience, credibility, ethics, fairness, honesty, honor *(good reputation)*, principle *(virtue)*, probity, rectitude, right *(righteousness)*, trustworthiness, truth, veracity, whole. SEE MAIN ENTRY
integument cover *(protection)*
integumentum veil
intellect caliber *(mental capacity)*, character *(personal quality)*, comprehension, mastermind, reason *(sound judgment)*, sense *(intelligence)*. SEE MAIN ENTRY
intellection apprehension *(perception)*, cognition, deliberation, knowledge *(awareness)*, ratiocination, reflection *(thought)*
intellectional faculty intelligence *(intellect)*
intellectual literate, mastermind, profound *(esoteric)*, sapient
intellectual ability sense *(intelligence)*
intellectual faculties judgment *(discernment)*
intellectual power caliber *(mental capacity)*, comprehension, intelligence *(intellect)*
intellectual powers intellect, judgment *(discernment)*
intellectual prodigy mastermind
intellectual property rights SEE MAIN ENTRY

intellectualism comprehension
intellectuality comprehension, education, intellect, intelligence *(intellect)*, sense *(intelligence)*
intellectualization concept, contemplation, ratiocination
intellectualize muse, ponder, reason *(conclude)*, study
intellectually deep profound *(esoteric)*
intellegentia comprehension, discrimination *(good judgment)*, insight, intellect, intelligence *(intellect)*
intellegere realize *(understand)*, understand
intellegi non potest incomprehensible
intelligence aptitude, caliber *(mental capacity)*, common sense, competence *(ability)*, discrimination *(good judgment)*, espionage, information *(knowledge)*, intellect, knowledge *(awareness)*, notification, reason *(sound judgment)*, report *(detailed account)*, sagacity, understanding *(comprehension)*. SEE MAIN ENTRY
intelligence agent spy
intelligencer harbinger, informant, informer *(a person who provides information)*, spy
intelligent discreet, perspicacious, rational, reasonable *(rational)*, sapient, sciential, sensible. SEE MAIN ENTRY
intelligent grip information *(knowledge)*
intelligibility coherence
intelligible clear *(apparent)*, cognizable, coherent *(clear)*, comprehensible, distinct *(clear)*, explicit, lucid, obvious, pellucid, scrutable, simple, solvable, unambiguous, unmistakable. SEE MAIN ENTRY
intelligibly fairly *(clearly)*
intemperance debauchery, dipsomania, exaggeration, greed, inebriation, waste
intemperate disorderly, dissolute, drastic, drunk, egregious, excessive, exorbitant, extreme *(exaggerated)*, gluttonous, hot-blooded, incendiary, inordinate, insatiable, lawless, prodigal, profligate *(extravagant)*, profuse, promiscuous, unconscionable, unreasonable, unrestrained *(not repressed)*, wanton. SEE MAIN ENTRY
intemperately unduly
intemperateness exaggeration
intempestivus untimely
intend allocate, attempt, plan, predetermine, purport, pursue *(strive to gain)*. SEE MAIN ENTRY
intendance generalship
intendancy generalship
intendant administrator, director, procurator, superintendent
intended aforethought, apparent *(presumptive)*, bona fide, deliberate, express, intentional, knowing, premeditated, prospective, purposeful, tactical, voluntary, willful
intended for a specific purpose express
intended for instruction didactic
intended for teaching didactic
intended for youth juvenile
intended result end *(intent)*, purpose
intended to bring about delay dilatory
intended to defer decision dilatory
intended to gain time dilatory
intendere exert, intend
intendment animus, end *(intent)*, plan
intense acute, close *(rigorous)*, drastic, eager, fervent, forcible, harsh, hot-blooded, intensive, major, potent, powerful, profound *(intense)*, purposeful, serious *(grave)*,

severe, strong, trenchant, vehement. SEE MAIN ENTRY
intense application　diligence *(care)*
intense desire　ardor, greed
intense study　diligence *(care)*
intense thought　diligence *(care)*
intensification　advance *(increase)*, aggravation *(exacerbation)*, augmentation, boom *(increase)*, exaggeration, growth *(increase)*
intensified　intense
intensify　accrue *(increase)*, aggravate *(exacerbate)*, compound, consolidate *(strengthen)*, develop, dwell *(linger over)*, enhance, enlarge, exacerbate, expand, heighten *(augment)*, magnify, reinforce. SEE MAIN ENTRY
intensity　degree *(magnitude)*, force *(strength)*, life *(vitality)*, main force, passion, pressure, rigor, severity, strength. SEE MAIN ENTRY
intensity of expression　emphasis
intensive　comprehensive, cumulative *(intensifying)*, radical *(extreme)*, resounding, thorough, unmitigated. SEE MAIN ENTRY
intent　animus, cause *(reason)*, circumspect, connotation, contemplation, content *(meaning)*, destination, earnest, forethought, goal, hot-blooded, idea, industrious, intense, objective, pertinacious, plan, point *(purpose)*, project, purpose, purposeful, reason *(basis)*, scienter, serious *(devoted)*, signification, spirit, volition, will *(desire)*. SEE MAIN ENTRY
intent on　solicitous
intent upon　decisive, insistent, resolute
intention　animus, cause *(reason)*, conatus, connotation, contemplation, content *(meaning)*, design *(intent)*, destination, end *(intent)*, expectation, forethought, goal, idea, objective, plan, point *(purpose)*, predetermination, project, prospect *(outlook)*, purpose, reason *(basis)*, resolution *(decision)*, scienter, signification, target. SEE MAIN ENTRY
intentional　deliberate, express, knowing, premeditated, purposeful, voluntary, willful. SEE MAIN ENTRY
intentional act　overt act
intentional deception　fraud
intentional distortion　lie
intentional exaggeration　lie
intentional exclusion of lessee　eviction
intentional killing　murder
intentional misstatement　falsehood, lie, misrepresentation, perjury, story *(falsehood)*
intentional relinquishment　waiver
intentional untruth　lie, story *(falsehood)*
intentional wrongdoing　malice
intentionality　animus, design *(intent)*
intentionally　knowingly, purposely
intentionally disregard　ignore
intentionally untrue　false *(not genuine)*
intentiveness　interest *(concern)*
intentivus　intensive
intentness　compulsion *(obsession)*, diligence *(care)*, diligence *(perseverance)*, industry *(activity)*, interest *(concern)*, observation, preoccupation, regard *(attention)*
intentus　earnest, intense, intent, vigilant
inter se congredi　meet
inter se dare　reciprocate
inter se repugnare　contradict
inter vivos　SEE MAIN ENTRY
interacting　correlative, interlocking
interaction　course
interactive　concerted, mutual *(reciprocal)*

interaffiliated　interrelated
interaffiliation　mutuality
interagency　medium
interagent　adjuster, advocate *(counselor)*, arbiter, arbitrator, factor *(commission merchant)*, go-between, instrumentality, liaison, medium, umpire. SEE MAIN ENTRY
interallied　associated, concurrent *(united)*, interrelated
interassociated　interrelated
interassociation　mutuality
interblend　combine *(join together)*, consolidate *(unite)*, desegregate, embody, incorporate *(include)*
interbreed　commingle
intercalate　enter *(insert)*, interject, interpose
intercalation　insertion, intervention *(interference)*
intercapedo　interruption, pause
intercede　arbitrate *(conciliate)*, impose *(intrude)*, interfere, interpose, intervene, mediate, negotiate, reconcile. SEE MAIN ENTRY
intercede for　assist, contribute *(assist)*, help
interceder　adjuster, advocate *(counselor)*, arbiter, arbitrator, go-between, intermediary, referee
intercedere　intervene, protest
intercept　avert, block, check *(restrain)*, clog, discontinue *(break continuity)*, disrupt, eavesdrop, foil, forestall, hamper, hijack, hinder, inhibit, interfere, interpose, interrupt, occlude, overhear, parry, prevent, stave, stay *(halt)*, stem *(check)*, stop, thwart. SEE MAIN ENTRY
interception　interruption, intervention *(interference)*, restraint
interceptor　embezzler
intercessio　veto
intercession　advocacy, arbitration, assistance, collective bargaining, interven-tion *(interference)*, mediation. SEE MAIN ENTRY
intercessor　adjuster, advocate *(counselor)*, amicus curiae, arbiter, arbitrator, counselor, intermediary, judge, jurist, liaison, referee, umpire
interchange　alternate *(take turns)*, barter, bequeath, change, commerce, communication *(discourse)*, consignment, contact *(association)*, contact *(communicate)*, conversation, conversion *(change)*, convert *(change use)*, crossroad *(intersection)*, devolution, devolve, displace *(replace)*, exchange, handle *(trade)*, mutuality, quid pro quo, reciprocate, reciprocity, replace, replacement, return *(respond)*, subrogation, trade *(commerce)*, trade, vary. SEE MAIN ENTRY
interchange ideas　converse
interchange information　converse
interchange of commodities　commerce
interchange of goods　commerce
interchange of information　conversation
interchange of opinions　conference, conversation
interchange of speech　conversation
interchange of thoughts　conversation
interchange of views　discourse, meeting *(conference)*
interchange opinions　converse
interchange regularly　alternate *(take turns)*
interchange successively　alternate *(take turns)*
interchange thoughts　communicate, converse

interchange views　confer *(consult)*, consult *(ask advice of)*, discuss
interchangeability　identity *(similarity)*, mutuality
interchangeable　akin *(germane)*, coequal, cognate, comparable *(equivalent)*, convertible, disjunctive *(alternative)*, equivalent, identical, negotiable, reciprocal
interchangeable commitment　mutual understanding
interchangeableness　par *(equality)*
interchanged　mutual *(reciprocal)*
interchanges　vicissitudes
intercipere　embezzle
interclasped　conjoint
interclude　deter, occlude
intercommunicate　communicate, contact *(communicate)*
intercommunication　communication *(discourse)*, contact *(association)*, conversation, notification, parley
intercommunion　consortium *(marriage companionship)*, contact *(association)*
interconnect　connect *(relate)*, contact *(touch)*, involve *(implicate)*, juxtapose, relate *(establish a connection)*
interconnected　interrelated, reciprocal, related, relative *(relevant)*
interconnection　chain *(nexus)*, coalescence, connection *(fastening)*, intersection, mutuality, nexus, privity, relation *(connection)*, relationship *(connection)*
interconnections　ties
intercourse　business *(commerce)*, commerce, communication *(discourse)*, contact *(association)*, dealings, exchange, interchange, sodality
intercross　cross *(intersect)*
intercrossing　crossroad *(intersection)*, intersection
intercurrent　intermediate
interdenominational　nonsectarian
interdependence　mutuality, relationship *(connection)*
interdependent　cognate, conjoint, correlative, inseparable, mutual *(collective)*, reciprocal, related
interdicere　forbid, inhibit, interdict
interdict　ban, bar *(obstruction)*, bar *(exclude)*, block, coerce, condemn *(ban)*, constraint *(restriction)*, debar, enjoin, forbid, inhibit, prohibit, prohibition, proscription, renounce, restrain, restrict, veto. SEE MAIN ENTRY
interdicted　illegitimate *(illegal)*, illicit
interdictio aquae et ignis　banishment
interdiction　canon, constraint *(restriction)*, decree, injunction, obviation, prohibition, proscription, refusal, restriction, veto
interdictive　prohibitive *(restrictive)*, restrictive
interdictory　prohibitive *(restrictive)*, restrictive
interdictum　prohibition
interest　activity, advocacy, appertain, behalf, benefit *(betterment)*, birthright, boom *(increase)*, business *(affair)*, claim *(right)*, commission *(fee)*, concern *(involve)*, contribution *(participation)*, dividend, dominion *(absolute ownership)*, engage *(involve)*, equity *(share of ownership)*, fee *(estate)*, holding *(property owned)*, immerse *(engross)*, market *(demand)*, motivate, nepotism, occupy *(engage)*, part *(portion)*, patronage *(support)*, prescription *(claim of title)*, profit, regard *(attention)*, regard *(esteem)*, remainder *(estate in*

property), revenue, significance, title *(right)*, weight *(importance)*, welfare. SEE MAIN ENTRY

interest certificate   coupon

interest group   constituency

interest in land   easement, estate *(property)*

interest in real estate   leasehold

interest in real property   freehold

interest of a lessee   leasehold

interested   eager, inquisitive, interrogative, one-sided, partial *(biased)*, receptive, unjust

interested party   privy, prospect *(prospective patron)*

interesting   attractive, moving *(evoking emotion)*, provocative, sapid

interests   affairs, dealings

interfere   arrest *(stop)*, censor, clog, constrict *(inhibit)*, counter, countervail, debar, defer *(put off)*, delay, disqualify, disrupt, disturb, encroach, encumber *(hinder)*, estop, fight *(counteract)*, forestall, hamper, hinder, hold up *(delay)*, impede, impose *(intrude)*, infringe, intercede, interpose, interrupt, intervene, intrude, mediate, militate, obtrude, obturate, overstep, parry, prevent, prohibit, tamper, thwart. SEE MAIN ENTRY

interfere with   bar *(hinder)*, block, collide *(clash)*, conflict, counteract, deter, disadvantage, discontinue *(break continuity)*, molest *(annoy)*, obstruct, oppugn, preclude, suspend

interfere with the law SEE MAIN ENTRY

interference   bar *(obstruction)*, barrier, check *(bar)*, collision *(dispute)*, conflict, damper *(stopper)*, deterrence, deterrent, disadvantage, embargo, encroachment, encumbrance, fetter, filibuster, frustration, handicap, hiatus, impediment, imposition *(excessive burden)*, infringement, intercession, interruption, intervention *(imposition into a lawsuit)*, intrusion, invasion, mediation, molestation, nuisance, obstruction, onus *(burden)*, opposition, prohibition, resistance, restraint, veto. SEE MAIN ENTRY

interfering   intrusive, mesne, obtrusive, preventive, prohibitive *(restrictive)*

interficere   dispatch *(put to death)*, kill *(defeat)*, kill *(murder)*, slay

interfuse   combine *(join together)*, consolidate *(unite)*, converge, desegregate, embody, incorporate *(include)*, intersperse, penetrate, pervade, unite

interfused   conjoint

interfusion   coalescence, incorporation *(blend)*

intericere   interject, interpose

interim   abeyance, cessation *(interlude)*, hiatus, interlocutory, interruption, interval, moratorium, pause, pendency, provisional, recess, respite *(interval of rest)*, shifting, temporary, tentative, time, transient. SEE MAIN ENTRY

interim agreement   modus vivendi

interim dividend   coupon

interimere   dispatch *(put to death)*, slay

interior   internal. SEE MAIN ENTRY

interire   perish

interjacence   arbitration, intervention *(interference)*

interjacent   intermediate, mesne

interjaculate   inject, interject

interject   comment, discontinue *(break continuity)*, enter *(insert)*, inject, interfere, interpose. SEE MAIN ENTRY

interjection   expletive, insertion, intercession, intervention *(imposition into a lawsuit)*, intervention *(interference)*, remark

interjection into a lawsuit   intervention *(imposition into a lawsuit)*

interknit   intertwine

interlace   commingle, conjoin, desegregate, implicate, incorporate *(include)*, intertwine

interlaced   complex, compound

interlacement   incorporation *(blend)*

interlard   commingle, desegregate, intersperse

interlarded   promiscuous

interlink   annex *(add)*, combine *(join together)*, connect *(join together)*, intertwine, join *(bring together)*

interlinked   coadunate, coherent *(joined)*, correlative, interrelated

interlinking   interlocking

interlock   bond *(hold together)*, conjoin, connect *(join together)*, engage *(involve)*, join *(bring together)*

interlocked   coadunate, coherent *(joined)*

interlocking   coalition. SEE MAIN ENTRY

interlocution   communication *(discourse)*, conference, conversation, discourse, parlance, parley, speech

interlocutor   adjuster, advocate *(counselor)*, spokesman

interlocutory SEE MAIN ENTRY

interlope   accroach, balk, encroach, impinge, impose *(intrude)*, infringe, intrude, obtrude

interloper   alien

interloping   encroachment, intervention *(interference)*, intrusion, intrusive, invasion

interlude   abeyance, hiatus, interruption, interval, lapse *(break)*, leave *(absence)*, lull, pause, pendency, recess, respite *(interval of rest)*, time

intermeddle   intercede, interfere, interpose, intervene, obtrude, tamper

intermeddling   intercession, intervention *(interference)*

intermedial   interlocutory, ministerial

intermediary   adjuster, advocate *(counselor)*, agent, arbiter, arbitrator, broker, clerical, deputy, factor *(commission merchant)*, forum *(medium)*, go-between, instrumentality, interagent, interlocutory, intermediate, liaison, medium, mesne, ministerial, procurator, referee, umpire, vicarious *(delegated)*. SEE MAIN ENTRY

intermediate   adjuster, advocate *(counselor)*, agent, arbiter, arbitrator, average *(midmost)*, go-between, instrumentality, interagent, intercede, interim, interpose, medium, mesne, ministerial, negotiate, procurator, referee. SEE MAIN ENTRY

intermediate agent   advocate *(counselor)*, go-between, interagent, medium

intermediate time   cessation *(interlude)*, pendency, respite *(interval of rest)*

intermediation   agency *(legal relationship)*, arbitration, collective bargaining, intercession, intervention *(interference)*

intermediator   adjuster, advocate *(counselor)*, arbiter, go-between, interagent, referee, umpire

intermedium   adjuster, advocate *(counselor)*, agent, broker, chain *(nexus)*, conduit *(intermediary)*, instrumentality, liaison, nexus, procurator, umpire

interminability   indestructibility, perpetuity

interminable   continual *(perpetual)*, durable, incessant, indeterminate, infinite, innumerable, open-ended, permanent, perpetual, profuse, unlimited. SEE MAIN ENTRY

interminably   ad infinitum

interminate   incessant

intermingle   commingle, confuse *(create disorder)*, desegregate, interject, intersperse, merge

intermingled   compound

intermissio   cessation *(interlude)*, cessation *(termination)*, halt, interruption, pause

intermission   abeyance, adjournment, cessation *(interlude)*, delay, extension *(postponement)*, halt, hiatus, interruption, interval, leave *(absence)*, lull, pause, pendency, recess, remission, respite *(interval of rest)*. SEE MAIN ENTRY

intermit   adjourn, cease, delay, desist, discontinue *(break continuity)*, disrupt, fluctuate, interfere, interrupt, pause, quit *(discontinue)*, recess, recur, suspend

intermittence   irregularity

intermittent   broken *(interrupted)*, disjunctive *(tending to disjoin)*, infrequent, periodic, sporadic. SEE MAIN ENTRY

intermittere   interrupt, neglect, pause, suspend

intermitti   abeyance

intermitting   disjunctive *(tending to disjoin)*, intermittent, sporadic

intermix   combine *(join together)*, commingle, denature, desegregate, diffuse, embody, incorporate *(include)*, intertwine, merge

intermixed   composite, conjoint, miscellaneous, promiscuous

intermixture   incorporation *(blend)*, integration *(amalgamation)*, melange, solution *(substance)*

intermutation   mutuality

intern   arrest *(apprehend)*, commit *(institutionalize)*, confine, constrain *(imprison)*, detain *(hold in custody)*, imprison, lock, shut

internal   domestic *(household)*, inherent, interior, intrinsic *(deep down)*, subjective. SEE MAIN ENTRY

internalize   accept *(embrace)*, understand

international compact   treaty

internecine   deadly, destructive, detrimental, harmful, lethal, noxious

internecive   lethal

interned   arrested *(apprehended)*

internee   captive, convict, hostage, prisoner

interning   commitment *(confinement)*

internment   apprehension *(act of arresting)*, arrest, bondage, captivity, commitment *(confinement)*, constraint *(imprisonment)*, detention, durance, incarceration. SEE MAIN ENTRY

internoscere   discriminate *(distinguish)*, distinguish

internuncio   advocate *(counselor)*, broker, plenipotentiary, referee

interpellare   interfere, interrupt

interpellate   cross-examine, examine *(interrogate)*

interpellation   citation *(charge)*, cross-examination, question *(inquiry)*

interpenetrate   break *(fracture)*, enter *(penetrate)*, intersperse, permeate, pervade

interpenetration   osmosis

interplay   mutuality, reciprocity

interpolare   falsification, falsify

interpolate   inject, interject, intersperse

interpolation   expletive, insertion, intervention *(interference)* *interponere*   interject, interpose

interpose   comment, discontinue *(break continuity)*, enter *(insert)*, impose *(intrude)*, inject, intercede, interfere, interject, interrupt, intersperse, intervene, introduce, obtrude. SEE MAIN ENTRY

interpose no obstacles   authorize

interposed   intermediate

interpositio   insertion

interposition   arbitration, collective bargaining, deterrent, hindrance, intercession, intervention *(imposition into a lawsuit)*, intervention *(interference)*, introduction. SEE MAIN ENTRY

interpres   broker, go-between

interpret   characterize, clarify, comment, construe *(comprehend)*, construe *(translate)*, define, determine, educate, elucidate, enlighten, explain, explicate, expound, illustrate, judge, read, recite, render *(depict)*, resolve *(solve)*, review, solve. SEE MAIN ENTRY

interpret falsely   slant

interpret incorrectly   misconceive, misread

interpretability   construction

interpretable   accountable *(explainable)*, determinable *(ascertainable)*

interpretari   construe *(translate)*, elucidate, explicate, interpret

interpretatio   construction, explanation, paraphrase

interpretation   clarification, comment, connotation, construction, content *(meaning)*, definition, diagnosis, explanation, meaning, paraphrase, rendition *(explication)*, signification, solution *(answer)*. SEE MAIN ENTRY

interpretational   interpretive

interpretative   demonstrative *(illustrative)*, discursive *(analytical)*. SEE MAIN ENTRY

interpreted   coherent *(clear)*

interpreter   judge

interpreters of the law   judiciary

interpretive   demonstrative *(illustrative)*, descriptive

interregnum   abeyance, anarchy, cessation *(interlude)*, duration, hiatus, interval, lull, pendency

interrelate   connect *(relate)*, involve *(implicate)*, relate *(establish a connection)*

interrelated   coadunate, cognate, coherent *(joined)*, collateral *(accompanying)*, correlative, mutual *(reciprocal)*, reciprocal, related, tangential. SEE MAIN ENTRY

interrelation   building *(business of assembling)*, chain *(nexus)*, coherence, connection *(relation)*, contact *(association)*, content *(structure)*, mutuality, nexus, proportion, relationship *(connection)*. SEE MAIN ENTRY

interrelation of parts   organization *(structure)*

interrelationship   relation *(connection)*, relationship *(connection)*

interritus   undaunted

interrogate   cross-examine, inquire, investigate, pose *(propound)*, probe. SEE MAIN ENTRY

interrogatio   inquiry *(request for information)*, interrogation

interrogation   cross-examination, cross-questioning, examination *(test)*, hearing, indagation, inquest, inquiry *(request for information)*, inquiry *(systematic investigation)*, investigation, question *(inquiry)*, test. SEE MAIN ENTRY

interrogational   interrogative

interrogative   inquisitive. SEE MAIN ENTRY

interrogativus   interrogative

interrogatories   SEE MAIN ENTRY

interrogatory   question *(inquiry)*

interrumpere   break *(fracture)*

interrupt   arrest *(stop)*, balk, cease, check *(restrain)*, close *(terminate)*, condemn *(ban)*, continue *(adjourn)*, cross *(intersect)*, defer *(put off)*, desist, discontinue *(break continuity)*, disorganize, disrupt, disturb, encumber *(hinder)*, estop, halt, hamper, hinder, hold up *(delay)*, impede, inhibit, interfere, interject, interpose, intervene, intrude, molest *(annoy)*, obstruct, obtrude, occlude, pause, preclude, prevent, recess, stall, stay *(halt)*, stem *(check)*, stop, suspend, thwart, toll *(stop)*, withstand. SEE MAIN ENTRY

interrupt work   strike *(refuse to work)*

interrupted   arrested *(checked)*, desultory, disconnected, disjointed, disjunctive *(tending to disjoin)*, intermittent

interrupting   obtrusive

interruption   abeyance, adjournment, cessation *(interlude)*, check *(bar)*, cloture, damper *(stopper)*, deferment, delay, disassociation, discontinuance *(act of discontinuing)*, disturbance, frustration, halt, hiatus, hindrance, impediment, interval, intervention *(interference)*, intrusion, lapse *(break)*, layoff, lull, molestation, obstruction, pause, pendency, recess, remission, respite *(interval of rest)*, split, stay, violation. SEE MAIN ENTRY

interruptive   intrusive, obtrusive

intersect   cross *(intersect)*, separate, split, traverse

intersecting road   crossroad *(intersection)*

intersection   crossroad *(intersection)*, meeting *(encounter)*. SEE MAIN ENTRY

intersperse   diffuse, dissolve *(disperse)*. SEE MAIN ENTRY

interstate commerce   commerce

interstice   hiatus, interruption, interval, rift *(gap)*, space

interthread   intertwine

intertwine   combine *(join together)*, connect *(join together)*, consolidate *(unite)*, implicate, join *(bring together)*, merge. SEE MAIN ENTRY

intertwined   inseparable, related

intertwist   annex *(add)*, combine *(join together)*, conjoin, intertwine, join *(bring together)*

interval   abeyance, cessation *(interlude)*, discontinuance *(act of discontinuing)*, duration, hiatus, moratorium, pause, pendency, period, point *(period of time)*, recess, remission, space, term *(duration)*, time. SEE MAIN ENTRY

interval of ease   reprieve

interval of rest   leave *(absence)*

interval of years   age

intervallum   interruption, interval, pause

intervene   arbitrate *(conciliate)*, check *(restrain)*, defer *(put off)*, discontinue *(break continuity)*, disrupt, estop, forestall, hold up *(delay)*, impose *(intrude)*, intercede, interfere, interject, interpose, mediate, obstruct, obtrude, parry, tamper. SEE MAIN ENTRY

intervener   actor, adjuster, advocate *(counselor)*, arbiter, interagent, medium, party *(litigant)*, referee

intervenient   intermediate, mesne

intervening   interlocutory, intermediate, mesne, ministerial

intervening agent   interagent

intervening cause   SEE MAIN ENTRY

intervening episode   cessation *(interlude)*

intervening party   amicus curiae

intervening period   cessation *(interlude)*, hiatus, pause, pendency, recess

intervening space   cessation *(interlude)*

intervening time   cessation *(interlude)*, interval

intervenire   interfere, intervene

intervenor   amicus curiae, arbitrator, litigant, umpire

intervention   agency *(legal relationship)*, arbitration, collective bargaining, intercession, invasion, mediation. SEE MAIN ENTRY

intervention to facilitate a compromise   mediation

interventional   interlocutory

interventionist   advocate *(counselor)*, arbitrator

interventor   advocate *(counselor)*

interventus   intervention *(interference)*

intervertere   embezzle

interview   appointment *(meeting)*, confrontation *(act of setting face to face)*, conversation, converse, examination *(test)*, examine *(interrogate)*, parley. SEE MAIN ENTRY

interviewers   press

interweave   combine *(join together)*, conjoin, connect *(join together)*, interject, intersperse, intertwine, join *(bring together)*

interwoven   complex, compound, interrelated, promiscuous, related

intestate individual   decedent

intestinus   internal

intimacy   confidence *(relation of trust)*, consortium *(marriage companionship)*, contact *(association)*, marriage *(intimate relationship)*, privacy, rapport, secret

intimate   advise, connote, consociate, familiar *(informed)*, hint, imply, indicate, infer, inseparable, mention, personal *(private)*, private *(confidential)*, purport, signify *(denote)*. SEE MAIN ENTRY

intimate connection   affiliation *(connectedness)*

intimated   assumed *(inferred)*

intimately allied   affiliated, cognate

intimately related   affiliated, cognate, consanguineous

intimation   cloud *(suspicion)*, clue, hint, implication *(inference)*, indication, insinuation, mention *(reference)*, premonition, reference *(allusion)*, report *(rumor)*, suggestion, suspicion *(uncertainty)*, symptom, tip *(clue)*. SEE MAIN ENTRY

intimidate   bait *(harass)*, browbeat, coerce, deter, discourage, frighten, harass, hector, menace, pressure, threaten. SEE MAIN ENTRY

intimidating   chilling effect, dictatorial, portentous *(ominous)*, sinister

intimidating force   menace

intimidation   admonition, coercion, deterrence, deterrent, fear, fright, menace, pressure, threat

intimus   intimate

intitle   delegate

intolerabilis   insufferable

intolerable   deplorable, insufferable, loathsome, objectionable, obnoxious, odious, offensive *(offending)*, onerous, oppressive, outrageous, painful, peccant *(culpable)*, unacceptable, undesirable, unendurable, unsatisfactory, unsavory, unsuitable. SEE MAIN ENTRY

intolerance   bias, cruelty, discrimination *(bigotry)*, exclusion, feud, hatred, ill will, incompatibility *(difference)*, inequity, ostracism, partiality, prejudice *(preconception)*, proscription, rejection, spite. SEE MAIN ENTRY

intolerant SEE MAIN ENTRY

intolerandus insufferable

intolerant adverse *(hostile),* bigot, callous, disdainful, dogmatic, draconian, illiberal, insolent, narrow, orgulous, parochial, provincial, relentless, remorseless, supercilious

intoleration rejection

intonate enunciate

intonation inflection, stress *(accent).* SEE MAIN ENTRY

intone enunciate

intorted circuitous

intoxicant alcohol

intoxicated drunk

intoxicating provocative

intoxicating liquor alcohol

intoxication dipsomania, inebriation, passion

intractable contumacious, difficult, disobedient, froward, immutable, incorrigible, indomitable, inexorable, inflexible, insubordinate, lawless, nonconsenting, obdurate, pertinacious, perverse, recalcitrant, renitent, restive, rigid, severe, unbending, uncontrollable, unruly, unyielding, willful. SEE MAIN ENTRY

intractableness contempt *(disobedience to the court)*

intransient permanent, perpetual

intransigence incompatibility *(difference),* tenacity

intransigency incompatibility *(difference)*

intransigent implacable, incorrigible, inflexible, irreconcilable, obdurate, purposeful, relentless, renitent, resolute, restive, steadfast, unbending, uncompromising, unyielding, willful

intransmutable definite, durable, indefeasible, irrevocable, permanent

intransparency density

intrare enter *(go in)*

intrepid heroic, spartan, undaunted

intrepidity audacity, confidence *(faith),* diligence *(perseverance),* prowess *(bravery)*

intrepidus undaunted

intricacy complex *(entanglement),* complication, entanglement *(confusion),* involution, predicament

intricate complex, compound, elaborate, incomprehensible, inextricable, labyrinthine, obscure *(abstruse),* recondite, sinuous. SEE MAIN ENTRY

intricate involvement imbroglio

intricate plot imbroglio

intricately wrought elaborate

intrigant confederate, conspirator, conspirer

intrigant copartner *(coconspirator)*

intrigue artifice, cabal, coax, collusion, complication, confederacy *(conspiracy),* connivance, connive, conspiracy, conspire, contrivance, contrive, deceive, deception, frame up, fraud, impress *(affect deeply),* indirection *(deceitfulness),* machination, maneuver, pettifoggery, plan, plot *(secret plan),* plot, scheme, secret, stratagem, strategy

intriguer conspirator, conspirer, copartner *(coconspirator)*

intriguery collusion, conspiracy, strategy

intriguing artful, attractive, collusive, insidious, machiavellian, perfidious, provocative, sapid, sly, subtle *(insidious),*

suggestive *(evocative),* tactical, unconscionable

intrinsic born *(innate),* central *(essential),* essential *(inherent),* implicit, ingrained, inherent, innate, native *(inborn),* organic, virtual. SEE MAIN ENTRY

intrinsic nature gist *(substance)*

intrinsical central *(essential),* essential *(inherent),* organic

intrinsicality character *(personal quality)*

intrinsicalness character *(personal quality)*

introduce adduce, bear *(adduce),* commence, enter *(insert),* establish *(launch),* extend *(offer),* herald, induct, infuse, initiate, inject, inseminate, instate, interject, interpose, invent *(produce for the first time),* launch *(initiate),* maintain *(commence),* move *(judicially request),* originate, pose *(propound),* precede, preface, propose, propound, submit *(give).* SEE MAIN ENTRY

introduce a change affect

introduce a system classify, organize *(arrange)*

introduce as an example cite *(state)*

introduce changes denature, modify *(alter),* qualify *(condition)*

introduce into office induct, instate

introduce new conditions qualify *(condition)*

introduce order codify, marshal, organize *(arrange)*

introduce order into fix *(arrange)*

introduced alleged

introduced to acquainted

introducer architect, author *(originator)*

introducere introduce, present *(introduce)*

introductio introduction

introduction appearance *(emergence),* birth *(beginning),* genesis, inflow, infusion, insertion, installation, nascency, onset *(commencement),* origination, outset, overture, preamble, preface, prelude. SEE MAIN ENTRY

introductory aforesaid, antecedent, elementary, inchoate, incipient, initial, last *(preceding),* original *(initial),* precursory, preliminary, preparatory, previous, prime *(original),* prior

introductory part preamble, preface

introductory statement preamble

introgression entrance, incursion, inflow, osmosis

introire enter *(go in)*

introitus entrance

intromit enter *(insert),* inject, interject

introspect muse, ponder

introspection contemplation. SEE MAIN ENTRY

introspective circumspect, cogitative, pensive, subjective

introversion introspection

intrude accroach, discontinue *(break continuity),* disrupt, disturb, encroach, impinge, infringe, interfere, interpose, interrupt, intervene, invade, obtrude, overstep, pervade, trespass. SEE MAIN ENTRY

intrude illegally encroach

intrude upon harass

intruder alien

intruding obtrusive

intrusion assault, disturbance, encroachment, incursion, infringement, interruption, intervention *(imposition into a lawsuit),* intervention *(interference),* invasion,

molestation, nuisance, onset *(assault).* SEE MAIN ENTRY

intrusive impertinent *(insolent),* obtrusive, presumptuous. SEE MAIN ENTRY

intrust delegate

intuit anticipate *(expect),* preconceive, presuppose

intuition belief *(state of mind),* common sense, comprehension, discretion *(quality of being discreet),* discrimination *(good judgment),* insight, instinct, judgment *(discernment),* sagacity

intuitional uncanny

intuitive acute, innate

intuitive truth principle *(axiom)*

intuitiveness insight

intwine combine *(join together)*

inundate immerse *(plunge into),* load, outpour, overcome *(overwhelm),* overload, overwhelm. SEE MAIN ENTRY

inundation cataclysm, inflow, overage, plethora, surfeit

inurbane provincial

inurbanity disrespect

inurbanus inelegant

inure accrue *(arise),* naturalize *(acclimate).* SEE MAIN ENTRY

inured impervious, inveterate, nonchalant, unaffected *(uninfluenced)*

inurement habituation

inusitate novel, unaccustomed, uncommon, unusual

inusitation desuetude, disuse

inusitatus eccentric, extraordinary, irregular *(not usual),* rare, sporadic, uncommon

inutile expendable, futile, ineffective, ineffectual, nugatory, unavailing, unfit

inutile check bad check

inutilis incompetent, ineffective, ineffectual, unfit

inutilitas inexpedience

inutility desuetude

invade accroach, assail, attack, break *(violate),* despoil, encroach, enter *(penetrate),* force *(break),* harry *(plunder),* impinge, impose *(intrude),* infringe, interfere, intrude, obtrude, occupy *(take possession),* overlap, overstep, pervade, preempt, trespass, violate. SEE MAIN ENTRY

invade unlawfully encroach

invader aggressor, assailant

invadere encroach, invade

invading intrusive, offensive *(taking the initiative)*

invalid disabled *(deprived of legal right),* disabled *(made incapable),* fallacious, false *(inaccurate),* faulty, helpless *(powerless),* illegal, inactive, inconsequential, ineffective, ineffectual, nugatory, null and void, otiose, patient, sophistic, unavailing, unsound *(fallacious),* untenable. SEE MAIN ENTRY

invalid check bad check

invalid trial mistrial

invalidate abate *(extinguish),* abolish, abrogate *(annul),* abrogate *(rescind),* annul, avoid *(cancel),* cancel, denature, destroy *(void),* disable, disarm *(divest of arms),* disavow, discharge *(release from obligation),* discontinue *(abandon),* disown *(deny the validity),* disprove, disqualify, frustrate, kill *(defeat),* negate, neutralize, nullify, obliterate, override, overrule, quash, recall *(call back),* refute, renege, repeal, rescind, revoke, vacate *(void),* vitiate, withdraw. SEE MAIN ENTRY

invalidate an attorney's license disbar
invalidated disabled *(deprived of legal right)*
invalidating cancellation
invalidation abatement *(extinguishment)*, abolition, ademption, annulment, avoidance *(cancellation)*, cancellation, counterargument, countermand, defeasance, defeat, disability *(legal disqualification)*, discharge *(annulment)*, discharge *(release from obligation)*, discontinuance *(act of discontinuing)*, dismissal *(termination of a proceeding)*, disqualification *(factor that disqualifies)*, disqualification *(rejection)*, dissolution *(termination)*, negation, rescision, reversal, revocation
invalidism disease
invalidity disability *(legal disqualification)*, disqualification *(factor that disqualifies)*, impuissance, nullity. SEE MAIN ENTRY
invalidus ineffective, ineffectual, powerless
invaluable beneficial, constructive *(creative)*, functional, inestimable, lucrative, practical, priceless, profitable, valuable. SEE MAIN ENTRY
invariability constant, regularity
invariable certain *(positive)*, chronic, constant *(adjective)*, constant *(noun)*, definite, durable, immutable, indefeasible, inflexible, obdurate, regular *(orderly)*, repetitious, stable, unalterable, uniform, unyielding
invariably always *(without exception)*. SEE MAIN ENTRY
invariant constant *(adjective)*, constant *(noun)*
invasion encroachment, entrance, foray, incursion, inflow, infringement, intrusion, onset *(assault)*, outbreak, violation. SEE MAIN ENTRY
invasion of a legal right injury, tort
invasion of a right infringement
invasive intrusive, obtrusive, offensive *(taking the initiative)*
invectio introduction
invective aspersion, condemnation *(blame)*, contumely, correction *(punishment)*, defamation, denunciation, diatribe, disparagement, harangue, libel, malediction, obloquy, outcry, phillipic, profanity, revilement, slander, vilification
invehere introduce
invehi in attack
inveigh demonstrate *(protest)*, denounce *(condemn)*, entice, lash *(attack verbally)*, protest. SEE MAIN ENTRY
inveigh against censure, condemn *(blame)*, contemn, decry, defame, impugn, reprimand, reproach
inveigle bait *(lure)*, betray *(lead astray)*, bilk, cheat, coax, convince, deceive, defraud, delude, dupe, entrap, hoodwink, illude, importune, influence, lure, palter, persuade, prevail *(persuade)*, trap. SEE MAIN ENTRY
inveiglement bribery, decoy, persuasion, seduction
invenire contrive, devise *(invent)*, discover, find *(discover)*, invent *(produce for the first time)*
invent compose, conjure, contrive, create, fabricate *(make up)*, find *(discover)*, forge *(produce)*, frame *(formulate)*, generate, initiate, lie *(falsify)*, make, manufacture, originate, palter, prevaricate, produce *(manufacture)*, scheme. SEE MAIN ENTRY
invented assumed *(feigned)*, fictitious, illusory, mendacious, unfounded, untrue

inventio contrivance
invention contrivance, creation, device *(mechanism)*, expedient, false pretense, falsehood, falsification, fiction, figment, formation, innovation, lie, myth, nascency, origination, pretense *(pretext)*, pretext, product, story *(falsehood)*, strategy, subreption. SEE MAIN ENTRY
invention of lies perjury
inventive fertile, original *(creative)*, productive, resourceful
inventiveness contrivance
inventor architect, author *(originator)*, pioneer
inventories assets
inventory check *(inspect)*, enumerate, index *(relate)*, inspection, invoice *(itemized list)*, itemize, roll, schedule, stock *(store)*, store *(depository)*, tabulate. SEE MAIN ENTRY
inventory expert comptroller
inventum invention
invenustus inelegant
inveracity bad faith, dishonesty, falsehood, improbity, story *(falsehood)*
inverse adverse *(opposite)*, antipode, antithesis, contra, contradictory, contrary, discordant, negative, opposite. SEE MAIN ENTRY
inversely contra
inversion antipode, reversal, subversion
inversus inverse
invert alter, disorganize, disorient, overthrow, overturn, upset
inverted disordered, inverse, opposite
invest admit *(give access)*, allow *(authorize)*, assign *(designate)*, bequeath, bestow, capitalize *(provide capital)*, clothe, commit *(entrust)*, confer *(give)*, constitute *(establish)*, contribute *(supply)*, delegate, deposit *(submit to a bank)*, embrace *(encircle)*, empower, enable, endue, enshroud, finance, induct, instate, lend, repose *(place)*, speculate *(chance)*, spend, supply, vest. SEE MAIN ENTRY
invest empower entrust
invest in purchase
invest in again refinance
invest money fund
invest the power charge *(empower)*
invest with devolve
invest with a body embody
invest with authoritative power charge *(empower)*, delegate
invest with matter embody
invest with power authorize, clothe, commit *(entrust)*
invested capital investment
invested money investment
invested property investment, securities, security *(stock)*, share *(stock)*, stock *(shares)*
invested sum principal *(capital sum)*
investigare examine *(interrogate)*, scrutinize, trace *(follow)*
investigate analyze, audit, canvass, check *(inspect)*, consider, deliberate, delve, discover, examine *(study)*, frisk, inquire, monitor, notice *(observe)*, peruse, probe, research, review, scrutinize, search, study, trace *(follow)*, treat *(process)*. SEE MAIN ENTRY
investigate judicially hear *(give a legal hearing)*
investigating committee commission *(agency)*
investigatio examination *(study)*, investigation
investigation analysis, cross-examination, cross-questioning, discovery, examination

(study), experiment, hearing, indagation, inquest, inquiry *(request for information)*, inquiry *(systematic investigation)*, interrogation, observation, probe, pursuit *(chase)*, pursuit *(effort to secure)*, question *(inquiry)*, research, review *(official reexamination)*, scrutiny, test, treatment. SEE MAIN ENTRY
investigation to uncover facts discovery
investigative inquisitive, interrogatory
investigator detective, spy
investing with authority delegation *(assignment)*
investiture delegation *(assignment)*, deputation *(selection of delegates)*, installation
investiture of title feoffment
investment advance *(allowance)*, advancement *(loan)*, binder, deputation *(selection of delegates)*, equity *(share of ownership)*, expenditure, fund, securities, security *(stock)*, share *(stock)*, stock *(shares)*, venture. SEE MAIN ENTRY
investment portfolio capital
investments capital, finance, personalty, portfolio, property *(possessions)*
investor backer, contributor *(giver)*, creditor, customer, grantor, patron *(influential supporter)*, shareholder
inveteracy behavior, constant, habituation
inveterate constant, durable, familiar *(customary)*, habitual, incorrigible, ingrained, pertinacious, stable, traditional. SEE MAIN ENTRY
inveterate habit habituation, practice *(custom)*
inveterate hatred feud
inveterate practice habit
inveterate strife feud
inveterateness habituation
inveteratus habitual, ingrained, inveterate, old
invictus indomitable, insuperable, invincible, irresistible
invidia disfavor, malice, rancor
invidiosus invidious, odious
invidious caustic, heinous, loathsome, malevolent, malicious, malignant, objectionable, obnoxious, odious, offensive *(offending)*, provocative, spiteful. SEE MAIN ENTRY
invidiousness malice
invidus jealous, malicious
invigilate police
invigorate develop, endue, fix *(repair)*, meliorate, nurture, recreate, renew *(refurbish)*, stimulate
invigorating medicinal, remedial, salubrious, salutary. SEE MAIN ENTRY
invigoration instigation, revival
invincible defensible, forcible, indomitable, inexpugnable, insuperable, insurmountable, irresistible, potent, powerful. SEE MAIN ENTRY
inviolability responsibility *(conscience)*. SEE MAIN ENTRY
inviolable clean, immune, indefeasible, inexpugnable, infrangible, invincible, lawful, private *(confidential)*, sacrosanct, secure *(free from danger)*, tenable, unalienable
inviolable refuge asylum *(hiding place)*
inviolableness inviolability
inviolate certain *(positive)*, clean, definite, durable, gross *(total)*, honest, intact, lawabiding, sacrosanct. SEE MAIN ENTRY
inviolatus inviolate
invious impervious
invisibility concealment, nonappearance
invisible covert, hidden, impalpable,

inconspicuous, indiscernible, intangible, obscure *(faint)*, undisclosed. SEE MAIN ENTRY

invisibleness nonappearance

invisus obnoxious, odious

invitatio invitation

invitation instigation, monition *(legal summons)*, overture, provocation, request, seduction. SEE MAIN ENTRY

invitation to combat defiance

invite call *(appeal to)*, call *(summon)*, motivate, offer *(propose)*, proffer, request, urge

invite competition challenge

invite the attention occupy *(engage)*

invite to contest challenge

inviting attractive, palatable, persuasive, provocative, sapid

invitingness amenity

invitus involuntary, reluctance

invocare invoke

invocate invoke

invocation call *(appeal)*, entreaty, laudation, petition, prayer, request, subpoena, summons

invocation of evil imprecation

invocatory plea call *(appeal)*

invocatory prayer call *(appeal)*

invoice charge *(assess)*, register. SEE MAIN ENTRY

invoke bear *(adduce)*, call *(appeal to)*, call *(summon)*. SEE MAIN ENTRY

involucrum veil

involuntarily unwillingly

involuntariness happenstance, instinct

involuntary compelling, fortuitous, innate, mandatory, obligatory, reluctant, unavoidable *(inevitable)*, unintentional, unwitting. SEE MAIN ENTRY

involuntary exile banishment

involuntary liquidation bankruptcy

involuntary loss of right forfeiture *(act of forfeiting)*

involuntary manslaughter SEE MAIN ENTRY

involuntary servitude bondage, subjection

involute elaborate, inextricable, labyrinthine, sinuous, snarl

involuted complex, inextricable, labyrinthine, sinuous

involution complex *(entanglement)*, complication. SEE MAIN ENTRY

involutional complex, sinuous

involutionary sinuous

involve appertain, apply *(pertain)*, bear *(adduce)*, comprehend *(include)*, comprise, confound, connote, consist, constitute *(compose)*, denounce *(inform against)*, embrace *(encircle)*, entail, immerse *(engross)*, implicate, imply, include, incorporate *(include)*, incriminate, interest, monopolize, occupy *(engage)*, perplex. SEE MAIN ENTRY

involve in criminal proceeding incriminate

involve in error misdirect

involve in guilt incriminate

involve in shame brand *(stigmatize)*, discredit, disgrace

involve in suspicion impugn

involve together commingle, pool

involved at risk, complex, compound, constructive *(inferential)*, difficult, disordered, elaborate, esoteric, inextricable, interested, intricate, labyrinthine, obscure *(abstruse)*, problematic, recondite, sinuous, tortuous *(bending)*. SEE MAIN ENTRY

involved situation imbroglio

involved state complication

involvement affiliation *(connectedness)*, association *(connection)*, complex *(entanglement)*, complication, embroilment, involution, preoccupation, quagmire, relationship *(connection)*. SEE MAIN ENTRY

involvere envelop

involving death fatal

involving in guilt incriminatory, inculpatory

involving risk dangerous

involving ruin fatal

invulnerability inviolability, protection, security *(safety)*

invulnerable certain *(positive)*, defensible, immune, indestructible, inexpugnable, infrangible, insuperable, invincible, permanent, safe, secure *(free from danger)*, tenable. SEE MAIN ENTRY

inward interior, intrinsic *(deep down)*

inward monitor conscience, responsibility *(conscience)*

inward perception impression

inwardly herein, wherein

inweave intertwine

inwrought born *(innate)*, ingrained

iocosus jocular

iocularis jocular

iota minimum, modicum, scintilla. SEE MAIN ENTRY

ipse actual

ipse dixit allegation, assertion, bigot, declaration

ipso facto SEE MAIN ENTRY

ipsum se inspicere introspection

ira resentment

iracund petulant

iracundus resentful

iram remittere relent

irascibility outburst

irascible contentious, disobedient, fractious, froward, perverse, petulant. SEE MAIN ENTRY

irascibleness outburst

ire passion, resentment

irenic nonmilitant, placid

irenical nonmilitant, placid

irk aggravate *(annoy)*, annoy, badger, bait *(harass)*, discommode, discompose, distress, disturb, irritate, molest *(annoy)*, offend *(insult)*, perturb, pique, plague, provoke. SEE MAIN ENTRY

irksome invidious, operose, oppressive, painful, provocative, vexatious. SEE MAIN ENTRY

iron fetter, relentless, staunch

iron grip adhesion *(affixing)*

iron rule oppression

iron will tenacity

iron-handed peremptory *(imperative)*

iron-hearted obdurate, spartan

ironbound ironclad

ironclad severe. SEE MAIN ENTRY

ironclad agreement contract. SEE MAIN ENTRY

ironhanded dictatorial, severe, stringent

ironia irony

ironic SEE MAIN ENTRY

ironical ironic

irony SEE MAIN ENTRY

irradiate radiate, spread

irrational arbitrary, disconnected, disproportionate, fatuous, ill-judged, illogical, injudicious, ludicrous, lunatic, misadvised, reckless, sophistic, thoughtless, unreasonable, unsound *(fallacious)*, untenable. SEE MAIN ENTRY

irrational conclusion non sequitur

irrational terror panic

irrebuttable unavoidable *(not voidable)*. SEE MAIN ENTRY

irreclaimable incorrigible, iniquitous, irredeemable, irretrievable, irreversible, irrevocable, lost *(taken away)*, obdurate, reprobate. SEE MAIN ENTRY

irreconcilability antithesis, conflict, contention *(opposition)*, difference, discrepancy, disparity, incompatibility *(difference)*, paradox. SEE MAIN ENTRY

irreconcilable adverse *(opposite)*, contradictory, discordant, disparate, disproportionate, dissenting, dissident, hostile, implacable, inapposite, inapt, incongruous, inconsistent, inept *(inappropriate)*, inimical, litigious, reluctant, repugnant *(incompatible)*, restive, uncompromising. SEE MAIN ENTRY

irreconcilable differences incompatibility *(difference)*. SEE MAIN ENTRY

irreconcilableness incompatibility *(difference)*

irrecoverable incorrigible, irredeemable, irremediable, irreparable, irretrievable, irreversible, lifeless *(dead)*, lost *(taken away)*. SEE MAIN ENTRY

irredeemable delinquent *(guilty of a misdeed)*, diabolic, incorrigible, irrecoverable, irremediable, irreparable, irretrievable, irreversible, irrevocable, lost *(taken away)*, reprobate. SEE MAIN ENTRY

irredeemable bill bad debt

irreducible certain *(positive)*, complex, inextricable, net, simple, succinct

irreformable incorrigible, irredeemable, irreversible

irrefragability certainty, certification *(certainness)*, certitude

irrefragable believable, categorical, certain *(fixed)*, certain *(positive)*, clear *(certain)*, cogent, conclusive *(determinative)*, convincing, definite, incontestable, incontrovertible, indefeasible, infallible, irrefutable, positive *(incontestable)*, uncontested, undeniable, undisputed, unequivocal, unimpeachable, unrefutable

irrefragably admittedly, fairly *(clearly)*

irrefragibility incontestability

irrefutability certainty, certification *(certainness)*, certitude, incontestability

irrefutable axiomatic, believable, categorical, certain *(fixed)*, certain *(positive)*, clear *(certain)*, cogent, conclusive *(determinative)*, convincing, credible, definite, definitive, factual, inappealable, incontestable, incontrovertible, indubious, irrebuttable, positive *(incontestable)*, provable, real, reliable, solid *(sound)*, sound, unavoidable *(not voidable)*, uncontested, undeniable, undisputed, unequivocal, unimpeachable, unrefutable. SEE MAIN ENTRY

irrefutably admittedly, fairly *(clearly)*

irregular anomalous, broken *(interrupted)*, casual, deviant, disjunctive *(tending to disjoin)*, disorderly, disparate, dissimilar, eccentric, extraordinary, haphazard, impermissible, incongruous, infrequent, intermittent, multifarious, nonconforming, novel, peculiar *(curious)*, random, sporadic, suspicious *(questionable)*, tortuous *(bending)*, unaccustomed, unequal *(unequivalent)*, unorthodox, unpredictable, unusual, variable. SEE MAIN ENTRY

irregularity deviation, disorder *(lack of order)*, diversity, entanglement *(confusion)*, exception *(exclusion)*, inequality, informality, misapplication, miscue, misdoing, nonconformity, quirk *(idiosyncrasy)*. SEE MAIN ENTRY

irrelated alien *(unrelated)*

irrelation difference, disparity, distinction *(difference)*, distortion

irrelative apart, disconnected, dissimilar, extraneous, gratuitous *(unwarranted)*, heterogeneous, impertinent *(irrelevant)*, inapposite, independent, irrelevant, unrelated. SEE MAIN ENTRY

irrelevance immateriality, inconsequence, insignificance

irrelevancy immateriality, inconsequence, insignificance, non sequitur

irrelevant collateral *(immaterial)*, expendable, extraneous, extrinsic, gratuitous *(unwarranted)*, immaterial, improper, inadmissible, inapplicable, inapposite, inappreciable, inappropriate, inconsequential, inconsiderable, irrelative, minor, needless, negligible, nugatory, null *(insignificant)*, paltry, peripheral, unessential, unfit, unnecessary, unrelated, unsuitable. SEE MAIN ENTRY

irreligious diabolic, mundane, profane

irremediable blameworthy, incorrigible, irrevocable. SEE MAIN ENTRY

irremedial irreversible

irremissible inexcusable, unjustifiable

irremovable durable, firm, fixed *(securely placed)*, immutable, indefeasible, indelible, inextricable, irreversible, irrevocable, permanent, stable

irrepair deterioration

irreparable incorrigible, irrecoverable, irredeemable, irremediable, irretrievable, irreversible, irrevocable. SEE MAIN ENTRY

irreparable harm SEE MAIN ENTRY

irrepealable conclusive *(determinative)*, irreversible, irrevocable, noncancellable

irreplaceability importance, need *(requirement)*

irreplaceable indispensable, inestimable, integral, priceless, vital

irreplaceable feature necessity, need *(requirement)*

irrepoachable honest

irrepproachable law-abiding

irreprehensible blameless, clean, inculpable, unimpeachable, unobjectionable. SEE MAIN ENTRY

irrepressible hot-blooded, indomitable, intractable, rampant, uncontrollable, unruly

irreproachable blameless, clean, incorruptible, inculpable, infallible, irreprehensible, meritorious, unimpeachable, unobjectionable

irreprovable blameless, clean, irreprehensible, unobjectionable

irresistable uncontrollable

irresistible certain *(positive)*, cogent, compelling, compulsory, definite, indomitable, inexpugnable, invincible, necessary *(inescapable)*, omnipotent, powerful, provocative, unavoidable *(inevitable)*. SEE MAIN ENTRY

irresistible compulsion necessity

irresistible impulse compulsion *(obsession)*, obsession

irresistible urge passion

irresoluble certain *(positive)*

irresolute capricious, doubtful, hesitant, insipid, mutable, noncommittal, passive, pliant, speculative, undecided, volatile. SEE MAIN ENTRY

irresoluteness ambivalence, indecision

irresolution ambivalence, doubt *(indecision)*, hesitation, incertitude, indecision, inertia, quandary

irresolved noncommittal, outstanding *(unresolved)*

irrespective SEE MAIN ENTRY

irrespective of regardless

irresponsibility anarchy, inconsideration, negligence, res ipsa loquitur

irresponsible capricious, careless, disobedient, heedless, ill-advised, lawless, misadvised, negligent, reckless, thoughtless, uncurbed, undependable, unreliable, untrustworthy, variable. SEE MAIN ENTRY

irresponsive unresponsive

irretrievable irrecoverable, irredeemable, irremediable, irreversible, irrevocable, lost *(taken away)*. SEE MAIN ENTRY

irretrievable debt bad debt

irrevealable clandestine, confidential

irreverant profane

irreverence bad repute, blasphemy, contempt *(disobedience to the court)*, disparagement, disrespect, expletive, ignominy, violation

irreverent contemptuous, impertinent *(insolent)*, pejorative, presumptuous, reprobate, supercilious

irreverent behavior blasphemy

irreversible certain *(positive)*, decisive, definite, indefeasible, indelible, ironclad, irrecoverable, irredeemable, irremediable, irreparable, irrevocable, noncancellable, permanent, stable, unalterable. SEE MAIN ENTRY

irreversible damage prejudice *(injury)*

irrevocability certitude

irrevocable certain *(positive)*, compulsory, conclusive *(determinative)*, decisive, definite, final, immutable, inappealable, indefeasible, indestructible, ironclad, irredeemable, irremediable, irreversible, lost *(taken away)*, necessary *(inescapable)*, permanent, stable, unavoidable *(inevitable)*, unavoidable *(not voidable)*. SEE MAIN ENTRY

irrevocable decision adjudication

irritable fractious, froward, petulant, querulous, sensitive *(easily affected)*

irritant aggravation *(annoyance)*

irritate affront, aggravate *(annoy)*, agitate *(activate)*, annoy, antagonize, badger, bait *(harass)*, disaffect, discommode, discompose, distress, exacerbate, harass, harrow, harry *(harass)*, hector, incense, inconvenience, molest *(annoy)*, offend *(insult)*, perturb, pique, plague, press *(goad)*, provoke, repel *(disgust)*. SEE MAIN ENTRY

irritating caustic, irksome, loathsome, offensive *(offending)*, painful, provocative, vexatious

irritation aggravation *(annoyance)*, dissatisfaction, instigation, molestation, nuisance, provocation, umbrage

irrupt encroach, intrude

irruption assault, encroachment, incursion, inflow, intrusion, outbreak, outburst

is composed of consist

is essentially consist

island isolate

isolate abstract *(separate)*, constrain *(imprison)*, detain *(hold in custody)*, dissociate, estrange, exclude, immure, insulate, jail, part *(separate)*, relegate, remove *(eliminate)*, seclude, select, sequester *(seclude)*, sever, split. SEE MAIN ENTRY

isolated alone *(solitary)*, apart, derelict *(abandoned)*, disconnected, discrete,

disjunctive *(tending to disjoin)*, exclusive *(singular)*, inapposite, individual, insular, obscure *(remote)*, private *(secluded)*, remote *(secluded)*, separate, singular, sole, solitary, sporadic

isolation exclusion, expulsion, ostracism, privacy, removal, segregation *(separation)*, severance

isolationist neutral

issuance apportionment, circulation, dispensation *(act of dispensing)*, distribution *(apportionment)*, output, publication *(disclosure)*, publicity. SEE MAIN ENTRY

issue accrue *(arise)*, administer *(tender)*, bestow, blood, cause of action, cessation *(termination)*, child, children, circulate, confer *(give)*, contention *(argument)*, denouement, derivation, descendant, dispense, disperse *(disseminate)*, disseminate, divide *(distribute)*, dole, effect, emanate, emerge, emit, ensue, evolve, exude, family *(household)*, impart, issuance, matter *(subject)*, mete, offshoot, offspring, outcome, outflow, outgrowth, output, point *(item)*, post, posterity, proceed *(go forward)*, product, progeny, promulgate, propagate *(spread)*, publication *(printed matter)*, publish, result, send, serial, serve *(deliver a legal instrument)*, signify *(inform)*, stem *(originate)*, subject *(topic)*, succession, supervene, tender, thesis, transmit, utter. SEE MAIN ENTRY

issue a command command, constrain *(compel)*, dictate, direct *(order)*, enact, instruct *(direct)*, require *(compel)*, subpoena, summon

issue a court directive subpoena, summon

issue a decree command, direct *(order)*, instruct *(direct)*, order

issue a fiat decree

issue a proclamation decree, notify

issue a pronouncement notify

issue a statement certify *(attest)*, posit, post, publish, speak

issue a ukase decree

issue a writ charge *(accuse)*, subpoena

issue an edict decree

issue an invitation call *(summon)*

issue an order command, dictate, direct *(order)*, enjoin, instruct *(direct)*, prescribe

issue counterfeit money forge *(counterfeit)*

issue for distribution publish

issue for public sale publish

issue forth arise *(originate)*, depart

issue of fact SEE MAIN ENTRY

issue one's fiat order

issue process subpoena, summon

issue rays radiate

issue threats coerce

issued positive *(prescribed)*

issued weapons armed

issueless barren, otiose, unproductive

it follows that consequently

itaque consequently

itch passion

item article *(commodity)*, article *(distinct section of a writing)*, component, count, detail, element, entity, entry *(record)*, member *(constituent part)*, object, particular, particularity, possession *(property)*, product, specification, technicality, term *(provision)*, title *(division)*, trait. SEE MAIN ENTRY

item in the indictment count

item of evidence exhibit

item of information particular

item of personalty possession *(property)*

item on the agenda issue *(matter in dispute)*, matter *(subject)*
itemization inventory, specification
itemize delineate, describe, designate, detail *(particularize)*, enumerate, impanel, index *(relate)*, specify, tabulate. SEE MAIN ENTRY
itemized detailed
itemized account bill *(invoice)*, invoice *(itemized list)*, tariff *(bill)*
itemized list inventory
itemized specification bill *(formal declaration)*
items circumstances, commodities, contents, goods
items for sale merchandise
items of business agenda
items of personalty possessions
iter course
iterare reiterate, renew *(begin again)*, repeat *(do again)*
iterate copy, reaffirm, recount, reiterate, repeat *(state again)*
iteration narration, recital, restatement
iterative incessant, insistent. SEE MAIN ENTRY
iterum reopen
itinerancy vagrancy
itinerant moving *(in motion)*. SEE MAIN ENTRY
itinerary plan
iubeo direction *(order)*
iubere order, pass *(approve)*
iucundus palatable
iudex judge, juror
iudicare criticize *(evaluate)*, judge, try *(conduct a trial)*
iudices jury
iudicialis forensic, judicial
iudicium court, criticism, determination, discretion *(quality of being discreet)*, discrimination *(good judgment)*, estimate *(idea)*, holding *(ruling of a court)*, insight, judgment *(discernment)*, judgment *(formal court decree)*, opinion *(belief)*, perception, sense *(intelligence)*, sentence, trial *(legal proceeding)*, tribunal, verdict
iudicium exercere judge
iungere connect *(join together)*
iurare swear
iureiurando adfirmare swear
iurgium altercation
iuridicialis forensic, juridical
iuris consultus jurist
iuris peritus jurist
iuris prudentia jurisprudence
iurisconsultus lawyer
iurisdictio judicature, jurisdiction
iurisperitus lawyer
ius law, right *(entitlement)*, statute
iusiurandum oath
iussum fiat, injunction, order *(judicial directive)*, regulation *(rule)*
iusta right *(entitlement)*
iuste fairly *(impartially)*
iustitia equity *(justice)*, fairness, justice
iustus equitable, just, justifiable, regular *(conventional)*, rightful, valid
iuvenilis juvenile *(adjective)*, juvenile *(noun)*

J

jab jostle *(bump into)*
jabber jargon *(unintelligible language)*, prattle

jabbering loquacious
jack up elevate
jackpot prize
jactation SEE MAIN ENTRY
jactitation jactation, rodomontade
jaculate impel, launch *(project)*, precipitate *(throw down violently)*, send
jaggedness irregularity
jail arrest *(apprehend)*, captivity, capture, cell, commit *(institutionalize)*, confine, constrain *(imprison)*, contain *(restrain)*, detain *(hold in custody)*, imprison, lock, penitentiary, prison, reformatory, restrain, seize *(apprehend)*. SEE MAIN ENTRY
jail inmate convict
jailbreak SEE MAIN ENTRY
jailed arrested *(apprehended)*, in custody
jailed person prisoner
jailer custodian *(warden)*, warden
jailhouse cell, penitentiary
jailing commitment *(confinement)*
jam block, imbroglio, impact
jam-packed replete
jammed inextricable, replete
jangle altercation, brawl *(noun)*, brawl *(verb)*, controversy *(argument)*, fracas, fray, noise
jangling altercation
jape SEE MAIN ENTRY
jar agitate *(perturb)*, bicker, collision *(accident)*, discompose, fracas, irritate, jostle *(bump into)*, perturb, strike *(collide)*
jargon language, phraseology. SEE MAIN ENTRY
jarring inapplicable, inapposite, inapt, incongruous, inconsistent, inept *(inappropriate)*, repugnant *(incompatible)*
jaundice bias, intolerance, predetermination, prejudice *(influence)*
jaundiced bilious, dyseptic, one-sided, parochial, partial *(biased)*, unequal *(unjust)*, unfair, unjust
jaunt perambulate
jaunty resilient
jealous resentful, suspicious *(distrustful)*. SEE MAIN ENTRY
jealousy resentment
jeer disdain, disparage, flout, hector, jape, mock *(deride)*, reject, ridicule. SEE MAIN ENTRY
jeering disdainful
jejune deficient, irksome, nugatory, otiose, pedestrian, prosaic, puerile, stale, unproductive. SEE MAIN ENTRY
jellification congealment
jeopardize compromise *(endanger)*, endanger, expose. SEE MAIN ENTRY
jeopardous noxious, precarious
jeopardy danger, hazard, peril, predicament, risk, threat, venture. SEE MAIN ENTRY
jest jape
jesting jocular
jet emit, outburst, outflow
jettison abandon *(relinquish)*, disown *(refuse to acknowledge)*, eject *(expel)*, evict, reject, relinquish. SEE MAIN ENTRY
jettisoned derelict *(abandoned)*
jibe comport *(agree with)*, concur *(agree)*
jilt rebuff, reject, spurn
jingoism intolerance
jitteriness trepidation
job appointment *(position)*, burden, business *(occupation)*, calling, career, employment, enterprise *(undertaking)*, labor *(work)*, livelihood, mission, occupation *(vocation)*, office, part *(role)*, position *(business status)*, post, profession *(vocation)*, project, province, pursuit *(occupation)*,

role, trade *(occupation)*, undertaking *(enterprise)*, work *(employment)*. SEE MAIN ENTRY
job action strike
job holder incumbent
job seeker candidate
jobation reprimand, reproach
jobber dealer
jobbery abuse *(corrupt practice)*, artifice, bribery, corruption, crime, gratuity *(bribe)*, improbity, pettifoggery
jobbing commercial
jobholder employee
jobless idle, otiose, unemployed
jockey maneuver
jocose jocular
jocular SEE MAIN ENTRY
jocularity life *(vitality)*
jocund jocular
jocundity life *(vitality)*
jog impetus, reminder, stimulate
jog the memory remind
join abut, accompany, adhere *(fasten)*, affiliate, affix, aggregate, amalgamate, annex *(add)*, append, bond *(hold together)*, border *(approach)*, border *(bound)*, cement, collect *(gather)*, commingle, congregate, connect *(join together)*, consolidate *(unite)*, conspire, contact *(touch)*, correspond *(be equivalent)*, enroll, espouse, federalize *(associate)*, federate, incorporate *(include)*, juxtapose, lock, meet, merge, organize *(unionize)*, participate, register, unite. SEE MAIN ENTRY
join as a third party implead
join battle with engage *(involve)*
join forces affiliate, combine *(act in concert)*, concur *(agree)*, connive, consolidate *(unite)*, conspire, cooperate, federalize *(associate)*, federate, involve *(participate)*, merge, participate, unite
join forces with consolidate *(unite)*
join in concur *(agree)*, contribute *(assist)*, cooperate, involve *(participate)*, participate
join in a compact confirm
join in a conversation discuss, speak
join in partnership with participate
join issue bicker, collide *(clash)*, discord, oppose, reason *(persuade)*, rebut, respond
join the majority conform
join together affiliate, concur *(agree)*, conjoin, converge, desegregate, organize *(unionize)*
join with combine *(act in concert)*, concur *(agree)*, connive, cooperate
joinder attachment *(act of affixing)*, merger. SEE MAIN ENTRY
joinder of a party SEE MAIN ENTRY
joined additional, associated, attached *(annexed)*, coadunate, collective, composite, concerted, concurrent *(united)*, conjoint, contiguous, correlative, inextricable, inseparable, interrelated, joint, promiscuous
joined in a union federal
joined together conjoint
joined with affiliated
joiner connection *(fastening)*
joining accession *(annexation)*, addition, attachment *(act of affixing)*, coalescence, combination, contact *(touching)*, joinder, marriage *(intimate relationship)*, matrimony, meeting *(encounter)*, union *(unity)*
joining place intersection
joining road crossroad *(intersection)*
joint common *(shared)*, concerted, concomitant, concordant, concurrent *(united)*, conjoint, connection *(fastening)*,

consensual, federal, harmonious, intersection, mutual (collective). SEE MAIN ENTRY

joint action concert, cooperative

joint agreement mutual understanding

joint and several in solido. SEE MAIN ENTRY

joint and several liability SEE MAIN ENTRY

joint concern cartel, coalition, company (enterprise), corporation, firm, merger, organization (association), pool

joint custody SEE MAIN ENTRY

joint discussion panel (discussion group)

joint effect synergy

joint effort coaction, collusion, conformity (agreement), conjunction, connivance, conspiracy

joint endeavor coalition

joint enterprise affiliation (connectedness), association (connection)

joint interest partnership

joint operation concert, cooperative

joint ownership pool

joint pact mutual understanding

joint participation coaction

joint planning collusion, conformity (agreement), connivance, conspiracy

joint possession cooperative, pool

joint-operator coactor

jointure dower

joke jape

joke about mock (deride)

joking jocular

jolly jocular

jolt bombshell, collision (accident), discompose, impetus, jostle (bump into), perturb, strike (collide)

joshing jocular

jot iota, minimum

jot down enter (record), note (record), record, set down

jottings script

journal calendar (record of yearly periods), dossier, record, register. SEE MAIN ENTRY

journalistic writers press

journalists press

journalize record

journey move (alter position), perambulate, quest

journey's end destination

journeying itinerant, moving (in motion)

journeyman artisan, practitioner

joust compete, fight (battle)

jovial jocular

joviality life (vitality)

joyful ecstatic, felicitous, jocular

joyless bleak (not favorable), bleak (severely simple), despondent, disconsolate, grave (solemn), lamentable, lugubrious, pessimistic

joylessness damper (depressant), pessimism

joyous ecstatic, felicitous, jocular

jubilant ecstatic

jubilee holiday

judge adjudge, adjudicate, arbitrate (adjudge), assess (appraise), bench, censor, conclude (decide), construe (comprehend), criticize (evaluate), decide, decree, deduce, deduct (conclude by reasoning), deem, deliberate, determine, diagnose, discern (discriminate), distinguish, estimate, evaluate, expect (consider probable), find (determine), gauge, guess, hear (give a legal hearing), hold (decide), intercede, jurist, magistrate, measure, opine, presume, presuppose, pronounce (pass judgment), rate, reason (conclude), rebuke, referee, speculate (conjecture), surmise, suspect (think),

try (conduct a trial), umpire, vote. SEE MAIN ENTRY

judge at random guess

judge before hearing prejudge

judge beforehand forejudge, preconceive, prejudge

judge erroneously misjudge

judge from premises infer

judge in advance forejudge, prejudge, presuppose

judge inaccurately misjudge

judge innocent palliate (excuse)

judge the future presage

judge with indulgence excuse

judge with uncertainty guess

judge wrongly misjudge

judged deliberate

judged by comparison comparative

judgelike judicial, juridical

judges tribunal

judge's chamber SEE MAIN ENTRY

judges of the facts jury

judgmatic determinative, discriminating (judicious), judicial, judicious, juridical. SEE MAIN ENTRY

judgment adjudication, alternative (option), apprehension (perception), arbitration, authority (documentation), belief (state of mind), caliber (mental capacity), choice (decision), common sense, concept, conclusion (determination), condemnation (punishment), consideration (contemplation), conviction (finding of guilt), conviction (persuasion), decision (election), decree, deliberation, determination, diagnosis, dialectic, dictate, direction (order), discipline (punishment), edict, estimate (idea), estimation (calculation), experience (background), fiat, finding, holding (ruling of a court), idea, inference, notion, opinion (belief), opinion (judicial decision), outcome, perception, position (point of view), pronouncement, prudence, recommendation, regard (esteem), relief (legal redress), res judicata, result, ruling, sagacity, sense (intelligence), sensibility, standpoint, verdict, vote. SEE MAIN ENTRY

judgment dissolving a marriage divorce

judgment for the defendant as a matter of law nonsuit

judgment of the court declaratory judgment

judgment on facts adjudication, determination, holding (ruling of a court), opinion (judicial decision). SEE MAIN ENTRY

judgment seat bench, court, tribunal

judicable determinable (ascertainable)

judicate adjudge, arbitrate (adjudge)

judication award

judicative judicial, juridical

judicator arbitrator, referee

judicatorial juridical

judicatory bench, board, chamber (body), forensic, forum (court), judicature, judiciary, jural, juridical, licit. SEE MAIN ENTRY

judicature bar (court), bench, council (assembly), forum (court), judgment (formal court decree), judicatory, judiciary. SEE MAIN ENTRY

judicial forensic, jural, juridical, licit, objective, open-minded, politic, unprejudiced. SEE MAIN ENTRY

judicial administrator clerk

judicial antecedent precedent

judicial assembly bench, court

judicial assertion dictum, judgment (formal court decree)

judicial assistant clerk

judicial authorization warrant (judicial writ)

judicial branch chamber (body), judiciary

judicial branch of government judiciary

judicial charge arraignment

judicial command mandate, order (judicial directive)

judicial comment dictum

judicial conclusion finding

judicial contest action (proceeding), case (lawsuit), controversy (lawsuit), lawsuit, suit, trial (legal proceeding). SEE MAIN ENTRY

judicial decision adjudication, award, decree, holding (ruling of a court)

judicial decision establishing a rule authority (documentation)

judicial decree mandate

judicial department chamber (body), judiciary

judicial determination ruling. SEE MAIN ENTRY

judicial examination hearing, voir dire

judicial forum bench, court, judiciary

judicial imperative subpoena

judicial inquiry inquest

judicial instruction order (judicial directive)

judicial investigation hearing

judicial murder capital punishment

judicial order mandate, warrant (judicial writ)

judicial order to refrain from an act injunction

judicial order to search search warrant

judicial outcome finding

judicial precedent authority (documentation)

judicial proceeding action (proceeding). SEE MAIN ENTRY

judicial process search warrant

judicial proclamation ruling

judicial pronouncement ruling

judicial reconsideration review (official reexamination)

judicial recorder clerk

judicial reexamination habeas corpus

judicial remark dictum

judicial reprimand admonition

judicial review SEE MAIN ENTRY

judicial secretary clerk

judicial sentence award

judicial separation of a husband and wife divorce

judicial tribunal bench, court, forum (court)

judicial validation of a will probate

judicial verdict finding

judicially determine adjudge

judiciary bar (court), bench, judicatory, jural, juridical, tribunal. SEE MAIN ENTRY

judicious careful, circumspect, determinative, discreet, impartial, judicial, juridical, nonpartisan, perspicacious, politic, preventive, provident (showing foresight), prudent, rational, reasonable (fair), reasonable (rational), sane, sapient, sensible, solid (sound), vigilant. SEE MAIN ENTRY

judiciousness discretion (quality of being discreet), discrimination (good judgment), judgment (discernment), prudence, reason (sound judgment), sense (intelligence). SEE MAIN ENTRY

judicium bench

jugglery deceit, machination, pettifoggery, ruse, subterfuge

juggling pettifoggery, prestidigitation

juicy pithy

jumble complex *(entanglement)*, confuse *(bewilder)*, confuse *(create disorder)*, discompose, entanglement *(confusion)*, jargon *(unintelligible language)*, melange, misinterpret, misunderstand, muddle, pandemonium, shambles, turmoil

jumbled complex, disconnected, disjointed, disordered, labyrinthine, miscellaneous, promiscuous

jump edge *(advantage)*, transition

jump in prices inflation *(decrease in value of currency)*

jump to a conclusion forejudge, preconceive, predetermine, prejudge, presuppose

jump to conclusions presume

jumpiness trepidation

jumping off point SEE MAIN ENTRY

junction adhesion *(affixing)*, attachment *(act of affixing)*, chain *(nexus)*, coalescence, coalition, collusion, combination, conjunction, connection *(abutment)*, connection *(fastening)*, connivance, consolidation, contact *(touching)*, crossroad *(intersection)*, intersection, joinder, meeting *(encounter)*, union *(unity)*. SEE MAIN ENTRY

junction of bodies contact *(touching)*

juncture case *(set of circumstances)*, connection *(fastening)*, contact *(touching)*, crossroad *(turning point)*, intersection, meeting *(encounter)*, occasion, period, point *(period of time)*, posture *(situation)*, situation. SEE MAIN ENTRY

jungle imbroglio

junior adolescent, inferior *(lower in position)*, juvenile, minor *(adjective)*, minor *(noun)*, secondary, subaltern, subordinate, subservient

juniority adolescence

junta cabal

jural forensic, juridical. SEE MAIN ENTRY

jurat juror. SEE MAIN ENTRY

jurgium brawl

juridic forensic, juridical, lawful, licit

juridical civic, forensic, judicial, jural. SEE MAIN ENTRY

jurisconsult advocate *(counselor)*, attorney, barrister, counsel, counselor, esquire, jurist, lawyer

jurisdiction agency *(legal relationship)*, ambit, area *(province)*, authority *(right)*, bailiwick, capacity *(authority)*, capacity *(sphere)*, charge *(custody)*, circuit, control *(supervision)*, custody *(supervision)*, department, direction *(guidance)*, domain *(sphere of influence)*, dominion *(supreme authority)*, generalship, government *(administration)*, judicature, occupation *(possession)*, power, predominance, primacy, province, realm, supervision, venue. SEE MAIN ENTRY

jurisdiction of the court judicature

jurisdictional forensic, justiciable

jurisdictional amount SEE MAIN ENTRY

jurisdictionally sound cognizable

jurisprudence law. SEE MAIN ENTRY

jurisprudent attorney, barrister, esquire, jurist, lawyer, licit

jurisprudential forensic, juridical, licit

jurist advocate *(counselor)*, attorney, barrister, counsel, counselor, esquire, judge, lawyer, magistrate. SEE MAIN ENTRY

juristic forensic, judicial, jural, juridical, legitimate *(rightful)*

juristical judicial

jurists bar *(body of lawyers)*

juror SEE MAIN ENTRY

jurors array *(jury)*

jury panel *(jurors)*. SEE MAIN ENTRY

jury charge instruction *(direction)*

jury deliberations SEE MAIN ENTRY

juryman juror

jurymen array *(jury)*, jury

jussive decretal

just bona fide, condign, conscientious, equal, equitable, ethical, evenhanded, honest, impartial, incorruptible, judicial, juridical, licit, mere, meritorious, moral, objective, open-minded, reasonable *(fair)*, rightful, solid *(sound)*, suitable, unbiased, unprejudiced, upright. SEE MAIN ENTRY

just as quasi

just begun inchoate

just cause compurgation

just claim cause of action, droit, right *(entitlement)*. SEE MAIN ENTRY

just compensation damages, out of pocket

just dealing fairness

just deserts discipline *(punishment)*

just division apportionment

just estimation appreciation *(perception)*

just the same as is

justice bench, condemnation *(punishment)*, court, disinterest *(lack of prejudice)*, equity *(justice)*, ethics, fairness, judge, jurist, magistrate, moderation, objectivity, principle *(virtue)*, probity, rectitude, retribution, right *(righteousness)*. SEE MAIN ENTRY

justice as distinguished from conformity to enactments or statutes equity *(justice)*

justice ascertained by natural reason equity *(justice)*

justice seat bench, court

justice under the law equity *(justice)*

justicer judge

justices judiciary

justiciable actionable, blameworthy, litigable, triable. SEE MAIN ENTRY

justifiability admissibility, legitimacy

justifiable admissible, allowable, defensible, juridical, just, pardonable, plausible, rational, reasonable *(rational)*, rightful, sensible, tenable. SEE MAIN ENTRY

justifiable excuse alibi

justification alibi, basis, capacity *(authority)*, compurgation, defense, determinant, excuse, explanation, ground, precedent, pretext, right *(entitlement)*, support *(corroboration)*. SEE MAIN ENTRY

justificatory palliative *(excusing)*

justificatory excuse alibi

justified allowed, clear *(free from criminal charges)*, condign, defensible, entitled, juridical, justifiable, pardonable, sound. SEE MAIN ENTRY

justifier advocate *(counselor)*, apologist, proponent

justify bear *(support)*, corroborate, defend, document, exculpate, excuse, extenuate, maintain *(sustain)*, palliate *(excuse)*, rationalize, reason *(persuade)*, sustain *(confirm)*, uphold, vindicate. SEE MAIN ENTRY

justifying palliative *(excusing)*

justly fairly *(impartially)*

justly claimable payable

justly complaining aggrieved *(victimized)*

justly responsible liable

justness candor *(impartiality)*, disinterest *(lack of prejudice)*, equity *(justice)*, fairness, integrity, justice, objectivity, propriety *(appropriateness)*, rectitude, right *(righteousness)*

jut project *(extend beyond)*

jut out project *(extend beyond)*

jutting prominent

juvenal juvenile

juvenile adolescent, child, infant, jejune *(lacking maturity)*, minor, puerile. SEE MAIN ENTRY

juvenile charge dependent

juvenile delinquent criminal. SEE MAIN ENTRY

juvenility adolescence

juxtapose adjoin, border *(approach)*, border *(bound)*, compare. SEE MAIN ENTRY

juxtaposed adjacent, proximate

juxtaposit adjoin, border *(approach)*, border *(bound)*

juxtaposition collation, connection *(abutment)*, contact *(touching)*, propinquity *(proximity)*. SEE MAIN ENTRY

juxtapositional immediate *(not distant)*

K

kaleidoscopic complex, protean

keen acute, bitter *(penetrating)*, close *(rigorous)*, cognizant, discriminating *(judicious)*, eager, fervent, incisive, intense, perceptive, perspicacious, ready *(willing)*, receptive, responsive, sapient, sedulous, sensitive *(discerning)*, sly, solicitous, subtle *(refined)*, trenchant, zealous. SEE MAIN ENTRY

keen sight perception

keen-eyed perspicacious

keen-sighted perspicacious

keen-witted perspicacious

keeness comprehension, perception

keenly aware vigilant

keenly sensitive acute

keenness insight, intelligence *(intellect)*, judgment *(discernment)*, predisposition, rigor, sagacity, sensibility

keensightedness sagacity

keep accompany, concern *(care)*, conserve, constrict *(inhibit)*, continue *(persevere)*, detain *(restrain)*, endure *(last)*, fulfill, fund, harbor, hoard, hold *(possess)*, jail, livelihood, obey, observe *(obey)*, occupy *(take possession)*, own, perform *(adhere to)*, possess, preserve, prolong, protect, remain *(continue)*, reserve, restrain, retain *(employ)*, retain *(keep in possession)*, save *(hold back)*, store, subsidize, sustenance, uphold, withhold. SEE MAIN ENTRY

keep a date rendezvous

keep a secret cloak

keep accounts note *(record)*, record

keep alive keep *(shelter)*, maintain *(carry on)*, perpetuate, preserve

keep aloof elude, estrange

keep aloof from forgo

keep an account deposit *(submit to a bank)*

keep an appointment rendezvous

keep an eye on observe *(watch)*, patrol

keep an eye upon survey *(examine)*

keep apart dichotomize, dissociate, estrange, insulate, isolate, part *(separate)*, seclude, separate, sever, withdraw

keep as captive constrain *(imprison)*, imprison

keep as one's own hold *(possess)*

keep at persist

keep at a distance eschew, estrange, rebuff

keep at a distance from avoid *(evade)*

keep at bay parry, repel *(drive back)*, repulse, stave, stem *(check)*

keep away   eschew, parry
keep away from   avoid (evade), forgo, shirk, shun
keep back   arrest (stop), check (restrain), constrain (restrain), constrict (inhibit), delay, detain (restrain), deter, discourage, encumber (hinder), forbear, hinder, hoard, impede, reserve, stall, strangle, suppress, withhold
keep behind bars   enclose, imprison
keep busy   occupy (engage)
keep clandestine   blind (obscure), conceal, enshroud, plant (covertly place)
keep clear of   avoid (evade), eschew, evade (elude), parry, shun
keep company with   accompany
keep count   enumerate
keep count of   poll
keep down   extinguish, repress, strangle, subject, suppress
keep driving   persevere
keep entirely to oneself   monopolize
keep faith   adhere (maintain loyalty)
keep for   hold (possess)
keep for future action   postpone
keep from   conceal, deny (refuse to grant), deter, discourage, forbear, forgo, prevent, refrain
keep from being successful   foil
keep from contact with others   isolate
keep from danger   ensconce
keep from entering   exclude
keep from happening   enjoin, prevent
keep from harm   ensure, preserve
keep from loss   conserve
keep from notice   enshroud
keep from proceeding   delay
keep from public view   seal (close)
keep from sight   camouflage
keep from view   camouflage, enshroud
keep going   adhere (persist), keep (continue), maintain (carry on), persevere, proceed (go forward), progress, remain (continue), sustain (prolong). SEE MAIN ENTRY
keep guard   patrol, police
keep guarded   ensconce
keep hidden   cloak, ensconce, enshroud, plant (covertly place)
keep hold of   occupy (take possession), retain (keep in possession)
keep house   inhabit, occupy (take possession)
keep in   circumscribe (surround by boundary), contain (enclose), enclose, encompass (surround), immure, inhibit, repress, stem (check), withhold
keep in bounds   condemn (ban), enjoin
keep in captivity   contain (restrain), immure, imprison
keep in check   balk, constrain (restrain), contain (restrain), control (restrain), fetter, immure, impede, repress
keep in confidence   seal (close)
keep in countenance   coax
keep in custody   confine, constrain (imprison), detain (hold in custody), enclose, immure, imprison. SEE MAIN ENTRY
keep in detention   constrain (imprison), detain (hold in custody), immure, imprison, seclude
keep in existence   conserve, perpetuate
keep in hand   hold (possess)
keep in ignorance   cloak
keep in mind   recall (remember), remember, retain (keep in possession)
keep in order   handle (manage), manage, police, rule (govern), superintend

keep in pay   retain (employ)
keep in perspective   discern (discriminate). SEE MAIN ENTRY
keep in private   seclude
keep in readiness   hold (possess)
keep in reserve   fund, garner, hoard, hold (possess), reserve, set aside (reserve)
keep in safety   cover (guard)
keep in secrecy   seal (close)
keep in service   employ (engage services)
keep in sight   monitor, observe (watch), regard (pay attention)
keep in solitude   isolate
keep in the dark   camouflage, obscure
keep in the shade   camouflage
keep in view   monitor, observe (watch), patrol, police
keep intact   preserve
keep moving   proceed (go forward), progress
keep off   deter, parry, stave
keep on   adhere (persist), bear (tolerate), hold (possess), maintain (carry on), persevere, persist, pursue (carry on), recur, remain (continue), stay (continue)
keep on hand   reserve
keep one guessing   obfuscate
keep one waiting   delay, hold up (delay), procrastinate
keep one's countenance   bear (tolerate)
keep one's distance   shun
keep one's word   perform (adhere to)
keep order   handle (manage), police, preside
keep orderly   police
keep out   bar (exclude), clog, condemn (ban), eliminate (exclude), exclude, reject, screen (select), seclude
keep out of harm's way   beware
keep out of sight   blind (obscure), conceal, cover (conceal), elude, enshroud, harbor, hide, lurk, suppress
keep out of the way   eschew
keep out of view   camouflage, hide
keep pace with   concur (coexist), reach
keep pending   adjourn, continue (adjourn), defer (put off), delay, hold up (delay)
keep posted   annunciate, convey (communicate), inform (notify)
keep prepared   hold (possess)
keep prisoner   constrain (imprison), contain (restrain), immure
keep quiet   rest (cease from action)
keep safe   conserve, ensconce, ensure, harbor, keep (shelter), preserve, save (conserve)
keep safe from harm   cover (guard)
keep score   poll
keep secret   camouflage, cloak, conceal, ensconce, harbor, hide, plant (covertly place), suppress, withhold
keep sound   preserve
keep subjugated   dominate
keep the peace.   SEE MAIN ENTRY
keep to   conform
keep to oneself   conceal, hide
keep under arrest   contain (restrain), detain (hold in custody), immure, imprison
keep under close watch   cover (guard)
keep under control   check (restrain), confine, contain (restrain), control (restrain), detain (hold in custody), detain (restrain), handle (manage), police, repress, restrain
keep under cover   ensconce, enshroud, hide, preserve

keep under surveillance   examine (study), scrutinize
keep undercover   cloak
keep underground   conceal
keep unimpaired   conserve
keep up   last, maintain (carry on), persevere, preserve, pursue (carry on), sustain (prolong)
keep vigil   patrol, police
keep watch   check (inspect), patrol, police, survey (examine)
keep watch over   preserve
keep within bounds   censor, condemn (ban), confine, detain (hold in custody), detain (restrain), immure, moderate (temper), restrain, trammel
keep within limits   curb, qualify (condition), restrict
keeper   caretaker (one caring for property), custodian (protector), guardian, holder
keeping   administration, charge (custody), compliance, conservation, constraint (imprisonment), control (supervision), custody (supervision), detention, retention, safekeeping, trust (custody), ward
keeping back   detention
keeping in   detention
keeping in custody   detention
keepsake   remembrance (commemoration), reminder, token
ken   apprehend (perceive), cognition, comprehend (understand), construe (comprehend), digest (comprehend), experience (background), find (discover), insight, knowledge (awareness), knowledge (learning), perceive, realization. SEE MAIN ENTRY
kept in custody   arrested (apprehended)
kept in prison   in custody
kept in remembrance   honorary
kept out   ineligible
kernel   main point
key   cardinal (basic), cardinal (outstanding), catchword, central (essential), clue, cornerstone, critical (crucial), explanation, fundamental, gravamen, indispensable, main point, major, material (important), necessary (required), primary, solution (answer), strategic, tip (clue). SEE MAIN ENTRY
key man   chairman, executive. SEE MAIN ENTRY
key person   caretaker (one fulfilling the function of office), executive
key point   landmark (significant change)
key woman   executive
keynote   cornerstone, corpus, highlight, main point
keystone   cornerstone, foundation (basis), gist (ground for a suit), gravamen, main point, mainstay
kick   beat (strike), impetus, spurn
kick out   evict, expel
kickback   graft, gratuity (bribe). SEE MAIN ENTRY
kicker   malcontent
kiddish   puerile
kidnap   abduct, carry away. SEE MAIN ENTRY
kidnapper   criminal
kidnapping   abduction
kill   destroy (efface), dispatch (put to death), eliminate (eradicate), execute (sentence to death), extinguish, prey, remove (eliminate), repress, slay, stifle. SEE MAIN ENTRY
kill by suffocation   extinguish
kill time   procrastinate
killer   criminal. SEE MAIN ENTRY

killing aberemurder, assassination, capital punishment, deadly, dispatch *(act of putting to death)*, fatal, homicide, lethal, manslaughter, murder, pernicious, pestilent. SEE MAIN ENTRY

killing with malice aforethought aberemurder

kin descendant, descent *(lineage)*, family *(common ancestry)*, house, kindred, next of kin, relation *(kinship)*, relative. SEE MAIN ENTRY

kind benevolent, blood, character *(personal quality)*, charitable *(lenient)*, class, color *(complexion)*, denomination, favorable *(expressing approval)*, form *(arrangement)*, humane, lenient, magnanimous, manner *(kind)*, philanthropic, propitious, race, style. SEE MAIN ENTRY

kind act favor *(act of kindness)*
kind office benevolence *(act of kindness)*
kind person benefactor, good samaritan, samaritan
kind regard favor *(partiality)*
kind treatment benevolence *(act of kindness)*

kindhearted benevolent, charitable *(lenient)*, humane, lenient, philanthropic, propitious. SEE MAIN ENTRY

kindhearte benevolence *(disposition to do good)*, consideration *(sympathetic regard)*, humanity *(humaneness)*

kindle agitate *(activate)*, burn, create, foment, generate, incite, induce, inspire, make, originate, provoke, spirit, stimulate. SEE MAIN ENTRY

kindle one's wrath incense
kindle wrath pique
kindliness benevolence *(disposition to do good)*, consideration *(sympathetic regard)*, largess *(generosity)*, philanthropy, pity, solace, understanding *(tolerance)*

kindly benevolent, humane, paternal, peaceable, philanthropic, propitious
kindly disposed benevolent
kindness affection, benefit *(conferment)*, benevolence *(disposition to do good)*, charity, clemency, consideration *(sympathetic regard)*, goodwill, help, humanity *(humaneness)*, largess *(generosity)*, lenience, philanthropy. SEE MAIN ENTRY

kindred affiliation *(bloodline)*, affinity *(family ties)*, akin *(related by blood)*, allied, analogous, blood, comparable *(capable of comparison)*, consanguineous, family *(common ancestry)*, house, interrelated, next of kin, propinquity *(kinship)*, related, relation *(kinship)*, relative *(relevant)*, relative, similar. SEE MAIN ENTRY

kindredship kinship, relationship *(family tie)*
kinetic impulsive *(impelling)*, moving *(in motion)*
kinfolk affiliation *(bloodline)*
king SEE MAIN ENTRY
kingdom domain *(sphere of influence)*, realm. SEE MAIN ENTRY
kink quirk *(idiosyncrasy)*, snarl
kinsfolk blood, kindred
kinship affiliation *(bloodline)*, affinity *(family ties)*, ancestry, blood, chain *(nexus)*, community, connection *(relation)*, contact *(association)*, family *(common ancestry)*, filiation, nexus, relationship *(family tie)*, resemblance. SEE MAIN ENTRY
kinsman blood, next of kin, relation *(kinship)*, relative
kinsmen affiliation *(bloodline)*, blood, family *(common ancestry)*, kindred

kinspeople kindred, next of kin
kinswoman blood
kismet predetermination
kith relative
kith and kin origin *(ancestry)*
kithless solitary
kleptomaniac SEE MAIN ENTRY
knack faculty *(ability)*, gift *(flair)*, propensity, skill
knave criminal, hoodlum
knavery artifice, collusion, corruption, deception, dishonesty, evasion, hoax, imposture, improbity, mischief, misdoing, pettifoggery. SEE MAIN ENTRY
knavish artful, deceptive, disreputable, false *(disloyal)*, immoral, iniquitous, lawless, machiavellian, perfidious, recreant, reprobate, tortuous *(corrupt)*, unconscionable
knavishness dishonesty, knavery
kneel to obey
kneeling prostration
knife lancinate, pierce *(lance)*
knifelike mordacious
knit connect *(join together)*, join *(bring together)*, related
knock impinge, jostle *(bump into)*, sully
knock about ill use
knock against collide *(crash against)*, impinge, jostle *(bump into)*
knock down beat *(strike)*. SEE MAIN ENTRY
knock into collide *(crash against)*, strike *(collide)*
knock out of shape mutilate
knot connection *(fastening)*, contort, intertwine, involution, snarl
knots ties
knotted complex, inextricable
knotty problematic, recondite
knotty point enigma
know appreciate *(comprehend)*, comprehend *(understand)*, conceive *(comprehend)*, digest *(comprehend)*, discern *(detect with the senses)*, find *(discover)*, identify, perceive, pierce *(discern)*, read, realize *(understand)*, recognize *(perceive)*, understand. SEE MAIN ENTRY
know again recall *(remember)*, recollect, remember
know by heart recall *(remember)*, remember
know entirely apprehend *(perceive)*
know of apprehend *(perceive)*
know well apprehend *(perceive)*
know-all bigot
know-how experience *(background)*, faculty *(ability)*, knowledge *(awareness)*, knowledge *(learning)*, prowess *(ability)*, science *(technique)*. SEE MAIN ENTRY
know-it-all bigot
knowable appreciable, ascertainable, cognizable, coherent *(clear)*, comprehensible, determinable *(ascertainable)*, discernible, perceivable, perceptible, ponderable, scrutable
knowing certain *(positive)*, cognizant, conscious *(aware)*, discriminating *(judicious)*, expert, familiar *(informed)*, intentional, judicial, learned, literate, omniscient, oracular, perceptive, perspicacious, politic, practiced, proficient, profound *(esoteric)*, qualified *(competent)*, rational, sapient, sciential, sensible, tactical, veteran. SEE MAIN ENTRY
knowing person expert, specialist, veteran
knowingly purposely. SEE MAIN ENTRY
knowledge apprehension *(perception)*,

caliber *(mental capacity)*, certainty, certification *(certainness)*, cognition, comprehension, concept, disclosure *(something disclosed)*, discrimination *(good judgment)*, edification, education, experience *(background)*, information *(knowledge)*, intelligence *(news)*, notification, realization, reason *(sound judgment)*, recognition, science *(study)*, scienter, skill, specialty *(special aptitude)*, understanding *(comprehension)*. SEE MAIN ENTRY
knowledge of facts information *(knowledge)*
knowledge of law jurisprudence
knowledgeable acquainted, acute, cognizant, expert, familiar *(informed)*, informed *(educated)*, knowing, learned, literate, omniscient, sciential, sensible, sophisticated
known apparent *(perceptible)*, cognizable, famous, illustrious, ordinary, outstanding *(prominent)*, prominent, proverbial, renowned, reputable, trite, unmistakable, usual. SEE MAIN ENTRY
known elsewhere as alias
known elsewhere by alias
known elsewhere under the name alias
known facts information *(knowledge)*, intelligence *(news)*
known in advance foreseeable
known name goodwill
known otherwise as alias
known previously as alias
known variously as alias
knuckle under succumb
kudos SEE MAIN ENTRY

L

"*lettre de change*" draft
labefactare invalidate
label brand, brand *(mark)*, call *(title)*, classify, define, denominate, denomination, denote, designation *(naming)*, designation *(symbol)*, device *(distinguishing mark)*, discriminate *(distinguish)*, earmark, heading, identification, identify, nominate, pigeonhole, rubric *(title)*, title *(designation)*, trademark. SEE MAIN ENTRY
label incorrectly mislabel
labeled entitled
labor employment, endeavor *(noun)*, endeavor *(verb)*, industry *(activity)*, job, persevere, struggle, work *(effort)*. SEE MAIN ENTRY
labor at one's vocation practice *(engage in)*
labor dispute strike
labor expense payroll
labor for attempt, pursue *(strive to gain)*, strive
labor in vain failure *(lack of success)*
labor saving economic
labor supply personnel
labor under bear *(tolerate)*
labor under a misapprehension err, miscalculate, misconceive, mistake, misunderstand. SEE MAIN ENTRY
labor under an error miscalculate
labor-saving economical
labor-saving device appliance
laborare labor
labored difficult, elaborate, painstaking, ponderous
laborer artisan, employee
laborers personnel
laboring force personnel
laborious difficult, faithful *(diligent)*,

843

industrious, onerous, operose, oppressive, painful, painstaking, sedulous. SEE MAIN ENTRY

laborious application pursuit *(effort to secure)*

laboriousness effort, industry *(activity)*

labyrinth complex *(entanglement)*, complication, confusion *(ambiguity)*, imbroglio, involution, snarl

labyrinthian labyrinthine, sinuous

labyrinthic labyrinthine

labyrinthine circuitous, complex, devious, difficult, indirect, inextricable, sinuous, tortuous *(bending)*. SEE MAIN ENTRY

lace connect *(join together)*, intertwine

lacerate damage, harrow, lancinate, mutilate, rend, sever

lacerated broken *(fractured)*

laches neglect. SEE MAIN ENTRY

lachrymose disconsolate

lack absence *(omission)*, dearth, defect, deficiency, deficit, delinquency *(shortage)*, disadvantage, failure *(falling short)*, foible, insufficiency, market *(demand)*, need *(deprivation)*, paucity, poverty, privation, require *(need)*, vice. SEE MAIN ENTRY

lack ability SEE MAIN ENTRY

lack belief in mistrust

lack candor feign, palter

lack confidence misdoubt

lack confidence in doubt *(distrust)*, mistrust, suspect *(distrust)*

lack conviction misdoubt

lack faith disbelieve, misdoubt

lack faith in mistrust

lack harmony disaccord, disagree

lack honesty cheat

lack information misunderstand

lack of ability inability

lack of accord discrepancy, inconsistency

lack of activity inertia

lack of agreement discrepancy, exception *(objection)*, incompatibility *(difference)*, incompatibility *(inconsistency)*, nonconformity, paradox

lack of allurement disincentive

lack of appreciation ingratitude

lack of attention disinterest *(lack of interest)*, negligence, res ipsa loquitur

lack of awareness insentience, nescience

lack of belief incredulity

lack of bias objectivity, tolerance

lack of candidness indirection *(deceitfulness)*

lack of capacity incapacity

lack of care disregard *(unconcern)*, inconsideration

lack of caution inconsideration

lack of certainty cloud *(suspicion)*, indecision, misgiving, qualm. SEE MAIN ENTRY

lack of certitude doubt *(indecision)*

lack of charm disincentive

lack of circumspection indiscretion

lack of clarity incoherence

lack of clearness confusion *(ambiguity)*

lack of competence inability

lack of complaint resignation *(passive acceptance)*

lack of comprehension insentience

lack of concern disinterest *(lack of interest)*

lack of concert discrepancy

lack of concord argument *(contention)*, contravention, controversy *(argument)*, discord

lack of confidence cloud *(suspicion)*, discredit, doubt *(indecision)*, doubt *(suspicion)*, misgiving, qualm. SEE MAIN ENTRY

lack of conformity discrepancy, exception *(objection)*

lack of congruence discrepancy

lack of congruity discrepancy

lack of connection difference

lack of conscience bad faith, corruption, dishonesty, dishonor *(shame)*, improbity, indirection *(deceitfulness)*

lack of consideration disregard *(unconcern)*, disrespect, inconsideration, indiscretion, ingratitude

lack of consonance discrepancy, incongruity

lack of control laxity. SEE MAIN ENTRY

lack of conviction doubt *(indecision)*, qualm

lack of corruption fairness

lack of courteousness disrespect

lack of courtesy disrespect

lack of decision indecision

lack of depth immateriality

lack of desire disincentive

lack of dexterity disqualification *(factor that disqualifies)*

lack of diligence laches, negligence

lack of discipline rebellion

lack of doubt credulity

lack of dubiety credulity

lack of dubiousness credulity

lack of due process lynch law

lack of education ignorance

lack of enthusiasm pessimism

lack of enticement disincentive

lack of equality inequality

lack of esteem discredit

lack of excess moderation

lack of expectation pessimism

lack of faith cloud *(suspicion)*, doubt *(indecision)*, doubt *(suspicion)*, incredulity, infidelity, suspicion *(mistrust)*

lack of feeling brutality

lack of fidelity bad faith, disloyalty

lack of fitness incapacity

lack of force impuissance

lack of funds failure *(bankruptcy)*

lack of good taste impropriety

lack of gratitude ingratitude

lack of harmony dissension, dissent *(difference of opinion)*, impugnation, incompatibility *(inconsistency)*, incongruity, paradox

lack of honesty dishonesty

lack of honor dishonor *(shame)*

lack of impetus disincentive

lack of incentive disincentive

lack of inducement disincentive

lack of integrity bad repute, dishonesty, improbity

lack of interest disregard *(unconcern)*, laxity

lack of jaundice objectivity

lack of judgment indiscretion

lack of justice lynch law

lack of knowledge ignorance, insentience, nescience

lack of learning ignorance, nescience

lack of legal sanction lynch law

lack of loyalty disloyalty, infidelity

lack of luxury austerity

lack of maintenance disrepair

lack of might impuissance

lack of motion inertia

lack of motivation disincentive

lack of movement inertia

lack of observation disregard *(unconcern)*

lack of order irregularity, pandemonium

lack of perception insentience

lack of personal jurisdiction SEE MAIN ENTRY

lack of piety blasphemy

lack of politeness disrespect

lack of possibility impossibility

lack of potentiality impossibility

lack of power impotence, impuissance, inability, incapacity, inefficacy

lack of prejudice fairness, objectivity, understanding *(tolerance)*

lack of principle bad faith, corruption, dishonesty, dishonor *(shame)*, improbity, knavery

lack of probity bad faith, corruption, dishonesty, dishonor *(shame)*, fraud, indirection *(deceitfulness)*, knavery

lack of proficiency disqualification *(factor that disqualifies)*

lack of propriety irregularity

lack of protection danger

lack of qualification disqualification *(factor that disqualifies)*

lack of regular order disorder *(lack of order)*

lack of relation disparity

lack of resemblance difference, discrepancy

lack of resistance resignation *(passive acceptance)*

lack of respect disrespect, ignominy, inconsideration

lack of reverence blasphemy, inconsideration

lack of safety danger

lack of skepticism credulity

lack of sophistication credulity

lack of sound silence

lack of spirit damper *(depressant)*

lack of stimulus disincentive

lack of strength fault *(weakness)*, impotence, impuissance, inefficacy, languor

lack of strictness lenience

lack of subject matter SEE MAIN ENTRY

lack of substance immateriality, impalpability

lack of suspicion credulity

lack of symmetry disparity, inequality, irregularity

lack of temptation disincentive

lack of thoroughness laxity

lack of toleration intolerance

lack of trust doubt *(suspicion)*, suspicion *(mistrust)*

lack of understanding opacity

lack of vigor impuissance

lack of warmth damper *(depressant)*

lack of warning surprise

lack resemblance differ *(vary)*

lack self-control carouse, overindulge

lack trust in mistrust

lackadaisical careless, dilatory, indolent, languid, lax, lifeless *(dull)*, otiose, phlegmatic, remiss, slipshod

lacking defective, deficient, delinquent *(overdue)*, devoid, essential *(required)*, faulty, imperfect, inadept, inadequate, insufficient, nonsubstantial *(not sufficient)*, paltry, peccable, perfunctory, save, void *(empty)*

lacking accord inconsistent

lacking activity stagnant

lacking agreement incongruous

lacking authority invalid

lacking caution imprudent

lacking clarity indistinct, nebulous, oblique *(evasive)*, opaque

lacking clearness ambiguous

lacking confidence hesitant
lacking content vacuous
lacking continuity desultory
lacking decency profligate (corrupt)
lacking dexterity inept (incompetent)
lacking dexterousness inept (incompetent)
lacking discretion ill-judged, injudicious
lacking elegance inelegant
lacking enthusiasm nonchalant
lacking experience inexperienced
lacking feeling insusceptible (uncaring)
lacking firmness insubstantial
lacking force invalid
lacking foresight improvident
lacking frankness disingenuous
lacking funds destitute, insolvent
lacking good taste inelegant
lacking grace inelegant
lacking harmony incongruous, inconsistent
lacking importance inapposite
lacking in quality poor (inferior in quality)
lacking individuality sequacious
lacking interest nonchalant
lacking judgment imprudent
lacking morals immoral
lacking nothing gross (total)
lacking order disjointed
lacking precision indistinct
lacking prejudice impartial
lacking principle profligate (corrupt)
lacking proficiency inexperienced
lacking proportion disproportionate
lacking prudence imprudent
lacking qualification incompetent
lacking refinement inelegant
lacking relevance inapposite
lacking remorse remorseless
lacking respect presumptuous
lacking self-confidence diffident
lacking shame profligate (corrupt)
lacking skill inept (incompetent), inexperienced
lacking stability insecure
lacking strength invalid
lacking substance insubstantial
lacking truth mendacious
lacking vigor indolent
lacking warmth nonchalant
lacking worth unworthy
lackluster inexpressive, lifeless (dull)
laconic brief, compact (pithy), concise, inarticulate, noncommittal, pithy, sententious, succinct, taciturn, unresponsive. SEE MAIN ENTRY
lactare dupe
lacuna hiatus, split
lade encumber (hinder), load
laden full, replete
lading cargo, freight
lading of a ship cargo
laedere harm, offend (insult)
lag delay, pause, procrastinate, stall. SEE MAIN ENTRY
laggard disinclined, indolent, lifeless (dull), otiose, truant
laggardness laches
lagging late (tardy), otiose
lagniappe contribution (donation), grant
laic civil (public), layman, profane
laical civil (public), profane
laid situated
laid bare naked (lacking embellishment)
laid down positive (prescribed)
laissez faire SEE MAIN ENTRY
lakeside littoral

lambaste beat (strike)
lamblike passive, patient, peaceable, pliable
lame defective, disable, imperfect, inadept, ineffective, ineffectual, insubstantial, maim, nonsubstantial (not sturdy), otiose, unable, unsatisfactory
lamed marred
lament deplore, languish, outcry, plaint, regret, repent. SEE MAIN ENTRY
lament with sympathize
lamenta plaint
lamentabilis lamentable
lamentable deplorable, gross (flagrant), regrettable. SEE MAIN ENTRY
lamentation disapprobation, plaint
lamentative querulous
lamenting disconsolate, querulous, remorseful, repentant
laming detriment
lampoon caricature, disparage, jape, mock (deride), parody, pillory, travesty
lampoonery ridicule
lance enter (penetrate), lancinate, launch (project), penetrate, split
lancinate harrow, rend. SEE MAIN ENTRY
land alight, circuit, curtilage, demesne, domain (land owned), fee (estate), freehold, holding (property owned), immovable, parcel, premises (buildings), property (land), real estate, realm, realty, region, territory. SEE MAIN ENTRY
land a blow beat (strike)
land and buildings estate (property)
land developer developer
land held by lease leasehold
land leased leasehold
landlocked SEE MAIN ENTRY
land owned realty
land revenue rent
landed proprietary
landed estate demesne, fee (estate), freehold, holding (property owned), real estate
landed interests property (land)
landed property demesne, fee (estate), freehold, property (land)
landed proprietor landowner
landholder landowner, tenant. SEE MAIN ENTRY
landing haven
landlord landholder, landowner, lessor, proprietor. SEE MAIN ENTRY
landmark cornerstone, crossroad (turning point), indicant, indicator. SEE MAIN ENTRY
landowner landholder, proprietor, tenant. SEE MAIN ENTRY
lands estate (property), fee (estate)
landscape scene
landslide (avalanche) SEE MAIN ENTRY
lane causeway, way (channel)
langour disinterest (lack of interest)
language discourse, phraseology, rhetoric (skilled speech), speech. SEE MAIN ENTRY
language of a particular profession jargon (technical language)
languens languid
languere languish
languescere languish
languid inactive, indolent, insipid, lifeless (dull), phlegmatic, powerless, torpid. SEE MAIN ENTRY
languidness disinterest (lack of interest), sloth
languish decay, degenerate, suffer (sustain loss). SEE MAIN ENTRY
languishing disconsolate, powerless

languor inaction, inertia. SEE MAIN ENTRY
languor languor
languorous languid, otiose, passive, phlegmatic, torpid
languourness lifeless (dull)
laniena shambles
lap embrace (encircle)
lap over overlap
lapidified ossified
lapis landmark (conspicuous object)
lapse abeyance, cease, cessation (interlude), cloture, decline (fall), default, degenerate, descent (declination), deteriorate, error, expire, halt, hiatus, interval, misdeed, nonpayment, oversight (carelessness), pendency, recrudescence, relapse, remission, respite (interval of rest), revert, stop, subside. SEE MAIN ENTRY
lapse in conduct delinquency (failure of duty)
lapse in judgment SEE MAIN ENTRY
lapse in time SEE MAIN ENTRY
lapsing regressive
lapsus lapse (expiration)
larcener burglar, hoodlum
larcenist hoodlum
larcenous SEE MAIN ENTRY
larceny burglary, conversion (misappropriation), embezzlement, housebreaking, misappropriation, theft. SEE MAIN ENTRY
larceny by force robbery
lard meliorate
lares household (domestic)
large broad, capacious, considerable, copious, extensive, gross (flagrant), major, ponderous, prodigious (enormous), substantial. SEE MAIN ENTRY
large amount plurality, sufficiency
large asset transfer bulk transfer
large enough ample
large number plurality, quantity
large quantity plurality
large scale far reaching
large undertaking campaign
large-scale broad, extensive
largehearted magnanimous
largeness capacity (maximum), degree (magnitude), latitude, mass (weight), measurement
larger number majority (greater part)
larger part majority (greater part)
largess benefit (conferment), bounty, consideration (recompense), donation, grant, philanthropy. SEE MAIN ENTRY
largesse contribution (donation), grant
largest part generality (bulk)
largiri bestow
largitas bounty
largitio largess (generosity)
larrup lash (strike)
lascivious dissolute, lecherous, lewd, licentious, obscene, prurient, salacious, scurrilous, suggestive (risqué). SEE MAIN ENTRY
lasciviousness debauchery
lascivire frisk
lascivus lascivious, wanton
lash beat (strike), denounce (condemn), handcuff, inveigh, punish, reprehend, reprimand. SEE MAIN ENTRY
lash back recriminate
lashing caustic, obloquy
lassitude inertia, languor, prostration
lassus languid
last continue (persevere), definitive, exist, extreme (last), final, keep (continue), persevere, persist, remain (continue), remain

(stay), resist *(withstand)*, stay *(continue)*, subsist, ultimate, withstand. SEE MAIN ENTRY.

last act   denouement

last minute   dilatory

last minute need   emergency

last of a series   end *(termination)*

last offer   ultimatum

last part   close *(conclusion)*, end *(termination)*

last stage   close *(conclusion)*, conclusion *(outcome)*

last stop   destination

lasting   chronic, constant, continuance, durable, indelible, indestructible, infallible, infinite, infrangible, irreversible, irrevocable, live *(existing)*, noncancellable, permanent, perpetual, persistent, solid *(sound)*, stable, standing, steadfast, strong. SEE MAIN ENTRY.

lasting a very short time   ephemeral

lasting period   duration

lasting reminder   monument

lastingness   indestructibility, life *(period of existence)*, longevity

latch   adhere *(fasten)*, shut

late   back *(in arrears)*, deceased, dilatory, former, lifeless *(dead)*, overdue, prior, remiss. SEE MAIN ENTRY.

late patens   comprehensive

late payment   delinquency *(shortage)*

latebra   evasion, subterfuge

lately   recent

latency   cessation *(interlude)*, inaction. SEE MAIN ENTRY.

lateness   delay

latent   blind *(concealed)*, covert, dormant, hidden, inactive, potential, secret, underlying, undisclosed. SEE MAIN ENTRY.

latent power   potential

later   ensuing, ex post facto, future, hereafter *(eventually)*, subsequent, successive, thereafter. SEE MAIN ENTRY.

later generations   posterity

later in time   ex post facto

later meditation   hindsight

later thought   hindsight

laterality   contour *(outline)*

latere   abscond, lurk

latest   contemporary, current, present *(current)*, prevailing *(current)*. SEE MAIN ENTRY.

latitare   lurk

latitude   coverage *(scope)*, freedom, informality, liberty, margin *(spare amount)*, purview, region, scope, space, territory, zone. SEE MAIN ENTRY.

latitudinarian   nonpartisan, open-minded

latitudinous   broad

latitudo   purview

latrocinium   robbery

latter   before mentioned, subsequent

latter day   current

latus   broad, extensive

laud   belaud, honor *(outward respect)*, honor, mention *(tribute)*, recommend

laudabilis   laudable, meritorious

laudable   exemplary, honest, meritorious, moral, professional *(stellar)*, scrupulous, unimpeachable, upright. SEE MAIN ENTRY.

laudatio   recommendation

laudation   doxology, honor *(outward respect)*, mention *(tribute)*, recommendation, reference *(recommendation)*, respect. SEE MAIN ENTRY.

laudatory   favorable *(expressing approval)*, meritorious

laudatus   laudable

laude dignus   laudable, meritorious

laugh at   disdain, disparage, flout, humili-

ate, jape, jeer, mock *(deride)*, pillory, spurn

laugh-provoking   ludicrous

laughable   ludicrous

laughing   jocular

launch   cast *(throw)*, cause, commence, create, discharge *(shoot)*, embark, generate, impel, incite, initiate, inspire, instate, maintain *(commence)*, originate, precipitate *(throw down violently)*, preface, project *(impel forward)*, send, undertake. SEE MAIN ENTRY.

launch again   renew *(begin again)*

launch an inquiry   SEE MAIN ENTRY.

launching   genesis, installation, nascency, onset *(commencement)*, outset

lavish   bestow, copious, excess, furnish, inordinate, liberal *(generous)*, philanthropic, prodigal, profuse, replete, superfluous, supply. SEE MAIN ENTRY.

lavishment   largess *(generosity)*

lavishness   largess *(generosity)*, philanthropy, waste

law   act *(enactment)*, brevet, canon, constitution, criterion, dictate, edict, enactment, holding *(ruling of a court)*, measure, ordinance, precept, prescription *(directive)*, principle *(axiom)*, regulation *(rule)*, rubric *(authoritative rule)*, rule *(legal dictate)*, statute. SEE MAIN ENTRY.

law and order   peace

law court   bench, judicatory, tribunal. SEE MAIN ENTRY.

law courts   judiciary

law enforcement agency   police

law enforcement agent   district attorney, marshal, peace officer

law enforcement agents   police

law enforcement body   police, posse

law firm   SEE MAIN ENTRY.

law of conduct   principle *(axiom)*

law of the case   holding *(ruling of a court)*. SEE MAIN ENTRY.

law officer   peace officer

law-abiding   clean, ethical, honest, lawful, legitimate *(rightful)*, licit, moral, obedient. SEE MAIN ENTRY.

law-breaker   delinquent

law-breaking   guilt

law-giving   decretal

law-making body   chamber *(body)*, legislature

law-making branch of government   legislature

law-revering   law-abiding

lawbreaker   convict, criminal, embezzler, felon, hoodlum, inmate, malefactor, offender, outlaw, recidivist, thief, vandal, wrongdoer. SEE MAIN ENTRY.

lawbreaker under suspension of sentence   probationer *(released offender)*

lawbreaking   bribery, culpable, delinquency *(misconduct)*, delinquent *(guilty of a misdeed)*, disobedient, disorderly, felonious, illegitimate *(illegal)*, larcenous, lawless, offense, racket, violation

lawful   allowable, allowed, choate lien, civic, clean, de jure, due *(regular)*, forensic, juridical, just, justifiable, legal, legitimate *(rightful)*, licit, permissible, rightful, statutory, unalienable, valid. SEE MAIN ENTRY.

lawful authority   hegemony. SEE MAIN ENTRY.

lawful cause   cause of action

lawful claim   due

lawful possession   dominion *(absolute ownership)*, interest *(ownership)*. SEE MAIN ENTRY.

lawful power   force *(legal efficacy)*. SEE MAIN ENTRY.

lawful vigor   force *(legal efficacy)*

lawfully   de jure, fairly *(impartially)*. SEE MAIN ENTRY.

lawfully sufficient   prima facie *(legally sufficient)*

lawfulness   legality, legitimacy, validity. SEE MAIN ENTRY.

lawgiver   lawmaker, legislator, politician

lawgivers   government *(political administration)*, legislature

lawgiving   legislative

lawless   broken *(unfulfilled)*, culpable, disobedient, disordered, disorderly, felonious, illegal, illicit, iniquitous, insubordinate, irresponsible, nonconforming, profligate *(corrupt)*, restive, sinister, uncontrollable, uncurbed, unlawful, unorthodox, unrestrained *(not repressed)*, unruly, unscrupulous, wrongful. SEE MAIN ENTRY.

lawless individual   malefactor, outlaw

lawlessness   anarchy, burglary, criminality, delinquency *(misconduct)*, disorder *(lack of order)*, illegality, irregularity, lynch law, misdeed, misdoing, misrule, offense, racket, revolution, riot, wrong

lawlike   licit

lawmaker   legislator, politician. SEE MAIN ENTRY.

lawmakers   chamber *(body)*, government *(political administration)*, legislature

lawmaking   codification, legislative, regulation *(management)*

laws   code, legislation *(enactments)*

laws of a profession   ethics

lawsuit   action *(proceeding)*, matter *(case)*, proceeding, suit, trial *(legal proceeding)*. SEE MAIN ENTRY.

lawyer   advocate *(counselor)*, attorney, barrister, counsel, counselor, esquire, jurist, practitioner, proctor, representative *(proxy)*. SEE MAIN ENTRY.

lawyers   bar *(body of lawyers)*

lax   careless, cursory, derelict *(negligent)*, improvident, indolent, negligent, peccable, perfunctory, promiscuous, remiss, slipshod, superficial, uncurbed. SEE MAIN ENTRY.

laxare   release

laxity   bad repute, dereliction, disinterest *(lack of interest)*, indifference, informality, laches, neglect, negligence, nonfeasance, nonperformance, omission, oversight *(carelessness)*. SEE MAIN ENTRY.

laxness   dereliction, laches, neglect, negligence, omission, oversight *(carelessness)*, sloth

lay   deposit *(place)*, profane, rest *(be supported by)*

lay a duty   tax *(levy)*

lay a duty on   exact, excise *(levy a tax)*

lay a duty upon   charge *(assess)*

lay a plan   program, scheme

lay a plot   frame *(charge falsely)*

lay a snare for   entrap

lay a trap   inveigle

lay a trap for   ambush, ensnare, entrap

lay a wager   bet, gamble, parlay *(bet)*

lay an embargo on   condemn *(ban)*, stop

lay an impost   assess *(tax)*

lay an information   complain *(charge)*

lay aside   abandon *(relinquish)*, continue *(adjourn)*, defer *(put off)*, dismiss *(put out of consideration)*, exclude, forgo, forswear, hold *(possess)*, hold up *(delay)*, keep *(shelter)*, neglect, postpone, pretermit, quit *(discontinue)*, reject, relinquish, renounce, select, set aside (reserve), suspend. SEE MAIN ENTRY

lay away   hold (possess), keep (shelter), reserve, store

lay bare   bare, betray (disclose), denude, disclose, divest, divulge, evidence, exhibit, expose, inform (betray), manifest, produce (offer to view), profess (avow)

lay before   communicate, offer (propose), pose (propound), proffer, propose, propound, tender

lay before the public   circulate, issue (publish), publish

lay blame upon   complain (charge), denounce (inform against), incriminate, reprehend

lay by   deposit (submit to a bank), hoard

lay charges against   denounce (inform against)

lay claim to   call (demand), exact, excise (levy a tax)

lay down   pose (propound), posit, stipulate. SEE MAIN ENTRY

lay down a plan   devise (invent). prearrange

lay down guide lines   organize (arrange)

lay down limits   demarcate

lay down one's office   demit

lay down the law   instruct (direct). SEE MAIN ENTRY

lay even money   bet

lay eyes on   discern (detect with the senses), observe (watch), pierce (discern)

lay hands on   attack, procure

lay hands upon   obtain

lay hold of   distrain, hijack, impropriate, pirate (take by violence), usurp

lay in ashes   pillage

lay in ruins   pillage, plunder

lay in store   fund, glean, hoard

lay into   attack

lay money down   bet

lay money on   gamble, parlay (bet), speculate (chance)

lay odds   bet

lay off   dislodge, dismiss (discharge), recess, suspend

lay on   levy

lay oneself open to   incur

lay open   bare, clarify, confess, denude, disabuse, disinter, divest, divulge, educe, elucidate, exhibit, expose, inform (betray), manifest, profess (avow), unveil

lay open to harm   expose

lay open to view   expose

lay out   demonstrate (establish), devise (invent), disburse (pay out), invest (fund), manifest, orchestrate, plan, prescribe, produce (offer to view), program

lay out a boundary   delimit

lay out money   spend

lay over   continue (adjourn), delay

lay plans   contrive, frame (formulate), maneuver

lay responsibility on   complain (charge)

lay responsibility upon   charge (accuse)

lay stress on   insist

lay the blame on   complain (charge), involve (implicate)

lay the foundation   build (construct), initiate, plan, plant (place firmly)

lay the foundation for   originate

lay the foundation of   generate

lay the foundations   cause, commence, create, establish (launch), instate, launch (initiate)

lay under embargo   enjoin

lay under restraint   arrest (apprehend), check (restrain), constrain (restrain), detain (restrain), hold up (delay), immure

lay up   fund, hoard

lay upon   impose (enforce)

lay waste   beat (defeat), damage, denude, despoil, destroy (efface), eliminate (eradicate), eradicate, extirpate, harry (plunder), loot, mistreat, pillage, plunder, spoil (impair), subvert. SEE MAIN ENTRY

lay waste to   extinguish

layer   SEE MAIN ENTRY

layer of society   class

laying aside   release

laying out   disbursement (act of disbursing)

layman   amateur. SEE MAIN ENTRY

laymen   public

layoff   dismissal (discharge), removal. SEE MAIN ENTRY

layout   arrangement (plan), array (order), configuration (form), design (construction plan), formation, method, order (arrangement), pattern, structure (composition)

lazare   expand

lazaretto   asylum (hospital)

laziness   inertia, laches, languor, laxity, sloth

lazy   idle, inactive, indolent, lax, lifeless (dull), otiose, phlegmatic, remiss, stagnant, torpid, truant

lead   advantage, clue, coax, command, conduct, control (regulate), direct (show), direct (supervise), dominate, edge (advantage), generalship, govern, guidance, influence, initiate, manage, manipulate (utilize skillfully), marshal, moderate (preside over), motivate, officiate, operate, originate, oversee, persuade, pioneer, plurality, preamble, precede, predominance, predominate (command), prescribe, preside, prevail (triumph), prevail upon, primacy, prior, prompt, protagonist, redound, regulate (manage), suggestion, superintend, tip (clue). SEE MAIN ENTRY

lead astray   bait (lure), brutalize, corrupt, debauch, delude, ensnare, entrap, illude, inveigle, misdirect, misguide, mislabel, mislead, misstate, pervert

lead by inducement   entrap

lead counsel   SEE MAIN ENTRY

lead in   preface

lead into captivity   immure

lead into danger by artifice   entrap

lead into error   delude, illude, misdirect, misguide, mislabel, mislead, misstate

lead into temptation   bait (lure), entrap

lead into trouble   mistreat

lead item   feature (special attraction)

lead on   entrap, inveigle

lead on by artifice   ensnare

lead one to   induce

lead one to expect   promise (raise expectations)

lead the way   initiate, instate, precede, preface

lead to   cause, conduce, engender

lead to a decision   arbitrate (adjudge)

lead to believe   assure (give confidence to), convert (persuade), convince, persuade

leadable   tractable

leaden   indolent, languid, lifeless (dull), otiose, ponderous, torpid

leadenness   sloth

leader   administrator, chairman, chief, demagogue, director, employer, forerunner, mastermind, official, patron (influential supporter), pioneer, protagonist, superintendent. SEE MAIN ENTRY

leader of affairs   official

leaders   management (directorate)

leadership   direction (guidance), generalship, guidance, hegemony, influence, management (directorate), management (supervision), predominance, primacy, supremacy. SEE MAIN ENTRY

leadership power   hierarchy (persons in authority)

leading   cardinal (outstanding), dominant, famous, important (significant), influential, initial, major, master, material (important), notable, noteworthy, paramount, precursory, prevailing (having superior force), primary, prime (most valuable), principal, prior, prominent, renowned, salient, sovereign (absolute), stellar. SEE MAIN ENTRY

leading case   SEE MAIN ENTRY

leading character   protagonist

leading inquiry   cross-examination

leading nowhere   blind (impassable)

leaf through   read

league   affiliation (amalgamation), association (alliance), band, cabal, cartel, chamber (body), coaction, coalescence, coalition, collusion, commingle, committee, company (assemblage), conciliation, confederacy (compact), conformity (agreement), connect (join together), connection (relation), connivance, consolidate (unite), consolidation, consortium (business cartel), consortium (marriage companionship), contribution (participation), cooperate, federalize (associate), federate, federation, organization (association), pact, partnership, party (political organization), pool (noun), pool (verb), society, sodality, syndicate, union (labor organization), unite. SEE MAIN ENTRY

league together   concur (agree), conspire, join (associate oneself with)

league with   combine (act in concert), conspire

leagued   affiliated, allied, associated, coadunate, collective, concurrent (united), conjoint, corporate (associate), federal, harmonious, joint, mutual (collective), partisan

leak   decrement, divulge, exude

leak into   penetrate

leakage   decrement, outflow

lean   gravitate, insufficient, minimal, rest (be supported by), select

lean against   abut, border (bound)

lean on   rely, trust

lean toward   discriminate (treat differently), prefer

leaning   character (personal quality), characteristic, conatus, conviction (persuasion), disposition (inclination), favor (partiality), favoritism, habit, inclination, inclined, inequity, nepotism, oblique (slanted), partiality, penchant, perspective, position (point of view), posture (attitude), preconception, predilection, predisposition, preference (choice), prejudice (preconception), proclivity, propensity, stand (position), standpoint, tendency. SEE MAIN ENTRY

leanness   dearth, poverty

leap   transition

leap of faith   SEE MAIN ENTRY

learn   apprehend (perceive), detect, discover, find (discover), gain, perceive, realize (understand), study, understand. SEE MAIN ENTRY

learn a habit   naturalize (acclimate), practice (train by repetition)

learn a lesson from profit
learn about ascertain
learn for a certainty discover
learn of discover
learn the answer solve
learnable ascertainable
learned cognizant, competent, didactic, expert, familiar (*informed*), informed (*educated*), literate, practiced, professional (*trained*), profound (*esoteric*), sapient, sciential. SEE MAIN ENTRY
learned counsel advocate (*counselor*), attorney, barrister, jurist
learned in the law forensic
learned man pedagogue
learned person mastermind, specialist
learned profession calling, profession (*vocation*)
learnedly knowingly
learner apprentice, disciple, neophyte, novice, probationer (*one being tested*), protégé
learning aptitude, common knowledge, comprehension, detection, discipline (*field of study*), edification, education, experience (*background*), information (*knowledge*), science (*study*). SEE MAIN ENTRY
lease convey (*transfer*), engage (*hire*), rent, sublet. SEE MAIN ENTRY
leased mercenary
leasehold property (*land*). SEE MAIN ENTRY
leaseholder landholder, lessee, lodger, occupant, tenant
leaser consumer, customer
leash handcuff, inhibit, limit, repress
leasing tenancy
least minimal. SEE MAIN ENTRY
least amount minimum
least part minimum
least quantity minimum
leave abscond, alight, bequeath, capacity (*authority*), charter (*sanction*), concession (*authorization*), consent, defect, demise, demit, depart, devise (*give*), disappear, discontinue (*abandon*), dispensation (*exception*), evacuate, fail (*neglect*), favor (*sanction*), forgo, forswear, franchise (*license*), freedom, furlough, give (*grant*), holiday, indulgence, liberty, license, move (*alter position*), option (*choice*), permission, permit, pretermit, quit (*evacuate*), relinquish, renounce, resign, retire (*conclude a career*), retire (*retreat*), retreat, secede, shun, sufferance, variance (*exemption*), withdraw, yield (*submit*). SEE MAIN ENTRY
leave a legacy bequeath, demise, descend. SEE MAIN ENTRY
leave a place move (*alter position*)
leave a will SEE MAIN ENTRY
leave alone neglect
leave an inference allude, imply
leave behind abandon (*physically leave*), surpass
leave by will bequeath, demise, devise (*give*)
leave defenseless endanger
leave destitute deprive, despoil
leave empty evacuate
leave in the lurch abandon (*physically leave*)
leave no choice necessitate
leave no option compel, constrain (*compel*), impose (*enforce*), necessitate
leave no trace disappear, expunge, perish
leave no trace of eradicate
leave no vestige of eradicate

leave nothing to be desired consummate
leave of absence furlough
leave off cease, desist, discontinue (*abandon*), discontinue (*break continuity*), forbear, interrupt, quit (*discontinue*), refrain, stop, suspend
leave one's country expatriate
leave out bar (*exclude*), block, censor, delete, disregard, eliminate (*exclude*), estrange, except (*exclude*), exclude, omit, overlook (*disregard*), pretermit, reject
leave out of consideration disregard
leave the impression demean (*deport oneself*)
leave the job strike (*refuse to work*)
leave to bequeath, devolve
leave to chance bet
leave undone omit, overlook (*disregard*), pretermit, shirk
leave unfinished quit (*discontinue*)
leave unlawfully defect
leave unprotected endanger, jeopardize
leave unregarded exclude
leaven determinant, imbue, penetrate, permeate
leavetaking egress
leaving abdication, desertion, discard, flight, resignation (*relinquishment*)
leaving no choice obligatory
leaving off moratorium
leaving out disregard (*unconcern*), omission, save
leavings surplus
lecherous depraved, immoral, lascivious, lewd, obscene, prurient, salacious, suggestive (*risqué*). SEE MAIN ENTRY
lechery debauchery, obscenity
lecture address (*talk to*), charge (*statement to the jury*), criticism, declaim, declamation, discourse (*noun*), discourse (*verb*), harangue, inculcate, instruct (*teach*), instruction (*teaching*), objurgation, peroration, rebuke, recital, recite, reprehend, reprimand (*noun*), reprimand (*verb*), reproach, speech. SEE MAIN ENTRY
lecturer pedagogue
lecturers faculty (*teaching staff*)
led astray blind (*not discerning*)
ledge border, margin (*outside limit*)
ledger account (*evaluation*), journal, register, roll. SEE MAIN ENTRY
lee refuge, safekeeping
leech parasite
leery suspicious (*distrustful*). SEE MAIN ENTRY
leeway freedom, margin (*spare amount*). SEE MAIN ENTRY
left derelict (*abandoned*). SEE MAIN ENTRY
left in penury bankrupt
left over residuary. SEE MAIN ENTRY
left to discretion discretionary
left to individual judgment discretionary
leftover balance (*amount in excess*), expendable, net, overage, remainder (*remaining part*), residual
legacy benefit (*conferment*), bequest, claim (*right*), dower, estate (*hereditament*), gift (*present*), grant, heritage, inheritance, will (*testamentary instrument*). SEE MAIN ENTRY
legal admissible, allowable, allowed, choate lien, civic, de jure, dué (*regular*), forensic, honest, jural, juridical, just, justifiable, lawful, legitimate (*rightful*), licit, permissible, rightful, statutory, valid. SEE MAIN ENTRY

legal abstract brief
legal action action (*proceeding*), cause (*lawsuit*), controversy (*lawsuit*), day in court, lawsuit, matter (*case*), proceeding, prosecution (*criminal trial*), suit. SEE MAIN ENTRY
legal administration bench
legal adversary litigant
legal adviser advocate (*counselor*), attorney, barrister, counsel, counselor, esquire, jurist
legal advisor lawyer
legal advocate lawyer
legal age majority (*adulthood*)
legal agreement lease, specialty (*contract*). SEE MAIN ENTRY
legal appointee attorney in fact
legal approval affirmance (*judicial sanction*)
legal argument answer (*judicial response*), case (*lawsuit*), controversy (*lawsuit*), lawsuit, plea. SEE MAIN ENTRY
legal arrangement before marriage antenuptial agreement
legal assertion cause of action
legal assistance maintenance (*support of spouse*). SEE MAIN ENTRY
legal authority judicature, jurisdiction
legal authorization affirmance (*judicial sanction*)
legal battle dispute
legal body corporation, corpus
legal call process (*summons*)
legal capacity capacity (*authority*)
legal cession grant
legal chicanery bunko
legal claim demand, right (*entitlement*). SEE MAIN ENTRY
legal code code, constitution, jurisprudence, law, pandect (*code of laws*)
legal command ordinance
legal competence competence (*ability*), majority (*adulthood*)
legal confinement commitment (*confinement*)
legal constraint commitment (*confinement*)
legal consultant lawyer
legal contest action (*proceeding*), day in court, lawsuit
legal controversy lawsuit
legal costs damages
legal counsel advice
legal course to adhere to adjective law
legal decision cognovit, judgment (*formal court decree*)
legal defender counselor
legal defense compurgation, justification, plea
legal dispute case (*lawsuit*), contention (*argument*), lawsuit, trial (*legal proceeding*). SEE MAIN ENTRY
legal dissolution of marriage divorce, separation
legal document agreement (*contract*), blank (*form*), brief, contract, policy (*contract*)
legal document to search search warrant
legal documents SEE MAIN ENTRY
legal enforcement of a lien fore-closure
legal entity corporation, corpus, partnership
legal epitome brief
legal estate effects, fee (*estate*), holding (*property owned*)

legal evidence admissible evidence, affirmance (*legal affirmation*), affirmation, corroboration. SEE MAIN ENTRY

legal expense cost (*expenses*)

legal expert jurist. SEE MAIN ENTRY

legal fitness competence (*ability*)

legal force validity

legal forum judiciary

legal heir legatee

legal immaturity minority (*infancy*), nonage. SEE MAIN ENTRY

ligdally in force SEE MAIN ENTRY

legal incapacity disability (*legal disqualification*), minority (*infancy*)

legal incompetence minority (*infancy*)

legal inquiry investigation

legal instructions charge (*statement to the jury*)

legal investigation inquest

legal issue case (*lawsuit*), contention (*argument*). SEE MAIN ENTRY

legal learning jurisprudence

legal liability damages, fine

legal mandate subpoena

legal maturity majority (*adulthood*)

legal memorandum brief

legal methods adjective law

legal minimum quorum

legal minority nonage

legal notice monition (*legal summons*), notification

legal nullification of marriage divorce

legal obligation liability

legal opponent litigant

legal order mittimus, precept, search warrant

legal philosophy jurisprudence

legal pledge adjuration, affirmance (*legal affirmation*), affirmation, asseveration, avowal, certification (*attested copy*), confirmation

legal power authority (*right*), droit, judicature, jurisdiction, prerogative, right (*entitlement*)

legal power to decide a case jurisdiction

legal practice jurisprudence

legal practitioner advocate (*counselor*), attorney, barrister, counsel, counselor, esquire, jurist, lawyer. SEE MAIN ENTRY

legal precedent jurisprudence. SEE MAIN ENTRY

legal procedure certiorari, proceeding

legal proceeding action (*proceeding*), controversy (*lawsuit*), suit. SEE MAIN ENTRY

legal proceedings case (*lawsuit*), cause (*lawsuit*), hearing, lawsuit, matter (*case*)

legal process certiorari, citation (*charge*), controversy (*lawsuit*), prosecution (*criminal trial*), search warrant, subpoena, summons, warrant (*judicial writ*). SEE MAIN ENTRY

legal profession bar (*body of lawyers*)

legal program agenda

legal ratification affirmance (*judicial sanction*)

legal recourse SEE MAIN ENTRY

legal redress recourse

legal relation of spouses to each other cohabitation (*married state*)

legal relationship privity

legal release from confinement discharge (*liberation*)

legal response SEE MAIN ENTRY

legal remedy suit

legal representative administrator, advocate (*counselor*), attorney in fact, counselor, executor, jurist

legal representation SEE MAIN ENTRY

legal residence address

legal responsibility liability, obligation (*duty*)

legal restraint constraint (*imprisonment*), detention, deterrence, deterrent, durance, embargo, estoppel, incarceration

legal right birthright, droit, freedom, jurisdiction, patent. SEE MAIN ENTRY

legal science jurisprudence

legal status of a married woman coverture

legal support maintenance (*support of spouse*)

legal tender cash, currency, money

legal termination of marriage divorce

legal title droit, right (*entitlement*), title (*right*)

ligally in force SEE MAIN ENTRY

legal trial day in court, hearing, inquiry (*systematic investigation*), prosecution (*criminal trial*)

legal union of a man and a woman cohabitation (*married state*)

legal vitality force (*legal efficacy*)

legal will testament

legal wrong tort

legalese jargon (*technical language*)

legalism legality. SEE MAIN ENTRY

legalist jurist

legalistic forensic, juridical

legality admissibility, legitimacy, sanction (*permission*), validity. SEE MAIN ENTRY

legalization consent, leave (*permission*), permit. SEE MAIN ENTRY

legalize allow (*authorize*), authorize, certify (*approve*), confirm, constitute (*establish*), formalize, legitimate, notarize, pass (*approve*), seal (*solemnize*), validate. SEE MAIN ENTRY

legalized allowable, allowed, choate lien, entitled, juridical, justifiable, lawful, legal, legitimate (*rightful*), licit, prescriptive, rightful, statutory, valid

legally de jure, fairly (*impartially*)

legally adequate prima facie (*legally sufficient*)

legally binding valid. SEE MAIN ENTRY

legally bound liable

legally determine try (*conduct a trial*)

legally discard a spouse divorce

legally enforceable triable. SEE MAIN ENTRY

legally incapable disabled (*deprived of legal right*)

legally in force SEE MAIN ENTRY

legally obliged to repay indebted

legally pursue sue

legally qualified eligible

legally responsible liable

legally restrain apprehend (*arrest*), arrest (*apprehend*)

legally restrain again rearrest

legally restrained arrested (*apprehended*)

legally sound permissible

legare leave (*give*)

legatary legatee

legate advocate (*counselor*), plenipotentiary

legatee beneficiary, devisee, donee, feoffee, heir, recipient, transferee. SEE MAIN ENTRY

legateship embassy

legati deputation (*delegation*)

legatio deputation (*delegation*), embassy, staff

legation delegation (*envoy*), deputation (*delegation*), embassy, mission

legatum bequest, legacy

legatus deputy, procurator

legend caption, fiction, inscription, myth, story (*narrative*). SEE MAIN ENTRY

legendary famous, fictitious, nonexistent, proverbial. SEE MAIN ENTRY

legendary story myth

legerdemain deception, knavery, maneuver (*trick*), prestidigitation

legere cull, select

leges facere legislate

legible coherent (*clear*), comprehensible

legibly fairly (*clearly*)

legion assemblage, band, quantity

legionary innumerable

legis violator lawbreaker

legislate authorize, constitute (*establish*), enact, govern, legalize, mandamus, pass (*approve*). SEE MAIN ENTRY

legislated due (*regular*), legitimate (*rightful*), licit, positive (*prescribed*)

legislating legislative

legislation act (*enactment*), amendment (*legislation*), bill (*proposed act*), canon, code, codification, edict, enactment, measure, ordinance, regulation (*rule*), rubric (*authoritative rule*), rule (*legal dictate*), statute. SEE MAIN ENTRY

legislative executive, statutory. SEE MAIN ENTRY

legislative act amendment (*legislation*)

legislative bill amendment (*legislation*)

legislative body chamber (*body*), congress, legislature

legislative cure remedial statute

legislative declaration bill (*formal declaration*)

legislative decree act (*enactment*), ordinance. SEE MAIN ENTRY

legislative draftsman lawmaker

legislative edict ordinance

legislative enactment measure, statute. SEE MAIN ENTRY

legislative mandate measure. SEE MAIN ENTRY

legislative precedent authority (*documentation*)

legislative process legislation (*lawmaking*)

legislative proclamation measure

legislative redress remedial statute

legislative sanction legalization

legislator lawmaker, politician. SEE MAIN ENTRY

legislatorial statutory

legislators government (*political administration*)

legislature chamber (*body*), congress. SEE MAIN ENTRY

legist advocate (*counselor*), attorney, barrister, counsel, counselor, esquire, jurist, lawyer, magistrate

legists bar (*body of lawyers*)

legitimacy admissibility, authority (*right*), honesty, legality, reality, validity. SEE MAIN ENTRY

legitimate admissible, allowable, allowed, authentic, authorize, bona fide, choate lien, constitute (*establish*), de jure, due (*regular*), ethical, fit, formalize, genuine, honest, justifiable, justify, lawful, legal, legalize, licit, official, permissible, plausible, proper, rational, real, reliable, right (*correct*), rightful, sanction, sane, scrupulous, sound, straightforward, tenable, true (*authentic*), upright, valid, veridical, viable, well-grounded. SEE MAIN ENTRY

legitimate puissance force (*legal efficacy*)

legitimately de jure, duly, in good faith

legitimateness legality, legitimacy, validity

849

legitimation legitimacy

legitimatization legalization

legitimatize allow (authorize), authorize, constitute (establish), formalize, legalize, legitimate, sanction, validate. SEE MAIN ENTRY

legitimization legitimacy

legitimize authorize, constitute (establish), pass (approve), sanction, validate. SEE MAIN ENTRY

legitimized choate lien, fully executed (signed)

legitimus justifiable, lawful, legal, licit

leisure furlough, holiday, leave (absence)

leisured unemployed

leisurely deliberate

lend bestow, capitalize (provide capital), finance, invest (fund), let (lease), loan, rent. SEE MAIN ENTRY

lend a hand facilitate, help, promote (organize)

lend aid help, serve (assist)

lend approval recommend

lend assistance contribute (assist)

lend force to compound

lend money to support (assist)

lend on security invest (fund), lease

lend one's aid capitalize (provide capital), subsidize

lend one's name to indorse

lend one's support to cooperate

lend oneself to cooperate, espouse, involve (participate), partake

lend support bear (support), capitalize (provide capital), help, preserve, recommend, subsidize

lend to again refinance

lender backer, creditor, obligee

lending assistance contributory

length extent, gamut. SEE MAIN ENTRY

length of life longevity

length of time duration, period

lengthen compound, continue (prolong), enlarge, expand, extend (enlarge), increase, keep (continue), project (extend beyond), prolong, spread, supplement, sustain (prolong). SEE MAIN ENTRY

lengthen out protract (stall)

lengthened protracted

lengthening continuance, continuation (prolongation), cumulative (increasing), development (progression)

lengthwise along

lengthy prolix, protracted, sesquipedalian. SEE MAIN ENTRY

lenience clemency, condonation, humanity (humaneness), indulgence, longanimity, moderation, pity. SEE MAIN ENTRY

leniency clemency, grace period, humanity (humaneness), indulgence, lenience, longanimity, moderation, pardon, pity. SEE MAIN ENTRY

lenient palliative (abating), perfunctory, permissive, placable. SEE MAIN ENTRY

lenify palliate (abate), relax, remit (relax), soothe

lenire allay, mitigate, mollify, pacify, soothe

lenis lenient

lenitive medicinal, narcotic, remedial

lenity clemency, humanity (humaneness), indulgence, lenience, moderation, pity

lentus flexible, intentional, malleable, phlegmatic, pliable, pliant, stagnant, torpid

leonine powerful

lese majesty rebellion

less save, subaltern. SEE MAIN ENTRY

less important minor, secondary, subordinate

less powerful inferior (lower in position)

less significant subordinate

less than necessary deficient

less than perfect faulty, peccable

less valuable inferior (lower in quality)

lessee consumer, customer, lodger, occupant, tenant. SEE MAIN ENTRY

lessen abridge (shorten), adulterate, allay, alleviate, assuage, attenuate, commute, curtail, debilitate, decrease, deduct (reduce), deplete, depreciate, depress, derogate, diminish, discount (minimize), ease, erode, expend (consume), extenuate, minimize, mitigate, moderate (temper), modify (moderate), mollify, palliate (abate), rebate, reduce, relax, remit (relax), retrench, soothe, subdue, subside. SEE MAIN ENTRY

lessen importance of demote

lessen in force mitigate

lessen in power impair

lessen in value impair. SEE MAIN ENTRY

lessen in worth degenerate

lessen one's reputation defame

lessen the labor facilitate

lessen the price of depreciate

lessen the reputation of derogate

lessen the self-confidence of discourage

lessen the strength of dilute

lessening abatement (reduction), attrition, curtailment, decline, decrease, decrement, deduction (diminution), derogatory, diminution, erosion, mitigating, mitigation, mollification, remission

lessening of price rebate

lesser ancillary (subsidiary), inferior (lower in position), inferior (lower in quality), mediocre, minimal, minor, secondary, subaltern, subordinate, subservient. SEE MAIN ENTRY

lesser group minority (outnumbered group)

lesser part minority (outnumbered group)

lesson caveat, correction (punishment), guidance. SEE MAIN ENTRY

lessor landlord, obligee, transferor. SEE MAIN ENTRY

let attorn, bestow, enable, engage (hire), grant (concede), lease, permit, rent, suffer (permit), vouchsafe. SEE MAIN ENTRY

let alone forswear, shun

let be leave (allow to remain)

let continue leave (allow to remain)

let down betray (lead astray), disappoint, disappointed, frustrate. SEE MAIN ENTRY

let drop divulge

let escape free, rescue

let fall outpour, precipitate (throw down violently), remark

let fly precipitate (throw down violently), project (impel forward)

let go acquitted, clear, disband, discharge (dismiss), discharge (liberate), disenthrall, disown (refuse to acknowledge), forfeit, free, leave (allow to remain), liberate, omit, palliate (excuse), release, relinquish, remit (release from penalty), renounce, surrender (give back), terminate, yield (submit). SEE MAIN ENTRY

let go free parole

let have present (make a gift)

let in receive (permit to enter)

let know apprise, communicate, confide (divulge), disabuse, inform (notify), mention, notify

let lapse discontinue (abandon)

let loose discharge (dismiss), discharge (liberate), disenthrall, extricate, free, liberate, pardon

let off absolve, acquit, acquitted, cast (throw), clear, excuse, palliate (excuse)

let one down fail (neglect)

let out communicate, disband, discharge (liberate), disengage, disenthrall, emit, free (not restricted), free, liberate, release, remit (release from penalty), rent, rescue, sublease, sublet. SEE MAIN ENTRY

let out of jail parole

let out of prison discharge (liberate), disenthrall, free, parole

let pass condone, forgo, omit, pretermit

let premises for a designated period lease

let ride overlook (disregard)

let slacken remit (relax)

let slide ignore, procrastinate

let slip betray (disclose), divulge, forfeit, ignore, omit, procrastinate

let stand leave (allow to remain). SEE MAIN ENTRY

let the matter stand procrastinate

let through receive (permit to enter)

let up diminution, ease, lessen, remit (relax), subside

letdown damper (depressant)

lethal deadly, deleterious, dire, fatal, insalubrious, malevolent, malignant, noxious, peccant (unhealthy), pernicious, pestilent, ruthless, toxic, virulent. SEE MAIN ENTRY

lethal instrument cudgel, gun

lethal instruments weapons

lethal weapon cudgel

lethal weapons weapons

lethality fatality

lethargic inactive, indolent, languid, lifeless (dull), otiose, phlegmatic, stagnant, torpid

lethargical inactive, languid, lifeless (dull), otiose, phlegmatic

lethargy inertia, languor, sloth

lethiferous deadly, fatal, insalubrious, lethal, pestilent

letter dispatch (message), inscribe, transmittal

letter in support reference (recommendation)

letter of credit draft. SEE MAIN ENTRY

letter of introduction reference (recommendation)

letter of recognition certification (certification of proficiency)

letter of recommendation reference (recommendation)

letter of the law SEE MAIN ENTRY

letter writing correspondence (communication by letters)

lettered cognizant, familiar (informed), informed (educated), learned, literate

letters correspondence (communication by letters), education

letting go layoff

letting off acquittal

lettre de cachet durance

letup cloture, pause, remission, respite (interval of rest)

levamentum mitigation

levant abscond, bilk, defraud, escape

levanter fugitive

levare assuage, elevate, extenuate

levatio mitigation

level balance (equality), coequal, commensurable, destroy (efface), extirpate, obliterate, pillage, regulate (adjust), subvert. SEE MAIN ENTRY

level of attendance draw (attendance)

level of development degree (station)

level of education civilization
level of excellence standard
level off compensate *(counterbalance)*, decrease
level with inform *(notify)*
level-headedness common sense, deliberation
levelheaded patient, prudent, rational, sane, sensible
levelheadedness sagacity, sanity
levelness regularity, uniformity
lever devastate
leverage advantage, clout, influence, latitude. SEE MAIN ENTRY
leviable ad valorem
leviathan prodigious *(enormous)*
levied attached *(seized)*. SEE MAIN ENTRY
levis capricious, frivolous, inconsiderable, negligible, slight, superficial, trivial, volatile
levy ad valorem, assess *(tax)*, attach *(seize)*, charge *(assess)*, collect *(recover money)*, confiscate, distrain, distraint, distress *(seizure)*, dun, duty *(tax)*, exact, excise, excise *(levy a tax)*, garnishment, imposition *(tax)*, impress *(procure by force)*, raise *(collect)*, require *(compel)*, requisition, sequester *(seize property)*, sequestration, tariff *(duties)*, tax, toll *(tax)*, toll *(exact payment)*. SEE MAIN ENTRY
levy a distress distrain
levy an excise on excise *(levy a tax)*
levy upon garnish
lewd depraved, immoral, lascivious, lecherous, licentious, obscene, promiscuous, prurient, salacious, scandalous, scurrilous, suggestive *(risqué)*, unrestrained *(not repressed)*, wanton. SEE MAIN ENTRY
lewdness debauchery, obscenity, perversion, pornography, vice
lex act *(enactment)*, canon, code, enactment, law, statute, term *(provision)*
lex loci SEE MAIN ENTRY
lex oblivionis indemnity
liabilities overhead
liability arrears, attornment, blame *(responsibility)*, burden, chance *(possibility)*, characteristic, charge *(lien)*, cloud *(incumbrance)*, debit, debt, delinquency *(shortage)*, detriment, disadvantage, drawback, due, duty *(obligation)*, encumbrance, excise, fault *(responsibility)*, fine, impairment *(drawback)*, impeachability, incumbrance *(lien)*, lien, penalty, probability, responsibility *(accountability)*, weight *(burden)*. SEE MAIN ENTRY
liability to disaster fatality
liability to err frailty
liability to injury danger, hazard, peril
liable accountable *(responsible)*, at fault, blameful, blameworthy, bound, inclined, possible, probable, prone, subject *(exposed)*, susceptible *(unresistent)*. SEE MAIN ENTRY
liable to conditional
liable to attack vulnerable
liable to be annulled voidable
liable to be completed determinable *(liable to be terminated)*
liable to be discontinued determinable *(liable to be terminated)*
liable to be dropped determinable *(liable to be terminated)*
liable to be ended determinable *(liable to be terminated)*
liable to be erroneous fallible
liable to come to an end determinable *(liable to be terminated)*

liable to disappear elusive
liable to err peccable
liable to expire determinable *(liable to be terminated)*
liable to mistake fallible
liable to prosecution actionable, blameful, blameworthy, justiciable
liable to question uncertain *(questionable)*
liable to sin peccable
liableness probability
liaison chain *(nexus)*, collusion, connection *(fastening)*, connection *(relation)*, connivance, contact *(association)*, nexus, relation *(connection)*. SEE MAIN ENTRY
liaisons ties
libation grant
libel aspersion, defamation, defame, denigrate, malign, slander, smear. SEE MAIN ENTRY
libelant accuser, claimant, complainant, contender, contestant, party *(litigant)*
libellus indictment, invoice *(itemized list)*, petition, schedule
libellus famosus libel
libelous calumnious, contemptuous, derogatory. SEE MAIN ENTRY
liber candid, exempt, free *(not restricted)*, independent, ingenuous, liberty, register
liberal ample, benevolent, broad, charitable *(benevolent)*, charitable *(lenient)*, copious, extensive, lenient, magnanimous, open-minded, permissive, philanthropic, prodigal, profuse, progressive *(advocating change)*, unbiased. SEE MAIN ENTRY
liberalis charitable *(lenient)*, liberal *(broad minded)*
liberalism latitude
liberalistic broad
liberalitas bounty, charity
liberality benefit *(conferment)*, benevolence *(disposition to do good)*, candor *(impartiality)*, clemency, disinterest *(lack of prejudice)*, largess *(generosity)*, lenience, philanthropy, tolerance. SEE MAIN ENTRY
liberalness charity, largess *(generosity)*
liberare absolve, acquit, disengage, exonerate, extricate, free, liberate, release, rescue
liberate absolve, acquit, clear, disencumber, disengage, disentangle, disenthrall, dissociate, enable, enfranchise, exclude, exculpate, excuse, exonerate, extricate, free, let *(permit)*, palliate *(excuse)*, pardon, parole, quit *(free of)*, redeem *(repurchase)*, release, relieve *(free from burden)*, remit *(release from penalty)*, rescue, save *(rescue)*. SEE MAIN ENTRY
liberate from connection disengage
liberate from oppression disenthrall
liberated exempt, free *(enjoying civil liberty)*, free *(not restricted)*, free *(relieved from a burden)*, liberal *(broad minded)*, sovereign *(independent)*, unbound. SEE MAIN ENTRY
liberatio acquittal, emancipation, liberation, release
liberation absolution, acquittal, compurgation, emancipation, exemption, exoneration, freedom, immunity, impunity, parole, probation, release, relief *(release)*, remission, suffrage. SEE MAIN ENTRY
liberation from foreign restraint liberty
liberi issue *(progeny)*
libertas freedom, latitude, liberty
liberticide oppression
libertinage debauchery

libertine dissolute, lascivious, lecherous, lewd, licentious, salacious, unrestrained *(not repressed)*
libertinism debauchery, vice
liberty capacity *(authority)*, charter *(sanction)*, dispensation *(exception)*, emancipation, exemption, freedom, furlough, immunity, informality, latitude, leave *(absence)*, leave *(permission)*, license, opportunity, option *(choice)*, parole, prerogative, privilege, suffrage. SEE MAIN ENTRY
liberty of action call *(option)*
liberty of approach admittance *(means of approach)*
liberty of choice franchise *(right to vote)*
liberty of choosing discretion *(power of choice)*
liberty of judgment discretion *(power of choice)*
liberty of use easement
liberty to enter ingress
liberty to vote franchise *(right to vote)*
libidinosus arbitrary, lascivious, licentious, prurient
libidinous dissolute, immoral, lascivious, lecherous, lewd, obscene, prurient, salacious, scurrilous, suggestive *(risqué)*, wanton
librate oscillate, vacillate
libretto script
libro balance *(equality)*
librum edere edit
license allow *(authorize)*, appoint, approval, authorize, bestow, brevet, capacity *(authority)*, certificate, certification *(certification of proficiency)*, certify *(approve)*, charter *(sanction)*, concession *(authorization)*, confirm, consent *(noun)*, consent *(verb)*, constitute *(establish)*, copyright, countenance, delegate, delegation *(assignment)*, discretion *(power of choice)*, dispensation *(exception)*, droit, empower, enable, enfranchise, entrust, exemption, freedom, grant *(concede)*, immunity, impunity, induct, indulgence, informality, invest *(vest)*, latitude, leave *(permission)*, let *(permit)*, liberty, option *(contractual provision)*, palliate *(excuse)*, patent, permission, permit *(noun)*, permit *(verb)*, prerogative, prescription *(claim of title)*, privilege, qualify *(meet standards)*, sanction *(permission)*, sanction, seal *(solemnize)*, sign, suffer *(permit)*, sufferance, suffrage, tolerance, warrant *(authorization)*. SEE MAIN ENTRY
licensed admissible, allowed, entitled, lawless, legitimate *(rightful)*, licit, official, permissible, privileged, qualified *(competent)*
licensee nominee *(delegate)*, transferee. SEE MAIN ENTRY
licensing of rights SEE MAIN ENTRY
licensor transferor. SEE MAIN ENTRY
licentia anarchy, freedom, latitude, leave *(permission)*, liberty
licentious depraved, disobedient, disorderly, disreputable, dissolute, immoral, lecherous, lewd, obscene, promiscuous, prurient, salacious, scandalous, scurrilous, uncurbed, unrestrained *(not repressed)*, wanton. SEE MAIN ENTRY
licentiousness debauchery, vice
licet permissible
licit allowable, allowed, de jure, due *(regular)*, honest, just, justifiable, law-abiding, lawful, legal, legitimate *(rightful)*, permissible, rightful, statutory, valid. SEE MAIN ENTRY
licitatio bid

licitly de jure

licitness droit, legitimacy

licitus permissible

lickerish lascivious, lecherous, prurient, salacious, suggestive *(risqué)*

lickerous salacious

lid cap. SEE MAIN ENTRY

lidless open *(unclosed)*

lie bear false witness, canard, deceive, deception, equivocate, evade *(deceive)*, fabricate *(make up)*, fake, false pretense, falsehood, falsify, fiction, figment, hoax, invent *(falsify)*, misguide, mislead, misrepresent, misrepresentation, misstate, misstatement, palter, perjure, posture *(attitude)*, pretend, pretense *(pretext)*, pretext, prevaricate, rest *(be supported by)*, story *(falsehood)*, subterfuge. SEE MAIN ENTRY

lie about feign

lie across cross *(intersect)*

lie adjacent to contact *(touch)*

lie against frame *(charge falsely)*, frame *(prearrange)*

lie beside adjoin

lie concealed lurk

lie contiguous to border *(bound)*

lie down repose *(rest)*

lie hidden lurk

lie in ambush lurk, prowl

lie in wait lurk, prowl

lie in wait for ambush

lie low lurk

lie near border *(approach)*

lie near to adjoin

lie next to border *(bound)*

lie over overlap

lief readily

liegeman subject *(object)*

lien encumbrance, hypothecation, security *(pledge)*. SEE MAIN ENTRY

lien on an estate encumbrance

lieutenant coadjutant, deputy, liaison, plenipotentiary, proctor, procurator, proxy, substitute

life entity, lifetime, practice *(professional business)*, spirit, survival. SEE MAIN ENTRY

life estate freehold

life span lifetime

life support SEE MAIN ENTRY

life's duration lifetime

life's work practice *(professional business)*

life-giving productive, salubrious

life-supporting vital

lifeblood main point. SEE MAIN ENTRY

lifeless dead, deceased, defunct, languid, mediocre, otiose, pedestrian, phlegmatic, ponderous, stagnant, torpid. SEE MAIN ENTRY

lifeless body corpse

lifeless object article *(commodity)*

lifelessness inertia, insentience, languor

lifelike descriptive, natural, realistic, suggestive *(evocative)*

lifelong durable

lifetime life *(period of existence)*, term *(duration)*. SEE MAIN ENTRY

lifework calling, career, employment, profession *(vocation)*, pursuit *(occupation)*

lift bolster, build *(augment)*, elevate, elevation, enhance, jostle *(pickpocket)*, promotion *(advancement)*, raise *(advance)*, steal, support *(assistance)*. SEE MAIN ENTRY

lift a ban facilitate. SEE MAIN ENTRY

lift controls disengage, quit *(free of)*

lift up heighten *(elevate)*

lifter thief

ligament chain *(nexus)*

ligation attachment *(act of affixing)*

ligature chain *(nexus)*, connection *(fastening)*

light deft, frivolous, jocular, minimal, negligible, slight, subtle *(refined)*, trivial. SEE MAIN ENTRY

light labor sinecure

light up burn

light upon find *(discover)*

light work sinecure

light-footed rapid

light-minded frivolous

lighten abate *(lessen)*, allay, alleviate, attenuate, commute, diminish, ease, extenuate, facilitate, lessen, mitigate, moderate *(temper)*, modify *(moderate)*, relieve *(free from burden)*. SEE MAIN ENTRY

lighten the labor disencumber

lightening abatement *(reduction)*, mitigation, mollification

lightness immateriality, informality

lightweight immaterial

likable palatable, preferable, sapid, savory

like akin *(germane)*, analogous, approximate, cognate, comparable *(capable of comparison)*, congruous, correlate, equal, equivalent, faithful *(true to fact)*, identical, related, relish, similar. SEE MAIN ENTRY

like better prefer

like in degree coequal, equal

like in quantity coequal, equal

like-kind SEE MAIN ENTRY

like quality analogy

like to desire

like-minded consensual

likeable attractive

liked popular, preferred *(favored)*

likelihood chance *(possibility)*, feasibility, possibility, presumption, probability, prospect *(outlook)*, supposition, weight *(credibility)*. SEE MAIN ENTRY

likeliness likelihood, probability, prospect *(outlook)*, supposition

likely apparent *(presumptive)*, appropriate, believable, circumstantial, convincing, deductible *(provable)*, fitting, future, ostensible, possible, potential, presumptive, probable, prone, prospective, suitable, viable. SEE MAIN ENTRY

likely client prospect *(prospective patron)*

likely customer prospect *(prospective patron)*

likely patron prospect *(prospective patron)*

likely person prospect *(prospective patron)*

likely to decrease taxes deductible *(capable of being deducted from taxes)*

likely to excite ill will invidious

likely to happen imminent

likely to harm dangerous

likeminded consenting

likemindedness concordance, understanding *(agreement)*

liken compare, conform, correspond *(be equivalent)*, measure

likeness analogy, appearance *(look)*, color *(complexion)*, conformity *(agreement)*, copy, correspondence *(similarity)*, counterpart *(parallel)*, duplicate, identity *(similarity)*, par *(equality)*, parity, peer, propinquity *(similarity)*, reflection *(image)*, relation *(connection)*, relationship *(connection)*, resemblance, semblance

likewise also

liking affinity *(regard)*, desire, disposition *(inclination)*, favor *(partiality)*, inclination, indorsement, partiality, penchant, predilection, predisposition, preference *(choice)*, proclivity, propensity, regard *(esteem)*

Lilliputian minimal

lilylivered recreant

limare file *(arrange)*

limber flexible, malleable, pliable, pliant

limelight publicity

limit abate *(lessen)*, abridge *(divest)*, ambit, bar *(obstruction)*, bar *(exclude)*, barrier, bind *(restrain)*, block, border, border *(bound)*, boundary, cap, capacity *(maximum)*, ceiling, censor, check *(restrain)*, commute, compel, condemn *(ban)*, confine, constrain *(imprison)*, constrain *(restrain)*, constrict *(inhibit)*, control *(restrain)*, curb, debar, defeasance, define, demarcate, detain *(restrain)*, deter, determine, diminish, disadvantage, discipline *(control)*, disfranchise, duration, edge *(border)*, enclose, enclosure, encumber *(hinder)*, end *(termination)*, enjoin, expiration, extent, extremity *(furthest point)*, frontier, gamut, guideline, hamper, hedge, impede, margin *(outside limit)*, maximum *(pinnacle)*, measurement, mete, moderate *(temper)*, modify *(moderate)*, obstruct, palliate *(abate)*, periphery, prevent, prohibit, prohibition, purview, qualify *(condition)*, quota, range, repress, restrain, restrict, retrench, scope, specialize, toll *(stop)*. SEE MAIN ENTRY

limit of endurance capacity *(maximum)*

limitable terminable

limitary qualified *(conditioned)*, restrictive

limitation abatement *(reduction)*, abridgment *(disentitlement)*, alienation *(transfer of title)*, bar *(obstruction)*, boundary, capacity *(maximum)*, censorship, check *(bar)*, clause, compulsion *(coercion)*, condition *(contingent provision)*, constraint *(restriction)*, control *(restriction)*, custody *(incarceration)*, damper *(stopper)*, detention, deterrence, deterrent, disadvantage, discipline *(obedience)*, enclosure, end *(termination)*, extent, fetter, flaw, foible, guideline, handicap, impairment *(drawback)*, impediment, mete, moderation, modification, obstacle, obstruction, periphery, prohibition, provision *(clause)*, purview, qualification *(condition)*, quota, reservation *(condition)*, restraint, restriction, term *(provision)*. SEE MAIN ENTRY

limitations configuration *(confines)*, confines, frontier, outline *(boundary)*

limitative conditional, prohibitive *(restrictive)*, restrictive

limited arrested *(checked)*, brief, certain *(specific)*, conditional, dependent, imperfect, infrequent, local, minimal, narrow, parochial, partial *(part)*, partial *(relating to a part)*, petty, private *(not public)*, privy, provisional, qualified *(conditioned)*, scarce, slight, specific, strict, temporary. SEE MAIN ENTRY

limited amount paucity

limited area region

limited choice dilemma

limited time period

limiting binding, determinative, mitigating, prohibitive *(restrictive)*, restrictive. SEE MAIN ENTRY

limitive determinative

limitless far reaching, indeterminate, infinite, innumerable, myriad, omnibus, open-ended, plenary, profuse, unbound, unlimited, unqualified (unlimited), unrestricted

limitlessly   ad infinitum

limits   area (province), boundary, capacity (sphere), configuration (confines), confines, outline (boundary), premises (buildings), purview. SEE MAIN ENTRY

limn   delineate, depict, portray

limp   insipid, languid, nonsubstantial (not sturdy)

limpid   clear (apparent), lucid, pellucid

line   ancestry, birth (lineage), blood, bloodline, business (occupation), calling, career, chain (series), derivation, descent (lineage), direction (course), employment, family (common ancestry), lineage, merchandise, occupation (vocation), origin (ancestry), parentage, policy (plan of action), polity, post, posterity, progeny, pursuit (occupation), race, range, stock in trade, trade (occupation), work (employment). SEE MAIN ENTRY

line drawn round   delineation

line of achievement   calling

line of action   action (performance), campaign, course, maneuver (tactic), manner (behavior), policy (plan of action), practice (custom), practice (procedure), procedure, process (course)

line of ancestors   bloodline, descent (lineage), family (common ancestry), origin (ancestry), parentage

line of business   calling, labor (work), position (business status), practice (professional business)

line of circumvallation   boundary, mete

line of conduct   behavior, campaign, course, manner (behavior), modus operandi, platform, policy (plan of action), practice (procedure)

line of credit   capital

line of demarcation   border, boundary, configuration (confines), crossroad (turning point), frontier, limit, mete, outline (boundary), periphery

line of descent   affiliation (bloodline), birth (lineage), degree (kinship), family (common ancestry), lineage, origin (ancestry)

line of duty   burden

line of goods   merchandise

line of proceeding   campaign, practice (custom)

line of sight   perspective

line of work   calling, labor (work), livelihood, position (business status), practice (professional business), profession (vocation), trade (occupation)

line up   allocate, file (arrange), fix (arrange), juxtapose, marshal, set down

lineage   affiliation (bloodline), affinity (family ties), ancestry, blood, bloodline, children, derivation, descendant, family (common ancestry), filiation, heritage, house, issue (progeny), kindred, off-spring, origin (ancestry), parentage, paternity, posterity, progeny, relationship (family tie), source, succession. SEE MAIN ENTRY

lineal   hereditary

lineal descendant   child

lineal descendants   issue (progeny)

lineament   color (complexion), feature (appearance), particularity, trait

lineamenta   contour (outline), design (construction plan)

lineaments   boundary, outline (boundary)

lineamentum   feature (appearance)

linear   direct (straight)

lined up   coextensive

lines   ambit, boundary, configuration (form), contour (outline), contour (shape), feature (appearance), script

lines of demarcation   confines

lineup   order (arrangement). SEE MAIN ENTRY

linger   continue (persevere), defer (put off), delay, last, loiter, pause, persist, procrastinate, prolong, remain (continue), remain (stay), stall

linger on   endure (last)

lingering   chronic, lasting, protracted

lingo   phraseology, speech

lingua   language

lingual   parol

linguistics   language

link   affiliation (connectedness), affix, appertain, association (connection), attach (join), broker, chain (nexus), combine (join together), commingle, connection (fastening), connection (relation), consolidate (unite), contact (association), contact (touch), engage (involve), go-between, implicate, implication (incriminating involvement), intermediary, join (bring together), kinship, liaison, lock, medium, member (constituent part), nexus, privity, propinquity (kinship), relate (establish a connection), relation (connection), relationship (connection), unite. SEE MAIN ENTRY

link together   connect (join together), connect (relate), involve (implicate)

linkage   affiliation (connectedness), affinity (family ties), association (connection), chain (nexus), coalescence, connection (fastening), connection (relation), contact (association), joinder, liaison, marriage (intimate relationship), relationship (connection). SEE MAIN ENTRY

linked   affiliated, akin (germane), associated, coadunate, cognate, concurrent (united), conjoint, correlative, interrelated, intimate, related

linking   joinder, marriage (intimate relationship)

links   chain (series), ties

lion's share   majority (greater part)

lionhearted   heroic, spartan

lionize   honor

lip   edge (border), margin (outside limit)

liquefacere   dissolve (disperse)

liquid assets   capital, estate (property)

liquidate   defray, destroy (efface), discharge (pay a debt), disorganize, dispatch (put to death), eliminate (eradicate), eradicate, extinguish, extirpate, kill (murder), obliterate, pay, remove (eliminate), slay. SEE MAIN ENTRY

liquidation   aberemurder, assassination, cancellation, composition (agreement in bankruptcy), discharge (payment), dispatch (act of putting to death), dissolution (termination), homicide, killing, murder, payment (act of paying)

liquidation of a debt   amortization

liquidator   recipient

liquor   alcohol

lis   action (proceeding), lawsuit, process (summons), suit

lis pendens   SEE MAIN ENTRY

lissome   flexible, malleable, pliable

list   bill (invoice), book, census, classify, codify, docket, enroll, enter (record), enumerate, file, file (place among official records), fix (arrange), impanel, index (cata-

log), index (relate), inscribe, inventory, itemize, organize (arrange), pigeonhole, poll, program (noun), program (verb), recite, record (noun), record (verb), register, roll, schedule, sequence, set down, specify, survey (poll), tabulate, tariff (bill). SEE MAIN ENTRY

list for jury duty   empanel

list jurors   empanel

list of appointments   calendar (record of yearly periods)

list of cases   docket

list of cases set down for hearing   calendar (list of cases)

list of causes arranged for trial   calendar (list of cases)

list of causes instituted in court   calendar (list of cases)

list of causes ready for trial   calendar (list of cases)

list of events   calendar (record of yearly periods)

list of goods   invoice (itemized list)

list of items   invoice (itemized list), tariff (bill)

list of items shipped   invoice (itemized list)

list of jurors   panel (jurors)

list of mercantile goods   invoice (itemized list)

list of paid employees   payroll

list of properties   inventory

list of receipts and payments   account (evaluation)

list of salaried employees   payroll

list of wages to be paid out   payroll

listen   attend (heed), concentrate (pay attention), eavesdrop, hear (give attention to), monitor, obey. SEE MAIN ENTRY

listen in on   overhear

listen stealthily   eavesdrop, overhear

listen to   heed, submit (yield)

listener   bystander

listing   census, docket, index (catalog), registration

listing of contents   index (catalog)

listless   despondent, idle, inactive, indolent, inexpressive, languid, lifeless (dull), otiose, phlegmatic, powerless, stagnant, torpid. SEE MAIN ENTRY

listlessness   disinterest (lack of interest), languor, sloth

literacy   education

literal   accurate, actual, authentic, exact, factual, faithful (true to fact), honest, narrow, orthodox, parochial, precise, strict, true (authentic), verbatim. SEE MAIN ENTRY

literal interpretation   connotation, content (meaning)

literal meaning   connotation, content (meaning). SEE MAIN ENTRY

literal sense   connotation, content (meaning)

literally   SEE MAIN ENTRY

literality   connotation, content (meaning)

literalize   construe (translate)

literally   faithfully, verbatim

literary   literate

literary artistry   phraseology

literary forgery   plagiarism

literary magazine   publication (printed matter)

literary person   author (writer)

literary piracy   plagiarism

literary publications   press

literary style   phraseology

literary theft   plagiarism

literate   familiar (informed), informed (educated), learned. SEE MAIN ENTRY

literati   faculty *(teaching staff)*
literatim   verbatim
literature   publication *(printed matter)*. SEE MAIN ENTRY
lithe   flexible, malleable, pliable, pliant
lithesome   malleable, pliable
litigable   actionable, justiciable. SEE MAIN ENTRY
litigant   accuser, actionable, actor, adversary, appellant, claimant, complainant, contender, contestant, disputant, petitioner, plaintiff, rival, suitor. SEE MAIN ENTRY
litigare   litigate
litigate   contend *(dispute)*. SEE MAIN ENTRY
litigate against   sue
litigate completely   exhaust *(try all possibilities)*
litigating counsel   SEE MAIN ENTRY
litigation   action *(proceeding)*, case *(lawsuit)*, cause *(lawsuit)*, complaint, contest *(dispute)*, controversy *(lawsuit)*, day in court, dispute, hearing, lawsuit, matter *(case)*, proceeding, prosecution *(criminal trial)*, suit, trial *(legal proceeding)*. SEE MAIN ENTRY
litigation of the charges   action *(proceeding)*
litigationist   litigant
litigator   contender, litigant, suitor. SEE MAIN ENTRY
litigatory   litigious
litigiosus   litigious
litigious   actionable, argumentative, contentious, forensic. SEE MAIN ENTRY
litterae   correspondence *(communication by letters)*, dispatch *(message)*, document
litteratus   learned
little   impalpable, inappreciable, minimal, minor, negligible, nominal, paltry, petty, remote *(small)*, scarce, slight, tenuous, trivial. SEE MAIN ENTRY
little by little   piecemeal
little chance   improbability
little one   infant
little-known   peculiar *(curious)*, recondite, unusual. SEE MAIN ENTRY
littleness   dearth
littoral   SEE MAIN ENTRY
livable   habitable
live   born *(alive)*, conscious *(awake)*, dwell *(reside)*, exist, inhabit, lodge *(reside)*, occupy *(take possession)*, reside, subsist. SEE MAIN ENTRY
live at   reside
live by   obey
live dissolutely   carouse
live idly   dissipate *(expend foolishly)*
live in   occupy *(take possession)*, remain *(occupy)*
live in sexual intimacy   cohabit
live in terror   fear
live on   endure *(last)*, exist, keep *(continue)*, last, persist
live through   bear *(tolerate)*
live together   cohabit
live under unfavorable conditions   languish
live up to   fulfill, keep *(fulfill)*
live with   cohabit
livelihood   business *(occupation)*, calling, career, employment, occupation *(vocation)*, revenue, support *(assistance)*, trade *(occupation)*. SEE MAIN ENTRY
liveliness   ardor, dispatch *(promptness)*, life *(vitality)*, spirit
lively   rapid, volatile
lively pace   dispatch *(promptness)*

liverish   petulant
livery of seisin   feoffment
livid   SEE MAIN ENTRY
lividus   jealous, spiteful
living   appointment *(position)*, bodily, born *(alive)*, business *(occupation)*, calling, conscious *(awake)*, durable, employment, extant, inhabitation *(act of dwelling in)*, live *(conscious)*, livelihood, present *(current)*, pursuit *(occupation)*, residential, sustenance, trade *(occupation)*, viable. SEE MAIN ENTRY
living as man and wife   coverture
living being   person
living by prey   predatory
living expenses   overhead
living image   alter ego
living on prey   rapacious
living place   abode, house, lodging, residence
living quarters   building *(structure)*, domicile, dwelling, habitation *(dwelling place)*, home *(domicile)*, house, inhabitation *(place of dwelling)*, residence
living soul   person
living space   inhabitation *(place of dwelling)*
living thing   entity
living together in sexual intimacy   cohabitation *(living together)*
living will   SEE MAIN ENTRY
livor   spite
load   burden, cargo, encumbrance, freight, impact, impede, incumbrance *(burden)*, onus *(burden)*, plethora, pressure, stress *(strain)*, tax *(overwork)*, weight *(burden)*. SEE MAIN ENTRY
load down   weigh
load to excess   overload
load up   hoard
loaded   full, ready *(prepared)*, replete
loaf   procrastinate
loafer   parasite
loafing   indolent, remiss
loan   capitalize *(provide capital)*, credit *(delayed payment)*, finance, invest *(fund)*, investment, lend, let *(lease)*. SEE MAIN ENTRY
loan applicant   obligor
loan at interest   investment
loan to again   refinance
loan transaction   mortgage
loanee   debtor, obligor
loath   averse, disinclined, disobedient, dissident, hesitant, renitent, restive
loathe   contemn, disdain. SEE MAIN ENTRY
loathe to   contra
loathed   undesirable
loathful   loathsome, obnoxious
loathing   alienation *(estrangement)*, hatred, malice, odium, phobia
loathsome   antipathetic *(distasteful)*, bad *(offensive)*, contemptible, disreputable, heinous, invidious, objectionable, obnoxious, odious, offensive *(offending)*, repugnant *(exciting aversion)*, repulsive, undesirable, unsavory. SEE MAIN ENTRY
loathsomeness   disrepute
lobby   bait *(lure)*, constituency, entrance, party *(political organization)*, special interest. SEE MAIN ENTRY
lobbyist   special interest. SEE MAIN ENTRY
local   chapter *(branch)*, domestic *(indigenous)*, native *(domestic)*, organ, provincial, regional. SEE MAIN ENTRY
local law   ordinance
local legislation   ordinance
local office   chapter *(branch)*

local representative   dealer
local rule   ordinance
locale   district, locality, location, part *(place)*, region, scene, seat, section *(vicinity)*, site, situs, territory, venue. SEE MAIN ENTRY
locality   community, district, environment, home *(domicile)*, location, region, scene, seat, section *(vicinity)*, site, situs, venue. SEE MAIN ENTRY
localize   restrict, site
localized   local, regional
locally born   native *(domestic)*
locare   contract, lease, rent
locate   allocate, deposit *(place)*, detect, discover, find *(discover)*, lodge *(house)*, pinpoint, plant *(place firmly)*, site. SEE MAIN ENTRY
locate oneself   lodge *(reside)*
located   situated
location   area *(province)*, locality, part *(place)*, region, scene, seat, section *(vicinity)*, site, situs, standpoint, structure *(edifice)*, venue. SEE MAIN ENTRY
lock   connect *(join together)*, fetter, fix *(make firm)*, occlude, seal *(close)*, shut. SEE MAIN ENTRY
lock in   immure, imprison, jail
lock out   bar *(exclude)*, eliminate *(exclude)*. SEE MAIN ENTRY
lock up   capture, commit *(institutionalize)*, confine, contain *(restrain)*, detain *(hold in custody)*, fetter, immure, imprison, jail, lock, restrain
locked   conjoint, impervious, inseparable
locker   coffer
locking up   commitment *(confinement)*
lockout   ostracism
lockup   penitentiary
loco movere   depose *(remove)*
loco parentis   SEE MAIN ENTRY
loco suo movere   displace *(remove)*
locomotive   moving *(in motion)*
locum vacuefacere   evacuate
locuples   unimpeachable
locus   address, circuit, locality
locus   location. SEE MAIN ENTRY
locus   position *(situation)*, post, purview, region, scene, scope, section *(vicinity)*
locus   situs
locus   space
locus classicus   cross section
locus qui petitur   objective
locus standi   character *(reputation)*
locutio   phraseology
locution   expression *(comment)*, parlance, phraseology, speech, term *(expression)*
lodge   chapter *(branch)*, deposit *(place)*, dwell *(reside)*, embed, fix *(make firm)*, harbor, inhabit, locate, occupy *(take possession)*, organ, remain *(occupy)*, remain *(stay)*, repose *(place)*, reside, stay *(rest)*. SEE MAIN ENTRY
lodge a complaint   accuse, blame, charge *(accuse)*, cite *(accuse)*, complain *(charge)*, denounce *(inform against)*, implicate, incriminate, indict, involve *(implicate)*, present *(prefer charges)*. SEE MAIN ENTRY
lodge together   cohabit
lodged   situated
lodger   habitant, inhabitant, lessee, occupant, resident, tenant. SEE MAIN ENTRY
lodging   address, building *(structure)*, chamber *(compartment)*, domicile, dwelling, habitation *(dwelling place)*, home

(*domicile*), house, household, inhabitation (*act of dwelling in*), inhabitation (*place of dwelling*), shelter (*protection*). SEE MAIN ENTRY

lodging house   building (*structure*)

lodging place   address, building (*structure*), dwelling, home (*domicile*), inhabitation (*place of dwelling*), lodging

lodging together   cohabitation (*living together*)

lodging together as husband and wife   cohabitation (*living together*)

lodgings   building (*structure*), premises (*buildings*), residence

lodgment   address, building (*structure*), domicile, dwelling, habitation (*act of inhabiting*), habitation (*dwelling place*), inhabitation (*act of inhabiting in*), inhabitation (*place of dwelling*), lodging, residence

loftiness   bombast, distinction (*reputation*), elevation, eminence, pretense (*ostentation*), rhetoric (*insincere language*)

lofty   grandiose, magnanimous, meritorious, orgulous, presumptuous, prominent, proud (*self-respecting*), remarkable, supercilious. SEE MAIN ENTRY

log   book, calendar (*record of yearly periods*), enter (*record*), journal, ledger, note (*record*), record (*noun*), record (*verb*), register

log book   register

logbook   calendar (*record of yearly periods*), journal, ledger

logic   common sense, data, dialectic, ratiocination, reason (*sound judgment*). SEE MAIN ENTRY

logic of discursive argument   dialectic

logical   apparent (*presumptive*), cogent, coherent (*clear*), colorable (*plausible*), consistent, convincing, deductive, discursive (*analytical*), normal (*sane*), persuasive, plausible, probable, rational, reasonable (*rational*), sane, sensible, solid (*sound*), tenable, valid, viable. SEE MAIN ENTRY

logical argumentation   dialectic

logical discussion   deliberation, dialectic

logical order   array (*order*), method, sequence

logical process   deduction (*conclusion*), dialectic, system

logical reasoning   rationale

logical relation   analogy

logical result   consequence (*conclusion*)

logical sequence   corollary, deduction (*conclusion*), dialectic

logically appealing   coherent (*clear*)

logically consistent   coherent (*clear*), consonant

logically then   consequently

logically unsound   illogical

logicalness   reason (*sound judgment*)

logomachic   argumentative

logomachical   argumentative

logomachy   fight (*argument*)

loiter   delay, pause, procrastinate, prowl. SEE MAIN ENTRY

loitering   truant

lone   exclusive (*singular*), only (*sole*), separate, singular, sole, solitary, unilateral. SEE MAIN ENTRY

lonely   derelict (*abandoned*), solitary

lonesome   derelict (*abandoned*), solitary

long   prolix, protracted, sesquipedalian. SEE MAIN ENTRY

long and short of it   SEE MAIN ENTRY

long-drawn (*protracted*)   SEE MAIN ENTRY

long for   desire, lack, need

long gone   dead

long life   longevity

long odds   improbability

long vehement speech   diatribe

long windedness   prolixity

long-continued   protracted

long-continuing   chronic, durable

long-delayed   back (*in arrears*), overdue

long-drawn   protracted

long-enduring   durable

long-established   conventional, customary, prescriptive, traditional

long-lasting   durable, incessant, permanent, stable, steadfast

long-lived   chronic, durable, stable

long-spun   prolix

long-standing   chronic, durable, inveterate, stable, traditional. SEE MAIN ENTRY

long-suffering   lenient, patient, resigned, stoical

long-winded   flatulent, loquacious, profuse, prolix, turgid, voluble

longanimity   lenience, resignation (*passive acceptance*), sufferance. SEE MAIN ENTRY

longanimous   lenient, patient, placable

longevity   age. SEE MAIN ENTRY

longevous   durable

longhand   handwriting, holographic, script

longiloquent   loquacious

longing   desire, eager, jealous, predisposition, will (*desire*)

longlivedness   longevity

longsighted   perspicacious

longstanding   chronic, prescriptive

longus   prolix

look   appear (*seem to be*), aspect, complexion, condition (*state*), configuration (*form*), demean (*deport oneself*), demeanor, deportment, feature (*appearance*), manner (*behavior*), notice (*observe*), observation, observe (*watch*), presence (*poise*), regard (*pay attention*), semblance, vision (*dream*). SEE MAIN ENTRY

look about for   canvass

look about one   beware

look after   concern (*care*), conduct, control (*regulate*), direct (*supervise*), foster, handle (*manage*), harbor, keep (*shelter*), maintain (*sustain*), manage, operate, overlook (*superintend*), oversee, preserve, protect, provide (*arrange for*), superintend

look ahead   plan

look ahead to   prognosticate

look around for   delve

look as if   appear (*seem to be*)

look askance at   disfavor

look at   discern (*detect with the senses*), note (*notice*), notice (*observe*), observe (*watch*), regard (*pay attention*), spy, survey (*examine*)

look at closely   scrutinize

look back   remember

look back upon   recall (*remember*), recollect

look behind the scenes   delve

look down on   condescend (*patronize*), disdain, disfavor, disparage, patronize (*condescend toward*)

look down upon   discriminate (*treat differently*), misprize, spurn

look for   delve, expect (*anticipate*), ferret, hunt, spy

look for flaws   check (*inspect*), examine (*study*)

look forward to   anticipate (*prognosticate*), expect (*anticipate*), forestall, prognosticate

look into   canvass, check (*inspect*), delve, examine (*study*), frisk, inquire, investigate, probe, research, scrutinize, search. SEE MAIN ENTRY

look on   discern (*detect with the senses*)

look out   beware, overlook (*superintend*), patrol

look out for   care (*be cautious*)

look over   check (*inspect*), examine (*study*), frisk, overlook (*superintend*), peruse, review, scrutinize, search. SEE MAIN ENTRY

look through   delve, examine (*study*), frisk, search

look to   focus, heed, rely, resort

look up   SEE MAIN ENTRY

look up information in   consult (*seek information from*)

look up to   honor, regard (*hold in esteem*)

look upon   deem, discern (*detect with the senses*), opine, regard (*pay attention*)

look with scorn on   disdain

look with scorn upon   condescend (*patronize*)

looked after   safe

looked for   foreseeable, forseen, immediate (*imminent*), prospective

looked toward   future

looker   bystander, witness

looker-on   bystander, eyewitness, witness

looking back   hindsight, retrospect

looking within   introspection

lookout   caretaker (*one caring for property*), spy, surveillance

loom   emerge, impend

looming   forthcoming, future, imminent, inevitable, instant, pending (*imminent*), prospective. SEE MAIN ENTRY

loop   detour

loophole   flaw, subterfuge. SEE MAIN ENTRY

loose   careless, discharge (*liberate*), disconnected, disencumber, disengage, disjunctive (*tending to disjoin*), dispel, free (*not restricted*), inaccurate, inexact, lax, lecherous, liberal (*not literal*), liberate, licentious, open-ended, promiscuous, salacious, separate, suggestive (*risqué*), unrestrained (*not repressed*). SEE MAIN ENTRY

loose rendering   paraphrase

loose statement   generality (*vague statement*)

loose thinking   non sequitur

loose translation   paraphrase

loosen   disencumber, disentangle, disenthrall, dissociate, ease, extricate, give (*yield*), remit (*relax*). SEE MAIN ENTRY

looseness   informality, laxity, vice

looseness of morals   perversion

loosing   discharge (*liberation*), discharge (*release from obligation*)

loot   despoil, jostle (*pickpocket*), pilfer, pillage, pirate (*take by violence*), plunder (*noun*), plunder (*verb*), prey, prize, rob, spoil (*pillage*), spoils. SEE MAIN ENTRY

looting   burglary, foray, housebreaking, spoliation, theft

lop   break (*separate*), curtail, retrench

lop off   sever

loquacious   profuse, voluble. SEE MAIN ENTRY

loquacity   prolixity, tautology

loquax   loquacious

loqui   generalize

lordliness   pride

lordly   dictatorial, disdainful, inflated (*vain*), orgulous, presumptuous, proud (*conceited*), supercilious, tyrannous

855

lordship dominion (*supreme authority*), hegemony, possession (*ownership*), supremacy

lore discipline (*field of study*), information (*knowledge*)

lose deplete, erode, fail (*lose*), forfeit, succumb, suffer (*sustain loss*). SEE MAIN ENTRY

lose an opportunity forfeit

lose by breach of condition forfeit

lose by default forfeit. SEE MAIN ENTRY

lose by failure to appear default, forfeit

lose control carouse

lose courage fear

lose ground retreat. SEE MAIN ENTRY

lose heart languish

lose identity merge

lose individuality merge

lose life decease, perish

lose luster tarnish

lose morale degenerate

lose no time hasten

lose one's life die

lose sight of neglect

lose spirit languish

lose strength languish

lose value depreciate

losel improvident

loss abridgment (*disentitlement*), bad debt, bankruptcy, calamity, consumption, cost (*penalty*), damage, damages, decline, decrease, decrement, defeat, deficiency, deficit, detriment, disadvantage, erosion, expense (*sacrifice*), failure (*lack of success*), forfeiture (*thing forfeited*), impairment (*damage*), injury, miscarriage, penalty, prejudice (*injury*), privation, toll (*effect*). SEE MAIN ENTRY

loss consequent to a default forfeiture (*thing forfeited*)

loss of affection estrangement. SEE MAIN ENTRY

loss of belief discredit

loss of credence discredit

loss of credit discredit

loss of fortune bankruptcy, poverty, privation

loss of freedom bondage, subjection

loss of health disease

loss of honor bad repute, disgrace, disrepute, ignominy, notoriety, opprobrium, scandal, shame

loss of identity merger

loss of life death, demise (*death*)

loss of opportunity SEE MAIN ENTRY

loss of power prostration

loss of reason insanity

loss of reputation attaint, bad repute, disgrace, dishonor (*shame*), disrepute, ignominy, infamy, notoriety, opprobrium, scandal, shame. SEE MAIN ENTRY

loss of repute discredit

loss of respect ignominy

loss of right disqualification (*rejection*), forfeiture (*act of forfeiting*), waiver

loss of standing opprobrium

loss of strength failure (*falling short*), fault (*weakness*), frailty

loss of value decline, decrease. SEE MAIN ENTRY

lost astray, disconsolate, incorrigible, irredeemable, irretrievable, reprobate. SEE MAIN ENTRY

lost cause SEE MAIN ENTRY

lost connection anacoluthon, non sequitur

lost labor miscarriage

lost to principle profligate (*corrupt*)

lost to virtue profligate (*corrupt*)

lot assemblage, bulk, conglomeration, entirety, lottery, parcel, plight, plot (*land*), posture (*situation*), predetermination, property (*land*), quantity, real estate, situation. SEE MAIN ENTRY

lottery SEE MAIN ENTRY

loud blatant (*obtrusive*), disorderly, flagrant, powerful, resounding, tawdry. SEE MAIN ENTRY

loud noise outcry

loud protest outcry

loudness noise

lounge rest (*be supported by*), rest (*cease from action*)

loutish opaque, provincial, uncouth

love affection, affinity (*regard*), predilection. SEE MAIN ENTRY

love of mankind philanthropy

loved popular

lovely elegant, sapid

loving zealous

low caitiff, depraved, heinous, ignoble, inelegant, lamentable, minimal, nominal, nonsubstantial (*not sufficient*), odious, offensive (*offending*), outrageous, poor (*inferior in quality*), scandalous, scarce, scurrilous, servile, subaltern, tainted (*corrupted*). SEE MAIN ENTRY

low comedy travesty

low estimation dishonor (*shame*), disparagement, disregard (*lack of respect*)

low grade mediocrity

low opinion disapproval, disparagement

low quality mediocrity

low regard bad repute

low spirited disconsolate

low spirits damper (*depressant*), pessimism

low standard bad repute

low standing ignominy

low valuation disparagement

low-class mediocre

low-grade inferior (*lower in quality*), mediocre, poor (*inferior in quality*)

low-level minor, subordinate

low-minded depraved, dissolute

low-priced nominal

low-quality marginal, mediocre

low-spirited lugubrious, pessimistic

low-spiritedness pessimism

lowborn caitiff, ignoble

lower debase, decrease, deduct (*reduce*), defame, demean (*make lower*), demote, denigrate, depreciate, depress, derogate, deteriorate, diminish, discount (*reduce*), disgrace, humiliate, inferior (*lower in position*), lessen, minimize, minor, modify (*moderate*), pervert, pillory, reduce, subaltern, subdue, subordinate, subservient. SEE MAIN ENTRY

lower in authority inferior (*lower in position*)

lower in price depreciate

lower in rank demote, inferior (*lower in position*), subaltern, subordinate

lower in reputation depreciate

lower in the scale inferior (*lower in position*)

lower in value debase, depreciate

lower morally taint (*corrupt*)

lower oneself condescend (*deign*), patronize (*condescend toward*)

lower price discount

lower the courage of discourage

lower the estimation of disparage

lower the sale price discount (*reduce*)

lower the standard adulterate

lower the value of depreciate

lowering decline, decrease, deduction (*diminution*), depression, diminution

lowest (*far below*) SEE MAIN ENTRY

lowest quantity minimum

lowliness prostration

lowly base (*inferior*), ignoble, inferior (*lower in position*), subaltern, subordinate

lowness bad character, depression

loyal constant, dependable, obedient, reliable, serious (*devoted*), staunch, steadfast. SEE MAIN ENTRY

loyalist disciple

loyally faithfully

loyalty adherence (*devotion*), allegiance, discipline (*obedience*), faith, fealty, fidelity, homage, rectitude, regard (*esteem*), trustworthiness. SEE MAIN ENTRY

lubric lascivious, lecherous

lubricious prurient

lubricity obscenity, pornography

lubricous lascivious, lecherous, lewd, licentious, obscene

lucent lucid

lucid cognizable, coherent (*clear*), comprehensible, distinct (*clear*), evident, explicit, manifest, normal (*sane*), obvious, palpable, pellucid, rational, reasonable (*rational*), sane, unambiguous, unmistakable. SEE MAIN ENTRY

lucidity competence (*sanity*), reason (*sound judgment*), sanity

lucidly fairly (*clearly*)

lucidus lucid

luck contingency, opportunity, prosperity, quirk (*accident*), welfare. SEE MAIN ENTRY

luckless ominous

lucky auspicious, fortuitous, propitious, prosperous

lucrari gain

lucrative gainful, profitable. SEE MAIN ENTRY

lucre boom (*prosperity*)

lucrosus gainful, lucrative

lucrum earnings, profit

luctatio struggle

lucubration pandect (*treatise*)

luculent comprehensible, lucid

ludibrio mock (*deride*)

ludicrous fatuous, inept (*inappropriate*), irrational, unreasonable. SEE MAIN ENTRY

ludicrous imitation parody

ludicrous presentation travesty

ludicrous representation ridicule

ludicrousness incongruity, inexpedience

ludificari flout, hoodwink

ludificatio hoax

luggage cargo

lugubrious despondent, lamentable. SEE MAIN ENTRY

lugubris lugubrious

lukewarm irresolute, languid, nonchalant, noncommittal, perfunctory

lukewarmness indifference

lull allay, alleviate, cessation (*interlude*), cloture, halt, hiatus, holiday, interruption, interval, lapse (*break*), mollification, mollify, moratorium, pause, peace, pendency, recess, remission, respite (*interval of rest*), soothe, subside. SEE MAIN ENTRY

lumbering ponderous

luminary mastermind

luminous cognizable, coherent (*clear*), notable, outstanding (*prominent*)

lump assemblage, entirety, part (*portion*), totality

lump sum payment SEE MAIN ENTRY

lump together commingle, compile, consolidate *(unite)*, hoard
lumpiness irregularity
lumpish lifeless *(dull)*, obtuse, opaque, ponderous, stagnant
lumpishness opacity, sloth
lunacy insanity, paranoia. SEE MAIN ENTRY
lunatic non compos mentis. SEE MAIN ENTRY
lunge at beat *(strike)*, strike *(assault)*
lupine predatory, rapacious
lurch oscillate
lure amenity, betray *(lead astray)*, cajole, coax, ensnare, entice, entrap, incentive, inveigle, persuade, prevail *(persuade)*, seduction, trap. SEE MAIN ENTRY
lure into a compromising act entrap
lurid licentious, obscene, salacious, suggestive *(risqué)*. SEE MAIN ENTRY
luridus lurid
luring attractive, bribery
lurk prowl. SEE MAIN ENTRY
lurking hidden, surreptitious
luscious nectarious, palatable, sapid, savory
lush fertile
lust debauchery, desire, passion
lust for need
lust for money greed
luster prestige, reputation
lusterless lifeless *(dull)*, ponderous
lustful dissolute, hot-blooded, lascivious, lecherous, lewd, obscene, prurient, salacious, suggestive *(risqué)*, wanton
lustiness life *(vitality)*, prowess *(bravery)*, puissance, sinew
lustless languid, powerless
lustrate decontaminate
lustrous outstanding *(prominent)*
lusty powerful, strong, vehement
luxate disjoint, dislocate. SEE MAIN ENTRY
luxuriant copious, fertile, productive, profuse, superfluous, wanton
luxuriate pullulate
luxuriate in relish
luxuriosus dissolute
luxurious replete, superfluous
luxury prosperity. SEE MAIN ENTRY
lyceum institute
lying deceit, deceptive, dishonest, dishonesty, disingenuous, falsification, improbity, insidious, mendacious, perfidious, subreption, untrue. SEE MAIN ENTRY
lymphatic languid, otiose, phlegmatic, ponderous
lynch law SEE MAIN ENTRY

M

macabre SEE MAIN ENTRY
macellum market *(business)*
macerate bait *(harass)*, plague
Machiavellian artful. SEE MAIN ENTRY
Machiavellism artifice
machina device *(contrivance)*, expedient, machination
machinari conjure, contrive
machinate connive, conspire, contrive, maneuver, plan, plot, scheme
machination artifice, cabal, connivance, contrivance, deception, device *(contrivance)*, expedient, frame up, hoax, maneuver *(trick)*, premeditation, ruse, scheme, stratagem, strategy, subterfuge. SEE MAIN ENTRY
machinator conspirator, copartner *(co-conspirator)*

machine appliance, expedient, instrument *(tool)*, make, syndicate, tool
machine like controlled *(automatic)*
machine-made industrial
machiner artisan
machinery conduit *(channel)*, facility *(instrumentality)*, instrument *(tool)*, instrumentality, medium SEE MAIN ENTRY
macroscopic perceivable, perceptible
macula defilement
maculare stain, sully
maculate pollute, stain, tarnish
maculation bad repute, flaw
mad deranged, lunatic, non compos mentis, outrageous, quixotic. SEE MAIN ENTRY
madcap hot-blooded, outrageous, precipitate
madden aggravate *(annoy)*, incense, irritate, obsess, offend *(insult)*, perturb, pique, provoke
maddened deranged, non compos mentis
maddening vexatious
made captive arrested *(apprehended)*
made fast fixed *(securely placed)*
made poorly insubstantial
made prisoner arrested *(apprehended)*
made public naked *(perceptible)*
made up mendacious
madhouse shambles
madness furor, insanity, lunacy, paranoia
maelstrom bluster *(commotion)*, commotion, disturbance, furor, shambles
maeror depression
maestus disconsolate
magazine depository, journal, publication *(printed matter)*
magic prestidigitation. SEE MAIN ENTRY
magical mysterious, uncanny
magister pedagogue, principal *(director)*
magisterial dogmatic, insolent, juridical, official, powerful, presumptuous, supercilious
magistracy bench, judiciary
magistrate bench, caretaker *(one fulfilling the function of office)*, judge, jurist. SEE MAIN ENTRY
magistrates court
magistrature bench
magistratus authorities, magistrate
magnanimity charity, clemency, condonation, indulgence, largess *(generosity)*, longanimity, philanthropy
magnanimous benevolent, charitable *(benevolent)*, lenient, liberal *(generous)*, meritorious, philanthropic, placable. SEE MAIN ENTRY
magnanimousness clemency, largess *(generosity)*
magnanimus magnanimous
magnate SEE MAIN ENTRY
magnetic attractive SEE MAIN ENTRY
magnetism draw *(attraction)*
magni momenti momentous
magnification aggravation *(exacerbation)*, augmentation, bombast, boom *(increase)*, distortion, exaggeration, extension *(expansion)*, hyperbole, laudation, overstatement SEE MAIN ENTRY
magnificent elegant, meritorious, proud *(self-respecting)* SEE MAIN ENTRY
magnified extreme *(exaggerated)*, inflated *(overestimated)*
magnify aggravate *(exacerbate)*, build *(augment)*, compound, develop, elaborate, enhance, enlarge, expand, extend *(enlarge)*, heighten *(augment)*, inflate,

intensify, overestimate, promote *(advance)*, supplement. SEE MAIN ENTRY
magnifying cumulative *(intensifying)*
magniloquence ardor, bombast, fustian, overstatement, peroration, rhetoric *(insincere language)*
magniloquent grandiose, inflated *(bombastic)*, orotund, sesquipedalian, turgid
magnitude amount *(quantity)*, bulk, caliber *(measurement)*, consequence *(significance)*, extent, importance, mass *(weight)*, materiality *(consequence)*, measurement, purview, weight *(importance)*. SEE MAIN ENTRY
magnitudo bulk, magnitude
magno rate
magnus considerable, extensive, gross *(total)*, important *(significant)*
maiden incipient, initial, original *(initial)*
maiestas treason
mail correspondence *(communication by letters)*, dispatch *(message)*, send. SEE MAIN ENTRY
mail again redirect
maim damage, disable, harm, mutilate, prejudice *(injure)*
maimed disabled *(made incapable)*, marred
maiming disabling
main cardinal *(basic)*, central *(essential)*, dominant, essential *(inherent)*, important *(significant)*, indispensable, leading *(ranking first)*, master, material *(important)*, noteworthy, paramount, primary, principal, prominent, salient, stellar, strength, substantive, vital. SEE MAIN ENTRY
main asset transfer bulk transfer
main attraction feature *(special attraction)*
main body cornerstone, corpus, generality *(bulk)*, majority *(greater part)*, principal *(capital sum)*
main business agenda
main character protagonist
main charge complaint, count, gist *(ground for a suit)*, indictment
main element cornerstone
main feature motif
main features contour *(outline)*
main focus SEE MAIN ENTRY
main force SEE MAIN ENTRY
main idea main point
main ingredient necessity
main interest specialty *(special aptitude)*
main item feature *(special attraction)*
main meaning context
main office headquarters
main part body *(main part)*, bulk, center *(essence)*, corpus, generality *(bulk)*, majority *(greater part)*, plurality
main point center *(essence)*, content *(meaning)*, cornerstone, gist *(ground for a suit)*, gravamen. SEE MAIN ENTRY
main thing cornerstone, main point
mainly a fortiori, ab initio, as a rule, generally, particularly. SEE MAIN ENTRY
mainspring cause *(reason)*, derivation, reason *(basis)*
mainstay abettor, backer, cornerstone, partisan, strength, support *(assistance)*. SEE MAIN ENTRY
maintain adhere *(persist)*, allege, argue, assert, authorize, avouch *(avow)*, avow, bear *(adduce)*, bear *(support)*, bestow, cite *(state)*, conserve, continue *(persevere)*, continue *(prolong)*, control *(regulate)*, corroborate, declare, defend, endure *(last)*, fund,

harbor, justify, keep *(continue)*, keep *(shelter)*, nurture, own, perpetuate, persevere, persist, plead *(allege in a legal action)*, posit, possess, preserve, profess *(avow)*, prolong, promote *(organize)*, propound, prosecute *(carry forward)*, protect, provide *(supply)*, pursue *(carry on)*, remain *(continue)*, remain *(occupy)*, reserve, resist *(withstand)*, retain *(employ)*, retain *(keep in possession)*, store, subsidize, subsist, supply, support *(assist)*, sustain *(prolong)*, uphold. SEE MAIN ENTRY

maintain a course   persevere

maintain a middle position   compromise *(settle by mutual agreement)*

maintain as conformable to duty   justify

maintain as conformable to justice   justify

maintain by affirmation   vouch

maintain by arguments   plead *(argue a case)*

maintain continuity   continue *(prolong)*

maintain under oath   swear

maintainable   defensible, justifiable, tenable

maintained   alleged, chronic, durable, lasting, plausible, safe

maintained in prison   in custody

maintainer   abettor, advocate *(counselor)*, advocate *(espouser)*, backer, benefactor, mainstay, partisan

maintaining   conservation, convincing

maintenance   aid *(help)*, aid *(subsistence)*, alimony, conservation, continuation *(prolongation)*, ecology, livelihood, longevity, preservation, promotion *(encouragement)*, provision *(something provided)*, security *(safety)*, support *(assistance)*, survival, sustenance. SEE MAIN ENTRY

maintenance allowance   alimony

maintenance of regularity   status quo

major numerus   majority *(greater part)*

major pars   majority *(greater part)*

majestic   important *(significant)*, outstanding *(prominent)*, proud *(self-respecting)*, solemn

majesty   eminence, prestige

major   cardinal *(outstanding)*, central *(essential)*, critical *(crucial)*, important *(significant)*, indispensable, key, material *(important)*, momentous. SEE MAIN ENTRY

major business asset transfer   bulk transfer

major event   cornerstone

major misfortune   calamity

major part   body *(main part)*, bulk, cornerstone, corpus, main point, majority *(greater part)*

majority   bulk, generality *(bulk)*, maturity, plurality, preponderance. SEE MAIN ENTRY

make   build *(construct)*, cause, color *(complexion)*, create, fabricate *(construct)*, forge *(produce)*, form, frame *(construct)*, gain, generate, impose *(enforce)*, manner *(kind)*, manufacture, occasion, originate, press *(constrain)*, produce *(manufacture)*, realize *(obtain as a profit)*, receive *(acquire)*, require *(compel)*, style. SEE MAIN ENTRY

make a bargain   agree *(contract)*, close *(agree)*, contract, handle *(trade)*

make a beginning   embark

make a benefaction   bestow

make a bequest   bequeath, demise, descend, devise *(give)*, leave *(give)*

make a bet   parlay *(bet)*

make a bid   attempt, endeavor, offer *(propose)*, proffer, strive

make a butt of   mock *(deride)*

make a change   affect, vary

make a choice   cast *(register)*, decide, discriminate *(distinguish)*, elect *(choose)*, resolve *(decide)*, select

make a circuit   detour

make a clean breast   betray *(disclose)*

make a common cause with   federalize *(associate)*

make a commotion   brawl

make a compact   settle

make a comparison   contrast, measure

make a complaint   cite *(accuse)*

make a compromise   compromise *(settle by mutual agreement)*

make a computation   calculate

make a condition   stipulate

make a confession   confess

make a deal   compromise *(settle by mutual agreement)*

make a decision   adjudge, adjudicate, arbitrate *(adjudge)*, cast *(register)*, choose, conclude *(decide)*, decide, determine, find *(determine)*, fix *(settle)*, hold *(decide)*, resolve *(decide)*, rule *(decide)*

make a declaration   declare

make a decree   instruct *(direct)*

make a deduction   derive *(deduce)*

make a demand   call *(demand)*, move *(judicially request)* SEE MAIN ENTRY

make a departure   evacuate, quit *(evacuate)*

make a detour   deviate

make a distinction   differentiate, discriminate *(distinguish)*, discriminate *(treat differently)*, select

make a duplicate of   copy

make a false show of   feign

make a finding   SEE MAIN ENTRY

make a fool of   delude, dupe, hoodwink, humiliate, illude, mock *(deride)*

make a formal proclamation   notice *(give formal warning)*

make a gaudy display   flaunt

make a generalization   generalize

make a getaway   escape

make a gift   give *(grant)*

make a good return   pay

make a hit   succeed *(attain)*

make a judgment   diagnose

make a legacy   demise, descend

make a likeness   delineate

make a list   enumerate

make a loan   bestow

make a member   enroll

make a memorandum   note *(record)*, record

make a mess of   muddle

make a mistake   err, miscalculate, misconceive, misconstrue, misinterpret, misjudge, mislead, misunderstand

make a mixture   combine *(join together)*

make a motion   move *(judicially request)*, pose *(propound)*, proffer, propose, propound, submit *(give)* SEE MAIN ENTRY

make a new beginning   continue *(resume)*

make a note   record

make a party to   implicate, incriminate, involve *(implicate)*

make a passage   penetrate

make a path for   facilitate

make a petition   call *(appeal to)*, move *(judicially request)*

make a place for   locate, lodge *(house)*, plant *(place firmly)*

make a plan   devise *(invent)*, maneuver, plot

make a positive statement   affirm *(claim)*

make a prediction   predict, presage, prognosticate, promise *(raise expectations)*

make a present   grant *(transfer formally)*

make a present of   bequeath, bestow

make a presentation   give *(grant)*

make a pretext of   pretend

make a proclamation   proclaim

make a profit   gain

make a prognosis   predict

make a promise   assure *(insure)*, pledge *(promise the performance of)*

make a proposition   offer *(propose)*

make a public announcement   issue *(publish)*

make a purchase   buy, procure

make a racket   brawl

make a reality   implement

make a rebuttal   converse, retort, return *(respond)* SEE MAIN ENTRY

make a reconnaissance   check *(inspect)*, spy

make a record   enroll

make a rejoinder   answer *(reply)*, controvert, dispute *(debate)*, respond, return *(respond)*

make a remark   observe *(remark)*

make a replica   copy

make a request   call *(appeal to)*, move *(judicially request)*, plead *(implore)*, pray, solicit

make a request for   desire

make a requisition   call *(appeal to)*, move *(judicially request)*, order, petition

make a resolute stand   hold out *(resist)*

make a resolution   conclude *(decide)*, determine, rule *(decide)*

make a sale   handle *(trade)*, sell, vend

make a selection   cast *(register)*, cull, decide, discriminate *(distinguish)*, elect *(choose)*, extract, select

make a shambles   pillage

make a shift with   displace *(replace)*

make a show   pretend

make a show of   fake, flaunt, profess *(pretend)*

make a showy appearance   flaunt

make a solemn declaration   affirm *(declare solemnly)*

make a solemn resolution   promise *(vow)*

make a spectacle   flaunt

make a speech   converse, declaim, discourse, recite, speak

make a spurious copy of   forge *(counterfeit)*

make a stand   repulse

make a stand against   counter, counteract, cross *(disagree with)*, fight *(counteract)*, repel *(drive back)*, resist *(oppose)*

make a start   preface

make a statement   avow, bear *(adduce)*, claim *(maintain)*, contend *(maintain)*, converse, declare, express, profess *(avow)*, speak. SEE MAIN ENTRY

make a suggestion   propose, submit *(give)*

make a summary of   digest *(summarize)*

make a survey   canvass, poll

make a testamentary disposition   leave *(give)*

make a transcript of   copy

make a transition   change

make a trial run   check *(inspect)*

make a try   attempt

make able   charge *(empower)*, empower, enable

make absolute   certify *(attest)*, support *(corroborate)*

make acceptable   rationalize

make accordant   attune

make accountable for   encumber *(financially obligate)*

make acknowledgment   return *(respond)*

make acquainted   convey *(communicate)*, present *(introduce)*

make acquainted with   forewarn, notice *(give formal warning)*

make active   implement, launch *(initiate)*

make adjustments   attune, modify *(alter)*

make again   reproduce

make agree   attune

make allowance   condone, rebate

make allowance for   discount *(reduce)*, extenuate, palliate *(excuse)*, provide *(arrange for)*

make allowances   rationalize

make allowances for   countenance, excuse

make allusion to   mention

make amends   propitiate, recoup *(reimburse)*, redeem *(satisfy debts)*, redress, refund, remedy, repay, repent, replace, restore *(return)*

make an accusation   complain *(charge)*

make an adjustment   compromise *(settle by mutual agreement)*

make an affidavit   depose *(testify)*, plead *(allege in a legal action)*

make an agenda   program

make an agreement   agree *(contract)*, close *(agree)* SEE MAIN ENTRY

make an agreement with   connive, conspire, cooperate, join *(associate oneself with)*

make an allusion   hint

make an allusion to   imply, remind

make an analysis   analyze, examine *(study)*

make an announcement   enunciate, notice *(give formal warning)*, notify, report *(disclose)*

make an antagonist of   antagonize

make an appearance   appear *(attend court proceedings)*, arise *(appear)*, emerge

make an arrest   capture

make an assertion   affirm *(claim)*, allege, argue, avouch *(avow)*, avow, bear *(adduce)*, claim *(maintain)*, contend *(maintain)*, express, plead *(allege in a legal action)*, profess *(avow)*

make an asseveration   affirm *(declare solemnly)*

make an attempt   endeavor, strive

make an attestation   affirm *(declare solemnly)*

make an authoritative request   call *(demand)*, exact

make an averment   affirm *(declare solemnly)*

make an avowal   promise *(vow)*

make an effort   endeavor, strive, try *(attempt)*, undertake

make an effort at   attempt

make an end of   cease, close *(terminate)*, conclude *(complete)*, dispatch *(dispose of)*, quit *(discontinue)*

make an engagement   promise *(vow)*

make an entrance   enter *(go in)*, pervade

make an entry   book, cast *(register)*, enter *(record)*, inscribe, note *(record)*, record

make an error   misinterpret, misjudge

make an escape   elude, flee

make an estimate   calculate, measure

make an estimation   gauge

make an examination   probe

make an example of   discipline *(punish)*

make an exception   except *(exclude)*, exclude

make an exit   depart, quit *(evacuate)*

make an expenditure   expend *(disburse)*

make an impact upon   impress *(affect deeply)*

make an impression on   impress *(affect deeply)*

make an incision   lancinate

make an incursion   encroach

make an inquiry   analyze

make an introduction   present *(introduce)*

make an investment   invest *(fund)*

make an issue   contend *(dispute)*

make an oath   promise *(vow)*

make an offer   proffer

make an onset against   attack

make an opening   capitalize *(seize the chance)*

make an order   instruct *(direct)*

make an overture   offer *(propose)*, proffer

make an uproar   brawl

make angry   affront, offend *(insult)*

make apparent   bare, characterize, delineate, elucidate

make appeal   call *(appeal to)*

make appeal to   sue

make application   call *(appeal to)*, demand, move *(judicially request)*, petition, request. SEE MAIN ENTRY

make application for   desire

make arrangements   arrange *(plan)*, deal, devise *(invent)*, frame *(formulate)*, maneuver, plan, plot, program, scheme

make aseptic   decontaminate

make ashamed   demean *(make lower)*, derogate

make available   disburse *(distribute)*, let *(lease)*, rent

make available for rent   sublease

make averse   alienate *(estrange)*

make aware   apprise, caution, convey *(communicate)*, enlighten, forewarn

make away with   dispatch *(put to death)*, distrain

make beautiful   embellish

make believe   assume *(simulate)*, fake, false *(not genuine)*, feign, invent *(falsify)*, pretend, prevaricate, profess *(pretend)*, simulate

make better   ameliorate, cultivate, emend, enhance, expurgate, meliorate, mollify, reform, remedy, renovate, repair, restore *(renew)*

make binding   validate

make blunt   obtund

make bold to ask   call *(appeal to)*, importune

make book   parlay *(bet)*

make brief   condense, constrict *(compress)*, decrease, digest *(summarize)*, minimize

make by mechanical industry   manufacture

make calm   lull

make capable   empower, enable, qualify *(meet standards)*

make capital   gain

make capital out of   profit

make captive   arrest *(apprehend)*, fetter, immure

make captive again   rearrest

make certain   ascertain, assure *(give confidence to)*, assure *(insure)*, certify *(attest)*,

document, ensure, find *(discover)*, reconfirm, verify *(confirm)* SEE MAIN ENTRY

make charges against   denounce *(inform against)*

make claims upon   call *(demand)*, charge *(assess)*, dun

make clear   characterize, clarify, comment, define, delineate, demonstrate *(establish)*, describe, detail *(particularize)*, elucidate, enlighten, evince, exhibit, explain, explicate, exposit, expound, interpret, manifest, profess *(avow)*, resolve *(solve)*, simplify *(clarify)*, stipulate SEE MAIN ENTRY

make clear by examples   exemplify

make cognizant   apprise

make comfortable   ease

make common cause   affiliate

make common cause with   combine *(act in concert)*, cooperate, involve *(participate)*

make compatible   arbitrate *(conciliate)*, reconcile

make compensation   bear the expense, contribute *(indemnify)*, cover *(provide for)*, outbalance, pay, quit *(repay)*, refund, return *(refund)*, satisfy *(discharge)*

make competent   qualify *(meet standards)*

make complete   conclude *(complete)*, replenish

make comprehensible   clarify

make compulsory   enforce

make concessions   compromise *(settle by mutual agreement)*

make concise   condense, digest *(summarize)*

make confident   assure *(give confidence to)*, convince

make conformable   adapt

make connection   contact *(communicate)*

make consistent   reconcile

make conspicuous   manifest

make contact   collide *(crash against)*, overlap

make contented   pander, reconcile

make contiguous   juxtapose

make conveyance of   grant *(transfer formally)*

make corporeal   embody

make corrections   edit, emend, fix *(repair)*, modify *(alter)*, rectify, review

make corrupt   pervert

make deductions   construe *(comprehend)*, reason *(conclude)*

make defense for   justify, support *(justify)*

make definite   stipulate

make deletions   redact

make delivery of legal process   serve *(deliver a legal instrument)*

make demands   exact, petition

make demands on   claim *(demand)*, dun, order

make dense   constrict *(compress)*

make denser   condense

make deposition   depose *(testify)*

make desirable   recommend

make despondent   depress

make different   change, vary

make difficult   perplex

make dim   obscure

make discontented   disaffect

make disease-free   decontaminate

make disloyal   disaffect

make dissatisfied   disappoint

make distasteful   discredit

make distinctions   discern *(discriminate)*, distinguish

make distinctive differentiate
make distribution of disburse *(distribute)*
make docile subdue
make durable establish *(entrench)*
make earnest entreaty call *(appeal to)*
make earnest petition for pray
make easier favor
make easy ease, facilitate, help, naturalize *(acclimate)*
make effective enforce
make elaborate embellish
make equal compensate *(counterbalance)*
make essential entail
make eternal perpetuate
make even juxtapose
make everlasting perpetuate
make evident bare, bear *(adduce)*, cite *(state)*, demonstrate *(establish)*, document, evince, exemplify, explain, illustrate, manifest, profess *(avow)*
make excessive demands tax *(overwork)*
make excessive use of abuse *(misuse)*
make exchanges barter
make excuses rationalize
make excuses for extenuate, justify
make expenditure bear the expense, disburse *(pay out)*, spend
make explanation of justify
make explicit clarify, explain, explicate, express
make extinct superannuate
make eyeless blind *(deprive of sight)*
make false pretenses palter
make false statements falsify, frame *(charge falsely)*, palter
make fast fix *(make firm)*, handcuff, lock
make faulty vitiate
make favorably inclined propitiate
make feeble debilitate
make final disposition of dispatch *(dispose of)*
make firm affirm *(uphold)*, cement, concentrate *(consolidate)*, confirm, consolidate *(strengthen)*, establish *(entrench)*, sustain *(confirm)*
make forbidden forbid
make formal formalize
make formal accusation against denounce *(inform against)*, indict
make formal application move *(judicially request)*
make formal request apply *(request)*
make foul pollute
make free acquit, disengage, disenthrall, extricate, parole
make free with assume *(seize)*
make friendly disarm *(set at ease)*
make full replenish
make fun of disparage, jape, jeer, mock *(deride)*, pillory
make germ-free decontaminate
make good fulfill, indemnify, keep *(fulfill)*, pay, recoup *(reimburse)*, redress, refund, reimburse, repair, restore *(return)*, return *(refund)*, satisfy *(discharge)*, substantiate, support *(corroborate)*
make good against anticipated loss indemnify
make good use of profit
make great magnify
make greater accumulate *(enlarge)*, compound, enlarge, expand, increase, inflate
make haste hasten, precipitate *(hasten)*
make havoc confound, disorganize, disorient, muddle, perturb, pillage

make headway develop, persist, proceed *(go forward)*, progress
make healthful decontaminate
make heavy load, overload
make higher build *(augment)*, elevate, heighten *(augment)*, heighten *(elevate)*
make hostile disaffect
make hygienic decontaminate
make ill infect
make illegal annul, prohibit
make illegible deface
make illegitimate disfranchise
make impact collide *(crash against)*, impinge
make imperfect vitiate
make important honor
make impossible condemn *(ban)*, disqualify, preclude
make improper use of abuse *(misuse)*
make improvement profit
make improvements edit, embellish, emend, enhance, meliorate, modify *(alter)*, repair, review
make impure adulterate, denature, infect, vitiate
make inactive close *(terminate)*, delay, desist, disable, disarm *(divest of arms)*, halt
make incapable disable
make inconspicuous blind *(obscure)*, conceal
make incumbent entail
make indifferent alienate *(estrange)*
make indirect reference allude
make indirect suggestion connote
make indiscernible blind *(obscure)*, conceal
make indispensable necessitate
make indistinct obnubilate, obscure
make ineffective neutralize, vitiate
make ineffectual override
make inescapable entail
make inevitable necessitate
make inferior in value degenerate
make inimical alienate *(estrange)*, disaffect
make innovations alter
make innoxious decontaminate
make inoperative avoid *(cancel)*
make inquiries probe
make inquiry delve
make inroads encroach, impinge SEE MAIN ENTRY
make inroads on impair
make insecure endanger
make insensitive brutalize
make inseperable lock
make intelligible clarify, construe *(translate)*, elucidate
make into convert *(change use)*
make into a statute enact
make into law legislate, pass *(approve)*
make intricate perplex
make its appearance issue *(send forth)*
make known advise, annunciate, apprise, bare, betray *(disclose)*, circulate, communicate, confide *(divulge)*, convey *(communicate)*, declare, disabuse, disclose, disinter, divulge, enlighten, exhibit, express, herald, impart, inform *(betray)*, inform *(notify)*, instruct *(teach)*, issue *(publish)*, manifest, mention, notice *(give formal warning)*, notify, phrase, post, present *(introduce)*, proclaim, produce *(offer to view)*, profess *(avow)*, promulgate, propagate *(spread)*, publish, relate *(tell)*, report *(disclose)*, reveal, signify *(inform)*, spread, unveil, utter SEE MAIN ENTRY
make known publicly annunciate

make languid debilitate
make larger build *(augment)*, compound, enlarge, expand, extend *(enlarge)*, heighten *(augment)*, increase, inflate, magnify
make last perpetuate
make lasting establish *(entrench)*
make lawful legalize, legitimate
make laws enact, legislate
make leeway outbalance
make legacies bequeath
make legal authorize, constitute *(establish)*, legalize, legislate, legitimate, pass *(approve)*, validate SEE MAIN ENTRY
make legitimate justify, legitimate, support *(justify)*
make less decrease, deduct *(reduce)*, diminish, minimize, moderate *(temper)*, reduce
make less concentrated dilute
make less confusing elucidate
make less extreme commute, modify *(moderate)*
make less friendly disaffect
make less harsh commute
make less important demote
make less intense commute, modify *(moderate)*
make less rigorous commute
make less rough commute
make less serious extenuate
make less severe commute, mitigate, modify *(moderate)*, palliate *(abate)*
make less violent obtund, remit *(relax)*
make level compensate *(counterbalance)*
make liable expose, subject
make liable to danger compromise *(endanger)*, endanger
make liable to injury endanger
make light of discount *(disbelieve)*, disparage, underestimate
make lighter commute
make little of decry, depreciate, derogate, minimize, misprize
make longer prolong
make lower in character degenerate
make lower in quality adulterate, denature
make lowly demean *(make lower)*, derogate, humiliate
make lucid clarify, elucidate, exposit
make manifest bare, elicit, evince, exemplify, explain
make manifold proliferate
make mention remark, speak
make mention of notice *(give formal warning)*, observe *(remark)*
make mild palliate *(abate)*
make milder commute
make mischief mistreat
make miserable distress
make money gain
make money by profit
make more attractive enhance
make more certain support *(corroborate)*
make more comprehensive expand, extend *(enlarge)*
make more fluid dilute
make more important magnify
make more liquid dilute
make more offensive aggravate *(exacerbate)*
make more serious aggravate *(exacerbate)*
make more severe aggravate *(exacerbate)*, exacerbate
make more valuable enhance
make much of belaud

make naked denude
make national nationalize
make national in character nationalize
make natural naturalize (acclimate)
make necessary constrain (compel), entail, indicate, necessitate, press (constrain)
make needed indicate
make nervous browbeat
make new renovate
make no racial distinctions desegregate
make note of remark
make notes comment
make nothing of misprize
make noxious taint (contaminate)
make null destroy (void), overrule
make null and void override SEE MAIN ENTRY
make objection except (object)
make objections remonstrate
make obligatory exact, force (coerce), impose (enforce)
make observations comment
make obsolete superannuate, supersede
make obvious educe, evidence, exemplify, exhibit, manifest, signify (inform)
make of greater value appreciate (increase)
make of no effect avoid (cancel)
make off abscond, avoid (evade), flee
make off with carry away, despoil, hijack, hold up (rob), loot, pilfer, poach
make official formalize
make one attach (join), conjoin, consolidate (unite)
make one a third party implead
make one feel small browbeat
make one lose one's temper incense
make one shudder repel (disgust)
make one sick repel (disgust)
make one's choice cast (register), choose, determine
make one's debut commence
make one's exit abandon (physically leave)
make one's home dwell (reside)
make one's home at lodge (reside), occupy (take possession)
make one's mark pass (satisfy requirements)
make one's oath certify (attest)
make one's own acquire (secure), adopt, buy, embrace (accept), appropriate
make one's point persuade
make one's selection cast (register), choose
make one's submission move (judicially request)
make oneself acquainted with ascertain
make oneself answerable promise (vow)
make oneself answerable for guarantee
make oneself felt persuade
make oneself scarce retreat
make oneself useful pander
make open affirmation avouch (avow)
make oral communication speak
make oral mention speak
make orderly file (arrange)
make out detect, discern (detect with the senses), hear (perceive by ear), note (notice), perceive, pierce (discern), read, realize (understand), recognize (perceive), solve, spy
make outdated superannuate
make over change, convert (change use), deliver, devolve, fix (repair), grant (transfer

formally), present (make a gift), reconstitute, reconstruct, recreate, reform, rehabilitate, renew (refurbish), renovate, transform
make over to another assign (transfer ownership)
make overtures hold out (deliberate on an offer)
make participator involve (implicate)
make pay exact
make payment bear (yield), bear the expense, compensate (remunerate), defray, disburse (pay out), expend (disburse), pay, quit (repay), remit (send payment), remunerate, repay, satisfy (discharge)
make payment for purchase
make payment in advance prepay
make peace negotiate, pacify, placate, propitiate, reconcile
make peace between arbitrate (conciliate), intercede
make pecuniary provision endow
make perfect renew (refurbish)
make permanent establish (entrench), perpetuate
make perpetual perpetuate
make plain demonstrate (establish), describe, elucidate, evidence, evince, exemplify, exhibit, explain, explicate, exposit, expound, express, illustrate, interpret, manifest, resolve (solve), signify (inform), simplify (clarify), simplify (make easier), solve, unveil
make possible enable, facilitate, let (permit), permit, proffer
make possible the avoidance of avert
make potent empower
make practicable enable
make preferable recommend
make preparations anticipate (expect), arrange (plan), plan, plot, provide (arrange for)
make prisoner arrest (apprehend), capture, fetter, hijack
make probable conduce
make proclamation annunciate
make progress ameliorate, develop, proceed (go forward), progress SEE MAIN ENTRY
make provision bear (yield), maintain (sustain), provide (arrange for)
make provision for bestow, cover (provide for), endue
make provisions forestall
make provisions for nurture
make public bare, betray (disclose), circulate, convey (communicate), denude, disclose, disseminate, divulge, notice (give formal warning), notify, post, proclaim, propagate (spread), publish, reveal, signify (inform), spread
make publicly known reveal
make pure decontaminate
make putrid taint (contaminate)
make rapid strides proceed (go forward)
make ready plan, provide (arrange for)
make ready for publication edit
make realize convince
make reference quote
make reference to bear (adduce), cite (state)
make rejoinder reply
make relevant connect (relate)
make remarks comment
make repairs emend
make reparation contribute (indemnify), discharge (pay a debt), indemnify, quit (repay), redress, reimburse, repay, restore (return), return (refund)

make reparations recoup (reimburse)
make repayment defray
make requisite entail
make requisition call (demand), exact
make requital repay
make resplendent embellish
make responsible for commit (entrust), encumber (financially obligate)
make restitution bear the expense, compensate (remunerate), contribute (indemnify), defray, discharge (pay a debt), indemnify, liquidate (determine liability), pay, quit (repay), recoup (reimburse), refund, reimburse, repay, restore (return), return (refund) SEE MAIN ENTRY
make restoration fix (repair)
make right rectify, regulate (adjust)
make rigid fix (make firm)
make rounds perambulate
make routine inure (accustom)
make sad depress
make safe cover (guard), maintain (sustain)
make salubrious decontaminate
make scandal smear
make secret arrangements conspire
make secret observations spy
make self-conscious embarrass
make sense cohere (be logically consistent)
make sense of elucidate, interpret
make sensible pierce (discern)
make sightless blind (deprive of sight)
make simple elucidate, exposit
make smaller constrict (compress), curtail, decrease, deduct (reduce), derogate, diminish, minimize, reduce
make solemn bear (adduce)
make solemn affirmation avouch (avow), confess, speak
make solemn declaration speak, testify
make solid concentrate (consolidate), consolidate (strengthen)
make someone a trustee of delegate
make someone guardian of delegate, entrust
make sorrowful distress
make sound fix (repair), remedy, renew (refurbish), renovate
make sport of disparage
make stable establish (entrench)
make steadfast establish (entrench)
make steady compensate (counterbalance)
make strong nurture
make submissive impose (subject), subdue, subject
make subordinate subject
make subservient subject
make suitable adapt, qualify (meet standards)
make supplication pray
make sure ascertain, assure (insure), certify (attest), ensure, verify (confirm)
make sure again reconfirm
make swollen inflate
make terms agree (contract), conclude (decide), contract, determine, dicker, haggle, negotiate, transact
make terse condense
make testamentary disposition demise
make testamentary dispositions devise (give)
make the best of endure (suffer), submit (yield), tolerate
make the effort attempt
make the most of capitalize (seize the chance), exploit (make use of)

make the round of circulate

make thin attenuate, dilute, diminish, erode, minimize

make toe the line discipline (control)

make too much of overestimate

make tractable subdue

make tumid inflate

make ugly deface

make unable to see blind (deprive of sight)

make unapparent blind (obscure), conceal

make unavoidable entail, necessitate

make unclean disgrace, sully

make uncomfortable embarrass

make understandable elucidate, exposit

make understood clarify

make uneasy discommode, discompose, disturb, perturb

make unfaithful disaffect

make unfit disable

make unfriendly alienate (estrange), antagonize

make unhappy distress

make uniform conform, juxtapose, regulate (adjust)

make unlawful enjoin, outlaw

make unlike distort

make unperceptible blind (obscure), conceal

make unrecognizable camouflage, disguise

make unsafe endanger

make unsightly deface

make unsound damage

make unwelcome eschew, ignore, repel (disgust)

make up compile, conceive (invent), conjure, consist, constitute (compose), contrive, create, devise (invent), feign, indemnify, invent (falsify), manufacture, originate, produce (manufacture), reconcile, replenish, structure (composition)

make up a lack replenish

make up for compensate (counterbalance), outbalance, recoup (reimburse), redeem (satisfy debts), redress, remunerate, repent

make up one's mind conclude (decide), decide, determine, resolve (decide)

make use of capitalize (seize the chance), exercise (use), exert, impropriate, manipulate (utilize skillfully), ply, profit, resort, wield

make use of without permission pirate (reproduce without authorization)

make useless disable, disarm (divest of arms), disqualify, maim, nullify

make valid approve, authorize, certify (approve), confirm, countenance, formalize, implement, indorse, notarize, validate

make valueless nullify

make visible embody, expose, manifest, produce (offer to view), unveil

make vivid characterize, delineate, describe, detail (particularize), illustrate

make void abrogate (annul), adeem, annul, avoid (cancel), cancel, discharge (release from obligation), invalidate, nullify, override, overrule, quash, repeal, revoke, supersede, vacate (void), vitiate SEE MAIN ENTRY

make vulnerable compromise (endanger), endanger

make war fight (battle)

make way yield (submit)

make way for demit, displace (replace)

make weak dilute

make well cure, renew (refurbish)

make whole cure, fix (repair), renew (refurbish), renovate, replenish, restore (renew)

make wholesome decontaminate

make wholly without effect avoid (cancel)

make wicked brutalize

make worse aggravate (exacerbate), degenerate, exacerbate, impair

make wrathful bait (harass), pique

make written application petition

make-believe delusive, fictitious, hypothetical, illusory, imitation, mendacious, pretext

maker architect, author (originator), contractor. SEE MAIN ENTRY

makeshift expedient, interim, provisional, replacement, stopgap, surrogate, temporary, vicarious (substitutional)

makeup character (personal quality), characteristic, configuration (form), content (structure), disposition (inclination), frame (mood), organization (structure), personality, temperament

making building (business of assembling), commission (act), manufacture, onset (commencement)

making amends collection (payment), penitent

making apparent clarification

making aware disclosure (act of disclosing)

making distinct clarification

making evident clarification

making intelligible definition

making less decrease, deduction (diminution)

making lucid clarification

making one concrescence

making over renewal

making perspicuous clarification

making precise clarification

making public disclosure (act of disclosing), divulgation

making ready preparation

making reference referral

making sense coherent (clear)

making specific clarification

making trenchant clarification

making useless avoidance (cancellation)

mala fides bad faith

maladjusted inappropriate, unfit

maladjustment disaccord

maladminister misgovern, misguide, mishandle (mismanage), mismanage

maladministration misconduct, misdoing, misrule, misusage, misuse. SEE MAIN ENTRY

maladroit incompetent, inept (incompetent)

malady disability (physical inability), disease, disorder (abnormal condition), pain SEE MAIN ENTRY

malaise pain

malapert brazen, impertinent (insolent), insolent, obtrusive, presumptuous

malapropism error, misapplication, misusage

malapropos impertinent (irrelevant), inapplicable, inapposite, inappropriate, inapt, inept (inappropriate), inopportune, irrelevant, unfavorable, unsuitable, untimely

malapropros unfit

malcontent actor, dissident. SEE MAIN ENTRY

male administrare misgovern

male computare miscalculate

male interpretari misinterpret

male iudicare misjudge

male moratus immoral

male parentage paternity

male regere misgovern

maledicent contemptuous, querulous

maledictio revilement, slander

malediction aspersion, blasphemy, contempt (disdain), denunciation, expletive, imprecation, phillipic, profanity, revilement, vilification. SEE MAIN ENTRY

maledictive profane

maledictory abusive, calumnious, profane

maledictum obloquy

malefaction delict, delinquency (misconduct), disregard (omission), fault (responsibility), guilt, illegality, misdeed, misdoing, misprision, offense, perversion SEE MAIN ENTRY

malefactor convict, criminal, delinquent, embezzler, felon, hoodlum, lawbreaker, offender, outlaw, racketeer, recidivist. SEE MAIN ENTRY

malefactor wrongdoer

malefactor under suspension of sentence probationer (released offender)

malefic adverse (negative), deleterious, detrimental, disadvantageous, disastrous, harmful, heinous, insalubrious, lethal, malevolent, malicious, malignant, noxious, peccant (unhealthy), pernicious, pestilent, sinister

maleficence vice

maleficent bad (offensive), dangerous, deleterious, delinquent (guilty of a misdeed), diabolic, disadvantageous, harmful, insalubrious, lethal, malevolent, malicious, malignant, peccant (culpable), peccant (unhealthy), pernicious, pestilent, ruthless, scathing, sinister SEE MAIN ENTRY

maleficial lethal, malicious, peccant (culpable), pernicious, sinister

maleficient adverse (negative)

maleficium crime, mischief, misdeed

malevolence alienation (estrangement), atrocity, bad repute, belligerency, feud, hatred, ill will, malediction, malice, odium, rancor, spite, vengeance SEE MAIN ENTRY

malevolent bad (offensive), calumnious, caustic, cold-blooded, contemptuous, convict, cruel, delinquent (guilty of a misdeed), diabolic, hoodlum, hostile, inimical, iniquitous, libelous, malicious, malignant, outrageous, pernicious, resentful, ruthless, scathing, sinister, spiteful, vicious, vindictive, virulent. SEE MAIN ENTRY

malevolentia ill will, malice, spite

malevolus malevolent, malicious, spiteful

malfeasance abuse (corrupt practice), blame (culpability), conversion (misappropriation), crime, delict, delinquency (misconduct), disloyalty, disservice, guilt, knavery, maladministration, misconduct, misdeed, misdemeanor, misprision, misrule, offense, tort, wrong. SEE MAIN ENTRY

malfeasant convict, criminal, delinquent (guilty of a misdeed), felonious, hoodlum, illegitimate (illegal), offender, recidivist, wrongdoer SEE MAIN ENTRY

malfeasor convict, delinquent, hoodlum, lawbreaker, recidivist

malformation irregularity

malformed blemished, faulty, inferior (lower in quality)

malfunction disorder (abnormal condition), irregularity

malice alienation (estrangement), cruelty, ill will, odium, rancor, resentment, spite. SEE MAIN ENTRY

malice aforethought cruelty

malice prepense cruelty

malicious caustic, cold-blooded, contemptuous, cruel, felonious, harmful, invidious, libelous, malevolent, malignant, mordacious, noxious, outrageous, resentful, scathing, sinister, spiteful, vicious, vindictive, virulent, wrongful. SEE MAIN ENTRY

malicious action mischief

malicious burning of property arson

malicious defamation libel

malicious falsehood libel

malicious gossip scandal

malicious prosecution SEE MAIN ENTRY

malicious publication libel

malicious report slander

maliciously defame libel

maliciousness cruelty, ill will, malice, odium, spite

malific bad (offensive)

malign bait (harass), brand (stigmatize), cold-blooded, complain (criticize), contemn, cruel, damage, decry, defame, denigrate, denounce (condemn), depreciate, derogate, destructive, disapprove (condemn), disastrous, discommend, discredit, dishonor (deprive of honor), disoblige, disparage, harass, harmful, humiliate, ill use, lessen, lethal, libel, malevolent, malignant, misrepresent, mistreat, outrageous, pernicious, pestilent, pillory, reproach, ruthless, sinister, smear, spiteful, stain, sully, toxic, unfavorable, vicious, virulent. SEE MAIN ENTRY

malignance cruelty, fatality, harm, ill will, spite, vice

malignancy corruption, cruelty, fatality, harm, ill will, spite

malignant bad (inferior), caustic, contemptuous, cruel, dangerous, deadly, deleterious, detrimental, diabolic, disadvantageous, fatal, lethal, libelous, malevolent, malicious, nefarious, noxious, offensive (offending), outrageous, peccant (unhealthy), pernicious, pestilent, resentful, ruthless, scathing, sinister, spiteful, vicious, vindictive, virulent. SEE MAIN ENTRY

maligned accused (attacked)

maligning contemptuous

malignitas malice, spite

malignity bad repute, cruelty, fatality, harm, malice, mischief, rancor, resentment, spite

malignus spiteful

malinger fake, pretend, shirk, shun

malison imprecation, malediction

malitia knavery

malleability amenability, discipline (obedience)

malleable facile, flexible, open (persuasible), passive, pliable, pliant, resilient, sequacious, tractable, yielding. SEE MAIN ENTRY

mallet cudgel

malpractice delinquency (failure of duty), disregard (omission), guilt, misapplication, misconduct, misdeed, misdoing, misprision, misusage, misuse, offense, wrong. SEE MAIN ENTRY

maltreat abuse (misuse), abuse (victimize), bait (harass), brutalize, damage, disoblige, endanger, exploit (take advantage of), harass, harm, harrow, ill use, inflict, misemploy, mistreat, persecute. SEE MAIN ENTRY

maltreatment abuse (physical misuse), atrocity, infliction, injustice, mischief, misuse, molestation, oppression

malum delinquency (misconduct)

malus bad (inferior), bad (offensive), dishonest

malversation abuse (corrupt practice), bad faith, bad repute, crime, criminality, delict, delinquency (misconduct), embezzlement, guilt, maladministration, misappropriation, misconduct, misdeed, misdemeanor, misdoing, misprision, misusage, offense

mammoth prodigious (enormous) SEE MAIN ENTRY

man character (an individual), humanity (mankind), mortality

man of business dealer

man of erudition expert

man of law advocate (counselor)

man of learning expert

man of letters author (writer), pedagogue

man of mark key man, paragon

man with a grievance actor

man-made artificial, synthetic

manacle constrain (imprison), contain (restrain), detain (restrain), fetter (noun), fetter (verb), hamper, handcuff (noun), handcuff (verb), restrain, restrict, trammel

manacles bondage

manage administer (conduct), arrange (methodize), assume (undertake), comport (behave), conduct, control (regulate), demean (deport oneself), direct (supervise), discipline (control), dominate, effectuate, execute (accomplish), function, govern, maneuver, manipulate (control unfairly), marshal, militate, moderate (preside over), officiate, operate, oversee, predominate (command), preside, program, provide (arrange for), rule (govern), succeed (attain), superintend, transact, wield. SEE MAIN ENTRY

manage badly misgovern, mishandle (mismanage)

manage poorly mismanage

manage unskillfully mismanage

manageability amenability

manageable corrigible, facile, flexible, malleable, obedient, pliable, pliant, resigned, sequacious, tractable, yielding SEE MAIN ENTRY

managed care SEE MAIN ENTRY

management administration, agency (legal relationship), auspices, authorities, board, bureaucracy, conduct, control (supervision), course, custody (supervision), direction (guidance), disposition (final arrangement), distribution (arrangement), dominion (supreme authority), economy (economic system), economy (frugality), employer, generalship, government (administration), guidance, hierarchy (persons in authority), maneuver (tactic), operation, oversight (control), policy (plan of action), regime, staff, strategy, supervision, supremacy, transaction, treatment, trust (custody), usage. SEE MAIN ENTRY

management of money finance

management of natural resources ecology

management of resources economy (economic system)

manager administrator, caretaker (one fulfilling the function of office), chief, comptroller, custodian (protector), director, employer, executive, factor (commission merchant), principal (director), proctor, procurator, proprietor, superintendent

manager's office headquarters

managerial administrative

managers hierarchy (persons in authority), management (supervision)

managership control (supervision), direction (guidance), generalship, management (supervision)

managing administrative, executive, ministerial

manare exude

mancus deficient

mandamus fiat. SEE MAIN ENTRY

mandare delegate, devolve, entrust, instruct (direct), invest (vest), trust

mandate act (enactment), agency (legal relationship), article (precept), assignment (designation), brevet, burden, canon, charge (command), citation (charge), command, decree, delegation (assignment), dictate, direction (order), directive, edict, instruction (direction), law, measure, mission, mittimus, monition (legal summons), order (judicial directive), ordinance, plebiscite, precept, prescribe, proclamation, referendum, regulation (rule), requirement, requisition, statute, subpoena, summons, writ. SEE MAIN ENTRY

mandate of a court warrant (judicial writ)

mandated legitimate (rightful), licit

mandated territory state (political unit)

mandatorily will shall

mandatory binding, compulsory, conclusive (determinative), decretal, essential (required), exigent, imperative, indispensable, involuntary, necessary (required), obligatory, peremptory (imperative), positive (prescribed), requisite, unavoidable (inevitable), unavoidable (not voidable). SEE MAIN ENTRY

mandatory factor necessity, need (requirement)

mandatum charge (command), commission (act), fiat, injunction, instruction (direction), mandate, order (judicial directive), warrant (authorization)

manere adhere (persist)

maneuver act (undertaking), connive, conspire, contrivance, contrive, device (contrivance), devise (invent), evasion, expedient, inveigle, machination, manage, manipulate (utilize skillfully), militate, operate, overt act, perpetrate, plot, ploy, ruse, scheme (noun), scheme (verb), step, stratagem, subterfuge, trap. SEE MAIN ENTRY

maneuverability latitude

maneuverable negotiable

maneuverer catalyst

maneuvering artifice, campaign, conspiracy, strategy, tactical

maneuvers campaign, strategy

manger liaison

mangle damage, deface, disable, mutilate, spoil (impair)

mangled broken (fractured), marred

manhandle abuse (misuse), abuse (victimize), ill use, mishandle (maltreat), mistreat, persecute

manhood majority (adulthood)

mania compulsion (obsession), furor, lunacy, market (demand), obsession, paranoia, passion

maniacal deranged, frenetic, lunatic, non compos mentis, outrageous

manic lunatic, non compos mentis. SEE MAIN ENTRY

manicae handcuff

manifest adduce, apparent (perceptible), apparent (presumptive), appreciable, axiomatic, bare, bear (adduce), bear (yield), bill (invoice), blatant (conspicuous), bodily, cite (state), clear (apparent), coherent (clear), comprehensible, conspicuous, convey (communicate), corroborate, demonstrate (establish), denude, depict, disabuse, discernible, discover, disinter, distinct (clear), divulge, document, elucidate, embody, emerge, establish (show), evidence, evident, evince, exemplify, exhibit, explain, explicit, expose, flagrant, gross (flagrant), illustrate, inventory, naked (perceptible), obvious, open (in sight), ostensible, overt, palpable, patent, pellucid, perceivable, perceptible, personify, produce (offer to view), prominent, prove, public (known), reveal, scrutable, signify (denote), tangible, unmistakable, unveil, visible (in full view). SEE MAIN ENTRY

manifest act overt act

manifest directly express

manifest itself appear (materialize), arise (appear), issue (send forth), occur (come to mind)

manifestation appearance (emergence), common knowledge, complexion, disclosure (something disclosed), embodiment, face value (first blush), illustration, indicant, proof, symbol, symptom, token. SEE MAIN ENTRY

manifestations indicia

manifesting contempt contemptuous

manifestly fairly (clearly)

manifesto brevet, canon, issuance, proclamation, pronouncement, report (detailed account), statement

manifestus apparent (perceptible), conspicuous, evident, flagrant, obvious, open (in sight), overt, palpable, patent, perceptible

manifold compound, diverse, miscellaneous, multifarious, multifold, myriad, reproduce, rife. SEE MAIN ENTRY

manifoldness diversity

manipulable pliable

manipulate capitalize (seize the chance), coax, control (regulate), employ (make use of), exercise (use), exert, exploit (make use of), exploit (take advantage of), handle (manage), ill use, manage, militate, operate, perpetrate, ply, rule (govern), scheme, tamper, wield. SEE MAIN ENTRY

manipulate improperly misemploy

manipulation act (undertaking), connivance, contrivance, machination, management (judicious use), maneuver (tactic), performance (workmanship), plot (secret plan), stratagem, strategy SEE MAIN ENTRY

mankind mortality

manliness prowess (bravery)

manly potent, spartan, strong

manner appearance (look), avenue (means of attainment), behavior, character (personal quality), color (complexion), complexion, conduct, conduit (channel), course, custom, degree (station), demeanor, deportment, facility (instrumentality), form (arrangement), instrumentality, means (opportunity), method, mode, modus operandi, parlance, posture (attitude), practice (custom), presence (poise), process (course), style, system, tenor, trait, usage. SEE MAIN ENTRY

manner of conduct dealings

manner of construction organization (structure)

manner of disposal disposition (transfer of property)

manner of expression phraseology

manner of life behavior

manner of living modus vivendi

manner of operating modus operandi

manner of presentation style

manner of proceeding policy (plan of action), practice (procedure), procedure

manner of speaking parlance

manner of working avenue (means of attainment), procedure

mannered formal, histrionic

mannerism characteristic, habit, identity (individuality), quirk (idiosyncrasy), specialty (distinctive mark), trait

mannerless disorderly

mannerliness decorum

mannerly civil (polite)

manners behavior, conduct, courtesy, decorum, propriety (correctness), protocol (etiquette)

manor demesne, domain (land owned), dominion (absolute ownership), homestead

manpower personnel

mansio stay

manslaughter homicide. SEE MAIN ENTRY

manslayer criminal

mansuetuda clemency

mansuetude amenability, comity

mantic portentous (ominous), prophetic

mantle enshroud, plant (covertly place), spread, veil

manual directory, hornbook, pandect (treatise) SEE MAIN ENTRY

manual of instruction hornbook

manufactural industrial

manufacture build (construct), building (business of assembling), business (commercial enterprise), composition (makeup), creation, devise (invent), engender, fabricate (construct), forge (produce), form, formation, frame (construct), generate, industry (business), invent (produce for the first time), make, originate, palter, performance (workmanship). SEE MAIN ENTRY

manufactured assumed (feigned), industrial, synthetic

manufactured for sale commercial, industrial

manufactured goods merchandise

manufactured product output

manufacturer author (originator)

manufacturing productive

manumissio emancipation, liberation

manumission emancipation, liberation, release, suffrage

manumit disengage, disenthrall, enfranchise, free, liberate, quit (free of), release, relieve (free from burden), rescue

manumitted clear (free from criminal charges), free (enjoying civil liberty), unbound

manumittere liberate

manus force (strength), handwriting, profession (vocation), violence

manuscript holographic, script

many ample, innumerable, manifold, miscellaneous, multifarious, multifold, multiple, myriad, rife

many sidedness multiplicity

map blueprint, delineate, delineation, design (construction plan), direction (course), scheme

map out devise (invent), frame (construct), frame (formulate), locate, plan,

prearrange, predetermine, program, scheme

mar adulterate, contaminate, damage, deface, eviscerate, frustrate, harm, impair, impede, mutilate, prejudice (injure), smear, spoil (impair), stain, sully, vice, vitiate

mar the appearance of deface

marathon SEE MAIN ENTRY

maraud despoil, foray, harry (plunder), hold up (rob), loot, onset (assault), pillage (noun), pillage (verb), plunder (noun), plunder (verb), prey, spoil (pillage)

marauder burglar, criminal, thief

marauding burglary, depredation, rapacious, spoliation

marble-hearted malignant, ruthless

marcescence decline

march demonstrate (protest), frontier, patrol, perambulate, periphery, progress, traverse

march off depart, part (leave)

march out evacuate

marcher pedestrian

marge border

margin balance (amount in excess), border, edge (border), extremity (furthest point), latitude, mete, outline (boundary), penumbra, periphery, plethora, scope, space, surplus. SEE MAIN ENTRY

marginal inappreciable, petty. SEE MAIN ENTRY

marginal annotation comment, note (brief comment)

marginalia notation. SEE MAIN ENTRY

margo edge (border)

marijuana cannabis

marital conjugal, nuptial

marital infidelity adultery

marital partner consort, spouse

maritus consort

mark attaint, attend (heed), brand, characterize, clue, color (complexion), consider, deface, degree (station), demarcate, denote, designate, designation (symbol), discriminate (distinguish), earmark, eminence, expression (manifestation), feature (characteristic), goal, heed, importance, impression, index (catalog), indicant, indication, indicator, inscribe, inscription, intention, interest (concern), label (noun), label (verb), magnitude, manifest, manifestation, monument, note (notice), note (record), notice (observe), objective, observe (watch), particularity, perceive, prestige, property (distinctive attribute), recognize (perceive), record, regard (pay attention), reputation, select, significance, signify (denote), smear, speciality, specialty (distinctive mark), stain, stamp, subscribe (sign), symbol, symptom, target, trademark, trait, witness (have direct knowledge of) SEE MAIN ENTRY

mark against confront (oppose)

mark down book, cast (register), decrease, deduct (reduce), discount (reduce), enter (record), note (record), rebate

mark incorrectly mislabel

mark limits delimit, demarcate

mark of Cain onus (stigma)

mark of disgrace stigma

mark of honor mention (tribute)

mark of identification caption, earmark, label

mark of identity earmark

mark of shame stigma

mark off border (bound), characterize, circumscribe (surround by boundary), delimit, hedge, measure

mark off by differences differentiate
mark out circumscribe *(surround by boundary)*, delimit, demarcate, designate, differentiate, distinguish, indicate, prescribe, specify, trace *(delineate)*
mark out a course arrange *(plan)*, plan
mark out for choose
mark that designates device *(distinguishing mark)*
mark the difference between discriminate *(distinguish)*
mark the limits define
mark the time of date
mark time pause
mark up cost *(price)*
markdown discount, rebate
marked certain *(particular)*, certain *(specific)*, considerable, conspicuous, distinct *(distinguished from others)*, distinctive, important *(significant)*, manifest, marred, momentous, notable, noteworthy, open *(in sight)*, outstanding *(prominent)*, palpable, particular *(specific)*, peculiar *(distinctive)*, perceptible, preferential, prominent, remarkable, resounding, salient, several *(separate)*, special, specific, stellar, uncommon, unusual
marked by consent consenting
marked by excessive effort elaborate
marked feature characteristic, property *(distinctive attribute)*
marked occurrence event
marked off the calendar SEE MAIN ENTRY
marked price cost *(price)*
marked quality characteristic, property *(distinctive attribute)*
marked superiority distinction *(reputation)*
marked time date
marked traits character *(personal quality)*
markedly fairly *(clearly)*, particularly
marker indication, label, landmark *(conspicuous object)*
market barter, deal, exchange, handle *(trade)*, mercantile, outlet, sell, store *(business)*, vend. SEE MAIN ENTRY
market place store *(business)*. SEE MAIN ENTRY
market price estimate *(approximate cost)*, expense *(cost)*, par *(face amount)*
marketable negotiable, valuable. SEE MAIN ENTRY
marketing commerce, retail, trade *(commerce)*
marks fingerprints, indicia
marks left by a person's finger fingerprints
maroon isolate, seclude
marred blemished, defective, deficient, dilapidated, imperfect, poor *(inferior in quality)*. SEE MAIN ENTRY
marriage cohabitation *(married state)*, matrimony. SEE MAIN ENTRY
marriage accord consortium *(marriage companionship)*
marriage compatibility consortium *(marriage companionship)*
marriage concord consortium *(marriage companionship)*
marriage lines coverture
marriage partner consort, spouse
marriage tie marriage *(wedlock)*, matrimony
marriage to a second partner digamy
married conjugal, nuptial
married life marriage *(wedlock)*, matrimony

married state coverture, marriage *(wedlock)*, matrimony
married status cohabitation *(married state)*, marriage *(wedlock)*, matrimony
married tie coverture
marring defacement
marring feature flaw
marrow consequence *(significance)*, gist *(substance)*, main point, substance *(essential nature)*
marrowless powerless
marry combine *(act in concert)*, connect *(join together)*, join *(bring together)*, unite
marshal allocate, arrange *(methodize)*, classify, file *(arrange)*, fix *(arrange)*, organize *(arrange)*, tabulate. SEE MAIN ENTRY
marshaling array *(order)*, disposition *(final arrangement)*, distribution *(arrangement)*
mart exchange, market *(business)*, store *(business)*
martial spartan
martial law force *(compulsion)*
martiality belligerency
martinet dictator
marvel phenomenon *(unusual occurrence)*
marvelous ineffable, meritorious, portentous *(eliciting amazement)*, prodigious *(amazing)*, remarkable, special, unusual
mask camouflage, cloak, conceal, cover *(pretext)*, cover *(conceal)*, denature, disguise *(noun)*, disguise *(verb)*, ensconce, enshroud, envelop, false pretense, hide, obliterate, obnubilate, obscure, plant *(covertly place)*, pretend, pretense *(pretext)*, pretext, ruse, screen *(guard)*, shroud, stifle, strangle, subterfuge, suppress, veil
masked blind *(concealed)*, clandestine, furtive, hidden, mysterious, stealthy
masquerade camouflage, deception, disguise *(noun)*, disguise *(verb)*, evasion, false pretense, hoax, palter, pretend, ruse, sham
masquerade as impersonate, pose *(impersonate)*
mass accumulate *(amass)*, agglomeration, aggregate *(noun)*, aggregate *(verb)*, amount *(quantity)*, assemblage, assembly, body *(collection)*, bulk, caliber *(measurement)*, chamber *(body)*, cohere *(adhere)*, collect *(gather)*, collection *(accumulation)*, compile, concentrate *(consolidate)*, conglomerate, conglomeration, congregate, congregation, conjoin, consolidate *(strengthen)*, corpus, cumulation, desegregate, entirety, generality *(bulk)*, hoard, join *(bring together)*, load, majority *(greater part)*, materiality *(physical existence)*, measurement, meet, quantity, selection *(collection)*, store, totality, unite, weight *(burden)*. SEE MAIN ENTRY
mass meeting assemblage, caucus, congregation
mass produce manufacture
mass produced industrial
massacre aberemurder, dispatch *(act of putting to death)*, dispatch *(put to death)*, homicide, kill *(murder)*, killing, murder, slay
massed collective, compact *(dense)*, populous, solid *(compact)*
masses populace, population
massing centralization
massive capacious, compact *(dense)*, copious, gross *(flagrant)*, major, ponderous, prodigious *(enormous)*, solid *(compact)*
master apprehend *(perceive)*, comprehend *(understand)*, construe *(comprehend)*,

defeat, dominant, dominate, employer, expert, gain, impose *(subject)*, manage, mastermind, moderate *(preside over)*, overcome *(surmount)*, oversee, overthrow, overwhelm, paramount, pass *(satisfy requirements)*, pedagogue, predominate *(command)*, prevail *(triumph)*, principal *(director)*, professional, proprietor, remember, repress, rule *(govern)*, sovereign *(absolute)*, specialist, subdue, subject, subjugate, succeed *(attain)*, superintendent, surmount, understand. SEE MAIN ENTRY
master craftsman artisan
master hand expert
master of ceremonies chairman
master of jurisprudence jurist
master plan arrangement *(plan)*, blueprint, direction *(course)*, method
master worker practitioner
master workman artisan
masterdom supremacy
masterful competent, deft, dictatorial, expert, indomitable, potent, practiced, proficient, tyrannous SEE MAIN ENTRY
masterfulness influence, puissance
masterless independent
masterly artful, capable, competent, deft, expert, practiced, subtle *(refined)*
mastermind administer *(conduct)*, direct *(supervise)*, expert, manage, operate, oversee, predominate *(command)*. SEE MAIN ENTRY
masters hierarchy *(persons in authority)*
mastership ability, clout, generalship, performance *(workmanship)*, power, prowess *(ability)*, specialty *(special aptitude)*, supremacy
mastery ability, advantage, apprehension *(perception)*, cognition, competence *(ability)*, control *(supervision)*, dominance, dominion *(supreme authority)*, efficiency, experience *(background)*, force *(strength)*, gift *(flair)*, hegemony, influence, knowledge *(learning)*, occupation *(possession)*, ownership, performance *(workmanship)*, power, predominance, prowess *(ability)*, science *(technique)*, seisin, skill, specialty *(special aptitude)*, supremacy SEE MAIN ENTRY
mastery of thought comprehension
mat snarl
match alter ego, coincide *(correspond)*, compare, comport *(agree with)*, conform, connect *(join together)*, connect *(relate)*, connection *(relation)*, contest *(competition)*, correlate, correspond *(be equivalent)*, counterpart *(parallel)*, countervail, duplicate, equipoise, identity *(similarity)*, join *(bring together)*, matrimony, measure, peer, recriminate, resemblance, retaliate, same, strife SEE MAIN ENTRY
match against confront *(oppose)*, counteract
match strength with compete
match wits with compete
matched coextensive, comparable *(equivalent)*, conjugal, correlative, equal, fit, uniform
matching agreed *(harmonized)*, analogous, coequal, commensurable, commensurate, comparable *(equivalent)*, comparative, congruous, harmonious, identical, pendent, similar
matchless absolute *(ideal)*, best, inestimable, invaluable, laudable, major, paramount, premium, priceless, prime *(most valuable)*, rare, renowned, select, singular,

sterling, superior *(excellent)*, superlative, unapproachable, unique, unusual
matchless effort main force
matchmaker broker
mate coadjutant, colleague, consociate, consort, contributor *(contributor)*, copartner *(business associate)*, correlate, counterpart *(complement)*, participant, peer, resemblance, same, spouse
mated conjugal, nuptial
material appreciable, article *(commodity)*, bodily, cardinal *(basic)*, concrete, considerable, corporal, corporeal, critical *(crucial)*, crucial, equipment, essential *(required)*, expedient, important *(significant)*, major, momentous, mundane, noteworthy, objective, paraphernalia *(apparatus)*, pertinent, physical, relative *(relevant)*, relevant, resource, subject *(topic)*, substance *(essential nature)*, substantive, tangible, virtual. SEE MAIN ENTRY
material assets estate *(property)*, merchandise, principal *(capital sum)*, property *(possessions)*
material existence body *(person)*, materiality *(physical existence)*
material figuration embodiment
material object article *(commodity)*
material part component, gravamen
material point cornerstone, issue *(matter in dispute)*, landmark *(significant change)*, main point SEE MAIN ENTRY
material point deduced by the pleadings issue *(matter in dispute)*
material product object
material representation embodiment
material substance object
material things which are owned estate *(property)*
material wealth possessions
materialistic mercenary
materiality corpus, importance, magnitude, relevance, significance. SEE MAIN ENTRY
materialization corpus, embodiment, manifestation, phenomenon *(manifestation)*, realization
materialize embody, emerge, form, occur *(happen)*, realize *(make real)*, substantiate
materialman SEE MAIN ENTRY
materialness consequence *(significance)*, importance, magnitude, materiality *(consequence)*, materiality *(physical existence)*, significance
materials goods, merchandise
materials of combat ammunition
materiate bodily, physical
maternal consanguineous
maternity SEE MAIN ENTRY
mating matrimony
matriarch parents
matriculate register
matriculation registration
matrilinear consanguineous
matrimonial conjugal, nuptial
matrimonium marriage *(wedlock)*, matrimony
matrimony cohabitation *(married state)*, coverture, marriage *(wedlock)*. SEE MAIN ENTRY
matrix pattern
matronage coverture
matronhood coverture
matronship coverture
matronymic call *(title)*
matted inextricable
matter article *(commodity)*, business *(affair)*, case *(lawsuit)*, content *(meaning)*,

corpus, entity, gist *(substance)*, happening, import, issue *(matter in dispute)*, materiality *(consequence)*, materiality *(physical existence)*, object, particular, point *(item)*, proceeding, significance, subject *(topic)*. SEE MAIN ENTRY
matter for judgment case *(lawsuit)*, controversy *(lawsuit)*, lawsuit
matter in dispute problem SEE MAIN ENTRY
matter in hand issue *(matter in dispute)*
matter in question issue *(matter in dispute)* SEE MAIN ENTRY
matter legally submitted to the jury evidence
matter of cognition content *(meaning)*
matter of concern cornerstone
matter of contention issue *(matter in dispute)*
matter of course behavior, custom, practice *(custom)*, procedure, rule *(guide)*. SEE MAIN ENTRY
matter of disputation discrepancy
matter of dubitation doubt *(indecision)*, doubt *(suspicion)*
matter of duty allegiance
matter of fact certification *(certainness)*, fait accompli, prosaic, unpretentious
matter of factness pragmatism
matter of importance cornerstone
matter of necessity requirement
matter of no consequence nonentity
matter of no importance nonentity
matter of record certificate SEE MAIN ENTRY
matter-of-fact pragmatic
mattering much important *(significant)*
matters affairs, dealings
matters of fact evidence
matters of state politics
matters to be attended to agenda
maturare expedite, hasten, mature, precipitate *(hasten)*
maturate conclude *(complete)*, mature, progress
maturation finality, growth *(evolution)*
mature accrue *(arise)*, develop, full, payable, progress, ready *(prepared)*, receivable, ripe. SEE MAIN ENTRY
mature consideration deliberation
mature person adult
mature reflection deliberation
mature responsibility discretion *(quality of being discreet)*
matured choate lien, elderly, old
maturely considered deliberate, premeditated
matureness majority *(adulthood)*, maturity, timeliness
maturing payable
maturitas maturity
maturity age, discretion *(quality of being discreet)*, experience *(background)*, finality, majority *(adulthood)*. SEE MAIN ENTRY
maturus expeditious, ripe
maudlin demonstrative *(expressive of emotion)*
maul beat *(strike)*, lash *(strike)*, mishandle *(maltreat)*, mistreat
maundering prolix
mawkish unsavory
maxim article *(precept)*, belief *(something believed)*, catchword, code, constant, constitution, doctrine, dogma, expression *(comment)*, holding *(ruling of a court)*, law, ordinance, precedent, prescription *(directive)*, principle *(axiom)*, rule *(legal dictate)*. SEE MAIN ENTRY
maxim effort main force

maximal cardinal *(outstanding)*, radical *(extreme)*, utmost
maxime particularly
maximize enhance, expand, increase, magnify, overestimate, parlay *(exploit successfully)*
maximizing cumulative *(intensifying)*
maximum best, ceiling, full, ultimate, utmost *(adjective)*, utmost *(noun)*. SEE MAIN ENTRY
maximum amount cap
mayhem commotion, outbreak, outburst, shambles
maze complex *(entanglement)*, entanglement *(confusion)*, ignorance, imbroglio, involution, snarl SEE MAIN ENTRY
mazy circuitous, inextricable, labyrinthine, sinuous, tortuous *(bending)*
meager de minimus, deficient, inappreciable, inconsiderable, insufficient, marginal, mediocre, minimal, negligible, nominal, nonsubstantial *(not sufficient)*, paltry, petty, poor *(inferior in quality)*, scarce, slight, trivial, unworthy SEE MAIN ENTRY
meagerness austerity, dearth, deficiency, deficit, immateriality, insufficiency, poverty
mean average *(midmost)*, base *(inferior)*, bespeak, brutal, connote, denote, heinous, ignoble, illiberal, inappreciable, inconsiderable, inimical, intend, intermediate, loathsome, machiavellian, malevolent, mediocre, mediocrity, mesne, moderation, odious, paltry, parsimonious, penurious, perverse, petty, petulant, poor *(inferior in quality)*, purport, represent *(portray)*, scandalous, scurrilous, servile, signify *(denote)*, slight, spiteful, vicious. SEE MAIN ENTRY
mean proportioned average *(midmost)*
mean-spirited caitiff
mean-tempered petulant
meander detour, deviate, digress, perambulate, prowl
meandering circuitous, discursive *(digressive)*, indirect, labyrinthine, moving *(in motion)*, protracted, sinuous, tortuous *(bending)*
meandrous circuitous, sinuous
meaning connotation, consequence *(significance)*, construction, contents, context, definition, design *(intent)*, essence, explanation, gist *(substance)*, import, intent, main point, paraphrase, purview, significance, signification, spirit, substance *(essential nature)*, sum *(tally)*, tenor. SEE MAIN ENTRY
meaningful cognizable, coherent *(clear)*, eloquent, pithy, sententious, suggestive *(evocative)*
meaningfulness content *(meaning)*, import
meaningless collateral *(immaterial)*, frivolous, immaterial, incomprehensible, inexpressive, minor, nominal, null *(insignificant)*, pedestrian, trivial, unessential, void *(invalid)* SEE MAIN ENTRY
meaningless saying platitude
meaninglessness incoherence
meanness inconsideration, mediocrity, mischief
means access *(opening)*, appliance, conduit *(channel)*, determinant, effects, expedient, facility *(instrumentality)*, forum *(medium)*, instrument *(tool)*, instrumentality, livelihood, medium, method, mode, modus operandi, money, organ, process *(course)*, recourse, reserve, resource, stopgap, substance *(material possessions)*, system, tool, use, way *(manner)*. SEE MAIN ENTRY

means of access access *(right of way)*, approaches, avenue *(means of attainment)*, entrance, ingress, portal
means of approach access *(right of way)*
means of attack ammunition
means of communication language
means of earning a living calling
means of entering entrance
means of entry ingress
means of escape loophole, outlet
means of exit egress
means of expression forum *(medium)*
means of identification fingerprints
means of livelihood employment, position *(business status)*, post, pursuit *(occupation)*
means of offense cudgel
means of proof evidence
means of protection panoply
means of proving a fact evidence
means of recognition indicia, symptom
means of restraint deterrence, deterrent, fetter
means of subsistence maintenance *(support of spouse)*
means of support business *(occupation)*, employment
means of sustaining life sustenance
means to an end contrivance, device *(contrivance)*, expedient
meant bona fide, express, implied, knowing, purposeful
meantime ad interim
meanwhile ad interim
measly paltry
measurable appreciable, determinable *(ascertainable)* SEE MAIN ENTRY
measure act *(undertaking)*, allot, amendment *(legislation)*, amount *(quantity)*, assess *(appraise)*, assessment *(estimation)*, bill *(proposed act)*, calculate, caliber *(measurement)*, capacity *(maximum)*, compare, coverage *(scope)*, criterion, criticize *(evaluate)*, degree *(magnitude)*, delimit, dimension, enactment, evaluate, expedient, extent, gauge, index *(gauge)*, magnitude, mass *(weight)*, measurement, mete *(noun)*, mete *(verb)*, moiety, parcel, part *(portion)*, prescription *(directive)*, procedure, proportion, proposal *(suggestion)*, quantity, quota, rate, ration, regulation *(rule)*, rubric *(authoritative rule)*, segment, share *(interest)*, standard, statute, stopgap, transaction, unit *(item)*. SEE MAIN ENTRY
measure according to weight weigh
measure for measure quid pro quo, reprisal, retribution
measure of value money
measure out administer *(tender)*, apportion, dole, mete
measure up qualify *(meet standards)*
measure up to conform
measured deliberate, periodic, regular *(orderly)*
measured size area *(surface)*, caliber *(measurement)*
measured time phase *(period)*
measureless indeterminate, inestimable, infinite, myriad, open-ended, profuse, unlimited, unqualified *(unlimited)*
measurelessly ad infinitum
measurement amount *(quantity)*, appraisal, appreciation *(perception)*, census, comparison, computation, degree *(magnitude)*, estimate *(approximate cost)*, estimation *(calculation)*, magnitude, mass *(weight)*, quantity, rating. SEE MAIN ENTRY

measurement across caliber *(measurement)*
measurements area *(surface)*
measures campaign, course, legislation *(enactments)*, means *(opportunity)*
measuring out apportionment
meat signification
meaty compact *(pithy)*, pithy, sententious
mechanic artisan
mechanical controlled *(automatic)*, industrial, perfunctory, routine, technical
mechanical aid device *(mechanism)*
mechanical construction instrument *(tool)*
mechanical drawing blueprint
mechanician artisan
mechanics lien SEE MAIN ENTRY
mechanism appliance, contrivance, expedient, facility *(instrumentality)*, forum *(medium)*, instrument *(tool)*, medium, ploy, tool
mechanism for evasion loophole
mechanistic controlled *(automatic)*
mechanized industrial
medal prize
meddle disrupt, disturb, infringe, intercede, interfere, interrupt, intervene, militate, obtrude, overstep, tamper SEE MAIN ENTRY
meddlesome obtrusive
meddling interest *(concern)*, intrusion, molestation, obtrusive
mederi cure
media press
media pars center *(central position)*
medial average *(midmost)*, central *(situated near center)*, intermediate
median average *(midmost)*, central *(situated near center)*, intermediate, mesne, norm
mediary agent, conduit *(intermediary)*, go-between, intermediary, spokesman
mediate adjudicate, average *(midmost)*, compromise *(settle by mutual agreement)*, intercede, interpose, mollify, negotiate, pacify, reconcile. SEE MAIN ENTRY
mediated agreed *(harmonized)*
mediating agency interagent, liaison, medium
mediation collective bargaining, conciliation, intercession, mollification, negotiation, reconciliation. SEE MAIN ENTRY
mediator adjuster, advocate *(counselor)*, arbiter, broker, conduit *(intermediary)*, go-between, interagent, intermediary, liaison, medium, referee, spokesman, umpire
mediatorial intermediate
mediatorship collective bargaining
mediatory intermediate
Medicaid SEE MAIN ENTRY
medical medicinal, remedial
medical case patient
medical preparation drug
medical segregation quarantine
medical treatment cure
medicament cure, drug, panacea
medicamentum drug, remedy
Medicare SEE MAIN ENTRY
medicare drug
medicate cure, drug, relieve *(give aid)*, remedy
medication drug, narcotic
medicative medicinal, remedial
medicina remedy *(that which corrects)*, remedy
medicinal remedial, salubrious, salutary. SEE MAIN ENTRY

medicinal component drug
medicinal ingredient drug
medicine cure, narcotic, panacea
mediocre average *(standard)*, fair *(satisfactory)*, imperfect, inferior *(lower in quality)*, marginal, nondescript, nonsubstantial *(not sturdy)*, ordinary, paltry, passable, pedestrian, poor *(inferior in quality)*, prosaic, trivial, usual. SEE MAIN ENTRY
mediocris mediocre, poor *(inferior in quality)*
mediocritas mediocrity
mediocriter fairly *(moderately)*
mediocrity SEE MAIN ENTRY
meditari practice *(train by repetition)*
meditate concentrate *(pay attention)*, deliberate, muse, ponder, reflect *(ponder)*, study
meditate on brood, consider
meditate upon devote, focus, weigh
meditated deliberate, intentional
meditation consideration *(contemplation)*, deliberation, hindsight, introspection, reflection *(thought)*
meditative circumspect, cogitative, deliberate, pensive, solemn, speculative
medium advocate *(counselor)*, agent, atmosphere, average *(midmost)*, broker, buffer zone, conduit *(channel)*, conduit *(intermediary)*, determinant, expedient, facility *(instrumentality)*, factor *(commission merchant)*, fair *(satisfactory)*, instrument *(tool)*, instrumentality, interagent, intermediary, intermediate, mediocre, tool. SEE MAIN ENTRY
medium of exchange cash, currency, money
medium of proof documentation, evidence
medius center *(central position)*, intermediate, neutral
medley assemblage, composite, diversity, integration *(amalgamation)*, melange, miscellaneous
medullosus pithy
meed appropriation *(donation)*, compensation, honorarium, pay, prize, profit, recompense, requital, reward, tip *(gratuity)*, wage
meek malleable, nonmilitant, obedient, obeisant, patient, placid, pliable, pliant, resigned, sequacious, servile, unobtrusive, unpretentious
meekness resignation *(passive acceptance)*
meet abut, adjoin, appropriate, border *(approach)*, caucus, coincide *(concur)*, collection *(assembly)*, collide *(crash against)*, concur *(agree)*, confront *(encounter)*, congregate, connect *(join together)*, consolidate *(unite)*, contact *(touch)*, convene, converge, discharge *(pay a debt)*, endure *(suffer)*, engage *(involve)*, felicitous, fulfill, keep *(fulfill)*, pay, reach, rendezvous, report *(present oneself)*, rightful, strike *(collide)*, suitable, unite. SEE MAIN ENTRY
meet an obligation satisfy *(discharge)*
meet charges disburse *(pay out)*
meet death decease, perish
meet end to end border *(bound)*
meet halfway compromise *(settle by mutual agreement)*, negotiate
meet in a body congregate
meet in conflict confront *(oppose)*
meet one's death die
meet payments liquidate *(determine liability)*

meet requirements pass (satisfy requirements), satisfy (fulfill)
meet the bill bear the expense, defray, disburse (pay out)
meet the bill ahead of time prepay
meet the demand avail (bring about)
meet the demands qualify (meet standards)
meet the expense of disburse (pay out), expend (disburse)
meet the specifications qualify (meet standards)
meet the wants of accommodate
meet with bear (tolerate), border (bound), contact (communicate), find (discover), incur
meet with a loss forfeit, lose (be deprived of)
meet with success prevail (triumph), succeed (attain)
meeting adjacent, assemblage, assembly, caucus, chamber (body), coalition, collection (assembly), collision (accident), company (assemblage), concurrent (united), conference, confrontation (act of setting face to face), congregation, contact (touching), contiguous, interview, parley, rendezvous, session. SEE MAIN ENTRY
meeting hall chamber (compartment)
meeting of events crossroad (turning point)
meeting of minds accordance (understanding), mutual understanding, understanding (agreement). SEE MAIN ENTRY
meeting of political leaders caucus
meeting of the minds agreement (concurrence)
meeting place intersection, rendezvous
meeting point intersection
meeting standards palatable
meetness expedience
megalopolis city
melancholia pessimism
melancholic despondent, disconsolate, pessimistic
melancholy despondent, disconsolate, lamentable, lugubrious, pessimism, pessimistic
melange SEE MAIN ENTRY
meld amalgamate, combine (join together), desegregate, incorporate (include), join (bring together), unite
melee affray
melee altercation, belligerency, bluster (commotion)
mêlée brawl
mêlée collision (dispute), commotion, confrontation (altercation)
melee fracas, fray, imbroglio, pandemonium, riot, turmoil
melior preferable, superior (excellent)
meliorate ameliorate, commute, cure, develop, embellish, emend, fix (repair), mitigate, modify (alter), mollify, progress, rectify, reform, rehabilitate, relieve (give aid), remedy, renew (refurbish), renovate, repair, restore (renew). SEE MAIN ENTRY
melioration amendment (correction), correction (change), development (progression), improvement, mollification, progress, reform, rehabilitation, renewal, reorganization, repair, solace
meliorative mitigating
melliferous nectarious
mellifluous eloquent
mellow mollify, orotund, pacify, ripe
melodramatic histrionic

melodramatics histrionics
melt burn
melt away decrease, disappear, dissolve (disperse), lessen, perish, subside
melt into one consolidate (unite), merge
member chapter (branch), element, ingredient, offshoot, organ, party (participant). SEE MAIN ENTRY
member of a governmental body legislator
member of a jury juror
member of a legislative body legislator
member of a legislature lawmaker
member of a partnership partner
member of Congress lawmaker
member of organized crime racketeer
member of parliament legislator
member of the Assembly lawmaker
member of the bar attorney, barrister, counsel, counselor, esquire, jurist
member of the family relative
member of the House lawmaker
member of the human race person
member of the legal profession advocate (counselor), counsel, counselor, esquire, jurist, lawyer SEE MAIN ENTRY
member of the police force peace officer
member of the Senate lawmaker
members constituency, personnel
members of the bar chamber (body)
members of the media press
members of the press press
membership affiliation (connectedness), constituency, roll
membrum clause, ingredient
memento remembrance (commemoration), reminder, token
memo entry (record), reminder
memoir account (report), memorandum, recollection, story (narrative)
memorability importance, materiality (consequence)
memorable famous, illustrious, important (significant), major, material (important), momentous, notable, noteworthy, outstanding (prominent), paramount, portentous (eliciting amazement), prominent, remarkable, salient, special, stellar, unusual SEE MAIN ENTRY
memorable part highlight
memorableness importance
memoranda calendar (record of yearly periods)
memorandum brief, entry (record), marginalia, notation, note (brief comment), notice (announcement), record, register, reminder. SEE MAIN ENTRY
memorandum of law brief SEE MAIN ENTRY
memoria account (report), recollection, remembrance (recollection)
memorial honorary, monument, remembrance (commemoration), reminder
memorialization ceremony, remembrance (commemoration)
memorialize honor, recall (remember), remember
memorize recall (remember), remember
memory hindsight, recognition, recollection, remembrance (recollection), retention, retrospect. SEE MAIN ENTRY
menace bait (harass), challenge, danger, endanger, frighten, hazard, hector, impend, intimidate, jeopardize, jeopardy, portend, threat, threaten. SEE MAIN ENTRY
menacing abusive, dangerous, formidable, imminent, insalubrious, noxious, ominous, pernicious, portentous (ominous), precarious, prophetic, sinister

mend ameliorate, amend, cure, develop, emend, fix (repair), meliorate, progress, reconcile, recreate, rectify, redress, reform, rehabilitate, remedy, renew (refurbish), renovate, repair, restore (renew), settle
mendable corrigible
mendacious deceptive, disingenuous, false (inaccurate), fictitious, lying, untrue. SEE MAIN ENTRY
mendaciousness bad faith, dishonesty, improbity, indirection (deceitfulness)
mendacity artifice, bad faith, deceit, deception, dishonesty, false pretense, falsification, fraud, improbity, indirection (deceitfulness), lie, misstatement, pretense (pretext), subreption SEE MAIN ENTRY
mendacium falsehood, lie, misstatement, story (falsehood)
mendax mendacious
mendicancy poverty, privation
mendicant parasite
mendicate request
mendicitas indigence
mendicity poverty, privation
mendicus poor (underprivileged)
mending correction (change), renewal, repair
mendosus faulty
mendum defect, flaw
menial base (inferior), ignoble, inferior (lower in position), servile, subservient
menology calendar (record of yearly periods)
mens intellect, intelligence (intellect), purpose, reason (sound judgment), understanding (comprehension)
mens rea SEE MAIN ENTRY
mensio measurement
mensura measurement
mensurable appreciable, determinable (ascertainable)
mensural appreciable
mensurate assess (appraise)
mensuration assessment (estimation), estimation (calculation), measurement
mental non compos mentis, vicarious (delegated)
mental aberration lunacy, paranoia
mental ability intellect, intelligence (intellect), understanding (comprehension)
mental abnormality insanity, lunacy
mental acuteness intellect, intelligence (intellect)
mental agony distress (anguish)
mental alienation insanity
mental and spiritual makeup character (personal quality)
mental attitude impression
mental balance competence (sanity), sanity
mental capacity apprehension (perception), competence (sanity), comprehension, intellect, intelligence (intellect), reason (sound judgment)
mental constitution disposition (inclination), frame (mood)
mental cultivation edification
mental decay insanity
mental deficiency insanity
mental derangement insanity
mental disease insanity, paranoia
mental dissociation lunacy
mental equilibrium competence (sanity), sanity
mental faculty intellect, intelligence (intellect), judgment (discernment)

mental giant mastermind
mental grasp comprehension, information *(knowledge)*
mental health competence *(sanity)*, sanity
mental hospital asylum *(hospital)*
mental illness lunacy
mental image concept, impression, notion, perception, phantom, recollection, remembrance *(recollection)*, sense *(feeling)*
mental imbalance lunacy
mental impression concept, perception
mental incapacity insanity
mental infirmities insanity
mental instability insanity
mental institution asylum *(hospital)*
mental outlook position *(point of view)*
mental picture recollection
mental poise common sense
mental representation concept
mental reservation ambivalence
mental sickness insanity, lunacy
mental toil labor *(exertion)*
mental unsoundness insanity
mental view impression, perspective
mentality caliber *(mental capacity)*, comprehension, intellect, intelligence *(intellect)*, sagacity, sense *(intelligence)*, temperament
mentally aberrant lunatic
mentally appreciate discern *(detect with the senses)*
mentally capable competent
mentally deficient non compos mentis
mentally diseased non compos mentis SEE MAIN ENTRY
mentally ill lunatic, non compos mentis
mentally sick non compos mentis
mentally sound normal *(sane)*, sane
mentally unbalanced lunatic
mentally unsound non compos mentis
mentation reflection *(thought)*
mentio mention *(reference)*
mention adduce, advise, allude, attribution, citation *(attribution)*, cite *(state)*, comment *(noun)*, comment *(verb)*, communicate, convey *(communicate)*, designate, disclose, disclosure *(act of disclosing)*, enumerate, expression *(comment)*, impart, indication, inform *(notify)*, innuendo, intimation, itemize, notice *(announcement)*, notice *(observe)*, notification, notify, observation, observe *(remark)*, refer *(direct attention)*, reference *(allusion)*, reference *(citation)*, referral, relate *(tell)*, remark *(noun)*, remark *(verb)*, report *(disclose)*, reveal, signify *(inform)*, specify, tip *(clue)*. SEE MAIN ENTRY
mention in detail itemize
mention one by one enumerate
mention specifically enumerate
mentioned aforesaid
mentioned previously aforesaid
mentioning reference *(citation)*
mentiri lie *(falsify)*
mentis acies perception
mentis compos sane
mentor mastermind
mentors faculty *(teaching staff)*
Mephistophelian diabolic
mephitic deadly, harmful, insalubrious, malignant, pernicious, pestilent
mercantile commercial, industrial, retail. SEE MAIN ENTRY
mercantile business commerce, industry *(business)*, trade *(commerce)*
mercantile relations commerce, trade *(commerce)*

mercantilism commerce
mercari buy
mercator dealer, merchant
mercatura commerce
mercaturam trade
mercatus market *(business)*, trade *(commerce)*
mercenarius mercenary
mercenary employee, illiberal, parsimonious, penurious, venal. SEE MAIN ENTRY
merces fee *(charge)*, pay, recompense, rent, wage
merces mutare barter
merces vetitae contraband
merchandise barter, cargo, commodities, deal, freight, handle *(trade)*, item, output, paraphernalia *(personal belongings)*, product, sell, stock in trade, trade. SEE MAIN ENTRY
merchandise list inventory
merchandise sent consignment
merchandise specification invoice *(itemized list)*
merchandiser dealer, merchant
merchandising business *(commerce)*, commerce, commercial, mercantile, trade *(commerce)*
merchant dealer, supplier, vendor. SEE MAIN ENTRY
merchantable marketable
merchantry business *(commerce)*, commerce, deal, exchange, trade *(commerce)*
merciful benevolent, charitable *(lenient)*, humane, lenient, placable, propitious, sensitive *(easily affected)*
mercifulness clemency, humanity *(humaneness)*, lenience, pity
merciless brutal, cruel, diabolic, harmful, harsh, inexorable, malevolent, malicious, obdurate, relentless, remorseless, ruthless, unrelenting, vicious SEE MAIN ENTRY
mercilessness atrocity, brutality, cruelty
mercurial capricious, inconsistent, irresolute, moving *(in motion)*, undependable, unpredictable, untrustworthy, variable, volatile
mercurialness inconsistency
mercy benevolence *(disposition to do good)*, clemency, condonation, consideration *(sympathetic regard)*, humanity *(humaneness)*, lenience, pity, understanding *(tolerance)*
mere marginal, minor, naked *(lacking embellishment)*, only *(no more than)*, simple. SEE MAIN ENTRY
merely only, purely *(simply)*, solely *(purely)*
merere earn
meretricious dishonest, disreputable, fraudulent, pretentious *(ostentatious)*, tawdry. SEE MAIN ENTRY
meretriciousness bad faith
merge amalgamate, annex *(add)*, attach *(join)*, bond *(hold together)*, cement, coincide *(concur)*, combine *(join together)*, commingle, conjoin, connect *(join together)*, consolidate *(unite)*, converge, desegregate, federalize *(associate)*, federate, include, incorporate *(include)*, join *(bring together)*, organize *(unionize)*, pool, unite SEE MAIN ENTRY
merge in desegregate
merged compound, concordant, concurrent *(united)*, conjoint, federal, joint, miscellaneous
merger accession *(annexation)*, affiliation *(amalgamation)*, cartel, coalescence, coalition, combination, concert, consolidation,

consortium *(business cartel)*, federation, integration *(amalgamation)*, integration *(assimilation)*, meeting *(encounter)*, syndicate, trust *(combination of businesses)*
merging centralization, coalescence, coalition, concerted, concordant
meridian pinnacle
merit caliber *(quality)*, consequence *(significance)*, credit *(recognition)*, earn, importance, probity, quality *(excellence)*, quality *(grade)*, rate, rectitude, right *(righteousness)*, significance, value, weight *(importance)*, worth SEE MAIN ENTRY
merit as compensation earn
merited condign, due *(owed)*, entitled, equitable, fair *(just)*, just, justifiable, rightful, suitable
meriting blame peccant *(culpable)*
meriting censure culpable
meriting condemnation culpable
meritless unworthy
meritoria lodging
meritorious cogent, conscientious, exemplary, high-minded, incorruptible, justifiable, laudable, major, moral, reputable, sterling, unimpeachable
meritoriousness merit, validity
meritum merit
meritus condign, equitable, just
merriment enjoyment *(pleasure)*
merry jocular
merrymaking jocular
merus genuine, unadulterated
merx commodities, merchandise
mesh intertwine
mesh together engage *(involve)*
mesh with comport *(agree with)*
meshing interlocking
mesial central *(situated near center)*, intermediate
mesne intermediate. SEE MAIN ENTRY
mess confuse *(create disorder)*, imbroglio, pollute, predicament, quagmire, quantity, shambles, snarl
mess up confuse *(create disorder)*, disrupt, spoil *(impair)*
message communication *(statement)*, disclosure *(something disclosed)*, intelligence *(news)*, issuance, note *(brief comment)*, notice *(announcement)*, notification, proclamation, report *(detailed account)*. SEE MAIN ENTRY
messenger forerunner, harbinger, informer *(a person who provides information)*, liaison, plenipotentiary, proxy, representative *(proxy)*, spokesman
messuage homestead
messy disordered
metabolize convert *(change use)*
metage measurement
metamorphic protean
metamorphose alter, change, convert *(change use)*, modify *(alter)*, transform
metamorphosis conversion *(change)*
metaphor example
metaphorical comparative
metaphysical incomprehensible
metari measure
metastasis transition
mete allocate, allot, apportion, assess *(appraise)*, bestow, calculate, disburse *(distribute)*, dispense, distribute, divide *(distribute)*, dole, measure, parcel, partition, periphery, split. SEE MAIN ENTRY
mete out administer *(tender)*, allot, apportion, arbitrate *(adjudge)*, assign *(allot)*, contribute *(supply)*, disperse *(disseminate)*,

869

dispose (apportion), divide (distribute), dole, inflict, partition, present (make a gift), prorate, render (administer)

meteoric brief, ephemeral, transient

meteorical ephemeral

meter measure

meterable appreciable

meterage measurement

metes confines, outline (boundary)

method act (undertaking), arrangement (ordering), arrangement (plan), array (order), avenue (means of attainment), campaign, conduct, conduit (channel), contrivance, course, device (contrivance), direction (course), disposition (final arrangement), expedient, facility (instrumentality), form (arrangement), instrumentality, key (solution), manner (behavior), means (opportunity), mode, modus operandi, policy (plan of action), practice (custom), practice (procedure), procedure, process (course), regularity, rule (guide), scheme, science (technique), strategy, style, system, technicality, usage. SEE MAIN ENTRY

method of action manner (behavior)

method of attack avenue (means of attainment)

method of business dealings

method of communication forum (medium)

method of expression forum (medium)

method of living modus vivendi

method of treatment cure

methodical precise, procedural, punctilious, regular (orderly), systematic

methodicalness array (order), regularity

methodization classification

methodize adjust (regulate), classify, codify, coordinate, disentangle, fix (arrange), orchestrate, organize (arrange), pigeonhole, regulate (adjust), sort, tabulate

methodology array (order), modus operandi, order (arrangement), procedure, process (course)

meticulosity diligence (perseverance), interest (concern)

meticulous accurate, careful, circumspect, close (rigorous), conscientious, detailed, discriminating (judicious), exact, faithful (diligent), literal, painstaking, particular (exacting), precise, punctilious, punctual, strict, subtle (refined), thorough. SEE MAIN ENTRY

meticulously faithfully

meticulousness caution (vigilance), diligence (care), particularity, rigor

metier calling, career, industry (business), pursuit (occupation), trade (occupation), work (employment)

meting out apportionment

metiri gauge

metropolis city

metropolitan civic, civil (public)

metropolitan area city

mettle character (personal quality), frame (mood), prowess (bravery), spirit

mettlesome undaunted

metuere fear

metus fear

metus timor misgiving

mew imprison

miasmal deleterious, destructive, harmful, insalubrious, malignant, peccant (unhealthy)

miasmatic destructive, insalubrious, malignant

miasmatical insalubrious, malignant

miasmic deadly, destructive, insalubrious

microscopic impalpable

mid average (midmost), intermediate

middle average (midmost), center (central position), central (situated near center), interior, intermediate, mediocre, mesne. SEE MAIN ENTRY

middle class average (midmost)

middle distance center (central position)

middle grade average (midmost)

middle ground compromise

middle man representative (proxy)

middle point center (central position)

middle position center (central position)

middle state mediocrity

middleman agent, broker, conduit (intermediary), dealer, factor (commission merchant), go-between, interagent, intermediary, medium, merchant, procurator

middlemost average (midmost), central (situated near center)

middling average (midmost), fair (satisfactory), imperfect, marginal, mediocre, nondescript, ordinary, passable, usual

midmost central (situated near center), intermediate

midmost point center (central position)

midpoint center (central position), norm

midst center (central position)

midway en route

mien appearance (look), aspect, behavior, complexion, conduct, demeanor, deportment, manner (behavior), presence (poise), semblance, state (condition)

miff aggravate (annoy)

miffed resentful

might degree (magnitude), dint, force (strength), influence, main force, potential, prowess (bravery), puissance, quality (excellence), severity, sinew, strength. SEE MAIN ENTRY

mightiness dint, dominance, eminence, force (strength), influence, potential, predominance, puissance, strength

mightless powerless

mighty efficient, grandiose, important (significant), in full force, inexpugnable, influential, irresistible, omnipotent, potent, powerful, predominant, prevailing (having superior force), prodigious (enormous), spartan, strong, vehement

migrate leave (depart), move (alter position), part (leave). SEE MAIN ENTRY

migration immigration

migratory moving (in motion), transient, unsettled

mild civil (polite), innocuous, lenient, patient, peaceable, permissive, placable, placid SEE MAIN ENTRY

mild-tempered patient

milden mollify, relax

mildewed stale

mildly fairly (moderately)

mildness amenity, humanity (humaneness), lenience, moderation

mileage space

milestone cornerstone, crossroad (turning point), event, landmark (significant change), step

milieu atmosphere, case (set of circumstances), environment, section (vicinity)

militancy belligerency

militant aggressor, contentious, litigious, offensive (taking the initiative), pugnacious, radical (favoring drastic change), spartan

militaristic offensive (taking the initiative), pugnacious

military evolutions strategy

military science strategy

military tribunal SEE MAIN ENTRY

militate influence, operate. SEE MAIN ENTRY

militate against counter, counteract, countervail, oppugn

milk exploit (take advantage of)

millstone incumbrance (burden)

mime impersonate, mock (imitate), parody

mimesis part (role)

mimic impersonate, jape, mock (imitate), pose (impersonate), pretend

mimicking caricature

mimicry caricature, parody, ridicule, travesty

minacious ominous, pending (imminent), portentous (ominous), prophetic

minacious force menace

minacity menace

minae threat

minatorial imminent, portentous (ominous), prophetic

minatory aleatory (perilous), dangerous, imminent, ominous, portentous (ominous), prophetic, sinister, unpropitious

mince the truth prevaricate

mind animus, attend (heed), beware, care (be cautious), care (regard), comprehension, conatus, concern (care), conscience, conviction (persuasion), frame (mood), hear (give attention to), heed, intellect, intelligence (intellect), intent, memory (retention), note (notice), obey, observe (watch), preserve, propensity, reason (sound judgment), regard (pay attention), submit (yield), will (desire). SEE MAIN ENTRY

mind set position (point of view)

minded prone

mindful careful, circumspect, cognizant, conscious (aware), discreet, faithful (diligent), familiar (informed), judicious, knowing, meticulous, particular (exacting), perceptive, politic, prudent, sensitive (discerning) SEE MAIN ENTRY

mindfulness caution (vigilance), comprehension, diligence (care), discretion (quality of being discreet), interest (concern), knowledge (awareness), notice (heed), observation, perception, realization, recollection, regard (attention), sense (feeling), sensibility

mindless blind (not discerning), heedless, irrational, lax, negligent, non compos mentis, oblivious, opaque, perfunctory, reckless, unaware

mindlessness disinterest (lack of interest), disregard (unconcern)

mine bomb, contrive, extract, fund

mingle combine (join together), confuse (create disorder), desegregate, join (associate oneself with), unite

mingle confusedly confound

mingled complex, compound, conglomerate, promiscuous

minglement incorporation (blend), melange

mingling concrescence, integration (amalgamation), integration (assimilation)

miniature model, tenuous

minify diminish, lessen

minim minimum, scintilla

minimal minor, remote (small). SEE MAIN ENTRY

minimalize discount (minimize)

minime suspicax unsuspecting

minimization curtailment, deduction *(diminution)*, understatement

minimize allay, commute, decrease, depreciate, dilute, diminish, disparage, lessen, misprize, palliate *(abate)*, reduce, remit *(relax)*, underestimate. SEE MAIN ENTRY

minimum minimal, minor, modicum, nominal, paucity. SEE MAIN ENTRY

minimum wage SEE MAIN ENTRY

minimus inappreciable

minister administer *(conduct)*, caretaker *(one fulfilling the function of office)*, contribute *(assist)*, deputy, incumbent, officiate, operate, pander, proctor, supply

minister to accommodate, aid, assist, attend *(take care of)*, bear *(yield)*, bestow, care *(regard)*, concern *(care)*, cure, foster, preserve, relieve *(give aid)*, remedy, serve *(assist)*, support *(assist)*

ministerial administrative, executive. SEE MAIN ENTRY

ministering angel samaritan

ministerium service *(assistance)*

ministers government *(political administration)*

ministrant ancillary *(auxiliary)*, benefactor, samaritan, subservient

ministrare supply

ministration administration, aid *(help)*, aid *(subsistence)*, attendance, behalf, bureaucracy, direction *(guidance)*, help, relief *(aid)*, service *(assistance)*

ministry aid *(help)*, aid *(subsistence)*, bureau, control *(supervision)*, department, relief *(aid)*

minor adolescent, child, collateral *(immaterial)*, dependent *(adjective)*, dependent *(noun)*, frivolous, immaterial, inappreciable, incidental, inconsequential, inconsiderable, infant, inferior *(lower in position)*, juvenile *(adjective)*, juvenile *(noun)*, minimal, negligible, nonessential, null *(insignificant)*, petty, secondary, slight, subaltern, subordinate, unessential. SEE MAIN ENTRY

minor amount modicum

minor officer of the law marshal

minor part detail

minor point technicality

minor under guardianship dependent

minor under protectorship dependent

minoris aestimare underestimate

minoris facere underestimate

minority adolescence, nonage, paucity. SEE MAIN ENTRY

minors children

mintage money

minted monetary

minuere curtail, diminish, extenuate

minui suffer *(sustain loss)*

minus save

minute accurate, capsule, conscientious, detailed, entry *(record)*, exact, impalpable, inconsiderable, meticulous, minimal, minor, negligible, nominal, notation, note *(brief comment)*, outline *(synopsis)*, paltry, paraphrase, petty, record, remote *(small)*, report *(detailed account)*, scarce, slight, summary, synopsis, tenuous, trivial

minute account specification

minute application diligence *(care)*

minute attention diligence *(care)*, interest *(concern)*, scrutiny

minute circumstance particularity

minute examination cross-examination

minute investigation indagation

minute part detail

minute quantity iota

minute study diligence *(care)*

minute thought diligence *(care)*

minutely careful meticulous

minutely correct punctilious, punctual

minuteness diligence *(care)*, interest *(concern)*, particularity

minutes register, transcript

minutia particular

minutiae circumstances, technicality

minutus paltry, petty

miracle phenomenon *(unusual occurrence)*

miraculous incomprehensible, ineffable, portentous *(eliciting amazement)*, prodigious *(amazing)*, remarkable, special, unprecedented

mirage deception, figment, phantom

miratio surprise

mire pollute

mirror copy, impersonate, mock *(imitate)*, reproduce

mirth-loving jocular

mirthful jocular

mirthless solemn

mirus eccentric

misaddress misdirect

misadminister misgovern, mismanage

misadministration maladministration, misconduct

misadventure accident *(misfortune)*, adversity, casualty, catastrophe, debacle, disaster, miscarriage, misfortune, quirk *(accident)*, tragedy

misadvise misdirect, misguide, misinform, mislead

misadvised ill-advised, ill-judged, inadvisable. SEE MAIN ENTRY

misalliance disaccord, incongruity, misjoinder

misanthropic cynical

misapplication abuse *(corrupt practice)*, catachresis, conversion *(misappropriation)*, distortion, exploitation, maladministration, misappropriation, misdoing, misrepresentation, misusage, misuse, waste. SEE MAIN ENTRY

misapplied inapplicable, inappropriate

misapplied name misnomer

misapply abuse *(misuse)*, bilk, convert *(misappropriate)*, embezzle, exploit *(take advantage of)*, misemploy, mismanage, pervert, purloin, slant

misapply funds defalcate

misapprehend err, misconceive, misconstrue, misinterpret, misjudge, misread, mistake, misunderstand

misapprehension catachresis, fallacy, misestimation, misjudgment

misappropriate abuse *(misuse)*, bilk, divert, embezzle, exploit *(take advantage of)*, hold up *(rob)*, impropriate, jostle *(pickpocket)*, misemploy, mismanage, peculate, pilfer, plagiarize, poach, purloin, rob. SEE MAIN ENTRY

misappropriate funds embezzle

misappropriate intrusted funds embezzle

misappropriate money defalcate

misappropriation abuse *(corrupt practice)*, embezzlement, larceny, misapplication, misusage, misuse, plagiarism, theft. SEE MAIN ENTRY

misappropriation of funds conversion *(misappropriation)*

misarrange disorganize

misarrangement disturbance

misbecoming inappropriate

misbegetting bar sinister

misbegot illegitimate *(born out of wedlock)*

misbegotten illegitimate *(born out of wedlock)*

misbehave disobey, lapse *(fall into error)*

misbehaved disorderly

misbehaving delinquent *(guilty of a misdeed)*, disobedient, disorderly

misbehavior bad repute, culpability, delinquency *(misconduct)*, disregard *(omission)*, fault *(responsibility)*, guilt, impropriety, malfeasance, miscarriage, mischief, misconduct, misdeed, misdoing, transgression, violation

misbelief error, fallacy

misbelieve doubt *(distrust)*, misdoubt

misbeliever heretic

misbelieving doubtful

misbrand mislabel

miscalculate err, misapprehend, misconceive, misinterpret, misjudge, mistake, misunderstand. SEE MAIN ENTRY

miscalculated fallacious, ill-judged, incorrect, inexact, inflated *(overestimated)*

miscalculation confusion *(ambiguity)*, error, fallacy, fault *(mistake)*, miscue, misestimation, misjudgment

miscalling misnomer

miscarriage accident *(misfortune)*, disaster, failure *(lack of success)*. SEE MAIN ENTRY

miscarriage of justice error, inequity, injustice, misjudgment

miscarry fail *(lose)*

miscellaneous composite, conglomerate, diverse, heterogeneous, manifold, multifarious, multiple, omnibus, promiscuous. SEE MAIN ENTRY

miscellaneous collection melange

miscellany assemblage, compilation, conglomeration, diversity, melange

miscere combine *(join together)*, disorganize, unite

mischance accident *(misfortune)*, adversity, calamity, casualty, catastrophe, debacle, fatality, miscarriage, misfortune, quirk *(accident)*

mischaracterize mislabel

mischief disservice, harm, misdoing. SEE MAIN ENTRY

mischief-maker delinquent, malefactor

mischievous harmful, malevolent, malicious, noxious, peccant *(culpable)*, pernicious, sinister, vicious, wrongful

miscitation catachresis

miscite bear false witness, distort, falsify, misrepresent

misclassify mislabel

miscolor camouflage, cloak, distort, falsify, misinform, misrepresent, slant

miscomprehend misapprehend

miscomputation error, misestimation, misjudgment

miscompute err, miscalculate, misjudge

misconceive misapprehend, miscalculate, misconstrue, misinterpret, misjudge, mistake, misunderstand. SEE MAIN ENTRY

misconception catachresis, confusion *(ambiguity)*, error, fallacy, misapplication, misestimation, misjudgment

misconduct blame *(culpability)*, crime, culpability, disregard *(omission)*, fault *(responsibility)*, guilt, indiscretion, maladministration, malpractice, miscarriage, mischief, misdeed, misdoing, misemploy, misfeasance, misguide, mishandle *(mismanage)*, mismanage, misprision, misrule, offense, transgression, vice. SEE MAIN ENTRY

misconduct oneself offend *(violate the law)*

misconducted misadvised

misconjecture error, miscalculate, misconceive, misestimation, misinterpret

misconstructed fallacious

misconstruction catachresis, distortion, fallacy, falsification, misapplication, misjudgment, misrepresentation

misconstrue distort, err, misapprehend, miscalculate, misconceive, misinterpret, misjudge, misread, mistake, misunderstand, slant. SEE MAIN ENTRY

misconstrued incorrect

miscounseled ill-advised

miscount error, miscalculate

miscreancy wrong

miscreant bad *(offensive)*, convict, delinquent, hoodlum, immoral, iniquitous, malefactor, nefarious, outlaw, profane, racketeer, sinister, wrongdoer

miscue SEE MAIN ENTRY

misdealing bribery, crime, disingenuous, disreputable, machiavellian, racket

misdeed crime, delinquency *(misconduct)*, disservice, fault *(responsibility)*, guilt, illegality, lapse *(expiration)*, malfeasance, misconduct, misdemeanor, misdoing, misfeasance, misprision, offense, onus *(blame)*, tort, transgression, vice, wrong. SEE MAIN ENTRY

misdeed punishable by imprisonment felony

misdeem misapprehend, miscalculate, misconceive, misinterpret, misjudge, misread, misunderstand

misdemeanant convict, criminal, culpable, delinquent, lawbreaker, malefactor, wrongdoer

misdemeanor crime, delict, guilt, misconduct, misdeed, misdoing, offense. SEE MAIN ENTRY

misdenominate mislabel

misdescribe distort, mislabel, mislead, misrepresent

misdesignate mislabel

misdirect convert *(misappropriate)*, corrupt, deceive, delude, disorient, distort, divert, dupe, ensnare, exploit *(take advantage of)*, illude, misemploy, misgovern, misguide, mishandle *(mismanage)*, misinform, mislabel, mislead, mismanage, palter, slant. SEE MAIN ENTRY

misdirected errant, inappropriate, misadvised

misdirection abuse *(corrupt practice)*, digression, distortion, maladministration, misrule

misdo misemploy, mismanage

misdoer delinquent, wrongdoer

misdoing crime, criminality, culpability, delinquency *(misconduct)*, disservice, guilt, infringement, malfeasance, mischief, misconduct, misdeed, misdemeanor, misfeasance, offense, tort, transgression, wrong. SEE MAIN ENTRY

misdoubt apprehension *(fear)*, cloud *(suspicion)*, doubt *(suspicion)*, doubt *(distrust)*, mistrust, suspect *(distrust)*, suspicion *(mistrust)*. SEE MAIN ENTRY

miseducate distort, misdirect, misguide, misinform, mislead

misemploy abuse *(misuse)*, convert *(misappropriate)*, exploit *(take advantage of)*, mishandle *(maltreat)*, mismanage, mistreat,

persecute. SEE MAIN ENTRY

misemploy funds defalcate

misemployment abuse *(corrupt practice)*, conversion *(misappropriation)*, misapplication, misappropriation, misusage, misuse, waste

miserabilis deplorable, moving *(evoking emotion)*

miserable deplorable, disconsolate, lamentable, lugubrious, paltry, pessimistic, poor *(inferior in quality)*

misereri sympathize

miseria adversity

misericordia humanity *(humaneness)*, pity

misericors humane

miserly illiberal, parsimonious, penurious

misery calamity, disaster, distress *(anguish)*, pain, pessimism, prostration

misesteem misjudge

misestimate distort, miscalculate, misconceive, misjudge, overestimate

misestimation misjudgment. SEE MAIN ENTRY

misexplain distort, misrepresent

misexplanation catachresis, distortion, misapplication

misexplication catachresis, misapplication

misexposition catachresis

misexpress distort

misfeasance bad faith, crime, delict, fault *(responsibility)*, guilt, infringement, maladministration, misconduct, misdeed, misdemeanor, misdoing, misprision, offense, tort, transgression. SEE MAIN ENTRY

misfeasor convict, delinquent, lawbreaker

misfigured fallacious, incorrect, inexact

misfire miscarriage

misfit misjoinder

misfortunate unfavorable

misfortune adversity, calamity, casualty, catastrophe, debacle, detriment, disaster, failure *(lack of success)*, fatality, hardship, harm, infliction, loss, plight, predicament, quagmire, tragedy, trouble. SEE MAIN ENTRY

misgive doubt *(distrust)*, misdoubt, mistrust, suspect *(distrust)*

misgiving apprehension *(fear)*, cloud *(suspicion)*, disturbance, doubt *(indecision)*, doubt *(suspicion)*, expectation, fear, fright, incertitude, premonition, qualm, reluctance, scruple, stress *(strain)*, suspicion *(mistrust)*. SEE MAIN ENTRY

misgovern exploit *(take advantage of)*, mismanage, mistreat. SEE MAIN ENTRY

misgovernment anarchy, lynch law, maladministration, malfeasance, misconduct, misrule

misguidance error, maladministration, misconduct, misrepresentation, misrule

misguide deceive, delude, dupe, ensnare, equivocate, fabricate *(make up)*, illude, lie *(falsify)*, misdirect, misgovern, misinform, mislabel, mislead, mismanage, misrepresent, misstate, palter, prevaricate. SEE MAIN ENTRY

misguided astray, ill-advised, inadvisable, injudicious, misadvised

mishandle abuse *(misuse)*, exploit *(take advantage of)*, ill use, maltreat, misemploy, misguide, mismanage, mistreat, persecute. SEE MAIN ENTRY

mishandling abuse *(corrupt practice)*, abuse *(physical misuse)*, maladministration, misapplication, misrule, misuse

mishap accident *(misfortune)*, adversity, casualty, catastrophe, debacle, misfortune, quirk *(accident)*, situation, tragedy

misidentify mislabel, misread, mistake

misinform betray *(lead astray)*, bilk, cloak, deceive, delude, distort, equivocate, fabricate *(make up)*, hoodwink, illude, lie *(falsify)*, misdirect, misguide, mislabel, mislead, misstate, palter, prevaricate. SEE MAIN ENTRY

misinformation distortion, false pretense, misstatement

misinformed misadvised

misinstruct distort, misdirect, misguide, misinform, mislead

misinstructed misadvised

misinstruction distortion, propaganda

misinterpret distort, err, misapprehend, misconceive, misconstrue, misjudge, misread, mistake, misunderstand, slant. SEE MAIN ENTRY

misinterpretation catachresis, distortion, error, fallacy, misapplication, misestimation, misjudgment

misinterpreted inexact

misjoinder SEE MAIN ENTRY

misjoined incongruous

misjudge err, misapprehend, miscalculate, misconceive, misconstrue, misinterpret, misprize, mistake, misunderstand, overestimate, underestimate. SEE MAIN ENTRY

misjudged incorrect, inopportune, untimely

misjudging credulous

misjudgment catachresis, error, fallacy, fault *(mistake)*, indiscretion, misapplication, miscue, misestimation, overstatement. SEE MAIN ENTRY

mislabel SEE MAIN ENTRY

mislaid lost *(taken away)*

mislay dislocate, disorient, lose *(be deprived of)*

mislead betray *(lead astray)*, brutalize, circumvent, cloak, confound, confuse *(bewilder)*, corrupt, deceive, defraud, delude, disorient, distort, divert, dupe, ensnare, equivocate, evade *(deceive)*, fabricate *(make up)*, fake, feign, hoodwink, illude, inveigle, lie *(falsify)*, misdirect, misguide, misinform, mislabel, misrepresent, misstate, obscure, overreach, palter, pervert, pettifog, pretend, prevaricate. SEE MAIN ENTRY

misleader decoy

misleading assumed *(feigned)*, deceptive, delusive, dishonest, disingenuous, equivocal, evasive, fallacious, false *(inaccurate)*, fictitious, fraudulent, illusory, incorrect, lying, meretricious, ostensible, propaganda, sophistic, specious, untrue

misleading enlargement exaggeration

misleading notion fallacy

misled astray, misadvised

misled by deception blind *(not discerning)*

mislike disaffect

mismanage convert *(misappropriate)*, exploit *(take advantage of)*, fail *(neglect)*, misemploy, misgovern, misguide, mistreat, muddle. SEE MAIN ENTRY

mismanagement abuse *(corrupt practice)*, incompetence, maladministration, malfeasance, misapplication, misconduct, misdoing, misrule, misusage, misuse

mismark mislabel

mismatch conflict, incongruity, misjoinder

mismatched different, disproportionate, dissimilar, inapplicable, inapt, incommensurate, incongruous, inept *(inappropriate)*, unrelated, unsuitable

mismated different, incongruous, opposite

misname mislabel

misnaming misnomer

misnomer SEE MAIN ENTRY

misperceive misunderstand

misplace dislocate, disorganize, disorient, lose *(be deprived of)*

misplaced anomalous, inapplicable, inappropriate, inapt, inept *(inappropriate)*, lost *(taken away)*

misprint error

misprision contempt *(disdain)*, crime, delict, delinquency *(failure of duty)*, dereliction, guilt, misconduct, misdoing, neglect, nonfeasance, offense. SEE MAIN ENTRY

misprize contemn, depreciate, derogate, discount *(disbelieve)*, disdain, disfavor, disparage, humiliate, minimize, underestimate. SEE MAIN ENTRY

mispronunciation misusage

misquotation catachresis, distortion, falsification, misrepresentation

misquote distort, falsify, misrepresent, slant

misread distort, misconstrue, misinterpret, misjudge, mistake, misunderstand. SEE MAIN ENTRY

misreading catachresis

misreckon distort, err, misapprehend, miscalculate, misconceive, misinterpret, misjudge, misunderstand

misreckoning error, misestimation

misrender palter, slant

misrendering catachresis, distortion

misreport bear false witness, distort, falsify, feign, misrepresent, misrepresentation, misstate, palter

misreported inaccurate, inexact

misrepresent cloak, deceive, delude, disguise, distort, equivocate, evade *(deceive)*, fabricate *(make up)*, fake, falsify, feign, invent *(falsify)*, lie *(falsify)*, misguide, misinform, misinterpret, mislabel, mislead, misrepresent, misstate, overestimate, palter, perjure, pervert, pretend, prevaricate, slant. SEE MAIN ENTRY

misrepresentation abuse *(corrupt practice)*, artifice, bad faith, catachresis, color *(deceptive appearance)*, deceit, deception, distortion, evasion, false pretense, falsehood, falsification, forgery, fraud, hoax, lie, misstatement, overstatement, perjury, pretense *(pretext)*, pretext, sham, sophistry, story *(falsehood)*, subreption, understatement. SEE MAIN ENTRY

misrepresentative evasive, fallacious, false *(not genuine)*, fictitious, lying, mendacious

misrepresented assumed *(feigned)*, mendacious, spurious

misrule anarchy, lynch law, maladministration, misemploy, misgovern, mismanage, mistreat, oppression. SEE MAIN ENTRY

miss fail *(neglect)*, ignore, lack, lose *(be deprived of)*, miscue, need, omit, overlook *(disregard)*, pretermit, require *(need)*. SEE MAIN ENTRY

miss an opportunity fail *(neglect)*

miss the mark fail *(lose)* SEE MAIN ENTRY

missend mismanage

misserved aggrieved *(victimized)*

misshape contort, deface, distort

misshapen blemished, repulsive

missile bomb

missing deficient, delinquent *(overdue)*, devoid, insufficient, lost *(taken away)*, truant, vacuous

missio release

mission agency *(legal relationship)*, assignment *(task)*, business *(affair)*, business *(occupation)*, calling, charge *(responsibility)*, charge *(empower)*, commitment *(responsibility)*, delegation *(envoy)*, deputation *(delegation)*, design *(intent)*, embassy, end *(intent)*, function, goal, job, objective, occupation *(vocation)*, purpose, role. SEE MAIN ENTRY

mission of the ambassador embassy

missive dispatch *(message)*, note *(brief comment)*

missives correspondence *(communication by letters)*

misspend dissipate *(expend foolishly)*, misemploy

misstate delude, equivocate, fabricate *(make up)*, falsify, feign, invent *(falsify)*, lie *(falsify)*, misguide, misinform, mislabel, mislead, misrepresent, palter, prevaricate, slant. SEE MAIN ENTRY

misstated inaccurate, inexact, mendacious

misstatement abuse *(corrupt practice)*, color *(deceptive appearance)*, error, false pretense, falsehood, falsification, lie, miscue, misestimation, misrepresentation, overstatement, perjury, pretext, story *(falsehood)*. SEE MAIN ENTRY

misstatement of fact misrepresentation. SEE MAIN ENTRY

misstep delinquency *(misconduct)*, fault *(mistake)*, indiscretion, lapse *(expiration)*, lapse *(fall into error)*, miscue

missum facere discharge *(dismiss)*

mist obfuscate

mistakable uncertain *(ambiguous)*

mistake catachresis, defect, err, error, failure *(lack of success)*, fallacy, indiscretion, lapse *(expiration)*, misapplication, misapprehend, miscalculate, miscarriage, misconstrue, miscue, misdeed, misestimation, misinterpret, misjudge, misjudgment, misread, misstatement, misunderstand, oversight *(carelessness)*, wrong. SEE MAIN ENTRY

mistake of the court injustice

mistaken errant, erroneous, fallacious, false *(inaccurate)*, faulty, illogical, improper, inaccurate, incorrect, misadvised, unsound *(fallacious)*

mistaken belief error

mistaken idea fallacy

mistaken judgment error

misteach distort, misdirect, misguide, misinform, mislead, misrepresent

misterm misnomer

misthink misjudge

misticket mislabel

mistimed inauspicious, inopportune, premature, untimely

mistiness indistinctness

mistitle mislabel

mistranslate distort, misinterpret, misread

mistranslated inexact

mistranslation catachresis, distortion, error, misapplication

mistreat abuse *(misuse)*, abuse *(victimize)*, exploit *(take advantage of)*, ill use, maltreat, misemploy, persecute. SEE MAIN ENTRY

mistreatment abuse *(physical misuse)*, disservice, misuse, molestation, oppression, violation, wrong

mistrust apprehension *(fear)*, cloud *(suspicion)*, disbelieve, discount *(disbelieve)*, discredit, doubt *(suspicion)*, doubt *(distrust)*, incredulity, misdoubt, misgiving, qualm, rejection, suspect *(distrust)*. SEE MAIN ENTRY

mistrustful cynical, doubtful, incredulous, leery, resentful, suspicious *(distrustful)*

mistrustfulness cloud *(suspicion)*, doubt *(suspicion)*, incredulity, misgiving

mistrusting doubtful

misty inconspicuous, indistinct, opaque, unclear

misunderstand err, misapprehend, misconceive, misconstrue, misinterpret, misjudge, misread, mistake

misunderstanding argument *(contention)*, catachresis, conflict, difference, error, fault *(mistake)*, incompatibility *(difference)*, misapplication, miscue, misestimation, misjudgment, rift *(disagreement)*. SEE MAIN ENTRY

misunderstood vague

misusage abuse *(corrupt practice)*, abuse *(physical misuse)*, catachresis, distortion, misapplication, misappropriation, mischief, misuse, waste. SEE MAIN ENTRY

misuse abuse *(corrupt practice)*, conversion *(misappropriation)*, convert *(misappropriate)*, dissipate *(expend foolishly)*, embezzle, endanger, exploit *(take advantage of)*, exploitation, harass, harm, harrow, ill use, manipulate *(control unfairly)*, misapplication, misappropriation, misemploy, mishandle *(maltreat)*, mishandle *(mismanage)*, mismanage, mistreat, misusage, molest *(annoy)*, persecute, perversion, pervert, purloin, taint *(corrupt)*, violation, waste. SEE MAIN ENTRY

misuse entrusted monies defalcate

misuse of funds misapplication

misuse of power oppression

misuse of words distortion, error, misapplication

misused aggrieved *(harmed)*

misventure disaster

mite modicum

mitigare allay, assuage, extenuate, mitigate, mollify

mitigate abate *(lessen)*, adjust *(resolve)*, allay, alleviate, ameliorate, assuage, commute, curb, decrease, dilute, diminish, ease, extenuate, justify, lessen, lull, meliorate, moderate *(temper)*, modify *(moderate)*, mollify, obtund, palliate *(abate)*, relax, relieve *(free from burden)*, remedy, remit *(relax)*, soothe, subside. SEE MAIN ENTRY

mitigating narcotic, palliative *(abating)*. SEE MAIN ENTRY

mitigating circumstance justification

mitigating circumstances extenuating circumstances

mitigatio mitigation

mitigation abatement *(reduction)*, decrease, diminution, excuse, extenuating circumstances, justification, moderation, mollification, relief *(release)*, remission, solace. SEE MAIN ENTRY

mitigative narcotic, palliative *(abating)*

mitiorem facere mitigate

mitis lenient

mittere cast *(throw)*, discharge *(shoot)*, dispatch *(send off)*, remit *(send payment)*, send

mittimus citation *(charge)*, commitment *(confinement)*. SEE MAIN ENTRY

mix agitate *(shake up)*, amalgamate, combine *(join together)*, commingle, conjoin, consolidate *(strengthen)*, consolidate *(unite)*, denature, desegregate, diffuse, incorporate *(include)*, integration *(amalgamation)*, intersperse, join *(bring together)*, merge, pool, solution *(substance)*, unite. SEE MAIN ENTRY

mix together   commingle

mix up   agitate *(shake up)*, confuse *(bewilder)*, confuse *(create disorder)*, discompose, disrupt, muddle, obfuscate, perplex

mix-up   embroilment, entanglement *(confusion)*

mixed   composite, compound, conglomerate, conjoint, dissimilar, diverse, heterogeneous, inextricable, joint, miscellaneous, multifarious, multiple, nonsectarian, promiscuous

mixed up   labyrinthine

mixing   concrescence

mixture   coalescence, coalition, consolidation, diversity, incorporation *(blend)*, melange, merger, solution *(substance)*

mixup   pandemonium

mnemonic   reminder

mnemonic device   reminder

moan   deplore, plaint

mob   assemblage, mass *(body of persons)*

mob law   anarchy

mob rule   anarchy, lynch law

mob swayer   demagogue

mobile   moving *(in motion)*, protean

mobilis   movable, volatile

mobilization   campaign

mobilize   call *(summon)*, consolidate *(unite)*, convene, dispatch *(send off)*, employ *(make use of)*, impel

mobilized   ready *(prepared)*

mobocracy   lynch law

mobster   hoodlum, racketeer

mock   copy, deceptive, delusive, disdain, disgrace, disparage, false *(not genuine)*, flout, harass, humiliate, illude, imitation, jape, jeer, meretricious, misrepresent, pillory, pose *(impersonate)*, quasi, sham, simulate, spurious, synthetic, untrue. SEE MAIN ENTRY

mockery   caricature, dishonor *(shame)*, disparagement, disrespect, falsification, irony, parody, pretense *(ostentation)*, ridicule, travesty

mocking   caustic, cynical, disdainful

mode   avenue *(means of attainment)*, conduit *(channel)*, course, form *(arrangement)*, habit, instrumentality, manner *(behavior)*, means *(opportunity)*, method, modus operandi, parlance, practice *(custom)*, practice *(procedure)*, procedure, style, tenor, usage, way *(channel)*. SEE MAIN ENTRY

mode of action   behavior, conduct

mode of behavior   conduct

mode of communication   forum *(medium)*

mode of expression   context, phraseology

mode of living   modus vivendi

mode of management   course, policy *(plan of action)*, practice *(procedure)*, system

mode of operation   avenue *(means of attainment)*, modus operandi, procedure, process *(course)*, strategy. SEE MAIN ENTRY

mode of procedure   course, expedient, maneuver *(tactic)*, modus operandi, practice *(custom)*

mode of proceeding   manner *(behavior)*

mode of reasoning   dialectic

mode of speech   phraseology

mode of use   procedure

model   absolute *(ideal)*, build *(construct)*, case *(example)*, code, copy, criterion, design *(construction plan)*, epitome, example, exemplar, exemplary, forge *(produce)*, form *(arrangement)*, illustration, instance, laudable, make, norm, paradigm, paragon, paramount, pattern, precedent, principle *(axiom)*, professional *(stellar)*, prototype, representative *(example)*, rule *(guide)*, sample, specimen, standard, style, symbol, typical. SEE MAIN ENTRY

model after   mock *(imitate)*

model instance   precedent

model of virtue   paragon

model oneself after   pose *(impersonate)*

moderari   control *(regulate)*, modify *(moderate)*

moderate   adjust *(regulate)*, allay, alleviate, alter, arbitrate *(conciliate)*, assuage, average *(standard)*, controlled *(restrained)*, curb, de minimus, ease, extenuate, fair *(satisfactory)*, imperfect, intercede, intermediate, judge, judicious, lenient, lessen, marginal, mediate, mediocre, minimal, mitigate, mollify, negligible, nominal, nonpartisan, obtund, officiate, palliate *(abate)*, passable, peaceable, regulate *(adjust)*, relax, relieve *(free from burden)*, remit *(relax)*, restrain, soothe, subdue, subside, usual. SEE MAIN ENTRY

moderate in severity   mitigate

moderated   qualified *(conditioned)*, tempered

moderately good   fair *(satisfactory)*

moderately large   major

moderateness   continence, moderation, neutrality, temperance

moderatio   control *(supervision)*, restraint, temperance

moderation   composure, continence, control *(restriction)*, lenience, mitigation, regulation *(management)*, remission, restraint, temperance. SEE MAIN ENTRY

moderatism   moderation

moderator   arbiter, arbitrator, chairman, go-between, intermediary, judge, magistrate

moderator   procurator

moderator   referee, umpire

modern   contemporary, novel, present *(current)*, progressive *(advocating change)*, sophisticated, unprecedented, unusual

modernist   pioneer

modernization   development *(progression)*, innovation, renewal

modernize   meliorate, modify *(alter)*, reconstruct, renew *(refurbish)*, renovate

modest   de minimus, diffident, inconsiderable, inconspicuous, insubstantial, marginal, mediocre, minimal, minor, negligible, nominal, paltry, slight, unaffected *(sincere)*, unobtrusive, unpretentious

modestly   fairly *(moderately)*

modesty   decorum, propriety *(correctness)*

modicum   minimum, paucity, scintilla. SEE MAIN ENTRY

modicus   reasonable *(fair)*, unpretentious

modifiable   ambulatory, open-ended, pliable, protean, provisional, variable

modification   abatement *(reduction)*, amendment *(correction)*, correction *(change)*, curtailment, innovation, qualification *(condition)*, transition, treatment. SEE MAIN ENTRY

modification of the law   amendment *(legislation)*

modifications   vicissitudes

modificatory   restrictive

modified   qualified *(conditioned)*, tempered

modified by conditions   conditional, dependent

modify   abate *(lessen)*, adapt, alter, amend, change, convert *(change use)*, influence, moderate *(temper)*, qualify *(condition)*, reform, relax, restrict, revise, transform, treat *(process)*, vary. SEE MAIN ENTRY

modify by excisions   delete, edit

modify sentence   commute

modifying   mitigating, palliative *(abating)*, restrictive

modifying cause   catalyst

modulate   adapt, alleviate, alter, change, lessen, limit, obtund, palliate *(abate)*, regulate *(adjust)*, relax

modulation   inflection, remission

modulatory   palliative *(abating)*

module   entity

modus   kind, method, mode, moderation, restriction, style

modus operandi   course

modus operandi   procedure. SEE MAIN ENTRY

modus vivendi   SEE MAIN ENTRY

moiety   segment. SEE MAIN ENTRY

moil   commotion

mold   character *(personal quality)*, delineate, disposition *(inclination)*, fabricate *(construct)*, facsimile, forge *(produce)*, form, frame *(construct)*, influence, make, manufacture, militate, model, norm, nurture, organize *(unionize)*, pattern, prototype, resemblance

moldable   facile, flexible, malleable, pliable, pliant, sequacious

molded together   inseparable

molder   decay

moldering   decadent

molding   creation, edge *(border)*, facsimile, manufacture

moldy   stale

moles   bulk

molest   abuse *(victimize)*, brutalize, debauch, distress, disturb, endanger, harrow, hector, irritate, misemploy, mishandle *(maltreat)*, mistreat, pique, plague, press *(goad)*. SEE MAIN ENTRY

molestation   abuse *(physical misuse)*, disturbance, mischief, nuisance. SEE MAIN ENTRY

moleste ferre   resent

molestia   dissatisfaction

molestus   irksome, oppressive

mollification   reconciliation. SEE MAIN ENTRY

mollify   allay, assuage, disarm *(set at ease)*, mitigate, moderate *(temper)*, modify *(moderate)*, pacify, placate, propitiate, reconcile, remedy, soothe, subdue. SEE MAIN ENTRY

mollifying   palliative *(abating)*

mollire   mollify

molliri   relent

mollis   malleable, pliant, resilient, sensitive *(easily affected)*, susceptible *(responsive)*

Molotov cocktail   bomb

moment   date, degree *(magnitude)*, emphasis, import, importance, interest *(concern)*, occasion, phase *(period)*, point *(period of time)*, significance, weight *(importance)*

moment of change   landmark *(significant change)*

momentarily   pro tempore

momentariness   insignificance

momentary   brief, ephemeral, immediate *(imminent)*, pending *(imminent)*, temporary, transient, transitory, volatile

momentous   cardinal *(outstanding)*, consequential *(substantial)*, considerable, critical *(crucial)*, crucial, decisive, important *(significant)*, key, major, material *(important)*, notable, noteworthy, remarkable, serious *(grave)*, stellar, strategic. SEE MAIN ENTRY

momentousness   importance, magnitude, materiality *(consequence)*, significance

momentum   headway, impetus

momentum   importance, stress *(strain)*

momumental   notable

monad   individual, unit *(item)*

monarchy   realm

monas   individual

monens   hortative

monere   admonish *(warn)*, caution

moneta   currency

monetary   commercial, financial, fiscal, mercantile, pecuniary. SEE MAIN ENTRY

monetary benefit   interest *(profit)*

monetary clause   ad damnum clause

monetary exchange   commerce

monetary gain   interest *(profit)*

monetary help   maintenance *(support of spouse)*

monetary remuneration   compensation, indemnification

monetary reservoir   bank

monetary return   pay

monetary theory   finance

monetary unit   cash

monetary value   expense *(cost)*

money   assets, capital, cash, currency, finance, payment *(remittance)*, possession *(property)*, principal *(capital sum)*, remuneration, substance *(material possessions)*. SEE MAIN ENTRY

money back   refund

money box   bank

money chest   coffer

money coming in   income, proceeds

money conscious   mercenary, provident *(frugal)*

money dealings   finance

money due   debt, setoff

money earned   earnings

money expended   cost *(expenses)*, expenditure, expense *(cost)*, overhead

money going out   disbursement *(funds paid out)*

money hungry   mercenary

money illegally acquired   graft

money in actual use   currency

money in bank   deposit

money invested   security *(stock)*

money matters   finance

money order   check *(instrument)*, draft, note *(written promise to pay)*

money owed   debt

money paid   collection *(payment)*

money paid for passage   fare

money saving   economic

money sent   remittance

money's worth   tariff *(bill)*

money-conscious   economical

money-making   finance, gainful, profitable

money-saving   economical

moneyed   opulent, prosperous, solvent

moneyless   bankrupt, destitute, insolvent, poor *(underprivileged)*

moneylessness   poverty

moneymaking   lucrative

moneys   cash

moneys borrowed   loan

moneys expended   disbursement *(funds paid out)*

moneys paid out   disbursement *(funds paid out)*

monger   broker, dealer, merchant, vendor

monitio   premonition

monition   admonition, caution *(warning)*, caveat, citation *(charge)*, deterrence, deterrent, dispatch *(message)*, guidance, indication, intelligence *(news)*, notice *(warning)*, notification, symptom, warning. SEE MAIN ENTRY

monitor   audit, bystander, chairman, check *(inspect)*, examine *(study)*, overhear, patrol, proctor, procurator, superintendent, symptom. SEE MAIN ENTRY

monitorial   hortative, prophetic

monitory   informatory, ominous, portentous *(ominous)*, presageful, prophetic

monitum   premonition

monitus   warning

monocratic   dictatorial

monohemerous   temporary

monolithical   solid *(compact)*

monologue   peroration

monomachy   contest *(dispute)*

monomania   obsession

monomaniac   bigot

monopolistic organization   trust *(combination of businesses)*

monopolium   monopoly

monopolize   immerse *(engross)*, occupy *(engage)*, possess. SEE MAIN ENTRY

monopolize the thoughts   occupy *(engage)*

monopoly   consortium *(business cartel)*, exclusion, franchise *(license)*, trust *(combination of businesses)*. SEE MAIN ENTRY

monosyllabic   inarticulate

monotone   prosaic

monotonous   insistent, jejune *(dull)*, lifeless *(dull)*, pedestrian, ponderous, prolix, prosaic, repeated, repetitious, stale, usual

monster   prodigious *(enormous)*

monstrosity   atrocity

monstrous   arrant *(onerous)*, bad *(offensive)*, delinquent *(guilty of a misdeed)*, diabolic, flagrant, gross *(flagrant)*, heinous, inexcusable, inordinate, malignant, nefarious, odious, offensive *(offending)*, outrageous, prodigious *(enormous)*, reprehensible, repulsive, unconscionable

monstrousness   bestiality, disrepute

monument   landmark *(conspicuous object)*, remembrance *(commemoration)*. SEE MAIN ENTRY

monumental   noteworthy, prodigious *(enormous)*, remarkable

monumentum   monument

mood   atmosphere, climate, disposition *(inclination)*, emotion, spirit, state *(condition)*, tenor

moodish   fractious

moody   despondent, disconsolate, fractious, froward, inconsistent, petulant, resentful, restive

moonshiner   bootlegger

moored   firm, stable

moot   debate, dubious, equivocal, pose *(propound)*, posit, problematic, propound, undecided. SEE MAIN ENTRY

moot point   problem, thesis

mope   brood

mora   check *(bar)*, delay

moral   blameless, clean, conscientious, ethical, high-minded, honest, incorruptible, just, law-abiding, meritorious, proper, reputable, scrupulous, signification, upright. SEE MAIN ENTRY

moral behavior   ethics

moral certainty   certitude

moral compulsion   coercion

moral conduct   ethics

moral consciousness   conscience, responsibility *(conscience)*

moral degeneracy   bad repute

moral excellence   principle *(virtue)*, probity

moral faculty   conscience, responsibility *(conscience)*

moral insensibility   brutality

moral judgment   ethics

moral necessity   duty *(obligation)*

moral obligation   allegiance, conscience, duty *(obligation)*, ethics, responsibility *(conscience)*

moral philosophy   ethics

moral practice   ethics

moral principles   conscience, ethics

moral qualities   character *(personal quality)*

moral rectitude   ethics, honor *(good reputation)*, principle *(virtue)*

moral responsibility   obligation *(duty)*

moral science   casuistry

moral sense   conscience, responsibility *(conscience)*

moral soundness   integrity

moral strength   ethics, integrity

moral tone   ethics

moral turpitude   bad repute

moral weakness   foible

morale   confidence *(faith)*

moralis   ethical

moralism   maxim

morality   ethics, integrity, principle *(virtue)*, probity, propriety *(correctness)*, rectitude, responsibility *(conscience)*, right *(righteousness)*

morally   fairly *(impartially)*

morally abandoned   reprobate

morally evil   profligate *(corrupt)*

morally impure   lewd

morally unrestrained   lewd

morals   conduct, ethics, probity, right *(righteousness)*

morari   pause

moratorium   adjournment, cancellation, cessation *(interlude)*, deferment, delay, discontinuance *(interruption of a legal action)*, extension *(postponement)*, hiatus, pause, pendency, reprieve. SEE MAIN ENTRY

moratory   late *(tardy)*

morbid   malignant, ominous, peccant *(unhealthy)*, pessimistic, pestilent

morbidly meditate   brood

morbiferous   deleterious, malignant, pernicious, pestilent

morbific   deleterious, harmful, insalubrious, malignant, peccant *(unhealthy)*, pernicious, pestilent

morbifical   insalubrious, malignant, pestilent

morbus   disease

mordacious   caustic, harsh, incisive, malignant, scathing, virulent. SEE MAIN ENTRY

mordant   astringent, bitter *(penetrating)*, harsh, incisive, mordacious, severe, trenchant

mordax   caustic, cynical, incisive, scathing

mordent   caustic

more additional, ancillary *(auxiliary)*
more advantageous preferable
more desirable preferable
more elevated superior *(higher)*
more in demand preferable
more or less inexact, on or about
more pleasing preferable
more popular preferable
more select preferable
more than due overdue
more than enough copious, excess, superfluous
more than half majority *(greater part)*
more than one multiple, several *(plural)*
more than one can tell innumerable
more than sufficient superfluous
more time extension *(postponement)*
morem gerere comply
moreover also
mores behavior, character *(personal quality)*
mores decorum
mori die
moribund decadent, in extremis
moronic fatuous, non compos mentis, obtuse, opaque
morose disconsolate, lugubrious, pessimistic
morosis incapacity
morosus fractious
morsel iota, minimum
mortal character *(an individual)*, conscious *(awake)*, deadly, ephemeral, lethal, live *(conscious)*, pernicious, person, pestilent
mortal body person
mortal remains corpse
mortalis person
mortalitas mortality
mortality death, demise *(death)*, fatality. SEE MAIN ENTRY
mortalness mortality
mortals humanity *(mankind)*
mortar cement
mortem obire die
mortgage cloud *(incumbrance)*, encumber *(financially obligate)*, encumbrance, hypothecation, pawn. SEE MAIN ENTRY
mortgage holder obligee
mortgaged fully secured
mortgagee creditor, obligee
mortgagor debtor, obligor
mortgatee backer
mortifer deadly, lethal
mortiferous deadly, fatal, insalubrious, lethal
mortification disgrace, embarrassment, ignominy
mortify badger, demean *(make lower)*, discompose, disgrace, embarrass, humiliate, offend *(insult)*, plague
mortuus dead, defunct
mos habit, practice *(procedure)*, usage
mosaic composite, compound, miscellaneous
most majority *(greater part)*, maximum *(pinnacle)*, utmost
most carefully selected group elite
most complete definitive
most considerable principal
most desirable best
most distant extreme *(last)*, ultimate
most eminent superlative
most excellent best
most frequently as a rule, generally
most important cardinal *(outstanding)*, master, principal

most important character protagonist
most important point emphasis
most influential leading *(ranking first)*
most often as a rule, generally
most powerful principal, sovereign *(absolute)*
most precise definitive
most recent last *(preceding)*
most remote extreme *(last)*, ultimate
mostly as a rule, purely *(simply)*, quasi
mot catchword
mote minimum
mother parents
mother country home *(place of origin)*
motherhood maternity
motherland home *(place of origin)*
motherliness maternity
motif content *(meaning)*, subject *(topic)*. SEE MAIN ENTRY
motile moving *(in motion)*
motion application, call *(appeal)*, campaign, circulation, course, overture, petition, prayer, procedure, proposal *(suggestion)*, recommendation, request, suggestion, transition. SEE MAIN ENTRY
motion docket calendar *(list of cases)*
motionless firm, idle, inactive, indolent, otiose, placid, rigid, stable, stagnant, static, torpid
motionlessness inaction, inertia
motivate cause, coax, evoke, further, impel, induce, influence, inspire, lobby, originate, persuade, prevail *(persuade)*, prevail upon, prompt, provoke, spirit, stimulate, urge. SEE MAIN ENTRY
motivated by a desire for money mercenary
motivated by greed mercenary
motivating provocative
motivating force catalyst, stimulus
motivating idea end *(intent)*, purpose
motivation catalyst, cause *(reason)*, determinant, end *(intent)*, impulse, incentive, instigation, origination, persuasion, provocation, rationale, reason *(basis)*
motivator abettor
motive animus, basis, cause *(reason)*, design *(intent)*, desire, determinant, end *(intent)*, ground, impetus, impulse, incentive, intent, moving *(in motion)*, origination, point *(purpose)*, provocation, purpose, rationale, reason *(basis)*, source, stimulus, target. SEE MAIN ENTRY
motiveless arbitrary and capricious
motley composite, compound, diverse, heterogeneous, miscellaneous, multifarious
motor road causeway
motorway causeway
motto expression *(comment)*, phrase
motus commotion, disturbance, insurrection, mutiny, rebellion, revolt, sedition
moulder degenerate
mouldering dilapidated
mount accrue *(increase)*, increase, originate, progress
mount guard protect
mounted accrued
mourn deplore, repent
mourn for regret
mourn with sympathize
mournful despondent, disconsolate, lamentable, lugubrious, querulous, solemn
mourning disconsolate
mouth entrance, enunciate, express, phrase, recite, utter
mouthpiece medium, protagonist, spokesman

mouthy flatulent, fustian, inflated *(bombastic)*
movable ambulatory, amenable, disposable, open *(persuasible)*, pliant, possession *(property)*, protean, receptive, suasible, susceptible *(responsive)*. SEE MAIN ENTRY
movable article of property chattel
movable property effects
movables chattel, commodities, merchandise, paraphernalia *(personal belongings)*, possessions, property *(possessions)*
movant petitioner
move act *(undertaking)*, carry *(transport)*, constrain *(compel)*, dislocate, displace *(remove)*, further, impress *(affect deeply)*, incite, influence, inspire, interest, maneuver *(tactic)*, maneuver, motivate, operate, operation, persuade, pose *(propound)*, prevail *(persuade)*, prevail upon, proffer, prompt, propose, propound, provoke, reach, reason *(persuade)*, recommend, remove *(transfer)*, spirit, step, stimulate, transport, undertaking *(enterprise)*, urge, vacate *(leave)*, venture. SEE MAIN ENTRY
move across cross *(intersect)*
move ahead continue *(persevere)*, endure *(last)*, keep *(continue)*, proceed *(go forward)*, progress, resume
move aimlessly loiter
move at an accelerated rate of speed race
move away part *(leave)*, quit *(evacuate)*
move back ebb, retreat
move backward regress
move by persuasion prevail upon
move fast hasten
move forward gain, impel, proceed *(go forward)*
move furtively lurk
move in waves fluctuate, oscillate
move into occupy *(take possession)*
move near approach
move off abandon *(physically leave)*
move on dispatch *(send off)*, leave *(depart)*, progress
move onward progress
move out evacuate, move *(alter position)*, part *(leave)*, vacate *(leave)*
move quickly hasten
move secretly prowl
move speedily hasten
move strongly impress *(affect deeply)*
move to locate
move to action constrain *(compel)*, motivate, stimulate
move to and fro oscillate, vacillate
move to anger provoke
move toward approach, border *(approach)*, gravitate
move under cover prowl
move up expedite, prefer, promote *(advance)*, raise *(advance)*
move up and down beat *(pulsate)*
moveant applicant *(petitioner)*
moved inclined
movement activity, band, campaign, circulation, course, denomination, dispatch *(promptness)*, operation, outflow, progress, transition, transmittal. SEE MAIN ENTRY
movement forward progress
movement of population immigration
movement toward adulthood growth *(evolution)*
movement toward maturity growth *(evolution)*
mover advocate *(counselor)*, catalyst, special interest

movere   impress *(affect deeply)*, influence

moving   convincing, eloquent, impulsive *(impelling)*, incisive, itinerant, persuasive, potent, prevailing *(having superior force)*, profound *(intense)*, progressive *(going forward)*, sensitive *(easily affected)*. SEE MAIN ENTRY

moving cause   motive

moving force   impetus

moving power   motive

moving spirit   catalyst, motive

movingly expressive   eloquent

mow down   obliterate

much   innumerable

much the same   approximate, comparable *(capable of comparison)*, pendent

much touted   renowned

much used   trite

muchness   quantity

muck   pollute

muckrake   disapprove *(condemn)*, expose

muckraking   disparagement

mucky   sordid

muddle   blind *(obscure)*, complex *(entanglement)*, confound, confuse *(bewilder)*, confuse *(create disorder)*, confusion *(turmoil)*, discompose, disorder *(lack of order)*, disorganize, disorient, embroilment, imbroglio, obfuscate, perplex, plight, quagmire, turmoil. SEE MAIN ENTRY

muddled   complex, labyrinthine

muddleheaded   opaque

muddy   opaque, pollute, unclear

muffle   cloak, disguise, repress, shroud, stifle, subdue, suppress

muffled   covert, indistinct

muffler   damper *(stopper)*

mug   assail

mulcere   soothe

mulct   bilk, deceive, defraud, deprive, dupe, exact, fine *(noun)*, fine *(verb)*, forfeiture *(thing forfeited)*, peculate, penalize, punishment, seize *(confiscate)*, steal, trover. SEE MAIN ENTRY

mulctuary   penal, punitive

mulish   inflexible, intractable, obdurate, pertinacious, recalcitrant, restive, uncontrollable

mull   muse

mull over   brood, consider, deliberate, ponder, reflect *(ponder)*, review, study, weigh

multa   fine, penalty

multare   fine, sentence

multifarious   composite, compound, diverse, manifold, miscellaneous, multifold, multiple. SEE MAIN ENTRY

multifariousness   difference, diversification, diversity

multifold   manifold, multiple. SEE MAIN ENTRY

multiform   compound, dissimilar, diverse, heterogeneous, manifold, miscellaneous, multifarious, multifold, protean

multiformity   diversification, diversity

multigenerous   multifarious, multifold

multilateral trade   commerce

multiloquent   voluble

multipartite   bicameral

multiphase   protean

multiple   composite, compound, manifold, multifold, repeated. SEE MAIN ENTRY

multiplex   complex, complex *(entanglement)*, composite, compound, manifold

multiplex   miscellaneous, multifarious, multifold, multiple

multiplicare   proliferate

multiplicate   manifold, multifold

multiplication   accession *(enlargement)*, growth *(increase)*

multiplicity   diversity, quantity. SEE MAIN ENTRY

multiplied   accrued

multiply   accrue *(increase)*, accumulate *(enlarge)*, bear *(yield)*, compound, enlarge, expand, heighten *(augment)*, increase, proliferate, propagate *(increase)*, pullulate, reproduce

multiplying   cumulative *(increasing)*, cumulative *(intensifying)*

multipotent   influential, powerful

multisyllabic   sesquipedalian

multitude   assemblage, assembly, body *(collection)*, collection *(assembly)*, conglomeration, congregation, mass *(body of persons)*, plurality, populace, quantity. SEE MAIN ENTRY

multitudinary   profuse

multitudinous   innumerable, manifold, multifold, multiple, multiplicity, myriad, populous, profuse, rife

multitudinousness   quantity

multitudo   mass *(body of persons)*, plurality

mum   laconic, speechless, taciturn, unresponsive

mummery   parody

mundane   civil *(public)*, material *(physical)*, physical, profane, prosaic. SEE MAIN ENTRY

mundivagant   moving *(in motion)*

mundus   clean

munerari   present *(make a gift)*

municipal   civic, civil *(public)*, local, public *(affecting people)*

municipal code   ordinance

municipal regulation   bylaw, ordinance

municipality   city, community

municipalization   condemnation *(seizure)*

municipalize   condemn *(seize)*

munificence   benevolence *(disposition to do good)*, charity, donation, goodwill, largess *(generosity)*, philanthropy

munificent   benevolent, charitable *(benevolent)*, liberal *(generous)*, nonprofit, philanthropic, profuse

munificus   liberal *(generous)*

muniment   ammunition, certificate, charter *(license)*, form *(document)*

muniments   deed

munimentum   safeguard

munition   ammunition, gun

munitions   bomb, weapons

munus   calling, department, duty *(obligation)*, function, gift *(present)*, office, post

munus obire   discharge *(perform)*

murder   assassination, destroy *(efface)*, dispatch *(act of putting to death)*, dispatch *(put to death)*, extinguish, homicide, killing, manslaughter, slay. SEE MAIN ENTRY

murder by stealth   assassination

murder victim   corpse

murderer   criminal, lawbreaker SEE MAIN ENTRY

murderous   deadly, diabolic, fatal, lethal, malignant, pernicious, pestilent, ruthless, sinister

murderous assault   killing

mure   detain *(hold in custody)*

murkiness   indistinctness

murky   obscure *(faint)*, privy, unclear

murmur   speak

muscle   sinew, strength

muscular   powerful

muse   brood, concentrate *(pay attention)*, consider, digest *(comprehend)*, observe *(remark)*, ponder, reflect *(ponder)*, speculate *(conjecture)*, study. SEE MAIN ENTRY

museful   cogitative, pensive

mushroom   proliferate

musing   contemplation, hindsight, introspection, pensive, preoccupation, reflection *(thought)*

must   requirement, requisite

muster   call *(summon)*, collect *(gather)*, collection *(assembly)*, convene, garner, levy, marshal, meet, raise *(collect)*, recruit, rendezvous *(noun)*, rendezvous *(verb)*, roll

muster up   call *(summon)*

mustering   company *(assemblage)*

musty   stale

mutabilis   mutable

mutabilitas   inconsistency

mutability   irregularity

mutable   aleatory *(uncertain)*, ambulatory, convertible, faithless, inconsistent, irresolute, noncommittal, pliable, protean, unpredictable, unsettled. SEE MAIN ENTRY

mutare   alter, innovation, modify *(alter)*, vary

mutate   convert *(change use)*, transform, vary

mute   inarticulate, moderate *(temper)*, repress, speechless, stifle, subdue, taciturn, unresponsive. SEE MAIN ENTRY

mutilare   mutilate

mutilate   damage, deface, destroy *(efface)*, disable, harm, maim, spoil *(impair)*. SEE MAIN ENTRY

mutilated   broken *(fractured)*, defective, imperfect, marred

mutilation   defacement, defect, detriment, harm

mutineer   insurgent, malcontent

mutineering   disloyalty, insurrection

mutinous   contumacious, disobedient, disorderly, insubordinate, irresponsible, lawless, radical *(favoring drastic change)*, recalcitrant, renitent, restive, unruly

mutinousness   disloyalty, outbreak

mutiny   defect, defiance, defy, desertion, disloyalty, disobey, infidelity, insurrection, outbreak, rebel, rebellion, resistance, revolt, secede, sedition, treason. SEE MAIN ENTRY

mutter   speak

mutual   cognate, collective, common *(shared)*, concordant, correlative, joint, reciprocal, related. SEE MAIN ENTRY

mutual accord   conciliation

mutual agreement   arrangement *(understanding)*, bargain, composition *(agreement in bankruptcy)*, conciliation, consensus, contract, indenture, pact, policy *(contract)*, quid pro quo. SEE MAIN ENTRY

mutual appreciation   rapport

mutual assent   agreement *(concurrence)*, arrangement *(understanding)*

mutual assistance   coaction, concert

mutual attraction   affection

mutual aversion   feud

mutual company   partnership

mutual concern   coalition

mutual concession   adjustment, composition *(agreement in bankruptcy)*, compromise, conciliation

mutual consideration   comity, quid pro quo

mutual dependence   mutuality

mutual exchange   interview

mutual exclusiveness   antithesis, difference

mutual forgiveness reconciliation
mutual friendliness rapprochement
mutual intercourse contact *(association)*
mutual ownership pool
mutual pledge agreement *(contract)*, bargain, compact, contract, pact, understanding *(agreement)*
mutual profit boom *(prosperity)*
mutual promise agreement *(concurrence)*, arrangement *(understanding)*, compact, contract, mutual understanding, pact
mutual relation mutuality
mutual relationship privity
mutual respect comity
mutual sympathy consensus
mutual transfer assignment *(transfer of ownership)*, delivery
mutual understanding accommodation *(adjustment)*, accord, adjustment, agreement *(concurrence)*, bargain, cartel, compatibility, conciliation, consensus, covenant, quid pro quo. SEE MAIN ENTRY
mutual undertaking arrangement *(understanding)*, bargain, contract, indenture, league, policy *(contract)*
mutuality coaction, rapport, rapprochement, reciprocity, relation *(connection)*, relationship *(connection)*. SEE MAIN ENTRY
mutuality of interest privity
mutually agreeable consensual
mutually agreed concerted
mutually assent agree *(contract)*
mutually opposed opposite
mutually related correlative
mutually understood consensual
mutuari borrow
mutus mute, speechless
mutuum loan
mutuus mutual *(reciprocal)*, reciprocal
muzzle constraint *(restriction)*, curb, disadvantage, disarm *(divest of arms)*, discipline *(control)*, hamper, inhibit, prevent, repress, restrict, stifle, strangle, withhold
myriad innumerable, manifold, multiple, profuse. SEE MAIN ENTRY
myriads quantity
mysterious covert, elusive, enigmatic, esoteric, evasive, furtive, hidden, inapprehensible, incomprehensible, indefinable, indefinite, indistinct, ineffable, inexplicable, inscrutable, obscure *(abstruse)*, oracular, peculiar *(curious)*, private *(confidential)*, privy, problematic, recondite, secret, surreptitious, uncanny, uncertain *(ambiguous)*, undisclosed, vague. SEE MAIN ENTRY
mysteriousness indistinctness
mystery enigma, problem, question *(issue)*, secret. SEE MAIN ENTRY
mystic covert, esoteric, hidden, inapprehensible, incomprehensible, inexplicable, mysterious, recondite
mystical covert, esoteric, hidden, inapprehensible, incomprehensible, inexplicable, mysterious, oracular, recondite, sacrosanct
mysticism mystery
mystification confusion *(ambiguity)*
mystified incognizant, lost *(disoriented)*
mystify confound, confuse *(bewilder)*, delude, disorient, elude, equivocate, hoodwink, obfuscate, perplex
mystifying enigmatic, labyrinthine, mysterious, peculiar *(curious)*, uncanny, uncertain *(ambiguous)*
myth fiction, figment, story *(falsehood)*. SEE MAIN ENTRY
mythic fictitious, illusory

mythical fictitious
mythological fictitious, illusory

N

nafarius heinous
nag annoy, bicker, browbeat, hector, importune, irritate, obsess, plague, request
nagging critical (faultfinding), petulant, querulous
naive credulous, inexperienced, ingenuous, puerile, unaccustomed, unaffected *(sincere)*, unsuspecting. SEE MAIN ENTRY
naiveness credulity
naivete credulity, nescience
naked manifest, perceivable, perceptible. SEE MAIN ENTRY
name appoint, assign *(designate)*, bear *(adduce)*, call *(title)*, call *(title)*, character *(reputation)*, cite *(state)*, classify, cognomen, define, delegate, denominate, denomination, denounce *(inform against)*, designate, designation *(symbol)*, distinction *(reputation)*, elect (choose), identify, induct, instate, invest *(vest)*, label, mention, nominate, notoriety, phrase, pigeonhole, prestige, reputation, select, specify, stipulate, term *(expression)*, title *(designation)*. SEE MAIN ENTRY
name expressly enumerate
name for office nominate
name inaccurately mistake
name incorrectly mislabel
name one by one enumerate
name to fill an appointment delegate
named aforesaid, before mentioned, said, select. SEE MAIN ENTRY
named representative nominee *(candidate)*, officer
nameless anonymous, ineffable
namely a savoir
namesake call *(title)*
naming appointment *(act of designating)*, call *(title)*, nomination, selection *(choice)*
nancisci obtain
narcissism pride
narcissistic orgulous
narcotic cannabis. see main entry
narcotic preparation drug
narcotic substance drug
narcotical narcotic
narcotize drug
narrare narrative
narrate communicate, convey *(communicate)*, detail *(particularize)*, inform *(notify)*, recite, recount, relate (tell)
narratio account *(report)*, narration, recital, story *(narrative)*
narration account *(report)*, recital, report (detailed account), representation *(statement)*, story *(narrative)*. SEE MAIN ENTRY
narrative description, descriptive, journal, narration, recital, representation *(statement)*, scenario, statement. SEE MAIN ENTRY
narrator informant
narrow attenuate, constrict *(compress)*, decrease, illiberal, limit, limited, minimal, moderate *(temper)*, one-sided, parochial, partial *(part)*, precise, provincial, qualify *(condition)*, reduce, restrict, restrictive, specialize, specific, tenuous, uncompromising. SEE MAIN ENTRY
narrow means indigence, poverty, privation
narrow reading SEE MAIN ENTRY
narrow search indagation, inquiry *(systematic investigation)*

narrow-minded dogmatic, illiberal, narrow, one-sided, parochial, partial *(biased)*, provincial, unbending
narrow-minded person pedant
narrow-mindedness intolerance, prejudice *(preconception)*
narrowing centralization, decrease
narrowness intolerance
nascence nascency
nascency birth *(beginning)*, origin *(source)*, origination. SEE MAIN ENTRY
nascent inchoate, incipient, initial, original *(initial)*, primary. SEE MAIN ENTRY
nastiness mischief
nasty bad *(offensive)*, bitter *(penetrating)*, harmful, heinous, loathsome, malignant, objectionable, obnoxious, odious, offensive *(offending)*, perverse, repulsive, severe, unsavory, vicious
nasty blow disaster
natal native *(inborn)*, original *(initial)*
nation nationality, polity, populace, population, public, state *(political unit)*. SEE MAIN ENTRY
national domestic *(indigenous)*, federal, public *(affecting people)*. SEE MAIN ENTRY
national culture civilization
national group nationality
national status nationality
nationality blood, polity. SEE MAIN ENTRY
nationalization condemnation *(seizure)*
nationalize condemn *(seize)*, naturalize *(make a citizen)*. SEE MAIN ENTRY
nationwide public *(affecting people)*
native born *(innate)*, citizen, domestic *(indigenous)*, domiciliary, hereditary, inhabitant, inherent, innate, intrinsic *(belonging)*, local, natural, organic, original *(initial)*, prime *(original)*, regional, resident. SEE MAIN ENTRY
native character disposition *(inclination)*
native environment home *(domicile)*
native ground home *(place of origin)*
native grown domestic *(indigenous)*
native hearth home *(place of origin)*
native land home *(place of origin)*, nationality
native reason common sense
native soil home *(place of origin)*
native tendency instinct
natives population
nativity birth *(emergence of young)*, genesis, nascency, nationality, origin *(source)*, origination
nativus natural
natura character *(personal quality)*, disposition *(inclination)*, essence
natura et ingenium gift *(flair)*
natural bodily, born *(innate)*, common *(customary)*, conventional, familiar *(customary)*, genuine, habitual, informal, ingenuous, inherent, innate, legitimate *(lawfully conceived)*, naive, native *(inborn)*, normal *(regular)*, organic, physical, prevailing *(current)*, real, realistic, regular *(conventional)*, simple, spontaneous, unaffected *(sincere)*, undistorted, unobtrusive, unpretentious, usual, veridical. SEE MAIN ENTRY
natural ability gift *(flair)*, specialty *(special aptitude)*
natural course practice *(custom)*
natural courtesy decorum
natural disposition tendency
natural fitness disposition *(inclination)*
natural impulse conatus
natural liking affinity *(regard)*
natural meaning connotation

natural quality   gift *(flair)*
natural right   equity *(justice)*
natural sagacity   common sense
natural science   ecology
natural sense   instinct, proclivity
natural state   matter of course
natural tendency   conatus, disposition *(inclination)*, instinct, predisposition
natural turn of mind   character *(personal quality)*
naturalistic   realistic
naturalize   adopt, inure *(accustom)*. SEE MAIN ENTRY
naturally   consequently, generally
naturalness   informality
nature   animus, center *(essence)*, character *(personal quality)*, characteristic, color *(complexion)*, complexion, composition *(makeup)*, consequence *(significance)*, content *(meaning)*, content *(structure)*, disposition *(inclination)*, essence, frame *(mood)*, kind, personality, posture *(attitude)*, predisposition, quality *(attribute)*, quality *(grade)*, spirit, temperament, tendency, tenor, trait. SEE MAIN ENTRY
nature study   ecology
naught   nullity
naughtiness   mischief
naughty   improper, iniquitous, peccant *(culpable)*, perverse, reprehensible, reprobate
naulum   fare
nauseate   repel *(disgust)*
nauseating   loathsome, obnoxious, offensive *(offending)*, repugnant *(exciting aversion)*, repulsive, unsavory
nauseous   loathsome, repulsive, unsavory
navigable   open *(accessible)*, passable
navigate   direct *(show)*, oversee
navus   active
ne plus ultra   absolute *(ideal)*
ne plus ultra   maximum *(pinnacle)*
ne'er-do-well   derelict
near   border *(approach)*, cognate, congruous, contiguous, forthcoming, future, immediate *(not distant)*, imminent, inevitable, instant, local, pending *(imminent)*, present *(current)*, proximate, quasi. SEE MAIN ENTRY
near at hand   close *(near)*, future, immediate *(imminent)*, imminent, instant, present *(attendant)*
near by   immediate *(not distant)*
near death   in extremis
near in time   present *(current)*
near one's end   in extremis
near relation   next of kin
nearby   close *(near)*, local, present *(attendant)*
nearest   proximate
nearest blood relation   next of kin
nearest relative by blood   next of kin
nearing   forthcoming, immediate *(imminent)*, imminent
nearing completion   determinable *(liable to be terminated)*
nearly   almost
nearly accurate   approximate, inexact
nearly allied   consanguineous
nearly correct   approximate, inexact
nearly equal   approximate *(adjective)*, approximate *(verb)*
nearly perfect   approximate *(adjective)*
nearly related   consanguineous
nearly resembling   approximate *(adjective)*
nearly rival   approximate *(verb)*
nearness   comparison, connection *(abutment)*, presence *(attendance)*, propinquity

(proximity), relation *(connection)*, relationship *(connection)*
nearness of blood   propinquity *(kinship)*
nearness of relation   propinquity *(kinship)*
neat   meticulous, unadulterated
nebulose   nebulous
nebulosity   indistinctness, opacity
nebulosus   nebulous
nebulous   debatable, elusive, enigmatic, equivocal, inconspicuous, indistinct, inexpressive, obscure *(faint)*, opaque, recondite, uncertain *(ambiguous)*, vague. SEE MAIN ENTRY
nebulousness   incomprehensible
necessaries   maintenance *(support of spouse)*
necessarii   kindred
necessarily   a priori, consequently
necessarily connected   appurtenant
necessarius   indispensable, inevitable, integral, requisite, unavoidable *(inevitable)*, urgent
necessary   binding, cardinal *(basic)*, central *(essential)*, compelling, compulsory, desideratum, essential *(required)*, exigent, fundamental, imperative, important *(urgent)*, indispensable, integral, mandatory, material *(important)*, need *(requirement)*, obligatory, peremptory *(imperative)*, primary, requisite, unavoidable *(inevitable)*, urgent. SEE MAIN ENTRY
necessary attribute   necessity, need *(requirement)*
necessary component   necessity, need *(requirement)*
necessary condition   prerequisite
necessary item   prerequisite
necessary party   SEE MAIN ENTRY
necessary to life   vital
necessitas   compulsion *(coercion)*, necessary, necessity
necessitate   call *(demand)*, coerce, compel, constrain *(compel)*, enforce, entail, exact, force *(coerce)*, impose *(enforce)*, press *(constrain)*, require *(compel)*, require *(need)*. SEE MAIN ENTRY
necessitated   bound, indispensable, mandatory, necessary *(required)*, obligatory, requisite
necessitation   duress, enforcement, force *(compulsion)*, requirement, requisition
necessities   necessary, sustenance
necessities of life   maintenance *(support of spouse)*
necessitous   destitute, exigent, impecunious, important *(urgent)*, mandatory, necessary *(required)*, poor *(underprivileged)*, urgent
necessitousness   emergency, indigence, necessary, need *(deprivation)*, poverty
necessitude   force *(compulsion)*, necessary, need *(deprivation)*, privation
necessitudo   affinity *(family ties)*
necessity   burden, coercion, compulsion *(coercion)*, desideratum, enforcement, exigency, force *(compulsion)*, market *(demand)*, necessary, need *(deprivation)*, need *(requirement)*, obligation *(duty)*, poverty, prerequisite, pressure, priority, privation, requirement, requisition, sine qua non. SEE MAIN ENTRY
necrosis   demise *(death)*
nectarean   savory
nectareous   palatable, sapid, savory. SEE MAIN ENTRY
need   absence *(omission)*, compulsion *(obsession)*, contribution *(indemnification)*,

dearth, deficiency, desideratum, emergency, entail, exigency, foible, force *(compulsion)*, indigence, insufficiency, lack, market *(demand)*, necessary, necessity, paucity, poverty, prerequisite, pressure, privation, requirement, requisition, stress *(strain)*. SEE MAIN ENTRY
need for action   emergency
needed   essential *(required)*, exigent, fundamental, important *(urgent)*, indispensable, integral, necessary *(required)*, requisite, vital
needed item   prerequisite
needful   destitute, essential *(required)*, exigent, imperative, integral, poor *(underprivileged)*, requisite
needfulness   emergency, priority
neediness   indigence, poverty, privation
needing   perfunctory
needing outside support   dependent
needle   annoy, harrow, harry *(harass)*, irritate, pique, plague, stimulus
needless   excess, excessive, expendable, extraneous, gratuitous *(unwarranted)*, injudicious, inordinate, nonessential, redundant, superfluous, undue *(excessive)*, unessential, unnecessary, unwarranted. SEE MAIN ENTRY
needlessness   redundancy
needy   destitute, impecunious, penurious, poor *(underprivileged)*
needy circumstances   indigence, poverty
nefandus   heinous
nefarious   bad *(offensive)*, blameful, blameworthy, contemptible, contemptuous, delinquent *(guilty of a misdeed)*, diabolic, dishonest, disreputable, felonious, flagrant, heinous, immoral, inexpiable, iniquitous, irregular *(improper)*, malignant, objectionable, obnoxious, outrageous, peccant *(culpable)*, profligate *(corrupt)*, reprehensible, reprobate, scandalous, sinister. SEE MAIN ENTRY
nefarious act   tortious act
nefariousness   atrocity, delinquency *(misconduct)*, disrepute
nefarius   felon, nefarious
nefas   atrocity
nefastus   inauspicious
negans   negative
negare   deny *(contradict)*, deny *(refuse to grant)*
negate   abolish, abrogate *(annul)*, adeem, annul, cancel, challenge, contradict, contravene, controvert, counter, counteract, countercharge, countervail, demonstrate *(protest)*, deny *(contradict)*, disaccord, disaffirm, disallow, disapprove *(reject)*, disavow, disobey, disown *(deny the validity)*, disprove, dissent *(withhold assent)*, fight *(counteract)*, gainsay, impugn, neutralize, nullify, oppose, prohibit, protest, rebut, recant, refute, repeal, repudiate, rescind, revoke, vacate *(void)*, vitiate. SEE MAIN ENTRY
negated   null *(invalid)*, null and void
negating   contradictory
negatio   denial, negation
negation   absence *(omission)*, ademption, annulment, answer *(judicial response)*, answer *(reply)*, antipode, cancellation, confutation, contradiction, contravention, counterargument, declination, defeasance, denial, disagreement, disapprobation, disapproval, discharge *(annulment)*, disclaimer, prohibition, refusal, rejection, renunciation, repudiation, rescision, retraction, revocation. SEE MAIN ENTRY

negation of allegations demurrer
negative challenge, contradict, contrary, disadvantageous, disapprove *(reject)*, disavow, disown *(deny the validity)*, dispute *(contest)*, dissent *(withhold assent)*, negate, opposite, perverse, prohibit, rebut, recusant, refuse, veto, vitiate. SEE MAIN ENTRY
negative answer denial, refusal
negative compulsion coercion
negative evidence answer *(judicial response)*, contradiction
negative result miscarriage
negativistic perverse
negatory antipathetic *(oppositional)*, contradictory, contrary, negative
neglect blame *(culpability)*, break *(violate)*, default, delinquency *(failure of duty)*, dereliction, desuetude, disinterest *(lack of interest)*, disobey, disregard *(omission)*, disregard *(unconcern)*, disregard, disrepair, disuse, eschew, exclude, ignore, inconsideration, indifference, laches, laxity, leave *(allow to remain)*, maladministration, mismanage, misprision, nonpayment, nonperformance, nonuse, omission, omit, overlook *(disregard)*, override, oversight *(carelessness)*, pretermit, procrastinate, rebuff, reject, rejection, repudiate, shirk, shun, spurn. SEE MAIN ENTRY
neglect of duty delict, nonfeasance
neglect of obligation delinquency *(failure of duty)*
neglect one's duty default
neglect to obey disoblige
neglect to perform omission
neglected derelict *(abandoned)*, outmoded
neglectful blameful, careless, derelict *(negligent)*, disobedient, heedless, improvident, imprudent, inadvertent, lax, negligent, oblivious, otiose, perfunctory, reckless, remiss, thoughtless, truant. SEE MAIN ENTRY
neglectful of obligation delinquent *(overdue)*
neglectfulness dereliction, disinterest *(lack of interest)*, disregard *(omission)*, disregard *(unconcern)*, laches, laxity, negligence, sloth
neglecting derelict *(negligent)*
neglection breach
neglector of duty delinquent
neglegens careless, heedless, lax, negligent, reckless, regardless, remiss, thoughtless
neglegentia laxity, neglect, negligence
neglegere disregard, ignore, neglect
negligence delinquency *(failure of duty)*, dereliction, disinterest *(lack of interest)*, disregard *(unconcern)*, fault *(responsibility)*, incompetence, inconsideration, indifference, inertia, laches, lapse *(expiration)*, laxity, maladministration, misconduct, misprision, neglect, nonfeasance, nonperformance, omission, oversight *(carelessness)*. SEE MAIN ENTRY
negligent blameful, blameworthy, careless, delinquent *(guilty of a misdeed)*, disobedient, heedless, improvident, inadvertent, indolent, injudicious, lax, oblivious, perfunctory, reckless, remiss, slipshod, thoughtless. SEE MAIN ENTRY
negligent act tort
negligent act of injury delict
negligent offense delict
negligent wrongdoing delict
negligibility inconsequence

negligible collateral *(immaterial)*, de minimus, expendable, inapposite, inappreciable, inconsiderable, insufficient, minor, nominal, nonessential, null *(insignificant)*, paltry, petty, slight, trivial, unessential. SEE MAIN ENTRY
negotia commerce
negotiable assignable, conditional, heritable. SEE MAIN ENTRY
negotiable instrument coupon, debenture, draft, letter of credit, note *(written promise to pay)*, security *(stock)*. SEE MAIN ENTRY
negotiable paper check *(instrument)*, draft, note *(written promise to pay)*, security *(stock)*
negotiables portfolio, securities, stock *(shares)*
negotiant adjuster, advocate *(counselor)*, agent, arbiter, arbitrator, broker, intermediary, liaison, medium
negotiate arbitrate *(conciliate)*, assign *(transfer ownership)*, close *(agree)*, compromise *(settle by mutual agreement)*, confer *(consult)*, deal, debate, deliberate, dicker, discuss, haggle, intercede, judge, lobby, mediate, reconcile, settle, trade, transact, treat *(process)*. SEE MAIN ENTRY
negotiated agreed *(harmonized)*, contractual, res judicata
negotiated agreement contract
negotiation adjustment, collective bargaining, commerce, compromise, conciliation, conference, counteroffer, deal, intercession, mediation, meeting *(conference)*, parley, settlement, trade *(commerce)*, transaction, treaty. SEE MAIN ENTRY
negotiation process mediation
negotiations conference
negotiator adjuster, advocate *(counselor)*, agent, arbiter, arbitrator, broker, conduit *(intermediary)*
negotiator dealer
negotiator go-between, interagent, intermediary, judge, liaison, medium, spokesman
negotium employment, occupation *(vocation)*, pursuit *(occupation)*, transaction
neighbor adjoin, border *(approach)*, juxtapose
neighborhood civic, community, district, local, locality, location, region, regional, section *(vicinity)*, site, venue, vicinity
neighboring adjacent, close *(near)*, contiguous, immediate *(not distant)*, proximate
neighborliness comity, concordance, consideration *(sympathetic regard)*, rapprochement
neighborly benevolent
neither more nor less coequal
nemesis punishment, reprisal, retribution, revenge, vengeance
neologism jargon *(technical language)*
neology jargon *(technical language)*
neophyte amateur, novice, probationer *(one being tested)*. SEE MAIN ENTRY
neophytism preparation
neoteric novel
neoterical novel
neoterism innovation
nepenthe drug
nepotism SEE MAIN ENTRY
nequam bad *(offensive)*
nequitia knavery
nerve audacity, confidence *(faith)*, prowess *(bravery)*, reassure, temerity
nerveless powerless
nervous suspicious *(distrustful)*, unsettled

nervousness hesitation, misgiving, panic, qualm, stress *(strain)*, trepidation
nervus sinew
nervy insolent
nescience ignorance. SEE MAIN ENTRY
nescient blind *(not discerning)*, incognizant, opaque, unaware
nescius unaware
nest habitation *(dwelling place)*
nest egg fund, store *(depository)*
net capture, earn, ensnare, gain, realize *(obtain as a profit)*, trap. SEE MAIN ENTRY
net profit dividend, proceeds
net quantity amount *(quantity)*, amount *(result)*
net return income
nettle aggravate *(annoy)*, badger, discompose, disturb, hector, incense, irritate, offend *(insult)*, pique, plague, provoke
network complex *(development)*, conjunction, league. SEE MAIN ENTRY
neutral dispassionate, equitable, evenhanded, impartial, independent, intermediate, liberal *(broad minded)*, noncommittal, nonmilitant, nonpartisan, objective, openminded, peaceable, unbiased, unprejudiced. SEE MAIN ENTRY
neutralism neutrality
neutrality candor *(impartiality)*, disinterest *(lack of prejudice)*, objectivity, peace. SEE MAIN ENTRY
neutralization of forces balance *(equality)*
neutralize compensate *(counterbalance)*, counteract, countervail, cross *(disagree with)*, disable, disarm *(divest of arms)*, disqualify, dissolve *(terminate)*, frustrate, negate, nullify, outbalance, prevent, remedy, vitiate. SEE MAIN ENTRY
neutralized ineffective, ineffectual
neutralizer offset
neutralizing preventive
neutrius partis neutral
never sine die
never again sine die
never cease keep *(continue)*, persist
never changing immutable
never ending continuous
never idle diligent, industrious
never late punctual
never the same atypical
never tiring diligent
never to be forgotten critical *(crucial)*
never varying immutable
never-ceasing chronic, permanent, perpetual
never-dying perpetual
never-ending continual *(perpetual)*, durable, incessant, permanent, protracted
never-endingness perpetuity
never-fading perpetual
never-failing infallible, perpetual
never-stopping chronic, permanent, perpetual
never-tiring painstaking, pertinacious
never-wearying pertinacious
nevertheless notwithstanding, regardless
new contemporary, current, de novo, inexperienced, novel, recent, sophisticated, unaccustomed, unacquainted, unprecedented, unsettled, unusual. SEE MAIN ENTRY
new arrival novice
new beginning continuation *(resumption)*
new departure creation
new device innovation
new edition revision *(corrected version)*
new energy resurgence

new hearing   rehearing
new idea   innovation
new method   innovation
new offer   counteroffer
new outbreak   recrudescence
new phase   innovation
new start   continuation (resumption), renewal
new version   revival
newborn   child
newcomer   neophyte, novice, probationer (one being tested), stranger, successor
newest   last (preceding)
newfangled   unprecedented, unusual
newly   anew, de novo
newly arrived   recent
newly come   novel
news   communication (statement), disclosure (something disclosed), dispatch (message), information (facts), notice (announcement), notification, publicity, report (detailed account), story (narrative). SEE MAIN ENTRY
news article   story (narrative)
news blackout   censorship
news business   press
news gatherers   press
news item   story (narrative)
news story   report (detailed account)
newsmen   press
newspaper   organ
newspaper report   story (narrative)
newspaper world   press
newspaperman   press
newspapers   press
newsworthy   notable, noteworthy
newswriters   press
newsy   informative, informatory
next   a savoir, ensuing, future, immediate (imminent), imminent, inevitable, proximate, subsequent, thereafter. SEE MAIN ENTRY
next generation   offspring
next in line   successor
next of kin   affiliation (bloodline), blood, kindred. SEE MAIN ENTRY
next to   adjacent, contiguous, immediate (not distant)
nexus   attachment (act of affixing), connection (fastening), contact (touching), liaison, privity, relation (connection), sequence. SEE MAIN ENTRY
nice   palatable
nice appreciation   decorum
niceness   amenity
nicety   decorum, discretion (quality of being discreet), nuance, specification
nickname   cognomen, sobriquet
niggard   penurious
niggardly   economical, illiberal, nonsubstantial (not sufficient), paltry, parsimonious, penurious, slight
niggling   inconsequential
nigh   approximate, close (near), forthcoming, future, immediate (imminent), present (attendant), present (current), proximate
night stick   cudgel
nihil   nonentity
nihil ad rem pertinet   irrelevant
nihilism   anarchy, lynch law
nihilist   insurgent, malcontent
nihilistic   disorderly, incendiary
nihility   nullity
nil   blank (emptiness)
nim   steal
nimble   alert (agile), deft, rapid
nimble-fingered   deft
nimble-witted   perspicacious

nimbleness   dispatch (promptness)
nimiety   plethora, redundancy, surfeit, surplus
nimious   inordinate
nimium   excess
nimius   excessive, gross (total), undue (excessive)
nip   foil, thwart
nip in the bud   deter
nisus   conatus
nisus   endeavor
nitid   lucid
no decision   deadlock
no longer conventional   outmoded
no longer customary   outdated, outmoded
no longer fashionable   outdated
no longer in perfect condition   marred
no longer in style   outdated
no longer in use   obsolete
no longer law   null (invalid), null and void
no longer living   dead, deceased, defunct
no longer prevailing   outdated, outmoded
no longer prevalent   outdated
no longer stylish   outdated
no longer young   old
no matter when   whenever
no matter who   whoever
no more   defunct
no one   nonentity
no relation   alien (unrelated), apart
no reputation   disrepute
no repute   dishonor (shame), disrepute
no standing   dishonor (shame)
nobilis   notorious
nobility   character (reputation), distinction (reputation), elite, eminence, prestige
noble   heroic, high-minded, illustrious, laudable, law-abiding, magnanimous, meritorious, moral, prominent, proud (self-respecting), reputable, scrupulous, sterling, superior (excellent). SEE MAIN ENTRY
noble-minded   magnanimous
nobleness   integrity, principle (virtue), right (righteousness)
nobody   nonentity
nocens   harmful, prejudicial
nocent   harmful, lethal, noxious, pernicious, pestilent
nocere   harm
nocuous   bad (offensive), deleterious, harmful, inadvisable, lethal, malignant, peccant (unhealthy), pestilent, sinister
nod   recognition
nod assent to   coincide (concur)
nod of approbation   approval
noesis   insight, perception
noise   outcry, pandemonium. SEE MAIN ENTRY
noise abroad   circulate, divulge, proclaim, propagate (spread)
noiseless   mute, speechless
noiselessness   silence
noisiness   brawl
noisome   deleterious, detrimental, fatal, harmful, harsh, heinous, insalubrious, malignant, noxious, objectionable, obnoxious, peccant (unhealthy), pernicious, pestilent, repugnant (exciting aversion), repulsive, sinister. SEE MAIN ENTRY
noisy   blatant (obtrusive), loquacious
noisy quarrel   altercation, fracas
noisy strife   commotion
nol-pros   quit (discontinue)
nolition   reluctance
nollo contendere   SEE MAIN ENTRY

nollo presequi   SEE MAIN ENTRY
nom de plume   sobriquet
nomad   migrant
nomadic   moving (in motion)
nomen   entry (record), prestige
nomen alienum   alias
nomen deferre   indict
nomenclature   call (title), classification, denomination
nominal   immaterial, inconsiderable, negligible, null (insignificant), trivial. SEE MAIN ENTRY
nominalness   insignificance
nominare   call (title), designate, nominate
nominate   charge (empower), delegate, designate, induct, instate, invest (vest), propose, select. SEE MAIN ENTRY
nominatio   nomination
nomination   appointment (act of designating), assignment (designation), deputation (selection of delegates), selection (choice). SEE MAIN ENTRY
nomination contest   primary
nominative competition   primary
nominative contest   primary
nominative election   primary
nominator   licensor
nomine   nominal
nominee   candidate, contender, licensee. SEE MAIN ENTRY
nomography   jurisprudence
nomology   jurisprudence
nomothetic   decretal, due (regular), lawful
nomothetical   de jure
non aptus   incongruous
non compos mentis   SEE MAIN ENTRY
non credere   disbelieve
non idoneus   inapposite, inappropriate, unsatisfactory
non legitimus   felonious, illegitimate (illegal), unlawful
non necessarius   needless, unnecessary
non obsequi   disobedient
non occurrence   noncompliance (nonobservance)
non rectus   indirect
non salable   unmarketable
non sequitur   anacoluthon. SEE MAIN ENTRY
non specific   unspecified
non valere   inapplicable
non verisimilis   improbability
non voluntarius   involuntary
non-esse   blank (emptiness)
non-executionary judgment   declaratory judgment
non-uniform   atypical
nonabolishable   noncancellable
nonabstract   actual
nonacceptance   declination, denial, disapproval, disdain, dishonor (nonpayment), exclusion, impugnation, negation, refusal, rejection. SEE MAIN ENTRY
nonactual   baseless
nonadherence   breach, contempt (disobedience to the court), dishonor (nonpayment)
nonadhering   broken (unfulfilled), nonconforming
nonadmission   bar (obstruction), disqualification (rejection), exclusion, ostracism, prohibition
nonadmission of employees   lockout
nonage   adolescence, minority (infancy). SEE MAIN ENTRY
nonaggresive   nonmilitant
nonaggressive   lax
nonagreement   disaccord, discord, discrepancy, disparity, dispute, dissension,

dissent (difference of opinion), dissent (nonconcurrence), exception (objection), impugnation, incompatibility (difference), negation, nonconformity, variance (disagreement)

nonaligned neutral, nonpartisan
nonannullable noncancellable
nonapparent covert
nonappearance absence (nonattendance), concealment, leave (absence). SEE MAIN ENTRY
nonapproval disapprobation, disapproval, disparagement, dissatisfaction, exception (objection), reversal
nonassent dissension, dissent (nonconcurrence)
nonattendance leave (absence), nonappearance
nonattendant truant
nonavailability desuetude
nonbeing absence (omission), nonentity, nullity
nonbelligerence neutrality
nonbelligerent neutral
noncancellable SEE MAIN ENTRY
nonchalance disinterest (lack of interest), indifference
nonchalant careless, casual, dispassionate, informal. SEE MAIN ENTRY
nonchallengeable noncontestable
noncitizen alien
noncohesive disconnected
noncombatance neutrality
noncombatant neutral, nonmilitant
noncombative nonmilitant, peaceable
noncomformity contest (dispute)
noncommittal guarded, neutral. SEE MAIN ENTRY
noncomplete clause SEE MAIN ENTRY
noncompletion breach, deficiency, delinquency (failure of duty), dishonor (nonpayment), failure (falling short), frustration, laxity, miscarriage, neglect, nonperformance
noncompletion of a task delinquency (failure of duty)
noncompliance contempt (disobedience to the court), declination, defiance, dishonor (nonpayment), disregard (omission), dissent (difference of opinion), dissidence, impugnation, informality, infraction, insurrection, negation, neglect, nonperformance, offense, refusal, resistance, revolt, sedition, transgression. SEE MAIN ENTRY
noncompliance with law crime
noncompliant disobedient, dissident, insubordinate, nonconforming, perverse
noncompulsory disjunctive (alternative), extraneous, needless, unnecessary
nonconcurrence dissension, dissidence, nonconformity
nonconformance resistance
nonconformant nonconsenting
nonconforming dissident, eccentric, individual, licentious. SEE MAIN ENTRY
nonconformism deviation
nonconformist deviant, dissident, eccentric, heretic, lawless, malcontent, novel, original (creative), recusant
nonconformity breach, deviation, difference, disaccord, discrepancy, disparity, dissent (nonconcurrence), dissidence, exception (exclusion), incompatibility (inconsistency), incongruity, inconsistency, inequality, informality, irregularity, noncompliance (nonobservance), quirk (idiosyncrasy), schism. SEE MAIN ENTRY

nonconformity to fact falsehood
nonconsent declination, denial, disagreement, disapproval, dissent (nonconcurrence), dissent (withhold assent), impugnation, negation, refusal
nonconsenting SEE MAIN ENTRY
nonconsideration exclusion
nonconstitutional illicit
noncontent nonconsenting
noncontestable SEE MAIN ENTRY
noncontinuance cloture
noncontinuous discrete, disjunctive (tending to disjoin)
noncontroversial incontestable, incontrovertible, unimpeachable
noncontrovertible noncontestable
noncooperating contentious, disinclined, hostile
noncooperation contempt (disobedience to the court), defiance, dereliction, disaccord, division (act of dividing), impugnation, nonperformance
noncooperative recalcitrant
noncooperator malcontent
noncorroboration negation
noncriminal civil (public)
nondebatable noncontestable
nondescript indefinite, usual. SEE MAIN ENTRY
nondisputable noncontestable
nondivisible indivisible, inseparable
nondomicile nonresidence
nondurable ephemeral, temporary
none the less notwithstanding
noneccliastical civil (public)
nonelastic immutable, inflexible
nonemployment disuse, nonuse
nonentity blank (emptiness), nullity. SEE MAIN ENTRY
nonerasable noncancellable
nonessential circumstantial, collateral (immaterial), excessive, expendable, extraneous, extrinsic, immaterial, inconsequential, inconsiderable, minor, needless, petty, slight, supplementary, tangential, trivial, unessential. SEE MAIN ENTRY
nonessentiality immateriality
nonesuch exemplar, paragon, phenomenon (unusual occurrence)
nonetheless regardless
nonexclusive competitive (open), generic
nonexistence absence (omission), blank (emptiness), nonentity, nullity
nonexistent fictitious, insubstantial. SEE MAIN ENTRY
nonexpectation bombshell, improbability
nonexpert unprofessional
nonfatal nontoxic
nonfeasance crime, delict, dereliction, dishonor (nonpayment), laches, laxity, misconduct, neglect, nonperformance, omission. SEE MAIN ENTRY
nonfertile barren
nonfinal interlocutory
nonfulfillment default, defeat, deficiency, delinquency (failure of duty), delinquency (shortage), dishonor (nonpayment), failure (falling short), frustration, laxity, miscarriage, mistrial, neglect, nonfeasance, nonperformance
nonfulfillment of one's hopes dissatisfaction
nonfulfilment abortion (fiasco), breach
nonfunctional expendable, otiose
nonfunctioning otiose
nongregarious unapproachable
nonhabitancy nonresidence

nonhabitation nonresidence
nonhampering laissez faire
nonidentical different, dissimilar
nonimitation deviation, difference
nonimitative original (initial)
nonimmunity danger
noninclusion bar (obstruction), dispensation (exception), disqualification (rejection), exception (exclusion), exclusion, omission, ostracism, prohibition, rejection, removal
noninfringement laissez faire
noninhabitance nonresidence
noninhabitancy nonresidence
nonintentional occurrence quirk (accident)
noninterference freedom, home rule, laissez faire, latitude, liberty, neutrality
noninterfering neutral
nonintermeddling laissez faire
noninterruption laissez faire
nonintervention home rule, laissez faire, latitude, neutrality
noninterventionist neutral
nonintrusion laissez faire
noninvolvement disinterest (lack of interest), disinterest (lack of prejudice), objectivity
nonirritating innocuous, nontoxic
nonjuring recusant
nonlegal felonious, illicit, impermissible, lawless
nonlethal nontoxic
nonliability condonation, dispensation (exception), immunity, impunity
nonliable clear (free from criminal charges)
nonliteral translation paraphrase
nonmalignant harmless, innocuous, nontoxic
nonmaterial impalpable
nonmilitant SEE MAIN ENTRY
nonmilitary civil (public)
nonobjective subjective
nonobligatory disjunctive (alternative)
nonobservance breach, contempt (disobedience to the court), default, delinquency (failure of duty), dereliction, desuetude, deviation, dishonor (nonpayment), disregard (omission), disregard (unconcern), dissent (nonconcurrence), failure (falling short), indifference, informality, infraction, infringement, neglect, offense, oversight (carelessness), repudiation, transgression, violation
nonobservance of law crime
nonobservance of rules infraction
nonobservant broken (unfulfilled), disorderly, dissident, heedless, lawless, nonconforming, recusant
nonoccupance nonresidence
nonoccupancy nonresidence
nonoccupation nonresidence
nonofficial private (not public)
nonpacific contentious
nonpareil exemplar, outstanding (prominent), paragon, phenomenon (unusual occurrence), primary, prime (most valuable), singular, superior (excellent), superlative, unique, unusual
nonparticipance neutrality
nonparticipant neutral
nonparticipating neutral, otiose
nonparticipation abstention, neutrality
nonpartisan impartial, independent, liberal (broad minded), neutral, objective, unbiased, unprejudiced. SEE MAIN ENTRY

nonpartisanship candor *(impartiality)*, disinterest *(lack of prejudice)*, neutrality, objectivity
nonpayer delinquent
nonpaying penurious
nonpayment debt, delinquency *(shortage)*. SEE MAIN ENTRY
nonpayment at maturity dishonor *(nonpayment)*
nonperformance breach, default, deficiency, delinquency *(failure of duty)*, dereliction, failure *(falling short)*, frustration, laches, laxity, miscarriage, neglect, nonfeasance. SEE MAIN ENTRY
nonperishable indelible, indestructible
nonpermanent interlocutory, provisional
nonpermanent agreement modus vivendi
nonpermanent arrangement modus vivendi
nonpertinent extraneous, gratuitous *(unwarranted)*
nonphased. SEE MAIN ENTRY
nonphysical immaterial, incorporeal, intangible
nonplus confound, confuse *(bewilder)*, confusion *(ambiguity)*, discompose, disorient, disturb, embarrass, obfuscate, perplex, perturb, quagmire, quandary
nonpoisonous harmless, nontoxic
nonporous solid *(compact)*
nonpractice nonperformance
nonpresence absence *(nonattendance)*, nonappearance, nonresidence
nonproblematical noncontestable
nonproducing barren
nonproductive barren
nonprofessional layman, volunteer
nonprofit SEE MAIN ENTRY
nonprohibitive permissive
nonprosecution compurgation, impunity
nonpublic private *(not public)*, privy
nonquestionable noncontestable
nonrational arbitrary
nonrecognition disdain, insentience
nonrecurrent desultory
nonrefutable noncontestable
nonrescindable noncancellable
nonresidence SEE MAIN ENTRY
nonresident foreign
nonresistance acquiescence, capitulation, compliance, deference, discipline *(obedience)*, resignation *(passive acceptance)*
nonresistant passive, resigned, susceptible *(unresistent)*
nonresisting obeisant, passive, patient, pliable, pliant
nonresponsibility dispensation *(exception)*
nonresumption impasse
nonretention alienation *(transfer of title)*, assignment *(transfer of ownership)*, cession, desuetude, devolution
nonretractable noncancellable
nonreversible indefeasible, irreversible, irrevocable, noncancellable, permanent
nonsacred mundane
nonscientific illogical
nonsectarian SEE MAIN ENTRY
nonsense jargon *(unintelligible language)*, platitude
nonsensical fatuous, incredible, inexpressive, irrational, ludicrous, lunatic, puerile, unreasonable
nonsensical language jargon *(unintelligible language)*
nonsensical talk jargon *(unintelligible language)*, prattle

nonsensicality non sequitur
nonsensicalness jargon *(unintelligible language)*, non sequitur
nonspecialist layman
nonspecific broad, generic, indefinite, indeterminate
nonspiritual material *(physical)*, mundane, physical
nonstandard anomalous
nonstop consecutive, continual *(connected)*, incessant
nonsubjective objective
nonsubjectivity objectivity
nonsubsistence blank *(emptiness)*
nonsubstantial intangible. SEE MAIN ENTRY
nonsuccess miscarriage, mistrial
nonsuit dismissal *(termination of a proceeding)*. SEE MAIN ENTRY
nonsystematic haphazard
nontampering laissez faire
nontenancy nonresidence
nontoxic harmless, innocuous. SEE MAIN ENTRY
nontransferable inalienable
nontranslucent opaque
nonuniform anomalous, desultory, deviant, disjointed, disordered, disparate, dissimilar, distinct *(distinguished from others)*, divergent, heterogeneous, individual, intermittent, miscellaneous, multifarious, nonconforming, protean, sporadic, unique
nonuniformity deviation, difference, discrepancy, disparity, distinction *(difference)*, diversity, exception *(exclusion)*, incompatibility *(inconsistency)*, inequality, nonconformity
nonuse abatement *(extinguishment)*, abolition, cancellation, desuetude, discontinuance *(act of discontinuing)*, disuse. SEE MAIN ENTRY
nonutilization nonuse
nonvenomous harmless, nontoxic
nonviolence moderation
nonviolent harmless, nonmilitant
nonvirulent harmless, nontoxic
nonworker parasite
norm code, criterion, cross section, example, law, paradigm, pattern, rule *(guide)*, standard. SEE MAIN ENTRY
norma canon, rule *(guide)*, standard
normal accustomed *(customary)*, average *(standard)*, common *(customary)*, conventional, customary, exemplary, familiar *(customary)*, habitual, mediocre, natural, ordinary, prevailing *(current)*, prevalent, regular *(conventional)*, routine, sane, typical, usual. SEE MAIN ENTRY
normalcy competence *(sanity)*, sanity
normality competence *(sanity)*, sanity
normalize adjust *(regulate)*, naturalize *(acclimate)*, regulate *(adjust)*
normally as a rule, generally, invariably
normalness competence *(sanity)*
normative average *(standard)*, exemplary
noscere recognize *(acknowledge)*
noscitare recognize *(perceive)*
noscitur a sociis SEE MAIN ENTRY
not abide conflict, disapprove *(reject)*
not abiding dissenting
not able unable
not able to be conveyed inalienable
not absolute conditional, qualified *(conditioned)*
not abundant scarce
not accept abrogate *(rescind)*, conflict, disagree, disallow, disapprove *(reject)*, dis-

avow, disbelieve, disclaim, disdain, disoblige, disown *(deny the validity)*, dissent *(withhold assent)*
not accepting dissenting
not accidental express
not according to law illegal, illegitimate *(illegal)*, illicit
not accountable immune, privileged
not admissible SEE MAIN ENTRY
not admit disapprove *(reject)*, disavow, disclaim, disown *(deny the validity)*, doubt *(distrust)*
not admitted inadmissible
not agree differ *(vary)*, dispute *(contest)*, dispute *(debate)*, dissent *(differ in opinion)*
not agreeing dissenting
not alien native *(domestic)*
not allow estop, forbid
not allowed illegal, illicit, inadmissible
not allowed by law unlawful
not answerable clear *(unencumbered)*, exempt, immune
not apocryphal authentic
not applicable irrelevant
not approve disapprove *(reject)*, disavow, dissent *(withhold assent)*
not approved illegal, illicit
not argued over uncontested
not ascertained indeterminate
not ashamed unabashed
not authenticated unsupported
not authorized by law illegal
not averruncated chronic
not axiomatic controversial, disputable
not badly fairly *(moderately)*
not baneful nontoxic
not believe disbelieve, doubt *(distrust)*
not belonging disordered
not biased impartial
not binding invalid, void *(invalid)*
not blamable inculpable
not bother with disregard
not budge hold out *(resist)*
not by chance express
not capable of annulment irreversible
not capable of being introduced as evidence inadmissible
not care for disfavor, neglect, pretermit
not certain conditional, uncertain *(ambiguous)*
not challenged uncontested
not charged gratuitous *(given without recompense)*
not charged for free *(at no charge)*, gratuitous *(given without recompense)*
not choosy indiscriminate
not clear ambiguous, nebulous, uncertain *(ambiguous)*
not clear to the mind intangible
not close remote *(secluded)*
not cohesive disjunctive *(tending to disjoin)*
not commercial residential
not committed to writing parol
not comparable alien *(unrelated)*, disparate, dissimilar
not compare with differ *(vary)*
not complete partial *(part)*
not completed partial *(part)*
not completely formed inchoate
not compliant contumacious
not comply disallow, disobey
not comply with disoblige
not compromise hold out *(resist)*
not compulsory disjunctive *(alternative)*
not concealed manifest

not confirm demur, disallow, disavow, disown *(deny the validity)*
not conform conflict, deviate, differ *(vary)*
not conforming dissenting
not conforming to the usual anomalous
not connected with immaterial
not consenting dissident
not consider disapprove *(reject)*, disdain, disregard, dissent *(withhold assent)*
not considered ineligible
not contradictory consistent
not cooperate disobey
not countenance disapprove *(reject)*, enjoin
not countenanced SEE MAIN ENTRY
not covered by law illegal, illicit
not current outdated
not dangerous nontoxic
not deadly nontoxic
not declared openly implicit
not decreased undiminished
not defend dissent *(withhold assent)*
not definite intangible
not deleterious nontoxic
not designated indeterminate
not discharged delinquent *(overdue)*
not disconcerted unabashed
not dispose of hold *(possess)*
not disposed reluctant
not disputed uncontested
not do justice to derogate
not domestic alien *(foreign)*
not easily governed intractable
not easily worn out durable
not eligible ineligible
not elusive tangible
not employed unemployed
not endowed with life defunct
not enough deficient, inadequate, insufficiency, insufficient
not enslaved free *(enjoying civil liberty)*
not entirely quasi
not equal to incapable
not equate differ *(vary)*
not equitable unfair. SEE MAIN ENTRY
not established unsupported
not evident underlying
not excessive reasonable *(fair)*
not existing defunct
not expressed implicit
not expressed by writing parol
not extinct extant
not extraordinary nondescript
not extreme reasonable *(fair)*
not false authentic, true *(authentic)*
not faulty true *(authentic)*
not fictitious actual, authentic, documentary, true *(authentic)*
not final inconclusive, interlocutory
not find tenable disbelieve
not fit unworthy
not fitting gratuitous *(unwarranted)*, unacceptable
not fixed aleatory *(uncertain)*, ambulatory, indeterminate
not fixed in extent indeterminate
not fluctuating fixed *(settled)*
not following disproportionate, gratuitous *(unwarranted)*
not for publication confidential
not foreign domestic *(indigenous)*, native *(domestic)*
not forfeitable indefeasible
not forget remember
not fully executed inchoate
not genuine synthetic

not give up hold out *(resist)*
not guilty acquitted, blameless, clean, clear *(free from criminal charges)*, inculpable, irreprehensible. SEE MAIN ENTRY
not have any part of conflict, disapprove *(reject)*
not hear disregard
not hear of dismiss *(put out of consideration)*
not heed disobey, disregard
not hold with dissent *(withhold assent)*
not honest dishonest, fraudulent
not honorable blameworthy. SEE MAIN ENTRY
not ideal faulty
not identical distinct *(distinguished from others)*
not imaginary actual
not immediate remote *(not proximate)*
not important immaterial
not imported domestic *(indigenous)*
not impossible allowable
not improbable credible
not improper allowable
not in action defunct
not in bondage free *(enjoying civil liberty)*
not in force defunct, void *(invalid)*
not in keeping disproportionate
not in use vacant
not in vogue outdated, outmoded
not inclined reluctant
not include censor, disregard
not included inadmissible
not including save
not indigenous alien *(foreign)*
not indigious foreign
not integrated disjunctive *(tending to disjoin)*
not intended unpremeditated
not lasting ephemeral
not legitimate want of jurisdiction
not lessened undiminished
not liable blameless, exempt, immune
not like disfavor
not limited by conditions unconditional
not listen disobey, disregard
not long past recent
not lost extant
not lying candid
not made certain indeterminate
not maintain disavow, disown *(deny the validity)*, disown *(refuse to acknowledge)*
not manifest impalpable, ulterior
not mature undue *(not owing)*
not merely supposed actual
not met delinquent *(overdue)*
not mind disobey
not modern old, outdated
not modified unqualified *(unlimited)*
not narrow-minded liberal *(broad minded)*
not native alien *(foreign)*, foreign
not natural artificial, synthetic
not naturalized alien *(foreign)*
not near remote *(secluded)*
not nearby remote *(secluded)*
not necessitated gratuitous *(unwarranted)*
not nervous secure *(confident)*
not obey disobey, disoblige
not objectionable allowable
not obscure manifest, naked *(perceptible)*
not observant of the law lawless
not observe dishonor *(refuse to pay)*, overstep

not occupied vacant
not odd nondescript
not of high standards unprofessional
not of material nature incorporeal
not on point irrelevant
not on time overdue
not open private *(not public)*
not openly expressed tacit
not owing solvent
not paid on time delinquent *(overdue)*
not part with hold *(possess)*
not partial competitive *(open)*, general, impartial
not particular generic, open-ended
not particularly designated indeterminate
not pass disavow
not pay default, dishonor *(refuse to pay)*
not perfect fallible
not perfectly accurate approximate
not permanent transitory
not permit enjoin
not permitted illegal, illegitimate *(illegal)*, illicit. SEE MAIN ENTRY
not permitting passage impervious
not permitting penetration impervious
not pernicious nontoxic
not pertaining to immaterial, irrelevant
not pertinent gratuitous *(unwarranted)*, immaterial, improper, irrelevant
not plain ambiguous, uncertain *(ambiguous)*
not plainly apparent implicit
not plentiful scarce
not pliable intractable
not positive indefinite
not possessing life dead
not precise indeterminate
not private public *(open)*
not privileged competitive *(open)*
not proceed with cancel, forbear
not protracted brief
not public residential, secret
not readily discerned impalpable
not readily salable unmarketable
not receivable as evidence inadmissible
not receivable in evidence inadmissible
not reciprocal unilateral
not reputable disreputable
not required elective *(voluntary)*
not resist comply
not respect contemn, decry, disdain, disfavor
not respectable blameworthy, disreputable
not responsible clean, clear *(unencumbered)*, exempt, immune, not guilty
not restorable chronic
not restricted exempt
not retain displace *(remove)*, waive
not reveal conceal
not right errant, improper
not satisfying deficient
not scared secure *(confident)*
not select general
not selective indiscriminate
not sensitive to insusceptible *(resistant)*
not settled indeterminate
not sharp indefinite
not significant irrelevant
not similar dissimilar
not singular nondescript
not speak well of censure, decry
not special generic, nondescript
not specific open-ended
not spiritual corporal
not spurious authentic

not straightforward mendacious
not subject immune, privileged
not subject to exempt
not subject to a payment gratuitous *(given without recompense)*
not subject to regulation free *(enjoying civil liberty)*
not submit hold out *(resist)*, oppose
not subordinate substantive
not substantiated unsupported. SEE MAIN ENTRY
not succeed fail *(lose)*
not sufficient insufficient
not suitable improper
not support counter, disapprove *(reject)*
not sure conditional, uncertain *(questionable)*
not tainted blameless
not take kindly to disapprove *(condemn)*
not tampered with authentic
not the same different, disparate, distinct *(distinguished from others)*
not think about disregard
not think of disregard
not thought much of disreputable
not to be abrogated indefeasible
not to be admitted inadmissible
not to be allowed inadmissible
not to be annulled indefeasible
not to be avoided obligatory
not to be believed disputable
not to be changed immutable
not to be communicated confidential
not to be delayed exigent
not to be disclosed confidential
not to be disputed demonstrable, inappealable
not to be evaded obligatory
not to be made void indefeasible
not to be moved immutable
not to be overlooked considerable, exigent
not to be quoted confidential, unofficial
not to be recommended blameworthy
not to be spoken of confidential
not to the point irrelevant
not to the purpose irrelevant
not too difficult practicable
not toxiferous nontoxic
not trouble oneself disregard
not true dishonest, fraudulent, illusory
not unique nondescript
not up to expectation inadequate
not up to normal deficient
not up to par deficient, unsatisfactory
not use neglect, waive
not vague tangible, unambiguous
not valid illegal, null *(invalid)*, null and void. SEE MAIN ENTRY
not varying fixed *(settled)*
not vital incidental, inconsequential, irrelevant, minor
not wanted inadmissible
not weaken hold out *(resist)*
not well off impecunious
not well-founded baseless
not whole semi
not wholly in part
not working unemployed
not worth considering inconsiderable
not worth mentioning minor
not worthy of notice inconsiderable
not written nuncupative, parol
not yet carried into operation executory
not yet due undue *(not owing)*
not yet payable undue *(not owing)*
not yield hold out *(resist)*, oppose

nota brand, stamp, stigma, symptom, trait
notabilis notable
notability character *(reputation)*, clout, distinction *(reputation)*, eminence, emphasis, feature *(characteristic)*, importance, materiality *(consequence)*, notoriety, prestige, reputation, significance, status
notable appreciable, cardinal *(outstanding)*, considerable, conspicuous, critical *(crucial)*, extraordinary, famous, illustrious, important *(significant)*, influential, major, manifest, momentous, noteworthy, obvious, outstanding *(prominent)*, palpable, paramount, perceivable, perceptible, portentous *(eliciting amazement)*, prominent, remarkable, renowned, reputable, salient, special, unusual. SEE MAIN ENTRY
notable disaster catastrophe
notable feature consequence *(significance)*
notableness materiality *(consequence)*
notably particularly
notam homini inurere brand *(mark)*
notare brand *(mark)*, characterize, designate
notarize SEE MAIN ENTRY
notary notary public. SEE MAIN ENTRY
notatio notice *(heed)*, notice *(observe)*, observation
notation comment, marginalia, memorandum, reminder, symbol. SEE MAIN ENTRY
note attend *(heed)*, book, capsule, check *(instrument)*, comment *(noun)*, comment *(verb)*, coupon, denote, designate, discern *(detect with the senses)*, dispatch *(message)*, distinction *(reputation)*, draft, eminence, emphasis, enter *(record)*, entry *(record)*, hear *(give attention to)*, heed, importance, indicant, indication, indicator, interest *(concern)*, invoice *(bill)*, itemize, marginalia, memorandum, mention *(reference)*, mention, muse, notation, notice *(announcement)*, notice *(observe)*, observation, observe *(watch)*, outline *(synopsis)*, perceive, perception, pierce *(discern)*, prestige, record *(noun)*, record *(verb)*, regard *(esteem)*, regard *(pay attention)*, remark *(noun)*, remark *(verb)*, remind, reminder, report *(detailed account)*, reputation, respect, set down, significance, study, summary, symbol, transmittal, witness *(have direct knowledge of)*. SEE MAIN ENTRY
note differences discriminate *(distinguish)*, distinguish
note down register
note of explanation comment
note the distinctions discern *(discriminate)*, secern
note the similarities and differences compare
note the time of date
notebook file
noted famous, illustrious, notable, notorious, outstanding *(prominent)*, popular, renowned. SEE MAIN ENTRY
notedness notoriety
notes caption, currency, register
noteworthiness distinction *(reputation)*, eminence, importance, prestige
noteworthy certain *(specific)*, considerable, distinctive, extraordinary, famous, important *(significant)*, influential, major, momentous, notable, outstanding *(prominent)*, particular *(specific)*, peculiar *(distinctive)*, portentous *(eliciting amazement)*, prodigious *(amazing)*, rare, remarkable, renowned, special, stellar, uncanny, uncommon, unusual. SEE MAIN ENTRY

nothing blank *(emptiness)*, nonentity, nullity. SEE MAIN ENTRY
nothing but mere
nothingness blank *(emptiness)*, nonentity, nullity
nothus bastard, illegitimate *(born out of wedlock)*
notice admonition, advice, appreciate *(comprehend)*, attend *(heed)*, caution *(warning)*, caveat, character *(reputation)*, citation *(charge)*, comment, consider, declaration, detect, discern *(detect with the senses)*, disclosure *(something disclosed)*, dispatch *(message)*, dun, find *(discover)*, hear *(perceive by ear)*, heed, information *(facts)*, intelligence *(news)*, issuance, monition *(warning)*, notification, observation, observe *(watch)*, perceive, perception, pierce *(discern)*, pronouncement, publication *(disclosure)*, publicity, recognition, recognize *(perceive)*, regard *(attention)*, regard *(pay attention)*, report *(detailed account)*, symptom, ultimatum, witness *(have direct knowledge of)*. SEE MAIN ENTRY
notice critically review
notice of an action lis pendens
notice of an appearance SEE MAIN ENTRY
notice of claim demand
notice of danger warning
notice of pending suit lis pendens
notice of right lis pendens
notice on file lis pendens
notice to appear citation *(charge)*, monition *(legal summons)*
noticeable apparent *(perceptible)*, appreciable, blatant *(conspicuous)*, conspicuous, determinable *(ascertainable)*, distinct *(clear)*, distinctive, evident, flagrant, manifest, naked *(perceptible)*, noteworthy, obvious, open *(in sight)*, ostensible, overt, palpable, patent, perceivable, perceptible, prominent, salient, scrutable
noticeably fairly *(clearly)*
notification admonition, advice, caveat, citation *(charge)*, communication *(statement)*, declaration, directive, disclosure *(act of disclosing)*, disclosure *(something disclosed)*, dispatch *(message)*, information *(facts)*, issuance, monition *(legal summons)*, monition *(warning)*, notice *(announcement)*, proclamation, profession *(declaration)*, pronouncement, publication *(disclosure)*, publicity, report *(detailed account)*, subpoena. SEE MAIN ENTRY
notification of legal action service *(delivery of legal process)*
notification to appear summons, venire
notificatory declaratory
notified acquainted, informed *(having information)*
notifier informant, informer *(a person who provides information)*
notify admonish *(advise)*, advise, alert, annunciate, apprise, communicate, contact *(communicate)*, convey *(communicate)*, correspond *(communicate)*, disabuse, disclose, disseminate, enlighten, enunciate, forewarn, herald, inform *(notify)*, issue *(publish)*, mention, notice *(give formal warning)*, portend, predict, promulgate, propagate *(spread)*, relate *(tell)*, report *(disclose)*, reveal, signify *(inform)*. SEE MAIN ENTRY
notify of danger caution
notify publicly issue *(publish)*
notify to appear subpoena, summon
notifying informatory

noting down   registration
notio   idea, notion
notion   apprehension *(perception)*, assumption *(supposition)*, concept, idea, impression, opinion *(belief)*, perception, sense *(feeling)*, suspicion *(uncertainty)*. SEE MAIN ENTRY
notional   allusive, delusive, fictitious, illusory, inconsistent, insubstantial, nonexistent, quixotic
notoriety   bad repute, character *(reputation)*, common knowledge, disgrace, dishonor *(shame)*, ill repute, infamy, opprobrium, prestige, publicity, reputation, scandal, stigma. SEE MAIN ENTRY
notorious   apparent *(perceptible)*, blatant *(conspicuous)*, conspicuous, disreputable, famous, flagrant, outrageous, overt, prominent, proverbial, public *(known)*, renowned, scandalous, unmistakable. SEE MAIN ENTRY
notorious criminal   outlaw
notoriousness   character *(reputation)*, stigma
notus   acquainted, familiar *(customary)*, notorious
notwithstanding   regardless. SEE MAIN ENTRY
nought   nonentity
nourish   abet, bear *(support)*, cultivate, foster, maintain *(sustain)*, nurture, preserve, promote *(organize)*, support *(assist)*, sustain *(prolong)*
nourishing   conservation, salubrious, salutary
nourishment   preservation, sustenance
nouveau riche   philistine
novare   innovation
novation   SEE MAIN ENTRY
novel   different, noteworthy, original *(creative)*, portentous *(eliciting amazement)*, recent, unaccustomed, uncommon, unique, unprecedented, unusual. SEE MAIN ENTRY
novelty   innovation
novice   amateur, apprentice, neophyte, probationer *(one being tested)*, protégé. SEE MAIN ENTRY
novitiate   apprentice, preparation, probationer *(one being tested)*
novus   eccentric, extraordinary, novel, unprecedented
now   instantly
now and forever   SEE MAIN ENTRY
now and then   sporadic
now to be accounted for   a savoir
now to be announced   a savoir
now to be described   a savoir
now to be enunciated   a savoir
now to be itemized   a savoir
now to be listed   a savoir
now to be mentioned   a savoir
now to be narrated   a savoir
now to be presented   a savoir
now to be read   a savoir
now to be recited   a savoir
now to be recounted   a savoir
now to be reported   a savoir
now to be set forth   a savoir
now to be stated   a savoir
now to follow   a savoir
nowhere to be found   lost *(taken away)*
noxia   guilt
noxious   bad *(inferior)*, contemptible, deadly, deleterious, detrimental, fatal, harmful, harsh, inimical, insalubrious, lethal, malignant, objectionable, obnoxious, offensive *(offending)*, peccant *(unhealthy)*, pernicious, pestilent, repul-

sive, sinister, tainted *(contaminated)*, toxic, unfavorable, virulent. SEE MAIN ENTRY
noxiousness   harm
noxius   deleterious, harmful, obnoxious, pernicious, prejudicial
nuance   difference, differential, technicality. SEE MAIN ENTRY
nubilous   indistinct
nucleation   centralization
nucleus   center *(essence)*, consequence *(significance)*, cornerstone, gravamen, main point, mainstay
nudge   jostle *(bump into)*
nugatorius   invalid, nugatory
nugatory   collateral *(immaterial)*, expendable, futile, inactive, inadequate, inconsequential, inconsiderable, ineffective, ineffectual, invalid, minor, negligible, null *(insignificant)*, null *(invalid)*, null and void, otiose, paltry, petty, powerless, slight, trivial, unavailing, unproductive, void *(invalid)*. SEE MAIN ENTRY
nugatory check   bad check
nugatory trial   mistrial
nugax   frivolous
nuisance   aggravation *(annoyance)*, disadvantage, mischief, molestation. SEE MAIN ENTRY
nuisance value   SEE MAIN ENTRY
null   inactive, ineffective, ineffectual, invalid, lifeless *(dead)*, nugatory, vacuous, void *(invalid)*. SEE MAIN ENTRY
null and void   nugatory, otiose, powerless, void *(invalid)*. SEE MAIN ENTRY
nullifiable   defeasible, voidable
nullification   abatement *(extinguishment)*, abolition, ademption, annulment, cancellation, countermand, defeasance, destruction, discharge *(annulment)*, discharge *(release from obligation)*, disclaimer, discontinuance *(act of discontinuing)*, dissolution *(termination)*, mistrial, negation, repudiation, rescission, retraction, reversal, revocation. SEE MAIN ENTRY
nullified   null *(invalid)*, null and void
nullifier   offset
nullify   abate *(extinguish)*, abolish, abrogate *(annul)*, abrogate *(rescind)*, adeem, alleviate, annul, balk, cancel, contravene, counteract, destroy *(void)*, disable, disavow, discharge *(release from obligation)*, disinherit, disown *(deny the validity)*, disprove, dissolve *(terminate)*, eliminate *(eradicate)*, expunge, extinguish, extirpate, frustrate, invalidate, kill *(defeat)*, negate, neutralize, obliterate, override, overrule, overthrow, quash, recall *(call back)*, recant, renege, repeal, repudiate, rescind, revoke, supersede, vacate *(void)*, vitiate, withdraw. SEE MAIN ENTRY
nullify a marriage   divorce
nullify one's gains   overreach
nullifying   avoidance *(cancellation)*, cancellation
nullity   blank *(emptiness)*, invalidity, mistrial, nonentity. SEE MAIN ENTRY
nullius filius   bastard
nullius momenti   immaterial
nullo modo fieri potest   impossible
numb   drug, insusceptible *(uncaring)*, obtund, torpid
number   amount *(quantity)*, calculate, contain *(comprise)*, enumerate, itemize, quantity, quota. SEE MAIN ENTRY
number of people   population
numbering   census, poll *(canvass)*
numberless   frequent, infinite, innumerable, myriad, profuse

numerare   pay
numerate   enumerate
numeration   amount *(quantity)*, census, computation, poll *(canvass)*
numerous   copious, frequent, manifold, multifarious, multifold, multiple, myriad, populous, profuse, rife. SEE MAIN ENTRY
numerousness   multiplicity
numerus   quantity
numismatical   monetary, pecuniary
nummarius   venal
nummary   financial, pecuniary
nummi   principal *(capital sum)*
nummulary   monetary
nummus   money
nunc pro tunc   SEE MAIN ENTRY
nuncupative   parol, verbal. SEE MAIN ENTRY
nundinae   market *(business)*
nundination   trade *(commerce)*
nuntiare   inform *(notify)*
nuntius   innuendo, intelligence *(news)*, intimation
nuptiae   marriage *(wedlock)*
nuptial   conjugal. SEE MAIN ENTRY
nuptial agreements   SEE MAIN ENTRY
nuptial bond   cohabitation *(married state)*, coverture, marriage *(wedlock)*, matrimony
nuptial state   matrimony
nuptial tie   cohabitation *(married state)*, marriage *(wedlock)*, matrimony
nuptialis   nuptial
nurse   cure, foster, maintain *(sustain)*, nurture, promote *(organize)*, protect
nursing   conservation
nursing home   asylum *(hospital)*
nursling   infant
nurture   abet, aid, assist, care *(regard)*, conjure, cultivate, discipline *(train)*, educate, foster, keep *(shelter)*, maintain *(sustain)*, mature, preservation, promote *(organize)*. SEE MAIN ENTRY
nurture a belief   opine
nutriment   sustenance
nutrire   foster, nurture
nutrition   sustenance
nutritious   salubrious, salutary
nutritive   salubrious, salutary

O

oafish   obtuse, opaque, provincial
oafishness   opacity
oath   adjuration, affirmation, asseveration, assurance, attestation, avouchment, confirmation, covenant, obligation *(duty)*, pledge *(binding promise)*, profession *(declaration)*, promise, undertaking *(pledge)*, vow. SEE MAIN ENTRY
oath-giving   affirmation
oath-taking   affirmation
obaeratus   indebted
obducere   envelop
obduracy   resolution *(decision)*, tenacity
obdurate   callous, cold-blooded, disobedient, implacable, incorrigible, inexorable, inflexible, insusceptible *(uncaring)*, intractable, pertinacious, recusant, relentless, remorseless, reprobate, resolute, restive, rigid, ruthless, severe, strict, unaffected *(uninfluenced)*, unalterable, unbending, uncompromising, uncontrollable, unrelenting, unyielding, willful. SEE MAIN ENTRY
obdurescere   insensible
obedience   adherence *(devotion)*, adhesion *(loyalty)*, allegiance, capitulation, compliance, deference, duty *(obligation)*, fealty,

homage, loyalty, resignation *(passive acceptance)*, servitude

obedient amenable, controlled *(restrained)*, faithful *(loyal)*, law-abiding, lawful, licit, loyal, obeisant, obsequious, passive, pliable, pliant, sequacious, servile, subservient, tractable, true *(loyal)*, yielding. SEE MAIN ENTRY

obediently faithfully, respectfully

obeisance conformity *(obedience)*, homage, honor *(outward respect)*, prostration, respect

obeisant obedient, passive, pliant, sequacious, servile, subservient. SEE MAIN ENTRY

obey abide, accede *(concede)*, adhere *(maintain loyalty)*, bear *(tolerate)*, comply, conform, fulfill, hear *(give attention to)*, heed, observe *(obey)*, pander, submit *(yield)*, surrender *(yield)*, yield *(submit)*. SEE MAIN ENTRY

obey orders conform

obey regulations conform

obey rules conform

obeyed powerful

obfuscate blind *(obscure)*, camouflage, confound, confuse *(bewilder)*, disorganize, disorient, muddle, obnubilate, obscure. SEE MAIN ENTRY

obfuscated lost *(disoriented)*, nebulous, opaque

obfuscation concealment, evasion, obscuration, opacity, pretext

object article *(commodity)*, cause *(reason)*, collide *(clash)*, complain *(criticize)*, condemn *(ban)*, conflict, confront *(oppose)*, connotation, content *(meaning)*, contest, counter, demonstrate *(protest)*, demur, deprecate, design *(intent)*, destination, determinant, differ *(disagree)*, disaccord, disaffirm, disagree, disallow, disapprove *(reject)*, disown *(deny the validity)*, dissent *(withhold assent)*, doubt *(distrust)*, end *(intent)*, entity, expostulate, fight *(counteract)*, goal, idea, intent, intention, item, motive, negate, oppose, oppugn, point *(purpose)*, predetermination, project, purpose, pursuit *(goal)*, reason *(basis)*, recipient, reject, remonstrate, reprehend, signification, target. SEE MAIN ENTRY

object frivolously cavil

object lesson admonition. SEE MAIN ENTRY

object of responsibility charge *(custody)*

object of study specialty *(special aptitude)*

object of the action gist *(ground for a suit)*

object produced as evidence exhibit

object submitted in proof of facts exhibit

object to challenge, complain *(criticize)*, criticize *(find fault with)*, disapprove *(condemn)*, discriminate *(treat differently)*, disfavor, dispute *(contest)*, except *(object)*, refuse. SEE MAIN ENTRY

objectify substantiate

objecting critical *(faultfinding)*, disobedient, dissenting, dissident, nonconsenting, remonstrative

objection admonition, complaint, condemnation *(blame)*, criticism, demurrer, denial, disadvantage, disagreement, disapprobation, disapproval, disparagement, dissent *(difference of opinion)*, dissent *(nonconcurrence)*, drawback, grievance, ground, misgiving, negation, nonconformity, opposition, outcry, reaction *(opposi-

tion)*, rejection, reluctance, remonstrance, reprimand, reproach, scruple, stricture. SEE MAIN ENTRY

objection to a pleading demurrer

objectionable bad *(inferior)*, bad *(offensive)*, blameful, blameworthy, contemptuous, disreputable, heinous, immoral, impermissible, improper, inadmissible, inadvisable, inappropriate, inapt, ineligible, inept *(inappropriate)*, inexcusable, iniquitous, injudicious, invidious, loathsome, obnoxious, odious, offensive *(offending)*, peccable, reprehensible, repugnant *(exciting aversion)*, repulsive, unacceptable, undesirable, undue *(excessive)*, unendurable, unfit, unjustifiable, unsatisfactory, unsavory, unsuitable, unwarranted. SEE MAIN ENTRY

objective actual, candid, cause *(reason)*, desideratum, design *(intent)*, destination, dispassionate, end *(intent)*, equitable, evenhanded, factual, fair *(just)*, focus, goal, impartial, intent, intention, just, liberal *(broad minded)*, mission, motive, neutral, nonpartisan, open-minded, point *(purpose)*, predetermination, project, purpose, pursuit *(goal)*, rational, substantive, target, unbiased, unprejudiced. SEE MAIN ENTRY

objective certainty certification *(certainness)*, certitude

objective certitude certainty

objective necessity compulsion *(coercion)*

objectivity candor *(impartiality)*, disinterest *(lack of prejudice)*, fairness, justice. SEE MAIN ENTRY

objector appellant, disputant, malcontent

objects commodities

objuration disparagement, imprecation

objurgate admonish *(warn)*, blame, castigate, censure, contemn, criticize *(find fault with)*, defame, deprecate, disapprove *(condemn)*, expostulate, lash *(attack verbally)*, rebuke, remonstrate, reprehend, reprimand, reproach

objurgation aspersion, bad repute, blame *(culpability)*, charge *(accusation)*, condemnation *(blame)*, contempt *(disdain)*, contumely, denunciation, diatribe, disapprobation, obloquy, remonstrance, reprimand, reproach, revilement, stricture. SEE MAIN ENTRY

objurgatory blameful, contemptible, critical *(faultfinding)*, derogatory, remonstrative, scandalous

oblation benefit *(conferment)*, grant

obliga agreement *(contract)*

obligare bind *(obligate)*, pledge *(promise the performance of)*

obligate compel, constrain *(compel)*, detail *(assign)*, encumber *(financially obligate)*, entail, exact, force *(coerce)*, guarantee, necessitate, press *(constrain)*, require *(compel)*. SEE MAIN ENTRY

obligate oneself contract, promise *(vow)*, undertake

obligated accountable *(responsible)*, bound, contractual, indebted, indentured, liable

obligation agreement *(contract)*, allegiance, arrears, assurance, bond, burden, charge *(cost)*, charge *(lien)*, charge *(responsibility)*, cloud *(incumbrance)*, commitment *(responsibility)*, compact, compulsion *(coercion)*, condition *(contingent provision)*, contract, coverage *(insurance)*, debit, debt, delinquency *(shortage)*, duress,

enforcement, excise, expense *(cost)*, incumbrance *(lien)*, job, liability, lien, mortgage, need *(requirement)*, pledge *(binding promise)*, policy *(contract)*, pressure, promise *(contract)*, provision *(clause)*, rate, recognizance, requirement, responsibility *(accountability)*, restriction, security *(stock)*, specialty *(contract)*, trust *(custody)*, undertaking *(commitment)*, undertaking *(pledge)*, weight *(burden)*. SEE MAIN ENTRY

obligation accrued due

obligation incurred cost *(expenses)*

obligation of investigation SEE MAIN ENTRY

obligation repudiated delict

obligatorily will shall

obligatoriness responsibility *(accountability)*

obligatory binding, choate lien, compelling, compulsory, conclusive *(determinative)*, contractual, essential *(required)*, imperative, indispensable, involuntary, mandatory, necessary *(required)*, peremptory *(imperative)*, positive *(prescribed)*, prescriptive, requisite, strict, unavoidable *(inevitable)*. SEE MAIN ENTRY

obligatus indebted

oblige accommodate, aid, assist, bear *(support)*, bestow, bind *(obligate)*, call *(demand)*, coerce, compel, constrain *(compel)*, delegate, detail *(assign)*, dictate, enjoin, exact, excise *(levy a tax)*, force *(coerce)*, help, impose *(enforce)*, impose *(subject)*, let *(permit)*, necessitate, order, pander, patronize *(condescend toward)*, press *(constrain)*, require *(compel)*, suffer *(permit)*, supply, tolerate. SEE MAIN ENTRY

obliged accountable *(responsible)*, bound, indebted, indentured, liable

obliged in law liable

obligee SEE MAIN ENTRY

obligement enforcement, obligation *(duty)*

obliging accommodation *(adjustment)*, beneficial, benevolent, binding, charitable *(lenient)*, civil *(polite)*, favorable *(expressing approval)*, malleable, obedient, obeisant, philanthropic, pliable, propitious, sequacious, yielding

obligingness amenability, benevolence *(disposition to do good)*, clemency, comity, consideration *(sympathetic regard)*, indulgence

obligor debtor. SEE MAIN ENTRY

oblinere smear

obliquation indirection *(indirect action)*

oblique circuitous, deceptive, deviant, indirect, labyrinthine, sinuous. SEE MAIN ENTRY

oblique allusion innuendo

oblique hint insinuation

obliqueness indirection *(deceitfulness)*, indirection *(indirect action)*

obliquitous deceptive, sinister

obliquity bad faith, bad repute, corruption, crime, deception, delinquency *(misconduct)*, improbity, indirection *(deceitfulness)*, indirection *(indirect action)*, vice, wrong

obliquus indirect, oblique *(slanted)*

obliterate abate *(extinguish)*, abolish, adeem, annul, cancel, deface, delete, destroy *(efface)*, dissolve *(terminate)*, eliminate *(eradicate)*, eradicate, expunge, extinguish, extirpate, negate, nullify, overthrow, overturn, quash, remove *(eliminate)*, repeal, rescind. SEE MAIN ENTRY

obliterated lost *(taken away)*, null *(invalid)*, null and void

obliteration abatement *(extinguishment)*, abolition, annulment, catastrophe,

887

censorship, defacement, destruction, dissolution (*termination*), obscuration, removal

obliteration of grievances pardon

oblitterare expunge

oblivion disregard (*unconcern*), nullity

obliviosus oblivious

oblivious careless, heedless, inadvertent, incognizant, lax, negligent, unaware. SEE MAIN ENTRY

obliviousness disinterest (*lack of interest*), disregard (*unconcern*), negligence

obloquial calumnious

obloquious calumnious

obloquy aspersion, attaint, bad repute, blame (*culpability*), contempt (*disdain*), contumely, criticism, defamation, degradation, denunciation, diatribe, disgrace, dishonor (*shame*), disparagement, disrepute, ignominy, infamy, malediction, notoriety, odium, opprobrium, ostracism, phillipic, profanity, reproach, revilement, scandal, shame, slander, stricture. SEE MAIN ENTRY

obnoxious bad (*offensive*), blameworthy, contemptuous, disreputable, heinous, invidious, loathsome, nefarious, objectionable, odious, offensive (*offending*), reprehensible, repugnant (*exciting aversion*), repulsive, undesirable, unendurable, unsavory. SEE MAIN ENTRY

obnoxiousness bad repute, disrepute, indecency

obnoxium reddere subject

obnoxius dependent, liable

obnubliate SEE MAIN ENTRY

oboediens obedient

oboedire obey

obreptitious collusive, sly, stealthy, surreptitious

obruere overwhelm

obrussa criterion

obscene depraved, lascivious, lewd, licentious, objectionable, prurient, repulsive, salacious, scurrilous, suggestive (*risqué*). SEE MAIN ENTRY

obscene art pornography

obscene literature pornography

obscenitas obscenity

obscenity debauchery, pornography, turpitude. SEE MAIN ENTRY

obscenus obscene

obscuration indistinctness, opacity. SEE MAIN ENTRY

obscure allusive, ambiguous, blind (*concealed*), camouflage, clandestine, cloak, complex, conceal, confound, cover (*conceal*), de minimus, debatable, difficult, disguise, disorganize, disorient, elusive, enigmatic, ensconce, enshroud, envelop, equivocal, esoteric, hidden, hide, impalpable, inapprehensible, incomprehensible, inconspicuous, indefinable, indefinite, indeterminate, inexplicable, inscrutable, minor, mysterious, nebulous, obfuscate, obliterate, obnubilate, opaque, oracular, plant (*covertly place*), privy, recondite, secret, shroud, stealthy, ulterior, uncertain (*ambiguous*), unclear, underlying, unspecified, vague. SEE MAIN ENTRY

obscure information secret

obscure meaning ambiguity

obscure question enigma

obscure statement enigma

obscured hidden, lost (*taken away*)

obscurity ambiguity, complication, concealment, indistinctness, mystery, nonappearance, obscuration, opacity, privacy

obscurus inconspicuous, indistinct, inscrutable, lurid

obsecrare appeal, plead (*implore*), request

obsecrate importune, solicit

obsecratio entreaty

obsecration call (*appeal*), claim (*legal demand*), dun, entreaty, imprecation, request

obsequens subservient, yielding

obsequi defer (*put off*), defer (*yield in judgment*), obey

obsequious law-abiding, passive, sequacious, servile, subservient, yielding. SEE MAIN ENTRY

obsequiousness allegiance, discipline (*obedience*)

obsequium compliance

obserere lock

observable appreciable, blatant (*conspicuous*), clear (*apparent*), conspicuous, determinable (*ascertainable*), discernible, manifest, naked (*perceptible*), obvious, open (*in sight*), ostensible, palpable, patent, perceivable, perceptible, scrutable, visible (*noticeable*)

observably particularly

observably different distinct (*distinguished from others*)

observance acquiescence, adherence (*devotion*), allegiance, ceremony, compliance, conformity (*obedience*), contemplation, custom, discharge (*performance*), discipline (*obedience*), habit, manner (*behavior*), notice (*heed*), practice (*procedure*), prescription (*custom*), remembrance (*commemoration*), scrutiny. SEE MAIN ENTRY

observance of form formality

observance of obligation allegiance

observant alert (*vigilant*), circumspect, conscientious, conscious (*aware*), law-abiding, obedient, perspicacious, punctilious, receptive, sensible, sensitive (*discerning*), vigilant

observant of decorum punctilious

observant of form formal

observantia homage, respect

observantly faithfully

observare heed, keep (*fulfill*), observe (*obey*), observe (*watch*), regard (*pay attention*)

observatio observation

observation apprehension (*perception*), comment, comprehension, concept, conclusion (*determination*), dictum, diligence (*care*), discovery, estimate (*idea*), examination (*study*), generalization, indagation, inference, inspection, judgment (*discernment*), notice (*heed*), outlook, perception, pronouncement, regard (*attention*), remark, research, scrutiny, sense (*intelligence*), statement, surveillance, test. SEE MAIN ENTRY

observation post standpoint

observe abide, bear (*tolerate*), check (*inspect*), comment, comply, conform, consider, detect, discern (*detect with the senses*), discover, examine (*study*), express, find (*discover*), fulfill, heed, keep (*fulfill*), mention, monitor, note (*notice*), notice (*observe*), obey, patrol, perceive, perform (*adhere to*), peruse, phrase, pierce (*discern*), police, probe, regard (*pay attention*), relate (*tell*), remark, scrutinize, spy, study, survey (*examine*), witness (*have direct knowledge of*). SEE MAIN ENTRY

observe discipline conform

observer bystander, eyewitness, spy, witness

observing circumspect

obses hostage

obses harass, occupy (*engage*). SEE MAIN ENTRY

obsessed fanatical, lunatic, pensive

obsessed with addicted

obsessing compelling

obsessio blockade (*barrier*)

obsession dipsomania, phobia, preoccupation, requirement. SEE MAIN ENTRY

obsessional compelling

obsessive compelling, fanatical

obsidio blockade (*barrier*)

obsistere withstand

obsolescence desuetude, disuse

obsolescent obsolete, outdated, outmoded

obsolete defunct, inactive, old, outdated, outmoded. SEE MAIN ENTRY

obsoleteness desuetude

obsoletus dilapidated, obsolete, stale

obstacle bar (*obstruction*), barrier, blockade (*barrier*), check (*bar*), complication, damper (*stopper*), deterrence, deterrent, detriment, disadvantage, drawback, encumbrance, fetter, handicap, hindrance, impasse, impediment, interruption, nuisance, obstruction, pitfall, predicament, problem, prohibition, restraint, stay. SEE MAIN ENTRY

obstare prevent, withstand

obstinacy contempt (*disobedience to the court*), contest (*dispute*), reluctance, resistance, resolution (*decision*), tenacity

obstinate contentious, contumacious, difficult, disobedient, froward, immutable, impervious, implacable, incorrigible, inexorable, inflexible, insusceptible (*uncaring*), intractable, obdurate, persistent, pertinacious, perverse, proud (*conceited*), purposeful, recalcitrant, recusant, relentless, resolute, restive, rigid, steadfast, unbending, uncompromising, uncontrollable, unruly, unyielding, willful

obstinatus inflexible, pertinacious, willful

obstreperous blatant (*obtrusive*), disobedient, disorderly, intractable, perverse, recalcitrant, uncontrollable, unruly

obstruct abrogate (*annul*), arrest (*stop*), balk, ban, bar (*hinder*), block, check (*restrain*), clog, condemn (*ban*), constrain (*restrain*), constrict (*inhibit*), contain (*restrain*), control (*restrain*), counter, curb, debar, defer (*put off*), delay, detain (*restrain*), deter, disadvantage, discontinue (*break continuity*), disrupt, estop, fight (*counteract*), foil, forbid, forestall, frustrate, halt, hamper, hinder, hold up (*delay*), impede, inconvenience, inhibit, interdict, interfere, interpose, interrupt, keep (*restrain*), lock, obturate, occlude, oppose, oppugn, preclude, prevent, prohibit, repulse, resist (*oppose*), restrain, restrict, shut, stall, stave, stay (*halt*), stem (*check*), stifle, stop, suppress, thwart, toll (*stop*), trammel, withstand. SEE MAIN ENTRY

obstruct action encumber (*hinder*)

obstruct by opposition discourage

obstruct one's vision blind (*deprive of sight*)

obstruct the course of descent escheat

obstruct the view of cloak, enshroud

obstruct work strike (*refuse to work*)

obstructed arrested (*checked*), blind (*impassable*), broken (*interrupted*), impervious

obstructer deterrent

obstructio obstruction

obstruction barrier, blockade *(barrier)*, check *(bar)*, cloud *(incumbrance)*, complication, constraint *(restriction)*, damper *(stopper)*, deadlock, deterrence, deterrent, disadvantage, encumbrance, estoppel, fetter, filibuster, frustration, halt, handicap, hindrance, impasse, impediment, impugnation, interruption, obstacle, onus *(burden)*, predicament, prohibition, resistance, restraint, stay, trouble. SEE MAIN ENTRY

obstruction of justice misprision

obstruction to congressional action filibuster

obstructionism constraint *(restriction)*, contempt *(disobedience to the court)*

obstructionist assailant, disputant, malcontent

obstructive deterrent, preventive, prohibitive *(restrictive)*

obstruent obstruction

obstupefacere confound

obsuration concealment

obtain accept *(take)*, acquire *(receive)*, attain, buy, derive *(receive)*, educe, engage *(hire)*, evoke, extract, gain, glean, induce, inherit, occupy *(take possession)*, perform *(adhere to)*, possess, preempt, procure, purchase, raise *(collect)*, reach, realize *(obtain as a profit)*, reap, receive *(acquire)*, recover, recruit, redeem *(repurchase)*, succeed *(attain)*. SEE MAIN ENTRY

obtain a mortgage borrow

obtain a return profit, realize *(obtain as a profit)*

obtain a victory beat *(defeat)*, earn

obtain again repossess

obtain by any means acquire *(secure)*

obtain by compulsion enforce, extort

obtain by course of law recover

obtain by force enforce, impose *(enforce)*

obtain by reasoning derive *(deduce)*

obtain by search find *(discover)*

obtain exclusive possession monopolize

obtain in an unlawful manner extort

obtain insurance insure

obtain knowledge of overhear

obtain money by false pretenses cheat

obtain money on false pretenses defraud, peculate

obtain money under false pretenses defalcate

obtain payment collect *(recover money)*

obtain the use of borrow

obtain under false pretenses peculate

obtain unlawfully extort

obtainable available, open *(accessible)*, possible, potential, practicable, vulnerable

obtainer consumer

obtaining by force extortion

obtaining by threat extortion

obtaining national defense secrets espionage

obtaining of classified information espionage

obtainment adverse possession, collection *(accumulation)*, distraint, receipt *(act of receiving)*, recovery *(repossession)*, takeover

obtainment of property acquisition

obtegere cover *(pretext)*

obtemperans obedient

obtemperare conform

obtest importune, petition, pray, request, solicit

obtestatio appeal, entreaty

obtestation call *(appeal)*, dun

obtrectare decry, defame, depreciate

obtrectatio disparagement

obtrectation bad repute

obtrude accroach, encroach, impinge, impose *(intrude)*, interpose, intervene, intrude, invade, overstep. SEE MAIN ENTRY

obtrude on compel

obtrusion deterrent, encroachment, intrusion

obtrusive brazen, bumptious, contemptuous, flagrant, intrusive, prominent. SEE MAIN ENTRY

obtrusiveness pretense *(ostentation)*

obtund assuage, impair, palliate *(abate)*, soothe, subdue. SEE MAIN ENTRY

obturate balk, deter, occlude. SEE MAIN ENTRY

obturation blockade *(limitation)*, obstruction

obtuse blind *(not discerning)*, fatuous, impervious, inexpressive, opaque, unaffected *(uninfluenced)*. SEE MAIN ENTRY

obtuseness ignorance, opacity

obtusus obtuse

obumbrate obfuscate

obverse adverse *(opposite)*, antipode, contra, contradictory, contraposition, contrary, counterpart *(complement)*

obviate balk, bar *(hinder)*, deter, estop, forestall, overrule, overthrow, prevent, remove *(eliminate)*, stay *(halt)*, supersede. SEE MAIN ENTRY

obviation SEE MAIN ENTRY

obvious absolute *(conclusive)*, apparent *(perceptible)*, arrant *(definite)*, blatant *(conspicuous)*, coherent *(clear)*, comprehensible, conspicuous, distinct *(clear)*, elementary, evident, explicit, flagrant, gross *(flagrant)*, lucid, manifest, naked *(perceptible)*, open *(in sight)*, ostensible, outright, overt, palpable, patent, pellucid, perceivable, perceptible, prominent, public *(known)*, salient, scrutable, stark, tangible, unambiguous, undeniable, unmistakable. SEE MAIN ENTRY

obvious interpretation connotation, content *(meaning)*

obvious meaning connotation, content *(meaning)*

obvious sense connotation, content *(meaning)*

obviously fairly *(clearly)*

occasio occasion, opportunity

occasion access *(opening)*, avail *(bring about)*, cause, chance *(fortuity)*, create, day in court, engender, entail, event, evoke, experience *(encounter)*, generate, happening, incident, inspire, occurrence, opportunity, particular, point *(period of time)*, prompt, provoke, qualification *(fitness)*. SEE MAIN ENTRY

occasional casual, infrequent, intermittent, periodic, sporadic, uncommon, unusual

occasioner author *(originator)*

occasions circumstances

occidere kill *(murder)*, perish, slay

occisio murder

occlude balk, bar *(exclude)*, bar *(hinder)*, block, clog, constrict *(inhibit)*, debar, hinder, lock, obstruct, seal *(close)*, shut, stop. SEE MAIN ENTRY

occlusion blockade *(limitation)*, damper *(stopper)*, deterrent, obstruction

occulere conceal

occult blind *(obscure)*, cloak, covert, elusive, esoteric, hidden, incomprehensible, inexplicable, inscrutable, mysterious, obfuscate, obnubilate, obscure, recondite, secret, uncertain *(ambiguous)*, undisclosed

occultare disguise

occultari abscond

occultate camouflage

occultation obscuration

occultism mystery

occultness mystery

occultus hidden, inscrutable, latent, mysterious, secret, stealthy

occupancy enjoyment *(use)*, habitation *(act of inhabiting)*, inhabitation *(act of dwelling in)*, occupation *(possession)*, ownership, possession *(ownership)*, seisin, tenancy, tenure. SEE MAIN ENTRY

occupant citizen, denizen, domiciliary, habitant, inhabitant, inmate, lessee, lodger, resident, tenant. SEE MAIN ENTRY

occupant of an office incumbent

occupare assume *(seize)*, encroach, invest *(fund)*, occupy *(engage)*, occupy *(take possession)*

occupatio occupation *(possession)*, pursuit *(occupation)*, taking

occupation appointment *(position)*, calling, capacity *(job)*, career, employment, enjoyment *(use)*, enterprise *(undertaking)*, function, habitation *(act of inhabiting)*, industry *(activity)*, inhabitation *(act of dwelling in)*, job, labor *(work)*, livelihood, occupancy, office, position *(business status)*, post, practice *(professional business)*, profession *(vocation)*, project, province, seisin, specialty *(special aptitude)*, tenancy, tenure, undertaking *(enterprise)*, work *(employment)*. SEE MAIN ENTRY

occupational technical

occupatum employ *(engage services)*

occupiable habitable

occupied full, pensive, populous, residential

occupier citizen, denizen, domiciliary, habitant, inhabitant, inmate, lessee, lodger, occupant, resident, tenant

occupy consist, dwell *(reside)*, engage *(involve)*, hold *(possess)*, immerse *(engross)*, inhabit, interest, monopolize, own, possess, preempt, reside. SEE MAIN ENTRY

occupy oneself with address *(direct attention to)*, commit *(perpetrate)*, devote, notice *(observe)*, ply

occupy the attention interest

occupy the chair manage, officiate, preside

occupy the mind with concentrate *(pay attention)*

occupy the thoughts with concentrate *(pay attention)*, focus, ponder

occupying situated

occupying the same domicile cohabitation *(living together)*

occur accrue *(arise)*, appear *(materialize)*, ensue, supervene. SEE MAIN ENTRY

occur again recur

occur at the same time concur *(coexist)*

occur concurrently concur *(coexist)*

occurrence appearance *(emergence)*, case *(example)*, case *(set of circumstances)*, contingency, development *(outgrowth)*, event, experience *(encounter)*, happening, incident, occasion, particular, predicament, situation. SEE MAIN ENTRY

occurrences circumstances

occurring current
occurring after death posthumous
occurring again periodic
occurring at the same time concurrent (at the same time)
occurring by chance fortuitous
occurring in an instant instantaneous
occurring simultaneously coincidental
occurring together coincidental
ochlocracy lynch law
oculis captus blind (not discerning)
odd dissimilar, eccentric, inappropriate, irregular (not usual), ludicrous, noteworthy, novel, original (creative), particular (specific), peculiar (curious), singular, unaccustomed, uncanny, uncommon, unique, unusual. SEE MAIN ENTRY
oddity exception (exclusion), irregularity, quirk (idiosyncrasy), speciality, specialty (distinctive mark), trait. SEE MAIN ENTRY
oddment discard
oddments balance (amount in excess)
oddness irregularity
odds advantage, contraposition, disaccord, disagreement, edge (advantage), embroilment, feud, probability, variance (disagreement)
odiosus irksome, odious, repulsive
odiosus molestus offensive (offending)
odious antipathetic (distasteful), bad (offensive), base (bad), blameworthy, contemptible, disgraceful, disreputable, gross (flagrant), heinous, invidious, libelous, loathsome, nefarious, notorious, objectionable, obnoxious, offensive (offending), outrageous, reprehensible, repugnant (exciting aversion), repulsive, scandalous, sordid. SEE MAIN ENTRY
odiousness bad repute, disrepute, odium
odium alienation (estrangement), attaint, bad repute, contempt (disdain), criticism, degradation, discredit, disgrace, disrepute, hatred, ignominy, ill will, infamy, malice, notoriety, obloquy, opprobrium. SEE MAIN ENTRY
odium rancor
odium scandal, shame
odorari trace (follow)
of construe (translate)
of a different kind dissimilar
of a previous fashion outdated, outmoded
of a previous style outdated, outmoded
of all sorts dissimilar
of an equal size commensurable
of any description whatever
of any kind or sort whatever
of bad character disreputable
of consequence cogent
of course consequently
of decisive importance critical (crucial)
of doubtful certainty disputable
of doubtful meaning equivocal
of equal dignity coequal
of equal duration commensurate
of equal extent commensurate
of equal force equivalent
of equal length or volume commensurable
of equal power coequal
of equal rank commensurate
of equal value equivalent
of equal weight equivalent
of every description miscellaneous
of everyday occurrence typical
of external origin alien (unrelated)
of foreign origin alien (foreign)

of frequent occurrence typical
of general utility beneficial, practical
of good omen auspicious
of great age outdated
of great consequence critical (crucial), decisive, important (significant)
of great extent copious, far reaching
of great import SEE MAIN ENTRY
of great magnitude important (significant)
of great scope complete (all-embracing), far reaching, omnibus
of great weight important (significant)
of greater influence superior (higher)
of hidden meaning enigmatic
of high standing important (significant)
of high station important (significant)
of higher rank superior (higher)
of highest excellence prime (most valuable)
of humble birth ignoble
of ill fame disreputable, notorious
of ill repute notorious
of illicit union illegitimate (born out of wedlock)
of importance considerable, critical (crucial), important (significant), indispensable
of inestimable value invaluable
of law jural
of lawful parentage legitimate (lawfully conceived)
of less importance inferior (lower in position)
of like rank coequal
of little account immaterial, inappreciable, negligible
of little consequence negligible, nonessential, paltry, trivial
of little importance inapposite, inappreciable, negligible, nonessential
of little moment collateral (immaterial)
of little value paltry
of little weight frivolous
of long duration chronic, durable
of long standing conventional, customary, durable
of loose morals brazen
of low character ignoble
of low extraction caitiff, ignoble
of low origin caitiff
of low station ignoble
of lower rank subaltern
of many kinds dissimilar
of mean extraction caitiff
of mean origin caitiff
of minor importance de minimus, inconsequential
of mixed character miscellaneous
of moment crucial
of necessity compelling, consequently
of no account de minimus, expendable, frivolous, inconsequential, minor, nonessential, null (insignificant), paltry, unessential
of no avail unavailing
of no binding force null (invalid), null and void
of no concern nonessential
of no consequence immaterial, inconsequential, inconsiderable, insubstantial, nonessential, unessential
of no effect null (insignificant), null (invalid), null and void
of no essential consequence immaterial
of no importance immaterial, nonessential
of no legal weight null and void
of no moment immaterial, inconsiderable, negligible, null (insignificant)

of no repute blameworthy
of no significance immaterial, negligible, nonessential
of no validity null (invalid), null and void
of no value null (insignificant)
of no weight null (invalid)
of note considerable, crucial
of old outdated
of one accord concurrent (united), consensual, consenting
of one mind consensual
of promise auspicious
of recent occurrence recent
of regular recurrence continual (connected)
of repute credible
of right de jure
of second rank minor
of service beneficial, disposable, effective (efficient)
of short duration provisional
of small account petty, slight
of small importance nonessential, slight
of small moment petty
of small value paltry
of sound judgment normal (sane)
of supreme importance crucial
of that kind cognate
of that sort cognate
of the best quality prime (most valuable)
of the blood consanguineous
of the moment current
of the old order outdated
of the old school outdated, outmoded
of the origin reputed authentic
of the present current
of the quality of a felon felonious
of the same degree equal
of the same family consanguineous, interrelated
of the same kind consanguineous
of the same mind collective, concordant, consensual
of the same rank coequal, equal
of the same stock akin (related by blood)
of this date current
of todays date current
of uncertain issue doubtful
of uncertain significance equivocal
of unknown authorship anonymous
of unsound mind deranged, lunatic, non compos mentis
of use disposable, effective (efficient)
of value beneficial
of various kinds miscellaneous
of vital importance critical (crucial), essential (required)
of which wherein
off stale
off guard heedless, negligent, unaware, unsuspecting
off the mark improper
off the point immaterial
off the record confidential, unofficial
off the subject impertinent (irrelevant), irrelevant
off the topic immaterial, irrelevant
off-center astray
off-color improper, suggestive (risqué)
off-the-record private (confidential)
offbeat unusual
offed SEE MAIN ENTRY
offence crime
offend affront, aggravate (annoy), annoy, antagonize, bait (harass), disoblige, distress, estrange, harry (harass), hector, humiliate, irritate, mistreat, persecute, pique, plague,

provoke, repel *(disgust)*, trespass. SEE MAIN ENTRY

offend against the law   violate

offended   aggrieved *(victimized)*, resentful

offender   convict, criminal, delinquent, felon, lawbreaker, malefactor, outlaw, pariah, racketeer, recidivist, wrongdoer. SEE MAIN ENTRY

offender against society   outlaw

offender against the law   malefactor

offender under suspension of sentence   probationer *(released offender)*

offendere   disoblige, offend *(insult)*

offending   delinquent *(guilty of a misdeed)*, felonious, offensive *(offending)*, repugnant *(exciting aversion)*

offensa   disfavor, dissatisfaction

offense   assault, crime, delict, delinquency *(misconduct)*, disrespect, exception *(objection)*, felony, foray, guilt, indiscretion, infraction, injury, injustice, misconduct, misdeed, misdemeanor, misdoing, misfeasance, misprision, onset *(assault)*, provocation, resentment, transgression, umbrage, violation, wrong. SEE MAIN ENTRY

offense against the law   crime, guilt, misdemeanor, misfeasance

offense against the state   crime

offense punishable by imprisonment   felony

offenseless   blameless

offensio   dissatisfaction, offense

offensive   antipathetic *(distasteful)*, bad *(offensive)*, blatant *(obtrusive)*, calumnious, contemptible, contemptuous, foray, gross *(flagrant)*, heinous, impertinent *(insolent)*, inelegant, insolent, invidious, lewd, litigious, loathsome, lurid, noxious, objectionable, obnoxious, obscene, odious, onset *(assault)*, outrageous, peccant *(culpable)*, presumptuous, profligate *(corrupt)*, pugnacious, reprehensible, repugnant *(exciting aversion)*, repulsive, salacious, scandalous, scurrilous, unacceptable, unbecoming, unendurable, unsatisfactory, unsavory, unseemly, vicious. SEE MAIN ENTRY

offensive action   battery

offensive office environment   SEE MAIN ENTRY

offensive to decency   obscene

offensive to modesty   obscene

offensively assertive   blatant *(obtrusive)*

offensively obtrusive   blatant *(obtrusive)*

offensiveness   guilt, obscenity

offer   adduce, administer *(tender)*, bear *(yield)*, bid, hold out *(deliberate on an offer)*, introduce, invitation, overture, pose *(propound)*, present *(introduce)*, present *(make a gift)*, proffer, proposal *(suggestion)*, propose, proposition, propound, remit *(submit for consideration)*, tender. SEE MAIN ENTRY

offer a discount   rebate

offer a job to   delegate

offer a post   delegate

offer a word of caution   forewarn, notice *(give formal warning)*

offer advice   exhort

offer an explanation   explain

offer an explanation of   interpret

offer an inducement   coax, suborn

offer an opinion   advise

offer an opinion to   counsel

offer as an exhibit   introduce

offer assurances to   assure *(give confidence to)*

offer collateral   ensure, pawn, pledge *(deposit)*

offer compensation   indemnify

offer counsel   admonish *(advise)*, advise, charge *(instruct on the law)*

offer evidence   present *(introduce)*

offer for consideration   move *(judicially request)*

offer for inspection   exhibit

offer for sale   handle *(trade)*, sell, vend

offer in defense   justify

offer in exchange   displace *(replace)*

offer performance   offer *(tender)*

offer reparation   indemnify

offer resistance   confront *(oppose)*, hold out *(resist)*, oppose, parry, resist *(oppose)*, withstand

offer sacrifice   propitiate

offer satisfaction   indemnify

offer to give   dedicate

offer to the public   issue *(publish)*, post

offered   unsolicited, voluntary

offered price   bid

offerer   client

offering   benefit *(conferment)*, bribe, contribution *(donation)*, dedication, donation, gratuity *(present)*, introduction, largess *(gift)*, tip *(gratuity)*

offering a problem   difficult

offering as an exhibit   introduction

offering evidence   probative

offerre   offer *(propose)*

offertory   benefit *(conferment)*

offhand   cursory, impulsive *(rash)*, informal, nonchalant, perfunctory, slipshod, unpremeditated

offhandedness   informality

office   agency *(commission)*, appointment *(position)*, bureau, business *(occupation)*, calling, career, chamber *(compartment)*, chapter *(branch)*, duty *(obligation)*, employment, firm, function, mission, occupation *(vocation)*, organ, position *(business status)*, post, profession *(vocation)*, province, pursuit *(occupation)*, sphere, title *(position)*, trade *(occupation)*, work *(employment)*. SEE MAIN ENTRY

office bearer   official

office force   personnel

office holder   clerk, functionary

office hunter   candidate

office seeker   candidate, politician

office worker   clerk

office-seeker   contender

officebearer   incumbent

officeholder   caretaker *(one fulfilling the function of office)*, incumbent, officer, official, politician

officeholders   authorities

officer   caretaker *(one fulfilling the function of office)*, functionary, incumbent, key man, magistrate, marshal, official, peace officer, proctor SEE MAIN ENTRY

officer in charge   caretaker *(one fulfilling the function of office)*

officer of court   counsel, counselor

officer of state   caretaker *(one fulfilling the function of office)*, legislator, politician

officer of the court   administrator, attorney, esquire. SEE MAIN ENTRY

officer of the law   marshal, peace officer

officer who carries out orders of the court   marshal

officers   management *(directorate)*, police

officers of instruction   faculty *(teaching staff)*

officers of the law   police

official   actual, certain *(fixed)*, choate lien, civic, clerk, ex officio, factual, formal, functionary, genuine, incumbent, indubious, legitimate *(rightful)*, magistrate, notary public, officer, politician, valid. SEE MAIN ENTRY

official announcement   charter *(declaration of rights)*

official bulletin   declaration

official call   monition *(legal summons)*, process *(summons)*, summons

official correspondence   dispatch *(message)*

official count   census

official court order   summons

official criminal charge   information *(charge)*

official document   charter *(license)*

official enumeration of inhabitants   census

official enumeration of the population   census

official headquarters of an ambassador   embassy

official inquiry   investigation

official misconduct   crime, criminality, delict, guilt, misfeasance, offense SEE MAIN ENTRY

official mission   embassy

official notice   citation *(charge)*, monition *(legal summons)*, process *(summons)*, summons

official order   mittimus, summons

official procedure   bureaucracy

official publication   document, proclamation

official receiver   assessor

official reception   ceremony

official reckoning   census

official recognition   mention *(tribute)*

official record   instrument *(document)*

official registration   census

official reply   answer *(judicial response)*

official representative   legislator, plenipotentiary

official writing   certificate, instrument *(document)*

officialdom   bureaucracy

officially utter   pronounce *(pass judgment)*

officially withdraw   repeal

officials   authorities, hierarchy *(persons in authority)*, management *(directorate)*

officiary   official

officiate   administer *(conduct)*, exercise *(discharge a function)*, govern, handle *(manage)*, manage, moderate *(preside over)*, operate, oversee, preside, rule *(govern)*. SEE MAIN ENTRY

officiate at   conduct

officiating   executive, ministerial

officiation   bureaucracy, direction *(guidance)*

officio fungi   officiate

officious   dictatorial, obtrusive

officium   courtesy, duty *(obligation)*, function, obligation *(duty)*, office, subjection

offprint   copy

offset   adeem, compensate *(counterbalance)*, contra, counteract, countervail, cover *(provide for)*, equipoise, negate, neutralize, nullify, outbalance, overreach, reaction *(opposition)*, setoff. SEE MAIN ENTRY

offset bad debts   redeem *(satisfy debts)*

offsetting   contribution *(indemnification)*

offsetting claim   setoff

offshoot   affiliate, consequence *(conclusion)*, corollary, descendant, development *(outgrowth)*, organ, outgrowth. SEE MAIN ENTRY

offshoots offspring
offspring affinity *(family ties)*, blood, child, children, descendant, family *(household)*, issue *(progeny)*, offshoot, outcome, outgrowth, posterity, product, progeny, succession. SEE MAIN ENTRY
oft repeated proverbial, trite
oft-repeated customary, frequent, ordinary, periodic, typical
often chronic. SEE MAIN ENTRY
often done frequent
often met with common *(customary)*
oftentime periodic
old antique, elderly, obsolete, outdated, outmoded, prior, stale, traditional, trite. SEE MAIN ENTRY
old age longevity
old campaigner veteran
old fashioned antique
old soldier veteran
old-fashioned defunct, obsolete, outdated, outmoded
old-time outdated
old-world outdated, outmoded
olden old, outdated
older antique
oldest prime *(original)*
oldness longevity
oligopoly monopoly
olio melange
omega close *(conclusion)*, end *(termination)*
omen anticipate *(prognosticate)*, caution *(warning)*, forerunner, harbinger, herald, indicant, indication, portend, precursor, predict, premonition, presage, threat, token, warning
ominate forewarn, portend, predict, presage, prognosticate
ominous aleatory *(perilous)*, bleak *(not favorable)*, dangerous, dire, imminent, inauspicious, insalubrious, oracular, pending *(imminent)*, portentous *(ominous)*, presageful, prophetic, suggestive *(evocative)*, unfavorable, unpropitious. SEE MAIN ENTRY
omission breach, default, deficiency, deficit, delinquency *(failure of duty)*, dereliction, desuetude, dishonor *(nonpayment)*, dispensation *(exception)*, exception *(exclusion)*, exclusion, failure *(falling short)*, fault *(mistake)*, flaw, infraction, laches, miscue, neglect, negligence, nonfeasance, nonperformance, offense, ostracism, rejection, removal, renunciation. SEE MAIN ENTRY
omission of a court injustice
omission of duty delinquency *(failure of duty)*
omission of obligation delinquency *(failure of duty)*
omission prohibited by law crime
omissive remiss
omit abrogate *(rescind)*, bar *(exclude)*, censor, delete, eliminate *(exclude)*, except *(exclude)*, exclude, fail *(neglect)*, forgo, forswear, ignore, neglect, obliterate, overlook *(disregard)*, pretermit, prohibit, relegate, remove *(eliminate)*, set aside *(annul)*. SEE MAIN ENTRY
omit using conserve
omit what is due default
omitted null *(invalid)*, null and void
omittere abandon *(withdraw)*, disregard, omit
omitting perfunctory, save
omnibus SEE MAIN ENTRY
omniform protean
omnino in toto

omnipotence force *(strength)*, influence, predominance, supremacy
omnipotens omnipotent
omnipotent compelling, in full force, indomitable, influential, irresistible, powerful, predominant, strong. SEE MAIN ENTRY
omnipresent ubiquitous
omnis total
omniscient expert, learned. SEE MAIN ENTRY
omnivorous gluttonous
omnivorousness greed
on a footing with coequal
on a level with coequal
on a par coequal, commensurate, equal
on a par with coequal, equivalent
on a proper scale commensurate
on a suitable scale commensurate
on account of ad hoc, in furtherance
on account of this a priori, consequently
on all counts in toto
on approval elective *(selective)*
on bad terms inimical
on behalf of in furtherance, in lieu of. SEE MAIN ENTRY
on call available, disposable, ready *(prepared)*
on condition that provided
on duty operative
on edge restive
on even terms commensurate, equal, pro rata
on familiar terms intimate
on fire perfervid
on guard alert *(vigilant)*, circumspect, noncommittal, provident *(showing foresight)*, safe, vigilant
on hand present *(attendant)*
on intimate terms familiar *(informed)*
on no occasion sine die
on oath promissory
on one side only ex parte
on one's deathbed in extremis
on one's guard careful
on one's word promissory
on one's word of honor promissory
on or about SEE MAIN ENTRY
on paper holographic, in writing
on par comparable *(equivalent)*
on presentation prima facie *(self-evident)*
on purpose purposely. SEE MAIN ENTRY
on record documentary
on schedule punctual
on that account a priori, consequently
on that ground a priori
on the agenda at issue, forthcoming
on the alert careful
on the anniversary per annum
on the application of one party ex parte
on the basis of a year per annum
on the brink of almost
on the confines of contiguous
on the contrary contra
on the decline regressive
on the docket forthcoming. SEE MAIN ENTRY
on the edge peripheral
on the edge of contiguous
on the face of the matter prima facie *(self-evident)*
on the first view prima facie *(self-evident)*
on the fringe of society derelict *(abandoned)*
on the grounds SEE MAIN ENTRY
on the horizon forthcoming, pending *(imminent)*, prospective
on the increase cumulative *(increasing)*

on the journey en route
on the level SEE MAIN ENTRY
on the market available
on the other hand contra. SEE MAIN ENTRY
on the record SEE MAIN ENTRY
on the road en route
on the same footing coequal
on the same level equal
on the same matter pari materia
on the spot present *(attendant)*, present *(current)*
on the verge of almost
on the wane decadent, dilapidated
on the way en route, imminent
on the whole as a rule, generally. SEE MAIN ENTRY
on this account consequently
on time prompt, punctual
once late *(defunct)*, whenever
once more anew, de novo
oncoming forthcoming, imminent, onset *(commencement)*, pending *(imminent)*
one exclusive *(singular)*, individual, indivisible, sole, unit *(item)*, whole *(unified)*
one after another consecutive
one after the other consecutive
one and all en banc, in solido
one and the same same
one at a time respectively
one authorized to deliver a verdict juror
one by one respectively
one called to the bar advocate *(counselor)*, counselor, jurist
one engaged in a manual enterprise artisan
one engaged in buying and selling dealer
one excluded from some privilege alien
one held in captivity captive
one held in confinement captive
one held in subjegation captive
one holding land of another tenant
one implicated in the commission of a crime offender
one instigating an action complainant
one not legally competent minor
one occupying another's land tenant
one occupying real property tenant
one of constituent *(part)*
one of an adjudgment body juror
one of several parts installment
one of several payments installment
one of successive parts installment
one of the clientele customer
one of the contents component
one of the purchasing public customer
one seeking cure patient
one seeking relief patient
one sided ex parte, inequitable. SEE MAIN ENTRY
one skilled in an industrial art artisan
one suspected of a crime suspect
one sworn to deliver a verdict juror
one thing in return for another quid pro quo
one to whom a fee is conveyed feoffee
one to whom seisin passes feoffee
one to whom something is entrusted trustee
one to whom title is passed feoffee
one trained in a mechanic trade artisan
one undergoing therapy patient
one undergoing treatment patient
one using real property tenant
one who affirms declarant
one who applies for relief petitioner
one who asserts declarant

one who asserts a demand claimant
one who attests deponent
one who bears witness bystander, deponent
one who breaks the law offender
one who brings an action plaintiff
one who claims a right claimant
one who commits a crime offender
one who commits larceny embezzler
one who dispenses justice judge
one who enfeoffs another feoffor
one who exacts assessor
one who files an application for relief petitioner
one who flees fugitive
one who formulates laws legislator
one who gives a corporeal hereditament feoffor
one who gives assistance good samaritan
one who gives evidence deponent
one who gives or makes laws legislator
one who gives testimony witness
one who handles property for another fiduciary
one who has attained legal majority adult
one who has land landholder
one who has no specialized training layman
one who has not come of age infant
one who has not reached his majority infant
one who helps another good samaritan
one who helps to pass laws legislator
one who imposes a charge assessor
one who inherits heir, legatee
one who is enfeoffed feoffee
one who is unfriendly foe
one who levies assessor
one who makes an affidavit deponent
one who obtains evidence first hand eyewitness
one who opposes foe, opponent
one who personally observes an occurrence eyewitness
one who proclaims declarant
one who receives beneficiary
one who remains holdover
one who renders aid good samaritan
one who requests relief petitioner
one who sells for factorage factor (commission merchant)
one who stays on holdover
one who supplies criminal information to the police informer (one providing criminal information)
one who testifies to what he has seen eyewitness
one who testifies under oath affirmant, deponent
one who transacts business for another fiduciary
one who transfers property by deed feoffor
one who transfers real property to another feoffor
one's due birthright
one's duty charge (responsibility)
one's own land demesne
one's people blood
one-sided ex parte, illiberal, interested, parochial, partial (biased), unequal (unjust), unfair, unilateral
one-sided conception distortion
one-sided view distortion
one-sidedness favoritism, inequity, intolerance, partiality, predetermination, prejudice (preconception)

one-time late (defunct), previous
one-track mind compulsion (obsession)
oneness agreement (concurrence), concordance, conformity (agreement), entity, facsimile, identity (individuality), identity (similarity), peace, personality, union (unity)
onerare encumber (financially obligate), load
onerous bad (offensive), operose, oppressive, ponderous. SEE MAIN ENTRY
onesidedness foregone conclusion
ongoing chronic, live (existing), open-ended, progressive (going forward), protracted. SEE MAIN ENTRY
onlooker bystander, eyewitness, witness
only exclusive (singular), mere, sole, solely (singly). SEE MAIN ENTRY
onrush onset (assault)
onset assault, birth (beginning), genesis, inception, nascency, origin (source), origination, outset, start, threshold (commencement). SEE MAIN ENTRY
onset with force assault
onslaught assault, battery, incursion, onset (assault), outbreak, violence
onus allegiance, burden, commitment (responsibility), duty (tax), handicap, imposition (excessive burden), incumbrance (burden), liability, penalty, requirement, weight (burden). SEE MAIN ENTRY
onus cargo, encumbrance, freight
onus imponere load
onus probandi cloud (suspicion)
onward vanward
onward motion progress
ooze exude, outflow
opacity density, indistinctness, obscuration. SEE MAIN ENTRY
opaque impervious, inapprehensible, indefinable, indefinite, obtuse. SEE MAIN ENTRY
opaqueness density, obscuration, opacity
open aleatory (uncertain), apparent (perceptible), available, bare, bona fide, break (separate), candid, commence, conspicuous, denude, direct (forthright), equivocal, establish (launch), evident, explicit, flagrant, generate, honest, impartial, indeterminate, ingenuous, initiate, launch (initiate), liberal (broad minded), liberal (not literal), manifest (adjective), manifest (verb), naive, naked (perceptible), obvious, open-minded, originate, outstanding (unresolved), overt, passable, patent, penetrable, perceivable, perceptible, preface, pullulate, receptive, reveal, scrutable, simple, split, spread, straightforward, suasible, subject (exposed), susceptible (unresistent), unaffected (sincere), unbiased, undecided, unmistakable, unprejudiced, unrestricted, unsettled, vacant, vulnerable. SEE MAIN ENTRY
open a passage admit (give access)
open a path admit (give access)
open a road admit (give access)
open a route admit (give access)
open a trade deal
open act overt act
open again reopen
open an account with deal
open an entryway admit (give access)
open an inlet admit (give access)
open breach feud
open contest competition
open court bench
open declaration avowal, oath
open discussion meeting (conference), panel (discussion group)

open enemy foe
open fire discharge (shoot)
open fire upon attack
open forum panel (discussion group)
open market market place, trade (commerce)
open mart market (business)
open out compound
open position access (opening)
open quarrel feud
open statement of affirmation avouchment
open the mind disabuse
open the way for facilitate
open to disposable
open to all general
open to attack helpless (defenseless)
open to choice disjunctive (alternative), elective (selective)
open to criticism blameful, blameworthy, reprehensible
open to debate debatable, disputable, litigious, polemic
open to discussion controversial, debatable, disputable, forensic, moot, pending (unresolved), polemic, uncertain (questionable)
open to dispute debatable
open to doubt controversial, debatable, disputable, doubtful, implausible, incredible, ludicrous, problematic, suspicious (questionable), unbelievable
open to error undependable
open to objection irregular (improper)
open to proof theoretical
open to question controversial, debatable, disputable, doubtful, dubitative, equivocal, indefinite, indeterminate, litigious, moot, pending (unresolved), polemic, suspicious (questionable), uncertain (questionable)
open to suggestion receptive
open to suggestions amenable
open to suspicion debatable, disputable, doubtful, implausible, incredible, unbelievable
open to the public competitive (open)
open to the vision evident
open to various interpretations ambiguous, uncertain (ambiguous)
open to view apparent (perceptible), evident, expose, perceivable, perceptible, present (introduce)
open up bare, exhibit, liberate, manifest, unveil
open-ended SEE MAIN ENTRY
open-handed philanthropic
open-handedness philanthropy
open-minded dispassionate, impartial, liberal (broad minded), objective, open (persuasible), progressive (advocating change), receptive, suasible, unbiased. SEE MAIN ENTRY
open-mindedness disinterest (lack of prejudice), objectivity
open-mouthed speechless
opened penetrable
openhanded benevolent, charitable (benevolent), donative, liberal (generous)
openhandedness largess (generosity)
openhearted liberal (generous)
opening access (right of way), admission (entry), admittance (means of approach), chance (fortuity), egress, entrance, first appearance, hiatus, inception, initial, loophole, margin (spare amount), occasion, onset (commencement), opportunity,

original *(initial)*, origination, outlet, outset, portal, preamble, preface, preliminary, prelude, preparatory, rift *(gap)*, start. SEE MAIN ENTRY

opening argument   opening statement
opening of negotiations   overture
opening statement   SEE MAIN ENTRY
openly   fairly *(clearly)*
openminded   unprejudiced
openmindedness   fairness
openness   candor *(straightforwardness)*, honesty, latitude
opera   effort, service *(assistance)*
operable   functional, practicable
operant   active, functional
operate   administer *(conduct)*, commit *(perpetrate)*, conduct, control *(regulate)*, employ *(make use of)*, exercise *(use)*, exert, exploit *(make use of)*, function, handle *(manage)*, manage, manipulate *(utilize skillfully)*, militate, ply, transact, wield. SEE MAIN ENTRY
operate jointly   concur *(agree)*
operating   active, in full force
operating company   corporation
operating expenses   overhead
operation   act *(undertaking)*, activity, calling, campaign, commission *(act)*, conduct, course, deal, enterprise *(undertaking)*, instrumentality, management *(judicious use)*, maneuver *(tactic)*, manner *(behavior)*, method, modus operandi, performance *(execution)*, performance *(workmanship)*, practice *(procedure)*, process *(course)*, scheme, system, transaction, undertaking *(enterprise)*, usage. SEE MAIN ENTRY
operational   effective *(operative)*, functional, operative, practical
operational before   retroactive
operative   constructive *(creative)*, functional, ministerial, potent, practical, prevailing *(having superior force)*, procedural, valuable, viable. SEE MAIN ENTRY
operative with respect to the past   nunc pro tunc
operator   actor, artisan, dealer
operire   close *(terminate)*, cover *(pretext)*
operose   difficult, diligent, industrious, oppressive, painstaking. SEE MAIN ENTRY
operosus   painstaking
opes   strength
opiate   cannabis, drug, narcotic *(adjective)*, narcotic *(noun)*
opifex   artisan
opinabilis   hypothetical
opinari   guess, opine
opine   advise, comment, construe *(comprehend)*, counsel, deem, determine, gauge, guess, presume, presuppose, surmise, suspect *(think)*. SEE MAIN ENTRY
opinio   belief *(state of mind)*, character *(reputation)*, conviction *(persuasion)*, expectation, faith, impression, presumption, reputation, supposition
opinio praeiudicata   prejudice *(preconception)*
opinion   adjudication, advice, apprehension *(perception)*, assumption *(supposition)*, award, belief *(state of mind)*, concept, conclusion *(determination)*, conjecture, conviction *(persuasion)*, decree, deduction *(conclusion)*, determination, dictum, estimate *(idea)*, estimation *(calculation)*, finding, guidance, holding *(ruling of a court)*, idea, impression, judgment *(discernment)*, judgment *(formal court decree)*, notion, observation, position *(point of view)*, posture

(attitude), presumption, prognosis, pronouncement, recommendation, regard *(esteem)*, sense *(feeling)*, stand *(position)*, standpoint, supposition, theory. SEE MAIN ENTRY
opinion of the court   finding, ruling
opinion of the jury   verdict
opinionated   dogmatic, illiberal, inexorable, inflexible, narrow, obdurate, parochial, prejudicial, pretentious *(pompous)*, uncontrollable, unyielding
opinionated person   bigot, pedant
opinionative   dogmatic, inexorable, inflexible, obdurate, parochial
opinionativeness   discrimination *(bigotry)*
opinionist   bigot
opitulari   assist
oppidan   civil *(public)*, denizen, resident
oppignerare   pawn
oppignerare   pledge *(promise the performance of)*
oppilate   obstruct, occlude
oppilation   damper *(stopper)*
opponent   adversary, contender, contestant, contradictory, disputant, foe, litigant, plaintiff, rival. SEE MAIN ENTRY
opponent in a lawsuit   litigant
opportune   appropriate, auspicious, convenient, favorable *(advantageous)*, felicitous, fit, fitting, proper, propitious, seasonable, suitable. SEE MAIN ENTRY
opportune moment   opportunity
opportune time   opportunity
opportuneness   expedience, feasibility, timeliness
opportunism   bribery
opportunist   machiavellian
opportunistic   mercenary
opportunities   choice *(alternatives offered)*
opportunity   access *(opening)*, behalf, call *(option)*, day in court, latitude, occasion, option *(choice)*, possibility, privilege. SEE MAIN ENTRY
opportunity to obtain goods on time   credit *(delayed payment)*
opportunus   eligible, opportune, seasonable
oppose   answer *(reply)*, antagonize, argue, block, challenge, collide *(clash)*, compensate *(counterbalance)*, compete, complain *(criticize)*, condemn *(ban)*, conflict, contend *(dispute)*, contest, contradict, contrast, contravene, controvert, counter, counteract, countervail, cross *(disagree with)*, defy, demonstrate *(protest)*, demur, deprecate, differ *(disagree)*, disaccord, disaffirm, disagree, disallow, disapprove *(reject)*, discourage, disobey, disown *(deny the validity)*, dissent *(differ in opinion)*, dissent *(withhold assent)*, engage *(involve)*, except *(object)*, expostulate, fight *(battle)*, fight *(counteract)*, forbid, frustrate, gainsay, grapple, hamper, impugn, negate, object, oppugn, parry, polarize, preclude, prevent, prohibit, proscribe *(prohibit)*, protest, rebel, rebut, refuse, refute, reject, remonstrate, renounce, repel *(drive back)*, repulse, restrain, stem *(check)*, thwart, trammel, withstand. SEE MAIN ENTRY
oppose as false   impugn
oppose by argument   dispute *(contest)*
oppose by contrary proof   countercharge
opposed   adverse *(hostile)*, antipathetic *(oppositional)*, averse, contradictory, contrary, different, discordant, disinclined, disobedient, hostile, inimical, negative,

opposite, reluctant, renitent, repugnant *(incompatible)*, unfavorable
opposed to   contra *(adverb)*, contra *(preposition)*. SEE MAIN ENTRY
opposer   adversary, contender, contestant, disputant, foe, opponent
opposing   antipathetic *(oppositional)*, competitive *(antagonistic)*, contradictory, contrary, contravention, discordant, disobedient, dissenting, dissident, hostile, inimical, litigious, negative, opposite, preventive, recalcitrant, renitent, repugnant *(incompatible)*
opposing causes   conflict
opposing counsel   SEE MAIN ENTRY
opposing litigant   opponent
opposing party   adversary, complainant, contestant, foe, opponent, party *(litigant)*. SEE MAIN ENTRY
opposing suit   counterclaim
opposite   antipathetic *(oppositional)*, antipode, antithesis, contra *(adverb)*, contra *(noun)*, contradictory, contraposition, contrary *(adjective)*, contrary *(noun)*, discordant, hostile, inverse, negative, offset, opponent, pertinent. SEE MAIN ENTRY
opposite camp   foe
opposite evidence   answer *(judicial response)*
opposite extreme   antipode, contradiction
opposite in character   contrary
opposite in nature   contrary
opposite number   peer
opposite pole   antipode, antithesis
opposite side   antipode, contraposition, foe, opponent
opposite to   contra
oppositely   contra
oppositeness   antipode, contradiction, contradistinction, difference, dissent *(difference of opinion)*
opposites   contradiction
opposition   antipode, antithesis, argument *(contention)*, belligerency, check *(bar)*, collision *(dispute)*, competition, condemnation *(blame)*, conflict, confrontation *(altercation)*, contender, contest *(competition)*, contest *(dispute)*, contestant, contradiction, contradistinction, contraposition, contrary, contravention, controversy *(argument)*, counterargument, criticism, defiance, deterrence, deterrent, difference, disaccord, disagreement, disapprobation, disapproval, discord, dispute, dissatisfaction, dissent *(difference of opinion)*, dissent *(nonconcurrence)*, dissidence, division *(act of dividing)*, exception *(objection)*, feud, will, impediment, impugnation, incompatibility *(difference)*, mutiny, negation, objection, offset, opponent, outcry, protest, rebellion, rebuff, rejection, remonstrance, restraint, revolt, rival, strife, struggle, variance *(disagreement)*. SEE MAIN ENTRY
opposition to allegations   demurrer
oppositional   contradictory, contrary, discordant, hostile
oppositionist   adversary, contender, contestant, disputant
oppositive   antipathetic *(oppositional)*, contradictory
opposure   confrontation *(altercation)*, contempt *(disdain)*
oppress   abuse *(victimize)*, badger, bait *(harass)*, brutalize, coerce, constrain *(restrain)*, contemn, discommode, dominate, exploit *(take advantage of)*, harass,

harry *(harass)*, ill use, maltreat, mistreat, overload, persecute, plague, pressure, prey, subdue, subject, tax *(overwork)*

oppressed aggrieved *(victimized)*

oppression adversity, burden, coercion, compulsion *(coercion)*, cruelty, encumbrance, extortion, force *(compulsion)*, grievance, ground, incumbrance *(burden)*, infliction, injustice, molestation, pressure, servitude, thrall, weight *(burden)*. SEE MAIN ENTRY

oppressive bad *(offensive)*, brutal, cruel, detrimental, dictatorial, disastrous, forcible, harsh, malignant, onerous, ponderous, severe, tyrannous. SEE MAIN ENTRY

oppressive act ground

oppressive exaction blackmail, coercion, extortion

oppressive taskmaster dictator

oppressor dictator, hoodlum

opprimere overwhelm, repress, stifle

opprobrious bad *(offensive)*, blameful, blameworthy, calumnious, contemptible, contemptuous, disgraceful, disreputable, heinous, insolent, loathsome, notorious, objectionable, obnoxious, offensive *(offending)*, outrageous, reprehensible, scandalous, scurrilous

opprobrium aspersion

opprobrium attaint, bad repute, blame *(culpability)*, contempt *(disdain)*, contumely, criticism, degradation, denunciation, disapprobation, discredit, disdain, disgrace, dishonor *(shame)*, disrepute, ignominy, infamy, notoriety, obloquy, odium, reproach, revilement, scandal, shame, slander, vilification. SEE MAIN ENTRY

oppugn answer *(reply)*, assail, assault, attack, collide *(clash)*, confront *(oppose)*, contest, contradict, counteract, disaffirm, disagree, disprove, gainsay, hold out *(resist)*, oppose, refute, repulse, resist *(oppose)*. SEE MAIN ENTRY

oppugnance resistance

oppugnancy belligerency, conflict, contest *(dispute)*, contravention, disagreement, impugnation, mutiny, opposition

oppugnant adversary, antipathetic *(oppositional)*, competitive *(antagonistic)*, contrary, discordant, hostile, malevolent, opposite, recalcitrant, recusant

oppugnare assail, attack, impugn

oppugnatio assault

oppugnation belligerency, defiance, opposition, resistance

opt decide, espouse

opt for choose, elect *(choose)*. SEE MAIN ENTRY

optative solicitous

optimal best

optimas prime *(most valuable)*

optimates elite

optimism confidence *(faith)*, faith, longanimity

optimistic sanguine

optimum ceiling, utmost

optimus best, superlative

option choice *(alternatives offered)*, conatus, discretion *(power of choice)*, election *(choice)*, franchise *(right to vote)*, latitude, preference *(choice)*, suffrage, volition, vote. SEE MAIN ENTRY

optional discretionary, disjunctive *(alternative)*, elective *(voluntary)*, extraneous, needless, nonessential, spontaneous, unnecessary, voluntary

optionally SEE MAIN ENTRY

optionality discretion *(power of choice)*

opulence boom *(prosperity)*, prosperity

opulency boom *(prosperity)*

opulent copious. SEE MAIN ENTRY

opulentus opulent

opus enterprise *(undertaking)*, performance *(workmanship)*, product, work *(effort)*

ora edge *(border)*

oracular indefinite, mysterious, omniscient, portentous *(ominous)*, profound *(esoteric)*, prophetic. SEE MAIN ENTRY

oral language, nuncupative, parol, verbal. SEE MAIN ENTRY

oral communication conversation, discourse, parlance, parley, speech. SEE MAIN ENTRY

oral contention argument *(contention)*, fight *(argument)*

oral declaration nuncupative

oral evidence affirmance *(legal affirmation)*, deposition. SEE MAIN ENTRY

oral examination interview

oral expression speech

oral statement under oath deposition

oral testimony nuncupative

orare plead *(implore)*, pray, sue

orate address *(talk to)*, declaim, discourse, recite

oratio language, speech

oration bombast, declamation, diatribe, discourse, peroration, recital, speech.

orationem attribuere personify

orationem facere discourse

orationem habere discourse

oratorical flatulent, inflated *(bombastic)*, nuncupative, orotund

oratorical display declamation, peroration

oratory declamation, parlance, phraseology, rhetoric *(skilled speech)*, speech

orb sphere, zone

orbis circuit

orbit ambit, area *(province)*, bailiwick, capacity *(sphere)*, circuit, province, purview, realm, scope, sphere

orbus orphan

orchestrate compose. SEE MAIN ENTRY

ordain award, bestow, command, constitute *(establish)*, decide, dictate, direct *(order)*, impose *(enforce)*, induct, invest *(vest)*, necessitate, nominate, order, pass *(approve)*, pass *(determine)*, predetermine, prescribe, require *(compel)*

ordain by law enact, pass *(approve)*

ordained entitled, inevitable, mandatory, necessary *(inescapable)*, positive *(prescribed)*, rightful

ordained by custom prescriptive

ordained by legislation legislative

ordaining legislative

ordainment designation *(naming)*, nomination, ordinance, selection *(choice)*

ordeal aggravation *(annoyance)*, burden, infliction, nuisance, pain, trouble

order adjudge, adjudicate, adjudication, agenda, appointment *(act of designating)*, arbitrate *(adjudge)*, arrange *(methodize)*, authority *(documentation)*, award *(noun)*, award *(verb)*, book, buy, call *(demand)*, canon, caveat, chain *(series)*, charge *(command)*, choice *(decision)*, class, classification, coerce, command, compel, constrain *(compel)*, control *(regulate)*, course, decree *(noun)*, decree *(verb)*, delegate, demand *(noun)*, demand *(verb)*, denomination, detail *(assign)*, determination, dictate *(noun)*, dictate *(verb)*, directive, disposition

(determination), disposition *(final arrangement)*, draft, edict, enact, enjoin, exact, fiat, finding, force *(coerce)*, form *(arrangement)*, formation, govern, hierarchy *(arrangement in a series)*, holding *(ruling of a court)*, impose *(enforce)*, injunction, insist, instruct *(direct)*, instruction *(direction)*, judgment *(formal court decree)*, law, legislate, lineup, manage, mandamus, mandate, manner *(kind)*, method, mittimus, modus operandi, monition *(legal summons)*, opinion *(judicial decision)*, orchestrate, ordinance, organization *(structure)*, organize *(arrange)*, peace, pigeonhole, precept, prescribe, prescription *(directive)*, press *(constrain)*, procedure, program, purchase, register, regularity, regulate *(adjust)*, regulate *(manage)*, regulation *(rule)*, request *(noun)*, request *(verb)*, require *(compel)*, requirement, requisition, rule *(guide)*, rule *(legal dictate)*, rule *(govern)*, ruling, scheme, sentence, sequence, society, sodality, sort, statute, subpoena *(noun)*, subpoena *(verb)*, succession, summon, system, uniformity, warrant *(judicial writ)*, writ. SEE MAIN ENTRY

order authorizing a search search warrant

order back recommit, remand

order by law legalize

order for payment draft

order not to do forbid

order of business calendar *(record of yearly periods)*

order of cases calendar *(list of cases)*

order of penalty sentence

order of succession hierarchy *(arrangement in a series)*

order of the court adjudication, award, decree, holding *(ruling of a court)*, ruling, sentence. SEE MAIN ENTRY

order of the day agenda, docket, practice *(custom)*, practice *(procedure)*

order on a bank check *(instrument)*

order to appear subpoena *(noun)*, subpoena *(verb)*, summon, summons

order to appear in court subpoena *(noun)*

order with authority command

ordered decretal, systematic

ordering allotment, array *(order)*, classification, disposition *(final arrangement)*, distribution *(arrangement)*

orderless casual, disjointed, disordered, disorderly, haphazard, indiscriminate, random, slipshod

orderliness decorum, diligence *(care)*, method, peace, regularity, system

orderly meticulous, normal *(regular)*, peaceable, right *(suitable)*, systematic, uniform

orderly arrangement classification, method

orderly arrangement of papers file

orderly combination system

orderly disposition method

ordinance act *(enactment)*, brevet, bylaw, canon, code, codification, dictate, direction *(order)*, directive, edict, enactment, law, precept, prescription *(directive)*, regulation *(rule)*, rubric *(authoritative rule)*, rule *(legal dictate)*, statute, writ. SEE MAIN ENTRY

ordinances legislation *(enactments)*

ordinare arrange *(methodize)*, fix *(arrange)*, organize *(arrange)*

ordinarily as a rule, generally, invariably

ordinariness mediocrity

895

ordinarius regular *(conventional)*

ordinary accustomed *(customary)*, average *(standard)*, common *(customary)*, conventional, customary, daily, familiar *(customary)*, general, habitual, household *(familiar)*, imperfect, informal, jejune *(dull)*, mediocre, mundane, nondescript, normal *(regular)*, orthodox, passable, pedestrian, poor *(inferior in quality)*, prevalent, prosaic, regular *(conventional)*, trite, typical, usual. SEE MAIN ENTRY

ordinary course practice *(custom)*
ordinary judgment common sense
ordinary manner custom
ordinary run norm
ordinary run of things matter of course
ordinary sense common sense
ordinary state matter of course
ordinary wear and tear SEE MAIN ENTRY
ordinate nominate
ordinatio disposition *(final arrangement)*
ordination appointment *(act of designating)*, brevet, citation *(charge)*, classification, dedication, delegation *(assignment)*, designation *(naming)*, dictate, installation, nomination, ordinance, selection *(choice)*
ordo class, degree *(station)*, order *(arrangement)*, regularity, sequence
organ chapter *(branch)*, publication *(printed matter)*. SEE MAIN ENTRY
organic bodily, born *(innate)*, fundamental, native *(inborn)*, natural, physical. SEE MAIN ENTRY
organic law constitution
organic remains corpse
organism entity, individual
organization array *(order)*, association *(connection)*, building *(business of assembling)*, bureaucracy, business *(commercial enterprise)*, campaign, cartel, centralization, chamber *(body)*, citation *(attribution)*, classification, committee, company *(enterprise)*, complex *(development)*, composition *(makeup)*, concern *(business establishment)*, content *(structure)*, corporation, denomination, disposition *(final arrangement)*, distribution *(arrangement)*, facility *(institution)*, firm, form *(arrangement)*, formation, institute, league, method, order *(arrangement)*, practice *(procedure)*, regulation *(management)*, scheme, society, sodality, structure *(composition)*, syndicate, system, union *(labor organization)*. SEE MAIN ENTRY
organization of a commercial concern incorporation *(formation of a business entity)*
organization of a company incorporation *(formation of a business entity)*
organization to aid the needy foundation *(organization)*
organize arrange *(methodize)*, classify, codify, compose, constitute *(establish)*, contrive, coordinate, create, disentangle, establish *(launch)*, fabricate *(construct)*, federalize *(associate)*, federate, file *(arrange)*, fix *(arrange)*, form, frame *(construct)*, frame *(formulate)*, make, marshal, orchestrate, pigeonhole, plan, plot, program, provide *(arrange for)*, regulate *(adjust)*, scheme, sort, tabulate. SEE MAIN ENTRY
organize a corporation incorporate *(form a corporation)*
organized systematic, tactical
organized body federation
organized body for charity foundation *(organization)*

organized group committee, party *(political organization)*, society
organized illegal activity racket
organized knowledge science *(study)*
organized labor union *(labor organization)*
organized observation experiment
organized refusal to work strike
organized society facility *(institution)*
organizer architect, author *(originator)*, chief, developer, promoter
organizer of business enterprises promoter
organizer of commercial enterprises promoter
organizing conception impression
orgiastic gluttonous
orgulous proud *(conceited)*. SEE MAIN ENTRY
orgy debauchery
orient apprise, inform *(notify)*
orientation guidance, perspective, standpoint
origin affiliation *(bloodline)*, ancestry, basis, birth *(beginning)*, bloodline, cause *(reason)*, derivation, descent *(lineage)*, determinant, embryo, family *(common ancestry)*, foundation *(basis)*, genesis, ground, inception, lineage, nascency, nationality, onset *(commencement)*, outset, parentage, paternity, progenitor, reason *(basis)*, source, start. SEE MAIN ENTRY
original authentic, causative, fertile, genuine, incipient, initial, native *(domestic)*, native *(inborn)*, natural, nonconforming, noteworthy, novel, old, organic, paradigm, particular *(individual)*, pattern, peculiar *(distinctive)*, preliminary, primary, primordial, productive, prototype, resourceful, rudimentary, sample, source, true *(authentic)*, underlying, undistorted, unique, unprecedented, unusual. SEE MAIN ENTRY
original meaning connotation
original sum principal *(capital sum)*
original work creation
originality identity *(individuality)*, legitimacy, nonconformity, personality
originally ab initio
originate accrue *(arise)*, build *(construct)*, cause, commence, compose, conceive *(invent)*, conjure, constitute *(establish)*, create, embark, engender, establish *(launch)*, forge *(produce)*, frame *(construct)*, frame *(formulate)*, generate, induce, initiate, inspire, invent *(produce for the first time)*, launch *(initiate)*, legislate, maintain *(commence)*, make, manufacture, produce *(manufacture)*, propagate *(increase)*, provoke, result, stem *(originate)*, unveil. SEE MAIN ENTRY
originate from evolve
originate in emanate
originating causal
origination ancestry, birth *(beginning)*, building *(business of assembling)*, creation, derivation, embryo, formation, genesis, inception, invention, manufacture, nascency, onset *(commencement)*, outset, source, start. SEE MAIN ENTRY
originative causal, causative, constructive *(creative)*, fertile, original *(creative)*, prime *(original)*, productive, rudimentary
originator architect, developer, predecessor. SEE MAIN ENTRY
origo ancestry, lineage, origin *(ancestry)*, origin *(source)*, primogenitor, source
ornament embellish, motif

ornamental aesthetic
ornamentation bombast, motif
ornamented elaborate, pretentious *(ostentatious)*
ornare provide *(supply)*
ornate elaborate, grandiose, meretricious, pretentious *(ostentatious)*
ornatus pretentious *(ostentatious)*
ornery malicious
orotund flatulent, fustian, grandiose, histrionic, turgid. SEE MAIN ENTRY
orotundity bombast, declamation, fustian, histrionics, peroration
orphan SEE MAIN ENTRY
orphaned solitary
orphaned child orphan
orphaned infant orphan
orphic recondite
orthodox conventional, dogmatic, parochial, popular, proper, rigid, strict, traditional, typical, uncompromising, uniform, usual. SEE MAIN ENTRY
orthodoxus orthodox
orthodoxy doctrine, dogma
ortus birth *(beginning)*
os impudens indiscretion
oscillate alternate *(fluctuate)*, beat *(pulsate)*, hesitate, vacillate. SEE MAIN ENTRY
oscillating irresolute, variable
oscillation hesitation, indecision, trepidation
oscitancy inertia, languor
oscitant lifeless *(dull)*, otiose, phlegmatic
osculate contact *(touch)*, juxtapose
osmose penetrate, permeate
osmosis SEE MAIN ENTRY
ossified solid *(compact)*. SEE MAIN ENTRY
ostendere evince, prove, reflect *(mirror)*
ostensibility probability
ostensible apparent *(presumptive)*, circumstantial, colorable *(plausible)*, evident, manifest, naked *(perceptible)*, overt, patent, plausible, probable, purported, putative, specious. SEE MAIN ENTRY
ostensible motive pretext
ostensible purpose pretense *(pretext)*, pretext
ostensible reason excuse, pretense *(pretext)*, pretext
ostensibly prima facie *(self-evident)*
ostent presence *(poise)*
ostentare flaunt
ostentatio pretense *(ostentation)*
ostentation bombast, histrionics, jactation, rodomontade
ostentatious elaborate, grandiose, histrionic, inflated *(bombastic)*, tawdry
ostentatiousness pretense *(ostentation)*
ostentum phenomenon *(unusual occurrence)*
ostium entrance
ostracism banishment, boycott, exclusion, expulsion, ignominy, prohibition, rejection, segregation *(isolation by races)*. SEE MAIN ENTRY
ostracization banishment
ostracize bar *(exclude)*, condemn *(ban)*, defame, denounce *(condemn)*, eliminate *(exclude)*, exclude, expel, ignore, isolate, proscribe *(denounce)*, reject, relegate, renounce, seclude, spurn, transport
other additional, alter ego, ancillary *(auxiliary)*
other choice alternative *(substitute)*
other extreme antipode, antithesis, contradiction, contrary
other half alter ego

other person   alter ego
other self   alter ego
other side   foe, opponent
other than   different
other wordly   immaterial
otherness   contraposition, nonconformity
otherwise   contra. SEE MAIN ENTRY
otherwise called   alias
otherwise known as   alias
otherwise known by   alias
otherwise named   alias
otherwordly   demote
otherworldliness   immateriality
otiose   futile, inactive, indolent, nugatory, passive, redundant, stagnant, torpid, unproductive. SEE MAIN ENTRY
otiosity   sloth
otiosus   idle, unemployed
otium   ease, inaction, peace
oust   deport *(banish)*, depose *(remove)*, disinherit, dislocate, dislodge, dismiss *(discharge)*, disown *(refuse to acknowledge)*, displace *(remove)*, dispossess, divest, eject *(evict)*, eject *(expel)*, eliminate *(exclude)*, evict, exclude, expel, reject, relegate, remove *(dismiss from office)*, supersede, supplant. SEE MAIN ENTRY
oust from office   depose *(remove)*
ouster   deportation, discharge *(dismissal)*, dismissal *(discharge)*, disqualification *(rejection)*, disseisin, eviction, expulsion, layoff, rejection. SEE MAIN ENTRY
ouster by paramount title   eviction
ousting   banishment, defeasance, discharge *(dismissal)*, removal
out of   devoid
out of accord   discordant
out of bounds   excessive, extreme *(exaggerated)*, illicit, impermissible, inordinate, undue *(excessive)*. SEE MAIN ENTRY
out of cash   poor *(underprivileged)*
out of character   inappropriate, inapt, incongruous, inept *(inappropriate)*, undesirable, unseemly, unsuitable
out of circulation   rare
out of control   uncontrollable, uncurbed, unruly
out of danger   safe
out of debt   solvent
out of employment   unemployed
out of fashion   defunct, outmoded
out of favor   blameful, repugnant *(exciting aversion)*
out of focus   indistinct, nebulous, unclear
out of funds   bankrupt, insolvent
out of hand   uncurbed
out of humor   petulant
out of joint   disproportionate
out of keeping   anomalous, disproportionate, inapplicable, inappropriate, inapt, incommensurate, incongruous, inept *(inappropriate)*, unbecoming, undesirable, unfit, unsuitable, untimely
out of limits   inordinate
out of line   nonconforming
out of money   bankrupt, destitute, impecunious, insolvent, poor *(underprivileged)*
out of one's bearings   astray
out of one's mind   lunatic, non compos mentis
out of one's reckoning   astray
out of one's senses   lunatic, non compos mentis
out of one's wits   non compos mentis
out of order   anomalous, defective, deviant, disjointed, disordered, disorderly, faulty, imperfect, irregular *(not usual)*, irrel-

evant. SEE MAIN ENTRY
out of place   disordered, disproportionate, immaterial, impertinent *(irrelevant)*, improper, inapplicable, inappropriate, inapt, incongruous, inept *(inappropriate)*, irregular *(improper)*, irregular *(not usual)*, irrelevant, peculiar *(curious)*, unbecoming, unfit, unseemly, unsuitable, untimely
out of pocket   SEE MAIN ENTRY
out of pocket expenses   SEE MAIN ENTRY
out of proportion   disparate, disproportionate, extreme *(exaggerated)*, inapt, incommensurate, inept *(inappropriate)*
out of reach   difficult, inaccessible, infeasible, insuperable, insurmountable, unapproachable, unattainable
out of sight   covert, hidden, inconspicuous, lost *(taken away)*
out of sorts   petulant
out of step   deviant, nonconforming, unorthodox
out of the common run   eccentric, prodigious *(amazing)*
out of the ordinary   anomalous, different, distinct *(distinguished from others)*, eccentric, extraordinary, irregular *(not usual)*, noteworthy, original *(creative)*, peculiar *(curious)*, peculiar *(distinctive)*, portentous *(eliciting amazement)*, prodigious *(amazing)*, rare, singular, specific, unaccustomed, unusual
out of the question   impossible, impracticable, ineligible, infeasible, insuperable, insurmountable, unattainable
out of the regular order   extraordinary
out of the way   circuitous, indirect, irrelevant, peculiar *(curious)*, remote *(secluded)*, scarce, uncommon
out of touch   inaccessible
out of use   obsolete, outmoded
out of view   blind *(concealed)*, hidden
out of work   unemployed
out-and-out   outright
out-of-date   obsolete, outdated, outmoded
out-of-fashion   outdated
out-of-sorts   restive
out-of-the-way   immaterial, private *(secluded)*, unapproachable
out-of-use   outdated
outbalance   countervail, outweigh. SEE MAIN ENTRY
outbreak   bluster *(commotion)*, brawl, embroilment, fracas, furor, inception, insurrection, mutiny, onset *(commencement)*, outburst, outset, rebellion, revolt, revolution, riot, start, strife, threshold *(commencement)*. SEE MAIN ENTRY
outburst   bluster *(commotion)*, furor, outbreak, outflow, riot, spate, strife, violence. SEE MAIN ENTRY
outcast   derelict *(abandoned)*, derelict, ineligible, notorious, pariah, undesirable
outclass   beat *(defeat)*, surpass
outcome   amount *(result)*, answer *(solution)*, cessation *(termination)*, choice *(decision)*, conclusion *(outcome)*, consequence *(conclusion)*, corollary, denouement, development *(outgrowth)*, effect, end *(termination)*, finding, holding *(ruling of a court)*, issuance, output, product, result. SEE MAIN ENTRY
outcry   disparagement, exception *(objection)*, expletive, noise, pandemonium, panic, plaint, protest. SEE MAIN ENTRY
outdated   obsolete, outmoded. SEE MAIN ENTRY

outdistance   transcend
outdo   beat *(defeat)*, outbalance, outweigh, overcome *(surmount)*, surmount, surpass, transcend
outer   peripheral
outer boundary   periphery
outer district   frontier
outer edge   edge *(border)*, extremity *(furthest point)*, frontier, limit
outer edges   confines
outer limit   ambit
outer line   limit
outer part   frontier, periphery
outer point   limit
outermost   extreme *(last)*, last *(final)*, peripheral
outface   defy, oppugn, parry
outfit   assemblage, band, clothe, furnish, supply
outfitter   materialman
outflank   beat *(defeat)*
outflow   issuance. SEE MAIN ENTRY
outgo   cost *(expenses)*, disbursement *(act of disbursing)*, disbursement *(funds paid out)*, expenditure, expense *(cost)*, issuance, outlay
outgrowth   amount *(result)*, boom *(prosperity)*, conclusion *(outcome)*, consequence *(conclusion)*, corollary, denouement, effect, offshoot, outcome, result. SEE MAIN ENTRY
outgush   outflow
outland   peripheral
outlander   alien
outlandish   eccentric, ludicrous, peculiar *(curious)*, prodigious *(amazing)*, unaccustomed, unusual
outlandishness   quirk *(idiosyncrasy)*
outlast   endure *(last)*, persevere, persist, remain *(continue)*, subsist
outlaw   ban, bar *(exclude)*, condemn *(ban)*, convict, criminal, debar, deport *(banish)*, disfranchise, eliminate *(exclude)*, exclude, expatriate, expel, felon, foe, forbid, hoodlum, isolate, lawless, malefactor, pariah, proscribe *(denounce)*, proscribe *(prohibit)*, recidivist, relegate, seclude, thief, wrongdoer. SEE MAIN ENTRY
outlawed   felonious, illegal, illegitimate *(illegal)*, illicit, impermissible, unlawful
outlawing   expulsion
outlawry   banishment, criminality, lynch law, prohibition
outlay   bear the expense, charge *(cost)*, cost *(expenses)*, disburse *(pay out)*, disbursement *(act of disbursing)*, disbursement *(funds paid out)*, expenditure, expense *(cost)*, invest *(fund)*, investment, maintenance *(upkeep)*, overhead, payment *(act of paying)*, price, spend. SEE MAIN ENTRY
outlet   catharsis, egress, issuance, loophole, market *(demand)*, store *(business)*. SEE MAIN ENTRY
outline   ambit, arrangement *(plan)*, blueprint, border, border *(bound)*, boundary, brief, capsule, characterize, circumscribe *(define)*, circumscribe *(surround by boundary)*, compendium, complexion, condense, configuration *(confines)*, configuration *(form)*, construe *(translate)*, delineate, delineation, demarcate, depict, describe, description, design *(construction plan)*, digest, digest *(summarize)*, dimension, direction *(course)*, edge *(border)*, form *(arrangement)*, hedge, inform *(notify)*, mete, mode, pandect *(treatise)*, pattern, periphery, plan, plot, portray, practice *(procedure)*, program *(noun)*, program *(verb)*,

project, prospectus, render *(depict)*, report *(disclose)*, represent *(portray)*, scenario, schedule, scheme, suggestion, summary, synopsis. SEE MAIN ENTRY

outline on the law   brief

outlined   compact *(pithy)*

outlined before hand   intentional

outlined beforehand   deliberate, express, premeditated

outlines   confines, frontier

outlive   endure *(last)*, last, remain *(continue)*, subsist

outlook   conviction *(persuasion)*, opinion *(belief)*, perspective, platform, position *(point of view)*, posture *(attitude)*, side, stand *(position)*, standpoint. SEE MAIN ENTRY

outlying   peripheral, provincial

outlying area   frontier

outlying borders   frontier

outlying districts   frontier

outmaneuver   beat *(defeat)*, circumvent, dupe, elude, ensnare, illude, pettifog, surmount, surpass, thwart

outmatch   surpass

outmode   succeed *(follow)*

outmoded   obsolete, outdated. SEE MAIN ENTRY

outmost   peripheral

outnumber   surpass

outplay   beat *(defeat)*, surpass

outpoint   beat *(defeat)*, outbalance

outpost   border, frontier, periphery

outpour   issuance, outburst, outflow. SEE MAIN ENTRY

outpouring   boom *(prosperity)*

output   product, profit, result. SEE MAIN ENTRY

outrage   abuse *(physical misuse)*, bait *(harass)*, cruelty, defilement, delinquency *(misconduct)*, dishonor *(shame)*, disregard *(lack of respect)*, disservice, disturb, flout, ground, harass, harrow, mischief, misdoing, offend *(insult)*, offense, persecute, perturb, vice, wrong. SEE MAIN ENTRY

outraged   resentful

outrageous   arrant *(onerous)*, deplorable, diabolic, disgraceful, disorderly, drastic, egregious, excessive, exorbitant, extreme *(exaggerated)*, flagrant, gross *(flagrant)*, heinous, inept *(inappropriate)*, inexcusable, inordinate, insolent, irrational, nefarious, notorious, offensive *(offending)*, presumptuous, scandalous, unconscionable, undue *(excessive)*, unwarranted. SEE MAIN ENTRY

outrageous act   misdeed

outrageousness   exaggeration

outrange   beat *(defeat)*

outrank   outweigh, predominate *(outnumber)*, surpass, transcend

outre   egregious

outreach   circumvent

outright   candid, stark, total, unequivocal, unqualified *(unlimited)*, wholly. SEE MAIN ENTRY

outrival   beat *(defeat)*, outbalance, outweigh, overcome *(surmount)*, predominate *(outnumber)*, surmount, surpass, transcend

outrivalry   competition

outrun   surpass. SEE MAIN ENTRY

outset   genesis, inception, nascency, onset *(commencement)*, origination, prelude, start. SEE MAIN ENTRY

outshine   overcome *(surmount)*, surpass, transcend

outside   alien *(foreign)*, alien *(unrelated)*, border, contour *(outline)*, exempt, extremity

(furthest point), extrinsic, foreign, peripheral, periphery

outside surface   periphery

outside the law   felonious, illegal, illegitimate *(illegal)*, illicit, impermissible

outside the question   immaterial

outsider   alien, pariah, stranger

outskirt   margin *(outside limit)*, penumbra

outskirts   border, edge *(border)*, frontier, periphery, vicinity

outsmart   dupe, overreach

outsourcing   SEE MAIN ENTRY

outspoken   brazen, candid, clear *(apparent)*, direct *(forthright)*, explicit, express, honest, ingenuous, parol, straightforward, unaffected *(sincere)*

outspokenness   candor *(straightforwardness)*

outspread   broad, deploy, expand, spread

outstanding   best, blatant *(conspicuous)*, critical *(crucial)*, delinquent *(overdue)*, due *(owed)*, extraordinary, famous, flagrant, important *(significant)*, infrequent, leading *(ranking first)*, major, master, momentous, notable, noteworthy, open *(in sight)*, overdue, particular *(specific)*, past due, payable, portentous *(eliciting amazement)*, preferential, principal, prominent, receivable, remarkable, renowned, residuary, salient, special, stellar, uncommon, unpaid, unsettled, unusual. SEE MAIN ENTRY

outstanding debt   arrears, bad debt, cloud *(incumbrance)*, delinquency *(shortage)*, due, nonpayment, obligation *(liability)*

outstanding feature   emphasis, gist *(ground for a suit)*, highlight, main point

outstanding item   feature *(special attraction)*

outstanding property   feature *(characteristic)*

outstanding quality   importance

outstream   outflow

outstretch   expand

outstretched   broad

outstrip   outbalance, overcome *(surmount)*, predominate *(outnumber)*, surpass, transcend

outvie   outbalance, surpass, transcend

outward   ostensible, specious, superficial

outward act   overt act

outward appearance   color *(deceptive appearance)*, complexion, feature *(appearance)*

outward flow   outflow

outward form   configuration *(form)*, formality, semblance

outward look   appearance *(look)*

outward perception   impression

outward show   appearance *(look)*, presence *(poise)*, pretense *(ostentation)*

outward sweep   outflow

outwardly seem   assume *(simulate)*

outweigh   convince, nullify, outbalance, override, predominate *(outnumber)*, surpass, transcend. SEE MAIN ENTRY

outweighing   preponderance

outwit   betray *(lead astray)*, circumvent, defeat, dupe, elude, ensnare, evade *(deceive)*, frustrate, hoodwink, illude, overreach

outwitting   fraud

outworn   obsolete, outdated, outmoded

ovation   respect

over   complete *(ended)*, de novo

over again   anew, de novo. SEE MAIN ENTRY

over against   contra

over all   throughout *(all over)*

over and above   a fortiori, also

over pass   traverse

over-all   complete *(all-embracing)*

over-coloring   distortion

over-harsh   brutal

overabound   overload

overabounding   profuse

overabundance   overage, plethora, surfeit, surplus

overabundant   excess, needless, rampant

overact   overreach

overacted   histrionic

overacting   histrionics

overage   surplus. SEE MAIN ENTRY

overall   comprehensive, omnibus. SEE MAIN ENTRY

overall theme   motif

overanxiety   apprehension *(fear)*

overanxious   diffident

overapprehensive   diffident

overassess   overestimate

overassessment   exaggeration, surcharge

overawe   browbeat, deter, intimidate

overbalance   outbalance, outweigh

overbear   beat *(defeat)*, browbeat, repress, subdue, subjugate

overbearing   brutal, dictatorial, disdainful, dogmatic, inflated *(vain)*, insolent, onerous, oppressive, orgulous, peremptory *(absolute)*, presumptuous, proud *(conceited)*, severe, supercilious, tyrannous

overbid   beat *(defeat)*

overblown   inflated *(bombastic)*

overboard   extreme *(exaggerated)*

overboldness   audacity

overburden   disadvantage, exploit *(take advantage of)*, harass, impact, mishandle *(maltreat)*, mistreat, overload, persecute, surcharge

overcalculate   overestimate

overcareful   meticulous

overcast   obnubilate, obscure

overcaution   hesitation

overcautious   careful

overcharge   exploitation, overdraw, premium *(excess value)*, surcharge, usury

overcharged   disproportionate, inordinate

overcloud   blind *(obscure)*, obnubilate, obscure

overcoloring   caricature

overcome   attach *(seize)*, beat *(defeat)*, carry away, defeat, disconsolate, drunk, hijack, impose *(subject)*, outbalance, override, overturn, overwhelm, prevail *(triumph)*, repress, subdue, subject, subjugate, suppress, surmount. SEE MAIN ENTRY

overcome another's resistence   prevail upon

overcome by argument   convince, impugn

overcome by liquor   drunk

overcoming   prevailing *(having superior force)*

overcommit   overextend

overconfidence   temerity

overconfident   precipitate, presumptuous, reckless

overconscientious   particular *(exacting)*

overcount   overestimate

overcritical   critical *(faultfinding)*, nonconsenting, particular *(exacting)*, querulous

overcriticalness   disparagement

overcrowd   impact

overdaring   audacity

overdevelop   overextend

overdo distort, overestimate, over-indulge, overload, overreach

overdone extreme (*exaggerated*), outrageous

overdose overload, surfeit

overdraft deficit

overdramatize distort

overdramatized pretentious (*pompous*)

overdraw dissipate (*expend foolishly*). SEE MAIN ENTRY

overdrawing caricature

overdrawn inflated (*overestimated*), past due

overdrive harass, ill use

overdue back (*in arrears*), dilatory, late (*tardy*), outstanding (*unpaid*), past due. SEE MAIN ENTRY

overdue bill arrears

overdue payment arrears, due

overeat overindulge

overemotional fanatical, sensitive (*easily affected*)

overemphasis exaggeration, histrionics, hyperbole

overenlargement hyperbole

overenthusiasm exaggeration

overenthusiastic fanatical

overestimate magnify. SEE MAIN ENTRY

overestimation caricature, overstatement

overexercise tax (*overwork*)

overexert overload, tax (*overwork*)

overexertion stress (*strain*)

overexpand overextend

overextend overdraw, overreach. SEE MAIN ENTRY

overfamiliar presumptuous

overfastidious particular (*exacting*)

overfatigue tax (*overwork*)

overfeed overload

overfill overload

overflood inundate

overflow balance (*amount in excess*), cataclysm, inundate, outflow, overage, plethora, surfeit, surplus

overflowing cataclysm, copious, demonstrative (*expressive of emotion*), excess, excessive, full, inordinate, profuse, replete, superfluous

overfullness surfeit

overgenerous profuse

overgorge overindulge

overgratify overindulge

overgrow overlap

overhang overlap, project (*extend beyond*)

overhanging imminent, pending (*imminent*)

overhasty careless, imprudent, premature, reckless

overhaul check (*inspect*), fix (*repair*), modify (*alter*), remedy, renew (*refurbish*), repair (*noun*), repair (*verb*), reparation (*keeping in repair*), revise, scrutinize

overhauled renascent

overhauling reorganization, revision (*process of correcting*)

overhead cost (*expenses*), expense (*cost*), maintenance (*upkeep*). SEE MAIN ENTRY

overhear eavesdrop. SEE MAIN ENTRY

overheat burn

overindulge carouse

overindulgence greed. SEE MAIN ENTRY

overjoyed ecstatic

overjudge overestimate

overlap contact (*touch*), encroachment. SEE MAIN ENTRY

overlaud overestimate

overlay overcome (*overwhelm*), overlap

overlie overlap

overload disadvantage, impact, overcome (*overwhelm*), plethora, surcharge, surfeit, tax (*overwork*). SEE MAIN ENTRY

overlook administer (*conduct*), check (*inspect*), condone, contemn, control (*regulate*), disregard, exclude, excuse, forgive, ignore, misprize, monitor, neglect, palliate (*excuse*), pardon, patrol, peruse, police, preside, pretermit, remit (*release from penalty*), review, superintend, survey (*examine*). SEE MAIN ENTRY

overlook an offense condone

overlooker chief, custodian (*protector*), principal (*director*)

overlooking condonation, disregard (*unconcern*), oblivious, oversight (*control*)

overly unduly

overly bold presumptuous

overly confident presumptuous

overly decorated pretentious (*ostentatious*)

overly hasty precipitate

overly liberal profligate (*extravagant*)

overly passionate perfervid

overly trustful credulous

overmaster beat (*defeat*), defeat, overthrow, repress, subject

overmastering abduction

overmatch beat (*defeat*), outbalance, overcome (*surmount*)

overmeasure balance (*amount in excess*), overage, overestimate, surplus

overmeticulous particular (*exacting*)

overmuch disproportionate, excess, excessive, exorbitant, inordinate, needless, redundant, superfluous, undue (*excessive*), unnecessary, unwarranted

overpass overstep, surmount, transcend

overplentiful needless

overplus balance (*amount in excess*), expendable, overage, plethora, redundancy, remainder (*remaining part*), surplus

overpoise outweigh

overpower beat (*defeat*), carry away, check (*restrain*), defeat, force (*coerce*), hijack, obsess, outweigh, overcome (*overwhelm*), overcome (*surmount*), override, overthrow, overturn, overwhelm, repress, subdue, subjugate, supplant, suppress, surmount, upset. SEE MAIN ENTRY

overpowered with emotion ecstatic

overpowering compelling, formidable, in full force, indomitable, invincible, irresistible, moving (*evoking emotion*), onerous, oppressive, powerful, predominant, severe, strong

overpowering fright panic

overpraise doxology, exaggeration, overestimate

overpraised inflated (*overestimated*)

overpriced inflated (*overestimated*)

overprize magnify, overestimate

overprized inflated (*overestimated*)

overproud inflated (*vain*), orgulous

overrate magnify, overestimate

overrated inflated (*overestimated*)

overreach betray (*lead astray*), impose (*intrude*). SEE MAIN ENTRY

override abolish, abrogate (*rescind*), beat (*defeat*), browbeat, cancel, foil, frustrate, insist, invalidate, negate, nullify, overlap, overrule, preclude, predominate (*command*), prevent, repeal, repudiate, rescind, revoke, supersede, thwart. SEE MAIN ENTRY

overriding compelling, primary, reversal

overrule abolish, abrogate (*rescind*), annul, cancel, disaffirm, disown (*deny the validity*), dominate, invalidate, negate, nullify, override, predominate (*command*), prevent, quash, reject, repeal, repudiate, rescind, subjugate, supersede, vacate (*void*), withdraw. SEE MAIN ENTRY

overruled null (*invalid*), null and void

overruling cancellation, cardinal (*basic*), compelling, considerable, critical (*crucial*), predominant, prevailing (*having superior force*), primary, rejection, rescision, reversal

overrun balance (*amount in excess*), despoil, harass, impinge, incursion, invade, overlap, overstep, overthrow, overwhelm, permeate, spread, surplus, trespass

overrunning cataclysm, intrusion

oversee administer (*conduct*), censor, check (*inspect*), conduct, control (*regulate*), direct (*supervise*), discipline (*control*), govern, maintain (*sustain*), manage, moderate (*preside over*), monitor, officiate, operate, overlook (*superintend*), police, predominate (*command*), preside, regulate (*manage*), rule (*govern*), superintend, survey (*examine*). SEE MAIN ENTRY

overseer administrator, caretaker (*one caring for property*), caretaker (*one fulfilling the function of office*), chairman, chief, custodian (*protector*), director, employer, guardian, official, principal (*director*), procurator, superintendent, warden

oversensitive hot-blooded

overset overthrow, overturn, prostration, subversion, subvert

overshadow minimize, obfuscate, obnubilate, obscure, outweigh, overcome (*surmount*), predominate (*command*), shroud, surpass, transcend. SEE MAIN ENTRY

overshadowing critical (*crucial*), dominant, important (*significant*), obscuration

overshoot overreach

overshy diffident

oversight administration, auspices, control (*supervision*), delinquency (*failure of duty*), direction (*guidance*), disregard (*unconcern*), error, failure (*falling short*), fault (*mistake*), inconsideration, laxity, management (*supervision*), miscue, neglect, negligence, nonpayment, omission, protection, supervision, surveillance. SEE MAIN ENTRY

overspend dissipate (*expend foolishly*), overdraw

overspread diffuse, dissipate (*spread out*), inundate, overlap, penetrate, permeate, pervade, radiate, spread

overstate distort, magnify, misrepresent, overestimate, slant

overstated extreme (*exaggerated*), inflated (*overestimated*)

overstatement bombast, distortion, exaggeration, hyperbole, misrepresentation. SEE MAIN ENTRY

overstep accroach, encroach, impinge, impose (*intrude*), infringe, transcend, trespass. SEE MAIN ENTRY

overstep boundaries impinge

overstepping encroachment, incursion, infraction, invasion, malfeasance

overstrain dissipate (*expend foolishly*), harass, overdraw, overload, tax (*overwork*)

overstress magnify

overstressed inflated (*overestimated*)

overstretch overdraw

overstuff overload

oversufficient needless

oversupply balance *(amount in excess)*, overage, plethora, redundancy, surfeit, surplus

oversweet nectarious

overt apparent *(perceptible)*, blatant *(conspicuous)*, candid, clear *(apparent)*, comprehensible, conspicuous, evident, lucid, manifest, naked *(perceptible)*, obvious, open *(in sight)*, ostensible, palpable, patent, pellucid, perceivable, perceptible, public *(known)*, salient, scrutable, unmistakable. SEE MAIN ENTRY

overt act SEE MAIN ENTRY

overtake beat *(defeat)*, invade, reach

overtask exploit *(take advantage of)*, mistreat, overload

overtax exploit *(take advantage of)*, harass, misemploy, mistreat, overcome *(overwhelm)*, overload, persecute

overtaxing onerous

overthrow beat *(defeat)*, commotion, debacle, defeat *(noun)*, defeat *(verb)*, destroy *(efface)*, dislodge, dissolution *(termination)*, eliminate *(eradicate)*, insurrection, invalidate, kill *(defeat)*, miscarriage, negate, overcome *(surmount)*, overturn, overwhelm, plunder, prostration, quash, rebel, rebellion, refute, repulse, rescision, revolt, revolution, sedition, subject, subjugate, subversion, subvert, supplant, suppress, surmount, upset. SEE MAIN ENTRY

overthrow of authority outbreak, revolution

overthrowing reversal

overtire exhaust *(deplete)*, tax *(overwork)*

overtone implication *(inference)*, innuendo, intimation, suggestion

overtop outbalance, outweigh, predominate *(outnumber)*, transcend

overtrump beat *(defeat)*

overtrustfulness credulity

overture bid, invitation, preface, prelude, proposal *(suggestion)*, proposition, threshold *(commencement)*. SEE MAIN ENTRY

overturn abolish, debacle, destroy *(efface)*, disaffirm, disorient, disrupt, disturb, extirpate, kill *(defeat)*, nullify, override, overrule, overthrow, prostration, quash, rebellion, revolt, subversion, subvert, surmount, upset, vitiate. SEE MAIN ENTRY

overturn of authority revolution

overturn of government revolution

overturning havoc

overuse exploit *(take advantage of)*, overload, tax *(overwork)*

overused trite

overvaluation exaggeration

overvalue magnify, overestimate

overvalued inflated *(overestimated)*

overview inquiry *(systematic investigation)*. SEE MAIN ENTRY

overweening disdainful, inflated *(vain)*, orgulous, presumptuous, proud *(conceited)*, supercilious

overweigh convince, outbalance, outweigh, overload

overweight ponderous

overwelm quash

overwhelm beat *(defeat)*, controvert, defeat, devastate, force *(coerce)*, hijack, immerse *(engross)*, inundate, overload, overthrow, overturn, subdue, subjugate, suppress, upset. SEE MAIN ENTRY

overwhelming compelling, formidable, indomitable, ineffable, invincible, irresistible, lurid, moving *(evoking emotion)*, omnipotent, oppressive, powerful, prodigious

(amazing), remarkable, resounding, strong. SEE MAIN ENTRY

overwhelming part bulk

overwork exploit *(take advantage of)*, harass, misemploy, mistreat, overload, persecute

overwrought demonstrative *(expressive of emotion)*, frenetic

overzealous extreme *(exaggerated)*, fanatical

owe overdraw. SEE MAIN ENTRY

owe money overdraw

owed delinquent *(overdue)*, receivable

owing accountable *(responsible)*, delinquent *(overdue)*, due *(owed)*, indebted, outstanding *(unpaid)*, payable, receivable, unpaid, unsettled

owing nothing solvent

own hold *(possess)*, occupy *(take possession)*, particular *(individual)*, personal *(individual)*, possess, profess *(avow)*, recognize *(acknowledge)*, remain *(occupy)*. SEE MAIN ENTRY

own exclusively monopolize

own up betray *(disclose)*, confess

owned jointly common *(shared)*

owner employer, holder, lessor, principal *(director)*, proprietor, shareholder, tenant. SEE MAIN ENTRY

owner of an estate in land landholder, landlord, landowner

owner of land landowner

owner of lands landlord

owner of real estate landowner

owner of real property landowner

owner of tenements landlord

owner of the fee landholder, landowner

owner of the fee simple absolute landholder

owner's mark brand

owner's sign brand

ownership adverse possession, claim *(right)*, dominion *(absolute ownership)*, enjoyment *(use)*, occupancy, occupation *(possession)*, property *(possessions)*, right *(entitlement)*, seisin, stake *(interest)*, substance *(material possessions)*, tenancy, title *(right)*. SEE MAIN ENTRY

P

pace patrol, perambulate, rate, step

pace off measure

pacem conciliare mediate

pacesetter pioneer

pachydermatous impervious, insusceptible *(uncaring)*

pacifiable placable

pacific harmonious, neutral, patient, peaceable, placid

pacificate mollify, pacify, placate, propitiate, soothe

pacification conciliation, expiation, mollification, peace, reconciliation

pacificatory nonmilitant, peaceable

pacifier go-between

pacifistic neutral, nonmilitant, peaceable

pacify allay, alleviate, assuage, disarm *(set at ease)*, ease, lull, moderate *(temper)*, mollify, palliate, placate, propitiate, reconcile, redress, soothe. SEE MAIN ENTRY

pacifying palliative *(abating)*

pacisci agree *(contract)*, close *(agree)*, covenant

pack assemblage, band, cargo, impact, load, overload, quantity

pack away hoard

pack close impact

pack in impact

pack tightly constrict *(compress)*

pack together impact

package bargaining collective bargaining

packages cargo, freight

packed compact *(dense)*, full, pithy, populous, replete, solid *(compact)*

packed together solid *(compact)*

packed with meaning sententious

packet assemblage

packman dealer

packwoman dealer

pact accordance *(compact)*, adjustment, agree *(contract)*, agreement *(contract)*, arrangement *(understanding)*, assurance, bargain, cartel, compact, condition *(contingent provision)*, contract, covenant, deal, guaranty, indenture, league, mutual understanding, obligation *(duty)*, peace, policy *(contract)*, promise, protocol *(agreement)*, settlement, specialty *(contract)*, stipulation, treaty, understanding *(agreement)*. SEE MAIN ENTRY

pact before marriage antenuptial agreement

pactio bargain, compact, covenant, pact, treaty

paction assurance, contract, pact, promise

pactum compact, confederacy *(compact)*, contract, covenant, indenture, league, pact, settlement, stipulation

pad inflate

padded profuse, prolix

padlock handcuff, lock

paean doxology

paedeutic disciplinary *(educational)*

paenitendus regrettable

paenitens repentant

paenitet contrite

page call *(summon)*

paid mercenary

pain aggravate *(annoy)*, annoy, distress *(anguish)*, distress, irritate, nuisance, offend *(insult)*, perturb, pique, plague. SEE MAIN ENTRY

pain and suffering SEE MAIN ENTRY

pain reliever narcotic

pain-killing narcotic

pained aggrieved *(harmed)*, disconsolate, resentful

painful cruel, insufferable, lamentable, loathsome, oppressive, pernicious, repugnant *(exciting aversion)*, severe. SEE MAIN ENTRY

painkiller drug, narcotic

painless innocuous

pains burden, effort, endeavor, labor *(exertion)*, struggle

painstaking careful, circumspect, conscientious, difficult, diligence *(care)*, diligent, elaborate, faithful *(diligent)*, industrious, meticulous, operose, particular *(exacting)*, pertinacious, precise, sedulous, thorough. SEE MAIN ENTRY

paint delineate, describe, portray

paint a picture delineate

pair connect *(join together)*, join *(bring together)*

pair with combine *(act in concert)*, commingle

paired attached *(annexed)*, concurrent *(united)*, conjoint, conjugal, correlative

palatable popular, sapid, savory. SEE MAIN ENTRY

palatial elaborate

palaver confer *(consult)*, conference, council *(assembly)*, speak, speech. SEE MAIN ENTRY

pale ambit, border, capacity *(sphere)*, circuit, district, locality, nebulous, obscure *(faint)*, outline *(boundary)*, periphery, sphere. SEE MAIN ENTRY

paleness indistinctness

palingenesis reconversion, revival

palinode retraction

pall veil

palladian omniscient

palladium bulwark, protection, safeguard, security *(safety)*

palliate abate *(lessen)*, allay, alleviate, ameliorate, assuage, commute, condone, cure, drug, extenuate, forgive, justify, lessen, lull, meliorate, mitigate, moderate *(temper)*, mollify, obtund, redress, relieve *(give aid)*, remedy, remit *(relax)*, soothe. SEE MAIN ENTRY

palliation abatement *(reduction)*, extenuating circumstances, justification, mitigation, moderation, mollification, relief *(release)*, solace

palliative cure, drug, medicinal, mitigating, narcotic *(adjective)*, narcotic *(noun)*, panacea, remedial, remedy *(that which corrects)*, salutary. SEE MAIN ENTRY

palliative circumstances extenuating circumstances

palm off foist

palm off fraudulently foist

palming prestidigitation

palmy prosperous

palmy days prosperity

palpability density, materiality *(physical existence)*

palpable actual, apparent *(perceptible)*, appreciable, arrant *(definite)*, bodily, coherent *(clear)*, comprehensible, concrete, corporal, corporeal, distinct *(clear)*, evident, lucid, manifest, material *(physical)*, obvious, overt, pellucid, perceivable, perceptible, physical, ponderable, sensible, substantive, tangible, unmistakable. SEE MAIN ENTRY

palpable episode fact

palpably fairly *(clearly)*

palpably false unbelievable

palpitate beat *(pulsate)*

palsied powerless

palter equivocate, evade *(deceive)*, fabricate *(make up)*, feign, haggle, lie *(falsify)*, misrepresent, perjure, pettifog, prevaricate. SEE MAIN ENTRY

palter with the truth distort

paltriness immateriality, inconsequence, insignificance

paltry de minimus, deficient, frivolous, inappreciable, inconsequential, inconsiderable, inferior *(lower in quality)*, insubstantial, insufficient, minimal, minor, negligible, nonsubstantial *(not sufficient)*, nugatory, null *(insignificant)*, petty, poor *(inferior in quality)*, scarce, slight, tenuous. SEE MAIN ENTRY

paltry few minority *(outnumbered group)*

pamper pander

pamper excessively overindulge

pampering indulgence, lenience, lenient

panacea cure. SEE MAIN ENTRY

panache pretense *(ostentation)*

pandect abstract, capsule, compendium, constitution, digest, hornbook, outline *(synopsis)*, summary. SEE MAIN ENTRY

pandemic general, omnibus, predominant, prevailing *(current)*, prevalent, rife. SEE MAIN ENTRY

pandemonium bluster *(commotion)*, brawl, commotion, confusion *(turmoil)*, disorder *(lack of order)*, embroilment, furor,

noise, outcry, panic, riot, shambles, turmoil. SEE MAIN ENTRY

pander SEE MAIN ENTRY

panegyric mention *(tribute)*

panegyrical favorable *(expressing approval)*

panel array *(jury)*, band, chamber *(body)*, jury, meeting *(conference)*. SEE MAIN ENTRY

panel of judges bench, chamber *(body)*, forum *(court)*, tribunal

pang pain

pangs of conscience remorse

panhandler parasite

panic fear, fright, frighten, pandemonium, phobia, trepidation. SEE MAIN ENTRY

panoplied armed, safe

panoply ammunition, protection. SEE MAIN ENTRY

panorama scene

panoramic comprehensive

pansophic learned, omniscient

pansophical omniscient

pantomine mock *(imitate)*

panurgic practiced

paper blank *(form)*, certificate, document, instrument *(document)*, pandect *(treatise)*

paper credit letter of credit

paper money check *(instrument)*, currency, debenture

papers credentials, data, dossier

paphian lascivious, salacious

par peer, similar

par worth. SEE MAIN ENTRY

paraclete advocate *(counselor)*

parade demonstrate *(protest)*, display, flaunt, histrionics, lineup, pretense *(ostentation)*, produce *(offer to view)*. SEE MAIN ENTRY

parade conspicuously flaunt

paradigm case *(example)*, example, exemplar, instance, model, pattern, prototype, sample, specimen, standard. SEE MAIN ENTRY

paradigma paradigm

paradigmatic exemplary

paradisiacal placid

paradox enigma. SEE MAIN ENTRY

paradoxical debatable, disputable, impossible, inconsistent, inexplicable, ironic, problematic. SEE MAIN ENTRY

paragon exemplar, expert, model, pattern, prototype, representative *(example)*, standard. SEE MAIN ENTRY

paragraph chapter *(division)*, clause, subheading, title *(division)*

parallel agreed *(harmonized)*, akin *(germane)*, analogous, coequal, coextensive, cognate, collateral *(accompanying)*, commensurable, comparable *(capable of comparison)*, compare, comparison, concerted, concomitant, concurrent *(at the same time)*, congruous, connection *(relation)*, consensual, consonant, constructive *(inferential)*, correlate, correlative, correspond *(be equivalent)*, equivalent, mutual *(reciprocal)*, peer, reciprocal, relate *(establish a connection)*, reproduce, resemblance, same, similar, tantamount. SEE MAIN ENTRY

parallel relation analogy

paralleling commensurate

parallelism analogy, identity *(similarity)*, parity, propinquity *(similarity)*

parallelize compare

paralogical sophistic

paralogism fallacy, non sequitur

paralogistic fallacious, illogical

paralogize distort

paralysis deadlock, inaction, inertia

paralysis of authority lynch law

paralytic disabled *(made incapable)*, powerless

paralyze debar, disable, disarm *(divest of arms)*, fetter, impair, impede, inhibit, prevent, stall

paralyzed disabled *(made incapable)*, helpless *(powerless)*, powerless

paralyzing chilling effect, disabling

parameter guideline

paramount absolute *(ideal)*, best, cardinal *(outstanding)*, central *(essential)*, critical *(crucial)*, dominant, important *(significant)*, influential, leading *(ranking first)*, major, master, material *(important)*, necessary *(required)*, noteworthy, outstanding *(prominent)*, peremptory *(imperative)*, predominant, preferential, prevailing *(having superior force)*, primary, prime *(most valuable)*, principal, professional *(stellar)*, salient, sovereign *(absolute)*, stellar, superior *(higher)*, superlative, vital. SEE MAIN ENTRY

paramount law constitution

paramountcy hegemony, importance, influence, predominance, preponderance, prestige, primacy, significance, stress *(accent)*, supremacy

paramountly a fortiori

paranoia insanity. SEE MAIN ENTRY

parapet bulwark

paraph sign

paraphernalia effects, goods. SEE MAIN ENTRY

paraphrase construe *(translate)*, elucidate, explain, plagiarize, quote, recapitulate, repeat *(state again)*, restatement. SEE MAIN ENTRY

paraphrased repeated

paraphrasis paraphrase

parasite SEE MAIN ENTRY

parasitize prey

paratus ready *(prepared)*

parcel installment, lot, moiety, part *(separate)*, property *(land)*, ration, real estate, reapportion, subdivide. SEE MAIN ENTRY

parcel of land plot *(land)*, section *(vicinity)*

parcel out allocate, allot, apportion, disburse *(distribute)*, dispense, disperse *(disseminate)*, dispose *(apportion)*, distribute, divide *(distribute)*, dole, marshal, mete, partition, prorate, sort, split. SEE MAIN ENTRY

parcel out again redistribute

parcel out to delegate

parceling out disbursement *(act of disbursing)*, distribution *(apportionment)*

parcelling division *(act of dividing)*

parcels paraphernalia *(personal belongings)*

parcener heir

parcere forbear

parch burn

parcus close *(rigorous)*, frugal, parsimonious

pardon absolution, absolve, acquit, acquittal, amnesty, clear, clemency, compurgation, condonation, condone, discharge *(release from obligation)*, discharge *(liberate)*, dispensation *(exception)*, emancipation, exculpate, excuse, exonerate, exoneration, extenuate, forgive, free, grace, grace period, impunity, indulgence, liberate, liberation, longanimity, overlook *(excuse)*, palliate *(excuse)*, purge *(wipe out by atonement)*, quit *(free of)*, release, remission, remit *(release from penalty)*, respite *(reprieve)*, vindicate. SEE MAIN ENTRY

pardonable allowable, defensible, justifiable. SEE MAIN ENTRY

pardoned clear *(free from criminal charges)*, free *(relieved from a burden)*

pardoning clemency, lenient, palliative *(excusing)*

pardonment release

pare curtail, decrease, denude, diminish, discount *(minimize)*, excise *(cut away)*, lessen, minimize, rebate, retrench

pare down curtail

paregoric narcotic

parens parents, progenitor

parent ancestor, author *(originator)*, derivation, precursor, primogenitor, progenitor, source. SEE MAIN ENTRY

parentage adoption *(affiliation)*, affiliation *(bloodline)*, affinity *(family ties)*, ancestry, birth *(lineage)*, blood, bloodline, citation *(attribution)*, derivation, descent *(lineage)*, family *(common ancestry)*, filiation, lineage, origin *(ancestry)*, origination, paternity, race, source. SEE MAIN ENTRY

parental paternal

parenthesis insertion

parenthesize interpose

parenthetic incidental, nonessential

parenthetical nonessential. SEE MAIN ENTRY

parenthetically among

parenthood maternity, origin *(ancestry)*

parentless child orphan

parents ancestry. SEE MAIN ENTRY

parents and children household

parere bear *(yield)*, comply, generate, heed, obey

pari materia SEE MAIN ENTRY

pariah derelict. SEE MAIN ENTRY

paring economy *(frugality)*

parity analogy, balance *(equality)*, correspondence *(similarity)*, equipoise, identity *(similarity)*, resemblance. SEE MAIN ENTRY

park locate, lodge *(house)*, stay *(rest)*

parkway causeway

parlance conference, language, phraseology, rhetoric *(skilled speech)*, speech. SEE MAIN ENTRY

parlay bet, build *(augment)*, compound. SEE MAIN ENTRY

parley communicate, confer *(consult)*, conference, confrontation *(act of setting face to face)*, consult *(ask advice of)*, conversation, converse, council *(assembly)*, deliberate, discourse, discuss, mediate, mediation, meet, meeting *(conference)*, negotiate, negotiation, session, speak, treat *(process)*. SEE MAIN ENTRY

parliament chamber *(body)*, council *(assembly)*, legislature

parliamentarian legislator

parlor chamber *(compartment)*

parlous aleatory *(perilous)*

parlous state peril

parochial illiberal, narrow, provincial, regional. SEE MAIN ENTRY

parochialis parochial

parody caricature, distort, jape, mock *(imitate)*, pose *(impersonate)*, travesty. SEE MAIN ENTRY

parol nuncupative. SEE MAIN ENTRY

parole discharge *(liberate)*, free, liberate, liberation, probation, undertaking *(pledge)*, verbal. SEE MAIN ENTRY

paroled free *(relieved from a burden)*, unbound

parolee convict, probationer *(released offender)*

paroxysm outbreak, outburst

parrot copy, impersonate, mock *(imitate)*, recite, repeat *(state again)*

parry avert, bicker, block, defense, dispute *(debate)*, divert, elude, equivocate, prevaricate, prevent, rebut, refute, repel *(drive back)*, reply, resist *(oppose)*, respond, retort. SEE MAIN ENTRY

parrying avoidance *(evasion)*

pars clause, constituent *(part)*, department, faction, ingredient, installment, item, proportion, segment, share *(interest)*, side, subdivision

pars interior chamber *(compartment)*

pars minima minimum

parsimonia economy *(frugality)*

parsimonious economical, frugal, illiberal, penurious, provident *(frugal)*. SEE MAIN ENTRY

part alienate *(estrange)*, alight, aspect, assignment *(task)*, bifurcate, break *(separate)*, chapter *(division)*, circuit, component, constituent *(part)*, courtroom, depart, department, detach, detail, dichotomize, disband, discontinue *(break continuity)*, disengage, disjoint, disperse *(scatter)*, dissociate, dissolve *(separate)*, divide *(separate)*, divorce, element, equity *(share of ownership)*, estrange, excerpt, factor *(ingredient)*, feature *(characteristic)*, ingredient, interest *(ownership)*, isolate, item, leave *(depart)*, lot, luxate, member *(constituent part)*, moiety, organ, phase *(aspect)*, proportion, province, quit *(evacuate)*, ration, region, remove *(eliminate)*, retire *(retreat)*, role, section *(division)*, section *(vicinity)*, segment, separate, sever, share *(interest)*, split, subdivision, title *(division)*, unit *(item)*. SEE MAIN ENTRY

part and parcel constituent *(part)*

part company avoid *(evade)*, disband, estrange, move *(alter position)*, separate, split

part exemplifying a mass cross section

part exemplifying a number cross section

part of the bargain counteroffer

part payment deposit, installment

part payment of a debt installment

part ways separate

part with abandon *(relinquish)*, alienate *(transfer title)*, attorn, bestow, cede, disown *(refuse to acknowledge)*, forfeit, forgo, forswear, jettison, lose *(be deprived of)*, parcel, relinquish, renounce, spend, surrender *(give back)*. SEE MAIN ENTRY

part with life die

partage split

partake contribute *(assist)*, engage *(involve)*, involve *(participate)*, participate. SEE MAIN ENTRY

partake in cooperate

partake in a symposium discuss

partake of contribute *(assist)*

partaken privy

partaker accessory, accomplice, participant, partner, party *(participant)*

parted discrete, disjunctive *(tending to disjoin)*, separate

partes office, part *(role)*, role

partes hominis agere impersonate

partial deficient, ex parte, illiberal, imperfect, inchoate, inequitable, interested, one-sided, parochial, partisan, preferential, prone, semi, unequal *(unjust)*, unjust. SEE MAIN ENTRY

partial change modification

partial excuse extenuating circumstances

partial payment installment

partial similarity analogy

partial to inclined, willing *(desirous)*

partial truth evasion

partialism favoritism

partiality affection, affinity *(regard)*, bias, favoritism, foregone conclusion, inclination, inequality, inequity, injustice, intolerance, nepotism, penchant, preconception, predetermination, predilection, predisposition, preference *(choice)*, prejudice *(preconception)*, proclivity, propensity, tendency. SEE MAIN ENTRY

partially in part, piecemeal

partible divisible, divisive, separable, severable

particeps participant, partner

particeps criminis abettor, accessory, accomplice, cohort, colleague, copartner *(coconspirator)*

participant accessory, accomplice, actor, contestant, contributor *(contributor)*, partisan, partner, privy. SEE MAIN ENTRY

participate assist, connive, contribute *(assist)*, cooperate, engage *(involve)*, espouse, federalize *(associate)*, federate, join *(associate oneself with)*, partake. SEE MAIN ENTRY

participate in commit *(perpetrate)*, compete

participate in an unlawful scheme conspire

participate surreptitiously connive

participate with combine *(act in concert)*

participating common *(shared)*, concurrent *(united)*

participation affiliation *(connectedness)*, assistance, association *(connection)*, collusion, connivance, contact *(association)*, coverage *(scope)*, integration *(assimilation)*, interest *(ownership)*, league, partnership

participation in fraud collusion

participator accessory, accomplice, colleague, confederate, consociate, contributor *(contributor)*, member *(individual in a group)*, participant, partner, party *(participant)*

participatory common *(shared)*, mutual *(collective)*

particle constituent *(part)*, element, iota, minimum, modicum, part *(portion)*, scintilla. SEE MAIN ENTRY

particular accurate, certain *(specific)*, circumspect, concrete, conscientious, detail, detailed, distinct *(clear)*, distinct *(distinguished from others)*, distinctive, exact, express, faithful *(diligent)*, feature *(characteristic)*, individual, item, meticulous, painstaking, peculiar *(distinctive)*, personal *(individual)*, point *(item)*, precise, proper, punctilious, singular, special, specific, specification, strict, technicality, term *(provision)*, unusual. SEE MAIN ENTRY

particular aptitude penchant

particular characteristic specialty *(distinctive mark)*

particular charge complaint, count

particular course of action procedure

particular item specialty *(distinctive mark)*

particular manner of proceeding course

particular matter specialty *(distinctive mark)*

particular object article *(commodity)*

particular object of pursuit specialty *(special aptitude)*

particular one individual

particular part component

particular point specialty *(distinctive mark)*

particular point of time date

particularity characteristic, color *(complexion)*, detail, differential, diligence *(care)*, habit, identity *(individuality)*, particular, personality, property *(distinctive attribute)*, quality *(attribute)*, quality *(grade)*, quirk *(idiosyncrasy)*, speciality, specialty *(distinctive mark)*, technicality, trait. SEE MAIN ENTRY

particularization designation *(naming)*, specification

particularize delineate, depict, describe, designate, detail *(particularize)*, differentiate, distinguish, itemize, portray, recount, relate *(tell)*, specify

particularized descriptive, detailed

particularly a fortiori. SEE MAIN ENTRY

particularness discretion *(quality of being discreet)*, particularity

particulars circumstances, description, story *(narrative)*

partim partial *(part)*, partial *(relating to a part)*

parting divergent, division *(act of dividing)*, egress, estrangement, leave *(absence)*, rift *(disagreement)*, rift *(gap)*, separation

parting with cession

partiri parcel, part *(separate)*

partisan addict, advocate *(espouser)*, backer, ex parte, inequitable, interested, one-sided, parochial, partial *(biased)*, party *(participant)*, political, politician, preferential, prejudicial, proponent. SEE MAIN ENTRY

partisan competition primary

partisan conflict faction

partisan contest primary

partisan election primary

partisan outlook posture *(attitude)*

partisanism bias, inequity, nepotism, politics

partisanship bias, constituency, faction, favor *(partiality)*, favoritism, indorsement, inequity, injustice, nepotism, partiality, predilection, prejudice *(preconception)*. SEE MAIN ENTRY

partitio division *(act of dividing)*

partition allot, allotment, apportion, apportionment, assign *(allot)*, assignment *(allotment)*, barrier, bifurcate, chapter *(division)*, classify, decentralization, demarcate, dichotomize, disassociation, dispensation *(act of dispensing)*, disperse *(disseminate)*, disperse *(scatter)*, distribution *(apportionment)*, divide *(separate)*, division *(act of dividing)*, parcel, part *(separate)*, schism, segregation *(separation)*, sever, split *(noun)*, split *(verb)*, subdivide, subdivision. SEE MAIN ENTRY

partitioned bipartite, disconnected, disjunctive *(tending to disjoin)*

partitioned space chamber *(compartment)*

partitionment apportionment

partly in part

partner accessory, accomplice, assistant, associate, coactor, coadjutant, coconspirator, cohort, colleague, confederate, connect *(join together)*, consociate, consort, conspirer, contributor *(contributor)*, copartner *(business associate)*, member *(individual in a group)*, participant, partisan, party *(participant)*. SEE MAIN ENTRY

partner in crime accessory, accomplice, coactor, coconspirator, conspirer, copartner *(coconspirator)*

partner in wrongdoing accomplice, coconspirator

partnered conjoint, conjugal, corporate *(associate)*

partnership affiliation *(connectedness)*, association *(connection)*, coaction, coalition, community, company *(enterprise)*, consortium *(business cartel)*, consortium *(marriage companionship)*, contribution *(participation)*, cooperative, firm, integration *(assimilation)*, league, matrimony, merger, pool, sodality, syndicate. SEE MAIN ENTRY

parts contents

parturient fertile

parturition birth *(emergence of young)*

partus embryo

party actor, amicus curiae, appellant, applicant *(petitioner)*, assemblage, character *(an individual)*, complainant, constituency, contender, contributor *(contributor)*, denomination, individual, litigant, participant, person, petitioner, privy, side. SEE MAIN ENTRY

party against whom a complaint is lodged defendant

party against whom charges are pending defendant

party answering a summons or bill respondent

party competition primary

party contest primary

party election primary

party in power management *(directorate)*

party leadership politics

party line platform, policy *(plan of action)*

party machine party *(political organization)*

party making an affidavit deponent

party member partisan, politician

party planks platform

party politics politics

party system politics

party to a suit accuser, appellant, claimant, complainant, contender, contestant, litigant, suitor

party to an instrument comaker

party to the suit plaintiff

party who is sued defendant

party who sues plaintiff

party-liner partisan

parum candidus disingenuous

parum clarus indistinct

parum distinctus inarticulate

parum insignis inconspicuous

parum procedere miscarriage

parvi facere disregard

parvo emere rate

parvus limited

pasquinade parody, ridicule

pass alienate *(transfer title)*, circulate, confirm, constitute *(establish)*, convey *(transfer)*, decide, enact, experience *(encounter)*, expire, exude, forgo, franchise *(license)*, give *(grant)*, grant *(transfer formally)*, incident, key *(passport)*, legislate, outbalance, penetrate, perambulate, perish, permit, plight, posture *(situation)*, predicament, pretermit, promote *(advance)*, surmount, surpass, transcend, transfer, transmit, traverse. SEE MAIN ENTRY

pass an opinion determine, find *(determine)*

pass and repass beat *(pulsate)*

pass away decease, die, expire, perish

pass back regress

pass by disdain, disregard, ignore, neglect, omit, reject

pass by devise descend

pass by inheritance descend

pass by operation of law descend

pass by succession descend

pass by will demise

pass censure on condemn *(blame)*, convict, denounce *(condemn)*

pass censure upon disapprove *(condemn)*

pass current circulate

pass down attorn, confer *(give)*, contribute *(supply)*, convey *(transfer)*, demise, endow, render *(deliver)*

pass down from generation to generation descend

pass for assume *(simulate)*, displace *(replace)*, impersonate, pose *(impersonate)*, profess *(pretend)*

pass from one to another circulate

pass from point to point traverse

pass in the mind occur *(come to mind)*

pass into enter *(go in)*

pass judgment adjudge, adjudicate, arbitrate *(adjudge)*, award, conclude *(decide)*, decide, decree, determine, find *(determine)*, hold *(decide)*, rule *(decide)*. SEE MAIN ENTRY

pass judgment upon sentence

pass laws legislate

pass off fake, pretend

pass off another's ideas as one's own plagiarize

pass off another's writings as one's own plagiarize

pass off as genuine foist

pass off for disguise, misrepresent

pass on abalienate, annunciate, comment, convey *(communicate)*, deliver, descend, die, perish, proceed *(go forward)*, transfer, transmit

pass on again recover

pass on information annunciate, notice *(give formal warning)*

pass on to bequeath

pass orders instruct *(direct)*

pass out disburse *(distribute)*, disperse *(disseminate)*, divide *(distribute)*, parcel

pass out of sight disappear

pass over alienate *(transfer title)*, condone, discount *(disbelieve)*, disdain, dismiss *(put out of consideration)*, exclude, excuse, grant *(transfer formally)*, ignore, neglect, omit, overlook *(disregard)*, override, pretermit, reject, remit *(release from penalty)*

pass over to bequeath

pass round circulate

pass sentence adjudicate, award, decide, determine, rule *(decide)*

pass sentence on condemn *(punish)*, convict

pass sentence upon judge, pronounce *(pass judgment)*

pass through endure *(suffer)*, perambulate, permeate, pervade, traverse

pass time in idleness loiter

pass title convey *(transfer)*

pass to devolve

pass to another lapse *(cease)*

pass under review censor, judge, notice *(observe)*, peruse

pass unfavorable judgment upon disapprove *(condemn)*

pass up disapprove *(reject)*, disavow, refuse. SEE MAIN ENTRY

pass upon award, rule *(decide)*

pass without notice ignore

passable admissible, allowable, average *(standard)*, fair *(satisfactory)*, imperfect, marginal, mediocre, pardonable, penetrable, unobjectionable. SEE MAIN ENTRY

passableness mediocrity

passably fairly (moderately)

passage access (right of way), admission (entry), admittance (means of approach), avenue (route), chapter (division), circulation, clause, conversion (change), entrance, entry (entrance), excerpt, fare, ingress, osmosis, progress, reconversion, transition, transmittal

passage at arms affray

passage money fare

passage out egress, outlet

passage taken from a book excerpt

passages approaches

passageway access (right of way), admission (entry), admittance (means of approach), avenue (route), entrance, portal

passbook ledger

passe outdated, outmoded

passed allowed

passed away dead, deceased, defunct, lifeless (dead)

passed down hereditary

passed on deceased, late (defunct), lifeless (dead)

passer-by bystander

passing brief, circulation, cursory, ephemeral, extremity (death), itinerant, moving (in motion), promotion (advancement), provisional, temporary, transient, transition, volatile

passing away death, demise (death), in extremis, transitory

passing into law legalization

passing judgment conviction (finding of guilt)

passing of seisin feoffment

passing over omission

passing word mention (reference)

passion affection, ardor, emotion, furor, obsession, penchant, propensity, spirit. SEE MAIN ENTRY

passionate demonstrative (expressive of emotion), eager, ecstatic, fanatical, fervent, hot-blooded, impulsive (rash), intense, serious (devoted), vehement, zealous

passionateness ardor

passionless cold-blooded, controlled (restrained), dispassionate, languid, lifeless (dull), nonchalant, perfunctory, phlegmatic, stoical

passive dormant, indolent, insensible, languid, lifeless (dull), obedient, otiose, patient, phlegmatic, pliant, resigned, sequacious, servile, stagnant, static, stoical, torpid, unobtrusive, yielding. SEE MAIN ENTRY

passive agreement acquiescence

passive consent acquiescence

passiveness capitulation, inaction, inertia, resignation (passive acceptance)

passivity capitulation, inaction, inertia, languor, resignation (passive acceptance), sloth

passport credentials, permit

password catchword

past back (in arrears), defunct, former, last (preceding), obsolete, old, outdated, outmoded, previous, prior. SEE MAIN ENTRY

past bearing insufferable, unendurable

past comprehension inapprehensible, inscrutable

past cure incorrigible, irredeemable, irremediable

past dispute categorical, certain (positive), cogent, inappealable, incontestable,

incontrovertible, indubious, irrefutable, positive (incontestable), uncontroverted, undeniable, undisputed

past due delinquent (overdue), late (tardy), outstanding (unpaid), overdue. SEE MAIN ENTRY

past enduring insufferable, unendurable

past help irremediable

past hope incorrigible, irrecoverable, irredeemable

past mending irredeemable, irremediable

past recall irredeemable, irretrievable

past the time for payment overdue

paste combine (join together)

pastiche melange

pastoral placid

pat suitable, usual

patch fix (repair), flaw, parcel, plot (land), repair, restore (renew)

patch up fix (repair), renew (refurbish), restore (renew)

patch up a quarrel placate

patching repair

patchwork melange

patefacere detect, manifest, reveal

patefactio common knowledge, disclosure (act of disclosing)

patens open (unclosed)

patent apparent (perceptible), appreciable, blatant (conspicuous), charter (license), clear (apparent), comprehensible, conspicuous, evident, explicit, lucid, manifest, naked (perceptible), obvious, open (in sight), ostensible, overt, palpable, pellucid, perceivable, perceptible, permit, unmistakable. SEE MAIN ENTRY

patently bad arrant (onerous)

patently offensive obscene

patere open (accessible)

paternal consanguineous. SEE MAIN ENTRY

paternal parentage paternity

paternity descent (lineage), filiation, parentage. SEE MAIN ENTRY

paternus hereditary, paternal

path access (right of way), admission (entry), admittance (means of approach), avenue (route), conduit (channel), outlet, way (channel). SEE MAIN ENTRY

pathetic deplorable, disconsolate, lamentable, paltry

pathfinder pioneer, precursor

pathless impervious

pathogenic contagious, insalubrious

pathway way (channel)

pati bear (tolerate), let (permit), suffer (permit)

patience composure, diligence (perseverance), indulgence, lenience, longanimity, moderation, resignation (passive acceptance), sufferance, temperament, temperance, tolerance, understanding (tolerance). SEE MAIN ENTRY

patiens patient, phlegmatic

patient charitable (lenient), lenient, peaceable, persistent, pertinacious, placid, resigned, sedulous, steadfast, stoical. SEE MAIN ENTRY

patient endurance longanimity, sufferance

patientia sufferance

patois phraseology

patriarch ancestor, parents, precursor, predecessor, primogenitor

patriarchal consanguineous, paternal

patriarchs ancestry

patriciate society

patrilinear consanguineous

patrimonial paternal, testamentary

patrimonium birthright, heritage

patrimony bequest, birthright, estate (hereditament), hereditament, heritage

patriotic faithful (loyal), loyal

patrius paternal

patrocinium patronage (power to appoint jobs)

patrol perambulate, police, protect, traverse. SEE MAIN ENTRY

patrolman peace officer, warden

patron abettor, advocate (counselor), advocate (espouser), backer, benefactor, client, consumer, contributor (giver), customer, donor, employer, good samaritan, guardian, member (individual in a group), partisan, promoter, proponent, samaritan, sponsor. SEE MAIN ENTRY

patron of professional servies client

patronage advantage, advocacy, aid (help), aid (subsistence), auspices, charge (custody), charity, control (supervision), favor (sanction), goodwill, guidance, help, nepotism, protection, safekeeping, support (assistance), trade (commerce). SEE MAIN ENTRY

patroness donor

patronize deign, finance, foster, help, nurture, prefer, preserve, promote (organize), protect, sponsor, subscribe (promise), subsidize, support (assist). SEE MAIN ENTRY

patronizer client, patron (regular customer)

patronizing inflated (vain), orgulous, proud (conceited), supercilious

patronus advocate (counselor), patron (influential supporter), spokesman

patronymic call (title)

pattern array (order), compose, configuration (form), constant, content (structure), contrive, create, criterion, delineation, example, exemplar, form (arrangement), habit, make, manner (behavior), model, modus operandi, motif, norm, order (arrangement), paradigm, practice (custom), prototype, rule (guide), specimen, stamp, standard, structure (composition), style, system. SEE MAIN ENTRY

pattern after copy, mock (imitate)

pattern bargaining collective bargaining

pattern of words phraseology

patterned boiler plate, periodic, regular (orderly)

patterning creation

patternless disordered

patulous open (unclosed)

patulus open (unclosed)

pauciloquent brief, laconic, mute, succinct, taciturn

paucitas paucity

paucity dearth, deficiency, deficit, delinquency (shortage), insignificance, insufficiency, need (deprivation), poverty. SEE MAIN ENTRY

paululum modicum

paulum modicum

pauperism bankruptcy, indigence, poverty, privation

pauperize deplete, deprive

pauperized bankrupt, impecunious, poor (underprivileged)

paupertas poverty

pause cease, cessation (interlude), defer (put off), delay, discontinuance (act of discontinuing), doubt (hesitate), extension (postponement), halt (noun), halt (verb), hesitate, hiatus, interruption, interval, lapse *(break)*, leave *(absence)*, lull, misdoubt, moratorium, pendency, procrastinate, qualm, recess *(noun)*, recess *(verb)*, remain *(stay)*, remission, reprieve, respite *(interval of rest)*, rest *(cease from action)*, stay *(rest)*, stop. SEE MAIN ENTRY

pausing dilatory, hesitant

pave the way expedite, facilitate, precede, provide *(arrange for)*

paved road causeway

paved way causeway

pavor consternation, fear, fright, panic

pawn captive, deposit, security *(pledge)*. SEE MAIN ENTRY

pax peace

pay advance *(allowance)*, commission *(fee)*, compensation, contribute *(supply)*, cover *(provide for)*, defray, disburse *(pay out)*, disbursement *(funds paid out)*, earnings, expend *(disburse)*, fund, income, indemnify, inure *(benefit)*, liquidate *(determine liability)*, offer *(tender)*, payment *(remittance)*, post, profit, recoup *(reimburse)*, remit *(send payment)*, remunerate, remuneration, requital, revenue, reward, satisfy *(discharge)*, spend, subsidize, tender, wage. SEE MAIN ENTRY

pay a debt quit *(repay)*

pay a price for buy

pay allegiance adhere *(maintain loyalty)*

pay an indemnity bear the expense, defray, quit *(repay)*

pay and settle liquidate *(determine liability)*

pay attention devote, hear *(give attention to)*, heed, notice *(observe)*, observe *(watch)*

pay attention to care *(be cautious)*, care *(regard)*, concern *(care)*, consider, note *(notice)*, observe *(obey)*, oversee

pay back bear *(yield)*, contribute *(indemnify)*, indemnify, quit *(repay)*, rebate, reciprocate, recoup *(reimburse)*, recriminate, refund, reimburse, repay, replace, retaliate, return *(refund)*

pay cash for buy

pay compensation bear the expense, defray, indemnify

pay damages bear the expense, compensate *(remunerate)*, contribute *(indemnify)*. SEE MAIN ENTRY

pay debts liquidate *(determine liability)*

pay deference honor

pay dividends disperse *(disseminate)*

pay for bear the expense, buy, compensate *(remunerate)*, defray, finance, fund, purchase, sponsor, subsidize

pay heed devote, observe *(watch)*

pay heed to note *(notice)*

pay homage honor

pay homage to regard *(hold in esteem)*, yield *(submit)*

pay honor dedicate

pay in advance prepay

pay in full bear the expense, compensate *(remunerate)*, discharge *(pay a debt)*, quit *(repay)*, satisfy *(discharge)*

pay in kind repay

pay little attention to minimize

pay little heed to minimize

pay load freight

pay no attention discount *(disbelieve)*, disregard, neglect

pay no attention to disobey, ignore, pretermit

pay no heed discount *(disbelieve)*

pay no heed to ignore, neglect

pay no mind discount *(disbelieve)*

pay no regard to dismiss *(put out of consideration)*, disregard, neglect, pretermit

pay off disburse *(pay out)*, discharge *(pay a debt)*, quit *(repay)*, satisfy *(discharge)*. SEE MAIN ENTRY

pay old debts quit *(repay)*

pay on demand bear the expense

pay one's way defray

pay out disperse *(disseminate)*, divide *(distribute)*, dole, expend *(disburse)*, mete

pay reparations defray, indemnify

pay respect to defer *(yield in judgment)*

pay respects honor

pay the bill bear the expense

pay the costs bear the expense, defray

pay the equivalent compensate *(remunerate)*

pay the penalty repent

pay the value compensate *(remunerate)*

pay towards subsidize

pay tribute belaud, bestow, honor, regard *(hold in esteem)*

pay up discharge *(pay a debt)*, satisfy *(discharge)*

pay wages bear the expense, compensate *(remunerate)*

pay-off commission *(fee)*

pay-out payoff *(payment in full)*

payable delinquent *(overdue)*, outstanding *(unpaid)*, receivable, unpaid. SEE MAIN ENTRY

payee beneficiary, heir, holder, recipient, transferee. SEE MAIN ENTRY

paying beneficial, compensatory, gainful, lucrative, productive, profitable

paying back contribution *(indemnification)*, expiation, reimbursement, restitution

paying for collection *(payment)*

paying guest tenant

paying off discharge *(payment)*

payload cargo

payment amortization, binder, charge *(cost)*, collection *(payment)*, commission *(fee)*, compensation, consideration *(recompense)*, contribution *(indemnification)*, correction *(punishment)*, cost *(expenses)*, deposit, disbursement *(funds paid out)*, downpayment, earnings, expenditure, expense *(cost)*, expiation, fee *(charge)*, handsel, honorarium, income, indemnification, indemnity, out of pocket, outlay, pay, payroll, pension, perquisite, price, prize, profit, rate, receipt *(voucher)*, recompense, reimbursement, relief *(legal redress)*, remittance, remuneration, rent, reparation *(indemnification)*, requital, restitution, retainer, retribution, revenue, reward, satisfaction *(discharge of debt)*, settlement, tip *(gratuity)*, toll *(effect)*, toll *(tax)*, trover, wage. SEE MAIN ENTRY

payment beforehand advance *(allowance)*

payment for delay demurrage

payment for expenses refund

payment for misconduct fine

payment for services payroll

payment for the right of carriage fare

payment in lieu composition *(agreement in bankruptcy)*

payment of damages compensation

payments overhead

payments past due arrears

payoff effect

payor transferor

payroll SEE MAIN ENTRY

peace composure, concordance, lull, reconciliation. SEE MAIN ENTRY

peace of mind composure

peace offering reparation *(indemnification)*

peace officer marshal. SEE MAIN ENTRY

peace officers police

peace-loving nonmilitant, peaceable

peaceable neutral, nonmilitant, patient, placid. SEE MAIN ENTRY

peaceful dispassionate, harmonious, neutral, nonmilitant, peaceable, placid

peaceful of mind complacent

peacefulness composure

peacelike peaceable

peacemaker go-between, intermediary, referee, umpire

peacemaking compromise, conciliation, intercession, reconciliation

peak ceiling, culmination, maximum *(amplitude)*, pinnacle

pealing resounding

peasant ignoble

pecability offense

peccability bad repute, blame *(culpability)*, culpability, delinquency *(misconduct)*, frailty, impeachability

peccable blameful, blameworthy, imperfect, profane, reprehensible, sinister. SEE MAIN ENTRY

peccadillo guilt, impropriety, malfeasance, misconduct, misdeed, misdemeanor, misdoing, misfeasance

peccancy culpability, delinquency *(misconduct)*, guilt, malfeasance, misdeed

peccans offender, peccant *(culpable)*

peccant bad *(offensive)*, blameful, blameworthy, culpable, delinquent *(guilty of a misdeed)*, disgraceful, errant, guilty, iniquitous, malignant, nefarious, objectionable, offensive *(offending)*, profane, profligate *(corrupt)*, reprehensible, reprobate, sinister. SEE MAIN ENTRY

peccare lapse *(fall into error)*, offend *(violate the law)*

peccatum error, fault *(responsibility)*, lapse *(expiration)*, misconduct, misdeed, offense, transgression

peculate bilk, cheat, convert *(misappropriate)*, defalcate, defraud, impropriate, loot, mulct *(defraud)*, poach, purloin, rob, steal. SEE MAIN ENTRY

peculation bad faith, bad repute, conversion *(misappropriation)*, embezzlement, larceny, misappropriation, misusage, theft

peculator embezzler, hoodlum, thief

peculiarity SEE MAIN ENTRY

peculiar anomalous, certain *(particular)*, certain *(specific)*, different, distinct *(distinguished from others)*, distinctive, eccentric, express, extraordinary, irregular *(not usual)*, ludicrous, nonconforming, noteworthy, novel, particular *(individual)*, particular *(specific)*, personal *(individual)*, prodigious *(amazing)*, remarkable, several *(separate)*, singular, specific, suspicious *(questionable)*, unaccustomed, uncanny, uncommon, unique, unusual. SEE MAIN ENTRY

peculiar expression phrase

peculiar feature aspect

peculiar idiom characteristic, specialty *(distinctive mark)*

peculiar temperament specialty *(distinctive mark)*

peculiaris specific

peculiarities color *(complexion)*, personality

peculiarity character *(personal quality)*, characteristic, differential, distinction *(differ-*

ence), feature *(characteristic)*, habit, identity *(individuality)*, irregularity, nonconformity, property *(distinctive attribute)*, quality *(attribute)*, quirk *(idiosyncrasy)*, speciality, specialty *(distinctive mark)*, technicality, trait

peculiarity of phrasing phraseology

peculiarly particularly

pecunia fund, income, money, remittance

pecunia praesens cash

pecuniae aversor embezzler

pecuniae residuae arrears

pecuniam mutuam dare capitalize *(provide capital)*

pecuniam redigere realize *(obtain as a profit)*

pecuniaria finance

pecuniarius pecuniary

pecuniary commercial, financial, fiscal, monetary. SEE MAIN ENTRY

pecuniary aid alimony, consideration *(recompense)*, pension

pecuniary assistance alimony

pecuniary burden charge *(cost)*, charge *(lien)*

pecuniary due debit

pecuniary management finance

pecuniary penalty amercement, fine, forfeiture *(thing forfeited)*

pecuniary punishment fine

pecuniary resource bank

pecuniary resources assets, capital, cash, possessions, property *(possessions)*

pecunious opulent, prosperous, solvent

pedagogic didactic, disciplinary *(educational)*

pedagogical disciplinary *(educational)*

pedagogue SEE MAIN ENTRY

pedagogy education, guidance, instruction *(teaching)*

pedant SEE MAIN ENTRY

pedantic dogmatic, inflated *(bombastic)*, learned, sesquipedalian

pedantical learned

pedantry diligence *(care)*

peddle barter, handle *(trade)*, sell, vend

peddler dealer, merchant, vendor

pedem referre retreat

pederasty sodomy

pedestal cornerstone

pedestrian inferior *(lower in quality)*, mundane, nondescript, ordinary, prevalent, prosaic, stale, usual. SEE MAIN ENTRY

pedestrianize perambulate

pedigree ancestry, blood, bloodline, descent *(lineage)*, origin *(ancestry)*, parentage

pedogogic informative

peel denude

peep spy

peer contributor *(contributor)*, copartner *(business associate)*, delve, spy. SEE MAIN ENTRY

peer at examine *(study)*, observe *(watch)*

peer into frisk, investigate, peruse, scrutinize

peerage society

peerless absolute *(ideal)*, best, inestimable, invaluable, laudable, noteworthy, outstanding *(prominent)*, paramount, premium, priceless, prime *(most valuable)*, rare, singular, sterling, superior *(excellent)*, superlative, unapproachable, unique, unusual

peeve bait *(harass)*, irritate

peevish fractious, froward, perverse, petulant, querulous, resentful, restive, sensitive *(easily affected)*

pejoration decline

pejorative calumnious, derogatory, libelous. SEE MAIN ENTRY

pelf spoils

pellicere lure

pellucid clear *(apparent)*, cognizable, coherent *(clear)*, comprehensible, distinct *(clear)*, lucid. SEE MAIN ENTRY

pellucidus lucid, pellucid

pelt beat *(strike)*, lash *(strike)*

pen close *(enclosed area)*, detain *(hold in custody)*, enclose, lock, note *(record)*, restrict

pen in confine, encompass *(surround)*

pen up repress

penal disciplinary *(punitory)*, punitive. SEE MAIN ENTRY

penal colony penitentiary, prison

penal institution jail, penitentiary, prison, reformatory

penal restraint bondage

penal retribution correction *(punishment)*, cost *(penalty)*, discipline *(punishment)*, forfeiture *(thing forfeited)*, penalty, punishment, sanction *(punishment)*

penal servitude bondage, correction *(punishment)*

penal settlement penitentiary

penalization condemnation *(punishment)*, conviction *(finding of guilt)*, correction *(punishment)*, cost *(penalty)*, forfeiture *(thing forfeited)*, punishment

penalize condemn *(punish)*, convict, demote, discipline *(punish)*, fine, mulct *(fine)*, punish. SEE MAIN ENTRY

penalizing punitive

penalty amercement, condemnation *(punishment)*, conviction *(finding of guilt)*, correction *(punishment)*, damages, disadvantage, discipline *(punishment)*, expense *(sacrifice)*, fine, forfeiture *(thing forfeited)*, imposition *(tax)*, infliction, punishment, reparation *(indemnification)*, reprisal, retribution, sanction *(punishment)*, sentence, surcharge, trover. SEE MAIN ENTRY

penalty for delay demurrage

penalty imposed on an offender punishment

penance cost *(penalty)*, discipline *(punishment)*, penalty, punishment

penance doer penitent

penates household *(domestic)*

penchant affection, animus, bias, characteristic, conatus, disposition *(inclination)*, favor *(partiality)*, favoritism, inclination, partiality, predilection, predisposition, proclivity, propensity, tendency. SEE MAIN ENTRY

pencraft handwriting

pendant addition, appendix *(accession)*, appurtenance, complement, correlate, counterpart *(complement)*

pendency cessation *(interlude)*. SEE MAIN ENTRY

pendent dependent. SEE MAIN ENTRY

pendere pay

pending ad interim, conditional, forthcoming, future, outstanding *(unresolved)*, undecided, unsettled, until. SEE MAIN ENTRY

pendulate alternate *(fluctuate)*, beat *(pulsate)*, fluctuate, oscillate

penes quos est reipublica government *(political administration)*

penetrabilis penetrable

penetrability danger

penetrable cognizable, coherent *(clear)*, comprehensible, passable, scrutable, vulnerable. SEE MAIN ENTRY

penetralia privacy

penetrare penetrate

penetrate break *(fracture)*, delve, encroach, impress *(affect deeply)*, interpose, invade, lancinate, permeate, pervade, pierce *(lance)*, solve, spread. SEE MAIN ENTRY

penetrating acute, incisive, interrogative, mordacious, perspicacious, potent, profound *(esoteric)*, profound *(intense)*, sensitive *(discerning)*, trenchant

penetration comprehension, encroachment, entrance, incursion, inflow, infusion, insertion, insight, judgment *(discernment)*, osmosis, perception, sagacity

penetrative trenchant

penitence remorse

penitent contrite, remorseful, repentant. SEE MAIN ENTRY

penitential contrite, penitent, remorseful, repentant

penitentiary cell, jail, prison, reformatory. SEE MAIN ENTRY

penitus defixus inveterate

penitus insitus inveterate

penmanship handwriting, script

penned holographic

penniless bankrupt, destitute, impecunious, insolvent, penurious, poor *(underprivileged)*

pennilessness indigence, poverty

penny-conscious frugal

penny-pinching parsimonious

penological disciplinary *(punitory)*

penology discipline *(punishment)*

penscript script

pensio installment

pension annuity, capitalize *(provide capital)*. SEE MAIN ENTRY

pensioner dependent, protégé

pensive cogitative, grave *(solemn)*, serious *(grave)*, solemn. SEE MAIN ENTRY

pensiveness contemplation, introspection, preoccupation

penumbra SEE MAIN ENTRY

penuria dearth, insufficiency

penurious illiberal, impecunious, parsimonious, poor *(underprivileged)*, provident *(frugal)*. SEE MAIN ENTRY

penury bankruptcy, dearth, deficiency, indigence, need *(deprivation)*, poverty, privation

people community, family *(common ancestry)*, humanity *(mankind)*, nationality, populace, population, race. SEE MAIN ENTRY

people delegated delegation *(envoy)*

peopled populous

peoples of the earth humanity *(mankind)*

pepper intersperse

per thereby

per annum SEE MAIN ENTRY

per capita SEE MAIN ENTRY

per contra contra

per day per diem

per diem SEE MAIN ENTRY

per head per capita

per miscere confound

per vim factus forcible

peragrare perambulate, prowl

perambulate SEE MAIN ENTRY

perceivable apparent *(perceptible)*, appreciable, blatant *(conspicuous)*, clear *(apparent)*, coherent *(clear)*, comprehensible, conspicuous, determinable *(ascertainable)*, discernible, distinct *(clear)*, evident, manifest, naked *(perceptible)*, obvious, open *(in sight)*, ostensible, palpable, patent, perceptible, tangible, visible *(noticeable)*. SEE MAIN ENTRY

perceivable dissimilarity distinction (difference), identity (individuality)
perceive appreciate (comprehend), comprehend (understand), conceive (comprehend), conjure, construe (comprehend), deem, detect, discern (detect with the senses), discover, find (discover), identify, judge, note (notice), notice (observe), observe (watch), pierce (discern), read, realize (understand), regard (pay attention), spy, understand. SEE MAIN ENTRY
perceive as true presume
perceive clearly differentiate, distinguish
perceive differences secern
perceive something audible hear (perceive by ear)
perceive the worth of appreciate (value)
perceived cognizable, foreseeable
perceived from accompanying words noscitur a sociis
perceived happening fact
perceiving reasonable (rational)
percellere disconcert
percent proportion, share (interest)
percentage commission (fee), moiety, part (portion), per capita, proportion, quota, ration, share (interest). SEE MAIN ENTRY
percentage compensation commission (fee)
percentage of ownership interest (ownership)
percept concept, idea
perceptible appreciable, ascertainable, bodily, clear (apparent), cognizable, coherent (clear), comprehensible, concrete, conspicuous, determinable (ascertainable), discernible, distinct (clear), evident, manifest, obvious, open (in sight), ostensible, overt, palpable, patent, perceivable, ponderable, scrutable, tangible, visible (in full view). SEE MAIN ENTRY
perceptibly fairly (clearly)
perception cognition, comprehension, concept, detection, discovery, discretion (quality of being discreet), discrimination (good judgment), estimate (idea), idea, impression, insight, judgment (discernment), knowledge (awareness), precognition, reaction (response), realization, reason (sound judgment), recognition, sagacity, scienter, sense (feeling), sense (intelligence), sensibility, understanding (comprehension), vision (dream). SEE MAIN ENTRY
perception of difference diagnosis
perceptive acute, cognizant, conscious (aware), discreet, discriminating (judicious), judicious, juridical, knowing, lucid, omniscient, perspicacious, politic, profound (esoteric), receptive, responsive, sapient, sensible, sensitive (discerning), sensitive (easily affected), subtle (refined), vicarious (delegated). SEE MAIN ENTRY
perceptiveness judgment (discernment), knowledge (awareness)
perceptivity sensibility
perch rest (be supported by), seat
percipere hear (perceive by ear), perceive
percipience cognition, insight, judgment (discernment), knowledge (awareness), perception, sagacity
percipiency insight, reason (sound judgment)
percipient circumspect, cognizant, conscious (aware), judicious, juridical, knowing, omniscient, perceptive, perspicacious, reasonable (rational), sensitive (discerning)
percolate permeate

percontatio inquiry (request for information), interrogation
percussion collision (accident)
percutere beat (strike)
perdere destroy (efface), lose (be deprived of), spoil (impair)
perdition adversity, destruction, miscarriage, subversion
perditus immoral, incorrigible, profligate (corrupt), reprobate
perdu hidden, recondite
perducere conduct
perdurable chronic, constant, durable, infinite, infrangible, permanent, perpetual, persistent, stable
perdure endure (last), last, persist, remain (continue), subsist
perduring live (existing), permanent
peregrinate perambulate, prowl
peregrine foreign
peregrinus alien, foreign
peremptory compelling, compulsory, decisive, dictatorial, dogmatic, inappealable, insistent, mandatory, severe, supercilious, tyrannous, unequivocal. SEE MAIN ENTRY
peremptory challenge SEE MAIN ENTRY
peremptory claim demand
peremptory demand dun
peremptory refusal rebuff
perennial chronic, consecutive, constant, continual (connected), continuous, immutable, incessant, indestructible, permanent, unremitting
perenniality perpetuity
perennis permanent, perpetual
pererration vagrancy
perfect absolute (ideal), accurate, amend, attain, best, blameless, cap, complete, consummate, definitive, develop, elaborate, enhance, faithful (true to fact), felicitous, finish, fulfill, infallible, intact, mature, meritorious, peremptory (absolute), pure, rectify, renew (refurbish), renovate, right (suitable), ripe, thorough, unblemished, unimpeachable. SEE MAIN ENTRY
perfect a routine practice (train by repetition)
perfect substitute alter ego
perfected choate lien, elaborate
perfected condition maturity
perfectible corrigible
perfection amendment (correction), maturity, progress. SEE MAIN ENTRY
perfectionism casuistry, particularity
perfectly purely (positively)
perfectly sure positive (confident)
perferre enact, endure (suffer)
perfervid eager, fervent, intense, vehement, zealous. SEE MAIN ENTRY
perfervor ardor
perficere consummate, dispatch (dispose of), perfect, perform (execute)
perfidia infidelity, treason
perfidiosus faithless, perfidious
perfidious bad (offensive), collusive, contemptible, dishonest, disingenuous, disobedient, evasive, faithless, false (disloyal), felonious, fraudulent, insidious, irresponsible, lying, machiavellian, malevolent, mendacious, outrageous, recreant, tortuous (corrupt), undependable, unreliable, untrue, untrustworthy. SEE MAIN ENTRY
perfidiousness bad faith, bad repute, corruption, dishonesty, disloyalty, indirection (deceitfulness), infidelity
perfidus faithless, false (disloyal), perfidious

perfidy artifice, bad faith, bad repute, breach, bribery, collusion, corruption, deceit, dishonesty, disloyalty, duplicity, false pretense, fraud, indirection (deceitfulness), infidelity, treason, turpitude
perforable penetrable
perforare pierce (lance)
perforate enter (penetrate), lancinate, penetrate, pervade, pierce (lance)
perforated penetrable
perforation split
perform abide, commit (perpetrate), comply, comport (behave), demonstrate (establish), dispatch (dispose of), effectuate, execute (accomplish), exercise (discharge a function), fulfill, function, implement, inflict, keep (fulfill), make, obey, observe (obey), officiate, operate, perpetrate, pretend, pursue (carry on), realize (make real), recite, render (administer), transact. SEE MAIN ENTRY
perform a circuit detour, deviate
perform a function avail (be of use)
perform by turns alternate (take turns), reciprocate
perform on militate
perform reciprocally alternate (take turns)
perform repeatedly practice (train by repetition)
perform responsively alternate (take turns), reciprocate
perform sentry duty patrol
perform the duties of practice (engage in)
perform the functions of practice (engage in)
performability feasibility
performable facile, possible, potential, practicable, viable
performance act (undertaking), conduct, course, finality, fruition, function, histrionics, infliction, operation, part (role), proceeding, process (course), realization, role, transaction. SEE MAIN ENTRY
performance of executive duties administration
performance owed obligation (duty)
performed complete (ended)
performer actor
performing active, operative
perfringere breach
perfugium refuge
perfunctoriness disinterest (lack of interest), laxity
perfunctory careless, casual, cursory, inadequate, informal, lax, superficial. SEE MAIN ENTRY
pergere continue (persevere)
periculum danger, experiment, hazard, risk, venture
peril danger, endanger, hazard, jeopardize, jeopardy, menace, pitfall, risk, threat, venture. SEE MAIN ENTRY
perilous dangerous, disastrous, insalubrious, insecure, noxious, ominous, peccant (unhealthy), portentous (ominous), precarious
perilousness danger, jeopardy
perimeter ambit, border, boundary, configuration (confines), confines, contour (outline), enclosure, frontier, guideline, limit, margin (outside limit), mete, outline (boundary), periphery, purview, range, zone. SEE MAIN ENTRY
perimeters realm
perimetric peripheral
perimetrical peripheral

perimetros periphery

period age, annum, cycle, date, duration, expiration, life *(period of existence)*, moratorium, tenure, term *(duration)*, time. SEE MAIN ENTRY

period of allowance grace period

period of being under legal age minority *(infancy)*

period of being under statutory age minority *(infancy)*

period of decrease decline

period of detention quarantine

period of existence lifetime

period of indulgence grace period

period of isolation quarantine

period of legal immaturity nonage

period of legal minority nonage

period of life lifetime

period of obligatory delay moratorium

period of rest lull

period of survival life *(period of existence)*, lifetime

period of testing probation

period of time date, duration, phase *(period)*

period of tolerance grace period

period of trial probation

periodic disjunctive *(tending to disjoin)*, habitual, infrequent, intermittent, regular *(orderly)*, repeated, sporadic. SEE MAIN ENTRY

periodic payment installment, premium *(insurance payment)*

periodic returns from property or labor income

periodical habitual, journal, organ, publication *(printed matter)*, regular *(orderly)*, serial, sporadic

periodicity frequency, regularity

peripatetic itinerant *(adjective)*, itinerant *(noun)*, moving *(in motion)*, pedestrian

peripheral collateral *(immaterial)*, expendable, extraneous, extrinsic, minor, nonessential, null *(insignificant)*. SEE MAIN ENTRY

peripheral group minority *(outnumbered group)*

periphery ambit, border, boundary, contour *(outline)*, edge *(border)*, frontier, margin *(outside limit)*, mete, outline *(boundary)*, zone. SEE MAIN ENTRY

periphrasis digression, indirection *(indirect action)*

periphrastic indirect, redundant, turgid

periphrastical indirect

perire perish

perish decease, die, expire, succumb. SEE MAIN ENTRY

perishable ephemeral, nonsubstantial *(not sturdy)*, temporary, transient

perished deceased, defunct, late *(defunct)*, lifeless *(dead)*, lost *(taken away)*

peritia experience *(background)*, skill

peritus acquainted, familiar *(informed)*, proficient

periurare perjure

periurium perjury

periurium facere perjure

perjure palter, prevaricate. SEE MAIN ENTRY

perjure oneself bear false witness, fabricate *(make up)*, frame *(charge falsely)*, lie *(falsify)*, misrepresent

perjured dishonest, fraudulent, lying, mendacious, perfidious

perjured testimony frame up

perjury deceit, dishonesty, falsification, fiction, hypocrisy, misstatement, subreption. SEE MAIN ENTRY

perlegere peruse

perlustrare perambulate

permanence constant, continuity, indestructibility, perpetuity, survival

permanent chronic, constant, continual *(perpetual)*, conventional, durable, fixed *(securely placed)*, fixed *(settled)*, immutable, indefeasible, indelible, indestructible, infinite, ingrained, irreversible, irrevocable, last *(final)*, noncancellable, perpetual, stable, standing, static, unalterable. SEE MAIN ENTRY

permanent attachment to real property fixture

permanent exclusion expulsion, ouster

permanent legal address home *(domicile)*

permanent resident inhabitant

permanent structure monument

permanere endure *(last)*, last, pursue *(carry on)*

permeable penetrable

permeare diffuse

permeate diffuse, imbue, penetrate, pervade, spread. SEE MAIN ENTRY

permeation infusion, osmosis

permeative ubiquitous

permetiri measure

permiscere confuse *(bewilder)*, muddle

permissibility admissibility, legitimacy

permissible admissible, allowable, allowed, lawful, legal, licit, potential. SEE MAIN ENTRY

permissible evidence admissible evidence

permissibleness legality

permissio leave *(permission)*

permission acquiescence, admittance *(acceptance)*, assent, capacity *(authority)*, charter *(sanction)*, concession *(authorization)*, consent, discretion *(power of choice)*, dispensation *(exception)*, favor *(sanction)*, franchise *(license)*, indorsement, indulgence, liberty, license, permit, privilege, sanction *(permission)*, sufferance, title *(right)*, warrant *(authorization)*. SEE MAIN ENTRY

permission to defer payment credit *(delayed payment)*

permission to rent lease

permissioned allowed

permissive SEE MAIN ENTRY

permit abide, accede *(concede)*, allow *(authorize)*, allow *(endure)*, approval, assent, authorize, bear, bestow, capacity *(authority)*, certify *(approve)*, charge *(empower)*, charter *(license)*, charter *(sanction)*, concede, concession *(authorization)*, condone, confirm, consent *(noun)*, consent *(verb)*, copyright, dispensation *(exception)*, empower, enable, enfranchise, exemption, franchise *(license)*, freedom, grant *(concede)*, invest *(vest)*, key *(passport)*, leave *(allow to remain)*, license, palliate *(excuse)*, patent, qualify *(meet standards)*, receive *(permit to enter)*, recognize *(acknowledge)*, sanction *(permission)*, sanction, tolerate, vouchsafe, warrant *(authorization)*, yield *(submit)*. SEE MAIN ENTRY

permit by law legalize

permit to borrow lend, loan

permit to vote enfranchise

permittance acquiescence, leave *(permission)*

permitted admissible, allowed, due *(regular)*, entitled, justifiable, lawful, licit, open *(accessible)*, pardonable, permissible, potential, privileged, public *(open)*, rightful, unrestricted

permitted by law legal

permittere concede, countenance, devolve, grant *(concede)*, grant *(transfer formally)*, suffer *(permit)*

permitting charitable *(lenient)*, consenting

permutable aleatory *(uncertain)*, ambulatory, convertible, protean

permutatio exchange, interchange

permutation exchange, mutuality

permute alternate *(take turns)*, change, convert *(change use)*

perniciosus deadly, detrimental, disastrous, fatal, pernicious

pernicious bad *(offensive)*, deadly, deleterious, destructive, detrimental, disadvantageous, disastrous, fatal, harmful, heinous, immoral, inadvisable, incendiary, inimical, iniquitous, insalubrious, lethal, malevolent, malicious, malignant, nefarious, noxious, objectionable, obnoxious, oppressive, pestilent, prejudicial, sinister, toxic, vicious, virulent. SEE MAIN ENTRY

perniciousness fatality, harm

perorate converse, declaim, discourse

peroratio peroration

peroration close *(conclusion)*. SEE MAIN ENTRY

perperam misunderstand

perperam accipere misconceive

perpetrate execute *(accomplish)*, operate, perform *(execute)*. SEE MAIN ENTRY

perpetration act *(undertaking)*, commission *(act)*, course, discharge *(performance)*, infliction, performance *(execution)*

perpetual chronic, constant, continuous, durable, habitual, immutable, incessant, indestructible, infinite, periodic, permanent, stable, standing, unlimited, unremitting. SEE MAIN ENTRY

perpetually invariably

perpetualness perpetuity

perpetuate continue *(prolong)*, establish *(entrench)*, keep *(continue)*, maintain *(carry on)*, persevere, preserve, prolong, remain *(continue)*, sustain *(prolong)*, uphold. SEE MAIN ENTRY

perpetuated lasting, permanent, perpetual, standing

perpetuating honorary

perpetuation continuance, continuation *(prolongation)*, longevity, perpetuity, preservation, remembrance *(commemoration)*

perpetuitas continuance, continuation *(prolongation)*, continuity, perpetuity

perpetuity continuity, indestructibility. SEE MAIN ENTRY

perpetuo comitari inseparable

perpetuus continual *(perpetual)*, incessant, indestructible

perplex agitate *(perturb)*, badger, bait *(harass)*, confound, confuse *(bewilder)*, discommode, discompose, disconcert, disorganize, disturb, obfuscate, perturb. SEE MAIN ENTRY

perplexed lost *(disoriented)*

perplexing complex, debatable, difficult, disputable, dubious, enigmatic, equivocal, indefinable, labyrinthine, mysterious, peculiar *(curious)*, problematic, recondite, uncertain *(ambiguous)*, vague

perplexing state of affairs imbroglio

perplexity cloud *(suspicion)*, complication, confusion *(ambiguity)*, dilemma, doubt *(indecision)*, enigma, ignorance, impasse, incertitude, paradox, predicament, quagmire, quandary

perplexus indistinct, labyrinthine

perquisite bounty, gratuity *(present)*, pay, prerogative, privilege, reward, tip *(gratuity)*. SEE MAIN ENTRY

perquisites bonus, paraphernalia *(personal belongings)*, revenue

perquisition examination *(study)*, indagation, probe, quest

perscribere record, register

perscrutari investigate, scrutinize

perscrutatio scrutiny

perscrutation indagation, probe

persecute abuse *(violate)*, badger, bait *(harass)*, brutalize, endanger, exploit *(take advantage of)*, harrow, harry *(harass)*, hector, ill use, irritate, maltreat, mishandle *(maltreat)*, mistreat, pique, plague, press *(goad)*, provoke. SEE MAIN ENTRY

persecuted aggrieved *(victimized)*

persecuting brutal, callous, illiberal, malignant

persecution abuse *(physical misuse)*, cruelty, infliction, injustice, intolerance, molestation, oppression

persecutor bigot

persequi prosecute *(carry forward)*

perseverance continuance, continuation *(prolongation)*, industry *(activity)*, longanimity, purpose, resolution *(decision)*, tenacity, tolerance

perseverant diligent, insistent, lasting, patient, persistent, relentless, sedulous, steadfast, strong, undaunted, unrelenting, unremitting, unyielding, zealous

perseverare continue *(persevere)*, keep *(continue)*

persevere adhere *(persist)*, bear *(tolerate)*, continue *(persevere)*, endeavor, endure *(last)*, hold out *(resist)*, insist, keep *(continue)*, last, maintain *(carry on)*, persist, prolong, pursue *(carry on)*, recur, remain *(continue)*, resist *(withstand)*, stay *(continue)*. SEE MAIN ENTRY

persevere at ply

persevere in prosecute *(carry forward)*

perseverence prowess *(bravery)*. SEE MAIN ENTRY

persevering chronic, diligent, durable, faithful *(diligent)*, indelible, indestructible, indomitable, industrious, inexorable, inflexible, insistent, live *(existing)*, painstaking, patient, permanent, persistent, pertinacious, purposeful, relentless, resolute, sedulous, steadfast, strong, undaunted, unrelenting, unremitting, unyielding

persist continue *(persevere)*, endure *(last)*, exist, hold out *(resist)*, insist, keep *(continue)*, last, maintain *(carry on)*, persevere, prosecute *(carry forward)*, pursue *(carry on)*, recur, remain *(continue)*, repeat *(do again)*, resist *(withstand)*, stay *(continue)*, subsist. SEE MAIN ENTRY

persist in adhere *(persist)*, bear *(tolerate)*

persistence continuance, continuation *(prolongation)*, diligence *(perseverance)*, industry *(activity)*, longevity, purpose, resolution *(decision)*, tenacity, tolerance, uniformity

persistency diligence *(perseverance)*, tenacity

persistent chronic, continual *(connected)*, diligent, durable, faithful *(diligent)*, frequent, immutable, incessant, indelible, industrious, inexorable, infinite, insistent, lasting, patient, permanent, perpetual, pertinacious, purposeful, relentless, repeated, resolute, sedulous, stable, steadfast, strong, undaunted, unrelenting, unremitting, unyielding, zealous. SEE MAIN ENTRY

persistent exertion diligence *(perseverance)*

persistere continue *(persevere)*, persevere, persist, pursue *(carry on)*

persisting chronic, durable, indelible, indestructible, inexorable, insistent, irrevocable, lasting, live *(existing)*, patient, permanent, pertinacious, undaunted

persisting in error perverse

persisting in fault perverse

persnickety particular *(exacting)*

person actor, character *(an individual)*, individual. SEE MAIN ENTRY

person accused of crime suspect

person affording evidence witness

person appointed to administer affairs trustee

person coming from a foreign country alien

person employing advice client

person entrusted with property of another fiduciary

person from foreign parts alien

person full of character individual

person in authority chairman, chief, incumbent, official, principal *(director)*

person in charge caretaker *(one fulfilling the function of office)*, chief, executor, principal *(director)*

person in possession holder, lessee

person in responsibility executor

person making a feoffment feoffor

person named to carry out the provisions of a will executor

person of age adult

person of experience veteran

person of importance key man

person of intellect mastermind

person of repute key man, paragon

person of voting age adult

person represented client

person represented by counsel client

person responsible official

person under 18 years of age minor

person under 18 years old infant

person under arrest captive, prisoner

person under guardianship dependent

person under legal age juvenile, minor

person under the age of majority infant

person who conveys a fee feoffor

person who flees justice fugitive

person who is not of full age infant, minor

person who makes a claim claimant

person who makes allegations declarant

person who writes author *(writer)*

person with a grievance claimant

personage body *(person)*, character *(an individual)*, individual, person

personal intimate, particular *(individual)*, private *(confidential)*, privy, several *(separate)*, subjective, unofficial. SEE MAIN ENTRY

personal allowance alimony

personal bearing behavior, conduct, deportment, manner *(behavior)*

personal bias prejudice *(preconception)*

personal characteristic identity *(individuality)*, specialty *(distinctive mark)*

personal chattels which are not in possession intangible

personal effect chattel

personal effects assets, movable, paraphernalia *(personal belongings)*, property *(possessions)*

personal equation characteristic

personal estate goods, paraphernalia *(personal belongings)*

personal gain earnings

personal hatred malice

personal identity personality

personal judgment assumption *(supposition)*, conviction *(persuasion)*, estimate *(idea)*

personal mark personality

personal matter confidence *(relation of trust)*, secret

personal presence appearance *(look)*

personal property effects, movable, paraphernalia *(personal belongings)*, personalty, possessions

personal property capable of being inherited hereditament

personal reasons motive

personal representative administrator, executor

personal resources assets, personalty, property *(possessions)*

personal right not reduced to possession intangible

personal security pledge *(security)*

personal style manner *(behavior)*

personal traits character *(personal quality)*

personal wrong tort

personality character *(an individual)*, character *(personal quality)*, disposition *(inclination)*, identity *(individuality)*, individual, presence *(poise)*, property *(distinctive attribute)*, temperament. SEE MAIN ENTRY

personalize call *(title)*

personalized private *(not public)*, subjective

personally in person

personally solicit lobby

personalty chattel, effects, estate *(property)*, movable, paraphernalia *(personal belongings)*, possessions

personate assume *(simulate)*, copy, feign, impersonate, mock *(imitate)*, pose *(impersonate)*

personation caricature, copy

personification embodiment

personify characterize, depict, embody, impersonate. SEE MAIN ENTRY

personifying exemplary

personnel copartner *(business associate)*

personnel employee, staff. SEE MAIN ENTRY

persons humanity *(mankind)*, populace, population, public

persons in office authorities

persons in power hierarchy *(persons in authority)*

persons of commanding influence authorities

persons summoned to attend the court as jurymen panel *(jurors)*

personship identity *(individuality)*

perspective aspect, opinion *(belief)*, outlook, standpoint, vision *(dream)*. SEE MAIN ENTRY

perspicacious acute, circumspect, cognizant, discriminating *(judicious)*, judicious, juridical, lucid, perceptive, sapient, sensitive *(discerning)*

perspicaciousness comprehension, experience *(background)*, perception, sagacity

perspicacitas sagacity

perspicacity caliber *(mental capacity)*, discretion *(quality of being discreet)*, discrimination *(good judgment)*, insight, judgment *(discernment)*, perception, sagacity, sense *(intelligence)*. SEE MAIN ENTRY

909

perspicax acute, perspicacious
perspicuity discrimination (good judgment)
perspicuous appreciable, clear (apparent), cognizable, coherent (clear), comprehensible, evident, explicit, lucid, manifest, obvious, open (in sight), ostensible, overt, palpable, patent, perceivable, perceptible, unambiguous, unmistakable. SEE MAIN ENTRY
perspicuousness judgment (discernment)
perspicuus comprehensible, distinct (clear), lucid, manifest, obvious
perstare persevere, persist
perstringere refer (direct attention)
persuable reasonable (rational)
persuadable amenable, open (persuasible), open-minded, pliable, receptive, suasible, susceptible (responsive)
persuade agitate (activate), assure (give confidence to), bait (lure), coax, convince, counsel, exhort, incite, induce, influence, inspire, inveigle, lobby, motivate, prejudice (influence), pressure, prevail upon, prompt, reason (persuade), recommend, urge. SEE MAIN ENTRY
persuade against caution, deter, discourage
persuade by argument convince
persuade not to work picket
persuade oneself presuppose
persuade to believe error delude
persuaded affirmative, certain (positive), definite, positive (confident)
persuadere convince, prevail (persuade), prevail upon
persuaders lobby
persuading hortative, moving (evoking emotion)
persuasibility amenability, credulity
persuasible amenable, credulous, open-minded, pliable, suasible
persuasio belief (state of mind), faith
persuasion belief (something believed), concept, conclusion (determination), credence, denomination, dogma, force (compulsion), guidance, idea, incentive, inducement, instigation, motive, opinion (belief), patronage (power to appoint jobs), pressure, propaganda, seduction, standpoint, surety (certainty). SEE MAIN ENTRY
persuasive believable, cogent, colorable (plausible), convincing, determinative, eloquent, hortative, prevailing (having superior force), provocative, sound, specious, strong. SEE MAIN ENTRY
persuasive facts evidence
persuasiveness inducement
persuasory persuasive
pert brazen, impertinent (insolent), insolent, presumptuous
pertain appertain, correspond (be equivalent), refer (direct attention), relate (establish a connection). SEE MAIN ENTRY
pertain to affiliate, concern (involve), connect (relate)
pertaining correlative, pertinent, relative (relevant)
pertaining to comparative, germane, incident, relevant
pertaining to business commercial
pertaining to financial matters fiscal
pertaining to government finances fiscal
pertaining to home household (domestic)
pertaining to law jural
pertaining to litigation actionable
pertaining to merchants commercial

pertaining to monetary receipts and expenditures fiscal
pertaining to one's household domestic (household)
pertaining to ownership proprietary
pertaining to property proprietary
pertaining to the courts forensic
pertaining to the family domestic (household), household (domestic)
pertaining to the home domestic (household)
pertaining to the law forensic
pertaining to the public revenues fiscal
pertaining to the public treasury fiscal
pertaining to the whole community common (shared)
pertaining to trade commercial
pertinacia tenacity
pertinacious diligent, faithful (diligent), inexorable, inflexible, insistent, intractable, obdurate, patient, persistent, purposeful, relentless, resolute, sedulous, steadfast, unrelenting, unremitting, unyielding. SEE MAIN ENTRY
pertinaciousness tenacity
pertinacity diligence (perseverance), tenacity
pertinax contumacious, froward, inflexible, pertinacious, willful
pertinence connection (relation), interest (concern), propriety (appropriateness), qualification (fitness), relation (connection), relationship (connection), relevance
pertinent akin (germane), applicable, apposite, appropriate, felicitous, fit, germane, interrelated, intrinsic (belonging), material (important), noteworthy, related, relative (relevant), relevant, suitable, tangential. SEE MAIN ENTRY
pertinent to comparative
pertinere concern (involve), relate (establish a connection)
pertinere ad apply (pertain)
pertness disrespect
perturb badger, bait (harass), discommode, discompose, disconcert, disorganize, disorient, disrupt, distress, disturb, embarrass, harrow, molest (annoy), obfuscate, perplex, pique, provoke, upset. SEE MAIN ENTRY
perturbance panic
perturbare confuse (bewilder), disconcert, disorganize, disturb
perturbate agitate (perturb), perturb
perturbatio confusion (turmoil)
perturbation apprehension (fear), commotion, confusion (ambiguity), consternation, distress (anguish), disturbance, embarrassment, instigation, misgiving, panic, quandary, trepidation, turmoil
perturbed frenetic, unsettled
perturbing enigmatic
perturbo perturb
perusal analysis, discovery, examination (study), indagation, inquiry (systematic investigation), inspection, scrutiny. SEE MAIN ENTRY
peruse check (inspect), examine (study), observe (watch), probe, read, regard (pay attention), scrutinize, study, survey (examine). SEE MAIN ENTRY
peruse carefully concentrate (pay attention)
pervade diffuse, enter (penetrate), imbue, obsess, penetrate, permeate, spread. SEE MAIN ENTRY

pervadere penetrate
pervading ubiquitous
pervagari perambulate
pervasive broad, ubiquitous
perverse arbitrary, contentious, contumacious, difficult, disobedient, fractious, froward, intractable, opposite, petulant, restive, sinister, unruly, unyielding, vicious. SEE MAIN ENTRY
perverseness contempt (disobedience to the court)
perversion abuse (corrupt practice), debauchment, distortion, lie, misapplication, misstatement, misusage, misuse, sodomy, travesty, vice. SEE MAIN ENTRY
perversion of integrity corruption
perversion of the truth evasion
perversion of truth false pretense, falsehood, indirection (deceitfulness), perjury, story (falsehood)
perversity bad repute
perversus incorrect, perverse
pervert abuse (misuse), adulterate, bear false witness, brutalize, camouflage, contort, corrupt, damage, debase, debauch, degenerate, denature, deteriorate, distort, falsify, harm, infect, invent (falsify), lie (falsify), misconceive, misconstrue, misemploy, misguide, mislead, mismanage, misread, misrepresent, misstate, mistreat, misunderstand, palter, pollute, prevaricate, slant, subvert, taint (corrupt), vitiate. SEE MAIN ENTRY
perverted depraved, dissolute, immoral, mendacious, perverse, tainted (corrupted)
pervicacious intractable, obdurate, pertinacious, recalcitrant, restive, unreasonable, unyielding
pervicax pertinacious
pervious amenable, disposable, open (persuasible), passable, penetrable, pliable, suasible
pervius penetrable
pervulgatus prevalent, trite
pessimism damper (depressant). SEE MAIN ENTRY
pessimistic cynical, despondent, disconsolate, ominous. SEE MAIN ENTRY
pest nuisance
pester annoy, badger, discompose, harass, harry (harass), hector, importune, irritate, molest (annoy), perturb, pique, plague, press (goad)
pestering vexatious
pestiferous contagious, dangerous, deadly, harmful, insalubrious, lethal, malignant, noxious, pernicious
pestilence nuisance
pestilens insalubrious, pestilent
pestilent insalubrious, lethal, noxious, peccant (unhealthy), toxic. SEE MAIN ENTRY
pestilential deleterious, detrimental, harmful, insalubrious, lethal, malignant, pernicious, pestilent
pet animal, popular
petard bomb
peter out perish, subside
petere petition, solicit
petit petty
petitio application, plea
petition appeal, application, apply (request), bill (formal declaration), call (appeal), call (appeal to), canvass, claim (demand), complaint, cross-examine, entreaty, importune, invitation, motion, move (judicially request), plead (implore), pray, prayer, press (beseech), request

(noun), request (verb), requisition, solicit, sue, suit. SEE MAIN ENTRY

petition for intercede, request

petition for release habeas corpus

petitionary solicitous

petitioner accuser, actor, appellant, applicant (petitioner), candidate, claimant, complainant, contender, litigant, malcontent, party (litigant), plaintiff, special interest, suitor, undersigned. SEE MAIN ENTRY

petitioner for legal redress complainant

petitioners lobby

petitor contestant, plaintiff

petrification congealment

petrified ossified

petrify browbeat, frighten, intimidate

pettifog cheat, circumvent. SEE MAIN ENTRY

pettifoggery artifice, bad faith, bribery, false pretense, knavery. SEE MAIN ENTRY

pettifogging bunko, hoax, immoral

pettiness immateriality

pettish fractious, petulant, querulous

petty de minimus, frivolous, illiberal, inappreciable, inconsequential, inconsiderable, insubstantial, minor, nominal, nugatory, null (insignificant), paltry, parsimonious, penurious, provincial, puerile, slight, tenuous, trivial. SEE MAIN ENTRY

petty detail technicality

petty dishonesty pettifoggery

petulans petulant

petulant argumentative, brazen, fractious, froward, perverse, querulous. SEE MAIN ENTRY

phalanx band, mass (body of persons)

phantasm phantom

phantasmal delusive, illusory

phantom SEE MAIN ENTRY

pharisaism hypocrisy

phase aspect, duration, transition. SEE MAIN ENTRY

phenomenal extraordinary, infrequent, noteworthy, portentous (eliciting amazement), prodigious (amazing), unusual

phenomenon experience (encounter), happening, occurrence, vision (dream). SEE MAIN ENTRY

philanthropic benevolent, charitable (benevolent), donative, humane, liberal (generous), magnanimous, meritorious, nonprofit. SEE MAIN ENTRY

philanthropic gift charity

philanthropic institution foundation (organization)

philanthropist benefactor, contributor (giver), donor, good samaritan, patron (influential supporter), samaritan

philanthropize bestow, dedicate

philanthropy benefit (conferment), benevolence (act of kindness), benevolence (disposition to do good), charity, dedication, donation, favor (act of kindness), goodwill, help, largess (generosity). SEE MAIN ENTRY

philippic denunciation

philippic outcry, revilement, stricture. SEE MAIN ENTRY

philistine ordinary. SEE MAIN ENTRY

philoprogenitive fertile, prolific

philosophaster pedant

philosophia moralis ethics

philosophic patient, stoical

philosophical cogitative, logical, profound (esoteric), theoretical

philosophize reason (conclude), speculate (conjecture)

philosophy doctrine, posture (attitude), principle (axiom), theory

philosophy of law jurisprudence

phlegm disinterest (lack of interest), languor, sloth

phlegmatic dispassionate, indolent, languid, lifeless (dull), obtuse, otiose, passive, stagnant, torpid. SEE MAIN ENTRY

phlegmatical languid, phlegmatic, stagnant

phobia apprehension (fear), fear, fright, panic, paranoia. SEE MAIN ENTRY

phoenix revival

phonate enunciate

phonation intonation, speech

phonic nuncupative, oral

phoniness falsification

phony bogus, fictitious, fraudulent, imitation, specious

photographic descriptive

photostat duplicate

phrase chapter (division), clause, denominate, express, observe (remark), relate (tell), speak, term (expression). SEE MAIN ENTRY

phraseology language, parlance, rhetoric (skilled speech), speech. SEE MAIN ENTRY

phrasing language, phraseology, rhetoric (skilled speech)

phrenetic fanatical

phrenetical fanatical

phylactery reminder

phylum race

physic drug (noun), drug (verb)

physical bodily, concrete, corporal, corporeal, mundane, tangible. SEE MAIN ENTRY

physical appearance demeanor

physical being body (person), materiality (physical existence)

physical condition health

physical derangement disease

physical element component

physical force compulsion (coercion)

physical hurt injury

physical limit capacity (maximum)

physical nature materiality (physical existence)

physical power force (strength)

physically strong powerful

physicalness materiality (physical existence)

physiognomy appearance (look), feature (appearance)

physique body (person), configuration (form)

piacular penitent

piaculum expiation

picayune inconsequential, insubstantial, minor, negligible, petty, trivial

pick alternative (option), appoint, choice (alternatives offered), choose, cull, decide, decision (election), discretion (power of choice), elect (choose), election (choice), extract, option (choice), prefer, reap, screen (select), select, volition, vote

pick a quarrel bicker

pick one's pockets jostle (pickpocket)

pick out appoint, choose, cull, eviscerate, except (exclude), extract, prefer

pick up elevate, gain, glean, heighten (elevate), obtain, overhear, procure, purchase, reap, receive (acquire)

picked preferable, select

picked out preferred (favored)

pickeer hold up (rob)

picket demonstrate (protest). SEE MAIN ENTRY

pickings spoils

pickle imbroglio

pickpocket hoodlum

pickpocketing larceny

picky particular (exacting)

pictorial descriptive, suggestive (evocative)

picture characterize, conceive (comprehend), concept, contour (outline), delineate, depict, describe, design (construction plan), detail (particularize), draw (depict), exemplify, portray, recount, render (depict), represent (portray), symbol, vision (dream)

picturize delineate

piddling inconsiderable, paltry, petty, puerile

piece commingle, component, constituent (part), detail, element, gun, item, lot, member (constituent part), minimum, moiety, parcel, part (portion), ration, repair, segment, story (narrative), unit (item)

piece of apparatus appliance

piece of architecture building (structure), edifice

piece of ground lot

piece of information item, particular

piece of land parcel, plot (land), premises (buildings)

piece of landed property estate (property)

piece of legislation measure

piece of news item

piece together combine (join together), consolidate (unite), devise (invent), fabricate (construct), frame (construct), join (bring together), make, merge, solve

pieced together conjoint

piecemeal SEE MAIN ENTRY

pierce break (fracture), enter (penetrate), impress (affect deeply), inject, lancinate, penetrate, pervade. SEE MAIN ENTRY

piercing acute, bitter (penetrating), caustic, harsh, incisive, interrogative, mordacious, perspicacious, profound (intense), trenchant

piercing of the corporate veil SEE MAIN ENTRY

pietas affection

pig-headed obdurate

pigeonhearted recreant

pigeonhole classify, defer (put off), file (arrange), hold up (delay), partition, postpone, procrastinate, set aside (reserve). SEE MAIN ENTRY

piger stagnant

piggish insatiable

pigheaded pertinacious

pignerare pawn

pignoration security (pledge)

pignus bail, mortgage, pledge (security), security (stock)

pignus judiciale charge (lien), cloud (incumbrance)

pignus legale cloud (incumbrance)

piker bettor

pile agglomeration, assemblage, collect (gather), collection (accumulation), cumulation, hoard, load, selection (collection)

pile up accumulate (amass), compound, hoard, keep (shelter), set aside (reserve), store

pileup collision (accident)

pilfer despoil, embezzle, hold up (rob), jostle (pickpocket), loot, peculate, poach, purloin, rob, steal. SEE MAIN ENTRY

pilferage larceny, misappropriation, theft

pilferer burglar, criminal, embezzler, thief

pilfering burglary, embezzlement, housebreaking, plagiarism, spoliation, theft

piling up cumulative (increasing)

911

pillage despoil, devastate, harry (plunder), havoc, hold up (rob), loot, pilfer, pirate (take by violence), plunder (noun), plunder (verb), prey, prize, rape, rob, seize (confiscate), spoils, spoliation, steal. SEE MAIN ENTRY

pillager burglar, criminal, thief, vandal

pillaging burglary, foray, predatory, rapacious, spoliation

pillar mainstay

pillory brand (stigmatize), defame, denigrate, denounce (condemn), disgrace, dishonor (deprive of honor), smear. SEE MAIN ENTRY

pilot administer (conduct), conduct, control (regulate), govern, manage, manipulate (utilize skillfully), moderate (preside over), officiate, operate, overlook (superintend), oversee, prescribe, preside, superintend

pilotage direction (guidance), management (supervision)

pilpulistic argumentative

pin fix (make firm)

pin down restrict

pinch constrict (compress), dearth, plight, predicament, privation, quagmire, retrench, stress (strain)

pinch hitter substitute

pinchbeck spurious

pinched impecunious, narrow

pine languish

pine away languish

pinion contain (restrain), handcuff (noun), handcuff (verb), restrict, trammel

pinnacle ceiling, culmination. SEE MAIN ENTRY

pinpoint designate, discover, locate. SEE MAIN ENTRY

pioneer commence, forerunner, initiate, originate, precede, precursor. SEE MAIN ENTRY

pious tartuffish, zealous

piquancy instigation

piquant hot-blooded, incisive, moving (evoking emotion), palatable, provocative, sapid, savory

pique affront, aggravate (annoy), annoy, badger, bait (harass), discommode, discompose, dissatisfaction, disturb, harrow, harry (harass), incense, interest, irritate, malice, molest (annoy), offend (insult), perturb, plague, provoke, resentment, stimulate, umbrage. SEE MAIN ENTRY

piqued bitter (reproachful), petulant, resentful

piracy pillage, robbery, spoliation

pirate abduct, copy, criminal, hijack, hold up (rob), impropriate, loot, pillage, plagiarize, plunder, poach, prey, seize (confiscate), spoil (pillage), steal, thief. SEE MAIN ENTRY

piratic larcenous

piratical larcenous, rapacious

piste brand

pistol gun

pit against alienate (estrange), counter, counteract

pit against one another polarize

pitch elevate, inflection, intonation, launch (project), precipitate (throw down violently)

pitch into attack

piteous deplorable, lamentable, lugubrious

pitfall hazard, trap, trouble. SEE MAIN ENTRY

pith center (essence), contents, corpus, essence, gist (substance), import, main point, significance, signification, subject (topic), substance (essential nature)

pith of a matter gist (ground for a suit)

pithless languid, powerless

pithy brief, concise, eloquent, laconic, sententious, succinct. SEE MAIN ENTRY

pithy saying catchword, maxim

pitiable deplorable, lamentable

pitiful deplorable, lamentable, paltry, poor (inferior in quality)

pitiless brutal, callous, cold-blooded, cruel, diabolic, harmful, harsh, implacable, inexorable, malevolent, relentless, remorseless, ruthless, severe, unaffected (uninfluenced), unrelenting, unresponsive

pitilessness brutality, malice

pittance paucity, ration

pitted blemished, marred

pitted-against SEE MAIN ENTRY

pitting of strength competition

pitting of strengths contest (competition)

pitting of wits competition

pity lenience, relent, sympathize. SEE MAIN ENTRY

pitying lenient

pivot cornerstone, crossroad (turning point)

pivotal cardinal (basic), causative, central (essential), critical (crucial), crucial, decisive, indispensable, material (important). SEE MAIN ENTRY

pivotal argument base (foundation)

pivotal point gravamen, main point. SEE MAIN ENTRY

placabilis peaceable, placable

placability amenability, benevolence (disposition to do good), lenience, longanimity

placable lenient, nonmilitant. SEE MAIN ENTRY

placableness lenience

placare pacify, placate, propitiate, soothe

placate disarm (set at ease), lull, mollify, pacify, propitiate, reconcile, soothe. SEE MAIN ENTRY

placation conciliation, mollification

placative nonmilitant

placatus dispassionate

place allocate, area (province), base (place), building (structure), case (set of circumstances), character (reputation), circuit, class, deploy, dispose (apportion), employ (engage services), fix (arrange), habitation (dwelling place), identify, inhabitation (place of dwelling), instate, levy, locality, locate, location, lodge (house), lodge (reside), marshal, organize (arrange), pigeonhole, pinpoint, plant (place firmly), position (situation), post, premises (buildings), prestige, recall (remember), recognize (perceive), recollect, region, remember, residence, role, scene, seat, set down, site (noun), site (verb), situs, source, stand (witness' place in court), status, territory. SEE MAIN ENTRY

place a cloud on encumber (financially obligate)

place a false construction on misinterpret

place a value on calculate, estimate, evaluate

place a wrong construction on misinterpret

place against contrast

place an erroneous construction on misinterpret

place an instrument in a place of deposit file (place among official records)

place at one's disposal extend (offer), present (make a gift)

place at ones disposal hold out (deliberate on an offer)

place authority vest

place before introduce, preface

place between interpose

place by itself isolate

place close together juxtapose

place control vest

place for safe keeping depository

place in a category classify, partition, pigeonhole

place in a dubious position compromise (endanger)

place in a former state reinstate

place in a receptacle deposit (place)

place in an office delegate

place in authority nominate

place in charge of delegate

place in command nominate

place in confinement arrest (apprehend), commit (institutionalize), imprison, jail

place in custody again rearrest

place in danger jeopardize

place in durance confine, contain (restrain), detain (hold in custody)

place in juxtaposition border (approach), compare, contrast

place in office elect (select by a vote), hire, induct, instate, nominate

place in official custody of the clerk file (place among official records)

place in order apportion, arrange (methodize), classify, file (arrange), fix (arrange), marshal, organize (arrange), sort

place in the condition of natural born subjects naturalize (make a citizen)

place in the foreground adduce

place in the possession of deliver

place in the protection of entrust

place in the record enter (record)

place into enter (insert), inject, interject

place limitations border (bound), clog

place near border (approach), juxtapose

place next to juxtapose

place of abode habitation (dwelling place), home (domicile), household, inhabitation (place of dwelling)

place of assignation rendezvous

place of birth home (place of origin)

place of business address, market (business), market place, office

place of business traffic market place

place of buying and selling market (business), market place

place of commerce market (business), market place

place of concealment cache (hiding place)

place of confinement jail, penitentiary

place of deposit cache (storage place), depository, treasury

place of detention penitentiary

place of dwelling abode, home (domicile)

place of education institute

place of employment office

place of entry entrance

place of existence home (domicile)

place of exit egress

place of habitation building (structure), house

place of immunity asylum (hiding place)

place of imprisonment penitentiary

place of jurisdiction venue

place of meeting rendezvous

place of occupancy domicile

place of one's domestic affections home (domicile)

place of protection refuge
place of refuge asylum (hiding place), home (domicile), shelter (protection)
place of residence apartment, domicile, dwelling, habitation (dwelling place), home (domicile), inhabitation (place of dwelling), lodging, residence
place of rest home (domicile), lodging
place of safety cache (storage place), haven, refuge
place of settlement homestead
place of trade market (business), market place
place of traffic market (business)
place on record cast (register), file (place among official records)
place out of bounds exclude
place outside the protection of the law outlaw
place parallel border (approach)
place permanently fix (make firm)
place reliance in trust
place reliance on confide (trust)
place side by side adjoin, juxtapose
place the blame for lodge (bring a complaint)
place the blame on impute, incriminate
place the responsibility for impute
place to live in home (domicile)
place trust in delegate, rely
place under a liquid immerse (plunge into)
place under arrest apprehend (arrest)
place under federal administration federalize (place under federal control)
place under federal rule federalize (place under federal control)
place under government control nationalize
place under interdiction enjoin
place under protective custody confine
place under the ban enjoin
place upon a list empanel
place where justice is administered court, judicatory
place where one lives home (domicile)
placed situated
placed in advance preferred (given priority)
placement arrogation, assignation, classification, disposition (final arrangement), distribution (apportionment), distribution (arrangement), installation, location, order (arrangement), organization (structure), rating, situs
placement against contraposition
placement opposite contraposition
placere interest
placet brevet
placid complacent, patient, peaceable, stoical. SEE MAIN ENTRY
placidity composure, longanimity
placidness composure
placidus dispassionate, peaceable, placid
placing array (order), introduction
placing in confinement commitment (confinement)
placing in office appointment (act of designating), assignment (designation), designation (naming)
placitum decision (judgment)
placitum decree, dogma
plagiarism counterfeit. SEE MAIN ENTRY
plagiarize copy, fake, pirate (reproduce without authorization), steal. SEE MAIN ENTRY
plagiary counterfeit

plague annoy, badger, bait (harass), discommode, discompose, disease, disturb, dun, embarrass, harass, harm, harrow, harry (harass), hector, ill use, importune, infliction, irritate, mistreat, molest (annoy), nuisance, obsess, persecute, perturb, pique, press (goad), prey, provoke, trouble. SEE MAIN ENTRY
plagued by conscience penitent
plagueful pestilent
plaguesome invidious
plain apparent (perceptible), arrant (definite), blatant (conspicuous), clear (apparent), coherent (clear), comprehensible, conspicuous, direct (forthright), elementary, evident, exact, explicit, express, flagrant, genuine, household (familiar), ingenuous, jejune (dull), lucid, manifest, mere, mundane, naive, naked (lacking embellishment), naked (perceptible), nondescript, obvious, only (no more than), open (in sight), ostensible, overt, palpable, patent, pedestrian, pellucid, perceivable, perceptible, prosaic, salient, scrutable, simple, stark, tangible, unaffected (sincere), unambiguous, unequivocal, unmistakable, unpretentious, usual, visible (in full view)
plain English plain language
plain interpretation explanation
plain language SEE MAIN ENTRY
plain meaning connotation, content (meaning)
plain sense common sense
plain speaking plain language
plain speech plain language
plain to be seen patent, perceivable
plain words plain language
plain-speaking bona fide, honest
plain-spoken straightforward
plainly fairly (clearly), only, purely (simply), solely (purely)
plainness honesty, informality
plainspeaking honesty
plainspoken unaffected (sincere)
plaint charge (accusation), complaint, denunciation, outcry. SEE MAIN ENTRY
plaintful querulous
plaintiff actor, claimant, complainant, litigant, party (litigant), suitor. SEE MAIN ENTRY
plaintiff's allegations pleading
plaintiff's initiatory pleading complaint
plaintive disconsolate, lugubrious, querulous
plait intertwine. SEE MAIN ENTRY
plan agenda, blueprint, building (business of assembling), calculate, campaign, conceive (invent), conspiracy, conspire, contemplation, content (structure), contour (outline), contrivance, contrive, course, delineation, design (construction plan), design (intent), device (contrivance), devise (invent), direction (course), enterprise (undertaking), expedient, forethought, form (arrangement), frame (construct), frame (formulate), frame (prearrange), goal, idea, intend, intent, intention, maneuver, method, model, motif, motive, order (arrangement), organization (structure), originate, pattern, platform, ploy, policy (plan of action), prearrange, predetermine, preparation, procedure, process (course), program (noun), program (verb), project, proposal (report), proposal (suggestion), propose, proposition, prospect (outlook), prospectus, provide (arrange for), purpose, purview, resolution (formal statement), resolve (decide), schedule, scheme (noun), scheme (verb), set down, stratagem, strategy,

structure (composition), subterfuge, system, target, undertaking (attempt), undertaking (enterprise), way (channel). SEE MAIN ENTRY
plan a crime conspire
plan an unlawful act conspire
plan mischief plot
plan of action platform, polity, practice (procedure), procedure, strategy
plan of attack design (intent), maneuver (tactic), strategy
plan of campaign policy (plan of action)
plan of offensive campaign
plan on anticipate (expect), expect (anticipate)
plan out devise (invent)
plan secretly conspire, plot
plan strategy maneuver
plan to commit a crime conspire
plane degree (station)
plane in toto
plane surface area (surface)
planless haphazard
planned aforethought, deliberate, express, foreseeable, forthcoming, future, intentional, knowing, premeditated, prospective, purposeful, strategic, tactical, willful
planned beforehand aforethought, premeditated
planned campaign maneuver (tactic), strategy
planned course of action forethought
planned disbursement budget
planned for future
planned in advance deliberate, express, premeditated
planned place of arrival destination
planner accessory, accomplice, architect, catalyst, coactor, conspirer, contractor, developer, promoter
planning agenda
planning ahead forethought
planning board commission (agency)
plans calendar (record of yearly periods)
plant deposit (place), embed, engender, establish (entrench), fix (make firm), frame up, inculcate, initiate, inseminate, insertion, instate, repose (place). SEE MAIN ENTRY
plant the evidence frame (prearrange)
planted situated
plastic flexible, pliable, pliant, sequacious, tractable
plasticity amenability
plat intertwine, plot (land)
platform policy (plan of action), polity, prospectus, stand (witness' place in court), strategy. SEE MAIN ENTRY
platitude SEE MAIN ENTRY
platitudinous ordinary, pedestrian, prosaic, trite
plaudit mention (tribute)
plausibility common sense, credibility, likelihood, possibility, probability
plausible apparent (presumptive), believable, convincing, defensible, justifiable, ostensible, persuasive, possible, presumptive, probable, rational, reasonable (rational), specious, tenable, viable. SEE MAIN ENTRY
plausible excuse alibi
play bet, latitude, parlay (bet), performance (workmanship), pretend
play a direct part affect
play a leading part predominate (command)
play a long shot bet
play a part involve (participate), mock (imitate), pose (impersonate)

play a part in participate
play a trick dupe
play a trick on delude
play act pretend
play against counter, counteract
play at cross purposes conflict, counteract
play down disparage
play false betray *(lead astray)*, cheat, illude, pretend
play favorites prefer
play for bet
play for money gamble
play for stakes gamble
play for time procrastinate
play havoc with disorganize, prejudice *(injure)*
play one false ensnare
play out discontinue *(abandon)*
play safe hedge
play the market invest *(fund)*, speculate *(chance)*
play the part assume *(simulate)*
play tricks upon jape
play truant flee
play up magnify
play upon dupe
play upon words distort
play-act simulate
playact palter
playbook script
player bettor
player for stakes bettor
playful jocular
playfulness mischief
plaza market place
plea advocacy, allegation, answer *(judicial response)*, argument *(pleading)*, call *(appeal)*, claim *(legal demand)*, contention *(argument)*, counterargument, entreaty, invitation, nollo contendere, petition, pleading, prayer, pretense *(pretext)*, request, response. SEE MAIN ENTRY
plea in being elsewhere alibi
plea in rebuttal answer *(judicial response)*, confutation, counterargument, rejoinder
plead address *(petition)*, adduce, allege, answer *(reply)*, answer *(respond legally)*, bear *(adduce)*, depose *(testify)*, exhort, importune, intercede, petition, pray, press *(beseech)*, pressure, reason *(persuade)*, respond, solicit, sue. SEE MAIN ENTRY
plead a cause against a third party implead
plead for advocate, bear *(support)*, call *(appeal to)*, defend, justify, request, side
plead guilty repent
plead in favor of advocate
plead one's case advocate, assert
plead one's cause advocate, assert, defend, justify
plead with call *(appeal to)*
pleader advocate *(counselor)*, apologist, attorney, claimant, counsel, intermediary, jurist, petitioner, proponent, suitor
pleading argument *(pleading)*, persuasion, plea, precatory. SEE MAIN ENTRY
pleading in a civil action complaint
pleadings matter *(case)*, plea
pleasant attractive, desirable *(pleasing)*, harmonious, jocular, palatable, sapid, savory
pleasantness amenity
please obey, pacify, pander, placate, propitiate, satisfy *(fulfill)*
pleased complacent, inclined, proud *(self-respecting)*

pleased with oneself inflated *(vain)*
pleasing attractive, harmonious, palatable, popular, sapid, savory
pleasingness amenity
pleasurable desirable *(pleasing)*, palatable, sapid
pleasure benefit *(betterment)*, satisfaction *(fulfilment)*, treat, will *(desire)*
pleasureful desirable *(pleasing)*
plebeian ordinary, uncouth
plebian ignoble
plebicola demagogue
plebis dux demagogue
plebiscite election *(selection by vote)*, poll *(casting of votes)*, referendum. SEE MAIN ENTRY
plebiscitum enactment
plebs populace
pledge adjuration, agree *(contract)*, agreement *(contract)*, allegiance, assurance, assure *(insure)*, avouch *(guarantee)*, bail, bear *(adduce)*, bind *(obligate)*, binder, bond *(secure a debt)*, charge *(lien)*, cloud *(incumbrance)*, commitment *(responsibility)*, compact, contract *(noun)*, contract *(verb)*, covenant, coverage *(insurance)*, deal, debenture, deposit, due, duty *(obligation)*, guarantee, guaranty, hostage, hypothecation, insurance, lien, loan, mortgage, oath, pact, pawn, profess *(avow)*, profession *(declaration)*, promise, promise *(vow)*, responsibility *(accountability)*, specialty *(contract)*, stipulate, subscribe *(promise)*, undertake, undertaking *(bond)*, undertaking *(commitment)*, underwrite, vouch, vow, warrant *(guaranty)*, warranty. SEE MAIN ENTRY
pledge for the payment of a debt mortgage
pledge of security mortgage
pledge one's credit promise *(vow)*
pledge one's honor promise *(vow)*
pledge one's word avouch *(guarantee)*, promise *(vow)*, undertake
pledge oneself promise *(vow)*
pledged agreed *(promised)*, bound, contractual, fully secured, loyal
pledged word contract, specialty *(contract)*, undertaking *(pledge)*
pledgee creditor
pledges ties
pledgor debtor, obligor
plenary complete *(all-embracing)*, detailed, full, gross *(total)*, radical *(extreme)*, thorough, unmitigated, unqualified *(unlimited)*. SEE MAIN ENTRY
plenipotent omnipotent, powerful
plenipotentiaries deputation *(delegation)*
plenipotentiary deputy, omnipotent, spokesman, substitute. SEE MAIN ENTRY
plenitude capacity *(maximum)*, sufficiency
plenitudinous replete
plenteous ample, copious, multiple, replete, rife
plentiful considerable, copious, liberal *(generous)*, ordinary, profuse, replete, rife, substantial, usual
plentifulness boom *(prosperity)*, plethora, quorum
plentitude boom *(prosperity)*, maximum *(amplitude)*
plenty overage, plethora, prosperity, quantity, quorum, store *(depository)*, sufficiency, surfeit
plenum body *(collection)*, chamber *(body)*, corpus, meeting *(conference)*, quorum, session

plenus full
pleonasm redundancy, tautology
pleonastic extraneous, needless, prolix, redundant, repetitious, turgid
pleonastical prolix, repetitious
plethora sufficiency. SEE MAIN ENTRY
plethoric excessive, full, replete, turgid
plexiform sinuous
pliability amenability, credulity
pliable amenable, facile, flexible, malleable, passive, pliant, resilient, sequacious, suasible, tractable, yielding. SEE MAIN ENTRY
pliancy amenability, compliance, credulity, discipline *(obedience)*
pliant amenable, facile, flexible, malleable, obedient, obeisant, passive, patient, pliable, resilient, sequacious, suasible, susceptible *(responsive)*, tractable, yielding. SEE MAIN ENTRY
plight case *(set of circumstances)*, condition *(state)*, emergency, imbroglio, position *(situation)*, posture *(situation)*, predicament, problem, promise *(vow)*, quagmire, quandary, situation, state *(condition)*. SEE MAIN ENTRY
plight one's honor promise *(vow)*
plight one's word promise *(vow)*
plod bear *(tolerate)*, labor, persevere, persist
plodding operose, painstaking, patient, pedestrian, pertinacious, stable, steadfast
plot cabal, campaign, confederacy *(conspiracy)*, connivance, connive, conspiracy, conspire, contrivance, contrive, delineate, delineation, forethought, location, lot, machination, maneuver *(trick)*, maneuver, parcel, plan *(noun)*, plan *(verb)*, prearrange, program, property *(land)*, real estate, ruse, scenario, scheme *(noun)*, scheme *(verb)*, section *(vicinity)*, stratagem. SEE MAIN ENTRY
plot an action in advance conspire
plot craftily conspire
plot of ground parcel, section *(vicinity)*
plot of land parcel, section *(vicinity)*
plot together conspire
plotted deliberate, premeditated, tactical
plotter coactor, conspirator, conspirer
plotting artful, collusion, collusive, insidious, machiavellian, malevolent, perfidious, sly
ploy artifice, machination, plot *(secret plan)*, stratagem. SEE MAIN ENTRY
pluck cull, eviscerate, prowess *(bravery)*
pluck out excise *(cut away)*, extirpate
plucking out avulsion, evulsion
pluckless languid, phlegmatic
plucky indomitable, spartan
plug clog, damper *(stopper)*, obstruction, occlude, shut, stem *(check)*, stop
plug away labor, persevere, persist
plug up block, clog
plum prize
plumb probe
plunder despoil, devastate, hijack, hold up *(rob)*, loot, pillage *(noun)*, pillage *(verb)*, pirate *(take by violence)*, prey, prize, rape, rob, spoil *(pillage)*, spoils, spoliation, steal. SEE MAIN ENTRY
plunder by stealth poach
plunderage burglary, pillage, rape, spoils, spoliation
plunderer burglar, criminal, vandal
plundering burglary, foray, havoc, housebreaking, larcenous, predatory, rapacious, robbery, spoliation
plunderous larcenous

plunge   decline, depress, risk, speculate (*chance*), venture
plunge ahead   race
plunge in   pierce (*lance*)
plunge into   embark, occupy (*engage*)
plunge into a liquid   immerse (*plunge into*)
plunger   bettor
plural   multiple
plurality   majority (*greater part*), mass (*body of persons*), multiplicity, preponderance. SEE MAIN ENTRY
plures esse   predominate (*outnumber*)
plus   advantage, also, balance (*amount in excess*), further
ply   cajole, employ (*make use of*), importune, labor, manipulate (*utilize skillfully*), occupy (*engage*), propensity, wield. SEE MAIN ENTRY
ply one's task   attempt
ply one's trade   labor
plying   bribery
poach   hold up (*rob*), impose (*intrude*), pilfer, purloin, steal. SEE MAIN ENTRY
poached trade   contraband
poached traffic   contraband
pock-marked   blemished
pocket   obtain, receive (*acquire*), steal
pococurante   careless, casual, cold-blooded, inactive, insusceptible (*uncaring*), lax, lifeless (*dull*), nonchalant
pococurantism   disinterest (*lack of interest*)
poena   expiation, penalty, punishment, retribution
poenalis   penal
poetic   original (*creative*)
poignant   bitter (*penetrating*), moving (*evoking emotion*)
point   case (*set of circumstances*), consequence (*significance*), content (*meaning*), contention (*argument*), degree (*station*), detail, direct (*show*), edge (*border*), end (*termination*), feature (*characteristic*), gist (*ground for a suit*), import, intent, issue (*matter in dispute*), item, location, matter (*subject*), motive, object, objective, occasion, particular, period, phase (*aspect*), phase (*period*), pinnacle, posture (*situation*), property (*distinctive attribute*), purpose, refer (*direct attention*), remark, signification, situs, standpoint, subject (*topic*), target, technicality, term (*provision*), tip (*clue*). SEE MAIN ENTRY
point at   denounce (*inform against*), strive
point at issue   matter (*subject*), subject (*topic*)
point in common   analogy
point in dispute   problem, question (*issue*)
point in question   issue (*matter in dispute*), matter (*subject*)
point of   connotation
point of cessation   destination
point of comparison   criterion, example, norm, precedent
point of concentration   focus
point of convergence   center (*central position*), focus
point of difference   characteristic, distinction (*difference*), specialty (*distinctive mark*)
point of disembarkation   destination
point of etiquette   decorum
point of no return   crossroad (*turning point*)
point of observation   outlook, perspective
point of resemblance   analogy

point of time   date, phase (*period*)
point of view   concept, conviction (*persuasion*), idea, opinion (*belief*), outlook, perception, perspective, platform, posture (*attitude*), side, stand (*position*), standpoint. SEE MAIN ENTRY
point out   apprise, bear (*adduce*), charge (*instruct on the law*), comment, convey (*communicate*), demonstrate (*establish*), denote, designate, direct (*show*), disabuse, discriminate (*distinguish*), enumerate, exhibit, explain, impart, indicate, inform (*notify*), instruct (*teach*), itemize, manifest, mention, quote, reason (*persuade*), remind, select, signify (*denote*), specify
point out an essential difference   distinguish
point to   allude, ascribe, attribute, bear (*adduce*), cite (*state*), connote, evince, exemplify, implicate, imply, indicate, mention, predict, presage
point to be settled   problem
point up   dwell (*linger over*)
point-blank   direct (*forthright*)
pointed   acute, compact (*pithy*), conspicuous, direct (*forthright*), eloquent, explicit, incisive, laconic, mordacious, persuasive, pithy, sententious, trenchant
pointedly   fairly (*clearly*), knowingly, purposely
pointer   indicant, indication, indicator, suggestion, tip (*clue*)
pointing out   designation (*naming*), reference (*citation*)
pointless   immaterial, inapposite, insipid, null (*insignificant*), pedestrian, unavailing, unreasonable
pointlessness   immateriality
points of comparison   analogy
poise   composure, confidence (*faith*), decorum, demeanor, deportment
poison   contaminate, degenerate, infect, pervert, pollute, taint (*contaminate*), virulent, vitiate
poisoned   deadly, peccant (*unhealthy*), tainted (*contaminated*)
poisoning   contaminate, detriment
poisonous   deadly, deleterious, fatal, harmful, incendiary, insalubrious, lethal, malevolent, malignant, noxious, obnoxious, peccant (*unhealthy*), pernicious, pestilent, ruthless, toxic, virulent
poke   delve, jostle (*bump into*), loiter
poke fun at   jape, mock (*deride*)
poke into   frisk, probe
poker-faced   inexpressive, inscrutable
polarity   antipode, antithesis, conflict, penchant, reaction (*opposition*)
polarize   SEE MAIN ENTRY
polarized   hostile
pole   cudgel, end (*termination*), extremity (*furthest point*)
polemic   argumentative, contention (*argument*), disputable, dispute, litigious. SEE MAIN ENTRY
polemical   argumentative, contentious, controversial, dissenting, forensic, litigious, polemic
polemicist   disputant
polemics   argument (*contention*), contest (*dispute*), controversy (*argument*), disaccord, disagreement, fight (*argument*), strife
polemist   contender
poles apart   distinct (*distinguished from others*)

police   censor, moderate (*preside over*), patrol, peace officer, regulate (*manage*), rule (*govern*). SEE MAIN ENTRY
police constable   peace officer
police force   police
police officer   peace officer
police officers   police
police tipper   informer (*one providing criminal information*)
policeman   peace officer
policewoman   peace officer
policy   course, direction (*course*), platform, polity, practice (*procedure*), principle (*axiom*), procedure, process (*course*), program, rule (*guide*), scheme, strategy, system. SEE MAIN ENTRY
policy-fixing meeting   caucus
polis   city
polish   amend, complete, cultivate, decorum, discretion (*quality of being discreet*), edit, embellish, enhance, meliorate, revise
polished   civil (*polite*), literate
polished manners   courtesy, decorum
polite   diplomatic, discreet, formal, obeisant
polite act   courtesy
polite regard   respect
politely   respectfully
politeness   comity, consideration (*sympathetic regard*), courtesy, decorum, deference, propriety (*correctness*), protocol (*etiquette*), respect
politic   diplomatic, discreet, favorable (*advantageous*), judicial, judicious, juridical, provident (*showing foresight*), prudent, sensible, solid (*sound*), strategic, subtle (*refined*), tactical. SEE MAIN ENTRY
political   civic, civil (*public*). SEE MAIN ENTRY
political affairs   politics
political agitator   malcontent
political aspirant   candidate
political body   congress
political community   government (*political administration*)
political competition   primary
political confluence   caucus
political contention   primary
political contestant   candidate
political corruption   graft
political disorder   anarchy
political division   state (*political unit*)
political election   primary
political independence   freedom, home rule, liberty
political influence   politics
political involvement   politics
political leaders   government (*political administration*)
political machine   party (*political organization*)
political maneuvers   politics
political methods   politics
political partisanship   politics
political prisoner   hostage
political process   politics
political regime   government (*political administration*)
political representative   nominee (*candidate*)
political rivalry   primary
political strategy   politics
political subdivision   venue
political system   regime
political upheaval   insurrection, revolt, revolution
politically independent   autonomous (*self governing*), sovereign (*independent*)

politician demagogue, lawmaker, legislator. SEE MAIN ENTRY

politicians government *(political administration)*

politico lawmaker, politician

politicos government *(political administration)*

politics SEE MAIN ENTRY

polity body *(collection)*, community, constituency, government *(political administration)*, nationality, policy *(plan of action)*, public, society, state *(political unit)*. SEE MAIN ENTRY

poll canvass, cast *(register)*, census, election *(selection by vote)*, inquiry *(request for information)*, plebiscite, primary, referendum, vote *(noun)*, vote *(verb)*. SEE MAIN ENTRY

pollage tax

polliceri promise *(vow)*

pollinate inseminate

pollinize inseminate

polluere stain

pollute abuse *(violate)*, adulterate, contaminate, corrupt, damage, debase, degenerate, denature, deteriorate, disgrace, harm, impair, infect, misemploy, mistreat, pervert, smear, stain, sully, taint *(contaminate)*, tarnish, vitiate. SEE MAIN ENTRY

polluted dissolute, harmful, profane, salacious, tainted *(contaminated)*

pollution contaminate, detriment, misusage, perversion

pollution control ecology

poltergeist phantom

poltroon recreant

poltroonish caitiff

polygamous SEE MAIN ENTRY

polymorphic protean

polymorphous protean

polysyllabic profundity bombast

pommel impinge

pomp pretense *(ostentation)*, solemnity

pomposity bombast, fustian, pretense *(ostentation)*, pride, rhetoric *(insincere language)*

pompous dictatorial, flatulent, formal, fustian, grandiose, inflated *(bombastic)*, inflated *(vain)*, orgulous, orotund, presumptuous, proud *(conceited)*, supercilious, turgid

pompous prolixity bombast

pompous speech rhetoric *(insincere language)*

pompousness pretense *(ostentation)*, rhetoric *(insincere language)*

ponder brood, concentrate *(pay attention)*, consider, debate, deliberate, doubt *(hesitate)*, muse, reason *(conclude)*, speculate *(conjecture)*, study, weigh. SEE MAIN ENTRY

ponder over deliberate

ponder reasons for and against deliberate

ponderable appreciable. SEE MAIN ENTRY

ponderare ponder

pondered deliberate, intentional

pondering cogitative, consideration *(contemplation)*, contemplation, deliberation, reflection *(thought)*

ponderosus ponderous

ponderous jejune *(dull)*, major, oppressive, pedestrian. SEE MAIN ENTRY

ponderousness weight *(burden)*

pondus importance, influence, pressure, stress *(strain)*, validity

ponere invest *(fund)*, propose

poniard pierce *(lance)*

pool combination, combine *(act in concert)*, concert, consolidation, consortium *(business cartel)*, contribution *(participation)*, cooperate, federalize *(associate)*, federation, fund, join *(associate oneself with)*, join *(bring together)*, league, partnership, syndicate, trust *(combination of businesses)*, unite. SEE MAIN ENTRY

pool one's interests federate

pooled common *(shared)*, conjoint

poor base *(inferior)*, deficient, deplorable, destitute, devoid, impecunious, imperfect, inadept, inadequate, inferior *(lower in quality)*, insubstantial, insufficient, lamentable, marginal, mediocre, negligible, paltry, perfunctory, slipshod, unfavorable, unsatisfactory. SEE MAIN ENTRY

poor administration maladministration

poor chance improbability

poor circumstances indigence, poverty

poor judgment error, indiscretion, misestimation, misjudgment

poor opinion disparagement

poor prospect improbability

poor quality work noncompliance *(improper completion)*

poor reputation ignominy

poor usage misapplication

poor visiblity indistinctness

poorly adapted disproportionate, unsuitable

poorly advised misadvised

poorly defined inconspicuous, unclear, vague

poorly done perfunctory

poorly off impecunious

poorly qualified inexperienced

poorly seen inconspicuous, unclear

poorly timed untimely

poorness dearth, indigence, mediocrity, poverty

populace community, nationality, population, public. SEE MAIN ENTRY

populacy population

popular common *(customary)*, common *(shared)*, competitive *(open)*, current, customary, familiar *(customary)*, famous, general, household *(familiar)*, illustrious, meritorious, ordinary, prescriptive, prevailing *(current)*, prevalent, proverbial, public *(known)*, regular *(conventional)*, renowned, rife, routine, sapid, select, typical, usual. SEE MAIN ENTRY

popular agitator demagogue

popular choice referendum

popular decision poll *(casting of votes)*, referendum, suffrage

popular favor character *(reputation)*, distinction *(reputation)*, reputation

popular regard affection

popular report hearsay

popular repute notoriety

popular ringleader catalyst

popular vote referendum

popularity character *(reputation)*, notoriety

popularize elucidate, explain

popularly believed consensual

populate dwell *(reside)*

populated populous

population community, populace, public, society. SEE MAIN ENTRY

populous compact *(dense)*, copious, manifold, rife. SEE MAIN ENTRY

populus public

pore over consider, notice *(observe)*, peruse, read, reflect *(ponder)*, study

pornographic lascivious, lewd, obscene, prurient, salacious, suggestive *(risqué)*

pornography obscenity. SEE MAIN ENTRY

porous penetrable

port complexion, conduct, deportment, destination, haven, manner *(behavior)*

portage carriage

portage fee fare

portal admittance *(means of approach)*, entrance, margin *(outside limit)*, outlet. SEE MAIN ENTRY

portare bear *(support)*

portend anticipate *(prognosticate)*, forewarn, indicate, predict, presage, prognosticate, promise *(raise expectations)*, threaten. SEE MAIN ENTRY

portendance caveat

portendere portend, presage

portending evil ominous, portentous *(ominous)*, sinister

portending happiness auspicious

portendment caveat

portent caution *(warning)*, forerunner, harbinger, indicant, indication, phenomenon *(unusual occurrence)*, precursor, premonition, significance, threat, token, warning

portention caveat

portentous dire, imminent, important *(significant)*, ominous, oracular, presageful, prophetic, unusual. SEE MAIN ENTRY

porter caretaker *(one caring for property)*

porterage carriage

portfolio dossier. SEE MAIN ENTRY

portio installment, share *(interest)*

portion allotment, article *(distinct section of a writing)*, assignment *(allotment)*, chapter *(division)*, commission *(fee)*, component, detail, dole, element, equity *(share of ownership)*, excerpt, factor *(ingredient)*, heritage, installment, interest *(ownership)*, lot, member *(constituent part)*, moiety, parcel, part *(separate)*, partition, phase *(aspect)*, proportion, prorate, quantity, quota, ration, region, segment, share *(interest)*, subdivide, title *(division)*. SEE MAIN ENTRY

portion off allocate

portion out allocate, allot, apportion, assign *(allot)*, dispense, disperse *(disseminate)*, distribute, divide *(distribute)*, measure, parcel, partition, reapportion

portion out again reassign

portion out equitably apportion

portioning division *(act of dividing)*

portorium tax, toll *(tax)*

portraiture representation *(statement)*

portray characterize, copy, delineate, denote, depict, describe, detail *(particularize)*, draw *(depict)*, exemplify, impersonate, mock *(imitate)*, pose *(impersonate)*, pretend, recite, recount, relate *(tell)*, render *(depict)*, reproduce, signify *(denote)*. SEE MAIN ENTRY

portray by example exemplify

portray falsely fake

portray in words delineate, describe

portrayal caricature, delineation, description, narration, part *(role)*, representation *(statement)*, story *(narrative)*, symbol

portus haven

poscere require *(compel)*

pose disguise, offer *(propose)*, palter, perplex, posit, position *(point of view)*, posture *(attitude)*, pretense *(ostentation)*, propose, propound, role. SEE MAIN ENTRY

pose as assume *(simulate)*, fake, impersonate, purport

posed specious

poser enigma

posit comment, infer, pose (propound), postulate, presume, presuppose, propound, surmise, suspect (think). SEE MAIN ENTRY

posited assumed (inferred), situated

position advantage, aspect, calling, capacity (job), career, case (set of circumstances), character (reputation), claim (assertion), class, condition (state), conviction (persuasion), degree (station), employment, file (arrange), job, livelihood, locality, locate, location, marshal, occupation (vocation), office, opinion (belief), opinion (judicial decision), outlook, perspective, platform, plight, post, posture (attitude), posture (situation), predicament, prestige, principle (axiom), profession (vocation), proposition, pursuit (occupation), reputation, role, seat, side, site (noun), site (verb), situation, situs, stand (position), stand (witness' place in court), standpoint, state (condition), status, supposition, thesis, trade (occupation), venue, work (employment). SEE MAIN ENTRY

position in society character (reputation), reputation

position of influence authority (power), patronage (power to appoint jobs)

position of power authority (power)

position paper pandect (treatise)

position together juxtapose

positioned situated

positions premises (hypotheses)

positive absolute (conclusive), actual, affirmative, authentic, axiomatic, categorical, certain (fixed), clear (certain), conclusive (determinative), convincing, decisive, definite, demonstrable, distinct (clear), dogmatic, explicit, express, incontrovertible, indubious, inexorable, irrefutable, obdurate, peremptory (absolute), pure, resounding, secure (confident), stark, strict, substantive, tangible, undisputed, unequivocal, unmistakable, unrefutable, well-grounded. SEE MAIN ENTRY

positive action course

positive assertion allegation, avouchment

positive declaration affirmance (legal affirmation), allegation, assertion, asseveration, averment

positive fact certification (certainness)

positive statement affirmance (legal affirmation), affirmation, allegation, assertion, asseveration, averment, avouchment, avowal, declaration

positively de facto, fairly (clearly), ipso facto

positively declared alleged

positively direct enjoin

positiveness belief (state of mind), certainty, certification (certainness), certitude, confidence (faith), conviction (persuasion), surety (certainty), weight (credibility)

positivistic dogmatic

positus situated

posse possibility

possess appropriate, comprehend (include), impropriate, keep (shelter), obsess, obtain, occupy (take possession), own, remain, retain (keep in possession). SEE MAIN ENTRY

possess authority handle (manage), rule (govern)

possess oneself of assume (seize), distrain

possessed diabolic, fanatical, frenetic, lunatic

possessed of immunity exempt, immune

possessed of knowledge cognizant

possessing double meaning equivocal

possessing merit meritorious

possessing unlimited power omnipotent

possessio domain (land owned), estate (property), holding (property owned), occupancy, possession (ownership), possession (property), possessions, retention, tenure

possession acquisition, chattel, compulsion (obsession), dominion (absolute ownership), enjoyment (use), habitation (act of inhabiting), holding (property owned), interest (ownership), item, occupancy, receipt (act of receiving), seisin, tenancy, title (right). SEE MAIN ENTRY

possession and control trust (custody)

possession of full rights emancipation

possessione depellere dispossess

possessions assets, commodities, effects, estate (property), goods, merchandise, movable, paraphernalia (personal belongings), personalty, property (possessions). SEE MAIN ENTRY

possessive jealous, mercenary

possessiveness greed

possessor bearer

possessor holder

possessor lessee, lodger, occupant, proprietor, tenant

possessor of descent heir

possessorship dominion (absolute ownership), ownership, seisin, tenancy

possibility access (opening), contingency, feasibility, likelihood, opportunity, potential, probability, proposal (suggestion), prospect (outlook), prospect (prospective patron), risk, suggestion. SEE MAIN ENTRY

possibility of injury risk

possibility of loss risk

possible conditional, contingent, convincing, debatable, future, plausible, potential, practicable, presumptive, probable, prospective, viable. SEE MAIN ENTRY

possible client prospect (prospective patron)

possible customer prospect (prospective patron)

possible patron prospect (prospective patron)

possibleness chance (possibility), likelihood, potential

possidere hold (possess), own, tenure

post annunciate, appointment (position), bond (secure a debt), book, calling, career, convey (communicate), dispatch (send off), employment, enter (record), induct, inform (notify), inscribe, issue (publish), itemize, location, notify, office, organ, pawn, pledge (deposit), position (business status), pursuit (occupation), record, register, role, seat, send, set down, situation, stand (witness' place in court), standpoint, title (position), trade (occupation), work (employment). SEE MAIN ENTRY

post mortem posthumous

post on redirect

post road causeway

postal communication dispatch (message)

postdate succeed (follow)

posted acquainted, cognizant, informed (having information), knowing, situated

posterior back (in reverse), ensuing

posterior subsequent

posteritas posterity

posterity descendant, heir, offspring, progeny, succession. SEE MAIN ENTRY

postern portal

posterus future

postfix attachment (thing affixed)

posthaste rapid

posthumous SEE MAIN ENTRY

postnote memorandum

postpone adjourn, continue (adjourn), defer (put off), delay, discontinue (break continuity), hold up (delay), impede, procrastinate, recess, stall, suspend. SEE MAIN ENTRY

postponed arrested (checked), late (tardy)

postponed payment bill (invoice)

postponement adjournment, cessation (interlude), continuance, deferment, delay, discontinuance (act of discontinuing), moratorium, pendency, reprieve

postponement of penalty reprieve

postscript addendum, allonge, codicil, insertion, rider

postulant claimant

postulare arraign

postulate assumption (supposition), avow, claim (legal demand), comment (noun), comment (verb), concept, condition (contingent provision), conjecture, deduction (conclusion), generalization, guess, hypothesis, infer, inference, maxim, opine, pose (propound), posit, presume, presumption, presuppose, principle (axiom), propose, proposition, propound, require (compel), supposition, suspicion (uncertainty), theory, thesis. SEE MAIN ENTRY

postulate of reason principle (axiom)

postulated assumed (inferred), presumptive, requisite, theoretical

postulates premises (hypotheses)

postulatio claim (legal demand), pretense (pretext), request, requisition

postulation condition (contingent provision), conjecture, conviction (persuasion), deduction (conclusion), generalization, hypothesis, inference, prolepsis, request, suspicion (uncertainty), thesis

postulational presumptive

postulatory theoretical

postulatum inference

posture appearance (look), aspect, case (set of circumstances), color (complexion), complexion, condition (state), conduct, conviction (persuasion), demeanor, deportment, disguise, manner (behavior), opinion (belief), outlook, position (point of view), position (situation), predicament, presence (poise), profess (pretend), role, situation, state (condition), status. SEE MAIN ENTRY

pot cannabis, stake (award)

potable palatable

potare carouse

potation alcohol, dipsomania, inebriation

potence dint, force (strength), main force, puissance, sinew

potency caliber (quality), clout, competence (ability), dint, efficiency, faculty (ability), force (strength), influence, leverage, main force, potential, power, prestige, puissance, quality (excellence), sinew, strength, validity, weight (importance). SEE MAIN ENTRY

potens influential, predominant

potent assertive, capable, cogent, compelling, considerable, convincing, efficient, in full force, indomitable, inexpugnable, influential, irresistible, omnipotent, operative, persuasive, powerful, predominant, prevailing *(having superior force)*, productive, sound, sovereign *(absolute)*, strong, valid, virtual. SEE MAIN ENTRY

potentia influence, predominance

potential chance *(possibility)*, constructive *(inferential)*, likelihood, possibility, possible, prospective, viable, virtual. SEE MAIN ENTRY

potentialis potential *(adjective)*, potential *(noun)*

potentiality ability, capacity *(aptitude)*, chance *(possibility)*, feasibility, likelihood, possibility, quality *(excellence)*

potentially liable at risk

potentiate empower

potestas ability, dominion *(supreme authority)*, license, opportunity, permission, possibility, power, warrant *(authorization)*

potestatem facere authorize, empower

potestates authorities

pother furor, hector, perplex, perturb, pique, plague, turmoil

potior preferable

potiorem outweigh

potpourri melange

poultice drug

pounce upon attack, oppugn, seize *(confiscate)*

pound beat *(pulsate)*, beat *(strike)*, cell, enclosure, lash *(strike)*, strike *(assault)*

pour forth emit, issue *(send forth)*, outpour, speak

pour in imbue, penetrate

pour out emit, issue *(send forth)*, outpour

pour out of emanate

pour over inundate

pourboire bonus, bounty

pourparler caucus

poverty dearth, deficiency, indigence, paucity, privation. SEE MAIN ENTRY

poverty-stricken bankrupt, destitute, impecunious, penurious, poor *(underprivileged)*

power advantage, capacity *(aptitude)*, capacity *(authority)*, catalyst, clout, control *(supervision)*, credit *(recognition)*, dint, dominance, dominion *(supreme authority)*, droit, faculty *(ability)*, force *(strength)*, government *(administration)*, hegemony, influence, jurisdiction, license, main force, management *(directorate)*, occupation *(possession)*, option *(contractual provision)*, patronage *(power to appoint jobs)*, potential, predominance, prerogative, pressure, prestige, primacy, puissance, quality *(excellence)*, range, realm, regime, right *(entitlement)*, sinew, strength, supremacy, title *(right)*, validity, warrant *(authorization)*, weight *(importance)*. SEE MAIN ENTRY

power of choice latitude, liberty, volition

power of choosing discretion *(power of choice)*, will *(desire)*

power of determination will *(desire)*

power of directing pressure

power of disposal dominion *(absolute ownership)*

power of entrance ingress

power of impelling clout, pressure

power over trust *(custody)*

power to choose latitude, liberty, option *(choice)*

power to grasp ideas comprehension

power to reason intellect, intelligence *(intellect)*

power to understand comprehension, understanding *(comprehension)*

power-crazed dictatorial

power-hungry dictatorial

power-mad dictatorial

powerful assertive, cogent, consequential *(substantial)*, considerable, convincing, decisive, drastic, efficient, eloquent, forcible, important *(significant)*, incisive, indomitable, inexpugnable, influential, intense, intensive, irresistible, omnipotent, persuasive, potent, predominant, prevailing *(having superior force)*, prominent, sound, sovereign *(absolute)*, strong, trenchant, valid, vehement, virtual. SEE MAIN ENTRY

powerfully expressive eloquent

powerfulness dint, force *(strength)*, influence, main force, potential, sinew

powerless harmless, inactive, inadequate, ineffective, ineffectual, inept *(incompetent)*, insipid, insubstantial, languid, nonsubstantial *(not sturdy)*, null *(insignificant)*, null *(invalid)*, otiose, unable, untenable. SEE MAIN ENTRY

powerless group minority *(outnumbered group)*

powerlessness disability *(physical inability)*, fault *(weakness)*, impotence, impuissance, inability, inefficacy, insentience

powerpacked powerful

powers hierarchy *(persons in authority)*

powers that be authorities, authority *(power)*, bureaucracy

practicability feasibility, potential

practicable appropriate, beneficial, effective *(efficient)*, functional, justifiable, potential, practical, probable, suitable, viable. SEE MAIN ENTRY

practicableness feasibility

practical beneficial, constructive *(creative)*, effective *(efficient)*, efficient, functional, ministerial, politic, practicable, pragmatic, purposeful, realistic, viable, virtual. SEE MAIN ENTRY

practical attitude pragmatism

practical demonstration illustration

practical discernment common sense

practical joke hoax

practical knowledge common sense, experience *(background)*

practical management administration

practical wisdom experience *(background)*

practicality common sense, expedience, feasibility, pragmatism, utility *(usefulness)*, utilization

practicalness pragmatism

practice business *(occupation)*, calling, conduct, course, custom, dealings, deportment, discipline *(training)*, employ *(make use of)*, employment, exercise *(discharge a function)*, exercise *(use)*, expedient, experience *(background)*, habit, manner *(behavior)*, method, mode, operate, operation, perform *(adhere to)*, ply, position *(business status)*, prescription *(custom)*, procedure, profession *(vocation)*, protocol *(etiquette)*, pursue *(carry on)*, pursuit *(occupation)*, qualify *(meet standards)*, resort, rule *(guide)*, system, trade *(occupation)*, usage, use. SEE MAIN ENTRY

practice chicanery cheat, circumvent, deceive, defraud, delude, dupe, illude, profess *(pretend)*

practice deception deceive, mislead

practice economy retrench

practice exclusively specialize

practice extravagance dissipate *(expend foolishly)*

practice fraud cheat, mulct *(defraud)*

practice fraud upon defraud, delude

practice gaming gamble

practice of spying on others espionage

practice upon one's credulity delude

practiced cognizant, competent, convincing, deft, expert, facile, familiar *(informed)*, literate, proficient, qualified *(competent)*, resourceful, veteran. SEE MAIN ENTRY

practiced hand expert, specialist, veteran

practiced individual professional

practicing lawyer jurist

practicing plural marriage polygamous

practitioner addict, attorney, esquire, expert, professional, specialist. SEE MAIN ENTRY

practitioner of the law jurist

praebere furnish, provide *(supply)*

praeceps precipitate

praeceptum maxim, precept, regulation *(rule)*, rule *(legal dictate)*

praecidere abridge *(shorten)*

praecipere forestall, instruct *(direct)*

praecipitare precipitate *(hasten)*, precipitate *(throw down violently)*

praecipue particularly

praecipuus cardinal *(basic)*, cardinal *(outstanding)*, salient, special

praecurrentia precursory

praecursor precursor

praeda plunder

praedabundus predatory

praedari plunder, prey

praedatorius predatory

praedial proprietary

praedicare declare, proclaim, publish

praedicatio declaration, publication *(disclosure)*

praedicere predict

praedium liberum freehold

praeesse superintend

praefari preface

praefatio preface

praefectus official, superintendent

praefinire predetermine

praegravare encumber *(financially obligate)*

praeiudicare preconceive, prejudge

praeiudicata opinio preconception

praematurus premature

praemeditatio premeditation

praemium prize, recompense, remuneration

praemium proponere reward

praemonere forewarn

praenomen call *(title)*

praenuntius forerunner, harbinger, precursor

praeoccupatio preoccupation

praeoptare prefer

praepollens predominant

praepollere predominate *(command)*

praeponere prefer

praepositio preference *(priority)*

praesagire presage

praesagium misgiving

praesciens foreseeable

praescribere instruct *(direct)*, prescribe

praescriptum instruction *(direction)*, precept, rule *(legal dictate)*

praesens immediate *(at once)*, imminent, instantaneous, present *(attendant)*, present *(current)*

praesentia presence *(attendance)*

praesertim particularly

praeses guardian

praesidere preside

praesidium patronage *(power to appoint jobs)*, protection

praestantia eminence

praestantior superior *(excellent)*

praestare ascendant, evince, indorse

praestituere predetermine

praeterire ignore, overlook *(superintend)*

praetermissio omission

praetermittere omit

praetervehi pass *(advance)*

praetextum pretext

praetextus color *(deceptive appearance)*

praetor judge

praetorium headquarters

praevaricatio collusion

praevenire forestall

praevertere anticipate *(prognosticate)*

pragmatic constructive *(inferential)*, effective *(efficient)*, functional, realistic. SEE MAIN ENTRY

pragmatic sanction charter *(sanction)*

pragmatism expedience. SEE MAIN ENTRY

pragmatize justify

praise advocacy, belaud, doxology, estimation *(esteem)*, honor *(outward respect)*, honor, laudation, mention *(tribute)*, recommend, recommendation, regard *(hold in esteem)*, remembrance *(commemoration)*, respect. SEE MAIN ENTRY

praised popular

praiseworthy exemplary, laudable, meritorious, moral, professional *(stellar)*

praiseworthy quality merit

praising favorable *(expressing approval)*

prankishness mischief

prate bombast, prattle

prattle jargon *(unintelligible language)*, prattle, speech. SEE MAIN ENTRY

prattling loquacious

prava rerum administratio maladministration

pravitas distortion

pravus immoral, sinister

praxis course, manner *(behavior)*

pray apply *(request)*, importune, request. SEE MAIN ENTRY

pray for petition

prayer call *(appeal)*, entreaty, petition, request. SEE MAIN ENTRY

pre-trial inquiries interrogatories

preach address *(talk to)*, declaim, educate, inculcate, recite

preaching instruction *(teaching)*, propaganda

preamble overture, preface *(noun)*, preface *(verb)*, prelude, threshold *(commencement)*. SEE MAIN ENTRY

preannounce anticipate *(prognosticate)*, predict, prognosticate

preannouncement prognosis

preapprehend preconceive

preapprehension bias, inequity, preconception, predetermination, predisposition

prearrange devise *(invent)*, frame *(prearrange)*, maneuver, plan, plot, predetermine. SEE MAIN ENTRY

prearrange fraudulently frame *(charge falsely)*, frame *(prearrange)*

prearranged aforethought, deliberate, express, intentional, premeditated, stated

prearrangement premeditation

precari pray

precarious aleatory *(perilous)*, debatable, insecure, noxious, uncertain *(questionable)*, unreliable, unsound *(not strong)*, untrustworthy, volatile, vulnerable. SEE MAIN ENTRY

precariousness danger, doubt *(indecision)*, hazard, jeopardy, peril, predicament, risk

precatio prayer

precatory SEE MAIN ENTRY

precaution caution, discretion *(quality of being discreet)*, panoply, preparation, prudence, safeguard. SEE MAIN ENTRY

precautional solid *(sound)*

precautionary circumspect, noncommittal, preparatory, preventive, provident *(showing foresight)*, prudent, solid *(sound)*

precautious careful, circumspect, discreet, noncommittal, provident *(showing foresight)*, prudent, solid *(sound)*, vigilant

precede antecede, preface. SEE MAIN ENTRY

precedence advantage, importance, magnitude, preference *(priority)*, prestige, priority, reputation, significance, supremacy. SEE MAIN ENTRY

precedent aforesaid, antecedent, authority *(documentation)*, before mentioned, code, criterion, finding, forerunner, holding *(ruling of a court)*, judgment *(formal court decree)*, last *(preceding)*, law, mode, model, pattern, precursor, precursory, preparatory, prescription *(custom)*, previous, prior, prototype, standard, stare decisis. SEE MAIN ENTRY

precedential exemplary

preceding aforesaid, antecedent, before mentioned, former, old, precursory, preferred *(given priority)*, preliminary, preparatory, previous, prior, said. SEE MAIN ENTRY

preceding instance precedent

precept act *(enactment)*, authority *(documentation)*, belief *(something believed)*, brevet, canon, charge *(command)*, citation *(charge)*, code, codification, constitution, dictate, direction *(order)*, directive, doctrine, dogma, edict, guidance, holding *(ruling of a court)*, injunction, instruction *(direction)*, law, mandate, maxim, order *(judicial directive)*, precedent, prescription *(directive)*, principle *(axiom)*, recommendation, regulation *(rule)*, rubric *(authoritative rule)*, rule *(legal dictate)*, technicality, writ. SEE MAIN ENTRY

preceptive decretal, disciplinary *(educational)*, informative, prescriptive

preceptor pedagogue

preceptoral disciplinary *(educational)*

precepts code, platform

precepts on securities blue sky law

preces entreaty, imprecation, request

precinct bailiwick, circuit, close *(enclosed area)*, department, district, province, region, territory

precincts confines, vicinity

preciosity bombast

precious inestimable, invaluable, premium, priceless, rare, sterling, valuable

preciousness bombast

precipitance dispatch *(promptness)*, haste, inconsideration

precipitancy dispatch *(promptness)*, haste, inconsideration

precipitant careless, impulsive *(rash)*, precipitate

precipitate careless, cause, evoke, expedite, hasten, heedless, impel, imprudent, impulsive *(rash)*, induce, injudicious, inspire, launch *(project)*, originate,

premature, reckless, thoughtless, unexpected. SEE MAIN ENTRY

precipitation congealment, dispatch *(promptness)*, haste

precipitous impulsive *(rash)*, precipitate

precipitousness dispatch *(promptness)*, haste

précis abridgment *(condensation)*

precis abstract, capsule, compendium, condense

precise absolute *(conclusive)*, accurate, actual, appropriate, brief, certain *(particular)*, certain *(specific)*, circumspect, close *(rigorous)*, coherent *(clear)*, conscientious, detailed, distinct *(clear)*, draconian, exact, explicit, express, factual, faithful *(true to fact)*, laconic, literal, meticulous, narrow, painstaking, particular *(exacting)*, positive *(incontestable)*, prompt, proper, punctilious, punctual, rigid, sententious, specific, strict, stringent, subtle *(refined)*, systematic, true *(authentic)*, unambiguous, verbatim. SEE MAIN ENTRY

precise amount face amount

precise moment point *(period of time)*

precisely faithfully

precisely bounded definite

precisely formulated specific

preciseness particularity, rigor

precisian precise

precision particularity, regularity, rigor, truth, veracity

precision tool appliance

preclude bar *(exclude)*, bar *(hinder)*, block, censor, clog, condemn *(ban)*, constrain *(restrain)*, debar, disable, disqualify, eliminate *(exclude)*, enjoin, estop, exclude, fight *(counteract)*, forbid, forestall, halt, hamper, impede, interdict, interfere, obstruct, occlude, preempt, prevent, prohibit, reject, restrict, stay *(halt)*, stop, supersede, thwart, withstand. SEE MAIN ENTRY

precluded barred

precluding unless

preclusion bar *(obstruction)*, blockade *(limitation)*, check *(bar)*, constraint *(restriction)*, damper *(stopper)*, deterrence, deterrent, disqualification *(rejection)*, embargo, estoppel, exception *(exclusion)*, exclusion, hindrance, impasse, obstacle, obstruction, ostracism, preemption, prohibition. SEE MAIN ENTRY

preclusion by act estoppel

preclusion by conduct estoppel

preclusion of work lockout

preclusive exclusive *(limited)*, preventive, prohibitive *(restrictive)*, restrictive

precognition SEE MAIN ENTRY

precognitive prophetic

precognize anticipate *(prognosticate)*, preconceive

preconceive anticipate *(expect)*, forejudge, opine, predetermine, prejudge, preordain, presume, presuppose. SEE MAIN ENTRY

preconceived aforethought, prejudicial

preconceived idea bias, foregone conclusion, inequity, preconception, prejudice *(preconception)*

preconceived liking preference *(choice)*

preconceived notion inequity, prejudice *(preconception)*

preconception bias, expectation, inequity, intolerance, opinion *(belief)*, partiality, predetermination, predisposition, prejudice *(preconception)*. SEE MAIN ENTRY

preconceptual prejudicial

preconcert orchestrate, plan, plot, pre-arrange, program

preconclude forejudge, preconceive, predetermine, prejudge, preordain, presuppose

preconclusion foregone conclusion, preconception, predetermination, predisposition

precondemn prejudge

precondition necessity, need (requirement), prerequisite, requirement, sine qua non

preconsider predetermine, prejudge, preordain

preconsideration forethought, predisposition, premeditation

preconsidered aforethought, deliberate, intentional, premeditated

precontrive plan, prearrange

precontrived premeditated

precurse portend

precursive aforesaid, antecedent, before mentioned, ominous, oracular, precursory, preliminary, previous, prophetic

precursor ancestor, ascendant, caution (warning), forerunner, harbinger, indicator, parents, pioneer, precedent, predecessor, primogenitor, progenitor. SEE MAIN ENTRY

precursory aforesaid, antecedent, before mentioned, elementary, incipient, last (preceding), ominous, oracular, original (initial), preliminary, preparatory, previous, prior. SEE MAIN ENTRY

predaceous larcenous

predacious predatory, rapacious

predate antecede, antedate

predative predatory

predatory larcenous, rapacious. SEE MAIN ENTRY

predatory incursion foray

predecessor ancestor, ascendant, forerunner, parents, pioneer, precedent, precursor, primogenitor, progenitor. SEE MAIN ENTRY

predecessors ancestry

predecide forejudge, preconceive, predetermine, prejudge, preordain, presuppose

predecision foregone conclusion, predetermination, predisposition

predecisive prejudicial

predeliberate preordain

predeliberated aforethought, deliberate, premeditated

predeliberation forethought, goal, plan, predetermination, premeditation

predesign contrive, frame (prearrange), plan, prearrange, scheme

predesigned deliberate, intentional, premeditated

predesigned conclusion foregone conclusion

predestinate prearrange, predetermine

predestination predetermination

predestine prearrange, predetermine, preordain

predestined forthcoming, future, inevitable

predeterminated premeditated

predetermination animus, bias, design (intent), foregone conclusion, forethought, goal, intent, preconception, predisposition, prejudice (preconception), premeditation. SEE MAIN ENTRY

predetermine anticipate (prognosticate), devise (invent), forejudge, frame (prearrange), necessitate, orchestrate, plan, prearrange, preconceive, prejudge, prejudice

preconclude (influence), preordain, presuppose, program, scheme

predetermined aforethought, deliberate, express, fixed (settled), intentional, premeditated, stated

predetermined conclusion foregone conclusion

predetermined course of events predetermination

predevised premeditated

predicament case (set of circumstances), complication, condition (state), confusion (ambiguity), deadlock, dilemma, emergency, entanglement (involvement), imbroglio, impasse, occurrence, peril, pitfall, plight, position (situation), posture (situation), problem, quagmire, quandary, situation, state (condition). SEE MAIN ENTRY

predicate ascribe, assume (suppose), attribute, avow, cite (state), claim (maintain), contend (maintain), declare, express, pose (propound), posit, postulate, propound, surmise

predication affirmance (authentication), affirmation, assertion, claim (assertion), pronouncement

predict anticipate (prognosticate), calculate, caution, expect (consider probable), forewarn, portend, preconceive, presage, prognosticate, promise (raise expectations). SEE MAIN ENTRY

predictable foreseeable, regular (conventional)

predicted foreseeable, forseen, forthcoming, future, imminent

predicting omniscient, oracular

prediction premonition, prognosis, prospect (outlook)

prediction of danger monition (warning)

prediction of misfortune misgiving

predictive oracular, prophetic, provident (showing foresight)

predictory prophetic

predilection affinity (regard), animus, bias, character (personal quality), characteristic, choice (decision), compulsion (obsession), conatus, conviction (persuasion), desire, disposition (inclination), favor (partiality), foregone conclusion, inclination, inequity, partiality, penchant, position (point of view), predisposition, preference (choice), prejudice (preconception), presumption, proclivity, propensity, standpoint, vote. SEE MAIN ENTRY

predispose anticipate (expect), bait (lure), convince, preconceive, predetermine, prejudice (influence), prevail upon, slant

predispose to conduce

predisposed inclined, parochial, partial (biased), partisan, prone, ready (willing), susceptible (unresistant)

predisposition affection, animus, bias, conatus, conviction (persuasion), disposition (inclination), foregone conclusion, habit, inclination, instinct, partiality, penchant, personality, position (point of view), predilection, prejudice (preconception), presumption, proclivity, propensity, tendency. SEE MAIN ENTRY

predispositional prejudicial

predominance advantage, dominance, force (strength), hegemony, influence, majority (greater part), occupation (possession), patronage (power to appoint jobs), power, precedence, preponderance, prestige, puissance, supremacy. SEE MAIN ENTRY

predominancy clout, dominance, influence, occupation (possession), predominance, primacy, supremacy

predominant cardinal (outstanding), causative, compelling, considerable, customary, dominant, forcible, influential, leading (ranking first), omnipotent, potent, prevailing (current), prevailing (having superior force), prevalent, primary, prime (most valuable), principal, rife, salient, sovereign (absolute), stellar. SEE MAIN ENTRY

predominant part bulk, generality (bulk), majority (greater part)

predominantly the same in strict conformity

predominate beat (defeat), dominate, outbalance, outweigh, prevail (be in force), prevail (triumph), rule (govern), surpass, transcend. SEE MAIN ENTRY

predominating dominant, master, prevailing (having superior force)

predominating influence hegemony

predomination predominance, preponderance, prestige, primacy, supremacy

predominent prominent, remarkable

preeminence advantage, character (reputation), eminence, precedence, preference (priority), preponderance, prestige, primacy, priority, reputation, significance, supremacy

preeminent absolute (ideal), best, cardinal (outstanding), compelling, conspicuous, dominant, famous, important (significant), influential, leading (ranking first), master, meritorious, notable, noteworthy, outstanding (prominent), paramount, primary, prime (most valuable), principal, professional (stellar), prominent, renowned

preeminently particularly

preeminently bad arrant (onerous)

preempt attach (seize), distrain, preclude, sequester (seize property). SEE MAIN ENTRY

preemption taking. SEE MAIN ENTRY

preengagement reservation (engagement)

preestablish contrive, prearrange, predetermine, preordain, program

preestimate preconception, prejudge, presuppose

preexamine canvass

preexist precede

preexistent aforesaid, antecedent, before mentioned, former, preexisting, previous, prior

preexisting old, preliminary. SEE MAIN ENTRY

prefabrication building (business of assembling)

preface caption, forerunner, overture, preamble, prelude. SEE MAIN ENTRY

prefatorial previous

prefatory antecedent, before mentioned, elementary, inchoate, incipient, initial, last (preceding), precursory, preliminary, preparatory, previous, prior

prefatory note preamble, preface

prefer choose, discriminate (treat differently), favor, proffer, promote (advance), relish, screen (select), select. SEE MAIN ENTRY

prefer a claim impeach, litigate, prosecute (charge), sue

prefer a petition call (appeal to), pray

prefer a request call (appeal to), plead (implore), pray

prefer a request to petition

prefer an appeal call (appeal to)

prefer charges accuse, arraign, book, complain (charge), impeach, incriminate, indict, involve (implicate), lodge (bring a complaint), present (prefer charges), prosecute (charge)

preferability choice (decision)

preferable preferred (favored), select, superior (excellent). SEE MAIN ENTRY

preference advantage, bias, choice (decision), conatus, discrimination (bigotry), disposition (inclination), election (choice), favor (partiality), favoritism, inclination, inequity, option (choice), partiality, patronage (power to appoint jobs), penchant, poll (casting of votes), position (point of view), precedence, predilection, predisposition, prejudice (preconception), prerogative, primary, priority, propensity, referendum, selection (choice), volition, vote, will (desire). SEE MAIN ENTRY

preferential adoptive, preferred (favored). SEE MAIN ENTRY

preferential treatment favor (partiality), inequity, nepotism, partiality

preferment behalf, preference (priority), progress, promotion (advancement)

preferment of charges complaint

preferred popular, preferable, preferential, select, superior (excellent). SEE MAIN ENTRY

preferred provider organization SEE MAIN ENTRY

preferred standing preference (priority). SEE MAIN ENTRY

preferring of charges accusation

preferror of charges complainant

prefigurate portend, presage, presuppose

prefiguration caution (warning), caveat, prognosis

prefigurative prophetic

prefigure forewarn, portend, presage, presuppose

prefigurement forerunner, prognosis

pregnability danger

pregnable disabled (made incapable), helpless (defenseless), indefensible, open (accessible), penetrable, powerless, untenable, vulnerable

pregnant eloquent, productive, replete, strategic

prehension adhesion (affixing), arrest, condemnation (seizure), disseisin, understanding (comprehension)

preindicate portend, predict, presage

preindication symptom

preindicative prophetic

preinstruct initiate

prejudge forejudge, opine, preconceive, predetermine, prejudice (influence), preordain, presume, presuppose. SEE MAIN ENTRY

prejudged conclusion foregone conclusion

prejudgment bias, foregone conclusion, inequity, intolerance, partiality, preconception, predetermination, predilection, prejudice (preconception)

prejudicate forejudge, prejudge

prejudication bias, preconception

prejudice bias, damage, detriment, disadvantage (noun), disadvantage (verb), discrimination (bigotry), drawback, exclusion, favor (partiality), favoritism, foregone conclusion, hatred, inclination, inequality, inequity, influence, injury, injustice, intolerance, ostracism, partiality, penchant, preconception, predetermination, predilection,

predisposition, preference (choice), proclivity, segregation (isolation by races), slant, tendency. SEE MAIN ENTRY

prejudiced disadvantaged, ex parte, exclusive (limited), illiberal, inequitable, interested, one-sided, parochial, partial (biased), subjective, unequal (unjust), unfair, unjust

prejudiced view foregone conclusion, preconception

prejudicial adverse (negative), detrimental, disadvantageous, unfavorable. SEE MAIN ENTRY

prejudicial delay laches

prelect declaim, discourse, inculcate, recite

prelection discourse, harangue, peroration

preliminaries preparation

preliminary antecedent, before mentioned, inchoate, last (preceding), original (initial), overture, precursory, preparatory, previous, prior. SEE MAIN ENTRY

preliminary comment preface

preliminary condition need (requirement), prerequisite

preliminary drawing design (construction plan)

preliminary negotiation overture

preliminary part prelude

preliminary statement preface

preliminary step preparation

prelude overture, preamble, preface (noun), preface (verb), threshold (commencement). SEE MAIN ENTRY

preludial last (preceding), precursory, preliminary, preparatory, prior

preluding aforesaid

preludious last (preceding), precursory

prelusion preamble, preface, prelude

prelusive antecedent, last (preceding), original (initial), precursory, preliminary, preparatory, previous, prior

prelusory aforesaid, antecedent, last (preceding), original (initial), precursory, preliminary, preparatory, previous

premature undue (not owing). SEE MAIN ENTRY

premeditate intend, plan, plot, ponder, prearrange, predetermine, scheme

premeditated aforethought, deliberate, express, intentional, willful. SEE MAIN ENTRY

premeditation conference, consideration (contemplation), deliberation, forethought, goal, predetermination. SEE MAIN ENTRY

premeditative circumspect

premier initial

premise assume (suppose), assumption (supposition), basis, foundation (basis), generalization, ground, inference, postulate (noun), postulate (verb), presumption, proposition, supposition, thesis

premised apparent (presumptive)

premises apartment, area (province), building (structure), part (place), property (land), structure (edifice). SEE MAIN ENTRY

premium bonus, bounty, gratuity (present), payment (remittance), perquisite, price, prize, profit, reward. SEE MAIN ENTRY

premium bond coupon

premium certificate coupon

premium for the use of money interest (profit)

premonish admonish (warn), anticipate (prognosticate), expostulate, forewarn, portend, predict, prognosticate

premonishment notice (warning), premonition

premonition caveat, misgiving, prognosis. SEE MAIN ENTRY

premonitive portentous (ominous)

premonitor indication, symptom

premonitory ominous, portentous (ominous), prophetic

premonitory sign harbinger, indication, symptom

premonstrate portend, predict, presage, prognosticate

premunition precaution, preparation

prenomen call (title)

prenotice prognosis

prenotification notice (warning), premonition, tip (clue)

prenotify caution

prenotion bias, foregone conclusion, inequity, precognition, preconception, predetermination

prentice neophyte

preoccupation compulsion (obsession), contemplation, interest (concern), obsession. SEE MAIN ENTRY

preoccupied oblivious

preoccupy immerse (engross), obsess, occupy (engage), preempt

preordain predetermine. SEE MAIN ENTRY

preordained inevitable

preorder prearrange

preordination foregone conclusion

preparation building (business of assembling), composition (makeup), creation, direction (guidance), discipline (training), edification, education, experience (background), instruction (teaching), manufacture, performance (workmanship), plan, precursor, prelude, provision (act of supplying), qualification (fitness). SEE MAIN ENTRY

preparation of laws legislation (lawmaking)

preparative preliminary, preparatory

preparatory precursory, preliminary, previous, prior. SEE MAIN ENTRY

prepare arrange (plan), charge (instruct on the law), compile, conceive (invent), contrive, devise (invent), discipline (train), educate, establish (launch), fix (arrange), forewarn, frame (construct), induct, initiate, instill, instruct (teach), make, nurture, originate, plan, plot, practice (train by repetition), prearrange, produce (manufacture), provide (arrange for), qualify (meet standards), scheme

prepare a complaint address (petition)

prepare a formal request address (petition)

prepare a petition address (petition)

prepare an estimate evaluate

prepare for anticipate (expect), expect (anticipate), forestall

prepare for crops cultivate

prepare for publication edit

prepare for the worst caution

prepare something specious fake

prepare the ground precede

prepared aforethought, alert (vigilant), circumspect, competent, defensible, discreet, expert, familiar (informed), fit, inclined, informed (educated), practiced, provident (showing foresight), prudent, resourceful, ripe, tactical

prepared announcement statement

prepared for sale commercial

prepared speech peroration

prepared text statement

preparedness diligence (care), maturity, prudence, qualification (fitness)

preparer   precursor
preparing   prospective
prepay   SEE MAIN ENTRY
prepense   aforethought, deliberate
prepollence   dominance, hegemony, influence, power, predominance, preponderance
prepollency   dominance, influence, power, predominance, preponderance
prepollent   influential, paramount, sovereign (absolute)
preponderance   dominance, generality (bulk), majority (greater part), plurality. SEE MAIN ENTRY
preponderancy   generality (bulk), plurality, preponderance
preponderant   cardinal (basic), cardinal (outstanding), compelling, dominant, influential, predominant, prevailing (having superior force), prevalent, prime (most valuable)
preponderate   beat (defeat), dominate, outbalance, outweigh, predominate (outnumber), prevail (be in force), prevail (triumph)
preponderating   prevailing (having superior force)
preponderation   generality (bulk), majority (greater part), preponderance
prepositional   preparatory
prepositive   before mentioned
prepossess   forejudge, preconceive, slant
prepossess unfavorably   prejudice (influence)
prepossessed   interested, one-sided, parochial, partial (biased), prejudicial, unequal (unjust), unjust
prepossessing   attractive, palatable, sapid
prepossession   compulsion (obsession), foregone conclusion, inequity, partiality, preconception, predetermination, predilection, predisposition, prejudice (preconception), preoccupation
preposterous   excessive, exorbitant, impossible, incredible, inept (inappropriate), inordinate, irrational, ludicrous, outrageous, prohibitive (costly), unconscionable, unreasonable, unseemly
prepotency   dint, dominance, influence, predominance
prepotent   dominant, forcible, influential, master, omnipotent, paramount, potent, sovereign (absolute)
prequisiteness   need (requirement)
prerequirement   condition (contingent provision), necessary, necessity, need (requirement)
prerequisite   attornment, compulsory, condition (contingent provision), important (urgent), integral, mandatory, necessary (required), necessary, necessity, obligatory, qualified (conditioned), requirement, requisite, sine qua non. SEE MAIN ENTRY
preresolution   predetermination, premeditation
preresolve   prearrange, predetermine, preordain
preresolved   aforethought, premeditated
prerogative   authority (right), birthright, capacity (authority), droit, enjoyment (use), franchise (license), franchise (right to vote), freedom, impunity, liberty, license, option (contractual provision), prescription (claim of title), privilege, right (entitlement), suffrage, title (right). SEE MAIN ENTRY
presage   anticipate (prognosticate), caution (warning), forerunner, forewarn,

harbinger, herald, indicant, indicate, indication, misgiving, portend, precognition, precursor, predict, premonition, prognosis, prognosticate, promise (raise expectations), threat, threaten, warning. SEE MAIN ENTRY
presaged   foreseen
presageful   inauspicious, ominous, portentous (ominous), prophetic, sinister. SEE MAIN ENTRY
presagement   prognosis
presaging   ominous, oracular, portentous (ominous), prophetic
presaging good fortune   auspicious
prescience   precognition
prescient   omniscient, prophetic, vigilant
prescribe   administer (conduct), admonish (advise), advise, advocate, allocate, assign (designate), authorize, call (demand), caution, command, constitute (establish), counsel, decree, define, detail (assign), dictate, direct (order), drug, enact, govern, impose (enforce), instruct (direct), order, pass (approve), recommend, require (compel), rule (govern), urge. SEE MAIN ENTRY
prescribe a task   instruct (direct)
prescribe by law   constitute (establish)
prescribe laws   legislate
prescribe punishment   condemn (punish), convict, determine, pronounce (pass judgment), sentence
prescribe the law   charge (instruct on the law)
prescribed   arrested (checked), boiler plate, certain (specific), fixed (settled), juridical, legal, licit, limited, mandatory, necessary (required), prescriptive, qualified (conditioned), stated, traditional
prescribed by law   lawful, legal
prescribed code of conduct   decorum
prescribed form   constant, criterion, custom, formality, law, matter of course, policy (plan of action), practice (procedure)
prescribed method of action   proceeding
prescribed mode of action   proceeding
prescribed procedure   ceremony
prescribed punishment   conviction (finding of guilt), fine, penalty, sentence
prescribed system   course
prescribed usage   practice (procedure)
prescriber   arbiter
prescript   act (enactment), bylaw, canon, citation (charge), code, dictate, direction (order), directive, fiat, injunction, mandate, measure, order (judicial directive), ordinance, precept, prescription (directive), regulation (rule), requirement
prescription   assignment (designation), brevet, bylaw, canon, citation (charge), cloud (incumbrance), code, codification, condition (contingent provision), constitution, dictate, direction (order), directive, drug, fiat, guidance, law, mandate, measure, order (judicial directive), practice (custom), recommendation, regulation (rule), requirement, rubric (authoritative rule), rule (legal dictate), title (right), usage. SEE MAIN ENTRY
prescriptive   compulsory, decretal, formal, legislative, orthodox, rightful, traditional, unalienable. SEE MAIN ENTRY
prescriptive right   droit
prescripts   legislation (enactments)
preselect   reserve
presence   attendance, behavior, complexion, conduct, demeanor, deportment, manner (behavior), phenomenon

(manifestation), posture (attitude), specter, vision (dream). SEE MAIN ENTRY
presence in court   appearance (coming into court)
presence of mind   common sense, composure, discretion (quality of being discreet), prudence
present   actual, adduce, allege, bear (adduce), benefit (conferment), bestow, confer (give), contribute (supply), contribution (donation), convey (transfer), current, de facto, dedicate, disclose, display, dole, donation, endow, endowment, endue, exhibit, expose, exposit, express, extant, extend (offer), fund, furnish, gift (present), give (grant), grant, grant (transfer formally), hold out (deliberate on an offer), impart, initiate, instruct (teach), introduce, largess (gift), leave (give), manifest, mete, offer (tender), pass (determine), pay, perquisite, phrase, plead (allege in a legal action), portray, pose (propound), post, produce (offer to view), proffer, pronounce (speak), propose, propound, provide (supply), recite, remark, remit (submit for consideration), render (deliver), replenish, serve (deliver a legal instrument), submit (give), supply, tender, unveil. SEE MAIN ENTRY
present a case   show cause
present an answer   appear (attend court proceedings)
present an opportunity   extend (offer)
present an ultimatum   call (demand), charge (assess)
present argument   show cause
present as proof   cite (state)
present as worthy   recommend
present cause   show cause
present day   contemporary, current
present facts   communicate
present falsely   pretend
present for acceptance   offer (tender)
present for acceptance or rejection   extend (offer)
present for consideration   exhibit
present for payment   tender
present formally   introduce
present information   inform (notify)
present itself   arise (appear), occur (come to mind)
present itself to the mind   occur (come to mind)
present money   fund
present money for safekeeping   deposit (submit to a bank)
present one's claim   call (demand), charge (assess), demand
present oneself   appear (attend court proceedings), comport (behave), demean (deport oneself), report (present oneself)
present reason   show cause
present reasons against   argue
present reasons for   argue
present reasons for and against   debate
present the appearance   appear (seem to be), demean (deport oneself)
present the meaning of   expound
present to the court for acceptance   introduce
present to the view   appear (materialize)
present to view   denude, disinter, exhibit
present varied opinions   debate, discuss
present with bias   prejudice (influence)
present-day   present (current)
present-time   present (current)
presentability   admissibility
presentable   admissible, passable

presentably fairly (moderately)

presentation account (report), application, benefit (conferment), bid, cession, claim (assertion), clarification, concession (authorization), contribution (donation), declaration, dedication, disclosure (something disclosed), dispensation (act of dispensing), donation, endowment, exhibit, experience (encounter), expression (manifestation), gift (present), gratuity (present), inheritance, installation, introduction, largess (gift), notice (announcement), overture, presence (poise), profession (declaration), program, proposal (suggestion), proposition, publicity, representation (statement), resolution (formal statement), reward, role, style

presentation of arguments and evidence hearing

presentation of basics opening statement

presentation of data opening statement

presentation of essentials opening statement

presentation of evidence corroboration

presentation of testimony hearing

presentation of the documentation opening statement

presentation of the evidence opening statement

presentation of the facts opening statement

presentation to the public publication (disclosure)

presentation to view disclosure (act of disclosing)

presented alleged

presenter contributor (giver), donor, grantor

presentient ominous, portentous (ominous), prophetic

presentiment apprehension (fear), expectation, fear, foregone conclusion, inequity, misgiving, precognition, preconception, premonition

presenting donative

presenting favorable conditions propitious

presenting few difficulties convenient

presenting information informatory

presently in due course, instantly

presentment charge (accusation), claim (legal demand), dedication, dispensation (act of dispensing), endowment, expression (manifestation), indictment, largess (gift). SEE MAIN ENTRY

preservation bulwark, conservation, continuation (prolongation), custody (supervision), defense, ecology, maintenance (support of spouse), panoply, protection, safekeeping, security (safety), shelter (protection), support (assistance), ward. SEE MAIN ENTRY

preservation from harm custody (supervision)

preservation from injury custody (supervision)

preservation of the same conditions status quo

preservative preventive, prophylactic, protective

preserve adhere (maintain loyalty), conserve, continue (prolong), ensconce, fund, harbor, hoard, hold (possess), keep (shelter), maintain (sustain), perpetuate, prolong, protect, protection, record, rescue, reserve, retain (keep in possession), save

(conserve), sustain (prolong), uphold. SEE MAIN ENTRY

preserve a memory remember

preserve permanently as a public record file (place among official records)

preserve public order police

preserve public tranquility police

preserved intact, lasting, permanent, safe

preserver guardian

preserving conservation

presettle prepay

preshow forewarn, portend, presage

preside direct (supervise), manage, officiate, overlook (superintend). SEE MAIN ENTRY

preside over administer (conduct), conduct, control (regulate), direct (supervise), dominate, govern, handle (manage), hear (give a legal hearing), manage, operate, regulate (manage), render (administer), rule (govern)

presidency management (directorate)

president chief, key man

presider chairman

presiding executive

presiding officer chairman, director

presidium board, management (directorate)

presignify caution, portend, predict, presage, prognosticate

press attach (seize), bait (lure), call (appeal to), call (demand), claim (demand), coax, coerce, compel, constrain (compel), constrict (compress), demand, desire, duress, enforce, exact, exhort, exigency, force (coerce), hasten, impact, impede, importune, impose (enforce), incite, inculcate, insist, jostle (bump into), lobby, motivate, plead (implore), pray, pressure (noun), pressure (verb), prompt, solicit, spirit, urge, weigh. SEE MAIN ENTRY

press a claim dun, sue

press advice on charge (instruct on the law)

press agentry publicity

press back repress

press by entreaty importune

press down depress

press earnestly insist

press in embed, inject

press in court litigate

press into service resort

press notice publicity, story (narrative)

press on impel, proceed (go forward), progress

press onward continue (persevere), endure (last), keep (continue), progress

press out distill

press together constrict (compress), impact

pressed by duty bound

pressed into smaller compass compact (dense)

pressed together cohesive (compact), compact (dense), solid (compact)

pressing compelling, compulsory, critical (crucial), crucial, essential (required), exigent, grave (important), imperative, important (urgent), indispensable, insistent, major, mandatory, obligatory, onerous, operose, peremptory (imperative), relentless, requisite, serious (grave), urgent, vital. SEE MAIN ENTRY

pressing concern requirement

pressing necessity emergency, exigency

pressing need emergency, prerequisite

pressing requirement market (demand)

pressure aggravation (annoyance), bribery, cajole, coerce, coercion, compel, compulsion (coercion), constrain (compel), constraint (restriction), dint, duress, encumbrance, enforcement, exigency, force (compulsion), force (strength), hasten, impetus, impulse, inducement, instigation, leverage, lobby, main force, persuasion, power, predicament, provocation, requirement, stress (strain), weight (burden). SEE MAIN ENTRY

pressure group faction, lobby, special interest

prestige advantage, character (reputation), clout, credit (recognition), distinction (reputation), eminence, importance, influence, power, precedence, primacy, reputation, respect, status. SEE MAIN ENTRY

prestigious outstanding (prominent)

prestigitation SEE MAIN ENTRY

presumable apparent (presumptive), believable, circumstantial, colorable (plausible), constructive (inferential), ostensible, plausible, presumptive, probable

presumably prima facie (self-evident), reputedly

presume assume (suppose), deem, expect (consider probable), fourjudge, guess, infer, intend, opine, postulate, preconceive, predetermine, prejudge, presuppose, prognosticate, read, surmise, suspect (think), trust. SEE MAIN ENTRY

presume on accroach

presumed assumed (inferred), constructive (inferential), deductible (provable), forseen, presumptive, putative, theoretical

presumed wrongdoer suspect

presuming obtrusive, presumptuous

presumption assumption (supposition), concept, condition (contingent provision), conjecture, disrespect, expectation, generalization, inequity, opinion (belief), position (point of view), preconception, predetermination, probability, prognosis, prospect (outlook), rationale, speculation (conjecture), supposition. SEE MAIN ENTRY

presumption of innocense SEE MAIN ENTRY

presumptive circumstantial, colorable (plausible), deductible (provable), probable, putative, speculative, theoretical. SEE MAIN ENTRY

presumptuous brazen, impertinent (insolent), insolent, obtrusive, orgulous, orotund, proud (conceited), supercilious. SEE MAIN ENTRY

presumptuousness contumely, disrespect, temerity

presupposal foregone conclusion, inference, preconception, predetermination

presuppose assume (suppose), forejudge, guess, opine, postulate, preconceive, predetermine, prejudge, presume, surmise, suspect (think). SEE MAIN ENTRY

presupposed assumed (inferred), presumptive

presupposition assumption (supposition), condition (contingent provision), conjecture, conviction (persuasion), foregone conclusion, generalization, idea, inference, opinion (belief), preconception, predetermination, presumption, prolepsis, theory

presurmise conjecture, expectation, foregone conclusion, forejudge, preconceive, preconception, predetermination, predetermine, prejudge, premonition, presume, presuppose

923

pretend claim *(demand)*, cloak, copy, evade *(deceive)*, fabricate *(make up)*, fake, false *(not genuine)*, feign, invent *(falsify)*, lie *(falsify)*, misrepresent, mock *(imitate)*, palter, prevaricate, purport, simulate, specious, spurious. SEE MAIN ENTRY

pretend not to see ignore

pretend to be assume *(simulate)*, impersonate, pose *(impersonate)*

pretended artificial, assumed *(feigned)*, deceptive, delusive, evasive, fictitious, hypothetical, illusory, imitation, mendacious, ostensible, purported, specious, synthetic, tartuffish

pretender fake, pedant

pretense appearance *(look)*, artifice, bad faith, color *(deceptive appearance)*, counterfeit, cover *(pretext)*, deceit, disguise, excuse, false pretense, falsehood, falsification, fraud, histrionics, hoax, hypocrisy, imposture, indirection *(deceitfulness)*, misstatement, pretext, rodomontade, role, sham, story *(falsehood)*, subterfuge. SEE MAIN ENTRY

pretense of virtue hypocrisy

pretension artifice, disguise, droit, hypocrisy, jactation, pretense *(ostentation)*, pretext, rhetoric *(insincere language)*, rodomontade

pretentious flatulent, fustian, grandiose, histrionic, inflated *(bombastic)*, inflated *(vain)*, orotund, tawdry. SEE MAIN ENTRY

pretentious speech fustian

pretentious talk rodomontade

pretentiousness bombast, pretense *(ostentation)*, rhetoric *(insincere language)*

preterition disregard *(omission)*

pretermission default, disregard *(omission)*, failure *(falling short)*, omission

pretermit defer *(put off)*, disregard, neglect. SEE MAIN ENTRY

preternatural mysterious, peculiar *(curious)*, uncanny

pretexed purported

pretext artifice, bad faith, color *(deceptive appearance)*, deception, disguise, evasion, excuse, false pretense, falsehood, ruse, stratagem, subterfuge. SEE MAIN ENTRY

pretexted assumed *(feigned)*

pretiosissimus invaluable, priceless

pretiosus valuable

pretium bribe, charge *(cost)*, price, ransom, worth

pretrial examination proceedings discovery

pretty attractive

pretty good passable

pretty well fairly *(moderately)*

prevail carry *(succeed)*, coax, continue *(persevere)*, convert *(persuade)*, dominate, endure *(last)*, last, outbalance, outweigh, pass *(satisfy requirements)*, persevere, persist, predominate *(command)*, remain *(continue)*, subsist, succeed *(attain)*, surpass, transcend. SEE MAIN ENTRY

prevail against resist *(withstand)*, withstand

prevail on govern. SEE MAIN ENTRY

prevail over beat *(defeat)*, defeat, kill *(defeat)*, operate, overcome *(surmount)*, override, prejudice *(influence)*, prescribe, surmount

prevail upon affect, bait *(lure)*, browbeat, coax, constrain *(compel)*, convince, exhort, incite, induce, influence, inspire, motivate, persuade, reason *(persuade)*, urge

prevail with arbitrate *(conciliate)*

prevailing accustomed *(customary)*, cardinal *(outstanding)*, coercion, common *(customary)*, convincing, current, customary, dominant, familiar *(customary)*, force *(compulsion)*, forcible, general, influential, leading *(ranking first)*, master, ordinary, orthodox, popular, potent, powerful, predominant, prevalent, prime *(most valuable)*, principal, regular *(conventional)*, rife, successful, typical, usual. SEE MAIN ENTRY

prevailing attitudes climate

prevailing conditions climate

prevailing form protocol *(etiquette)*

prevailing idea motif

prevailing standards climate

prevailing style mode

prevailing taste custom, mode

prevalence boom *(prosperity)*, custom, frequency, mode, preponderance, usage

prevalent common *(customary)*, conventional, current, customary, dominant, extensive, familiar *(customary)*, frequent, general, habitual, household *(familiar)*, influential, master, material *(important)*, ordinary, popular, predominant, present *(current)*, prevailing *(current)*, proverbial, rampant, regular *(conventional)*, rife, routine, typical, usual. SEE MAIN ENTRY

prevaricate bear false witness, cheat, circumvent, deceive, equivocate, evade *(deceive)*, fabricate *(make up)*, feign, invent *(falsify)*, lie *(falsify)*, mislead, misrepresent, misstate, palter, pettifog, pretend. SEE MAIN ENTRY

prevaricating deceptive, disingenuous, disreputable, equivocal, mendacious, oblique *(evasive)*, untrue

prevarication ambivalence, deceit, deception, dishonesty, evasion, false pretense, falsehood, falsification, fiction, fraud, indirection *(deceitfulness)*, lie, perjury, story *(falsehood)*, subreption, subterfuge

prévenance comity

prevene antecede

prevenience expectation

prevenient aforesaid, antecedent, before mentioned, precursory, preliminary, previous, prior, said

prevent arrest *(stop)*, avert, balk, ban, bar *(exclude)*, bar *(hinder)*, block, censor, clog, condemn *(ban)*, constrain *(restrain)*, counter, counteract, countervail, debar, delay, detain *(restrain)*, disqualify, disrupt, eliminate *(exclude)*, enjoin, estop, exclude, fight *(counteract)*, foil, forbid, forestall, frustrate, halt, hamper, impede, inhibit, interdict, interfere, interpose, keep *(restrain)*, obstruct, obturate, occlude, oppose, parry, preclude, prohibit, proscribe *(prohibit)*, repel *(drive back)*, resist *(oppose)*, restrain, restrict, stave, stay *(halt)*, stem *(check)*, stifle, stop, suppress, thwart, withstand. SEE MAIN ENTRY

prevent crime police

prevent from being discovered enshroud

prevent from being seen enshroud

prevent offenses against the state police

prevent passage clog, shut

prevent publication censor

prevent temporarily hinder

preventative offset, preventive, prophylactic, restrictive

prevented arrested *(checked)*

preventing prohibitive *(restrictive)*

prevention bar *(obstruction)*, barrier, constraint *(restriction)*, control *(restriction)*, damper *(stopper)*, deterrence, deterrent, disadvantage, fetter, frustration, halt,

impediment, obstruction, obviation, prohibition, restraint, stay, veto. SEE MAIN ENTRY

prevention of accomplishment frustration

prevention of congressional action filibuster

prevention of waste economy *(frugality)*

preventive barrier, prohibitive *(restrictive)*, prophylactic, protective, restrictive, salutary. SEE MAIN ENTRY

preventive custody constraint *(imprisonment)*, detention

preventive detention constraint *(imprisonment)*

preventive measure panoply, safeguard

preventive measures precaution

preview precursor

previous aforesaid, antecedent, before mentioned, former, last *(preceding)*, late *(defunct)*, precursory, preexisting, preliminary, prior, said. SEE MAIN ENTRY

previous consideration forethought

previous deliberation premeditation

previous design forethought

previous reflection forethought, premeditation

previous to heretofore, theretofore

previously heretofore

previously called alias

previously in mind aforethought

previously mentioned previous, said

previously named said. SEE MAIN ENTRY

previously referred to said

previously specified aforesaid

prevision premonition

prewarn admonish *(warn)*, caution, forewarn, presage

prewarning caveat, premonition

prey pillage, prize, victim. SEE MAIN ENTRY

prey on plague, plunder

prey on the mind obsess

prey upon bait *(harass)*, endanger, harass, loot

preyed upon aggrieved *(harmed)*

preying rapacious

price bid, charge *(cost)*, collection *(payment)*, evaluate, expenditure, expense *(cost)*, fare, fee *(charge)*, gratuity *(bribe)*, par *(face amount)*, rate *(noun)*, rate *(verb)*, recompense, value, worth. SEE MAIN ENTRY

price charged face value *(price)*

price increase inflation *(decrease in value of currency)*

price list tariff *(bill)*

price of a ticket fare

price of corruption gratuity *(bribe)*

price of passage fare

price of redemption ransom

price of retaking ransom

price of retrieval ransom

priceless inestimable, invaluable, prime *(most valuable)*, rare. SEE MAIN ENTRY

pricing charge *(assess)*

prick enter *(penetrate)*, lancinate, penetrate, pierce *(lance)*, provocation

pricking bitter *(penetrating)*

pride SEE MAIN ENTRY

prideful inflated *(vain)*, orgulous, pretentious *(pompous)*, proud *(conceited)*, supercilious

prig steal

prim formal, pretentious *(pompous)*

prima facie content *(meaning)*. SEE MAIN ENTRY

primacy advantage, dominance, dominion *(supreme authority)*, emphasis, force *(strength)*, importance, magnitude, power, precedence, prestige, priority, regime, significance, stress (accent), supremacy. SEE MAIN ENTRY

primal cardinal (basic), central (essential), incipient, initial, original (initial), prime (original), primordial, principal, rudimentary, underlying

primarily a fortiori, ab initio, particularly

primarius leading (ranking first)

primary cardinal (basic), causative, central (essential), critical (crucial), dominant, elementary, essential (inherent), essential (required), fundamental, important (significant), inchoate, incipient, indispensable, initial, integral, leading (ranking first), master, material (important), organic, original (initial), paramount, preliminary, prime (original), primordial, principal, rudimentary, salient, simple, stellar, substantive, ultimate, underlying, vital. SEE MAIN ENTRY

primary constituent necessity

primary element center (essence), consequence (significance), content (meaning)

primary meaning connotation, content (meaning), gist (substance)

primary rights SEE MAIN ENTRY

primate chief

prime bonus

prime cardinal (basic), cardinal (outstanding), dominant, edify, educate, important (significant), initiate, instruct (teach), leading (ranking first), major, master, meritorious, necessary (required), notable, original (initial), paramount, premium, primary, primordial, principal, professional (stellar), ripe, salient, select, sterling, superlative. SEE MAIN ENTRY

prime constituent center (essence), main point, sine qua non

prime ingredient center (essence), main point, sine qua non

prime ingredients character (personal quality)

prime motive derivation

prime mover aggressor, architect, author (originator), determinant, promoter, protagonist, reason (basis)

primed acquainted, fit, informed (having information), ready (prepared), ripe

primer hornbook

primeval incipient, original (initial), prime (original), primordial

primigenial original (initial), primordial

primitive brutal, elementary, incipient, obsolete, organic, original (initial), outdated, outmoded, prime (original), primordial, rudimentary

primogenitor ancestor, derivation, progenitor. SEE MAIN ENTRY

primogenitors parentage

primogeniture birthright

primordial original (initial), prime (original), rudimentary. SEE MAIN ENTRY

primus cardinal (basic), cardinal (outstanding), elementary, fundamental, initial, primary, prime (original), principal

princeliness philanthropy

princely charitable (benevolent), liberal (generous), magnanimous, meritorious, outstanding (prominent), philanthropic

princeps chief, leading (ranking first), principal

principal accomplice, assets, cardinal (basic), cash, central (essential), chairman, chief, corpus, critical (crucial), director, dominant, fundamental, important (significant), leading (ranking first), major, material

(important), necessary (required), noteworthy, outstanding (prominent), paramount, predominant, primary, prime (most valuable), professional (stellar), prominent, protagonist, salient, stellar, substantive, superlative, vital. SEE MAIN ENTRY

principal backer mainstay

principal character protagonist

principal item feature (special attraction)

principal maintainer mainstay

principal part body (main part), bulk, center (essence), cornerstone, generality (bulk), gist (ground for a suit), gravamen, majority (greater part), principal (capital sum)

principal person chief

principal point gist (ground for a suit), main point

principal support mainstay

principal supporter mainstay

principal sustainer mainstay

principal thoroughfare avenue (route)

principalis fundamental, primary, principal

principally ab initio, as a rule, generally, particularly

principatus predominance, supremacy

principia premises (hypotheses)

principium maxim

principium origin (source)

principle article (precept), basis, belief (something believed), color (complexion), conscience, consequence (significance), conviction (persuasion), cornerstone, corpus, criterion, doctrine, dogma, generality (vague statement), ground, honor (good reputation), integrity, law, maxim, precept, prescription (directive), probity, reason (basis), rectitude, right (righteousness), rule (legal dictate), substance (essential nature), thesis, veracity. SEE MAIN ENTRY

principle of law stare decisis

principle part component

principled bona fide, conscientious, equitable, ethical, high-minded, honest, juridical, just, law-abiding, meritorious, moral, reputable, scrupulous, strict

principles code, ethics, honesty, pandect (code of laws), platform, policy (plan of action), polity

principles of government constitution

principles of morality ethics

print brand (mark), circulate, copy (noun), copy (verb), impression, issue (publish), post, publish, stamp

printed holographic

printing publication (printed matter), script

prints fingerprints

prior aforesaid, antecedent, back (in arrears), before mentioned, former

prior last (preceding)

prior precursory, preexisting, preferred (given priority), preliminary, preparatory, previous, said. SEE MAIN ENTRY

prior condition prerequisite

prior determination premeditation

prior instance authority (documentation), precedent

prior measure precaution, preparation

prior planning forethought

prior right prerogative, priority

prior thought forethought

prior to heretofore, theretofore

priority importance, magnitude, materiality (consequence), precedence, preferential, prerogative, privilege, significance. SEE MAIN ENTRY

prison bondage, captivity, cell, constraint (imprisonment), detention, jail, penitentiary, reformatory. SEE MAIN ENTRY

prison house cell, prison

prisonbreaker fugitive

prisoner captive, convict, hostage, inmate. SEE MAIN ENTRY

prisoner at the bar convict

prisoner behind bars convict

prisoner of state convict

prisonhouse jail, penitentiary

pristine initial, original (initial), primordial

pristinus former

privacy concealment, confidence (relation of trust), obscuration. SEE MAIN ENTRY

private blind (concealed), confidence (relation of trust), confidential, covert, esoteric, furtive, interior, internal, intimate, obscure (remote), personal (individual), privy, remote (secluded), residential, secret, several (separate), solitary, surreptitious. SEE MAIN ENTRY

private affair confidence (relation of trust), secret

private communication secret

private enterprise business (commercial enterprise), commerce

private language jargon (technical language)

private matter secret

private property possessions

private understanding contract

private war feud

private wrong tort

privateering larcenous

privately alone (solitary), in person

privateness privacy

privation abridgment (disentitlement), bankruptcy, cost (penalty), curtailment, dearth, deficiency, denial, detriment, expense (sacrifice), foreclosure, indigence, injury, loss, need (deprivation), paucity, poverty. SEE MAIN ENTRY

privation of seisin disseisin

privatus personal (private), private (not public)

privilege advantage, allow (authorize), authorize, birthright, capacity (authority), charter (sanction), claim (right), concession (authorization), dispensation (exception), droit, easement, empower, enable, exclusion, exemption, franchise (license), franchise (right to vote), free, freedom, grant (concede), immunity, impunity, invest (vest), let (permit), liberty, license, option (contractual provision), palliate (excuse), patent, permit, prerogative, prize, right (entitlement), sanction. SEE MAIN ENTRY

privilege to publish copyright

privilege to reproduce copyright

privileged entitled, exempt, free (not restricted), immune, preferential, rightful, unalienable. SEE MAIN ENTRY

privileged class elite, society

privileged communication confidence (relation of trust), secret

privileged information secret

privity chain (nexus), nexus. SEE MAIN ENTRY

privy mysterious, personal (private), private (confidential), secret, stealthy. SEE MAIN ENTRY

privy council bench

privy to familiar (informed)

prizable valuable

prize bounty, consideration (recompense), honor, hush money, paragon, prefer, preferential, premium (excess value),

prime *(most valuable)*, profit, raise *(advance)*, recognition, recommend, regard *(hold in esteem)*, reward, select, spoils, stake *(award)*. SEE MAIN ENTRY
pro forma   SEE MAIN ENTRY
pro life   SEE MAIN ENTRY
pro rata   per capita. SEE MAIN ENTRY
pro re valere   equivalent
pro tem   pro tempore
pro tempore   SEE MAIN ENTRY
pro-choice   SEE MAIN ENTRY
probabilis   plausible
probabilitas   likelihood
probability   chance *(possibility)*, expectation, likelihood, possibility, presumption, prospect *(outlook)*, supposition. SEE MAIN ENTRY
probable   apparent *(presumptive)*, believable, circumstantial, constructive *(inferential)*, deductible *(provable)*, foreseeable, future, possible, presumptive, reasonable *(rational)*. SEE MAIN ENTRY
probable cause   SEE MAIN ENTRY
probare   approve, establish *(show)*, evince, prove, recommend, verify *(confirm)*, vindicate
probate   SEE MAIN ENTRY
probatio   probation. SEE MAIN ENTRY
probation   examination *(test)*, preparation. SEE MAIN ENTRY
probationary   tentative
probationer   apprentice, novice. SEE MAIN ENTRY
probative   tentative
probative matter   evidence
probatory   probative
probe   analysis, analyze, audit, canvass, check *(inspect)*, consider, cross-examination, cross-examine, cross-questioning, delve, examine *(interrogate)*, examine *(study)*, frisk, hearing, hunt, indagation, inquire, inquiry *(request for information)*, inquiry *(systematic investigation)*, interrogation, investigate, investigation, penetrate, peruse, pursuit *(chase)*, pursuit *(effort to secure)*, question *(inquiry)*, research, scrutinize, scrutiny, search, study, trace *(follow)*, traverse, trial *(experiment)*. SEE MAIN ENTRY
probe into   research
probe to the bottom   delve
prober   detective
probing   interrogative, judgment *(discernment)*
probitas   honesty, integrity, probity, rectitude
probity   candor *(impartiality)*, conscience, credibility, ethics, fairness, good faith, honesty, honor *(good reputation)*, integrity, justice, principle *(virtue)*, rectitude, right *(righteousness)*, trustworthiness, truth, veracity. SEE MAIN ENTRY
problem   disadvantage, enigma, foible, grievance, hindrance, impasse, issue *(matter in dispute)*, matter *(subject)*, misfortune, nuisance, pitfall, plight, quagmire, question *(issue)*, thesis, trouble. SEE MAIN ENTRY
problematic   debatable, difficult, disputable, doubtful, inauspicious, uncertain *(questionable)*. SEE MAIN ENTRY
problematical   controversial, debatable, inauspicious, moot, problematic, uncertain *(questionable)*, undecided, vague
probrosus   disgraceful, scandalous, scurrilous
probrum   discredit, infamy, reproach
probus   honest, moral, upright

procacious   bumptious, impertinent *(insolent)*, insolent
procacity   temerity
procedural   SEE MAIN ENTRY
procedural law   adjective law
procedure   agenda, avenue *(means of attainment)*, campaign, conduct, constant, course, direction *(course)*, expedient, form *(arrangement)*, maneuver *(tactic)*, manner *(behavior)*, matter of course, method, mode, modus operandi, operation, policy *(plan of action)*, polity, practice *(custom)*, proceeding, process *(course)*, rule *(guide)*, scheme, step, strategy, system. SEE MAIN ENTRY
proceed   accrue *(arise)*, arise *(occur)*, continue *(resume)*, develop, emanate, ensue, occur *(happen)*, pass *(advance)*, progress, pursue *(carry on)*, redound, remain *(continue)*, reopen, result, resume, stem *(originate)*. SEE MAIN ENTRY
proceed against civilly   prosecute *(charge)*
proceed against criminally   prosecute *(charge)*
proceed by stratagem   circumvent, devise *(invent)*, maneuver
proceed from   arise *(originate)*, result
proceed to   assume *(undertake)*
proceed with   conduct, discharge *(perform)*, maintain *(carry on)*, prosecute *(carry forward)*, transact
proceeding   business *(affair)*, continuation *(resumption)*, day in court, event, expedient, experience *(encounter)*, happening, incident, lawsuit, manner *(behavior)*, occurrence, operation, procedure, progressive *(going forward)*, step, suit, transaction, trial *(legal proceeding)*. SEE MAIN ENTRY
proceeding from antecedent to consequent   a priori
proceeding without cessation   continual *(connected)*
proceeding without interruption   continual *(connected)*
proceedings   affairs, case *(lawsuit)*, cause *(lawsuit)*, dealings, matter *(case)*, record, register, strategy
proceeds   commission *(fee)*, earnings, income, output, product, profit, rent, revenue. SEE MAIN ENTRY
process   avenue *(means of attainment)*, conduit *(channel)*, course, expedient, instrumentality, manufacture, method, mode, modus operandi, operation, practice *(procedure)*, procedure, proceeding, search warrant, step, subpoena, system, transaction, treatment, warrant *(judicial writ)*. SEE MAIN ENTRY
process in law   controversy *(lawsuit)*
process of extinguishment of rights   foreclosure
process of governing   bureaucracy
process of proving   proof
processing   treatment
procession   chain *(series)*, order *(arrangement)*, sequence, serial, succession
proclaim   affirm *(claim)*, annunciate, appoint, argue, avouch *(avow)*, avow, bear *(adduce)*, certify *(attest)*, circulate, command, communicate, convey *(communicate)*, declaim, declare, decree, disclose, divulge, enunciate, express, herald, inform *(notify)*, issue *(publish)*, manifest, notify, observe *(remark)*, plead *(allege in a legal action)*, posit, post, prescribe, profess *(avow)*, promulgate, pronounce *(speak)*,

propagate *(spread)*, publish, report *(disclose)*, signify *(inform)*, speak, utter. SEE MAIN ENTRY
proclaimed   alleged, public *(known)*
proclaimer   harbinger, informant, informer *(a person who provides information)*
proclaimor   declarant
proclamation   adjudication, avouchment, canon, charge *(command)*, charter *(declaration of rights)*, communication *(statement)*, declaration, decree, dictate, directive, disclosure *(act of disclosing)*, disclosure *(something disclosed)*, divulgation, issuance, notice *(announcement)*, notification, order *(judicial directive)*, ordinance, publication *(disclosure)*, publicity, report *(detailed account)*. SEE MAIN ENTRY
proclamatory   declaratory
proclivis   inclined, prone
proclivitas   predisposition, proclivity, propensity, tendency
proclivity   affinity *(regard)*, bias, character *(personal quality)*, characteristic, conatus, conviction *(persuasion)*, desire, disposition *(inclination)*, favor *(partiality)*, favoritism, frame *(mood)*, habit, inclination, instinct, liability, partiality, penchant, position *(point of view)*, predisposition, preference *(choice)*, propensity, standpoint, tendency. SEE MAIN ENTRY
procrastinare   procrastinate
procrastinate   defer *(put off)*, hesitate, hold up *(delay)*, neglect, protract *(prolong)*, stall. SEE MAIN ENTRY
procrastinating   dilatory
procrastination   cessation *(interlude)*, deferment, delay, laches, neglect, pause
procrastinative   dilatory, indolent, remiss
procrastinatory   dilatory
procreant   fertile
procreare   propagate *(increase)*
procreate   bear *(yield)*, create, produce *(manufacture)*, propagate *(increase)*, pullulate, reproduce
procreation   creation
procreative   causative, fertile, prolific
procreator   ancestor, ascendant, parents, predecessor, primogenitor, progenitor
procreators   ancestry
proctor   advocate *(counselor)*, deputy, director, factor *(commission merchant)*, plenipotentiary, procurator, superintendent. SEE MAIN ENTRY
proctorage   supervision
proctorship   control *(supervision)*
procurable   disposable, open *(accessible)*
procuracy   agency *(legal relationship)*, delegation *(envoy)*
procurare   administer *(conduct)*, administer *(tender)*, oversee, superintend
procuratio   administration, government *(administration)*, supervision
procuration   acquisition, agency *(legal relationship)*, delegation *(assignment)*, deputation *(selection of delegates)*, recovery *(repossession)*
procurator   agent, attorney, barrister, deputy, director jurist, proctor. SEE MAIN ENTRY
procurator   factor *(commission merchant)*, proxy
procuratory   vicarious *(delegated)*
procure   acquire *(secure)*, attain, buy, coax, contrive, derive *(receive)*, educe, engage *(hire)*, evoke, gain, glean, hire, lobby, obtain, occupy *(take possession)*, pander, purchase, raise *(collect)*, realize

(obtain as a profit), reap, receive *(acquire)*, recover. SEE MAIN ENTRY

procure another to commit perjury   suborn

procure by effort   earn

procure indirectly   suborn

procure title to   buy, purchase

procurement   acquisition, adverse possession, provision *(act of supplying)*, recovery *(repossession)*, takeover

procurer   consumer, go-between

prod   coax, coerce, constrain *(compel)*, impel, jostle *(bump into)*, press *(goad)*, pressure, prompt, remind, reminder, spirit, stimulate, stimulus, urge

prodding   provocation

prodere   betray *(disclose)*, deliver, give *(grant)*

prodesse   avail *(be of use)*, contribute *(assist)*

prodigal   dissolute, improvident, inordinate, liberal *(generous)*, needless, portentous *(eliciting amazement)*, profligate *(extravagant)*, profuse, superfluous, unrestrained *(not repressed)*. SEE MAIN ENTRY

prodigality   delinquency *(misconduct)*, inconsideration, largess *(generosity)*, misapplication, neglect, waste

prodigalize   dissipate *(expend foolishly)*

prodigious   far reaching, noteworthy, portentous *(eliciting amazement)*, special, unusual. SEE MAIN ENTRY

prodigium   phenomenon *(unusual occurrence)*

prodigy   mastermind

prodition   bad repute, bribery

prodromal   before mentioned

prodrome   precursor

produce   adduce, avail *(bring about)*, bear *(adduce)*, bear *(yield)*, build *(construct)*, cargo, cause, commodities, compose, conjure, constitute *(compose)*, create, develop, discharge *(perform)*, effectuate, engender, evoke, exhibit, fabricate *(construct)*, form, formulate, frame, frame *(construct)*, frame *(formulate)*, furnish, generate, germinate, goods, induce, inspire, invent *(produce for the first time)*, make, manufacture, merchandise, occasion, offer *(tender)*, originate, output, perpetrate, proceeds, product, profit, propagate *(increase)*, provide *(supply)*, pullulate, realize *(make real)*, realize *(obtain as a profit)*. SEE MAIN ENTRY

produce a change   affect

produce a good effect   profit

produce a good result   profit

produce an effect   affect

produce an example   illustrate

produce an instance   exemplify, quote

produce conviction   convince

produce counterfeit money   forge *(counterfeit)*

produce equilibrium   compensate *(counterbalance)*

produce evidence   verify *(confirm)*

produce injury   inflict

produce rapidly   proliferate

produce the evidence   bear *(adduce)*

produced   alleged

produced materials   commodities

producer   author *(originator)*, derivation, determinant, maker

producere   adduce, promote *(advance)*

producing   creation

producing a powerful effect   forcible

producing abundantly   copious

producing boredom   lifeless *(dull)*

producing ennui   lifeless *(dull)*

product   amount *(result)*, conclusion *(outcome)*, consequence *(conclusion)*, development *(outgrowth)*, effect, invention, item, outcome, output, proceeds, result

product of imagination   fiction, idea

product of the imagination   figment

production   boom *(increase)*, boom *(prosperity)*, building *(business of assembling)*, business *(commerce)*, composition *(makeup)*, creation, discharge *(performance)*, disclosure *(act of disclosing)*, formation, fruition, industry *(business)*, manifestation, manufacture, operation, origination, outcome, output, performance *(execution)*, performance *(workmanship)*, realization. SEE MAIN ENTRY

production and distribution   commerce

productive   beneficial, causal, causative, constructive *(creative)*, copious, effective *(efficient)*, efficient, fertile, gainful, lucrative, operative, original *(creative)*, potent, profitable, prolific, purposeful. SEE MAIN ENTRY

productiveness   creation, efficiency, utility *(usefulness)*

productivity   boom *(prosperity)*, creation, utility *(usefulness)*

products   commodities, goods, stock in trade. SEE MAIN ENTRY

proelium committere   fight *(battle)*

proem   overture, preamble, preface, prelude

proemial   elementary, incipient, original *(initial)*, preliminary, preparatory, prior

profanation   blasphemy, profanity

profane   abuse *(violate)*, contaminate, debase, diabolic, mundane, obscene, pollute. SEE MAIN ENTRY

profane interjection   expletive

profane language   profanity

profane oath   blasphemy

profaneness   blasphemy, profanity

profanity   imprecation. SEE MAIN ENTRY

profanus   profane

profectio   start

proferre   adduce, postpone, publish, quote

profess   affirm *(claim)*, allege, annunciate, assert, assume *(simulate)*, assure *(insure)*, avouch *(avow)*, avow, bear *(adduce)*, claim *(maintain)*, concede, contend *(maintain)*, declare, depose *(testify)*, enunciate, palter, posit, pretend, purport, testify. SEE MAIN ENTRY

professed   alleged, ostensible, purported, putative, specious

professed belief   doctrine, dogma, principle *(axiom)*

professed purpose   pretense *(pretext)*, pretext

professio   profession *(declaration)*

profession   admission *(disclosure)*, affirmation, appointment *(position)*, assertion, asseveration, averment, avowal, business *(occupation)*, calling, career, conviction *(persuasion)*, cover *(pretext)*, declaration, disclosure *(act of disclosing)*, disclosure *(something disclosed)*, employment, expression *(comment)*, industry *(business)*, job, labor *(work)*, livelihood, mission, occupation *(vocation)*, office, position *(business status)*, post, pretext, pronouncement, pursuit *(occupation)*, testimony, trade *(occupation)*, work *(employment)*. SEE MAIN ENTRY

profession of faith   principle *(axiom)*

professional   ethical, expert *(adjective)*, expert *(noun)*, learned, practitioner, specialist, technical. SEE MAIN ENTRY

professional advice   holding *(ruling of a court)*

professional decision   holding *(ruling of a court)*

professional error of judgment   malpractice

professional ethics   conscience

professional fee   retainer

professional force   staff

professional language   jargon *(technical language)*

professional laxness   malpractice

professional misconduct   malpractice

professional neglect   malpractice

professional negligence   malpractice

professional staff   staff

professional standards   ethics

professional vocabulary   jargon *(technical language)*

professionalism   specialty *(special aptitude)*

professor   pedagogue, specialist

professorate   faculty *(teaching staff)*

professorial   learned

professors   faculty *(teaching staff)*

proffer   adduce, bestow, bid, contribute *(supply)*, extend *(offer)*, give *(grant)*, hold out *(deliberate on an offer)*, introduce, invitation, offer *(propose)*, offer *(tender)*, overture, pose *(propound)*, present *(make a gift)*, proposal *(suggestion)*, propose, propound, remit *(submit for consideration)*, tender. SEE MAIN ENTRY

proffer payment   offer *(tender)*

proffered   unsolicited

proficere   profit, progress

proficiency   ability, caliber *(mental capacity)*, capacity *(aptitude)*, competence *(ability)*, efficiency, experience *(background)*, facility *(easiness)*, faculty *(ability)*, force *(strength)*, gift *(flair)*, knowledge *(learning)*, performance *(workmanship)*, potential, prowess *(ability)*, science *(technique)*, skill, specialty *(special aptitude)*

proficient   artful, capable, cognizant, competent, deft, effective *(efficient)*, efficient, expert, familiar *(informed)*, informed *(educated)*, learned, literate, practiced, professional *(trained)*, qualified *(competent)*, resourceful, sciential, specialist, veteran. SEE MAIN ENTRY

proficient person   expert, specialist

proficient practitioner   professional

proficisci   leave *(depart)*

proficuous   beneficial

profile   brief, characterize, configuration *(form)*, contour *(outline)*, contour *(shape)*, cross section, delineate, delineation, description, outline *(boundary)*

profit   advantage, avail *(bring about)*, bear *(yield)*, behalf, benefit *(betterment)*, boom *(prosperity)*, capitalize *(seize the chance)*, collect *(recover money)*, commission *(fee)*, dividend, earn, earnings, edification, gain, inure *(benefit)*, output, pay, perquisite, proceeds, prosperity, realization, realize *(obtain as a profit)*, reap, revenue, succeed *(attain)*, utility *(usefulness)*, worth. SEE MAIN ENTRY

profit and loss account   budget

profit and loss statement   ledger

profit by   employ *(make use of)*, exploit *(make use of)*

profit by cheating   prey

profit by swindling   prey

profit from conversion of assets   income

profit from money loaned   interest *(profit)*
profit from sale   income
profit making   boom *(prosperity)*
profitability   utility *(usefulness)*
profitable   beneficial, constructive *(creative)*, copious, effective *(efficient)*, favorable *(advantageous)*, fertile, functional, gainful, lucrative, practical, productive, salutary, successful, valuable. SEE MAIN ENTRY
profitableness   expedience, feasibility, worth
profiteering   exploitation, graft, mercenary
profiteri   avow, declare, offer *(propose)*
profiting   prosperous
profitless   barren, disadvantageous, futile, ineffective, ineffectual, unavailing, unproductive
profits   earnings, income
profits from employment   earnings
profits of commerce   income
profligacy   bad repute, debauchery, delinquency *(misconduct)*, vice
profligate   delinquent *(guilty of a misdeed)*, depraved, disreputable, dissolute, immoral, improvident, iniquitous, lawless, lecherous, lewd, licentious, nefarious, obscene, prodigal, profuse, promiscuous, reprobate, salacious, scandalous, tainted *(corrupted)*, unscrupulous, vicious, wrongdoer. SEE MAIN ENTRY
profligatus   profligate *(extravagant)*, reprobate
profluence   boom *(prosperity)*
profluency   boom *(prosperity)*
profluent   progressive *(going forward)*
profound   convincing, esoteric, intense, learned, obscure *(abstruse)*, recondite, sapient. SEE MAIN ENTRY
profound application   diligence *(care)*
profound attention   diligence *(care)*
profound study   diligence *(care)*
profound thought   diligence *(care)*, preoccupation
profugus   fugitive
profundity   sagacity
profuse   copious, excess, excessive, inordinate, liberal *(generous)*, loquacious, manifold, multiple, prolific, replete, rife, superfluous, undue *(excessive)*, voluble. SEE MAIN ENTRY
profuseness   boom *(prosperity)*, plethora, sufficiency, surfeit, tautology
profusion   boom *(prosperity)*, overage, plethora, quantity, spate, store *(depository)*, sufficiency, surfeit, waste
profusive   copious
profusus   profuse
progenerate   propagate *(increase)*, reproduce
progenerative   fertile
progenies   issue *(progeny)*, offspring, progeny
progenitive   prolific
progenitor   ancestor, ascendant, derivation, forerunner, parents, predecessor. SEE MAIN ENTRY
progenitors   lineage, parentage
progenitorship   paternity
progeniture   bloodline
progeny   child, children, descendant, family *(household)*, offspring, posterity, succession. SEE MAIN ENTRY
prognose   predict
prognosis   caution *(warning)*. SEE MAIN ENTRY
prognostic   caution *(warning)*, harbinger, indicant, indication, indicator, menace,

oracular, precursor, prophetic, provident *(showing foresight)*, symptom, warning
prognosticate   expect *(consider probable)*, forewarn, herald, portend, predict, presage, promise *(raise expectations)*. SEE MAIN ENTRY
prognostication   prognosis
prognosticative   precursory, prophetic
program   arrange *(methodize)*, arrange *(plan)*, calendar *(record of yearly periods)*, campaign, course, direction *(course)*, docket, enterprise *(undertaking)*, method, plan, platform, policy *(plan of action)*, polity, practice *(procedure)*, procedure, prospectus, register, schedule, set down, strategy, system, undertaking *(enterprise)*. SEE MAIN ENTRY
program of action   arrangement *(plan)*, device *(contrivance)*, method, proposition, scheme
program of business   agenda
program of operation   agenda
progredi   progress
progress   accession *(enlargement)*, accrue *(arise)*, advance *(progression)*, advancement *(improvement)*, augmentation, boom *(increase)*, boom *(prosperity)*, civilization, continue *(persevere)*, develop, development *(progression)*, edification, endure *(last)*, enlarge, evolve, expand, germinate, growth *(evolution)*, headway, increase, inflow, keep *(continue)*, move *(alter position)*, pass *(advance)*, persist, proceed *(go forward)*, promotion *(advancement)*, pursue *(strive to gain)*, reform, remain *(continue)*, renew *(begin again)*, resume, succeed *(attain)*, transition. SEE MAIN ENTRY
progress to maturity   development *(progression)*
progressing   live *(existing)*
progression   accession *(enlargement)*, advance *(progression)*, advancement *(improvement)*, array *(order)*, boom *(increase)*, boom *(prosperity)*, chain *(series)*, civilization, continuity, cycle, gamut, headway, hierarchy *(arrangement in a series)*, order *(arrangement)*, progress, promotion *(advancement)*, reform, sequence, serial, step, succession, way *(manner)*
progressive   continuous, corrigible, direct *(uninterrupted)*, liberal *(broad minded)*, radical *(favoring drastic change)*, sophisticated. SEE MAIN ENTRY
progressive course   process *(course)*
progressive growth   development *(progression)*
progressiveness   boom *(prosperity)*
progressivism   reform
progressus   advance *(progression)*, development *(progression)*, progress
prohibere   avert, debar, exclude, hinder, preclude, prevent, stop
prohibit   abolish, abrogate *(annul)*, abrogate *(rescind)*, ban, bar *(exclude)*, bar *(hinder)*, block, censor, clog, condemn *(ban)*, constrain *(restrain)*, contain *(restrain)*, control *(restrain)*, counter, curb, debar, deny *(refuse to grant)*, disfranchise, disqualify, dissent *(withhold assent)*, eliminate *(exclude)*, enjoin, estop, exclude, fetter, forbid, forestall, halt, inhibit, interdict, interfere, keep *(restrain)*, lock, negate, obstruct, occlude, oppose, preclude, prevent, refuse, reject, repel *(drive back)*, repress, restrain, restrict, revoke, stay *(halt)*, stop, suppress, withhold. SEE MAIN ENTRY
prohibit by legal injunction   enjoin

prohibited   barred, illegal, illegitimate *(illegal)*, illicit, impermissible, improper, inadmissible, irregular *(improper)*, unauthorized, unlawful
prohibited articles   contraband
prohibited by law   illegal, illegitimate *(illegal)*
prohibited import   contraband
prohibiting   penal
prohibition   bar *(obstruction)*, barrier, censorship, check *(bar)*, coercion, constraint *(imprisonment)*, constraint *(restriction)*, control *(restriction)*, countermand, denial, deterrence, embargo, estoppel, exclusion, fetter, halt, injunction, limitation, obstacle, obstruction, ostracism, proscription, refusal, rejection, restraint, restriction, temperance, veto. SEE MAIN ENTRY
prohibitionary   restrictive
prohibitive   exclusive *(limited)*, inordinate, preventive, restrictive. SEE MAIN ENTRY
prohibitory   prohibitive *(restrictive)*, restrictive
project   arrange *(plan)*, campaign, cast *(throw)*, contrive, device *(contrivance)*, emanate, endeavor, enterprise *(undertaking)*, impel, overlap, plan, prearrange, precipitate *(throw down violently)*, predetermine, program *(noun)*, program *(verb)*, proposition, propound, pursuit *(occupation)*, scheme *(noun)*, scheme *(verb)*, send, undertaking *(business)*, undertaking *(enterprise)*, venture. SEE MAIN ENTRY
projected   forthcoming, prospective, speculative
projected campaign   project
projected goal   design *(intent)*
projected law   bill *(proposed act)*
projected scheme   project
projecting   prominent
projection   design *(construction plan)*, plan
projector   architect
prolatio   extension *(expansion)*
prolegomenon   preamble, preface
prolepsis   SEE MAIN ENTRY
proles   offspring
proletarian   ignoble
proletariat   populace
proliferate   bear *(yield)*, increase, propagate *(increase)*, pullulate, reproduce. SEE MAIN ENTRY
proliferation   augmentation, boom *(increase)*, boom *(prosperity)*
proliferative   productive, prolific
proliferous   productive, prolific
prolific   beneficial, copious, fertile, productive, profuse, rampant. SEE MAIN ENTRY
prolix   flatulent, loquacious, profuse, prosaic, protracted, turgid. SEE MAIN ENTRY
prolixity   SEE MAIN ENTRY
prolocutor   procurator, spokesman
prologue   preamble, prelude, threshold *(commencement)*
prolong   compound, conserve, defer *(put off)*, delay, dwell *(linger over)*, expand, hold up *(delay)*, increase, keep *(continue)*, last, maintain *(carry on)*, perpetuate, persevere, preserve, procrastinate, remain *(continue)*, stay *(continue)*. SEE MAIN ENTRY
prolongate   dwell *(linger over)*
prolongation   adjournment, advance *(increase)*, boom *(increase)*, continuance, deferment, delay, extension *(postponement)*, longevity, survival
prolonged   chronic, continuous, prolix, protracted

prolonged outburst of denunciation diatribe

prolusion preface

promenade perambulate

prominence character (reputation), clout, consequence (significance), distinction (reputation), eminence, emphasis, honor (outward respect), importance, materiality (consequence), notoriety, prestige, reputation, significance, status, stress (accent), weight (importance). SEE MAIN ENTRY

prominens prominent

prominent appreciable, blatant (conspicuous), clear (apparent), conspicuous, critical (crucial), famous, flagrant, illustrious, important (significant), influential, leading (ranking first), manifest, momentous, naked (perceptible), notable, noteworthy, notorious, obtrusive, obvious, open (in sight), palpable, paramount, particular (specific), patent, perceivable, perceptible, primary, prime (most valuable), principal, remarkable, renowned, reputable, salient, stellar, unusual. SEE MAIN ENTRY

prominent aspect main point

prominent detail highlight

prominent object landmark (conspicuous object)

prominent part highlight

prominent point main point

prominently fairly (clearly), particularly

promiscuous haphazard, immoral, indiscriminate, lascivious, licentious, random. SEE MAIN ENTRY

promiscuus indiscriminate, miscellaneous, promiscuous

promise agree (contract), allegiance, assurance, assure (insure), bestow, bind (obligate), bond, bond (secure a debt), commitment (responsibility), compact, condition (contingent provision), contract (noun), contract (verb), cosign, covenant, coverage (insurance), depose (testify), duty (obligation), ensure, expectation, guarantee, insurance, oath, obligation (duty), pact, pledge (binding promise), possibility, potential, predict, presage, probability, proffer, prognosis, prognosticate, prospect (outlook), recognizance, responsibility (accountability), security (pledge), stipulate, stipulation, swear, testament, undertake, undertaking (pledge), underwrite, vouch, vow, warrant (guaranty), warranty. SEE MAIN ENTRY

promise ill impend

promise solemnly pledge (promise the performance of)

promise to contribute subscribe (promise)

promise to pay coverage (insurance)

promise to pay another's debt guaranty

promise to set aside reservation (engagement)

promise under seal specialty (contract)

promised contractual, forseen, forthcoming, indentured, prospective

promising auspicious, favorable (advantageous), possible, probable, promissory, propitious, viable

promising to underwrite promissory

promisor surety (guarantor)

promissory SEE MAIN ENTRY

promissory note bond, draft, security (pledge)

promissory oath pledge (binding promise)

promissory obligation bill (formal declaration)

promissum pledge (binding promise), promise, vow

promittere hold out (deliberate on an offer), proffer

promote advocate, aid, ameliorate, assist, avail (be of use), bear (support), capitalize (provide capital), conduce, continue (persevere), cultivate, develop, elevate, enhance, expedite, facilitate, favor, foment, foster, further, hasten, heighten (augment), help, honor, inure (benefit), lobby, motivate, notify, nurture, originate, prefer, preserve, prompt, propagate (spread), provoke, raise (advance), recommend, sanction, serve (assist), side, sponsor, subsidize, support (assist), sustain (prolong), urge. SEE MAIN ENTRY

promote a cause defend

promote public health and safety police

promote racial harmony desegregate

promote racial mixing desegregate

promoter abettor, advocate (espouser), backer, benefactor, coactor, conspirer, developer, disciple, partisan, patron (influential supporter), sponsor. SEE MAIN ENTRY

promoting beneficial

promoting health salutary

promotion advance (progression), advancement (improvement), advocacy, aid (help), behalf, benefit (betterment), development (progression), elevation, headway, progress, propaganda, publicity, relief (aid), support (assistance). SEE MAIN ENTRY

promotor coactor

promovere promote (advance)

prompt abet, acute, advocate, agitate (activate), cause, coax, convince, counsel, enjoin, evoke, exhort, expeditious, hint, immediate (at once), impel, incite, indication, induce, influence, initiate, inspire, instantaneous, instruct (direct), motivate, originate, persuade, prevail (persuade), provoke, punctual, ready (prepared), recommend, remind, reminder, spirit, stimulate, summary, urge. SEE MAIN ENTRY

prompte readily

prompted inclined

prompter abettor, advocate (counselor), catalyst, special interest

prompting advice, cause (reason), guidance, impulsive (impelling), incentive, inducement, instigation, invitation, moving (evoking emotion), persuasion, provocation, suggestion

promptitude dispatch (promptness)

promptly as soon as feasible, forthwith, instantly, readily

promptuary bank, cache (storage place), repository

prompture suggestion

promptus expeditious, prompt, ready (prepared)

promulgare promulgate

promulgate annunciate, bear (adduce), circulate, convey (communicate), decree, diffuse, disclose, disseminate, divulge, enunciate, herald, inform (notify), issue (publish), notify, posit, proclaim, propagate (spread), report (disclose), reveal, signify (inform), spread. SEE MAIN ENTRY

promulgate a decree instruct (direct)

promulgate an order command, instruct (direct)

promulgated alleged, public (known)

promulgatio notice (announcement), notice (give formal warning), notification

promulgation charter (declaration of rights), declaration, divulgation, issuance,

notification, proclamation, pronouncement, publication (disclosure), publicity

promulgatory declaratory

prone inclined, partial (biased), ready (willing), subject (exposed). SEE MAIN ENTRY

prone to addicted

prone to believe credulous

prone to display of feeling demonstrative (expressive of emotion)

prone to emotional display demonstrative (expressive of emotion)

prone to error fallible

prone to inaccuracy fallible

proneness affection, bias, character (personal quality), characteristic, conatus, disposition (inclination), favor (partiality), favoritism, frame (mood), inclination, instinct, liability, penchant, position (point of view), predilection, predisposition, preference (choice), proclivity, propensity, tendency

proneness to error frailty

pronounce adjudicate, affirm (claim), affirm (declare solemnly), allege, annunciate, argue, assert, avouch (avow), avow, award, certify (attest), communicate, convey (communicate), decide, declare, decree, determine, enunciate, express, issue (publish), judge, pass (determine), phrase, posit, profess (avow), recite, rule (decide), speak, try (conduct a trial), utter. SEE MAIN ENTRY

pronounce a judgment conclude (decide), determine

pronounce as an official act find (determine)

pronounce distinctly enunciate

pronounce formally adjudge, arbitrate (adjudge)

pronounce free from guilt exonerate

pronounce guilty determine, sentence

pronounce in a distinct manner enunciate

pronounce innocent of wrong excuse

pronounce judgment arbitrate (adjudge), award, condemn (punish), convict, deem, opine, pass (determine), rule (decide), sentence

pronounce legal authorize, certify (approve), legalize, notarize

pronounce not guilty acquit, clear, vindicate

pronounce on award

pronounce sentence condemn (punish), convict

pronounced alleged, clear (apparent), conspicuous, distinct (clear), evident, flagrant, lucid, manifest, nuncupative, obvious, open (in sight), palpable, prominent, salient, unmistakable, verbal

pronouncement adjudication, affirmance (authentication), affirmance (legal affirmation), affirmation, allegation, assertion, asseveration, averment, avouchment, avowal, award, charter (declaration of rights), choice (decision), conclusion (determination), confession, declaration, decree, determination, dictum, disposition (determination), edict, fiat, finding, holding (ruling of a court), issuance, judgment (formal court decree), law, notice (announcement), notification, observation, opinion (judicial decision), order (judicial directive), proclamation, profession (declaration), publication (disclosure), remark, resolution (formal statement), ruling, sentence, speech, statement, surety (certainty). SEE MAIN ENTRY

pronouncement by a court   award, holding *(ruling of a court)*

pronouncement of a jury   verdict

pronunciamento   canon, issuance, pronouncement

pronunciamiento   decree

pronunciation   speech, stress *(accent)*

pronuntiare   enunciate, issue *(publish)*, proclaim, pronounce *(pass judgment)*

pronuntiatio   declamation, publication *(disclosure)*

pronus   prone, propensity

prooemium   preface, prelude

proof   certification *(attested copy)*, certification *(certainness)*, confirmation, corroboration, counterargument, data, design *(construction plan)*, document, documentation, evidence, ground, safe, strength, testimony, token. SEE MAIN ENTRY

proof by a witness   deposition, testimony

proof legally presented at trial   evidence

proof of absence   alibi

proof of authority   credentials

proof of delivery   receipt *(proof of receiving)*

proof of facts   evidence

proof of guilt   conviction *(finding of guilt)*

proof of identity   identification

proof of payment   receipt *(proof of receiving)*

proof of the validity of a will   probate

proof of the will   probate

prop   bear *(support)*, bolster, elevate, help, mainstay, reinforcement, rest *(be supported by)*, uphold

propaedeutic   didactic, informative

propaedeutical   informative

propaedeutics   education

propaganda   persuasion. SEE MAIN ENTRY

propagandist   advocate *(espouser)*

propagandistic   persuasive

propagandize   convert *(persuade)*, convince, inculcate, instill, misinform, persuade, prevail *(persuade)*, promote *(organize)*

propagare   extend *(enlarge)*

propagate   bear *(yield)*, circulate, diffuse, disperse *(disseminate)*, disseminate, notify, originate, proclaim, produce *(manufacture)*, proliferate, promulgate, reproduce, spread. SEE MAIN ENTRY

propagated   public *(known)*

propagatio   extension *(expansion)*

propagation   maternity, publication *(disclosure)*, publicity, report *(detailed account)*, transmittal

propagator   advocate *(espouser)*

propel   cast *(throw)*, constrain *(compel)*, dispatch *(send off)*, impel, launch *(project)*, move *(alter position)*, precipitate *(throw down violently)*, project *(impel forward)*, provoke, send, spirit, stimulate, urge. SEE MAIN ENTRY

propel oneself   proceed *(go forward)*

propellant   impetus

propellants   ammunition

propense   prone, ready *(willing)*

propenseness   predisposition, propensity

propensio   penchant

propensio animi   bias

propension   character *(personal quality)*, penchant, predisposition, propensity

propensity   affinity *(regard)*, animus, aptitude, bias, character *(personal quality)*, characteristic, conatus, conviction *(persuasion)*, desire, disposition *(inclination)*, favor *(partiality)*, frame *(mood)*, habit, inclination,

instinct, partiality, penchant, position *(point of view)*, predilection, predisposition, preference *(choice)*, proclivity, standpoint, tendency. SEE MAIN ENTRY

propensus   inclined, propensity

proper   accurate, admissible, allowable, applicable, appropriate, due *(regular)*, eligible, equitable, evenhanded, fit, fitting, formal, honest, juridical, just, justifiable, lawful, legal, licit, meritorious, moral, official, orthodox, permissible, precise, reasonable *(fair)*, reasonable *(rational)*, relevant, right *(suitable)*, rightful, seasonable, several *(separate)*, suitable, tenable, unprejudiced. SEE MAIN ENTRY

proper behavior   protocol *(etiquette)*

proper for judicial examination   justiciable

proper for judicial review   justiciable

proper formality   propriety *(correctness)*

proper name   call *(title)*

proper occasion   opportunity

proper thing to do   decorum

proper time   opportunity, timeliness

proper title   heading

proper to be examined in courts of justice   justiciable

proper to public debate   forensic

properantia   haste

properare   hasten

properatio   dispatch *(promptness)*, haste

properly   as a matter of right, fairly *(impartially)*

properly qualified   competent

properly timed   punctual, seasonable

properness   decorum, propriety *(appropriateness)*, propriety *(correctness)*

propertied   opulent

properties   commodities

property   assets, capital, characteristic, chattel, demesne, differential, domain *(land owned)*, dominion *(absolute ownership)*, effects, fee *(estate)*, freehold, goods, holding *(property owned)*, interest *(ownership)*, land, merchandise, money, paraphernalia *(personal belongings)*, parcel, personalty, plot *(land)*, possessions, premises *(buildings)*, principal *(capital sum)*, quality *(attribute)*, quality *(grade)*, real estate, realty, remainder *(estate in property)*, resource, securities, share *(stock)*, specialty *(distinctive mark)*, stock *(shares)*, substance *(material possessions)*, territory, trait. SEE MAIN ENTRY

property holder   landholder, landowner, lessee

property illegally acquired   graft

property leased   leasehold

property obtained by descent   inheritance

property obtained by devise   inheritance

property owner   landholder, landowner, lessor, shareholder

property permanently affixed to the realty   immovable

property right   lien

property saved   salvage

property which may descend to an heir   hereditament

prophesied   foreseeable, forseen

prophesy   anticipate *(prognosticate)*, expect *(consider probable)*, forewarn, portend, predict, presage, prognosis, prognosticate, promise *(raise expectations)*

prophetic   oracular, portentous *(ominous)*. SEE MAIN ENTRY

prophetical   portentous *(ominous)*, prophetic

prophylactic   preventive, protective, remedial, salutary. SEE MAIN ENTRY

prophylaxis   deterrence

propiatory   penitent

propietory owner   landlord

propinquitas   affinity *(family ties)*, relationship *(family tie)*

propinquity   blood, connection *(relation)*, corollary, kinship, relation *(connection)*, vicinity. SEE MAIN ENTRY

propinquus   approximate, close *(near)*, related, relation *(kinship)*, relative

propitiable   nonmilitant

propitiare   propitiate

propitiate   arbitrate *(conciliate)*, disarm *(set at ease)*, mollify, pacify, placate, reconcile, redeem *(satisfy debts)*, redress, soothe. SEE MAIN ENTRY

propitiated   agreed *(harmonized)*

propitiating   compensatory

propitiation   collection *(payment)*, conciliation, expiation, mollification, reconciliation

propitiator   go-between, intermediary, referee

propitiatory   nonmilitant

propitious   auspicious, beneficial, favorable *(advantageous)*, fitting, opportune, seasonable, viable. SEE MAIN ENTRY

propitiousness   expedience, opportunity

propitius   propitious

propone   hold out *(deliberate on an offer)*

proponent   advocate *(espouser)*, apologist. SEE MAIN ENTRY

proponere   exhibit, issue *(publish)*

proporting   distribution *(apportionment)*

proportion   allotment, caliber *(measurement)*, coordinate, differential, quota, ration, regularity, share *(interest)*. SEE MAIN ENTRY

proportionable   cognate, proportionate

proportional   commensurable, commensurate, congruous, harmonious, proportionate, relative *(comparative)*

proportionate   adequate, commensurable, commensurate, congruous, correlative, dispense, harmonious, pro rata, relative *(comparative)*, suitable. SEE MAIN ENTRY

proportionately   per capita, pro rata

proportioned   coextensive, elegant

proportionment   apportionment

proportions   area *(surface)*, degree *(magnitude)*, dimension, magnitude

proposal   advice, agenda, application, bid, bill *(proposed act)*, campaign, conspiracy, invitation, measure, motion, motive, nomination, overture, plan, platform, policy *(plan of action)*, prescription *(directive)*, program, project, proposition, recommendation, request, resolution *(formal statement)*, strategy, suggestion. SEE MAIN ENTRY

propose   advise, advocate, argue, counsel, extend *(offer)*, hold out *(deliberate on an offer)*, initiate, intend, move *(judicially request)*, nominate, plan, pose *(propound)*, posit, present *(introduce)*, proffer, propound, raise *(advance)*, recommend, remit *(submit for consideration)*, resolve *(decide)*, submit *(give)*, tender. SEE MAIN ENTRY

propose a motion   move *(judicially request)*

propose a question   inquire

propose an action formally   move *(judicially request)*

propose as a candidate   nominate

propose legal instructions   charge *(instruct on the law)*

proposed   apparent *(presumptive)*, tentative

proposed act   measure

proposed action   agenda, design *(intent)*, plan, platform, policy *(plan of action)*, strategy

proposed enactment   bill *(proposed act)*

proposed law   bill *(proposed act)*

proposed measure   motion

proposed regulation   bill *(proposed act)*

proposed rule   bill *(proposed act)*

proposed sequence of action   design *(intent)*

proposed statute   bill *(proposed act)*

proposer of a law   lawmaker

proposer of legislation   lawmaker

propositio   proposition

proposition   advice, affirmance *(legal affirmation)*, agenda, application, basis, bid, business *(affair)*, claim *(assertion)*, clause, contention *(argument)*, invitation, issue *(matter in dispute)*, matter *(subject)*, measure, motion, overture, plan, platform, policy *(plan of action)*, principle *(axiom)*, project, proposal *(suggestion)*, question *(issue)*, rationale, recommendation, resolution *(formal statement)*, strategy, suggestion, theory, thesis, ultimatum. SEE MAIN ENTRY

propositional   apparent *(presumptive)*

propositum   intention, matter *(subject)*, object, project, purpose, strategy

propound   adduce, admonish *(advise)*, advocate, allege, annunciate, argue, assert, avouch *(avow)*, avow, bear *(adduce)*, claim *(maintain)*, defend, hold *(decide)*, issue *(publish)*, offer *(propose)*, posit, postulate, proffer, propose, submit *(give)*, utter. SEE MAIN ENTRY

propounded   alleged

proprietary   ownership, proprietor. SEE MAIN ENTRY

proprietary rights   occupation *(possession)*

proprietas   character *(personal quality)*, characteristic, feature *(characteristic)*, property *(distinctive attribute)*, trait

proprieties   protocol *(etiquette)*

proprietor   employer, landholder, landlord, landowner, principal *(director)*, tenant

proprietorship   adverse possession, dominion *(absolute ownership)*, enjoyment *(use)*, interest *(ownership)*, occupancy, occupation *(possession)*, ownership, possession *(ownership)*, tenancy, title *(right)*

propriety   admissibility, aptitude, behalf, behavior, conduct, decorum, deportment, expedience, formality, integrity, justice, qualification *(fitness)*, rectitude, right *(righteousness)*

proprius   distinctive, essential *(required)*, individual, inherent, innate, particular *(specific)*, specific, typical

propugnaculum   bulwark, safeguard

propulsare   parry, repulse, stave

propulsion   impetus

propulsive   compelling, impulsive *(impelling)*

propulsive force   impetus

prorate   allocate, allot, apportion, charge *(assess)*, disburse *(distribute)*, distribute, divide *(distribute)*, parcel, partition. SEE MAIN ENTRY

prorogare   prolong

prorogate   postpone

prorogation   adjournment, cloture, deferment, delay, dissolution *(termination)*

prorogue   adjourn, continue *(adjourn)*, defer *(put off)*, postpone, procrastinate, recess

prorsus   in toto

proruption   outbreak, outburst

prosaic   average *(standard)*, jejune *(dull)*, languid, lifeless *(dull)*, mediocre, mundane, nondescript, ordinary, pedestrian, ponderous, stale, trite, typical, usual. SEE MAIN ENTRY

prosaical   mediocre, ordinary, prosaic

proscribe   ban, bar *(hinder)*, block, border *(bound)*, censor, condemn *(ban)*, constrain *(restrain)*, debar, eliminate *(exclude)*, enjoin, exclude, forbid, forswear, inhibit, interdict, limit, order, outlaw, prohibit, reject, relegate, renounce, repudiate, restrain, restrict, sentence. SEE MAIN ENTRY

proscribed   barred, illegal, illegitimate *(illegal)*, illicit, impermissible, unauthorized

proscribed form   procedure

proscribed person   pariah

proscribere   outlaw, proscribe *(prohibit)*

proscriptio   proscription

proscription   bar *(obstruction)*, boycott, check *(bar)*, constraint *(restriction)*, deterrence, deterrent, direction *(order)*, injunction, limitation, mandate, obstacle, obstruction, ostracism, prohibition, refusal, rejection, renunciation, restraint, veto. SEE MAIN ENTRY

proscriptive   prohibitive *(restrictive)*, restrictive

proscriptus   outlaw

proscrit   discard

prosecute   accuse, arraign, complain *(charge)*, incriminate, lodge *(bring a complaint)*, pursue *(carry on)*. SEE MAIN ENTRY

prosecute an inquiry   delve

prosecute one's case   plead *(argue a case)*

prosecute to a conclusion   close *(terminate)*, conclude *(complete)*, consummate, follow-up

prosecuting attorney   district attorney, prosecutor. SEE MAIN ENTRY

prosecution   action *(proceeding)*, arraignment, complainant, complaint, cross-examination, proceeding, prosecutor, pursuit *(chase)*. SEE MAIN ENTRY

prosecutor   accuser, complainant, district attorney, jurist. SEE MAIN ENTRY

prosecutorial complaint   information *(charge)*

proselyte   partisan, persuade

proselytism   persuasion

proselytize   convert *(persuade)*, persuade

prosequi   pursue *(chase)*

prospect   chance *(possibility)*, contemplation, customer, expectation, likelihood, motive, opportunity, possibility, potential, probability. SEE MAIN ENTRY

prospection   expectation

prospective   apparent *(presumptive)*, forthcoming, future, immediate *(imminent)*, imminent, pending *(imminent)*, proximate. SEE MAIN ENTRY

prospective buyer   patron *(regular customer)*

prospective client   prospect *(prospective patron)*

prospective customer   prospect *(prospective patron)*

prospector   speculator

prospectus   issuance, plan, program, proposition. SEE MAIN ENTRY

prosper   auspicious

prosper   earn, gain, prevail *(triumph)*, progress, succeed *(attain)*

prospering   successful

prosperitas   prosperity

prosperity   welfare. SEE MAIN ENTRY

prosperous   beneficial, opulent, successful. SEE MAIN ENTRY

prosperous issue   boom *(prosperity)*

prosperous outcome   boom *(prosperity)*

prosperousness   boom *(prosperity)*, prosperity, welfare

prosperus   favorable *(advantageous)*, prosperous

prospicience   expectation

prostitute   betray *(lead astray)*, corrupt, deteriorate, misemploy, mistreat, pervert, pollute

prostitution   misusage, perversion

prostrate   disable, helpless *(powerless)*, overcome *(overwhelm)*, overthrow, servile, subservient

prostration   impuissance. SEE MAIN ENTRY

prosy   jejune *(dull)*, mundane, pedestrian, prolix, prosaic, stale, usual

protagonist   abettor, backer. SEE MAIN ENTRY

protean   aleatory *(uncertain)*, mutable, pliable, variable. SEE MAIN ENTRY

protect   care *(be cautious)*, care *(regard)*, conceal, conserve, cover *(guard)*, defend, ensconce, enshroud, ensure, envelop, foster, harbor, hedge, keep *(shelter)*, maintain *(sustain)*, patrol, police, preserve, save *(rescue)*, screen *(guard)*, shroud, side, sponsor, support *(assist)*, sustain *(prolong)*, uphold. SEE MAIN ENTRY

protect against loss   insure

protect from injury   preserve

protected   exempt, guarded, immune, impervious, inexpugnable, insusceptible *(resistant)*, safe, secure *(free from danger)*

protecting   conservation, preventive

protection   adoption *(affiliation)*, advantage, auspices, behalf, blackmail, bulwark, charge *(custody)*, conservation, coverage *(insurance)*, custody *(supervision)*, defense, direction *(guidance)*, ecology, gratuity *(bribe)*, haven, immunity, impunity, inviolability, lodging, panoply, patronage *(support)*, precaution, preservation, refuge, reinforcement, safeguard, safekeeping, security *(safety)*, shield, support *(assistance)*, surveillance, trust *(custody)*, veil, ward. SEE MAIN ENTRY

protection against loss   indemnity, insurance

protection money   bribe

protective   paternal, preventive, prophylactic, salutary. SEE MAIN ENTRY

protective covering   panoply

protective custody   constraint *(imprisonment)*, detention, preservation, safekeeping

protective device   barrier

protective fire   barrage

protective order   SEE MAIN ENTRY

protective outfit   panoply

protector   advocate *(counselor)*, apologist, backer, benefactor, guardian, peace officer, proponent, samaritan, shield, sponsor, warden

protectorship   adoption *(affiliation)*, auspices, control *(supervision)*, management *(supervision)*, patronage *(support)*

protectory   cache *(hiding place)*

protegé   disciple. SEE MAIN ENTRY

proteiform   pliable, protean

protervitas   audacity

protest   admonition, avow, challenge, complain *(criticize)*, complaint, conflict, confront *(oppose)*, contention *(opposition)*, counter, counteract, cross *(disagree with),* demur, denial, deprecate, differ *(disagree),* disaccord *(noun),* disaccord *(verb),* disaffirm, disagree, disallow, disapprobation, disapprove *(reject),* disavow, disown *(deny the validity),* disparagement, dissension, dissent *(withhold assent),* drawback, except *(object),* exception *(objection),* expostulate, fight *(counteract),* gainsay, impugnation, negate, negation, nonconformity, object, objection, oppose, opposition, oppugn, outcry, picket, prohibit, reaction *(opposition),* refuse, reject, remonstrance, remonstrate, renounce, reprehend, repudiate, resist *(oppose),* resistance. SEE MAIN ENTRY

protest against counter, counteract, decry, denounce *(condemn),* inveigh, reproach

protest against a ruling exception *(objection)*

protest frivolously cavil

protestant dissident, heretic, recusant, reluctant

protestation avowal, complaint, contention *(opposition),* criticism, denial, disapprobation, disapproval, dissension, drawback, exception *(objection),* impugnation, negation, nonconformity, opposition, outcry, remonstrance

protested bill bad debt

protester malcontent

protesting dissenting, dissident, nonconsenting, remonstrative

prothonotary clerk

protocol bill *(proposed act),* decorum, mode, practice *(procedure),* rule *(guide),* treaty. SEE MAIN ENTRY

protogenic primordial

protomorphic rudimentary

protoplast prototype

prototypal primordial

prototype constant, exemplar, model, paradigm, pattern, rule *(guide),* sample, standard. SEE MAIN ENTRY

protract compound, continue *(prolong),* delay, enlarge, extend *(enlarge),* hold up *(delay),* increase, last, procrastinate, prolong, sustain *(prolong).* SEE MAIN ENTRY

protracted chronic, profuse, prolix. SEE MAIN ENTRY

protraction adjournment, advance *(increase),* boom *(increase),* continuance, continuation *(prolongation),* continuity, filibuster, longevity

protrude overlap, project *(extend beyond)*

protrudent salient

protruding obtrusive, prominent, salient

protrusive obtrusive, prominent, salient

protuberant obtrusive, prominent, salient

protuberate project *(extend beyond)*

proud disdainful, inflated *(vain),* supercilious. SEE MAIN ENTRY

proud contempt disdain

provable convincing. SEE MAIN ENTRY

prove ascertain, bear *(adduce),* cite *(state),* confirm, convince, corroborate, demonstrate *(establish),* disabuse, document, establish *(show),* evince, manifest, reason *(persuade),* substantiate, support *(corroborate),* sustain *(confirm),* testify, validate, verify *(confirm).* SEE MAIN ENTRY

prove acceptable satisfy *(fulfill)*

prove blameless exonerate

prove false disprove, rebut, refute

prove guiltless exculpate

prove inadequate fail *(lose)*

prove innocent absolve, acquit, clear

prove not guilty absolve, exculpate, exonerate

prove one's point convince

prove the contrary contradict, disprove, negate

prove the truth of justify

prove the validity of a will probate

prove to be a participant in involve *(implicate)*

prove to be wrong disprove

prove to the contrary disprove

prove treacherous defect

prove unreliable fail *(neglect)*

prove unsatisfactory fail *(lose)*

prove useless fail *(lose)*

prove warranted justify

proved dependable, reliable, unrefutable, valid

proved innocent acquitted

proved strength proof

provehere promote *(advance),* raise *(advance)*

proven dependable, irrefutable, official, sound, undeniable, unrefutable

proven name goodwill

provenance birth *(lineage),* derivation, genesis, origination, source

provender replenish

provenience derivation, origination, source

proverb maxim, phrase

proverbial trite. SEE MAIN ENTRY

proverbial saying maxim

provide accommodate, avail *(bring about),* bear *(yield),* bequeath, bestow, clothe, dispense, enable, endow, endue, fund, furnish, give *(grant),* hoard, impart, lend, make, pander, present *(make a gift),* procure, produce *(manufacture),* recruit, render *(administer),* replenish, sell, stipulate, supply, transmit, yield *(produce a return).* SEE MAIN ENTRY

provide against forestall

provide an answer respond

provide an opportunity extend *(offer)*

provide capital finance, invest *(fund)*

provide capital again refinance

provide capital for capitalize *(provide capital),* subsidize

provide financing subsidize

provide for bear *(support),* capitalize *(provide capital),* expect *(anticipate),* fund, maintain *(sustain),* nurture, plan, preserve, sponsor, subsidize, support *(assist)*

provide funds finance

provide funds for capitalize *(provide capital),* subsidize

provide funds for again refinance

provide justification palliate *(excuse),* support *(justify)*

provide means enable

provide money finance, fund, invest *(fund)*

provide money for capitalize *(provide capital),* subsidize

provide refuge harbor

provide safety harbor

provide sanctuary harbor, preserve

provide subvention finance

provide the answer countercharge, resolve *(solve)*

provide the means implement

provide the wherewithal fund

provide with administer *(tender),* lend, render *(administer)*

provide with a motive motivate

provide with an alibi excuse

provide with documents document

provide with information instruct *(teach)*

provide with nomenclature call *(title),* identify, label

provide with proof document

provided SEE MAIN ENTRY

provided with arms armed

provided without charge free *(at no charge),* gratuitous *(given without recompense)*

providence discretion *(quality of being discreet),* economy *(frugality),* precaution, preparation, provision *(act of supplying),* prudence

provident acute, careful, economical, frugal, judicious, juridical, politic, preparatory, preventive, prudent, vigilant. SEE MAIN ENTRY

providentia forethought

providential auspicious, favorable *(advantageous),* fitting, fortuitous, opportune, propitious, prosperous

provider materialman, supplier

providere provide *(arrange for)*

providing donative

providing evidence probative

providing proof probative

providing sanctuary conservation

providus circumspect, vigilant

province ambit, bailiwick, capacity *(sphere),* circuit, coverage *(scope),* department, district, division *(administrative unit),* domain *(sphere of influence),* jurisdiction, locality, part *(role),* pursuit *(occupation),* purview, realm, region, role, section *(vicinity),* sphere, territory. SEE MAIN ENTRY

provincia department, province, sphere

provincial local, naive, narrow, parochial, regional. SEE MAIN ENTRY

provincialism prejudice *(preconception)*

proving cogent, convincing

provise stipulation

provision accommodation *(adjustment),* aid, alimony, article *(distinct section of a writing),* attornment, bear *(yield),* bestow, budget, clause, condition *(contingent provision),* contribution *(donation),* dispensation *(act of dispensing),* donation, endowment, forethought, fund, furnish, inheritance, limitation, precaution, preparation, principle *(axiom),* qualification *(condition),* ration, replenish, reservation *(condition),* reserve, resource, safeguard, stock *(store),* supply, title *(division),* ultimatum. SEE MAIN ENTRY

provision for damages ad damnum clause

provision of the law statute

provisional conditional, contingent, dubious, empirical, interim, interlocutory, qualified *(conditioned),* restrictive, speculative, subject *(conditional),* surrogate, temporary, tentative, transient, transitory, uncertain *(questionable),* vicarious *(substitutional).* SEE MAIN ENTRY

provisional hypothesis proposition

provisional measure stopgap

provisional settlement modus vivendi

provisionally pro tempore, provided

provisionary conditional, qualified *(conditioned)*

provisioner supplier

provisioning equipment

provisions ammunition, cargo, maintenance *(support of spouse),* merchandise, stock in trade, store *(depository),* sustenance

provisions of a law legislation *(enactments)*

proviso arrangement (*understanding*), article (*distinct section of a writing*), attornment, clause, condition (*contingent provision*), need (*requirement*), option (*contractual provision*), prerequisite, provision (*clause*), qualification (*condition*), requirement, reservation (*condition*), salvo, specification, term (*provision*), ultimatum

provisory conditional, dependent, interim, interlocutory, provisional, qualified (*conditioned*), restrictive, tentative, transient

provocare defy

provocateur catalyst

provocatio appeal, defiance

provocation aggravation (*annoyance*), catalyst, incentive, inducement, influence, instigation, motive, reason (*basis*), stimulus. SEE MAIN ENTRY

provocative catalyst, impertinent (*insolent*), incentive, inducement, invitation, moving (*evoking emotion*), offensive (*taking the initiative*), persuasive, presumptuous, provocation, salacious, sapid, suggestive (*evocative*), suggestive (*risqué*), vexatious. SEE MAIN ENTRY

provocator aggressor, demagogue

provoke aggravate (*annoy*), agitate (*activate*), annoy, antagonize, badger, bait (*harass*), bait (*lure*), cause, coax, contrive, discommode, discompose, evoke, exacerbate, foment, generate, harass, harrow, harry (*harass*), hector, incense, incite, inspire, irritate, lobby, mistreat, molest (*annoy*), occasion, offend (*insult*), originate, persecute, perturb, pique, plague, press (*goad*), prompt, spirit, stimulate, urge. SEE MAIN ENTRY

provoke desire lure, motivate

provoke hatred alienate (*estrange*), incense

provoke hatred against disaffect

provoke ire incense

provoked aggrieved (*harmed*), bitter (*reproachful*)

provoker demagogue

provoking moving (*evoking emotion*), offensive (*taking the initiative*), persuasive, provocative, sapid, vexatious

provost plenipotentiary

prowess ability, efficiency, skill. SEE MAIN ENTRY

prowl lurk, perambulate, pursue (*chase*). SEE MAIN ENTRY

prowl after hunt

prowler burglar

prowling burglary, stealthy

proxies deputation (*delegation*)

proximal adjacent, approximate, close (*near*), contiguous, proximate

proximate approximate, border (*approach*), close (*near*), contiguous, immediate (*not distant*), present (*attendant*). SEE MAIN ENTRY

promixate cause SEE MAIN ENTRY

proximate to situated

proximity presence (*attendance*), propinquity (*similarity*), vicinity

proximity of blood degree (*kinship*)

proximus proximate, related

proxy agency (*legal relationship*), agent, attorney in fact, conduit (*intermediary*), deputy, plenipotentiary, proctor, procurator, replacement, substitute, surrogate. SEE MAIN ENTRY

proxyship delegation (*assignment*)

prudence caution (*vigilance*), common sense, continence, deliberation, diligence

(*care*), discretion (*quality of being discreet*), discrimination (*good judgment*), economy (*frugality*), expedience, precaution, preparation, sagacity, sense (*intelligence*), temperance. SEE MAIN ENTRY

prudens circumspect, deliberate, discreet, judicious, knowing, politic, prudent, reasonable (*rational*), sensible, tactical

prudent acute, careful, circumspect, deliberate, diplomatic, discreet, economical, frugal, guarded, judicial, judicious, juridical, noncommittal, politic, provident (*frugal*), provident (*showing foresight*), responsive, safe, sensible, solid (*sound*), vigilant. SEE MAIN ENTRY

prudent conduct management (*judicious use*)

prudentia caution (*vigilance*), discretion (*quality of being discreet*), discrimination (*good judgment*), prudence, sagacity, sense (*intelligence*)

prudential judicial, judicious, juridical, politic, provident (*showing foresight*), prudent, solid (*sound*)

prudently contrived politic

prune decrease, diminish, minimize, retrench

prurience pornography

prurient dissolute, immoral, lascivious, lecherous, lewd, salacious. SEE MAIN ENTRY

pry delve, force (*break*), hunt, research, spy

pry into examine (*study*), frisk, inquire, peruse, probe, scrutinize, search

prying encroachment, interest (*concern*), interrogative, obtrusive

pseudo false (*not genuine*), imitation, quasi, spurious, surrogate, synthetic

pseudonym sobriquet

pseudonymous quasi

psyche spirit

psychiatric hospital asylum (*hospital*)

psychiatric ward asylum (*hospital*)

psychological habits character (*personal quality*)

psychologically abnormal non compos mentis

psychopathic non compos mentis

psychotic non compos mentis

puberty adolescence

pubes adult

pubescence adolescence

pubescent juvenile, minor

public blatant (*conspicuous*), civic, common (*shared*), competitive (*open*), conspicuous, famous, manifest, national, open (*accessible*), overt, patent, political, populace, population. SEE MAIN ENTRY

public address peroration

public announcement canon, charter (*declaration of rights*), declaration, issuance, proclamation, publication (*disclosure*)

public attorney district attorney, jurist

public avowal proclamation

public building edifice

public business utility (*public service*)

public company utility (*public service*)

public corporation utility (*public service*)

public declaration avouchment

public disclosure common knowledge

public disgrace dishonor (*shame*)

public distribution publicity

public disturbance commotion

public domain SEE MAIN ENTRY

public economy finance

public enemy convict, criminal, foe, outlaw

public esteem character (*reputation*), distinction (*reputation*)

public favor goodwill, prestige

public industry utility (*public service*)

public inquest hearing

public knowledge common knowledge

public manners conduct

public notice common knowledge, declaration, notoriety, proclamation, publicity

public office holder official

public opinion poll (*canvass*)

public opponent foe

public pleader district attorney

public proceeding hearing

public prosecutor complainant, district attorney, prosecutor

public recognition mention (*tribute*)

public relations publicity

public reproach bad repute, infamy

public revenue finance

public sale auction

public sale of property auction

public servant caretaker (*one fulfilling the function of office*), legislator, politician

public servants government (*political administration*)

public service nonprofit, politics

public speaking declamation, rhetoric (*skilled speech*)

public spirit philanthropy

public statement charter (*declaration of rights*)

public support goodwill

public treasury bank

public uprising revolution

public wrong crime

public-spirited philanthropic

publicare condemn (*seize*), confiscate

publication charter (*declaration of rights*), declaration, disclosure (*act of disclosing*), disclosure (*something disclosed*), issuance, pandect (*treatise*), proclamation, pronouncement, publicity. SEE MAIN ENTRY

publicist attorney, barrister, promoter

publicists press

publicity issuance, notice (*announcement*), notification, notoriety, promotion (*encouragement*), story (*narrative*). SEE MAIN ENTRY

publicize annunciate, bare, communicate, correspond (*communicate*), denude, disseminate, divulge, herald, issue (*publish*), notify, proclaim, promulgate, propagate (*spread*), publish, spread, utter

publicized notorious

publicizer harbinger

publicly accuse condemn (*blame*), denounce (*condemn*), denounce (*inform against*)

publicly indecent lewd

publicly known common (*customary*)

publicly owned national

publicly recognized standing character (*reputation*)

publicness common knowledge

publicus common (*shared*), official, political, public (*known*)

publish annunciate, apprise, bear (*adduce*), circulate, convey (*communicate*), disclose, disseminate, divulge, enunciate, expose, herald, inform (*notify*), manifest, notice (*give formal warning*), notify, post, proclaim, promulgate, propagate (*spread*), report (*disclose*), reveal, signify (*inform*), speak, spread, utter. SEE MAIN ENTRY

publish a falsehood libel

publish abroad disseminate

published patent, public *(known)*
publishers press
puckishness mischief
pudency embarrassment
pueri child, children
puerile inept *(incompetent)*, jejune *(lacking maturity)*. SEE MAIN ENTRY
puerile person juvenile
puerilis juvenile *(adjective)*, juvenile *(noun)*, puerile
puerility adolescence, minority *(infancy)*. SEE MAIN ENTRY
puff up inflate
puffed inflated *(enlarged)*
puffed up inflated *(enlarged)*, proud *(conceited)*, supercilious, turgid
puffery overstatement, rodomontade
puffy inflated *(enlarged)*
pugilatio fight *(battle)*
pugilist contender
pugna affray, fight *(argument)*, fray
pugnacious argumentative, conten-tious, hostile, litigious, perverse, petulant, polemic, querulous, spartan. SEE MAIN ENTRY
pugnaciousness belligerency
pugnacity belligerency
pugnare contend *(dispute)*
pugnax contentious
puisne inferior *(lower in position)*
puissance clout, dint, influence, main force, potential, power, predominance, quality *(excellence)*, strength, validity. SEE MAIN ENTRY
puissant cogent, compelling, considerable, efficient, in full force, indomitable, inexpugnable, influential, irresistible, omnipotent, potent, powerful, predominant
puissant prevailing *(having superior force)*
puissant strong
puling querulous
pull draw *(attraction)*, draw *(extract)*, educe, evulsion, extract, predominance, pressure, stress *(strain)*
pull aside divert
pull back retreat, withdraw
pull different ways bicker
pull down derogate, subvert
pull in discipline *(control)*, inhibit
pull into shape frame *(formulate)*
pull out abandon *(withdraw)*, disinter, educe, eviscerate, extirpate, extract, leave *(depart)*, quit *(evacuate)*, relinquish, renege, secede
pull strings influence, lobby, manipulate *(control unfairly)*
pull strings for prefer
pull the strings predominate *(command)*
pull together cooperate, unite
pull up disinter
pull up by the roots extirpate, obliterate
pull wires manipulate *(control unfairly)*
pullalare pullulate
pulling out evulsion
pullulate germinate, increase, propagate *(increase)*. SEE MAIN ENTRY
pulsare beat *(strike)*
pulse beat *(pulsate)*
pulseless lifeless *(dead)*
pulverize break *(fracture)*, destroy *(efface)*
pulverized broken *(fractured)*
pummel beat *(strike)*, fight *(battle)*, lash *(strike)*
pump up inflate
punch beat *(strike)*
punctilio decorum, formality, particular, protocol *(etiquette)*

punctilious accurate, close *(rigorous)*, conscientious, detailed, diligent, draconian, exact, meticulous, painstaking, particular *(exacting)*, precise, rigid, strict. SEE MAIN ENTRY
punctiliously faithfully
punctiliousness decorum, particularity
punctual exact, expeditious, instant, precise, prompt. SEE MAIN ENTRY
punctuality dispatch *(promptness)*, regularity
punctualness dispatch *(promptness)*
punctuate discontinue *(break continuity)*, interrupt, reaffirm
punctuated disjunctive *(tending to disjoin)*
punctum vote
punctum temporis instant
puncture break *(fracture)*, debunk, enter *(penetrate)*, lancinate, penetrate, pierce *(lance)*
pundit mastermind
pungent bitter *(acrid tasting)*, caustic, incisive, mordacious, trenchant
punic faith bad faith
punire condemn *(punish)*
punish beat *(strike)*, convict, fine, inflict, mulct *(fine)*, penalize, repay, reprehend. SEE MAIN ENTRY
punish by pecuniary penalty fine
punish with death execute *(sentence to death)*
punishable culpable, delinquent *(guilty of a misdeed)*, illegal, impermissible
punishable act tortious act
punishable by law illicit
punishable offense misdemeanor
punishing cruel, disciplinary *(punitory)*, harsh, penal, punitive
punishing experience condemnation *(punishment)*
punishment condemnation *(punishment)*, conviction *(finding of guilt)*, cost *(penalty)*, expiation, forfeiture *(act of forfeiting)*, forfeiture *(thing forfeited)*, infliction, penalty, reprisal, retribution, revenge, sentence, vengeance. SEE MAIN ENTRY
punishment fixed by law penalty
punishment prescribed by law penalty
punishment without trial lynch law
punition condemnation *(punishment)*, conviction *(finding of guilt)*, correction *(punishment)*, punishment, reprisal
punitive disciplinary *(punitory)*, penal, severe, vindictive. SEE MAIN ENTRY
punitive action reprisal, retribution, revenge
punitive damages SEE MAIN ENTRY
punitory penal, punitive, vindictive
punt bet
punter bettor
puny negligible, null *(insignificant)*, paltry, petty
pupil disciple, neophyte, novice, protégé
purblind opaque
purchasable mercenary, venal
purchase acquire *(secure)*, buy, deal, leverage, procure, takeover, trade *(commerce)*, trade, transaction. SEE MAIN ENTRY
purchase from patronize *(trade with)*
purchase money price
purchase on time credit *(delayed payment)*
purchase on trust credit *(delayed payment)*
purchase price cost *(price)*
purchase without a guaranty caveat emptor

purchase without a warranty caveat emptor
purchased at one's risk caveat emptor
purchaser client, consumer, customer, patron *(regular customer)*
purchaser of goods consumer
purchaser of goods from another customer
purchaser of stolen goods fence
purchaser of stolen property fence
pure absolute *(ideal)*, authentic, blameless, clean, clear *(apparent)*, genuine, honest, inculpable, inviolate, moral, natural, original *(initial)*, pellucid, simple, stark, sterling, theoretical, true *(authentic)*, unadulterated, unblemished, upright. SEE MAIN ENTRY
pure in heart clean
pure-hearted clean
purebred genuine
purely only, solely *(purely)*. SEE MAIN ENTRY
purgare absolve, acquit, justify, vindicate
purgatio justification
purgation absolution, acquittal, catharsis, clemency, confession
purgatorial penitent
purge absolve, catharsis, clear, decontaminate, deplete, deportation, discharge *(liberate)*, dismiss *(discharge)*, displace *(remove)*, eliminate *(eradicate)*, eradicate, exclusion, exonerate, expel, expulsion, expurgate, extirpate, free, oust, pardon, removal, remove *(eliminate)*. SEE MAIN ENTRY
purge oneself confess
purged clear *(free from criminal charges)*
purified sacrosanct
purify decontaminate, expurgate, fix *(repair)*, meliorate
purify by removing the foreign and nonessential distill
purifying medicinal, remedial
puritanic severe, uncompromising
puritanical draconian, rigid, severe, strict, stringent, tartuffish, uncompromising
purity honor *(good reputation)*, integrity, rectitude
purlieu bailiwick, periphery, vicinity
purlieus border, locality, location, part *(place)*, region, section *(vicinity)*
purloin abduct, bilk, carry away, cheat, defalcate, deprive, despoil, embezzle, hold up *(rob)*, impropriate, jostle *(pickpocket)*, loot, peculate, pilfer, pirate *(reproduce without authorization)*, plunder, poach, rob, steal. SEE MAIN ENTRY
purloiner embezzler, hoodlum, thief
purloining embezzlement, theft
purloinment burglary, theft
purport amount *(result)*, bespeak, connotation, consequence *(significance)*, content *(meaning)*, context, cornerstone, design *(intent)*, gist *(substance)*, import, intent, main point, materiality *(consequence)*, meaning, point *(purpose)*, pretend, signification, signify *(denote)*, spirit, substance *(essential nature)*, tenor, value. SEE MAIN ENTRY
purported ostensible, putative, specious. SEE MAIN ENTRY
purpose animus, basis, cause *(reason)*, contemplation, content *(meaning)*, cornerstone, design *(intent)*, destination, end *(intent)*, forethought, function, goal, ground, idea, impetus, intend, intent, intention, mission, motive, object, objective, plan, predetermination, project, pursuit *(goal)*, purview, reason *(basis)*, resolution *(decision)*, resolve *(decide)*, signification,

undertaking (attempt), use, volition, will (desire). SEE MAIN ENTRY

purpose in view   design (intent)

purposed   aforethought, deliberate, intentional, tactical, willful

purposeful   decisive, deliberate, earnest, express, industrious, intense, intentional, knowing, persistent, pertinacious, resolute, serious (devoted), tactical, voluntary, willful. SEE MAIN ENTRY

purposefully   knowingly, purposely

purposefulness   diligence (perseverance)

purposeless   arbitrary and capricious, casual, expendable, nugatory, random, unavailing, unintentional, unwitting, vacuous

purposely   SEE MAIN ENTRY

purposive   aforethought, express, purposeful

purse   reward, stake (award), treasury

purser   comptroller

pursuance   course, endeavor, industry (activity)

pursuant to   SEE MAIN ENTRY

pursue   adhere (persist), approach, assume (undertake), attempt, bait (harass), chase, continue (persevere), delve, desire, endeavor, exercise (discharge a function), follow-up, hunt, inquire, keep (continue), maintain (carry on), persevere, ply, practice (engage in), prosecute (carry forward), race, remain (continue), research, resume, search, specialize, strive, study, trace (follow), undertake. SEE MAIN ENTRY

pursue a claim   sue

pursue a course   perform (execute)

pursue an inquiry   audit, canvass, investigate, probe, research

pursue in court   litigate

pursue relentlessly   persist

pursuer   addict

pursuit   activity, assignment (task), business (occupation), calling, career, course, design (intent), employment, endeavor, enterprise (undertaking), function, industry (activity), industry (business), inquiry (systematic investigation), labor (work), livelihood, market (demand), mission, objective, occupation (vocation), operation, position (business status), post, practice (professional business), probe, profession (vocation), project, quest, research, specialty (special aptitude), struggle, trade (occupation), undertaking (business), undertaking (enterprise), work (employment). SEE MAIN ENTRY

pursuit by a law enforcement agency   prosecution (criminal trial)

pursuits   affairs

purulent   toxic

purus   clean, pure, unblemished, unconditional

purvey   bear (yield), fund, furnish, pander, provide (supply), replenish, supply

purveyance   provision (act of supplying)

purveyor   supplier

purview   area (province), coverage (scope), jurisdiction, scope. SEE MAIN ENTRY

push   cajole, coerce, constrain (compel), dispatch (send off), exhort, foray, force (coerce), impact, impel, impetus, importune, impulse, incite, jostle (bump into), launch (project), main force, pressure (noun), pressure (verb), project (impel forward), promote (organize), prompt, provoke, spirit, stimulus, struggle, urge. SEE MAIN ENTRY

push ahead   expedite, proceed (go forward)

push aside   divert, doubt (hesitate), hold up (delay), ignore, misprize, postpone, procrastinate, relegate

push away   dispel, eject (expel), parry, stave

push back   repel (drive back), repulse

push forward   expedite, facilitate

push into   browbeat

push on   hasten, move (alter position), proceed (go forward), progress

push out   dislodge, eject (expel)

push through   dispatch (send off), expedite

push together   impact

push too far   incense, tax (overwork)

push toward   pursue (strive to gain)

push up   promote (advance)

pushing   impulsive (impelling)

pushy   eager, obtrusive

pusillanimity   fear

pusillanimous   caitiff, recreant

pusillus   paltry

put   deposit (place), dispose (incline), impute, introduce, locate, lodge (house), phrase, plant (place firmly), raise (advance), repose (place), situated, submit (give). SEE MAIN ENTRY

put a barrier around   enclose, include

put a damper on   discourage

put a false appearance on   misrepresent

put a false appearance upon   disguise

put a false construction on   distort, misconceive, misread, misrepresent, misunderstand

put a false construction upon   perjure, profess (pretend)

put a false sense on   distort, misconstrue, mistake

put a mark on   brand (mark)

put a mark upon   label

put a meaning on   comment, construe (translate)

put a restraint upon   check (restrain)

put a stop to   cease, check (restrain), clog, close (terminate), condemn (ban), constrain (restrain), desist, deter, eliminate (eradicate), enjoin, estop, finish, hold up (delay), interrupt, quit (discontinue), strangle, toll (stop)

put a wrong construction on   misread, misunderstand

put aboard   load

put about   circulate

put across   explain

put ahead   conduce

put along side   border (approach)

put alongside   compare, juxtapose

put an approximate price on   estimate

put an embargo on   bar (hinder), condemn (ban)

put an end to   abate (extinguish), annul, cancel, cease, check (restrain), condemn (ban), destroy (void), discontinue (abandon), dispatch (put to death), eliminate (eradicate), enjoin, estop, expunge, extinguish, extirpate, finish, halt, interrupt, quash, quit (discontinue), stay (halt), stop, subvert, terminate

put an erroneous construction on   distort, misunderstand

put an indication on   brand (mark)

put an interpretation   construe (translate)

put an obligation upon   commit (entrust)

put aside   abandon (relinquish), defer (put off), eliminate (exclude), except (exclude),

exclude, forfeit, hoard, hold up (delay), isolate, keep (shelter), postpone, pretermit, reserve, select, set aside (reserve), waive

put asunder   disconnected, divorce

put at a disadvantage   embarrass, penalize

put at ease   assure (give confidence to)

put at hazard   compromise (endanger), pawn

put at interest   deposit (submit to a bank)

put at stake   pawn

put away   keep (shelter), preserve, retain (keep in possession), set aside (reserve)

put back   reconstitute, reinstate, renew (begin again), replace, restore (return)

put back into service   reinstate

put before   instruct (teach)

put behind bars   imprison, jail, lock

put beside   juxtapose

put between   interject, intersperse

put beyond the protection of the law   outlaw

put by   store

put close together   juxtapose

put confidence in   rely, trust

put down   cast (register), defeat, demean (make lower), derogate, dispatch (put to death), enter (record), humiliate, kill (defeat), quash, repress, stifle, subdue, subjugate

put faith in   confide (trust), rely

put first   preface

put forth   argue, communicate, emit, exert, extend (offer), issue (publish), move (judicially request), offer (propose), pass (determine), plead (allege in a legal action), posit, postulate, present (introduce), profess (avow), propound, publish, pullulate, submit (give). SEE MAIN ENTRY

put forth an effort   attempt, strive

put forth effort   try (attempt)

put forth for acceptance   offer (propose)

put forth for consideration   offer (propose)

put forward   alleged, circulate, claim (maintain), conduce, declare, extend (offer), flaunt, hold out (deliberate on an offer), introduce, issue (publish), move (judicially request), offer (propose), plead (allege in a legal action), pose (propound), posit, postulate, prefer, profess (avow), proffer, propose, propound, submit (give), tender

put forward for consideration   extend (offer), introduce, offer (propose)

put forward in opposition   object

put goods in   load

put in   enter (insert), interpose, introduce

put in a bad light   defame, denounce (condemn), pillory

put in a cell   constrain (imprison), imprison

put in a claim for   call (demand), desire

put in a conspicuous place   expose

put in accord   arbitrate (conciliate)

put in action   apply (put in practice), employ (make use of), enforce, execute (accomplish), exercise (use), exert, manipulate (utilize skillfully)

put in an affidavit   avouch (avow), plead (allege in a legal action)

put in an appearance   appear (attend court proceedings), emerge, issue (send forth), report (present oneself)

put in array   classify, file (arrange), organize (arrange)

put in bodily fear   menace

put in care of   charge (empower), confide (trust)

put in charge entrust
put in check balk, counter
put in commission assign *(designate)*, delegate, invest *(vest)*
put in concealment blind *(obscure)*, camouflage, plant *(covertly place)*
put in condition fix *(repair)*
put in custody commit *(institutionalize)*
put in danger expose
put in durance arrest *(apprehend)*
put in duress arrest *(apprehend)*, seize *(apprehend)*
put in execution commence
put in fear browbeat, intimidate, menace
put in for request
put in force administer *(conduct)*, authorize, constitute *(establish)*, effectuate, enact, enforce, execute *(accomplish)*, implement, impose *(enforce)*, legislate, pass *(approve)*, perform *(adhere to)*, perform *(execute)*
put in good condition fix *(repair)*
put in hazard endanger
put in in a bad light denigrate
put in irons fetter, handcuff, imprison, trammel
put in jeopardy compromise *(endanger)*, endanger
put in motion agitate *(shake up)*, dispatch *(send off)*, establish *(launch)*, exercise *(discharge a function)*, impel, launch *(initiate)*, move *(alter position)*
put in one's hands delegate
put in operation apply *(put in practice)*, capitalize *(seize the chance)*, employ *(make use of)*, enforce
put in opposition confront *(oppose)*, oppose, polarize
put in order classify, emend, file *(arrange)*, fix *(arrange)*, fix *(repair)*, marshal, orchestrate, organize *(arrange)*, pigeonhole, regulate *(adjust)*, repair, restore *(renew)*, settle, sort
put in other words construe *(translate)*, elucidate, explain
put in pawn pledge *(deposit)*
put in peril expose
put in place locate
put in pledge pawn
put in possession bequeath, devolve, grant *(transfer formally)*, instate, seize *(confiscate)*, vest
put in practice exercise *(use)*, exploit *(make use of)*, implement, perform *(adhere to)*, ply
put in production manufacture
put in proper order fix *(arrange)*
put in readiness arrange *(methodize)*
put in repair fix *(repair)*, restore *(renew)*
put in restraint apprehend *(arrest)*
put in safekeeping delegate
put in shape fix *(repair)*
put in slyly foist
put in stealthily foist
put in the hands of commit *(entrust)*, endow
put in the place of change, displace *(replace)*, supersede
put in uniform clothe
put in view expose
put in words communicate, enunciate, express
put in writing enter *(record)*, inscribe, note *(record)*, record
put into inject
put into a cage imprison
put into a receptacle enclose
put into a systematic form orchestrate

put into a temper incense
put into action exercise *(discharge a function)*, expedite, exploit *(make use of)*, perpetrate
put into bodily form embody
put into circulation circulate, diffuse, dispel, issue *(publish)*, publish
put into condition remedy
put into disorder confound
put into effect enact, enforce, exercise *(discharge a function)*, implement, operate, pass *(approve)*, perpetrate, ply, render *(administer)*
put into execution enforce
put into force inflict
put into isolation confine
put into language phrase
put into motion cast *(throw)*
put into operation exploit *(make use of)*, manipulate *(utilize skillfully)*
put into practice exercise *(discharge a function)*, operate, transact
put into shape formulate, frame *(formulate)*, organize *(arrange)*, remedy, renew *(refurbish)*, repair
put into the hands of deliver
put into words observe *(remark)*, phrase, relate *(tell)*, speak
put money down bet
put off adjourn, delay, deter, hold up *(delay)*, pause, postpone, pretermit, procrastinate, stall, stave, suspend
put off a decision doubt *(hesitate)*
put off the scent misdirect
put off the track divert, obfuscate
put off to a future time hold up *(delay)*
put on betray *(lead astray)*, levy, pretend, prevaricate, specious
put on a false front pretend
put on a firm basis establish *(entrench)*
put on a pedestal elevate, honor
put on an act fake
put on board load
put on deceitfully assume *(simulate)*
put on display produce *(offer to view)*
put on guard caution, forewarn, portend
put on one's guard alert, notice *(give formal warning)*
put on paper note *(record)*, record
put on payroll hire
put on record cast *(register)*, enter *(record)*, file *(place among official records)*, note *(record)*, record, set down
put on sale sell
put on speed hasten
put on the retired list discharge *(dismiss)*
put on the scale weigh
put on the stage produce *(offer to view)*
put on trial hear *(give a legal hearing)*, impeach, sue
put one's case plead *(argue a case)*
put one's mind to concentrate *(pay attention)*
put one's trust in swear
put one's veto to condemn *(ban)*
put one's veto upon bar *(hinder)*
put oneself out endeavor
put out depose *(remove)*, disadvantage, disappointed, discompose, dislodge, disoblige, displace *(remove)*, eject *(evict)*, exclude, expel, extinguish, issue *(publish)*, oust, perturb, provoke, publish, remove *(dismiss from office)*
put out at interest invest *(fund)*
put out of action disable
put out of combat disarm *(divest of arms)*

put out of commission impair
put out of countenance bait *(harass)*, humiliate, pique
put out of house by legal process evict
put out of humor irritate, provoke
put out of joint luxate
put out of matrimony divorce
put out of mind dismiss *(put out of consideration)*
put out of order disorganize, upset
put out of place luxate
put out of possession depose *(remove)*, eject *(evict)*
put out of sight blind *(obscure)*, cloak, cover *(conceal)*, hide, plant *(covertly place)*
put out of the way dispatch *(put to death)*
put out of wedlock divorce
put over continue *(adjourn)*
put over to a future date continue *(adjourn)*
put pressure on bait *(harass)*, browbeat, coerce, constrain *(compel)*, enforce, insist, lobby, press *(constrain)*, press *(goad)*
put questions to examine *(interrogate)*
put right disabuse, edit, emend, help, redress, repair, restore *(renew)*
put side by side juxtapose
put something across bilk
put something over bilk, dupe, illude
put something over on betray *(lead astray)*
put straight disabuse
put the blame on charge *(accuse)*, convict, impeach
put through attain, pass *(approve)*, prosecute *(carry forward)*
put through a deal dicker
put through paces discipline *(train)*
put to call *(appeal to)*, pose *(propound)*
put to a wrong use convert *(misappropriate)*
put to advantage capitalize *(seize the chance)*
put to death destroy *(efface)*, dispatch *(put to death)*, execute *(sentence to death)*, extinguish, kill *(murder)*, slay
put to death according to law execute *(sentence to death)*
put to flight repel *(drive back)*, repulse
put to inconvenience discommode
put to press publish
put to rest lull
put to rights rectify
put to rout beat *(defeat)*
put to service capitalize *(seize the chance)*, employ *(make use of)*, exploit *(make use of)*
put to shame brand *(stigmatize)*, denigrate, humiliate, pillory, reproach, sully
put to sleep drug, lull
put to the proof prove
put to the test probe, prove
put to the vote choose
put to use apply *(put in practice)*, employ *(make use of)*, exercise *(use)*, exploit *(make use of)*, profit, resort
put to work employ *(engage services)*, engage *(hire)*, exercise *(use)*, exploit *(make use of)*, hire, retain *(employ)*
put to wrong use exploit *(take advantage of)*
put together affix, annex *(add)*, attach *(join)*, cement, collect *(gather)*, commingle, connect *(join together)*, consolidate *(strengthen)*, consolidate *(unite)*, constitute *(compose)*, create, devise *(invent)*, fabricate

(construct), forge *(produce)*, form, formulate, frame *(construct)*, incorporate *(include)*, join *(bring together)*, make, manufacture

put under an injunction condemn *(ban)*, enjoin, forbid

put under an interdiction condemn *(ban)*, enjoin

put under arrest apprehend *(arrest)*, confine, constrain *(imprison)*, detain *(hold in custody)*, immure

put under contract engage *(hire)*

put under duress kidnap

put under embargo enjoin

put under lock and key imprison

put under obligation compel, constrain *(compel)*, force *(coerce)*, press *(constrain)*

put under prohibition condemn *(ban)*

put under restraint arrest *(apprehend)*, check *(restrain)*, coerce, confine, constrain *(imprison)*, constrain *(restrain)*, control *(restrain)*, detain *(hold in custody)*, fetter, hold up *(delay)*, imprison, jail, restrict

put under suspicion compromise *(endanger)*

put under the ban enjoin

put under water immerse *(plunge into)*

put up build *(construct)*, invest *(fund)*, nominate, pledge *(deposit)*, proffer

put up a front fake

put up a petition move *(judicially request)*

put up a request call *(appeal to)*, plead *(implore)*

put up a sign post

put up a struggle parry

put up for sale handle *(trade)*, sell, vend

put up petitions pray

put up the money finance, lend, sponsor

put up with authorize, bear *(tolerate)*, endure *(suffer)*, forbear, submit *(yield)*, suffer *(permit)*, tolerate

put upon record inscribe

putare impression

putative plausible, presumptive. SEE MAIN ENTRY

putrefaction deterioration, spoilage

putrefied tainted *(contaminated)*

putrefy decay, degenerate, infect, spoil *(impair)*, taint *(contaminate)*

putrescence spoilage

putrid loathsome, offensive *(offending)*, tainted *(contaminated)*

putridity deterioration

putting in custody commitment *(confinement)*

putting in order disposition *(determination)*

putting off deferment, delay

putting out expulsion

putting together accession *(annexation)*

puzzle complication, confound, confuse *(bewilder)*, confusion *(ambiguity)*, dilemma, disconcert, disturb, enigma, hoodwink, involution, muddle, mystery, obfuscate, paradox, perplex, pose *(propound)*, problem, question *(issue)*, secret

puzzle out solve

puzzle over doubt *(hesitate)*, ponder, reflect *(ponder)*, speculate *(conjecture)*

puzzled lost *(disoriented)*

puzzlement ambiguity, cloud *(suspicion)*, confusion *(ambiguity)*, dilemma, quandary

puzzling debatable, difficult, elusive, enigmatic, equivocal, esoteric, hidden, inapprehensible, incomprehensible, indefinable, inexplicable, inexpressive, inscrutable,

labyrinthine, mysterious, opaque, peculiar *(curious)*, problematic, recondite, uncertain *(ambiguous)*

puzzling alternative dilemma

puzzling problem enigma

pylon portal

pyramid build *(augment)*, parlay *(exploit successfully)*

pyromania arson

pyrotic caustic

pythonic ominous, portentous *(ominous)*, prophetic

Q

quack fake

quackery abortion *(fiasco)*, fraud, hypocrisy

quadrate comport *(agree with)*

quadrate with cohere *(adhere)*

quaerere investigate, speculate *(conjecture)*

quaesitor judge

quaestio inquest, inquiry *(systematic investigation)*, interrogation, question *(inquiry)*, subject *(topic)*, trial *(legal proceeding)*

quaestuosus gainful, lucrative

quaestus earnings, income, profit

quaff carouse

quagmire impasse, pitfall, plight, quandary. SEE MAIN ENTRY

quaint eccentric, nonconforming, novel, outdated, outmoded

quake beat *(pulsate)*, cataclysm

quaking trepidation

qualification caliber *(mental capacity)*, capacity *(aptitude)*, capacity *(authority)*, clause, condition *(contingent provision)*, control *(restriction)*, correction *(change)*, degree *(academic title)*, discipline *(training)*, discretion *(quality of being discreet)*, doubt *(indecision)*, drawback, education, experience *(background)*, extenuating circumstances, faculty *(ability)*, gift *(flair)*, limitation, modification, necessary, necessity, performance *(workmanship)*, potential, preparation, propensity, provision *(clause)*, reservation *(condition)*, restriction, salvo, sine qua non, specialty *(special aptitude)*, term *(provision)*. SEE MAIN ENTRY

qualifications competence *(ability)*

qualified admissible, capable, competent, conditional, deft, dependent, desirable *(qualified)*, eligible, entitled, expert, familiar *(informed)*, fit, literate, practiced, professional *(trained)*, proficient, sciential, suitable, veteran. SEE MAIN ENTRY

qualified endorsement without recourse

qualified person expert, mastermind, specialist

qualified practitioner professional

qualify allay, allow *(authorize)*, alter, delegate, discipline *(train)*, empower, enable, enfranchise, extenuate, instill, instruct *(teach)*, lessen, moderate *(temper)*, modify *(alter)*, modify *(moderate)*, palliate *(abate)*, pass *(satisfy requirements)*, restrict, satisfy *(fulfill)*, specialize, validate. SEE MAIN ENTRY

qualifying mitigating, palliative *(excusing)*, preparatory, restrictive

qualifying factors circumstances

qualifying reasons extenuating circumstances

qualities character *(personal quality)*, temperament

quality characteristic, color *(complexion)*, complexion, condition *(state)*, differential, feature *(characteristic)*, gift *(flair)*, intonation, merit, meritorious, premium, property *(distinctive attribute)*, select, speciality, specialty *(distinctive mark)*, status, sterling, trait, value, weight *(importance)*, worth. SEE MAIN ENTRY

quality of being certain certainty

quality of being equal and fair equity *(justice)*

quality of being singular identity *(individuality)*

quality of execution performance *(workmanship)*

quality of work performance *(workmanship)*

quality-minded particular *(exacting)*

qualm apprehension *(fear)*, doubt *(indecision)*, doubt *(suspicion)*, fear, hesitation, misgiving, scruple, suspicion *(mistrust)*. SEE MAIN ENTRY

qualmish diffident, disinclined, hesitant

qualmishness doubt *(indecision)*, doubt *(suspicion)*

qualms reluctance

quandary complication, confusion *(ambiguity)*, deadlock, dilemma, disturbance, doubt *(indecision)*, imbroglio, impasse, incertitude, indecision, plight, predicament, problem, quagmire. SEE MAIN ENTRY

quantification appraisal, measurement, rating

quantified definite

quantify calculate, measure, pinpoint, rate

quantitas quantity

quantity bulk, conglomeration, corpus, extent, measurement, part *(portion)*, quota, ration, selection *(collection)*, unit *(item)*. SEE MAIN ENTRY

quantity produced output

quantum bulk, proportion, quantity, quota

quantum meruit SEE MAIN ENTRY

quarantine captivity, confine, constraint *(imprisonment)*, contain *(enclose)*, detain *(hold in custody)*, detention, durance, exclude, immure, insulate, isolate, ostracism, seclude, sequester *(seclude)*. SEE MAIN ENTRY

quarantine station captivity

quarrel altercation, argument *(contention)*, bicker, brawl, challenge, collide *(clash)*, commotion, conflict *(noun)*, conflict *(verb)*, confrontation *(altercation)*, contend *(dispute)*, contention *(opposition)*, contest *(dispute)*, contradict, contravention, controversy *(argument)*, disaccord *(noun)*, disaccord *(verb)*, disagree, disagreement, dissension, dissent *(differ in opinion)*, dissidence, embroilment, feud, fight *(argument)*, fracas, fray, incompatibility *(difference)*, object, outbreak, split, strife, struggle, variance *(disagreement)*

quarrel noisily brawl

quarrel over contest, dispute *(contest)*

quarreling abusive, argument *(contention)*, conflict, contention *(opposition)*, discord, dissenting, dissident

quarrelsome argumentative, contentious, disorderly, dissenting, fractious, litigious, negative, petulant, polemic, pugnacious, querulous

quarrelsomeness contention *(opposition)*

quarry extract, victim

quarter circuit, deposit *(place)*, disjoint, district, dwell *(reside)*, harbor, indulgence, lenience, locality, locate, location, lodge quartered

(house), lodge *(reside)*, part *(place)*, pity, region, territory

quartered situated

quarters building *(structure)*, domicile, dwelling, habitation *(dwelling place)*, home *(domicile)*, house, inhabitation *(place of dwelling)*, lodging, premises *(buildings)*, residence

quash abate *(extinguish)*, abolish, abrogate *(annul)*, cancel, censor, condemn *(ban)*, contain *(restrain)*, discharge *(release from obligation)*, disinherit, dissolve *(terminate)*, eliminate *(eradicate)*, enjoin, expunge, extinguish, extirpate, invalidate, kill *(defeat)*, negate, nullify, obliterate, overcome *(surmount)*, overthrow, overwhelm, prohibit, refute, repeal, rescind, revoke, subjugate, suppress, upset, vacate *(void)*, vitiate, withdraw. SEE MAIN ENTRY

quash the conviction clear

quashed invalid, lifeless *(dead)*, null *(invalid)*, null and void

quashing avoidance *(cancellation)*, deterrence, dismissal *(termination of a proceeding)*, rescision

quasi imitation. SEE MAIN ENTRY

quasi pendent

quasi spurious, synthetic

quaver beat *(pulsate)*

queer eccentric, irregular *(not usual)*, ludicrous, noteworthy, peculiar *(curious)*, prodigious *(amazing)*, singular, unaccustomed

queerness quirk *(idiosyncrasy)*

quell abate *(extinguish)*, allay, alleviate, arrest *(stop)*, assuage, beat *(defeat)*, cancel, cease, condemn *(ban)*, contain *(restrain)*, decrease, defeat, destroy *(efface)*, deter, diminish, eliminate *(eradicate)*, enjoin, expunge, extinguish, extirpate, halt, impede, kill *(defeat)*, lull, moderate *(temper)*, mollify, obliterate, obtund, overcome *(surmount)*, override, overthrow, overturn, overwhelm, pacify, palliate *(abate)*, prevail *(triumph)*, prohibit, quash, remit *(relax)*, repress, restrain, soothe, stay *(halt)*, stem *(check)*, stifle, stop, strangle, subdue, subject, subjugate, suppress

quell suspicion disarm *(set at ease)*

quelling palliative *(abating)*

quench allay, assuage, cancel, deter, discourage, extinguish, inhibit, quash, repress, satisfy *(fulfill)*, soothe, stifle, suppress

quenchless hot-blooded, indomitable, insatiable

querela grievance, plaint

queribundus querulous

querimonia complaint, grievance, plaint

querimonious querulous

querulous fractious, froward, litigious, particular *(exacting)*, petulant, reluctant, resentful. SEE MAIN ENTRY

querulousness dissatisfaction

querulus querulous

query challenge, check *(inspect)*, cross-examination, cross-examine, cross-questioning, dispute *(contest)*, doubt *(distrust)*, examine *(interrogate)*, impugn, inquire, inquiry *(request for information)*, interrogation, pose *(propound)*, question *(inquiry)*

quest agency *(legal relationship)*, attempt, campaign, cross-examination, delve, discovery, endeavor, hunt, indagation, inquest, probe, pursue *(chase)*, pursuit *(chase)*, pursuit *(effort to secure)*, research *(noun)*, research *(verb)*, undertaking

(attempt), undertaking *(enterprise)*, venture. SEE MAIN ENTRY

question analyze, canvass, challenge, check *(inspect)*, consult *(ask advice of)*, contest, cross-examine, disbelieve, discount *(disbelieve)*, doubt *(indecision)*, doubt *(distrust)*, enigma, examine *(interrogate)*, hesitate, impugn, incertitude, incredulity, inquire, inquiry *(request for information)*, inquiry *(systematic investigation)*, investigate, issue *(matter in dispute)*, matter *(subject)*, misdoubt, mistrust, pose *(propound)*, probe, problem, qualm, scruple, scrutinize, suspect *(distrust)*, suspicion *(uncertainty)*, thesis. SEE MAIN ENTRY

question and answer interview

question at issue conflict, controversy *(argument)*, issue *(matter in dispute)*

question in one's mind doubt *(suspicion)*

question the truth of dispute *(contest)*

question under oath examine *(interrogate)*. SEE MAIN ENTRY

questionability cloud *(suspicion)*, ill repute, improbability

questionable blameworthy, contestable, controversial, debatable, disputable, doubtful, dubious, dubitative, equivocal, implausible, indefinite, lewd, ludicrous, moot, outrageous, problematic, speculative, tentative, unbelievable, undecided, unethical, unscrupulous, unsound *(fallacious)*, unsustainable, untenable, untrustworthy, vague. SEE MAIN ENTRY

questionableness ill repute

questionary form *(document)*, poll *(canvass)*

questioned moot

questioning conversation, cross-examination, cross-questioning, cynical, dissenting, doubtful, incorrigible, incredulous, indagation, inquest, inquisitive, interest *(concern)*, interrogation, interrogative, interrogatories, investigation, leery, research, skeptical, test

questioning integrity impeachment

questioning under oath examination *(test)*

questioning witness's veracity impeachment

questionless axiomatic, certain *(positive)*, clear *(certain)*, decisive, definite, incontrovertible, irrefutable, undisputed, unimpeachable

questionlessness certainty

questionnaire blank *(form)*, form *(document)*, poll *(canvass)*. SEE MAIN ENTRY

questions interrogatories

queue assemblage, lineup. SEE MAIN ENTRY

qui conventui praeest chairman

qui facit actor

qui oppugnat assailant

qui sibi placet complacent

qui vulnerari potest vulnerable

quibble equivocate, haggle, prevaricate, tergiversate. SEE MAIN ENTRY

quibbling excuse salvo

quick alert *(agile)*, artful, born *(alive)*, brief, cursory, deft, expeditious, facile, immediate *(at once)*, impulsive *(rash)*, instantaneous, live *(conscious)*, perfunctory, perspicacious, precipitate, proficient, prompt, rapid, ready *(prepared)*, summary, volatile. SEE MAIN ENTRY

quick discharge dispatch *(promptness)*

quick judgment discretion *(quality of being discreet)*

quick of apprehension perceptive, sapi-

ent, sensitive *(discerning)*

quick riddance dispatch *(promptness)*

quick sense perception

quick-tempered hot-blooded, sensitive *(easily affected)*

quick-witted acute, perspicacious, sapient

quicken expedite, facilitate, precipitate *(hasten)*, promise *(raise expectations)*

quickening acceleration, cumulative *(intensifying)*, revival

quickly forthwith, instantly, readily

quickly executed summary

quickly performed summary

quickness dispatch *(promptness)*, efficiency, facility *(easiness)*, haste, judgment *(discernment)*, sagacity, skill

quickness of perception intelligence *(intellect)*

quid center *(essence)*

quid pro quo collection *(payment)*. SEE MAIN ENTRY

quidam certain *(specific)*

quiddity center *(essence)*, character *(personal quality)*, content *(meaning)*, essence, gist *(substance)*, main point

quies ease, inaction

quiescence cessation *(interlude)*, composure, inaction, inertia, languor, lull, peace, silence. SEE MAIN ENTRY

quiescency abeyance, lull, silence

quiescent dormant, lifeless *(dull)*, mute, passive, patient, peaceable, placid, stagnant, static

quiet allay, alleviate, diffident, diminish, dormant, ease, inconspicuous, laconic, lifeless *(dull)*, lull *(noun)*, lull *(verb)*, moderate *(temper)*, moderation, mollify, mute, obtund, pacify, palliate *(abate)*, patient, peace, peaceable, placate, placid, private *(secluded)*, remit *(relax)*, repress, silence, solemn, soothe, speechless, static, strangle, subdue, subside, taciturn, unobtrusive, unpretentious. SEE MAIN ENTRY

quiet down lull

quieten lull

quieting palliative *(abating)*

quietly persevering patient

quietness peace, silence

quietude composure, privacy, silence

quietus denouement

quietus extremity *(death)*

quietus inactive, placid

quietus release, remission

quintessence center *(essence)*, character *(personal quality)*, characteristic, consequence *(significance)*, content *(meaning)*, cornerstone, corpus, essence, gist *(substance)*, main point, spirit. SEE MAIN ENTRY

quintessential best

quirk compulsion *(obsession)*, speciality, specialty *(distinctive mark)*. SEE MAIN ENTRY

quit abandon *(physically leave)*, abandon *(relinquish)*, abandon *(withdraw)*, cease, comport *(behave)*, defect, demean *(deport oneself)*, demit, discontinue *(abandon)*, evacuate, forfeit, forgo, forswear, halt, leave *(depart)*, part *(leave)*, pay, recoup *(reimburse)*, relinquish, remise, renege, renounce, resign, retire *(conclude a career)*, retreat, secede, shirk, stop, vacate *(leave)*, withdraw, yield *(submit)*. SEE MAIN ENTRY

quit of free *(relieved from a burden)*

quit work strike *(refuse to work)*

quitclaim cede, remise. SEE MAIN ENTRY

quite the contrary contra

938

quittance acquittal, amnesty, collection (*payment*), compensation, contribution (*indemnification*), expiation, honorarium, payment (*act of paying*), payment (*remittance*), quitclaim, receipt (*proof of receiving*), recompense, remission, remittance, remuneration, reparation (*indemnification*), reprieve, requital, restitution, revenge, reward, satisfaction (*discharge of debt*), trover, wage

quitting abdication, desertion, resignation (*relinquishment*)

quiver beat (*pulsate*)

quivering trepidation

quixotic SEE MAIN ENTRY

quixotical quixotic

quiz check (*inspect*), cross-examine, examination (*test*), examine (*interrogate*), inquire, test. SEE MAIN ENTRY

quizzical inquisitive, interrogative, ironic, skeptical, suspicious (*distrustful*)

quo nihil efficitur inconclusive

quod abalienari non potest inalienable

quod comprehendi incomprehensible

quod contra dicitur objection

quod contra leges fit illegal, illicit

quod defendi non potest indefensible

quod eodem tempore est contemporaneous

quod est admirabile contraque opinionem omnium paradox

quod everti non potest indestructible

quod ex lege legal, licit

quod fieri non potest impracticable

quod fieri non potest impossible

quod indecorum est impropriety

quod nihil ad rem est impertinent (*irrelevant*)

quod nihil excusationis habet inexcusable

quod refutari non potest inappealable, incontrovertible

quod restat remainder (*remaining part*)

quod satis est sufficiency

quod tangi non potest impalpable

quondam former, prior

quorum minimum. SEE MAIN ENTRY

quota quorum, ration. SEE MAIN ENTRY

quotation attribution, bid, charge (*cost*), citation (*attribution*), cost (*price*), estimate (*approximate cost*), excerpt, price, rate, reference (*citation*), value, worth

quote cite (*state*), excerpt, extract, recite, refer (*direct attention*), repeat (*state again*). SEE MAIN ENTRY

quoted passage excerpt, reference (*citation*)

quoted price bid, cost (*price*), face value (*price*), tariff (*bill*)

quotidian daily

quotidianus customary, ordinary

quotidie daily

quoting reference (*citation*)

quotum proportion, share (*interest*)

R

rabble-rouser demagogue, malcontent

rabid deranged, extreme (*exaggerated*), fanatical, outrageous, vehement, zealous

rabidity furor, passion

race competition, contest (*competition*), descent (*lineage*), hasten, origin (*ancestry*), strife. SEE MAIN ENTRY

race hatred discrimination (*bigotry*)

race prejudice discrimination (*bigotry*)

racial balance integration (*assimilation*)

racial harmonization integration (*assimilation*)

racial harmony integration (*assimilation*)

racial prejudice segregation (*isolation by races*)

racialism discrimination (*bigotry*), segregation (*isolation by races*)

racism discrimination (*bigotry*), intolerance, segregation (*isolation by races*)

rack plague

rack the brains ponder

racket bluster (*commotion*), brawl, bunko, commotion, disorder (*lack of order*), noise, outcry, pandemonium. SEE MAIN ENTRY

racketeer malefactor, outlaw. SEE MAIN ENTRY

rackety disorderly

racking insufferable

racy lurid, suggestive (*risqué*)

radiant ecstatic, illustrious

radiare radiate

radiate cast (*throw*), circulate, deploy, diffuse, dispel, disseminate, dissipate (*spread out*), dissolve (*disperse*), emanate, emit, pervade, spread, transmit. SEE MAIN ENTRY

radiating divergent

radical demagogue, drastic, extreme (*exaggerated*), fanatical, insurgent, malcontent, outrageous, total, unusual, vital. SEE MAIN ENTRY

radically new measure innovation

radicated permanent

radius boundary

raffish blatant (*obtrusive*), caitiff, ignoble

raffle bet, lottery

rag mock (*deride*)

rage furor, mode, outbreak, outburst, passion, style, violence

rage against inveigh

raging disorderly, lunatic, outrageous, severe

raid attack, bait (*harass*), depredation, despoil, devastate, encroach, encroachment, foray, harry (*plunder*), impinge, incursion, invade, invasion, loot, onset (*assault*), outbreak, pillage (*noun*), pillage (*verb*), plunder (*noun*), plunder (*verb*), prey, spoil (*pillage*), spoliation

raider burglar, vandal

raiding burglary, housebreaking, predatory

rail demonstrate (*protest*), inveigh

rail at flout, reprimand, reproach

railing aspersion, diatribe

raillery ridicule

rainmaker SEE MAIN ENTRY

raise accrue (*increase*), adopt, ameliorate, boom (*increase*), build (*augment*), build (*construct*), collect (*recover money*), compound, develop, discipline (*train*), elevate, enhance, enlarge, excise (*levy a tax*), expand, foster, frame (*construct*), heighten (*augment*), heighten (*elevate*), honor, increase, increment, levy, magnify, meliorate, originate, parlay (*exploit successfully*), prefer, produce (*manufacture*), promote (*advance*), promotion (*advancement*), recruit, uphold. SEE MAIN ENTRY

raise a demand necessitate

raise a hue and cry against censure, decry, impugn

raise a question challenge, doubt (*distrust*)

raise a question as to impugn

raise a suspicion doubt (*distrust*)

raise above the proper value inflate

raise aloft elevate, heighten (*elevate*)

raise anger incense

raise apprehension dissuade, frighten

raise apprehensions browbeat, menace

raise contributions collect (*recover money*)

raise expectations assure (*give confidence to*)

raise frivolous objection to cavil

raise funds collect (*recover money*)

raise hopes promise (*raise expectations*)

raise objections challenge, counter, demur, differ (*disagree*), disaffirm, disagree, dissent (*withhold assent*), protest, remonstrate

raise objections frivolously cavil

raise one's voice against challenge, decry, dissent (*withhold assent*), impugn, inveigh

raise questions impugn

raise specious objection to cavil

raise spirits invoke

raise taxes toll (*exact payment*)

raise to a higher position elevate

raise to distinction honor

raise troops recruit

raise up one's voice pray

raised prominent

raised path causeway

raised road causeway

raised voice outcry

raison d'être basis SEE MAIN ENTRY

rake off decrease

rake through frisk

rakeoff gratuity (*bribe*)

rakish dissolute, lecherous, licentious

rally assemblage, call (*summon*), caucus, coax, collection (*assembly*), combine (*act in concert*), congregate, convene, help, incite, join (*bring together*), meet, provoke, reassure, stimulate

rally around side

rally round cooperate

rally to bear (*support*), maintain (*sustain*)

ram constrict (*compress*), impact

ram in inject

ramble detour, digress, perambulate, prowl

rambler itinerant

rambling circuitous, desultory, discursive (*digressive*), indirect, labyrinthine, loquacious, profuse, prolix, sinuous, voluble

rambling talk jargon (*unintelligible language*)

ramification organ

ramified divergent

ramify bifurcate, radiate, spread

rammed compact (*dense*)

rampage bluster (*commotion*), brawl (*noun*), brawl (*verb*), commotion, confusion (*turmoil*), outburst, pandemonium, passion, violence

rampageous uncontrollable

rampancy passion

rampant disorderly, hot-blooded, predominant, prevailing (*current*), prevalent, rife, uncontrollable, unrestrained (*not repressed*), unruly, vehement. SEE MAIN ENTRY

rampart barrier, buffer zone, bulwark, mainstay, security (*safety*), shield

ramshackle dilapidated

rancid loathsome, stale, tainted (*contaminated*)

rancor alienation (*estrangement*), cruelty, feud, ill will, malice, odium, spite, umbrage, vengeance. SEE MAIN ENTRY

rancorous bitter *(reproachful)*, caustic, harsh, hostile, invidious, malevolent, malignant, mordacious, negative, relentless, ruthless, scathing, spiteful, vindictive, virulent

random astray, desultory, discursive *(digressive)*, disordered, disorderly, fortuitous, haphazard, indiscriminate, unpredictable. SEE MAIN ENTRY

random luck act of god, happenstance

random sample cross section

randomness incoherence

range area *(province)*, capacity *(aptitude)*, chain *(series)*, circuit, classify, coverage *(scope)*, degree *(magnitude)*, direction *(course)*, extent, file *(arrange)*, fix *(arrange)*, gamut, hierarchy *(arrangement in a series)*, jurisdiction, latitude, magnitude, perambulate, prowl, purview, region, scene, scope, sort, space, sphere. SEE MAIN ENTRY

range of choice latitude

range of meaning connotation, context

range of view coverage *(scope)*, perspective

range of vision perspective

range together juxtapose

ranger migrant

ranging discursive *(digressive)*

rank calculate, class, classify, codify, condition *(state)*, credit *(recognition)*, criticize *(evaluate)*, degree *(station)*, depraved, estimate, evaluate, excessive, fertile, file *(arrange)*, fix *(arrange)*, gauge, loathsome, marshal, materiality *(consequence)*, measure, obnoxious, odious, organize *(arrange)*, pigeonhole, precedence, prestige, productive, quality *(excellence)*, rate, rating, repulsive, reputation, sort, status, tabulate, title *(position)*, unmitigated

rank first surpass

ranking classification, degree *(station)*, master, outstanding *(prominent)*, rating

rankle affront, aggravate *(annoy)*, annoy, bait *(harass)*, harass, irritate

rankling malice, resentment

ransack despoil, devastate, foray, harry *(plunder)*, loot, pillage *(noun)*, pillage *(verb)*, pirate *(take by violence)*, plunder, prey, spoil *(pillage)*, spoliation

ransom blackmail, extricate, free, pay, redeem *(repurchase)*, rescue. SEE MAIN ENTRY

ransomed free *(relieved from a burden)*

rant bombast, declaim, fustian, outpour, reprimand, rodomontade

rant at reproach

ranter bigot, demagogue

ranting bluster *(speech)*, fustian, incoherence, lunatic

rap beat *(strike)*

rapacious confiscatory, insatiable, larcenous, mercenary, predatory. SEE MAIN ENTRY

rapaciousness desire, extortion

rapacity bad repute, extortion, larceny, pillage

rapax rapacious

rape molest *(subject to indecent advances)*. SEE MAIN ENTRY

rapere rape, seize *(apprehend)*

rapid cursory, expeditious, impulsive *(rash)*, instantaneous, precipitate, summary. SEE MAIN ENTRY

rapidity dispatch *(promptness)*, haste

rapidly instantly

rapidus rapid

rapina pillage, plunder, robbery

rapine depredation, larceny, pillage, plunder, rape, spoliation

rapport accordance *(understanding)*, compatibility, concert, concordance, connection *(relation)*, contact *(association)*, peace, rapprochement, relationship *(connection)*, understanding *(agreement)*. SEE MAIN ENTRY

rapprochement arbitration, comparison

rapprochement reconciliation. SEE MAIN ENTRY

rapscallion degenerate, malefactor

rapt ecstatic, pensive

rapt attention diligence *(care)*, obsession, preoccupation

raptorial predatory

rapture passion

rapturous ecstatic

raptus abduction

rare extraordinary, individual, inestimable, infrequent, meritorious, nonconforming, notable, noteworthy, novel, obscure *(remote)*, original *(creative)*, peculiar *(curious)*, portentous *(eliciting amazement)*, priceless, remarkable, scarce, select, singular, special, sporadic, unaccustomed, uncanny, uncommon, unique, unprecedented, unusual, valuable. SEE MAIN ENTRY

rare occurrence improbability, phenomenon *(unusual occurrence)*

rarefy cultivate, decontaminate

rareness dearth, paucity

rari aditus inaccessible, unapproachable

rarity exception *(exclusion)*, improbability, irregularity, phenomenon *(unusual occurrence)*, specialty *(distinctive mark)*

rarus infrequent, rare, scarce, sporadic, uncommon

rascal malefactor

rascality artifice, deception, ill repute, improbity, knavery, mischief, misdoing

rascally artful, lawless, machiavellian, profligate *(corrupt)*, reprobate, sinister, unconscionable

rash blind *(not discerning)*, careless, heedless, hot-blooded, ill-advised, ill-judged, impolitic, improvident, imprudent, irresponsible, negligent, precipitate, premature, presumptuous, spontaneous, thoughtless, unpolitic, unpremeditated

rashness audacity, haste, inconsideration, indiscretion, inexpedience, neglect, temerity

rasp erode, irritate

rasure annulment, cancellation

ratable ad valorem

rate amount *(sum)*, assess *(appraise)*, assessment *(levy)*, calculate, caliber *(quality)*, charge *(cost)*, charge *(assess)*, classify, criticize *(evaluate)*, differential, duty *(tax)*, earnings, estimate *(approximate cost)*, estimate, evaluate, expense *(cost)*, frequency, gauge, inveigh, measure, organize *(arrange)*, par *(face amount)*, pigeonhole, price, rebuke, reprehend, worth. SEE MAIN ENTRY

rate below the true value underestimate

rate incorrectly misjudge

rate of pay wage

rate too low underestimate

rather than in lieu of

rather well fairly *(moderately)*

ratification acceptance, acknowledgment *(acceptance)*, adoption *(acceptance)*, affirmance *(authentication)*, affirmation, approval, assent, certification *(attested copy)*, charter *(sanction)*, confirmation, consent, corroboration, indorsement, jurat, legalization, proof, sanction *(permission)*, stamp, subscription, support *(corroboration)*. SEE MAIN ENTRY

ratified allowed, choate lien, nunc pro tunc

ratified agreement contract

ratifier surety *(guarantor)*, undersigned

ratify accept *(assent)*, accredit, acknowledge *(respond)*, affirm *(uphold)*, agree *(comply)*, approve, assent, attest, bear *(adduce)*, bestow, certify *(approve)*, certify *(attest)*, concur *(agree)*, confirm, consent, corroborate, cosign, countenance, countersign, embrace *(accept)*, endorse, fix *(make firm)*, indorse, pass *(approve)*, recommend, sanction, seal *(solemnize)*, sign, subscribe *(sign)*, substantiate, support *(corroborate)*, sustain *(confirm)*, validate. SEE MAIN ENTRY

rating assessment *(estimation)*, class, disapprobation, estimate *(approximate cost)*, estimation *(calculation)*, measurement, reprimand, reproach, status. SEE MAIN ENTRY

ratio differential, proportion, quota, share *(interest)*. SEE MAIN ENTRY

ratio account *(evaluation)*, expedient, ground, method, mode, motive, phase *(aspect)*, process *(course)*, reason *(basis)*, reference *(allusion)*, reflection *(thought)*, scheme *(noun)*, scheme *(verb)*, style, theoretical, theory

ratio decidendi authority *(documentation)*

ratio iudiciorum judicatory

ratiocinari reason *(conclude)*

ratiocinate debate, deduce, deliberate, ponder, reason *(conclude)*

ratiocinatio ratiocination

ratiocination contemplation, deduction *(conclusion)*, deliberation, dialectic, judgment *(discernment)*. SEE MAIN ENTRY

ratiocinative deductible *(provable)*, discursive *(analytical)*, logical, pensive, rational, reasonable *(rational)*, sensible

ratiocinatory discursive *(analytical)*, logical, pensive

ration allocate, allot, allotment, budget, disburse *(distribute)*, dispense, distribute, divide *(distribute)*, dole, mete, moiety, parcel, provision *(something provided)*, quota, reapportion, share *(interest)*. SEE MAIN ENTRY

rational colorable *(plausible)*, conscious *(aware)*, convincing, deductive, discriminating *(judicious)*, discursive *(analytical)*, judicial, judicious, juridical, justifiable, logical, lucid, normal *(sane)*, plausible, possible, pragmatic, reasonable *(rational)*, sane, sapient, sensible, solid *(sound)*, tenable. SEE MAIN ENTRY

rational faculty common sense, intellect, intelligence *(intellect)*, judgment *(discernment)*, sense *(intelligence)*

rationale argument *(pleading)*, basis, cause *(reason)*, construction, explanation, ground, motive, reason *(basis)*. SEE MAIN ENTRY

rationalism dialectic

rationalistic discursive *(analytical)*

rationality coherence, common sense, competence *(sanity)*, comprehension, discrimination *(good judgment)*, intellect, intelligence *(intellect)*, judgment *(discernment)*, pragmatism, ratiocination, reason *(sound judgment)*, sagacity, sanity, sense *(intelligence)*

rationalization deduction *(conclusion)*, dialectic, excuse, justification, ratiocination

rationalize comment, deduce, deduct *(conclude by reasoning)*, ponder, reason *(conclude)*. SEE MAIN ENTRY

rationalizing dialectic
rationcinate construe (comprehend), deduct (conclude by reasoning)
ratione praeditus rational
rationem inire embark
rationem rei responsibility (accountability)
rationes dispungere audit
rationi consentaneus reasonable (fair)
rationing control (restriction), distribution (apportionment), division (act of dividing)
rationis expers irrational
rationis particeps reasonable (rational)
rattle confuse (bewilder), discompose, perplex
rattle the saber brandish
ratum facere sanction
ravage beat (defeat), catastrophe, consumption, damage, debacle, despoil, destroy (efface), devastate, disaster, extirpate, harm, harry (plunder), havoc, loot, obliterate, overthrow, pillage, plunder, prejudice (injure), prey, prostration, rape, spoil (pillage), wear and tear
ravagement defilement
ravager aggressor, assailant, vandal
ravaging depredation, disastrous, larcenous, predatory
rave against lash (attack verbally)
ravel ascertain, disorganize, elucidate, snarl
raveled disordered, inextricable, labyrinthine, problematic
raven despoil, prey
ravening predatory, rapacious
ravenous eager, gluttonous, predatory, rapacious
ravenousness greed
ravin plunder, spoils
raving bluster (speech), bombast, frenetic, incoherence, insanity, lunatic, non compos mentis, zealous
ravish abduct, carry away, mishandle (maltreat), molest (subject to indecent advances), prey
ravishing attractive, provocative
ravishment abduction, rape
raw imperfect, incomplete, inept (incompetent), inexperienced, mordacious, premature, puerile, unaccustomed, unversed
raw materials commodities
rawness ignorance, nescience
raze abolish, destroy (efface), devastate, eliminate (eradicate), expunge, extinguish, extirpate, obliterate, plunder
razzia foray, pillage, plunder
re carere dispense
re liber free (relieved from a burden)
re multari forfeit
re uti avail (bring about)
re vacuus devoid
re-charged double jeopardy
re-litigated double jeopardy
re-prosecuted double jeopardy
re-tried double jeopardy
reach abut, accede (succeed), attain, capacity (aptitude), capacity (maximum), capacity (sphere), contact (communicate), contact (touch), coverage (scope), degree (magnitude), extent, gamut, impress (affect deeply), jurisdiction, magnitude, obtain, pass (satisfy requirements), purview, range, scope, succeed (attain). SEE MAIN ENTRY
reach a compromise settle
reach a conclusion infer
reach a decision decide

reach a new high surpass
reach a peak culminate
reach a verdict decide
reach an official decision rule (decide)
reach beyond overreach
reach manhood develop
reach of mind caliber (mental capacity), comprehension, intellect, intelligence (intellect)
reach one's goal attain
reach over overlap, overreach
reach the end of exhaust (deplete)
reach the goal consummate
reach the highest point culminate
reach the zenith culminate
reach to adjoin
reach too far overreach
reachable available, disposable, open (accessible), passable, public (open), vulnerable
reacknowledge reconfirm
reacquire collect (recover money), reclaim, recoup (regain), recover, repossess
react perceive, reply, respond, return (respond)
reacting responsive
reaction answer (reply), consequence (conclusion), effect, emotion, estimate (idea), impression, opinion (belief), repercussion, reply, reprisal, response. SEE MAIN ENTRY
reactionary hostile, illiberal, malcontent, renitent
reactionist malcontent
reactivate reconstitute
reactivation recrudescence
reactive responsive, sensitive (easily affected), susceptible (responsive)
read peruse, predict, study. SEE MAIN ENTRY
read as one pari materia
read back repeat (state again)
read in tandem pari materia
read incorrectly misread
read the future predict
read together pari materia
read up on research
read with respect of another pari materia
readable cognizable
readapt attune
readdress redirect
readily SEE MAIN ENTRY
readily impressed susceptible (responsive)
readily influenced pliant
readily mastered facile
readily perceived palpable
readily seen palpable
readily wrought tractable
readiness amenability, diligence (care), dispatch (promptness), facility (easiness), faculty (ability), gift (flair), inclination, maturity, opportunity, plan, predisposition, preparation, proclivity, propensity, qualification (fitness)
readiness to believe credulity
readiness to give largess (generosity)
reading declamation, rendition (explication)
reading matter publication (printed matter)
readjust adapt, attune, modify (alter), redress, rehabilitate, remedy, renovate, repair
readjust downward depreciate
readjustment accommodation (adjustment), correction (change), reconversion,

rehabilitation, renewal, reorganization, reparation (keeping in repair)
readminister redistribute
readmit renew (begin again)
ready artful, available, competent, discipline (train), eager, expeditious, facile, fit, inclined, instant, present (current), proficient, prompt, prone, provide (arrange for), provident (showing foresight), punctual, ripe, willing (desirous), zealous. SEE MAIN ENTRY
ready ability facility (easiness)
ready cash capital
ready for use disposable, effective (operative)
ready money cash, currency
ready-tongued voluble
readying discipline (training), preparation
reaffirm avouch (avow), certify (attest), plead (allege in a legal action), reconfirm, reiterate, repeat (state again). SEE MAIN ENTRY
reaffirmation recital, restatement SEE MAIN ENTRY
reaffirmed nunc pro tunc
real absolute (conclusive), actual, apparent (perceptible), authentic, bona fide, certain (positive), concrete, convincing, corporeal, de facto, definite, documentary, factual, faithful (true to fact), genuine, legitimate (rightful), material (physical), natural, objective, peremptory (absolute), physical, ponderable, pure, realistic, reliable, rightful, sterling, substantial, substantive, tangible, true (authentic), veridical. SEE MAIN ENTRY
real content gist (substance)
real episode fact
real estate demesne, domain (land owned), estate (property), fee (estate), holding (property owned), immovable, land, parcel, premises (buildings), property (land), realty. SEE MAIN ENTRY
real estate trespass encroachment
real experience fact
real interpretation connotation
real meaning connotation
real property demesne, domain (land owned), fee (estate), freehold, holding (property owned), immovable, property (land), real estate, realty
real property capable of being inherited hereditament
real property holder landholder, landowner
real property owner landholder, landowner
real property subject to a lease leasehold
real security bond, charge (lien), cloud (incumbrance), hostage, lien, mortgage, pledge (security)
real sense connotation
real size area (surface)
realignment transition
realism pragmatism, truth
realistic accurate, actual, candid, descriptive, factual, faithful (true to fact), natural, pragmatic, reasonable (rational), sane, true (authentic). SEE MAIN ENTRY
realistic attitude pragmatism
realisticness pragmatism
reality fact, fait accompli, gist (substance), honesty, materiality (physical existence), substance (essential nature), truth, validity. SEE MAIN ENTRY
realizable cognizable, coherent (clear), comprehensible, disposable, passable, possible, potential, practicable

941

realization acquisition, appreciation (increased value), cessation (termination), cognition, commission (act), comprehension, conclusion, determination), creation, denouement, development (outgrowth), discharge (performance), embodiment, end (termination), fait accompli, fruition, insight, knowledge (awareness), occurrence, outcome, perception, performance (execution), phenomenon (manifestation), profit, recognition, satisfaction (fulfilment), sense (feeling), understanding (comprehension). SEE MAIN ENTRY

realization in advance advancement (loan)

realize accomplish, acquire (secure), appreciate (comprehend), apprehend (perceive), attain, avail (bring about), collect (recover money), commit (perpetrate), complete, comprehend (understand), conceive (comprehend), conjure, construe (comprehend), consummate, detect, discern (detect with the senses), discharge (perform), discover, dispatch (dispose of), earn, effectuate, execute (accomplish), find (discover), fulfill, gain, implement, invent (produce for the first time), note (notice), notice (observe), obtain, pass (satisfy requirements), perceive, pierce (discern), procure, produce (manufacture), profit, reap, receive (acquire), recognize (acknowledge), recover, solve, substantiate, succeed (attain). SEE MAIN ENTRY

realize in cash liquidate (convert into cash)

realize the worth of appreciate (value)

realized cognizable, complete (ended), fully executed (consummated)

realized from accompanying words noscitur a sociis

reallocate reapportion, reassign

reallocation reclassification, removal

reallot reapportion, reassign, redistribute

reallotment reclassification

really purely (positively)

realm ambit, area (province), bailiwick, capacity (sphere), circuit, coverage (scope), demesne, department, district, domain (sphere of influence), jurisdiction, part (role), province, region, scope, sphere, territory. SEE MAIN ENTRY

realness honesty, legitimacy, reality, validity

realtor broker

realty demesne, domain (land owned), estate (property), fee (estate), freehold, holding (property owned), property (land), real estate. SEE MAIN ENTRY

reanalysis reclassification

reanalyze reexamine

reanimate recall (call back), recreate, renew (refurbish), renovate, restore (renew), resurrect

reanimated renascent

reanimation recrudescence, renewal, repair, resurgence, revival

reap acquire (receive), attain, earn, gain, procure, profit, realize (obtain as a profit), receive (acquire), succeed (attain). SEE MAIN ENTRY

reap profits gain

reap rewards gain

reap the benefit of capitalize (seize the chance), gain

reap the fruits profit

reappear recur, return (go back)

reappearance recrudescence, resurgence, revival

reappearing periodic, renascent

reappoint reapportion, reassign, reinstate

reapportion redistribute. SEE MAIN ENTRY

reapportionment reclassification

reappraise reassess

reappreciate reassess

reapprise reassess

reappropriate reassign

reapprove reconfirm

rear discipline (train), educate, foster, last (final), nurture

rearmost back (in reverse), final

rearrange alter, convert (change use), disturb, edit, modify (alter), reapportion, reconstruct, redistribute, reform, restore (renew)

rearrangement exchange, interchange, reclassification, renewal, reorganization

rearrest SEE MAIN ENTRY

rearward back (in reverse)

reason analyze, answer (solution), basis, common sense, competence (sanity), comprehension, construe (comprehend), contention (argument), debate, deduce, deduct (conclude by reasoning), deliberate, derive (deduce), discrimination (good judgment), end (intent), excuse, gist (ground for a suit), ground, impetus, incentive, infer, intellect, intelligence (intellect), justice, justification, motive, point (item), point (purpose), ponder, postulate, rationale, rationalize, read, reflect (ponder), sagacity, sanity, sense (intelligence), solution (answer), stimulus, treat (process), understanding (comprehension). SEE MAIN ENTRY

reason about discuss, treat (process)

reason against oppugn

reason earnestly against expostulate

reason for action motive

reason for disapproval objection

reason for legal pursuit cause of action

reason for relief cause of action

reason for which suit is commenced gist (ground for a suit)

reason out deliberate, solve

reason the point deliberate

reason to believe clue

reason to complain grievance

reason upon argue

reason with counsel, discuss

reasonability admissibility, competence (sanity)

reasonable adequate, amenable, colorable (plausible), considerable, convincing, discriminating (judicious), equitable, fair (satisfactory), impartial, judicial, judicious, just, justifiable, logical, normal (sane), objective, open-minded, ostensible, peaceable, placable, plausible, possible, practicable, pragmatic, probable, rational, receptive, right (correct), right (suitable), rightful, sane, sensible, solid (sound), suitable, tenable, unprejudiced, upright, viable. SEE MAIN ENTRY

reasonable chance likelihood, opportunity, probability, prospect (outlook)

reasonable claim cause of action

reasonable excuse justification

reasonable ground likelihood

reasonable presumption likelihood

reasonable prospect likelihood

reasonable supposition presumption

reasonableness common sense, equity (justice), expedience, fairness, feasibility, justice, moderation, pragmatism, probability, propriety (appropriateness), sanity

reasonably anticipated foreseeable

reasonably good fair (satisfactory)

reasonably sufficient adequate

reasoned deductive, deliberate, intentional, judicial, logical, premeditated

reasoned judgment adjudication, conclusion (determination), deduction (conclusion), determination

reasoning contemplation, dialectic, discursive (analytical), judgment (discernment), justification, pensive, ratiocination, rational, rationale, reflection (thought), speculation (conjecture)

reasoning faculties judgment (discernment)

reasoning faculty intellect, intelligence (intellect)

reasoning power intellect, intelligence (intellect), judgment (discernment), sagacity

reasonless deranged, irrational, lunatic, misadvised

reassemble recall (call back)

reassembling repair

reassembly collection (assembly)

reassert avouch (avow), plead (allege in a legal action), reaffirm, reiterate, repeat (state again)

reassertation recital

reassertion restatement

reassess SEE MAIN ENTRY

reassessment rehearing

reassign reapportion, recover, redistribute, relocate, remand. SEE MAIN ENTRY

reassignment reclassification

reassort reapportion, redistribute

reassorting reclassification

reassortment reclassification

reassume recoup (regain)

reassurance assurance, certainty, certification (attested copy), coverage (insurance), solace, surety (certainty), trust (confidence)

reassure assure (give confidence to), certify (attest), corroborate, insure. SEE MAIN ENTRY

reassure oneself ascertain

reassured positive (confident), sanguine, secure (confident)

reassurement certification (attested copy)

reassuring favorable (expressing approval), propitious

reauthenticate reconfirm

reave hold up (rob), pillage, plunder

reawaken renew (refurbish)

reawakening revival

rebate discount (reduce), refund (noun), refund (verb), reimburse, reimbursement, repay, restitution. SEE MAIN ENTRY

rebegin continue (resume)

rebel defect, defy, demagogue, disobey, fight (battle), insurgent, malcontent, pariah, resist (oppose), secede, strike (refuse to work). SEE MAIN ENTRY

rebellio insurrection

rebellion anarchy, commotion, defiance, disloyalty, disturbance, infidelity, insurrection, mutiny, outbreak, outburst, resistance, revolt, revolution, riot, sedition, subversion, treason. SEE MAIN ENTRY

rebellion against the government treason

rebellious contumacious, disobedient, disorderly, dissident, fractious, froward, impertinent (insolent), insubordinate, intractable, irresponsible, lawless, pugnacious, radical (favoring drastic change), recalcitrant, recusant, restive, unruly

rebelliousness defiance

rebellis insurgent

rebirth reconversion, renewal, resurgence, revival

reborn renascent

rebound reaction (opposition), reflect (mirror), repercussion, return (go back)

rebounding resounding

rebuff abrogate (annul), censure, check (bar), confront (oppose), contemn, contempt (disdain), controvert, counter, counteract, decline (reject), disallow, disapprove (condemn), disapprove (reject), disdain (noun), disdain (verb), disfavor, disoblige, disown (refuse to acknowledge), disrespect, dissent (withhold assent), eliminate (exclude), exclude, fight (counteract), impeach, parry, reaction (opposition), rebut, refusal, refuse, reject, rejection, renounce, renunciation, repel (drive back), repulse, resist (oppose), resistance, reversal, shun, spurn. SEE MAIN ENTRY

rebuffing negative

rebuild copy, fix (repair), reclaim, reconstitute, reconstruct, recreate, rehabilitate, renew (refurbish), renovate, repair, reproduce, restore (renew), resurrect

rebuilding rehabilitation, reorganization, reparation (keeping in repair)

rebukable reprehensible

rebuke admonish (warn), admonition, aspersion, bad repute, blame (culpability), blame, castigate, censure, complain (criticize), condemn (blame), condemnation (blame), criticize (find fault with), denounce (condemn), denunciation, diatribe, disapprobation, disapprove (condemn), disparagement, exception (objection), impeachment, lash (attack verbally), objection, objurgation, odium, outcry, penalize, rebuff (noun), rebuff (verb), remonstrance, remonstrate, reprehend, reprimand (noun), reprimand (verb), reproach (noun), reproach (verb), reversal, stricture. SEE MAIN ENTRY

rebuking critical (faultfinding), remonstrative

rebut answer (reply), answer (respond legally), contradict, contravene, controvert, countercharge, countervail, disaccord, disaffirm, disallow, disown (deny the validity), disprove, dispute (debate), gainsay, impugn, negate, oppose, refute, reply, respond, retaliate, retort, return (respond). SEE MAIN ENTRY

rebut the charge countercharge

rebuttal answer (judicial response), answer (reply), argument (pleading), confutation, contradiction, contravention, counterargument, defense, denial, disagreement, plea, pleading, reply, response SEE MAIN ENTRY

rebutter confutation, counterargument

rebutting contradictory, contrary, negative

rebutting evidence answer (judicial response), contradiction

recalcitrance contempt (disobedience to the court), contest (dispute), defiance, resistance, revolt, tenacity

recalcitrancy defiance

recalcitrant adverse (hostile), contentious, contumacious, deviant, disinclined, disobedient, disorderly, dissident, fractious, incorrigible, indomitable, insubordinate, insusceptible (uncaring), intractable, lawless, nonconsenting, obdurate, recusant, reluctant, renitent, restive, uncontrollable, unreasonable, unruly, unyielding, vicious. SEE MAIN ENTRY

recalcitrantly unwillingly

recalcitrate confront (oppose), disobey, oppose, oppugn, rebel, resist (oppose)

recalcitration defiance, opposition, reaction (opposition)

recalculate reassess

recall abjuration, abrogate (rescind), ademption, annul, cancel, cancellation, countermand, defeasance, depose (remove), disavow, discharge (annulment), discharge (release from obligation), disinherit, hindsight, nullify, recant, reclaim, recognition, recognize (perceive), recollect, recollection, redeem (repurchase), remember, remembrance (recollection), renege, repeal, repossess, rescind, rescision, retain (keep in possession), retraction, retrospect, revocation, revoke, withdraw. SEE MAIN ENTRY

recall to life cure, resurrect

recalling cancellation, memory (retention)

recalling to mind honorary

recant abrogate (rescind), cancel, disaffirm, disavow, disclaim, disinherit, disown (deny the validity), negate, nullify, renounce, repent, repudiate, rescind, revoke, tergiversate, vacate (void), withdraw. SEE MAIN ENTRY

recantare recant

recantation abjuration, abolition, bad faith, cancellation, countermand, denial, disclaimer, negation, rejection, renunciation, repudiation, rescision, retraction, reversal, revocation

recap scenario, summary

recapitulate compile, copy, digest (summarize), itemize, quote, recite, recount, reiterate, repeat (state again), review. SEE MAIN ENTRY

recapitulated compact (pithy)

recapitulation account (report), capsule, compendium, digest, hornbook, narration, outline (synopsis), paraphrase, recital, report (detailed account), restatement, retrospect, review (official reexamination), scenario, statement, story (narrative), summary, synopsis

recapitulatory repetitious

recapture rearrest, recoup (regain), recover, recovery (repossession), redeem (repurchase), repossess, rescue, salvage

recast alter, change, convert (change use), modify (alter), reconstruct, recreate, reform (noun), reform (verb), revise, tempered, transform

recasting reorganization

recede decrease, depart, diminish, ebb, erode, escheat, regress, retire (retreat), retreat, revert, subside, withdraw

recede from view disappear

recedence capitulation

recedere ebb, retire (retreat)

receding regressive

receipt acceptance, binder, quitclaim, realization. SEE MAIN ENTRY

receipt for payment binder

receipt in full payment (act of paying)

receipted payment collection (payment), satisfaction (discharge of debt)

receipts capital, earnings, income, proceeds, profit, revenue

receivable delinquent (overdue), passable. SEE MAIN ENTRY

receival acquisition

receive accept (take), congregate, draw (extract), embrace (encircle), endure (suffer), gain, hold (possess), inherit, instate, obtain, partake, possess, procure, realize (obtain as a profit), reap, tolerate. SEE MAIN ENTRY

receive a false idea misconstrue

receive a false impression err, misapprehend, miscalculate, misconceive, misconstrue, misinterpret, misread, mistake

receive a legacy inherit

receive a wrong idea misinterpret

receive a wrong impression misconceive, misread, mistake, misunderstand

receive an endowment inherit

receive an incorrect impression misinterpret, misread

receive an instrument officially file (place among official records)

receive as right inherit

receive by bequest inherit

receive by devise inherit

receive by law of descent inherit

receive by succession inherit

receive compensation earn

receive information overhear

receive information aurally hear (perceive by ear)

receive knowledge of overhear

receive money collect (recover money)

receive notice beware

receive payment collect (recover money)

receive property as an heir inherit

receive with approval accept (take)

received common (customary), popular

received maxim principle (axiom)

receiver assignee, bearer, beneficiary, catchall, disciple, fence, feoffee, heir, holder, recipient. SEE MAIN ENTRY

receiver of stolen goods fence

receiver of stolen property fence

receiving acquisition, assumption (adoption), receptive

recent current, novel, present (current). SEE MAIN ENTRY

receptacle catchall, coffer, depository, enclosure, receiver, repository, treasury

receptaculum depository, refuge, repository, shelter (protection)

reception acquisition, adoption (acceptance), assumption (adoption), ceremony, entrance, receipt (act of receiving)

reception room chamber (compartment)

receptive available, inclined, liberal (broad minded), open (persuasible), openminded, passive, penetrable, perceptive, pliable, pliant, responsive, suasible, susceptible (responsive), willing (not averse). SEE MAIN ENTRY

receptiveness acceptance, amenability

receptor receiver

recertify reconfirm

recess abeyance, adjourn, adjournment, cloture, continue (adjourn), defer (put off), discontinuance (act of discontinuing), discontinue (break continuity), extension (postponement), furlough, halt, hiatus, holiday, interruption, interval, lapse (break), leave (absence), lull, moratorium, pause, pendency, remission, respite (interval of rest), rest (cease from action). SEE MAIN ENTRY

recession capitulation, decline, erosion, outflow

recessive regressive

rechannel recover

recharge reassess, replenish

recharging renewal

recheck reconfirm, reexamine, review

recidere relapse (noun), relapse (verb)

recidivate relapse, return (go back). SEE MAIN ENTRY

recidivation recrudescence, relapse

recidivism relapse, reversion *(act of returning)*. SEE MAIN ENTRY

recidivist convict, criminal, delinquent, felon, malefactor, outlaw. SEE MAIN ENTRY

recidivistic regressive

recidivous incorrigible, regressive, reprobate

recipe system

recipere admit *(give access)*, enfranchise

recipience acquisition, assumption *(adoption)*, receipt *(act of receiving)*

recipient assignee, bearer, beneficiary, devisee, donee, grantee, heir, holder, legatee, payee, receiver, receptive, subject *(object)*, transferee, trustee. SEE MAIN ENTRY

recipient of a fee feoffee

recipient of stolen goods fence

recipient of stolen property fence

reciprocal coequal, cognate, common *(shared)*, complement, correlate, correlative, counterpart *(complement)*, equivalent, related, same. SEE MAIN ENTRY

reciprocal action reaction *(response)*, repercussion

reciprocal agreement mutual understanding

reciprocal commitment mutual understanding

reciprocal concession composition *(agreement in bankruptcy)*

reciprocal exchange interchange

reciprocal feeling consortium *(marriage companionship)*

reciprocal trade commerce

reciprocality mutuality, quid pro quo, reciprocity

reciprocalize correspond *(be equivalent)*

reciprocally attached conjoint

reciprocalness mutuality, reciprocity

reciprocate beat *(pulsate)*, repay, retaliate, return *(respond)*. SEE MAIN ENTRY

reciprocating mutual *(reciprocal)*

reciprocation exchange, interchange, mutuality, quid pro quo, reciprocity, reply, reprisal, retribution, revenge

reciprocative convertible, mutual *(reciprocal)*, reciprocal, responsive

reciprocator correlate

reciprocity comity, exchange, mutuality, quid pro quo, rapprochement, relationship *(connection)*. SEE MAIN ENTRY

reciprocity of obligation agreement *(concurrence)*

recision abolition, retraction

recission revocation

recital account *(report)*, declamation, delineation, disclosure *(act of disclosing)*, disclosure *(something disclosed)*, discourse, instruction *(teaching)*, mention *(reference)*, narration, report *(detailed account)*, restatement, specification, speech, statement, story *(narrative)*. SEE MAIN ENTRY

recitation declamation, declaration, delineation, disclosure *(act of disclosing)*, discourse, instruction *(teaching)*, mention *(reference)*, narration, parlance, peroration, proclamation, recital, reference *(citation)*, remark, report *(detailed account)*, rhetoric *(skilled speech)*, speech, statement, story *(narrative)*

recite allege, assert, cite *(state)*, converse, convey *(communicate)*, declaim, delineate, depict, detail *(particularize)*, discourse, discuss, inform *(notify)*, mention, phrase, pronounce *(speak)*, quote, recapitulate, recount, relate *(tell)*, remark, repeat *(state again)*, report *(disclose)*, speak, utter. SEE MAIN ENTRY

recite a spell invoke

recite an incantation invoke

recited aforesaid, repeated, verbal

reckless careless, heedless, hot-blooded, ill-advised, ill-judged, impolitic, improvident, imprudent, impulsive *(rash)*, injudicious, misadvised, negligent, precipitate, prodigal, profligate *(extravagant)*, profuse, remiss, thoughtless, unpolitic, wanton. SEE MAIN ENTRY

reckless expenditure misapplication

reckless homocide manslaughter

recklessness audacity, inconsideration, indiscretion, neglect, negligence, temerity

reckon assess *(appraise)*, calculate, consider, criticize *(evaluate)*, determine, estimate, evaluate, guess, infer, judge, measure, opine, presuppose, rate, speculate *(conjecture)*, suspect *(think)*

reckon among contain *(comprise)*

reckon from some point in time date

reckon on expect *(anticipate)*

reckon up sum

reckon with pay

reckoner accountant, comptroller

reckoning accounting, amount *(sum)*, appraisal, assessment *(estimation)*, bill *(invoice)*, census, computation, consideration *(contemplation)*, consideration *(recompense)*, contribution *(indemnification)*, cost *(price)*, determination, dun, estimate *(approximate cost)*, estimate *(idea)*, estimation *(calculation)*, expiation, invoice *(bill)*, measurement, pay, payment *(act of paying)*, recovery *(award)*

reclaim claim *(demand)*, collect *(recover money)*, cure, fix *(repair)*, meliorate, purge *(wipe out by atonement)*, reconstruct, recoup *(regain)*, recover, redeem *(repurchase)*, reform, rehabilitate, renew *(refurbish)*, repossess, rescue. SEE MAIN ENTRY

reclaimable corrigible

reclaimed renascent, repentant

reclaimed materials salvage

reclamare remonstrate

reclamatio remonstrance

reclamation compensation, progress, recovery *(award)*, recovery *(repossession)*, redemption, reform, rehabilitation, renewal, replacement, replevin, restitution, revival, salvage

reclass reassess, redistribute

reclassification SEE MAIN ENTRY

reclassify reapportion, redistribute

recline repose *(rest)*, rest *(be supported by)*

reclusive solitary

recognition acknowledgment *(acceptance)*, adoption *(acceptance)*, appreciation *(perception)*, apprehension *(perception)*, approval, assent, certification *(certification of proficiency)*, character *(reputation)*, charter *(sanction)*, cognition, comprehension, concession *(compromise)*, franchise *(license)*, identification, knowledge *(awareness)*, notice *(heed)*, notoriety, perception, realization, reason *(sound judgment)*, recollection, remembrance *(recollection)*, respect, reward, scienter, sense *(intelligence)*, understanding *(comprehension)*. SEE MAIN ENTRY

recognizable apparent *(perceptible)*, appreciable, arrant *(definite)*, ascertainable, cognizable, coherent *(clear)*, comprehensible, conspicuous, discernible, distinct *(clear)*, explicit, manifest, naked *(perceptible)*, obvious, open *(in sight)*, palpable, pellucid, perceivable, perceptible, ponderable,

prominent, solvable, unambiguous, unmistakable, visible *(noticeable)*

recognizably fairly *(clearly)*

recognizance binder, concession *(compromise)*, guaranty, identification, remembrance *(recollection)*, specialty *(contract)*. SEE MAIN ENTRY

recognize acknowledge *(verify)*, admit *(concede)*, appreciate *(comprehend)*, apprehend *(perceive)*, assent, authorize, bear *(tolerate)*, bestow, comprehend *(understand)*, concede, confirm, countenance, detect, diagnose, discern *(detect with the senses)*, find *(discover)*, grant *(concede)*, hear *(perceive by ear)*, heed, identify, notice *(observe)*, perceive, pierce *(discern)*, realize *(understand)*, recall *(remember)*, recollect, remember, spy, witness *(have direct knowledge of)*. SEE MAIN ENTRY

recognize as different distinguish

recognize as distinct discern *(discriminate)*

recognize as separate differentiate, discriminate *(distinguish)*

recognize authority of acknowledge *(verify)*

recognize the worth of appreciate *(value)*

recognized allowed, common *(customary)*, customary, familiar *(customary)*, famous, household *(familiar)*, influential, master, ordinary, orthodox, outstanding *(prominent)*, predominant, prescriptive, proverbial, public *(known)*, putative, renowned, right *(suitable)*, salient

recognized because of continued possession prescriptive

recognized by law jural, legitimate *(rightful)*

recognized by the law legal

recognized condition necessity

recognized from accompanying words noscitur a sociis

recognized maxim principle *(axiom)*

recognized principles polity

recognized through use prescriptive

recoil rebuff, refuse, repercussion, retreat, revert

recoil from eschew, shun

recoil from with pride disdain

recoiling reluctance, resilient

recolere resume

recollect identify, recall *(remember)*, recognize *(perceive)*, remember, retain *(keep in possession)*. SEE MAIN ENTRY

recollection hindsight, identification, memory *(retention)*, recognition, retrospect. SEE MAIN ENTRY

recollective suggestive *(evocative)*

recommence continue *(resume)*, proceed *(continue)*, renew *(begin again)*, reopen, resume

recommencement continuation *(resumption)*, renewal

recommend admonish *(advise)*, advise, advocate, authorize, bestow, coax, counsel, countenance, exhort, incite, indorse, instruct *(direct)*, offer *(propose)*, prefer, prompt, propose, propound, refer *(send for action)*, urge. SEE MAIN ENTRY

recommend against expostulate

recommend points of law charge *(instruct on the law)*

recommend to pardon condone

recommendable desirable *(qualified)*

recommendation advice, advocacy, auspices, determination, dictum, direction (guidance), guidance, holding (ruling of a court), judgment (formal court decree), patronage (support), proposal (suggestion), proposition, suggestion, tip (clue). SEE MAIN ENTRY

recommendations credentials

recommendatory advisory, favorable (expressing approval)

recommended preferential

recommender arbiter

recommission reassign

recommit confine, rearrest, remand. SEE MAIN ENTRY

recommit to custody commit (institutionalize)

recommitment rendition (restoration)

recompensation in value compensation

recompense alimony, bear the expense, brokerage, collect (recover money), collection (payment), commission (fee), compensate (remunerate), compensation, contribute (indemnify), contribution (indemnification), cover (provide for), damages, disburse (pay out), disbursement (funds paid out), discharge (payment), discharge (pay a debt), earnings, expiation, fee (charge), honorarium, indemnification, indemnify, indemnity, pay (noun), pay (verb), payment (act of paying), payment (remittance), payroll, perquisite, price, prize, quit (repay), reciprocate, recoup (reimburse), recovery (award), refund (noun), refund (verb), reimburse, reimbursement, relief (legal redress), remedy (legal means of redress), remit (send payment), remittance, remunerate, remuneration, reparation (indemnification), repay, requital, restitution, restore (return), retainer, revenue, reward, satisfaction (discharge of debt), satisfy (discharge), trover, wage. SEE MAIN ENTRY

recompense for past loss indemnify

recompenser insurer

recompensive compensatory

recompose reconstruct

reconcilable apposite, concordant, congruous, consonant, correlative, placable, suitable

reconcile adapt, agree (comply), arbitrate (conciliate), comport (agree with), compromise (settle by mutual agreement), conform, correspond (be equivalent), disarm (set at ease), mediate, mollify, pacify, placate, propitiate, rationalize, settle, unite. SEE MAIN ENTRY

reconcile oneself to submit (yield)

reconciled agreed (harmonized), consensual, patient, resigned

reconcilement accordance (compact), accordance (understanding), adjustment, conciliation, condonation, consensus, intercession, rapprochement, reconciliation

reconciler adjuster, arbiter, arbitrator, go-between, intermediary, referee, umpire

reconciliatio accommodation (adjustment)

reconciliation accordance (compact), accordance (understanding), adjustment, arrangement (understanding), compatibility, concession (compromise), conciliation, expiation, intercession, mediation, mollification, pact, peace, rapprochement, settlement. SEE MAIN ENTRY

reconcinnare renew (refurbish)

recondite complex, difficult, equivocal, esoteric, hidden, inapprehensible, incomprehensible, inexplicable, learned, mysteri-

ous, nebulous, oblique (evasive), obscure (abstruse), opaque, private (confidential), privy, profound (esoteric), secret. SEE MAIN ENTRY

recondite knowledge secret

reconditeness ambiguity

recondition change, fix (repair), reconstitute, reconstruct, rehabilitate, renew (refurbish), renovate, repair, restore (renew), resurrect, transform

reconditioned renascent

reconditioning repair, reparation (keeping in repair)

reconditus recondite

reconfine rearrest

reconfirm SEE MAIN ENTRY

reconfirmed nunc pro tunc

reconnaissance examination (study), inspection, observation, research

reconnoiter check (inspect), examine (study), investigate, observe (watch), oversee, patrol, perambulate, spy, study, survey (examine)

reconnoiterer spy

reconnoitering discovery

reconsider appeal, reexamine, review, revise. SEE MAIN ENTRY

reconsideration appeal, hindsight, retrospect, review (official reexamination)

reconstitute convert (change use), reconstruct, reform, rehabilitate, reinforce, reinstate, renew (refurbish), renovate, reproduce, restore (renew). SEE MAIN ENTRY

reconstituted renascent

reconstitution reclassification, reform, rehabilitation, renewal, reorganization, replacement

reconstruct alter, change, convert (change use), copy, emend, fix (repair), modify (alter), reconstitute, recreate, reform, rehabilitate, renew (refurbish), renovate, repair, repeat (do again), reproduce, restore (renew), revise, transform. SEE MAIN ENTRY

reconstructed renascent, tempered

reconstruction conversion (change), correction (change), reform, rehabilitation, remembrance (recollection), renewal, reorganization, repair, reparation (keeping in repair), replacement

reconvene recall (call back)

reconversion SEE MAIN ENTRY

reconvert reconstitute, rehabilitate, renew (refurbish), renovate, transform

record account (report), bill (invoice), book, calendar (list of cases), calendar (record of yearly periods), cast (register), ceiling, date, deed, docket, document, documentation, dossier, enroll, evidence, file, form (document), impanel, index (relate), inscribe, inscription, instrument (document), inventory, journal, ledger, marginalia, memorandum, notation, note (brief comment), register (noun), register (verb), render (depict), report (detailed account), roll, set down, story (narrative), transcript. SEE MAIN ENTRY

record book ledger

record keeper clerk

record keeping registration

record of credits and debits ledger

record of money transactions ledger

record of proceedings docket

record of the court file

record of yearly periods calendar (record of yearly periods)

record the vote poll

record-breaking best

recordari recall (remember), recollect, remember

recordatio recollection

recordation SEE MAIN ENTRY

recorded documentary, in writing

recorded expression of a formal judgment award, holding (ruling of a court)

recorded information dossier, file

recorded item entry (record)

recorded material document, documentation, dossier

recorder accountant, amanuensis, clerk, notary public

recording record, registration, transcript

recording secretary amanuensis

records credentials, proof

recount census, converse, convey (communicate), delineate, depict, detail (particularize), disabuse, inform (notify), itemize, mention, notify, quote, recapitulate, recite, relate (tell), repeat (state again), report (disclose). SEE MAIN ENTRY

recountal narration, recital, restatement, story (narrative)

recounted narrative

recounting narration, recital, report (detailed account), restatement

recoup collect (recover money), outbalance, recover, redeem (repurchase), repossess, restore (return). SEE MAIN ENTRY

recoupable deductible (capable of being deducted from taxes)

recouping recovery (repossession)

recoupment compensation, expiation, indemnity, recompense, recovery (award), refund, reimbursement, replevin, restitution, salvage, satisfaction (discharge of debt), setoff, trover

recourse alternative (option), tool. SEE MAIN ENTRY

recourse to some higher power appeal

recourse to the principles of natural justice equity (justice)

recover collect (recover money), cure, hold (possess), obtain, occupy (take possession), reap, reclaim, recoup (regain), redeem (repurchase), renew (refurbish), repossess, rescue. SEE MAIN ENTRY

recover knowledge recognize (perceive)

recover knowledge of recall (remember), remember

recover property evict

recoverable corrigible

recovery adverse possession, boom (prosperity), compensation, cure, damages, expiation, improvement, out of pocket, progress, recompense, redemption, reform, repair, replacement, replevin, restitution, resurgence, revival, salvage, trover. SEE MAIN ENTRY

recovery of property replevin

recovery of property from another's possession eviction

recreance sedition

recreancy bad faith, desertion, disloyalty, infidelity, lapse (expiration), recidivism, sedition

recreant caitiff, convict, criminal, degenerate, delinquent, disgraceful, disreputable, faithless, false (disloyal), felon, iniquitous, lawless, peccable, reprehensible, reprobate, untrue. SEE MAIN ENTRY

recreare reassure

recreate copy, portray, reconstruct, renew (refurbish), renovate, repeat (do again), reproduce, restore (renew). SEE MAIN ENTRY

recreated renascent

recreation enjoyment *(pleasure)*, reform, rehabilitation, revival

recreation time leave *(absence)*

recremental excess

recrementitial excess

recrementitious excess

recriminate answer *(respond legally)*, blame, censure, charge *(accuse)*, countercharge, denounce *(condemn)*, dispute *(contest)*, impeach, reprehend, reprimand, return *(respond)*. SEE MAIN ENTRY

recrimination answer *(judicial response)*, charge *(accusation)*, condemnation *(blame)*, contention *(opposition)*, denunciation, incrimination

recriminative critical *(faultfinding)*

recrudesce recur, relapse

recrudescence relapse, renewal. SEE MAIN ENTRY

recrudescency recrudescence, relapse, renewal

recruit disciple, employ *(engage services)*, enroll, hire, induct, novice, prospect *(prospective patron)*, retain *(employ)*, supply, volunteer. SEE MAIN ENTRY

rectifiable corrigible

rectification accommodation *(adjustment)*, adjustment, collection *(payment)*, compensation, correction *(change)*, reform, relief *(legal redress)*, remedial statute, remedy *(legal means of redress)*, reorganization, repair, reparation *(keeping in repair)*, revision *(process of correcting)*

rectify adjust *(resolve)*, ameliorate, amend, attune, cure, disabuse, edit, emend, fix *(repair)*, meliorate, modify *(alter)*, purge *(purify)*, redress, reform, regulate *(adjust)*, rehabilitate, remedy, renew *(refurbish)*, repair, restore *(renew)*, revise, settle. SEE MAIN ENTRY

rectilineal direct *(straight)*

rectitude conscience, credibility, ethics, fairness, good faith, honor *(good reputation)*, integrity, justice, merit, principle *(virtue)*, probity, propriety *(correctness)*, right *(righteousness)*, trustworthiness, veracity. SEE MAIN ENTRY

rectus direct *(forthright)*, proper, right *(righteousness)*

recumbency abeyance, prostration

recumbent inactive, passive

recuperare recover

recuperate cure, progress

recuperation cure, rehabilitation, resurgence, revival

recuperative medicinal, remedial, salubrious

recuperatory medicinal

recur occur *(happen)*, repeat *(do again)*. SEE MAIN ENTRY

recurrence continuation *(resumption)*, cycle, frequency, habit, recrudescence, redundancy, regularity, relapse, renewal, resurgence, revival

recurrent chronic, consecutive, habitual, incessant, insistent, intermittent, iterative, periodic, repeated, repetitious, routine, sporadic, typical, usual

recurring chronic, habitual, intermittent, iterative, periodic, regular *(orderly)*, repeated, repetitious, routine, sporadic

recurring period cycle

recurring theme motif

recusancy contempt *(disobedience to the court)*, contest *(dispute)*, defiance, disagreement, dissidence, nonconformity, resistance, schism, sedition, violation

recusant contumacious, disobedient, dissenting, dissident, insubordinate, lawless, malcontent, nonconsenting, radical *(favoring drastic change)*, recalcitrant, restive. SEE MAIN ENTRY

recusare decline *(reject)*, protest

recusatio protest, refusal

red neck bigot

red tape bureaucracy

redact edit, formulate, revise. SEE MAIN ENTRY

redaction correction *(change)*

redargue disaccord

redarguere disprove, rebut, refute

redargution confutation

reddere refund, reimburse, render *(deliver)*, repay, restore *(return)*, return *(refund)*

reddition restitution

rede advice

redeem buy, collect *(recover money)*, cure, defray, discharge *(pay a debt)*, disenthrall, extricate, free, fulfill, indemnify, liberate, liquidate *(convert into cash)*, outbalance, pardon, purchase, purge *(wipe out by atonement)*, reclaim, recoup *(regain)*, recover, reform, refund, rehabilitate, renovate, repossess, rescue, restore *(return)*, save *(conserve)*. SEE MAIN ENTRY

redeemable corrigible, payable, receivable

redeemable part coupon

redeemer benefactor, customer, good samaritan

redeliberate reconsider

redelivery replevin

redemption discharge *(payment)*, freedom, indemnification, indemnity, liberation, progress, ransom, recovery *(repossession)*, rehabilitation, replevin, restitution, salvage. SEE MAIN ENTRY

redemption slip coupon

redemptive compensatory

redesign renew *(refurbish)*

redetain rearrest

redimire intertwine

redintegrare renew *(begin again)*

redintegrate fix *(repair)*, rehabilitate, renew *(refurbish)*, renovate, restore *(renew)*

redintegrated renascent

redintegration reconversion, rehabilitation, repair, revival

redire return *(go back)*

redirect divert. SEE MAIN ENTRY

redisperse reapportion

redistribute reapportion, reassign, subdivide. SEE MAIN ENTRY

redistributing reclassification

redistribution reclassification

redistrict reapportion

reditus proceeds, rent, revenue

redivide reapportion, reassign, redistribute, subdivide

redivivus renascent

redo emend, reconstitute, reconstruct, recreate, reform, renew *(refurbish)*, repeat *(do again)*, reproduce, restore *(renew)*, transform

redolent suggestive *(evocative)*

redone repeated

redouble accrue *(increase)*, accumulate *(enlarge)*, expand, intensify, reinforce, reiterate

redoubled repeated

redoubling augmentation, renewal

redoubtable formidable, indomitable, inexpugnable

redound result. SEE MAIN ENTRY

redraft edit, redact

redress adjust *(resolve)*, collection *(payment)*, compensate *(remunerate)*, contribution *(indemnification)*, cure *(noun)*, cure *(verb)*, disbursement *(funds paid out)*, equity *(justice)*, fix *(repair)*, habeas corpus, help, recompense, recourse, recovery *(award)*, rectify, reform, reimburse, reimbursement, remedy, renew *(refurbish)*, repair, reparation *(indemnification)*, repent, requital, restitution, restore *(return)*, satisfaction *(discharge of debt)*, trover. SEE MAIN ENTRY

redressible wrong cause of action

reduce abate *(lessen)*, abridge *(shorten)*, abstract *(summarize)*, allay, alleviate, assuage, attenuate, beat *(defeat)*, commute, condense, constrict *(compress)*, curtail, debilitate, decrease, demean *(make lower)*, demote, deplete, depose *(remove)*, depress, derogate, digest *(summarize)*, diminish, discount *(minimize)*, divest, erode, expend *(consume)*, extenuate, impair, lessen, minimize, mitigate, moderate *(temper)*, modify *(moderate)*, mollify, palliate *(abate)*, rebate, relax, remit *(relax)*, restrict, retrench, subdue, subjugate. SEE MAIN ENTRY

reduce a punishment commute

reduce expenses retrench

reduce forces disarm *(divest of arms)*

reduce in asperity commute

reduce in intensity attenuate

reduce in quality debase

reduce in severity allay

reduce in strength attenuate, disarm *(divest of arms)*, extenuate

reduce tension ease

reduce the armament disarm *(divest of arms)*

reduce the edge obtund

reduce the mark-up discount *(reduce)*

reduce the purchasing value of depreciate

reduce the strength of depreciate, dilute

reduce the violence obtund

reduce to a code codify

reduce to a digest codify

reduce to a formula formulate

reduce to ashes deflagrate

reduce to chaos mismanage

reduce to extreme purity and strength distill

reduce to inferior rank demote

reduce to method regulate *(adjust)*

reduce to nothing annul, destroy *(efface)*, extinguish

reduce to nought annul

reduce to order arrange *(methodize)*, classify, codify, file *(arrange)*, orchestrate, organize *(arrange)*, pigeonhole, sort

reduce to subjection repress

reduce to the ranks demote, humiliate

reduce volume constrict *(compress)*

reduced brief, inferior *(lower in position)*, insolvent, minimal, nominal, poor *(underprivileged)*. SEE MAIN ENTRY

reduced circumstances poverty, privation

reduced in means destitute

reduced to a writing in writing

reduced to beggary poor *(underprivileged)*

reducing mitigating

reducing to order   classification
reductio ad absurdum   counterargument
reduction   abatement *(reduction)*, abridgment *(condensation)*, abstract, capsule, curtailment, decrease, deduction *(diminution)*, deterioration, diminution, discount, erosion, mitigation, moderation, mollification, rebate, refund, relief *(release)*, remission
reduction in rank   degradation
reduction to order   method
redundance   overage, redundancy, sufficiency, surfeit, surplus
redundancy   overage, prolixity, surplus, tautology. SEE MAIN ENTRY
redundant   excess, excessive, expendable, extraneous, inordinate, iterative, needless, nonessential, profuse, prolix, repetitious, superfluous, turgid, unnecessary. SEE MAIN ENTRY
redundantia   redundancy
redundare   redound
redundent   repeated
reduplicate   copy, plagiarize, repeat *(do again)*, reproduce
reduplicated   repeated
reduplicative   repeated, repetitious
reecho   copy
reechoed   repetitious
reeducation   rehabilitation
reeking   offensive *(offending)*
reel off   recite
reembark   renew *(begin again)*, reopen
reenact   repeat *(do again)*
reenactment   duplicate
reendorse   reconfirm
reendorsed   nunc pro tunc
reenforce   reconfirm, relieve *(give aid)*
reengage   reassign
reenter   renew *(begin again)*, return *(go back)*
reestablish   continue *(resume)*, copy, reclaim, reconfirm, reconstitute, reconstruct, recreate, reform, rehabilitate, reinforce, reinstate, relocate, renovate, reopen, restore *(return)*, return *(go back)*
reestablished   nunc pro tunc, renascent
reestablishment   continuation *(resumption)*, reclassification, reconversion, rehabilitation, renewal, reorganization, resurgence, revival
reestimate   reassess
reevaluate   reassess, reconsider
reexamination   appeal, cross-examination, cross-questioning, hindsight, rehearing, retrospect
reexamine   appeal, audit, check *(inspect)*, cross-examine, reconsider, review, revise. SEE MAIN ENTRY
reface   meliorate
refashion   amend, convert *(change use)*, copy, fix *(repair)*, reconstruct, recreate, reform, rehabilitate, renew *(refurbish)*, renovate, reproduce, restore *(renew)*
refashioned   renascent
refellere   controvert, disprove, refute
refer   appertain, apply *(pertain)*, assign *(transfer ownership)*, confer *(consult)*, delegate, hint, pertain, quote, relegate, remit *(submit for consideration)*, submit *(give)*. SEE MAIN ENTRY
refer back   recommit
refer to   allude, appeal, ascribe, bear *(adduce)*, cite *(state)*, concern *(involve)*, connote, consult *(seek information from)*, denote, mention, specify
refer to for information   consult *(seek information from)*

refer to legal authorities   cite *(state)*
referable to   comparative
referee   adjudicate, arbiter, arbitrate *(conciliate)*, arbitrator, decide, determine, go-between, hear *(give a legal hearing)*, intercede, intermediary, judge *(noun)*, judge *(verb)*, mediate, negotiate, umpire. SEE MAIN ENTRY
reference   attribution, citation *(attribution)*, connection *(relation)*, connotation, derivation, documentation, excerpt, guidance, indication, innuendo, insinuation, intimation, recommendation, referral, relation *(connection)*, relevance, reminder. SEE MAIN ENTRY
reference book   directory
reference form   form *(document)*
reference work   directory
references   credentials
referendary   arbitrator
referendum   election *(selection by vote)*, plebiscite, poll *(casting of votes)*. SEE MAIN ENTRY
referent   mention *(reference)*
referential   comparative, leading *(guiding)*, suggestive *(evocative)*
referment   reference *(allusion)*, reference *(citation)*, referral
referral   reference *(citation)*. SEE MAIN ENTRY
referre   enter *(record)*, move *(judicially request)*, recapitulate, recount, refer *(send for action)*, render *(deliver)*, report *(disclose)*, restore *(return)*, submit *(give)*
referrence   delegation *(assignment)*
referrential   pertinent
referring   comparative, delegation *(assignment)*, germane, pertinent, relative *(relevant)*
referring to   relevant
reficere   fix *(repair)*, reconstruct, renew *(refurbish)*, renovate, repair
refill   replenish, supply
refilled   replete
refinance   SEE MAIN ENTRY
refine   amend, clarify, compound, cultivate, decontaminate, develop, edit, elaborate, emend, enhance, expurgate, meliorate, modify *(alter)*, perfect, purge *(purify)*, reform. SEE MAIN ENTRY
refined   aesthetic, choate lien, civil *(polite)*, discreet, elegant, meritorious, punctilious
refined discrimination   discretion *(quality of being discreet)*
refined manners   decorum
refined taste   decorum
refinement   amendment *(correction)*, amenity, civilization, clarification, courtesy, decorum, development *(progression)*, discretion *(quality of being discreet)*, presence *(poise)*, propriety *(correctness)*, reform
refining   revision *(process of correcting)*
refinish   renew *(refurbish)*
refit   fix *(repair)*, rehabilitate, renew *(refurbish)*, renovate, repair, restore *(renew)*
refitting   renewal, repair
reflect   brood, characterize, deliberate, muse, pause, radiate, rationalize, reason *(conclude)*. SEE MAIN ENTRY
reflect again   reconsider
reflect discredit upon   discommend, disgrace, dishonor *(deprive of honor)*
reflect dishonor upon   discredit, disgrace
reflect honor on   dedicate
reflect honor upon   bestow
reflect over   deliberate
reflect poorly upon   denigrate, disparage

reflect shame upon   disgrace
reflect upon   brand *(stigmatize)*, consider, deliberate, denounce *(condemn)*, ponder, study, weigh
reflecting   circumspect, discreet, judicious, juridical
reflection   apprehension *(perception)*, bad repute, comment, concept, consideration *(contemplation)*, contemplation, criticism, deliberation, dialectic, discredit, hindsight, idea, impression, innuendo, introspection, memory *(retention)*, observation, opinion *(belief)*, penumbra, remark, repercussion, resemblance. SEE MAIN ENTRY
reflective   aforethought, circumspect, cogitative, deliberate, pensive, profound *(esoteric)*, rational, solemn SEE MAIN ENTRY
reflex   controlled *(restrained)*, repercussion
reflex action   instinct
refluence   outflow
refluent   regressive
reflux   decrease, outflow
refocillate   recreate
reform   ameliorate, amend, change, convert *(change use)*, convert *(persuade)*, correction *(change)*, development *(progression)*, emend, fix *(repair)*, meliorate, modify *(alter)*, progress, reconstitute, reconstruct, recreate, rectify, redeem *(satisfy debts)*, repair *(noun)*, repair *(verb)*, repent, reproduce, restore *(renew)*, revision *(process of correcting)*, transform. SEE MAIN ENTRY
reform school   reformatory
reformable   corrigible
reformation   amendment *(correction)*, correction *(change)*, development *(progression)*, reform, rehabilitation, renewal, reorganization, repair
reformational   corrigible, disciplinary *(punitory)*, progressive *(advocating change)*
reformative   disciplinary *(punitory)*, medicinal, progressive *(advocating change)*, remedial, repentant
reformatory   corrigible, disciplinary *(punitory)*, jail, penitentiary, prison, progressive *(advocating change)*, repentant. SEE MAIN ENTRY
reformed   penitent, renascent, repentant
reformed character   penitent
reformer   insurgent, malcontent
reformers   lobby
refractoriness   contempt *(disobedience to the court)*
refractory   contumacious, difficult, disobedient, disorderly, fractious, froward, hostile, incorrigible, indomitable, inflexible, insubordinate, intractable, lawless, obdurate, perverse, recalcitrant, restive, uncontrollable, unruly, unyielding, vicious
refrain   cease, desist, eschew, forbear, shun, stop, withhold. SEE MAIN ENTRY
refrain from   avoid *(evade)*, forgo, forswear, waive
refrain from action   forbear
refrain from noticing   ignore
refrain from punishing   condone
refrain from using   conserve
refrain from working   strike *(refuse to work)*
refraining   avoidance *(evasion)*
refraining from involvement   laissez faire
refraining from utterance   mute
refrainment   abstention
refresh   meliorate, reassure, reconstruct, recreate, renew *(refurbish)*, renovate, repair, replenish, restore *(renew)*

refresh one's memory recall (remember)
refresh the memory remind
refreshed renascent
refreshing palatable, sapid, unusual
refreshment enjoyment (pleasure), renewal, revival, solace, treat
refuel replenish
refuge asylum (hiding place), asylum (protection), bulwark, cache (hiding place), haven, home (domicile), inhabitation (place of dwelling), lodging, protection, shelter (protection), shelter (tax benefit), shield. SEE MAIN ENTRY
refugee alien
refugee prisoner fugitive
refugium refuge
refulgent lucid
refund bear the expense, compensate (remunerate), consideration (recompense), defray, discharge (payment), discharge (pay a debt), indemnify, indemnity, quit (repay), rebate (noun), rebate (verb), reciprocate, recoup (reimburse), reimburse, reimbursement, repay, replace, replacement, restitution, restore (return). SEE MAIN ENTRY
refunding compensatory
refundment refund
refurbish fix (repair), meliorate, reconstruct, rehabilitate, reinforce, renew (refurbish), renovate, repair
refurbishment reparation (keeping in repair)
refusal bar (obstruction), declination, disapproval, disclaimer, exclusion, negation, noncompliance (nonobservance), ostracism, prohibition, rebuff, rejection, renunciation, repudiation, resistance. SEE MAIN ENTRY
refusal of agreement dissension
refusal of approval veto
refusal of bail bondage
refusal of consent declination
refusal to accept dishonor (nonpayment)
refusal to answer demurrer
refusal to be provoked longanimity
refusal to become involved laissez faire
refusal to believe cloud (suspicion), doubt (suspicion)
refusal to comply mutiny
refusal to do business boycott
refusal to furnish work lockout
refusal to obey disregard (omission), infraction
refusal to obey orders contempt (disobedience to the court)
refusal to pay default, dishonor (nonpayment), nonpayment
refusal to sanction veto
refuse abrogate (annul), ban, bar (exclude), censor, condemn (ban), constrain (restrain), debar, decline (reject), disaffirm, disallow, disapprove (reject), disavow, dismiss (put out of consideration), disobey, disoblige, dissent (withhold assent), forbid, forgo, forswear, hold out (resist), prohibit, proscribe (prohibit), protest, rebuff, refrain, reject, renounce, shirk, spurn, waive, withhold. SEE MAIN ENTRY
refuse approval forbid
refuse assent disaccord, disagree, dissent (withhold assent)
refuse assent to disapprove (reject)
refuse bail imprison
refuse consent disapprove (reject), forbid, hold out (resist)
refuse credence disavow, disbelieve, disown (deny the validity), impugn
refuse payment dishonor (refuse to pay)

refuse permission ban, censor, interdict, prohibit, proscribe (prohibit)
refuse to accept contest, contradict, decline (reject), disaccord, disavow, disown (deny the validity), except (object), reject, repudiate, spurn
refuse to acknowledge deny (contradict), disaccord, disavow, disbelieve, ignore, repudiate
refuse to admit contest, deny (contradict), disaccord, disavow, disbelieve, disown (deny the validity), dissent (withhold assent), exclude, gainsay, ignore
refuse to agree disagree
refuse to allow deny (contradict), deny (refuse to grant), disallow, forbid, inhibit
refuse to associate with isolate
refuse to authorize forbid
refuse to believe disbelieve, doubt (distrust)
refuse to bestow deny (refuse to grant)
refuse to confirm disapprove (reject)
refuse to conform cross (disagree with), rebel
refuse to consent disaccord
refuse to consider exclude, reject
refuse to corroborate disallow, disavow, disown (deny the validity)
refuse to credit disbelieve
refuse to disclose withhold
refuse to give deny (refuse to grant)
refuse to give permission forbid
refuse to give up endure (last), persevere, persist
refuse to grant constrain (restrain), disallow
refuse to hear disregard, ignore
refuse to honor dishonor (refuse to pay)
refuse to honor a commitment renege
refuse to honor a promise renege
refuse to include exclude
refuse to know disregard
refuse to notice ignore
refuse to obey disobey
refuse to oblige disoblige
refuse to permit deny (refuse to grant), forbid
refuse to ratify disapprove (reject)
refuse to receive disapprove (reject)
refuse to recognize disown (refuse to acknowledge), neglect
refuse to regard disregard
refuse to sanction disapprove (reject)
refuse to see exclude
refuse to submit resist (withstand), withstand
refuse to supply deny (refuse to grant)
refuse to support rebel, secede
refuse to sustain overrule
refuse to tolerate persecute
refuse to trust doubt (distrust)
refuse to waste conserve
refuse to yield endure (last), persevere, resist (oppose)
refused inadmissible
refusing disinclined, dissident, nonconsenting, reluctant
refusing to admit dissenting
refusing to agree dissenting, irreconcilable
refusing to harmonize irreconcilable
refusing to obey contumacious
refusing to relent persistent
refutability cloud (suspicion)
refutable contestable, controversial, debatable, defeasible, disputable, dubious, dubitative, litigable, untenable

refutal answer (reply), contradiction
refutare controvert
refutation answer (judicial response), argument (pleading), confutation, contradiction, counterargument, defeat, demurrer, denial, negation, opposition, plea, repudiation
refutative contradictory, contrary
refutatory contradictory, contrary
refute answer (reply), avoid (cancel), conflict, contradict, contravene, controvert, countercharge, countervail, cross (disagree with), debate, defeat, disaccord, disaffirm, disagree, disallow, disown (deny the validity), disprove, dispute (contest), dispute (debate), gainsay, impugn, invalidate, negate, oppose, oppugn, overthrow, parry, rebut, reply. SEE MAIN ENTRY
refute by argument countercharge
refuting contradictory, contrary, dissenting, negative
regain collect (recover money), reclaim, recover, redeem (repurchase), repossess
regaining recovery (repossession)
regainment recovery (repossession)
regard affection, appertain, apply (pertain), aspect, caution (vigilance), character (reputation), complexion, concern (interest), concern (involve), consider, consideration (sympathetic regard), credit (recognition), deem, defer (yield in judgment), deference, diligence (care), discern (detect with the senses), estimation (esteem), hear (give attention to), heed, homage, honor (good reputation), honor (outward respect), honor, interest (concern), keep (fulfill), mention (tribute), note (notice), notice (heed), notice (observe), observation, observe (watch), opine, outlook, perceive, perception, prestige, presuppose, prudence, recognition, reputation, respect, surmise, worth. SEE MAIN ENTRY
regard as apprehend (perceive)
regard as axiomatic postulate, presume
regard as wrong disapprove (condemn)
regard carefully check (inspect), concentrate (pay attention), examine (study), focus, scrutinize
regard indulgently excuse
regard likely expect (consider probable)
regard studiously peruse
regard unfavorably disfavor
regard upon deliberate
regard with blame disapprove (condemn)
regard with favor favor
regard with kindness favor
regard with proud contempt disdain
regard with sorrow deplore
regard with suspicion doubt (distrust), mistrust
regardful careful, circumspect, cognizant, conscientious, conscious (aware), discreet, judicious, meticulous, obedient, painstaking, particular (exacting), politic, preventive, prudent, vigilant
regardfully respectfully
regardfulness discretion (quality of being discreet), interest (concern), notice (heed)
regarding pertinent, wherein
regardless careless, cursory, derelict (negligent), inadvertent, insusceptible (uncaring), lax, negligent, perfunctory, thoughtless. SEE MAIN ENTRY
regardless of irrespective
regardlessness disregard (lack of respect), disregard (omission), disregard (unconcern), inconsideration, negligence

regauge reassess

regency dominion *(supreme authority)*, hegemony, hierarchy *(persons in authority)*, predominance, regime

regeneracy revival

regenerate change, convert *(change use)*, cure, fix *(repair)*, meliorate, penitent, reclaim, reconstitute, reconstruct, recreate, reform, renew *(begin again)*, renew *(refurbish)*, renovate, repeat *(do again)*, restore *(renew)*, resurrect, transform

regenerated renascent

regenerateness reconversion

regeneration development *(progression)*, reconversion, reform, rehabilitation, renewal, resurgence, revival

regenesis reconversion, resurgence, revival

regent plenipotentiary, sovereign *(absolute)*, substitute

regere direct *(supervise)*, govern, manage

regignere reproduce

regime hierarchy *(persons in authority)*, management *(directorate)*, system, tenure. SEE MAIN ENTRY

regimen control *(supervision)*

regimen regime, regulation *(rule)*, system

regiment control *(regulate)*, manage, marshal, orchestrate, organize *(arrange)*, oversee

regimentation distribution *(arrangement)*, form *(arrangement)*, regulation *(management)*

regio direction *(course)*, district, region, section *(vicinity)*, territory

region area *(province)*, bailiwick, capacity *(sphere)*, circuit, coverage *(scope)*, district, division *(administrative unit)*, domain *(sphere of influence)*, locality, location, parcel, province, realm, scope, seat, section *(vicinity)*, sphere, territory, vicinity, zone. SEE MAIN ENTRY

regional local, native *(domestic)*, parochial, provincial. SEE MAIN ENTRY

register account *(evaluation)*, book, calendar *(list of cases)*, calendar *(record of yearly periods)*, date, digest *(comprehend)*, docket, document, empanel, enroll, enter *(record)*, file, file *(place among official records)*, form *(document)*, impanel, inscribe, inventory, itemize, join *(associate oneself with)*, journal, ledger, marginalia, notary public, notation, poll *(canvass)*, poll, program, record *(noun)*, record *(verb)*, roll, set down, subscribe *(promise)*, survey *(poll)*, tabulate. SEE MAIN ENTRY

register of cases calendar *(list of cases)*

register one's vote cast *(register)*

registered person member *(individual in a group)*

registerer notary public

registering census

registrar accountant, clerk, comptroller, notary public

registration census, entry *(record)*, poll *(canvass)*, reservation *(engagement)*, subscription. SEE MAIN ENTRY

registration book register

registry docket, file, form *(document)*, ledger, registration, roll

règlement act *(enactment)*

reglement bylaw

regnancy government *(administration)*

regnant dominant, master, paramount, powerful, predominant

régnant prevailing *(having superior force)*

regnant rife, sovereign *(absolute)*

regnare rule *(govern)*

regradation reclassification

regrade retreat

regrater broker

regress decline, deteriorate, escheat, recidivate, relapse *(noun)*, relapse *(verb)*, reversion *(act of returning)*, revert. SEE MAIN ENTRY

regression decline, lapse *(expiration)*, recidivism, recrudescence, relapse, reversion *(act of returning)*

regressive decadent. SEE MAIN ENTRY

regret deplore, dissatisfaction, refuse, remorse, repent. SEE MAIN ENTRY

regret profoundly deplore

regretful contrite, penitent, remorseful, repentant

regretfulness remorse

regrets refusal

regrettable deplorable, lamentable. SEE MAIN ENTRY

regretted regrettable

regretting contrite, repentant

regroup redistribute

regrouping reclassification

regula canon, law, maxim, principle *(axiom)*, rule *(guide)*, standard

regular accustomed *(customary)*, chronic, consistent, constant, continual *(connected)*, conventional, customary, daily, familiar *(customary)*, general, habitual, household *(familiar)*, mundane, natural, ordinary, periodic, prevailing *(current)*, prevalent, punctual, repeated, routine, systematic, traditional, typical, uniform, usual. SEE MAIN ENTRY

regular arrangement method

regular employment pursuit *(occupation)*

regular performance norm

regular procedure matter of course

regular proceeding process *(course)*

regular recurrence regularity

regular return cycle, regularity

regularity arrangement *(ordering)*, array *(order)*, constant, form *(arrangement)*, frequency, method, organization *(structure)*, system, uniformity. SEE MAIN ENTRY

regularity of action method

regularity of recurrence cycle, frequency

regularize adapt, codify, coordinate, modify *(alter)*, naturalize *(acclimate)*, regulate *(adjust)*

regularly as a rule, generally, invariably

regularness regularity

regulate administer *(conduct)*, arbitrate *(conciliate)*, arrange *(methodize)*, attune, check *(inspect)*, conduct, determine, direct *(supervise)*, discipline *(control)*, file *(arrange)*, fix *(arrange)*, govern, handle *(manage)*, manage, manipulate *(utilize skillfully)*, marshal, mitigate, moderate *(preside over)*, modify *(moderate)*, officiate, operate, orchestrate, organize *(arrange)*, oversee, palliate *(abate)*, police, preclude, prescribe, preside, prohibit, qualify *(condition)*, rule *(govern)*, superintend. SEE MAIN ENTRY

regulated periodic, regular *(orderly)*, safe, systematic

regulated by conditional, dependent

regulating adjustment, leading *(guiding)*

regulation act *(enactment)*, administration, boiler plate, bureaucracy, bylaw, canon, check *(bar)*, codification, condition *(contingent provision)*, constitution, control *(supervision)*, criterion, custody *(supervision)*, dictate, direction *(guidance)*, direction *(order)*, discipline *(training)*, disposition

(final arrangement), edict, enactment, familiar *(customary)*, fiat, government *(administration)*, instruction *(direction)*, law, management *(supervision)*, mandate, measure, moderation, ordinance, ordinary, precept, prescription *(directive)*, principle *(axiom)*, quota, requirement, restriction, rubric *(authoritative rule)*, rule *(legal dictate)*, statute, supervision, supremacy, writ. SEE MAIN ENTRY

regulation by a system classification

regulation by law code, edict

regulation by statute code, edict, legalization

regulation of finances economy *(economic system)*

regulations code, legislation *(enactments)*, mode, protocol *(etiquette)*. SEE MAIN ENTRY

regulative administrative

regulatory civic, disciplinary *(punitory)*

rehabilitate cure, fix *(repair)*, meliorate, reconstruct, recreate, rectify, reform, reinstate, renew *(refurbish)*, renovate, repair, restore *(renew)*. SEE MAIN ENTRY

rehabilitated renascent

rehabilitation correction *(change)*, improvement, progress, reconversion, remedy *(legal means of redress)*, rendition *(restoration)*, renewal, reorganization, repair, reparation *(keeping in repair)*. SEE MAIN ENTRY

rehash copy, repeat *(state again)*, restatement

rehear appeal, reconsider

rehearing appeal. SEE MAIN ENTRY

rehearsal discipline *(training)*, preparation

rehearse practice *(train by repetition)*, recite, review

rehearsed repeated

rehire reinstate

rei adiacere abut

rei adversari militate

rei deditus addicted

rei obstare militate

reicere rebuff, reject, repudiate

reidentification remembrance *(recollection)*

reidentify recognize *(perceive)*, remember

reiectio rejection, renunciation

reify substantiate

reign dominion *(supreme authority)*, govern, government *(administration)*, hegemony, influence, jurisdiction, power, predominance, predominate *(command)*, preside, prevail *(triumph)*, regime, rule *(govern)*, term *(duration)*. SEE MAIN ENTRY

reign of terror lynch law, oppression

reign over dominate, handle *(manage)*

reigning influential, master, paramount, powerful, predominant, rife, sovereign *(absolute)*

reimburse bear the expense, compensate *(remunerate)*, contribute *(indemnify)*, defray, disburse *(pay out)*, indemnify, pay, quit *(repay)*, rebate, reciprocate, refund, remunerate, repay, replace, restore *(return)*, return *(refund)*, satisfy *(discharge)*. SEE MAIN ENTRY

reimbursement collection *(payment)*, commission *(fee)*, compensation, consideration *(recompense)*, contribution *(indemnification)*, damages, disbursement *(funds paid out)*, discharge *(payment)*, honorarium, indemnification, indemnity, pay, payment (act of paying), payment (remittance), rebate, receipt (voucher), recompense, refund, remittance, remuneration, reparation (indemnification), restitution, satisfaction (discharge of debt). SEE MAIN ENTRY

reimbursing compensatory

reimprison rearrest

rein constraint (restriction), damper (stopper), disadvantage, fetter, hamper, oversee, subdue

rein in constrict (inhibit), detain (restrain), discipline (control), inhibit, repress, stem (check), withhold

reinaugurate reinstate

reincarcerate remand

reincarnate resurrect

reincarnation revival

reindoctrination rehabilitation

reinfection recrudescence

reinforce accumulate (enlarge), aid, assist, bear (support), bear (yield), compound, corroborate, develop, enhance, heighten (augment), help, preserve, side, supplement, support (assist), support (corroborate), sustain (confirm), sustain (prolong). SEE MAIN ENTRY

reinforced strong

reinforcement aid (help), assistance, augmentation, boom (increase), help, mainstay, relief (aid). SEE MAIN ENTRY

reinless lawless, uncurbed

reinquire reexamine

reinquiry rehearing, review (official reexamination)

reins bondage

reins of government bureaucracy

reinstall reassign, reinstate, renew (begin again), replace, restore (return)

reinstate continue (resume), proceed (continue), reclaim, remit (release from penalty), renew (begin again), replace, restore (return), surrender (give back). SEE MAIN ENTRY

reinstatement continuation (resumption), rehabilitation, renewal, replacement, restitution

reinstitute continue (resume), renew (begin again), reopen, repeat (do again)

reinstitution continuation (resumption)

reinstitutionalize remand

reinsurance coverage (insurance)

reinsure certify (attest)

reintegrate reconstitute, rehabilitate, renew (refurbish)

reintroduce renew (begin again)

reinvest refinance, reinstate

reinvest with restore (return)

reinvestigate reexamine

reinvigorate fix (repair), meliorate, recruit, rehabilitate, reinforce, remedy, renew (refurbish), renovate, restore (renew)

reinvigoration rehabilitation, renewal

reipublicae forma organization (association), polity

reissue circulate, copy, redistribute, renewal

reiterant iterative, repetitious

reiterate copy, dwell (linger over), quote, reaffirm, recapitulate, recite, recount, repeat (state again), review. SEE MAIN ENTRY

reiterated repeated

reiteration narration, platitude, recital, redundancy, restatement. SEE MAIN ENTRY

reiterative frequent, incessant, insistent, repetitious

reive hold up (rob)

rejail rearrest

reject abrogate (annul), bar (exclude), censor, challenge, condemn (ban), contemn, decry, defect, demonstrate (protest), demur, deny (refuse to grant), deprecate, differ (disagree), disaccord, disaffirm, disallow, disavow, disbelieve, discard, disclaim, discriminate (treat differently), disdain, disfavor, dismiss (put out of consideration), disobey, disoblige, disown (deny the validity), disqualify, dissent (withhold assent), eliminate (exclude), eschew, exclude, expel, fight (counteract), forgo, forswear, gainsay, ignore, oppose, outlaw, overrule, prohibit, proscribe (denounce), rebuff, refuse, relegate, relinquish, remove (eliminate), renounce, repudiate, repulse, resign, select, set aside (annul), spurn, waive. SEE MAIN ENTRY

reject as erroneous deny (contradict)

reject as inadmissable disapprove (reject)

reject as untrue disbelieve

reject by subsequent action overrule

reject by subsequent decision overrule

rejected derelict (abandoned), disreputable, inadmissible, ineligible, obsolete, outdated, outmoded, poor (inferior in quality), undesirable, unsatisfactory

rejecting disqualification (rejection), negative

rejection abandonment (repudiation), abjuration, bar (obstruction), boycott, breach, check (bar), criticism, declination, denial, disapprobation, disapproval, disclaimer, disdain, dishonor (nonpayment), dismissal (termination of a proceeding), disparagement, disqualification (rejection), exception (objection), exclusion, expulsion, impugnation, intolerance, layoff, negation, nonconformity, objection, ostracism, prohibition, proscription, rebuff, refusal, removal, renunciation, repudiation, reversal, veto. SEE MAIN ENTRY

rejective reluctant

rejoice in relish

rejoicing enjoyment (pleasure)

rejoin acknowledge (respond), answer (reply), answer (respond legally), countercharge, meet, rebut, reply, respond, retort, return (respond). SEE MAIN ENTRY

rejoinder answer (judicial response), answer (reply), confutation, contradiction, counterargument, counterclaim, reaction (response), reply, response. SEE MAIN ENTRY

rejoining responsive

rejudge reassess, reconsider

rejuvenate cure, fix (repair), recreate, renew (refurbish), renovate, repair, restore (renew), resurrect

rejuvenated renascent

rejuvenation renewal, reparation (keeping in repair), resurgence, revival

rejuvenescence revival

rekindle renew (refurbish), resurrect

relabi relapse

relapse crossroad (turning point), decline, escheat, lapse (expiration), recidivate, recidivism, recrudescence, regress, renewal, repeat (do again), return (go back), reversion (act of returning). SEE MAIN ENTRY

relapsing regressive

relate admit (concede), allege, allude, appertain, apply (pertain), assert, communicate, compare, connect (relate), contact (communicate), converse, convey (communicate), correspond (be equivalent), correspond (communicate), delineate, depict, depose (testify), detail (particularize), disabuse, divulge, impart, inform (notify), involve (implicate), involve (participate), notify, pertain, phrase, recapitulate, recite, recount, refer (direct attention), remark, repeat (state again). SEE MAIN ENTRY

relate ideas converse

relate to affiliate, concern (involve)

related affiliated, akin (germane), allied, analogous, associated, coadunate, cognate, collateral (accompanying), comparable (capable of comparison), consanguineous, consonant, correlative, germane, interrelated, pertinent, relative (relevant), relevant, similar, tangential. SEE MAIN ENTRY

related by affinity next of kin

related to incident

relatedness association (connection), chain (nexus), connection (relation), degree (kinship)

relater informer (a person who provides information)

relating akin (germane), germane, pertinent, reference (citation), relative (relevant)

relating to apposite, cognate, comparative, correlative, incident

relating to a penalty penal

relating to a will testate

relating to accounts fiscal

relating to method procedural

relating to money matters fiscal

relating to moral action ethical

relating to one side only ex parte

relating to the family domestic (household)

relating to the home domestic (household)

relating to the management of revenue fiscal

relating to the mechanics of a lawsuit procedural

relating to traffic industrial

relatio report (detailed account)

relation affiliation (bloodline), affiliation (connectedness), affinity (family ties), analogy, association (connection), attribution, chain (nexus), collation, contact (association), correlate, delineation, disclosure (act of disclosing), kinship, mention (reference), narration, nexus, privity, proportion, recital, relationship (connection), relationship (family ties), relative, relevance, report (detailed account), representation (statement), story (narrative). SEE MAIN ENTRY

relation by birth kindred

relation by blood affinity (family ties), kindred, next of kin

relation by consanguinity kindred

relational comparative, pertinent, relative (relevant)

relations blood, dealings, kindred, next of kin

relationship affiliation (bloodline), affiliation (connectedness), affinity (family ties), association (connection), chain (nexus), connection (relation), contact (association), filiation, kinship, nexus, privity, propinquity (kinship), proportion, rapport, relation (connection), relation (kinship), relevance. SEE MAIN ENTRY

relationship between persons degree (kinship)

relative apposite, cognate, commensurable, commensurate, comparative, consanguineous, correlative, germane, proportionate, related, relation (kinship), relevant. SEE MAIN ENTRY

relative estimate comparison, proportion
relative estimation comparison
relative position aspect, degree *(station)*, relation *(connection)*
relative quantity differential
relative to incident
relative to the manner of proceeding procedural
relativeness analogy
relatives kindred, next of kin
relativity analogy, chain *(nexus)*, proportion
relator complainant, informant
relax ease, impair, lull, mollify, recess, relent, relieve *(free from burden)*, repose *(rest)*, rest *(cease from action)*, soothe, subside. SEE MAIN ENTRY
relax severity commute
relaxation enjoyment *(pleasure)*, informality, leave *(absence)*, mitigation, mollification, pause, remission, respite *(interval of rest)*
relaxation of control freedom
relaxation of law dispensation *(exception)*. SEE MAIN ENTRY
relaxed informal
relay deliver, disseminate, pass *(advance)*, send
relay ideas converse
release absolution, acquit, acquittal, amnesty, assign *(transfer ownership)*, authorize, bestow, catharsis, cede, cession, clear, clemency, composition *(agreement in bankruptcy)*, condone, deed, disband, discharge *(liberation)*, discharge *(dismiss)*, discharge *(liberate)*, disencumber, disengage, disentangle, disenthrall, dismiss *(discharge)*, dispel, disposition *(transfer of property)*, dissociate, emancipation, enable, enfranchise, excuse, exemption, exoneration, extricate, exude, free, freedom, immunity, issuance, issue *(publish)*, layoff, let *(permit)*, liberate, liberation, notice *(announcement)*, notification, palliate *(excuse)*, pardon *(noun)*, pardon *(verb)*, parole *(noun)*, parole *(verb)*, privilege, probation, proclaim, publication *(disclosure)*, publicity, quit *(free of)*, receipt *(proof of receiving)*, redeem *(repurchase)*, redemption, relieve *(free from burden)*, relinquish, remise, remission, remit *(release from penalty)*, report *(detailed account)*, rescue, respite *(reprieve)*, settlement, terminate, vindicate, waiver. SEE MAIN ENTRY
release conditionally parole
release from an obligation exonerate
release from attachment disengage
release from bondage disenthrall
release from charge immunity
release from custody discharge *(liberation)*, emancipation, liberate
release from debt satisfaction *(discharge of debt)*
release from duty immunity
release from employment dismissal *(discharge)*
release from imprisonment parole
release from imputation absolve
release from liability exemption, exonerate
release from matrimonial status divorce
release from matrimony divorce
release from obligation dispensation *(exception)*, excuse, exemption, palliate *(excuse)*
release from penalty pardon
release from pressure ease

release from prison parole SEE MAIN ENTRY
release from punishment absolution, pardon *(noun)*, pardon *(verb)*
release from restraint disenthrall, extricate, free
release from wedlock divorce
released clear *(free from criminal charges)*, exempt, free *(relieved from a burden)*, immune, public *(known)*, unbound
released convict probationer *(released offender)*
released criminal probationer *(released offender)*
released felon probationer *(released offender)*
released lawbreaker probationer *(released offender)*
released malefactor probationer *(released offender)*
released prisoner probationer *(released offender)*
released transgressor probationer *(released offender)*
released wrongdoer probationer *(released offender)*
releasing from custody liberation
releasor licensor
relegate assign *(transfer ownership)*, bar *(exclude)*, delegate, detail *(assign)*, dislodge, remand, remit *(submit for consideration)*, seclude, set aside *(annul)*. SEE MAIN ENTRY
relegate to commit *(entrust)*
relegatio banishment
relegation assignment *(transfer of ownership)*, proscription, rejection, removal
relent comply, condone, relax, submit *(yield)*, succumb, surrender *(yield)*, yield *(submit)*. SEE MAIN ENTRY
relentless callous, close *(rigorous)*, cold-blooded, cruel, dictatorial, diligent, draconian, faithful *(diligent)*, immutable, implacable, inexorable, inflexible, ironclad, malicious, obdurate, patient, persistent, pertinacious, recalcitrant, remorseless, resolute, rigid, ruthless, sedulous, serious *(devoted)*, severe, stable, steadfast, unalterable, unbending, uncompromising, unrelenting, unyielding. SEE MAIN ENTRY
relentlessness cruelty, diligence *(perseverance)*, rigor, severity
relet sublet
relevance connection *(relation)*, consequence *(significance)*, importance, interest *(concern)*, materiality *(consequence)*, propriety *(appropriateness)*, qualification *(fitness)*, relation *(connection)*, relationship *(connection)*, significance. SEE MAIN ENTRY
relevancy relationship *(connection)*. SEE MAIN ENTRY
relevant akin *(germane)*, applicable, apposite, appropriate, congruous, correlative, felicitous, fit, fitting, germane, important *(significant)*, interrelated, material *(important)*, pertinent, proper, related, suitable, valuable. SEE MAIN ENTRY
relevant fact evidence
relevant instance illustration
relevant material evidence
relevant to all general
relevy reassess
reliability adhesion *(loyalty)*, candor *(straightforwardness)*, certainty, certification *(certainness)*, constant, credibility, honor *(good reputation)*, loyalty, trustworthiness. SEE MAIN ENTRY
reliable accurate, authentic, believable,

bona fide, candid, certain *(fixed)*, certain *(positive)*, cogent, conscientious, constant, convincing, credible, definite, dependable, diligent, factual, faithful *(loyal)*, fiduciary, honest, incorruptible, indestructible, infallible, loyal, meritorious, official, positive *(incontestable)*, reputable, safe, scrupulous, secure *(sound)*, solid *(sound)*, stable, staunch, steadfast, strong, tenable, true *(authentic)*, true *(loyal)*. SEE MAIN ENTRY
reliableness certification *(certainness)*
reliably faithfully
reliance confidence *(faith)*, credence, credit *(delayed payment)*, faith, mainstay, prospect *(outlook)*, security *(safety)*, trust *(confidence)*, weight *(credibility)*. SEE MAIN ENTRY
reliance on principle *(axiom)*, surety *(certainty)*
reliant dependent
relic holdover, reminder, token
relief abatement *(reduction)*, aid *(help)*, aid *(subsistence)*, benefit *(betterment)*, benevolence *(act of kindness)*, charity, contour *(outline)*, contour *(shape)*, cure, help, immunity, mitigation, mollification, panacea, reinforcement, remedial statute, remedy *(legal means of redress)*, remedy *(that which corrects)*, remission, reparation *(indemnification)*, replacement, service *(assistance)*, solace, substitute, support *(assistance)*. SEE MAIN ENTRY
relief from exoneration
relieve abate *(lessen)*, aid, allay, alleviate, assist, assuage, commute, cure, demote, diminish, discharge *(dismiss)*, discharge *(liberate)*, discharge *(release from obligation)*, disencumber, disentangle, divest, ease, excuse, exonerate, extricate, free, help, meliorate, mitigate, mollify, pacify, palliate *(abate)*, redress, release, remedy. SEE MAIN ENTRY
relieve from accusation exonerate
relieve of dispossess
relieve of blame exonerate
relieve of burden vindicate
relieve of complication disentangle
relieve of liability exonerate
relieve of obligation disengage
relieve of responsibility discharge *(release from obligation)*
relieve of something detrimental cure
relieve pressure soothe
relieved free *(relieved from a burden)*, prominent
relieved from liability exempt
reliever backer
relieving curative, mitigating, palliative *(abating)*
religiosus conscientious, scrupulous
religious sacrosanct, solemn
religious order denomination, society
religiously faithfully
relinquish bestow
relinquere leave *(give)*, relinquish
relinquish annul, attorn, cease, cede, confer *(give)*, contribute *(supply)*, convey *(transfer)*, demit, disavow, discontinue *(abandon)*, disown *(refuse to acknowledge)*, forfeit, forgo, forswear, lapse *(cease)*, leave *(allow to remain)*, quit *(discontinue)*, release, remise, remit *(relax)*, renounce, resign, retire *(conclude a career)*, secede, set aside *(annul)*, surrender *(give back)*, vacate *(leave)*, vacate *(void)*, waive, withdraw, yield *(submit)*. SEE MAIN ENTRY
relinquish life die, perish

951

relinquished derelict (abandoned)

relinquishing claim to cession

relinquishment abandonment (desertion), abandonment (discontinuance), abdication, cancellation, capitulation, cession, concession (compromise), denial, dereliction, desuetude, disclaimer, disposition (transfer of property), expense (sacrifice), pardon, release, remission, renunciation, waiver SEE MAIN ENTRY

relinquishment by gift disposition (transfer of property)

reliquum remainder (remaining part)

reliquus balance (amount in excess)

relish enjoyment (pleasure), penchant, propensity. SEE MAIN ENTRY

relishable palatable, preferable, sapid

relive recall (remember), recollect, remember

reload replenish

relocate remove (transfer). SEE MAIN ENTRY

reluct contend (dispute), demonstrate (protest), fight (battle), oppugn, parry

reluctance disincentive, doubt (indecision), hesitation, misgiving, resistance, scruple. SEE MAIN ENTRY

reluctance to believe cloud (suspicion), doubt (suspicion), incredulity

reluctant averse, disinclined, disobedient, hesitant, renitent, restive. SEE MAIN ENTRY

reluctant to punish placable

reluctantly unwillingly

reluctate oppugn, parry, resist (oppose)

relume burn

rely SEE MAIN ENTRY

rely on confide (trust), rely, trust

rely on fortune bet

rely upon confide (trust)

relying on based on

relying upon subject (conditional)

rem administrare administer (conduct)

rem amittere forfeit

rem attingere abut

rem bene succeed (attain)

rem concedere waive

rem dissimulare connive, disguise

rem faciliorem reddere facilitate

rem hereditate accipere inherit

rem hominem flagitare importune

rem homini adsignare assign (allot)

rem integram relinquere abeyance

rem invenire detect

rem longius prosequi dwell (linger over)

rem praestare vouch

rem pro re pacisci barter

rem re mutare barter

rem relinquere abandon (withdraw)

rem sibi adrogare assume (seize)

rem simulare appearance (look)

rem tempore tribuere date

rem tempori adsignare date

rem testari attest

remade renascent

remail redirect

remain cease, dwell (reside), endure (last), exist, halt, inhabit, keep (continue), last, lodge (reside), persevere, persist, reside, resist (withstand), stay (continue), stay (rest), subsist. SEE MAIN ENTRY

remain alive endure (last), exist, subsist

remain firm determine, hold out (resist)

remain hidden elude

remain unchanged persist

remain unconverted disbelieve

remain undiscovered elude

remain valid endure (last)

remainder balance (amount in excess), complement, discard, dower, holdover, overage, residual, surplus. SEE MAIN ENTRY

remainder over reversion (remainder of an estate)

remaining durable, habitation (act of inhabiting), lasting, live (existing), net, permanent, persistent, residuary, superfluous

remaining course alternative (option)

remaining courses choice (alternatives offered)

remaining options choice (alternatives offered)

remaining period unexpired term

remaining portion balance (amount in excess), holdover, remainder (remaining part)

remaining time unexpired term

remains balance (amount in excess), corpse, remainder (remaining part), residual, salvage

remake change, convert (change use), copy, fix (repair), reconstitute, reconstruct, recreate, reform, rehabilitate, renew (refurbish), renovate, repeat (do again), reproduce, restore (renew), transform

remaking reform, rehabilitation, reorganization

remand bondage, confine, constraint (imprisonment), detain (hold in custody), recommit, relegate, remit (submit for consideration). SEE MAIN ENTRY

remand to custody commit (institutionalize)

remanded arrested (apprehended)

remanded into custody arrested (apprehended)

remanding to custody commitment (confinement)

remanent superfluous

remanere remain (stay)

remark acknowledge (respond), comment (noun), comment (verb), convey (communicate), dictum, disclosure (something disclosed), express, expression (comment), mention (reference), muse, observation, phrase, pronouncement, speak, statement. SEE MAIN ENTRY

remark on mention

remark upon comment

remarkable considerable, conspicuous, egregious, extraordinary, famous, illustrious, important (significant), major, material (important), meritorious, momentous, nonconforming, notable, noteworthy, outstanding (prominent), paramount, peculiar (curious), perceivable, portentous (eliciting amazement), prime (most valuable), prodigious (amazing), prominent, renowned, salient, singular, special, unaccustomed, uncanny, uncommon, unusual. SEE MAIN ENTRY

remarkably particularly

remarriage digamy

remeasure reapportion, reassess

remediable corrigible

remediable by an action at law actionable

remedial curative, medicinal, progressive (advocating change), salubrious, salutary. SEE MAIN ENTRY

remedial justice equity (justice)

remedial measure remedial statute, remedy (legal means of redress), remedy (that which corrects)

remedial statute SEE MAIN ENTRY

remediless inoperable (incurable), irredeemable, irremediable, irreparable, irreversible, irrevocable

remedium relief (release), remedy (that which corrects), remedy

remedy adjust (resolve), alleviate, amend, amendment (correction), assuage, correction (change), cure (noun), cure (verb), disabuse, drug, emend, fix (repair), habeas corpus, help (noun), help (verb), panacea, recourse, rectify, redress, reform, regulate (adjust), relief (legal redress), relieve (give aid), remedial statute, repair (noun), repair (verb), reparation (indemnification), reparation (keeping in repair), restore (renew). SEE MAIN ENTRY

remember occur (come to mind), recognize (perceive), recollect, retain (keep in possession), review. SEE MAIN ENTRY

remember with sorrow repent

rememberable notable

remembrance contribution (donation), hindsight, impression, memory (commemoration), monument, recognition, recollection, reminder, retrospect, reward, token. SEE MAIN ENTRY

rememoration retrospect

remind advise, notify, prompt. SEE MAIN ENTRY

remind oneself remember

reminder admonition, monument, note (brief comment), notice (announcement), suggestion. SEE MAIN ENTRY

remindful suggestive (evocative)

reminisce recall (remember), recollect, remember

reminiscence recollection, remembrance (recollection), retrospect

reminiscent suggestive (evocative)

reminiscential suggestive (evocative)

reminisci recollect, remember

remise alienate (transfer title), cede, pass (advance). SEE MAIN ENTRY

remiss careless, delinquent (guilty of a misdeed), delinquent (overdue), derelict (negligent), dilatory, disobedient, improvident, lax, negligent, oblivious, overdue, perfunctory, slipshod, thoughtless, truant. SEE MAIN ENTRY

remissio abatement (extinguishment), abatement (reduction), remission

remission absolution, acquittal, cessation (interlude), collection (payment), diminution, discontinuance (act of discontinuing), exoneration, halt, lull, pause, relief (release). SEE MAIN ENTRY

remission of guilt pardon

remissness culpability, dereliction, disregard (omission), laches, laxity, neglect, negligence, omission, oversight (carelessness)

remissus languid, lax, negligent

remit absolve, acquit, alleviate, bear (yield), bear the expense, bequeath, bestow, compensate (remunerate), condone, contribute (indemnify), contribute (supply), defray, delay, deliver, diminish, discontinue (break continuity), dispatch (send off), excuse, free, give (grant), lessen, lull, offer (tender), present (make a gift), recommit, reimburse, reinstate, relax, release, relent, remand, remise, remunerate, restore (return), satisfy (discharge), subside, suspend, transmit. SEE MAIN ENTRY

remit a penalty exonerate

remit the penalty palliate (excuse)

remit to custody commit (institutionalize)

remittal recovery (award)

remittance amortization, benefit (conferment), collection (payment), consideration (recompense), delivery, disbursement (funds paid out), discharge (payment), expenditure, expense (cost), installment, pay, payment (act of paying), payment (remittance), pension, transmittal. SEE MAIN ENTRY

remittance for delay   demurrage
remitted   clear (free from criminal charges)
remittent   intermittent, periodic, sporadic
remitter   restitution
remittere   abate (lessen), remand, remit (relax)
remitting   compensatory
remitting to custody   commitment (confinement)
remnant   balance (amount in excess), discard, end (termination), overage
remodel   convert (change use), emend, modify (alter), reconstitute, reconstruct, recreate, reform, renew (refurbish), renovate, restore (renew), transform
remodeling   development (progression), rehabilitation, reorganization, repair
remold   convert (change use), modify (alter), reconstitute, reconstruct, revise, transform
remolded   tempered
remonstrance   admonition, blame (culpability), complaint, criticism, diatribe, disapprobation, disapproval, discredit, dispute, dissension, exception (objection), objection, opposition, protest, reply, reprimand. SEE MAIN ENTRY
remonstrant   remonstrative
remonstrate   admonish (warn), argue, blame, castigate, caution, censure, challenge, complain (criticize), demonstrate (protest), denounce (condemn), deter, disaccord, disagree, disapprove (condemn), discourage, dissuade, expostulate, fault, oppose, oppugn, protest, reason (persuade), reprimand. SEE MAIN ENTRY
remonstrate against   decry
remonstrate with   rebuke
remonstration   disapprobation, disapproval, dispute, opposition, protest
remonstrative   hortative. SEE MAIN ENTRY
remora   handicap, obstacle, obstruction. SEE MAIN ENTRY
remorseful   contrite, penitent, repentant. SEE MAIN ENTRY
remorseful person   penitent
remorsefulness   remorse
remorseless   brutal, callous, cold-blooded, cruel, incorrigible, obdurate, relentless, ruthless, sinister, unaffected (uninfluenced), unrelenting. SEE MAIN ENTRY
remorselessness   cruelty
remote   foreign, immaterial, impertinent (irrelevant), inaccessible, inapposite, inappropriate, inconsequential, irrelevant, private (secluded), remote (secluded), solitary, unapproachable. SEE MAIN ENTRY
remote cause   SEE MAIN ENTRY
remote district   frontier
remotion   removal
remotus   remote (not proximate)
removable   deductible (capable of being deducted from taxes), defeasible, moving (in motion)
removal   absence (nonattendance), avoidance (cancellation), banishment, deduction (diminution), defeasance, deportation, discharge (dismissal), distress (seizure), eviction, evulsion, exception (exclusion), exclusion, expropriation (divestiture), expulsion, flight, foreclosure, homicide,

layoff, leave (absence), loss, obviation, ouster, rejection, replacement. SEE MAIN ENTRY
removal from a job   dismissal (discharge)
removal from a position   dismissal (discharge)
removal from employment   discharge (dismissal)
removal from office   dismissal (discharge)
removal of a cause out of court   dismissal (termination of a proceeding)
removal of discrimination   integration (assimilation)
removal of errors   correction (change), revision (process of correcting)
remove   abscond, abstract (separate), adeem, bowdlerize, cancel, carry away, debar, deduct (reduce), delete, deport (banish), detach, discharge (dismiss), discharge (release from obligation), disencumber, disinter, dislocate, dislodge, dismiss (discharge), dispel, dispossess, dissociate, divest, eject (evict), eject (expel), eliminate (eradicate), eliminate (exclude), eradicate, evacuate, evict, except (exclude), excise (cut away), exclude, expel, expunge, extirpate, extract, hold up (rob), impound, move (alter position), obliterate, oust, overthrow, part (leave), reject, relegate, rescind, retire (retreat), retrench, revoke, seclude, sequester (seclude), succeed (follow), superannuate, supersede, supplant, suspend, transfer, transport, vacate (leave), withdraw. SEE MAIN ENTRY
remove a disability   enable
remove a hindrance   disencumber
remove a restraint   disencumber
remove all sign of   expunge
remove all trace of   expunge
remove an essential part   eviscerate
remove an impediment   disencumber
remove bodily   carry away
remove doubt   ascertain, reassure
remove errors   edit, emend
remove falsehood   disabuse
remove faults   amend
remove fear   reassure
remove from   abandon (physically leave)
remove from legal office   disbar
remove from life   dispatch (put to death)
remove from office   demote, discharge (dismiss), dismiss (discharge), oust
remove from premises   eject (evict)
remove from private ownership   nationalize
remove from the practice of law   disbar
remove from the roll of attorneys   disbar
remove misunderstanding   resolve (solve)
remove one's anxieties   lull
remove one's fears   lull
remove oneself   flee, quit (evacuate), retreat, secede
remove pollutants   decontaminate
remove suspicion   disarm (set at ease)
remove the errors   fix (repair)
remove the obstacles   permit
remove the traces   obliterate
remove unhealthy agents   decontaminate
remove utterly   eradicate
removed   alone (solitary), apart, discrete, distinct (distinguished from others), inaccessible, insular, insusceptible (uncaring), irrelative, obscure (remote), private (secluded), remote (not proximate), remote (secluded), separate, solitary, unapproachable
removed from bondage   free (enjoying civil liberty), sovereign (independent)

removere   remove (transfer), seclude
rempublicam gubernare   administer (conduct)
remunerari   compensate (remunerate), remunerate
remunerate   bear the expense, contribute (indemnify), defray, disburse (pay out), indemnify, pay, quit (repay), recoup (reimburse), reimburse, remit (send payment), repay, satisfy (discharge). SEE MAIN ENTRY
remunerate for injury   compensate (remunerate)
remuneratio   recompense, remuneration
remuneration   advance (allowance), alimony, annuity, boom (prosperity), brokerage, collection (payment), commission (fee), compensation, consideration (recompense), contribution (indemnification), disbursement (funds paid out), earnings, fee (charge), honorarium, income, indemnification, indemnity, out of pocket, pay, payment (remittance), payroll, pension, perquisite, profit, recompense, recovery (award), reimbursement, remittance, rent, requital, restitution, retainer, revenue, reward, satisfaction (discharge of debt), wage. SEE MAIN ENTRY
remuneration for injury   compensation
remuneration for injury suffered   damages
remunerative   beneficial, compensatory, gainful, lucrative, productive, profitable, valuable. SEE MAIN ENTRY
remunerator   insurer
renaissance   reconversion, renewal, resurgence, revival
renascence   renewal, resurgence, revival
renascent   SEE MAIN ENTRY
rencounter   conflict, confrontation (act of setting face to face), confrontation (altercation), fight (battle), struggle
rend   break (fracture), destroy (efface), dichotomize, disjoint, disperse (scatter), force (break), lancinate, luxate, separate, sever, split. SEE MAIN ENTRY
rend asunder   disrupt, sever
render   administer (tender), allocate, avail (bring about), bear (yield), bear the expense, bequeath, bestow, cede, construe (translate), contribute (supply), define, discharge (perform), dispense, offer (tender), pay, present (make a gift), proffer, rebate, recite, recount, remit (send payment), satisfy (discharge), supply, tender, transact, yield (produce a return). SEE MAIN ENTRY
render a decision   pass (determine)
render a document imperfect   mutilate
render a judgment   pass (determine). SEE MAIN ENTRY
render a service   accommodate, function
render a service to   promote (organize)
render a task easier   facilitate
render accordant   adapt, attune, comport (agree with), conform, regulate (adjust)
render an account   convey (communicate), depict
render an account of   speak
render an attorney's license null and void   disbar
render assistance   enable, facilitate, help, relieve (give aid), subsidize
render averse   deter, disaffect, discourage, dissuade
render better   emend, meliorate, nurture, repair
render broad   expand
render central   focus
render certain   ascertain, assure (give confidence to), assure (insure)

render chaotic   degenerate
render clear   explicate
render compatible   arbitrate *(conciliate)*
render competent   empower, enable
render complete   conclude *(complete)*, consummate
render concordant   arbitrate *(conciliate)*, reconcile
render deathless   perpetuate
render defective   vitiate
render definite   ascertain
render different   convert *(change use)*, transform
render difficult   encumber *(hinder)*, hinder
render dim   blind *(obscure)*
render evil   brutalize, pervert
render eyeless   blind *(deprive of sight)*
render feeble   impair
render few   deduct *(reduce)*, diminish
render filthy   pollute
render flustered   embarrass
render free   clear, discharge *(liberate)*, disenthrall, quit *(free of)*
render harmless   decontaminate, disarm *(divest of arms)*
render help   aid, contribute *(assist)*, serve *(assist)*
render helpless   disable
render honor to   dedicate
render humble   humiliate
render ill at ease   embarrass
render illegible   deface, expunge, obliterate
render impassable   stop
render imperceptible   obliterate
render imperfect   mutilate
render impossible   forbid. SEE MAIN ENTRY
render impotent   disable, disqualify
render impure   taint *(contaminate)*
render in a better form   modify *(alter)*
render incompetent   disable
render ineffective   destroy *(void)*
render inefficacious   vitiate
render inert   dissolve *(terminate)*, neutralize
render inimical   antagonize
render innocuous   disarm *(divest of arms)*
render inoperative   neutralize, vacate *(void)*
render insufficient   deplete
render intelligible   clarify, comment, construe *(translate)*, solve
render invalid   cancel, frustrate, nullify, repeal, rescind
render invisible   blind *(obscure)*, cloak, conceal, enshroud, hide, plant *(covertly place)*, shroud
render judgment   adjudicate
render larger   expand
render less   decrease, discount *(minimize)*, minimize
render less difficult   commute, ease, facilitate
render less excusable   aggravate *(exacerbate)*
render less painful   soothe
render less tolerable   aggravate *(exacerbate)*
render lip service   palter
render manifest   exemplify
render more compact   condense
render necessary   call *(demand)*, necessitate
render neutral   neutralize
render no longer opposed   arbitrate *(conciliate)*
render null   extirpate, perish
render null and void   abolish, adeem, annul, disown *(deny the validity)*, frustrate, negate. SEE MAIN ENTRY

render payment   disburse *(pay out)*, expend *(disburse)*
render powerless   disable, disarm *(divest of arms)*, handcuff, stall
render precise   characterize, define
render putrid   decay
render safe   assure *(insure)*, hedge, police
render sanitary   decontaminate
render service   pander
render sightless   blind *(deprive of sight)*
render smaller   diminish
render solid   consolidate *(strengthen)*, fix *(make firm)*
render spurious   adulterate, fake
render sterile   decontaminate
render strong   nurture
render suspect   impugn
render threadlike   attenuate
render uncertain   blind *(obscure)*, confuse *(bewilder)*, disorganize, disorient, perplex
render unclean   infect, smear
render unfit   disable, disqualify
render up   abandon *(relinquish)*, restore *(return)*, surrender *(give back)*
render useful   capitalize *(seize the chance)*, inure *(benefit)*
render useless   cancel, eliminate *(eradicate)*
render vain   foil
render visionless   blind *(deprive of sight)*
render void   adeem, annul, cancel, discharge *(release from obligation)*
render weak   debilitate, dilute, disarm *(divest of arms)*
render worse   aggravate *(exacerbate)*, exacerbate
renderable   accountable *(explainable)*
rendered stable   fixed *(securely placed)*
rendering   delivery, design *(construction plan)*, explanation, paraphrase, rendition *(explication)*
rendering explicit   clarification
rendering incisive   clarification
rendering legal advice   representation *(acting for others)*
rendering legal assistance   representation *(acting for others)*
rendering unequivocal   clarification
rendering unmistakable   clarification
rendering void   avoidance *(cancellation)*
rendezvous   appointment *(meeting)*, meeting *(encounter)*, session. SEE MAIN ENTRY
rending   separation
rendition   delineation, explanation, narration, paraphrase, performance *(execution)*, recital. SEE MAIN ENTRY
renegade   fugitive, insurgent, malcontent, pariah, recreant
renege   abandon *(withdraw)*, annul, cancel, default, defect, deny *(refuse to grant)*, nullify, refuse, renounce, rescind, revoke, tergiversate, withdraw. SEE MAIN ENTRY
renew   amend, continue *(resume)*, cure, fix *(repair)*, meliorate, proceed *(continue)*, recollect, reconstitute, reconstruct, recreate, recur, reform, rehabilitate, relapse, remedy, renovate, reopen, repair, repeat *(do again)*, replenish, reproduce, resume, resurrect. SEE MAIN ENTRY
renew memories   remind
renewable   corrigible
renewal   continuation *(resumption)*, recrudescence, reform, rehabilitation, repair, reparation *(keeping in repair)*, replacement, resurgence, revival. SEE MAIN ENTRY
renewed   renascent, repeated
renitant   contumacious

renitence   reaction *(opposition)*, reluctance, resistance
renitency   conflict, reaction *(opposition)*, reluctance
renitent   adverse *(hostile)*, disinclined, disobedient, hostile, insusceptible *(uncaring)*, recalcitrant, reluctant, restive, rigid, unbending, unyielding. SEE MAIN ENTRY
renounce   abandon *(relinquish)*, abrogate *(annul)*, cede, decline *(reject)*, defect, demit, deny *(refuse to grant)*, disaffirm, disapprove *(reject)*, disavow, disclaim, discontinue *(abandon)*, disdain, disinherit, disown *(refuse to acknowledge)*, eliminate *(exclude)*, exclude, forbear, forfeit, forgo, forswear, leave *(allow to remain)*, negate, overrule, quit *(discontinue)*, rebel, rebuff, recant, refrain, refuse, reject, relinquish, repel *(drive back)*, repudiate, rescind, resign, revoke, set aside *(annul)*, spurn, surrender *(give back)*, tergiversate, waive, yield *(submit)*. SEE MAIN ENTRY
renounce citizenship   expatriate
renounce claim to   cede, forgo
renounce rights of citizenship   expatriate
renouncement   abandonment *(repudiation)*, abjuration, ademption, denial, desertion, disclaimer, rebuff, refusal, renunciation, repudiation, resignation *(relinquishment)*, reversal, revocation
renovare   continue *(resume)*, recreate, renew *(refurbish)*
renovate   convert *(change use)*, fix *(repair)*, meliorate, reconstitute, reconstruct, recreate, rectify, reform, rehabilitate, renew *(refurbish)*, restore *(renew)*, transform. SEE MAIN ENTRY
renovated   renascent
renovatio   renewal
renovation   correction *(change)*, development *(progression)*, reform, rehabilitation, renewal, repair, reparation *(keeping in repair)*, replacement
renovize   renovate
renown   character *(reputation)*, distinction *(reputation)*, eminence, notoriety, prestige, reputation
renowned   conspicuous, famous, household *(familiar)*, illustrious, influential, notable, noteworthy, notorious, outstanding *(prominent)*, prodigious *(amazing)*, prominent, public *(known)*, reputable. SEE MAIN ENTRY
rent   charge *(cost)*, lease, let *(lease)*, rift *(gap)*, schism, split, sublease, sublet. SEE MAIN ENTRY
rent out   lease, let *(lease)*, sublease, sublet
rent payer   lessee, lodger, tenant
rental   rent
rentee   lessee
renter   lessee, lodger, occupant, tenant
renting   tenancy
renueve   decline *(reject)*
renumeration   proceeds
renunciate   disallow
renunciation   abandonment *(repudiation)*, abdication, abjuration, ademption, cancellation, confutation, continence, declination, denial, desertion, disclaimer, disdain, expense *(sacrifice)*, rebuff, refusal, rejection, repudiation, rescision, resignation *(relinquishment)*, retraction, reversal, waiver. SEE MAIN ENTRY
renunciatory   ambulatory
renuntiare   report *(disclose)*, revoke
renuntiatio   report *(detailed account)*
reobtain   recoup *(regain)*, recover

reoccupation salvage
reoccupy reclaim
reoccur recur
reoccurrence relapse
reopen appeal, continue (resume), renew (begin again). SEE MAIN ENTRY
reopening appeal, continuation (resumption), renewal
reordering reclassification
reorganization development (progression), progress, reclassification, reconversion, rehabilitation, repair, replacement. SEE MAIN ENTRY
reorganize alter, change, convert (change use), emend, meliorate, reconstitute, reconstruct, recreate, reform, reinforce, renew (begin again), renovate, restore (renew), resurrect, transform, vary
repair correction (change), cure, emend, maintenance (upkeep), meliorate, rectify, redress, reform (noun), reform (verb), rehabilitate, rehabilitation, remedy, renew (refurbish), renewal, renovate, reparation (keeping in repair), restore (renew). SEE MAIN ENTRY
repairable corrigible
repaired renascent
repairing correction (change)
reparable corrigible
reparare fix (repair), recover, repair
reparation collection (payment), compensation, consideration (recompense), contribution (indemnification), damages, discharge (payment), indemnification, justice, payment (remittance), recompense, recovery (award), redemption, rehabilitation, reimbursement, relief (legal redress), remedy (legal means of redress), remittance, rendition (restoration), repair, replacement, requital, restitution, retribution, satisfaction (discharge of debt), satisfaction (fulfilment), trover. SEE MAIN ENTRY
reparation for loss out of pocket
reparative compensatory, curative, remedial, salubrious, salutary
reparative measure remedy (legal means of redress)
reparatory remedial, salutary
repartee answer (reply)
repartition dispensation (act of dispensing), distribution (apportionment), reapportion, redistribute
repast treat
repay bear the expense, compensate (remunerate), defray, disburse (pay out), discharge (pay a debt), indemnify, rebate, reciprocate, recoup (reimburse), refund, reimburse, remit (send payment), remunerate, replace, restore (return), retaliate, return (refund), satisfy (discharge). SEE MAIN ENTRY
repay for a loss compensate (remunerate)
repay in kind retaliate
repaying compensatory
repayment collection (payment), commission (fee), compensation, consideration (recompense), contribution (indemnification), disbursement (funds paid out), discharge (payment), expiation, indemnification, indemnity, out of pocket, pay, rebate, recompense, recovery (award), refund, reimbursement, reparation (indemnification), reprisal, requital, restitution, retribution, revenge, satisfaction (discharge of debt), vengeance
repayment for injury sustained damages
repayment for loss damages

repeal abate (extinguish), abatement (extinguishment), abolish, abolition, abrogate (rescind), adeem, ademption, annul, cancel, cancellation, countermand, defeasance, discharge (annulment), discharge (release from obligation), discharge (release from obligation), discontinue (abandon), dissolution (termination), invalidate, negate, negation, nullify, overrule, quash, renege, repudiate, repudiation, rescind, rescision, retraction, reversal, revocation, revoke, supersede, vacate (void), withdraw. SEE MAIN ENTRY
repealed lifeless (dead), null (invalid), null and void
repeat circulate, copy, insist, mock (imitate), propagate (spread), quote, reaffirm, recapitulate, recite, recount, recur, reflect (mirror), reiterate, relate (tell), renew (begin again), reopen, reproduce, speak. SEE MAIN ENTRY
repeat by rote recite
repeat from memory recite
repeat offender recidivist
repeated consecutive, continuous, frequent, habitual, incessant, insistent, iterative, ordinary, periodic, persistent, repetitious, routine, usual. SEE MAIN ENTRY
repeated relapse into crime recidivism
repeatedly invariably
repeatedly recognized common (customary)
repeater gun
repeating chronic, repetitious
repel alienate (estrange), antagonize, arrest (stop), confront (oppose), counter, decline (reject), deter, disapprove (reject), disavow, discourage, disfavor, disoblige, exclude, forswear, hold out (resist), oppose, outlaw, parry, rebuff, refuse, refute, reject, renounce, repulse, resist (oppose), spurn, stave, stem (check), withstand. SEE MAIN ENTRY
repelled averse
repellence repudiation
repellent antipathetic (distasteful), contemptible, contemptuous, insusceptible (resistant), loathsome, obnoxious, odious, offensive (offending), repugnant (exciting aversion), repulsive, sordid, undesirable
repellere parry, rebuff, rebut, repel (drive back), repulse, stave
repelling loathsome, offensive (offending), repugnant (exciting aversion), repulsive, unsavory
repent reform, regret. SEE MAIN ENTRY
repentance remorse
repentant contrite, penitent, remorseful. SEE MAIN ENTRY
repentant person penitent
repenting remorseful. SEE MAIN ENTRY
repercuss repel (drive back), repulse
repercussion conclusion (outcome), effect, outgrowth, reaction (response). SEE MAIN ENTRY
repercussive resounding
reperire detect, invent (produce for the first time)
reperta invention
repertory cache (storage place), depository, treasury
repetere renew (begin again), resume
repetition copy, duplicate, frequency, habit, narration, redundancy, relapse, renewal, restatement, tautology
repetitional insistent, repeated, repetitious

repetitionary insistent, repeated, repetitious
repetitious chronic, incessant, iterative, repeated. SEE MAIN ENTRY
repetitive chronic, consecutive, frequent, iterative, prolix, redundant, repeated, repetitious
repetitiveness cycle, frequency
rephrase construe (translate), elucidate, explain, quote, recapitulate, reiterate, repeat (state again)
rephrasing restatement
repine complain (criticize), deplore, languish, regret
repiner malcontent
repititious redundant
replace accede (succeed), change, convert (change use), cover (provide for), discharge (dismiss), disinherit, rebate, reconstitute, recoup (regain), recoup (reimburse), redistribute, refund, reimburse, reinstate, relocate, remand, remove (dismiss from office), renew (refurbish), renovate, repay, replenish, represent (substitute), restore (return), succeed (follow), superannuate, supersede, supplant. SEE MAIN ENTRY
replace with displace (replace)
replaceable corrigible, expendable
replacement alternative (substitute), correction (change), cover (substitute), defeasance, discharge (dismissal), exchange, novation, preemption, refund, reimbursement, reparation (keeping in repair), restitution, stopgap, subrogation, substitute, succedaneum, successor. SEE MAIN ENTRY
replacing acting, subrogation
replay restatement
replenish bear (yield), bestow, provide (supply), recruit, reinforce, renew (refurbish), supply. SEE MAIN ENTRY
replenished replete
replenishment reinforcement, renewal
replere replenish
replete copious, detailed, full, intact, profuse, rife. SEE MAIN ENTRY
repleteness plethora
repletion overage, plethora, sufficiency, surfeit
repletus full
replevied attached (seized)
replevin reclaim, recoup (regain), recovery (repossession), redeem (repurchase), redemption. SEE MAIN ENTRY
replevy attach (seize), distrain, reclaim, recoup (regain), recover, recovery (repossession), redeem (repurchase), repossess, sequester (seize property)
replica copy, counterpart (parallel), duplicate, facsimile, fake, model, resemblance, semblance
replicate copy, repeat (do again), reproduce, retort
replication acknowledgment (acceptance), answer (judicial response), answer (reply), counterargument, reply, response
replier respondent
reply acknowledge (respond), acknowledgment (acceptance), answer (respond legally), confutation, correspond (communicate), counterargument, countercharge, plea, pleading, reaction (response), rebut, rejoinder, respond, response, retort, return (respond). SEE MAIN ENTRY
reply to a charge answer (judicial response)
replying responsive
reponder reconsider

reponere repay, replace, reserve

report annunciate, apprise, betray *(disclose)*, bill *(invoice)*, book, canvass, comment, communication *(statement)*, conclusion *(determination)*, convey *(communicate)*, delineate, delineation, depict, detail *(particularize)*, disabuse, disclose, disclosure *(something disclosed)*, dispatch *(message)*, disseminate, divulge, document, enlighten, enter *(record)*, entry *(record)*, file, finding, form *(document)*, hearsay, herald, holding *(ruling of a court)*, inform *(notify)*, intelligence *(news)*, issuance, judgment *(formal court decree)*, memorandum, mention *(reference)*, mention, narration, notice *(announcement)*, notification, notify, observation, opinion *(judicial decision)*, outline *(synopsis)*, portray, post, proclaim, promulgate, pronouncement, propagate *(spread)*, publication *(disclosure)*, publicity, publish, quote, recital, recite, record, recount, relate *(tell)*, rendition *(explication)*, repeat *(state again)*, repercussion, report *(disclose)*, representation *(statement)*, reputation, review *(critical evaluation)*, scenario, signify *(inform)*, speak, statement, story *(narrative)*, summary, tip *(clue)*. SEE MAIN ENTRY

report against accuse, denounce *(inform against)*, inform *(betray)*

report inaccurately misinform

report intended to delude canard

reported alleged, documentary, narrative, public *(known)*, putative, stated

reportedly reputedly

reporter bystander, deponent, informant, informer *(a person who provides information)*, spy, witness

reporters press

reporting informatory

repose abeyance, composure, desist, leave *(absence)*, lull, pause, peace, prostration, recess, remain *(stay)*, rest *(cease from action)*, stay *(rest)*. SEE MAIN ENTRY

reposeful complacent, placid

reposing inactive

reposit deposit *(place)*, hoard, repose *(place)*, store

reposition relocate

repository arsenal, bank, cache *(storage place)*, catchall, depository, hoard, recipient, treasury. SEE MAIN ENTRY

repossess reclaim, recoup *(regain)*, recover, redeem *(repurchase)*. SEE MAIN ENTRY

repossession redemption, replevin, salvage

reprehend admonish *(warn)*, blame, castigate, cavil, censure, charge *(accuse)*, complain *(charge)*, complain *(criticize)*, condemn *(blame)*, criticize *(find fault with)*, decry, defame, denounce *(condemn)*, disapprove *(condemn)*, discredit, fault, lash *(attack verbally)*, protest, rebuke, remonstrate, reprimand, reproach. SEE MAIN ENTRY

reprehendendus reprehensible

reprehendere blame, censure, criticize *(find fault with)*, rebuke, reprehend, reprimand

reprehensibility culpability, guilt

reprehensible bad *(offensive)*, blameful, blameworthy, contemptible, delinquent *(guilty of a misdeed)*, disreputable, gross *(flagrant)*, guilty, heinous, inexcusable, inexpiable, iniquitous, loathsome, nefarious, obnoxious, odious, offensive *(offending)*, outrageous, peccable, peccant *(culpable)*, scandalous, sinister, unjustifiable, unseemly, vicious. SEE MAIN ENTRY

reprehensio blame *(culpability)*, reprimand, stricture

reprehension bad repute, blame *(culpability)*, condemnation *(blame)*, conviction *(finding of guilt)*, criticism, denunciation, diatribe, disapprobation, disapproval, discredit, disparagement, impugnation, objurgation, onus *(blame)*, reprimand, reproach, revilement, stricture

reprehensive critical *(faultfinding)*

represent advise, bare, bear *(adduce)*, characterize, comport *(behave)*, connote, construe *(comprehend)*, convey *(communicate)*, copy, delineate, denote, depict, draw *(depict)*, exemplify, illustrate, impersonate, lobby, manifest, portray, purport, render *(depict)*, replace, signify *(denote)*, simulate, specify. SEE MAIN ENTRY

represent as assume *(simulate)*

represent as resembling compare

represent by diagram delineate

represent by outlines delineate

represent by words describe

represent falsely cheat, falsify, lie *(falsify)*, misrepresent, palter

represent fictitiously feign, profess *(pretend)*

represent fraudulently misrepresent

represent in words portray, relate *(tell)*

represent incorrectly mislabel, misrepresent

represent oneself demean *(deport oneself)*

represent oneself to be impersonate

represent pictorially delineate

represent to oneself conjure

representation agency *(legal relationship)*, assertion, brief, color *(deceptive appearance)*, concept, copy, cross section, definition, delineation, deputation *(delegation)*, design *(construction plan)*, designation *(symbol)*, disclosure *(act of disclosing)*, disguise, duplicate, election *(selection by vote)*, embodiment, example, illustration, indicant, manifestation, model, narration, paraphrase, part *(role)*, performance *(workmanship)*, profession *(declaration)*, proxy, recital, rendition *(explication)*, resemblance, role, sample, semblance, substitute, suggestion, symbol. SEE MAIN ENTRY

representation by words delineation

representation in language expression *(comment)*. SEE MAIN ENTRY

representational descriptive, detailed, realistic, representative, vicarious *(substitutional)*

representative acting, advocate *(counselor)*, agent, broad, broker, case *(example)*, conduit *(intermediary)*, congruous, demonstrative *(illustrative)*, deputy, descriptive, employee, epitome, example, exemplary, factor *(commission merchant)*, functionary, general, indicant, instance, intermediary, lawmaker, legislator, liaison, nominee *(delegate)*, normal *(regular)*, ordinary, plenipotentiary, politician, proctor, procurator, proxy, realistic, replacement, sample, several *(separate)*, specimen, spokesman, substitute, surrogate, typical, usual. SEE MAIN ENTRY

representative in Congress lawmaker

representative of the decedent executor

representative sampling cross section

representative section cross section

representative selection case *(example)*, cross section, example, excerpt, instance, sample, specimen

representatives chamber *(body)*, commission *(agency)*, committee, delegation *(envoy)*, deputation *(delegation)*, government *(political administration)*

representing acting, congruous, in lieu of

repress allay, ban, bar *(hinder)*, bind *(restrain)*, capture, clog, condemn *(ban)*, confine, constrain *(restrain)*, constrict *(inhibit)*, contain *(restrain)*, counteract, curb, deter, disadvantage, dominate, enjoin, extinguish, hamper, hold up *(delay)*, inhibit, interdict, kill *(defeat)*, limit, moderate *(temper)*, overturn, prevent, prohibit, quash, restrain, restrict, stifle, stop, strangle, subdue, subject, suppress, trammel, withhold. SEE MAIN ENTRY

repressed arrested *(checked)*

repressing limiting

repressing emotion stoical

repression censorship, coercion, constraint *(restriction)*, control *(restriction)*, deterrence, deterrent, disadvantage, discipline *(obedience)*, duress, fetter, force *(compulsion)*, oppression, prohibition, restraint

repressive dictatorial, prohibitive *(restrictive)*, restrictive

repressive governor dictator

reprieve abeyance, absolution, absolve, acquit, acquittal, amnesty, clear, clemency, compurgation, condonation, condone, discharge *(liberation)*, discharge *(release from obligation)*, emancipation, excuse, exoneration, forgive, grace, grace period, immunity, impunity, palliate *(excuse)*, pardon *(noun)*, pardon *(verb)*, parole, postpone, release, relief *(release)*, remission, remit *(release from penalty)*, stay, stay *(halt)*, vindicate. SEE MAIN ENTRY

reprieved blameless, clear *(free from criminal charges)*, free *(relieved from a burden)*

reprimand admonish *(warn)*, admonition, bad repute, blame, castigate, censure, complain *(criticize)*, condemn *(punish)*, condemnation *(blame)*, criticism, criticize *(find fault with)*, denounce *(condemn)*, denunciation, diatribe, disapprobation, disapprove *(condemn)*, discipline *(punishment)*, disparagement, fault, impeach, impeachment, lash *(attack verbally)*, objurgation, outcry, penalize, punish, punishment, rebuff, rebuke, remonstrance, reprehend, reproach *(noun)*, reproach *(verb)*. SEE MAIN ENTRY

reprimanded blameful, blameworthy

reprimanding remonstrative

reprimere restrain, stifle, suppress

reprint copy *(noun)*, copy *(verb)*, transcript

reprisal conviction *(finding of guilt)*, counterattack, exchange, penalty, reaction *(opposition)*, requital, retribution, revenge, vengeance. SEE MAIN ENTRY

reproach admonition, aspersion, attaint, bad repute, blame *(culpability)*, blame, castigate, censure, charge *(accusation)*, complain *(charge)*, complain *(criticize)*, condemn *(blame)*, condemnation *(blame)*, contemn, contempt *(disdain)*, contempt *(disobedience to the court)*, contumely, criticism, criticize *(find fault with)*, denigrate, denounce *(condemn)*, denunciation, diatribe, disapprobation, disapproval, disapprove *(condemn)*, discredit, disgrace, dishonor *(shame)*, dishonor *(deprive of honor)*, disparagement, guilt, ignominy, impeach, impeachment, incrimination, indictment, infamy, lash *(attack verbally)*, notoriety, objurgation, obloquy, odium, onus *(stigma)*, opprobrium, outcry, rebuff, rebuke, remonstrance, remonstrate, reprehend, reprimand *(noun)*, reprimand *(verb)*, revilement, scandal, shame, slander, stigma, stricture. SEE MAIN ENTRY

reproach oneself   regret

reproachability   bad character

reproachable   blameful, blameworthy, delinquent *(guilty of a misdeed)*, guilty, reprehensible

reproachableness   culpability

reproached   accused *(attacked)*, disreputable

reproachful   blameful, contemptible, contemptuous, critical *(faultfinding)*, ignoble, remonstrative

reproachful accusation   incrimination

reproaching   contemptuous

reprobacy   bad faith, delinquency *(misconduct)*

reprobate   bad *(offensive)*, blame, blameful, blameworthy, censure, complain *(charge)*, condemn *(ban)*, convict, criminal, criticize *(find fault with)*, delinquent *(guilty of a misdeed)*, delinquent, denounce *(condemn)*, disapprove *(condemn)*, disgraceful, dissolute, felon, immoral, incorrigible, inexcusable, iniquitous, judge, lecherous, lewd, malefactor, nefarious, peccable, peccant *(culpable)*, perverse, rebuff, recidivist, recreant, reject, reprehend, reprehensible, reprimand, reproach, sentence, spurn, tainted *(corrupted)*, vandal, vicious, wrongdoer. SEE MAIN ENTRY

reprobation   abandonment *(repudiation)*, admonition, bad repute, blame *(culpability)*, condemnation *(blame)*, contempt *(disdain)*, conviction *(finding of guilt)*, correction *(punishment)*, denunciation, di-scredit, disdain, disparagement, impugnation, ostracism, outcry, phillipic, rejection, remonstrance, renunciation, reprimand, reproach, revilement, stricture

reprobative   blameful, blameworthy, contemptible, critical *(faultfinding)*, remonstrative

reprobatory   remonstrative

reprobe   reexamine

reproduce   bear *(yield)*, copy, mock *(imitate)*, portray, proliferate, propagate *(increase)*, pullulate, quote, recreate, reflect *(mirror)*, rehabilitate, reiterate, render *(depict)*, renew *(refurbish)*, repeat *(do again)*, trace *(delineate)*. SEE MAIN ENTRY

reproduce fraudulently   forge *(counterfeit)*

reproduce in kind   proliferate

reproduce rapidly   proliferate

reproduced   renascent, repeated

reproducing   plagiarism

reproduction   boom *(increase)*, copy, counterpart *(parallel)*, duplicate, facsimile, fake, maternity, plagiarism, renewal, replacement, resemblance, revival, sham, transcript

reproof   admonition, aspersion, bad repute, blame *(culpability)*, charge *(accusation)*, condemnation *(blame)*, contempt *(disdain)*, conviction *(finding of guilt)*, criticism, denunciation, diatribe, disapprobation, discipline *(punishment)*, disparagement, impeachment, objurgation, ostracism, rebuff, remonstrance, reprimand, reproach, revilement, stricture. SEE MAIN ENTRY

reprovable   blameful, blameworthy, guilty, reprehensible

reproval   contempt *(disdain)*, correction *(punishment)*, disapprobation, objurgation, remonstrance, reprimand

reprove   admonish *(warn)*, advise, blame, browbeat, castigate, censure, comment, complain *(criticize)*, condemn *(blame)*, condemn *(punish)*, criticize *(find fault with)*, denigrate, deter, disapprove *(condemn)*, discipline *(punish)*, discourage, fault, impeach, lash *(attack verbally)*, penalize, rebuff, rebuke, remonstrate, reprehend, reprimand, reproach

reproved   accused *(attacked)*

reproving   critical *(faultfinding)*, remonstrative

reptilian   heinous

republic   polity

republish   copy

repudiare   disclaim, disown *(deny the validity)*, disown *(refuse to acknowledge)*, reject, repudiate

repudiate   abandon *(relinquish)*, abolish, abrogate *(annul)*, abrogate *(rescind)*, adeem, annul, answer *(reply)*, cancel, challenge, condemn *(blame)*, contemn, contradict, controvert, cross *(disagree with)*, decline *(reject)*, default, defect, demur, deny *(contradict)*, deprecate, differ *(disagree)*, disaccord, disaffirm, disagree, disallow, disapprove *(condemn)*, disapprove *(reject)*, disavow, disclaim, disdain, dishonor *(refuse to pay)*, disinherit, disobey, disoblige, disown *(deny the validity)*, disown *(refuse to acknowledge)*, dissent *(withhold assent)*, except *(object)*, exclude, forfeit, forswear, gainsay, ignore, invalidate, leave *(allow to remain)*, negate, nullify, oust, overrule, picket, prohibit, proscribe *(prohibit)*, protest, rebuff, rebut, recall *(call back)*, recant, refuse, refute, reject, renounce, repel *(drive back)*, repulse, rescind, resign, revoke, secede, set aside *(annul)*, spurn, waive. SEE MAIN ENTRY

repudiated   broken *(unfulfilled)*, derelict *(abandoned)*

repudiating   dissenting, negative

repudiatio   denial, rejection, renunciation, repudiation

repudiation   abandonment *(desertion)*, abjuration, abolition, ademption, breach, cancellation, condemnation *(blame)*, confutation, contempt *(disobedience to the court)*, countermand, declination, default, denial, desertion, disapprobation, disapproval, discharge *(annulment)*, disclaimer, discredit, disdain, disqualification *(rejection)*, dissent *(nonconcurrence)*, exclusion, impugnation, infringement, negation, nonpayment, ouster, prohibition, protest, rebuff, refusal, rejection, renunciation, rescision, retraction, reversal, revocation. SEE MAIN ENTRY

repudiation of a marriage   divorce

repudiation of employment   lockout

repudiation of one's duty   delinquency *(failure of duty)*

repudiation of payment   dishonor *(nonpayment)*

repudiation of the allegations   demurrer

repudiative   ambulatory

repudiatory   ambulatory

repudium   divorce

repugn   disaccord, disagree, expostulate, oppose

repugnance   antipode, contempt *(disdain)*, disapprobation, incompatibility *(difference)*, malice, odium, phobia, reluctance, resistance

repugnancy   disapprobation

repugnans   contradictory, repugnant *(exciting aversion)*

repugnant   adverse *(hostile)*, antipathetic *(distasteful)*, averse, bad *(offensive)*, contemptible, contemptuous, contradictory, heinous, inimical, loathsome, malevolent, negative, objectionable, obnoxious, odious, offensive *(offending)*, repulsive, unacceptable, unfavorable, unsavory. SEE MAIN ENTRY

repugnantia   contradiction, incongruity

repugnare   conflict, object

repugning   dissenting

repulsa   defeat, rebuff

repulse   beat *(defeat)*, block, contemn, disallow, disavow, disdain *(noun)*, disdain *(verb)*, disfavor, disown *(refuse to acknowledge)*, dissent *(withhold assent)*, eliminate *(exclude)*, exclude, fight *(counteract)*, kill *(defeat)*, oppose, parry, rebuff *(noun)*, rebuff *(verb)*, refusal, reject, rejection, renounce, repel *(disgust)*, repel *(drive back)*, resist *(oppose)*, spurn, stem *(check)*, withstand. SEE MAIN ENTRY

repulsion   contempt *(disobedience to the court)*, disdain, malice, renunciation, resistance

repulsive   antipathetic *(distasteful)*, bad *(offensive)*, contemptible, contemptuous, contumacious, loathsome, lurid, objectionable, obnoxious, odious, offensive *(offending)*, repugnant *(exciting aversion)*, undesirable. SEE MAIN ENTRY

repulsiveness   odium

repurchase   redemption

reputability   distinction *(reputation)*, honesty, honor *(good reputation)*, integrity, probity, rectitude, regard *(esteem)*

reputable   conscientious, credible, dependable, high-minded, honest, incorruptible, influential, law-abiding, meritorious, moral, outstanding *(prominent)*, reliable, renowned, scrupulous, unimpeachable. SEE MAIN ENTRY

reputableness   character *(reputation)*, credit *(recognition)*

reputare   reconsider, weigh

reputation   credit *(recognition)*, notoriety, prestige, regard *(esteem)*. SEE MAIN ENTRY

repute   character *(reputation)*, credit *(recognition)*, distinction *(reputation)*, eminence, honesty, honor *(good reputation)*, importance, notoriety, prestige, regard *(esteem)*, reputation, respect

reputed   putative SEE MAIN ENTRY

reputedly   SEE MAIN ENTRY

request   application, call *(appeal)*, call *(appeal to)*, canvass, charge *(command)*, claim *(demand)*, demand, desire, dun *(noun)*, dun *(verb)*, entreaty, importune, invitation, lobby, mandate, market *(demand)*, motion, move *(judicially request)*, petition *(noun)*, petition *(verb)*, plead *(implore)*, prayer, press *(beseech)*, pressure, require *(need)*, requirement, requisition, solicit, subpoena, urge. SEE MAIN ENTRY

request another decision   appeal

request for another decision   appeal

request for payment   bill *(invoice)*

request for relief   petition, prayer

request for retrial   appeal

request for review   appeal

request for the aid of the court   prayer

request reexamination   appeal

request reopening of a case   appeal

request the presence of   call *(summon)*

request to appear   summons

request to perform   demand

requested important *(urgent)*, popular
requesting insistent
requestion reexamine
require appoint, bind *(obligate)*, call *(demand)*, claim *(demand)*, coerce, command, compel, constrain *(compel)*, decree, demand, dictate, dun, enforce, enjoin, entail, exact, force *(coerce)*, impose *(enforce)*, impose *(subject)*, insist, instruct *(direct)*, lack, levy, necessitate, need, order, prescribe, press *(constrain)*, request, tax *(levy)*, tax *(overwork)*. SEE MAIN ENTRY
require a tax excise *(levy a tax)*
require authoritatively dictate, exact
require compliance impose *(enforce)*, subpoena, summon
require of others call *(demand)*
require to attend subpoena, summon
required binding, bound, compulsory, exigent, forcible, fundamental, imperative, important *(urgent)*, indispensable, integral, mandatory, obligatory, positive *(prescribed)*, requisite, urgent, vital
required assumption presumption
required by custom prescriptive
required by law legal
required item necessity, need *(requirement)*
required legal assumption presumption
required manner practice *(procedure)*
required to attend venire
requirement appointment *(act of designating)*, article *(precept)*, burden, call *(appeal)*, call *(option)*, canon, charge *(command)*, claim *(legal demand)*, compulsion *(coercion)*, condition *(contingent provision)*, demand, desideratum, dictate, directive, duress, enforcement, exigency, instruction *(direction)*, mandate, market *(demand)*, necessary, necessity, ordinance, precept, prerequisite, provision *(clause)*, qualification *(condition)*, request, requisition, sine qua non, ultimatum, writ. SEE MAIN ENTRY
requirement of polite society decorum
requirement to appear process *(summons)*
requirement to attend subpoena
requirere require *(need)*
requiring perfunctory
requiring immediate attention exigent, imperative
requiring immediate care exigent
requiring no effort convenient
requiring prompt action exigent
requisite attornment, binding, burden, central *(essential)*, compulsory, condition *(contingent provision)*, demand, desideratum, essential *(required)*, fundamental, imperative, important *(urgent)*, indispensable, integral, mandatory, necessary *(required)*, necessary, necessity, need *(requirement)*, obligatory, positive *(prescribed)*, prerequisite, primary, qualification *(condition)*, requirement, requisition, reservation *(condition)*, substantive, ultimatum, vital. SEE MAIN ENTRY
requisiteness need *(requirement)*, priority
requisition application, arrogation, call *(appeal)*, call *(option)*, call *(demand)*, canon, charge *(command)*, claim *(demand)*, desideratum, dun, exact, excise *(levy a tax)*, importune, mandate, market *(demand)*, monition *(legal summons)*, move *(judicially request)*, petition *(noun)*, petition *(verb)*, pray, prayer, request *(noun)*, request *(verb)*, require *(compel)*, requirement. SEE MAIN ENTRY

requisition to the court application
requisitioned necessary *(required)*
requisitory confiscatory, requisite
requital collection *(payment)*, compensation, consideration *(recompense)*, contribution *(indemnification)*, exchange, expiation, honorarium, indemnification, interchange, recompense, remuneration, reprisal, restitution, retribution, revenge, reward, satisfaction *(discharge of debt)*, trover. SEE MAIN ENTRY
requite defray, disburse *(pay out)*, indemnify, reciprocate, recoup *(reimburse)*, recriminate, refund, reimburse, remit *(send payment)*, remunerate, repay, retaliate, retort, satisfy *(discharge)*
requited reciprocal
requitement contribution *(indemnification)*, indemnification, indemnity, recompense, requital, restitution, retribution, reward, satisfaction *(discharge of debt)*, trover. SEE MAIN ENTRY
rerank reassess
res article *(commodity)*, article *(distinct section of a writing)*, commodities
res corpus
res effects, fact, issue *(matter in dispute)*, item, matter *(subject)*, occurrence, point *(item)*, possession *(property)*, possessions, substance *(essential nature)*
res adversae adversity
res arcana secret
res atrox atrocity
res commodata loan
res cuius actio est actionable
res ficta fiction
res ipsa loquitor SEE MAIN ENTRY
res judicata adjudication. SEE MAIN ENTRY
res mira phenomenon *(unusual occurrence)*
res occulta mystery, secret
res repetundae extortion
res secundae prosperity
res simillima counterpart *(parallel)*
res summa main point
res venales merchandise
resanction reconfirm
rescind abate *(extinguish)*, abolish, adeem, annul, cancel, disavow, discharge *(release from obligation)*, disclaim, disinherit, disown *(deny the validity)*, invalidate, negate, nullify, overrule, quash, recall *(call back)*, recant, renege, repeal, revoke, vacate *(void)*, vitiate, withdraw. SEE MAIN ENTRY
rescind an attorney's license to practice disbar
rescinded null *(invalid)*, null and void
rescindere abrogate *(rescind)*, invalidate, quash, repeal, rescind, revoke
rescinding cancellation
rescindment abatement *(extinguishment)*, abolition, ademption, annulment, cancellation, countermand, defeasance, rescision, retraction, revocation
rescission abandonment *(repudiation)*, abolition, ademption, avoidance *(cancellation)*, cancellation, countermand, defeasance, discharge *(annulment)*, discharge *(release from obligation)*, dissolution *(termination)*, negation, repudiation, reversal. SEE MAIN ENTRY
rescribere answer *(reply)*
rescript canon, citation *(charge)*, correction *(change)*, dictate, direction *(order)*, directive, fiat, issuance, law, monition *(legal summons)*, order *(judicial directive)*,

proclamation, requirement, revision *(corrected version)*, transcript
rescrutinize reexamine
rescuable corrigible
rescue aid *(help)*, aid, clear, disencumber, disenthrall, extricate, free, help, liberate, liberation, palliate *(excuse)*, preserve, quit *(free of)*, ransom, recovery *(repossession)*, redeem *(repurchase)*, redemption, relief *(aid)*, salvage. SEE MAIN ENTRY
rescue from imprisonment disenthrall
rescue from oppression disenthrall
rescue from slavery disenthrall
rescued free *(relieved from a burden)*
rescuer benefactor, good samaritan
research analysis, analyze, audit, canvass, delve, examination *(study)*, examine *(study)*, experiment, indagation, inquire, inquiry *(systematic investigation)*, investigation, peruse, probe, quest, scrutinize, scrutiny, study, test. SEE MAIN ENTRY
reseat reinstate
resell recover
resemblance analogy, comparison, correspondence *(similarity)*, identity *(similarity)*, parity, propinquity *(similarity)*, relation *(connection)*, same, semblance. SEE MAIN ENTRY
resemble appear *(seem to be)*, approximate, correspond *(be equivalent)*, demean *(deport oneself)*
resembling akin *(germane)*, analogous, comparable *(capable of comparison)*, congruous, correlative, identical, similar
resembling truth specious. SEE MAIN ENTRY
resent contemn
resentful bitter *(reproachful)*, malevolent, malicious, malignant, restive, spiteful, vindictive. SEE MAIN ENTRY
resentfulness resentment
resentive resentful
resentment dissension, ground, ill will, malice, odium, rancor, spite, umbrage. SEE MAIN ENTRY
reservation adjournment, condition *(contingent provision)*, doubt *(indecision)*, limitation, misgiving, modification, objection, provision *(clause)*, qualification *(condition)*, registration, restriction, retention, salvo, selection *(choice)*. SEE MAIN ENTRY
reservations reluctance
reservatory repository, treasury
reserve adjourn, bank, cash, composure, cumulation, doubt *(indecision)*, engage *(hire)*, fund *(noun)*, fund *(verb)*, garner, hoard, hold up *(delay)*, keep *(shelter)*, margin *(spare amount)*, misgiving, predetermine, provision *(something provided)*, register, resource, restraint, retain *(employ)*, retain *(keep in possession)*, save *(hold back)*, stock *(store)*, stopgap, store *(depository)*, store, strangle, treasury, withhold. SEE MAIN ENTRY
reserve fund resource, treasury
reserved diffident, discreet, formal, guarded, inarticulate, laconic, mute, noncommittal, private *(not public)*, privy, taciturn, unapproachable, unobtrusive, unresponsive
reserved amount margin *(spare amount)*
reserves assets, capital, hoard
reservoir arsenal, cache *(storage place)*, depository, fund, repository, stock *(store)*, store *(depository)*, sufficiency
reset adjust *(regulate)*
resettle relocate
reshape camouflage, convert *(change use)*, distort, modify *(alter)*, reform, repair

reshaped tempered
reship redirect
reside dwell *(reside)*, lodge *(reside)*, remain *(occupy)*. SEE MAIN ENTRY
reside in inhabit, occupy *(take possession)*
reside together cohabit
residence abode, address, apartment, building *(structure)*, domicile, dwelling, habitation *(act of inhabiting)*, habitation *(dwelling place)*, headquarters, home *(domicile)*, homestead, house, household, inhabitation *(place of dwelling)*, lodging, occupancy, occupation *(possession)*, seat. SEE MAIN ENTRY
residencer citizen
residences premises *(buildings)*
residency abode, domicile, inhabitation *(place of dwelling)*, residence, tenancy
resident citizen, constituent *(member)*, denizen, domiciliary, habitant, inhabitant, inmate, lessee, lodger, occupant, tenant. SEE MAIN ENTRY
residential habitable, household *(domestic)*. SEE MAIN ENTRY
residential building development *(building)*
residentiary denizen, habitant, household *(domestic)*, inhabitant, lodger, occupant, resident
residents populace, population
resider citizen, habitant, lodger, occupant, resident
residere subside
residing habitation *(act of inhabiting)*
residing together cohabitation *(living together)*
residual balance *(amount in excess)*, net, residuary, superfluous. SEE MAIN ENTRY
residual estate remainder *(estate in property)*
residual portion balance *(amount in excess)*
residual time unexpired term
residuals remainder *(remaining part)*
residuary alluvion, net, residual, superfluous. SEE MAIN ENTRY
residue balance *(amount in excess)*, overage, remainder *(remaining part)*, residual, reversion *(remainder of an estate)*, surplus
residuum balance *(amount in excess)*
residuum remainder *(remaining part)*
residuum residual
residuum surplus
resign abandon *(relinquish)*, cede, defect, demit, depart, discontinue *(abandon)*, forgo, leave *(depart)*, quit *(discontinue)*, reconcile, relent, relinquish, remise, renounce, retire *(conclude a career)*, secede, submit *(yield)*, succumb, surrender *(give back)*, withdraw, yield *(submit)*. SEE MAIN ENTRY
resign oneself bear *(tolerate)*
resign oneself to comply, endure *(suffer)*
resignation abdication, acceptance, capitulation, cession, desertion, longanimity, renunciation, sufferance, tolerance. SEE MAIN ENTRY
resigned complacent, passive, patient, stoical. SEE MAIN ENTRY
resignedness acquiescence, capitulation
resilient corrigible. SEE MAIN ENTRY
resist challenge, collide *(clash)*, conflict, confront *(oppose)*, contest, counter, counteract, countervail, cross *(disagree with)*, decline *(reject)*, defy, demonstrate *(protest)*, disaccord, disaffirm, disallow, disapprove *(reject)*, disobey, dissent *(withhold assent)*,

fight *(battle)*, fight *(counteract)*, hamper, hold up *(delay)*, object, oppose, oppugn, parry, rebel, rebuff, refuse, repel *(drive back)*, repulse, stem *(check)*, withstand. SEE MAIN ENTRY
resist change persevere
resist lawful authority rebel
resist openly defy
resistance conflict, contempt *(disobedience to the court)*, contention *(opposition)*, contest *(dispute)*, contravention, defiance, deterrence, disadvantage, disapproval, fight *(battle)*, impediment, impugnation, mutiny, negation, opposition, protest, reaction *(opposition)*, rebellion, rebuff, refusal, reluctance, revolt, struggle. SEE MAIN ENTRY
resistance against attack defense
resistance movement rebellion
resistance to authority contempt *(disobedience to the court)*, sedition
resistance to change inertia
resistance to government insurrection, revolution
resistant antipathetic *(oppositional)*, contumacious, disobedient, dissident, durable, inexorable, infrangible, nonconsenting, recalcitrant, recusant, renitent, rigid, unbending
resistence collision *(dispute)*
resister adversary, disputant, malcontent
resistere counteract, hold out *(resist)*, withstand
resisting chronic, cohesive *(sticking)*, disorderly, dissenting, indomitable, opposite, renitent, spartan, unyielding
resisting authority contumacious
resisting control contumacious, restive
resistive adverse *(hostile)*, disobedient, insubordinate, intractable, negative, opposite, perverse, preventive, recalcitrant, unruly
resistless forcible, indomitable, inexpugnable, invincible, irresistible, passive, resigned, susceptible *(unresistent)*, unavoidable *(inevitable)*
resite relocate
resolute decisive, definite, diligent, earnest, faithful *(loyal)*, fanatical, heroic, indomitable, inexorable, inflexible, loyal, obdurate, patient, peremptory *(absolute)*, persistent, pertinacious, purposeful, relentless, sedulous, serious *(devoted)*, spartan, staunch, steadfast, strong, true *(loyal)*, unalterable, unbending, uncompromising, undaunted, unyielding. SEE MAIN ENTRY
resolutely faithfully
resoluteness prowess *(bravery)*, resolution *(decision)*, spirit, tenacity, will *(desire)*
resolution act *(enactment)*, adhesion *(loyalty)*, adjudication, animus, answer *(solution)*, arbitration, award, bill *(proposed act)*, choice *(decision)*, conclusion *(determination)*, consequence *(conclusion)*, decision *(judgment)*, declaration, decree, denouement, determination, diligence *(perseverance)*, disposition *(determination)*, finding, forethought, goal, holding *(ruling of a court)*, intent, intention, judgment *(formal court decree)*, key *(solution)*, opinion *(judicial decision)*, outcome, project, proposition, purpose, result, ruling, solution *(answer)*, spirit, suggestion, tenacity, volition, will *(desire)*. SEE MAIN ENTRY
resolution by a jury verdict
resolution of the court finding
resolvable determinable *(ascertainable)*, solvable

resolve animus, arbitrate *(adjudge)*, arrange *(methodize)*, ascertain, choice *(decision)*, choose, conclude *(decide)*, conclusion *(determination)*, contemplation, decide, design *(intent)*, determination, determine, discharge *(perform)*, endeavor, find *(determine)*, fix *(settle)*, forethought, goal, hold *(decide)*, intend, intent, intention, judge, plan *(noun)*, plan *(verb)*, predetermination, purpose, reason *(conclude)*, resolution *(decision)*, rule *(decide)*, settle, solve. SEE MAIN ENTRY
resolve a discord attune
resolve beforehand prearrange, predetermine, prejudge, preordain
resolve into change
resolved decisive, deliberate, indomitable, inexorable, inflexible, intense, intentional, patient, peremptory *(absolute)*, persistent, pertinacious, purposeful, res judicata, resolute, sedulous, serious *(devoted)*, spartan, steadfast, uncompromising, unrelenting, unyielding
resonance intonation
resonant full, orotund
resort device *(contrivance)*, expedient, refuge, resource, stopgap. SEE MAIN ENTRY
resort to employ *(make use of)*, exploit *(make use of)*
resort to arms belligerency, fight *(battle)*
resort to superior authority appeal
resounding powerful. SEE MAIN ENTRY
resource chattel, expedient, help, holding *(property owned)*, instrumentality, means *(funds)*, possession *(property)*, recourse, reserve, tool. SEE MAIN ENTRY
resourceful artful, competent, deft, original *(creative)*, practiced, productive. SEE MAIN ENTRY
resourcefulness common sense, discretion *(quality of being discreet)*, efficiency
resourceless helpless *(defenseless)*
resources advantage, assets, capital, cash, effects, estate *(property)*, finance, fund, goods, livelihood, means *(funds)*, money, paraphernalia *(personal belongings)*, personalty, possessions, principal *(capital sum)*, property *(possessions)*, provision *(something provided)*, reserve, stock in trade, substance *(material possessions)*
respect abide, character *(reputation)*, comity, complexion, comply, concede, concern *(care)*, concern *(involve)*, consideration *(sympathetic regard)*, courtesy, credit *(recognition)*, decorum, defer *(yield in judgment)*, deference, estimation *(esteem)*, fealty, heed, homage, honor, keep *(fulfill)*, mention *(tribute)*, obey, observe *(obey)*, particular, perform *(adhere to)*, prestige, regard *(esteem)*, regard *(hold in esteem)*, reputation, worth. SEE MAIN ENTRY
respectability character *(reputation)*, decorum, distinction *(reputation)*, honesty, honor *(good reputation)*, propriety *(correctness)*, reputation
respectable considerable, ethical, fair *(satisfactory)*, high-minded, honest, incorruptible, influential, law-abiding, moral, proper, reliable, reputable, upright
respected influential, outstanding *(prominent)*, popular, prominent, reputable
respectful civil *(polite)*, obedient, obeisant, servile
respectful deportment decorum
respectfulness comity, deference
respectfully SEE MAIN ENTRY
respecting relative *(relevant)*, wherein

respective certain (specific), particular (individual), specific

respectively per capita, pro rata. SEE MAIN ENTRY

respectlessness ingratitude

respectus regard (esteem), retrospect

respicere consider, regard (hold in esteem)

respite abeyance, adjournment, cessation (interlude), clemency, continue (adjourn), defer (put off), deferment, extension (postponement), furlough, halt, hiatus, immunity, interruption, interval, leave (absence), lull, moratorium, pause, pendency, recess, relief (aid), relief (release), remission, remit (release from penalty), reprieve, stay, stay (halt). SEE MAIN ENTRY

respite from impending punishment reprieve

resplendent illustrious

respond answer (reply), correspond (communicate), countercharge, obey, rebut, reciprocate, remark, reply, retort. SEE MAIN ENTRY

respond conclusively countercharge

responded to reciprocal

respondence answer (reply), response

respondent contender, defendant, litigant, open (persuasible), party (litigant), responsive. SEE MAIN ENTRY

responder respondent

respondere answer (reply), reply, retort, return (respond)

responsal response

response acknowledgment (acceptance), answer (reply), consequence (conclusion), counterargument, effect, emotion, impression, plea, rejoinder, repercussion, reply, sensibility. SEE MAIN ENTRY

response to an action appearance (coming into court)

responsibility agency (legal relationship), allegiance, assignment (task), burden, business (affair), competence (ability), duty (obligation), function, integrity, job, labor (work), liability, obligation (duty), onus (blame), onus (burden), part (role), position (business status), rectitude, requirement, trust (custody), weight (burden). SEE MAIN ENTRY

responsible actionable, amenable, blameful, blameworthy, bound, causative, competent, culpable, dependable, diligent, liable, lucid, moral, normal (sane), reliable, sane, solid (sound), true (loyal)

responsible for at fault

responsibleness charge (responsibility)

responsibly faithfully

responsio reply

responsive favorable (expressing approval), flexible, open (persuasible), openminded, perceptive, pliable, pliant, receptive, resilient, sensitive (discerning), suasible, willing (not averse). SEE MAIN ENTRY

responsive allegations pleading

responsive offer counteroffer

responsive to change flexible, resilient

responsiveness amenability, sensibility

responsum reply

respublica community, realm

rest abeyance, cessation (interlude), complement, composure, deposit (place), desist, extension (postponement), furlough, halt (noun), halt (verb), hiatus, holiday, inaction, inertia, interval, leave (absence), lodge (reside), lull, moratorium, pause (noun), pause (verb), recess (noun), recess (verb), relief (release), remain (stay),

remainder (remaining part), remission, repose (rest), respite (interval of rest), stop. SEE MAIN ENTRY

rest assured opine

rest in peace die

rest period pause

restate construe (translate), copy, elucidate, explain, quote, reaffirm, recapitulate, reiterate, repeat (state again). SEE MAIN ENTRY

restate briefly review

restated repeated

restatement narration, paraphrase, recital, redundancy, summary. SEE MAIN ENTRY

restation relocate

rested on based on

restful placid

restiff restive

resting dormant, inactive, static

resting place destination, haven, home (domicile)

restinguere extinguish

restituere fix (repair), reconstruct, redress, rehabilitate, reinstate

restitute bear the expense, recoup (reimburse), replace, restore (renew)

restitution collection (payment), consideration (recompense), contribution (indemnification), damages, disbursement (funds paid out), discharge (payment), expiation, indemnification, indemnity, out of pocket, payment (act of paying), payment (remittance), recompense, recovery (award), refund, rehabilitation, reimbursement, relief (legal redress), remedy (legal means of redress), remuneration, rendition (restoration), reparation (indemnification), replacement, requital, satisfaction (discharge of debt), trover. SEE MAIN ENTRY

restitutive compensatory, medicinal, remedial

restitutory compensatory

restive adverse (hostile), contumacious, disinclined, disobedient, disorderly, fractious, froward, insubordinate, intractable, lawless, recalcitrant, recusant, uncontrollable, unruly, willful. SEE MAIN ENTRY

restiveness contempt (disobedience to the court), disturbance

restless frenetic, moving (in motion), restive, unsettled

restlessness commotion, diligence (perseverance), disturbance, outburst, trepidation

restock replenish

restorable corrigible

restoral reparation (keeping in repair)

restoration acquittal, collection (payment), compensation, continuation (resumption), contribution (indemnification), correction (change), damages, indemnification, indemnity, out of pocket, progress, reconversion, recovery (repossession), redemption, rehabilitation, reimbursement, relief (legal redress), renewal, reorganization, repair, reparation (indemnification), reparation (keeping in repair), replacement, restitution, resurgence, revival

restoration of harmony arrangement (understanding), reconciliation

restoration to health cure

restorative curative, cure, medicinal, palliative (abating), panacea, remedial, remedy (that which corrects), salubrious, salutary

restorative agent panacea

restore bear (yield), bestow, continue (resume), contribute (indemnify), cure,

emend, fix (repair), indemnify, meliorate, quit (repay), rebate, reconstitute, reconstruct, recoup (reimburse), recreate, rectify, redress, reform, refund, rehabilitate, reimburse, reinstate, remand, remedy, renew (refurbish), renovate, repair, repay, resurrect, return (refund), surrender (give back). SEE MAIN ENTRY

restore courage to reassure

restore equilibrium adjust (regulate), regulate (adjust)

restore harmony arbitrate (conciliate), attune, disarm (set at ease), mediate, pacify, placate, reconcile, settle

restore one's faith assure (give confidence to)

restore permission authorize

restore to a state of peace pacify

restore to a state of tranquillity pacify

restore to assurance reassure

restore to confidence reassure

restore to equilibrium compensate (counterbalance)

restore to friendship reconcile

restore to liberty enfranchise

restore to office reinstate

restore to power reinstate

restored renascent

restrain allay, apprehend (arrest), arrest (apprehend), arrest (stop), balk, ban, bar (hinder), block, border (bound), cancel, capture, censor, check (restrain), clog, commit (institutionalize), condemn (ban), confine, constrain (imprison), constrain (restrain), constrict (inhibit), continue (adjourn), curb, debar, deter, diminish, discipline (control), discourage, disqualify, enclose, enjoin, estop, fetter, foil, forbear, forbid, govern, halt, hamper, hinder, hold up (delay), immure, impede, imprison, inhibit, interdict, jail, limit, lock, mitigate, moderate (temper), mollify, obstruct, occlude, police, preclude, prevent, prohibit, proscribe (prohibit), repress, restrict, rule (govern), stay (halt), stem (check), stifle, stop, strangle, subdue, subjugate, suppress, thwart, toll (stop), trammel, withhold. SEE MAIN ENTRY

restrain by injunction enjoin

restrain motion fetter

restrain movement fetter

restrained arrested (apprehended), arrested (checked), bound, controlled (restrained), frugal, limited, passive, patient, peaceable, reasonable (fair), taciturn, unobtrusive

restraining compulsory, limiting, preventive, prohibitive (restrictive), restrictive

restraining device barrier

restraining order injunction

restraint apprehension (act of arresting), arrest, bar (obstruction), barrier, bondage, captivity, censorship, check (bar), cloud (incumbrance), coercion, commitment (confinement), composure, compulsion (coercion), constraint (restriction), continence, control (restriction), custody (incarceration), damper (stopper), detention, deterrence, deterrent, disadvantage, discipline (obedience), disincentive, durance, embargo, estoppel, fetter, force (compulsion), handicap, hindrance, impediment, incarceration, incumbrance (lien), injunction, limitation, moderation, obstacle, obstruction, prohibition, propriety (correctness), quota, restriction, retention, servitude, stay, temperance, veto. SEE MAIN ENTRY

restraint of movement quarantine

restraints confines

restrengthen compound

restrict abridge *(divest)*, bar *(exclude)*, block, border *(bound)*, capture, censor, check *(restrain)*, clog, compel, condemn *(ban)*, confine, constrain *(imprison)*, constrain *(restrain)*, constrict *(inhibit)*, contain *(restrain)*, control *(restrain)*, debar, detain *(restrain)*, deter, disadvantage, discipline *(control)*, disfranchise, disqualify, enclose, enjoin, estop, exclude, fetter, forbid, halt, hamper, hinder, impede, inhibit, interdict, jail, keep *(restrain)*, limit, lock, modify *(moderate)*, occlude, preclude, prevent, prohibit, proscribe *(prohibit)*, qualify *(condition)*, repress, restrain, specialize, toll *(stop)*, trammel, withhold. SEE MAIN ENTRY

restrict access condemn *(ban)*, confine, constrain *(restrain)*, picket, police

restrict in area constrict *(compress)*

restricted arrested *(checked)*, certain *(specific)*, conditional, confidential, dependent, exclusive *(limited)*, limited, local, narrow, partial *(biased)*, personal *(private)*, private *(not public)*, privy, qualified *(conditioned)*, regional, specific, without recourse. SEE MAIN ENTRY

restricted goods contraband

restricted to a small area parochial

restricted to a small scope parochial

restricting limiting

restriction abridgment *(disentitlement)*, arrest, barrier, blockade *(limitation)*, bondage, censorship, check *(bar)*, commitment *(confinement)*, compulsion *(coercion)*, condition *(contingent provision)*, constraint *(imprisonment)*, custody *(incarceration)*, damper *(stopper)*, decrease, detention, deterrence, deterrent, disadvantage, duress, economy *(frugality)*, embargo, enclosure, encumbrance, estoppel, fetter, force *(compulsion)*, guideline, hindrance, impediment, incarceration, injunction, limitation, moderation, modification, obstacle, obstruction, prohibition, provision *(clause)*, qualification *(condition)*, quota, reservation *(condition)*, restraint, salvo, veto. SEE MAIN ENTRY

restriction on movement bondage, detention, durance

restriction on personal liberty incarceration

restrictive arbitrary and capricious, binding, compulsory, exclusive *(limited)*, limiting, preventive, proprietary. SEE MAIN ENTRY

restrictive practice constraint *(restriction)*, control *(restriction)*

restrictus parsimonious

restringe restrict

restructuring reorganization

restudy reexamine

restyle change, convert *(change use)*, transform

restyling revision *(process of correcting)*

resubstantiate reconfirm

result adjudication, answer *(solution)*, award, conclusion *(determination)*, conclusion *(outcome)*, consequence *(conclusion)*, denouement, destination, determination, development *(outgrowth)*, effect, emanate, end *(termination)*, ensue, evolve, finding, follow-up, holding *(ruling of a court)*, issuance, judgment *(formal court decree)*, occur *(happen)*, outcome, outgrowth, output, proceeds, product, redound, stem *(originate)*, supervene, toll *(effect)*. SEE MAIN ENTRY

result ascertained conclusion *(determination)*, determination

result from accrue *(arise)*

result in produce *(manufacture)*

result of judicial inquest conclusion *(determination)*

resultance conclusion *(outcome)*, outgrowth

resultant amount *(result)*, ancillary *(subsidiary)*, consequential *(deducible)*, constructive *(creative)*, deductive, derivative, development *(outgrowth)*, effect, end *(termination)*, ensuing, outcome, outgrowth, residuary, result

resultant action conclusion *(outcome)*, consequence *(conclusion)*, effect

resulting ancillary *(subsidiary)*, derivative, ensuing

resulting from contingent, dependent

resultless futile, otiose

resume brief. SEE MAIN ENTRY

resumé capsule, dossier

resume proceed *(continue)*, recur, renew *(begin again)*, reopen, repeat *(do again)*, return *(go back)*

resumption recrudescence, renewal, resurgence, revival. SEE MAIN ENTRY

resupply replenish

resurge renew *(refurbish)*

resurgence recrudescence, resurgence, revival. SEE MAIN ENTRY

resurgent corrigible, renascent

resurrect disinter, renew *(refurbish)*, renovate, repair. SEE MAIN ENTRY

resurrected renascent

resurrection rehabilitation, renewal, repair, resurgence, revival

resuscitate cure, recall *(call back)*, remedy, renew *(refurbish)*, restore *(renew)*, resurrect. SEE MAIN ENTRY

resuscitated renascent

resuscitation rehabilitation, renewal, resurgence, revival

retabulating reclassification

retail recount, vend. SEE MAIN ENTRY

retail store market *(business)*

retailer dealer, merchant, vendor

retain continue *(prolong)*, detain *(hold in custody)*, employ *(engage services)*, enclose, engage *(hire)*, fund, hire, hoard, hold *(possess)*, keep *(shelter)*, occupy *(take possession)*, own, perpetuate, possess, prolong, recall *(remember)*, remain *(occupy)*, remember, reserve, save *(hold back)*, store, understand. SEE MAIN ENTRY

retain exclusive control monopolize

retain exclusive possession monopolize

retain in custody impound

retain the impression of recognize *(perceive)*

retain the services of employ *(engage services)*

retainer compensation, consociate, deposit, downpayment, honorarium. SEE MAIN ENTRY

retainer of counsel client

retaining reservation *(engagement)*

retaining fee compensation, retainer

retainment employment, reservation *(engagement)*, retention

retake attach *(seize)*, reclaim, recoup *(regain)*, recover, rescue

retaking replevin

retaliate answer *(reply)*, penalize, punish, rebut, reciprocate, recriminate, repay, resist *(oppose)*, return *(respond)*. SEE MAIN ENTRY

retaliation counterattack, exchange, interchange, reaction *(opposition)*, reprisal, requital, retribution, revenge, vengeance

retaliative malevolent, reciprocal, ruthless, vindictive

retaliatory disciplinary *(punitory)*, malevolent, penal, punitive, reciprocal, vindictive

retaliatory punishment revenge

retard bar *(hinder)*, block, check *(restrain)*, clog, condemn *(ban)*, constrict *(inhibit)*, control *(restrain)*, curb, debar, defer *(put off)*, delay, diminish, disadvantage, discontinue *(break continuity)*, encumber *(hinder)*, enjoin, foil, hamper, hinder, hold up *(delay)*, impede, inhibit, interfere, interrupt, keep *(restrain)*, obstruct, occlude, preclude, prevent, procrastinate, protract *(prolong)*, stall, stem *(check)*, thwart, trammel, withstand. SEE MAIN ENTRY

retard decay keep *(shelter)*

retard flow shut

retardant preventive

retardare hinder, impede

retardation check *(bar)*, damper *(stopper)*, delay, deterrent, disadvantage, encumbrance, filibuster, hindrance, impediment, restraint

retarded arrested *(checked)*, disadvantaged, late *(tardy)*

retardment check *(bar)*, disadvantage, filibuster, hindrance, impediment

retax reassess

retell copy, quote, reaffirm, recapitulate, recite, recount, reiterate, relate *(tell)*, repeat *(state again)*, review

retelling narration, recital, redundancy, restatement

retentio detention, retention

retention apprehension *(act of arresting)*, arrest, enjoyment *(use)*, occupancy, occupation *(possession)*, remembrance *(recollection)*, reservation *(engagement)*. SEE MAIN ENTRY

retentive memory retrospect

rethink reconsider

reticent discreet, guarded, inarticulate, laconic, mute, noncommittal, taciturn, unobtrusive, unresponsive

reticular sinuous

reticulate intertwine

retinere detain *(restrain)*, hold up *(delay)*, keep *(fulfill)*, keep *(restrain)*, restrain, withhold

retire abandon *(withdraw)*, demit, depart, discharge *(dismiss)*, discontinue *(abandon)*, dislodge, ebb, flee, leave *(depart)*, part *(leave)*, quit *(discontinue)*, quit *(evacuate)*, recess, rest *(cease from action)*, retreat, secede, seclude, sequester *(seclude)*, superannuate, supplant, withdraw. SEE MAIN ENTRY

retire from office demit

retire from sight seclude

retired former, obsolete, outmoded

retirement abandonment *(desertion)*, cessation *(termination)*, end *(termination)*, expiration, layoff, leave *(absence)*, obscuration, privacy, removal, resignation *(relinquishment)*

retirement benefits pension

retirement income annuity, pension

retirement of a debt discharge *(payment)*

retiring diffident, inconspicuous, unobtrusive, unpretentious

retold repeated

retort answer *(reply)*, answer *(reply)*, confutation, counterargument, counterattack, countercharge, plea, rebut, recriminate, refute, rejoinder, reply *(noun)*, reply *(verb)*, respond, response, return *(respond)*. SEE MAIN ENTRY

retort a charge recriminate

retortion counterattack

retouch emend, enhance, fix *(repair)*, renew *(refurbish)*, repair, restore *(renew)*

retouching repair

retrace copy, recall *(remember)*, reexamine, repeat *(do again)*, review. SEE MAIN ENTRY

retrace one's steps return *(go back)*

retract abandon *(withdraw)*, abolish, abrogate *(annul)*, abrogate *(rescind)*, adeem, annul, cancel, disaffirm, disavow, discharge *(release from obligation)*, disclaim, disinherit, disown *(deny the validity)*, invalidate, negate, nullify, overrule, recant, renege, repeal, repudiate, rescind, revoke, secede, vacate *(void)*, withdraw

retractare recant, revise

retractation defeasance, discharge *(annulment)*, negation, repudiation, retraction, revocation. SEE MAIN ENTRY

retracting cancellation

retraction abjuration, abolition, ademption, annulment, breach, cancellation, correction *(change)*, countermand, defeasance, denial, negation, renunciation, repudiation, rescission, reversal, revocation. SEE MAIN ENTRY

retractory willful

retranslate construe *(translate)*

retransmit recover

retread repair

retreat abandon *(physically leave)*, abandon *(withdraw)*, asylum *(hiding place)*, avoid *(evade)*, avoidance *(evasion)*, chamber *(compartment)*, decline, disappear, ebb, evacuate, flee, flight, give *(yield)*, haven, leave *(absence)*, leave *(depart)*, part *(leave)*, privacy, quit *(evacuate)*, refuge, removal, renege, resign, return *(go back)*, revert, seclude, shelter *(protection)*, vacate *(leave)*, withdraw. SEE MAIN ENTRY

retrench curtail, decrease, diminish. SEE MAIN ENTRY

retrenchment curtailment, decrease

retrial appeal, rehearing

retribution condemnation *(punishment)*, conviction *(finding of guilt)*, correction *(punishment)*, discipline *(punishment)*, justice, punishment, relief *(legal redress)*, reprisal, revenge, vengeance. SEE MAIN ENTRY

retributive compensatory, disciplinary *(punitory)*, penal, punitive, reciprocal, vindictive

retributive action sanction *(punishment)*

retributive justice condemnation *(punishment)*, conviction *(finding of guilt)*, correction *(punishment)*, discipline *(punishment)*, penalty, punishment, reprisal, retribution

retributive punishment revenge, vengeance

retrievable corrigible

retrieval compensation, out of pocket, recovery *(repossession)*, redemption, replevin, restitution, salvage, trover

retrieve collect *(recover money)*, reap, reclaim, recoup *(regain)*, recover, redeem *(repurchase)*, remedy, repossess, rescue

retrievement trover

retroaction decline, reaction *(opposition)*, repercussion, reversion *(act of returning)*

retroactive ex post facto. SEE MAIN ENTRY

retroactive effect nunc pro tunc

retrocede escheat, regress, relapse, retire *(retreat)*, retreat

retrocedent regressive

retrocession decline, relapse, reversion *(act of returning)*

retrogradation decline, degradation, deterioration, lapse *(expiration)*, recidivism, relapse, reversion *(act of returning)*

retrograde decadent, decay, depreciate, deteriorate, recidivate, regress, regressive, relapse, return *(go back)*, revert

retrogress decay, degenerate, deteriorate, regress, relapse, revert

retrogression decline, degradation, deterioration, lapse *(expiration)*, recidivism, reconversion, relapse, reversion *(act of returning)*

retrogressive back *(in reverse)*, bad *(offensive)*, decadent, regressive

retrospect hindsight, recall *(remember)*, recapitulate, recollect, remembrance *(recollection)*. SEE MAIN ENTRY

retrospection hindsight, recollection, remembrance *(recollection)*

retrospective back *(in reverse)*

retrospective effect nunc pro tunc

retrospectively heretofore

retroversion reconversion, relapse, reversion *(act of returning)*

retrovert escheat, relapse, revert

retrude repel *(drive back)*, repulse

retry appeal, reconsider

return annuity, answer *(reply)*, answer *(reply)*, bear *(yield)*, benefit *(betterment)*, commission *(fee)*, compensate *(remunerate)*, compensation, consideration *(recompense)*, continuation *(resumption)*, contribute *(indemnify)*, contribution *(indemnification)*, discharge *(payment)*, dividend, escheat, indemnification, indemnity, output, pay, payment *(act of paying)*, perquisite, poll *(canvass)*, proceed *(continue)*, profit, quit *(repay)*, reaction *(response)*, rebate, reciprocate, reciprocity, recommit, recompense, reconversion, recoup *(reimburse)*, recovery *(repossession)*, recrudescence, recur, redemption, refund *(noun)*, refund *(verb)*, regress, rehabilitation, reinstate, relapse *(noun)*, relapse *(verb)*, remand, remuneration, rendition *(restoration)*, renewal, rent, reparation *(indemnification)*, repay, repeat *(do again)*, reply *(noun)*, reply *(verb)*, reprisal, requital, response, restitution, retaliate, retort, retribution, revenue, reversion *(act of returning)*, revert, revival, reward, salvage, satisfaction *(discharge of debt)*, surrender *(give back)*, trover, yield *(produce a return)*. SEE MAIN ENTRY

return an accusation recriminate

return an answer respond

return in money income

return money paid out indemnify

return on capital income

return the charge recriminate

return to continue *(resume)*, renew *(begin again)*, reopen, resume

return to prison remand

return to the original state fix *(repair)*

returned reciprocal

returned check bad check

returning chronic, incessant, periodic

returning at intervals chronic, periodic

returns earnings, proceeds

retusus obtuse

réunion assemblage

reunion collection *(assembly)*, conciliation, congregation, meeting *(conference)*, rapprochement, reconciliation

reunite call *(summon)*, collect *(gather)*, conjoin, convene, meet, pacify, reconcile

reus criminal

reutter recapitulate, reiterate

reuttered repeated

revalidate reconfirm

revalidated nunc pro tunc

revalue reassess

revamp amend, convert *(change use)*, edit, emend, fix *(repair)*, modify *(alter)*, reconstruct, recreate, redact, rehabilitate, renew *(refurbish)*, renovate, repair, revise, transform

revamping renewal, reparation *(keeping in repair)*

revampment amendment *(correction)*, correction *(change)*

reveal adduce, admit *(concede)*, apprise, bare, betray *(disclose)*, circulate, communicate, confess, construe *(translate)*, convey *(communicate)*, declare, denude, depict, detect, disabuse, disclose, disinter, display, divulge, enlighten, evidence, exhibit, explain, explicate, expose, expound, find *(discover)*, impart, inform *(betray)*, inform *(notify)*, interpret, issue *(publish)*, locate, manifest, mention, notice *(give formal warning)*, notify, produce *(offer to view)*, profess *(avow)*, promulgate, publish, relate *(tell)*, report *(disclose)*, resolve *(solve)*, signify *(denote)*, signify *(inform)*, speak, unveil, utter. SEE MAIN ENTRY

reveal itself arise *(appear)*, occur *(come to mind)*

reveal oneself report *(present oneself)*

reveal something private confide *(divulge)*

reveal the answer resolve *(solve)*

reveal to public notice exhibit

revealed comprehensible, evident, manifest, naked *(perceptible)*, obvious, open *(in sight)*, overt, palpable, patent, pellucid, perceivable, perceptible, public *(known)*

revealing demonstrative *(illustrative)*, descriptive, disclosure *(act of disclosing)*, informative, informatory

revealment admission *(disclosure)*, confession, disclosure *(act of disclosing)*, disclosure *(something disclosed)*, discovery, expression *(manifestation)*, publication *(disclosure)*, publicity

revel carouse

revel in relish

revelation admission *(disclosure)*, answer *(solution)*, communication *(statement)*, declaration, disclosure *(something disclosed)*, discovery, exhibit, expression *(manifestation)*, information *(knowledge)*, manifestation, notice *(announcement)*, notification, publication *(disclosure)*, publicity, report *(detailed account)*, testimony, vision *(dream)*

revelatory informatory

revelry treat

revenant phantom, specter

revenge counterattack, penalize, rancor, repay, reprisal, retaliate, retribution, vengeance. SEE MAIN ENTRY

revengeful malevolent, malignant, resentful, ruthless, spiteful, vindictive

revengefulness belligerency, rancor, reprisal, revenge, spite, vengeance

revenue boom *(prosperity)*, capital, duty *(tax)*, earnings, finance, income, money, pay, perquisite, proceeds, profit, rent, resource, substance *(material possessions)*, wage. SEE MAIN ENTRY

reverberant resounding

reverberating resounding

reverberation reaction (response), repercussion

reverberatory resounding

revere honor, regard (hold in esteem)

revered outstanding (prominent), reputable, sacrosanct

reverence courtesy, estimation (esteem), fealty, homage, honor (outward respect), honor, interest (concern), regard (esteem), regard (hold in esteem), respect

reverenced reputable

reverend sacrosanct

reverent obeisant

reverenter respectfully

reverential obedient, obeisant, sequacious, solemn

reverently respectfully

reverie contemplation, figment, introspection, preoccupation, reflection (thought)

reversal annulment, cancellation, countermand, defeasance, discharge (annulment), negation, nollo prosequi, reconversion, recrudescence, relapse, repudiation, rescision, retraction, reversion (act of returning), revocation. SEE MAIN ENTRY

reverse abrogate (annul), abrogate (rescind), adverse (opposite), annul, antipathetic (oppositional), antipode, antithesis, cancel, contra, contradict, contradictory, contraposition, contrary, counteract, counterpart (complement), debacle, disaffirm, discharge (release from obligation), disown (deny the validity), escheat, hostile, invalidate, inverse, misfortune, negate, negative, nullify, opposite, override, overrule, overthrow, overturn, plight, quash, recant, recrudescence, regress, regressive, relapse (noun), relapse (verb), renege, repeal, repudiate, rescind, retreat, reversion (act of returning), revert, revoke, tragedy, trouble, upset, vacate (void), vitiate, withdraw

reverse direction return (go back)

reversed back (in reverse), inverse, null (invalid), null and void, opposite, regressive

reverseless indefeasible, indelible, irreversible, irrevocable, permanent

reversible ambulatory, capricious, convertible

reversing cancellation

reversion continuation (resumption), decline, defeasance, devolution, heritage, lapse (expiration), nollo prosequi, recidivism, reconversion, recovery (repossession), recrudescence, relapse, remainder (remaining part), restitution, resurgence, reversal. SEE MAIN ENTRY

reversion rights SEE MAIN ENTRY

reversion to the government escheatment

reversion to the state escheatment

reversional ambulatory, regressive

reversionary regressive

reversionary estate remainder (estate in property)

revert disorganize, escheat, recur, regress, relapse, repeat (do again), return (go back), revoke. SEE MAIN ENTRY

revert to the state escheat

reverti lapse (cease), return (go back)

reverting reversion (act of returning)

revest reinstate, restore (return)

review account (report), analysis, analyze, appeal (noun), appeal (verb), audit, canvass, capsule, censor, check (inspect), comment, compendium, consideration (contemplation), contemplation, criticism,

criticize (evaluate), cross-questioning, deliberate, digest, diligence (care), discretion (power of choice), discuss, evaluate, examination (study), examine (study), frisk, habeas corpus, hindsight, hornbook, indagation, inquest, inspection, investigate, judge, judgment (discernment), monitor, muse, narration, notice (observe), observe (watch), overlook (superintend), peruse, ponder, probe (noun), probe (verb), recall (remember), recapitulate, recital, recollect, reconsider, reexamine, reiterate, remember, repeat (state again), report (detailed account), restatement, retrospect, revise, revision (process of correcting), scenario, scrutinize, scrutiny, study, summary, survey (examine), survey (poll), synopsis, test, trial (experiment). SEE MAIN ENTRY

review of things past hindsight

reviewer juror

reviewers of fact jury

revile attack, blame, condemn (blame), contemn, decry, defame, denigrate, denounce (condemn), derogate, disapprove (condemn), discommend, flout, inveigh, lash (attack verbally), libel, malign, rebuke, reprimand, reproach

revilement bad repute, contempt (disdain), contumely, criticism, denunciation, diatribe, disapprobation, discredit, disdain, disparagement, libel, malediction, obloquy, outcry, phillipic, rejection, reprimand, reproach, slander, vilification. SEE MAIN ENTRY

revilement of religion blasphemy

reviling abusive, aspersion, contemptuous, diatribe

revindication recovery (repossession)

revisable corrigible

revisal amendment (correction), correction (change), revision (process of correcting)

revise adapt, amend, change, convert (change use), edit, emend, modify (alter), qualify (condition), rectify, reform, remedy, renew (refurbish), review, transform, treat (process). SEE MAIN ENTRY

revise one's thoughts reconsider

revised current, tempered

revised edition correction (change), revision (corrected version)

revising reorganization

revision amendment (correction), correction (change), development (progression), innovation, reform, renewal, reorganization. SEE MAIN ENTRY

revisional ambulatory, corrigible

revisionist malcontent

revisit return (go back)

revisory ambulatory

revitalize renew (refurbish), resurrect

revival recrudescence, rehabilitation, renewal, repair, resurgence. SEE MAIN ENTRY

revival in the mind remembrance (recollection)

revive change, copy, cure, develop, fix (repair), meliorate, recall (call back), recall (remember), recollect, recreate, rehabilitate, reinstate, remedy, renew (begin again), renew (refurbish), renovate, reopen, repair, restore (renew), resurrect

revived de novo, renascent

revivement rehabilitation

revivification recrudescence, rehabilitation, renewal, resurgence, revival

revivified renascent

revivify cure, fix (repair), recall (call back), rehabilitate, remedy, renovate, restore (renew), resurrect

revivifying remedial

reviviscence recrudescence, revival

reviviscency recrudescence

reviviscent salubrious

revocable ambulatory, defeasible, voidable

revocare recall (call back)

revocatio revocation

revocation abatement (extinguishment), abjuration, abolition, ademption, annulment, cancellation, countermand, defeasance, denial, discharge (annulment), discharge (release from obligation), disclaimer, dissolution (termination), mistrial, negation, repudiation, rescision, retraction, reversal. SEE MAIN ENTRY

revocation of orders countermand

revocatory ambulatory

revoke abate (extinguish), abolish, abrogate (rescind), adeem, annul, bear false witness, cancel, debar, disavow, discharge (release from obligation), discontinue (abandon), disinherit, disown (deny the validity), dissolve (terminate), invalidate, kill (defeat), negate, nullify, override, overrule, prohibit, proscribe (prohibit), recall (call back), recant, refuse, renege, repeal, repudiate, rescind, vacate (void), withdraw. SEE MAIN ENTRY

revoke one's license to practice law disbar

revoked null (invalid), null and void

revokement abjuration, abolition, ademption, annulment, cancellation, countermand, defeasance, dissolution (termination), negation, rescision, reversal, revocation

revoking cancellation, revocation

revolt conflict, contest (dispute), defect, defiance, disagree, disloyalty, disobey, disturbance, fight (battle), infidelity, insurrection, mutiny, outbreak, outburst, overthrow, protest, rebel, rebellion, reject, rejection, repel (disgust), resistance, revolution, riot, secede, sedition, strike (refuse to work), subversion, treason. SEE MAIN ENTRY

revolted averse

revolter insurgent, malcontent

revolting bad (offensive), heinous, loathsome, lurid, objectionable, obnoxious, odious, offensive (offending), repugnant (exciting aversion), repulsive, unsavory

revolution anarchy, cycle, defiance, disturbance, innovation, insurrection, mutiny, outbreak, outburst, rebellion, resistance, revolt, sedition, subversion, treason. SEE MAIN ENTRY

revolutionary demagogue, disorderly, incendiary, insubordinate, insurgent, lawless, malcontent, radical (favoring drastic change), restive

revolutionist insurgent, malcontent

revolutionize change, disobey, overthrow, rebel, reform, transform

revolve muse

revolve in the mind ponder, reflect (ponder), study

revolver gun

revulsion contempt (disdain), disapprobation, hatred, odium

reward benefit (conferment), bonus, bounty, commission (fee), compensate (remunerate), compensation, consideration (recompense), disburse (pay out), earnings, fee (charge), grant, gratuity (present), pay (noun), pay (verb), perquisite, prize, profit, recognition, recompense, remunerate, remuneration, repay, requital, retribution, revenue, tip (gratuity). SEE MAIN ENTRY

reward for a loss compensate *(remunerate)*

reward for an injury compensate *(remunerate)*

reward for injury compensation

reward for loss compensation

reward for service bounty, compensation, honorarium, perquisite, wage

reward of labor earnings

reward of office earnings

rewarder donor, grantor

rewardful compensatory, lucrative

rewarding compensatory, gainful, lucrative, profitable, valuable

reweigh reconsider

reword construe *(translate)*, quote, recapitulate, recount, reiterate, repeat *(state again)*, review

reworded repeated

rewording paraphrase, rendition *(explication)*, restatement

rework amend, edit, emend, modify *(alter)*, reconsider, reconstruct, redact, reform, renew *(refurbish)*, revise

rewrite amend, copy, correction *(change)*, edit, emend, modify *(alter)*, redact, revise, revision *(corrected version)*. SEE MAIN ENTRY

rewriting revision *(process of correcting)*

rezone reapportion, reassign

rhapsodical ecstatic

rhetoric bombast, declamation, fustian, language, parlance, phraseology, speech. SEE MAIN ENTRY

rhetorica rhetoric *(skilled speech)*

rhetorical flatulent, inflated *(bombastic)*, orotund, turgid, voluble

rhetorical discourse peroration

rhetorical phrase expletive

rhetorical presentation discourse

rhetorical word expletive

rhetoricalness bombast

rhetorize declaim

rhythm regularity

rhythmic intermittent, periodic, regular *(orderly)*

rhythmical periodic

rialto market *(business)*

ribald blameworthy, blatant *(obtrusive)*, disreputable, inelegant, lascivious, lewd, obscene, offensive *(offending)*, prurient, salacious, scurrilous, suggestive *(risqué)*

ribaldry obscenity

rich copious, elaborate, eloquent, fertile, full, nectarious, opulent, productive, profuse, prolific, prosperous, resounding, savory, strong, successful. SEE MAIN ENTRY

riches assets, cash, hoard, money, prosperity, substance *(material possessions)*

richly endowed opulent

richness boom *(prosperity)*, plethora, prosperity

rickety imperfect

ricochet repercussion

rid dislodge, eject *(evict)*, extirpate, free *(relieved from a burden)*, relieve *(free from burden)*, relinquish

rid of deception disabuse

rid of defects emend

rid oneself of forgo, jettison, renounce

riddance catharsis, deportation, estrangement, exclusion, layoff, privation, rejection, removal

riddle enigma, mystery, penetrate, problem

riddled penetrable

rider addendum, allonge, amendment *(legislation)*, appendix *(supplement)*. SEE MAIN ENTRY

ridicile discommend

ridicula imitatio parody

ridicule contemn, contempt *(disdain)*, decry, derogate, disdain, disgrace, dishonor *(shame)*, disparage, disparagement, disrespect, flout, humiliate, illude, impeach, jape, jeer, libel, malign, minimize, misprize, mock *(deride)*, offend *(insult)*, parody, pillory, smear, travesty. SEE MAIN ENTRY

ridicule irresponsibly cavil

ridiculing cynical, disdainful

ridiculous fatuous, incredible, inept *(inappropriate)*, irrational, ludicrous, unreasonable, untenable

ridiculousness incongruity

ridiculum ridicule

ridiculus jocular

rife general, ordinary, populous, predominant, prevailing *(current)*, prevalent, profuse, rampant, replete, usual. SEE MAIN ENTRY

rifle despoil, gun, loot, pirate *(take by violence)*, plunder, poach, steal

rifler burglar

rift alienation *(estrangement)*, disaccord, disassociation, dissension, estrangement, flaw, hiatus, schism, split, strife. SEE MAIN ENTRY

rig furnish, manipulate *(control unfairly)*

right accurate, actual, allowable, applicable, appropriate, birthright, capacity *(authority)*, cause of action, certain *(positive)*, condign, cure, dominion *(absolute ownership)*, droit, due, eligible, emend, equitable, equity *(share of ownership)*, ethical, exact, factual, fairness, fit, fix *(repair)*, franchise *(license)*, honest, intangible, interest *(ownership)*, juridical, just, justice, liberty, license, licit, option *(contractual provision)*, patent, possession *(ownership)*, prerogative, prescription *(claim of title)*, privilege, proper, propriety *(appropriateness)*, qualification *(fitness)*, real, reasonable *(rational)*, rectify, rectitude, redress, remedy, repair, rightful, share *(interest)*, sound, stake *(interest)*, suitable, title *(right)*, true *(authentic)*, truth, undistorted. SEE MAIN ENTRY

right answer solution *(answer)*

right arm mainstay

right away instantly

right dealing equity *(justice)*

right hand mainstay

right note decorum

right now instantly

right of action cause of action

right of choice discretion *(power of choice)*, franchise *(right to vote)*, latitude, liberty, option *(choice)*, patronage *(power to appoint jobs)*

right of entry access *(right of way)*, ingress

right of future enjoyment reversion *(remainder of an estate)*

right of future possession reversion *(remainder of an estate)*

right of literary property copyright

right of ownership interest *(ownership)*

right of passage easement

right of possession dominion *(absolute ownership)*, fee *(estate)*, ownership

right of put and call call *(option)*

right of recovery cause of action

right of representation franchise *(right to vote)*

right of retention possession *(ownership)*

right of succession reversion *(remainder of an estate)*

right of use easement

right of way easement

right thing to do decorum

right time opportunity

right to adjudicate authority *(right)*

right to buy or sell option *(contractual provision)*

right to command authority *(right)*

right to control SEE MAIN ENTRY

right to counsel SEE MAIN ENTRY

right to decide freedom

right to determine authority *(right)*

right to die SEE MAIN ENTRY

right to dispose of property charge *(lien)*

right to enforce charge on property mechanics lien

right to enforce charge upon property lien

right to enter ingress

right to life SEE MAIN ENTRY

right to personal things intangible

right to precedence priority

right to preference priority

right to privacy SEE MAIN ENTRY

right to profits accruing patent

right to property dominion *(absolute ownership)*

right to recovery intangible

right to relief cause of action

right to remain silent SEE MAIN ENTRY

right to retain occupation *(possession)*

right to settle issues authority *(right)*

right to vote suffrage

right, title and interest in land estate *(property)*

right-hand man assistant

right-minded clean, high-minded, law-abiding, meritorious, moral

right-of-way priority

righteous clean, conscientious, equitable, ethical, high-minded, just, law-abiding, meritorious, moral, proper, pure, reputable, right *(correct)*, upright

righteously fairly *(impartially)*

righteousness equity *(justice)*, ethics, honor *(good reputation)*, integrity, justice, merit, principle *(virtue)*, probity, rectitude

rightful actual, allowed, appropriate, blameless, bona fide, due *(regular)*, felicitous, genuine, juridical, just, legal, legitimate *(rightful)*, licit, right *(correct)*, sound, suitable, true *(authentic)*, unalienable. SEE MAIN ENTRY

rightful possession dominion *(absolute ownership)*, interest *(ownership)*

rightful power authority *(right)*, prerogative

rightful strength force *(legal efficacy)*

rightfully as a matter of right, duly, fairly *(impartially)*

rightfulness equity *(justice)*, fairness, justice, legality, legitimacy, principle *(virtue)*

righting correction *(change)*

rightly fairly *(impartially)*

rightness expedience, fairness, honesty, propriety *(appropriateness)*, qualification *(fitness)*

rights and privileges birthright

rigid close *(rigorous)*, draconian, exact, factual, firm, fixed *(securely placed)*, formal, inflexible, ironclad, irreconcilable, literal, meticulous, narrow, orthodox, particular *(exacting)*, pertinacious, precise, provincial, punctilious, relentless, renitent, severe, solid *(compact)*, static, strict, stringent, unalterable, unbending, uncompromising, unmitigated, unrelenting, unyielding. SEE MAIN ENTRY

rigid control   censorship
rigid routine   bureaucracy
rigidity   formality, rigor
rigidly   faithfully, invariably
rigidness   formality, particularity, rigor
rigidus   inflexible, rigid, stark, strict, unbending
rigor   severity. SEE MAIN ENTRY
rigorist   bigot
rigorous   accurate, callous, draconian, harsh, inflexible, intense, ironclad, meticulous, onerous, oppressive, particular *(exacting)*, precise, punctilious, rigid, severe, strict, stringent, unrelenting
rigorous proof   certification *(certainness)*
rigorous search   indagation, probe
rigorousness   rigor, severity
rile   badger, bait *(harass)*, disaffect, discompose, harry *(harass)*, incense, irritate, offend *(insult)*, pique
rim   border, boundary, edge *(border)*, frontier, limit, margin *(outside limit)*, mete, outline *(boundary)*, periphery
rima   rift *(gap)*, split
rimari   ferret, probe *(noun)*, probe *(verb)*
ring   cabal, enclose, encompass *(surround)*, hedge, league, syndicate
ringing   resounding
ringleader   demagogue, pioneer
riot   anarchy, belligerency, bluster *(commotion)*, brawl *(noun)*, brawl *(verb)*, disorder *(lack of order)*, embroilment, fracas, imbroglio, insurrection, outbreak, pandemonium, rebel, rebellion, sedition. SEE MAIN ENTRY
rioter   insurgent, malcontent
riotous   disobedient, disorderly, drunk, lawless, licentious, uncontrollable, unruly
rip   lancinate, rend, split *(noun)*, split *(verb)*
rip out   eviscerate
riparian   fluvial, littoral
ripe   ready *(prepared)*. SEE MAIN ENTRY
ripe to submit for judicial review   justiciable
ripen   develop, mature, progress
ripeness   opportunity
ripening   growth *(evolution)*
riposte   answer *(reply)* counterattack, countercharge, reply, response, retort, return *(respond)*
ripping out   avulsion, evulsion
rise   advancement *(improvement)*, appearance *(emergence)*, appreciate *(increase)*, appreciation *(increased value)*, augmentation, boom *(increase)*, build *(augment)*, commence, disobey, elevation, emerge, genesis, growth *(increase)*, inception, increase, increment, inflate, inflation *(increase)*, nascency, onset *(commencement)*, origination, outset, progress *(noun)*, progress *(verb)*, promotion *(advancement)*, pullulate, rebel, result, start, stem *(originate)*. SEE MAIN ENTRY
rise above   outbalance, outweigh, overcome *(surmount)*, predominate *(outnumber)*, surmount, surpass, transcend
rise against   confront *(oppose)*
rise and fall   fluctuate
rise from   accrue *(arise)*
rise in arms   rebel
rise in hostility before   accost
rise in value   appreciate *(increase)*, appreciation *(increased value)*
risible   ludicrous
rising   insurrection, outbreak, outburst, progressive *(going forward)*, prominent, prosperous, rebellion, revolt, sedition

rising generation   children
rising insubordination   commotion
rising prices   boom *(prosperity)*
risk   bet, compromise *(endanger)*, danger, endanger, endeavor, expose, gamble, hazard, invest *(fund)*, jeopardize, jeopardy, parlay *(bet)*, pawn, peril, pitfall, speculate *(chance)*, threat, venture. SEE MAIN ENTRY
risk exposure to harm   endanger
risk one's money   invest *(fund)*
risk taker   speculator
risk-taker   bettor
risk-taking   hot-blooded, impulsive *(rash)*
riskful   aleatory *(perilous)*, precarious
risks   pitfall
risky   aleatory *(perilous)*, dangerous, impulsive *(rash)*, insalubrious, insecure, noxious, precarious, speculative, toxic, vulnerable
risky undertaking   venture
risqué   brazen
risque   improper, lewd, lurid, obscene, salacious, scurrilous
rite   ceremony, custom, form *(arrangement)*, formality
ritual   behavior, ceremony, custom, form *(arrangement)*, formal, formality, process *(course)*, propriety *(correctness)*, remembrance *(commemoration)*, routine, solemn, way *(manner)*
ritualism   behavior
ritualistic   formal
ritualistically   pro forma
ritualize   formalize
ritually   pro forma
ritus   ceremony, formality
rival   adversary, antagonize, compete, competitive *(antagonistic)*, conflict, confront *(oppose)*, contend *(dispute)*, contender, contestant, counteract, disputant, foe, jealous, outbalance, peer, resist *(oppose)*, surpass, transcend. SEE MAIN ENTRY
rivaling   comparative, competitive *(antagonistic)*
rivalry   belligerency, competition, conflict, contention *(opposition)*, contest *(competition)*, impugnation, strife
rivalship   contest *(competition)*
rive   break *(separate)*, dichotomize, disjoint, disperse *(scatter)*, force *(break)*, lancinate, luxate, rend, separate, sever, split
riven   broken *(fractured)*
riverine   fluvial
rivery   fluvial
rivet the attention   occupy *(engage)*
rivet the mind   occupy *(engage)*
rivet the thoughts   occupy *(engage)*
riveted   immutable, stable, steadfast
rixa   affray, altercation, brawl
rixari   brawl, dispute *(contest)*
road   access *(right of way)*, admission *(entry)*, admittance *(means of approach)*, avenue *(route)*, causeway, course, way *(channel)*
roadway   admission *(entry)*, avenue *(route)*, causeway, way *(channel)*
roam   perambulate, prowl
roamer   itinerant, pedestrian
roaming   discursive *(digressive)*, moving *(in motion)*, shifting, transient, vagrancy
roar   barrage, pandemonium
rob   defalcate, deprive, despoil, harry *(plunder)*, hold up *(rob)*, impropriate, loot, peculate, pilfer, pillage, pirate *(take by violence)*, plunder, prey, purloin, spoil *(pillage)*, steal. SEE MAIN ENTRY
rob of freedom   subjugate

robber   burglar, criminal, outlaw, thief, vandal
robbery   burglary, housebreaking, plunder, spoliation, theft. SEE MAIN ENTRY
robbing   burglary
robe   clothe
roborant   medicinal, remedial, salubrious, salutary
robur   strength
robust   durable, strong
robustness   health, puissance, sinew, strength
robustus   strong
rock   lull, oscillate, vacillate
rocklike   durable
rodomontade   bombast, exaggeration, fustian, jactation. SEE MAIN ENTRY
rogare   petition, pray, request, sue
rogatio   bill *(proposed act)*, motion, proposition, question *(inquiry)*, request
rogue   convict, delinquent, hoodlum, malefactor
roguery   deception, improbity, knavery, mischief, misdoing
roguish   false *(disloyal)*, immoral, jocular, machiavellian, reprobate, unscrupulous
roguishness   knavery, mischief
roil   agitate *(activate)*, annoy, badger, discompose, disturb, hector, pique, plague, provoke
roisterer   hoodlum
role   agency *(legal relationship)*, assignment *(task)*, capacity *(job)*, conduct, duty *(obligation)*, function, job, office, position *(business status)*, profession *(vocation)*. SEE MAIN ENTRY
roll   docket, file, record, register, schedule. SEE MAIN ENTRY
roll back   decrease, diminish
roll into one   collect *(gather)*, consolidate *(unite)*
roll on   proceed *(go forward)*
roll out   spread
roll-over clause   SEE MAIN ENTRY
rollicking   jocular
rolling   fluvial
rolling in riches   opulent
romance   figment
romantic   quixotic
rompish   jocular
roof   ceiling, shelter *(protection)*
rookie   novice
room   capacity *(maximum)*, chamber *(compartment)*, coverage *(scope)*, dwell *(reside)*, freedom, inhabit, latitude, margin *(spare amount)*, part *(place)*, scope, space
room for improvement   foible
room in which a court of law is held   courtroom
room in which a lawcourt is held   courtroom
room to spare   margin *(spare amount)*
room together   cohabit
room used for the application of the laws   courtroom
room used for the public administration of justice   courtroom
room where justice is administered   courtroom
roomer   inmate, lessee, lodger, occupant
rooming together   cohabitation *(living together)*
rooms   lodging
roomy   capacious
roorback   canard
root   basis, bloodline, cause *(reason)*, derivation, determinant, embed, establish

(entrench), fix *(make firm)*, foundation *(basis)*, genesis, gist *(substance)*, gravamen, ground, hunt, origin *(source)*, origination, plant *(place firmly)*, reason *(basis)*, source
root of dissension contention *(argument)*
root out destroy *(efface)*, disinter, extirpate, ferret, solve
root up disinter
rooted firm, fixed *(settled)*, habitual, immutable, indelible, ingrained, inveterate, organic, permanent, prescriptive, situated, stable, steadfast, traditional
rooted belief conviction *(persuasion)*
rootless baseless, solitary
rope handcuff
rope off demarcate, isolate, seclude
roseate auspicious, propitious
roster record, register, roll
rot decay, degenerate, spoil *(impair)*, spoilage, taint *(contaminate)*
rotate oscillate, vary
rotation cycle, order *(arrangement)*, sequence
rotten heinous, marred, odious, profligate *(corrupt)*, repulsive, stale, tainted *(contaminated)*, tainted *(corrupted)*
rotting decadent, dissolution *(disintegration)*
rough astringent, blatant *(obtrusive)*, brutal, disorderly, harsh, hoodlum, imperfect, impertinent *(insolent)*, inelegant, inexact, mishandle *(maltreat)*, mordacious, provincial, severe, stringent, uncouth
rough calculation estimate *(approximate cost)*, estimation *(calculation)*
rough cast design *(construction plan)*
rough copy design *(construction plan)*
rough draft delineation
rough guess estimate *(approximate cost)*, estimation *(calculation)*
rough outline configuration *(form)*
rough representation design *(construction plan)*
rough sketch contour *(outline)*
roughness irregularity
round chain *(series)*, cycle, stabilize
round body sphere
round table panel *(discussion group)*, session
round up convene, cull
round-about astray
roundabout circuitous, devious, discursive *(digressive)*, indirect, labyrinthine, oblique *(evasive)*, sinuous, tortuous *(bending)*
roundabout action indirection *(indirect action)*
roundabout course detour
roundabout way digression
roundaboutness indirection *(indirect action)*
roundly wholly
rouse agitate *(activate)*, bait *(harass)*, coax, disturb, evoke, exhort, foment, hasten, impel, impress *(affect deeply)*, incite, interest, motivate, persuade, perturb, pique, prompt, provoke, spirit, stimulate, urge
rouser demagogue
rousing moving *(evoking emotion)*, persuasive
rout beat *(defeat)*, debacle, defeat, dispel, miscarriage, overcome *(surmount)*, prostration, repel *(drive back)*, repulse, subjugate, surmount
rout out expel, purge *(purify)*
route access *(right of way)*, admission *(entry)*, admittance *(means of approach)*,

conduit *(channel)*, course, direction *(course)*, send, way *(channel)*
routes approaches
routine accustomed *(customary)*, behavior, conventional, custom, customary, daily, familiar *(customary)*, habit, habitual, manner *(behavior)*, matter of course, method, mode, modus operandi, mundane, normal *(regular)*, operation, perfunctory, practice *(custom)*, practice *(procedure)*, procedure, process *(course)*, regular *(conventional)*, rule *(guide)*, system, systematic, trite, usage, usual. SEE MAIN ENTRY
routine event matter of course
routine happening matter of course
routine procedure custom
routinely invariably
rove digress, perambulate, prowl
rover itinerant, migrant, pedestrian
roving circuitous, discursive *(digressive)*, moving *(in motion)*, shifting, transient, vagrancy
row affray, altercation, bluster *(commotion)*, brawl *(noun)*, brawl *(verb)*, chain *(series)*, commotion, confrontation *(altercation)*, disaccord, embroilment, fight *(argument)*, fracas, fray, imbroglio, pandemonium, riot, strife, trouble, turmoil
rowdiness brawl, fracas
rowdy blatant *(obtrusive)*, disorderly, pugnacious, uncontrollable, unruly
royal outstanding *(prominent)*, sovereign *(absolute)*
rub contact *(touch)*
rub away diminish, erode
rub off deface, obliterate
rub out censor, deface, delete, destroy *(efface)*, expunge, extirpate, obliterate
rub the wrong way irritate
rubber check bad check
rubbery resilient
rubbing away erosion
rubric article *(precept)*, bylaw, caption, code, constitution, dictate, direction *(order)*, law, measure, precept, prescription *(directive)*, principle *(axiom)*, statute, title *(designation)*. SEE MAIN ENTRY
rubricate embellish
ruckus noise
ruction brawl, commotion, fracas, fray, noise, pandemonium
rude blatant *(obtrusive)*, brazen, caitiff, caustic, contemptuous, disdainful, disorderly, impertinent *(insolent)*, inelegant, insolent, obtrusive, offensive *(offending)*, perverse, presumptuous, provincial, uncouth, unseemly
rude behavior disrespect
rude reproach disparagement
rudeness contempt *(disobedience to the court)*, contumely, disparagement, disregard *(lack of respect)*, disrespect, ingratitude, rebuff, temerity
rudiment cornerstone, element, embryo, foundation *(basis)*, necessity
rudimental elementary, inchoate, incipient, original *(initial)*, rudimentary, ultimate
rudimentary cardinal *(basic)*, elementary, fundamental, inchoate, incipient, initial, minimal, organic, original *(initial)*, prime *(original)*, primordial, simple, ultimate, underlying. SEE MAIN ENTRY
rudimentary state embryo
rudis inexperienced, novice, uncouth, unversed
rue deplore, regret, remorse, repent

rueful contrite, despondent, lamentable, penitent, remorseful, repentant
ruffian aggressor, delinquent, hoodlum, malefactor
ruffianism brutality, misdoing
ruffianly disorderly
ruffle aggravate *(annoy)*, agitate *(shake up)*, annoy, badger, discompose, disconcert, disorient, disrupt, disturb, harry *(harass)*, incense, irritate, molest *(annoy)*, perturb, pique, plague
rugged brutal, powerful, severe, solid *(sound)*, strong
ruggedness health
ruin bankruptcy, betray *(lead astray)*, catastrophe, consumption, damage *(noun)*, damage *(verb)*, debacle, debauch, decay, decline, defeat, despoil, destroy *(efface)*, destruction, deterioration, detriment, devastate, disable, disaster, dissolution *(termination)*, extinguish, failure *(lack of success)*, fatality, foil, harm *(noun)*, harm *(verb)*, havoc, impair, loss, miscarriage, mischief, misemploy, misfortune, obliterate, overturn, pervert, pillage, plunder, prejudice *(injure)*, prostration, spoil *(impair)*, stain, subversion, subvert, thwart, upset
ruin one's eyesight blind *(deprive of sight)*
ruin one's prospects disappoint
ruinable destructible
ruinate despoil, destroy *(efface)*, pillage, spoil *(impair)*
ruination adversity, bankruptcy, catastrophe, consumption, damage, debacle, defeat, defilement, destruction, deterioration, detriment, disaster, disrepair, dissolution *(termination)*, havoc, prostration, subversion, waste, wear and tear
ruined bad *(inferior)*, bad *(offensive)*, bankrupt, depraved, dilapidated, imperfect, insolvent, irredeemable, irremediable, irreparable, marred, poor *(underprivileged)*
ruiner vandal
ruining disastrous, fatal
ruinous adverse *(negative)*, bad *(offensive)*, deadly, deleterious, diabolic, dire, disastrous, fatal, harmful, insalubrious, malevolent, malignant, noxious, pernicious, regrettable
ruinous price toll *(effect)*
ruinousness adversity, disaster
rule act *(enactment)*, adjudge, adjudicate, arbitrate *(adjudge)*, array *(order)*, award, belief *(something believed)*, brevet, bureaucracy, bylaw, canon, codification, coerce, command, conclude *(decide)*, condition *(contingent provision)*, constant, control *(regulate)*, criterion, decide, decree, determine, dictate *(noun)*, dictate *(verb)*, direct *(order)*, direct *(supervise)*, direction *(order)*, doctrine, dogma, dominate, dominion *(supreme authority)*, edict, enactment, enjoin, fiat, find *(determine)*, govern, government *(administration)*, habit, handle *(manage)*, hegemony, hold *(decide)*, influence, instruction *(direction)*, law, legislate, manage, mandamus, mandate, manipulate *(control unfairly)*, matter of course, maxim, measure *(noun)*, measure *(verb)*, method, mode, norm, occupation *(possession)*, operate, opinion *(judicial decision)*, order *(judicial directive)*, order, ordinance, oversee, pass *(determine)*, pattern, police, power, practice *(procedure)*, precedent, precept, predominance, predominate *(command)*, prescription *(directive)*, preside, prevail *(triumph)*, primacy, principle

(axiom), procedure, pronounce *(pass judgment)*, regime, regulate *(manage)*, rubric *(authoritative rule)*, ruling, stare decisis, statute, subject, superintend, supremacy, technicality, try *(conduct a trial)*, wield. SEE MAIN ENTRY

rule against   overrule
rule dishonestly   misgovern
rule for future determinations   precedent
rule for future guidance   precedent
rule of action   platform, policy *(plan of action)*, principle *(axiom)*
rule of conduct   canon, law
rule of might   oppression
rule of proceeding   formality
rule on   judge
rule out   delete, deter, dismiss *(put out of consideration)*, disqualify, eliminate *(exclude)*, exclude, negate, obliterate, overrule, prevent
rule over   dominate, predominate *(command)*, subjugate
rule upon   adjudicate
rule-abiding   obedient
ruled   positive *(prescribed)*
ruler   arbitrator
rulers   authorities, hierarchy *(persons in authority)*
rulership   government *(administration)*
rules   code, mode, protocol *(etiquette)*
rules and regulations   codification, criterion
rules of business   practice *(procedure)*
rules of conduct   decorum
rules of war   strategy
ruling   act *(enactment)*, adjudication, authority *(documentation)*, award, canon, central *(essential)*, code, conclusion *(determination)*, condition *(contingent provision)*, conviction *(finding of guilt)*, decree, determination, dictate, dominant, edict, enactment, finding, influential, judgment *(formal court decree)*, mandate, master, measure, omnipotent, opinion *(judicial decision)*, order *(judicial directive)*, potent, powerful, predominant, prescription *(directive)*, prevailing *(having superior force)*, primary, principal, pronouncement, requirement, rubric *(authoritative rule)*, sentence, sovereign *(absolute)*, verdict. SEE MAIN ENTRY
ruling of the court   award, decree
ruling passion   obsession
ruling power   government *(political administration)*
ruling whim   obsession
rulings   codification, legislation *(enactments)*
ruminant   cogitative, pensive
ruminate   brood, concentrate *(pay attention)*, consider, deliberate, muse, ponder, reflect *(ponder)*, speculate *(conjecture)*, study, weigh
rumination   consideration *(contemplation)*, contemplation, deliberation, dialectic, hindsight, reflection *(thought)*, speculation *(conjecture)*. SEE MAIN ENTRY
ruminative   cogitative, pensive
rummage   delve
rumor   canard, circulate
rumor   hearsay
rumor   spread
rumor about   circulate
rumored   reputedly
rumpere   infringe, violate
rumpus   bluster *(commotion)*, fray, furor, imbroglio, pandemonium, riot, turmoil

run   abscond, chain *(series)*, conduct, exude, flee, function, hierarchy *(arrangement in a series)*, manage, manipulate *(utilize skillfully)*, market *(demand)*, moderate *(preside over)*, officiate, operate, race, rule *(govern)*. SEE MAIN ENTRY
run a race   race
run across   find *(discover)*
run afoul of   collide *(clash)*
run after   chase, hunt, pursue *(chase)*
run against   collide *(clash)*, conflict, counteract, fight *(counteract)*, jostle *(bump into)*, oppugn
run at   attack
run at cross purposes   conflict
run at cross-purposes   collide *(clash)*
run away   abandon *(physically leave)*, abscond, defect, escape, evacuate, flee, leave *(depart)*, quit *(evacuate)*, retreat
run away with   jostle *(pickpocket)*, kidnap
run checks on   check *(inspect)*, poll, probe
run counter   check *(restrain)*, confront *(oppose)*, counteract
run counter to   antagonize, collide *(clash)*, conflict, confront *(oppose)*, contradict, contravene, counteract, countervail, cross *(disagree with)*, discord, disaffirm, except *(object)*, fight *(counteract)*, oppugn
run down   brutalize, decrease, defame, degenerate, denigrate, deplete, depreciate, derogate, diminish, disapprove *(condemn)*, disparage, lessen, minimize, misprize, mistreat, old, pillory, pursue *(chase)*, reprehend, reprimand, sully, underestimate
run foul of   collide *(clash)*
run from   shirk
run in opposition to   conflict, counter, counteract
run in pursuit   chase
run into   impinge, pervade
run into debt   overdraw
run into each other   collide *(crash against)*
run its course   cease
run low   diminish
run of luck   prosperity
run of the mill   mediocre, prevalent, regular *(conventional)*, trite
run off   flee, publish
run off with   carry away, hold up *(rob)*, jostle *(pickpocket)*, kidnap, poach
run on   keep *(continue)*, persevere
run out   close *(terminate)*, expire, lapse *(cease)*, terminate
run over   inundate, invade, overlap, overstep, recapitulate, repeat *(state again)*, review
run parallel to   correspond *(be equivalent)*
run riot   brawl
run swiftly   race
run tests on   check *(inspect)*
run the chance   incur
run the risk   bet
run through   exhaust *(deplete)*, penetrate, permeate, pervade, pierce *(lance)*, spend
run together   collide *(crash against)*, commingle
runabout   itinerant
runagate   fugitive
runaway   elusive, fugitive
rundle   step
rung   degree *(station)*, step
runic   mysterious
runner   bootlegger, candidate
running   consecutive, continuous, fluvial,

management *(judicious use)*
running account   ledger
running away   flight
running counter to   dissenting, opposition
running expense   cost *(expenses)*
running expenses   maintenance *(upkeep)*
running out   expiration
runoff   outflow
runthrough   hornbook
rupture   alienation *(estrangement)*, break *(fracture)*, controversy *(argument)*, disassociation, disrupt, embroilment, estrangement, feud, force *(break)*, rend, rift *(gap)*, schism, separate, separation, sever, split, variance *(disagreement)*
ruptured   broken *(fractured)*
ruse   artifice, bunko, canard, deception, device *(contrivance)*, evasion, expedient, fake, false pretense, fraud, hoax, imposture, machination, maneuver *(trick)*, plot *(secret plan)*, ploy, pretense *(pretext)*, pretext, stratagem, subterfuge. SEE MAIN ENTRY
rush   dispatch *(promptness)*, dispatch *(send off)*, expedite, haste, hasten, outbreak, outburst, precipitate *(hasten)*, race, spate. SEE MAIN ENTRY
rush off   dispatch *(send off)*
rush through   hasten
rush to a conclusion   presuppose
rush to conclusion   prejudge
rush upon   assail, attack, inundate
rushed   perfunctory, precipitate
rushing   rapid
rushing in   incursion
rustic   inelegant, ingenuous, simple, uncouth
rusticate   retreat
rusty   old
ruth   lenience, pity
ruthful   placable
ruthless   brutal, cold-blooded, cruel, diabolic, draconian, harsh, malevolent, malicious, malignant, relentless, remorseless, severe, uncompromising, unrelenting, unscrupulous. SEE MAIN ENTRY
ruthlessness   atrocity, brutality, cruelty, oppression, rancor, severity, violence
ruttish   lecherous, lewd, licentious, salacious
rutty   lewd

S

sabotage   damage, disable, disloyalty, pillage, spoil *(impair)*, subversion
saboteurs   conspirers. SEE MAIN ENTRY
saccharine   nectarious
sack   depredation, despoil, devastate, foray, harry *(plunder)*, havoc, hold up *(rob)*, loot, pillage *(noun)*, pillage *(verb)*, pirate *(take by violence)*, plunder *(noun)*, plunder *(verb)*, spoliation
sacrament of marriage   matrimony
sacramental   sacrosanct, solemn
sacred   ineffable, infrangible, inviolate, sacrosanct, solemn
sacrifice   abandon *(relinquish)*, cost *(penalty)*, extirpate, forbear, forfeit, forswear, lose *(be deprived of)*, loss, relinquish, renunciation, suffer *(sustain loss)*, waive, yield *(submit)*. SEE MAIN ENTRY
sacrifice pride   condescend *(deign)*
sacrificed   lost *(taken away)*
sacrilege   blasphemy
sacrilegious   profane

sacrilegiousness blasphemy

sacrosanct infrangible. SEE MAIN ENTRY

sad deplorable, despondent, disconsolate, grave *(solemn),* lamentable, lugubrious, pessimistic, regrettable, remorseful

sadden depress, discourage, distress

saddening lamentable

saddle disadvantage, encumber *(hinder),* load, overcome *(overwhelm),* overload

saddle with tax *(overwork)*

sadistic brutal, cruel, diabolic, ruthless

sadness damper *(depressant),* distress *(anguish)*

saepire enclose

safe bank, cache *(storage place),* coffer, depository, guarded, immune, impervious, indubious, inexpugnable, innocuous, intact, nontoxic, reliable, repository, salutary, secure *(free from danger),* solid *(sound),* treasury. SEE MAIN ENTRY

safe conduct protection, security *(safety)*

safe deposit box coffer

safe haven SEE MAIN ENTRY

safe place cache *(hiding place),* cache *(storage place),* refuge

safe retreat cache *(hiding place)*

safe workplace SEE MAIN ENTRY

safe-deposit box depository

safe-deposite vault bank

safebreaker burglar

safecracker burglar

safeguard asylum *(protection),* auspices, barrier, bear *(support),* bulwark, concern *(care),* conserve, cover *(protection),* cover *(guard),* coverage *(insurance),* custody *(supervision),* defend, discretion *(quality of being discreet),* ensconce, ensure, foster, guarantee, guaranty, guardian, harbor, hedge, keep *(shelter),* maintain *(sustain),* panoply, patrol, police, precaution, preparation, preserve, protect, protection, rescue, save *(rescue),* screen *(guard),* security *(safety),* shield, ward. SEE MAIN ENTRY

safeguarded guarded, safe

safeguarding conservation, preservation, preventive, prophylactic, protective

safehold asylum *(hiding place)*

safekeeper guardian

safekeeping charge *(custody),* conservation, custody *(incarceration),* custody *(supervision),* preservation, protection, ward. SEE MAIN ENTRY

safeness security *(safety)*

safety asylum *(protection),* inviolability, preservation, protection, refuge, shelter *(protection),* trust *(custody).* SEE MAIN ENTRY

safety from prosecution immunity

safety valve SEE MAIN ENTRY

safety valve provisions SEE MAIN ENTRY

sag give *(yield),* languish

saga account *(report),* report *(detailed account),* story *(narrative).* SEE MAIN ENTRY

sagacious cognizant, discriminating *(judicious),* judicial, judicious, juridical, learned, lucid, omniscient, perspicacious, politic, profound *(esoteric),* prudent, rational, reasonable *(rational),* resourceful, sapient, sensible, solid *(sound),* subtle *(refined).* SEE MAIN ENTRY

sagaciousness insight, perception, sagacity, sense *(intelligence)*

sagacitas perception, sagacity

sagacity caliber *(mental capacity),* common sense, comprehension, discretion *(quality of being discreet),* discrimination *(good judgment),* insight, intelligence

(intellect), judgment *(discernment),* perception, reason *(sound judgment),* sense *(intelligence).* SEE MAIN ENTRY

sagax acute, judicious, perceptive, perspicacious

sage cognizant, expert, judicial, judicious, juridical, learned, lucid, mastermind, oracular, pedagogue, perspicacious, profound *(esoteric),* prudent, rational, sapient, sensible, solid *(sound)*

sage maxim principle *(axiom)*

sage reflection maxim

sageness comprehension

sagesse discretion *(quality of being discreet)*

said aforesaid, before mentioned, oral, stated. SEE MAIN ENTRY

said again repeated

said aloud oral

said in a preceding part aforesaid

sainted sacrosanct

saintly laudable

sake advantage, reason *(basis)*

salable disposable, marketable, negotiable, valuable

salable commodities merchandise

salable commodity item, product

salacious depraved, dissolute, immoral, lascivious, lecherous, lewd, lurid, obscene, prurient, scurrilous, suggestive *(risqué).* SEE MAIN ENTRY

salaciousness obscenity, pornography

salacity debauchery, obscenity, pornography

salaried worker employee

salary commission *(fee),* compensate *(remunerate),* compensation, earnings, honorarium, income, pay, payment *(remittance),* payroll, recompense, revenue, wage

sale conveyance, disposition *(transfer of property),* trade *(commerce),* transaction. SEE MAIN ENTRY

sale by bid auction

sale by outcry auction

sale proceeds income

sale to the highest bidder auction

sales trade *(commerce)*

salesman dealer, vendor

salesmanship persuasion

salesperson dealer, merchant

saleswoman dealer

salience emphasis, importance, interest *(concern),* materiality *(consequence),* significance

saliency emphasis

salient arrant *(definite),* clear *(apparent),* distinctive, evident, important *(significant),* manifest, material *(important),* notable, noteworthy, open *(in sight),* outstanding *(prominent),* palpable, paramount, perceivable, perceptible, prominent, remarkable. SEE MAIN ENTRY

salient characteristic aspect

salient feature main point

salient point content *(meaning),* cornerstone, feature *(characteristic),* gist *(ground for a suit),* gravamen, highlight, landmark *(significant change),* main point, significance. SEE MAIN ENTRY

salient quality feature *(characteristic)*

salire frisk

salle chamber *(compartment)*

sally outburst

salubrious beneficial, medicinal, remedial, safe, salutary. SEE MAIN ENTRY

salubriousness health

salubrity health

salus health, maintenance *(upkeep),* security *(safety)*

salutaris beneficial, remedial, salutary

salutary beneficial, contributory, favorable *(advantageous),* medicinal, profitable, prophylactic, remedial, salubrious. SEE MAIN ENTRY

salutation remembrance *(commemoration)*

salute honor, recognize *(acknowledge),* salvo

salutiferous beneficial, medicinal, remedial, salubrious, salutary

salvage recover, recovery *(repossession),* rehabilitate, renew *(refurbish),* renewal, renovate, repair, reparation *(keeping in repair),* replevin, rescue, save *(conserve).* SEE MAIN ENTRY

salvageable corrigible

salvaged renascent

salvation discharge *(liberation),* emancipation, mainstay, preservation, protection, redemption, rehabilitation, release, relief *(aid),* safekeeping, salvage, security *(safety)*

salve assuage, cure *(noun),* cure *(verb),* pacify, placate, relieve *(give aid),* soothe

salvo barrage, discharge *(shot),* reservation *(condition).* SEE MAIN ENTRY

salvus intact

samaritan SEE MAIN ENTRY

Samaritanism benevolence *(disposition to do good)*

same analogous, cognate, equal, equivalent, similar, uniform. SEE MAIN ENTRY

same conditions status quo

same line of descent family *(common ancestry)*

same strain family *(common ancestry)*

sameness constant, correspondence *(similarity),* facsimile, identity *(similarity),* par *(equality),* parity, regularity, resemblance, semblance

sample case *(example),* check *(inspect),* cross section, example, exemplary, illustration, instance, model, paradigm, partake, pattern, poll, prototype, representative, representative *(example),* specimen. SEE MAIN ENTRY

samples selection *(collection)*

sanare cure

sanatio cure

sanative medicinal, remedial, salutary

sanatory medicinal, remedial, salubrious, salutary

sancire confirm, sanction

sanctification elevation

sanctified inviolate, sacrosanct, solemn

sanctify authorize, elevate, purge *(purify)*

sanctify by custom inure *(accustom)*

sanctimonious tartuffish

sanctimoniousness blasphemy, hypocrisy

sanctimony hypocrisy

sanctio enactment, ratification

sanction abide, accept *(assent),* acceptance, accredit, acquiescence, adoption *(acceptance),* advantage, advocacy, advocate, allow *(authorize),* appoint, approval, approve, assent *(noun),* assent *(verb),* authority *(documentation),* authorize, bear *(support),* bear *(tolerate),* bestow, bind *(obligate),* brevet, capacity *(authority),* certify *(approve),* concede, concession *(authorization),* concur *(agree),* confirm, confirmation, consent *(noun),* consent *(verb),* constitute *(establish),* copyright, corroborate, countenance, countersign, decree, delegate, discretion *(power of choice)*, dispensation *(exception)*, droit, embrace *(accept)*, empower, enable, endorse, enfranchise, favor, fiat, force *(compulsion)*, franchise *(license)*, grant *(concede)*, indorse, indorsement, indulgence, invest *(vest)*, leave *(permission)*, legality, legalization, legalize, legislate, legitimate, let *(permit)*, liberty, license, option *(contractual provision)*, pass *(approve)*, permission, permit *(noun)*, permit *(verb)*, prefer, prerogative, privilege, promote *(organize)*, qualify *(meet standards)*, ratification, reassure, recommend, recommendation, right *(entitlement)*, seal *(solemnize)*, sign, subscription, sufferance, sustain *(confirm)*, title *(right)*, tolerate, uphold, validate, vest, warrant *(authorization)*. SEE MAIN ENTRY

sanction a claim authorize
sanction by law legalize
sanctionability admissibility
sanctionable admissible, allowable, licit
sanctionableness admissibility, legality
sanctioned admissible, allowable, allowed, due *(regular)*, entitled, juridical, justifiable, lawful, legal, legitimate *(rightful)*, licit, official, permissible, privileged, rightful, statutory, traditional, valid
sanctioned by custom legitimate *(rightful)*
sanctioned by law de jure, jural, lawful, legitimate *(rightful)*, permissible
sanctioned by legal authority legitimate *(rightful)*
sanctioned by the law allowed
sanctioned effectiveness force *(legal efficacy)*
sanctioned potency force *(legal efficacy)*
sanctions codification
sanctitas inviolability
sanctity good faith, honesty
sanctuary asylum *(hiding place)*, asylum *(protection)*, bulwark, haven, preservation, protection, refuge, security *(safety)*, shelter *(protection)*, shield
sanctum sanctorum asylum *(hiding place)*
sanctus conscientious, incorruptible, inculpable, irreprehensible, moral, unimpeachable
sane lucid, rational, sensible. SEE MAIN ENTRY
sanemindedness competence *(sanity)*
saneness competence *(sanity)*, sanity
sang-froid dispassionate
sanguinary deadly, ruthless
sanguine SEE MAIN ENTRY
sanguine expectation faith
sanguineness belief *(state of mind)*, confidence *(faith)*, faith
sanguineous sanguine
sanguis blood
sanitary remedial, salutary
sanitary cordon quarantine
sanitas health
sanitize decontaminate
sanitorium asylum *(hospital)*
sanity reason *(sound judgment)*. SEE MAIN ENTRY
sans pareil best
sansculottic insubordinate
sanus sane
sap eviscerate, exhaust *(deplete)*, impair
sap the strength of debilitate
sapid palatable, savory. SEE MAIN ENTRY

sapience caliber *(mental capacity)*, common sense, judgment *(discernment)*, sagacity, sense *(intelligence)*
sapiency sagacity
sapiens judicious, sapient
sapient acute, discriminating *(judicious)*, judicial, judicious, juridical, learned, literate, omniscient, oracular, perspicacious, prudent, reasonable *(rational)*, sensible, solid *(sound)*. SEE MAIN ENTRY
sapiential sensible
sapless languid, powerless
saporous sapid
sarcasm diatribe, irony, ridicule
sarcastic bitter *(reproachful)*, cynical, incisive, insolent, ironic, offensive *(offending)*, trenchant
sarcastical cynical, incisive, ironic
sardonic bitter *(reproachful)*, cynical, disdainful, ironic
satanic cruel
satanic diabolic
satanic heinous, malevolent, malignant, sinister
sate assuage, satisfy *(fulfill)*
sated full
satellite offshoot, partisan
satiate assuage, pacify, satisfy *(fulfill)*
satiate to excess overindulge
satiated full, replete
satiation plethora, surfeit
satietas surfeit
satiety plethora, sufficiency, surfeit
satire caricature, distortion, irony, parody, ridicule
satiric incisive, ironic
satirical incisive, ironic
satirize jape, mock *(deride)*, mock *(imitate)*
satisdatio warranty
satisfactio reparation *(indemnification)*
satisfaction amortization, benefit *(betterment)*, compensation, conciliation, consideration *(recompense)*, contribution *(indemnification)*, discharge *(payment)*, enjoyment *(pleasure)*, expiation, fruition, indemnification, offset, out of pocket, payment *(act of paying)*, pride, proof, recompense, recovery *(award)*, refund, relief *(legal redress)*, remuneration, reparation *(indemnification)*, requital, restitution, retribution, revenge, settlement, surfeit, trover. SEE MAIN ENTRY
satisfaction for damage compensation
satisfaction for injury compensation
satisfaction in full payoff *(payment in full)*
satisfactorily fairly *(moderately)*
satisfactoriness mediocrity, sufficiency
satisfactory adequate, ample, competent, eligible, mediocre, palatable, prima facie *(legally sufficient)*, right *(suitable)*, suitable, unobjectionable
satisfactory evidence proof
satisfactory notice adequate notice
satisfiable placable
satisfied certain *(positive)*, complacent, definite, full, indubious, peaceable, positive *(confident)*, proud *(self-respecting)*, replete, successful
satisfy assuage, assure *(give confidence to)*, compensate *(remunerate)*, comply, contribute *(indemnify)*, convince, disarm *(set at ease)*, discharge *(pay a debt)*, fulfill, keep *(fulfill)*, liquidate *(determine liability)*, obey, observe *(obey)*, pacify, pander, pay, perform *(adhere to)*, placate, propitiate,

reassure, recoup *(reimburse)*, redeem *(satisfy debts)*, redress, refund, reimburse, remedy, remit *(send payment)*, remunerate, repay, restore *(return)*, return *(refund)*, supply, vouchsafe. SEE MAIN ENTRY
satisfy a claim defray
satisfy by evidence convince, persuade
satisfy by proof convince, persuade
satisfy desires pander
satisfy in advance prepay
satisfy in full discharge *(pay a debt)*
satisfy oneself ascertain
satisfy requirements pass *(satisfy requirements)*
satisfy to excess overindulge
satisfying adequate, compensatory, sapid
saturate imbue, inject, inundate, overload, penetrate, permeate, pervade, replenish
saturated drunk, full, replete
saturation maximum *(amplitude)*, osmosis, plethora, sufficiency, surfeit
saturnine disconsolate, grave *(solemn)*, lugubrious
satyric dissolute, lascivious, prurient, salacious
satyrical lascivious, salacious
sauciness disrespect
saucy brazen, impertinent *(insolent)*, insolent, obtrusive, offensive *(offending)*, presumptuous
saunter perambulate
savage assail, brutal, cold-blooded, cruel, disorderly, harsh, hot-blooded, malevolent, malicious, malignant, mistreat, ruthless, severe, vicious
savageness brutality, cruelty
savagery atrocity, bestiality, brutality, cruelty, severity, violence
savant expert, mastermind, specialist
save conserve, deposit *(submit to a bank)*, extricate, free, fund, garner, glean, hold *(possess)*, keep *(shelter)*, maintain *(sustain)*, perpetuate, preserve, protect, release, remedy, renew *(refurbish)*, rescue, reserve, retain *(keep in possession)*, store, sustain *(prolong)*, unless. SEE MAIN ENTRY
save from disencumber
save from loss conserve
save harmless indemnify
save up fund, hoard, set aside *(reserve)*
saved free *(relieved from a burden)*
saved from bondage free *(enjoying civil liberty)*
saving conservation, economical, economy *(frugality)*, hoard, penurious, preservation, provident *(frugal)*, prudent, reservation *(engagement)*
saving clause loophole, reservation *(condition)*, salvo
savings capital, fund, reserve, store *(depository)*
savior samaritan
savoir faire common sense, discretion *(quality of being discreet)*
savor partake, relish
savorless insipid, stale
savory palatable, sapid. SEE MAIN ENTRY
saw maxim, phrase
say allege, claim *(maintain)*, comment, communicate, contend *(maintain)*, converse, declare, enunciate, express, observe *(remark)*, phrase, posit, pronounce *(speak)*, purport, referendum, relate *(tell)*, remark, speak, speech, suffrage
say again recapitulate, reiterate, repeat *(state again)*

say by heart   recite
say in advance   preface
say in defense   support *(justify)*
say in reply   answer *(reply)*, counter-charge, retort, return *(respond)*
say less than the truth   perjure
say no   challenge
say no to   ban
say over   repeat *(state again)*
say repeatedly   reiterate
say-so   SEE MAIN ENTRY
say under oath   depose *(testify)*, witness *(attest to)*
say yes   concur *(agree)*
saying   catchword, expression *(comment)*, maxim, phrase, remark
scab   pariah
scabrous   lurid, obscene, salacious, scurrilous
scaena   scene
scaenicus   histrionic, histrionics
scald   burn
scalding   caustic
scale   caliber *(measurement)*, chain *(series)*, differential, index *(gauge)*, magnitude, surmount
scale down   decrease, diminish, discount *(minimize)*, minimize
scale of prices   tariff *(bill)*
scaled   proportionate
scamp   degenerate, derelict, malefactor
scamper   race
scampish   disorderly, profligate *(corrupt)*
scampishness   knavery
scan   analyze, canvass, check *(inspect)*, frisk, investigate, monitor, observe *(watch)*, patrol, peruse, probe, read, regard *(pay attention)*, research, scrutinize, search, study, survey *(examine)*
scandal   defamation, discredit, disgrace, dishonor *(shame)*, ignominy, infamy, notoriety, odium, opprobrium, shame, slander. SEE MAIN ENTRY
scandalize   contemn, defame, discredit, disgrace, libel, pillory, repel *(disgust)*
scandalizing   flagrant
scandalous   arrant *(onerous)*, bad *(offensive)*, blameworthy, calumnious, contemptuous, delinquent *(guilty of a misdeed)*, disgraceful, disorderly, flagrant, ignoble, inexpiable, iniquitous, lewd, libelous, licentious, nefarious, notorious, outrageous, peccant *(culpable)*, regrettable, vicious. SEE MAIN ENTRY
scandalum magnatum   stigma
scant   deficient, inadequate, inappreciable, insubstantial, insufficient, marginal, minimal, minor, negligible, nonsubstantial *(not sufficient)*, paltry, petty, poor *(inferior in quality)*, remote *(small)*, scarce, slight, tenuous
scant of   devoid
scant respect   disparagement
scantiness   austerity, dearth, deficit, delinquency *(shortage)*, insignificance, insufficiency, need *(deprivation)*, paucity, poverty
scantity   poverty
scantling   minimum
scantness   dearth, insufficiency, paucity, poverty
scanty   de minimus, deficient, imperfect, inappreciable, insufficient, marginal, minimal, negligible, nominal, nonsubstantial *(not sufficient)*, paltry, partial *(relating to a part)*, petty, trivial
scapegrace   degenerate
scar   deface, defacement, onus *(stigma)*, stigma

scarce   barren, deficient, infrequent, insufficient, minimal, nonsubstantial *(not sufficient)*, paltry, rare, uncommon, unusual. SEE MAIN ENTRY
scarcely   almost
scarceness   dearth, insignificance, paucity, poverty
scarcity   dearth, deficiency, deficit, delinquency *(shortage)*, indigence, insufficiency, need *(deprivation)*, paucity, poverty
scare   browbeat, discourage, fear, fright, frighten, intimidate, menace, start, trepidation
scared   caitiff
scarify   lash *(attack verbally)*
scarifying   critical *(faultfinding)*
scarlet   lewd, licentious, salacious
scarred   married
scathe   damage, disable, harm *(noun)*, harm *(verb)*, lash *(attack verbally)*, persecute
scathed   marred
scatheful   adverse *(negative)*, malevolent, malignant, noxious, scathing, sinister
scatheless   inviolate, safe
scathing   bitter *(penetrating)*, critical *(faultfinding)*, harsh, incisive, mordacious, trenchant. SEE MAIN ENTRY
scatter   break *(fracture)*, deploy, diffuse, disband, disburse *(distribute)*, dislocate, disorganize, dispel, dispense, dissipate *(spread out)*, dissociate, dissolve *(disperse)*, distribute, intersperse, radiate, repel *(drive back)*, spread
scatter abroad   disperse *(disseminate)*, disperse *(scatter)*
scatter thinly   dissipate *(spread out)*
scatter to the winds   dissipate *(spread out)*
scatter widely   dissipate *(spread out)*
scatterbrained   fatuous, thoughtless
scattered   disconnected, sporadic
scattering   circulation, decentralization, havoc
scavenge   prowl
sceleratus   criminal, felon, guilty
scelestus   felon
scenario   SEE MAIN ENTRY
scene   locality, location, region, territory, vicinity. SEE MAIN ENTRY
scene of destruction   shambles
scene of disorder   shambles
scent   clue, trace *(follow)*
scepter   supremacy
schedule   agenda, arrange *(plan)*, book, calendar *(list of cases)*, calendar *(record of yearly periods)*, docket, empanel, impanel, invoice *(itemized list)*, plan *(noun)*, plan *(verb)*, policy *(contract)*, program *(noun)*, program *(verb)*, register *(noun)*, register *(verb)*, roll, scheme, set down. SEE MAIN ENTRY
schedule of affairs   agenda
schedule of articles   inventory
schedule of duties   tariff *(duties)*
schedule of events   calendar *(record of yearly periods)*
schedule of items and their respective prices   invoice *(itemized list)*
scheduled   forthcoming, future, prospective
scheduling   codification, economy *(frugality)*
schema   arrangement *(plan)*
schematic arrangement   array *(order)*
schematism   arrangement *(ordering)*
schematize   arrange *(methodize)*, coordinate, devise *(invent)*

scheme   agenda, arrangement *(plan)*, artifice, avenue *(means of attainment)*, blueprint, cabal, campaign, circumvent, codification, connivance, connive, conspiracy, conspire, contrivance, contrive, course, design *(intent)*, device *(contrivance)*, devise *(invent)*, direction *(course)*, endeavor, enterprise *(undertaking)*, expedient, forethought, form *(arrangement)*, frame *(formulate)*, goal, hoax, intend, intent, machination, maneuver *(tactic)*, maneuver *(trick)*, maneuver, mode, organization *(structure)*, plan *(noun)*, plan *(verb)*, platform, plot *(secret plan)*, plot, ploy, policy *(plan of action)*, practice *(procedure)*, procedure, process *(course)*, program, project, proposal *(suggestion)*, proposition, prospectus, racket, ruse, stratagem, strategy, suggestion, system. SEE MAIN ENTRY
scheme of arrangement   configuration *(form)*, method
schemeful   collusive
schemer   architect, coactor, conspirator, conspirer
schemery   collusion, confederacy *(conspiracy)*, strategy
scheming   artful, collusion, collusive, deceptive, devious, diplomatic, dishonest, disingenuous, evasive, fraudulent, insidious, machiavellian, perfidious, recreant, sinister, sly, unconscionable, untrue
schism   alienation *(estrangement)*, contention *(opposition)*, difference, disaccord, disassociation, discord, dissension, dissent *(difference of opinion)*, dissidence, division *(act of dividing)*, estrangement, fight *(argument)*. SEE MAIN ENTRY
schisma   schism
schismatic   contentious, divisive, heretic, hostile, polemic, recusant
schismatize   conflict
scholar   disciple, expert, pedagogue, specialist
scholarly   didactic, diligent, disciplinary *(educational)*, learned, literate, profound *(esoteric)*
scholarship   education, knowledge *(learning)*
scholastic   didactic, disciplinary *(educational)*, informative, literate
scholium   clarification, comment, note *(brief comment)*
school   discipline *(train)*, edify, educate, instill, institute, instruct *(teach)*, organization *(association)*, practice *(train by repetition)*, style
school oneself   study
schooled   familiar *(informed)*, informed *(educated)*, knowing, learned, literate, sciential
schooling   discipline *(training)*, edification, education, experience *(background)*, guidance, instruction *(teaching)*
schoolman   pedagogue
schoolmaster   pedagogue
schoolteacher   pedagogue
science   SEE MAIN ENTRY
science of law   jurisprudence
science of legal relations   jurisprudence
science of monetary relations   finance
science of oratory   rhetoric *(skilled speech)*
science of teaching   education
science of wealth   finance
sciens   expert, familiar *(informed)*, knowing, proficient

scienter SEE MAIN ENTRY

scientia knowledge *(learning)*, science *(study)*, skill

sciential SEE MAIN ENTRY

scientific objective, precise, real, sound, technical, valid

scientific determination diagnosis

scindere split

scintilla iota, minimum. SEE MAIN ENTRY

sciolist pedant

sciolistic superficial

scion child, descendant, heir, offshoot, offspring, posterity, successor

scions progeny

scissile destructible, divisible, severable

scission decentralization, division *(act of dividing)*, severance, split

scissura split

scissure rift *(gap)*, split

scitum resolution *(decision)*

scoff derogate, disdain *(noun)*, disdain *(verb)*, disparage, flout, humiliate, jape, jeer, mock *(deride)*

scoff at contemn, discommend, reject

scoffing cynical, disregard *(lack of respect)*, disrespect, impertinent *(insolent)*, skeptical

scofflaw delinquent

scold castigate, denounce *(condemn)*, disapprove *(condemn)*, fault, inveigh, rebuke, remonstrate, reprehend, reprimand, reproach

scolding critical *(faultfinding)*, criticism, diatribe, disparagement, objurgation, obloquy, outcry, rebuff, reprimand, reproach

sconce fine, penalty

scope area *(province)*, capacity *(aptitude)*, capacity *(maximum)*, capacity *(sphere)*, connotation, content *(meaning)*, contents, context, degree *(magnitude)*, extent, gamut, intent, latitude, magnitude, opportunity, province, purview, range, region, scene, space, sphere. SEE MAIN ENTRY

scope of vision perspective

scorch burn, deflagrate

scorching bitter *(penetrating)*

score bill *(invoice)*, calculate, carry *(succeed)*, census, computation, inveigh, poll, sum *(tally)*

score a success attain, succeed *(attain)*

scorify burn

scorn affront, contemn, contempt *(disdain)*, decry, disapprove *(reject)*, disavow, disdain *(noun)*, disdain *(verb)*, dishonor *(shame)*, disoblige, disown *(refuse to acknowledge)*, disparage, disparagement, disregard *(lack of respect)*, disrespect, exclude, flout, forswear, humiliate, ignore, illude, infamy, minimize, misprize, mock *(deride)*, odium, pillory, rebuff, rejection, renounce, repulse, ridicule, shame, spurn, vilification

scorn of the consequences audacity

scorned derelict *(abandoned)*, undesirable

scornful bitter *(reproachful)*, contemptuous, cynical, disdainful, inflated *(vain)*, orgulous, pejorative, supercilious

scornful imitation ridicule

scornful insolence contumely

scornful treatment contumely

scornfulness contumely, disdain

scorning disdain

scorse trade

scot tax

scotch stem *(check)*

scoundrel convict, hoodlum, malefactor, wrongdoer

scoundrelism corruption, knavery

scoundrelly sinister

scour decontaminate, frisk, perambulate, purge *(purify)*, search

scourge catastrophe, disaster, discipline *(punishment)*, discipline *(punish)*, disease, harm *(noun)*, harm *(verb)*, lash *(strike)*, nuisance, persecute, plague, punish

scourging correction *(punishment)*

scout forerunner, observe *(watch)*, patrol, pioneer, precede, precursor, reject, search, spurn, spy

scramble bluster *(commotion)*, brawl, commingle, competition, confound, disorganize, disorient, dispatch *(promptness)*, fracas, fray, muddle, race

scrambled composite, miscellaneous, promiscuous

scrap bicker, brawl, reject, salvage

scrape entanglement *(involvement)*, erode, imbroglio, misdeed, misdoing, plight, predicament, quagmire

scrape together glean

scraping obsequious

scrapped derelict *(abandoned)*

scrappy sporadic

scratch deface, defacement

scratch out censor, deface, delete, destroy *(efface)*, expunge, obliterate

scratched marred

scrawl script

scream outcry

screaming blatant *(obtrusive)*, flagrant

screed declamation, philippic

screen blind *(obscure)*, buffer zone, camouflage, cloak, conceal, cover *(pretext)*, cover *(conceal)*, disguise *(noun)*, disguise *(verb)*, ensconce, enshroud, envelop, harbor, hedge, hide, lodge *(house)*, maintain *(sustain)*, obfuscate, obliterate, obnubilate, obscure, panoply, plant *(covertly place)*, preserve, protect, safeguard, shelter *(protection)*, shield, shroud, sort, suppress, veil. SEE MAIN ENTRY

screen from observation blind *(obscure)*, camouflage

screen from sight blind *(obscure)*, camouflage

screen off insulate

screen out reject, seclude

screened allusive, blind *(concealed)*, clandestine, covert, hidden, immune, impalpable, indiscernible, latent, mysterious, safe

screened from danger safe

screening protective

scriba clerk, notary public

scribbled holographic

scribe amanuensis, clerk, inscribe, notary public, note *(record)*

scribere legislate

scrimmage affray, brawl *(noun)*, brawl *(verb)*, fight *(battle)*, fray, struggle

scrimping austerity, parsimonious

scrinium portfolio

script handwriting, scenario. SEE MAIN ENTRY

scription handwriting, script

scriptor author *(writer)*

scriptorial holographic

scriptory in writing

scriptural holographic

scrivener amanuensis, clerk, notary public

scrofulous lurid, salacious

scrounger parasite

scrub decontaminate, poor *(inferior in quality)*

scrubby ignoble, poor *(inferior in quality)*

scrumptious palatable, sapid

scruple demur, doubt *(hesitate)*, hesitate, hesitation, misdoubt, qualm, refuse. SEE MAIN ENTRY

scruples conscience, integrity, reluctance, responsibility *(conscience)*

scrupulosity honesty, particularity

scrupulous accurate, bona fide, candid, careful, clean, close *(rigorous)*, conscientious, credible, equitable, evenhanded, exact, factual, fair *(just)*, high-minded, honest, impartial, incorruptible, just, lawabiding, literal, meticulous, moral, orthodox, painstaking, particular *(exacting)*, precise, punctilious, punctual, reliable, reputable, right *(correct)*, straightforward, strict, undistorted, upright, vigilant. SEE MAIN ENTRY

scrupulously fairly *(impartially)*, faithfully

scrupulousness adhesion *(loyalty)*, fairness, honesty, honor *(good reputation)*, integrity, particularity, principle *(virtue)*, probity, rectitude, responsibility *(conscience)*, rigor

scrupulus embarrassment

scrutable cognizable, coherent *(clear)*, solvable. SEE MAIN ENTRY

scrutari probe *(noun)*, probe *(verb)*

scrutation indagation, scrutiny

scrutinization analysis, investigation

scrutinize analyze, audit, canvass, check *(inspect)*, concentrate *(pay attention)*, consider, criticize *(evaluate)*, discern *(detect with the senses)*, examine *(study)*, frisk, inquire, investigate, monitor, notice *(observe)*, observe *(watch)*, overlook *(superintend)*, oversee, peruse, probe, regard *(pay attention)*, research, review, search, spy, study, survey *(examine)*. SEE MAIN ENTRY

scrutinizing circumspect, inquisitive, interrogative

scrutiny analysis, contemplation, crossexamination, cross-questioning, diligence *(care)*, discovery, examination *(study)*, indagation, inquiry *(request for information)*, inquiry *(systematic investigation)*, inspection, interrogation, investigation, notice *(heed)*, observation, perception, probe, question *(inquiry)*, regard *(attention)*, research, review *(official reexamination)*, surveillance, test, trial *(experiment)*. SEE MAIN ENTRY

scud race

scuffle affray, altercation, belligerency, brawl *(noun)*, brawl *(verb)*, commotion, confrontation *(altercation)*, fight *(battle)*, fight *(battle)*, fracas, fray, struggle

sculpture contour *(shape)*

scurrile calumnious, libelous, salacious, scurrilous

scurrilis scurrilous

scurrility aspersion, bad repute, contempt *(disdain)*, contumely, diatribe, disapprobation, expletive, slander

scurrillity obscenity

scurrilous blatant *(obtrusive)*, calumnious, ignoble, lewd, libelous, malignant, salacious, scandalous. SEE MAIN ENTRY

scurry dispatch *(promptness)*

scurvy iniquitous, objectionable, odious, poor *(inferior in quality)*

scuttlebutt report *(rumor)*

scutum shield

se abstinere refrain
se applicare recourse
se conferre recourse
se coniungere join (associate oneself with)
se continere refrain
se defendere answer (reply)
se interponere intrude, mediate
se opponere confront (oppose)
se recipere retreat
se rei dedere address (talk to)
se submittere condescend (deign)
seaboard littoral
seacoast littoral
seal bar (hinder), brand, brand (mark), complete, conclude (complete), conclude (decide), confirm, confirmation, determine, fix (settle), lock, notarize, occlude, sanction (permission), shut, sign, stamp, subscribe (sign), symbol, validate. SEE MAIN ENTRY
seal of secrecy censorship
seal the doom of determine
seal up contain (enclose), immure, repress
sealed blind (impassable), impervious, necessary (inescapable), undisclosed
sealed record SEE MAIN ENTRY
sealing off blockade (enclosure)
sear burn, deflagrate
search audit, canvass, chase, cross-examination, delve, endeavor, examination (study), experiment, ferret, indagation, inquest, inquire, inquiry (request for information), inquiry (systematic investigation), interrogation, investigation, market (demand), peruse, probe, pursue (chase), pursuit (chase), pursuit (effort to secure), quest, question (inquiry), research (noun), research (verb), scrutinize, scrutiny, survey (examine), test, trace (follow), undertaking (attempt), undertaking (enterprise). SEE MAIN ENTRY
search for delve, hunt
search for an answer consult (seek information from)
search for information inquiry (request for information)
search into check (inspect), inquire, investigate, probe, scrutinize, study
search into facts cross-examination, inquest
search laboriously delve
search made for useful military information espionage
search one's pockets frisk
search out hunt, locate, spy
search through delve, frisk
search warrant SEE MAIN ENTRY
searching inquisitive, interrogative, quest, vigilant
searching examination probe
searching inquiry analysis, cross-examination, hearing, investigation
searching investigation indagation
seared callous, impervious
searing insufferable, scathing
seashore littoral
seaside littoral
season duration, inure (accustom), lifetime, mature, moderate (temper), period, phase (period), term (duration)
seasonable apposite, favorable (advantageous), fit, fitting, opportune, prompt, proper, propitious, punctual, relevant, suitable
seasonableness timeliness

seasonal intermittent, periodic, regular (orderly). SEE MAIN ENTRY
seasoned elderly, expert, practiced, ripe, sapid, veteran
seasoning experience (background)
seat address, embed, headquarters, instate, locality, standpoint, venue. SEE MAIN ENTRY
seat of judgment bench
seat of justice bar (court), bench
seated situated
secede defect, leave (depart), quit (discontinue), renege, withdraw. SEE MAIN ENTRY
secede from abandon (physically leave), relinquish
secern SEE MAIN ENTRY
secernere distinguish, isolate
secession desertion, lapse (expiration), resignation (relinquishment), revolt, schism
seclude blind (obscure), camouflage, cloak, conceal, condemn (ban), confine, cover (conceal), ensconce, enshroud, harbor, hide, immure, insulate, isolate, protect, shroud. SEE MAIN ENTRY
seclude oneself lurk, retire (retreat), retreat
secluded clandestine, covert, evasive, hidden, obscure (remote), secret, separate, solitary, unapproachable
secludere seclude
seclusion concealment, exclusion, obscuration, privacy, quarantine
seclusive private (secluded), remote (secluded)
second abet, abettor, advocate, aid, approve, assist, assistant, backer, bear (support), concur (agree), confirm, countersign, deputy, endorse, help, indorse, justify, point (period of time), proctor, promote (organize), recommend, replacement, side, support (assist), uphold. SEE MAIN ENTRY
second best poor (inferior in quality)
second examination review (official reexamination)
second legal marriage digamy
second marriage digamy
second nature habit
second rank circumstantial
second self alter ego
second thoughts hesitation, hindsight
second time de novo
second to none best, cardinal (outstanding), paramount, premium, primary, superior (excellent), superlative
second view hindsight
second-rate inferior (lower in quality), mediocre, poor (inferior in quality)
second-story thief burglar
secondary ancillary (subsidiary), circumstantial, collateral (immaterial), contributory, deputy, derivative, extrinsic, incidental, inferior (lower in position), minor, null (insignificant), pendent, peripheral, plenipotentiary, replacement, slight, subaltern, subordinate, subservient, subsidiary, succedaneum, supplementary, unessential. SEE MAIN ENTRY
secondary evidence hearsay
secondary group minority (outnumbered group)
secondary implied meaning connotation
secondary rights SEE MAIN ENTRY
seconded SEE MAIN ENTRY
seconder advocate (counselor), advocate (espouser), assistant, backer, benefactor, colleague, partisan, proponent

secondhand evidence hearsay
seconding accommodation (backing), advocacy, help
secrecy concealment, confidence (relation of trust), evasion, mystery, obscuration, privacy
secret anonymous, clandestine, confidence (relation of trust), confidential, covert, enigma, enigmatic, esoteric, furtive, hidden, inscrutable, interior, intimate, mysterious, mystery, personal (private), private (confidential), privy, recondite, seal (close), sequester (seclude), sly, stealthy, surreptitious, ulterior, uncanny, undisclosed. SEE MAIN ENTRY
secret agent spy
secret approval connivance
secret association collusion
secret communication confidence (relation of trust)
secret fraudulent understanding collusion
secret group cabal
secret observation espionage
secret place cache (hiding place)
secret plot cabal
secret storehouse cache (storage place)
secret understanding collusion
secret understanding for fraud collusion
secret watching espionage
secretary amanuensis, clerk
secrete blind (obscure), camouflage, cloak, conceal, cover (conceal), emit, ensconce, enshroud, exude, harbor, hide, plant (covertly place)
secrete oneself lurk
secreted blind (concealed), hidden
secretion concealment
secretive clandestine, evasive, furtive, laconic, mysterious, noncommittal, oblique (evasive), sly, stealthy, surreptitious, taciturn, unresponsive
secretiveness concealment, evasion, mystery, privacy
secretness evasion
secretus mysterious, secret, separate
sect class, denomination, side, society, split
sectarian heretic, one-sided, parochial, partisan (adjective), partisan (noun), specific
sectarianism intolerance, schism
sectarism schism
sectarist pariah
sectary advocate (espouser), backer, pariah, partisan
section article (distinct section of a writing), chamber (compartment), chapter (branch), chapter (division), circuit, clause, component, constituent (part), cross (intersect), decentralization, denomination, department, detail, dichotomize, disjoint, district, divide (separate), division (act of dividing), element, heading, ingredient, installment, locality, location, member (constituent part), moiety, organ, parcel, part (place), part (portion), part (separate), partition, phase (aspect), pigeonhole, province, region, segment, separate, share (interest), split, subdivision, subheading, territory, title (division). SEE MAIN ENTRY
section head caption
sectional broken (fractured), local, partial (part), partial (relating to a part), provincial, regional
sectionalism intolerance

sectionalize dichotomize, divide *(separate)*, parcel, partition, separate

sector chapter *(division)*, component, constituent *(part)*, department, ingredient, locality, parcel, region, segment, subdivision

secular civil *(public)*, material *(physical)*, mundane, profane

secundarius secondary

secundum leges fit legal

secundus fair *(satisfactory)*, prosperous

securable available, disposable, open *(accessible)*

secure accept *(take)*, adhere *(fasten)*, affix, arrest *(apprehend)*, attach *(join)*, attach *(seize)*, attain, bar *(hinder)*, bind *(restrain)*, bond *(hold together)*, bond *(secure a debt)*, buy, cement, certain *(positive)*, collect *(recover money)*, combine *(join together)*, conserve, convincing, cosign, cover *(guard)*, definite, derive *(receive)*, detain *(hold in custody)*, earn, educe, employ *(engage services)*, engage *(hire)*, ensconce, ensure, evoke, fetter, firm, fix *(make firm)*, fixed *(securely placed)*, gain, guarantee, handcuff, harbor, hijack, hold *(possess)*, inexpugnable, infallible, infrangible, inviolate, keep *(shelter)*, lock, maintain *(sustain)*, obtain, permanent, police, positive *(confident)*, possess, preserve, procure, protect, purchase, reap, receive *(acquire)*, recover, reliable, repossess, restrict, retain *(employ)*, retain *(keep in possession)*, safe, seal *(close)*, shut, solid *(sound)*, sponsor, stabilize, stable, steadfast, strong, succeed *(attain)*, underwrite, vouch. SEE MAIN ENTRY

secure against damage indemnify

secure against loss assure *(insure)*, indemnify, insure

secure by force constrain *(compel)*

secure exclusive control monopolize

secure exclusive possession monopolize

secure for a consideration buy, purchase

secure from capture inexpugnable, invincible

secure payment collect *(recover money)*

secure retreat asylum *(hiding place)*

secure the services of hire

secure with chains fetter

secured firm, guarded

secured by law inalienable

secured debenture security *(stock)*

securely fixed firm

securement distraint

secureness certainty, security *(safety)*

securing accession *(annexation)*

securities portfolio. SEE MAIN ENTRY

securities law blue sky law

securities oversight blue sky law

securities rules blue sky law

securities statutes blue sky law

security accommodation *(backing)*, assurance, asylum *(protection)*, bail, binder, bond, bulwark, certainty, charge *(lien)*, check *(instrument)*, cloud *(incumbrance)*, confidence *(faith)*, deposit, guaranty, handsel, hostage, hypothecation, indemnity, inviolability, letter of credit, lien, mainstay, mortgage, pledge *(security)*, precaution, preservation, protection, recognizance, refuge, reliance, safeguard, safekeeping, share *(stock)*, shelter *(protection)*, shelter *(tax benefit)*, shield, specialty *(contract)*, stock *(shares)*, undertaking *(bond)*, under-

taking *(pledge)*, ward, warrant *(guaranty)*. SEE MAIN ENTRY

security against damage indemnity

security against loss coverage *(insurance)*, indemnity, insurance

security against violence inviolability

security for a debt mortgage

security officer peace officer

security on property charge *(lien)*, cloud *(incumbrance)*, lien, mechanics lien

securus safe

secus procedere miscarriage

sedare allay, assuage, lull

sedate peaceable, phlegmatic, solemn

sedateness composure, decorum, moderation

sedative drug, narcotic *(adjective)*, narcotic *(noun)*, palliative *(abating)*

sedentary inactive, torpid

sedes dwelling, foundation *(basis)*, inhabitation *(place of dwelling)*, residence, seat

sediment alluvion

seditio insurrection, mutiny, rebellion, revolt, sedition

sedition anarchy, bad faith, bad repute, defiance, disloyalty, infidelity, insurrection, mutiny, rebellion, resistance, revolt, subversion, treason. SEE MAIN ENTRY

seditionary insurgent, malcontent

seditionem rebel

seditionist malcontent

seditiosus insubordinate

seditious lawless, nonconsenting, restive

seditiousness bad faith, disloyalty, infidelity, sedition

seduce bait *(lure)*, betray *(lead astray)*, brutalize, corrupt, entice, inveigle, lure, mislead, persuade, prevail *(persuade)*, suborn

seducement bribery, seduction

seduction debauchery, debauchment, rape. SEE MAIN ENTRY

seductive attractive, provocative, suggestive *(risqué)*

sedulity diligence *(perseverance)*, industry *(activity)*

sedulous active, diligent, faithful *(diligent)*, industrious, painstaking, patient, persistent, pertinacious, purposeful, relentless, resolute, stable, steadfast, unrelenting, unremitting, unyielding, zealous. SEE MAIN ENTRY

sedulousness diligence *(perseverance)*, industry *(activity)*

sedulus industrious, painstaking, sedulous

see apprehend *(perceive)*, comprehend *(understand)*, conceive *(comprehend)*, detect, discern *(detect with the senses)*, discover, note *(notice)*, notice *(observe)*, observe *(watch)*, perceive, pierce *(discern)*, realize *(understand)*, recognize *(perceive)*, regard *(pay attention)*, spy, witness *(have direct knowledge of)*

see about check *(inspect)*

see as distinct discern *(discriminate)*

see at a glance discern *(detect with the senses)*

see in retrospect recall *(remember)*

see the difference diagnose, discern *(discriminate)*, discriminate *(distinguish)*

see through construe *(comprehend)*, dispatch *(dispose of)*, execute *(accomplish)*, follow-up, implement

see to attend *(take care of)*, handle *(manage)*, maintain *(sustain)*, manage, superintend

seeable appreciable, discernible, manifest, open *(in sight)*, ostensible, palpable, perceivable, perceptible, scrutable, visible *(in full view)*

seed children, embryo, inseminate, posterity, progeny

seedy poor *(inferior in quality)*

seek apply *(request)*, chase, delve, endeavor, ferret, frisk, hunt, petition, probe, pursue *(chase)*, pursue *(strive to gain)*, request, research, search, strive, trace *(follow)*, try *(attempt)*

seek a clue delve

seek accord close *(agree)*

seek advice confer *(consult)*, counsel, refer *(send for action)*

seek as due claim *(demand)*

seek by request sue

seek counsel consult *(ask advice of)*

seek facts from consult *(seek information from)*

seek guidance consult *(ask advice of)*

seek information inquire

seek information regarding investigate, probe

seek legal redress litigate

seek redress address *(petition)*

seek reexamination appeal

seek reference of a case from one court to another appeal

seek review of a case appeal

seek the opinion of consult *(ask ad-vice of)*

seek to attempt

seek to attain pursue *(strive to gain)*

seek to persuade counsel

seeker candidate, special interest, suitor

seeking inquisitive, quest

seeking to avoid evasive

seeking to elude evasive

seeking to evade evasive

seem comport *(behave)*, demean *(deport oneself)*, pretend

seem like appear *(seem to be)*

seem to be demean *(deport oneself)*

seeming apparent *(presumptive)*, colorable *(plausible)*, constructive *(inferential)*, deceptive, ostensible, plausible, presumptive, probable, specious

seeming contradiction paradox

seemingly prima facie *(self-evident)*, reputedly

seemingly but not actually quasi

seemingly fair colorable *(plausible)*

seemingly sound colorable *(plausible)*

seemingly valid colorable *(plausible)*

seemingly worthy of acceptance plausible

seemliness conduct, decorum, expedience, propriety *(appropriateness)*

seemly appropriate, felicitous, fit, fitting, proper, right *(suitable)*, rightful, seasonable, suitable

seep exude, outflow, permeate

seep in penetrate, pervade

seepage osmosis

seer bystander, eyewitness

seesaw beat *(pulsate)*, oscillate, vacillate

seethe burn

segment chapter *(division)*, component, constituent *(part)*, cross *(intersect)*, dichotomize, disjoint, divide *(separate)*, element, factor *(ingredient)*, installment, member *(constituent part)*, moiety, parcel *(noun)*, parcel *(verb)*, part *(portion)*, partition, section *(division)*, separate, sever, share *(interest)*, split, subdivision, subheading. SEE MAIN ENTRY segmental

segmental partial (relating to a part)
segmentation disassociation, division (act of dividing), split
segmentum segment
segnitia sloth
segregare seclude
segregate classify, demarcate, differentiate, dissociate, divide (separate), estrange, exclude, insulate, isolate, relegate, remove (eliminate), screen (select), seclude, select, separate, sequester (seclude), sever, sort, split
segregated remote (secluded), separate
segregation discrimination (differentiation), division (act of dividing), estrangement, exception (exclusion), exclusion, expulsion, intolerance, ostracism, quarantine, removal, selection (choice), severance, split. SEE MAIN ENTRY
seigniory domain (land owned)
seignorage dominion (absolute ownership)
seisin dominion (absolute ownership), enjoyment (use), holding (property owned), inheritance, interest (ownership), land, ownership, paraphernalia (personal belongings), possession (ownership). SEE MAIN ENTRY
seiunctio segregation (separation)
seiungere detach, isolate
seize abridge (divest), adopt, annex (arrogate), apprehend (arrest), arrest (apprehend), capture, carry away, confiscate, construe (comprehend), deprive, despoil, distrain, divest, embrace (accept), garnish, grapple, harry (plunder), hijack, impound, impress (procure by force), impropriate, kidnap, levy, loot, obsess, obtain, occupy (take possession), pilfer, pirate (take by violence), plunder, possess, preempt, prey, procure, purloin, receive (acquire), repossess, rob, takeover, usurp. SEE MAIN ENTRY
seize again rearrest
seize and appropriate confiscate, garnish
seize as forfeited to the public treasury confiscate
seize by authority confiscate
seize by legal warrant arrest (apprehend)
seize for public use nationalize
seize for the government nationalize
seize from private control federalize (place under federal control)
seize from state control federalize (place under federal control)
seize legally book
seize power federalize (place under federal control), usurp
seize summarily attach (seize)
seize the advantage beat (defeat)
seize wrongfully infringe
seized arrested (apprehended)
seized articles contraband
seized goods contraband
seizing attachment (seizure), confiscatory, distress (seizure)
seizure adverse possession, apprehension (act of arresting), appropriation (taking), arrest, arrogation, disseisin, garnishment, infringement, levy, occupation (possession), onset (assault), plunder, sequestration, taking
seizure and appropriation distraint
seizure and transference extradition
seizure of a privilege forfeiture (act of forfeiting)

seizure of private property for public use expropriation (right of eminent domain)
seizure of property by the government expropriation (right of eminent domain)
seizure of property in the public interest expropriation (right of eminent domain)
seizure to procure satisfaction of a debt distraint
sejunction division (act of dividing)
seldom happening infrequent
seldom met with scarce, uncommon
seldom occurring infrequent
seldom seen infrequent, rare
select adopt, appoint, best, cast (register), certain (specific), choose, compile, cull, decide, delegate, designate, digest (summarize), edit, elect (choose), exclusive (limited), extract, inestimable, meritorious, nominate, particular (specific), personal (individual), prefer, preferential, premium, prime (most valuable), private (not public), rare, recruit, restrictive, specialize, specific, specify, valuable. SEE MAIN ENTRY
select and arrange compile
select as one's own adopt
select body elite
select boundaries locate
select few elite
select for office elect (select by a vote)
select jurors empanel
select passage excerpt
selected particular (specific), preferable, preferential, preferred (favored), select
selectee licensee, nominee (delegate)
selection adoption (acceptance), alternative (option), appointment (act of designating), assignment (designation), assumption (adoption), choice (alternatives offered), choice (decision), compilation, decision (election), designation (naming), discretion (power of choice), election (choice), excerpt, manner (kind), nomination, nominee (candidate), option (choice), patronage (power to appoint jobs), poll (casting of votes), preference (choice), primary, referendum, volition, vote. SEE MAIN ENTRY
selection for office by vote election (selection by vote)
selection of words phraseology
selective adoptive, discretionary, discriminating (distinguishing), discriminating (judicious), disjunctive (alternative), exclusive (limited), particular (exacting), preferential, restrictive
selectiveness particularity
selector licensor
self identity (individuality)
self consistent consonant
self-abasing obeisant, repentant
self-abnegation capitulation
self-absorption introspection
self-accusation confession, remorse
self-accusatory remorseful, repentant
self-accusing contrite, penitent
self-acting spontaneous
self-admiration pride
self-admiring pretentious (pompous)
self-applauding inflated (vain), orgulous, pretentious (pompous), proud (conceited)
self-applause pride
self-approval pride
self-assertive obtrusive
self-assurance composure, surety (certainty)
self-assured assertive, positive (confident)
self-centered inflated (vain)

self-centred orgulous
self-command composure, continence, discipline (obedience)
self-communing pensive, reflection (thought)
self-communion introspection
self-condemnation confession, remorse
self-condemnatory contrite, remorseful, repentant
self-condemned penitent
self-confident positive (confident)
self-conquest discipline (obedience)
self-conscious diffident, histrionic
self-consciousness embarrassment
self-consequence consequence (significance)
self-consistent consistent
self-contained autonomous (independent)
self-containment home rule
self-content complacent
self-contradiction paradox
self-contradictory illogical, impossible
self-control continence, longanimity, moderation, restraint, sufferance, temperance, will (desire)
self-controlled controlled (restrained), dispassionate, nonchalant, patient, stoical
self-convicted contrite, penitent, repentant
self-conviction remorse, surety (certainty)
self-counsel introspection, reflection (thought)
self-criticism remorse
self-denial austerity, continence, discipline (obedience), restraint, temperance
self-denouncing repentant
self-denunciatory contrite
self-derived power home rule
self-determination discretion (power of choice), freedom, home rule, liberty, suffrage
self-determined autonomous (self governing), nonpartisan, sovereign (independent), spontaneous
self-determined being character (an individual)
self-directing autonomous (self governing), free (enjoying civil liberty), nonpartisan, sovereign (independent)
self-direction discipline (obedience), home rule, liberty
self-discipline continence, will (desire)
self-disciplined stoical
self-doubt doubt (indecision)
self-effacing diffident, unobtrusive
self-esteem pride
self-esteeming pretentious (pompous)
self-evident apparent (perceptible), axiomatic, certain (positive), clear (apparent), coherent (clear), comprehensible, conspicuous, convincing, discernible, distinct (clear), ostensible, palpable
self-evident proposition principle (axiom)
self-evident truth principle (axiom)
self-exaltation pride
self-examination introspection
self-existent peremptory (absolute)
self-explanatory comprehensible
self-flattering orgulous
self-glorification jactation, pride
self-glorifying inflated (vain), orgulous, pretentious (pompous)
self-governed sovereign (independent)

974

self-governing free *(enjoying civil liberty)*, independent, nonpartisan

self-government freedom, home rule, liberty, suffrage

self-importance consequence *(significance)*, pride

self-important consequential *(substantial)*, inflated *(vain)*, orgulous, pretentious *(pompous)*, proud *(conceited)*

self-imposed task campaign

self-inspection introspection

self-knowledge introspection

self-lauding inflated *(vain)*, orgulous

self-legislation home rule

self-magnifying orgulous

self-mastery discipline *(obedience)*

self-possession composure, sufferance

self-praising orgulous

self-regulation discipline *(obedience)*

self-reliance home rule

self-reliant autonomous *(independent)*, independent, spartan

self-reproach remorse

self-reproachful contrite, penitent, repentant

self-reproaching remorseful

self-reproof remorse

self-reproving repentant

self-respect integrity

self-restraint austerity, composure, continence, discipline *(obedience)*, sufferance, temperance

self-rule freedom

self-ruling autonomous *(self governing)*, free *(enjoying civil liberty)*, sovereign *(independent)*

self-sacrifice philanthropy

self-satisfaction pride

self-satisfied complacent, inflated *(vain)*, orgulous, pretentious *(pompous)*, proud *(conceited)*

self-scrutiny introspection

self-seeking venal

self-study introspection

self-subsistence home rule

self-subsistent independent

self-sufficiency home rule

self-sufficient autonomous *(independent)*, insular

self-support home rule

self-supporting autonomous *(independent)*, independent

self-willed pertinacious, perverse, voluntary

selfhood identity *(individuality)*, personality

selfish illiberal, insatiable, mercenary, parsimonious, penurious, thoughtless

selfishness greed

selfless dispassionate, liberal *(generous)*, philanthropic

selflessness largess *(generosity)*, philanthropy

selfness identity *(individuality)*, personality

selfsameness resemblance. SEE MAIN ENTRY

sell deal, handle *(trade)*, liquidate *(convert into cash)*, persuade, trade, vend. SEE MAIN ENTRY

sell assets liquidate *(convert into cash)*

sell at the market handle *(trade)*

sell below par discount *(reduce)*

sell into slavery subjugate

sell out betray *(disclose)*, betray *(lead astray)*

seller creditor, dealer, merchant, supplier, vendor

selling alienation *(transfer of title)*

selling price price

selvedge border

semantics meaning

semaphore indicator

semasiology meaning

semblance analogy, complexion, correspondence *(similarity)*, disguise, face value *(first blush)*, facsimile, identity *(similarity)*, parity, presence *(poise)*, pretense *(pretext)*, pretext, propinquity *(similarity)*, reflection *(image)*, resemblance. SEE MAIN ENTRY

semi SEE MAIN ENTRY

seminal original *(initial)*

seminar conference, meeting *(conference)*, panel *(discussion group)*, parley

semiprocessed inchoate

sempiternal constant, continual *(perpetual)*, durable, infinite, permanent, perpetual

sempiternus indelible, perpetual

senate legislature

senator lawmaker, legislator

senatus consultum decree

send consign, delegate, deliver, dispatch *(send off)*, dispel, displace *(remove)*, project *(impel forward)*, radiate, refer *(send for action)*, remand, remit *(submit for consideration)*, remove *(transfer)*, transfer, transmit, transport. SEE MAIN ENTRY

send a final demand charge *(assess)*

send a message correspond *(communicate)*, transmit

send abroad diffuse

send an order instruct *(direct)*

send an order for call *(demand)*

send as deputy delegate

send away deport *(banish)*, dislodge, dismiss *(discharge)*, dispatch *(send off)*, displace *(remove)*, evacuate, expatriate, rebuff, relegate, repulse

send back disavow, recommit, reflect *(mirror)*, remand, restore *(return)*

send flying dispel, launch *(project)*, precipitate *(throw down violently)*

send for call *(summon)*, request, subpoena, summon

send forth cast *(throw)*, circulate, diffuse, discharge *(shoot)*, dispatch *(send off)*, emit, launch *(project)*, outpour, precipitate *(throw down violently)*, radiate, remove *(transfer)*, send

send forward redirect

send headlong impel, launch *(project)*, precipitate *(throw down violently)*

send home dispel

send money remit *(send payment)*

send off cast *(throw)*, dismiss *(discharge)*, launch *(project)*, project *(impel forward)*

send on redirect, transmit

send on a commission delegate

send on a mission delegate

send on an errand delegate

send out delegate, emit, issue *(publish)*, outpour, send

send payment remit *(send payment)*

send regrets refuse

send through the mail dispatch *(send off)*

send to an asylum commit *(institutionalize)*

send to jail arrest *(apprehend)*, commit *(institutionalize)*, confine, imprison

send to prison apprehend *(arrest)*, commit *(institutionalize)*, constrain *(imprison)*, immure, imprison, jail

send to the bottom immerse *(plunge into)*

send word communicate, inform *(notify)*

sending consignment, delivery, transmittal

sending away deportation

sending to another state for trial extradition

sending to jail commitment *(confinement)*

senescence deterioration

senescent elderly

senility caducity

senior adult, chief, principal *(director)*, superior *(higher)* SEE MAIN ENTRY

senior court appellate court

senior statesman veteran

seniority age, authority *(power)*, longevity, precedence, predominance, preference *(priority)*, primacy, priority

sensation emotion, impression, reaction *(response)*, sense *(feeling)*, sensibility

sensational blatant *(conspicuous)*, lurid, moving *(evoking emotion)*

sensationalism exaggeration

sense apprehend *(perceive)*, apprehension *(perception)*, competence *(sanity)*, comprehension, connotation, construction, content *(meaning)*, contents, context, detect, expedience, gist *(substance)*, import, impression, intellect, intelligence *(intellect)*, main point, meaning, perceive, perception, prudence, reaction *(response)*, reason *(sound judgment)*, sagacity, sanity, signification, spirit, substance *(essential nature)*, tenor, understanding *(comprehension)*. SEE MAIN ENTRY

sense of danger apprehension *(fear)*

sense of disgrace ignominy

sense of duty adhesion *(loyalty)*, allegiance, charge *(responsibility)*, commitment *(responsibility)*, conscience, responsibility *(conscience)*

sense of language parlance

sense of moral right conscience

sense of obligation responsibility *(conscience)*

sense of proportion perspective

sense of responsibility adhesion *(loyalty)*, honor *(good reputation)*

sense of right and wrong conscience, ethics, responsibility *(conscience)*

sense of shame disgrace, ignominy

sense perception impression

senseless fatuous, frivolous, ill-advised, impolitic, inexpressive, insensible, irrational, ludicrous, lunatic, misadvised, non compos mentis, obtuse, opaque, puerile, unpolitic, unreasonable, unsound *(fallacious)*, vacuous

senseless prate platitude

senseless talk jargon *(unintelligible language)*

senselessness inexpedience, insentience

senses competence *(sanity)*

sensibility cognition, perception, pragmatism, realization, reason *(sound judgment)*. SEE MAIN ENTRY

sensible colorable *(plausible)*, conscious *(aware)*, discreet, familiar *(informed)*, functional, judicial, judicious, justifiable, lucid, normal *(sane)*, perceptive, perspicacious, physical, plausible, politic, pragmatic, prudent, rational, reasonable *(rational)*, responsive, sane, sapient, solid *(sound)*, viable. SEE MAIN ENTRY

sensible to cognizant

sensibleness common sense, expedience, pragmatism, reason *(sound judgment)*, sanity

sensilis sensitive *(discerning)*

sensitive charitable *(lenient)*, circumspect, discreet, hot-blooded, moving *(evoking emotion)*, open *(persuasible)*, perceptive, receptive, responsive, susceptible *(responsive)*, susceptible *(unresistent)*. SEE MAIN ENTRY

sensitiveness discretion *(quality of being discreet)*, emotion, sensibility

sensitivity discretion *(quality of being discreet)*, insight, sensibility, understanding *(tolerance)*

sensory experience perception

sensory perception impression

sensu carere insensible, insusceptible *(uncaring)*

sensual dissolute, mundane, obscene, physical, salacious

sensuous lascivious, physical

sensus content *(meaning)*, sense *(feeling)*

sent to prison arrested *(apprehended)*

sentence adjudge, adjudication, clause, condemn *(punish)*, condemnation *(punishment)*, convict, conviction *(finding of guilt)*, decide, decree, determination, discipline *(punish)*, finding, holding *(ruling of a court)*, judge, judgment *(formal court decree)*, opinion *(judicial decision)*, penalize, penalty, punish, ruling, verdict. SEE MAIN ENTRY

sentenced blameworthy

sentencing commitment *(confinement)*, conviction *(finding of guilt)*

sententia content *(meaning)*, conviction *(persuasion)*, expression *(comment)*, holding *(ruling of a court)*, meaning, motion, opinion *(judicial decision)*, resolution *(decision)*, standpoint, tenor, verdict, vote

sententiam dicere comment

sententiosus sententious

sententious axiomatic, brief, compact *(pithy)*, incisive, laconic, pithy, proverbial, succinct. SEE MAIN ENTRY

sententious saying maxim

sententious utterance maxim

sentient conscious *(aware)*, perceptive, responsive, sensitive *(discerning)*

sentiment affection, conviction *(persuasion)*, emotion, idea, notion, opinion *(belief)*, position *(point of view)*, posture *(attitude)*, reaction *(response)*, spirit

sentimental sensitive *(easily affected)*

sentimental attachment affection

sentimentality affection

sentinel guardian, protect

sentire perceive

sentry caretaker *(one caring for property)*, guardian, warden

separabilis severable

separable divisible, divisive, moving *(in motion)*, severable. SEE MAIN ENTRY

separable part of a certificate coupon

separare apart, detach, divide *(separate)*, part *(separate)*, separate, sever

separate alienate *(estrange)*, alone *(solitary)*, apart, bifurcate, bipartite, classify, cross *(intersect)*, cull, demarcate, detach, dichotomize, different, disaffect, disband, disconnected, discontinue *(abandon)*, discontinue *(break continuity)*, discrete, discriminate *(distinguish)*, disengage, disentangle, disjoint, disjunctive *(tending to disjoin)*, disorganize, disparate, disperse *(scatter)*, dissociate, distill, distinct *(distinguished from others)*, distinguish, divide *(separate)*, estrange, except *(exclude)*,

excise *(cut away)*, exclusive *(singular)*, extract, extrinsic, foreign, impertinent *(irrelevant)*, individual, insular, insulate, interrupt, irrelative, isolate, liberate, luxate, particular *(individual)*, particular *(specific)*, private *(secluded)*, purge *(purify)*, relegate, remove *(eliminate)*, screen *(select)*, secede, seclude, sequester *(seclude)*, sequester *(seize property)*, sever, singular, sole, solitary, sort, split, sporadic, subdivide, substantive, unrelated, withdraw. SEE MAIN ENTRY

separate as different differentiate

separate existence entity

separate from quit *(evacuate)*

separate in two dichotomize

separate into categories organize *(arrange)*

separate maintenance alimony, estrangement

separate oneself retire *(retreat)*

separate oneself from part *(leave)*

separate paragraph item

separate part chamber *(compartment)*, chapter *(division)*, section *(division)*

separate ticket coupon

separated apart, bicameral, bipartite, broken *(fractured)*, disconnected, discrete, inaccessible, individual, irrelative, peculiar *(distinctive)*, remote *(secluded)*, separate, solitary, unapproachable

separately respectively

separateness difference, nonconformity, privacy

separating divergent

separatio separation

separation alienation *(estrangement)*, decentralization, dichotomy, disassociation, discrimination *(differentiation)*, dissolution *(disintegration)*, diversification, division *(act of dividing)*, estrangement, evulsion, exception *(exclusion)*, exclusion, expulsion, hiatus, liberation, ostracism, privacy, quarantine, removal, rift *(gap)*, schism, section *(division)*, selection *(choice)*, severance, split, subdivision. SEE MAIN ENTRY

separation by races segregation *(isolation by races)*

separation money alimony

separatism nonconformity

separatist heretic

separative discriminating *(distinguishing)*, distinctive

separatus distinct *(distinguished from others)*, particular *(specific)*, separate

seperate select

sept family *(common ancestry)*

septic deleterious, peccant *(unhealthy)*

sequacious passive, pliable, pliant, resilient. SEE MAIN ENTRY

sequel codicil, development *(outgrowth)*, effect, follow-up, outgrowth

sequela codicil

sequence array *(order)*, chain *(series)*, continuity, cycle, method, order *(arrangement)*, outcome, succession. SEE MAIN ENTRY

sequence of events calendar *(record of yearly periods)*

sequent consecutive, corollary, derivative, future, outcome, proximate, subsequent, successive

sequential ancillary *(subsidiary)*, consecutive, consequential *(deducible)*, continuous, ensuing, narrative, subsequent, successive

sequester attach *(seize)*, collect *(recover money)*, confiscate, deprive, distrain,

exclude, garnish, impound, impress *(procure by force)*, insulate, isolate, remove *(eliminate)*, seclude, seize *(confiscate)*, withdraw. SEE MAIN ENTRY

sequestered attached *(seized)*, privy, remote *(secluded)*

sequestrate attach *(seize)*, condemn *(seize)*, confiscate, deprive, distrain, garnish, impound, impress *(procure by force)*, remove *(eliminate)*, seize *(confiscate)*, sequester *(seize property)*, withdraw

sequestrating confiscatory

sequestration attachment *(seizure)*, disseisin, distraint, distress *(seizure)*, expropriation *(divestiture)*, privation, removal, taking. SEE MAIN ENTRY

sequi pursue *(chase)*, pursue *(strive to gain)*

serendipitous beneficial

serendipity happenstance

serene complacent, patient, peaceable, phlegmatic, placid

serenity composure, peace

serere propagate *(spread)*

serial cognate, consecutive, intermittent, journal, periodic, progressive *(going forward)*. SEE MAIN ENTRY

serialization distribution *(arrangement)*, sequence

serialized consecutive

seriate classify, consecutive

seriatim consecutive

seriation hierarchy *(arrangement in a series)*

series assemblage

series chain *(series)*

series hierarchy *(arrangement in a series)*

series sequence

series serial, succession

series of events proceeding, program

series of measures process *(course)*

serious chronic, critical *(crucial)*, dangerous, dire, earnest, exigent, grave *(important)*, grave *(solemn)*, important *(significant)*, insistent, major, momentous, pensive, pernicious, persistent, pertinacious, purposeful, resolute, solemn, steadfast, urgent. SEE MAIN ENTRY

serious accident casualty

serious calamity catastrophe

serious infraction of the law crime

serious thought consideration *(contemplation)*

seriously purely *(positively)*

seriously dangerous deadly

seriousness consequence *(significance)*, contemplation, degree *(magnitude)*, diligence *(care)*, import, importance, magnitude, severity, significance, solemnity, weight *(importance)*

serius grave *(important)*, serious *(grave)*

sermo discourse, language

sermon declamation, diatribe, instruction *(teaching)*, objurgation, peroration, reprimand, speech

sermonize address *(talk to)*, declaim, discourse, inculcate, speak

serpentiform circuitous

serpentile circuitous

serpentine artful, circuitous, devious, indirect, insidious, labyrinthine, sinuous, subtle *(insidious)*, tortuous *(bending)*

serpentoid circuitous

serried compact *(dense)*, solid *(compact)*

servant employee

servantry personnel

servants personnel, staff

servare conserve, preserve

serve abet, accommodate, aid, assist, attend *(take care of)*, avail *(be of use)*, bestow, care *(regard)*, contribute *(assist)*, dispense, divide *(distribute)*, fulfill, function, help, inure *(benefit)*, obey, officiate, order, pander, perform *(execute)*, promote *(organize)*, provide *(arrange for)*, supply. SEE MAIN ENTRY

serve as exercise *(discharge a function)*
serve as a substitute succeed *(follow)*
serve in the capacity of perform *(execute)*
serve notice caution, communicate, contact *(communicate)*, notify
serve the people rule *(govern)*
serve the purpose satisfy *(fulfill)*
serve with a writ call *(summon)*
service adhesion *(loyalty)*, agency *(legal relationship)*, aid, avail *(be of use)*, benevolence *(act of kindness)*, bureaucracy, employment, fix *(repair)*, help, homage, maintain *(sustain)*, maintenance *(upkeep)*, office, post, profit, promotion *(encouragement)*, purpose, repair, reparation *(keeping in repair)*, servitude, usage, use, utility *(usefulness)*, worth. SEE MAIN ENTRY
service road causeway
serviceability means *(opportunity)*, use, utility *(usefulness)*, utilization
serviceable constructive *(creative)*, convenient, disposable, effective *(efficient)*, functional, instrumental, ministerial, operative, passable, practical, pragmatic, profitable, subservient, valuable
serviceableness worth
services agency *(legal relationship)*
serviceway easement
servicing provision *(act of supplying)*
servile dependent, ignoble, obedient, obsequious, passive, pliable, pliant, sequacious, subaltern, subservient
servilis servile
servility amenability, discipline *(obedience)*, fealty, homage
serving adequate, part *(portion)*, provision *(act of supplying)*, ration
serving as a deterrent exemplary
serving as a model exemplary
serving as a pattern exemplary
serving as a sample exemplary
serving as a warning exemplary
serving as an adjunct ancillary *(auxiliary)*
serving as an aid ancillary *(auxiliary)*
serving as an instance exemplary
serving to commemorate honorary
serving to declare declaratory
serving to distinguish distinctive
servire serve *(assist)*
servitium servitude
servitude adhesion *(loyalty)*, bondage, homage, restraint, subjection, thrall. SEE MAIN ENTRY
servitus servitude, subjection, thrall
sescenti myriad
sesquipedalian turgid. SEE MAIN ENTRY
sesquipedalian words bombast
sesquipedalianism fustian
sesquipedalism bombast
sesquipedality bombast
session caucus, chamber *(body)*, congregation, meeting *(conference)*, phase *(period)*, term *(duration)*. SEE MAIN ENTRY
session of the court forum *(court)*
sessions bar *(court)*
set adjust *(resolve)*, assemblage, assess *(appraise)*, assign *(designate)*, cement,

chain *(series)*, chronic, class, confederacy *(compact)*, crystallize, customary, deposit *(place)*, designate, embed, firm, fix *(make firm)*, fix *(settle)*, fixed *(securely placed)*, formal, habitual, inexorable, ingrained, instate, inveterate, levy, locate, permanent, pertinacious, plant *(place firmly)*, positive *(prescribed)*, prescribe, prescriptive, prevalent, ready *(prepared)*, repose *(place)*, resolute, rigid, routine, situated, society, stabilize, unyielding, usual
set a figure evaluate
set a name to subscribe *(sign)*
set a price on estimate, evaluate
set a question at rest find *(determine)*
set a snare for entrap
set a task bind *(obligate)*, direct *(order)*
set a trap for ambush, dupe, ensnare, entrap, hunt
set a value on calculate, estimate, evaluate, gauge, measure, rate
set about assume *(undertake)*, endeavor, occupy *(engage)*, undertake
set above others prefer
set abroach dispel
set adrift derelict *(abandoned)*
set afloat originate
set afoot initiate
set against alienate *(estrange)*, antagonize, counter, counteract, disaffect, discourage, estrange, oppose
set an earlier date antedate
set apart allocate, characterize, choose, dedicate, demarcate, designate, devote, different, disconnected, discriminate *(distinguish)*, distinct *(distinguished from others)*, distinguish, estrange, except *(exclude)*, exclude, exempt, hoard, hold *(possess)*, insulate, isolate, label, preferred *(favored)*, relegate, remove *(eliminate)*, reserve, sacrosanct, seclude, select, separate *(adjective)*, separate *(verb)*, sequester *(seize property)*, set aside *(reserve)*, sever
set apart as different differentiate
set apart for special use dedicate
set aright fix *(repair)*
set as a goal intend, pursue *(strive to gain)*
set aside abandon *(relinquish)*, abolish, abrogate *(rescind)*, allocate, annul, cancel, dedicate, defer *(put off)*, designate, devote, disapprove *(reject)*, disavow, discharge *(release from obligation)*, disclaim, dismiss *(put out of consideration)*, disown *(deny the validity)*, dispel, eliminate *(exclude)*, exclude, hoard, hold *(possess)*, hold up *(delay)*, isolate, leave *(allow to remain)*, negate, null *(invalid)*, null and void, override, overrule, postpone, rebuff, reject, repeal, repudiate, rescind, reserve, seclude, sequester *(seize property)*, succeed *(follow)*, supersede, vacate *(void)*, waive. SEE MAIN ENTRY
set astir foment, inspire, promise *(raise expectations)*
set asunder disconnected, dispel, dissolve *(separate)*
set at ease assure *(give confidence to)*, satisfy *(fulfill)*
set at large clear, disencumber, disenthrall, extricate, free, liberate, release
set at liberty acquit, clear, discharge *(liberate)*, disengage, disenthrall, enfranchise, extricate, free, liberate, pardon, parole, quit *(free of)*, release
set at naught counteract, disavow, lessen, minimize, misprize, underestimate

set at nought decry, disown *(deny the validity)*, spurn
set at odds alienate *(estrange)*, antagonize, disaffect
set at rest complete *(ended)*, conclude *(complete)*, dispatch *(dispose of)*, settle, through
set at variance alienate *(estrange)*, estrange
set back check *(restrain)*, constrict *(inhibit)*, delay, hinder
set before pose *(propound)*
set bounds limit
set bounds to demarcate
set by hoard
set conflagration arson
set down alight, avow, browbeat, enter *(record)*, express, formulate, itemize, note *(record)*, record, render *(deliver)*. SEE MAIN ENTRY
set down to attribute
set eyes on discern *(detect with the senses)*
set firmly embed, plant *(place firmly)*
set foot in enter *(go in)*
set for a later time continue *(adjourn)*
set form formality, matter of course, procedure
set format procedure
set forth allege, alleged, argue, assert, cite *(state)*, commence, communicate, contend *(maintain)*, declare, delineate, demonstrate *(establish)*, depict, detail *(particularize)*, exhibit, exposit, expound, express, interject, issue *(publish)*, manifest, pass *(determine)*, plead *(allege in a legal action)*, portray, posit, present *(introduce)*, proclaim, profess *(avow)*, proffer, promulgate, propose, propound, quit *(evacuate)*, reason *(persuade)*, recite, recount, relate *(tell)*, render *(depict)*, report *(disclose)*, signify *(inform)*, stated, trace *(delineate)*. SEE MAIN ENTRY
set forth evidence bare
set forth in a will testamentary
set forth in words express
set forth the character of characterize
set forth the meaning interpret
set free absolve, acquit, clear, condone, discharge *(liberate)*, disencumber, disengage, disentangle, disenthrall, dismiss *(discharge)*, dissociate, enfranchise, exculpate, exonerate, extricate, free *(relieved from a burden)*, free, liberate, palliate *(excuse)*, pardon, parole, quit *(free of)*, release, relieve *(free from burden)*, rescue, unbound, vindicate
set going create, dispatch *(send off)*, establish *(launch)*, impel, initiate, launch *(initiate)*, originate
set going again renew *(begin again)*
set guidelines organize *(arrange)*
set in remain *(stay)*
set in array organize *(arrange)*
set in motion expedite, exploit *(make use of)*, generate, impel, implement, incite, launch *(initiate)*, launch *(project)*, maintain *(commence)*, manipulate *(utilize skillfully)*, motivate, originate, preface, undertake
set in operation commence, establish *(launch)*, maintain *(commence)*
set in opposition contrast
set in order apportion, arrange *(methodize)*, classify, coordinate, distribute, file *(arrange)*, fix *(arrange)*, marshal, orchestrate, organize *(arrange)*
set in place locate, settle

977

set limitations constrict *(inhibit)*
set limits constrict *(inhibit)*
set little store by underestimate
set loose release, rescue
set moving impel
set no store by disbelieve, flout
set no value on decry
set of facts case *(set of circumstances)*
set of maneuvers strategy
set of questions examination *(test)*
set of rules codification, law, protocol *(etiquette)*
set of standards protocol *(etiquette)*
set of tactics program
set of terms article *(precept)*, counteroffer, settlement
set off abandon *(physically leave)*, compensate *(counterbalance)*, countervail, demarcate, differentiate, discriminate *(distinguish)*, offset, outbalance, part *(leave)*. SEE MAIN ENTRY
set off against contrast
set off by opposition contrast
set one back deter, hold up *(delay)*, impede
set one's hand and seal notarize
set one's hand and seal to certify *(attest)*
set one's name to sign
set oneself against conflict, confront *(oppose)*, disapprove *(condemn)*
set out allocate, depart, embark, leave *(depart)*, manifest, part *(leave)*, produce *(offer to view)*, quit *(evacuate)*
set out to attempt
set phrase expression *(comment)*
set purpose animus, design *(intent)*, goal, intention, objective, project
set right attune, debunk, disabuse, emend, fix *(repair)*, inform *(notify)*, rectify, redress, regulate *(adjust)*, reveal
set side by side compare, juxtapose
set store by honor
set straight disabuse, emend, inform *(notify)*, informed *(having information)*, redeem *(satisfy debts)*, reform, remedy
set terms contract
set the date date
set to brawl, fight *(battle)*
set to music orchestrate
set to rights file *(arrange)*, rectify
set to work employ *(engage services)*, engage *(hire)*, exert, exploit *(make use of)*, hire, manipulate *(utilize skillfully)*, occupy *(engage)*
set too high an estimate overestimate
set up build *(construct)*, capitalize *(provide capital)*, constitute *(establish)*, create, devise *(invent)*, establish *(launch)*, fabricate *(construct)*, frame *(construct)*, frame *(formulate)*, initiate, make, marshal, organize *(unionize)*, originate, plan, plant *(place firmly)*, structure *(composition)*
set up an inquiry analyze, canvass, delve
set up housekeeping lodge *(reside)*
set up in business capitalize *(provide capital)*, finance
set upon accost, assail, assault, earnest, oppugn, persistent
set upon with force assault, attack
set upon with violence assail, assault
set-off counterclaim, drawback
set-to affray, controversy *(argument)*, fracas
setback adversity, casualty, damper *(depressant)*, debacle, decline, defeat,

delay, disadvantage, disaster, hindrance, impediment, misfortune, plight, relapse, toll *(effect)*, trouble
setdown disgrace
setoff indemnity
setting atmosphere, case *(set of circumstances)*, posture *(situation)*, scene, site, vicinity
setting a price appraisal
setting apart appropriation *(allotment)*, dedication, discrimination *(differentiation)*, segregation *(separation)*
setting aside avoidance *(cancellation)*, repudiation
setting aside for a particular purpose dedication
setting aside of specific property levy
setting forth narration, representation *(statement)*
setting forth in words expression *(comment)*
setting free discharge *(liberation)*, emancipation, parole, release
setting the value appraisal
settle accommodate, adjudge, adjudicate, adjust *(resolve)*, administer *(conduct)*, agree *(comply)*, agree *(contract)*, arbitrate *(adjudge)*, arbitrate *(conciliate)*, arrange *(methodize)*, award, choose, close *(agree)*, compromise *(settle by mutual agreement)*, concede, conclude *(complete)*, conclude *(decide)*, decide, deposit *(place)*, determine, discharge *(pay a debt)*, dwell *(reside)*, embed, hold *(decide)*, intercede, judge, liquidate *(determine liability)*, locate, lodge *(reside)*, lull, mediate, negotiate, pacify, pay, plant *(place firmly)*, reconcile, recoup *(reimburse)*, refund, reimburse, remit *(send payment)*, remunerate, repose *(place)*, repose *(rest)*, reside, rest *(cease from action)*, return *(refund)*, rule *(decide)*, satisfy *(discharge)*, settle, stabilize, stipulate, subside, sustain *(confirm)*. SEE MAIN ENTRY
settle a debt quit *(repay)*
settle a dispute mediate
settle accounts discharge *(pay a debt)*, satisfy *(discharge)*
settle accounts with collect *(recover money)*, compensate *(remunerate)*
settle accounts with the debtors and creditors liquidate *(determine liability)*
settle amicably accommodate
settle an account quit *(repay)*
settle by authoritative decision arbitrate *(adjudge)*
settle by conciliation mediate
settle by covenant agree *(contract)*
settle by decree rule *(decide)*
settle differences arbitrate *(conciliate)*, compromise *(settle by mutual agreement)*, mediate, pacify
settle disputes negotiate
settle firmly consolidate *(strengthen)*
settle in occupy *(take possession)*
settle in advance prepay
settle in one's mind conclude *(decide)*, determine
settle on elect *(choose)*
settle on by deliberate will resolve *(decide)*
settle order on notice settle
settle terms stipulate
settle upon conclude *(decide)*, descend, determine, fund, leave *(give)*, resolve *(decide)*
settled absolute *(conclusive)*, agreed *(harmonized)*, categorical, certain *(fixed)*,

certain *(positive)*, certain *(specific)*, chronic, complete *(ended)*, contractual, definite, durable, firm, immutable, incontrovertible, indefeasible, ingrained, irrevocable, necessary *(inescapable)*, prescriptive, resolute, serious *(devoted)*, situated, stable, standing, stated, steadfast, through, unalterable, unavoidable *(not voidable)*, unyielding
settled belief conviction *(persuasion)*
settled decision adjudication, holding *(ruling of a court)*
settled determination intention
settled disposition practice *(custom)*
settled judgment conviction *(persuasion)*
settled law code
settled method formality. SEE MAIN ENTRY
settled principle law, principle *(axiom)*
settled procedure method, system
settled purpose animus, design *(intent)*, objective
settled upon preferred *(favored)*
settled without appeal clear *(certain)*
settlement accommodation *(adjustment)*, accord, accordance *(compact)*, adjustment, agreement *(concurrence)*, agreement *(contract)*, alimony, alluvion, arbitration, arrangement *(understanding)*, bargain, choice *(decision)*, compensation, composition *(agreement in bankruptcy)*, compromise, concession *(compromise)*, conciliation, consequence *(conclusion)*, consideration *(recompense)*, contract, denouement, descent *(declination)*, determination, discharge *(payment)*, disposition *(determination)*, disposition *(final arrangement)*, dower, expiation, habitation *(act of inhabiting)*, habitation *(dwelling place)*, honorarium, nollo contendere, outcome, pact, pay, payment *(act of paying)*, payoff *(payment in full)*, recompense, reconciliation, refund, remuneration, reparation *(indemnification)*, restitution, satisfaction *(discharge of debt)*, treaty. SEE MAIN ENTRY
settlement by authoritative decision holding *(ruling of a court)*, opinion *(judicial decision)*
settlement by mutual agreement composition *(agreement in bankruptcy)*
settlement of an estate administration
settlement of differences conciliation
settlement of difficulties mediation
settlement of dispute mediation
settlement on account composition *(agreement in bankruptcy)*, discharge *(payment)*
settler domiciliary, habitant, inhabitant, migrant, pioneer, referee, resident
settling conclusion *(determination)*
settlings alluvion
setup content *(structure)*, device *(contrivance)*, method, order *(arrangement)*
sever break *(separate)*, detach, dichotomize, disband, discontinue *(abandon)*, discontinue *(break continuity)*, disengage, disjoint, dissociate, dissolve *(separate)*, divide *(separate)*, divorce, estrange, excise *(cut away)*, interrupt, isolate, luxate, part *(separate)*, partition, rend, separate, split, subdivide. SEE MAIN ENTRY
sever one's connections secede
sever the unity of possession partition
severable divisible, divisive, separable. SEE MAIN ENTRY
several diverse, manifold, multiple. SEE MAIN ENTRY
severally respectively

severance decentralization, dichotomy, dismissal *(discharge)*, division *(act of dividing)*, estrangement, exception *(exclusion)*, interruption, schism, separation, split. SEE MAIN ENTRY

severance of relations estrangement

severe astringent, bitter *(penetrating)*, brutal, callous, caustic, close *(rigorous)*, critical *(faultfinding)*, crucial, cruel, dictatorial, draconian, drastic, harsh, incisive, inexorable, insufferable, intense, mordacious, onerous, oppressive, pejorative, precise, relentless, rigid, scathing, serious *(grave)*, spartan, strict, trenchant, tyrannous, uncompromising, unmitigated, unrelenting. SEE MAIN ENTRY

severe censure denunciation

severe discipline austerity

severed bipartite, broken *(fractured)*, disconnected, disjunctive *(tending to disjoin)*, separate

severence disassociation

severitas austerity, rigor, severity, solemnity

severity austerity, cruelty, oppression, violence. SEE MAIN ENTRY

severus rigid, serious *(grave)*, severe, solemn, strict

sex-ridden lascivious

sexton caretaker *(one caring for property)*

sexual assault rape SEE MAIN ENTRY

sexual deviation sodomy

sexual unfaithfulness of a married person adultery

sexually abuse molest *(subject to indecent advances)*

sexually assault molest *(subject to indecent advances)*

sexual harassment SEE MAIN ENTRY

sexually impure lewd

sexually indecent lewd

sexually indulgent lecherous

sexy obscene, salacious, suggestive *(risqué)*

shabby decadent, dilapidated, inferior *(lower in quality)*, penurious, poor *(inferior in quality)*, slipshod

shabby work noncompliance *(improper completion)*

shackle arrest *(apprehend)*, constrain *(imprison)*, contain *(restrain)*, detain *(restrain)*, disadvantage, encumber *(hinder)*, estop, fetter *(noun)*, fetter *(verb)*, hamper, handcuff *(noun)*, handcuff *(verb)*, hinder, hindrance, impede, impediment, lock, obstruction, repress, restrain, restraint, restrict, trammel

shade blind *(obscure)*, camouflage, cloak, conceal, ensconce, enshroud, hide, minimum, nuance, obfuscate, obnubilate, obscuration, obscure, penumbra, phantom, plant *(covertly place)*, protect, screen *(guard)*, veil

shade into consolidate *(unite)*

shade of difference differential, nuance

shade of meaning nuance

shaded impalpable

shadiness ill repute, improbity, knavery

shading obscuration

shadow alter ego, blind *(obscure)*, cloak, conceal, damper *(depressant)*, ensconce, hide, indistinctness, nuance, obnubilate, penumbra, specter, spy, trace *(follow)*

shadowed nebulous

shadowiness indistinctness

shadowing obscuration

shadowy blind *(concealed)*, dubious, elusive, equivocal, impalpable, inconspicuous, intangible, mysterious, nebulous, obscure *(faint)*, opaque, unclear, vague

shady furtive, machiavellian, unethical

shady reputation disrepute, opprobrium, turpitude

shake beat *(pulsate)*, brandish, discompose, disturb, intersperse, jostle *(bump into)*, perturb

shake off dispel

shake one's faith deter

shake up agitate *(perturb)*, churn, discompose, disturb, perturb

shakedown blackmail

shaking trepidation

shaky diffident, insecure, precarious

shall SEE MAIN ENTRY

shallow barren, cursory, fatuous, frivolous, puerile, superficial, trivial, volatile

shallowness immateriality, insignificance

sham artifice, bogus, cloak, colorable *(specious)*, cover *(pretext)*, deceit, deception, deceptive, delusive, disguise, duplicity, evasion, fabricate *(make up)*, fake, false *(not genuine)*, false pretense, feign, fictitious, forgery, fraud, fraudulent, hoax, imitation, imposture, invent *(falsify)*, mendacious, meretricious, misrepresent, pretend, pretense *(ostentation)*, pretense *(pretext)*, pretext, prevaricate, profess *(pretend)*, recreant, role, ruse, spurious, subterfuge. SEE MAIN ENTRY

shambles havoc. SEE MAIN ENTRY

shame attaint, bad repute, defame, degradation, demean *(make lower)*, denigrate, derogate, discredit, disgrace *(noun)*, disgrace *(verb)*, disparage, disrepute, embarrass, embarrassment, expose, humiliate, ignominy, ill repute, infamy, notoriety, obloquy, odium, onus *(stigma)*, opprobrium, ostracism, reproach, scandal, stigma, sully, tarnish. SEE MAIN ENTRY

shame into browbeat

shamefacedness disgrace

shameful arrant *(onerous)*, contemptible, depraved, diffident, disgraceful, disreputable, gross *(flagrant)*, heinous, ignoble, inexcusable, inexpiable, iniquitous, nefarious, notorious, obscene, paltry, peccant *(culpable)*, profligate *(corrupt)*, reprehensible, salacious, scandalous, unseemly

shameful notoriety disgrace

shamefulness bad repute, defilement, dishonor *(shame)*, disrepute

shameless arrant *(onerous)*, brazen, contemptible, depraved, dishonest, disreputable, dissolute, flagrant, immoral, impertinent *(insolent)*, insolent, lascivious, lewd, machiavellian, notorious, obscene, outrageous, presumptuous, profane, profligate *(corrupt)*, prurient, remorseless, reprobate, salacious, scurrilous, suggestive *(risqué)*, tainted *(corrupted)*, unabashed, vicious

shamelessness temerity

shanghai abduct, carry away, kidnap

shanghaiing abduction

shape body *(main part)*, build *(construct)*, color *(complexion)*, complexion, compose, condition *(state)*, configuration *(form)*, create, criterion, delineate, delineation, devise *(invent)*, dimension, fabricate *(construct)*, feature *(appearance)*, forge *(produce)*, form *(arrangement)*, form, formalize, formulate, frame *(construct)*, frame *(formulate)*, influence, make, militate, mode, motif, organization *(structure)*, pattern, phenomenon *(manifestation)*, posture *(situation)*, specter, state *(condition)*, structure *(composition)*, style, vision *(dream)*. SEE MAIN ENTRY

shape a course arrange *(plan)*, plan

shape out a course contrive

shape up crystallize, develop

shapeless disordered, indefinite, indeterminate

shapelessness confusion *(turmoil)*

shaping building *(business of assembling)*, creation, determinative

share allocate, allot, apportion, assign *(allot)*, claim *(right)*, contribute *(supply)*, convey *(communicate)*, disburse *(distribute)*, dispensation *(act of dispensing)*, dispense, distribute, divide *(distribute)*, dividend, dole, engage *(involve)*, holding *(property owned)*, interest *(ownership)*, involve *(participate)*, member *(constituent part)*, moiety, part *(portion)*, partake, participate, partition, pool, proportion, quota, ration, reciprocate, segment, split, stake *(interest)*, subdivide. SEE MAIN ENTRY

share an address cohabit

share and share alike per capita

share bed and board cohabit

share buyer customer

share grief sympathize

share in cooperate, partake, participate

share of profits commission *(fee)*

share out mete

share secrets confide *(divulge)*

share sorrow sympathize

share-out coupon

shared concurrent *(united)*, joint, mutual *(collective)*

shared among several common *(shared)*

shared by two or more common *(shared)*

shareholder contributor *(contributor)*, member *(individual in a group)*, participant. SEE MAIN ENTRY

shareholding contribution *(participation)*

sharer contributor *(contributor)*, copartner *(business associate)*, member *(individual in a group)*, participant, partner, party *(participant)*

shares securities

sharing cognate, contribution *(participation)*, distribution *(apportionment)*, division *(act of dividing)*

sharp acute, artful, bitter *(acrid tasting)*, caustic, cheat, close *(rigorous)*, cognizant, deft, distinct *(clear)*, harsh, incisive, intensive, machiavellian, mordacious, mulct *(defraud)*, perceptive, perspicacious, politic, profound *(intense)*, resourceful, responsive, sapient, scathing, severe, sly, subtle *(refined)*, trenchant, vigilant

sharp censure reprimand

sharp criticism reproach

sharp practice artifice, knavery, maneuver *(trick)*, misdoing, pettifoggery, ruse

sharp sight perception

sharp words reprimand

sharp-edged acute

sharp-sighted perspicacious

sharp-tempered fractious

sharp-witted acute, artful, perspica-cious

sharpen enhance, intensify

sharpening cumulative *(intensifying)*

sharper bettor

sharply defined precise

sharpness discretion *(quality of being discreet)*, insight, perception, propensity, rigor, sagacity, sensibility, severity

sharpness of mind judgment (discernment)

shatter break (fracture), discompose, disintegrate, extinguish, extirpate, force (break), overcome (overwhelm), overthrow, rend

shattered broken (fractured), disabled (made incapable)

shave decrease, minimize

shave off diminish

she who has expired decedent

sheaf assemblage

sheath cover (protection)

sheathe cover (guard), ensconce, enshroud, envelop, protect, shroud

shed cast (throw), denude, eliminate (exclude), emit, outpour, radiate

shed light on clarify SEE MAIN ENTRY

shed light upon comment, elucidate, enlighten, explain, explicate, exposit, resolve (solve), solve

shed tears over deplore

sheepish diffident

sheer absolute (complete), mere, naked (lacking embellishment), outright, pure, stark, thorough, unmitigated

sheer force main force

sheer power main force

sheer terror panic

sheet of flame conflagration

shell bomb, frame (structure)

shelling barrage

shelter asylum (hiding place), asylum (protection), building (structure), bulwark, cache (hiding place), cloak, cover (protection), cover (guard), dwelling, ensconce, enshroud, harbor, haven, hedge, hide, house, immure, keep (shelter), lodging, maintain (sustain), panoply, preserve, protect, protection, receive (permit to enter), refuge, safekeeping, screen (guard), security (safety), shield, shroud, veil. SEE MAIN ENTRY

shelter for the afflicted asylum (hospital)

sheltered blind (concealed), covert, guarded, immune, safe, secure (free from danger)

sheltering conservation, protective

shelterless helpless (defenseless)

shelve continue (adjourn), defer (put off), delay, hold up (delay), postpone, pretermit, procrastinate, protract (stall), reserve, retire (retreat), set aside (reserve), superannuate, suspend

shepherd protect

sheriff peace officer

shibboleth catchword

shield blind (obscure), bulwark, conceal, conserve, cover (protection), cover (guard), defend, disguise (noun), disguise (verb), ensconce, enshroud, envelop, harbor, hedge, lodge (house), maintain (sustain), obfuscate, panoply, preserve, protect, protection, safeguard, save (rescue), screen (guard), shelter (protection), veil. SEE MAIN ENTRY

shield from danger preserve

shield from injury preserve

shielded exempt, guarded, immune, impervious, safe

shielding conservation, preservation, preventive, protective

shift conversion (change), convert (change use), convey (transfer), conveyance, digress, diversification, divert, equivocate, exchange, expedient, fluctu-

ate, hoax, innovation, maneuver, oscillate, palter, period, phase (period), pretext, prevaricate, reconversion, removal, remove (transfer), replacement, ruse, stratagem, subterfuge, tergiversate, transfer, transform, transition, vacillate, vary

shift from its place displace (remove)

shift in topic digression

shift the blame recriminate

shifting discursive (digressive), faithless, moving (in motion), sporadic, temporary, variable. SEE MAIN ENTRY

shiftless idle, improvident, indolent, irresponsible, remiss, truant

shiftlessness sloth, vagrancy

shifty dishonest, disingenuous, evasive, fraudulent, furtive, machiavellian, perfidious, sly, subtle (insidious), undependable, unreliable, unscrupulous, untrue, untrustworthy

shillelagh cudgel

shindy riot

shining illustrious

shining example exemplar

ship consign, deliver, dispatch (send off), send, transmit, transport

shipload cargo

shipment cargo, carriage, consignment, delivery, freight

shipments outflow

shipper carrier, dealer

shipping cargo, carriage, consignment

shirk default, disobey, fail (neglect), neglect, refuse, shun. SEE MAIN ENTRY

shirk one's duty default

shirking disinclined, truant

shiver beat (pulsate), break (fracture), rend, split

shivered broken (fractured)

shoal plurality, superficial

shock bombshell, collision (accident), frighten, intimidate, overwhelm, perturb, repel (disgust), repercussion, stimulus, surprise, upset

shock with sudden fear frighten

shock-proof callous

shocking arrant (onerous), deplorable, disgraceful, flagrant, gross (flagrant), heinous, immoral, loathsome, lurid, notorious, odious, offensive (offending), outrageous, portentous (eliciting amazement), reprehensible, repulsive, scandalous, unexpected

shoddiness disrepute

shoddy inferior (lower in quality), poor (inferior in quality), tawdry

shoot emit, inject, launch (project), precipitate (throw down violently), send

shoot at attack

shoot forth pullulate

shoot forward project (impel forward)

shoot upward expand

shop business (commercial enterprise), market (business), store (business), trade

shop at patronize (trade with)

shop goods merchandise

shop with patronize (trade with)

shopkeeper dealer, merchant

shoplift steal

shopman dealer, merchant

shopper consumer, customer, patron (regular customer)

shopperson dealer

shopping center market (business), market place

shopwoman dealer

shopworn stale, trite

shore margin (outside limit)

shore up bolster, maintain (carry on)

short brief, caustic, compact (pithy), concise, cursory, deficient, delinquent (overdue), devoid, ephemeral, impecunious, imperfect, inadequate, incommensurate, insufficient, laconic, minimal, perfunctory, petulant, poor (underprivileged), scarce, succinct, transient. SEE MAIN ENTRY

short fall insufficiency

short letter note (brief comment)

short measure delinquency (shortage), insufficiency

short of devoid, save

short of cash impecunious

short of funds impecunious, indebted

short of money destitute, impecunious, poor (underprivileged)

short supply dearth, deficiency, delinquency (shortage), insufficiency

short version summary

short-lived ephemeral, temporary, transient, volatile

short-tempered fractious, hot-blooded, petulant

short-term acting, brief

shortage absence (omission), dearth, deficiency, deficit, delinquency (shortage), insufficiency, need (deprivation), paucity, poverty

shortcoming breach, decrement, defect, deficiency, deficit, disadvantage, disqualification (factor that disqualifies), failure (falling short), fault (weakness), flaw, foible, frailty, handicap, inability, insufficiency, lapse (expiration), onus (blame), vice

shorten abstract (summarize), commute, condense, constrict (compress), curtail, decrease, digest (summarize), diminish, discount (minimize), lessen, minimize, reduce, retrench

shortened compact (pithy), concise, minimal

shortening curtailment, decrease, decrement, deduction (diminution)

shortening of time acceleration

shortly in due course, instantly

shortness deficit, delinquency (shortage), disrespect

shortness of supply need (deprivation)

shortsighted ill-advised, ill-judged, imprudent, misadvised

shotgun gun

shoulder assume (undertake), bear (support), bolster, maintain (sustain), underwrite

shout outcry

shove impact, impel, impetus, jostle (bump into)

shove aside avert

show adduce, appearance (look), argue, bare, bear (adduce), betray (disclose), brandish, cite (state), clarify, color (deceptive appearance), demean (deport oneself), demonstrate (establish), denote, denude, depict, designate, detail (particularize), discipline (train), disinter, display, document, edify, educate, emerge, evince, exhibit, explain, expose, express, expression (manifestation), flaunt, histrionics, hypocrisy, illustrate, indicate, instruct (teach), manifest, manifestation, performance (workmanship), phenomenon (manifestation), portray, present (introduce), pretense (ostentation), pretense (pretext), pretext, produce (offer to view), prove, purport, render (depict), represent (portray), semblance, signify *(denote)*, specify, testify, unveil. SEE MAIN ENTRY

show a difference differentiate

show a relationship connect *(relate)*

show affinity connect *(relate)*

show an aversion discriminate *(treat differently)*

show an image reflect *(mirror)*

show as cognate connect *(relate)*

show as kindred connect *(relate)*

show bias discriminate *(treat differently)*

show by example demonstrate *(establish)*, exemplify, illustrate

show cause SEE MAIN ENTRY

show clearly prove

show clemency relax, remit *(release from penalty)*

show concern for deplore

show consideration for favor

show contempt for flout

show contrast differ *(vary)*

show correspondence compare

show courtesy defer *(yield in judgment)*

show determination adhere *(persist)*

show devotion adhere *(maintain loyalty)*

show disagreement demonstrate *(protest)*

show disapproval blame, demonstrate *(protest)*

show disrespect humiliate

show evidence cite *(state)*

show favor bestow, vouchsafe

show favor to favor

show forbearance bear *(tolerate)*

show grounds for show cause

show hostility collide *(clash)*, menace

show ill will antagonize, ill use, mistreat

show improvement develop

show in receive *(permit to enter)*

show indecision alternate *(fluctuate)*, vacillate

show indignation resent

show indirectly imply

show itself arise *(appear)*, occur *(come to mind)*

show manner comport *(behave)*

show mercy condone, palliate *(excuse)*, relent, remit *(release from penalty)*, sympathize

show mien comport *(behave)*

show no mercy persecute

show no pity persecute

show no respect minimize

show off expose, flaunt

show oneself report *(present oneself)*

show opinion publicly demonstrate *(protest)*

show opposition demonstrate *(protest)*

show phases change

show pity relax

show preference discriminate *(treat differently)*, prefer

show prejudice discriminate *(treat differently)*

show promise portend

show proof cite *(state)*

show regard for observe *(obey)*

show regret for repent

show relation connect *(relate)*

show reluctance challenge

show resemblance connect *(relate)*

show respect defer *(yield in judgment)*, honor

show signs evince

show signs of promise *(raise expectations)*

show similarity connect *(relate)*

show tenderness sympathize

show the fallacy of disprove

show the meaning of construe *(comprehend)*

show to be an abettor involve *(implicate)*

show to be analagous compare

show to be false disprove

show to be just justify

show to be similar compare

show unfair bias favor

show up emerge

show variety deviate, differ *(vary)*, fluctuate, vary

showable manifest

shower barrage, sufficiency

shower upon bestow, load

showiness pretense *(ostentation)*

showing apparent *(perceptible)*, clear *(apparent)*, demonstrative *(illustrative)*, disclosure *(act of disclosing)*, evident, exhibit, explanation, expression *(manifestation)*, illustration, lineup, manifestation, perceivable, perceptible, proof, salient, visible *(in full view)*

showing homage obeisant

showing lack of judgment injudicious

showing of criminal defendants lineup

showing of criminals for inspection and identification lineup

showing of possible suspects lineup

showing of suspected criminals lineup

showing poor judgment ill-judged, injudicious

showmanship histrionics

shown clear *(apparent)*, ostensible, perceptible

showpiece sample

showy elaborate, flagrant, grandiose, histrionic, inflated *(vain)*, meretricious, orotund, pretentious *(ostentatious)*, prominent, tawdry

shred iota

shrewd artful, judicious, machiavellian, perceptive, perspicacious, politic, practiced, prudent, resourceful, sapient, sensible, sly, subtle *(insidious)*

shrewd diagnosis discretion *(quality of being discreet)*

shrewdness discretion *(quality of being discreet)*, discrimination *(good judgment)*, forethought, insight, perception, prudence, sagacity, sense *(intelligence)*

shrewish fractious, petulant, querulous

shrine monument, reminder

shrink abridge *(shorten)*, commute, condense, constrict *(compress)*, decrease, deduct *(reduce)*, depreciate, depress, diminish, disoblige, ebb, erode, lessen, minimize, reduce, retreat, shirk, subside

shrink from eschew, mistrust, shun

shrinkage curtailment, decline, decrease, decrement, deduction *(diminution)*, diminution, erosion

shrinking decrease, diffident, disinclined, hesitant, reluctant, unobtrusive

shrive clear, excuse, forgive, palliate *(excuse)*, purge *(wipe out by atonement)*, redeem *(satisfy debts)*

shrivel decay, degenerate

shriver penitent

shroud blind *(obscure)*, camouflage, cloak, conceal, cover *(conceal)*, disguise, ensconce, enshroud, envelop, harbor, hide, obfuscate, obliterate, obnubilate, obscure, plant *(covertly place)*, protect, screen *(guard)*, suppress, veil. SEE MAIN ENTRY

shrouded blind *(concealed)*, clandestine, covert, esoteric, furtive, hidden, impalpable, inconspicuous, secret, stealthy

shrouded in mystery esoteric, inexplicable, problematic

shrug off ignore

shrunk compact *(pithy)*

shuck denude

shuffle beat *(pulsate)*, bilk, equivocate, evade *(deceive)*, exchange, palter, prevaricate

shun avoid *(evade)*, default, disapprove *(reject)*, disavow, discriminate *(treat differently)*, disdain, elude, eschew, forgo, forswear, leave *(allow to remain)*, neglect, refrain, refuse, reject, repulse, shirk, spurn, stave. SEE MAIN ENTRY

shunned derelict *(abandoned)*, undesirable

shunning avoidance *(evasion)*, boycott, disapprobation, disapproval, elusive, reluctant

shunt avert, divert, set aside *(annul)*

shut blind *(impassable)*, impervious, obturate, occlude. SEE MAIN ENTRY

shut away remote *(secluded)*

shut down close *(terminate)*, conclude *(complete)*, discontinue *(abandon)*, shut

shut in bind *(restrain)*, border *(bound)*, circumscribe *(surround by boundary)*, confine, contain *(enclose)*, detain *(hold in custody)*, enclose, encompass *(surround)*, fetter, jail, keep *(restrain)*, occlude. SEE MAIN ENTRY

shut off ban, bar *(hinder)*, block, clog, occlude

shut out ban, bar *(exclude)*, barred, condemn *(ban)*, debar, discharge *(dismiss)*, eliminate *(exclude)*, exclude, lock, prohibit, relegate, restrict, seclude, select

shut up block, immure, jail, keep *(restrain)*, lock

shut-in patient

shut-off blind *(impassable)*

shutdown blockade *(limitation)*, close *(conclusion)*, halt, strike

shutter protect

shutting out renunciation

shy deficient, diffident, guarded, hesitant, insufficient, precipitate *(throw down violently)*

shy at refuse

shy away from avoid *(evade)*, shun

shy from mistrust

shy of leery

shyness reluctance

sib interrelated, relative

sibi adsumere usurp

sibylic prophetic

sibylline oracular, portentous *(ominous)*, prophetic

sick individual patient

sick person patient

sicken degenerate, disable, languish, repel *(disgust)*

sickening heinous, loathsome, objectionable, odious, offensive *(offending)*, repulsive, unsavory

sickling patient

sickly languid, powerless, unsound *(not strong)*

sickness disability *(physical inability)*, disease, disorder *(abnormal condition)*, pain, prostration

side border, choose, edge *(border)*, faction, phase *(aspect)*. SEE MAIN ENTRY

side against counter, counteract, disapprove *(reject)*, fight *(counteract)*, oppugn

side by side along, contiguous
side issue development (outgrowth)
side road causeway
side with concur (agree), conform, cooperate, espouse, involve (participate), join (associate oneself with), maintain (sustain), unite
side-partner consociate
sidelong indirect
sidereal stellar
sideslip digression
sidestep avoidance (evasion), detour, digress, digression, parry
sidetrack digress, divert
siege assault, barrage, belligerency, invasion, onset (assault), outbreak
sieve screen (select), sort
sift analyze, censor, cull, discriminate (distinguish), screen (select), scrutinize, select, sort, study
sifting analysis
sigh plaint
sigh for deplore
sight appearance (look), detect, discern (detect with the senses), notice (observe), perception, phenomenon (manifestation), phenomenon (unusual occurrence), recognize (perceive), scene, spy, witness (have direct knowledge of). SEE MAIN ENTRY
sight draft check (instrument)
sighted perceivable, perceptible
sighting detection, discovery
sightly attractive
sigil brand, stamp
sigmoid circuitous
sign authorize, brand, brand (mark), call (title), clue, designation (symbol), device (distinguishing mark), earmark, expression (manifestation), forerunner, harbinger, index (catalog), indicant, indication, indicator, indorse, label, manifestation, notarize, phenomenon (manifestation), precursor, premonition, seal (solemnize), symbol, symptom, threat, title (designation), token, witness (attest to). SEE MAIN ENTRY
sign a name to subscribe (sign)
sign and seal notarize
sign away alienate (transfer title), cede, devolve, forgo, relinquish
sign in empanel, register
sign legally notarize
sign on join (associate oneself with)
sign one's name on indorse
sign over alienate (transfer title), assign (transfer ownership), grant (transfer formally), lend
sign up employ (engage services), enroll, recruit, register
signal admonition, clue, contact (communicate), denote, direct (order), forewarn, illustrious, important (significant), indicant, indicate, indication, manifestation, material (important), momentous, notable, noteworthy, notify, particular (specific), peculiar (curious), remarkable, symbol, symptom
signal by which one is summoned process (summons)
signalize indicate
signally particularly
signatory surety (guarantor), undersigned
signature call (title), indicant, subscription
signboard indicant
signed contractual
signed and delivered instrument deed

signed and sealed contractual
signed notice receipt (proof of receiving)
signer affiant, surety (guarantor), undersigned
signet brand, trademark
significance clout, connotation, construction, content (meaning), degree (magnitude), distinction (reputation), import, importance, interest (concern), magnitude, main point, materiality (consequence), meaning, notoriety, point (purpose), prestige, purpose, relevance, signification, spirit, stress (accent), substance (essential nature), tenor, validity, value, weight (importance). SEE MAIN ENTRY
significant central (essential), consequential (substantial), considerable, constructive (creative), critical (crucial), crucial, decisive, determinative, indispensable, key, major, material (important), momentous, necessary (required), notable, noteworthy, outstanding (prominent), paramount, prominent, remarkable, salient, special, strategic, substantial, unusual, valuable
significant detail necessity
significant event landmark (significant change)
significant feature highlight
significant occurrence landmark (significant change)
significant part content (meaning)
significare allude, denote, express, hint, imply, indicate, portend, purport
significatio content (meaning), hint, import, indication, innuendo, insinuation, intimation, meaning, significance, signification
signification assignment (designation), connotation, consequence (significance), content (meaning), corpus, designation (naming), implication (inference), import, manifestation, meaning, significance, substance (essential nature), symbol, tenor, title (designation). SEE MAIN ENTRY
signified implied
signify allude, bear (adduce), bespeak, communicate, connote, construe (translate), convey (communicate), denominate, denote, depict, designate, evidence, exemplify, hint, indicate, inform (notify), manifest, notify, portend, predict, presage, prognosticate, promise (raise expectations), purport, refer (direct attention), represent (portray). SEE MAIN ENTRY
signify assent acknowledge (respond), concur (agree)
signing up registration
signit stamp
signory domain (sphere of influence)
signpost indication, landmark (conspicuous object)
signs indicia
signum stamp, symbol
silence allay, concealment, lull (noun), lull (verb), peace, placate, repress, stifle, stop, strangle, subdue, suppress. SEE MAIN ENTRY
silent inarticulate, mute, noncommittal, speechless, stealthy, tacit, taciturn
silentium silence
silhouette configuration (form), contour (outline), contour (shape), delineate, delineation
sill threshold (entrance)
silly fatuous, frivolous, inept (inappropriate), ludicrous, puerile, superficial, vacuous

silly talk jargon (unintelligible language)
similar akin (germane), analogous, approximate, cognate, commensurable, commensurate, comparable (capable of comparison), congruous, consonant, correlative, equal, equivalent, identical, pendent, same, tantamount, uniform. SEE MAIN ENTRY
similar appearance analogy
similar form analogy
similar item cover (substitute)
similar relation analogy
similar to comparative
similarity analogy, conformity (agreement), identity (similarity), par (equality), parity, relation (connection), resemblance, same, semblance
similarly also
similative congruous
simile example
similis analogous, similar
similitude analogy, correlate, correspondence (similarity), identity (similarity), propinquity (similarity), relation (connection), resemblance, semblance
similitudinous comparative
similitudo analogy, resemblance
similtude parity
simoniacal mercenary
simple coherent (clear), comprehensible, credulous, elementary, facile, fatuous, genuine, household (familiar), ingenuous, innocuous, lucid, mere, mundane, naive, naked (lacking embellishment), narrow, nominal, obtuse, only (no more than), opaque, ordinary, pellucid, puerile, pure, rudimentary, stark, unadulterated, unaffected (sincere), unobtrusive, unpretentious, unsuspecting. SEE MAIN ENTRY
simple job sinecure
simple meaning connotation
simple-minded non compos mentis, obtuse, opaque, simple
simpleness credulity, ignorance
simplex candid, categorical, honest, ingenuous, naive, open (persuasible), simple, straightforward, unaffected (sincere), unconditional, unpretentious
simplicity credulity, honesty, ignorance, informality, opacity
simplification clarification, definition, explanation, illustration, paraphrase
simplified elementary, simple
simplify clarify, elucidate, enlighten, explain, explicate, exposit, expound, facilitate, interpret. SEE MAIN ENTRY
simplistic statement generality (vague statement)
simply only, solely (purely)
simul simultaneous
simulacrum color (deceptive appearance)
simulacrum deception
simulacrum disguise
simulacrum distortion
simulacrum embodiment
simulacrum imitation, semblance, sham
simulare feign, pretend
simulate copy, disguise, fake, feign, forge (counterfeit), misrepresent, mock (imitate), pose (impersonate), pretend, profess (pretend), reflect (mirror). SEE MAIN ENTRY
simulated artificial, false (not genuine), imitation, specious, spurious, surrogate
simulatio disguise, pretext
simulation color (deceptive appearance), copy, counterfeit, decoy, disguise, fake,

false pretense, plagiarism, pretense *(pretext)*, pretext, sham
simulatione pretense *(pretext)*
simulative artificial
simulatus false pretense, ostensible
simultaneity synchronism
simultaneous coincidental, collateral *(accompanying)*, concerted, concomitant, contemporaneous, instant, instantaneous. SEE MAIN ENTRY
simultaneous discharge of shots salvo
simultaneousness synchronism
simultas feud
sin guilt, misdeed, transgression, trespass, vice, wrong
sin-laden diabolic
since thereafter
sincere candid, direct *(forthright)*, earnest, faithful *(loyal)*, fervent, genuine, honest, ingenuous, pure, reliable, scrupulous, serious *(devoted)*, simple, straightforward, true *(loyal)*, veridical. SEE MAIN ENTRY
sincerely faithfully
sinceritas honesty
sincerity candor *(straightforwardness)*, honesty, integrity, probity, truth, veracity
sincerus genuine, honest, real, simple, unadulterated
sine certamine uncontested
sine corpore immaterial
sine die SEE MAIN ENTRY
sine nomine anonymous
sine qua non center *(essence)*, cornerstone. SEE MAIN ENTRY
sinecure SEE MAIN ENTRY
sinere let *(permit)*, suffer *(permit)*
sinew prowess *(bravery)*. SEE MAIN ENTRY
sinewless languid, powerless
sinewy powerful
sinful arrant *(onerous)*, bad *(offensive)*, delinquent *(guilty of a misdeed)*, depraved, diabolic, disgraceful, immoral, iniquitous, malignant, nefarious, outrageous, peccant *(culpable)*, profane, profligate *(corrupt)*, reprehensible, reprobate, salacious, sinister
sinfulness guilt, vice
sing out proclaim
sing the praises of belaud
singe burn, deflagrate
single exclusive *(singular)*, express, individual, particular *(individual)*, particular *(specific)*, simple, singular, sole, solitary, sporadic, unilateral, unique, whole *(unified)*
single case particular
single item entity
single out cull, differentiate, except *(exclude)*, extract, label, prefer, screen *(select)*, select
single piece entity
single-minded intense, pertinacious, purposeful, steadfast
single-mindedness adhesion *(loyalty)*, diligence *(care)*, loyalty, obsession
singled out preferred *(favored)*
singlehearted faithful *(loyal)*
singleness identity *(individuality)*, particularity, purpose, uniformity
singleness of heart loyalty
singleness of purpose diligence *(perseverance)*
singleton item
singly only, respectively, retail
singula detail
singular certain *(particular)*, certain *(specific)*, different, distinct *(distinguished from others)*, distinctive, eccentric, extraordinary, individual, infrequent, irregular *(not*

usual), nonconforming, notable, noteworthy, novel, only *(sole)*, original *(creative)*, particular *(individual)*, particular *(specific)*, peculiar *(curious)*, peculiar *(distinctive)*, personal *(private)*, portentous *(eliciting amazement)*, prodigious *(amazing)*, rare, remarkable, renowned, several *(separate)*, sole, special, unaccustomed, uncanny, uncommon, unilateral, unique, unprecedented, unusual. SEE MAIN ENTRY
singularis individual, rare, remarkable, singular, unique
singularity differential, feature *(characteristic)*, identity *(individuality)*, irregularity, nonconformity, particularity, personality, property *(distinctive attribute)*, quality *(attribute)*, quirk *(idiosyncrasy)*, speciality, specialty *(distinctive mark)*, technicality, trait
singularly particularly
sinister arrant *(onerous)*, bad *(offensive)*, blameworthy, diabolic, dire, heinous, malevolent, malignant, nefarious, odious, ominous, pernicious, portentous *(ominous)*, unfavorable, unpropitious. SEE MAIN ENTRY
sinistrous disastrous
sink decay, decrease, degenerate, depreciate, depress, ebb, immerse *(plunge into)*, invest *(fund)*, languish, subside
sink away perish
sink back relapse
sink in penetrate
sink into enter *(penetrate)*
sink to a lower condition degenerate
sinkage decline
sinking decadent, decline, decrease, depression, descent *(declination)*, relapse
sinless blameless, incorruptible, inculpable, innocent, irreprehensible, not guilty, pure, unblemished, unimpeachable
sinlessness innocence
sinner convict, offender, wrongdoer
sinning diabolic, iniquitous
sinuate circuitous, sinuous, tortuous *(bending)*
sinuated tortuous *(bending)*
sinuation involution
sinuosity complication, involution
sinuosus sinuous
sinuous circuitous, complex, devious, indirect, labyrinthine, oblique *(evasive)*, tortuous *(bending)*. SEE MAIN ENTRY
sire ascendant, author *(originator)*, generate, originate, progenitor, propagate *(increase)*, reproduce
sired in wedlock legitimate *(lawfully conceived)*
sisyphean operose
sit in conclave deliberate
sit in council deliberate
sit in judgment adjudge, adjudicate, arbitrate *(adjudge)*, decide, determine, find *(determine)*, hear *(give a legal hearing)*, judge, try *(conduct a trial)*
site building *(structure)*, circuit, habitation *(dwelling place)*, locality, location, part *(place)*, pinpoint, scene, seat, situs, venue. SEE MAIN ENTRY
sitting session
sitting room chamber *(compartment)*
situate allocate, deposit *(place)*, establish *(entrench)*, locate, lodge *(house)*, pinpoint, plant *(place firmly)*, site
situated SEE MAIN ENTRY
situated at the farthest limit extreme *(last)*

situation aspect, capacity *(job)*, career, case *(set of circumstances)*, condition *(state)*, degree *(station)*, employment, environment, experience *(encounter)*, livelihood, locality, occasion, occupation *(vocation)*, occurrence, office, perspective, plight, position *(business status)*, post, predicament, pursuit *(occupation)*, region, site, situs, standpoint, state *(condition)*, status, title *(position)*, trade *(occupation)*. SEE MAIN ENTRY
situations circumstances
situs circuit, site. SEE MAIN ENTRY
situs locality, situated, situation
sizable appreciable, considerable, major, prodigious *(enormous)*, substantial
sizableness mass *(weight)*
size arrange *(methodize)*, bulk, calculate, caliber *(measurement)*, classify, dimension, extent, magnitude, mass *(weight)*, maximum *(amplitude)*, measure, measurement, sort, space. SEE MAIN ENTRY
size up gauge
sizzle burn
skeleton capsule, configuration *(form)*, contour *(outline)*, design *(construction plan)*, foundation *(basis)*, frame *(structure)*, outline *(synopsis)*, summary
skeleton plan delineation
skeptic heretic
skeptical cynical, dubious, inconvincible, incredulous, leery, suspicious *(distrustful)*. SEE MAIN ENTRY
skepticalness doubt *(suspicion)*, incredulity, misgiving
skepticism cloud *(suspicion)*, doubt *(suspicion)*, incredulity, misgiving, qualm, reluctance, suspicion *(mistrust)*
sketch abridge *(shorten)*, abridgment *(condensation)*, blueprint, brief, capsule, contour *(outline)*, contrive, delineate, delineation, depict, description, design *(construction plan)*, draw *(depict)*, frame *(construct)*, frame *(formulate)*, indicate, narration, outline *(synopsis)*, portray, program, prospectus, render *(depict)*, scenario, story *(narrative)*, trace *(delineate)*
sketch in outline delineate
sketch out arrange *(plan)*, delineate, devise *(invent)*
sketchy deficient, inchoate, partial *(relating to a part)*, perfunctory, unclear
skewer penetrate, pierce *(lance)*
skill ability, capacity *(aptitude)*, competence *(ability)*, discretion *(quality of being discreet)*, efficiency, experience *(background)*, facility *(easiness)*, faculty *(ability)*, gift *(flair)*, knowledge *(learning)*, performance *(workmanship)*, potential, propensity, prowess *(ability)*, qualification *(fitness)*, science *(technique)*, specialty *(special aptitude)*. SEE MAIN ENTRY
skilled competent, deft, efficient, expert, facile, familiar *(informed)*, learned, literate, practiced, professional *(trained)*, proficient, qualified *(competent)*, veteran
skilled hand expert, specialist
skilled in commerce commercial
skilled laborer artisan
skilled occupation career
skilled person specialist
skilled practitioner expert, professional, specialist
skilled technician professional
skilled worker artisan, specialist
skillful artful, capable, competent, deft, effective *(efficient)*, efficient, expert, facile,

familiar *(informed)*, practiced, professional *(trained)*, proficient, qualified *(competent)*, resourceful, sciential, subtle *(refined)*, tactical

skillful in handling others diplomatic

skillful management strategy

skillful treatment management *(judicious use)*

skillfulness competence *(ability)*, efficiency, experience *(background)*, faculty *(ability)*, gift *(flair)*, performance *(workmanship)*, prowess *(ability)*, science *(technique)*, specialty *(special aptitude)*

skim border *(approach)*, read, review

skimpy deficient, marginal, petty, scarce

skin denude

skin-deep superficial

skip ignore, neglect, omit, pretermit

skirmish affray, collision *(dispute)*, commotion, confront *(oppose)*, confrontation *(altercation)*, contend *(dispute)*, contest *(dispute)*, disaccord, fight *(battle)*, fight *(battle)*, fray

skirt border, border *(approach)*, detour, digress, embrace *(encircle)*, margin *(outside limit)*, outline *(boundary)*

skirting circuitous

skirts confines, edge *(border)*, periphery

skittish restive

skulduggery bunko, knavery

skulk lurk, prowl

skulking recreant, sly, stealthy

skyrocket increase

skyscraper edifice

slab part *(portion)*

slack careless, derelict *(negligent)*, indolent, languid, lax, negligent, otiose, remiss, truant

slack off subside

slacken alleviate, commute, decrease, delay, ease, hold up *(delay)*, impede, lessen, moderate *(temper)*, pause, relax, subdue, subside

slackening mollification

slackness informality, laxity, neglect, negligence, sloth

slake allay, assuage, satisfy *(fulfill)*, soothe

slam beat *(strike)*

slam into collide *(crash against)*

slander aspersion, defamation, defame, denigrate, disparage, libel, malign, smear, tarnish, vilification. SEE MAIN ENTRY

slanderous calumnious, derogatory

slant aspect, character *(personal quality)*, complexion, favoritism, inclination, intolerance, misrepresent, outlook, perspective, position *(point of view)*, prejudice *(preconception)*, prejudice *(influence)*, side, stand *(position)*, tendency. SEE MAIN ENTRY

slanted inclined, one-sided, prejudicial

slanting oblique *(slanted)*

slap beat *(strike)*, lash *(strike)*, strike *(assault)*

slapp suit SEE MAIN ENTRY

slapdash cursory, superficial

slash commute, decrease, deduct *(reduce)*, lancinate, minimize, rebate, rend, split

slash prices discount *(reduce)*

slashing incisive, mordacious

slate docket, lash *(attack verbally)*, program, punish, rebuke, reprehend, reproach, set down

slatternly sordid

slaughter aberemurder, dispatch *(put to death)*, eliminate *(eradicate)*, extinguish,

homicide, kill *(murder)*, killing, slay

slaughtering killing, lethal

slaughterous deadly, fatal

slave captive

slavery bondage, captivity, restraint, servitude, subjection, thrall

slavish loyal, obsequious, pliable, pliant, sequacious, servile, subservient

slavishness bondage

slay destroy *(efface)*, dispatch *(put to death)*, execute *(sentence to death)*, extinguish, kill *(murder)*. SEE MAIN ENTRY

slaying aberemurder, assassination, homicide, killing

sleave involution

sleazy poor *(inferior in quality)*, tawdry

sleep repose *(rest)*

sleep at lodge *(reside)*

sleeping dormant

sleepless industrious

sleepy torpid

sleight false pretense, imposture, maneuver *(trick)*

sleight of hand prestidigitation

sleightful delusive, evasive

slender insubstantial, insufficient, minimal, slight, subtle *(refined)*, tenuous

slender means poverty

sleuth research, spy

slice part *(portion)*, ration, rend, segment, share *(interest)*, split

slick deft, machiavellian

slide ebb

slide back relapse

slight affront, aspersion, bad repute, brief, contemn, de minimus, deficient, delinquency *(failure of duty)*, depreciate, discommend, discount *(disbelieve)*, disdain, disoblige, disparage, disregard *(lack of respect)*, disrespect, flout, frivolous, humiliate, ignore, impalpable, inappreciable, inconsequential, inconsiderable, insubstantial, insufficient, lessen, minimal, minimize, minor, misprize, neglect *(noun)*, neglect *(verb)*, negligible, nominal, nonsubstantial *(not sturdy)*, nugatory, offend *(insult)*, omit, paltry, pardonable, petty, pretermit, rebuff *(noun)*, rebuff *(verb)*, reject, rejection, remote *(small)*, spurn, superficial, tenuous, trivial, underestimate. SEE MAIN ENTRY

slight change modification

slight indication hint

slight mention hint

slight trace suggestion

slighting calumnious, contemptuous, derogatory, pejorative

slighting language disparagement

slim insubstantial, insufficient, minimal, remote *(small)*, slight, trivial

sling project *(impel forward)*

slink lurk, prowl

slink away shirk

slip coupon, delinquency *(failure of duty)*, deviate, ebb, err, error, failure *(falling short)*, fault *(mistake)*, indiscretion, label, lapse *(expiration)*, lapse *(fall into error)*, miscalculate, miscue, misdeed, misdoing, misstatement, omission, oversight *(carelessness)*, receipt *(proof of receiving)*, transgression

slip and fall case SEE MAIN ENTRY

slip away elude, escape, leave *(depart)*, move *(alter position)*, retreat

slip away from abandon *(physically leave)*

slip back ebb, escheat, recidivate, relapse

slip from virtue lapse *(fall into error)*

slip into penetrate

slip off move *(alter position)*

slip out elude, evade *(elude)*

slip up miscalculate, mistake

slippery deceptive, elusive, evasive, insecure, machiavellian, perfidious, precarious, sly, undependable, untrustworthy

slipshod careless, cursory, inaccurate, lax, negligent. SEE MAIN ENTRY

slipshodness disorder *(lack of order)*

slit lancinate, sever, split *(noun)*, split *(verb)*

sliver minimum

slivered broken *(fractured)*

slogan catchword, phrase

sloping oblique *(slanted)*

sloppiness laxity

sloppy careless, repulsive, slipshod

slot split

sloth inaction, inertia, languor, laxity, neglect. SEE MAIN ENTRY

slothful idle, inactive, indolent, lax, lifeless *(dull)*, negligent, otiose, remiss, truant

slough denude, jettison

slovenliness laxity, neglect

slovenly disorderly, lax, negligent, slipshod, sordid

slow check *(restrain)*, constrict *(inhibit)*, delay, deliberate, hesitant, languid, late *(tardy)*, obtuse, otiose, phlegmatic, torpid

slow down alleviate, check *(restrain)*, delay, diminish, encumber *(hinder)*, hinder, impede, moderate *(temper)*, obstruct, prolong

slow in understanding opaque

slow motion languor

slow pace languor

slow to believe inconvincible, incredulous

slow to take offense peaceable

slow up delay, hold up *(delay)*

slow-moving deliberate, ponderous

slow-paced deliberate

slow-wittedness opacity

slowed down arrested *(checked)*

slowing down decrease

slowness delay, hesitation, languor, opacity

slug beat *(strike)*

sluggish despondent, inactive, indolent, languid, lax, lifeless *(dull)*, otiose, phlegmatic, ponderous, stagnant, torpid

sluggishness inaction, inertia, languor, sloth

slumber repose *(rest)*

slumbering dormant

slumberous narcotic

slump decline, decrease *(noun)*, decrease *(verb)*, depress, depression, languish

slur aspersion, brand *(stigmatize)*, contemn, defamation, defame, denounce *(condemn)*, denunciation, depreciate, discommend, discredit, disgrace *(noun)*, disgrace *(verb)*, dishonor *(shame)*, dishonor *(deprive of honor)*, disparage, ignominy, libel *(noun)*, libel *(verb)*, malign, notoriety, obloquy, onus *(stigma)*, opprobrium, reproach, scandal, slander, smear, spurn, stigma, sully, tarnish

slur over ignore, minimize

slush fund hush money

sly artful, covert, deceptive, devious, disingenuous, furtive, insidious, machiavellian, mendacious, secret, stealthy, subtle *(insidious)*, unscrupulous. SEE MAIN ENTRY

slyness artifice, evasion, indirection *(deceitfulness)*, knavery

smack beat *(strike)*

small brief, deficient, impalpable, inappreciable, inconsiderable, minimal, minor, negligible, nominal, null *(insignificant)*, paltry, petty, remote *(small)*, slight, tenuous, trivial

small amount iota, minimum, modicum, scintilla

small cavity cell

small chance improbability

small group minority *(outnumbered group)*

small hope improbability

small number minority *(outnumbered group)*, paucity

small parcel of land lot

small part member *(constituent part)*, segment

small percentage minority *(outnumbered group)*

small proportion minority *(outnumbered group)*

small quantity iota, minimum, minority *(outnumbered group)*, modicum, paucity, scintilla

small room cell

small-minded parochial, parsimonious, provincial

smaller minor

smaller group minority *(outnumbered group)*

smaller part minority *(outnumbered group)*

smallest minimal

smallness inconsequence, insignificance

smallness of number dearth

smart omniscient, rapid, resourceful

smarten embellish

smarting bitter *(penetrating)*, painful

smartness perception, sagacity, sense *(intelligence)*

smash break *(fracture)*, debacle, defeat, extirpate, force *(break)*, obliterate, spoil *(impair)*, strike *(assault)*, strike *(collide)*, subdue

smash into collide *(crash against)*

smash up collide *(clash)*

smear attaint, brand *(stigmatize)*, contemn, deface, defacement, defamation, defame, denigrate, denounce *(condemn)*, denunciation, disgrace, dishonor *(shame)*, dishonor *(deprive of honor)*, disparage, libel *(noun)*, libel *(verb)*, malign, pillory, slander, spread, stain, stigma, sully, tarnish, vilification. SEE MAIN ENTRY

smearing calumnious, defilement, pejorative

smelt burn

smirch attaint, brand, brand *(stigmatize)*, defamation, defame, denigrate, derogate, disgrace *(noun)*, disgrace *(verb)*, dishonor *(deprive of honor)*, ignominy, infect, malign, onus *(stigma)*, opprobrium, pillory, pollute, shame, smear, stain, stigma, sully, tarnish

smirched tainted *(contaminated)*

smite beat *(strike)*, harm, impress *(affect deeply)*, kill *(murder)*, lash *(strike)*, plague, punish, strike *(assault)*

smoke out expose

smoke screen disguise, subterfuge

smokiness indistinctness

smoky indistinct

smolder burn

smoldering dormant

smooth allay, alleviate, deft, facile, facilitate, help, machiavellian, moderate *(temper)*, mollify, pacify, placate, placid, practiced, soothe

smooth over disarm *(set at ease)*

smoothe expedite

smoothly diplomatic, readily

smoothness facility *(easiness)*, uniformity

smother assuage, extinguish, hamper, inhibit, prohibit, repress, stifle, strangle, subdue, suppress, withhold

smudge brand *(stigmatize)*, deface, defacement, onus *(stigma)*, stain, sully, tarnish

smug complacent, pretentious *(pompous)*

smuggle hide

smuggled commerce contraband

smuggled goods contraband

smuggled trade contraband

smuggled traffic contraband

smuggler bootlegger, criminal

smugness pride

smut obscenity, pornography

smutch onus *(stigma)*

smuttiness obscenity

smutty profane, prurient, salacious, suggestive *(risqué)*

snag block, complex *(entanglement)*, damper *(stopper)*, entanglement *(confusion)*, impediment, obstacle, obstruct, obstruction, snarl, trouble

snakelike circuitous, tortuous *(bending)*

snaky circuitous, malevolent, sinuous

snap impulsive *(rash)*, rend, split, spontaneous, unpremeditated

snap back retort

snappish fractious, perverse, petulant

snappy expeditious, petulant

snare ambush, artifice, bait *(lure)*, deceive, deception, ensnare, entrap, hunt, inveigle, mislead, pitfall, ruse, trap *(noun)*, trap *(verb)*

snaring bribery

snarl altercation, complex *(entanglement)*, confuse *(create disorder)*, entanglement *(confusion)*, involution, perplex, perturb. SEE MAIN ENTRY

snarled complex, inextricable, labyrinthine, problematic

snarling perverse, petulant

snatch hijack, kidnap, poach, purloin, steal, trap

snatching appropriation *(taking)*, distress *(seizure)*

sneak cloak, deceive, lurk, prowl

sneak off escape

sneak thief burglar, criminal

sneakiness deceit, fraud

sneaking clandestine, devious, furtive, machiavellian, perfidious, recreant, sly, stealthy

sneaky covert, deceptive, evasive, fraudulent, furtive, lying, machiavellian, perfidious, sly, stealthy, surreptitious

sneer disdain, disparage, disrespect, flout, humiliate, jeer, mock *(deride)*, ridicule, spurn

sneer at denigrate, derogate, discommend, disdain, minimize, misprize

sneering cynical, disdainful

snicker mock *(deride)*

snigger mock *(deride)*

sniggering ridicule

snobbery pride

snobbish disdainful, exclusive *(limited)*, pretentious *(pompous)*

snobby disdainful, exclusive *(limited)*

snoop spy *(noun)*, spy *(verb)*

snooper spy *(noun)*

snooty disdainful

snowy clean

snub affront, curb, disdain, disregard *(lack of respect)*, disregard, disrespect, humiliate, ignore, offend *(insult)*, ostracism, rebuff *(noun)*, rebuff *(verb)*, reject, rejection, repulse, shun, spurn

snuff out obliterate, stifle, strangle

so-called ostensible, purported, specious

so-so mediocre

soak imbue, immerse *(plunge into)*, overload, permeate, pervade

soak through penetrate

soaked full

sober deliberate, disconsolate, discriminating *(judicious)*, earnest, grave *(solemn)*, lucid, major, moderate *(temper)*, objective, peaceable, pensive, phlegmatic, prudent, rational, sane, sensible, serious *(grave)*, solemn

sober-minded sane

sober-mindedness common sense

sobered penitent

soberness solemnity, temperance

sobriety common sense, continence, deliberation, moderation, reason *(sound judgment)*, sagacity, solemnity, temperance

sobriquet call *(title)*, cognomen. SEE MAIN ENTRY

sociable amicable, harmonious

social civil *(public)*, public *(affecting people)*

social adjustment civilization

social behavior conduct

social climber philistine

social code decorum

social conduct decorum

social elevation civilization

social graces conduct, decorum

social group public, sodality

social procedures decorum

social rank class

social responsibility obligation *(duty)*

social security SEE MAIN ENTRY

social status class

social usage custom, decorum

socialize nationalize

societal civil *(public)*, national, public *(affecting people)*

societas association *(connection)*, combination, company *(assemblage)*, confederacy *(compact)*, league, partnership, syndicate

societas clandestina cabal

society chamber *(body)*, civilization, coalition, community, confederacy *(compact)*, institute, league, nationality, populace, population, public, sodality. SEE MAIN ENTRY

socius associate, consort, partner

socius criminis accessory, accomplice, cohort, colleague, copartner *(coconspirator)*

sodalis associate

sodalitas facility *(institution)*, foundation *(organization)*, institute

sodality body *(collection)*, cartel, coalition, corporation, league, organization *(association)*, partnership, society, union *(labor organization)*. SEE MAIN ENTRY

sodomy SEE MAIN ENTRY

soft charitable *(lenient)*, flexible, lenient, malleable, pliant, yielding

soft job   sinecure

soften   allay, alleviate, assuage, commute, ease, extenuate, give *(yield)*, mitigate, moderate *(temper)*, modify *(moderate)*, mollify, obtund, palliate *(abate)*, propitiate, relax, relent, remit *(relax)*, soothe, subdue

softened   malleable

softening   mitigating, mitigation, mollification, palliative *(abating)*

softening circumstances   extenuating circumstances

softhearted   benevolent, charitable *(lenient)*, lenient, placable, sensitive *(easily affected)*

softheartedness   benevolence *(disposition to do good)*, lenience

softness   lenience, mollification

soil   brand *(stigmatize)*, debase, deface, denigrate, depreciate, disgrace, infect, onus *(stigma)*, pervert, pillory, pollute, smear, stain, sully, taint *(contaminate)*, tarnish

soiled   blemished, tainted *(contaminated)*

soiling   defacement

sojourn   dwell *(reside)*, habitation *(act of inhabiting)*, inhabit, inhabitation *(act of dwelling in)*, lodge *(reside)*, reside, stop

sojourner   denizen, habitant, inhabitant, lodger, occupant, resident

sojournment   habitation *(act of inhabiting)*, presence *(attendance)*

solace   alleviate, assuage, assure *(give confidence to)*, benefit *(betterment)*, reassure, sympathize. SEE MAIN ENTRY

solatium   compensation, consideration *(recompense)*, expiation, pay, payment *(remittance)*, recompense, reward, satisfaction *(discharge of debt)*

solatium   solace

solatium   trover

solder   cement, connect *(join together)*

soldier-like   spartan

soldierly   heroic, spartan

soldiership   strategy

sole   exclusive *(singular)*, individual, singular, solitary, unique. SEE MAIN ENTRY

sole control of a commodity   monopoly

solecism   catachresis, irregularity, misuse

solecistic   anomalous, faulty, incorrect

solecistical   faulty, incorrect

solely   only. SEE MAIN ENTRY

solemn   critical *(crucial)*, earnest, important *(significant)*, major, sacrosanct, serious *(grave)*. SEE MAIN ENTRY

solemn affirmation   affidavit, affirmation, averment, oath

solemn agreement   testament

solemn appropriation   dedication

solemn assertion   assurance, vow

solemn averment   affirmance *(legal affirmation)*, affirmation, asseveration, attestation, avouchment, confirmation, declaration, surety *(certainty)*

solemn avowal   adjuration, affirmance *(legal affirmation)*, affirmation, asseveration, attestation, avouchment, confirmation, declaration, oath, surety *(certainty)*

solemn declaration   affirmation, asseveration, attestation, avouchment, certification *(attested copy)*, commitment *(responsibility)*, confirmation, deposition, jurat, oath, pledge *(binding promise)*, surety *(certainty)*, vow

solemn entreaty   call *(appeal)*, prayer

solemn feeling   solemnity

solemn invocation   oath

solemn mockery   blasphemy

solemn observance   ceremony

solemn promise   assurance, testament, vow

solemn request   petition

solemn word   pledge *(binding promise)*

solemn writing   instrument *(document)*

solemnity   ceremony, formality, importance. SEE MAIN ENTRY

solemnization   ceremony, remembrance *(commemoration)*

solemnize   formalize, keep *(fulfill)*

solemnly affirm   avouch *(avow)*, certify *(attest)*

solemnly promise   assure *(insure)*

solemnly request   petition

solicit   apply *(request)*, bait *(lure)*, call *(appeal to)*, desire, importune, inquire, lobby, petition, plead *(implore)*, pray, pressure, pursue *(strive to gain)*, request, urge. SEE MAIN ENTRY

solicitation   SEE MAIN ENTRY

solicit earnestly   importune

solicit insistently   bait *(harass)*, importune

solicit votes   lobby

solicitant   applicant *(petitioner)*, claimant, petitioner

solicitation   call *(appeal)*, dun, entreaty, instigation, invitation, persuasion, request, seduction

solicitor   advocate *(counselor)*, agent, attorney, barrister, claimant, counsel, counselor, esquire, jurist, lawyer, petitioner, practitioner, procurator, representative *(proxy)*, special interest, suitor

solicitorial   forensic, juridical

solicitors   bar *(body of lawyers)*

solicitous   benevolent, interested, protective, zealous. SEE MAIN ENTRY

solicitousness   benevolence *(disposition to do good)*, consideration *(sympathetic regard)*

solicitude   benevolence *(disposition to do good)*, concern *(interest)*, consideration *(sympathetic regard)*, interest *(concern)*, precaution

solid   authentic, axiomatic, bodily, cogent, cohesive *(compact)*, compact *(dense)*, compound, concrete, corporeal, dependable, firm, fixed *(securely placed)*, indomitable, inflexible, infrangible, intact, material *(physical)*, meritorious, ossified, secure *(sound)*, sound, stable, staunch, strong, substantive, tangible, unyielding, valid, well-grounded, whole *(undamaged)*. SEE MAIN ENTRY

solid substance   corpus

solid vote   consensus

solidarity   coaction, conciliation, confederacy *(compact)*, corpus, integration *(assimilation)*, merger

solidification   adhesion *(affixing)*, agglomeration, coalescence, congealment, consolidation

solidified   compact *(dense)*, concrete, ossified, solid *(compact)*

solidify   amalgamate, cement, cohere *(adhere)*, consolidate *(strengthen)*, consolidate *(unite)*, crystallize, establish *(entrench)*, fix *(make firm)*, unite

solidity   certainty, common sense, congealment, density, materiality *(physical existence)*, strength

solidness   congealment

solidus   concrete, durable, firm, solid *(sound)*

soliloquize   recite

soliloquy   peroration

solitariness   privacy

solitary   derelict *(abandoned)*, exclusive *(singular)*, individual, insular, nonconforming, only *(sole)*, private *(secluded)*, remote *(secluded)*, separate, sole. SEE MAIN ENTRY

solitary abode   cell

solitude   privacy

solitudo   privacy

solitus   accustomed *(customary)*, typical

sollemnis   periodic

sollers   resourceful

sollertia   skill

sollicitare   harass, molest *(annoy)*, perplex, pique

sollicitudo   concern *(interest)*, misgiving, trouble

sollicitus   solicitous

solo   alone *(solitary)*, apart, solitary

soluble   solvable

solus   apart, sole, solitary

solutio   solution *(answer)*

solution   conclusion *(determination)*, denouement, determination, disposition *(determination)*, explanation, finding, opinion *(judicial decision)*, outcome, panacea, remedy *(legal means of redress)*. SEE MAIN ENTRY

solution to difficulties   panacea

solutus   exempt, free *(not restricted)*, independent

solvable   determinable *(ascertainable)*. SEE MAIN ENTRY

solve   adjust *(resolve)*, ascertain, construe *(comprehend)*, elucidate, explain, expound, find *(discover)*, interpret, remedy, settle. SEE MAIN ENTRY

solvent   solid *(sound)*, solution *(substance)*

solvere   annul, defray, disburse *(pay out)*, disengage, free

somatic   bodily, corporal, physical, tangible

somatical   bodily

somber   bleak *(not favorable)*, bleak *(severely simple)*, despondent, disconsolate, grave *(solemn)*, lifeless *(dull)*, lugubrious, ominous, portentous *(ominous)*, solemn

sombrous   bleak *(not favorable)*, bleak *(severely simple)*

some   several *(plural)*

somebody   character *(an individual)*, person

someone   character *(an individual)*, person

something added   appurtenance, augmentation

something constructively affixed to real property   fixture

something equivalent   quid pro quo

something for something   quid pro quo

something immovable from realty   fixture

something like   cognate, pendent

something of value   consideration *(recompense)*

something over and above   bonus

something owed   due

something owing   mortgage

something physically annexed to realty   fixture

something produced by capital   income

something to be imitated   example

somewhat   fairly *(moderately)*, in part

somewhere about   on or about

somnifacient narcotic

somniferous narcotic

somnific narcotic

somnolence languor

somnolency languor

somnolent torpid

sonitus noise

sonorous orotund, resounding, sesquipedalian

sons progeny

soon in due course, instantly

soon to be prospective

soon to happen prospective

sooner than due premature

sooner than intended premature

soothe allay, alleviate, assuage, cure, lessen, lull, moderate *(temper)*, mollify, pacify, placate, propitiate, relieve *(give aid)*, remedy, remit *(relax)*, sympathize. SEE MAIN ENTRY

soother narcotic

soothing medicinal, mitigation, mollification, narcotic, palliative *(abating)*, placid, remedial

soothsay predict, presage, prognosticate

sop bribe, gratuity *(bribe)*

sophism fallacy, non sequitur

sophistic deceptive, ill-founded, illogical, illusory, incorrect, specious. SEE MAIN ENTRY

sophistical deceptive, fallacious, ill-founded, illogical, illusory, incorrect, sophistic, specious, subtle *(insidious)*, unsound *(fallacious)*

sophistical excuse evasion

sophisticate denature, evade *(deceive)*, expert, mislead, pervert, prevaricate, veteran

sophisticated elegant, practiced, subtle *(refined)*, veteran. SEE MAIN ENTRY

sophistication civilization, experience *(background)*, perversion

sophistry casuistry, fallacy, non sequitur, subterfuge. SEE MAIN ENTRY

sophomoric inexperienced

soporiferous narcotic

soporific drug, narcotic *(adjective)*, narcotic *(noun)*, pedestrian

sorcery prestidigitation

sordid penurious, poor *(inferior in quality)*. SEE MAIN ENTRY

sordidus illiberal, sordid

sore bitter *(penetrating)*, pain, painful, resentful

soreness pain, resentment, umbrage

sorosis sodality

sorriness remorse

sorrow distress *(anguish)*, pain, plaint, remorse, tragedy

sorrow for regret

sorrow over deplore

sorrowful bitter *(reproachful)*, contrite, deplorable, despondent, disconsolate, grave *(solemn)*, lamentable, lugubrious, penitent, pessimistic, remorseful, repentant

sorrowfulness pessimism

sorry contrite, deplorable, ignoble, lamentable, nonsubstantial *(not sturdy)*, paltry, penitent, poor *(inferior in quality)*, remorseful, repentant

sorry plight predicament

sors capital, lottery, principal *(capital sum)*

sort class, classify, codify, distribute, file *(arrange)*, fix *(arrange)*, form *(arrangement)*, kind, manner *(kind)*, organize *(arrange)*, pigeonhole, screen *(select)*, tab-

ulate. SEE MAIN ENTRY

sort out cull, diagnose, differentiate, discriminate *(distinguish)*, fix *(arrange)*, part *(separate)*, select

sort systematically fix *(arrange)*

sortable applicable, fit

sortie affray, incursion

sortitio lottery

sottish drunk

sought after popular

soul center *(essence)*, consequence *(significance)*, essence, person, personality, spirit, substance *(essential nature)*

soul-searching contrite

soul-stirring profound *(intense)*

soulless cold-blooded

sound authentic, cogent, communicate, credible, defensible, discriminating *(judicious)*, durable, fiduciary, firm, fixed *(securely placed)*, honest, indomitable, intact, intonation, inviolate, judicious, juridical, justifiable, legitimate *(rightful)*, licit, logical, lucid, meritorious, noise, normal *(sane)*, persuasive, phrase, plausible, positive *(incontestable)*, pragmatic, pronounce *(speak)*, rational, reasonable *(rational)*, reliable, safe, sane, scrupulous, secure *(sound)*, sensible, stable, staunch, strong, thorough, true *(authentic)*, unblemished, undeniable, utter, valid, viable, well-grounded. SEE MAIN ENTRY

sound forth proclaim

sound judgment discretion *(quality of being discreet)*, expedience

sound mind competence *(sanity)*

sound moral principle integrity

sound out inquire

sound perception common sense

sound reasoning discretion *(quality of being discreet)*, discrimination *(good judgment)*. SEE MAIN ENTRY

sound sense common sense

sound stewardship economy *(frugality)*

sound the alarm alert, caution

sound thinking pragmatism

sound understanding common sense, sanity

sounded oral

sounding resounding

soundless mute, speechless

soundlessness lull, silence

soundmindedness competence *(sanity)*, sanity

soundness certainty, competence *(sanity)*, health, honesty, legitimacy, quality *(excellence)*, sanity, strength, validity, welfare

soundness of body health

soundness of mind competence *(sanity)*

sour aggravate *(annoy)*, bitter *(acrid tasting)*, dyseptic, petulant, severe, spoil *(impair)*, stale

sour-tempered bitter *(reproachful)*, dyseptic, petulant

source authority *(power)*, basis, cause *(reason)*, citation *(attribution)*, connotation

source derivation

source determinant, documentation, embryo, genesis, inception, informant, informer *(a person who provides information)*, onset *(commencement)*, origination, parentage, progenitor, prototype, reason *(basis)*, reference *(citation)*, resource, spy, start. SEE MAIN ENTRY

source material derivation, reference *(citation)*

source of danger peril

source of income livelihood

source of perplexity problem

source of risk hazard, peril

soured bitter *(acrid tasting)*, stale

sourish bitter *(acrid tasting)*

souse immerse *(plunge into)*, permeate

souvenir remembrance *(commemoration)*, reminder, token

sovereign autonomous *(self governing)*, dominant, free *(enjoying civil liberty)*, government *(political administration)*, independent, master, national, nonpartisan, omnipotent, paramount, powerful, predominant, superlative. SEE MAIN ENTRY

sovereign state nationality

sovereign unit state *(political unit)*

sovereignty bureaucracy, capacity *(authority)*, dominance, dominion *(supreme authority)*, hierarchy *(persons in authority)*, home rule, influence, jurisdiction, polity, predominance, primacy, regime, supremacy

sow diffuse, dissipate *(spread out)*, distribute, inseminate, plant *(place firmly)*, spread

sow dissension alienate *(estrange)*, disaffect

sow the seeds of cause

space arrange *(methodize)*, atmosphere, coverage *(scope)*, distribute, extent, latitude, margin *(spare amount)*, pause, range, region, scope. SEE MAIN ENTRY

space of time duration, phase *(period)*

space-saving compact *(dense)*

spacious broad, capacious, open *(unclosed)*

spaciousness capacity *(maximum)*, extent, space

span comprehend *(include)*, connect *(relate)*, duration, encompass *(include)*, extent, gamut, include, life *(period of existence)*, lifetime, magnitude, measure, measurement, period, phase *(period)*, purview, range, scope, space, term *(duration)*

span of years lifetime

spangle embellish

spar bicker, compete, contend *(dispute)*, fight *(battle)*

spare ancillary *(auxiliary)*, balance *(amount in excess)*, bear *(tolerate)*, bestow, condone, conserve, dole, excess, excessive, expendable, fund, insufficient, keep *(shelter)*, needless, nonessential, overage, palliate *(excuse)*, preserve, release, relent, relinquish, remit *(release from penalty)*, residuary, superfluous, supplementary, surplus, sustain *(prolong)*, unnecessary

spare no effort endeavor, persevere

spare no pains endeavor

spared clear *(free from criminal charges)*, free *(relieved from a burden)*, immune

spargere disseminate, spread

sparing conservation, deficient, devoid, economical, economy *(frugality)*, frugal, illiberal, lenient, parsimonious, penurious, placable, provident *(frugal)*, prudent, release, scarce

sparing no pains painstaking

sparing of words brief, inarticulate, laconic, sententious, taciturn

sparing use temperance

spark iota, scintilla

sparkle spirit

sparring belligerency

sparse barren, deficient, infrequent, insufficient, petty, scarce, sporadic

sparseness delinquency *(shortage),* insignificance, insufficiency, paucity, poverty

sparsity dearth, deficiency, delinquency *(shortage),* paucity

spartan draconian

spartan frugal, stoical. SEE MAIN ENTRY

spasm outbreak, outburst

spasmodic broken *(interrupted),* desultory, disjointed, disjunctive *(tending to disjoin),* intermittent, periodic, sporadic, unpredictable, variable

spat bicker, brawl, contend *(dispute)*

spate plethora. SEE MAIN ENTRY

spatium magnitude, space

spatium interiectum interval

spatium temporis term *(duration)*

spatter defame, diffuse, pillory, pollute, stain, sully

spawn create, engender, offspring, proliferate, propagate *(increase),* reproduce

spe depellere disappoint

speak avow, communicate, convey *(communicate),* declaim, discourse, enunciate, express, phrase, recite, relate *(tell),* remark, utter. SEE MAIN ENTRY

speak about report *(disclose)*

speak against cross *(disagree with),* disapprove *(reject),* gainsay, protest

speak clearly enunciate

speak derisively jeer

speak disparagingly of decry

speak evil defame

speak evil of derogate, malign, smear

speak falsely bear false witness, feign, misrepresent, perjure, prevaricate

speak for plead *(argue a case),* promote *(organize),* represent *(substitute),* uphold

speak formally pronounce *(speak)*

speak highly of recommend

speak ill defame

speak ill of censure, complain *(criticize),* decry, defame, denigrate, denounce *(condemn),* derogate, discommend, dishonor *(deprive of honor),* disparage, malign, pillory, reproach, sully

speak in favor of advocate, justify

speak logically reason *(persuade)*

speak of bespeak, circulate, connote, discuss, mention

speak of slightingly defame

speak on discuss

speak on oath attest

speak one's mind communicate

speak out disclose, manifest

speak publicly declaim

speak rhetorically declaim

speak slightingly jeer, lessen

speak slightingly of decry, derogate, discommend, misprize

speak the truth disclose

speak to address *(talk to)*

speak up for plead *(argue a case)*

speak well of recommend

speak with converse

speaker amicus curiae, chairman, plenipotentiary, spokesman

speaking conversation

speaking by delegated authority acting

speaking for another representation *(acting for others)*

spear penetrate, pierce *(lance)*

special ad hoc, certain *(particular),* certain *(specific),* considerable, distinct *(distinguished from others),* distinctive, exclusive *(singular),* extraordinary, individual, momentous, nonconforming, notable, noteworthy, outstanding *(prominent),* particular *(individual),* particular *(specific),* peculiar *(distinctive),* preferential, preferred *(favored),* rare, remarkable, singular, specific, technical, uncommon, unique, unusual. SEE MAIN ENTRY

special ability gift *(flair)*

special attention emphasis

special attraction feature *(special attraction)*

special case exception *(exclusion)*

special characteristic specialty *(distinctive mark)*

special concern emphasis

special dispensation variance *(exemption)*

special endowment gift *(flair)*

special favor distinction *(reputation)*

special interest SEE MAIN ENTRY

special interest group lobby

special interests lobby

special intonation emphasis

special item specialty *(distinctive mark)*

special line of work specialty *(special aptitude)*

special marking distinction *(difference)*

special matter specialty *(distinctive mark)*

special occurrence phenomenon *(unusual occurrence)*

special point detail, particular, particularity, specialty *(distinctive mark),* specification, technicality

special points circumstances

special price discount

special privilege dispensation *(exception),* exemption, immunity, license

special privileges patronage *(support)*

special project specialty *(special aptitude)*

special right prerogative

special significance emphasis

special skill specialty *(special aptitude)*

special study specialty *(special aptitude)*

specialist expert, mastermind, practitioner, professional. SEE MAIN ENTRY

speciality characteristic, identity *(individuality),* technicality. SEE MAIN ENTRY

specialization calling, pursuit *(occupation),* specialty *(special aptitude)*

specialize practice *(engage in),* restrict, select, study. SEE MAIN ENTRY

specialize in occupy *(engage),* practice *(engage in)*

specialized professional *(trained),* technical

specialized administrative unit bureau

specialized language jargon *(technical language)*

specialized terminology jargon *(technical language)*

specialized unit bureau

specialized vocabulary jargon *(technical language)*

specializer expert, specialist

specially particularly

specially prepared express

specially provided for privileged

specially selected premium, prime *(most valuable)*

specially trained person expert

specialness speciality

specialties commodities

specialty bailiwick, business *(occupation),* caliber *(mental capacity),* calling, capacity *(sphere),* career, characteristic, department, employment, feature *(special attraction),* identity *(individuality),* merchandise, occupation *(vocation),* penchant, position *(business status),* practice *(professional business),* profession *(vocation),* province, pursuit *(occupation),* trade *(occupation),* trait, work *(employment).* SEE MAIN ENTRY

specie cash, currency, money

species apparent *(perceptible),* appearance *(look),* color *(complexion)*

species denomination, kind, manner *(kind)*

species pretext, semblance

species of proof evidence

specific actual, certain *(particular),* concrete, descriptive, detailed, exact, explicit, express, particular *(individual),* particular, personal *(individual),* point *(item),* precise, regional, said, special, technical, technicality. SEE MAIN ENTRY

specific aptness penchant

specific confinement limitation

specific curtailment limitation

specific moment point *(period of time)*

specific quality characteristic, identity *(individuality),* particularity, penchant, property *(distinctive attribute),* specialty *(distinctive mark)*

specifically particularly

specification assignment *(designation),* caption, clarification, classification, clause, condition *(contingent provision),* delineation, description, designation *(naming),* detail, diagnosis, item, limitation, particular, prerequisite, provision *(clause),* qualification *(condition),* report *(detailed account),* requirement, reservation *(condition),* selection *(choice),* stipulation, technicality, term *(provision),* ultimatum. SEE MAIN ENTRY

specification of details bill *(formal declaration)*

specifications pattern

specificity identity *(individuality)*

specificness specialty *(distinctive mark)*

specifics data, information *(facts)*

specified aforesaid, certain *(particular),* certain *(specific),* conditional, express, stated

specified income payable for life annuity, pension

specified period of time date

specify allocate, allot, amplify, annunciate, assign *(designate),* call *(title),* characterize, cite *(state),* classify, communicate, convey *(communicate),* define, delineate, denominate, depict, describe, designate, detail *(particularize),* diagnose, disabuse, distinguish, enumerate, explain, identify, index *(relate),* interject, itemize, label, mention, nominate, pinpoint, portray, postulate, qualify *(condition),* quote, report *(disclose),* select, signify *(inform),* stipulate. SEE MAIN ENTRY

specify in greater detail amplify

specify limits border *(bound)*

specify the particulars of delineate

specify the peculiarities of characterize

specimen case *(example),* entity, example, illustration, instance, model, representative *(example).* SEE MAIN ENTRY

specimen paragon, pattern, sample

speciosus specious

specious deceptive, delusive, ostensible, purported, sophistic, untenable. SEE MAIN ENTRY

specious argument non sequitur

specious reasoning non sequitur, sophistry

speciously attractive meretricious

speckled marred

spectacle phenomenon (*manifestation*), phenomenon (*unusual occurrence*), scene, vision (*dream*)

spectacular conspicuous

spectare aspect, observe (*watch*), survey (*examine*), witness (*have direct knowledge of*)

spectator bystander, eyewitness

spectator et testis eyewitness

specter phantom, reflection (*image*), spirit, vision (*dream*). SEE MAIN ENTRY

spectral immaterial, insubstantial

speculari spy

speculate bet, gamble, guess, invest (*fund*), muse, opine, parlay (*bet*), ponder, postulate, presume, presuppose, prognosticate, reflect (*ponder*), surmise, suspect (*think*). SEE MAIN ENTRY

speculate with endanger

speculation conjecture, consideration (*contemplation*), contemplation, estimate (*idea*), estimation (*calculation*), hypothesis, inference, investment, opinion (*belief*), postulate, presumption, prospect (*outlook*), rationale, reflection (*thought*), risk, sense (*feeling*), supposition, suspicion (*uncertainty*), theory, thesis, venture. SEE MAIN ENTRY

speculatist bettor

speculative cogitative, controversial, debatable, deliberate, disputable, doubtful, dubious, hypothetical, indeterminate, inquisitive, insecure, moot, pensive, presumptive, putative, tentative, theoretical, undecided, unpredictable, unsettled, unsound (*fallacious*). SEE MAIN ENTRY

speculator bettor. SEE MAIN ENTRY

speculator spy

speculatory presumptive, speculative, theoretical

speech declamation, discourse, language, parlance, peroration, phraseology, remark. SEE MAIN ENTRY

speech-making rhetoric (*skilled speech*)

speechification declamation

speechless mute, taciturn. SEE MAIN ENTRY

speechlessness silence

speechmaker spokesman

speed dispatch (*promptness*), dispatch (*send off*), expedite, haste, help, precipitate (*hasten*), promote (*organize*), race

speed along dispatch (*send off*), hasten

speed on its way dispatch (*send off*)

speed track causeway

speed up expedite, facilitate, precipitate (*hasten*)

speeded adjudication accelerated judgment

speedily instantly

speediness dispatch (*promptness*)

speedup acceleration

speedway causeway

speedy brief, cursory, expeditious, immediate (*at once*), instant, instantaneous, perfunctory, precipitate, prompt, rapid, ready (*prepared*), summary

speedy completion dispatch (*promptness*)

speedy disposition dispatch (*promptness*)

speedy transaction dispatch (*promptness*)

speedy trial SEE MAIN ENTRY

spell duration, hiatus, interval, period, phase (*period*), prognosticate, recess, respite (*interval of rest*), term (*duration*)

spell danger caution

spell out clarify, comment, define, describe, elucidate, enlighten, explain, explicate, exposit, expound

spellbind coax

spellbinding eloquent

spend bestow, consume, defray, deplete, disburse (*pay out*), dissipate (*expend foolishly*), exert, exhaust (*deplete*), expend (*consume*), expend (*disburse*), pay. SEE MAIN ENTRY

spend lavishly dissipate (*expend foolishly*)

spend more than one has overdraw

spend one's time in occupy (*engage*)

spend wastefully dissipate (*expend foolishly*)

spendable disposable

spending outlay, payment (*act of paying*)

spendings disbursement (*funds paid out*), expenditure, overhead

spendthrift improvident, prodigal, profligate (*extravagant*), profuse

spent irredeemable, irretrievable, powerless

sperare expect (*anticipate*)

spernere disdain

spes chance (*possibility*), expectation

sphaera sphere

sphere ambit, area (*province*), bailiwick, circuit, coverage (*scope*), department, district, jurisdiction, position (*business status*), province, pursuit (*occupation*), purview, range, realm, region, scene, scope, zone. SEE MAIN ENTRY

sphere of activity calling

sphere of occupation appointment (*position*)

spheroid sphere

sphinx-like mysterious

sphinxian mysterious

spice spirit

spicy obscene, salacious, suggestive (*risqué*)

spike penetrate, pierce (*lance*)

spill outflow, outpour

spill over inundate

spin out prolong

spineless irresolute, obsequious, powerless

spiral sinuous

spiral inflation boom (*prosperity*)

spiriferous circuitous

spirit ardor, complexion, connotation, content (*meaning*), disposition (*inclination*), emotion, frame (*mood*), gist (*substance*), gravamen, life (*vitality*), motivate, phantom, prowess (*bravery*), specter, tenor. SEE MAIN ENTRY

spirit away abduct, carry away, hold up (*rob*), kidnap, purloin

spirit of the law equity (*justice*)

spirited alert (*agile*), eager, expeditious, fervent, trenchant, unrestrained (*not repressed*), volatile. SEE MAIN ENTRY

spiritedness life (*vitality*)

spiriting away abduction

spiritless caitiff, disconsolate, grave (*solemn*), inactive, inexpressive, insensible, insipid, lifeless (*dull*), nonchalant, otiose, pedestrian, phlegmatic, prosaic, recreant, torpid

spiritlessness disinterest (*lack of interest*)

spirits alcohol

spiritual incorporeal, intangible, sacrosanct, solemn

spiritual upbuilding edification

spirituality immateriality

spiritualness immateriality

spit pierce (*lance*)

spite antagonize, cruelty, disoblige, harass, harrow, ill will, malice, mistreat, plague, rancor, resentment. SEE MAIN ENTRY

spiteful bilious, bitter (*reproachful*), contemptuous, cruel, dyseptic, harmful, hostile, invidious, malevolent, malicious, malignant, mordacious, outrageous, pejorative, perverse, petulant, resentful, scathing, sinister, vicious, vindictive, virulent. SEE MAIN ENTRY

spitefulness ill will, malice, rancor, spite

splash pretense (*ostentation*), sully

splay deploy, radiate, spread

spleen resentment, umbrage

spleenful bilious, fractious, malevolent, malignant, perverse, petulant

spleeny fractious, perverse

splendid elegant, illustrious, meritorious, premium, prime (*most valuable*), proud (*self-respecting*), sterling

splendidus illustrious

splendor prestige

splendorous illustrious

splenetic bitter (*reproachful*), fractious, froward, perverse, petulant, querulous, resentful, restive

splenetical petulant

splice combine (*join together*), connection (*fastening*), intertwine, join (*bring together*)

spliced conjoint

splinter break (*fracture*), rend, separate, sever, split

splinter party faction

splintered broken (*fractured*)

split alienation (*estrangement*), apportion, bifurcate, break (*separate*), controversy (*argument*), cross (*intersect*), detach, dichotomize, dichotomy, disaccord (*noun*), disaccord (*verb*), disagree, disassociation, discord, discrepancy, disjoint, divide (*separate*), division (*act of dividing*), divisive, estrangement, feud, force (*break*), isolate, mete, part (*separate*), partial (*part*), rend, rift (*disagreement*), rift (*gap*), schism, separate (*adjective*), separate (*verb*), separation, sever, sort, subdivide, variance (*disagreement*). SEE MAIN ENTRY

split again reapportion

split hairs bicker, pettifog

split off break (*separate*)

split up disintegrate, disperse (*scatter*), disrupt, dissolve (*separate*), dissolve (*terminate*), divorce, parcel, partition, prorate, separate

splitting division (*act of dividing*)

splotch defacement, stain

splurge pretense (*ostentation*), spend

spoil adulterate, corrupt, damage, decay, deface, depreciate, deteriorate, disable, eviscerate, foil, frustrate, harm, hold up (*rob*), infect, loot, misemploy, mismanage, pervert, pillage, pirate (*take by violence*), pollute, prejudice (*injure*), prey, prize, stain, sully, taint (*contaminate*), thwart, vitiate. SEE MAIN ENTRY

spoil excessively overindulge

spoil the look of deface

spoilage decrement, dissolution (*disintegration*). SEE MAIN ENTRY

spoilate pirate *(take by violence)*
spoiled decadent, marred, stale, tainted *(contaminated)*
spoiler burglar, vandal
spoiling burglary, damage, decadent
spoils plunder, stake *(award)*. SEE MAIN ENTRY
spoken nuncupative, oral, verbal
spoken expression language
spoken in confidence confidential
spoken language speech
spoken out loud oral
spoken word language, parlance, speech
spokesman advocate *(counselor)*, advocate *(espouser)*, go-between, informer *(a person who provides information)*, interagent, liaison, plenipotentiary, procurator, proponent, representative *(proxy)*. SEE MAIN ENTRY
spokesperson liaison, medium, plenipotentiary
spokeswoman advocate *(counselor)*, advocate *(espouser)*
spolia spoils
spoliare spoil *(pillage)*
spoliate despoil, harry *(plunder)*, loot, pillage, plunder, prey, spoil *(pillage)*
spoliatio robbery
spoliation depredation, deterioration, dissolution *(disintegration)*, havoc, pillage, plunder, rape. SEE MAIN ENTRY
spoliatory predatory
sponge parasite
spongy resilient
sponsio guarantee, recognizance
sponsor avouch *(guarantee)*, backer, bestow, capitalize *(provide capital)*, creditor, espouse, finance, guarantee, guardian, invest *(fund)*, nurture, partisan, patron *(influential supporter)*, promote *(organize)*, promoter, proponent, protect, surety *(guarantor)*, underwrite. SEE MAIN ENTRY
sponsor again refinance
sponsorship accommodation *(backing)*, advocacy, aid *(help)*, appropriation *(donation)*, auspices, behalf, favor *(sanction)*, goodwill, guidance, indorsement, patronage *(support)*, promotion *(encourage-ment)*
spontaneity impulse
spontaneous elective *(voluntary)*, fortuitous, impulsive *(rash)*, informal, ingenuous, prompt, unaffected *(sincere)*, unintentional, unpremeditated. SEE MAIN ENTRY
spontaneous inclination impulse
spontaneus spontaneous
sporadic broken *(interrupted)*, infrequent, intermittent, periodic. SEE MAIN ENTRY
sporadical sporadic
sport bet, contest *(competition)*, flaunt, ridicule
sport with dupe
sporting fair *(just)*
sporting event contest *(competition)*
sportive jocular
sportsmanlike fair *(just)*
spot deface, defacement, detect, discern *(detect with the senses)*, locality, location, notice *(observe)*, onus *(stigma)*, part *(place)*, position *(situation)*, quagmire, region, seat, stain, standpoint, stigma, sully, tarnish, witness *(have direct knowledge of)*
spotless absolute *(ideal)*, clean, inviolate, irreprehensible, moral, pure, unblemished, unimpeachable

spotlight publicity
spotted blemished, marred
spotting detection
spotty sporadic
spousal marriage *(wedlock)*, matrimony
spousal support SEE MAIN ENTRY
spouse consort. SEE MAIN ENTRY
spout exude, outflow, outlet, outpour, recite
sprawl expand, spread
spray barrage, discharge *(shot)*
spread accumulate *(enlarge)*, augmentation, boom *(increase)*, cast *(throw)*, circulate, circulation, coverage *(scope)*, deploy, diffuse, disburse *(distribute)*, dispel, disperse *(disseminate)*, dissipate *(spread out)*, dissolve *(disperse)*, distribute, division *(act of dividing)*, enlarge, expand, growth *(increase)*, herald, increase, inflate, inflated *(enlarged)*, inflation *(increase)*, issue *(publish)*, magnify, pervade, post, proliferate, promulgate, publish, radiate, scope, utter. SEE MAIN ENTRY
spread a report circulate, disseminate
spread about diffuse
spread abroad circulate, diffuse, disperse *(disseminate)*, divulge, post, proclaim, promulgate, propagate *(spread)*, public *(known)*
spread an evil report malign
spread around diffuse
spread far and wide diffuse, disseminate
spread out compound, disperse *(disseminate)*, expand, far-reaching, open *(unclosed)*, prolix
spread out in area extend *(enlarge)*
spread out in battle formation deploy
spread over dissipate *(spread out)*, expand, overlap
spread through permeate, pervade
spread too far overextend
spread too thin overextend
spread widely diffuse, disperse *(scatter)*
spread-out extensive
spreading boom *(increase)*, broad, circulation, contagious, extension *(expansion)*, extensive, rampant
spreading abroad divulgation
spree carouse
sprightliness life *(vitality)*
sprightly alert *(agile)*, jocular, resilient, volatile
spring accrue *(arise)*, derivation, ensue, fund, origination, proceed *(go forward)*, reason *(basis)*, redound, result, source, stem *(originate)*
spring forth arise *(originate)*
spring from emanate, evolve
spring up arise *(originate)*, issue *(send forth)*, pullulate, supervene
spring upon attack
springhead derivation, source
springy resilient
sprinkle dissipate *(spread out)*, distribute, intersperse, spread
sprinkling minimum
sprint race
sprite phantom, specter
sprout germinate, outgrowth, proliferate, pullulate, stem *(originate)*
sprout from redound
sprouting boom *(increase)*, growth *(evolution)*
spruce up embellish
spry alert *(agile)*
spun out prolix

spunk resolution *(decision)*
spunkless languid, phlegmatic
spur abet, agitate *(activate)*, bait *(harass)*, catalyst, cause *(reason)*, exhort, hasten, impel, impetus, incentive, motivate, precipitate *(hasten)*, prevail upon, provocation, provoke, spirit, stimulate, stimulus, urge
spur of necessity compulsion *(coercion)*, force *(compulsion)*
spur on incite, prompt
spurious artificial, assumed *(feigned)*, bogus, deceptive, delusive, dishonest, disingenuous, disreputable, erroneous, false *(not genuine)*, fictitious, fraudulent, imitation, lying, mendacious, meretricious, specious, synthetic, unfounded, untrue. SEE MAIN ENTRY
spurious issue bastard
spuriousness bad faith, false pretense
spurn bar *(exclude)*, condescend *(patronize)*, contemn, decline *(reject)*, decry, demonstrate *(protest)*, disallow, disapprove *(reject)*, disavow, disclaim, discommend, discount *(disbelieve)*, disdain, disoblige, disown *(refuse to acknowledge)*, disregard, disrespect, dissent *(withhold assent)*, eliminate *(exclude)*, exclude, fight *(counteract)*, flout, forswear, humiliate, mock *(deride)*, rebuff *(noun)*, rebuff *(verb)*, refuse, reject, renounce, repel *(drive back)*, repudiate, repulse, set aside *(annul)*, shun. SEE MAIN ENTRY
spurning denial, disdain, negative, rejection, renunciation
spurt acceleration, dispatch *(promptness)*, emit, outburst, outflow, outpour, race
spy conspirator, discern *(detect with the senses)*, informant, observe *(watch)*, recognize *(perceive)*. SEE MAIN ENTRY
spy against subvert
spy upon spy
spying espionage
squabble affray, altercation, bicker, brawl *(noun)*, brawl *(verb)*, confrontation *(altercation)*, contend *(dispute)*, contest *(dispute)*, controversy *(argument)*, disaccord *(noun)*, disaccord *(verb)*, embroilment, fight *(argument)*, fight *(battle)*, fracas, strife
squad assemblage, band
squalid destitute, repulsive, sordid
squall fracas
squander consume, lose *(be deprived of)*, misemploy, mishandle *(mismanage)*, overdraw
squandered irredeemable, lost *(taken away)*
squandering consumption, improvident, misapplication, prodigal, profligate *(extravagant)*, profuse, waste
square close *(enclosed area)*, compensate *(counterbalance)*, fair *(just)*, market place, parcel, pay, refund, regulate *(adjust)*, rightful, upright
square accounts discharge *(pay a debt)*, pay, repay
square measure dimension
square with comport *(agree with)*
squash depress, extinguish, kill *(defeat)*, obliterate, repress, stifle
squat inhabit, lodge *(reside)*, reside, rest *(be supported by)*, usurp
squatter habitant
squeal divulge
squealer informer *(one providing criminal information)*

squeamish   disinclined, reluctant
squeamishness   reluctance
squeeze   constrain (compel), constrict (compress), exact, impact
squeeze out   distill
squeeze together   consolidate (strengthen)
squeezed together   compact (dense)
squelch   abolish, counteract, defeat, extinguish, quash, refute, stifle, strangle
squib   parody, ridicule
squirt   emit
stab   enter (penetrate), lancinate, penetrate, pierce (lance)
stabbing   bitter (penetrating)
stabile   stable
stabilire   establish (entrench), instate
stabilis   constant (adjective), constant (noun), durable, firm, immovable, immutable, permanent, solid (sound), stable, steadfast
stabilitate   establish (entrench)
stability   certainty, composure, constant, equipoise, indestructibility, prowess (bravery), responsibility (conscience), security (safety), uniformity
stabilization   balance (equality)
stabilize   adjust (regulate), compensate (counterbalance), establish (entrench), fix (make firm), settle. SEE MAIN ENTRY
stable   certain (fixed), constant, demonstrable, dependable, durable, firm, fixed (securely placed), indelible, indomitable, infallible, irrevocable, permanent, perpetual, rational, regular (orderly), reliable, secure (free from danger), secure (sound), solid (sound), static, staunch, steadfast, strong, unalterable, unyielding. SEE MAIN ENTRY
stable equilibrium   balance (equality)
stable state   status quo
stabulare   stall
stack   assemblage, bulk, hoard, load, store (depository)
staff   committee, cudgel, employ (engage services), hire, mainstay, personnel, unit (department). SEE MAIN ENTRY
staff members   staff
staff person   employee
staff with   engage (hire)
stage   degree (station), direct (supervise), duration, period, phase (period), point (period of time), portray, scene, term (duration)
stage of advancement   degree (station)
stage of life   age
stage setting   scene
stagecraft   histrionics
stagger   overcome (overwhelm), vacillate
staggering   incredible, ineffable, portentous (eliciting amazement), unbelievable
staggering belief   ludicrous
stagnans   stagnant
stagnant   inactive, indolent, languid, lifeless (dull), static, torpid. SEE MAIN ENTRY
stagnate   languish
stagnating   barren, otiose, stagnant
stagnation   desuetude, inaction, inertia, languor
stagy   histrionic
staid   earnest, phlegmatic, solemn
stain   attaint, brand, brand (stigmatize), damage, debase, deface, defacement, demean (make lower), denigrate, depreciate, derogate, discredit (noun), discredit (verb), disgrace (noun), disgrace (verb), dishonor (shame), dishonor (deprive of

honor), disparage, disrepute, flaw, humiliate, ignominy, infamy, infect, onus (stigma), opprobrium, pervert, pillory, pollute, scandal, shame, smear, stigma, sully, tarnish. SEE MAIN ENTRY
stain one's reputation   malign
stain the character of   defame
stained   blemished, marred, tainted (contaminated)
stainless   absolute (ideal), blameless, clean, honest, infallible, inviolate, irreprehensible, meritorious, pure, unblemished, unimpeachable
stainlessness   honesty
stake   bet, binder, bond (secure a debt), claim (right), compromise (endanger), deposit, dominion (absolute ownership), downpayment, endanger, equity (share of ownership), gamble, guarantee, guaranty, holding (property owned), interest (ownership), jeopardize, lien, loan, parlay (bet), pawn, pledge (security), pledge (deposit), right (entitlement), risk, speculate (chance), title (right). SEE MAIN ENTRY
stake money   handsel, pledge (security)
stake one's credit   promise (vow)
stake out   border (bound), demarcate
stale   dilapidated, languid, lifeless (dull), mundane, obsolete, old, ordinary, outdated, outmoded, pedestrian, prosaic, repetitious, trite, usual. SEE MAIN ENTRY
stale comment   platitude
stalemate   abeyance, check (restrain), deadlock, draw (tie), halt, impasse, impede, stall
staleness   disuse
stalk   approach, hunt, perambulate, pursuit (chase)
stall   arrest (stop), balk, block, chamber (compartment), clog, constrict (inhibit), continue (adjourn), debar, defer (put off), delay (noun), delay (verb), detain (restrain), disadvantage, extension (postponement), hold up (delay), impasse, inconvenience, obstruct, pause, postpone, procrastinate, remit (relax), stand (witness' place in court), stem (check), stop, store (business), suspend. SEE MAIN ENTRY
stall for time   delay
stalling   filibuster
stalwart   cohort, colleague, heroic, indomitable, pertinacious, powerful, purposeful, sedulous, spartan, stable, staunch, strong, undaunted
stalwartness   strength
stamina   force (strength), health, longanimity, prowess (bravery), puissance, sinew, strength, tenacity, tolerance
stamp   brand, brand (mark), embed, indicant, indicator, label (noun), label (verb), seal (solemnize), speciality, specialty (distinctive mark), tenor, validate. SEE MAIN ENTRY
stamp incorrectly   mislabel
stamp of approval   confirmation, indorsement, ratification, sanction (permission)
stamp out   eliminate (eradicate), eradicate, extirpate, obliterate
stamped   monetary
stamped with approval   permissible, popular
stampede   panic
stance   manner (behavior), opinion (belief)
stanch   cease, firm, incorruptible, indomitable, infallible, occlude, pertina-

cious, reliable, resolute, solid (sound), stable, stem (check), stop, true (loyal), unyielding
stanchly   faithfully
stanchness   adhesion (loyalty), fidelity, loyalty
stand   bear (tolerate), desist, endure (last), endure (suffer), halt, lie (be sustainable), opine, opinion (belief), outlook, remain (stay), resist (withstand), resistance, stay (rest), thesis, tolerate. SEE MAIN ENTRY
stand against   counter, counteract, disapprove (reject), fight (counteract), oppugn
stand aghast   fear
stand aloof   eschew
stand apart   deviate
stand around   loiter
stand aside   abandon (withdraw), demit, quit (discontinue), resign, retire (conclude a career)
stand behind   espouse, preserve, sanction, side, sponsor, subsidize
stand between   intercede, part (separate)
stand by   adhere (maintain loyalty), adjoin, assist, contribute (assist), countenance, help, indorse, keep (fulfill), maintain (sustain), recommend, side, subsidize, uphold
stand clear   eschew
stand down   demit
stand facing   confront (encounter)
stand fast   endure (last), hold out (resist), persevere, remain (continue), remain (stay), resist (withstand), subsist, withstand
stand firm   adhere (persist), bear (adduce), claim (maintain), confront (oppose), hold out (resist), insist, last, maintain (sustain), persevere, remain (continue), resist (withstand), withstand
stand firm against   oppose
stand for   connote, denote, exemplify, indicate, replace, represent (portray), signify (denote)
stand guard   patrol, police
stand in   replacement
stand in awe   fear
stand in for   displace (replace)
stand in need of   require (need)
stand in relation   concern (involve)
stand in relation to   pertain
stand in stead of   supersede
stand in the place of   represent (substitute)
stand in the way   balk, bar (hinder), block, check (restrain), delay, estop, hinder, hold up (delay), impede, inconvenience, interpose, obstruct
stand in the way of   clog
stand off   deadlock
stand one's ground   maintain (sustain)
stand opposite   confront (encounter)
stand out   project (extend beyond)
stand out in opposition   contrast
stand over   discipline (control), moderate (preside over)
stand sentinel   patrol, police
stand still   halt, pause, rest (cease from action)
stand the cost   bear the expense, defray
stand the cost of   disburse (pay out)
stand the hazard   bet
stand the strain   bear (tolerate)
stand the test   pass (satisfy requirements)
stand together   conform, cooperate
stand up against   challenge, defy
stand up for   defend, espouse, justify, plead (argue a case), support (justify), uphold

stand up to disown *(deny the validity)*, fight *(battle)*, fight *(counteract)*, oppugn, resist *(withstand)*, withstand

stand-in alter ego, cover *(substitute)*, substitute, surrogate

standard broad, bylaw, canon, code, constant, conventional, cornerstone, criterion, customary, decorum, designation *(symbol)*, epitome, example, exemplar, familiar *(customary)*, general, habitual, household *(familiar)*, law, mediocre, model, mundane, norm, normal *(regular)*, ordinary, paradigm, paragon, pattern, popular, precedent, prevalent, principle *(axiom)*, pro forma, prototype, rate, regular *(conventional)*, repeated, representative, routine, rule *(guide)*, stare decisis, typical, uniform, usual. SEE MAIN ENTRY

standard for comparison exemplar, paragon

standard for imitation exemplar

standard letter form *(document)*

standard of comparison criterion, example, sample

standard of criticism criterion, pattern

standard of judgment criterion, pattern

standard of perfection exemplar

standard of value money

standard practice constant

standard procedure avenue *(means of attainment)*, constant, modus operandi. SEE MAIN ENTRY

standardization uniformity

standardization of laws codification

standardize adapt, adjust *(regulate)*, conform, orchestrate, organize *(arrange)*, regulate *(adjust)*

standardized boiler plate, industrial, normal *(regular)*, systematic, typical

standardness mediocrity

standards conscience, ethics

standards of conduct ethics

standards of professional behavior ethics

standby colleague

standing caliber *(quality)*, case *(set of circumstances)*, character *(reputation)*, class, credit *(recognition)*, degree *(station)*, eminence, extant, honor *(good reputation)*, lasting, posture *(situation)*, prestige, quality *(excellence)*, quality *(grade)*, reputation, situation, stagnant, state *(condition)*, static, status. SEE MAIN ENTRY

standing apart distinct *(distinguished from others)*

standing by ready *(prepared)*

standing committee commission *(agency)*

standing in the place of acting

standing order decree, law, rule *(guide)*, rule *(legal dictate)*

standing out conspicuous, evident, manifest, noteworthy, obvious, patent, salient

standing out clearly evident

standoff draw *(tie)*

standoffish unapproachable

standpoint conviction *(persuasion)*, outlook, perspective, position *(point of view)*, posture *(attitude)*, side, stand *(position)*. SEE MAIN ENTRY

standstill cessation *(interlude)*, check *(bar)*, cloture, deadlock, desuetude, halt, hiatus, impasse, interruption, lull, moratorium, pause, remission

staple item, stock in trade

staples commodities, goods, merchandise, provision *(something provided)*

star feature *(special attraction)*, master

starched formal, punctilious, rigid

starchy rigid

stare abide, continue *(prolong)*

stare scrutinize

stare decisis SEE MAIN ENTRY

staring stark

stark naked *(lacking embellishment)*, palpable, severe, unmitigated. SEE MAIN ENTRY

starlike stellar

starring outstanding *(prominent)*

starry stellar

start arise *(originate)*, cause, commence, conceive *(invent)*, create, embark, embryo, establish *(launch)*, generate, genesis, impel, impetus, inception, incite, initiate, launch *(initiate)*, maintain *(commence)*, nascency, onset *(commencement)*, originate, origination, outset, overt act, postulate, preface, prelude, stem *(originate)*, threshold *(commencement)*, undertake, unveil. SEE MAIN ENTRY

start a corporation incorporate *(form a corporation)*

start a fight attack

start a lawsuit litigate

start a war attack

start afresh resume

start again relapse, renew *(begin again)*, resume

start an action complain *(charge)*, litigate

start forward again resume

start fresh relapse

start out arise *(originate)*, depart, embark

start over reopen

start up induct

starting elementary, incipient, initial, nascency, original *(initial)*, preliminary, preparatory, prime *(original)*, rudimentary

starting before retroactive

starting point base *(foundation)*, derivation, embryo, inception, onset *(commencement)*, origin *(source)*, origination, outset, postulate

startle disconcert, disturb, frighten, menace, upset

startler bombshell

startling lurid, peculiar *(curious)*, portentous *(eliciting amazement)*, prodigious *(amazing)*, unanticipated, uncommon, unexpected, unforeseeable, unusual

starvation poverty, privation

starved deficient, poor *(underprivileged)*

stash deposit *(place)*

state acknowledge *(declare)*, adduce, affirm *(claim)*, allege, annunciate, aspect, assert, avouch *(avow)*, avow, caliber *(quality)*, case *(set of circumstances)*, claim *(maintain)*, comment, contend *(maintain)*, converse, convey *(communicate)*, declare, disabuse, enunciate, exposit, express, inform *(notify)*, interject, issue *(publish)*, mention, notify, observe *(remark)*, phase *(period)*, phrase, plead *(allege in a legal action)*, plight, polity, pose *(propound)*, posit, position *(situation)*, posture *(situation)*, predicament, proclaim, profess *(avow)*, pronounce *(speak)*, public *(affecting people)*, publish, purport, quagmire, recite, recount, relate *(tell)*, remark, remind, report *(disclose)*, signify *(inform)*, situation, speak, status, stipulate, swear, testify, utter, verify *(swear)*. SEE MAIN ENTRY

state a fact testify

state a grievance complain *(charge)*

state a truth testify

state affairs politics

state again reiterate

state an untruth misrepresent

state as fact bear *(adduce)*

state as true allege, assert, avouch *(avow)*, avow

state authoritatively command

state by items itemize

state by way of objection object

state directly express

state emphatically certify *(attest)*, contend *(maintain)*, plead *(allege in a legal action)*, speak

state falsely misrepresent

state fully expound

state highway causeway

state hospital asylum *(hospital)*

state in detail expound, specify

state in nonexplicit terms imply

state incorrectly misstate

state institution asylum *(hospital)*

state management bureaucracy, government *(administration)*

state managers government *(political administration)*

state misleadingly misstate

state occasion ceremony

state of a married woman coverture

state of affairs case *(set of circumstances)*, circumstances, plight, posture *(situation)*

state of anxiety fear

state of being condition *(state)*

state of being different difference

state of being equal parity

state of being public common knowledge

state of being unused desuetude

state of disorder disturbance

state of doubt quandary

state of equilibrium balance *(equality)*

state of excitability ardor

state of excitement affection

state of feeling frame *(mood)*

state of health health

state of inaction deadlock, impasse

state of indebtedness arrears, cloud *(incumbrance)*, mortgage

state of indecision deadlock

state of inertia deadlock

state of matrimony cohabitation *(married state)*, coverture

state of mind frame *(mood)*

state of neutralization deadlock

state of no progress impasse

state of not being satisfied dissatisfaction

state of order array *(order)*, system

state of refinement civilization

state of siege belligerency

state of suspense doubt *(indecision)*

state of terror panic

state of violence shambles

state of war belligerency

state on oath bear *(adduce)*

state one's case plead *(argue a case)*, speak

state one's terms dicker

state opposition demonstrate *(protest)*, object

state positively affirm *(claim)*

state precisely specify

state servant caretaker *(one fulfilling the function of office)*

state something in detail elaborate

state systematically formulate

state the meaning of define

state the meaning precisely   define
state under oath   swear
state with conviction   affirm (claim), argue, avouch (avow), avow, certify (attest), express, speak
state's attorney   district attorney, prosecution (government agency), prosecutor
statecraft   government (administration)
stated   alleged, assumed (inferred), certain (positive), certain (specific), convincing, definite, nuncupative, verbal. SEE MAIN ENTRY
stated as a premise   theoretical
stated authoritatively   positive (prescribed)
stated in a writing   in writing
stated in writing   in writing
stated maintenance   pension
stated term   condition (contingent provision)
stated terms   contract
statehood   nationality
stateliness   solemnity
stately   elegant, proud (self-respecting), solemn
statement   account (evaluation), acknowledgment (avowal), admission (disclosure), affidavit, affirmation, allegation, amount (sum), assertion, attestation, avowal, bill (invoice), budget, caption, census, certification (attested copy), claim (assertion), comment, confession, declaration, dictum, disclosure (something disclosed), dispatch (message), dun, expression (comment), invoice (bill), issuance, ledger, mention (reference), note (brief comment), notice (announcement), notification, observation, postulate, proclamation, profession (declaration), pronouncement, prospectus, publication (disclosure), recital, remark, rendition (explication), report (detailed account), resolution (formal statement), speech, suggestion, testimony, title (division). SEE MAIN ENTRY
statement alleged in defense   plea
statement alleged in justification   plea
statement by way of illustration   dictum
statement of a cause of action   count
statement of account   budget, invoice (bill)
statement of belief   principle (axiom)
statement of claim   demand
statement of debits and credits   account (evaluation)
statement of defense   argument (pleading), justification, plea, pleading
statement of facts   averment, avouchment, bill (formal declaration), declaration, testimony. SEE MAIN ENTRY
statement of general truth   maxim
statement of indebtedness   bill (invoice)
statement of meaning   definition
statement of obligations   invoice (bill)
statement of particulars   specification
statement of pecuniary transactions   account (evaluation)
statement of position   principle (axiom)
statement of the case   brief
statement of the costs   estimate (approximate cost)
statement of the plaintiff's cause   complaint
statement offered in proof   argument (pleading)
statement on oath   affirmance (legal affirmation), affirmation, averment, avowal, deposition, pledge (binding promise)

statement particularizing debts due   invoice (bill)
statement recorded in a book   entry (record)
statement tending to prove a point   argument (pleading)
statement under oath   affidavit, deposition
statement which answers the charges   plea
statement which confirms information on an affidavit   jurat
statements on behalf of the defense   plea
statements that describe   delineation
statemongers   government (political administration)
stateroom   chamber (compartment)
statesman   politician
statesmanship   discretion (quality of being discreet), government (administration), politics
statesmen   government (political administration)
static   certain (fixed), dormant, immutable, inactive, permanent, rigid, stagnant, torpid. SEE MAIN ENTRY
static condition   status quo
statical   static
statim   instantly
station   appointment (position), base (place), building (structure), caliber (quality), character (reputation), class, condition (state), department, locality, locate, location, lodge (house), lodge (reside), office, plant (place firmly), plight, position (business status), position (situation), post, posture (situation), prestige, reputation, seat, situation, stand (witness' place in court), standpoint, state (condition), status, title (position), venue
stationary   firm, permanent, stable, stagnant, standing, static, steadfast
stationed   situated
statistic   computation, poll (canvass)
statistical inquiry   census, investigation
statistician   accountant, actuary
statistics   census, information (facts)
statuere   constitute (establish), determine, establish (launch), fix (settle), instate, resolve (decide)
stature   capacity (authority), elevation, magnitude
status   caliber (quality), case (set of circumstances), character (reputation), class, credit (recognition), degree (station), honor (good reputation), precedence, prestige, quality (excellence), rating, reputation, situation, title (position)
status   condition (state), phase (aspect), position (situation), posture (situation), state (condition)
status quo   SEE MAIN ENTRY
statutable   law-abiding, lawful, legitimate (rightful), licit
statute   act (enactment), authority (documentation), canon, code, codification, constitution, edict, enactment, law, measure, ordinance, precept, prescription (directive), regulation (rule), rubric (authoritative rule), rule (legal dictate). SEE MAIN ENTRY
statute book   code, codification, pandect (code of laws)
statute law   code, codification
statutes   legislation (enactments)
statutory   due (regular), forensic, law-abiding, lawful, legal, legislative, legitimate (rightful), licit, rightful, valid. SEE MAIN ENTRY

statutory cogency   force (legal efficacy)
statutory law   enactment
staunch   constrict (inhibit), dependable, faithful (loyal), loyal, purposeful, steadfast, strong. SEE MAIN ENTRY
staunch belief   conviction (persuasion), faith
staunch loyalty   faith
staunchness   constant
stave in   break (fracture)
stave off   avert, contain (restrain), defer (put off), deter, dissuade, forestall, hold up (delay), parry, postpone, prevent, procrastinate, repel (drive back), thwart, withstand
stay   abeyance, adjournment, arrest (stop), balk, ban, bar (hinder), barrier, block, cease, cessation (interlude), clog, cloture, cohere (adhere), constrict (inhibit), continuance, continue (adjourn), curb, defer (put off), delay (noun), delay (verb), desist, detain (restrain), dwell (reside), encumbrance, endure (last), estop, exist, extension (postponement), forestall, halt (noun), halt (verb), impede, inhabit, inhabitation (act of dwelling in), keep (continue), keep (restrain), last, lodge (reside), lull, mainstay, obstruct, occupy (take possession), pause (noun), pause (verb), persevere, persist, postpone, preclude, prevent, prohibit, prohibition, remain (continue), remission, repress, reprieve, reside, resist (withstand), respite (interval of rest), rest (cease from action), restraint, stem (check), stop, subsist, suspend, toll (stop), uphold, withstand. SEE MAIN ENTRY
stay alive   exist, subsist
stay away   shirk
stay away from   shun
stay incognito   prowl
stay of execution   reprieve, respite (reprieve)
stay on   continue (persevere), last
stay order   injunction
stay together   cohabit, consolidate (unite)
stayed   arrested (checked)
staying   durable, infallible, lasting, live (existing), permanent, persistent
staying power   diligence (perseverance), resolution (decision), sinew
stead   behalf, help (noun), help (verb), site
steadfast   chronic, constant, continual (connected), dependable, diligent, durable, faithful (loyal), firm, fixed (securely placed), immutable, indelible, industrious, inexorable, inflexible, loyal, patient, permanent, persistent, pertinacious, purposeful, relentless, reliable, resolute, sedulous, serious (devoted), solid (sound), stable, staunch, strong, true (loyal), uncompromising, unrelenting, unyielding. SEE MAIN ENTRY
steadfast belief   faith
steadfastly   faithfully
steadfastness   adherence (devotion), adhesion (loyalty), allegiance, constant, diligence (perseverance), faith, fealty, fidelity, industry (activity), loyalty, resolution (decision), tenacity
steadily   faithfully, in good faith, invariably
steadiness   constant, diligence (perseverance), indestructibility, longanimity, moderation, regularity, resolution (decision)
steady   bear (support), consecutive, constant, continual (connected), continuous, controlled (restrained), dependable, direct (uninterrupted), dispassionate, establish (entrench), firm, fixed (securely placed),

immutable, incessant, industrious, inexorable, infallible, loyal, patient, permanent, persistent, pertinacious, punctual, purposeful, regular (orderly), reliable, resolute, serious (devoted), solid (sound), stabilize, stable, staunch, steadfast, strong, true (loyal), undaunted, uniform, unyielding, well-grounded

steady advance progress

steady application diligence (perseverance)

steady demand market (demand)

steal acquire (secure), carry away, convert (misappropriate), defalcate, deprive, despoil, impropriate, jostle (pickpocket), loot, lurk, mulct (defraud), peculate, pilfer, pillage, pirate (reproduce without authorization), pirate (take by violence), plagiarize, plunder, poach, prowl, purloin, rob, spoil (pillage), usurp. SEE MAIN ENTRY

steal away abscond, elude, escape, kidnap

stealer burglar, hoodlum, thief

stealing acquisition, burglary, embezzlement, housebreaking, misappropriation, plagiarism, robbery, theft

stealth evasion

stealthful stealthy

stealthiness concealment, evasion

stealthy artful, clandestine, covert, evasive, furtive, insidious, machiavellian, mysterious, privy, sly, subtle (insidious), surreptitious. SEE MAIN ENTRY

steamship company carrier

steeled impervious

steeled against callous

steely rigid, unaffected (uninfluenced)

steep immerse (plunge into), oblique (slanted), permeate, pervade

steeped in poison deadly

steeped in vice vicious

steepness elevation

steer administer (conduct), direct (show), direct (supervise), govern, manage, manipulate (utilize skillfully), militate, moderate (preside over), officiate, operate, overlook (superintend), oversee, prescribe, preside, regulate (manage), superintend

steer clear shirk

steer clear of shun

steer for pursue (strive to gain)

steerage direction (guidance), management (judicious use), regulation (management), supervision

steered direct (straight)

steering guidance, leading (guiding), management (supervision)

steering committee management (directorate)

steeve load

stellar leading (ranking first), master, principal. SEE MAIN ENTRY

stem block, bloodline, cease, check (restrain), confront (oppose), constrict (inhibit), derivation, enjoin, halt, obstruct, parentage, race, repulse, resist (oppose), source, stay (halt), stop, withstand. SEE MAIN ENTRY

stenographic copy transcript

stentorian powerful

step act (undertaking), degree (station), expedient, operation, perambulate, phase (period), procedure, proceeding, venture. SEE MAIN ENTRY

step aside deviate

step-by-step SEE MAIN ENTRY

step down alight, diminish, quit (discontinue), resign

step in enter (go in), intercede, intervene

step up expand, increase, intensify

step up to approach

stepping up a pace acceleration

steps campaign

steps in the prosecution of an action proceeding

stereotyped boiler plate, familiar (customary), mundane, ordinary, routine, trite, typical, usual

stereotyped saying platitude

sterile barren, ineffective, ineffectual, otiose, unproductive

sterilis unproductive

sterilize decontaminate

sterilized pure

sterling genuine, high-minded, honest, laudable, meritorious, priceless, professional (stellar). SEE MAIN ENTRY

stern astringent, bitter (penetrating), harsh, particular (exacting), relentless, rigid, serious (grave), severe, solemn, strict, stringent, unapproachable, unbending, unrelenting, unyielding

sternly just inexorable

sternness cruelty, rigor, severity

stew imbroglio

steward caretaker (one caring for property), proctor, procurator, substitute, superintendent, supplier

stewards management (directorate)

stewardship control (supervision), custody (supervision), generalship, government (administration), management (supervision), supervision, surveillance

stick bond (hold together), cement, cohere (adhere), cudgel, lancinate, pierce (lance)

stick at refuse

stick close cohere (adhere)

stick in enter (insert), plant (place firmly)

stick on to cohere (adhere)

stick out project (extend beyond)

stick to adhere (fasten), adhere (persist), keep (continue), maintain (carry on), maintain (sustain), persevere, persist, pursue (carry on)

stick together adhere (fasten), cohere (adhere), combine (join together), consolidate (unite)

stick up hold up (rob)

stick up for side

sticker brand, label

stickiness adhesion (affixing)

sticking coherent (joined), cohesive (sticking)

sticking out manifest

sticking together adherence (adhesion), coherence, coherent (joined)

stickle haggle, refuse, remonstrate

stickler bigot

stickling restive

stickup man burglar

stiff close (rigorous), draconian, formal, immutable, indomitable, inflexible, ossified, ponderous, potent, precise, punctilious, renitent, restrictive, rigid, severe, solid (compact), strict, stringent, strong, unbending, unyielding

stiffen fix (make firm)

stiffened ossified

stiffness formality

stifle arrest (stop), cloak, clog, constrict (inhibit), debar, diminish, extinguish, fore-

stall, impair, inhibit, keep (restrain), repress, restrain, restrict, stop, suppress, thwart, withhold. SEE MAIN ENTRY

stifle competition monopolize

stifled clandestine

stifling censorship, deadly, disadvantage, oppressive

stigma attaint, bad repute, brand, discredit, disgrace, dishonor (shame), disparagement, ignominy, infamy, notoriety, obloquy, opprobrium, reproach, scandal, shame. SEE MAIN ENTRY

stigmatism brand

stigmatization denunciation, notoriety

stigmatize charge (accuse), defame, denigrate, denounce (condemn), discredit, disgrace, dishonor (deprive of honor), disparage, humiliate, incriminate, involve (implicate), lessen, pillory, smear, stain, sully, tarnish

stigmatizing calumnious

still allay, alleviate, assuage, dead, dormant, idle, lull, moderate (temper), mollify, mute, notwithstanding, pacify, palliate (abate), peaceable, placate, placid, regardless, repress, soothe, stagnant, stall, standing, static, stifle, strangle, suppress

still existing extant

still in debate pending (unresolved)

still to be found extant

stillare distill

stilling palliative (abating)

stillness abeyance, inaction, insentience, lull, pause, peace, silence

stilted formal, histrionic, inflated (bombastic), orotund, pretentious (pompous), turgid

stiltedness formality

stimulant catalyst, cause (reason), drug, impulse, incentive, inducement, motive, provocation, stimulus

stimulare spirit

stimulate abet, agitate (activate), bait (lure), cause, coax, develop, elicit, evoke, exhort, expedite, foment, foster, impel, incite, induce, influence, inspire, motivate, originate, promise (raise expectations), prompt, provoke, renew (begin again), spirit, urge. SEE MAIN ENTRY

stimulated inclined

stimulater inducement

stimulating causative, constructive (creative), impulsive (impelling), moving (evoking emotion), provocative, remedial, salubrious

stimulation aggravation (exacerbation), cause (reason), development (progression), inducement, instigation, motive, origination, provocation, reason (basis), stimulus

stimulative inducement, moving (evoking emotion), provocative, stimulus

stimulator catalyst, stimulus

stimulus cause (reason), impetus, incentive, inducement, motive, origination, provocation. SEE MAIN ENTRY

stimulus instigation

sting affront, aggravate (annoy), irritate, pique, provoke, stimulus

stinginess austerity

stinging bitter (penetrating), caustic, harsh, incisive, mordacious, offensive (offending), scathing, severe, trenchant

stinging words diatribe

stingy illiberal, nonsubstantial (not sufficient), parsimonious, penurious, provident (frugal)

stint assignment *(task)*, austerity, insufficiency, period

stinted devoid, limited, slight

stinting frugal, illiberal, limiting, parsimonious

stintless liberal *(generous)*

stipend alimony, annuity, commission *(fee)*, consideration *(recompense)*, endowment, honorarium, loan, pay, payment *(remittance)*, payroll, pension, perquisite, subsidy, wage

stipendium campaign, pay

stipulari stipulate

stipulate agree *(contract)*, bear *(adduce)*, designate, determine, mention, posit, promise *(vow)*, select, signify *(inform)*, specify. SEE MAIN ENTRY

stipulated agreed *(promised)*, contractual, stated

stipulatio stipulation

stipulation adjustment, agreement *(contract)*, assignment *(designation)*, attornment, bargain, clause, compact, condition *(contingent provision)*, consent, contract, covenant, designation *(naming)*, indenture, option *(contractual provision)*, pact, prerequisite, promise, protocol *(agreement)*, provision *(clause)*, qualification *(condition)*, reservation *(condition)*, security *(pledge)*, selection *(choice)*, specialty *(contract)*, specification, term *(provision)*, ultimatum, undertaking *(pledge)*. SEE MAIN ENTRY

stipulation to compensate for loss insurance

stipulative conditional

stipulatory qualified *(conditioned)*

stir agitate *(shake up)*, commingle, commotion, discompose, emotion, foment, furor, impress *(affect deeply)*, incite, industry *(activity)*, interest, noise, outburst, pandemonium, perturb, prompt, provoke, turmoil

stir to anger irritate

stir up agitate *(activate)*, churn, disrupt, disturb, engender, foment, incite, motivate, perturb, pique, press *(goad)*, promote *(organize)*, provoke, spirit, stimulate

stirps ancestry, family *(common ancestry)*

stirps issue *(progeny)*, lineage, offspring, parentage

stirps race

stirring momentous, moving *(evoking emotion)*, noteworthy, portentous *(eliciting amazement)*, provocative, sapid, solemn

stock average *(standard)*, blood, bloodline, boiler plate, cargo, commodities, cumulation, derivation, descent *(lineage)*, familiar *(customary)*, family *(common ancestry)*, fund *(noun)*, fund *(verb)*, furnish, garner, goods, hoard, household *(familiar)*, kindred, merchandise, nationality, nondescript, ordinary, origin *(ancestry)*, parentage, possessions, posterity, prevailing *(current)*, prevalent, progeny, prosaic, provide *(supply)*, provision *(something provided)*, race, regular *(conventional)*, repeated, replenish, reserve, resource, routine, stock in trade, store *(depository)*, store, supply, trite, typical, usual. SEE MAIN ENTRY

stock agreement call *(option)*

stock book inventory

stock company corporation

stock in trade commodities, goods, merchandise, possessions, product, resource. SEE MAIN ENTRY

stock list inventory

stock market exchange

stock pile reserve

stock saying catchword

stock sheet inventory

stock up hoard

stockade bulwark, jail

stocked replete

stockholder member *(individual in a group)*, shareholder

stockholder of record shareholder

stockholding share *(stock)*

stockowner shareholder

stockpile accumulate *(amass)*, collection *(accumulation)*, cumulation, fund, garner, hoard *(noun)*, hoard *(verb)*, provision *(something provided)*, store *(depository)*, store

stockroom cache *(storage place)*

stocks portfolio, securities

stocks and bonds portfolio

stodgy lifeless *(dull)*, pedestrian

stoic patient, resigned, spartan, unaffected *(uninfluenced)*

stoical controlled *(restrained)*, dispassionate, patient, phlegmatic, resigned, spartan, unaffected *(uninfluenced)*. SEE MAIN ENTRY

stoicism continence, discipline *(obedience)*, longanimity, resignation *(passive acceptance)*, sufferance, tolerance

stolen article contraband

stolen articles plunder

stolen goods contraband, plunder, spoils

stolid dispassionate, jejune *(dull)*, opaque, phlegmatic, ponderous

stolidity opacity

stolidness opacity

stomach endure *(suffer)*, tolerate

stomachus resentment

stony insensible, obdurate, ossified, phlegmatic, rigid, severe, unaffected *(uninfluenced)*

stony-hearted brutal, malignant, relentless, ruthless, severe

stool pigeon informant

stoop comply, condescend *(deign)*, decline *(fall)*, deign, succumb, vouchsafe

stop adjourn, balk, ban, bar *(hinder)*, barrier, block, blockade *(barrier)*, cease, cessation *(interlude)*, check *(bar)*, check *(restrain)*, clog, close *(terminate)*, cloture, conclude *(complete)*, condemn *(ban)*, constrict *(inhibit)*, contain *(restrain)*, debar, delay, desist, destination, desuetude, detain *(restrain)*, deter, deterrence, discontinuance *(act of discontinuing)*, discontinue *(abandon)*, disqualify, disrupt, dissolve *(terminate)*, dwell *(reside)*, embargo, encumbrance, end *(termination)*, enjoin, estop, expiration, expire, finality, finish, forbear, forbid, forestall, forgo, halt *(noun)*, halt *(verb)*, hesitate, hiatus, hold up *(delay)*, impasse, impede, impediment, inhibit, interdict, interfere, interrupt, interruption, keep *(restrain)*, kill *(defeat)*, lapse *(cease)*, leave *(allow to remain)*, lock, lodge *(reside)*, lull, moratorium, obstacle, obstruct, obstruction, occlude, palliate *(abate)*, parry, preclude, prevent, prohibit, prohibition, quash, quit *(discontinue)*, recess *(noun)*, recess *(verb)*, refrain, remission, remit *(relax)*, reprieve, resist *(oppose)*, respite *(interval of rest)*, rest *(cease from action)*, restrain, restraint, restrict, shut, stall, stay, stay *(halt)*, stay *(rest)*, stem *(check)*, stifle, strangle, suppress, suspend, terminate, thwart, withstand. SEE MAIN ENTRY

stop an advance halt

stop and consider pause

stop at nothing persevere

stop in progress by hindrances impede

stop look and listen beware

stop payment default, dishonor *(refuse to pay)*

stop short balk, clog, halt

stop the progress of estop

stop the way estop

stop to consider doubt *(hesitate)*

stop up block, clog, obstruct, obturate, occlude, shut

stop work cease, rest *(cease from action)*, strike *(refuse to work)*

stopgap expedient, substitute, temporary. SEE MAIN ENTRY

stopover halt

stoppage abeyance, bar *(obstruction)*, blockade *(limitation)*, cessation *(termination)*, check *(bar)*, close *(conclusion)*, cloture, damper *(stopper)*, deadlock, defeasance, deferment, desuetude, discontinuance *(act of discontinuing)*, embargo, encumbrance, end *(termination)*, expiration, extremity *(death)*, filibuster, finality, halt, hiatus, impediment, interruption, layoff, lull, miscarriage, moratorium, obstacle, obviation, pause, prohibition, recess, remission, restraint, stay, strike

stoppage of use desuetude

stoppage of work lockout

stopped arrested *(checked)*, broken *(interrupted)*

stopped-up blind *(impassable)*

stopper bar *(obstruction)*, check *(bar)*, damper *(stopper)*, obstacle, obstruction, obturate, shut, stop

stopping-place destination

stopple damper *(stopper)*, stop

storage arsenal, cache *(storage place)*, coffer, conservation, cumulation, depository, preservation

store business *(commercial enterprise)*, collection *(accumulation)*, conceal, cumulation, deposit *(place)*, depository, fund *(noun)*, fund *(verb)*, garner, hoard *(noun)*, hoard *(verb)*, keep *(shelter)*, load, market *(business)*, merchandise, provision *(something provided)*, quantity, replenish, repose *(place)*, reserve *(noun)*, reserve *(verb)*, resource, stock in trade, sufficiency, treasury. SEE MAIN ENTRY

store away reserve

store in the archives file *(place among official records)*

store of knowledge education

store of provisions cache *(storage place)*

store secretly hoard

store up accumulate *(amass)*, conserve, hoard, reserve, set aside *(reserve)*

storehouse bank, cache *(storage place)*, depository, repository, reserve, store *(depository)*, treasury

storehouse for safekeeping cache *(storage place)*

storekeeper dealer, merchant

storeroom cache *(storage place)*, repository

storm assail, attack, barrage, bluster *(commotion)*, cataclysm, demonstrate *(protest)*, furor, incursion, onset *(assault)*, pandemonium, passion, strike *(assault)*, turmoil. SEE MAIN ENTRY

storm against inveigh

stormer aggressor

storming barrage

stormless placid

stormy disorderly, severe, unruly

story falsehood, figment, item, myth, recital, scenario, statement. SEE MAIN ENTRY

storylike narrative

storytelling narration

stout firm, heroic, indomitable, ponderous, powerful, spartan, strong

stout heart prowess (*bravery*)

stout-hearted spartan

stouthearted heroic, undaunted

stoutness puissance, strength

stow deposit (*place*), garner, hoard, load

stow away harbor, hide, hoard, store

straddle pause, tergiversate

strages havoc

straggle spread

straight clean, direct (*uninterrupted*), ethical, naked (*lacking embellishment*), right (*direct*), straightforward, unadulterated, unbending, undistorted

straight course rectitude, right (*righteousness*)

straight-out SEE MAIN ENTRY

straight-thinking pragmatic

straightaway direct (*straight*), forthwith, right (*direct*)

straighten fix (*repair*), organize (*arrange*), rectify

straighten out arrange (*methodize*), disabuse, disentangle, fix (*arrange*), fix (*settle*), negotiate, regulate (*adjust*), settle

straightforward absolute (*conclusive*), bona fide, candid, clear (*apparent*), cognizable, coherent (*clear*), compact (*pithy*), credible, direct (*forthright*), explicit, honest, ingenuous, irreprehensible, law-abiding, lucid, outright, pellucid, right (*direct*), simple, unaffected (*sincere*), unequivocal, upright. SEE MAIN ENTRY

straightforwardness probity, rectitude

straightness rectitude

straightway instantly

strain aggravation (*annoyance*), ancestry, blood, bloodline, burden, descent (*lineage*), distill, distort, effort, encumber (*hinder*), endeavor (noun), endeavor (*verb*), exert, exhaust (*deplete*), family (*common ancestry*), feud, force (*break*), harass, ill will, labor (*exertion*), labor, mistreat, overextend, overload, overstep, pressure, purge (*purify*), race, screen (*select*), strive, struggle, tax (*overwork*), try (*attempt*), work (*effort*)

strain of invective diatribe

strain out distill

strain the meaning distort

strain the sense distort

strain the truth distort, perjure

strained relations contest (*dispute*), disaccord, discord

strained sense catachresis, distortion

straining operose

strait emergency, entanglement (*involvement*), plight, quagmire

strait-laced provincial, severe, stringent

straitened poor (*underprivileged*)

straitened circumstances poverty

straitened means privation

straitlaced restrictive, rigid, strict, unbending

straits poverty, predicament

strange eccentric, extraneous, extrinsic, foreign, incongruous, ineffable, inexplicable, irregular (*not usual*), irrelative, ludicrous, mysterious, noteworthy, novel, obscure (*remote*), peculiar (*curious*), prodigious (*amazing*), rare, remarkable, suspicious (*questionable*), unaccustomed, unacquainted, uncanny, uncommon, uncouth, unrelated, unusual

strange behavior quirk (*idiosyncrasy*)

strange occurrence quirk (*idiosyncrasy*)

strange person stranger

strangeness irregularity, nonconformity, quirk (*idiosyncrasy*)

stranger alien. SEE MAIN ENTRY

strangle extinguish, inhibit, repress, stifle, suppress. SEE MAIN ENTRY

strangulare strangle

strangulate constrict (*inhibit*), stifle

strangulation blockade (*limitation*), constraint (*restriction*)

strap fetter, handcuff

strapped impecunious, poor (*underprivileged*)

strapping powerful, strong

stratagem act (*undertaking*), artifice, campaign, contrivance, deception, design (*intent*), device (*contrivance*), expedient, false pretense, hoax, instrumentality, machination, maneuver (*tactic*), maneuver (*trick*), operation, plot (*secret plan*), ploy, policy (*plan of action*), practice (*procedure*), pretext, ruse, scheme, trap. SEE MAIN ENTRY

strategem plan, subterfuge

strategic cardinal (*basic*), critical (*crucial*), diplomatic, necessary (*required*), subtle (*refined*), tactical. SEE MAIN ENTRY

strategic item necessity, need (*requirement*)

strategical necessary (*required*), strategic, tactical

strategics contrivance

strategist catalyst, coactor, conspirator, conspirer, expert, mastermind

strategists management (*directorate*)

strategy campaign, design (*intent*), direction (*course*), discretion (*quality of being discreet*), expedient, forethought, machination, maneuver (*tactic*), plan, practice (*procedure*), procedure, process (*course*), program, proposition, ruse, scheme, stratagem, system. SEE MAIN ENTRY

stratification order (*arrangement*)

stratum class

stray detour, deviant, deviate, digress, lapse (*fall into error*), miscalculate, prowl, random, sporadic

strayed lost (*disoriented*)

straying astray, deviation, discursive (*digressive*), divergent, indirection (*indirect action*), shifting, truant

streak frame (*mood*)

stream issue (*send forth*), outflow, outpour

stream of abuse diatribe

stream of correspondence dispatch (*message*)

stream out emanate

streaming copious, fluvial

streamline simplify (*make easier*)

streamy fluvial

street avenue (*route*), causeway

street number address

street vendor dealer

strenghten sustain (*confirm*)

strength amount (*quantity*), degree (*magnitude*), dint, emphasis, faculty (*ability*), health, main force, mainstay, potential, predominance, protection, prowess (*brav-

ery*), puissance, sinew, tenacity, tolerance, validity. SEE MAIN ENTRY

strength of character discipline (*obedience*)

strength of will diligence (*perseverance*), discipline (*obedience*)

strengthen aid, bear (*support*), compound, concentrate (*consolidate*), corroborate, develop, document, edify, empower, enable, endue, enforce, enhance, establish (*entrench*), heighten (*augment*), help, intensify, justify, magnify, nurture, reassure, recruit, reinforce, side, supplement, support (*corroborate*), sustain (*prolong*)

strengthened insusceptible (*resistant*), protective

strengthener reinforcement

strengthening boom (*increase*), consolidation, corroboration, cumulative (*increasing*), cumulative (*intensifying*), development (*progression*), enforcement, help, remedial, support (*corroboration*)

strengthful strong

strengthless helpless (*powerless*), languid, nonsubstantial (*not sturdy*), null (*invalid*), null and void, powerless

strengthlessness impotence, impuissance

strenuous difficult, intense, intensive, onerous, operose, oppressive, painstaking SEE MAIN ENTRY

strenuous effort endeavor, pursuit (*effort to secure*)

strenuousness effort, industry (*activity*)

strenuus spartan

strepitus noise

stress aggravation (*annoyance*), argue, assert, certify (*attest*), compulsion (*coercion*), contend (*maintain*), duress, dwell (*linger over*), emphasis, enunciate, force (*compulsion*), inflection, insist, plead (*allege in a legal action*), pressure (noun), pressure (*verb*), pronounce (*speak*), reaffirm, remind, work (*effort*). SEE MAIN ENTRY

stressed alleged

stretch capacity (*maximum*), capacity (*sphere*), develop, distort, distortion, duration, embellish, enlarge, exaggeration, expand, extend (*enlarge*), extent, falsify, gamut, increase, inflate, magnify, magnitude, overextend, overstep, period, phase (*period*), prolong, purview, range, scope, slant, space, spread, stress (*strain*), sustain (*prolong*)

stretch a point magnify

stretch out deploy, expand, extend (*enlarge*), spread

stretch the meaning distort

stretch the truth fabricate (*make up*), perjure, prevaricate

stretch too far overextend

stretchable flexible, malleable, pliable

stretched inflated (*enlarged*)

stretching continuation (*prolongation*), extension (*expansion*)

strew diffuse, dispel, disperse (*disseminate*), disseminate, dissipate (*spread out*), spread

stricken disconsolate

strict astringent, close (*rigorous*), conscientious, draconian, drastic, exact, explicit, factual, faithful (*true to fact*), inflexible, intense, ironclad, literal, meticulous, narrow, orthodox, painstaking, particular (*exacting*), precise, punctilious, punctual, rigid, severe, stringent, tyrannous, unbending, uncompromising. SEE MAIN ENTRY

strict construction SEE MAIN ENTRY
strict control force (compulsion)
strict disciplinarian dictator
strict examination indagation, probe
strict honesty integrity
strict inquiry analysis, examination (study), hearing, indagation, investigation
strict interpretation explanation
strict isolation quarantine
strict meaning SEE MAIN ENTRY
strict order array (order)
strict procedure bureaucracy
strict search indagation
striction deterrence, hindrance
strictly faithfully
strictly defined definite
strictly honest clean
strictly to the letter verbatim
strictness austerity, particularity, rigor, severity
stricture admonition, aspersion, bad repute, condemnation (blame), correction (punishment), denunciation, discredit, obloquy, obstruction, ostracism, outcry, reprimand, revilement, slander. SEE MAIN ENTRY
stride perambulate, step
strident discordant, harsh
stridulous harsh
strife altercation, argument (contention), belligerency, competition, contention (opposition), contest (dispute), controversy (argument), disaccord, disagreement, discord, dispute, dissension, dissidence, embroilment, feud, fight (argument), fray, labor (exertion), outbreak, outburst, resistance, revolt, variance (disagreement), work (effort). SEE MAIN ENTRY
strike assault (noun), assault (verb), attack, beat (pulsate), boycott, collide (crash against), contact (touch), defiance, fight (battle), find (discover), impact, impinge, impress (affect deeply), inflict, mistreat, onset (assault), reach, rebel, rebellion, resist (oppose), resistance, revolt. SEE MAIN ENTRY
strike a balance adjust (regulate), compensate (counterbalance), compromise (settle by mutual agreement), discharge (pay a debt)
strike a bargain barter, close (agree), dicker, settle
strike a light burn
strike against collide (crash against), jostle (bump into)
strike at accost, collide (crash against), contend (dispute), oppugn
strike back conflict, confront (oppose), counter, recriminate, resist (oppose), retaliate
strike forcibly against each other collide (crash against)
strike hard impress (affect deeply)
strike home impress (affect deeply)
strike in with involve (participate)
strike off decrease, deduct (reduce), delete, discount (reduce), rebate
strike off the roll discharge (dismiss)
strike off the roll of lawyers disbar
strike one as being appear (seem to be)
strike out annul, deface, delete, edit, eliminate (eradicate), eradicate, expunge, expurgate, obliterate, redact
strike sightless blind (deprive of sight)
strike the first blow attack
strike together jostle (bump into)
strike visionless blind (deprive of sight)

strike with overwhelming fear frighten, menace
striking arrant (definite), clear (apparent), conspicuous, distinct (clear), eloquent, flagrant, insistent, manifest, notable, obvious, open (in sight), palpable, particular (specific), portentous (eliciting amazement), powerful, prodigious (amazing), prominent, remarkable, salient, special, unusual
striking part highlight
striking qualities character (personal quality)
striking together collision (accident)
strikingly particularly
string assemblage, handcuff, sequence
string out dispel, protract (stall)
stringency austerity, rigor, severity
stringent astringent, close (rigorous), compulsory, draconian, harsh, inflexible, ironclad, particular (exacting), relentless, rigid, severe, strict, uncompromising. SEE MAIN ENTRY
strip abridge (divest), deduct (reduce), demote, denude, deprive, despoil, disarm (divest of arms), divest, erode, expose, harry (plunder), loot, minimize, pillage, plunder, prey, remove (eliminate), unveil
strip of disguise expose
strip of right disqualify
stripling juvenile
strive attempt, compete, contend (dispute), endeavor, exert, labor, oppose, try (attempt), undertake. SEE MAIN ENTRY
strive against conflict, dispute (contest), oppose, oppugn, repel (drive back), resist (oppose)
strive for pursue (strive to gain)
striver contender
striving competitive (antagonistic), struggle
striving for effect flagrant, histrionic
striving for superiority competition
stroke calamity, expedient, maneuver (tactic), operation
stroll perambulate, prowl
strong assertive, categorical, cogent, cohesive (compact), compelling, convincing, disorderly, drastic, durable, firm, forcible, in full force, indomitable, inexpugnable, influential, infrangible, insusceptible (resistant), intense, intensive, irresistible, omnipotent, orotund, persuasive, potent, powerful, predominant, prevailing (having superior force), profound (intense), reliable, resilient, resounding, secure (sound), solid (sound), sound, spartan, stable, staunch, steadfast, substantial, tenable, unyielding, valid, vehement, well-grounded. SEE MAIN ENTRY
strong arm tactics coercion
strong aversion odium
strong connection adhesion (loyalty)
strong contrast antithesis
strong demand market (demand)
strong discomfort pain
strong dissension dissension
strong feeling passion
strong language expletive
strong point specialty (special aptitude)
strong probability presumption
strong request dun
strong-minded inexorable, obdurate, purposeful, unbending
strong-willed earnest, hot-blooded, inexorable, inflexible, obdurate, persistent, pertinacious, purposeful, resolute, steadfast
strongbox coffer, treasury

stronghold bulwark, mainstay, protection, refuge, shelter (protection)
strongly attached close (intimate), intimate
strongroom bank
structural fundamental, organic
structural composition configuration (form)
structural design configuration (form)
structure body (main part), complex (development), composition (makeup), configuration (form), construction, contour (outline), contour (shape), corpus, delineation, edifice, fabricate (construct), form, formation, motif, order (arrangement), temperament. SEE MAIN ENTRY
structures premises (buildings)
structuring building (business of assembling)
struggle affray, campaign, commotion, compete, conflict, confront (oppose), confrontation (altercation), contend (dispute), contention (opposition), contest (competition), contest, effort, embroilment, endeavor (noun), endeavor (verb), engage (involve), fight (battle), grapple, labor, onus (burden), opposition, persevere, pursuit (effort to secure), resistance, strife, strive, work (effort). SEE MAIN ENTRY
struggle against dispute (contest), fight (battle)
struggle for pursue (strive to gain)
struggle for superiority competition
struggler candidate
strut flaunt, perambulate
strutting inflated (vain)
stub coupon, receipt (proof of receiving)
stubborn callous, chronic, contentious, difficult, disobedient, fractious, froward, impervious, incorrigible, indomitable, inexorable, inflexible, insusceptible (uncaring), intractable, obdurate, persistent, pertinacious, perverse, pugnacious, purposeful, recalcitrant, relentless, resolute, restive, rigid, severe, unbending, uncontrollable, unrelenting, unruly, unyielding
stubborn person bigot
stubbornly disobedient contumacious
stubbornly rebellious contumacious
stubbornness defiance, diligence (perseverance), tenacity
stuck inextricable
student disciple, neophyte, novice, protégé
studere adhere (maintain loyalty), favor, study
studied aforethought, deliberate, elaborate, intentional, literate, nonchalant, premeditated, purposeful, tactical, willful
studies education
studiosus partial (biased), zealous
studious diligent, industrious, learned, literate, pensive
studiously purposely
studiousness diligence (care), interest (concern)
studium ardor, inclination, interest (concern), predilection, predisposition, pursuit (chase), regard (esteem)
study analysis, analyze, audit, brood, canvass, check (inspect), consider, consideration (contemplation), contemplation, deliberate, deliberation, diligence (care), hornbook, indagation, inquire, inquiry (systematic investigation), inspection, knowledge (learning), monitor, observation, overlook (superintend), pandect (treatise),

peruse, ponder, preoccupation, probe, read, reason *(conclude)*, reflect *(ponder)*, reflection *(thought)*, research *(noun)*, research *(verb)*, review *(official reexamination)*, review, scrutinize, scrutiny, subject *(topic)*, survey *(examine)*, test, treatment, trial *(experiment)*, weigh. SEE MAIN ENTRY

study book hornbook

study deeply concentrate *(pay attention)*

study in detail investigate, probe

study in silence muse

study of ecosystems ecology

study of environs ecology

study of surroundings ecology

study quietly muse

study systematically examine *(study)*

stuff load

stuffed compact *(dense)*, full, replete

stuffy orotund, pedestrian

stultification constraint *(restriction)*

stultify balk, check *(restrain)*, clog, deter, disable, foil, frustrate, thwart

stultus irrational

stumble miscalculate, miscue, mistake

stumble on find *(discover)*, locate

stumbling incompetent

stumbling block bar *(obstruction)*, barrier, blockade *(barrier)*, complication, deadlock, deterrence, disadvantage, handicap, obstacle

stump confuse *(bewilder)*

stumper enigma, problem

stun drug, impress *(affect deeply)*, overcome *(overwhelm)*, overwhelm

stunned speechless

stunt lessen

stupefacient drug, narcotic

stupefaction bombshell

stupefactive narcotic

stupefied insensible, lifeless *(dull)*, phlegmatic, speechless, torpid

stupefy confuse *(bewilder)*, drug, lull, muddle, obfuscate

stupendous grandiose, portentous *(eliciting amazement)*, prodigious *(enormous)*, remarkable, special

stuperous torpid

stupid fatuous, impolitic, incompetent, inexpressive, irrational, obtuse, opaque, thoughtless, torpid, unpolitic, vacuous

stupidity opacity

stupidness opacity

stupor inertia, insentience, prostration, sloth

stuprare dishonor *(deprive of honor)*

stuprate debauch

stupration rape

stuprum debauchery, seduction

sturdiness health, prowess *(bravery)*, strength

sturdy durable, firm, indestructible, inexpugnable, solid *(sound)*, stable, strong

style call *(title)*, character *(personal quality)*, cognomen, color *(complexion)*, complexion, conduct, custom, denominate, form *(arrangement)*, habit, identify, manner *(behavior)*, manner *(kind)*, means *(opportunity)*, mode, modus operandi, motif, nominate, parlance, personality, phrase, phraseology, practice *(custom)*, presence *(poise)*, property *(distinctive attribute)*, structure *(composition)*, temperament, usage. SEE MAIN ENTRY

style of arrangement content *(structure)*, organization *(structure)*

style of penmanship handwriting

styleless outdated, outmoded

stylish current, elegant, popular

stymie balk, clog, constrict *(inhibit)*, debar, delay, disadvantage, estop, forestall, frustrate, hamper, imbroglio, inconvenience, keep *(restrain)*, obstruct, parry, stay *(halt)*, stifle, stop, thwart. SEE MAIN ENTRY

sua sponte free *(enjoying civil liberty)*. SEE MAIN ENTRY

sua voluntate free *(enjoying civil liberty)*

suable actionable

suadere advocate

suasible amenable, open *(persuasible)*, pliable. SEE MAIN ENTRY

suasion instigation, persuasion

suasive cogent, convincing, hortative, persuasive

suasor advocate *(counselor)*, spokesman

suavis palatable

suavity courtesy

sub hasta vendere auction

subaltern ancillary *(subsidiary)*, assistant, ignoble, inferior *(lower in position)*, minor, secondary, slight, subordinate, subservient. SEE MAIN ENTRY

subalternate subaltern

subauscultare overhear

subcategory subdivision

subcenturio subaltern

subclass subdivision

subcommittee caucus

subconscious perception impression

subdere foist

subditus false *(not genuine)*

subdivide apportion, break *(separate)*, codify, dichotomize, disjoint, file *(arrange)*, parcel, part *(separate)*, partition, pigeonhole, sever, sort, split. SEE MAIN ENTRY

subdivided bipartite

subdivisible divisible

subdivision affiliate, chapter *(branch)*, chapter *(division)*, class, component, constituent *(part)*, decentralization, denomination, department, detail, dichotomy, lot, member *(constituent part)*, offshoot, organ, part *(portion)*, province, section *(division)*, segment, split, subheading. SEE MAIN ENTRY

subdivisional local, regional

subdivisive divisive

subdolous deceptive, machiavellian, surreptitious

subdolus sly

subdual control *(restriction)*, subjection

subduce withdraw

subducere steal

subduct decrease, deduct *(reduce)*, discount *(reduce)*, except *(exclude)*, excise *(cut away)*, retrench, withdraw

subduction curtailment, decrease, deduction *(diminution)*

subdue allay, alleviate, arrest *(stop)*, beat *(defeat)*, browbeat, capture, confine, constrain *(restrain)*, contain *(restrain)*, control *(restrain)*, defeat, diminish, disarm *(set at ease)*, dominate, extinguish, foil, halt, impose *(subject)*, lessen, lull, moderate *(temper)*, modify *(moderate)*, mollify, overcome *(surmount)*, override, overthrow, overturn, overwhelm, pacify, palliate *(abate)*, prevail *(triumph)*, quash, repress, restrain, stifle, strangle, subject, subjugate, suppress, surmount. SEE MAIN ENTRY

subdued dispassionate, passive, placid, solemn, unobtrusive

subduing bondage, mitigating, palliative *(abating)*

subgrade poor *(inferior in quality)*

subgroup chapter *(division)*, class, classification, part *(portion)*, section *(division)*, subdivision, subheading

subhead caption

subheading caption, subdivision. SEE MAIN ENTRY

subicere forge *(counterfeit)*, hint, subject

subiectio forgery

subiectus subject *(conditional)*

subigere compel

subit occur *(come to mind)*

subitaneous unexpected, unforeseeable

subitus instantaneous

subiungere subdue

subject article *(commodity)*, article *(distinct section of a writing)*, captive, compel, constrain *(compel)*, content *(meaning)*, contents, dependent, dominate, inferior *(lower in position)*, object, passive, question *(issue)*, require *(compel)*, servile, subdue, subjugate, subordinate, subservient, thesis. SEE MAIN ENTRY

subject for inquiry issue *(matter in dispute)*, matter *(subject)*

subject matter content *(meaning)*, contents, context, matter *(subject)*, tenor. SEE MAIN ENTRY

subject of controversy discrepancy

subject of dispute cause *(lawsuit)*, conflict, controversy *(argument)*, discrepancy, problem

subject of inquiry question *(inquiry)*

subject of thought contents

subject to conditional, contingent, dependent, incident, liable, provided

subject to a charge encumber *(financially obligate)*

subject to a handicap penalize

subject to a liability encumber *(financially obligate)*

subject to a pecuniary penalty fine

subject to action of court of justice justiciable

subject to analysis examine *(study)*

subject to another jurisdiction foreign

subject to argument debatable, disputable

subject to authority impose *(subject)*

subject to be concluded determinable *(liable to be terminated)*

subject to being abrogated defeasible

subject to being annulled defeasible

subject to being cancelled defeasible

subject to being divested defeasible

subject to being invalidated defeasible

subject to being repealed defeasible

subject to being retracted defeasible

subject to being revoked defeasible, voidable

subject to being taken away defeasible

subject to being withdrawn defeasible

subject to cancellation determinable *(liable to be terminated)*, voidable

subject to chance conditional, insecure

subject to change ambulatory, conditional, indefinite, insecure, mutable, provisional

subject to contention debatable, forensic

subject to contravention debatable

subject to control impose *(subject)*

subject to controversy debatable, disputable, forensic, moot, polemic

subject to dependence impose *(subject)*

subject to discontinuance determinable *(liable to be terminated)*

subject to examination analyze, audit, canvass, cross-examine, monitor

subject to influence impose (subject)
subject to loss endanger
subject to measurement determinable (ascertainable)
subject to penalty condemn (punish), penalize, punish
subject to preference disjunctive (alternative)
subject to pressure enforce
subject to punishment discipline (punish), penalize
subject to questioning examine (interrogate)
subject to revisal corrigible
subject to scrutiny check (inspect), examine (study), frisk, inquire, monitor, peruse, probe
subject to strain distress
subject to termination determinable (liable to be terminated)
subject to terms conditional, contingent, provisional, qualified (conditioned), without recourse
subject to verification inconclusive
subjected subordinate
subjection acquiescence, allegiance, bondage, captivity, duress, force (compulsion), homage, oppression, prostration, servitude, thrall. SEE MAIN ENTRY
subjection to responsibility (accountability)
subjection to death mortality
subjection to fate fatality
subjection to force compulsion (coercion)
subjective partial (biased), personal (private). SEE MAIN ENTRY
subjective belief credence
subjectivity intolerance, prejudice (preconception)
subjoin affix, annex (add), append, attach (join), compound, connect (join together), join (bring together)
subjoined attached (annexed)
subjoiner adjoiner
subjoining accession (annexation)
subjugate abduct, beat (defeat), coerce, confine, constrain (restrain), defeat, discipline (control), dominate, impose (subject), jail, manage, overcome (surmount), overthrow, overwhelm, repress, restrain, subdue, subject, surmount. SEE MAIN ENTRY
subjugated to inferior (lower in position)
subjugation abduction, bondage, captivity, duress, force (compulsion), oppression, servitude, subjection, thrall
subjunction accession (annexation), addition, attachment (act of affixing), rider
sublation removal
sublease rent, sublet. SEE MAIN ENTRY
sublet lease, rent, sublease. SEE MAIN ENTRY
sublevatio relief (release)
sublimate elevate, purge (purify)
sublime illustrious, meritorious, outstanding (prominent)
sublunar mundane
sublunary mundane
submerge censor, immerse (engross), immerse (plunge into), overcome (overwhelm), overwhelm
submerged latent
submerse immerse (plunge into)
submission acquiescence, adhesion (loyalty), allegiance, amenability, application, argument (pleading), assent, bid, capitulation, compliance, concession

(compromise), conciliation, conformity (obedience), deference, discipline (obedience), homage, longanimity, proposal (suggestion), proposition, prostration, rendition (restoration), resignation (passive acceptance), servitude, subjection, sufferance, thrall, tolerance
submission to a court's jurisdiction appearance (coming into court)
submissive malleable, obedient, obeisant, obsequious, passive, patient, pliable, pliant, powerless, resigned, sequacious, servile, subordinate, subservient, tractable, yielding
submissive to correction corrigible
submissively faithfully, respectfully
submissiveness acquiescence, adhesion (loyalty), amenability, capitulation, conformity (obedience), deference, discipline (obedience), homage, loyalty, resignation (passive acceptance)
submit abide, accede (concede), admonish (advise), advise, argue, bear (adduce), bestow, cede, concede, conform, counsel, defer (yield in judgment), extend (offer), forbear, give (grant), hear (give attention to), hold out (deliberate on an offer), index (docket), introduce, move (judicially request), obey, offer (propose), offer (tender), pose (propound), posit, proffer, propose, propound, refer (send for action), render (deliver), serve (assist), succumb, surrender (yield), tender. SEE MAIN ENTRY
submit a formal request move (judicially request)
submit for determination defer (yield in judgment)
submit in evidence exhibit
submit in judgment to defer (yield in judgment)
submit oneself to appear (attend court proceedings)
submit the case rest (end a legal case)
submit to allow (endure), bear (tolerate), comply, concede, endure (suffer), tolerate
submit without complaint forbear
submittal acquiescence, capitulation, cession, deference
suborder class
subordinate ancillary (subsidiary), assistant, coadjutant, dependent, derivative, employee, extrinsic, impose (subject), incidental, inferior (lower in position), minor, obsequious, passive, pliant, secondary, sequacious, servile, slight, subaltern, subject (conditional), subject, subservient, subsidiary, supplementary, tangential. SEE MAIN ENTRY
subordinate group minority (outnumbered group)
subordinate part adjunct, member (constituent part)
subordinate position subordinate
subordination allegiance, array (order), bondage, conformity (obedience), servitude, subjection
subordination to rules discipline (obedience)
suborn bait (lure), coax, convince, corrupt, inveigle, persuade, taint (corrupt). SEE MAIN ENTRY
subornare suborn
subornation gratuity (bribe)
subornative persuasive
subpoena call (summon), charge (command), citation (charge), direction (order), monition (legal summons), process (summons), serve (deliver a legal instrument),

summon, venire, warrant (judicial writ). SEE MAIN ENTRY
subpoema duces tecum SEE MAIN ENTRY
subrent lease, rent, sublease, sublet
subreption deceit, fraud, misstatement. SEE MAIN ENTRY
subreptitious collusive
subrogate change, replace, succeed (follow), supersede, supplant
subrogation replacement. SEE MAIN ENTRY
subscribe attest, bear (adduce), close (agree), corroborate, enroll, hear (give attention to), join (associate oneself with), notarize, register, sign, subsidize. SEE MAIN ENTRY
subscribe to abide, accede (concede), advocate, agree (comply), assent, assure (insure), authorize, coincide (concur), concur (agree), contribute (assist), countenance, defer (yield in judgment), embrace (accept), espouse, indorse, maintain (sustain), profess (avow), promote (organize), sanction, sponsor
subscriber affiant, contributor (giver), donor, notary public, proponent, surety (guarantor), undersigned
subscribere sign
subscript addendum, codicil, rider
subscription advance (allowance), advocacy, affirmance (judicial sanction), aid (help), confirmation, consent, favor (sanction), grant, sanction (permission), vow. SEE MAIN ENTRY
subsection department, subheading
subsequent consecutive, derivative, ensuing, future, prospective, proximate, secondary, successive. SEE MAIN ENTRY
subsequent meditation hindsight
subsequent reflection hindsight
subsequently thereafter
subsequently set down a savoir
subserve aid, assist, avail (be of use), foster, inure (benefit), pander, promote (organize), subsidize
subservience adhesion (loyalty), bondage, homage, servitude
subserviency subjection
subservient dependent, inferior (lower in position), obedient, obeisant, obsequious, passive, pliant, subordinate, subsidiary. SEE MAIN ENTRY
subside decrease, diminish, ebb, lessen. SEE MAIN ENTRY
subsidence decline, decrease, descent (declination), lull, remission
subsidiarius subsidiary
subsidiary affiliate, appurtenance, appurtenant, chapter (branch), circumstantial, contingent, derivative, extraneous, extrinsic, incident, incidental, inferior (lower in position), minor, offshoot, organ, pendent, secondary, slight, subaltern, subordinate, subservient, supplementary. SEE MAIN ENTRY
subsidiary group minority (outnumbered group)
subsidiary law code
subsidium help, relief (aid), support (assistance)
subsidization alimony, pension
subsidize assist, capitalize (provide capital), contribute (supply), endow, finance, fund, maintain (sustain), pay, supplement, support (assist). SEE MAIN ENTRY
subsidize again refinance
subsidizer backer
subsidy aid (help), aid (subsistence), alimony, annuity, assistance, benefit

(conferment), commission *(fee)*, consideration *(recompense)*, contribution *(donation)*, donation, endowment, grant, loan, maintenance *(support of spouse)*, payment *(act of paying)*, pension, perquisite. SEE MAIN ENTRY

subsist continue *(persevere)*, endure *(last)*, exist, last, remain *(continue)*, stay *(continue)*. SEE MAIN ENTRY

subsist of contain *(comprise)*

subsistence aid *(help)*, livelihood, maintenance *(support of spouse)*, subsidy, support *(assistance)*, sustenance

subsistence level austerity, poverty

subsistent extant, inherent

subsistere halt

subspecies class

substance amount *(quantity)*, article *(commodity)*, body *(main part)*, bulk, capsule, center *(essence)*, connotation, consequence *(significance)*, construction, content *(meaning)*, contents, contour *(shape)*, cornerstone, corpus, element, essence, gist *(ground for a suit)*, gravamen, import, importance, main point, materiality *(physical existence)*, meaning, money, object, point *(purpose)*, property *(possessions)*, reality, significance, signification, spirit, structure *(composition)*, sum *(tally)*, value. SEE MAIN ENTRY

substance of a charge complaint

substandard deficient, perfunctory, poor *(inferior in quality)*

substantiable deductible *(provable)*

substantial actual, appreciable, capacious, cardinal *(basic)*, cogent, cohesive *(compact)*, concrete, considerable, convincing, corporal, corporeal, critical *(crucial)*, durable, far reaching, firm, grave *(important)*, important *(significant)*, major, material *(important)*, material *(physical)*, meritorious, momentous, opulent, organic, outstanding *(prominent)*, physical, pithy, prodigious *(enormous)*, secure *(sound)*, solid *(sound)*, sound, stable, staunch, substantive, tangible, valid. SEE MAIN ENTRY

substantial cause gravamen

substantial cause shown SEE MAIN ENTRY

substantial form contour *(shape)*

substantial meaning connotation, content *(meaning)*, gist *(substance)*

substantial number bulk

substantial part bulk

substantial part of a complaint gist *(ground for a suit)*

substantial quantity bulk

substantial rise of prices inflation *(decrease in value of currency)*

substantiality certainty, character *(personal quality)*, cornerstone, corpus, embodiment, importance, materiality *(consequence)*, materiality *(physical existence)*, reality, significance, strength

substantialize embody, substantiate

substantially as a rule

substantially true candid

substantialness materiality *(physical existence)*, reality, strength

substantiate affirm *(uphold)*, attest, bear *(adduce)*, cite *(state)*, corroborate, demonstrate *(establish)*, document, establish *(show)*, maintain *(sustain)*, probate, prove, quote, realize *(make real)*, seal *(solemnize)*, support *(corroborate)*, sustain *(confirm)*, uphold, validate, verify *(confirm)*, witness *(attest to)*. SEE MAIN ENTRY

substantiated incident fact

substantiation affirmance *(authentication)*, affirmation, attestation, certification

(attested copy), confirmation, corroboration, documentation, evidence, jurat, proof, ratification, realization, reference *(citation)*, reference *(recommendation)*, support *(corroboration)*. SEE MAIN ENTRY

substantiative demonstrative *(illustrative)*. SEE MAIN ENTRY

substantive actual, appreciable, cardinal *(basic)*, concrete, corporeal, de facto, necessary *(required)*, organic, physical, ponderable, solid *(sound)*, substantial, tangible, virtual

substantive issue SEE MAIN ENTRY

substituere replace

substantive issue SEE MAIN ENTRY

substitutable equivalent, expendable

substitute agent, alienate *(transfer title)*, alternate *(take turns)*, change, commute, conduit *(intermediary)*, convert *(change use)*, cover *(provide for)*, delegate, deputy, devolve, disjunctive *(alternative)*, displace *(replace)*, exchange, false *(not genuine)*, imitation, liaison, offset, plenipotentiary, procurator, provisional, proxy, quid pro quo, replace, replacement, representative *(proxy)*, secondary, stopgap, succedaneum, supersede, supplant, surrogate, transform. SEE MAIN ENTRY

substitute for succeed *(follow)*

substitutes choice *(alternatives offered)*

substituting for acting

substitution contribution *(indemnification)*, cover *(substitute)*, devolution, exchange, novation, preemption, proxy, recompense, replacement, representation *(acting for others)*, representative *(proxy)*, stopgap, subrogation, substitute, succedaneum

substitution of counsel SEE MAIN ENTRY

substitutional disjunctive *(alternative)*, surrogate

substitutive convertible, disjunctive *(alternative)*

substructure foundation *(basis)*

subsume classify, comprise, encompass *(include)*, include, pigeonhole

subterfuge artifice, bad faith, color *(deceptive appearance)*, concealment, contrivance, cover *(pretext)*, deception, evasion, excuse, expedient, false pretense, hoax, imposture, machination, maneuver *(trick)*, pretense *(pretext)*, pretext, ruse, scheme, stratagem. SEE MAIN ENTRY

subterranean clandestine

subtile imponderable, subtle *(refined)*

subtilis acute, exact

subtilize clarify, differentiate

subtitle caption

subtle artful, discreet, furtive, impalpable, inconspicuous, insidious, obscure *(faint)*, politic, recondite, sly, surreptitious. SEE MAIN ENTRY

subtle communication reference *(allusion)*

subtle difference differential, nuance

subtle maneuver device *(contrivance)*

subtlety discretion *(quality of being discreet)*, evasion, nuance, subterfuge, technicality

subtract abridge *(shorten)*, curtail, decrease, deduct *(reduce)*, dilute, diminish, discount *(reduce)*, eradicate, except *(exclude)*, excise *(cut away)*, lessen, minimize, rebate, remove *(eliminate)*, retrench, withdraw

subtract from derogate

subtraction curtailment, decrease, decrement, deduction *(diminution)*, discount, exception *(exclusion)*, removal. SEE MAIN ENTRY

suburbs vicinity

subvenire assist, help

subvention alimony, annuity, benefit *(conferment)*, contribution *(donation)*, dispensation *(act of dispensing)*, donation, grant, help, pension, subsidy

subventionize subsidize

subversion bad faith, counterargument, disloyalty, mutiny, rebellion, revolt, sedition, treason. SEE MAIN ENTRY

subversionary harmful

subversive activities subversion

subversive activity bad faith, disloyalty, espionage

subversives SEE MAIN ENTRY

subvert corrupt, destroy *(efface)*, disturb, harm, overthrow, overturn, pervert, supplant, upset. SEE MAIN ENTRY

subverter insurgent

subvertere abolish, overturn, subvert, upset

succedaneum alternative *(substitute)*, stopgap. SEE MAIN ENTRY

succedere succeed *(follow)*, supersede

succeed accomplish, attain, avail *(bring about)*, carry *(succeed)*, complete, discharge *(perform)*, dispatch *(dispose of)*, displace *(replace)*, effectuate, ensue, execute *(accomplish)*, gain, implement, pass *(satisfy requirements)*, prevail *(triumph)*, reach, replace, supersede, supervene, supplant. SEE MAIN ENTRY

succeed in reaching attain, earn

succeed to inherit

succeeding consecutive, ensuing, future, proximate, subsequent, successive

succeeding generation descendant

succeeding generations posterity, progeny

success advantage, benefit *(betterment)*, fruition, progress, prosperity, satisfaction *(fulfilment)*, welfare

successful auspicious, effective *(efficient)*, felicitous, lucrative, operative, prevailing *(having superior force)*, profitable, prosperous. SEE MAIN ENTRY

successful remedial treatment cure

successfulness prosperity

succession birth *(lineage)*, bloodline, chain *(series)*, continuity, cycle, devolution, frequency, hierarchy *(arrangement in a series)*, sequence, subrogation. SEE MAIN ENTRY

succession of acts course

succession of property inheritance

succession of property rights devolution

successions vicissitudes

successive consecutive, direct *(uninterrupted)*, disjunctive *(tending to disjoin)*, ensuing, periodic, progressive *(going forward)*, regular *(orderly)*, repeated. SEE MAIN ENTRY

successive phases vicissitudes

successive portion installment, serial

successive relationship privity

successively gaining in force cumulative *(increasing)*

successively waxing in force cumulative *(increasing)*

successiveness continuity

successless disappointed, unavailing

successlessness miscarriage

successor descendant, devisee, heir, offspring, replacement, transferee. SEE MAIN ENTRY

successors posterity

successorship succession

succinct brief, compact (pithy), concise, laconic, pithy, proverbial, sententious. SEE MAIN ENTRY

succor abet, accommodation (backing), aid (help), aid, alleviate, assist, assistance, avail (be of use), bear (support), benefit (betterment), benevolence (act of kindness), bolster, contribute (assist), contribution (donation), favor, foster, help (noun), help (verb), nurture, relief (aid), relieve (give aid), remedy, serve (assist), service (assistance), soothe, support (assistance)

succorer benefactor, good samaritan, samaritan, sponsor

succulent palatable, sapid

succumb accede (concede), cede, comply, concede, decease, expire, fail (lose), hear (give attention to), languish, lose (undergo defeat), obey, perish, quit (discontinue), relent, submit (yield), surrender (yield), yield (submit). SEE MAIN ENTRY

succumb to death die

succumbere succumb

succurrere help

succeed in winning beat (defeat)

such being the case consequently

sudden brief, immediate (at once), impulsive (rash), precipitate, spontaneous, summary, unanticipated, unexpected, unforeseeable, unforeseen

sudden attack assault, bombshell, foray

sudden burst bombshell

sudden contact collision (accident)

sudden death fatality

sudden desire impulse

sudden excursion outburst

sudden fear consternation, panic

sudden force impulse

sudden happening accident (chance occurrence)

sudden misfortune disaster

sudden peril emergency

sudden terror fright

suddenness dispatch (promptness)

sue appeal, call (appeal to), claim (demand), complain (charge), importune, litigate, prosecute (charge). SEE MAIN ENTRY

sue a third party implead

sue for request

suffer abide, allow (endure), bear (tolerate), consent, forbear, languish, let (permit), permit, recognize (acknowledge), sanction, tolerate, vouchsafe. SEE MAIN ENTRY

suffer a deprivation lose (be deprived of)

suffer a relapse relapse

suffer by comparison lose (undergo defeat)

suffer death die

suffer defeat lose (undergo defeat), quit (discontinue), yield (submit)

suffer loss decrease, lose (be deprived of)

suffer pain endure (suffer)

suffer privation lack

suffer to occur allow (endure), authorize

sufferable allowable, permissible

sufferance acquiescence, charter (sanction), consent, dispensation (exception), franchise (license), indulgence, leave (permission), longanimity, resignation (passive acceptance), sanction (permission), tolerance, understanding (tolerance). SEE MAIN ENTRY

suffered allowable

sufferer victim

suffering adversity, discipline (punishment), distress (anguish), hardship, misfortune, pain, prostration, sanction (punishment), sufferance, toll (effect), trouble

suffering privation poor (underprivileged)

suffice avail (bring about), bear (tolerate), fulfill, satisfy (fulfill)

suffice to defray cover (provide for)

sufficience quorum

sufficiency admissibility, competence (ability), minimum, quorum, satisfaction (fulfilment), store (depository). SEE MAIN ENTRY

sufficient adequate, ample, commensurate, competent, fair (satisfactory), operative, suitable. SEE MAIN ENTRY

sufficient amount minimum

sufficient evidence proof

sufficient for the purpose adequate

sufficient foundation SEE MAIN ENTRY

sufficient in law legal

sufficient notice adequate notice

sufficient number quorum

sufficient on its face prima facie (legally sufficient)

sufficient on the pleadings prima facie (legally sufficient)

sufficient proof SEE MAIN ENTRY

sufficient quantity quorum

sufficient to make out a case prima facie (legally sufficient)

sufficiently strong prima facie (legally sufficient)

sufficientness sufficiency

sufficing adequate, commensurate

suffisant complacent

suffix codicil

sufflate inflate

sufflation inflation (increase)

suffocate extinguish, impede, repress, stifle

suffocating deadly, oppressive

suffragari favor, support (assist)

suffrage discretion (power of choice), franchise (right to vote). SEE MAIN ENTRY

suffragia election (choice)

suffragium suffrage, vote

suffragium ferre vote

suffuscus dun

suffuse penetrate, permeate, pervade, spread

sugary nectarious

suggest admonish (advise), advise, advocate, allude, bespeak, charge (instruct on the law), coax, connote, convey (communicate), counsel, denote, evidence, hint, hold out (deliberate on an offer), implicate, imply, indicate, instruct (direct), mention, nominate, offer (propose), pose (propound), postulate, present (introduce), proffer, promise (raise expectations), prompt, propose, propound, purport, raise (advance), recommend, refer (direct attention), remark, remind, signify (denote), submit (give). SEE MAIN ENTRY

suggest a proposed claim counsel

suggest a proposed contention counsel

suggest conclusions of law charge (instruct on the law)

suggest itself occur (come to mind)

suggested constructive (inferential), implicit, implied, tacit

suggested meaning implication (inference)

suggested plan suggestion

suggester catalyst, special interest

suggestibility credulity

suggestible open (persuasible), pliant

suggesting advisory, demonstrative (illustrative), precatory

suggestio falsi color (deceptive appearance)

suggestion advice, advocacy, connotation, expedient, guidance, hint, hypothesis, implication (inference), indicant, indication, innuendo, insinuation, intimation, mention (reference), notion, nuance, plan, possibility, postulate, proposal (suggestion), proposition, recommendation, reference (allusion), reminder, request, suspicion (uncertainty), tip (clue). SEE MAIN ENTRY

suggestive allusive, apparent (presumptive), circumstantial, demonstrative (illustrative), implicit, leading (guiding), lewd, portentous (ominous), precatory, provocative, prurient, salacious. SEE MAIN ENTRY

sui generus SEE MAIN ENTRY

sui iuris sovereign (independent)

suit accommodate, action (proceeding), agree (comply), calculate, call (appeal), case (lawsuit), cause (lawsuit), chain (series), claim (legal demand), clothe, comport (agree with), concur (agree), conform, entreaty, matter (case), proceeding, prosecution (criminal trial), satisfy (fulfill), trial (legal proceeding). SEE MAIN ENTRY

suit at law action (proceeding), case (lawsuit), cause (lawsuit), lawsuit, matter (case), proceeding, trial (legal proceeding)

suit in equity lawsuit

suit in law action (proceeding), controversy (lawsuit), suit

suit one's purpose avail (be of use)

suit to extinguish the equity of redemption foreclosure

suitability admissibility, aptitude, competence (ability), decorum, expedience, propriety (appropriateness), qualification (fitness), relevance, timeliness, use, utility (usefulness)

suitable adequate, admissible, allowable, allowed, applicable, apposite, appropriate, available, commensurate, competent, condign, consonant, constructive (creative), convenient, correlative, desirable (qualified), disposable, eligible, entitled, fair (just), fair (satisfactory), favorable (advantageous), felicitous, fit, fitting, habitable, harmonious, just, justifiable, opportune, pertinent, practical, prima facie (legally sufficient), proper, qualified (competent), reasonable (fair), relative (relevant), relevant, right (suitable), rightful, scient\[sic\], seasonable, valuable, viable. SEE MAIN ENTRY

suitable circumstance chance (fortuity), opportunity

suitable for living in habitable

suitable for use functional

suitable notice adequate notice

suitable occasion opportunity

suitable time occasion, opportunity, timeliness

suitableness decorum, expedience, propriety (appropriateness), qualification (fitness), relevance

suite chain (series)

suited agreed (harmonized), apposite, appropriate, capable, convenient, correlative, fit, fitting, opportune, proper, sciential, suitable

suited to youth juvenile

suitedness qualification *(fitness)*

suiting congruous, felicitous, harmonious

suitor appellant, claimant, complainant, contender, contestant, litigant, party *(litigant)*, plaintiff, special interest. SEE MAIN ENTRY

sulk brood

sulky resentful, restive

sullen despondent, resentful, restive

sullied blemished, marred, tainted *(contaminated)*

sully brand *(stigmatize)*, contaminate, debauch, deface, defame, denigrate, depreciate, derogate, disapprove *(condemn)*, disgrace, disparage, humiliate, infect, pillory, pollute, smear, stain, taint *(contaminate)*, tarnish, vitiate. SEE MAIN ENTRY

sullying defilement

sum aggregate, amount *(quantity)*, amount *(result)*, computation, consideration *(recompense)*, content *(meaning)*, corpus, entirety, expenditure, expense *(cost)*, face amount, face value *(price)*, import, principal *(capital sum)*, quantity, substance *(essential nature)*, totality. SEE MAIN ENTRY

sum and substance capsule, center *(essence)*, content *(meaning)*, context, corpus, gist *(ground for a suit)*, gist *(substance)*, gravamen, materiality *(consequence)*, scenario

sum asked for cost *(price)*

sum charged expense *(cost)*

sum derived from a sale proceeds

sum entrusted loan

sum of money fund

sum of money borrowed loan

sum of money lent loan

sum owed debt

sum owing debit

sum paid for carrying a passenger fare

sum shown face amount

sum stated face amount

sum total aggregate, amount *(result)*, corpus, in solido, principal *(capital sum)*, quantity, sum *(total)*, whole

sum up condense, criticize *(evaluate)*, digest *(summarize)*, recapitulate, repeat *(state again)*, review

sumere presume

sumless innumerable, myriad

summa amount *(quantity)*

summarily dispossess eject *(evict)*

summariness dispatch *(promptness)*

summarium epitome, summary, synopsis

summarization narration. SEE MAIN ENTRY

summarize abridge *(shorten)*, condense, extract, lessen, recapitulate, recount, repeat *(state again)*, review

summarized brief, compact *(pithy)*, concise, laconic, sententious

summary abridgment *(condensation)*, abstract, account *(report)*, brief *(adjective)*, brief *(noun)*, capsule, compact *(pithy)*, compendium, concise, cursory, decisive, digest, direct *(forthright)*, narration, pandect *(treatise)*, paraphrase, pithy, prompt, proposal *(report)*, prospectus, recital, report *(detailed account)*, restatement, scenario, statement, succinct, sum *(tally)*, synopsis. SEE MAIN ENTRY

summary of facts story *(narrative)*

summary on the law brief

summary punishment by mob lynch law

summate sum

summation account *(report)*, amount *(sum)*, computation, corpus, denouement, outline *(synopsis)*, synopsis

summed up compact *(pithy)*

summing up recital

summisse respectfully

summit caucus, ceiling, culmination, meeting *(conference)*, panel *(discussion group)*, paragon, parley, pinnacle

summit conference parley

summit talk parley

summital cardinal *(basic)*

summitry negotiation

summon convene, evoke, invoke, prosecute *(charge)*, request, require *(compel)*, serve *(deliver a legal instrument)*, subpoena. SEE MAIN ENTRY

summon back recall *(call back)*

summon by incantation invoke

summon forth call *(summon)*, educe, elicit, evoke

summon to court subpoena

summon up evoke, recall *(remember)*, recollect, remember

summons charge *(accusation)*, charge *(command)*, direction *(order)*, invitation, monition *(legal summons)*, subpoena, venire, warrant *(judicial writ)*. SEE MAIN ENTRY

summons to appear and answer monition *(legal summons)*

summus ascendant, extreme *(last)*, paramount, unqualified *(unlimited)*

sumptio assumption *(supposition)*, postulate

sumptious profuse

sumptuary financial, pecuniary

sumptuous elaborate

sumptus outlay, waste

sumptus minuere retrench

sunder bifurcate, break *(separate)*, disband, discontinue *(abandon)*, discontinue *(break continuity)*, disengage, disjoint, disrupt, dissociate, dissolve *(separate)*, divide *(separate)*, divorce, estrange, interrupt, isolate, lancinate, luxate, part *(separate)*, rend, separate, sever, split, subdivide

sunderance disassociation, division *(act of dividing)*, interruption, severance, split

sundered disconnected, discrete, separate

sundering estrangement, separation

sundry composite, diverse, manifold, miscellaneous, multiple, several *(plural)*

sung famous

sunset law SEE MAIN ENTRY

sunshine laws SEE MAIN ENTRY

suo arbitrio discretion *(power of choice)*

super superlative

superable possible

superabundance boom *(prosperity)*, plethora, redundancy, sufficiency, surfeit, surplus

superabundant copious, excess, excessive, expendable, inordinate, multiple, needless, redundant, superfluous, unwarranted

superadd compound, supplement

superadded additional

superannuate SEE MAIN ENTRY

superannuated antique, old, outdated, outmoded, powerless

superare beat *(defeat)*, defeat, outweigh, predominate *(command)*, prevail *(triumph)*

superb meritorious, portentous *(eliciting amazement)*, preferential, premium, prime *(most valuable)*, professional *(stellar)*, sterling

superbia intolerance

superbire rampant

superbus supercilious

supercharge overload

supercherie bunko

supercilious cynical, disdainful, insolent, orgulous, presumptuous, proud *(conceited)*. SEE MAIN ENTRY

superciliousness disdain, disrespect, pride

superego conscience

supereminence eminence, primacy

supereminent cardinal *(outstanding)*, master, outstanding *(prominent)*, paramount, primary, prime *(most valuable)*, principal

supererogate surpass

supererogative excess, superfluous, unnecessary

supererogatory excess, excessive, expendable, inordinate, needless, nonessential, superfluous, unnecessary

superexcellent superior *(excellent)*, superlative

superficial artificial, careless, casual, cursory, frivolous, inconsequential, insubstantial, minor, nominal, nugatory, null *(insignificant)*, perfunctory, pretentious *(ostentatious)*, remote *(small)*, trivial. SEE MAIN ENTRY

superficially pro forma

superficies area *(surface)*

superfine best, premium, subtle *(refined)*, superlative

superfluity balance *(amount in excess)*, boom *(prosperity)*, exaggeration, plethora, redundancy, remainder *(remaining part)*, surfeit, surplus

superfluous disproportionate, excess, excessive, expendable, extraneous, gratuitous *(unwarranted)*, inordinate, needless, nonessential, profuse, redundant, undue *(excessive)*, unessential, unnecessary, unwarranted. SEE MAIN ENTRY

superfluousness balance *(amount in excess)*, exaggeration, plethora, tautology

superfund SEE MAIN ENTRY

superhighway causeway

superimpose overlap

superinduce affect, cause

superintend administer *(conduct)*, check *(inspect)*, conduct, control *(regulate)*, direct *(supervise)*, discipline *(control)*, govern, handle *(manage)*, manage, officiate, operate, oversee, patrol, police, prescribe, preside, regulate *(manage)*, rule *(govern)*. SEE MAIN ENTRY

superintendence administration, agency *(legal relationship)*, auspices, charge *(custody)*, control *(supervision)*, custody *(supervision)*, direction *(guidance)*, government *(administration)*, jurisdiction, management *(supervision)*, occupation *(possession)*, oversight *(control)*, regulation *(management)*, safekeeping, supervision, supremacy, surveillance

superintendency generalship

superintendent caretaker *(one caring for property)*, caretaker *(one fulfilling the function of office)*, director, employer, guardian, official, principal *(director)*, procurator, warden. SEE MAIN ENTRY

superintendents management *(directorate)*

superintending administrative

superior absolute *(ideal)*

superior ascendant

superior best, chief, disdainful, dominant, employer, important *(significant)*, inflated *(vain)*, irresistible, meritorious, notable, outstanding *(prominent)*,

paramount, predominant, preferable, preferential, premium, prime *(most valuable)*, principal *(director)*. SEE MAIN ENTRY
superior prior
superior professional *(stellar)*, select, special, sterling, superlative, unapproachable, valuable
superior group elite
superior individual paragon
superior situation advantage
superiority advantage, dint, distinction *(reputation)*, edge *(advantage)*, eminence, hegemony, importance, influence, merit, precedence, predominance, preponderance, prestige, pride, primacy, priority, quality *(excellence)*, status, strength, stress *(accent)*, supremacy, value
superiority in number plurality
superlatio exaggeration
superlative absolute *(ideal)*, best, bombast, cardinal *(outstanding)*, exaggeration, meritorious, outstanding *(prominent)*, paramount, portentous *(eliciting amazement)*, premium, prime *(most valuable)*, rare, sterling, superior *(excellent)*, unapproachable, utmost. SEE MAIN ENTRY
supernatural mysterious, peculiar *(curious)*, uncanny
supernatural being spirit
supernormal best, extraordinary, mysterious, prodigious *(amazing)*, unusual
supernumerary ancillary *(auxiliary)*, copious, excess, excessive, expendable, needless, redundant, superfluous, unwarranted
superplus balance *(amount in excess)*, surplus
supersaturate overload
supersaturated inordinate
supersaturation overage, plethora, surfeit, surplus
superscription caption, heading, inscription, label, rubric *(title)*, title *(designation)*
supersede abolish, abrogate *(rescind)*, accede *(succeed)*, annul, disinherit, dislodge, displace *(replace)*, leave *(allow to remain)*, override, overrule, replace, succeed *(follow)*, supplant, upset. SEE MAIN ENTRY
superseded null *(invalid)*, null and void, outdated, outmoded
supersedence preemption
superseder alternative *(substitute)*
supersedere forbear
superseding cause SEE MAIN ENTRY
supersedure replacement, subrogation
supersession cancellation, defeasance, preemption, replacement, subrogation
superstruct build *(construct)*
superstructure building *(structure)*
supervacaneous superfluous
supervacaneus redundant, superfluous, unnecessary
supervacuus superfluous, unnecessary
supervene ensue, succeed *(follow)*. SEE MAIN ENTRY
supervenient additional, extraneous, incidental, needless, nonessential, supplementary
supervenire intervene, supervene
supervention preemption
supervise administer *(conduct)*, care *(regard)*, check *(inspect)*, conduct, control *(regulate)*, discipline *(control)*, govern, handle *(manage)*, manage, moderate *(preside over)*, officiate, operate, overlook *(superintend)*, oversee, police, predominate *(command)*, preside, regulate *(manage)*, rule *(govern)*, superintend. SEE MAIN ENTRY

supervise communications censor
supervising administrative, leading *(guiding)*
supervising director chief
supervision administration, agency *(legal relationship)*, auspices, charge *(custody)*, direction *(guidance)*, generalship, guidance, jurisdiction, observation, oversight *(carelessness)*, oversight *(control)*, protection, regime, regulation *(management)*, safekeeping, supremacy, surveillance. SEE MAIN ENTRY
supervisor administrator, caretaker *(one caring for property)*, chairman, director, employer, guardian, official, principal *(director)*, procurator, superintendent, warden
supervisor of accounts comptroller
supervisor of an estate administrator
supervisors management *(directorate)*
supervisorship generalship
supervisory administrative, leading *(guiding)*, predominant
supervisory official warden
supine inactive, indolent, insensible, languid, lifeless *(dull)*, otiose, passive, phlegmatic, ponderous, stagnant, torpid
supineness disinterest *(lack of interest)*, inertia, languor, sloth
suppeditare defray, furnish, provide *(supply)*, supply
suppeditate supply
supplant abolish, accede *(succeed)*, dislodge, displace *(replace)*, replace, succeed *(follow)*, supersede. SEE MAIN ENTRY
supplantation replacement, subrogation
supplanter alternative *(substitute)*, replacement, substitute
supplanting exchange, preemption, subrogation
supple flexible, malleable, obedient, passive, pliable, pliant, servile, yielding
supplement accrue *(increase)*, addendum, addition, additive, adjunct, affix, aid, allonge, amendment *(correction)*, amendment *(legislation)*, annex *(add)*, append, appurtenance, attach *(join)*, attachment *(thing affixed)*, augmentation, boom *(increase)*, codicil, complement, compound, corollary, correlate, enlarge, expand, extend *(enlarge)*, increase, increment, insertion, offshoot, reinforce, reinforcement, replenish, rider. SEE MAIN ENTRY
supplement to a will codicil
supplemental additional, ancillary *(auxiliary)*, collateral *(accompanying)*, expendable, extrinsic, incidental, nonessential, pendent, subsidiary, superfluous, supplementary, unnecessary. SEE MAIN ENTRY
supplementary additional, ancillary *(auxiliary)*, collateral *(accompanying)*, expendable, extraneous, incidental, nonessential, subsidiary, unnecessary. SEE MAIN ENTRY
supplementary device attachment *(thing affixed)*
supplementation accession *(annexation)*, accession *(enlargement)*, addendum, continuation *(resumption)*, development *(progression)*, extension *(expansion)*, insertion
supplementum reinforcement
supplere replenish
suppletive supplementary
suppletory supplementary
supplex petitioner
suppliant special interest, suitor
supplicant petitioner, suitor
supplicate call *(appeal to)*, desire,

importune, plead *(implore)*, pray, press *(beseech)*, request, solicit, sue
supplication call *(appeal)*, entreaty, intercession, prayer, request
supplicatory solicitous
supplicium execute *(sentence to death)*
supplied with arms armed
supplier contributor *(giver)*, materialman. SEE MAIN ENTRY
supplies equipment, goods, merchandise, paraphernalia *(apparatus)*, store *(depository)*, sustenance
supply bear *(yield)*, bestow, clothe, contribute *(supply)*, cumulation, dole, endow, endue, fund *(noun)*, fund *(verb)*, furnish, give *(grant)*, hoard, lend, maintain *(sustain)*, pander, present *(make a gift)*, provision *(something provided)*, quantity, recruit, replenish, reserve, resource, stock *(store)*, stock in trade, store *(depository)*, sufficiency, yield *(produce a return)*. SEE MAIN ENTRY
supply accommodations for lodge *(house)*
supply aid abet, assist, bear *(support)*, capitalize *(provide capital)*, inure *(benefit)*, lend, nurture, serve *(assist)*, subsidize
supply an equivalent replace
supply base headquarters
supply deficiencies replenish
supply funds loan
supply money finance
supply on hand stock in trade
supply or furnish with reference index *(relate)*
supply support bear *(support)*, capitalize *(provide capital)*, subsidize
supply the necessities of support *(assist)*
supply the wants of accommodate
supply with a subsidy capitalize *(provide capital)*
supply with an epithet call *(title)*
supply with means enable, endow
supplying commercial, donative
supplying another's place representation *(acting for others)*
supponere foist, forge *(counterfeit)*
support abet, abettor, accommodate, accommodation *(backing)*, adhere *(maintain loyalty)*, adhesion *(loyalty)*, advantage, advocacy, advocate *(espouser)*, advocate, affirm *(uphold)*, aid *(help)*, aid *(subsistence)*, aid, alimony, allegiance, allow *(authorize)*, approval, approve, assist, assistance, attest, auspices, base *(foundation)*, basis, bear *(tolerate)*, behalf, benevolence *(act of kindness)*, bolster, bulwark, capitalize *(provide capital)*, care *(regard)*, certification *(attested copy)*, charity, charter *(sanction)*, choose, concur *(agree)*, confederate, confirm, confirmation, conform, consent *(noun)*, consent *(verb)*, conservation, contribute *(assist)*, cornerstone, corroborate, corroboration, cosign, countenance, countersign, coverage *(insurance)*, defend, defense, demonstrate *(establish)*, document, documentation, ecology, embrace *(accept)*, enable, encourage, endorse, enforcement, espouse, expedite, favor *(sanction)*, favor, fealty, finance, foster, foundation *(basis)*, frame *(structure)*, goodwill, grant *(concede)*, ground, guarantee, guaranty, help *(noun)*, help *(verb)*, indorse, indorsement, invest *(fund)*, involve *(participate)*, justify, keep *(continue)*, keep *(shelter)*, let *(permit)*, livelihood, loyalty,

mainstay, maintain *(sustain)*, nurture, palliate *(excuse)*, partisan, pass *(approve)*, patronage *(support)*, patronize *(trade with)*, pay *(noun)*, pay *(verb)*, pension, preservation, preserve, promote *(organize)*, protect, protection, prove, quote, reassure, recommend, recommendation, reinforce, reinforcement, reliance, relief *(aid)*, resource, safekeeping, sanction *(permission)*, sanction, seal *(solemnize)*, security *(safety)*, service *(assistance)*, shelter *(protection)*, side, sponsor, subscribe *(promise)*, subsidize, substantiate, sustain *(confirm)*, sustenance, underwrite, uphold, verify *(confirm)*, vouch. SEE MAIN ENTRY

support again refinance
support an analogy correspond *(be equivalent)*
support the expense of disburse *(pay out)*, expend *(disburse)*
supportability corroboration
supportable convincing, deductible *(provable)*, defensible, provable, tenable
supportable by law valid
supported by authority allowed
supporter abettor, accomplice, advocate *(espouser)*, apologist, assistant, backer, benefactor, coactor, coadjutant, coconspirator, cohort, confederate, contributor *(giver)*, copartner *(coconspirator)*, disciple, partisan, patron *(influential supporter)*, patron *(regular customer)*, promoter, proponent, surety *(guarantor)*, undersigned
supporting ancillary *(auxiliary)*, instigation, propitious, underlying
supporting evidence corroboration, documentation. SEE MAIN ENTRY
supporting structure foundation *(basis)*
supportive benevolent, demonstrative *(illustrative)*
supposable apparent *(presumptive)*, colorable *(plausible)*, constructive *(inferential)*, ostensible, possible, theoretical
supposal assumption *(supposition)*, condition *(contingent provision)*, conjecture, deduction *(conclusion)*, estimate *(idea)*, estimation *(calculation)*, generalization, hypothesis, inference, postulate, supposition
suppose anticipate *(expect)*, deduce, deduct *(conclude by reasoning)*, deem, estimate, expect *(consider probable)*, gauge, generalize, guess, infer, opine, presume, presuppose, reason *(conclude)*, speculate *(conjecture)*, surmise, suspect *(think)*. SEE MAIN ENTRY
supposed apparent *(presumptive)*, assumed *(inferred)*, hypothetical, ostensible, plausible, presumptive, probable, putative
supposedly reputedly
supposition concept, condition *(contingent provision)*, conjecture, conviction *(persuasion)*, deduction *(conclusion)*, estimate *(idea)*, estimation *(calculation)*, generalization, ground, hypothesis, idea, inference, notion, opinion *(belief)*, perception, postulate, presumption, prognosis, proposition, speculation *(conjecture)*, suspicion *(uncertainty)*, theory, thesis. SEE MAIN ENTRY
suppositional apparent *(presumptive)*, assumed *(inferred)*, disputable, doubtful, dubious, hypothetical, ill-founded, illusory, indefinite, moot, plausible, presumptive, speculative, theoretical, unfounded, unsupported

suppositionary apparent *(presumptive)*
suppositious debatable
suppositious check bad check
supposititious presumptive, unfounded, unsupported
suppositive apparent *(presumptive)*, hypothetical, presumptive, theoretical
suppress abate *(lessen)*, abolish, allay, arrest *(stop)*, ban, beat *(defeat)*, camouflage, censor, check *(restrain)*, cloak, clog, coerce, conceal, condemn *(ban)*, confine, constrain *(restrain)*, constrict *(inhibit)*, contain *(restrain)*, control *(restrain)*, counter, countervail, curb, debar, defeat, detain *(restrain)*, disadvantage, eliminate *(eradicate)*, enjoin, ensconce, expurgate, extinguish, fetter, forestall, hamper, hide, hold up *(delay)*, inhibit, keep *(restrain)*, limit, moderate *(temper)*, negate, obliterate, obscure, obstruct, overthrow, overturn, overwhelm, palliate *(abate)*, prevail *(triumph)*, prohibit, quash, repress, restrain, restrict, revoke, shroud, stay *(halt)*, stem *(check)*, stifle, stop, strangle, subdue, subject, subjugate, trammel, withhold. SEE MAIN ENTRY
suppress competition monopolize
suppressed arrested *(checked)*, clandestine, hidden, inadmissible, inconspicuous, undisclosed
suppressing limiting
suppressio veri color *(deceptive appearance)*
suppression abatement *(reduction)*, bar *(obstruction)*, censorship, concealment, constraint *(restriction)*, control *(restriction)*, countermand, defeasance, deterrence, deterrent, disadvantage, dissolution *(termination)*, fetter, obstacle, oppression, prohibition, quota, removal, restraint, servitude
suppression of sound silence
suppression of the truth concealment
suppression of truth bad faith, false pretense, misstatement, story *(falsehood)*
suppressive dictatorial, prohibitive *(restrictive)*, restrictive
supprimere suppress, withhold
supputation census
supremacy advantage, authority *(power)*, capacity *(authority)*, dominance, dominion *(supreme authority)*, eminence, force *(strength)*, hegemony, importance, influence, possession *(ownership)*, power, precedence, predominance, primacy, priority, regime, significance. SEE MAIN ENTRY
supreme absolute *(ideal)*, best, cardinal *(outstanding)*, central *(essential)*, crucial, definitive, dictatorial, dominant, final, important *(significant)*, influential, leading *(ranking first)*, major, master, meritorious, omnipotent, outstanding *(prominent)*, paramount, predominant, prevailing *(having superior force)*, primary, prime *(most valuable)*, principal, sovereign *(absolute)*, superior *(excellent)*, superlative, ultimate, unapproachable, utmost
supreme authority predominance, supremacy
supreme contempt disdain
supreme law constitution
supremely particularly
supremeness power, primacy, supremacy
suppression of evidence SEE MAIN ENTRY
surcease cease, cessation *(termination)*, close *(terminate)*, conclude *(complete)*, desist, expire, quit *(discontinue)*

surcharge overload. SEE MAIN ENTRY
sure affirmative, axiomatic, believable, certain *(fixed)*, certain *(positive)*, clear *(certain)*, constant, dependable, dogmatic, explicit, incontrovertible, indubious, inevitable, infallible, irrefutable, necessary *(inescapable)*, pertinacious, positive *(confident)*, positive *(incontestable)*, real, reliable, safe, secure *(confident)*, stable, staunch, true *(loyal)*, unambiguous, unavoidable *(inevitable)*, unequivocal, unmistakable, unrefutable
sure assumption certitude
sure presumption certainty, certitude
sure to happen inevitable
surely admittedly, fairly *(clearly)*
sureness certainty, certification *(certainness)*, certitude, confidence *(faith)*, conviction *(persuasion)*, credence, faith, reliance, surety *(certainty)*, trust *(confidence)*
surety accommodation *(backing)*, assurance, bail, bond, certainty, certitude, confidence *(faith)*, coverage *(insurance)*, credence, deposit, downpayment, faith, guaranty, insurer, recognizance, safeguard, security *(pledge)*, sponsor, warrant *(guaranty)*. SEE MAIN ENTRY
surface bare, cursory, dimension, emerge, issue *(send forth)*, ostensible, side, superficial
surfeit balance *(amount in excess)*, overage, overload, plethora, satisfy *(fulfill)*, sufficiency, surplus, tautology. SEE MAIN ENTRY
surfeited full, replete
surge growth *(increase)*, increase, increment, inflate, inflation *(increase)*, inundate, issue *(send forth)*
surging fluvial
surly fractious, froward, harsh, impertinent *(insolent)*, perverse, petulant, resentful
surmisable colorable *(plausible)*, ostensible, presumptive, probable
surmisal estimate *(idea)*, estimation *(calculation)*
surmise anticipate *(expect)*, apprehend *(perceive)*, assumption *(supposition)*, concept, conclusion *(determination)*, conjecture, deduce, deduct *(conclude by reasoning)*, deduction *(conclusion)*, deem, estimate *(idea)*, estimation *(calculation)*, expect *(consider probable)*, gauge, generalize, guess, hypothesis, idea, infer, inference, opine, opinion *(belief)*, perception, postulate *(noun)*, postulate *(verb)*, preconceive, presume, presumption, presuppose, prognosticate, rationale, speculate *(conjecture)*, speculation *(conjecture)*, supposition, suspect *(think)*, suspicion *(uncertainty)*, theory. SEE MAIN ENTRY
surmised approximate, inexact
surmount beat *(defeat)*, defeat, kill *(defeat)*, negotiate, overthrow, overwhelm, prevail *(triumph)*, transcend. SEE MAIN ENTRY
surmount obstacles succeed *(attain)*
surmountable possible
surname call *(title)*
surpass beat *(defeat)*, outbalance, outweigh, override, predominate *(outnumber)*, prevail *(triumph)*, surmount, transcend. SEE MAIN ENTRY
surpassing best, infringement, preferable, superlative
surplus balance *(amount in excess)*, bonus, boom *(prosperity)*, excess, excessive, expendable, needless, net, overage, plethora, profuse, redundancy, redundant, remainder *(estate in property)*, remainder

(remaining part), residual, residuary, superfluous, surfeit, unnecessary. SEE MAIN ENTRY

surplus time unexpired term

surplusage balance *(amount in excess)*, bonus, overage, plethora, surfeit, surplus

surprisal bombshell. SEE MAIN ENTRY

surprise bombshell, fortuitous, overwhelm, unforeseeable, unforeseen. SEE MAIN ENTRY

surprise package bombshell

surprised unaware

surprising coincidental, fortuitous, noteworthy, peculiar *(curious)*, portentous *(eliciting amazement)*, prodigious *(amazing)*, remarkable, unaccustomed, unanticipated, uncommon, unexpected, unusual

surrebut rebut, reply, retort, return *(respond)*

surrebuttal answer *(judicial response)*, counterargument, reply

surrebutter answer *(judicial response)*, counterargument, response

surrejoin answer *(respond legally)*, rebut, reply, retort, return *(respond)*

surrejoinder answer *(judicial response)*, confutation, counterargument, response

surrender abandon *(relinquish)*, abandonment *(discontinuance)*, abdication, accede *(concede)*, alienate *(transfer title)*, alienation *(transfer of title)*, bear *(yield)*, cancellation, capitulation, cede, cession, concession *(compromise)*, deliver, delivery, desuetude, discontinue *(abandon)*, disposition *(transfer of property)*, expense *(sacrifice)*, forfeit, forgo, give *(grant)*, give *(yield)*, introduce, leave *(allow to remain)*, obey, perish, prostration, quit *(discontinue)*, relinquish, remise, render *(deliver)*, rendition *(restoration)*, renounce, resign, resignation *(passive acceptance)*, resignation *(relinquishment)*, submit *(yield)*, succumb, vacate *(leave)*, waive, waiver, withdraw, yield *(submit)*. SEE MAIN ENTRY

surrender of an individual extradition

surrender of control abdication

surrender to another assign *(transfer ownership)*

surrendered resigned

surrendered to addicted

surrendering obeisant

surreptitious clandestine, collusive, covert, dishonest, disingenuous, evasive, fraudulent, furtive, hidden, insidious, mysterious, privy, secret, sly, stealthy, unobtrusive. SEE MAIN ENTRY

surreptitiousness bad faith, deceit, dishonesty, false pretense, fraud, improbity

surripere pilfer, purloin, steal

surrogate attorney in fact, conduit *(intermediary)*, deputy, judge, plenipotentiary, proctor, proxy, replace, replacement, substitute. SEE MAIN ENTRY

surrogation replacement, subrogation

surround border *(bound)*, circumscribe *(surround by boundary)*, contain *(enclose)*, delimit, detain *(hold in custody)*, embrace *(encircle)*, enclose, enshroud, envelop, hedge, include

surrounded by difficulties difficult

surrounding blockade *(enclosure)*, local

surrounding area periphery

surrounding facts circumstances

surrounding influence climate

surrounding space periphery

surroundings atmosphere, circumstances, climate, context, environment, locality, scene, section *(vicinity)*, vicinity

surveillance bondage, contemplation, direction *(guidance)*, espionage, inspection, management *(supervision)*, notice *(heed)*, observation, precaution, scrutiny, supervision. SEE MAIN ENTRY

survey analysis, analyze, appraisal, assessment *(estimation)*, canvass, check *(inspect)*, compendium, delineate, digest *(summarize)*, estimate, examination *(study)*, examine *(study)*, gauge, inquire, inquiry *(request for information)*, inquiry *(systematic investigation)*, inspection, investigate, measure, measurement, monitor, observation, observe *(watch)*, overlook *(superintend)*, pandect *(treatise)*, peruse, poll *(canvass)*, poll, question *(inquiry)*, regard *(pay attention)*, research, retrospect, review *(official reexamination)*, review, scrutinize, scrutiny, study, test. SEE MAIN ENTRY

survey carefully traverse

survey of time past hindsight

surveyable appreciable, determinable *(ascertainable)*

surveying discovery

surviorship longevity

survival life *(period of existence)*, longevity. SEE MAIN ENTRY

survival studies ecology

survivance longevity

survive endure *(last)*, exist, keep *(continue)*, last, persevere, persist, remain *(continue)*, subsist. SEE MAIN ENTRY

surviving durable, extant, lasting, live *(existing)*, net, outstanding *(unpaid)*, permanent, perpetual

survivor heir

susceptibility bias, character *(personal quality)*, credulity, danger, peril, predisposition, probability, sensibility, tendency. SEE MAIN ENTRY

susceptible liable, open *(accessible)*, open *(persuasible)*, penetrable, pliant, receptive, responsive, sensitive *(easily affected)*, subject *(exposed)*, vulnerable, willing *(not averse)*. SEE MAIN ENTRY

susceptible of apportionment divisible

susceptible of division divisible

susceptible of proof provable

susceptibleness peril

susceptive pliant, sensitive *(easily affected)*, susceptible *(responsive)*

susceptivity credulity, peril

suscipere assume *(undertake)*, incur, undertake

suspect assume *(suppose)*, controversial, debatable, deem, disbelieve, discount *(disbelieve)*, disputable, doubt *(distrust)*, dubitative, expect *(consider probable)*, guess, incredible, infer, leery, ludicrous, misdoubt, mistrust, opine, presume, presumptive, presuppose, surmise, suspicious *(questionable)*, unbelievable, uncertain *(questionable)*. SEE MAIN ENTRY

suspected criminal suspect

suspecting cynical, inconvincible, incredulous, leery, skeptical, suspicious *(distrustful)*

suspectum reddere incriminate

suspend adjourn, arrest *(stop)*, balk, bar *(exclude)*, cancel, cease, close *(terminate)*, continue *(adjourn)*, debar, defer *(put off)*, desist, discharge *(dismiss)*, discontinue *(abandon)*, discontinue *(break continuity)*, dismiss *(discharge)*, disrupt, forestall, halt, hold up *(delay)*, impede, inhibit, interrupt, leave *(allow to remain)*, negate, nullify,

obstruct, palliate *(abate)*, pause, postpone, pretermit, procrastinate, prohibit, quit *(discontinue)*, recess, remit *(relax)*, remove *(dismiss from office)*, revoke, stop, toll *(stop)*. SEE MAIN ENTRY

suspend charges pardon

suspend from the practice of law disbar

suspend from the profession of law disbar

suspend operation close *(terminate)*

suspend work strike *(refuse to work)*

suspended arrested *(checked)*, broken *(interrupted)*, disjunctive *(tending to disjoin)*, dormant, inactive, null *(invalid)*, null and void, static

suspended animation inaction

suspended judgment doubt *(indecision)*

suspense doubt *(indecision)*, expectation, pendency, remission

suspenseful conditional, pending *(unresolved)*

suspension abandonment *(discontinuance)*, abeyance, adjournment, cancellation, cessation *(interlude)*, check *(bar)*, cloture, deferment, delay, desuetude, discontinuance *(act of discontinuing)*, disuse, expulsion, extension *(postponement)*, halt, hiatus, inaction, interruption, lull, moratorium, nonuse, ostracism, pause, pendency, remission, rescision, respite *(interval of rest)*, solution *(substance)*, stay

suspension of activity extension *(postponement)*

suspension of business failure *(bankruptcy)*

suspension of consciousness insentience

suspension of disbelief credence

suspension of employment layoff

suspension of execution reprieve

suspension of hostilities peace

suspension of punishment reprieve

suspension of work furlough, leave *(absence)*, strike

suspicari surmise, suspect *(think)*

suspicio doubt *(suspicion)*, notion, suspicion *(mistrust)*

suspicion apprehension *(fear)*, conjecture, idea, incredulity, inference, opinion *(belief)*, qualm, speculation *(conjecture)*, suggestion, supposition. SEE MAIN ENTRY

suspicionem habere suspect *(think)*

suspiciosus suspicious *(distrustful)*

suspicious cynical, debatable, disputable, disreputable, guarded, implausible, inconvincible, incredible, incredulous, jealous, leery, resentful, skeptical, unbelievable, uncertain *(questionable)*, vigilant. SEE MAIN ENTRY

suspiciousness bad faith, bad repute, doubt *(suspicion)*, incredulity, suspicion *(mistrust)*

sustain adhere *(persist)*, affirm *(uphold)*, aid, allow *(authorize)*, allow *(endure)*, approve, authorize, bear *(adduce)*, bear *(support)*, bear *(tolerate)*, bolster, care *(regard)*, certify *(attest)*, concur *(agree)*, confirm, conserve, continue *(persevere)*, continue *(prolong)*, corroborate, countenance, defend, demonstrate *(establish)*, document, endure *(last)*, endure *(suffer)*, finance, foster, fund, harbor, help, indorse, justify, keep *(continue)*, keep *(shelter)*, last, nurture, pass *(approve)*, perpetuate, persevere, persist, preserve, prolong, promote *(organize)*, protect, provide *(supply)*, reaffirm, reassure, remain *(continue)*, retain *(keep in possession)*, side, sponsor, subsidize, supply, support *(assist)*, support *(corroborate)*, uphold, vouch, witness *(attest to)*. SEE MAIN ENTRY

sustain by authority   authorize

sustain damage   suffer *(sustain loss)*

sustainable   convincing, deductible *(provable)*, provable

sustainable in law   valid

sustained   chronic, constant, continual *(connected)*, continuous, durable, habitual, incessant, lasting, live *(existing)*, permanent, persistent, safe

sustained action   continuance

sustained by   dependent

sustained trial   endeavor, pursuit *(effort to secure)*

sustainer   abettor, backer, benefactor, mainstay, partisan

sustaining   conservation, continuation *(prolongation)*, corroboration, salutary

sustainment   aid *(help)*, aid *(subsistence)*, ecology, livelihood, tolerance

sustenance   aid *(help)*, aid *(subsistence)*, alimony, behalf, continuation *(prolongation)*, contribution *(donation)*, ecology, help, livelihood, mainstay, maintenance *(support of spouse)*, relief *(aid)*, support *(assistance)*. SEE MAIN ENTRY

sustentare   sustain *(prolong)*, uphold

sustentation   alimony, conservation, sustenance

sustentative   salubrious, salutary

sustinere   bear *(tolerate)*, endure *(suffer)*, preserve, sustain *(prolong)*, uphold

swaddle   envelop

swag   contraband, spoils

swagger   flaunt, jactation, pride, rodomontade

swaggering   bluster *(speech)*, inflated *(vain)*, insolent

swallow   consume, endure *(suffer)*, tolerate

swallow up   obliterate, overcome *(overwhelm)*

swamp   immerse *(plunge into)*, inundate, overcome *(overwhelm)*

swank   jactation

swap   barter, exchange, interchange, replace, replacement, trade *(commerce)*

swarm   assemblage, mass *(body of persons)*, meet

swarming   populous, profuse, rife

swashbuckling   rodomontade

swatch   sample

swathe   enshroud, envelop

sway   advantage, authority *(power)*, bailiwick, beat *(pulsate)*, coax, convert *(persuade)*, convince, dint, dispose *(incline)*, dominance, dominate, dominion *(supreme authority)*, force *(strength)*, government *(administration)*, hegemony, induce, influence *(noun)*, influence *(verb)*, inspire, inveigle, lobby, manage, motivate, oscillate, patronage *(power to appoint jobs)*, persuade, power, predominance, predominate *(command)*, prejudice *(influence)*, preside, pressure, prestige, prevail *(persuade)*, prevail upon, primacy, supremacy, vacillate, wield. SEE MAIN ENTRY

swayable   open *(persuasible)*, pliable, pliant, suasible, susceptible *(responsive)*

swayed   one-sided, partial *(biased)*, partisan

swaying   convincing, persuasive

swear   acknowledge *(declare)*, assure

(insure), attest, avouch *(avow)*, avow, bear *(adduce)*, certify *(attest)*, depose *(testify)*, evidence, plead *(allege in a legal action)*, promise *(vow)*, testify, witness *(attest to)*. SEE MAIN ENTRY

swear an affidavit   certify *(attest)*

swear an oath   avouch *(avow)*, promise *(vow)*

swear by   trust

swear falsely   bear false witness, cloak, frame *(charge falsely)*, lie *(falsify)*, perjure

swear in   delegate

swear off   forgo, refrain, renounce

swear the truth   avouch *(avow)*

swear to   vouch

swear under oath   depose *(testify)*

swearer   affiant, bystander, deponent, juror, witness

swearing   adjuration, affirmation, attestation, averment, avouchment, blasphemy, certification *(attested copy)*, confirmation, expletive, imprecation, oath, profanity

swearing off   denial, renunciation

sweep   coverage *(scope)*, extent, gamut, range, scope, space

sweep aside   rescind

sweep away   eliminate *(eradicate)*, eradicate, obliterate

sweep out   purge *(purify)*

sweep through   patrol, perambulate

sweeping   broad, complete *(all-embracing)*, comprehensive, extensive, far reaching, general, generic, inclusive, omnibus, outright, prevailing *(current)*, prevalent, radical *(extreme)*, thorough, unqualified *(unlimited)*

sweeping change   revolution

sweepstake   lottery

sweet   attractive, nectarious, sapid, savory

sweet-tempered   benevolent

swell   accrue *(increase)*, accumulate *(enlarge)*, boom *(increase)*, build *(augment)*, develop, enlarge, expand, extend *(enlarge)*, growth *(increase)*, increase, inflate, inflation *(increase)*, magnify, proliferate, spread

swell the ranks   recruit

swelled   inflated *(enlarged)*, turgid

swelling   accession *(enlargement)*, boom *(increase)*, cumulative *(increasing)*, growth *(increase)*, inflation *(increase)*, orotund, plethora

swelling utterance   bombast

swerve   depart, detour, deviate, deviation, digress, digression, divert, indirection *(indirect action)*, oscillate

swerving   deviation

swift   brief, expeditious, impulsive *(rash)*, instantaneous, precipitate, prompt, rapid, ready *(prepared)*, summary

swift execution   dispatch *(promptness)*

swift rate   dispatch *(promptness)*

swiftly   instantly

swiftness   haste

swindle   bait *(lure)*, betray *(lead astray)*, bilk, bunko, cheat, circumvent, deceive, deception, defalcate, defraud, delude, dupe, embezzle, embezzlement, fake, false pretense, hoax, hoodwink, illude, imposture, larceny, misappropriation, mislead, mulct *(defraud)*, peculate, purloin

swindled   aggrieved *(harmed)*

swindler   criminal, delinquent, embezzler, outlaw, thief

swindling   fraud, imposture, larceny, theft

swing   beat *(pulsate)*, beat *(strike)*, brandish, fluctuate, oscillate, vacillate, wield

switch   alternate *(take turns)*, barter, change, conversion *(change)*, convert *(change use)*, displace *(replace)*, lash *(strike)*, reciprocate, remove *(transfer)*, replace, replacement, subrogation, transform

switch around   change

switched off   disconnected

swollen   full, fustian, inflated *(enlarged)*, orotund, pretentious *(pompous)*, proud *(conceited)*, supercilious, turgid

swollen diction   bombast

swollen language   fustian

swoon   prostration

sworn   agreed *(promised)*. SEE MAIN ENTRY

sworn declarant   SEE MAIN ENTRY

sworn enemy   foe

sworn evidence   affidavit, affirmance *(legal affirmation)*, affirmation, attestation, certification *(attested copy)*, deposition

sworn pledge   oath

sworn promise   oath

sworn statement   adjuration, affidavit, affirmation, asseveration, oath

sycophant   parasite

sycophantic   obsequious, sequacious, servile, subservient

syllabus   capsule, compendium, outline *(synopsis)*, pandect *(treatise)*, plan, program, prospectus, summary

syllogism   corollary

symbiosis   coalescence

symbol   device *(distinguishing mark)*, earmark, indicant, indication, indicator, manifestation, representative *(example)*, substitute, suggestion, token, trademark. SEE MAIN ENTRY

symbolic   nominal, representative, suggestive *(evocative)*

symbolical   representative

symbolization   connotation

symbolize   connote, denote, depict, exemplify, personify, replace, represent *(portray)*, signify *(denote)*

symbolized   tacit

symbols   indicia

symbolum   symbol

symmetric   equal

symmetrical   coequal, coextensive, equal, regular *(orderly)*

symmetrical scales   balance *(equality)*

symmetry   analogy, arrangement *(ordering)*, balance *(equality)*, constant, correspondence *(similarity)*, equipoise, parity, proportion, regularity, uniformity

sympathetic   charitable *(lenient)*, concerted, concordant, consensual, lenient, open *(persuasible)*, patient, propitious, receptive, sensitive *(easily affected)*, susceptible *(responsive)*, vicarious *(delegated)*

sympathetic perception   discretion *(quality of being discreet)*

sympathize   relent, sponsor. SEE MAIN ENTRY

sympathize with   concur *(agree)*

sympathizer   advocate *(espouser)*, backer, disciple, partisan, proponent, samaritan, sponsor

sympathizing   benevolent, charitable *(lenient)*, vicarious *(delegated)*

sympathy   affinity *(regard)*, concordance, condonation, goodwill, humanity *(humaneness)*, lenience, pity, sensibility, solace, tolerance, understanding *(tolerance)*

symphonize   orchestrate

symphysis   concrescence

symposiac parley
symposiarch chairman
symposium assemblage, conference, meeting *(conference)*, panel *(discussion group)*, parley
symptom indicant, indication, indicator, manifestation, symbol, warning. SEE MAIN ENTRY
symptomatology diagnosis
synchronal commensurate, concurrent *(at the same time)*, consonant, contemporaneous, simultaneous
synchronic simultaneous
synchronical simultaneous
synchronism SEE MAIN ENTRY
synchronistic concurrent *(at the same time)*, contemporaneous, simultaneous
synchronistical concurrent *(at the same time)*, simultaneous
synchronization consensus
synchronize coincide *(concur)*, conform, coordinate
synchronized congruous, consonant
synchronous concurrent *(at the same time)*, congruous, contemporaneous, simultaneous
syncophantic vexatious
syncretize combine *(act in concert)*, embody, federalize *(associate)*, unite
syndic functionary, procurator
syndicate amalgamate, association *(alliance)*, business *(commercial enterprise)*, cartel, coalition, combine *(act in concert)*, committee, confederacy *(compact)*, consortium *(business cartel)*, corporation, enterprise *(economic organization)*, federation, institute, merger, organization *(association)*, partnership, pool, trust *(combination of businesses)*. SEE MAIN ENTRY
synergetic associated, joint. SEE MAIN ENTRY
synergic concerted, concomitant, concurrent *(united)*, consensual
synergism collusion, synergy
synergy collusion, concert. SEE MAIN ENTRY
syngrapha bill *(invoice)*, bond, instrument *(document)*
synod council *(assembly)*, meeting *(conference)*, session
synonym call *(title)*, definition, same
synonymity identity *(similarity)*, propinquity *(similarity)*
synonymous coequal, coextensive, cognate, congruous, equivalent, identical, same, similar, tantamount
synopsis abridgment *(condensation)*, abstract, brief, capsule, compendium, digest, pandect *(treatise)*, paraphrase, prospectus, restatement, scenario, summary. SEE MAIN ENTRY
synopsize abridge *(shorten)*, abstract *(summarize)*, condense
synoptic broad, compact *(pithy)*, comprehensive, concise, succinct
syntaxis classification
synthesis building *(business of assembling)*, centralization, coalescence, composition *(makeup)*, embodiment, formation, manufacture
synthesize consist, consolidate *(unite)*, embody, make
synthetic assumed *(feigned)*, false *(not genuine)*, imitation, spurious. SEE MAIN ENTRY
system arrangement *(plan)*, array *(order)*, avenue *(means of attainment)*, bureaucracy, codification, complex *(development)*, course, device *(contrivance)*,

doctrine, form *(arrangement)*, hierarchy *(arrangement in a series)*, institute, means *(opportunity)*, method, mode, modus operandi, order *(arrangement)*, practice *(procedure)*, procedure, process *(course)*, program, rule *(guide)*, scheme, strategy, usage. SEE MAIN ENTRY
system of belief doctrine
system of distributing wealth economy *(economic system)*
system of drill discipline *(training)*
system of exchanges commerce
system of government polity
system of knowledge education, science *(study)*
system of law code
system of laws codification, jurisprudence
system of morals ethics
system of reckoning time calendar *(record of yearly periods)*
system of regulations codification
system of rules code, protocol *(etiquette)*
systematic arrangement of cases calendar *(list of cases)*
systematic arrangement of laws codification
systematic search indagation, investigation
systematic secret observation of the words and conduct of others espionage
systematic training discipline *(training)*, education
systematical systematic
systematically invariably
systematization arrangement *(ordering)*, array *(order)*, centralization, classification, distribution *(arrangement)*, form *(arrangement)*, formation, order *(arrangement)*, organization *(structure)*, regulation *(management)*
systematization of laws codification
systematize adjust *(regulate)*, arrange *(methodize)*, classify, codify, conform, contrive, coordinate, distribute, file (arrange), fix *(arrange)*, frame *(construct)*, marshal, orchestrate, organize *(arrange)*, pigeonhole, police, regulate *(adjust)*, sort, tabulate
systematized tactical
systemic physical
systemize codify
systemless haphazard, indiscriminate

T

T.N.T. bomb
tab invoice *(bill)*
tabernacle domicile, dwelling, habitation *(dwelling place)*
tabescere languish
tabid dil apidated
table calendar *(record of yearly periods)*, continue *(adjourn)*, defer *(put off)*, delay, doubt *(hesitate)*, hold up *(delay)*, postpone, procrastinate, suspend
table of cases calendar *(list of cases)*
table of charges tariff *(bill)*
tables census
tabling deferment
taboo ban, exclude, forbid, illicit, inhibit, prohibition, proscribe *(prohibit)*, restraint, restrict, veto
tabula document, instrument *(document)*, inventory, roll, schedule

tabula rasa blank *(emptiness)*
tabulae register
tabular register of the year calendar *(record of yearly periods)*
tabulas referre register
tabulate book, cast *(register)*, codify, enter *(record)*, enumerate, fix *(arrange)*, itemize, pigeonhole, poll, record, register, sort, survey *(poll)*. SEE MAIN ENTRY
tabulation census, codification, poll *(canvass)*, registration
tacere speechless
tacit allusive, constructive *(inferential)*, covert, implicit, implied, indirect, undisclosed. SEE MAIN ENTRY
tacit assent acquiescence
tacit inference implication *(inference)*
tacitly assumed constructive *(inferential)*
taciturn inarticulate, laconic, mute, noncommittal, unresponsive. SEE MAIN ENTRY
taciturnitas silence
taciturnus taciturn
tacitus implicit, tacit
tack avenue *(means of attainment)*
tack together combine *(join together)*
tackle attack, endeavor, grapple, occupy *(engage)*, ply, strive, try *(attempt)*, undertake
tact consideration *(sympathetic regard)*, courtesy, decorum, discretion *(quality of being discreet)*, prudence
tactful diplomatic, judicious, politic, subtle *(refined)*
tactfulness discretion *(quality of being discreet)*
tactic expedient, machination, method, plan, plot *(secret plan)*, stratagem
tactical strategic. SEE MAIN ENTRY
tactician mastermind
tactics artifice, campaign, contrivance, direction *(course)*, manner *(behavior)*, modus operandi, practice *(procedure)*, procedure, process *(course)*, scheme, strategy. SEE MAIN ENTRY
tactile bodily, material *(physical)*, palpable, tangible
taction contact *(touching)*
tactless thoughtless, unpolitic
tactlessness disrespect, impropriety, indiscretion
tactual tangible
taeter loathsome
tag brand, brand *(mark)*, call *(title)*, catchword, classify, label *(noun)*, label *(verb)*, nominate, pigeonhole, rate, title *(designation)*
tag incorrectly mislabel
tail end *(termination)*
tail end extremity *(furthest point)*
tailor conform, transform
tailor-made fit
taint adulterate, attaint, bad repute, brand, brand *(stigmatize)*, contaminate *(noun)*, contaminate *(verb)*, contemn, corrupt, damage, debase, defame, degenerate, depreciate, derogate, deteriorate, disadvantage, discredit *(noun)*, discredit *(verb)*, disease, disgrace *(noun)*, disgrace *(verb)*, dishonor *(shame)*, dishonor *(deprive of honor)*, disparage, disrepute, humiliate, ignominy, impair, infamy, infect, misemploy, notoriety, onus *(stigma)*, opprobrium, pervert, pillory, pollute, prejudice *(injure)*, reproach, scandal, shame, smear, stain, stigma, sully, tarnish. SEE MAIN ENTRY
tainted blameworthy, blemished, imperfect, marred, odious, peccable, peccant

(unhealthy), sinister, unsound *(not strong)*. SEE MAIN ENTRY

taintless absolute *(ideal)*, blameless, clean, pure, unblemished

take acquire *(secure)*, adopt, apprehend *(arrest)*, appropriate, attach *(seize)*, carry *(transport)*, derive *(receive)*, despoil, endure *(suffer)*, excise *(levy a tax)*, gain, hijack, impound, impress *(procure by force)*, inherit, loot, obtain, partake, pilfer, plunder, preempt, procure, profit, purloin, reap, receive *(acquire)*, seize *(apprehend)*, seize *(confiscate)*, sequester *(seize property)*, spoils, transport, trust, usurp. SEE MAIN ENTRY

take a beating lose *(undergo defeat)*

take a break rest *(cease from action)*

take a breather pause

take a census poll

take a chance bet, gamble, parlay *(bet)*, speculate *(chance)*, try *(attempt)*

take a circuitous route detour

take a constitutional perambulate

take a crack at endeavor

take a decisive step choose, conclude *(decide)*, determine

take a different course deviate

take a dim view of disapprove *(condemn)*

take a fancy to prefer

take a lease rent

take a life slay

take a part in participate

take a part of participate

take a recess recess

take a rest recess

take a roll call poll

take a roundabout course detour

take a share of partake

take a stand posit, resolve *(decide)*

take a stand against counter, disagree, oppose, rebut

take a temporary route detour

take a turn reciprocate

take a vow promise *(vow)*

take a walk perambulate

take account of note *(notice)*, ponder

take action complain *(charge)*, endeavor, execute *(accomplish)*, implement, militate, perform *(execute)*, strive

take advantage deceive

take advantage of bait *(lure)*, bilk, capitalize *(seize the chance)*, defraud, delude, dupe, employ *(make use of)*, ensnare, exploit *(make use of)*, illude, manipulate *(control unfairly)*, mislead

take after copy, mock *(imitate)*

take alarm fear

take amiss misapprehend, resent

take an account of calculate

take an active part in contribute *(assist)*, partake, participate

take an advance borrow

take an airing perambulate

take an alternate highway detour

take an alternate route detour

take an indirect way detour

take an interest in participate

take an oath promise *(vow)*

take another's place displace *(replace)*

take apart break *(separate)*, disjoint, dissolve *(separate)*

take as an axiom postulate

take as an heir inherit

take as one's own assume *(seize)*, impropriate

take authority hold *(possess)*

take away abduct, abridge *(divest)*, abridge *(shorten)*, adeem, carry away, decrease, deduct *(reduce)*, depreciate, deprive, dilute, diminish, dislodge, displace *(remove)*, distrain, divest, excise *(cut away)*, hijack, hold up *(rob)*, jostle *(pickpocket)*, kidnap, lessen, plunder, remove *(eliminate)*, withdraw

take away an essential part eviscerate

take away from confiscate, disinherit

take back adeem, bear false witness, disavow, disclaim, recall *(call back)*, recant, recoup *(regain)*, repossess, rescind, withdraw

take back again collect *(recover money)*

take birth arise *(originate)*

take by assault capture, carry away, hijack

take by authority apprehend *(arrest)*, arrest *(apprehend)*

take by craft ensnare

take by descent inherit

take by force abduct, capture, despoil, hijack, kidnap, levy, pirate *(take by violence)*, rob

take by fraud defalcate, defraud, dupe, embezzle, purloin

take by illegal methods poach

take by inheritance inherit

take by stealth carry away

take by strategem ensnare

take by succession inherit

take by theft hold up *(rob)*

take by unfair methods poach

take captive apprehend *(arrest)*, arrest *(apprehend)*, capture, carry away, constrain *(imprison)*, detain *(hold in custody)*, hijack, immure

take care beware, heed

take care of assume *(undertake)*, concern *(care)*, conduct, control *(regulate)*, cover *(guard)*, foster, keep *(shelter)*, maintain *(sustain)*, operate, preserve, preside, protect, serve *(assist)*, support *(assist)*

take charge assume *(undertake)*, command, govern, preside, takeover, usurp

take charge of arrest *(apprehend)*, conduct, maintain *(sustain)*, manage, moderate *(preside over)*, operate

take cognizance notice *(observe)*

take cognizance of hear *(perceive by ear)*, heed, note *(notice)*, observe *(watch)*, regard *(pay attention)*, witness *(have direct knowledge of)*

take command direct *(supervise)*, federalize *(place under federal control)*, govern, hold *(possess)*, takeover

take control federalize *(place under federal control)*

take control of accept *(take)*

take counsel confer *(consult)*, consult *(ask advice of)*

take counsel with oneself deliberate

take disciplinary action condemn *(punish)*

take dishonestly hold up *(rob)*, purloin

take down demean *(make lower)*, demote, enter *(record)*, note *(record)*, record

take effect occur *(happen)*

take employment occupy *(engage)*

take evasive action counter, elude, parry

take evidence investigate

take exception complain *(criticize)*, conflict, cross *(disagree with)*, demur, differ *(disagree)*, differ *(vary)*, disaccord, disagree, disapprove *(reject)*, dispute *(con-*

test), dissent *(differ in opinion)*, except *(object)*, expostulate, object, oppugn, protest, remonstrate, reprehend

take exception to challenge, complain *(criticize)*, confront *(oppose)*, contest, denounce *(condemn)*, disapprove *(condemn)*, disapprove *(reject)*, disclaim, gainsay, oppose, reject, renounce, resent

take exception to the allegations demurrer

take feloniously embezzle, hold up *(rob)*, purloin

take flight abscond, disappear, escape, evacuate, flee, move *(alter position)*, quit *(evacuate)*, retreat

take for deem

take for granted assume *(suppose)*, guess, postulate, presume, presuppose, suspect *(think)*, trust

take for oneself impropriate

take for public use condemn *(seize)*

take forcibly carry away

take form crystallize, develop, evolve

take fright fear

take from adeem, diminish, discount *(reduce)*, occupy *(take possession)*

take heed beware

take hold of accept *(take)*, grapple, sequester *(seize property)*

take illegally convert *(misappropriate)*, pirate *(reproduce without authorization)*, poach

take in acquire *(receive)*, betray *(lead astray)*, bilk, comprehend *(include)*, comprehend *(understand)*, defraud, delude, dupe, embrace *(encircle)*, encompass *(include)*, entrap, illude, include, incorporate *(include)*, instate, mislead, realize *(understand)*, reap, receive *(acquire)*, receive *(permit to enter)*, recruit, seize *(apprehend)*

take in exchange displace *(replace)*

take in hand undertake

take into account calculate, consider, discuss, heed, notice *(observe)*, provide *(arrange for)*

take into consideration appreciate *(comprehend)*, concern *(care)*, deliberate, muse, notice *(observe)*

take into custody apprehend *(arrest)*, arrest *(apprehend)*, book, capture, confine, constrain *(imprison)*, detain *(hold in custody)*, distrain, enclose, immure, impound, jail, restrain, seize *(apprehend)*

take into employ employ *(engage services)*

take into legal custody impound

take into one's employ engage *(hire)*

take into preventive custody arrest *(apprehend)*

take into protective custody arrest *(apprehend)*

take into service employ *(engage services)*, engage *(hire)*, hire

take issue collide *(clash)*, differ *(disagree)*, differ *(vary)*, disagree

take issue with antagonize, contradict, counter, counteract, demurrer, disown *(deny the validity)*, dispute *(contest)*, dissent *(differ in opinion)*, gainsay, impugn, oppose. SEE MAIN ENTRY

take it to be deem

take its course occur *(happen)*

take leave abandon *(physically leave)*, dissociate, leave *(depart)*, part *(leave)*, quit *(evacuate)*, retire *(conclude a career)*, retire *(retreat)*

take leave of quit *(evacuate)*
take liberties infringe
take life dispatch *(put to death)*
take lodgings lodge *(reside)*
take measures frame *(formulate)*, perpetrate, plan, plot, provide *(arrange for)*
take minutes record
take no account of disregard, flout, override
take no denial compel, constrain *(compel)*, insist, persevere, persist, press *(constrain)*
take no interest disregard
take no note ignore, neglect
take no note of disregard
take no notice dismiss *(put out of consideration)*, ignore, neglect, overlook *(disregard)*
take no notice of disregard
take no part in refrain
take no stock in disbelieve
take note heed, observe *(watch)*, spy
take note of concern *(care)*, peruse
take notice appreciate *(comprehend)*, heed, note *(notice)*, observe *(watch)*, perceive, regard *(pay attention)*
take notice of attend *(heed)*
take off decrease, deduct *(reduce)*, diminish, discount *(reduce)*, rebate
take off on mock *(imitate)*
take offense resent
take offensive action attack
take on adopt, attempt, contend *(dispute)*, embark, endeavor, engage *(involve)*, fight *(battle)*, grapple, hire, occupy *(engage)*
take on cargo load
take on character crystallize
take on credit borrow
take on loan borrow
take on oneself assume *(undertake)*
take on the aspect appear *(seem to be)*
take on the manner appear *(seem to be)*, demean *(deport oneself)*
take one to court prosecute *(charge)*
take one's choice choose
take one's departure abandon *(physically leave)*, part *(leave)*
take one's leave abandon *(physically leave)*
take one's life away dispatch *(put to death)*
take one's meaning construe *(comprehend)*
take one's oath affirm *(declare solemnly)*, attest, avow, bear *(adduce)*, certify *(attest)*, testify, witness *(attest to)*
take one's stand against antagonize, counteract
take oneself away quit *(evacuate)*
take order crystallize
take orders obey
take origin arise *(originate)*
take out delete, distill, except *(exclude)*, excise *(cut away)*, exclude, expunge, extract, remove *(eliminate)*, select
take out of context abstract *(separate)*
take out of the place of interment disinter
take over accroach, annex *(arrogate)*, appropriate, attach *(seize)*, condemn *(seize)*, confiscate, distrain, hold *(possess)*, impound, impropriate, manage, obtain, occupy *(take possession)*, preempt, preside, prevail *(triumph)*, succeed *(follow)*, supplant. SEE MAIN ENTRY
take over another's duties displace *(replace)*

take pains endeavor, strive
take part combine *(act in concert)*, compete, engage *(involve)*, involve *(participate)*, join *(associate oneself with)*, occupy *(engage)*, participate
take part in conspire, cooperate, espouse, partake
take part in a demonstration picket
take part with assist, conspire, cooperate
take patiently allow *(endure)*, bear *(tolerate)*, endure *(suffer)*, tolerate
take place arise *(occur)*, occur *(happen)*, supervene
take pleasure in relish
take poorly resent
take possession acquire *(secure)*, annex *(arrogate)*, collect *(recover money)*, condemn *(seize)*, evict, obtain, possess, receive *(acquire)*, takeover, usurp
take possession for public use eminent domain
take possession of accept *(take)*, adopt, attach *(seize)*, capture, confiscate, distrain, hold up *(rob)*, impound, impress *(procure by force)*, impropriate, preempt, procure, repossess, seize *(confiscate)*. SEE MAIN ENTRY
take precautions beware, care *(be cautious)*, caution, forestall
take precedence beat *(defeat)*, override, surpass, transcend
take precedence over outweigh
take prisoner apprehend *(arrest)*, arrest *(apprehend)*, capture, carry away, confine, detain *(hold in custody)*, hijack, restrain, seize *(apprehend)*
take prisoner again rearrest
take responsibility underwrite
take responsibility for sponsor
take retribution retaliate
take revenge retaliate
take rooms lodge *(reside)*
take shape crystallize, develop, evolve
take sides bicker, involve *(participate)*
take something from derogate
take steps devise *(invent)*, frame *(formulate)*, maneuver, perform *(execute)*, plot, proceed *(go forward)*, provide *(arrange for)*, strive
take stock calculate, check *(inspect)*, observe *(watch)*, survey *(poll)*
take stock of criticize *(evaluate)*, examine *(study)*, muse, notice *(observe)*, peruse
take summarily annex *(arrogate)*, attach *(seize)*, confiscate
take surreptitiously abduct
take the chair officiate
take the chances of bet
take the dimensions calculate
take the edge off obtund
take the first step embark, launch *(initiate)*, originate
take the initiative attack, commence, initiate, originate
take the lead command, initiate, launch *(initiate)*, originate, precede, predominate *(command)*
take the necessary measure SEE MAIN ENTRY
take the offensive attack, fight *(battle)*, oppugn
take the opportunity capitalize *(seize the chance)*
take the part of assume *(simulate)*, impersonate, pose *(impersonate)*, represent *(substitute)*, side, support *(assist)*

take the place of accede *(succeed)*, displace *(replace)*, succeed *(follow)*, supersede, supplant
take the semblance of assume *(simulate)*
take the stand testify
take the yield reap
take time stall
take time out pause, recess, rest *(cease from action)*
take to prefer
take to account impeach
take to court litigate, sue
take to mean understand
take to one's heels flee
take to oneself embrace *(accept)*, impropriate
take to pieces break *(separate)*, disable
take to safety rescue
take to task castigate, condemn *(blame)*, denounce *(condemn)*, disapprove *(condemn)*, discipline *(punish)*, fault, lash *(attack verbally)*, punish, rebuke, reprehend, reproach
take training practice *(train by repetition)*
take trouble strive
take umbrage alienate *(estrange)*, resent
take under consideration deliberate, ponder
take unlawful possession rob
take unlawfully steal
take up adopt, assume *(undertake)*, discharge *(pay a debt)*, embark, embrace *(accept)*, endeavor, espouse, immerse *(engross)*, levy, occupy *(engage)*, ply, specialize, undertake
take up abode locate, reside
take up again continue *(resume)*, proceed *(continue)*, resume
take up an inquiry canvass, probe
take up an option choose
take up arms fight *(battle)*, rebel
take up in conference discuss
take up membership join *(associate oneself with)*
take up one's abode dwell *(reside)*
take up quarters lodge *(reside)*
take up residence dwell *(reside)*, inhabit, reside
take up residence in lodge *(reside)*, occupy *(take possession)*
take upon oneself endeavor, pledge *(promise the performance of)*, promise *(vow)*, undertake
take vengeance retaliate
take vengeance on punish
take warning beware
take wing disappear
take without proof assume *(suppose)*, presume
take wrongfully hold up *(rob)*, purloin
take wrongly misapprehend
take-off travesty
take-over disseisin, sequestration
take-over of property eviction
taken lost *(taken away)*, preferred *(favored)*
taken advantage of aggrieved *(victimized)*
taken by force by the authorities arrested *(apprehended)*
taken for granted apparent *(presumptive)*, assumed *(inferred)*, ordinary, tacit
taken into custody arrested *(apprehended)*
taken prisoner arrested *(apprehended)*
takeover condemnation *(seizure)*

taker bearer, customer, extortionist, grantee, payee, volunteer

taking acquisition, apprehension *(act of arresting)*, arrogation, confiscatory, disseisin, distress *(seizure)*, plagiarism. SEE MAIN ENTRY

taking away abduction, removal
taking back retraction
taking by undue exercise of power blackmail, extortion
taking counsel deliberation
taking different courses divergent
taking effect before retroactive
taking exception dissenting
taking for public use expropriation *(right of eminent domain)*
taking hold apprehension *(act of arresting)*
taking information interrogation
taking issue with dissenting
taking of human life murder
taking of life aberemurder
taking of private land by the government expropriation *(right of eminent domain)*
taking of property for public use condemnation *(seizure)*
taking on assumption *(adoption)*
taking possession appropriation *(taking)*, condemnation *(seizure)*, disseisin
taking the law in one's own hands lynch law
taking the place of another vicarious *(delegated)*
taking without compensation disseisin
takings earnings, spoils
tale falsehood, myth, narration, story *(narrative)*
tale telling narration
talebearer informant
talent aptitude, caliber *(mental capacity)*, capacity *(aptitude)*, competence *(ability)*, faculty *(ability)*, gift *(flair)*, penchant, performance *(workmanship)*, potential, proclivity, propensity, sense *(intelligence)*, skill, specialty *(special aptitude)*. SEE MAIN ENTRY
talented artful, deft, practiced, proficient, resourceful, veteran
talesmen jury
talion punishment, reprisal
talionic disciplinary *(punitory)*, punitive
talk communicate, conversation, converse, declaim, declamation, discourse *(noun)*, discourse *(verb)*, interview, language, parlance, parley, peroration, phrase, recite, recount, report *(detailed account)*, report *(rumor)*, scandal, speak, speech, utter. SEE MAIN ENTRY
talk about discuss, mention, remark
talk down to condescend *(patronize)*, patronize *(condescend toward)*
talk insincerely palter
talk into convert *(persuade)*, exhort, induce, influence, motivate, prevail upon
talk it over discuss
talk nonsense prattle
talk of circulate, discuss
talk out discuss
talk out of dissuade, expostulate
talk over confer *(consult)*, consult *(ask advice of)*, discourse, discuss, reason *(persuade)*
talk together discourse, discuss
talkative demonstrative *(expressive of emotion)*, flatulent, loquacious, voluble
talked about renowned
talked of famous, illustrious, notable

talked-about household *(familiar)*
talked-of household *(familiar)*
talking loquacious
talking big bluster *(speech)*
talks conference
tall story myth
tall talk rodomontade
tallage assessment *(levy)*, duty *(tax)*
tallness elevation
tally account *(evaluation)*, amount *(sum)*, bill *(invoice)*, calculate, census, comport *(agree with)*, computation, poll *(canvass)*, poll, record
tally sheet inventory
tame alleviate, dominate, harmless, insipid, jejune *(dull)*, lifeless *(dull)*, malleable, moderate *(temper)*, obedient, passive, peaceable, pedestrian, phlegmatic, placid, prosaic, resigned, soothe, subdue, subject, subjugate
tameable corrigible
tamper disturb. SEE MAIN ENTRY
tamper with adulterate, contaminate, damage, denature, falsify, pervert, suborn, vitiate
tangency connection *(abutment)*, contact *(touching)*
tangent close *(near)*, proximate, tangential
tangential proximate. SEE MAIN ENTRY
tangere adjoin, affect
tangibility embodiment, materiality *(physical existence)*
tangible actual, apparent *(perceptible)*, appreciable, bodily, certain *(positive)*, concrete, corporal, corporeal, de facto, manifest, material *(physical)*, palpable, perceivable, perceptible, physical, substantive. SEE MAIN ENTRY
tangible assets estate *(property)*, merchandise, principal *(capital sum)*, property *(possessions)*
tangible form embodiment
tangible object entity
tangible proof fact
tangibles estate *(property)*, property *(possessions)*
tangibly fairly *(clearly)*
tangle complex *(entanglement)*, disorganize, engage *(involve)*, implicate, intertwine, involution, perplex, snarl
tangled complex, compound, disordered, disorderly, inextricable, intricate, labyrinthine, problematic, recondite, sinuous
tangly inextricable
tangy palatable
tankage capacity *(maximum)*
tantalization bribery, incentive, seduction
tantalize bait *(lure)*, interest, lure
tantalized eager
tantalizing provocative, sapid
tantamount coequal, comparable *(equivalent)*, equal, equivalent, identical. SEE MAIN ENTRY
tantamount to constructive *(inferential)*, virtual
tap impinge
tap the lines eavesdrop
taper attenuate, converge, decrease, diminish, lessen
taper off subside
tapering narrow
tar brand *(stigmatize)*
tardare delay, hold up *(delay)*
tardiness delay
tardus phlegmatic

tardy back *(in arrears)*, dilatory, overdue, remiss
targe panoply
target design *(intent)*, destination, end *(intent)*, goal, intention, object, objective, purpose, pursuit *(goal)*, victim. SEE MAIN ENTRY
tariff duty *(tax)*, excise, fare, imposition *(tax)*, levy, tax. SEE MAIN ENTRY
tarnish attaint, brand *(stigmatize)*, contaminate, debase, deface, defacement, defame, demean *(make lower)*, denigrate, depreciate, derogate, discredit *(noun)*, discredit *(verb)*, disgrace *(noun)*, disgrace *(verb)*, dishonor *(shame)*, dishonor *(deprive of honor)*, disparage, humiliate, ignominy, infamy, infect, onus *(stigma)*, opprobrium, pillory, pollute, reproach, scandal, shame, smear, stain, stigma, sully, taint *(corrupt)*. SEE MAIN ENTRY
tarnished blemished, disgraceful, marred
tarnished honor attaint, disgrace, dishonor *(shame)*, ignominy, scandal, shame
tarriance delay
tarry delay, dwell *(reside)*, lodge *(reside)*, loiter, pause, procrastinate, prolong, reside, stop
tarrying deferment
tart astringent, bitter *(acrid tasting)*, caustic
Tartuffish SEE MAIN ENTRY
task act *(undertaking)*, agency *(legal relationship)*, burden, business *(affair)*, calling, campaign, capacity *(job)*, charge *(responsibility)*, duty *(obligation)*, duty *(tax)*, employment, endeavor, enterprise *(undertaking)*, exact, function, job, labor *(work)*, mission, operation, part *(role)*, post, project, pursuit *(occupation)*, role, specialty *(special aptitude)*, tax *(overwork)*, trade *(occupation)*, undertaking *(business)*, undertaking *(enterprise)*, venture, work *(employment)*. SEE MAIN ENTRY
task undertaken undertaking *(attempt)*
taskmaster employer, principal *(director)*, superintendent
taste discretion *(quality of being discreet)*, mode, partake, partiality, predilection, predisposition, propensity, propriety *(correctness)*, sensibility, style
tasteful aesthetic, attractive, elegant, felicitous, fit, palatable, proper
tastefulness decorum
tasteless disreputable, inelegant, insipid, jejune *(dull)*, pedestrian, stale, tawdry
tastelessness indecency
tasty nectarious, palatable, sapid, savory
tattle betray *(disclose)*, divulge, inform *(notify)*, report *(rumor)*
taught informed *(educated)*, knowing
taunt badger, bait *(harass)*, denigrate, discompose, disparage, jape, jeer, mock *(deride)*, offend *(insult)*, pique, plague, press *(goad)*, provocation, provoke, ridicule
taunting critical *(faultfinding)*, instigation
taut firm, rigid
tautness stress *(strain)*
tautologic redundant
tautological iterative, redundant
tautology redundancy. SEE MAIN ENTRY
tawdry blatant *(obtrusive)*, meretricious, poor *(inferior in quality)*, pretentious *(ostentatious)*. SEE MAIN ENTRY
tax assessment *(levy)*, charge *(cost)*, charge *(assess)*, encumber *(hinder)*, exact, excise, excise *(levy a tax)*, exhaust

(deplete), fine, force (coerce), impose (enforce), levy (noun), levy (verb), rebuke, reproach, require (compel), tariff (duties), toll (exact payment). SEE MAIN ENTRY

tax collector   assessor
tax gatherer   assessor
tax haven   shelter (tax benefit)
tax man   assessor
tax on demand   duty (tax)
tax one's energies   strive
tax receiver   assessor
tax sanctuary   shelter (tax benefit)
tax taker   assessor
taxation   ad valorem, duty (tax), excise, levy, tax
taxer   assessor
taxing   onerous, oppressive
taxis   classification
teach   communicate, convey (communicate), disabuse, edify, educate, elucidate, enlighten, explain, impart, inculcate, inform (notify), initiate, instill, nurture. SEE MAIN ENTRY
teach a lesson to   punish
teach by example   demonstrate (establish)
teach by examples   illustrate
teach wickedness   brutalize, pervert
teachable   corrigible, malleable, pliable, sequacious, tractable
teacher   pedagogue
teachers   faculty (teaching staff)
teaching   didactic, direction (guidance), discipline (field of study), doctrine, edification, education, experience (background), guidance, informatory, maxim, precept, preparation, propaganda
teaching body   faculty (teaching staff)
teaching personnel   faculty (teaching staff)
teachings   doctrine
team   band
team of employees   personnel
team up   federalize (associate), involve (participate)
team up with   combine (act in concert), join (associate oneself with)
teammate   coadjutant, contributor (contributor), member (individual in a group), partner
teamwork   coaction, concert, contribution (participation), cooperative
teamworker   contributor (contributor), partner
tear   divide (separate), lancinate, mutilate, race, rend, separate, sever, split
tear apart   disjoint, mutilate
tear assunder   part (separate)
tear asunder   force (break), rend
tear away   deprive
tear down   obliterate, refute
tear into   attack
tear loose   extricate
tear off   denude
tear oneself away   part (leave)
tear out   eliminate (eradicate), eviscerate, excise (cut away), extirpate
tear to pieces   extirpate
tear up   disorganize
tearable   divisible
tearful   disconsolate, lugubrious, querulous
tearing   division (act of dividing), separation
tearing away   avulsion
tearing down   destruction
tearing off   avulsion

tearless   callous
tease   badger, bait (harass), bait (lure), cajole, discompose, harrow, harry (harass), hector, irritate, jape, mock (deride), molest (annoy), offend (insult), perplex, pique, plague, press (goad), provoke
teaser   enigma
technic   instrumentality. SEE MAIN ENTRY
technical   industrial. SEE MAIN ENTRY
technical term   technicality
technicality   detail. SEE MAIN ENTRY
technician   artisan, expert, specialist
technique   avenue (means of attainment), discretion (quality of being discreet), expedient, facility (instrumentality), instrumentality, method, mode, modus operandi, performance (workmanship), specialty (special aptitude), strategy, style, system, treatment
technological   industrial
technology   SEE MAIN ENTRY
tectum   ceiling, habitation (dwelling place), inhabitation (place of dwelling)
tectus   inscrutable
tedious   jejune (dull), lifeless (dull), mundane, onerous, pedestrian, ponderous, prolix, prosaic, repetitious, trite, usual
teem   propagate (increase), pullulate
teeming   copious, full, manifold, populous, productive, profuse, prolific, replete, rife
teemless   barren
teen   juvenile
teenager   adolescent, juvenile, minor
teeter   beat (pulsate)
teetotalism   temperance
tegere   cloak, shroud
telegram   dispatch (message)
telegraphic   laconic, sententious
telescope   abridge (shorten), abstract (summarize), constrict (compress)
telescoped   compact (pithy)
telic   purposeful
tell   annunciate, apprise, betray (disclose), communicate, constrain (compel), convey (communicate), declare, depict, detail (particularize), direct (order), disclose, divulge, enunciate, express, herald, impart, inform (notify), instruct (direct), mention, notify, observe (remark), order, phrase, posit, proclaim, profess (avow), pronounce (speak), propagate (spread), publish, recite, recount, remark, remind, report (disclose), reveal, signify (inform), speak, utter. SEE MAIN ENTRY
tell a falsehood   fabricate (make up), falsify, lie (falsify), misguide, mislead, misrepresent, misstate, perjure, prevaricate
tell a lie   bear false witness, fabricate (make up), misguide, misstate, perjure, prevaricate
tell a secret   confide (divulge)
tell again   recapitulate, repeat (state again)
tell all   confess
tell an untruth   lie (falsify), misguide, mislead, misstate, prevaricate
tell apart   differentiate, discriminate (distinguish)
tell details   detail (particularize)
tell falsehoods about   frame (charge falsely)
tell fortunes   predict, prognosticate
tell from   differentiate
tell fully   detail (particularize)
tell how   explain
tell in detail   recount

tell lies   misrepresent
tell lies about   frame (charge falsely)
tell of   bespeak, connote, evidence, signify (denote)
tell on   betray (disclose)
tell over   repeat (state again)
tell particulars   detail (particularize)
tell secrets   inform (betray)
tell the future   predict
tell the meaning   define
tell the meaning of   denote
tell the truth   bare, disabuse
tell vividly   delineate, depict, portray
tell with assurance of secrecy   confide (divulge)
teller   bystander, deponent, harbinger, informer (a person who provides information)
telling   caveat, cogent, conversation, demonstrative (illustrative), determinative, disclosure (act of disclosing), eloquent, incisive, informatory, noteworthy, persuasive, potent, powerful, recital, strategic, trenchant
tellurian   mundane
telluric   mundane
temblor   cataclysm
temerarious   careless, hot-blooded, impolitic, improvident, imprudent, impulsive (rash), injudicious, lax, negligent, remiss, unpolitic
temerarius   heedless, ill-advised, imprudent, injudicious, precipitate
temeritas   temerity
temerity   audacity. SEE MAIN ENTRY
temerous   negligent, reckless
temper   abate (lessen), adapt, adjust (regulate), allay, alleviate, alter, animus, assuage, character (personal quality), commute, complexion, curb, disposition (inclination), extenuate, frame (mood), lessen, mitigate, modify (moderate), mollify, palliate (abate), passion, posture (attitude), qualify (condition), regulate (adjust), relax, soothe, spirit, subdue
temperament   character (personal quality), color (complexion), conatus, condition (state), disposition (inclination), frame (mood), personality, posture (attitude), predisposition, property (distinctive attribute), spirit, tendency, trait. SEE MAIN ENTRY
temperamental   fractious, sensitive (easily affected)
temperance   austerity, clemency, constraint (restriction), continence, longanimity, moderation, prudence, restraint. SEE MAIN ENTRY
temperantia   continence, control (supervision), moderation, temperance
temperare   control (restrain), forbear, modify (moderate)
temperate   charitable (lenient), controlled (restrained), dispassionate, judicious, normal (sane), peaceable, reasonable (fair)
temperateness   continence, moderation, temperance
temperatio   organization (structure)
tempered   reasonable (fair). SEE MAIN ENTRY
tempering   abatement (reduction), mitigating, palliative (abating)
tempermental   demonstrative (expressive of emotion)
tempest   bluster (commotion), commotion, furor, outburst, turmoil
tempestivus   ripe, seasonable
tempestuous   disorderly, outrageous, severe, vehement. SEE MAIN ENTRY

template pattern

tempo rate

temporal civil (public), corporeal, ephemeral, material (physical), mundane, physical, profane, temporary, transient, transitory

temporarily pro tempore

temporarily established provisional

temporary acting, brief, ephemeral, interim, interlocutory, provisional, tentative, transient, transitory, vicarious (substitutional). SEE MAIN ENTRY

temporary accommodation loan

temporary agreement modus vivendi

temporary arrangement modus vivendi, stopgap

temporary closing lockout

temporary deprivation layoff

temporary discharge layoff

temporary escape reprieve

temporary existence mortality

temporary expedient replacement, stopgap, substitute

temporary halt moratorium

temporary inaction cessation (interlude)

temporary possession occupancy, tenancy

temporary quiet lull

temporary refuge asylum (hiding place)

temporary relief moratorium, reprieve

temporary route detour

temporary settlement modus vivendi

temporary stillness lull

temporary stop extension (postponement), hiatus, pendency

temporary stoppage respite (interval of rest)

temporary substitute stopgap

temporary suspension extension (postponement), layoff

temporary suspension of the execution of a sentence reprieve

temporis intervallum interim

temporis spatium duration

temporize delay, stall, suspend

tempt bait (lure), cajole, coax, entice, entrap, interest, inveigle, lure, motivate, prompt

temptare attempt, try (attempt)

temptation bribery, cause (reason), hush money, incentive, provocation, seduction

tempted eager

temptestuousness bluster (commotion)

tempting attractive, bribery, palatable, persuasive, provocative, sapid, savory

tempus date, emergency, occasion

temulentus drunk

tenability credibility

tenable believable, colorable (plausible), convincing, defensible, inexpugnable, persuasive, reasonable (rational). SEE MAIN ENTRY

tenableness credibility

tenacious chronic, cohesive (sticking), diligent, dogmatic, durable, indestructible, indivisible, industrious, inexorable, infallible, inflexible, inseparable, insistent, intractable, obdurate, patient, permanent, persistent, purposeful, relentless, resolute, sedulous, serious (devoted), stable, steadfast, strong, unrelenting, unremitting, unyielding, willful

tenaciousness adherence (adhesion), adherence (devotion), adhesion (loyalty), diligence (perseverance), strength, tenacity

tenacitas tenacity

tenacity adherence (adhesion), adherence (devotion), adhesion (loyalty), dili-

gence (perseverance), industry (activity), longanimity, purpose, resolution (decision), retention, rigor, strength. SEE MAIN ENTRY

tenancy duration, enjoyment (use), habitation (act of inhabiting), inhabitation (act of dwelling in), ownership, possession (ownership), seisin, term (duration), time. SEE MAIN ENTRY

tenant denizen, dwell (reside), habitant, inhabit, inhabitant, lessee, lodge (reside), lodger, occupant, reside, resident. SEE MAIN ENTRY

tenant-landlord agreement lease

tenantable habitable

tenanted populous

tenantless devoid

tenantry inhabitation (act of dwelling in)

tenative interim

tenax close (rigorous), parsimonious, penurious

tend care (regard), concern (care), contribute (assist), dispose (incline), foster, gravitate, keep (shelter), pander, prefer, preserve, serve (assist)

tend to conduce

tend to show evidence

tend toward discriminate (treat differently), gravitate

tendency animus, aptitude, bias, character (personal quality), characteristic, color (complexion), conatus, direction (course), disposition (inclination), habit, inclination, instinct, mode, penchant, position (point of view), predilection, predisposition, probability, proclivity, propensity, quality (grade), standpoint, temperament, tenor. SEE MAIN ENTRY

tendency to change the mind indecision

tendency to waver indecision

tender benevolent, bestow, bid, cede, confer (give), contribute (indemnify), contribute (supply), dispense, extend (offer), introduce, invitation, overture, pay, pose (propound), present (make a gift), proffer, proposal (suggestion), propose, proposition, propound, remit (send payment), remit (submit for consideration), satisfy (discharge), submit (give). SEE MAIN ENTRY

tender age nonage

tender feeling affection

tender in advance prepay

tender offer SEE MAIN ENTRY

tender one's resignation abandon (withdraw), demit, resign, retire (conclude a career)

tender passion affection

tender payment disburse (pay out)

tender performance offer (tender)

tenderfoot neophyte

tenderhearted sensitive (easily affected)

tenderness affection, affinity (regard), benevolence (disposition to do good), consideration (sympathetic regard)

tending inclined, prone

tending to attract attention conspic-uous

tending to cause death deadly, malignant, pernicious, pestilent

tending to elude elusive

tending to escape elusive

tending to evade evasive

tending to excite lustful desires obscene

tending to impair prejudicial

tending to obstruct prejudicial

tending to slip away elusive

tenement estate (property)

tenere detain (restrain), hold (possess), interest, occupy (engage), own, possess, restrain, retain (keep in possession)

tenet article (precept), belief (something believed), concept, conviction (persuasion), doctrine, dogma, idea, law, precept, principle (axiom), rule (legal dictate), thesis

tenets platform

tenor complexion, condition (state), connotation, content (meaning), context, degree (magnitude), gist (substance), import, main point, meaning, mode, signification, spirit, substance (essential nature), temperament. SEE MAIN ENTRY

tense rigid

tenseness stress (strain)

tension conflict, discaccord, feud, ill will, pressure, stress (strain)

tensity stress (strain)

tentative conditional, hesitant, interlocutory, problematic, provisional, speculative, uncertain (questionable), undecided, unsettled, vicarious (substitutional). SEE MAIN ENTRY

tentative approach proposition

tentative explanation hypothesis

tentative law hypothesis

tentative statement proposition, suggestion

tentativeness hesitation

tenuis inconsiderable, negligible, petty, poor (inferior in quality), slight

tenuitas poverty

tenuous illusory, insubstantial, marginal, nonsubstantial (not sturdy), null (insignificant), slight. SEE MAIN ENTRY

tenure domain (land owned), duration, enjoyment (use), occupancy, occupation (possession), ownership, period, phase (period), seisin, tenancy, term (duration), time, title (right). SEE MAIN ENTRY

tenure by lease leasehold

tepidity disinterest (lack of interest)

tergiversari equivocate, prevaricate

tergiversate abandon (relinquish), defect, equivocate, leave (depart), palter, prevaricate, quit (discontinue), rebel, recant, secede. SEE MAIN ENTRY

tergiversating false (disloyal), regressive, undependable, unreliable, untrustworthy

tergiversatio evasion

tergiversation breach, evasion, reversal, revolt, sedition

tergiversator pariah

term call (title), call (title), clause, condition (contingent provision), define, denominate, denomination, duration, expiration, finality, identify, label, life (period of existence), lifetime, option (contractual provision), period, phase (period), phrase, provision (clause), purview, qualification (condition), session, technicality, tenure, time, title (division). SEE MAIN ENTRY

term of activity life (period of existence)

term of effectiveness life (period of existence)

term of imprisonment captivity

term of life age

term of reference article (distinct section of a writing)

terminable defeasible, determinable (liable to be terminated). SEE MAIN ENTRY

terminal border, conclusive (settled), destination, end (termination), extreme (last), final, finality, last (final), mete, ultimate

terminal point destination, end (termination), extremity (furthest point), objective

terminally ill in extremis
terminare finish, limit
terminate abate *(extinguish)*, abolish, abrogate *(rescind)*, adjourn, annul, cancel, cap, cease, complete, conclude *(complete)*, consummate, culminate, decide, desist, destroy *(void)*, discontinue *(abandon)*, eliminate *(eradicate)*, expire, extinguish, finish, halt, lapse *(cease)*, liquidate *(convert into cash)*, obstruct, overthrow, palliate *(abate)*, quash, quit *(discontinue)*, rest *(cease from action)*, result, shut, slay, stop. SEE MAIN ENTRY
terminate a trial rest *(end a legal case)*
terminate business affairs liquidate *(convert into cash)*
terminate work strike *(refuse to work)*
terminated complete *(ended)*, dead, defunct, through
terminated trial mistrial
terminating final, last *(final)*
termination abatement *(extinguishment)*, adjournment, barrier, border, cancellation, close *(conclusion)*, conclusion *(outcome)*, denouement, destination, desuetude, discharge *(performance)*, discontinuance *(act of discontinuing)*, discontinuance *(interruption of a legal action)*, effect, end *(termination)*, expiration, extremity *(death)*, extremity *(furthest point)*, finality, frontier, halt, lapse *(expiration)*, layoff, moratorium, rescision, resignation *(relinquishment)*, result. SEE MAIN ENTRY
termination of a pregnancy abortion *(feticide)*
termination of an action dismissal *(termination of a proceeding)*, nonsuit
termination of cohabitation estrangement
termination of employment layoff
termination of life death, homicide
termination of marital cohabitation separation
termination of membership expulsion
terminational complete *(ended)*, definitive, final, last *(final)*
terminative complete *(ended)*, conclusive *(settled)*, definitive, extreme *(last)*, final, last *(final)*, ultimate
terminology denomination, language, parlance, phraseology
terminus boundary
terminus cessation *(termination)*
terminus close *(conclusion)*, denouement
terminus destination, end *(termination)*, extremity *(furthest point)*, finality
terminus limit
terminus mete, periphery
termless indeterminate, infinite, openended, unlimited
termly intermittent
termor lodger
terms adjustment, arrangement *(understanding)*, case *(set of circumstances)*, compromise, posture *(situation)*, premises *(hypotheses)*, settlement
terms for agreement contract
terms imposed circumstances
terms proposed counteroffer, proposition
terra district
terra firma cornerstone
terrae filius nonentity
terrain land, locality, parcel, region, territory, zone
terrene mundane
terrestrial mundane

terrible deplorable, dire, formidable, gross *(flagrant)*, heinous, lamentable, loathsome, nefarious, pestilent, regrettable, sinister. SEE MAIN ENTRY
terrible accident disaster
terrifc meritorious. SEE MAIN ENTRY
terrific prodigious *(enormous)*
terrify endanger, frighten, intimidate, menace
terrifying formidable
territorial local, regional
territorial division district
territorial range of authority jurisdiction
territorial shape dimension
territory area *(province)*, bailiwick, capacity *(sphere)*, circuit, district, domain *(sphere of influence)*, dominion *(absolute ownership)*, estate *(property)*, freehold, jurisdiction, locality, location, parcel, possessions, property *(land)*, province, purview, realm, region, scope, section *(vicinity)*, site, space, venue, vicinity, zone. SEE MAIN ENTRY
territory for defense buffer zone
terror fear
terror fright
terror panic, phobia, trepidation
terrorism anarchy, lynch law. SEE MAIN ENTRY
terrorist assailant, criminal. SEE MAIN ENTRY
terrorist activity SEE MAIN ENTRY
terrorize bait *(harass)*, coerce, endanger, frighten, harass, intimidate, threaten
terse cohesive *(compact)*, compact *(pithy)*, laconic, pithy, sententious, succinct
test attempt, canon, check *(inspect)*, criterion, endeavor, experiment, indagation, question *(inquiry)*, research, survey *(poll)*, trial *(experiment)*, try *(attempt)*, venture. SEE MAIN ENTRY
test case criterion
test of endurance contest *(competition)*
testable deductible *(provable)*, incontrovertible, irrefutable
testament certificate, codicil, will *(testamentary instrument)*. SEE MAIN ENTRY
testamentary heritable. SEE MAIN ENTRY
testamentary declaration testament
testamentary decree testament
testamentary disposition bequest, conveyance, demise *(conveyance)*
testamentary gift bequest, legacy
testamentum testament, will *(testamentary instrument)*
testari depose *(testify)*, testify, witness *(attest to)*
testate SEE MAIN ENTRY
testator contributor *(giver)*, decedent, grantor
tested conclusive *(determinative)*, definite, dependable, genuine, indubious, meritorious, safe
testee subject *(object)*
testem facere attest
testificari attest, depose *(testify)*, testify, witness *(attest to)*
testificatio attestation
testification affirmation, attestation, averment, avouchment, certification *(attested copy)*, corroboration, deposition, reference *(recommendation)*
testification under oath affidavit
testified to alleged
testifier affiant, affirmant, bystander, deponent, eyewitness, witness
testify acknowledge *(verify)*, affirm *(declare solemnly)*, avouch *(avow)*, avow,

bear *(adduce)*, bespeak, certify *(attest)*, inform *(notify)*, manifest, posit, promise *(vow)*, verify *(swear)*, vouch. SEE MAIN ENTRY
testify against inform *(betray)*
testify to attest, corroborate, establish *(show)*, report *(disclose)*, witness *(attest to)*
testimonial affirmation, deposition, monument, recommendation, remembrance *(commemoration)*, reminder, respect
testimonial averment admission *(disclosure)*
testimonials credentials
testimonium affirmation
testimonium attestation, deposition, evidence *(noun)*, evidence *(verb)*, proof, testimony
testimonium dicere witness *(attest to)*
testimonium per tabulas datum affidavit
testimony adjuration, admission *(disclosure)*, affirmance *(legal affirmation)*, affirmation, attestation, avowal, certification *(attested copy)*, corroboration, deposition, disclosure *(something disclosed)*, proof, reference *(recommendation)*, statement. SEE MAIN ENTRY
testing trial *(experiment)*
testing program experiment, research
testis witness
testy fractious, perverse, petulant, querulous, spiteful
tether fix *(make firm)*, handcuff, restrict, trammel
tethered fixed *(securely placed)*
text content *(meaning)*, contents, context, hornbook, meaning, phraseology, scenario, script, subject *(topic)*
textbook hornbook
textual literal
thalamus chamber *(compartment)*
thankful indebted
thankless undesirable, unrequited
thanklessness ingratitude
thanks recognition
that being so consequently
that being the case consequently
that is a savoir
that is to say a savoir
that may be determined determinable *(ascertainable)*
that which a person owes to another obligation *(duty)*
that which attaches attachment *(act of affixing)*
that which furnishes proof evidence
that which is comprehended coverage *(scope)*
that which is decided holding *(ruling of a court)*
that which is due from a person obligation *(duty)*
that which is owed debit
that which is owing due, obligation *(liability)*, responsibility *(accountability)*
that which is proper decorum
that which tends to prove evidence
thaumaturgy mystery
the accused defendant
the act of tracing delineation
the bench forum *(court)*
the case basic facts
the court judge
the deceased dead
the defense litigant
the defunct dead
the departed dead
the entirety in solido

the facts in the matter   basic facts
the facts of the case   basic facts
the following   a savoir
the government   prosecution *(government agency)*
the late   dead
the late lamented   dead
the legal fraternity   bar *(body of lawyers)*
the most possible   utmost
the other side   contra
the outvoted   minority *(outnumbered group)*
the people   district attorney, prosecution *(government agency)*
the prosecuting attorney   prosecution *(government agency)*
the prosecution   contender, district attorney
the state   district attorney, prosecution *(government agency)*
the succeeding   a savoir
the unforeseen   bombshell
the whole   sum *(total)*
the whole story   basic facts
theater   scene
theatralis   pretentious *(pompous)*
theatrecraft   histrionics
theatric   histrionic
theatrical   grandiose, histrionic, meretricious, orotund
theatricalism   histrionics
theatricality   histrionics, pretense *(ostentation)*
theatricalness   histrionics
theft   burglary, conversion *(misappropriation)*, embezzlement, housebreaking, larceny, misappropriation, plunder, robbery, spoliation. SEE MAIN ENTRY
theft of money entrusted to one's care   embezzlement
theft of money entrusted to one's management   embezzlement
theistic   sacrosanct
theme   content *(meaning)*, motif, question *(issue)*, subject *(topic)*, thesis
theme of inquiry   question *(inquiry)*
themes   contents
then   late *(defunct)*
then again   also
theologic   sacrosanct
theological   sacrosanct
theorem   inference, postulate, prescription *(directive)*, principle *(axiom)*, supposition
theorems   premises *(hypotheses)*
theoretical   debatable, disputable, indefinite, intangible, moot, nonexistent, presumptive, speculative. SEE MAIN ENTRY
theorization   generalization, speculation *(conjecture)*
theorize   assume *(suppose)*, derive *(deduce)*, generalize, guess, opine, ponder, postulate, presume, presuppose, prognosticate, rationalize, reason *(conclude)*, reflect *(ponder)*, speculate *(conjecture)*, surmise, suspect *(think)*
theory   assumption *(supposition)*, concept, conjecture, conviction *(persuasion)*, deduction *(conclusion)*, generalization, hypothesis, idea, inference, opinion *(belief)*, perception, proposition, rationale, speculation *(conjecture)*, supposition, thesis. SEE MAIN ENTRY
theory of business   finance
theory of fiscal relations   finance
therapeutic   curative, cure, medicinal,

palliative *(abating)*, remedial, salubrious, salutary
therapeutical   medicinal, salubrious
therapy   treatment
there   SEE MAIN ENTRY
thereafter   ex post facto. SEE MAIN ENTRY
thereby   SEE MAIN ENTRY
therefore   consequently
therein   herein, wherein
theretofore   SEE MAIN ENTRY
thersitical   scandalous
thesaurus   treasury
theses   premises *(hypotheses)*
thesis   conjecture, contents, deduction *(conclusion)*, hypothesis, inference, opinion *(belief)*, postulate, proposition, subject *(topic)*, supposition, theory. SEE MAIN ENTRY
thews   sinew
thick   cohesive *(compact)*, compact *(dense)*, impervious, obtuse, opaque, ossified, populous, rife, solid *(compact)*
thick-headed   opaque
thick-skinned   callous, impervious
thick-witted   opaque
thick-wittedness   opacity
thicken   crystallize
thickened   ossified
thickening   congealment
thicket   assemblage
thickheaded   obtuse
thickheadedness   opacity
thickly settled   populous
thickness   caliber *(measurement)*, congealment, density, opacity
thief   burglar, convict, criminal, embezzler, hoodlum, lawbreaker, outlaw. SEE MAIN ENTRY
thieve   carry away, defalcate, despoil, embezzle, hold up *(rob)*, impropriate, loot, pilfer, pillage, pirate *(take by violence)*, plunder, purloin, steal
thievery   burglary, conversion *(misappropriation)*, embezzlement, housebreaking, larceny, misappropriation, plagiarism, racket, robbery, spoliation, theft
thieving   larcenous
thievish   furtive, larcenous, stealthy
thievishness   dishonesty
thin   deficient, dilute, diminish, excise *(cut away)*, extenuate, insubstantial, insufficient, jejune *(dull)*, lessen, minimal, minimize, narrow, nonsubstantial *(not sufficient)*, reduce, slight, tenuous
thin out   deploy, dilute, diminish, lessen
thin with liquid   dilute
thing   article *(commodity)*
things   effects
things as they are   status quo
things for sale   goods
think   deduce, deduct *(conclude by reasoning)*, deem, expect *(consider probable)*, guess, muse, opine, presume, presuppose, rationalize, reason *(conclude)*, reflect *(ponder)*, speculate *(conjecture)*, surmise. SEE MAIN ENTRY
think about   consider, devote, digest *(comprehend)*, muse, regard *(pay attention)*, study
think ahead   plan, scheme
think anxiously   brood
think back   remember
think back to   recall *(remember)*
think better   prefer
think better of   reconsider, repent
think carefully   deliberate
think credible   assume *(suppose)*
think deeply   ponder

think differently   differ *(disagree)*, differ *(vary)*, disagree
think highly of   recommend, regard *(hold in esteem)*
think ill of   disapprove *(condemn)*
think intensely   concentrate *(pay attention)*
think it over   doubt *(hesitate)*
think likely   assume *(suppose)*, deduce, deduct *(conclude by reasoning)*, expect *(consider probable)*, guess, presume
think little of   disparage, disregard, minimize
think logically   rationalize
think no more of   dismiss *(put out of consideration)*
think nothing of   disdain, disregard, minimize
think of   conjure, initiate, invent *(produce for the first time)*, recollect
think on   ponder
think one deserves   claim *(demand)*
think out   calculate, scheme, solve
think over   brood, deliberate, muse, pause, reconsider
think probable   assume *(suppose)*
think reprehensible   disapprove *(condemn)*
think through   reason *(conclude)*
think too little of   underestimate
think twice   beware, hesitate, pause
think unworthy of notice   disdain
think up   conjure, create, frame *(formulate)*, invent *(produce for the first time)*, make, originate
think well of   regard *(hold in esteem)*
think wrong   disapprove *(condemn)*
thinkable   colorable *(plausible)*, plausible, possible, potential, viable
thinker   mastermind
thinking   assumption *(supposition)*, circumspect, cogitative, conviction *(persuasion)*, dialectic, opinion *(belief)*, ratiocination, rational, reason *(sound judgment)*, reflection *(thought)*, sapient, sensible
thinking out   deliberation
thinly scattered   scarce
thinness   immateriality, paucity
thinning out   erosion
thirst   desire, need *(deprivation)*
thirst for   need
thorny   impracticable, precarious
thorough   accurate, circumspect, complete *(all-embracing)*, comprehensive, conscientious, definitive, detailed, diligent, faithful *(diligent)*, industrious, ingrained, intensive, judicious, meticulous, outright, painstaking, particular *(exacting)*, plenary, precise, punctilious, radical *(extreme)*, scrupulous, systematic, total, unmitigated. SEE MAIN ENTRY
thoroughfare   causeway
thoroughgoing   circumspect, complete *(all-embracing)*, comprehensive, diligent, intensive, meticulous, particular *(exacting)*, radical *(extreme)*, systematic, thorough, total, trenchant
thoroughgoingness   diligence *(care)*
thoroughly   in toto, purely *(positively)*
thoroughness   caution *(vigilance)*, diligence *(care)*
those holding power   authorities
those in command   authorities
those in control   authorities
those of influence   authorities
those who rule   authorities

though regardless

thought apprehension *(perception)*, concept, consideration *(sympathetic regard)*, contemplation, deliberation, idea, notice *(heed)*, notion, opinion *(belief)*, perspective, point *(item)*, proposal *(suggestion)*, ratiocination, reason *(sound judgment)*, remark, suggestion, theory. SEE MAIN ENTRY

thought beforehand forethought

thought out intentional, premeditated

thought-out deliberate

thought-provoking sapid, suggestive *(evocative)*

thoughtful benevolent, careful, circumspect, cogitative, deliberate, discreet, discriminating *(judicious)*, earnest, intentional, judicial, judicious, pensive, politic, profound *(esoteric)*, provident *(showing foresight)*, prudent, rational, sensible

thoughtful regard consideration *(sympathetic regard)*

thoughtfulness benevolence *(disposition to do good)*, consideration *(sympathetic regard)*, contemplation, courtesy, deliberation, discretion *(quality of being discreet)*, discrimination *(good judgment)*, forethought, interest *(concern)*, introspection, largess *(generosity)*

thoughtless blind *(not discerning)*, careless, casual, cursory, derelict *(negligent)*, fatuous, heedless, hot-blooded, ill-judged, impolitic, improvident, imprudent, impulsive *(rash)*, inadvertent, injudicious, irrational, irresponsible, lax, misadvised, negligent, oblivious, perfunctory, perverse, precipitate, reckless, remiss, slipshod, unpremeditated, unwitting, vacuous. SEE MAIN ENTRY

thoughtlessness disinterest *(lack of interest)*, disregard *(lack of respect)*, inconsideration, indiscretion, ingratitude, laxity, neglect, oversight *(carelessness)*, temerity

thoughts of the past hindsight, retrospect

thrall captive, durance, servitude, subjection. SEE MAIN ENTRY

thralldom bondage, custody *(incarceration)*, durance, servitude, thrall

thrash beat *(strike)*, lash *(strike)*

thrashing battery

thrasonical orgulous

thread nexus

threadbare trite

threadbare phrase platitude

threat apprehension *(fear)*, coercion, danger, dun, duress, hazard, jeopardy, menace, peril, pitfall, ultimatum, warning. SEE MAIN ENTRY

threaten bait *(harass)*, brandish, challenge, coerce, compel, endanger, exact, forewarn, frighten, hector, impend, intimidate, jeopardize, menace, portend, presage, promise *(raise expectations)*. SEE MAIN ENTRY

threatening abusive, chilling effect, dangerous, formidable, imminent, insalubrious, noxious, ominous, pending *(imminent)*, pestilent, portentous *(ominous)*, precarious, pugnacious, sinister, unpropitious

threatening harm imminent

threatful ominous

thresh beat *(strike)*

threshold cornerstone, entrance, margin *(outside limit)*, onset *(commencement)*, outline *(boundary)*, outset, start. SEE MAIN ENTRY

thrift austerity, economy *(frugality)*, moderation, prudence

thriftiness austerity, economy *(frugality)*, moderation

thriftless improvident, prodigal, profligate *(extravagant)*, profuse

thrifty economic, economical, frugal, parsimonious, provident *(frugal)*, prudent

thrifty use management *(judicious use)*

thrill enjoyment *(pleasure)*, passion

thrilled ecstatic, proud *(self-respecting)*

thrilling moving *(evoking emotion)*, provocative

thrive gain, germinate, increase, prevail *(triumph)*, proliferate, succeed *(attain)*

thriving cumulative *(increasing)*, prosperous, successful

thriving condition prosperity

thriving conditions boom *(prosperity)*

thriving economy boom *(prosperity)*

throb beat *(pulsate)*

throbbing painful

throe outbreak, outburst

throng assemblage, collection *(assembly)*, congregate, mass *(body of persons)*, meet

thronged populous

throttle occlude, shut, stifle

throttle down curb

through arrant *(definite)*, complete *(ended)*, hereby, thereby. SEE MAIN ENTRY

through and through outright

through road causeway

through the medium of hereby, thereby

throughout ad interim, wholly. SEE MAIN ENTRY

throughway way *(channel)*

throw emit, impel, launch *(project)*, project *(impel forward)*, send

throw a veil over camouflage, conceal

throw aside forgo, reject

throw away abandon *(relinquish)*, dislodge, dispel, jettison, relinquish

throw back reflect *(mirror)*, repulse

throw dishonor upon brand *(stigmatize)*, disgrace

throw doubt upon impugn

throw down overthrow, precipitate *(throw down violently)*, subvert

throw headlong precipitate *(throw down violently)*

throw into confusion agitate *(perturb)*, confound, confuse *(bewilder)*, confuse *(create disorder)*, discompose, disconcert, dislocate, disorganize, disorient, misdirect, muddle, obfuscate, perturb

throw into disorder confuse *(create disorder)*, disorganize, disorient

throw into prison arrest *(apprehend)*, immure

throw light upon define, elucidate, explain, explicate, exposit, interpret, resolve *(solve)*, solve

throw off abandon *(relinquish)*, dispel, emit, repel *(drive back)*

throw off heat radiate

throw off the scent obfuscate

throw oneself upon attack

throw open admit *(give access)*, manifest

throw open to inquiry canvass

throw out discharge *(dismiss)*, dislodge, displace *(remove)*, eject *(evict)*, eject *(expel)*, eliminate *(exclude)*, emit, exclude, expel, oust, pose *(propound)*, propound, radiate, reject, relegate

throw out of gear luxate

throw out of joint dislocate

throw out of order agitate *(shake up)*, dislocate, disorganize, disorient, muddle

throw over overthrow

throw overboard jettison

throwback reversion *(act of returning)*

throwing out disqualification *(rejection)*, expulsion

thrown away lost *(taken away)*

thrown overboard derelict *(abandoned)*

thrust emphasis, foray, gravamen, impetus, impinge, impulse, launch *(project)*, onset *(assault)*, operation, project *(impel forward)*

thrust at accost, assail, assault, oppugn

thrust back repel *(drive back)*

thrust in impact, inject, interject, interpose, intrude, plant *(place firmly)*

thrust oneself intrude

thrust oneself in impose *(intrude)*

thrust out deport *(banish)*, dislodge, eject *(evict)*, eject *(expel)*, eliminate *(exclude)*, evict, exclude, expel, oust

thrust under immerse *(plunge into)*

thrust upon surreptitiously foist

thrustful compelling, decisive

thrusting out deportation

thruway causeway

thug assailant

thumb peruse

thumb through read

thumbnail sketch brief

thump beat *(pulsate)*

thumping prodigious *(enormous)*

thunder barrage, outbreak, outburst

thunder against inveigh, reprimand

thunder forth proclaim

thunderbolt bombshell

thunderclap bombshell

thunderous resounding

thunderstruck speechless

thus a fortiori, consequently

thusly a priori, consequently

thwart annoy, arrest *(stop)*, avert, balk, bar *(hinder)*, beat *(defeat)*, block, check *(restrain)*, circumvent, condemn *(ban)*, constrict *(inhibit)*, contain *(restrain)*, contravene, counter, countervail, defeat, deter, disadvantage, discontinue *(break continuity)*, discourage, disrupt, encumber *(hinder)*, enjoin, estop, fight *(counteract)*, foil, forestall, frustrate, halt, hamper, hold up *(delay)*, impede, inconvenience, interdict, interfere, interrupt, keep *(restrain)*, kill *(defeat)*, obstruct, occlude, oppugn, overreach, override, parry, preclude, prevent, prohibit, repulse, resist *(oppose)*, stay *(halt)*, stem *(check)*, stop, toll *(stop)*, trammel, withstand. SEE MAIN ENTRY

thwarted disappointed

thwarted expectation frustration

thwarter deterrence, deterrent

thwarting defeat, disadvantageous, frustration, preventive

ticket brand, coupon, fare, key *(passport)*, label *(noun)*, label *(verb)*, pigeonhole, trademark

ticket incorrectly mislabel

ticket of leave permit

ticklish insecure, precarious

tidal wave cataclysm

tide outflow

tide over continue *(adjourn)*

tide turning SEE MAIN ENTRY

tidewater littoral

tidings intelligence *(news)*, report *(detailed account)*, story *(narrative)*

tidy compact (*pithy*), meticulous

tie adherence (*adhesion*), adherence (*devotion*), adhesion (*loyalty*), attachment (*act of affixing*), chain (*nexus*), charge (*lien*), combine (*join together*), connect (*join together*), connection (*fastening*), connection (*relation*), contact (*association*), deadlock, fetter (*noun*), fetter (*verb*), handcuff, kinship, liaison, marriage (*intimate relationship*), nexus, prevent, privity, propinquity (*kinship*), relate (*establish a connection*), relation (*connection*), relationship (*connection*), restrain, trammel

tie down fetter

tie in with correspond (*be equivalent*), involve (*implicate*), pertain

tie one's hands handcuff

tie the hands of handcuff

tie together intertwine

tie up constrict (*inhibit*), encumber (*hinder*), handcuff, restrict, trammel

tie-in relation (*connection*), relevance

tied bound, cohesive (*sticking*), compound, equal, inextricable, interrelated, related

tied down indentured

tied in with relevant

tied together conjoint

tier degree (*station*)

ties SEE MAIN ENTRY

ties of blood affiliation (*bloodline*), degree (*kinship*), filiation

ties of family blood

ties of race affiliation (*bloodline*)

tiff bicker, brawl

tight cohesive (*compact*), compact (*dense*), fixed (*securely placed*), illiberal, impervious, parsimonious, solid (*compact*)

tight situation predicament, problem, quagmire

tight spot imbroglio, predicament

tight-lipped mute

tighten adhere (*fasten*), constrict (*compress*)

tightfisted illiberal

tightly knit compact (*dense*)

tightness stress (*strain*)

til until

till ad interim, bank, coffer, cultivate, treasury

tilt bicker, compete

tilted oblique (*slanted*)

timbre intonation

time annum, chance (*fortuity*), date (*noun*), date (*verb*), duration, life (*period of existence*), lifetime, occasion, opportunity, period, phase (*period*), point (*period of time*), term (*duration*), timeliness. SEE MAIN ENTRY

time ahead prospect (*outlook*)

time during which anything occurs date

time from birth to death life (*period of existence*)

time interval period

time of life age

time of war belligerency

time off furlough, holiday

time out halt, pause, recess

time payment loan

time saving economic

time stretch period

time without end perpetuity

time worn antique

time-honored conventional, familiar (*customary*), illustrious, inveterate, prescriptive, traditional

time-saving economical

timed punctual

timeful seasonable

timeless durable, incessant, infinite

timelessness perpetuity

timeliness dispatch (*promptness*), expedience. SEE MAIN ENTRY

timely apposite, appropriate, favorable (*advantageous*), felicitous, fitting, opportune, prompt, propitious, punctual, seasonable, suitable

timely care precaution

timere fear

timeserving undependable

timetable calendar (*list of cases*), calendar (*record of yearly periods*), schedule

timeworn dilapidated, obsolete, old, stale

timid diffident, hesitant, irresolute, recreant

timidity fear

timor fear

timorous diffident, recreant

timorousness fear

tincture minimum, penetrate

tinge minimum, stain

tingere imbue

tingling ecstatic

tinker repair

tinsel meretricious, tawdry

tint stain

tiny impalpable, minimal, remote (*small*), tenuous

tip bonus, bounty, edge (*border*), end (*termination*), extremity (*furthest point*), gratuity (*present*), herald, inform (*notify*), intelligence (*news*), perquisite, pinnacle, recommendation, reward, suggestion. SEE MAIN ENTRY

tip off notify

tip over upset

tipped informed (*having information*), oblique (*slanted*)

tipper informant, informer (*a person who provides information*)

tipping oblique (*slanted*)

tipple carouse

tipster bystander, informant, informer (*one providing criminal information*), informer (*a person who provides information*)

tiptop superlative

tirade bombast, declamation, denunciation, diatribe, disparagement, harangue, obloquy, philippic, revilement, stricture

tire exhaust (*deplete*), succumb

tire out tax (*overwork*)

tired languid, lifeless (*dull*)

tiredness languor, prostration

tireless diligent, faithful (*diligent*), industrious, persistent, undaunted

tirelessness diligence (*perseverance*)

tiresome irksome, jejune (*dull*), lifeless (*dull*), operose, painful, pedestrian, prolix, prosaic, vexatious

tiring irksome, operose, oppressive

tiro probationer (*one being tested*)

titallative sapid

titanic prodigious (*enormous*), strong

tithe tax, toll (*tax*)

titillate bait (*lure*), interest

titillating attractive, provocative, salacious, sapid, suggestive (*risqué*)

title caption, claim (*right*), degree (*academic title*), denominate, denomination, designation (*symbol*), dominion (*absolute ownership*), fee (*estate*), heading, interest (*ownership*), label, nominate, ownership,

possession (*ownership*), prerogative, privilege, prize, right (*entitlement*), seisin, stake (*interest*), subheading, term (*expression*). SEE MAIN ENTRY

title deed debenture

title impairment incumbrance (*lien*)

title incorrectly mislabel

title of honor degree (*academic title*)

titleholder landholder, landowner

tittle iota, minimum, scintilla

titular nominal

titulary nominal

titulus inscription

to until

to a certain extent in part, quasi

to a degree fairly (*moderately*), in part

to a limited extent fairly (*moderately*), in part

to all appearances prima facie (*self-evident*)

to all intents and purposes as a rule

to be future, prospective

to be believed convincing

to be decided disputable

to be depended on credible, official

to be expected foreseeable, probable

to be had available, disposable

to be paid delinquent (*overdue*), due (*owed*)

to be relied upon credible

to be similiar correspond (*be equivalent*)

to be supposed apparent (*presumptive*)

to be trusted official

to blame delinquent (*guilty of a misdeed*), guilty

to bring to completion consummate

to bring together desegregate

to come forthcoming, future, immediate (*imminent*), inevitable, prospective

to each according to his share per capita, pro rata

to infinity ad infinitum

to no end unavailing

to no purpose unavailing

to one's advantage beneficial

to one's liking attractive

to some extent fairly (*moderately*)

to that end a priori, consequently

to the contrary contra

to the end throughout (*all over*)

to the letter faithfully, literal, verbatim

to the point applicable, apposite, brief, cogent, cohesive (*compact*), compact (*pithy*), concise, explicit, felicitous, germane, laconic, pertinent, relevant, sententious, succinct

to the purpose apposite, effective (*efficient*), felicitous, fit, pertinent, practical, relevant

to the same degree equal

to the time when until

to this day through (*until now*)

to wit a savoir

toady pander, truckle

toadying obsequious, sequacious, subservient

toast honor

toddler infant

together along, conjoint, en masse, intact

together with also

togetherness integration (*assimilation*)

toil effort, endeavor (*noun*), endeavor (*verb*), industry (*activity*), labor (*work*), labor, persevere, strive, work (*effort*)

toil unceasingly persist

toiler employee

toilsome onerous, operose, oppressive
token binder, bounty, brand, clue, coupon, denote, designation *(symbol)*, device *(distinguishing mark)*, expression *(manifestation)*, guaranty, indicant, indication, indicator, money, nominal, null *(insignificant)*, perquisite, precursor, prize, remembrance *(commemoration)*, security *(pledge)*, specialty *(distinctive mark)*, symbol, symptom. SEE MAIN ENTRY
token payment binder, installment, pledge *(security)*
tokens indicia
told acquainted, informed *(having information)*, narrative, oral, parol, stated
told in confidence confidential
tolerability admissibility, mediocrity
tolerable admissible, allowable, allowed, considerable, fair *(satisfactory)*, imperfect, marginal, mediocre, passable, permissible, reasonable *(fair)*, unobjectionable
tolerableness mediocrity
tolerably fairly *(moderately)*
tolerance acceptance, benevolence *(disposition to do good)*, charter *(sanction)*, clemency, composure, consent, disinterest *(lack of prejudice)*, dispensation *(exception)*, franchise *(license)*, goodwill, indulgence, leave *(permission)*, lenience, longanimity, permission, privilege, resignation *(passive acceptance)*, sanction *(permission)*, sufferance, temperance. SEE MAIN ENTRY
tolerans patient
tolerant benevolent, charitable *(lenient)*, dispassionate, lenient, liberal *(broad minded)*, nonmilitant, open-minded, patient, peaceable, permissive, receptive, resigned, stoical, unbiased, unprejudiced
tolerantia tolerance
tolerantly fairly *(impartially)*
tolerare bear *(tolerate)*, endure *(suffer)*, tolerate
tolerate abide, accept *(assent)*, allow *(endure)*, authorize, concede, condescend *(deign)*, condone, consent, endure *(suffer)*, forbear, let *(permit)*, palliate *(excuse)*, permit, receive *(permit to enter)*, recognize *(acknowledge)*, resist *(withstand)*, sanction, submit *(yield)*, suffer *(permit)*, vouchsafe. SEE MAIN ENTRY
tolerated allowable, allowed
tolerating permissive
toleratio sufferance
toleration acceptance, approval, charter *(sanction)*, clemency, consent, disinterest *(lack of prejudice)*, dispensation *(exception)*, indulgence, lenience, longanimity, resignation *(passive acceptance)*, sanction *(permission)*, sufferance, temperance, tolerance, understanding *(tolerance)*
toll assessment *(levy)*, charge *(cost)*, duty *(tax)*, exact, excise, fare, fee *(charge)*, imposition *(tax)*, levy, price, tax. SEE MAIN ENTRY
tollere abolish, cancel
tome publication *(printed matter)*
tonality intonation
tone character *(personal quality)*, color *(complexion)*, complexion, inflection, intonation, manner *(behavior)*, means *(opportunity)*, parlance, phraseology, property *(distinctive attribute)*, stress *(accent)*, style, tenor
tone down allay, commute, diminish, moderate *(temper)*, modify *(moderate)*, mollify, subdue

tone of voice intonation
tongue language, speech
tongue lash reproach
tongue-lashing denunciation, diatribe, malediction, obloquy, phillipic
tongue-tied inarticulate, mute, speechless
tonguey loquacious
tonic cure, medicinal, panacea, remedial, salubrious, salutary
tonnage cargo
too also
too difficult insurmountable
too early premature
too familiar trite
too few insufficiency
too hard difficult, impracticable, insurmountable
too little deficient, insufficient, nonsubstantial *(not sufficient)*
too many overage
too much disproportionate, overage
too small nonsubstantial *(not sufficient)*
too soon premature
too zealous perfervid
tool appliance, device *(mechanism)*, embellish, expedient, facility *(instrumentality)*, instrumentality, medium, resource. SEE MAIN ENTRY
tools paraphernalia *(apparatus)*
toothsome palatable
top cardinal *(outstanding)*, ceiling, culminate, culmination, leading *(ranking first)*, major, outbalance, outweigh, paramount, pinnacle, prime *(most valuable)*, surmount, surpass, transcend
top-match SEE MAIN ENTRY
top people elite
top person key man
top-flight master, renowned
top-level best, major
top-level meeting caucus
top-notch best, premium, select
top-rank notable
top-secret confidential
topic caption, context, heading, matter *(subject)*, question *(issue)*, thesis
topic for discussion matter *(subject)*
topic under consideration issue *(matter in dispute)*
topical current, present *(current)*
topical outline hornbook
topics affairs, contents
toploftiness pride
toplofty insolent, supercilious
topmost best, leading *(ranking first)*, primary
topmost point culmination
topping superior *(excellent)*
topple obliterate, overthrow, overturn, subvert, upset
torment annoy, badger, bait *(harass)*, discompose, distress *(anguish)*, distress, endanger, harass, harrow, harry *(harass)*, hector, ill use, inflict, infliction, irritate, mistreat, molest *(annoy)*, obsess, oppression, pain, persecute, pique, plague, press *(goad)*, prey, provoke, trouble. SEE MAIN ENTRY
tormenting caustic, painful
tormentum gun
torpedo bomb
torpescence sloth
torpescent lifeless *(dull)*, otiose, torpid
torpid dormant, inactive, indolent, insipid, jejune *(dull)*, languid, lifeless *(dull)*, otiose, phlegmatic, powerless, stagnant, static. SEE MAIN ENTRY

torpidity inaction, languor, sloth
torpidness languor
torpor inaction, inertia, languor, sloth
torporifc narcotic
torporific insensible, obtuse, stagnant, torpid
torquere harrow, harry *(harass)*
torrefy deflagrate
torrent outbreak, outburst, spate
torrid hot-blooded
torsion involution
torsional tortuous *(bending)*
tort delict, delinquency *(misconduct)*, misconduct. SEE MAIN ENTRY
tortile circuitous, sinuous, tortuous *(bending)*
tortility involution
tortious illicit
tortious act SEE MAIN ENTRY
tortiously illegally
tortuose indirect. SEE MAIN ENTRY
tortuosity involution
tortuous caustic, circuitous, complex, cruel, devious, labyrinthine, machiavellian, sinuous. SEE MAIN ENTRY
tortuousness involution
torture badger, cruelty, endanger, ill use, inflict, infliction, irritate, mistreat, pique, plague, prey, punish
torturous insufferable, painful
torturous interference SEE MAIN ENTRY
toss beat *(pulsate)*, cast *(throw)*, launch *(project)*, precipitate *(throw down violently)*, send
toss aside forswear
toss out jettison
toss overboard jettison
toss up bet
tot infant
total absolute *(complete)*, aggregate *(noun)*, aggregate *(verb)*, amount *(quantity)*, categorical, collective, complete *(all-embracing)*, comprehensive, comprise, computation, corpus, detailed, entirety, face amount, face value *(price)*, full, in solido, inclusive, maximum *(amplitude)*, outright, peremptory *(absolute)*, plenary, poll, pure, radical *(extreme)*, stark, sum, survey *(poll)*, thorough, unqualified *(unlimited)*, whole *(undamaged)*, whole *(unified)*. SEE MAIN ENTRY
total loss miscarriage
totalitarian dictator, dictatorial
totalitarianism oppression
totality aggregate, complex *(development)*, corpus, entirety, finality, in solido, principal *(capital sum)*, quantity, sum *(total)*, whole. SEE MAIN ENTRY
totalize calculate
totally in toto, purely *(positively)*, wholly
totalness entirety, totality
tote carry *(transport)*, transport
totem designation *(symbol)*
totter vacillate
tottering insecure, precarious
totus entirety, total
touch abut, adjoin, appertain, apply *(pertain)*, connect *(join together)*, correspond *(be equivalent)*, disarm *(set at ease)*, impinge, impress *(affect deeply)*, interest, minimum, nuance, overlap, reach, suggestion
touch off launch *(initiate)*
touch on connote, indicate, refer *(direct attention)*
touch up embellish, emend, enhance, fix *(repair)*, meliorate, modify *(alter)*, repair, revise

touch upon allude, comment, mention, pertain

touchable palpable, tangible

touched lunatic

touching adjacent, close *(near)*, contiguous, moving *(evoking emotion)*, persuasive, profound *(intense)*, proximate, tangential, wherein

touchstone standard

touchy fractious, perverse, petulant, querulous, resentful, sensitive *(easily affected)*

tough durable, indestructible, indomitable, insusceptible *(resistant)*, insusceptible *(uncaring)*, ossified, pertinacious, rigid, severe, strong, unyielding. SEE MAIN ENTRY

toughen inure *(accustom)*

toughened callous, incorrigible, insusceptible *(uncaring)*, ossified

toughness main force, strength, tenacity

tour perambulate, period, phase *(period)*

touring moving *(in motion)*

tournament contest *(competition)*

tourner la loi circumvent

tourney contest *(competition)*, fight *(battle)*, oppose

tournure contour *(outline)*

tousle agitate *(shake up)*, discompose

tout bystander, inform *(notify)*

tout au contraire contradictory

tout le contraire contrary

towardly seasonable

tower edifice

tower above overcome *(surmount)*, transcend

tower of strength mainstay

tower over surpass

towering prodigious *(enormous)*, salient

town civic, community

townsman denizen, habitant, resident

toxic deadly, deleterious, detrimental, fatal, harmful, insalubrious, lethal, malignant, noxious, peccant *(unhealthy)*, pernicious, pestilent, virulent. SEE MAIN ENTRY

toxic tort SEE MAIN ENTRY

toxicant deadly, pernicious, pestilent

toxiferous lethal, malignant, pernicious, pestilent

trace copy, deduce, deduct *(conclude by reasoning)*, delineate, derive *(deduce)*, detect, ferret, find *(discover)*, follow-up, hint, hunt, impression, indication, iota, locate, minimum, pursue *(chase)*, research, scintilla, search, solve, suggestion, suspicion *(uncertainty)*. SEE MAIN ENTRY

trace out delineate

trace the outline of delineate

trace to ascribe

traceable deductible *(provable)*

tracing copy, delineation, outline *(boundary)*, pattern

tracing back derivation

track chase, delve, detect, follow-up, investigate, pursue *(chase)*, research, search, trace *(follow)*

track down ferret, hunt, locate, search, trace *(follow)*

track mentally investigate

tract district, land, lot, pandect *(treatise)*, parcel, plot *(land)*, property *(land)*, province, section *(vicinity)*, territory, thesis

tract of land premises *(buildings)*

tractabilis palpable, tangible, tractable

tractability amenability, compliance, credulity

tractable amenable, corrigible, facile, flexible, malleable, obedient, open *(persuasible)*, passive, patient, pliable, pliant, receptive, resigned, resilient, sequacious, servile, suasible, subservient, willing *(not averse)*, yielding. SEE MAIN ENTRY

tractableness compliance

tractare manage, manipulate *(utilize skillfully)*, wield

tractate pandect *(treatise)*

tractatio management *(supervision)*

tractile pliable, pliant, tractable

traction stress *(strain)*

tractus region

tradable marketable

trade barter, business *(commerce)*, business *(occupation)*, buy, calling, career, commerce, commercial, deal *(noun)*, deal *(verb)*, dealings, devolve, dicker, employment, exchange, handle *(trade)*, industry *(business)*, interchange, job, labor *(work)*, livelihood, mercantile, occupation *(vocation)*, office, position *(business status)*, practice *(professional business)*, profession *(vocation)*, pursuit *(occupation)*, reciprocate, sale, vend, work *(employment)*. SEE MAIN ENTRY

trade association union *(labor organization)*

trade by exchange barter

trade fair market *(business)*

trade in handle *(trade)*, sell

trade name brand

trade off barter

trade secret SEE MAIN ENTRY

trade sign trademark

trade with deal

trademark brand, denomination, designation *(symbol)*, device *(distinguishing mark)*, indicant, symbol. SEE MAIN ENTRY

trader broker, dealer, merchant, speculator, supplier, vendor

tradere deliver, surrender *(yield)*

tradesman artisan, dealer, vendor

tradesperson dealer, merchant

tradeswoman dealer

trading business *(commerce)*, commerce, commercial

trading house market *(business)*

trading place market place

trading post market *(business)*

tradition custom, habit, myth, prescription *(custom)*, propriety *(correctness)*, solemnity, usage

tradition-bound conventional

traditional accustomed *(customary)*, common *(customary)*, conventional, customary, familiar *(customary)*, formal, habitual, hereditary, ordinary, orthodox, prescriptive, proverbial, regular *(conventional)*, standing, typical, usual. SEE MAIN ENTRY

traditionalism custom

traditionalist philistine

traditionality custom

traditionally invariably

traditionary traditional

traditive prescriptive, traditional

traduce defame, denigrate, denounce *(condemn)*, deprecate, depreciate, derogate, discommend, disoblige, disparage, lessen, libel, malign, pillory, reproach, smear, sully

traducement aspersion, bad repute, defamation, denunciation, dishonor *(shame)*, obloquy, revilement, slander, vilification

traducere transfer

traducing libelous

traffic business *(commerce)*, commerce, deal, dealings, exchange, trade *(commerce)*, trade

traffic by exchange barter

traffic in deal, handle *(trade)*, sell

traffic of commodities commerce

traffic with communicate, patronize *(trade with)*

trafficker dealer

tragedy adversity, calamity, casualty, catastrophe, debacle, disaster, fatality, misfortune. SEE MAIN ENTRY

tragic deplorable, dire, disastrous, fatal, lamentable

tragical deplorable, dire, disastrous

tragoedia tragedy

trahere derive *(receive)*, prolong

traiectio exaggeration

trail chase, delve, follow-up, hunt, pursue *(chase)*, search, spy, stem *(originate)*, trace *(follow)*

trail blazer pioneer

trailing subsequent

train chain *(series)*, cultivate, edify, educate, empower, foster, inculcate, initiate, instill, instruct *(teach)*, nurture, specialize, succession

train by instruction discipline *(train)*

train in study

train of thought idea

trained competent, expert, familiar *(informed)*, informed *(educated)*, literate, practiced, professional *(trained)*, proficient, qualified *(competent)*, resourceful, sciential, technical, veteran

trained person expert, practitioner, professional, specialist

trained personnel expert

trainee neophyte, novice, protégé

trainer pedagogue

training competence *(ability)*, direction *(guidance)*, disciplinary *(educational)*, edification, education, experience *(background)*, guidance, instruction *(teaching)*, preparation

trainload cargo

trait character *(personal quality)*, characteristic, differential, feature *(characteristic)*, habit, particularity, property *(distinctive attribute)*, quality *(attribute)*, specialty *(distinctive mark)*, symptom. SEE MAIN ENTRY

traitor conspirer, insurgent, malcontent

traitoriousness disloyalty

traitorous disobedient, faithless, false *(disloyal)*, perfidious, recreant, untrue

traitorousness bad faith, infidelity

traits personality

traject deliver, project *(impel forward)*

trammel bar *(hinder)*, block, check *(bar)*, confine, constrain *(imprison)*, constraint *(restriction)*, contain *(restrain)*, control *(restrain)*, curb, debar, detain *(hold in custody)*, detain *(restrain)*, disadvantage, enclose, enclosure, encumber *(hinder)*, fetter *(noun)*, fetter *(verb)*, hamper, handcuff *(noun)*, handcuff *(verb)*, hinder, impede, impediment, obstacle, obstruct, obstruction, occlude, repress, restrain, restrict. SEE MAIN ENTRY

tramontane stranger

tramp perambulate, prowl, step, traverse

tramper derelict

trample spurn, subjugate

trample on damage, mistreat, violate

trample upon beat *(defeat)*, break *(violate)*

trance insentience, preoccupation

trangression infringement

tranmission conveyance

tranquil complacent, dispassionate, patient, peaceable, placid

tranquil mind composure

tranquility longanimity, peace, solace

tranquilization mollification, remission

tranquilize allay, alleviate, assuage, disarm *(set at ease)*, lull, moderate *(temper)*, mollify, pacify, placate, propitiate, remit *(relax)*, soothe, subdue

tranquilizer narcotic

tranquilizing narcotic, palliative *(abating)*

tranquillitas composure, ease

tranquillity composure, lull

tranquillus dispassionate, placid

transact commit *(perpetrate)*, conduct, dicker, discharge *(perform)*, execute *(accomplish)*, manage, negotiate, perform *(adhere to)*, perpetrate, trade. SEE MAIN ENTRY

transact business handle *(trade)*

transact business with patronize *(trade with)*

transact with patronize *(trade with)*

transaction act *(undertaking)*, agreement *(contract)*, business *(commerce)*, commission *(act)*, deal, event, exchange, interchange, occurrence, operation, proceeding, process *(course)*, sale, trade *(commerce)*, treatment, undertaking *(business)*. SEE MAIN ENTRY

transactions affairs, dealings

transcedent sacrosanct

transcend beat *(defeat)*, outbalance, outweigh, overcome *(surmount)*, overstep, prevail *(triumph)*, surmount, surpass. SEE MAIN ENTRY

transcendant prime *(most valuable)*

transcendence infringement, supremacy

transcendency supremacy

transcendent best, notable, outstanding *(prominent)*, paramount, primary, superior *(excellent)*, superlative

transcendental mysterious, obscure *(abstruse)*, paramount, recondite

transcendere surmount

transcending infringement

transcribe copy, enter *(record)*

transcript copy, record. SEE MAIN ENTRY

transcript of minutes of commitment mittimus

transcript of testimony deposition

transcription record, transcript

transcursion transgression

transect dichotomize

transfer abalienate, assignment *(transfer of ownership)*, attorn, bear *(yield)*, cargo, carriage, cede, cession, confer *(give)*, consign, consignment, convert *(change use)*, conveyance, copy, deed, defect, delegate, delivery, demise *(conveyance)*, deport *(banish)*, devise *(give)*, devolution, devolve, dispatch *(send off)*, dispensation *(act of dispensing)*, displace *(remove)*, displace *(replace)*, disposition *(transfer of property)*, exchange, give *(grant)*, grant *(transfer formally)*, impart, move *(alter position)*, reassign, refer *(send for action)*, relegate, remand, removal, replacement, sale, send, subrogation, supplant, transmit, transmittal, transport. SEE MAIN ENTRY

transfer again recover

transfer among the living inter vivos

transfer back recover

transfer by deed abalienate, deliver

transfer by will abalienate, demise

transfer by writing grant *(transfer formally)*

transfer control to the government nationalize

transfer for a consideration sell

transfer for sale consign

transfer of property conveyance, devolution, feoffment

transfer of property as security for a debt mortgage

transfer of security mortgage

transfer of title conveyance

transfer ownership alienate *(transfer title)*, bequeath, demise, devolve, grant *(transfer formally)*, pass *(advance)*

transfer ownership to the government nationalize

transfer property deliver

transfer right deliver

transfer title convey *(transfer)*, pass *(advance)*

transfer to devolve

transfer to an earlier date antedate

transfer to another assign *(transfer ownership)*

transfer to another authority extradition

transferable assignable, contagious, heritable, negotiable

transferee assignee, bearer, consumer, devisee, feoffee, heir, legatee, licensee, payee, recipient. SEE MAIN ENTRY

transference alienation *(transfer of title)*, assignment *(transfer of ownership)*, carriage, consignment, conveyance, deed, delivery, demise *(conveyance)*, devolution, disposition *(transfer of property)*, extradition, removal, subrogation, takeover, transition, transmittal

transferor carrier, feoffor, licensor. SEE MAIN ENTRY

transferral delivery

transferre transfer

transferred bailment

transferred by a legacy testamentary

transferred by bequest testamentary

transferred by devise testamentary

transferring consignment

transfigere pierce *(lance)*

transfiguration development *(progression)*

transfigure affect, change, convert *(change use)*, denature, distort, meliorate, modify *(alter)*, transform, vary

transfix pierce *(lance)*

transform adapt, alter, change, convert *(change use)*, denature, distort, meliorate, modify *(alter)*, renew *(begin again)*, vary. SEE MAIN ENTRY

transformable convertible, protean

transformation conversion *(change)*, development *(progression)*, reconversion, reorganization, transition

transformations vicissitudes

transformed tempered

transfuse deliver, inject, permeate, pervade

transfuse the sense construe *(translate)*

transgredi pass *(advance)*

transgress accroach, break *(violate)*, contravene, disobey, encroach, impose *(intrude)*, infringe, lapse *(fall into error)*, offend *(violate the law)*, overstep, trespass, violate

transgress established bounds impinge

transgressed broken *(unfulfilled)*

transgressing blameworthy, culpable, delinquent *(guilty of a misdeed)*, diabolic, felonious, guilty, peccant *(culpable)*

transgression bad repute, breach, contravention, criminality, culpability, delinquency *(misconduct)*, disregard *(omission)*, encroachment, fault *(responsibility)*, felony, guilt, illegality, infraction, injustice, invasion, malfeasance, mischief, misconduct, misdeed, misdemeanor, misdoing, misfeasance, misprision, offense, onus *(blame)*, tort, vice, violation, wrong. SEE MAIN ENTRY

transgressive disobedient, lawless, unlawful

transgressor convict, criminal, degenerate, delinquent, felon, lawbreaker, malefactor, offender, outlaw, recidivist, vandal, wrongdoer. SEE MAIN ENTRY

transhipment removal

transient acting, brief, ephemeral, interim, interlocutory, lodger, moving *(in motion)*, mutable, profane, provisional, shifting, temporary, transitory, unsettled, volatile. SEE MAIN ENTRY

transient arrangement modus vivendi

transientness insignificance, mortality

transigere transact

transire omit, pass *(advance)*

transit circulation, reconversion, transition

transitio transition

transition circulation, conversion *(change)*, reconversion. SEE MAIN ENTRY

transitional intermediate, mesne, moving *(in motion)*, progressive *(going forward)*, provisional, temporary

transitive temporary

transitorily pro tempore

transitoriness mortality

transitory brief, ephemeral, interlocutory, profane, provisional, shifting, temporary, transient, volatile. SEE MAIN ENTRY

translatable accountable *(explainable)*, determinable *(ascertainable)*

translate define, deliver, elucidate, explain, explicate, interpret, render *(depict)*, transform

translate incorrectly misread

translate into action exercise *(discharge a function)*

translate orally interpret

translaticius conventional, ordinary

translation construction, definition, explanation, paraphrase, rendition *(explication)*, restatement

translocate deliver, move *(alter position)*

translocation carriage, extradition, removal, transmittal

transmigration circulation, immigration, transition

transmigratory moving *(in motion)*

transmissible assignable, contagious, hereditary, heritable, negotiable

transmission alienation *(transfer of title)*, assignment *(transfer of ownership)*, circulation, consignment, contact *(association)*, conveyance, delivery, demise *(conveyance)*, devolution, osmosis, publication *(disclosure)*, transmittal

transmission of knowledge declaration, notification

transmission of title feoffment

transmissive contagious

transmit annunciate, assign *(transfer ownership)*, bestow, cede, circulate,

1019

communicate, confer *(give)*, consign, contribute *(supply)*, convey *(communicate)*, convey *(transfer)*, correspond *(communicate)*, delegate, deliver, demise, descend, devise *(give)*, devolve, dispatch *(send off)*, disseminate, give *(grant)*, grant *(transfer formally)*, impart, issue *(send forth)*, leave *(give)*, notify, pass *(advance)*, propagate *(spread)*, radiate, redirect, remit *(submit for consideration)*, remove *(transfer)*, send, transfer, transport. SEE MAIN ENTRY

transmit by will   devise *(give)*

transmit disease   infect

transmit payment   remit *(send payment)*

transmittable   assignable

transmittal   assignment *(transfer of ownership)*, conveyance, delivery, demise *(conveyance)*, remittance. SEE MAIN ENTRY

transmittance   delivery, transmittal

transmittere   transfer, transmit, transport

transmittible   negotiable

transmogrify   alter, change, convert *(change use)*, transform

transmutable   convertible

transmutation   conversion *(change)*, transition

transmute   alter, change, convert *(change use)*, denature, modify *(alter)*, transform, vary

transparent   clear *(apparent)*, direct *(forthright)*, evident, explicit, ingenuous, lucid, manifest, obvious, open *(in sight)*, pellucid, perceivable, unambiguous. SEE MAIN ENTRY

transpierce   enter *(penetrate)*, lancinate, penetrate, pierce *(lance)*

transpiration   experience *(encounter)*, happening

transpire   arise *(occur)*, ensue, occur *(happen)*, pass *(advance)*

transplacement   removal

transplant   consign, deliver, transport

transplantation   insertion, removal, transmittal

transplendent   illustrious

transport   carry *(transport)*, consign, convey *(transfer)*, deliver, deport *(banish)*, expatriate, move *(alter position)*, passion, relegate, transfer, transmit. SEE MAIN ENTRY

transport back   recover

transport company   carrier

transportable property   movable

transportables   movable

transportare   transport

transportation   carriage, removal, transmittal

transportation charge   fare

transportation fee   fare

transportation of commodities   commerce

transportation of goods   commerce

transported   ecstatic

transposable   convertible

transposal   delivery, exchange

transpose   convert *(change use)*, convey *(transfer)*, displace *(replace)*, move *(alter position)*

transposed   inverse

transposition   delivery, exchange, replacement

transshape   convert *(change use)*, transform

transshipment   carriage

transubstantiate   change, convert *(change use)*, modify *(alter)*, transform

transudation   outflow

trap   ambush, artifice, bait *(lure)*, deceive, deception, decoy, dupe, ensnare, entrap, frame up, hunt, imposture, inveigle, lock, maneuver *(trick)*, mislead, obstruct, occlude, pitfall, stratagem. SEE MAIN ENTRY

trapping   chattel

trappings   paraphernalia *(personal belongings)*

trashy   inferior *(lower in quality)*, poor *(inferior in quality)*, trivial

traumatize   damage

travail   disaster, effort, endeavor, hardship, labor, strive

travel   perambulate. SEE MAIN ENTRY

travel over   traverse

travelable   passable

traveled   passable

traveling   moving *(in motion)*, progressive *(going forward)*

traveller   itinerant

travelling   itinerant

traversable   passable

traversal   contravention, counterargument, demurrer, disapproval, impugnation, intersection, negation, opposition, prohibition

traverse   answer *(reply)*, balk, circumvent, collide *(clash)*, contest, contradict, contravene, counteract, countervail, cross *(disagree with)*, cross *(intersect)*, demonstrate *(protest)*, demur, deny *(contradict)*, disaccord, disaffirm, disagree, disavow, disobey, disown *(deny the validity)*, disprove, dispute *(contest)*, fight *(counteract)*, gainsay, hinder, negate, oppugn, patrol, perambulate, prohibit, protest, refuse, refute, reject, repel *(drive back)*, thwart. SEE MAIN ENTRY

traverse the outline of   delineate

traversing   negative

travesty   caricature, distortion, jape, mock *(imitate)*, parody, ridicule. SEE MAIN ENTRY

treacherous   aleatory *(perilous)*, bad *(offensive)*, collusive, cruel, dangerous, detrimental, dishonest, faithless, false *(disloyal)*, fraudulent, harmful, insecure, insidious, insubordinate, irresponsible, lying, machiavellian, malevolent, malicious, malignant, nefarious, perfidious, pernicious, precarious, recreant, ruthless, sinister, sly, tortuous *(corrupt)*, undependable, unreliable, unscrupulous, untrue, untrustworthy, vicious, virulent

treacherous killing   assassination

treacherousness   bad faith, dishonesty, false pretense, improbity

treachery   bad faith, collusion, deceit, disloyalty, false pretense, fraud, infidelity, knavery, machination, pettifoggery, sedition, treason

tread   perambulate, step

tread on   mistreat, spurn

treading warily   diffident

treason   disloyalty, infidelity, mutiny, rebellion, sedition. SEE MAIN ENTRY

treasonable   faithless, false *(disloyal)*, perfidious, recreant, untrue

treasonable activities   disloyalty

treasonable alliance   confederacy *(conspiracy)*, conspiracy

treasonous   disobedient, faithless, false *(disloyal)*, insubordinate, perfidious

treasure   cash, conserve, foster, fund, garner, hoard, keep *(shelter)*, money, possession *(property)*, possessions, preserve, protect, regard *(hold in esteem)*, store

(depository), store, substance *(material possessions)*, sufficiency

treasure house   treasury

treasure up   hoard

treasured   valuable

treasurehouse   repository

treasurer   comptroller

treasury   arsenal, coffer, repository, selection *(collection)*, store *(depository)*. SEE MAIN ENTRY

treasury note   check *(instrument)*

treat   adjust *(resolve)*, comment, cure, drug, enjoyment *(pleasure)*, manage, relieve *(give aid)*, remedy. SEE MAIN ENTRY

treat abusively   mishandle *(maltreat)*

treat as a special case   except *(exclude)*, exclude

treat as human   personify

treat badly   mistreat

treat cruelly   ill use

treat differently   favor

treat ill   mishandle *(maltreat)*

treat improperly   mishandle *(maltreat)*, violate

treat in a condescending way   patronize *(condescend toward)*

treat poorly   persecute

treat rudely   ignore

treat thoroughly   exhaust *(try all possibilities)*

treat unfairly   ill use

treat unkindly   ill use

treat with contempt   disdain, flout, mock *(deride)*

treat with derision   mock *(deride)*

treat with discourtesy   offend *(insult)*

treat with disdain   flout, spurn

treat with disfavor   disgrace

treat with disrespect   humiliate, mock *(deride)*

treat with indignity   disoblige, humiliate, offend *(insult)*

treat with indulgence   bear *(tolerate)*, forbear

treat with insolence   hector, jeer

treat with partiality   favor, prefer

treat with reserve   mistrust

treat with scorn   mock *(deride)*

treat without due respect   disregard

treat without reverence   violate

treated   tempered

treatise   hornbook

treatise on the law   hornbook

treatment   analysis, design *(construction plan)*, expedient, management *(judicious use)*, pandect *(treatise)*, practice *(procedure)*, process *(course)*, relief *(aid)*, usage. SEE MAIN ENTRY

treaty   bargain, compact, league, mutual understanding, pact, peace, promise, protocol *(agreement)*, stipulation. SEE MAIN ENTRY

treaty-making   negotiation

trek   perambulate, traverse

trekker   migrant

tremble   beat *(pulsate)*

trembling   trepidation

tremendous   far reaching, major, portentous *(eliciting amazement)*, prodigious *(enormous)*

tremor   cataclysm, trepidation

tremulous   diffident

tremulousness   trepidation

trench on   intrude, overstep

trench upon   impinge

trenchant   active, acute, bitter *(penetrating)*, brief, caustic, cogent, compelling, concise, eloquent, incisive, mordacious, pithy, potent, powerful, scathing, succinct. SEE MAIN ENTRY

trend bias, conatus, direction *(course)*, gravitate, mode, style, tendency, tenor

trend downward decline *(fall)*

trending inclined

trepan bait *(lure)*, deception, ensnare

trepidatio trepidation

trepidation apprehension *(fear)*, cloud *(suspicion)*, consternation, disturbance, fear, fright, misgiving, panic, phobia, stress *(strain)*, suspicion *(mistrust)*. SEE MAIN ENTRY

trepidity trepidation

trespass accroach, breach, break *(violate)*, delinquency *(misconduct)*, disobey, disregard *(omission)*, encroach, encroachment, impinge, impose *(intrude)*, infraction, infringe, infringement, intrude, intrusion, invade, invasion, lapse *(fall into error)*, misdeed, misdoing, obtrude, offend *(violate the law)*, overstep, transgression, violate, violation, wrong. SEE MAIN ENTRY

trespasser malefactor

trespassing disobedient, housebreaking, infringement, intrusive, peccant *(culpable)*

triable illicit, justiciable. SEE MAIN ENTRY

triable act tortious act

trial action *(proceeding)*, cause *(lawsuit)*, conatus, contest *(competition)*, cross-examination, day in court, discipline *(punishment)*, distress *(anguish)*, effort, endeavor, experiment, grievance, hearing, indagation, infliction, inquiry *(systematic investigation)*, inspection, lawsuit, matter *(case)*, misfortune, nuisance, plight, predicament, preliminary, proceeding, prosecution *(criminal trial)*, quagmire, stress *(strain)*, suit, tentative, test, trouble, undertaking *(attempt)*, undertaking *(enterprise)*, venture. SEE MAIN ENTRY

trial at the bar hearing

trial balloon SEE MAIN ENTRY

trial by jury hearing

trial in court hearing

trial list calendar *(list of cases)*

trial of a case action *(proceeding)*

trial of superiority competition

trial of the issues action *(proceeding)*

tribe affinity *(family ties)*, assemblage, band, blood, family *(common ancestry)*, house, origin *(ancestry)*, parentage, progeny, society

tribuere attribute, render *(deliver)*

tribulation burden, distress *(anguish)*, misfortune, quagmire, trouble

tribunal bar *(court)*, bench, board, chamber *(body)*, council *(assembly)*, court, forum *(court)*, judicatory, judicature, judiciary, jury. SEE MAIN ENTRY

tributary contributory, inferior *(lower in position)*

tribute bounty, contribution *(donation)*, duty *(tax)*, gift *(present)*, honor *(outward respect)*, payment *(remittance)*, recognition, recommendation, remembrance *(commemoration)*, respect, reward, tax

trick artifice, bait *(lure)*, betray *(lead astray)*, bilk, bunko, canard, circumvent, deceive, deception, decoy, defraud, delude, device *(contrivance)*, dupe, ensnare, evade *(deceive)*, evasion, expedient, fake, false pretense, foist, hoax, hoodwink, illude, imposture, inveigle, knavery, machination, maneuver, mislead, misrepresent, mulct *(defraud)*, overreach, pettifog, plot *(secret plan)*, ploy, pretense *(pretext)*,

pretext, racket, ruse, sham, stratagem, subterfuge. SEE MAIN ENTRY

trickery artifice, collusion, deceit, deception, duplicity, falsification, frame up, fraud, hoax, hypocrisy, imposture, knavery, pettifoggery, prestidigitation, pretense *(pretext)*, pretext, ruse, sham

trickiness deception, dishonesty, fraud, improbity, knavery, pettifoggery

trickish fraudulent, machiavellian

trickle distill, exude, paucity

tricksy jocular

tricky deceptive, delusive, devious, disingenuous, evasive, fraudulent, illusory, insidious, intricate, lying, machiavellian, perfidious, sly, sophistic, strategic, subtle *(insidious)*, surreptitious, unconscionable

tried conclusive *(determinative)*, convincing, dependable, expert, indubious, loyal, reliable, staunch, steadfast, true *(loyal)*, veteran

tried for the same crime double jeopardy

trier array *(jury)*

trier of fact juror

trier of the facts array *(jury)*

triers of fact jury, panel *(jurors)*

trifle palter, paucity, pettifog, scintilla, technicality

trifle amount modicum

trifle with mock *(deride)*

trifling collateral *(immaterial)*, de minimus, expendable, frivolous, inappreciable, inconsequential, inconsiderable, insubstantial, marginal, minor, negligible, nominal, nonessential, nugatory, null *(insignificant)*, paltry, petty, slight, superficial, tenuous, trivial, unessential

trigger launch *(initiate)*, originate

trim abridge *(shorten)*, color *(complexion)*, commute, compact *(pithy)*, curtail, decrease, deduct *(reduce)*, edit, embellish, lessen

trimming curtailment, reprimand

trip misguide, overreach

trip and fall case SEE MAIN ENTRY

trip up entrap

triste disconsolate

tristis grave *(important)*, solemn

tristitia depression, solemnity

trite inexpressive, lifeless *(dull)*, mediocre, mundane, nondescript, ordinary, pedestrian, prosaic, stale. SEE MAIN ENTRY

trite expression phrase, platitude

trite phrase platitude

trite remark platitude

trite saying platitude

tritus customary, trite

triumph carry *(succeed)*, kill *(defeat)*, pass *(satisfy requirements)*, reach, succeed *(attain)*, supremacy

triumph over beat *(defeat)*, defeat, overcome *(surmount)*, overwhelm, subdue, subject, subjugate, surmount, surpass

triumphal prevailing *(having superior force)*

triumphant prevailing *(having superior force)*, successful

trivia detail

trivial collateral *(immaterial)*, de minimus, frivolous, immaterial, inapposite, inconsequential, inconsiderable, insubstantial, mediocre, minor, negligible, nominal, nonessential, nugatory, null *(insignificant)*, paltry, peripheral, petty, remote *(small)*, slight, superficial, tenuous, unessential, usual. SEE MAIN ENTRY

triviality immateriality, inconsequence, insignificance, mediocrity, platitude, technicality

troop assemblage, band

trope call *(title)*

trophy prize

troth adherence *(devotion)*, adhesion *(loyalty)*, faith, loyalty, profession *(declaration)*, reliance, undertaking *(pledge)*

trothless faithless, false *(disloyal)*, perfidious

trouble aggravate *(annoy)*, agitate *(perturb)*, annoy, badger, bait *(harass)*, burden, disaster, discommode, discompose, disorient, distress *(anguish)*, distress, disturb, embarrass, emergency, encumber *(hinder)*, fracas, grievance, harass, hector, inconvenience, mischief, misfortune, molest *(annoy)*, nuisance, obsess, pandemonium, perplex, persecute, perturb, pique, plague, plight, predicament, press *(goad)*, problem, quagmire, strife, turmoil. SEE MAIN ENTRY

trouble maker delinquent

trouble oneself endeavor, strive

trouble-maker demagogue

troubled disconsolate, pessimistic, unsettled

troublemaker malcontent

troublesome difficult, froward, invidious, irksome, operose, oppressive, painful, perverse, problematic, uncontrollable, undesirable, unruly, vexatious

troubling painful

troublous bad *(offensive)*, harmful

trounce beat *(strike)*, browbeat, defeat, lash *(strike)*, punish, reprehend, reprimand

troupe assemblage, band, body *(collection)*, organization *(association)*

trover recovery *(repossession)*. SEE MAIN ENTRY

trow presuppose, surmise

truancy absence *(nonattendance)*, dereliction, nonappearance, nonperformance

truant disobedient. SEE MAIN ENTRY

truce cessation *(interlude)*, conciliation, halt, interruption, interval, lull, pause, peace, treaty

trucidare kill *(defeat)*

truck trade *(commerce)*

truckage carriage

truckle SEE MAIN ENTRY

truckle to pander

truckling servile, subservient

truckload cargo

truculence atrocity, brutality

truculency brutality

truculent brutal, cold-blooded, harsh, hostile, malevolent, malicious, malignant, offensive *(offending)*, perverse, relentless, ruthless, sinister

trudge perambulate

true absolute *(conclusive)*, accurate, actual, authentic, candid, convincing, credible, de facto, definite, dependable, direct *(straight)*, documentary, factual, faithful *(loyal)*, faithful *(true to fact)*, genuine, honest, incontrovertible, literal, loyal, positive *(incontestable)*, proper, pure, real, reliable, rightful, serious *(devoted)*, solid *(sound)*, sound, staunch, steadfast, sterling, unadulterated, undistorted, unrefutable, unyielding, valid, veridical. SEE MAIN ENTRY

true believer disciple

true bill accusation

true charge accusation

true dimensions area *(surface)*

true incident   fact

true meaning   connotation, gist *(substance)*

true to fact   exact, literal

true to form   normal *(regular)*

true to life   descriptive, natural

true to nature   undistorted

true to scale   candid

true to the facts   actual, candid, certain *(positive)*, honest

true to the letter   actual, verbatim

true to type   typical

truehearted   honest, loyal, moral, true *(loyal)*

trueness   adhesion *(loyalty)*, allegiance, fidelity, loyalty, validity

truism   platitude, postulate, principle *(axiom)*

truly   admittedly, de facto, faithfully, in good faith, ipso facto

trump   outbalance

trump up   fabricate *(make up)*, frame *(prearrange)*, invent *(falsify)*, misrepresent, palter, perjure

trump up a charge   frame *(charge falsely)*

trumped up   colorable *(specious)*, ill-founded, lying, unfounded, untrue

trumped up story   myth

trumped-up   fictitious

trumped-up charge   frame up

trumped-up story   frame up

trumpery   deception, falsification

trumpet   circulate, herald, inform *(notify)*, proclaim, propagate *(spread)*, publish

truncare   mutilate

truncate   commute, condense, deduct *(reduce)*, excise *(cut away)*, mutilate, remove *(eliminate)*

truncheon   beat *(strike)*, cudgel, lash *(strike)*

trunk road   causeway

truss   bear *(support)*

trust   agency *(legal relationship)*, cartel, charge *(custody)*, commit *(entrust)*, commitment *(responsibility)*, confederacy *(compact)*, confidence *(faith)*, consortium *(business cartel)*, credence, credulity, entrust, expectation, faith, league, loan, mission, office, pool, prospect *(outlook)*, protégé, reliance, rely, security *(safety)*. SEE MAIN ENTRY

trust to chance   bet, parlay *(bet)*

trust to keep secret   confide *(divulge)*

trust with   delegate

trustable   dependable, incorruptible

trusted   authentic, convincing, credible, dependable, fiduciary, intimate, undisputed

trustee   administrator, comptroller, executor, fiduciary, guardian, nominee *(delegate)*, receiver, representative *(proxy)*, substitute, transferee. SEE MAIN ENTRY

trustees   commission *(agency)*, committee

trusteeship   charge *(custody)*, custody *(supervision)*, ward

truster   disciple

trustful   sanguine, unsuspecting

trustfulness   credulity

trustiness   adhesion *(loyalty)*, fidelity, honor *(good reputation)*, probity

trusting   convincing, credulous, naive, positive *(confident)*, sanguine, unsuspecting

trustingly   faithfully

trustless   irresponsible

trustworthily   faithfully

trustworthiness   adhesion *(loyalty)*, certification *(certainty)*, credibility, fidelity, honesty, honor *(good reputation)*, integrity, loyalty, principle *(virtue)*, probity, rectitude, responsibility *(conscience)*, trust *(confidence)*, veracity, weight *(credibility)*. SEE MAIN ENTRY

trustworthy   accurate, authentic, believable, bona fide, candid, cogent, conscientious, convincing, credible, demonstrable, dependable, diligent, factual, faithful *(loyal)*, fiduciary, harmless, high-minded, honest, incorruptible, infallible, ingenuous, law-abiding, loyal, moral, official, positive *(incontestable)*, real, reliable, reputable, safe, scrupulous, secure *(sound)*, solid *(sound)*, staunch, steadfast, tenable, thorough, true *(authentic)*, true *(loyal)*, upright

trusty   believable, conscientious, dependable, incorruptible, infallible, law-abiding, loyal, reliable, secure *(sound)*, solid *(sound)*, staunch, true *(loyal)*

truth   fact, honesty, maxim, principle *(virtue)*, probity, reality, right *(righteousness)*, validity, veracity. SEE MAIN ENTRY

truth telling   credible

truth-speaking   straightforward

truth-telling   veridical

truthful   accurate, actual, candid, credible, direct *(forthright)*, honest, ingenuous, literal, precise, real, realistic, reliable, right *(correct)*, scrupulous, sound, straightforward, true *(authentic)*, unaffected *(sincere)*, undistorted, upright, valid, veridical. SEE MAIN ENTRY

truthfully   faithfully

truthfulness   credibility, honesty, integrity, probity, veracity

truthless   dishonest, disingenuous, evasive, fallacious, false *(inaccurate)*, fraudulent, lying, mendacious, untrue

truthlessness   bad faith, dishonesty, improbity

try   adjudicate, adopt, attempt, check *(inspect)*, endeavor *(noun)*, endeavor *(verb)*, exert, harrow, harry *(harass)*, hear *(give a legal hearing)*, judge, pursuit *(effort to secure)*, resort, strive, test, undertake. SEE MAIN ENTRY

try a case   hear *(give a legal hearing)*, judge

try conclusions   reason *(conclude)*

try for   pursue *(strive to gain)*, strive

try hard   attempt

try one's best   attempt, pursue *(strive to gain)*, strive

try one's fortune   bet

try one's luck   bet, gamble, speculate *(chance)*

try one's patience   badger, bait *(harass)*, provoke

try the cause   adjudicate, hear *(give a legal hearing)*

try the patience   discompose, pique, plague

try to find   hunt

try to obtain   pursue *(strive to gain)*

try to overtake   chase

trying   onerous, operose, oppressive, painful, severe, vexatious

trying situation   predicament

tryout   experiment, test

tryst   appointment *(meeting)*, rendezvous

tueri   preserve

tuitio   preservation

tuition   direction *(guidance)*, edification, education, experience *(background)*, guidance

tuitionary   disciplinary *(educational)*

tumble   agitate *(shake up)*, disorganize, subvert, upset

tumid   flatulent, fustian, grandiose, inflated *(bombastic)*, inflated *(enlarged)*, orotund, pretentious *(pompous)*, turgid

tumidity   bombast

tumidness   bombast

tumidus   inflated *(bombastic)*, inflated *(enlarged)*, pretentious *(pompous)*

tumult   affray, anarchy, belligerency, bluster *(commotion)*, brawl, commotion, confusion *(turmoil)*, disorder *(lack of order)*, disturbance, embroilment, entanglement *(confusion)*, fracas, fray, furor, imbroglio, noise, outcry, pandemonium, revolution, riot, turmoil

tumultuary   disordered, disorderly

tumultuous   disordered, disorderly. SEE MAIN ENTRY

tumultuous assault   affray

tumultuousness   bluster *(commotion)*, disorder *(lack of order)*

tumultus   affray, commotion, disturbance, revolt, riot

tune   adjust *(regulate)*

tune down   diminish

tunnel   penetrate

turba   band, commotion, riot, turmoil

turbare   muddle

turbatio   disturbance

turbid   inextricable, opaque, unclear

turbulence   bluster *(commotion)*, commotion, confusion *(turmoil)*, disorder *(lack of order)*, disturbance, embroilment, furor, irregularity, pandemonium, revolution, severity, turmoil

turbulency   turmoil

turbulent   disordered, disorderly, hot-blooded, unruly, vehement

turbulentus   insubordinate

turgent   turgid

turgescence   bombast, inflation *(increase)*, plethora, rodomontade

turgescent   orotund, pretentious *(pompous)*, proud *(conceited)*

turgid   flatulent, fustian, grandiose, inflated *(bombastic)*, inflated *(enlarged)*, orotund, pretentious *(pompous)*, proud *(conceited)*. SEE MAIN ENTRY

turgid language   fustian

turgidity   bombast, inflation *(increase)*

turgidness   inflation *(increase)*

turgidus   inflated *(enlarged)*

turmoil   affray, anarchy, bluster *(commotion)*, brawl, commotion, conflict, disorder *(lack of order)*, disturbance, embroilment, emotion, fracas, fray, furor, havoc, imbroglio, misrule, outcry, pandemonium, panic, riot, shambles. SEE MAIN ENTRY

turn   alter, avert, contort, contour *(shape)*, convert *(change use)*, crossroad *(turning point)*, deviate, digress, gift *(flair)*, occurrence, opportunity, oscillate, posture *(situation)*, predisposition, prejudice *(influence)*, proclivity, quirk *(accident)*, slant, spoil *(impair)*, tendency, transform, transition. SEE MAIN ENTRY

turn a deaf ear to   ignore

turn adrift   dispel, evict

turn against   antagonize, confront *(oppose)*, rebel

turn aside   avert, deter, detour, deviate, discourage, divert, eschew, estop, expostulate, impede, parry, prevent, shun, stave, thwart

turn attention devote

turn attention to note *(notice)*

turn away abandon *(relinquish)*, alienate *(estrange)*, avert, decline *(reject)*, depose *(remove)*, disaffect, disapprove *(reject)*, disclaim, disfavor, dismiss *(discharge)*, exclude, parry, prevent, rebuff, repulse

turn away from disavow, eschew, shun

turn awry distort

turn back disavow, escheat, parry, regress, revert

turn down decline *(reject)*, disapprove *(reject)*, disoblige, refuse, spurn

turn from change, disapprove *(reject)*, disavow, discourage, disfavor, refuse, renounce

turn from a purpose dissuade

turn from sin redeem *(satisfy debts)*

turn in retire *(retreat)*

turn informer betray *(disclose)*, denounce *(inform against)*

turn into change, evolve, vary

turn into cash realize *(obtain as a profit)*

turn into money liquidate *(convert into cash)*, realize *(obtain as a profit)*

turn loose discharge *(dismiss)*, discharge *(liberate)*, disenthrall, free, liberate, parole

turn of expression phrase, phraseology

turn of mind disposition *(inclination)*, position *(point of view)*, spirit

turn of the tide crossroad *(turning point)*

turn off alienate *(estrange)*, shut

turn on recriminate

turn one's back on abandon *(physically leave)*, ignore, quit *(evacuate)*, relinquish

turn one's back upon disdain

turn one's gaze upon peruse

turn out deport *(banish)*, depose *(remove)*, discharge *(dismiss)*, disinherit, dislodge, dismiss *(discharge)*, displace *(remove)*, dispossess, eject *(evict)*, eliminate *(exclude)*, evict, exclude, expel, expose, fabricate *(construct)*, formulate, make, manufacture, oust, produce *(manufacture)*, remove *(dismiss from office)*, result, supplant

turn out by industrial process manufacture

turn out of doors evict

turn out of house and home evict

turn out of one's way deviate

turn out of possession eject *(evict)*

turn over alienate *(transfer title)*, attorn, cede, consign, deal, deliver, devolve, give *(grant)*, lend, muse, reflect *(ponder)*, serve *(deliver a legal instrument)*, subvert

turn over for safekeeping entrust

turn over in one's mind consider

turn over in the mind ponder, reason *(conclude)*, speculate *(conjecture)*

turn over to commit *(entrust)*, delegate, relegate

turn renegade tergiversate

turn selfishly to one's own account exploit *(take advantage of)*

turn state's evidence confess

turn tail retreat

turn the attention to observe *(watch)*, occupy *(engage)*

turn the eyes on observe *(watch)*

turn the leaves of peruse

turn the mind to occupy *(engage)*

turn the tables on recriminate

turn to call *(appeal to)*, consult *(ask advice of)*

turn to account employ *(make use of)*, exercise *(use)*, expend *(consume)*, exploit *(make use of)*, gain, inure *(benefit)*, profit

turn to for help resort

turn to for support resort

turn to good account capitalize *(seize the chance)*

turn to one's advantage capitalize *(seize the chance)*

turn to scorn disdain

turn to the side avert

turn to use employ *(make use of)*

turn up discover, disinter, emerge

turn upside down overthrow, upset

turnabout reversal, reversion *(act of returning)*

turnaround reversion *(act of returning)*

turned about inverse

turned around back *(in reverse)*

turned to bone ossified

turning circuitous, critical *(crucial)*, indirect, sinuous, strategic, tortuous *(bending)*

turning aside obviation

turning over to a foreign state extradition

turning to account exploitation

turnkey warden

turnout result

turnpike causeway

turns on SEE MAIN ENTRY

turpis disgraceful, obscene, scandalous, vicious

turpitude bad faith, bad repute, corruption, defilement, delinquency *(misconduct)*, discredit, dishonor *(shame)*, disrepute, guilt, knavery, misconduct, misdoing, perversion, shame, vice, wrong. SEE MAIN ENTRY

turpitudinous bad *(offensive)*

turpitudo disgrace, dishonor *(shame)*, ignominy, obscenity

tussle affray, belligerency, commotion, fight *(battle)*, fight *(battle)*, fracas, grapple, struggle

tutari protect

tutela charge *(custody)*, protection

tutelage aid *(help)*, auspices, charge *(custody)*, direction *(guidance)*, edification, education, guidance, instruction *(teaching)*, patronage *(support)*, protection, safekeeping, ward

tutelar guardian

tutelary protective

tutor edify, educate, enlighten, instill, instruct *(teach)*, nurture, pedagogue

tutored familiar *(informed)*

tutorial didactic, disciplinary *(educational)*

tutoring direction *(guidance)*, education, guidance, instruction *(teaching)*

tutors faculty *(teaching staff)*

tutus safe

twaddle prattle

tweaking SEE MAIN ENTRY

twelve months annum

twice-bereaved child orphan

twice-told repeated

twin alter ego, correlate, counterpart *(parallel)*, duplicate, identical, same, similar

twine contort

twine together intertwine

twinge of conscience qualm

twining circuitous

twist camouflage, complex *(entanglement)*, contort, disorganize, distort, distortion, falsify, intertwine, involution, mutilate, palter, prejudice *(influence)*,

quirk *(accident)*, quirk *(idiosyncrasy)*, slant, snarl, tendency

twist and turn contort

twist the meaning distort, misinterpret, misstate, misunderstand

twist the meaning of camouflage, misread, misrepresent

twist the sense distort

twist the truth pretend, prevaricate

twist the words distort, misconstrue

twistable malleable

twisted disordered, inextricable, labyrinthine, peccable, sinuous, tortuous *(bending)*, unreasonable

twisting circuitous, indirect, labyrinthine, sinuous, tortuous *(bending)*

twit jape, jeer, mock *(deride)*

two-faced faithless, false *(disloyal)*, machiavellian, recreant, tartuffish, undependable, unreliable, unscrupulous, untrue, untrustworthy

two-facedness duplicity

two-part trial SEE MAIN ENTRY

two-sided bilateral, mutual *(reciprocal)*, reciprocal

two-way mutual *(reciprocal)*

type case *(example)*, characteristic, class, classification, classify, color *(complexion)*, criterion, denomination, designation *(symbol)*, form *(arrangement)*, instance, kind, manner *(kind)*, personality, pigeonhole, resemblance, style

typical average *(standard)*, boiler plate, broad, common *(customary)*, conventional, customary, demonstrative *(illustrative)*, familiar *(customary)*, general, habitual, mediocre, mundane, natural, nondescript, normal *(regular)*, ordinary, orthodox, prevailing *(current)*, prevalent, regular *(conventional)*, representative, usual. SEE MAIN ENTRY

typical component epitome

typical example representative *(example)*, sample

typical instance example, representative *(example)*

typical part epitome

typical performance norm

typicus typical

typification epitome

typify depict, exemplify, personify, represent *(portray)*, signify *(denote)*

typifying exemplary, representative

tyrannical brutal, cruel, dictatorial, oppressive, relentless, severe, strict, stringent, tyrannous

tyrannical leader dictator

tyrannize bait *(harass)*, harass, mishandle *(maltreat)*, mistreat, tax *(overwork)*

tyrannized aggrieved *(harmed)*

tyrannous brutal, dictatorial. SEE MAIN ENTRY

tyranny cruelty, injustice, oppression, severity, thrall

tyrant dictator

tyro neophyte, novice

tyrranize brutalize, dominate

U

uber productive

ubiquitary present *(current)*, ubiquitous

ubiquitous broad, present *(current)*. SEE MAIN ENTRY

ugly loathsome, odious, repulsive, scandalous

ukase citation *(charge)*, declaration, decree, directive, fiat, order *(judicial directive)*, requirement

ulciscendi cupidus vindictive

ulcisci punish, retaliate

ullage deficiency

ulterior additional, undisclosed. SEE MAIN ENTRY

ultimate categorical, ceiling, conclusive *(determinative)*, conclusive *(settled)*, definitive, extreme *(last)*, final, forthcoming, future, last *(final)*, prospective. SEE MAIN ENTRY

ultimate cause derivation, determinant, gist *(ground for a suit)*

ultimate end design *(intent)*

ultimate motive determinant

ultimate point extremity *(furthest point)*

ultimate purpose intention, object

ultimate result issuance

ultimately hereafter *(eventually)*, in due course

ultimatum canon, charge *(command)*, claim *(legal demand)*, condition *(contingent provision)*, demand, dictate, dun, mandate, notice *(warning)*, requirement, warning. SEE MAIN ENTRY

ultimus extreme *(last)*, final, ultimate

ultio revenge, vengeance

ultra vires SEE MAIN ENTRY

ultracritical critical *(faultfinding)*

ultraist radical *(favoring drastic change)*

ultramodern sophisticated

ultrareligious fanatical

ululant blatant *(obtrusive)*

umbrage alienation *(estrangement)*, dissatisfaction, malice, offense, resentment. SEE MAIN ENTRY

umbrageous mysterious, resentful

umpirage collective bargaining

umpire decide, go-between, intercede, judge *(noun)*, judge *(verb)*, mediate, negotiate, referee, rule *(decide)*. SEE MAIN ENTRY

unabashed brazen, impertinent *(insolent)*, insolent, presumptuous. SEE MAIN ENTRY

unabated undiminished, unremitting

unabetted alone *(unsupported)*, solitary, unsupported

unable disabled *(deprived of legal right)*, helpless *(powerless)*, inadept, inadequate, incapable, incompetent, inept *(incompetent)*, otiose, powerless, unfit, unqualified *(not competent)*. SEE MAIN ENTRY

unable to be annulled irrevocable, unavoidable *(not voidable)*

unable to be bought inalienable, incorruptible

unable to be corrected irremediable

unable to be discredited unimpeachable

unable to be disposed of inalienable

unable to be evaded compulsory

unable to be expressed ineffable

unable to be fixed irremediable

unable to be investigated inscrutable

unable to be overcome invincible

unable to be pacified irreconcilable

unable to be quelled invincible

unable to be remedied irremediable

unable to be spoken ineffable

unable to be subjugated invincible

unable to exist without dependent

unable to find the way lost *(disoriented)*

unable to make both ends meet bankrupt

unable to make ends meet impecunious, poor *(underprivileged)*

unable to pay indebted, insolvent

unable to pay matured debts bankrupt

unable to resist eager

unable to satisfy creditors bankrupt

unable to speak mute, speechless

unable to utter articulate sound mute

unable to yield barren

unabridged full, gross *(total)*, intact, thorough

unabridgedly in toto

unacceptable blameful, ineligible, inferior *(lower in quality)*, invidious, nonsubstantial *(not sufficient)*, objectionable, repugnant *(exciting aversion)*, undesirable, unendurable, unsatisfactory, unsuitable. SEE MAIN ENTRY

unacceptableness bad repute

unacceptance disapproval

unaccepted outdated, outmoded, unorthodox

unaccessible inaccessible

unaccidental voluntary

unaccommodating disinclined, froward, invidious, perverse, restive, thoughtless

unaccompanied alone *(unsupported)*, separate, singular, sole, solitary

unaccomplished amateur, executory, inadept

unaccountable arbitrary, clear *(unencumbered)*, immune, inapprehensible, incomprehensible, indefinable, inexplicable, inscrutable, lawless, mysterious, nonconforming, peculiar *(curious)*, prodigious *(amazing)*, uncanny, uncurbed, unforeseeable, unpredictable. SEE MAIN ENTRY

unaccredited unauthorized

unaccustomed extraordinary, inexperienced, nonconforming, peculiar *(curious)*, prodigious *(amazing)*, special, unacquainted, uncommon, unusual. SEE MAIN ENTRY

unachievability impossibility

unachievable difficult, impossible, impracticable, inaccessible, infeasible, insuperable, insurmountable, unattainable

unacknowledged anonymous, unrequited, unspecified

unacquaintance ignorance

unacquainted blind *(not discerning)*, incognizant, inexperienced, insensible, unaccustomed, unaware, unversed. SEE MAIN ENTRY

unacquirability unavailability

unacquirable inaccessible, unattainable

unacquired devoid

unactivated lifeless *(dull)*

unactivity neglect

unactual delusive, illusory, nominal

unadaptable nonconforming, otiose, rigid

unadapted improper, incompetent, ineligible, inexperienced, unfit, unqualified *(not competent)*

unadjustable irreconcilable, nonconforming

unadjusted outstanding *(unresolved)*, unsettled

unadministered executory

unadorned clear *(apparent)*, naked *(lacking embellishment)*, nondescript, simple

unadroit amateur, inadept, inept *(incompetent)*

unadult juvenile

unadulterate decontaminate

unadulterated authentic, genuine, honest, naked *(lacking embellishment)*, natural,
pure, simple, sterling, true *(authentic)*. SEE MAIN ENTRY

unadulteration honesty

unadvantageous deleterious

unadventurous careful, safe

unadvertised ulterior

unadvisable adverse *(negative)*, disadvantageous, inappropriate, injudicious

unadvised hot-blooded, imprudent, impulsive *(rash)*, incognizant, unaware

unaffected bona fide, direct *(forthright)*, dispassionate, exempt, genuine, honest, impartial, impervious, inexpressive, ingenuous, insensible, insusceptible *(uncaring)*, irreconcilable, naive, neutral, nonchalant, simple, straightforward, true *(authentic)*, unpretentious. SEE MAIN ENTRY

unaffected by immune

unaffected by injury intact, inviolate

unaffectedness candor *(straightforwardness)*, honesty, informality

unaffiliated alien *(unrelated)*, apart, disconnected, extraneous, foreign, independent, irrelative, separate, unrelated

unaffirmative negative

unaffirmed debatable, disputable, unauthorized

unafraid secure *(confident)*, spartan, unabashed, undaunted

unaggressive harmless, nonmilitant

unaging immutable

unagitated peaceable, phlegmatic, placid

unagreeing discordant

unagressive languid

unaided alone *(unsupported)*, helpless *(defenseless)*, solitary, unilateral, unsupported

unaimed haphazard, indiscriminate, random

unaired undisclosed

unalarmed undaunted

unalert negligent

unalertness neglect, negligence

unalienable SEE MAIN ENTRY

unalike atypical, dissimilar, heterogeneous

unallayed persistent, undiminished

unalleviated chronic

unallied alien *(unrelated)*, apart, disconnected, extraneous, foreign, impertinent *(irrelevant)*, inapposite, independent, individual, irrelative, irrelevant, separate, unrelated

unallocated unclaimed

unallowable impermissible, improper, inexcusable, inexpiable, unjustifiable

unallowed felonious, illegitimate *(illegal)*, illicit, *ultra vires*, unlawful

unalloyed genuine, simple, sterling, unadulterated

unalluring undesirable, unsavory

unalterability indestructibility

unalterable firm, immutable, indefeasible, indelible, inevitable, inexorable, inflexible, ironclad, irreconcilable, irreversible, irrevocable, necessary *(inescapable)*, obdurate, peremptory *(absolute)*, permanent, resolute, rigid, stable, steadfast, unalienable. SEE MAIN ENTRY

unalterableness resistance

unalterably invariably

unaltered certain *(positive)*, durable, intact, inviolate, unaffected *(uninfluenced)*, uniform

unambiguity certification *(certainness)*, certitude

unambiguous accurate, axiomatic, categorical, certain *(fixed)*, certain *(positive)*, clear *(apparent)*, coherent *(clear)*, comprehensible, conclusive *(determinative)*, demonstrable, direct *(forthright)*, distinct *(clear)*, explicit, express, incontestable, incontrovertible, lucid, pellucid, precise, unequivocal, unmistakable. SEE MAIN ENTRY
unambiguously fairly *(clearly)*
unambitious diffident, lax
unamenable impervious, inflexible
unamiable bitter *(reproachful)*
unamicable malevolent
unample deficient
unamusing pedestrian
unanimated inexpressive, insipid, languid, lifeless *(dead)*
unanimity accordance *(understanding)*, agreement *(concurrence)*, compatibility, concert, conciliation, consensus, peace, rapprochement, understanding *(agreement)*
unanimous concordant, consensual, harmonious
unanimously in toto
unannexed disconnected, discrete, disjunctive *(tending to disjoin)*, individual
unannounced undisclosed, unexpected
unanswerable certain *(fixed)*, cogent, immune, incontrovertible, irrefutable, positive *(incontestable)*, sound, uncurbed, undeniable, undisputed, unequivocal, unrefutable
unanswered unrequited
unanswering unresponsive
unanticipated impulsive *(rash)*, premature, unexpected, unforeseeable, unforeseen. SEE MAIN ENTRY
unanticipated event accident *(chance occurrence)*
unanxious peaceable, phlegmatic, secure *(confident)*
unapologizing incorrigible
unapparent blind *(concealed)*, hidden, impalpable, inconspicuous, indiscernible, intangible, latent, obscure *(abstruse)*, obscure *(faint)*, potential, undisclosed
unappealable certain *(fixed)*, final
unappealing objectionable, unacceptable, undesirable
unappeasability contention *(opposition)*
unappeasable implacable, insatiable, irreconcilable, relentless, remorseless, uncontrollable, unrelenting
unappetizing bitter *(acrid tasting)*, repugnant *(exciting aversion)*, unsavory
unapplied theoretical, unclaimed
unappreciable paltry
unappreciativeness ingratitude
unapprehensive careless, lax, phlegmatic, spartan, unabashed, undaunted
unapprised blind *(not discerning)*, unaware
unapprized incognizant, unacquainted, unwitting
unapproachability unavailability
unapproachable difficult, disdainful, inaccessible, remote *(secluded)*, unattainable. SEE MAIN ENTRY
unapproached best, paramount
unappropriated unclaimed
unapprovable undesirable
unapproved unauthorized, unorthodox
unapproving hostile, nonconsenting
unapt disproportionate, impertinent *(irrelevant)*, inadept, inadequate, inapplicable, inapposite, inappropriate, inapt, incompe-

tent, inept *(inappropriate)*, inept *(incompetent)*, irrelevant, powerless, unbecoming, unsatisfactory, unseemly, unsuitable
unaptness disqualification *(factor that disqualifies)*, impropriety
unarm disarm *(divest of arms)*
unarmed helpless *(defenseless)*, powerless
unarmored helpless *(defenseless)*
unaroused dormant, insensible, insusceptible *(uncaring)*, lifeless *(dull)*, nonchalant
unarranged casual, complex, disordered, haphazard, random
unartificial natural
unascertained debatable, disputable, dubious, inconclusive, indefinite, outstanding *(unresolved)*, pending *(unresolved)*, provisional, unconfirmed, undecided
unashamed brazen, dissolute, unabashed
unasked unsolicited
unasked for unclaimed
unaspiring lax
unassailability incontestability, inviolability, security *(safety)*
unassailable categorical, certain *(positive)*, clear *(certain)*, defensible, definitive, immune, inappealable, incontestable, inexpugnable, infallible, insuperable, insurmountable, invincible, irreprehensible, safe, secure *(free from danger)*, tenable, unimpeachable. SEE MAIN ENTRY
unassembled disordered
unassenting dissident, involuntary
unassertive obsequious, passive, pliant, resigned, sequacious, servile, subservient
unassimilated discrete, individual
unassisted alone *(unsupported)*, solitary, unsupported
unassociated alien *(unrelated)*, apart, disconnected, discrete, disjunctive *(tending to disjoin)*, extraneous, foreign, independent, individual, irrelative, remote *(secluded)*, separate, unrelated
unassumed honest
unassuming diffident, direct *(forthright)*, honest, inconspicuous, ordinary, unaffected *(sincere)*, unobtrusive, unpretentious
unassumingly respectfully
unassumingness informality
unassured conditional, dubious, hesitant, insecure, noncommittal, precarious, provisional
unassured purchase caveat emptor
unatonable inexcusable, inexpiable
unattach disengage, remove *(eliminate)*
unattached apart, disconnected, discrete, free *(not restricted)*, independent, individual, irrelative, moving *(in motion)*, separate, sovereign *(independent)*, unrelated, unsettled
unattackability security *(safety)*
unattackable defensible, immune, inexpugnable, insuperable, insurmountable, safe, secure *(free from danger)*, tenable
unattainability impossibility, unavailability
unattainable impossibility, impossible, inaccessible, infeasible, insuperable, insurmountable, unapproachable. SEE MAIN ENTRY
unattended alone *(unsupported)*, separate, sole, solitary. SEE MAIN ENTRY
unattended to perfunctory
unattested unconfirmed, uncorroborated, unfounded, unsupported
unattractive unacceptable, undesirable, unsavory

unauthentic artificial, assumed *(feigned)*, bogus, dishonest, dubious, fraudulent, illusory, imitation, invalid, spurious, unsound *(fallacious)*, unsustainable
unauthenticated dubious, unconfirmed, uncorroborated, unfounded, unsupported, untrustworthy
unauthenticity bad faith
unauthorative uncorroborated
unauthoritative dubious, ineffective, ineffectual, unofficial
unauthorization illegality
unauthorized disorderly, felonious, illegal, illegitimate *(illegal)*, illicit, impermissible, improper, irregular *(improper)*, null *(invalid)*, null and void, ultra vires, unlawful, unofficial, unwarranted, wrongful. SEE MAIN ENTRY
unauthorized assumption of property conversion *(misappropriation)*
unauthorized borrowing plagiarism
unauthorized copy counterfeit
unauthorized reproduction fake
unavailability absence *(omission)*, impossibility. SEE MAIN ENTRY
unavailable difficult, inaccessible, scarce, unattainable
unavailing disadvantageous, expendable, futile, ineffective, ineffectual, needless, nugatory, null *(insignificant)*, otiose, powerless, unproductive. SEE MAIN ENTRY
unavoidable certain *(fixed)*, certain *(positive)*, compelling, compulsory, exigent, forthcoming, imperative, important *(urgent)*, indispensable, inevitable, irrevocable, mandatory, necessary *(inescapable)*, obligatory, peremptory *(imperative)*, undeniable. SEE MAIN ENTRY
unavowed ulterior
unawaited unexpected
unawaited event bombshell
unawakened dormant
unaware heedless, incognizant, insensible, lax, oblivious, reckless, unacquainted, unsuspecting, unwitting. SEE MAIN ENTRY
unawareness ignorance, insentience, nescience
unawares unknowingly
unawed unabashed
unbacked unsound *(not strong)*, unsupported
unbalance discompose, disorganize, disorient, disturb, inequality, obsess
unbalanced deranged, disproportionate, inequitable, insecure, *non compos mentis*, partial *(biased)*, unequal *(unequivalent)*, unsettled
unbalanced mind insanity
unbar disencumber, disengage, disenthrall
unbarred open *(accessible)*, public *(open)*
unbased baseless, ill-founded, insubstantial
unbearable deplorable, insufferable, intolerable, loathsome, objectionable, obnoxious, odious, offensive *(offending)*, onerous, oppressive, painful, repulsive, unendurable. SEE MAIN ENTRY
unbeatable indomitable, inexpugnable, infallible, insuperable, insurmountable, invincible, irresistible, premium. SEE MAIN ENTRY
unbeaten prosperous, successful
unbecoming improper, inapposite, inappropriate, inapt, incongruous, inept *(inappropriate)*, objectionable, undesirable, undue *(excessive)*, unfit, unseemly, unsuitable. SEE MAIN ENTRY

unbefitting disproportionate, improper, inapposite, inappropriate, inapt, inept *(inappropriate)*, unbecoming, undesirable, undue *(excessive)*, unfit, unprofessional, unsatisfactory, unseemly
unbefriended helpless *(defenseless)*
unbeguile disabuse
unbeholdable indiscernible, intangible
unbelief cloud *(suspicion)*, doubt *(suspicion)*, suspicion *(mistrust)*
unbelievable debatable, disputable, doubtful, implausible, impossible, incredible, ludicrous, remarkable, suspicious *(questionable)*, uncanny. SEE MAIN ENTRY
unbeliever heretic
unbelieving cynical, inconvincible, incredulous, leery, skeptical
unbellicose nonmilitant, peaceable
unbelligerent nonmilitant, peaceable
unbend condescend *(deign)*, relent
unbending callous, draconian, firm, formal, immutable, implacable, inexorable, inflexible, insusceptible *(uncaring)*, intractable, ironclad, irreconcilable, obdurate, orthodox, parochial, pertinacious, precise, relentless, resolute, rigid, severe, strict, unalterable, uncompromising, unrelenting, unyielding. SEE MAIN ENTRY
unbenevolent cruel, scathing, sinister
unbent direct *(straight)*
unbeseeming unbecoming, unsuitable
unbetraying loyal, true *(loyal)*
unbias candor *(impartiality)*
unbiased broad, discriminating *(judicious)*, dispassionate, equal, equitable, evenhanded, factual, fair *(just)*, honest, impartial, judicial, juridical, just, liberal *(broad minded)*, neutral, nonpartisan, objective, open-minded, receptive, undistorted, unprejudiced. SEE MAIN ENTRY
unbiased impulse common sense
unbiasedly fairly *(impartially)*
unbiasedness disinterest *(lack of prejudice)*, fairness
unbidden lawless, spontaneous, unsolicited, voluntary, willing *(uncompelled)*
unbigoted equitable, impartial, judicial, just, liberal *(broad-minded)*, neutral, nonpartisan, objective, open-minded, unbiased, unprejudiced
unbind break *(separate)*, disband, disencumber, disengage, disenthrall, dissociate, divide *(separate)*, extricate, free, liberate, remove *(eliminate)*, rescue, separate, sever, split
unbinding liberation
unblamable blameless, clean, inculpable, innocent, irreprehensible, pardonable, unimpeachable
unblameworthy blameless, inculpable, irreprehensible, unimpeachable, unobjectionable
unblemished absolute *(ideal)*, blameless, clean, incorruptible, intact, inviolate, irreprehensible, not guilty, pure, unimpeachable. SEE MAIN ENTRY
unblenched undaunted
unblenching heroic, spartan
unblended simple
unblest profane
unblindfold disabuse
unblocked open *(accessible)*
unblurred clear *(apparent)*, cognizable, coherent, clear *(clear)*, conspicuous
unblushing brazen, callous, lascivious, nonchalant, salacious, unabashed
unboastful diffident

unbodied incorporeal
unbolt disengage, parole
unborn nonexistent
unborrowed native *(domestic)*, original *(creative)*
unbosom divulge
unbought free *(at no charge)*, gratis, gratuitous *(given without recompense)*, impartial, just, loyal
unbound clear *(unencumbered)*, exempt, free *(not restricted)*, independent, sovereign *(independent)*, uncurbed, unqualified *(unlimited)*, unrestricted. SEE MAIN ENTRY
unbounded absolute *(complete)*, competitive *(open)*, excessive, indefinite, indeterminate, infinite, open-ended, unconditional, unlimited, unmitigated, unrestrained *(not in custody)*, unrestricted
unbowdlerized salacious
unbreakable indivisible, inexpugnable, infrangible, ironclad
unbreathed undisclosed
unbribable honest, incorruptible, just, law-abiding
unbribed clean, evenhanded, impartial, just, loyal
unbridgeable insuperable
unbridled clear *(unencumbered)*, disorderly, dissolute, free *(not restricted)*, hot-blooded, incendiary, independent, inordinate, intemperate, lecherous, open-ended, prodigal, profuse, uncurbed, unrestrained *(not in custody)*, unrestrained *(not repressed)*, unrestricted, unruly
unbridled authority SEE MAIN ENTRY
unbroadened provincial
unbroken consecutive, continual *(connected)*, continuous, direct *(straight)*, direct *(uninterrupted)*, gross *(total)*, incessant, intact, inviolate, safe, unremitting
unbroken line chain *(series)*
unbroken order array *(order)*
unbruised intact
unbuckle disengage
unburden alleviate, disencumber, ease, free, mitigate, release, relieve *(free from burden)*
unburdened clear *(free from criminal charges)*, clear *(unencumbered)*, free *(relieved from a burden)*
unbury disinter
unbusied inactive
unbusinesslike inexperienced, unprofessional
uncage parole
uncalculated fortuitous, imprudent, unintentional, unpremeditated
uncalculating careless, impulsive *(rash)*, injudicious, negligent, precipitate
uncalled for disproportionate, excessive, extraneous, gratuitous *(unwarranted)*, inapplicable, inappropriate, nonessential
uncalled-for exorbitant, expendable, inordinate, needless, otiose, redundant, superfluous, unclaimed, undue *(excessive)*, unessential, unnecessary, unsolicited, unwarranted
uncamouflaged obvious, patent
uncandid devious, disingenuous, lying, mendacious, sly, untrue
uncanny mysterious. SEE MAIN ENTRY
uncanonical unorthodox
uncaptivating insipid, lifeless *(dull)*, pedestrian
uncarcerated person SEE MAIN ENTRY
uncared for derelict *(abandoned)*
uncareful slipshod

uncaring callous, cold-blooded, heedless, lax, nonchalant, obdurate, oblivious, obtuse, perfunctory, phlegmatic, slipshod, unaffected *(uninfluenced)*
uncase denude, unveil
uncatholic parochial
uncaught free *(not restricted)*, unbound
uncaused baseless
unceasing chronic, continual *(connected)*, continual *(perpetual)*, continuous, durable, incessant, industrious, infinite, live *(existing)*, open-ended, patient, permanent, perpetual, persistent, standing, undiminished, unremitting
uncensored intact, lurid
uncensurable blameless, clear *(free from criminal charges)*, irreprehensible, laudable, meritorious, unimpeachable, unobjectionable
unceremonial informal
unceremonious informal, presumptuous
unceremoniousness informality
uncertain ambiguous, approximate, capricious, casual, conditional, controversial, debatable, difficult, disputable, dubious, elusive, equivocal, fallible, hesitant, inconclusive, inconvincible, indefinite, indeterminate, insecure, intangible, irresolute, leery, moot, mutable, nebulous, noncommittal, pending *(unresolved)*, precarious, problematic, reluctant, shifting, skeptical, speculative, sporadic, subject *(conditional)*, suspicious *(questionable)*, unclear, unconfirmed, undecided, undependable, unforeseeable, unpredictable, unsettled, untrustworthy, vague. SEE MAIN ENTRY
uncertain event condition *(contingent provision)*, contingency
uncertain state doubt *(indecision)*
uncertainness doubt *(indecision)*, hesitation, incertitude, quandary
uncertainty ambivalence, chance *(possibility)*, confusion *(ambiguity)*, contingency, dilemma, doubt *(indecision)*, hazard, hesitation, improbability, incertitude, incredulity, indecision, jeopardy, misgiving, peril, possibility, qualm, quandary, reluctance, risk, scruple, speculation *(risk)*, venture. SEE MAIN ENTRY
uncertainty of meaning ambiguity
uncertified controversial, dubious, unauthorized, unconfirmed, unsupported
unchain break *(separate)*, disencumber, disengage, disenthrall, dissociate, free, liberate, parole, rescue
unchained free *(not restricted)*, unbound, uncurbed
unchaining liberation, release
unchallengeable axiomatic, clear *(certain)*, conclusive *(determinative)*, equitable, evenhanded, incontrovertible, indefeasible, inexpugnable, irrebuttable, irrefutable, irreprehensible, just, positive *(incontestable)*, sound, tenable, unalienable, uncontested, undisputed, unimpeachable
unchallenged accurate, consensual, permissible, uncontested, uncontroverted, undisputed, unequivocal
unchangeability indestructibility
unchangeable categorical, certain *(positive)*, conclusive *(determinative)*, consonant, durable, fixed *(settled)*, immutable, inappealable, indefeasible, indelible, inevitable, inflexible, infrangible, ironclad, irreconcilable, irredeemable, irreversible, irrevocable, loyal, noncancellable,

obdurate, orthodox, patient, permanent, stable, unalterable, unavoidable *(not voidable)*, unbending, uncompromising, unyielding

unchangeableness constant

unchangeably invariably

unchanged consonant, infallible, literal, regular *(conventional)*, unaffected *(uninfluenced)*

unchanging certain *(fixed)*, consistent, consonant, constant, continual *(connected)*, definite, dependable, equal, fixed *(settled)*, immutable, inexorable, infallible, ironclad, loyal, permanent, persistent, resolute, stable, standing, steadfast, uniform, unremitting

uncharacteristic improper, novel

uncharged free *(at no charge)*

uncharitable exclusive *(limited)*, illiberal, mordacious, parsimonious, scathing

uncharitableness rancor

uncharming pedestrian

unchartered illegal, impermissible, ultra vires, unauthorized, unsettled

unchary impulsive *(rash)*

unchaste dissolute, immoral, lascivious, lecherous, lewd, licentious, obscene, peccable, promiscuous, prurient, salacious

unchastised clear *(free from criminal charges)*

unchastity obscenity, vice

unchecked exempt, free *(not restricted)*, independent, intemperate, live *(existing)*, permanent, persistent, rampant, unbound, unconditional, unconfirmed, uncurbed, unlimited, unqualified *(unlimited)*, unrestrained *(not in custody)*, unrestrained *(not repressed)*, unrestricted. SEE MAIN ENTRY

uncheerful grave *(solemn)*, pessimistic

uncheerfulness pessimism

uncheery grave *(solemn)*, pessimistic

unchivalrous ignoble, illiberal

unchosen ineligible

uncircumscribed far reaching, omnipotent

uncircumspect careless, derelict *(negligent)*, hot-blooded, imprudent, impulsive *(rash)*, lax, negligent, reckless, remiss

uncircumspection indiscretion

uncivil blatant *(obtrusive)*, contemptuous, disdainful, disorderly, impertinent *(insolent)*, offensive *(offending)*, perverse, uncouth

uncivilized brutal, caitiff, disorderly, vicious

unclaimed anonymous, derelict *(abandoned)*. SEE MAIN ENTRY

unclarified equivocal, opaque

unclarity opacity

unclasp disengage

unclassifiable individual, nonconforming, nondescript, unusual

unclassified complex, disjointed, disordered, miscellaneous, peculiar *(curious)*

unclean insalubrious, lewd, prurient, repulsive, salacious, tainted *(contaminated)*

unclean hands SEE MAIN ENTRY

uncleanliness defilement

uncleanness defilement

unclear difficult, elusive, equivocal, impalpable, inarticulate, incomprehensible, inconspicuous, indefinable, indefinite, indeterminate, indistinct, inexact, inscrutable, nebulous, oblique *(evasive)*, obscure *(faint)*, opaque, pending *(unresolved)*, uncertain *(ambiguous)*, unspecified, vague. SEE MAIN ENTRY

unclearness confusion *(ambiguity)*, incoherence, indistinctness, obscuration, opacity

unclever inadept, inept *(incompetent)*, unversed

unclinch break *(separate)*

uncloak bare, denude, expose, find *(discover)*, reveal, unveil

unclog disencumber

unclogged open *(unclosed)*

unclosed competitive *(open)*, penetrable

unclothe bare, denude

unclouded clear *(apparent)*, comprehensible, conspicuous, distinct *(clear)*, manifest, open *(in sight)*, perceivable, pure

uncoerced autonomous *(independent)*, free *(not restricted)*, voluntary

uncohesive desultory, disconnected, disjointed

uncoil spread

uncollaborated unsupported

uncollected outstanding *(unpaid)*, payable, unpaid, unsettled

uncollectible debt bad debt

uncolored accurate, factual, fair *(just)*, genuine, honest, impartial, just, objective, open-minded, true *(authentic)*, unbiased, unprejudiced

uncombined simple, unadulterated

uncomely unbecoming

uncomfortable egregious, lamentable, oppressive, painful

uncomfortableness dissatisfaction

uncomforting callous, harsh

uncommanded unauthorized

uncommendable blameful, blameworthy, disorderly, inappropriate, objectionable, peccable, reprehensible, scandalous, sinister, unethical

uncommissioned unauthorized

uncommitted impartial, independent, neutral, noncommittal, nonpartisan

uncommon anomalous, distinct *(distinguished from others)*, distinctive, eccentric, extraordinary, individual, infrequent, momentous, nonconforming, noteworthy, novel, original *(creative)*, particular *(specific)*, peculiar *(distinctive)*, prodigious *(amazing)*, rare, remarkable, scarce, singular, special, specific, unaccustomed, uncanny, unique, unorthodox, unusual. SEE MAIN ENTRY

uncommonly particularly

uncommonness paucity

uncommunicated undisclosed

uncommunicative laconic, mute, noncommittal, phlegmatic, surreptitious, taciturn, unresponsive

uncommunicativeness loophole

uncompassionate callous, cruel, draconian, inexorable, obdurate, relentless, remorseless, ruthless, unaffected *(uninfluenced)*, unrelenting, unresponsive

uncompassionateness cruelty

uncompelled autonomous *(independent)*, impartial, nonpartisan, spontaneous, voluntary

uncompensated due *(owed)*, unpaid, unrequited

uncomplaining patient, resigned

uncomplaisant perverse, reluctant, restive

uncompleted deficient, executory, imperfect, inchoate, incipient, insufficient, partial *(part)*, partial *(relating to a part)*, rudimentary

uncomplex elementary

uncompliant broken *(unfulfilled)*, disobedient, lawless, perverse, recalcitrant, recusant, restive, unruly

uncomplicate simplify *(make easier)*

uncomplicated elementary, naked *(lacking embellishment)*, simple

uncomplimentary critical *(faultfinding)*, derogatory, pejorative

uncomplimentary remark disparagement

uncomplying contumacious, disobedient, insubordinate, lawless, nonconsenting, recalcitrant, reluctant, restive, unruly

uncompounded simple, unadulterated

uncomprehended hidden

uncomprehending blind *(not discerning)*, obtuse, opaque

uncomprehension nescience

uncompromising close *(rigorous)*, dictatorial, draconian, formal, immutable, implacable, inexorable, inflexible, ironclad, irreconcilable, obdurate, orthodox, particular *(exacting)*, patient, pertinacious, precise, punctilious, purposeful, radical *(favoring drastic change)*, relentless, resolute, rigid, scathing, sedulous, serious *(devoted)*, severe, stable, steadfast, strict, stringent, thorough, tyrannous, unbending, unrelenting, unyielding, willful. SEE MAIN ENTRY

uncompromisingness rigor

unconceal bare, expose, find *(discover)*, manifest, unveil

unconcealed comprehensible, evident, manifest, naked *(perceptible)*, obvious, open *(in sight)*, overt, palpable, patent, pellucid, perceivable, perceptible, salient, scrutable, unmistakable

unconcern dereliction, disinterest *(lack of interest)*, indifference, laxity, neglect, negligence, sloth

unconcerned careless, casual, cold-blooded, controlled *(restrained)*, derelict *(negligent)*, heedless, insusceptible *(uncaring)*, lax, negligent, neutral, nonchalant, obdurate, perfunctory, phlegmatic, reckless, remiss, secure *(confident)*, thoughtless, torpid, truant, unabashed, unaffected *(uninfluenced)*, undaunted, unresponsive. SEE MAIN ENTRY

unconcise prolix

unconcluded outstanding *(unresolved)*, pending *(unresolved)*

unconcrete intangible

unconcreteness impalpability

uncondemned blameless, clear *(free from criminal charges)*

unconditional absolute *(complete)*, categorical, complete *(all-embracing)*, comprehensive, outright, peremptory *(absolute)*, strict, unlimited, unmitigated, unqualified *(unlimited)*, unrestricted. SEE MAIN ENTRY

unconditional authority SEE MAIN ENTRY

unconditional inheritance fee *(estate)*

unconditionally purely *(positively)*

unconditioned absolute *(conclusive)*, categorical, peremptory *(absolute)*

uncondoling callous

unconfident dubious, hesitant, insecure

unconfined broad, competitive *(open)*, exempt, free *(not restricted)*, open-ended, plenary, unbound, unconditional, uncurbed, unlimited, unrestrained *(not in custody)*, unrestricted. SEE MAIN ENTRY

unconfirmable unsustainable

unconfirmed debatable, disputable, dubious, ill-founded, inconclusive, provisional, speculative, uncertain *(questionable)*, uncorroborated, unsupported. SEE MAIN ENTRY

unconfirmed account hearsay

unconfirmed report hearsay, report *(rumor)*

unconformable disparate, disproportionate, dissident, dissimilar, inapplicable, inapposite, inappropriate, incommensurate, irreconcilable, irregular *(not usual)*, lawless, nonconforming, original *(creative)*, peculiar *(curious)*, peculiar *(distinctive)*, recusant, repugnant *(incompatible)*, rigid, unique, unorthodox, unrelated. SEE MAIN ENTRY

unconforming eccentric, peculiar *(distinctive)*, recusant

unconformity breach, controversy *(argument)*, deviation, difference, disaccord, disagreement, discrepancy, disparity, dissent *(difference of opinion)*, dissidence, distinction *(difference)*, diversity, exception *(exclusion)*, incompatibility *(inconsistency)*, incongruity, inconsistency, inequality, irregularity, nonconformity, quirk *(idiosyncrasy)*, variance *(disagreement)*

unconfused coherent *(clear)*, comprehensible, distinct *(distinguished from others)*, unambiguous

unconfusedly fairly *(clearly)*

unconfusing explicit, unmistakable

unconfutability certainty

unconfutable clear *(certain)*, convincing, incontrovertible, irrefutable, positive *(incontestable)*, solid *(sound)*, sound, unimpeachable, unrefutable

unconfuted certain *(positive)*, cogent, definite

uncongenial inapposite, inapt, incongruous, inept *(inappropriate)*, offensive *(offending)*, unsuitable

unconnected alien *(unrelated)*, apart, collateral *(immaterial)*, desultory, disconnected, discrete, disjunctive *(tending to disjoin)*, foreign, gratuitous *(unwarranted)*, impertinent *(irrelevant)*, inapposite, inconsequential, independent, individual, irrelative, irrelevant, obscure *(remote)*, remote *(secluded)*, separate, solitary, unrelated. SEE MAIN ENTRY

unconquerable formidable, indomitable, inexpugnable, infallible, insuperable, insurmountable, invincible, irresistible, powerful, spartan

unconquered independent, sovereign *(independent)*

unconscienced recreant, unconscionable

unconscientious inaccurate

unconscientiousness bad faith, neglect

unconscionable excessive, exorbitant, immoral, inordinate, outrageous, perfidious, prohibitive *(costly)*, reprobate, unethical, unwarranted, usurious. SEE MAIN ENTRY

unconscionable delay laches

unconscionable rate of interest usury

unconscionability SEE MAIN ENTRY

unconscious blind *(not discerning)*, incognizant, insensible, involuntary, oblivious, torpid, unaware, unintentional, unsuspecting, unwitting

unconsciously unknowingly

unconsciousness disregard *(unconcern)*, ignorance, insentience

unconsecrated profane

unconsenting disinclined, disobedient, dissenting, dissident, nonconsenting, recusant, reluctant, restive

unconsentingly unwillingly

unconsidered haphazard, ill-advised, ill-judged, impulsive *(rash)*, injudicious, irrational, misadvised, unpremeditated

unconsolable disconsolate

unconsoling callous, harsh

unconsonant hostile, inapplicable, inapposite, inappropriate, inapt, inept *(inappropriate)*

unconspicuous unobtrusive

unconstitutional illegal, illicit, impermissible, unauthorized, unlawful

unconstitutionality prohibition

unconstrained absolute *(complete)*, autonomous *(independent)*, candid, clear *(unencumbered)*, direct *(forthright)*, ingenuous, lawless, open-ended, simple, spontaneous, unbound, uncurbed, unqualified *(unlimited)*, unrestrained *(not in custody)*, unrestrained *(not repressed)*, unrestricted, voluntary, willful

unconstraint freedom, honesty, informality, latitude, liberty

uncontained unrestricted

uncontaminated pure, unadulterated

uncontemplated unanticipated, unexpected

uncontemporary outdated

uncontentious nonmilitant, peaceable

uncontestable arrant *(definite)*, irrefutable, manifest, palpable, unmistakable

uncontested axiomatic, categorical, clear *(certain)*, conclusive *(determinative)*, consensual, definite, definitive, indubious, uncontroverted. SEE MAIN ENTRY

uncontradictable incontestable, incontrovertible

uncontradicted consensual, uncontested, uncontroverted

uncontrite incorrigible

uncontrived spontaneous, straightforward

uncontrollable hot-blooded, incorrigible, inexorable, intractable, necessary *(inescapable)*, obdurate, recalcitrant, restive, unavoidable *(inevitable)*, unruly, unyielding. SEE MAIN ENTRY

uncontrolled autonomous *(independent)*, capricious, disorderly, drunk, exempt, impulsive *(rash)*, independent, intemperate, irresponsible, lawless, licentious, open-ended, rampant, sensitive *(easily affected)*, sovereign *(independent)*, spontaneous, unbound, uncurbed, unlimited, unqualified *(unlimited)*, unrestrained *(not repressed)*, unrestricted

uncontroversial clear *(certain)*, consensual, inappealable, irrefutable, uncontested, undisputed, unrefutable

uncontroverted consensual, uncontested. SEE MAIN ENTRY

unconventional anomalous, deviant, divergent, eccentric, individual, informal, irregular *(not usual)*, licentious, nonconforming, novel, original *(creative)*, peculiar *(curious)*, prodigious *(amazing)*, unaccustomed, uncommon, unorthodox, unusual

unconventionality exception *(exclusion)*, informality, nonconformity, quirk *(idiosyncrasy)*

unconversable unresponsive

unconversant blind *(not discerning)*, inexperienced, unaccustomed, unacquainted, unversed

unconverted negative

unconveyed undisclosed

unconvinced incredulous, leery, negative, undecided

unconvincing doubtful, implausible, incredible, ludicrous, problematic, suspicious *(questionable)*, unbelievable

uncooperated reluctant

uncooperative adverse *(hostile)*, contentious, disinclined, disobedient, froward, hostile, perverse, recalcitrant, unresponsive

uncoordinated disordered, incongruous, random, slipshod

uncopied honest, original *(creative)*

uncorked open *(unclosed)*

uncorrectable chronic

uncorrectness misestimation

uncorroborated baseless, inconclusive, unconfirmed, unsupported. SEE MAIN ENTRY

uncorrupt blameless, conscientious, credible, decontaminate, ethical, even-handed, high-minded, impartial, incorruptible, inculpable, just, moral, pure, reputable, straightforward, upright

uncorrupted blameless, clean, dispassionate, ethical, evenhanded, fair *(just)*, high-minded, impartial, inviolate, just, law-abiding, literal, moral, pure, unadulterated

uncorruptibility rectitude

uncorruptible credible

uncountable innumerable, myriad

uncounted innumerable, multiple, myriad

uncounterfeited authentic, bona fide, genuine, honest, unaffected *(sincere)*, veridical

uncouple break *(separate)*, detach, disband, disjoint, dissociate, dissolve *(separate)*, divide *(separate)*, divorce, separate, sever

uncoupled disconnected

uncoupling division *(act of dividing)*, separation

uncourageous caitiff, recreant

uncourteous uncouth

uncourtliness disrespect

uncourtly disorderly, inelegant, presumptuous, provincial, uncouth

uncouth blatant *(obtrusive)*, ignoble, impertinent *(insolent)*, inelegant, provincial. SEE MAIN ENTRY

uncovenanted purchase caveat emptor

uncover bare, betray *(disclose)*, convey *(communicate)*, denude, detect, disabuse, disclose, discover, disinter, divest, divulge, evidence, exhibit, expose, find *(discover)*, inform *(betray)*, locate, manifest, present *(introduce)*, produce *(offer to view)*, reveal, unveil

uncovered apparent *(perceptible)*, clear *(apparent)*, conspicuous, distinct *(clear)*, helpless *(defenseless)*, open *(in sight)*, open *(unclosed)*, overt, palpable

uncovering disclosure *(act of disclosing)*, discovery, expression *(manifestation)*, manifestation

uncovery disclosure *(act of disclosing)*

uncreated nonexistent

uncreative trite

uncredulousness cloud *(suspicion)*, doubt *(suspicion)*

uncringing unabashed

uncritical casual, favorable *(expressing approval)*, indiscriminate, promiscuous, unnecessary

uncritical acceptance credulity

uncrown overthrow

uncrowning abdication

unctious subservient

unculpable blameless, clean, pardonable

uncultivated idle, ignoble, inelegant, natural, uncouth

uncultured blatant (obtrusive), imperfect, inelegant, uncouth

uncurbed clear (unencumbered), disorderly, dissolute, free (not restricted), independent, inordinate, intemperate, intractable, irresponsible, lawless, licentious, prodigal, profuse, unrestrained (not in custody), unrestrained (not repressed), unruly. SEE MAIN ENTRY

uncurrent outdated, outmoded

uncurtain bare, denude, manifest, reveal, unveil

uncurtained palpable

uncustomarily particularly

uncustomary anomalous, extraordinary, informal, infrequent, nonconforming, noteworthy, novel, original (creative), peculiar (curious), portentous (eliciting amazement), prodigious (amazing), rare, singular, special, unaccustomed, uncommon, unprecedented, unusual

uncut gross (total), intact, undiminished

undamaged intact, safe, undiminished

undaring judicious, noncommittal, safe

undaunted diligent, heroic, indomitable, patient, persistent, pertinacious, relentless, resolute, spartan, steadfast, unabashed. SEE MAIN ENTRY

undauntedness audacity, diligence (perseverance)

undebased unadulterated

undebatable undisputed

undecayed intact

undeceitful direct (forthright)

undeceitfulness honesty

undeceive debunk, disabuse, inform (notify), reveal

undeceived conscious (aware), informed (having information)

undeceiving direct (forthright)

undeceptive direct (forthright), unaffected (sincere)

undeceptiveness honesty, probity

undecided aleatory (uncertain), conditional, controversial, debatable, disputable, equivocal, hesitant, impartial, indefinite, indeterminate, irresolute, moot, mutable, noncommittal, outstanding (unresolved), pending (unresolved), pliant, problematic, provisional, tentative, uncertain (questionable), unsettled. SEE MAIN ENTRY

undecidedness ambivalence, doubt (indecision), qualm

undecipherability incoherence

undecipherable complex, inapprehensible, indistinct, inexplicable, inexpressive

undeciphered hidden, mysterious

undeclared implied, tacit, undisclosed

undecorated naked (lacking embellishment), simple

undeducted from gross (total)

undefaced intact

undefeatable indefeasible, insuperable, insurmountable

undefeated prosperous, successful

undefended helpless (defenseless), open (accessible), susceptible (unresistent), untenable

undefiled blameless, inviolate, pure, unadulterated, unblemished

undefinable inapprehensible, ineffable. SEE MAIN ENTRY

undefined equivocal, inconspicuous, indefinite, indeterminate, indistinct, nebu-

lous, open-ended, unclear, unspecified, vague

undeflected direct (straight)

undefrayed delinquent (overdue)

undeft inadept, inept (incompetent)

undeftness disqualification (factor that disqualifies), inability, incompetence

undelectable unsavory

undeleted gross (total)

undeliberate unintentional

undemanded unclaimed

undemanding facile, lax, lenient

undemanding chore sinecure

undemanding job sinecure

undemanding task sinecure

undemocratic dictatorial

undemolished intact

undemonstrable debatable, disputable, problematic, unsustainable, untenable

undemonstrated debatable, disputable, dubious, inconclusive, speculative, unconfirmed, uncorroborated, unsupported

undemonstrative controlled (restrained), dispassionate, passive, phlegmatic, placid, stoical

undeniability certainty, certitude, incontestability

undeniable axiomatic, believable, categorical, certain (fixed), certain (positive), clear (certain), cogent, conclusive (determinative), convincing, credible, definite, definitive, evident, factual, incontestable, incontrovertible, indefeasible, indubious, irrefutable, lucid, necessary (inescapable), noncontestable, obvious, official, positive (incontestable), real, reliable, uncontested, undisputed, unequivocal, unimpeachable, unmistakable, unrefutable. SEE MAIN ENTRY

undeniable fact fait accompli

undeniably admittedly, fairly (clearly)

undenied accurate

undenominational nonsectarian

undependability dishonesty, improbity

undependable dishonest, disobedient, faithless, fallible, false (disloyal), insecure, irresponsible, machiavellian, perfidious, precarious, recreant, unpredictable, unreliable, untrustworthy. SEE MAIN ENTRY

under inferior (lower in position), subaltern

under a sense of impending death in extremis

under a vow bound

under advisement at issue

under arms armed

under arrest arrested (apprehended), in custody. SEE MAIN ENTRY

under average poor (inferior in quality)

under ban illicit, impermissible

under compulsion bound

under consideration at issue, pending (unresolved)

under control bailment, systematic

under cover safe

under discussion debatable, disputable, moot

under examination at issue, debatable

under fiduciary control in trust

under inquiry controversial

under legal obligation actionable, liable

under lock and key in custody

under necessity bound

under oath promissory. SEE MAIN ENTRY

under obligation accountable (responsible), actionable, bound, indebted, indentured, liable

under one's hand holographic

under par minimal

under shelter immune

under surveillance guarded

under the circumstances consequently

under the control of conditional

under the influence of addicted

under the influence of liquor drunk

under the mark minimal

under the surface internal, latent

underage juvenile

underage person minor

underbid haggle

underbred ignoble

undercover cache (hiding place), clandestine, collusive, confidential, covert, furtive, hidden, mysterious, private (confidential), sly, stealthy, surreptitious, unobtrusive

undercover agent spy

undercover man bystander, spy

undercover work espionage

underestimate depreciate, derogate, discount (minimize), lessen, minimize, misprize. SEE MAIN ENTRY

underestimating pejorative

underestimation disregard (lack of respect), understatement

undergo allow (endure), bear (tolerate), endure (suffer), tolerate

undergo eclipse disappear

undergo evolution evolve

undergo the cost of disburse (pay out)

undergo the expense of disburse (pay out)

undergrade poor (inferior in quality)

underground clandestine, covert, furtive, hidden, surreptitious, unobtrusive

underground activity sedition

underhand clandestine, covert, furtive, machiavellian, mysterious, oblique (evasive), sly, stealthy, subtle (insidious), surreptitious, unscrupulous

underhand dealing bad faith, collusion, dishonesty, evasion, knavery, pettifoggery

underhand participation connivance

underhand practice pettifoggery

underhanded clandestine, collusive, deceptive, dishonest, disingenuous, false (disloyal), fraudulent, hidden, insidious, machiavellian, oblique (evasive), sly, unethical. SEE MAIN ENTRY

underhanded act maneuver (trick)

underhanded complicity connivance

underhanded practice deceit

underhandedness deceit, dishonesty, false pretense, fraud, illegality, improbity, indirection (deceitfulness)

underived original (creative), primordial

underlease rent

underlet rent, sublease, sublet

underlie inspire

underline insist, reaffirm

underling assistant, coadjutant

underlining emphasis

underlying cardinal (basic), central (essential), fundamental, latent, organic, original (initial), primary, rudimentary, substantive, virtual. SEE MAIN ENTRY

underlying principle basis, cause (reason), foundation (basis)

undermine check (restrain), corrupt, countervail, debilitate, disable, disarm (divest of arms), discommode, disqualify, foil, frustrate, hamper, hold up (delay), impair, invalidate, overreach, plot, pollute, rebel, smear, subvert, supplant, thwart. SEE MAIN ENTRY

1029

undermine one's belief deter, impugn
undermining detrimental
undermost cardinal *(basic)*, underlying
underpin bolster
underpinning foundation *(basis)*
underplot collusion, connivance, conspiracy, machination
underpraise depreciate, minimize
underprice discount *(reduce)*, minimize, underestimate
underprize depreciate, misprize, underestimate
underrate depreciate, derogate, discommend, disparage, lessen, minimize, misprize, underestimate
underreckon depreciate, derogate, minimize, misprize, underestimate
underripe premature
underscoring emphasis
undersell discount *(reduce)*
undersign corroborate, cosign, indorse, notarize, seal *(solemnize)*, sign, subscribe *(sign)*, witness *(attest to)*
undersigned SEE MAIN ENTRY
undersized minimal
understand agree *(comply)*, appreciate *(comprehend)*, apprehend *(perceive)*, conceive *(comprehend)*, construe *(comprehend)*, deduce, deduct *(conclude by reasoning)*, digest *(comprehend)*, discover, find *(discover)*, infer, interpret, perceive, pierce *(discern)*, presume, presuppose, read, recognize *(perceive)*, resolve *(solve)*, solve, surmise, suspect *(think)*, sympathize. SEE MAIN ENTRY
understand by construe *(comprehend)*
understand fully comprehend *(understand)*
understand improperly misconstrue
understand incorrectly miscalculate, misinterpret, misread
understand the meaning of construe *(comprehend)*
understand wrongly misunderstand
understandability coherence
understandable ascertainable, cognizable, coherent *(clear)*, comprehensible, elementary, explicit, lucid, obvious, pardonable, pellucid, perceptible, ponderable, reasonable *(rational)*, scrutable, simple, unambiguous. SEE MAIN ENTRY
understandable language plain language
understandably fairly *(clearly)*
understanding accord, accordance *(understanding)*, adjustment, affection, agreement *(concurrence)*, agreement *(contract)*, apprehension *(perception)*, attornment, bargain, belief *(state of mind)*, benevolence *(disposition to do good)*, benevolent, caliber *(mental capacity)*, charitable *(lenient)*, cognition, cognizant, common sense, compact, comprehension, concept, conciliation, concordance, conscious *(aware)*, consideration *(sympathetic regard)*, consortium *(marriage companionship)*, construction, contract, conviction *(persuasion)*, covenant, deal, discrimination *(good judgment)*, estimate *(idea)*, experience *(background)*, humanity *(humaneness)*, inference, information *(knowledge)*, insight, intellect, intelligence *(intellect)*, judgment *(discernment)*, juridical, knowing, knowledge *(awareness)*, league, lenience, longanimity, notion, omniscient, option *(contractual provision)*, pact, patient, perception, perceptive,

perspicacious, placable, policy *(contract)*, promise, protocol *(agreement)*, quid pro quo, rapport, rapprochement, rational, realization, reason *(sound judgment)*, receptive, reconciliation, sagacity, sane, sanity, scienter, sense *(feeling)*, sense *(intelligence)*, sensible, sensitive *(discerning)*, settlement, specialty *(contract)*, stipulation, term *(provision)*, tolerance, treaty, vicarious *(delegated)*. SEE MAIN ENTRY
understanding before marriage antenuptial agreement
understandings dealings
understate discount *(minimize)*, distort, minimize, misrepresent
understatement SEE MAIN ENTRY
understood assumed *(inferred)*, clear *(apparent)*, cognizable, coherent *(clear)*, consensual, constructive *(inferential)*, contractual, familiar *(customary)*, implicit, implied, indirect, lucid, prescriptive, tacit
understood by a select few esoteric
understood by the initiated esoteric
understood from accompanying words noscitur a sociis
understudy replace, replacement, substitute
understudy for displace *(replace)*
undertake agree *(contract)*, attempt, close *(agree)*, commence, contract, embark, endeavor, engage *(involve)*, generate, incur, initiate, launch *(initiate)*, maintain *(commence)*, occupy *(engage)*, originate, participate, pledge *(promise the performance of)*, ply, practice *(engage in)*, promise *(vow)*, strive, try *(attempt)*, underwrite. SEE MAIN ENTRY
undertake by contract contract
undertake responsibility answer *(be responsible)*
undertaking activity, agreement *(contract)*, appointment *(position)*, assumption *(adoption)*, bail, burden, business *(affair)*, business *(occupation)*, calling, campaign, charge *(responsibility)*, commitment *(responsibility)*, contract, covenant, coverage *(insurance)*, endeavor, enterprise *(undertaking)*, expedient, indenture, industry *(business)*, job, labor *(work)*, livelihood, maneuver *(tactic)*, mission, occupation *(vocation)*, operation, part *(role)*, plan, pledge *(binding promise)*, post, practice *(professional business)*, proceeding, profession *(vocation)*, project, prosecution *(criminal trial)*, pursuit *(effort to secure)*, pursuit *(occupation)*, role, specialty *(contract)*, transaction, vow, work *(effort)*. SEE MAIN ENTRY
undertakings dealings
undervaluation disregard *(lack of respect)*, understatement
undervalue depreciate, derogate, discommend, discount *(minimize)*, discount *(reduce)*, disparage, humiliate, lessen, minimize, misprize, underestimate
underworker assistant
underworld activity racket
underworld character criminal, outlaw, racketeer
underworld gangster racketeer
underwrite assure *(insure)*, authorize, avouch *(guarantee)*, bond *(secure a debt)*, close *(agree)*, cosign, ensure, guarantee, indorse, promise *(vow)*, sign, sponsor, subscribe *(sign)*, subsidize, vouch. SEE MAIN ENTRY
underwrite again refinance
underwrite against loss insure

underwriter insurer, surety *(guarantor)*
underwriting coverage *(insurance)*
undeserved disproportionate, undue *(excessive)*, unjust
undeserving disproportiate, unworthy
undeserving of censure irreprehensible
undesignated anonymous, unspecified
undesigned fortuitous, inadvertent, random, unexpected, unforeseen, unintentional, unpremeditated, unwitting
undesigned occurrence accident *(chance occurrence)*, quirk *(accident)*
undesigning direct *(forthright)*, ingenuous, simple, straightforward, unaffected *(sincere)*
undesirability bad character, detriment, disqualification *(factor that disqualifies)*, inexpedience
undesirable antipathetic *(distasteful)*, bad *(inferior)*, bad *(offensive)*, delinquent, deplorable, gratuitous *(unwarranted)*, ill-advised, improper, imprudent, inadvisable, inappropriate, inapt, ineligible, inept *(inappropriate)*, inferior *(lower in quality)*, injudicious, inopportune, loathsome, needless, objectionable, repugnant *(exciting aversion)*, sordid, unacceptable, unendurable, unfit, unsatisfactory, unsavory, unsuitable. SEE MAIN ENTRY
undesirableness inexpedience
undesired unacceptable, unsolicited
undesirous averse
undespairing sanguine
undestroyable indelible, indestructible, infallible, noncancellable, permanent, perpetual
undestroyed chronic, extant, intact, inviolate, lasting, live *(existing)*
undestructive nontoxic
undetached interested, one-sided, partisan
undetachment bias, inequity, nepotism, predetermination
undetected blind *(concealed)*, hidden, latent, potential, undisclosed
undetermination ambivalence
undetermined casual, conditional, debatable, disputable, dubious, equivocal, indefinite, irresolute, moot, outstanding *(unresolved)*, pending *(unresolved)*, problematic, provisional, speculative, uncertain *(questionable)*, undecided, unsettled, vague
undeterminedness doubt *(indecision)*
undeveloped deficient, dormant, imperfect, inadequate, inexperienced, juvenile, latent, partial *(relating to a part)*, premature, rudimentary
undeveloped stage embryo
undeviating accurate, boiler plate, certain *(positive)*, comparable *(equivalent)*, consistent, consonant, constant, direct *(straight)*, equal, exact, factual, immutable, industrious, intense, literal, loyal, patient, persistent, pertinacious, purposeful, regular *(conventional)*, relentless, resolute, right *(direct)*, rigid, sedulous, sequacious, stable, steadfast, straightforward, unalterable, undistorted, uniform, unrelenting, unyielding
undeviatingly faithfully, invariably
undevout profane
undexterous inadept
undextrous amateur
undifferentiating indiscriminate
undignified blatant *(obtrusive)*, disreputable, inappropriate, inelegant, unbecoming, unprofessional, unseemly

undiligent negligent

undiluted honest, unadulterated

undiminished complete *(all-embracing)*, gross *(total)*, intact, outright, plenary, whole *(undamaged)*. SEE MAIN ENTRY

undiminished quantity entirety

undiplomatic impolitic, unpolitic

undirected astray, casual, discursive *(digressive)*, fortuitous, haphazard, indiscriminate, random

undiscernable impalpable

undiscernible inconspicuous, indefinite, intangible, nebulous

undiscerning blind *(not discerning)*, cursory, heedless, ill-judged, inadvertent, injudicious, insensible, oblivious, obtuse, perfunctory, promiscuous, unaware

undischarged unpaid

undisciplined capricious, disobedient, disordered, disorderly, inexperienced, intractable, irresponsible, lawless, licentious, uncurbed, unrestrained *(not repressed)*, unversed

undisclosable private *(confidential)*

undisclosed clandestine, covert, esoteric, furtive, hidden, mysterious, personal *(private)*, potential, privy, secret, stealthy, surreptitious, ulterior. SEE MAIN ENTRY

undiscordant consonant

undiscouraged patient, persistent, undaunted

undiscoverability mystery

undiscoverable inapprehensible, indiscernible, inexplicable, inscrutable

undiscovered latent, potential

undiscriminating promiscuous

undisguise bare

undisguised accurate, apparent *(perceptible)*, authentic, bona fide, candid, clear *(apparent)*, coherent *(clear)*, conspicuous, distinct *(clear)*, evident, explicit, factual, genuine, honest, ingenuous, lucid, manifest, naked *(lacking embellishment)*, obvious, open *(in sight)*, overt, palpable, patent, pellucid, realistic, true *(authentic)*, undistorted, unmistakable

undisguising direct *(forthright)*, honest

undismayed unabashed, undaunted

undispassionate one-sided, partisan

undispassionateness bias, inequity

undisputable indefeasible, sound

undisputed accurate, axiomatic, categorical, certain *(fixed)*, certain *(positive)*, clear *(certain)*, consensual, convincing, definite, definitive, factual, general, resounding, true *(authentic)*, uncontested, uncontroverted, unequivocal, unimpeachable. SEE MAIN ENTRY

undissembling bona fide, candid, honest, straightforward

undissimulating honest

undissolvable inseparable

undissolved solid *(compact)*

undistinctive usual

undistinguished marginal, mediocre, mundane, nondescript, obscure *(faint)*, ordinary, unpretentious, usual

undistorted accurate, authentic, bona fide, candid, direct *(straight)*, distinct *(clear)*, factual, genuine, honest, literal, realistic, sound, straightforward, true *(authentic)*, unadulterated. SEE MAIN ENTRY

undistracted pertinacious, steadfast

undisturbed dispassionate, inviolate, patient, peaceable, phlegmatic, placid, sane, secure *(confident)*, stoical

undiversified uniform

undividable indivisible, inseparable

undivided complete *(all-embracing)*, concurrent *(united)*, gross *(total)*, intact, outright, total, undiminished

undivided attention diligence *(care)*, diligence *(perseverance)*, interest *(concern)*, obsession

undividedly in toto

undividedness entirety, integration *(assimilation)*, whole

undivisible whole *(unified)*

undivulgable private *(confidential)*

undivulged esoteric, hidden, secret, ulterior, undisclosed

undo abolish, abrogate *(annul)*, beat *(defeat)*, betray *(lead astray)*, counteract, denude, disengage, disorganize, disown *(deny the validity)*, dissociate, dissolve *(separate)*, dissolve *(terminate)*, frustrate, invalidate, liberate, overreach, overrule, part *(separate)*, subvert, upset, vitiate. SEE MAIN ENTRY

undoable impracticable, inoperable *(impracticable)*

undogmatic open-minded

undoing annulment, defeasance, defeat, destruction, detriment, disaster, dissolution *(disintegration)*, prostration, reversal

undone irredeemable, irreparable

undoubtable cogent, irrefutable, noncontestable, palpable, real

undoubted absolute *(conclusive)*, axiomatic, certain *(positive)*, clear *(certain)*, cogent, conclusive *(determinative)*, decisive, definitive, uncontested, uncontroverted, undisputed, unimpeachable, unmistakable

undoubtedly admittedly, fairly *(clearly)*

undoubtful certain *(positive)*, indubious

undoubting affirmative, certain *(positive)*, credulous, definite, pertinacious, positive *(confident)*, sanguine, unsuspecting

undramatic insipid, jejune *(dull)*

undrape bare, denude, expose, manifest, unveil

undress denude, expose, unveil

undrilled inexperienced, unversed

undue disproportionate, drastic, excess, excessive, exorbitant, extreme *(exaggerated)*, gratuitous *(unwarranted)*, improper, inadmissible, inapposite, inappropriate, inapt, inept *(inappropriate)*, inordinate, outrageous, prohibitive, redundant, unauthorized, unfit, unreasonable, unseemly, unwarranted, usurious, wrongful. SEE MAIN ENTRY

undue amount overage, plethora

undue delay laches. SEE MAIN ENTRY

undue expansion of currency inflation *(decrease in value of currency)*

undue influence coercion, pressure. SEE MAIN ENTRY

undueness breach, exaggeration, inequity

undulate beat *(pulsate)*, circuitous, oscillate, vacillate

undulated circuitous

undulating circuitous

undulative circuitous

undulatory circuitous, tortuous *(bending)*

unduly arbitrary and capricious. SEE MAIN ENTRY

unduteousness breach, nonperformance

undutiful broken *(unfulfilled)*, disobedient, irresponsible, untrue

undutifulness breach, contempt *(disobedience to the court)*, infidelity, nonperformance

undying chronic, constant, durable, immutable, incessant, indestructible, infallible, infinite, permanent, persistent. SEE MAIN ENTRY

unearned increment gratuity *(present)*

unearth ascertain, betray *(disclose)*, delve, detect, disclose, discover, disinter, educe, expose, ferret, find *(discover)*, locate, manifest, probe, research, reveal, solve, trace *(follow)*

unearthing detection, discovery

unearthly intangible, nonsubstantial *(not sturdy)*, uncanny

unease pain, scruple

uneasiness apprehension *(fear)*, concern *(interest)*, distress *(anguish)*, embarrassment, fear, misgiving, qualm, scruple, trepidation

uneasiness of mind dissatisfaction

uneasy restive, unsettled

uneconomical improvident, prodigal, prolix

unedited intact

uneducated unversed

uneffective unqualified *(not competent)*

unelaborate unpretentious

unelapsed period unexpired term

unelevated insipid

unembarrassed brazen, unabashed

unembellished naked *(lacking embellishment)*, simple

unembodied incorporeal

unembroidered honest, literal, undistorted

unemotional clinical, cold-blooded, controlled *(restrained)*, dispassionate, inexpressive, insusceptible *(uncaring)*, phlegmatic, unresponsive. SEE MAIN ENTRY

unemotional consideration common sense

unemphatic insipid

unemployable impracticable

unemployed idle, inactive, otiose, truant, vacant. SEE MAIN ENTRY

unemployment disuse, inaction

unemployment insurance SEE MAIN ENTRY

unempowered inadequate, incapable, ineffectual, powerless, unauthorized

unenclosed open *(accessible)*

unencumbered exempt, free *(relieved from a burden)*, immune, independent, unbound, unrestrained *(not in custody)*. SEE MAIN ENTRY

unendangered safe

unended live *(existing)*

unending chronic, continual *(perpetual)*, continuous, direct *(uninterrupted)*, durable, far reaching, immutable, incessant, infinite, myriad, open-ended, permanent, perpetual, protracted, rife, unlimited

unendorsed unauthorized, unofficial

unendorsed purchase caveat emptor

unendowed disabled *(deprived of legal right)*, disabled *(made incapable)*, inadept, powerless

unendowment incompetence

unendurable insufferable, intolerable, loathsome, objectionable, obnoxious, odious, offensive *(offending)*, oppressive, painful. SEE MAIN ENTRY

unenduring ephemeral, temporary, transient, transitory

unenforceable void *(invalid)*

unengaged unemployed

unenlightened blind *(not discerning)*, ill-judged, incognizant, insensible, opaque, unacquainted, unaware

unenlightenment ignorance, nescience
unenlivened jejune *(dull)*, lifeless *(dull)*, nondescript, pedestrian
unenslaved free *(enjoying civil liberty)*, independent, sovereign *(independent)*
unentangled free *(not restricted)*
unenterprising careful, indolent, lax, lifeless *(dull)*
unentertaining insipid, jejune *(dull)*, lifeless *(dull)*, pedestrian, prosaic
unenthralled free *(enjoying civil liberty)*, independent
unenthusiastic disinclined, lifeless *(dull)*, nonchalant, perfunctory
unentitled impermissible, ineligible, unauthorized, unwarranted
unequal broken *(interrupted)*, disparate, disproportionate, heterogeneous, incommensurate, incompetent, insufficient, partial *(biased)*, peculiar *(distinctive)*, unconscionable, unfair, unjust. SEE MAIN ENTRY
unequal to deficient, inadept, inadequate
unequaled absolute *(ideal)*, best, cardinal *(outstanding)*, leading *(ranking first)*, noteworthy, paramount, premium, priceless, prime *(most valuable)*, professional *(stellar)*, rare, select, singular, superior *(excellent)*, superlative, unapproachable, unique, unprecedented, unusual
unequalled extraordinary, inestimable, invaluable
unequalness difference
unequipped incapable, incompetent, ineligible, powerless, unfit, unqualified *(not competent)*
unequivocal absolute *(conclusive)*, axiomatic, categorical, certain *(positive)*, clear *(apparent)*, clear *(certain)*, cogent, cognizable, coherent *(clear)*, conclusive *(determinative)*, constant, credible, decisive, definite, demonstrable, distinct *(clear)*, dogmatic, evident, explicit, express, incontestable, incontrovertible, indubious, irrefutable, lucid, official, outright, palpable, peremptory *(absolute)*, positive *(incontestable)*, precise, reliable, unambiguous, unmistakable, unrefutable, vehement. SEE MAIN ENTRY
unequivocally fairly *(clearly)*, purely *(positively)*
unequivocalness belief *(state of mind)*, certainty, certitude, incontestability, surety *(certainty)*
uneradicated lasting
unerasable chronic, indelible, permanent, perpetual
unerased lasting
unerring absolute *(conclusive)*, accurate, actual, certain *(fixed)*, certain *(positive)*, clean, clear *(certain)*, definite, effective *(efficient)*, exact, factual, incorruptible, inculpable, infallible, irreprehensible, literal, moral, positive *(incontestable)*, precise, reliable, secure *(sound)*, solid *(sound)*, strict, unblemished. SEE MAIN ENTRY
unerringly faithfully
unerroneous actual, factual, real
unescorted solitary
unessayed unsettled
unessential collateral *(immaterial)*, expendable, extraneous, extrinsic, gratuitous *(unwarranted)*, immaterial, inapposite, inconsequential, inconsiderable, irrelevant, minor, needless, negligible, nonessential, null *(insignificant)*, petty,

remote *(small)*, secondary, slight, superfluous, supplementary, unnecessary. SEE MAIN ENTRY
unestablished inconclusive, unconfirmed, unfounded
unethical dishonest, disingenuous, disreputable, fraudulent, immoral, machiavellian, profligate *(corrupt)*, unconscionable, unprofessional, unscrupulous. SEE MAIN ENTRY
unethical use exploitation
unevasible necessary *(inescapable)*
unevasive clear *(apparent)*, cognizable
uneven broken *(interrupted)*, disordered, disorderly, disparate, disproportionate, inequitable, one-sided, partial *(biased)*, sporadic, unequal *(unequivalent)*, unfair, unpredictable, variable
unevenness diversity, flaw, incoherence, inequality, irregularity
uneventful mundane, unavailing
unevident impalpable, inconspicuous, ulterior, unclear
unexact indefinite
unexacted unclaimed
unexacting casual, flexible
unexaggerated authentic, bona fide, exact, factual, honest, literal, naked *(lacking embellishment)*, sound, true *(authentic)*, undistorted
unexalted mundane
unexamined perfunctory
unexampled extraordinary, original *(creative)*, peculiar *(curious)*, portentous *(eliciting amazement)*, prodigious *(amazing)*, rare, renowned, singular, special, uncommon, unique, unprecedented
unexcelled absolute *(ideal)*, cardinal *(outstanding)*, leading *(ranking first)*, paramount, professional *(stellar)*, select, superior *(excellent)*, superlative, unapproachable
unexceptionability admissibility
unexceptionable admissible, clean, irreprehensible, mediocre, unimpeachable, unobjectionable
unexceptional average *(standard)*, fair *(satisfactory)*, familiar *(customary)*, nondescript, normal *(regular)*, ordinary, regular *(conventional)*, typical, usual
unexceptionality mediocrity
unexcercised unversed
unexcessiveness temperance
unexcitable controlled *(restrained)*, peaceable, phlegmatic
unexcited dispassionate, nonchalant, peaceable, phlegmatic, placid, unaffected *(uninfluenced)*
unexciting insipid, jejune *(dull)*, mediocre, nondescript, ordinary, trite
unexclusive comprehensive
unexcused delay laches
unexecuted executory, inchoate
unexempt from actionable, subject *(exposed)*
unexercised inactive
unexisting devoid, nonexistent
unexpectant unsuspecting
unexpected coincidental, fortuitous, impulsive *(rash)*, nonconforming, original *(creative)*, peculiar *(curious)*, precipitate, unanticipated, unforeseeable, unforeseen, unintentional, unprecedented, unpredictable, unusual, unwitting. SEE MAIN ENTRY
unexpected event bombshell, surprise
unexpected happening emergency
unexpected misfortune accident

(chance occurrence)
unexpected occurrence accident *(chance occurrence)*, happenstance, surprise
unexpectedness chance *(possibility)*
unexpended net
unexpired term SEE MAIN ENTRY
unexplainable inapprehensible, inexplicable, mysterious, undefinable
unexplained dubious, equivocal, hidden, mysterious, undisclosed
unexplained delay laches
unexplicit impalpable, unclear
unexplored unsettled
unexplored ground mystery
unexposed blind *(concealed)*, hidden, immune, latent, potential, safe, undisclosed
unexpressed implicit, indirect, potential, tacit, ulterior, undisclosed
unexpressive mute
unexpurgated gross *(total)*, intact, lurid, salacious
unextravagant reasonable *(fair)*
unextreme reasonable *(fair)*
unfabricated authentic, factual, genuine, honest, true *(authentic)*
unfacile inadept, inept *(incompetent)*
unfactual inaccurate, incorrect, lying
unfactualness error
unfaded intact, undiminished
unfading chronic, durable, indelible, indestructible, infallible, live *(existing)*, permanent, perpetual
unfailing certain *(fixed)*, certain *(positive)*, credible, definite, dependable, durable, faithful *(loyal)*, inevitable, infallible, lasting, live *(existing)*, loyal, permanent, perpetual, persistent, reliable, secure *(sound)*, solid *(sound)*, stable, staunch, steadfast, true *(loyal)*, unremitting
unfair inequitable, iniquitous, one-sided, partial *(biased)*, sinister, unconscionable, unequal *(unjust)*, unethical, unjust, unreasonable, unscrupulous, unwarranted, wrongful. SEE MAIN ENTRY
unfair action injustice
unfair choice dilemma
unfair judgment misjudgment
unfairly call to account frame *(charge falsely)*
unfairness bad faith, discrimination *(bigotry)*, grievance, inequality, inequity, injustice, misjudgment, nepotism, prejudice *(injury)*, wrong
unfaith bad faith
unfaithful broken *(unfulfilled)*, derelict *(negligent)*, dishonest, disobedient, faithless, false *(disloyal)*, fraudulent, perfidious, recreant, untrue, untrustworthy
unfaithfulness adultery, bad faith, breach, dereliction, disloyalty, infidelity
unfaithworthiness bad faith
unfaithworthy irresponsible, precarious
unfaked authentic, bona fide, genuine, honest, undistorted, veridical
unfallacious actual, real, true *(authentic)*
unfallen blameless, irreprehensible
unfalse actual, credible, true *(loyal)*
unfaltering continuous, definite, diligent, direct *(uninterrupted)*, industrious, inexorable, infallible, patient, persistent, pertinacious, purposeful, relentless, resolute, sedulous, serious *(devoted)*, stable, staunch, steadfast, undaunted
unfamiliar extraordinary, foreign, incognizant, inexperienced, inexplicable,

noteworthy, novel, peculiar *(curious)*, prodigious *(amazing)*, rare, recondite, special, unaccustomed, unacquainted, uncanny, uncommon, unprecedented, unusual, unversed

unfamiliar with unaware

unfamiliarity ignorance, insentience

unfamiliarly particularly

unfashionable deviant, eccentric, nonconforming, obsolete, original *(creative)*, outdated, outmoded, unorthodox

unfasten detach, disencumber, disengage, disentangle, disjoint, free, liberate, remove *(eliminate)*, sever

unfastened discrete, free *(not restricted)*, insecure, moving *(in motion)*, open *(unclosed)*, unbound

unfathomability mystery

unfathomable complex, inapprehensible, inarticulate, incomprehensible, indefinable, indeterminate, inexpressive, innumerable, inscrutable, myriad, mysterious, opaque, profound *(intense)*, unlimited

unfathomableness mystery, opacity

unfavorable adverse *(negative)*, averse, bleak *(not favorable)*, deleterious, derogatory, disadvantageous, disastrous, harmful, inadvisable, inapposite, inauspicious, inimical, inopportune, lamentable, noxious, prejudicial, regrettable, sinister, unpropitious, unsatisfactory, unsuitable, untimely. SEE MAIN ENTRY

unfavorable circumstance disadvantage

unfavorable remark stricture

unfavorable to health insalubrious, peccant *(unhealthy)*

unfavorable verdict conviction *(finding of guilt)*

unfavorableness disadvantage

unfavorably known notorious

unfearing unabashed, undaunted

unfeasable insuperable

unfeasibility impossibility

unfeasible impossible, impracticable, inoperable *(impracticable)*, insurmountable, unattainable

unfeeling brutal, callous, cold-blooded, cruel, dispassionate, harsh, insensible, insusceptible *(uncaring)*, lifeless *(dead)*, lifeless *(dull)*, malevolent, malicious, nonchalant, obdurate, obtuse, perfunctory, phlegmatic, relentless, ruthless, severe, torpid, unaffected *(uninfluenced)*, unresponsive

unfeelingness brutality, ingratitude, insentience

unfeigned authentic, bona fide, genuine, honest, naive, real, straightforward, true *(authentic)*

unfeigning direct *(forthright)*, genuine, honest, unaffected *(sincere)*

unfenced open *(accessible)*

unfertile barren, lifeless *(dull)*, otiose

unfetter break *(separate)*, disencumber, disengage, disentangle, disenthrall, extricate, free, liberate, parole, release, rescue

unfettered clear *(unencumbered)*, free *(not restricted)*, independent, lawless, unbound, unrestrained *(not in custody)*, unrestrained *(not repressed)*, unrestricted

unfettering freedom, liberation, release

unficticious veridical

unfictitious authentic, genuine, honest, true *(authentic)*, undistorted

unfigurative literal

unfilled available, insatiable, vacant, vacuous, void *(empty)*

unfilled place access *(opening)*

unfinalized inchoate, partial *(relating to a part)*

unfinished defective, deficient, executory, imperfect, inchoate, insufficient, interim, outstanding *(unresolved)*, partial *(part)*, partial *(relating to a part)*, rudimentary, semi

unfirm insubstantial

unfit amateur, bad *(inferior)*, bad *(offensive)*, detrimental, disabled *(deprived of legal right)*, disabled *(made incapable)*, disqualify, faulty, ill-advised, improper, inadept, inadequate, inadmissible, inapplicable, inapposite, inappropriate, inapt, incapable, incompetent, incongruous, ineligible, inept *(inappropriate)*, injudicious, inopportune, insufficient, powerless, unable, unbecoming, undesirable, undue *(excessive)*, unqualified *(not competent)*, unsatisfactory, unseemly, unsuitable, unworthy. SEE MAIN ENTRY

unfitness disability *(legal disqualification)*, disability *(physical inability)*, disqualification *(factor that disqualifies)*, illegality, impotence, impropriety, inability, incapacity, incompetence, incongruity, inexpedience

unfitted disabled *(made incapable)*, inadept, inadequate, inadmissible, inapplicable, inappropriate, incompetent, ineligible, insufficient, unbecoming

unfittedness disqualification *(factor that disqualifies)*

unfitting disproportionate, improper, inadvisable, inapplicable, inapposite, inappropriate, inapt, incongruous, ineligible, inept *(inappropriate)*, unfit, unprofessional, unseemly, unsuitable

unfittingness impropriety, incongruity, inexpedience

unfix disengage, free

unfixable irremediable

unfixed casual, debatable, disputable, free *(not restricted)*, indeterminate, irresolute, pending *(unresolved)*, unbound, undecided, unsettled, unspecified

unflagging faithful *(diligent)*, industrious, infallible, patient, permanent, persistent, pertinacious, purposeful, sedulous, stable, steadfast. SEE MAIN ENTRY

unflappable nonchalant

unflattering calumnious, derogatory, harsh, pejorative

unfledged inexperienced, jejune *(lacking maturity)*, juvenile

unfleshly incorporeal, intangible

unflimsy strong

unflinching heroic, indomitable, patient, pertinacious, purposeful, relentless, resolute, spartan, stable, steadfast, unabashed, undaunted

unflowing stagnant

unfluctuating equal

unflustered phlegmatic

unfold bare, betray *(disclose)*, clarify, construe *(translate)*, crystallize, denude, deploy, develop, disabuse, disclose, educe, elucidate, evolve, expand, explain, explicate, expose, exposit, expound, find *(discover)*, interpret, manifest, produce *(offer to view)*, recount, reveal, simplify *(clarify)*, solve, spread, unveil

unfold the meaning of explicate

unfold the sense of explicate

unfolding denouement, detection, development *(progression)*, disclosure

(act of disclosing), explanation, growth *(evolution)*, happening, manifestation

unfoldment disclosure *(act of disclosing)*

unfool disabuse

unforbidden admissible, allowable, allowed, permissible, unrestricted

unforced ingenuous, nonpartisan, spontaneous, voluntary, willing *(uncompelled)*

unforeseeable unpredictable. SEE MAIN ENTRY

unforeseen fortuitous, haphazard, unanticipated, unexpected, unintentional. SEE MAIN ENTRY

unforeseen accident casualty

unforeseen adversity misfortune

unforeseen circumstance complication

unforeseen circumstances SEE MAIN ENTRY

unforeseen condition emergency

unforeseen contingency surprise

unforeseen event quirk *(accident)*, surprise

unforeseen occurrence accident *(chance occurrence)*, contingency, emergency, happenstance, quirk *(accident)*, surprise

unforewarned unaware

unforfeitable inalienable

unforgettable indelible, notable, noteworthy, outstanding *(prominent)*, remarkable, special

unforgivable inexcusable, inexpiable, peccant *(culpable)*, unjustifiable

unforgiving callous, implacable, irreconcilable, obdurate, relentless, remorseless, resentful, ruthless, unrelenting, vindictive

unforgoable obligatory

unforgotten indelible

unformed premature

unforthcoming noncommittal

unfortified disabled *(made incapable)*, helpless *(defenseless)*, indefensible, open *(accessible)*, powerless, untenable

unfortunate adverse *(negative)*, deplorable, derelict *(abandoned)*, dire, harmful, inopportune, lamentable, ominous, regrettable, unfavorable, unpropitious, unsuitable. SEE MAIN ENTRY

unfortunate accident casualty

unfortunate consequence cost *(penalty)*

unfortunate event accident *(misfortune)*, disaster

unfortunate occurrence casualty

unfortunate occurrence misfortune

unfortunate person victim

unfounded baseless, delusive, erroneous, fallacious, false *(inaccurate)*, fictitious, gratuitous *(unwarranted)*, ill-founded, illogical, inaccurate, insubstantial, sophistic, specious, unsupported, untrue, unwarranted. SEE MAIN ENTRY

unfounded conclusion non sequitur

unfounded story canard

unfrequent infrequent

unfrequented private *(secluded)*, remote *(secluded)*

unfriended derelict *(abandoned)*

unfriendliness alienation *(estrangement)*, estrangement, ill will, incompatibility *(difference)*, ostracism, rancor

unfriendly adverse *(hostile)*, antipathetic *(oppositional)*, contentious, inimical, malevolent, perverse, pugnacious, recusant, unfavorable, vicious, virulent

unfriendly feeling ill will

unfrightened secure *(confident)*, undaunted

unfrock denude

unfrugal improvident, prodigal
unfruitful barren, disadvantageous, futile, ineffective, ineffectual, nugatory, otiose, unproductive
unfruitfulness inefficacy
unfulfilled deficient, executory
unfulfillment nonperformance
unfulfillment of an assignment delinquency *(failure of duty)*
unfulfillment of duty delinquency *(failure of duty)*
unfunctional impracticable
unfurl bare, deploy, spread
unfurled open *(unclosed)*
unfurnished deficient, void *(empty)*
unfussy inaccurate
ungainly incompetent, inelegant, inept *(incompetent)*, uncouth
ungallant perverse
ungallantness disrespect
ungarbled honest, literal
ungarrulous laconic, taciturn
ungathered outstanding *(unpaid)*
ungenerous illiberal, parsimonious, penurious
ungenteel blatant *(obtrusive)*, disorderly, ignoble, inelegant, presumptuous, unbecoming, unseemly
ungentle brutal, caustic, disorderly, harsh, hot-blooded, scathing, severe
ungentlemanlike disorderly
ungentlemanliness disrespect
ungentlemanly blatant *(obtrusive)*, disorderly, illiberal, uncouth
ungenuine artificial, assumed *(feigned)*, bogus, dishonest, disingenuous, fraudulent, imitation, mendacious, spurious
ungenuineness bad faith
ungermane alien *(unrelated)*, inapplicable, inapposite, inappropriate, inconsequential, nonessential, peripheral, unrelated
ungerminating barren
ungettable unattainable
ungifted amateur, inadept
ungiving insusceptible *(uncaring)*
unglue disengage
ungodly mundane, profane
ungovernable contumacious, disobedient, froward, hot-blooded, incorrigible, indomitable, insubordinate, intractable, lawless, obdurate, perverse, recalcitrant, restive, uncontrollable, unruly, unyielding
ungoverned disorderly, lawless, licentious, uncurbed, unrestrained *(not repressed)*
ungraceful inelegant, provincial
ungracious abusive, blatant *(obtrusive)*, harsh, impertinent *(insolent)*, invidious, offensive *(offending)*, perverse, severe
ungraciousness disrespect
ungratefulness ingratitude
ungratifying nonsubstantial *(not sufficient)*, unsatisfactory
ungrounded baseless, erroneous, fallacious, false *(inaccurate)*, ill-founded, illogical, incorrect, insubstantial, nonsubstantial *(not sturdy)*, sophistic, unfounded, unsound *(fallacious)*
ungrudging benevolent, dispassionate, liberal *(generous)*, magnanimous, philanthropic
ungrudgingness philanthropy
unguaranteed purchase caveat emptor
unguarded careless, helpless *(defenseless)*, improvident, imprudent, indefensible, lax, open *(accessible)*, perfunctory,

unaware, unsuspecting, untenable, vulnerable. SEE MAIN ENTRY
unguardedness danger
unguided astray, haphazard, ill-judged, random
unguilty blameless, clean
unhabitual unusual
unhabituated inexperienced, unaccustomed
unhallow pollute
unhallowed mundane, profane
unhamper disencumber, disengage, disentangle, extricate
unhampered clear *(unencumbered)*, free *(not restricted)*, unrestrained *(not in custody)*, unrestrained *(not repressed)*
unhandsome unbecoming, unseemly
unhandy impracticable, incompetent, inept *(incompetent)*
unhappiness damper *(depressant)*, dissatisfaction, distress *(anguish)*, pessimism
unhappiness with one's lot dissatisfaction
unhappy bitter *(reproachful)*, deplorable, despondent, disconsolate, lamentable, lugubrious, pessimistic, regrettable
unharmable secure *(free from danger)*
unharmed intact, inviolate, safe
unharmonious hostile, inapplicable, inapposite, inappropriate
unharmoniousness conflict, discord
unharness disencumber, extricate, parole
unharnessing release
unhasty deliberate
unhazarded safe
unhazardous harmless, nontoxic, reliable
unhealable chronic
unhealthful deleterious, insalubrious, pernicious, pestilent
unhealthiness disease
unhealthy deadly, deleterious, detrimental, disadvantageous, harmful, inadvisable, insalubrious, lethal, noxious, pernicious, pestilent, unsound *(not strong)*
unhealthy air air pollution
unhealthy situation peril
unheard diffident, ineffable
unheard of extraordinary, implausible, ludicrous, noteworthy, novel, original *(creative)*, peculiar *(curious)*, portentous *(eliciting amazement)*, prodigious *(amazing)*, uncanny, uncommon, unprecedented, unusual. SEE MAIN ENTRY
unhearing heedless, insensible
unheeded perfunctory
unheedful derelict *(negligent)*, heedless, inadvertent, negligent, perfunctory
unheedfulness disregard *(lack of respect)*, disregard *(unconcern)*, neglect
unheeding derelict *(negligent)*, heedless, inadvertent, lax, negligent, oblivious, perfunctory, reckless, remiss, unaware
unhelpful detrimental, disadvantageous, inadvisable, perverse
unheralded undisclosed, unexpected, unforeseen
unheroic peccable
unhesitating categorical, certain *(positive)*, clear *(certain)*, decisive, definite, immediate *(at once)*, positive *(confident)*, prompt, purposeful, secure *(confident)*, stable, steadfast
unheterodox orthodox
unhidden comprehensible, conspicuous, distinct *(clear)*, evident, manifest, obvious,

open *(in sight)*, overt, palpable, patent, pellucid, perceivable, perceptible, scrutable
unhindered clear *(unencumbered)*, free *(not restricted)*, independent, unbound, uncurbed, unrestrained *(not in custody)*, unrestrained *(not repressed)*
unhinge confuse *(bewilder)*, discompose, disjoint, impair, luxate, obsess
unhinged lunatic
unhistorical fictitious
unhitch disengage
unholiness blasphemy
unholy mundane, profane
unhook disengage
unhopeful despondent
unhostile amicable, nonmilitant, propitious
unhouse displace *(remove)*
unhurried deliberate
unhurriedness deliberation
unhurt intact, inviolate, safe, whole *(undamaged)*
unhygienic insalubrious, peccant *(unhealthy)*
unicus singular, sole, unique
unidealism pragmatism
unidealistic mercenary, pragmatic, realistic
unidentical different, dissimilar, diverse
unidentifiable nondescript
unidentified anonymous
unification accession *(annexation)*, affiliation *(amalgamation)*, centralization, coalescence, coalition, combination, confederacy *(compact)*, consolidation, federation, incorporation *(blend)*, incorporation *(formation of a business entity)*, integration *(amalgamation)*, joinder, league, meeting *(encounter)*, merger, pool, relationship *(connection)*, sodality, union *(unity)*
unified coadunate, collective, concurrent *(united)*, conjoint, consonant, intact, joint, mutual *(collective)*
unifier connection *(fastening)*
uniform boiler plate, clothe, coequal, comparable *(equivalent)*, concordant, consistent, consonant, equal, identical, proportionate, regular *(orderly)*, repeated, routine, same, similar, systematic. SEE MAIN ENTRY
uniformity adjustment, agreement *(concurrence)*, arrangement *(ordering)*, array *(order)*, conciliation, conformity *(agreement)*, consensus, constant, correspondence *(similarity)*, identity *(similarity)*, method, parity, regularity, resemblance, semblance, union *(unity)*. SEE MAIN ENTRY
uniformly invariably
unify amalgamate, cohere *(adhere)*, collect *(gather)*, combine *(join together)*, conjoin, consolidate *(strengthen)*, conspire, crystallize, desegregate, federalize *(associate)*, federate, include, join *(bring together)*, merge, organize *(unionize)*, pool, unite
unilateral ex parte *(adjective)*, ex parte *(adverb)*. SEE MAIN ENTRY
unimaginable implausible, impossible, incomprehensible, incredible, ineffable, infeasible, peculiar *(curious)*, prodigious *(amazing)*, unbelievable
unimaginative lifeless *(dull)*, mundane, obtuse, ordinary, parochial, pedestrian, prosaic, sequacious, stale, trite, usual
unimagined actual, factual, real, sound, true *(authentic)*

unimitated distinct *(distinguished from others)*, distinctive, genuine, individual, noteworthy, original *(creative)*, peculiar *(distinctive)*, uncommon, unique
unimitative eccentric, special
unimpaired complete *(all-embracing)*, intact, inviolate, safe, undiminished, whole *(undamaged)*
unimparted undisclosed
unimpassioned dispassionate, insipid, insusceptible *(uncaring)*, jejune *(dull)*, languid, lifeless *(dull)*, nonchalant, open-minded, phlegmatic, placid, prosaic, stoical
unimpeachability certainty, certification *(certainness)*, certitude, incontestability
unimpeachable absolute *(conclusive)*, accurate, actual, axiomatic, believable, blameless, certain *(positive)*, clean, clear *(certain)*, conclusive *(determinative)*, definite, definitive, demonstrable, ethical, factual, genuine, inappealable, incontestable, incontrovertible, incorruptible, infallible, irrebuttable, irrefutable, irreprehensible, just, laudable, law-abiding, loyal, meritorious, not guilty, official, positive *(incontestable)*, provable, real, reputable, secure *(sound)*, solid *(sound)*, sound, true *(authentic)*, unalienable, undeniable, unobjectionable, unrefutable, upright. SEE MAIN ENTRY
unimpeached inculpable
unimpeded exempt, free *(not restricted)*, free *(relieved from a burden)*, passable, uncurbed, unrestrained *(not in custody)*
unimperiled secure *(free from danger)*
unimportance immateriality, inconsequence, insignificance, mediocrity
unimportant collateral *(immaterial)*, expendable, frivolous, futile, immaterial, inapposite, inappreciable, inconsequential, inconsiderable, inferior *(lower in position)*, insubstantial, irrelevant, mediocre, minimal, minor, negligible, nominal, nonessential, nugatory, null *(insignificant)*, paltry, peripheral, petty, remote *(small)*, secondary, slight, tenuous, trivial, unessential, unnecessary
unimposing diffident, unobtrusive
unimpressed callous, nonchalant, unaffected *(uninfluenced)*
unimpressible callous, cold-blooded, dispassionate, inexorable, insusceptible *(uncaring)*, stoical, unresponsive, unyielding
unimpressionable callous, clinical, dispassionate, unresponsive
unimpressive poor *(inferior in quality)*, usual
unimprison free
unimprovable irremediable
uninclined disinclined, reluctant
unincreased undiminished
unindebted compensatory, solvent
unindoctrinated unversed
uninduced nonpartisan
uninfluenceable impervious, unresponsive, unyielding
uninfluenced dispassionate, fair *(just)*, impartial, impervious, independent, judicial, just, liberal *(broad minded)*, loyal, neutral, nonpartisan, objective, open-minded, unbiased, unprejudiced
uninfluential ineffective, ineffectual, minor, null *(insignificant)*, powerless
uninfluential group minority *(outnumbered group)*
uninformed blind *(not discerning)*, incognizant, inexperienced, unacquainted, unaware, unversed, unwitting

uninformedness nescience
uninhabited devoid, solitary, unsettled, vacant, void *(empty)*
uninhibited candid, intemperate, uncurbed
uninhibitedness freedom, latitude, liberty
uniniquitous blameless
uninitiated incompetent, inexperienced, unaccustomed, unversed
uninjured intact, inviolate, safe, unblemished
uninjurious harmless, innocuous, nontoxic, salutary
uninspired insipid, jejune *(dull)*, languid, lifeless *(dull)*, mundane, perfunctory, unaffected *(uninfluenced)*
uninspiring insipid, jejune *(dull)*, lifeless *(dull)*, mediocre, pedestrian, prosaic
uninstructed incognizant
unintellectualism illiteracy
unintellectuality ignorance
unintelligence ignorance, nescience
unintelligent fatuous, irrational, obtuse, opaque, vacuous
unintelligibility ambiguity, incoherence, opacity
unintelligible ambiguous, disconnected, equivocal, inapprehensible, inarticulate, incomprehensible, indefinite, indistinct, inexplicable, inexpressive, inscrutable, mysterious, nebulous, obscure *(abstruse)*, opaque, recondite, uncertain *(ambiguous)*, unclear
unintelligible talk jargon *(unintelligible language)*
unintelligibleness obscuration
unintended fortuitous, haphazard, inadvertent, involuntary, unexpected, unforeseeable, unforeseen, unintentional, unpremeditated, unwitting
unintentional fortuitous, haphazard, inadvertent, involuntary, spontaneous, unexpected, unpremeditated, unwitting. SEE MAIN ENTRY
unintentional happening contingency
unintentional homicide manslaughter
unintentional mistake oversight *(carelessness)*
unintentional murder manslaughter
unintentional omission oversight *(carelessness)*
unintentionality quirk *(accident)*
unintentionally unknowingly
uninterested cold-blooded, derelict *(negligent)*, insusceptible *(uncaring)*, languid, lax, nonchalant, perfunctory, unresponsive
uninteresting insipid, lifeless *(dull)*, mediocre, mundane, nondescript, pedestrian, prosaic, stale, usual
unintermitted continual *(connected)*
unintermitted continuance perpetuity
unintermittedness continuity
unintermittent continuous, incessant, unremitting
unintermitting chronic, continuous, durable, incessant, relentless
uninterrupted chronic, consecutive, constant, continual *(connected)*, continuous, durable, incessant, permanent, perpetual, progressive *(going forward)*, unremitting
uninterrupted connection continuity
uninterrupted existence perpetuity
uninterrupted in course consecutive
uninterruptedness continuity, perpetuity
uninterruption continuity

uninured unaccustomed
uninvented genuine, honest
uninventive lifeless *(dull)*, pedestrian
uninvited unsolicited
uninvited attendance intrusion
uninvited entry intrusion
uninviting antipathetic *(distasteful)*, bleak *(severely simple)*, objectionable, repulsive, unacceptable, undesirable, unsavory
uninvolved clean, cognizable, dispassionate, irreprehensible, neutral, noncommittal, not guilty, perfunctory, simple
union accession *(annexation)*, adhesion *(affixing)*, adhesion *(loyalty)*, affiliation *(amalgamation)*, assemblage, association *(alliance)*, cabal, cartel, centralization, chain *(nexus)*, chamber *(body)*, coaction, coalescence, coalition, cohabitation *(married state)*, coherence, collusion, combination, compatibility, composition *(makeup)*, conciliation, confederacy *(compact)*, conformity *(agreement)*, conjunction, connection *(abutment)*, connection *(fastening)*, consensus, consolidation, consortium *(business cartel)*, contact *(association)*, contact *(touching)*, contribution *(participation)*, cooperative, corporation, coverture, federation, incorporation *(blend)*, incorporation *(formation of a business entity)*, institute, integration *(amalgamation)*, intersection, joinder, league, marriage *(intimate relationship)*, matrimony, meeting *(encounter)*, melange, merger, nexus, pact, pool, reconciliation, relationship *(connection)*, session, society, sodality, syndicate. SEE MAIN ENTRY
union of action coaction
union of factions coalition
unionize consolidate *(unite)*, federalize *(associate)*, federate
unions ties
unique certain *(particular)*, different, distinct *(distinguished from others)*, distinctive, eccentric, exclusive *(singular)*, extraordinary, individual, inestimable, irregular *(not usual)*, nonconforming, noteworthy, novel, only *(sole)*, original *(creative)*, particular *(individual)*, particular *(specific)*, peculiar *(distinctive)*, portentous *(eliciting amazement)*, prodigious *(amazing)*, rare, remarkable, renowned, scarce, several *(separate)*, singular, sole, special, specific, unaccustomed, unapproachable, uncommon, unprecedented, unusual. SEE MAIN ENTRY
unique feature distinction *(difference)*
uniquely particularly
uniqueness characteristic, difference, distinction *(difference)*, identity *(individuality)*, irregularity, nonconformity, particularity, personality, specialty *(distinctive mark)*
unirritable dispassionate
unison accordance *(compact)*, agreement *(concurrence)*, concert, consensus, consent, rapprochement, synchronism, union *(unity)*
unisonant consonant
unisonous consonant
unit band, component, entity, factor *(ingredient)*, ingredient, item, member *(constituent part)*, organ. SEE MAIN ENTRY
unit of being entity
unit of composition component, ingredient
unite accumulate *(amass)*, adhere *(fasten)*, affiliate, affix, aggregate, agree *(comply)*, amalgamate, annex *(add)*, attach *(join)*, bond *(hold together)*, border

(approach), call (summon), cement, cohere (adhere), coincide (concur), collect (gather), combine (act in concert), combine (join together), commingle, compile, concentrate (consolidate), congregate, conjoin, connect (join together), conspire, contact (touch), convene, converge, correspond (be equivalent), desegregate, federalize (associate), federate, include, incorporate (include), involve (participate), join (associate oneself with), join (bring together), lock, meet, merge, organize (unionize), pool, reconcile, relate (establish a connection). SEE MAIN ENTRY

unite by compact federate
unite efforts concur (agree)
unite efforts with participate
unite for a common purpose organize (unionize)
unite in a federation federate
unite in a league federalize (associate), federate
unite ones efforts cooperate
unite with concur (agree), cooperate, participate, side
united affiliated, associated, attached (annexed), coadunate, coherent (joined), cohesive (sticking), collective, composite, compound, concerted, concordant, concurrent (united), conglomerate, conjoint, conjugal, consensual, federal, harmonious, indivisible, infrangible, inseparable, interrelated, joint, mutual (collective), nuptial, solid (compact). SEE MAIN ENTRY
united action coaction, conjunction, synergy
united body faction
united front merger
uniting accession (annexation), concerted, concordant, concrescence
unity accordance (compact), adhesion (affixing), affiliation (amalgamation), agreement (concurrence), cartel, centralization, coalition, coherence, compatibility, complex (development), concert, conciliation, concordance, consent, identity (similarity), peace, propinquity (similarity), rapprochement, relationship (connection), totality, uniformity. SEE MAIN ENTRY
unius diei ephemeral
universal boiler plate, collective, common (shared), competitive (open), comprehensive, familiar (customary), general, generic, nonsectarian, prevailing (current), prevalent, proverbial, rife, total, ubiquitous, uniform, unlimited, usual, whole (unified). SEE MAIN ENTRY
universal cure panacea
universal forgiveness of past offenses amnesty
universal principle doctrine
universal remedy panacea
universality generality (bulk), whole
universalize generalize
universally always (without exception)
universally known common (customary)
universally recognized familiar (customary), famous, household (familiar)
universe generalize
university institute
universus total
univocal definite, unambiguous
unjaundiced impartial, neutral, objective, open-minded, reasonable (rational), receptive, unbiased, undistorted, unprejudiced
unjealous dispassionate

unjoined apart, disconnected, discrete, disjunctive (tending to disjoin), individual
unjoint disjoint, displace (remove), luxate
unjoyful pessimistic
unjust delinquent (guilty of a misdeed), inequitable, iniquitous, one-sided, partial (biased), peccant (culpable), prejudicial, severe, unconscionable, unfair, unjustifiable, unreasonable, unscrupulous, unwarranted, wrongful. SEE MAIN ENTRY
unjust acquisition graft
unjust action injustice
unjust burden imposition (excessive burden)
unjust decision inequity
unjust deed ground
unjust enrichment SEE MAIN ENTRY
unjust opinion misjudgment
unjust performance malfeasance
unjust requirement imposition (excessive burden)
unjustifiable baseless, blameful, blameworthy, disproportionate, immoral, indefensible, inexcusable, inexpiable, iniquitous, peccant (culpable), reprehensible, sinister, unequal (unjust), unjust, unreasonable, untenable, unwarranted, wanton. SEE MAIN ENTRY
unjustified arbitrary, gratuitous (unwarranted), illegal, partial (biased), unauthorized, undue (excessive), unjustifiable, unwarranted
unjustly call to account frame (charge falsely)
unjustly involve frame (charge falsely)
unjustly severe tyrannous
unjustness ground, inequity, nepotism
unkempt disordered, inelegant
unkind caustic, cold-blooded, cruel, harsh, invidious, malevolent, mordacious, pernicious, ruthless, scathing, severe
unkindly harsh
unkindness cruelty, disservice, ill will, inconsideration, severity
unknot break (separate), disengage, disentangle, extricate
unknowable inapprehensible, incomprehensible, inexplicable, inscrutable
unknowing blind (not discerning), incognizant, insensible, unacquainted, unaware, unintentional, unversed, unwitting
unknowingly SEE MAIN ENTRY
unknowingness ignorance, nescience
unknowledgeable unversed
unknown anonymous, blind (concealed), clandestine, covert, defunct, disputable, hidden, inexplicable, mysterious, obscure (remote), secret, surreptitious, ulterior, undisclosed, unprecedented. SEE MAIN ENTRY
unknown information secret
unknown person stranger
unlace disengage
unladylike blatant (obtrusive), disorderly, unbecoming
unlatch disengage
unlatched open (unclosed)
unlavish economical, provident (frugal)
unlawful broken (unfulfilled), delinquent (guilty of a misdeed), felonious, illegal, illegitimate (illegal), illicit, immoral, impermissible, unauthorized, unscrupulous, unwarranted, wrongful. SEE MAIN ENTRY
unlawful acquisition larceny
unlawful act burglary, miscarriage, offense, tortious act
unlawful action malfeasance

unlawful appropriation conversion (misappropriation)
unlawful bait bribe
unlawful begetting bar sinister
unlawful breaking and entering burglary
unlawful carnal connection adultery
unlawful carnal knowledge adultery
unlawful carnality adultery
unlawful combination conspiracy
unlawful compensation bribe
unlawful compulsion coercion
unlawful contrivance conspiracy
unlawful conversion larceny
unlawful departure desertion
unlawful detention detainer
unlawful encouragement bribery
unlawful entry intrusion
unlawful force violence
unlawful gain graft
unlawful gift bribe
unlawful gratuity bribe
unlawful hitting battery
unlawful homicide aberemurder, assassination
unlawful invasion encroachment
unlawful killing murder
unlawful obstruction nuisance
unlawful obtainer extortionist
unlawful plan conspiracy
unlawful practice guilt
unlawful restriction detainer
unlawful retention detainer
unlawful scheme conspiracy
unlawful sexual intercourse sodomy
unlawful striking battery
unlawful taking extortion, larceny
unlawful touching battery
unlawful use of another's property conversion (misappropriation)
unlawful use of power misfeasance
unlawfully illegally
unlawfully begotten illegitimate (born out of wedlock)
unlawfully deprive purloin
unlawfully seize kidnap
unlawfulness burglary, criminality, illegality, injustice, prohibition
unlearned jejune (lacking maturity), unversed
unlearnedness ignorance, illiteracy, nescience
unleash free
unlegalized illicit
unlegislated illicit
unless SEE MAIN ENTRY
unlessened undiminished
unlettered unversed
unliable immune
unliberal parochial
unlicensed felonious, illegitimate (illegal), impermissible, inexperienced, ultra vires, unauthorized, unlawful
unlikable objectionable, undesirable
unlike different, disparate, dissimilar, distinct (distinguished from others), distinctive, diverse, heterogeneous, peculiar (distinctive), unequal (unequivalent), unrelated. SEE MAIN ENTRY
unlike others distinct (distinguished from others)
unlikelihood improbability
unlikeliness improbability
unlikely disputable, doubtful, dubious, implausible, impossible, incredible, infeasible, unbelievable, unfit
unlikely to cause harm innocuous

unlikely to cause injury innocuous

unlikeness contraposition, deviation, difference, discrepancy, disparity, distinction *(difference)*, distortion, diversity, identity *(individuality)*, incompatibility *(inconsistency)*, incongruity, inconsistency, inequality, nonconformity, specialty *(distinctive mark)*

unlimited absolute *(complete)*, copious, dictatorial, far reaching, indefinite, indeterminate, infinite, innumerable, inordinate, intemperate, myriad, omnibus, openended, peremptory *(absolute)*, perpetual, plenary, unbound, unrestrained *(not in custody)*, unrestrained *(not repressed)*, unrestricted. SEE MAIN ENTRY

unlimited in power omnipotent

unlimited inheritance fee *(estate)*

unlimited sovereignty home rule

unlink detach

unlinked disconnected

unliquidated delinquent *(overdue)*, outstanding *(unpaid)*

unliquidated claim liability, obligation *(liability)*

unlively grave *(solemn)*, jejune *(dull)*, lifeless *(dull)*, pedestrian, ponderous

unload alleviate, deplete, diminish, disencumber, dislodge, ease, relieve *(free from burden)*, remove *(eliminate)*, vend

unlock disencumber, disengage, disenthrall, dissociate, find *(discover)*, solve

unlocked open *(accessible)*, open *(unclosed)*

unlooked for fortuitous, unanticipated, unexpected, unforeseeable

unloose break *(separate)*, diffuse, disencumber, disengage, disentangle, dissociate, extricate, liberate, part *(separate)*, rescue, separate

unloosen disjoint, extricate

unloquacious laconic, mute, taciturn

unlovable odious

unloyal broken *(unfulfilled)*, faithless

unloyalty bad faith

unlucid blind *(not discerning)*

unlucky dire, harmful, inauspicious, ominous, regrettable, unfavorable

unlucky accident misfortune

unlucky happening misfortune

unlucky person victim

unmaintainable unsustainable, untenable

unmake annul, destroy *(void)*, disorganize, extirpate, obliterate

unmaking cancellation, destruction

unmalleable immutable, inflexible, intractable, ironclad, obdurate, rigid, uncontrollable

unmanacle disenthrall, free

unmanageable contumacious, disobedient, disordered, disorderly, fractious, froward, impossible, impracticable, incorrigible, indomitable, inexorable, inflexible, intractable, obdurate, perverse, ponderous, recalcitrant, restive, uncontrollable, unruly, unyielding, wanton. SEE MAIN ENTRY

unmanifested latent, potential

unmanly ignoble, recreant, unseemly

unmanned devoid

unmannered disorderly, offensive *(offending)*

unmannerliness disrespect

unmannerly brazen, disdainful, disorderly, impertinent *(insolent)*, inelegant, insolent, obtrusive, offensive *(offending)*, perverse, uncouth

unmannerly conduct disrespect

unmarked intact, usual

unmarketable SEE MAIN ENTRY

unmarketable check bad check

unmarred intact, pure, unblemished, unimpeachable

unmarry divorce, separate

unmask admit *(concede)*, bare, betray *(disclose)*, clarify, detect, disabuse, disclose, divulge, expose, find *(discover)*, inform *(betray)*, manifest, produce *(offer to view)*, report *(disclose)*, reveal, unveil

unmasked naked *(lacking embellishment)*, obvious, palpable, patent, scrutable

unmasking admission *(disclosure)*, disclosure *(act of disclosing)*, manifestation

unmasterable insuperable, insurmountable

unmatched different, disparate, dissimilar, diverse, heterogeneous, inestimable, leading *(ranking first)*, only *(unrepeated)*, original *(creative)*, paramount, premium, prime *(most valuable)*, solitary, superlative, unequal *(unequivalent)*, unique, unprecedented, unrelated, unusual

unmatured premature

unmeaningful null *(insignificant)*

unmeant fortuitous, inadvertent, unintentional, unpremeditated, unwitting

unmeasured copious, indeterminate, infinite, innumerable, intemperate, openended

unmeditated involuntary

unmeet improper, inappropriate, inapt, inept *(inappropriate)*, unbecoming, undesirable, unseemly

unmelting callous

unmemorable usual

unmentionable confidential, ineffable

unmentioned tacit, ulterior, undisclosed

unmerciful brutal, callous, cold-blooded, cruel, harsh, inexorable, malignant, obdurate, relentless, remorseless, ruthless, severe, unrelenting

unmeretricious elegant

unmerited undue *(excessive)*, unjust

unmetaphorical literal

unmethodical capricious, casual, desultory, disordered, disorderly, haphazard, indiscriminate, informal, unpredictable

unmeticulous casual, inexact, slipshod

unmilitant harmless, nonmilitant, peaceable

unmindful blind *(not discerning)*, careless, casual, cold-blooded, cursory, derelict *(negligent)*, disobedient, dispassionate, heedless, impulsive *(rash)*, inadvertent, incognizant, insensible, lax, negligent, nonchalant, oblivious, perfunctory, reckless, remiss, thoughtless, unaware, unwitting

unmindfully unknowingly

unmindfulness disinterest *(lack of interest)*, disregard *(lack of respect)*, disregard *(unconcern)*, neglect, negligence

unmingled pure, simple, sterling, unadulterated

unmistakability certainty

unmistakable absolute *(conclusive)*, arrant *(definite)*, axiomatic, certain *(fixed)*, certain *(positive)*, clear *(apparent)*, clear *(certain)*, cognizable, coherent *(clear)*, comprehensible, conclusive *(determinative)*, conspicuous, definite, demonstrable, evident, explicit, factual, incontrovertible, irrefutable, lucid, manifest, naked *(perceptible)*, obvious, open *(in sight)*, palpable, particular *(specific)*, perceivable, percepti-

ble, positive *(incontestable)*, salient, unambiguous, unequivocal. SEE MAIN ENTRY

unmistakableness surety *(certainty)*

unmistakably fairly *(clearly)*

unmistakably bad arrant *(onerous)*

unmistaken accurate, actual, proper, real, true *(authentic)*

unmitigable hot-blooded, relentless

unmitigated absolute *(conclusive)*, categorical, chronic, comprehensive, disorderly, drastic, gross *(flagrant)*, harsh, intensive, outright, pure, rigid, severe, stark, thorough, unqualified *(unlimited)*. SEE MAIN ENTRY

unmitigating chronic

unmixed absolute *(conclusive)*, pure, simple, strong, unadulterated

unmodern obsolete

unmodest brazen

unmodifiable irrevocable, permanent, unalterable

unmodified unqualified *(unlimited)*

unmolested safe

unmoneyed bankrupt, destitute, impecunious, poor *(underprivileged)*

unmoral immoral

unmotivated fortuitous

unmovable firm, impervious, inexorable, inflexible, permanent, pertinacious

unmoved callous, cold-blooded, impervious, inexpressive, insensible, insusceptible *(uncaring)*, irreconcilable, nonchalant, peaceable, placid, steadfast, stoical, unaffected *(uninfluenced)*, unresponsive

unmoved by entreaties inexorable

unmoved by pity relentless

unmoving firm, inactive, rigid, stagnant, static

unmuddied clean

unmurmuring patient

unmuzzled uncurbed

unnamable ineffable

unnamed anonymous, unspecified

unnatural anomalous, artificial, cruel, diabolic, histrionic, illegitimate *(born out of wedlock)*, irregular *(not usual)*, peculiar *(curious)*, synthetic, unaccustomed, uncanny, unusual

unnatural carnal intercourse sodomy

unnatural habit perversion

unnatural sexual intercourse sodomy

unnaturalized alien *(foreign)*

unnaturalness bestiality, false pretense, irregularity, pretense *(ostentation)*

unnavigable impervious

unneat slipshod

unnecessary circumstantial, excess, excessive, expendable, extraneous, gratuitous *(unwarranted)*, inconsequential, inordinate, minor, needless, nonessential, null *(insignificant)*, otiose, redundant, superfluous, undue *(excessive)*, unessential, unwarranted. SEE MAIN ENTRY

unnecessary addition expletive

unnecessary inclusion expletive

unnecessary loss waste

unnecessary prolongation laches

unneeded excess, excessive, expendable, extraneous, gratuitous *(unwarranted)*, needless, nonessential, otiose, undue *(excessive)*, unessential, unnecessary

unnerve disable, discommode, discourage, disturb, frighten, intimidate, menace, perturb, upset

unnerved disconsolate, powerless, unsettled

unnerving formidable

unnervous dispassionate
unnotable petty
unnoteworthiness immateriality, inconsequence, insignificance, mediocrity
unnoteworthy average *(standard)*, inapposite, mediocre, minor, negligible, nonessential
unnoticeable impalpable, inconspicuous, indiscernible, minor
unnoticed inconspicuous, latent
unnoticing heedless, inadvertent, oblivious
unnourishing deficient
unnumberable myriad
unnumbered infinite, innumerable, multiple, myriad, profuse
unobjectionability admissibility
unobjectionable admissible, allowable, blameless, clean, fair *(satisfactory)*, innocuous, irreprehensible, mediocre, nontoxic, palatable, pardonable, unimpeachable. SEE MAIN ENTRY
unobliging thoughtless
unobnoxious innocuous
unobscure comprehensible, palpable
unobscured palpable
unobservable impalpable
unobservance breach, contempt *(disobedience to the court)*, neglect, negligence
unobservant blind *(not discerning)*, broken *(unfulfilled)*, careless, derelict *(negligent)*, heedless, inadvertent, lax, oblivious, perfunctory, reckless, thoughtless, unaware, unorthodox
unobserved blind *(concealed)*, defunct, hidden, inconspicuous
unobserving blind *(not discerning)*, lax
unobstructed clear *(unencumbered)*, free *(not restricted)*, open *(accessible)*, open *(in sight)*, passable, patent, unbound, uncurbed, unrestrained *(not in custody)*, unrestricted
unobtrusive diffident
unobtainability impossibility, unavailability
unobtainable impossible, inaccessible, infeasible, insuperable, scarce, unapproachable, unattainable
unobtainableness impossibility
unobtrusive covert, furtive, inconspicuous, unpretentious. SEE MAIN ENTRY
unobvious impalpable, inconspicuous, ulterior, unclear
unoccupied devoid, idle, open *(accessible)*, otiose, solitary, unemployed, unsettled, vacant, vacuous, void *(empty)*
unoffended dispassionate
unoffending blameless, clean, innocent, innocuous, irreprehensible
unofficered devoid
unofficial informal, interim, private *(not public)*, uncorroborated. SEE MAIN ENTRY
unopened impervious
unoperative ineffective, ineffectual
unopinionated impartial, liberal *(broad minded)*
unopinioned impartial
unopposed consensual
unopposing passive
unordered casual, indeterminate
unordinary extraordinary, momentous, nonconforming, novel, original *(creative)*, unaccustomed
unorganized casual, complex, disordered, haphazard, indiscriminate, random, slipshod

unoriginal familiar *(customary)*, lifeless *(dull)*, ordinary, pedestrian, prosaic, trite, usual
unornamented naked *(lacking embellishment)*
unorthodox deviant, eccentric, informal, nonconforming, novel, original *(creative)*, peculiar *(curious)*, skeptical, uncommon, unusual. SEE MAIN ENTRY
unorthodoxness nonconformity
unorthodoxy blasphemy, deviation, informality, irregularity, nonconformity, quirk *(idiosyncrasy)*
unostentatious diffident, inconspicuous, unobtrusive, unpretentious
unovercomable insuperable
unowed undue *(not owing)*
unowned derelict *(abandoned)*
unpacifiable implacable
unpacific contentious, offensive *(taking the initiative)*, pugnacious
unpaid delinquent *(overdue)*, due *(owed)*, free *(at no charge)*, gratuitous *(given without recompense)*, overdue, payable, receivable, unsettled. SEE MAIN ENTRY
unpaid amount delinquency *(shortage)*
unpaid bill arrears
unpaid debt arrears, obligation *(liability)*
unpaid dues nonpayment
unpaid for gratis, gratuitous *(given without recompense)*
unpaid worker volunteer
unpainstaking inaccurate
unpaired dissimilar, solitary
unpalatable bitter *(acrid tasting)*, loathsome, objectionable, odious, offensive *(offending)*, repugnant *(exciting aversion)*, repulsive, undesirable, unendurable, unsavory. SEE MAIN ENTRY
unparalled renowned
unparalleled best, cardinal *(outstanding)*, extraordinary, inestimable, invaluable, leading *(ranking first)*, major, nonconforming, noteworthy, only *(unrepeated)*, original *(creative)*, outstanding *(prominent)*, paramount, portentous *(eliciting amazement)*, premium, prime *(most valuable)*, rare, remarkable, singular, special, superior *(excellent)*, superlative, unapproachable, uncommon, unique, unprecedented, unusual. SEE MAIN ENTRY
unpardonable blameful, felonious, inexcusable, inexpiable, peccant *(culpable)*, reprehensible, unjustifiable
unpardoning callous
unparticular casual, indiscriminate
unpassable impervious
unpassionate dispassionate
unpatent impalpable
unpatriotic faithless
unpatterned disordered
unpayable irredeemable
unpeaceful contentious, litigious, offensive *(taking the initiative)*, pugnacious
unpeacefulness belligerency
unpent free *(not restricted)*
unpeopled devoid
unperceivability nonappearance
unperceivable impalpable, inconspicuous, indiscernible, intangible
unperceived blind *(concealed)*, hidden, ulterior
unperceiving blind *(not discerning)*, heedless
unperceptive inadvertent, insensible
unperfected partial *(relating to a part)*

unperfidious bona fide, candid, loyal, true *(loyal)*
unperfidiousness responsibility *(conscience)*
unperforated impervious
unperformability impossibility
unperformable impracticable, insurmountable, unattainable
unperformed executory, partial *(part)*
unperilous reliable
unperjured accurate, bona fide, candid, honest, straightforward, true *(authentic)*, veridical
unpermitted unauthorized
unpersevering otiose, truant
unpersuadable inexorable
unpersuaded disinclined
unperturbed cold-blooded, dispassionate, patient, phlegmatic
unperverted undistorted
unphysical intangible
unpierceable impervious
unpin disengage
unpitying callous, cruel, harsh, obdurate, relentless, remorseless, ruthless, unrelenting
unplagiarized authentic
unplain equivocal, impalpable, inarticulate, indefinable, indistinct, obscure *(faint)*, opaque, unclear
unplainness indistinctness, opacity
unplanned coincidental, fortuitous, haphazard, spontaneous, unforeseeable, unpremeditated
unplanned happening quirk *(accident)*
unplausible suspicious *(questionable)*
unpleasant bitter *(acrid tasting)*, deplorable, invidious, loathsome, objectionable, obnoxious, odious, offensive *(offending)*, outrageous, painful, repugnant *(exciting aversion)*, repulsive, unacceptable, undesirable, unendurable, unsatisfactory, unsavory
unpleasant sound noise
unpleasing deplorable, objectionable, obnoxious, offensive *(offending)*, unacceptable, undesirable, unsavory
unplentiful scarce
unpliable immutable, inflexible, unyielding
unpliant inflexible, ironclad, rigid, strong, unalterable, unbending
unplug detach
unpoetic prosaic
unpoetical mundane, pedestrian, prosaic
unpointed jejune *(dull)*
unpolished blatant *(obtrusive)*, caitiff, imperfect, impertinent *(insolent)*, inelegant, provincial, uncouth
unpolite perverse
unpoliteness disrespect
unpolitic SEE MAIN ENTRY
unpollute decontaminate
unpolluted inviolate, pure
unpopular odious, repugnant *(exciting aversion)*, unacceptable, undesirable
unpopularity ill repute, ill will, odium
unpopulated bleak *(exposed and barren)*
unpositive conditional
unpossessed derelict *(abandoned)*, unclaimed, vacant
unpossessed of devoid
unpowerful incapable
unpracticability impossibility
unpracticed inexperienced, outdated, outmoded, unaccustomed, unversed
unpraiseworthy blameful, blameworthy, unbecoming, unseemly

unprecedented extraordinary, nonconforming, noteworthy, novel, portentous *(eliciting amazement)*, prodigious *(amazing)*, renowned, singular, special, uncommon, unforeseeable, unique, unusual. SEE MAIN ENTRY

unprecise approximate, casual, faulty, liberal *(not literal)*

unpreciseness misestimation, misjudgment

unpredictability chance *(possibility)*, happenstance

unpredictable conditional, debatable, fallible, haphazard, undependable, unforeseeable, unreliable. SEE MAIN ENTRY

unpredicted fortuitous, unexpected, unforeseeable, unforeseen

unprejudice disinterest *(lack of prejudice)*

unprejudiced dispassionate, equal, equitable, evenhanded, factual, fair *(just)*, impartial, judicial, juridical, just, liberal *(broad minded)*, neutral, nonpartisan, objective, reasonable *(rational)*, receptive, unbiased, undistorted. SEE MAIN ENTRY

unprejudicedness candor *(impartiality)*

unpremeditated fortuitous, haphazard, impulsive *(rash)*, inadvertent, involuntary, random, spontaneous, unexpected, unintentional, unwitting. SEE MAIN ENTRY

unpremeditated murder manslaughter

unpremeditation inconsideration, quirk *(accident)*

unprepared impulsive *(rash)*, lax, premature, spontaneous, unaware, unfit, unpremeditated, unqualified *(not competent)*, unversed, vulnerable

unprepared for precipitate, unexpected, unforeseeable

unpreparedness disqualification *(factor that disqualifies)*, laxity

unpreparing improvident

unprepossessed dispassionate, impartial, neutral, open-minded, unprejudiced

unprepossessing repulsive

unpresentable blatant *(obtrusive)*, unseemly

unpretended bona fide, genuine, honest, true *(authentic)*

unpretending direct *(forthright)*, genuine, honest, unaffected *(sincere)*, veridical

unpretentious bona fide, diffident, direct *(forthright)*, genuine, honest, inconspicuous, simple, unaffected *(sincere)*. SEE MAIN ENTRY

unpretentiousness candor *(straightforwardness)*

unprevalent unusual

unpreventable certain *(fixed)*, compulsory, inevitable, necessary *(inescapable)*, unavoidable *(inevitable)*

unprevented free *(not restricted)*, unbound, uncurbed, unrestrained *(not in custody)*

unprincipaled dissolute

unprincipled baseless, delinquent *(guilty of a misdeed)*, depraved, diabolic, dishonest, disingenuous, disreputable, false *(disloyal)*, heinous, illicit, immoral, inexcusable, iniquitous, lawless, machiavellian, peccable, peccant *(culpable)*, perfidious, profligate *(corrupt)*, reprehensible, reprobate, sinister, unconscionable, unethical, unfair, unjust, unscrupulous, vicious

unprincipled politician demagogue

unprintable profane, salacious

unprocessed inchoate

unproclaimed undisclosed

unprocreant barren

unprocurable inaccessible, unattainable

unproductive barren, futile, ineffective, ineffectual, inept *(incompetent)*, nugatory, otiose, unavailing. SEE MAIN ENTRY

unproductive trial mistrial

unproductivity miscarriage

unprofaned inviolate

unprofessional unethical SEE MAIN ENTRY

unprofessional conduct incompetence, malpractice, misconduct

unprofessional treatment malpractice

unproficiency disqualification *(factor that disqualifies)*, inability, incapacity, incompetence, maladministration

unproficient inadept, inept *(incompetent)*, unversed

unprofitability detriment, inexpedience

unprofitable barren, detrimental, disadvantageous, expendable, futile, idle, inadvisable, ineffective, ineffectual, injudicious, needless, nugatory, otiose, unavailing, unproductive

unprogressive decadent, static

unprogressiveness inaction

unprohibited admissible, allowable, allowed, lawful, licit, permissible, public *(open)*

unprolific barren, otiose, unproductive

unprolonged brief

unpromising inauspicious, ominous, pessimistic, sinister, unfavorable, unfit, unpropitious, untimely

unprompted impulsive *(rash)*, spontaneous, voluntary

unprompted will conatus

unpronounceable ineffable

unpronounced impalpable, implicit, inconspicuous, tacit, undisclosed

unpropitiating implacable

unpropitious adverse *(hostile)*, antipathetic *(oppositional)*, detrimental, dire, disadvantageous, harmful, inauspicious, inimical, inopportune, ominous, pernicious, portentous *(ominous)*, regrettable, sinister, unfavorable, untimely. SEE MAIN ENTRY

unprosperous impecunious, poor *(underprivileged)*

unprosperousness poverty

unprotected dangerous, helpless *(defenseless)*, indefensible, insecure, open *(in sight)*, precarious, susceptible *(unresistent)*, untenable, vulnerable

unprovable unsustainable

unproved inconclusive, theoretical, unconfirmed, unsupported

unproved theory hypothesis

unproven debatable, disputable, inconclusive, speculative, theoretical, unconfirmed, uncorroborated, unfounded, unsupported

unprovided deficient, devoid

unprovided for poor *(underprivileged)*

unproviding improvident

unprovocativeness disincentive

unprovoked gratuitous *(unwarranted)*, wanton

unpublicized undisclosed

unpublished secret, undisclosed

unpugnacious nonmilitant, peaceable

unpunctilious casual

unpunctual back *(in arrears)*, dilatory, late *(tardy)*, untimely

unpunctuality irregularity

unpunishable immune

unpunished clear *(free from criminal charges)*

unpurposed unwitting

unpurposeful unintentional, unpremeditated

unpushing diffident

unqualification certainty, disability *(legal disqualification)*

unqualified absolute *(complete)*, affirmative, categorical, certain *(positive)*, clear *(certain)*, complete *(all-embracing)*, comprehensive, decisive, definite, demonstrable, disabled *(deprived of legal right)*, disabled *(made incapable)*, free *(not restricted)*, inadept, inadmissible, inapplicable, inapt, incapable, incompetent, ineligible, inept *(inappropriate)*, inept *(incompetent)*, inexperienced, insufficient, omnibus, outright, peremptory *(absolute)*, plenary, positive *(incontestable)*, powerless, stark, thorough, total, unable, unconditional, unequivocal, unfit, unmitigated, unrestricted, unversed, unworthy. SEE MAIN ENTRY

unqualifiedness disability *(legal disqualification)*, disqualification *(factor that disqualifies)*, incompetence

unquashable noncancellable

unquelled disorderly, hot-blooded

unquenchable indomitable, insatiable, powerful

unquenched hot-blooded

unquestionability certainty, certification *(certainness)*, incontestability

unquestionable absolute *(conclusive)*, accurate, authentic, axiomatic, believable, categorical, certain *(fixed)*, certain *(positive)*, clear *(certain)*, cogent, conclusive *(determinative)*, de facto, decisive, definitive, demonstrable, evident, factual, genuine, incontestable, incontrovertible, indefeasible, inevitable, infallible, irrebuttable, irrefutable, lucid, manifest, noncontestable, obvious, palpable, pellucid, peremptory *(absolute)*, positive *(incontestable)*, probable, real, reliable, solid *(sound)*, tenable, true *(authentic)*, uncontested, undeniable, unequivocal, unimpeachable, unmistakable, unrefutable. SEE MAIN ENTRY

unquestionableness certainty, certification *(certainness)*, certitude, surety *(certainty)*

unquestionably admittedly, fairly *(clearly)*

unquestioned axiomatic, certain *(fixed)*, certain *(positive)*, clear *(certain)*, consensual, decisive, definite, infallible, proverbial, uncontested, uncontroverted, undisputed

unquestioning categorical, credulous, positive *(confident)*, unsuspecting

unquestioning acceptance faith

unquestioning belief credulity

unquiet restive

unratified unauthorized, unconfirmed, uncorroborated

unravel ascertain, clarify, construe *(translate)*, detect, discover, disengage, disentangle, elucidate, explain, extricate, find *(discover)*, interpret, resolve *(solve)*, separate, simplify *(make easier)*, solve, spread

unraveled elementary

unraveling denouement

unraveling of plot denouement

unravelment development *(progression)*, evulsion

unreachable impervious, inaccessible, unapproachable, unattainable
unreacting unresponsive
unread unversed
unreadable inapprehensible, pedestrian, unclear
unready back *(in arrears)*, late *(tardy)*, premature, unqualified *(not competent)*
unreal artificial, assumed *(feigned)*, bogus, delusive, dishonest, erroneous, false *(not genuine)*, fictitious, fraudulent, hypothetical, illusory, impalpable, inaccurate, insubstantial, nonexistent, spurious, unsound *(fallacious)*, untrue
unrealistic infeasible, quixotic, subjective
unreality figment, myth, phantom
unrealizable impracticable, inaccessible, insurmountable
unrealized possible, potential
unrealizing incognizant, insensible, unaware
unreasonable arbitrary, baseless, contumacious, disproportionate, drastic, excessive, exorbitant, extreme *(exaggerated)*, fanatical, ill-advised, ill-judged, impolitic, impossible, impracticable, improper, inexcusable, inexpiable, infeasible, inordinate, irrational, ludicrous, misadvised, oppressive, outrageous, partial *(biased)*, perverse, prohibitive *(costly)*, sophistic, unconscionable, undue *(excessive)*, unfair, unjust, unjustifiable, unsound *(fallacious)*, untenable, unwarranted, usurious. SEE MAIN ENTRY
unreasonable amplification exaggeration
unreasonable bias prejudice *(preconception)*
unreasonable delay laches
unreasonable fear paranoia
unreasonable fright paranoia
unreasonably resolute fanatical
unreasoned arbitrary, injudicious, irrational, unsound *(fallacious)*
unreasoned alarm phobia
unreasoned fear phobia
unreasoning fatuous, ill-judged, irrational, opaque, thoughtless, vacuous
unreasoning fear panic
unreceivable inadmissible
unreceptive impervious
unrecognizable impalpable, inapprehensible, incomprehensible, indiscernible, indistinct, inexplicable, unclear
unrecognizing oblivious
unrecompensed gratis, gratuitous *(given without recompense)*, outstanding *(unpaid)*, unpaid, unrequited
unreconciled adverse *(hostile)*, contradictory, disinclined, irreconcilable, polemic
unrecoverable irretrievable
unredeemable profligate *(corrupt)*
unredeemed diabolic
unreduced complete *(all-embracing)*, gross *(total)*, intact, undiminished, whole *(undamaged)*
unrefined blatant *(obtrusive)*, disreputable, impertinent *(insolent)*, improper, inelegant, provincial, uncouth, unseemly
unreflecting blind *(not discerning)*, irrational, misadvised, thoughtless
unreflective thoughtless
unreformable incorrigible
unrefreshed languid
unrefutability incontestability
unrefutable clear *(certain)*, convincing, inappealable, positive *(incontestable)*, solid *(sound)*, unimpeachable. SEE MAIN ENTRY

unrefuted accurate, actual, certain *(positive)*, definite, factual
unregarded indiscernible, perfunctory
unregenerate lascivious, lecherous, profligate *(corrupt)*, remorseless, reprobate
unregretful incorrigible
unregretting incorrigible
unregular intermittent
unregulated disorderly
unrehearsed fortuitous, spontaneous, unpremeditated
unreined free *(not restricted)*, independent, intemperate, lawless, licentious, uncurbed, unrestrained *(not repressed)*
unrelated alien *(unrelated)*, different, disconnected, dissimilar, extraneous, foreign, gratuitous *(unwarranted)*, heterogeneous, immaterial, impertinent *(irrelevant)*, inapposite, inconsequential, individual, irrelative, irrelevant. SEE MAIN ENTRY
unrelatedness difference, inconsequence
unrelaxed rigid
unrelaxing industrious, patient, persistent, pertinacious
unrelenting brutal, callous, cold-blooded, constant, cruel, dictatorial, diligent, faithful *(diligent)*, immutable, implacable, inexorable, inflexible, ironclad, obdurate, patient, pertinacious, recalcitrant, relentless, remorseless, resolute, rigid, ruthless, sedulous, severe, unbending, uncompromising, undaunted, vindictive. SEE MAIN ENTRY
unreliability dishonesty, improbity, knavery
unreliable capricious, dangerous, debatable, dishonest, disobedient, disputable, dubious, faithless, fallible, false *(disloyal)*, false *(inaccurate)*, fraudulent, insecure, irresponsible, mutable, perfidious, precarious, recreant, uncertain *(questionable)*, undependable, unpredictable, unsound *(not strong)*, untrustworthy, variable. SEE MAIN ENTRY
unrelievable chronic
unreligious profane
unreluctant willing *(not averse)*
unremarkable mediocre, nondescript, usual
unremarkableness mediocrity
unremedied chronic
unremittent chronic
unremitting chronic, close *(rigorous)*, consecutive, continual *(connected)*, continuous, diligent, faithful *(diligent)*, incessant, industrious, patient, persistent, pertinacious, relentless, sedulous, stable, strong, uncompromising. SEE MAIN ENTRY
unremorseful remorseless
unremorsefulness cruelty
unremoved lasting, present *(attendant)*, present *(current)*
unremunerated unpaid, unrequited
unremunerative unproductive
unrenowned obscure *(remote)*
unrepaid unrequited
unrepair deterioration
unrepealable irrevocable, permanent, perpetual
unrepealed lasting
unrepeated desultory, unique
unrepentant incorrigible, profligate *(corrupt)*, recusant, remorseless
unrepining resigned
unreplenished devoid, inadequate
unreplying unresponsive

unrepresentative anomalous, atypical
unrepressed disorderly, hot-blooded, uncurbed, unrestrained *(not repressed)*
unreproachable blameless
unreproached blameless, inculpable
unreproved blameless, inculpable
unrequested unsolicited
unrequired expendable, needless, nonessential, redundant, unnecessary
unrequisitioned unclaimed
unrequited outstanding *(unpaid)*, unpaid. SEE MAIN ENTRY
unresembling dissimilar
unresentful placable
unreserve honesty
unreserved absolute *(complete)*, bona fide, brazen, candid, complete *(all-embracing)*, comprehensive, direct *(forthright)*, ingenuous, public *(open)*, unaffected *(sincere)*, unqualified *(unlimited)*, unrestrained *(not repressed)*
unreservedly in toto
unresigned recusant
unresistant passive, yielding
unresisting obedient, obeisant, passive, patient, peaceable, resigned, servile, stoical, yielding
unresistingness capitulation
unresolved debatable, disputable, doubtful, dubious, equivocal, hesitant, indefinite, indeterminate, irresolute, noncommittal, undecided, unsettled
unrespectability bad character, bad repute, ignominy, notoriety
unrespectable disreputable, ignoble, notorious
unrespected blameworthy
unresponding unresponsive
unresponsive cold-blooded, dispassionate, impervious, insensible, insusceptible *(uncaring)*, lifeless *(dull)*, noncommittal, obdurate, perfunctory, phlegmatic, unaffected *(uninfluenced)*. SEE MAIN ENTRY
unrest confusion *(turmoil)*, disorder *(lack of order)*, disturbance, embroilment, strife, trepidation, turmoil
unrestful restive
unrestorable irreversible, irrevocable
unrestored languid
unrestrainable uncontrollable
unrestrained absolute *(complete)*, capricious, clear *(unencumbered)*, competitive *(open)*, demonstrative *(expressive of emotion)*, direct *(forthright)*, dissolute, exempt, free *(not restricted)*, gluttonous, immune, informal, ingenuous, inordinate, intemperate, irresponsible, lecherous, licentious, privileged, prodigal, profligate *(extravagant)*, rampant, unbound, uncurbed, unlimited, unqualified *(unlimited)*, unrestricted, unruly, unscrupulous, voluntary. SEE MAIN ENTRY
unrestraint debauchery, freedom, honesty, latitude
unrestricted absolute *(complete)*, autonomous *(independent)*, competitive *(open)*, complete *(all-embracing)*, comprehensive, copious, dictatorial, exempt, general, immune, omnibus, open *(accessible)*, open-ended, peremptory *(absolute)*, plenary, public *(open)*, sovereign *(independent)*, unbound, unconditional, unlimited, unqualified *(unlimited)*. SEE MAIN ENTRY
unrestricted inheritance fee *(estate)*
unretarded undiminished
unreturnable irreversible
unreturned unrequited

unrevealable private (confidential)
unrevealed blind (concealed), clandestine, confidential, furtive, hidden, impalpable, inscrutable, latent, mysterious, personal (private), privy, secret, stealthy, ulterior, undisclosed
unrevengeful placable
unreversed live (existing)
unrevised inexact
unrevived lifeless (dead)
unrevoked live (existing)
unrewarded barren, due (owed), unpaid, unrequited
unrewarding barren, needless, unproductive
unriddle ascertain, elucidate, explicate, expound, solve
unrighteous blameworthy, culpable, diabolic, immoral, iniquitous, lawless, nefarious, peccable, peccant (culpable), reprehensible, reprobate, sinister, vicious
unrighteousness guilt, injustice, misdoing, offense, wrong
unrigorous liberal (not literal)
unrigorousness informality, laxity
unripe inexperienced, premature
unripeness minority (infancy)
unrivaled absolute (ideal), best, paramount, premium, prime (most valuable), professional (stellar), superlative, unique, unprecedented, unusual
unrivaled effort main force
unrivalled leading (ranking first), superior (excellent)
unrobe denude, unveil
unroll spread
unromantic pragmatic, realistic
unroot disinter, eradicate
unrooted unsettled
unrooting evulsion
unroutine unusual
unruffled callous, controlled (restrained), dispassionate, nonchalant, patient, peaceable, phlegmatic, placid, stoical
unruliness anarchy, commotion, contempt (disobedience to the court), defiance, disturbance, irregularity, lynch law, misrule, outbreak, outburst, pandemonium, riot
unruly disobedient, disordered, disorderly, fractious, froward, indomitable, insubordinate, intemperate, intractable, licentious, perverse, restive, uncontrollable, uncurbed, vicious. SEE MAIN ENTRY
unsacred mundane, profane
unsacredness blasphemy
unsafe aleatory (perilous), dangerous, deadly, destructible, harmful, insalubrious, insecure, noxious, precarious, speculative, susceptible (unresistent), toxic, unsound (not strong), untrustworthy, vulnerable
unsafe object hazard
unsafety jeopardy, peril
unsagacious unpolitic
unsaid implicit, tacit, undisclosed
unsaintly profane
unsalable barren, unmarketable
unsalaried unpaid
unsame dissimilar
unsanctified mundane, profane
unsanctioned illegal, illegitimate (illegal), illicit, impermissible, null (invalid), null and void, ultra vires, unauthorized, unlawful, unwarranted
unsanitary insalubrious
unsated insatiable
unsatisfaction dissatisfaction

unsatisfactoriness mediocrity
unsatisfactory antipathetic (distasteful), deficient, deleterious, deplorable, detrimental, faulty, imperfect, inadequate, inadvisable, inferior (lower in quality), nonsubstantial (not sufficient), objectionable, paltry, poor (inferior in quality), unacceptable, undesirable, unfavorable, unsuitable. SEE MAIN ENTRY
unsatisfied delinquent (overdue), disappointed, insatiable, outstanding (unpaid), payable. SEE MAIN ENTRY
unsatisfied hopes frustration
unsatisfying nonsubstantial (not sufficient), unsatisfactory, unsuitable
unsavory bitter (acrid tasting), disreputable, insipid, loathsome, objectionable, offensive (offending), repugnant (exciting aversion), repulsive, unendurable. SEE MAIN ENTRY
unsay disclaim, recall (call back), recant
unsaying retraction
unscarred intact
unscathed intact, inviolate, safe
unscholarliness ignorance, illiteracy
unscholarly unprofessional
unschooled inexperienced, naive, unversed
unscientific illogical, inexact
unscintillating insipid, pedestrian
unscramble ascertain, clarify, elucidate, explain, find (discover), interpret, resolve (solve), solve
unscratched intact
unscreen bare, denude, disclose, find (discover), manifest, produce (offer to view)
unscreened obvious, palpable
unscrew disengage
unscrupulous arrant (onerous), delinquent (guilty of a misdeed), depraved, diabolic, dishonest, disingenuous, disreputable, faithless, false (disloyal), fraudulent, immoral, insidious, lawless, machiavellian, peccant (culpable), perfidious, recreant, sly, tortuous (corrupt), unconscionable, unethical. SEE MAIN ENTRY
unscrupulous agitator demagogue
unscrupulous haranguer demagogue
unscrupulousness bad faith, bad repute, corruption, dishonesty, fraud, improbity
unseal bare, disclose, reveal, unveil
unsealed open (accessible), open (unclosed)
unsearchable inscrutable
unsearchableness opacity
unseasonable improper, inapposite, inappropriate, inapt, inept (inappropriate), inopportune, premature, undue (not owing), unsuitable, untimely
unseasoned inexperienced, juvenile, unaccustomed
unseat demote, depose (remove), discharge (dismiss), dislocate, dislodge, dismiss (discharge), displace (remove), disturb, divest, oust, overthrow, supplant
unseating discharge (dismissal), removal
unsecluded open (in sight)
unseconded alone (unsupported), solitary, unsupported
unsecurable inaccessible, unattainable
unseeable inconspicuous, indiscernible, intangible
unseeableness nonappearance
unseeing blind (not discerning), blind (sightless), heedless, inadvertent, incognizant, insensible

unseeminglyness indecency
unseemliness impropriety
unseemly blatant (obtrusive), brazen, delinquent (guilty of a misdeed), disgraceful, disorderly, disproportionate, ill-advised, illicit, improper, inappropriate, inapt, inelegant, inept (inappropriate), notorious, objectionable, slipshod, unbecoming, uncouth, undesirable, undue (excessive), unfit, unprofessional, unsatisfactory, unsuitable, wrongful. SEE MAIN ENTRY
unseen blind (concealed), clandestine, covert, furtive, hidden, inconspicuous, latent, potential, secret, stealthy, surreptitious, ulterior, underlying, undisclosed, unobtrusive
unselected miscellaneous
unselective promiscuous
unselfconscious ingenuous
unselfish benevolent, charitable (benevolent), humane, liberal (generous), magnanimous, meritorious, philanthropic
unselfish person good samaritan
unselfishness benevolence (disposition to do good), charity, consideration (sympathetic regard), disinterest (lack of prejudice), humanity (humaneness), largess (generosity), philanthropy
unsensible ill-judged, impolitic, inadvisable, irrational, misadvised, unreasonable
unsensibleness inexpedience
unsentimental dispassionate, pragmatic
unsentimentality pragmatism
unseparated composite
unsepulcher disinter
unserious frivolous
unserviceable impracticable, ineffective, ineffectual, nugatory, otiose, unavailing
unserviceable check bad check
unsettle agitate (perturb), confuse (bewilder), confuse (create disorder), discompose, dislocate, disorganize, disorient, disrupt, disturb, inconvenience, muddle, obfuscate, perplex, perturb, upset
unsettled aleatory (uncertain), conditional, debatable, delinquent (overdue), deranged, disorderly, disputable, due (owed), frenetic, hesitant, inconclusive, indefinite, indeterminate, insecure, irresolute, lunatic, moot, moving (in motion), mutable, non compos mentis, noncommittal, outstanding (unpaid), outstanding (unresolved), payable, pending (unresolved), precarious, problematic, protean, provisional, restive, speculative, tentative, uncertain (questionable), unconfirmed, undecided, unpaid, unsound (not strong), unspecified, vague, variable. SEE MAIN ENTRY
unsettled in one's mind non compos mentis
unsettled in opinion doubtful
unsettled opinion doubt (indecision), indecision
unsettlement confusion (turmoil), disturbance, doubt (indecision)
unsevered complete (all-embracing), intact, undiminished
unshacking liberation
unshackle disencumber, disengage, disenthrall, extricate, free, liberate, parole, rescue
unshackled free (not restricted), independent, uncurbed, unrestrained (not in custody), unrestricted
unshackling emancipation
unshaded candid, patent

unshakable certain *(positive)*, dogmatic, incontrovertible, indubious, pertinacious, safe

unshakable opinion conviction *(persuasion)*

unshakable trust faith

unshakeable infrangible, ironclad, stable, staunch

unshaken constant, definite, dispassionate, inexorable, patient, pertinacious, positive *(confident)*, resolute, secure *(confident)*, stable, steadfast, unabashed, undaunted

unshaken belief credence

unshape deface, mutilate

unshared personal *(private)*, solitary

unshatterable infrangible

unshattered intact

unsheathe bare, denude, evidence, expose, withdraw

unsheltered bleak *(exposed and barren)*, dangerous, helpless *(defenseless)*, insecure, open *(in sight)*, precarious

unshield bare

unshielded helpless *(defenseless)*, insecure, open *(accessible)*, open *(in sight)*, precarious, vulnerable

unshifting chronic, fixed *(settled)*, permanent, unremitting

unshocked nonchalant

unshorn gross *(total)*

unshortened gross *(total)*

unshown unconfirmed

unshrewd unpolitic

unshrinking heroic, indomitable, pertinacious, purposeful, relentless, spartan, unabashed, undaunted

unshroud bare, denude, disclose, find *(discover)*, manifest, reveal

unshrouded palpable

unshut open *(unclosed)*

unsightliness defacement

unsightly poor *(inferior in quality)*, repulsive, unseemly

unsigned anonymous

unsimilar dissimilar

unsimulated authentic, bona fide, genuine, honest, real, unaffected *(sincere)*

unskilled amateur, incompetent, inexperienced, unaccustomed, unversed

unskilled person novice

unskilled practitioner layman

unskillful inadept, incapable, incompetent, inept *(incompetent)*

unskillfulness abortion *(fiasco)*, disqualification *(factor that disqualifies)*, inability, incapacity, inefficacy

unslackening chronic

unslanted objective, unbiased, unprejudiced

unslantedness disinterest *(lack of prejudice)*

unsleeping industrious, vigilant

unslumbering vigilant

unsmoothness irregularity

unsnap disengage

unsober drunk

unsociable disdainful, taciturn, unapproachable, unresponsive

unsociableness ostracism

unsoftened unmitigated

unsoftening unrelenting

unsoiled blameless, clean, unblemished

unsolicited SEE MAIN ENTRY

unsolicitous cold-blooded, heedless, remiss

unsolicitousness disinterest *(lack of interest)*

unsolid insubstantial, intangible, nonsubstantial *(not sturdy)*

unsolidity impalpability

unsolvable insurmountable

unsolved doubtful, equivocal, pending *(unresolved)*

unsophisticated credulous, elementary, honest, inexperienced, ingenuous, naive, provincial, simple, unadulterated, unaffected *(sincere)*, usual

unsophistication credulity

unsorted disjointed, haphazard, miscellaneous

unsought unclaimed, undesirable, unsolicited

unsound bad *(inferior)*, baseless, defective, deficient, dubious, erroneous, fallacious, false *(inaccurate)*, faulty, ill-judged, illogical, imperfect, impolitic, improper, inaccurate, inadvisable, inconsequential, incorrect, injudicious, insecure, insubstantial, insufficient, irrational, misadvised, *non compos mentis*, nonsubstantial *(not sturdy)*, peccable, precarious, sophistic, unreasonable, unreliable, untenable, untrustworthy. SEE MAIN ENTRY

unsound argument fallacy

unsound check bad check

unsound mind insanity

unsoundness disability *(physical inability)*, disease, frailty, inexpedience, invalidity

unsoundness of mind insanity, lunacy

unsparing benevolent, charitable *(benevolent)*, close *(rigorous)*, copious, liberal *(generous)*, philanthropic, profuse, relentless, ruthless, severe, trenchant, unqualified *(unlimited)*, unrelenting

unsparingness philanthropy

unsparkling insipid, lifeless *(dull)*, pedestrian

unspeakable ineffable, offensive *(offending)*, profane, remarkable

unspecific indiscriminate

unspecified anonymous, broad, collective, generic, indefinite, indeterminate, inexact, nonsectarian, vague. SEE MAIN ENTRY

unspecious authentic, bona fide, honest

unspeciousness honesty

unspent net, residuary

unspiced insipid

unspied latent, surreptitious

unspirited inactive, insipid, jejune *(dull)*, languid, lifeless *(dull)*, nonchalant

unspiritual civil *(public)*, corporeal, lecherous, material *(physical)*, mundane, physical

unspoiled intact

unspoken implicit, implied, tacit

unsporting unfair

unspotted blameless, clean, infallible, inviolate, pure, unblemished

unspurious authentic, bona fide, factual, genuine, honest, real, true *(authentic)*

unspuriousness honesty

unstable aleatory *(uncertain)*, capricious, dangerous, ephemeral, faithless, fallible, inconsistent, indefinite, insecure, irresponsible, mutable, *non compos mentis*, nonsubstantial *(not sturdy)*, peccable, precarious, temporary, transient, transitory, undependable, unpredictable, unreliable, unsettled, unsound *(not strong)*, untrustworthy, variable, volatile

unstaffed devoid

unstaid moving *(in motion)*, unsettled

unstained clean, inviolate, pure

unstated tacit

unstationary moving *(in motion)*

unsteadfast faithless, false *(disloyal)*, insecure, irresolute, mutable, noncommittal, precarious, undependable, unpredictable, untrustworthy, variable

unsteadfastness bad faith, disloyalty

unsteadiness doubt *(indecision)*, inconsistency, indecision, irregularity

unsteady broken *(interrupted)*, dangerous, disorderly, inconsistent, infrequent, insecure, irresolute, irresponsible, mutable, noncommittal, powerless, precarious, sporadic, undependable, unpredictable, unreliable, unsettled, unsound *(not strong)*, variable, volatile

unstereotyped informal

unstick detach, disengage

unstinted absolute *(complete)*, full, profuse, unqualified *(unlimited)*

unstinting benevolent, charitable *(benevolent)*, copious, liberal *(generous)*, philanthropic, profuse

unstirred callous, dispassionate, inactive, insusceptible *(uncaring)*, nonchalant, obdurate, unaffected *(uninfluenced)*

unstirring placid, stagnant

unstoppable infallible

unstopped chronic, continual *(connected)*, continual *(perpetual)*, continuous, direct *(uninterrupted)*, free *(not restricted)*, live *(existing)*, rampant

unstoppered open *(unclosed)*

unstopping chronic, persistent

unstraightforward devious, disingenuous, oblique *(evasive)*

unstraightforward action indirection *(indirect action)*

unstraightforwardness dishonesty, improbity, indirection *(deceitfulness)*

unstrain ease

unstrained harmonious

unstrained meaning connotation

unstrap disengage

unstrengthened dangerous, helpless *(defenseless)*, insipid, languid, powerless

unstrict flexible, inaccurate, informal, lax, lenient, liberal *(not literal)*

unstrictness latitude

unstruck unaffected *(uninfluenced)*

unstrung powerless

unstudied casual, ingenuous, perfunctory, simple, spontaneous, unpremeditated, unversed

unsturdy nonsubstantial *(not sturdy)*

unstylish outdated, outmoded

unsubduable indomitable, inexpugnable, insurmountable, invincible

unsubdued undaunted

unsubject immune

unsubjected free *(enjoying civil liberty)*, independent, sovereign *(independent)*

unsubmissive contumacious, disobedient, disorderly, incorrigible, indomitable, intractable, lawless, nonconforming, nonconsenting, recalcitrant, recusant, renitent, restive, uncontrollable, unruly

unsubmissiveness contempt *(disobedience to the court)*

unsubsiding chronic

unsubstantial baseless, delusive, erroneous, futile, ill-founded, illusory, immaterial, impalpable, imponderable, incorporeal, insubstantial, intangible, negligible, nominal, nonsubstantial *(not sturdy)*, null (insignificant), otiose, precarious, slight, tenuous, unfounded, unsound (fallacious), unsound (not strong), untrue

unsubstantiality blank (emptiness), immateriality, nonentity

unsubstantialness impalpability, nonentity

unsubstantiated baseless, implausible, inconclusive, theoretical, unconfirmed, uncorroborated, unsupported

unsuccessful disappointed, futile, inadept, ineffective, ineffectual, otiose, regrettable, unavailing, unproductive

unsuccessful attempt failure (lack of success)

unsuccessful trial mistrial

unsuccessfulness frustration

unsuccessive broken (interrupted), desultory, disjointed, disjunctive (tending to disjoin), intermittent, sporadic

unsufferable painful

unsufficing deficient, inadequate, insufficient, nonsubstantial (not sufficient)

unsuitability disability (legal disqualification), disqualification (factor that disqualifies), impropriety, incongruity, inexpedience, misdoing

unsuitable bad (inferior), bad (offensive), detrimental, disproportionate, gratuitous (unwarranted), ill-advised, imperfect, improper, inadmissible, inadvisable, inapplicable, inapposite, inappropriate, inapt, incapable, incompetent, incongruous, inconsistent, ineligible, inept (inappropriate), injudicious, inopportune, irrelevant, objectionable, unacceptable, unauthorized, unbecoming, undesirable, undue (excessive), unfit, unprofessional, unsatisfactory, unseemly, wrongful. SEE MAIN ENTRY

unsuitable action impropriety

unsuitable for practical use impracticable

unsuitableness disability (legal disqualification), impropriety, incompatibility (inconsistency), inconsistency

unsuitably timed untimely

unsuited gratuitous (unwarranted), improper, inapplicable, inapposite, inappropriate, incapable, ineligible, inept (inappropriate), inopportune, insufficient, unbecoming, unfavorable, unfit, unqualified (not competent), unsuitable

unsuitedness disability (legal disqualification)

unsullied blameless, clean, irreprehensible, pure, unblemished

unsunderable indivisible, inseparable

unsupplied deficient, devoid, void (empty)

unsupportable baseless, ill-founded, illusory, insubstantial, unfounded

unsupported baseless, helpless (defenseless), ill-founded, inconclusive, powerless, solitary, unauthorized, unconfirmed, uncorroborated, unfounded. SEE MAIN ENTRY

unsupported by evidence inconclusive

unsupposed actual

unsuppressed chronic, intemperate, lawless, uncurbed, unmitigated, unrestrained (not in custody), unrestrained (not repressed)

unsure aleatory (uncertain), conditional, controversial, debatable, disputable, doubtful, dubious, equivocal, fallible, hesitant, inconclusive, indefinite, insecure, leery, noncommittal, precarious, skeptical,

uncertain (questionable), undecided, undependable, unpredictable, vague. SEE MAIN ENTRY

unsure of oneself diffident

unsureness doubt (indecision), hazard, hesitation, incertitude, indecision, peril, suspicion (uncertainty)

unsurmountable insurmountable

unsurpassable inestimable, prime (most valuable)

unsurpassed absolute (ideal), cardinal (outstanding), dominant, infallible, leading (ranking first), paramount, premium, primary, prime (most valuable), professional (stellar), superior (excellent), superlative, unapproachable. SEE MAIN ENTRY

unsurprising usual

unsusceptibility resistance

unsusceptible callous, cold-blooded, dispassionate, immune, obdurate, phlegmatic

unsusceptible of change certain (positive)

unsuspected blind (concealed), covert, latent, surreptitious

unsuspected event surprise

unsuspecting credulous, definite, incognizant, insensible, naive, secure (confident), unaware, unsuspecting, unwitting. SEE MAIN ENTRY

unsuspectingly unknowingly

unsuspectingness credulity

unsuspicious credulous, definite, ingenuous, naive, unsuspecting

unsuspiciousness credulity

unsustainable baseless, debatable, disputable, doubtful, dubitative, erroneous, ill-founded, illogical, insubstantial, untenable. SEE MAIN ENTRY

unsustained baseless, debatable, disputable, unsupported

unswayable impervious, inflexible

unswayed dispassionate, fair (just), impartial, judicial, just, liberal (broad minded), loyal, neutral, nonpartisan, objective, open-minded, receptive, unaffected (uninfluenced), unbiased, unprejudiced

unsweet bitter (acrid tasting)

unswerving purposeful

unswerving constant, direct (straight), industrious, loyal, patient, persistent, pertinacious, relentless, resolute, right (correct), right (direct), sedulous, serious (devoted), stable, steadfast, straightforward, true (loyal), undistorted, uniform, unremitting

unswerving fidelity adhesion (loyalty)

unswervingly faithfully

unsymmetric irregular (not usual)

unsymmetrical disproportionate, irregular (not usual)

unsympathetic callous, cold-blooded, cruel, harsh, insusceptible (uncaring), obdurate, relentless, ruthless, unaffected (uninfluenced), unrelenting, unresponsive

unsympathizing callous, cruel

unsynthetic authentic, genuine, honest, natural, real, sterling, unaffected (sincere), veridical

unsystematic capricious, casual, desultory, discursive (digressive), disjointed, disordered, disorderly, haphazard, indiscriminate, sporadic, unpredictable

untactful impolitic, unpolitic

untaint decontaminate

untainted absolute (ideal), blameless, infallible, pure, unblemished, unimpeachable

untaken available, unclaimed

untalented amateur, inadept

untalkative laconic, mute, taciturn

untalked of undisclosed

untamed brutal, lawless, unmitigated, vicious

untangle ascertain, elucidate, explain, explicate, rectify, resolve (solve), solve

untarnishable incorruptible

untarnished absolute (ideal), clean, pure, unblemished

untasteful inelegant, unbecoming, unseemly

untastefulness indecency

untaught spontaneous, unversed

untaught state ignorance

untaxed free (at no charge)

untempered intemperate, unmitigated

untenable baseless, disabled (deprived of legal right), doubtful, helpless (defenseless), ill-founded, illogical, implausible, inadequate, indefensible, insubstantial, invalid, ludicrous, nonsubstantial (not sturdy), sophistic, unbelievable, unfounded, unreasonable, unsound (fallacious), unsupported, unsustainable, vulnerable. SEE MAIN ENTRY

untenableness invalidity

untenanted devoid, vacant, void (empty)

untender harsh

unterrified undaunted

untested inconclusive, novel

untested opinion theory

unthankfulness ingratitude

unthinkability impossibility

unthinkable implausible, impossible, incomprehensible, incredible, infeasible, ludicrous, prodigious (amazing), unbelievable

unthinking careless, fatuous, heedless, ill-judged, impolitic, impulsive (rash), inadvertent, involuntary, irrational, lax, misadvised, negligent, opaque, perfunctory, reckless, remiss, spontaneous, superficial, thoughtless, unintentional, unpremeditated, unwitting, vacuous

unthinkingness disregard (unconcern)

unthorough cursory, lax, negligent, partial (relating to a part), perfunctory

unthought of perfunctory, unanticipated, unexpected, unforeseeable, unforeseen

unthoughtful ill-judged, irrational, lax, misadvised, thoughtless

unthoughtfulness inexpedience, temerity

unthreatened immune, safe, secure (free from danger)

unthreatening harmless

unthriftiness waste

unthrifty improvident, prodigal, profligate (extravagant), profuse

untidiness laxity

untidy disordered, disorderly, lax, slipshod

untie break (separate), disencumber, disengage, disentangle, disenthrall, extricate, free, liberate, remove (eliminate), separate, sever, split

untied free (not restricted), unbound

until ad interim. SEE MAIN ENTRY

until the conclusion of throughout (during)

untimeliness impropriety, inexpedience

untimely improper, inapposite, inappropriate, inapt, inauspicious, inept (inappropriate), inopportune, overdue, premature, regrettable, undue (not owing), unexpected, unfavorable, unsuitable. SEE MAIN ENTRY

untimid undaunted

untiring diligent, faithful *(diligent)*, incessant, industrious, painstaking, patient, persistent, pertinacious, resolute, sedulous, stable, steadfast, unremitting

untitled ignoble

untold esoteric, hidden, indefinite, innumerable, multiple, myriad, mysterious, personal *(private)*, secret, tacit, undisclosed, unlimited

untolerating parochial

untomb disinter

untorn intact

untouchable dispassionate, immune, impalpable, inalienable, intangible

untouched cold-blooded, immune, impartial, insensible, insusceptible *(uncaring)*, intact, inviolate, natural, nonchalant, obdurate, pure, unadulterated, unaffected *(uninfluenced)*

untoward adverse *(hostile)*, deplorable, detrimental, disproportionate, inadvisable, inapposite, inappropriate, inapt, inauspicious, inept *(inappropriate)*, lawless, perverse, regrettable, uncontrollable, unfavorable, unpropitious, unruly, unsatisfactory, unsuitable

untraceable irretrievable

untractable fractious, immutable

untraditional divergent, unprecedented, unusual

untrained disorderly, incompetent, inexperienced, unaccustomed

untrained individual novice

untrained person layman

untrammel disencumber, rescue

untrammeled clear *(unencumbered)*, free *(not restricted)*, unbound, unrestrained *(not in custody)*, unrestricted

untransferable unalienable

untranslatable indefinable, ineffable, undefinable

untransparent equivocal, opaque

untraveled provincial

untreacherous candid, incorruptible, loyal, true *(loyal)*

untreacherousness responsibility *(conscience)*

untried inconclusive, inexperienced, moot, novel, unaccustomed, unconfirmed, unsettled

untrodden unsettled

untroubled cold-blooded, harmonious, peaceable, phlegmatic, placid, positive *(confident)*. SEE MAIN ENTRY

untrue bogus, broken *(unfulfilled)*, colorable *(specious)*, deceptive, delusive, dishonest, erroneous, faithless, fallacious, false *(disloyal)*, false *(inaccurate)*, fictitious, fraudulent, inaccurate, incorrect, invalid, lying, mendacious, perfidious, recreant, spurious, unfounded, unreliable, unsound *(fallacious)*, unsustainable, untrustworthy. SEE MAIN ENTRY

untrue declaration falsehood

untrue statement misrepresentation, story *(falsehood)*

untrue story myth

untrueness bad faith

untrustful cynical, suspicious *(distrustful)*

untrustiness bad faith

untrusting incredulous, skeptical, suspicious *(distrustful)*

untrustworthiness bad faith, dishonesty, improbity, indirection *(deceitfulness)*, knavery

untrustworthy dangerous, dishonest, disingenuous, disreputable, faithless, fallible, false *(disloyal)*, fraudulent, inaccurate, insecure, irresponsible, machiavellian, perfidious, precarious, recreant, sinister, suspicious *(distrustful)*, uncertain *(questionable)*, undependable, unreliable, unsound *(not strong)*, unsustainable, untrue. SEE MAIN ENTRY

untrusty irresponsible

untruth canard, deceit, deception, defamation, dishonesty, false pretense, falsehood, fiction, figment, lie, misrepresentation, misstatement, myth, perjury, pretense *(pretext)*, pretext, story *(falsehood)*, subreption, subterfuge

untruthful dishonest, disingenuous, disreputable, evasive, fraudulent, lying, machiavellian, mendacious, perfidious, untrue

untruthful report canard, fiction

untruthfulness bad faith, deceit, deception, dishonesty, false pretense, falsification, fraud, improbity, indirection *(deceitfulness)*, misrepresentation, misstatement

unturned direct *(straight)*, straightforward

untutored inexperienced

untutored intelligence instinct

untwist disentangle, simplify *(clarify)*

untying division *(act of dividing)*, liberation, release

untypical anomalous, dissimilar, infrequent, unusual

ununiformity inequality, irregularity

unus sole

unusable expendable, impracticable, inapplicable, otiose, unfit

unused defunct, expendable, idle, inexperienced, novel, unemployed, vacant

unusual anomalous, different, distinct *(distinguished from others)*, eccentric, extraordinary, foreign, individual, infrequent, irregular *(not usual)*, lurid, momentous, nonconforming, noteworthy, novel, original *(creative)*, particular *(individual)*, particular *(specific)*, patent, peculiar *(distinctive)*, portentous *(eliciting amazement)*, rare, remarkable, scarce, singular, special, specific, unaccustomed, uncommon, unexpected, unforeseeable, unique, unorthodox, unprecedented. SEE MAIN ENTRY

unusual circumstance phenomenon *(unusual occurrence)*

unusual happening phenomenon *(unusual occurrence)*

unusual incident phenomenon *(unusual occurrence)*

unusual occurrence surprise

unusual task onus *(burden)*

unusually particularly

unusualness irregularity, quirk *(idiosyncrasy)*

unutilized vacant

unutterable ineffable

unutterable contempt disdain

unvalidated unconfirmed, uncorroborated, unsupported

unvanquishable insurmountable, invincible

unvanquished independent, prevailing *(having superior force)*, sovereign *(independent)*, successful

unvaried boiler plate, equal, literal, ordinary, pedestrian, prosaic, stale, uniform, usual

unvarnished accurate, genuine, honest, literal, naked *(lacking embellishment)*, simple, true *(authentic)*, unadulterated

unvarnished truth honesty

unvarying certain *(positive)*, chronic, comparable *(equivalent)*, constant, continual *(perpetual)*, equal, fixed *(settled)*, invariably, normal *(regular)*, permanent, persistent, regular *(orderly)*, steadfast, uniform, unremitting

unveil admit *(concede)*, bare, clarify, denude, detect, disabuse, disclose, disinter, divulge, educe, exhibit, expose, find *(discover)*, manifest, present *(introduce)*, produce *(offer to view)*, reveal. SEE MAIN ENTRY

unveiled comprehensible, naked *(lacking embellishment)*, palpable, scrutable

unveiling admission *(disclosure)*, denouement, disclosure *(act of disclosing)*, manifestation

unvenal incorruptible

unvendible unmarketable

unventilated impervious

unventured unsettled

unveracious dishonest, evasive, false *(inaccurate)*, fraudulent, incorrect, lying, mendacious, untrue

unveraciousness bad faith

unveracity bad faith, deception, false pretense, misrepresentation

unveridical mendacious

unverifiable controversial, debatable, disputable, dubious, hypothetical, unsustainable

unverified inconclusive, unconfirmed, uncorroborated, unsupported

unverified comments hearsay

unverified news hearsay, report *(rumor)*

unverified supposition conjecture

unverity bad faith

unversed blind *(not discerning)*, inexperienced, unaccustomed, unacquainted, unaware. SEE MAIN ENTRY

unvexed complacent, patient

unviable impracticable, insurmountable

unvindictive placable

unviolated clean, inviolate

unvirtuous bad *(offensive)*, blameworthy, delinquent *(guilty of a misdeed)*, diabolic, dishonest, dissolute, fraudulent, immoral, lewd, peccable, peccant *(culpable)*, profane, promiscuous, prurient, salacious

unvirtuousness delinquency *(misconduct)*

unvisited solitary

unvivid insipid, lifeless *(dull)*, pedestrian

unvocal inarticulate, mute, speechless, taciturn

unvocalizing mute

unvoiced implicit, tacit, undisclosed

unvoidable noncancellable

unwakened dormant

unwanted derelict *(abandoned)*, ineligible, needless, otiose, unacceptable, undesirable, unsolicited

unwariness disregard *(unconcern)*, inconsideration, indiscretion, neglect, negligence

unwarlike nonmilitant

unwarned unaware, unsuspecting

unwarped direct *(straight)*, nonpartisan, objective, open-minded, unbiased, undistorted, unprejudiced

unwarrantable disproportionate, felonious, illegal, illicit, improper, indefensible, inexcusable, lawless, untenable, unwarranted

unwarrantable intrusion nuisance
unwarranted baseless, disproportionate, exorbitant, extreme *(exaggerated)*, ill-founded, illegal, illicit, inconsequential, inexcusable, irregular *(improper)*, irrelevant, lawless, nonessential, outrageous, profuse, prohibitive *(costly)*, sophistic, ultra vires, unauthorized, unconscionable, undue *(excessive)*, unfounded, unjust, unlawful, unreasonable, unsound *(fallacious)*. SEE MAIN ENTRY
unwarranted conclusion anacoluthon, non sequitur
unwarranted purchase caveat emptor
unwary careless, heedless, hot-blooded, impolitic, improvident, imprudent, injudicious, lax, misadvised, negligent, reckless, unaware, unpolitic
unwasteful economical, frugal
unwastefulness austerity
unwatchful derelict *(negligent)*, heedless, lax, negligent, perfunctory, reckless, remiss, thoughtless
unwatchfulness disregard *(unconcern)*, laxity, neglect, negligence
unwavering certain *(positive)*, constant, definite, diligent, faithful *(diligent)*, faithful *(loyal)*, fixed *(settled)*, indomitable, industrious, inexorable, infallible, intense, loyal, patient, permanent, persistent, pertinacious, positive *(confident)*, purposeful, resolute, stable, staunch, steadfast, straightforward, true *(loyal)*, unalterable, unrelenting, unyielding
unweakened powerful, undiminished
unwearied patient, unremitting
unwearying diligent, incessant, patient, persistent, pertinacious, sedulous
unweighable imponderable
unweighed casual, perfunctory
unwelcome invidious, unacceptable, undesirable, unsatisfactory, unsolicited
unwelcome suggestion intrusion
unwell unsound *(not strong)*
unwholesome detrimental, harmful, immoral, insalubrious, noxious, obnoxious, obscene, peccant *(unhealthy)*, pernicious, sinister
unwholesome condition disease
unwieldy impracticable, onerous, ponderous
unwilled involuntary
unwilling adverse *(hostile)*, averse, disinclined, disobedient, dissident, evasive, intractable, involuntary, nonconsenting, recalcitrant, recusant, reluctant, remiss, renitent, restive. SEE MAIN ENTRY
unwilling to accept inconvincible, incredulous
unwilling to care insusceptible *(uncaring)*
unwilling to give parsimonious
unwilling to pay penurious
unwillingness contempt *(disobedience to the court)*, declination, disincentive, hesitation, refusal, reluctance, resistance, scruple
unwillingness to believe incredulity
unwillingly SEE MAIN ENTRY
unwind spread
unwise detrimental, disadvantageous, fatuous, ill-advised, ill-judged, impolitic, imprudent, inadvisable, inapt, inept *(inappropriate)*, injudicious, irrational, misadvised, puerile, reckless, unfit, unpolitic, unreasonable. SEE MAIN ENTRY
unwiseness indiscretion, inexpedience

unwished undesirable, unsolicited
unwitnessed unconfirmed
unwitting incognizant, insensible, unintentional. SEE MAIN ENTRY
unwittingly unknowingly
unwitty pedestrian
unwonted different, nonconforming, original *(creative)*, unforeseeable, unusual
unworkability impossibility
unworkable impossible, impracticable, infeasible, inoperable *(impracticable)*, insurmountable, otiose. SEE MAIN ENTRY
unworldliness ignorance
unworldly incorporeal, inexperienced, naive
unworn intact, undiminished
unworried nonchalant, phlegmatic
unworthiness frailty
unworthy blameful, blameworthy, contemptible, delinquent *(guilty of a misdeed)*, disgraceful, disreputable, ignoble, odious, peccant *(culpable)*, poor *(inferior in quality)*, reprehensible, scandalous, undesirable, unethical, unfit, unsatisfactory. SEE MAIN ENTRY
unworthy of belief suspicious *(questionable)*
unworthy of confidence untrustworthy
unworthy of consideration inappreciable, inconsiderable
unworthy of notice inappreciable, inconsiderable
unworthy of regard negligible, petty
unworthy of respect notorious
unworthy of serious consideration de minimus, paltry, puerile
unworthy of serious notice frivolous
unworthy of trust untrustworthy
unwrap bare, denude, expose, unveil
unwritten nuncupative, oral, parol, prescriptive, verbal
unwritten law custom, equity *(justice)*
unyielding barren, callous, chronic, disobedient, disobedient, durable, fanatical, firm, formidable, froward, immutable, impervious, implacable, impossible, indelible, indestructible, indomitable, industrious, inexorable, inexpugnable, infallible, inflexible, insusceptible *(resistant)*, insusceptible *(uncaring)*, intractable, invincible, ironclad, irreconcilable, obdurate, oppressive, parsimonious, particular *(exacting)*, patient, permanent, persistent, pertinacious, perverse, recalcitrant, relentless, resolute, restive, rigid, sedulous, serious *(devoted)*, severe, solid *(compact)*, stable, staunch, steadfast, strict, stringent, strong, unaffected *(uninfluenced)*, unalterable, unbending, uncompromising, unmitigated, unproductive, unrelenting, unruly, willful. SEE MAIN ENTRY
unyieldingness resistance, rigor, tenacity
unyoke disencumber, dissociate, divorce, separate
unzealous disinclined
up for discussion arguable, debatable
up in arms inimical, resentful
up in the air debatable
up to effective *(efficient)*, proficient, sciential, until
up to date contemporary, current, progressive *(advocating change)*, sophisticated
up to par palatable
up to standard fairly *(moderately)*
up to the mark coequal
up to the minute contemporary, current, sophisticated

up to the time of until
up to this time heretofore
up-to-date novel, present *(current)*, prevailing *(current)*, recent
up-to-the-minute novel, present *(current)*
upbear bear *(support)*
upbraid blame, castigate, cavil, censure, complain *(criticize)*, condemn *(blame)*, criticize *(find fault with)*, denounce *(condemn)*, disapprove *(condemn)*, fault, harass, impeach, lash *(attack verbally)*, rebuke, remonstrate, reprehend, reprimand, reproach. SEE MAIN ENTRY
upbraiding critical *(faultfinding)*, criticism, denunciation, diatribe, objurgation, outcry, reprimand, reproach, revilement
upbringing education, instruction *(teaching)*
upbuild build *(construct)*, edify
upcoming forthcoming, future, immediate *(imminent)*, imminent, instant, pending *(imminent)*, prospective, proximate
updated version revision *(corrected version)*
upend overthrow, overturn, upset
upgrade ameliorate, amend, elevate, enhance, inure *(benefit)*, meliorate, promote *(advance)*
upgrading boom *(prosperity)*
upgrowth boom *(increase)*, boom *(prosperity)*, development *(progression)*
upheaval bluster *(commotion)*, cataclysm, commotion, confusion *(turmoil)*, disaster, furor, havoc, mutiny, outburst, rebellion, revolution, shambles, strife, subversion, turmoil. SEE MAIN ENTRY
uphill operose
uphold adhere *(maintain loyalty)*, advocate, aid, approve, bear *(support)*, bolster, certify *(approve)*, concur *(agree)*, confirm, continue *(prolong)*, corroborate, defend, demonstrate *(establish)*, document, espouse, establish *(show)*, indorse, justify, maintain *(sustain)*, pass *(approve)*, preserve, promote *(organize)*, prove, reassure, recommend, sanction, side, sponsor, subsidize, substantiate, support *(assist)*, sustain *(confirm)*, sustain *(prolong)*, underwrite, vouch, witness *(attest to)*. SEE MAIN ENTRY
uphold in evidence corroborate, establish *(show)*, support *(corroborate)*, sustain *(confirm)*
upholder abettor, advocate *(counselor)*, advocate *(espouser)*, apologist, backer, benefactor, mainstay, partisan, patron *(influential supporter)*, proponent
upholding conservation, corroboration
upkeep alimony, conservation, maintenance *(support of spouse)*, overhead, preservation, promotion *(encouragement)*, safekeeping, support *(assistance)*, sustenance. SEE MAIN ENTRY
uplift edify, elevate, elevation, enhance, heighten *(elevate)*, meliorate, promotion *(advancement)*, raise *(advance)*, reassure, reform
uplifting edification
upmost prominent
upper circles elite
upper class society
upper classes elite
upper extremity maximum *(pinnacle)*, pinnacle
upper hand advantage, edge *(advantage)*, predominance
upper limit capacity *(maximum)*

1045

upperhand supremacy

uppermost best, cardinal (basic), cardinal (outstanding), primary

uppish proud (conceited), supercilious

uppity proud (conceited), supercilious

upraise elevate, enhance, heighten (elevate), raise (advance), uphold

upright blameless, clean, conscientious, credible, dependable, equitable, ethical, evenhanded, fair (just), high-minded, incorruptible, innocent, irreprehensible, just, law-abiding, licit, meritorious, moral, pure, reliable, reputable, right (correct), scrupulous, sterling, straightforward, unaffected (sincere), unimpeachable. SEE MAIN ENTRY

upright distance elevation

upright moral character integrity

uprighteousness justice

uprightly faithfully

uprightness candor (straightforwardness), conscience, credibility, equity (justice), ethics, fairness, good faith, honesty, honor (good reputation), integrity, merit, principle (virtue), probity, rectitude, responsibility (conscience), right (righteousness), trustworthiness

uprightness of character integrity

uprisen disorderly

uprising anarchy, commotion, defiance, disturbance, insurrection, mutiny, outbreak, rebellion, resistance, revolt, revolution, riot, sedition, subversion. SEE MAIN ENTRY

uproar bluster (commotion), brawl, commotion, confusion (turmoil), disorder (lack of order), disturbance, embroilment, fracas, fray, furor, imbroglio, noise, outbreak, outburst, outcry, pandemonium, riot, shambles, turmoil. SEE MAIN ENTRY

uproarious disorderly

uproariousness noise, pandemonium

uproot destroy (efface), dislodge, eliminate (eradicate), eradicate, evict, exclude, extirpate, overthrow, overturn, reject, remove (eliminate), supplant

uprooting evulsion, rejection

ups and downs vicissitudes

upset agitate (perturb), annoy, beat (defeat), counterargument, debacle, defeat, disaster, discommode, discompose, disconcert, discourage, dislocate, disorganize, disorient, disrupt, distress, disturb, embarrass, foil, harrow, hold up (delay), kill (defeat), muddle, obfuscate, override, overrule, overthrow, overturn, perplex, perturb, pique, prostration, rebellion, subversion, subvert, supplant, surmount, unsettled. SEE MAIN ENTRY

upsetting oppressive, unsatisfactory

upshot amount (result), conclusion (outcome), consequence (conclusion), denouement, development (outgrowth), effect, end (termination), holding (ruling of a court), issuance, outcome, result

upstanding high-minded, law-abiding, moral, right (correct), upright

upstandingness honesty, integrity, rectitude

upsurge advance (progression), boom (increase), boom (prosperity), inflate, inflation (increase)

upswing headway

uptrend development (progression)

upturn in prices inflation (decrease in value of currency)

upward curve boom (prosperity)

upward trend boom (prosperity)

uranic stellar

urban civic, civil (public)

urban district city

urban place city

urbana record

urbane civil (polite), sophisticated

urbanitas courtesy

urbanity courtesy

urbanization city, development (building)

urbs city

urge abet, admonish (advise), advocate, argue, assert, bait (harass), bait (lure), cajole, call (appeal to), caution, charge (instruct on the law), coax, compel, constrain (compel), counsel, demand, desire (noun), desire (verb), exact, exhort, foment, force (coerce), hold out (deliberate on an offer), impel, impetus, importune, incite, inculcate, influence, insist, inspire, inveigle, lobby, motivate, persuade, petition, plead (implore), pray, press (beseech), pressure, prevail (persuade), prevail upon, promote (organize), prompt, provocation, reason (persuade), recommend, request, solicit, stimulus. SEE MAIN ENTRY

urge against expostulate, forewarn, remonstrate

urge as a reason allege

urge forward compel, constrain (compel), expedite, impel, precipitate (hasten), press (constrain)

urge in court litigate

urge not to dissuade

urge on agitate (activate), expedite, hasten, spirit

urge persistently pray

urge reasons for assert, defend, justify, plead (argue a case)

urge repeatedly pray

urge to take heed forewarn

urge upon offer (propose), tender

urgency compulsion (coercion), dispatch (promptness), emergency, exigency, force (compulsion), haste, importance, necessity, need (requirement), pressure, priority, requirement, stress (accent), stress (strain). SEE MAIN ENTRY

urgent compulsory, critical (crucial), crucial, essential (required), exigent, grave (important), imperative, indispensable, insistent, mandatory, necessary (required), obligatory, peremptory (imperative), provocative, requisite, vehement, vital. SEE MAIN ENTRY

urgent need exigency

urgent request prayer

urgent requirement necessity, need (requirement)

urger demagogue

urgere impel, press (beseech), urge

urging impulsive (impelling), inducement, influence, instigation, invitation

urging by force compulsion (coercion)

urging by moral constraint compulsion (coercion)

urging by physical constraint compulsion (coercion)

usability utility (usefulness), utilization

usable applicable, available, beneficial, constructive (creative), disposable, effective (operative), eligible, functional, malleable, passable, ripe, viable. SEE MAIN ENTRY

usage consumption, custom, function, management (judicious use), manner (behavior), means (opportunity), mode,

phraseology, practice (custom), prescription (custom), procedure, use. SEE MAIN ENTRY

use apply (put in practice), consumption, employ (make use of), exert, exhaust (deplete), expend (consume), exploit (make use of), exploitation, function, handle (manage), help, impropriate, manipulate (control unfairly), manipulate (utilize skillfully), means (opportunity), ownership, parlay (exploit successfully), patronize (trade with), ply, practice (custom), prescription (custom), profit, purpose, resort, spend, treat (process), usage, utility (usefulness), value, wield, worth. SEE MAIN ENTRY

use and title patent

use another's services employ (engage services)

use arguments plead (argue a case)

use as an agent employ (engage services)

use badly exploit (take advantage of), ill use

use carefully conserve

use dispiteously mishandle (maltreat), mistreat, persecute

use evasions tergiversate

use false evidence frame (prearrange)

use for one's own needs bilk

use force upon coerce

use frugally conserve

use hard mistreat, tax (overwork)

use improperly abuse (misuse), exploit (take advantage of)

use in support of propositions of law cite (state)

use of words parlance, phraseology

use one's authority police

use one's best endeavors attempt

use one's discretion choose

use one's imagination compose

use one's influence lobby

use one's option choose

use premises rent

use selfishly exploit (take advantage of)

use sparingly conserve

use subterfuge tergiversate

use threats threaten

use thriftily conserve

use trickery palter

use up consume, deplete, diminish, dissipate (expend foolishly), exhaust (deplete), expend (consume), spend

use up available remedies exhaust (try all possibilities)

use violence force (coerce)

use wrongfully infringe

use wrongly abuse (misuse), exploit (take advantage of), ill use, misemploy, mishandle (maltreat), mishandle (mismanage), mistreat

useable operative, purposeful

used dilapidated, old, trite

used as a deterrent exemplary

used as a model exemplary

used as a specimen exemplary

used by all common (shared)

used to familiar (informed)

used up irredeemable

used with another thing appurtenant

useful applicable, beneficial, constructive (creative), contributory, convenient, disposable, effective (efficient), favorable (advantageous), functional, gainful, instrumental, lucrative, ministerial, operative, potent, practical, pragmatic, productive,

profitable, purposeful, salutary, subservient, valuable, viable. SEE MAIN ENTRY
useful office   service *(assistance)*
usefulness   consequence *(significance)*, expedience, feasibility, importance, service *(assistance)*, use, utilization, value
useless   disabled *(made incapable)*, expendable, futile, impracticable, inadequate, incapable, incompetent, ineffective, ineffectual, inept *(incompetent)*, invalid, needless, nugatory, null *(insignificant)*, null *(invalid)*, null and void, otiose, paltry, powerless, redundant, superfluous, trivial, unable, unavailing, unfit, unproductive, unsatisfactory, void *(invalid)*. SEE MAIN ENTRY
useless check   bad check
useless consumption   waste
useless expenditure   misapplication
useless trial   mistrial
user   customer
usher   conduct, harbinger, precursor
usher in   herald, induct, initiate, introduce, originate, precede, preface, receive *(permit to enter)*
using   through *(by means of)*
using evasion   evasive
using the help of   through *(by means of)*
using up   consumption
usitatus   current, customary, habitual
usuage   enjoyment *(use)*
usual   accustomed *(customary)*, average *(standard)*, common *(customary)*, conventional, customary, daily, familiar *(customary)*, frequent, general, habitual, household *(familiar)*, jejune *(dull)*, lifeless *(dull)*, mediocre, mundane, nondescript, normal *(regular)*, ordinary, orthodox, pedestrian, prescriptive, prevailing *(current)*, pro forma, prosaic, regular *(conventional)*, rife, routine, typical. SEE MAIN ENTRY
usual custom   matter of course, practice *(custom)*
usual manner   custom
usual method   practice *(custom)*
usual occurrence   matter of course
usual practice   matter of course
usual procedure   habit, matter of course
usual thing   matter of course
usual way   practice *(procedure)*
usually   as a rule, generally, invariably
usually understood   common *(customary)*
usualness   frequency
usufruct   benefit *(betterment)*
usufructuary   beneficiary
usura   interest *(profit)*
usurious   mercenary. SEE MAIN ENTRY
usurp   abridge *(divest)*, accroach, adopt, annex *(arrogate)*, assume *(seize)*, attach *(seize)*, condemn *(seize)*, depose *(remove)*, deprive, dislodge, impropriate, infringe, invade, levy, overstep, preempt, seize *(confiscate)*, steal, supplant, takeover, trespass. SEE MAIN ENTRY
usurp for public use   eminent domain
usurpation   arrogation, assumption *(seizure)*, distress *(seizure)*, infringement
usurpatory   confiscatory
usurped   attached *(seized)*
usury   exploitation. SEE MAIN ENTRY
usus   misuse, practice *(procedure)*, routine, use
usus perversus   abuse *(corrupt practice)*, misapplication
utensil   appliance, device *(mechanism)*, expedient, instrument *(tool)*, tool
utensils   paraphernalia *(apparatus)*

utile   functional
utilis   beneficial, profitable, salutary
utilitarian   beneficial, disposable, effective *(efficient)*, functional, practical, pragmatic, purposeful, subservient, valuable
utilitarianism   casuistry
utilitas   expedience, use
utility   advantage, appliance, behalf, benefit *(betterment)*, expedience, feasibility, function, help, instrument *(tool)*, profit, propriety *(appropriateness)*, use, value, worth. SEE MAIN ENTRY
utilizable   applicable, disposable, functional, practical
utilization   benefit *(betterment)*, consumption, enjoyment *(use)*, exploitation, management *(judicious use)*, usage, use. SEE MAIN ENTRY
utilization for profit   exploitation
utilize   adopt, apply *(put in practice)*, capitalize *(seize the chance)*, consume, employ *(make use of)*, exercise *(use)*, exert, exploit *(make use of)*, manipulate *(utilize skillfully)*, ply, profit, resort, wield. SEE MAIN ENTRY
utilize for profit   bilk, capitalize *(seize the chance)*
utmost   cardinal *(basic)*, cardinal *(outstanding)*, ceiling, extreme *(last)*, maximum *(amplitude)*, primary, prime *(most valuable)*, superlative. SEE MAIN ENTRY
utmost care   diligence *(care)*
utmost extent   ceiling, pinnacle
utmost height   ceiling, culmination, pinnacle
utmost point   extremity *(furthest point)*
utopian   quixotic
utter   absolute *(complete)*, arrant *(definite)*, comment, communicate, complete *(all-embracing)*, confess, converse, declare, disclose, disseminate, enunciate, express, gross *(flagrant)*, mention, observe *(remark)*, outright, phrase, proclaim, profess *(avow)*, pronounce *(speak)*, publish, pure, recite, relate *(tell)*, remark, reveal, speak, stark, thorough, total, unconditional, unequivocal, unmitigated, unqualified *(unlimited)*. SEE MAIN ENTRY
utter a falsehood   bear false witness, misrepresent, palter, perjure
utter again   repeat *(state again)*
utter an oath   swear
utter contempt   disdain
utter disapproval   denunciation
utter force   main force
utter formally   pronounce *(pass judgment)*, pronounce *(speak)*
utter forth   pronounce *(speak)*, speak
utter invective   inveigh
utter judicial sentence   pronounce *(pass judgment)*
utter judicial sentence against   convict, determine
utter reliability   certification *(certainness)*
utter with conviction   certify *(attest)*, claim *(maintain)*, contend *(maintain)*, issue *(publish)*, posit, speak
utter words   speak
utterance   comment, communication *(statement)*, confession, disclosure *(something disclosed)*, observation, parlance, phrase, pronouncement, publicity, remark, speech, statement. SEE MAIN ENTRY
uttered   nuncupative, oral, parol, stated, verbal
uttered with conviction   alleged
uttering   disclosure *(act of disclosing)*

utterly   in toto, purely *(positively)*, wholly
utterly disperse   dispel
utterly illogical   irrational
utterly overlook   ignore
utterly senseless   *non compos mentis*
uttermost   ceiling, extreme *(last)*

V

vacancy   access *(opening)*, blank *(emptiness)*
vacant   available, barren, devoid, idle, inexpressive, thoughtless, vacuous, void *(empty)*. SEE MAIN ENTRY
vacate   abolish, abrogate *(rescind)*, adeem, avoid *(cancel)*, cancel, cease, depart, disappear, discontinue *(abandon)*, dismiss *(discharge)*, disown *(deny the validity)*, evacuate, leave *(depart)*, move *(alter position)*, negate, nullify, quash, quit *(evacuate)*, recant, relinquish, renege, repeal, rescind, resign, retire *(conclude a career)*, retire *(retreat)*, retreat, revoke, secede, withdraw. SEE MAIN ENTRY
vacate office   abandon *(withdraw)*, demit
vacate one's seat   demit
vacated   null *(invalid)*, null and void, open *(accessible)*
vacating   abandonment *(desertion)*, abdication, avoidance *(cancellation)*
vacatio   exemption, immunity
vacation   abdication, abolition, ademption, avoidance *(cancellation)*, cancellation, countermand, defeasance, furlough, holiday, leave *(absence)*, pause, recess *(noun)*, recess *(verb)*, resignation *(relinquishment)*. SEE MAIN ENTRY
vacatur   ademption, cancellation, revocation. SEE MAIN ENTRY
vaccinate   inject
vacillant   irresolute
vacillare   vacillate
vacillate   alternate *(fluctuate)*, beat *(pulsate)*, doubt *(hesitate)*, hesitate, oscillate, pause, tergiversate, vary. SEE MAIN ENTRY
vacillating   capricious, dubious, faithless, hesitant, inconsistent, irresolute, irresponsible, moving *(in motion)*, mutable, noncommittal, shifting, undecided, undependable, unreliable, unsettled, volatile
vacillation   ambivalence, doubt *(indecision)*, hesitation, incertitude, inconsistency, indecision
vacillatory   irresolute, undecided
vacuefacere   vacate *(leave)*
vacuitas   exemption
vacuity   nullity, opacity
vacuous   barren, devoid, fatuous, inexpressive, jejune *(dull)*, opaque, thoughtless, vacant, void *(empty)*. SEE MAIN ENTRY
vacuousness   blank *(emptiness)*
vacuum   blank *(emptiness)*, need *(deprivation)*
vacuus   blank *(emptiness)*, free *(relieved from a burden)*, idle, unemployed, vacant, void *(empty)*
vadimonium   guarantee
vadimonium deserere   default
vadium   promise, security *(pledge)*
vadium mortuum   charge *(lien)*, cloud *(incumbrance)*
vadium vivum   charge *(lien)*
vafer   sly
vagabond   moving *(in motion)*
vagabondage   vagrancy
vagabondism   vagrancy

vagari   err, prowl
vagarious   capricious
vagary   notion, quirk *(idiosyncrasy)*
vagrancy   SEE MAIN ENTRY
vagrant   derelict, indirect, moving *(in motion)*, variable
vague   allusive, ambiguous, broad, debatable, disputable, dubious, equivocal, evasive, impalpable, imponderable, inapprehensible, inarticulate, incomprehensible, inconspicuous, indefinite, indeterminate, indistinct, inexact, inexpressive, inscrutable, insubstantial, intangible, nebulous, noncommittal, oblique *(evasive)*, obscure *(faint)*, opaque, open-ended, problematic, uncertain *(ambiguous)*, unclear, undecided, undefinable, unspecified. SEE MAIN ENTRY
vague impression   hint
vague suggestion   hint
vagueness   ambiguity, confusion *(ambiguity)*, doubt *(indecision)*, ignorance, incertitude, indistinctness, obscuration, opacity
vagus   discursive *(digressive)*
vail   largess *(gift)*
vain   baseless, futile, ineffective, ineffectual, invalid, nugatory, orgulous, otiose, presumptuous, pretentious *(pompous)*, proud *(conceited)*, unavailing
vain attempt   abortion *(fiasco)*, failure *(lack of success)*, miscarriage. SEE MAIN ENTRY
vain effort   abortion *(fiasco)*, miscarriage
vain pretensions   pride
vainglorious   grandiose, inflated *(bombastic)*, orgulous, orotund, pretentious *(pompous)*, proud *(conceited)*, supercilious
vainglorious boasting   rodomontade
vainglory   bombast, jactation, pride, rodomontade
valens   strong
valere   avail *(be of use)*
valetudo   health
valiancy   prowess *(bravery)*
valiant   heroic, indomitable, spartan, undaunted. SEE MAIN ENTRY
valid   accurate, actual, adequate, allowed, authentic, certain *(positive)*, cogent, convincing, de facto, deductible *(provable)*, demonstrable, documentary, effective *(efficient)*, effective *(operative)*, factual, genuine, honest, lawful, legal, legitimate *(rightful)*, licit, official, operative, persuasive, potent, real, reasonable *(rational)*, right *(correct)*, right *(suitable)*, rightful, solid *(sound)*, substantial, suitable, true *(authentic)*, unrefutable, viable. SEE MAIN ENTRY
valid notice   adequate notice
valid potentiality   force *(legal efficacy)*
validate   accredit, affirm *(uphold)*, approve, attest, authorize, bear *(adduce)*, certify *(approve)*, certify *(attest)*, confirm, constitute *(establish)*, corroborate, cosign, demonstrate *(establish)*, document, endorse, establish *(show)*, formalize, indorse, legalize, legitimate, notarize, pass *(approve)*, prove, quote, sanction, seal *(solemnize)*, sign, substantiate, support *(corroborate)*, sustain *(confirm)*, verify *(confirm)*, witness *(attest to)*. SEE MAIN ENTRY
validate a will   probate
validated   allowed, choate lien
validation   acknowledgment *(avowal)*, affirmance *(authentication)*, affirmation, approval, avowal, certification *(attested copy)*, confirmation, consent, corroboration, documentation, evidence, legalization, ratification, sanction *(permission)*, stamp, subscription, support *(corroboration)*. SEE MAIN ENTRY
validation of a testament   probate
validification   attestation, corroboration, reference *(recommendation)*
validity   honesty, legality, legitimacy, quality *(excellence)*, strength, weight *(credibility)*. SEE MAIN ENTRY
validity proceedings   probate
validly   admittedly
validus   compelling
valor   prowess *(bravery)*
valorization   ad valorem, rating
valorize   calculate, gauge
valorous   heroic, spartan, undaunted. SEE MAIN ENTRY
valorousness   prowess *(bravery)*
valuable   beneficial, chattel, considerable, constructive *(creative)*, crucial, functional, gainful, important *(significant)*, inestimable, instrumental, invaluable, lucrative, material *(important)*, meritorious, possession *(property)*, practical, priceless, productive, profitable, purposeful, sterling, subservient. SEE MAIN ENTRY
valuables   assets, estate *(property)*, property *(possessions)*
valuate   assess *(appraise)*, calculate, gauge
valuation   account *(evaluation)*, appraisal, appreciation *(perception)*, assessment *(estimation)*, census, charge *(cost)*, computation, conclusion *(determination)*, cost *(price)*, estimate *(approximate cost)*, estimation *(calculation)*, expense *(cost)*, idea, measurement, par *(face amount)*, price, rate, rating, regard *(esteem)*, value, worth. SEE MAIN ENTRY
value   amount *(sum)*, assess *(appraise)*, calculate, caliber *(quality)*, charge *(cost)*, charge *(assess)*, cost *(price)*, criticize *(evaluate)*, degree *(magnitude)*, emphasis, estimate *(approximate cost)*, estimate, evaluate, expense *(cost)*, gauge, honor, importance, judge, magnitude, materiality *(consequence)*, measure, merit, par *(face amount)*, prefer, price, quality *(excellence)*, rate *(noun)*, rate *(verb)*, recommend, regard *(esteem)*, regard *(hold in esteem)*, significance, signification, utility *(usefulness)*, weight *(importance)*, worth. SEE MAIN ENTRY
value added tax   ad valorem
value in exchange   par *(face amount)*
value incorrectly   misconceive
value received   income, proceeds, profit
valued at   ad valorem
valueless   barren, expendable, futile, needless, negligible, nugatory, null *(insignificant)*, null *(invalid)*, null and void, otiose, paltry, poor *(inferior in quality)*, unavailing, unfit
valueless check   bad check
values   ethics
vamp   modify *(alter)*, repair
vandal   SEE MAIN ENTRY
vandalism   defacement, pillage
vandalize   damage
vandimonium deserere   default
vanguard   forerunner, pioneer, precursor
vanish   depart, disappear, dissipate *(spread out)*, evacuate, expire, leave *(depart)*, perish, quit *(evacuate)*
vanished   defunct, irretrievable, lost *(taken away)*
vanishing   elusive, ephemeral, transient
vanishment   nonappearance
vanitas   nullity
vanity   jactation, pride
vanload   cargo
vanquish   beat *(defeat)*, defeat, demean *(make lower)*, foil, humiliate, kill *(defeat)*, overcome *(surmount)*, overturn, overwhelm, repress, restrain, subdue, subject, subjugate, succeed *(attain)*, suppress, surmount, upset. SEE MAIN ENTRY
vanquishment   defeat, prostration
vantage   edge *(advantage)*, leverage
vantage point   perspective, stand *(position)*, standpoint
vanus   delusive, fallacious, futile, illusory, unavailing, unfounded, void *(invalid)*
vanward   SEE MAIN ENTRY
vapid   insipid, jejune *(dull)*, languid, lifeless *(dull)*, prosaic, stale
vapid expression   platitude
vapidity   opacity
vapor   phantom
vaporable   volatile
vaporing   inflated *(vain)*, rodomontade
vaporizable   volatile
vaporize   disappear
vaporize and condense   distill
vaporous   immaterial, volatile
variability   deviation, diversity, irregularity
variable   aleatory *(uncertain)*, ambulatory, atypical, broken *(interrupted)*, capricious, faithless, inconsistent, mutable, open-ended, periodic, pliable, protean, sporadic, undependable, unpredictable, untrustworthy. SEE MAIN ENTRY
variableness   irregularity
variance   alienation *(estrangement)*, argument *(contention)*, conflict, contest *(dispute)*, contradiction, contravention, controversy *(argument)*, deviation, difference, digression, disaccord, disagreement, discord, discrepancy, disparity, dispute, dissent *(difference of opinion)*, dissent *(nonconcurrence)*, dissidence, distinction *(difference)*, estrangement, feud, fight *(argument)*, incompatibility *(difference)*, incompatibility *(inconsistency)*, incongruity, inconsistency, inequality, nonconformity, nuance, rift *(disagreement)*, split, strife. SEE MAIN ENTRY
variant   deviant, different, differential, discordant, distinction *(difference)*, divergent, diverse, heterogeneous, peculiar *(distinctive)*, variable
variare   vary
variation   deviation, difference, digression, discrepancy, disparity, distinction *(difference)*, diversification, diversity, inequality, innovation, irregularity, modification, nonconformity. SEE MAIN ENTRY
variations   vicissitudes
varied   complex, composite, compound, conglomerate, different, disparate, dissimilar, diverse, heterogeneous, miscellaneous, multifarious, multifold, multiple. SEE MAIN ENTRY
variegate   alter, change, vary
variegated   composite, compound, dissimilar, diverse, heterogeneous, manifold, miscellaneous, multifarious, multifold, promiscuous
variegation   difference, diversity
varietal   different
varietas   difference
variety   class, color *(complexion)*, denomination, difference, diversity, kind, manner *(kind)*, nonconformity, selection *(collection)*

variety store market *(business)*

variform dissimilar, heterogeneous, miscellaneous, multifold

various different, dissimilar, diverse, heterogeneous, manifold, miscellaneous, multifarious, multiple

variously called alias

variously known as alias

variousness diversity

varius discursive *(digressive)*, manifold, miscellaneous, multifarious, unsettled

varnish embellish, invent *(falsify)*, mislead, slant

varnished mendacious

vary alter, alternate *(fluctuate)*, change, collide *(clash)*, conflict, convert *(change use)*, detour, deviate, differ *(vary)*, disaccord, disagree, fluctuate, modify *(alter)*, oscillate, replace, transform. SEE MAIN ENTRY

vary from depart

varying desultory, different, dissenting, divergent, diverse, heterogeneous, protean, shifting. SEE MAIN ENTRY

vassal dependent

vassalage thrall

vast capacious, extensive, far reaching, general, inclusive, prodigious *(enormous)*, unlimited

vastatio havoc

vastness degree *(magnitude)*, gamut, magnitude, measurement, space

vasty capacious

vatic ominous, oracular, prophetic

vaticinal foreseeable, ominous, oracular, prophetic

vaticinari predict

vaticinate anticipate *(prognosticate)*, forewarn, portend, predict, presage, prognosticate

vaticination prognosis

vault bank, coffer, depository, surmount, treasury

vaunt jactation

vauntful inflated *(vain)*

vaunting orgulous

vecordia insanity

vectigal duty *(tax)*, income, revenue, tax, toll *(tax)*

vectura fare

veer detour, deviate, digress, divert, slant, vary

vegatating lifeless *(dull)*

vegetate germinate, languish, pullulate

vegetating insensible

vegetation inaction, inertia, languor

vegetative inactive, lifeless *(dull)*

vehemence force *(compulsion)*, outburst, passion, violence

vehemens compelling

vehement categorical, demonstrative *(expressive of emotion)*, eager, fervent, forcible, hot-blooded, incisive, insistent, intense, intensive, powerful. SEE MAIN ENTRY

vehement condemnation denunciation

vehement desire passion

vehement speech harangue

vehicle expedient, forum *(medium)*, go-between, instrument *(tool)*, instrumentality, interagent, intermediary, medium, tool. SEE MAIN ENTRY

vehicle for escape loophole

vehiculum carriage

veil blind *(obscure)*, camouflage, cloak, conceal, cover *(conceal)*, disguise, ensconce, enshroud, envelop, hide, obfuscate, obnubilate, obscure, plant *(covertly*

place), protect, screen *(guard)*, shroud, suppress. SEE MAIN ENTRY

veil the brightness blind *(obscure)*

veiled allusive, clandestine, covert, enigmatic, equivocal, esoteric, furtive, hidden, impalpable, inconspicuous, indiscernible, latent, mysterious, oblique *(evasive)*, obscure *(faint)*, personal *(private)*, secret, stealthy, surreptitious

veiled information secret

veiled observation insinuation

veiled remark insinuation

vein phraseology, tenor

velare cover *(pretext)*, cover *(conceal)*, shroud

velitation confrontation *(altercation)*, contention *(opposition)*

velleity will *(desire)*

vellicare cavil

velocity haste, rate

velox rapid

venal bad *(offensive)*, blameful, blameworthy, lawless, machiavellian, mercenary, penurious, unjust. SEE MAIN ENTRY

venalis marketable, mercenary, venal

venality bad faith, bad repute, bribery, corruption, disloyalty

venari hunt

vend barter, handle *(trade)*, sell. SEE MAIN ENTRY

vendee consumer, customer, patron *(regular customer)*

vendere sell

vendetta feud, rancor, reprisal, revenge, vengeance

vendible item, marketable, negotiable

vendibles commodities, goods, merchandise, stock in trade

venditation jactation

vendition sale

vendor dealer, merchant. SEE MAIN ENTRY

vendor of stolen goods fence

vendor of stolen property fence

vendue auction

veneer cover *(protection)*, disguise

venemous malicious, scathing, spiteful

venerable antique, outstanding *(prominent)*, popular, sacrosanct, solemn. SEE MAIN ENTRY

venerate defer *(yield in judgment)*, honor, regard *(hold in esteem)*

venerated reputable, sacrosanct

venerating obedient

veneration estimation *(esteem)*, fealty, homage, honor *(outward respect)*, interest *(concern)*, regard *(esteem)*, respect

vengeance punishment, rancor, reprisal, retribution, revenge, spite. SEE MAIN ENTRY

vengeful resentful, ruthless, vindictive. SEE MAIN ENTRY

vengefulness rancor, reprisal, resentment, retribution, revenge, vengeance

venia amnesty, indulgence, pardon, remission

venial allowable

venire SEE MAIN ENTRY

venom malice, odium, rancor, resentment, severity, spite

venomous bitter *(penetrating)*, bitter *(reproachful)*, caustic, dangerous, deadly, deleterious, fatal, harmful, insalubrious, lethal, malevolent, malignant, peccant *(unhealthy)*, pejorative, pernicious, perverse, pestilent, resentful, ruthless, sinister, toxic, vicious, virulent

venomousness rancor

vent bare, convey *(communicate)*, denude, disabuse, disclose, expose, express, exude, outlet, outpour, promulgate, propagate *(spread)*, relate *(tell)*, reveal, signify *(inform)*, spread, utter

ventilate bare, circulate, consult *(ask advice of)*, proclaim, propagate *(spread)*, publish, relate *(tell)*

ventilate a question reason *(persuade)*

ventilated public *(known)*

ventilation catharsis, publicity, report *(detailed account)*

venture activity, attempt, bet, business *(commercial enterprise)*, compromise *(endanger)*, embark, endeavor *(noun)*, endeavor *(verb)*, enterprise *(undertaking)*, experience *(encounter)*, experiment, invest *(fund)*, investment, livelihood, mission, occupation *(vocation)*, occurrence, offer *(propose)*, operation, parlay *(bet)*, presume, project, pursuit *(effort to secure)*, pursuit *(occupation)*, risk, speculate *(chance)*, speculate *(conjecture)*, speculation *(risk)*, strive, try *(attempt)*, undertake, undertaking *(business)*, undertaking *(enterprise)*. SEE MAIN ENTRY

venture a conjecture postulate

venture a supposition postulate

venture capital capitalize *(provide capital)*

venture on commence

venture upon assume *(undertake)*

venturer bettor, speculator

ventures business *(commerce)*

venturesome aleatory *(perilous)*, hot-blooded, imprudent, impulsive *(rash)*, insecure, resourceful

venturesomeness temerity

venturous aleatory *(perilous)*, imprudent, impulsive *(rash)*, insecure

venue locality. SEE MAIN ENTRY

venustus felicitous

veracious accurate, actual, bona fide, candid, certain *(positive)*, clean, credible, demonstrable, dependable, direct *(forthright)*, documentary, factual, honest, incontrovertible, ingenuous, literal, real, realistic, reliable, right *(correct)*, sound, straightforward, strict, true *(authentic)*, undistorted, unrefutable, upright, veridical. SEE MAIN ENTRY

veraciously faithfully

veraciousness honesty, probity, veracity

veracity credibility, honesty, probity, reality, rectitude, truth, validity. SEE MAIN ENTRY

verbal loquacious, nuncupative, oral, parol. SEE MAIN ENTRY

verbal abuse malediction, obloquy, philippic, revilement

verbal assault barrage, malediction

verbal attack malediction, vilification

verbal communication discourse

verbal conflict argument *(contention)*

verbal contention contest *(dispute)*, dispute

verbal contest fight *(argument)*

verbal controversy dispute

verbal engagement contest *(dispute)*, dispute

verbal evidence affirmance *(legal affirmation)*

verbal exposition discourse

verbal expression speech

verbal intercourse conversation, discourse, interview, language, parlance, parley, speech

verbal onslaught   diatribe
verbal portraiture   delineation
verbalism   expression *(comment)*, term *(expression)*
verbalize   communicate, enunciate, express, phrase, pronounce *(speak)*, relate *(tell)*, remark
verbatim   accurate, exact, faithfully, literal. SEE MAIN ENTRY
verberare   beat *(strike)*, lash *(strike)*
verbiage   bombast, fustian, language, prattle, prolixity, tautology
verbose   flatulent, inflated *(bombastic)*, loquacious, profuse, prolific, prolix, redundant, voluble
verbosity   fustian, prolixity, tautology
verbosus   loquacious, prolix
verbum   expression *(comment)*, term *(expression)*, verbal
verdant   inexperienced
verdict   adjudication, answer *(solution)*, award, conclusion *(determination)*, consequence *(conclusion)*, conviction *(finding of guilt)*, decision *(judgment)*, decree, determination, finding, holding *(ruling of a court)*, result, ruling, sentence. SEE MAIN ENTRY
verdict after judicial inquiry   finding
verdict of not guilty   acquittal, compurgation
verecunde   respectfully
verecundia   homage
verecundus   diffident
vereri   fear
verge   border, border *(approach)*, boundary, dispose *(incline)*, edge *(border)*, extremity *(furthest point)*, limit, margin *(outside limit)*, outline *(boundary)*, periphery, side
verge on   abut, approach, connect *(join together)*
verge upon   border *(approach)*, contact *(touch)*
verging   contiguous, immediate *(not distant)*, proximate
verging on   adjacent
veri similis   probable
veri similitudo   likelihood, probability
veridical   bona fide, candid, cogent, direct *(forthright)*, factual, genuine, honest, reliable, straightforward, true *(authentic)*. SEE MAIN ENTRY
veridicality   honesty, integrity, veracity
verifiability   corroboration
verifiable   accurate, ascertainable, authentic, certain *(positive)*, deductible *(provable)*, determinable *(ascertainable)*, indubious, provable, tangible, true *(authentic)*, veridical
verifiable excuse   alibi
verifiable happening   fact
verificate   SEE MAIN ENTRY
verification   acknowledgment *(acceptance)*, affirmance *(authentication)*, affirmation, approval, attestation, avowal, certainty, certification *(attested copy)*, confirmation, consent, corroboration, document, documentation, evidence, experiment, jurat, proof, reference *(recommendation)*, support *(corroboration)*. SEE MAIN ENTRY
verificative   demonstrative *(illustrative)*, probative
verificative excuse   alibi
verificatory   provable
verified   official
verify   affirm *(uphold)*, ascertain, assure *(insure)*, attest, avouch *(guarantee)*, bear

(adduce), certify *(attest)*, check *(inspect)*, confirm, corroborate, demonstrate *(establish)*, depose *(testify)*, document, ensure, establish *(show)*, evidence, find *(discover)*, identify, prove, quote, recognize *(perceive)*, reveal, seal *(solemnize)*, substantiate, support *(corroborate)*, sustain *(confirm)*, testify, validate, witness *(attest to)*. SEE MAIN ENTRY
verify a testament   probate
verify again   reconfirm
verifying   convincing, demonstrative *(illustrative)*
verifying statement   jurat
verisimilar   believable, circumstantial, credible, probable
verisimilis   colorable *(plausible)*, plausible
verisimilitude   credibility, probability
verisimilous   probable
veritable   absolute *(conclusive)*, actual, authentic, candid, de facto, definite, documentary, genuine, honest, real, sound, true *(authentic)*, unrefutable, valid
veritably   admittedly
veritas   reality, truth, veracity
verity   honesty, reality, truth, validity, veracity
vermicular   tortuous *(bending)*
vermiculate   tortuous *(bending)*
vermiculated   tortuous *(bending)*
vernacular   language, native *(domestic)*, ordinary, prevailing *(current)*, prevalent, regional, usual
vernal   juvenile
vernile   servile
versant   learned
versari   employ *(engage services)*
versari in re   concern *(involve)*
versatile   artful, mutable, pliable, protean, resourceful. SEE MAIN ENTRY
versatility   ability, amenability
verse maker   author *(writer)*
versed   cognizant, competent, expert, familiar *(informed)*, informed *(educated)*, learned, qualified *(competent)*
version   construction, paraphrase
versus   contra
versus   contra
versutus   artful
vertex   ceiling, crossroad *(intersection)*
verus   actual, authentic, candid, essential *(required)*, real, right *(righteousness)*, sterling, true *(authentic)*
verve   ardor, emotion, life *(vitality)*, passion, spirit
very   stark. SEE MAIN ENTRY
very fine   impalpable, premium
very thorough   complete *(all-embracing)*
vesanus   frenetic
vesicate   burn
vest   admit *(give access)*, bestow, dedicate, empower. SEE MAIN ENTRY
vest in   bequeath, commit *(entrust)*, delegate, repose *(place)*. SEE MAIN ENTRY
vest with a title   authorize
vested   immutable, prescriptive
vested interest   birthright, claim *(right)*, equity *(share of ownership)*, prescription *(claim of title)*, right *(entitlement)*, title *(right)*
vested interest in land   fee *(estate)*, freehold
vested right   birthright, charter *(sanction)*, droit, due, prerogative, prescription *(claim of title)*
vestibule   entrance
vestigium   indication

vestire   clothe
vestis mutata   disguise
vetare   condemn *(ban)*, disallow, forbid
veteran   expert *(adjective)*, expert *(noun)*, practiced, specialist. SEE MAIN ENTRY
vetitus   felonious, illegal, illicit, unlawful
veto   ban, countermand, debar, decline *(reject)*, disapproval, disapprove *(reject)*, disavow, exclude, forbid, forestall, inhibit, interdict, negate, nonconformity, prevent, prohibit, prohibition, protest, refusal, refuse, reject, rejection, renunciation, repudiation, restraint, restrict, stem *(check)*. SEE MAIN ENTRY
vetoed   impermissible
vetus   old, stale
vetustus   old
vex   affront, aggravate *(annoy)*, annoy, badger, bait *(harass)*, discommode, discompose, distress, disturb, embarrass, harass, harrow, harry *(harass)*, hector, incense, inconvenience, irritate, mistreat, molest *(annoy)*, obsess, offend *(insult)*, perplex, perturb, pique, plague, press *(goad)*, provoke, repel *(disgust)*. SEE MAIN ENTRY
vexare   harass, harrow, harry *(harass)*, molest *(annoy)*, persecute, pique, plague
vexatio   molestation, oppression
vexation   burden, damage, dissatisfaction, distress *(anguish)*, grievance, molestation, nuisance, provocation
vexatious   invidious, operose, oppressive, perverse, provocative. SEE MAIN ENTRY
vexed   aggrieved *(harmed)*, bitter *(reproachful)*
vexed question   dilemma, problem
vexing   provocative, unsatisfactory
via   direction *(course)*, facility *(instrumentality)*, method, mode
via   through *(from beginning to end)*
viability   feasibility, possibility
viable   live *(conscious)*, permissible, possible, virtual. SEE MAIN ENTRY
viableness   possibility
viatical settlement   SEE MAIN ENTRY
vibrant   strong. SEE MAIN ENTRY
vibrare   brandish
vibrate   beat *(pulsate)*, vacillate
vicar   deputy, proctor, spokesman
vicarial   surrogate
vicarious   derivative, secondary, surrogate. SEE MAIN ENTRY
vicarius   deputy, proxy, representative *(proxy)*, surrogate
vice   bad repute, flaw, foible, guilt, mens rea, mischief, misdoing, sodomy, wrong. SEE MAIN ENTRY
vice versa   contra, contrary
vice-ridden   profane, profligate *(corrupt)*
vicegerent   deputy
viceregent   procurator
viceroy   plenipotentiary
vicinage   area *(province)*, locality, location, propinquity *(proximity)*, region, section *(vicinity)*
vicinal   adjacent, close *(near)*, present *(attendant)*, proximate
vicinitas   section *(vicinity)*
vicinity   area *(province)*, locality, location, region, site. SEE MAIN ENTRY
vicinus   adjacent
vicious   bad *(offensive)*, brutal, cruel, dangerous, delinquent *(guilty of a misdeed)*, diabolic, harmful, heinous, hostile, inexcusable, inexpiable, iniquitous, malevolent, malicious, malignant, noxious, peccant *(culpable)*, pernicious, profligate

(corrupt), reprehensible, reprobate, ruthless, severe, spiteful, tainted (corrupted), unjustifiable, unscrupulous. SEE MAIN ENTRY

viciousness bestiality, cruelty, delinquency (misconduct), guilt, malice, spite

vicissitudes circumstances. SEE MAIN ENTRY

vicissitudinous unpredictable

vicissitudo reciprocity

vicitimize ill use

victim cadaver, captive, corpse, patient, subject (object). SEE MAIN ENTRY

victima victim

victimization abuse (physical misuse), atrocity, bunko, cruelty, oppression

victimize bait (harass), betray (lead astray), bilk, deceive, defeat, dupe, endanger, ensnare, exploit (take advantage of), extort, harass, illude, inveigle, mishandle (maltreat), mistreat, palter, persecute, prey, slay. SEE MAIN ENTRY

victorious prevailing (having superior force), successful

victory supremacy

victual nurture, supply

victualer supplier

victuals sustenance

victus livelihood, maintenance (support of spouse), sustenance

videlicet a savoir

videor apparent (perceptible)

videre witness (have direct knowledge of). SEE MAIN ENTRY

videri appear (seem to be)

vie strive

vie for endeavor

vie with compete, contend (dispute), contest, fight (battle), grapple

view advice, apprehend (perceive), apprehension (perception), aspect, assumption (supposition), complexion, concept, conclusion (determination), conviction (persuasion), coverage (scope), credence, design (intent), detect, discern (detect with the senses), estimate (idea), idea, intent, notice (observe), notion, observation, observe (watch), opine, opinion (belief), perception, perspective, pierce (discern), platform, position (point of view), posture (attitude), purview, reaction (response), recognize (perceive), regard (pay attention), scene, scrutinize, side, spy, stand (position), standpoint, study, surmise, survey (examine), suspect (think), theory, witness (have direct knowledge of). SEE MAIN ENTRY

view as deem

view from all sides ponder

view retrospectively review

view with a scornful eye disdain, flout

view with deliberation ponder

view with disfavor censure, deprecate, disapprove (condemn), discommend, disfavor, expostulate

view with dissatisfaction resent

view with favor countenance

view with regret deplore

viewable apparent (perceptible), discernible, perceivable, perceptible, visible (in full view)

viewer bystander, eyewitness

viewership bystander

viewless inconspicuous

viewpoint aspect, conviction (persuasion), idea, opinion (belief), outlook, perception, perspective, position (point of view), posture (attitude), side, stand (position), standpoint. SEE MAIN ENTRY

vigil notice (heed), precaution, surveillance

vigilance diligence (care), notice (heed), precaution, prudence, regard (attention), surveillance, ward

vigilans vigilant

vigilant careful, circumspect, conscious (aware), discreet, guarded, leery, meticulous, protective, provident (showing foresight). SEE MAIN ENTRY

vigilence diligence (perseverance)

vignette brief

vigor ardor, diligence (perseverance), dint, effort, force (strength), health, industry (activity), life (vitality), main force, prowess (bravery), puissance, sinew, spirit, strength

vigorless powerless

vigorous active, compelling, forcible, indomitable, intense, intensive, irresistible, potent, powerful, resolute, resounding, strong, trenchant. SEE MAIN ENTRY

vigorous enunciation emphasis

vigorously effective drastic

vigorousness ardor, effort, force (strength), sinew

vile arrant (onerous), bad (offensive), blameful, caitiff, contemptible, contemptuous, deplorable, depraved, disgraceful, heinous, ignoble, iniquitous, loathsome, machiavellian, malignant, nefarious, objectionable, obnoxious, obscene, odious, offensive (offending), paltry, peccant (culpable), profligate (corrupt), reprobate, repulsive, scurrilous, vicious. SEE MAIN ENTRY

vileness delinquency (misconduct), dishonor (shame), disrepute, obscenity, shame, turpitude, vice

vilification aspersion, bad repute, condemnation (blame), contumely, denunciation, diatribe, dishonor (shame), disparagement, disrespect, impeachment, imprecation, libel, malediction, obloquy, opprobrium, outcry, phillipic, profanity, reproach, revilement, scandal, slander. SEE MAIN ENTRY

vilify brand (stigmatize), condemn (blame), contemn, decry, defame, denigrate, denounce (condemn), derogate, discommend, dishonor (deprive of honor), disparage, humiliate, inveigh, lash (attack verbally), lessen, libel, malign, pillory, reprimand, reproach, smear, sully, tarnish

vilifying calumnious, libelous, pejorative

vilipend blame, brand (stigmatize), censure, contemn, decry, defame, denigrate, denounce (condemn), deprecate, derogate, disapprove (condemn), discommend, disoblige, disparage, lash (attack verbally), lessen, malign, reprimand, reproach, smear, sully

vilipendency bad repute, disapprobation, disparagement, disrespect

vilis paltry

villa estate (property)

villager habitant, resident

villain convict, criminal, hoodlum, malefactor, wrongdoer

villainous bad (offensive), contemptible, delinquent (guilty of a misdeed), felonious, heinous, inexpiable, iniquitous, malevolent, malignant, nefarious, notorious, obnoxious, outrageous, peccant (culpable), recreant, reprehensible, sinister, unscrupulous, vicious. SEE MAIN ENTRY

villainousness corruption, delinquency (misconduct), knavery

villainy atrocity, corruption, delinquency (misconduct), knavery, mischief, misdeed, misdoing, wrong

vim industry (activity), life (vitality), spirit

vincere beat (defeat), defeat, establish (show), outweigh, overrule, predominate (command), prevail (triumph)

vincibility danger

vincible disabled (made incapable), helpless (defenseless), inadequate, indefensible, penetrable, powerless, untenable, vulnerable

vincibleness danger

vincula fetter, incarceration

vincula ties

vinculo matrimonii cohabitation (married state)

vinculum chain (series), fetter

vinculum nexus

vindicable defensible, justifiable, pardonable, tenable, unobjectionable

vindicate absolve, acquit, bear (adduce), bear (support), clear, condone, exculpate, excuse, exonerate, extenuate, forgive, free, justify, liberate, maintain (sustain), palliate (excuse), pardon, rationalize, remit (release from penalty), substantiate, support (corroborate), support (justify), sustain (confirm), uphold. SEE MAIN ENTRY

vindicate a right claim (demand)

vindicate a title claim (demand)

vindicate from unjust reproach exculpate

vindicated acquitted, blameless, clear (free from criminal charges)

vindicating palliative (excusing)

vindicatio assertion

vindication absolution, acquittal, advocacy, compurgation, condonation, corroboration, exoneration, indemnity, justification, liberation, pardon, reason (basis), support (corroboration)

vindicative palliative (excusing)

vindicator proponent

vindicatory defensible, palliative (excusing), vindictive

vindicta revenge, vengeance

vindictive implacable, malevolent, malicious, malignant, punitive, relentless, resentful, ruthless, severe, spiteful. SEE MAIN ENTRY

vindictive oath imprecation

vindictiveness rancor, reprisal, resentment, retribution, revenge, spite, vengeance

vinegarish bitter (acrid tasting)

vintage age, old

violare infringe, offend (violate the law), violate

violate betray (lead astray), contravene, damage, debauch, disobey, encroach, endanger, impinge, impose (intrude), infringe, invade, misemploy, mishandle (maltreat), mistreat, molest (subject to indecent advances), overstep, pollute, taint (corrupt), trespass. SEE MAIN ENTRY

violate a confidence betray (disclose), inform (betray)

violate a contract infringe

violate a law infringe

violate a privilege infringe

violate a regulation infringe

violate one's oath defect

violate rules mismanage

violate the confidence of inform (betray)

violate the truth falsify

violated broken *(unfulfilled)*
violating disobedient
violatio infraction, infringement
violation abuse *(corrupt practice)*, abuse *(physical misuse)*, breach, contravention, debauchment, defilement, delict, delinquency *(misconduct)*, disregard *(omission)*, encroachment, guilt, incursion, infraction, infringement, invasion, irregularity, misdeed, misdoing, misprision, misusage, misuse, offense, perversion, rape, rebellion, sedition, transgression, wrong. SEE MAIN ENTRY
violation of a contract infringement
violation of a duty delict
violation of a law infringement
violation of a legal duty tort
violation of a privilege infringement
violation of a regulation infringement
violation of allegiance bad faith, disloyalty, treason
violation of an oath perjury
violation of another's rights assault
violation of duty bad faith, default
violation of law breach, crime, felony, guilt, infraction, misdemeanor, misfeasance, offense
violation of oath infidelity
violation of orders contempt *(disobedience to the court)*, infraction, offense
violation of professional code malpractice
violation of professional duty malpractice
violation of right injustice, wrong
violation of the law illegality
violation of the marriage vows adultery
violation of trust dishonesty, disloyalty
violative broken *(unfulfilled)*, disobedient, lawless
violator aggressor, assailant, offender
violator of laws malefactor
violator of the law outlaw
violence affray, belligerency, brutality, commotion, cruelty, embroilment, havoc, infliction, infringement, injury, outburst, passion, severity, strife. SEE MAIN ENTRY
violent brutal, demonstrative *(expressive of emotion)*, disorderly, drastic, extreme *(exaggerated)*, forcible, hot-blooded, malignant, pernicious, pestilent, precipitate, severe, strong, uncontrollable, vehement, virulent. SEE MAIN ENTRY
violent anger passion
violent animosity malice
violent behavior outbreak
violent change revolution
violent contact collision *(accident)*
violent death fatality, homicide, killing, murder
violent disagreement dissension
violent separation avulsion
violent upheaval cataclysm
violentia violence
viperine dangerous
viperous dangerous, malevolent, spiteful
vires ability, strength
virgin unadulterated
virile potent, spartan, strong
virility strength
virtual constructive *(inferential)*. SEE MAIN ENTRY
virtue caliber *(quality)*, ethics, honesty, honor *(good reputation)*, integrity, merit, probity, rectitude, right *(righteousness)*, veracity

virtueless bad *(offensive)*, base *(bad)*, delinquent *(guilty of a misdeed)*, diabolic, inexpiable, peccable, profane, salacious
virtuosity performance *(workmanship)*, prowess *(ability)*, specialty *(special aptitude)*
virtuoso expert, specialist
virtuous blameless, clean, conscientious, ethical, evenhanded, high-minded, incorruptible, inculpable, innocent, innocuous, irreprehensible, just, laudable, law-abiding, meritorious, moral, proper, pure, reputable, right *(correct)*, right *(suitable)*, sterling, upright
virtuous conduct ethics
virtuously faithfully
virtuousness ethics, integrity, principle *(virtue)*
virtus merit, prowess *(bravery)*, worth
virulence fatality, force *(strength)*, harm, rancor, severity, spite
virulency fatality, spite
virulent antipathetic *(distasteful)*, bitter *(penetrating)*, caustic, chronic, dangerous, deleterious, fatal, harsh, insalubrious, lethal, malevolent, malicious, malignant, mordacious, noxious, peccant *(unhealthy)*, pernicious, pestilent, ruthless, scathing, sinister, spiteful, toxic, vicious. SEE MAIN ENTRY
virulently inimical malignant
virus disease
vis compulsion *(coercion)*, efficiency, essence, faculty *(ability)*, force *(strength)*, impetus, import, importance, influence, life *(vitality)*, meaning, power, pressure, significance, signification, stock *(store)*
vis-à-vis antipode, contra, contrary, hostile
visa permission, permit
visage aspect, complexion, feature *(appearance)*, presence *(poise)*, semblance
viscidity adhesion *(affixing)*
viscosity adhesion *(affixing)*
viscous coherent *(joined)*
visé confirmation
visible apparent *(perceptible)*, appreciable, bodily, clear *(apparent)*, coherent *(clear)*, conspicuous, discernible, distinct *(clear)*, evident, extant, flagrant, manifest, naked *(perceptible)*, obvious, open *(in sight)*, ostensible, overt, palpable, patent, perceivable, perceptible, prominent, remarkable, salient, tangible, unmistakable. SEE MAIN ENTRY
visible effect impression
visible form embodiment
visible sign symbol
visible token indicant
visibly fairly *(clearly)*
vision phantom, phenomenon *(manifestation)*, sagacity, standpoint. SEE MAIN ENTRY
visionary delusive, illusory, impossible, infeasible, insubstantial, nonexistent, quixotic, theoretical
visioned original *(creative)*
visionless blind *(sightless)*
visit appointment *(meeting)*, attend *(be present at)*, inhabit
visit punishment discipline *(punish)*, penalize
visitation adversity, misfortune, presence *(attendance)*
visor enshroud, veil
vista aspect, scene, vision *(sight)*
visual discernible, perceivable, perceptible

visual examination inspection
visual impact face value *(first blush)*
visualization concept, perception
visualize compose, conceive *(comprehend)*, conjure, discern *(detect with the senses)*, invent *(produce for the first time)*
visualized distinct *(clear)*
visualizing original *(creative)*
vita life *(period of existence)*
vita decedere die
vital born *(alive)*, cardinal *(basic)*, central *(essential)*, compulsory, critical *(crucial)*, crucial, exigent, fundamental, important *(urgent)*, indispensable, integral, live *(conscious)*, major, mandatory, material *(important)*, necessary *(required)*, obligatory, primary, requisite, strategic, substantive, urgent, viable. SEE MAIN ENTRY
vital center seat
vital concern main point, sine qua non
vital element center *(essence)*
vital essence spirit
vital part center *(essence)*, consequence *(significance)*, ingredient, necessity, need *(requirement)*, prerequisite, requirement, substance *(essential nature)*
vital principle gist *(substance)*
vital statistics census
vitalic vital
vitalis vital
vitality ardor, force *(strength)*, health, prowess *(bravery)*, puissance, spirit, strength
vitalization birth *(beginning)*
vitalize generate, stimulate
vitalized born *(alive)*
vitalness need *(requirement)*, priority
vitals necessary, necessity
vitare avoid *(evade)*, eschew, shun
vitiare adulterate, corrupt, debase, debauch, falsification, falsify, vitiate
vitiate abolish, adulterate, annul, contaminate, corrupt, damage, debase, debauch, degenerate, denature, deteriorate, disable, dissolve *(terminate)*, infect, invalidate, neutralize, nullify, pervert, pollute, revoke, spoil *(impair)*, subvert, sully, taint *(corrupt)*. SEE MAIN ENTRY
vitiated depraved, profligate *(corrupt)*, reprobate, stale, tainted *(corrupted)*
vitiation annulment, contaminate, damage, debauchment, fault *(weakness)*, invalidity, perversion, rescision
vitiis inficere infect
vitiosus faulty, vicious
vitium fallacy, flaw, foible, guilt
vitriol disapprobation
vitriolic bitter *(reproachful)*, malevolent, malignant, mordacious, scathing
vituperare blame, censure, condemn *(blame)*, decry, rebuke, reprimand
vituperate castigate, condemn *(blame)*, contemn, defame, denigrate, denounce *(condemn)*, impeach, inveigh, lash *(attack verbally)*, malign, pillory, rebuke, reprimand, reproach
vituperatio blame *(culpability)*, obloquy, reprimand
vituperation aspersion, condemnation *(blame)*, contumely, denunciation, diatribe, disparagement, imprecation, malediction, obloquy, outcry, philippic, profanity, revilement, stricture, vilification
vituperative calumnious, contemptuous, harsh, libelous, pejorative
vivacity ardor, life *(vitality)*, spirit
vivid acute, clear *(apparent)*, coherent *(clear)*, descriptive, detailed, distinct

(clear), eloquent, intense, profound *(intense)*, strong, suggestive *(evocative)*. SEE MAIN ENTRY

vividly   fairly *(clearly)*

vividness   strength

vivification   birth *(emergence of young)*, revival

vivified   conscious *(awake)*

vivify   generate, heighten *(augment)*, stimulate

vixenish   petulant, querulous

vizard   veil

vocable   term *(expression)*

vocabulary   language, parlance, phraseology

vocabulum   term *(expression)*

vocal   nuncupative, oral, parol

vocal embodiment of thought   expression *(comment)*

vocalism   intonation

vocalization   parlance, speech

vocalize   communicate, enunciate, observe *(remark)*, phrase, pronounce *(speak)*, remark

vocalized   oral

vocare   call *(title)*

vocation   appointment *(position)*, business *(occupation)*, calling, career, employment, job, labor *(work)*, livelihood, mission, position *(business status)*, post, practice *(professional business)*, profession *(vocation)*, pursuit *(occupation)*, specialty *(special aptitude)*, trade *(occupation)*, work *(employment)*

vocational   technical

voces   outcry

vociferance   noise

vociferate   interject

vociferatio   outcry

vociferation   noise, outcry, pandemonium

vociferous   blatant *(obtrusive)*, loquacious

vogue   custom, market *(demand)*, mode, style, usage

vogue word   catchword

voice   circulate, communicate, disclose, divulge, enunciate, express, intonation, mention, observe *(remark)*, phrase, poll *(casting of votes)*, pronounce *(speak)*, propose, propound, recite, referendum, remark, report *(disclose)*, reveal, signify *(inform)*, spokesman, suffrage, utter. SEE MAIN ENTRY

voice change   inflection

voice disapproval   reprehend

voiced   nuncupative, oral, parol, stated, verbal

voiceless   mute, speechless

voicing   expression *(comment)*

void   abate *(extinguish)*, abolish, abrogate *(annul)*, abrogate *(rescind)*, absence *(omission)*, adeem, annul, avoid *(cancel)*, barren, blank *(emptiness)*, cancel, defunct, deplete, discontinue *(abandon)*, disown *(deny the validity)*, eliminate *(eradicate)*, eradicate, inactive, ineffective, ineffectual, inexpressive, invalid, lifeless *(dead)*, nugatory, null *(invalid)*, null and void, nullify, nullity, overrule, recall *(call back)*, recant, repeal, rescind, revoke, supersede, vacant, vacuous. SEE MAIN ENTRY

void check   bad check

void of   deficient, devoid

void of contents   barren

void of feeling   insensible

void of reason   irrational

void of suspicion   certain *(positive)*, credible, naive

void of taste   insipid

void of truth   dishonest, fraudulent, mendacious

void the license of an attorney   disbar

void trial   mistrial

voidable   defeasible. SEE MAIN ENTRY

voidance   abatement *(extinguishment)*, abolition, ademption, annulment, avoidance *(cancellation)*, cancellation, countermand, defeasance, discharge *(annulment)*, discharge *(release from obligation)*, dissolution *(termination)*, exclusion, repudiation, rescision, retraction, reversal

voiding   cancellation, reversal

voidness   invalidity

voir dire   SEE MAIN ENTRY

volaticus   volatile

volatile   brief, ephemeral, inconsistent, irresolute, mutable, temporary, transient, transitory, variable. SEE MAIN ENTRY

volatility   inconsistency

volcanic   vehement

volcano   outburst

volens   voluntary

volitient   deliberate, spontaneous, voluntary

volition   animus, conatus, discretion *(power of choice)*, election *(choice)*, forethought, intent, purpose, will *(desire)*. SEE MAIN ENTRY

volitional   deliberate, discretionary, spontaneous, voluntary, willful, willing *(desirous)*

volitionally   purposely

volitionary   voluntary

volitive   deliberate, discretionary, permissive, spontaneous, willful

volley   barrage, discharge *(shot)*, salvo

voluble   loquacious. SEE MAIN ENTRY

volume   bulk, capacity *(maximum)*, coverage *(scope)*, degree *(magnitude)*, magnitude, publication *(printed matter)*, quantity

voluminous   capacious, copious

voluntarily   purposely, readily

voluntariness   conatus, purpose

voluntarius   spontaneous, voluntary

voluntary   consenting, deliberate, gratis, gratuitous *(given without recompense)*, spontaneous, unsolicited, willful, willing *(not averse)*. SEE MAIN ENTRY

voluntary acknowledgment   admission *(disclosure)*

voluntary activity   conatus

voluntary association   affiliation *(amalgamation)*, merger

voluntary attestment under oath   affidavit

voluntary conveyance   largess *(gift)*

voluntary decision   alternative *(option)*

voluntary exile   privacy

voluntary oversight   connivance

voluntary relinquishment   waiver

voluntary work   campaign

voluntary worker   volunteer

voluntas   inclination, volition, will *(desire)*

volunteer   hold out *(deliberate on an offer)*, pose *(propound)*, proffer, tender, unpaid. SEE MAIN ENTRY

volunteered   unsolicited

volute   sinuous

voracious   eager, gluttonous, predatory, rapacious

voraciousness   greed

voracity   greed

votary   addict, advocate *(counselor)*, advocate *(espouser)*, colleague, disciple, partisan, proponent

vote   cast *(register)*, decide, franchise *(right to vote)*, plebiscite, poll *(casting of votes)*, primary, referendum, suffrage. SEE MAIN ENTRY

vote against   disapprove *(reject)*, protest, reject

vote down   disapprove *(reject)*, fight *(counteract)*

vote favorably   pass *(approve)*

vote for   confirm, side

vote in   legislate, pass *(approve)*

vote into office   elect *(select by a vote)*, nominate

vote of confidence   adhesion *(loyalty)*

vote to accept   adopt

vote-casting   election *(selection by vote)*

voted   consensual

voter   constituent *(member)*

voters   constituency

voting age   majority *(adulthood)*

voting district   constituency

voting list   constituency

voting power   franchise *(right to vote)*

votum   prayer

vouch   affirm *(declare solemnly)*, avouch *(avow)*, avouchment, avow, certify *(attest)*, contend *(maintain)*, depose *(testify)*, posit, promise *(vow)*, seal *(solemnize)*, swear, vow. SEE MAIN ENTRY

vouch for   accredit, affirm *(uphold)*, assure *(insure)*, attest, authorize, avouch *(guarantee)*, bear *(adduce)*, certify *(attest)*, confirm, corroborate, cosign, depose *(testify)*, guarantee, indorse, recommend, side, sponsor, support *(corroborate)*, underwrite, verify *(swear)*, witness *(attest to)*

vouch for as genuine   certify *(attest)*

vouched   alleged

vouched for   promissory

voucher   affiant, affirmant, assurance, bond, certificate, corroboration, coupon, deponent, draft, guaranty, note *(written promise to pay)*, permit, receipt *(proof of receiving)*, reference *(recommendation)*, security *(pledge)*, surety *(guarantor)*, warrant *(authorization)*, warranty

vouchers   credentials

vouching   adjuration, advocacy, averment, deposition, reference *(recommendation)*

vouchsafe   accede *(concede)*, allow *(authorize)*, authorize, bestow, cede, condescend *(deign)*, deign, give *(grant)*, grant *(concede)*, let *(permit)*, patronize *(condescend toward)*, present *(make a gift)*, sanction. SEE MAIN ENTRY

vouchsafed   allowed

vouchsafement   concession *(authorization)*, consent, disposition *(transfer of property)*, indulgence, leave *(permission)*, license, privilege, sanction *(permission)*

vouchsafer   contributor *(giver)*, donor

vow   adjuration, asseveration, assurance, assure *(insure)*, avouch *(avow)*, avouchment, avow, bear *(adduce)*, claim *(maintain)*, commitment *(responsibility)*, oath, pledge *(binding promise)*, pledge *(promise the performance of)*, profession *(declaration)*, promise, promise *(vow)*, surety *(certainty)*, swear, undertake, undertaking *(pledge)*, verify *(swear)*. SEE MAIN ENTRY

vox   call *(appeal)*, expression *(comment)*, verbal

voyager   itinerant

voyaging   moving *(in motion)*

vulgar   blatant *(obtrusive)*, caitiff, depraved, ignoble, impertinent *(insolent)*,

inelegant, lewd, licentious, lurid, meretricious, obnoxious, obscene, odious, poor *(inferior in quality)*, profane, scurrilous, tawdry, unbecoming, uncouth, unseemly. SEE MAIN ENTRY
vulgare propagate *(spread)*
vulgarian blatant *(obtrusive)*
vulgarity indecency, obscenity, pornography, profanity
vulgarize corrupt, debase
vulgus mass *(body of persons)*
vulnerability danger, frailty, jeopardy, liability, peril, risk
vulnerable destructible, helpless *(defenseless)*, inadequate, indefensible, insecure, liable, open *(accessible)*, penetrable, precarious, subject *(exposed)*, susceptible *(unresistent)*, untenable. SEE MAIN ENTRY
vulnerable point fault *(weakness)*, peril
vulnerableness frailty
vulnerary medicinal
vulpine artful, insidious, machiavellian, sly, subtle *(insidious)*, surreptitious
vulturine predatory, rapacious
vulturish predatory
vulturous predatory, rapacious
vying competitive *(antagonistic)*
vying for ascendance competition
vying with comparative, contravention

W

wag brandish
wage commission *(fee)*, exercise *(discharge a function)*, fee *(charge)*, income, payment *(remittance)*, perquisite, ply, recompense. SEE MAIN ENTRY
wage earner employee
wage war engage *(involve)*, fight *(battle)*
wager bet, gamble, lottery, parlay *(bet)*, pawn, risk, speculate *(chance)*, speculation *(risk)*, stake *(award)*, venture
wagerer bettor, speculator
wages compensation, earnings, income, pay, payroll, revenue
waggery mischief
waggish jocular
waggishness mischief
waggle brandish
waif orphan
wail outcry, plaint
wailful querulous
wait cessation *(interlude)*, defer *(put off)*, deferment, delay, discontinue *(break continuity)*, forbear, halt *(noun)*, halt *(verb)*, hesitate, last, moratorium, pause, procrastinate, remain *(stay)*, respite *(interval of rest)*, stay, stay *(rest)*. SEE MAIN ENTRY
wait for anticipate *(expect)*, expect *(anticipate)*, forestall
wait on pander, serve *(assist)*
wait upon attend *(take care of)*
waiting expectation, ready *(prepared)*
waiting period moratorium
waive abrogate *(rescind)*, discontinue *(abandon)*, discontinue *(break continuity)*, forbear, forfeit, forgo, forswear, leave *(allow to remain)*, refrain, reject, relinquish, remit *(release from penalty)*, renounce, surrender *(give back)*, yield *(submit)*. SEE MAIN ENTRY
waive privilege condescend *(deign)*
waive punishment condone
waived exempt
waiver cancellation, cession, quitclaim, rejection, release, renunciation. SEE MAIN ENTRY

wake incite, inspire
wake up foment
wakeful vigilant
wakefulness diligence *(care)*
waken foment
walk patrol, perambulate
walk a beat patrol
walk away move *(alter position)*, quit *(evacuate)*
walk in enter *(go in)*
walk of life business *(occupation)*, calling, position *(business status)*, profession *(vocation)*
walk off move *(alter position)*
walk off with hold up *(rob)*, jostle *(pickpocket)*, poach
walk out quit *(evacuate)*, secede, strike *(refuse to work)*
walk through perambulate
walker pedestrian
walkout strike
wall barrier. SEE MAIN ENTRY
wall in enclose, encompass *(surround)*, envelop, restrain, restrict
wall of flame conflagration
wall up block, immure
walled in area enclosure
wallow carouse
wan disconsolate, languid
wander digress, perambulate
wander about prowl
wander aimlessly loiter
wander from the subject deviate
wanderer derelict, itinerant, migrant
wandering circuitous, discursive *(digressive)*, incoherence, indirect, itinerant, labyrinthine, lost *(disoriented)*, lunatic, moving *(in motion)*, prolix, shifting, truant, unsettled, vagrancy
wane decline, decline *(fall)*, decrease *(noun)*, decrease *(verb)*, degenerate, deteriorate, diminish, ebb, end *(termination)*, lessen, outflow, relapse, subside
waning attrition, decrease, old
want absence *(omission)*, conatus, dearth, deficiency, desideratum, desire *(noun)*, desire *(verb)*, exigency, failure *(falling short)*, foible, indigence, insufficiency, lack, market *(demand)*, need *(deprivation)*, need, paucity, poverty, privation, request, require *(need)*, requirement, requisition, will *(desire)*. SEE MAIN ENTRY
want of ability disqualification *(factor that disqualifies)*, inability
want of activity inertia
want of adaptation incompatibility *(difference)*
want of agreement incompatibility *(difference)*, incompatibility *(inconsistency)*
want of attention disinterest *(lack of interest)*
want of authority want of jurisdiction
want of capacity inability. SEE MAIN ENTRY
want of caution audacity, impropriety, temerity
want of certainty cloud *(suspicion)*
want of circumspection impropriety
want of comprehension insanity
want of confidence cloud *(suspicion)*, doubt *(indecision)*, doubt *(suspicion)*, fear, qualm
want of consideration ingratitude
want of duty laches, maladministration
want of esteem disrepute, disrespect
want of faith cloud *(suspicion)*, doubt *(indecision)*, doubt *(suspicion)*, incredulity
want of fidelity story *(falsehood)*

want of forbearance discrimination *(bigotry)*, intolerance
want of formality informality
want of harmony conflict, impugnation, inconsistency, opposition
want of integrity dishonesty
want of interest disinterest *(lack of interest)*
want of jurisdiction SEE MAIN ENTRY
want of knowledge ignorance. SEE MAIN ENTRY
want of legal capacity disability *(legal disqualification)*
want of legal qualification disability *(legal disqualification)*
want of loyalty disloyalty
want of method irregularity, pandemonium
want of moral strength frailty
want of notice disregard *(unconcern)*
want of originality platitude
want of power inability
want of principle abuse *(corrupt practice)*, bad repute, corruption, perversion
want of reason insanity
want of respect disparagement
want of sensibility insentience
want of skill disqualification *(factor that disqualifies)*, inability
want of success abortion *(fiasco)*
want of thought disregard *(lack of respect)*, disregard *(unconcern)*, negligence
want of toleration intolerance
want of transparency opacity
want of trust doubt *(suspicion)*
wantage dearth, need *(deprivation)*
wanted important *(urgent)*, indispensable, popular, requisite
wanting defective, deficient, delinquent *(overdue)*, destitute, devoid, faulty, imperfect, inadept, inadequate, insufficient, marginal, nonsubstantial *(not sufficient)*, paltry, partial *(part)*, partial *(relating to a part)*, perfunctory, poor *(inferior in quality)*, scarce, solicitous, unsatisfactory, vacuous, void *(empty)*
wanting discretion imprudent
wanting in candor disingenuous
wanting in probity dishonest, fraudulent
wanting in proportion disproportionate
wanton flagrant, hot-blooded, imprudent, lascivious, lecherous, lewd, licentious, malicious, needless, obscene, outrageous, prodigal, profuse, promiscuous, prurient, reckless, salacious, suggestive *(risqué)*, unrestrained *(not repressed)*, unruly, unscrupulous. SEE MAIN ENTRY
wanton destruction waste
wanton disregard malice
wantonly wicked conduct atrocity
wantonness delinquency *(misconduct)*, vice
war contend *(dispute)*, contest *(dispute)*, fight *(battle)*, strife
war hammer cudgel
war of words argument *(contention)*, contest *(dispute)*, fight *(argument)*
war with engage *(involve)*
ward bailiwick, charge *(custody)*, control *(supervision)*, dependent, district, division *(administrative unit)*, juvenile, minor, orphan, preservation, protect, protégé, region. SEE MAIN ENTRY
ward off avert, contain *(restrain)*, counter, debar, deter, estop, forestall, parry, prevent, repel *(drive back)*, repulse, shun, stall, stave, stop, thwart

warden caretaker (one caring for property), guardian, superintendent. SEE MAIN ENTRY

wardenship auspices, control (supervision)

warder guardian, warden

warding off defense, preventive

wardship adoption (affiliation), auspices, charge (custody), control (supervision), custody (supervision), management (supervision), preservation, protection, safekeeping

ware cargo, item

warehouse cache (storage place), depository, repository, store

wares cargo, commodities, merchandise, stock in trade

warfare belligerency, campaign, fight (battle), outbreak, strife

wariness caution (vigilance), deliberation, diligence (care), discretion (quality of being discreet), doubt (suspicion), notice (heed), precaution

warlike disorderly, inimical, litigious, malevolent, offensive (taking the initiative), pugnacious, spartan

warlikeness belligerency

warm benevolent, charitable (lenient), moving (evoking emotion)

warmhearted benevolent, humane

warmheartedness benevolence (disposition to do good)

warmth affection

warmth of feeling ardor

warn advise, alert, apprise, caution, counsel, deter, discourage, exhort, forewarn, herald, inform (notify), notice (give formal warning), notify, portend, predict, presage, remind, remonstrate, reprimand. SEE MAIN ENTRY

warn against admonish (warn)

warn beforehand forewarn

warn in advance forewarn

warned informed (having information)

warner informer (a person who provides information)

warning admonition, advice, caveat, deterrent, forerunner, harbinger, hortative, indication, indicator, intelligence (news), notification, precaution, precursor, premonition, remonstrance, remonstrative, reprimand, symptom, threat, tip (clue), ultimatum. SEE MAIN ENTRY

warning notice dun

warning sign caveat, symptom

warp corrupt, deface, distort, mutilate, pervert, predisposition, prejudice (influence), propensity, slant, tendency

warped defective, depraved, dissolute, faulty, imperfect, one-sided, peccable, tainted (corrupted), unjust, unsound (not strong)

warped idea misestimation

warped impression misestimation

warped judgment distortion, misestimation

warrant affirm (uphold), allow (authorize), assure (insure), authorize, avouch (guarantee), award, basis, bear (adduce), bind (obligate), bond, bond (secure a debt), brevet, canon, capacity (authority), certificate, certify (attest), charge (empower), citation (charge), claim (maintain), commitment (responsibility), concession (authorization), confirmation, consent (noun), consent (verb), contend (maintain), corroborate, coverage (insurance),

delegate, delegation (assignment), direction (order), dispensation (exception), draft, droit, empower, ensure, fiat, grant (concede), guarantee, guaranty, indorsement, injunction, justify, leave (permission), let (permit), license, monition (legal summons), order, permit (noun), permit (verb), pledge (promise the performance of), power, precept, prerogative, privilege, promise (vow), proof, reassure, requirement, right (entitlement), sponsor, subscribe (promise), surety (certainty), undertaking (pledge), uphold, validate, verify (swear), vouch, vow, witness (attest to). SEE MAIN ENTRY

warrant of commitment mittimus

warrantability admissibility

warrantable admissible, allowable, colorable (plausible), defensible, justifiable, licit, permissible, reasonable (rational), tenable

warrantableness admissibility, legality

warranted admissible, agreed (promised), allowed, condign, entitled, fully secured, juridical, justifiable, legal, licit, rightful, valid

warranted by law lawful

warranting advocacy

warrantor backer, surety (guarantor)

warranty assurance, bond, certainty, consent, contract, covenant, coverage (insurance), guaranty, pact, pledge (binding promise), promise, recognizance, security (pledge), specialty (contract), warrant (guaranty). SEE MAIN ENTRY

warranty against loss insurance

wartime belligerency

wary alert (vigilant), circumspect, deliberate, diffident, guarded, inconvincible, leery, noncommittal, provident (showing foresight), prudent, skeptical, suspicious (distrustful), vigilant

wash permeate

wash away purge (purify)

waspish fractious, perverse, petulant, querulous, resentful

wastage consumption, decrement, spoilage, waste, wear and tear

waste barren, bleak (exposed and barren), consume, consumption, decrement, degenerate, deplete, destroy (efface), deteriorate, diminish, discard, dissipate (expend foolishly), erode, erosion, exhaust (deplete), expend (consume), havoc, impair, lose (be deprived of), loss, misapplication, misemploy, mishandle (mismanage), mistreat, pillage, prey, prostration, spoil (pillage), spoilage. SEE MAIN ENTRY

waste away decay, diminish, ebb, languish, lessen

waste time procrastinate

wasted futile, irredeemable, lost (taken away), otiose, stale, unavailing, unsound (not strong)

wasteful barren, careless, improvident, inordinate, intemperate, needless, prodigal, profligate (extravagant), profuse, superfluous, unavailing, unproductive

wasteful expenditure misapplication

wastefulness consumption, misapplication, waste

wasting decadent, deleterious, fatal, waste

wasting away decadent

wastrel degenerate, derelict

watch charge (custody), check (inspect), concern (care), custody (supervision), har-

bor, heed, monitor, note (notice), notice (heed), notice (observe), observation, oversee, patrol, peruse, police, precaution, preserve, regard (attention), regard (pay attention), safekeeping, scrutinize, spy, superintend, surveillance, survey (examine), ward, witness (have direct knowledge of). SEE MAIN ENTRY

watch closely examine (study)

watch diligently police

watch for expect (anticipate)

watch out beware

watch out for care (be cautious)

watch over attend (take care of), care (be cautious), care (regard), cover (guard), ensconce, foster, keep (shelter), maintain (sustain), overlook (superintend), oversee, preserve, protect

watch secretly spy

watched over guarded

watcher bystander, eyewitness, spy

watchful alert (vigilant), careful, circumspect, conscious (aware), diligent, discreet, guarded, leery, meticulous, noncommittal, precise, preventive, protective, provident (showing foresight), suspicious (distrustful), vigilant

watchful care oversight (control)

watchfulness caution (vigilance), deliberation, diligence (care), discretion (quality of being discreet), notice (heed), observation, oversight (control), precaution, prudence, regard (attention), surveillance, ward

watchman caretaker (one caring for property), guardian, warden

watchword catchword, indicant, phrase

water dilute

water down denature, lessen

waterfront littoral

waterlog permeate

watermark brand

waterproof impervious

watershed crossroad (turning point)

waterside littoral

watertight impervious

wave beat (pulsate), brandish, display, flaunt, fluctuate

wave brazenly flaunt

wave conspicuously flaunt

wave ostentatiously flaunt

waver alternate (fluctuate), beat (pulsate), doubt (hesitate), fluctuate, hesitate, misdoubt, oscillate, pause, vacillate, vary

wavering capricious, doubt (indecision), dubious, faithless, hesitant, hesitation, intermittent, irresolute, irresponsible, moving (in motion), mutable, noncommittal, shifting, sporadic, undecided, undependable, unpredictable, unreliable, unsettled, untrustworthy, variable, volatile. SEE MAIN ENTRY

wax expand, inflate, proliferate, pullulate

waxen flexible

waxing inflation (increase)

way access (right of way), admission (entry), admittance (means of approach), avenue (means of attainment), avenue (route), conduct, conduit (channel), demeanor, deportment, direction (course), expedient, facility (instrumentality), form (arrangement), habit, instrumentality, key (solution), manner (behavior), method, mode, modus operandi, ploy, practice (custom), practice (procedure), presence (poise), procedure, process (course), state (condition), style, system, temperament, treatment. SEE MAIN ENTRY

way in access (*right of way*), entrance, ingress

way of acting behavior, conduct

way of approach access (*right of way*)

way of doing things design (*intent*), practice (*procedure*)

way of escape loophole

way of life behavior, modus vivendi

way of living modus vivendi

way of operation procedure

way of thinking conviction (*persuasion*), outlook, perspective, position (*point of view*), posture (*attitude*), principle (*axiom*)

way out egress, loophole, outlet

way over land easement

way through access (*right of way*)

way to ingress

wayfaring itinerant, moving (*in motion*), vagrancy

waylay accost, ambush, assail, attack, carry away, ensnare, jostle (*pickpocket*), kidnap

waymark landmark (*conspicuous object*)

ways approaches, conduct, deportment, means (*opportunity*), policy (*plan of action*), presence (*poise*)

ways and means avenue (*means of attainment*), modus operandi, process (*course*)

wayward disobedient, disorderly, dissolute, eccentric, froward, insubordinate, intractable, lawless, opposite, peccable, perverse, restive, unruly, unyielding, variable

waywardness delinquency (*misconduct*)

weak defective, deficient, dependent, fallible, harmless, helpless (*powerless*), imperfect, inactive, inadequate, incapable, inconclusive, indistinct, ineffective, ineffectual, insipid, insubstantial, insufficient, invalid, jejune (*dull*), languid, lifeless (*dull*), marginal, nonsubstantial (*not sturdy*), obscure (*faint*), poor (*inferior in quality*), powerless, unsatisfactory, unsound (*not strong*), untenable, vulnerable. SEE MAIN ENTRY

weak group minority (*outnumbered group*)

weak point disadvantage, fault (*weakness*), flaw, foible, frailty, vice

weak side foible, frailty

weak spot flaw

weak-eyed blind (*sightless*)

weak-minded caitiff

weaken adulterate, alleviate, attenuate, countervail, damage, debase, debilitate, denature, deplete, depreciate, depress, derogate, deteriorate, dilute, diminish, disable, disadvantage, disarm (*divest of arms*), encumber (*hinder*), erode, eviscerate, exhaust (*deplete*), extenuate, impair, languish, lapse (*fall into error*), lessen, moderate (*temper*), mollify, obtund, prejudice (*injure*), relapse, relax, remit (*relax*), tax (*overwork*), vitiate. SEE MAIN ENTRY

weaken in force attenuate

weaken the resolution of discourage

weakened decadent, disadvantaged, old

weakening damage, decrease, disabling, mitigation, operose, relapse

weakly nonsubstantial (*not sturdy*)

weakness caducity, defect, deficiency, detriment, disability (*physical inability*), disadvantage, disease, flaw, foible, frailty, impotence, impuissance, incapacity, inefficacy, languor, penchant, predisposition, propensity, prostration, vice

weakness of character foible

weal boom (*prosperity*), prosperity, welfare

wealth assets, boom (*prosperity*), economy (*economic system*), effects, finance, income, means (*funds*), money, personalty, possessions, principal (*capital sum*), prosperity, resource, store (*depository*), substance (*material possessions*), sufficiency. SEE MAIN ENTRY

wealthy prosperous, successful. SEE MAIN ENTRY

wean alienate (*estrange*), withdraw

wean away disaffect

weapon bomb, cudgel, gun

weaponless powerless

weapons ammunition. SEE MAIN ENTRY

wear consumption, degenerate, depreciate, endure (*last*), erode, erosion, flaunt, keep (*continue*), usage

wear and tear decrement, defacement. SEE MAIN ENTRY

wear away consume, decay, degenerate, diminish, erode, expire, languish, lessen, spend

wear down diminish, erode, harass, prevail (*persuade*), tax (*overwork*)

wear down by friction erode

wear out consume, deplete, diminish, exhaust (*deplete*), impair, misemploy, mistreat, spend, tax (*overwork*)

wear the aspect appear (*seem to be*)

weariful irksome

weariness inertia, languor, prostration

wearing chronic, irksome, operose, oppressive

wearing away attrition, erosion

wearing down by friction erosion

wearisome irksome, jejune (*dull*), lifeless (*dull*), mundane, onerous, operose, oppressive, ordinary, painful, pedestrian, ponderous, prolix, prosaic, trite, vexatious

weary exhaust (*deplete*), lugubrious, otiose, tax (*overwork*)

weary load onus (*burden*)

wearying irksome, lifeless (*dull*), operose, ponderous

weather atmosphere, bear (*tolerate*), endure (*last*), endure (*suffer*), erode, maintain (*sustain*), resist (*withstand*), withstand

weatherbeaten dilapidated

weathered old

weave incorporate (*include*)

weave a plot scheme

web intertwine, involution

wed connect (*join together*), join (*bring together*), unite

wedded composite, concurrent (*united*), conjoint, conjugal, nuptial

wedded state cohabitation (*married state*), coverture, marriage (*wedlock*), matrimony

wedded status cohabitation (*married state*)

wedded to addicted

wedding marriage (*wedlock*)

wedding a second time digamy

wedge impact

wedged inextricable

wedlock cohabitation (*married state*), matrimony

weed cannabis, delete, edit, eliminate (*exclude*), excise (*cut away*), exclude, expurgate, screen (*select*)

weed out diminish, eliminate (*eradicate*), eradicate, expel, extirpate, lessen, reject, select

ween opine, surmise

weep exude

weep over deplore, regret, repent

weeping disconsolate, outcry, repentant

weigh assess (*appraise*), brood, compare, consider, criticize (*evaluate*), debate, deliberate, determine, diagnose, digest (*comprehend*), estimate, gauge, judge, measure, muse, pause, ponder, rate, reason (*conclude*), reflect (*ponder*), review, speculate (*conjecture*), study, survey (*examine*). SEE MAIN ENTRY

weigh against countervail

weigh down disadvantage, encumber (*hinder*), load, overcome (*overwhelm*), overload, overwhelm, tax (*overwork*)

weigh in the mind deliberate

weigh more than outweigh

weigh on harass

weigh on the mind obsess

weigh out mete

weighable appreciable, ponderable

weighed deliberate, tactical

weighing contemplation, deliberation, discrimination (*differentiation*), estimation (*calculation*), judgment (*discernment*), reflection (*thought*)

weight burden, clout, corpus, degree (*magnitude*), dint, dominance, eminence, emphasis, import, importance, incumbrance (*burden*), influence, interest (*concern*), load, magnitude, materiality (*consequence*), onus (*burden*), power, predominance, pressure, prestige, primacy, significance, stress (*accent*). SEE MAIN ENTRY

weight of numbers majority (*greater part*), plurality

weight of the evidence SEE MAIN ENTRY

weighted inequitable, unfair

weightiness import, importance, interest (*concern*), magnitude, materiality (*consequence*), significance

weightless intangible

weighty cogent, compelling, consequential (*substantial*), critical (*crucial*), determinative, dominant, grave (*important*), important (*significant*), key, major, material (*important*), momentous, onerous, oppressive, persuasive, ponderous, potent, powerful, predominant, prevailing (*having superior force*), prominent, serious (*grave*), solid (*sound*), sound, urgent

weird mysterious, peculiar (*curious*), prodigious (*amazing*), uncanny

welcome desirable (*pleasing*), embrace (*accept*), palatable, sapid

welcoming receptive

weld cement, join (*bring together*), lock, merge

welded conjoint, inseparable

welfare advantage, behalf, benefit (*betterment*), boom (*prosperity*). SEE MAIN ENTRY

well fund, source

well based well-grounded

well being prosperity

well defined visible (*in full view*)

well done professional (*stellar*)

well enough fairly (*moderately*)

well established fixed (*settled*)

well founded well-grounded

well off prosperous. SEE MAIN ENTRY

well provided for opulent

well thought of popular, reputable

well thought out strategic

well to do prosperous

well-acquainted familiar (*informed*)

well-adapted apposite, politic

well-advised cognizant, discreet, discriminating *(judicious)*, juridical, politic, prudent, reasonable *(rational)*, sensible

well-armed armed

well-balanced proportionate

well-based authentic, true *(authentic)*

well-behaved civil *(polite)*, malleable, obedient

well-being benefit *(betterment)*, boom *(prosperity)*, health, welfare. SEE MAIN ENTRY

well-bred civil *(polite)*, proper

well-brought up civil *(polite)*

well-built solid *(sound)*, stable, strong

well-chosen felicitous

well-chosen moment crossroad *(turning point)*

well-conducted moral

well-considered aforethought, circumspect, deliberate, judicious, premeditated

well-constructed solid *(sound)*

well-defined absolute *(conclusive)*, accurate, certain *(specific)*, clear *(apparent)*, coherent *(clear)*, conspicuous, definite, distinct *(clear)*, manifest, obvious, perceivable, perceptible, precise, tangible, unambiguous, unmistakable

well-deserved condign

well-developed explicit, ripe

well-devised politic, premeditated

well-disciplined spartan

well-disposed inclined, peaceable, prone, propitious

well-doer benefactor

well-done meritorious, right *(suitable)*

well-drawn descriptive, distinct *(clear)*

well-earned condign

well-educated cognizant, familiar *(informed)*, informed *(educated)*, learned, literate

well-established ingrained, solid *(sound)*

well-expressed felicitous

well-fitted competent, fit

well-fixed opulent

well-founded actual, authentic, axiomatic, believable, cogent, convincing, de facto, legitimate *(rightful)*, presumptive, provable, reasonable *(rational)*, solid *(sound)*, sound, tenable, true *(authentic)*. SEE MAIN ENTRY

well-founded opinion conviction *(persuasion)*

well-grounded actual, authentic, believable, cogent, cognizant, convincing, credible, de facto, informed *(educated)*, justifiable, legitimate *(rightful)*, presumptive, provable, rational, solid *(sound)*, sound, stable, tenable, true *(authentic)*, valid. SEE MAIN ENTRY

well-grounded hope likelihood, prospect *(outlook)*

well-grounded possibility likelihood

well-informed cognizant, knowing, learned, literate, omniscient, politic

well-intentioned benevolent, meritorious, propitious

well-judged politic

well-knit cohesive *(compact)*

well-known blatant *(conspicuous)*, common *(customary)*, customary, familiar *(customary)*, famous, household *(familiar)*, illustrious, important *(significant)*, influential, master, mundane, prevailing *(current)*, prevalent, prominent, proverbial, public *(known)*, renowned, reputable, salient, trite, usual. SEE MAIN ENTRY

well-liked popular

well-made solid *(sound)*, strong

well-mannered civil *(polite)*

well-marked clear *(apparent)*, coherent *(clear)*, conspicuous, definite, distinct *(clear)*, manifest, perceivable, perceptible, prominent

well-matched concurrent *(united)*, uniform

well-meaning benevolent, propitious

well-meant benevolent

well-off opulent, successful

well-ordered systematic

well-organized systematic

well-paying gainful, lucrative, profitable

well-performed right *(suitable)*

well-planned artful, tactical

well-pleased proud *(self-respecting)*

well-populated populous

well-posted knowing

well-principled honest, law-abiding

well-provided copious, full, replete

well-qualified expert, fit, practiced, professional *(trained)*, proficient

well-read cognizant, informed *(educated)*, learned, literate

well-received popular

well-recognized household *(familiar)*, influential

well-regarded influential

well-regulated regular *(orderly)*, right *(suitable)*, systematic

well-rounded informed *(educated)*, learned

well-satisfied proud *(self-respecting)*

well-seen clear *(apparent)*, conspicuous, manifest, prominent

well-situated opulent, prosperous, successful

well-spoken civil *(polite)*

well-stocked copious, full, replete

well-suited appropriate, fit, qualified *(competent)*, sciential

well-supplied full, rife

well-taught learned, literate

well-thought-out tactical

well-timed felicitous, fit, opportune, punctual, seasonable

well-timed initiative crossroad *(turning point)*

well-to-do opulent, successful

well-trained learned

well-trodden familiar *(customary)*, mundane, ordinary, routine, usual

well-versed cognizant, familiar *(informed)*, informed *(educated)*, knowing, proficient

well-wisher proponent, samaritan

well-worn ordinary

well-written cognizable

wellhead source

wellspring origin *(source)*, origination, source

welter commotion, imbroglio, shambles, turmoil

wergild reparation *(indemnification)*

whack lash *(strike)*

whatever SEE MAIN ENTRY

whatsoever whatever.. SEE MAIN ENTRY

wheedle inveigle

whelm overcome *(overwhelm)*

when ad interim, whenever

whenever SEE MAIN ENTRY

whereabouts locality, scene. SEE MAIN ENTRY

whereby hereby, thereby. SEE MAIN ENTRY

wherefore consequently, reason *(basis)*

wherein herein. SEE MAIN ENTRY

whereon wherein

whereupon wherein

wherewithal assets, expedient, instrumentality, means *(funds)*, means *(opportunity)*, money, resource, substance *(material possessions)*, sufficiency

whet stimulate, stimulus

whet one's interest interest

whichever whatever

while ad interim, duration, period. SEE MAIN ENTRY

whilom former

whim notion

whimpering querulous

whimsical arbitrary and capricious, capricious, original *(creative)*

whine plaint

whiner malcontent

whining querulous

whiny petulant, querulous

whip beat *(strike)*, churn, punish

whirl commotion

whisper imply, report *(rumor)*, suggestion, tip *(clue)*

whit iota, minimum, scintilla

white clean

whittle abridge *(shorten)*, diminish

whiz race

whoever SEE MAIN ENTRY

whole absolute *(complete)*, aggregate, amount *(quantity)*, collective, corpus, detailed, entirety, full, gross *(total)*, intact, inviolate, plenary, principal *(capital sum)*, pure, radical *(extreme)*, safe, total, totality, undiminished. SEE MAIN ENTRY

whole attention diligence *(care)*, obsession

whole mind diligence *(care)*

whole range gamut

wholeness body *(collection)*, corpus, entirety, finality, sum *(total)*, whole

wholesale destruction conflagration

wholesale trader dealer

wholesaler dealer

wholesome clean, remedial, salubrious, salutary, unaffected *(sincere)*

wholesomeness health

wholly in toto, solely *(singly)*. SEE MAIN ENTRY

wholly inadequate SEE MAIN ENTRY

whomever whoever

whomsoever whoever

whopping prodigious *(enormous)*

whorled circuitous

whosoever whoever

wicked arrant *(onerous)*, bad *(offensive)*, base *(bad)*, contemptible, delinquent *(guilty of a misdeed)*, depraved, diabolic, felonious, harmful, heinous, ignoble, illicit, immoral, impermissible, incorrigible, inexpiable, iniquitous, irregular *(improper)*, malevolent, malicious, malignant, nefarious, outrageous, peccant *(culpable)*, pernicious, perverse, profane, profligate *(corrupt)*, reprehensible, reprobate, scandalous, sinister, tainted *(corrupted)*, unjust, unjustifiable, unscrupulous, vicious. SEE MAIN ENTRY

wicked action misdeed

wicked deed misdeed, misdemeanor, misdoing

wickedness atrocity, corruption, delinquency *(misconduct)*, dishonor *(shame)*, disrepute, mischief, misdoing, perversion, turpitude, vice, wrong

wide broad, capacious, comprehensive, copious, extensive, far reaching, generic, inclusive, liberal *(not literal)*, open *(unclosed)*

wide awake vigilant

wide currency coverage *(scope)*

wide of the mark improper

wide open penetrable

wide-awake careful

wide-embracing complete *(all-embracing)*

wide-open open-ended, patent

wide-reaching comprehensive, extensive, omnibus

widely accepted prevailing *(current)*, prevalent

widely extended extensive

widely known common *(customary)*, household *(familiar)*, illustrious, prevalent, proverbial, public *(known)*, trite

widely read informed *(educated)*, learned, literate

widely recognized predominant

widely used conventional

widen accrue *(increase)*, compound, deploy, develop, enlarge, expand, extend *(enlarge)*, increase, magnify, project *(extend beyond)*, spread, supplement

widening augmentation, cumulative *(increasing)*, extension *(expansion)*

widespread broad, collective, common *(customary)*, comprehensive, current, extensive, familiar *(customary)*, far reaching, general, household *(familiar)*, omnibus, ordinary, predominant, prevailing *(current)*, prevalent, rampant, rife. SEE MAIN ENTRY

widow's estate dower

widow's portion dower

width caliber *(measurement)*, extent, gamut

wield brandish, employ *(make use of)*, exercise *(use)*, exert, exploit *(make use of)*, handle *(manage)*, manipulate *(utilize skillfully)*, militate, ply. SEE MAIN ENTRY

wield authority govern, handle *(manage)*, manage, preside

wield influence prevail upon

wield restraint over hold *(possess)*

wielding power forcible

wieldy flexible

wife consort, spouse

wifedom coverture

wild disobedient, disorderly, ill-judged, licentious, ludicrous, lunatic, outrageous, precipitate, promiscuous, rampant, reckless, uncontrollable, unrestrained *(not repressed)*, unruly, vehement

wild being animal

wild confusion riot

wild uproar pandemonium

wild-fire conflagration

wildness furor, irregularity, pandemonium, violence

wile artifice, bunko, contrivance, deception, device *(contrivance)*, false pretense, hoax, imposture, machination, maneuver *(trick)*, ploy, pretext, ruse, stratagem

wiles knavery

wiliness artifice, dishonesty, fraud

will animus, choose, conatus, contribute *(supply)*, decision *(election)*, demise, descend, design *(intent)*, desire, determine, discretion *(power of choice)*, elect *(choose)*, forethought, give *(grant)*, latitude, leave *(give)*, predetermination, purpose, resolution *(decision)*, resolve *(decide)*, tenacity, testament, volition. SEE MAIN ENTRY

will addendum codicil

will and bequeath descend, devise *(give)*

will power discipline *(obedience)*, resolution *(decision)*

will supplement codicil

will to bequeath, devise *(give)*

will validation proceeding probate

will verification proceeding probate

willed deliberate

willful arbitrary and capricious, deliberate, disobedient, express, froward, hot-blooded, inexorable, inflexible, intentional, intractable, obdurate, pertinacious, premeditated, purposeful, recalcitrant, restive, spontaneous, unbending, uncontrollable, unruly, unyielding, voluntary. SEE MAIN ENTRY

willful abandonment desertion

willful burning of property arson

willful disregard contempt *(disobedience to the court)*

willful distortion of the truth perjury

willful falsehood perjury

willful telling of a falsehood perjury

willful telling of a lie perjury

willfully purposely

willfully contrary froward

willfully disregard ignore

willfully disrespectful contumacious

willfulness forethought

willing available, consenting, eager, favorable *(expressing approval)*, inclined, malleable, obedient, obeisant, pliable, pliant, prone, receptive, resigned, solicitous, tractable, zealous. SEE MAIN ENTRY

willing consent assent

willing help aid *(help)*, charity

willing to forgive lenient, placable

willing to yield to influence of others flexible

willingly purposely, readily

willingness acquiescence, adhesion *(loyalty)*, amenability, assent, conformity *(obedience)*, consent, deference, goodwill, predisposition, sanction *(permission)*, volition. SEE MAIN ENTRY

willingness to comply compliance

willingness to forgive clemency, condonation

willingness to please consideration *(sympathetic regard)*

willingness to purchase market *(demand)*

willowy flexible

willpower strength

wilt languish, perish

wilted dilapidated, stale

wily artful, collusive, deceptive, delusive, devious, disingenuous, fraudulent, insidious, machiavellian, politic, sly, subtle *(insidious)*, surreptitious

wily device contrivance, machination

win acquire *(receive)*, carry *(succeed)*, earn, gain, inveigle, obtain, prevail *(triumph)*, reap, receive *(acquire)*, succeed *(attain)*

win an argument convert *(persuade)*

win back recoup *(regain)*, recover

win over convert *(persuade)*, convince, disarm *(set at ease)*, persuade, placate, prejudice *(influence)*, prevail *(persuade)*, prevail upon, propitiate, reason *(persuade)*, reconcile

win the battle beat *(defeat)*

wind contort

wind up close *(terminate)*, complete, expire, finish, terminate

windfall profit

winding circuitous, indirect, labyrinthine, sinuous, tortuous *(bending)*

window-dressing pretense *(ostentation)*

windup close *(conclusion)*, defeasance, denouement

windy loquacious, orotund

wing affiliate, organ, protection

winged rapid

winning popular, prevailing *(having superior force)*, prize, sapid, successful

winning over persuasion

winnings earnings, profit, spoils, stake *(award)*

winnow cull, distinguish, screen *(select)*, select, separate

winsome sapid

wipe away deface, expunge

wipe off expunge

wipe out delete, destroy *(efface)*, dissolve *(terminate)*, eliminate *(eradicate)*, expunge, extinguish, extirpate, obliterate, rescind, revoke, stop

wipe out illiteracy educate

wiretap eavesdrop

wiry resilient, strong

wisdom caliber *(mental capacity)*, cognition, common sense, comprehension, discretion *(quality of being discreet)*, experience *(background)*, information *(knowledge)*, insight, intelligence *(intellect)*, knowledge *(learning)*, reason *(sound judgment)*, sagacity, sense *(intelligence)*, understanding *(comprehension)*. SEE MAIN ENTRY

wise cognizant, conduct, discreet, discriminating *(judicious)*, expert, favorable *(advantageous)*, fit, judicial, judicious, learned, manner *(behavior)*, omniscient, oracular, perceptive, perspicacious, politic, profound *(esoteric)*, prudent, rational, reasonable *(rational)*, sapient, sensible, solid *(sound)*

wise man mastermind

wise saying maxim

wiseness sense *(intelligence)*

wish conatus, desire, end *(intent)*, market *(demand)*, predisposition, purpose, request, volition, will *(desire)*

wish for desire, lack

wishful eager

wistful pensive

with along

with a high degree of certainty high probability

with a valid will testate

with alacrity expeditious

with all reasonable speed forthwith

with all respect respectfully

with allegiance faithfully

with an executed will testate

with an iron hand dictatorial

with assurance fairly *(clearly)*

with authority as a matter of right

with cause for cause

with certainty fairly *(clearly)*

with compliance respectfully

with confidence fairly *(clearly)*

with constancy faithfully

with deference respectfully

with dispatch expeditious

with due deference respectfully

with due respect respectfully

with fealty faithfully

with fidelity faithfully

with force of law obligatory

with forethought aforethought, deliberate, express, premeditated, purposely

with free will purposely
with full effect in full force
with full force in full force
with funds solvent
with good credit solvent
with good faith faithfully
with intent purposely
with justice fairly (impartially)
with justification for cause
with knowledge knowingly
with license liberal (not literal)
with meager funds poor (underprivileged)
with means opulent
with no exception complete (all-embracing), total
with no mistake exact
with nothing missing intact
with premeditation purposely
with reasonable dispatch forthwith, immediate (at once)
with reference to apposite, comparative, pertinent
with regard to comparative
with relation to comparative
with scanty funds poor (underprivileged)
with secret design clandestine
with simplicity ingenuous
with speed expeditious, instantly
with the aid of thereby
with the end in sight determinable (liable to be terminated)
with the greater force a fortiori
with the highest respect respectfully
with the stipulation provided
with the understanding provided
with this proviso provided
with validity de facto
withdraw abolish, abscond, adeem, annul, cancel, cease, debar, deduct (reduce), demit, depart, diminish, disavow, discontinue (abandon), disengage, disinherit, disinter, dissociate, ebb, evacuate, excise (cut away), extract, flee, forfeit, hold up (rob), invalidate, leave (depart), part (leave), quash, quit (discontinue), quit (evacuate), recall (call back), recant, recess, refrain, refuse, relinquish, remove (eliminate), renege, repeal, repudiate, rescind, resign, retire (retreat), retreat, revoke, secede, seclude, sequester (seclude), superannuate, vacate (leave). SEE MAIN ENTRY
withdraw clandestinely abscond
withdraw from eschew, forgo, forswear, stop
withdraw from association disband
withdraw from observation conceal
withdraw from one's native land expatriate
withdraw one's objections concede
withdraw one's support defect
withdraw the affections of alienate (estrange), disaffect
withdrawal abandonment (desertion), abandonment (discontinuance), abdication, absence (nonattendance), ademption, alienation (estrangement), cancellation, cloture, countermand, deduction (diminution), defeasance, discontinuance (act of discontinuing), discontinuance (interruption of a legal action), egress, estrangement, evulsion, exception (exclusion), outflow, privacy, recess, removal, renunciation, repudiation, rescision, resignation (relinquishment), retraction, revocation, schism, severance

withdrawal of a sentence reprieve
withdrawal of the charge compurgation, exoneration
withdrawing cancellation
withdrawment ademption
withdrawn inarticulate, null (invalid), null and void, taciturn, unapproachable. SEE MAIN ENTRY
wither decay, decline (fall), degenerate, diminish, languish, perish
withered ineffective, ineffectual, stale
withering bitter (penetrating), consumption, decadent, dilapidated, harsh, regressive, scathing, supercilious
withheld arrested (checked)
withhold arrest (stop), condemn (ban), constrain (restrain), constrict (inhibit), debar, defer (put off), deny (refuse to grant), disinherit, forbear, hamper, hide, hoard, hold up (delay), inhibit, keep (restrain), refrain, repress, reserve, restrain, retain (keep in possession), stifle, strangle. SEE MAIN ENTRY
withhold action forbear
withhold approval disaccord, disallow
withhold approval from disapprove (reject)
withhold assent demur, differ (disagree), differ (vary), disaccord, disbelieve, expostulate, hold out (resist)
withhold consent disoblige, forbid, hold out (resist), refuse
withhold judgment doubt (hesitate), misdoubt
withhold one's assent disapprove (reject)
withhold payment default, dishonor (refuse to pay)
withhold permission ban, censor, disapprove (reject), forbid
withhold reliance doubt (distrust)
withholding reservation (engagement)
withholding approval dissenting
withholding assent dissenting
withholding of patronage boycott
within herein, wherein
within appropriate time provided timeliness
within boundary lines internal
within bounds fairly (moderately)
within reach available, disposable, facile, open (accessible), passable, possible, practicable, present (attendant)
within reason fairly (moderately)
within sight of almost
within the bounds of possiblity practicable
within the law allowed, de jure, jural, juridical, law-abiding, lawful, legal, legitimate (rightful), licit, permissible, rightful, statutory
within the range of possibility possible
within the realm of possibility plausible, possible
withold conceal
withold information conceal
without devoid, peripheral, save, unless
without a bend direct (straight)
without a name anonymous
without a penny poor (underprivileged)
without a preference impartial
without a shade of doubt categorical
without a shred of evidence SEE MAIN ENTRY
without a sign of life dead
without a stain clean
without a wait instantly

without adequate ability incompetent
without adequate determining principle arbitrary
without aid helpless (defenseless)
without airs unpretentious
without animation languid
without any lapse of time instantly
without appeal categorical, final, irrevocable, mandatory, obligatory
without assent unwillingly
without authority illegal, illicit, null (invalid), null and void, powerless, unofficial
without base baseless
without basis baseless, gratuitous (unwarranted), ill-founded, illogical, insubstantial, unfounded, unsupported
without bearings lost (disoriented)
without belief incredulous, leery
without bias fairly (impartially)
without blame blameless
without blemish infallible
without body incorporeal
without bound indeterminate, profuse
without cause baseless
without caution reckless
without ceasing incessant
without ceremony informal, unofficial
without cessation continuous
without charge gratis, gratuitous (given without recompense)
without choice compulsory, mandatory, obligatory
without circumlocution direct (straight)
without companions solitary
without company solitary
without comparison best, prime (most valuable)
without compensation gratuitous (given without recompense)
without compulsion voluntary
without concern perfunctory
without conditions unconditional
without confusion simple
without connection foreign, impertinent (irrelevant), irrelative
without consent involuntary, unwillingly
without consequence null (insignificant)
without consideration arbitrary, gratis, gratuitous (given without recompense), heedless, oblivious, thoughtless
without constraint voluntary
without content devoid
without contents void (empty)
without context alien (unrelated)
without cost free (at no charge)
without current stagnant
without date sine die
without deductions gross (total)
without defect unblemished
without defense blameful, blameworthy, inexcusable, inexpiable
without delay as soon as feasible, immediate (at once), instant, instantaneous, instantly, prompt
without depth immaterial
without dexterity inadept
without difference equivalent, same
without distinction comparable (equivalent), fairly (impartially), identical
without divergence direct (straight)
without doubt decisive, definitive, demonstrable, indubious, undisputed
without effect ineffective, ineffectual
without employment unemployed
without end ad infinitum, durable, indeterminate, infinite, permanent, perpetual, profuse

without enthusiasm   perfunctory
without equal   inestimable
without error   exact
without exaggeration   literal
without exception   invariably
without excuse   blameful, inexcusable, inexpiable, peccant *(culpable)*, unjustifiable
without exit   blind *(impassable)*
without experience   inexperienced
without faith   inconvincible, incredulous, leery
without fault   blameless
without favor   fairly *(impartially)*
without favoritism   impartial
without force   helpless *(powerless)*, insipid, languid, nonsubstantial *(not sturdy)*, powerless
without foresight   improvident
without form   intangible
without formality   informal
without foundation   gratuitous *(unwarranted)*, ill-founded, illogical, insubstantial, nonsubstantial *(not sturdy)*, unfounded, unsupported
without funds   impecunious
without guile   ingenuous
without harm   innocent
without heart   cold-blooded
without hesitation   instantly
without honor   perfidious, recreant
without hope   irredeemable
without insight   blind *(not discerning)*
without integrity   immoral, unscrupulous
without interruption   continuous, incessant
without issue   barren
without judgment   irrational
without judicial authority   want of jurisdiction
without knowledge   inexperienced
without law   lawless
without legal authority   illegally
without legal effect   null *(invalid)*, null and void
without legal efficacy   invalid
without legal force   null *(invalid)*, null and void, void *(invalid)*
without legal sanction   illegally
without life   dead, defunct, lifeless *(dead)*
without limit   indeterminate, infinite, profuse
without limitation   peremptory *(absolute)*
without limits   open-ended
without loss   intact, undiminished, whole *(undamaged)*
without meaning   null *(insignificant)*
without measure   indeterminate, infinite
without method   disordered
without modesty   proud *(conceited)*
without monetary inducement   gratis
without monetary reward   gratis
without money   impecunious
without motion   stagnant
without nerves   dispassionate
without notice   instantly, unaware
without novelty   stale
without number   infinite, myriad, unlimited
without offense   innocent
without omission   in toto, total
without omissions   complete *(all-embracing)*
without order   haphazard
without originality   sequacious
without parallel   paramount, superlative
without particularizing   generally
without pecuniary gain   gratis

without perceptible time lapse   instantaneous
without physical substance   intangible
without pity   ruthless
without plausibility   insubstantial
without potency   null *(invalid)*, null and void
without power of appeal   inappealable
without power of choice   involuntary
without power to harm   innocuous
without precision   inexact
without prejudice   fairly *(impartially)*
without price   inestimable, invaluable, priceless
without probity   dishonest, fraudulent
without prudence   impulsive *(rash)*, reckless
without qualification   absolute *(complete)*
without question   decisive, definitive, indubious, undisputed
without rational basis   capricious
without reality   baseless, insubstantial, unfounded
without reason   arbitrary, baseless, irrational, ludicrous
without recompense   gratis
without recourse   SEE MAIN ENTRY
without reference   irrespective
without reference to   irrelevant
without regard   insusceptible *(uncaring)*
without regard to   regardless. SEE MAIN ENTRY
without regrets   relentless
without relation   alien *(unrelated)*, heterogeneous, irrelative
without reliance in   suspect *(distrust)*
without reproach   blameless, clean
without repute   notorious
without reservations   unconditional
without reserve   categorical, demonstrative *(expressive of emotion)*
without resources   destitute, devoid
without respect or regard to   irrespective
without respect to   regardless
without restraint   inordinate. SEE MAIN ENTRY
without results   unproductive
without reward   gratis
without rhyme or reason   irrational
without risk   harmless, immune, nontoxic, safe
without scruples   unscrupulous
without shame   unabashed
without significance   null *(insignificant)*
without sound basis   ill-founded
without specified limits   open-ended
without spirit   languid
without stain   unblemished
without stint   profuse
without stopping   incessant
without strings   unrestricted
without substance   ill-founded, immaterial, incorporeal, null *(insignificant)*, unfounded
without substantial cause   arbitrary
without succor   helpless *(defenseless)*
without suspicion   unsuspecting
without taste   inelegant, insipid
without tendency to harm   innocuous
without the appearance of life   dead
without the name of the author   anonymous
without thought   impulsive *(rash)*
without truth   dishonest, disingenuous, fraudulent

without value   null *(invalid)*, null and void
without vanity   diffident
without vitality   powerless
without warmth   cold-blooded, dispassionate
without warranty   as is
without weight   immaterial, ineffective, ineffectual
without will   involuntary
withstand   allow *(endure)*, collide *(clash)*, counteract, defy, endure *(last)*, endure *(suffer)*, hold out *(resist)*, last, parry, repel *(drive back)*, repulse. SEE MAIN ENTRY
withstanding   resistance
witless   fatuous, irrational, obtuse, opaque
witlessly   unknowingly
witness   attest, avow, bystander, bystander, corroboration, declarant, deponent, depose *(testify)*, discern *(detect with the senses)*, indicator, informant, notarize, note *(notice)*, notice *(observe)*, perceive, pierce *(discern)*, regard *(pay attention)*, subscribe *(sign)*, verify *(swear)*, vouch. SEE MAIN ENTRY
witness against   informer *(one providing criminal information)*
witness as to character   bystander
witness box   stand *(witness' place in court)*
witness stand   stand *(witness' place in court)*
witness to   bear *(adduce)*
witness to a crime   bystander
witness who gives testimony   deponent
witnessing   attestation, observation, reference *(recommendation)*
wittingly   knowingly, purposely
witty   jocular
wizardry   prowess *(ability)*
wobbly   insubstantial, nonsubstantial *(not sturdy)*
woe   disaster, distress *(anguish)*, pain, plaint, tragedy
woebegone   disconsolate, lugubrious
woeful   blameworthy, dire, disconsolate, lamentable, lugubrious, regrettable
wolfish   predatory, rapacious
womanhood   majority *(adulthood)*
wonder   phenomenon *(unusual occurrence)*, reflect *(ponder)*, surprise
wonder about   ponder, speculate *(conjecture)*
wonderful   meritorious, noteworthy, portentous *(eliciting amazement)*, prodigious *(amazing)*, remarkable, special
wondering   incredulous
wonderment   phenomenon *(unusual occurrence)*, surprise
wonderwork   phenomenon *(unusual occurrence)*
wondrous   noteworthy, portentous *(eliciting amazement)*, prodigious *(amazing)*, remarkable
wont   custom, manner *(behavior)*, usage
wonted   boiler plate, conventional, customary, familiar *(customary)*, habitual, inveterate, ordinary, orthodox, prescriptive, prevailing *(current)*, regular *(conventional)*, usual
wontedness   custom
woo   persuade, prevail *(persuade)*
wooden   rigid
word   canon, disclosure *(something disclosed)*, intelligence *(news)*, phrase, pledge *(binding promise)*, profession *(declaration)*, promise, remark, term *(expression)*, undertaking *(pledge)*, vow. SEE MAIN ENTRY

word for word faithfully, literal, verbatim *(adjective)*, verbatim *(adverb)*

word group phrase

word of command instruction *(direction)*

word of explanation comment, note *(brief comment)*

word of honor pledge *(binding promise)*, profession *(declaration)*, vow

word picture delineation

wordage language, parlance

wordiness fustian, prolixity

wording language, phraseology, rhetoric *(skilled speech)*

wordless mute, speechless, tacit

wordlessness silence

words speech

wordy flatulent, loquacious, profuse, prolific, prolix, redundant, turgid, voluble

work activity, appointment *(position)*, assignment *(task)*, burden, business *(occupation)*, calling, career, cultivate, duty *(obligation)*, effectuate, employ *(make use of)*, employment, endeavor, exert, exploit *(make use of)*, function *(noun)*, function *(verb)*, industry *(activity)*, industry *(business)*, job, labor, livelihood, manage, manipulate *(utilize skillfully)*, militate, mission, occupation *(vocation)*, office, operate, perform *(execute)*, performance *(execution)*, performance *(workmanship)*, perpetrate, ply, position *(business status)*, post, profession *(vocation)*, publication *(printed matter)*, pursuit *(occupation)*, role, strive, struggle, wield. SEE MAIN ENTRY

work a change adapt, affect

work a cure remedy

work against antagonize, collide *(clash)*, counter, counteract, countervail, fight *(counteract)*, hinder, interfere

work as a team cooperate, federalize *(associate)*

work at endeavor, occupy *(engage)*, practice *(engage in)*, practice *(train by repetition)*

work at cross purposes counter

work done fait accompli

work evil mistreat

work for foster, help, pursue *(strive to gain)*, serve *(assist)*

work for a judge clerk

work for hire SEE MAIN ENTRY

work force personnel

work hard labor, strive

work in interject, intersperse

work in the service of pander

work in unison combine *(act in concert)*

work into a passion incense, provoke

work jointly concur *(agree)*

work on lobby, treat *(process)*

work out calculate, compose, devise *(invent)*, dispatch *(dispose of)*, fix *(settle)*, implement, maneuver, negotiate, perpetrate, plan, plot, program, scheme, settle, solve

work out differences mediate

work out in detail develop

work over emend, modify *(alter)*, redact, revise

work party personnel

work place office

work side by side with cooperate

work stoppage lockout, strike

work to excess overload

work together combine *(act in concert)*, consolidate *(unite)*, cooperate, federalize *(associate)*, involve *(participate)*, participate

work toward conduce

work unceasingly adhere *(persist)*, persevere, persist

work unflaggingly persevere, persist

work up churn, compose, foment, frame *(formulate)*, perturb, pique, provoke, scheme, stimulate

work upon affect, constrain *(compel)*, influence, motivate

workability feasibility, potential

workable demonstrable, determinable *(ascertainable)*, fit, functional, operative, possible, potential, practicable, practical, solvable, viable

workableness feasibility

workaday household *(familiar)*, ordinary, prevailing *(current)*, regular *(conventional)*, usual

workday mundane

worked up frenetic

worker apprentice, artisan, employee

worker of iniquity criminal, delinquent

workers personnel, staff

workfellow contributor *(contributor)*, partner

working active, effective *(operative)*, functional, operative

working ability performance *(workmanship)*

working arrangement modus vivendi

working assets capital, cash

working capital finance, money, principal *(capital sum)*

working in concert association *(connection)*

working people personnel

working plan device *(contrivance)*, method

working proposition device *(contrivance)*

working together coaction, connivance

workingman artisan

workingwoman artisan

workless idle, unemployed

workman artisan, employee

workwoman artisan

world-wide nonsectarian, ubiquitous. SEE MAIN ENTRY

world-wise veteran

worldliness experience *(background)*

worldly civil *(public)*, material *(physical)*, mundane, physical, profane

worldly belongings possessions

worldly substance effects

worldly wisdom common sense

worldly-minded mundane

worldwide prevailing *(current)*, prevalent, rife

worn dilapidated, old, trite, unsound *(not strong)*

worn out decadent, dilapidated, old, stale, trite

worrisome problematic

worry agitate *(perturb)*, apprehension *(fear)*, badger, bait *(harass)*, concern *(interest)*, discommode, discompose, distress *(anguish)*, distress, disturb, embarrass, fear, harry *(harass)*, hector, interest *(concern)*, mistreat, molest *(annoy)*, nuisance, pain, perplex, perturb, pique, plague, press *(goad)*, qualm. SEE MAIN ENTRY

worsen aggravate *(exacerbate)*, decay, degenerate, depreciate, deteriorate, exacerbate, harm, impair

worsening aggravation *(exacerbation)*

worship honor *(outward respect)*, regard *(hold in esteem)*, respect

worshiped sacrosanct

worshipful solemn

worst dire, subdue, subject, upset

worth advantage, amount *(sum)*, benefit *(betterment)*, caliber *(quality)*, charge *(cost)*, connotation, credit *(recognition)*, emphasis, estimate *(approximate cost)*, expense *(cost)*, face value *(price)*, magnitude, materiality *(consequence)*, merit, par *(face amount)*, prestige, price, quality *(excellence)*, quality *(grade)*, rate, respect, significance, signification, value. SEE MAIN ENTRY

worth a great deal opulent

worth considering material *(important)*

worth imitating meritorious

worthiness expedience, honesty, integrity, merit, qualification *(fitness)*, rectitude, right *(righteousness)*, value, worth

worthless barren, contemptible, delinquent *(guilty of a misdeed)*, expendable, frivolous, futile, ignoble, immaterial, inconsequential, inconsiderable, ineffective, ineffectual, insubstantial, needless, nugatory, null *(insignificant)*, null *(invalid)*, null and void, otiose, paltry, petty, poor *(inferior in quality)*, reprobate, trivial, unable, unavailing, unproductive, unsound *(fallacious)*, unworthy

worthless argument fallacy

worthless check bad check

worthless person degenerate

worthless trial mistrial

worthlessness immateriality

worthwhile beneficial, gainful, laudable, lucrative, meritorious, productive, profitable, purposeful

worthy capable, condign, constructive *(creative)*, desirable *(qualified)*, entitled, exemplary, fit, high-minded, justifiable, laudable, meritorious, moral, premium, qualified *(competent)*, reputable, scrupulous, sterling, suitable, unimpeachable, upright, valuable

worthy of attention extraordinary

worthy of belief authentic, credible, fiduciary

worthy of blame culpable, sinister

worthy of choice preferable, qualified *(competent)*

worthy of confidence credible, loyal, official

worthy of consideration considerable, major

worthy of contempt disgraceful

worthy of credence convincing, credible, fiduciary, plausible

worthy of estimation laudable

worthy of fame meritorious

worthy of imitation exemplary

worthy of note remarkable

worthy of notice influential, notable, noteworthy, paramount, salient

worthy of praise meritorious

worthy of regard extraordinary

worthy of remark major, notable, noteworthy, paramount, salient

worthy of trust reliable

would-be specious

wound damage, disable, harm, inflict, infliction, maim, mistreat, mutilate, offend *(insult)*, prejudice *(injure)*, provoke

wound the feelings affront

woundable vulnerable

wounded aggrieved *(harmed)*, marred

wounded pride resentment

wounding harmful, offensive *(offending)*

woven compound

wrack prostration

wraith phantom

wrangle altercation, argument (contention), belligerency, bicker, brawl (noun), brawl (verb), challenge, collide (clash), conflict (noun), conflict (verb), confront (oppose), confrontation (altercation), contend (dispute), contest (dispute), contravention, controversy (argument), debate, dicker, disaccord, disagree, dispute, dispute (debate), dissidence, fight (argument), fracas, haggle, oppugn, strife

wrangler disputant, malcontent

wrangling altercation, argument (contention), contention (opposition), contentious, discord, dissension, dissenting, hostile

wrap clothe, cover (guard), encompass (surround), ensconce, enshroud, envelop, hide, obnubilate, obscure, plant (covertly place), shroud

wrap around envelop

wrapper enclosure

wrath ill will, malice, passion, resentment, umbrage

wreak inflict

wreathe intertwine

wreathed tortuous (bending)

wreck damage (noun), damage (verb), debacle, despoil, destroy (efface), devastate, disable, mutilate, obliterate, pillage, prejudice (injure), prostration, spoil (impair)

wrecker vandal

wrecking activities defacement

wrench contort, deprive, distort, exact, force (break), luxate, sever

wrench away from confiscate

wrench the meaning distort

wrench the sense distort

wrenching extortion

wrest contort, deprive, exact, extort, levy, seize (confiscate), sequester (seize property), slant, succeed (attain), usurp

wrest away from confiscate

wrest from abridge (divest), acquire (secure), coerce

wrest property from evict

wrester extortionist

wresting avulsion, extortion

wresting money by force extortion

wrestle compete, grapple

wrestle with confront (oppose), fight (battle)

wretched deplorable, derelict (abandoned), disconsolate, heinous, lamentable, lugubrious, obnoxious, paltry, peccant (culpable), pessimistic, poor (inferior in quality)

wretchedness disrepute, distress (anguish), pessimism, prostration

wring distill, exact, extort, press (constrain)

wring away from confiscate

wringing extortion

wrinkle artifice, contort

writ brevet, canon, certificate, charge (command), citation (charge), direction (order), directive, document, habeas corpus, monition (legal summons), precept, process (summons), search warrant, subpoena, summons. SEE MAIN ENTRY

writ for deliverance from illegal confinement habeas corpus

writ of summons citation (charge)

writ to gain freedom habeas corpus

write communicate, compile, compose, correspond (communicate), frame

(construct), inscribe, note (record), record, subscribe (sign)

write a prescription prescribe

write about treat (process)

write down book, enter (record), note (record), record

write in enter (record)

write notes for edit

write off obliterate. SEE MAIN ENTRY

write up report (disclose)

write-off bad debt

write-up publicity

writer amanuensis

writhe beat (pulsate), contort

writing charter (declaration of rights), communication (statement), entry (record), handwriting, instrument (document), memory (commemoration), proposal (report), publication (printed matter), script, testament

writing delivered as the evidence of an agreement instrument (document)

writing that discredits libel

writing which gives formal expression to a legal act instrument (document)

writings correspondence (communication by letters)

written documentary, holographic

written accusation indictment, information (charge), libel

written agreement covenant, lease

written announcement resolution (formal statement)

written application for relief petition

written assurance vow

written authorization proxy

written certificate bill (formal declaration)

written characters script

written complaint bill (formal declaration)

written constitution code

written contract certificate

written copy transcript

written declaration under oath deposition

written declaration upon oath affidavit

written discourse publication (printed matter)

written document form (document)

written evidence affirmance (legal affirmation), certificate, certification (attested copy)

written expression language

written formal expression instrument (document)

written instrument coupon

written instrument of contingency escrow

written law act (enactment), code, codification, constitution, statute

written material document, record

written matter inscription, script

written notification to appear in court summons

written off derelict (abandoned)

written order holding (ruling of a court), instruction (direction), mandate

written permission charter (license), license

written pledge covenant

written precept of imprisonment mittimus

written record entry (record), register

written requests for information interrogatories

written requirement specification

written statement averment

written statement of defense pleading

written statement under oath affidavit

written statements of accusation pleading

written terms contract

written word language

wrong abuse (violate), affront, arrant (onerous), at fault, blame (culpability), blameworthy, crime, culpable, damage (noun), damage (verb), delict, delinquency (misconduct), disservice, errant, erroneous, fallacious, false (inaccurate), faulty, felonious, grievance, ground, guilt, harm, harrow, heinous, illicit, immoral, impermissible, improper, inaccurate, inadmissible, inadvisable, inapplicable, inapposite, incorrect, infraction, infringement, iniquitous, injury, injustice, inopportune, irregular (improper), mendacious, mens rea, mischief, misconduct, misdeed, misdemeanor, misdoing, misfeasance, mishandle (maltreat), mistreat, nefarious, objectionable, offense, peccant (culpable), persecute, perverse, prejudice (injury), prejudice (injure), reprehensible, sinister, sophistic, tort, transgression, unethical, unfit, unjust, unjustifiable, unseemly, unsound (fallacious), unsustainable, untenable, untrue, vice, vicious, violation, wrongful. SEE MAIN ENTRY

wrong application misapplication

wrong arising from affirmative action misfeasance

wrong course detour, error

wrong designation misnomer

wrong doing infringement

wrong estimation misjudgment

wrong implementation noncompliance (improper completion)

wrong impression error, misestimation

wrong interpretation catachresis, distortion, misapplication

wrong name misnomer

wrong reasoning non sequitur

wrong statement misstatement

wrong usage catachresis, misapplication

wrong use abuse (corrupt practice), misapplication, misusage, misuse

wrong verdict injustice

wrong-doer delinquent

wrongdoer convict, criminal, felon, hoodlum, lawbreaker, malefactor, offender, recidivist. SEE MAIN ENTRY

wrongdoer released from prison probationer (released offender)

wrongdoing criminality, culpability, delinquency (misconduct), felony, guilt, injustice, knavery, mens rea, mischief, misconduct, misdeed, misfeasance, offense, tort, transgression, turpitude, vice

wronged aggrieved (victimized)

wrongful arrant (onerous), blameful, blameworthy, felonious, illegal, illegitimate (illegal), illicit, impermissible, improper, irregular (improper), lawless, outrageous, peccant (culpable), unauthorized, unjust, unlawful, unscrupulous, unwarranted. SEE MAIN ENTRY

wrongful act tort, tortious act. SEE MAIN ENTRY

wrongful action malfeasance

wrongful action of a public official misprision

wrongful appropriation embezzlement

wrongful assumption conversion (misappropriation)

wrongful conduct   malfeasance. SEE MAIN ENTRY

wrongful conversion of property   misappropriation

wrongful displacement   asportation

wrongful dispossession   disseisin

wrongful entry   encroachment

wrongful exaction   extortion

wrongful exercise of dominion   conversion (misappropriation)

wrongful impoundment   detainer

wrongful ingress   encroachment

wrongful keeping   detainer

wrongful performance of a normally legal act   misfeasance

wrongful removal   asportation

wrongful taking   larceny, theft

wrongful transfer   asportation

wrongful use   misapplication, misappropriation. SEE MAIN ENTRY

wrongfully   illegally

wrongfulness   infringement, misdoing, misfeasance, offense

wrongheaded   perverse

wrongly advised   misadvised

wrongly timed   inappropriate

wrongness   error

wrongous   unlawful

wrought up   frenetic

wrought with labor   elaborate

Y

yard   close (enclosed area), curtilage

yardage   space

yardstick   criterion. SEE MAIN ENTRY

yarn   myth

yawning   open (unclosed), penetrable

year   annum

yearly   per annum

yearly payment   annuity, premium (insurance payment)

yearn for   lack, need

yearning   desire, eager, predisposition, solicitous, will (desire)

years   age, longevity

years of existence   lifetime

yeilding   resignation (passive acceptance)

yell   outcry

yellow   recreant

yen   desire

yet   notwithstanding

yet to be   forthcoming

yield   abandon (relinquish), abide, accede (concede), accommodate, accrue (arise), acknowledge (verify), allow (endure), bestow, cede, concede, concur (agree), condescend (deign), condone, confer (give), confess, conform, consent, defer (yield in judgment), engender, forfeit, forgo, forswear, fund, furnish, germinate, grant (concede), hear (give attention to), let (permit), lose (undergo defeat), obey, outcome, outgrowth, output, proceeds, produce (manufacture), product, profit, quit (discontinue), redound, relax, release, relent, relinquish, resign, result, revenue, succumb, supply, vouchsafe, waive. SEE MAIN ENTRY

yield assent   accede (concede), agree (comply), certify (approve), coincide (concur), conform, grant (concede), permit

yield gain   inure (benefit)

yield in opinion to   defer (yield in judgment)

yield passage to   admit (give access)

yield profit   inure (benefit)

yield results   make

yield returns   gain, profit

yield to   comply, observe (obey), recognize (acknowledge)

yield to the wishes of others   truckle

yielding   amenable, capitulation, cession, charitable (lenient), compliance, concession (compromise), conformity (obedience), consenting, constructive (creative), disposition (transfer of property), facile, fertile, flexible, lenient, malleable, obedient, obeisant, obsequious, operative, passive, patient, permissive, pliable, pliant, powerless, productive, prolific, release, renunciation, resignation (relinquishment), resigned, resilient, sequacious, subjection, susceptible (unresistent), tractable, willing (not averse). SEE MAIN ENTRY

yielding abundantly   copious

yieldingness   amenability, compliance

yoke   bondage, curb, fetter, incorporate (include), join (bring together), lock, subjection, thrall

young   child, inexperienced, juvenile, progeny

young boy   child

young descendant   child

young girl   child

young people   children

young person   adolescent, infant, juvenile, minor

younger generation   children, offspring

youngling   adolescent, child, juvenile, minor

youngster   adolescent, child, infant, juvenile, minor

youngsters   children

your honor   judge. SEE MAIN ENTRY

youth   adolescence, adolescent, child, children, infant, juvenile, minor, minority (infancy), nonage

youthful   inexperienced, juvenile

youthfulness   minority (infancy)

Z

zeal   adhesion (loyalty), ardor, compulsion (obsession), diligence (perseverance), emotion, industry (activity), life (vitality), loyalty, passion, predisposition, purpose, spirit

zealot   addict, bigot, partisan

zealotist   partisan

zealotry   resolution (decision)

zealous   eager, earnest, faithful (loyal), fanatical, fervent, hot-blooded, industrious, intense, intensive, painstaking, pertinacious, purposeful, ready (willing), resolute, sedulous, serious (devoted), steadfast, thorough, true (loyal), unyielding, vehement, willing (desirous). SEE MAIN ENTRY

zealous advocates   lobby

zealous attachment   affection

zealousness   diligence (perseverance), industry (activity)

zenith   ceiling, culmination, pinnacle

zero   blank (emptiness)

zest   enjoyment (pleasure), life (vitality)

zestful   eager, fervent, ready (willing)

zestfulness   life (vitality)

zigzag   circuitous, indirect, indirection (indirect action), sinuous, tortuous (bending)

zonal   regional

zone   area (province), circuit, coverage (scope), demarcate, department, district, division (administrative unit), enclosure, insulate, locality, location, purview, region, scope, territory, vicinity. SEE MAIN ENTRY

zoning laws   SEE MAIN ENTRY